CARSWELL

CONSOLIDATED ONTARIO SECURITIES ACT, REGULATIONS AND RULES 2016

With Policy Statements, Blanket Orders and Notices

60th Edition

Borden Ladner Gervais LLP

THOMSON REUTERS

ISSN 1189-7082

ISBN 978-0-7798-7091-2 (60th edition)

A cataloguing record for this publication is available from Library and Archives Canada.

Printed in the United States by Thomson Reuters.

TELL US HOW WE'RE DOING

Scan the QR code to the right with your smartphone to send your comments regarding our products and services. Free QR Code Readers are available from your mobile device app store. You can also email us at carswell.feedback@thomsonreuters.com

THOMSON REUTERS

THOMSON REUTERS CANADA, A DIVISION OF THOMSON REUTERS CANADA LIMITED

One Corporate Plaza
2075 Kennedy Road
Toronto, Ontario
M1T 3V4

Customer Relations
Toronto 1-416-609-3800
Elsewhere in Canada/U.S. 1-800-387-5164
Fax 1-416-298-5082
www.carswell.com
Contact www.carswell.com/email

Summary Table of Contents

INTRODUCTION

This book contains the text of the *Securities Act*, R.S.O. 1990, c. S. 5 (as amended), proclaimed in force December 31, 1991, together with the Regulations made under the Act and the Rules (including National and Multilateral Instruments) made under the Act.

This Act is the successor to the *Securities Act*, R.S.O. 1980, c. 466, which in turn is the successor to the *Securities Act*, 1978, proclaimed in force from September 15, 1979 (see the 10th edition of this book). The 1978 Act succeeded the *Securities Act*, R.S.O. 1970, c. 426, which originated in the *Securities Act*, 1966.

Also included in this book are National, Multilateral and Ontario Securities Commission (OSC) policy statements, certain OSC Blanket Orders, Recognitions, Designations and Assignments, OSC notices, Canadian Securities Administrators notices and intergovernmental agreements.

Generally, rules (including instruments), policy statements and notices have been ordered in accordance with the current national numbering system. The old consecutively numbered National Policies and the old OSC Policies are in their own sections. Although the latter were grouped by topic, the current numbering system categorizes the topics differently. At the beginning of these sections, we have provided a summary of the status of those policies. The OSC notices that do not have numbers under the national numbering system follow as in previous editions.

This edition is current to May 28, 2016, with the exceptions of CSA Staff Notice 31-343, which is current as at November 26, 2015, National Instrument 24-102 and Companion Policy 24-102CP, which are current as at December 3, 2015, CSA Staff Notice 13-315 (Revised), which is current as at December 10, 2015, OSC Staff Notice 13-706 and the Investment Funds Practitioner - December 2015, which are current as at December 17, 2015, OSC Staff Notice 11-739 (Revised) and CSA Staff Notice 52-306 (Revised), which are current as at January 14, 2016, CSA Staff Notice 45-314 and Summary of Key Capital Raising Prospectus Exemptions in Ontario, which are current as at January 28, 2016, OSC Staff Notices 81-729 and 51-726 and National Instrument 24-102, which are current as at February 18, 2016, Multilateral Instruments 11-102, 13-102, 61-101 and 62-104, National Policy 62-203, National Instruments 43-101, 62-103, 62-104, Companion Policies 55-104CP and 61-101CP and OSC Rules 13-502, 14-501, 48-501, 71-801, 71-802, and 91-502, which are current as at February 25, 2016. Lastly, OSC Staff Notice 33-723 is current as at September 23, 2005.

This work reproduces only the official English language version of the *Securities Act* and of the Regulation. As these have official French versions, the reader is advised that reference to the official French language material may be warranted in appropriate circumstances.

Securities law and practice is updated on a continuing basis in *Securities Law and Practice* (3rd ed.), edited by Borden Ladner Gervais LLP, an annual subscription service, and *SecuritiesPartner Plus*, a CD-ROM service, both published by Carswell, as well as *SecuritiesSource*, an online service part of WestlawNext® Canada.

Philippe Tardif

June 6, 2016

TABLE OF CONTENTS

SECURITIES ACT

INTERPRETATION

PART I — THE COMMISSION (SS. 2–3.12)

PART II — (S. 4)

PART III — APPOINTMENT OF EXPERTS (S. 5)

PART IV — EXECUTIVE DIRECTOR AND SECRETARY (SS. 6, 7)

PART V — ADMINISTRATIVE PROCEEDINGS, REVIEWS AND APPEALS (SS. 8–10)

PART VI — INVESTIGATIONS AND EXAMINATIONS (SS. 11–18)

PART VII — RECORD-KEEPING AND COMPLIANCE REVIEWS (SS. 19–20.1)

PART VIII — SELF-REGULATION (SS. 21–21.11)

Table of Contents

Table of Contents

Table of Contents

Table of Contents

SCHEDULE [1]

1015 — GENERAL REGULATION

PART I — GENERAL

Interpretation

Financial Statements

PART II — CONTINUOUS DISCLOSURE

Non-Financial Matters

Other Disclosure

Financial Matters — Interim Financial Disclosure

Annual Financial Disclosure

Finance Companies

Miscellaneous

PART III — PROSPECTUS REQUIREMENTS

Further Exemptions

Table of Contents

Table of Contents

Table of Contents

261/02 — TORONTO STOCK EXCHANGE INC.

85/05 — EXEMPTIONS RESPECTING THE ONTARIO FINANCING AUTHORITY

Rules (including National Instruments) and Policies, Recognition and Designation Orders and Notices with the Numbering System for the Policy Reformulation Project

I — Procedure and Related Matters

1.1 — General

Table of Contents

Table of Contents

II — Certain Capital Market Participants

2.1 — Stock Exchanges

2.3 — Trading Rules

Table of Contents

Table of Contents

Table of Contents

3.2 — Registration Exemptions

3.3 — Ongoing Requirements Affecting Registrants

Table of Contents

3.4 — Fitness for Registration

3.5 — Non-Resident Registrants

IV — Distribution Requirements

4.1 — Prospectus Contents — Non-Financial Matters

4.3 — Prospectus Filing Matters

4.4 — Alternative Forms of Prospectus

Table of Contents

4.6 — Requirements Affecting Distributions by Certain Issuers

4.7 — Advertising and Marketing

4.8 — Distribution Restrictions

V — Ongoing Requirements for Issuers and Insiders

5.1 — Disclosure — General

Table of Contents

Table of Contents

5.2 — Financial Disclosure

Table of Contents

Table of Contents

7.2 — Distributions Outside The Jurisdiction

VIII — Investment Funds

8.1 — Investment Fund Distributions

Table of Contents

IX — Derivatives

9.1 — Trades in Derivatives

Table of Contents

Ontario Securities Commission Rules of Procedure

Procedures for Opportunities to be Heard Before Director's Decisions on Registration Matters

Practice Guideline — Electronic Copies of Written Submissions

Policy Statements (Old Numbering System)

National Policies

National Policy Statements

Uniform Act Policies

O.S.C. Policies

1 — General

2 — Ontario Securities Commission Procedure and Related Matters

4 — Registration

O.S.C. Blanket Orders, Recognitions, Designations and Assignments

1.0 — Procedure and Related Matters

2.0 — Certain Capital Market Participants

O.S.C. Notices

O.S.C. Notices

Table of Contents

A NOTE ON CROSS-REFERENCES

In order to assist the reader, we have inserted after certain provisions of the Act and the Regulation cross-references to other sections of the Act and regulation as well as the Rules, Policy Statements, Blanket Orders and Notices. References are indicated with the following abbreviations:

BOR — Ontario Securities Commission Blanket Orders, Recognitions, Designations and Assignments

CSAN — Canadian Securities Administrators Notices

MI — Multilateral Instrument

MPS — Multilateral Policy Statement

NI — National Instrument

NPS — National Policy Statement

OPS — Ontario Securities Commission Policy Statement

OSA — Ontario *Securities Act*, R.S.O. 1990, c. S-5, as amended

OSCN — Ontario Securities Commission Notice

Reg. — R.R.O. 1990, Regulation 1015 — Securities Act Regulation, as amended

Rule — Ontario Securities Commission Rule (other than National Instrument or Multilateral Instrument)

References to the Ontario *Securities Act* are to section numbers. References to Regulation 1015 are either to section numbers or Forms. Unless otherwise indicated, all NI, MI, Rule, NPS and OPS references are to the given Instrument, Rule or Policy as a whole, and not to any specific paragraph therein, unless otherwise indicated.

SECURITIES ACT

R.S.O. 1990, c. S.5, as am. S.O. 1992, c. 18, s. 56; 1993, c. 27, Sched.; 1994, c. 11, ss. 349–381; 1994, c. 33; 1997, c. 10, ss. 36–41; 1997, c. 19, s. 23; 1997, c. 31, s. 179; 1997, c. 43, Sched. F, s. 13; 1999, c. 6, s. 60; 1999, c. 9, ss. 193–222; 2001, c. 23, ss. 209–218; 2002, c. 18, Sched. H, ss. 6–14; 2002, c. 22, ss. 177–189; 2004, c. 8, ss. 46, 47(1), item 7 (Fr.); 2004, c. 16, Sched. D, s. 1, Table (Fr.); 2004, c. 17, s. 32, Table; 2004, c. 31, Sched. 34; 2005, c. 5, s. 64; 2005, c. 31, Sched. 20; 2006, c. 8, s. 144; 2006, c. 19, Sched. C, s. 1(1), (2); 2006, c. 21, Sched. F, s. 136(1), Table 1; 2006, c. 29, s. 65; 2006, c. 33, Sched. Z.5; 2006, c. 35, Sched. C, s. 121; 2007, c. 7, Sched. 7, s. 191, Sched. 38, ss. 1, 2 (Fr.), 3–6, 7 (Fr.), 8, 9(1)–(3) (Fr.), (4), 10, 11 (Fr.), 12 (Fr.), 13(1) (Fr.), (2), (3) (Fr.), (4), 14, 15; 2008, c. 19, Sched. R; 2009, c. 18, Sched. 26; 2009, c. 34, Sched. S, ss. 1–8, 9 (Fr.); 2010, c. 1, Sched. 26, ss. 1, 2, 3 (Fr.), 4–6, 7 (Fr.), 8, 9; 2010, c. 26, Sched. 18 [ss. 1(1), (5), (13), 19–22, 28, 31(1), 35(2) not in force at date of publication.]; 2011, c. 9, Sched. 38; 2012, c. 8, Sched. 55 [s. 3 conditions not yet satisfied.]; 2013, c. 2, Sched. 13; 2014, c. 7, Sched. 28 [ss. 4, 14, 17 not in force at date of publication.]; 2015, c. 20, Sched. 39, ss. 1, 2(1), (2), (3) (Fr.), (4), (5), (6) (Fr.), (7), 3, 4(1), (2), (3) (Fr.), (4), (5) (Fr.), (6) (Fr.), (7), (8); 2015, c. 38, Sched. 18, ss. 1–3, 4(1) (Fr.), (2), (3), 5–10; 2016, c. 5, Sched. 26 [ss. 2, 3 not in force at date of publication.].

INTERPRETATION

1. (1) Definitions — In this Act,

"adviser" means a person or company engaging in or holding himself, herself or itself out as engaging in the business of advising others as to the investing in or the buying or selling of securities;

Proposed Amendment — 1(1) "adviser"

"adviser" means a person or company engaging in or holding himself, herself or itself out as engaging in the business of advising others as to the investing in or the buying or selling of securities or derivatives;

2010, c. 26, Sched. 18, s. 1(1) [Not in force at date of publication.]

OSA 1(1)"adviser"

Related Provisions: OSA 34, 25(3).

Rules: NI 31-103; Rule 35-502.

Policies and Orders: OSCN 41; OSCN 81-708; NPS 31-103CP.

"alternative trading system" means a marketplace that,

(a) is not a recognized quotation and trade reporting system or a recognized exchange,

(b) does not require an issuer to enter into an agreement to have its securities traded on the marketplace,

(c) does not provide, directly or through one or more subscribers, a guarantee of a two-sided market for a security or derivative on a continuous or reasonably continuous basis,

(d) does not set requirements governing the conduct of subscribers, other than conduct in respect of the trading by those subscribers on the marketplace, and

(e) does not discipline subscribers other than by exclusion from participation in the marketplace;

OSA 1(1)"alternative trading system"

Related Provisions: OSA 21.0.1.

"associate", where used to indicate a relationship with any person or company means,

(a) any company of which such person or company beneficially owns, directly or indirectly, voting securities carrying more than 10 per cent of the voting rights attached to all voting securities of the company for the time being outstanding,

(a.1) [Repealed 2015, c. 38, Sched. 18, s. 1(2).]

(b) any partner of that person or company,

(c) any trust or estate in which such person or company has a substantial beneficial interest or as to which such person or company serves as trustee or in a similar capacity,

(d) any relative of that person who resides in the same home as that person,

(e) any person who resides in the same home as that person and to whom that person is married or with whom that person is living in a conjugal relationship outside marriage, or

(f) any relative of a person mentioned in clause (e) who has the same home as that person;

"chief compliance officer" means, in respect of a registrant that is a registered dealer, registered adviser or registered investment fund manager, an individual designated by the registrant,

(a) to establish and maintain policies and procedures to assess, monitor and report on the registrant's compliance with Ontario securities law, and

(b) to fulfill such other compliance functions as may be prescribed by the regulations;

OSA 1(1)"chief compliance officer"

Related Provisions: OSA 25(6).

Rules: NI 31-103.

"clearing agency" means,

    (a) with respect to securities, a person or company that,

        (i) acts as an intermediary in paying funds or delivering securities, or both, in connection with trades and other transactions in securities,

        (ii) provides centralized facilities for the clearing of trades and other transactions in securities, including facilities for comparing data respecting the terms of settlement of a trade or transaction, or

        (iii) provides centralized facilities as a depository of securities,

    but does not include,

        (iv) the Canadian Payments Association or its successors,

        (v) an exchange or a quotation and trade reporting system,

        (vi) a registered dealer, or

        (vii) a bank, trust company, loan corporation, insurance company, treasury branch, credit union or caisse populaire that, in the normal course of its authorized business in Canada, engages in an activity described in subclause (a)(i), but does not also engage in an activity described in subclause (a)(ii) or (iii), and

    (b) with respect to derivatives, a person or company that provides centralized facilities for the clearing and settlement of trades in derivatives that, with respect to a contract, instrument or transaction,

        (i) enables each party to the contract, instrument or transaction to substitute, through novation or otherwise, the credit of the clearing agency for the credit of the parties,

        (ii) arranges or provides, on a multilateral basis, for the settlement or netting of obligations resulting from such contracts, instruments or transactions executed by participants in the clearing agency, or

        (iii) otherwise provides clearing services or arrangements that mutualize or transfer among participants in the clearing agency the credit risk arising from such contracts, instruments or transactions executed by the participants,

    but does not include a person or company solely because the person or company arranges or provides for,

        (iv) settlement, netting or novation of obligations resulting from agreements, contracts or transactions on a bilateral basis and without a central counterparty,

        (v) settlement or netting of cash payments through the Automated Clearing Settlement System or the Large Value Transfer System, or

        (vi) settlement, netting or novation of obligations resulting from a sale of a commodity in a transaction in the spot market;

    (c) [Repealed 2010, c. 26, Sched. 18, s. 1(3).]

    (d) [Repealed 2010, c. 26, Sched. 18, s. 1(3).]

    (e) [Repealed 2010, c. 26, Sched. 18, s. 1(3).]

    (f) [Repealed 2010, c. 26, Sched. 18, s. 1(3).]

    (g) [Repealed 2010, c. 26, Sched. 18, s. 1(3).]

OSA 1(1)"clearing agency"

Related Provisions: OSA 21.2.

"Commission" means the Ontario Securities Commission;

OSA 1(1)"Commission"

Related Provisions: OSA Part I.

"company" means any corporation, incorporated association, incorporated syndicate or other incorporated organization;

"contract" includes a trust agreement, declaration of trust or other similar instrument;

"contractual plan" means any contract or other arrangement for the purchase of shares or units of a mutual fund by payments over a specified period or by a specified number of payments where the amount deducted from any one of the payments as sales charges is larger than the amount that would have been deducted from such payment for sales charges if deductions had been made from each payment at a constant rate for the duration of the plan;

"control person" means,

    (a) a person or company who holds a sufficient number of the voting rights attached to all outstanding voting securities of an issuer to affect materially the control of the issuer, and, if a person or company holds more than 20 per cent of the voting rights attached to all outstanding voting securities of an issuer, the person or company is deemed, in the absence of evidence to the contrary, to hold a sufficient number of the voting rights to affect materially the control of the issuer, or

(b) each person or company in a combination of persons or companies, acting in concert by virtue of an agreement, arrangement, commitment or understanding, which holds in total a sufficient number of the voting rights attached to all outstanding voting securities of an issuer to affect materially the control of the issuer, and, if a combination of persons or companies holds more than 20 per cent of the voting rights attached to all outstanding voting securities of an issuer, the combination of persons or companies is deemed, in the absence of evidence to the contrary, to hold a sufficient number of the voting rights to affect materially the control of the issuer;

"credit rating" means an assessment that is publicly disclosed or distributed by subscription concerning the creditworthiness of an issuer,

    (a) as an entity, or

    (b) with respect to specific securities or a specific pool of securities or assets;

"credit rating organization" means a person or company that issues credit ratings;

OSA 1(1)"credit rating organization"

Related Provisions: OSA Part IX.

"dealer" means, except for the purposes described in subsection (1.2), a person or company engaging in or holding himself, herself or itself out as engaging in the business of trading in securities as principal or agent;

Proposed Amendment — 1(1) "dealer"

"dealer" means, except for the purposes described in subsection (1.2), a person or company engaging in or holding himself, herself or itself out as engaging in the business of trading in securities or derivatives as principal or agent;

2010, c. 26, Sched. 18, s. 1(5) [Not in force at date of publication.]

OSA 1(1)"dealer"

Related Provisions: OSA Part XI.

Rules: NI 31-103.

Policies and Orders: NPS 31-103CP.

"debt security" means a bond, debenture, note or similar instrument representing indebtedness, whether secured or unsecured;

"decision" means, in respect of a decision of the Commission or a Director, a direction, decision, order, ruling or other requirement made under a power or right conferred by this Act or the regulations;

OSA 1(1)"decision"

Related Provisions: OSA 8, 9.

"derivative" means an option, swap, futures contract, forward contract or other financial or commodity contract or instrument whose market price, value, delivery obligations, payment obligations or settlement obligations are derived from, referenced to or based on an underlying interest (including a value, price, rate, variable, index, event, probability or thing), but does not include,

    (a) a commodity futures contract as defined in subsection 1(1) of the *Commodity Futures Act*,

    (b) a commodity futures option as defined in subsection 1(1) of the *Commodity Futures Act*,

    (c) a contract or instrument that, by reason of an order of the Commission under subsection (10), is not a derivative, or

    (d) a contract or instrument in a class of contracts or instruments prescribed by the regulations not to be derivatives;

OSA 1(1)"derivative"

Related Provisions: OSA Part XV.1.

"designated credit rating organization" means a credit rating organization that is designated by the Commission under Part IX;

"designated derivative" means a derivative,

    (a) that, by reason of an order of the Commission under subsection (11), is a designated derivative, or

    (b) that belongs to a class of derivatives prescribed by the regulations;

OSA 1(1)"designated derivative"

Rules: Rule 91-506.

"designated trade repository" means a trade repository that is designated by the Commission under section 21.2.2;

OSA 1(1)"designated trade repository"

Rules: Rule 91-507.

"Director" means the Executive Director of the Commission, a Director or Deputy Director of the Commission, or a person employed by the Commission in a position designated by the Executive Director for the purpose of this definition;

OSA 1(1)"Director"

Related Provisions: OSA Part IV.

Policies and Orders: BOR 1.3.

"director" means a director of a company or an individual performing a similar function or occupying a similar position for any person;

"distribution", where used in relation to trading in securities, means,

    (a) a trade in securities of an issuer that have not been previously issued,

(b) a trade by or on behalf of an issuer in previously issued securities of that issuer that have been redeemed or purchased by or donated to that issuer,

(c) a trade in previously issued securities of an issuer from the holdings of any control person,

(d) a trade by or on behalf of an underwriter in securities which were acquired by that underwriter, acting as underwriter, prior to the 15th day of September, 1979 if those securities continued on that date to be owned by or for that underwriter, so acting,

(e) a trade by or on behalf of an underwriter in securities which were acquired by that underwriter, acting as underwriter, within eighteen months after the 15th day of September, 1979, if the trade took place during that eighteen months, and

(f) any trade that is a distribution under the regulations,

and on and after the 15th day of March, 1981, includes a distribution as referred to in subsections 72(4), (5), (6) and (7), and also includes any transaction or series of transactions involving a purchase and sale or a repurchase and resale in the course of or incidental to a distribution and "distribute", "distributed" and "distributing" have a corresponding meaning;

OSA 1(1)"distribution"

Related Provisions: OSA Part XV, XVI.

Definitions: OSA 1(1)"control person".

Rules: NI 45-102.

Policies and Orders: OPS 1.5.

"distribution company" means a person or company distributing securities under a distribution contract;

OSA 1(1)"distribution company"

Related Provisions: OSA Part XXI.

"distribution contract" means a contract between an investment fund or its trustees or other legal representative and a person or company under which that person or company is granted the right to purchase the shares or units of the investment fund for distribution or to distribute the shares or units of the investment fund on behalf of the investment fund;

OSA 1(1)"distribution contract"

Related Provisions: OSA Part XXI.

"distribution to the public", where used in relation to trading in securities, means a distribution that is made for the purpose of distributing to the public securities issued by an issuer, whether such trades are made directly or indirectly to the public through an underwriter or otherwise;

"economic exposure" in relation to a reporting issuer means the extent to which the economic or financial interests of a person or company are aligned with the trading price of securities of the reporting issuer or the economic or financial interests of the reporting issuer;

"economic interest in a security" means,

(a) a right to receive or the opportunity to participate in a reward, benefit or return from a security, or

(b) an exposure to a loss or a risk of loss in respect of a security;

"form of proxy" means a written or printed form that, upon completion and execution by or on behalf of a security holder, becomes a proxy;

OSA 1(1)"form of proxy"

Related Provisions: OSA Part XIX.

Rules: NI 51-102, Part 9, NI 81-106, Part 12.

"forward-looking information" means disclosure regarding possible events, conditions or financial performance that is based on assumptions about future economic conditions and courses of action and includes future oriented financial information with respect to prospective financial performance, financial position or cash flows that is presented either as a forecast or a projection;

OSA 1(1)"forward-looking information"

Related Provisions: OSA 132.1, 138.4.

Rules: NI 51-102, Parts 4A and 4B.

Policies and Orders: CSAN 51-330.

"individual" means a natural person, but does not include a partnership, unincorporated association, unincorporated syndicate, unincorporated organization, trust, or a natural person in his or her capacity as trustee, executor, administrator or other legal personal representative;

"insider" means,

(a) a director or officer of a reporting issuer,

(b) a director or officer of a person or company that is itself an insider or subsidiary of a reporting issuer,

(c) a person or company that has,

(i) beneficial ownership of, or control or direction over, directly or indirectly, securities of a reporting issuer carrying more than 10 per cent of the voting rights attached to all the reporting issuer's outstanding voting securities, excluding, for the purpose of the calculation of the percentage held, any securities held by the person or company as underwriter in the course of a distribution, or

(ii) a combination of beneficial ownership of, and control or direction over, directly or indirectly, securities of a reporting issuer carrying more than 10 per cent of the voting rights attached to all the reporting issuer's outstanding voting securities, excluding, for the purpose of the calculation of the percentage held, any securities held by the person or company as underwriter in the course of a distribution,

(d) a reporting issuer that has purchased, redeemed or otherwise acquired a security of its own issue, for so long as it continues to hold that security,

(e) a person or company designated as an insider in an order made under subsection (11),

(f) a person or company that is in a class of persons or companies designated under subparagraph 40 v of subsection 143(1);

OSA 1(1)"insider"

Related Provisions: OSA 1(2)–(9), Part XXI, 76, 134.

Regulations: Reg.: Part VIII.

Policies and Orders: CSAN 55-314.

"investment fund" means a mutual fund or a non-redeemable investment fund;

OSA 1(1)"investment fund"

Rules: NI 81-106.

"investment fund manager" means a person or company that directs the business, operations or affairs of an investment fund;

OSA 1(1)"investment fund manager"

Related Provisions: OSA 25(4).

Rules: NI 31-103; Rule 81-802.

"issuer" means a person or company who has outstanding, issues or proposes to issue, a security;

OSA 1(1)"issuer"

Related Provisions: OSA 53(2).

"management company" means a person or company who provides investment advice, under a management contract;

OSA 1(1)"management company"

Related Provisions: OSA Part XXI.

"management contract" means a contract under which an investment fund is provided with investment advice, alone or together with administrative or management services, for valuable consideration;

OSA 1(1)"management contract"

Related Provisions: OSA Part XXI.

"market participant" means,

(a) a registrant,

(b) a person or company exempted from the requirement to be registered under this Act,

(c) a reporting issuer,

(c.1) a person or company that has issued securities to a registrant or through a registrant acting as agent,

(c.2) a director, officer or promoter of a person or company described in clause (c) or (c.1),

(d) a manager or custodian of assets, shares or units of an investment fund,

(e) a recognized clearing agency,

(f) a recognized commodity futures exchange,

(g) a recognized exchange,

(h) a recognized quotation and trade reporting system,

(i) a recognized self-regulatory organization,

(i.1) a person or company that is exempt from the requirement under section 21, 21.1, 21.2 or 21.2.1 to be recognized by the Commission,

(j) a designated credit rating organization,

(k) a designated trade repository,

(l) a transfer agent for securities of an issuer,

(m) a registrar for securities of an issuer,

(n) the Canadian Investor Protection Fund,

(o) the Ontario Contingency Trust Fund,

(o.1) the MFDA Investor Protection Corporation,

(p) the general partner of a market participant, or

(q) any other person or company or member of a class of persons or companies prescribed by the regulations;

OSA 1(1)"market participant"

Related Provisions: OSA 127.

Rules: Rule 23-501, 24-501, 81-802.

"marketplace" means any of the following, but does not include an inter-dealer bond broker:

1. An exchange.

2. A quotation and trade reporting system.

3. A person or company not included in paragraph 1 or 2 that,

   i. constitutes, maintains or provides a market or facility for bringing together buyers and sellers of securities or derivatives,

   ii. brings together the orders for securities or derivatives of multiple buyers and sellers, and

   iii. uses established non-discretionary methods under which the orders interact with each other, and the buyers and sellers entering the orders agree to the terms of a trade.

4. With respect to securities, a dealer who executes a trade of an exchange-traded security outside a marketplace described in paragraph 1, 2 or 3;

"material change",

(a) when used in relation to an issuer other than an investment fund, means,

   (i) a change in the business, operations or capital of the issuer that would reasonably be expected to have a significant effect on the market price or value of any of the securities of the issuer, or

   (ii) a decision to implement a change referred to in subclause (i) made by the board of directors or other persons acting in a similar capacity or by senior management of the issuer who believe that confirmation of the decision by the board of directors or such other persons acting in a similar capacity is probable, and

(b) when used in relation to an issuer that is an investment fund, means,

   (i) a change in the business, operations or affairs of the issuer that would be considered important by a reasonable investor in determining whether to purchase or continue to hold securities of the issuer, or

   (ii) a decision to implement a change referred to in subclause (i) made,

   (A) by the board of directors of the issuer or the board of directors of the investment fund manager of the issuer or other persons acting in a similar capacity,

   (B) by senior management of the issuer who believe that confirmation of the decision by the board of directors or such other persons acting in a similar capacity is probable, or

   (C) by senior management of the investment fund manager of the issuer who believe that confirmation of the decision by the board of directors of the investment fund manager of the issuer or such other persons acting in a similar capacity is probable;

OSA 1(1)"material change"

Related Provisions: OSA 76.

Rules: NI 51-102, Part 7; NI 81-106, Part 11.

Policies and Orders: NPS 51-201.

"material fact", when used in relation to securities issued or proposed to be issued, means a fact that would reasonably be expected to have a significant effect on the market price or value of the securities;

OSA 1(1)"material fact"

Related Provisions: OSA Part XVIII.

Policies and Orders: NPS 51-201.

"Minister" means the Minister of Finance or such other member of the Executive Council to whom the administration of this Act may be assigned;

OSA 1(1)"Minister"

Related Provisions: OSA 11(5), 122(7).

"misrepresentation" means,

(a) an untrue statement of material fact, or

(b) an omission to state a material fact that is required to be stated or that is necessary to make a statement not misleading in the light of the circumstances in which it was made;

OSA 1(1)"misrepresentation"

Related Provisions: OSA 61(2)(a), Part XXIII and Part XXIII.1.

"mutual fund" means an issuer whose primary purpose is to invest money provided by its security holders and whose securities entitle the holder to receive on demand, or within a specified period after demand, an amount computed by reference to the value of a proportionate interest in the whole or in part of the net assets, including a separate fund or trust account, of the issuer;

OSA 1(1)"mutual fund"

Related Provisions: OSA Part XXI.

Rules: NI 81-101, 81-102, 81-106.

"mutual fund in Ontario" means a mutual fund that is a reporting issuer or that is organized under the laws of Ontario, but does not include a private mutual fund;

OSA 1(1)"mutual fund in Ontario"

Related Provisions: OSA 111.

Rules: NI 81-106.

"non-redeemable investment fund" means an issuer,

    (a) whose primary purpose is to invest money provided by its security holders,

    (b) that does not invest,

        (i) for the purpose of exercising or seeking to exercise control of an issuer, other than an issuer that is a mutual fund or a non-redeemable investment fund, or

        (ii) for the purpose of being actively involved in the management of any issuer in which it invests, other than an issuer that is a mutual fund or a non-redeemable investment fund, and

    (c) that is not a mutual fund;

"offering memorandum" means a document, together with any amendments to that document, purporting to describe the business and affairs of an issuer that has been prepared primarily for delivery to and review by a prospective purchaser so as to assist the prospective purchaser to make an investment decision in respect of securities being sold in a distribution to which section 53 would apply but for the availability of one or more of the exemptions contained in Ontario securities law, but does not include a document setting out current information about an issuer for the benefit of a prospective purchaser familiar with the issuer through prior investment or business contacts.

OSA 1(1)"offering memorandum"

Related Provisions: OSA 130.1.

Rules: Rules 14-501, 45-501.

"officer", with respect to an issuer or registrant, means,

    (a) a chair or vice-chair of the board of directors, a chief executive officer, a chief operating officer, a chief financial officer, a president, a vice-president, a secretary, an assistant secretary, a treasurer, an assistant treasurer and a general manager,

    (b) every individual who is designated as an officer under a by-law or similar authority of the registrant or issuer, and

    (c) every individual who performs functions similar to those normally performed by an individual referred to in clause (a) or (b);

"Ontario securities law" means,

    (a) this Act,

    (b) the regulations, and

    (c) in respect of a person or company, a decision of the Commission or a Director to which the person or company is subject;

"person" means an individual, partnership, unincorporated association, unincorporated syndicate, unincorporated organization, trust, trustee, executor, administrator, or other legal representative;

"portfolio manager" [Repealed 2009, c. 18, Sched. 26, s. 1(4).]

"portfolio securities", where used in relation to a mutual fund, means securities held or proposed to be purchased by the mutual fund;

OSA 1(1)"portfolio securities"

Related Provisions: OSA 119.

"private company" means a company in whose constating document,

    (a) the right to transfer its shares is restricted,

    (b) the number of its shareholders, exclusive of persons who are in its employment and exclusive of persons who, having been formerly in the employment of the company, were, while in that employment, and have continued after termination of that employment to be, shareholders of the company, is limited to not more than fifty, two or more persons who are the joint registered owners of one or more shares being counted as one shareholder, and

    (c) any invitation to the public to subscribe for its securities is prohibited;

"private mutual fund" means a mutual fund that is,

    (a) operated as an investment club, where,

        (i) its shares or units are held by not more than fifty persons and its indebtedness has never been offered to the public,

        (ii) it does not pay or give any remuneration for investment advice or in respect of trades in securities, except normal brokerage fees, and

        (iii) all of its members are required to make contributions in proportion to the shares or units each holds for the purpose of financing its operations, or

    (b) administered by a trust company registered under the *Loan and Trust Corporations Act* and consists of a common trust fund as defined in section 1 of that Act;

OSA 1(1)"private mutual fund"

Rules: NI 45-106, s. 2,20, 2.21.

"promoter" means,

(a) a person or company who, acting alone or in conjunction with one or more other persons, companies or a combination thereof, directly or indirectly, takes the initiative in founding, organizing or substantially reorganizing the business of an issuer, or

(b) a person or company who, in connection with the founding, organizing or substantial reorganizing of the business of an issuer, directly or indirectly, receives in consideration of services or property, or both services and property, 10 per cent or more of any class of securities of the issuer or 10 per cent or more of the proceeds from the sale of any class of securities of a particular issue, but a person or company who receives such securities or proceeds either solely as underwriting commissions or solely in consideration of property shall not be deemed a promoter within the meaning of this definition if such person or company does not otherwise take part in founding, organizing, or substantially reorganizing the business;

OSA 1(1)"promoter"

Related Provisions: OSA 58.

"proxy" means a completed and executed form of proxy by means of which a security holder has appointed a person or company as the security holder's nominee to attend and act for and on the security holder's behalf at a meeting of security holders;

OSA 1(1)"proxy"

Related Provisions: OSA Part XIX.

Rules: NI 51-102, Part 9; NI 81-106, Part 12.

"published market" means, with respect to a class of securities, a market in Canada or outside of Canada on which the securities are traded, if the prices at which they have been traded on that market are regularly,

(a) disseminated electronically, or

(b) published in a newspaper or business or financial publication of general and regular paid circulation;

"quotation and trade reporting system" means a person or company that operates facilities that permit the dissemination of price quotations for the purchase and sale of securities and reports of completed transactions in securities for the exclusive use of registered dealers, but does not include an exchange or a registered dealer;

"recognized clearing agency" means a clearing agency recognized by the Commission under section 21.2;

"recognized commodity futures exchange" means a person or company that is registered or recognized by the Commission as a commodity futures exchange under the *Commodity Futures Act* or that is exempted from the requirement to be registered or recognized by order of the Commission;

"recognized exchange" means a person or company recognized by the Commission under section 21;

"recognized quotation and trade reporting system" means a quotation and trade reporting system recognized by the Commission under section 21.2.1;

"recognized self-regulatory organization" means a self-regulatory organization recognized by the Commission under section 21.1 or recognized as a self-regulatory body by the Commission under the *Commodity Futures Act*;

"recognized stock exchange" [Repealed 2010, c. 26, Sched. 18, s. 1(10).]

"register" [Repealed 1994, c. 11, s. 350(7).]

"registrant" means a person or company registered or required to be registered under this Act;

"regulations" means the regulations made under this Act and, unless the context otherwise indicates, includes the rules;

"related derivative" means, with respect to a security, a derivative that is related to the security because the derivative's market price, value, delivery obligations, payment obligations or settlement obligations are, in a material way, derived from, referenced to or based on the market price, value, delivery obligations, payment obligations or settlement obligations of the security;

"related financial instrument" means an agreement, arrangement or understanding to which an insider of a reporting issuer is a party, the effect of which is to alter, directly or indirectly, the insider's,

(a) economic interest in a security of the reporting issuer, or

(b) economic exposure to the reporting issuer;

"reporting issuer" means an issuer,

(a) that has issued voting securities on or after the 1st day of May, 1967 in respect of which a prospectus was filed and a receipt therefor obtained under a predecessor of this Act or in respect of which a securities exchange take-over bid circular was filed under a predecessor of this Act,

(b) that has filed a prospectus and for which the Director has issued a receipt under this Act,

(b.1) that has filed a securities exchange take-over bid circular under this Act before December 14, 1999,

(c) any of whose securities have been at any time since the 15th day of September, 1979 listed and posted for trading on any exchange in Ontario recognized by the Commission, regardless of when such listing and posting for trading commenced,

(d) to which the *Business Corporations Act* applies and which, for the purposes of that Act, is offering its securities to the public,

(e) that is the company whose existence continues following the exchange of securities of a company by or for the account of such company with another company or the holders of the securities of that other company in connection with,

    (i) a statutory amalgamation or arrangement, or

    (ii) a statutory procedure under which one company takes title to the assets of the other company that in turn loses its existence by operation of law, or under which the existing companies merge into a new company,

where one of the amalgamating or merged companies or the continuing company has been a reporting issuer for at least twelve months, or

(f) that is designated as a reporting issuer in an order made under subsection 1(11);

OSA 1(1)"reporting issuer"

Related Provisions: OSA 1(10), 1(11), 53(2).

"representative" means,

    (a) in respect of a registered dealer, an individual who trades securities on behalf of the dealer, whether or not the individual is employed by the dealer, or

    (b) in respect of a registered adviser, an individual who provides advice on behalf of the adviser with respect to investing in, buying or selling securities, whether or not the individual is employed by the adviser;

Proposed Amendment — 1(1) "representative"

"representative" means,

    (a) in respect of a registered dealer, an individual who trades securities or derivatives on behalf of the dealer, whether or not the individual is employed by the dealer, or

    (b) in respect of a registered adviser, an individual who provides advice on behalf of the adviser with respect to investing in securities or buying or selling securities or derivatives, whether or not the individual is employed by the adviser;

2010, c. 26, Sched. 18, s. 1(13) [Not in force at date of publication.]

"rules" means,

    (a) the rules made under section 143, and

    (b) orders, rulings and policies listed in the Schedule;

"salesperson" [Repealed 2009, c. 18, Sched. 26, s. 1(5).]

"security" includes,

    (a) any document, instrument or writing commonly known as a security,

    (b) any document constituting evidence of title to or interest in the capital, assets, property, profits, earnings or royalties of any person or company,

    (c) any document constituting evidence of an interest in an association of legatees or heirs,

    (d) any document constituting evidence of an option, subscription or other interest in or to a security,

    (e) a bond, debenture, note or other evidence of indebtedness or a share, stock, unit, unit certificate, participation certificate, certificate of share or interest, preorganization certificate or subscription other than,

        (i) a contract of insurance issued by an insurance company licensed under the *Insurance Act*, and

        (ii) evidence of a deposit issued by a bank listed in Schedule I, II or III to the *Bank Act* (Canada), by a credit union or league to which the *Credit Unions and Caisses Populaires Act, 1994* applies, by a loan corporation or trust corporation registered under the *Loan and Trust Corporations Act* or by an association to which the *Cooperative Credit Associations Act* (Canada) applies,

    (f) any agreement under which the interest of the purchaser is valued for purposes of conversion or surrender by reference to the value of a proportionate interest in a specified portfolio of assets, except a contract issued by an insurance company licensed under the *Insurance Act* which provides for payment at maturity of an amount not less than three quarters of the premiums paid by the purchaser for a benefit payable at maturity,

    (g) any agreement providing that money received will be repaid or treated as a subscription to shares, stock, units or interests at the option of the recipient or of any person or company,

    (h) any certificate of share or interest in a trust, estate or association,

    (i) any profit-sharing agreement or certificate,

    (j) any certificate of interest in an oil, natural gas or mining lease, claim or royalty voting trust certificate,

    (k) any oil or natural gas royalties or leases or fractional or other interest therein,

    (l) any collateral trust certificate,

    (m) any income or annuity contract not issued by an insurance company,

    (n) any investment contract,

    (o) any document constituting evidence of an interest in a scholarship or educational plan or trust, and

(p) any commodity futures contract or any commodity futures option that is not traded on a commodity futures exchange registered with or recognized by the Commission under the *Commodity Futures Act* or the form of which is not accepted by the Director under that Act,

whether any of the foregoing relate to an issuer or proposed issuer;

OSA 1(1)"security"

Policies and Orders: OSCN 44; CSAN 46-303.

"self-regulatory organization" means a person or company that is organized for the purpose of regulating the operations and the standards of practice and business conduct, in capital markets, of its members and their representatives with a view to promoting the protection of investors and the public interest;

"senior officer" [Repealed 2006, c. 33, Sched. Z.5, s. 1(5).]

"trade" or **"trading"** includes,

(a) any sale or disposition of a security for valuable consideration, whether the terms of payment be on margin, instalment or otherwise, but does not include a purchase of a security or, except as provided in clause (d), a transfer, pledge or encumbrance of securities for the purpose of giving collateral for a debt made in good faith,

(b) any participation as a trader in any transaction in a security through the facilities of any exchange or quotation and trade reporting system,

(b.1) entering into a derivative or making a material amendment to, terminating, assigning, selling or otherwise acquiring or disposing of a derivative, or

(b.2) a novation of a derivative, other than a novation with a clearing agency,

(c) any receipt by a registrant of an order to buy or sell a security,

(d) any transfer, pledge or encumbrancing of securities of an issuer from the holdings of any person or company or combination of persons or companies described in clause (c) of the definition of "distribution" for the purpose of giving collateral for a debt made in good faith, and

(e) any act, advertisement, solicitation, conduct or negotiation directly or indirectly in furtherance of any of the foregoing;

OSA 1(1)"trade"

Related Provisions: OSA Part XII, Part XIII.

Regulations: Reg.: Part VI.

Policies and Orders: OPS 1.5, 31-706, 57-602.

"trade repository" means a person or company that collects and maintains reports of completed trades by other persons and companies;

OSA 1(1)"trade repository"

Related Provisions: OSA 21.2.2.

Rules

Rule 91-507

"ultimate designated person" means, in respect of a registrant that is a registered dealer, registered adviser or registered investment fund manager, an individual designated by the registrant,

(a) to supervise the registrant's activities that are directed towards ensuring compliance with Ontario securities law by the registrant and by each individual acting on the registrant's behalf, and

(b) to fulfill such other functions as may be prescribed by the regulations in order to otherwise promote compliance with Ontario securities law;

OSA 1(1)"ultimate designated person"

Related Provisions: OSA 25(5).

Rules: NI 31-103.

"underwriter" means a person or company who, as principal, agrees to purchase securities with a view to distribution or who, as agent, offers for sale or sells securities in connection with a distribution and includes a person or company who has a direct or indirect participation in any such distribution, but does not include,

(a) a person or company whose interest in the transaction is limited to receiving the usual and customary distributor's or seller's commission payable by an underwriter or issuer,

(b) a mutual fund that, under the laws of the jurisdiction to which it is subject, accepts its shares or units for surrender and resells them,

(c) a company that, under the laws of the jurisdiction to which it is subject, purchases its shares and resells them, or

(d) a bank listed in Schedule I, II or III to the *Bank Act* (Canada) with respect to securities described in paragraph 1 of subsection 35(2) or to such banking transactions as are designated by the regulations;

OSA 1(1)"underwriter"

Related Provisions: OSA 25(1)(b).

Rules: NI 31-103; NI 45-106, s. 2.33.

Policies and Orders: OPS 1.5; OSCN 46-701.

"voting security" means any security other than a debt security of an issuer carrying a voting right either under all circumstances or under some circumstances that have occurred and are continuing.

(1.1) Same — For the purposes of this Act, any of "business combination", "consultant", "disclosure controls and procedures", "exchange-traded security", "future-oriented financial information", "going private transaction", "insider bid", inter-dealer bond broker", "internal controls", "offer to acquire", "offeror", "penny stocks", "related party transactions" and "reverse take-overs" may be defined in the regulations or the rules and, if so defined, has the defined meaning.

OSA 1(1.1)

Rules: Rule 14-501, s. 1.1(3); 62-504, s. 1.1, MI 61-101, s. 1.1.

(1.1.1) Purchase and sale of a derivative — For the purposes of this Act,

(a) a person or company purchases a derivative by entering into, making a material amendment to or otherwise acquiring a derivative;

(b) a person or company sells a derivative by making a material amendment to, terminating, assigning or otherwise disposing of a derivative; and

(c) a novation of a derivative, other than a novation with a clearing agency, is deemed to be the purchase and sale of a derivative.

OSA 1(1.1.1)

Definitions: OSA 1(1)"derivative".

(1.2) Meaning of "dealer" for purposes of Parts XV and XVI and s. 133 — For the purposes of Parts XV and XVI and section 133,

"dealer" means a person or company that trades in securities in the capacity of principal or agent.

OSA 1(1.2)

Definitions: OSA 1(1)"dealer".

(2) Affiliated companies — A company shall be deemed to be an affiliate of another company if one of them is the subsidiary of the other or if both are subsidiaries of the same company or if each of them is controlled by the same person or company.

OSA 1(2)

Related Provisions: OSA 89(2).

(3) Controlled companies — A company shall be deemed to be controlled by another person or company or by two or more companies if,

(a) voting securities of the first-mentioned company carrying more than 50 per cent of the votes for the election of directors are held, otherwise than by way of security only, by or for the benefit of the other person or company or by or for the benefit of the other companies; and

(b) the votes carried by such securities are entitled, if exercised, to elect a majority of the board of directors of the first-mentioned company.

OSA 1(3)

Related Provisions: OSA 89(3).

(4) Subsidiary companies — A company shall be deemed to be a subsidiary of another company if,

(a) it is controlled by,

(i) that other, or

(ii) that other and one or more companies each of which is controlled by that other, or

(iii) two or more companies each of which is controlled by that other; or

(b) it is a subsidiary of a company that is that other's subsidiary.

OSA 1(4)

Related Provisions: OSA 89(1).

(5) Beneficial ownership of securities — A person shall be deemed to own beneficially securities beneficially owned by a company controlled by the person or by an affiliate of such company.

(6) Idem — A company shall be deemed to own beneficially securities beneficially owned by its affiliates.

(7) Insider of mutual fund — Every management company and every distribution company of a mutual fund that is a reporting issuer and every insider of such management company or distribution company shall be deemed to be an insider of the mutual fund.

(8) [Repealed 2006, c. 33, Sched. Z.5, s. 1(8).]

(9) [Repealed 2006, c. 33, Sched. Z.5, s. 1(8).]

(10) Relieving orders — If the Commission is satisfied that it would not be prejudicial to the public interest, it may make an order that, for the purposes of Ontario securities law,

(a) a person or company is not,

(i) an insider, or

(ii) a reporting issuer;

(b) a contract or instrument is not a derivative; or

(c) a derivative is not a designated derivative.

OSA 1(10)

Definitions: OSA 1(1)"reporting issuer"; OSA 1(1)"insider"; OSA 1(1)"derivative"; OSA 1(1)"designated derivative".

Rules: Rule 13-502, App. C, Item E(4).

Policies and Orders: OPS 2.1; BOR 1.2, 1.3; CSAN 12-307; OSCN 12-703.

(11) Designation — If the Commission considers that it is in the public interest, it may make an order that, for purposes of Ontario securities law,

(a) a person or company is an insider of a reporting issuer if the person or company would reasonably be expected to have, in the ordinary course, access to material information about the business, operations, assets or revenues of the issuer;

(b) a person or company is a reporting issuer; or

(c) a derivative is a designated derivative.

OSA 1(11)

Definitions: OSA 1(1)"reporting issuer"; OSA 1(1)"insider"; OSA 1(1)"derivative"; OSA 1(1)"designated derivative".

Rules: Rule 13-502, App. C, Item E.1.

Policies and Orders: OPS 12-602, 2.1.

(12) Terms and conditions — An order under subsection (10) may be made subject to such terms and conditions as the Commission may impose.

(13) Who may apply — An order under subsection (10) or (11) may be made on application by an interested person or by the Director.

(14) Hearing — The Commission shall not make an order under subsection (10) or (11) without giving the person or company that would be subject to the order an opportunity to be heard.

(15) Extended meaning for purposes of subs. (14) — A person or company that is a party to a contract, instrument or derivative referred to in clause (10)(b) or (c) or (11)(c) is deemed, for the purpose of subsection (14), to be a person or company that would be subject to an order made under subsection (10) or (11).

1994, c. 11, s. 350; 1994, c. 33, s. 1; 1997, c. 19, ss. 23(1), 34; 1999, c. 6, s. 60(1); 1999, c. 9, s. 193; 2001, c. 23, s. 209; 2002, c. 22, s. 177; 2004, c. 31, Sched. 34, s. 1; 2005, c. 5, s. 64(1); 2006, c. 8, s. 144; 2006, c. 33, Sched. Z.5, s. 1; 2007, c. 7, Sched. 38, s. 1; 2009, c. 18, Sched. 26, s. 1; 2010, c. 1, Sched. 26, s. 1; 2010, c. 26, Sched. 18, s. 1(2)–(4), (6)–(12), (14)–(21); 2014, c. 7, Sched. 28, s. 1; 2015, c. 38, Sched. 18, s. 1

1.1 Purposes — The purposes of this Act are,

(a) to provide protection to investors from unfair, improper or fraudulent practices; and

(b) to foster fair and efficient capital markets and confidence in capital markets.

1994, c. 33, s. 2

PART I — THE COMMISSION (SS. 2–3.12)

2. [Repealed 1997, c. 10, s. 36.]

2.1 Principles to consider — In pursuing the purposes of this Act, the Commission shall have regard to the following fundamental principles:

1. Balancing the importance to be given to each of the purposes of this Act may be required in specific cases.

2. The primary means for achieving the purposes of this Act are,

　　i. requirements for timely, accurate and efficient disclosure of information,

　　ii. restrictions on fraudulent and unfair market practices and procedures, and

　　iii. requirements for the maintenance of high standards of fitness and business conduct to ensure honest and responsible conduct by market participants.

3. Effective and responsive securities regulation requires timely, open and efficient administration and enforcement of this Act by the Commission.

4. The Commission should, subject to an appropriate system of supervision, use the enforcement capability and regulatory expertise of recognized self-regulatory organizations.

5. The integration of capital markets is supported and promoted by the sound and responsible harmonization and co-ordination of securities regulation regimes.

6. Business and regulatory costs and other restrictions on the business and investment activities of market participants should be proportionate to the significance of the regulatory objectives sought to be realized.

1994, c. 33, s. 2

2.2 Authority in extraordinary circumstances — **(1) Notice to Minister** — The Commission shall notify the Minister if, in its opinion, there are extraordinary circumstances that may require immediate action to be taken under this section in the public interest.

(2) Criteria — For the purposes of this section, each of the following events constitutes extraordinary circumstances:

1. A major market disturbance characterized by or constituting sudden fluctuations of securities prices that threaten fair and orderly capital markets.

2. A major market disturbance characterized by or constituting a substantial disruption in the system for clearance and settlement of transactions.

3. A major disruption in the functioning of capital markets or of a significant segment of the markets, including a major disruption in the availability of capital to market participants.

4. A major disruption in the transmission, execution or processing of securities transactions.

5. A substantial threat of such a major market disturbance or major disruption.

(3) Order to suspend trading — The Commission may, without notice or a hearing, make an order under this subsection to suspend trading in a security or related derivative or to suspend all trading on a recognized exchange or otherwise,

(a) if, in the opinion of the Commission, there are extraordinary circumstances requiring immediate action to be taken in the public interest; and

(b) if, in the opinion of the Commission, the order is necessary to maintain or restore fair and orderly securities markets, to ensure prompt, accurate and safe clearance and settlement of transactions in securities or to assist in doing so in another jurisdiction.

(4) Terms and conditions — The order may be subject to such terms and conditions as the Commission may impose.

(5) Duration of order — The order takes effect immediately and expires no later than 10 days after the day on which it is made.

(6) Notice and publication of order — The Commission shall promptly issue a news release describing the details of the order and shall publish the order in its Bulletin.

(7) Opportunity to be heard — The Commission shall give an opportunity to be heard to persons and companies who are directly affected by the order and who consider themselves aggrieved by it, and the opportunity to be heard may be oral or in writing in the discretion of the Commission.

(8) Revocation or variation of order — The Commission may make an order revoking or varying the order under subsection (3) but cannot vary it to provide for an expiry later than the date specified in subsection (5).

(9) Commission regulation — Subject to the approval of the Minister, the Commission may make a regulation relating to any matter governed by Ontario securities law, despite any other provision of this Act,

(a) if, in the opinion of the Commission, there are extraordinary circumstances requiring immediate action to be taken in the public interest; and

(b) if, in the opinion of the Commission, the regulation is necessary to maintain or restore fair and orderly securities markets, to ensure prompt, accurate and safe clearance and settlement of transactions in securities or to assist in doing so in another jurisdiction.

(10) Same — The Commission is not precluded from making a regulation under subsection (9) that has substantially the same effect as an order previously made under subsection (3) in respect of the same extraordinary circumstances.

(11) Duration of regulation — Upon being approved by the Minister, the regulation comes into force immediately, despite section 22 of the *Legislation Act, 2006*, and it is revoked no later than 30 days after the day on which it comes into force.

(12) Extension of duration of regulation — Despite subsection (11), an amendment to the regulation may provide that it remains in effect for a further period of up to 30 days, and the regulation may be so amended more than once.

(13) Notice and publication of regulation — When the regulation comes into force, the Commission shall promptly issue a news release describing the details of the regulation and shall publish the regulation in its Bulletin together with a statement setting out the substance and purpose of the regulation and the nature of the extraordinary circumstances.

(14) Same, amendment of regulation — Subsection (13) applies, with necessary modifications, with respect to any amendment to the regulation.

(15) Additional information — As soon as practicable after the regulation comes into force, the Commission shall publish in its Bulletin a description of the particular circumstances upon which the Commission based its decision to make the regulation.

(16) Regulation of the L.G. in C. — The Lieutenant Governor in Council may make a regulation relating to any matter governed by Ontario securities law, despite any other provision of this Act,

(a) if, in the opinion of the Lieutenant Governor in Council, there are extraordinary circumstances requiring immediate action to be taken in the public interest; and

(b) if, in the opinion of the Lieutenant Governor in Council, the regulation is necessary to maintain or restore fair and orderly securities markets, to ensure prompt, accurate and safe clearance and settlement of transactions in securities or to assist in doing so in another jurisdiction.

(17) Regulation of L.G. in C. prevails — A regulation made under subsection (16) prevails over a regulation made under subsection (9), and a regulation made under subsection (16) may revoke a regulation made under subsection (9).

(18) Interpretation — This section does not limit the authority of the Commission under any other section of this Act.

2009, c. 18, Sched. 26, s. 2; 2010, c. 26, Sched. 18, s. 2

3. (1) Commission continued — The Ontario Securities Commission is continued as a corporation without share capital under the name Ontario Securities Commission in English and Commission des valeurs mobilières de l'Ontario in French.

(2) Composition — The Commission is composed of at least nine and not more than 16 members.

(3) Deficiency in number — If there are fewer than nine but at least two members in office, the Commission shall be deemed to be properly constituted for a period not exceeding 90 days after the deficiency in the number of members first occurs.

(4) Appointment — The members shall be appointed by the Lieutenant Governor in Council for such term of office not exceeding five years as the Lieutenant Governor in Council determines. A member may be reappointed.

(5) Chair and Vice-Chairs — The Lieutenant Governor in Council shall, by order, designate a member of the Commission as Chair and may designate up to three members as Vice-Chairs.

(6) Same — The Chair and each Vice-Chair holds office for the term specified by the Lieutenant Governor in Council which shall not exceed his or her term as a member of the Commission.

(7) Duties of Chair — The Chair is the chief executive officer of the Commission and shall devote his or her full time to the work of the Commission.

(8) Duties of members — The members (other than the Chair) shall devote such time as may be necessary for the due performance of their duties as members.

(9) Protection from liability — A member is not liable for an act, an omission, an obligation or a liability of the Commission or its employees. A member is not liable for any act that in good faith is done or omitted in the performance or intended performance of his or her duties as a member of the Commission under this or any other Act.

(10) Acting Chair — If the office of Chair is vacant or if the Chair is absent or is unable to act for any reason, a Vice-Chair shall act as Chair.

(11) Quorum — Two members of the Commission constitute a quorum.

(12) Crown agency — The Commission is an agent of Her Majesty in right of Ontario, and its powers may be exercised only as an agent of Her Majesty.

1997, c. 10, s. 37; 2009, c. 34, Sched. S, s. 1; 2012, c. 8, Sched. 55, s. 1

3.1 (1) Board of directors — The Commission shall have a board of directors composed of the members of the Commission.

(2) Duties — The board of directors shall oversee the management of the financial and other affairs of the Commission.

(3) Presiding officer — The Chair shall preside over board meetings and, in his or her absence, a Vice-Chair shall do so. In the absence of the Chair and Vice-Chairs, the members in attendance may appoint one of their number to preside at a meeting.

(4) Meetings — Subject to the by-laws of the Commission, the board of directors may meet at any place in Canada.

1997, c. 10, s. 37

3.2 (1) Powers of the Commission — The Commission has the capacity and the rights, powers and privileges of a natural person.

(2) Duties — The Commission is responsible for the administration of this Act and shall perform the duties assigned to it under this Act and any other Act.

(3) By-laws — Subject to the approval of the Minister, the Commission may make by-laws,

    (a) governing the administration, management and conduct of the affairs of the Commission;

    (b) governing the appointment of an auditor;

    (c) setting out the powers, functions and duties of the Chair, each Vice-Chair and the officers employed by the Commission;

    (d) delegating to employees of the Commission the exercise or performance of any power or duty conferred or imposed on an officer of the Commission under this Act and fixing the terms or conditions of the delegation;

    (e) governing the remuneration and benefits of the Chair, each Vice-Chair and the other members of the Commission;

    (f) governing the time, place and method for holding meetings of the board of directors and the procedure at such meetings;

    (g) governing the appointment, operation or dissolution of committees of the board of directors and delegating duties of the board to the committees; and

    (h) governing the refund of fees paid to the Commission under this or any other Act and authorizing employees of the Commission to approve refunds subject to such conditions and in such circumstances as the Commission considers appropriate.

(4) Notice to Minister — The Commission shall deliver to the Minister a copy of every by-law passed by it.

(5) Minister's review — Within 60 days after delivery of the by-law, the Minister may approve, reject or return it to the Commission for further consideration.

(6) Effect of approval — A by-law that is approved by the Minister becomes effective on the date of the approval or on such later date as the by-law may provide.

(7) Effect of rejection — A by-law that is rejected by the Minister does not become effective.

(8) Effect of return for further consideration — A by-law that is returned to the Commission for further consideration does not become effective under the Commission returns it to the Minister and the Minister approves it.

(9) Expiry of review period — If within the 60-day period the Minister does not approve, reject or return the by-law for further consideration, the by-law becomes effective on the 75th day after it is delivered to the Minister or on such later date as the by-law may provide.

(10) Publication — The Commission shall publish the by-law in its Bulletin as soon as practicable after the by-law becomes effective.

(11) Part III (Regulations) of the *Legislation Act, 2006* not to apply — Part III (Regulations) of the *Legislation Act, 2006* does not apply to by-laws made by the Commission.

1997, c. 10, s. 37; 2006, c. 21, Sched. F, s. 136(1), Table 1

3.3 (1) Borrowing power — The Commission shall not, without the approval of the Lieutenant Governor in Council, borrow money, pledge, mortgage or hypothecate any of its property, or create or give a security interest in any of its property.

(2) Short term loans permitted — Despite subsection (1), the Commission may borrow money for periods of not more than two years to meet the short term needs of the Commission, and shall do so only on such terms and conditions, whether with or without security, as the Minister may approve.

(3) Purchases and loans by Province — The Minister, on behalf of Ontario, may purchase securities of or make loans to the Commission in such amounts, at such times and on such terms and conditions as the Lieutenant Governor in Council considers expedient.

(4) Same — The Minister may pay from the Consolidated Revenue Fund the money necessary for a purchaser or loan made under subsection (3).

1997, c. 10, s. 37

3.4 (0.1) Fees — The Commission may collect and enforce the payment of such fees as may be prescribed by the regulations.

(1) Authority re income — Despite the *Financial Administration Act*, the fees payable to the Commission under this or any other Act, the revenue from the exercise of a power conferred or the discharge of a duty imposed on the Commission under this or any other Act, and the investments held by the Commission do not form part of the Consolidated Revenue Fund and, subject to this section, shall be applied to carrying out the powers conferred and duties imposed on the Commission under this or any other Act.

(2) Exceptions — The Commission shall pay into the Consolidated Revenue Fund money received by the Commission pursuant to an order under paragraph 9 or 10 of subsection 127(1) of this Act or paragraph 9 or 10 of subsection 60(1) of the *Commodity Futures Act* or as a payment to settle enforcement proceedings commenced by the Commission, other than money,

    (a) to reimburse the Commission for costs incurred or to be incurred by it; or

    (b) that is designated under the terms of the order or settlement,

        (i) for allocation to or for the benefit of third parties, or

        (ii) for use by the Commission for the purpose of educating investors or promoting or otherwise enhancing knowledge and information of persons regarding the operation of the securities and financial markets.

(2.1) Same — The Minister may establish guidelines respecting the allocation of money received by the Commission pursuant to an order described in subsection (2) or money received by the Commission as a payment to settle enforcement proceedings commenced by the Commission.

(3) Surplus — When ordered to do so by the Minister, the Commission shall pay into the Consolidated Revenue Fund such of its surplus funds as are determined by the Minister.

(4) Same — In determining the amount of a payment to be made under subsection (3), the Minister shall allow such reserves for the future needs of the Commission as he or she considers appropriate, and shall ensure that the payment will not impair the Commission's ability to pay its liabilities, to meet its obligations as they become due or to fulfil its contractual commitments.

1997, c. 10, s. 37; 2002, c. 22, s. 178; 2004, c. 31, Sched. 34, s. 2; 2009, c. 18, Sched. 26, s. 3; 2012, c. 8, Sched. 55, s. 2

OSA 3.4

Related Provisions: OSA 127.

3.5 (1) Powers re hearings — The Commission may hold hearings in or outside Ontario.

(2) Joint hearings — The Commission may hold hearings in conjunction with other bodies empowered by statute to administer or regulate trading in securities, derivatives or commodities, and may consult with those bodies during the course of, or in connection with, the hearing.

OSA 3.5(2)

Rules: Rules of Procedure 13.

(3) Powers of one commissioner — Despite subsection 3(11) and subject to subsection (4), any two or more members of the Commission may in writing authorize one member of the Commission to exercise any of the powers and perform any of the duties of the Commission, including the power to conduct contested hearings on the merits, and a decision of the member shall have the same force and effect as if made by the Commission.

OSA 3.5(3)
Policies and Orders: BOR 1.4, 1.5.

(4) Eligibility to sit on hearing — No member who exercises a power or performs a duty of the Commission under Part VI except section 17 in respect of a matter under investigation or examination shall sit on a hearing by the Commission that deals with the matter, except with the written consent of the parties to the proceeding.

1997, c. 10, s. 37; 1999, c. 9, s. 194; 2010, c. 26, Sched. 18, s. 3; 2011, c. 9, Sched. 38, s. 1

OSA 3.5(4)
Policies and Orders: BOR 1.4.

3.6 (1) Commission staff — The Commission may employ such persons as it considers necessary to enable it effectively to perform its duties and exercise its powers under this or any other Act.

(2) Officers — The Commission shall appoint from among its employees an Executive Director and a Secretary as officers of the Commission, and may appoint from among its employees such other officers as it considers necessary.

(3) Status of members — The members of the Commission are not its employees, and the Chair and Vice-Chairs shall not hold any other office in the Commission or be employed by it in any other capacity.

(4) Conflict of interest, indemnification — Sections 132 (conflict of interest) and 136 (indemnification) of the *Business Corporations Act* apply with necessary modifications with respect to the Commission as if the Minister were its sole shareholder.

(5) [Repealed 2006, c. 35, Sched. C, s. 121.]

(6) Public Service Pension Plan not to apply — The Public Service Pension Plan established under the *Public Service Pension Act* does not apply to the members and employees of the Commission, except as authorized by order of the Lieutenant Governor in Council.

(7) Agreement for services — The Commission and a ministry of the Crown may enter into agreements for the provision by employees of the Crown of any service required by the Commission to carry out its duties and powers. The Commission shall pay the agreed amount for services provide to it.

1997, c. 10, s. 37; 2006, c. 35, Sched. C, s. 121

3.7 (1) Memorandum of understanding — Every five years beginning with the Commission's 1998-99 fiscal year, the Commission and the Minister shall enter into a memorandum of understanding setting out,

(a) the respective roles and responsibilities of the Minister and the Chair;

(b) the accountability relationship between the Commission and the Minister;

(c) the responsibility of the Commission to provide to the Minister business plans, operational budgets and plans for proposed significant changes in the operations or activities of the Commission; and

(d) and other matter that the Minister may require.

(2) Same — The Commission shall comply with the memorandum of understanding in exercising its powers and performing its duties under this Act, but the failure to do so does not affect the validity of any action taken by the Commission or give rise to any rights or remedies by any person.

(3) Publication of memorandum — The Commission shall publish the memorandum of understanding in its Bulletin as soon as practicable after the memorandum is entered into.

1997, c. 10, s. 37

OSA 3.7
Policies and Orders: IA 9.

3.8 (1) Minister's request for information — The Commission shall promptly give the Minister such information about its activities, operations and financial affairs as the Minister requests.

(2) Examination — The Minister may designate a person to examine any financial or accounting procedures, activities or practices of the Commission. The person designated shall do so and report the results of the examination to the Minister.

(3) Duty to assist, etc. — The members and employees of the Commission shall give the person designated by the Minister all the assistance and co-operation necessary to enable him or her to complete the examination.

1997, c. 10, s. 37

3.9 (1) Fiscal year — The fiscal year of the Commission begins on April 1.

(2) Financial statements — The Commission shall prepare annual financial statements in accordance with generally accepted accounting principles. The financial statements must present the financial position, financial performance and changes in the financial position of the Commission for its most recent fiscal year.

(3) Auditors — The Commission shall appoint one or more auditors licensed under the *Public Accounting Act, 2004* to audit the financial statements of the Commission for each fiscal year.

(4) Auditor General — The Auditor General may also audit the financial statements of the Commission.

1997, c. 10, s. 37; 2004, c. 8, s. 46; 2004, c. 17, s. 32, Table; 2010, c. 1, Sched. 26, s. 2

3.10 (1) Annual report — Within six months after the end of each fiscal year, the Commission shall deliver to the Minister an annual report, including the Commission's audited financial statements, on the affairs of the Commission for that fiscal year.

(2) Report to be laid before Assembly — Within one month after receiving the Commission's annual report, the Minister shall lay the report before the Assembly by delivering the report to the Clerk.

(3) Review by standing or select committee — After the annual report is laid before the Assembly, a standing or select committee of the Assembly shall be empowered to review the report and to report the committee's opinions and recommendations to the Assembly.

1997, c. 10, s. 37; 2005, c. 31, Sched. 20, s. 1

3.11 Collection of personal information — The Commission may collect personal information within the meaning of section 38 of the *Freedom of Information and Protection of Privacy Act* for the purpose of carrying out its duties and exercising its powers under this or any other Act.

1997, c. 10, s. 37

3.12 Non-application of certain Acts — The *Corporations Act* and the *Corporations Information Act* do not apply with respect to the Commission.

Proposed Amendment — Conditional Amendment — 3.12

On the coming into force of S.O. 2010, c. 15, s. 4(1) [Not in force at date of publication.], s. 3.12 is replaced with the following:

> 3.12 Non-application of certain Acts — The *Not-for-Profit Corporations Act, 2010* and the *Corporations Information Act* do not apply with respect to the Commission.

2012, c. 8, Sched. 55, s. 3 [Conditions not yet satisfied.]

1997, c. 10, s. 37

PART II — (S. 4)

[Heading repealed 2009, c. 34, Sched. S, s. 2.]

4. [Repealed 2009, c. 34, Sched. S, s. 2.]

PART III — APPOINTMENT OF EXPERTS (S. 5)

5. (1) Appointment of experts — The Commission may appoint one or more experts to assist the Commission in such manner as it may consider expedient.

(2) Submissions to experts — The Commission may submit any agreement, prospectus, financial statement, report or other document to one or more experts appointed under subsection (1) for examination, and the Commission has the like power to summon and enforce the attendance of witnesses before the expert and to compel them to produce documents, records and things as is vested in the Commission, and subsection 13(1) applies with necessary modifications.

(3) Payment of experts — An expert appointed under subsection (1) shall be paid such amounts for services and expenses as the Lieutenant Governor in Council may determine.

1994, c. 11, s. 353

OSA 5

Definitions: OSA 1(1)"Commission".

Policies and Orders: BOR 1.4.

PART IV — EXECUTIVE DIRECTOR AND SECRETARY (SS. 6, 7)

6. (1) Executive Director — There shall be an Executive Director of the Commission.

(2) Chief administrative officer — Subject to the direction of the Commission, the Executive Director is the chief administrative officer of the Commission.

(3) Assignment of powers and duties — A quorum of the Commission may assign any of its powers and duties under this Act, except powers and duties under section 8 and Part VI, to the Executive Director or to another Director.

(4) Same — The Executive Director may assign any of his or her powers and duties to another Director, other than powers and duties assigned to the Executive Director by the Commission.

(5) Revocation of assignment — The Commission may revoke, in whole or in part, an assignment of powers and duties made under subsection (3) and the Executive Director may revoke, in whole or in part, an assignment of powers and duties made under subsection (4).

(6) Terms and conditions — An assignment under this section may be subject to such terms and conditions as are set out in the assignment.

(7) Absence or incapacity of Executive Director — If the Executive Director is absent or incapable of acting, the Commission may designate another individual to act as Executive Director.

1994, c. 11, s. 354; 1997, c. 10, s. 38

OSA 6

Related Provisions: OSA 7, 8, 11–17, 25, 26, 31, 38(3), 50(3), 51, 58, 59, 61(1), 61(2), 61(4), 63(4), 64(1), 64(2), 68, 141(1).

Definitions: OSA 1(1)"Director"; 1(1)"Commission".

Policies and Orders: BOR 1.2, 1.3.

7. (1) Secretary — There shall be a Secretary to the Commission.

(2) Powers and duties — The Secretary,

   (a) may accept service of all notices and other documents on behalf of the Commission;

   (b) when authorized by the Commission, may sign a decision made by the Commission as a result of a hearing;

   (c) may certify under his or her hand a decision made by the Commission or a document, record or thing used in connection with a hearing by the Commission if certification is required for a purpose other than that stated in subsection 9(3);

   (d) may exercise such other powers as are vested in the Secretary by this Act or the regulations; and

   (e) shall perform such duties as are imposed on the Secretary by this Act or the regulations or by the Commission.

(3) Acting Secretary — If the Secretary is absent for any reason, the Commission may designate another individual to act in the capacity of Secretary and the individual designated has all the powers and duties of the Secretary.

(4) Certification by Secretary — A certificate purporting to be signed by the Secretary is, without proof of the office or signature, admissible in evidence, so far as it is revlevant, for all purposes in any action, prosecution or other proceeding.

1994, c. 11, s. 354

OSA 7

Definitions: OSA 1(1)"person"; 1(1)"company".

Policies and Orders: BOR 1.1, 1.5.

PART V — ADMINISTRATIVE PROCEEDINGS, REVIEWS AND APPEALS (SS. 8–10)

8. (1) Review of decision — Within 30 days after a decision of the Director, the Commission may notify the Director and any person or company directly affected of its intention to convene a hearing to review the decision.

OSA 8(1)

Related Provisions: OSA 26, 61.

Definitions: OSA 1(1)"decision".

(2) Review of Director's decisions — Any person or company directly affected by a decision of the Director may, by notice in writing sent by registered mail to the Commission within thirty days after the mailing of the notice of the decision, request and be entitled to a hearing and review thereof by the Commission.

(3) Power on review — Upon a hearing and review, the Commission may by order confirm the decision under review or make such other decision as the Commission considers proper.

(4) Stay — Despite the fact that a person or company requests a hearing and review under subsection (2), the decision under review takes effect immediately, but the Commission may grant a stay until disposition of the hearing and review.

1994, c. 11, s. 355; 1999, c. 9, s. 195

OSA 8(4)

Related Provisions: OSA 3(4).

OSA 8

Definitions: OSA 1(1)"decision"; 1(1)"Director"; 1(1)"Commission"; 1(1)"person"; 1(1)"company".

Rules: Rules of Procedure 2.2, 14.

9. (1) Appeal — A person or company directly affected by a final decision of the Commission, other than a decision under section 74, may appeal to the Divisional Court within thirty days after the later of the making of the final decision or the issuing of the reasons for the final decision.

OSA 9(1)

Related Provisions: 74.

Definitions: OSA 1(1)"decision".

(2) Stay — Despite the fact that an appeal is taken under this section, the decision appealed from takes effect immediately, but the Commission or the Divisional Court may grant a stay until disposition of the appeal.

(3) Certification of documents — The Secretary shall certify to the Divisional Court,

(a) the decision that has been reviewed by the Commission;

(b) the decision of the Commission, together with any statement of reasons therefor;

(c) the record of the proceedings before the Commission; and

(d) all written submissions to the Commission or other material that is relevant to the appeal.

(4) Respondent on appeal — The Commission is the respondent to an appeal under this section.

(4.1) Minister — The Minister is entitled to be heard by counsel or otherwise on the argument of an appeal under this section, whether or not the Minister is named as a party to the appeal.

(5) Powers of court on appeal — Where an appeal is taken under this section, the court may by its order direct the Commission to make such decision or to do such other act as the Commission is authorized and empowered to do under this Act or the regulations and as the court considers proper, having regard to the material and submissions before it and to this Act and the regulations, and the Commission shall make such decision or do such act accordingly.

(6) Further decisions — Despite an order of the court on an appeal, the Commission may make any further decision upon new material or where there is a significant change in the circumstances, and every such decision is subject to this section.

1994, c. 11, s. 356

OSA 9

Related Provisions: OSA 74.

Definitions: OSA 1(1)"person"; 1(1)"company"; 1(1)"decision"; 1(1)"Minister".

Rules: Rules of Procedure 2.3, 15.

10. [Repealed 1994, c. 11, s. 357.]

PART VI — INVESTIGATIONS AND EXAMINATIONS (SS. 11–18)

11. (1) Investigation order — The Commission may, by order, appoint one or more persons to make such investigation with respect to a matter as it considers expedient,

(a) for the due administration of Ontario securities law or the regulation of the capital markets in Ontario; or

(b) to assist in the due administration of the securities or derivatives laws or the regulation of the capital markets in another jurisdiction.

(2) Contents of order — An order under this section shall describe the matter to be investigated.

(3) Scope of investigation — For the purposes of an investigation under this section, a person appointed to make the investigation may investigate and inquire into,

(a) the affairs of the person or company in respect of which the investigation is being made, including any trades, communications, negotiations, transactions, investigations, loans, borrowings or payments to, by, on behalf of, or in relation to or connected with the person or company and any property, assets or things owned, acquired or alienated in whole or in part by the person or company or by any other person or company acting on behalf of or as agent for the person or company; and

(b) the assets at any time held, the liabilities, debts, undertakings and obligations at any time existing, the financial or other conditions at any time prevailing in or in relation to or in connection with the person or company, and any relationship that may at any time exist or have existed between the person or company and any other person or company by reason of investments, commissions promised, secured or paid, interests held or acquired, the loaning or borrowing of money, stock or other property, the transfer, negotiation or holding of stock, interlocking directorates, common control, undue influence or control or any other relationship.

(4) Right to examine — For the purposes of an investigation under this section, a person appointed to make the investigation may examine any documents or other things, whether they are in the possession or control of the person or company in respect of which the investigation is ordered or of any other person or company.

(5) Minister may order investigation — Despite subsection (1), the Minister may, by order, appoint one or more persons to make such investigation as the Minister considers expedient,

(a) for the due administration of Ontario securities law or the regulation of the capital markets in Ontario; or

(b) to assist in the due administration of the securities or derivatives laws or the regulation of the capital markets in another jurisdiction.

(6) Same — A person appointed under subsection (5) has, for the purpose of the investigation, the same authority, powers, rights and privileges as a person appointed under subsection (1).

1994, c. 11, s. 358; 2010, c. 26, Sched. 18, s. 4

OSA 11

Related Provisions: OSA 16, 127.

Definitions: OSA 1(1)"Commission"; 1(1)"person"; 1(1)"company"; 1(1)"Ontario securities law"; 1(1)"derivative".

ACT

Policies and Orders: BOR 1.4.

12. (1) Financial examination order — The Commission may, by order, appoint one or more persons to make such examination of the financial affairs of a market participant as it considers expedient,

    (a) for the due administration of Ontario securities law or the regulation of the capital markets in Ontario; or

    (b) to assist in the due administration of the securities or derivatives laws or the regulation of the capital markets in another jurisdiction.

(2) Contents of order — An order under subsection (1) shall describe the matter to be examined.

(3) Right to examine — For the purposes of an examination under this seciton, a person appointed to conduct the examination may examine any documents or other things, whether they are in the possession or control of the market participant or any other person or company.

1994, c. 11, s. 358; 2010, c. 26, Sched. 18, s. 5

OSA 12

Related Provisions: OSA 16.

Definitions: OSA 1(1)"Commission"; 1(1)"market participant"; 1(1)"person"; 1(1)"company".

Policies and Orders: BOR 1.4.

13. (1) Power of investigator or examiner — A person making an investigation or examination under section 11 or 12 has the same power to summon and enforce the attendance of any person and to compel him or her to testify on oath or otherwise, and to summon and compel any person or company to produce documents and other things, as is vested in the Superior Court of Justice for the trial of civil actions, and the refusal of a person to attend or to answer questions or of a person or company to produce such documents or other things as are in his, her or its custody or possession makes the person or company liable to be committed for contempt by the Superior Court of Justice as if in breach of an order of that court.

(2) Rights of witness — A person or company giving evidence under subsection (1) may be represented by counsel and may claim any privilege to which the person or company is entitled.

(3) Inspection — A person making an investigation or examination under section 11 or 12 may, on production of the order appointing him or her, enter the business premises of any person or company named in the order during business hours and inspect any documents or other things that are used in the business of that person or company and that relate to the matters specified in the order, except those maintained by a lawyer in respect of his or her client's affairs.

(4) Authorization to search — A person making an investigation or examination under section 11 or 12 may apply to a judge of the Ontario Court of Justice in the absence of the public and without notice for an order authorizing the person or persons named in the order to enter and search any building, receptacle or place specified and to seize anything described in the authorization that is found in the building, receptacle or place and to bring it before the judge granting the authorization or another judge to be dealt with by him or her according to law.

(5) Grounds — No authorization shall be granted under subsection (4) unless the judge to whom the application is made is satisfied on information under oath that there are reasonable and probable grounds to believe that there may be in the building, receptacle or place to be searched anything that may reasonably relate to the order made under section 11 or 12.

(6) Power to enter, search and seize — A person named in an order under subsection (4) may, on production of the order, enter any building, receptacle or place specified in the order between 6 a.m. and 9 p.m., search for and seize anything specified in the order, and use as much force as is reasonably necessary for that purpose.

(7) Expiration — Every order under subsection (4) shall name the date that it expires, and the date shall be not later than fifteen days after the order is granted.

(8) Application — Section 159 and 160 of the *Provincial Offences Act* apply to searches and seizures under this section with such modifications as the circumstances require.

(9) Private residences — For the purpose of subsections (4), (5) and (6), "building, receptacle or place" does not include a private residence.

1994, c. 11, s. 358; 2006, c. 19, Sched. C, s. 1(1), (2)

OSA 13

Related Provisions: OSA 11, 12, 16, 17(3), 17(6), 122.

Definitions: OSA 1(1)"person"; 1(1)"company".

Regulations: Reg.: Form 1.

14. (1) Copying — Anything seized or produced under this Part shall be made available for inspection and copying by the person or company from which it was obtained, if practicable.

(2) Return — Anything seized or produced under this Part shall be returned to the person or company from which it was obtained when,

    (a) retention is no longer necessary for the purposes of an investigation, examination, proceeding or prosecution; or

    (b) the Commission so orders.

1994, c. 11, s. 358

OSA 14

Definitions: OSA 1(1)"person"; 1(1)"company"; 1(1)"Commission".

15. (1) Report of investigation or examination — A person appointed under subsection 11(1) or 12(1) shall, at the request of the Chair of the Commission or of a member of the Commission involved in making the appointment, provide a report to the Chair or member, as the case may be, of any testimony given and any documents or other things obtained under section 13.

(2) Same — A person appointed under subsection 11(5) shall, at the request of the Chair of the Commission, provide a report to the Chair of any testimony given and any documents or other things obtained under section 13.

(3) Report privileged — A report provided under this section is privileged.

1994, c. 11, s. 358

OSA 15

Related Provisions: OSA 11(1), 12(1), 13, 11(5), 16.

Definitions: OSA 1(1)"Commission".

16. (1) Non — disclosure — Except in accordance with section 17, no person or company shall disclose at any time, except to his, her or its counsel,

(a) the nature or content of an order under section 11 or 12; or

(b) the name of any person examined or sought to be examined under section 13, any testimony given under section 13, any information obtained under section 13, the nature or content of any questions asked under section 13, the nature or content of any demands for the production of any document or other thing under section 13, or the fact that any document or other thing was produced under section 13.

(2) Confidentiality — If the Commission issues an order under section 11 or 12, all reports provided under section 15, all testimony given under section 13 and all documents and other things obtained under section 13 relating to the investigation or examination that is the subject of the order are for the exclusive use of the Commission or of such other regulator as the Commission may specify in the order, and shall not be disclosed or produced to any other person or company or in any other proceeding except as permitted under section 17.

1994, c. 11, s. 358; 2002, c. 18, Sched. H, s. 7

OSA 16

Related Provisions: OSA 17, 11, 12, 13, 15.

Definitions: OSA 1(1)"person"; 1(1)"company".

Policies and Orders: OSCN 15-703.

17. (1) Disclosure by Commission — If the Commission considers that it would be in the public interest, it may make an order authorizing the disclosure to any person or company of,

(a) the nature or content of an order under section 11 or 12;

(b) the name of any person examined or sought to be examined under section 13, any testimony given under section 13, any information obtained under section 13, the nature or content of any questions asked under section 13, the nature or content of any demands for the production of any document or other thing under section 13, or the fact that any document or other thing was produced under section 13; or

(c) all or part of a report provided under section 15.

(2) Opportunity to object — No order shall be made under subsection (1) unless the Commission has, where practicable, given reasonable notice and an opportunity to be heard to,

(a) persons and companies named by the Commission; and

(b) in the case of disclosure of testimony given or information obtained under section 13, the person or company that gave the testimony or from which the information was obtained.

(2.1) Order without notice — Despite subsection (2), if the Commission considers that it would be in the public interest, it may make an order without notice and without giving an opportunity to be heard authorizing the disclosure of the things described in clauses (1)(a) to (c) to any entity referred to in paragraph 1, 3, 4 or 5 of section 153.

(3) Disclosure to police — Without the written consent of the person from whom the testimony was obtained, no order shall be made under subsection (1) or (2.1) authorizing the disclosure of testimony given under subsection 13(1) to,

(a) a municipal, provincial, federal or other police force or to a member of a police force; or

(b) a person responsible for the enforcement of the criminal law of Canada or of any other country or jurisdiction.

(4) Terms and conditions — An order under subsection (1) or (2.1) may be subject to terms and conditions imposed by the Commission.

(5) Disclosure by court — A court having jurisdiction over a prosecution under the *Provincial Offences Act* initiated by the Commission may compel production to the court of any testimony given or any document or other thing obtained under section 13, and after inspecting the testimony, document or thing and providing all interested parties with an opportunity to be heard, the court may order the release of the testimony, document or thing to the defendant if the court determines that it is relevant to the prosecution, is not protected by privilege and is necessary to enable the defendant to make full answer and defence, but the making of an order under this subsection does not determine whether the testimony, document or thing is admissible in the prosecution.

(6) Disclosure in investigation or proceeding — A person appointed to make an investigation or examination under this Act may disclose or produce anything mentioned in subsection (1), but may do so only in connection with,

(a) a proceeding commenced or proposed to be commenced before the Commission or the Director under this Act; or

(b) an examination of a witness, including an examination of a witness under section 13.

(7) Disclosure to police — Without the written consent of the person from whom the testimony was obtained, no disclosure shall be made under subsection (6) of testimony given under subsection 13(1) to,

(a) a municipal, provincial, federal or other police force or to a member of a police force; or

(b) a person responsible for the enforcement of the criminal law of Canada or of any other country or jurisdiction.

1994, c. 11, s. 358; 1999, c. 9, s. 196; 2001, c. 23, s. 210; 2013, c. 2, Sched. 13, s. 1; 2016, c. 5, Sched. 26, s. 1

OSA 17

Related Provisions: OSA 11, 12, 13, 15, 16.

Definitions: OSA 1(1)"Commission".

Rules: Rules of Procedure.

Policies and Orders: BOR 1.4; OSCN 15-703.

18. Prohibition on use of compelled testimony — Testimony given under section 13 shall not be admitted in evidence against the person from whom the testimony was obtained in a prosecution for an offence under section 122 or in any other prosecution governed by the *Provincial Offences Act*.

1994, c. 11, s. 358

OSA 18

Related Provisions: OSA 13, 122.

OSA Part VI

Regulations: Reg.: 163.

Rules: Rules of Procedure 4.

PART VII — RECORD-KEEPING AND COMPLIANCE REVIEWS (SS. 19–20.1)

19. (1) Record-keeping — Every market participant shall keep the following records:

1. Such books, records and other documents as are necessary for the proper recording of its business transactions and financial affairs and the transactions that it executes on behalf of others.

2. Such books, records and other documents as may otherwise be required under Ontario securities law.

3. Such books, records and other documents as may reasonably be required to demonstrate compliance with Ontario securities law.

(2) Record of transaction — Without limiting the generality of subsection (1), every recognized exchange shall keep a record of the time at which each transaction on the recognized exchange took place and shall supply to any client of a member of the recognized exchange, on production of a written confirmation of a transaction with the member, particulars of the time at which the transaction took place and verification or otherwise of the matters set forth in the written confirmation.

(3) Provision of information to Commission — Every market participant shall deliver to the Commission at such time or times as the Commission or any member, employee or agent of the Commission may require,

(a) any of the books, records and documents that are required to be kept by the market participant under Ontario securities law; and

(b) except where prohibited by law, any filings, reports or other communications made to any other regulatory agency whether within or outside of Ontario.

1994, c. 11, s. 358; 1999, c. 9, s. 197; 2010, c. 26, Sched. 18, s. 6; 2015, c. 20, Sched. 39, s. 1

OSA 19

Definitions: OSA 1(1)"market participant"; 1(1)"recognized exchange"; 1(1)"Commission".

Rules: Rule 35-502, s. 3.3(2).

20. (1) Compliance reviews — The Commission may designate in writing one or more persons to review the books, records and documents of a market participant for the purpose of determining whether Ontario securities law is being complied with.

(1.1) [Repealed 2014, c. 7, Sched. 28, s. 2.]

(2) Same, exemption from prospectus requirement — The Commission may designate in writing one or more persons to review the books, records and documents of an issuer that has distributed securities in reliance on an exemption from the prospectus requirement for the purpose of determining whether the issuer has complied with the requirements, conditions and restrictions of the exemption relied on for the distribution.

(3) Same, derivatives — The Commission may designate in writing one or more persons for the purpose of reviewing the books, records and documents that are required to be kept by a person or company under the regulations with respect to derivatives.

(4) Powers of compliance reviewer — A person conducting a compliance review may, on production of his or her designation, do the following:

1. In respect of a compliance review under subsection (1) or (2),

   i. enter the business premises of any market participant or issuer referred to in subsection (2) during business hours, and

   ii. inquire into and examine the books, records and documents of the market participant or issuer, and make copies of the books, records and documents.

2. In respect of a compliance review under subsection (3),

   i. enter the business premises of any person or company during business hours, and

   ii. inquire into and examine the books, records and documents of the person or company that are required to be kept under the regulations with respect to derivatives, and make copies of the books, records and documents.

(5) Fees — A person or company in respect of which a compliance review is conducted under this section shall pay the Commission such fees as may be prescribed by the regulations.

1994, c. 11, s. 358; 2010, c. 26, Sched. 18, s. 7; 2014, c. 7, Sched. 28, s. 2

OSA 20

Related Provisions: OSA 19.

Definitions: OSA 1(1)"Commission"; 1(1)"market participant".

Policies and Orders: BOR 1.4; OSCN 11-758, 11-763, 33-724, 33-725, 33-728, 33-729, 33-730, 33-731, 33-732, 33-733, 33-734, 33-736.

20.1 (1) Continuous disclosure reviews — The Commission or any member, employee or agent of the Commission may conduct a review of the disclosures that have been made or that ought to have been made by a reporting issuer or mutual fund in Ontario, on a basis to be determined at the discretion of the Commission or the Director.

(1.1) Same, issuer other than reporting issuer or mutual fund in Ontario — The Commission or any member, employee or agent of the Commission may conduct a review of an issuer other than a reporting issuer or mutual fund in Ontario for the purpose of determining whether disclosure requirements under Ontario securities law applicable to the issuer are being complied with, on a basis to be determined at the discretion of the Commission or the Director.

(2) Information and documents — An issuer that is subject to a review under this section shall, at such time or times as the Commission or Director may require, deliver to the Commission or Director any information and documents relevant to the review.

(3) Freedom of Information and Protection of Privacy Act — Despite the *Freedom of Information and Protection of Privacy Act*, information and documents obtained pursuant to a review under this section are exempt from disclosure under that Act if the Commission determines that the information and documents should be maintained in confidence.

(4) Prohibition on certain representations — An issuer, or any person or company acting on behalf of an issuer, shall not make any representation, written or oral, that the Commission has in any way passed upon the merits of the disclosure record of the issuer.

2002, c. 22, s. 179; 2014, c. 7, Sched. 28, s. 3

OSA 20.1

Policies and Orders: OSCN 51-703, 51-706, 51-713, 51-716, 81-705, 81-709, 81-717; CSAN 51-310, 51-316, 51-332, 51-337, 51-339, 52-315, 52-325.

PART VIII — SELF-REGULATION (SS. 21–21.11)

21. (1) Exchanges — No person or company shall carry on business as an exchange in Ontario unless recognized by the Commission under this section.

(1.1) Exception, commodity futures exchange — Subsection (1) does not apply to a person or company with respect to carrying on business as a commodity futures exchange if the person or company is registered to do so under the *Commodity Futures Act*.

(2) Recognition — The Commission may, on the application of a person or company proposing to carry on business as an exchange in Ontario, recognize the person or company if the Commission is satisfied that to do so would be in the public interest.

(3) Same — A recognition under this section shall be made in writing and shall be subject to such terms and conditions as the Commission may impose.

(4) Standards and conduct — A recognized exchange shall regulate the operations and the standards of practice and business conduct of its members and their representatives in accordance with its by-laws, rules, regulations, policies, procedures, interpretations and practices.

(5) Commission's powers — The Commission may, if it considers it in the public interest, make any decision with respect to,

(a) the manner in which a recognized exchange carries on business;

(b) the trading of securities or derivatives on or through the facilities of a recognized exchange;

(c) any security or derivative listed or posted for trading on a recognized exchange;

(d) issuers, whose securities are listed or posted for trading on a recognized exchange, to ensure that they comply with Ontario securities law; or

(e) any by-law, rule, regulation, policy, procedure, interpretation or practice of a recognized exchange.

1994, c. 11, s. 358; 2010, c. 26, Sched. 18, s. 8

OSA 21

Definitions: OSA 1(1)"person"; 1(1)"company"; 1(1)"Commission"; 1(1)"recognized exchange"; 1(1)"trading"; 1(1)"security"; 1(1)"issuer".

Regulations: Reg.: 108, 110, 145.

Rules: Rule 13-502, App. B.1 and E.1.

Policies and Orders: BOR 1.2, 1.3; OSCN 21-705, 21-706, 21-707.

Recognitions: CNSX Markets. (2013) 36 O.S.C.B. 10881; Maple Group Acquisition Corporation, TMX Group Inc., TSX Inc., Alpha Trading Systems Limited Partnership, Alpha Trading Systems Inc., Alpha Market Services Inc. and Alpha Exchange Inc. (2012) 35 O.S.C.B. (Supp. 3) 5 as varied by 35 O.S.C.B. 11197.

Exemptions: Bourse de Montréal Inc.: (2012) 35 O.S.C.B. 7136; ICE Futures Canada, Inc.: (2012) 35 O.S.C.B. 8999; ICE Futures Europe: (2006) 29 O.S.C.B. 7223; ICE Futures U.S., Inc.: (2009) 32 O.S.C.B. 7378; Natural Gas Exchange Inc.: (2012) 35 O.S.C.B. 7173; TSX Venture Exchange Inc.: (2012) 35 O.S.C.B. 7088; various swap execution facilities: (2013) O.S.C.B. 9789-9854; SwapEx LLC: (2013) 36 O.S.C.B. 10679; ICAP Global Derivatives Limited: (2014) 37 O.S.C.B. 5095 (Interim).

21.0.1 Alternative trading systems — The Commission may, if it considers it in the public interest, make any decision with respect to,

(a) the manner in which an alternative trading system carries on business in Ontario;

(b) the trading of securities or derivatives on or through the facilities of the alternative trading system; or

(c) any by-law, rule, regulation, policy, procedure, interpretation or practice of the alternative trading system.

2010, c. 26, Sched. 18, s. 9

OSA 21.0.1

Rules: Rule 13-502, App. B.1 and E.2.

Policies and Orders: OSCN 21-705, 21-706.

21.1 (1) Self-regulatory organizations — The Commission may, on the application of a self-regulatory organization, recognize the self-regulatory organization if the Commission is satisfied that to do so would be in the public interest.

(2) Same — A recognition under this section shall be made in writing and shall be subject to such terms and conditions as the Commission may impose.

(3) Standards and conduct — A recognized self-regulatory organization shall regulate the operations and the standards of practice and business conduct of its members and their representatives in accordance with its by-laws, rules, regulations, policies, procedures, interpretations and practices.

(4) Commission's powers — The Commission may, if it is satisfied that to do so would be in the public interest, make any decision with respect to any by-law, rule, regulation, policy, procedure, interpretation or practice of a recognized self-regulatory organization.

1994, c. 11, s. 358

OSA 21.1(4)

Regulations: Reg.: 110.

Rules: Rule 13-502, App. C, Item E.

Policies and Orders: BOR 1.2, 1.3.

Recognitions: Investment Dealers Association: (2008) 31 O.S.C.B. 5675, surrendered (2014) 37 O.S.C.B. 3939; Investment Industry Regulatory Organization of Canada: (2010) 33 O.S.C.B. 5027; Market Regulation Services Inc.: (2008) 31 O.S.C.B. 5678; Mutual Fund Dealers Association: (2008) 31 O.S.C.B. 12002.

21.2 Clearing agencies — (0.1) Prohibition — No person or company shall carry on business in Ontario as a clearing agency unless the person or company is recognized by the Commission under this section as a clearing agency.

(1) Clearing agencies — The Commission may, on the application of a clearing agency, recognize the clearing agency if the Commission is satisfied that to do so would be in the public interest.

(2) Same — A recognition under this section shall be made in writing and shall be subject to such terms and conditions as the Commission may impose.

(3) Commission's powers — The Commission may make decisions with respect to any of the following matters if the Commission is satisfied that it is in the public interest to do so:

1. Any by-law, rule, regulation, policy, procedure, interpretation or practice of a recognized clearing agency.

2. The manner in which a recognized clearing agency carries on its business.

1994, c. 11, s. 358; 2005, c. 31, Sched. 20, s. 2

OSA 21.2

Definitions: OSA 1(1)"Commission"; 1(1)"clearing agency"; 1(1)"decision"; 1(1)"recognized clearing agency".

Rules: Rule 91-502, 13-502, App. B.1 and E.1.

Policies and Orders: OSCN 24-702; BOR 1.2, 1.3.

Recognitions: Canadian Depository for Securities Limited and CDS Clearing and Depository Services Inc.: (2013) 36 O.S.C.B. 92 as varied by 36 O.S.C.B. 5095 and 36 O.S.C.B. 6966; FundSERV Inc.: (2012) 35 O.S.C.B. 3634; Canadian Derivatives Clearing Corporation: (2014) 37 O.S.C.B. 3915.

Exemptions: Chicago Merchantile Exchange Inc.: (2013) 36 O.S.C.B. 6735; CLS Bank International and CLS Services Ltd.: (2011) 34 O.S.C.B. 2553; CME Clearing Europe Limited: (2012) 35 O.S.C.B. 9820; ICE Clear Canada, Inc.: (2011) 34 O.S.C.B. 2077; LCH. Clearnet Limited.: (2013) 36 O.S.C.B. 9157; Omgeo Canada Matching Ltd.: (2011) 34

O.S.C.B. 2069; Options Clearing Corporation: (2012) 35 O.S.C.B. 9831; SS&C Technologies Canada Corp.: (2011) 34 O.S.C.B. 2073; Canadian Derivatives Clearing Corporation (interim): (2012) 35 O.S.C.B. 1908 as varied (2013) 36 O.S.C.B. 2321 and 36 O.S.C.B. 5976; ICE Clear Credit LLC (interim): (2013) 36 O.S.C.B. 612; CMEG Exchanges: (2013) 36 O.S.C.B. 10472; Market Access SGF Corporation: (2013) 36 O.S.C.B. 11385.

21.2.1 (1) Quotation and trade reporting system — The Commission may, on the application of a quotation and trade reporting system, recognize the quotation and trade reporting system if the Commission is satisfied that to do so is in the public interest.

(2) Same — A recognition under this section shall be made in writing and is subject to such terms and conditions as the Commission may impose.

(3) Commission's powers — The Commission may, if it is satisfied that to do so is in the public interest, make any decision with respect to any by-law, rule, regulation, policy, procedure, interpretation or practice of a recognized quotation and trade reporting system.

1997, c. 19, s. 23(2)

OSA 21.2.1(3)

Policies and Orders: BOR 1.2, 1.3.

Recognitions: none.

21.2.2 (1) Trade repository designation — The Commission may, on the application of a person or company proposing to carry on business as a trade repository in Ontario, designate the person or company if the Commission considers it in the public interest.

(2) Further requirements — A designation under this section must be made in writing and is subject to such terms and conditions as the Commission may impose.

(3) Commission's powers — The Commission may, if it considers it in the public interest, make any decision with respect to,

(a) the manner in which a designated trade repository carries on business; or

(b) any by-law, rule, regulation, policy, procedure, interpretation or practice of a designated trade repository.

2010, c. 26, Sched. 18, s. 10

OSA 21.2.2

Definitions: OSA 1(1)"trade repository".

Rules: Rule 13-502, App. B.1, Item F, Rule 91-507.

Designations: none.

21.3 (1) Council, committee or ancillary body — A recognized exchange, a recognized quotation and trade reporting system or a recognized self-regulatory organization may, with the prior approval of the Commission and on such terms and conditions as the Commission determines to be necessary or appropriate in the public interest, establish a council, committee or ancillary body and assign to it regulatory or self-regulatory powers or responsibilities or both.

(2) Inclusion — A council, committee or ancillary body that exercises the powers or assumes the responsibilities of a recognized exchange, recognized quotation and trade reporting system or recognized self-regulatory organization is also included in,

(a) the recognition of the recognized exchange, recognized quotation and trade reporting system or recognized self-regulatory organization;

(b) any suspension, restriction or termination of the recognition of the recognized exchange, recognized quotation and trade reporting system or recognized self-regulatory organization; and

(c) any imposition of terms or conditions on the recognition of the recognized exchange, recognized quotation and trade reporting system or recognized self-regulatory organization.

(3) Same — The provisions of Ontario securities law that apply to recognized exchanges, recognized quotation and trade reporting systems and recognized self-regulatory organizations also apply with necessary modifications to the council, committee or ancillary body.

1997, c. 19, s. 23(3); 2010, c. 26, Sched. 18, s. 11

OSA 21.3

Rules: Rule 13-502, App. C, Item E(1).

Definitions: OSA 1(1)"Commission"; 1(1)"recognized quotation and trade reporting system"; 1(1)"recognized exchange"; 1(1)"recognized self-regulatory organization".

21.4 Voluntary surrender — On application by a recognized exchange, recognized self-regulatory organization, recognized quotation and trade reporting system, recognized clearing agency or designated trade repository, the Commission may accept the voluntary surrender of the recognition or designation, and may impose terms and conditions applicable to the acceptance, if the Commission is satisfied that the surrender of the recognition or designation is not prejudicial to the public interest.

1997, c. 19, s. 23(3); 2010, c. 26, Sched. 18, s. 12

OSA 21.4

Definitions: OSA 1(1)"recognized exchange"; 1(1)"Commission"; 1(1)"recognized quotation and trade reporting system"; 1(1)"recognized self-regulatory organization"; 1(1)"recognized clearing agency"; 1(1)"designated trade repository".

21.5 (1) Assignment of powers and duties — The Commission may, on such terms and conditions as it may impose, assign to a recognized exchange or recognized self-regulatory organization any of the powers and duties of the Commission under Part XI or the regulations related to that Part.

(2) Same — The Executive Director may, with the approval of the Commission, assign to a recognized exchange or recognized self-regulatory organization any of the powers and duties of the Director under Part XI or the regulations related to that Part.

(3) Revocation of assignment — The Commission or, with the approval of the Commission, the Executive Director may at any time revoke, in whole or in part, an assignment of powers and duties made under this section.

1994, c. 11, s. 358; 2010, c. 26, Sched. 18, s. 13

OSA 21.5

Related Provisions: OSA Part XI.

Definitions: OSA 1(1)"Commission"; 1(1)"recognized exchange"; 1(1)"recognized self-regulatory organization".

Policies and Orders: BOR 2.3.

21.6 Contravention of Ontario securities law — No by-law, rule, regulation, policy, procedure, interpretation or practice of a recognized exchange, recognized self-regulatory organization, recognized quotation and trade reporting system, recognized clearing agency or designated trade repository shall contravene Ontario securities law, but a recognized exchange, recognized self-regulatory organization, recognized quotation and trade reporting system, recognized clearing agency or designated trade repository may impose additional requirements within its jurisdiction.

1997, c. 19, s. 23(4); 2010, c. 26, Sched. 18, s. 14

OSA 21.6

Definitions: OSA 1(1)"recognized quotation and trade reporting system"; 1(1)"recognized exchange"; 1(1)"recognized self-regulatory organization"; 1(1)"recognized clearing agency"; 1(1)"designated trade repository"; 1(1)"Ontario securities law".

21.7 (1) Review of decisions — The Executive Director or a person or company directly affected by, or by the administration of, a direction, decision, order or ruling made under a by-law, rule, regulation, policy, procedure, interpretation or practice of a recognized exchange, recognized self-regulatory organization, recognized quotation and trade reporting system, recognized clearing agency or designated trade repository may apply to the Commission for a hearing and review of the direction, decision, order or ruling.

(2) Procedure — Section 8 applies to the hearing and review of the direction, decision, order or ruling in the same manner as it applies to a hearing and review of a decision of the Director.

1994, c. 11, s. 358; 1997, c. 19, s. 23(5); 2010, c. 26, Sched. 18, s. 15

OSA 21.7

Related Provisions: OSA 8.

Definitions: OSA 1(1)"person"; 1(1)"company"; 1(1)"recognized quotation and trade reporting system"; 1(1)"recognized exchange"; 1(1)"recognized self-regulatory organization"; 1(1)"recognized clearing agency"; 1(1)"designated trade repository"; 1(1)"decision".

Rules: Rules of Procedure 2.2, 14.

21.8 Auditors — (1) Exchanges — Every recognized exchange shall appoint an auditor for the exchange.

(2) Recognized self-regulatory organization auditor — At the request of the Commission, a recognized self-regulatory organization shall appoint an auditor for the self-regulatory organization.

(3) Recognized clearing agency auditor — At the request of the Commission, a recognized clearing agency shall appoint an auditor for the clearing agency.

1994, c. 11, s. 358; 2005, c. 31, Sched. 20, s. 3; 2010, c. 26, Sched. 18, s. 16

OSA 21.8

Definitions: OSA 1(1)"recognized exchange"; 1(1)"Commission"; 1(1)"recognized self-regulatory organization".

21.9 (1) Auditor of member — Every recognized exchange and every recognized self-regulatory organization shall cause each of its members to appoint an auditor.

(2) Selection of auditor — The auditor of a member shall be chosen from the panel of auditing firms selected under subsection (3).

(3) Panel of auditors — Every recognized exchange and recognized self-regulatory organization shall select a panel of auditing firms for their members.

(4) Auditor — No person shall be appointed as an auditor under subsection (1) unless the person has practised as an auditor in the securities industry in Canada for five years or more.

(5) Examination and report — The auditor of a member shall make an examination, in accordance with generally accepted auditing standards, of the annual financial statements and regulatory filings of the member as called for by the by-laws, rules, regulations, policies, procedures, interpretations or practices applicable to the member, and shall report on the financial affairs of the member to the recognized exchange or recognized self-regulatory organization, as the case may be, in accordance with professional reporting standards.

1994, c. 11, s. 358; 2010, c. 26, Sched. 18, s. 17

OSA 21.9

Definitions: OSA 1(1)"recognized exchange"; 1(1)"recognized self-regulatory organization".

21.10 (1) Auditor of registrant — Every registrant that is not subject to section 21.9 shall appoint an auditor who satisfies such requirements as may be established by the Commission.

(2) Examination and report — The auditor of a registrant that is not subject to section 21.9 shall make an examination of the annual financial statements and other regulatory filings of the registrant, in accordance with generally accepted auditing standards, and shall prepare a report on the financial affairs of the registrant in accordance with professional reporting standards.

(3) Filing with Commission — The registrant shall file the report with the Commission together with its annual financial statements and other regulatory filings.

(4) Delivery of financial statements — A registrant that is not subject to section 21.9 shall deliver to the Commission annual audited financial statements, prepared in accordance with generally accepted accounting principles, and other regulatory filings as prescribed by the regulations, within ninety days after the end of its financial year or as otherwise prescribed by the regulations.

(5) Certification of financial statements — The annual financial statements and regulatory filings delivered to the Commission shall be certified by the registrant or an officer or partner of the registrant.

(6) Additional information — The registrant shall deliver to the Commission such other information as the Commission may require in such form as it may require.

1994, c. 11, s. 358

OSA 21.10

Related Provisions: OSA 21.9.

Definitions: OSA 1(1)"registrant"; 1(1)"Commission".

Rules: Rule 35-502, Part 4.

21.11 (1) Restriction on shareholdings in The Toronto Stock Exchange Inc. — Without the prior approval of the Commission, no person or company and no combination of persons or companies acting jointly or in concert shall beneficially own or exercise control or direction over more than 5 per cent, or such other percentage as may be prescribed under subsection (5), of any class or series of voting shares of The Toronto Stock Exchange Inc.

(2) Sale of restricted shares — The Toronto Stock Exchange Inc. may sell any shares held contrary to the restriction in subsection (1) in accordance with section 45 of the *Business Corporations Act*, with necessary modifications.

(3) Transition — Despite subsection (1), if a person or company beneficially owns or exercises control or direction over more than 5 per cent, or such other percentage as may be prescribed under subsection (5), of any class or series of voting shares of The Toronto Stock Exchange Inc. as a result of the issue of shares by The Toronto Stock Exchange Inc. in connection with the continuance of The Toronto Stock Exchange under the *Business Corporations Act*, the person or company may continue to beneficially own or exercise control or direction over the shares, but shall not vote or cause to permit to be voted any shares of any class or series of voting shares in excess of the 5 per cent level or the prescribed level, as the case may be, without the prior approval of the Commission.

(4) Approval — The Commission may, by order, give its approval to a person, company or transaction, for the purposes of subsection (1) or (3), and may impose such terms and conditions on the approval as the Commission considers appropriate.

(5) Regulations — The Commission may, by regulation, prescribe a percentage for the purposes of subsection (1) and (3) and may prescribe different percentages for different classes of persons or companies.

(6) Non-application of s. 42 *Business Corporations Act* — Section 42 of the *Business Corporations Act* does not apply to The Toronto Stock Exchange Inc.

1999, c. 9, s. 198

OSA 21.11

Regulations: O. Reg 261/02 generally.

OSA Part VIII

Rules: Rule 31-507.

Policies and Orders: CSAN 24-303.

PART IX — CREDIT RATING ORGANIZATIONS (SS. 22–24)

[Heading added 2010, c. 26, Sched. 18, s. 18.]

22. (1) Application for designation — A credit rating organization may apply to the Commission to be designated by the Commission if the credit rating organization wants its credit ratings to satisfy,

　　(a) a requirement in Ontario securities law that a credit rating be given by a credit rating organization designated by the Commission; or

　　(b) a condition for an exemption under Ontario securities law.

(2) Designation — The Commission may designate a credit rating organization, subject to any terms and conditions the Commission considers advisable, if,

　　(a) an application for designation is made by the credit rating organization or the Director; and

　　(b) the Commission considers it in the public interest to designate the credit rating organization.

(3) Cancellation of designation — The Commission may, if it considers it in the public interest, cancel the designation of a credit rating organization or impose or change the terms and conditions of the designation.

(4) Right to hearing — The Commission shall not, without giving the credit rating organization an opportunity to be heard, refuse to designate a credit rating organization, cancel its designation or impose or change the terms and conditions to which the designation is subject.

(5) Same — If the Director applies to the Commission for the designation of a credit rating organization, the Commission shall not designate the credit rating organization without giving the credit rating organization an opportunity to be heard.

1994, c. 11, s. 358; 2010, c. 26, Sched. 18, s. 18

OSA 22

Rules: NI 25-101.

Policies and Orders: NPS 11-205.

Designations: DBRS Limited: (2012) 35 O.S.C.B. 10322; Fitch, Inc.: (2012) 35 O.S.C.B. 10317; Moody's Canada Inc.: (2012) 35 O.S.C.B. 10329; Standard & Poor's Ratings Services (Canada), a business unit of McGraw-Hill Companies (Canada) Corporation: (2012) 35 O.S.C.B. 10325.

23. Duty to comply with prescribed requirements — A designated credit rating organization shall comply with such requirements as may be prescribed by the regulations, including requirements,

(a) relating to the establishment, publication and enforcement by the credit rating organization of a code of conduct applicable to its directors, officers and employees and the minimum requirements to be included in the code of conduct;

(b) prohibiting conflicts of interest between the credit rating organization and a person or company whose securities are being rated and establishing procedures to be followed if conflicts of interest arise or to avoid conflicts of interest.

1994, c. 11, s. 358; 2010, c. 26, Sched. 18, s. 18

24. (1) Commission not involved in credit rating — Nothing in this Part shall be construed as authorizing the Commission to direct or regulate the content of credit ratings or methodologies used to determine credit ratings.

(2) Same — No credit rating organization and no person or company acting on its behalf shall make any written or oral representation that the Commission has in any way passed upon the merits of a credit rating or the methodologies used to determine the credit rating.

1994, c. 11, s. 358; 2010, c. 26, Sched. 18, s. 18

OSA Part IX

Rules: NI 25-101.

Policies and Orders: NPS 11-205.

PART X

[Heading repealed 1994, c. 11, s. 358.]

[23, 24.]

[Note: ss. 23, 24 have been re-enacted under Part IX.]

PART XI — REGISTRATION (SS. 25–33.1)

25. Registration — **(1) Dealers** — Unless a person or company is exempt under Ontario securities law from the requirement to comply with this subsection, the person or company shall not engage in or hold himself, herself or itself out as engaging in the business of trading in securities unless the person or company,

Proposed Amendment — 25(1) opening words

(1) Dealers — Unless a person or company is exempt under Ontario securities law from the requirement to comply with this subsection, the person or company shall not engage in or hold himself, herself or itself out as engaging in the business of trading in securities or derivatives unless the person or company,

2010, c. 26, Sched. 18, s. 19(1) [Not in force at date of publication.]

(a) is registered in accordance with Ontario securities law as a dealer; or

(b) is a representative registered in accordance with Ontario securities law as a dealing representative of a registered dealer and is acting on behalf of the registered dealer.

OSA 25(1)

Related Provisions: OSA 26, 27, 74, 140, Part XII.

Definitions: OSA 1(1)"trading"; 1(1)"security"; 1(1)"dealer"; 1(1)"representative".

Rules: Rules 35-101, 35-502, 35-503, 45-501, 91-501 91-502, 91-503; NI 31-103, 31-101, 45-106, 71-101.

Policies and Orders: NPS 31-201; OSCN 81-708.

Proposed Addition — 25(1.1)

(1.1) If trading in derivatives — Despite subsection (1), if the regulations provide that a person or company trading in derivatives must be registered in a category of registration prescribed by the regulations or that the person or company must comply with prescribed requirements when trading derivatives on his, her or its own account, or both, the person or company shall not trade in derivatives unless,

　　(a) the person or company,

　　　　(i) is, if required by the regulations, registered in the applicable category under the regulations, and

　　　　(ii) is in compliance with such requirements as may be prescribed by the regulations; or

　　(b) the person or company is exempt under Ontario securities law from the requirement to comply with this subsection.

2010, c. 26, Sched. 18, s. 19(2) [Not in force at date of publication.]

(2) Same, underwriters — Unless a person or company is exempt under Ontario securities law from the requirement to comply with this subsection, the person or company shall not act as an underwriter unless the person or company,

　　(a) is registered in accordance with Ontario securities law as a dealer and is authorized under section 26 or 27 to act as an underwriter in the circumstances; or

　　(b) is a representative registered in accordance with Ontario securities law as a dealing representative of a registered dealer described in clause (a) and is acting on behalf of the registered dealer.

OSA 25(2)

Related Provisions: OSA 26, 27.

Definitions: OSA 1(1)"underwriter"; 1(1)"representative".

(3) Same, advisers — Unless a person or company is exempt under Ontario securities law from the requirement to comply with this subsection, the person or company shall not engage in the business of, or hold himself, herself or itself out as engaging in the business of, advising anyone with respect to investing in, buying or selling securities unless the person or company,

Proposed Amendment — 25(3) opening words

(3) Same, advisers — Unless a person or company is exempt under Ontario securities law from the requirement to comply with this subsection, the person or company shall not engage in the business of, or hold himself, herself or itself out as engaging in the business of, advising anyone with respect to investing in securities or buying or selling securities or derivatives unless the person or company,

2010, c. 26, Sched. 18, s. 19(3) [Not in force at date of publication.]

　　(a) is registered in accordance with Ontario securities law as an adviser;

　　(b) is a representative registered in accordance with Ontario securities law as an advising representative of a registered adviser and is acting on behalf of the registered adviser; or

　　(c) is a representative registered in accordance with Ontario securities law as an associate advising representative of a registered adviser and is acting on behalf of the registered adviser under the supervision of a registered advising representative of the registered adviser.

OSA 25(3)

Definitions: OSA 1(1)"adviser"; 1(1)"security"; 1(1)"representative".

(4) Same, investment fund managers — Unless a person or company is exempt under Ontario securities law from the requirement to comply with this subsection, the person or company shall not act as an investment fund manager unless the person or company is registered in accordance with Ontario securities law as an investment fund manager.

OSA 25(4)

Definitions: OSA 1(1)"investment fund manager".

(5) Same, ultimate designated person — If a registrant that is a registered dealer, registered adviser or registered investment fund manager is required under the regulations to designate an individual as his, her or its ultimate designated person, the individual must be registered in accordance with Ontario securities law as the ultimate designated person of the registrant.

OSA 25(5)

Definitions: OSA 1(1)"ultimate designated person".

(6) Same, chief compliance officer — If a registrant that is a registered dealer, registered adviser or registered investment fund manager is required under the regulations to designate an individual as his, her or its chief compliance officer, the individual must be registered in accordance with Ontario securities law as the chief compliance officer of the registrant.

OSA 25(6)

Definitions: OSA 1(1)"chief compliance officer".

(7) Commission guidelines re engaged in a business — The Commission may, by the adoption of a policy under section 143.8, establish guidelines setting out criteria to be considered in determining whether a person or company is engaged in a business when trading securities or providing advice with respect to investing in, buying or selling securities.

| **Proposed Amendment — 25(7)** |

(7) Commission guidelines re engaged in a business — The Commission may, by the adoption of a policy under section 143.8, establish guidelines setting out criteria to be considered in determining whether a person or company is engaged in a business when he, she or it,

    (a) is trading securities or derivatives;

    (b) is providing advice with respect to investing in securities; or

    (c) is providing advice with respect to buying or selling securities or derivatives.

                      2010, c. 26, Sched. 18, s. 19(4) [Not in force at date of publication.]

                          1994, c. 11, s. 359; 1999, c. 9, s. 199; 2009, c. 18, Sched. 26, s. 4

OSA 25(7)

Policies and Orders: NPS 31-103CP.

OSA 25

Regulations: Reg. 85/05.

Rules: NI 31-103, 31-102, 33-109, 35-101.

Policies and Orders: NPS 31-201, 31-103CP; OSCN 33-734.

26. (1) Application for registration, etc. — An application for registration, reinstatement of registration or an amendment to an existing registration must contain such information in such form as the Director may reasonably require and must be accompanied by such fee as may be required by the regulations.

(2) Dealer registration categories — A person or company making an application under subsection (1) with respect to registration as a dealer under this Act shall do the following:

    1. Apply to be registered in one or more of the following categories:

        i. investment dealer,

        ii. mutual fund dealer,

        iii. scholarship plan dealer,

        iv. exempt market dealer,

        v. restricted dealer, limited to the trading and underwriting activities authorized under section 27 for the person's or company's registration,

        vi. such other category of dealer as may be prescribed by the regulations.

    2. Provide such information as the Director may require to verify that the activities of the person or company will be within the permitted activities prescribed by the regulations for the particular category or categories of dealer registration for which the person or company has applied.

(3) Permitted underwriting, investment dealer — A person or company registered under this Act as an investment dealer may act as an underwriter in respect of any distribution of securities unless the regulations provide otherwise.

(4) Permitted underwriting, exempt market dealer — A person or company registered under this Act as an exempt market dealer may act as an underwriter with respect to a distribution of securities made under an exemption from the prospectus requirements under this Act or the regulations unless the regulations provide otherwise.

(5) Permitted underwriting, other — A person or company registered under this Act in a category referred to in subparagraph 1 vi of subsection (2) may act as an underwriter in respect of any distribution of securities if the regulations so provide.

(6) Adviser registration categories — A person or company making an application under subsection (1) with respect to registration as an adviser shall indicate for which of the following categories of adviser registration he, she or it is applying and shall provide such information as the Director may require to verify that the activities of the person or company will be within the permitted activities for that category of adviser registration:

    1. Portfolio manager, authorized to provide advice to a client with respect to investing in, buying or selling any type of security, with or without discretionary authority granted by the client to manage the client's portfolio.

    2. Restricted portfolio manager, limited to the advising activities authorized under section 27 for the person's or company's registration.

    3. Such other category of adviser as may be prescribed by the regulations.

(7) Prescribed category — If one or more categories of registration are prescribed by the regulations, a person or company applying for registration in a category prescribed by the regulations shall so indicate and provide such information as the Director may require to verify that the category is appropriate for the applicant.

                          1999, c. 9, s. 200; 2009, c. 18, Sched. 26, s. 4

OSA 26

Related Provisions: OSA 8, 27.

Definitions: OSA 1(1)"Director"; 1(1)"trade"; 1(1)"security".

Rules: NI 31-103, 33-109.

Policies and Orders: OSCN 33-730; NPS 31-103CP, 33-109CP, 34-202.

27. (1) Registration, etc. — On receipt of an application by a person or company and all information, material and fees required by the Director and the regulations, the Director shall register the person or company, reinstate the registration of the person or company or amend the registration of the person or company, unless it appears to the Director,

    (a) that, in the case of a person or company applying for registration, reinstatement of registration or an amendment to a registration, the person or company is not suitable for registration under this Act; or

    (b) that the proposed registration, reinstatement of registration or amendment to registration is otherwise objectionable.

(2) Matters to be considered — In considering for the purposes of subsection (1) whether a person or company is not suitable for registration, the Director shall consider,

    (a) whether the person or company has satisfied,

        (i) the requirements prescribed in the regulations relating to proficiency, solvency and integrity, and

        (ii) such other requirements for registration, reinstatement of registration or an amendment to a registration, as the case may be, as may be prescribed by the regulations; and

    (b) such other factors as the Director considers relevant.

(3) Terms and conditions — The Director may, in his or her discretion, impose terms and conditions on the registration, reinstatement of registration or amendment of registration of any person or company and, without limiting the generality of the foregoing,

    (a) may restrict the duration of the registration; and

    (b) may restrict the person or company to,

        (i) trading only specified securities or specified classes of securities or securities of specified classes of issuers,

Proposed Amendment — 27(3)(b)(i)

        (i) trading only specified securities or derivatives, specified classes of securities or derivatives or securities of specified classes of issuers,

2010, c. 26, Sched. 18, s. 20(1) [Not in force at date of publication.]

        (ii) underwriting only specified securities or specified classes of securities or securities of specified classes of issuers, or

        (iii) providing advice with respect to investing in, buying or selling only specified securities or specified classes of securities or securities of specified classes of issuers.

Proposed Amendment — 27(3)(b)(iii)

        (iii) providing advice with respect to,

            (A) investing in, buying or selling only specified securities or specified classes of securities or securities of specified classes of issuers, or

            (B) buying or selling only specified derivatives or specified classes of derivatives.

2010, c. 26, Sched. 18, s. 20(2) [Not in force at date of publication.]

(4) Right to require audit or review — The Commission or the Director may, at any time, require a registrant that is a registered dealer, registered adviser or registered investment fund manager to direct its auditor, at the registrant's expense, to conduct any audit or financial review required by the Commission or the Director and deliver to the Commission as soon as practicable a report of the findings of the audit or review.

1994, c. 11, s. 360; 2009, c. 18, Sched. 26, s. 4

OSA 27

Rules: NI 31-103, 33-109.

Policies and Orders: NPS 31-103CP, 33-109CP.

28. Revocation or suspension of registration or imposition of terms and conditions — The Director may revoke or suspend the registration of a person or company or impose terms or conditions of registration at any time during the period of registration of the person or company if it appears to the Director,

    (a) that the person or company is not suitable for registration or has failed to comply with Ontario securities law; or

    (b) that the registration is otherwise objectionable.

2009, c. 18, Sched. 26, s. 4

29. (1) Automatic suspension, person or company — The registration of a person or company in a particular category of registration is suspended if any of the following events occurs:

    1. A fee imposed on the person or company under this Act or the regulations relating to a particular category of registration of the person or company remains unpaid more than 30 days after the day it is due.

    2. The membership of the person or company in a self-regulatory organization is suspended or terminated if,

        i. the membership of the person or company relates to the particular category of registration, and

        ii. the membership of the person or company is a condition of registration under Ontario securities law.

3. The approval by a self-regulatory organization of the person as a representative of a registered dealer is revoked or suspended by the self-regulatory organization if,

  i. the approval of the representative relates to the particular category of registration in which the representative is registered under Ontario securities law, and

  ii. the membership of the dealer in the self-regulatory organization is a condition of the dealer's registration under Ontario securities law.

OSA 29(1)

Rules: Rule 13-502.

(2) Automatic suspension, representatives of suspended dealer or adviser — A registered representative's registration in a particular category with respect to a particular registered dealer or registered adviser is suspended when the corresponding category of registration of that dealer or adviser is suspended.

(3) Automatic suspension, representative ceasing to represent registrant — The registration of a representative with respect to a registrant that is a registered dealer, registered advisor or registered investment fund manager is suspended at the time the representative ceases, by reason of any of the following events, to have the authority to act on behalf of the registrant in a capacity that requires the representative to be registered:

  1. The employment of the representative by the registrant is terminated.

  2. The representative's employment functions change.

  3. The partnership or agency relationship of the representative with the registrant changes or is terminated.

(4) Automatic suspension, chief compliance officer or ultimate designated person — The registration of an individual as a chief compliance officer or ultimate designated person is suspended at the time the individual ceases to be the chief compliance officer or ultimate designated person of the registered dealer, registered adviser or registered investment fund manager that designated the individual.

(5) Revocation after automatic suspension — The registration of a person or company that is suspended under subsection (1), (2), (3) or (4) and not reinstated is revoked on the second anniversary of the suspension.

(6) Exception — Despite subsection (5), if a proceeding is commenced under section 122 or 128 or under the rules of a self-regulatory organization with respect to a registrant, or a hearing is commenced under section 127 with respect to the activities of the registrant, the registrant's registration continues to remain suspended until an order has been made by the court or a decision is made by the Commission or self-regulatory organization in the proceeding or hearing.

1994, c. 11, s. 361; 2009, c. 18, Sched. 26, s. 4; 2009, c. 34, Sched. S, s. 3

OSA 29

Rules: NI 31-103, 33-109.

30. (1) Surrender of registration — On application by a person or company for the surrender of his, her or its registration, the Director may accept the application and revoke the registration if the Director is satisfied,

  (a) that all financial obligations of the person or company to his, her or its clients have been discharged;

  (b) that all requirements, if any, prescribed by the regulations for the surrender of registration have been fulfilled or the Director is satisfied that they will be fulfilled in an appropriate manner; and

  (c) that the surrender of the registration is not prejudicial to the public interest.

(2) Conditions — The Director may impose such terms and conditions on the surrender of a registration as the Director considers appropriate in the circumstances.

2009, c. 18, Sched. 26, s. 4

OSA 30

Rules: Rule 13-502, App. C, Item E(4.1).

31. Right to be heard — The Director shall not do any of the following without giving a person or company an opportunity to be heard:

  1. Refuse to register the person or company.

  2. Amend the registration of the person or company.

  3. Refuse to reinstate the registration of the person or company after the registration is suspended.

  4. Refuse a request from the person or company to amend his, her or its registration.

  5. Impose terms and conditions on the registration under subsection 27(3) or section 28, either as a condition of registration or at any time during the period in which the person or company is registered.

  6. Suspend or revoke the registration of the person or company under section 28.

  7. Impose terms and conditions under subsection 30(2) on the surrender of registration of the person or company.

2009, c. 18, Sched. 26, s. 4; 2009, c. 34, Sched. S, s. 4

OSA 31

Policies and Orders: OSCN 34-701; Procedures for Opportunities to be Heard.

32. (1) Duty to comply with Ontario securities law — Every person and company registered under this Act shall comply at all times with Ontario securities law, including such regulations that apply to them as may be made relating to,

    (a) proficiency standards;

    (b) business conduct;

    (c) in the case of a registrant that is a registered dealer, registered adviser or registered investment fund manager, submission of information respecting ownership, management, directors, officers and any other persons or companies exercising control of the registrant;

    (d) opening accounts and reporting trades;

    (e) record-keeping;

    (f) custody of clients' assets;

    (g) conflicts of interest;

    (h) tied selling and referral arrangements;

    (i) client complaints;

    (j) appointment of auditors and preparation and filing of financial information;

    (k) procedures to be followed when a relationship is terminated between a representative and a registered dealer or registered adviser or when the representative commences a new association with a different registered dealer or registered adviser; and

    (l) reinstatement of registration.

(2) Duty to establish controls, etc. — Every registrant that is a registered dealer, registered adviser or registered investment fund manager shall establish and maintain systems of control and supervision in accordance with the regulations for controlling his, her or its activities and supervising his, her or its representatives.

1999, c. 9, s. 201; 2009, c. 18, Sched. 26, s. 4

OSA 32

Rules: Rule 31-103.

33. Address for service — Except as otherwise permitted or required by the regulations, all notices under this Act or the regulations are sufficiently served for all purposes on a registrant or applicant if they are sent by ordinary letter mail or delivered to the last address for service provided to the Commission.

1999, c. 9, s. 202; 2009, c. 18, Sched. 26, s. 4

33.1 Further information — The Director may require further information or material to be submitted by an applicant or registrant within a specified time and,

    (a) may require verification by affidavit or otherwise of any information or material submitted; or

    (b) may require,

        (i) the applicant or registrant,

        (ii) any partner of the applicant or registrant,

        (iii) any officer, director, governor or trustee of the applicant or registrant or any person performing a similar function, or

        (iv) any employee of the applicant or registrant,

to submit to examination under oath by a person designated by the Director.

2009, c. 18, Sched. 26, s. 4

OSA Part XI

Related Provisions: OSA Part XII.

Regulations: Reg.: 110.

Rules: Rule 35-502; NI 31-102, 31-103, 33-109.

Policies and Orders: NPS 11-204.

PART XII — EXEMPTIONS FROM REGISTRATION REQUIREMENTS (SS. 34–35.3)

34. (1) Exemption from registration requirements, advisers — Each of the following persons and companies is exempt from the requirement to be registered as an adviser under this Act while engaging in the business of providing advice with respect to investing in or buying or selling securities:

Proposed Amendment — 34(1) opening words

(1) Exemption from registration requirements, advisers — Each of the following persons and companies is exempt from the requirement to be registered as an adviser under this Act while engaging in the business of providing advice with respect to investing in securities or buying or selling securities or derivatives:

2010, c. 26, Sched. 18, s. 21(1) [Not in force at date of publication.]

1. A person or company that engages in or holds himself, herself or itself out as engaging in the business of providing advice, either directly or through publications or other media, with respect to investing in or buying or selling securities, including any class of securities and the securities of a class of issuers, that are not purported to be tailored to the needs of anyone receiving the advice.

Proposed Amendment — 34(1), para. 1

1. A person or company that engages in or holds himself, herself or itself out as engaging in the business of providing advice, either directly or through publications or other media, with respect to investing in securities or buying or selling securities or derivatives, including any class of securities or derivatives and the securities of a class of issuers, that are not purported to be tailored to the needs of anyone receiving the advice.

2010, c. 26, Sched. 18, s. 21(1) [Not in force at date of publication.]

2. Such persons or companies as may be prescribed by the regulations or whose activities are prescribed by the regulations.

(2) Conditions and restrictions — The regulations may prescribe conditions and restrictions that apply to an exemption under paragraph 2 of subsection (1).

(3) Requirement to disclose interest — If an adviser described in paragraph 1 of subsection (1) recommends investing in, buying, selling or holding a specified security or class of securities or the securities of a specified class of issuers in which any of the following has a financial or other interest, either directly or indirectly, the adviser must disclose the interest concurrently with providing the advice:

Proposed Amendment — 34(3) opening words

(3) Requirement to disclose interest — If an adviser described in paragraph 1 of subsection (1) recommends investing in, buying, selling or holding a specified security or class of securities or the securities of a specified class of issuers, or buying or selling a specified derivative or specified class of derivatives, in which any of the following has a financial or other interest, either directly or indirectly, the adviser must disclose the interest concurrently with providing the advice:

2010, c. 26, Sched. 18, s. 21(2) [Not in force at date of publication.]

1. The adviser.

2. A partner, director or officer of the adviser.

3. A person or company that would be an insider of the adviser if the adviser were a reporting issuer.

(4) Same — If the adviser's financial or other interest includes an interest in an option described in clause (b) of the definition of "financial or other interest" in subsection (5), the disclosure required by subsection (3) must include a description of the terms of the option.

(5) Interpretation — For the purpose of subsection (3),

"**financial or other interest**" in a security includes,

(a) ownership, beneficial or otherwise, in the security or in another security issued by the same issuer,

(b) an option in respect of the security or in respect of another security issued by the same issuer,

(c) a commission or other compensation received or expected to be received from any person or company in connection with a trade in the security,

(d) a financial arrangement with any person or company regarding the security, and

(e) a financial arrangement with any underwriter or other person or company who has an interest in the security.

Proposed Amendment — 34(5)

(5) Interpretation — For the purpose of subsection (3),

"**financial or other interest**" in a security or derivative includes,

(a) an ownership interest, beneficial or otherwise, in the security or derivative,

(b) an ownership interest, beneficial or otherwise, in another security issued by the same issuer,

(c) an option in respect of the security or in respect of another security issued by the same issuer,

(d) a commission or other compensation received or expected to be received from any person or company in connection with a trade in the security or the derivative,

(e) a financial arrangement with any person or company regarding the security or derivative,

(f) a financial arrangement with an underwriter or other person or company who has an interest in the security or derivative, and

(g) in the case of a derivative and except as otherwise prescribed by the regulations, a material interest, financial or otherwise, in the derivative's underlying interest.

2010, c. 26, Sched. 18, s. 21(3) [Not in force at date of publication.]

1994, c. 11, s. 363; 2009, c. 18, Sched. 26, s. 5

OSA 34

Rules: NI 31-103, 8.23–8.26; Rule 35-502, Part 7.

35. (1) Exemption from registration requirements, dealers — A person or company is exempt from the requirement to be registered under this Act to act as a dealer when trading in the following types of securities or acting as an underwriter in respect of their distribution:

　　1. Debt securities issued by or guaranteed by the Government of Canada or the government of a province or territory of Canada.

　　2. Debt securities that are,

　　　　i. issued by a municipal corporation in Canada for elementary, secondary or vocational school purposes,

　　　　ii. issued or guaranteed by a municipal corporation in Canada, or

　　　　iii. secured by or payable out of rates or taxes levied under the law of a province or territory of Canada on property in the province or territory and collectible by or through the municipality in which the property is situated.

　　3. Debt securities that are issued by a corporation established under regulations made under subsection 248(1) of the *Education Act*.

(2) Same — A person or company is exempt from the requirement to be registered under this Act to act as a dealer when trading in or acting as an underwriter in respect of the distribution of a security evidencing indebtedness that is secured by or under a security agreement, as defined in subsection 1(1) of the *Personal Property Security Act*, or that is secured in a similar manner in accordance with comparable legislation of another province or territory of Canada that provides for the granting of security in personal property.

(3) Exception to exemption — The exemption described in subsection (2) does not apply with respect to a trade to an individual or with respect to underwriting such a trade.

(4) Exemption if other legislation applies — The following persons and companies are exempt, in the circumstances indicated, from the requirement to be registered under this Act to act as a dealer when trading in securities that evidence indebtedness secured by a mortgage or charge on real property in Canada or when acting as an underwriter in respect of their distribution:

　　1. A person or company that is licensed under the *Mortgage Brokerages, Lenders and Administrators Act, 2006* or that is exempt from the requirement to be licensed under that Act, if the real property is in Ontario.

　　2. A person or company that is licensed or registered under comparable legislation in the province or territory of Canada, other than Ontario, in which the real property is located or that is exempt from any legislative requirement to be licensed or registered.

(5) Prescribed securities — A person or company is exempt from the requirement to be registered under this Act to act as a dealer when trading in such types of securities as may be prescribed in the regulations that are traded in accordance with the regulations or when acting as an underwriter in respect of their distribution.

Proposed Addition — 35(5.1)

(5.1) Prescribed derivatives — A person or company is exempt from the requirement to be registered under this Act to act as a dealer when trading in such classes of derivatives as may be prescribed by the regulations.

2010, c. 26, Sched. 18, s. 22(1) [Not in force at date of publication.]

(6) Conditions and restrictions — The regulations may prescribe conditions and restrictions that apply to an exemption under subsection (5).

Proposed Amendment — 35(6)

(6) Conditions and restrictions — The regulations may prescribe conditions and restrictions that apply to an exemption under subsection (5) or (5.1).

2010, c. 26, Sched. 18, s. 22(2) [Not in force at date of publication.]

1994, c. 11, s. 364; 1997, c. 19, s. 23(6)–(8); 1997, c. 31, s. 179; 1999, c. 6, s. 60(2); 1999, c. 9, s. 203; 2001, c. 23, s. 211; 2005, c. 5, s. 64(2); 2006, c. 29, s. 65; 2007, c. 7, Sched. 7, s. 191; 2009, c. 18, Sched. 26, s. 5

OSA 35

Related Provisions: OSA 73.

Rules: NI 31-103, 8.1–8.22; Rule 45-501, Parts 3 and 4.

35.1 (1) Exemption from registration requirement, financial institutions — Each of the following financial institutions is exempt from the requirement to be registered under this Act to act as a dealer, underwriter, adviser or investment fund manager if the financial institution, in so acting, limits its activities to only those activities not prohibited by its governing legislation:

　　1. A bank listed in Schedule I, II or III to the *Bank Act* (Canada).

　　2. An association to which the *Cooperative Credit Associations Act* (Canada) applies or a central cooperative credit society for which an order has been made under subsection 473(1) of that Act.

　　3. A loan corporation, trust company, trust corporation, insurance company, treasury branch, credit union, caisse populaire, financial services cooperative or credit union league or federation that is authorized by a statute of Canada or Ontario to carry on business in Canada or Ontario, as the case may be.

　　4. Business Development Bank of Canada.

(2) Conditions and restrictions — An exemption under subsection (1) is subject to such conditions and restrictions as may be prescribed by a regulation made by the Lieutenant Governor in Council.

(3) Additional exemptions — Such other financial institutions as may be prescribed by regulation are exempt from the requirement to be registered under this Act to act as a dealer, underwriter, adviser or investment fund manager.

(4) Conditions and restrictions — An exemption under subsection (3) is subject to such conditions and restrictions as may be prescribed by regulation.

2009, c. 18, Sched. 26, s. 5

OSA 35.1

Related Provisions: OSA 143(1)8, 143(2)(a.0.1).

35.2 (1) Exemption from registration requirements, international adviser or dealer — The regulations shall provide that a person or company is exempt from the requirement to be registered under this Act to act as a dealer or adviser, as the case may be, if the person or company acts as a dealer or adviser in a jurisdiction outside Canada.

(2) Conditions and restrictions — The regulations may prescribe conditions and restrictions that apply to an exemption under subsection (1).

2009, c. 18, Sched. 26, s. 5

OSA 35.2

Rules: NI 31-103, 8.18 and 8.26; Rule 35-502, Part 7.

35.3 Additional exemptions by regulation — The regulations may prescribe exemptions from the requirement to be registered under this Act in addition to the exemptions provided under sections 34 to 35.2.

2009, c. 18, Sched. 26, s. 5

OSA Part XII

Related Provisions: OSA 143(1)8.

Rules: NI 31-103, Part 8; NI 35-101; NI 45-106, Part 3; Rules 35-502, 35-507, 35-501, Part 3.

PART XIII — TRADING IN SECURITIES AND DERIVATIVES GENERALLY (SS. 36–50)

[Heading amended 2010, c. 26, Sched. 18, s. 23.]

36. (1) Confirmation of trade — Subject to the regulations, every registered dealer who has acted as principal or agent in connection with the purchase or sale of a security or derivative shall promptly send by ordinary letter mail or deliver to the customer a written confirmation of the transaction containing the information required by the regulations.

(2) Disclosure of trade information to Commission — Every person or company that has acted as an agent in connection with the purchase or sale of a security or derivative shall promptly disclose to the Commission, on receipt of a written request from the Commission, the name of every person or company from, to or through whom the security or derivative was bought or sold.

(3) [Repealed 2009, c. 18, Sched. 26, s. 6.]

(4) [Repealed 2009, c. 18, Sched. 26, s. 6.]

(5) [Repealed 2009, c. 18, Sched. 26, s. 6.]

(6) [Repealed 2009, c. 18, Sched. 26, s. 6.]

(7) [Repealed 2009, c. 18, Sched. 26, s. 6.]

1997, c. 19, s. 23(9); 2009, c. 18, Sched. 26, s. 6; 2010, c. 26, Sched. 18, s. 23

OSA 36

Related Provisions: OSA 143(1)8.2.

Definitions: OSA 1(1)"security"; 1(1)"dealer"; 1(1)"derivative"; 1(1)"person"; 1(1)"company".

Rules: NI 31-103, s. 14.12, 14.13; Rule 56-501, s. 2.2.

Policies and Orders: OPS 13-601; NPS 11-201.

37. (1) Order prohibiting calls to residences — The Commission may by order suspend, cancel, restrict or impose terms and conditions on the right of any person or company named or described in the order to call at a residence or telephone from a location in Ontario to a residence located in or out of Ontario for the purpose of trading in any security or derivative or in any class of securities or derivatives.

(2) Hearing — The Commission shall not make an order under subsection (1) without giving the person or company affected an opportunity to be heard.

(3) "residence" defined — In this section, **"residence"** includes any building or part of a building in which the occupant resides either permanently or temporarily and any premises appurtenant thereto.

(4) What constitutes calls — For the purposes of this section, a person or company shall be deemed conclusively to have called or telephoned where an officer, director employee or agent of the person or company calls or telephones on its behalf.

1994, c. 33, s. 3; 2009, c. 18, Sched. 26, s. 7; 2010, c. 26, Sched. 18, s. 24

OSA 37

Definitions: OSA 1(1)"officer"; 1(1)"director"; 1(1)"person"; 1(1)"company"; 1(1)"Commission".

38. (1) Representations prohibited — No person or company, with the intention of effecting a trade in a security, other than a security that carries an obligation of the issuer to redeem or purchase, or a right of the owner to require redemption or purchase, shall make any representation, written or oral, that he, she or it or any person or company,

(a) will resell or repurchase; or

(b) will refund all or any of the purchase price of,

such security.

(1.1) Representation prohibited, derivatives — No person or company, with the intention of effecting a trade in a derivative, shall make any representation, written or oral, that he, she or it or any other person or company will refund any amount paid in respect of the derivative, unless the terms of the derivative provide for a refund or provide a right to a party to require a refund.

(2) Future value — No person or company, with the intention of effecting a trade in a security or derivative, shall give any undertaking, written or oral, relating to the future value or price of the security or derivative.

(3) Listing — Subject to the regulations, no person or company, with the intention of effecting a trade in a security or derivative, shall, except with the written permission of the Director, make any written or oral representation that the security or derivative will be listed on an exchange or quoted on a quotation and trade reporting system, or that application has been or will be made to list the security or derivative on an exchange or quote the security or derivative on a quotation and trade reporting system, unless,

(a) in the case of securities, application has been made to list or quote the securities and other securities issued by the same issuer are already listed on an exchange or quoted on a quotation and trade reporting system; or

(b) the exchange or quotation and trade reporting system has granted approval to the listing or quoting of the securities or derivatives, conditional or otherwise, or has consented to, or indicated that it does not object to, the representation.

OSA 38(3)

Rules: NI 45-101, s. 9.1; Rule 13-502, App. C, Item E(4.1).

(4) Application of section — This section does not apply to a representation referred to in subsection (1) or (1.1) if the representation is contained in an enforceable written agreement and,

(a) in the case of a representation in respect of a security, the security has a total acquisition cost of more than $50,000; or

(b) in the case of a representation in respect of a derivative, the derivative is in a class of derivatives prescribed by the regulations.

1999, c. 9, s. 204; 2010, c. 26, Sched. 18, s. 25

OSA 38

Definitions: OSA 1(1)"person"; 1(1)"company"; 1(1)"issuer"; 1(1)"trade"; 1(1)"security"; 1(1)"derivative"; 1(1)"quotation and trade reporting system"; 1(1)"Director".

39. [Repealed 2009, c. 18, Sched. 26, s. 8.]

40. [Repealed 2009, c. 18, Sched. 26, s. 8.]

41. [Repealed 2009, c. 18, Sched. 26, s. 8.]

42. [Repealed 1999, c. 9, s. 205.]

43. Use of name of another registrant — No registrant shall use the name of another registrant on letterheads, forms, advertisements or signs, as correspondent or otherwise, unless the registrant is a partner, officer or agent of or is authorized so to do in writing by the other registrant.

OSA 43

Definitions: OSA 1(1)"registrant"; 1(1)"officer".

44. (1) Representation of registration — No person or company shall represent that he, she or it is registered under this Act unless the representation is true and, when making the representation, the person or company specifies his, her or its category of registration.

(2) Representation prohibited — No person or company shall make a statement about any matter that a reasonable investor would consider relevant in deciding whether to enter into or maintain a trading or advising relationship with the person or company if the statement is untrue or omits information necessary to prevent the statement from being false or misleading in the circumstances in which it is made.

2009, c. 18, Sched. 26, s. 9

OSA 44

Definitions: OSA 1(1)"person"; 1(1)"company".

Policies and Orders: OSCN 33-734, s. 3.2.

45. [Repealed 2009, c. 18, Sched. 26, s. 10.]

46. Prohibited representation re Commission approval — No person or company shall make a written or oral representation that the Commission has in any way passed on the financial standing, fitness or conduct of a registrant or on the merits of an issuer or a security, derivative or underlying interest of a derivative.

2010, c. 26, Sched. 18, s. 26

OSA 46

Definitions: OSA 1(1)"person"; 1(1)"company"; 1(1)"Commission"; 1(1)"registrant"; 1(1)"security"; 1(1)"derivative"; 1(1)"issuer".

47. (1) Margin contracts — Where a person, or a partner or employee of a partnership, or a director, officer or employee of a company, after the person or the partnership or company has contracted as a registered dealer with any customer to buy and carry upon margin any securities of any issuer either in Canada or elsewhere, and while such contract continues, sells or causes to be sold securities of the same issuer for any account in which,

(a) the person;

(b) the firm or a partner thereof; or

(c) the company or a director thereof,

has a direct or indirect interest, if the effect of such sale would, otherwise than unintentionally, be to reduce the amount of such securities in the hands of the dealer or under the dealer's control in the ordinary course of business below the amount of such securities that the dealer should be carrying for all customers, any such contract with a customer is, at the option of the customer, voidable and the customer may recover from the dealer all money paid with interest thereon or securities deposited in respect thereof.

(2) Exercise of option — The customer may exercise such option by a notice to that effect sent by prepaid mail addressed to the dealer at the dealer's address for service in Ontario.

OSA 47

Definitions: OSA 1(1)"person"; 1(1)"director"; 1(1)"officer"; 1(1)"dealer"; 1(1)"security"; 1(1)"company".

48. Declaration as to short position — Any person or company who places an order for the sale of a security through an agent acting for him, her or it that is a registered dealer and who,

(a) at the time of placing the order, does not own the security; or

(b) if acting as agent, knows the principal does not own the security,

shall, at the time of placing the order to sell, declare to the agent that he, she or it or the principal, as the case may be, does not own the security.

OSA 48

Definitions: OSA 1(1)"person"; 1(1)"company"; 1(1)"security"; 1(1)"dealer".

49. (1) Shares in name of registrant not to be voted — Subject to subsection (4), voting securities of an issuer registered in the name of,

(a) a registrant or in the name of the registrant's nominee; or

(b) a custodian or in the name of the custodian's nominee, where such issuer is a mutual fund that is a reporting issuer,

that are not beneficially owned by the registrant or the custodian, as the case may be, shall not be voted by the registrant or custodian at any meeting of security holders of the issuer.

(2) Forwarding of information by registrant — Forthwith after receipt of a copy of a notice of a meeting of security holders of an issuer, the registrant or custodian shall, where the name and address of the beneficial owner of securities registered in the name of the registrant or custodian are known, send or deliver to each beneficial owner of such security so registered at the record date for notice of meeting a copy of any notice, financial statement, information circular or other material but the registrant or custodian is not required to send or deliver such material unless the issuer or the beneficial owner of such securities has agreed to pay the reasonable costs to be incurred by the registrant or custodian in so doing.

OSA 49(2)

Rules: Rule 56-501, s. 2.2.

(3) Copies of information — At the request of a registrant or custodian, the person or company sending material referred to in subsection (2) shall forthwith furnish to the registrant or custodian, at the expense of the sender, the requisite number of copies of the material.

(4) Voting of shares — A registrant or custodian shall vote or give a proxy requiring a nominee to vote any voting securities referred to in subsection (1) in accordance with any written voting instructions received from the beneficial owner.

(5) Proxies — A registrant or custodian shall, if requested in writing by a beneficial owner, give to the beneficial owner or his, her or its nominee a proxy enabling the beneficial owner or the nominee to vote any voting securities referred to in subsection (1).

(6) "custodian" defined — For the purpose of this section, **"custodian"** means custodian of securities issued by a mutual fund held for the benefit of plan holders under a custodial agreement or other arrangement.

OSA 49

Definitions: OSA 1(1)"voting security"; 1(1)"issuer"; 1(1)"registrant"; 1(1)"mutual fund"; 1(1)"proxy".

Rules: NI 54-101.

50. (1) Submission of advertising — The Commission may, after giving the registered dealer an opportunity to be heard, and upon being satisfied that the registered dealer's past conduct with respect to the use of advertising and sales literature affords reasonable grounds for belief that it is necessary for the protection of the public to do so, order that the registered dealer shall deliver to the Commission at least seven days before it is used, copies of all advertising and sales literature which the registered dealer proposes to use in connection with trading in securities or derivatives.

(2) Definitions — For the purposes of this section,

"advertising" includes television and radio commercials, newspaper and magazine advertisements and all other sales material generally disseminated through the communications media;

"sales literature" includes audio and visual recordings in any media, written matter and all other material designed for use in a presentation to a purchaser, whether such material is given or shown to the purchaser, but does not include,

    (a) preliminary prospectuses,

    (b) prospectuses, and

    (c) disclosure documents, in respect of derivatives, that satisfy the requirements prescribed by the regulations.

(3) Prohibition of advertising — Where the Commission has issued an order pursuant to subsection (1), the Director may prohibit the use of the advertising and sales literature so delivered or may require that deletions or changes be made prior to its use.

(4) [Repealed 1994, c. 11, s. 365.]

1994, c. 11, s. 365; 2010, c. 26, Sched. 18, s. 27

OSA 50

Definitions: OSA 1(1)"dealer"; 1(1)"Commission".

Rules: NI 81-102, Part 15.

Policies and Orders: NPS 42.

OSA Part XIII

Rules: NI 31-103.

PART XIV — PROSPECTING SYNDICATES (S. 51)

51. (1) Agreements — Upon the filing of a prospecting syndicate agreement and the issuance of a receipt therefor by the Director, the liability of the members of the syndicate or parties to the agreement is limited to the extent provided by the terms of the agreement where,

    (a) the sole purpose of the syndicate is the financing of prospecting expeditions, preliminary mining development, or the acquisition of mining properties, or any combination thereof;

    (b) the agreement clearly sets out,

        (i) the purpose of the syndicate,

        (ii) the particulars of any transaction effected or in contemplation involving the issue of units for a consideration other than cash,

        (iii) the maximum amount, not exceeding 25 per cent of the sale price, that may be charged or taken by a person or company as commission upon the sale of units in the syndicate,

        (iv) the maximum number of units in the syndicate, not exceeding $33\frac{1}{3}$ per cent of the total number of units of the syndicate, that may be issued in consideration of the transfer to the syndicate of mining properties,

        (v) the location of the principal office of the syndicate and that the principal office shall at all times be maintained in Ontario and that the Director and the members of the syndicate shall be notified immediately of any change in the location of the principal office,

        (vi) that a person or company holding mining properties for the syndicate shall execute a declaration of trust in favour of the syndicate with respect to such mining properties,

        (vii) that after the sale for cash of any issued units of the syndicate no mining properties shall be acquired by the syndicate other than by staking unless such acquisition is approved by members of the syndicate holding at least two-thirds of the issued units of the syndicate that have been sold for cash,

        (viii) that the administrative expenditures of the syndicate, including, in addition to any other items, salaries, office expenses, advertising and commissions paid by the syndicate with respect to the sale of its units, shall be limited to one-third of the total amount received by the treasury of the syndicate from the sale of its units,

        (ix) that a statement of the receipts and disbursements of the syndicate shall be furnished to the Director and to each member annually,

        (x) that 90 per cent of the vendor units of the syndicate shall be escrowed units and may be released upon the consent of the Director and that any release of such units shall not be in excess of one vendor unit for each unit of the syndicate sold for cash,

        (xi) that no securities, other than those of the syndicate's own issue, and no mining properties owned by the syndicate or held in trust for the syndicate shall be disposed of unless such disposal is approved by members of the syndicate holding at least two-thirds of the issued units of the syndicate other than escrowed units; and

    (c) the agreement limits the capital of the syndicate to a sum not exceeding $250,000.

(2) Receipt for filed agreement — The Director may in his or her discretion issue a receipt for a prospecting syndicate agreement filed under this section and is not required to determine whether it is in conformity with clauses (1)(a), (b) and (c).

(3) Application — After a receipt is issued by the Director for a prospecting syndicate agreement, the requirements of the *Business Names Act* as to filing do not apply to the prospecting syndicate.

(4) Prohibition of trading by dealer — No registered dealer shall trade in a security issued by a prospecting syndicate either as agent for the prospecting syndicate or as principal.

(5) Receipt — The Director shall not refuse to issue a receipt under subsection (1) without giving the person or company who filed the prospecting syndicate agreement an opportunity to be heard.

OSA 51

Definitions: OSA 1(1)"Director"; 1(1)"person"; 1(1)"company"; 1(1)"security"; 1(1)"dealer".

Policies and Orders: OPS 13-601.

OSA Part XIV

Rules: Rule 13-502, App. C, Item D.

PART XV — PROSPECTUSES — DISTRIBUTION (SS. 52–64)

52. "distribution" extended meaning — To but not including the 15th day of March, 1981, for the purposes of sections 54 to 64, **"distribution"** means only a distribution that is a distribution to the public.

53. (1) Prospectus required — No person or company shall trade in a security on his, her or its own account or on behalf of any other person or company if the trade would be a distribution of the security, unless a preliminary prospectus and a prospectus have been filed and receipts have been issued for them by the Director.

(2) Filing without distribution — A preliminary prospectus and a prospectus may be filed in accordance with this Part to enable the issuer to become a reporting issuer, despite the fact that no distribution is contemplated.

2006, c. 33, Sched. Z.5, s. 2

OSA 53

Related Provisions: OSA 55, 74.

Definitions: OSA 1(1)"person"; 1(1)"company"; 1(1)"trade"; 1(1)"security"; 1(1)"distribution"; 1(1)"reporting issuer".

Rules: NI 13-101, NI 41-101 to Rule 48-501; NI 71-101 to Rule 72-501; NI 81-101 to NI 81-105; Rules 91-501 to 91-503.

Policies and Orders: OPS 1.5, 13-601; NPS 41-201 to OSCN 48-701.

54. (1) Preliminary prospectus — A preliminary prospectus shall substantially comply with the requirements of Ontario securities law respecting the form and content of a prospectus, except that the report or reports of the auditor or accountant required by the regulations need not be included.

(2) Idem — A preliminary prospectus may exclude information with respect to the price to the underwriter and offering price of any securities and other matters dependent upon or relating to such prices.

1994, c. 11, s. 366

OSA 54

Definitions: OSA 1(1)"underwriter"; 1(1)"security".

55. Receipt for preliminary prospectus — The Director shall issue a receipt for a preliminary prospectus forthwith upon the filing thereof.

OSA 55

Definitions: OSA 1(1)"Director".

Policies and Orders: OSCN 41-701.

56. (1) Prospectus — A prospectus shall provide full, true and plain disclosure of all material facts relating to the securities issued or proposed to be distributed and shall comply with the requirements of Ontario securities law.

(2) Supplemental material — The prospectus shall contain or be accompanied by such financial statements, reports or other documents as are required by this Act or the regulations.

1994, c. 11, s. 367

OSA 56

Definitions: OSA 1(1)"security"; 1(1)"distribution".

Regulations: Reg.: Part III.

Rules: NI 41-101, 44-101, 44-102, 44-103, 81-101, 81-102, Rule 41-801 and 81-803.

Policies and Orders: NPS 11-202.

57. (1) Amendment to preliminary prospectus on material change — Where a material adverse change occurs after a receipt is obtained for a preliminary prospectus filed in accordance with subsection 53(1) and before the receipt for the prospectus is obtained or, where a material change occurs after the receipt for the prospectus is obtained but prior to the completion of the distribution under such prospectus, an amendment to such preliminary prospectus or prospectus, as the case may be, shall be filed as soon as practicable and in any event within ten days after the change occurs.

(2) Same, additional securities — If, after a receipt for a prospectus or for an amendment to a prospectus is issued but before the distribution under the prospectus or amendment is completed, securities in addition to those previously disclosed in the prospectus or amendment are to be distributed, the issuer making the distribution shall file an amendment to the prospectus disclosing the additional securities as soon as practicable and, in any event, within 10 days after the decision to increase the number of securities offered is made.

(2.1) Receipt — The Director shall issue a receipt for an amendment to a prospectus that must be filed under subsection (1) or (2) unless the Director refuses in accordance with subsection 61(2) to issue the receipt.

(2.2) Restriction — Unless otherwise permitted by regulation, an issuer shall not proceed with a distribution or an additional distribution until a receipt is issued for an amendment to the prospectus that must be filed under subsection (1) or (2).

(3) Notice of amendment — An amendment to a preliminary prospectus referred to in subsection (1) shall, forthwith after it has been filed, be forwarded to each recipient of the preliminary prospectus according to the record maintained under section 67.

2007, c. 7, Sched. 38, s. 3

OSA 57

Related Provisions: OSA 67.

Definitions: OSA 1(1)"material change"; 1(1)"security"; 1(1)"distribution"; 1(1)"Commission".

Rules: NI 41-101, 44-101, 71-101, 81-101; Rule 41-801.

Policies and Orders: OPS 13-601.

58. (1) Certificate by issuer — Subject to subsection (3) of this section and subsection 63(2) and subject to any waiver or variation consented to in writing by the Director, a prospectus filed under subsection 53(1) or subsection 62(1) shall contain a certificate in the prescribed form, signed by the chief executive officer, the chief financial officer, and, on behalf of the board of directors, any two directors of the issuer, other than the foregoing, duly authorized to sign, and any person or company who is a promoter of the issuer.

OSA 58(1)

Related Provisions: OSA 63(2), 53(1), 62(1).

(2) Idem — Subject to subsection (3) of this section and subsection 63(2), a prospectus filed under subsection 53(2) shall contain a certificate in the prescribed form, signed by the chief executive officer, the chief financial officer, and, on behalf of the board of directors, any two directors of the issuer, other than the foregoing, duly authorized to sign, and any person or company who is a promoter of the issuer.

OSA 58(2)

Related Provisions: OSA 53(2).

(3) Idem — Where the issuer has only three directors, two of whom are the chief executive officer and the chief financial officer, the certificate may be signed by all the directors of the issuer.

(4) Idem — Where the Director is satisfied upon evidence or on submissions that either, or both of, the chief executive officer or chief financial officer of the issuer is for adequate cause not available to sign a certificate in a prospectus, the Director may permit the certificate to be signed by any other responsible officer or officers of the issuer in lieu of either, or both of, the chief executive officer or chief financial officer.

(5) Idem — With the consent of the Director, a promoter or a guarantor need not sign the certificate in a prospectus.

(6) Certificate of promoter — The Director may, in his or her discretion, require any person or company who was a promoter of the issuer within the two preceding years or who is a guarantor of the securities being distributed to sign the certificate required by subsection (1) or (2) subject to such conditions as the Director may consider proper.

(7) Idem — With the consent of the Director, a promoter or a guarantor may sign a certificate in a prospectus by his, her or its agent duly authorized in writing.

1999, c. 9, s. 206; 2007, c. 7, Sched. 38, s. 4

OSA 58

Definitions: OSA 1(1)"person"; 1(1)"company"; 1(1)"promoter"; 1(1)"issuer"; 1(1)"Director".

Rules: NI 41-101, 44-101, 44-102, 44-103, 81-101.

Policies and Orders: OPS 41-501CP, s. 5.1.

59. (1) Certificate of underwriter — Subject to subsection 63(2), where there is an underwriter, a prospectus shall contain a certificate in the prescribed form, signed by the underwriter or underwriters who, with respect to the securities offered by the prospectus, are in a contractual relationship with the issuer or security holder whose securities are being offered by the prospectus.

OSA 59(1)

Related Provisions: OSA 63(2).

(2) Idem — With the consent of the Director, an underwriter may sign a certificate in a prospectus by his, her or its agent duly authorized in writing.

2007, c. 7, Sched. 38, s. 5

OSA 59

Related Provisions: OSA 130(1)(b), 140(1).

Definitions: OSA 1(1)"underwriter"; 1(1)"security"; 1(1)"issuer"; 1(1)"Director".

Rules: NI 41-101, 44-101, 44-102, 44-103, 81-101.

60. Statement of rights — Every prospectus shall contain a statement of the rights given to a purchaser by sections 71 and 130.

OSA 60

Related Provisions: OSA 71, 130.

Rules: NI 41-101, Part 18.

61. (1) Issuance of receipt — Subject to subsection (2) of this section and subsection 63(4), the Director shall issue a receipt for a prospectus filed under this Part unless it appears to the Director that it is not in the public interest to do so.

OSA 61(1)

Related Provisions: OSA 63(4).

(2) Refusal of receipt — The Director shall not issue a receipt for a prospectus or an amendment to a prospectus if it appears to the Director that,

(a) the prospectus or any document required to be filed with it,

(i) does not comply in any substantial respect with any of the requirements of this Act or the regulations,

(ii) contains any statement, promise, estimate or forward-looking information that is misleading, false or deceptive, or

(iii) contains a misrepresentation;

(b) an unconscionable consideration has been paid or given or is intended to be paid or given for any services or promotional purposes or for the acquisition of property;

(c) the aggregate of,

(i) the proceeds from the sale of the securities under the prospectus that are to be paid into the treasury of the issuer, and

(ii) the other resources of the issuer,

is insufficient to accomplish the purpose of the issue stated in the prospectus;

OSA 61(2)(c)

Policies and Orders: CSAN 41-307.

(d) the issuer cannot reasonably be expected to be financially responsible in the conduct of its business because of the financial condition of,

(i) the issuer,

(ii) any of the issuer's officers, directors, promoters, or control persons, or

(iii) the investment fund manager of the issuer or any of the investment fund manager's officers, directors or control persons;

(e) the business of the issuer may not be conducted with integrity and in the best interests of the security holders of the issuer because of the past conduct of,

(i) the issuer,

(ii) any of the issuer's officers, directors, promoters, or control persons, or

(iii) the investment fund manager of the issuer or any of the investment fund manager's officers, directors or control persons;

(f) a person or company that has prepared or certified any part of the prospectus, or that is named as having prepared or certified a report or valuation used in connection with the prospectus, is not acceptable;

(g) an escrow or pooling agreement in the form that the Director considers necessary or advisable with respect to the securities has not been entered into; or

OSA 61(2)(g)

Policies and Orders: NPS 46-201; CSAN 41-305.

(h) adequate arrangements have not been made for the holding in trust of the proceeds payable to the issuer from the sale of the securities pending the distribution of the securities.

(3) Hearing — The Director shall not refuse to issue a receipt under subsection (1) or (2) without giving the person or company who filed the prospectus an opportunity to be heard.

(4) Referral to Commission — Where it appears to the Director that a preliminary prospectus, *pro forma* prospectus, or prospectus raises a material question involving the public interest under subsection (1) or a new or novel question of interpretation under subsection (2) that might result in the Director refusing to issue a receipt under subsection (1) or (2), the Director may refer the question to the Commission for determination.

(5) Form of question — The Director shall state the question in writing setting out the facts upon which the question is based.

(6) Filing of question — The question, together with any additional material, shall be lodged by the Director with the Secretary of the Commission, and a copy of the question shall forthwith be served by the Secretary upon any interested person or company.

(7) Hearing by Commission — The Commission, after giving the parties an opportunity to be heard, shall consider and determine the question and refer the matter back to the Director for final consideration under subsections (1) and (2).

(8) Decision of Commission — Subject to any order of the Divisional Court made under section 9, the decision of the Commission on the question is binding on the Director.

2006, c. 33, Sched. Z.5, s. 3

OSA 61(8)

Related Provisions: OSA 9.

OSA 61

Related Provisions: OSA 8.

Definitions: OSA 1(1)"Director"; 1(1)"misrepresentation"; 1(1)"security"; 1(1)"issuer"; 1(1)"officer"; 1(1)"director"; 1(1)"promoter"; 1(1)"person"; 1(1)"company"; 1(1)"distribution"; 1(1)"Commission".

Regulations: Reg.: 238.

Policies and Orders: OSCN 41-701.

62. (1) Refiling of prospectus — In this section,

"lapse date" means, with reference to a security that is being distributed under subsection 53(1) or this section, the date that is 12 months after the date of the most recent propsectus relating to the security.

OSA 62(1)

Related Provisions: OSA 53(1).

(1.1) Same — No distribution of a security to which subsection 53(1) applies shall continue after the lapse date, unless a new prospectus that complies with this Part is filed and a receipt for the new prospectus is obtained from the Director.

(2) Idem — A distribution may be continued for a further twelve months after a lapse date if,

(a) a *pro forma* prospectus prepared in accordance with the regulations is filed not less than thirty days prior to the lapse date of the previous prospectus;

(b) a prospectus is filed not later than ten days following the lapse date of the previous prospectus; and

(c) a receipt for the prospectus is obtained from the Director within the twenty days following the lapse date of the previous prospectus.

(3) Idem — The continued distribution of securities after the lapse date does not contravene subsection (1.1) unless and until any of the conditions of subsection (2) are not complied with.

(4) Failure to refile — Subject to any extension granted under subsection (5), all trades completed in reliance upon subsection (2) after the lapse date may be cancelled at the option of the purchaser within ninety days of the purchaser's first knowledge of the failure to comply with such conditions where any of the conditions to the continuation of a distribution under subsection (2) are not complied with.

(5) Extension of time — The Commission may, upon an application of a reporting issuer, extend, subject to such terms and conditions as it may impose, the times provided by subsection (2) where in its opinion it would not be prejudicial to the public interest to do so.

1997, c. 19, s. 23(10); 2001, c. 23, s. 212

OSA 62(5)

Policies and Orders: OPS 2.1.

OSA 62

Related Provisions: OSA 72.

Definitions: OSA 1(1)"distribution"; 1(1)"security"; 1(1)"Director"; 1(1)"Commission".

Rules: NI 44-102, 71-101.

Policies and Orders: OPS 13-601; ON BOR 1.2, 1.3.

63. (1) Forms of prospectus — A person or company may, if permitted by the regulations, file a short form of preliminary prospectus, short form of prospectus, pro forma prospectus, preliminary simplified prospectus, simplified prospectus or pro forma simplified prospectus under section 53 or 62 in the prescribed form and any such prospectus that complies with the applicable regulations shall, for the purposes of section 56, be considered to provide sufficient disclosure of all material facts relating to the securities issued or proposed to be distributed under the prospectus.

OSA 63(1)

Related Provisions: OSA 53, 62, 56.

(2) Alternative certificates — A short form prospectus may contain one or more forms of certificate to be signed as alternatives to the forms of certificate set out in subsections 58(1) and (2) and subsection 59(1) and, where any such certificate in a short form prospectus is used in accordance with the regulations, it is not necessary to use the alternative certificate required by subsections 58(1) and (2) and subsection 59(1), as the case may be.

OSA 63(2)

Related Provisions: OSA 58(1), (2), 59(1).

(3) Summary statement — A person or company may, if permitted by the regulations, file a summary statement as a separate document in the prescribed form together with a prospectus filed under section 53 or 62.

OSA 63(3)

Related Provisions: OSA 53, 62.

(4) Refusal of summary statement — Where a summary statement is filed with a prospectus, the Director shall not issue a receipt for the prospectus if it appears to the Director that the summary statement does not comply with the regulations applicable thereto.

(5) Delivery of summary statement — A summary statement filed with a prospectus for which a receipt has been issued may be sent or delivered by a dealer to a purchaser of securities instead of a prospectus as required in section 71, and, where a dealer so elects, the provisions of sections 71 and 133 with respect to a prospectus apply with necessary modifications to a summary statement.

OSA 63(5)

Related Provisions: OSA 71, 133.

Definitions: OSA 1(1)"Director"; 1(1)"misrepresentation"; 1(1)"security"; 1(1)"issuer"; 1(1)"prospectus"; 1(1)"promoter"; 1(1)"company"; 1(1)"person".

(6) Delivery of prospectus on request — Every summary statement sent or delivered to a purchaser shall contain a statement informing the purchaser that a copy of the prospectus which was filed with the summary statement will be provided to the purchaser on request, and each person or company who signs or causes to be signed, as the case may be, the certificate contained in the prospectus shall ensure compliance with any such request.

(7) Summary statement without force and effect — Where, during the distribution or distribution to the public of a security under a prospectus, an order is made to cease trading in the security, or the receipt issued by the Director for the prospectus is revoked or the prospectus lapses or the use of a prospectus is otherwise prohibited by the Act, the regulations or by a decision of the Commission or an order of a court, a summary statement filed with the prospectus shall cease to have force and effect for the purposes of section 71 unless the Director otherwise orders.

OSA 63(7)

Related Provisions: OSA 71.

(8) Liability not affected — Nothing in this section shall be construed to provide relief from liability arising under section 130 where a misrepresentation is contained in a prescribed short form prospectus and, for the purposes of section 130, where a misrepresentation is contained in a summary statement filed with a prospectus, the misrepresentation shall be deemed to be contained in the prospectus.

2006, c. 33, Sched. Z.5, s. 4

OSA 63(8)

Related Provisions: OSA 130.

OSA 63

Definitions: OSA 1(1)"person"; 1(1)"company"; 1(1)"material fact"; 1(1)"distribution"; 1(1)"distribution to the public"; "Director"; 1(1)"Commission"; 1(1.2)"dealer".

Rules: Rules 41-801, 44-801, s. 1.1; NI 81-101.

Policies and Orders: OPS 13-601.

64. (1) Orders to furnish information re distribution to public — Where a person or company proposing to make a distribution of previously issued securities of an issuer is unable to obtain from the issuer of the securities information or material that is necessary for the purpose of complying with this Part or the regulations, the Director may order the issuer of the securities to furnish to the person or company that proposes to make the distribution such information and material as the Director considers necessary for the purposes of the distribution, upon such terms and subject to such conditions as the Director considers proper, and all such information and material may be used by the person or company to whom it is furnished for the purpose of complying with this Part and the regulations.

(2) Idem — Where a person or company proposing to make a distribution of previously issued securities of an issuer is unable to obtain any or all of the signatures to the certificates required by this Act or the regulations, or otherwise to comply with this Part or the regulations, the Director may, upon being satisfied that all reasonable efforts have been made to comply with this Part and the regulations and that no person or company is likely to be prejudicially affected by such failure to comply, make such order waiving any of the provisions of this Part or the regulations as the Director considers advisable, upon such terms and subject to such conditions as he or she considers proper.

OSA 64

Definitions: OSA 1(1)"person"; 1(1)"company"; 1(1)"distribution"; 1(1)"security"; 1(1)"issuer"; 1(1)"Director".

OSA Part XV

Related Provisions: OSA Part XVII.

Rules: NI 41-101, 44-101, 44-102, 44-103, 81-101.

Policies and Orders: NPS 41-101CP, 44-101CP, 44-102CP, 44-103CP, 81-101CP.

Proposed Addition — 64.1, 64.2

PART XV.1 — TRADING IN DERIVATIVES (SS. 64.1, 64.2)

[Heading added 2010, c. 26, Sched. 18, s. 28. Not in force at date of publication.]

64.1 (1) Disclosure document, designated derivative — No person or company shall trade a designated derivative unless a disclosure document that satisfies the requirements prescribed by the regulations,

(a) has been filed and accepted by the Director; and

(b) has been delivered in accordance with the regulations.

(2) Exception — Subsection (1) does not apply in respect of,

(a) a trade described in clause (e) of the definition of ""trade" or "trading"" in subsection 1 (1); or

(b) a trade that is otherwise exempt under this Act or the regulations.

(3) Acceptance of disclosure document — The Director shall accept the filed disclosure document unless,

(a) the Director considers that it would not be in the public interest to accept the disclosure document; or

(b) the Director is prohibited by the regulations from accepting it.

(4) Opportunity to be heard — The Director shall not refuse to accept a disclosure document that satisfies the requirements prescribed by the regulations without giving the person or company that filed the disclosure document an opportunity to be heard.

(5) Part XV not applicable — Part XV and the regulations made for the purposes of that Part do not apply in respect of,

(a) a designated derivative; or

(b) a derivative that is traded on,

(i) an exchange, under standardized terms determined by the exchange, or

(ii) any other marketplace, if any conditions prescribed by the regulations are satisfied.

2010, c. 26, Sched. 18, s. 28 [Not in force at date of publication.]

OSA 64.1

Definitions: OSA 1(1)"designated derivative"; 1(1)"marketplace".

64.2 (1) Deemed to be securities for certain purposes — If authorized by the regulations, a derivative that belongs to a class of derivatives prescribed by the regulations is deemed to be a security for such purposes as may be prescribed by the regulations, and such provisions of this Act and the regulations as may be prescribed by the regulations apply to or in respect of the derivative in the manner and to the extent prescribed by the regulations.

(2) Not void for failure to comply with Act, etc. — Unless the terms of the derivative provide otherwise, a derivative transaction is not void, voidable or unenforceable, and no counterparty to the transaction is entitled to rescind the transaction, solely by reason that the transaction failed to comply with this Act or the regulations.

2010, c. 26, Sched. 18, s. 28 [Not in force at date of publication.]

PART XVI — DISTRIBUTION — GENERALLY (SS. 65–71)

65. (1) "waiting period" defined — In this section,

"waiting period" means the period prescribed by regulation or, if no period is prescribed, the period between the Director's issuance of a receipt for a preliminary prospectus relating to the offering of a security and the Director's issuance of a receipt for the prospectus.

OSA 65(1)

Rules: NI 41-101, s. 1.1.

(2) Distribution of material during waiting period — Despite section 53, but subject to Part XIII, it is permissible during the waiting period,

(a) to distribute a notice, circular, advertisement or letter to or otherwise communicate with any person or company identifying the security proposed to be issued, stating the price thereof, if then determined, the name and address of a person or company from whom purchases of the security may be made and containing such further information as may be permitted or required by the regulations, if every such notice, circular, advertisement, letter or other communication states the name and address of a person or company from whom a preliminary prospectus may be obtained;

(b) to distribute a preliminary prospectus; and

(c) to solicit expressions of interest from a prospective purchaser if, prior to such solicitation or forthwith after the prospective purchaser indicates an interest in purchasing the security, a copy of the preliminary prospectus is forwarded to him, her or it.

2007, c. 7, Sched. 38, s. 6

OSA 65(2)

Related Provisions: OSA 53, Part XIII.

OSA 65
Related Provisions: OSA 66–69, 53.
Definitions: OSA 1(1)"Director"; 1(1)"security"; 1(1)"person"; 1(1)"company".
Rules: NI 41-101, 44-101.

66. Distribution of preliminary prospectus — Any dealer distributing a security to which section 65 applies shall, in addition to the requirements of clause 65(2)(c), send a copy of the preliminary prospectus to each prospective purchaser who, without solicitation, indicates an interest in purchasing the security and requests a copy of such preliminary prospectus.

OSA 66
Related Provisions: OSA 65, 65(2)(c).
Definitions: OSA 1(1)"security".

67. Distribution list — Any dealer distributing a security to which section 65 applies shall maintain a record of the names and addresses of all persons and companies to whom the preliminary prospectus has been forwarded.

OSA 67
Definitions: OSA 1(1)"security"; 1(1)"person"; 1(1)"company"; 1(1)"distribution"; 1(1.2)"dealer".
Policies and Orders: NPS 47-201.

68. Defective preliminary prospectus — Where it appears to the Director that a preliminary prospectus is defective in that it does not substantially comply with the requirements of Ontario securities law as to form and content, the Director may, without giving notice, order that the trading permitted by subsection 65(2) in the security to which the preliminary prospectus relates shall cease until a revised preliminary prospectus satisfactory to the Director is filed and forwarded to each recipient of the defective preliminary prospectus according to the record maintained under section 67.

1994, c. 11, s. 368

OSA 68
Related Provisions: OSA 65(2), 67.
Definitions: OSA 1(1)"trade"; 1(1)"security".

69. Material given on distribution — From the date of the issuance by the Director of a receipt for a prospectus relating to a security, a person or company trading in the security in a distribution, either on his, her or its own account or on behalf of any other person or company, may distribute the prospectus, any document filed with or referred to in the prospectus and any notice, circular, advertisement, or letter of the nature described in clause 65(2)(a) or in the regulations, but shall not distribute any other printed or written material respecting the security that is prohibited by the regulations.

OSA 69
Related Provisions: OSA 65(2)(a).
Definitions: OSA 1(1)"distribution"; 1(1)"Director"; 1(1)"security"; 1(1)"person"; 1(1)"company"; 1(1)"trade".
Rules: NI 41-101, 44-101.

70. (1) Order to cease trading — Where it appears to the Commission, after the filing of a prospectus under this Part and the issuance of a receipt therefor, that any of the circumstances set out in subsection 61(2) exist, the Commission may order that the distribution of the securities under the prospectus shall cease.

OSA 70(1)
Related Provisions: OSA 61(2), OSA 127.
Regulations: Reg.: 239.

(2) Hearing — No order shall be made under subsection (1) without a hearing unless in the opinion of the Commission the length of time required for a hearing could be prejudicial to the public interest, in which event a temporary order may be made which shall expire fifteen days from the date of the making thereof unless the hearing is commenced in which case the Commission may extend the order until the hearing is concluded.

(3) Notice — A notice of every order made under this section shall be served upon the issuer to whose securities the prospectus relates, and forthwith upon the receipt of the notice,

    (a) distribution of the securities under prospectus by the person or company named in the order shall cease; and

    (b) any receipt issued by the Director for the prospectus is revoked.

OSA 70
Definitions: OSA 1(1)"trade"; 1(1)"Commission"; 1(1)"distribution"; 1(1)"security"; 1(1)"person"; 1(1)"company".

71. (1) Obligation to deliver prospectus — A dealer not acting as agent of the purchaser who receives an order or subscription for a security offered in a distribution to which subsection 53(1) or section 62 is applicable shall, unless the dealer has previously done so, send by prepaid mail or deliver to the purchaser the latest prospectus and any amendment to the prospectus filed either before entering into an agreement of purchase and sale resulting from the order or subscription or not later than midnight on the second day, exclusive of Saturdays, Sundays, and holidays, after entering into such agreement.

OSA 71(1)

Related Provisions: OSA 53(1), 62.

(1.1) Same, investment fund securities — Subsection (1) does not apply to the dealer in respect of a purchase and sale of an investment fund security offered in a distribution described in that subsection if the regulations prescribe a disclosure document that is required in respect of the purchase and sale and the time and manner in which the disclosure document is to be sent or delivered to a purchaser.

Proposed Addition — 71(1.2), (1.3)

(1.2) Exchange traded funds — Subsection (1) does not apply in respect of a distribution of a prescribed investment fund security trading on an exchange or an alternative trading system.

(1.3) Obligation to deliver prospectus — A dealer acting as agent of the purchaser who receives an order from the purchaser for a purchase of a prescribed investment fund security trading on an exchange or an alternative trading system shall send or deliver to the purchaser a prescribed disclosure document in accordance with the regulations.

2014, c. 7, Sched. 28, s. 4(1) [Not in force at date of publication.]

(2) Withdrawal from purchase — An agreement of purchase and sale referred to in subsection (1) is not binding upon the purchaser if the dealer from whom the purchaser purchases the security receives written or telegraphic notice evidencing the intention of the purchaser not to be bound by the agreement of purchase and sale not later than midnight on the second day, exclusive of Saturdays, Sundays and holidays, after receipt by the purchaser of,

    (a) the latest prospectus and any amendment to the prospectus; or

    (b) the prescribed disclosure document referred to in subsection (1.1).

Proposed Addition — 7(2.1)

(2.1) Same, exchange traded funds — A purchase referred to in subsection (1.3) is not binding on the purchaser in the circumstances prescribed by the regulations.

2014, c. 7, Sched. 28, s. 4(2) [Not in force at date of publication.]

(3) Application of subs. (2) — Subsection (2) does not apply if the purchaser is a registrant or if the purchaser sells or otherwise transfers beneficial ownership of the security referred to in subsection (2), otherwise than to secure indebtedness, before the expiration of the time referred to in subsection (2).

(4) Time of receipt — For the purpose of this section, where the latest prospectus, any amendment to the prospectus or the prescribed disclosure document referred to in subsection (1.1) is sent by prepaid mail, it shall be deemed conclusively to have been received in the ordinary course of mail by the person or company to whom it was addressed.

Proposed Amendment — 71(4)

(4) Time of receipt — For the purpose of this section, where the latest prospectus, any amendment to the prospectus or the prescribed disclosure document referred to in subsection (1.1) or (1.3) is sent by prepaid mail, it shall be deemed conclusively to have been received in the ordinary course of mail by the person or company to whom it was addressed.

2014, c. 7, Sched. 28, s. 4(3) [Not in force at date of publication.]

(5) Receipt of prospectus, disclosure document by agent — The receipt of the latest prospectus, any amendment to the prospectus or the prescribed disclosure document referred to in subsection (1.1) by a dealer who is acting as agent of or who thereafter commences to act as agent of the purchaser with respect to the purchase of a security to which subsection (1) or (1.1) applies shall, for the purpose of this section, be receipt by the purchaser as of the date on which the agent received such latest prospectus, amendment to the prospectus or prescribed disclosure document, as the case may be.

(6) Receipt of notice by agent — The receipt of the notice referred to in subsection (2) by a dealer who acted as agent of the vendor with respect to the sale of the security referred to in subsection (1) shall, for the purpose of this section, be receipt by the vendor as of the date on which the agent received such notice.

(7) Dealer as agent — For the purpose of this section, a dealer shall not be considered to be acting as agent of the purchaser unless the dealer is acting solely as agent of the purchaser with respect to the purchase and sale in question and has not received and has no agreement to receive compensation from or on behalf of the vendor with respect to the purchase and sale.

Proposed Amendment — 71(7)

(7) Dealer as agent — For the purpose of this section, except subsection (1.3), a dealer shall not be considered to be acting as agent of the purchaser unless the dealer is acting solely as agent of the purchaser with respect to the purchase and sale in question and has not received and has no agreement to receive compensation from or on behalf of the vendor with respect to the purchase and sale.

2014, c. 7, Sched. 28, s. 4(4) [Not in force at date of publication.]

(8) Onus of proof — The onus of proving that the time for giving notice under subsection (2) has expired is upon the dealer from whom the purchaser has agreed to purchase the security.

2011, c. 9, Sched. 38, s. 2

OSA 71

Related Provisions: OSA 73(2), 57.

Definitions: OSA 1(1)"security"; 1(1)"distribution"; 1(1)"registrant"; 1(1.2)"dealer".

Rules: NI 81-101, s. 3.2.

Policies and Orders: NPS 11-201.

PART XVII — EXEMPTIONS FROM THE PROSPECTUS REQUIREMENT (SS. 72–74)

[Heading amended 2009, c. 18, Sched. 26, s. 11.]

72. Definition — In this Part,

"prospectus requirement" means sections 53 and 62.

1994, c. 11, s. 369; 1997, c. 19, s. 23(11), (12); 1999, c. 6, s. 60(3); 1999, c. 9, s. 207; 2001, c. 23, s. 213; 2005, c. 5, s. 64(3); 2006, c. 33, Sched. Z.5, s. 5; 2009, c. 18, Sched. 26, s. 11

73. Exemption, debt securities of governments in Canada — The prospectus requirement does not apply to a distribution of any of the following debt securities:

1. Debt securities issued or guaranteed by the Government of Canada or the government of a province or territory of Canada.

2. Debt securities that are,

   i. issued by a municipal corporation in Canada for elementary, secondary or vocational school purposes,

   ii. issued or guaranteed by a municipal corporation in Canada, or

   iii. secured by or payable out of rates or taxes levied under the law of a province or territory of Canada on property in the province or territory and collectible by or through the municipality in which the property is situated.

3. Debt securities that are issued by a corporation established under regulations made under subsection 248(1) of the *Education Act*.

1993, c. 27, Sched.; 2009, c. 18, Sched. 26, s. 12

OSA 73

Related Provisions: OSA 143(1)(a.0.1).

Rules: NI 45-106; Rule 45-501.

73.1 Exemption, securities of financial institutions — (1) Debt securities — The prospectus requirement does not apply to a distribution of a debt security that is issued or guaranteed by any of the following financial institutions:

1. A bank listed in Schedule I, II or III to the *Bank Act* (Canada).

2. An association to which the *Cooperative Credit Associations Act* (Canada) applies or a central cooperative credit society for which an order has been made under subsection 473(1) of that Act.

3. A loan corporation, trust company, trust corporation, insurance company, treasury branch, credit union, caisse populaire, financial services cooperative or credit union league or federation that is authorized by a statute of Canada or Ontario to carry on business in Canada or Ontario, as the case may be.

4. Such other financial institutions as may be prescribed by the regulations.

(2) Exception, subordinated debt securities — The exemption under paragraph 1, 2 or 3 of subsection (1) from the prospectus requirement does not apply to debt securities issued or guaranteed by a financial institution described in the paragraph that are subordinate in right of payment to deposits held by the issuer or guarantor of those debt securities.

(3) Conditions and restrictions — The exemption under subsection (1) with respect to a financial institution described in paragraph 1, 2 or 3 of that subsection is subject to such conditions and restrictions as may be prescribed by a regulation made by the Lieutenant Governor in Council.

OSA 73.1(3)

Related Provisions: OSA 143(1)20.

(4) Same — The exemption under subsection (1) with respect to a financial institution referred to in paragraph 4 of that subsection is subject to such conditions and restrictions as may be prescribed by the regulations.

(5) Report — Without limiting the generality of subsection (4), the regulations may prescribe reporting requirements that apply in connection with the exemption under subsection (1) with respect to a financial institution referred to in paragraph 4 of that subsection.

(6) Other securities — The prospectus requirement does not apply to a distribution of any of the following securities:

1. Securities issued by a corporation to which the *Co-operative Corporations Act* applies.

2. Membership shares and patronage shares, within the meaning of the *Credit Unions and Caisses Populaires Act, 1994*, of a credit union.

3. Securities issued to its members by a credit union to which the *Credit Unions and Caisses Populaires Act, 1994* applies.

4. Securities issued to its members or to the members of its member credit unions by a league to which the *Credit Unions and Caisses Populaires Act, 1994* applies.

2009, c. 18, Sched. 26, s. 12(2)

73.2 Exemption, where other legislation applies — (1) Secured by or under a security agreement — Subject to subsection (2), the prospectus requirement does not apply to a distribution of a security evidencing indebtedness that is secured by or under a security agreement, as defined in subsection 1(1) of the *Personal Property Security Act*, or that is secured in a similar manner in accordance with comparable legislation of another province or territory of Canada that provides for the granting of security in personal property.

(2) Exception to exemption — The exemption under subsection (1) from the prospectus requirement does not apply to a distribution to an individual.

(3) Distribution by licensed mortgage brokerage, etc. — The prospectus requirement does not apply to a distribution of a security evidencing indebtedness secured by a mortgage or charge on real property in Canada if the distribution is made by a person or company,

(a) that is licensed under the *Mortgage Brokerages, Lenders and Administrators Act, 2006* or is exempt from the requirement to be licensed under that Act, if the real property is in Ontario; or

(b) that is licensed or registered under comparable legislation in the province or territory of Canada, other than Ontario, in which the real property is located, or is exempt from any legislative requirement to be licensed or registered in the province or territory.

2009, c. 18, Sched. 26, s. 12(2)

73.3 Exemption, accredited investor — (1) Definition — For the purposes of this section,

"accredited investor" means,

(a) a financial institution described in paragraph 1, 2 or 3 of subsection 73.1(1),

(b) the Business Development Bank of Canada,

(c) a subsidiary of any person or company referred to in clause (a) or (b), if the person or company owns all of the voting securities of the subsidiary, except the voting securities required by law to be owned by directors of that subsidiary,

(d) a person or company registered under the securities legislation of a province or territory of Canada as an adviser or dealer, except as otherwise prescribed by the regulations,

(e) the Government of Canada, the government of a province or territory of Canada, or any Crown corporation, agency or wholly owned entity of the Government of Canada or of the government of a province or territory of Canada,

(f) a municipality, public board or commission in Canada and a metropolitan community, school board, the Comité de gestion de la taxe scolaire de l'Île de Montréal or an intermunicipal management board in Quebec,

(g) any national, federal, state, provincial, territorial or municipal government of or in any foreign jurisdiction, or any agency of that government,

(h) a pension fund that is regulated by either the Office of the Superintendent of Financial Institutions (Canada) or a pension commission or similar regulatory authority of a province or territory of Canada,

(i) a person or company that is recognized or designated by the Commission as an accredited investor,

(j) such other persons or companies as may be prescribed by the regulations.

(2) Exemption — The prospectus requirement does not apply to a distribution of a security if the purchaser purchases the security as principal and is an accredited investor.

(3) Status as principal — The regulations may prescribe circumstances in which a person or company is deemed to be purchasing a security as principal for the purposes of an exemption under this section.

(4) Conditions and restrictions — The regulations may prescribe conditions and restrictions that apply to an exemption under this section.

(5) Report — Without limiting the generality of subsection (4), the regulations may prescribe reporting requirements that apply in connection with an exemption under this section.

(6) Interpretation — For the purposes of the definition of "accredited investor" in subsection (1), the regulations may define "foreign jurisdiction" and "subsidiary".

2009, c. 18, Sched. 26, s. 12(2)

OSA 73.3

Rules: NI 45-106, 2.3.

73.4 Exemption, private issuer — (1) Definition — For the purposes of this section,

"private issuer" has the meaning prescribed by the regulations.

(2) Exemption — The prospectus requirement does not apply to a distribution of a security of a private issuer to a person or company who purchases the security as principal and who satisfies the criteria prescribed by regulation.

(3) Conditions and restrictions — The regulations may prescribe conditions and restrictions that apply to an exemption under this section. 2009, c. 18, Sched. 26, s. 12(2)

73.5 Exemption, government incentive securities — (1) Definition — For the purposes of this section,

"government incentive security" means a security that enables the holder to receive a grant or other monetary or tax benefit pursuant to a provision of an Act or regulation of Canada, Ontario or another province or territory of Canada, and that is prescribed by the regulations as a government incentive security.

(2) Exemption — The prospectus requirement does not apply to a distribution of a government incentive security.

(3) Conditions and restrictions — The regulations may prescribe conditions and restrictions that apply to an exemption under this section.

(4) Report — Without limiting the generality of subsection (3), the regulations may prescribe reporting requirements that apply in connection with an exemption under this section.

2009, c. 18, Sched. 26, s. 12(2)

73.6 (1) Additional exemptions by regulation — The regulations may prescribe exemptions from the prospectus requirement in addition to the exemptions provided under sections 73 to 73.5.

(2) Report — Without limiting the generality of subsection (1), the regulations may prescribe reporting requirements that apply in connection with an exemption authorized by that subsection.

2009, c. 18, Sched. 26, s. 12(2)

73.7 (1) Resale of securities, deemed distribution — The regulations may provide that the first trade in a security previously distributed under an exemption from the prospectus requirement is deemed to be a distribution unless it is carried out in accordance with the regulations.

(2) Distribution by a control person — Without limiting the generality of subsection (1), the regulations shall prescribe the circumstances in which a distribution by a control person is exempted from the prospectus requirement.

2009, c. 18, Sched. 26, s. 13

OSA 73.7

Rules: NI 45-102.

74. (1) Exemption order — Upon the application of an interested person or company, the Commission may make the following rulings if the Commission is satisfied that to do so would not be prejudicial to the public interest:

1. A ruling that any person or company is not subject to section 25.

2. A ruling that any trade, intended trade, security, person or company is not subject to section 53.

OSA 74(1)

Related Provisions: OSA 25, 53.

(1.1) Terms and conditions — In a ruling under subsection (1), the Commission may impose such terms and conditions as are considered necessary.

(2) Determination of whether distribution has ceased — Where doubt exists whether a distribution of any security has been concluded or is currently in progress, the Commission may determine the question and rule accordingly.

(3) Ruling final — A decision of the Commission under this section is final and there is no appeal therefrom.

2009, c. 18, Sched. 26, s. 14

OSA 74

Definitions: OSA 1(1)"person"; 1(1)"company"; 1(1)"trade"; 1(1)"security"; 1(1)"distribution"; 1(1)"Commission".

Rules: Rules Part III, IV, VII, VIII and IX.

Policies and Orders: OPS 2.1, 13-601.

OSA Part XVII

Related Provisions: OSA 143(1)20.

Rules: NI 45-106, 45-102; Rule 45-501.

PART XVIII — CONTINUOUS DISCLOSURE (SS. 75–83.1)

75. (1) Publication of material change — Subject to subsection (3), where a material change occurs in the affairs of a reporting issuer, it shall forthwith issue and file a news release authorized by a senior officer disclosing the nature and substance of the change.

(2) Report of material change — Subject to subsection (3), the reporting issuer shall file a report of such material change in accordance with the regulations as soon as practicable and in any event within ten days of the date on which the change occurs.

OSA 75(2)

Regulations: Reg.: 3.

(3) Exception — A reporting issuer may, instead of complying with subsection (1), promptly file with the Commission the report required under subsection (2), marked as confidential, and its written reasons for doing so if,

(a) the reporting issuer reasonably believes that a disclosure required under subsections (1) and (2) would be unduly detrimental to its interests; or

(b) the material change consists of a decision made by the senior management of the reporting issuer to implement a change and the senior management,

(i) believes that confirmation by the board of directors of the decision to implement the change is probable, and

(ii) has no reason to believe that any person or company with knowledge of the material change has purchased or sold the reporting issuer's securities or traded a related derivative.

(4) Idem — Where a report has been filed with the Commission under subsection (3), the reporting issuer shall advise the Commission in writing where it believes the report should continue to remain confidential within ten days of the date of filing of the initial report and every ten days thereafter until the material change is generally disclosed in the manner referred to in subsection (1) or, if the material change consists of a decision of the type referred to in clause (3)(b), until that decision has been rejected by the board of directors of the issuer.

(5) Requirement to disclose subsequently — A reporting issuer that has filed a report under subsection (3) shall promptly disclose the material change in the manner referred to in subsection (1) if the reporting issuer becomes aware or has reasonable grounds to believe that a person or company having knowledge of the material change is purchasing or selling securities of the reporting issuer or trading a related derivative.

1994, c. 11, s. 349; 2002, c. 22, s. 180; 2004, c. 31, Sched. 34, s. 3; 2010, c. 26, Sched. 18, s. 29

OSA 75

Related Provisions: OSA 72(8), 82.

Definitions: OSA 1(1)"material change"; 1(1)"reporting issuer"; 1(1)"Commission"; 1(1)"related derivative".

Rules: NI 13-101, 51-102, Part 7, 81-106, Part 11, 71-102; Rules 51-801, 71-802, 81-801.

Policies and Orders: OPS 13-601, 52-601, 57-603, 51-801CP; OSCN 51-708, 53-701, 52-710; NPS 51-201, 51-102CP.

76. (1) Trading where undisclosed change — No person or company in a special relationship with an issuer shall purchase or sell securities of the issuer with the knowledge of a material fact or material change with respect to the issuer that has not been generally disclosed.

(2) Tipping — No issuer and no person or company in a special relationship with an issuer shall inform, other than in the necessary course of business, another person or company of a material fact or material change with respect to the issuer before the material fact or material change has been generally disclosed.

(3) Same — No person or company that is considering or evaluating whether, or that proposes,

(a) to make a take-over bid, as defined in Part XX, for the securities of an issuer;

(b) to become a party to a reorganization, amalgamation, merger, arrangement or similar business combination with an issuer; or

(c) to acquire a substantial portion of the property of an issuer,

shall inform another person or company of a material fact or material change with respect to the issuer before the material fact or material change has been generally disclosed except where the information is given in the necessary course of business relating to the take-over bid, business combination or acquisition.

OSA 76(3)

Related Provisions: OSA 89(1).

Proposed Addition — 76(3.1)

(3.1) Recommendation — No issuer, no person or company in a special relationship with an issuer, and no person or company that is considering or evaluating whether, or that proposes to take one or more of the actions described in clause (3)(a), (b) or (c) shall recommend or encourage, other than in the necessary course of business, another person or company to purchase or sell securities of the issuer with the knowledge of a material fact or material change with respect to the issuer that has not been generally disclosed.

2016, c. 5, Sched. 26, s. 2(1) [Not in force at date of publication.]

(4) Defence — No person or company shall be found to have contravened subsection (1), (2) or (3) if the person or company proves that the person or company reasonably believed that the material fact or material change had been generally disclosed.

Proposed Amendment — 76(4)

(4) Defence — No person or company shall be found to have contravened subsection (1), (2), (3) or (3.1) if the person or company proves that the person or company reasonably believed that the material fact or material change had been generally disclosed.

2016, c. 5, Sched. 26, s. 2(2) [Not in force at date of publication.]

(5) Definition — For the purposes of this section,

"insider" includes a person or company that would be an insider of an issuer if the issuer were a reporting issuer;

"issuer" means,

(a) a reporting issuer, or

(b) any other issuer whose securities are publicly traded;

"person or company in a special relationship with an issuer" means,

(a) a person or company that is an insider, affiliate or associate of,

(i) the issuer,

ACT

(ii) a person or company that is considering or evaluating whether to make a take-over bid, as defined in Part XX, or that proposes to make a take-over bid, as defined in Part XX, for the securities of the issuer, or

(iii) a person or company that is considering or evaluating whether to become a party, or that proposes to become a party, to a reorganization, amalgamation, merger or arrangement or similar business combination with the issuer or to acquire a substantial portion of its property,

(b) a person or company that is engaging in any business or professional activity, that is considering or evaluating whether to engage in any business or professional activity, or that proposes to engage in any business or professional activity if the business or professional activity is,

(i) with or on behalf of the issuer, or

(ii) with or on behalf of a person or company described in subclause (a)(ii) or (iii),

(c) a person who is a director, officer or employee of,

(i) the issuer,

(ii) a subsidiary of the issuer,

(iii) a person or company that controls, directly or indirectly, the issuer, or

(iv) a person or company described in subclause (a)(ii) or (iii) or clause (b),

(d) a person or company that learned of the material fact or material change with respect to the issuer while the person or company was a person or company described in clause (a), (b) or (c);

(e) a person or company that learns of a material fact or material change with respect to the issuer from any other person or company described in this subsection, including a person or company described in this clause, and knows or ought reasonably to have known that the other person or company is a person or company in such a relationship;

"reporting issuer" [Repealed 2015, c. 20, Sched. 39, s. 2(7).]

OSA 76(5)

Related Provisions: OSA 89(1).

(6) Idem — For the purpose of subsection (1), a security of the issuer shall be deemed to include,

Proposed Amendment — 76(6) opening words

(6) Idem — For the purpose of subsections (1) and (3.1), a security of the issuer shall be deemed to include,

2016, c. 5, Sched. 26, s. 2(3) [Not in force at date of publication.]

(a) a put, call, option or other right or obligation to purchase or sell securities of the issuer;

(b) a security, the market price of which varies materially with the market price of the securities of the issuer; or

(c) a related derivative.

2010, c. 26, Sched. 18, s. 30; 2013, c. 2, Sched. 13, s. 2; 2015, c. 20, Sched. 39, s. 2(1), (2), (4), (5), (7)

OSA 76

Definitions: OSA 1(1)"person"; 1(1)"company"; 1(1)"reporting issuer"; 1(1)"material fact"; 1(1)"material change"; 1(1)"security"; 1(1)"associate"; 1(1)"director"; 1(1)"officer"; 1(1)"related derivative".

Regulations: Reg.: 175.

Policies and Orders: OPS 33-601; NPS 51-201.

77. (1) Interim financial reports — Every reporting issuer that is not a mutual fund shall file within sixty days of the date to which it is made up an interim financial report,

(a) where the reporting issuer has not completed its first financial year, for the periods commencing with the beginning of that year and ending nine, six and three months respectively before the date on which that year ends, but no interim financial report is required to be filed for any period that is less than three months in length;

(b) where the reporting issuer has completed its first financial year, to the end of each of the three-month, six-month and nine-month periods of the current financial year that commenced immediately following the last financial year, including a comparative statement to the end of each of the corresponding periods in the last financial year,

made up and certified as required by the regulations and in accordance with generally accepted accounting principles.

(2) Idem — Every mutual fund in Ontario shall file within sixty days of the date to which it is made up an interim financial report,

(a) where the mutual fund in Ontario has not completed its first financial year, for the period commencing with the beginning of that year and ending six months before the date on which that year ends but, if the first financial year is less than six months in length, no interim financial report is required to be filed;

(b) where the mutual fund in Ontario has completed its first financial year, for the six-month period of the current financial year that commenced immediately following the last financial year,

made up and certified as required by the regulations and in accordance with generally accepted accounting principles.

2002, c. 18, Sched. H, s. 9; 2010, c. 1, Sched. 26, s. 4

OSA 77(2)

Rules: NI 81-104, Part 8.

OSA 77

Related Provisions: OSA 72(8).

Definitions: OSA 1(1)"reporting issuer"; 1(1)"mutual fund"; 1(1)"mutual fund in Ontario".

Regulations: Reg.: 161.

Rules: Rules 51-801, 71-802, 81-801; NI 13-101, 51-102, Part 4, 52-107, 52-109, 71-101, 71-102, 81-106, Parts 2 and 3.

Policies and Orders: OPS 13-601, 51-603, 51-801CP; OSCN 52-710, 51-102CP, 81-106CP.

78. (1) Comparative financial statements — Every reporting issuer that is not a mutual fund and every mutual fund in Ontario shall file annually within 140 days from the end of its last financial year comparative financial statements relating separately to,

> (a) the period that commenced on the date of incorporation or organization and ended as of the close of the first financial year or, if the reporting issuer or mutual fund has completed a financial year, the last financial year, as the case may be; and

> (b) the period covered by the financial year next preceding the last financial year, if any,

made up and certified as required by the regulations and in accordance with generally accepted accounting principles.

(2) Auditor's report — Every financial statement referred to in subsection (1) shall be accompanied by a report of the auditor of the reporting issuer or mutual fund prepared in accordance with the regulations.

(3) Auditor's examination — The auditor of a reporting issuer or mutual fund shall make such examinations as will enable the auditor to make the report required by subsection (2).

(4) "auditor" defined — For the purposes of this Part, **"auditor"**, where used in relation to the reporting issuer or mutual fund, includes the auditor of the reporting issuer or mutual fund and any other independent public accountant.

OSA 78

Related Provisions: OSA 72(8).

Definitions: OSA 1(1)"reporting issuer"; 1(1)"mutual fund"; 1(1)"mutual fund in Ontario".

Rules: NI 13-101, 51-102, Part 4, 52-107, 52-108, 52-109, 52-110, 71-101, 71-102, 81-106, Parts 2 and 3; Rules 51-801, 71-802.

Policies and Orders: OPS 13-601, 51-603, 51-801CP, 81-801CP; NPS 51-102CP, 71-102CP, 81-106CP; CSAN 42-301, 52-302 to OSCN 52-716.

79. (1) Delivery of financial statements to security holders — Every reporting issuer or mutual fund in Ontario that is required to file a financial statement under section 77 or 78 shall send a true copy of the financial statement to every holder of its securities whose latest address, as shown on its books, is in Ontario.

(2) Deadline — The reporting issuer or mutual fund in Ontario shall send the true copy of the financial statement no later than the end of the period during which it is required to file the financial statement under section 77 or 78.

(3) Exception — Despite subsection (1), a reporting issuer or mutual fund in Ontario is not required to send a copy of the financial statement to a security holder who holds its evidence of indebtedness only.

(4) Deemed compliance — If the laws of a reporting issuer's jurisdiction of incorporation, organization or continuance impose requirements corresponding to the requirements in subsections (1) and (2), compliance with the requirements imposed by that jurisdiction shall be deemed to be compliance with the requirements in subsections (1) and (2).

2002, c. 18, Sched. H, s. 10

OSA 79

Related Provisions: OSA 77, 78.

Definitions: OSA 1(1)"reporting issuer"; 1(1)"mutual fund in Ontario"; 1(1)"security".

Rules: NI 44-101, 51-102, Part 4, 54-102, 71-101, 71-102, 81-106, Part 2; Rule 44-801, 51-801, 71-802, 81-801.

Policies and Orders: OPS 51-801CP, 52-601; NPS 71-102CP, 81-106CP.

80. Relief against certain requirement — Upon the application of a reporting issuer or other interested person or company or upon the motion of the Commission, the Commission may, where in the opinion of the Commission to do so would not be prejudicial to the public interest, make an order on such terms and conditions as the Commission may impose,

> (a) [Repealed 1999, c. 9, s. 208(2).]

> (b) exempting, in whole or in part, any reporting issuer from a requirement of this Part or the regulations relating to a requirement of this Part,

>> (i) if such requirement conflicts with a requirement of the laws of the jurisdiction under which the reporting issuer is incorporated, organized or continued,

>> (ii) if the reporting issuer ordinarily distributes financial information to holders of its securities in a form, or at times, different from those required by this Part, or

>> (iii) if otherwise satisfied in the circumstances of the particular case that there is adequate justification for so doing.

1994, c. 33, s. 4; 1999, c. 9, s. 208

OSA 80

Definitions: OSA 1(1)"reporting issuer"; 1(1)"Commission"; 1(1)"security".

Rules: NI 44-101, 51-102, 71-101, 71-102, 81-106; 13-502, App. C, Item E(3).

Policies and Orders: OPS 2.1, 52-601; OSCN 52-710; NPS 51-102CP, 71-102CP.

81. (1) Filing of information circular — Where the management of a reporting issuer is required to send an information circular under clause 86(1)(a), the reporting issuer shall forthwith file a copy of such information circular certified in accordance with the regulations.

OSA 81(1)

Related Provisions: OSA 86(1)(a).

(2) Idem — In any case where subsection (1) is not applicable, the reporting issuer shall file annually within 140 days from the end of its last financial year a report prepared and certified in accordance with the regulations.

OSA 81

Definitions: OSA 1(1)"reporting issuer".

Regulations: Reg.: 181.

Rules: NI 13-101, 51-102, Part 9, 71-101, 71-102, 81-106, Part 12; Rules 51-801, 71-802, 81-801.

Policies and Orders: OPS 13-601, 51-801CP, 81-801CP.

82. Filing of documents filed in another jurisdiction — Where the laws of the jurisdiction in which the reporting issuer was incorporated, organized or continued require the reporting issuer to file substantially the same information in that jurisdiction as is required by this Part, the reporting issuer may comply with the filing requirements of this Part by filing copies of the news release, timely disclosure report, information circular or financial statements and auditor's report, as the case may be, required by that jurisdiction provided such releases, reports, circulars or statements are manually signed or certified in accordance with the regulations.

1994, c. 11, s. 349

OSA 82

Definitions: OSA 1(1)"reporting issuer".

Rules: NI 71-102; Rule 71-802.

Policies and Orders: NPS 71-102CP.

83. List of reporting issuers in default — The Commission may publish a list of reporting issuers who are in default of any requirement of this Act or the regulations.

2006, c. 33, Sched. Z.5, s. 6; 2010, c. 1, Sched. 26, s. 5

OSA 83

Definitions: OSA 1(1)"Commission"; 1(1)"reporting issuer"; 1(1)"regulations".

Policies and Orders: CSAN 51-322; OPS 51-601.

83.1 [Repealed 2006, c. 33, Sched. Z.5, s. 6.]

OSA Part XVIII

Rules: NI 51-102, 52-107, 52-108, 52-109, 52-110, 71-101, 71-102, 81-106; Rule 51-801, 71-801, 71-802, 81-801.

Policies and Orders: OPS 51-801CP, 81-801CP; NPS 12-203, 51-201, 51-102CP, 81-106CP, 51; OSCN 52-710.

PART XIX — PROXIES AND PROXY SOLICITATION (SS. 84–88)

84. Definitions — In this Part,

"information circular" means an information circular prepared in accordance with the regulations;

"solicit" and **"solicitation"** include,

(a) any request for a proxy whether or not accompanied by or included in a form of proxy,

(b) any request to execute or not to execute a form of proxy or to revoke a proxy,

(c) the sending or delivery of a form of proxy or other communication to a security holder under circumstances reasonably calculated to result in the procurement, withholding or revocation of a proxy,

(d) the sending or delivery of a form of proxy to a security holder under section 85,

but do not include,

(e) the sending or delivery of a form of proxy to a security holder in response to an unsolicited request made by the security holder or on the security holder's behalf,

(f) the performance by any person or company of ministerial acts or professional services on behalf of a person or company soliciting a proxy, or

(g) such other activities as may be prescribed in the regulations.

2005, c. 31, Sched. 20, s. 4

OSA 84

Related Provisions: OSA 85.

Definitions: OSA 1(1)"proxy"; 1(1)"security"; 1(1)"form of proxy".

Rules: NI 51-102; Rule 51-801.

85. Mandatory solicitation of proxies — Subject to section 88, if the management of a reporting issuer gives or intends to give to holders of its voting securities notice of a meeting, the management shall, concurrently with or prior to giving the notice to the security holders whose latest address as shown on the books of the reporting issuer is in Ontario, send to each such security holder who is entitled to notice of meeting, at the security holder's latest address as shown on the books of the reporting issuer, a form of proxy for use at the meeting that complies with the regulations.

2001, c. 23, s. 214

OSA 85

Related Provisions: OSA 85.

Definitions: OSA 1(1)"reporting issuer"; 1(1)"voting security"; 1(1)"form of proxy".

Rules: NI 51-102, s. 9.1, 81-106, s. 12.2.

86. (1) Information circular — Subject to subsection (2) and section 88, no person or company shall solicit proxies from holders of its voting securities whose latest address as shown on the books of the reporting issuer is in Ontario unless,

(a) in the case of a solicitation by or on behalf of the management of a reporting issuer, an information circular, either as an appendix to or as a separate document accompanying the notice of the meeting, is sent to each such security holder of the reporting issuer whose proxy is solicited at the security holder's latest address as shown on the books of the reporting issuer; or

(b) in the case of any other solicitation, the person or company making the solicitation, concurrently with or prior thereto, delivers or sends an information circular to each such security holder whose proxy is solicited.

OSA 86(1)

Related Provisions: OSA 88.

Rules: NI 51-102, s. 9.1, 81-106, s. 12.4; Rule 51-801, s. 3.10, 81-801, s. 3.10.

(2) Application of subs. (1) — Subsection (1) does not apply to,

(a) any solicitation, otherwise than by or on behalf of the management of a reporting issuer, where the total number of security holders whose proxies are solicited is not more than fifteen, two or more persons or companies who are the joint registered owners of one or more securities being counted as one security holder;

(a.1) any solicitation, otherwise than by or on behalf of the management of a reporting issuer, in such other circumstances as may be prescribed in the regulations;

(b) any solicitation by a person or company made under section 49; or

(c) any solicitation by a person or company in respect of securities of which he, she or it is the beneficial owner.

2001, c. 23, s. 215; 2005, c. 31, Sched. 20, s. 5

OSA 86(2)

Related Provisions: OSA 49.

OSA 86

Related Provisions: OSA 81.

Definitions: OSA 1(1)"person"; 1(1)"company"; 1(1)"reporting issuer"; 1(1)"voting security"; 1(1)"proxy".

Rules: NI 51-102, Part 9, 81-106, Part 12; Rule 51-801, 81-801.

87. Voting where proxies — The chair at a meeting has the right not to conduct a vote by way of ballot on any matter or group of matters in connection with which the form of proxy has provided a means whereby the person or company whose proxy is solicited may specify how such person or company wishes the securities registered in his, her or its name to be voted unless,

(a) a poll is demanded by any security holder present at the meeting in person or represented thereat by proxy; or

(b) proxies requiring that the securities represented thereby be voted against what would otherwise be the decision of the meeting in relation to such matters or group of matters total more than 5 per cent of all the voting rights attached to all the securities entitled to be voted and be represented at the meeting.

OSA 87

Definitions: OSA 1(1)"person"; 1(1)"company"; 1(1)"security"; 1(1)"form of proxy".

88. (1) Compliance with laws of other jurisdiction — Where a reporting issuer is complying with the requirements of the laws of the jurisdiction under which it is incorporated, organized or continued and the requirements are substantially similar to the requirements of this Part, the requirements of this Part do not apply.

(2) Exemption by order — Subject to subsection (1), upon the application of any interested person or company, the Commission may,

(a) if a requirement of this Part conflicts with a requirement of the laws of the jurisdiction under which the reporting issuer is incorporated, organized or continued; or

(b) if otherwise satisfied in the circumstances of the particular case that there is adequate justification for so doing,

make an order on such terms and conditions as the Commission may impose, exempting, in whole or in part, a person or company from the requirements of this Part and of section 81.

1994, c. 11, s. 370

OSA 88(2)

Related Provisions: OSA 81.

Policies and Orders: OPS 2.1.

OSA 88

Definitions: OSA 1(1)"reporting issuer"; 1(1)"person"; 1(1)"company"; 1(1)"Commission".

Rules: NI 51-102, 71-101, 71-102, 81-106; Rule 51-801, 71-802, 81-801.

Policies and Orders: NPS 51-102CP, 71-102CP, 81-106CP; OPS 51-801CP, 81-801CP.

OSA Part XIX

Rules: NI 51-102, Part 9, 54-101, 81-106, Part 12.

Policies and Orders: NPS 11-201, Part 4, 51-102CP, 71-102CP, 81-106CP; OPS 51-801CP, 81-801CP.

PART XX — TAKE-OVER BIDS AND ISSUER BIDS (SS. 89–105.1)

Interpretation

[Heading added 2007, c. 7, Sched. 38, s. 8.]

89. Definitions — In this Part,

"interested person" means,

(a) an offeree issuer,

(b) a security holder, director or officer of an offeree issuer,

(c) an offeror,

(d) the Director, and

(e) any person or company not referred to in clauses (a) to (d) who, in the opinion of the Commission or the Superior Court of Justice, as the case may be, is proper to make an application under section 104 or 105, as the case may be;

"issuer bid" means a direct or indirect offer to acquire or redeem a security or a direct or indirect acquisition or redemption of a security that is,

(a) made by the issuer of the security; and

(b) within a prescribed class of offers, acquisitions or redemptions;

"offeree issuer" means an issuer whose securities are the subject of a take-over bid, an issuer bid or an offer to acquire;

"take-over bid" means a direct or indirect offer to acquire a security that is,

(a) made by a person or company other than the issuer of the security; and

(b) within a prescribed class of offers to acquire.

2007, c. 7, Sched. 38, s. 8; 2015, c. 38, Sched. 18, s. 2

OSA 89

Definitions: OSA 1(1)"security"; 1(1)"issuer"; 1(1)"person"; 1(1)"company".

Rules: NI 62-104.

Offeree Issuer and Offeror Obligations

[Heading added 2015, c. 38, Sched. 18, s. 2.]

90. Making a bid — A person or company must not make a take-over bid or an issuer bid, whether alone or acting jointly or in concert with one or more persons or companies, except in accordance with the regulations.

2007, c. 7, Sched. 38, s. 8; 2015, c. 38, Sched. 18, s. 2

OSA 90

Definitions: OSA 1(1)"security"; 1(1)"person"; 1(1)"company".

91. (1) Recommendation relating to take-over bid — If a take-over bid has been made, the board of directors of the offeree issuer shall,

(a) determine whether to recommend acceptance or rejection of the take-over bid or determine not to make a recommendation; and

(b) make the recommendation, or a statement that they are not making a recommendation, in accordance with the regulations.

(2) Individual recommendation — An individual director or officer of the offeree issuer may recommend acceptance or rejection of the take-over bid if the recommendation is made in accordance with the regulations.

(3) [Repealed 2015, c. 38, Sched. 18, s. 2.]

2007, c. 7, Sched. 38, s. 8; 2015, c. 38, Sched. 18, s. 2

OSA 91

Definitions: OSA 1(1)"associate"; 1(1)"person"; 1(1)"company"; 1(1)"dealer"; OSA 89(1)"offeror"; OSA 89(2)"affiliate".

92. [Repealed 2015, c. 38, Sched. 18, s. 2.]

[Heading repealed 2015, c. 38, Sched. 18, s. 2.]

93. [Repealed 2015, c. 38, Sched. 18, s. 2.]

93.1 [Repealed 2015, c. 38, Sched. 18, s. 2.]

93.2 [Repealed 2015, c. 38, Sched. 18, s. 2.]

93.3 [Repealed 2015, c. 38, Sched. 18, s. 2.]

93.4 [Repealed 2015, c. 38, Sched. 18, s. 2.]

[Heading repealed 2015, c. 38, Sched. 18, s. 2.]

94. [Repealed 2015, c. 38, Sched. 18, s. 2.]

94.1 [Repealed 2015, c. 38, Sched. 18, s. 2.]

94.2 [Repealed 2015, c. 38, Sched. 18, s. 2.]

94.3 [Repealed 2015, c. 38, Sched. 18, s. 2.]

94.4 [Repealed 2015, c. 38, Sched. 18, s. 2.]

94.5 [Repealed 2015, c. 38, Sched. 18, s. 2.]

94.6 [Repealed 2015, c. 38, Sched. 18, s. 2.]

94.7 [Repealed 2015, c. 38, Sched. 18, s. 2.]

94.8 [Repealed 2015, c. 38, Sched. 18, s. 2.]

[Heading repealed 2015, c. 38, Sched. 18, s. 2.]

95. [Repealed 2015, c. 38, Sched. 18, s. 2.]

95.1 [Repealed 2015, c. 38, Sched. 18, s. 2.]

95.2 [Repealed 2015, c. 38, Sched. 18, s. 2.]

96. [Repealed 2015, c. 38, Sched. 18, s. 2.]

96.1 [Repealed 2015, c. 38, Sched. 18, s. 2.]

96.2 [Repealed 2015, c. 38, Sched. 18, s. 2.]

[Heading repealed 2015, c. 38, Sched. 18, s. 2.]

97. [Repealed 2015, c. 38, Sched. 18, s. 2.]

97.1 [Repealed 2015, c. 38, Sched. 18, s. 2.]

97.2 [Repealed 2015, c. 38, Sched. 18, s. 2.]

97.3 [Repealed 2015, c. 38, Sched. 18, s. 2.]

[Heading repealed 2015, c. 38, Sched. 18, s. 2.]

98. [Repealed 2015, c. 38, Sched. 18, s. 2.]

98.1 [Repealed 2015, c. 38, Sched. 18, s. 2.]

98.2 [Repealed 2015, c. 38, Sched. 18, s. 2.]

98.3 [Repealed 2015, c. 38, Sched. 18, s. 2.]

98.4 [Repealed 2015, c. 38, Sched. 18, s. 2.]

98.5 [Repealed 2015, c. 38, Sched. 18, s. 2.]

98.6 [Repealed 2015, c. 38, Sched. 18, s. 2.]

98.7 [Repealed 2015, c. 38, Sched. 18, s. 2.]

99. [Repealed 2015, c. 38, Sched. 18, s. 2.]

99.1 [Repealed 2015, c. 38, Sched. 18, s. 2.]

[Heading repealed 2015, c. 38, Sched. 18, s. 2.]

100. [Repealed 2015, c. 38, Sched. 18, s. 2.]

100.1 [Repealed 2015, c. 38, Sched. 18, s. 2.]

100.2 [Repealed 2015, c. 38, Sched. 18, s. 2.]

100.3 [Repealed 2015, c. 38, Sched. 18, s. 2.]

100.4 [Repealed 2015, c. 38, Sched. 18, s. 2.]

100.5 [Repealed 2015, c. 38, Sched. 18, s. 2.]

100.6 [Repealed 2015, c. 38, Sched. 18, s. 2.]

[Heading repealed 2015, c. 38, Sched. 18, s. 2.]

101. [Repealed 2015, c. 38, Sched. 18, s. 2.]

101.1 [Repealed 2015, c. 38, Sched. 18, s. 2.]

101.2 [Repealed 2015, c. 38, Sched. 18, s. 2.]

101.3 [Repealed 2015, c. 38, Sched. 18, s. 2.]

101.4 [Repealed 2015, c. 38, Sched. 18, s. 2.]

101.5 [Repealed 2015, c. 38, Sched. 18, s. 2.]

101.6 [Repealed 2015, c. 38, Sched. 18, s. 2.]

101.7 [Repealed 2015, c. 38, Sched. 18, s. 2.]

[Heading repealed 2015, c. 38, Sched. 18, s. 2.]

102. [Repealed 2015, c. 38, Sched. 18, s. 2.]

102.1 [Repealed 2015, c. 38, Sched. 18, s. 2.]

102.2 [Repealed 2015, c. 38, Sched. 18, s. 2.]

Applications and Exemptions

[Heading added 2007, c. 7, Sched. 38, s. 8.]

103. [Repealed 2015, c. 38, Sched. 18, s. 3.]

104. (1) Application to the Commission — On application by an interested person, if the Commission considers that a person or company has not complied with, or is not complying with, a requirement under this Part or the regulations related to this Part, the Commission may make an order,

(a) restraining the distribution of any document or any communication used or issued in connection with a take-over bid or an issuer bid;

(b) requiring an amendment to or variation of any document or any communication used or issued in connection with a take-over bid or an issuer bid and requiring the distribution of amended, varied or corrected documents or communications;

(c) directing any person or company to comply with a requirement under this Part or the regulations related to this Part;

(d) restraining any person or company from contravening a requirement under this Part or the regulations related to this Part; and

(e) directing the directors and officers of any person or company to cause the person or company to comply with or to cease contravening a requirement under this Part or the regulations related to this Part.

(1.1) Notice to Director — If, in a proceeding under subsection (1), the Director is not the applicant, the Director shall be given notice of the application and may appear at the proceeding as a party.

(2) Exemptions — On application by an interested person and subject to such terms and conditions as the Commission may impose, if the Commission is satisfied that it would not be prejudicial to the public interest, the Commission may,

(a) [Repealed 2015, c. 38, Sched. 18, s. 4(3).]

(b) vary any time period set out in this Part or the regulations related to this Part; and

(c) exempt a person or company from any of the requirements of this Part or the regulations related to this Part.

1994, c. 11, s. 372; 2006, c. 33, Sched. Z.5, s. 7; 2007, c. 7, Sched. 38, s. 8; 2015, c. 38, Sched. 18, s. 4(2), (3)

OSA 104

Definitions: OSA 103"interested person"; OSA 1(1)"Commission"; 1(1)"person"; 1(1)"company"; OSA 89(1)"take-over bid"; 89(1)"issuer bid".

Rules: Rule 62-504, s. 8.1; Rules of Procedure 2.4, 16.

105. (1) Application to the court — On application by an interested person, if the Superior Court of Justice is satisfied that a person or company has not complied with a requirement under this Part or the regulations related to this Part, the Superior Court of Justice may make such interim or final order as the Court thinks fit, including, without limitation, an order,

(a) compensating any interested person who is a party to the application for damages suffered as a result of a contravention of a requirement of this Part or the regulations related to this Part;

(b) rescinding a transaction with any interested person, including the issue of a security or an acquisition and sale of a security;

(c) requiring any person or company to dispose of any securities acquired under or in connection with a take-over bid or an issuer bid;

(d) prohibiting any person or company from exercising any or all of the voting rights attaching to any securities; or

(e) requiring the trial of an issue.

(2) Notice to Director — If, in a proceeding under subsection (1), the Director is not the applicant, the Director shall be given notice of the application and may appear at the proceeding as a party.

2006, c. 19, Sched. C, s. 1(1); 2006, c. 33, Sched. Z.5, s. 8; 2007, c. 7, Sched. 38, s. 8; 2015, c. 38, Sched. 18, s. 5

OSA 105

Definitions: OSA 103"interested person"; OSA 1(1)"person"; 1(1)"company"; OSA 89(1)"take-over bid"; 89(1)"issuer bid".

[Heading repealed 2015, c. 38, Sched. 18, s. 6.]

105.1 [Repealed 2015, c. 38, Sched. 18, s. 6.]

OSA Part XX

Rules: MI 61-101, NI 62-103, Rule 62-504.

Policies and Orders: NPS 62-202, 62-203; OPS 62-602; CSAN 62-304.

PART XXI — INSIDER TRADING AND SELF-DEALING (SS. 106–121.1)

106. (1) Definitions — In this Part,

"investment fund" means, except in sections 111, 112, 116 and 121.1, an investment fund that is a reporting issuer;

"mutual fund" means a mutual fund that is a reporting issuer;

"related investment funds" includes more than one investment fund under common management;

"related person or company", in relation to an investment fund, means a person in whom, or a company in which, the investment fund, its management company and its distribution company are prohibited by the provisions of this Part from making any investment.

OSA 106(1)

Related Provisions: OSA 111.

(2) Same — For the purpose of this Part,

(a) any issuer in which an investment fund holds in excess of 10 per cent of the voting securities or in which the investment fund and related investment funds hold in excess of 20 per cent of the voting securities shall be deemed to be a related person or company of that investment fund or of each of those investment funds; and

(b) the acquisition or disposition by an insider of a put, call or other transferable option with respect to a security shall be deemed to be a change in the beneficial ownership of the security to which such put, call or other transferable option relates.

2006, c. 33, Sched. Z.5, s. 9; 2014, c. 7, Sched. 28, s. 5

OSA 106

Definitions: OSA 1(1)"investment fund"; 1(1)"mutual fund"; 1(1)"reporting issuer"; 1(1)"person"; 1(1)"company"; 1(1)"security"; 1(1)"voting security"; 1(1)"issuer".

107. (1) Insider reporting — Within 10 days of becoming an insider or within such other time period as may be prescribed, a person or company who becomes an insider of a reporting issuer, other than a mutual fund, shall file a report disclosing, in the prescribed manner and form, any direct or indirect beneficial ownership of or control or direction over securities of the reporting issuer and any interest in, or right or obligation associated with, a related financial instrument and the insider shall make such other disclosure as may be required by the regulations.

(2) Same — Within 10 days, or within such other time period as may be prescribed, of any change in the direct or indirect beneficial ownership of, or control or direction over, securities of the reporting issuer or any interest in, or right or obligation associated with, a related financial instrument, an insider of a reporting issuer, other than a mutual fund, shall file a report disclosing, in the prescribed manner and form, such change and the insider shall make such other disclosure as may be required by the regulations.

(3) [Repealed 2006, c. 33, Sched. Z.5, s. 10.]

1999, c. 9, s. 214; 2006, c. 33, Sched. Z.5, s. 10

OSA 107

Definitions: OSA 1(1)"person"; 1(1)"company"; 1(1)"reporting issuer"; 1(1)"insider"; 1(1)"security"; 1(1)"director"; 1(1)"officer".

Regulations: Reg.: 241.

Rules: NI 55-102, 55-104, 71-102.

Policies and Orders: OPS 13-601; BOR 1.2, 1.3; CSAN 55-309, 55-310, 55-311, 55-312, 55-314, 55-315, 55-316.

108. [Repealed 2006, c. 33, Sched. Z.5, s. 10.]

109. Report of transfer by insider — Where voting securities are registered in the name of a person or company other than the beneficial owner and the person or company knows that they are beneficially owned by an insider and that the insider has failed to file a report of such ownership with the Commission as required by this Part, the person or company shall file a report in accordance with the regulations except where the transfer was for the purpose of giving collateral for a genuine debt.

OSA 109

Definitions: OSA 1(1)"voting security"; 1(1)"person"; 1(1)"company"; 1(1)"Commission".

Regulations: Reg.: 168; Reg.: Form 37.

Rules: Rule 55-502.

Policies and Orders: OPS 13-601; ON BOR 1.2, 1.3; OSCN 55-502.

110. (1) Definition — For the purposes of sections 111, 112, 113, 114 and 115,

"investment" means a purchase of any security of any class of securities of an issuer including bonds, debentures, notes, or other evidences of indebtedness thereof, and a loan to persons or companies but does not include an advance or loan, whether secured or unsecured, that is made by an investment fund, its management company or its distribution company that is merely ancillary to the main business of the investment fund, its management company or its distribution company.

(2) Interpretation — For the purposes of sections 111, 112, 113, 114 and 115,

(a) a person or company or a group of persons or companies has a significant interest in an issuer, if,

(i) in the case of a person or company, he, she or it, as the case may be, owns beneficially, either directly or indirectly, more than 10 per cent, or

(ii) in the case of a group of persons or companies, they own beneficially, either individually or together and either directly or indirectly, more than 50 per cent,

of the outstanding shares or units of the issuer;

(b) a person or company or a group of persons or companies is a substantial security holder of an issuer if that person or company or group of persons or companies owns beneficially, either individually or together or directly or indirectly, voting securities to which are attached more than 20 per cent of the voting rights attached to all the voting securities of the issuer for the time being outstanding, but in computing the percentage of voting rights attached to voting securities owned by an underwriter, there shall be excluded any voting securities acquired by the underwriter as such in a distribution of such securities but the exclusion ceases to have effect on completion or cessation of the distribution by the underwriter;

OSA 110(2)(b)

Regulations: Reg.: 242.

(c) where a person or company or group of persons or companies owns beneficially, directly or indirectly, or pursuant to this clause is deemed to own beneficially, voting securities of an issuer, that person or company or group of persons or companies shall be deemed to own beneficially a proportion of voting securities of any other issuer that are owned beneficially, directly or indirectly, by the first mentioned issuer, which proportion shall equal the proportion of the voting securities of the first mentioned issuer that are owned beneficially, directly or indirectly, or that pursuant to this clause are deemed to be owned beneficially, by that person or company or group of persons or companies.

2014, c. 7, Sched. 28, s. 6

OSA 110

Definitions: OSA 1(1)"security"; 1(1)"issuer"; 1(1)"person"; 1(1)"company"; 1(1)"management company"; 1(1)"distribution"; 1(1)"voting security"; 1(1)"underwriter"; OSA 106(1)"mutual fund".

111. (1) Loans of investment funds — No investment fund shall knowingly make an investment by way of loan to,

(a) any officer or director of the investment fund, its management company or distribution company or an associate of any of them;

(b) any individual, where the individual or an associate of the individual is a substantial security holder of the investment fund, its management company or distribution company.

(2) Investments of investment funds, etc. — No investment fund shall knowingly make an investment,

(a) in any person or company who is a substantial security holder of the investment fund, its management company or its distribution company;

(b) in any person or company in which the investment fund, alone or together with one or more related investment funds, is a substantial security holder; or

(c) in an issuer in which any of the following has a significant interest:

(i) any officer or director of the investment fund, its management company or distribution company or an associate of any of them; or

(ii) any person or company who is a substantial security holder of the investment fund, its management company or its distribution company.

(3) Divesting of prohibited loans and investments — No mutual fund in Ontario or its management company or its distribution company shall knowingly hold an investment made after September 15, 1979 and before the day this section comes into force if the investment is an investment described in this section.

(4) Same — No investment fund or its management company or its distribution company shall knowingly hold an investment made on or after the day this section comes into force if the investment is an investment described in this section.

(5) Interpretation — In this section,

"investment fund" means a mutual fund in Ontario or a non-redeemable investment fund that is a reporting issuer.

2014, c. 7, Sched. 28, s. 7

OSA 111

Definitions: OSA 1(1)"mutual fund in Ontario"; 1(1)"officer"; 1(1)"director"; 1(1)"individual"; 1(1)"security"; 1(1)"associate"; 1(1)"management company"; 1(1)"distribution company"; 1(1)"issuer"; 1(1)"distribution"; OSA 106(1)"investment fund"; 106(1)"related investment funds"; OSA 110(1)"investment".

Regulations: Reg.: 242.

Rules: NI 81-102, Part 2.

Policies and Orders: OSCN 33-733, 33-734.

112. Indirect investment — No investment fund or its management company or its distribution company shall knowingly enter into any contract or other arrangement that results in its being directly or indirectly liable or contingently liable in respect of any investment by way of loan to, or other investment in, a person or company to whom it is by section 111 prohibited from making a loan or in which it is prohibited from making any other investment, and for the purpose of section 111 any such contract or other arrangement shall be deemed to be a loan or an investment, as the case may be.

2014, c. 7, Sched. 28, s. 8

OSA 112

Definitions: OSA 1(1)"management company"; 1(1)"distribution company"; 1(1)"person"; 1(1)"company"; OSA 106(1)"investment fund"; OSA 110(1)"investment".

Regulations: Reg.: 242.

113. Relieving orders — Upon an application of an interested person or company, the Commission may, where it is satisfied,

(a) that a class of investment or a particular investment represents the business judgment of responsible persons uninfluenced by considerations other than the best interests of an investment fund; or

(b) that a particular investment is in fact in the best interests of an investment fund,

OSA 113(b)

Related Provisions: OSA 111, 112.

order, subject to such terms and conditions as it may impose, that section 111 or 112 does not apply to the class of investment, particular investment, contract or other arrangement, as the case may be.

2014, c. 7, Sched. 28, s. 9

OSA 113

Definitions: OSA 1(1)"person"; 1(1)"company"; 1(1)"Commission"; OSA 106(1)"investment fund"; OSA 110(1)"investment".

Policies and Orders: OPS 2.1.

114. Exception to cl. 110(2)(c) — Despite clause 110(2)(c), an investment fund is not prohibited from making an investment in an issuer only because a person or company or a group of persons or companies who own beneficially, directly or indirectly, or are deemed to own beneficially, voting securities of the investment fund or its management company or its distribution company are by reason thereof deemed to own beneficially voting securities of the issuer.

2014, c. 7, Sched. 28, s. 10

OSA 114

Definitions: OSA 1(1)"issuer"; 1(1)"person"; 1(1)"company"; 1(1)"voting security"; 1(1)"management company"; 1(1)"distribution company"; OSA 106(1)"investment fund".

Regulations: Reg.: 242.

115. (1) Fees on investment — No investment fund shall make any investment in consequence of which a related person or company of the investment fund will receive any fee or other compensation except fees paid pursuant to a contract which is disclosed in any preliminary prospectus or prospectus, or any amendment to either of them, that is filed by the investment fund and is accepted by the Director.

(2) Relieving orders — The Commission may, upon the application of an investment fund and where it is satisfied that it would not be prejudicial to the public interest to do so, order, subject to such terms and conditions as it may impose, that subsection (1) does not apply to the investment fund.

2014, c. 7, Sched. 28, s. 11

OSA 115(2)

Policies and Orders: OPS 2.1.

OSA 115

Definitions: OSA 1(1)"Director"; OSA 106(1)"investment fund"; 106(1)"related person or company"; OSA 110(1)"investment".

Regulations: Reg.: 242.

116. Standard of care, investment fund managers — Every investment fund manager,

(a) shall exercise the powers and discharge the duties of their office honestly, in good faith and in the best interests of the investment fund; and

(b) shall exercise the degree of care, diligence and skill that a reasonably prudent person would exercise in the circumstances.

2006, c. 33, Sched. Z.5, s. 11

OSA 116

Definitions: OSA 1(1)"person"; 1(1)"company"; OSA 106(1)"investment fund manager".

Rules: NI 81-102, s. 4.4; 81-107; Rule 81-802.

Policies and Orders: OSCN 33-734.

117. (1) Filing by management companies — Every management company shall, in respect of each investment fund to which it provides services or advice, file a report prepared in accordance with the regulations of any of the following within 30 days after the end of the month in which it occurs:

1. Every transaction of purchase or sale of securities between the investment fund and any related person or company.

2. Every loan received by the investment fund from, or made by the investment fund to, any of its related persons or companies.

3. Every purchase or sale effected by the investment fund through any related person or company with respect to which the related person or company received a fee either from the investment fund or from the other party to the transaction or from both.

4. Any transaction in which, by arrangement other than an arrangement relating to insider trading in portfolio securities, the investment fund is a joint participant with one or more of its related persons or companies.

(2) Relieving orders — The Commission may, on the application of the management company of an investment fund and where it is of the opinion that it would not be prejudicial to the public interest to do so, order, subject to such terms and conditions as it may impose, that subsection (1) does not apply to any transaction or class of transactions.

2014, c. 7, Sched. 28, s. 12

OSA 117(2)

Policies and Orders: OPS 2.1.

OSA 117

Definitions: OSA 1(1)"management company"; 1(1)"security"; OSA 106(1)"investment fund"; 106(1)"related person or company".

Regulations: Reg.: 169; Reg.: Form 38.

Rules: NI 81-102, Part 2.

Policies and Orders: OPS 13-601.

118. [Repealed 2009, c. 18, Sched. 26, s. 15.]

119. Trades by mutual fund insiders — No person or company that has access to information concerning the investment program of a mutual fund or the investment portfolio managed for a client by a registered adviser or registered dealer through discretionary authority provided by the client shall purchase or sell securities of an issuer for his, her or its own account if,

(a) the portfolio securities of the mutual fund or the investment portfolio managed for the client by the registered adviser or registered dealer include securities of that issuer; and

(b) the person or company has used the information for his, her or its direct benefit or advantage.

2009, c. 18, Sched. 26, s. 16

OSA 119

Related Provisions: OSA 134(3.1).

Definitions: OSA 1(1)"person"; 1(1)"company"; 1(1)"portfolio securities"; 1(1)"security"; 1(1)"issuer"; OSA 106(1)"mutual fund".

Policies and Orders: CSAN 33-720.

120. Publication of summaries of reports — The Commission shall summarize in or as a part of a monthly periodical available to the public on payment of a reasonable fee the information contained in every report filed in compliance with this Part.

OSA 120

Definitions: OSA 1(1)"Commission".

121. (1) Filing in other jurisdiction — Where the laws of the jurisdiction in which the reporting issuer is incorporated, organized or continued require substantially the same reports in that jurisdiction as are required by this Part, the filing requirements of this Part may be complied with by filing the reports required by the laws of such jurisdiction manually signed or certified in accordance with the regulations.

(2) Exemptions by order of Commission — Subject to subsection (1), the Commission may,

(a) upon the application of an interested person or company,

(i) if a requirement of this Part conflicts with a requirement of the laws of the jurisdiction under which the reporting issuer is incorporated, organized or continued, or

(ii) if otherwise satisfied in the circumstances of the particular case that there is adequate justification for so doing; or

(b) of its own motion,

make an order on such terms and conditions as seem to the Commission just and expedient, exempting in whole or in part, a person or company, from the requirements of this Part.

1994, c. 33, s. 6

OSA 121(2)

Rules: NI 55-101.

Policies and Orders: OPS 2.1; CSAN 55-306.

OSA 121

Definitions: OSA 1(1)"reporting issuer"; 1(1)"person"; 1(1)"company".

Rules: NI 71-101, 71-102; Rule 71-801, 71-802.

Policies and Orders: OPS 13-601.

121.1 Authorized exceptions to prohibitions — If the regulations so provide, a body established under subsection 121.4(1) by an investment fund may approve a transaction that is prohibited under this Part and, in that case, the prohibition does not apply to the transaction.

2005, c. 31, Sched. 20, s. 6

OSA 121.1

Rules: NI 81-107.

Policies and Orders: OPS 81-802 CP.

OSA Part XXI

Regulations: Reg.: Part VIII.

Rules: NI 55-102, 55-104, 71-101, 71-102, 81-102, 81-107, 33-103, Parts 13 and 14; Rules 55-502, 71-801, 71-802.

Policies and Orders: CSAN 55-310 to CSAN 55-316; CSAN 81-310; OPS 55-701, 81-802CP.

PART XXI.1 — GOVERNANCE AND OTHER REQUIREMENTS (SS. 121.2–121.4)

[Heading added 2005, c. 31, Sched. 20, s. 7.]

121.2 Definition — In this Part,

"prescribed" means prescribed in the regulations.

2005, c. 31, Sched. 20, s. 7

OSA 121.2

Definitions: OSA 1(1)"regulations".

121.3 Governance of reporting issuers — For the purposes of this Act, a reporting issuer shall comply with such requirements as may be prescribed with respect to the governance of reporting issuers, including requirements relating to,

(a) the composition of its board of directors and qualifications for membership on the board, including matters respecting the independence of members;

(b) the establishment of specified types of committees of the board of directors, the mandate, functioning and responsibilities of each committee, the composition of each committee and the qualifications for membership on the committee, including matters respecting the independence of members;

(c) the establishment and enforcement of a code of business conduct and ethics applicable to its directors, officers and employees and applicable to persons or companies that are in a special relationship with the reporting issuer, including the minimum requirements for such a code; and

(d) procedures to regulate conflicts of interest between the interests of the reporting issuer and those of a director or officer of the issuer.

2005, c. 31, Sched. 20, s. 7

OSA 121.3

Related Provisions: OSA 143(1) 56.1.

Rules: NI 52-110, NI 58-101.

121.4 (1) Oversight, etc., of investment funds — If required to do so by the regulations, an investment fund shall establish and maintain a body for the purposes of overseeing activities of the investment fund and the investment fund manager, reviewing or approving prescribed matters affecting the investment fund, including transactions referred to in section 121.1, and disclosing information to security holders of the fund, to the investment fund manager and to the Commission.

(2) Same — The body has such powers and duties as may be prescribed.

2005, c. 31, Sched. 20, s. 7

OSA 121.4

Related Provisions: OSA 121.1, 143(1) 62.

Rules: NI 81-107.

Policies and Orders: OPS 81-802CP.

Proposed Addition — 121.5

PART XXI.2 — PROTECTION FROM REPRISALS (S. 121.5)

[Heading added 2016, c. 5, Sched. 26, s. 3. Not in force at date of publication.]

121.5 (1) No reprisals — No person or company, or person acting on behalf of a person or company, shall take a reprisal against an employee of the person or company because the employee has,

(a) sought advice about providing information, expressed an intention to provide information, or provided information to the person or company, the Commission, a recognized self-regulatory organization or a law enforcement agency about an act of the person or company, or person acting on behalf of the person or company, that has occurred, is ongoing or is about to occur, and that the employee reasonably believes is contrary to Ontario securities law or a by-law or other regulatory instrument of a recognized self-regulatory organization; or

(b) in relation to information provided under clause (a), cooperated, testified or otherwise assisted, or expressed an intention to cooperate, testify or otherwise assist in,

(i) an investigation by the Commission, a recognized self-regulatory organization or a law enforcement agency, or

(ii) a proceeding of the Commission or a recognized self-regulatory organization, or a judicial proceeding.

(2) Same — For the purposes of subsection (1), a reprisal is any measure taken against an employee that adversely affects his or her employment and includes but is not limited to,

(a) ending or threatening to end the employee's employment;

(b) demoting, disciplining or suspending, or threatening to demote, discipline or suspend an employee;

(c) imposing or threatening to impose a penalty related to the employment of the employee; or

(d) intimidating or coercing an employee in relation to his or her employment.

(3) Prohibition re agreements — A provision in an agreement, including a confidentiality agreement, between a person or company and an employee of the person or company is void to the extent that it precludes or purports to preclude the employee from,

(a) providing information described in clause (1)(a) to the Commission, a recognized self-regulatory organization or a law enforcement agency; or

(b) in relation to information provided under clause (1)(a), cooperating, testifying or otherwise assisting, or expressing an intention to cooperate, testify or otherwise assist in,

(i) an investigation by the Commission, a recognized self-regulatory organization or a law enforcement agency, or

(ii) a proceeding of the Commission or a recognized self-regulatory organization, or a judicial proceeding.

2016, c. 5, Sched. 26, s. 3 [Not in force at date of publication.]

PART XXII — ENFORCEMENT (SS. 122–129.2)

122. (1) Offences, general — Every person or company that,

(a) makes a statement in any material, evidence or information submitted to the Commission, a Director, any person acting under the authority of the Commission or the Executive Director or any person appointed to make an investigation or examination under this Act that, in a material respect and at the time and in the light of the circumstances under which it is made, is misleading or untrue or does not state a fact that is required to be stated or that is necessary to make the statement not misleading;

(b) makes a statement in any application, release, report, preliminary prospectus, prospectus, return, financial statement, information circular, take-over bid circular, issuer bid circular or other document required to be filed or furnished under Ontario securities law that, in a material respect and at the time and in the light of the circumstances under which it is made, is misleading or untrue or does not state a fact that is required to be stated or that is necessary to make the statement not misleading; or

Proposed Amendment — 122(1)(b)

(b) makes a statement in any application, release, report, preliminary prospectus, prospectus, return, financial statement, information circular, take-over bid circular, issuer bid circular, disclosure document in respect of a designated derivative or other document required to be filed or furnished under Ontario securities law that, in a material respect and at the time and in the light of the circumstances under which it is made, is misleading or untrue or does not state a fact that is required to be stated or that is necessary to make the statement not misleading; or

2010, c. 26, Sched. 18, s. 31(1) [Not in force at date of publication.]

(c) contravenes Ontario securities law,

is guilty of an offence and on conviction is liable to a fine of not more than $5 million or to imprisonment for a term of not more than five years less a day, or to both.

(1.1) Exemption — Clauses 122(1)(a) and (b) do not apply to a statement made or given to the Commission in a submission in respect of a proposed rule or policy.

(2) Defence — Without limiting the availability of other defences, no person or company is guilty of an offence under clause (1)(a) or (b) if the person or company did not know and in the exercise of reasonable diligence could not have known that the statement was misleading or untrue or that it omitted to state a fact that was required to be stated or that was necessary to make the statement not misleading in light of the circumstances in which it was made.

(3) Directors and officers — Every director or officer of a company or of a person other than an individual who authorizes, permits or acquiesces in the commission of an offence under subsection (1) by the company or person, whether or not a charge has been laid or a finding of guilt has been made against the company or person in respect of the offence under subsection (1), is guilty of an offence and is liable on conviction to a fine of not more than $5 million or to imprisonment for a term of not more than five years less a day, or to both.

(4) Fine for contravention of s. 76 — Despite subsection (1) and in addition to any imprisonment imposed under subsection (1), a person or company who is convicted of contravening subsection 76(1), (2) or (3) is liable to a minimum fine equal to the profit made or the loss avoided by the person or company by reason of the contravention and a maximum fine equal to the greater of,

(a) $5 million; and

(b) the amount equal to triple the amount of the profit made or the loss avoided by the person or company by reason of the contravention.

OSA 122(4)

Related Provisions: OSA 76.

(5) Same — If it is not possible to determine the profit made or loss avoided by the person or company by reason of the contravention, subsection (4) does not apply but subsection (1) continues to apply.

(6) Definitions: "loss avoided", "profit made" — In subsections (4) and (5),

"loss avoided" means,

(a) in respect of a security, other than anything deemed to be a security under subsection 76(6), the amount by which the amount received for the security sold in contravention of subsection 76(1) exceeds the average trading price of the security in the 20 trading days following general disclosure of the material fact or the material change, and

(b) in respect of anything deemed to be a security under subsection 76(6), such amount as may be prescribed by or determined in accordance with a regulation made by the Lieutenant Governor in Council;

"profit made" means,

(a) in respect of a security, other than anything deemed to be a security under subsection 76(6), and except in respect of a short sale, the amount by which the average trading price of the security in the 20 trading days following general disclosure of the material fact or the material change exceeds the amount paid for the security purchased in contravention of subsection 76(1),

(b) in respect of a short sale, the amount by which the amount received for the security sold in contravention of subsection 76(1) exceeds the average trading price of the security in the twenty trading days following general disclosure of the material fact or the material change,

(b.1) in respect of anything deemed to be a security under subsection 76(6), such amount as may be prescribed by or determined in accordance with a regulation made by the Lieutenant Governor in Council, or

(c) the value of any consideration received for informing another person or company of a material fact or material change with respect to the reporting issuer in contravention of subsection 76(2) or (3).

OSA 122(6)

Related Provisions: OSA 76.

(7) Consent of Commission — No proceeding under this section shall be commenced except with the consent of the Commission.

(8) Trial by provincial judge — The Commission or an agent for the Commission may by notice to the clerk of the court having jurisdiction in respect of an offence under this Act require that a provincial judge preside over the proceeding.

> 1994, c. 11, s. 373; 1994, c. 33, s. 7; 2002, c. 18, Sched. H, s. 11; 2002, c. 22, ss. 181, 188(3); 2010, c. 26, Sched. 18, s. 31(2)–(4)

OSA 122

Related Provisions: OSA 29(6).

Definitions: OSA 1(1)"person"; 1(1)"company"; 1(1)"Commission"; 1(1)"Director"; 1(1)"Ontario securities law"; 1(1)"director"; 1(1)"officer"; 1(1)"security"; 1(1)"material fact"; 1(1)"material change"; 1(1)"reporting issuer".

Policies and Orders: BOR 1.4.

122.1 (1) Additional remedies — If a person or company is convicted of an offence under this Act, the court may, in addition to any penalty, order the convicted person or company to make restitution or pay compensation in relation to the offence to an aggrieved person or company.

(2) Notice — If a court makes an order for restitution or compensation, it shall cause a copy of the order or a notice of the content of the order to be given to the person or company to whom the restitution or compensation is ordered to be paid.

(3) Filing — An order for restitution or compensation may be filed with a local registrar of the Superior Court of Justice and the responsibility for filing shall be on the person or company to whom the restitution or compensation is ordered to be paid.

(4) Enforcement — An order for restitution or compensation filed under subsection (3) may be enforced as if it were an order of the court.

(5) Post judgment interest — Section 129 of the *Courts of Justice Act* applies in respect of an order for restitution or compensation filed under subsection (3) and, for that purpose, the date of filing shall be deemed to be the date of the order.

(6) Limitation — A person or company is not entitled to participate in a proceeding in which an order may be made under this section solely on the basis that the person or company has a right of action against a defendant to the proceeding or that the person or company may be entitled to receive an amount under the order.

(7) Civil remedies protected — A civil remedy for an act or omission is not affected by reason only that an order for restitution or compensation under this section has been made in respect of that act or omission.

> 2006, c. 33, Sched. Z.5, s. 12

123. [Repealed 1994, c. 11, s. 373.]

124. Information containing more than one offence — An information in respect of any contravention of this Act may be for one or more offences, and no information, summons, warrant, conviction or other proceeding in any prosecution is objectionable or insufficient by reason of the fact that it relates to two or more offences.

125. (1) Execution of warrant issued in another province — Where a provincial judge, magistrate or justice of another province or territory of Canada issues a warrant for the arrest of any person on a charge of contravening any provision of a statute of such province or territory similar to this Act, any provincial judge or justice of Ontario within whose jurisdiction that person is or is suspected to be, may, upon satisfactory proof of the handwriting of the provincial judge, magistrate or a justice who issued the warrant, make an endorsement thereon in the form prescribed by the regulations, and a warrant so endorsed is sufficient authority to the person bringing the warrant and to all other persons to whom it was originally directed and to all police officers to execute the warrant within that jurisdiction and to take the person arrested thereunder either out of or anywhere in Ontario and to rearrest such person anywhere in Ontario.

(2) Prisoner in transit — Any police officer of Ontario or of any other province or territory of Canada who is passing through Ontario and who has in custody a person arrested in another province or territory under a warrant endorsed under subsection (1) is entitled to hold, take and rearrest the accused anywhere in Ontario under such warrant without proof of the warrant or the endorsement thereof.

> 1994, c. 11, s. 374

OSA 125

Definitions: OSA 1(1)"person".

Regulations: Reg.: 160; Reg.: Form 39.

126. (1) Freeze direction — If the Commission considers it expedient for the due administration of Ontario securities law or the regulation of the capital markets in Ontario or expedient to assist in the due administration of the securities laws or the regulation of the capital markets in another jurisdiction, the Commission may,

(a) direct a person or company having on deposit or under its control or for safekeeping any funds, securities or property of any person or company to retain those funds, securities or property;

(b) direct a person or company to refrain from withdrawing any funds, securities or property from another person or company who has them on deposit, under control or for safekeeping; or

(c) direct a person or company to maintain funds, securities or property, and to refrain from disposing of, transferring, dissipating or otherwise dealing with or diminishing the value of those funds, securities or property.

(1.1) Duration — A direction under subsection (1) applies until the Commission in writing revokes the direction or consents to release funds, securities or property from the direction, or until the Superior Court of Justice orders otherwise.

(2) Application — A direction under subsection (1) that names a bank or other financial institution shall apply only to the branches of the bank or other financial institution identified in the direction.

(3) Exclusions — A direction under subsection (1) shall not apply to funds, securities or property in a recognized clearing agency or to securities in process of transfer by a transfer agent unless the direction so states.

(4) Certificate of pending litigation — The Commission may order that a direction under subsection (1) be certified to a land registrar or mining recorder and that it be registered or recorded against the lands or claims identified in the direction, and on registration or recording of the certificate it shall have the same effect as a certificate of pending litigation.

(5) Review by court — As soon as practicable, but not later than 10 days after a direction is issued under subsection (1), the Commission shall serve and file a notice of application in the Superior Court of Justice to continue the direction or for such other order as the court considers appropriate.

(5.1) Grounds for continuance or other order — An order may be made under subsection (5) if the court is satisfied that the order would be reasonable and expedient in the circumstances, having due regard to the public interest and,

(a) the due administration of Ontario securities law or the securities laws of another jurisdiction; or

(b) the regulation of capital markets in Ontario or another jurisdiction.

(6) Notice — A direction under subsection (1) may be made without notice but, in that event, copies of the direction shall be sent forthwith by such means as the Commission may determine to all persons and companies named in the direction.

(7) Clarification or revocation — A person or company directly affected by a direction may apply to the Commission for clarification or to have the direction varied or revoked.

1994, c. 11, s. 375; 2006, c. 19, Sched. C, s. 1(1); 2010, c. 26, Sched. 18, s. 32; 2014, c. 7, Sched. 28, s. 13

OSA 126

Related Provisions: OSA 127.

Definitions: OSA 1(1)"Commission"; 1(1)"Ontario securities law"; 1(1)"person"; 1(1)"company"; 1(1)"recognized clearing agency".

Policies and Orders: BOR 1.4.

126.1 (1) Fraud and market manipulation — A person or company shall not, directly or indirectly, engage or participate in any act, practice or course of conduct relating to securities, derivatives or the underlying interest of a derivative that the person or company knows or reasonably ought to know,

(a) results in or contributes to a misleading appearance of trading activity in, or an artificial price for, a security, derivative or underlying interest of a derivative; or

(b) perpetrates a fraud on any person or company.

(2) Attempts — A person or company shall not, directly or indirectly, attempt to engage or participate in any act, practice or course of conduct that is contrary to subsection (1).

2002, c. 22, s. 182; 2010, c. 26, Sched. 18, s. 33; 2013, c. 2, Sched. 13, s. 3

126.2 (1) Misleading or untrue statements — A person or company shall not make a statement that the person or company knows or reasonably ought to know,

(a) in a material respect and at the time and in the light of the circumstances under which it is made, is misleading or untrue or does not state a fact that is required to be stated or that is necessary to make the statement not misleading; and

(b) would reasonably be expected to have a significant effect on the market price or value of a security, derivative or underlying interest of a derivative.

(2) Same — A breach of subsection (1) does not give rise to a statutory right of action for damages otherwise than under Part XXIII or XXIII.1.

2002, c. 22, s. 182; 2004, c. 31, Sched. 34, s. 4; 2010, c. 26, Sched. 18, s. 34

127. (1) Orders in the public interest — The Commission may make one or more of the following orders if in its opinion it is in the public interest to make the order or orders;

1. An order that the registration or recognition granted to a person or company under Ontario securities law be suspended or restricted for such period as is specified in the order or be terminated, or that terms and conditions be imposed on the registration or recognition.

OSA 127(1)1

Policies and Orders: OPS 34-601, 34-602.

2. An order that trading in any securities by or of a person or company or that trading in any derivatives by a person or company cease permanently or for such period as is specified in the order.

OSA 127(1)2

Policies and Orders: OPS 1.4; NPS 12-202, 12-203, 62-203, s. 2.3; CSAN 11-319.

2.1 An order that the acquisition of any securities by a particular person or company is prohibited permanently or for the period specified in the order.

3. An order that any exemptions contained in Ontario securities law do not apply to a person or company permanently or for such period as is specified in the order.

4. An order that a market participant submit to a review of his, her or its practices and procedures and institute such changes as may be ordered by the Commission.

5. If the Commission is satisfied that Ontario securities law has not been complied with, an order that a release, report, preliminary prospectus, prospectus, return financial statement, information circular, take-over bid circular, issuer bid circular, offering memorandum, proxy solicitation or any other document described in the order,

Proposed Amendment — 127(1), para. 5 opening words

5. If the Commission is satisfied that Ontario securities law has not been complied with, an order that a release, report, preliminary prospectus, prospectus, return, financial statement, information circular, take-over bid circular, issuer bid circular, offering memorandum, proxy solicitation, disclosure document in respect of a derivative or any other document described in the order,

2010, c. 26, Sched. 18, s. 35(2) [Not in force at date of publication.]

i. be provided by a market participant to a person or company,

ii. not be provided by a market participant to a person or company, or

iii. be amended by a market participant to the extent that amendment is practicable.

6. An order that a person or company be reprimanded.

7. An order that a person resign one or more positions that the person holds as a director or officer of an issuer.

8. An order that a person is prohibited from becoming or acting as director or officer of any issuer.

8.1 An order that a person resign one or more positions that the persons holds as a director or officer of a registrant.

8.2 An order that a person is prohibited from becoming or acting as a director or officer of a registrant.

8.3 An order that a person resign one or more positions that the person holds as a director or officer of an investment fund manager.

8.4 An order that a person is prohibited from becoming or acting as a director or officer of an investment fund manager.

8.5 An order that a person or company is prohibited from becoming or acting as a registrant, as an investment fund manager or as a promoter.

9. If a person or company has not complied with Ontario securities law, an order requiring the person or company to pay an administrative penalty of not more than $1 million for each failure to comply.

10. If a person or company has not complied with Ontario securities law, an order requiring the person or company to disgorge to the Commission any amounts obtained as a result of the non-compliance.

OSA 127(1)

Related Provisions: OSA 3.4(2).

Policies and Orders: BOR 1.2, 1.3.

(2) Terms and conditions — An order under this section may be subject to such terms and conditions as the Commission may impose.

(3) Cease trading order — The Commission may make an order under paragraph 2 of subsection (1) despite the delivery of a report to it under subsection 75(3).

(3.1) Exception — A person or company is not entitled to participate in a proceeding in which an order may be made under paragraph 9 or 10 of subsection (1) solely on the basis that the person or company may be entitled to receive any amount paid under the order.

(4) Hearing requirement — No order shall be made under this section without a hearing, subject to section 4 of the *Statutory Powers Procedure Act*.

(4.1) No hearing required — Despite subsection (4), the Commission may make an order under paragraph 2 or 2.1 of subsection (1) without giving the person or company that is subject to the order an opportunity to be heard if the person or company fails to file a record required to be filed under this Act.

(4.2) Contents of order — An order made under subsection (4.1) must include a reference to the record that was not filed.

(4.3) Revocation of order — Subject to subsection (4.6), the Commission shall revoke an order made under subsection (4.1) as soon as practicable after the record referred to in the order is filed.

(4.4) Notice of order — The Commission shall publish a notice of every order made under subsection (4.1) as soon as practicable after the order is made.

(4.5) Notice of revocation — The Commission shall publish a notice of every order revoked under subsection (4.3) as soon as practicable after the order is revoked.

(4.6) Additional information — If an order made under subsection (4.1) has been in effect for more than 90 days and the Commission is of the opinion that it would be in the public interest to do so, the Commission may require that, before it revokes the order, in addition to filing the record referred to in the order, the person or company that is the subject of the order concurrently file or deliver such additional records or information about the person or company as the Commission requests.

(5) Temporary orders — Despite subsection (4), if in the opinion of the Commission the length of time required to conclude a hearing could be prejudicial to the public interest, the Commission may make a temporary order under paragraph 1, 2 or 3 of subsection (1) or subparagraph ii of paragraph 5 of subsection (1).

(6) Period of temporary order — The temporary order shall take effect immediately and shall expire on the fifteenth day after its making unless extended by the Commission.

(7) Extension of temporary order — The Commission may extend a temporary order until the hearing is concluded if a hearing is commenced within the fifteen-day period.

(8) Same — Despite subsection (7), the Commission may extend a temporary order under paragraph 2 of subsection (1) for such period as it considers necessary if satisfactory information is not provided to the Commission within the fifteen-day period.

(9) Notice of temporary order — The Commission shall give written notice of every temporary order made under subsection (5), together with a notice of hearing, to any person or company directly affected by the temporary order.

(10) Inter-jurisdictional enforcement — Without limiting the generality of subsections (1) and (5), an order may be made under subsection (1) or (5) in respect of a person or company if any of the following circumstances exist:

1. The person or company has been convicted in any jurisdiction of an offence arising from a transaction, business or course of conduct related to securities or derivatives.

2. The person or company has been convicted in any jurisdiction of an offence under a law respecting the buying or selling of securities or derivatives.

3. The person or company has been found by a court in any jurisdiction to have contravened the laws of the jurisdiction respecting the buying or selling of securities or derivatives.

4. The person or company is subject to an order made by a securities regulatory authority, derivatives regulatory authority or financial regulatory authority, in any jurisdiction, that imposes sanctions, conditions, restrictions or requirements on the person or company.

5. The person or company has agreed with a securities regulatory authority, derivatives regulatory authority or financial regulatory authority, in any jurisdiction, to be made subject to sanctions, conditions, restrictions or requirements.

1994, c. 11, s. 375; 1999, c. 9, s. 215; 2002, c. 22, s. 183; 2004, c. 31, Sched. 34, s. 5; 2005, c. 31, Sched. 20, s. 8; 2008, c. 19, Sched. R, s. 1; 2010, c. 26, Sched. 18, s. 35(1), (3)–(6); 2015, c. 20, Sched. 39, s. 3

OSA 127

Related Provisions: OSA 126, 129.2, 29(6).

Definitions: OSA 1(1)"Commission"; 1(1)"person"; 1(1)"company"; 1(1)"security"; 1(1)"derivative"; 1(1)"market participant".

Rules: Rules of Procedure.

Policies and Orders: BOR 1.4, OSCN 15-902.

127.1 (1) Payment of investigation costs — If, in respect of a person or company whose affairs were the subject of an investigation, the Commission,

(a) is satisfied that the person or company has not complied with, or is not complying with, Ontario securities law; or

(b) considers that the person or company has not acted in the public interest,

the Commission may, after conducting a hearing, order the person or company to pay the costs of the investigation.

(2) Payment of hearing costs — If, in respect of a person or company whose affairs were the subject of a hearing, the Commission, after conducting the hearing,

(a) is satisfied that the person or company has not complied with, or is not complying with, Ontario securities law; or

(b) considers that the person or company has not acted in the public interest, the Commission may order the person or company to pay the costs of or related to the hearing that are incurred by or on behalf of the Commission.

(3) Payment of costs where offence — Where a person or company is guilty of an offence under this Act or the regulations, the Commission may, after conducting a hearing, order the person or company to pay the costs of any investigation carried out in respect of that offence.

(4) Costs — For the purposes of subsections (1), (2) and (3), the costs that the Commission may order the person or company to pay include, but are not limited to, all or any of the following:

1. Costs incurred in respect of services provided by persons appointed or engaged under section 5, 11 or 12.
2. Costs of matters preliminary to the hearing.
3. Costs for time spent by the Commision or the staff of the Commission.
4. Any fee paid to a witness.
5. Costs of legal services provided to the Commission.

1999, c. 9, s. 216

OSA 127.1

Related Provisions: OSA 11, 12, 127.

Definitions: OSA 1(1) "Commission"; 1(1) "Ontario securities law".

Rules: Rules of Procedure 18.

Policies and Orders: OPS 51-601, 57-603; OSCN 15-702; CSAN 57-301.

128. (1) Applications to court — The Commission may apply to the Superior Court of Justice for a declaration that a person or company has not complied with or is not complying with Ontario securities law.

(2) Prior hearing not required — The Commission is not required, before making an application under subsection (1), to hold a hearing to determine whether the person or company has not complied with or is not complying with Ontario securities law.

(3) Remedial powers of court — If the court makes a declaration under subsection (1), the court may, despite the imposition of any penalty under section 122 and despite any order made by the Commission under section 127, make any order that the court considers appropriate against the person or company, including, without limiting the generality of the foregoing, one or more of the following orders:

1. An order that the person or company comply with Ontario securities law.

2. An order requiring the person or company to submit to a review by the Commission of his, her or its practices and procedures and to institute such changes as may be directed by the Commission.

3. An order directing that a release, report, preliminary prospectus, prospectus, return, financial statement, information circular, takeover bid circular, issuer bid circular, offering memorandum, proxy solicitation or any other document described in the order,

    i. be provided by the person or company to another person or company,

    ii. not be provided by the person or company to another person or company, or

    iii. be amended by the person or company to the extent that amendment is practicable.

4. An order rescinding any transaction entered into by the person or company relating to trading in securities including the issuance of securities.

5. An order requiring the issuance, cancellation, purchase, exchange or disposition of any securities by the person or company.

6. An order prohibiting the voting or exercise of any other right attaching to securities by the person or company.

7. An order prohibiting the person from acting as officer or director or prohibiting the person or company from acting as promoter of any market participant permanently or for such period as is specified in the order.

8. An order appointing officers and directors in place of or in addition to all or any of the officers and directors of the company then in office.

9. An order directing the person or company to purchase securities of a security holder.

10. An order directing the person or company to repay to a security holder any part of the money paid by the security holder for securities.

11. An order requiring the person or company to produce to the court or an interested person financial statements in the form required by Ontario securities law, or an accounting in such other form as the court may determine.

12. An order directing rectification of the registers or other records of the company.

13. An order requiring the person or company to compensate or make restitution to an aggrieved person or company.

14. An order requiring the person or company to pay general or punitive damages to any other person or company.

15. An order requiring the person or company to disgorge to the Minister any amounts obtained as a result of the non-compliance with Ontario securities law.

16. An order requiring the person or company to rectify any past non-compliance with Ontario securities law to the extent that rectification is practicable.

OSA 128(3)

Related Provisions: OSA 122, 127, 127.1.

(4) Interim Orders — On an application under this section the court may make such interim orders as it considers appropriate.

1993, c. 27, Sched.; 1994, c. 11, s. 375; 2006, c. 19, Sched. C, s. 1(1)

OSA 128

Related Provisions: OSA 29(6).

Definitions: OSA 1(1)"person"; 1(1)"company"; 1(1)"Ontario securities law"; 1(1)"security"; 1(1)"officer"; 1(1)"director".

Policies and Orders: BOR 1.4.

129. (1) Appointment of receiver, etc — The Commission may apply to the Superior Court of Justice for an order appointing a receiver, receiver and manager, trustee or liquidator of all or any part of the property of any person or company.

(2) Grounds — No order shall be made under subsection (1) unless the court is satisfied that,

(a) the appointment of a receiver, receiver and manager, trustee or liquidator of all or any part of the property of the person or company is in the best interests of the creditors of the person or company or of persons or companies any of whose property is in the possession or under the control of the person or company or the security holders of or subscribers to the person or company; or

(b) it is appropriate for the due administration of Ontario securities law.

(3) Application without notice — The court may make an order under subsection (1) on an application without notice, but the period of appointment shall not exceed fifteen days.

(4) Motion to continue order — If an order is made without notice under subsection (3), the Commission may make a motion to the court within fifteen days after the date of the order to continue the order or for the issuance of such other order as the court considers appropriate.

(5) Powers of receiver, etc — A receiver, receiver and manager, trustee or liquidator of the property of a person or company appointed under this section shall be the receiver, receiver and manager, trustee or liquidator of all or any part of the property belonging to the person or company or held by the person or company on behalf of or in trust for any other person or company, and, if so directed by the court, the receiver, receiver and manager, trustee or liquidator has the authority to wind up or manage the business and affairs of the person or company and has all powers necessary or incidental to that authority.

(6) Directors' powers cease — If an order is made appointing a receiver, receiver and manager, trustee or liquidator of the property of a person or company under this section, the powers of the directors of the company that the receiver, receiver and manager, trustee or liquidator is authorized to exercise may not be exercised by the directors until the receiver, receiver and manager, trustee or liquidator is discharged by the court.

(7) Fees and expenses — The fees charged and expenses incurred by a receiver, receiver and manager, trustee or liquidator appointed under this section in relation to the exercise of powers pursuant to the appointment shall be in the discretion of the court.

(8) Variation or discharge of order — An order made under this section may be varied or discharged by the court on motion.

1994, c. 11, s. 375; 2006, c. 19, Sched. C, s. 1(1)

OSA 129

Definitions: OSA 1(1)"Commission"; 1(1)"person"; 1(1)"company"; 1(1)"Ontario securities law".

Policies and Orders: BOR 1.4.

129.1 Limitation period — Except where otherwise provided in this Act, no proceeding under this Act shall be commenced later than six years from the date of the occurrence of the last event on which the proceeding is based.

1994, c. 11, s. 375; 1999, c. 9, s. 217

129.2 Directors and officers — For the purposes of this Act, if a company or a person other than an individual has not complied with Ontario securities law, a director or officer of the company or person who authorized, permitted or acquiesced in the non-compliance shall be deemed to also have not complied with Ontario securities law, whether or not any proceeding has been commenced against the company or person under Ontario securities law or any order has been made against the company or person under section 127.

2002, c. 22, s. 184

PART XXIII — CIVIL LIABILITY (SS. 130–138)

130. (1) Liability for misrepresentation in prospectus — Where a prospectus, together with any amendment to the prospectus, contains a misrepresentation, a purchaser who purchases a security offered by the prospectus during the period of distribution or during distribution to the public has, without regard to whether the purchaser relied on the misrepresentation, a right of action for damages against,

(a) the issuer or a selling security holder on whose behalf the distribution is made;

(b) each underwriter of the securities who is required to sign the certificate required by section 59;

(c) every director of the issuer at the time the prospectus or the amendment to the prospectus was filed;

(d) every person or company whose consent to disclosure of information in the prospectus has been filed pursuant to a requirement of the regulations but only with respect to reports, opinions or statements that have been made by them; and

(e) every person or company who signed the prospectus or the amendment to the prospectus other than the persons or companies included in clauses (a) to (d), or, where the purchaser purchased the security from a person or company referred to in clause (a) or (b) or from another underwriter of the securities, the purchaser may elect to exercise a right of rescission against such person, company or underwriter, in which case the purchaser shall have no right of action for damages against such person, company or underwriter.

(2) Defence — No person or company is liable under subsection (1) if he, she or it proves that the purchaser purchased the securities with knowledge of the misrepresentation.

(3) Idem — No person or company, other than the issuer or selling security holder, is liable under subsection (1) if he, she or it proves,

(a) that the prospectus or the amendment to the prospectus was filed without his, her or its knowledge or consent, and that, on becoming aware of its filing, he, she or it forthwith gave reasonable general notice that it was so filed;

(b) that, after the issue of a receipt for the prospectus and before the purchase of the securities by the purchaser, on becoming aware of any misrepresentation in the prospectus or an amendment to the prospectus he, she or it withdrew the consent thereto and gave reasonable general notice of such withdrawal and the reason therefor;

(c) that, with respect to any part of the prospectus or the amendment to the prospectus purporting to be made on the authority of an expert or purporting to be a copy of or an extract from a report, opinion or statement of an expert, he, she or it had no reasonable grounds to believe and did not believe that there had been a misrepresentation or that such part of the prospectus or the amendment to the prospectus did not fairly represent the report, opinion or statement of the expert or was not a fair copy of or extract from the report, opinion or statement of the expert;

(d) that, with respect to any part of the prospectus or the amendment to the prospectus purporting to be made on his, her or its own authority as an expert or purporting to be a copy of or an extract from his, her or its own report, opinion or statement as an expert but that contains a misrepresentation attributable to failure to represent fairly his, her or its report, opinion or statement as an expert,

(i) the person or company had, after reasonable investigation, reasonable grounds to believe and did believe that such part of the prospectus or the amendment to the prospectus fairly represented his, her or its report, opinion or statement, or

(ii) on becoming aware that such part of the prospectus or the amendment to the prospectus did not fairly represent his, her or its report, opinion or statement as an expert, he, she or it forthwith advised the Commission and gave reasonable general notice that such use had been made and that he, she or it would not be responsible for that part of the prospectus or the amendment to the prospectus; or

(e) that, with respect to a false statement purporting to be a statement made by an official person or contained in what purports to be a copy of or extract from a public official document, it was a correct and fair representation of the statement or copy of or extract from the document, and he, she or it had reasonable grounds to believe and did believe that the statement was true.

(4) Idem — No person or company, other than the issuer or selling security holder, is liable under subsection (1) with respect to any part of the prospectus or the amendment to the prospectus purporting to be made on his, her or its own authority as an expert or purporting to be a copy of or an extract from his, her or its own report, opinion or statement as an expert unless he, she or it,

(a) failed to conduct such reasonable investigation as to provide reasonable grounds for a belief that there had been no misrepresentation; or

(b) believed there had been a misrepresentation.

(5) Idem — No person or company, other than the issuer or selling security holder, is liable under subsection (1) with respect to any part of the prospectus or the amendment to the prospectus not purporting to be made on the authority of an expert and not purporting to be a copy of or an extract from a report, opinion or statement of an expert unless he, she or it,

(a) failed to conduct such reasonable investigation as to provide reasonable grounds for a belief that there had been no misrepresentation; or

(b) believed there had been a misrepresentation.

(6) Limitation re underwriters — No underwriter is liable for more than the total public offering price represented by the portion of the distribution underwritten by the underwriter.

(7) Limitation in action for damages — In an action for damages pursuant to subsection (1), the defendant is not liable for all or any portion of such damages that the defendant proves do not represent the depreciation in value of the security as a result of the misrepresentation relied upon.

(8) Joint and several liability — All or any one or more of the persons or companies specified in subsection (1) are jointly and severally liable, and every person or company who becomes liable to make any payment under this section may recover a contribution from any person or company who, if sued separately, would have been liable to make the same payment provided that the court may deny the right to recover such contribution where, in all the circumstances of the case, it is satisfied that to permit recovery of such contribution would not be just and equitable.

(9) Limitation re amount recoverable — In no case shall the amount recoverable under this section exceed the price at which the securities were offered to the public.

(10) No derogation of rights — The right of action for rescission or damages conferred by this section is in addition to and without derogation from any other right the purchaser may have at law.

2004, c. 31, Sched. 34, s. 6; 2006, c. 33, Sched. Z.5, s. 13

OSA 130

Definitions: OSA 1(1)"misrepresentation"; 1(1)"security"; 1(1)"distribution"; 1(1)"distribution to the public"; 1(1)"issuer"; 1(1)"underwriter"; 1(1)"person"; 1(1)"company"; 1(1)"Commission".

130.1 (1) Liability for misrepresentation in offering memorandum — Where an offering memorandum contains a misrepresentation, a purchaser who purchases a security offered by the offering memorandum during the period of distribution has, without regard to whether the purchaser relied on the misrepresentation, the following rights:

    1. The purchaser has a right of action for damages against the issuer and a selling security holder on whose behalf the distribution is made.

    2. If the purchaser purchased the security from a person or company referred to in paragraph 1, the purchaser may elect to exercise a right of rescission against the person or company. If the purchaser exercises this right, the purchaser ceases to have a right of action for damages against the person or company.

(2) Defence — No person or company is liable under subsection (1) if he, she or it proves that the purchaser purchased the securities with knowledge of the misrepresentation.

(3) Limitation in action for damages — In an action for damages pursuant to subsection (1), the defendant is not liable for all or any portion of the damages that the defendant proves do not represent the depreciation in value of the security as a result of the misrepresentation relied upon.

(4) Joint and several liabililty — Subject to subsection (5), all or any one or more of the persons or companies specified in subsection (1) are jointly and severally liable, and every person or company who becomes liable to make any payment under this section may recover a contribution from any person or company who, if sued separately, would have been liable to be make the same payment, unless the court rules that, in all the circumstances of the case, to permit recovery of the contribution would not be just and equitable.

(5) Same — Despite subsection (4), an issuer shall not be liable where it is not receiving any proceeds from the distribution of the securities being distributed and the misrepresentation was not based on information provided by the issuer, unless the misrepresentation,

    (a) was based on information that was previously publicly disclosed by the issuer;

    (b) was a misrepresentation at the time of its previous public disclosure; and

    (c) was not subsequently publicly corrected or superseded by the issuer prior to the completion of the distribution of the securities being distributed.

(6) Limitation re amount recoverable — In no case shall the amount recoverable under this section exceed the price at which the securities were offered.

(7) No derogation of rights — The right of action for rescission or damages conferred by this section is in addition to and without derogation from any other right the purchaser may have at law.

(8) Application — This section applies only with respect to an offering memorandum which has been furnished to a prospective purchaser in connection with a distribution of a security under an exemption from section 53 of the Act that is specified in the regulations for the purposes of this section.

1999, c. 9, s. 218; 2001, c. 23, s. 216; 2004, c. 31, Sched. 34, s. 7

OSA 130.1

Definitions: OSA 1(1)"offering memorandum"; 1(1)"misrepresentation".

Rules: Rules 45-501, Part 5.

Policies and Orders: OPS 45-501CP, Part 5; OSCN 45-705.

131. (1) Liability for misrepresentation in circular — Where a take-over bid circular sent to the security holders of an offeree issuer as required by the regulations related to Part XX, or any notice of change or variation in respect of the circular, contains a misrepresentation, a security holder may, without regard to whether the security holder relied on the misrepresentation, elect to exercise a right of action for rescission or damages against the offeror or a right of action for damages against,

    (a) every person who at the time the circular or notice, as the case may be, was signed was a director of the offeror;

    (b) every person or company whose consent in respect of the circular or notice, as the case may be, has been filed pursuant to a requirement of the regulations but only with respect to reports, opinions or statements that have been made by the person or company; and

    (c) each person who signed a certificate in the circular or notice, as the case may be, other than the persons included in clause (a).

OSA 131(1)

Related Provisions: OSA Part XX.

(2) Same — Where a directors' circular or a director's or officer's circular delivered to the security holders of an offeree issuer as required by the regulations related to Part XX, or any notice of change or variation in respect of the circular, contains a misrepresentation, a security holder has, without regard to whether the security holder relied on the misrepresentation, a right of action for damages against every director or officer who signed the circular or notice that contained the misrepresentation.

OSA 131(2)

Related Provisions: OSA Part XX.

(3) Idem — Subsection (1) applies with necessary modifications where an issuer bid circular or any notice of change or variation in respect thereof contains a misrepresentation.

(4) Defence — No person or company is liable under subsection (1), (2) or (3) if the person or company proves that the security holder had knowledge of the misrepresentation.

(5) Idem — No person or company, other than the offeror, is liable under subsection (1), (2) or (3) if he, she or it proves,

(a) that the take-over bid circular, issuer bid circular, directors' circular or director's or officer's circular, as the case may be, was sent without his, her or its knowledge or consent and that, on becoming aware of it, he, she or it forthwith gave reasonable general notice that it was so sent;

(b) that, after the sending of the take-over bid circular, issuer bid circular, directors' circular or director's or officer's circular, as the case may be, on becoming aware of any misrepresentation in the take-over bid circular, issuer bid circular, directors' circular or director's or officer's circular, he, she or it withdrew the consent thereto and gave reasonable general notice of the withdrawal and the reason therefor;

(c) that, with respect to any part of the circular purporting to be made on the authority of an expert or purporting to be a copy of or an extract from a report, opinion or statement of an expert, he, she or it had no reasonable grounds to believe and did not believe that there had been a misrepresentation or that such part of the circular did not fairly represent the report, opinion or statement of the expert or was not a fair copy of or extract from the report, opinion or statement of the expert;

(d) that, with respect to any part of the circular purporting to be made on his, her or its own authority as an expert or purporting to be a copy of or an extract from his, her or its own report, opinion or statement as an expert, but that contains a misrepresentation attributable to failure to represent fairly his, her or its report, opinion or statement as an expert,

(i) the person or company had, after reasonable investigation, reasonable grounds to believe and did believe that such part of the circular fairly represented his, her or its report, opinion or statement as an expert, or

(ii) on becoming aware that such part of the circular did not fairly represent his, her or its report, opinion or statement as an expert, he, she or it forthwith advised the Commission and gave reasonable general notice that such use had been made and that he, she or it would not be responsible for that part of the circular; or

(e) that, with respect to a false statement purporting to be a statement made by an official person or contained in what purports to be a copy of or extract from a public official document, it was a correct and fair representation of the statement or copy of or extract from the document and he, she or it had reasonable grounds to believe and did believe that the statement was true.

(6) Idem — No person or company, other than the offeror, is liable under subsection (1), (2) or (3) with respect to any part of the circular purporting to be made on his, her or its own authority as an expert or purporting to be a copy of or an extract from his, her or its own report, opinion or statement as an expert unless he, she or it,

(a) failed to conduct such reasonable investigation as to provide reasonable grounds for a belief that there had been no misrepresentation; or

(b) believed there had been a misrepresentation.

(7) Idem — No person or company, other than the offeror, is liable under subsection (1), (2) or (3) with respect to any part of the circular not purporting to be made on the authority of an expert and not purporting to be a copy of or an extract from a report, opinion or statement of an expert unless he, she or it,

(a) failed to conduct such reasonable investigation as to provide reasonable grounds for a belief that there had been no misrepresentation; or

(b) believed there had been a misrepresentation.

(8) Joint and several liability — All or any one or more of the persons or companies specified in subsection (1), (2) or (3) are jointly and severally liable, and every person or company who becomes liable to make any payment under this section may recover a contribution from any person or company who, if sued separately, would have been liable to make the same payment provided that the court may deny the right to recover such contribution where, in all the circumstances of the case, it is satisfied that to permit recovery of such contribution would not be just and equitable.

(9) Limitation of damages — In an action for damages pursuant to subsection (1), (2) or (3) based on a misrepresentation affecting a security offered by the offeror company in exchange for securities of the offeree company, the defendant is not liable for all or any portion of such damages that the defendant proves do not represent the depreciation in value of the security as a result of the misrepresentation.

(10) Deemed issuer bid circular — Where the offeror in an issuer bid made in the normal course through the facilities of a designated exchange in reliance on an exemption set out in the regulations related to Part XX is required by the by-laws, regulations or policies of the applicable designated exchange to file with it or deliver to security holders of the offeree issuer a disclosure document, the disclosure document shall be deemed, for the purposes of this section, to be an issuer bid circular delivered to the security holders as required by Part XX or the regulations related to Part XX.

OSA 131(10)

Related Provisions: OSA Part XX, 93(1)(a), 93(3)(e).

(11) No derogation of rights — The right of action for rescission or damages conferred by this section is in addition to and without derogation from any other right the security holders of the offeree issuer may have at law.

2004, c. 31, Sched. 34, s. 8; 2007, c. 7, Sched. 38, s. 9(4); 2010, c. 26, Sched. 18, s. 36; 2015, c. 38, Sched. 18, s. 7

OSA 131

Definitions: OSA 1(1)"security"; 1(1)"misrepresentation"; 1(1)"person"; 1(1)"director"; 1(1)"company".

132. Standard of reasonableness — In determining what constitutes reasonable investigation or reasonable grounds for belief for the purposes of sections 130 and 131, the standard of reasonableness shall be that required of a prudent person in the circumstances of the particular case.

OSA 132

Related Provisions: OSA 130, 131.

Definitions: OSA 1(1)"person".

132.1 (1) Defence to liability for misrepresentation — A person or company is not liable in an action under section 130, 130.1 or 131 for a misrepresentation in forward-looking information if the person or company proves all of the following things:

1. The document containing the forward-looking information contained, proximate to that information,

   i. reasonable cautionary language identifying the forward-looking information as such, and identifying material factors that could cause actual results to differ materially from a conclusion, forecast or projection in the forward-looking information, and

   ii. a statement of the material factors or assumptions that were applied in drawing a conclusion or making a forecast or projection set out in the forward-looking information.

2. The person or company had a reasonable basis for drawing the conclusions or making the forecasts and projections set out in the forward-looking information.

(2) Exception — Subsection (1) does not relieve a person or company of liability respecting forward-looking information in a financial statement or forward-looking information in a document released in connection with an initial public offering.

2004, c. 31, Sched. 34, s. 9

OSA 132.1

Definitions: OSA 1(1)"forward-looking information".

Policies and Orders: OPS 51-604; CSAN 51-320.

133. Liability of dealer or offeror — Each of the following has a right of action for rescission or damages against the dealer or offeror who failed to comply with the applicable requirement:

1. A purchaser of a security to whom a prospectus was required to be sent or delivered but was not sent or delivered in compliance with subsection 71(1).

2. A purchaser of an investment fund security to whom a prescribed disclosure document referred to in subsection 71(1.1) was required to be sent or delivered but was not sent or delivered in compliance with the regulations.

Proposed Addition — 133, para. 2.1

2.1 A purchaser of a prescribed investment fund security trading on an exchange or an alternative trading system to whom a prescribed disclosure document referred to in subsection 71(1.3) was required to be sent or delivered but was not sent or delivered in compliance with the regulations.

2014, c. 7, Sched. 28, s. 14 [Not in force at date of publication.]

3. A security holder to whom a take-over bid and take-over bid circular or an issuer bid and an issuer bid circular, or any notice of change or variation to any such bid or circular, were required by the regulations related to Part XX to be sent or delivered but were not sent or delivered in compliance with that Part.

2007, c. 7, Sched. 38, s. 10; 2011, c. 9, Sched. 38, s. 3; 2015, c. 38, Sched. 18, s. 8

OSA 133

Related Provisions: OSA 71(1), 71(1.3), Part XX.

Definitions: OSA 1(1)"investment fund"; OSA 1(1)"security"; OSA 1(1.2)"dealer".

Rules: NI 81-101, s. 3.2.

134. (1) Liability where material fact or change undisclosed — Every person or company in a special relationship with an issuer who purchases or sells securities of the issuer with knowledge of a material fact or material change with respect to the issuer that has not been generally disclosed is liable to compensate the seller or purchaser of the securities, as the case may be, for damages as a result of the trade unless,

   (a) the person or company in the special relationship with the issuer proves that the person or company reasonably believed that the material fact or material change had been generally disclosed; or

   (b) the material fact or material change was known or ought reasonably to have been known to the seller or purchaser, as the case may be.

(2) Idem, tipping — Every,

   (a) issuer;

   (b) person or company in a special relationship with an issuer;

   (c) person or company that is considering or evaluating whether to make a take-over bid, as defined in Part XX, or that proposes to make a take-over bid, as defined in Part XX, for the securities of the issuer, and

OSA 134(2)(c)

Related Provisions: OSA Part XX.

(c.1) person or company that is considering or evaluating whether to become a party, or that proposes to become a party, to a reorganization, amalgamation, merger or arrangement or similar business combination with the issuer or to acquire a substantial portion of its property,

and who informs another person or company of a material fact or material change with respect to the issuer that has not been generally disclosed is liable to compensate for damages any person or company that thereafter sells securities of the issuer to or purchases securities of the issuer from the person or company that received the information unless,

(d) the person or company who informed the other person or company proves that the informing person or company reasonably believed the material fact or material change had been generally disclosed;

(e) the material fact or material change was known or ought reasonably to have been known to the seller or purchaser, as the case may be;

(f) in the case of an action against an issuer or a person in a special relationship with the issuer, the information was given in the necessary course of business; or

(g) in the case of an action against a person or company described in clause (c) or (c.1), the information was given in the necessary course of business relating to the take-over bid, business combination or acquisition.

(3) Liability for improper use of information, mutual funds — A person or company is accountable to a mutual fund in Ontario for any benefit or advantage received or receivable as a result of a purchase or sale of securities of an issuer if,

(a) the portfolio securities of the mutual fund include securities of that issuer; and

(b) the person or company,

(i) has access to information concerning the investment program of the mutual fund, and

(ii) uses that information for his, her or its direct benefit or advantage to purchase or sell securities of that issuer for his, her or its own account.

(3.1) Same, discretionary investment portfolios — A person or company is accountable to a client of a registrant for any benefit or advantage received or receivable as a result of a purchase or sale of securities of an issuer if,

(a) an investment portfolio is managed for the client by the registrant through discretionary authority provided by the client;

(b) the portfolio securities of the investment portfolio include securities of that issuer;

(c) the registrant is a registered adviser or registered dealer; and

(d) the person or company has,

(i) access to information concerning the investment portfolio, and

(ii) uses that information for his, her or its direct benefit or advantage to purchase or sell securities of that issuer.

(4) Accountability for gain — Every person or company who is an insider, affiliate or associate of an issuer that,

(a) sells or purchases the securities of the issuer with knowledge of a material fact or material change with respect to the issuer that has not been generally disclosed; or

(b) communicates to another person, other than in the necessary course of business, knowledge of a material fact or material change with respect to the issuer that has not been generally disclosed,

is accountable to the issuer for any benefit or advantage received or receivable by the person or company as a result of the purchase, sale or communication, as the case may be, unless the person or company proves that the person or company reasonably believed that the material fact or material change had been generally disclosed.

(5) Liability, joint and several — Where more than one person or company in a special relationship with an issuer is liable under subsection (1) or (2) as to the same transaction or series of transactions, their liability is joint and several.

(6) Measure of damages — In assessing damages under subsection (1) or (2), the court shall consider,

(a) if the plaintiff is a purchaser, the price paid by the plaintiff for the security less the average market price of the security in the twenty trading days following general disclosure of the material fact or material change; or

(b) if the plaintiff is a vendor, the average market price of the security in the twenty trading days following general disclosure of the material fact or material change less the price received by the plaintiff for the security,

but the court may instead consider such other measures of damages as may be relevant in the circumstances.

(7) Definition — For the purposes of this section,

"issuer" means,

(a) a reporting issuer, or

(b) any other issuer whose securities are publicly traded;

"a person or company in a special relationship with an issuer" has the same meaning as in subsection 76(5).

"reporting issuer" [Repealed 2015, c. 20, Sched. 39, s. 4(8).]

OSA 134(7)

Related Provisions: OSA 76(5).

(8) Idem — For the purposes of subsections (1) and (2), a security of the issuer shall be deemed to include,

    (a) a put, call, option or other right or obligation to purchase or sell securities of the issuer;

    (b) a security, the market price of which varies materially with the market price of the securities of the issuer; or

    (c) a related derivative.

        2009, c. 18, Sched. 26, s. 17; 2010, c. 26, Sched. 18, s. 37; 2013, c. 2, Sched. 13, s. 4; 2015, c. 20, Sched. 39, s. 4(1), (2), (4), (7), (8)

OSA 134

Definitions: OSA 1(1)"person"; 1(1)"company"; 1(1)"reporting issuer"; 1(1)"material fact"; 1(1)"material change"; 1(1)"trade"; 1(1)"security"; 1(1)"mutual fund in Ontario"; 1(1)"portfolio manager"; 1(1)"portfolio securities"; 1(1)"issuer"; 1(1)"insider"; 1(1)"associate"; 1(1)"related derivative".

Regulations: Reg.: 175.

Rules: NI 55-101.

Policies and Orders: OPS 33-601; NPS 51-201.

135. (1) Action by Commission on behalf of issuer — Upon application by the Commission or by any person or company who was at the time of a transaction referred to in subsection 134(1) or (2) or is at the time of the application a security holder of the reporting issuer, a judge of the Superior Court of Justice may, if satisfied that,

    (a) the Commission or the person or company has reasonable grounds for believing that the reporting issuer has a cause of action under subsection 134(4); and

OSA 135(1)(a)

Related Provisions: OSA 134(1).

    (b) either,

        (i) the reporting issuer has refused or failed to commence an action under section 134 within sixty days after receipt of a written request from the Commission or such person or company so to do, or

        (ii) the reporting issuer has failed to prosecute diligently an action commenced by it under section 134,

make an order, upon such terms as to security for costs and otherwise as to the judge seems fit, requiring the Commission or authorizing such person or company or the Commission to commence or continue an action in the name of and on behalf of the reporting issuer to enforce the liability created by subsection 134(4).

OSA 135(1)(b)

Related Provisions: OSA 134.

(2) Action by Commission on behalf of mutual fund — Upon the application by the Commission or any person or company who was at the time of a transaction referred to in subsection 134(3) or is at the time of the application a security holder of the mutual fund, a judge of the Superior Court of Justice may, if satisfied that,

    (a) the Commission or the person or company has reasonable grounds for believing that the mutual fund has a cause of action under subsection 134(3); and

    (b) the mutual fund has either,

        (i) refused or failed to commence an action under subsection 134(3) within sixty days after receipt of a written request from the Commission or the person or company so to do, or

        (ii) failed to prosecute diligently an action commenced by it under subsection 134(3),

make an order, upon terms as to security for costs or otherwise as to the judge seems proper, requiring the Commission or authorizing the person or company or the Commission to commence and prosecute or to continue an action in the name of and on behalf of the mutual fund to enforce the liability created by subsection 134(3).

OSA 135(2)

Related Provisions: OSA 134(3).

(3) Costs — Where an action under subsection 134(3), (3.1) or (4) is,

    (a) commenced;

    (b) commenced and prosecuted; or

    (c) continued,

by a board of directors of a reporting issuer, the trial judge or, on motion to the Superior Court of Justice, a judge of the Court may order that the costs properly incurred by the board of directors in commencing, commencing and prosecuting or continuing the action, as the case may be, shall be paid by the reporting issuer, if the judge is satisfied that there were apparent grounds for believing the action was in the best interests of the reporting issuer and the security holders thereof.

OSA 135(3)

Related Provisions: OSA 134(3), (4).

(4) Action by Commission on behalf of security holder of the reporting issuer — Where an action under subsection 134(3), (3.1) or (4) is,

(a) commenced;

(b) commenced and prosecuted; or

(c) continued,

by a person or company who is a security holder of the reporting issuer, the trial judge or, on motion to the Superior Court of Justice, a judge of the Court may order that the costs properly incurred by such person or company in commencing, commencing and prosecuting or continuing the action, as the case may be, shall be paid by the reporting issuer, if the judge is satisfied that,

(d) the reporting issuer failed to commence the action or had commenced it but had failed to prosecute it diligently; and

(e) there are apparent grounds for believing that the continuance of the action is in the best interests of the reporting issuer and the security holders thereof.

OSA 135(4)

Regulated Provisions: OSA 134(3), (4).

(5) Idem — Where an action under subsection 134(3), (3.1) or (4) is,

(a) commenced;

(b) commenced and prosecuted; or

(c) continued,

by the Commission, the trial judge or, on motion to the Superior Court of Justice, a judge of the Court shall order the reporting issuer to pay all costs properly incurred by the Commission in commencing, commencing and prosecuting or continuing the action, as the case may be.

OSA 135(5)

Related Provisions: OSA 134(3), (4).

(6) Idem — In determining whether there are apparent grounds for believing that an action or its continuance is in the best interests of a reporting issuer and the security holders thereof, the judge shall consider the relationship between the potential benefit to be derived from the action by the reporting issuer and the security holders thereof and the cost involved in the prosecution of the action.

(7) Notice of application — Notice of every application under subsection (1) or (2) shall be given to the Commission, the reporting issuer or the mutual fund, as the case may be, and each of them may appear and be heard thereon.

(8) Order to co-operate — Every order made under subsection (1) or (2) requiring or authorizing the Commission to commence and prosecute or continue an action shall provide that the reporting issuer or mutual fund, as the case may be, shall co-operate fully with the Commission in the commencement and prosecution or continuation of the action, and shall make available to the Commission all books, records, documents and other material or information known to the reporting issuer or mutual fund or reasonably ascertainable by the reporting issuer or mutual fund relevant to such action.

(9) Appeal — An appeal lies to the Divisional Court from any order made under this section.

2006, c. 19, Sched. C, s. 1(1); 2009, c. 18, Sched. 26, s. 18

OSA 135

Definitions: OSA 1(1)"person"; 1(1)"company"; 1(1)"reporting issuer"; 1(1)"security"; 1(1)"mutual fund"; 1(1)"Commission".

136. (1) Disclosure of intended status as principal — If, contrary to Ontario securities law, a registered dealer fails to disclose to a person or company with whom it effects a purchase or sale of a security that it intended to act as principal in respect of the purchase or sale, the person or company may rescind the contract effecting the purchase or sale by mailing or delivering written notice of the rescission to the registered dealer within 60 days after the date of delivery of the security to or by the person or company, as the case may be.

(2) Disclosure of actual status as principal — If, contrary to Ontario securities law, a registered dealer fails to disclose to a person or company that it has acted as principal in respect of a purchase or sale of a security, the person or company may rescind the contract effecting the purchase or sale by mailing or delivering written notice of the rescission to the registered dealer within seven days after the date of the delivery to the person or company of the written confirmation of the contract.

(3) Service — For the purposes of subsection (2), a confirmation sent by ordinary letter mail is deemed to be delivered to the person or company to whom it was addressed in the ordinary course of mail.

(4) Exception — Subsections (1) and (2) do not allow the rescission of a contract effecting the purchase of a security by a person or company if the person or company no longer owns the security.

(5) Onus — In an action respecting a rescission to which subsection (1) or (2) applies, the onus of proving that a registered dealer disclosed that he, she or it acted or intended to act as principal is on the registered dealer.

(6) Limitation period — No action respecting a rescission shall be commenced under this section after the expiration of a period of 90 days from the date of delivery of the notice under subsection (1) or (2).

2009, c. 18, Sched. 26, s. 19

OSA 136

Definitions: OSA 1(1)"person"; 1(1)"company"; 1(1)"security"; 1(1)"dealer".

137. (1) Rescission of purchase of mutual fund security — Every purchaser of a security of a mutual fund in Ontario may, where the amount of the purchase does not exceed the sum of $50,000, rescind the purchase by notice given to the registered dealer from whom the purchase was made within forty-eight hours after receipt of the confirmation for a lump sum purchase or within sixty days after receipt of the confirmation for the initial payment under a contractual plan but, subject to subsection (5), the amount the purchaser is entitled to recover on exercise of this right to rescind shall not exceed the net asset value of the securities purchased, at the time the right is exercised.

(2) Idem — The right to rescind a purchase made under a contractual plan may be exercised only with respect to payments scheduled to be made within the time specified in subsection (1) for rescinding a purchase made under a contractual plan.

(3) Notice — The notice mentioned in subsection (1) shall be in writing, and may be given by prepaid mail, telegram or other means.

(4) Service — A confirmation sent by prepaid mail shall be deemed conclusively to have been received in the ordinary course of mail by the person or company to whom it was addressed.

(5) Reimbursement — Every registered dealer from whom the purchase was made shall reimburse the purchaser who has exercised the right of rescission in accordance with this section for the amount of sales charges and fees relevant to the investment of the purchaser in the mutual fund in respect of the shares or units of which the notice of exercise of the right of rescission was given.

OSA 137

Definitions: OSA 1(1)"security"; 1(1)"contractual plan"; 1(1)"dealer"; 1(1)"mutual fund".

Regulations: Reg.: 95(2).

Rules: NI 81-102.

138. Limitation periods — Unless otherwise provided in this Act, no action shall be commenced to enforce a right created by this Part more than,

    (a) in the case of an action for rescission, 180 days after the date of the transaction that gave rise to the cause of action; or

    (b) in the case of any action, other than an action for rescission, the earlier of,

        (i) 180 days after the plaintiff first had knowledge of the facts giving rise to the cause of action, or

        (ii) three years after the date of the transaction that gave rise to the cause of action.

PART XXIII.1 — CIVIL LIABILITY FOR SECONDARY MARKET DISCLOSURE (SS. 138.1–138.14)

[Heading added 2002, c. 22, s. 185.]

Interpretation and Application

[Heading added 2002, c. 22, s. 185.]

138.1 Definitions — In this Part,

"compensation" means compensation received during the 12-month period immediately preceding the day on which the misrepresentation was made or on which the failure to make timely disclosure first occurred, together with the fair market value of all deferred compensation including, without limitation, options, pension benefits and stock appreciation rights, granted during the same period, valued as of the date that such compensation is awarded;

"control person" [Repealed 2006, c. 33, Sched. Z.5, s. 14(1).]

"core document" means,

    (a) a prospectus, a take-over bid circular, an issuer bid circular, a directors' circular, a notice of change or variation in respect of a take-over bid circular, issuer bid circular or directors' circular, a rights offering circular, management's discussion and analysis, an annual information form, an information circular, annual financial statements and an interim financial report of the responsible issuer, where used in relation to,

        (i) a director of a responsible issuer who is not also an officer of the responsible issuer,

        (ii) an influential person, other than an officer of the responsible issuer or an investment fund manager where the responsible issuer is an investment fund, or

        (iii) a director or officer of an influential person who is not also an officer of the responsible issuer, other than an officer of an investment fund manager,

    (b) a prospectus, a take-over bid circular, an issuer bid circular, a directors' circular, a notice of change or variation in respect of a take-over bid circular, issuer bid circular or directors' circular, a rights offering circular, management's discussion and analysis, an annual information form, an information circular, annual financial statements, an interim financial report and a material change report required by subsection 75(2) or the regulations of the responsible issuer, where used in relation to,

        (i) a responsible issuer or an officer of the responsible issuer,

        (ii) an investment fund manager, where the responsible issuer is an investment fund, or

        (iii) an officer of an investment fund manager, where the responsible issuer is an investment fund, or

    (c) such other documents as may be prescribed by regulation for the purposes of this definition;

"document" means any written communication, including a communication prepared and transmitted only in electronic form,

(a) that is required to be filed with the Commission, or

(b) that is not required to be filed with the Commission and,

(i) that is filed with the Commission,

(ii) that is filed or required to be filed with a government or an agency of a government under applicable securities or corporate law or with any exchange or quotation and trade reporting system under its by-laws, rules or regulations, or

(iii) that is any other communication the content of which would reasonably be expected to affect the market price or value of a security of the responsible issuer;

"expert" means a person or company whose profession gives authority to a statement made in a professional capacity by the person or company, including, without limitation, an accountant, actuary, appraiser, auditor, engineer, financial analyst, geologist or lawyer, but not including a designated credit rating organization;

"failure to make timely disclosure" means a failure to disclose a material change in the manner and at the time required under this Act or the regulations;

"forward-looking information" [Repealed 2004, c. 31, Sched. 34, s. 10(3).]

"influential person" means, in respect of a responsible issuer,

(a) a control person,

(b) a promoter,

(c) an insider who is not a director or officer of the responsible issuer, or

(d) an investment fund manager, if the responsible issuer is an investment fund;

"issuer's security" means a security of a responsible issuer and includes a security,

(a) the market price or value of which, or payment obligations under which, are derived from or based on a security of the responsible issuer, and

(b) which is created by a person or company on behalf of the responsible issuer or is guaranteed by the responsible issuer;

"liability limit" means,

(a) in the case of a responsible issuer, the greater of,

(i) 5 per cent of its market capitalization (as such term is defined in the regulations), and

(ii) $1 million,

(b) in the case of a director or officer of a responsible issuer, the greater of,

(i) $25,000, and

(ii) 50 per cent of the aggregate of the director's or officer's compensation from the responsible issuer and its affiliates,

(c) in the case of an influential person who is not an individual, the greater of,

(i) 5 per cent of its market capitalization (as defined in the regulations), and

(ii) $1 million,

(d) in the case of an influential person who is an individual, the greater of,

(i) $25,000, and

(ii) 50 per cent of the aggregate of the influential person's compensation from the responsible issuer and its affiliates,

(e) in the case of a director or officer of an influential person, the greater of,

(i) $25,000, and

(ii) 50 per cent of the aggregate of the director's or officer's compensation from the influential person and its affiliates,

(f) in the case of an expert, the greater of,

(i) $1 million, and

(ii) the revenue that the expert and the affiliates of the expert have earned from the responsible issuer and its affiliates during the 12 months preceding the misrepresentation, and

(g) in the case of each person who made a public oral statement, other than an individual referred to in clause (d), (e) or (f), the greater of,

(i) $25,000, and

(ii) 50 per cent of the aggregate of the person's compensation from the responsible issuer and its affiliates;

"management's discussion and analysis" means the section of an annual information form, annual report or other document that contains management's discussion and analysis of the financial condition and financial performance of a responsible issuer as required under Ontario securities law;

"public oral statement" means an oral statement made in circumstances in which a reasonable person would believe that information contained in the statement will become generally disclosed;

"**release**" means, with respect to information or a document, to file with the Commission or any other securities regulatory authority in Canada or an exchange or to otherwise make available to the public;

"**responsible issuer**" means,

(a) a reporting issuer, or

(b) any other issuer with a real and substantial connection to Ontario, any securities of which are publicly traded;

"**trading day**" means a day during which the principal market (as defined in the regulations) for the security is open for trading.

     2002, c. 22, s. 185; 2004, c. 31, Sched. 34, s. 10; 2006, c. 33, Sched. Z.5, s. 14; 2010, c. 1, Sched. 26, s. 6; 2010, c. 26, Sched. 18, s. 38

OSA 138.1

Definitions: OSA 1(1) "control person".

Regulations: Reg.: 248–251.

138.2 Application — This Part does not apply to,

(a) the purchase of a security offered by a prospectus during the period of distribution;

(b) the acquisition of an issuer's security pursuant to a distribution that is exempt from section 53 or 62, except as may be prescribed by regulation;

OSA 138.2(b)

Regulations: Reg.: 252(1).

(c) the acquisition or disposition of an issuer's security in connection with or pursuant to a take-over bid or issuer bid, except as may be prescribed by regulation; or

OSA 138.2(c)

Regulations: Reg.: 252(2).

(d) such other transactions or class of transactions as may be prescribed by regulation.

     2002, c. 22, s. 185; 2004, c. 31, Sched. 34, s. 11

Liability

[Heading added 2002, c. 22, s. 185.]

138.3 Liability for secondary market disclosure — (1) Documents released by responsible issuer — Where a responsible issuer or a person or company with actual, implied or apparent authority to act on behalf of a responsible issuer releases a document that contains a misrepresentation, a person or company who acquires or disposes of the issuer's security during the period between the time when the document was released and the time when the misrepresentation contained in the document was publicly corrected has, without regard to whether the person or company relied on the misrepresentation, a right of action for damages against,

(a) the responsible issuer;

(b) each director of the responsible issuer at the time the document was released;

(c) each officer of the responsible issuer who authorized, permitted or acquiesced in the release of the document;

(d) each influential person, and each director and officer of an influential person, who knowingly influenced,

    (i) the responsible issuer or any person or company acting on behalf of the responsible issuer to release the document, or

    (ii) a director or officer of the responsible issuer to authorize, permit or acquiesce in the release of the document; and

(e) each expert where,

    (i) the misrepresentation is also contained in a report, statement or opinion made by the expert,

    (ii) the document includes, summarizes or quotes from the report, statement or opinion of the expert, and

    (iii) if the document was released by a person or company other than the expert, the expert consented in writing to the use of the report, statement or opinion in the document.

(2) Public oral statements by responsible issuer — Where a person with actual, implied or apparent authority to speak on behalf of a responsible issuer makes a public oral statement that relates to the business or affairs of the responsible issuer and that contains a misrepresentation, a person or company who acquires or disposes of the issuer's security during the period between the time when the public oral statement was made and the time when the misrepresentation contained in the public oral statement was publicly corrected has, without regard to whether the person or company relied on the misrepresentation, a right of action for damages against,

(a) the responsible issuer;

(b) the person who made the public oral statement;

(c) each director and officer of the responsible issuer who authorized, permitted or acquiesced in the making of the public oral statement;

(d) each influential person, and each director and officer of the influential person, who knowingly influenced,

    (i) the person who made the public oral statement to make the public oral statement, or

    (ii) a director or officer of the responsible issuer to authorize, permit or acquiesce in the making of the public oral statement; and

(e) each expert where,

(i) the misrepresentation is also contained in a report, statement or opinion made by the expert,

(ii) the person making the public oral statement includes, summarizes or quotes from the report, statement or opinion of the expert, and

(iii) if the public oral statement was made by a person other than the expert, the expert consented in writing to the use of the report, statement or opinion in the public oral statement.

(3) Influential persons — Where an influential person or a person or company with actual, implied or apparent authority to act or speak on behalf of the influential person releases a document or makes a public oral statement that relates to a responsible issuer and that contains a misrepresentation, a person or company who acquires or disposes of the issuer's security during the period between the time when the document was released or the public oral statement was made and the time when the misrepresentation contained in the document or public oral statement was publicly corrected has, without regard to whether the person or company relied on the misrepresentation, a right of action for damages against,

(a) the responsible issuer, if a director or officer of the responsible issuer, or where the responsible issuer is an investment fund, the investment fund manager, authorized, permitted or acquiesced in the release of the document or the making of the public oral statement;

(b) the person who made the public oral statement;

(c) each director and officer of the responsible issuer who authorized, permitted or acquiesced in the release of the document or the making of the public oral statement;

(d) the influential person;

(e) each director and officer of the influential person who authorized, permitted or acquiesced in the release of the document or the making of the public oral statement; and

(f) each expert where,

(i) the misrepresentation is also contained in a report, statement or opinion made by the expert,

(ii) the document or public oral statement includes, summarizes or quotes from the report, statement or opinion of the expert, and

(iii) if the document was released or the public oral statement was made by a person other than the expert, the expert consented in writing to the use of the report, statement or opinion in the document or public oral statement.

(4) Failure to make timely disclosure — Where a responsible issuer fails to make a timely disclosure, a person or company who acquires or disposes of the issuer's security between the time when the material change was required to be disclosed in the manner required under this Act or the regulations and the subsequent disclosure of the material change has, without regard to whether the person or company relied on the responsible issuer having complied with its disclosure requirements, a right of action for damages against,

(a) the responsible issuer;

(b) each director and officer of the responsible issuer who authorized, permitted or acquiesced in the failure to make timely disclosure; and

(c) each influential person, and each director and officer of an influential person, who knowingly influenced,

(i) the responsible issuer or any person or company acting on behalf of the responsible issuer in the failure to make timely disclosure, or

(ii) a director or officer of the responsible issuer to authorize, permit or acquiesce in the failure to make timely disclosure.

(5) Multiple roles — In an action under this section, a person who is a director or officer of an influential person is not liable in that capacity if the person is liable as a director or officer of the responsible issuer.

(6) Multiple misrepresentations — In an action under this section,

(a) multiple misrepresentations having common subject matter or content may, in the discretion of the court, be treated as a single misrepresentation; and

(b) multiple instances of failure to make timely disclosure of a material change or material changes concerning common subject matter may, in the discretion of the court, be treated as a single failure to make timely disclosure.

(7) No implied or actual authority — In an action under subsection (2) or (3), if the person who made the public oral statement had apparent authority, but not implied or actual authority, to speak on behalf of the issuer, no other person is liable with respect to any of the responsible issuer's securities that were acquired or disposed of before that other person became, or should reasonably have become, aware of the misrepresentation.

2002, c. 22, s. 185; 2004, c. 31, Sched. 34, s. 12; 2006, c. 33, Sched. Z.5, s. 15

OSA 138.3

Definitions: OSA 1(1)"misrepresentation"; 138.1"document", "expert", "failure to make timely disclosure", "influential person", "issuer's security", "public oral statement", "release", "responsible issuer".

138.4 Burden of proof and defences — **(1) Non-core documents and public oral statements** — In an action under section 138.3 in relation to a misrepresentation in a document that is not a core document, or a misrepresentation in a public oral statement, a person or company is not liable, subject to subsection (2), unless the plaintiff proves that the person or company,

(a) knew, at the time that the document was released or public oral statement was made, that the document or public oral statement contained the misrepresentation;

(b) at or before the time that the document was released or public oral statement was made, deliberately avoided acquiring knowledge that the document or public oral statement contained the misrepresentation; or

(c) was, through action or failure to act, guilty of gross misconduct in connection with the release of the document or the making of the public oral statement that contained the misrepresentation.

OSA 138.4(1)

Definitions: OSA 1(1)"forward-looking information".

(2) Same — A plaintiff is not required to prove any of the matters set out in subsection (1) in an action under section 138.3 in relation to an expert.

(3) Failure to make timely disclosure — In an action under section 138.3 in relation to a failure to make timely disclosure, a person or company is not liable, subject to subsection (4), unless the plaintiff proves that the person or company,

(a) knew, at the time that the failure to make timely disclosure first occurred, of the change and that the change was a material change;

(b) at the time or before the failure to make timely disclosure first occurred, deliberately avoided acquiring knowledge of the change or that the change was a material change; or

(c) was, through action or failure to act, guilty of gross misconduct in connection with the failure to make timely disclosure.

(4) Same — A plaintiff is not required to prove any of the matters set out in subsection (3) in an action under section 138.3 in relation to,

(a) a responsible issuer;

(b) an officer of a responsible issuer;

(c) an investment fund manager; or

(d) an officer of an investment fund manager.

(5) Knowledge of the misrepresentation or material change — A person or company is not liable in an action under section 138.3 in relation to a misrepresentation or a failure to make timely disclosure if that person or company proves that the plaintiff acquired or disposed of the issuer's security,

(a) with knowledge that the document or public oral statement contained a misrepresentation; or

(b) with knowledge of the material change.

(6) Reasonable investigation — A person or company is not liable in an action under section 138.3 in relation to,

(a) a misrepresentation if that person or company proves that,

(i) before the release of the document or the making of the public oral statement containing the misrepresentation, the person or company conducted or caused to be conducted a reasonable investigation, and

(ii) at the time of the release of the document or the making of the public oral statement, the person or company had no reasonable grounds to believe that the document or public oral statement contained the misrepresentation; or

(b) a failure to make timely disclosure if that person or company proves that,

(i) before the failure to make timely disclosure first occurred, the person or company conducted or caused to be conducted a reasonable investigation, and

(ii) the person or company had no reasonable grounds to believe that the failure to make timely disclosure would occur.

(7) Factors to be considered by court — In determining whether an investigation was reasonable under subsection (6), or whether any person or company is guilty of gross misconduct under subsection (1) or (3), the court shall consider all relevant circumstances, including,

(a) the nature of the responsible issuer;

(b) the knowledge, experience and function of the person or company;

(c) the office held, if the person was an officer;

(d) the presence or absence of another relationship with the responsible issuer, if the person was a director;

(e) the existence, if any, and the nature of any system designed to ensure that the responsible issuer meets its continuous disclosure obligations;

(f) the reasonableness of reliance by the person or company on the responsible issuer's disclosure compliance system and on the responsible issuer's officers, employees and others whose duties would in the ordinary course have given them knowledge of the relevant facts;

(g) the period within which disclosure was required to be made under the applicable law;

(h) in respect of a report, statement or opinion of an expert, any professional standards applicable to the expert;

(i) the extent to which the person or company knew, or should reasonably have known, the content and medium of dissemination of the document or public oral statement;

(j) in the case of a misrepresentation, the role and responsibility of the person or company in the preparation and release of the document or the making of the public oral statement containing the misrepresentation or the ascertaining of the facts contained in that document or public oral statement; and

(k) in the case of a failure to make timely disclosure, the role and responsibility of the person or company involved in a decision not to disclose the material change.

(8) Confidential disclosure — A person or company is not liable in an action under section 138.3 in respect of a failure to make timely disclosure if,

(a) the person or company proves that the material change was disclosed by the responsible issuer in a report filed on a confidential basis with the Commission under subsection 75(3) or the regulations;

(b) the responsible issuer had a reasonable basis for making the disclosure on a confidential basis;

(c) where the information contained in the report filed on a confidential basis remains material, disclosure of the material change was made public promptly when the basis for confidentiality ceased to exist;

(d) the person or company or responsible issuer did not release a document or make a public oral statement that, due to the undisclosed material change, contained a misrepresentation; and

(e) where the material change became publicly known in a manner other than the manner required under this Act or the regulations, the responsible issuer promptly disclosed the material change in the manner required under this Act or the regulations.

(9) Forward-looking information — A person or company is not liable in an action under section 138.3 for a misrepresentation in forward-looking information if the person or company proves all of the following things:

1. The document or public oral statement containing the forward-looking information contained, proximate to that information,

i. reasonable cautionary language identifying the forward-looking information as such, and identifying material factors that could cause actual results to differ materially from a conclusion, forecast or projection in the forward-looking information, and

ii. a statement of the material factors or assumptions that were applied in drawing a conclusion or making a forecast or projection set out in the forward-looking information.

2. The person or company had a reasonable basis for drawing the conclusions or making the forecasts and projections set out in the forward-looking information.

OSA 138.4(9)

Definitions: OSA 1(1)"forward-looking information".

Rules: NI 51-102, Parts 4A and 4B.

Policies and Orders: OPS 51-604; CSAN 51-330.

(9.1) Same — The person or company shall be deemed to have satisfied the requirements of paragraph 1 of subsection (9) with respect to a public oral statement containing forward-looking information if the person who made the public oral statement,

(a) made a cautionary statement that the oral statement contains forward-looking information;

(b) stated that,

(i) the actual results could differ materially from a conclusion, forecast or projection in the forward-looking information, and

(ii) certain material factors or assumptions were applied in drawing a conclusion or making a forecast or projection as reflected in the forward-looking information; and

(c) stated that additional information about,

(i) the material factors that could cause actual results to differ materially from the conclusion, forecast or projection in the forward-looking information, and

(ii) the material factors or assumptions that were applied in drawing a conclusion or making a forecast or projection as reflected in the forward-looking information,

is contained in a readily-available document or in a portion of such a document and has identified that document or that portion of the document.

OSA 138.4(9.1)

Policies and Orders: OPS 51-604.

(9.2) Same — For the purposes of clause (9.1)(c), a document filed with the Commission or otherwise generally disclosed shall be deemed to be readily available.

(10) Exception — Subsection (9) does not relieve a person or company of liability respecting forward-looking information in a financial statement required to be filed under this Act or the regulations or forward-looking information in a document released in connection with an initial public offering.

(11) Expert report, statement or opinion — A person or company, other than an expert, is not liable in an action under section 138.3 with respect to any part of a document or public oral statement that includes, summarizes or quotes from a report, statement or opinion made by the expert in respect of which the responsible issuer obtained the written consent of the expert to the use of the report, statement or opinion, if the consent had not been withdrawn in writing before the document was released or the public oral statement was made, if the person or company proves that,

(a) the person or company did not know and had no reasonable grounds to believe that there had been a misrepresentation in the part of the document or public oral statement made on the authority of the expert; and

(b) the part of the document or oral public statement fairly represented the report, statement or opinion made by the expert.

(12) Same — An expert is not liable in an action under section 138.3 with respect to any part of a document or public oral statement that includes, summarizes or quotes from a report, statement or opinion made by the expert, if the expert proves that the written consent previously provided was withdrawn in writing before the document was released or the public oral statement was made.

(13) Release of documents — A person or company is not liable in an action under section 138.3 in respect of a misrepresentation in a document, other than a document required to be filed with the Commission, if the person or company proves that, at the time of release of the document, the person or company did not know and had no reasonable grounds to believe that the document would be released.

(14) Derivative information — A person or company is not liable in an action under section 138.3 for a misrepresentation in a document or a public oral statement, if the person or company proves that,

(a) the misrepresentation was also contained in a document filed by or on behalf of another person or company, other than the responsible issuer, with the Commission or any other securities regulatory authority in Canada or an exchange and was not corrected in another document filed by or on behalf of that other person or company with the Commission or that other securities regulatory authority in Canada or exchange before the release of the document or the public oral statement made by or on behalf of the responsible issuer;

(b) the document or public oral statement contained a reference identifying the document that was the source of the misrepresentation; and

(c) when the document was released or the public oral statement was made, the person or company did not know and had no reasonable grounds to believe that the document or public oral statement contained a misrepresentation.

(15) Where corrective action taken — A person or company, other than the responsible issuer, is not liable in an action under section 138.3 if the misrepresentation or failure to make timely disclosure was made without the knowledge or consent of the person or company and, if, after the person or company became aware of the misrepresentation before it was corrected, or the failure to make timely disclosure before it was disclosed in the manner required under this Act or the regulations,

(a) the person or company promptly notified the board of directors of the responsible issuer or other persons acting in a similar capacity of the misrepresentation or the failure to make timely disclosure; and

(b) if no correction of the misrepresentation or no subsequent disclosure of the material change in the manner required under this Act or the regulations was made by the responsible issuer within two business days after the notification under clause (a), the person or company, unless prohibited by law or by professional confidentiality rules, promptly and in writing notified the Commission of the misrepresentation or failure to make timely disclosure.

2002, c. 22, s. 185; 2004, c. 31, Sched. 34, s. 13; 2006, c. 33, Sched. Z.5, s. 16; 2010, c. 26, Sched. 18, s. 39

OSA 138.4

Definitions: OSA 1(1)"forward-looking information", "material change", "misrepresentation", "person", "company"; 138.1"core document", "document", "expert", "failure to make timely disclosure", "public oral statement", "release", "responsible issuer".

Policies and Orders: OPS 51-604.

Damages
[Heading added 2002, c. 22, s. 185.]

138.5 (1) Assessment of damages — Damages shall be assessed in favour of a person or company that acquired an issuer's securities after the release of a document or the making of a public oral statement containing a misrepresentation or after a failure to make timely disclosure as follows:

1. In respect of any of the securities of the responsible issuer that the person or company subsequently disposed of on or before the 10th trading day after the public correction of the misrepresentation or the disclosure of the material change in the manner required under this Act or the regulations, assessed damages shall equal the difference between the average price paid for those securities (including any commissions paid in respect thereof) and the price received upon the disposition of those securities (without deducting any commissions paid in respect of the disposition), calculated taking into account the result of hedging or other risk limitation transactions.

2. In respect of any of the securities of the responsible issuer that the person or company subsequently disposed of after the 10th trading day after the public correction of the misrepresentation or the disclosure of the material change in the manner required under this Act or the regulations, assessed damages shall equal the lesser of,

i. an amount equal to the difference between the average price paid for those securities (including any commissions paid in respect thereof) and the price received upon the disposition of those securities (without deducting any commissions paid in respect of the disposition), calculated taking into account the result of hedging or other risk limitation transactions, and

ii. an amount equal to the number of securities that the person disposed of, multiplied by the difference between the average price per security paid for those securities (including any commissions paid in respect thereof determined on a per security basis) and,

A. if the issuer's securities trade on a published market, the trading price of the issuer's securities on the principal market (as those terms are defined in the regulations) for the 10 trading days following the public correction of the misrepresentation or the disclosure of the material change in the manner required under this Act or the regulations, or

B. if there is no published market, the amount that the court considers just.

3. In respect of any of the securities of the responsible issuer that the person or company has not disposed of, assessed damages shall equal the number of securities acquired, multiplied by the difference between the average price per security paid for those securities (including any commissions paid in respect thereof determined on a per security basis) and,

i. if the issuer's securities trade on a published market, the trading price of the issuer' securities on the principal market (as those terms are defined in the regulations) for the 10 trading days following the public correction of the misrepresentation or the disclosure of the material change in the manner required under this Act or the regulations, or

ii. if there is no published market, the amount that the court considers just.

(2) Same — Damages shall be assessed in favour of a person or company that disposed of securities after a document was released or a public oral statement made containing a misrepresentation or after a failure to make timely disclosure as follows:

1. In respect of any of the securities of the responsible issuer that the person or company subsequently acquired on or before the 10th trading day after the public correction of the misrepresentation or the disclosure of the material change in the manner required under this Act or the regulations, assessed damages shall equal the difference between the average price received upon the disposition of those securities (deducting any commissions paid in respect of the disposition) and the price paid for those securities (without including any commissions paid in respect thereof), calculated taking into account the result of hedging or other risk limitation transactions.

2. In respect of any of the securities of the responsible issuer that the person or company subsequently acquired after the 10th trading day after the public correction of the misrepresentation or the disclosure of the material change in the manner required under this Act or the regulations, assessed damages shall equal the lesser of,

    i. an amount equal to the difference between the average price received upon the disposition of those securities (deducting any commissions paid in respect of the disposition) and the price paid for those securities (without including any commissions paid in respect thereof), calculated taking into account the result of hedging or other risk limitation transactions, and

    ii. an amount equal to the number of securities that the person disposed of, multiplied by the difference between the average price per security received upon the disposition of those securities (deducting any commissions paid in respect of the disposition determined on a per security basis) and,

        A. if the issuer's securities trade on a published market, the trading price of the issuer's securities on the principal market (as those terms are defined in the regulations) for the 10 trading days following the public correction of the misrepresentation or the disclosure of the material change in the manner required under this Act or the regulations, or

        B. if there is no published market, the amount that the court considers just.

3. In respect of any of the securities of the responsible issuer that the person or company has not acquired, assessed damages shall equal the number of securities that the person or company disposed of, multiplied by the difference between the average price per security received upon the disposition of those securities (deducting any commissions paid in respect of the disposition determined on a per security basis) and,

    i. if the issuer's securities trade on a published market, the trading price of the issuer's securities on the principal market (as such terms are defined in the regulations) for the 10 trading days following the public correction of the misrepresentation or the disclosure of the material change in the manner required under this Act or the regulations, or

    ii. if there is no published market, then the amount that the court considers just.

(3) Same — Despite subsections (1) and (2), assessed damages shall not include any amount that the defendant proves is attributable to a change in the market price of securities that is unrelated to the misrepresentation or the failure to make timely disclosure.

2002, c. 22, s. 185; 2004, c. 31, Sched. 34, s. 14; 2006, c. 33, Sched. Z.5, s. 17

OSA 138.5

Regulations: Reg.: 251.

Definitions: OSA 1(1)"material change", "misrepresentation"; 138.5"document", "failure to make timely disclosure", "issuer's security", "public oral statement", "release".

138.6 (1) Proportionate liability — In an action under section 138.3, the court shall determine, in respect of each defendant found liable in the action, the defendant's responsibility for the damages assessed in favour of all plaintiffs in the action, and each such defendant shall be liable, subject to the limits set out in subsection 138.7(1), to the plaintiffs for only that portion of the aggregate amount of damages assessed in favour of the plaintiffs that corresponds to that defendant's responsibility for the damages.

(2) Same — Despite subsection (1), where, in an action under section 138.3 in respect of a misrepresentation or a failure to make timely disclosure, a court determines that a particular defendant, other than the responsible issuer, authorized, permitted or acquiesced in the making of the misrepresentation or the failure to make timely disclosure while knowing it to be a misrepresentation or a failure to make timely disclosure, the whole amount of the damages assessed in the action may be recovered from that defendant.

(3) Same — Each defendant in respect of whom the court has made a determination under subsection (2) is jointly and severally liable with each other defendant in respect of whom the court has made a determination under subsection (2).

(4) Same — Any defendant against whom recovery is obtained under subsection (2) is entitled to claim contribution from any other defendant who is found liable in the action.

2002, c. 22, s. 185; 2004, c. 31, Sched. 34, s. 15

OSA 138.6

Definitions: OSA 1(1)"misrepresentation"; 138.1"failure to make timely disclosure", "responsible issuer".

138.7 (1) Limits on damages — Despite section 138.5, the damages payable by a person or company in an action under section 138.3 is the lesser of,

(a) the aggregate damages assessed against the person or company in the action; and

(b) the liability limit for the person or company less the aggregate of all damages assessed after appeals, if any, against the person or company in all other actions brought under section 138.3, and under comparable legislation in other provinces or territories in Canada in respect of that misrepresentation or failure to make timely disclosure, and less any amount paid in settlement of any such actions.

(2) Same — Subsection (1) does not apply to a person or company, other than the responsible issuer, if the plaintiff proves that the person or company authorized, permitted or acquiesced in the making of the misrepresentation or the failure to make timely disclosure while knowing that it was a misrepresentation or a failure to make timely disclosure, or influenced the making of the misrepresentation or the failure to make timely disclosure while knowing that it was a misrepresentation or a failure to make timely disclosure.

2002, c. 22, s. 185; 2004, c. 31, Sched. 34, s. 16

OSA 138.7

Definitions: OSA 1(1)"misrepresentation"; 138.1"liability limit", "failure to make timely disclosure".

Procedural Matters
[Heading added 2002, c. 22, s. 185.]

138.8 (1) Leave to proceed — No action may be commenced under section 138.3 without leave of the court granted upon motion with notice to each defendant. The court shall grant leave only where it is satisfied that,

(a) the action is being brought in good faith; and

(b) there is a reasonable possibility that the action will be resolved at trial in favour of the plaintiff.

(2) Same — Upon an application under this section, the plaintiff and each defendant shall serve and file one or more affidavits setting forth the material facts upon which each intends to rely.

(3) Same — The maker of such an affidavit may be examined on it in accordance with the rules of court.

(4) Copies to be sent to the Commission — A copy of the application for leave to proceed and any affidavits and factums filed with the court shall be sent to the Commission when filed.

(5) Requirement to provide notice — The plaintiff shall provide the Commission with notice in writing of the date on which the application for leave is scheduled to proceed, at the same time such notice is given to each defendant.

(6) Same, appeal of leave decision — If any party appeals the decision of the court with respect to whether leave to commence an action under section 138.3 is granted,

(a) each party to the appeal shall provide a copy of its factum to the Commission when it is filed; and

(b) the appellant shall provide the Commission with notice in writing of the date on which the appeal is scheduled to be heard, at the same time such notice is given to each respondent.

2002, c. 22, s. 185; 2004, c. 31, Sched. 34, s. 17; 2009, c. 34, Sched. S, s. 6

138.9 (1) Notice — A person or company that has been granted leave to commence an action under section 138.3 shall,

(a) promptly issue a news release disclosing that leave has been granted to commence an action under section 138.3;

(b) send a written notice to the Commission within seven days, together with a copy of the news release;

(c) send a copy of the statement of claim or other originating document to the Commission when filed; and

(d) provide the Commission with notice in writing of the date on which the trial of the action is scheduled to proceed, at the same time such notice is given to each defendant.

(2) Appeal — If any party to an action under section 138.3 appeals the decision of the court,

(a) each party shall provide a copy of its factum to the Commission when it is filed; and

(b) the appellant shall provide the Commission with notice in writing of the date on which the appeal is scheduled to be heard, at the same time such notice is given to each respondent.

2002, c. 22, s. 185; 2004, c. 31, Sched. 34, s. 18; 2009, c. 34, Sched. S, s. 7

OSA 138.9

Definitions: OSA 1(1)"Commission".

138.10 Restriction on discontinuation, etc., of action — An action under section 138.3 shall not be discontinued, abandoned or settled without the approval of the court given on such terms as the court thinks fit including, without limitation, terms as to costs, and in determining whether to approve the settlement of the action, the court shall consider, among other things, whether there are any other actions outstanding under section 138.3 or under comparable legislation in other provinces or territories in Canada in respect of the same misrepresentation or failure to make timely disclosure.

2002, c. 22, s. 185; 2004, c. 31, Sched. 34, s. 19

138.11 Costs — Despite the *Courts of Justice Act* and the *Class Proceedings Act, 1992*, the prevailing party in an action under section 138.3 is entitled to costs determined by a court in accordance with applicable rules of civil procedure.

2002, c. 22, s. 185; 2004, c. 31, Sched. 34, s. 20

138.12 Power of the Commission — The Commission may intervene in an action under section 138.3, in an application for leave to commence the action under section 138.8 and in any appeal from the decision of the court in the action or with respect to whether leave is granted to commence the action.

2002, c. 22, s. 185; 2004, c. 31, Sched. 34, s. 21; 2009, c. 34, Sched. S, s. 8

OSA 138.12

Definitions: OSA 1(1)"Commission".

138.13 No derogation from other rights — The right of action for damages and the defences to an action under section 138.3 are in addition to, and without derogation from, any other rights or defences the plaintiff or defendant may have in an action brought otherwise than under this Part.

2002, c. 22, s. 185; 2004, c. 31, Sched. 34, s. 22

138.14 (1) Limitation period — No action shall be commenced under section 138.3,

    (a) in the case of misrepresentation in a document, later than the earlier of,

        (i) three years after the date on which the document containing the misrepresentation was first released, and

        (ii) six months after the issuance of a news release disclosing that leave has been granted to commence an action under section 138.3 or under comparable legislation in the other provinces or territories in Canada in respect of the same misrepresentation;

    (b) in the case of a misrepresentation in a public oral statement, later than the earlier of,

        (i) three years after the date on which the public oral statement containing the misrepresentation was made, and

        (ii) six months after the issuance of a news release disclosing that leave has been granted to commence an action under section 138.3 or under comparable legislation in another province or territory of Canada in respect of the same misrepresentation; and

    (c) in the case of a failure to make timely disclosure, later than the earlier of,

        (i) three years after the date on which the requisite disclosure was required to be made, and

        (ii) six months after the issuance of a news release disclosing that leave has been granted to commence an action under section 138.3 or under comparable legislation in another province or territory of Canada in respect of the same failure to make timely disclosure.

(2) Suspension of limitation period — A limitation period established by subsection (1) in respect of an action is suspended on the date a notice of motion for leave under section 138.8 is filed with the court and resumes running on the date,

    (a) the court grants leave or dismisses the motion and,

        (i) all appeals have been exhausted, or

        (ii) the time for an appeal has expired without an appeal being filed; or

    (b) the motion is abandoned or discontinued.

2002, c. 22, s. 185; 2004, c. 31, Sched. 34, s. 23; 2014, c. 7, Sched. 28, s. 15

OSA 138.14

Definitions: OSA 1(1)"misrepresentation"; 138.1"document", "failure to make timely disclosure", "public oral statement", "release".

Part XXIII.1

Regulations: Reg.: Part XVI.

PART XXIV — GENERAL PROVISIONS (SS. 139–154)

139. Admissibility in evidence of certified statements — A statement as to,

    (a) the registration or non-registration of any person or company;

    (b) the filing or non-filing of any document or material required or permitted to be filed;

    (c) any other matter pertaining to such registration, non-registration, filing or non-filing, or to any such person, company, document or material; or

    (d) the date the facts upon which any proceedings are to be based first came to the knowledge of the Commission,

purporting to be certified by the Commission or a member thereof or by the Director is, without proof of the office or signature of the person certifying, admissible in evidence, so far as relevant, for all purposes in any action, proceeding or prosecution.

OSA 139

Definitions: OSA 1(1)"person"; 1(1)"company"; 1(1)"Commission".

140. (1) Filing and inspection of material — Where Ontario securities law requires that material be filed, the filing shall be effected by depositing the material, or causing it to be deposited, with the Commission and all material so filed shall, subject to subsection (2), be made available by the Commission for public inspection during the normal business hours of the Commission.

(2) Idem — Despite subsection (1), the Commission may hold material or any class of material required to be filed by Ontario securities law in confidence so long as the Commission is of the opinion that the material so held discloses intimate financial, personal or other information and that the desirability of avoiding disclosure thereof in the interests of any person or company affected outweighs the desirability of adhering to the principle that material filed with the Commission be available to the public for inspection.

1994, c. 11, s. 376; 1999, c. 9, s. 219

OSA 140(2)

Policies and Orders: OPS 2.1; BOR 1.2, 1.3.

OSA 140

Related Provisions: OSA 36(5), 51(1), 72(3).

Definitions: OSA 1(1)"Commission"; 1(1)"person"; 1(1)"company".

Regulations: Reg.: 113.

Policies and Orders: OPS 13-601.

141. (1) Immunity of Commission and officers — No action or other proceeding for damages shall be instituted against the Commission or any member thereof, or any employee or agent of the Commission for any act done in good faith in the performance or intended performance of any duty or in the exercise or the intended exercise of any power under Ontario securities law, or for any neglect or default in the performance or exercise in good faith of such duty or power.

(2) Immunity re intended compliance — No person or company has any rights or remedies and no proceedings lie or shall be brought against any person or company for any act or omission of the last-mentioned person or company done or omitted in compliance with Ontario securities law.

(3) Liability of Crown — Subsection (1) does not, by reason of subsections 5(2) and (4) of the *Proceedings Against the Crown Act*, relieve the Crown of liability in respect of a tort committed by the Commission or any person referred to in subsection (1) to which the Crown would otherwise be subject.

1994, c. 11, s. 377; 2010, c. 26, Sched. 18, s. 40

OSA 141

Definitions: OSA 1(1)"Commission"; 1(1)"person"; 1(1)"company".

142. (1) Application to Her Majesty — Subject to subsections (2) and (3), this Act applies to,

(a) Her Majesty in right of Canada;

(b) Her Majesty in right of Ontario; and

(c) Her Majesty in right of any other province or territory of Canada,

and agents and servants thereof.

(2) Exceptions — Subsections 13(1), (3) and (4), sections 20, 60, 122, 126, 126.1, 126.2, 129, 130, 130.1, 131, 134 and 135, Part XXIII.1 and section 139 do not apply to,

(a) Her Majesty in right of Canada;

(b) Her Majesty in right of Ontario;

(c) Her Majesty in right of any other province or territory of Canada; or

(d) an agent or servant of Her Majesty, as referred to in clause (a), (b) or (c), where the matter arises from the performance of a duty or the exercise of a power as an agent or servant thereof or from any neglect or default in the performance or exercise of such duty or power.

OSA 142(2)

Related Provisions: OSA 13(1), (3), (4), 20, 60, 122, 126, 126.1, 126.2, 129, 130, 130.1, 131, 134, 135, 139, Part XXIII.1.

Policies and Orders: OSCN 91-701.

(2.1) Exception, market participant — The definition of **"market participant"** in subsection 1(1) does not include,

(a) Her Majesty in right of Canada;

(b) Her Majesty in right of Ontario;

(c) Her Majesty in right of any other province or territory of Canada; or

(d) an agent or servant of Her Majesty, as referred to in clause (a), (b) or (c).

(3) Exception, derivatives — Rules made under paragraph 11, paragraph 19.3 and subparagraphs 35 i, iii, iv, v and vii of subsection 143(1) do not apply to derivatives traded by,

(a) Her Majesty in right of Ontario or the Ontario Financing Authority when acting as agent for Her Majesty in right of Ontario;

(b) Her Majesty in right of Canada;

(c) Her Majesty in right of any other province or territory of Canada; or

(d) an agent or servant of Her Majesty in right of Ontario prescribed by the Lieutenant Governor in Council.

(4) Conditions and restrictions — An agent or servant of Her Majesty in right of Ontario prescribed under clause 142(3)(d) shall comply with such conditions and restrictions relating to the exception as may be prescribed by the Lieutenant Governor in Council.

1994, c. 11, s. 378; 2002, c. 22, s. 186; 2004, c. 31, Sched. 34, s. 24; 2010, c. 26, Sched. 18, s. 41; 2014, c. 7, Sched. 28, s. 16; 2015, c. 38, Sched. 18, s. 9; 2016, c. 5, Sched. 26, s. 4

143. (1) Rules — The Commission may make rules in respect of the following matters:

1. Prescribing requirements in respect of applications for registration and the renewal, amendment, expiration or surrender of registration and in respect of suspension, revocation or reinstatement of registration.

1.1 Requiring registered dealers, registered advisers or registered investment fund managers to designate an ultimate designated person and prescribing classes of individuals or the qualifications required of individuals who are eligible to be designated as ultimate designated persons.

1.2 Prescribing additional functions required to be performed by an ultimate designated person in respect of the registrant by whom he or she is designated, including requiring the ultimate designated person,

  i. to supervise the activities of the registrant that are directed towards ensuring compliance with Ontario securities law by the registrant and individuals acting on the registrant's behalf,

  ii. to otherwise promote compliance by the registrant and by individuals acting on the registrant's behalf with Ontario securities law.

1.3 Requiring registered dealers, registered advisers or registered investment fund managers to designate a chief compliance officer and prescribing classes of individuals or the qualifications required of individuals who are eligible to be designated as chief compliance officers.

1.4 Prescribing additional functions required to be performed by a chief compliance officer in respect of the registrant by whom he or she is designated, including requiring the chief compliance officer,

  i. to establish and maintain policies and procedures for assessing compliance with Ontario securities law by the registrant and individuals acting on the registrant's behalf,

  ii. to monitor and assess compliance by the registrant and by individuals acting on the registrant's behalf with Ontario securities law,

  iii. to report to the registrant's ultimate designated person or to its board of directors or partners with respect to compliance matters,

  iv. to submit an annual report to the board of directors of the registrant or to the registrant's partners setting out the chief compliance officer's assessment of the level of compliance by the registrant and the individuals acting on its behalf with Ontario securities law.

1.5 Prescribing circumstances in which a suspended registration is or may be reinstated.

1.6 Prescribing activities in which a person or company whose registration is suspended or restricted may engage or activities in which he, she or it is prohibited from engaging.

2. Prescribing categories or subcategories of registration, classifying registrants into categories or sub-categories, prescribing the criteria a person or company must satisfy to qualify for registration in a particular category or sub-category of registration, prescribing requirements for registrants or prescribing terms and conditions on registration, reinstatement of registration, amendment of registration or registration in a particular category or sub-category of registration, including,

  i. standards of practice and business conduct of registrants in dealing with their customers and clients and prospective customers and clients,

  ii. requirements that are advisable for the prevention or regulation of conflicts of interest,

  iii. requirements in respect of membership in a self-regulatory organization, and

  iv. requirements that persons and companies registered under this Act be bonded or insured on terms acceptable to the Director.

3. Extending any requirements prescribed under paragraph 2 to unregistered directors, partners, representatives and officers of registrants.

4. Prescribing requirements in respect of the residence in Ontario or Canada of registrants.

5. Governing the provision of notice to the Director of,

  i. a proposed change in beneficial ownership of, or direct or indirect control or direction over, securities of a person or company registered under this Act,

  ii. a proposed change in beneficial ownership of, or direct or indirect control or direction over, securities of a person or company of which a person or company registered under this Act is a subsidiary, or

  iii. a proposed change in ownership of a substantial portion of the assets of a person or company registered under this Act.

OSA 143(1)5

Related Provisions: OSA 127(1)1.

5.1 Authorizing the Director to make an order that a proposed change described in subparagraph 5 i or iii must not be effected until the change has been approved by the Director.

6. Prescribing requirements for persons and companies in respect of calling at or telephoning to residences for the purposes of trading in securities.

7. Prescribing requirements in respect of the disclosure or furnishing of information to the public or the Commission by persons and companies registered under this Act, by their directors, partners or officers or by persons or companies that beneficially own, directly or indirectly, or exercise direct or indirect control or direction over at least 10 per cent of the voting securities of persons and companies registered under this Act or providing for exemptions from or varying the requirements under this Act in respect of the disclosure or furnishing of information to the public or the Commission by any of them.

8. Prescribing any matter referred to in Part XII (Exemptions from Registration Requirements) as required by the regulations or prescribed by or in the regulations, other than the matters referred to in subsection 35.1(2).

OSA 143(1)8

Related Provisions: OSA 35.1(2), Part XII.

8.1 Respecting the exemption of any person or company from any requirement under this Act or the regulations that is comparable to a requirement established by a self-regulatory organization and prescribing conditions that must be satisfied for the exemption to apply.

8.2 Exempting registered dealers from the requirement under subsection 36(1) to send a customer a written confirmation of a transaction.

OSA 143(1)8.2

Related Provisions: OSA 36.

9. [Repealed 2009, c. 18, Sched. 26, s. 20(11).]

10. Prescribing requirements in respect of the books, records and other documents required by subsection 19(1) to be kept by market participants, including the form in which and the period for which the books, records and other documents are to be kept.

OSA 143(1)10

Related Provisions: OSA 19(1).

10.1 Prescribing a class of instruments, certificates, agreements, documents or other things that are not securities for the purposes of the Act.

11. Regulating the listing or trading of publicly traded securities or the trading of derivatives, including rules,

    i. relating to clearing and settling trades,

    ii. requiring the reporting of trades and quotations, and

    iii. prescribing classes of derivatives in respect of which trades must be cleared or settled through a clearing agency.

12. Regulating recognized exchanges, recognized self-regulatory organizations, recognized quotation and trade reporting systems, alternative trading systems, recognized clearing agencies and designated trade repositories, including,

    i. prescribing requirements in respect of the review or approval by the Commission of any by-law, rule, regulation, policy, procedure, interpretation or practice,

    ii. prescribing restrictions on the ownership, control and direction of a recognized exchange, clearing agency or alternative trading system.

13. Regulating trading in or advising about securities or derivatives to prevent trading or advising that is fraudulent, manipulative, deceptive or unfairly detrimental to investors.

14. Regulating trading or advising in penny stocks, including prescribing requirements in respect of additional disclosure and suitability for investment.

15. Prescribing categories or subcategories of issuers for purposes of the prospectus requirements under this Act, the regulations and the rules and classifying issuers into categories or subcategories.

16. Regulating in respect of, or varying this Act to facilitate, expedite or regulate in respect of, the distribution of securities, or the issuing of receipts, including by establishing,

    i. requirements in respect of distributions of securities by means of a prospectus incorporating other documents by reference,

    ii. requirements in respect of distributions of securities by means of a simplified or summary prospectus or other form of disclosure document,

    iii. requirements in respect of distributions of securities on a continuous or delayed basis,

    iv. requirements in respect of pricing of distributions of securities after the issuance of a receipt for the prospectus filed in relation thereto,

    v. procedures for the issuing of receipts for prospectuses after expedited or selective review thereof,

    vi. provisions for the incorporation by reference of certain documents in a prospectus and the effect, including from a liability and evidentiary perspective, of modifying or superseding statements,

    vii. requirements for the form of a prospectus certificate, including providing for alternative forms in circumstances other than those referred to in subsection 63(2) of this Act,

    viii. provisions for eligibility requirements to obtain a receipt for, or distribute under, a particular form of prospectus and the loss of that eligibility, and

    ix. provisions for varying withdrawal rights.

16.1 Prescribing requirements for the certification of prospectuses by persons and companies in relation to the following:

    i. if the issuer is a trust, requiring individuals who perform functions for the issuer similar to those performed by a chief executive officer or chief financial officer of an issuer to certify the prospectus,

    ii. if the issuer is a trust and its business or a material part of its business is conducted through a person or company other than the issuer, requiring a director and the chief executive officer and the chief financial officer of the person or company, or individuals who perform functions for the person or company similar to those performed by a chief executive officer or chief financial officer, to certify the prospectus,

    iii. if the issuer is a limited partnership, requiring the general partner of the issuer and individuals who perform functions for the issuer similar to those performed by a chief executive officer or a chief financial officer of an issuer to certify the prospectus, and

    iv. if the issuer is not organized as a company, trust or limited partnership, requiring persons or companies that perform functions similar to those performed by persons or companies described in subparagraph i, ii or iii or section 58 to certify the prospectus.

17. Prescribing requirements for the escrow of securities in connection with distributions.

18. Designating activities, including the use of documents or advertising, in which registrants or issuers are permitted to engage or are prohibited from engaging in connection with distributions.

19. Prescribing which distributions and trading in relation to the distributions are distributions and trading outside Ontario.

19.1 Prescribing one or more classes of contracts or instruments that are not derivatives for the purpose of prescribed provisions of Ontario securities law and prescribing those provisions.

19.2 Prescribing one or more classes of derivatives that are designated derivatives for the purposes of prescribed provisions of Ontario securities law and prescribing those provisions.

19.3 Prescribing registration requirements in respect of persons or companies trading in derivatives.

19.4 Prescribing derivatives or classes of derivatives that are deemed to be securities for the purposes of prescribed provisions of this Act, the regulations and the rules and prescribing those provisions.

19.5 Prescribing circumstances in which a material interest in a derivative's underlying interest is not a financial or other interest for the purposes of section 34.

19.6 Prescribing one or more classes of derivatives for the purpose of clause 38(4)(b).

19.7 Prescribing one or more conditions for the purposes of subclause 64.1(5)(b)(ii).

20. Prescribing any matter referred to in Part XVII (Exemptions from Prospectus Requirements) as required by the regulations or prescribed by or in the regulations, other than the matters referred to in subsection 73.1(3).

OSA 143(1)20

Related Provisions: OSA 73.1, Part XVII.

21. Prescribing the circumstances in which the Director must refuse to issue a receipt for a prospectus and prohibiting the Director from issuing a receipt in those circumstances.

22. Prescribing requirements in respect of the preparation and dissemination and other use, by reporting issuers, of documents providing for continuous disclosure that are in addition to the requirements under this Act, including requirements in respect of,

     i. an annual report,

     ii. an annual information form, and

     iii. supplemental analysis of financial statements.

22.1 Respecting the preparation, form and content requirements applicable to the public dissemination of forward-looking information by reporting issuers where the dissemination is not part of a required filing.

23. Exempting reporting issuers from any requirement of Part XVIII (Continuous Disclosure),

     i. if the requirement conflicts with a requirement of the laws of the jurisdiction under which the reporting issuers are incorporated, organized or continued,

     ii. if the reporting issuers ordinarily distribute financial information to holders of their securities in a form, or at times, different from those required by Part XVIII, or

     iii. under circumstances that the Commission considers justify the exemption.

OSA 143(1)23

Related Provisions: OSA Part XVIII.

24. Requiring issuers or other persons and companies to comply, in whole or in part, with Part XVIII (Continuous Disclosure), or rules made under paragraph 22.

OSA 143(1)24

Related Provisions: OSA Part XVIII.

25. Prescribing requirements in respect of financial accounting, reporting and auditing for purposes of this Act, the regulations and the rules, including,

     i. defining accounting principles and auditing standards acceptable to the Commission,

     ii. financial reporting requirements for the preparation and dissemination of future-oriented financial information and *pro forma* financial statements,

     iii. standards of independence and other qualifications for auditors,

     iv. requirements respecting a change in auditors by a reporting issuer or a registrant,

     v. requirements respecting a change in the financial year of an issuer or in an issuer's status as a reporting issuer under this Act, and

     vi. defining auditing standards for attesting to and reporting on a reporting issuer's internal controls.

26. Prescribing requirements for the validity and solicitation of proxies prescribing activities for the purposes of clause (g) of the definition of "solicit" and "solicitation" in section 84 and prescribing circumstances for the purposes of clause 86(2)(a.1).

27. Providing for the application of Part XVIII (Continuous Disclosure) and Part XIX (Proxies and Proxy Solicitation) in respect of registered holders or beneficial owners of voting securities or equity securities of reporting issuers or other persons or companies on behalf of whom the securities are held, including requirements for reporting issuers, recognized clearing agencies, registered holders, registrants and other persons or companies who hold securities on behalf of persons or companies but who are not the registered holders.

OSA 143(1)27

Related Provisions: OSA Part XVIII, XIX.

28. Regulating take-over bids, issuer bids, insider bids, going-private transactions, business combinations and related party transactions, including,

   i. providing for the matters that, under Part XX, may be specified by regulation or required by the regulations or that, under Part XX, must or may be determined or done in accordance with the regulations,

   ii. establishing different classes of take-over bids and issuer bids and prescribing requirements in respect of each such class,

   iii. restricting the ability of a person or company to acquire or sell a security before, during or after an offer to acquire, acquisition, redemption, related party transaction, business combination or similar transaction,

   iv. prescribing the disclosure, certification, delivery or dissemination of any circular, notice, report or other document required to be filed or delivered to a person or company,

   v. prescribing requirements relating to the conduct or management of the affairs of an issuer, and its directors and officers, before, during or after an offer to acquire, acquisition, redemption, related party transaction, business combination or similar transaction,

   vi. prescribing requirements, prohibitions, restrictions and thresholds in respect of early warning,

   vii. prescribing requirements respecting defensive tactics in connection with take-over bids,

   viii. prescribing requirements to be met by a person or company that acquires an interest or right in or to, or a right or obligation associated with, a related financial instrument,

   ix. varying any or all of the time periods in the regulations related to Part XX,

   x. prescribing exemptions from the requirements of Part XX or the regulations related to it, and

   xi. removing or varying exemptions from the requirements of Part XX or the regulations related to it.

OSA 143(1)28

Related Provisions: OSA Part XX.

29. Providing for exemptions from any requirement of section 76 or from liability under section 134 and prescribing standards or criteria for determining when a material fact or material change has been generally disclosed.

OSA 143(1)29

Related Provisions: OSA 76, 134.

30. Prescribing time periods under section 107 of the Act or varying or providing for exemptions from any requirement of Part XXI (Insider Trading and Self-Dealing).

OSA 143(1)30

Related Provisions: OSA 107, Part XXI.

30.1 Regulating the disclosure or furnishing of information to the public or the Commission by insiders, including,

   i. prescribing filing requirements for the reporting by insiders of their respective direct or in direct beneficial ownership of, or control or direction over, securities of a reporting issuer or changes in ownership, control or direction,

   ii. prescribing requirements respecting the reporting by insiders of any interest in or right or obligation associated with a related financial instrument or changes in such interests, rights or obligations,

   iii. prescribing requirements respecting the reporting by insiders of any agreement, arrangement or understanding that alters, directly or indirectly, an insider's economic interest in a security or an insider's economic exposure to a reporting issuer or changes in such agreements, arrangements or understandings.

30.2 Prescribing requirements in respect of a reporting issuer to facilitate compliance by insiders of the reporting issuer with this Act and with the rules made under paragraph 30.1.

30.3 Requiring that reports under paragraph 30.1 shall also provide information for the period of up to six months before a person or company became an insider.

31. Regulating investment funds and the distribution and trading of the securities of investment funds, including,

   i. varying Part XV or Part XVIII by prescribing additional disclosure requirements in respect of investment funds and requiring or permitting the use of particular forms or types of additional offering or other documents in connection with the funds,

   ii. prescribing permitted investment policy and investment practices for investment funds and prohibiting or restricting certain investments or investment practices for investment funds,

   ii.1 prescribing requirements for investment funds in respect of derivatives,

   iii. prescribing requirements governing the custodianship of assets of investment funds,

   iv. prescribing minimum initial capital requirements for investment funds making a distribution and prohibiting or restricting the reimbursement of costs in connection with the organization of a fund,

   v. prescribing matters affecting investment funds that require the approval of security holders of the fund, the Commission or the Director, including, in the case of security holders, the level of approval,

   vi. prescribing requirements in respect of the calculation of the net asset value of investment funds,

   vii. prescribing requirements in respect of the content and use of sales literature, sales communications or advertising relating to investment funds or the securities of investment funds,

   viii. designating mutual funds as private mutual funds and prescribing requirements for private mutual funds,

ix. respecting sales charges imposed by a distribution company or contractual plan service company under a contractual plan on purchasers of shares or units of an investment fund, and commissions or sales incentives to be paid to registrants in connection with the securities of an investment fund,

x. prescribing the circumstances in which a plan holder under a contractual plan has the right to withdraw from the contractual plan,

xi. prescribing procedures applicable to investment funds, registrants and any other person or company in respect of sales and redemption of investment fund securities and payments for sales and redemptions,

xii. prescribing requirements in respect of, or in relation to, promoters, advisers or persons and companies who administer or participate in the administration of the affairs of investment funds.

OSA 143(1)31

Related Provisions: OSA Part XV, XVIII.

32. Respecting fees payable by an issuer to an adviser as consideration for investment advice, alone or together with administrative or management services provided to a mutual fund or non-redeemable investment fund.

33. Prescribing requirements relating to the qualification of a registrant to act as an adviser to an investment fund.

34. Regulating commodity pools, including,

i. varying Part XV (Prospectuses — Distribution) or XVIII (Continuous Disclosure) to prescribe additional disclosure requirements in respect of commodity pools and requiring or permitting the use of particular forms or types of additional offering or other documents in connection with commodity pools,

ii. prescribing requirements in respect of, or in relation to, promoters, advisers, persons and companies who administer or participate in the administration of the affairs of commodity pools,

iii. prescribing standards in relation to the suitability of investors in commodity pools,

iv. prohibiting or restricting the payment of fees, commissions or compensation by commodity pools or holders of securities of commodity pools and restricting the reimbursement of costs in connection with the organization of commodity pools,

v. prescribing requirements with respect to the voting rights of security holders, and

vi. prescribing requirements in respect of the redemption of securities of a commodity pool.

OSA 143(1)34

Related Provisions: OSA Part XV, XVIII.

35. Prescribing requirements relating to derivatives, including,

i. requirements for disclosure documents relating to designated derivatives,

ii. record keeping and reporting requirements,

iii. requirements in respect of persons or companies trading in derivatives, including requirements in respect of margin, collateral, capital, clearing and settlement,

iv. requirements that one or more classes of derivatives be traded on a recognized exchange or an alternative trading system,

v. requirements relating to position limits for derivatives transactions,

vi. requirements that one or more classes of derivatives not be traded in Ontario,

vii. transparency requirements relating to the public dissemination of, or public access to, transaction level data,

viii. transparency requirements other than those referred to in subparagraph vii.

36. Varying this Act with respect to foreign issuers to facilitate distributions, compliance with requirements applicable or relating to reporting issuers and the making of take-over bids, issuer bids, insider bids, going-private transactions, business combinations and related party transactions where the foreign issuers are subject to requirements of the laws of other jurisdictions that the Commission considers are adequate in light of the purposes and principles of this Act.

37. Regulating labour sponsored investment fund corporations registered under Part III (Labour Sponsored Investment Fund Corporations) of the *Community Small Business Investment Funds Act*, and the distribution and trading of the securities of the corporations and varying this Act in respect of the corporations and,

i. prescribing proficiency requirements that apply in respect of registrants trading in securities of the corporations,

ii. requiring or prohibiting the use of particular forms or types of offering documents for or in respect of the securities of the corporations,

iii. prescribing disclosure requirements for or in respect of the securities of the corporations,

iv. exempting the corporations from specified requirements or restrictions that ordinarily apply to or in respect of mutual funds, and

v. prescribing insider reporting requirements for or in respect of the corporations.

38. Prescribing requirements in respect of reverse take-overs including requirements for disclosure that are substantially equivalent to that provided by a prospectus.

39. Requiring or respecting the media, format, preparation, form, content, execution, certification, dissemination and other use, filing and review of all documents required under or governed by this Act, the regulations or the rules and all documents determined by the regulations or the rules to be ancillary to the documents, including,

i. applications for registration and other purposes,

ii. preliminary prospectuses and prospectuses,

iii. interim financial reports and financial statements,

iv. proxies and information circulars, and

v. take-over bid circulars, issuer bid circulars and directors' circulars.

39.1 Governing the approval of any document described in paragraph 39.

40. Respecting the designation or recognition of any person, company or jurisdiction if advisable for purposes of this Act, including,

i. recognizing exchanges, self-regulatory organizations and clearing agencies,

ii. designating, for purposes of subsection 88(1), the jurisdictions whose requirements are substantially similar to the requirements of Part XIX,

iii. designating a person or company for the purpose of the definition of "market participant",

iv. designating classes of persons or companies not to be insiders for the purpose of the definition of "insider", and

v. designating classes of persons or companies for the purpose of clause (f) of the definition of "insider" in subsection 1(1), if the persons or companies would reasonably be expected to have, in the ordinary course, access to material information about the business, operations, assets or revenue of the issuer, to be insiders.

41. Respecting the conduct of the Commission and its employees in relation to duties and responsibilities and discretionary powers under this Act, including

i. the conduct of investigations and examinations carried out under Part VI (Investigations and Examinations), and

ii. the conduct of hearings.

42. Establishing conditions for any exemption that the Commission is authorized to give by subsection 46(4) or 190(6) or section 113 of the *Business Corporations Act* and, despite those provisions, dispensing with applications for exemption when the conditions are met.

43. Prescribing the fees payable to the Commission, including those for filing, for applications for registration or exemptions, for trades in securities, in respect of audits made by the Commission, and in connection with the administration of Ontario securities law.

44. Varying this Act to permit or require the use of an electronic or computer-based system for the filing, delivery or deposit of,

i. documents or information required under or governed by this Act, the regulations or rules, and

ii. documents determined by the regulations or rules to be ancillary to documents required under or governed by this Act, the regulations or rules.

45. Establishing requirements for and procedures in respect of the use of an electronic or computer-based system for the filing, delivery or deposit of documents or information.

46. Providing for electronic signatures for the signing of documents and prescribing the circumstances in which persons or companies shall be deemed to have signed or certified documents on an electronic or computer-based system for any purpose of this Act, the regulations or the rules.

47. Regulating scholarship plans and the distribution and trading of the securities of scholarship plans.

48. Specifying the conditions under which any particular type of trade that would not otherwise be a distribution shall be a distribution.

49. Permitting or requiring, or varying this Act to permit or require, methods of filing or delivery, to or by the Commission, issuers, registrants, security holders or others, of documents, information, notices, books, records, things, reports, orders, authorizations or other communications required under or governed by Ontario securities law.

50. Providing for exemptions from or varying the requirements set out in Part XIII.

OSA 143(1)50

Related Provisions: OSA Part XIII.

51. [Repealed 2009, c. 18, Sched. 26, s. 20(13).]

52. Providing for exemptions from or varying the requirements under this Act in respect of amendments to prospectuses or preliminary prospectuses, or prescribing circumstances under which an amendment to a preliminary prospectus or prospectus must be filed.

52.1 Permitting a distribution or additional distribution under subsection 57(2.2) to proceed without a receipt for an amendment.

53. Providing for exemptions from or varying the requirements of section 62, 65 or 71.

OSA 143(1)53

Related Provisions: OSA 62, 65, 71.

54. Prescribing the disclosure document that is required in respect of the purchase and sale of an investment fund security for the purpose of subsection 71(1.1), requiring dealers to provide the disclosure document to purchasers and prescribing the time and manner for sending or delivering the disclosure document.

Proposed Addition — 143(1), para. 54.1

54.1 Prescribing investment fund securities trading on an exchange or an alternative trading system for the purpose of subsection 71(1.2), prescribing the disclosure document that is required in respect of prescribed investment fund securities under subsection 71(1.3), prescribing the time and manner for sending or delivering the disclosure document, and prescribing the circumstances in which a purchase is not binding on a purchaser for the purpose of subsection 71(2.1).

2014, c. 7, Sched. 28, s. 17 [Not in force at date of publication.]

55. Specifying exemptions and circumstances that shall be subject to section 130.1.

OSA 143(1)55

Related Provisions: OSA 130.1.

55.1 Prescribing documents for the purposes of the definition of "core document" in subsection 138.1(1).

55.2 Providing for the application of Part XXIII.1 to the acquisition of an issuer's security pursuant to a distribution that is exempt from section 53 or 62 and to the acquisition or disposition of an issuer's security in connection with or pursuant to a take-over bid or issuer bid.

55.2.1 Prescribing transactions or classes of transactions for the purposes of clause 138.2(d).

55.3 Prescribing the meaning of "market capitalization", "trading price" and "principal market" and such other terms as are used in Part XXIII.1 and are not otherwise defined in this Act.

56. Prescribing, providing for exemptions from or varying any or all of the time periods in this Act or the regulations.

56.1 Prescribing requirements with respect to the governance of reporting issuers for the purposes of section 121.3.

57. Requiring reporting issuers to appoint audit committees and prescribing requirements relating to the functioning and responsibilities of audit committees, including requirements in respect of,

    i. the standard of review to be applied by audit committees in their review of documents filed under Ontario securities law,

    ii. the certification or other evidence of review by audit committees,

    iii. the scope and content of an audit committee's review, and

    iv. the composition of audit committees and the qualifications of audit committee members, including independence requirements.

58. Requiring reporting issuers to devise and maintain a system of internal controls related to the effectiveness and efficiency of their operations, including financial reporting and asset control, sufficient to provide reasonable assurances that,

    i. transactions are executed in accordance with management's general or specific authorization,

    ii. transactions are recorded as necessary to permit preparation of financial statements in accordance with generally accepted accounting principles or any other criteria applicable to those statements,

    iii. transactions are recorded as necessary to maintain accountability for assets,

    iv. access to assets is permitted only in accordance with management's general or specific authorization, and

    v. the recorded accountability for assets is compared with the existing assets at reasonable intervals and appropriate action is taken with respect to any differences.

59. Requiring reporting issuers to devise and maintain disclosure controls and procedures sufficient to provide reasonable assurances that,

    i. information required to be disclosed under Ontario securities law is recorded, processed, summarized and reported, within the time periods specified under Ontario securities law, and

    ii. information required to be disclosed under Ontario securities law is accumulated and communicated to the reporting issuer's management, including its chief executive and financial officers, as appropriate, to allow timely decisions regarding required disclosure.

60. Requiring chief executive officers and chief financial officers of reporting issuers, or persons performing similar functions, to provide a certification that addresses the reporting issuer's internal controls, including a certification that addresses,

    i. the establishment and maintenance of the internal controls,

    ii. the design of the internal controls, and

    iii. the evaluation of the effectiveness of the internal controls.

61. Requiring chief executive officers and chief financial officers of reporting issuers, or persons performing similar functions, to provide a certification that addresses the reporting issuer's disclosure controls and procedures, including a certification that addresses,

    i. the establishment and maintenance of the disclosure controls and procedures,

    ii. the design of the disclosure controls and procedures, and

    iii. the evaluation of the effectiveness of the disclosure controls and procedures.

62. Requiring investment funds to establish and maintain a body for the purposes described in subsection 121.4(1), prescribing its powers and duties and prescribing requirements relating to,

    i. the mandate and functioning of the body,

    ii. the composition of the body and qualifications for membership on the body, including matters respecting the independence of members, and the process for selecting the members,

    iii. the standard of care that applies to members of the body when exercising their powers, performing their duties and carrying out their responsibilities,

    iv. the disclosure of information to security holders of the investment fund, to the investment fund manager and to the Commission, and

    v. matters affecting the investment fund that require review by the body or the approval of the body.

63. Prescribing requirements in respect of credit rating organizations, including requirements relating to,

    i. the disclosure or furnishing of information to the Commission by a credit rating organization,

ii. the establishment, publication and enforcement of a code of conduct applicable to directors, officers and employees of credit rating organizations, including minimum requirements to be included in the code,

iii. prohibitions against and procedures regarding conflicts of interest between a credit rating organization and the person or company whose securities it is rating,

iv. the maintenance of books and records necessary for the conduct of a credit rating organization's business and the issuance and maintenance of credit ratings,

v. the appointment by credit rating organizations of one or more compliance officers and any minimum standards that must be met or qualifications a compliance officer must have.

(2) Regulations — The Lieutenant Governor in Council may make regulations in respect of,

(0.a) any matter referred to in this Act as being prescribed by or determined in accordance with regulations made by the Lieutenant Governor in Council;

(a) any matter in respect of which the Commission may make rules, with necessary modifications;

(a.0.1) the matters described in subsections 35.1(2) and 73.1(3);

OSA 143(2)(a.0.1)

Related Provisions: OSA 35.1(2), 73(3).

(a.1) the administration and distribution of amounts disgorged under paragraph 10 of subsection 127(1);

(b) any matter advisable for carrying out the purposes of this Act.

(3) Revoking or amending regulations — Subject to the approval of the Minister, the Commission, concurrently with making a rule, may make a regulation that amends or revokes any provision of a regulation made by the Lieutenant Governor in Council under this Act or by the Commission under this subsection that in the opinion of the Commission is necessary or advisable to effectively implement the rule.

(4) Effective date — A regulation made under subsection (3) is not effective before the rule referred to in that subsection comes into force.

(5) Retroactive — Subject to subsection (4), a regulation made under subsection (3), if it so provides, is effective with reference to a period before it was filed.

(6) Incorporation by reference — A regulation or rule may incorporate by reference, and require compliance with, one or more provisions of an Act or regulation and all or part of any standard, procedure or guideline.

(7) Classes — Regulations or rules in respect of registrants, issuers, other persons or companies, securities, trades, or other matters or things, may be made in respect of any class or category of registrants, issuers, other persons or companies, securities, trades or other matters or things.

(8) Scope — A regulation or a rule may be general or particular in its application, may be limited as to time or place or both and may exclude any place from the application of the regulation or rule.

(9) Exemptions — Without limiting the authority of the Commission under section 147 a regulation or rule may authorize the Commission or the Director to grant an exemption to it.

(10) Same — An exemption or a removal of an exemption,

(a) may be granted or made in whole or in part; and

(b) may be granted or made subject to conditions or restrictions.

(11) Part III (Regulations) of the *Legislation Act, 2006* does not apply — Part III (Regulations) of the *Legislation Act, 2006* does not apply to the rules.

(12) Same — A regulation made under subsection (3) is subject to Part III (Regulations) of the *Legislation Act, 2006*.

(13) L.G. in C. prevails — If there is a conflict or an inconsistency between a regulation made by the Lieutenant Governor in Council under this Act and a rule, the regulation prevails but in all other respects a rule has the same force and effect as a regulation.

1994, c. 33, s. 8; 1997, c. 19, s. 23(13)–(15); 1997, c. 43, Sched. F, s. 13; 1999, c. 9, s. 220; 2001, c. 23, s. 217; 2002, c. 18, Sched. H, s. 12; 2002, c. 22, s. 187; 2004, c. 31, Sched. 34, s. 25; 2005, c. 31, Sched. 20, s. 9; 2006, c. 21, Sched. F, s. 136(1), Table 1; 2006, c. 33, Sched. Z.5, s. 18; 2007, c. 7, Sched. 38, s. 13(2), (4); 2009, c. 18, Sched. 26, s. 20; 2010, c. 1, Sched. 26, s. 8; 2010, c. 26, Sched. 18, s. 42; 2011, c. 9, Sched. 38, s. 4; 2015, c. 38, Sched. 18, s. 10; 2016, c. 5, Sched. 26, s. 5

OSA 142(2.1)(b)

Related Provisions: OSA 1(1)"market participant".

OSA 142(3)

Related Provisions: OSA 143(1).

OSA 143

Definitions: OSA 1(1)"person"; 1(1)"company"; 1(1)"private mutual fund"; 1(1)"underwriter"; 1(1)"trade"; 1(1)"security"; 1(1)"issuer"; 1(1)"registrant"; 1(1)"recognized clearing agency"; 1(1)"material fact"; 1(1)"material change"; 1(1)"distribution"; 1(1)"mutual fund"; 1(1)"recognized exchange"; 1(1)"recognized quotation and trade reporting system"; 1(1)"recognized self-regulatory organization"; 1(1)"derivative"; 1(1)"alternative trading system"; 1(1)"credit rating organization"; 1(1)"designated trade repository".

143.1 (1) Deemed rules — Every order and ruling of the Commission and every policy relating to an order or ruling that is listed in the Schedule shall be deemed to be a rule validly made under this Act and to have come into force on the day this section comes into force.

(2) Amended orders or rulings — For the purposes of subsection (1), a reference to an order, ruling or policy, whether or not it is referred to in the Schedule as amended, is a reference to the order, ruling or policy as it existed on November 16, 1994.

(3) Revocation — Every rule that became a rule by virtue of subsection (1) is revoked on the second anniversary of the day on which this section comes into force.

1994, c. 33, s. 8

143.2 (1) Publication — The Commission shall publish in its Bulletin notice of every rule that it proposes to make under section 143.

(2) Notice — The notice must include the following:

1. The proposed rule.

2. A statement of the substance and purpose of the proposed rule.

3. A summary of the proposed rule.

4. A reference to the authority under which the rule is proposed or a statement that the Commission is seeking legislative amendments to provide the requisite rule-making authority.

5. A discussion of all alternatives to the proposed rule that were considered by the Commission and the reasons for not proposing the adoption of the alternatives considered.

6. A reference to any significant unpublished study, report or other written materials on which the Commission relies in proposing the rule.

7. A description of the anticipated costs and benefits of the proposed rule.

8. A reference to every regulation or provision in a regulation to be amended or revoked under subsection 143(3).

(3) Exception — The Commission does not have to make reference to written material that, in the opinion of the Commission, should be held in confidence because it discloses intimate financial, personal or other information and the desirability of avoiding disclosure of the substance of it or its existence in the interests of any person or company affected outweighs the desirability of making it or knowledge of its existence available to the public.

(4) Representations — Upon publication of a notice under subsection (1), the Commission shall invite, and shall give a reasonable opportunity to, interested persons and companies to make written representations with respect to the proposed rule within a period of at least 90 days after the publication.

(5) Exceptions to notice requirement — Publication of a notice is not required if,

(a) all persons and companies who would be subject to the proposed rule are named, the information set out in subsection (2) is sent to each of them and they and any other person or company whose interests are likely to be substantially affected by the proposed rule are given an opportunity to make written representations with respect to it;

(b) the proposed rule grants an exemption or removes a restriction and is not likely to have a substantial effect on the interests of persons or companies other than those who benefit under it;

(c) what is proposed is only an amendment that does not materially change an existing rule;

(d) the Commission,

(i) believes that there is an urgent need for the proposed rule and that, without it, there is a substantial risk of material harm to investors or to the integrity of the capital markets, and

(ii) has the approval of the Minister to make the rule without publication of notice; or

(e) the proposed rule remakes an order, ruling or policy that was deemed to be a rule by the operation of section 143.1 without materially changing the effect or intent of the rule.

(6) Publication — When a rule to which clause (5)(d) applies comes into force, the Commission shall publish in its Bulletin a statement setting out the substance and purpose of the rule and the nature of the urgency and the risk.

(7) Changes to proposal — If, following publication of the notice and consideration of the submissions, the Commission proposes material changes to the proposed rule, the Commission shall publish in its Bulletin notice of the proposed changes.

(8) Notice — The notice must include the following:

1. The proposed rule with the changes incorporated.

2. A concise statement of the purpose of the changes.

3. The reasons for the changes.

(9) Representations re changes — Upon publication of a notice of changes, the Commission shall invite, and shall give a reasonable opportunity to, interested persons and companies to make written representations with respect to the changes within such period as the Commission considers appropriate.

(10) Making rule — In cases where a notice and comment process is required, the Commission may make the rule only at the end of the notice and comment process and after considering all representations made as a result of that process.

(11) Inspection of material — Section 140 applies to all written representations made under this section as if they were material required to be filed.

(12) Interpretation — In this section and in section 143.3, **"rule"** includes an amendment to and a revocation of a rule.

1994, c. 33, s. 8; 1997, c. 19, s. 23(16); 2006, c. 33, Sched. Z.5, s. 19

143.3 (1) Delivery of rules to Minister — The Commission must deliver to the Minister a copy of every rule made by it together with the following:

1. A copy of the notices published under section 143.2, unless publication of notice was not required, and copies of all documents referred to in the notices.

2. A summary of the representations made and other documents submitted in respect of the rule as proposed.

3. All other material information that was considered by the Commission in connection with the making of the rule.

(2) Publication — The Commission shall publish in its Bulletin every rule made by it as soon after the rule is made as practicable together with the following:

1. The date on which a rule and the material required under subsection (1) were delivered to the Minister.

2. The date the rule is to come into force if an action is not taken by the Minister under subsection (3).

3. A statement of the substance and purpose of the rule.

4. A summary of the written comments received during the comment periods if notice and comment were required.

5. A statement of the Commission setting out its response to the significant issues and concerns brought to the attention of the Commission during the comment periods.

(3) Action by Minister — Within 60 days after a rule is delivered to the Minister, the Minister may,

(a) approve the rule,

(b) reject the rule; or

(c) return it to the Commission for further consideration.

1994, c. 33, s. 8

143.4 (1) When rules effective — A rule that is approved by the Minister comes into force 15 days after it is approved unless there is a later day specified in the rule in which case it comes into force on that later day.

(2) Same — If the Minister does not approve a rule, reject it or return it to the Commission for further consideration and a coming into force day,

(a) that is at least 75 days after the rule is delivered to the Minister is specified in the rule, the rule comes into force on the specified day;

(b) is not specified in the rule, the rule comes into force on the 75th day after the rule is delivered to the Minister; or

(c) that is within 75 days after the rule is delivered to the Minister is specified in the rule, the rule comes into force on the 75th day after the rule is delivered to the Minister.

(3) Same — A rule that is returned to the Commission for further consideration cannot come into force until it is returned by the Commission to the Minister at which time this section applies as if the rule were delivered for the first time.

(4) Same — A rule that is rejected by the Minister does not come into force.

(5) Same — A rule to which clause 143.2(5)(d) (urgency provision) applies that is approved by the Minister comes into force on the day it is published in the Commission's Bulletin.

(6) Revocation by operation of law — Every rule to which clause 143.2(5)(d) applies is revoked on the 275th day after it comes into force.

(7) Publication — The Commission shall publish every rule that comes into force in *The Ontario Gazette* and in its Bulletin.

(8) Deemed notice — Every person or company affected by a rule shall be deemed to have notice of it when it is published in the Commission's Bulletin.

1994, c. 33, s. 8

143.5 (1) Returned for consideration — If the Minister returns a rule to the Commission for further consideration, the Minister may specify what is to be considered, the conditions that apply and the process to be followed.

(2) Same — Subject to any instruction that the Commission receives under subsection (1), the Commission shall consider any rule returned to it in the manner and following the process that it feels is appropriate.

1994, c. 33, s. 8

143.6 Publication — The Commission shall publish in its Bulletin notice of,

(a) any action taken by the Minister under subsection 143.3(3) in respect of every rule that the Commission has delivered to the Minister; and

(b) any matters specified by the Minister under subsection 143.5(1) to be considered.

1994, c. 33, s. 8

143.7 (1) Studies — The Minister may in writing require the Commission,

(a) to study and make recommendations in respect of any matter of a general nature under or affecting this Act, the regulations or the rules; and

(b) to consider making a rule in respect of a matter specified by the Minister.

(2) Publication — The Commission shall publish in its Bulletin notice of every requirement from the Minister made under subsection (1).

(3) Notice — The notice must include the following:

1. A statement of the substance of the requirement.

2. A reference to every unpublished study, report or other written materials provided to the Commission by the Minister other than materials that the Minister has asked the Commission to treat as confidential.

1994, c. 33, s. 8

143.8 (1) Policy — In this Act, **"policy"** means a written statement of the Commission of,

(a) principles, standards, criteria or factors that relate to a decision or exercise of a discretion by the Commission or the Director under this Act, the regulations or the rules;

(b) the manner in which a provision of this Act, the regulations or the rules is interpreted or applied by the Commission or the Director;

(c) the practices generally followed by the Commission or the Director in the performance of duties and responsibilities under this Act; and

(d) something that is not of a legislative nature.

OSA 143.8(1)

Policies and Orders: OSCN 11-722.

(2) Publication — The Commission shall publish in its Bulletin notice of the proposed adoption of a policy.

(3) Notice — The notice must include the following:

1. The proposed policy.

2. A statement of the purpose of the proposed policy.

3. A summary of the proposed policy.

4. A reference to any significant unpublished study, report, decision or other written materials on which the Commission relies in proposing the policy.

5. A reference to any provision of this Act, a regulation or a rule to which the proposed policy relates.

(4) Exception — The Commission does not have to make reference to written material that, in the opinion of the Commission, should be held in confidence because it discloses intimate financial, personal or other information and the desirability of avoiding disclosure of the substance of it or its existence in the the interests of any person or company affected outweighs the desirability of making it or knowledge of its existence available to the public.

(5) Representations — Upon publication of the notice, the Commission shall invite, and shall give a reasonable opportunity to, interested persons and companies to make written representations with respect to the proposed policy within a period of at least 60 days after the publication.

(6) Exceptions to notice requirement — Publication of a notice is not required if the proposed policy would make no material substantive change to an existing policy.

(7) Changes to proposal — If, following publication of the notice, the Commission proposes material changes to the proposed policy, the Commission shall publish in its Bulletin,

(a) the proposed policy with the changes incorporated;

(b) a concise statement of the purpose for the changes; and

(c) the reasons for the changes.

(8) Representations re changes — Upon publication of a notice of change, the Commission shall invite, and shall give a reasonable opportunity to, interested persons and companies to make written representations with respect to the change within such period as the Commission considers appropriate.

(9) Publication in Bulletin — The Commission shall publish in its Bulletin every policy adopted by it as soon after the policy is adopted as practicable together with the following:

1. The date and the policy comes into effect.

2. A statement of the substance and purpose of the policy.

3. A summary of the written comments received during the comments periods.

4. A statement of the Commission setting out its response to the significant issues and concerns brought to the attention of the Commission during the comment periods and the reasons for any changes made to the proposed policy following its publication.

(10) Inspection of material — Section 140 applies to all written representations made under this section as if they were material required to be filed.

(11) Restriction — The Commission shall not adopt a policy that, by reason of its prohibitive or mandatory character, is of a legislative nature.

(12) Interpretation — In this section, **"policy"** includes a change to and a rescission of a policy.

1994, c. 33, s. 8

143.9 (1) Priorities — The Commission shall, by June 30, 1995, and each year thereafter, within 90 days after the end of its financial year, deliver to the Minister and publish in its Bulletin a statement of the Chair of the Commission setting out the proposed priorities of the Commission in connection with the administration of this Act, the regulations and the rules, together with a summary of the reasons for the adoption of the priorities.

(1.1) Same — The statement referred to in subsection (1) shall also outline in general terms the Commission's anticipated expenditures for the next financial year by category for any category expected to exceed 10 per cent of the overall expenditures for the year.

(2) Same — The Commission shall, at least 60 days before the publication date of the statement, publish a notice in its Bulletin inviting interested persons or companies to make written representations as to the matters that should be identified as priorities.

1994, c. 33, s. 8; 1997, c. 10, s. 39

OSA 143.9

Policies and Orders: OSCN 11-767.

143.10 (1) Memorandum of understanding — The Commission must first deliver to the Minister and then publish in the Commission's Bulletin every agreement, memorandum of understanding or arrangement between the Commission and,

    (a) another securities, derivatives or financial regulatory authority;

    (b) any self-regulatory body or organization; or

    (c) any jurisdiction.

(1.1) Exception — Despite subsection (1), the Commission is not required to publish an agreement, memorandum of understanding or arrangement if the principal purpose of the agreement, memorandum of understanding or arrangement relates to,

    (a) the provision of products or services by a party not named in subsection (1);

    (b) the sharing of costs incurred by a party named in subsection (1); or

    (c) the provision of services by, or the temporary transfer of, an employee of a party named in subsection (1).

(2) Minister's option — The Minister may approve or reject the agreement, memorandum of understanding or arrangement within 60 days after it is published in the Bulletin or, if publication under subsection (1) is not required, within 60 days after it is delivered to the Minister.

(3) Coming into effect — If the Minister approves the agreement, memorandum of understanding or arrangement, it comes into effect on the date specified in the agreement, memorandum of understanding or arrangement or, if no date is specified, on the day it is approved.

(4) Same — If the Minister does not approve or reject the agreement, memorandum of understanding or arrangement within the 60-day period described in subsection (2), it comes into effect on the date specified in it or, if no date is specified, upon the expiry of that 60-day period.

(5) Same — If the Minister rejects the agreement, memorandum of understanding or arrangement before it comes into effect by the operation of subsection (4), it does not come into effect.

(6) [Repealed 2007, c. 7, Sched. 38, s. 14(4).]

1994, c. 33, s. 8; 2006, c. 33, Sched. Z.5, s. 20; 2007, c. 7, Sched. 38, s. 14; 2010, c. 26, Sched. 18, s. 43

143.11 General orders prohibited — The Commission shall not make any orders or rulings of general application.

1994, c. 33, s. 8

143.12 Review by Select or Standing Committee — (1) Appointment of first advisory committee — On or before May 31, 2007, the Minister shall appoint an advisory committee to review the legislation, regulations and rules relating to matters dealt with by the Commission and the legislative needs of the Commission.

(1.1) Appointment of subsequent advisory committees — The Minister shall appoint an advisory committee to perform the functions described in subsection (1) not later than 48 months after the appointment of the previous advisory committee appointed under subsection (1) or this subsection.

(2) Same — The committee shall review the legislation, regulations and rules relating to matters dealt with by the Commission and the legislative needs of the Commission and solicit the views of the public in respect of these matters by means of a notice and comment process.

(3) Report — The committee shall prepare for the Minister a report of its review and its recommendations.

(4) Same — The Minister shall table the report in the Legislature.

(5) Committee review — Upon the report being tabled, a select or standing committee of the Legislative Assembly shall be appointed to review the report, hear the opinions of interested persons or companies and make recommendations to the Legislative Assembly regarding amendments to this Act.

1994, c. 33, s. 8; 2004, c. 31, Sched. 34, s. 26

143.13 Confidential information — The Minister is entitled to keep confidential any information or documents received from the Commission that the Commission was entitled to keep confidential.

1994, c. 33, s. 8

143.14 Electronic communication — The Commission shall be deemed to have complied with a requirement under Ontario securities law to publish or otherwise make available a notice, rule or other information if the Commission provides the notice, rule or information in electronic form through an electronic medium or posts it on its web site.

2002, c. 18, Sched. H, s. 13

144. (1) Revocation or variation of decision — The Commission may make an order revoking or varying a decision of the Commission, on the application of the Executive Director or a person or company affected by the decision, if in the Commission's opinion the order would not be prejudicial to the public interest.

(2) Terms and conditions — The order may be made on such terms and conditions as the Commission may impose.

1994, c. 11, s. 380

OSA 144

Definitions: OSA 1(1)"Commission"; 1(1)"person"; 1(1)"company".

Rules: Rule 13-502, App. C, Item E(1) and E(4.1); Rules of Procedure 2.3, 15.

Policies and Orders: OPS 2.1; NPS 12-202; BOR 1.2, 1.3, 1.4.

145. Continuation of registration — Every registration made and receipt for a prospectus issued under *The Securities Act*, being chapter 426 of the Revised Statutes of Ontario, 1970, and in effect immediately before the 15th day of September, 1979, continues in the same manner as if made or issued under this Act.

146. (1) No privilege — Despite subsection 33(4) of the *Evidence Act*, the Commission may by order compel a bank or officer of a bank, in an investigation, financial examination or hearing under Ontario securities law to which the bank is not a party, to produce any book or record the contents of which can be proved under section 33 of the *Evidence Act* or to appear as a witness to prove the matters, transactions and accounts contained in the book or record.

(2) Definitions — In subsection (1), **"bank"** and **"officer of a bank"** have the same meanings as in subsection 33(4) of the *Evidence Act*.

1994, c. 11, s. 381

OSA 146

Related Provisions: OSA 11, 127.

Definitions: OSA 1(1)"Commission"; 1(1)"Ontario securities law".

Policies and Orders: BOR 1.4.

147. Exemption — Except where exemption applications are otherwise provided for in Ontario securities law, the Commission may, on the application of an interested person or company and if in the Commission's opinion it would not be prejudicial to the public interest, make an order on such terms and conditions as it may impose exempting the person or company from any requirement of Ontario securities law.

1994, c. 11, s. 381

OSA 147

Definitions: OSA 1(1)"Commission"; 1(1)"Ontario securities law"; 1(1)"person"; 1(1)"company".

Rules: Rule 35-502, Part 4, 13-502, App. C, Item E(1).

Policies and Orders: BOR 1.2, 1.3.

148. [Repealed 1997, c. 10, s. 40.]

OSA 148

Definitions: OSA 1(1)"Commission"; 1(1)"Director"; 1(1)"person"; 1(1)"company"; 1(1)"Minister".

149. Costs — Nothing shall preclude a court from ordering costs payable to the Commission and in the event that costs are awarded to the Commission, a counsel fee may be awarded despite the fact that the Commission was represented by Commission staff.

1994, c. 11, s. 381

OSA 149

Definitions: OSA 1(1)"Commission".

150. Decision under more than one provision — Nothing in this Act shall be construed as limiting the Commission's ability to make a decision under more than one provision of Ontario securities law in respect of the same conduct or matter.

1994, c. 11, s. 381

OSA 150

Definitions: OSA 1(1)"decision"; 1(1)"Commission"; 1(1)"Ontario securities law".

151. (1) Enforcement of Commission decision — On filing with the Superior Court of Justice, a decision made by the Commission or by a Director pursuant to subsection 6(3) shall be deemed to be an order of the Superior Court of Justice and is enforceable as an order of that court.

(2) Filing decision — A decision of a Director may not be filed with the court under subsection (1) until the time permitted for an application to review the Director's decision pursuant to subsection 8(2) has expired or, if the decision has been appealed, the Commission has confirmed it.

1994, c. 11, s. 381; 2006, c. 19, Sched. C, s. 1(1)

OSA 151(2)

Related Provisions: OSA 8(2).

OSA 151

Definitions: OSA 1(1)"Commission"; 1(1)"Director".

152. (1) Application for letters of request — The Commission may apply to the Superior Court of Justice for an order,

(a) appointing a person to take the evidence of a witness outside of Ontario for use in a proceeding before the Commission; and

(b) providing for the issuance of a letter of request directed to the judicial authorities of the jurisdiction in which the witness is to be found, requesting the issuance of such process as is necessary to compel the person to attend before the person appointed under clause (a) to give testimony on oath or otherwise and to produce documents and things relevant to the subject matter of the proceeding.

(2) Practice and procedure — The practice and procedure in connection with an appointment under this section, the taking of evidence and the certifying and return of the appointment shall, as far as possible, be the same as those that govern similar matters in civil proceedings in the Superior Court of Justice.

(3) Admissibility of evidence — The making of an order under subsection (1) does not determine whether evidence obtained pursuant to the order is admissible in the proceeding before the Commission.

(4) Reciprocal assistance — If it is made to appear to the Superior Court of Justice that a court or tribunal of competent jurisdiction outside of Ontario has, on behalf of a securities commission or other body empowered by statute to administer or regulate trading in securities or derivatives, duly authorized, by commission, order or other process, the obtaining of the testimony of a witness outside the jurisdiction of the securities commission or other body and within Ontario for use at a proceeding before the securities commission or other body, the Superior Court of Justice may order the examination of the witness before the person appointed in the manner and form directed by the commission, order or other process, and may, by the same or by subsequent order, command the attendance of the witness for the purpose of being examined, or the production of a writing or other document or thing mentioned in the order, and may give all such directions as to the time and place of the examination and all other matters connected with the examination as seem proper.

1994, c. 11, s. 381; 2006, c. 19, Sched. C, s. 1(1); 2010, c. 26, Sched. 18, s. 44

OSA 152

Definitions: OSA 1(1)"Commission".

Policies and Orders: BOR 1.4.

153. Exchange of information — Despite the *Freedom of Information and Protection of Privacy Act*, the Commission may provide information to and receive information from the following entities, both in Canada and elsewhere, and the information received by the Commission is exempt from disclosure under that Act if the Commission determines that the information should be maintained in confidence:

1. Other securities, derivatives or financial regulatory authorities.

2. Exchanges.

2.1 Trade repositories.

2.2 Clearing agencies.

2.3 Alternative trading systems.

3. Self-regulatory bodies or organizations.

4. Law enforcement agencies.

5. Governmental or regulatory authorities not mentioned in paragraphs 1 to 4.

6. Any person or entity, other than an employee of the Commission, who provides services to the Commission.

1999, c. 9, s. 221; 2002, c. 18, Sched. H, s. 14; 2010, c. 26, Sched. 18, s. 45

154. Disclosure — The disclosure of information to the Commission or a trade repository that is made in good faith by a person or company in compliance or attempted compliance with Ontario securities law,

(a) does not constitute a breach of any contractual provision to which the person or company or any other person or company is subject; and

(b) does not constitute any other basis of liability against the person or company or any other person or company.

2010, c. 26, Sched. 18, s. 46

OSA 154

Definitions: OSA 1(l)"trade repository".

SCHEDULE [1]

The number in square brackets has been editorially added by Carswell

Part A

Blanket Ruling	Date Issued
In The Matter of Certain Reporting Issuers, 1980 O.S.C.B. 166	10/04/80
In The Matter of The Automatic Investment of Dividends or Distributions in Shares or Units of Mutual Funds (1983), 6 O.S.C.B. 1078	11/05/83
In The Matter of Certain Proposed Amendements (1983), 6 O.S.C.B. 3508	19/10/83
In The Matter of Discount Brokerage and The Role of Financial Institutions (1984), 7 O.S.C.B. 458	10/01/84
In The Matter of Order Execution Access Dealers (1984), 7 O.S.C.B. 1520	10/02/84
In The Matter of Certain Reporting Issuers (1984), 7 O.S.C.B. 1913	27/04/84
In The Matter of Certain Reporting Issuers (1984), 7 O.S.C.B. 3247	24/07/84
In the Matter of Zero Coupon Strip Bonds (1984), 7 O.S.C.B. 4085	25/09/84
In The Matter of Eurosecurity Financings (1984), 7 O.S.C.B. 4897	22/11/84
In The Matter of Trades in Securities of a Private Company Under the Execution Act (1985), 8 O.S.C.B. 127	04/01/85
In The Matter of Certain Reporting Issuers (1985), 8 O.S.C.B. 2915	12/07/85
In The Matter of The Mandatory Investment of Dividends or Distributions In Shares or Units of Mutual Funds (1985), 8 O.S.C.B. 4308	16/10/85
In The Matter of a Policy of The Toronto Stock Exchange on Small Shareholder Selling and Purchase Arrangements (1987), 10 O.S.C.B. 1455	02/03/87
In The Matter of a Policy of The Montreal Exchange on Small Shareholder Selling and Purchase Arrangements (1987), 10 O.S.C.B. 4938	18/08/87
In The Matter of Certain Proposed Amendments (1987), 10 O.S.C.B. 5936	22/09/87
In The Matter of The Business Corporations Act, 1982, S.O. 1982, chapter 4, as amended and In The Matter of The Canadian Depository for Securities (1988), 11 O.S.C.B. 542	25/11/87
In The Matter of Trading in Recognized Options Cleared Through Recognized Clearing Organizations (1988), 11 O.S.C.B. 4895	01/12/88
In The Matter of The Securities Act R.S.O. 1980, chapter 466, as amended (1989), 12 O.S.C.B. 2735	07/07/89
In The Matter of The Toronto Stock Exchange (1990), 13 O.S.C.B. 3007	12/07/90
In The Matter of Self-Directed Registered Education Savings Plans (1990), 13 O.S.C.B. 4793	22/10/90
In The Matter of The Toronto Stock Exchange (1991), 14 O.S.C.B. 881	27/02/91
In The Matter of The Recognized Options Rationalization Order (1991), 14 O.S.C.B. 2157	30/04/91
In The Matter of an Assignment to the Director Pursuant to Section 6 of The Securities Act (1991), 14 O.S.C.B. 3439	25/06/91
In The Matter of First Prospectuses Filed by National Policy Statement No. 36 Mutual Funds and In The Matter of Universal Money Market Fund (1991), 14 O.S.C.B. 3475	03/07/91
In The Matter of Mutual Fund Securities (1991), 14 O.S.C.B. 3763	24/07/91
In The Matter of The Recognized Options Rationalization Order (1991), 14 O.S.C.B. 4234	14/08/91
In The Matter of Self-Directed Registered Education Savings Plans (1992), 15 O.S.C.B. 613	05/12/91
In The Matter of Certain Advisers (1992), 15 O.S.C.B. 1955	05/05/92
In The Matter of Certain Members of The Toronto Stock Exchange (1992), 15 O.S.C.B. 3354	14/07/92
In The Matter of The Limitations on a Registrant Underwriting Securities of a Related Issuer or Connected Issuer of The Registrant (1992), 15 O.S.C.B. 3645	30/07/92
In The Matter of Going Private Transactions (1993), 16 O.S.C.B. 3428	30/06/93

In The Matter of Insider Bids, Issuer Bids and Take-Over Bids in Anticipation of Going Private Transactions (1993), 16 O.S.C.B. 3429	30/06/93
In The Matter of Real Return Bond Strip Bonds (1994), 17 O.S.C.B. 2875	23/11/93
In The Matter of Dividend Reinvestment and Stock Dividend Plans (1993), 16 O.S.C.B. 5928	26/11/93
In The Matter of Ontario Regulation 638/93 and The Disclosure of Executive Compensation and of Indebtedness of Directors, Executive Officers and Senior Officers (1993), 16 O.S.C.B. 5913	01/12/93
Blanket Permission Under Section 81 of The Regulation Under The Securities Act (Ontario) (1993), 16 O.S.C.B. 5914	01/12/93
Blanket Permission — International Offerings made by way of Private Placement in Ontario — Subsection 38(3) of The Securities Act (Ontario) (1993), 16 O.S.C.B. 5938	01/12/93
In The Matter of Regulation 1015, R.R.O. 1990, as amended and In The Matter of Certain International Offerings by Private Placement in Ontario (1993), 16 O.S.C.B. 5931	01/12/93
In The Matter of Networking Arrangements Governed by the Principles of Regulation (1993), 16 O.S.C.B. 6168	15/12/93
In The Matter of a Proposal of the Toronto Stock Exchange to Foster Capital Formation for Junior Resource and Industrial Enterprises (1994), 17 O.S.C.B. 347	10/01/94
In The Matter of Dividend Reinvestment Plans (1994), 17 O.S.C.B. 1178	02/03/94
In The Matter of Ontario Regulation 638/93 and The Disclosure of Executive Compensation and of Indebtedness of Directors, Executive Officers and Senior Officers (1994), 17 O.S.C.B. 1176	08/03/94
Blanket Permission Under Section 81 of The Regulation Under The Securities Act (Ontario) (1994), 17 O.S.C.B. 1187	08/03/94
In The Matter of Trades by Issuers In Connection With Securities Exchange Issuer Bids and In The Matter of Trades by Holders of Securities of a Company to Another Company In Connection With an Amalgamation, an Arrangement or a Specified Statutory Procedure (1994), 17 O.S.C.B. 1975	20/04/94
In The Matter of Trades by Issuers Upon Exercise of Certain Conversion or Exchange Rights and In The Matter of The First Trade in Securities Acquired Upon Exercise of Such Conversion or Exchange Rights (1994), 17 O.S.C.B. 2876	07/06/94
In The Matter of Certain Amendments to Regulation 1015 of The Revised Regulations of Ontario 1990 made under The Securities Act (Financial intermediary registration exemption)	08/11/94
In The Matter of Certain Amendments to Regulation 1015 of The Revised Regulations of Ontario 1990 made under The Securities Act (Corporate sponsored plans)	08/11/94
In The Matter of Trades by an Issuer in Securities of its own issue to Senior Officers, Directors, Personal Holding Companies and Registered Retirement Savings Plans and a Controlling Shareholder in Securities of an Issuer to Employees, Senior Officers, Directors, Personal Holding Companies and Registered Retirement Savings Plans	14/11/94
In The Matter of the First Trade in Securities Acquired Pursuant to Certain Exemptions, 26/04/94, 170SCB-1978 "Resale Ruling", amended, 14/11/94	14/11/94
In The Matter of Trading in Securities of Labour Sponsored Investment Fund Corporations (Blanket Order/ordonnance générale)	10/11/94

Part B

Blanket Ruling and Related Policy Statements

Blanket Ruling and Related Policy Statement	*Date Issued*
In The Matter of a Simplified Prospectus Qualification System for Mutual Funds (1984), 7 O.S.C.B. 5333 [including National Policy Statement No. 36 (1984), 7 O.S.C.B. 5355 and National Policy Statement No. 39/y compris l'instruction générale canadienne no 36 (1984), 7 O.S.C.B. 5355 et l'instruction générale canadienne no 39]	18/12/84
In The Matter of Certain Reporting Issuers (1988), 11 O.S.C.B. 1029 [including National Policy Statement No. 41 (1987), 10 O.S.C.B. 6307/y compris l'instruction générale canadienne no 41 (1987), 10 O.S.C.B. 6307]	01/03/88
In The Matter of Rules for Shelf Prospectus Offerings and for Pricing Offerings after the Prospectus Is Receipted (1991), 14 O.S.C.B. 1824 [including National Policy Statement No. 44 (1991), 14 O.S.C.B. 1844/y compris l'instruction générale canadienne no 44 (1991), 14 O.S.C.B. 1844]	02/05/91

In The Matter of Regulation 910, R.R.O. 1980, as amended and In The Matter of The Multijurisdictional   24/06/91
Disclosure System (1991), 14 O.S.C.B. 2863 [including National Policy Statement No. 45 (1991), 14
O.S.C.B. 2889/y compris l'instruction générale canadienne no 45 (1991), 14 O.S.C.B. 2889]

In The Matter of The Prompt Offering Qualification System (1993), 16 O.S.C.B. 731, 16 O.S.C.B. 732;   17/02/93 & 25/02/93
16 O.S.C.B. 949 [including National Policy Statement No. 47 (1993), 16 O.S.C.B. 765/y compris
l'instruction générale canadienne no 47 (1993), 16 O.S.C.B. 765]

In The Matter of National Policy Statement No. 47 and The Solicitation of Expressions of Interest   09/06/93
(1993), 16 O.S.C.B. 2832 [including National Policy Statement No. 47 (1993), 16 O.S.C.B. 765/y compris l'instruction générale canadienne no 47 (1993), 16 O.S.C.B. 765]

In The Matter of Certain Trades in Securities of Junior Resource Issuers (1988), 11 O.S.C.B. 1522   30/03/88
[including Ontario Policy No. 5.2 (1988), 11 O.S.C.B. 563/y compris la politique de l'Ontario no 5.2
(1988), 11 O.S.C.B. 563]

1994, c. 33, s. 9

ONT. REG. 1015 — GENERAL REGULATION

made under the *Securities Act*

R.R.O. 1990, Reg. 1015, as am. O. Reg. 249/92; 455/92; 457/92; 496/92; 592/92; 209/93; 638/93; 80/95; 13/96; 549/96; 247/97; 507/97; 88/98; 130/98; 149/98; 165/98; 166/98; 268/98; 542/98; 568/98; 657/98; 662/98; 1/99; 322/99; 3/00; 108/00; 133/00; 222/00; 342/00; 468/00 [Corrected Gaz. 133:48, November 25/00.]; 601/00; 631/00; 632/00 [Corrected Gaz. 134:3, January 20/01.]; 636/00; 683/00; 689/00; 67/01; 91/01; 126/01; 273/01; 388/01; 393/01; 423/01; 424/01; 504/01; 290/02; 16/03; 48/03; 56/04, ss. 1–14; 57/04; 72/04; 215/05; 346/05; 453/05; 491/05; 500/06; 562/07; 589/07; 31/08; 357/09; 358/09; 141/10; 437/10; 64/14; 130/16.

PART I — GENERAL

Interpretation

1. (1) Every term used in this Regulation that is,

(a) defined in section 1 of the Act is used in this Regulation as so defined unless it is otherwise defined in this Regulation or the context otherwise requires;

(b) defined in a Part of the Act for purposes of that Part, is used as so defined in those sections of this Regulation that relate to the subject matter of that Part; and

(c) defined only for a Part or section of this Regulation is, unless otherwise provided, so defined only for the purposes of such Part or section.

(2) In this Regulation,

"debt security" [Repealed O. Reg. 357/09, s. 1.]

"finance company" [Repealed O. Reg. 357/09, s. 1.]

"industrial company" [Repealed O. Reg. 357/09, s. 1.]

"insurance company" means an issuer licensed under the *Insurance Act*;

"natural resource company" means a mining, gas, oil or exploration issuer designated by the Director as a natural resource company;

ON Reg. 1015:1(2)"natural resource company"

Definitions: OSA 1(1)"Director".

"variable insurance contract" [Repealed O. Reg. 357/09, s. 1.]

(3) [Repealed O. Reg. 437/10, s. 1(1).]

(4) Except as otherwise provided in National Instrument 52-107 *Acceptable Accounting Principles and Auditing Standards,* in National Instrument 71-101 *The Multijurisdictional Disclosure System* and in Ontario Securities Commission Rule 71-801 *The Multijurisdictional Disclosure System,* where an issuer is incorporated or organized in a jurisdiction other than Canada or a province or territory of Canada, **"generally accepted accounting principles"** may, at the option of the issuer, mean such principles as prescribed in the incorporating jurisdiction by or pursuant to applicable legislation or where a recommendation has been made by an association in that jurisdiction equivalent to the Canadian Institute of Chartered Accountants, the principles recommended by that association, but where an option is exercised under this subsection, the notes to the financial statements shall state which option has been applied in the choice of generally accepted accounting principles.

ON Reg. 1015:1(4)

Definitions: OSA 1(1)"issuer".

Rules: Rule 71-801; NI 44-101, 52-107, 71-101, 81-106, s. 2.6.

Policies and Orders: OSCN 52-701 to 52-714, 71-508; CSAN 42-301, 52-320, 52-321, 52-324.

(5) Where the Act or this Regulation requires the disclosure of the number or percentage of securities beneficially owned by a person and, by virtue of subsection 1(5) of the Act, one or more companies will also have to be shown as beneficially owning the securities, a statement disclosing all the securities beneficially owned by the person or deemed to be beneficially owned, and indicating whether the ownership is direct or indirect and, if indirect, indicating the name of the controlled company or company affiliated with the controlled company through which the securities are indirectly owned and the number or percentage of the securities so owned by the company, shall be deemed sufficient disclosure without disclosing the name of any other company which is deemed to beneficially own the same securities.

ON Reg. 1015:1(5)

Related Provisions: OSA 1(5).

Definitions: OSA 1(1)"security"; 1(1)"person"; 1(1)"company".

(6) Where the Act or this Regulation requires the disclosure of the number or percentage of securities beneficially owned by a company and, by virtue of subsection 1(6) of the Act, one or more other companies will also have to be shown as beneficially owning the securities, a statement disclosing all securities beneficially owned or deemed to be beneficially owned by the parent company and indicating whether the ownership is direct or indirect and, if indirect, indicating the name of the subsidiary through which the securities are indirectly owned and the number or percentage of the securities so owned, shall be deemed sufficient disclosure without disclosing the name of any other company which is deemed to beneficially own the same securities.

ON Reg. 1015:1(6)

Related Provisions: OSA 1(6).

Definitions: OSA 1(1)"company"; 1(1)"security".

(7) A company shall be deemed to be another's holding company or parent company if that other is its subsidiary.

O. Reg. 80/95, s. 1; 568/98, s. 1; 632/00, s. 1; 72/04, s. 1; 491/05, s. 1; 357/09, s. 1; 437/10, s. 1

ON Reg. 1015:1(7)

Definitions: OSA 1(1)"company".

Financial Statements

2. [Repealed O. Reg. 437/10, s. 2.]

PART II — CONTINUOUS DISCLOSURE

[Heading amended O. Reg. 56/04, s. 1.]

Non-Financial Matters

3. (1) [Repealed O. Reg. 215/05, s. 2(1).]

(1.1) Every report required to be filed under subsection 75(2) of the Act by a reporting issuer shall be prepared in accordance with Form 51-102F3 of National Instrument 51-102 *Continuous Disclosure Obligations* except that,

(a) the reference in Item 3 of the Form to section 7.1 of National Instrument 51-102 shall be read as if it were a reference to subsection 75(1) of the Act; and

(b) the references in Items 6 and 7 of the Form to subsection 7.1(2), (5) or (7) of National Instrument 51-102 shall be read as if they were references to subsection 75(3), (4) or (5), respectively, of the Act.

(1.2) [Repealed O. Reg. 64/14, s. 1.]

(2) The requirements in this section apply except as otherwise provided in National Instrument 71-101 *The Multijurisdictional Disclosure System* and in Ontario Securities Commission Rule 71-801 *The Multijurisdictional Disclosure System*.

O. Reg. 568/98, s. 3; 56/04, s. 2; 215/05, s. 2; 64/14, s. 1

ON Reg. 1015:3(2)

Rules: NI 71-101; Rule 71-801.

Amended: (2014) 37 O.S.C.B. 1638.

4. Where the reporting issuer files,

(a) the report required by subsection 75(2) of the Act in reliance on,

(i) subsection 75(3) of the Act, or

(ii) Item 7 of Form 51-102F3 of National Instrument 51-102 *Continuous Disclosure Obligations*; or

(iii) [Repealed O. Reg. 215/05, s. 3.]

(b) the notification required by subsection 75(4) of the Act,

everything that is required to be filed thereby shall be designated as confidential and refer to section 75 of the Act.

O. Reg. 56/04, s. 3; 215/05, s. 3; 64/14, s. 2

ON Reg. 1015:4

Related Provisions: OSA 75(2)–(4).

Definitions: OSA 1(1) "reporting issuer".

Rules: NI 51-102, 81-106.

Amended: (2014) 37 O.S.C.B. 1638.

Other Disclosure

5. [Revoked O. Reg. 56/04, s. 4.]

6. [Repealed O. Reg. 215/05, s. 4.]

Financial Matters — Interim Financial Disclosure

6.1 [Revoked O. Reg. 636/00, s. 1.]

7. [Revoked O. Reg. 636/00, s. 2.]

8. [Revoked O. Reg. 636/00, s. 3.]

9. [Revoked O. Reg. 636/00, s. 4.]

Annual Financial Disclosure

9.1 [Revoked O. Reg. 636/00, s. 5.]

10. [Revoked O. Reg. 636/00, s. 6.]

11. [Revoked O. Reg. 636/00, s. 7.]

Finance Companies

12. [Revoked O. Reg. 507/97, s. 1.]

Miscellaneous

13. [Revoked O. Reg. 636/00, s. 8.]

PART III — PROSPECTUS REQUIREMENTS

Further Exemptions

14. [Revoked O. Reg. 662/98, s. 1.]

15. [Revoked O. Reg. 130/98, s. 2.]

16. [Revoked O. Reg. 662/98, s. 1.]

17. [Revoked O. Reg. 662/98, s. 1.]

18. [Revoked O. Reg. 662/98, s. 1.]

19. [Revoked O. Reg. 662/98, s. 1.]

20. [Revoked O. Reg. 662/98, s. 1.]

21. [Revoked O. Reg. 662/98, s. 1.]

Restriction of Exemptions

22. [Revoked O. Reg. 662/98, s. 1.]

23. [Revoked O. Reg. 662/98, s. 1.]

24. [Revoked O. Reg. 662/98, s. 1.]

25. [Revoked O. Reg. 662/98, s. 1.]

26. [Revoked O. Reg. 662/98, s. 1.]

27. [Revoked O. Reg. 662/98, s. 1.]

28. [Revoked O. Reg. 662/98, s. 1.]

29. [Revoked O. Reg. 662/98, s. 1.]

30. [Revoked O. Reg. 662/98, s. 1.]

31. [Revoked O. Reg. 662/98, s. 1.]

32. [Revoked O. Reg. 662/98, s. 1.]

Filing Requirements

33. [Revoked O. Reg. 91/01, s. 1.]

34. [Revoked O. Reg. 632/00, s. 3.]

35. [Revoked O. Reg. 632/00, s. 3.]

36. [Revoked O. Reg. 632/00, s. 3.]

Content of Prospectuses — Non-Financial Matters

37. [Revoked O. Reg. 632/00, s. 3.]

38. [Repealed O. Reg. 453/05, s. 1.]

Finance Companies

39. [Revoked O. Reg. 632/00, s. 5.]

Format

40. [Revoked O. Reg. 632/00, s. 5.]

41. [Revoked O. Reg. 632/00, s. 5.]

42. [Revoked O. Reg. 632/00, s. 5.]

43. If a prospectus is required to be filed in respect of an issuer bid, the information required in Form 62-104F2 in National Instrument 62-104 *Take-Over Bids and Issuer Bids*, other than the certificate in Item 31 of Part 2 of the form, shall be included in the prospectus.

O. Reg. 589/07, s. 1; 130/16, s. 1

ON Reg. 1015:43

Related Provisions: OSA Part XV; OSA 89(1)"issuer bid".

Rules: Rule 62-504.

44. [Repealed O. Reg. 31/08, s. 1.]

45. [Revoked O. Reg. 632/00, s. 6.]

46. [Revoked O. Reg. 632/00, s. 6.]

47. [Revoked O. Reg. 632/00, s. 6.]

48. [Revoked O. Reg. 632/00, s. 6.]

49. [Revoked O. Reg. 632/00, s. 6.]

50. [Revoked O. Reg. 631/00, s. 1.]

51. [Revoked O. Reg. 631/00, s. 1.]

52. [Revoked O. Reg. 632/00, s. 7.]

Content of Prospectus — Financial Matters

53. [Revoked O. Reg. 632/00, s. 7.]

54. [Repealed O. Reg. 31/08, s. 1.]

55. [Revoked O. Reg. 632/00, s. 7.]

56. [Revoked O. Reg. 632/00, s. 7.]

57. [Revoked O. Reg. 632/00, s. 7.]

58. [Revoked O. Reg. 632/00, s. 7.]

59. [Revoked O. Reg. 632/00, s. 7.]

60. [Repealed O. Reg. 562/07, s. 1.]

61. [Revoked O. Reg. 632/00, s. 8.]

62. [Revoked O. Reg. 632/00, s. 8.]

63. [Revoked O. Reg. 632/00, s. 8.]

64. [Revoked O. Reg. 632/00, s. 8.]

65. [Revoked O. Reg. 632/00, s. 8.]

66. [Revoked O. Reg. 632/00, s. 8.]

Reporting Requirements

67. [Revoked O. Reg. 662/98, s. 1.]

68. [Revoked O. Reg. 662/98, s. 1.]

69. (1) [Revoked O. Reg. 423/01, s. 1.]

(2) [Repealed O. Reg. 491/05, s. 2.]

(3) [Revoked O. Reg. 662/98, s. 1.]

(4) [Revoked O. Reg. 657/98, s. 1.]

(5) [Revoked O. Reg. 657/98, s. 1.]

O. Reg. 80/95, s. 11; 657/98, s. 1; 662/98, s. 1; 423/01, s. 1; 491/05, s. 2

70. [Revoked O. Reg. 423/01, s. 2.]

Statement of Material Facts

71. [Repealed O. Reg. 491/05, s. 3.]

72. [Repealed O. Reg. 491/05, s. 3.]

73. [Repealed O. Reg. 491/05, s. 3.]

74. [Repealed O. Reg. 491/05, s. 3.]

75. [Repealed O. Reg. 491/05, s. 3.]

76. [Repealed O. Reg. 491/05, s. 3.]

77. [Repealed O. Reg. 491/05, s. 3.]

Options

78. [Repealed O. Reg. 491/05, s. 3.]

Escrow Agreement

79. [Repealed O. Reg. 453/05, s. 2.]

Certificate — Portion of Distribution Underwritten

80. [Revoked O. Reg. 632/00, s. 10.]

Prospectus Requirements — Variation Permitted

81. [Revoked O. Reg. 632/00, s. 10.]

Restriction in Use of Terms

82. [Revoked O. Reg. 632/00, s. 10.]

PART IV

[Heading repealed O. Reg. 358/09, s. 1.]

[Heading repealed O. Reg. 358/09, s. 1.]

83. [Repealed O. Reg. 215/05, s. 5.]

[Heading repealed O. Reg. 358/09, s. 1.]

84. [Repealed O. Reg. 215/05, s. 5.]

[Heading repealed O. Reg. 358/09, s. 1.]

85. [Repealed O. Reg. 215/05, s. 5.]

[Heading repealed O. Reg. 358/09, s. 1.]

86. [Repealed O. Reg. 215/05, s. 5.]

[Heading repealed O. Reg. 358/09, s. 1.]

87. [Repealed O. Reg. 215/05, s. 5.]

88. [Repealed O. Reg. 215/05, s. 5.]

89. [Repealed O. Reg. 215/05, s. 5.]

90. [Repealed O. Reg. 215/05, s. 5.]

91. [Repealed O. Reg. 215/05, s. 5.]

92. [Repealed O. Reg. 215/05, s. 5.]

93. [Repealed O. Reg. 215/05, s. 5.]

94. [Repealed O. Reg. 215/05, s. 5.]

95. [Repealed O. Reg. 358/09, s. 1.]

PART V — REGISTRATION REQUIREMENTS

[Heading repealed O. Reg. 358/09, s. 2.]

96. [Repealed O. Reg. 358/09, s. 2.]

[Heading repealed O. Reg. 357/09, s. 2.]

97. [Repealed O. Reg. 357/09, s. 2.]

[Heading repealed O. Reg. 358/09, s. 2.]

98. [Repealed O. Reg. 358/09, s. 2.]

99. [Repealed O. Reg. 358/09, s. 2.]

100. [Repealed O. Reg. 358/09, s. 2.]

101. [Repealed O. Reg. 358/09, s. 2.]

[Heading repealed O. Reg. 358/09, s. 2.]

102. [Repealed O. Reg. 358/09, s. 2.]

103. [Repealed O. Reg. 358/09, s. 2.]

104. [Repealed O. Reg. 358/09, s. 2.]

105. [Repealed O. Reg. 357/09, s. 2.]

106. [Repealed O. Reg. 358/09, s. 2.]

Conditions of Registration — Capital Requirements

107. [Repealed O. Reg. 358/09, s. 2.]

108. [Repealed O. Reg. 358/09, s. 2.]

109. [Repealed O. Reg. 358/09, s. 2.]

110. (1) Every dealer, other than an exempt market dealer as defined in National Instrument 31-103 *Registration Requirements and Exemptions*, shall participate in a compensation fund or contingency trust fund approved by the Commission and established by,

(a) a recognized self-regulatory organization referred to in section 21.1 of the Act;

(b) a recognized stock exchange; or

(c) a trust corporation registered under the *Loan and Trust Corporations Act*.

(2) The Commission may vary the amount required to be contributed by any participant where in its opinion it would not be prejudicial to the public interest to do so, provided that the variation is published by the Commission in a publication published by it prior to the variation taking effect.

O. Reg. 453/05, s. 7; 358/09, s. 3

ON Reg. 1015:110

Definitions: OSA 1(1)"dealer"; 1(1)"adviser"; 1(1)"security"; 1(1)"Commission"; 1(1)"recognized stock exchange".

Related Provisions: OSA 21, 21.1.

Rules: NI 31-103; Rule 13-502, App. C, Item E(1).

Approvals: Canadian Investor Protection Fund: (2008) 31 O.S.C.B. 9522; MFDA Investor Protection Corporation: (2006) 29 O.S.C.B. 7055.

111. [Repealed O. Reg. 358/09, s. 4.]

112. [Repealed O. Reg. 358/09, s. 4.]

[Heading repealed O. Reg. 358/09, s. 4.]

113. [Repealed O. Reg. 358/09, s. 4.]

Conditions of Registration — New Accounts and Supervision

114. [Revoked O. Reg. 1/99, s. 1.]

115. [Repealed O. Reg. 358/09, s. 4.]

[Heading repealed O. Reg. 358/09, s. 4.]

116. [Repealed O. Reg. 358/09, s. 4.]

117. [Repealed O. Reg. 358/09, s. 4.]

118. [Repealed O. Reg. 358/09, s. 4.]

119. [Repealed O. Reg. 358/09, s. 4.]

120. [Repealed O. Reg. 358/09, s. 4.]

121. [Repealed O. Reg. 358/09, s. 4.]

122. [Repealed O. Reg. 358/09, s. 4.]

[Heading repealed O. Reg. 358/09, s. 4.]

123. [Repealed O. Reg. 358/09, s. 4.]

Conditions of Registration — Proficiency Requirements

124. [Revoked O. Reg. 468/00, s. 2.]

125. [Revoked O. Reg. 1/99, s. 1.]

126. [Revoked O. Reg. 468/00, s. 3.]

127. [Repealed O. Reg. 358/09, s. 4.]

[Heading revoked O. Reg. 393/01, s. 1.]

128. [Revoked O. Reg. 393/01, s. 1.]

[Heading revoked O. Reg. 16/03, s. 1.]

129. [Revoked O. Reg. 16/03, s. 1.]

[Heading repealed O. Reg. 358/09, s. 4.]

130. [Repealed O. Reg. 358/09, s. 4.]

131. [Repealed O. Reg. 358/09, s. 4.]

132. [Repealed O. Reg. 358/09, s. 4.]

133. [Repealed O. Reg. 358/09, s. 4.]

Examination

134. A summons for an examination under section 33.1 of the Act shall be in Form 8.

O. Reg. 357/09, s. 3

ON Reg. 1015:134

Related Provisions: OSA 33.1.

Regulations: Reg.: Form 8.

Rules: Rule 35-502, s. 3.9.

Amendments to Registration

135. [Repealed O. Reg. 453/05, s. 10.]

136. [Revoked O. Reg. 16/03, s. 3.]

137. [Repealed O. Reg. 453/05, s. 10.]

138. [Repealed O. Reg. 453/05, s. 10.]

Reporting to Ontario Securities Commission

139. [Repealed O. Reg. 358/09, s. 4.]

140. [Repealed O. Reg. 358/09, s. 4.]

141. [Repealed O. Reg. 358/09, s. 4.]

142. [Repealed O. Reg. 358/09, s. 4.]

143. [Repealed O. Reg. 357/09, s. 4.]

144. [Repealed O. Reg. 358/09, s. 4.]

145. [Repealed O. Reg. 358/09, s. 4.]

146. [Repealed O. Reg. 357/09, s. 4.]

147. (1) [Repealed O. Reg. 453/05, s. 15(1).]

(2) [Repealed O. Reg. 358/09, s. 4.]

O. Reg. 453/05, s. 15; 358/09, s. 4

Further Exemptions from Registration Requirements

148. [Repealed O. Reg. 491/05, s. 6.]

149. [Revoked O. Reg. 424/01, s. 1.]

150. [Repealed O. Reg. 491/05, s. 7.]

151. [Repealed O. Reg. 491/05, s. 7.]

ON Reg. 1015:Part V

Related Provisions: OSA Part XI.

Rules: NI 31-101 to Rule 35-503.

Policies and Orders: NPS 31-201 to OSCN 34-701; OPS 4.3.

PART VI — OVER-THE-COUNTER TRADING

General

152. In this Part,

"approved market-maker" means a registered dealer who is approved under this Regulation to act as a market-maker in a security;

"COATS security" means,

(a) a share of a company,

(b) a right or warrant, but not an option, to purchase a share of a company, or

(c) any combination of a share of a company and a right or warrant, but not an option, to purchase a share of a company,

but does not include,

(d) a security of a private issuer as defined in subsection 2.4(1) of National Instrument 45-106 *Prospectus and Registration Exemptions*,

(d.1) a security that, under subsection 2.13(1), 2.20(1), 2.21(1), 2.34(2), 2.35(1), 2.36(2), 2.37(1) or 2.38(1) of National Instrument 45-106 *Prospectus and Registration Exemptions*, is exempt from registration,

(d.2) a security that, under subsection 2.4(1), 2.5(1) or 2.6(1) or (2) of Ontario Securities Commission Rule 45-501 *Ontario Prospectus and Registration Exemptions*, is exempt from registration, or

(d.3) [Repealed O. Reg. 491/05, s. 8(3).]

(e) a security that is traded on a marketplace as defined in National Instrument 21-101 *Marketplace Operation*;

"COAT System" means the system developed for trading in the over-the-counter market and known as the Canadian Over-the-Counter Automated Trading System.

O. Reg. 393/01, s. 2; 424/01, s. 2; 491/05, s. 8

ON Reg. 1015:152

Related Provisions: OSA 35(2).

Definitions: OSA 1(1)"dealer"; 1(1)"company"; 1(1)"security"; 1(1)"Commission".

153. The Commission, itself or through an agent, shall operate the COAT System and for such purpose it shall develop computer software and provide and operate computer facilities.

Trade Reporting

154. (1) Every purchase or sale in Ontario of a COATS security made by a registered dealer, as principal or agent, shall be reported on the COAT System except a trade that is,

(a) made through the facilities of a stock exchange or other organized market recognized by the Commission for the purpose of this Part;

(b) a distribution by or on behalf of an issuer; or

(c) a trade made in reliance on an exemption set out in section 2.3, 2.7, 2.8, 2.10 or 2.15 of National Instrument 45-106 *Prospectus and Registration Exemptions*.

ON Reg 1015:154(1)

Policies and Orders: BOR 2.1.

(2) Every purchase or sale in a COATS security that is required to be reported under subsection (1) shall be reported on the COAT System in accordance with the following provisions:

1. The registered dealer, if any, through or by whom the sale is made shall report the trade.

2. Where the sale is not made by or through a registered dealer, the registered dealer by or through whom the purchase is made shall report the trade.

3. The report shall be made in accordance with the requirements of the COAT System.

O. Reg. 424/01, s. 3; 491/05, s. 9

ON Reg. 1015:154

Definitions: OSA 1(1)"dealer"; 1(1)"trade".

Market-Making

155. (1) A registered dealer, other than a security issuer, mutual fund dealer or scholarship plan dealer, may apply to the Director for approval to act as a market-maker in a COATS security of a class that trades in Ontario.

(2) An application for approval to act as a market-maker in a security shall be in Form 41 and shall be filed with the Director.

ON Reg. 1015:155(2)

Regulations: Reg.: Form 41.

ON Reg. 1015:155

Definitions: OSA 1(1)"dealer"; 1(1)"issuer"; 1(1)"mutual fund"; 1(1)"trade"; 1(1)"Director".

156. (1) A registered dealer shall not post quotations for a security on the COAT System,

(a) unless the dealer has been approved by the Director to act as a market-maker in the security;

(b) until the day and time set out in the Director's approval; and

(c) unless the Director has determined that it is not contrary to the public interest for the security to be quoted on the COAT System.

(2) Once an approved market-maker has posted a quotation on the COAT System with respect to a security, the market-maker, so long as it is an approved market-maker in the security, shall make continuous and uninterrupted quotations with respect to the security from 9.30 a.m. to 5.00 p.m. on any day that is not a Saturday or holiday and, where it does not make continuous and uninterrupted quotes, it shall be deemed to have ceased being an approved market-maker in the security.

(3) An approved market-maker shall not quote an ask price for a security on the COAT System unless a bid price for the security is also quoted by the market-maker.

ON Reg. 1015:156

Definitions: OSA 1(1)"dealer"; 1(1)"Director"; 1(1)"security".

General

157. The Director may direct registered dealers to discontinue quoting or trading, or both, in a security in which a trade would be reportable on the COAT System in order to assist in the dissemination of information and to re-establish orderly trading.

ON Reg. 1015:157

Definitions: OSA 1(1)"Director"; 1(1)"security".

158. Every registered dealer shall pay the applicable COAT System fees.

ON Reg. 1015:158

Definitions: OSA 1(1)"dealer".

159. (1) The forms, fees and other requirements of the Commission's agent in the operation of the COAT System, including the fees charged to commercial vendors of information for information reported thereon, are subject to the approval of the Commission and the forms, fees and other requirements, and any amendment to any of them, shall be published by the Commission in the month following the approval.

(2) The Commission may inspect all books, documents, correspondence and other records of any description maintained in relation to the COAT System by a registered dealer and by the Commission's agent.

ON Reg. 1015:159

Definitions: OSA 1(1)"Commission"; 1(1)"dealer".

PART VII — ONTARIO SECURITIES COMMISSION PROCEDURE AND RELATED MATTERS

Endorsement of Warrants

160. The endorsement of a warrant by a provincial judge or justice of Ontario provided for by section 125 of the Act shall be in accordance with Form 39.

O. Reg. 80/95, s. 14; 56/04, s. 6

ON Reg. 1015:160

Related Provisions: OSA 125.

Regulations: Reg.: Form 39.

Execution and Certification of Documents

161. Except as otherwise provided in the Act, section 174 of this Regulation, Ontario Securities Commission Rule 11-501 *Electronic Delivery of Documents to the Ontario Securities Commission*, Ontario Securities Commission Rule 55-502 *Facsimile Filing or Delivery of Section 109 Reports*, National Instrument 55-102 *System for Electronic Disclosure by Insiders (SEDI)* or National Instrument 71-102 *Continuous Disclosure and Other Exemptions Relating to Foreign Issuers*,

(a) every document required or permitted to be filed with the Commission by an individual that is required to be signed or certified shall be manually signed and shall include below the signature the name of the individual in typewritten or printed form;

(b) subject to clause (c) every document required or permitted to be filed with the Commission by a company or person, other than an individual, that is required to be signed or certified, shall be manually signed by an officer or director of the company or person or, subject to clause (d), by the attorney or agent of such person or company and shall include below the signature the name of the officer, director, attorney or agent in typewritten or printed form;

ON Reg. 1015:161(b)

Regulations: Reg.: 181.

(c) where a partner signs or certifies on behalf of a professional partnership, the partner is not required to sign his or her name but if an individual other than a partner signs or certifies, the individual shall sign his or her name manually and the name of the individual shall be included below his or her signature in typewritten or printed form; and

(d) where a document required or permitted to be filed with the Commission by an individual, company or person has been executed by an attorney or agent of the individual, company or person, a duly completed power of attorney or document of authority authorizing the signing of the document shall be filed with the document unless the Director permits the filing of the document without the power of attorney or document of authority.

O. Reg. 80/95, s. 15; 166/98, s. 1; 388/01, s. 1; 57/04, s. 1; 64/14, s. 3

Fees and Filing

ON Reg. 1015:161

Related Provisions: OSA 11.

Definitions: OSA 1(1)"individual"; 1(1)"company"; 1(1)"person"; 1(1)"officer"; 1(1)"director"; 1(1)"Commission".

Regulations: Reg.: 174, 246.

Rules: Rule 55-502; NI 55-102.

Amended: (2014) 37 O.S.C.B. 1638.

162. (1) [Revoked O. Reg. 165/98, s. 1.]

(2) Where any material that is filed is not prepared in accordance with the Act or this Regulation, the Director may, or the Commission may require the Director to, return the material to the person or company that is required to comply with the provisions.

(3) Where any material is returned to a person or company under subsection (2), the fee paid upon the filing of the material shall not be refunded without the consent of the Commission.

O. Reg. 80/95, s. 15; 165/98, s. 1

ON Reg. 1015:162

Definitions: OSA 1(1)"Director"; 1(1)"Commission"; 1(1)"person"; 1(1)"company".

Investigations

163. The following practices and procedures apply to investigations conducted under the Act:

1. Every summons issued by a person under subsection 11(4) or section 13 of the Act shall be served personally on the individual summoned who shall be paid the like fees and allowances for his or her attendance before the person as are paid for the attendance of a witness summoned to attend before the Supreme Court.

2. Every summons to a witness to appear before a person appointed to make an investigation under section 11 or 13 of the Act shall be in Form 1.

3. The service of a summons on a witness, the payment or tender of fees and allowances to the witness and the service of a notice on a witness may be proved by an affidavit in Form 2.

ON Reg. 1015:163

Related Provisions: OSA Part VI.

Definitions: OSA 1(1)"individual".

PART VIII — INSIDER TRADING

General

164. The disclosure required by section 40 of the Act with respect to a person or company that would be an insider of the adviser if the adviser were a reporting issuer is required only where such person or company participates in the formulation of, or has access prior to implementation to, investment decisions made on behalf of or the advice given to clients of the adviser.

ON Reg. 1015:164

Definitions: OSA 1(1)"person"; 1(1)"company"; 1(1)"insider"; 1(1)"adviser"; 1(1)"issuer"; 1(1)"decision".

165. [Revoked O. Reg. 13/96, s. 1.]

166. [Repealed O. Reg. 141/10, s. 1.]

167. [Repealed O. Reg. 141/10, s. 1.]

168. Every report required to be filed under section 109 of the Act shall be prepared in accordance with Form 37.

ON Reg. 1015:168

Related Provisions: OSA 109.

Regulations: Reg.: Form 37.

169. Every report required to be filed under section 117 of the Act shall be prepared in accordance with Form 38.

ON Reg. 1015:169

Related Provisions: OSA 117.

Regulations: Reg.: Form 38.

170. [Repealed O. Reg. 141/10, s. 1.]

171. [Repealed O. Reg. 141/10, s. 1.]

172. [Revoked O. Reg. 126/01, s. 1.]

173. (1) A person or company that is required under this Part and under Part XXI of the Act to file a report prepared in accordance with Form 55-102 (made under National Instrument 55-102 *System for Electronic Disclosure by Insiders (SEDI)*) shall be deemed to have complied with such requirements if a report prepared in accordance with Form 55-102 (made under National Instrument 55-102 *System for Electronic Disclosure by Insiders (SEDI)*) is filed in a Canadian jurisdiction other than Ontario with a securities commission or other agent that has been designated by the Commission for the purpose of accepting such filings.

(2) This section does not apply to insiders who are required by National Instrument 55-102 *System for Electronic Disclosure by Insiders (SEDI)* to file the report in electronic format.

O. Reg. 388/01, s. 2

ON Reg. 1015:173

Related Provisions: OSA Part XXI.

Rules: NI 55-102.

174. (1) A report prepared in accordance with Form 55-102 F6 (made under National Instrument 55-102 *System for Electronic Disclosure by Insiders (SEDI)*) that is filed with the Commission may contain the facsimile signature of the individual, officer, director, agent or attorney required to sign the form, if an original manually signed copy is filed concurrently with a securities commission in Canada designated by the Commission for the purpose of accepting such filings.

(2) This section does not apply to insiders who are required by National Instrument 55-102 *System for Electronic Disclosure by Insiders (SEDI)* to file the report in electronic format.

O. Reg. 388/01, s. 3

ON Reg. 1015:174

Definitions: OSA 1(1)"Commission"; 1(1)"officer"; 1(1)"director".

Regulations: Reg.: 161.

Rules: NI 55-102.

Insider Trading

175. (1) A person or company that purchases or sells securities of a reporting issuer with knowledge of a material fact or material change with respect to the reporting issuer that has not been generally disclosed is exempt from subsection 76(1) of the Act and from liability under section 134 of the Act, where the person or company proves that,

(a) no director, officer, partner, employee or agent of the person or company who made or participated in making the decision to purchase or sell the securities of the reporting issuer had actual knowledge of the material fact or material change; and

(b) no advice was given with respect to the purchase or sale of the securities to the director, officer, partner, employee or agent of the person or company who made or participated in making the decision to purchase or sell the securities by a director, partner, officer, employee or agent of the person or company who had actual knowledge of the material fact or the material change,

but this exemption is not available to an individual who had actual knowledge of the material fact or change.

ON Reg. 1015:175(1)

Related Provisions: OSA 76(1), 134.

(2) A person or company that purchases or sells securities of a reporting issuer with knowledge of a material fact or material change with respect to the reporting issuer that has not been generally disclosed is exempt from subsection 76(1) of the Act and from liability under section 134 of the Act, where the person or company proves that,

(a) the purchase or sale was entered into as agent of another person or company pursuant to a specific unsolicited order from that other person or company to purchase or sell;

(b) the purchase or sale was made pursuant to participation in an automatic dividend reinvestment plan, share purchase plan or other similar automatic plan that was entered into by the person or company prior to the acquisition of knowledge of the material fact or material change; or

(c) the purchase or sale was made to fulfil a legally binding obligation entered into by the person or company prior to the acquisition of knowledge of the material fact or material change.

ON Reg. 1015:175(2)

Related Provisions: OSA 76(1), 134.

(3) In determining whether a person or company has sustained the burden of proof under subsection (1), it shall be relevant whether and to what extent the person or company has implemented and maintained reasonable policies and procedures to prevent contraventions of subsection 76(1) of the Act by persons making or influencing investment decisions on its behalf and to prevent transmission of information concerning a material fact or material change contrary to subsection 76(2) or (3) of the Act.

ON Reg. 1015:175(3)

Related Provisions: OSA 76(1)–(3).

(4) A person or company who purchases or sells a security of a reporting issuer as agent or trustee for a person or company who is exempt from subsection 76(1) of the Act and from liability under section 134 of the Act by reason of clause 2(b) or (c), is also exempt from subsection 76(1) of the Act and from liability under section 134 of the Act.

ON Reg. 1015:175(4)

Related Provisions: OSA 76(1), 134.

(5) A person or company is exempt from subsections 76(1), (2) and (3) of the Act where the person or company proves that such person or company reasonably believed that,

(a) the other party to a purchase or sale of securities; or

(b) the person or company informed of the material fact or material change,

as the case may be, had knowledge of the material fact or material change.

ON Reg. 1015:175(5)

Related Provisions: OSA 76(1)–(3).

ON Reg. 1015:175

Definitions: OSA 1(1)"person"; 1(1)"company"; 1(1)"security"; 1(1)"reporting issuer"; 1(1)"material fact"; 1(1)"material change"; 1(1)"director"; 1(1)"officer".

Policies and Orders: OPS 33-601; OSCN 55-701.

ON Reg. 1015:Part VIII

Related Provisions: OSA Part XXI.

Rules: NI 55-101, 55-102, 55-103; Rule 55-502.

Policies and Orders: CSAN 55-308 to 55-312.

PART IX
[Heading repealed O. Reg. 215/05, s. 6.]

176. [Repealed O. Reg. 215/05, s. 6.]

177. [Repealed O. Reg. 215/05, s. 6.]

178. [Repealed O. Reg. 215/05, s. 6.]

179. [Repealed O. Reg. 215/05, s. 6.]

180. [Repealed O. Reg. 215/05, s. 6.]

181. [Repealed O. Reg. 215/05, s. 6.]

PART X — TAKE-OVER BIDS AND ISSUER BIDS

182. [Repealed O. Reg. 222/00, s. 1.]

183. [Repealed O. Reg. 589/07, s. 2.]

184. [Repealed O. Reg. 589/07, s. 2.]

185. [Repealed O. Reg. 589/07, s. 2.]

186. [Repealed O. Reg. 589/07, s. 2.]

187. [Repealed O. Reg. 589/07, s. 2.]

188. [Repealed O. Reg. 589/07, s. 2.]

189. [Repealed O. Reg. 589/07, s. 2.]

190. [Revoked O. Reg. 80/95, s. 22.]

191. [Revoked O. Reg. 80/95, s. 22.]

192. [Revoked O. Reg. 80/95, s. 22.]

193. [Repealed O. Reg. 589/07, s. 2.]

194. [Repealed O. Reg. 589/07, s. 2.]

195. [Repealed O. Reg. 589/07, s. 2.]

196. [Repealed O. Reg. 589/07, s. 2.]

197. [Revoked O. Reg. 133/00, s. 1.]

198. [Repealed O. Reg. 589/07, s. 2.]

199. [Revoked O. Reg. 133/00, s. 1.]

200. [Repealed O. Reg. 589/07, s. 2.]

201. [Repealed O. Reg. 589/07, s. 2.]

202. [Repealed O. Reg. 589/07, s. 2.]

203. [Repealed O. Reg. 589/07, s. 2.]

203.1 [Revoked O. Reg. 48/03, s. 1.]

203.2 [Revoked O. Reg. 48/03, s. 2.]

PART XI — UNIVERSAL REGISTRATION

Interpretation

204. [Repealed O. Reg. 358/09, s. 4.]

205. [Repealed O. Reg. 357/09, s. 4.]

Registration of Market Intermediaries

206. [Repealed O. Reg. 491/05, s. 11.]

Limited Market Dealer Registration

[Heading repealed O. Reg. 358/09, s. 4.]

207. [Revoked O. Reg. 149/98, s. 4.]

208. [Repealed O. Reg. 358/09, s. 4.]

Financial Intermediary Dealer Registration

209. (1) [Repealed O. Reg. 358/09, s. 4.]

(2) [Repealed O. Reg. 358/09, s. 4.]

(3) [Repealed O. Reg. 358/09, s. 4.]

(4) [Repealed O. Reg. 358/09, s. 4.]

(5) [Repealed O. Reg. 358/09, s. 4.]

(6) [Repealed O. Reg. 358/09, s. 4.]

(7) [Repealed O. Reg. 358/09, s. 4.]

(8) [Repealed O. Reg. 358/09, s. 4.]

(9) [Repealed O. Reg. 358/09, s. 4.]

(10) [Repealed O. Reg. 357/09, s. 4.]

O. Reg. 273/01, s. 1; 357/09, s. 4; 358/09, s. 4

[Heading repealed O. Reg. 358/09, s. 4.]

210. [Repealed O. Reg. 358/09, s. 4.]

[Heading repealed O. Reg. 358/09, s. 4.]

211. [Repealed O. Reg. 358/09, s. 4.]

PART XII

[Heading repealed O. Reg. 358/09, s. 5.]

[Heading repealed O. Reg. 358/09, s. 5.]

212. [Repealed O. Reg. 358/09, s. 5.]

[Heading repealed O. Reg. 358/09, s. 5.]

213. [Repealed O. Reg. 358/09, s. 5.]

214. [Repealed O. Reg. 358/09, s. 5.]

215. [Repealed O. Reg. 358/09, s. 5.]

216. [Repealed O. Reg. 358/09, s. 5.]

[Heading repealed O. Reg. 358/09, s. 5.]

217. [Repealed O. Reg. 358/09, s. 5.]

[Heading repealed O. Reg. 358/09, s. 5.]

218. [Repealed O. Reg. 358/09, s. 5.]

PART XIII — CONFLICTS OF INTEREST

Interpretation

219. [Repealed O. Reg. 358/09, s. 6.]

220. [Repealed O. Reg. 357/09, s. 4.]

General Duties

221. [Revoked O. Reg. 1/99, s. 1.]

222. [Revoked O. Reg. 1/99, s. 1.]

[Heading repealed O. Reg. 358/09, s. 6.]

223. [Repealed O. Reg. 358/09, s. 6.]

Limitations on Underwriting

224. [Revoked O. Reg. 504/01, s. 2.]

[Heading repealed O. Reg. 358/09, s. 6.]

225. [Repealed O. Reg. 358/09, s. 6.]

[Heading repealed O. Reg. 358/09, s. 6.]

226. [Repealed O. Reg. 358/09, s. 6.]

[Heading repealed O. Reg. 358/09, s. 6.]

227. [Repealed O. Reg. 358/09, s. 6.]

[Heading repealed O. Reg. 358/09, s. 6.]

228. [Repealed O. Reg. 358/09, s. 6.]

Limitations on Networking

229. [Revoked O. Reg. 273/01, s. 3.]

[Heading repealed O. Reg. 358/09, s. 6.]

230. [Repealed O. Reg. 358/09, s. 6.]

Miscellaneous

231. [Repealed O. Reg. 357/09, s. 4.]

232. [Repealed O. Reg. 358/09, s. 6.]

233. [Repealed O. Reg. 357/09, s. 4.]

PART XIV — LABOUR SPONSORED INVESTMENT FUND CORPORATIONS

234. In this Part,

"eligible investment" means an eligible investment as defined in section 204.8 of the *Income Tax Act* (Canada);

"employee organization" and **"labour sponsored investment fund corporation"** have the meanings specified in the *Labour Sponsored Venture Capital Corporations Act, 1992;*

"Labour Sponsored Investment Fund Course" [Revoked O. Reg. 468/00, s. 5.]

O. Reg. 455/92, s. 1; 209/93, s. 1; 468/00, s. 5

ON Reg. 1015:234

Definitions: OSA 1(1)"person"; 1(1)"trade".

123

235. Despite the definition of "promoter" in subsection 1(1) of the Act, if an employee organization incorporates a company to incorporate, organize and register another company as a labour sponsored investment fund corporation, the employee organization and its members shall be deemed not to be a promoter of the labour sponsored investment fund corporation.

O. Reg. 455/92, s. 1

ON Reg. 1015:235

Definitions: OSA 1(1)"promoter"; Reg.: 234"employee organization".

236. [Revoked O. Reg. 468/00, s. 6.]

237. [Repealed O. Reg. 31/08, s. 1.]

238. (1) The Director shall not refuse to issue a receipt for a prospectus of a labour sponsored investment fund corporation under subsection 61(1) or (2) of the Act if the circumstance forming the basis for a refusal under subsection 61(1) or (2) of the Act is permitted under the *Labour Sponsored Venture Capital Corporations Act, 1992* or this Part.

ON Reg. 1015:238(1)

Related Provisions: OSA 61(1), (2).

(2) Despite subsection 61(1) of the Act, the Director shall not issue a receipt for a prospectus of a labour sponsored investment fund corporation if,

(a) it appears to the Director that the corporation is in contravention of this Part; or

(b) the Director receives notice from the Minister of Revenue that the Minister of Revenue has served notice under section 31 of the *Labour Sponsored Venture Capital Corporations Act, 1992* of a proposal to revoke the registration of the labour sponsored investment fund corporation.

ON Reg. 1015:238(2)

Related Provisions: OSA 61(1).

(3) Clause (2)(b) ceases to apply if the Director receives notice from the Minister of Revenue that the Minister of Revenue will not revoke the registration of the labour sponsored investment fund corporation.

(4) The Director shall not refuse to issue a receipt under clause (2)(a) before giving the labour sponsored investment fund corporation that filed the prospectus an opportunity to be heard.

(5) Immediately after making a decision to refuse to issue a receipt under clause (2)(a), the Director shall notify the Commission of the decision.

(6) Within thirty days of the Director's decision to refuse to issue a receipt under clause (2)(a), the Commission may notify the Director and any person or company directly affected by the Director's decision of the Commission's intention to convene a hearing to review the decision.

O. Reg. 455/92, s. 1

ON Reg. 1015:238

Definitions: OSA 1(1)"Director"; 1(1)"decision"; 1(1)"person"; 1(1)"company"; 1(1)"distribution"; Reg.: 234"labour sponsored investment fund corporation".

239. The Commission shall not make an order under subsection 70(1) of the Act requiring that the distribution of securities under a prospectus of a labour sponsored investment fund corporation cease, if the circumstance forming the basis for an order under subsection 70(1) of the Act is permitted under the *Labour Sponsored Venture Capital Corporations Act, 1992* or this Part.

O. Reg. 455/92, s. 1

ON Reg. 1015:239

Related Provisions: OSA 70(1).

Definitions: OSA 1(1)"Commission"; 1(1)"distribution"; 1(1)"security"; Reg.: 234"labour sponsored investment fund corporation".

240. (1) If a rule, policy or practice of the Commission or the Director pertaining to mutual funds conflicts with a provision of the *Labour Sponsored Venture Capital Corporations Act, 1992* pertaining to labour sponsored investment fund corporations, the rule, policy or practice of the Commission or the Director pertaining to mutual funds shall not apply to labour sponsored investment fund corporations.

(2) Without limiting the generality of subsection (1), a rule, policy or practice of the Commission or the Director respecting any of the following subjects shall not apply to labour sponsored investment fund corporations:

1. The incorporation and initial capitalization of mutual funds.

2. Investment restrictions on mutual funds.

3. The borrowing of money by mutual funds.

4. The making of illiquid investments by mutual funds.

5. The lending of money by mutual funds.

6. The guaranteeing by mutual funds of debts or obligations of other persons or companies.

7. The management or control of other issuers by mutual funds.

8. The sale or redemption of securities of mutual funds.

9. [Repealed O. Reg. 215/05, s. 7(2).]

O. Reg. 455/92, s. 1; 3/00, s. 5; 215/05, s. 7

ON Reg. 1015:240

Definitions: OSA 1(1)"mutual fund"; 1(1)"Commission"; 1(1)"Director"; Reg.: 234"labour sponsored investment fund corporation".

Policies and Orders: OSCN 81-706.

241. For the purpose of subsection 107(1) of the Act, a labour sponsored investment fund corporation shall be deemed not to be a mutual fund.

O. Reg. 455/92, s. 1

ON Reg. 1015:241

Related Provisions: OSA 107(1).

Definitions: OSA 1(1)"mutual fund"; Reg.: 234"labour sponsored investment fund corporation".

242. Despite clause 110(2)(b) of the Act, for the purposes of sections 111 to 115 of the Act, an eligible investment of a labour sponsored investment fund corporation shall be deemed not to be an investment by the labour sponsored investment fund corporation in a person or company in which it is a substantial securityholder.

O. Reg. 455/92, s. 1

ON Reg. 1015:242

Related Provisions: OSA 110(2)(b), 111–115.

Definitions: OSA 1(1)"person"; 1(1)"company"; Reg.: 234"eligible investment"; 1(1)"labour sponsored investment fund corporation".

243. When a labour sponsored investment fund corporation provides to its shareholders a quarterly or annual share valuation in accordance with its undertaking under clause 14(1)(h) of the *Labour Sponsored Venture Capital Corporations Act, 1992*, the corporation shall file with the Commission a copy of the valuation and a copy of all reports prepared by or for the corporation about the valuation.

O. Reg. 455/92, s. 1

ON Reg. 1015:243

Definitions: OSA 1(1)"Commission"; Reg.: 234"labour sponsored investment fund corporation".

Rules: NI 81-106, Part 8.

244. A labour sponsored investment fund corporation is exempt from the requirements of Part IV that are inconsistent with the *Labour Sponsored Venture Capital Corporations Act, 1992* or the regulations made under that Act.

O. Reg. 455/92, s. 1

ON Reg. 1015:244

Definitions: Reg.: 234"labour sponsored investment fund corporation".

Regulations: Reg.: Part IV.

245. The Commission may exempt any person or company from a requirement of this Regulation that relates to labour sponsored investment fund corporations or may vary a provision of this Regulation that relates to labour sponsored investment fund corporations as it applies to any person or company, if the Commission is satisfied that to do so would not be prejudicial to the public interest, having regard to the spirit and intent of the *Labour Sponsored Venture Capital Corporations Act, 1992*.

O. Reg. 455/92, s. 1

ON Reg. 1015:245

Definitions: OSA 1(1)"Commission"; 1(1)"person"; 1(1)"company"; Reg.: 234"labour sponsored investment fund corporation".

PART XV — ELECTRONIC FILING

246. Despite the requirement for manual or facsimile signatures in section 11, and sections 64, 93, 161 and 181, a document to be filed in electronic format under the rule entitled National Instrument 13-101 — System for Electronic Document Analysis and Retrieval (SEDAR) that is subject to any of those provisions shall be signed in the manner required under that rule.

O. Reg. 549/96, s. 3; 636/00, s. 9

ON Reg. 1015:246

Regulations: Reg.: 161.

Rules: NI 13-101.

247. Despite the requirement to file in duplicate or triplicate in subsections 6(1) and 12(1), and section 203, a document to be filed in electronic format under the rule entitled National Instrument 13-101 — System for Electronic Document Analysis and Retrieval (SEDAR) that is subject to any of those provisions shall be filed in the manner required under that rule.

O. Reg. 549/96, s. 3; 423/01, s. 3

ON Reg. 1015:247

Rules: NI 13-101.

PART XVI — CIVIL LIABILITY FOR SECONDARY MARKET DISCLOSURE

[Heading added O. Reg. 453/05, s. 19.]

248. In this Part,

"equity security" means a security of an issuer that carries a residual right to participate in the earnings of the issuer and, on liquidation or winding up of the issuer, in its assets.

O. Reg. 130/16, s. 2

249. For the purposes of Part XXIII.1 of the Act, **"market capitalization"** means, in respect of an issuer, the amount determined as follows:

1. For each class of equity securities for which there is a published market, determine the sum of the number of outstanding securities of the class at the close of trading on each of the 10 trading days before the day on which the misrepresentation was made or the failure to make timely disclosure first occurred.

2. Divide the sum determined under paragraph 1 by 10.

3. Multiply the quotient determined under paragraph 2 for each class by the trading price of the securities of the class on the principal market for the securities for the 10 trading days before the day on which the misrepresentation was made or the failure to make timely disclosure first occurred.

4. Add the amounts determined under paragraph 3 for each class of equity securities for which there is a published market.

5. For each class of equity securities not traded on a published market, determine the fair market value of the outstanding securities of that class as of the day on which the misrepresentation was made or the failure to make timely disclosure first occurred.

6. Add the amounts determined under paragraph 5 for each class of equity securities not traded on a published market.

7. Add the amount determined under paragraph 4 to the amount determined under paragraph 6 to determine the market capitalization of the issuer.

O. Reg. 453/05, s. 19

250. For the purposes of Part XXIII.1 of the Act,

"principal market" means, in respect of a class of securities of a responsible issuer,

(a) the published market in Canada on which the greatest volume of trading in securities of that class occurred during the 10 trading days before the day on which the misrepresentation was made or the failure to make timely disclosure first occurred, or

(b) the published market on which the greatest volume of trading in securities of that class occurred during the 10 trading days before the day on which the misrepresentation was made or the failure to make timely disclosure first occurred, if securities of that class are not traded during those 10 trading days on a published market in Canada.

O. Reg. 453/05, s. 19

251. For the purposes of Part XXIII.1 of the Act, **"trading price"** means, in respect of a security of a class of securities for which there is a published market, the amount determined under the following rules:

1. Subject to paragraphs 2 and 3, the trading price of the security is the volume weighted average price of securities of that class on the published market during the period for which the trading price is to be determined.

2. Subject to paragraph 3, if there was trading in the securities of that class in the published market on fewer than half of the trading days during the period for which the trading price of the securities is to be determined, the trading price of the security is determined as follows:

    i. Calculate the sum of the average of the highest bid and lowest ask prices for each trading day in the period on which there were no trades in securities of that class in the published market.

    ii. Divide the amount determined under subparagraph i by the number of trading days on which there were no trades in securities of that class in the published market.

    iii. Add to the amount determined under subparagraph ii the volume weighted average price of securities of that class on the published market for those trading days on which securities of that class were traded.

    iv. Divide by two the amount determined under subparagraph iii.

3. If there were no trades of securities of that class in the published market during the period for which the trading price is to be determined, the trading price of the security is the fair market value of the security.

O. Reg. 453/05, s. 19

252. (1) Part XXIII.1 of the Act applies to the acquisition of an issuer's security pursuant to an exemption from section 53 or 62 of the Act that is set out in clause 72(7)(b) of the Act, which exemption is prescribed for the purposes of clause 138.2(b) of the Act.

(2) Part XXIII.1 of the Act applies to the acquisition or disposition of an issuer's security in connection with or pursuant to a take-over bid that is exempt under section 4.1, 4.4 or 4.5 of National Instrument 62-104 Take-Over Bids and Issuer Bids or an issuer bid that is exempt under section 4.8, 4.10 or 4.11 of National Instrument 62-104 Take-Over Bids and Issuer Bids.

O. Reg. 453/05, s. 19; 589/07, s. 4; 130/16, s. 3

Related Provisions: OSA Part XXIII.1.

Schedule 1 [Heading revoked O. Reg. 48/03, s. 3.]

[Revoked O. Reg. 48/03, s. 3.]

Form 1 — Summons to a Witness Before a Person Appointed Under Section..........of the Act

RE:................................

TO:................................

You are hereby summoned and required to attend before me at an examination to be held at .... in the .... of .... on ....day the .... day of ...., 19.......... at the hour of .... o'clock in the .... noon (local time), and so from day to day until the examination is concluded to give evidence on oath in connection with an investigation ordered by .... and to bring with you and produce at such time and place ....

Dated this..........day of.........., 19..........

ONTARIO SECURITIES COMMISSION

(Signature)

Name . . . .

Title . . . .

Form 1

Regulations: Reg.: 163.

Form 2 — Affidavit of Service

Securities Act

Province of Ontario)
)
.... of ....)
)
)
)
)
)

IN THE MATTER OF THE *SECURITIES ACT*

AND

IN THE MATTER OF . . . .

I, ...of the .... of ....in the .... of ....make oath and say that:

1. I did on the..........day of ...., 19..........personally serve................................ at about...................................with a true copy of the summons annexed hereto by delivering the same to and leaving the same with .... at the................................of . . . . . . in the................................. of ....

2. I did at the same time and place produce and pay the sum of..........Dollars conduct money.

3. To effect such service I necessarily travelled .... miles.

SWORN before me at the . . . .)
of . . . . in the ....)
of . . . . , this ....)
day of . . . . , 19 ....)
A Commissioner, etc.

. . . .
(signature)

Form 2

Regulations: Reg.: 163.

Form 3 [Repealed O. Reg. 358/09, s. 7.]

[Repealed O. Reg. 358/09, s. 7.]

Form 4 [Heading revoked O. Reg. 16/03, s. 6.]

[Revoked O. Reg. 16/03, s. 6.]

Form 5 [Repealed O. Reg. 358/09, s. 7.]

[Repealed O. Reg. 358/09, s. 7.]

Form 6 [Repealed O. Reg. 358/09, s. 7.]

[Repealed O. Reg. 358/09, s. 7.]

Form 7 [Repealed O. Reg. 453/05, s. 22.]

[Repealed O. Reg. 453/05, s. 22.]

Form 8 — Summons to a Witness Before a Person Designated under Section 31 of the Act

Securities Act

RE: ....

TO: ....

You are hereby summoned and required by the Director to attend before me .... at an examination to be held at .... in the .... of .... on .... day the .... day of .... 19.......... at the hour of............................. o'clock in the .... noon (local time), and so from day until the examination is concluded, to give evidence on oath and to bring with you and produce at such time and place ....

Dated at ...., this .... day of ...., 19..........

ONTARIO SECURITIES COMMISSION

....

(Signature)

Form 8

Related Provisions: OSA 31.

Regulations: Reg.: 134.

Form 9 [Repealed O. Reg. 358/09, s. 7.]

[Repealed O. Reg. 358/09, s. 7.]

Form 10 [Repealed O. Reg. 357/09, s. 5.]

[Repealed O. Reg. 357/09, s. 5.]

Form 11 [Revoked O. Reg. 424/01, s. 6.]

[Revoked O. Reg. 424/01, s. 6.]

Form 12 [Revoked O. Reg. 632/00, s. 11.]

[Revoked O. Reg. 632/00, s. 11.]

Form 13 [Revoked O. Reg. 632/00, s. 11.]

[Revoked O. Reg. 632/00, s. 11.]

Form 14 [Revoked O. Reg. 632/00, s. 11.]

[Revoked O. Reg. 632/00, s. 11.]

Form 15 [Repealed O. Reg. 31/08, s. 2.]

[Repealed O. Reg. 31/08, s. 2.]

Form 16 [Revoked O. Reg. 91/01, s. 6.]

[Revoked O. Reg. 91/01, s. 6.]

Form 17 [Repealed O. Reg. 453/05, s. 22.]

[Repealed O. Reg. 453/05, s. 22.]

Form 18 [Repealed O. Reg. 453/05, s. 22.]

[Repealed O. Reg. 453/05, s. 22.]

Form 19 [Repealed O. Reg. 453/05, s. 22.]

[Repealed O. Reg. 453/05, s. 22.]

Form 20 [Revoked O. Reg. 662/98, s. 3.]

[Revoked O. Reg. 662/98, s. 3.]

Form 21 [Revoked O. Reg. 662/98, s. 3.]

[Revoked O. Reg. 662/98, s. 3.]

Form 22 [Revoked O. Reg. 423/01, s. 5.]

[Revoked O. Reg. 423/01, s. 5.]

Form 23 [Revoked O. Reg. 423/01, s. 5.]

[Revoked O. Reg. 423/01, s. 5.]

Form 24 [Repealed O. Reg. 491/05, s. 13.]

[Repealed O. Reg. 491/05, s. 13.]

Form 25 [Repealed O. Reg. 491/05, s. 13.]

[Repealed O. Reg. 491/05, s. 13.]

Form 26 [Repealed O. Reg. 491/05, s. 13.]

[Repealed O. Reg. 491/05, s. 13.]

Form 27 [Repealed O. Reg. 215/05, s. 8.]

[Repealed O. Reg. 215/05, s. 8.]

Form 28 [Revoked O. Reg. 56/04, s. 14(2).]

[Revoked O. Reg. 56/04, s. 14(2).]

Form 29 [Revoked O. Reg. 507/97, s. 4.]

[Revoked O. Reg. 507/97, s. 4.]

Form 30 [Repealed O. Reg. 215/05, s. 9.]

[Repealed O. Reg. 215/05, s. 9.]

Form 31 [Repealed O. Reg. 589/07, s. 3.]

[Repealed O. Reg. 589/07, s. 3.]

Form 32 [Repealed O. Reg. 589/07, s. 3.]

[Repealed O. Reg. 589/07, s. 3.]

Form 33 [Repealed O. Reg. 589/07, s. 3.]

[Repealed O. Reg. 589/07, s. 3.]

Form 34 [Repealed O. Reg. 589/07, s. 3.]

[Repealed O. Reg. 589/07, s. 3.]

Form 35 [Repealed O. Reg. 589/07, s. 3.]

[Repealed O. Reg. 589/07, s. 3.]

Form 36 — Insider Report

[Revoked O. Reg. 13/96, s. 1; Replaced by ON Rule 55-501F]

Form 37 — Report by a Registered Owner of Securities Beneficially Owned by an Insider

Securities Act

NOTE: THIS REPORT IS ONLY REQUIRED WHERE:

1. VOTING SECURITIES ARE TRANSFERRED INTO THE NAME OF A PERSON OR COMPANY OTHER THAN THE BENEFICIAL OWNER:

2. THE PERSON OR COMPANY KNOWS THAT:

(a) THEY ARE BENEFICIALLY OWNED BY AN INSIDER, AND

(b) THE INSIDER HAS FAILED TO FILE A REPORT OF SUCH OWNERSHIP WITH THE ONTARIO SECURITIES COMMISSION AS REQUIRED BY PART XX OF THE ACT; AND

3. THE TRANSFER WAS NOT FOR THE PURPOSE OF GIVING COLLATERAL FOR A DEBT MADE IN GOOD FAITH.

1. State the relationship between the undersigned and the insider.

2. Certificate (Instruction 1):

The undersigned hereby certifies that:

1. attached as an exhibit is an unexecuted insider trading report in respect of voting securities that are registered in the name of the undersigned but beneficially owned by the insider named in the report, and

2. the report has, in respect of such voting securities, been completed to the best of my information and belief.

. . . .

Date of Report   Signature (Instruction 2)

Instructions

1. Use as the exhibit the form of report the insider has failed to file as required by Part XX of the Act. Complete the report only in respect of voting securities. If required information is not known by the person or company completing the attached report mark "Not known" or "Complete information not known".

2. Please print the name and office of the person or company executing this report or on whose behalf this report is executed.

Form 37

Related Provisions: OSA Part XX, 109.

Definitions: OSA 1(1)"security"; 1(1)"insider"; 1(1)"voting security"; 1(1)"person"; 1(1)"company".

Regulations: Reg.: 168.

Rules: Rule 55-502.

Form 38 — Report under Section 117 of the Act

Securities Act

NAME OF THE MUTUAL FUND FOR WHICH THE MANAGEMENT COMPANY PROVIDES SERVICES AND ADVICE . . . .

. . . .

NAME OF THE MANAGEMENT COMPANY . . . .

. . . .

DATE OF THE TRANSACTION . . . .

. . . .

CATEGORY OF THE TRANSACTION (INSTRUCTION 1) . . . .

. . . .

PARTIES TO THE TRANSACTION . . . .

. . . .

NATURE OF THE TRANSACTION (INSTRUCTION 2) . . . .

. . . .

. . . .

The undersigned hereby certifies that the information given in this report is true and complete in every respect.

. . . .

Date of Report   Name of Management Company

                                  By . . . .

                                                          Signature

                                  . . . .

                                                       Official Capacity

Instructions

Instruction 1

Categorize each transaction as being a transaction of purchase and sale of securities between the mutual fund and a related person or company, a transaction or purchase and sale of securities resulting in a related person or company receiving a fee, a loan between the mutual fund and a related person or company or a transaction to which the mutual fund and a related person or company of the mutual fund are joint participants.

Instruction 2

Where the transaction is categorized as a purchase or sale of securities between the mutual fund and a related person or company, state the issuer of the securities purchased or sold, the class or designation of the securities, the amount or number of securities and the consideration.

Where the transaction is categorized as a purchase or sale of securities resulting in a related person or company receiving a fee, state the issuer of the securities purchased or sold, the class or designation of the securities, the amount or number of the securities, the consideration, the name of the related person or company receiving a fee, the name of the person or company that paid the fee to the related person or company and the amount of the fee received by the related person or company.

Where the transaction is categorizied as a loan between the mutual fund and a related person or company, state the name of the lender, the name of the borrower, the amount of money loaned, the terms of the loan and the purpose of the loan.

Where the transaction is categorized as one to which the mutual fund and one or more of its related persons or companies are joint participants, state terms of participation and the purpose of the transaction.

Form 38

Related Provisions: OSA 117.

Definitions: OSA 1(1)"management company"; 1(1)"mutual fund"; 1(1)"security"; 1(1)"person"; 1(1)"company".

Regulations: Reg.: 169.

Form 39 — Endorsement of Warrant

Securities Act

Province of Ontario)

....)

(territorial jurisdiction))

Pursuant to subsection 12(1) of the *Securities Act* and pursuant to application this day made to me, I hereby authorize the execution of this warrant within the said territorial jurisdiction.

Dated this .... day of .... 19..........,

at.................................

....

(a Provincial Judge or Justice in
and for the Province of Ontario)

Form 39

Related Provisions: OSA 12(1), 125(1).

Regulations: Reg.: 160.

Form 40 [Revoked O. Reg. 56/04, s. 14(4).]

[Revoked O. Reg. 56/04, s. 14(4).]

Form 41[1]

Form 42 [Revoked O. Reg. 48/03, s. 4.]

[Revoked O. Reg. 48/03, s. 4.]

Form 43 [Revoked O. Reg. 48/03, s. 4.]

[Revoked O. Reg. 48/03, s. 4.]

Form 44 [Revoked O. Reg. 48/03, s. 4.]

[Revoked O. Reg. 48/03, s. 4.]

Form 45 [Repealed O. Reg. 31/08, s. 2.]

[Repealed O. Reg. 31/08, s. 2.]

FORMS

---

[1]Editor's Note: Form 41, entitled "Application for Approval to be a Market-Maker in a COATS Security," while still in effect, is no longer used, as COATS has been superseded.

Ont. Reg. 261/02 — Toronto Stock Exchange Inc.

made under the *Securities Act*

O. Reg. 261/02

1. Restriction on shareholdings — Ten per cent is prescribed, for the purposes of subsection 21.11(1) of the Act, as the maximum percentage of any class or series of voting shares of The Toronto Stock Exchange Inc. that any person or company or combination of persons or companies acting jointly or in concert is permitted to beneficially own or exercise control or direction over, without the prior approval of the Commission.

ONT. REG. 85/05 — EXEMPTIONS RESPECTING THE ONTARIO FINANCING AUTHORITY

made under the *Securities Act*

O. Reg. 85/05, as am. O. Reg. 355/09.

1. Exemption re s. 25 of the Act — The Ontario Financing Authority is exempt from the requirements of section 25 of the Act in respect of any activities relating to trading, advising or acting as an underwriter or an investment fund manager if the activities are carried out in the fulfilment of its duties and responsibilities under the *Capital Investment Plan Act*.

O. Reg. 355/09, s. 1

2. [Repealed O. Reg. 355/09, s. 1.]

3. [Repealed O. Reg. 355/09, s. 1.]

RULES (INCLUDING NATIONAL INSTRUMENTS) AND POLICIES, RECOGNITION AND DESIGNATION ORDERS AND NOTICES WITH THE NATIONAL NUMBERING SYSTEM

The following section publishes the rules of the OSC and all of the policies, recognition and designation orders and notices for which a number has been assigned in accordance with the current five-digit numbering system used by the Canadian Securities' Administrators, as described in CSAN 11-312. Those National Policies, OSC Policies, Blanket Orders, Recognitions, Designations and Assignments and OSC Notices which have been assigned numbers according to the old numbering system, or which have not been assigned numbers, can be found in their own sections of the book.

RULES

PART I — PROCEDURE AND RELATED MATTERS
1.1 — General

See also BOR 1.1, 1.2, 1.3, 1.4, 1.5.

Multilateral Instrument 11-102 — Passport System

Date: March 17, 2008, as amended effective September 28, 2009, April 30, 2010, January 1, 2011, May 6, 2011, April 20, 2012, July 1, 2012, May 5, 2015, December 8, 2015 and April 3, 2016

31 O.S.C.B. 1009, 33 O.S.C.B. 645, 33 O.S.C.B. (Supp. 5) 36, 34 O.S.C.B. 5172, 8322 and 38 O.S.C.B. (Supp. 3) 28. [amendments are not always published in the O.S.C.B.]

[Editor's note: MI 11-102 and its Companion Policy have been adopted in all jurisdictions except Ontario. Although they are not in force in Ontario, they are included in this book to assist readers in interpreting NPS 11-202, 11-203, 11-204 and 11-205 which have numerous references to MI 11-102 and the Companion Policy. This version reflects the amendments as issued by the British Columbia Securities Commission, found in British Columbia Securities Act and Rules Annotated *and on WestlawNext Canada.]*

Table of Contents

4B.6 Deemed designation of a credit rating organization

PART 5 EFFECTIVE DATE

5.1 Effective date

APPENDIX A [Repealed]

APPENDIX B Prospectus provisions

APPENDIX C [Repealed]

APPENDIX D Equivalent provisions

PART 1 — DEFINITIONS

1.1 Definitions — In this Instrument,

"category" means a category of registration set out in NI 31-103;

"equivalent provision" means, for a provision listed in Appendix D below the name of a jurisdiction, the provision set opposite that provision below the name of another jurisdiction;

"firm" means a person or company that is registered, or is seeking registration, as a dealer, adviser or investment fund manager;

"foreign firm" means a firm that has its head office outside Canada;

"foreign individual" means an individual whose working office is outside Canada;

"Form 33-109F2" means Form 33-109F2 *Change or Surrender of Individual Categories* under NI 33-109;

"Form 33-109F4" means Form 33-109F4 *Registration of Individuals and Review of Permitted Individuals* under NI 33-109;

"Form 33-109F5" means Form 33-109F5 *Change of Registration Information* under NI 33-109;

"Form 33-109F6" means Form 33-109F6 *Firm Registration* under NI 33-109;

"national prospectus instrument" means

    (a) National Instrument 41-101 General Prospectus Requirements,

    (b) National Instrument 44-101 Short Form Prospectus Distributions,

    (c) National Instrument 44-102 *Shelf Distributions*,

    (d) National Instrument 44-103 *Post-Receipt Pricing*,

    (d.1) National Instrument 71-101 *The Multijurisdictional Disclosure System*, or

    (e) National Instrument 81-101 Mutual Fund Prospectus Disclosure;

"NI 31-103" means National Instrument 31-103 *Registration Requirements, Exemptions and Ongoing Registrant Obligations*;

"NI 33-109" means National Instrument 33-109 *Registration Information*;

"preliminary prospectus" includes an amendment to a preliminary prospectus;

"principal jurisdiction" means, for a person or company, the jurisdiction of the principal regulator;

"principal regulator" means, for a person or company, the securities regulatory authority or regulator determined in accordance with Part 3, 4 or 4A, as applicable;

"prospectus" includes an amendment to a prospectus;

"SEDAR" has the same meaning as in National Instrument 13-101 *System for Electronic Document Analysis and Retrieval*.

"sponsoring firm" has the same meaning as in NI 33-109;

"working office" means the office of the sponsoring firm where an individual does most of his or her business.

1.2 Language of documents — Québec — In Québec, nothing in this Instrument shall be construed as relieving a person from requirements relating to the language of documents.

PART 2 — [REPEALED]

PART 3 — PROSPECTUS

3.1 Principal regulator for prospectus — (1) For the purposes of this section, the specified jurisdictions are British Columbia, Alberta, Saskatchewan, Manitoba, Ontario, Québec, New Brunswick and Nova Scotia.

(2) Subject to subsection (3) and section 3.2, for the purposes of a prospectus filing subject to this Part the principal regulator is the securities regulatory authority or regulator of the jurisdiction in which

    (a) the issuer's head office is located, if the issuer is not an investment fund, or

    (b) the investment fund manager's head office is located, if the issuer is an investment fund.

(3) If the jurisdiction identified under paragraph (2)(a) or (b) is not a specified jurisdiction, the principal regulator is the securities regulatory authority or regulator of the specified jurisdiction with which the issuer or, in the case of an investment fund, the investment fund manager, has the most significant connection.

3.2 Discretionary change of principal regulator for prospectus — If a person or company receives written notice from a securities regulatory authority or regulator that specifies a principal regulator, the securities regulatory authority or regulator specified in the notice is the principal regulator as of the later of

    (a) the date the person or company receives the notice, and

    (b) the effective date specified in the notice, if any.

3.3 Deemed issuance of receipt — (1) Subject to section 3.5(1), a receipt for a preliminary prospectus is deemed to be issued if

(a) the preliminary prospectus is filed under a provision set out in Appendix B and under a national prospectus instrument,

(b) at the time of filing the preliminary prospectus, the filer indicates on SEDAR that it is filing the preliminary prospectus under this Instrument,

(c) the local jurisdiction is not the principal jurisdiction for the preliminary prospectus, and

(d) the preliminary prospectus is filed with the principal regulator and the principal regulator issues a receipt for it.

(2) A receipt for a prospectus is deemed to be issued if

(a) the prospectus is filed under a provision set out in Appendix B and under a national prospectus instrument,

(b) subject to section 3.5(2), the filer

(i) complied with paragraph (1)(b) at the time of filing the related preliminary prospectus, or

(ii) indicated on SEDAR that it filed the related pro forma prospectus under this Instrument at the time of filing the related pro forma prospectus,

(c) the local jurisdiction is not the principal jurisdiction for the prospectus, and

(d) the prospectus is filed with the principal regulator and the principal regulator issues a receipt for the prospectus.

3.4 [Repealed]

3.5 Transition for section 3.3 — (1) Section 3.3(1) does not apply in respect of a receipt issued on or after March 17, 2008 if the receipt relates to an amendment, filed after March 17, 2008, to a preliminary prospectus and the preliminary prospectus was filed before March 17, 2008.

(2) Section 3.3(2)(b) does not apply in respect of a receipt issued on or after March 17, 2008 if

(a) the receipt relates to an amendment to a prospectus whose related preliminary prospectus or pro forma prospectus was filed before March 17, 2008, and

(b) the filer indicated on SEDAR that it filed the amendment under this Instrument at the time of filing the amendment.

PART 4 — DISCRETIONARY EXEMPTIONS

4.1 Specified jurisdiction — For the purposes of this Part, the specified jurisdictions are British Columbia, Alberta, Saskatchewan, Manitoba, Ontario, Québec, New Brunswick and Nova Scotia.

4.2 Principal regulator — general — Subject to sections 4.3 to 4.6, the principal regulator for an application for an exemption is,

(a) for an application made with respect to an investment fund, the securities regulatory authority or regulator of the jurisdiction in which the investment fund manager's head office is located, or

(b) for an application made with respect to a person or company other than an investment fund, the securities regulatory authority or regulator of the jurisdiction in which the person or company's head office is located.

4.3 Principal regulator — exemptions related to insider reporting and take-over bids — Subject to sections 4.4 to 4.6, the principal regulator for an application for an exemption from

(a) a provision related to insider reporting listed in Appendix D is the securities regulatory authority or regulator of the jurisdiction in which the head office of the reporting issuer is located, or

(b) a provision related to take-over bids listed in Appendix D is the securities regulatory authority or regulator of the jurisdiction in which the head office of the issuer whose securities are subject to the take-over bid is located.

4.4 Principal regulator — head office not in a specified jurisdiction — Subject to sections 4.4.1, 4.5 and 4.6, if the jurisdiction identified under section 4.2 or 4.3, as applicable, is not a specified jurisdiction, the principal regulator for the application is the securities regulatory authority or regulator of the specified jurisdiction with which

(a) in the case of an application for an exemption from a provision related to insider reporting listed in Appendix D, the reporting issuer has the most significant connection,

(b) in the case of an application for an exemption related to a provision related to take-over bids listed in Appendix D, the issuer whose securities are subject to the take-over bid has the most significant connection, or

(c) in any other case, the person or company or, in the case of an investment fund, the investment fund manager, has the most significant connection.

4.4.1 Principal regulator for discretionary exemption application made with an application for registration — Subject to sections 4.5 and 4.6, if a firm or individual makes an application for exemption from a requirement listed below in connection with an application for registration in the principal jurisdiction, the principal regulator for the application for exemption is the principal regulator as determined under section 4A.1:

(a) a requirement in Parts 3 and 12 of NI 31-103;

(b) a requirement in Part 2 of NI 33-109.

4.5 Principal regulator — exemption not sought in principal jurisdiction — (1) Subject to section 4.6 and subsection (2), if a person or company is not seeking an exemption in the jurisdiction of the principal regulator, as determined under section 4.2, 4.3, 4.4 or 4.4.1, as applicable, the principal regulator for the application is the securities regulatory authority or regulator in the specified jurisdiction

(a) in which the person or company is seeking the exemption, and

(b) with which

(i) in the case of an application for an exemption from a provision related to insider reporting, the reporting issuer has the most significant connection,

(ii) in the case of an application for an exemption from a provision related to take-over bids, the issuer whose securities are subject to the take-over bid has the most significant connection, or

(iii) in any other case, the person or company, or in the case of an investment fund, the investment fund manager, has the most significant connection.

(2) Subject to section 4.6, if at any one time a person or company is seeking more than one exemption and not all of the exemptions are needed in the jurisdiction of the principal regulator, as determined under section 4.2, 4.3, 4.4 or 4.4.1 or subsection (1), as applicable, the person or company may make the application to the securities regulatory authority or regulator in the specified jurisdiction

(a) in which the person or company is seeking all of the exemptions, and

(b) with which

(i) in the case of an application for an exemption from a provision related to insider reporting, the reporting issuer has the most significant connection,

(ii) in the case of an application for exemption from a provision related to take-over bids, the issuer whose securities are subject to the take-over bid has the most significant connection, or

(iii) in any other case, the person or company, or in the case of an investment fund, the investment fund manager, has the most significant connection.

(3) If a person makes an application under subsection (2), the securities regulatory authority or regulator under that subsection is the principal regulator for the application.

4.6 Discretionary change of principal regulator for discretionary exemption applications — If a person or company receives written notice from a securities regulatory authority or regulator that specifies a principal regulator for the person or company's application, the securities regulatory authority or regulator specified in the notice is the principal regulator for the application.

4.7 Passport application of discretionary exemptions — (1) If an application is made in the principal jurisdiction for an exemption from a provision of securities legislation listed in Appendix D, the equivalent provision of the local jurisdiction does not apply if

(a) the local jurisdiction is not the principal jurisdiction for the application,

(b) the principal regulator for the application granted the exemption and the exemption is in effect,

(c) the person or company that made the application gives notice to the securities regulatory authority or regulator that this subsection is intended to be relied upon for the equivalent provision of the local jurisdiction, and

(d) the person or company relying on the exemption complies with any terms, conditions, restrictions or requirements imposed by the principal regulator as if they were imposed in the local jurisdiction.

(2) For the purpose of paragraph (1)(c), the person or company may give the notice referred to in that paragraph by giving it to the principal regulator.

4.8 Availability of passport for discretionary exemptions applied for before March 17, 2008 — (1) If, before March 17, 2008, an application was made in a specified jurisdiction for an exemption from a provision of securities legislation listed in Appendix D, the equivalent provision of the local jurisdiction does not apply if

(a) the local jurisdiction is not the specified jurisdiction,

(b) the securities regulatory authority or regulator in the specified jurisdiction granted the exemption whether the order was made before, on or after March 17, 2008,

(c) subject to subsection (3), the person or company that made the application gives notice to the securities regulatory authority or regulator that this subsection is intended to be relied upon for the equivalent provision of the local jurisdiction, and

(d) the person or company relying on the exemption complies with any terms, conditions, restrictions or requirements imposed by the securities regulatory authority or regulator in the specified jurisdiction as if they were imposed in the local jurisdiction.

(2) For the purpose of paragraph (1)(c), the person or company may give the notice referred to in that paragraph by giving it to the securities regulatory authority or regulator that would be the principal regulator under Part 4 if an application were to be made under that Part at the time the notice is given.

(3) Paragraph (1)(c) does not apply to a reporting issuer in respect of an exemption from a CD requirement, as defined in Multilateral Instrument 11-101 *Principal Regulator System*, if, before March 17, 2008,

(a) the principal regulator, identified under that Instrument, granted the exemption, and

(b) the reporting issuer filed the notice of principal regulator under section 2.2 or 2.3 of that Instrument.

PART 4A — REGISTRATION

4A.1 Principal regulator for registration — (1) Subject to subsections (2) and (3) and section 4A.2, for the purposes of this Part, the principal regulator is the securities regulatory authority or regulator of the jurisdiction in which,

(a) for a firm, the firm's head office is located, or

(b) for an individual, the individual's working office is located.

(2) The principal regulator for a foreign firm is the securities regulatory authority or regulator in the jurisdiction of Canada the firm identified

(a) in item 2.2(b) of its most recently submitted Form 33-109F6, or

(b) in its most recently submitted Form 33-109F5, if the change noted in that form relates to item 2.2(b) of Form 33-109F6.

(3) The principal regulator for a foreign individual is the principal regulator for the individual's sponsoring firm.

4A.2 Discretionary change of principal regulator for registration — If a securities regulatory authority or regulator gives written notice that specifies a principal regulator for the firm or individual, the securities regulatory authority or regulator specified in the notice is the principal regulator for the firm or individual as of the later of

(a) the date the firm or individual receives the notice, and

(b) the effective date specified in the notice, if any.

4A.3 Firm registration — (1) Subject to subsection (4), if a firm is registered in a category in its principal jurisdiction, the firm is registered in the same category in the local jurisdiction if

(a) the firm has submitted a completed Form 33-109F6 in accordance with NI 33-109, and

(b) in the case of a category for which securities legislation requires that the firm be a member of a self-regulatory organization, the firm is a member of the self-regulatory organization or is exempt from the requirement.

(2) A firm that makes a submission under subsection (1)(a) must pay the required fee at the time it makes the submission.

(3) For the purpose of subsection (1), the firm may make the submission by giving it to the principal regulator.

(4) Subsection (1) does not apply to a firm registered in the category of restricted dealer.

4A.4 Individual registration — (1) If an individual acting on behalf of a sponsoring firm is registered in a category in his or her principal jurisdiction, the individual is registered in the same category in the local jurisdiction if

(a) the sponsoring firm is registered in the local jurisdiction in the same category as in the firm's principal jurisdiction,

(b) the individual has submitted a completed Form 33-109F2 or a completed Form 33-109F4 in accordance with NI 33-109, and

(c) in the case of a category for which securities legislation requires that the individual be a member or an approved person of a self-regulatory organization, the individual is a member or approved person of the self-regulatory organization or is exempt from the requirement.

(2) An individual who makes a submission under subsection (1)(b) must pay the required fee at the time the individual makes the submission.

4A.5 Terms and conditions of registration — (1) If a firm or individual is registered in the same category in the principal jurisdiction and in the local jurisdiction, a term, condition, restriction or requirement imposed on the registration in the principal jurisdiction applies as if it were imposed in the local jurisdiction.

(2) A term, condition, restriction or requirement that applies in the local jurisdiction under subsection (1) continues to apply until the earlier of the date

(a) the securities regulatory authority or regulator that imposed the term, condition, restriction or requirement cancels or revokes it, or

(b) the term, condition, restriction or requirement expires.

4A.6 Suspension — If a firm's or individual's registration in the principal jurisdiction is suspended, the firm's or individual's registration in the local jurisdiction is suspended.

4A.7 Termination — If a firm's or individual's registration in the principal jurisdiction is cancelled, revoked or terminated, as applicable, the firm's or individual's registration in the local jurisdiction is cancelled, revoked or terminated, as applicable.

4A.8 Surrender — If a firm or individual is registered in the same category in the local jurisdiction and the principal jurisdiction, and the firm or individual applies to surrender the registration in the principal jurisdiction, the firm's or individual's registration in that category in the local jurisdiction is cancelled, revoked or terminated, as applicable, if the principal regulator accepts the firm's or individual's surrender of registration in the principal jurisdiction.

4A.9 Transition — terms and conditions in non-principal jurisdictions — (1) Subject to subsection (2), section 4A.5 does not apply to a firm or individual until October 28, 2009 if the firm or individual was registered in the local jurisdiction before September 28, 2009.

(2) Section 4A.5 does not apply to a firm or individual after October 28, 2009 if

(a) on or before October 28, 2009, the firm or individual applies to the securities regulatory authority or regulator for an exemption from section 4A.5, and

(b) the securities regulatory authority or regulator has not issued a decision rejecting the application and the application has not been withdrawn.

(3) Subject to subsection (4), if a firm or individual was registered in the same category in the principal jurisdiction and the local jurisdiction before September 28, 2009, a term, condition, restriction or requirement imposed on the registration in the local jurisdiction before October 28, 2009, if any, does not apply to the firm or individual on or after October 28, 2009 unless the term, condition, restriction or requirement was

(a) agreed to under a settlement agreement between the firm or individual and the securities regulatory authority or regulator, or

(b) imposed in a decision relating to the firm or individual made by the securities regulatory authority or regulator following a hearing.

(4) If a firm or individual applies for an exemption under subsection (2), subsection (3) does not apply unless

(a) the securities regulatory authority or regulator has issued a decision rejecting the application, or

(b) the application has been withdrawn.

4A.10 Notice of principal regulator for foreign firm — (1) If a foreign firm was registered in a category in the local jurisdiction and another jurisdiction of Canada before September 28, 2009, the firm must submit the information required in item 2.2(b) of Form 33-109F6 by submitting a Form 33-109F5 on or before October 28, 2009.

(2) For the purposes of subsection (1), the foreign firm may make the submission by giving it to the principal regulator.

PART 4B — APPLICATION TO BECOME A DESIGNATED RATING ORGANIZATION

4B.1 Specified jurisdiction — For the purposes of this Part, the specified jurisdictions are British Columbia, Alberta, Saskatchewan, Manitoba, Ontario, Québec, Nova Scotia and New Brunswick.

4B.2 Principal regulator — general — Subject to sections 4B.3 to 4B.5, the principal regulator for an application by a credit rating organization to become a designated rating organization is

(a) the securities regulatory authority or regulator of the jurisdiction in which the head office of the credit rating organization is located,

(b) if the head office for a credit rating organization is not in a jurisdiction of Canada, the securities regulatory authority or regulator of the jurisdiction in which the largest branch office of the credit rating organization is located, or

(c) if neither the head office or a branch office of the credit rating organization is located in a jurisdiction of Canada, the securities regulatory authority or regulator of the jurisdiction with which the credit rating organization has the most significant connection.

4B.3 **Principal regulator — head office not in a specified jurisdiction** — Subject to section 4B.5, if the jurisdiction identified under section 4B.2 is not a specified jurisdiction, the principal regulator for the application is the securities regulatory authority or regulator of the specified jurisdiction with which the credit rating organization has the most significant connection.

4B.4 **Principal regulator — designation not sought in principal jurisdiction** — Subject to section 4B.5 if a credit rating organization is not seeking to become a designated rating organization in the jurisdiction of the principal regulator, as determined under section 4B.2 or 4B.3, as applicable, the principal regulator for the designation is the securities regulatory authority or regulator in the specified jurisdiction

(a) in which the credit rating organization is seeking the designation, and

(b) with which the credit rating organization has the most significant connection.

4B.5 **Discretionary change of principal regulator for application for designation** — If a credit rating organization receives written notice from a securities regulatory authority or regulator that specifies a principal regulator for the credit rating organization's application, the securities regulatory authority or regulator specified in the notice is the principal regulator for the designation.

4B.6 **Deemed designation of a credit rating organization** — (1) If an application to become a designated rating organization is made by a credit rating organization in the principal jurisdiction, the credit rating organization is deemed to be a designated rating organization in a local jurisdiction if

(a) the local jurisdiction is not the principal jurisdiction for the application,

(b) the principal regulator for the application designated the credit rating organization and that designation is in effect,

(c) the credit rating organization that applied to be designated gives notice to the securities regulatory authority or regulator that this subsection is intended to be relied upon for the designation in the local jurisdiction, and

(d) the credit rating organization complies with any terms, conditions, restrictions or requirements imposed by the principal regulator as if they were imposed in the local jurisdiction.

(2) For the purpose of paragraph (1)(c), the credit rating organization may give the notice referred to in that paragraph by giving it to the principal regulator.

PART 5 — EFFECTIVE DATE

5.1 **Effective date** — This Instrument comes into force on March 17, 2008.

APPENDIX A — [REPEALED]

APPENDIX B — PROSPECTUS PROVISIONS

Jurisdiction	Securities Act provisions
British Columbia	sections 61(1) (*Prospectus required*) and 62 (*Voluntary filing of prospectus*)
Alberta	section 110 (*Filing prospectus*)
Saskatchewan	section 58 (*Prospectus required*)
Manitoba	sections 37(1) (*Prohibition as to trading*) and 37(1.1) (*Voluntary filing of non-offering prospectus*)
Ontario	section 53 (*Prospectus required*)
Québec	sections 11 (*Prospectus required*), 12 (*Distribution outside Québec*), and 68 (para 2) (*Voluntary filing of prospectus*)
New Brunswick	section 71 (*Filing of preliminary prospectus and prospectus required and voluntary filing of prospectus*)
Nova Scotia	sections 58(1) (*Prospectus required*) and 58(2) (*Prospectus to enable issuer to become a reporting issuer where no distribution is contemplated*)
Prince Edward Island	sections 94 (*Prospectus required*) and 95 (*Filing prospectus without distribution*)
Newfoundland and Labrador	sections 54.(1) (*Prospectus required*) and 54.(2) (*Prospectus to enable issuer to become a reporting issuer where no distribution is contemplated*)
Yukon	sections 94 (*Prospectus required*) and 95 (*Filing prospectus without distribution*)
Northwest Territories	sections 94 (*Prospectus required*) and 95 (*Filing prospectus without distribution*)
Nunavut	sections 94 (*Prospectus required*) and 95 (*Filing prospectus without distribution*)

APPENDIX C — [REPEALED]

APPENDIX D — EQUIVALENT PROVISIONS

All references are to provisions of the *Securities Act* of the relevant jurisdiction unless otherwise noted. All references to 'NI' are to 'National Instruments". All references to 'MI' are to 'Multilateral Instruments'.

Provision	British Columbia	Alberta	Saskatchewan	Manitoba	Québec	Nova Scotia	New Brunswick	Prince Edward Island	Newfoundland and Labrador	Yukon	Northwest Territories	Nunavut	Ontario
SEDAR							NI 13-101						
Marketplace operation			NI 21-101 (only Parts 3, 4, 7, 8, 11 and 13 and sections 5.1(1), 5.1(2), 5.9, 5.10, 6.1, 6.2, 6.3, 6.7, 6.9 and 6.11, as those parts and sections apply to an ATS)										
Trading rules			NI 23-101 (only Parts 4 and 8-11)										
Use of client brokerage commissions							NI 23-102						
Electronic trading and direct electronic access to marketplaces			NI 23-103 (only sections 3(1), 3(2), 3(3)(a) to 3(7), 4, 4.2, 4.3, 4.4(a)(ii), 4.4(a)(iii), 4.4(a)(v) to 4.4(a)(vii), 4.4(b), 4.5, 4.7, and 5(3))										
Institutional trade matching and settlement							NI 24-101						
Designated rating organizations							NI 25-101						
National registration database (NRD)							NI 31-102						
Registration requirements							NI 31-103 (except as noted below)						
Dealing representative category						s.2.1(1)(a) of NI 31-103							s. 25(1)(b)
Advising representative category						s.2.1(1)(b) of NI 31-103							s. 25(3)(b)
Associate advising representative category						s.2.1(1)(c) of NI 31-103							s. 25(3)(c)
Ultimate designated person registration	s.2.1(1)(d) of NI 31-103	ss. 75(2)(c) and 75.1 of Securities Act and s.2.1(1)(d) of NI 31-103	s. 27(3) of Securities Act and s.2.1(1)(d) of NI 31-103		Paragraph 2 of s. 149 of Securities Act and s. 2.1(1)(d) of NI 31-103	s.2.1(1)(d) of NI 31-103			ss. 26(2)(c) and 26.1 of Securities Act and s.2.1(1)(d) of NI 31-103	s. 87 of Securities Act and s.2.1(1)(d) of NI 31-103	s. 87 of Securities Act and s.2.1(1)(d) of NI 31-103	s. 87 of Securities Act and s.2.1(1)(d) of NI 31-103	s. 25(5)
Chief compliance officer registration	s.2.1(1)(e) of NI 31-103	ss. 75(2)(c) and 75.1 of Securities Act and s.2.1(1)(e) of NI 31-103	s. 27(3) of Securities Act and s.2.1(1)(e) of NI 31-103		Paragraph 2 of s. 149 of Securities Act and s.2.1(1)(e) of NI 31-103	s.2.1(1)(e) of NI 31-103			ss. 26(2)(c) and 26.1 of Securities Act and s.2.1(1)(e) of NI 31-103	s. 87 of Securities Act and s.2.1(1)(e) of NI 31-103	s. 87 of Securities Act and s.2.1(1)(e) of NI 31-103	s. 87 of Securities Act and s.2.1(1)(e) of NI 31-103	s. 25(6)
Dealing representative of a mutual fund must be approved person	s.3.15(2) of NI 31-103		s.3.15(2) of NI 31-103		n/a				s.3.15(2) of NI 31-103				

Provision	British Columbia	Alberta	Saskatchewan	Manitoba	Québec	Nova Scotia	New Brunswick	Prince Edward Island	Newfoundland and Labrador	Yukon	Northwest Territories	Nunavut	Ontario
Employment, partnership or agency relationship ends						s.6.1 of NI 31-103							s. 29(3)
Suspension of IIROC approval for individual						s.6.2 of NI 31-103							s.29(1), paragraph 3
Suspension of MFDA approval for individual			s.6.3 of NI 31-103		n/a				s.6.3 of NI 31-103				s. 29(1), paragraph 3
Sponsoring firm suspended						s.6.4 of NI 31-103							s. 29(2)
Revocation of a suspended registration — individual						s.6.6 of NI 31-103							s.29(5)
Exception for individuals involved in a hearing						s.6.7 of NI 31-103							s. 29(6)
Dealer categories						s.7.1(1) of NI 31-103							s. 26(2)
Adviser categories						s.7.2(1) of NI 31-103							s. 26(6)
Investment fund manager category						s.7.3 of NI 31-103							s.25(4)
MFDA membership for mutual fund dealers			s.9.2 of NI 31-103		n/a					s.9.2 of NI 31-103			
Suspension or revocation of IIROC membership						s.10.2 of NI 31-103							s. 29(1) paragraph 2
Suspension of MFDA firm membership			s.10.3 of NI 31-103		n/a				s.10.3 of NI 31-103				s. 29(1), paragraph 2
Revocation of a suspended registration — firm						s.10.5 of NI 31-103							s. 29(5)
Exception for firms involved in a hearing						s.10.6 of NI 31-103							s. 29(6)

Part 1:
PROCEDURE

Provision	British Columbia	Alberta	Saskatchewan	Manitoba	Québec	Nova Scotia	New Brunswick	Prince Edward Island	Newfoundland and Labrador	Yukon	Northwest Territories	Nunavut	Ontario
Provide records to regulator			s.11.6(1)(c) of NI 31-103										s. 19(3)
Insurance — scholarship plan dealer only		s.12.3 of NI 31-103			n/a				s.12.3 of NI 31-103				
Complaint handling		s.13.15 of NI 31-103			s.168.1.1 of *Securities Act* and s.13.15 of NI 31-103				s.13.15 of NI 31-103				
Dispute resolution service		s.13.16 of NI 31-103			s.168.1.3 of *Securities Act* and s.13.16 of NI 31-103				s.13.16 of NI 31-103				
Underwriting conflicts							NI 33-105						
Registrant information							NI 33-109						
Prospectus disclosure requirements							NI 41-101 (except as noted below)						
Certificate of issuer						s.5.3(1) of NI 41-101							s. 58
Certificate of corporate issuer						s.5.4(1) of NI 41-101							s. 58
Certificate of issuer involved in reverse takeover						s.5.8 of NI 41-101							n/a
Certificate of underwriter						s.5.9(1) of NI 41-101							s. 59(1)
Certificate of promoter						s.5.11(1) of NI 41-101							s. 58
Delivery of amendments						s.6.4 of NI 41-101							s. 57(3)
Amendment to a preliminary prospectus						s.6.5(1) of NI 41-101							s. 57(1)
Amendment to a final prospectus						s.6.6(1) of NI 41-101							s. 57(1)
Amendment to a final prospectus						s.6.6(2) of NI 41-101							s. 57(2)
Regulator must issue receipt						s.6.6(3) of NI 41-101							s. 57(2.1)

Provision	British Columbia	Alberta	Saskatchewan	Manitoba	Québec	Nova Scotia	New Brunswick	Prince Edward Island	Newfoundland and Labrador	Yukon	Northwest Territories	Nunavut	Ontario
Regulator must not refuse a receipt						s.6.6(4) of NI 41-101							ss. 57(2.1) and 61(3)
Prohibition against distribution						s.6.6(5) of NI 41-101							s. 57(2.2)
Distribution of preliminary prospectus and distribution list						s.16.1 of NI 41-101							ss.66 and 67
Lapse date						s.17.2 of NI 41-101							s. 62
Statement of rights						s.18.1 of NI 41-101							s.60
Disclosure standards for mineral projects							NI 43-101						
Short form prospectus distribution requirements							NI 44-101						
Shelf prospectus requirements							NI 44-102						
Post receipt pricing							NI 44-103						
Rights offering requirements							[Repealed]						
Resale of securities							NI 45-102						
Standards of disclosure for oil and gas activities							NI 51-101						
Continuous disclosure obligations						NI 51-102 (except as noted below)							
Publication of material change						s.7.1 of NI 51-102							s. 75 of *Securities Act* and s. 15 3(1.1) of Regulation 1015 (General)
Accounting principles and auditing standards requirements						NI 52-107 (except as noted below)							
Acceptable accounting principles						s.3.2 of NI 52-107							s.3.2 of NI 52-107
Auditor oversight							NI 52-108						
Certification of disclosure in annual and interim filings							NI 52-109						
Audit committees							NI 52-110						

Part 1: PROCEDURE

Provision	British Columbia	Alberta	Saskatchewan	Manitoba	Québec	Nova Scotia	New Brunswick	Prince Edward Island	Newfoundland and Labrador	Yukon	Northwest Territories	Nunavut	Ontario
Communication with beneficial owners							NI 54-101						
System for electronic disclosure by insiders (SEDI)							NI 55-102						
Insider reporting requirements							NI 55-104 (except as noted below)							NI 55-104 (except as noted below)
Primary insider reporting requirement							Part 3 of NI 55-104							s. 107
Disclosure of corporate governance practices							NI 58-101						
Protection of minority security holders in special transactions			n/a		MI 61-101				n/a				MI 61-101
Early warning reports and other take-over bid and insider reporting requirements							NI 62-103						
Take-over bid and issuer bid requirements							NI 62-104						
Multi-jurisdictional disclosure system							NI 71-101						
Mutual fund prospectus disclosure							NI 81-101 (except as noted below)						
Amendment to a preliminary simplified prospectus						s.2.2.1(1) of NI 81-101							s. 57(1)
Delivery of amendments						s.2.2.2 of NI 81-101							s. 57(3)
Amendment to a simplified prospectus						s.2.2.3(1) of NI 81-101							s. 57(1)
Amendment to a simplified prospectus						s.2.2.3(2) of NI 81-101							s. 57(2)
Regulator must issue receipt						s.2.2.3(3) of NI 81-101							s. 57(2.1)
Regulator must not refuse a receipt						s.2.2.3(4) of NI 81-101							ss. 57(2.1) and 61(3)
Lapse date						s.2.5 of NI 81-101							s. 62

Provision	British Columbia	Alberta	Saskatchewan	Manitoba	Québec	Nova Scotia	New Brunswick	Prince Edward Island	Newfoundland and Labrador	Yukon	Northwest Territories	Nunavut	Ontario
Statement of rights							s.2.8 of NI 81-101						s. 60
Distribution of preliminary simplified prospectus and distribution list							s.3.2(3) of NI 81-101						ss. 66 and 67
Certificate of mutual fund						s.5.1.3(1) of NI 81-101							s. 58
Certificate of promoter						s.5.1.6(1) of NI 81-101							s. 58
Certificate of corporate mutual fund						s.5.1.7(1) of NI 81-101							s. 58
Mutual fund requirements							NI 81-102						
Commodity pools							NI 81-104						
Mutual fund sales practices							NI 81-105						
Investment fund continuous disclosure							NI 81-106						
Independent review committee							NI 81-107						
Registration													
Dealer/underwriter registration requirement	ss.34(1)(a) and 34(1)(d)	ss.75(1)(a) and 75(2)(a)	s.27(2)(a)	ss.6(1)(a) and 6(1)(d)	ss.148 and 149	ss.31(1) and 31(4)	ss.45(a) and 45(d)	ss.86(1)(a) and 86(2)	s.26(1)(a)	ss.86(1)(a) and 86(2)	ss.86(1)(a) and 86(2)	ss.86(1)(a) and 86(2)	ss. 25(1) and (2)
Adviser registration requirement	s.34(1)(b)	ss.75(1)(b) and 75(2)(b)	s.27(2)(b)	s.6(1)(b)	ss.148 and 149	ss.31(2) and 31(4)	s.45(b)	s.86(1)(b)	s.26(1)(b)	s.86(1)(b)	s.86(1)(b)	s.86(1)(b)	s. 25(3)
Investment fund manager registration requirement	s.34(1)(c)	s.75(1)(c)	s.27(2)(c)	s.6(1)(c)	s.148	ss.31(3) and 31(4)	s.45(c)	s.86(3)	s.26(1)(c)	s.86(3)	s.86(3)	s.86(3)	s. 25(4)
Compensation or contingency trust fund	s.23 of Securities Rules	s.28 of ASC Rules (General)	s.23 of Regulations	n/a	s.196 of Securities Regulation	s.27 of General Securities Rules		n/a	s.98 of Regulation		n/a	n/a	s. 110 of Regulation 1015 (General)
Requirements when using registration exemptions													
Offering memorandum in required form						s.3.9(5) of NI 45-106					n/a		n/a
Requirement to file offering memorandum within prescribed time						s.3.9(17) of NI 45-106							n/a
Trading in Securities Generally													
Registered dealer acting as principal	s.51		n/a	s.70			n/a		s.40		n/a	n/a	s. 39

Provision	British Columbia	Alberta	Saskatchewan	Manitoba	Québec	Nova Scotia	New Brunswick	Prince Edward Island	Newfoundland and Labrador	Yukon	Northwest Territories	Nunavut	Ontario
Disclosure of investor relations activities	s.52						s.62				n/a		
Use of name of another registrant	s.53	s.99	s.49	s.73	n/a	s.49	s.63	n/a	s.44		n/a		s. 43
Trading in Exchange Contracts													
Trading exchange contracts on an exchange in jurisdiction	s.58	s.106 & 107	s.40		n/a		s.70.1				n/a		
Trading exchange contracts on an exchange outside jurisdiction	s.59	s.108 & 109	s.41		n/a		s.70.2				n/a		
Prospectus													
Prospectus requirement	s.61	s.110	s.58	s.37	ss.11 and 12	s.58	s.71(1)	s.94	s.54	s.94	s.94	s.94	s. 53
Contents of prospectus (full, true & plain disclosure)	s.63	s.113	s.61	s.41	ss.13 and 20	s.61	s.74	s.99	s.57	s.99	s.99	s.99	s. 56
Waiting period communications	s.78	s.123	s.73	s.38	ss.21 & 22	s.70	s.82	s.97	s.66	s.97	s.97	s.97	s. 65(2)
Obligation to send prospectus	s.83	s.129	s.79	s.64	ss.29, 30, 31 and 32	s.76	s.88	s.101(1)	s.72	s.101(1)	s.101(1)	s.101(1)	s. 71(1)
Requirements when using prospectus exemptions													
Offering memorandum in required form	s. 2.9(5) of NI 45-106	s.2.9(5) & s.2.9(5.1) of NI 45-106	s.2.9(5) & s.2.9(5.1) of NI 45-106	s.2.9(5) of NI 45-106	s.2.9(5) and s.2.9(5.1) of NI 45-106	s.2.9(5) and s.2.9(5.1) of NI 45-106	s.2.9(5) and s.2.9(5.1) of NI 45-106	s.2.9(5) of NI 45-106	s.2.9(5) of NI 45-106	s.2.9(5) of NI 45-106	s.2.9(5) of NI 45-106	s.2.9(5) of NI 45-106	s. 2.9(5) s.2.9(5.1) of NI 45-106
Requirement to file offering memorandum within prescribed time						s. 2.9(14) of NI 45-106		s. 2.9(5) of NI 45-106					
Filing report of exempt distribution	ss.6.1 and 6.3 of NI 45-106	s.129.1 of ASC Rules (General) and ss.6.1 and 6.3 of NI 45-106	ss.6.1 and 6.3 of NI 45-106	s.7 of Regulation and ss.6.1 and 6.3 of NI 45-106				ss.6.1 and 6.3 of NI 45-106		ss.6.1 and 6.3 of NI 45-106			
Continuous Disclosure													
Voting if proxies provided	s.118	s.157	s.96	s.105	n/a	s.93	ss.102 and 103(2)	n/a	s.88		n/a		s. 87
Shares in name of registrant not to be voted	s.182 of Securities Rules	s.104	s.55	s.79	ss.164 and 165	s.55	s.103(3)–(7)	s.163	s.50	s.163	s.163	s.163	s. 49
Insider Reporting													
Insider reporting requirements	s. 87	s. 182	s. 116	s. 109	s. 89.3	s. 113	s. 135	s. 1 of Local Rule 55-501	s. 108	s. 1 of Local Rule 55-501	s. 2 of Local Rule 55-501	s.1 of Local Rule 55-501	s. 107
Take-Over Bids and Issuer Bids													

Provision	British Columbia	Alberta	Saskatchewan	Manitoba	Québec	Nova Scotia	New Brunswick	Prince Edward Island	Newfoundland and Labrador	Yukon	Northwest Territories	Nunavut	Ontario
Directors must make recommendation on bid	s.99(1)	s.160	s.100	s.90	ss.113 & 114	s.97	s.124	s.108(1)	s.92	s.108(1)	s.108(1)	s.108(1)	ss. 95 and 96
Investment Funds — Self Dealing													
Investments of mutual funds	s.6 of BC Instrument 81-513 *Self-Dealing*	s.185	s.120	n/a	n/a	s.119	s.137	n/a	s.112		n/a		s. 111
Indirect investment	s.7 of BC Instrument 81-513 *Self-Dealing*	s.186	s.121		n/a	s.120	s.138	n/a	s.113		n/a		s. 112
Fees on investment for mutual fund	s.8 of BC Instrument 81-513 *Self-Dealing*	s.189	s.124		n/a	s.123	s.141	n/a	s.116		n/a		s. 115
Report of mutual fund manager	s.9 of BC Instrument 81-513 *Self-Dealing*	s.191	s.126		n/a	s.125	s.143	n/a	s.118		n/a		s. 117
General													
Restrictions on transactions with responsible persons	n/a		n/a			s.126		n/a	s.119	n/a	n/a		s. 119
Principal Trading Prohibitions		s.193	s.128		n/a	s.127		n/a	s.120		n/a		
Public inspection of records	s.169(3)	s.221(3)	s.152(2)	s.134	n/a	s.148(1)	s.198(3)	s.26(1)	s.140(1)	s.26(1)	s.26(1)	s.26(1)	s. 140(1)

Companion Policy 11-102CP — Passport System

[See Editor's note at the beginning of MI 11-102.]

Table of Contents

PART 1 — GENERAL

1.1 Definitions — In this Policy,

"CP 33-109" means Companion Policy 33-109CP *Registration Information*;

"domestic firm" means a firm whose head office is in Canada;

"domestic individual" means an individual whose working office is in Canada;

"MI 11-101" means Multilateral Instrument 11-101 *Principal Regulator System*;

"non-principal jurisdiction" means, for a person or company, a jurisdiction other than the principal jurisdiction;

"non-principal regulator" means, for a person or company, the securities regulatory authority or regulator of a jurisdiction other than the principal jurisdiction;

"NP 11-202" means National Policy 11-202 *Process for Prospectus Reviews in Multiple Jurisdictions*;

"NP 11-203" means National Policy 11-203 *Process for Exemptive Relief Applications in Multiple Jurisdictions*;

"NP 11-204" means National Policy 11-204 *Process for Registration in Multiple Jurisdictions*;

"NP 11-205" means National Policy 11-205 *Process for Designation of Credit Rating Organizations in Multiple Jurisdictions*;

"NRD" has the same meaning as in NI 31-102;

"NRD format" has the same meaning as in NI 31-102;

"SRO" means self regulatory organization; and

"T&C" means a term, condition, restriction or requirement imposed by a securities regulatory authority or regulator on the registration of a firm or an individual.

1.2 **Additional definitions** — Terms used in this policy and that are defined in NP 11-202, NP 11-203, NP 11-204 and NP 11-205 have the same meanings as in those national policies.

1.3 **Purpose** — (1) **General** — Multilateral Instrument 11-102 *Passport System* (the Instrument) and this policy implement the passport system contemplated by the *Provincial/Territorial Memorandum of Understanding Regarding Securities Regulation*.

The Instrument gives each market participant a single window of access to the capital markets in multiple jurisdictions. It enables a person or company to deal only with its principal regulator to

- get deemed receipts in other jurisdictions (except Ontario) for a preliminary prospectus and prospectus,

- obtain automatic exemptions in other jurisdictions (except Ontario) equivalent to most types of discretionary exemptions granted by the principal regulator, or

- register automatically in other jurisdictions (except Ontario).

The Instrument also enables a credit rating organization to obtain a deemed designation as a designated rating organization in other jurisdictions (except Ontario).

(2) **Process** — NP 11-202, NP 11-203, NP 11-204 and NP 11-205 set out the processes for a market participant in any jurisdiction to obtain a deemed prospectus receipt, an automatic exemption, an automatic registration or a deemed designation as a designated rating organization in a passport jurisdiction. These policies also set out processes for a market participant in a passport jurisdiction to get a prospectus receipt or a discretionary exemption from the OSC or to register in Ontario or to obtain designation as a designated rating organization in Ontario.

NP 11-203 also sets out the process for seeking exemptive relief in multiple jurisdictions that falls outside the scope of the Instrument. NP 11-203 applies to a broad range of exemptive relief applications, not just discretionary exemption applications from the provisions listed in Appendix D of the Instrument. For example, NP 11-203 applies to an application to be designated a reporting issuer, mutual fund, non-redeemable investment fund or insider. However, it does not apply to an application to be designated as a designated rating organization, specifically covered in NP 11-205. It also applies to an application for a discretionary exemption from a provision not listed in Appendix D of the Instrument.

Please refer to NP 11-202, NP 11-203, NP 11-204 and NP 11-205 for more details on these processes.

(3) **Interpretation of the Instrument** — As with all national or multilateral instruments, you should read the Instrument from the perspective of the local jurisdiction in which you seek a deemed prospectus receipt, an automatic exemption or registration or a deemed designation as a designated rating organization. For example, if the Instrument does not specify where you file a document, it means that you must file it in the local jurisdiction. In this policy, we generally use the term 'non-principal jurisdiction' instead of 'local jurisdiction'.

To get a deemed receipt for a prospectus in the non-principal jurisdiction, a filer must file the prospectus in the jurisdiction through SEDAR. Similarly, to get an automatic exemption based on a discretionary exemption granted in the principal jurisdiction, a filer must give notice under section 4.7(1)(c) of the Instrument to the securities regulatory authority or regulator in the non-principal jurisdiction. Under section 4.7(2) of the Instrument, a filer can satisfy the latter requirement by giving notice to the principal regulator instead of the securities regulatory authority or regulator in the non-principal jurisdiction.

To register in the non-principal jurisdiction, a firm or individual must make the required submission in the non-principal jurisdiction. To streamline the process, section 4A.3(3) of the Instrument allows a firm to make its submission to the principal regulator instead of the non-principal regulator. Submissions for individuals are made through NRD. If the principal regulator imposes a T&C on a firm's or individual's registration, or suspends, terminates or accepts the surrender of registration of the firm or individual, that decision applies automatically in the non-principal jurisdiction, whether or not the firm or individual registered in the non-principal jurisdiction under the Instrument.

To obtain a deemed designation as a designated rating organization in another jurisdiction, a credit rating organization must give notice under section 4B.6(1)(c) of the Instrument to the securities regulatory authority or regulator in the non-principal jurisdiction. Under section 4B.6(2) of the Instrument, a credit rating organization can satisfy the latter requirement by giving notice to the principal regulator instead of the securities regulatory authority or regulator in the non-principal jurisdiction.

(4) **Operation of law** — The provisions of the Instrument on prospectus receipt, discretionary exemptions, registration and designation as a designated rating organization produce automatic legal outcomes in the non-principal jurisdiction that result from a decision made by the principal regulator. The effect is to make the law of the non-principal jurisdiction apply to a market participant as if the non-principal regulator had made the same decision as the principal regulator.

(5) **Applicable requirements** — A market participant must comply with the law of each jurisdiction in which it files a prospectus, is a reporting issuer, seeks registration, is registered or seeks designation as a designated rating organization.

- Most prospectus, continuous disclosure, registration requirements and requirements relating to designated rating organizations are harmonized and are in rules or regulations commonly referred to as 'national instruments'. The securities regulatory authorities and regulators intend to interpret and apply the harmonized requirements in national instruments in a consistent way, and we have put practices and procedures in place to achieve this objective.

- Some jurisdictions have non-harmonized requirements in Securities Acts or local rules or regulations. In addition, some national instruments contain requirements or carve-outs for specific jurisdictions, which are apparent on the face of the instruments.

- Registrants will be subject to a few non-harmonized requirements. Section 4A.5 contains a description of these requirements.

(6) Ontario — The OSC has not adopted the Instrument, but the Instrument provides that the OSC can be a principal regulator for purposes of a prospectus filing under Part 3, a discretionary exemption application under Part 4, registration under Part 4A, or an application for designation as a designated rating organization under Part 4B. Consequently, Ontario market participants have direct access to passport as follows:

- When the OSC issues a receipt for a prospectus to an issuer whose principal jurisdiction is Ontario, a deemed receipt is automatically issued in each passport jurisdiction where the market participant filed the prospectus under the Instrument.

- When the OSC grants a discretionary exemption to a market participant whose principal jurisdiction is Ontario, the person obtains an automatic exemption from the equivalent provision of securities legislation of each passport jurisdiction for which the person gives the notice described in section 4.7(1)(c) of the Instrument.

- A firm or individual whose principal jurisdiction is Ontario and who is registered in a category in Ontario is automatically registered in the same category in a passport jurisdiction when the firm or individual makes the required submission under the Instrument.

- When the OSC designates a credit rating organization as a designated rating organization, the credit rating organization obtains a deemed designation in each passport jurisdiction for which the credit rating organization gives the notice described in section 4B.6(1)(c) of the Instrument.

1.4 Language of documents — Québec — The Instrument does not relieve issuers filing in Québec from the linguistic obligations prescribed by Québec law, including the specific obligations in the Québec *Securities Act* (e.g. section 40.1). For example, where a prospectus is filed in several jurisdictions including Québec, the prospectus must be in French or in French and English.

PART 2 — [REPEALED]

PART 3 — PROSPECTUS

3.1 Principal regulator for prospectus — For a prospectus filing subject to Part 3 of the Instrument, the principal regulator is the principal regulator identified under section 3.1 of the Instrument. Under this section, the principal regulator must be the securities regulatory authority or regulator in a specified jurisdiction. Section 3.1(1) of the Instrument specifies the following jurisdictions for purposes of that section: British Columbia, Alberta, Saskatchewan, Manitoba, Ontario, Québec, New Brunswick and Nova Scotia.

Section 3.4 of NP 11-202 gives guidance on how to identify the principal regulator for a prospectus filing subject to Part 3 of the Instrument.

3.2 Discretionary change in principal regulator for prospectus — Section 3.2 of the Instrument permits the securities regulatory authority or regulator to change the principal regulator for a prospectus filing subject to Part 3 of the Instrument on its own motion or on application. Section 3.5 of NP 11-202 gives guidance on the process for, and considerations leading to, a discretionary change in principal regulator for a prospectus filing subject to Part 3 of the Instrument.

3.3 Deemed issuance of receipt — Section 3.3 of the Instrument deems a receipt to be issued for a preliminary prospectus or prospectus in the non-principal jurisdiction if certain conditions are met. A deemed receipt in the non-principal jurisdiction has the same legal effect as a receipt issued in the principal jurisdiction.

To rely on section 3.3 of the Instrument in the non-principal jurisdiction, a filer must file on SEDAR the preliminary prospectus or the pro forma prospectus, and the prospectus, in both the non-principal jurisdiction and the principal jurisdiction. When filing, the filer must also indicate that it is filing the preliminary prospectus or pro forma prospectus under the Instrument. Under the law of the non-principal jurisdiction, these filings trigger the obligation to file supporting documents (e.g., consents and material contracts) and to pay required fees.

NP 11-202 sets out the process for making a waiver application for a prospectus filing subject to Part 3 of the Instrument.

If the principal regulator refuses to issue a receipt for a prospectus, it will notify the filer and the non-principal regulators by sending a refusal letter through SEDAR. In these circumstances, the Instrument will no longer apply to the filing and the filer may deal separately with the local securities regulatory authority or regulator in any non-principal jurisdiction in which the prospectus was filed to determine if the local securities regulatory authority or regulator would issue a local receipt.

3.4 [Repealed]

3.5 Transition for section 3.3 — Section 3.3 of the Instrument applies to a preliminary prospectus or pro forma prospectus and their related prospectus, and to an amendment to a prospectus, filed on or after March 17, 2008.

Section 3.5(1) of the Instrument removes the deemed receipt that would otherwise be available in the non-principal jurisdiction under section 3.3 of the Instrument if a preliminary prospectus amendment is filed after March 17, 2008 and the related preliminary prospectus was filed before March 17, 2008.

Section 3.5(2) provides an exemption from the requirement in section 3.3(2)(b) of the Instrument to indicate on SEDAR, at the time of filing the preliminary prospectus or pro forma prospectus, that the preliminary prospectus or pro forma prospectus is filed under Instrument. This means there is a deemed receipt in the non-principal jurisdiction for a prospectus amendment if the related preliminary prospectus or pro forma prospectus was filed before March 17, 2008 and the filer indicated on SEDAR that it filed the amendment under the Instrument at the time of filing the amendment.

PART 4 — DISCRETIONARY EXEMPTIONS

4.1 Application — Part 4 of the Instrument applies to an application for a discretionary exemption from a provision listed in Appendix D of the Instrument. Part 4 does not apply to a discretionary exemption application from a provision not listed in Appendix D of the Instrument or to other types of exemptive relief applications. For example, Part 4 does not apply to an application to designate a person to be a reporting issuer, mutual fund, non-redeemable investment fund or insider.

4.2 Principal regulator for discretionary exemption applications — For purposes of a discretionary exemption application under Part 4 of the Instrument, the principal regulator is the principal regulator identified under sections 4.1 to 4.5 of the Instrument. Except under section 4.4.1, the principal regulator must be the securities regulatory authority or regulator in a specified jurisdiction. Section 4.1 of the Instrument specifies the following jurisdictions for this purpose: British Columbia, Alberta, Saskatchewan, Manitoba, Ontario, Québec, New Brunswick and Nova Scotia.

Section 4.4.1 of the Instrument provides that the principal regulator for an application for exemption from a requirement in Parts 3 and 12 of NI 31-103 and Part 2 of NI 33-109 made in connection with an application for registration in the principal jurisdiction is the principal regulator as determined under section 4A.1 of the Instrument. The securities regulatory authority or regulator of each jurisdiction may be a principal regulator under section 4A.1 of the Instrument.

Section 3.6 of NP 11-203 gives guidance on how to identify the principal regulator for a discretionary exemption application under Part 4 of the Instrument.

4.3 Discretionary change of principal regulator for discretionary exemption applications — Section 4.6 of the Instrument permits the securities regulatory authority or regulator to change the principal regulator for a discretionary exemption application under Part 4 of the Instrument on its own motion or on application. Section 3.7 of NP 11-203 gives guidance on the process for, and considerations leading to, a discretionary change in principal regulator for a discretionary exemption application under Part 4 of the Instrument.

4.4 Passport application of discretionary exemptions — Section 4.7(1) of the Instrument exempts a person or company from an equivalent provision of securities legislation in the non-principal jurisdiction if the principal regulator for the application grants the discretionary exemption, the filer gives the notice required under paragraph (c) of that section and other conditions are met. The equivalent provisions from which an automatic exemption is available under section 4.7(1) of the Instrument are set out in Appendix D of the Instrument.

If the principal regulator revokes or cancels the discretionary exemption or it expires under a sunset clause, the exemption in section 4.7 is no longer available in the non-principal jurisdiction.

A discretionary exemption under section 4.7(1) of the Instrument is available in the passport jurisdictions for which the filer gives the required notice when filing the application. However, the discretionary exemption can become available later in other passport jurisdictions if the circumstances warrant. For example, if a reporting issuer obtains a discretionary exemption from a national continuous disclosure requirement in its principal jurisdiction and an automatic exemption under section 4.7(1) in three non-principal jurisdictions in 2008 and the issuer becomes a reporting issuer in a fourth non-principal jurisdiction in 2009, the issuer could obtain an automatic exemption in the new jurisdiction. To obtain the automatic exemption in the new jurisdiction, the issuer would have to give the notice referred to in section 4.7(1)(c) of the Instrument in respect of that jurisdiction and meet the other condition of the exemption.

Under section 4.7(2) of the Instrument the filer may give the required notice to the principal regulator instead of the non-principal regulator.

A filer should identify in the application all the exemptions required and give notice for all the jurisdictions in which section 4.7(1) of the Instrument is intended to be relied upon. If an exemption is required in a non-principal jurisdiction when the filer files the application, but the filer does not give the required notice for that jurisdiction until after the principal regulator grants the exemption, the securities regulatory authority or regulator of the non-principal jurisdiction will take appropriate action. This could include removing the exemption, in which case the filer may have an opportunity to be heard in that jurisdiction in appropriate circumstances.

A principal regulator's decision to vary a decision the principal regulator previously made to exempt a person or company from a provision set out in Appendix D of the Instrument has automatic effect in a non-principal jurisdiction if

- the person or company applied in the principal jurisdiction to have the decision varied and gave the notice required under section 4.7(1)(c) of the Instrument in respect of the non-principal jurisdiction,
- the principal regulator grants the exemption and the exemption is in effect, and
- the other conditions of section 4.7(1) of the Instrument are met.

If the principal regulator for an application for exemption from a filing requirement under section 6.1 of National Instrument 45-106 *Prospectus Exemptions* (NI 45-106) grants an exemption under section 4.7(1) of the Instrument, a person or company has an automatic exemption in a non-principal jurisdiction under the section only if

- the filing requirement arises from the person or company relying on one of the provisions referred to in section 6.1 of NI 45-106 in the principal jurisdiction,
- the person or company is relying on the equivalent exemption in the non-principal jurisdiction, and
- the person or company complies with the conditions of section 4.7(1) of the Instrument.

Because, under the Instrument, a person or company files an application for a discretionary exemption only in the principal jurisdiction to obtain an automatic exemption in multiple jurisdictions, the filer is required to pay fees only in the principal jurisdiction.

NP 11-203 sets out the process for seeking exemptive relief in multiple jurisdictions, including the process for seeking a discretionary exemption under Part 4 of the Instrument.

4.5 Availability of passport for discretionary exemptions applied for before March 17, 2008 — Under section 4.8(1) of the Instrument, an exemption from the equivalent provision is automatically available in the local jurisdiction if

- an application was made in a specified jurisdiction before March 17, 2008 for an exemption from a provision of securities legislation that is now listed in Appendix D of the Instrument,
- the securities regulatory authority or regulator in the specified jurisdiction granted the exemption before, on or after March 17, 2008, and
- certain other conditions are met.

These conditions include giving the notice required under section 4.8(1)(c). Section 4.8(2) permits the filer to give the required notice to the securities regulatory authority or regulator that would be the principal regulator for the application under Part 4 if an application were to be made under that Part at the time the notice is given, instead of to the non-principal regulator.

Under section 4.1, the specified jurisdictions are British Columbia, Alberta, Saskatchewan, Manitoba, Ontario, Québec, New Brunswick and Nova Scotia.

A specified jurisdiction for purposes of section 4.8 of the Instrument is a principal jurisdiction under MI 11-101.

The combined effect of sections 4.8(1) and 4.8(3) is to make an exemption from a CD requirement granted by the principal regulator before March 17, 2008 under MI 11-101 automatically available in the non-principal jurisdiction, even though the decision of the principal regulator under MI 11-101 does not refer to the non-principal jurisdiction. To benefit from this, however, the reporting issuer must comply with the terms and conditions of the decision of the principal regulator under MI 11-101. Only exemptions granted from CD requirements that are now listed in Appendix D of the Instrument become available in the non-principal jurisdiction in this way.

Appendix A of this policy lists the CD requirements from which a reporting issuer could get an exemption under section 3.2 of MI 11-101. Appendix D of the Instrument sets out the list of equivalent provisions.

PART 4A — REGISTRATION

4A.1 Application — The Instrument permits a firm or individual to register automatically in a non-principal jurisdiction based on its principal jurisdiction registration. It also makes some types of regulatory decisions by a firm's or individual's principal regulator apply automatically in each non-principal jurisdiction where the firm or individual is registered, whether or not the firm or individual is registered automatically under the Instrument.

Permitted individual — The Instrument does not apply to "permitted individuals" under NI 33-109 because these individuals are not registered under securities legislation. The Instrument applies to a permitted individual only if the permitted individual becomes registered in a category in his or her principal jurisdiction and seeks registration in the same category in a non-principal jurisdiction.

Restricted dealers and their representatives — Section 4A.3 of the Instrument does not apply to a firm registered in the category of "restricted dealer" under NI 31-103. To register in a non-principal jurisdiction, a restricted dealer must apply directly to the non-principal regulator. Automatic registration under the Instrument does not apply to restricted dealers because there are no standard requirements for this category and most firms registered as restricted dealers operate in a single jurisdiction. However, if a restricted dealer registers directly in the same category in a non-principal jurisdiction, the provisions of the Instrument relating to T&Cs (section 4A.5), suspension (section 4A.6), termination (section 4A.7) and surrender (section 4A.8) apply to the firm.

All the provisions of the Instrument apply to the dealing representatives of a restricted dealer. This includes automatic registration under section 4A.4 of the Instrument if the representative's sponsoring firm is registered as a restricted dealer in the representative's principal jurisdiction and the non-principal jurisdiction in which the representative seeks registration. It also includes the provisions of the Instrument relating to T&Cs (section 4A.5), suspension (section 4A.6), termination (section 4A.7) and surrender (section 4A.8).

4A.2 Registration by SRO — The securities regulatory authority or regulator in some jurisdictions has delegated, assigned or authorized an SRO to perform all or part of its registration function. The instrument applies to the decisions made by SROs under these arrangements. For more details, refer to section 3.5 of NP 11-204.

4A.3 Principal regulator for registration — The principal regulator of a firm or individual is the securities regulatory authority or regulator identified under section 4A.1 of the Instrument. The securities regulatory authority or regulator of any jurisdiction can be a principal regulator for registration. Section 3.6 of NP 11-204 gives guidance on how to identify the principal regulator of a firm or individual under Part 4A of the Instrument.

4A.4 Discretionary change of principal regulator for registration — Section 4A.2 of the Instrument permits the securities regulatory authority or regulator to change the principal regulator for the purpose of Part 4A of the Instrument. Section 3.7 of NP 11-204 gives guidance on the process for a discretionary change of principal regulator for registration under Part 4A of the Instrument.

4A.5 Registration — Sections 4A.3 and 4A.4 of the Instrument are available for firms or individuals required to be registered under NI 31-103, except for firms registering as restricted dealers.

A firm or individual who registers in a non-principal jurisdiction under section 4A.3 or 4A.4 of the Instrument must comply with all applicable requirements of the non-principal jurisdiction, including the obligation to pay the required fees in that jurisdiction and any non-harmonized requirements.

In Québec, firms and individuals in the mutual fund and scholarship plan sectors are subject to a specific regulatory framework that also applies under passport:

- mutual fund firms registered in Québec are not required to be members of the Mutual Fund Dealers Association of Canada (MFDA) and are under the direct supervision of the Autorité des marchés financiers, as are scholarship plan firms,

- individuals in the mutual fund and scholarship plan sectors are required to be members of the Chambre de la sécurité financière,

- firms and individuals must maintain professional liability insurance, and

- firms must contribute to the Fonds d'indemnisation des services financiers which provides financial compensation to investors who are victims of fraudulent tactics or embezzlement committed by these firms or individuals.

In addition, in Québec, an individual who is a representative of an investment dealer cannot concurrently be employed by a financial institution and carry on business as a representative in a Québec branch of a financial institution unless he or she is a representative specialized in mutual funds or scholarship plans.

In British Columbia, investment dealers that trade in the U.S. over-the-counter markets must comply with local requirements to manage the risks of trading these securities, retain records and report quarterly to the Commission.

To register in a non-principal jurisdiction — Before making a submission under section 4A.3 or 4A.4, the firm or individual should ensure that the firm's or individual's principal jurisdiction is correctly identified in the firm's or individual's latest submission under NI 33-109.

Firm — Under section 4A.3(1) of the Instrument, if a firm is registered in its principal jurisdiction in a category set out in NI 31-103, other than the category of "restricted dealer", the firm is registered in the same category in a non-principal jurisdiction if the firm

    (a) has submitted a completed Form 33-109F6 in accordance with NI 33-109, and

    (b) is a member of an SRO if required for that category.

A firm should refer to Part 4 and section 5.2 of NP 11-204 for guidance on how to make its submission under the Instrument.

Under section 4A.3(3) of the Instrument, a firm may make the relevant submission by giving it to its principal regulator instead of the non-principal regulator. In a jurisdiction where the principal regulator has delegated, assigned or authorized an SRO to register firms, the firm should make the submission by giving it to the relevant office of the SRO.

To register under section 4A.3(1) of the Instrument, the firm must be a member of an SRO if required in the local jurisdiction for that category of registration. This condition does not apply if the firm has an exemption in the local jurisdiction from the requirement to be a member of the SRO. All jurisdictions require investment dealers to be members of the Investment Industry Regulatory Organization of Canada. All jurisdictions, except Québec, require mutual fund dealers to be members of the MFDA. A mutual fund dealer whose principal jurisdiction is Québec must be a member of the MFDA before it can register in another jurisdiction.

Individual — Under section 4A.4 of the Instrument, if an individual acting on behalf of a sponsoring firm is registered in his or her principal jurisdiction in a category set out in NI 31-103, the individual is registered in the same category in a non-principal jurisdiction if

    (a) the individual's sponsoring firm is registered in the non-principal jurisdiction in the same category as in the firm's principal jurisdiction,

(b) the individual submitted a completed Form 33-109F2 or Form 33-109F4 in accordance with NI 33-109, and

(c) the individual is a member or an approved person of an SRO if required for that category.

Section 5.2 of NP 11-204 provides guidance on how to make a submission.

To register under section 4A.4 of the Instrument, the individual must be a member or an approved person of an SRO if required in the local jurisdiction for that category of registration. This condition does not apply if the individual has an exemption in the local jurisdiction from the requirement to be a member or approved person of the SRO. Québec legislation requires individuals who are representatives of mutual fund or scholarship plan dealers to be members of the Chambre de la sécurité financière. Other jurisdictions require individuals who are representatives of mutual fund dealers to be approved persons under the rules of the MFDA.

For greater certainty, if an individual is registered in a category in his or her principal jurisdiction for more than one sponsoring firm, each sponsoring firm must be registered in the same category in the non-principal jurisdiction in which the individual seeks registration under section 4A.4 of the Instrument.

4A.6 Terms and conditions of registration — Section 4A.5(1) of the Instrument provides that, if a firm or individual is registered in the same category in the principal jurisdiction and in the non-principal jurisdiction, a T&C imposed on the registration in the principal jurisdiction applies to the firm or individual as if it were imposed in the non-principal jurisdiction (i.e., by operation of law). Under section 4A.5(2) of the Instrument, a T&C continues to apply until the earlier of the date the securities regulatory authority or regulator that imposed it, cancels or revokes it, or it expires.

Under section 4A.5 of the Instrument, if the principal regulator amends or adds a T&C to a category in which a firm or individual is registered, the amended or additional T&C automatically applies to the firm's or individual's registration in the same category in the non-principal jurisdiction.

In the event of a change of principal regulator, and for each category in which a firm or an individual is registered in the non-principal jurisdiction under section 4A.3 or 4A.4 of the Instrument, the firm's or individual's

- original principal regulator will revoke any T&C it imposed, and
- new principal regulator will adopt any T&C's that are appropriate.

This will enable the new principal regulator to amend the firm's or individual's T&Cs in appropriate circumstances and result in any T&C amended by the new principal regulator applying automatically in a non-principal jurisdiction as if it had been imposed in that jurisdiction (i.e., by operation of law).

4A.7 Suspension — Under section 4A.6 of the Instrument, if a firm's or an individual's registration in the principal jurisdiction is suspended, the firm's or individual's registration is automatically suspended in any non-principal jurisdiction where the firm or individual is registered. For greater certainty, a suspension of registration is a suspension of a firm's or individual's trading or advising privileges and the firm or individual remains registered under securities legislation. A firm's or individual's registration is suspended on the same day in the principal jurisdiction and the non-principal jurisdiction. NRD will show the same suspension date in each relevant jurisdiction.

A firm's or individual's registration is suspended in the non-principal jurisdiction for as long as the firm's or individual's registration is suspended in the principal jurisdiction. If the principal regulator lifts a firm's or individual's suspension, the firm or individual may resume trading or advising in the non-principal jurisdiction on the date NRD shows that the suspension has been lifted. Any T&C imposed by the principal regulator when it lifts a suspension applies automatically in the non-principal jurisdiction under section 4A.5 of the Instrument.

4A.8 Termination — Under section 4A.7 of the Instrument, if a firm's or individual's registration in the principal jurisdiction is cancelled, revoked or terminated, as applicable, the firm's or individual's registration in the non-principal jurisdiction is automatically cancelled, revoked or terminated, as applicable. A firm's or individual's registration is terminated on the same date in the principal jurisdiction and the non-principal jurisdiction. NRD will show the same termination date in each relevant jurisdiction.

4A.9 Surrender — Under section 4A.8 of the Instrument, a firm's or individual's registration is automatically cancelled, revoked or terminated, as applicable, in a category in **all** non-principal jurisdictions in which the firm or individual is registered if the firm or individual applies to surrender registration in the category in its principal jurisdiction and the principal regulator accepts the surrender.

A firm should submit an application to surrender registration in one or more categories in the firm's principal jurisdiction and Ontario, if Ontario is a non-principal jurisdiction. The application should identify any non-principal jurisdiction where the firm is registered in the same category(ies). In a jurisdiction where the principal regulator has delegated, assigned or authorized an SRO to perform registration functions, a firm should submit its application to surrender to the relevant office of the SRO. A firm should refer to Appendix B of CP 33-109 for guidance on how to submit its application for surrender to the principal regulator or the relevant office of the SRO.

An individual should make the relevant NRD submission under NI 33-109 to surrender registration.

If a firm or individual applies to surrender a category in the principal jurisdiction, the principal regulator may suspend registration in the category pending surrender, or impose a T&C. See section 4A.7 of this Policy for guidance on suspension of registration.

If the principal regulator imposes a T&C, section 4A.5 of the Instrument provides that the T&C applies in each non-principal jurisdiction where a firm or individual is registered in the same category as if the T&C had been imposed in the non-principal jurisdiction.

The Instrument does not deal with a firm or individual that seeks to surrender a category in a non-principal jurisdiction only. If a firm or individual seeks to surrender a category in a non-principal jurisdiction, other than Ontario,

- the firm may still submit its application by giving it to the principal regulator only or, if the principal regulator has delegated, assigned or authorized an SRO to perform registration functions, the relevant office of the SRO in the principal jurisdiction,
- the individual should make the relevant NRD submission under NI 33-109,
- the firm's or individual's submission should indicate the non-principal jurisdiction where the firm or individual is applying to surrender registration, and
- the fact that a securities regulatory authority, regulator or SRO accepts the surrender of registration of a firm or individual in the non-principal jurisdiction does not affect the registration of the firm or individual in another jurisdiction.

4A.10 Transition — terms and conditions in non-principal jurisdiction — The purpose of section 4A.9(1) of the Instrument is to delay until October 28, 2009 the automatic application of section 4A.5 of the Instrument in a non-principal jurisdiction in which a firm or individual is registered on September 28, 2009. This gives the firm or individual time to make an application under section 4A.9(2) of the Instrument for an exemption from having a T&C imposed by the principal regulator apply automatically in the non-principal jurisdiction.

A firm or individual should apply for the exemption contemplated in section 4A.9(2) of the Instrument separately in each non-principal jurisdiction because the purpose of the exemption application is to give the firm or individual an opportunity to be heard on the automatic application in the non-principal jurisdiction of a T&C imposed by the principal regulator. For this reason, a firm or individual should not make the application under NP 11-203.

If a firm or individual does not apply for an exemption under section 4A.9(2) of the Instrument in a non-principal jurisdiction,

- a T&C imposed by the principal regulator automatically applies on October 28, 2009 in the non-principal jurisdiction, and
- a T&C previously imposed by the non-principal regulator ceases to apply unless it is enforcement related.

4A.11 Transition — notice of principal regulator for foreign firm — Under section 4A.10(1) of the Instrument, a foreign firm registered in a category in multiple jurisdictions before September 28, 2009 is required to submit the information to identify its principal jurisdiction in item 2.2(b) in Form 33-109F6 by submitting a Form 33-109F5 on or before October 28, 2009. This information will determine the foreign firm's principal regulator under section 4A.1 of the Instrument.

Section 4A.10(2) of the Instrument permits the foreign firm to make this submission to a non-principal regulator by giving it only to its principal regulator. In a jurisdiction where the principal regulator has delegated, assigned or authorized an SRO to perform registration functions, the foreign firm should make the submission to the relevant office of the SRO. Foreign firms should refer to Appendix B of CP 33-109 for guidance on how to make a submission.

Because the principal regulator for a foreign individual is the same as the principal regulator for the individual's sponsoring firm, the Instrument does not require the foreign individual to make a submission to identify the individual's principal regulator.

PART 4B — APPLICATION TO BECOME A DESIGNATED RATING ORGANIZATION

4B.1 Application — Part 4B of the Instrument only applies to an application for designation as a designated rating organization. Designated rating organizations applying for a discretionary exemption from a provision of National Instrument 25-101 *Designated Rating Organizations* should refer to Part 4 of the Instrument.

4B.2 Principal regulator for application for designation — For purposes of an application for designation as a designated rating organization under Part 4B of the Instrument, the principal regulator is the principal regulator identified under sections 4B.2 to 4B.5 of the Instrument. The principal regulator must be the securities regulatory authority or regulator in a specified jurisdiction. Section 4B.1 of the Instrument specifies the following jurisdictions for this purpose: British Columbia, Alberta, Saskatchewan, Manitoba, Ontario, Québec, Nova Scotia and New Brunswick.

Section 7 of NP 11-205 gives guidance on how to identify the principal regulator for an application for designation as a designated rating organization under Part 4B of the Instrument.

4B.3 Discretionary change of principal regulator for application for designation — Section 4B.5 of the Instrument permits the securities regulatory authority or regulator to change the principal regulator for an application for designation as a designated rating organization under Part 4B of the Instrument on its own motion or on application. Section 8 of NP 11-205 gives guidance on the process for, and considerations leading to, a discretionary change in principal regulator for an application for designation as a designated rating organization under Part 4B of the Instrument.

4B.4 Passport application of designation — Section 4B.6(1) of the Instrument provides that a credit rating organization is deemed to be designated as a designated rating organization in the non-principal jurisdiction if the principal regulator for the application grants the designation, the credit rating organization gives the notice required under paragraph (c) of that section and other conditions are met.

A deemed designation under section 4B.6(1) of the Instrument is available in the passport jurisdictions for which the credit rating organization gives the required notice when filing the application for designation. Credit rating organizations should give the notice in paragraph (c) of that section for all passport jurisdictions. However, the deemed designation can become available later in other passport jurisdictions if the circumstances warrant. To obtain the deemed designation in the new jurisdiction, the credit rating organization would have to give the notice referred to in section 4B.6(1)(c) of the Instrument in respect of that jurisdiction and meet the other conditions of the designation.

Because, under the Instrument, a credit rating organization makes an application for designation only in the principal jurisdiction to obtain a deemed designation in multiple jurisdictions, the credit rating organization is required to pay fees only in the principal jurisdiction.

NP 11-205 sets out the process for seeking designation as a designated rating organization in multiple jurisdictions under Part 4B of the Instrument.

PART 5 — EFFECTIVE DATE

5.1 Effective date — The Instrument applies to continuous disclosure documents, prospectuses and discretionary exemption applications filed on or after March 17, 2008.

The Instrument applies to an individual or firm seeking registration outside its principal jurisdiction on or after September 28, 2009. In addition, it applies to an individual or firm that is registered on that date unless the individual or firm requests and obtains an exemption under section 4A.9(2).

The Instrument applies to applications for designation as a designated rating organization filed on or after April 20, 2012.

APPENDIX A — CD REQUIREMENTS UNDER MI 11-101

For ease of reference, this appendix reproduces the definition of CD requirements in MI 11-101 even though some references might no longer be relevant because sections were repealed after September 19, 2005 when MI 11-101 came into force.

British Columbia:

Securities Act: section 85 and 117

Securities Rules: section 144 (except as it relates to fees), 145 (except as it relates to fees, 152 and 153

sections 2, 3 and 189 as they relate to a filing under another CD requirement, as defined in MI 11-101

Alberta:

Securities Act: sections 146, 149 (except as it relates to fees), 150, 152 and 157.1

*Securities Commission
Rules (General):* except as it relates to a prospectus, section 143–169, 196 and 197

Saskatchewan:

The Securities Act, 1988: section 84, 86–88, 90, 94 and 95

The Securities Regulations: section 117–138.1 and 175 as it relates to a filing under another CD requirement, as defined under MI 11-101

Manitoba:

Securities Act: sections 101(1), 102(1), 104, 106(3), 119, 120 (except as it relates to fees) and 121–130

Securities Regulation: sections 38–40 and 80–87

Québec:

Securities Act: sections 73 excluding the filing requirement of a statement of material change, 75 excluding the filing requirement, 76, 77 excluding the filing requirement, 78, 80–82.1, 83.1, 87, 105 excluding the filing requirement, 106 and 107 excluding the filing requirement

Securities Regulation: sections 115.1–119, 119.4, 120–138 and 141–161

Regulations: No. 14, No. 48, Q-11, Q-17 (Title IV) and 62–102

A document filed with or delivered to the Autorité des marchés financiers, delivered to securityholder in Québec or disseminated in Québec under section 3.2 of the Instrument, is deemed, for the purposes of securities legislation in Québec, to be a document filed, delivered or disseminated under Chapter II of Title III or section 84 of the *Securities Act* (Québec).

New Brunswick:

Securities Act: sections 89(1)–(4), 90, 91, 100 and 101

Nova Scotia:

Securities Act: section 81, 83, 84 and 91

General Securities Rules: sections 9, 140(2), 140(3) and 141

Newfoundland and Labrador:

Securities Act: except as they relate to fees, sections 76, 78–80, 82, 86 and 87

Securities Regulations: sections 4–14 and 71–80

Yukon:

Securities Act: section 22(5) except as it relates to filing a new or amended prospectus

All jurisdictions:

(a) National Instrument 43-101 *Standards of Disclosure for Mineral Projects*, except as it relates to a prospectus,

(b) National Instrument 51-101 *Standards of Disclosure for Oil and Gas Activities*, except as it relates to a prospectus,

(c) National Instrument 51-102 *Continuous Disclosure Obligations*,

(d) National Instrument 52-107 *Acceptable Accounting Principles and Auditing Standards*,

(e) National Instrument 52-108 *Auditor Oversight*,

(f) National Instrument 52-109 *Certification of Disclosure in Issuers' Annual and Interim Filings*,

(g) National Instrument 52-110 *Audit Committees*, except in British Columbia

(h) BC Instrument 52-509 *Audit Committees*, only in British Columbia

(i) National Instrument 54-101 *Communication with Beneficial Owners of Securities of a* Reporting *Issuer*,

(j) National Instrument 58-101 *Disclosure of Corporate Governance Practices*,

(k) section 8.5 of National Instrument 81-104 *Commodity Pools*, and

(l) National Instrument 81-106 *Investment Fund Continuous Disclosure*.

National Policy 11-201 — Electronic Delivery of Documents

Date: **December 17, 1999, as amended February 14, 2003 and November 18, 2011**

22 O.S.C.B. 8163, 26 O.S.C.B. 1437 and 34 O.S.C.B. 11603

Table of Contents

PART 1 — GENERAL

1.1 Definitions — In this Policy

"delivered" means transmitted, sent, delivered or otherwise communicated, and "deliver", "delivery" and similar words have corresponding meanings;

"electronic commerce legislation" means the statutes listed in Appendix A and any other federal, provincial or territorial statute of Canada concerning the regulation of electronic commerce, and the regulations, rules, forms and schedules under those statutes, as amended from time to time;

"electronic delivery" includes the delivery of documents by facsimile, e-mail, optical disk, the Internet or other electronic means;

"electronic signature" means electronic information that a person creates or adopts in order to execute or sign a document and that is in, attached to or associated with the document;

"proxy document" means a document relating to a meeting of a reporting issuer, and includes an information circular, a form of proxy, a request for voting instructions, and voting instructions.

1.1.1 Further Definitions — Terms used in this policy that are defined in National Instrument 14-101 *Definitions* have the same meaning as in that instrument.

1.2 Purpose of this Policy — (1) The purpose of this Policy is to provide guidance to securities industry participants who want to use electronic delivery to fulfill delivery requirements in securities legislation.

(2) The Canadian Securities Administrators (the CSA or we) recognize that information technology is an important and useful tool in improving communications to investors. We want provisions of securities legislation that impose delivery requirements to be applied in a manner that accommodates technological developments without undermining investor protection.

1.3 Other Legislation and Rules — (1) Electronic commerce legislation generally prescribes a legal framework for electronic delivery and addresses consent to electronic delivery. The provisions of electronic commerce legislation may vary from jurisdiction to jurisdiction and may not be equally in force in all jurisdictions.

(2) Electronic delivery of documents may also be subject to corporate legislation, SRO rules or stock exchange rules that either directly impose requirements for electronic delivery or incorporate by reference requirements for electronic delivery from electronic commerce legislation. An issuer's constating documents, such as its articles of incorporation, may also limit electronic delivery.

(3) Documents required to be delivered under securities laws, including documents sent electronically, may be subject to the protections of privacy legislation. Securities industry participants may need to take additional steps to preserve the confidentiality of personal information under that legislation.

1.4 **Application of this Policy** — (1) Parts 2 and 3 of this Policy apply to documents required to be delivered under securities legislation. These include prospectuses, financial statements, trade confirmations, account statements and proxy-related materials that are delivered by securities industry participants or those acting on their behalf, such as transfer agents. Part 4 of this Policy provides additional guidance that only applies to the use of proxy documents in electronic format.

(2) This Policy does not apply to deliveries where the method of delivery prescribed by securities legislation does not permit electronic delivery.

(3) This Policy does not apply to documents filed with or delivered by or to a securities regulatory authority or regulator.

(4) For guidance on using electronic communication to trade securities, refer to National Policy 47-201 *Trading Securities Using the Internet and Other Electronic Means* and, in Québec, *Notice 47-201 relating to Trading Securities Using the Internet and Other Electronic Means*.

PART 2 — ELECTRONIC DELIVERY OF DOCUMENTS

2.1 **Basic Components of Electronic Delivery of Documents** — (1) Subject to applicable electronic commerce or other legislation, we believe that the delivery requirements of securities legislation can generally be satisfied through electronic delivery if each of the following elements is met:

1. The recipient of the document receives notice that the document has been, or will be, delivered electronically as described in section 2.3.

2. The recipient of the document has easy access to the document, as described in section 2.4.

3. The document that is received by the recipient is the same as the document delivered by the deliverer, as described in section 2.5.

4. The deliverer of the document has evidence that the document has been delivered, as described in section 2.6.

If any one of these components is absent, however, the effectiveness of the delivery may be uncertain.

(2) The components of electronic delivery listed above are compatible with the legal framework for electronic delivery under electronic commerce legislation.

2.2 **Consent to Electronic Delivery** — (1) Electronic commerce legislation may require the consent of a recipient to electronic delivery. Securities legislation does not require a deliverer to obtain the consent of the intended recipient nor does it prescribe the form or content of any consent. However, the process of obtaining express consent, and then delivering the document in accordance with that consent, may enable the deliverer to achieve some of the basic components of electronic delivery set out in section 2.1. An express consent may give rise to the inferences that, if a document is sent by electronic delivery in accordance with the terms of a consent:

(a) the recipient will receive notice of the electronic delivery of the document;

(b) the recipient has the necessary technical ability and resources to access the document; and

(c) the recipient will actually receive the document.

(2) A deliverer may effect electronic delivery without the benefit of an express consent. However, if a deliverer does not obtain an express consent, it may be more difficult to demonstrate that the intended recipient had notice of, and access to, the document, and that the intended recipient actually received the document.

2.3 **Notice** — (1) An intended recipient should have notice of the electronic delivery. Notice can be given in any manner, electronic or non-electronic, that advises the recipient of the proposed electronic delivery.

(2) A deliverer intending to effect electronic delivery by permitting intended recipients to access a document posted to a website should not assume that the availability of the document will be known to recipients without separate notice of its availability.

2.4 **Access** — (1) A recipient of an electronically delivered document should have easy access to the document.

(2) Deliverers should take reasonable steps to ensure that electronic access to documents is not burdensome or overly complicated for recipients. The electronic systems employed by deliverers should be sufficiently powerful to ensure quick downloading, appropriate formatting and general availability.

(3) A document should remain available to recipients for whatever period of time is appropriate and relevant, given the nature of the document.

(4) A document delivered electronically should be delivered using appropriate electronic formats and methods of electronic delivery that enable the recipient to store and retain a permanent record of it which may be used for subsequent reference, and print it, as is the case with paper delivery.

2.5 **Delivery of an Unaltered Document** — A deliverer should take reasonable steps to prevent alteration or corruption of a document during electronic delivery. This may include adopting security measures to protect against third-party tampering with the document. Deficiencies in the completeness or integrity of a document delivered electronically may raise questions as to whether the document has in fact been delivered.

2.6 **Effecting Delivery** — (1) A deliverer should have internal processes to show that a document delivery has been attempted.

(2) A deliverer of a document should not conclude that electronic delivery has been effected if the deliverer has any reason to believe that a document has not been received, such as receiving a notification of delivery failure. If electronic delivery is attempted but cannot be accomplished for any reason, delivery should be attempted by an alternative method, such as by paper delivery.

PART 3 — MISCELLANEOUS ELECTRONIC DELIVERY MATTERS

3.1 **Form and Content of Documents** — (1) For the sake of consistency, documents delivered electronically may follow the formatting requirements set out in the SEDAR Filer Manual. This includes altering the document to be delivered electronically from the paper version in accordance with these formatting requirements.

(2) As with documents filed under SEDAR, documents proposed to be delivered electronically should be recreated in electronic format, rather than scanned into electronic format. This is recommended because scanned documents can be difficult to transmit, store and retrieve on a cost-efficient basis and may be difficult to view upon retrieval.

3.2 **Confidentiality of Documents** — Some documents that may be sent by electronic delivery, such as trade confirmations, are confidential to the recipients. Deliverers should take all reasonably necessary steps to ensure that the confidentiality of those documents is preserved in the electronic delivery process.

3.3 Hyperlinks — (1) The hyperlink function can provide the ability to access information instantly, in the same document or in a different document on the same or another website.

(2) The use of hyperlinks within a document may not be appropriate for the reasons described in subsection (3), unless the hyperlink is to another point in that same document.

(3) A deliverer that provides a hyperlink in a document to information outside the document risks incorporating that hyperlinked information into the document and thereby becoming legally responsible for the accuracy of that hyperlinked information. Also, the existence of hyperlinks in a document delivered electronically to a separate document raises the question of which documents are being delivered — only the base document, or the base document and documents to which the base document is linked.

(4) For documents delivered electronically that contain hyperlinks to other documents, deliverers are encouraged to clearly distinguish which documents are governed by statutory disclosure requirements and which are not. This may be effected, for example, by the use of appropriate headings on each page of the documents.

(5) Paragraph 7.2(e) of the SEDAR Filer Manual prohibits hyperlinks between documents.

(6) An attempt to deliver documents by referring an intended recipient to a third party provider of the document, such as SEDAR, will alone likely not constitute valid delivery of the document.

3.4 Multimedia Communications — (1) Multimedia communications are sometimes used to present information in varied combinations of text, graphics, video, animation and sound.

We recommend that no information presented through multimedia communications be included in disclosure documents required by statute unless it can be reproduced identically in non-electronic form. This will ensure that all recipients receive the same statutorily required information, regardless of their multimedia capabilities.

(2) Securities industry participants may use multimedia communications to compile and disseminate publicly available information.

(3) Multimedia communications are subject to provisions in securities legislation regarding misleading or untrue statements and promotional or advertising restrictions. These provisions may be relevant, for example, when the multimedia communications appear on a deliverer's website or are hyperlinked to a deliverer's website.

3.5 Timing of Electronic Delivery — Electronic delivery of materials to recipients should be made in accordance with the timing specified in securities legislation.

PART 4 — PROXY DOCUMENTS

4.1 Proxy Delivery Requirements — (1) Securities legislation and securities directions contain provisions relating to the proxy solicitation process that have raised questions as to whether the electronic delivery of proxy documents is permitted, and whether proxy documents can be in electronic format. We have identified two types of requirements in securities law that affect the use of proxy documents in electronic format:

     1. Requirements in certain securities directions or securities legislation that

         (a) a form of proxy or proxy be in written or printed form (the "written proxy requirements"); and

         (b) a registered holder of voting securities vote or give a proxy in respect of such voting securities in accordance with any written voting instructions provided by the beneficial owner of such voting securities (the "written voting instructions requirements") (collectively with the written proxy requirements, the "in writing requirements").

     2. Requirements in securities legislation that a proxy be executed (the "proxy execution requirements").

(2) Securities industry participants who are required by securities legislation to deliver proxy documents and wish to use an electronic delivery method should refer to Part 2 of this Policy, which sets out the principles for delivering documents electronically.

(3) Merely making proxy documents available for access on a website will not constitute delivery of these documents in accordance with the four components of effective delivery that are set out in Part 2 of this Policy.

4.2 The In Writing Requirements — (1) Forms of proxy, proxies and voting instructions in electronic format (including an electronic format that makes use of the telephone) will generally satisfy the in writing requirements if the electronic format used

         (a) ensures the integrity of the information contained in the forms of proxy and proxies; and

         (b) enables the recipient to maintain a permanent record of this information for subsequent reference.

(2) In order to ensure the integrity of information, the electronic format of the form of proxy, proxy or voting instructions should not permit the information in the document to be easily corrupted or changed. For example, the written proxy requirements generally would not be satisfied by sending an e-mail with a form of proxy in Word format attached, as this format could be easily tampered with.

(3) In order to assist a recipient to retain a permanent record of the information so as to be usable for subsequent reference, appropriate electronic formats and methods of electronic delivery should be used that include the ability to store and print the record.

4.3 Proxy Execution Requirements — (1) The proxy execution requirements are normally satisfied by a security holder's signature. The use of a signature indicates adoption of the information in the completed proxy, and permits authentication of the security holder's identity. We are of the view that the use of a manual signature is one method, but not the only method, of executing a proxy.

(2) The proxy execution requirements may be satisfied through the security holder using an electronic signature to execute a proxy, including a proxy in electronic format that satisfies the in writing requirements (see section 4.2). Any technology or process adopted for executing a proxy should create a reliable means of identifying the person using the signature and establishing that the person incorporated, attached or associated it to the proxy. The security holder's electronic signature should result from the security holder's use of a technology or process that permits the following to be verified or proven:

     1. a security holder used the technology or process to incorporate, attach or associate the security holder's signature to the proxy;

     2. the identity of the specific security holder using the technology or process; and

     3. the electronic signature resulting from a security holder's use of the technology or process is unique to the security holder.

PART 5 — EFFECTIVE DATE

5.1 Prior policy — National Policy 11-201 *Delivery of Documents by Electronic Means* is replaced by the Policy.

5.2 Effective Date — The Policy comes into effect on November 18, 2011.

APPENDIX A — ELECTRONIC COMMERCE LEGISLATION

Alberta

Electronic Transactions Act, S.A. 2001, c. E-55

British Columbia

Electronic Transactions Act, S.B.C. 2001, c.10

Manitoba

The Electronic Commerce and Information Act, S.M. 2000, c. E55

New Brunswick

Electronic Transactions Act, S.N.B. 2001, c. E-55

Newfoundland and Labrador

Electronic Commerce Act, S.N.L. 2001, c. E-52

Northwest Territories

Electronic Transactions Act, S.N.W.T. 2011, c. 13

Nova Scotia

Electronic Commerce Act, S.N.S. 2000 c. 26

Nunavut

Electronic Commerce Act, S.Nu. 2004, c. 7

Ontario

Electronic Commerce Act, S.O. 2000, c. 17

Prince Edward Island

Electronic Commerce Act, S.P.E.I. 2001, c. E-41

Quebec

An Act to establish a legal framework for information technology, R.S.Q. 2001, c. C-1.1

Saskatchewan

The Electronic Information and Documents Act, S.S. 2000, c. E-7.22

Yukon

Electronic Commerce Act, S.Y. 2000, c. 10

Adoption by OSC: (1999) 22 O.S.C.B. 8160; Request for Comments: (1998) 21 O.S.C.B. 7782 and (1997) 20 O.S.C.B. 3075.

Adoption of amendment by OSC: (2003) 26 O.S.C.B. 1437; Request for Comments: (2002) 25 O.S.C.B. 5359.

Adoption of amendment by OSC: (2011) 34 O.S.C.B. 11603; Request for Comments: (2011) 34 O.S.C.B. 5065.

Policies and Orders: NPS 47-201.

National Policy 11-202 — Process for Prospectus Reviews in Multiple Jurisdictions

Date: March 17, 2008, as amended effective September 28, 2009 and February 19, 2014

31 O.S.C.B. 1051, 32 O.S.C.B. (Supp. 4) 350 and 37 O.S.C.B. 1637

Table of Contents

PART 1 — APPLICATION

1.1 Scope and application — This policy describes procedures for the filing and review of a preliminary prospectus, prospectus and related materials in more than one Canadian jurisdiction.

PART 2 — DEFINITIONS

2.1 Definitions — In this policy,

"CP 11-102" means Companion Policy 11-102CP *Passport System* to MI 11-102;

"dual prospectus" means a prospectus described in section 3.3 of this policy;

"dual review" means the review under this policy of a dual prospectus;

"filer" means

(a) a person or company filing a prospectus, or

(b) an agent of a person or company referred to in paragraph (a);

"long form prospectus" includes a simplified prospectus and annual information form for a mutual fund;

"materials" mean the documents required under a national prospectus instrument;

"MI 11-102" means Multilateral Instrument 11-102 *Passport System*;

"NI 13-101" means National Instrument 13-101 *System for Electronic Document Analysis and Retrieval* (SEDAR);

"NP 11-203" means National Policy 11-203 *Process for Exemptive Relief Applications in Multiple Jurisdictions*;

"OSC" means the regulator in Ontario;

"passport jurisdiction" means the jurisdiction of a passport regulator;

"passport prospectus" means a prospectus described in section 3.2 of this policy;

"passport regulator" means a regulator that has adopted MI 11-102;

"pre-filing" means a consultation with the principal regulator for a prospectus filing, initiated before the filing of materials, regarding the interpretation of securities legislation or securities directions or their application to a particular offering or proposed offering;

"regulator" means a securities regulatory authority or regulator;

"shelf prospectus" means a prospectus filed under National Instrument 44-102 *Shelf Distributions*;

"short form prospectus" means a prospectus filed under National Instrument 44-101 *Short Form Prospectus Distributions*; and

"waiver application" means a request for an exemption from securities legislation, if the exemption would be evidenced by the issuance of a receipt under this policy.

2.2 Further definitions — Terms used in this policy and that are defined in MI 11-102, NI 13-101, or National Instrument 14-101 *Definitions* have the same meanings as in those instruments.

PART 3 — OVERVIEW AND PRINCIPAL REGULATOR

3.1 Overview — This policy deals with prospectuses filed in multiple jurisdictions in the following circumstances:

(a) The principal regulator is passport regulator and the prospectus is not filed in Ontario. This is a "passport prospectus."

(b) The principal regulator is the OSC and the prospectus is also filed in a passport jurisdiction. This is also a "passport prospectus."

(c) The principal regulator is a passport regulator and the prospectus is also filed in Ontario. This is a "dual prospectus."

3.2 Passport Prospectus — (1) If the principal regulator is a passport regulator and the prospectus is not filed in Ontario, only the principal regulator will review the prospectus. Under MI 11-102, the issuance of a receipt by the principal regulator will trigger a deemed receipt in each other passport jurisdiction where the prospectus is filed.

(2) If the principal regulator is the OSC and the prospectus is also filed in a passport jurisdiction, only the OSC will review the prospectus. Under MI 11-102, the issuance of the OSC receipt will trigger a deemed receipt in each passport jurisdiction where the prospectus is filed.

3.3 Dual Prospectus — If the principal regulator is a passport regulator and the prospectus is also filed in Ontario, the principal regulator will review the prospectus, and the OSC, as a non-principal regulator, will coordinate its review with the principal regulator. The receipt of the principal regulator will trigger a deemed receipt in each other passport jurisdiction where the prospectus is filed and will evidence the receipt of the OSC, if the OSC has made the same decision as the principal regulator.

3.4 Principal Regulator — (1) For purposes of a prospectus filing under this policy, the principal regulator is identified in the same manner as in section 3.1 of MI 11-102. This section summarizes section 3.1 of MI 11-102 and provides guidance for identifying the principal regulator for a prospectus filing. The same guidance also applies to a related pre-filing.

(2) For purposes of a waiver application related to a prospectus filing under this policy, the principal regulator is identified in the same manner as in sections 4.1 to 4.5 of MI 11-102. A filer should refer to section 3.6 of NP 11-203 for guidance on how to identify the principal regulator for a waiver application related to a prospectus filing under this policy.

(3) In most circumstances, the principal regulator for a waiver application and the principal regulator for the related prospectus filing will be the same. If the principal regulator is not the same, the regulators may initiate a discretionary change of principal regulator under section 3.5 of this policy. Alternatively, the filer may apply for a discretionary change of principal regulator under that section.

(4) The principal regulator for a prospectus filing under this policy is the regulator of the jurisdiction in which

(a) the issuer's head office is located, if the issuer is not an investment fund, or

(b) the investment fund manager's head office is located, if the issuer is an investment fund.

(5) If the regulator identified under subsection (4) is not in a specified jurisdiction, the principal regulator is the regulator in the specified jurisdiction with which the issuer, or in the case of an investment fund, the investment fund manager, has the most significant connection.

(6) For purposes of this section, a specified jurisdiction is one of British Columbia, Alberta, Saskatchewan, Manitoba, Ontario, Québec, New Brunswick or Nova Scotia.

(7) The factors an issuer, or in the case of an investment fund, the investment fund manager, should consider in identifying the principal regulator based on its most significant connection are, in order of influential weight:

(a) location of management;

(b) location of assets and operations;

(c) location of trading market or quotation system in Canada;

(d) location of securities holders, if the securities are not traded or quoted on a trading market or quotation system in Canada;

(e) location of underwriter;

(f) location of legal counsel; and

(g) location of transfer agent.

The connecting factors in (e) to (g) are not relevant for a Canadian issuer, or Canadian investment fund manager, because it will have a significant connection to a specified jurisdiction based on the connecting factors in (a) to (d). Regulators will generally object to a Canadian issuer, or Canadian investment fund manager, identifying a principal regulator based on the factors in (e) to (g).

(8) A filer should refer to section 3.6 of NP 11-203 for additional guidance if the filer

(a) is seeking a waiver application exemption but does not seek it from the regulator that would normally be the principal regulator for the waiver application, or

(b) is seeking more than one exemption and does not seek all of the exemptions from the regulator that would normally be the principal regulator for the waiver application.

3.5 Discretionary change in principal regulator — (1) If the principal regulator identified under section 3.4 of this policy thinks that it is not the appropriate principal regulator, it will first consult with the filer and the appropriate regulator and then give the filer a written notice of the new principal regulator and the reasons for the change. The regulator specified in the notice will be the principal regulator as of the later of the date the filer receives the notice and the effective date specified in the notice, if any.

(2) A filer may request a discretionary change of principal regulator for a prospectus filing if the filer believes that the principal regulator identified under section 3.4 of this policy is not the appropriate principal regulator.

(3) When a filer requests a discretionary change in principal regulator under subsection (2), the principal regulator will consult with the appropriate regulator.

(4) Regulators do not anticipate changing a principal regulator except in exceptional circumstances and will give a written notice when approving a request.

(5) A filer that requests a discretionary change of principal regulator under subsection (2) should do so at least 30 days before filing the related materials. If the filer submits the request at least 30 days before filing the related materials, the regulators will use their best efforts to resolve the request within 30 days of receiving it. If the request is not resolved when the filer files the related materials, the principal regulator determined under section 3.4 of this policy will be the principal regulator for the prospectus filing. If the regulators subsequently agree to the change, they will give the filer notice and the change of principal regulator will apply to the filer's future prospectus filings.

(6) A filer should submit a written request for a change in principal regulator to its current principal regulator and include the reasons for requesting the change.

(7) The guidance in this section also applies to a pre-filing.

(8) A filer should refer to section 3.7 of NP 11-203 for guidance on a discretionary change of principal regulator for a waiver application related to a prospectus filing under this policy.

PART 4 — FILING MATERIALS

4.1 Election to file under this policy, identification of principal regulator and payment of fees — The filer should indicate in its electronic filing on SEDAR the principal regulator for the prospectus offering and that it is filing materials under this policy and MI 11-102. If the principal regulator is not in the jurisdiction of the issuer's head office (or, in the case of an investment fund, the jurisdiction of the investment fund manager's head office), the filer should also indicate the connecting factor used to identify the principal regulator. If the filer files a prospectus in paper format under NI 13-101, the filer should include this information in the cover letter for the prospectus. In all cases, the filer should pay the required fees in each jurisdiction in which it files the prospectus.

4.2 Filing for distribution to purchasers only in jurisdictions outside principal jurisdiction — If a filer proposes to distribute its securities by prospectus only to purchasers in jurisdictions other than the jurisdiction of its principal regulator, the filer should file the materials with, and pay the required fees to, the principal regulator. The principal regulator will review the materials of the filer.

4.3 Blacklined document — A filer should file on SEDAR, as much in advance of filing final materials as possible, a draft final prospectus (the French language version in Québec), blacklined against the preliminary prospectus to show all proposed changes. A filer should also file with the final materials a copy of the final prospectus blacklined against the preliminary prospectus to show all changes made.

4.4 Seasoned Prospectuses — If a pro forma or preliminary prospectus is filed within two years of the date that a final receipt was issued for a prospectus of the same issuer, a filer (other than a filer that files under National Instrument 81-101 *Mutual Fund Prospectus Disclosure*) may identify the pro forma or preliminary prospectus as a seasoned prospectus. When filing a seasoned prospectus, the filer should also file

(a) a copy of the seasoned prospectus blacklined against the preceding prospectus of the filer to show all changes made, and

(b) a certificate certifying that the blacklined prospectus indicates all differences between the content of the seasoned prospectus and that of the filer's previous prospectus.

PART 5 — REVIEW OF MATERIALS

5.1 General — The principal regulator will review the materials in accordance with its securities legislation and securities directions and based on its review procedures, analysis and precedents.

5.2 Passport prospectus — The filer will deal only with the principal regulator, who will provide comments to, and receive responses from, the filer on the materials.

5.3 Dual prospectus — (1) The OSC will also review the materials and will advise the principal regulator of any concerns relating to the materials that, if left unresolved, would cause the OSC to opt out of the dual review.

(2) The filer will deal only with the principal regulator, who will provide comments to, and receive responses from, the filer and will issue the prospectus receipt if the relevant conditions are satisfied. However, in exceptional circumstances, the principal regulator may refer the filer to the OSC.

5.4 Review period for preliminary long form prospectuses and pro forma prospectuses — (1) The principal regulator will use its best efforts to review the materials relating to a preliminary long form prospectus or pro forma prospectus and provide a first comment letter within 10 working days of the date of the preliminary receipt or of receiving the pro forma prospectus and related materials in acceptable form. The principal regulator may provide further comments as a result of the filer's responses or the continuing review of the materials.

(2) In the case of a dual prospectus, the OSC will, within five working days of the date of the preliminary receipt or of receiving the pro forma prospectus and related materials in acceptable form, use its best efforts to:

(a) advise the principal regulator of any concerns with the materials that, if left unresolved, would cause the OSC to opt out of the dual review; or

(b) indicate on SEDAR that it is clear to receive final materials.

5.5 Review period for preliminary short form prospectuses and preliminary shelf prospectuses — (1) The principal regulator will use its best efforts to review the materials relating to a preliminary short form prospectus or preliminary shelf prospectus and provide a first comment letter within three working days of the date of the preliminary receipt. The principal regulator may provide further comments as a result of the filer's responses or the continuing review of the materials.

(2) In the case of a dual prospectus, the OSC will, within two working days of the date of the preliminary receipt, use its best efforts to:

(a) advise the principal regulator of any concerns with the materials that, if left unresolved, would cause the OSC to opt out of the dual review; or

(b) indicate on SEDAR that it is clear to receive final materials.

(3) If the principal regulator does not think it can review a preliminary short form prospectus or preliminary shelf prospectus adequately within the time-period contemplated in subsection (1) because it is too complex, the principal regulator may decide to apply the time-period for long form prospectuses. In that case, the principal regulator will notify the filer and, in the case of a dual prospectus, the OSC, within one working day of issuing the receipt for the preliminary short form prospectus or the preliminary shelf prospectus. Filers should submit a pre-filing to resolve any issues that may cause a delay in the review of a preliminary short form prospectus or preliminary shelf prospectus.

5.6 Novel and substantive issue — If a prospectus is filed for an offering that involves a novel and substantive issue or raises a novel policy concern and the issues were not resolved in a pre-filing, the complexity of the issue or concern may delay the review of the prospectus.

5.7 Form of response — The filer should provide written responses to the principal regulator's comment letter.

PART 6 — OPTING OUT OF A DUAL REVIEW

6.1 Opting Out — (1) The OSC can opt out of a dual review at any time before the principal regulator issues a final receipt for the materials. The OSC will provide notice of its decision to opt out to the filer and the principal regulator by indicating that it has opted out on SEDAR.

(2) The OSC will provide to the principal regulator written reasons for its decision to opt out of the dual review. The principal regulator will forward the reasons to the filer and will use its best efforts to resolve opt-out issues with the filer and the OSC.

(3) If the principal regulator is able to resolve the OSC's opt-out issues with the filer and the OSC, the OSC may opt back in. If the principal regulator is unable to resolve the OSC's opt-out issues, the principal regulator's final receipt will not evidence that the OSC has issued a receipt and the filer should deal with the OSC outside the dual review to resolve any outstanding issues.

PART 7 — RECEIPTS

7.1 Effect of prospectus receipt — (1) Under MI 11-102, a filer that receives a receipt for a preliminary prospectus or prospectus from the principal regulator will be deemed to have a receipt for the preliminary prospectus or prospectus in a passport jurisdiction if certain conditions are met, including that

(a) the filer filed the preliminary prospectus or prospectus in the passport jurisdiction, and

(b) the regulator of the passport jurisdiction is not the principal regulator for the prospectus filing.

To assist filers, the principal regulator will list in its receipt the passport jurisdictions where the prospectus has been filed under MI 11-102 and indicate that a receipt is deemed to be issued in each of those jurisdictions, if the conditions of MI 11-102 have been satisfied.

(2) In the case of a dual prospectus, the principal regulator's receipt for a preliminary prospectus will also evidence that the OSC has issued a receipt. The principal regulator's receipt for a final prospectus will also evidence that the OSC has issued a receipt, if the OSC has indicated on SEDAR that is it "clear for final".

(3) If a pro forma prospectus or an amended and restated preliminary prospectus is filed in the principal jurisdiction and a preliminary prospectus is filed in a non-principal jurisdiction, the principal regulator will issue a document that evidences that the regulator in the non-principal jurisdiction issued a receipt for the preliminary prospectus.

7.2 Conditions to issuance of preliminary receipt — The principal regulator will issue a preliminary receipt if:

(1) the principal regulator determines that the filer has filed acceptable materials; and

(2) the filer provides a letter to the principal regulator with the materials confirming the following, to the best of its knowledge and belief:

(a) The filer filed the materials (including all required translations) with, and paid the required fees to, the principal regulator and all non-principal regulators.

(b) The filer delivered all documents required to be delivered under the securities legislation of each jurisdiction in which the filer filed the materials.

(c) The filer is not subject to a cease trade order issued by the regulator of any jurisdiction in which the filer filed the materials.

(d) Where an underwriter is required to sign a certificate, at least one underwriter that signed the certificate is registered, or has filed an application for registration or for exemption from registration, in each jurisdiction in which the filer will offer securities to purchasers.

(e) Where an underwriter is required to sign a certificate in a jurisdiction in which the filer is making the distribution and none of the underwriters that signed the certificate is registered in that jurisdiction, but one of them has filed an application for registration or for exemption from

Part 1:
PROCEDURE

registration, that underwriter filed an undertaking with the principal regulator not to solicit in that jurisdiction until it is registered or exempt from registration.

(f) If the filer plans to distribute the securities itself, the filer is registered in each jurisdiction in which the filer will offer securities to purchasers, has filed an application for registration or for exemption from registration, or is not required to be registered.

(g) If the filer has filed an application for registration or exemption from registration in a jurisdiction, the filer filed an undertaking with the principal regulator not to solicit in that jurisdiction until the filer is registered or exempted from registration.

7.3 Conditions to issuance of final receipt for a prospectus — The principal regulator will issue a final receipt for a prospectus if:

(1) the principal regulator is satisfied that all of its comments have been resolved;

(2) in the case of a dual prospectus, the OSC indicates on SEDAR that it is clear to receive final materials or opts out of the dual review;

(3) the principal regulator determines that the filer filed acceptable materials; and

(4) the filer provides a letter to the principal regulator with the materials confirming the following, to the best of its knowledge and belief:

(a) The filer filed the materials (including all required translations and any undertaking the principal regulator requested) with, and paid the required fees to, the principal regulator and all non-principal regulators, except the OSC if the prospectus is a dual prospectus and the OSC has opted out of the dual review.

(b) The filer delivered all documents required to be delivered under the securities legislation of each jurisdiction in which the filer filed the materials.

(c) The filer is not subject to a cease trade order issued by the regulator of any jurisdiction in which the filer filed the materials.

(d) Where an underwriter is required to sign a certificate, at least one underwriter that signed the certificate is registered or is exempt from registration in each jurisdiction in which the filer will offer securities to purchasers.

(e) If the filer plans to distribute the securities itself, the filer is registered in each jurisdiction in which the filer will offer securities to purchasers, has an exemption from registration, or is not required to be registered.

(f) The filer has applied for and received all necessary exemptions from applicable securities legislation from the principal regulator and also from the OSC, in the case of a dual prospectus for which the OSC has not opted out of the dual review.

7.4 Translations — The filer is responsible for ensuring the accuracy of any required translations.

PART 8 — PRE-FILINGS AND WAIVER APPLICATIONS

8.1 General — (1) A filer seeking a pre-filing interpretation or a waiver application exemption before the issuance of a receipt should submit the pre-filing or waiver application sufficiently in advance of the filing of the related materials to avoid delays in the issuance of the receipt.

(1.1) Despite subsection (1), in Ontario prefilings and waiver applications are submitted in accordance with Ontario Securities Commission Rule 11-501 *Electronic Delivery of Documents to the Ontario Securities Commission*.

(2) The time required to review a pre-filing or waiver application will depend on whether it is routine or involves a novel and substantive issue or raises a novel policy concern.

(3) Annex A to the policy lists examples of pre-filings and waiver applications.

8.2 Procedure — (1) A filer should submit a pre-filing or waiver application by letter to the principal regulator. The pre-filing or waiver application should:

(a) identify the principal regulator for the pre-filing or waiver application and the basis for that determination;

(b) identify the non-principal regulators from which the filer requires the pre-filing interpretation or exemption,

(c) describe the subject matter of the pre-filing or waiver application, set out the interpretation or exemption sought, and provide supporting documentation; and

(d) in the case of a pre-filing or waiver application relating to a dual prospectus, provide the information set out in paragraph (c) that is relevant for Ontario.

(2) Filing the waiver application under subsection (1) with the principal regulator will satisfy the requirement to give notice in section 4.7(1)(c) of MI 11-102 to each passport regulator from which the filer seeks the exemption.

(3) For a routine pre-filing or waiver application,

(a) the principal regulator alone will review the pre-filing or waiver application and supporting documentation in accordance with its securities legislation and securities directions and based on its review procedures, analysis and precedents, and

(b) the principal regulator will use its best efforts to advise the filer of the disposition of the pre-filing or waiver application within four working days from receiving it.

(4) If the principal regulator determines that a pre-filing or waiver application for a passport prospectus involves a novel and substantive issue or raises a novel policy concern, the principal regulator may provide copies or a description of the pre-filing or waiver application to other regulators for discussion purposes.

(5) If the principal regulator determines that a pre-filing or waiver application for a dual prospectus involves a novel and substantive issue or raises a novel policy concern,

(a) The principal regulator will direct the filer to submit the pre-filing or waiver application in writing to the OSC if the filer has not already submitted it under paragraph (6).

(b) The principal regulator will use its best efforts to review the pre-filing or waiver application and supporting documentation and send its proposed disposition to the OSC within four working days from the date the principal regulator receives the pre-filing or waiver application.

(c) The OSC will use its best efforts to advise the principal regulator whether it agrees or disagrees with the principal regulator's proposed disposition within two working days from the date the OSC receives the principal regulator's proposed disposition.

(d) The principal regulator will advise the filer of the disposition of the pre-filing or waiver application if the OSC agrees with the proposed disposition.

(e) The principal regulator will use its best efforts to resolve the outstanding issues with the filer and the OSC if the OSC disagrees with the proposed disposition.

(f) If the principal regulator is unable to resolve the OSC's outstanding issues, the principal regulator will advise the filer of how it disposed of the pre-filing or waiver application and to deal separately with the OSC to resolve the outstanding issues.

(6) If it is apparent to the filer that a pre-filing or waiver application for a dual prospectus involves a novel and substantive issue or raises a novel policy concern, the filer may accelerate the process by initially submitting the pre-filing or waiver application to both the principal regulator and the OSC.

8.3 Information to be provided with related materials — (1) When filing a preliminary or pro forma prospectus after submitting a pre-filing or waiver application, a filer should always indicate on SEDAR that it submitted a pre-filing or waiver application in the principal jurisdiction and, if applicable, in Ontario.

(2) If the principal regulator for the filer's pre-filing or waiver application is different from the principal regulator for the filer's related prospectus filing, the filer should also indicate the name of the principal regulator for the pre-filing or waiver application in the cover letter for the prospectus.

(3) In addition, when filing a preliminary prospectus or pro forma prospectus after receiving the disposition for a pre-filing or waiver application, the filer should include in the cover letter for the prospectus:

(a) the name of the principal regulator for the pre-filing or waiver application, if it is different from the principal regulator for the prospectus filing;

(b) a description of the subject matter of the pre-filing or waiver application;

(c) the relevant provisions of the securities legislation in the principal jurisdiction;

(d) how the principal regulator for the pre-filing or waiver application disposed of the pre-filing or waiver application; and

(e) in the case of a pre-filing or waiver application relating to a dual prospectus,

(i) the information set out in paragraph (c) that is relevant for Ontario;

(ii) if the OSC disagrees with the principal regulator's proposed disposition, how the OSC disposed of the matter; and

(iii) if the filer did not seek an interpretation or an exemption in any passport jurisdiction, the subject matter of the pre-filing or waiver application and the disposition by the OSC.

8.4 Effect of prospectus receipt when waiver application submitted — (1) If a filer submitted a waiver application for a prospectus filing and the disclosure in the prospectus reflects that the principal regulator granted an exemption, the principal regulator's final receipt

(a) evidences that the principal regulator has granted the exemption, and

(b) results in an equivalent exemption in each passport jurisdiction that the filer identified in its waiver application under section 8.2(1)(b) of this policy and in which the filer filed the prospectus.

(2) If the principal regulator for the waiver application is different from the principal regulator for the related prospectus, the principal regulator for the waiver application will advise the principal regulator for the related prospectus of the disposition of the waiver application. If the principal regulator for the waiver application grants the exemption, the final receipt of the principal regulator for the related prospectus will

(a) evidence that the principal regulator for the waiver application has granted the exemption, and

(b) result in an equivalent exemption in each passport jurisdiction that the filer identified in its waiver application under section 8.2(1)(b) of this policy and in which the filer filed the prospectus.

(3) In the case of a waiver application relating to a dual prospectus, the principal regulator's final receipt will also evidence that the OSC has granted the exemption if the OSC has indicated on SEDAR that it is "clear for final".

8.5 Resolution of pre-filing — (1) The fact that the principal regulator issued the final receipt for a prospectus filing for which a filer submitted a pre-filing confirms that the pre-filing was satisfactorily resolved.

(2) If the principal regulator for a pre-filing is different from the principal regulator for the related prospectus, the principal regulator for the pre-filing will advise the principal regulator for the related prospectus of its interpretation.

PART 9 — APPLICATIONS

9.1 Applications in multiple jurisdictions — In many instances, filers require exemptions not contemplated under Part 8 to file materials or to facilitate a distribution of securities. NP 11-203 is available for these types of exemption applications.

9.2 Timing of application — A filer requiring an exemption before the issuance of a receipt should file its application sufficiently in advance of the filing of the related materials to avoid delays in the issuance of the receipt.

9.3 Additional information to be provided — When filing an application, the filer should indicate in a cover letter for the application that it has filed or will file related materials. When filing the related materials for a dual prospectus, the filer should indicate on SEDAR it has made or is making the application in Ontario.

PART 10 — AMENDMENTS

10.1 Conditions to issuance of receipt for preliminary prospectus amendments — The principal regulator will issue a preliminary prospectus amendment receipt if:

(1) the principal regulator determines that the filer has filed acceptable materials; and

(2) the filer provides a letter to the principal regulator with the materials confirming the following, to the best of its knowledge and belief:

(a) The filer filed the materials (including all required translations) with, and paid the required fees to, the principal regulator and all non-principal regulators.

(b) The filer delivered all documents required to be delivered under the securities legislation of each jurisdiction in which the filer filed the materials.

(c) The filer is not subject to a cease trade order issued by the regulator of any jurisdiction in which the filer filed the materials.

(d) Where an underwriter is required to sign a certificate, at least one underwriter that signed the certificate is registered, or has filed an application for registration or for exemption from registration, in each jurisdiction in which the filer will offer securities to purchasers.

(e) Where an underwriter is required to sign a certificate in a jurisdiction in which the filer is making the distribution and none of the underwriters that signed the certificate is registered in that jurisdiction, but one of them has filed an application for registration or for exemption from registration, that underwriter filed an undertaking with the principal regulator not to solicit in that jurisdiction until it is registered or exempt from registration.

(f) If the filer plans to distribute the securities itself, the filer is registered in each jurisdiction in which the filer will offer securities to purchasers, has filed an application for registration or for exemption from registration, or is not required to be registered.

(g) If the filer has filed an application for registration or exemption from registration in a jurisdiction, the filer filed an undertaking with the principal regulator not to solicit in that jurisdiction until the filer is registered or exempted from registration.

10.2 Receipt for preliminary prospectus amendments — (1) Under MI 11-102, a filer that receives a receipt for a preliminary prospectus amendment from the principal regulator will be deemed to have a receipt for the preliminary prospectus amendment in a passport jurisdiction if certain conditions are met, including that

(a) the filer filed the preliminary prospectus amendment in the passport jurisdiction, and

(b) the regulator in the passport jurisdiction is not the principal regulator for the prospectus filing.

To assist filers, the principal regulator will list in its receipt the passport jurisdictions in which it understands the filer has a deemed receipt.

(2) In the case of a dual prospectus, the principal regulator's receipt for a preliminary prospectus amendment will also evidence that the OSC has issued a receipt.

10.3 Review period for preliminary prospectus amendments — (1) If a filer files a preliminary prospectus amendment before the principal regulator issues its comment letter relating to the preliminary prospectus materials, the principal regulator may be unable to complete its review of the preliminary prospectus materials and issue its comment letter within the time-period indicated in section 5.4(1) or 5.5(1) of this policy, as applicable. The principal regulator will use its best efforts to issue its comment letter on the later of the date that is

(a) in the case of a long form prospectus, five working days after the date of the receipt for the preliminary prospectus amendment and the original due date for the comment letter; and

(b) in the case of a short form prospectus or a shelf prospectus, three working days after the date of the receipt for the preliminary prospectus amendment and the original due date for the comment letter.

Similarly, in the case of a dual prospectus, if a filer files a preliminary prospectus amendment before the OSC completes its review under section 5.4(2) or 5.5(2) of this policy, the OSC may be unable to complete its review within the relevant time-periods. The OSC will use its best efforts to advise the principal regulator by the later of

(a) the date that is three working days after the date of the receipt for the preliminary prospectus amendment, and

(b) the original due date for advising the principal regulator

of any concerns with the materials that, if left unresolved, would cause it to opt out of the dual review.

(2) If a filer files a preliminary long form prospectus amendment after the principal regulator has issued its comment letter,

(a) the principal regulator will use its best efforts to review the materials and issue a comment letter within three working days of the date of the receipt for the preliminary long form prospectus amendment; and

(b) in the case of a dual prospectus, the OSC will use its best efforts to advise the principal regulator, within three working days of the date of the receipt for the preliminary long form prospectus amendment, of any concerns with the materials that, if left unresolved, would cause it to opt out of the dual review.

(3) If a filer files a preliminary short form prospectus amendment or preliminary shelf prospectus amendment after the principal regulator has issued its comment letter,

(a) the principal regulator will use its best efforts to review the materials and issue a comment letter within two working days of the date of the receipt for the preliminary short form prospectus amendment or preliminary shelf prospectus amendment; and

(b) in the case of a dual prospectus, the OSC will use its best efforts to advise the principal regulator, within two working days of the date of the receipt for the preliminary short form prospectus amendment or preliminary shelf prospectus amendment, of any concerns with the materials that, if left unresolved, would cause it to opt out of the dual review.

(4) The time periods in subsections (2) and (3) may not apply in circumstances where it would be more appropriate for the principal regulator and, in the case of a dual prospectus, the OSC, to review the amendment materials at a different stage of the review process. For example, the principal regulator and the OSC may wish to defer reviewing the amendment materials until after receiving and reviewing the filer's responses to comments already issued on the preliminary prospectus materials.

10.4 Review period for prospectus amendments — (1) If a filer files a long form prospectus amendment,

(a) the principal regulator will use its best efforts to review the materials and issue a comment letter within three working days of the date of receiving the materials in acceptable form; and

(b) in the case of a dual prospectus, the OSC will use its best efforts to advise the principal regulator within three working days of the date of receiving the materials in acceptable form of any concerns with the materials that, if left unresolved, would cause it to opt out of the dual review.

(2) If a filer files a short form prospectus amendment or shelf prospectus amendment,

(a) the principal regulator will use its best efforts to review the materials and issue a comment letter within two working days of the date of receiving the materials in acceptable form; and

(b) in the case of a dual prospectus, the OSC will use its best efforts to advise the principal regulator within two working days of the date of receiving the materials in acceptable form of any concerns with the materials that, if left unresolved, would cause it to opt out of the dual review.

10.5 Conditions to issuance of prospectus amendment receipt — The principal regulator will issue a prospectus amendment receipt if:

(1) the principal regulator is satisfied that all of its comments have been resolved;

(2) in the case of a dual prospectus, the OSC indicates on SEDAR that it is clear to receive amendments to final materials or opts out of the dual review;

(3) the principal regulator determines that the filer filed acceptable materials; and

(4) the filer provides a letter to the principal regulator with the materials confirming the following, to the best of its knowledge and belief:

(a) The filer filed the materials (including all required translations and any undertaking the principal regulator requested) with, and paid the required fees to, the principal regulator and all non-principal regulators, except the OSC if the amendment relates to a dual prospectus and the OSC has opted out of the dual review.

(b) The filer delivered all documents required to be delivered under the securities legislation of each jurisdiction in which the filer filed the materials.

(c) The filer is not subject to a cease trade order issued by the regulator of any jurisdiction in which the filer filed the materials;

(d) Where an underwriter is required to sign a certificate and the amendment relates to the removal of an underwriter, at least one underwriter that signed the certificate is registered or is exempt from registration in each jurisdiction in which the filer will offer securities to purchasers.

(e) The filer has applied for and received all necessary exemptions from applicable securities legislation from the principal regulator, and from the OSC in the case of a dual prospectus for which the OSC has not opted out of the dual review.

10.6 Prospectus amendment receipt — (1) Under MI 11-102, a filer that receives a receipt for a prospectus amendment from the principal regulator will be deemed to have a receipt for the prospectus amendment in a passport jurisdiction if certain conditions are met, including that

(a) the filer filed the prospectus amendment in the passport jurisdiction, and

(b) the regulator in the passport jurisdiction is not the principal regulator for the prospectus filing.

To assist filers, the principal regulator will list in its receipt the passport jurisdictions in which it understands the filer has a deemed receipt.

(2) In the case of a dual prospectus, the principal regulator's receipt for a prospectus amendment will also evidence that the OSC has issued a receipt, if the OSC has indicated on SEDAR that it is "clear" for the amendment to final.

PART 11 — HOLIDAYS

11.1 Holidays — A receipt issued under this Policy is deemed to be issued in a non-principal passport jurisdiction on the date of the receipt issued by the principal regulator even if the non-principal passport regulator is closed on that date. For a dual prospectus, the receipt from the principal regulator will also evidence that the OSC has issued a receipt if the OSC is open on the date of the principal regulator's receipt and has not opted-out. If the OSC is not open on the date of the principal regulator's receipt, the principal regulator will issue a second receipt that evidences that the OSC has issued a receipt on the next day that the OSC is open.

PART 12 — EFFECTIVE DATE AND TRANSITION

12.1 Effective date — This policy comes into effect on March 17, 2008.

12.2 Prospectus filed before March 17, 2008 — The process set out in National Policy 43-201 Mutual Reliance Review System for Prospectuses will continue to apply to

(a) a preliminary prospectus, pro forma prospectus, preliminary prospectus amendment or prospectus amendment filed before March 17, 2008,

(b) a prospectus, other than a prospectus amendment, whose related preliminary prospectus or pro forma prospectus was filed before March 17, 2008, and

(c) a pre-filing or waiver application filed before March 17, 2008 if it relates to a prospectus whose related preliminary prospectus or pro forma prospectus was filed before March 17, 2008.

ANNEX A — EXAMPLES OF PRE-FILINGS AND WAIVER APPLICATIONS DEALT WITH UNDER PART 8 OF NATIONAL POLICY 11-202

Matters relating to:

1. Financial statement and other prospectus requirements

2. Escrow requirements for a prospectus

3. Confidentiality of material contracts

4. NI 81-101 *Mutual Fund Prospectus Disclosure*

5. Confidential pre-filing of a prospectus for review purposes

Adoption by OSC: (2008) 31 O.S.C.B. 1234 and 1009; Request for Comments: (2007) 30 O.S.C.B. 7527.

Adoption of Amendments by OSC: (2009) 32 O.S.C.B. (Supp. 4) 350, 32 O.S.C.B. (Supp. 2) 424 and (2008) 31 O.S.C.B. 12070; Request for Comments: (2008) 31 O.S.C.B. 7171.

Adoption of Amendments by OSC: (2013) 36 O.S.C.B. 10503; Request for Comments: (2013) 36 O.S.C.B. 3929.

Adoption of Amendments by OSC: (2014) 37 O.S.C.B. 1637.

Policies and Orders: CSAN 13-315; NPS 11-203, 11-204.

Part 1: PROCEDURE

National Policy 11-203 — Process For Exemptive Relief Applications In Multiple Jurisdictions

Date: March 17, 2008, as amended effective September 28, 2009, July 31, 2012, February 19, 2014, September 22, 2014 and January 13, 2016

31 O.S.C.B. 1066, 32 O.S.C.B. (Supp. 4) 351, 35 O.S.C.B. 4503, 37 O.S.C.B. 1637, 37 O.S.C.B. (Supp. 4) 131 and 38 O.S.C.B. (Supp. 4) 36

Table of Contents

Annex A — Form of decision for passport application

Annex B — Form of decision for dual application

Annex C — Form of decision for coordinated review application

Annex D — Form of decision for hybrid application

PART 1 — APPLICATION

1.1 Application — This policy describes the process for the filing and review of an application for exemptive relief in more than one Canadian jurisdiction.

PART 2 — DEFINITIONS

2.1 Definitions — In this policy

"AMF" means the regulator in Québec;

"application" means a request for exemptive relief other than a pre-filing or waiver application as those terms are defined in NP 11-202;

"coordinated review" means the review under this policy of a coordinated review application;

"coordinated review application" means an application described in section 3.4 of this policy;

"CP 11-102" means Companion Policy 11-102CP *Passport System* to MI 11-102;

"dual application" means an application described in section 3.3 of this policy;

"dual review" means the review under this policy of a dual application;

"exemption" means any discretionary exemption to which Part 4 of MI 11-102 applies;

"exemptive relief" means any approval, decision, declaration, designation, determination, exemption, extension, order, ruling, permission, recognition, revocation, waiver or other relief sought under securities legislation or securities directions;

"filer" means

   (a) a person or company filing an application, or

   (b) an agent of a person or company referred to in paragraph (a);

"hybrid application" means an application comprised of both

   (a) a passport application or dual application, and

   (b) a coordinated review application;

"MI 11-102" means Multilateral Instrument 11-102 *Passport System*;

"notified passport jurisdiction" means a passport jurisdiction for which a filer gave the notice referred to in section 4.7(1)(c) of MI 11-102

"NP 11-202" means National Policy 11-202 *Process for Prospectus Reviews in Multiple Jurisdictions*;

"NP 11-204"means National Policy 11-204 *Process for Registration in Multiple Jurisdictions*;

"OSC" means the regulator in Ontario;

"passport application" means an application described in section 3.2 of this policy;

"passport jurisdiction" means the jurisdiction of a passport regulator;

"passport regulator" means a regulator that has adopted MI 11-102;

"pre-filing" means a consultation with the principal regulator for an application, initiated before the filing of the application, regarding the interpretation of securities legislation or securities directions or their application to a particular transaction or matter or proposed transaction or matter; and

"regulator" means a securities regulatory authority or regulator.

2.2 Further definitions — Terms used in this policy that are defined in MI 11-102 or National Instrument 14-101 *Definitions* have the same meanings as in those instruments.

PART 3 — OVERVIEW, PRINCIPAL REGULATOR AND GENERAL GUIDELINES

3.1 Overview — This policy applies to any application for exemptive relief in multiple jurisdictions. These are the possible types of applications:

   (a) The principal regulator is a passport regulator and the filer does not seek an exemption in Ontario. This is a "passport application."

   (b) The principal regulator is the OSC and the filer also seeks an exemption in a passport jurisdiction. This is also a "passport application."

   (c) The principal regulator is a passport regulator and the filer also seeks an exemption in Ontario. This is a "dual application."

   (d) An application for any type of exemptive relief not covered by Part 4 of MI 11-102. This is a "coordinated review application."

3.2 Passport application — (1) If the principal regulator is a passport regulator and the filer does not seek an exemption in Ontario, the filer files the application only with, and pays fees only to, the principal regulator. Only the principal regulator reviews the application. The principal regulator's decision to grant an exemption automatically results in an equivalent exemption in the notified passport jurisdictions.

(2) If the principal regulator is the OSC and the filer also seeks an equivalent exemption in a passport jurisdiction, the filer files the application only with, and pays fees only to, the OSC. Only the OSC reviews the application. The OSC's decision to grant the exemption automatically results in an equivalent exemption in the notified passport jurisdictions.

3.3 Dual application — If the principal regulator is a passport regulator and the filer also seeks an exemption in Ontario, the filer files the application with, and pays fees to, both the principal regulator and the OSC. The principal regulator reviews the application and the OSC, as a non-principal regulator, coordinates its review with the principal regulator. The principal regulator's decision to grant the exemption automatically results in an equivalent exemption in the notified passport jurisdictions and, if the OSC has made the same decision as the principal regulator, evidences the decision of the OSC.

3.4 Coordinated review application — If the application is outside the scope of MI 11-102 (see section 4.1 of CP 11-102 for details on the types of applications that fall outside the scope of MI 11-102), the filer files the application and pays fees in each jurisdiction where the exemptive relief is required. The principal regulator reviews the application, and each non-principal regulator coordinates its review with the principal regulator. The decision of the principal regulator to grant exemptive relief evidences the decision of each non-principal regulator that has made the same decision as the principal regulator.

3.5 Hybrid applications — The processes and outcomes applicable to a passport application, dual application or a coordinated review application under this policy also apply to a hybrid application. For a hybrid application, the filer should follow the processes for both a coordinated review application and either a passport application or dual application, as appropriate.

3.6 Principal regulator — (1) For any application under this policy, the principal regulator is identified in the same manner as in sections 4.1 to 4.5 of MI 11-102. This section summarizes sections 4.1 to 4.5 of MI 11-102 and provides guidance on identifying the principal regulator for an application under this policy.

(2) For the purpose of this section, a specified jurisdiction is one of British Columbia, Alberta, Saskatchewan, Manitoba, Ontario, Québec, New Brunswick or Nova Scotia.

(3) Except as provided in subsections (4) to (9) and (11) of this section and in section 3.7 of this policy, the principal regulator for an exemptive relief application is

    (a) for an application made for an investment fund, the regulator of the jurisdiction in which the investment fund manager's head office is located; or

    (b) for an application made for a person or company other than an investment fund, the regulator of the jurisdiction in which the person or company's head office is located.

(4) Except as provided in subsections (6) to (9) and (11) of this section and in section 3.7 of this policy, the principal regulator for an application for exemptive relief from a provision of securities legislation related to insider reporting is the regulator in the jurisdiction in which the head office of the reporting issuer, not the insider, is located.

(5) Except as provided in subsections (6) to (9) and (11) of this section and in section 3.7 of this policy, the principal regulator for an application for exemptive relief from a provision of securities legislation related to take-over bids is the regulator in the jurisdiction in which the head office of the issuer whose securities are subject to the take-over bid, not the person or company that is making the take-over bid, is located.

(6) Except as provided in subsections (7), (8), (9) and (11) of this section and section 3.7 of this policy, if the jurisdiction identified under subsection (3), (4) or (5) is not a specified jurisdiction, the principal regulator for the application is the regulator of the specified jurisdiction with which

    (a) in the case of an application for exemptive relief from a provision of securities legislation related to insider reporting, the reporting issuer has the most significant connection,

    (b) in the case of an application for exemptive relief from a provision of securities legislation related to take-over bids, the issuer whose securities are subject to the take-over bid has the most significant connection, or

    (c) in any other case, the person or company or, in the case of an investment fund, the investment fund manager, has the most significant connection.

(7) Except as provided in subsections (8), (9) and (11) of this section and section 3.7 of this policy, if a firm or individual makes an application for exemptive relief from a requirement in Parts 3 and 12 of NI 31-103 or Part 2 of NI 33-109 in connection with an application for registration in the principal jurisdiction, the principal regulator for the exemptive relief application is the principal regulator as determined under section 3.6 of NP 11-204. Under section 3.6 of NP 11-204 the securities regulatory authority or regulator of any jurisdiction can be a principal regulator.

(8) Except as provided in subsections (9) and (11) of this section, and section 3.7 of this policy, if a person or company is not seeking exemptive relief in the jurisdiction of the principal regulator, as determined under subsections (3), (4), (5), (6) or (7), the principal regulator for the application is the regulator in the specified jurisdiction

    (a) in which the person or company is seeking exemptive relief, and

    (b) with which

        (i) in the case of an application for exemptive relief from a provision of securities legislation related to insider reporting, the reporting issuer has the most significant connection,

        (ii) in the case of an application for exemptive relief from a provision of securities legislation related to take-over bids, the issuer whose securities are subject to the take-over bid has the most significant connection, or

        (iii) in any other case, the person or company or, in the case of an investment fund, the investment fund manager, has the most significant connection.

(9) Except as provided in subsection (11) of this section and section 3.7 of this policy, if at any one time a person or company is seeking more than one item of exemptive relief and not all of the exemptive relief is needed in the jurisdiction of the principal regulator, as determined under subsection (3), (4), (5), (6), (7) or (8), the person or company may make an application to the regulator in the specified jurisdiction

    (a) in which the person or company is seeking all of the exemptive relief, and

    (b) with which

        (i) in the case of an application for exemptive relief from a provision of securities legislation related to insider reporting, the reporting issuer has the most significant connection,

        (ii) in the case of an application for exemptive relief from a provision of securities legislation related to take-over bids, the issuer whose securities are subject to the take-over bid has the most significant connection, or

        (iii) in any other case, the person or company or, in the case of an investment fund, the investment fund manager, has the most significant connection.

That regulator will be the principal regulator for the application.

(10) Except as provided in subsection (11) of this section, the factors a filer should consider in identifying the principal regulator for the application based on the most significant connection test are, in order of influential weight:

    (a) location of reporting issuer status or registration status,

    (b) location of management,

    (c) location of assets and operations,

    (d) location of majority of security holders or clients, and

    (e) location of trading market or quotation system in Canada.

(11) In the case of an application for exemptive relief from a provision of Multilateral Instrument 51-105 *Issuers Quoted in the U.S. Over-the-Counter Markets*, the factors a filer should consider in identifying the principal regulator for the application are set out in Part 5 of Companion Policy 51-105CP.

3.7 Discretionary change in principal regulator — (1) If the principal regulator identified under section 3.6 of this policy thinks it is not the appropriate principal regulator, it will first consult with the filer and the appropriate regulator and then give the filer a written notice of the new principal regulator and the reasons for the change.

(2) A filer may request a discretionary change of principal regulator for an application if

    (a) the filer believes the principal regulator identified under section 3.6 of this policy is not the appropriate principal regulator,

    (b) the location of the head office changes over the course of the application,

    (c) the most significant connection to a specified jurisdiction changes over the course of the application, or

    (d) the filer withdraws its application in the principal jurisdiction because no exemptive relief is required in that jurisdiction.

(3) Regulators do not anticipate changing a principal regulator except in exceptional circumstances.

(4) A filer should submit a written request for a change in principal regulator to its current principal regulator and include the reasons for requesting the change.

3.8 General guidelines — (1) A filer should identify the exemptive relief that is appropriate and necessary in the principal jurisdiction and each non-principal jurisdiction to which the filer applies or for which it gives notice under section 4.7(1)(c) of MI 11-102.

(2) The terms, conditions, restrictions and requirements of a decision will reflect the securities legislation and securities directions of the principal jurisdiction.

(3) A decision will generally provide exemptive relief for the entire transaction or matter that is the subject of the application to ensure the transaction or matter gets uniform treatment in all jurisdictions. This means that, if the transaction or matter is comprised of a series of trades, the decision will generally exempt all the trades in the series and the filer will not rely on statutory exemptions for some trades and on the decision for others.

(4) The regulators are not prepared to extend the availability of a non-harmonized exemption set out in National Instrument 45-106 *Prospectus Exemptions* (NI 45-106) to a non-principal jurisdiction where the non-harmonized exemption is not available under that rule. If a filer makes a passport application or a dual application that would have that effect, the principal regulator will request that the filer provide a representation that no person or company will rely on the exemption in that non-principal jurisdiction. For example, jurisdictions have adopted different types of offering memorandum exemptions under NI 45-106. A principal regulator would not grant an exemption that would have the effect of allowing the use of a type of offering memorandum exemption that is not available under NI 45-106 in a non-principal jurisdiction, unless the filer gave a representation that no person or company would offer the securities relying on that type of offering memorandum exemption in the non-principal jurisdiction.

(5) Regulators will generally send communications to filers by e-mail or facsimile.

PART 4 — PRE-FILINGS

4.1 General — (1) A filer should submit a pre-filing sufficiently in advance of an application to avoid any delays in the issuance of a decision on the application.

(2) The principal regulator will treat the pre-filing as confidential except that it:

    (a) may provide copies or a description of the pre-filing to other regulators for discussion purposes if the pre-filing involves a novel and substantive issue or raises a novel policy concern, and

    (b) may have to release the pre-filing under freedom of information and protection of privacy legislation.

4.2 Procedure for passport application pre-filing — A filer should submit a pre-filing for a passport application by letter to the principal regulator and should

    (a) identify in the pre-filing the principal regulator for the application and each passport jurisdiction for which the filer intends to give the notice referred to in section 4.7(1)(c) of MI 11-102, and

    (b) submit the pre-filing to the principal regulator only.

4.3 Procedure for dual application pre-filing — (1) A filer submitting a pre-filing for a dual application should identify in the pre-filing the principal regulator, each passport jurisdiction for which the filer intends to give the notice referred to in section 4.7(1)(c) of MI 11-102, and Ontario.

(2) The filer should submit the pre-filing only to the principal regulator. If the pre-filing is routine, the filer will deal only with the principal regulator to resolve the pre-filing.

(3) If the principal regulator determines that a pre-filing submitted as a routine pre-filing involves a novel and substantive issue or raises a novel policy concern, it will advise the filer and direct the filer to submit the pre-filing to the OSC.

(4) If it is apparent to the filer that a pre-filing involves a novel and substantive issue or raises a novel policy concern, the filer may accelerate this process by submitting the pre-filing to both the principal regulator and the OSC.

(5) If a pre-filing involves a novel and substantive issue or raises a novel policy concern, the principal regulator will arrange with the OSC to discuss it within seven business days, or as soon as practicable after the OSC receives the pre-filing.

4.4 Procedure for coordinated review application pre-filing — (1) A filer submitting a pre-filing for a coordinated review application should identify in the pre-filing the principal regulator and all non-principal jurisdictions where the filer intends to file the application.

(2) The filer should submit the pre-filing only to the principal regulator. If the pre-filing is routine, the filer will deal only with the principal regulator to resolve the pre-filing.

(3) If the principal regulator determines that a pre-filing submitted as a routine pre-filing involves a novel and substantive issue or raises a novel policy concern, it will advise the filer and direct the filer to submit the pre-filing to each non-principal regulator.

(4) If it is apparent to the filer that a pre-filing involves a novel and substantive issue or raises a novel policy concern, the filer may accelerate this process by submitting the pre-filing to the principal regulator and each non-principal regulator with whom the filer intends to file the application.

(5) If a pre-filing involves a novel and substantive issue or raises a novel policy concern, the principal regulator will arrange with the non-principal regulators to discuss the pre-filing within seven business days, or as soon as practicable after all non-principal regulators receive the pre-filing.

4.5 Disclosure in related application — The filer should include in the application that follows a pre-filing,

(a) a description of the subject matter of the pre-filing and the approach taken by the principal regulator, and

(b) any alternative approach proposed by a non-principal regulator that was involved in discussions and that disagreed with the principal regulator.

PART 5 — FILING MATERIALS

5.1 Election to file under this policy and identification of principal regulator — In its application, the filer should indicate whether it is filing a passport application, dual application, coordinated review application or hybrid application under this policy and identify the principal regulator for the application. If submitting a hybrid application, the filer should indicate whether it includes a passport application or a dual application.

5.2 Materials to be filed with application — (1) For a passport application, the filer should remit to the principal regulator the fees payable under the securities legislation of the principal regulator, and file the following materials with the principal regulator only:

(a) a written application drafted in accordance with the procedures of the principal regulator as to format and content in which the filer:

(i) states the basis for identifying the principal regulator under section 3.6 of this policy,

(ii) identifies whether another application in connection with the same transaction or matter has been filed in one or more jurisdictions, the reasons for that application, and the principal regulator for that application,

(iii) sets out, for any related pre-filing, the information referred to in section 4.5 of this policy,

(iv) sets out, under separate headings, each provision of securities legislation listed in Appendix D of MI 11-102 below the name of the principal jurisdiction from which the filer and other relevant party seek an exemption,

(v) gives notice of the non-principal passport jurisdictions for which section 4.7(1) of MI 11-102 is intended to be relied upon for each equivalent provision of the local jurisdiction,

(vi) sets out any request for confidentiality,

(vii) sets out references to previous decisions of the principal regulator or other regulators that would support granting the exemption, or indicates that the exemption sought is novel and has not been previously granted;

(viii) includes a verification statement that authorizes the filing of the application and confirms the truth of the facts in the application; and

(ix) states that the filer and other relevant party is not in default of securities legislation in any jurisdiction or, if the filer is in default, the nature of the default;

(b) supporting materials; and

(c) a draft form of decision with terms, conditions, restrictions or requirements, including

(i) a representation stating that the filer and other relevant party are not in default of securities legislation in any jurisdiction or, if the filer or other relevant party is in default, the nature of the default; and

(ii) resale restrictions, if applicable, based on the securities legislation and securities directions of the principal jurisdiction.

(2) For a dual application, the filer should remit the fees payable under the securities legislation of the principal regulator and the OSC to each of them, as appropriate, and file the following materials with both the principal regulator and the OSC:

(a) a written application drafted in accordance with the procedures of the principal regulator as to format and content in which the filer:

(i) states the basis for identifying the principal regulator under section 3.6 of this policy,

(ii) identifies whether another application in connection with the same transaction or matter has been filed in one or more jurisdictions, the reasons for the application, and the principal regulator for that application,

(iii) sets out, for any related pre-filing, the information referred to in section 4.5 of this policy,

(iv) sets out, under separate headings, each provision of securities legislation listed in Appendix D of MI 11-102 below the name of the principal jurisdiction from which the filer and other relevant party seek an exemption, the relevant provisions of securities legislation in Ontario and an analysis of any differences between the applicable provisions in the principal jurisdiction and Ontario,

(v) gives notice of the non-principal passport jurisdictions for which section 4.7(1) of MI 11-102 is intended to be relied upon for each equivalent provision of the local jurisdiction,

(vi) sets out any request for confidentiality,

(vii) sets out any request to shorten the review period (see section 6.2(3) of this policy) or the opt-out period (see section 7.2(4) of this policy) and provides supporting reasons,

(viii) sets out references to previous decisions of the principal regulator or other regulators that would support granting the exemption, or indicates that the exemption sought is novel and has not been previously granted;

(ix) includes a verification statement that authorizes the filing of the application and confirms the truth of the facts in the application; and

(x) states that the filer and any relevant party are not in default of securities legislation in any jurisdiction or, if the filer or other relevant party is in default, the nature of the default;

(b) supporting materials; and

(c) a draft form of decision with terms, conditions, restrictions or requirements, including

(i) a representation stating that the filer and other relevant party are not in default of securities legislation in any jurisdiction or if the filer or relevant party is in default, the nature of the default; and

(ii) resale restrictions, if applicable, based on the securities legislation and securities directions of the principal jurisdiction.

(3) For a coordinated review application, the filer should remit the fees payable under the securities legislation of the principal regulator and each non-principal regulator from whom the filer or other relevant parties seek exemptive relief to each of them, as appropriate, and file the following materials with the principal regulator and each of the non-principal regulators:

(a) a written application drafted in accordance with the procedures of the principal regulator as to format and content in which the filer:

(i) states the basis for identifying the principal regulator section 3.6 of this policy,

(ii) identifies whether another application in connection with the same transaction or matter has been filed in one or more jurisdictions, the reasons for the application, and the principal regulator for that application,

(iii) sets out, for any related pre-filing, the information referred to in section 4.5 of this policy,

(iv) sets out, under separate headings, each provision of securities legislation in the principal jurisdiction from which the filer and other relevant party are seeking exemptive relief, the relevant provisions of securities legislation in each non-principal jurisdiction, and an analysis of any differences between the applicable provisions in the principal jurisdiction and each non-principal jurisdiction,

(v) sets out any request for confidentiality,

(vi) sets out any request to shorten the review period (see section 6.2(3) of this policy) or the opt-out period (see section 7.2(4) of this policy) and provides supporting reasons,

(vii) sets out references to previous decisions of the principal regulator or other regulators that would support granting the exemptive relief, or indicates that the exemptive relief sought is novel and has not been previously granted;

(viii) includes a verification statement that authorizes the filing of the application and confirms the truth of the facts in the application; and

(ix) states that the filer and any other relevant party are not in default of securities legislation in any jurisdiction or if the filer or other relevant party is in default, the nature of the default;

(b) supporting materials; and

(c) a draft form of decision with terms, conditions, restrictions or requirements, including

(i) a representation stating that the filer and any other relevant party are not in default of securities legislation in any jurisdiction or if the filer or other relevant party is in default, the nature of the default; and

(ii) resale restrictions, if applicable, based on the securities legislation and securities directions of the principal jurisdiction.

(4) For a hybrid application, the filer should pay the fees, file the application with each regulator and, for each type of application, set out the exemption or exemptive relief sought and submit the relevant information and materials, all as described in this section.

(5) A filer should file an application sufficiently in advance of any deadline to ensure that staff have a reasonable opportunity to complete the review and make recommendations for a decision.

(6) A filer making a passport application or a dual application should identify in the application all the exemptions required and give the required notice for all the passport jurisdictions for which section 4.7(1) of MI 11-102 is intended to be relied upon. The notice given under subsection (1)(a)(v) or (2)(a)(v) above satisfies the notice requirement of section 4.7(1)(c) of MI 11-102.

(7) A filer seeking exemptive relief in Québec should file a French language version of the draft decision when the AMF is acting as principal regulator.

5.3 Materials to be filed to make an exemption available in an additional passport jurisdiction under sections 4.7 and 4.8 of MI 11-102 — (1) Under section 4.7(1) of MI 11-102, an exemption from a provision of securities legislation listed in Appendix D of that Instrument granted by the principal regulator under a passport application or dual application can become available in a non-principal passport jurisdiction for which the filer did not give the notice referred to in section 5.2(1)(a)(v) or 5.2(2)(a)(v) of this policy in the initial application if certain conditions are met. One of the conditions is that the filer give the notice under section 4.7(1)(c) of MI 11-102 for the additional non-principal passport jurisdiction.

(2) Under section 4.8(1) of MI 11-102, an exemption from a provision of securities legislation that is now listed in Appendix D of that Instrument and that was granted before March 17, 2008 by the regulator in a specified jurisdiction, as defined in that section, can also become available in a non-principal passport jurisdiction if certain conditions are met. One of the conditions is that the filer gives the notice under section 4.8(1)(c) of MI 11-102 for the non-principal passport jurisdiction. Under section 4.8(3), the filer is not required to give this notice if the exemption relates to a CD requirement, as defined in Multilateral Instrument 11-101 *Principal Regulator System*, that is now listed in Appendix D of MI 11-102 and other conditions are met. For more guidance on section 4.8(1) of MI 11-102, refer to section 9.3 of this policy and section 4.5 of CP 11-102.

(3) For greater certainty, a filer may not rely on section 4.7 or 4.8 of MI 11-102 to obtain an automatic exemption from a provision of Ontario's securities legislation listed in Appendix D of MI 11-102. A filer may rely on section 4.7 and 4.8 of MI 11-102 only in a passport jurisdiction.

(4) The filer should give the notice referred to in subsection (1) to the principal regulator for the initial application and the notice referred to in subsection (2) to the regulator that would be the principal regulator under Part 4 of MI 11-102 if an application were to be made under that Part at the time the notice is given. The notice should

(a) list each relevant non-principal passport jurisdiction for which notice is given that section 4.7(1) or 4.8(1) of MI 11-102 is intended to be relied upon,

(b) include the date of the decision of

(i) the principal regulator for the initial application, if the notice is given under section 4.7(1)(c) of MI 11-102, or

(ii) the regulator of the specified jurisdiction that granted the application, if the notice is given under section 4.8(1)(c) of MI 11-102,

Part 1: PROCEDURE

(c) include the citation for the regulator's decision,

(d) describe the exemption the regulator granted, and

(e) confirm that the exemption is still in effect.

(5) If an exemption sought in a passport application or a dual application is required in a non-principal jurisdiction at the time the filer files the application, but the filer does not give the notice required under section 4.7(1)(c) of MI 11-102 for that jurisdiction until after the principal regulator grants the exemption, the regulator of the non-principal passport jurisdiction will take appropriate action. This could include removing the exemption, in which case the filer would have an opportunity to be heard in that jurisdiction in appropriate circumstances.

(6) The regulator that receives the notice referred to in subsection (1) or (2) will send a copy of the notice and its decision to the regulator in the relevant non-principal passport jurisdiction.

5.4 Request for confidentiality — (1) A filer requesting that the regulators hold an application and supporting materials in confidence during the application review process should provide a substantive reason for the request in its application.

(2) If a filer is requesting that the regulators hold the application, supporting materials, or decision in confidence after the effective date of the decision, the filer should describe the request for confidentiality separately in its application, and pay any required fee:

(a) in the principal jurisdiction, if the filer is making a passport application,

(b) in the principal jurisdiction and in Ontario, if the filer is making a dual application, or

(c) in each jurisdiction, if the filer is making a coordinated review application.

(3) Any request for confidentiality should explain why the request is reasonable in the circumstances and not prejudicial to the public interest and when any decision granting confidentiality could expire.

(4) Communications on requests for confidentiality will normally take place by e-mail. If a filer is concerned with this practice, the filer may request in the application that all communications take place by facsimile or telephone.

5.5 Filing — A filer should send the application materials in paper together with the fees to

(a) the principal regulator, in the case of a passport application,

(b) the principal regulator and the OSC, in the case of a dual application, or

(c) each regulator from which the filer seeks exemptive relief, in the case of a coordinated review application.

The filer should also provide an electronic copy of the application materials, including the draft decision document, by e-mail or on CD ROM. Filing the application concurrently in all required jurisdictions will make it easier for the principal regulator and non-principal regulators, if applicable, to process the application expeditiously. In British Columbia, an electronic filing system is available for filing and tracking exemptive relief applications. Filers should file an application in British Columbia using that system instead of e-mail. Filers should file applications related to National Instrument 81-102 *Investment Funds* on SEDAR. Filers should file applications related to individual proficiency requirements in NI 31-103 on NRD.

Filers should send pre-filing and application materials by e-mail using the relevant address or addresses listed below:

British Columbia	www.bcsc.bc.ca (click on BCSC e-services and follow the steps)
Alberta	legalapplications@seccom.ab.ca
Saskatchewan	exemptions@gov.sk.ca
Manitoba	exemptions.msc@gov.mb.ca
Ontario	https://www.osc.gov.on.ca/filings
Québec	dispenses-passeport@lautorite.qc.ca
New Brunswick	Passport-passeport@nbsc-cvmnb.ca
Nova Scotia	nsscexemptions@gov.ns.ca
Prince Edward Island	CCIS@gov.pe.ca
Newfoundland and Labrador	securitiesexemptions@gov.nl.ca
Yukon	Corporateaffairs@gov.yk.ca
Northwest Territories	SecuritiesRegistry@gov.nt.ca
Nunavut	legal.registries@gov.nu.ca

5.6 Incomplete or deficient material — If the filer's materials are deficient or incomplete, the principal regulator may ask the filer to file an amended application. This will likely delay the review of the application.

5.7 Acknowledgment of receipt of filing — (1) After the principal regulator receives a complete and adequate application, the principal regulator will send the filer an acknowledgment of receipt of the application. The principal regulator will send a copy of the acknowledgement to any other regulator with whom the filer has filed the application. The acknowledgement will identify the name, phone number, fax number and e-mail address of the individual reviewing the application.

(2) For a dual application, coordinated review application or hybrid application, the principal regulator will tell the filer, in the acknowledgement, the end date of the review period identified in section 6.2(3) of this policy.

5.8 Withdrawal or abandonment of application — (1) If a filer withdraws an application at any time during the process, the filer is responsible for notifying the principal regulator and any non-principal regulator with whom the filer filed the application and for providing an explanation of the withdrawal.

(2) If at any time during the review process, the principal regulator determines that a filer has abandoned an application, the principal regulator will notify the filer that it will mark the application as "abandoned". In that case, the principal regulator will close the file without further notice to the filer unless the filer provides acceptable reasons not to close the file in writing within 10 business days. If the filer does not, the principal regulator will notify the filer and any non-principal regulator with whom the filer filed the application that the principal regulator has closed the file.

PART 6 — REVIEW OF MATERIALS

6.1 Review of passport application — (1) The principal regulator will review any passport application in accordance with its securities legislation and securities directions and based on its review procedures, analysis and considering previous decisions.

(2) The filer will deal only with the principal regulator, who will provide comments to and receive responses from the filer.

6.2 Review and processing of dual application or coordinated review application — (1) The principal regulator will review any dual application or coordinated review application in accordance with its securities legislation and securities directions, based on its review procedures, analysis and considering previous decisions. The principal regulator will consider any comments from a non-principal regulator with whom the filer filed the application. Please refer to section 5.2(2) of this policy for guidance on the non-principal regulator with whom a filer should file a dual application, and to section 5.2(3) for similar guidance for a coordinated review application.

(2) The filer will generally deal only with the principal regulator, who will be responsible for providing comments to the filer once it has considered the comments from the non-principal regulators and completed its own review. However, in exceptional circumstances, the principal regulator may refer the filer to a non-principal regulator with whom the filer has filed the application.

(3) A non-principal regulator with whom the filer has filed the application will have seven business days from receiving the acknowledgement referred to in section 5.7(1) of this policy to review the application. In exceptional circumstances, if the filer filed the dual application or coordinated review application concurrently in the non-principal jurisdictions and shows that it is necessary and reasonable in the circumstances for the application to receive immediate attention, the principal regulator may abridge the review period. A non-principal regulator that disagrees with abridging the review period may notify the filer and the principal regulator and request the filer to withdraw the application in that jurisdiction. In that case, the application will proceed as a local application without the need to file a new application and pay any additional related fees.

(4) Exceptional circumstances when the principal regulator may abridge the review period include:

(a) where exemptive relief is sought for a contested take-over bid and delay would prejudice the filer's position, and

(b) other situations in which the filer is responding to a critical event beyond its control and could not have applied for the exemptive relief earlier.

(5) Unless the filer provides compelling reasons as to why it did not start the application process sooner, the principal regulator will not consider the following circumstances as exceptional:

(a) the mailing of a management information circular for a scheduled meeting of security holders to consider a transaction,

(b) the filing of a prospectus where the receipt for the prospectus cannot evidence the exemptive relief,

(c) the closing of a transaction,

(d) the filing of a continuous disclosure document shortly before the date on which its filing is required, or

(e) other situations in which the deadline was known before filing the application and the filer could have filed the application earlier.

While staff will attempt to accommodate transaction timing where possible, filers planning time-sensitive transactions should build sufficient regulatory approval time into their transaction schedules.

The fact that a filer may consider an application as routine is not a compelling argument for requesting an abridgement.

(6) Filers should provide sufficient information in an application to enable staff to assess how quickly they should handle the application. For example, if the filer has committed to take certain steps by a specific date and needs to have staff's view or a decision by that date, the filer should explain why staff's view or the exemptive relief is required by the specific date and identify these time constraints in its application.

(7) A non-principal regulator with whom the filer has filed the dual application or coordinated review application will advise the principal regulator, before the expiration of the review period, of any substantive issues that, if left unresolved, would cause staff to recommend that the non-principal regulator opt out of the review. The principal regulator may assume that a non-principal regulator does not have comments on the application if the principal regulator does not receive them within the review period.

(8) A non-principal regulator with whom the filer has filed the dual application or coordinated review application will notify the filer and the principal regulator and request that the filer withdraw the application if staff of the non-principal regulator think that no exemptive relief is required under its securities legislation.

PART 7 — DECISION-MAKING PROCESS

7.1 Passport application — (1) After completing the review process and after considering the recommendation of its staff, the principal regulator will determine whether to grant or deny the exemption a filer sought in a passport application.

(2) If the principal regulator is not prepared to grant the exemption a filer sought in its passport application based on the information before it, it will notify the filer accordingly.

(3) If a filer receives a notice under subsection (2) and this process is available in the principal jurisdiction, the filer may request the opportunity to appear before, and make submissions to, the principal regulator.

7.2 Dual application or coordinated review application — (1) After completing the review process and after considering the recommendation of its staff, the principal regulator will determine whether to grant or deny the exemption a filer sought in a dual application or the exemptive relief the filer sought in a coordinated review application and immediately circulate its decision to the non-principal regulators with whom the filer filed the application.

(2) Each non-principal regulator with whom the filer filed the dual application or coordinated review application will have five business days from receipt of the principal regulator's decision to confirm whether it has made the same decision and is opting in or is opting out of the dual review or coordinated review.

(3) If the non-principal regulator is silent, the principal regulator will consider that the non-principal regulator has opted out.

(4) If the filer shows that it is necessary and reasonable in the circumstances, the principal regulator may request, but cannot require, the non-principal regulators to abridge the opt-out period. In some circumstances, abridging the opt-out period may not be feasible. For example, in many jurisdictions, only a panel of the regulator that convenes according to a schedule can make some types of decisions.

(5) The principal regulator will not send the filer a decision for a dual application or coordinated review application before the earlier of

(a) the expiry of the opt-out period, or

(b) receipt from a non-principal regulator with whom the filer filed the application of the confirmation referred to in subsection (2).

(6) If the principal regulator is not prepared to grant the exemption a filer sought in its dual application or the exemptive relief the filer sought in its coordinated review application based on the information before it, it will notify the filer and all non-principal regulators with whom the filer filed the application.

(7) If a filer receives a notice under subsection (6) and this process is available in the principal jurisdiction, the filer may request the opportunity to appear before, and make submissions to, the principal regulator. The principal regulator may hold a hearing on its own, or jointly or concurrently with the non-principal regulators with whom the filer filed the application. After the hearing, the principal regulator will send a copy of the decision to the filer and all non-principal regulators with whom the filer filed the application.

(8) A non-principal regulator electing to opt out will notify the filer, the principal regulator and any other non-principal regulator with whom the filer filed the application and give its reasons for opting out. The filer may deal directly with the non-principal regulator to resolve outstanding issues and obtain a decision without having to file a new application or pay any additional related fees. If the filer and non-principal regulator resolve all outstanding issues, the non-principal regulator may opt back into the dual review or coordinated review by notifying the principal regulator and the other non-principal regulators with whom the filer filed the application within the opt-out period referred to in subsection (2).

PART 8 — DECISION

8.1 Effect of decision made under passport application — (1) The decision of the principal regulator under a passport application to grant an exemption from a provision of securities legislation listed below the name of the principal jurisdiction in Appendix D of MI 11-102 is the decision of the principal regulator. Under MI 11-102, a filer is automatically exempt from the equivalent provision of each notified passport jurisdiction as a result of the principal regulator for the application granting the exemption.

(2) Except in the circumstances described in section 5.3(1) or (2) of this policy, the exemption is effective in each notified passport jurisdiction on the date of the principal regulator's decision (even if the regulator in the notified passport jurisdiction is closed on that date). In the circumstances described in section 5.3(1) of this policy, the exemption is effective in the relevant non-principal passport jurisdiction on the date the filer gives the notice under section 4.7(1)(c) or 4.8(1)(c) of MI 11-102 for that jurisdiction (even if the regulator in that jurisdiction is closed on that date).

8.2 Effect of decision made under dual application — (1) The decision of the principal regulator under a dual application to grant an exemption from a provision of securities legislation listed below the name of the principal jurisdiction in Appendix D of MI 11-102 is the decision of the principal regulator. Under MI 11-102, a filer is automatically exempt from an equivalent provision of each notified passport jurisdiction as a result of the principal regulator for the application granting the exemption. The decision of the principal regulator under a dual application also evidences the OSC's decision, if the OSC has confirmed that it has made the same decision as the principal regulator.

(2) The principal regulator will not issue the decision until the earlier of

(a) the date that the OSC confirms that it has made the same decision as the principal regulator, or

(b) the date the opt-out period referred to in section 7.2(2) of this policy has expired.

8.3 Effect of decision made under coordinated review application — (1) The decision of the principal regulator under a coordinated review application to grant exemptive relief from a provision of securities legislation in the principal jurisdiction is the decision of the principal regulator and evidences the decision of each non-principal regulator that has confirmed that it has made the same decision as the principal regulator.

(2) The principal regulator will not issue the decision until the earlier of

(a) the date that the principal regulator has received confirmation from each non-principal regulator that it has made the same decision as the principal regulator, or

(b) the date the opt-out period referred to in section 7.2(2) of this policy has expired.

8.4 Listing non-principal jurisdictions — (1) For convenience, the decision of the principal regulator on a passport application or a dual application will refer to the notified passport jurisdictions, but it is the filer's responsibility to ensure that it gives the required notice for each jurisdiction for which section 4.7(1) of MI 11-102 is intended to be relied upon.

(2) The decision of the principal regulator on a dual application or a coordinated review application will contain wording that makes it clear that the decision evidences and sets out the decision of each non-principal regulator that has made the same decision as the principal regulator.

(3) For a coordinated review application for which Québec is not the principal jurisdiction, the AMF will issue a local decision concurrently with and in addition to the principal regulator's decision. The AMF decision will contain the same terms and conditions as the principal regulator's decision. No other local regulator will issue a local decision.

8.5 Form of decision — (1) Except as described in subsection (2), the decision will be in the form set out in:

(a) Annex A, for a passport application,

(b) Annex B, for a dual application,

(c) Annex C, for a coordinated review application, or

(d) Annex D, for a hybrid application.

(2) A principal regulator may issue a less formal decision where it is appropriate.

(3) If the decision is to deny the exemptive relief, the decision will set out reasons.

8.6 Issuance of decision — The principal regulator will send the decision to the filer and to all non-principal regulators.

PART 9 — EFFECTIVE DATE AND TRANSITION

9.1 Effective date — This policy comes into effect on March 17, 2008.

9.2 Exemptive relief applications filed before March 17, 2008 — The process set out in National Policy 12-201 *Mutual Reliance Review System for Exemptive Relief Applications* (MRRS) will continue to apply to an exemptive relief application and any related pre-filing filed in multiple jurisdictions before March 17, 2008.

9.3 Availability of passport for exemptions applied for before March 17, 2008 — (1) Section 4.8(1) of MI 11-102 provides that an exemption from the equivalent provision is automatically available in the local jurisdiction if

(a) an application was made in a specified jurisdiction before March 17, 2008 for an exemption from a provision of securities legislation that is now listed in Appendix D of MI 11-102,

(b) the regulator in the specified jurisdiction granted the exemption before, on or after March 17, 2008, and

(c) certain other conditions are met, including giving the required notice for the additional non-principal passport jurisdiction; refer to section 5.3 of this policy for information on where to give the required notice and what information the notice should contain.

(2) A specified jurisdiction for purposes of section 4.8 of MI 11-102 is a principal jurisdiction under Multilateral Instrument 11-101 *Principal Regulator System*. Therefore, section 4.8(1) applies to an exemption from a CD requirement, as defined in Multilateral Instrument 11-101 *Principal Regulator System*, which the principal regulator under that Instrument granted to a reporting issuer before March 17, 2008 if the exemption relates to a CD requirement that is now listed in Appendix D of MI 11-102. In this case, however, section 4.8(3) exempts a reporting issuer from having to give the notice required in section 4.8(1)(c). Refer to section 4.5 of the CP 11-102 for guidance on the effect of section 4.8 of MI 11-102.

(3) For greater certainty, a filer may not rely on section 4.8 of MI 11-102 to obtain an automatic exemption from a provision of Ontario's securities legislation listed in Appendix D of MI 11-102. A filer may rely on section 4.8 of MI 11-102 only in a passport jurisdiction.

9.4 Revocation or variation of MRRS decisions made before March 17, 2008 — (1) A filer that wants the regulators to revoke an MRRS decision made before March 17, 2008 should make a coordinated review application.

(2) A filer that wants the regulators to vary an MRRS decision made before March 17, 2008 should make a coordinated review application. However, in the case of an MRRS decision that gave exemptive relief from a provision set out in Appendix D of MI 11-102, the filer should instead request new relief by making a passport application or dual application and referencing the MRRS decision in the new application and the proposed decision document.

(3) If a filer makes a passport application or a dual application under subsection (2), the filer must give the notice required under section 4.7(1)(c) of MI 11-102 and meet the other conditions of that section for the principal regulator's decision to have effect automatically in a non-principal passport jurisdiction. A filer may give the notice in the application it files with the principal regulator.

ANNEX A — FORM OF DECISION FOR PASSPORT APPLICATION

[Citation:*[neutral citation]*

[Date of decision]]

In the Matter of the Securities Legislation of [name of principal jurisdiction] (the Jurisdiction) and In the Matter of the Process for Exemptive Relief Applications in Multiple Jurisdictions and In the Matter of [name(s) of filer(s) and other relevant parties, including definitions as required] (the Filer(s))

Decision

Background

The principal regulator in the Jurisdiction has received an application from the Filer(s) for a decision under the securities legislation of the Jurisdiction of the principal regulator (the Legislation) for [*describe the exemption sought (the Exemption Sought) by referring to the relevant requirement(s) or provision(s) listed in the first column of Appendix D to MI 11-102.*]

Under the Process for Exemptive Relief Applications in Multiple Jurisdictions (for a passport application):

(a) the [*name of the principal regulator*] is the principal regulator for this application, and

(b) the Filer(s) has(have) provided notice that section 4.7(1) of Multilateral Instrument 11-102 *Passport System* (MI 11-102) is intended to be relied upon in [*names of non-principal passport jurisdictions*].

Interpretation

Terms defined in National Instrument 14-101 *Definitions* and MI 11-102 have the same meaning if used in this decision, unless otherwise defined. [*Add additional definitions here.*]

Representations

This decision is based on the following facts represented by the Filer(s):

[*Insert material representations necessary to explain why the principal regulator came to this decision. Include the location of the Filer's head office and, if appropriate, the connecting factor the filer used to identify the principal regulator for the application. State that the filer and any other relevant party is not in default of securities legislation in any jurisdiction or, if the filer or other relevant party is in default, set out the nature of the default.*]

Decision

The principal regulator is satisfied that the decision meets the test set out in the Legislation for the principal regulator to make the decision.

The decision of the principal regulator under the Legislation is that the Exemption Sought is granted provided that:

[*Insert numbered terms, conditions, restrictions or requirements. These should include references to the relevant requirement(s) or provision(s) listed in the first column of Appendix D to MI 11-102.*]

[*If any exemption has an effective date after the date of the decision, state here.*]

...................(Name of signatory for the principal regulator)

.... (Title)

.... (*Name of principal regulator*)

(*justify signature block*)

ANNEX B — FORM OF DECISION FOR A DUAL APPLICATION

[Citation:[*neutral citation*]

[*Date of decision*]]

In the Matter of the Securities Legislation of [name of principal jurisdiction] and Ontario (the Jurisdictions) and In the Matter of the Process for Exemptive Relief Applications in Multiple Jurisdictions and In the Matter of [name(s) of filer(s) and other relevant parties, including definitions as required] (the Filer(s))

Decision

Background

The securities regulatory authority or regulator in each of the Jurisdictions (Decision Maker) has received an application from the Filer(s) for a decision under the securities legislation of the Jurisdictions (the Legislation) for [*describe the exemption sought (the Exemption Sought) by referring to the relevant requirement(s) or provision(s) listed in the first column of Appendix D to MI 11-102.*]

Under the Process for Exemptive Relief Applications in Multiple Jurisdictions (for a dual application):

(a) the [*name of the principal regulator*] is the principal regulator for this application,

(b) the Filer(s) has(have) provided notice that section 4.7(1) of Multilateral Instrument 11-102 *Passport System* (MI 11-102) is intended to be relied upon in [*names of non-principal passport jurisdictions*], and

(c) the decision is the decision of the principal regulator and evidences the decision of the securities regulatory authority or regulator in Ontario.

Interpretation

Terms defined in National Instrument 14-101 *Definitions* and MI 11-102 have the same meaning if used in this decision, unless otherwise defined. [*Add additional definitions here.*]

Representations

This decision is based on the following facts represented by the Filer(s):

[*Insert material representations necessary to explain why the Decision Makers came to this decision. Include the location of the Filer's head office and, if appropriate, the connecting factor the filer used to identify the principal regulator for the application. State that the filer and any other relevant party is not in default of securities legislation in any jurisdiction or, if the filer or other relevant party is in default, set out the nature of the default.*]

Decision

Each of the Decision Makers is satisfied that the decision meets the test set out in the Legislation for the Decision Maker to make the decision.

The decision of the Decision Makers under the Legislation is that the Exemption Sought is granted provided that:

[*Insert numbered terms, conditions, restrictions or requirements. These should include references to the relevant requirement(s) or provision(s) listed in the first column of Appendix D to MI 11-102.*]

[*If any exemption has an effective date after the date of the decision, state here.*]

.... (*Name of signatory for the principal regulator*)

.... (*Title*)

.... (*Name of principal regulator*)

(*justify signature block*)

ANNEX C — FORM OF DECISION FOR COORDINATED REVIEW APPLICATION

[Citation:[*neutral citation*]

[*Date of decision*]]

In the Matter of the Securities Legislation of [name of jurisdictions participating in decision] (the Jurisdictions) and In the Matter of the Process for Exemptive Relief Applications in Multiple Jurisdictions and In the Matter of [name(s) of filer(s) and other relevant parties, including definitions as required] (the Filer(s))

Decision

Background

The securities regulatory authority or regulator in each of the Jurisdictions (Decision Maker) has received an application from the Filer(s) for a decision under the securities legislation of the Jurisdictions (the Legislation) for [*describe the exemptive relief sought (the Exemptive Relief Sought) in words (e.g., that the filer is not a reporting issuer). Do not use statutory references. Include defined terms as necessary.*]

Under the Process for Exemptive Relief Applications in Multiple Jurisdictions (for a coordinated review application):

(a) the [*name of the principal regulator*] is the principal regulator for this application, and

(b) the decision is the decision of the principal regulator and evidences the decision of each other Decision Maker.

Interpretation

Terms defined in National Instrument 14-101 Definitions have the same meaning if used in this decision, unless otherwise defined. [*Add additional definitions here.*]

Representations

This decision is based on the following facts represented by the Filer(s):

[Insert material representations necessary to explain why the Decision Makers came to this decision. Include the location of the Filer's head office and, if appropriate, the connecting factor the filer used to identify the principal regulator for the application. State that the filer and any other relevant party is not in default of securities legislation in any jurisdiction or, if the filer or other relevant party is in default, set out the nature of the default. Do not use statutory references.]

Decision

Each of the Decision Makers is satisfied that the decision meets the test set out in the Legislation for the Decision Maker to make the decision.

The decision of the Decision Makers under the Legislation is that the Exemptive Relief Sought is granted provided that:

[Insert numbered terms, conditions, restrictions or requirements. These should be generic and without statutory references to the Legislation of the Jurisdictions.]

[If any exemptive relief has an effective date after the date of the decision, state here.]

.... (*Name of signatory for the principal regulator*)

.... (*Title*)

.... (*Name of principal regulator*)

(*justify signature block*)

ANNEX D — FORM OF DECISION FOR HYBRID APPLICATION

[Citation:[*neutral citation*]

[*Date of decision*]]

In the Matter of the Securities Legislation of [name of principal jurisdiction (for a passport application), or of principal jurisdiction and Ontario (for a dual application), and name of each jurisdiction participating in coordinated review application decision] and In the Matter of the Process for Exemptive Relief Applications in Multiple Jurisdictions and In the Matter of [name(s) of filer(s) and other relevant parties, including definitions as required,] (the Filer(s))

Decision

Background

[If you are making a passport application, insert:]

The securities regulatory authority or regulator in .... has received an application from the Filer(s) for a decision under the securities legislation of the jurisdiction of the principal regulator (the Legislation) for *[describe the exemption sought (the Passport Exemption) by referring to the relevant requirement(s) or provision(s) listed in the first column of Appendix D to MI 11-102].*

OR

[If you are making a dual application, insert:]

The securities regulatory authority or regulator in .... and Ontario (Dual Exemption Decision Makers) have received an application from the Filer(s) for a decision under the securities legislation of those jurisdictions (the Legislation) for *[describe the exemption sought (the Dual Exemption) by referring to the relevant requirement(s) or provision(s) listed in the first column of Appendix D to MI 11-102.]*

AND

[For your coordinated review application, insert:]

The securities regulatory authority or regulator in each of .... (the Jurisdictions) (Coordinated Exemptive Relief Decision Makers) has received an application from the Filer(s) for a decision under the securities legislation of the Jurisdictions (the Legislation) for *[describe the exemptive relief sought (the Coordinated Exemptive Relief) in words (e.g., that the filer is not a reporting issuer). Do not use statutory references. Include defined terms as necessary.]*

Under the Process for Exemptive Relief Applications in Multiple Jurisdictions (for a hybrid application):

(a) the *[name of the principal regulator]* is the principal regulator for this application,

(b) the Filer(s) has(ve) provided notice that section 4.7(1) of Multilateral Instrument 11-102 *Passport System* (MI 11-102) is intended to be relied upon in *[names of non-principal passport jurisdictions]*,

(c) the decision is the decision of the principal regulator, *[if you are making a dual application, insert: "and the decision evidences the decision of the securities regulatory authority or regulator in Ontario,"]* and

(d) the decision evidences the decision of each Coordinated Exemptive Relief Decision Maker.

Interpretation

Terms defined in MI 11-102 and National Instrument 14-101 *Definitions* have the same meaning if used in this decision, unless otherwise defined. *[Add additional definitions here.]*

Representations

This decision is based on the following facts represented by the Filer(s):

[Insert material representations necessary to explain why the Decision Makers came to this decision. Include the location of the Filer's head office and, if appropriate, the connecting factor the filer used to identify the principal regulator for the application. State that the filer and any other relevant party is not in default of securities legislation in any jurisdiction or, if the filer or other relevant party is in default, set out the nature of the default. Do not use statutory references.]

Decision

Each of the principal regulator [*if you are making a dual application, insert*: ", the securities regulatory authority or regulator in Ontario,"] and the Coordinated Exemptive Relief Decision Makers is satisfied that the decision meets the test set out in the Legislation for the relevant regulator or securities regulatory authority to make the decision.

[*If you are making a passport application, insert:*]

The decision of the principal regulator under the Legislation is that the Passport Exemption is granted provided that:

> [*Insert numbered terms, conditions, restrictions or requirements. These should include references to the relevant requirement(s) or provision(s) listed in the first column of Appendix D to MI 11-102.*]

OR

[*If you are making a dual application, insert:*]

The decision of the Dual Exemption Decision Makers under the Legislation is that the Dual Exemption is granted provided that:

> [*Insert numbered terms, conditions, restrictions or requirements. These should include references to the relevant requirement(s) or provision(s) listed in the first column of Appendix D to MI 11-102.*]

AND

[*For your coordinated application, insert:*]

The decision of the Coordinated Review Decision Makers under the Legislation is that the Coordinated Exemptive Relief is granted provided that:

> [*Insert numbered terms, conditions, restrictions or requirements. These should be generic and without statutory references to the Legislation of the Jurisdictions.*]

> [*If any exemption or exemptive relief has an effective date after the date of the decision, state here.*]

.... (*Name of signatory for the principal regulator*)

.... (*Title*)

.... (*Name of principal regulator*)

(*justify signature block*)

Adoption by OSC: (2008) 31 O.S.C.B. 1009; Request for Comments: (2007) 31 O.S.C.B. 1066.

Adoption of Amendments by OSC: (2009) 32 O.S.C.B. (Supp. 4) 351, 32 O.S.C.B. (Supp. 2) 424 and (2008) 31 O.S.C.B. 12070; Request for Comments: (2008) 31 O.S.C.B. 7171.

Adoption of Amendments by OSC: (2012) 35 O.S.C.B. 4503.

Adoption of Amendments by OSC: (2013) 36 O.S.C.B. 10503; Request for Comments: (2013) 36 O.S.C.B. 3929.

Adoption of Amendments by OSC: (2014) 37 O.S.C.B. (Supp. 4) 131; Request for Comments: (2013) 36 O.S.C.B. (Supp. 3).

Adoption of Amendments by OSC: (2014) 37 O.S.C.B. 1637.

Policies and Orders: CSAN 13-315; NPS 11-202, 11-204, 12-203.

National Policy 11-204 — Process for Registration in Multiple Jurisdictions

Date: September 28, 2009

32 O.S.C.B. (Supp. 4) 339

Table of Contents

PART 5 PASSPORT REGISTRATION

    5.1 Application

    5.2 Filing of materials

    5.3 Registration

PART 6 INTERFACE REGISTRATION

    6.1 Application

    6.2 Filing materials

    6.3 Decision-making process

    6.4 Decision

    6.5 Opportunity to be heard

PART 1 — APPLICATION

1.1 Application — This policy describes procedures for a firm or individual to register in more than one Canadian jurisdiction.

PART 2 — DEFINITIONS

2.1 Definitions — In this policy,

"IIROC" means the Investment Industry Regulatory Organization of Canada;

"interface registration" means a registration described in section 3.3 of this policy;

"MI 11-102" means Multilateral Instrument 11-102 *Passport System*;

"NI 31-102" means National Instrument 31-102 *National Registration Database*;

"NRD" has the same meaning as in NI 31-102;

"NRD submission" has the same meaning as in NI 31-102;

"OSC" means the regulator in Ontario;

"passport jurisdiction" means the jurisdiction of a passport regulator;

"passport registration" means a registration described in section 3.2 of this policy;

"passport regulator" means a regulator that has adopted MI 11-102;

"permitted individual" has the same meaning as in NI 33-109;

"regulator" means a securities regulatory authority or regulator; and

"SRO" means self-regulatory organization.

2.2 Further definitions — Terms used in this policy and that are defined in National Instrument 14-101 *Definitions*, MI 11-102 or Companion Policy 11-102CP *Passport System* have the same meanings as in those instruments and policy.

2.3 Interpretation — Unless the context indicates otherwise, a reference in this policy to a 'regulator', 'principal regulator', or the OSC is a reference to the SRO to whom the regulator, principal regulator, or OSC has delegated, assigned or authorized the performance of all or part of its registration function or to the relevant office of that SRO for the jurisdiction of the regulator or principal regulator.

PART 3 — OVERVIEW AND PRINCIPAL REGULATOR

3.1 Overview — This policy deals with a firm's or individual's registration in multiple jurisdictions in the following circumstances:

    (i) The firm or individual is seeking registration or is registered in the firm's or individual's principal jurisdiction (including Ontario) and the firm or individual seeks registration in another jurisdiction (excluding Ontario). This is a "passport registration."

    (ii) The firm or individual is seeking registration or is registered in the firm's or individual's principal jurisdiction, the principal regulator is a passport regulator, and the firm or individual seeks registration in Ontario. This is an "interface registration."

3.2 Passport registration — Under MI 11-102, if a firm or individual seeks registration or is registered in the firm's or individual's principal jurisdiction (including Ontario) and seeks registration in another jurisdiction (excluding Ontario), the firm or individual makes a submission to register in the other jurisdiction. Only the principal regulator reviews the firm's or individual's submission and the firm or individual's sponsoring firm deals only with the firm's or individual's principal regulator. The principal regulator reviews the firm's or individual's submission to register in the other jurisdiction only to ensure that it is complete. The other regulator does not conduct a review of the firm or individual.

3.3 Interface registration — If a firm or individual seeks registration or is registered in the firm's or individual's principal jurisdiction, the principal regulator is a passport regulator, and the firm or individual seeks registration in Ontario, the firm or individual submits an application to register in Ontario. The principal regulator will review the firm's or individual's application to register in Ontario and the OSC will decide whether to opt in or opt out of the principal regulator's determination. The firm or the individual's sponsoring firm will generally deal only with the firm's or the individual's principal regulator.

3.4 Registration in passport jurisdictions and Ontario — If a firm or individual whose principal regulator is a passport regulator seeks registration in a non-principal passport jurisdiction and in Ontario, the firm or individual should refer to the processes for

    • a passport registration, to register in the non-principal passport jurisdiction, and

    • an interface registration, to register in Ontario.

Part 1: PROCEDURE

3.5 Registration by SRO — In some jurisdictions, the regulator has delegated, assigned or authorized an SRO to perform all or part of its registration function. The SRO continues to perform these functions in the relevant jurisdictions for a passport registration or an interface registration under this policy. At the date of this policy, the following arrangements apply to registration of IIROC member firms and their representatives.

(a) If Alberta, Saskatchewan, British Columbia or Newfoundland and Labrador is the principal jurisdiction of a firm or individual, the firm or the individual's sponsoring firm should deal with the office of IIROC, instead of the regulator, in or for that jurisdiction.

(b) If Ontario or Québec is the principal jurisdiction of an individual, the individual's sponsoring firm should deal with the office of IIROC, instead of the regulator, in or for that jurisdiction in respect of the individual.

3.6 Principal regulator — (1) For purposes of a passport registration and an interface registration under this policy, the principal regulator of a firm or individual is identified in the same manner as in section 4A.1 of MI 11-102. This section summarizes section 4A.1 of MI 11-102 and provides guidance for identifying a firm's or individual's principal regulator. The regulator of any jurisdiction can be a principal regulator for registration under this policy.

If a firm or individual makes an application for exemptive relief from a requirement in Parts 3 and 12 of NI 31-103 or Part 2 of NI 33-109 in connection with an application for registration in the principal jurisdiction, the principal regulator for the application for exemptive relief is identified in the same manner as in section 4.4.1 of MI 11-102. If a firm or individual makes any other application for exemptive relief from a registration requirement, the principal regulator is identified in the same manner as in sections 4.1 to 4.4 of MI 11-102. If a firm or individual is not seeking the relief, or is seeking more than one item of relief and not all of the items of relief, in its principal jurisdiction, the principal regulator is identified in the same manner as in section 4.5 of MI 11-102. A firm or individual should refer to section 3.6 of NP 11-203 for further guidance on how to identify the principal regulator for exemptive relief application purposes.

(2) Subject to subsection (5) of this section and section 3.7 of this policy, the principal regulator of a firm is the regulator in the jurisdiction where the firm has its head office, unless the firm's head office is outside Canada. A firm identifies its head office in item 2.1 *Head office address* of Form 33-109F6 and this information is reflected on NRD.

(3) For greater certainty, a firm is a domestic firm if it is a legal entity and has a head office in Canada. For example, a Canadian subsidiary of a foreign firm is a domestic firm. A Canadian branch office of a foreign firm is not.

(4) Subject to subsection (7) of this section and section 3.7 of this policy, the principal regulator of an individual is the regulator in the jurisdiction where the individual has his or her working office, unless the individual's working office is outside Canada. The working office of a domestic individual is the office of the sponsoring firm where the individual does most of his or her business. A domestic individual identifies his or her working office in item 9 *Location of Employment* of Form 33-109F4 and this information is reflected on NRD.

(5) Subject to section 3.7 of this policy, if the head office of a firm is outside Canada, the principal regulator for the foreign firm is the regulator in the jurisdiction of Canada the firm identified as its principal jurisdiction in its most recently filed Form 33-109F5 or Form 33-109F6. These forms require a foreign firm to identify its principal jurisdiction in Canada. If the foreign firm is not registered in a jurisdiction of Canada or has not completed its first financial year since being registered, the principal jurisdiction is the jurisdiction of Canada in which the firm expects most of its clients to be resident at the end of its current financial year. In all other circumstances, it is the jurisdiction in which most of the firm's clients were resident at the end of its most recently completed financial year.

(6) Subject to section 3.7 of this policy, if the working office of an individual is outside Canada, the principal regulator of the foreign individual is the principal regulator of the individual's sponsoring firm.

(7) A firm should notify the regulator by providing the information about its head office or principal jurisdiction in Form 33-109F6 in accordance with NI 33-109 if

- in the case of a domestic firm, the firm changes the jurisdiction of its head office,
- in the case of a foreign firm, the jurisdiction in which most of the firm's clients were resident at the end of its most recently completed financial year changes.

NI 33-109 provides that the firm may make this submission to a non-principal regulator by giving it only to its principal regulator. A firm should refer to Appendix B of CP 33-109 for guidance on how to make this submission.

(9) In the event of a change in a domestic individual's working office, the individual should make the NRD Submission for a *Location of Employment Change* in accordance with NI 33-109.

(10) Under MI 11-102, a foreign firm registered in a non-principal passport jurisdiction before September 28, 2009 must submit the information required in item 2.2(b) of Form 33-109F6 by submitting a Form 33-109F5 on or before October 28, 2009. A foreign firm may make its submission to a non-principal passport regulator by giving it only to its principal regulator. Foreign firms should refer to Appendix B of CP 33-109 for guidance on how to make this submission.

(11) Under MI 11-102, the principal regulator for a foreign individual is the same as the principal regulator for the individual's sponsoring firm. For that reason, the foreign individual is not required to make a submission to identify the individual's principal regulator.

3.7 Discretionary change of principal regulator — (1) If a regulator thinks that the principal regulator identified under section 3.6 of this policy is inappropriate, the regulator will give the firm or individual written notice of the appropriate principal regulator for the firm or individual and the reasons for the change. The regulator specified in the notice will be the firm or individual's principal regulator as of the later of the date the firm or individual receives the notice and the effective date specified in the notice, if any. To streamline the process, the regulators will give the written notice relating to the principal regulator of an individual to the individual's sponsoring firm.

(2) Regulators do not generally expect changing the principal regulator for a domestic firm or domestic individual. Regulators anticipate changing the principal regulator for a foreign firm only in exceptional circumstances. Regulators may change the principal regulator for a foreign individual if the foreign individual is not registered in his or her sponsoring firm's principal jurisdiction or if the individual's principal regulator under this policy does not correspond to his or her principal regulator as shown on NRD. Regulators will give written notice of a change in principal regulator.

PART 4 — GENERAL GUIDANCE FOR FIRMS AND INDIVIDUALS

4.1 Effect of submission — (1) If an individual makes an NRD submission for the individual in relation to a passport registration or an interface registration in a non-principal jurisdiction, this has the effect of submitting the current information in the individual's entire Form 33-109F4 in the jurisdiction.

(2) Because firms do not file or submit their Form 33-109F6 on NRD, the form requires instead that the firm make a solemn declaration or affirmation that, among other things,

- the information provided on the form is true and complete, and
- with respect to a submission made in respect of a non-principal jurisdiction, at the date of the submission,
    - the firm has filed or submitted all information required to be filed or submitted in relation to the firm's registration in its principal jurisdiction,
    - the information is true and complete.

In addition, the form requires the firm to authorize its principal regulator to give each non-principal regulator access to any information the firm has filed or submitted to the principal regulator under securities legislation of the principal jurisdiction in relation to the firm's registration in that jurisdiction.

Should a regulator discover that a firm made a false declaration or affirmation, the regulator may take appropriate enforcement action against the firm.

4.2 Fees — (1) A firm or an individual must submit any required fees for the firm or the individual under applicable securities legislation in the principal jurisdiction and the non-principal passport jurisdiction when making the relevant submission. A submission is not considered complete unless the required fees are submitted under applicable securities legislation in relevant jurisdictions.

(2) A firm may pay the fee related to a submission by sending a cheque to the relevant regulator or submitting payment to each relevant regulator directly on NRD. A domestic individual must pay the fee related to a submission to each relevant regulator by submitting it on NRD. A foreign individual must pay the fee related to a submission by sending a cheque to the relevant regulator or submitting payment to each relevant regulator directly on NRD.

4.3 Firm submissions — A firm should refer to Appendix B of CP 33-109 for guidance on how to make a submission under section 5.2(1) to (3) or section 6.2(1) or (2) of this policy.

PART 5 — PASSPORT REGISTRATION

5.1 Application — (1) This part applies to a firm or individual seeking registration in any category (other than a firm seeking registration as a restricted dealer) in a non-principal passport jurisdiction. To register in a non-principal jurisdiction, a restricted dealer must apply directly to the non-principal passport regulator. This part applies to an individual seeking registration in a non-principal passport jurisdiction to act on behalf of a restricted dealer if the restricted dealer is registered as such in that jurisdiction and its principal jurisdiction.

(2) A firm seeking registration as a restricted dealer must complete the entire Form 33-109F6 and submit it, along with all supporting materials, in each jurisdiction where it seeks registration as such.

5.2 Filing of materials — (1) For a firm — Under MI 11-102, a firm that seeks registration in a non-principal passport jurisdiction in a category for which the firm is registered or is concurrently seeking registration in its principal jurisdiction (including Ontario) should complete the entire Form 33-109F6 or the items of Form 33-109F6 specified in section 1.3 of the form for the firm's particular situation. The firm should submit the F6 or relevant items together with any supporting materials. Making the submission to the principal regulator satisfies the firm's obligation under MI 11-102 to make the submission to the regulator in the non-principal passport jurisdiction.

(2) For an individual — Under MI 11-102, an individual who seeks registration in a non-principal passport jurisdiction in a category for which the individual is registered or is concurrently seeking registration in his or her principal jurisdiction (including Ontario) should submit a completed Form 33-109F4, or in some cases a completed Form 33-109F2, for the individual in accordance with NI 33- 109.

(3) NI 33-109 requires a completed Form 33-109F4 or completed Form 33-109F2 to be submitted on NRD. NRD automatically submits the relevant form to the appropriate regulators. In some circumstances, it is not necessary to complete the entire form. For example, it is not necessary to complete the entire form for an individual to seek registration in the same category in an additional jurisdiction, to add or remove a category of registration, or to register in a category with an additional or a new sponsoring firm. In those circumstances, the relevant NRD submission indicates which items of the form to complete.

(4) Making an NRD submission under subsection (3) satisfies the individual's obligation under MI 11-102 to submit a completed Form 33-109F4.

(5) Fees in non-principal jurisdiction — Fees required for a firm or individual to register automatically in a non-principal passport jurisdiction under MI 11-102 are prescribed in the fee regulation of each jurisdiction. If the principal regulator refuses to register the firm or individual, the regulator in any non-principal passport jurisdiction in respect of which a submission was made will return the fees submitted in relation to the submission.

5.3 Registration — (1) NRD will record a firm's or an individual's category of registration in the principal jurisdiction, any T&C imposed by the principal regulator, and any exemption from Parts 3 and 12 of NI 31-103 or Part 2 of NI 33-109 granted by the principal regulator.

(2) Under MI 11-102, a firm or individual that is registered in a category in the firm's or individual's principal jurisdiction is automatically registered in a non-principal passport jurisdiction in the same category as in the firm's or the individual's principal jurisdiction if the firm or individual submitted the relevant completed NI 33-109 form and is a member or approved person of an SRO if that is required for that category of registration.

For a mutual fund dealer based in Québec, the SRO condition means that the firm must be a member of the Mutual Fund Dealers Association of Canada (MFDA) before it can register in another jurisdiction. However, this condition does not apply if the firm has an exemption in the local jurisdiction from the requirement to be a member of the MFDA.

For a representative of a mutual fund dealer or scholarship plan dealer whose working office is outside Québec, the SRO condition means that he or she must be a member of the Chambre de la sécurité financière before he or she can become registered in Québec. This condition does not apply if the individual has an exemption in Québec from the requirement to be a member of the Chambre.

For a representative of a mutual fund dealer whose working office is in Québec, the SRO conditions means that he or she must be an approved person of the MFDA before he or she can become registered outside of Québec. This condition does not apply if the individual has an exemption in the relevant jurisdiction from the requirement to be an approved person of the MFDA.

If a firm or individual is registered in the same category in the principal jurisdiction and in the non-principal passport jurisdiction, MI 11-102 provides that a T&C imposed on the registration in the principal jurisdiction applies as if it were imposed in the non-principal passport jurisdiction. The T&C applies until the earlier of the date that the regulator that imposed it cancels or revokes it, or the T&C expires.

Part 1:
PROCEDURE

(3) NRD will record for each non-principal passport jurisdiction in respect of which the firm or individual made the relevant submission

- the firm's or the individual's automatic registration in the same category as in the principal jurisdiction,
- any T&C imposed by the principal regulator that applies automatically to the firm or individual in the non-principal jurisdiction, and
- any exemption from Parts 3 and 12 of NI 31-103 or Part 2 of NI 33-109 granted by the principal regulator that applies automatically in the non-principal jurisdiction.

If a firm or individual made the relevant submission to register concurrently in the principal jurisdiction and one or more non-principal passport jurisdictions, NRD will show the same registration date in the principal jurisdiction and the non-principal passport jurisdiction(s).

If a firm or individual is already registered in the principal jurisdiction when the firm or individual makes the relevant submission in respect of a non-principal jurisdiction, NRD will show the date the submission is made in respect of the non-principal passport jurisdiction as the registration date in the non-principal passport jurisdiction for an individual. For a firm, NRD may show a different registration date in the non-principal passport jurisdiction. If that is the case, the registration date in the non-principal passport jurisdiction is the date on which the relevant submission was made in respect of the non-principal passport jurisdiction. The principal regulator will confirm the firm's registration date in the non-principal passport jurisdiction outside NRD.

(4) The principal regulator may grant or have granted a discretionary exemption application from a requirement of Parts 3 and 12 of NI 31-103 or Part 2 of NI 33-109 in connection with an application to register in the principal jurisdiction. In that case, the exemption applies automatically in the non-principal passport jurisdiction in which the firm or individual is registered automatically under MI 11-102 if certain conditions are met. The conditions are set out section 4.7 of MI 11-102. Among other things, section 4.7(1)(c) of MI 11-102 requires the applicant to give notice of intention to rely on the exemption in the non-principal jurisdiction.

PART 6 — INTERFACE REGISTRATION

6.1 **Application** — (1) This part applies to a firm or an individual seeking registration in any category (other than a firm seeking registration as a restricted dealer) in Ontario when Ontario is a non-principal jurisdiction. To register in Ontario, a restricted dealer must apply directly to the OSC. This part applies to an individual seeking registration in Ontario to act on behalf of a restricted dealer if the restricted dealer is registered as such in Ontario and its principal jurisdiction.

(2) A firm seeking registration as a restricted dealer in Ontario must complete the entire Form 33-109F6 and submit it, along with all supporting materials, directly to the OSC whether Ontario is the firm's principal jurisdiction or non-principal jurisdiction.

6.2 **Filing materials** — (1) For a firm — If a firm seeks registration in Ontario in a category for which it is concurrently seeking registration in its principal jurisdiction, the firm should complete the entire Form 33-109F6 and submit it to its principal regulator and the OSC. Supporting materials that are required under Form 33-109F6 may be submitted to the OSC by giving them to the principal regulator.

(2) If a firm is registered in a category in its principal jurisdiction and subsequently seeks registration in the same category in Ontario, the firm should complete the items of Form 33-109F6 specified in section 1.3 of the form and submit the form to the principal regulator and the OSC.

Supporting materials that are required under Form 33-109F6 may be submitted to the OSC by giving them to the principal regulator.

(3) If a firm seeks to add a category in its principal jurisdiction and in Ontario, the firm must complete the items of Form 33-109F6 specified in section 1.3 of the form and submit the form to its principal regulator and the OSC.

Supporting materials that are required under Form 33-109F6 may be submitted to the OSC by giving them to the principal regulator.

(4) For an individual — Under NI 33-109, an individual who seeks registration is required to submit a completed Form 33-109F4, or in some cases a completed Form 33-109F2, through NRD. NRD automatically submits the relevant form to the appropriate regulators. In some circumstances, it is not necessary to complete the entire form. For example, it is not necessary to complete the entire form for an individual to seek registration in the same category in an additional jurisdiction, to add or remove a category of registration, or to register in a category with an additional or a new sponsoring firm. In those circumstances, the relevant NRD submission indicates which items of the form to complete.

(5) Making an NRD submission under subsection (4) satisfies the individual's obligation to submit a completed Form 33-109F4.

6.3 **Decision-making process** — (1) If a firm or individual seeks registration in the principal jurisdiction and in Ontario, the firm or the individual's sponsoring firm will generally deal only with the principal regulator.

(2) The principal regulator will submit to the OSC (or the Ontario office of IIROC, for an individual seeking registration as a representative of an investment dealer) an interface document containing its proposed determination. The OSC will advise the principal regulator whether it opts in to, or opts out of, the principal regulator's proposed determination generally within one business day from receiving the interface document. The Ontario office of IIROC will generally do this within one business day from receiving the interface document.

(3) The OSC may impose a local T&C on a firm's or an individual's registration without opting out.

(4) If the OSC opts out, it will give the principal regulator written reasons for its decision and the principal regulator will forward the reasons to the firm or the individual's sponsoring firm and use its best efforts to resolve the opt-out issues with the firm or the sponsoring firm of the individual and the OSC.

(5) If the principal regulator is able to resolve the OSC's opt-out issues with the firm or the individual's sponsoring firm before NRD shows the firm or individual as being registered in the principal jurisdiction, the OSC may opt back into the interface registration. In that case, the OSC will notify the principal regulator and the firm or the individual's sponsoring firm that it has opted back in. If the principal regulator is unable to resolve the OSC's opt-out issues, the firm or individual's sponsoring firm should deal with the OSC directly to resolve them.

6.4 **Decision** — (1) NRD will record a firm or individual's category of registration in the principal jurisdiction, any T&C that applies in the principal jurisdiction, and any exemption from Part 4 of NI 31-103 or Part 2 of NI 33-109 granted by the principal regulator. If the OSC opts in, NRD will also record that the firm or individual is registered in the same category in Ontario, including the date when the registration takes effect, and that the OSC has adopted the same T&C and granted the same exemption from Divisions 1 and 2 of Part 3 and Part 12 of NI 31-103 [or Part 2 of NI 33-109] as the principal regulator.

(2) If the OSC imposes a local T&C on a firm's or an individual's registration, NRD will also record any T&C applicable in Ontario only.

6.5 Opportunity to be heard — (1) If the principal regulator of a firm or an individual that seeks registration in the principal jurisdiction and, concurrently, in Ontario is not prepared to grant registration or is prepared to grant registration with a T&C, the principal regulator will

- send the firm or the individual's sponsoring firm a copy of the principal regulator's proposed T&C, if applicable, and
- notify the firm or the individual's sponsoring firm that it has the right to request an opportunity to be heard from the principal regulator.

If the OSC opts in to the determination of the principal regulator to refuse registration or impose a T&C, the principal regulator will forward to the firm or the individual's sponsoring firm the OSC's notification that the firm or individual has the right to request an opportunity to the heard from the OSC.

(2) If a firm or individual exercises the right to request an opportunity to be heard from the principal regulator or from the principal regulator and the OSC, the principal regulator will notify the OSC.

(3) If the firm or the individual's sponsoring firm also requests an opportunity to be heard in Ontario, the principal regulator and the OSC will decide whether to provide an opportunity to be heard separately, jointly or concurrently. After the firm or individual had an opportunity to be heard and the principal regulator makes a decision, the principal regulator will send to the OSC a new interface document setting out its proposed determination, if applicable.

(4) If a firm or individual is registered in the principal jurisdiction and, subsequently, applies to register in Ontario, and the OSC decides to refuse registration or impose a local T&C, the OSC will send the principal regulator for the firm or the individual

- a copy of the T&C, if applicable, and
- the OSC's notification that the firm or individual has the right to request an opportunity to be heard in Ontario.

The principal regulator will forward these documents to the firm or individual's sponsoring firm. Thereafter, the firm or the individual will deal directly with the OSC.

Adoption by OSC: (2009) 32 O.S.C.B. (Supp. 4) 339, 32 O.S.C.B. (Supp. 2) 424 and (2008) 31 O.S.C.B. 12070; Request for Comments: (2008) 31 O.S.C.B. 7171.

Rules: NI 31-103, 33-109.

National Policy 11-205 — Process for Designation of Credit Rating Organizations in Multiple Jurisdictions

Date: April 20, 2012, as amended February 19, 2014

35 O.S.C.B. 2383 and 37 O.S.C.B. 1637

Table of Contents

Part 1:
PROCEDURE

PART 7 DECISION

21. Effect of decision made under passport application

22. Effect of decision made under dual application

23. Listing non-principal jurisdictions

24. Issuance of decision

PART 8 EFFECTIVE DATE

25. Effective date

PART 1 — APPLICATION

1. Application — This policy describes the process for the filing and review of an application to become a designated rating organization in more than one jurisdiction of Canada.

PART 2 — DEFINITIONS

2. Definitions — In this policy

"AMF" means the regulator in Québec;

"application" means an application to become a designated rating organization;

"dual application" means an application described in section 6 of this policy;

"dual review" means the review under this policy of a dual application;

"filer" means

(a) a person or company filing an application, or

(b) an agent of a person or company referred to in paragraph (a);

"MI 11-102" means Multilateral Instrument 11-102 *Passport System;*

"NI 25-101" means National Instrument 25-101 *Designated Rating Organizations;*

"notified passport jurisdiction" means a passport jurisdiction for which a filer gave the notice referred to in section 4B.6(1)(c) of MI 11-102;

"OSC" means the regulator in Ontario;

"passport application" means an application described in section 5 of this policy;

"passport jurisdiction" means the jurisdiction of a passport regulator;

"passport regulator" means a regulator that has adopted MI 11-102;

"regulator" means a securities regulatory authority or regulator.

3. Further definitions — Terms used in this policy that are defined in MI 11-102, National Instrument 14-101 *Definitions* or NI 25-101 have the same meanings as in those instruments.

PART 3 — OVERVIEW, PRINCIPAL REGULATOR AND GENERAL GUIDELINES

4. Overview — This policy applies to an application to become a designated rating organization in multiple jurisdictions. These are the possible types of applications:

(a) The principal regulator is a passport regulator and the filer does not seek a designation in Ontario. This is a "passport application."

(b) The principal regulator is the OSC and the filer also seeks a designation in a passport jurisdiction. This is also a "passport application."

(c) The principal regulator is a passport regulator and the filer also seeks a designation in Ontario. This is a "dual application."

5. Passport application — (1) If the principal regulator is a passport regulator and the filer does not seek a designation in Ontario, the filer files the application only with, and pays fees only to, the principal regulator. Only the principal regulator reviews the application. The principal regulator's decision to grant the designation automatically results in a deemed designation in the notified passport jurisdictions.

(2) If the principal regulator is the OSC and the filer also seeks designation in a passport jurisdiction, the filer files the application only with, and pays fees only to the OSC. Only the OSC reviews the application. The OSC's decision to grant the designation automatically results in a deemed designation in the notified passport jurisdictions.

6. Dual application — Designation sought in passport jurisdiction and Ontario — If the principal regulator is a passport regulator and the filer also seeks a designation in Ontario, the filer files the application with, and pays fees to the principal regulator and the OSC. The principal regulator reviews the application and the OSC, as non-principal regulator, coordinates its review with the principal regulator. The principal regulator's decision to grant the designation automatically results in a deemed designation in the notified passport jurisdictions and, if the OSC has made the same decision as the principal regulator, evidences the decision of the OSC.

7. Principal regulator for an application — (1) For an application under this policy, the principal regulator is identified in the same manner as in sections 4B.2 to 4B.5 of MI 11-102.

(2) If the filer cannot determine its principal regulator under 4B.2(a) or (b) of MI 11-102, section 4B.2(c) of MI 11-102 requires that the filer determine its principal regulator by determining the specified jurisdiction with which the filer has the most significant connection. Section 4B.3 and 4B.4 also establish circumstances in which the filer may need to determine its principal regulator.

(3) For the purpose of this section, a specified jurisdiction is one of British Columbia, Alberta, Saskatchewan, Manitoba, Ontario, Québec, Nova Scotia and New Brunswick.

(4) The factors a filer should consider in identifying the principal regulator for the application based on the most significant connection test are, in order of influential weight:

    (a) jurisdiction where the filer generated the majority of its credit rating related revenue in the 3-year period preceding the date of its application, or

    (b) jurisdiction where the filer issued the most initial ratings in the 3-year period preceding the date of its application.

8. Discretionary change in principal regulator — (1) If the principal regulator identified under section 7 of this policy thinks it is not the appropriate principal regulator, it will first consult with the filer and the appropriate regulator and then give the filer a written notice of the new principal regulator and the reasons for the change.

(2) A filer may request a discretionary change of principal regulator for an application if

    (a) the filer concludes that the principal regulator identified under section 7 of this policy is not the appropriate principal regulator,

    (b) the location of the head office changes over the course of the application,

    (c) the most significant connection to a specified jurisdiction changes over the course of the application, or

    (d) the filer withdraws its application in the principal jurisdiction because it does not want to be designated in that jurisdiction.

(3) Regulators do not anticipate changing a principal regulator except in exceptional circumstances.

(4) A filer should submit a written request for a change in principal regulator to its current principal regulator and include the reasons for requesting the change.

PART 4 — FILING MATERIALS

9. Election to file under this policy and identification of principal regulator — In an application, the filer should indicate whether it is filing a passport application or a dual application and identify the principal regulator for the application.

10. Materials to be filed with application — (1) For a passport application, the filer should remit to the principal regulator the fees payable under the securities legislation of the principal regulator, and file the following materials with the principal regulator only:

    (a) a written application in which the filer:

        (i) states the basis for identifying the principal regulator under section 7 of this policy,

        (ii) gives notice of the non-principal passport jurisdictions for which section 4B.6 of MI 11-102 is intended to be relied upon,

        (iii) states that the filer and any relevant party is not in default of securities legislation applicable to credit rating organizations in any jurisdiction of Canada or in any jurisdiction in which the filer operates or, if the filer is in default, the nature of the default;

    (b) the materials required by Part 2 of NI 25-101;

    (c) other supporting materials.

(2) For a dual application, the filer should remit the fees payable under the securities legislation of the principal regulator and the OSC, and file the following materials with the principal regulator and the OSC:

    (a) a written application in which the filer:

        (i) states the basis for identifying the principal regulator under section 7 of this policy,

        (ii) gives notice of the non-principal passport jurisdictions for which section 4B.6 of MI 11-102 is intended to be relied upon;

        (iii) states that the filer is not in default of securities legislation applicable to credit rating organizations in any jurisdiction of Canada or in any jurisdiction in which the filer operates or, if the filer is in default, the nature of the default;

    (b) the materials required by Part 2 of NI 25-101;

    (c) other supporting materials.

11. Language — A filer seeking a designation in Québec should file a French language version of the draft decision when the AMF is acting as principal regulator.

12. Materials to be filed to make a designation available in an additional passport jurisdiction under section 4B.6 of MI 11-102 — (1) Under section 4B.6 of MI 11-102, the principal regulator's decision to grant the designation under a passport application or dual application can become available in a non-principal passport jurisdiction for which the filer did not give the notice referred to in section 10(1)(a)(ii) or 10(2)(a)(ii) of this policy in the initial application if certain conditions are met. One of the conditions is that the filer gives the notice under section 4B.6(1)(c) of MI 11-102 for the additional non-principal passport jurisdiction.

(2) For greater certainty, a filer may not rely on section 4B.6 of MI 11-102 to obtain an automatic designation under the provision of Ontario's securities legislation.

(3) The filer should give the notice referred to in subsection (1) to the principal regulator for the initial application. The notice should

    (a) list each relevant non-principal passport jurisdiction for which notice is given that section 4B.6 of MI 11-102 is intended to be relied upon,

    (b) include the date of the decision of the principal regulator for the initial application, if the notice is given under section 4B.6(1)(c) of MI 11-102,

    (c) include the citation for the principal regulator's decision, and

    (d) confirm that the designation is still in effect.

(4) The regulator that receives the notice referred to in section 10 will send a copy of the notice and its decision to the regulator in the relevant non-principal passport jurisdiction.

13. Filing — A filer should send the application materials in paper together with the fees to

    (a) the principal regulator, in the case of a passport application, and

    (b) the principal regulator and the OSC in the case of a dual application.

Part 1:
PROCEDURE

The filer should also provide an electronic copy of the application materials, including the draft decision document, by e-mail or on CD ROM. Filing the application concurrently in all required jurisdictions will make it easier for the principal regulator and non-principal regulators, if applicable, to process the application expeditiously.

Filers should send application materials by e-mail using the relevant address or addresses listed below:

British Columbia www.bcsc.bc.ca (click on BCSC e-services and follow the steps

Alberta	legalapplications@asc.ca
Saskatchewan	exemptions@sfsc.gov.sk.ca
Manitoba	exemptions.msc@gov.mb.ca
Ontario	https://www.osc.gov.on.ca/filings
Québec	Dispenses-Passeport@lautorite.qc.ca
New Brunswick	Passport-passeport@nbsc-cvmnb.ca
Nova Scotia	nsscexemptions@gov.ns.ca
Prince Edward Island	CCIS@gov.pe.ca
Newfoundland and Labrador	securitiesexemptions@gov.nl.ca
Yukon	corporateaffairs@gov.yk.ca
Northwest Territories	securitiesregistry@gov.nt.ca
Nunavut	legalregistries@gov.nu.ca

14. Incomplete or deficient material — If the filer's materials are deficient or incomplete, the principal regulator may ask the filer to file an amended application. This will likely delay the review of the application.

15. Acknowledgment of receipt of filing — After the principal regulator receives a complete and adequate application, the principal regulator will send the filer an acknowledgment of receipt of the application. The principal regulator will send a copy of the acknowledgement to any other regulator with whom the filer has filed the application. The acknowledgement will identify the name, phone number, fax number and e-mail address of the individual reviewing the application.

16. Withdrawal or abandonment of application — (1) If a filer withdraws an application at any time during the process, the filer is responsible for notifying the principal regulator and any non-principal regulator with whom the filer filed the application and for providing an explanation of the withdrawal.

(2) If at any time during the review process, the principal regulator determines that a filer has abandoned an application, the principal regulator will notify the filer that it will mark the application as "abandoned". In that case, the principal regulator will close the file without further notice to the filer unless the filer provides acceptable reasons not to close the file in writing within 10 business days. If the filer does not, the principal regulator will notify the filer and any non-principal regulator with whom the filer filed the application that the principal regulator has closed the file.

PART 5 — REVIEW OF MATERIALS

17. Review of passport application — (1) The principal regulator will review any passport application in accordance with its securities legislation and securities directions and based on its review procedures, analysis and considering previous decisions.

(2) The filer will deal only with the principal regulator, who will provide comments to and receive responses from the filer.

18. Review and processing of dual application — (1) The principal regulator will review any dual application in accordance with its securities legislation and securities directions, and based on its review procedures, analysis and considering previous decisions. Please refer to section 10(2) of this policy for guidance on filing an application with the OSC as non-principal regulator with whom a filer should file a dual application.

(2) The filer will generally deal only with the principal regulator, who will be responsible for providing comments to the filer once it has completed its own review. However, in exceptional circumstances, the principal regulator may refer the filer to the OSC as non-principal regulator.

PART 6 — DECISION-MAKING PROCESS

19. Passport application — (1) After completing the review process and after considering the recommendation of its staff, the principal regulator will determine whether to grant or deny the designation sought in a passport application.

(2) If the principal regulator is not prepared to grant the designation based on the information before it, it will notify the filer accordingly.

(3) If a filer receives a notice under subsection (2) and this process is available in the principal jurisdiction, the filer may request the opportunity to appear before, and make submissions to, the principal regulator.

20. Dual application — (1) After completing the review process and after considering the recommendation of its staff, the principal regulator will determine whether to grant or deny the designation sought in a dual application and immediately circulate its decision to the OSC.

(2) The OSC will have at least 10 business days from receipt of the principal regulator's decision to confirm whether it has made the same decision and is opting in or is opting out of the dual review.

(3) If the OSC is silent, the principal regulator will consider that the OSC has opted out.

(4) If the filer shows that it is necessary and reasonable in the circumstances, the principal regulator may request, but cannot require, the OSC to abridge the opt-out period.

(5) The principal regulator will not send the filer a decision for a dual application before the earlier of

    (a) the expiry of the opt-out period, or

    (b) receipt from the OSC of the confirmation referred to in subsection (2).

(6) If the principal regulator is not prepared to grant the designation a filer sought in its dual application based on the information before it, it will notify the filer and the OSC.

(7) If a filer receives a notice under subsection (6) and this process is available in the principal jurisdiction, the filer may request the opportunity to appear before, and make submissions to, the principal regulator. The principal regulator may hold a hearing on its own, or jointly or concurrently with the OSC. After the hearing, the principal regulator will send a copy of the decision to the filer and the OSC.

(8) If the OSC elects to opt out it will notify the filer and the principal regulator and give its reasons for opting out. The filer may deal directly with the OSC to resolve outstanding issues and obtain a decision without having to file a new application or pay any additional related fees. If the filer and the OSC resolve all outstanding issues, the OSC may opt back into the dual review by notifying the principal regulator within the opt-out period referred to in subsection (2).

PART 7 — DECISION

21. **Effect of decision made under passport application** — (1) The decision of the principal regulator under a passport application is the decision of the principal regulator. Under MI 11-102, a filer is automatically designated in the notified passport jurisdictions as a result of the decision of the principal regulator making the designation.

(2) Except in the circumstances described in section 12(1) of this policy, the designation is effective in each notified passport jurisdiction on the date of the principal regulator's decision (even if the regulator in the notified passport jurisdiction is closed on that date). In the circumstances described in section 12(1) of this policy, the designation is effective in the relevant non-principal passport jurisdiction on the date the filer gives the notice under section 4B.6(1)(c) of MI 11-102 for that jurisdiction (even if the regulator in that jurisdiction is closed on that date).

22. **Effect of decision made under dual application** — (1) The decision of the principal regulator under a dual application is the decision of the principal regulator. Under MI 11-102, a filer is automatically designated in the notified passport jurisdictions as a result of the decision of principal regulator making the designation. The decision of the principal regulator under a dual application also evidences the OSC's decision, if the OSC has confirmed that it has made the same decision as the principal regulator.

(2) The principal regulator will not issue the decision until the earlier of

    (a) the date that the OSC confirms that it has made the same decision as the principal regulator, or

    (b) the date the opt-out period referred to in section 20(2) of this policy has expired.

23. **Listing non-principal jurisdictions** — (1) For convenience, the decision of the principal regulator on a passport application or a dual application will refer to the notified passport jurisdictions, but it is the filer's responsibility to ensure that it gives the required notice for each jurisdiction for which section 4B.6(1) of MI 11-102 is intended to be relied upon.

(2) The decision of the principal regulator on a dual application will contain wording that makes it clear that the decision evidences and sets out the decision of the OSC to the effect that it has made the same decision as the principal regulator.

(3) For a dual application for which Québec is not the principal jurisdiction, the AMF will issue a local decision concurrently with and in addition to the principal regulator's decision. The AMF decision will contain the same terms and conditions as the principal regulator's decision. No other local regulator will issue a local decision.

24. **Issuance of decision** — The principal regulator will send the decision to the filer and to all non-principal regulators.

PART 8 — EFFECTIVE DATE

25. **Effective date** — This policy comes into effect on April 20, 2012.

Adoption by OSC: (2012) 35 O.S.C.B. 3294 and 2383; Request for Comments: (2011) 34 O.S.C.B. 3249 and (2010) 33 O.S.C.B. 6153.

Adoption of Amendments by OSC: (2013) 36 O.S.C.B. 10503; Request for Comments: (2013) 36 O.S.C.B. 3929.

Adoption of Amendments by OSC: (2014) 37 O.S.C.B. 1637.

CSA Notice 11-302 — Withdrawal of CSA Notices

Date: **December 21, 2001**

24 O.S.C.B. 7629

[Not reproduced]

CSA Notice 11-305 — Withdrawal of CSA Staff Notice 42-301 and 52-302

Date: **January 16, 2004**

27 O.S.C.B. 711

[Not reproduced]

CSA Notice 11-309 — Withdrawal of CSA Notices

Date: **March 3, 2006**

29 O.S.C.B. 1807

[Not reproduced]

CSA Notice 11-310 — Withdrawal of CSA Notices

Date: **December 5, 2008**

31 O.S.C.B. 11532

[Not reproduced]

CSA Staff Notice 11-312 (Revised) — National Numbering System

Date: **February 6, 2009, with correction published May 1, 2009; revised February 19, 2010**[1]

32 O.S.C.B. 1211 and 32 O.S.C.B. 3677; 33 O.S.C.B. 1515

The Canadian Securities Administrators (CSA) follows a system in which securities regulatory instruments are assigned numbers that indicate the type and subject matter of the instrument.

The numbering system was designed so as to:

(i) convey as much information as possible about the particular instrument so that a user knows what type of instrument it is, whether the instrument is national or local and what subject matter it relates to;

(ii) permit all National Instruments, National Policies and CSA Notices to have the same numbers in all jurisdictions (as is currently the case); and

(iii) be flexible enough to permit Local Rules, Policies, Notices and implementing instruments of all jurisdictions to be numbered in accordance with the numbering system without affecting the numbering of National Instruments, National Policies and CSA Notices.

Under the numbering system, each instrument is assigned a five digit number, with a hyphen appearing between the second and third digit. There are four components to the number assigned to a document:

- The first digit represents the broad subject area.

- The second digit represents a sub-category of the broad subject area.

- The third digit represents the type of the document.

- The last two digits represent the number of the document within its document type in its sub-category (in sequential order starting at 01).

More specifically, these four components may be described as follows:

- The **first** digit relates to the subject matter category into which the instrument has been classified. The nine subject matter categories are:

    1. Procedures and Related Matters

    2. Certain Capital Market Participants (Self-Regulatory Organizations, Exchanges and Market Operations)

    3. Registration Requirements and Related Matters (Dealers, Advisers and other Registrants)

    4. Distribution Requirements (Prospectus Requirements and Prospectus Exemptions)

    5. Ongoing Requirements for Issuers and Insiders (Continuous Disclosure)

    6. Take-over Bids and Special Transactions

    7. Securities Transactions Outside the Jurisdiction

    8. Investment Funds

    9. Derivatives

    For example, in the context of 54-101, the number "5" indicates that the instrument relates to Ongoing Requirements for Issuers and Insiders.

- The **second** digit relates to the sub-category of the subject matter category into which the instrument has been classified (see the "sub-category" column of the table below).

    Using the 54-101 example, within the Ongoing Requirements for Issuers and Insiders category, a sub-category for instruments dealing with Proxy Solicitation is denoted by the number "4". Accordingly, all instruments dealing with this matter commence with the numbers "54".

- The **third** digit classifies the document as one of nine types of documents:

    1. National[2] Instrument/Multilateral Instrument and any related Companion Policy or Form(s)

    2. National Policy/Multilateral Policy

    3. CSA Notice

    4. CSA Concept Proposal or Discussion Paper

    5. Local Rule, Regulation or Blanket Order or Ruling and any related Companion Policy or Form(s), except an Implementing Instrument described below.

    6. Local Policy

    7. Local Notice

---

[1]This Notice contains minor revisions to CSA Staff Notice 11-312, as published on February 6, 2009. The publishing of this staff notice coincided with the withdrawal of OSC Staff Notice 11-724 *Numbering System for Policy Reformulation Project* (19 O.S.C.B. 4258).

[2]A National Instrument or Policy is an instrument or policy that has been adopted by all CSA jurisdictions, whereas a Multilateral Instrument or Policy is an instrument or policy that has not been adopted by one or more CSA jurisdictions.

8. Implementing Instrument[3]

9. Miscellaneous

Using the same example, the third digit in 54-101 indicates that the type of instrument is a National Instrument or Multilateral Instrument (or a related Companion Policy or Form).

- The **fourth** and **fifth** digits represent a number assigned to instruments of the same type in consecutive order from 01 to 99 within a particular sub-category.

  Again, using the example 54-101, the number "01" indicates that the instrument is the first document of its type in the sub-category "Proxy Solicitation".

A Companion Policy or Form that is related to an Instrument or Local Rule will have the same number as the Instrument or Local Rule to which it relates, followed by "CP" in the case of a Companion Policy or "F" in the case of a Form. If there is more than one Form related to a particular instrument, the Forms will be numbered consecutively (F1, F2, F3, etc.).

Category, Sub-Category and Document Type Numbers

Category (1st digit)	Sub-Category (2nd digit)	Document Type (3rd digit)
1 — Procedure and Related Matters	1 — General 2 — Applications 3 — Filings with Securities Regulatory Authority 4 — Definitions 5 — Hearings and Enforcement	1 — National or Multilateral Instrument (Rule) and any related Companion Policy and Form 2 — National or Multilateral Policy 3 — CSA Notice or CSA Staff Notice 4 — CSA Concept Proposal or Discussion Paper
2 — Certain Capital Market Participants	1 — Stock Exchanges 2 — Other Markets 3 — Trading Rules 4 — Clearing and Settlement 5 — Other Participants	5 — Local Rule, Regulation or Blanket Order or Ruling and any related Companion Policy or Form 6 — Local Policy 7 — Local Notice
3 — Registration and Related Matters	1 — Registration Requirements 2 — Registration Exemptions 3 — Ongoing Requirements Affecting Registrants 4 — Fitness for Registration 5 — Non-Resident Registrants	8 — Implementing Instrument (Local Rule that gives effect to a National or Multilateral Instrument) 9 — Miscellaneous item (e.g., a Form that does not relate to another Instrument or Policy)
4 — Distribution Requirements	1 — Prospectus Contents — Non-Financial Matters 2 — Prospectus Contents — Financial Matters 3 — Prospectus Filing Matters 4 — Alternative Forms of Prospectus 5 — Prospectus Exempt Distributions 6 — Requirements Affecting Distributions by Certain Issuers 7 — Advertising and Marketing 8 — Distribution Restrictions	
5 — Ongoing Requirements for Issuers and Insiders	1 — Disclosure — General 2 — Financial Disclosure 3 — Timely Disclosure 4 — Proxy Solicitation 5 — Insider Reporting 6 — Restricted Shares 7 — Cease Trading Orders	

---

[3]For this purpose, an Implementing Instrument is a local rule making consequential changes relating to the implementation of a National Instrument/Multilateral Instrument.

Category (1st digit)	Sub-Category (2nd digit)	Document Type (3rd digit)
	8 — Corporate Governance	
6 — Take-Over Bids and Special Transactions	1 — Special Transactions 2 — Take-over Bids	
7 — Securities Transactions Outside the Jurisdictions	1 — International Issuers 2 — Distributions Outside the Jurisdiction	
8 — Investment Funds	1 — Investment Fund Distributions	
9 — Derivatives[4]	1 — Trades in Derivatives	

CSA Notice 11-313 — Withdrawal of Staff Notices and Policies

Date: February 19, 2010

33 O.S.C.B. 1518

[Not reproduced]

CSA Staff Notice 11-314 — Update of CSA Instruments

Date: May 6, 2011

34 O.S.C.B. 5171

[Not reproduced]

CSA Staff Notice 11-316 — Notice of Local Amendments — British Columbia

Date: April 13, 2012

35 O.S.C.B. 3589

[Not reproduced; amendments incorporated in NI 45-106]

CSA Staff Notice 11-317 — Withdrawal of Notices

Date: June 21, 2012

35 O.S.C.B. 5679

[Not reproduced]

CSA Staff Notice 11-318 — Guidance for Cease Trade Order Database Users

Date: August 23, 2012

35 O.S.C.B. 7725

Introduction and Purpose

Staff of the Canadian Securities Administrators (CSA Staff or we) are publishing this Staff Notice (the Notice) to highlight recent and upcoming changes to the Cease Trade Order Database (CTO Database). It provides guidance to CTO Database users and, in particular, to members of the investment industry in Canada.

Background

A cease trade order (CTO or Order) is a decision issued by a provincial or territorial securities regulatory authority or similar regulatory body against a company or an individual. Orders are issued for different reasons such as failing to meet disclosure requirements or as a result of an enforcement action that involves an investigation of potential wrongdoing. The purpose of the CTO Database is twofold: provide stakeholders with a publicly searchable database containing all Orders issued by participating CSA members, regardless of whether their effect is temporary or indefinite, and disseminate such Orders to its subscribers.

---

[4]Please note that in Québec, derivatives regulations will be made under the *Derivatives Act* (Québec) and not the *Securities Act* (Québec).

The CTO Database classifies Orders as either "Active" or "Inactive":

- Active Orders are decisions that are in effect. An Active Order's status may be either issued or amended.

- An Inactive Order's status may be either expired or revoked. An expired CTO has reached its end date as specified in the Order. A revoked CTO has been revoked by the provincial or territorial securities regulatory authority which originally issued it.

The CTO Database includes both Active CTOs and CTOs that have become inactive following either their expiry or revocation. CTOs issued against companies that have since dissolved or been discontinued remain active until expressly revoked or until they have expired. This content allows for a comprehensive database with an ability to provide historical data.

Substance of Implemented Changes

1. — Stock Symbols

Removal of stock symbols from the CTO Database: When an issuer is de-listed, stock symbols can be reused and reassigned to a new issuer. An issuer that is not subject to a CTO could be re-assigned the stock symbol of a cease-traded issuer that has been de-listed. These situations can create confusion among members of the investment industry when determining whether a trade can be executed, based solely on a stock symbol. Consequently, CSA staff has agreed that it would be preferable to have all stock symbols removed from the CTO Database.

2. — Security Identifiers

Use of CUSIP numbers: The CTO Database uses the CUSIP number as a security identifier. These numbers are assigned by CUSIP Global Services, managed on behalf of the American Bankers Association by S&P Capital IQ, to securities trading in Canada and the United States. Other securities identifiers, such as SEDOL (which identifies securities trading in the United Kingdom) and ISIN (international security identifier which is formed by adding CA in front of the CUSIP number), are not available through the CTO Database.

The CUSIP number is nine characters long. The first six characters identify the issuer, the seventh and eighth characters identify the type of security and the last digit is used as a check digit. Historically, the CTO Database did not require a certain number of characters when entering the CUSIP number, which resulted in CUSIP numbers being entered inconsistently into the database. As a result, going forward, the CTO Database has been modified to require, and only provide, the first six digits of the CUSIP number when a CUSIP number is entered. Since Orders that ban trading in securities of an issuer generally apply to all the securities of the issuer, including additional CUSIP characters to identify the type of security was not deemed necessary.

The CUSIP numbers are automatically retrieved from a list provided by S&P Capital IQ. However, in some instances, when the company name is uploaded to the CTO Database it does not exactly match the company name on the S&P Capital IQ list. In these instances, no CUSIP number will be available through the CTO Database. Also, no CUSIP number will be assigned to Orders that ban trading by certain individuals and/or companies. It remains the obligation of users to conduct the necessary due diligence to determine whether or not a specific trade can be executed. As such, we emphasize the importance of reading all decisions to fully understand their scope.

3. — Date Format

Standardized Date Format: We have standardized the date format in the CTO Database for the Issued Date, the Expiry Date as well as for search results downloaded into an Excel spreadsheet. All of these dates are now under the same format: YYYY/MM/DD.

4. — Company Names

Consistency in Company Names: We have implemented a mechanism to reduce as much as possible certain inconsistencies with respect to the format of company names. In spite of this modification to the CTO Database, sometimes these inconsistencies originate from the Orders themselves and under certain circumstances may continue to be unavoidable. Company names are entered in the database exactly as they appear on the Orders. If a company that is subject to a CTO changes its name, the CTO Database will not be changed unless there is an Order amending the original CTO.

5. — French Spelling

French Spelling: The CTO Database includes CTOs against companies with French names. In the past, when users downloaded search results for Orders against companies with French names, the results were often displayed incorrectly due to the use of accents (e.g."Systèmes Mécaniques Inc." appeared in the search results spreadsheet as "SystAtilde;"mes MAtilde;©caniques Inc."). This problem has been corrected and downloaded search results should now display correctly.

6. — Intra-day CTOs

Issuance of Intra-day CTOs: Under normal circumstances, dissemination of Orders through the CTO Database is automated. All Orders uploaded late at night or early in the morning are disseminated before the markets open and Orders uploaded during market hours are disseminated in the evening, once the markets close. However, some exceptional situations require Canadian securities regulatory authorities to issue cease trade Orders during market hours. The decision to disseminate an Order through the CTO Database during market hours rests entirely with the securities regulatory authority that issues the Order.

Upon receipt of a request from a securities regulatory authority to disseminate a CTO against a Canadian listed issuer during market hours, CSA staff will inform IIROC Market Surveillance staff before disseminating that Order to facilitate timely implementation and communication of a regulatory action.

7. — Notifications

Notifications of Expiration of Orders: We have changed the date and time of these notifications. The database will now send emails notifying subscribers of the expiration of Orders between 11:45 p.m. ET and 11:58 p.m. ET on the same date the Order expires. Therefore, if an Order expires on May 25, 2012, it is uploaded into the CTO database with a May 25, 2012 expiration date and the database will send the notification on May 25, 2012 between 11:45 p.m. ET and 11:58 p.m. ET.

Members of the investment industry will need to review their internal protocols to determine whether this change has an impact on their systems. This change has no legal impact on the scope of decisions.

Substance of Upcoming Changes

1. — Categories of Orders

Two Categories of Orders: Later this fall, CTOs will be classified into two new distinct groups:

(i) Orders that ban trading in securities of a reporting issuer or a non-reporting issuer, regardless of whether the Order resulted from a continuous disclosure default or an enforcement action, and;

(ii) Orders that ban trading by certain individuals and/or companies, regardless of whether the Order resulted from a continuous disclosure default of the issuer (such as a management cease trader order) or an enforcement action.

Some Orders may fall under both categories, in which circumstance, they will appear in both categories and two distinct notifications, one for each category, will be sent out to subscribers.

Orders classified under the first category ban trading in the securities of an issuer and those under the second category prevent certain individuals and/or companies from trading either in securities of a specific issuer or from trading in all securities.

This new categorization is intended as a tool to simplify the classification of Orders and enhance search results. However, it remains the obligation of users to conduct the necessary due diligence before trading to determine whether or not a specific trade can be executed. As such, we cannot overstate the importance of reading all decisions to fully understand their scope.

CSA Staff Notice 11-319 — Extension of Consultation Period — Consultation Paper 25-401: Potential Regulation of Proxy Advisory Firms

Date: August 16, 2012

35 O.S.C.B. 7724

On June 21, 2012, the Canadian Securities Administrators published for comment Consultation Paper 25-401 *Potential Regulation of Proxy Advisory Firms* (the Consultation Paper). The Consultation Paper discusses certain concerns raised about the services provided by proxy advisory firms and their potential impact on Canadian capital markets and considers whether, and how, these concerns should be addressed by Canadian securities regulators. The comment period is scheduled to close on August 20, 2012. We have received feedback from several stakeholders that it would be beneficial for stakeholders to have additional time to review the Consultation Paper and prepare comments. We therefore are extending the comment period from August 20, 2012 to **September 21, 2012**.

CSA Staff Notice 11-320 — Notice of Local Amendments — Nova Scotia and Yukon

Date: November 15, 2012

35 O.S.C.B. 10227

[Not reproduced]

CSA Staff Notice 11-321 — Business Continuity Planning — Industry Testing Exercise

Date: February 7, 2013

36 O.S.C.B. 1412

Introduction

Business continuity is an ongoing priority for securities industry participants and regulatory authorities. Various events over the past few years, such as flu outbreaks, natural disasters, black-outs and marketplace system problems heightened that priority by highlighting the risk of operational disruptions to the financial system.

Substance and Purpose

Staff of the Canadian Securities Administrators (CSA Staff or we) support and encourage the industry's efforts to identify the challenges and address the potential impact of incidents that could disrupt normal business operations. Securities regulations require that business continuity plans be tested regularly, to reflect current or potential developments. Subsection 12.4(2) of National Instrument 21-101 *Marketplace Operation* requires marketplaces to test their business continuity and disaster recovery plans on a reasonably frequent basis and, in any event, at least annually. In addition, subsection 11.1(b) of National Instrument 31-103 *Registration Requirements, Exemptions and Ongoing Registrant Obligations* requires a registered firm to establish, maintain and apply policies and procedures that establish a system of controls and supervision sufficient to manage the risks associated with its business in accordance with prudent business practices. Dealer Member Rules of the Investment Industry Regulatory Organization of Canada (IIROC) requires Dealer Members to establish and maintain a business continuity plan and conduct an annual review and a test of their business continuity plan to determine whether any modifications are necessary. In addition, clearing agencies are expected to have procedures to ensure business continuity including regularly testing their business continuity plans.

We are of the view that dealers, marketplaces, self-regulatory organizations and clearing agencies should participate regularly in industry-wide testing.

As stated in IIROC Notice 12-0279 issued on September 24, 2012, IIROC has set the date for a market wide test on October 5, 2013. IIROC expects all Dealer Members and major service providers to participate in this test and it will share the results of the test with all participants.

CSA Staff encourage all dealers, marketplaces and clearing agencies to participate in the October, 2013 market-wide exercise organized by IIROC. Participation in this exercise may lead to the discovery of potential system and operational problems that could undermine the integrity of the capital markets.

CSA Staff Notice NI 11-322 — Extension of Consultation Period — Proposed Amendments to 62-104, NI 61-103 — Proposed Changes to NPS 62-203 — Proposed NI 62-105 — Proposed Companion Policy 62-105 CP

Date: June 3, 2013

36 O.S.C.B. 5655

[Not reproduced]

CSA Staff Notice 11-323 — Withdrawal of Notices and Policies

Date: September 12, 2013

36 O.S.C.B. 8942

[Not reproduced]

CSA Staff Notice NI 11-324 — Extension of Comment Period — Proposed Amendments to NI 81-102, NPS 81-102CP and Related Consequential Amendments and Other Matters Concerning NI 81-104 and Securities Lending, Repurchases and Reverse Repurchases by Investment Funds

Date: June 25, 2013

36 O.S.C.B. 6424

[Not reproduced]

CSA Staff Notice 11-326 — Cyber Security

Effective: September 26, 2013

36 O.S.C.B. 9289

Strong and tailored cyber security measures are an important element of issuers', registrants and regulated entities'[1] controls in promoting the reliability of their operations and the protection of confidential information. The risk of a major cyber attack on key Financial Market Infrastructure (FMI) has been highlighted by the International Organization of Securities Commissions (IOSCO) and the World Federation of Exchanges (WFE) in a recent report issued July 16, 2013.[2]

The IOSCO report defines cyber crime as a *"harmful activity, executed by one group (including both grassroots groups or nationally coordinated groups) through computers, IT systems and/or the internet and targeting the computers, IT infrastructure and internet presence of another entity."* Although cyber threats have existed in the past, more recently two major types of cyber threats, Denial of Service (DoS) attacks and Advanced Persistent Threats (APT), have increased in frequency and sophistication.

To manage the risks of a cyber threat, issuers, registrants and regulated entities should be aware of the challenges of cyber crime and should take the appropriate protective and security hygiene measures necessary to safeguard themselves and their clients or stakeholders.

Specifically:

- Issuers, registrants and regulated entities who have not considered the risks of cyber crime to date should consider how they can best address the risks of cyber crime. Steps they could take include:

  - educating staff on the importance of, and their role in, ensuring the security of their firm s and client information and computer security;

  - following guidance and best practices from industry associations and recognized information security organizations; and

  - as appropriate, conducting regular third party vulnerability and security tests and assessments.

---

[1]Regulated entities include self-regulatory organizations, marketplaces, clearing agencies and information processors.

[2]"Cyber-crime, securities markets and systemic risk", joint staff working paper of the IOSCO Research Department and World Federation of Exchanges, July 16, 2013.

- Issuers, registrants and regulated entities that have already taken steps to address the issue should review their cyber security risk control measures on a regular basis.

Issuers should consider whether the cyber crime risks to them, any cyber crime incidents they may experience, and any controls they have in place to address these risks, are matters they need to disclose in a prospectus or a continuous disclosure filing.

Registrants should consider whether their risk management systems allow them to manage the risks of cyber crime in accordance with prudent business practices.

Regulated entities, especially those that are key market infrastructure entities, should consider the measures necessary to manage the risks of cyber crime.

Future Action

The CSA will consider these issues in its reviews of issuer disclosure and in its oversight of registrants and regulated entities.

CSA Staff Notice 11-327 — Extension of Consultation Period — Proposed National Policy 25-201 Guidance for Proxy Advisory Firms

Date: June 12, 2014

Citation: 37 O.S.C.B. 5549

[Not reproduced]

CSA Staff Notice 11-328 — Notice of Local Amendments in Alberta and the Adoption of Multilateral Amendments in Yukon

Date: March 12, 2015

38 O.S.C.B. 2279

[Not reproduced]

CSA Staff Notice 11-329 — Withdrawal of Notices and Revocation of Omnibus/Blanket Orders

Date: July 16, 2015

38 O.S.C.B. 6358

This Notice formally withdraws a number of CSA notices and announces the revocation and withdrawal of parallel orders and a policy. The withdrawn materials may remain available for historical research purposes on some CSA members' websites.

CSA Staff Notices

CSA staff have determined that the following CSA Staff Notices are no longer required and accordingly they are or have been withdrawn.

CSA Staff Notice 31-313	*NI 31-103 Registration Requirements and Exemptions and Related Instruments Frequently Asked Questions as of December 18, 2009*
CSA Staff Notice 31-314	*NI 31-103 Registration Requirements and Exemptions and Related Instruments Frequently Asked Questions as of February 5, 2010*
CSA Staff Notice 31-315	*Omnibus/blanket orders exempting registrants from certain provisions of National Instrument 31-103 Registration Requirements and Exemptions*
CSA Staff Notice 31-326	*Outside Business Activities*
CSA Staff Notice 31-327	*Broker-Dealer Registration in the Exempt Market Dealer Category*
CSA Staff Notice 31-328	*Revocation of Omnibus/Blanket Orders Exempting Registrants from Certain Provisions of National Instrument 31-103 Registration Requirements, Exemptions and Ongoing Registrant Obligations*
CSA Staff Notice 31-329	*Omnibus/Blanket Orders Exempting Registrants from Certain Provisions of National Instrument 31-103 Registration Requirements, Exemptions and Ongoing Registrant Obligations and Related Staff Positions*
CSA Staff Notice 31-330	*Omnibus/Blanket Orders Extending Certain Transition Provisions Relating to the Investment Fund Manager Registration Requirement and the Obligation to Provide Dispute Resolution Services*
CSA Staff Notice 31-331	*Follow-Up to Broker Dealer Registration in the Exempt Market Dealer Category*
CSA Staff Notice 31-333	*Follow-Up to Broker Dealer Registration in the Exempt Market Dealer Category*

CSA Staff Notice 31-335	*Extension of Interim Relief for Members of the Investment Industry Regulatory Organization of Canada from the Requirement in section 14.2(1) of National Instrument 31-103 Registration Requirements, Exemptions and Ongoing Registrant Obligations in Respect of the Provision of Relationship Disclosure Information to Existing Clients*

This Notice also announces the relevant securities regulators have revoked a number of parallel orders and withdrawn a multilateral policy that are no longer required.

Omnibus/blanket order and policy	Status
Exemption from the requirement to register for international advisers	**This order is revoked.**[1] The order provided relief from restrictions on the registration exemption for international advisers in section 8.26 of NI 31-103 tied to the definition of "Canadian permitted client". Section 8.26 was amended effective January 11, 2015 to remove these restrictions.
Exemption from the requirement to register for international dealers	**This order is revoked.**[2] The order provided relief from restrictions on the registration exemption for international dealers in section 8.18 of NI 31-103 tied to the definition of "Canadian permitted client". Section 8.18 was amended effective January 11, 2015 to remove these restrictions.
Continuation of transition provisions for persons and companies adding a jurisdiction	**This order is revoked.**[3] The order provided relief from certain provisions in NI 31-103 to a person or company registered in a jurisdiction of Canada on and since the date NI 31-103 came into force that applied for registration in another jurisdiction after the date NI 31-103 came into force. The order is no longer required because certain transition and grandfathering provisions in NI 31-103 are spent and others have been amended.
Exemption from time limits on examination requirements for dealing representatives of scholarship plan dealers	**This order is revoked.**[4] The order provided relief from time limits on examination requirements in NI 31-103 for representatives of scholarship plan dealers registered in a jurisdiction of Canada on and since the date NI 31-103 came into force. Section 3.3 of NI 31-103 was amended effective January 11, 2015 to provide equivalent relief.
Transitional Relief from the Requirement to Register as an Investment Fund Manager	**This order is revoked.**[5] The order provided relief from the investment fund manager registration requirement in the local jurisdiction to a person or company registered in another jurisdiction of Canada as an investment fund manager until December 31, 2012 or while a registration application in the local jurisdiction was being processed if applied for by December 31, 2012. This order also provided relief from the investment fund manager registration requirement in the local jurisdiction to a person or company whose head office was not in a jurisdiction of Canada until December 31, 2012 or while a registration application in the local jurisdiction was being processed. The order is no longer required because the relief has expired.

Notes:

1 Local orders: BC: BCI 31-523; AB: BO 31-521; SK: GO 31-917; MB: BO 31-517; ON: no local order was issued and this was instead addressed in the OSC Staff position set out in CSA Staff Notice 31-329; QC: Décision n° 2011-PDG-0153; NB: Blanket Order 31-521; NS: Blanket Order No. 31-522

2 Local orders: BC: BCI 32-524; AB: BO 31-520; SK: GO 31-916; MB: BO 31-516; ON: no local order was issued and this was instead addressed in the OSC Staff position set out in CSA Staff Notice 31-329; QC: Décision n° 2011-PDG-0152; NB: Blanket Order 31-520; NS: Blanket Order No. 31-521

3 Local orders: BC: BCI 32-509; AB: BO 31-506; SK: GO 31-904; MB: BO 31-512; ON: *In the Matter of Jonathan Boulduc (the "Lead Filer") and Certain Other Persons or Companies Registered under the Act*, (2010) 33 OSCB 1773; QC: Décision n° 2010-PDG-0039; NB: Blanket Order 31-504; NS: Blanket Order No. 31-507

4 Local orders: BC: BCI 32-512; AB: BO 31-509; SK: GO 31-907; MB: BO 31-509; ON: *In the Matter of Laurence Ginsberg (the "Lead Filer") and Dealing Representatives of Exempt Market Dealers and Scholarship Plan Dealers*, (2010) 33 OSCB 1776; QC: Décision n° 2010-PDG-0042; NB: Blanket Order 31-507; NS: Blanket Order No. 31-510

5 Local orders: BC: BCI 31-508; AB: BO 31-524; SK: GO 31-920; MB: Commission Order No. 6550, dated July 5, 2012; ON: The two aspects of relief were addressed in the following two separate decisions, the first of which has not been revoked as it remains relevant to

Part 1: PROCEDURE

certain outstanding registration applications: *In the Matter of Fédération des Caisses Desjardins du Québec (the Lead Filer) and Persons or Companies Acting as an Investment Fund Manager in Ontario and Registered as an Investment Manager in the Jurisdiction of Canada in which their Head Office is Located at the Date of this Decision,* (2012) 35 OSCB 6293, and *In the Matter of Capital International, Inc. (the Lead Filer) and Persons or Companies Acting as an Investment Fund Manager in Ontario Without a Head Office in a Jurisdiction of Canada at the Date of this Decision,* (2012) 35 OSCB 6295; QC: Décision n° 2012-PDG-0133; NB: Blanket Order 31-524 (previously revoked); NS: Blanket Order No. 31-525

Questions

Please refer your questions to any of the following people:
[Omitted.]

OSC Rule 11-501 — Electronic Delivery Of Documents To The Ontario Securities Commission

Date: February 19, 2014, amended December 8, 2015, January 13, 2015 and January 16, 2016.

36 O.S.C.B. 10503, 38 O.S.C.B. 8330, 38 O.S.C.B. (Supp. 4) 53 and 38 OSCB (Supp-3) 53.

1. Interpretation — (1) In this Rule

"form filer" means a person or company required or permitted by Ontario securities law to file or deliver a required document with the Ontario Securities Commission;

"NRD" has the meaning ascribed to it in National Instrument 31-102 *National Registration Database*;

"required document" means

    (a) a document listed in Appendix A; or

    (b) any other document required to be filed with or delivered to the Ontario Securities Commission under Ontario securities law by

        (i) a market participant, or

        (ii) another person or company exempted from a requirement of Ontario securities law by reason of section 147 of the Act or an application otherwise provided for in Ontario securities law;

"SEDAR" has the meaning ascribed to it in National Instrument *13-101 System for Electronic Document Analysis and Retrieval (SEDAR)*;

"SEDI" has the meaning ascribed to it in National Instrument 55-102 *System for Electronic Disclosure by Insiders (SEDI)*.

(2) In this Rule, unless the context otherwise requires, "document" includes "information", "material" and "notice" as those words are used in Ontario securities law.

(3) In this Rule, a reference to a document that is required or permitted to be delivered includes a document that is required or permitted to be deposited with, or delivered, furnished, sent, provided or submitted to, the Ontario Securities Commission under Ontario securities law.

(4) The transmission of a document in electronic format to the Ontario Securities Commission under section 2 of this Rule constitutes

    (a) if the document is required or permitted to be filed under Ontario securities law, the filing of that document under Ontario securities law; and

    (b) if the document is required or permitted to be delivered to the Ontario Securities Commission under Ontario securities law, the delivery of that document.

2. Electronic filing — (1) Each required document of a person or company must be transmitted to the Ontario Securities Commission electronically by the person or company following the steps set out at https://www.osc.gov.on.ca/filings.

(2) Subsection 2(1) does not apply to any required document that is

    (a) filed or delivered through SEDAR, SEDI or NRD;

    (b) filed or delivered under the Ontario Securities Commission Rules of Procedure; or

    (c) filed or delivered under Part V, Part VI or Part VII of the Securities Act.

3. Temporary technical difficulties exemption — (1) If unanticipated technical difficulties prevent the timely transmission of a required document, the form filer may transmit the document by e-mail as soon as practical and in any event no later than 2 business days after the day on which the filing was required.

(2) A filing under subsection (1) must include the following legend at the top of the first page:

    THIS REPORT IS BEING FILED UNDER A TEMPORARY TECHNICAL DIFFICULTIES EXEMPTION

(3) In addition to filing or delivery under subsection (1), a copy of each completed required document of a form filer must be transmitted under section 2 as soon as practical after the unanticipated technical difficulty has been resolved and in any event no later than 3 business days after resolution of the technical difficulties.

(4) If a document is filed or delivered as required under this section, the date by which the document is required to be filed or delivered under Ontario securities law is deemed to be the date on which the document is filed electronically under section 2.

4. Exemption — The Director may grant an exemption from the provisions of this Rule, in whole or in part, subject to such conditions or restrictions as may be imposed in the exemption.

5. Effective Date — This Rule comes into force on February 19, 2014.

Appendix A

Document Reference	Description of Document
Securities Act, s. 1(10)	Applications to the Commission under clause 1(10) of the *Securities Act*
Securities Act, s. 1(11)	Applications to the Commission under clause 1(11) of the *Securities Act*
Securities Act, Part VIII	Applications to the Commission for recognition or designation under Part VIII of the *Securities Act*
Securities Act, s. 21.4	Applications to the Commission for the voluntary surrender of a recognition or designation under section 21.4 of the *Securities Act*
Securities Act, s. 75(3) 51-102, s. 7.1(2), 81-106, s. 11.2(4)	Confidential material change reports permitted to be filed under subsection 75(3) of the *Securities Act*, subsection 7.1(2) of National Instrument 51-102 *Continuous Disclosure Obligations*, or subsection 11.2(2) of NI 81-106 *Investment Fund Continuous Disclosure*
Securities Act, s. 75(4) 51-102, s. 7.1(5), 81-106, s. 11.2(4)	The notification required under subsection 75(4) of the *Securities Act*, subsection 7.1(5) of NI 51-102 *Continuous Disclosure Obligations*, or subsection 11.2(4) of NI 81-106 *Investment Fund Continuous Disclosure*
Securities Act, Part XXIII.1	Notices and other documents to be sent to the Commission under Part XXIII.1 of the *Securities Act*
Securities Act, s. 144	Applications to the Commission to vary or revoke a recognition or designation granted under Part VIII of the *Securities Act*
11-202	Pre-filings or waiver applications within the meaning of National Policy 11-202 *Process for Prospectus Reviews in Multiple Jurisdictions*
11-203	Pre-filings, as defined in National Policy 11-203 Process for *Exemptive Relief Applications in Multiple Jurisdictions*
11-203	Applications, as defined in National Policy 11-203 *Process for Exemptive Relief Applications in Multiple Jurisdictions*
11-205	Applications to become Designated Rating Organization, under the process set out in National Policy 11-205 *Process for Designation of Credit Rating Organizations in Multiple Jurisdictions*
12-202	Applications to vary or revoke a CTO as defined in National Policy 12-202 *Revocation of a Compliance-related Cease Trade Order*
13-101 s. 2.1	Documents to be filed with the Commission by issuers not required to comply with National Instrument 13-101 *System for Electronic Document Analysis and Retrieval* in accordance with section 2.1 of that Instrument
13-101 s. 2.3	Documents to be filed with the Commission in paper format under section 2.3 of National Instrument 13-101 *System for Electronic Document Analysis and Retrieval*
13-502F4	Form 13-502F4 *Capital Markets Participation Fee Calculation*
13-502F5	Form 13-502F5 *Adjustment of Fee for Registrant Firms and Unregistered Exempt International Firms*
13-503F1	Form 13-503F1 *Capital Markets Participation Fee Calculation (Firms registered only under the Commodity Futures Act)*
13-503F2	Form 13-503F2 *Adjustment of Fee for Registrant Firms registered only under the Commodity Futures Act*
13-502F8	Form 13-502F8 *Designated Rating Organizations — Participation Fee*
21-101F1	Form 21-101F1 *Information Statement Exchange or Quotation and Trade Reporting System*
21-101F2	Form 21-101F2 *Initial Operation Report Alternative Trading System*
21-101F3	Form 21-101F3 *Quarterly Report of Alternative Trading System Activities*
21-101F4	Form 21-101F4 *Cessation of Operations Report for Alternative Trading System*
21-101F5	Form 21-101F5 *Initial Operation Report for Information Processor*
21-101F6	Form 21-101F6 *Cessation of Operations Report for Information Processor*
24-101F1	Form 24-101F1 *Registered Firm Exception Report of DAP/RAP Trade Reporting and Matching*
24-101F2	Form 24-101F2 *Clearing Agency — Quarterly Operations Report of Institutional Trade Reporting and Matching*
24-101F3	Form 24-101F3 *Matching Service Utility — Notice of Operations*

Part 1:
PROCEDURE

Document Reference	Description of Document
24-101F4	Form 24-101F4 *Matching Service Utility — Notice of Cessation of Operations*
24-101F5	Form 24-101F5 *Matching Service Utility — Quarterly Operations Report of Institutional Trade Reporting and Matching*
25-101F1	Form 25-101F1 *Designated Rating Organization Application and Annual Filing*
25-101F2	Form 25-101F2 *Submission to Jurisdiction and Appointment of Agent for Service of Process*
31-103 s. 11.9	Notice of acquisition pursuant to section 11.9 of National Instrument 31-103 *Registration Requirements, Exemptions and Ongoing Registrant Obligations*
31-103 s. 11.10	Notice of acquisition pursuant to section 11.10 of National Instrument 31-103 Registration *Requirements, Exemptions and Ongoing Registrant Obligations*
31-103 s. 12.2	Notice of repayment or termination of subordination agreement pursuant to section 12.2 of National Instrument 31-103 *Registration Requirements, Exemptions and Ongoing Registrant Obligations*
31-103 s. 12.7	Notice of change, claim or cancellation of insurance policy pursuant to section 12.7 of National Instrument 31-103 *Registration Requirements, Exemptions and Ongoing Registrant Obligations*
31-103F1	Form 31-103F1 *Calculation of Excess Working Capital*, together with associated financial information as required by sections 12.12, 12.13 and 12.14 of National Instrument 31-103 *Registration Requirements, Exemptions and Ongoing Registrant Obligations*
31-103F2	Form 31-103F2 *Submission to Jurisdiction and Appointment of Agent for Service*
31-103F3	Form 31-103F3 *Use of Mobility Exemption*
31-317	CSA Staff Notice: 31-317 (Revised) *Reporting Obligations Related to Terrorist Financing*
32-102F1	Form 32-102F1 *Submission to Jurisdiction and Appointment of Agent for Service for International Investment Fund Manager*
32-102F2	Form 32-102F2 *Notice of Regulatory Action*
33-109F5	Form 33-109F5 *Change of Registration Information*
33-109F6	Form 33-109F6 *Firm Registration*
33-506F5	Form 33-506F5 *Change of Registration Information (Commodity Futures Act)*
33-506F6	Form 33-506F6 *Firm Registration (Commodity Futures Act)*
35-101F1	Form 35-101F1 *Form of Submission to Jurisdiction and Appointment of Agent for Service of Process by Broker-Dealer*
35-101F2	Form 35-101F2 *Form of Submission to Jurisdiction and Appointment of Agent for Service of Process by Agents of the Broker-Dealer*
43-101F1	Form 43-101F1 *Technical Report*
45-106F1	Form 45-106F1 *Report of Exempt Distribution*
45-106F15	Form 45-106F15 *Rights Offering Circular for Reporting Issuers*
45-106 s. 2.1.2	Notice and materials sent pursuant to section 2.1.2 of National Instrument 45-106 *Prospectus Exemptions*
45-106F2	Form 45-106F2 *Offering Memorandum for Non-Qualifying Issuers* or any amendment to a previously filed Form 45-106F2
45-106F3	Form 45-106F3 *Offering Memorandum for Qualifying Issuers* or any amendment to a previously filed Form 45-106F3
45-106 s. 2.9(17.1)	45-106 s. 2.9(17.1) Filing of marketing materials pursuant to subsection 2.9(17.1) of National Instrument 45-106 *Prospectus Exemptions*
45-106F16	Form 45-106F16 *Notice of Use of Proceeds*
45-106 s. 2.9(17.13)	Delivery of a notice of change in financial year end pursuant to subsection 2.9(17.13) of National Instrument 45-106 *Prospectus Exemptions*
45-106 s. 2.9(17.5)	Delivery of annual financial statements pursuant to subsection 2.9 (17.5) of National Instrument 45-106 *Prospectus Exemptions*
45-106 s. 2.42(2)(a)	Notice to the Commission given pursuant to paragraph 2.42(2)(a) of National Instrument 45-106 *Prospectus Exemptions*
45-106 s. 4.1(4)	Letters filed with the Commission pursuant to subsection 4.1(4) of National Instrument 45-106 *Prospectus Exemptions*

Document Reference	Description of Document
45-108 s. 12(1)(a)	A term sheet made available to a purchaser pursuant to clause 12(1)(a) of Multilateral Instrument 45-108 *Crowdfunding*
45-108 s. 12(1)(c)	Materials summarizing the information in a crowdfunding offering document made available to a purchaser pursuant to clause 12(1)(c) of Multilateral Instrument 45-108 *Crowdfunding*
45-108F1	Form 45-108F1 *Crowdfunding Offering Document*
45-501F1	Form 45-501F1 *Report of Exempt Distribution*
45-501 s. 5.4	Delivery of an offering memorandum or any amendment to a previously delivered offering memorandum in accordance with section 5.4 of OSC Rule 45-501 *Ontario Prospectus and Registration Exemptions*
71-101F1	Form 71-101F1 *Forms of Submission to Jurisdiction and Appointment of Agent for Service of Process*
81-102 s. 5.8(3)	Notice to the Commission by a manager under subsection 5.8(3) of National Instrument 81-102 *Mutual Funds*
81-102 s. 6.7(3)	Delivery of custodian compliance reports under subsection 6.7(3) of National Instrument 81-102 *Mutual Funds*
81-102 s. 12.1(2), 12.1(3)	Compliance reports under subsection 12.1(2) or 12.1(3) of National Instrument 81-102 *Mutual Funds*
81-106 s. 2.11(c)	Notice to the Commission that a mutual fund is relying on the exemption not to file its financial statements in section 2.11 of National Instrument 81-106 *Investment Fund Continuous Disclosure*
91-507, Part 4	OTC Derivative Trade Reporting (not already reported to repository) pursuant to Part 4 of OSC Rule 91-507 *Trade Repositories and Derivatives Data Reporting*
Business Corporations Act, s. 1(6)	Applications to the Commission under subsection 1(6) of the *Business Corporations Act*
Business Corporations Act, s. 46(4)	Applications to the Commission under subsection 46(4) of the *Business Corporations Act*
Business Corporations Act, s. 113	Applications to the Commission under section 113 of the *Business Corporations Act*
Business Corporations Act, s. 158(1.1)	Applications to the Commission under subsection 158(1.1) of the *Business Corporations Act*
Business Corporations Act, s. 190(6)	Applications to the Commission under subsection 190(6) of the *Business Corporations Act*
Ont. Reg. 289/00 generally made under the Business Corporations Act, s. 4(b)	Applications to the Commission for consents under subsection 4(b) of Ont. Reg. 289/00 generally made under the *Business Corporations Act*

Final Rule: (2014) 37 O.S.C.B. 1631; Approval by OSC: (2013) 36 O.S.C.B. 10503; Request for Comments: (2013) 36 O.S.C.B. 3929
Adoption of Amendments by OSC: 38 O.S.C.B. (Supp. 3) 53.

OSC Policy 11-601 — The Securities Advisory Committee to the OSC

Date: February 1, 2002
25 O.S.C.B. 683

A. — General

1. The Ontario Securities Commission (the "Commission") has established an advisory committee composed of practising securities lawyers, named "The Securities Advisory Committee to the OSC" ("SAC").

B. — Terms of Reference

1. SAC provides advice to the Commission and Commission staff on a variety of matters including legislative and policy initiatives and important capital markets trends.

2. At the request of the Commission or Commission staff, SAC provides advice and comments on the legal, regulatory and market implications of any aspect of Commission rules, policies, operations, and administration.

3. On its own initiative, SAC may report to the Commission or Commission staff at any time on issues the members consider should be addressed by the Commission or of which the Commission should be aware.

4. SAC may report annually to the Chairman of the Commission on its activities for the preceding year.

5. SAC generally meets at least monthly.

C. — Composition of SAC

1. SAC will consist of up to 12 members. Members of SAC will generally be expected to serve minimum terms of two years, except where they are appointed for the purpose of completing the unexpired term of a former member. Terms may extend to, but will not exceed, three

years. Terms may be staggered so that a certain number of the members may retire in any one year. Except in transition periods, members will not be re-appointed on the expiry of their terms.

2. SAC will select one member to act as Chairman. The Chairman's term may be one or two years and, in the former case, may be renewed.

D. — Appointment Criteria

1. Individuals appointed to SAC should have an excellent knowledge of "Ontario securities law" (the legislation and policies for which the OSC is responsible), and significant practice experience in the securities area. Expertise in an area of special interest to the Commission at the time an appointment is made may also be a factor in selection. SAC members are expected to have excellent technical abilities and a strong interest in the development of securities regulatory policy.

2. SAC members will be selected with a view to ensuring that SAC is reasonably representative of the full spectrum of securities law practice.

3. SAC members should be in a position to make the time commitment that SAC's work entails. Members who find themselves unable to make this time commitment may be asked to resign in order that their places may be filled by more active members.

E. — Application Process

1. In order to replace SAC members whose terms expire, the Commission will first publish a notice soliciting new applications for membership and setting a deadline for submissions. When the selection process is complete, a notice of the new members will be published.

2. Securities law practitioners interested in serving on SAC should apply in writing to the General Counsel, indicating areas of practice and relevant experience.

3. The General Counsel will review all applications for membership and recommend new members to the Chairman of the Commission. The Chairman of the Commission, on the advice of the General Counsel and, if requested, of the current SAC Chairman, will make the final decision as to SAC membership.

F. — Liaison Between SAC and Commission

1. The General Counsel serves as the liaison between SAC and the Commission. The General Counsel will attend SAC meetings. Matters are referred to SAC by the Office of the General Counsel on behalf of Commission staff. Commission staff are expected to attend SAC meetings in appropriate cases. In addition to attendance at SAC meetings, Commission staff may work directly with SAC on particular projects.

2. All material submitted by the Commission to SAC is confidential, as are all SAC proceedings. Material shall not be distributed to or discussed with anyone who is not a member of SAC, unless the prior consent of the General Counsel has been obtained.

3. Commission staff will ensure that material is submitted to SAC in a timely fashion, so that sufficient opportunity for review and comment is provided.

Adoption by OSC: (2002) 25 O.S.C.B. 683; amending and renumbering OSC Policy 1.7; Notice: (1985) 8 O.S.C.B. 906; Final: (1985) 8 O.S.C.B. 943; replaced (1991) 14 O.S.C.B. 4133.

OSC Staff Notice 11-706 — Withdrawal of Staff Notices

Date: **October 6, 2000**

23 O.S.C.B. 6861

[Not reproduced]

OSC Staff Notice 11-709 — Assignment of Notice Numbers

Date: **April 20, 2001**

24 O.S.C.B. 2405

[Not reproduced]

OSC Staff Notice 11-710 — Withdrawal of Staff Accounting Communiqués

Date: **April 20, 2001**

24 O.S.C.B. 2406

[Not reproduced]

OSC Staff Notice 11-712 — Withdrawal of CSA Notices

Date: **April 20, 2001**

24 O.S.C.B. 2406

[Not reproduced]

OSC Notice 11-722 — Recommendations of the Committee on Staff Communications

Date: 1995/08/11

18 O.S.C.B. 3617; assigned number: (2003) 26 O.S.C.B. 2319

The Ontario Securities Commission recently struck a Committee on Staff Communications (the "Committee") to provide recommendations to senior management of the Commission and to the Commission itself regarding the procedures for and content of communications from OSC staff to the public. The recommendations of the Committee were accepted by the Commission on July 25, 1995 and are effective immediately.

Background

The practice concerning the involvement of the Commission in staff communications has been varied. In light of the *Securities Amendment Act, 1994* ("Bill 190"), the Commission created the Committee in order to determine the appropriate procedure and the respective roles of staff and the Commission on staff communications. The members of the Committee were Jack Geller, Morley Carscallen, John Stransman (of Stikeman, Elliott), Patricia O'Malley (of KPMG Peat Marwick Thorne), Brenda Eprile, Susan Wolburgh Jenah, Randee Pavalow and Craig Wright.

The content of staff communications may involve (i) factors which relate to the exercise of a discretion by staff, (ii) the manner in which the *Securities Act* (the "Act"), the regulations, rules or policies are interpreted by staff, or (iii) the practices generally followed by staff in the performance of its responsibilities. The publication of staff communications in a timely manner is critical to the goals of transparency and efficiency. It is essential that staff views be published so that the public is aware of such views. It is also important, however, that staff have the benefit of the Commission's input and knowledge of the Commission's concerns, if any, and that the Commission be kept informed of staff's views and the reasons supporting such views.

Summary of Recommendations

The recommendations of the Committee, as accepted by the Commission, are summarized below:

(i) — At What Point in the Process Should the Commission be Involved in a Staff Communication?

Neither the Commission nor individual Commissioners should be involved in a proposed staff communication until a consensus on the issues has been reached at the staff level, unless staff wishes to discuss a proposed communication with Commissioners who have indicated a view on the issue or who have extensive experience with respect to the issue.

(ii) — Impact of Bill 190: Commission Policy versus Staff Notice

The procedural difference which flows from an instrument being designated as a policy rather than a staff notice is clear: policies must be published for comment, whereas staff notices can be published immediately without any notice and comment requirement. However, often it is difficult to distinguish between those instruments which should be characterized as staff notices and those instruments which should be characterized as Commission policy. The definition of "policy" in subsection 143.8(1) of the Act is extremely broad and arguably could apply to all instruments which are not rules, but it is clear that there is and should be room for communications which are less than Commission policy but still warrant publication. The Ontario Task Force on Securities Regulation recognized the importance of these less formal instruments in providing valuable information to the public and endorsed the "frequent articulation of actual practices" of staff.

There are many factors which should be taken into account in determining whether a particular instrument is a staff notice or a policy. The Commission has adopted the following criteria which are subject to change over time. These criteria are not necessarily comprehensive or determinative. Many are quite subjective.

- If staff's views on a particular issue have "crystallized", the instrument is more likely to be a policy; if the views are still being formed and developed by staff (even though there may be a consensus at the staff level), then the instrument is more likely to be a staff notice. Part of the rationale for this criterion is that an uncrystallized view is likely to change or to be further developed and so the flexibility of a staff notice is more appropriate. In this regard, staff notices may describe staff views on one or more historical events (and therefore be based on a specific set of facts). These staff views may change and "crystallize" as staff deals with different factual circumstances. Policies, on the other hand, tend to be more future-oriented in the sense that they may be based on a broader range of factual circumstances or be without an historical "anchor".

- If the issue addressed by the instrument occurs frequently and has a broad impact on market participants, the instrument is more likely to be a policy than a staff notice. Statements which have a frequent and broad impact on market participants should be subjected to a comment period. Similarly, if a communication is permissive rather than restrictive, it is more likely to be a notice than a policy since there is perhaps less need for a comment period. (However, the converse of this criterion is not necessarily true; — statement that is restrictive would not necessarily be a policy).

- Items which are primarily of an administrative or procedural nature are more likely to be notices rather than policies.

- If the Commission has been extensively involved in an instrument and subscribes to its content, the instrument is more likely to be a policy. On the other hand, if the Commission has had limited involvement and/or there has been no effort to seek consensus among Commissioners, the instrument should probably be a staff notice.

The decision as to whether a communication should be a notice or a policy rests with staff, under the supervision of the Executive Director and the Chair (acting as chief executive officer of the Commission). The Commission has the ability to reverse the decision of staff when the instrument is presented to the Commission and may choose to adopt an instrument as Commission policy, notwithstanding staff's earlier determination that the instrument should be a staff notice.

(iii) — Procedures for Bringing Staff Communications to the Commission's Attention

There is considerable merit in bringing the issues addressed in a proposed staff notice before the Commission prior to publication because staff will obtain the views and comments of the Commission and will be informed of any significant disagreements which the Commission may have with respect to the proposed notice. Similarly, the Commission will benefit from being informed of staff's views and the reasoning behind such views. However, to the extent that the Commission becomes involved in drafting the staff notice, the instrument may become Commission policy by virtue of the Commission's involvement. Accordingly, proposed staff notices should be brought to the Commission's attention in concept only. Under this procedure, staff will describe the issue to the Commission and discuss the content of the proposed staff notice, but the text of the staff notice will not be presented to the Commissioners for their comment. In most cases, it will be appropriate for staff to provide the Commissioners with a background memorandum on the issues being addressed in the proposed staff notice in order to facilitate the oral presentation.

Only in exceptional circumstances should a staff notice be published prior to the Commission being informed of the issues. These rare circumstances include emergencies where the publication of the staff view is so urgent that it is not practicable to wait for the next Commission meeting. Even in these circumstances, however, staff should speak to the Chair or a Vice-Chair to inform them of staff's intentions. Minor matters which do not warrant discussion at a full Commission meeting (such as minor administrative matters) need not be presented to Commissioners prior to publication.

(iv) — What if Some Commissioners Disagree with Staff's Views?

A staff notice does not require a consensus of the Commission in order to be published. While it is important for staff to know the extent to which any Commissioners disagree with staff on a particular matter, and staff would be wise to take this disagreement into account in deciding whether to proceed with the publication of the notice, it is ultimately staff's decision (under the supervision of the Executive Director and the Chair, acting as chief executive officer of the Commission) whether or not to publish the staff notice in the face of such disagreement. In this regard, it is important to note that staff notices emanate from staff and are not approved (or non-disapproved) by the Commission. Accordingly, views expressed in a staff notice do not necessarily represent the views of the Commission or any individual Commissioners. Commissioners remain free to disagree with and rule against the staff views if and when the matter comes before a panel of Commissioners for a determination.

(v) — Reasonable Apprehension of Bias

Before presenting an issue to the Commission that will be the subject of a staff notice, staff should consider whether the issue may potentially raise concerns in the mind of a particular market participant (or group of market participants) that the Commission has prejudged their case. Where these situations arise, it may be appropriate for staff to consult with the Chair or a Vice Chair to obtain their views on whether there is a risk of bias. In the limited circumstances where this risk is sufficiently great, it may be necessary to publish the notice without presentation before or discussion at a full Commission meeting. However, given the level of Commission involvement in staff notices, the frequency of these concerns should be rare.

(vi) — Should Advisory Boards be Consulted on Staff Communications?

In the past, many staff communications have been submitted to the Securities Advisory Committee or the Financial Disclosure Advisory Board prior to publication. The practice of consulting such advisory boards or other interested parties prior to the publication of staff communications has often been extremely helpful and should be continued in circumstances where it is reasonably expected that such bodies would have strong views or particular expertise with respect to the proposed staff communication. The involvement of the advisory boards should not, however, be an automatic procedure but rather should be addressed on a case by case basis.

(vii) — Frequency of Staff Notices

The views of staff should be published on a much more frequent and timely basis. It is important that any views of staff or decisions made by staff which may have an impact on market participants be communicated to the public. OSC staff should be more aggressive in identifying such issues and publishing notices. While certain notices should be published as soon as they are developed, other less urgent notices should be collected and published together on a periodic basis (such as every 6 months).

Conclusion

It is expected that the implementation of these recommendations will result in better and more consistent procedures for publishing staff communications and in improved communication between staff, the Commission and the public.

For further information contact: Executive Director

OSC Notice 11-723 — Policy Reformulation Project

Date: 1996/05/10

19 O.S.C.B. 2310; assigned number: (2003) 26 O.S.C.B. 2319

This issue of the Bulletin contains the proposed rule in respect of the System For Electronic Document Analysis And Retrieval ("SEDAR"). This is the first substantive proposed rule that is being made in more than one Canadian jurisdiction. SEDAR is being described as a "National Instrument" by each jurisdiction. The adoption of National Instruments and National Policies (as described below) represents a continuation on the part of the Canadian Securities Administrators of their efforts in promoting and maintaining harmonization and consistency among jurisdictions in the context of the new rule or regulation making regimes that have now come into effect in several provinces. To assist market participants in understanding this aspect of the Policy Reformulation Project, a brief explanation is provided as to the concept of National Instruments and National Policies, and their development.

1. Those existing National Policy Statements that will be maintained as part of the Policy Reformulation Project will be replaced by National Instruments and National Policies. National Instruments will be legislative in nature and will be adopted as rules in Ontario and in most cases as rules or regulations in other jurisdictions in which the securities commission or similar body has rule or regulation making power and as policies in jurisdictions without rule or regulation making power. The manner in which a National Instrument will be made by a particular jurisdiction will vary depending on the legislative framework in place in the jurisdiction.

2. National Policies will not be legislative in nature but will set out principles or criteria relating to the exercise of discretion by the applicable securities commission or similar body or their staff, the manner in which they interpret their respective statutes and the practices generally followed by them in the performance of their duties. National Policies will be adopted as policies by all jurisdictions that adopt them.

3. A National Instrument will be made as a rule in Ontario under subsection 143(1) of the *Securities Act* (Ontario), as it is legislative in nature.

4. A National Policy will be adopted as a policy in Ontario under section 143.8 of the *Securities Act* (Ontario).

5. National Instruments and National Policies are being drafted generically so that, to the extent practicable, they can be adopted or made in the same form by each jurisdiction. Accordingly, a National Instrument or National Policy will not generally refer to a particular jurisdiction or the legislation of a particular jurisdiction. Instead, National Instruments and National Policies will make use of terms such as "securities legislation", "securities regulatory authority" and "local jurisdiction". It is contemplated that a National Instrument will be made setting out definitions of certain terms that will be used with common meaning in National Instruments and National Policies. That proposed National Instrument will define terms adopted on a national basis such as those referred to above and other terms relevant to the understanding of a National Instrument or National Policy. Until this National Instrument is published for comment, proposed National Instruments will set out the meanings of any common terms in a footnote. The proposed National Instrument for definitions will also provide that a term used in a National Instrument and defined in the securities legislation of the applicable jurisdiction, the definition of which is not restricted to a specific portion of the securities legislation, will, for the purposes of that jurisdiction, have the meaning given to it in the securities legislation of that jurisdiction.

6. A user applying a National Instrument to matters in Ontario will read "securities legislation" to mean the Ontario statute, regulation and rules, "securities regulatory authority" to mean the Ontario Securities Commission and "local jurisdiction" to mean Ontario. A user applying a National Instrument with respect to matters in another jurisdiction will read "securities legislation" as that term is defined for that jurisdiction in the proposed National Instrument for definitions, "securities regulatory authority" to mean the securities commission or similar body in that jurisdiction and "local jurisdiction" to mean that jurisdiction. Generally, a National Instrument will not refer to "distributing securities in the local jurisdiction" or "filing in the local jurisdiction". Instead, it will refer to "distributing securities" or "filing". In that regard, a National Instrument should be read the same way as a user read a statute, regulation or rule adopted locally which generally do not refer to the jurisdiction making them but apply based on activity in or a connection to the jurisdiction.

7. Each jurisdiction may opt out of or amend a particular provision of a National Instrument. A local instrument may be used to vary local legislation or create exemptions under this local legislation if necessary to give proper effect to the National Instrument.

8. Each National Instrument that is of a prohibitive or mandatory nature (as opposed to exemptive in nature) will contain a provision allowing one or both of the appropriate securities regulatory authority or specified staff members in a particular jurisdiction to grant an exemption to the National Instrument.

Reference: Policy Coordinator

OSC Staff Notice 11-728 — Withdrawal of Staff Notices

Date: March 21, 2003 as corrected May 9, 2003

26 O.S.C.B. 2321 and 26 O.S.C.B. 3498

[Not reproduced]

OSC Staff Notice 11-729 — Withdrawal of Staff Notice

Date: June 4, 2003

26 O.S.C.B. 4137

[Not reproduced]

OSC Staff Notice 11-737 — Securities Advisory Committee — Vacancies

Date: August 27, 2004, September 17, 2004, July 15, 2005, November 23, 2007, July 25, 2008, September 25, 2009, September 24, 2010, November 11, 2011, October 11, 2012, October 24, 2013, October 23, 2014

27 O.S.C.B. 7407, 27 O.S.C.B. 7925, 28 O.S.C.B. 5955, 30 O.S.C.B. 9638, 31 O.S.C.B. 7406, 32 O.S.C.B. 7548, 33 O.S.C.B. 8472, 34 O.S.C.B. 11281, 35 O.S.C.B. 9189, 36 O.S.C.B. 10274 and 37 O.S.C.B. 9529

[Not reproduced]

OSC Notice 11-774 — Statement of Priorities; Request for Comments Regarding Statement of Priorities for Financial Year to End of March 31, 2017

Date: February 18, 2016

39 O.S.C.B. 1459

[Not reproduced]

OSC Staff Notice 11-739 (Revised) — Policy Reformulation Table of Concordance and List of New Instruments

Date: April 14, 2016

(2016), 39 O.S.C.B. 3584

The following revisions have been made to the Table of Concordance and List of New Instruments. A full version of the Table of Concordance and List of New Instruments as of March 31, 2016 has been posted to the OSC Website at www.osc.gov.on.ca.

Table of Concordance

Item Key
The third digit of each instrument represents the following: 1-National/Multilateral Instrument; 2-National/Multilateral Policy; 3-CSA Notice; 4-CSA Concept Release; 5-Local Rule; 6-Local Policy; 7-Local Notice; 8-Implementing Instrument; 9-Miscellaneous

Reformulation

Instrument	Title	Status
	None	

New Instruments

Instrument	Title	Status
21-316	Information Processor for Corporate Debt Securities	*Published January 7, 2016*
45-106	Prospectus Exemptions — Amendments	*Ministerial approval published January 7, 2016*
11-742	Securities Advisory Committee (Revised)	*Ministerial approval published January 7, 2016*
52-107	Acceptable Accounting Principles and Auditing Standards — Amendments	*Ministerial approval published January 7, 2016*
45-102	Resale of Securities — Amendments	*Ministerial approval published January 7, 2016*
11-203	Process for Exempt Relief Applications in Multiple Jurisdictions — Amendments	*Commission approval published January 7, 2016*
11-501	Electronic Delivery of Documents to the Ontario Securities Commission — Amendments	*Ministerial approval published January 7, 2016*
13-502	Fees — Amendments	*Ministerial approval published January 7, 2016*
45-501	Ontario Prospectus and Registration Exemptions — Amendments	*Ministerial approval published January 7, 2016*
11-739	Policy Reformulation — Table of Concordance and List of New Instruments — Revised	*Published January 14, 2016*
52-306	Non-GAAP Financial Measures — Revised	*Published January 14, 2016*
45-108	Crowdfunding	*Ministerial approval published January 14, 2016*
11-501	Electronic Delivery of Documents to the Ontario Securities Commission — Amendments	*Ministerial approval published January 14, 2016*
45-501	Ontario Prospectus and Registration Exemptions — Amendments	*Ministerial approval published January 14, 2016*
94-102	Derivatives Customer Clearing and Protection of Customer Collateral and Positions	*Published for comment January 21, 2016*
45-314	Updated List of Current CSA Exempt Market Initiatives (Revised)	*Published January 28, 2016*
81-729	Summary Report for Investment Fund and Structured Product Issuers	*Published February 18, 2016*

Instrument	Title	Status
51-726	Report on Staff's Review of Insider Reporting and User Guides for Insiders and Issuers	*Published February 18, 2016*
24-102	Clearing Agency Requirements	*Ministerial approval published February 18, 2016*
94-101	Mandatory Central Counterparty Clearing of Derivatives and Proposed Companion Policy CP Mandatory Central Counterparty Clearing of Derivatives	*Published for comment February 25, 2016*
43-101CP	Standards of Disclosure for Mineral Projects — Amendments	*Published February 25, 2016*
62-104	Take-Over Bids and Issuer Bids — Amendments	*Commission approval published February 25, 2016*
62-203	Take-Over Bids and Issuer Bids — Amendments	*Commission approval published February 25, 2016*
11-102	Passport System — Amendments	*Commission approval published February 25, 2016*
13-102	System Fees for SEDAR and NRD — Amendments	*Commission approval published February 25, 2016*
43-101	Standards of Disclosure for Mineral Projects — Amendments	*Commission approval published February 25, 2016*
55-104CP	Insider Reporting Requirements and Exemptions — Amendments	*Commission approval published February 25, 2016*
61-101	Protection of Minority Security Holders in Special Transactions — Amendments	*Commission approval published February 25, 2016*
61-101CP	Protection of Minority Security Holders in Special Transactions	*Commission approval published February 25, 2016*
62-103	The Early Warning System and Related Take-Over Bid and Insider Reporting Issues — Amendments	*Commission approval published February 25, 2016*
62-504	Take-Over Bids and issuer Bids — Repeal	*Commission approval published February 25, 2016*
13-502	Fees — Amendments	*Commission approval published February 25, 2016*
14-501	Definitions — Amendments	*Commission approval published February 25, 2016*
48-501	Trading During Distributions, Formal Bids and Share Exchange Transactions — Amendments	*Commission approval published February 25, 2016*
71-801	Implementing the Multijurisdictional Disclosure System — Amendments	*Commission approval published February 25, 2016*
71-802	Implementing National Instrument 71-103 Continuous Disclosure and Other Exemptions Relating to Foreign Issuers — Amendments	*Commission approval published February 25, 2016*
91-502	Trades in Recognized Options — Amendments	*Commission approval published February 25, 2016*
11-206	Process for Cease to be a Reporting Issuer Applications	*Commission approval published March 3, 2016*
11-207	Failure-to-File Cease Trade Orders and Revocations in Multiple Jurisdictions	*Commission approval published March 3, 2016*
12-202	Revocation of Certain Cease Trade Orders (replacing current NP 12-202)	*Commission approval published March 3, 2016*
12-203	Management Cease Trader Orders (replacing current NP 12-203)	*Commission approval published March 3, 2016*
11-774	Statement of Priorities — Request for Comments Regarding Statement of Priorities for Financial Year to End March 31, 2017	*Published for comment March 10, 2016*
54-304	Final Report on Review of the Proxy Voting Infrastructure and Request for Comments on Proposed Meeting Vote Reconciliation Protocols	*Published for comment March 31, 2016*

For further information, contact:

Darlene Watson

Project Specialist

Ontario Securities Commission

416-593-8148

April 14, 2016

Policy Reformulation
Table of Concordance and List of New Instruments

The following revisions have been made to the Table of Concordance and List of New Instruments. A full version of the Table of Concordance and List of New Instruments as of December 31, 2015 has been posted to the OSC Website at www.osc.gov.on.ca.

Table of Concordance

Item Key
The third digit of each instrument represents the following: 1-National/Multilateral Instrument; 2-National/Multilateral Policy; 3-CSA Notice; 4-CSA Concept Release; 5-Local Rule; 6-Local Policy; 7-Local Notice; 8-Implementing Instrument; 9-Miscellaneous

Reformulation

Instrument	Title	Status
	None	

New Instruments

Instrument	Title	Status
58-307	Staff Review of Women on Boards and in Executive Officer Positions — Compliance with NI 58-101 Disclosure of Corporate Governance Practices	*Published October 1, 2015*
21-101	Marketplace Operation — Amendments	*Ministerial approval published October 1, 2015*
23-101	Trading Rules — Amendments	*Ministerial approval published October 1, 2015*
21-706	Marketplaces' Initial Operations and Material System Changes	*Published October 1, 2015*
3-502	Fees — Amendments	*Commission approval published October 1, 2015*
11-739	Policy Reformulation Table of Concordance and New Instruments (Revised)	*Published October 8, 2015*
45-714	Summaries of Exempt Distribution Information	*Published October 15, 2015*
11-737	Securities Advisory Committee (Revised)	*Published October 22, 2015*
45-106	Prospectus Exemptions — Amendments (Offering Memorandum)	*Commission approval published October 29, 2015*
52-107	Acceptable Accounting Principles and Auditing Standards — Amendments (Offering Memorandum)	*Commission approval published October 29, 2015*
45-102	Resale of Securities — Amendments (Offering Memorandum)	*Commission approval published October 29, 2015*
11-203	Process for Exempt Relief Applications in Multiple Jurisdictions — Amendments (Offering Memorandum)	*Commission approval published October 29, 2015*
11-501	Requirement for the Electronic Delivery of Documents to the Ontario Securities Commission — Amendments (Offering Memorandum)	*Commission approval published October 29, 2015*
13-502	Fees — Amendments (Offering Memorandum)	*Commission approval published October 29, 2015*
45-501	Exempt Distributions — Amendments (Offering Memorandum)	*Commission approval published October 29, 2015*
15-601	Whistleblower Policy	*Request for comment published October 29, 2015*
48-501	Trading During Distributions, Formal Bids and Share Exchange Transactions — Amendments	*Ministerial approval of amendments published October 29, 2015*
45-108	Crowdfunding	*Commission approval published November 5, 2015*
45-102	Resale of Securities — Amendments (Crowdfunding)	*Commission approval published November 5, 2015*
11-501	Requirement for Electronic Delivery of Documents to the Ontario Securities Commission — Amendments (Crowdfunding)	*Commission approval published November 5, 2015*
51-345	Disclosure of Abandonment and Reclamation Costs in National Instrument 51-101 Standards of Disclosure for Oil and Gas Activities and Related Forms	*Published November 5, 2015*
11-773	The Investor Perspective	*Published November 5, 2015*

Instrument	Title	Status
41-101	General Prospectus Requirements — Amendments (Aequitas)	*Ministerial approval published November 5, 2015*
44-101	Short Form Prospectus Distribution — Amendments (Aequitas)	*Ministerial approval published November 5, 2015*
45-106	Prospectus Exemptions — Amendments (Aequitas)	*Ministerial approval published November 5, 2015*
51-102	Continuous Disclosure Obligations — Amendments (Aequitas)	*Ministerial approval published November 5, 2015*
52-109	Certification of Disclosure in Issuers' Annual and Interim Filings (Aequitas)	*Ministerial approval published November 5, 2015*
52-110	Audit Committees — Amendments (Aequitas)	*Ministerial approval published November 5, 2015*
58-101	Disclosure of Corporate Governance Practices — Amendments (Aequitas)	*Ministerial approval published November 5, 2015*
61-101	Protection of Minority Security Holders in Special Transactions — Amendments (Aequitas)	*Ministerial approval published November 5, 2015*
71-102	Continuous Disclosure and Other Exemptions Relating to Foreign Issuers — Amendments (Aequitas)	*Ministerial approval published November 5, 2015*
81-101	Mutual Fund Prospectus Disclosure — Amendments (Aequitas)	*Ministerial approval published November 5, 2015*
46-201	Escrow for Initial Public Offerings — Amendments (Aequitas)	*Ministerial approval published November 5, 2015*
56-501	Restricted Shares — Amendments (Aequitas)	*Ministerial approval published November 5, 2015*
31-343	Conflicts of interest in distributing securities of related or connected issuers	*Published November 26, 2015*
91-507	Trade Repositories and Derivatives Trade Reporting — Amendments	*Ministerial approval published November 5, 2015*
24-102	Clearing Agency Requirements	*Commission approval published December 3, 2015*
45-106	Prospectus Exemptions — Amendments (Rights Offerings)	*Commission approval published December 3, 2015*
41-101	General Prospectus Requirements — Amendments (Rights Offerings)	*Commission approval published December 3, 2015*
44-101	Short Form Prospectus Distributions — Amendments (Rights Offerings)	*Commission approval published December 3, 2015*
45-102	Resale of Securities — Amendments (Rights Offerings)	*Ministerial approval published December 3, 2015*
45-101	Rights Offerings — Amendments (Rights Offerings)	*Ministerial approval of repeal published December 3, 2015*
13-101	System for Electronic Document Analysis and Retrieval (SEDAR) — Amendments (Rights Offerings)	*Ministerial approval published December 3, 2015*
13-102	System Fees for SEDAR and NRD — Amendments (Rights Offerings)	*Ministerial approval published December 3, 2015*
11-501	Electronic Delivery of Documents to the Ontario Securities Commission — Amendments (Rights Offerings)	*Ministerial approval published December 3, 2015*
13-502	Fees — Amendments (Rights Offerings)	*Ministerial approval published December 3, 2015*
61-101	Protection of Minority Security Holders in Special Transactions — Amendments (Rights Offerings)	*Ministerial approval published December 3, 2015*
13-502	Fees — Amendments	*Ministerial approval published December 3, 2015*
24-102CP	Clearing Agency Requirements — Amendments	*Ministerial approval published December 3, 2015*
13-315	Securities Regulatory Authority Closed Dates 2016 (Revised)	*Published December 10, 2015*
81-102	Investment Funds — Amendments (CSA Mutual Fund Risk Classification Methodology)	*Request for comment published December 10, 2015*

Part 1:
PROCEDURE

Instrument	Title	Status
81-101	Mutual Fund Prospectus Disclosure — Amendments (CSA Mutual Fund Risk Classification Methodology)	*Request for comment published December 10, 2015*
41-101	General Prospectus Requirements — Amendments (CSA Mutual Fund Risk Classification Methodology)	*Request for comment published December 10, 2015*
13-706	SEDAR Filer Manual Update	*Published December 17, 2015*

For further information, contact:

Darlene Watson

Project Specialist

Ontario Securities Commission

416-593-8148

January 14, 2016

OSC Staff Notice 11-742 (Revised) — Securities Advisory Committee

Date: January 7, 2016

39 O.S.C.B. 10

[Not reproduced]

OSC Staff Notice 11-752 — Limited Market Dealer Initiative — Compliance Team

Date: May 20, 2005

28 O.S.C.B. 4517

The Compliance team of the Ontario Securities Commission (OSC) has commenced a new initiative regarding limited market dealers (LMD). This initiative developed from our efforts to evolve our Compliance mandate in 2004. In the past, we have monitored LMDs as part of our reviews of those investment counsel/portfolio managers (ICPM) who are also registered as LMDs. This initiative is the first step in our plan to enhance our oversight of LMDs.

Currently there are approximately 550 LMDs registered with the OSC. The spectrum of LMDs is very broad and includes LMDs registered as mutual fund dealers, as investment dealers, as ICPMs or solely as LMDs. These differences give rise to various business models and potentially different risks facing these firms.

Our initiative will have three phases: information gathering, program development and finally, on-site focussed reviews of a sample of LMDs. We are currently at the information gathering stage and anticipate performing on-site reviews in September. An industry report will be issued in 2006, documenting the results of our reviews and recommending changes (if any) to the existing legislation which applies to LMDs.

In an effort to broaden our understanding of this registration category, including the various business models and risks facing these firms, we will be sending a survey to all LMDs in Phase 1. The survey will consist of a series of questions which will require written responses. All LMDs will be required to complete the survey. We also intend to hold several focus groups in Phase 1. Each focus group will include 15–20 LMDs, representing a cross section of the population. Meetings will be 2 hours in length to ensure adequate coverage of the issues. We view this as a very important step in our initiative and would encourage firms to participate. If you are interested in attending one of our focus groups, please send an email to compliance@osc.gov.on.ca. Once meeting dates and times have been determined, those individuals expressing interest will be contacted.

We hope that this initiative will assist LMDs in enhancing their compliance structure and will result in a more effective regulatory regime.

OSC Staff Notice 11-753 (Revised) — Notice of Statement of Priorities for Financial Year to End March 31, 2012

Date: June 17, 2005, June 30, 2006, June 29, 2007, June 27, 2008, June 26, 2009, March 26, 2010 and June 17, 2011

28 O.S.C.B. 5317, 29 O.S.C.B. 5338, 30 O.S.C.B. 5809, 31 O.S.C.B. 6445, 32 O.S.C.B. 5171, 33 O.S.C.B. 2532 and 34 O.S.C.B. 6694

[Not reproduced]

OSC Notice 11-754 — Multilateral Instrument 11-101 Principal Regulator System, Form 11-101F1 Principal Regulator Notice under Multilateral Instrument 11-101, Companion Policy 11-101CP Principal Regulator System, Amendments to National Policy 43-201 Mutual Reliance Review System for Prospectuses and Annual Information Forms, Amendments to National Policy 12-201 Mutual Reliance Review System for Exemptive Relief Applications, Amendments to National Instrument 51-101 Standards of Disclosure for Oil and Gas Activities, and Multilateral Instrument 81-104 Commodity Pools

Date: August 26, 2005

28 O.S.C.B. 7135

Introduction

On May 27, 2005, the Ontario Securities Commission ("we" or the "Commission"), published a notice regarding proposed Multilateral Instrument 11-101 *Principal Regulator System* (MI 11-101), Form 11-101F1 *Notice of Principal Regulator under Multilateral Instrument 11-101*, Companion Policy 11-101CP *Principal Regulator System*. The notice also discussed proposed amendments to:

- National Policy 43-201 *Mutual Reliance Review System for Prospectuses and Annual Information Forms* (MRRS Prospectus Policy),

- National Policy 31-201 *National Registration System* (NRS Policy),

- National Instrument 51-101 *Standards of Disclosure for Oil and Gas Activities* (NI 51-101), and

- Multilateral Instrument 81-104 *Commodity Pools* (MI 81-104).

Other members of the Canadian Securities Administrators ("CSA") published a similar notice on May 27, 2005, but, unlike the Commission, indicated their intention to adopt MI 11-101.

Nine comment letters were submitted in connection with the May 27, 2005 notices. Five comment letters were addressed to the Commission and another four comment letters were addressed solely to the other CSA members. The comment letters received by the Commission are posted on the Commission's website at www.osc.gov.on.ca. We have considered the comments and thank all the commenters. For a summary of all comments and responses by the other members of the CSA, please see the following CSA member websites:

> www.albertasecurities.com
>
> www.bcsc.bc.ca
>
> www.lautorite.qc.ca

Notice of Amendments

For the reasons set out in the Commission's Notice dated May 27, 2005, we are not adopting MI 11-101, or its related Form and Companion Policy. Other members of the CSA, however, will be adopting MI 11-101 in their respective jurisdictions effective September 19, 2005. The text for MI 11-101 and related materials can be found on the CSA member websites noted above.

The Commission, together with the other members of the CSA, is adopting amendments to the MRRS Prospectus Policy, and National Policy 12-201 *Mutual Reliance Review System for Exemptive Relief Applications* (the "MRRS Applications Policy")(discussed below). The amendments to the MRRS Prospectus Policy and MRRS Applications Policy will also take effect on September 19, 2005.

In the Notice of May 27, the Commission also proposed an amendment to National Policy 31-201 *National Registration System* (NP 31-201) to shorten the decision-making process. The amendment would have reduced the opt-in period in NP 31-201 from five business days to two business days. NP 31-201 has been in effect since April 4 of this year. The CSA have decided not to make the proposed amendment at this time because we need more experience with the system to determine whether it is practical to reduce the opt-in period. The CSA will, therefore, monitor the operation of the system and reconsider the proposed amendment on the first anniversary of NP 31-201.

The British Columbia Securities Commission (BCSC) has also adopted amendments to remove B.C. only carve-outs in sections 2.1.3 and 3.6 of NI 51-101, and in section 8.6 of MI 81-104, to become effective September 19, 2005.

Changes Introduced to the Existing Regulatory System by MI 11-101

The fact that we have not adopted MI 11-101 will not affect the current filing requirements or mutual reliance practices for reporting issuers. All reporting issuers, regardless of where their head office is located, will continue to have to file, deliver and disseminate continuous disclosure information and will continue to pay filing fees in each province or territory where they are reporting issuers. In addition, they will continue to have to file prospectuses with, and obtain receipts from, the securities regulator in each jurisdiction in which they undertake a public offering.

Other than the mobility exemption for registrants (discussed below), the principal change for issuers introduced by MI 11-101 will be to reduce the number of securities regulators that may be involved in an application for relief from certain continuous disclosure requirements, or certain processing prospectus related disclosure or eligibility requirements. In this regard, for reporting issuers in Ontario that have a head office outside Ontario, they will continue to rely on the mutual reliance review systems ("MRRS"), but only two securities regulators will be involved — the OSC and the securities regulator located in the "participating principal jurisdiction" under MI 11-101. For reporting issuers with a head office in Ontario, they will continue to rely on MRRS in each jurisdiction where the relief is required. Considering that the current practice under MRRS enables market participants to deal with one regulator (i.e., their principal regulator), the changes introduced by MI 11-101 should, from an issuer's perspective, be marginal.

Commitment to Achieving Greater Efficiencies

Several commenters supported the Commission's decision not to publish MI 11-101 and many urged us to continue working to develop a set of harmonized, if not uniform, requirements. Some commenters also expressed the view that, rather than trying to get multiple regulators to act as one, it would be more efficient to create a single regulator with a single and consistent set of regulatory standards across the country. In this regard, the Commission continues to be committed to enhancing the efficiency and effectiveness of the Canadian regulatory system and developing harmonized requirements. We continue to work with other CSA members to develop greater uniformity in our regulatory requirements and practices.

In addition, we note that as a result of the collective efforts of all CSA members, the following rules or requirements will become uniform across the country on September 19, 2005 when the BCSC adopts them:

- Multilateral Instrument 52-109 *Certification of Disclosure in Issuers' Annual and Interim Filings* (MI 52-109),

- The requirements in National Instrument 51-101 *Standards of Disclosure for Oil and Gas Activities* (NI 51-101) respecting Form 51-101F3 and responsibilities by the Board of Directors to review certain procedures, statements and appointments,

- The disclosure requirement in Multilateral Instrument 81-104 *Commodity Pools* (MI 81-104) respecting the minimum and maximum levels of leverage experienced in a particular financial period, and

- The requirements in National Instrument 51-102 *Continuous Disclosure Obligations* (MI 51-102) respecting Business Acquisition Reports and restricted share disclosure.

We fully support initiatives that will further streamline our current administrative and review processes, as well as lead to greater harmonization in our regulatory requirements. Accordingly, we are amending, together with other CSA members, the MRRS Prospectus Policy and the MRRS Applications Policy (see discussion below).

We also support, in principle, the mobility registration exemption contained in MI 11-101. This exemption will permit registrants to continue to work with their existing clients who relocate to another jurisdiction. As a result of the comments we received, the Commission will study the feasibility of introducing a similar exemption for registrants whose clients move to Ontario. In the interim, the Commission will, in the appropriate cases, consider and grant applications for exemptive relief from the registration requirements based on the same type of restrictions listed under the mobility exemption in MI 11-101.

Amendments to the MRRS Prospectus Policy

The MRRS Prospectus Policy establishes the mutual reliance review system ("MRRS") for the review and clearance of prospectuses (including long-form, short-form and mutual fund prospectuses), prospectus amendments, waiver applications, and pre-filing discussions. The MRRS remains an important component of the Commission's focus on harmonization and streamlining regulatory requirements and processes that benefit market participants. Under the MRRS Prospectus Policy, each non-principal regulator relies primarily on the review and analysis of the principal regulator in reaching its own decision to grant a receipt.

A blacklined version of the MRRS Prospectus Policy is attached showing the amendments made by the CSA.

Summary of Comments and Changes

The commenters generally welcomed and supported the proposed changes to the prospectus review and clearance system.

To facilitate the review and clearance of prospectus filings, we have streamlined the MRRS Prospectus Policy by reducing the time it takes to review a prospectus by ensuring the non-principal regulators do their review at the same time (instead of after) the principal regulator does its review. We estimate this will shorten the prospectus review process for long form prospectuses by five business days and for short form prospectuses by one to two business days. The result should be quicker access to the capital markets for market participants.

In addition, we have extended the list of jurisdictions that can act as principal regulator under the MRRS Prospectus Policy by including New Brunswick.

We are also making changes that will virtually eliminate the need for issuers to deal with non-principal regulators on any comments. One of these changes requires the principal regulator to forward potential opt-out issues raised by a non-principal regulator to the filer and attempt to resolve those issues with the non-principal regulator and the filer (i.e., the filer would no longer be required to deal directly with a non-principal regulator).

Additional Changes

In addition to the changes we published for comment on May 27, we have amended the pre-filing procedures under the MRRS Prospectus Policy. We made these amendments even though we did not publish them for comment because they relate to internal CSA processes. The amendments shorten the timelines for the review of pre-filings and waiver applications and impose a time limit for the review of these applications by the principal regulator. We made these changes to encourage issuers to use the pre-filing and waiver application process when filing prospectuses that raise novel and substantive issues or raise a novel public policy concern.

Review of AIFs Pending Changes to National Instrument 44-101

The amendments to the MRRS Prospectus Policy streamline the process for reviewing annual information forms. They do not distinguish between the review process for initial and renewal annual information forms because the CSA expects to eliminate this distinction in the restatement of National Instrument 44-101 *Short Form Prospectus Distributions* later this year. Until that happens, we will continue to review initial and renewal annual information forms as we did prior to amending the MRRS Prospectus Policy.

Amendments to the MRRS Applications Policy

The MRRS Applications Policy establishes the MRRS for the review of applications for exemptive relief that are filed in more than one jurisdiction. Under the MRRS Applications Policy, each non-principal regulator relies primarily on the review and analysis of the principal regulator in reaching its own decision on whether to grant relief.

A blacklined version of the MRRS Applications Policy is attached showing the amendments made by the CSA.

The Commission, together with the other CSA, amended the MRRS Applications Policy even though we did not publish it for comment. The amendments will clarify the interplay between the MRRS Applications Policy and MI 11-101 and are not material. The amendments include:

- appending a template decision document for filers to use when they require a decision from their principal regulator under MI 11-101, and

- changing the list of jurisdictions willing to act as principal regulator to remove Newfoundland and Labrador, which has indicated it no longer wishes to act as such, and adding New Brunswick.

These amendments take effect on September 19, 2005.

[Attachments omitted]

OSC Staff Notice 11-755 — Notice of Withdrawal of Ontario Securities Commission Staff Notices

Date: September 9, 2005

28 O.S.C.B. 7478

[Not reproduced]

OSC Notice 11-756 — Assignment of Notice Numbers

Date: December 23, 2005

28 O.S.C.B. 10298

[Not reproduced]

OSC Staff Notice 11-757 — Withdrawal of OSC Notices

Date: February 10, 2006

29 O.S.C.B. 1192

[Not reproduced]

OSC Staff Notice 11-758 — Review of Limited Market Dealers

Date: June 16, 2006

28 O.S.C.B. 4902

Overview

The limited market dealer (LMD) category of registration was created in Ontario in 1987 when the Ontario Securities Commission (OSC) implemented the "universal registration" system. At that time, the OSC extended registration requirements to all market intermediaries, including LMDs that operate in the exempt market under prospectus and registration exemptions.

LMDs are subject to some of the conditions of registration that apply to investment dealers under Ontario securities law, such as know your client, and suitability and supervisory functions. However, they are not subject to other conditions, such as proficiency, minimum capital requirements and filing of financial statements.

The LMD category is diverse and includes three main groups:

- LMDs that are not registered in any other registration category (sole LMDs)

- LMDs that are also registered as Investment Counsel Portfolio Managers (ICPMs)

- LMDs that are also members of the Mutual Fund Dealers Association (MFDA)

As of January 31, 2006, approximately 550 LMDs were registered with the OSC. Approximately 46% of these were sole LMDs, 40% were also registered as ICPMs, 13% were also mutual fund dealers and 1% were also registered in other categories.

Historically, the OSC's Compliance team monitored LMDs to a limited extent as part of its reviews of ICPMs that are also registered as LMDs. We initiated this review as a result of an increase in the number of firms registered as LMDs, and also to address specific areas of concern, including suitability, trade supervision and sales practices.

In 2005, the OSC conducted its first compliance review of LMDs. Our goals were to better understand their business operations, review their compliance with securities law and identify any regulatory gaps. This was a first step in enhancing compliance oversight and helping LMDs develop stronger compliance and internal controls. The results of this review will also assist the CSA Registration Reform Steering Committee in harmonizing registration requirements by identifying any specific risks this category poses to investor protection.

Part 1:
PROCEDURE

We identified a significant number of deficiencies as a result of our review. The 10 most frequent deficiencies were identified in at least 25% of our sample. The most significant deficiency — not collecting and documenting know your client (KYC) and suitability information — was identified in almost 80% of the LMDs reviewed. Without the necessary documentation, determining the suitability of a particular investment becomes more difficult.

For LMDs with significant deficiencies, we have taken further action including referring the matter to Enforcement, and closely monitoring the LMD. Approximately two thirds of the LMDs with deficiencies have resolved their issues to our satisfaction. We will continue to follow up with the remaining LMDs to ensure that all deficiencies are dealt with appropriately and within a reasonable time frame. If deficiencies cannot be resolved within a reasonable time frame, further action may be taken such as imposing terms and conditions on registration, or referring the matter to Enforcement. Commencing in the current fiscal year, we also intend to conduct regular compliance field reviews of LMDs to review their compliance with securities law.

This notice describes how we conducted the review and provides a summary of the results.

Information gathering

The Compliance team gathered information about the business operations of LMDs through a focus group, individual meetings and a written survey.

Focus group and individual meetings

The Compliance team held a focus group with representatives from LMDs in June 2005. All LMDs were invited and participation was voluntary. The firms that attended included a cross-section of the LMD population.

We also held individual meetings with other representatives from LMDs, on a voluntary basis. As well, we met with the MFDA, the Investment Dealers Association of Canada (IDA), and the Limited Market Dealers Association to hear their views on the LMD registration category.

LMD survey

We developed a written survey as our primary tool for gathering information. The survey consisted of structured questions and focused on key information about LMDs and their business operations, including corporate/management structure, products distributed, size of business, client base, policies and procedures, books and records, compliance with legislation, referral arrangements, outsourced functions, and custody and lending activities.

Specific criteria were developed for each question to ensure that the surveys were evaluated consistently. The survey was risk weighted and resulted in a risk score that translated into a risk ranking of high, medium high, medium low or low.

The survey excluded LMDs that were also members of the MFDA. The MFDA conducted a separate survey of all of its members, including approximately 75 LMDs in June 2005. The MFDA is addressing any issues identified from its survey through its oversight process.

In July 2005, we sent the survey to the remaining 475 LMDs who were not members of the MFDA. Almost all of the firms completed and returned the survey. We determined that 106 of these firms were inactive and excluded them from our overall results. The majority of the inactive firms were not using their LMD registration or were in the start-up phase of their business cycle.

We identified eight different business models from the survey (see Appendix 1):

- Firms registered as sole LMDs were distributed across five business models.

- Firms dually registered as LMDs and ICPMs were primarily distributed across two business models.

- A small number of LMDs were operating as Inter-Dealer Bond Brokers (IDBs).

Although the majority of LMDs operated under one business model, some operated under two or more business models.

Compliance reviews

We analysed the information we gathered in the first phase to conduct a focused compliance review of a sample of LMDs.

Objective

We had three objectives for the reviews:

    1. To gain insight into the business operations of LMDs, including the type of exempt products they distribute and the nature of their clients

    2. To assess LMDs' compliance with securities law

    3. To identify any regulatory gaps

Scope

The reviews focused on areas with the greatest overall regulatory risk to investors:

- KYC and suitability
- Know your product
- Disclosure to investors
- Referral arrangements

- Custody

- Compliance and supervision structure

Sample selection

We selected 21 LMDs for review, representing 6% of registered LMDs (excluding inactive firms, members of the MFDA and IDBs). Risk ranking was a key factor in determining the sample. The majority of the sample consisted of LMDs with a risk ranking of "high". We also made specific selections to ensure that the various business models were adequately represented. A proportionately higher weighting of sole LMDs was selected as a result of our preliminary analysis of the surveys.

How the reviews were conducted

Our review teams were primarily made up of Compliance staff, but we also drew on resources and expertise from other branches in the OSC, including Corporate Finance, Investment Funds and Enforcement. The reviews began in mid-October 2005 and were largely completed by December 2005. We performed on-site visits of all 21 LMDs in the sample. We later determined that two of these firms were inactive. Our results are based on 19 reviews.

Results

We identified a significant number of compliance deficiencies during our reviews (see Appendix 2). The majority were identified in firms registered as sole LMDs. Very few deficiencies were identified in LMDs that are registered as ICPMs, or provide mergers and acquisitions services.

We found that LMDs may have roles outside the scope of their LMD registration. For example, an LMD may also be the issuer, ICPM or fund manager of non-prospectus qualified investment funds. We identified a number of deficiencies stemming from these other roles.

Common deficiencies

The following is a discussion of the 10 most frequent deficiencies we identified. To assist LMDs in understanding the deficiencies, we have included the applicable legislation and suggested practices to address each deficiency. We encourage all LMDs to use this as a self-assessment tool to strengthen their compliance with Ontario securities law.

1. — Not collecting and documenting KYC and suitability information

Almost 80% of the LMDs reviewed were deficient in this area. Examples included:

- No KYC and suitability information was collected or documented

- KYC forms were not signed by the clients

- No evidence that KYC forms were reviewed

In most cases, LMDs had documents from clients confirming that they were accredited investors. However, they did not collect and document KYC and suitability information (e.g. investment objectives and risk tolerance). The fact that a client is an accredited investor does not mean that any investment product is suitable for him or her. Without the necessary documentation, determining the suitability of a particular investment becomes more difficult.

Applicable legislation

It is the dealer's obligation to collect and document KYC information and assess the suitability of client trades as required by section 1.5 of OSC Rule 31-505 — *Conditions of Registration* (OSC Rule 31-505).

Suggested practices

At a minimum, the KYC form should contain the investor's name, address, investment objectives, risk tolerance, investment restrictions, investment time frame, annual income and net worth. The KYC form should be signed and dated by the client and reviewed by the compliance officer.

2. — No or inadequate filing of regulatory forms and/or statement of policies

Over 60% of the LMDs reviewed were deficient in this area. Examples included:

- No statement of policies

- The most current statement of policies was not filed with the OSC

- Statements of policies did not include all related issuers

- Exempt distribution reports were not filed with the OSC

- Offering memoranda, where distributed, were not filed with the OSC

Applicable legislation

Section 223 of R.R.O. 1990, Regulation 1015 made under the Act (the Regulation) requires a dealer to prepare and file a statement of policies with the OSC, as well as provide a copy to its clients. The statement should outline the activities of the dealer in respect of related or connected issuers.

Section 6.1 of National Instrument 45-106 — *Prospectus Exemptions* (NI 45-106) requires the issuer of the security to file Form 45-106F1 with the OSC for a trade made in reliance on certain exemptions from the prospectus requirement within 10 days of the distribution. If a trade is made in a security of a mutual fund or non-redeemable investment fund (investment funds), the filing requirement is within 30 days after the financial year end of the investment funds.

Section 6.4 of revised OSC Rule 45-501 — *Ontario Prospectus and Registration Exemptions* (OSC Rule 45-501) requires the seller to deliver a copy of the offering memorandum to the OSC within 10 days of the distribution if the trade is made in reliance on certain exemptions from the prospectus requirement.

Suggested practices

LMDs should prepare and file a current statement of policies with the OSC and distribute a copy to clients. The statement of policies should include a complete listing of related issuers and a concise description of the nature of the relationship with each related issuer. LMDs that are issuers should refer to section 6 of NI 45-106 for reporting requirements. LMDs acting as sellers should refer to section 6.4 of revised OSC Rule 45-501 as noted previously.

3. — Misleading marketing materials/websites

Over 40% of the LMDs reviewed were deficient in this area. Examples included:

- Websites and marketing materials with incorrect information (e.g. brochures with an incorrect description of LMD activities and the products or services provided)

- Marketing materials that claimed "superior methodology" and "high returns" without any support to substantiate these claims

- Websites with outdated materials

- Certain salespersons who were incorrectly held out as officers and directors of the LMD in marketing materials

- Back-tested and pro-forma performance data (i.e. simulated historical and future trading performance that does not represent actual results) that was presented to clients.

Applicable legislation

Section 2.1 of OSC Rule 31-505 requires dealers to deal fairly, honestly, and in good faith with their clients. Section 45 of the *Securities Act (Ontario)* (Act) states that no person or company who is not registered shall hold himself, herself or itself out as being registered.

Suggested practices

LMDs should establish and enforce procedures for reviewing and approving marketing materials and websites. This is to ensure that all marketing materials and websites contain accurate and up-to-date information. All claims made in marketing materials and websites should be adequately supported. Back-tested performance data can be quite misleading to investors because it is typically presented as actual results of the funds or the investment strategy. Back-tested data can be constructed to achieve a desired outcome and is difficult to verify.

4. — Ineffective compliance officer

Over 35% of the LMDs reviewed were deficient in this area. Examples included:

- Compliance officers who did not understand their roles and responsibilities (e.g. no review of clients' trades for suitability or marketing materials for appropriate disclosure)

- A lack of understanding of securities legislation

Applicable legislation

Paragraph 1.3 of OSC Rule 31-505 requires dealers to designate a registered partner or officer as the compliance officer who is responsible for discharging the obligations of the dealer under Ontario securities law. It also requires the designated compliance officer to be responsible for opening new accounts and supervising trades for each client.

Suggested practices

LMDs should clearly define the roles and responsibilities of their compliance officers. A compliance officer should fully understand his or her roles and responsibilities and LMDs should take the necessary steps, including providing additional training, to ensure that these responsibilities are met.

5. — Registration issues

Over 35% of the LMDs reviewed were deficient in this area. Examples included:

- LMDs acting as an ICPM without registration

- Individuals acting as salespersons without registration

Most of the LMDs were only involved in the distribution of investment fund units. However, some LMDs performed multiple roles and were affiliated with the issuer. For example, some LMDs were acting as general partners or portfolio managers for their funds. These LMDs were actively involved in providing investment advice and managing the funds' portfolios, but were not registered as ICPMs. In all cases, the individual who managed the funds' portfolios did not meet the proficiency requirements of an ICPM under Part 3 of OSC Rule 31-502 — Proficiency Requirements for Registrants.

We also identified a number of cases where an individual employee or a third-party financial planner was selling investment products for LMDs without registration.

Applicable legislation

Section 25 of the Act prohibits trading in securities or acting as an adviser unless you are appropriately registered with the OSC.

Suggested practices

LMDs should review their current business activities and obtain the appropriate registration for all registerable activities. They should also review their business arrangements with third parties to ensure that each party to the agreement is appropriately registered to carry out its responsibilities.

6. — Inadequate disclosure and/or misleading statements in offering memoranda

Over 35% of the LMDs reviewed were deficient in this area. Examples included:

- Risk factors that were inadequately disclosed or not disclosed

- Inadequate disclosure of conflicts of interest

- Back-tested and pro-forma performance data (i.e. simulated historical or future trading performance that does not represent actual results) was presented to clients (see common deficiency no.3)

- Statutory right of action for damages against the issuer and selling security holder, and right of rescission was not disclosed

Some of the LMDs or their affiliates were acting as fund managers, general partners or issuers. Clients were given various types of disclosure documents, such as an offering memorandum, an investment summary or other offering document. We consider these documents to be offering memoranda as defined in subsection 1(1) of the Act.

Applicable legislation

Subsection 2.1(1) of OSC Rule 31-505 requires a dealer to deal fairly, honestly and in good faith with its clients.

For certain exemptions from the prospectus requirement, section 6.3 of revised OSC Rule 45-501 requires the right of action (set out in section 130.1 of the Act) for damages against the issuer and a selling security holder, and the right of rescission to be described in the offering memorandum.

Suggested practices

LMDs or their affiliates should disclose all relevant information to their clients, including, but not limited to, risk factors, conflicts of interest and rights of action for damages or rescission in offering memoranda. This information is critical to clients when making investment decisions.

7. — Lack of written policies and procedures manual

Over 35% of the LMDs reviewed were deficient in this area. Examples included:
- No written policies and procedures manual
- Missing procedures for some major areas of the business
- Insufficient detail about policies and procedures

Applicable legislation

Section 1.2 of OSC Rule 31-505 requires dealers to develop and enforce written procedures for dealing with clients that conform to prudent business practice and enable them to serve clients adequately. The policies and procedures should be in sufficient detail, updated periodically and made available to all staff. In addition, the relevant regulatory requirements should be outlined in the policies and procedures.

Suggested practices

LMDs should develop and enforce written policies and procedures manuals that are tailored to their operations. At a minimum, the following areas should be covered:

- Role of the compliance officer, including reviewing and approving new accounts and supervising trades

- Supervision and training of registered salespersons

- Collection and documentation of KYC and suitability information

**Part 1:
PROCEDURE**

- Prospectus exemptions available to investors and their application
- Maintenance of books and records
- Handling of client money in trust accounts
- Review and approval of marketing materials and websites
- Dealing with conflicts of interest
- Personal trading

8. — Inadequate books and records

Over 30% of the LMDs reviewed were deficient in this area. The following are examples of books and records that were not maintained:

- Monthly and annual financial statements
- KYC forms
- Trade blotter and trade confirmations
- Signed subscription and accredited investor forms
- Bank reconciliations for both trust and operating bank accounts
- Marketing materials

Applicable legislation

Subsection 19(1) of the Act requires a market participant to keep books, records and other documents for the proper recording of its business transactions and financial affairs, and the transactions that it executes on behalf of others.

Suggested practices

LMDs should determine the appropriate books and records to be maintained in their operations. At a minimum, they should maintain records of client information, KYC forms, agreements with third parties, a trade blotter and financial statements.

9. — No written agreements with salespersons or third parties

Over 30% of LMDs did not have written agreements with salespersons or promoters.

Applicable legislation

Subsection 19(1) of the Act requires a market participant to keep books, records and other documents for the proper recording of its business transactions and financial affairs, and the transactions that it executes on behalf of others.

Suggested practices

LMDs should establish written agreements with salespersons or third parties. The agreements should clearly define the roles and responsibilities of each party and ensure that each party to the agreement is appropriately registered to carry out its responsibilities.

10. — No written referral agreement and inadequate disclosure to clients

Over 25% of the LMDs reviewed were deficient in this area. Examples included:

- No written agreement for third-party referral arrangements
- Inadequate disclosure to clients about the arrangement and the amount of fees paid to third parties

Applicable legislation

Subsection 19(1) of the Act requires a market participant to keep books, records and other documents for the proper recording of its business transactions and financial affairs, and the transactions that it executes on behalf of others.

Subsection 2.1(1) of OSC Rule 31-505 requires a dealer to deal fairly, honestly and in good faith with its clients. LMDs should provide adequate disclosure to clients regarding any conflicts of interest.

Suggested practices

LMDs should establish written agreements with referring parties. The agreements should clearly define the roles and responsibilities of each party and the amount of the fee. LMDs should also provide written disclosure to clients that includes the nature of the referral arrangement, the amount of the fee paid and any potential conflicts of interest.

Our response

As a result of these reviews, the OSC has taken steps to help address the deficiencies and improve compliance oversight.

When further action beyond a deficiency report is necessary, the Compliance team may, among other things:

- Refer the matter to Enforcement
- Closely monitor the LMD
- Impose terms and conditions on registration

Where appropriate, we referred matters resulting from the reviews to Enforcement. We continue to monitor some LMDs. We have suspended a few of the LMDs we reviewed because of registration renewal issues. These suspensions were made independently of our initiative.

Compliance deficiency reports were sent to the LMDs reviewed, where applicable. Each LMD was required to provide a written response, effectively an action plan, to all deficiencies identified in our report within 30 days. Approximately two thirds of the LMDs with deficiencies have resolved their deficiencies to our satisfaction. We will continue to follow up with the remaining LMDs to ensure that all deficiencies are dealt with appropriately and within a reasonable time frame. If deficiencies cannot be resolved within a reasonable time frame, further action, as noted above, may be taken such as imposing terms and conditions on registration, or referring the matter to Enforcement.

Commencing in the current fiscal year, the Compliance team will be conducting regular compliance field reviews of LMDs to review their compliance with securities law.

As noted previously, the results of this initiative will assist the CSA Registration Reform Steering Committee in harmonizing registration requirements. As a result, registration requirements may not be extended to some of the currently registered LMDs, for example, those providing mergers and acquisitions services. Also, due to the nature and frequency of the deficiencies identified, increased regulation of LMDs is being considered, including requirements for proficiency, books and records, filing of audited financial statements, and maintaining insurance and minimum capital, similar to those applicable to other registrants.

We expect that this initiative will assist LMDs in enhancing their compliance structure and will result in a more effective regulatory regime.

Appendix 1 — Summary of LMD business models

Model	% of LMDs surveyed*	Business objectives	Type of investors	Products
1. Sole LMD (mergers and acquisitions)	13.1%	Provides assistance in mergers and acquisitions and disposition of corporations	Institutional	No products distributed Only services provided as previously discussed
2. Sole LMD (private placement)	24.7%	Provides advice on capital structuring to raise financing Distributes new issues to accredited investors	Institutional and high net worth (accredited investors)	Shares, corporate debt, units of trusts, etc. (depends on the investment vehicle used to structure the private placement)
3. Sole LMD (relationship facilitator)	9.7%	Facilitates relationships between investors and registrants Does not distribute securities Provides advice on the suitability of the investment opportunity; this is done when the initial matching of the two parties occurs	Institutional and high net worth (accredited investors)	No products distributed Only services provided as previously discussed
4. Sole LMD (distributes exempt products)	21.3%	Distributes non-prospectus qualified products	Institutional and high net worth (accredited investors)	Pooled funds, hedge funds, etc.
5. Sole LMD (full-service)	3.1%	Distributes non-prospectus qualified and other types of investment products	Institutional and high net worth (accredited investors)	Pooled funds, hedge funds, etc. and other investment products (e.g. equities, fixed income, etc.)
6. ICPM (integrated)	28.4%	LMD is used to: facilitate the investment management of discretionary client accounts distribute products that are developed and managed (on a discretionary basis) in-house	Institutional and high net worth (accredited investors)	Pooled funds, hedge funds, etc.

Model	% of LMDs surveyed*	Business objectives	Type of investors	Products
7. ICPM (non-integrated)	24.4%	LMD is used to distribute products that are developed and managed (on a discretionary basis) in-house The products are distributed to investors who do not have a managed account with the registrant	Institutional and high net worth (accredited investors)	Pooled funds, hedge funds, etc.
8. Inter-dealer bond broker (IDB)	0.6%	Acts as an intermediary and matches buyers and sellers of government and Canadian bonds anonymously Recognized by the IDA as an IDB	Institutional (e.g. major banks, IDA member firms and international dealers)	Canadian federal bonds, provincial bonds, corporate bonds, T-Bills, repurchase agreements, federal and provincial government derivatives, forward currency swaps, overnight interest rate swaps, etc.

Notes:
* Based on active LMD population identified from surveys submitted. The total of the percentages is greater than 100% because some LMDs operate under multiple business models.

Appendix 2 — Top 10 most frequent deficiencies

Deficiency type	Number of deficiencies identified in LMD sample	% of total active LMD sample
Not collecting and documenting KYC and suitability information	15	79%
No or inadequate filing of regulatory forms and/or statement of policies	12	63%
Misleading marketing materials/website	8	42%
Ineffective compliance officer	7	37%
Registration issues	7	37%
Inadequate disclosure and/or misleading statements in offering memoranda	7	37%
Lack of written policies and procedures manual	7	37%
Inadequate books and records	6	32%
No written agreements with salespersons or third parties	6	32%
No written referral agreement and inadequate disclosure to clients	5	26%

OSC Staff Notice 11-759 — Business Continuity Planning

Date: January 5, 2007

30 O.S.C.B. 7

Business continuity is an ongoing priority for financial industry participants and financial regulatory authorities. Recent acts of terrorism, the 2003 outbreaks of Severe Acute Respiratory Syndrome (SARS), the Avian Flu, and various widespread natural disasters have served to heighten that priority by underlining the substantial risk of major operational disruptions to the financial system.

The Ontario Securities Commission (OSC) is part of the global efforts to identify the challenges and address the potential impact of any incidents that could disrupt normal business operations.

To aid the financial community's efforts in developing sound business continuity practices, the International Joint Forum[1] published a paper in August 2006 entitled *High-Level Principles for Business Continuity*.[2] In the paper, the Joint Forum states that financial regulatory authorities and financial industry participants have a shared interest in promoting the operational integrity of the financial system to major disruptions. This interest is the result of multiple factors, including:

• the pivotal role that financial intermediation plays in facilitating and promoting national and global economic activity;

[1]Represents: Basel Committee on Banking Supervision, International Organization of Securities Commissions, International Association of Insurance Supervisors and the Bank for International Settlements.

[2]The paper is a revised version of the draft issued for consultation in December 2005. The paper is available on the websites of the Bank for International Settlements (BIS), the International Organization of the Securities Commission (IOSCO) and the International Association of Insurance Supervisors (IAIS).

- the concentration of clearing and settlement processes in most financial systems;

- deepening interdependencies among financial industry participants within and across jurisdictions; and

- the importance of public confidence in the ability of financial systems to function smoothly.

The Joint Forum paper defines business continuity management as "... a whole-of-business approach that includes policy, standards and procedures for ensuring that specified operations can be maintained or recovered in a timely fashion in the event of a disruption". It also indicates that "... effective business continuity management concentrates on the impact, as opposed to the source, of the disruption, which affords financial industry participants and financial authorities greater flexibility to address a broad range of disruptions".

OSC Staff believe that financial industry participants as well as financial regulatory authorities should regularly test their business continuity plans, evaluate their effectiveness, and update their business continuity management.

OSC Staff Notice 11-760 — Report on Mutual Fund Sales Practices under Part 5 of NI 81-105 Mutual Fund Sales Practices

Date: April 27, 2007

30 O.S.C.B. 3892

Executive Summary

Introduction

In the fall of 2006, OSC staff conducted a focused review of the marketing and educational practices of fund managers under Part 5 of National Instrument 81-105 *Mutual Fund Sales Practices* (NI 81-105). This report summarizes our findings and provides guidance to industry participants on complying with these requirements.

Background

NI 81-105 regulates the sales practices of industry participants in connection with the distribution of publicly offered securities of mutual funds. This includes the manager and the principal distributor of the mutual fund, as well as dealers and their sales representatives.

The intention of NI 81-105 is to reduce conflicts between the interests of investors and those of dealers, their sales representatives and managers. NI 81-105 came into force in May 1998 in response to the concern that certain sales practices and compensation arrangements common in the industry at the time could be perceived as inducing dealers and their sales representatives to sell mutual fund securities based on the incentives they were receiving, rather than on what was suitable for, and in the best interests of, investors.

By prohibiting certain sales practices and compensation arrangements, NI 81-105 establishes a minimum standard of conduct for industry participants to follow in their sales practices.

We last reviewed industry sales practices under NI 81-105 in October 1998 as part of a national compliance review. In our view, sufficient time had passed to warrant a review of Part 5 of NI 81-105, which deals with the following marketing and educational practices:

- cooperative marketing practices (section 5.1)

- mutual fund sponsored conferences (section 5.2)

- third party sponsored educational events (section 5.3)

- industry association sponsored events (section 5.4)

- participating dealer sponsored events (section 5.5) and

- promotional items and business promotion activities (section 5.6)

Purpose of the review

The goals of the review were to:

- confirm our understanding of how managers are interpreting and complying with Part 5 of NI 81-105

- review and assess managers' policies, procedures and practices relating to sales practices

- assess whether additional guidance to industry participants is necessary and

- determine whether NI 81-105 is meeting our objectives, or whether amendments are necessary

Scope of the review

We reviewed a sample of 20 managers with assets under management totaling $306 billion as at July 31, 2006. The managers varied in size from $6 million to $67 billion in assets under management.

The review teams consisted of staff from the Compliance team of the Capital Markets Branch and staff from the Investment Funds Branch. We conducted onsite reviews of the managers included in the sample during the period from September to December 2006. We reviewed samples of documentation dating from August 1, 2005 to July 31, 2006 that related to events sponsored by managers.

Each manager that we reviewed received a report in February 2007, which set out the specific deficiencies staff noted during their reviews. The managers were required to respond in writing to staff within 30 days of receiving the report and explain how they were going to correct the deficiencies.

Key findings

Overall, the managers we reviewed substantially complied with Part 5 of NI 81-105. While the deficiency reports sent to each manager identified areas for improvement, none of the deficiencies warranted enforcement action.

We identified the following three areas of deficiency that were common to the managers in the sample:

1. — Primary purpose test

Meeting the primary purpose test under Part 5 is essential to managers deciding to accept or reject a cooperative marketing request.

Primary purpose tests were not met because broader topics such as financial planning or investing in securities were included in the sales communications, investor conferences or seminars organized under section 5.1. In addition, significant time was spent on practice management sessions, motivational speakers, award ceremonies, sessions on general business operations or recreational activities for conferences or events organized under sections 5.2 to sections 5.6.

2. — Policies and procedures

Policies and procedures for sales practices were inadequate because there was not enough detail to ensure compliance with Part 5. For example, policies and procedures simply repeated the provisions of NI 81-105 and did not provide guidelines or processes to assist managers in reviewing and approving requests and reimbursing expenses.

In some instances, the managers had detailed policies and procedures in place but they did not consistently adhere to them.

Additionally, some managers' policies and procedures under Part 5 did not appropriately capture events hosted or attended by dealers and sales representatives who distribute both mutual fund securities and non-mutual fund securities, such as segregated funds and closed-end funds.

3. — Monitoring promotional items and business promotion activities

Managers did not adequately monitor promotional items and business promotion activities. They did not have adequate processes in place to:

- monitor the total dollar amount of benefits given to individual sales representatives as promotional items or in promotion activities or

- track the frequency with which these benefits were provided to individual sales representatives.

Specific deficiencies relating to each section of Part 5 of NI 81-105 are described below under Detailed findings.

Conclusion

We recognize that managers engage in a variety of sales practices and must use their judgment when applying the principles set out in NI 81-105, in particular under Part 5. To meet their standard of care under securities legislation, we expect managers to develop policies and procedures specific to their businesses and to apply them consistently to their sales practices.

In particular, we expect managers to maintain documentation to support decisions to provide sponsorship under Part 5. See Appendix A for a list of guidelines managers may want to consider including in their policies and procedures manual.

We believe the spirit and intent of NI 81-105 remain relevant today and strike the right balance between protecting investors, and fostering fair and efficient capital markets. As a result, we are not proposing any amendments to NI 81-105 at this time.

We will, however, continue to review cooperative marketing and other sales practices as part of our regular reviews of fund managers. We expect industry participants to look to the guidance included in this report in meeting the requirements under Part 5 of NI 81-105.

Detailed findings

The following pages describe the deficiencies we observed for each section of Part 5 and our guidance for managers to meet the requirements. In many cases, the specific guidance noted under a section will also apply to other sections of Part 5.

Section 5.1 — Cooperative marketing practices

Section 5.1 permits managers to pay the costs of sales communications, investor conferences and seminars that dealers organize and present to investors, within certain parameters.

Deficiencies

We observed the following deficiencies:

- *Primary purpose.* Sales communications and investor conferences and seminars did not meet the primary purpose of promoting or providing educational information concerning a mutual fund, a mutual fund family or mutual funds generally. Instead, the sales communications and seminars dealt with the broader topic of investing generally.

- *Documentation.* There was inadequate supporting documentation to demonstrate:

  - that sales communications and investor conferences and seminars met the primary purpose test

- that the manager reviewed requests from dealers for financial support

- that manager sponsorship of investor conferences and seminars was disclosed to the attendees in writing

- that the 50% contribution limit on mutual fund organizations was met when more than one manager paid direct costs who managers made payments to

- *Payments.* Managers paid for items that dealers used for client appreciation purposes, for example, golf tournaments, tickets to sporting events, books on investing and gift certificates.

   Managers made cooperative payments directly to sales representatives instead of to dealers.

- *Policies and procedures.* In some instances, events were not identified and tracked under the appropriate section of Part 5. In other instances, the review process for sponsorship requests was handled solely by the manager's sales department with no independent oversight by, for example, the manager's compliance department.

   Managers did not follow the guidelines in their policies and procedures for paying for cooperative marketing under section 5.1.

- *Disclosure.* Sales communications did not disclose manager sponsorship.

Guidance

We expect managers to consider the following:

Primary purpose

The primary purpose for sales communications, investor seminars and conferences in section 5.1 is more limited in scope than in other sections of Part 5 and may not include topics on financial planning or investing in securities. Managers require exemptive relief if they want to sponsor seminars or conferences on broader topics under this section.

We expect managers to have internal policies and procedures to evaluate the content of sales communications and investor conferences or seminars under this section. Managers may want to consider developing an internal percentage benchmark to assess whether the primary purpose test is met. For example, if the amount of time spent on permitted topics at an investor seminar or conference exceeds a certain percentage, the event meets the primary purpose requirement.

If the investor seminar or conference is a lunch or dinner presentation, looking solely at the time allotted to the educational portion of the event may not be an appropriate way to evaluate whether the primary purpose test is met. In this instance, we expect managers to consider the whole event, including:

- the content of the presentations

- the cost of meals or refreshments and

- any other costs

Managers may want to consider setting an internal dollar amount per person per event as a general guideline for sponsoring lunch or dinner seminars and conferences. If the costs appear excessive compared to the purpose of the event, the objective of the event may be viewed as client appreciation, which is not permitted by section 5.1.

Documentation

We expect managers to maintain documentation to support their decisions on providing sponsorship. We expect the documentation to include:

- a copy of the written communication identifying the manager as a sponsor

- final copies of any advertisement, newsletter or transcripts for television or radio advertisements

- a final agenda that sets out the topics covered and the time allotted to each topic

- evidence that sponsorship by multiple managers in total did not exceed 50% of the direct costs and

- copies of all invoices and receipts

Payments

Paragraph 5.1(c) specifies that the participating dealer — not the sales representative — must provide the manager with invoices and receipts associated with the event. Section 5.1 also requires managers to make reimbursement cheques payable to dealers, not to sales representatives.

Disclosure

Paragraph 5.1(e) specifies that attendees of investor seminars and conferences must be informed in writing of the manager's sponsorship. We do not consider verbally introducing the manager as a sponsor at the investor seminar or conference to fulfill this requirement.

If the manager has not been identified in the invitation to the seminar or conference as a sponsor, we expect the manager to be clearly identified in writing as a sponsor on items such as signs, posters and banners.

We consider using the fund company's logo instead of the manager's full legal name on a sales communication to satisfy the disclosure requirement in paragraph 5.1(e) if:

- the logo is easily identifiable and

Part 1: PROCEDURE

- it is clear that the manager is sponsoring the event

The following are acceptable disclosure statements:

- "paid in part by XXX"
- "sponsored in part by XXX"
- "a portion of the costs has been paid by XXX" and
- "brought to you by XXX"

(where XXX is the fund manager's full legal name or its logo)

Section 5.2 — Mutual fund sponsored conferences

Section 5.2 permits managers to organize educational conferences or seminars for sales representatives of dealers, subject to certain conditions.

Deficiencies

We observed the following deficiencies:

- *Primary purpose.* Conferences and seminars did not meet the primary purpose test because significant parts of the conference were devoted to topics not permitted in paragraph 5.2(a) or to recreational activities.
- *Documentation.* There was a lack of documentation to support how the conferences and seminars met the primary purpose test.
- *Policies and procedures.* Managers did not follow their policies and procedures for assessing whether a conference or seminar met the requirements of section 5.2.
- *Payments.* Managers paid expenses that sales representatives incurred to attend the conference, such as arrival and departure ground transportation costs, and personal incidental expenses.
- *Participants.* Managers influenced which sales representatives attended the conference. Clients were invited to conferences and seminars with their sales representative.

Guidance

We expect managers to consider the following:

Primary purpose

Conferences or seminars for sales representatives of dealers may include organized recreational activities and free time, including entertainment in the evenings. However, the primary purpose of the conference or seminar must be to provide educational information as described in paragraph 5.2(a).

We do not consider it appropriate for events under section 5.6 to be combined with events under section 5.2.

When determining primary purpose, we expect managers to consider the whole event including:

- the content of the presentations
- how much of the business day is spent on permitted educational topics (allowing for reasonable breaks, meals and time to travel between activities)
- the cost of meals or refreshments and
- any other costs

We expect the time spent on permitted educational topics to be proportionate to the time spent on other topics or activities, such as practice management, recreational activities or entertainment. If the organized recreational activities and free time appear excessive, the overall objective of the event may be viewed as business promotion, which is not permitted by section 5.2.

We consider topics that help sales representatives meet their obligations as registrants to be permissible educational information under section 5.2. An example is "how to ensure compliance with securities legislation". Topics that relate to practice management are not permissible.

We expect managers to have internal policies and procedures to evaluate the content of conferences or seminars and ensure compliance under section 5.2. This can include:

- comparing the conference or seminar agenda to an internal percentage benchmark to assess whether the primary purpose test will be met and
- reviewing agenda items by topic and the amount of time allotted to each topic

In addition, managers should consider having people who are not involved in organizing the events review them.

Documentation

We expect managers to maintain documentation that supports their decisions to provide sponsorship under this section. We expect the documentation to include:

- the budget for the event

- a final agenda that sets out the topics covered and the time allotted to each topic

- a final list of the attendees

- evidence that:

  - the conference or seminar complies with section 5.2

  - the manager's internal guidelines for the section have been met and

- copies of all invoices and receipts

Payments

We expect managers to maintain a budget for all conferences and seminars, and to ensure that the costs incurred are directly attributable to the conference or seminar.

Participants

Paragraph 5.2(b) specifies that the selection of sales representatives be made exclusively by the dealer. Managers may contact sales representatives directly only if they have the permission of the dealer and they invite all of the dealer's sales representatives.

We view the invitation and attendance of clients of sales representatives to conferences or seminars as client appreciation, which is not permitted by section 5.2.

Section 5.3 — Third party sponsored educational events

Section 5.3 permits managers to pay the registration fees for sales representatives attending conferences, seminars or courses offered by organizations that are not members of the mutual fund organization or the dealer, within certain parameters.

Deficiencies

We observed the following deficiencies:

- *Primary purpose*. Courses did not meet the primary purpose test. While there were educational components dealing with financial planning and investing, the course content focused primarily on topics not permitted in paragraph 5.3(a).

- *Policies and procedures*. Managers did not follow their policies and procedures. For example, managers did not comply with their internal policies to reimburse only 50% of the total cost of a course, but reimbursed the full amount.

- *Documentation*. We noted a lack of documentation that supported the managers' assessment that the conferences, seminars and courses met the primary purpose test, and the managers' pre-approval decisions and reimbursement of expenses.

  In addition, managers relied on the dealer to confirm that the events met the requirements of section 5.3 or to maintain all documentation which, by itself, is not sufficient.

- *Payments*. Managers reimbursed sales representatives for items other than the registration fee for the conference, seminar or course, such as dinners and course material.

Guidance

We expect managers to consider the following:

Primary purpose

It is the manager's responsibility to assess whether the primary purpose test is met under section 5.3. We expect managers to have internal policies and procedures to evaluate the content of a third party conference, seminar or course under this section.

When determining primary purpose, we expect managers to consider the whole event including:

- the content of the presentations and

- how much of the business day is spent on permitted educational topics (allowing for reasonable breaks, meals and time to travel between activities)

Certain organizations, such as the Canadian Securities Institute and the Investment Funds Institute of Canada, offer courses that normally meet the primary purpose test in paragraph 5.3(a). However, due to the variety of courses that may be offered, we expect managers to review the content of each conference, seminar and course before providing sponsorship.

Documentation

We do not consider a manager's standard of care under securities legislation to be satisfied by relying solely on third party certifications that the regulatory requirements under Part 5 have been met. We expect managers to carry out their own due diligence to determine compliance with this section and NI 81-105.

**Part 1:
PROCEDURE**

Payments

Section 5.3 permits managers to pay only the registration fees. Accordingly, managers should review invoices carefully to ensure they are paying only for expenses covered under this section.

Section 5.4 — Industry association sponsored events

Section 5.4 permits managers to pay to a trade or industry association the costs or expenses incurred relating to a conference, seminar or course organized by them, subject to certain conditions.

Deficiencies

We observed the following deficiencies:

- *Primary purpose.* Managers did not adequately review the content of the conference, seminar or course to determine primary purpose.

- *Documentation.* We noted a lack of documentation that supported how the conference, seminar or course met the primary purpose test, and how the manager assessed the total direct costs of the conference, seminar or course to ensure compliance with the sponsorship limit in paragraph 5.4(2)(b). In some cases there was no documentation relating to the event, for example, there were no invoices for the costs of the conference.

- *Payments.* Managers paid more than 10 per cent of the total direct costs of the conference.

Guidance

We expect managers to consider the following:

Primary purpose

When determining primary purpose, we expect managers to consider the whole event including:

- the content of the presentations

- how much of the business day is spent on permitted educational topics (allowing for reasonable breaks, meals and time spent traveling between activities)

- the cost of meals or refreshments and

- any other costs

Managers may want to consider reviewing agenda items by topic and the amount of time allotted to each topic.

It is the manager's responsibility to ensure that the industry association sponsoring the event has obtained exemptive relief to receive cooperative support under section 5.4.

Documentation

We expect managers to maintain documentation that supports their decisions to provide sponsorship and their compliance with this section. In particular, we expect managers to have records that they have not paid more than 10% of the total direct costs of the event as set out in paragraph 5.4(2)(b).

Section 5.5 — Participating dealer sponsored events

Section 5.5 permits managers to pay the costs of conferences and seminars organized and presented by dealers (that are not investor conferences or seminars referred to in section 5.1), within certain parameters.

Deficiencies

We observed the following deficiencies:

- *Primary purpose.* Conferences and seminars did not meet the primary purpose of providing educational information about financial planning, investing in securities, mutual fund industry matters, the managers' mutual funds or mutual funds generally because significant portions of the content of the events were devoted to topics not captured in paragraph 5.5(a) or significant parts of the day were devoted to recreational activities.

  Managers did not adequately review the content of the conference or seminar to determine primary purpose. For example, a manager reviewed only the content of the sessions that its staff presented, but did not look into the content of the other sessions presented at a multi-day conference.

  Managers did not follow their policies and procedures for determining primary purpose when processing requests from affiliated dealers.

- *Documentation.* There was inadequate documentation to support managers' pre-approval decision and its reimbursement of expenses. Managers sponsored events that did not meet the primary purpose test under their policies and procedures, with no documentation to demonstrate why the decision was made.

- *Processes.* Managers did not implement procedures to handle requests for pre-approval in a timely manner.

- *Payments.* Managers paid more than 10% of the total direct costs of the conference or seminar.

Guidance

We expect managers to consider the following:

Primary purpose

Conferences or seminars may include organized recreational activities and free time, including entertainment in the evenings. However, to meet the primary purpose test in section 5.5, the overall purpose of the conference or seminar must be to provide educational information described in paragraph 5.5(a).

When determining primary purpose, we expect managers to consider the whole event, including:

- the content of the presentations

- how much of the business day is spent on permitted educational topics (allowing for reasonable breaks, meals and time to travel between activities)

- the cost of meals or refreshments and
- any other costs

Documentation

We expect managers to maintain documentation to support their decisions to provide sponsorship under this section. We expect the documentation to include:

- a final agenda that sets out the topics covered and the time allotted to each topic

- records that:

  - the conference or seminar complied with section 5.5

  - the manager's internal policies and procedures for its pre-approval and final consideration and approval were met

  - the manager's total sponsorship did not exceed 10% of the direct costs

  - sponsorship by multiple managers in total did not exceed 66% of the direct costs

- the total costs of the event and the amount paid by the manager and

- copies of all invoices and receipts

We do not consider a manager's standard of care under securities legislation to be satisfied by relying solely on third party certifications that the regulatory requirements under Part 5 have been met. We expect managers to carry out their own due diligence to ensure compliance with section 5.5 and NI 81-105.

Payments

Section 5.5 permits a manager to pay the direct costs incurred by the dealer in organizing and presenting the conference or seminar. Direct costs do not include the travel, accommodation or personal incidental expenses of attendees.

We recognize conferences and seminars often take many months to organize, and the details of the events, such as agenda items, estimated costs, the total number of sponsors and the amount of their contributions, may change. However, we expect managers to review a final agenda that sets out the topics covered and the time allotted to each topic, costs, list of sponsors, etc. when determining whether to reimburse the dealer under this section.

Section 5.6 — Promotional items and business promotion activities

Section 5.6 permits managers to provide to sales representatives non-monetary benefits of a promotional nature if the benefits are not too extensive or frequent, and subject to certain conditions.

Deficiencies

We observed the following deficiencies:

- *Policies and procedures.* Managers did not have adequate guidelines for the frequency and extent of promotional items and business promotion activities they provided to sales representatives or adequate processes to effectively monitor them. For example, promotional items and promotion activities provided to sales representatives were often tracked separately.

  Managers did not follow the dollar thresholds and frequency limits in their policies and procedures. For example, managers exceeded their quarterly and annual dollar limits per sales representative.

- *Non-monetary benefits.* The non-monetary benefits provided to individual sales representatives were too frequent or too excessive.

Guidance

We expect managers to consider the following:

Policies and procedures

231

We expect managers to have internal processes and monitoring procedures to assess whether the requirements of this section will be met. Among other things, managers should consider including the following items in their policies and procedures:

- an annual dollar limit that can be spent on a per sales representative basis, for example, $1,000

- frequency limits for benefits on a quarterly and annual basis and

- internal guidelines for dollar amounts for different types of promotional items and events, such as trinkets, sports events, concerts, etc.

Participants

We view the attendance of clients of sales representatives at promotional activities intended for sales representatives as client appreciation, which is not permitted by section 5.6.

Appendix A

Managers may want to consider including the following items in their policies and procedures manual on sales practices to help them comply with Part 5 of NI 81-105:

Section 5.1 — Cooperative marketing practices

- guidelines for ensuring the primary purpose test is met
- procedures for:
    - ensuring that no more than 50% of the total direct costs are paid by all mutual fund organizations in total
    - obtaining receipts for expenditures incurred by the dealer
    - ensuring the manager's sponsorship is disclosed in writing
- processes to ensure managers make payments to dealers, not to sales representatives

Section 5.2 — Mutual fund sponsored conferences

- guidelines for:
    - ensuring the primary purpose test is met
    - ensuring the manager does not influence the selection of sales representatives of dealers
    - appropriate costs associated with an event
- permitted locations to hold conferences and seminars
- processes to ensure the manager does not pay for travel, accommodation or personal incidental expenses of sales representatives attending an event

Section 5.3 — Third party sponsored educational events

- guidelines for ensuring:
    - the primary purpose test is met
    - the manager does not influence the selection of sales representatives of dealers
- procedures for obtaining receipts for registration fees
- permitted locations for conferences and seminars

Section 5.4 — Industry association sponsored events

- guidelines for ensuring:
    - the primary purpose test is met
    - the manager does not influence the selection of sales representatives of dealers
- procedures for ensuring that no more than 10% of the total direct costs are paid by all members of a mutual fund family in aggregate
- permitted locations for conferences and seminars

Section 5.5 — Participating dealer sponsored events

- guidelines for ensuring:
    - the primary purpose test is met
    - the manager does not influence the selection of sales representatives of dealers

- procedures for ensuring:
  - no more than 10% of the total direct costs are paid by all members of a mutual fund family in total
  - no more than 66% of the total direct costs are paid by all members of sponsoring mutual fund families in total
- permitted locations to hold conferences and seminars

Section 5.6 — Promotional items and business promotion activities

- guidelines for assessing the frequency and extent of promotional items and promotion activities
- processes for monitoring the non-monetary benefits that individual sales representatives receive

OSC Notice 11-762 (Revised) — Request for Comments Regarding Statement of Priorities for Fiscal Year Ending March 31, 2010

Date: May 1, 2009
32 O.S.C.B. 3771

[Not reproduced]

OSC Staff Notice 11-763 — A Focused Review of the Securities Valuation and Expense Allocation Practices of Fund Managers

Date: July 25, 2008
31 O.S.C.B. 7402

Overview

In late 2007, OSC staff conducted a focused review of the securities valuation and operating expense allocation practices of fund managers. This notice is a summary of the review, our observations and suggested practices.

We selected a sample of 26 fund managers with assets under management totalling $159 billion as at September 30, 2007. These fund managers vary in size and offer a wide variety of products, including mutual funds, pooled funds, closed-end funds and labour sponsored investment funds.

The review teams consisted of staff from the Compliance team of the Compliance and Registrant Regulation Branch and staff from the Investment Funds Branch. Starting in November 2007, we conducted the reviews at the fund managers' offices and assessed their practices from October 1, 2006 to September 30, 2007.

Purpose of the review

Our objectives were to review and assess:

- the appropriateness of the methodologies that fund managers use to value the securities in their funds' portfolios
- the practices fund managers follow in charging expenses to their funds. We focused on the operating expense component of the management expense ratio (MER).[1] We did not review the management fee component.

Securities valuation

Scope of the review

Our review included:

- reviewing and assessing the adequacy and appropriateness of fund managers' policies and procedures for valuing different types of securities
- testing the valuation of different types of securities
- reviewing the documentation to support securities valuation, particularly securities that do not have readily available market prices, such as privately issued securities, illiquid securities, certain types of derivatives and restricted securities
- comparing the disclosure of the valuation policies in offering documents against actual practices
- assessing the fund managers' oversight of suppliers where services were outsourced

---

[1]MER is calculated by taking the total of the management fees, operating expenses and any performance fees, and dividing it by the fund's average assets for the period. Brokerage commissions and transaction costs are excluded from the MER calculation. The trailing commission paid to dealers and advisory fees paid to portfolio managers are usually included in the management fees of conventional mutual funds.

Observations

Overall, the fund managers in our sample:

- had adequate policies and procedures for valuing portfolio securities

- were using appropriate valuation methodologies, particularly for securities that do not have readily available market prices

- were following practices that were consistent with the disclosure of their valuation policies

- were adequately overseeing service providers, including procedures to ensure service providers were following the fund manager's valuation policies

Policies and procedures

Fund managers generally had detailed policies and procedures on valuation, which they disclosed in the funds' offering documents. Their policies and procedures covered all types of securities in their funds' portfolios and provided guidance on the entire process of securities valuation.

Fund managers ensured that the valuation of assets and liabilities, and the calculation of net asset value (NAV) of the funds were prudently carried out. Their internal policies also covered situations where they might consider using estimated fair values instead of market prices.

Valuation of portfolios

The valuation methodologies used by the fund managers depended on the type of security and the availability of market quotations. Most securities in the fund portfolios were highly liquid exchange traded securities. The fund managers generally used an electronic price feed from an independent pricing vendor to price these securities. Most fund managers also validated these prices through a secondary pricing source, such as another independent pricing vendor, a custodian or a broker.

Fund managers in our sample had sound processes to fair value securities that did not have readily available market quotations, for example, privately issued securities. In general, they used acquisition cost until an arm's length transaction occurred that justified a change in value, for example, a new round of financing or a comparable third-party transaction. They clearly documented how they estimated fair value and the information they used to make the estimate.

As an added control, some fund managers had a valuation committee that met regularly to review the portfolios for appropriateness and reasonability.

Oversight of service providers

Many of the fund managers in our sample outsourced the valuation function. Fund managers typically maintained adequate oversight of these providers, although their approaches varied.

For example, fund managers:

- reviewed daily price variance reports for price changes above a pre-determined tolerance level (i.e. 5% to 10%)

- used stale price reports that identified all securities whose closing price had remained constant for the last five business days

- completed a reasonability review of the funds' NAV using a report showing the daily NAV, prior day NAV and the day-over-day dollar change and percentage change. Reasonableness was generally based on the movement of a fund's NAV compared to a broader market index.

We assessed the adequacy of fund managers' oversight by:

- reviewing their monitoring procedures

- testing a sample of their prices against an independent pricing source

- reviewing the service providers' CICA Handbook Section 5970 Report on Key Internal Controls and Safeguards, if the service providers chose to have their control procedures audited by an independent party

We noted that the fund managers in our sample had effective controls relating to the valuation of securities by their service providers.

Suggested practices

Fund managers should develop and enforce written policies and procedures that include, at a minimum, the following:

- valuation methodologies for all types of securities held in the funds' portfolios

- procedures to obtain prices from different pricing sources and process to be followed for securities that do not have readily available market prices

- procedures to identify and handle situations where prices obtained from the normal pricing sources may not be accurate, e.g. stale securities, halted securities or significant market events

- procedures to investigate price variances over a pre-determined tolerance level

- procedures to review and approve the valuation at the end of each valuation day prior to finalizing the calculation of NAV

- procedures for the identification, rectification and accounting treatment for NAV errors

Fund managers are ultimately responsible for those functions that they have outsourced to service providers. Fund managers should:

- enter into agreements that clearly outline the service providers' roles and responsibilities

- establish and document procedures to monitor service providers to ensure outsourced functions are performed properly, for example:

  - procedures to ensure that fund managers' valuation policies and procedures are being followed

  - guidelines on the frequency of communication between fund managers and service providers

  - the types and frequency of reports to be provided by service providers

- maintain records of their review of the outsourced functions

Fund manager should also consider establishing a valuation committee to independently review the securities in the funds' portfolios to ensure that valuation is done appropriately

Expense allocation practices

Scope of the review

Operating expenses[2] are incurred in the daily operation of a fund and include expenses such as accounting, audit, legal, transfer agent and custodial fees. Our review focused on the types of operating expenses fund managers charged to their funds and how fund managers allocated these expenses.

Our review included:

- reviewing and assessing fund managers' policies and procedures on accumulating and allocating operating expenses to the funds

- selecting samples of different types of operating expenses and reviewing documentation to assess whether the expenses were reasonable, appropriate and allocated fairly to various funds

- comparing expense disclosure in offering documents against the types of operating expenses actually charged

Observations

Overall, the fund managers in our sample:

- followed prudent practices relating to operating expenses

- used appropriate methodologies for allocating operating expenses to various funds

- clearly disclosed the types of operating expenses charged, including specific or unique expenses, such as the fixed administration fee

Allocating operating expenses

We noted that fund-specific operating expenses were easy to allocate to individual funds because they were supported by invoices that provided a breakdown of the expenses by fund. These included many of the standard operating expenses such as legal, audit, valuation and custodial fees.

In general, operating expenses that could not be directly linked to a particular fund were accumulated and allocated to the relevant funds. For example, some administrative expenses, such as accounting and information technology support, were accumulated and allocated to the funds that had used the services. Fund managers based their allocations on one or more appropriate factors, such as the number of fund investors, fund mandate, assets under management, the number of portfolio transactions or the number of classes in a fund.

Disclosure

The offering documents we reviewed contained appropriate disclosure relating to operating expenses. The disclosure included a general statement that each fund must pay all of its operating expenses and an itemized list of the types of operating expenses that could be charged to the fund. Fund managers used the term "administration expense" as a collective term for general expenses incurred to support the day-to-day administration of the funds that could not be easily itemized.

Suggested practices

Fund managers should establish and enforce written policies and procedures that include, at a minimum, the following:

- the types of expenses that should be borne by the funds

- procedures to ensure that invoices are reviewed and approved by an authorized person before they are processed for payment

- procedures to independently review expenses charged to the funds for accuracy and appropriateness

- a process to ensure that only those expenses disclosed in the offering documents are charged to the funds

---

[2]Operating expenses make up the "ER" portion of the MER.

Fund managers should also develop and document procedures used to budget and accrue for expenses in the funds, for example:

- procedures to prepare and approve the funds' budgets at the beginning of each fiscal year to ensure that only reasonable and appropriate expenses will be charged to the funds

- procedures to monitor accrued amounts versus actual amounts on a periodic basis and guidelines on when an adjustment to the accruals should be made

When allocating expenses to the funds, fund managers should:

- clearly document the method used

- determine the appropriate factors to be used for the allocation and how they are applied for each type of expense

- ensure the allocation method is fair and reasonable to all funds

OSC Staff Notice 11-764 — Business Continuity Planning — Industry Testing Exercise

Date: February 11, 2011

34 O.S.C.B. 1479

Business continuity is an ongoing priority for industry participants and regulatory authorities. Various events that have occurred over the past few years, such as the different flu outbreaks, natural disasters, black-outs or marketplaces' system problems that impacted a part or the industry as a whole, have served to heighten that priority by highlighting the risk of operational disruptions to the financial system.

Staff of the Ontario Securities Commission (OSC Staff or we) encourage the industry's efforts to identify the challenges and address the potential impact of any incidents that could disrupt normal business operations. This practice is consistent with securities legislation. Specifically, securities regulations require that business continuity plans be tested regularly, to reflect current or potential developments. Subsection 12.1(b) of National Instrument 21-101 *Marketplace Operation* requires marketplaces to test their business continuity and disaster recovery plans on a reasonably frequent basis and, in any event, at least annually. In addition, subsection 11.1(b) of National Instrument 31-103 *Registration Requirements and Exemptions* requires a registered firm to establish, maintain and apply policies and procedures that establish a system of controls and supervision sufficient to manage the risks associated with its business in accordance with prudent business practices. Rule 17.16 of the Dealer Member Rules of the Investment Industry Regulatory Organization of Canada (IIROC), approved by the recognizing regulators of IIROC, requires Dealer Members to establish and maintain a business continuity plan and conduct an annual review and a test of their business continuity plan to determine whether any modifications are necessary. In addition, clearing agencies are expected to have procedures to ensure business continuity including regularly testing their business continuity plans.

We are of the view that dealers, marketplaces, self-regulatory organizations and clearing agencies should participate regularly in industry-wide testing. We are considering whether it is necessary to make such testing mandatory through rule proposals or additional requirements in the recognition orders of various entities.

As stated in IIROC Notice 10-0332 issued on December 16, 2010, IIROC has set the date for a market wide test on September 10, 2011. IIROC expects all Dealer Members and major service providers to participate in this test and it will share the results of the test with all participants.

In light of the above and the existing requirements, OSC Staff encourage all dealers, marketplaces and clearing agencies to participate in the September 2011 market-wide exercise organized by IIROC. Participation in this exercise may facilitate the discovery of any potential communication issues, points of failure between industry participants within and across different jurisdictions or other issues with services provided by third-party service providers.

OSC Notice 11-765 — 2011-2012 Statement of Priorities Draft for Comment

Date: February 25, 2011

34 O.S.C.B. 2265

[Not reproduced]

OSC Notice 11-766 — Statement of Priorities — Request for Comment Regarding Statement of Priorities for Financial Year to End March 31, 2013

Date: March 30, 2012

30 O.S.C.B. 3007

[Not reproduced]

OSC Notice 11-767 — Notice of Statement of Priorities for Financial Year to End March 31, 2013

Date: June 28, 2012

35 O.S.C.B. 5927

[Not reproduced]

OSC Notice 11-768 — Notice of Statement of Priorities for Financial Year to End March 31, 2014

Date: June 27, 2013

36 O.S.C.B. 3423; correction 36 O.S.C.B. 6663

[Not reproduced]

OSC Notice 11-769 — Statement of Priorities — Request for Comments Regarding the Statement of Priorities for Financial Year to End March 31, 2015

Date: April 3, 2014

(2014), 37 O.S.C.B. 3339

[Not reproduced]

OSC Notice 11-770 — Notice of Statement of Priorities for Financial Year to End March 31, 2015

Date: June 26, 2014

37 O.S.C.B. 5182

The *Securities Act* (Act) requires the Ontario Securities Commission (OSC or Commission) to deliver to the Minister of Finance by June 30th of each year a statement of the Commission setting out its priorities for its current financial year in connection with the administration of the Act, the regulations and rules, together with a summary of the reasons for the adoption of the priorities.

In the notice published by the Commission on April 2, 2014, the Commission set out its draft Statement of Priorities (SoP) and invited public input in advance of finalizing and publishing the 2014-2015 Statement of Priorities. Twelve responses were received and carefully considered. We appreciate the time and effort taken by all of the commenters to review the SoP and provide their thoughtful and helpful feedback. A high level summary of the comments, and our replies to them, is set out below.

The responses were broadly supportive of the overall direction of the OSC goals and priorities and included:

a. Support for improved regulatory harmonization including pursuit of a national regulator and greater Canadian Securities Administrators (CSA) cooperation.

b. Positive acknowledgement of the OSC's ongoing efforts to keep pace with national and international developments.

c. Endorsement of budget controls to the extent that they do not impair the OSC's capacity to achieve its mandate.

Concerns were raised about the slow progress on various initiatives. While we understand, we are constrained by the fact that policy development is a complex process which takes time to do well. We believe that it is appropriate to undertake research and complete a careful assessment of consequences and potential impacts prior to implementing regulatory policies that can have profound impacts on our markets, market participants and investors. Our process often also requires considerable consultation with our CSA counterparts and other regulators, which is important for harmonization across Canada. Comments on the pace of regulatory development varied depending on whether the commenter supported or opposed the initiative. For some initiatives we heard that we are proceeding too quickly, while for others commenters expressed frustration at the perceived lack of progress.

The comments focussed on a wide range of issues. We address notable comments in the following section:

a. Investor advocates suggested that the SoP is too focused on capital formation and not enough attention is being placed on investor issues.

We respectfully disagree. The majority of our priorities for 2014-2015 have considerable impact on investor protection. In particular, this year the OSC will work on three transformative initiatives that are squarely focused on investor protection as it relates to mutual fund fees, final phases of the point of sale disclosure project and a best interests standard for advisors. Important work is also planned to address shareholder democracy which is a key area for investors. We would also note that, where issues were raised that the SoP did not include specific investor-related initiatives (for example, in relation to seniors) as a priority, in almost every instance these issues are being addressed within the OSC's business plan. We remain focused on investor protection and we believe that the SoP strikes an appropriate balance in addressing these important areas of focus.

b. Some commenters wanted to see greater evidence of the results of our efforts to engage and communicate with investors. Specifically, concern was expressed that we have not published the findings of our "OSC in the Community" work.

We launched OSC in the Community in 2013 as a new way to engage directly with investors and civic leaders in their community and we committed to publishing a list of what we heard from investors. The OSC has spoken with hundreds of investors across the province and highlights of the feedback from Ontarians have been published in OSC Investor Voice, a new online publication about the OSC's conversations with investors highlighting what we have heard and how we are responding to the issues.

c. A number of commenters highlighted seniors' issues as an area requiring more focus. One commenter suggested that the OSC create a Seniors Advisory Committee.

We agree that seniors are a very important and growing segment of investors. Our Office of the Investor (OI) is becoming increasingly active in this area. As seniors are a key segment of investors we will look to work with the Investor Advisory Panel (IAP) to ensure that the views and issues related to this very important group are brought forward and addressed.

The OI and the IAP will be holding a round table consultation this Fall to explore senior investment issues and possible solutions. The OI also participated in the Financial Consumer Agency of Canada's seniors' financial literacy consultations.

Part 1: PROCEDURE

d. Commenters recommended that the Commission define more clearly and specifically the timing and plans for delivering on the Statement of Priorities.

The SoP sets out the work that we expect to complete within the year against each initiative. We publish a report card detailing our progress against each initiative following the end of our fiscal year. The report card will be published on our website following delivery of the SoP to the Minister.

Policy initiatives can have profound impacts on our markets, market participants and investors. We believe we must thoroughly research and carefully assess potential impacts prior to implementing policies. As a result many of our initiatives have a multi-year time horizon. In these cases, it is very difficult to provide full project timetables. For many projects, such as our initiative on a Best Interest Duty, the work required will depend in part on the outcome of the research we conduct this year. Once this research and analysis has been completed we will publish the results and our decision on how we plan to move forward, including timing.

The OSC is committed to achieving harmonized, national regulatory solutions where practical. As a result, for many of our policy projects where we must collaborate with other regulators, timelines and completion dates are often not entirely within our control. While we will continue to seek CSA-wide solutions that address regulatory issues, we may be forced to introduce Ontario-only solutions if consensus cannot be achieved that addresses the issues in a timely manner.

e. A number of commenters suggested adding an initiative aimed at establishing a regulatory framework for advisors with a focus on proficiency.

We are reviewing the impact that advisor titles and proficiency standards have on investor protection as part of our Best Interest Duty initiative.

f. We received comments seeking improvements to dispute resolution and an approach to provide compensation to Ontario investors who suffer losses because of violations of the Act

The OSC believes having one dispute-resolution service for the securities industry is important for investors. We have taken steps to improve dispute resolution through the introduction of amendments to National Instrument 31-103 *Registration Requirements, Exemptions and Ongoing Registrant Obligations* (NI 31-103) and Companion Policy 31-103CP *Registration Requirements, Exemptions and Ongoing Registrant Obligations* that require all registered dealers and advisers outside of Quebec to use Ombudsman for Banking Services and Investments (OBSI) as their provider of dispute-resolution services by August 1, 2014.

The CSA has committed to continue to work with OBSI to ensure it has the capacity to effectively discharge its mandate. Participating CSA members (the OSC included) and OBSI have entered into a memorandum of understanding (MOU) that creates an oversight framework for OBSI to monitor performance against the standards set out by the CSA. Included in the MOU is a commitment to an independent evaluation of OBSI's operations and practices by August 1, 2016. We strongly support this process and expect registrants to abide by their obligations. If experience indicates that this process is not achieving the desired outcomes, we will consider additional actions to achieve this important protection for investors.

Some commenters have suggested that the OSC should compel payments to investors. The OSC does not have this authority and would need legislation to expand its powers in order to force binding decisions.

g. Commenters also noted that the SoP did not specifically mention shareholder democracy issues such as rights plans, majority voting, access proxy, say on pay and defensive tactics.

Work is underway on all of these issues. As a result we do not think it is necessary to further highlight these issues.

h. We heard from some commenters that they want to see a priority added to address the issue of uneven regulation of interchangeable investments. One commenter suggested merging the OSC and the Financial Services Commission of Ontario (FSCO) to achieve consistency in regulatory approaches across retail managed investment products.

We agree that consistent regulation of like products is an important objective and we strive for that outcome whenever possible. We continue to advocate for harmonized approaches with other regulators, however, any solution involving changes to the current division of regulation across the OSC and FSCO is a government decision and not within the OSC's control.

i. Opposition was raised by an investor advocate (FAIR Canada) to our priority to reduce regulatory burden.

We believe that industry compliance costs are ultimately borne by investors. If compliance costs can be reduced by removing regulatory requirements that do not impair our ability to achieve our regulatory goals, we believe that this contributes to more efficient markets. We remain committed to this priority as we believe that it benefits market participants and investors.

The specific actions we have identified under our priority to reduce regulatory burden relate to addressing fees paid to us, performing solid regulatory impact analyses before introducing new policy, reducing filings or eliminating requirements that are no longer necessary or appropriate, and enhancing how we receive data from market participants. Our objective is to appropriately reduce the time and costs associated with compliance but not at the expense of investor protection or good compliance. For example, we would consider eliminating requirements to file certain forms or information if we found we no longer required the information or if changes in market structure have made a particular requirement redundant.

j. A number of commenters suggested adding an initiative aimed at establishing a one-stop information source for investors where they could obtain information (e.g. registration, disciplinary and background).

Ontario became part of the National Registration System in 2013. Proposals to improve the system, including potential changes to its content to better support investors, will be considered by the CSA this year.

k. Support for our initiative aimed to improve capital formation was mixed. While some commenters favoured the move to expand opportunities for capital formation through new exemptions, others were concerned about whether the amount of research conducted to assess the potential impact on markets and investors has been sufficient. Questions were also raised about the ability to assure compliance with the investor-protection features in the new capital raising proposals.

A number of rules and multi-lateral instruments related to proposed prospectus exemptions are currently out for public comment. With those publications we have released analysis and data on the potential impacts on the market and market participants. We will be undertaking a comprehensive review of all feedback to determine next steps on these proposals. As part of this process preliminary work is underway to develop an oversight framework to monitor compliance with any new capital raising exemption requirements.

l. One commenter suggested that we should add a priority focusing on structured product regulation.

Through our operational work, review of alternative asset classes, strategies and complex products remain a priority focus. The next phase of the CSA's Modernization of Investment Fund Product proposals will be focused on alternative funds, with a specific focus on differentiating how we regulate these types of products and considering the appropriate proficiency for the sale of such products.

In response to comments we previously received about having too many priorities our objective in the last two years has been to limit the number of priorities in the SoP. This in turn has allowed us to be as transparent and accountable as we can about what we will deliver on those priorities, when we will deliver, and how we will measure our performance. In keeping with this goal to remain focused and committed to the highest priority items, we do not propose to add any additional priorities to our 2014-2015 SoP. However, beyond our twelve highest priorities, the OSC must also continue its core work and support of other important but lower priority initiatives. Several specific suggested priorities will be pursued as part of our core work.

All of the comment letters are available on our website www.osc.gov.on.ca. The Statement of Priorities will serve as the guide for the Commission's operations. Following delivery of the Statement of Priorities to the Minister, we will also publish on our website a report on our progress against our 2013-2014 priorities.

Ontario Securities Commission — 2014-2015 — Statement of Priorities

June 26, 2014

Introduction

We are pleased to present the Ontario Securities Commission (OSC or Commission) Chair's proposed Statement of Priorities for the Commission commencing April 1, 2014. The Statement of Priorities is required by the *Securities Act* (Ontario) and requires the OSC to publish the statement in its Bulletin and to deliver it to the Minister by June 30 of each year. This statement also supports the OSC's commitment to delivering its regulatory services effectively and with accountability.

This Statement of Priorities sets out the OSC's strategic goals and the specific initiatives that will be pursued in support of each of these goals in the fiscal year beginning each April. The statement also presents the environmental factors that the OSC considered in setting these goals. The OSC remains committed to its Vision and Mandate:

OSC Vision

To be an effective and responsive securities regulator — fostering a culture of integrity and compliance and instilling investor confidence in the capital markets.

OSC Mandate

The OSC's mandate (established by statute) is to provide protection to investors from unfair, improper or fraudulent practices and to foster fair and efficient capital markets and confidence in capital markets.

Our Environment — Risks and Challenges

The regulatory framework for Ontario's capital markets is designed to provide protection to investors while fostering fair and efficient capital markets. Public confidence in these markets can be affected by many factors, including the stability of the financial system, the economic health of the country and the volatility in the marketplace. There are a wide range of issues and risks that challenge the OSC's ability to achieve its vision/mandate.

As we move away from defined benefit pension plans, individual investors are facing more complex investment choices and are being forced to assume greater risks for their investments and retirement savings. A survey by the Investor Education Fund (2012) identified a number of key findings regarding the investor/advisor relationship:

a. Investors often have limited financial literacy and advisors are the key influence on investors' decision-making

b. Investors don't understand or consider different types of advisor registration and licensing.

c. Knowledge of mutual fund fees and what affects them is minimal. Their complexity makes it difficult for investors to assess potential conflicts of interest.

d. Most clients believe the advisor has a legal duty to put the client's interests ahead of his or her own.

A well-functioning investor/advisor relationship is critical to the economic well-being of Ontarians and ultimately to achieving healthy capital markets. The OSC will need to promote a framework that protects investors, where reliance by investors on their advisors is well placed, the advice being provided is suitable and any conflicts are managed appropriately. The Ontario Government is currently examining the need for more consistent proficiency standards for individuals who offer financial advice and planning services. The OSC will work with the government as this initiative evolves.

The OSC will also need to continue to seek ways to promote investor protection and support those efforts through investor focused policy initiatives, investor education and initiatives to deliver clearer and more understandable information to investors. Through achievement of these outcomes the OSC will continue to foster investors' confidence to invest in our capital markets.

Capital formation and efficient access to capital for issuers is critical to the economic prosperity of Ontario. The OSC must balance the need to take action to support this vital market function with its mandate to protect investors. Smaller participants are facing challenges raising capital through traditional sources, such as bank financing. To support capital formation the OSC needs to find ways to improve access by small and medium enterprises to capital raising alternatives such as private equity and "angel" investors. Other alternatives such as "crowd funding" can provide additional options to fund start-up enterprises. Actions in these areas will also help to address competition to attract smaller issuers that is emerging from other jurisdictions.

The OSC needs to act to address the international, national and interprovincial nature of the markets it regulates. The OSC must remain responsive to market developments with timely regulatory responses that maintain the competitiveness and attractiveness of Ontario capital markets to investors and capital. Capital markets are increasingly international and capital flows are not constrained by borders. It is critical that the OSC continue to play an active role in international organizations such as IOSCO to influence and promote changes to international securities regulation that are most beneficial to Ontario markets and participants. Greater harmonization and streamlined regulatory requirements that are aligned with international standards can enhance the quality and reputation of our markets and promote capital inflows.

Currently the financial industry, market participants and investors are facing many challenges from globalization, structural changes within our markets as well as ongoing financial innovation. These changes all generate increased complexity and have given rise to new areas of regulatory focus such as the regulation of derivative markets, regulatory changes needed to oversee electronic trading and the effects of rapidly evolving technology including social media on our markets. Domestic market evolution also continues to present issues. For example, smaller retail focused financial firms and issuers continue to experience pressure on their current business models due to market conditions and increasing competition from larger entities. The OSC will need to focus on regulatory solutions and market structures that address market evolution, foster competition and meet the needs of market participants and investors.

To address national and interprovincial issues it remains important for the OSC to continue to work with its Canadian Securities Administrators (CSA) partners to harmonize the rules and their application across the country where possible. Concurrently, the OSC supports the significant efforts underway between BC, Ontario and the Federal Governments to implement a cooperative securities regulator that will deliver more efficient and effective regulation of the capital markets and effectively oversee sources of systemic risk. The resource implications for the OSC's role in this initiative are currently unclear but are expected to be substantial.

The increasing regulatory burden continues to present challenges for market participants as the complexity of regulatory requirements and the resources required to comply continue to grow. The OSC will need to examine whether the existing rules are still effective and determine whether they inhibit or promote high-quality capital markets and deliver a system that protects investors and promotes their confidence. It is important to continue to seek less intrusive regulatory solutions and opportunities to avoid undue burdens on business. The OSC must look for ways to lower the regulatory costs while achieving its mandate, as they are a critical component affecting the competiveness and efficiency of Ontario's capital markets.

We continue to believe that effective consultation is necessary to ensure the development of good regulatory policy and decision making. We will continue to consult through our various advisory committees, public comment processes and other initiatives such as "OSC in the Community" and issue-specific public roundtables.

OSC Regulatory Goals for 2014 - 2015

1. Deliver strong investor protection
2. Deliver responsive regulation
3. Deliver effective enforcement and compliance
4. Support and promote financial stability
5. Run a modern, accountable and efficient organization

Key OSC Regulatory Priorities for 2014 - 2015

The OSC strives to be as responsive, innovative and collaborative as possible in its policy responses to other regulators. The OSC remains committed to enhanced co-operation and information-sharing with the CSA, working with its partners in the International Organization of Securities Commissions (IOSCO) and collaborating with other international agencies and governments.

In this environment, the OSC must use its finite resources as efficiently as possible. This Statement of Priorities identifies the most important areas where the OSC intends to focus its resources and actions in 2014-2015. Each of the proposed priorities has been aligned under one of the five OSC regulatory goals.

Summary of 2014-2015 OSC Priorities

Deliver strong investor protection	
Issue/Priority	**Proposed Actions**
1. Best Interest Duty to Investors	a. Complete the joint OSC/IIROC/MFDA mystery shop research sweep of advisors to gauge the suitability of advice currently being provided to investors
	b. Conduct research on advisor compensation to study the alignment of compensation with client's interests and inform our assessment of the need for a best interest duty
	c. Evaluate the options and recommend an approach for this project

2. **Embedded Fees in Mutual Funds**	a.	Complete third-party research to determine whether and to what extent the perceived conflicts of interests associated with various forms of commission compensation (including product imbedded commissions) influence advisor behaviour. The research will aim to:
	i.	quantify the degree to which various forms of compensation for distribution affect fund sales
	ii.	assess whether the use of fee-based compensation materially changes the advice given to the client and has the potential to lead to enhanced long-term investment outcomes relative to the use of commission compensation (including embedded commissions)
	b.	Encourage expansion of product choices across distribution platforms
3. **Point of Sale Disclosure for Investors**		The CSA Point of Sale (POS) initiative for mutual funds will:
	a.	Publish final rules introducing pre-sale delivery of the Fund Facts. Work with the CSA to consider mandating a risk classification methodology to improve the comparability of risk ratings of mutual funds in the Fund Facts
	b,	Publish rules for comment by December 2014 that create a new summary disclosure document for ETFs and require it to be delivered. Legislative changes may be necessary before rules can be finalized

Deliver responsive regulation

Issue/Priority		Proposed Actions
4. **Market Structure Evolution**	a.	Publish proposals to update the order protection rule to respond to the evolution of the Canadian capital market structure
5. **Improve Capital Formation**	a.	Complete our review of stakeholder feedback on the following proposed new capital raising prospectus exemptions (offering memorandum, family, friends and business associates, existing security holder and crowd funding exemptions)
	b.	Subject to considering the feedback received, develop and publish proposed rules implementing these exemptions
	c.	Develop proposals for streamlining the existing rights offering exemption to improve its efficiency and effectiveness for reporting issuers
6. **Regulation of Fixed Income Securities**	a.	Review transparency in the corporate bond market and develop a proposal to increase post trade information available to the market.
7. **Corporate Governance — Women on Boards**	a.	Complete review of stakeholder feedback on our proposed disclosure requirements requiring TSX-listed and other non-venture issuers to provide disclosure regarding the representation of women on boards and in executive management positions
	b.	Subject to considering the feedback received, develop and publish proposed rules requiring disclosure about the number of women on boards and in executive management positions
8. **Shareholder Democracy**	a.	Publish a progress report with preliminary recommendations on the status of our review of the proxy voting system
	b.	Review the feedback received on CSA Consultation Paper 54-401 Review of the Proxy Voting Infrastructure through the comment letter process and the related OSC roundtable to target specific concerns and potential solutions

Deliver effective enforcement and compliance

Issue/Priority		Proposed Actions
9. **Serious Securities-related Misconduct**	a.	Bring forward more cases involving fraudulent activity that harms investors and affects the integrity of our market by leveraging strategic partnerships with law enforcement agencies, the Ministry of the Attorney General and relevant international regulatory authorities
	b.	Bring forward more cases where issuer or registrant misconduct is harming market integrity or eroding confidence in Ontario's capital markets.
	c.	Select registrants for compliance reviews that are most likely to have material compliance issues, are new registrant firms, or are involved in a specific topic or industry sector that is of concern
	d.	Issue and analyze a Risk Assessment Questionnaire to gather information necessary to risk rate our registrant population

Support and promote financial stability

Issue/Priority		Proposed Actions
	a.	Develop rules for the clearing of OTC derivatives and implement trade reporting rules for OTC derivatives
	b.	Work with CSA colleagues to create a harmonised and efficient OTC derivatives regime in Canada

Part 1: PROCEDURE

		c.	Develop and implement a web portal for trade reports that are unable to be accepted by a designated trade repository
10.	Systemic Risk to Financial Markets	d.	Develop a plan for implementing data analysis for systemic risk oversight and market conduct purposes including the development of analytical tools and the creation of snapshot descriptions of the Canadian OTC derivatives market
		e.	Pursue a leadership role internationally to influence the development of global securities regulation that works for Canada
		f.	Work with the Ontario, B.C. and Federal governments to support the creation of a Co-operative Capital Markets Regulator

Run a modern, accountable and efficient organization

Issue/Priority		Proposed Actions	
11.	Reduce Regulatory Burden	a.	Review current fee rule and issues arising due to market evolution and develop a proposed fee rule for approval by the Minister
		b.	Complete a regulatory impact analysis for all proposed policy projects.
		c.	Review filing requirements to identify opportunities to cease collection of data that is not used, lightly used, or readily available elsewhere
		d.	Implement electronic solutions to ease submission of data for market participants
12.	Timely and Fair Adjudication	a.	Implement an on-line Electronic Case Management System to receive and distribute electronic filings to improve access to the tribunal and make the hearing process more understandable and efficient
		b.	Enhance accessibility for respondents and the public by holding electronic hearings (where practical)
		c.	Adopt and implement a guideline for the timely release of decisions within 6 months, where practical

Deliver strong investor protection

Protection of investors continues to be a fundamental element of everything the OSC does. The OSC's Office of the Investor works to strengthen the OSC's investor engagement and ensure investor issues are directly considered in policy and operational activities. Our increasing engagement with investors has improved our understanding of their needs and has informed how the OSC undertakes its outreach and education, regulatory policy, compliance oversight and enforcement work. Seniors represent a growing segment of Ontario's investors. The Office of the Investor will continue to focus on outreach to seniors and bring attention to seniors' issues in policy development, compliance and enforcement.

The Office of the Investor is continuing to lead outreach to investors across Ontario to hear their concerns and issues and to provide them with resources and tips to help them become more informed and protected investors. The OSC wants investors to be able to make more informed investment decisions. More effective disclosure, prepared in easy-to-understand formats, can help investors better understand investment products, risks, costs and performance. These initiatives and outreach efforts provide a better understanding of investor issues and enhance the OSC's ability to better protect investors.

Many Ontarians work with an advisor or dealer to achieve their investment and retirement goals. Registered firms and individuals are expected to meet their responsibilities to clients with respect to know your client, know your product and suitability. Investors should be able to expect financial services and products that meet their needs from firms that treat them fairly. Findings from studies commissioned by the Investor Education Fund, Investor Advisory Panel and others have concluded that mutual fund investors often have little knowledge about what they are buying, the fees they are paying or how their advisors are paid. These findings are further supported by Ombudsman for Banking Services and Investments cases that show that suitability can be a problem and investors often have no understanding of the risks they are assuming. Interactions with investors at OSC in the Community events have confirmed these findings as well as investor appetite for simpler and easier to understand information relating to their investments.

To address these issues, the OSC needs to examine the investor experience and quality of advice being provided to investors in order to better understand the impact, if any, that issues such as incentive structures and embedded commissions may be having on the nature of advice being provided to investors. Research in this crucial area will allow the OSC to identify if there are issues to address and opportunities for improvements.

The OSC will undertake the priorities set out below toward achieving the following outcomes for investors:

1. Investors are provided with clear information before, during and after the point of sale of financial services and products

2. Advice provided to investors is clear, and suitable for their needs

3. The goals of firms and the investors they deal with are aligned

Best Interest Duty to Investors

Priority 1 Issue	Investors expect the OSC to clearly demonstrate and communicate how they are protecting their interests. Investors expect a fair and transparent client/advisor relationship. The OSC will take steps to examine and better understand the potential impacts on dealers, advisors and investors of imposing a best interest duty.	
	a.	Complete the joint OSC/IIROC/MFDA mystery shop research sweep of advisors to gauge the suitability of advice currently being provided to investors

Action Plan	b.	Conduct research on advisor compensation to study the alignment of compensation with client's interests and inform our assessment of the need for a best interest duty
	c.	Evaluate the options and recommend an approach for this project
Success Measures/ Expected Outcomes	a.	Mystery shop research completed on time and within budget. Data collected, analysed and areas for potential remediation identified
	b.	Report on mystery shop published including guidance issued on what constitutes non-compliant advice, compliant advice and good advice. Key findings used to inform targeting of future OSC suitability sweeps and best interest duty policy development
	c.	Status of advisor compensation research published
	d.	Options evaluated and recommendations developed

Embedded Fees in Mutual Funds

Priority 2 Issue	Investors are at risk if advisors fail to provide suitable investment advice or manufacturers fail to offer product choices due to compensation structures. The OSC will undertake a targeted analysis of how compensation models influence advisor behaviour to inform a decision on whether or not to cap or ban embedded commissions and other types of compensation arrangements.	
Action Plan	a.	Complete third-party research to determine whether and to what extent the perceived conflicts of interests associated with various forms of commission compensation (including product imbedded commissions) influence advisor behaviour. The research will aim to:
	i.	quantify the degree to which various forms of compensation for distribution affect fund sales
	ii.	assess whether the use of fee-based compensation materially changes the advice given to the client and has the potential to lead to enhanced long-term investment outcomes relative to the use of commission compensation (including embedded commissions)
	b.	Encourage expansion of product choices across distribution platforms
Success Measures/Expected Outcomes	a.	Research completed as per plan (on time and within budget) by early 2015
	b.	Actionable results identified and a recommendation made about whether or not to cap or ban embedded commissions
	c.	Staff notice setting out key findings and status will be published by early 2015

Point of Sale Disclosure for Investors

Priority 3 Issue	Investor protection can be improved by providing more meaningful and accessible information to investors to support more informed investment decisions. The OSC will publish rules introducing pre-sale delivery of Fund Facts for mutual funds and introduce a new summary disclosure document and delivery regime for ETFs.	
Action Plan		The CSA Point of Sale (POS) initiative for mutual funds will:
	a.	Publish final rules introducing pre-sale delivery of the Fund Facts. Work with the CSA to consider mandating a risk classification methodology to improve the comparability of risk ratings of mutual funds in the Fund Facts
	b.	Publish rules for comment by December 2014 that create a new summary disclosure document for ETFs and require it to be delivered. Legislative changes may be necessary before rules can be finalized
Success Measures/ Expected Outcomes	a.	Positive feedback from stakeholders on the consultation process
	b.	Final rules will be published by March 2015, subject to Minister approval
	Note: Effectiveness of pre-sale delivery of Fund Facts to be considered in 2015-2016 following implementation (i.e. costs savings to industry stakeholders on delivery; greater investor awareness of key risks and costs).	

Part 1: PROCEDURE

Deliver responsive regulation

Market Structure Evolution

The overall objective of market regulation is to ensure that markets remain fair and that all participants have confidence in both the resiliency and integrity of the market. Global capital markets continue to undergo significant technological change and rapid evolution. The OSC has responded to these changes with collaborative policy responses with the CSA and through the implementation of appropriate international best practices to support fair, efficient and orderly markets in Ontario.

In addition, the OSC plans to review the effects of its rules post-implementation to determine if the rules are achieving the desired outcomes. As an example, the order protection rule appears to have had a number of unintended consequences that may be creating inefficiencies and additional costs in the market. This rule will be examined and changes to address these issues will be proposed during the coming year.

Priority 4 Issue		The OSC needs to address issues that arise as a result of the evolution of the market including the impact of the order protection rule.
Action Plan	a.	Publish proposals to update the order protection rule to respond to the evolution of the Canadian capital market structure
Success Measures/ Expected Outcomes	a.	Proposed changes to update the order protection rule are published
	b.	Industry feedback confirms that the proposed changes to the order protection rule will improve efficiency and are aligned with current market needs

Improve Capital Formation

The OSC recognizes that cost-effective access to capital is critical to companies of all sizes to grow and develop. The OSC has heard from stakeholders that the current capital raising options in Ontario may not be meeting the needs of companies, particularly start-ups and small and medium enterprises (SMEs). It is critical for the OSC to consider ways to support this important sector. The OSC has also heard from stakeholders that investors may want increased access to investment opportunities in the exempt market.

The OSC has considered a broader range of capital raising options, particularly for smaller companies. These options are more tailored to start-ups and SMEs and will improve the rule harmonization with other CSA regulators. The OSC is also considering options that provide greater access to exempt market products for all investors while maintaining important investor protections. If appropriate, the OSC will propose changes to its current rules.

Priority 5 Issue		The current capital raising regime in Ontario needs to better meet the needs of market participants, especially SMEs. The OSC will look at options to expand opportunities for businesses to raise capital.
Action Plan	a.	Complete our review of stakeholder feedback on the following proposed new capital raising prospectus exemptions (offering memorandum, family, friends and business associates, existing security holder and crowd funding exemptions)
	b.	Subject to considering the feedback received, develop and publish proposed rules implementing these exemptions
	c.	Develop proposals for streamlining the existing rights offering exemption to improve its efficiency and effectiveness for reporting issuers
Success Measures/ Expected Outcomes	a.	Rule amendments delivered to Minister for approval and publication of amendments in final form
	b.	Proposals for streamlining the existing rights offering exemption published for public comment

Regulation of Fixed Income Securities

The Canadian fixed income market is similar to the equity market in terms of value of assets outstanding. The fixed income market (particularly the corporate bond market) has substantially increased in size in the last decade and there is a large presence of retail investors invested in this market directly and indirectly. Debt financings are also an important source of financing for Canadian corporations.

In Canada, corporate bond trading is subject to limited post-trade transparency for both regulators and retail investors. The OSC needs to take steps to better understand the significant issues (e.g. access, sales practices and disclosure) affecting fixed income securities and those who invest in them, and to identify opportunities where changes to regulatory approaches could improve market transparency and better protect investor interests.

Priority 6 Issue		Fixed income is a significant but less transparent segment of our capital markets. Retail participation is high as investors seek opportunities for higher yields. The OSC will examine ways to improve the transparency of this market.
Action Plan	a.	Review transparency in the corporate bond market and develop a proposal to increase post trade information available to the market.
Success Measures/ Expected Outcomes	a.	The proposal will be published by March 2015.

Corporate Governance — Women on Boards

Effective corporate governance is a fundamental part of a Board's responsibility and it is key to maintaining investor confidence. The OSC continues to seek opportunities to improve the focus of boards on good governance practices. More diverse board composition may encourage greater effectiveness and better corporate decision making. The OSC has proposed to require greater transparency for investors and other stakeholders regarding the representation of women on boards and in senior management. This transparency is intended to assist investors when making investment and voting decisions.

Priority 7 Issue		There are growing expectations for better board governance and transparency, including increased transparency regarding the representation of women in leadership roles at reporting issuers.
Action Plan	a.	Complete review of stakeholder feedback on our proposed disclosure requirements requiring TSX-listed and other non-venture issuers to provide disclosure regarding the representation of women on boards and in executive management positions
	b.	Subject to considering the feedback received, develop and publish proposed rules requiring disclosure about the number of women on boards and in executive management positions
Success Measures/ Expected Outcomes	a.	Rule amendments delivered to the Minister of Finance for approval and final amendments published
	b.	The criteria and process to select senior management and the Board will be more transparent to shareholders

Shareholder Democracy

The ability to vote on certain key decisions is a fundamental shareholder right. By voting, shareholders elect directors, approve or disapprove major matters and make their views known on matters such as executive compensation. Shareholder voting plays an important role in the fairness and efficiency of our capital markets. Recently, some issuers and investors have raised concerns about the reliability and accuracy of the proxy voting infrastructure that records shareholder votes. The OSC believes it is critical that the proxy voting infrastructure records votes accurately and reliably, and it is necessary for market confidence that it is perceived to be fair.

Priority 8 Issue		The OSC is taking a leadership role in looking for ways forward with the proxy voting system, and improving the accuracy and reliability of the proxy voting infrastructure.
Action Plan	a.	Publish a progress report with preliminary recommendations on the status of our review of the proxy voting system
	b.	Review the feedback received on CSA Consultation Paper 54-401 Review of the Proxy Voting Infra-structure through the comment letter process and the related OSC roundtable to target specific concerns and potential solutions
Success Measures/ Expected Outcomes	a.	Progress report published by December 2014
	b.	Significant stakeholder engagement on the issues and positive stakeholder feedback on the consultation process

Deliver effective enforcement and compliance

Serious Securities-related Misconduct

To promote public confidence in capital markets, the OSC must use its authority to address significant non-compliance and misconduct. The OSC continues to intensify its enforcement presence and is exploring new opportunities to bolster investor and market participant trust in our markets.

The OSC continues to pursue more fraud cases before the courts, where it can seek jail sentences for violations of the *Securities Act* (Ontario) and breaches of Commission orders. The OSC is also considering various new policy initiatives to strengthen its enforcement regime including no-enforcement action agreements, no-contest settlements, and a credit for co-operation program with enhanced public disclosure of the credit granted for co-operating with the OSC.

As the regulatory agenda increases the OSC must effectively allocate its resources. As enforcement consumes the greatest proportion of OSC resources it is particularly important to maximize the enforcement impact on activities with the most detrimental impact on investors. The OSC Joint Serious Offences Team (JSOT) has been formed with the cooperation of law enforcement agencies and the Ministry of the Attorney General and the OSC is leveraging their different powers, authorities and skill sets to address these issues.

Effective Compliance

The OSC conducts compliance reviews of registered firms primarily to assess compliance with Ontario securities law, but also to help regis-trants improve their understanding of the regulatory requirements and our expectations, and to help us to learn about a specific industry topic or practice.

The OSC will continue to focus on firms that are most likely to have material compliance issues or risk of harm to investors or would have a significant effect on the capital markets if there is a compliance breach due to their size or market penetration. In addition to reviewing individual firms, the OSC will continue to conduct issue specific compliance reviews (sweeps). Sweeps allow us to respond on a timely basis to industry-wide concerns or issues. The OSC regularly performs sweeps of newly registered firms to assess if they are off to a good start and to help them to understand their requirements and our expectations.

Priority 9 Issue	The OSC needs to better demonstrate the effectiveness and efficiency of its enforcement and compliance efforts. The OSC will seek to limit potential harm to investors by focusing enforcement efforts on cases involving fraud, manipulation and other serious securities related misconduct. The OSC will focus its compliance oversight on registrants that are most likely to have material compliance issues, including risk of harm to investors, or significant effect on the capital markets if there is a compliance breach.
Action Plan	a. Bring forward more cases involving fraudulent activity that harms investors and affects the integrity of our market by leveraging strategic partnerships with law enforcement agencies, the Ministry of the Attorney General and relevant international regulatory authorities b. Bring forward more cases where issuer or registrant misconduct is harming market integrity or eroding confidence in Ontario's capital markets. c. Select registrants for compliance reviews that are most likely to have material compliance issues, are new registrant firms, or are involved in a specific topic or industry sector that is of concern d. Issue and analyze a Risk Assessment Questionnaire to gather information necessary to risk rate our registrant population

Success Measures/ Expected Outcomes	a. The OSC JSOT will:
	  i. Increase the number of cases investigated for fraudulent activity and recidivist offenders
	  ii. Work with law enforcement to proactively use Criminal Code tools in JSOT investigations
	
	b. Visible and effective enforcement actions in cases of unacceptable or egregious issuer or registrant misconduct will result in improved market conduct and have a deterrent effect on future misconduct
	
	c. Increase the number of reviews of registrants that reveal significant compliance issues
	
	d. Respond on a timely basis to industry wide compliance issues or concerns

Support and Promote Financial Stability

Ontario's financial markets are part of the Canadian and international capital markets, closely linked by technology, investment flows, risk-management practices, cross border transactions and the global business models of market participants. The OSC must align its regulatory framework to adhere to important global reforms and standards, including G20 commitments (OTC derivatives and systemic risk) that seek to promote financial system resilience. The OSC actively participates in the development of international securities regulation and plays a leadership role as a key member of the IOSCO Executive, which sets internationally recognized standards for the securities sector. This role is critical to allow the OSC to develop and implement timely, aligned regulatory responses that maintain the competitiveness and attractiveness of Ontario capital markets to investors and capital.

One of the key outcomes from the 2008 financial crisis was the understanding of the need for increased regulatory coordination and oversight of the OTC derivatives markets. As the trading of OTC derivatives could be a significant source of systemic risk in Canada a globally and nationally coordinated OTC derivatives regime benefits Ontario capital markets. Regulatory oversight of the OTC derivatives markets should result in earlier identification of potential risks and increase the ability of regulators to respond to systemic risk and market misconduct. This will also ensure Canada can meet its international commitments in this area.

Priority 10 Issue	Increasingly interconnected global financial markets present systemic risk to financial market stability. OTC derivatives represent a significant potential source of systemic risk in Canada. The OSC will develop and implement an OTC derivatives regulatory framework to reduce potential risks to the financial system posed by unregulated entities. The OSC supports implementation of a cooperative securities regulator that will deliver more efficient and effective regulation of the capital markets and effectively oversee sources of systemic risk.
	a. Develop rules for the clearing of OTC derivatives and implement trade reporting rules for OTC derivatives b. Work with CSA colleagues to create a harmonised and efficient OTC derivatives regime in Canada c. Develop and implement a web portal for trade reports that are unable to be accepted by a designated trade repository

Action Plan	d.	Develop a plan for implementing data analysis for systemic risk oversight and market conduct purposes including the development of analytical tools and the creation of snapshot descriptions of the Canadian OTC derivatives market
	e.	Pursue a leadership role internationally to influence the development of global securities regulation that works for Canada
	f.	Work with the Ontario, B.C. and Federal governments to support the creation of a Co-operative Capital Markets Regulator
Success Measures/	a.	Clearing and reporting rules for OTC derivatives that align with international standards and meet G20 commitments will be in place
Expected Outcomes	b.	Systems for oversight and to facilitate systemic analysis of the Ontario derivatives markets will be in place on time and within budget

Run a modern, accountable and efficient organization

Reduce Regulatory Burden

All market participants are operating in challenging economic times and have to deal with intense competition, uneven global economic growth and slowly recovering financial markets. Smaller market participants are struggling to adjust to market volatility and market structure changes. Recognizing these challenges the OSC is looking for ways to reduce the regulatory burden in both time and the costs of compliance. Market participants expect the OSC to use its limited resources efficiently, so improving our efficiency is a top priority. In February the OSC implemented a targeted, one-time fee reduction to address market conditions and assist smaller market participants. The OSC has also committed to review its current fee rule and issues arising due to market evolution and develop a proposed fee rule for approval by the Minister.

Where regulatory requirements may no longer be appropriate or required due to market evolution there is an opportunity to reduce regulatory burden. The OSC is committed to assessing the impacts of its proposed policy and operational changes to try to ensure that any proposed regulation is proportionate and fit for purpose, does not act as an unnecessary barrier to new firms entering the industry and does not constrain innovation and growth. The OSC will improve its policy development process by completing a regulatory impact analysis prior to initiating any proposed policy projects.

Priority 11 Issue	Market participants continue to identify regulatory burden as a significant issue. The OSC will look for ways to reduce regulatory burden on market participants.
Action Plan	a.	Review current fee rule and issues arising due to market evolution and develop a proposed fee rule for approval by the Minister
	b.	Complete a regulatory impact analysis for all proposed policy projects.
	c.	Review filing requirements to identify opportunities to cease collection of data that is not used, lightly used, or readily available elsewhere
	d.	Implement electronic solutions to ease submission of data for market participants
Success Measures/	a.	At least two opportunities identified where filing requirements could be reduced or eliminated
Expected Outcomes	b.	At least 95% of capital and financial statement filings by registrants received electronically

Timely and Fair Adjudication

Timely and fair adjudication processes are a key requirement of the regulatory framework. The OSC is looking for ways to reduce costs, improve the efficiency of the adjudication process and to modernize our hearing process. Improved timeliness benefits respondents and reduces the risk of offenders avoiding sanction due to unreasonable delays in the process.

Priority 12 Issue	The OSC needs to improve its adjudicative processes through more transparent policies, practices and procedures and more timely dissemination of its orders, decisions and reasons.
Action Plan	a.	Implement an on-line Electronic Case Management System to receive and distribute electronic filings to improve access to the tribunal and make the hearing process more understandable and efficient
	b.	Enhance accessibility for respondents and the public by holding electronic hearings (where practical)
	c.	Adopt and implement a guideline for the timely release of decisions within 6 months, where practical
Success Measures/	a.	The Electronic Case Management System will be implemented on time and within budget.
Expected Outcomes	b.	Hearings will be held electronically, as appropriate
	c.	The efficiency and timeliness of tribunal adjudicative hearing and deliberation processes will be improved. Decisions will be released within six months, where practical

Part 1: PROCEDURE

2014-2015 Financial Outlook

OSC Revenues and Surplus

The OSC is forecasting 2014-2015 revenues to increase by 2.7% from 2013-2014 revenues. The forecast reflects fee increases set out in the OSC's fee rules (13-502 and 13-503), which became effective April 1, 2013. The fee increases are necessary to meet the OSC's evolving regulatory responsibilities, many of which are driven by work at the international level. To maintain competitive capital markets in Canada, the OSC must align its regulatory framework to be consistent with important global reforms and standards including G20 commitments (derivatives and systemic risk), increasingly complex international enforcement files, changing oversight responsibilities related to market infrastructure entities and new complex products.

In February, the OSC announced an opportunity for one-time relief on participation fees for certain small registered firms and reporting issuers ("Participants"). Eligible Participants were required to apply for relief. The total financial impact of the relief provided was $391,000.

Although the OSC experienced a surplus in 2014, it expects to operate at a deficit in 2014-2015. As a result, the OSC's general surplus as at March 31, 2015 is expected to be approximately $4.9 million. The OSC maintains a $20 million reserve that may be used to fund operations.

2014-2015 Budget Approach

The 2014-2015 OSC Budget is focused on investment in the key strategies identified in the 2012-2015 OSC Strategic Plan, while at the same time maintaining fiscal responsibility. In setting this budget the OSC has taken a strategic approach to assess areas where resources can be reduced, or the work can be done differently or more efficiently and has refocused resources to priority areas. This resulted in decreased budgets for certain program areas and an OSC Budget for 2014-2015 which is lower than the 2013-2014 budget.

2014-15 Budget Comparisons

(thousands)	2013/2014 Budget	2013/2014 Actual	2014/2015 Budget	2014-15 Budget to 2013-14 Budget		2014-15 Budget to 2013-14 Actual	
Revenues	101,160	98,677	101,325	165	0.2%	2,648	2.7%
Expenses	103,552	97,155	102,976	(577)	-0.6%	5,821	6.0%
Excess (Deficiency) of Revenue compared with Expenses	(2,392)	1,522	(1,651)	741		(3,173)	
Capital Expenditures	5,661	6,940	3,349	(2,312)		(3,591)	

The OSC continues to face challenges to continue to improve its capacity to keep up with market developments, innovation and investor concerns. Increased use of technology is a key element of the OSC's strategy. As a result, the budget reflects the need to invest resources to update and improve the OSC Information Technology infrastructure. The budget also includes resources for work toward the successful implementation of the Common Market Regulator.

The budget reflects a decrease of 0.6% from the 2013-2014 budget. Salaries and benefits, which comprise $77.9 million or 75.7% of the budget, reflect an increase of $3.5 million or 4.7% over 2013-2014 spending due to budgeting of full-year costs for vacancies and staff hired throughout 2013-2014 and new positions approved to achieve the OSC's strategic initiatives.

The significant decrease in the capital budget primarily reflects the fact that the build-out of recently acquired additional space that took place in 2012-2013 and 2013-2014 is now complete. The budget also includes an investment to support upgrading and expansion of our information technology, including completion of the network replacement. In addition, funds have been allocated to implement a refresh of our mobile devices program.

OSC Notice 11-771 — Statement of Priorities — Request for Comments Regarding Statement of Priorities for Financial Year to End March 31, 2016

Date: April 2, 2015

38 O.S.C.B. 2953

[Not reproduced]

OSC Notice 11-772 — Notice of Statement of Priorities for Financial Year to End March 31, 2016

Date: June 18, 2015

38 O.S.C.B. 5434

The *Securities Act* (Act) requires the Ontario Securities Commission (OSC or Commission) to deliver to the Minister of Finance by June 30th of each year a statement of the Commission setting out its priorities for its current financial year in connection with the administration of the Act, the regulations and rules, together with a summary of the reasons for the adoption of the priorities.

In the notice published on April 2, 2015, the Commission set out its draft Statement of Priorities (SoP) and invited public input in advance of finalizing and publishing the 2015-2016 Statement of Priorities. Seventeen responses, focussed on a wide range of issues, were received.

We appreciate the time and effort taken by all of the commenters to review the SoP and provide their thoughtful and helpful feedback. The responses were broadly supportive of the overall direction of the OSC goals and priorities and included:

    a. Support for the OSC's demonstrated commitment to consultation and investor protection

    b. Support for improved regulatory harmonization including pursuit of a national regulator and greater CSA cooperation

    c. Positive acknowledgement of the OSC's ongoing efforts to keep pace with national and international developments

Specific support was noted for the various proposals including the whistleblower program, the review of fixed income and timely and fair adjudication.

A number of comments focused on the pace of regulatory development for various initiatives. These comments varied depending on whether the commenter supported or opposed the initiative. For some initiatives we heard that we may be proceeding too quickly, while for others commenters expressed frustration at the perceived lack of progress. The OSC is mindful of these concerns and will work to address the timeliness of its policy development processes where practical. The OSC is committed to achieving harmonized, national regulatory solutions where practical. As a result, for many of our policy projects where we must collaborate with other regulators, timelines and completion dates are often not entirely within our control. While we will continue to seek CSA-wide solutions that address regulatory issues, we may be forced to introduce Ontario-only solutions if consensus cannot be achieved that addresses the issues in a timely manner.

A high level summary of the comments, and our replies to them, is set out below:

a. Our proposed priority on Best Interest Duty received the most attention. Comments covered a range of issues including concerns about the pace of progress and more clarity on the expected timing on finalizing an approach. A number of comments were also provided on related issues such as proficiency and titles.

We have clarified our proposed direction and the expected timing to bring this issue to a final resolution. As noted last year, we will be reviewing the impact that advisor titles and proficiency standards have on investor protection as part of this priority.

b. A number of commenters highlighted seniors' issues as a growing area of risk requiring more focus. One commenter suggested that the OSC create a Seniors Advisory Committee.

On April 1, 2015 the OSC merged the OSC Office of the Investor and the Investor Education Fund to form the Office of the Investor Policy, Education and Outreach (OIPEO) to provide an enhanced structure to deliver investor protection. Work is underway in the newly integrated OIPEO to develop a strategy and identify key focus areas to achieve critical investor protection outcomes.

We agree that seniors are an extremely important and growing segment of investors that demand attention. Other issues such as fraud prevention and education were also identified as potential risk areas. We are confident that the OIPEO plan that will be finalized in 2015 will be a comprehensive blueprint to address these and other key investor protection issues. The OIPEO will work closely with the Investor Advisory Panel (IAP) to ensure that the views and issues related to seniors and other important investor groups are brought forward and addressed.

c. A number of specific enforcement and compliance priorities were suggested including increased focus on unsuitable investment advice, use of titles and the need to set timelines for completing audits of all registrants. One commenter suggested the need for nationwide enforcement bans.

The OSC will consider these suggestions in managing its enforcement and compliance resources in 2015/2016 and beyond.

d. A number of commenters suggested adding an initiative to make registration checks easier and improve access for investors to obtain information (e.g. registration, discipline history and background).

Ontario became part of the National Registration System in 2013. Proposals to improve the system, including potential changes to its content to better support investors are being developed. Implementation of further enhancements to the system is expected later in 2015.

e. Some commenters were critical of current options for investors to seek compensation from losses, and want to see more done to provide protection to investors when they have suffered losses due to breaches of securities laws.

The OSC is pursuing various methods for effecting compensation for investors, one example was the distribution of frozen funds to harmed investors through the Civil Remedies for Illicit Activities Office.

The OSC does not have the authority to make OBSI decisions binding. The OSC is closely monitoring the recent steps taken to improve dispute resolution through the introduction of amendments to National Instrument 31-103 *Registration Requirements, Exemptions and Ongoing Registrant Obligations* (NI 31-103) and Companion Policy 31-103CP *Registration Requirements, Exemptions and Ongoing Registrant Obligations*. Participating CSA members (the OSC included) and OBSI have entered into a memorandum of understanding (MOU) that creates a framework for OBSI to monitor performance against the standards set out by the CSA. Included in the MOU is a commitment to an independent evaluation of OBSI's operations and practices. We strongly support this process and expect registrants to abide by their obligations.

f. One commenter suggested that the Women on Boards initiative should be broadened to include other forms of diversity.

We value diversity and believe that a strong board with diverse thinking can enhance corporate governance. At this point, being in the first year of this initiative, we have elected to focus our efforts on studying the impact of the new rule relating to Women on Boards and in Senior Management positions. In three years' time, we will conduct an analysis and come to a determination as to what, if any, additional policy measures are appropriate.

g. One commenter noted that the SoP did not specifically mention shareholder democracy issues such as, proxy voting and say on pay. They also proposed the addition of priorities related to environmental, social and governance (ESG) disclosure.

The OSC, together with the CSA, is continuing its work on improving the proxy voting infrastructure. On the January 29, 2015, the CSA published CSA Staff Notice 54-303 *Progress Report on Review of the Proxy Voting Infrastructure* in which we described the results of our findings and next steps, including overseeing the development of industry protocols to improve vote reconciliation practices. We are also continuing to monitor developments in respect of say-on-pay in Canada and other jurisdictions to determine whether it would be necessary and appropriate to mandate say-on-pay under securities regulation. Companies already have an obligation disclose material environmental and governance issues. We have not concluded that it is appropriate at this time to mandate additional ESG disclosures. As a result we will not be amending the SoP to include these issues.

h. We heard from some commenters that want to see a priority added to address potential risks arising from regulatory arbitrage opportunities. A number of commenters urged the OSC to take a more active role in discussions being led by the Ministry of Finance related to financial planning. One solution suggested was to merge the OSC and FSCO to achieve consistency in regulatory approaches across retail managed investment products.

We agree that consistent regulation of like products is an important objective and we strive for that outcome whenever practical. The OSC will be actively monitoring the discussions related to financial planning to understand and, if necessary, provide input on issues that affect investors and market participants. We continue to advocate for harmonized approaches with other regulators, however, any solution involving changes to the current division of regulation across the OSC and FSCO is a government decision and not within the OSC's control.

i. One commenter expressed concern about compliance costs and specifically that the OSC is proposing to raise fees by 13.9% in the upcoming year.

In the revised OSC fee rules, which became effective April 6, 2015, the rates for participation fees, which account for over 80% of OSC revenues were maintained at the 2014 levels and are expected to remain at these levels for three years. Fee revenues increased due to changes in the market activity and a decision to address market participant requests to return to calculating their fees based on their current fiscal year results. Additional details on the current OSC fee rule can be sourced at: https://www.osc.gov.on.ca/en/SecuritiesLaw_rule_20150205_13-502_noc-approval-rev-rep.htm

j. Some commenters were opposed to the current OSC capital formation initiatives including crowdfunding primarily due to concerns about investor protection. Some commenters favoured the move to expand opportunities for capital formation through new exemptions and the need for support for small and medium enterprises (SMEs).

The OSC believes that providing increased opportunities for capital raising, particularly for start-ups and small and medium enterprises (SMEs), is an important element of fostering fair and efficient capital markets. In proposing new prospectus exemptions, the OSC has considered changes to the exempt market regulatory regime as a whole. The OSC has proposed strong investor protection measures, while supporting the capital raising needs of businesses. Some of the key investor protection measures include:

- Limits on the amount investors can invest in securities acquired under a proposed offering memorandum exemption and proposed crowdfunding exemption

- The introduction of risk acknowledgment forms to both the accredited investor exemption and family, friends and business associates exemption

- Ongoing disclosure requirements for non-reporting issuers that raise money in reliance on certain prospectus exemptions

- Requiring that crowdfunding be conducted through registered portals that have certain gatekeeper responsibilities

k. Some commenters suggested that the exempt market initiatives move forward at a faster pace and seemingly in the absence of the rigorous research that has been required for the investor protection initiatives. Concerns were expressed about whether the amount of research conducted to assess the potential impact on markets and investors has been sufficient.

The various OSC exempt market initiatives have moved at an appropriate speed given the complexity of each project and collaboration with our CSA colleagues where appropriate. In developing proposals for new prospectus exemptions, the OSC engaged in extensive research and consultation, including:

- The commissioning of third-party research to gain insight into retail investors' views on investing in SMEs

- Creating an OSC advisory committee made up of volunteers from industry, the securities bar, academia and investor advocates, to advise the OSC on exempt market reform

- Hosting five public town halls and holding 46 targeted stakeholder consultations, including with other Canadian and foreign regulators.

We have also continued to monitor developments in exempt market reform in jurisdictions outside of Canada. The OSC has also reviewed and considered the feedback received from over 800 submissions in response to proposals published for comment in March, 2014. Together, these extensive consultations have informed our proposals.

l. One commenter expressed concern that regulators have chosen to rely on a risk acknowledgement form (for this and other exemptions such as the Accredited Investor exemption) and have done so without any empirical testing to determine whether it helps protect investors.

The OSC has drawn on its extensive experience in developing targeted retail disclosure documents such as Fund Facts, in adopting a revised risk acknowledgment form for the accredited investor exemption. The risk acknowledgment form highlights the key risks associated with investing in the exempt market, describes the individual categories of accredited investor in a plain language and asks investors to confirm the category to which they belong. We believe the risk acknowledgment form will provide improved investor protection.

m. Questions were raised about the OSC's capacity to assure compliance and investor protection in both the public and the expanded exempt markets.

The OSC is also sensitive to the need for a strong compliance focus in the exempt market. The OSC is developing programs for the oversight of the expanded exempt markets and is very mindful of the need to do this effectively to provide appropriate protections for investors. The OSC will be carefully monitoring the impact and the outcomes achieved by these measures to determine if any additional actions are required.

The OSC's primary focus is effective delivery on its core regulatory work. In our SoP we try to only set out our highest priorities and to try to be as transparent and accountable as we can about what we will deliver on those priorities, including when we will deliver and how we will measure our performance. The OSC will also focus resources on several other important initiatives that have been identified for inclusion by various commenters. However, in keeping with our goal to remain focused on and committed to our core work and highest priority items, we will not be adding any additional priorities to our 2015-2016 SoP.

All of the comment letters are available on our website www.osc.gov.on.ca. The Statement of Priorities will serve as the guide for the Commission's operations. Following delivery of the Statement of Priorities to the Minister, we will also publish on our website a report on our progress against our 2014-2015 priorities.

2015-2016 OSC Statement of Priorities

Introduction

We are pleased to present the OSC Chair's Statement of Priorities (SoP) for the Commission for the year commencing April 1, 2015. The *Securities Act* (Ontario) requires the Ontario Securities Commission (OSC) to publish the SoP in its Bulletin and to deliver it to the Minister by June 30 of each year. This SoP also supports the OSC's commitment to delivering its regulatory services effectively and with accountability.

This SoP sets out the OSC's strategic goals and the specific initiatives that the OSC will pursue in support of each of these goals in 2015-2016. The SoP also describes the environmental factors that the OSC has considered in setting these goals.

OSC Vision

To be an effective and responsive securities regulator — fostering a culture of integrity and compliance and instilling investor confidence in the capital markets.

OSC Mandate

The OSC's mandate (established by statute) is to provide protection to investors from unfair, improper or fraudulent practices and to foster fair and efficient capital markets and confidence in capital markets.

Our Environment — Challenges and Issues

Capital market structures and products continue to evolve at a rapid pace. The regulatory framework for Ontario's capital markets is designed to provide protection to investors while fostering fair and efficient capital markets. A wide range of issues and risks challenges the OSC's ability to achieve its vision and mandate. Public confidence in these markets can be affected by many factors, including the stability of the financial system, the economic health of the country and the volatility in the marketplace. Key challenges and issues that may influence our policy agenda and affect our operations and how we use our resources are set out below.

Globalization continues to have wide-ranging impacts on our capital markets. Extreme mobility of capital heightens the need for the OSC to support the competitiveness of Ontario capital markets and the importance of regulatory alignment both domestically and around the world. It creates a strong need for engagement and appropriate coordination with foreign regulators to achieve effective cross-jurisdiction enforcement or mutual reliance in other areas that can deliver better regulatory outcomes. The OSC must also remain focused on seeking proportionate regulatory solutions and opportunities to avoid or reduce undue burdens on business as regulatory burden is a key component affecting the competitiveness and efficiency of Ontario's capital markets. Over- or under-regulation may deter innovation, capital raising, and productive and appropriate risk taking.

Harmonization and Coordination need to be key focus areas for the OSC given the international, national and interprovincial nature of the markets it regulates and because capital flows are not constrained by borders. The OSC also works with the Canadian Securities Administrators (CSA) to harmonize rules and their application across the country where practicable. The OSC continues to play an active role in international organizations such as the International Organization of Securities Commissions (IOSCO) to influence and promote changes to international securities regulation to benefit Ontario markets and participants.

The OSC is working with the Ontario Government and other participating jurisdictions to implement a cooperative capital markets regulatory regime to deliver more efficient and effective regulation of the capital markets. The OSC must balance the need to maintain an engaged and effective OSC regulatory presence while contributing to a smooth transition to a Capital Markets Regulatory Authority (CMRA) that addresses the needs of investors and market participants.

Ongoing Structural Changes in our Financial System will continue to introduce a range of challenges. Evolving business models, growth in exempt market activities (including crowdfunding) and the expanding use of social media and mobile technology will continue to pose regulatory challenges.

Financial markets are increasingly dispersed and complex and the complexity of financial products, markets and technology continues to evolve at a rapid pace. For example, growth in clearing through derivatives clearing organizations and new requirements for uncleared swaps and monitoring have implications in terms of market concentration and investor choice. The transparency, fairness and liquidity of fixed income markets can also affect the cost of capital and investor alternatives. Investors also must deal with complexities and variations in the design of investment funds, retail products and hybrid securities.

Digital evolution continues to disrupt and transform the capital markets landscape. This evolution can be seen in a wide range of examples that challenge the OSC's ability to maintain an effective and efficient regulatory framework to support rapidly evolving market structures and processes. Evolving market channels (e.g. automated financial advice) could redefine client wealth management expectations as well as the fees charged for advice. Increased dependence on digital connectivity, combined with exponential growth in data, creates challenges with data management and raises potential exposure to resilience issues and disruptions, including cyber security issues.

Demographics, including a growing seniors' population, will continue to generate a range of investor-focused issues. Expectations that the OSC will support and protect investors continue to grow and are reinforced by increasingly active investor advocacy groups. The OSC will need to continue to reach out and connect with investors and understand their needs, to advance investor interests and to educate investors about market changes.

Reliance on advice is expected to continue to grow to meet changing investor risk profiles and more complex investment choices and structural shifts, such as the continuing shift from defined benefit to defined contribution pension plans. In addition, new Exempt Market offerings are expected to attract many new investors to the capital markets who are inexperienced and would benefit from the advice of investment professionals. As a result, issues related to market conduct, firms' compliance cultures and how advisors meet the interests of their clients will continue to remain important areas of focus. Investors are seeking an environment where reliance on their advisors is well-placed, the advice being provided is suitable, and any conflicts are managed appropriately. Through achievement of these outcomes, the OSC will foster investors' confidence to invest in our capital markets.

A well-functioning investor/advisor relationship is critical to the economic well-being of Ontarians and ultimately to achieving healthy capital markets. The Ontario Government is currently examining policy alternatives for more tailored regulation of financial planning, including analysis of relevant issues (e.g. sufficiency of regulatory frameworks, proficiency and education requirements and the use of multiple titles). Better alignment of the interests of firms and investors can be achieved by improving standards of financial advice, raising competency and increasing transparency regarding financial advice.

Human capital continues to be an area of strategic focus for the OSC. The OSC operates in a competitive environment where attracting, motivating and retaining top talent is a key challenge. It will be critically important for the OSC to invest in data and information systems and continue to provide the right tools and training to leverage the talents of its people.

Increasing regulatory burden affects the competiveness and efficiency of Ontario's capital markets. Regulatory burden continues to present challenges for market participants as the complexity of regulatory requirements and the resources required to comply continue to grow. The OSC will need to examine whether the existing rules remain effective, and determine whether they inhibit or promote high-quality capital markets and deliver a system that protects investors and promotes their confidence. The OSC must balance the costs of complying with the regulatory protections that safeguard investor needs with the concern that these costs may induce market participants to access non-traditional, less regulated markets for capital.

OSC 2015-2016 Regulatory Goals

1. Deliver strong investor protection — *The OSC will champion investor protection, especially for retail investors*

2. Deliver responsive regulation — *The OSC will identify important issues and deal with them in a timely way*

3. Deliver effective compliance, supervision and enforcement — *The OSC will deliver effective compliance oversight and pursue fair, vigorous and timely enforcement*

4. Promote financial stability through effective oversight — *The OSC will continue to identify, address and mitigate systemic risk and promote stability by implementing programs to effectively oversee and supervise our capital markets including the OTC derivatives market, the fixed income market, and key infrastructure entities such as clearing agencies.*

5. Be an innovative, accountable and efficient organization — *The OSC will be an innovative and efficient organization through excellence in the execution of its operations, and will demonstrate accountability in fulfilling its mandate and achieving its goals*

The OSC has accomplished much in moving its regulatory agenda forward and has made a number of key advances in the way it approaches its work. The OSC has made important advances in providing guidance to market participants and investors and in using open and consultative processes to assess and address issues. The OSC has significantly grown the level of its cooperation with many entities, including Federal Finance, the Office of the Superintendent of Financial Institutions and the Heads of Agencies, in order to achieve more harmonized and coordinated outcomes. The amount of enforcement activity conducted with police and other enforcement bodies continues to expand, resulting in more successes across a broader range of enforcement actions. The impact of the OSC's efforts internationally is growing, resulting in timely insight, understanding and input into emerging regulatory issues.

Confidence in fair and efficient markets is a prerequisite for economic growth. The OSC is the largest regulator in the largest market in Canada. Our actions have implications for Ontario, for the rest of Canada and, given the global nature of capital markets, internationally. The OSC remains committed to promoting safe, trustworthy and efficient markets in Ontario and has identified a broad range of initiatives to improve the regulatory framework in Ontario. Although the OSC SoP is focused on our plan for 2015-2016, in some cases these initiatives are ongoing from prior years and/or will not be completed within 2015-2016. Initiatives often span more than one year for various reasons including:

- The nature and complexity of most issues warrant careful analysis and review of potential options and implications

- Consultation contributes to better outcomes; however, consultation takes time. This is particularly true in achieving national consensus with other regulators on harmonized approaches

- Regulatory choices can have fundamental and profound impacts on industry. The cost of being wrong can be very significant and the impacts on industry are usually difficult, if not impossible, to reverse

In some instances, specific priorities are not carried forward to the SoP in the following year. This does not necessarily mean that work on the initiative has stopped but rather that its priority relative to other initiatives no longer warrants inclusion in the SoP, the remaining work is minimal, or the next steps involve integrating the changes into the OSC's daily operations.

This document sets out the most important priority areas where the OSC intends to focus resources and actions in 2015-2016. It is important to note that the majority of OSC resources are focused on delivering the core regulatory work (authorizations, reviews, compliance and enforcement) undertaken by the OSC to maintain high standards of regulation in Ontario's capital markets. A smaller proportion of OSC resources are applied to our high profile work on SoP initiatives. Each of the proposed priorities has been aligned under one of the five OSC regulatory goals.

Goal 1 — Deliver strong investor protection

The OSC is strongly committed to delivering on its mandate to protect investors and is proposing a number of initiatives to enhance investor protection. Investors need to be confident in the market and products they invest in. A key step to achieving this outcome is to improve the alignment of the interests of advisors and firms with those of investors. Know your client (KYC), know your product (KYP) and suitability are among the most fundamental obligations owed to a client. This is particularly important given the degree to which investors rely on advice.

Investors need to be confident that the advice they receive involving financial products and services is unbiased and of high quality. Investors need to better understand the cost of advice and be assured that compensation structures will not adversely affect the quality of advice they receive or their long term investment outcomes. At a more fundamental level it is important to achieve greater consistency in the level and type of disclosure across similar products. To maximize the value of improved disclosure the OSC also needs to proactively inform and educate investors so they are better prepared and able to invest.

Investor profiles are diverse and this raises complex challenges. Aging demographics raise a number of investor protection issues. Older Canadians are facing challenges to achieve sufficient investment returns either for their own retirement or for aging parents. New investors, in particular those attracted by new investment alternatives provided by Exempt Markets, may be inexperienced and require expert support and guidance. Other vulnerable investor groups can also be at risk as they strive to support education costs for children or to meet lifestyle consumption goals. As each of these groups searches for yield and/or capital appreciation, its members can become susceptible to fraud and other investment risks that can have life-changing outcomes. The wide disparity in the level of financial literacy and understanding among investor groups is a key source of risk that needs to be addressed through outreach, education and regulation.

Achieving consensus on harmonized approaches to improve investors' confidence and trust in our markets, and the advisors and firms they interact with, will take more than one year to achieve. The priorities set out below are designed to improve the alignment of the expectations of investors and the actions of their advisors and assist investors to more effectively meet the challenging environment they face.

Putting the Interests of Investors First

Priority Issue	Advance regulatory reforms that put the interests of investors first	
Action Plan/Next Steps	a.	Develop and evaluate regulatory provisions to create a best interest duty
	b.	Develop and evaluate targeted regulatory reforms and/or guidance under NI 31-103 to improve the advisor/client relationship
	c.	Finalize analysis of advisor compensation practices and address those practices that are inconsistent with current regulatory requirements
Success Measures/Expected Outcomes	a.	Analysis of approaches for creating a best interest duty completed and proposals developed
	b.	Analysis of targeted amendments and/or guidance to NI 31-103 completed
	c.	Staff Notice of compensation review findings including expectations for compliance and best practices

Reviewing Compensation Arrangements in Mutual Funds and Empowering Investors through Better Disclosure

Priority Issue	Determine what regulatory action is needed to address embedded commissions and other types of compensation arrangements and improve retail investment product disclosure	
Action Plan/Next Steps	a.	Complete third-party research to determine how mutual fund compensation models may influence advisor behaviour
	b.	Review and evaluate with the CSA the research results and publish the findings
	c.	Support implementation of pre-sale delivery of Fund Facts for mutual funds and continue to work with the CSA to implement the Point of Sale initiative; specifically, publish rules for comment:
	i.	to introduce a mandated CSA risk classification methodology to improve the comparability of risk ratings of mutual funds in the Fund Facts
	ii.	to introduce a new summary disclosure document for ETFs (ETF Facts) and require it to be delivered
	a.	Third-party research completed and Staff Notice setting out key findings published

| Success Measures/Expected Outcomes | b. | Actionable results identified by the OSC including a recommendation made about embedded commissions and other types of compensation arrangements |
| | c. | Rules to introduce a mandated CSA risk classification methodology and to introduce a new summary disclosure document for ETFs published for comment |

Improve Education, Outreach and Advocacy for Investors

Priority Issue		Advance investor protection and support to retail investors by expanding the OSC's investor engagement, education and outreach
	a.	Improve the OSC's investor focus by integrating the OSC Office of the Investor with the OSC Investor Education Fund to create the new Office of Investor Policy, Education and Outreach, to:
	i.	establish and implement the OSC's investor education strategy
Action Plan/Next Steps	ii.	better inform investors about market events, product innovations and key OSC regulatory and supervisory activities by publishing alerts and bulletins and working with investor networks and organizations on education and outreach campaigns
	iii.	refresh and expand outreach programs, such as OSC in the Community, with a focus on potentially vulnerable investors
	b.	Obtain a better understanding of investor issues and needs through targeted research, seminars and roundtables
	c.	Respond to the issues identified at the 2014/15 seniors roundtable by:
	i.	completing targeted research to improve the OSC's understanding of seniors' financial needs and challenges
	ii.	collaborating with SROs and investor and industry associations to identify ways to be more responsive to seniors
Success Measures/Expected Outcomes	a.	Existing partnerships strengthened and new external relationships created to inform and advance investor focused issues
	b.	Specific recommendations from the seniors roundtable addressed
	c.	Relationships with key senior stakeholder organizations and networks established and strengthened

Goal 2 — Deliver responsive regulation

To meet the OSC's mandate the bulk of its resources are focused on delivering our core regulatory functions. As a gatekeeper to the markets, the OSC vets potential participants to confirm that they are suitable to participate in our markets and interact with investors or to raise capital in our markets. Compliance and enforcement activities continue to play a central role in maintaining and enhancing trust in Ontario's capital markets. Effective registration and compliance oversight regimes, combined with timely enforcement, help deter misconduct and non-compliance by registrants and market participants.

Within the context of today's capital markets, we continue to believe that a national securities regulator will enhance investor protection, foster efficient rulemaking and globally competitive markets in Canada, strengthen our capacity to identify and manage systemic risk and solidify Canada's international reputation for regulating its financial system. While working with the participating jurisdictions to transition smoothly to the CMRA it will be critical for the OSC to maintain high standards of regulation and to keep stakeholders informed and engaged throughout the transition period. The OSC will also need to work with the CSA to seek harmonized approaches to regulation as much as possible.

Our regulatory framework needs to remain current, responsive to the continuing evolution of market structures and products, and supportive of capital formation in Ontario. The OSC must carefully balance the desire to broaden investment alternatives and improve access to capital with the need to maintain appropriate investor protections. To support the implementation of a regulatory framework to expand exempt markets and achieve this balance, the OSC will implement effective oversight and supervision processes. The OSC will need to work effectively with IIROC to achieve outcomes that best respond to these issues.

Where regulatory solutions are not achieving desired outcomes the OSC will need to take action to make necessary changes to achieve appropriate outcomes. Where access and transparency of markets are not sufficient, the OSC will need to look for solutions to improve the fairness and integrity of those markets where the needs of investors and those seeking capital can be achieved with mutual benefit.

The OSC introduced disclosure requirements in 2014 to promote the transparency and representation of women on Boards and in executive and senior management positions at senior exchange-listed issuers. The OSC continues to strongly support this outcome and will seek to maintain momentum on this issue to achieve better corporate decision-making.

Women on Boards and in Executive and Senior Management Positions

Priority Issue		Continue efforts to promote transparency and representation of women on Boards and in executive and senior management positions for senior exchange-listed issuers
	a.	Receive and review issuer disclosures on representation of women on Boards and in executive and senior management positions
Action Plan	b.	Publish results of the disclosure review
	c.	Hold consultation roundtable to discuss results
Success Measures/	a.	Disclosure review completed and results are published
Expected Outcomes	b.	Continued improvement in the transparency of Board selection and composition for senior exchange-listed issuers

Improve Access to Capital

Priority Issue		Foster capital formation in Ontario while maintaining appropriate investor safeguards
	a.	Develop and publish rules to implement the following:
	i.	offering memorandum exemption from prospectus requirements
	ii.	crowdfunding regime
	iii.	modernized prospectus-exempt rights offering regime
Action Plan/Next Steps	iv.	new reporting requirements regarding exempt market distributions
	b.	With the CSA, develop an enhanced and harmonized report of exempt distributions to facilitate better monitoring of new prospectus exemptions
	c.	Conduct compliance and pre-registration reviews focussing on these new exemptions and EMD portal business models. Meet with SROs to ensure our approaches to oversight are consistent and opportunities for regulatory arbitrage are minimized
	a.	Rules, companion policy and guidance for the proposed new exemptions published for comment and delivered to the Minister for approval
Success Measures/Expected Outcomes	b.	Significant areas of non-compliance identified are appropriately addressed by registrants. Reduction in non-compliance by registrants
	c.	Improved ability to monitor exempt market activity more efficiently

Market Structure Evolution

Priority Issue		Respond to issues (market data fees, trading fees) arising from the implementation of the Order Protection Rule (OPR)
Action Plan/Next Steps	a.	OPR framework amended in response to comments received from publication in 2014/2015, including finalizing approaches for dealing with trading fees and market data fees
Success Measures/Expected Outcomes	a.	Final changes to update the OPR framework, including approaches for dealing with trading fees and market data fees, are published

Goal 3 — Deliver effective compliance, supervision and enforcement

Effective compliance and strong enforcement are the cornerstones of protecting investors and fostering confidence in capital markets. The importance of effective compliance and supervision continues to grow as domestic market structures, processes and products (expansion of exempt market, new markets) and international (IOSCO, PFMI) guidelines and responsibilities evolve. As part of its core work the OSC will

Part 1:
PROCEDURE

continue to undertake targeted compliance reviews of high risk and new registrants, specifically, online advice and portal business models. We will also conduct targeted prospectus and continuous disclosure reviews of issuers, investment funds and structured products that respond to market developments and product innovations, and publish OSC staff guidance as warranted.

The OSC continues to seek innovative approaches to identify serious breaches of Ontario securities law. Effective enforcement in today's increasingly complex markets requires new tools, enhanced computer forensics and other technological support. The OSC recently announced its intention to pursue a whistleblower program to achieve more timely, actionable information to deter misconduct. Through this initiative the OSC hopes to minimize harm to investors and better preserve the integrity of Ontario capital markets.

The OSC needs to reduce its enforcement timelines, including more timely issuance of its orders, decisions and reasons. A key to achieving this outcome will be measures to improve access to the tribunal and make the hearing process more streamlined, accessible and efficient.

Enhance Compliance through Effective Inspections, Supervision and Oversight

Priority Issue	Protect investors and foster confidence in our markets by confirming compliance with our regulatory framework	
Action Plan/Next Steps	a.	Develop and implement programs to effectively oversee an expanded exempt market in Ontario including a risk based supervision program for issuers and registrants and tailored pre-registration reviews and compliance examination programs
	b.	Implement data analysis for systemic risk oversight and market conduct purposes including the development of analytical tools and the creation of snapshot descriptions of the Canadian OTC derivatives market
Success Measures/Expected Outcomes	a.	New supervision programs in place and initial results of programs and reports on exempt market activity developed and published
	b.	Systems for oversight and to facilitate systemic analysis of the Ontario derivatives markets will be in place
	c.	Compliance program for the trade reporting rule in place. Reviews of largest derivatives participants commenced

Earlier Identification of Fraud and Other Violations

Priority Issue	Deter misconduct by seeking more timely, actionable information that will allow the OSC to pursue impactful cases of misconduct and serious breaches of securities law	
Action Plan/ Next Steps	a.	Complete consultations on proposed OSC whistleblower program
	b.	Respond to comments and publish OSC whistleblower policy, if appropriate
Success Measures/Expected Outcomes	a.	OSC whistleblower program launched, if appropriate

Enhance Enforcement and Adjudicative Processes

Priority Issue	Achieve better outcomes from OSC enforcement and adjudicative processes by introducing better tools, analytics and approaches	
Action Plan/Next Steps	a.	Improve technological support to Enforcement staff, including the Joint Serious Offences Team, through enhanced computer forensics and the capacity to conduct e-discoveries and e-hearings
Success Measures/Expected Outcomes	a.	The OSC's e-hearing directive and applicable case management guidelines result in reduced case timelines

Timely, Fair and Efficient Adjudication

Priority Issue	The OSC will improve its case management and adjudicative processes through more transparent policies, practices and procedures and more timely issuance of its orders, decisions and reasons	
Action Plan/Next Steps	a.	Continue the implementation of its Electronic Case Management System and Hearing system and use of technology to enhance accessibility for respondents and the public by holding electronic hearings
	b.	Implement and monitor adherence to its internal guideline for the timely release of decisions within six months
	c.	Adhere to newly adopted Case Management Practice Directive regarding a new Case Management Timeline for Enforcement Proceedings

Goal 4 — Promote financial stability through effective oversight

Capital markets have become increasingly interconnected by technology, business models and investment flows. The interconnectedness of markets creates the potential for systemic risk within the wider financial framework, and securities regulators have assumed an important role in maintaining its stability. Success in managing this complex area will have a significant impact on market confidence and ultimately the health of our capital markets. It is critical for the OSC to work with other financial market regulators to design and build a regulatory framework and operational programs to effectively oversee and supervise the OTC derivatives market and its participants.

There are approximately $500 billion in corporate bonds outstanding in Canada and almost $500 billion in corporate bonds traded in the Canadian secondary market in 2014. In Canada, corporate bond trading is subject to limited post-trade transparency for both regulators and investors. The OSC is taking steps to enhance regulation in the fixed income market and to identify opportunities where changes to regulatory approaches could improve market transparency and better protect investor interests.

Promote Financial Stability through Effective Oversight

Priority Issue	Advance OSC systemic risk oversight and analytic capabilities	
Action Plan/ Next Steps	a.	Develop rules for the clearing of OTC derivatives
	b.	Develop a registrant regulation framework for derivatives market participants
	c.	Implement rules and a compliance program for OTC derivatives trade reporting
	d.	Implement rule/policy framework for clearing agencies to incorporate CPMI/IOSCO revised standards
	e.	Develop recommendations to implement Principle 14 Segregation and Portability under the CPMI IOSCO Principles for Financial Market Infrastructures
Success Measures/Expected Outcomes	a.	Clearing and reporting rules for OTC derivatives that align with international standards and meet G20 commitments will be in place
	b.	National Instrument for Registration of Derivatives Dealers published for comment
	c.	Notice that outlines recommendations for implementation of segregation and portability (other than for OTC derivatives) published

Regulation of the Fixed Income Market

Priority Issue	Enhance regulation in the fixed income market by increasing transparency, improving market integrity and evaluating access	
Action Plan	a.	Publish a regulatory plan, working with IIROC, that addresses key issues identified in the fixed income review, including requirements to increase post trade transparency
Success Measures/ Expected Outcomes	a.	Plan published and implementation of proposed changes underway
	b.	Improved post-trade transparency allowing more informed decision-making among all market participants

Goal 5 — Be an innovative, accountable and efficient organization

Securities regulators are facing growing pressures to respond appropriately to market issues while avoiding over-regulation. The need for a cost-effective regulatory framework is critical as capital moves more quickly across multiple marketplaces that span jurisdictional borders. The OSC is strengthening its core functions, including compliance and enforcement, and adjusting how it works to develop the capacity to efficiently deliver the right regulation for investors, market participants and markets. The OSC needs to continue its efforts to upgrade procedures, practices and systems as part of a commitment to robust processes and high-quality execution, including:

- Implementing a consistent organizational approach for managing risks

- Increasing reliance on research and analytics in the way we work, including conducting regulatory impact analyses prior to initiating proposed policy projects

- Expanding the use of technology to gather and analyze data and other information, including information required for compliance and adjudicative matters

Management and staff will continue these efforts to reposition the organization as a more proactive and agile securities regulator that fosters the integrity of capital markets in Ontario.

Harmonization and coordination are key elements in achieving cost-effective regulation. Increasingly, the OSC must deal with regulatory matters that are international, not just provincial or national, in their scope, such as the oversight of emerging markets issuers and the regulation of OTC derivatives. More than ever before, the OSC regulates within the context of a global marketplace, which underlines the imperative of engaging with our international counterparts, especially through IOSCO, to deliver proactive regulation. The OSC needs to provide leadership to the multinational reform agenda on matters that promote the convergence of stronger international market conduct standards that

Part 1: PROCEDURE

benefit investors and market participants. Participation in international regulatory fora allows the OSC to obtain timely insight and understanding of emerging compliance and regulatory issues to develop an informed, proactive oversight approach.

Effectively Influence the International Regulatory Agenda

Priority Issue	Influence the international regulatory agenda to reflect the needs of Ontario's markets	
Action Plan/Next Steps	a.	Enhance our ability to influence and shape the international standard setting process by seeking leadership roles within IOSCO (e.g., Chair committees and task forces)
	b.	Perform greater proactive analyses of risks/issues identified by other jurisdictions globally by participating in bi-lateral meetings with key regulatory partners
Success Measures/Expected Outcomes	a.	Other regulators seek our views and advice in developing regulatory standards because of the value we bring
	b.	Ontario's interests are reflected in international initiatives that relate to issues affecting our markets
	c.	Canadian regulatory framework keeps pace with global regulatory developments. Harmonized regulatory approaches internationally and within the CSA, where applicable, reduce regulatory burden on our market participants

Proactive use of Data and Research

Priority Issue	Improve policy development and regulatory outcomes by increasing the integration of economic and quantitative analysis, including regulatory impact analyses, in the development of policies and rules	
Action Plan/Next Steps	a.	Continue to develop data collection, management and assessment practices
	b.	Demonstrate enhanced use of economic analysis, research and data analysis within the OSC including completing a regulatory impact analysis for proposed policy projects
Success Measures/ Expected Outcomes	a.	Use of research reflected in OSC policy initiatives and OSC publications
	b.	Completion of one major research project

2015-2016 Financial Outlook

OSC Revenues and Surplus

The OSC is forecasting 2015-2016 revenues to increase by 11.4% from 2014-2015 actual revenues. The forecast reflects fee rates set out in the OSC's fee rules (13-502 and 13-503), which became effective April 6, 2015. The key change to the new fee rules is the return to the previous method of calculating participation fees. Under the new rules, we will use the most recent financial year information, as opposed to a reference fiscal year. As a result, fees due to the OSC will become less predictable as the amount payable by market participants will increase or decrease based on actual changes in business conditions and performance. Under the new fee rules, the OSC expects to generate a surplus of $6.6 million in 2015-2016 to add to its expected 2014-2015 ending surplus of $14.3 million, for a total surplus of $20.9 million as at March 2016. When the new fee rules were developed and published, the OSC advised that they would be relatively revenue neutral over the three-year period, with an expected surplus in 2015-2016, a smaller surplus in 2016-2017 and a deficit in 2017-2018. This is because revenues are expected to be relatively flat over the term of the rule, while expenses are expected to increase each year. The budget approved by the OSC Board for 2015-2016 is in line with this expectation. As a result, the above-noted ending general surplus is expected to be $19.2 million by the end of 2017-2018.

2015-2016 Budget Approach

Our regulatory framework needs to remain current and responsive to the continuing evolution of market structures and products and supportive of capital formation in Ontario. The OSC must carefully balance the desire to improve access to capital with the need to retain appropriate investor protections. The 2015-2016 SoP sets out the OSC's key priorities to meet these challenges. Achievement of these priorities is a key driver of the proposed increases to the 2015-2016 OSC Budget as this will require focused investments in the following four areas:

- improving education, outreach and advocacy through creation of the new Office of Investor Policy, Education and Outreach

- development of a new regulatory framework (including supervision and oversight) for the derivatives market

- enhanced oversight of the exempt market

- improving the OSC's information technology, in particular to support a greater reliance on data and research.

The budget reflects an increase of 6.0% from the 2014-2015 budget. Salaries and benefits, which comprise $80.7 million or 73.9% of the budget, represent an increase of $4.8 million or 5.9% over 2014-2015 spending. The key reasons for this increase are:

- approval of new positions to support the investments noted above

- underspending in 2014-2015 by maintaining vacancies for longer than planned as a cost control measure and due to some shifting or deferring of priorities as a result of the CMRA initiative. Therefore, budgeting of full-year costs for vacancies and staff hired throughout 2014-2015 contributes to the increase.

The OSC will maintain fiscal responsibility in its other operating areas as evidenced by the fact that budget amounts will decrease, or remain flat in approximately 40% of its operating branches. The budget also includes resources for work toward the successful implementation of the CMRA.

The capital budget primarily reflects the build-out of recently acquired additional space, as well as the cost to support the OSC's information technology needs, including a data warehouse to support Derivatives oversight.

(thousands)	2014-15 Budget	2014-2015 Actual	2015-2016 Budget	2015-2016 Budget to 2014-2015 Budget		2015-2016 Budget to 2014-2015 Actual	
Revenues	$101,325	$103,936	$115,782	$14,457	14.3%	$11,846	11.4%
Expenses	$102,976	$95,875	$109,182	$6,206	6.0%	$13,307	13.9%
Deficiency of Revenue Compared with Expenses	($1,651)	$8,061	$6,600	$8,251		($1,461)	
Capital Expenditures	$3,349	$1,616	$3,101	($248)		$1,485	

OSC Staff Notice 11-773 — The Investor Perspective

Date: November 5, 2015

38 O.S.C.B. 9258

[Not reproduced]

1.2 — Applications

See also OPS 2.1 and NPS 11-203.

National Policy 12-201 — Mutual Reliance Review System for Exemptive Relief Applications

Date: November 19, 1999 as amended July 12, 2002, August 2, 2004 and September 19, 2005

22 O.S.C.B. 7298, 25 O.S.C.B. 4447, 27 O.S.C.B. 6987 and 28 O.S.C.B. 7166

[Rescinded (2008) 31 O.S.C.B. 1009; replaced by NPS 11-203]

Adopted: (1999) 22 O.S.C.B. 7293; Request for Comments: (1998) 21 O.S.C.B. 7211 and (1998) 21 O.S.C.B. 621; Amendment to Policy: 25 O.S.C.B. 4445; Amendment to Schedule A to Policy: 27 O.S.C.B. 6987; Amendment to Policy: 28 O.S.C.B. 7166.

National Policy 12-202 — Revocation of a Compliance-related Cease Trade Order

Date: July 27, 2007 as amended effective March 17, 2008, December 15, 2008 and January 1, 2011

30 O.S.C.B. 6735, 31 O.S.C.B. (Supp. 2) 257, 31 O.S.C.B. 11350, 33 O.S.C.B. (Supp. 5) 37

Table of Contents

PART 1 — INTRODUCTION

This policy provides guidance for issuers that are subject to a CTO (as defined below) issued as a result of failing to comply with continuous disclosure requirements.

This policy explains what an issuer should do to apply for a partial or full revocation of a CTO. It describes what the issuer should file, the general type of review that the securities regulatory authorities (or "we") will perform, and explains some of the factors that we will consider when determining whether to grant a full or partial revocation of the CTO.

Although this policy provides guidance to issuers applying for a revocation order, the policy also applies, where the context permits, to a securityholder or other party applying for a revocation order.

PART 2 — DEFINITIONS

In this policy:

"annual meeting requirement" means the requirement in applicable corporate legislation or any equivalent non-corporate requirement to hold an annual meeting of securityholders;

"application" means an application for a partial or full revocation of a CTO submitted to the applicable jurisdictions (see Appendix A for section references); in British Columbia, if the CTO has been in effect for 90 days or less, the filing of the required continuous disclosure documents constitutes the application;

"CTO" means a cease trade order issued against an issuer or its management or insiders prohibiting trading in the securities of the issuer as a result of a failure to comply with continuous disclosure requirements;

"MD&A" means management's discussion and analysis as defined in National Instrument 51-102 *Continuous Disclosure Obligations*;

"MRFP" means management's report on fund performance as defined in National Instrument 81-106 *Investment Fund Continuous Disclosure*; and

"NI 52-109" means National Instrument 52-109 *Certification of Disclosure in Issuers' Annual and Interim Filings*;

"partial revocation order" means an order that permits one or more issuers or individuals to conduct specific trades when a CTO is in effect.

In Quebec, "trade" is not defined in the *Securities Act* ("QSA"). This policy covers all securities transactions that may be the object of an order provided for in paragraph 3 of section 265 QSA.

Terms defined in National Instrument 14-101 *Definitions* have the same meaning in this policy.

PART 3 — QUALIFICATION AND CRITERIA FOR REVOCATION

3.1 Full revocations — (1) Filing requirements — Generally, we will not exercise our discretion to grant a full revocation order, subject to subsections 3.1(2) and 3.1(3), unless the issuer has filed all of its outstanding continuous disclosure. The most common deficiencies relate to disclosure required under:

(a) National Instrument 51-102 *Continuous Disclosure Obligations*;

(b) National Instrument 52-109 *Certification of Disclosure in Issuers' Annual and Interim Filings*;

(c) National Instrument 81-106 *Investment Fund Continuous Disclosure*;

(d) National Instrument 43-101 *Standards of Disclosure for Mineral Projects*;

(e) National Instrument 51-101 *Standards of Disclosure for Oil and Gas Activities*;

(f) National Instrument 52-110 *Audit Committees*; and

(g) National Instrument 58-101 *Disclosure of Corporate Governance Practices*.

(2) Exceptions to interim filing requirements — In exercising our discretion to revoke a CTO, we may elect not to require the issuer to file certain outstanding interim financial reports, interim MD&A, interim MRFP or interim certificates under NI 52-109, subject to subsection 3.1(3), if the issuer has filed:

(a) all outstanding audited annual financial statements, annual MD&A, annual MRFP and annual certificates under NI 52-109 required to be filed under applicable securities legislation;

(b) all outstanding annual information forms, information circulars and material change reports required to be filed under applicable securities legislation; and

(c) all outstanding interim financial reports (which include the applicable comparatives from the prior fiscal year), interim MD&A, interim MRFP and interim certificates under NI 52-109 for all interim periods in the current fiscal year required to be filed under applicable securities legislation.

(3) Exceptions to annual filing requirements — In certain cases, an issuer seeking a revocation order may consider that the length of time that has elapsed since the date of the CTO may make the preparation and filing of all outstanding disclosure impractical, or of limited use to investors. This may particularly apply to disclosure for periods that ended more than three years before the date of the application, or periods prior to a significant change in the issuer's business. An issuer seeking a revocation order in these circumstances should make detailed submissions explaining its position. In appropriate cases, we will consider whether the filing of certain outstanding disclosure might not be necessary as a precondition of a revocation order. The factors we may consider include:

(a) age of information to be contained in the continuous disclosure filing — information from older periods may be less relevant than information from more recent periods;

(b) access to records — lack of access to records may hinder compliance with some filing requirements;

(c) activity during the period — if an issuer was inactive or changed its business at any time while it was cease-traded, disclosure of information from or prior to this time may be less relevant;

(d) length of time the CTO has been in effect; and

(e) whether the historical disclosure relates to significant transactions or litigation.

We generally consider that disclosure for periods within the most recent three financial years of the issuer provides useful information for investors. We generally do not consider the time and cost required to prepare disclosure to be a compelling factor in our determination of the disclosure to be provided in connection with an application to revoke a CTO.

(4) Outstanding fees — Before we will issue a revocation order, the issuer must pay all outstanding fees to each relevant jurisdiction. Outstanding fees generally include, where applicable, all activity and participation fees, and late filing fees.

Depending on how long the CTO has been in effect, and whether the issuer filed its continuous disclosure documents in a timely manner while it was cease-traded, the amount of outstanding fees can be considerable. Before submitting an application, issuers should contact the relevant regulators to confirm the fees that will be payable.

(5) Annual meeting — An issuer that applies for the revocation of a CTO should ensure that it has complied with the annual meeting requirement.

If the issuer has not complied with the annual meeting requirement, we will generally not exercise our discretion to issue a revocation order unless the issuer provides an undertaking to the relevant securities regulatory authorities to hold the annual meeting within three months after the date on which the CTO is revoked.

Any such undertaking will not, however, relieve the issuer from any obligation it may have under the relevant legislation containing the annual meeting requirement.

(6) Recurring CTOs — An issuer that has been subject to another CTO within the 12-month period before the date of the current CTO should provide a detailed explanation in its application of the reasons for the multiple defaults.

In addition, we may request that the issuer provide to us information relating to disclosure controls and procedures that the issuer applies to ensure compliance with continuous disclosure requirements.

(7) News release — When a revocation order is issued, if the revocation of the CTO is a "material change", the issuer is required by securities legislation to issue and file a news release and material change report. If the revocation of the CTO is not a material change, the issuer should consider issuing a news release that announces the revocation of the CTO and outlines the issuer's future plans.

If the issuer has ceased to carry on an active business, or its business purpose has been abandoned, the news release should disclose this. The news release should also describe the issuer's future plans or state that the issuer has no future plans.

3.2 Partial revocations — (1) Permitted transactions — We will consider granting partial revocation orders to permit certain transactions involving trades in securities of the issuer, such as private placements or share-for-debt transactions, to allow the issuer to recapitalize or to raise sufficient funds to prepare and file outstanding continuous disclosure documents. We will generally not exercise our discretion to grant a partial revocation order unless the issuer intends to subsequently apply for a full revocation order and reasonably anticipates having sufficient resources after the proposed transaction to bring its continuous disclosure and fees up to date.

Other circumstances may arise that warrant a partial revocation order. For example, we will generally grant a partial revocation order to permit a securityholder to sell securities for a nominal amount solely to establish a tax loss.

Issuers may wish to consult their legal counsel to determine whether a particular transaction constitutes a trade and therefore requires an application for a partial revocation order. For example, in most jurisdictions, a disposition of securities by way of a bona fide gift, made in good faith and not as part of a plan or scheme to evade requirements of securities legislation, would generally not be considered a "trade" under provincial and territorial securities legislation. As such, where applicable, a partial revocation order would not typically be required in these circumstances. However, after the gift, the securities may remain subject to the CTO depending on the terms of the CTO.

(2) Acts in furtherance of a trade — The definition of trade, where applicable, includes acts in furtherance of a trade. In any particular case, it is a question of legal interpretation whether a step taken by an issuer or other party is an act in furtherance of a trade, and therefore a breach of the CTO. Issuers should consult their legal counsel whenever there is doubt as to whether a proposed action is an act in furtherance of a trade. An issuer must obtain a partial revocation order before carrying out an act in furtherance of a trade.

(3) Continuing effect of CTO — Following the completion of the trades permitted by a partial revocation of a CTO against an issuer, all securities of the issuer may remain subject to the CTO until a full revocation is granted, depending on the terms of the CTO.

PART 4 — APPLICATIONS

4.1 Application for a full revocation — An issuer requesting a full revocation order should submit an application, with the application fees, to the securities regulatory authorities in all jurisdictions where the issuer's securities are cease-traded. The application should include the following information:

    (a) the jurisdictions where the issuer's securities are cease-traded;

    (b) details of any revocation applications currently in progress in the other jurisdictions;

    (c) copies of any draft material change report or news release as discussed in section 3.1(7);

    (d) confirmation that all continuous disclosure documents have been filed with the relevant securities regulatory authorities or a description of the documents that will be filed;

    (e) confirmation that the issuer's SEDAR and SEDI profiles are up-to-date;

    (f) a draft revocation order; and

    (g) a completed personal information form and authorization in the form set out in Appendix A of National Instrument 41-101 *General Prospectus Requirements* for each current and incoming director, executive officer and promoter of the issuer.

If the promoter is not an individual, the issuer should provide the information for each director and executive officer of the promoter.

If the issuer is an investment fund, the issuer should also provide personal information for each director and executive officer of the manager of the investment fund.

All applications for full revocation will result in some level of review of the issuer's continuous disclosure record for compliance. If the CTO has been in effect for more than 90 days, this review will be similar to the full review under the harmonized continuous disclosure review program described in CSA Staff Notice 51-312 (Revised)–*Harmonized Continuous Disclosure Requirements*.

4.2 Application for a partial revocation — (1) General — An issuer requesting a partial revocation order should submit an application, with the application fees, to the securities regulatory authorities in all jurisdictions where the issuer's securities are cease-traded and where the proposed trades would occur. The application should include the following information:

    (a) the jurisdictions where the issuer's securities are cease-traded and where the proposed trades would occur;

    (b) details of any revocation applications currently in progress in the other jurisdictions;

    (c) a description of the proposed trades and their purpose;

    (d) a draft partial revocation order that includes:

        (i) a condition that the applicant will obtain and provide to the relevant securities regulatory authorities signed and dated acknowledgements from all participants in the proposed trades, which clearly state that the issuance of a partial revocation order does not guarantee the issuance of a full revocation order in the future; and

(ii) a condition that the applicant will provide a copy of the CTO and partial revocation order to all participants in the proposed trades;

(e) use of proceeds information as discussed in section 4.2(2), in the case of a proposed exempt financing;

(f) if applicable, details of the exemptions the issuer intends to rely on to complete the proposed trades; and

(g) if the proposed trades are the result of a decision by a court, a copy of the relevant court order.

(2) **Use of Proceeds** — If the purpose of a proposed partial revocation of a CTO is to permit an issuer to carry out an exempt financing, the application and the offering document, if any, should disclose:

(a) an estimate, reasonably supported, of the amount the issuer expects to raise from the financing; and

(b) a reasonably detailed explanation of the purpose of the financing and how the issuer plans to use the funds.

The issuer should also provide in the application and any proposed offering document an estimate, reasonably supported, of the total amount the issuer will need to apply for a full revocation order. That amount would include the funds needed to prepare and file the documents required to bring the issuer's continuous disclosure up to date and pay all outstanding fees.

APPENDIX A

Section references for an application under local securities legislation.

British Columbia:

Securities Act: sections 164 and 171.

Alberta:

Securities Act: section 214.

Saskatchewan:

The Securities Act, 1988: subsection 158(4).

Manitoba:

Securities Act: subsection 148(1).

Ontario:

Securities Act: section 144.

Quebec:

Securities Act: section 265.

New Brunswick:

Securities Act: section 206.

Nova Scotia:

Securities Act: section 151.

Prince Edward Island:

Securities Act: section 31.

Newfoundland and Labrador:

Securities Act: section 142.1.

Yukon:

not applicable.

Northwest Territories:

Securities Act: section 43.1.

Nunavut:

Securities Act: section 43.1.

Adoption by OSC: (2007) 30 O.S.C.B. 6733; Request for Comments: 30 O.S.C.B. 73.

Adoption of Amendment to Policy: (2008) 31 O.S.C.B. (Supp. 2) 257 and (2007) 30 O.S.C.B. (Supp. 7) 1 (Dec. 21, 2007); Request for Comments: (2006) 29 O.S.C.B. (Supp. 3) 1 (Dec. 22, 2006).

Adoption of Amendmenty to Policy: (2010) 33 O.S.C.B. (Supp. 5) 37 and 33 O.S.C.B. (Supp. 3) 1.

National Policy 12-203 — Cease Trade Orders for Continuous Disclosure Defaults

Date: August 29, 2008, as amended effective January 1, 2011

31 O.S.C.B. 8375 and 33 O.S.C.B. (Supp. 5) 37

PART 1 — INTRODUCTION

1.1 What is the purpose of the policy? — This policy provides guidance to issuers, investors and other market participants as to how the Canadian Securities Administrators (CSA or we) will generally respond to certain types of serious continuous disclosure defaults (referred to as specified defaults in this policy) by a reporting issuer.

The policy provides guidance on the following questions:

1. When will a CSA securities regulatory authority or regulator (a CSA regulator) respond to a specified default by issuing a cease trade order (CTO)? What do we mean by the term "CTO"? Why do we issue CTOs?

2. When will a CSA regulator respond to a specified default by issuing a management cease trade order (MCTO)? What do we mean by the term "MCTO"? Why do we issue MCTOs?

3. If a CSA regulator issues an MCTO, what other actions will we ordinarily take in these circumstances? What do we expect from defaulting reporting issuers in these circumstances?

The guidance in this policy represents general guidance only. Each CSA regulator will decide how to respond to a specified default, including whether to issue a CTO (and if so, whether to issue a general CTO or an MCTO), on a case-by-case basis after considering all relevant facts and circumstances.

1.2 What is the scope of the policy? —

(a) Application — This policy describes how the CSA regulators will ordinarily respond to a specified default by a reporting issuer. The term "specified default" is defined in part 2 of this policy and is based on the harmonized list of deficiencies developed by the CSA and described in CSA Notice 51-322 *Reporting Issuer Defaults* (CSA Notice 51-322). This notice describes the list of deficiencies that will generally result in a reporting issuer being noted in default of the securities laws of a particular jurisdiction.

The definition of "specified default" does not include certain defaults described in CSA Notice 51-322, such as a failure to file a material change report, or a failure to file technical disclosure or other reports required by National Instrument 43-101 *Standards of Disclosure for Mineral Projects* (NI 43-101) or National Instrument 51-101 *Standards of Disclosure for Oil and Gas Activities* (NI 51-101).

We have omitted these items from the definition because these filings will generally be non-periodic in nature, and in some cases it may be unclear whether the issuer has triggered a filing requirement. However, a CSA regulator may apply this policy if a reporting issuer is in default of a continuous disclosure requirement that is not included in the definition of specified default.

Similarly, a CSA regulator may apply this policy if a reporting issuer has made a required filing but the required filing is deficient in terms of content (a content deficiency). Examples of content deficiencies are set out in section 2 of CSA Notice 51-322.

(b) Mutual reliance principles — In deciding how to respond to a specified default, the CSA regulators will generally follow principles of mutual reliance. The issuer's principal regulator (PR) will normally be the one to decide whether to issue a CTO. The determination as to which regulator will act as PR will be based upon the principles set out in part 3 of National Policy 11-203 *Process for exemptive relief applications in multiple jurisdictions* (NP 11-203). This means that the PR will usually be the regulator in the jurisdiction where the reporting issuer's head office is located.

An issuer that wishes to apply for an MCTO under this policy must apply in the issuer's PR jurisdiction and send a copy of the application to the non-principal regulators in each other jurisdiction in which it is a reporting issuer. The issuer's PR will determine whether to issue a general CTO or an MCTO and, in the case of the latter, the appropriate scope of the MCTO. Non-principal regulators will ordinarily make the same decision as the PR on these questions. However, each regulator may still impose a general CTO if it believes it is appropriate.

(c) MCTOs issued under this policy are not a "penalty" or "sanction" for disclosure purposes — The CSA regulators do not consider MCTOs issued under this policy to be a "penalty or sanction" for the purposes of disclosure obligations in Canadian securities legislation relating to penalties or sanctions. They are not issued as part of an enforcement process and the regulators do not intend them to suggest a finding of fault or wrongdoing on the part of any individual named in the MCTO. For example, a defaulting issuer's board of directors might invite an individual to serve as an officer or director of the issuer to assist the issuer in remedying its default. The individual might have no prior involvement with the defaulting reporting issuer. The fact that the PR may subsequently name the individual in an MCTO does not mean the individual had any responsibility for the default, which occurred before the individual joined the issuer.

However, issuers are required to disclose MCTOs issued under this policy in accordance with the following disclosure requirements:

- Section 16.2 of Form 41-101F1 *Information Required in a Prospectus*,
- Item 16 of Form 44-101F1 *Short Form Prospectus*,
- Subsection 10.2(1) of Form 51-102F2 *Annual Information Form*, and
- Subsection 7.2 of Form 51-102F5 *Information Circular*.

If an issuer is required to include disclosure of an MCTO in a public filing, the issuer may supplement the disclosure with additional information explaining the circumstances of the MCTO.

(d) Regulators may consider other action, including enforcement action — If a reporting issuer is in default of a continuous disclosure requirement, the CSA regulators may also consider taking enforcement action against the reporting issuer, the directors and officers of the reporting issuer, or any other responsible party. Accordingly, nothing in this policy should be interpreted as limiting the discretion of the CSA regulators in responding to such a default through enforcement action.

PART 2 — DEFINITIONS AND INTERPRETATION

In this policy:

"alternative information guidelines" means the guidelines relating to a default announcement and default status report described in part 4 of this policy;

"cease trade order" and "CTO" mean an order under a provision of Canadian securities legislation, set out in Appendix A, that prohibits trading in securities of a reporting issuer, whether direct or indirect, by the persons or companies identified in the order, for such period as is specified in the order;

"default announcement" means a news release and report as described in section 4.3 of this policy;

"default status report" means a news release as described in section 4.4 of this policy;

"management cease trade order" and "MCTO" mean a CTO issued under this policy that prohibits trading in securities of a reporting issuer, whether direct or indirect, by

(a) the chief executive officer (CEO) of the reporting issuer,

(b) the chief financial officer (CFO) of the reporting issuer,

(c) at the discretion of the PR, the members of the board of directors of the reporting issuer or other persons or companies who had, or may have had, access directly or indirectly to any material fact or material change with respect to the reporting issuer that has not been generally disclosed, and

(d) in the case of a reporting issuer that does not have a CEO, CFO and/or a board of directors, individuals who perform similar functions to any of such positions;

"principal regulator" and "PR" mean an issuer's principal regulator as determined in accordance with part 3 of National Policy 11-203 *Process for exemptive relief applications in multiple jurisdictions* (NP 11-203).

"specified default" means a failure by a reporting issuer to comply with a specified requirement; and

"specified requirement" means the requirement to file within the time period prescribed by securities legislation

    (a) annual financial statements;

    (b) an interim financial report;

    (c) annual or interim management's discussion and analysis (MD&A) or annual or interim management report of fund performance (MRFP);

    (d) annual information form (AIF); or

    (e) certification of filings under National Instrument 52-109 Certification of Disclosure in Issuers' Annual and Interim Filings.

In certain jurisdictions, the CSA regulators may issue cease trade orders and management cease trade orders that prohibit both trading in and acquisitions of securities of a reporting issuer. In these jurisdictions, references in this policy to a "trade" refers to both a trade in or acquisition of securities of the reporting issuer.

In Quebec, "trade" is not defined in the *Securities Act* (QSA). This policy covers all securities transactions that may be the object of an order provided for in paragraph 3 of section 265 of the QSA.

PART 3 — REGULATORY RESPONSES TO A SPECIFIED DEFAULT

3.1 Issuance of a general CTO or an MCTO — In the jurisdictions where the issuer is a reporting issuer, the CSA regulators will respond to a specified default by noting the issuer in default on their default lists. For more information about the CSA default lists, please refer to CSA Notice 51-322.

The CSA regulators will then ordinarily respond to a specified default in one of two ways:

- The issuer's PR may issue a CTO.
- Alternatively, if an issuer applies under part 4 of this policy, and demonstrates that it is able to comply with this policy, the issuer's PR may issue an MCTO instead.

The issuer's PR will decide whether to proceed with a CTO (including whether to issue an MCTO) after considering the principles, factors and criteria described in part 4 of this policy and any other facts and circumstances the PR considers relevant. If the issuer's PR decides an MCTO is appropriate, it will similarly decide whether to extend it to the issuer's board of directors or other persons or companies.

If the issuer's PR issues a CTO, the non-principal regulators in the jurisdictions in which the issuer is a reporting issuer will generally issue similar CTOs to ensure the CTO is effective in their jurisdictions. If the issuer's PR issues an MCTO, the non-principal regulators in the jurisdictions in which the issuer is a reporting issuer will generally issue similar MCTOs in respect of persons or companies named in the MCTO who reside in their jurisdiction.

The CSA regulators will generally not grant exemptive relief to a reporting issuer to extend a continuous disclosure filing deadline to enable an issuer to avoid a default. The deadlines relating to the specified requirements represent the CSA's view as to reasonable and appropriate deadlines that should apply to reporting issuers in a consistent manner. While we recognize that issuers may sometimes face difficulties in complying with filing deadlines due to circumstances beyond their control, we do not believe it is appropriate to vary a filing deadline simply to allow an issuer to avoid being in default. The CSA regulators will consider the issuer's circumstances in deciding what action, if any, is appropriate to respond to a default.

If a defaulting reporting issuer is insolvent and is the subject of a stay of proceedings or similar order under the *Companies' Creditors Arrangement Act*, R.S.C. 1985, c. C-36, as amended, or the *Bankruptcy and Insolvency Act*, R.S.C. 1985, c. B-3, as amended, or similar legislation, the CSA regulators will generally note the issuer in default but take no other action until the relevant stay is lifted, provided the issuer complies with the alternative information guidelines. In situations where this is not the case, or where the default is expected to continue for an extended period, the CSA regulators will determine whether further action is warranted after considering all relevant factors and circumstances.

3.2 Why do we issue cease trade orders in response to a specified default? — Historically, if a reporting issuer has failed to comply with a specified requirement, such as the requirement to file audited annual financial statements, the CSA regulators have generally responded to this default by issuing a CTO.

The CSA regulators have historically taken this action for the following reasons:

- Without adequate continuous disclosure, there may not be sufficient information in the securities marketplace to properly support informed trading decisions regarding securities of the issuer.

- The integrity and fairness, or confidence in the integrity and fairness, of the capital markets, may be compromised if trading in securities of the reporting issuer is permitted to continue during the period of default (when there is heightened potential that some people may have access to information that would normally be reflected in the continuous disclosure document that the reporting issuer is in default of filing).

We acknowledge that a CTO can impose a burden on issuers and investors because

- existing investors are unable to sell their securities, and prospective investors are unable to purchase securities of the issuer, while the CTO remains in effect, and

- issuers are generally unable to access financing while the CTO remains in effect.

Nevertheless, if a reporting issuer is in default of a specified requirement, our overriding concern is generally investor protection. Investors and prospective investors should be able to make an informed investment decision about the securities of the defaulting reporting issuer.

The practice of responding to a specified default with a CTO has a significant positive effect on general compliance. The prospect of a CTO creates a strong incentive for the reporting issuer's management to ensure that the reporting issuer does not go into default. Similarly, the issuance of a CTO once the issuer is in default creates a strong incentive on the part of management to diligently rectify the filing default.

Finally, a CTO represents a rapid, public response by the CSA regulators to a serious continuous disclosure default by a reporting issuer. This sends a message to issuers and investors that filing deadlines are important and that there will be serious consequences for a failure to file, helping to preserve integrity and fairness in the securities marketplace.

PART 4 — APPLICATIONS FOR AN MCTO AS AN ALTERNATIVE TO A GENERAL CTO

4.1 Eligibility criteria — A CTO is an appropriate response to a specified default that is not likely to be rectified within a relatively short time and where the circumstances leading to the default are likely to continue. These circumstances include issuers that no longer have an active business, are insolvent, or have lost a majority of their board of directors.

If the outstanding filing is expected to be filed relatively quickly, and the default is not expected to be recurring, an MCTO may be an appropriate response to the default.

Issuers satisfying all of the following criteria are usually eligible for an MCTO:

- The outstanding filings will be filed as soon as they are available and within a reasonable period. In most cases, we expect this to be within two months. However, in exceptional circumstances, as determined by the PR, we may permit an issuer to take longer than two months to address the default.
- The issuer is generating revenue from its principal business or, if it is in the development stage, the issuer is actively pursuing the development of its products or properties.
- The issuer has the necessary financial and human resources, including a reasonable number of directors and officers in place, to address the default in a timely and effective manner and comply with all other continuous disclosure requirements (other than requirements reasonably linked to the specified default) for the duration of the default.
- The issuer's securities are listed on a Canadian stock exchange and there is an active, liquid market for those securities. Thinly traded issuers will generally not be considered eligible for an MCTO.
- The issuer is not on the defaulting reporting issuer list in any CSA jurisdiction for any reason other than the failure to comply with the specified requirement (and any other requirement that is reasonably linked to the specified requirement).

4.2 Contents of application — If an issuer satisfies the eligibility criteria set out above, it should contact its PR at least two weeks before the due date for the required filings and apply in writing for an MCTO instead of a general CTO against the issuer.

We acknowledge that there will be situations where an issuer, notwithstanding the exercise of reasonable diligence, will be unable to determine whether it can comply with a specified requirement at least two weeks before its due date. However, we believe that, in most cases, an issuer exercising reasonable diligence should be able to make this determination at least two weeks in advance of the deadline.

If an issuer, notwithstanding the exercise of reasonable diligence, is not able to make this determination at least two weeks before its due date, the issuer should include a brief explanation of the reasons for the delayed filing in its application.

In its application, the issuer should

- identify the specified default, the reasons for the default and the anticipated duration of the default;
- explain how the issuer satisfies each of the eligibility criteria described above;
- set out a detailed remediation plan that explains how the issuer proposes to remedy the default and includes a realistic timetable for remedying the default;
- include consents signed by the CEO and the CFO (or equivalent) to the issuance of an MCTO (see Appendix C);
- include a copy of the proposed or actual default announcement (see section 4.3);
- confirm that the issuer will comply with the alternative information guidelines described in sections 4.3 and 4.4 of this policy;
- include a copy of the issuer undertaking described in section 4.7 of this policy; and
- briefly describe the issuer's blackout policies and other policies and procedures relating to insider trading.

The issuer should send copies of the application to the regulators in all jurisdictions in which the issuer is a reporting issuer.

We will consider an issuer's history of complying with its continuous disclosure obligations when evaluating the issuer's request for an MCTO.

4.3 Alternative information guidelines — Default Announcement — If a reporting issuer determines that it will not comply, or subsequently determines that it has not complied, with a specified requirement, this will often represent a material change that the issuer should immediately communicate to the securities marketplace by way of a news release and material change report in accordance with part 7 of NI 51-102 Continuous Disclosure Obligations. In determining whether a failure to comply with a specified requirement is a material change, the issuer should consider both the events leading to the failure and the failure itself.

If the circumstances leading to the default, or the default, do not represent a material change, the issuer should nevertheless consider whether the circumstances involve important information that should be immediately communicated to the marketplace by way of news release.

The regulators will generally not exercise their discretion to issue an MCTO unless the issuer issues and files a default announcement containing the information set out below. If the default involves a material change, the material change report may contain this information, in which case a separate default announcement is not necessary. The default announcement should be authorized by the CEO or the CFO (or equivalent) of the reporting issuer, be approved by the board or audit committee and be prepared and filed with the CSA regulators on SEDAR in the same manner as a news release and material change report referred to in part 7 of NI 51-102. An issuer will usually be able to determine that it will not comply with a specified requirement at least two weeks before its due date and, as soon as it makes this determination, should issue the default announcement.

The default announcement should:

(i) identify the relevant specified requirement and the (anticipated) default;

(ii) disclose in detail the reason(s) for the (anticipated) default;

(iii) disclose the current plans of the reporting issuer to remedy the default, including the date it anticipates remedying the default;

(iv) confirm that the reporting issuer intends to satisfy the provisions of the alternative information guidelines so long as it remains in default of a specified requirement;

(v) disclose relevant particulars of any insolvency proceeding to which the reporting issuer is subject, including the nature and timing of information that is required to be provided to creditors, and confirm that the reporting issuer intends to file with the CSA regulators throughout the period in which it is in default, the same information it provides to its creditors when the information is provided to the creditors and in the same manner as it would file a material change report under part 7 of NI 51-102; and

(vi) subject to section 4.5 of this policy, disclose any other material information concerning the affairs of the reporting issuer that has not been generally disclosed.

A default announcement is not needed if the issuer is in default of a previous specified requirement, has followed the provisions of section 4.3 regarding a default announcement of that earlier default and is complying with the provisions of section 4.4 regarding default status reports.

4.4 Alternative information guidelines — Default Status Reports — After the default announcement, and during the period of the MCTO, the regulators will generally exercise their discretion to issue a general CTO unless the defaulting reporting issuer issues bi-weekly default status reports, in the form of news releases, containing the following information:

(i) any material changes to the information contained in the default announcement or subsequent default status reports, including a description of all actions taken to remedy the default and the status of any investigations into any events which may have contributed to the default;

(ii) particulars of any failure by the defaulting reporting issuer in fulfilling its stated intentions with respect to satisfying the provisions of the alternative information guidelines;

(iii) information regarding any (anticipated) specified default subsequent to the default which is the subject of the default announcement; and

(iv) subject to section 4.5 of this policy, any other material information concerning the affairs of the reporting issuer that has not been generally disclosed.

Where there are no changes otherwise required to be disclosed in items (i) to (iv), this fact should be disclosed in a default status report.

To keep the market continuously informed of any developments during the period of default, the issuer should issue default status reports every two weeks following the default announcement. If a CSA regulator, at any time, issues a general CTO against an issuer, default status reports will no longer be necessary.

Every default status report should be prepared, authorized, filed and communicated to the securities marketplace in the same manner as that specified in section 4.3 for a default announcement.

4.5 Confidential material information — The alternative information guidelines in this policy supplement the material change reporting requirements in NI 51-102 and should be interpreted in a similar manner. Similar to the procedures in NI 51-102, an issuer may omit confidential material information from default status announcement or default status reports if in the opinion of the issuer, and if that opinion is arrived at in a reasonable manner, disclosure of the applicable material information would be unduly detrimental to the interests of the reporting issuer.

4.6 Compliance with other continuous disclosure requirements — The alternative disclosure described in sections 4.3 and 4.4 of this policy supplement the issuer's disclosure record during the period of default. It does not provide an alternative to the continuous disclosure requirements under Canadian securities legislation.

If a reporting issuer is in default of a specified requirement, the issuer must still comply with all other applicable continuous disclosure requirements, other than requirements reasonably linked to the specified requirement in question. For example, an issuer that has not filed its financial statements on time will also be unable to comply with the requirement to file management's discussion and analysis under NI 51-102. However, failure to comply with a requirement to file audited financial statements in accordance with the requirements of part 4 of NI 51-102 does not excuse compliance with other requirements of NI 51-102 such as the requirement to file an Annual Information Form in accordance with part 6 of NI 51-102 or material change reports in accordance with part 7 of NI 51-102.

4.7 Issuer undertaking to cease certain trading activities — The reporting issuer should include with the application an undertaking that, for so long as the issuer is in default of the specified requirement in question, the issuer will not, directly or indirectly, issue securities to or acquire securities from an insider or employee of the issuer except in accordance with legally binding obligations to do so existing as of the date of the continuous disclosure default. The issuer should address the undertaking to the securities regulatory authorities of each jurisdiction in which the issuer is a reporting issuer.

4.8 Information respecting defaulting reporting issuers subject to insolvency proceedings — As explained in section 3.1, if a defaulting reporting issuer is insolvent and under Court protection, the CSA will generally note the issuer in default but take no other action until the relevant stay is lifted provided the issuer complies with the alternative information guidelines.

If a defaulting reporting issuer is the subject of insolvency proceedings but not under court protection, we will consider an application for an MCTO in cases where

(a) the issuer retains title to its assets,

(b) the issuer's directors and officers continue to manage the affairs of the issuer, and

(c) the issuer

(i) files a default announcement,

(ii) files default status reports,

(iii) files a report disclosing the information it provides to its creditors

• simultaneously with delivery to its creditors, and

• in the same manner as a report of a material change referred to in part 7 of NI 51-102; and

(iv) otherwise complies with this policy.

If the issuer chooses to file the information provided to creditors with a material change report, then, for purposes of filing on SEDAR, this must be contained in the same electronic document as the material change report.

4.9 Financial information in default announcements and default status reports — Any unaudited financial information that is communicated to the marketplace should, except in certain circumstances involving insolvency, be directly derived from financial statements prepared and presented in accordance with generally accepted accounting principles. In default announcements and default status reports, this information should be accompanied by cautionary language that the information has been prepared by management of the defaulting reporting issuer and is unaudited.

4.10 Default correction announcement — Once the specified default is remedied, the reporting issuer should consider communicating that information to the securities marketplace in the same manner as that specified in this policy for a default announcement.

PART 5 — TRADING BY MANAGEMENT AND OTHER INSIDERS DURING THE PERIOD OF DEFAULT

Issuers in default of a specified requirement should closely monitor and generally restrict trading by management and other insiders due to the increased risk that such persons may have access to material undisclosed information. Such information may include information that would otherwise have been reflected in the continuous disclosure filing that is the subject of the default, information about any investigation into the events that may have led to the default, and information about the status of remediation activities.

We remind management and other insiders that they should carefully consider the insider trading prohibitions under securities legislation before entering into any transaction involving securities of the issuer in default.

The CSA have articulated in National Policy 51-201 *Disclosure Standards* detailed best practices for issuers for disclosure and information containment and have provided an interpretation of insider trading laws. Issuers should adopt written disclosure policies to assist directors, officers and employees and other representatives in discharging timely disclosure obligations. Written disclosure policies should also provide guidance on how to maintain the confidentiality of corporate information and to prevent improper trading on inside information. Adopting the CSA best practices may assist issuers to take all reasonable steps to preserve the confidentiality of non-public information.

We also remind issuers and other market participants that an officer or other insider of a reporting issuer in default will generally be unable to sell securities acquired from the issuer on an exempt basis because of the resale restrictions in section 2.5(2)(7) and s. 2.6(3)(5) of National Instrument 45-102 *Resale of Securities*.

PART 6 — EFFECT OF A CTO ISSUED BY A REGULATOR IN ONE JURISDICTION ON TRADING IN ANOTHER JURISDICTION

Presently, all marketplaces (including exchanges, alternative trading systems and quotation and trade reporting systems) in Canada have retained Investment Industry Regulatory Organization of Canada (IIROC) as their regulation services provider. Under the Universal Market Integrity Rules (UMIR), which have been adopted by IIROC, if a securities commission issues a CTO with respect to an issuer whose securities are traded on a marketplace, IIROC imposes a regulatory halt on trading of those securities on all marketplaces for which IIROC acts as the regulation services provider. Such halt is taken whether or not the CSA regulator that issued the CTO is the PR of the issuer and once the halt is imposed by IIROC, no person subject to UMIR may trade those securities on any marketplace in Canada, over-the-counter or on a foreign organized regulated market. Therefore, the remainder of the guidance in this part deals with market participants who are not otherwise subject to the jurisdiction of IIROC.

Market participants should be cautious about trading in a security in one jurisdiction if a CSA regulator in another jurisdiction has issued a CTO. In most cases, if an issuer's PR issued a CTO in response to a failure by the issuer to comply with a material continuous disclosure requirement, the non-principal regulator will issue a reciprocal CTO on similar terms and conditions.

Continuous disclosure obligations reflect the minimum requirements we feel are necessary to generate sufficient public disclosure to permit investors to make informed investment decisions. The issuance of a CTO by the issuer's PR will generally mean that an issuer has not met the required standard and that there is a significant risk of harm to investors if trading is allowed to continue. Accordingly, market participants should carefully consider the existence of the material continuous disclosure default, and the determination of the issuer's PR, before effecting a trade in a non-principal regulator jurisdiction. Although a trade in one jurisdiction may not violate a CTO in another jurisdiction, the trading activity may still be contrary to the public interest and therefore subject to enforcement or other administrative proceedings.

If a market participant intends to execute a trade in securities of a cease-traded issuer on an exchange or marketplace outside of Canada, the market participant should carefully consider whether the trade may nevertheless be considered to be or include a trade within one or more jurisdictions in Canada where a CTO is in effect. For example, a transaction may be a trade in another jurisdiction if "acts in furtherance of the trade" occur within that jurisdiction. A transaction may also be a trade in another jurisdiction if there are connecting factors or other facts and circumstances that indicate that the securities may not "come to rest" outside Canada but may be resold to investors in a jurisdiction where a CTO is in effect.

PART 7 — EFFECTIVE DATE

This policy comes into force on September 1, 2008.

APPENDIX A — STATUTORY PROVISIONS FOR CEASE TRADE ORDERS

Jurisdiction	Legislative reference
British Columbia	Sections 161 and 164 of the *Securities Act* (British Columbia)
Alberta	Sections 33.1 and 198 of the *Securities Act* (Alberta)
Saskatchewan	Section 134.1 of *The Securities Act, 1988*
Manitoba	Sections 147.1 and 148 of the *Securities Act* (Manitoba)
Ontario	Section 127 of the *Securities Act* (Ontario)
Quebec	Section 265 of the *Securities Act* (Quebec)
Newfoundland and Labrador	Section 127(1) of the *Securities Act* (Newfoundland and Labrador)
Nova Scotia	Section 134 of the *Securities Act* (Nova Scotia)
New Brunswick	Section 188.2 of the *Securities Act* (New Brunswick)

APPENDIX B — LISTS OF DEFAULTING REPORTING ISSUERS

Certain securities regulatory authorities maintain lists that identify those reporting issuers that have been noted in default in the relevant jurisdiction. The lists identify the name of the reporting issuer, and the nature and description of the default. The lists, together with the harmonized categories of default and nomenclature used to identify each category, can be found on the following websites:

www.bcsc.bc.ca

www.albertasecurities.com

www.sfsc.gov.sk.ca

www.msc.gov.mb.ca

www.osc.gov.on.ca

www.lautorite.qc.ca

www.nbsc-cvmnb.ca

www.gov.ns.ca/nssc

Certain securities regulatory authorities have also published policies or notices containing information relating to defaults by reporting issuers. These local polices or notices are:

Alberta: Alberta Securities Commission Policy 51-601 — *Reporting Issuers List*

Saskatchewan: Saskatchewan Policy Statement 51-601 — *Reporting Issuers in Default*

Manitoba: Manitoba Securities Commission Local Policy 51-601 — *Reporting Issuers List*

Ontario: Ontario Securities Commission Policy 51-601 — *Reporting Issuer Defaults*

Quebec: AMF Notice on Reporting Issuer Defaults

New Brunswick: New Brunswick Securities Commission Policy 51-601 — *Reporting Issuers List*

Nova Scotia: Nova Scotia Securities Commission Policy 51-601 — *Reporting Issuers List*

APPENDIX C — SAMPLE FORM OF CONSENT

Consent

To: [*Name of Issuer's Principal Regulator*], as principal regulator,

And to: [*Name(s) of other CSA regulator(s) in whose jurisdiction(s) the Issuer is a reporting issuer*] (collectively with the principal regulator, the CSA regulators)

Re: *Consent to issuance of management cease trade order*

I, [*name of individual providing the consent*] hereby confirm as follows:

1. I am the [*name of position with the Issuer, e.g., the chief executive officer or chief financial officer*] of [*name of Issuer*] (the Issuer).

2. The Issuer is a [*nature of entity, e.g., a corporation incorporated under the Canada Business Corporations Act*] with a head office located in [*province or territory*].

3. The Issuer is a reporting issuer in [*identify all jurisdictions in which the issuer is a reporting issuer*]. The Issuer's principal regulator, as determined in accordance with part 3 of National Policy 11-203 *Process for exemptive relief applications in multiple jurisdictions* (NP 11-203) is [*name of principal regulator*].

4. The Issuer [*is*] [*is not*] [*delete as applicable*] a "venture issuer" as defined in National Instrument 51-102 *Continuous Disclosure Obligations* (NI 51-102). The Issuer has a financial year ending [*state the issuer's year end, e.g., December 31*].

5. On or about [*identify the deadline for filing*] (the filing deadline), the Issuer will be required to file [*briefly describe the required filings, e.g.,*

     a. audited annual financial statements for the year ended December 31, 2007, as required by Part 4 of NI 51-102;

     b. management's discussion and analysis (MD&A) relating to the audited annual financial statements, as required by Part 5 of NI 51-102; and

     c. CEO and CFO certificates relating to the audited annual financial statements, as required by National Instrument 52-109 Certification of Disclosure in Issuers' Annual and Interim Filings (collectively, the required filings).

6. The Issuer has determined that it may not be able to make the required filings by the filing deadline. The Issuer wishes to apply to the CSA regulators for a management cease trade order (an MCTO) as an alternative to a general cease trade order in accordance with National Policy 12-203 *Cease Trade Orders for Continuous Disclosure Defaults* (NP 12-203).

7. I am providing this consent in support of the Issuer's application for an MCTO in accordance with Part 4 of NP 12-203.

8. I hereby consent to the issuance of an MCTO against me by the Issuer's principal regulator under the applicable statutory authority listed in Appendix A to NP 12-203.

9. Specifically, I understand that the MCTO will prohibit me from trading in or acquiring securities of the Issuer, directly or indirectly, until two full business days following the receipt by the principal regulator of all filings the Issuer is required to make under the securities legislation of the principal regulator or until further Order of the principal regulator.

10. I hereby further consent to the issuance of any substantially similar MCTO that another CSA regulator may consider necessary to issue by reason of the default described above.

11. I hereby waive any requirement of a hearing, as may be provided for under the applicable statutory authority listed in Appendix A to NP 12-203, and any corresponding notice of hearing, in respect of the issuance of the MCTO.

DATED this .... day of [DATE]

by: ....

Name:

Title:

Adoption by OSC: (2008) 31 O.S.C.B. 8375; Request for Comments: (2008) 31 O.S.C.B. 3573.

Adoption of Amendment by OSC: (2010) 33 O.S.C.B. (Supp. 3) 1 and 33 O.S.C.B. (Supp. 5) 37.

Policies and Orders: CSAN 11-318.

CSA Staff Notice 12-307 — Applications for a Decision that an Issuer is not a Reporting Issuer

Date: September 12, 2003, revised February 4, 2005, November 1, 2006, March 7, 2008 and July 26, 2012

26 O.S.C.B. 6348, 28 O.S.C.B. 1189, 29 O.S.C.B. 8582, 31 O.S.C.B. 2770 and 35 O.S.C.B. 6794

Purpose

This Notice provides information and guidance on coordinated review applications that may be made under National Policy 11-203 *Process for Exemptive Relief Applications in Multiple Jurisdictions* (NP 11-203) for a decision that an issuer is not a reporting issuer (a decision). Among other things, this Notice covers:

- how an issuer can apply for a decision under a simplified procedure if it meets certain conditions,

- how an issuer can apply for a decision if it is not eligible to use the simplified procedure,

- how an issuer can describe the decision it wants in a way that addresses legislative differences between jurisdictions,

- how a foreign issuer with a small securityholder presence in Canada can apply for a decision, and

- the procedure for dissolved issuers.

In this Notice, "securityholder" means, for a security, the beneficial owner of the security.

The Simplified Procedure

The local securities regulatory authority or regulator (the Decision Maker) in each of Alberta, Saskatchewan, Manitoba, Ontario, Québec, New Brunswick, Prince Edward Island, Nova Scotia, Newfoundland and Labrador, Yukon, the Northwest Territories and Nunavut (the Jurisdictions) has adopted a simplified procedure for certain coordinated review applications (NP 11-203 describes the process for a coordinated review application) in which an issuer is seeking a decision that it is not a reporting issuer under the securities legislation of the Jurisdictions (the Legislation).

The simplified procedure is available to a reporting issuer:

- that is not a reporting issuer in British Columbia (including an issuer that has voluntarily surrendered its reporting issuer status under British Columbia Instrument 11-502 *Voluntary Surrender of Reporting Issuer Status*),

- that is seeking a decision that it is not a reporting issuer, from the Decision Maker in each of the Jurisdictions in which it is a reporting issuer,

- whose outstanding securities, including debt securities, are beneficially owned, directly or indirectly, by fewer than 15 securityholders in each of the jurisdictions of Canada and fewer than 51 securityholders in total worldwide,

- whose securities, including debt securities, are not traded in Canada or another country on a marketplace as defined in National Instrument 21-101 *Marketplace Operation* or any other facility for bringing together buyers and sellers of securities where trading data is publicly reported, and

- that is not in default of any of its obligations under the Legislation as a reporting issuer.

A reporting issuer may request a decision under the simplified procedure by submitting, to each of the Jurisdictions in which it is seeking the decision, the fees applicable under the Legislation, a draft decision document and a letter in duplicate prepared by or on behalf of the issuer that:

- states that the issuer is seeking a decision of the Decision Makers that it is not a reporting issuer,

- references the simplified procedure in this Notice, and

- includes representations that the applicant meets each of the criteria set out in the simplified procedure in this Notice.

Schedule 1 includes a sample application letter and form of decision document. In some cases, staff may request additional information from the reporting issuer. The reporting issuer should make its application in paper and electronic format as described in section 5.5 of NP 11-203.

The procedure will simplify the process in certain routine circumstances for a reporting issuer submitting a coordinated review application under NP 11-203 for decision that it is not a reporting issuer.

Applying for relief in British Columbia

The simplified procedure is not available in British Columbia. If a reporting issuer has no more than 50 securityholders (both debt and equity) and its securities are not traded through any exchange or market, it may surrender its status as a reporting issuer in that province by filing with the British Columbia Securities Commission the notice described in British Columbia Instrument 11-502 *Voluntary Surrender of Reporting Issuer Status*. The issuer would then apply for relief in other jurisdictions using the simplified procedure under this Notice.

Part 1:
PROCEDURE

OTC reporting issuers

The simplified procedure and the modified approach described in this Notice are not available to a reporting issuer that is an OTC reporting issuer under Multilateral Instrument 51-105 *Issuers Quoted in the U.S. Over-the-Counter Markets*.

What to do when the simplified procedure in this Notice and BC Instrument 11-502 is not available

If an issuer cannot meet all of the simplified procedure criteria in this Notice or in BC Instrument 11-502 (if the issuer is a reporting issuer in British Columbia), the issuer should submit an application under the standard procedure for a coordinated review application under NP 11-203 using the form of decision document attached as Annex C to NP 11-203. The reporting issuer should submit its application to each jurisdiction where the issuer is a reporting issuer.

An issuer wanting to avoid the minimum 10-day waiting period under BC Instrument 11-502 (which is a condition precedent to the other jurisdictions making a decision under the simplified procedure) should follow the standard procedure for a coordinated review application.

How to describe the decision the issuer wants

The legislation varies among the jurisdictions in how it authorizes regulators to terminate reporting issuer status. An issuer should include the language in the legislation of its principal regulator in its draft decision document. Where Québec is not the principal regulator and the issuer requires a decision in Québec, the issuer should also include the wording "revoke the issuer's status as a reporting issuer" in its draft decision document if the language in the legislation of the principal regulator uses the phrase "ceased to be a reporting issuer". The form of decision document in Schedule 1 to this Notice sets out the applicable language for each principal regulator.

Going-private transactions

Where the issuer is in the process of completing a going-private transaction following which it will want to stop being a reporting issuer, the issuer may apply for relief using the simplified procedure in this Notice prior to completing the transaction. A jurisdiction cannot make a decision until the transaction is complete and the issuer can represent that it has satisfied all the criteria for the simplified procedure.

Successor reporting issuers

In circumstances where an issuer has exchanged its securities with another party (or that party's securityholders) in connection with a statutory arrangement or procedure, the issuer should consider whether any other party in the transaction will or has become a reporting issuer following the exchange. If so, the issuer should disclose the name of that party in its application to stop being a reporting issuer and provide a brief summary of the statutory arrangement or procedure and the parties involved.

Issuers subject to business corporations legislation in certain jurisdictions

In certain jurisdictions of Canada, the local business corporations legislation:

- contains certain provisions that apply to reporting issuers that were incorporated, continued or amalgamated under the business corporations legislation, and

- provides that if a reporting issuer no longer wants those provisions to apply to it, it must obtain an order from the Decision Maker that it is no longer a public company for the purposes of the business corporations legislation.

Issuers should review their business corporations legislation to determine if they need to make a separate application to the relevant Decision Maker for an order under the business corporations legislation. A decision obtained under the simplified procedure in this Notice or a coordinated review application under NP 11-203 is only for the purposes of securities legislation.

Foreign issuers

Foreign-incorporated issuers often seek decisions that they are not reporting issuers under applicable securities legislation when they have a declining numbers of securityholders in Canada. In general, these issuers do not meet the criteria for the simplified procedure in this Notice because they typically have many beneficial securityholders in jurisdictions in Canada, and their securities are listed on one or more exchanges outside of Canada. However, they wish to cease being reporting issuers in Canada because their securities are not listed on an exchange in Canada and they do not intend to make any further distributions of securities in Canada.

Past approach

In the past, CSA staff have recommended a decision that a foreign issuer is not a reporting issuer where the issuer could demonstrate that Canadian ownership of its securities is *de minimis* compared to the total ownership by non-Canadian securityholders. In past decisions, this has been demonstrated when an issuer had:

- fewer than 300 beneficial securityholders in Canada, and

- a small percentage of total securityholdings beneficially owned by Canadian residents.

Modified approach

We have adopted a modified approach for applications by issuers that report in the U.S. and are listed on a U.S. exchange. If such an issuer meets the following criteria, CSA staff will generally recommend a decision that the issuer is not a reporting issuer:

1. The issuer makes a representation that residents of Canada do not:

   (a) directly or indirectly beneficially own more than 2% of each class or series of outstanding securities (including debt securities) of the issuer worldwide, and

   (b) directly or indirectly comprise more than 2% of the total number of securityholders of the issuer worldwide.

CSA staff realize that some filers have difficulty making representations on the beneficial ownership of securities by residents of Canada. CSA staff will not generally recommend granting the relief without the issuer satisfying the "2% test". In addition, staff will not generally recommend granting the relief where a representation is qualified or limited to the knowledge of the issuer, unless the issuer can fully demonstrate that it has made diligent enquiry to support the representation and why it cannot give an unqualified representation.

2. The issuer files continuous disclosure reports under U.S. securities laws and is listed on a U.S. exchange.

3. In the 12 months before applying for the decision, the issuer has not taken any steps that indicate there is a market for its securities in Canada. Steps that would indicate there is a market in Canada include conducting a prospectus offering in Canada, or establishing or maintaining a listing on a Canadian marketplace or exchange.

4. The issuer provides advance notice to Canadian resident securityholders in a news release that it has applied to securities regulatory authorities for a decision that it is not a reporting issuer in Canada and, if that decision is made, the issuer will no longer be a reporting issuer in any jurisdiction of Canada.

5. The issuer undertakes to concurrently deliver to its Canadian securityholders, all disclosure the issuer would be required under U.S. securities law or exchange requirements to deliver to U.S. resident securityholders.

Non-U.S. issuers that are listed on a major foreign exchange and meet the 2% test may also apply using the modified approach, provided that the issuer demonstrates that Canadian securityholders will receive adequate disclosure under the foreign securities law or exchange requirements.

Reporting issuer that has been dissolved or terminated

A reporting issuer does not need to apply for a decision that it is not a reporting issuer if it is:

- a corporation that was dissolved under applicable corporate legislation,

- a limited partnership that was dissolved under applicable limited partnership legislation,

- a trust that was terminated under its declaration of trust, or

- another form of business organization that was dissolved or terminated under its applicable governing legislation or constating or establishing document.

In each case, it will be sufficient if an agent files evidence of the dissolution or termination with the securities regulatory authority in each jurisdiction where the issuer was a reporting issuer.

For a corporation, sufficient evidence includes a copy of the certificate and articles of dissolution.

For a limited partnership, sufficient evidence typically includes:

- a copy of the declaration of dissolution or similar document filed under applicable limited partnership legislation, and

- a written representation from the general partner about the effective date of dissolution under applicable limited partnership legislation.

For a trust, sufficient evidence typically includes:

- a copy of the resolution authorizing the termination of the trust,

- a report on voting results indicating that the resolution was passed,

- a written representation that the trust no longer exists (it is sufficient if this representation is provided by filing counsel or former trustees or officers),

- a copy of the change in corporate structure notice filed under section 4.9 of National Instrument 51-102 *Continuous Disclosure Obligations*, and

- evidence such as a copy of a news release or written submission from filing counsel that the trust has no securities outstanding and none listed on an exchange.

If an issuer has commenced dissolution proceedings but still exists, it will remain a reporting issuer in the absence of a decision that it is not a reporting issuer.

Schedule 1 — Example of an Application Letter under the Simplified Procedure

[Enter date]

[List name of the principal regulator and each non-principal regulator]

Dear Sirs/Mesdames:

Re: [Enter name of applicant] (the Applicant) — application for a decision under the securities legislation of [list the jurisdictions] (the Jurisdictions) that the Applicant is not a reporting issuer

We are applying to the **[identify principal regulator]** as principal regulator **[on behalf of the Applicant]** for a decision under the securities legislation (the Legislation) of the Jurisdictions that the Applicant is not a reporting issuer.

In this application, "securityholder" means, for a security, the beneficial owner of the security.

Under the simplified procedure in CSA Staff Notice 12-307, the Applicant represents that:

- the outstanding securities of the Applicant, including debt securities, are beneficially owned, directly or indirectly, by fewer than 15 securityholders in each of the jurisdictions of Canada and fewer than 51 securityholders in total worldwide;

- no securities of the Applicant, including debt securities, are traded in Canada or another country on a marketplace as defined in National Instrument 21-101 *Marketplace Operation* or any other facility for bringing together buyers and sellers of securities where trading data is publicly reported;

- the Applicant is applying for a decision that it is not a reporting issuer in all of the jurisdictions of Canada in which it is currently a reporting issuer; and

- the Applicant is not in default of any of its obligations under the Legislation as a reporting issuer.

[Enter name of Applicant]

[Signature of the person who has signing authority]

Example of a Decision Document under the Simplified Procedure

[Enter date]

[Enter name and address of Applicant]

Dear Sirs/Mesdames:

Re: [Enter name of applicant] (the Applicant) — application for a decision under the securities legislation of [list the jurisdictions] (the Jurisdictions) that the Applicant is not a reporting issuer

The Applicant has applied to the local securities regulatory authority or regulator (the Decision Maker) in each of the Jurisdictions for a decision under the securities legislation (the Legislation) of the Jurisdictions that the Applicant is not a reporting issuer.

In this decision, "securityholder" means, for a security, the beneficial owner of the security.

The Applicant has represented to the Decision Makers that:

(a) the outstanding securities of the Applicant, including debt securities, are beneficially owned, directly or indirectly, by fewer than 15 securityholders in each of the jurisdictions of Canada and fewer than 51 securityholders in total worldwide;

(b) no securities of the Applicant, including debt securities, are traded in Canada or another country on a marketplace as defined in National Instrument 21-101 *Marketplace Operation* or any other facility for bringing together buyers and sellers of securities where trading data is publicly reported;

(c) the Applicant is applying for a decision that it is not a reporting issuer in all of the jurisdictions of Canada in which it is currently a reporting issuer; and

(d) the Applicant is not in default of any of its obligations under the Legislation as a reporting issuer.

[If the principal regulator is Ontario, insert:]

Each of the Decision Makers is satisfied that the test contained in the Legislation that provides the Decision Maker with the jurisdiction to make the decision has been met and orders that the Applicant is not a reporting issuer.

OR

[If the principal regulator is Saskatchewan or New Brunswick, insert:]

Each of the Decision Makers is satisfied that the test contained in the Legislation that provides the Decision Maker with the jurisdiction to make the decision has been met and orders that the Applicant is not to be a reporting issuer.

OR

[If the principal regulator is Alberta or Nova Scotia, insert:]

Each of the Decision Makers is satisfied that the test contained in the Legislation that provides the Decision Maker with the jurisdiction to make the decision has been met and orders that the Applicant is deemed to have ceased to be a reporting issuer **[if a decision is also sought in Quebec, add:]** and that the Applicant's status as a reporting issuer is revoked.

OR

[If the principal regulator is Manitoba, insert:]

Each of the Decision Makers is satisfied that the test contained in the Legislation that provides the Decision Maker with the jurisdiction to make the decision has been met and makes an order declaring that the Applicant has ceased to be a reporting issuer **[if a decision is also sought in Quebec, add:]** and revoking the Applicant's status as a reporting issuer.

OR

[If principal regulator is Quebec, insert:]

Each of the Decision Makers is satisfied that the test contained in the Legislation that provides the Decision Maker with the jurisdiction to make the decision has been met and orders that the Applicant's status as a reporting issuer is revoked.

.... **(Name of signatory for the principal regulator)**

.... **(Title)**

.... **(Name of principal regulator)**

OSC Policy 12-602 — Designating an Issuer in Certain Other Canadian Jurisdictions as a Reporting Issuer in Ontario

Date: **June 29, 2001, as amended effective March 31, 2003 and March 16, 2007**

24 O.S.C.B. 3914, 26 O.S.C.B. 888 and 30 O.S.C.B. 2641

Part 1 — Application

1.1 The procedures set forth in this Policy Statement apply to applications made to the Ontario Securities Commission (the "Commission") under clause 1(11)(b) of the *Securities Act* (Ontario) (the "Act") for a designation order that an issuer is a reporting issuer for purposes of Ontario securities law (a "Designation Order") where the applicant issuer is a reporting issuer in certain other Canadian jurisdictions.

1.2 Notwithstanding section 1.1 of this Policy Statement, sections 1.3 and 1.4 of Part 1 and Parts 4 and 5 of this Policy Statement apply to all applications made under clause 1(11)(b) of the Act.

1.3 The procedures set forth in OSC Policy 2.1 *Applications to the Ontario Securities Commission*, or any successor instrument, apply to all applications made under clause 1(11)(b) of the Act except to the extent modified by this Policy Statement.

1.4 Notwithstanding anything contained in this Policy Statement, the Commission retains its discretion to act in the public interest with respect to its consideration of all applications made under clause 1(11)(b) of the Act.

Part 2 — Issuers Listed on the TSX Venture Exchange

2.1 Unless it is otherwise prejudicial to the public interest to do so, upon application under clause 1(11)(b) of the Act, a Designation Order will generally be granted by the Commission to an issuer whose securities are listed and posted for trading on the TSX Venture Exchange ("TSX-V") if:

    (1) the issuer is in good standing in all jurisdictions in which it is a reporting issuer or a reporting issuer equivalent; and

    (2) the issuer is in good standing under the rules, regulations and policies of the TSX-V.

2.2 In order to independently assess the "good standing" referred to in subsection 2.1(1), staff may review the applicant issuer's continuous disclosure record and request that any deficiencies in that record be addressed prior to any recommendation under clause 1(11)(b) of the Act being made.

Part 3 — Issuers Not Listed on the TSX Venture Exchange

3.1 Unless it is otherwise prejudicial to the public interest to do so, upon application under clause 1(11)(b) of the Act, a Designation Order will generally be granted by the Commission to an issuer who is a reporting issuer in British Columbia, Alberta, Saskatchewan, Quebec or Nova Scotia or is a reporting issuer equivalent in Manitoba (the "Relevant Jurisdictions") and whose securities are not listed on the TSX-V if:

    (1) the issuer has been a reporting issuer or a reporting issuer equivalent, as applicable, in one or more Relevant Jurisdictions for at least 12 months prior to the date of the application; and

    (2) the issuer is in good standing in all jurisdictions in which it is a reporting issuer or a reporting issuer equivalent.

3.2 In order to independently assess the "good standing" referred to in subsection 3.1(2), staff may review the applicant issuer's continuous disclosure record and request that any deficiencies in that record be addressed prior to any recommendation under clause 1(11)(b) of the Act being made.

Part 4 — Application Procedure

4.1 An application made under clause 1(11)(b) of the Act should include:

    (1) if applicable, particulars of the jurisdictions in which the issuer is a reporting issuer or a reporting issuer equivalent and the date the issuer became a reporting issuer in each such jurisdiction;

    (2) if applicable, particulars of the stock exchanges or trading or quotation systems on which the issuer's securities are traded or quoted;

    (3) particulars of any penalties or sanctions imposed against the issuer by a court relating to Canadian securities legislation or by a Canadian securities regulatory authority and the grounds on which they were imposed or the terms of the settlement agreement and the circumstances that gave rise to the settlement agreement;

    (4) particulars of any penalties or sanctions imposed and the grounds on which they were imposed or the terms of the settlement agreement and the circumstances that gave rise to the settlement agreement, if a director or officer of the issuer, or a shareholder holding sufficient securities of the issuer to affect materially the control of the issuer has (i) been subject to any penalties or sanctions imposed by a court relating to Canadian securities legislation or by a Canadian securities regulatory authority or has entered into a settlement agreement with a Canadian securities regulatory authority, or (ii) been subject to any other penalties or sanctions imposed by a court or regulatory body that would be likely to be considered important to a reasonable investor making an investment decision;

(5) particulars of:

(i) any known ongoing or concluded investigations by:

(a) a Canadian securities regulatory authority; or

(b) a court or regulatory body, other than a Canadian securities regulatory authority, that would be likely to be considered important to a reasonable investor making an investment decision; and

(ii) any bankruptcy or insolvency proceedings, or other proceedings, arrangements or compromises with creditors, or the appointment of a receiver, receiver manager or trustee, within the 10 years before the date of the application;

relating to the issuer, a director or officer of the issuer, or a shareholder holding sufficient securities of the issuer to affect materially the control of the issuer;

(6) particulars of:

(i) any cease trade or similar orders, or orders that denied access to any exemptions under Ontario securities law, for a period of more than 30 consecutive days, within the 10 years before the date of the application; and

(ii) any bankruptcy or insolvency proceedings, or other proceedings, arrangements or compromises with creditors, or the appointment of a receiver, receiver manager or trustee, within the 10 years before the date of the application;

relating to any other issuer which a director or officer of the issuer making the application, or a shareholder holding sufficient securities of such issuer to affect materially the control of such issuer, was a director or officer of at the time of such event;

(7) confirmation that the issuer is not on the default list of the securities regulatory authority in each jurisdiction in which the issuer is a reporting issuer or a reporting issuer equivalent;

(8) for security check purposes, a completed *Authorization of Indirect Collection of Personal Information* in the form attached hereto as Appendix A for each director, executive officer and promoter, if any, and each director and executive officer of the promoter, if any, of the issuer; and

(9) the filing fee prescribed under Rule 13-502 *Fees*.

Part 5 — SEDAR

5.1 Immediately upon receipt of a Designation Order, the issuer will be expected to amend its SEDAR Profile to indicate that it is a reporting issuer in Ontario.

Appendix A — Authorization of Indirect Collection of Personal Information

The attached Schedule 1 contains information concerning the name, position with or relationship to the applicant, name and address of employer, if other than the applicant, residential address, passport number and date of issuance, date and place of birth and citizenship of each director, executive officer, promoter, if any, and each director and executive officer of the promoter, if any, of the applicant named below (the "Issuer"). The Issuer hereby confirms that each person or company listed on Schedule 1

(a) has been notified by the Issuer

(i) of the Issuer's delivery to the Commission of the information pertaining to the person or company as set out in Schedule 1,

(ii) that such information is being collected indirectly by the Commission under the authority granted to it under the *Securities Act* (Ontario),

(iii) that such information is being collected for the purpose of enabling the Commission to discharge its obligations under the provisions of the *Securities Act* (Ontario) that permits the Commission to refuse to grant an order that an issuer be a reporting issuer for the purposes of Ontario securities law where it would be prejudicial to the public interest, and

(iv) that the title, business address and business telephone number of the public official who can answer questions about the Commission's indirect collection of the information is:

Administrative Assistant to the Director of Corporate Finance

Ontario Securities Commission

20 Queen Street West

19th Floor, Box 55

Toronto, Ontario M5H 3S8

(416) 593-8086

(b) has authorized the indirect collection of the information by the Commission.

Date: ....

.... *Name of Issuer*

Per:.........

.... Name

.... Official Capacity

(Please print the name of the individual whose signature appears in the official capacity)

Schedule 1 Personal Information to Appendix A

Authorization of Indirect Collection of Personal Information

[Name of Issuer]

Name and Position with or Relationship to Issuer	Name and Address of Employer, if other than Issuer	Residential Address [If Residential Address is outside North America provide Passport No. and Date of Issuance]	Date and Place of Birth	Citizenship
....	....	....	....	....

Adoption by OSC: 24 O.S.C.B. 3914 (June 29, 2001); Request for Comments: 24 O.S.C.B. 1531 (March 9, 2001).

Amendment to Policy: 26 O.S.C.B. 4375 and 888.

Amendment to Policy: 30 O.S.C.B. 2641.

Policies and Orders: BOR 1.2.

OSC Staff Notice 12-703 — Applications for a Decision that an Issuer is not a Reporting Issuer

Date: April 25, 2003, March 23, 2007 and July 26, 2012

26 O.S.C.B. 3107, 30 O.S.C.B. 2532 and 35 O.S.C.B. 6802

Purpose

This Notice provides information and guidance on applications that may be made under subclause 1(10)(a)(ii) of the *Securities Act* (Ontario)(the Act) for an order that an issuer is not a reporting issuer (a decision).

This Notice applies to an issuer that only requires a decision in Ontario. If a decision is required in more than one jurisdiction of Canada, please see the guidance in CSA Staff Notice 12-307 *Applications for a Decision that an Issuer is not a Reporting Issuer*.

Among other things, this Notice covers:

• how an issuer can apply for a decision under a simplified procedure if it meets certain conditions,

• how an issuer can apply for a decision if it is not eligible to use the simplified procedure,

• how a foreign issuer with a small securityholder presence in Canada can apply for a decision, and

• the procedure for dissolved issuers.

In this Notice, "securityholder" means, for a security, the beneficial owner of the security.

The Simplified Procedure

The Ontario Securities Commission (the Commission) has adopted a simplified procedure for certain applications under subclause 1(10)(a)(ii) of the Act in which an issuer is seeking a decision that it is not a reporting issuer. Pursuant to an assignment of certain of the Commission's powers that was made under subsection 6(3) of the Act, a decision under the simplified procedure can be made by the Director under the Act. The Director does not have the power to grant relief to a reporting issuer that does not meet the conditions for the simplified procedure (only the Commission may grant relief to such a reporting issuer).

The simplified procedure is available to a reporting issuer:

• whose outstanding securities, including debt securities, are beneficially owned, directly or indirectly, by fewer than 15 securityholders in Ontario and fewer than 51 securityholders in total worldwide,

• whose securities, including debt securities, are not traded in Canada or another country on a marketplace as defined in National Instrument 21-101 *Marketplace Operation* or any other facility for bringing together buyers and sellers of securities where trading data is publicly reported,

• that is not in default of any of its obligations as a reporting issuer, and

• that will not be a reporting issuer in any jurisdiction of Canada immediately following the director making a decision that the issuer is not a reporting issuer.

A reporting issuer may request a decision under the simplified procedure by submitting, a draft decision document and a letter in duplicate prepared by or on behalf of the issuer that:

• states that the issuer is seeking a decision of the Director that it is not a reporting issuer,

• references the simplified procedure in this Notice, and

• includes representations that the applicant meets each of the criteria set out in the simplified procedure in this Notice.

Schedule 1 includes a sample application letter and form of decision document. In some cases, staff may request additional information from the reporting issuer. The reporting issuer should make its application in paper and electronic format to:

Ontario Securities Commission

20 Queen Street West

Suite 1903, Box 55

Part 1: PROCEDURE

Toronto, ON

M5H 3S8

Attention: Applications Administrator

The issuer should provide an electronic copy of the application letter and form of decision document by email to: applications@osc.gov.on.ca. The application should be accompanied by the signed verification statement referred to in section D(e) of OSC Policy 2.1 *Applications to the Ontario Securities Commission*. If confidentiality is requested, the application should comply with section C.2 of OSC Policy 2.1.

What to do when the simplified procedure in this Notice is not available

If an issuer cannot meet all of the simplified procedure criteria in this Notice, the issuer should submit an application under the standard procedure for an application under OSC Policy 2.1 using a more detailed application letter and form of decision document.

Going-private transactions

Where the issuer is in the process of completing a going-private transaction following which it will want to stop being a reporting issuer, the issuer may apply for relief using the simplified procedure in this Notice prior to completing the transaction. The Director cannot make a decision until the transaction is complete and the issuer can represent that it has satisfied all the criteria for the simplified procedure.

Successor reporting issuers

In circumstances where an issuer has exchanged its securities with another party (or that party's securityholders) in connection with a statutory arrangement or procedure, the issuer should consider whether any other party in the transaction will or has become a reporting issuer following the exchange. If so, the issuer should disclose the name of that party in its application to stop being a reporting issuer and provide a brief summary of the statutory arrangement or procedure and the parties involved.

Issuers subject to the *Business Corporations Act* (Ontario)

The *Business Corporations Act* (Ontario)(the OBCA):

- contains certain provisions that apply to reporting issuers that were incorporated, continued or amalgamated under the OBCA (the OBCA refers to these reporting issuers as "offering corporations"), and

- provides, in subsection 1(6), that if an offering corporation no longer wants those provisions to apply to it, it must obtain an order from the Commission deeming it to have ceased to be offering its securities to the public.

If an offering corporation requires an order under subsection 1(6) of the OBCA, it must make a separate application to the Commission. A decision obtained under the simplified procedure in this Notice or other application under subclause 1(10)(a)(ii) of the Act is only for the purposes of securities legislation.

Foreign issuers

Foreign-incorporated issuers often seek decisions that they are not reporting issuers under applicable securities legislation when they have a declining numbers of securityholders in Canada. In general, these issuers do not meet the criteria for the simplified procedure in this Notice because they typically have many beneficial securityholders in jurisdictions in Canada, and their securities are listed on one or more exchanges outside of Canada. For guidance on how such a foreign issuer can obtain a decision that the issuer is not a reporting issuer, please see the guidance under the heading "Foreign issuers" in CSA Staff Notice 12-307.

Reporting issuer that has been dissolved or terminated

A reporting issuer does not need to apply for a decision that it is not a reporting issuer if it is:

- a corporation that was dissolved under applicable corporate legislation,

- a limited partnership that was dissolved under applicable limited partnership legislation,

- a trust that was terminated under its declaration of trust, or

- another form of business organization that was dissolved or terminated under its applicable governing legislation or constating or establishing document.

In each case, it will be sufficient if an agent files evidence of the dissolution or termination with the Commission.

For a corporation, sufficient evidence includes a copy of the certificate and articles of dissolution.

For a limited partnership, sufficient evidence typically includes:

- a copy of the declaration of dissolution or similar document filed under applicable limited partnership legislation, and

- a written representation from the general partner about the effective date of dissolution under applicable limited partnership legislation.

For a trust, sufficient evidence typically includes:

- a copy of the resolution authorizing the termination of the trust,

- a report on voting results indicating that the resolution was passed,

- a written representation that the trust no longer exists (it is sufficient if this representation is provided by filing counsel or former trustees or officers),

- a copy of the change in corporate structure notice filed under section 4.9 of National Instrument 51-102 *Continuous Disclosure Obligations*, and

- evidence such as a copy of a news release or written submission from filing counsel that the trust has no securities outstanding and none listed on an exchange.

If an issuer has commenced dissolution proceedings but still exists, it will remain a reporting issuer in the absence of a decision that it is not a reporting issuer.

Schedule 1 — Example of an Application Letter under the Simplified Procedure

[Enter date]

Ontario Securities Commission

20 Queen Street West

Suite 1903, Box 55

Toronto, ON

M5H 3S8

Attention: Applications Administrator

Dear Sirs/Mesdames:

Re: [Enter name of applicant] (the Applicant) — application for an order under subclause 1(10)(a)(ii) of the *Securities Act* (Ontario)(the Act) that the Applicant is not a reporting issuer

We are applying to the Ontario Securities Commission **[on behalf of the Applicant]** for an order under subclause 1(10)(a)(ii) of the Act that the Applicant is not a reporting issuer.

In this application, "securityholder" means, for a security, the beneficial owner of the security.

Under the simplified procedure in OSC Staff Notice 12-703, the Applicant represents that:

- the outstanding securities of the Applicant, including debt securities, are beneficially owned, directly or indirectly, by fewer than 15 securityholders in Ontario and fewer than 51 securityholders in total worldwide;

- no securities of the Applicant, including debt securities, are traded in Canada or another country on a marketplace as defined in National Instrument 21-101 *Marketplace Operation* or any other facility for bringing together buyers and sellers of securities where trading data is publicly reported;

- the Applicant is not in default of any of its obligations under the Act as a reporting issuer; and

- the Applicant will not be a reporting issuer in any jurisdiction in Canada immediately following the Director granting the relief requested.

[Enter name of Applicant]

[Signature of the person who has signing authority]

Example of a Decision Document under the Simplified Procedure

[Enter date]

[Enter name and address of Applicant]

Dear Sirs/Mesdames:

Re: [Enter name of applicant] (the Applicant) — application for an order under subclause 1(10)(a)(ii) of the *Securities Act* (Ontario)(the Act) that the Applicant is not a reporting issuer

The Applicant has applied to the Ontario Securities Commission for an order under subclause 1(10)(a)(ii) of the Act that the Applicant is not a reporting issuer.

In this order, "securityholder" means, for a security, the beneficial owner of the security.

The Applicant has represented to the Commission that:

(a) the outstanding securities of the Applicant, including debt securities, are beneficially owned, directly or indirectly, by fewer than 15 securityholders in Ontario and fewer than 51 securityholders in total worldwide;

(b) no securities of the Applicant, including debt securities, are traded in Canada or another country on a marketplace as defined in National Instrument 21-101 *Marketplace Operation* or any other facility for bringing together buyers and sellers of securities where trading data is publicly reported;

(c) the Applicant is not in default of any of its obligations under the Legislation as a reporting issuer; and

(d) the Applicant will not be a reporting issuer in any jurisdiction of Canada immediately following the Director granting the relief requested.

The Director is satisfied that it would not be prejudicial to the public interest to grant the requested relief and orders that the Applicant is not a reporting issuer.

.... [Name of signatory]

[Title]

Ontario Securities Commission

Policies and Orders: CSAN 12-307.

OSC Staff Notice 12-704 — Materials to be Provided on a Compact Disc or 3.25" Disk or Exemptive Relief Applications

Date: April 7, 2006

29 O.S.C.B. 2904

In addition to materials filed in paper format, applicants for exemptive relief are asked to provide the following materials on a compact disc or a 3.25" disk in Microsoft Word format:

- a copy of the application; and

- a draft form of the decision document.

Filers do not need to provide these materials if the Commission is a non-principal regulator.

Filers are reminded to review National Policy 12-201 *Mutual Reliance Review System for Exemptive Relief Applications* and O.S.C. Policy 2.1 *Applications to the Ontario Securities Commission* for additional guidance relating to application filings.

1.3 — Filings With Securities Regulatory Authority

National Instrument 13-101 — System for Electronic Document Analysis and Retrieval (SEDAR)

Amended: September 7, 1999, September 30, 2003, March 30, 2004, June 1, 2005, November 1, 2006, January 1, 2011, May 6, 2011, May 14, 2013, October 12, 2013 and December 8, 2015.

19 O.S.C.B. (Supp) 1, 22 O.S.C.B. 540, 26 O.S.C.B. 5546, 27 O.S.C.B. 3602, 28 O.S.C.B. (Supp-1) 49, 29 O.S.C.B. 8851, 33 O.S.C.B. (Supp. 5) 35, 33 O.S.C.B. 11435, 34 O.S.C.B. 5171, 36 O.S.C.B. 4940, 36 O.S.C.B. 9607 and 38 O.S.C.B. 8323.

Table of Contents

Part 1 — Definitions and Interpretation

1.1 — Definitions

In this Instrument

"cover page information" means the information that is specified in the SEDAR Filer Manual and that is required to be filed as part of an electronic filing;

"electronic filer" means a person or company referred to in subsection 2.1(1) that is required to comply with this Instrument;

"electronic filing" means a document that is filed under securities legislation or securities directions in electronic format or the act of filing a document under securities legislation or securities directions in electronic format, as the context indicates;

"electronic format" means the computerized format of a document prepared and transmitted in accordance with the standards, procedures and guidelines contained in the SEDAR Filer Manual;

"filer profile" means a set of information providing a profile of an electronic filer;

"filing agent" means a person or company that is authorized to make an electronic filing on behalf of an electronic filer;

"filing service subscriber" means an electronic filer or a filing agent that enters into an agreement with the SEDAR filing service contractor to make electronic filings through SEDAR;

"foreign issuer (SEDAR)" means an issuer that is incorporated or organized under the laws of a foreign jurisdiction, unless

    (a) voting securities carrying more than 50 percent of the votes for the election of directors are held by persons or companies whose last address as shown on the books of the issuer is in Canada and either

        (i) the majority of the senior officers or directors of the issuer are citizens or residents of Canada, or

        (ii) assets of the issuer representing more than 50 percent of the total of all assets of the issuer are located in Canada, or

        (iii) the business of the issuer is administered principally in Canada; or

    (b) the issuer has a class of its equity securities listed and posted for trading on a stock exchange in Canada and does not have any of its equity securities listed and posted for trading on a stock exchange or quoted in a published market in any foreign jurisdiction;

"paper format" means the format of a document printed on paper;

"SEDAR" means the computer system for the transmission, receipt, acceptance, review and dissemination of documents filed in electronic format known as the System for Electronic Document Analysis and Retrieval;

"SEDAR Filer Manual" means the SEDAR Filer Manual incorporated by reference in this Instrument under section 4.1;

"SEDAR filer software" means the software provided under license to electronic filers and filing agents by the SEDAR filing service contractor;

"SEDAR filing service contractor" means the Alberta Securities Commission or a successor appointed by the securities regulatory authority to provide services in respect of electronic filings;

"supporting document" means a document required to be filed in support of, or otherwise in connection with, a filing made under securities legislation or securities directions; and

"third party filer" means a person or company required to file a document because of an activity relating to or affecting an issuer or the issuer's securityholders.

1.2 — Interpretation

(1) In this Instrument, unless the context otherwise requires, **"document"** includes "information" and "material" as those words are used in securities legislation or securities directions, as applicable.

(2) In this Instrument, a reference to a document that is required or permitted to be filed includes a document that is required or permitted to be deposited or filed with, or delivered, furnished, provided or submitted to, the securities regulatory authority under securities legislation or securities directions, as applicable.

(3) The filing of a document in electronic format with the securities regulatory authority under this Instrument constitutes

    (a) if the document is required or permitted to be filed only under this Instrument, the filing of that document under securities legislation or securities directions, as applicable;

(b) if the document is otherwise required or permitted to be filed under securities legislation or securities directions, the filing of that document under securities legislation or securities directions, as applicable; and

(c) if the document is required or permitted to be delivered, furnished, provided or submitted to the securities regulatory authority under securities legislation or securities directions, the delivery of that document.

(4) In this Instrument, a reference to a "SEDAR Form" refers to one of the several SEDAR forms appended to the SEDAR Filer Manual.

Part 2 — Electronic Filing Requirements

2.1 — Filers Required to Make Electronic Filings

(1) The following persons or companies shall comply with this Instrument:

1. Every issuer, other than a foreign issuer (SEDAR), that is required or otherwise is proposing to file a document under securities legislation or securities directions.

2. Every foreign issuer (SEDAR) that files a notice of election to become an electronic filer in the manner provided in subsection (2), unless it has elected to cease making electronic filings in the manner provided in subsection (4).

3. Every third party filer that makes a filing of a type to which this Instrument applies concerning an issuer that is required to comply with this Instrument.

(2) A foreign issuer (SEDAR) that is required or otherwise is proposing to file a document under securities legislation or securities directions may elect to become subject to this Instrument by filing in paper format on SEDAR Form 5 a notice of election to become an electronic filer.

(3) A foreign issuer (SEDAR) that files a notice of election to become an electronic filer shall comply with this Instrument for at least two years after filing the notice of election.

(4) A foreign issuer (SEDAR) that files a notice of election to become an electronic filer may elect to cease complying with this Instrument at any time after the expiry of the two-year period by filing a notice to this effect in electronic format at least 30 days before making a filing that does not comply with this Instrument.

(5) A person or company that is not required to comply with this Instrument shall not file any document through SEDAR.

2.2 — Documents to be Filed in Electronic Format

(1) An electronic filer that is required or otherwise is proposing to file any of the following documents shall file the documents in electronic format in accordance with this Instrument:

1. A document listed in Appendix A.

2. An amendment or supplement to a document filed in electronic format.

3. A supporting document, written correspondence or other written material relating to a document filed in electronic format.

4. A document required to be filed because it was sent by an issuer to its securityholders.

5. A document required to be filed because it was filed with a governmental agency or a stock exchange located outside the local jurisdiction.

6. A document that is required by securities legislation or securities directions other than this Instrument to be filed in electronic format.

(2) An electronic filer may file an application or request for exemptive relief from, or approval under, securities legislation in electronic format if

(a) the application or request relates to a prospectus filed or to be filed in electronic format; and

(b) the exemptive relief or approval being sought is reasonably required to facilitate a distribution of securities to which the prospectus relates.

(3) Despite paragraph 3 of subsection (1), the appendices or other supplemental materials forming part of a mining report filed as a supporting document may be filed in paper format.

2.3 — Documents to be Filed in Paper Format

(1) The following shall not be filed in electronic format:

1. A document that is required or permitted to be filed on a confidential basis under securities legislation or securities directions unless the securities legislation or securities directions require the confidential filing to be made in electronic format.

2. A document for which confidential treatment is requested under securities legislation or securities directions or is claimed under applicable freedom of information legislation.

3. An oil and gas report that is prepared and filed as a supporting document, except for any part that is a summary of the report, provided that this paragraph 3 does not apply to a statement or report referred to in section 2.1 of National Instrument 51-101 *Standards of Disclosure for Oil and Gas Activities*.

4. A document, other than one referred to in paragraphs 1, 2 or 3, that is not required or permitted to be filed in electronic format under section 2.2, unless the securities regulatory authority has approved the filing of the document in electronic format.

(2) If a document that was filed in paper format under paragraph 1 of subsection (1) ceases to remain confidential because the subject matter of the document is generally disclosed, the electronic filer shall file a copy of the document in electronic format within 10 days following general disclosure.

(3) If a confidential treatment request made pursuant to securities legislation in respect of a document filed in paper format under paragraph 2 of subsection (1) is rejected, the electronic filer shall file a copy of the document in electronic format within 10 days following the rejection.

2.4 — Manner of Effecting Electronic Filings

A document that is filed in electronic format shall be transmitted electronically using the SEDAR filer software in the manner required by the SEDAR Filer Manual.

2.5 — Filing Service Subscribers

Before making an electronic filing through SEDAR, the electronic filer or its filing agent shall become a filing service subscriber by furnishing an Application For SEDAR Filing Services on SEDAR Form 1 to the SEDAR filing service contractor and entering into the Filing Service Subscriber's Agreement on SEDAR Form 2.

2.6 — Hours for Transmission of Electronic Filings

Electronic filings may be transmitted through SEDAR to the securities regulatory authority on any business day between the hours of 7:00 a.m. and 11:00 p.m. Eastern Standard Time or Eastern Daylight Savings Time, whichever is in effect in Toronto, Ontario, Canada, and on any other day or at any other time that is provided in the SEDAR Filer Manual or that the securities regulatory authority announces by press release.

2.7 — Date of Filing

(1) A document filed in electronic format is, for purposes of securities legislation or securities directions, filed on the day that the electronic transmission of the document is completed.

(2) Despite subsection (1), a document filed in electronic format is, for purposes of Quebec securities legislation or Quebec securities directions, filed on the day that the document is retrieved in electronic format from SEDAR by the Commission des valeurs mobilières du Québec instead of on the day that the electronic transmission of the document is completed.

(3) Despite subsections (1) and (2), for purposes of a time period in securities legislation or securities directions that begins on or immediately after the date of the filing of a document filed in electronic format, the date of the filing of the document is the day on which the electronic transmission of the document is completed unless it is not completed on a business day by 5:00 p.m. local time in the city where the securities regulatory authority is located, in which case the date of the filing is the next business day.

2.8 — Payment of Filing Fees

(1) The fees payable to the securities regulatory authority for the filing of a document in electronic format shall be paid by an electronic payment authorized at the time the filing is made.

(2) A filing service subscriber shall make the payment referred to in subsection (1) by transmitting instructions through SEDAR in the manner set out in the SEDAR Filer Manual for the purpose of effecting an electronic funds transfer from the filing service subscriber to the securities regulatory authority.

Part 3 — Electronic Filing Exemptions

3.1 — Temporary Hardship Exemption

(1) If unanticipated technical difficulties prevent the timely preparation and transmission of an electronic filing, an electronic filer may file the document in paper format under cover of SEDAR Form 3 no later than two business days after the day on which the electronic filing was required or permitted.

(2) An electronic filer shall include the following legend in capital letters at the top of the first page of a document filed by it in paper format under this section:

> IN ACCORDANCE WITH SECTION 3.1 OF NATIONAL INSTRUMENT 13-101 — SYSTEM FOR ELECTRONIC DOCUMENT ANALYSIS AND RETRIEVAL (SEDAR), THIS (SPECIFY DOCUMENT) IS BEING FILED IN PAPER FORMAT UNDER A TEMPORARY HARDSHIP EXEMPTION.

(3) The requirements of securities legislation and securities directions relating to paper format filings and the payment of applicable filing fees apply to a filing under subsection (1) except that signatures to the paper format document may be in typed form rather than manual format.

(4) If a paper format document is filed in the manner and within the time prescribed in this section, the specific date by which the document is required to be filed under securities legislation or securities directions is extended to the date on which the filing is made in paper format.

(5) If an electronic filer makes a paper format filing under this section, the electronic filer shall file a copy of the paper format document in electronic format within three business days after the paper format document is filed.

(6) The electronic filer shall include the following statement in capital letters at the top of the first page of the electronic format copy of the document:

> THIS DOCUMENT IS A COPY OF THE (SPECIFY DOCUMENT) FILED ON (DATE) UNDER A TEMPORARY HARDSHIP EXEMPTION UNDER SECTION 3.1 OF NATIONAL INSTRUMENT 13-101 — SYSTEM FOR ELECTRONIC DOCUMENT ANALYSIS AND RETRIEVAL (SEDAR).

3.2 — Continuing Hardship Exemption

(1) An electronic filer may make an application for a continuing hardship exemption if an electronic filing cannot be made without undue burden or expense.

(2) An application for a continuing hardship exemption shall be filed in paper format contemporaneously with the filing of a similar application in another jurisdiction in which the electronic filing is required or proposed to be made and at least 20 days before the earliest date on which the electronic filing is required or proposed to be made, as applicable.

(3) An application for a continuing hardship exemption shall include the following:

> 1. A list of the jurisdictions, other than the local jurisdiction, in which the application is being made.
>
> 2. A list of the documents for which the exemption is being sought and, if applicable, the length of time for which the exemption is being requested.
>
> 3. The reason for requesting the exemption from filing the documents in electronic format and, if applicable, the justification for the length of time for which the exemption is being requested.

(4) The regulator or, if authorized to grant an exemption under section 7.1, the securities regulatory authority may grant or deny a continuing hardship exemption and shall notify the electronic filer in writing of a decision to grant or deny the exemption as soon as practicable after making its decision.

(5) If the application for a continuing hardship exemption is denied, the electronic filer shall make any required electronic filing on the required or the proposed filing date, as applicable.

(6) If the application for a continuing hardship exemption is granted, the electronic filer shall file the document for which the continuing hardship exemption is granted in paper format on the required or the proposed filing date, as applicable.

(7) An electronic filer that files a document in paper format under a continuing hardship exemption shall include the following legend in capital letters at the top of the first page of the document:

> IN ACCORDANCE WITH SECTION 3.2 OF NATIONAL INSTRUMENT 13-101 — SYSTEM FOR ELECTRONIC DOCUMENT ANALYSIS AND RETRIEVAL (SEDAR), THIS (SPECIFY DOCUMENT) IS BEING FILED IN PAPER FORMAT UNDER A CONTINUING HARDSHIP EXEMPTION.

(8) If a continuing hardship exemption is granted for a limited period, the exemption may be conditional upon the filing of the electronic format copy of the document that is the subject of the exemption upon the expiration of the period for which the exemption is granted.

3.3 — Exemption for Pre-Existing Documents

(1) Despite subsection 2.2(1), any supporting document, written correspondence or other written material relating to a document required to be filed in electronic format may be filed in paper format if the supporting document, written correspondence or other written material was prepared and issued, published or distributed before January 1, 1997.

(2) An electronic filer filing a supporting document, written correspondence or other written material in paper format under subsection (1) shall do so under cover of SEDAR Form 4 no later than two business days after the date of filing the electronic format document to which it relates.

(3) The requirements under securities legislation for paper format filings apply to a filing under subsection (1).

Part 4 — Preparation and Transmission of Electronic Filings

4.1 — SEDAR Filer Manual

(1) The most recent version of the SEDAR Filer Manual: Standards, Procedures and Guidelines for Electronic Filing with the Canadian Securities Administrators, as approved by the regulator or the securities regulatory authority, is incorporated by refernce in this Instrument.

(2) An electronic filing shall be prepared and transmitted in accordance with the standards, procedures and guidelines set forth in the SEDAR Filer Manual.

4.2 — Cover Page Information

(1) An electronic filing shall be accompanied by the cover page information required for the particular electronic filing.

(2) The cover page information shall be filed in the form and manner required by the SEDAR Filer Manual.

4.3 — Signatures

(1) A signature to or within any electronic filing shall be presented in typed form rather than manual form.

(2) An electronic filing that is required to be signed or certified shall be signed by means of an electronic entry of the name of the person or company required to sign or certify the electronic filing that is executed, adopted or authorized by the person or company as a signature.

(3) No prospectus, take-over bid circular, issuer bid circular, directors' circular, officers' circular or annual information form for a mutual fund, or amendment or supplement to any of these documents, that contains a certificate signed by a person or company, shall be filed in electronic format unless that person or company has manually signed a certificate of authentication on SEDAR Form 6.

(4) An electronic filer that makes an electronic filing to which subsection (3) applies shall file the manually signed certificate of authentication required under that subsection with the SEDAR filing service contractor at one of its offices listed in the SEDAR Filer Manual within three business days after the electronic filing is made.

4.4 — Incorporation by Reference

(1) The following documents shall not be incorporated by reference into an electronic filing:

1. A document filed in paper format in contravention of this Instrument.

2. A document filed in paper format under a temporary hardship exemption for which a required confirming electronic copy has not been filed.

(2) Subject to subsection (3), if an electronic filing incorporates by reference all or part of a document filed previously in paper format, the document or the part incorporated by reference shall be filed in electronic format as a supporting document to the electronic filing.

(3) Subsection (2) does not apply to an electronic filing made by a person or company that has been an electronic filer for less than one year.

4.5 — Maps and Photographs

(1) If a document to be filed in electronic format contains or is supplemented by a map or photograph and that map or photograph exceeds 8-1/2 inches by 11 inches or 21.5 centimetres by 28 centimetres, the map or the photograph, as applicable, shall be omitted from the electronic filing.

(2) If a map or photograph is omitted from an electronic filing, the electronic filer shall include a reference to the omitted map or photograph in the electronic filing.

(3) An electronic filer shall make a paper format copy of each map or photograph that is omitted from an electronic filing and shall retain that copy for six years after the date of the electronic filing.

(4) Upon request made by the securities regulatory authority within the six year period, an electronic filer shall deliver to the securities regulatory authority a paper format copy of a map or photograph omitted from an electronic filing.

4.6 — Red Ink

An electronic filer may satisfy any requirement that information be presented in red ink in a document to be filed in electronic format by presenting the information in the electronic format version of the document in bold face type and capital letters.

4.7 — Format of Documents and Number of Copies

A requirement in securities legislation or securities directions relating to the format in which a document to be filed must be printed or specifying the number of copies of a document that must be filed does not apply to an electronic filing made in accordance with this Instrument.

4.8 — Production of Electronic Format Documents By The Securities Regulatory Authority

(1) Subject to subsections (2) and (3), a document required or permitted to be issued or delivered by the securities regulatory authority under securities legislation or securities directions in response to or for an electronic filing may be issued or delivered solely in electronic format in accordance with this Instrument.

(2) The securities regulatory authority may satisfy any requirement that a document filed in electronic format be made available for public inspection by making available a printed copy or other output of the electronic filing readable by sight.

(3) The securities regulatory authority may satisfy any requirement to produce or make available an original or certified copy of a document filed in electronic format by providing a printed copy or other output of the electronic filing readable by sight that contains or is accompanied by a certification by the regulator that the printed copy or output is a copy of the document filed in electronic format.

4.9 — Official Copy of Electronic Format Documents

(1) For purposes of securities legislation, securities directions or any other related purpose, the official copy of a document filed in electronic format by an electronic filer or issued or delivered in electronic format by the securities regulatory authority is the electronic format version stored in SEDAR.

(2) Despite subsection (1), for purposes of Quebec securities legislation or Quebec securities directions, the official copy of a document filed in electronic format by an electronic filer is the electronic format version of the document retrieved from SEDAR by the Commission des valeurs mobilières du Québec instead of the electronic format version stored in SEDAR.

Part 5 — Filer Profiles

5.1 — Electronic Filing of Filer Profile Information

(1) An electronic filer shall file a filer profile in electronic format through SEDAR before making any other electronic filing.

(2) A filer profile shall be in the form required by and contain the information set out in the SEDAR Filer Manual.

(3) An electronic filer shall ensure that the information contained in its filer profile is correct in all material respects and shall file an amended filer profile in electronic format within 10 days following any change in the information contained in its filer profile.

5.2 — Liability for Filer Profile Information

A filer profile is not considered to be incorporated by reference in, or to otherwise form part of, any document that is subject to the civil liability provisions of securities legislation.

Part 6 — Joint Filings

6.1 — Joint Filings

An electronic filer shall file in electronic format in accordance with this Instrument a document that is to be filed jointly by an electronic filer and another person or company that is not an electronic filer.

Part 7 — Exemption

7.1 — Exemption

(1) The regulator or the securities regulatory authority may grant an exemption to this Instrument, in whole or in part, subject to such conditions or restrictions as may be imposed in the exemption.

(2) Despite subsection (1), in Ontario only the regulator may grant such an exemption.

Appendix A — Mandated Electronic Filings

Applicable Filing	Applicable Jurisdictions*
I *Mutual Fund Issuers*	
A. Securities Offerings	
1. Preliminary Simplified Prospectus, Annual Information Form and Fund Facts	
2. Pro Forma Simplified Prospectus, Annual information Form and Fund Facts	
3. Final Simplified Prospectus, Annual Information Form and Fund Facts	
4. Preliminary Long Form Prospectus	
5. Pro Forma Long Form Prospectus	
6. Final Long Form Prospectus	
7. Initial Fund Facts	
B. Continuous Disclosure	
1. Annual Financial Statements	
2. Interim Financial Statements/Report	
3. Annual Report	Que
4. Compliance Reports — Sale and Redemption of Securities	
5. Compliance Reports — Commingling of Money	
6. News Release	
7. Material Change Report	
8.1 Annual Management Report of Fund Performance	
8.2 Interim Management Report of Fund Performance	
9. Notice of Securityholders' Meeting and Record Date	
10. Management Proxy Circular/Information Circular	
11. Change of Auditor Filings	
12. Change in Year End Filings	
13. Labour Sponsored Investment Fund Valuation Reports	
14. Report of Management Company–Transactions with related persons or companies (Form 81-903F–British Columbia, Form 38–Alberta and Ontario, Form 36–Saskatchewan, Form 39–Nova Scotia, and Form 37–Newfoundland)	BC, Alta, Sask, Ont, NS and Nfld
15. Annual Information Form	
16. Change in Legal Structure Filings	
17. Material Contracts	
18. Report by Independent Review Committee	
19. Manager — transactions in securities of related issuers	
20. Manager — transactions under Part 4 of NI 81-102	
21. Manager — notification under Part 5 of NI 81-107	
C. Exemption and Other Applications	
1. Applications Pursuant to a National Instrument or National Policy Regulating Mutual Funds	
II *Other Issuers (Reporting/Non-reporting)*	
A. Securities Offerings	
(a) General Filings:	
1. [repealed]	

Applicable Filing		Applicable Jurisdictions*
2.	[repealed]	
3.	[repealed]	
4.	Preliminary Short Form Prospectus	
5.	Final Short Form Prospectus	
6.	[repealed]	
6.1	Base Short Form PREP Prospectus	
6.2	Base Long Form PREP Prospectus	
7.	Preliminary Base Shelf Prospectus	
8.	Final Base Shelf Prospectus	
9.	Shelf Prospectus Supplement	
10.	Preliminary Prospectus — Multijurisdictional Disclosure System ("MJDS")	
11.	Final Prospectus — MJDS	
12.	Prospectus Supplement — MJDS	
13.	Preliminary Long Form Prospectus	
14.	Pro Forma Long Form Prospectus	
15.	Final Long Form Prospectus	
16.	Supplemented Long Form PREP Prospectus	
16.1	Supplemented Short Form PREP Prospectus	
17.	[repealed]	
18.	[repealed]	
19.	Rights Offering — Circular	
20.	Rights Offering — Minimal Connection	
1.	Prospectus — Distribution outside Québec (QC sec. 12 Act)	Que
B.	Continuous Disclosure	
(a)	General Filings:	
1.	News Release	
2.	Material Change Report	
3.	Annual Financial Statements	
4.	Interim Financial Statements/Report	
5.	Annual Report	Que
6.	Annual Information Form (Non-POP System)	
7.	Management's Discussion & Analysis	BC, Ont & Que
8.1	Annual Management Report of Fund Performance	
8.2	Interim Management Report of Fund Performance	
9.	Notice of Securityholders' Meeting and Record Date	
10.	Management Proxy Circular/Information Circular	
11.	Report of Finance Company (Form 29 — British Columbia, Alberta, and Ontario, Form 27 — Saskatchewan)	BC, Alta, Sask & Ont
12.	Change of Auditor Filings	
13.	Future Oriented Financial Information Filings	
14.	Change in Year End Filings	
15.	Form 1 (Resale Rule)	
16.	Oil and Gas Annual Disclosure (NI 51-101)	
17.	Change in Corporate/Legal Structure Filings	
18.	Material Documents/Contracts	
19.	Report by Independent Review Committee	
20.	Manager — transactions in securities of related issuers	
21.	Manager — transactions under Part 4 of NI 81-102	
22.	Manager — notification under Part 5 of NI 81-107	
(b)	Ontario Filings:	
1.	Junior Natural Resource Issuer Filings	Ont
C.	Securities Acquisitions	
1.	Issuer Bid Circular	

Applicable Filing		Applicable Jurisdictions*
2.	Notice of Change or Variation	
3.	Issuer Bid Reports	Ont & Que
D.	Going Private and Related Party Transactions	
1.	Going Private Transaction Filings	Ont & Que
2.	Related Party Transaction Filings	Ont & Que
III	*Third Party Filers*	
1.	Take-over Bid Circular	
2.	Notice of Change or Variation	
3.	Directors' Circular	
4.	Director's or Officer's Circular	
5.	Take-over Bid Reports	Ont & Que
6.	Securities Acquisition (Early Warnings) Press Release and Report	BC, Alta, Sask, Man, Ont, Que, NB, NS, Nfld, NWT, Nun, PEI, & YT
7.	Proxy Solicitation Materials	

Notes:

* **"Applicable Jurisdiction"** *means a jurisdiction in which the particular filing is specifically required by securities legislation or securities directions. All jurisdictions are applicable unless otherwise indicated.*

Final Rule: (1996) O.S.C.B. (Supp.) 1 (December 20, 1996); Notice of Approval by OSC: (1996) O.S.C.B. (Supp.) 3 (November 15, 1996); Request for Comments: (1996) 19 O.S.C.B. 2345.

Amendment to Rule: (1999) 22 O.S.C.B. 540; Approval by OSC: (1999) 22 O.S.C.B. 3833; Request for Comments: (1999) 22 O.S.C.B. 1279.

Amendment to Rule: (2003) 26 O.S.C.B. 5546; Approval by OSC: (2003) 26 O.S.C.B. 5517; Request for Comments: (2003) 26 O.S.C.B. 587.

Amendment to Rule: (2004) 27 O.S.C.B. 3602; Approval by OSC: (2003) 26 O.S.C.B. 8217; Request for Comments: (2003) 26 O.S.C.B. 991.

Amendment to Rule: (2005) 28 O.S.C.B. 4972; Approval by OSC: (2005) 28 O.S.C.B. (Supp-1) 49; Request for Comments: (2004) 27 O.S.C.B. 5157; (2002) 25 O.S.C.B. 6273.

Amendment to Rule: (2006) 29 O.S.C.B. 8851; Approval by OSC: (2006) 29 O.S.C.B. (Supp-1) 1; Request for Comments: (2005) 28 O.S.C.B. (Supp-1) 1 and (2004) 27 O.S.C.B. 465.

Amendment to Rule: (2010) 33 O.S.C.B. (Supp. 5) 35; Approval by OSC: (2010) 33 O.S.C.B. (Supp. 3) 1.

Amendment to Rule: (2010) 33 O.S.C.B. 11435; Approval by OSC: (2010) 33 O.S.C.B. (Supp. 4) 1.

Amendment to Rule: CSAN 11-314.

Amendment to Rule: (2013) 36 O.S.C.B. 4940; Approval by OSC: (2013) 36 (Supp. 2) 1; Request for Comments: (2011) 34 O.S.C.B. (Aupp. 4) 1.

Amendment to Rule: (2013) 36 O.S.C.B. 9607; Approval by OSC: (2013) 36 O.S.C.B. 8569 (correction) and 7217; Request for Comments: (2013) 36 O.S.C.B. 1081

Policies and Orders: CSAN 13-117, 13-138

MULTILATERAL INSTRUMENT 13-102 — SYSTEM FEES FOR SEDAR AND NRD

Date: October 12, 2013, amended December 8, 2015
36 O.S.C.B. 9601 and December 8, 2015

PART 1 — DEFINITIONS AND INTERPRETATION

1. Definitions: — (1) In this Instrument,

"annual information form" means an "AIF" as defined by National Instrument 51-102 *Continuous Disclosure Obligations* or an annual information form for the purposes of Part 9 of National Instrument 81-106 *Investment Fund Continuous Disclosure*;

"initial filer profile" means a filer profile filed in accordance with subsection 5.1(1) of National Instrument 13-101 *System for Electronic Document Analysis and Retrieval (SEDAR)*;

"issuer bid" means an issuer bid to which Part 2 of National Instrument 62-104 *Take-Over Bids and Issuer Bids* applies;

"shelf prospectus" means a prospectus filed under National Instrument 44-102 *Shelf Distributions*;

"take-over bid" means a take-over bid to which Part 2 of National Instrument 62-104 *Take-Over Bids and Issuer Bids* applies.

(2) In this Instrument, a term referred to in Column 1 of the following table has the meaning ascribed to it in the Instrument referred to in Column 2 opposite that term.

Column 1 Defined Term	Column 2 Instrument
CPC instrument	National Instrument 45-106 *Prospectus Exemptions*
firm filer	National Instrument 31-102 *National Registration Database*
individual filer	National Instrument 31-102 *National Registration Database*
long form prospectus	National Instrument 41-101 *General Prospectus Requirements*
MJDS prospectus	National Instrument 71-101 *The Multijurisdictional Disclosure System*
NRD	National Instrument 31-102 *National Registration Database*
principal jurisdiction	Multilateral Instrument 11-102 *Passport System*
principal regulator	Multilateral Instrument 11-102 *Passport System*
rights offering circular	Section 2.1 of National Instrument 45-106 *Prospectus Exemptions*
SEDAR	National Instrument 13-101 *System for Electronic Document Analysis and Retrieval (SEDAR)*
short form prospectus	National Instrument 41-101 *General Prospectus Requirements*
sponsoring firm	National Instrument 33-109 *Registration Information*, in Form 33-109F4 *Registration of Individuals and Review of Permitted Individuals*

2. Inconsistency with other instruments — If there is any conflict or inconsistency between this Instrument and National Instrument 13-101 *System for Electronic Document Analysis and Retrieval (SEDAR)* or National Instrument 31-102 *National Registration Database*, this Instrument prevails.

PART 2 — SEDAR SYSTEM FEES

3. Local system fees — In Québec, a person or company making the type of filing described in Column C of Appendix A with the Autorité des marchés financiers must pay to the Autorité des marchés financiers the system fee specified in Column D of that Appendix.

4. System fees — (1) A person or company making a filing, in the local jurisdiction, of the type described in Column B of Appendix B, and of the category referred to in Column A of that Appendix, must pay to the securities regulatory authority the system fee specified in Column C or D of that Appendix, as the case may be.

(2) Despite subsection (1), if a person or company pays a fee referred to in item 1 or 2 of Appendix B, the person or company is not required to pay a fee with respect to any other filing referred to in that item made during the calendar year in which the payment was made.

(3) Despite subsection (1), in the calendar year that a person or company files its initial filer profile, the fee referred to in item 1 or 2 of Appendix B is prorated in accordance with the following formula:

$$A \times B / 12,$$

where

A = the amount referred to in item 1 or 2 of Appendix B, as applicable, and

B = the number of months remaining in the calendar year following the month in which the initial filer profile was filed.

PART 3 — NRD SYSTEM FEES

5. Enrolment Fee — If the local jurisdiction is a firm filer's principal jurisdiction, the firm filer must pay to the securities regulatory authority an enrolment fee of $500 upon enrolment in NRD.

6. NRD submission fee — (1) A firm filer must pay an NRD system fee in respect of an individual filer to the securities regulatory authority in the local jurisdiction if

(a) the firm filer is the sponsoring firm for the individual filer, and

(b) through the filing of a Form 33-109F4 *Registration of Individuals and Review of Permitted Individuals*, the individual filer registers or reactivates their registration in the local jurisdiction.

(2) The NRD system fee payable to the securities regulatory authority under subsection (1) by a sponsoring firm in respect of an individual filer is,

(a) if the securities regulatory authority is the principal regulator of the individual filer, $75.00, and

(b) in any other case, $20.50.

7. Annual NRD system fee — On December 31 of each year, a firm filer must pay an annual NRD system fee to the securities regulatory authority in the local jurisdiction equal to the total of the following:

(a) if the securities regulatory authority in the local jurisdiction is the principal regulator of one or more individuals who are individual filers on that date, and for which the firm filer is the sponsoring firm in that jurisdiction,

$75.00 × the number of those individuals, and

(b) if there are individual filers on that date for which the securities regulatory authority in the local jurisdiction is not the principal regulator, and for which the firm filer is the sponsoring firm in that jurisdiction,

$20.50 × the number of those individuals

PART 4 — PAYMENT OF FEES

8. Means of payment — A fee under section 3, 4, 6 or 7 must be paid through SEDAR or NRD, as the case may be.

PART 5 — EXEMPTION

9. Exemption — (1) The regulator or the securities regulatory authority may grant an exemption from this Instrument, in whole or in part, subject to such conditions or restrictions as may be imposed in the exemption.

(2) Despite subsection (1), in Ontario, only the regulator may grant such an exemption.

(3) Except in Ontario, an exemption referred to in subsection (1) is granted under the statute referred to in Appendix B of National Instrument 14-101 *Definitions*, opposite the name of the local jurisdiction.

PART 6 — EFFECTIVE DATE

10. Effective Date — This Instrument comes into force on October 12, 2013.

APPENDIX A — LOCAL SEDAR SYSTEM FEES

(Section 3)

Column A	Column B	Column C	Column D
Local Jurisdiction	Category of Filing	Type of Filing	System Fee
Québec	Securities Offerings	Prospectus distribution to person outside Québec, if made from within Québec (section 12 of *Securities Act* (Québec))	$130.00

APPENDIX B — OTHER SEDAR SYSTEM FEES

(Section 4)

Item	Column A	Column B	Column C	Column D
	Category of Filing	Type of Filing	System Fee Payable to Principal Regulator	System Fee Payable to Each Other Securities Regulatory Authority
1	Annual filing fee for continuous disclosure — investment funds *Note: Excludes the annual information form and all other filings listed separately in items 3 to 21.*	Initial filer profile or annual financial statements (for investment funds)	$495.00	N/A
2	Annual filing fee for continuous disclosure	Initial filer profile or annual financial statements (for reporting issuers other than investment funds)	$705.00	$74.00
	Note: Excludes the annual information form and all other filings listed separately in items 3 to 21.			

Item	Column A	Column B	Column C	Column D
	Category of Filing	**Type of Filing**	**System Fee Payable to Principal Regulator**	**System Fee Payable to Each Other Securities Regulatory Authority**
3	Investment fund issuers / securities offerings	Simplified prospectus, annual information form and fund facts (National Instrument 81-101 *Mutual Fund Prospectus Disclosure*)	$585.00, which applies in total to a combined filing, if one annual information form and one simplified prospectus are used to qualify the investment fund securities of more than one investment fund for distribution	$162.50, which applies in total to a combined filing, if one annual information form and one simplified prospectus are used to qualify the investment fund securities of more than one investment fund for distribution
4	Long form prospectus	$715.00	$212.50	5
5	Investment fund issuers / continuous disclosure	Annual information form (National Instrument 81-106 *Investment Fund Continuous Disclosure*) for investment fund if not a short form prospectus issuer	$455.00	N/A
6	Investment fund issuers / continuous disclosure	Annual information form (National Instrument 81-106 *Investment Fund Continuous Disclosure*) for investment fund if short form prospectus issuer	$2,655.00	N/A
7	Investment fund issuers / exemptions and other applications	Exemptions and other applications (National Instrument 81-102 *Mutual Funds*)	$195.00	$40.00
8		Exemptions and other applications in connection with a prospectus filing	$195.00	$82.50
9	Other issuers / securities offerings	Short form prospectus (National Instrument 44-101 *Short Form Prospectus Distributions*)	$390.00	$115.00
10		Shelf prospectus	$390.00	$115.00
11		MJDS Prospectus (National Instrument 71-101 *The Multijurisdictional Disclosure System*)	$390.00	$115.00
12		Long form prospectus	$715.00	$212.50
13		Rights offering circular	$325.00	$115.00
14		Prospectus governed by CPC instrument (TSX Venture Exchange)	$715.00	$212.50
15	Other issuers / continuous disclosure	Annual information form, if neither an investment fund nor a short form prospectus issuer	$455.00	N/A

Part 1:
PROCEDURE

Item	Column A	Column B	Column C	Column D
	Category of Filing	Type of Filing	System Fee Payable to Principal Regulator	System Fee Payable to Each Other Securities Regulatory Authority
16		Annual information form, if a short form prospectus issuer (other than an investment fund)	$2,655.00	N/A
17	Exemptions and other applications (if not an investment fund)	Exemptions and other applications in connection with prospectus filing	$195.00	$82.50
18	Other issuers / going private / related party transactions	Going private transaction filings	$325.00	$115.00
19		Related party transaction filings	$325.00	$115.00
20	Other issuers/securities acquisitions	Issuer bid filings	$195.00	$82.50
21	Third party filers/third party filings	Take-over bid filings	$195.00	$82.50

Final Rule: (2013) 26 O.S.C.B. 9601; Approval by OSC: (2013) 36 O.S.C.B. 7217; Request for Comments: (2013) 36 O.S.C.B. 1081

CSA Staff Notice 13-315 (Revised) — Securities Regulatory Authority Closed Dates 2016*

Date: December 10, 2015

38 O.S.C.B. 1026

We have a review system for prospectuses (including long form, short form and mutual fund prospectuses), prospectus amendments, prefilings, and waiver applications. It is described in National Policy 11-202 *Process for Prospectus Reviews in Multiple Jurisdictions* (**NP 11-202**).

Under NP 11-202, a filer that receives a receipt from the principal regulator will be deemed to have a receipt in each passport jurisdiction where the prospectus was filed. However, the principal regulator's receipt will only evidence that the OSC has issued a receipt if the OSC is open on the date of the principal regulator's receipt and has indicated that it is "clear for final". If the OSC is not open on the date of the principal regulator's receipt, the principal regulator will issue a second receipt that evidences that the OSC has issued a receipt on the next day that the OSC is open.

The following is a list of the closed dates of the securities regulatory authorities for 2016 and January 2017. Issuers should note these dates in structuring their affairs.

1. Saturdays and Sundays (all)
2. Friday, January 1 (all)
3. Monday, January 4 (QC)
4. Monday, February 8 (BC)
5. Monday, February 15 (AB, SK, MB, ON, PE, NS)
6. Friday, February 26 (YT)
7. Monday, March 14 (NL)
8. Friday, March 25 (all)
9. Monday, March 28 (all except AB, SK, ON)
10. Monday, May 23 (all)
11. Tuesday, June 21 (NT)
12. Friday, June 24 (QC)

---

*Bracketed information indicates those jurisdictions that are closed on the particular date.

13. Monday, June 27 (NL)

14. Friday, July 1 (all)

15. Monday, July 11 (NU, NL)

16. Friday, July 29 (SK)

17. Monday, August 1 (all except YT, QC, NL, PE)

18. Wednesday, August 3 (NL**)

19. Monday, August 15 (YT)

20. Friday, August 19 (PE)

21. Monday, September 5 (all)

22. Monday, October 10 (all)

23. Friday, November 11 (all except AB, ON, QC)

24. Friday, December 23 (QC, NT)

25. Friday, December 23 after 12:00 p.m. (NB, PE, NS), after 1:00 p.m. (YT, BC), after 3:00 p.m. (NU)

26. Monday, December 26 (all)

27. Tuesday, December 27 (all)

28. Friday, December 30 (NT, QC)

29. Friday, December 30 after 12:00 p.m. (NB), after 1:00 p.m. (BC), after 3:00 p.m. (NU)

30. Monday, January 2, **2017** (all)

31. Tuesday, January 3, **2017** (QC)

CSA Staff Notice 13-317 — Amendments to the SEDAR Filer Manual

Date: December 10, 2010

33 O.S.C.B. 11337

[Not reproduced]

CSA Staff Notice 13-318 — www.SEDAR.com

Date: March 28, 2013

36 O.S.C.B. 3425

Introduction and Purpose

Staff of the Canadian Securities Administrators (CSA, Staff or we) are publishing this Staff Notice (the Notice) to highlight changes to the SEDAR website (the Website or SEDAR.com) to be implemented on April 6, 2013. As a result of the changes, public filings and updates to the reporting issuer profiles made on the System for Electronic Document Analysis and Retrieval (SEDAR) will now be accessible on the website within 15 minutes of the original submission instead of the following day.

Background

SEDAR is the electronic system used for the transmission, receipt, review, acceptance and dissemination of most securities related information filed with Canadian securities regulatory authorities. Filing on SEDAR is mandatory for most reporting issuers — both public companies and investment funds in Canada. SEDAR enables industry to file securities offering and continuous disclosure documents and remit filing fees electronically between 7 a,m, and 11 p,m, Eastern Time and SEDAR.com provides free access to these public filings.

The Website was originally built to support access to public documents on a daily basis, so that documents made public on SEDAR would appear on the website the following day.

Changes to Timing of Document Accessibility on SEDAR.com

As part of its ongoing efforts to enhance investor awareness and in response to feedback from market participants, the CSA has recently implemented enhancements to the architecture of the SEDAR.com website, which have made it possible to support more timely replication of public filings from SEDAR to SEDAR.com.

As of April 6, 2013, replication of publicly available filings to SEDAR.com will occur every 15 minutes during SEDAR business hours. As a result, documents made public on SEDAR will now be accessible on the Website within 15 minutes of the original submission. New reporting issuer profiles that are made public, as well as updates to existing profiles, will also appear on SEDAR.com within 15 minutes.

We remind filers that they should ensure that documents filed on SEDAR are complete and accurate and comply with applicable privacy and securities laws before they are filed.

Part 1: PROCEDURE

**Weather permitting, otherwise observed on the first following acceptable weather day, such determination made on morning of holiday.

Additional Changes to SEDAR.com

In order to support the above noted enhancements to the website, we will also implement the following changes on SEDAR.com:

- *Announcement* — Include an announcement informing SEDAR.com users of the changes to the replication process on the following pages: Homepage, New Filings, Search Database, Company Profiles, Web Links, About SEDAR, Site Help, Site Map and Search Help. We will also add additional information regarding the changes to SEDAR.com to the Homepage.

- *New Filings Page* — Include a time stamp with text advising users of when a filing was last updated on the New Filings page.

- *Public Company and Investment Funds Filings Pages* — Add a new column to indicate the time of filing as well as the date of filing to the list appearing on these pages.

- *Frequently Asked Questions (FAQ)* — Update the answers to the frequently asked questions to reflect the changes to the replication process.

- *Terms of Use* — Update the Terms of Use for SEDAR.com to reflect the changes to the replication process.

CSA Staff Notice 13-319 — SEDAR Filer Manual Update

Date: January 9, 2014

37 O.S.C.B. 420

Introduction

National Instrument 13-101 *System for Electronic Document Analysis and Retrieval (SEDAR)* (NI 13-101) incorporates by reference the SEDAR Filer Manual (the Manual). A new service agreement has been entered into with CGI Information Systems and Management Consultants Inc. ("CGI") for ongoing hosting and operations of the SEDAR system and this change will be reflected in a new version of the Manual. Staff of the CSA are issuing this Notice to inform users that a new version of the Manual will be available on January 13, 2014.

Manual Version 8.5

The new version of the Manual provides updated and new guidance on a number of matters, notably:

- Updated contact information for the CSA Service Desk
- Updated SEDAR forms to provide the correct contact information
- Updated SEDAR Filer Manual and SEDAR forms 1 and 2 to provide the correct SEDAR Software licensing information
- Updated Appendix B Categories and Types of Electronic Filings to correspond with SEDAR version 8.5.
- Revised Appendix D SEDAR System Fees in order to refer users to Multilateral Instrument 13-102 *System Fees for SEDAR and NRD* and similar regulations

The version number of the Manual is 8.5, to correspond with the most current SEDAR release, SEDAR version 8.5, to be implemented on January 13, 2014. Manual Version 8.5 will be accessible on the SEDAR website at www.sedar.com.

For more information

Please contact the CSA Service Desk at 1-800-219-5381 or your local securities regulator, for inquiries after January 13, 2014.

CSA Staff Notice 13-320 — Regarding Implementation of Multilateral Instrument 13-102 *System Fees for SEDAR and NRD* and Related Consequential Amendments to CSA National System Rules

Date: October 8, 2013

36 O.S.C.B. 9717

[Not reproduced]

CSA Staff Notice 13-321 — Update on new service provider for the operation of the CSA National Systems and implementation of Related Consequential Amendments to CSA National Systems Rules

Date: November 21, 2013

Citation: 36 O.S.C.B. 11197

[Not reproduced]

CSA Staff Notice 13-322 — Service Transition Cutover Date for Information Management Services and implementation of Related Consequential Amendments to CSA National Systems Rules

Date: **January 9, 2014**

Citation: **37 O.S.C.B. 424**

[Not reproduced]

OSC Rule 13-501 — Payment of Fees

Date: **March 13, 1998**

21 O.S.C.B. 1699

1.1 Fees — Fees payable under Ontario securities law shall be paid to the "Ontario Securities Commission".

Final Rule: (1998) 21 O.S.C.B. 2925; Approval by OSC: (1998) 21 O.S.C.B. 1699; Request for Comments: (1997) 20 O.S.C.B. 6116.

Rules: Rule 13-502.

Policies and Orders: OSCN 13-317.

OSC Rule 13-502 — Fees

Date: **March 31, 2003, as amended effective December 1, 2003 and September 14, 2005; replaced effective April 1, 2006, as amended effective February 1, 2008 (by Rule 62-504) and March 17, 2008; replaced effective June 1, 2009, as amended effective September 28, 2009, April 5, 2010, January 1, 2011 and April 1, 2013; replaced effective April 6, 2015, amended December 15, 2015 and January 16, 2016**

26 O.S.C.B. 4339, 27 O.S.C.B. 7747, 28 O.S.C.B. (Supp-4) 139, 29 O.S.C.B. 2333, 31 O.S.C.B. (Supp. 2) 260, 32 O.S.C.B. 4445, 32 O.S.C.B. (Supp. 4) 381, 33 O.S.C.B. 2837, 33 O.S.C.B. (Supp. 5) 39, 36 O.S.C.B. 1274, 38 O.S.C.B. 1045, 38 O.S.C.B. 8534 and 38 O.S.C.B. (Supp. 3) 54

Table of Contents

PART 1 — INTERPRETATION

1.1 Definitions — In this Rule

"Canadian trading share" in relation to a person or company that is a specified regulated entity for a specified period, means the average in the specified period of the following:

(a) the share of the person or company of the total dollar values of trades of exchange-traded securities in Canada,

(b) the share of the person or company of the total trading volume of exchange-traded securities in Canada, and

(c) the share of the person or company of the total number of trades of exchange-traded securities in Canada;

"capitalization" in relation to a reporting issuer, means the capitalization of the reporting issuer determined in accordance with section 2.8, 2.9 or 2.10, as the case may be;

"capital markets activities" means activities for which registration is required, or activities for which an exemption from registration is required under the *Act* or under the *Commodity Futures Act*, or would be so required if those activities were carried on in Ontario;

"Class 1 reporting issuer" means a reporting issuer, other than a Class 3A reporting issuer or a Class 3B reporting issuer, that at the end of its previous financial year, has securities listed or quoted on a marketplace;

"Class 2 reporting issuer" means a reporting issuer other than a Class 1 reporting issuer, a Class 3A reporting issuer or a Class 3B reporting issuer;

"Class 3A reporting issuer" means a reporting issuer that is not incorporated under the laws of Canada or a province or territory and that

(a) had no securities listed or quoted on any marketplace at the end of its previous financial year, or

(b) had securities listed or quoted on a marketplace at the end of its previous financial year and all of the following apply:

(i) at the end of its previous financial year, securities registered in the names of persons or companies resident in Ontario represented less than 1% of the market value of all of the reporting issuer's outstanding securities for which it or its transfer agent or registrar maintains a list of registered owners;

(ii) the reporting issuer reasonably believes that, at the end of its previous financial year, securities beneficially owned by persons or companies resident in Ontario represented less than 1% of the market value of all its outstanding securities;

(iii) the reporting issuer reasonably believes that none of its securities traded on a marketplace in Canada during its previous financial year;

(iv) the reporting issuer has not issued any of its securities in Ontario in the last 5 years, other than

(A) to its employees or to employees of one or more of its subsidiaries, or

(B) to a person or company exercising a right previously granted by the reporting issuer or its affiliate to convert or exchange its previously issued securities without payment of any additional consideration;

"Class 3B reporting issuer" means a reporting issuer that

(a) is not a Class 3A reporting issuer, and

(b) is a designated foreign issuer or an SEC foreign issuer as those terms are defined in National Instrument 71-102 *Continuous Disclosure and Other Exemptions Relating to Foreign Issuers*;

"generally accepted accounting principles"in relation to a person or company, means the generally accepted accounting principles used to prepare the financial statements of the person or company in accordance with Ontario securities law;

"highest trading marketplace"means

(a) the marketplace on which the highest volume in Canada of the class or series was traded in the previous financial year and which discloses regularly the prices at which those securities have traded,

(b) if the class or series was not traded in the previous financial year on a marketplace in Canada, the marketplace on which the highest volume in the United States of America of the class or series was traded in the previous financial year and which discloses regularly the prices at which those securities have traded, or

(c) if the class or series was not traded in the previous financial year on a marketplace in Canada or the United States of America, the marketplace on which the highest volume of the class or series was traded in the previous financial year and which discloses regularly the prices at which those securities have traded;

"IIROC" means the Investment Industry Regulatory Organization of Canada;

"interim period" has the same meaning as in NI 51-102;

"MFDA" means the Mutual Fund Dealers Association of Canada;

"net assets" in relation to a person or company, means the total assets minus the total liabilities of the person or company, determined in accordance with the generally accepted accounting principles applying to the person or company;

"NI 31-103" means National Instrument 31-103 *Registration Requirements, Exemptions and Ongoing Registrant Obligations*;

"NI 33-109" means National Instrument 33-109 *Registration Information*;

"NI 45-106" means National Instrument 45-106 *Prospectus Exemptions*;

"NI 51-102" means National Instrument 51-102 *Continuous Disclosure Obligations*;

"NI 52-107" means National Instrument 52-107 *Acceptable Accounting Principles and Auditing Standards*;

"NI 55-102" means National Instrument 55-102 *System for Electronic Disclosure by Insiders (SEDI)*;

"Ontario percentage" means, in relation to a person or company for a previous financial year,

(a) in the case of a person or company that has a permanent establishment in Ontario in the previous financial year and no permanent establishment elsewhere, 100%,

(b) in the case of a person or company that has a permanent establishment in Ontario and elsewhere in the previous financial year and has taxable income in the previous financial year that is positive, the percentage of the taxable income that is taxable income earned in the year in Ontario, and

(c) in any other case, the percentage of the total revenues of the person or company for the previous financial year attributable to capital markets activities in Ontario;

"parent" means a person or company of which another person or company is a subsidiary;

"permanent establishment" means a permanent establishment as defined in subsection 400(2) of the *Income Tax Regulations* (Canada);

"permitted individual" has the same meaning as in NI 33-109;

"previous financial year" means,

(a) for a registrant or an unregistered capital markets participant, the financial year of the registrant or participant ending in the then current calendar year, or

(b) in all other cases, the most recently completed financial year of the person or company;

"principal regulator" has the same meaning as in NI 33-109;

"registrant firm" means a registered dealer, registered adviser or registered investment fund manager;

"specified Ontario revenues" in relation to a person or company for a financial year, means the specified Ontario revenues of the person or company calculated for the financial year under section 3.5 or 3.6, as the case may be;

"specified period" means the period beginning on April 1 of the previous calendar year and ending on March 31 of the calendar year;

"specified trading period" means, in respect of a reporting issuer's financial year, each period that is an interim period in the financial year and the period commencing on the first day of the financial year and ending on the last day of the financial year;

"specified regulated entity" means a person or company described in Column A of Appendix B.1 of the rule;

"subsidiary" subject to subsection 1(4) of the *Act*, a subsidiary of a person or company as determined in accordance with the generally accepted accounting principles applying to the person or company;

"taxable income" means taxable income as determined under the *Income Tax Act* (Canada);

"taxable income earned in the year in Ontario", in relation to a person or company for a financial year, means the taxable income of the person or company earned in the financial year in Ontario as determined under Part IV of the *Income Tax Regulations* (Canada);

"unregistered capital markets participant" means,

    (a) an unregistered investment fund manager; or

    (b) an unregistered exempt international firm;

"unregistered exempt international firm" means a dealer or adviser that is not registered under the Act if one or both of the following apply:

    (a) the dealer or adviser is exempt from the dealer registration requirement and the underwriter registration requirement only because of section 8.18 [*International dealer*] of NI 31-103;

    (b) the dealer or adviser is exempt from the adviser registration requirement only because of section 8.26 [*International adviser*] of NI 31-103;

"unregistered investment fund manager" means an investment fund manager of one or more investment funds that is not registered as an investment fund manager in accordance with Ontario securities law, other than an investment fund manager that does not have a place of business in Ontario, and one or more of the following apply:

    (a) none of the investment funds has security holders who are residents in Ontario;

    (b) the investment fund manager and the investment funds have not, at any time after September 27, 2012, actively solicited Ontario residents to purchase securities of any of the investment funds.

1.2 Interpretation of "listed or quoted" — In this Rule, a reporting issuer is deemed not to have securities listed or quoted on a marketplace that lists or quotes the reporting issuer's securities unless the reporting issuer or an affiliate of the reporting issuer applied for, or consented to, the listing or quotation.

PART 2 — CORPORATE FINANCE PARTICIPATION FEES

DIVISION 1 — GENERAL

2.1 Application — This Part does not apply to an investment fund that has an investment fund manager.

2.2 Participation Fee — (1) A reporting issuer that is a Class 1 reporting issuer or a Class 2 reporting issuer must, after each of its financial years, pay the participation fee shown in Appendix A opposite the capitalization of the reporting issuer for the previous financial year.

(2) A reporting issuer that is a Class 3A reporting issuer must, after each of its financial years, pay a participation fee of $1,070.

(3) A reporting issuer that is a Class 3B reporting issuer must, after each of its financial years, pay the participation fee shown in Appendix A.1 opposite the capitalization of the reporting issuer for the previous financial year.

(4) Despite subsections (1) to (3), a participation fee is not payable by a participant under this section if the participant became a reporting issuer in the period that begins immediately after the time that would otherwise be the end of the previous financial year in respect of the participation fee and ends at the time the participation fee would otherwise be required to be paid under section 2.3.

2.3 Time of Payment — A reporting issuer must pay the participation fee required under section 2.2 by the earlier of

    (a) the date on which its annual financial statements for its previous financial year are required to be filed under Ontario securities law, and

    (b) the date on which its annual financial statements for its previous financial year are filed.

2.4 Participation fee exemptions for subsidiaries — (1) Section 2.2 does not apply to a reporting issuer that is a subsidiary if all of the following apply:

    (a) at the end of the subsidiary's previous financial year, the parent of the subsidiary was a reporting issuer;

    (b) the audited financial statements of the parent prepared in accordance with NI 52-107 require the consolidation of the parent and the subsidiary;

    (c) the parent has paid a participation fee under subsection 2.2(1) calculated based on the capitalization of the parent for the previous financial year;

    (d) in the case of a parent that is a Class 1 reporting issuer, the capitalization of the parent for the previous financial year included the capitalization of the subsidiary as required under paragraph 2.8(1)(c);

    (e) in the previous financial year,

        (i) the net assets and total revenues of the subsidiary represented more than 90% of the consolidated net assets and total revenues of the parent in the parent's previous financial year, or

        (ii) the subsidiary was entitled to rely on an exemption or waiver from the requirements in subsections 4.1(1), 4.3(1), 5.1(1) or section 5.2, and section 6.1 of NI 51-102.

(2) A reporting issuer referred to in subsection (1) must file a completed Form 13-502F6 that contains a certification signed by an officer of the reporting issuer, by the earlier of

    (a) the date on which its annual financial statements for its previous financial year are required to be filed under Ontario securities law, or would have been required to be filed under Ontario securities law absent an exemption or waiver described in subparagraph (1)(e)(ii), and

    (b) the date on which it files its annual financial statements for its previous financial year.

2.5 Participation fee estimate for Class 2 reporting issuers — (1) If the annual financial statements of a Class 2 reporting issuer are not available by the date referred to in paragraph 2.3(a) the Class 2 reporting issuer must, on that date,

    (a) file a completed Form 13-502F2 showing a good faith estimate of the information required to calculate its capitalization as at the end of the previous financial year, and

    (b) pay the participation fee shown in Appendix A opposite the estimated capitalization.

(2) A Class 2 reporting issuer that estimated its capitalization under subsection (1) must, when it files its annual financial statements for the previous financial year,

    (a) calculate its capitalization under section 2.9,

    (b) pay the participation fee shown in Appendix A opposite the capitalization, less the participation fee paid under subsection (1), and

    (c) file a completed Form 13-502F2A that contains a certification signed by an officer of the reporting issuer.

(3) If the amount paid by a reporting issuer under subsection (1) exceeds the participation fee calculated under subsection (2), the issuer is entitled to a refund from the Commission of the amount overpaid.

(4) A request for a refund under subsection (3) must be made to the Commission by the same date on which the form referred to in paragraph 2(c) is required to be filed.

2.6 Filing report and certification — (1) At the time that it pays the participation fee required by this Part,

    (a) a Class 1 and a Class 3B reporting issuer must file a completed Form 13-502F1;

    (b) a Class 2 reporting issuer must file a completed Form 13-502F2; and

    (c) a Class 3A reporting issuer must file a completed Form 13-502F3A.

(2) A form required to be filed under subsection (1) must contain a certification signed by an officer of the reporting issuer.

2.7 Late fee — (1) A reporting issuer that is late in paying a participation fee under this Part must pay an additional late fee of 0.1% of the unpaid portion of the participation fee for each business day on which any portion of the participation fee was due and unpaid.

(2) If a late fee calculated under subsection (1) is less than $100, it is deemed to be nil.

DIVISION 2 — CALCULATING CAPITALIZATION

2.8 Class 1 reporting issuers — (1) The capitalization of a Class 1 reporting issuer for the previous financial year is the total of all of the following:

    (a) for each class or series of the reporting issuer's equity securities listed or quoted on a marketplace,

        (i) the sum of the market value of the securities listed or quoted on a marketplace at the end of the last trading day of each specified trading period in the previous financial year of the reporting issuer, calculated for each specified trading period as follows:

$$A \times B$$

    in which,

        "A" is equal to the closing price of the security in the class or series on the last trading day of the specified trading period in which such security was listed or quoted on the highest trading marketplace, and

        "B" is equal to the number of securities in the class or series of such security outstanding at the end of the specified trading period,

        (ii) divided by the number of specified trading periods in the reporting issuer's previous financial year in which the security of the reporting issuer was listed or quoted on a marketplace at the end of the last trading day of a specified trading period;

    (b) the fair value of the outstanding debt securities of the reporting issuer at the end of the previous financial year that are,

        (i) listed or quoted on a marketplace,

        (ii) traded over the counter, or

        (iii) available for purchase or sale without regard to a statutory hold period;

    (c) the capitalization for the previous financial year of a subsidiary that is exempt under subsection 2.4(1), calculated in accordance with paragraphs (1)(a) and (1)(b), and excluding any securities of the subsidiary held by the parent that have been included in the capitalization of the parent for the previous financial year.

2.9 Class 2 reporting issuers — (1) The capitalization of a Class 2 reporting issuer for the previous financial year is the total of all of the following items, as shown in its audited statement of financial position as at the end of the previous financial year:

    (a) retained earnings or deficit;

    (b) contributed surplus;

    (c) share capital or owners' equity, options, warrants and preferred shares;

    (d) non-current borrowings, including the current portion;

    (e) finance leases, including the current portion;

    (f) non-controlling interest;

    (g) items classified on the statement of financial position as non-current liabilities, and not otherwise referred to in this subsection;

    (h) any other item forming part of equity not otherwise referred to in this subsection.

(2) Despite subsection (1), a reporting issuer may calculate its capitalization using unaudited annual financial statements if it is not required to prepare, and does not ordinarily prepare, audited annual financial statements.

(3) Despite subsection (1), a reporting issuer that is a trust that issues only asset-backed securities through pass-through certificates may calculate its capitalization using the monthly filed distribution report for the last month of the previous financial year if it is not required to prepare, and does not ordinarily prepare, audited annual financial statements.

2.10 Class 3B reporting issuers — (1) The capitalization of a Class 3B reporting issuer must be determined under section 2.8, as if it were a Class 1 reporting issuer.

2.11 Reliance on Published Information — (1) Subject to subsection (2), in determining its capitalization, a reporting issuer may rely on information made available by a marketplace on which its securities trade.

Part 1:
PROCEDURE

(2) If a reporting issuer reasonably believes that the information made available by a marketplace is incorrect, the issuer must make a good faith estimate of the information required.

PART 3 — CAPITAL MARKETS PARTICIPATION FEES

DIVISION 1 — GENERAL

3.1 Participation fee — Registrant firms and unregistered capital markets participants — (1) A registrant firm or an unregistered capital markets participant must, by December 31 in each year, pay the participation fee shown in Appendix B opposite the specified Ontario revenues for the previous financial year of the firm or participant.

(2) A registrant firm or an unregistered capital markets participant must, by December 1 in each year, file a completed Form 13-502F4 showing the information required to determine the participation fee referred to in subsection (1).

(3) Despite subsection (2), a firm that becomes registered, or provides notification that it qualifies as an unregistered capital markets participant, between December 1 and 31, must file a completed Form 13-502F4 within 60 days of the date of registration or notification.

(4) Subsection (1) does not apply to a person or company that ceased at any time in the financial year to be an unregistered investment fund manager if the person or company did not become a registrant firm in the year.

(5) Despite subsection (1), the participation fee for an unregistered investment fund manager payable by December 31, 2015 is nil provided that:

(a) The unregistered investment fund manager has a financial year ending in 2015 between January 1 and the day immediately prior to the effective date of this Rule, and

(b) The unregistered investment fund manager paid the applicable participation fee for the financial year referred to in paragraph (a) within 90 days of its financial year end.

3.2 Estimating specified Ontario revenues for late financial year end — (1) If the annual financial statements of a registrant firm or an unregistered capital markets participant for a previous financial year are not completed by December 1 in the calendar year in which the previous financial year ends, the firm or participant must,

(a) by December 1, file a completed Form 13-502F4 showing a good faith estimate of the information required to calculate its specified Ontario revenues as at the end of the previous financial year, and

(b) by December 31, pay the participation fee shown in Appendix B opposite its estimated specified Ontario revenues for the previous financial year.

(2) A registrant firm or an unregistered capital markets participant that estimated its specified Ontario revenues for a previous financial year under subsection (1) must, not later than 90 days after the end of the previous financial year,

(a) calculate its specified Ontario revenues,

(b) determine the participation fee shown in Appendix B opposite the specified Ontario revenues, and

(c) if the participation fee determined under paragraph (b) exceeds the participation fee paid under subsection (1), pay the balance owing and file a completed Form 13-502F4 and Form 13-502F5.

(3) A registrant firm or unregistered capital markets participant that pays an amount under subsection (1) that exceeds the participation fee determined under subsection (2) is entitled to a refund from the Commission of the excess.

(4) A request for a refund under subsection (3) must be made to the Commission by the same date on which the form referred to in paragraph (2)(c) is required to be filed.

3.3 Certification — A form required to be filed under section 3.1 or 3.2 must contain a certification signed by

(a) the chief compliance officer of the registrant or the unregistered capital markets participant, or

(b) in the case of an unregistered capital markets participant without a chief compliance officer, an individual acting in a similar capacity.

3.4 Late fee — (1) A person or company that is late in paying a participation fee under this Part must pay an additional late fee of 0.1% of the unpaid portion of the participation fee for each business day on which any portion of the participation fee was due and unpaid.

(2) A late fee calculated under subsection (1) is deemed to be nil if it is less than $100.

DIVISION 2 — CALCULATING SPECIFIED ONTARIO REVENUES

3.5 Calculating specified Ontario revenues for IIROC and MFDA members — (1) The specified Ontario revenues for a previous financial year of a registrant firm that was an IIROC or MFDA member at the end of the previous financial year is calculated by multiplying

(a) the registrant firm's total revenues for the previous financial year, less the portion of the total revenue not attributable to capital markets activities,

by

(b) the registrant firm's Ontario percentage for the previous financial year.

(2) For the purpose of paragraph (1)(a), "total revenues" for a previous financial year means,

(a) for a registrant firm that was an IIROC member at the end of the previous financial year, the amount shown as total revenue for the previous financial year on Statement E of the *Joint Regulatory Financial Questionnaire and Report* filed with IIROC by the registrant firm; and

(b) for a registrant firm that was an MFDA member at the end of the previous financial year, the amount shown as total revenue for the previous financial year on Statement D of the MFDA *Financial Questionnaire and Report* filed with the MFDA by the registrant firm.

3.6 Calculating specified Ontario revenues for others — (1) The specified Ontario revenues for a previous financial year of a registrant firm that was not a member of IIROC or the MFDA at the end of the previous financial year, or an unregistered capital markets participant, is calculated by multiplying

(a) the firm's total revenues, as shown in the audited financial statements prepared in accordance with NI 52-107 for the previous financial year, less deductions permitted under subsection (2),

by

(b) the firm's Ontario percentage for the previous financial year.

(2) For the purpose of paragraph (1)(a), a person or company may deduct the following items, if earned in the previous financial year, from its total revenues:

(a) revenues not attributable to capital markets activities;

(b) redemption fees earned on the redemption of investment fund securities sold on a deferred sales charge basis;

(c) administration fees earned relating to the recovery of costs from investment funds managed by the person or company for operating expenses paid on behalf of the investment funds by the person or company;

(d) advisory or sub-advisory fees paid during the financial year by the person or company to

(i) a registrant firm, as "registrant firm" is defined in this Rule or in Rule 13-503 *(Commodity Futures Act) Fees*, or

(ii) an unregistered exempt international firm;

(e) trailing commissions paid during the financial year by the person or company to a registrant firm described in subparagraph (d)(i).

(3) Despite subsection (1), an unregistered capital markets participant may calculate its gross revenues using unaudited financial statements if it is not required to prepare, and does not ordinarily prepare, audited financial statements.

PART 4 — PARTICIPATION FEES FOR SPECIFIED REGULATED ENTITIES

4.1 Recognized exchange — (1) A recognized exchange must, no later than April 30 in each calendar year, pay the participation fee shown in Column B of Appendix B.1 opposite the corresponding Canadian trading share of the exchange for the specified period in Rows A1 to A6 of Column A.

(2) If there are two or more recognized exchanges, each of which is related to each other,

(a) the obligation under subsection (1) and Appendix B.1 must be calculated as if the recognized exchanges are a single entity, and

(b) each recognized exchange is jointly and severally liable in respect of the obligation.

4.2 Recognized quotation and trade reporting system — A recognized quotation and trade reporting system must, no later than April 30 in each calendar year, pay the participation fee shown in Column B of Appendix B.1 opposite the corresponding Canadian trading share of the quotation and trade reporting system for the specified period in Rows A1 to A6 of Column A.

4.3 (1) An alternative trading system described in Row C1 in Column A of Appendix B.1 must, no later than April 30 in each calendar year, pay a participation fee equal to the lesser of

(a) the participation fee set for the alternative trading system in Column B of Appendix B.1 as if it were a recognized exchange, opposite the corresponding Canadian trading share of the alternative trading system for the specified period in Rows A1 to A6 of Column A, less the capital markets participation fee paid under section 3.1 or 3.2 by the person or company on its specified Ontario revenues in the preceding financial year, and

(b) $17,000

(2) An alternative trading system described in Row C2 in Column A of Appendix B.1 must, no later than April 30 in each calendar year, pay a participation fee equal to the lesser of

(a) $30,000, less the capital markets participation fee paid under section 3.1 or 3.2 by the person or company on its specified Ontario revenues in the preceding financial year, and

(b) $8,750

(3) An alternative trading system described in row C3 in Column A of Appendix B.1 must, no later than April 30 in each calendar year, pay a participation fee equal to the lesser of

(a) $30,000, less the capital markets participation fee paid under section 3.1 or 3.2 by the person or company on its specified Ontario revenues in the preceding financial year, and

(b) $17,000

(4) If the amount determined under paragraph 1(a), 2(a) or 3(a) is negative, the amount must be refunded to the person or company not later than June 1 in the calendar year.

(5) If there are two or more alternative trading systems that trade the same asset class, each of which is related to each other,

(a) the obligation under subsections (1) to (3) and Appendix B.1 must be calculated as if the alternative trading systems are a single entity, and

(b) each alternative trading system is jointly and severally liable in respect of the obligation.

(6) If there are two or more alternative trading systems, each of which is related to each other and each of which trades different asset classes, then each alternative trading system must pay a participation fee as determined under subsection (1), (2) or (3).

4.4 Recognized clearing agencies — A recognized clearing agency must, no later than April 30 in each calendar year, pay the aggregate of the participation fees shown in Column B of Appendix B.1 opposite the services described in Rows D1 to D6 of Column A that are provided by the clearing agency in the specified period.

4.5 Other specified regulated entities — A person or company described in row B1, E1 or F1 in Column A of Appendix B.1 must, no later than April 30 in each calendar year, pay the participation fee shown in Column B of Appendix B.1 opposite the corresponding description in Row B1, E1 or F1, as the case may be.

Part 1:
PROCEDURE

4.6 Participation fee on recognition, designation, etc. — (1) A person or company must, on the date it first becomes a specified regulated entity, pay a participation fee of

$$A \times B \div C, \text{ where}$$

"A" is

(i) in the case of a recognized exchange, a recognized quotation and trade reporting system or an alternative trading system, $30,000,

(ii) in the case of an exchange exempt from recognition under the Act, $10,000,

(iii) in the case of a recognized clearing agency, the aggregate of the participation fees shown in Column B of Appendix B.1 opposite the services described in Rows D1 to D6 of Column A that are to be provided by the clearing agency in the specified period,

(iv) in the case of a clearing agency exempt from recognition under the Act, $10,000,

(v) in the case of a designated trade repository, $30,000,

"B" is the number of complete months remaining from the month in which the person or company first became a specified regulated entity until March 31, and

"C" is 12

(2) If a person or company first becomes a specified regulated entity between January 1 and March 31 of a calendar year, the fee required to be paid under subsection (1) is in addition to the fee required to be paid by the person or company in the same calendar year under section 4.1 to section 4.5.

4.7 A payment made under section 4.1 to section 4.6 must be accompanied by a completed Form 13-502F7.

4.8 (1) A person or company that is late paying a participation fee under this Part must pay an additional late fee of 0.1% of the unpaid portion of the participation fee for each business day on which any portion of the participation fee was due and unpaid.

(2) If the late fee calculated under subsection (1) is less than $100, it is deemed to be nil.

PART 5 — PARTICIPATION FEES FOR DESIGNATED CREDIT RATING ORGANIZATIONS

5.1 Payment of participation fee — (1) A designated credit rating organization must, after each financial year,

(a) pay a participation fee of $15,000, and

(b) file a completed Form 13-502F8.

(2) A designated credit rating organization must comply with subsection (1) by the earlier of

(a) the date on which it is required to file a completed Form 25-101FI *Designated Rating Organization Application and Annual Filing* in respect of the financial year under National Instrument 25-101 *Designated Rating Organizations*, and

(b) the date on which it files a completed Form 25-101FI *Designated Rating Organization Application and Annual Filing* in respect of the financial year.

5.2 Late fee — (1) A designated credit rating organization that is late paying a participation fee under this Part must pay an additional late fee of 0.1% of the unpaid portion of the participation fee for each business day on which any portion of the participation fee was due and unpaid.

(2) If a late fee calculated under subsection (1) is less than $100, it is deemed to be nil.

PART 6 — ACTIVITY FEES

6.1 Activity fees — General — A person or company must, when filing a document or taking an action described in any of Rows A to O of Column A of Appendix C, pay the activity fee shown opposite the description of the document or action in Column B.

6.2 Information request — A person or company that makes a request described in any of Rows P1 to P3 of Column A of Appendix C must pay the fee shown opposite the description of the request in Column B of Appendix C before receiving the document or information requested.

6.3 Investment fund families and affiliated registrants — Despite section 6.1, only one activity fee must be paid for an application made by or on behalf of

(a) two or more investment funds that have

(i) the same investment fund manager, or

(ii) investment fund managers that are affiliates of each other; or

(b) two or more registrants that

(i) are affiliates of each other, and

(ii) make an application described in item E of Column A of Appendix C in respect of a joint activity.

6.4 Late fee — (1) A person or company that files or delivers a form or document listed in Row A or B of Column A of Appendix D after the form or document was required to be filed or delivered must, when filing or delivering the form or document, pay the late fee shown in Column B of Appendix D opposite the description of the form or document.

(2) A person or company that files a Form 55-102F2 *Insider Report* after it was required to be filed must pay the late fee shown in Row C of Column B of Appendix D on receiving an invoice from the Commission.

(3) Subsection (2) does not apply to the late filing of Form 55-102F2 *Insider Report* by an insider of a reporting issuer if

(a) the head office of the reporting issuer is located outside Ontario; and

(b) the insider is required to pay a late fee for the filing in another province or territory.

PART 7 — CURRENCY CONVERSION

7.1 Canadian dollars — If a calculation under this Rule requires the price of a security, or any other amount, as it was on a particular date and that price or amount is not in Canadian dollars, it must be converted into Canadian dollars using the daily noon exchange rate for that date as posted on the Bank of Canada website.

PART 8 — EXEMPTION

8.1 Exemption — he Director may grant an exemption from the provisions of this Rule, in whole or in part, subject to such conditions or restrictions as may be imposed in the exemption.

PART 9 — REVOCATION AND EFFECTIVE DATE

9.1 Revocation — Rule 13-502 *Fees*, which came into force on June 1, 2009, is revoked.

9.2 Effective date — This Rule comes into force on [April 6, 2015].

APPENDIX A — CORPORATE FINANCE PARTICIPATION FEES

Capitalization for the Reference Fiscal Year	Participation Fee (effective April 6, 2015)
under $10 million	$890
$10 million to under $25 million	$1,070
$25 million to under $50 million	$2,590
$50 million to under $100 million	$6,390
$100 million to under $250 million	$13,340
$250 million to under $500 million	$29,365
$500 million to under $1 billion	$40,950
$1 billion to under $5 billion	$59,350
$5 billion to under $10 billion	$76,425
$10 billion to under $25 billion	$89,270
$25 billion and over	$100,500

APPENDIX A.1 — CORPORATE FINANCE PARTICIPATION FEES FOR CLASS 3B ISSUERS

Capitalization for the Reference Fiscal Year	Participation Fee (effective April 6, 2015)
under $10 million	$890
$10 million to under $25 million	$1,070
$25 million to under $50 million	$1,195
$50 million to under $100 million	$2,135
$100 million to under $250 million	$4,450
$250 million to under $500 million	$9,780
$500 million to under $1 billion	$13,650
$1 billion to under $5 billion	$19,785
$5 billion to under $10 billion	$25,460

Capitalization for the Reference Fiscal Year	Participation Fee (effective April 6, 2015)
$10 billion to under $25 billion	$29,755
$25 billion and over	$33,495

APPENDIX B — CAPITAL MARKETS PARTICIPATION FEES

Specified Ontario Revenues for the Reference Fiscal Year	Participation Fee (effective April 6, 2015)
under $250,000	$835
$250,000 to under $500,000	$1,085
$500,000 to under $1 million	$3,550
$1 million to under $3 million	$7,950
$3 million to under $5 million	$17,900
$5 million to under $10 million	$36,175
$10 million to under $25 million	$74,000
$25 million to under $50 million	$110,750
$50 million to under $100 million	$221,500
$100 million to under $200 million	$367,700
$200 million to under $500 million	$745,300
$500 million to under $1 billion	$962,500
$1 billion to under $2 billion	$1,213,800
$2 billion and over	$2,037,000

APPENDIX B.1 — PARTICIPATION FEES FOR SPECIFIED REGULATED ENTITIES

Part 3.1 of the Rule

Row	Specified Regulated Entity (Column A)	Participation Fee (Column B)
	A. Recognized exchange and recognized quotation and trade reporting system	
A1	A person or company with a Canadian trading share for the specified period of up to 5%.	$30,000
A2	A person or company with a Canadian trading share for the specified period of 5% to up to 15%.	$50,000
A3	A person or company with a Canadian trading share for the specified period of 15% to up to 25%.	$135,000
A4	A person or company with a Canadian trading share for the specified period of 25% to up to 50%.	$275,000
A5	A person or company with a Canadian trading share for the specified period of 50% to up to 75%.	$400,000
A6	A person or company with a Canadian trading share for the specified period of 75% or more.	$500,000
	B. Exchanges Exempt from Recognition under the Act	

Row	Specified Regulated Entity (Column A)	Participation Fee (Column B)
B1	A person or company that is exempted by the Commission from the application of subsection 21(1) of the *Act*.	$10,000

C. Alternative Trading Systems

C1	Each alternative trading system for exchange-traded securities only.	Lesser of (a) The amount in A1 to A6 determined based on Canadian trading share of alternative trading system less capital markets participation fee paid in respect of previous year, and (b) $17,000
C2	Each alternative trading system only for unlisted debt or securities lending.	Lesser of (a) $30,000 less capital markets participation fee paid in respect of the previous year, and (b) $8,750
C3	Each alternative trading system not described in Row C1 or C2.	Lesser of (a) $30,000 less capital markets participation fee paid in respect of the previous year, and (b) $17,000

D. Recognized Clearing Agencies–Services

D1	Matching services, being the provision of facilities for comparing data respecting the terms of settlement of a trade or transaction.	$10,000
D2	Netting services, being the provision of facilities for the calculation of the mutual obligations of participants for the exchange of securities and/or money.	$20,000
D3	Settlement services, being services that ensure that securities are transferred finally and irrevocably from one participant to another in exchange for a corresponding transfer of money and/or *vice versa*.	$20,000
D4	Acting as a central clearing counterparty by providing novation services, if the Commission does not place reliance on another regulator for direct oversight.	$150,000
D5	Acting as a central clearing counterparty by providing novation services, if the Commission places reliance on another regulator for direct oversight.	$70,000
D6	Depositary services, being the provision of centralized facilities as a depository for securities.	$20,000

E. Clearing Agencies Exempt from Recognition under the Act

E1	Each clearing agency that is exempted by the Commission from the application of subsection 21.2(1) of the *Act*.	$10,000

F. Trade Repositories

F1	Each designated trade repository designated under subsection 21.2.2(1) of the *Act*.	$30,000

Part 1: PROCEDURE

Appendix C — Activity Fees

Row	Document or Activity (Column A)	Fee (Column B)
	A. Prospectus Filings	
A1	Preliminary or Pro Forma Prospectus in Form 41-101F1 (including if PREP procedures are used)	$3,800
A2	Additional fee(s) for Preliminary or Pro Forma Prospectus of an issuer that is accompanied by, or incorporates by reference, technical report(s) that has not or have not been previously incorporated by reference in a Preliminary or Pro Forma Prospectus	$2,500 for each technical report
A3	Preliminary Short Form Prospectus in Form 44-101F1 (including if shelf or PREP procedures are used) or a Registration Statement on Form F-9 or F-10 filed by an issuer that is incorporated or that is organized under the laws of Canada or a jurisdiction in Canada province or territory in connection with a distribution solely in the United States under MJDS as described in the companion policy to National Instrument 71-101 *The Multijurisdictional Disclosure System*.	$3,800
A4	Prospectus Filing by or on behalf of certain investment Funds	
(a)	Preliminary or Pro Forma Simplified Prospectus and Annual Information Form in Form 81-101F1 and Form 81-101F2	The greater of
		(i) $3,800 for a prospectus, and
		(ii) $400 for each mutual fund in a prospectus.
(b)	Preliminary or Pro Forma Prospectus in Form 41-101F2 or Scholarship Plan Prospectus in Form 41-101F3	The greater of
		(i) $3,800 for a prospectus, and
		(ii) $650 for each investment fund in a prospectus.
A5	Review of prospectus supplement in relation to a specified derivative (as defined in National Instrument 44-102 *Shelf Distributions*).	$3,800
A6	Filing of prospectus supplement in relation to a specified derivative (as defined in National Instrument 44-102 *Shelf Distributions*) for which the amount payable is determined with reference to the price, value or level of an underlying interest that is unrelated to the operations or securities of the issuer.	$500
	B. Fees relating to exempt distributions under OSC Rule 45-501 *Ontario Prospectus and Registration Exemptions* **and NI 45-106**	
B1	Application for recognition, or renewal of recognition, as an accredited investor	$500
B2	Filing of a Form 45-501F1 or Form 45-106F1 for a distribution of securities of an issuer under an exemption from the prospectus requirement other than section 2.9 [*Offering memorandum*] of NI 45-106	$500
B2.1	Filing of a Form 45-106F1 for a distribution of securities of an issuer under section 2.9 [*Offering memorandum*] of NI 45-106	Greater of (i) $500 or (ii) 0.025% of the gross proceeds realized by the issuer from the distribution in Ontario
B3	Filing of a rights offering circular in Form 45-106F15	$3,800

Row	Document or Activity (Column A)	Fee (Column B)
		(plus an additional fee of $2,000 in connection with any application or filing described in any of Rows B1 to B3 if neither the applicant nor the filer or an issuer of which the applicant or filer is a wholly owned subsidiary is subject to, or is reasonably expected to become subject to, a participation fee under this Rule)
	C. **Notice of exemption**	
C1	Provision of Notice under paragraph 2.42(2)(a) of NI 45-106	$2,000
	D. **Syndicate Agreement**	
D1	Filing of Prospecting Syndicate Agreement	$500
	E. **Applications for specifically enumerated relief, approval, recognition, designation, etc.**	
E1	An application for relief from this Rule.	$1,800
E2	An application for relief from any of the following:	$1,800
	(a) National Instrument 31-102 *National Registration Database*;	
	(b) NI 33-109	
	(c) section 3.11 [*Portfolio manager — advising representative*] of NI 31-103;	
	(d) section 3.12 [*Portfolio manager — associate advising representative*] of NI 31-103;	
	(e) section 3.13 [*Portfolio manager — chief compliance officer*] of NI 31-103;	
	(f) section 3.14 [*Investment fund manager — chief compliance officer*] of NI 31-103;	
	(g) section 9.1 [*IIROC membership for investment dealers*] of NI 31-103;	
	(h) section 9.2 [*MFDA membership for mutual fund dealers*] of NI 31-103.	
E3	An application for relief from any of the following:	$500
	(a) section 3.3 [*Time limits on examination requirements*] of NI 31-103;	
	(b) section 3.5 [*Mutual fund dealer — dealing representative*] of NI 31-103;	
	(c) section 3.6 [*Mutual fund dealer — chief compliance officer*] of NI 31-103;	
	(d) section 3.7 [*Scholarship plan dealer — dealing representative*] of NI 31-103;	
	(e) section 3.8 [*Scholarship plan dealer — chief compliance officer*] of NI 31-103;	
	(f) section 3.9 [*Exempt market dealer — dealing representative*] of NI 31-103,	
	(g) section 3.10 [*Exempt market dealer — chief compliance officer*] of NI 31-103.	
E4	An application under subparagraph 1(10)(a)(ii) of the *Act*	$1,000
E5	An application	Nil

Part 1:
PROCEDURE

Row	Document or Activity (Column A)	Fee (Column B)
	(a) under section 30 or subsection 38(3) of the *Act* or subsection 1(6) of the *Business Corporations Act*,	
	(b) under subsection 144(1) of the *Act* for an order to partially revoke a cease-trade order to permit trades solely for the purpose of establishing a tax loss, as contemplated under section 3.2 of National Policy 12-202 *Revocation of a Compliance-related Cease Trade Order*, and	
	(c) under subsections 144(1) and 127(4.3) of the *Act* to revoke a cease trade order made under subsection 127(4.1) of the *Act* that has been in effect for 90 days or less.	
E6	An application other than a pre-filing, where the discretionary relief or regulatory approval is evidenced by the issuance of a receipt for the applicants' final prospectus (such as certain applications under National Instrument 41-101 *General Prospectus Requirements* or National Instrument 81-101 *Mutual Fund Prospectus Disclosure*).	(a) $4,800 for an application for relief from, or approval under, one section of the *Act*, a regulation or a rule (b) $7,000 for an application for relief from, or approval under, two or more sections of the *Act*, a regulation or a rule
E7	An application for approval under subsection 213(3) of the *Loan and Trust Corporations Act*	$1,500
E8	An application (a) made under subsection 46(4) of the *Business Corporations Act* for relief from the requirements under Part V of that Act (b) for consent to continue in another jurisdiction under paragraph 4(b) of Ont. Reg. 289/00 made under the *Business Corporations Act* *Note: These fees are in addition to the fee payable to the Minister of Finance as set out in the Schedule attached to the Minister's Fee Orders relating to applications for exemption orders made under the Business Corporations Act to the Commission.*	$400
F.	**Market Regulation Recognitions and Exemptions**	
F1	An application for recognition of an exchange under section 21 of the *Act*	$110,000
F2	An application for exemption from the requirement to be recognized as an exchange under section 21 of the *Act*	$83,000
F3	An application by a marketplace that trades OTC derivatives, including swap execution facilities, for exemption from the requirement to be recognized under section 21 of the *Act*	$20,000
F4	An application by clearing agencies for recognition under section 21.2 of the *Act*	$110,000
F5	An application for exemption from the requirement to be recognized as a clearing agency under section 21.2 of the *Act*	$83,000 (plus an additional fee of $100,000 in connection with an application described in any of Rows F1 to F5 that (a) reflects a merger of an exchange or clearing agency, (b) reflects an acquisition of a major part of the assets of an exchange or clearing agency, or

Row	Document or Activity (Column A)	Fee (Column B)
		(c) involves the introduction of a new business that would significantly change the risk profile of an exchange or clearing agency, or reflects a major reorganization or restructuring of an exchange or clearing agency).
	G. Initial Filing for ATS	
G1	Review of the initial Form 21-101F2 of a new alternative trading system	$55,000
	H. Trade Repository	
H1	Application for designation as a trade repository under section 21.2.2 of the *Act*	$83,000
	I. Pre-Filings	
I1	Each pre-filing relating to the items described in Rows F1 to F5, G1 and H1 of Appendix C	One-half of the otherwise applicable fee that would be payable if the corresponding formal filing had proceeded at the same time as the pre-filing.
I2	Any other pre-filing *Note: The fee for a pre-filing under this section will be credited against the applicable fee payable if and when the corresponding formal filing (e.g., an application or a preliminary prospectus) is actually proceeded with; otherwise, the fee is nonrefundable.*	The applicable fee that would be payable if the corresponding formal filing had proceeded at the same time as the pre-filing.
	J. Take-Over Bid and Issuer Bid Documents	
J1	Filing of a take-over bid or issuer bid circular under subsection 2.10(2), (3) or (4) of NI 62-104, the filing of an information circular by a person or company in connection with a solicitation that is not made by or on behalf of management, or the filing of an information circular in connection with a special meeting to be held to consider the approval of a going private transaction, reorganization, amalgamation, merger, arrangement, consolidation or similar business combination (other than a second step business combination in compliance with MI 61-101).	$4,500 (plus $2,000 if neither the offeror nor an issuer of which the offeror is a wholly-owned subsidiary is subject to, or reasonably expected to become subject to, a participation fee under this Rule)
J2	Filing of a notice of change or variation under section 2.13 of NI 62-104	Nil
	K. Registration-Related Activity	
K1	New registration of a firm in one or more categories of registration	$1,300
K2	Addition of one or more categories of registration	$700
K3	Registration of a new representative as a dealer and/or adviser on behalf of a registrant firm	$200 per individual, unless the individual makes an application to register in the same category of registration within three months of terminating employment with a previous firm.
K4	Review of permitted individual	$100 per individual, unless the individual is already registered as a dealer and/or adviser on behalf of a registrant firm
K5	Change in status from not being a representative on behalf of a registrant firm to being a representative on behalf of the registrant firm	$200 per individual
K6	Registration as a chief compliance officer or ultimate designated person of a registrant firm, if the individual is not registered as a representative on behalf of the registrant firm	$200 per individual
K7	Registration of a new registrant firm, or the continuation of registration of an existing registrant firm, resulting from or following an amalgamation of one or more registrant firms	$1,000

Part 1:
PROCEDURE

Row	Document or Activity (Column A)	Fee (Column B)
K8	Application for amending terms and conditions of registration	$800
	L. Registrant Acquisitions	
L1	Notice required under section 11.9 [*Registrant acquiring a registered firm's securities or assets*] or 11.10 [*Registered firm whose securities are acquired*] of NI 31-103	$3,600
	M. Certified Statements	
M1	Request for certified statement from the Commission or the Director under section 139 of the Act	$100
	N. Designated Rating Organizations	
N1	An application for designation of a credit rating organization under section 22 of the *Act*	$15,000
N2	An application for a variation of a designation of a credit rating organization under subsection 144(1) of the *Act* if the application	$15,000
	(a) reflects a merger of a credit rating organization,	
	(b) reflects an acquisition of a major part of the assets of a credit rating organization,	
	(c) involves the introduction of a new business that would significantly change the risk profile of a credit rating organization, or	
	(d) reflects a major reorganization or restructuring of a credit rating organization	
N3	Any other application for a variation of a designation of a credit rating organization under subsection 144(1) of the *Act*	$4,800
	O. Any Application not otherwise Listed in this Rule	
O1	An application for	$4,800
	(a) relief from one section of the Act, a regulation or a rule, or	
	(b) recognition or designation under one section of the Act, a regulation or a rule.	
O2	An application for	$7,000
	(a) relief from two or more sections of the Act, a regulation or a rule made at the same time, or	
	(b) recognition or designation under two or more sections of the *Act*, a regulation or a rule made at the same time.	
O3	An application made under O1 or O2 if none of the following is subject to, or is reasonably expected to become subject to, a participation fee under this Rule or OSC Rule 13-503 (*Commodity Futures Act*) Fees:	The amount in O1 or O2 is increased by $2,000
	(i) the applicant;	
	(ii) an issuer of which the applicant is a wholly owned subsidiary;	
	(iii) the investment fund manager of the applicant);	
O4	An application under subsection 144(1) of the *Act* if the application	The amount in O1 or O2 is increased by $100,000
	(a) reflects a merger of an exchange or clearing agency,	

Row	Document or Activity (Column A)	Fee (Column B)
	(b) reflects an acquisition of a major part of the assets of an exchange or clearing agency,	
	(c) involves the introduction of a new business that would significantly change the risk profile of an exchange or clearing agency, or	
	(d) reflects a major reorganization or restructuring of an exchange or clearing agency.	
	P. Requests to the Commission	
P1	Request for a copy (in any format) of Commission public records	$0.50 per image
P2	Request for a search of Commission public records	$7.50 for each 15 minutes search time spent by any person
P3	Request for one's own individual registration form.	$30

APPENDIX D — ADDITIONAL FEES FOR LATE DOCUMENT FILINGS

	Document (Column A)	Late Fee (Column B)
A.	Fee for late filing or delivery of any of the following forms documents:	For each form or document required to be filed or delivered, $100 for every business day following the date the form or document was required to be filed or delivered until the
	(a) Annual financial statements and interim financial information;	
	(b) Annual information form filed under NI 51-102 or National Instrument 81-106 *Investment Fund Continuous Disclosure*;	date the form or document is filed or delivered, subject to a maximum aggregate late fee of,
	(c) Notice under section 11.9 [*Registrant acquiring a registered firm's securities or assets*] of NI 31-103;	(a) if the person or company is subject to a participation fee under Part 3 of the
	(d) Form 33-109F1;	Rule and the estimated specified Ontario revenues for the previous
	(e) Form 33-109F5, if the Commission is the principal regulator for the registrant firm or the individual and the filing is made for the purpose of amending:	financial year are greater than or equal to $500 million, $10,000 for all forms or documents required to be filed or delivered by the person or company in
	(i) one or more of items 10, 12, 13, 14, 15, 16, or 17 of Form 33-109F4, or	the calendar year, or
	(ii) one or more of items 1, 2, 3, 4, 5.3, 5.4, 5.5, 5.8, 5.9, 5.10, 5.11, 5.12, 6, 7, or 8 of Form 33-109F6 if the information being amended relates to the registrant firm and not a specified affiliate (as defined in Form 33-109F6) of the registrant firm;	(b) in all other cases, $5,000 for all forms or documents required to be filed or delivered by the person or company in the calendar year.
	(f) Any form or document required to be filed or delivered by a registrant firm or individual in connection with the registration of the registrant firm or individual under the Act with respect to	
	(i) terms and conditions imposed on a registrant firm or individual, or	
	(ii) an order of the Commission;	
	(g) Form 13-502F1;	
	(h) Form 13-502F2;	
	(i) Form 13-502F3A;	
	(j) Form 13-502F4;	

Part 1:
PROCEDURE

Document (Column A)		Late Fee (Column B)
	(k) Form 13-502F5;	
	(l) Form 13-502F6;	
	(m) Form 13-502F7;	
	(n) Form 13-502F8	
B.	Fee for late filing or delivery of Form 33-109F5 if the Commission is the principal regulator for the registrant firm and the filing is made for the purpose of amending Form 33-109F6 for information of a specified affiliate (as defined in Form 33-109F6) of the registrant firm.	$100
C.	Fee for late filing Forms 45-501F1 and 45-106F1	$100 for every business day following the date the form was required to be filed by a person or company until the date the form is filed, to a maximum of $5,000 for all forms required to be filed by the person or company in the calendar year.
D.	Fee for late filing of Form 55-102F2 — *Insider Report*	$50 per calendar day per insider per issuer (subject to a maximum of $1,000 per issuer within any one year beginning on April 1st and ending on March 31st). The late fee does not apply to an insider if (a) the head office of the issuer is located outside Ontario, and (b) the insider is required to pay a late fee for the filing in a jurisdiction in Canada other than Ontario.

Final Rule: (2003) 26 O.S.C.B. 4339. Approval by OSC: (2003) 26 O.S.C.B. 867; Request for Comments: (2002) 25 O.S.C.B. 4067; (2001) 14 O.S.C.B. 1971.

Amendment to Rule: (2003) 26 O.S.C.B. 7747. Approval by OSC: (2003) 26 O.S.C.B. 6481; Request for Comments: (2003) 26 O.S.C.B. 3768.

Amendment to Rule: (2005) 28 O.S.C.B. (Supp-4) 139; Approval by OSC: (2005) 28 O.S.C.B. (Supp-3) 221; Request for Comments: (2004) 27 O.S.C.B. (Supp-3) 1.

Revised Rule: (2006) 29 O.S.C.B. 2333; Approval by OSC: (2006) 29 O.S.C.B. 597; Request for Comments: (2005) 28 O.S.C.B. 6663.

Revised Rule: (2009) 32 O.S.C.B. 4445; Approval by OSC: (2009) 32 O.S.C.B. 2207; Request for Comments: (2008) 31 O.S.C.B. 9553.

Amendment to Rule: (2009) 32 O.S.C.B. (Supp. 4) 381; Approval by OSC: (2009) 32 O.S.C.B. (Supp. 2) 1; Request for Comments: (2008) 31 O.S.C.B. 2279.

Amendment to Rule: (2010) 33 O.S.C.B. 2837; Approval by OSC: (2010) 33 O.S.C.B. 721; Request for Comments: (2009) 32 O.S.C.B. 7831.

Amendment to Rule: (2010) 33 O.S.C.B. (Supp. 5) 39; Approval by OSC: (2010) 33 O.S.C.B. (Supp. 3) 1.

Amendment to Rule: (2013) 36 O.S.C.B. 1247; Approval by OSC: (2012) 35 O.S.C.B. 11563; Request for Comments: (2012) 35 O.S.C.B. 7801.

Amendment to Rule: (2015) 38 O.S.C.B. 1045.

Related Provisions: OSA 3.4(0.1).

Rules: Rule 13-501.

Policies and Orders: OPS 13-502CP; OSCN 33-741.

Form 13-502F1 — Class 1 and Class 3B Reporting Issuers — Participation Fee

Management Certification

I, ..., an officer of the reporting issuer noted below have examined this Form 13-502F1 (the **Form**) being submitted hereunder to the Ontario Securities Commission and certify that to my knowledge, having exercised reasonable diligence, the information provided in the Form is complete and accurate.

(s)..........

Name: ....
Date:

Title:

Reporting Issuer Name: ....

End date of previous financial year: ....

Type of Reporting Issuer: ❏ **Class 1 reporting issuer** ❏ **Class 3B reporting issuer**

Highest Trading Marketplace: ....
(refer to the definition of "highest trading marketplace" under OSC Rule 13-502 *Fees*)

Market value of listed or quoted equity securities:
(in Canadian Dollars — refer to section 7.1 of OSC Rule 13-502 *Fees*)

Equity Symbol

1ˢᵗ Specified Trading Period (dd/mm/yy) ....
(refer to the definition of "specified trading period" under OSC Rule 13-502
Fees) .... to ....

Closing price of the security in the class or series on the last trading day of
the specified trading period in which such security was listed or quoted on the
highest trading marketplace $..........(i)

Number of securities in the class or series of such security outstanding at the
end of the last trading day of the specified trading period ....(ii)

Market value of class or series (i) × (ii) $..........(A)

2ⁿᵈ Specified Trading Period (dd/mm/yy)
(refer to the definition of "specified trading period" under OSC Rule 13-502
Fees) .... to ....

Closing price of the security in the class or series on the last trading day of
the specified trading period in which such security was listed or quoted on the
highest trading marketplace $..........(iii)

Number of securities in the class or series of such security outstanding at the
end of the last trading day of the specified trading period ....(iv)

Market value of class or series (iii) × (iv) $..........(B)

3ʳᵈ Specified Trading Period (dd/mm/yy)
(refer to the definition of "specified trading period" under OSC Rule 13-502
Fees) .... to ....

Closing price of the security in the class or series on the last trading day of
the specified trading period in which such security was listed or quoted on the
highest trading marketplace $ ....(v)

Number of securities in the class or series of such security outstanding at the
end of the last trading day of the specified trading period ....(vi)

Market value of class or series (v) × (vi) $..........(C)

4ᵗʰ Specified Trading Period (dd/mm/yy)
(refer to the definition of "specified trading period" under OSC Rule 13-502
Fees) .... to ....

Part 1:
PROCEDURE

Equity Symbol

Closing price of the security in the class or series on the last trading day of
the specified trading period in which such security was listed or quoted on the
highest trading marketplace   ....(vii)

Number of securities in the class or series of such security outstanding at the
end of the last trading day of the specified trading period   ....(viii)

Market value of class or series   (vii) × (viii) $..........(D)

5th Specified Trading Period (dd/mm/yy)

(if applicable — refer to the definition of "specified trading period" under OSC
Rule 13-502 *Fees*)   .... to ....

Closing price of the security in the class or series on the last trading day of
the specified trading period in which such security was listed or quoted on the
highest trading marketplace $..........(ix)

Number of securities in the class or series of such security outstanding at the
end of the last trading day of the specified trading period   ....(x)

Market value of class or series   (ix) × (x) $..........(E)

Average Market Value of Class or Series

(Calculate the simple average of the market value of the class or series of
security for each applicable specified trading period (i.e. A through E above))

                                                                            $.......... (1)

(Repeat the above calculation for each other class or series of equity securities of the reporting issuer (and a subsidiary pursuant to
paragraph 2.8(1)(c) of OSC Rule 13-502 *Fees*, if applicable) that was listed or quoted on a marketplace at the end of the previous
financial year)

Fair value of outstanding debt securities:

(See paragraph 2.8(1)(b), and if applicable, paragraph 2.8(1)(c) of OSC Rule
13-502 *Fees*) $.......... (2)

(Provide details of how value was determined)

Capitalization for the previous financial year   (1) + (2) $..........

Participation Fee

(For Class 1 reporting issuers, from Appendix A of OSC Rule 13-502 *Fees*,
select the participation fee)

(For Class 3B reporting issuers, from Appendix A.1 of OSC Rule 13-502
Fees, select the participation fee)

Late Fee, if applicable

(As determined under section 2.7 of OSC Rule 13-502 *Fees*) $..........

Total Fee Payable

(Participation Fee plus Late Fee) $..........

Form 13-502F2 — Class 2 Reporting Issuers — Participation Fee

Management Certification

I, ..., an officer of the reporting issuer noted below have examined this Form 13-502F2 (the **Form**) being submitted hereunder to the Ontario Securities Commission and certify that to my knowledge, having exercised reasonable diligence, the information provided in the Form is complete and accurate.

(s)..........

Name: Date:

Title:

Reporting Issuer Name: ....

End date of previous financial year: ....

Financial Statement Values:

> (Use stated values from the audited financial statements of the reporting issuer as of the end of its previous financial year)

Retained earnings or deficit $ _____ (A)

Contributed surplus $ _____ (B)

Share capital or owners' equity, options, warrants and preferred shares (whether such shares are classified as debt or equity for financial reporting purposes) $ _____ (C)

Non-current borrowings (including the current portion) $ _____ (D)

Finance leases (including the current portion) $ _____ (E)

Non-controlling interest $ _____ (F)

Items classified on the statement of financial position as non-current liabilities (and not otherwise listed above) $ _____ (G)

Any other item forming part of equity and not set out specifically above $ _____ (H)

Capitalization for the previous financial year

(Add items (A) through (H)) $ _____

Participation Fee

(From Appendix A of OSC Rule 13-502 *Fees*, select the participation fee beside the capitalization calculated above) $ _____

Late Fee, if applicable

(As determined under section 2.7 of OSC Rule 13-502 *Fees*) $ _____

Total Fee Payable

(Participation Fee plus Late Fee) $ _____

Form 13-502F2A — Adjustment of Fee Payment for Class 2 Reporting Issuers

Management Certification

I, ..., an officer of the reporting issuer noted below have examined this Form 13-502F2A (the **Form**) being submitted hereunder to the Ontario Securities Commission and certify that to my knowledge, having exercised reasonable diligence, the information provided in the Form is complete and accurate.

(s)..........   ....

Name: Date:

Title:

Reporting Issuer Name: ....

Financial year end date used to cal- ....
culate capitalization:

State the amount of participation fee paid under subsection 2.2(1) of OSC

Rule 13-502 *Fees*: $ _____ (i)

Show calculation of actual capitalization based on audited financial statements:

Financial Statement Values:

Retained earnings or deficit $ _____ (A)

Contributed surplus $ _____ (B)

Share capital or owners' equity, options, warrants and preferred shares (whether such shares are classified as debt or
equity for financial reporting purposes $ _____ (C)

Non-current borrowings (including the current portion) $ _____ (D)

Finance leases (including the current portion) $ _____ (E)

Non-controlling interest $ _____ (F)

Items classified on the statement of financial position as non-current liabilities (and not otherwise listed above) $ _____ (G)

Any other item forming part of equity and not set out specifically above $ _____ (H)

Capitalization
(Add items (A) through (H)) $ _____

Participation Fee
(From Appendix A of OSC Rule 13-502 *Fees*, select the participation fee beside the capitalization calculated above) $ _____ (ii)

Refund due (Balance owing)
(Indicate the difference between (i) and (ii) and enter nil if no difference)
(i) - (ii) = $ _____

Form 13-502F3A — Class 3A Reporting Issuers — Participation Fee

Management Certification

I, ..., an officer of the reporting issuer noted below have examined this Form 13-502F3A (the **Form**) being submitted hereunder to the Ontario Securities Commission and certify that to my knowledge, having exercised reasonable diligence, the information provided in the Form is complete and accurate.
(s)..........
Name: Date:
Title:

Reporting Issuer Name: ....
    (Class 3A reporting issuer cannot be incorporated or organized under the laws of Canada or a province or territory of Canada)
Financial year end date: ....

Indicate, by checking the appropriate box, which of the following criteria the issuer meets:

❏ (a) had no securities listed or quoted on any marketplace at the end of its previous financial year, or

❏ (b) had securities listed or quoted on a marketplace at the end of its previous financial year and all of the following apply:

(i) at the end of its previous financial year, securities registered in the names of persons or companies resident in Ontario represented less than 1% of the market value of all of the reporting issuer's outstanding securities for which it or its transfer agent or registrar maintains a list of registered owners;

(ii) the reporting issuer reasonably believes that, at the end of its previous financial year, securities beneficially owned by persons or companies resident in Ontario represented less than 1% of the market value of all its outstanding securities;

(iii) the reporting issuer reasonably believes that none of its securities traded on a marketplace in Canada during its previous financial year;

(iv) the reporting issuer has not issued any of its securities in Ontario in the last 5 years, other than

(A) to its employees or to employees of one or more of its subsidiaries, or

(B) to a person or company exercising a right previously granted by the reporting issuer or its affiliate to convert or exchange its previously issued securities without payment of any additional consideration;

Participation Fee

(From subsection 2.2(2) of OSC Rule 13-502 *Fees*) $ 1,195

Late Fee, if applicable

(As determined under section 2.7 of OSC Rule 13-502 *Fees*) $

Total Fee Payable

(Participation Fee plus Late Fee) $

Form 13-502F4 — Capital Markets Participation Fee Calculation

General Instructions

1. This form must be completed and returned to the Ontario Securities Commission by December 1 each year, as required by section 3.1 or 3.2 of OSC Rule 13-502 *Fees* (the Rule), except in the case where firms register after December 1 in a calendar year or provide notification after December 1 in a calendar year of their status as an unregistered capital markets participant. In these exceptional cases, this form must be filed within 60 days of registration or notification after December 1.

2. This form is to be completed by firms registered under the *Securities Act* or by firms that are registered under both the *Securities Act* and the *Commodity Futures Act*. This form is also completed by unregistered capital markets participants.

3. For firms registered under the *Commodity Futures Act*, the completion of this form will serve as an application for the renewal of both the firm and all its registered individuals wishing to renew under the *Commodity Futures Act*.

4. IIROC members must complete Part I of this form and MFDA members must complete Part II. Unregistered capital markets participants and registrant firms that are not IIROC or MFDA members must complete Part III.

5. IIROC Members may refer to Statement E of the Joint Regulatory Financial Questionnaire and Report for guidance.

6. MFDA members may refer to Statement D of the MFDA Financial Questionnaire and Report for guidance.

7. If a firm's permanent establishments are situated only in Ontario, all of the firm's total revenue for the previous financial year is attributed to Ontario. If permanent establishments are situated in Ontario and elsewhere, the percentage attributed to Ontario for a previous financial year will ordinarily be the percentage of the firm's taxable income that is allocated to Ontario for Canadian income tax purposes for the same financial year. For firms that do not have a permanent establishment in Ontario, the percentage attributable to Ontario will be based on the proportion of total revenues generated from capital markets activities in Ontario.

8. All figures must be expressed in Canadian dollars. All figures other than the participation fee must be rounded to the nearest thousand.

9. Information reported on this form must be certified by the chief compliance officer or equivalent to attest to its completeness and accuracy.

Chief Compliance Officer Certification

I, ..., of the registrant firm / unregistered capital markets participant noted below have examined this Form 13-502F4 (the **Form**) being submitted hereunder to the Ontario Securities Commission and certify that to my knowledge, having exercised reasonable diligence, the information provided in the Form is complete and accurate.

(s).......... ....

Name: Date:

Title:

1. — Firm Information

Firm NRD number: ....

Firm legal name: ....

2. — Contact Information for Chief Compliance Officer

Please provide the name, e-mail address, phone number and fax number for your Chief Compliance Officer.

Name: ....

E-mail address: ....

Phone: .... Fax: ....

3. — Membership Status (one selection)

❑ The firm is a member of the Mutual Fund Dealers Association (MFDA).

❑ The firm is a member of the Investment Industry Regulatory Organization of Canada (IIROC).

For a firm that does not hold membership with the MFDA or IIROC:

  ❑ The firm is an unregistered investment fund manager only

    ❑ All other firms

4. — Financial Information

Is the firm providing a good faith estimate under section 3.2 of the Rule?

❑ Yes ❑ No (one selection)

If no, end date of previous financial year: ..../   ..../   ....

                                                     yyyy   mm   dd

If yes, end date of financial year for which the good faith estimate is provided: ..../   ..../   ....

                                                     yyyy   mm   dd

5. — Participation Fee Calculation

Previous financial year

$

Note: Dollar amounts stated in thousands, rounded to the neared thousand.

Part I — IIROC Members

1.   Total revenue for previous financial year from Statement E of the Joint
       Regulatory Financial Questionnaire and Report $..........

2.   Less revenue not attributable to capital markets activities $..........

3.   Revenue subject to participation fee (line 1 less line 2) $..........

4.   Ontario percentage for previous financial year
          (See definition of "Ontario percentage" in the Rule)   ....%

5.   Specified Ontario revenues (line 3 multiplied by line 4) $..........

6.   Participation fee (From Appendix B of the Rule, select the participation fee
          opposite the specified Ontario revenues calculated above) $..........

Part II — MFDA Members

1.   Total revenue for previous financial year from Statement D of the MFDA
       Financial Questionnaire and Report $..........

2.   Less revenue not attributable to capital markets activities $..........

3.   Revenue subject to participation fee (line 1 less line 2) $..........

Previous financial year
$

4. Ontario percentage for previous financial year
(See definition of "Ontario percentage" in the Rule) ....%

5. Specified Ontario revenues (line 3 multiplied by line 4) $.........

6. Participation fee
(From Appendix B of the Rule, select the participation fee opposite the specified Ontario revenues
calculated above) $.........

Part III — Advisers, Other Dealers, and Unregistered Capital Markets Participants Notes:

1. Total revenues is defined as the sum of all revenues reported on the audited financial statements, except where unaudited financial statements are permitted in accordance with subsection 3.6(3) of the Rule. Audited financial statements should be prepared in accordance with NI 52-107. Items reported on a net basis must be adjusted for purposes of the fee calculation to reflect gross revenues.

2. Redemption fees earned upon the redemption of investment fund units sold on a deferred sales charge basis are permitted as a deduction from total revenue on this line.

3. Administration fees permitted as a deduction are limited solely to those that are otherwise included in total revenues and represent the reasonable recovery of costs from the investment funds for operating expenses paid on their behalf by the registrant firm or unregistered capital markets participant.

4. Where the advisory services of a registrant firm, within the meaning of this Rule or OSC Rule 13-503 (*Commodity Futures Act*) *Fees*, or of an unregistered exempt international firm, are used by the person or company to advise on a portion of its assets under management, such sub-advisory costs are permitted as a deduction on this line to the extent that they are otherwise included in gross revenues.

5. Trailer fees paid to registrant firms or unregistered exempt international firms described in note 4 are permitted as a deduction on this line to the extent they are otherwise included in gross revenues.

1. Total revenue for previous financial year (note 1) $.........

Less the following items:

2. Revenue not attributable to capital markets activities $.........

3. Redemption fee revenue (note 2) $.........

4. Administration fee revenue (note 3) $.........

5. Advisory or sub-advisory fees paid to registrant firms or unregistered
exempt international firms (note 4) $.........

6. Trailer fees paid to registrant firms or unregistered exempt international firms
(note 5) $.........

7. Total deductions (sum of lines 2 to 6) $.........

8. Revenue subject to participation fee (line 1 less line 7) $.........

9. Ontario percentage for previous financial year
(See definition of "Ontario percentage" in the Rule) ....%

10. Specified Ontario revenues (line 8 multiplied by line 9) $.........

Previous financial year

$

11.   Participation fee

(From Appendix B of the Rule, select the participation fee beside the specified Ontario revenues calculated above) $..........

Form 13-502F5 — Adjustment of Fee for Registrant Firms and Unregistered Capital Markets Participants

Firm name: ....

End date of previous completed financial year: ....

Note: Paragraph 3.2(2)(c) of OSC Rule 13-502 *Fees* (the Rule) requires that this form must be filed concurrent with a completed Form 13-502F4 that shows the firm's actual participation fee calculation.

1.   Estimated participation fee paid under section 3.2 of the Rule: $..........

2.   Actual participation fee calculated under paragraph 3.2(2)(b) of the Rule: $..........

3.   Refund due (Balance owing):

(Indicate the difference between lines 1 and 2) $..........

Form 13-502F6 — Subsidiary Exemption Notice

Management Certification

I, ..., an officer of the subsidiary noted below have examined this Form 13-502F6 (the **Form**) being submitted hereunder to the Ontario Securities Commission and certify that to my knowledge, having exercised reasonable diligence, the information provided in the Form is complete and accurate.

(s)..........   ....

Name: Date:

Title:

Name of Subsidiary: ....

Name of Parent: ....

End Date of Subsidiary's Previous Financial Year: ....

The reporting issuer (subsidiary) meets the following criteria set out under subsection 2.4(1) of OSC Rule 13-502 *Fees*:

(a) at the end of the subsidiary's previous financial year, a parent of the subsidiary was a reporting issuer;

(b) the audited financial statements of the parent prepared in accordance with NI 52-107 require the consolidation of the parent and the subsidiary;

(c) the parent has paid a participation fee under subsection 2.2(1) calculated based on the capitalization of the parent for its previous financial year;

(d) in the case of a parent that is a Class 1 reporting issuer, the capitalization of the parent for its previous financial year included the capitalization of the subsidiary as required under paragraph 2.8(1)(c);

(e) in its previous financial year,

(i) the net assets and total revenues of the subsidiary represented more than 90% of the consolidated net assets and total revenues of the parent for the parent's previous financial year, or

(ii) the subsidiary was entitled to rely on an exemption or waiver from the requirements in subsections 4.1(1), 4.3(1) and 5.1(1) and sections 5.2 and 6.1 of NI 51-102.

If paragraph e(i) above applies, complete the following table:

	Net Assets for previous financial year	Total Revenues for previous financial year	
Reporting Issuer (Subsidiary)	$..........	$..........	(A)
Reporting Issuer (Parent)	$..........	$..........	(B)
Percentage (A/B)	..........%	..........%	

Form 13-502F7 — Specified Regulated Entities — Participation Fee

Name of Specified Regulated Entity: ....

Applicable Calendar Year: .... (2014 or later)

Type of Specified Regulated Entity: (check one)

❑ Recognized exchange or recognized quotation and trade reporting system (complete (1) below)

❑ Alternative trading system (complete (2) or (3) below, as applicable)

❑ Recognized clearing agency (complete (4) below)

❑ Exempt exchange, Exempt clearing agency or Designated Trade Repository (complete (5) below, as applicable)

(1) — Participation Fee for applicable calendar year — Recognized exchange or recognized quotation and trade reporting system

Filer should enter their Canadian trading share for the specified period below:

Canadian Trading Share Description	..........% (To be Entered by Filer)
Line 1: the share in the specified period of the total dollar values of trades of exchange-traded securities	
Line 2: the share in the specified period of the total trading volume of exchange-traded securities	
Line 3: the share in the specified period of the total number of trades of exchange-traded securities	
Line 4: Average of Lines 1, 2 & 3 above	
Line 5: Filer is required to Pay the Amount from the corresponding column in the table below based on the average calculated on Line 4 above:	$..........
Canadian trading share for the specified period of up to 5%	$30,000
Canadian trading share for the specified period of 5% to up to 15%	$50,000
Canadian trading share for the specified period of 15% to up to 25%	$135,000
Canadian trading share for the specified period of 25% to up to 50%	$275,000
Canadian trading share for the specified period of 50% to up to 75%.	$400,000
Canadian trading share for the specified period of 75% or more	$500,000

(2) — Participation Fee for applicable calendar year — Alternative trading system for exchange-traded securities

Line 6: If operating an alternative trading system for exchange-traded securities, enter participation fee based on your Canadian trading share (Line 5)	$..........
Line 7: Enter amount of capital markets participation fee paid based on Form 13-502F4 on December 31 of the prior year	$..........
Line 8: Subtract Line 7 from Line 6. If positive, enter the lesser of this amount and $17,000. If zero or negative, there is no Part 4 fee payable and there is a refund due to you of the amount determined	$..........

(3) — Participation fee for applicable calendar year — other alternative trading system

Line 9: If operating as an alternative trading system that is not for exchange-traded securities, enter $30,000	$..........
Line 10: Enter amount of capital markets participation fee based on Form 13-502F4 on December 31 of the prior year	$..........
Line 11: Subtract Line 10 from Line 9. If positive, enter	
(a) The lesser of this amount and $8,750 if trading in debt or securities lending	

(b)   The lesser of this amount and $17,000 if you are a trading system other than that described in Line 6 or (a) above. $..........

If zero or negative, there is no Part 4 participation fee payable and there is a refund due to you.

(4) — Participation Fee for applicable calendar year — Recognized clearing agency

For services offered in Ontario Market the filer should enter the corresponding amount in the Fees Payable Column:

Services:	Fee Payable
Line 12: Matching services, being the provision of facilities for comparing data respecting the terms of settlement of a trade or transaction. Enter $10,000	$..........
Line 13: Netting services, being the provision of facilities for the calculation of the mutual obligations of participants for the exchange of securities and/or money. Enter $20,000	$..........
Line 14: Settlement services, being services that ensure that securities are transferred finally and irrevocably from one participant to another in exchange for a corresponding transfer of money and/or *vice versa*. Enter $20,000.	$..........
Line 15: Acting as a central clearing counterparty by providing novation services, if the Commission does not place reliance on another regulator for direct oversight. Enter $150,000	$..........
Line 16: Acting as a central clearing counterparty by providing novation services, if the Commission places reliance on another regulator for direct oversight. Enter $70,000.	$..........
Line 17: Depositary services, being the provision of centralized facilities as a depositary for securities. Enter $20,000.	$..........
Line 18: Total Participation Fee Payable (Sum of Lines 12–17):	$..........

(5) — Participation Fee for applicable calendar year for other types of specified regulated entities:

Line 19: Filer is required to pay the amount below, as applicable.	$..........
(a) If operating as an Exempt Exchange or Exempt Clearing Agency, enter $10,000	
(b) If operating as a Designated Trade Repository, enter $30,000	

(6) — Prorated Participation Fee:

Line 20: If this is the first time paying a participation fee as a specified regulated entity, prorate the amount under subsection 4.6(1) of the Rule.	$..........

(7) — Late Fee

Line 21: Unpaid portion of Participation Fee from Sections (1), (2), (3), (4), (5), (6)	$..........
Line 22: Number of Business Days Late	$..........
Line 23: Fee Payable is as follows: Amount from Line 21*[Amount from Line 22*0.1%]	$..........

(8) — Total Fee Payable

Line 24: Aggregate Participant Fee from Sections (1), (2), (3), (4), (5), (6)	$..........
Line 25: Late Fee from Line 23	$..........
Line 26: Fee Payable is amount from Line 24 plus amount from Line 25	$..........

Form 13-502F8 — Designated Credit Rating Organizations — Participation Fee

Name of Designated Credit Rating Organization:

Financial year end date: ....

Participation Fee in respect of the financial year

(From subsection 5.1(1) of OSC Rule 13-502 *Fees*) $15,000

Late Fee, if applicable

(From Section 5.2 of OSC Rule 13-502 *Fees*) $..........

Total Fee Payable

(Participation Fee plus Late Fee) $..........

Companion Policy 13-502CP — Fees

PART 1 — PURPOSE OF COMPANION POLICY

1.1 Purpose of Companion Policy — The purpose of this Companion Policy is to state the views of the Commission on various matters relating to OSC Rule 13-502 *Fees* (the "Rule"), including an explanation of the overall approach of the Rule and a discussion of various parts of the Rule.

PART 2 — PURPOSE AND GENERAL APPROACH OF THE RULE

2.1 Purpose and general approach of the Rule — (1) The purpose of the Rule is to establish a fee regime that creates a clear and streamlined fee structure.

(2) The fee regime of the Rule is based on the concepts of "participation fees" and "activity fees".

2.2 Participation fees — (1) Reporting issuers, registrant firms and unregistered capital markets participants, as well as specified regulated entities and designated rating organizations, are required to pay participation fees annually.

(2) Participation fees are designed to cover the Commission's costs not easily attributable to specific regulatory activities. The participation fee required of a person or company under Parts 2 and 3 of the Rule is based on a measure of the person's or company's size, which is used as a proxy for its proportionate participation in the Ontario capital markets. In the case of a reporting issuer, the participation fee is based on the issuer's capitalization, which is used to approximate its proportionate participation in the Ontario capital markets. In the case of a registrant firm or unregistered capital markets participant, the participation fee is based on the firm's revenues attributable to its capital markets activity in Ontario.

(3) Participation fees under Part 4 of the Rule are generally fixed annual amounts payable each calendar year. In the case of specified regulated entities to which Part 4 of the Rule applies, participation fees are generally specified for a particular organization or type of organization in Appendix B.1. The level of participation fees for recognized clearing agencies is determined by reference to the services they provide.

(4) Participation fees for designated rating organizations under Part 5 of the Rule are $15,000 per financial year.

(5) A person or company may be subject to participation fees under more than one part of the Rule. There is no cap on multiple participation fees except as described in subsection 2.7(2).

2.3 Application of participation fees — Although participation fees are determined with reference to information from a financial year of the payor generally ending before the time of their payment, they are applied to the costs of the Commission of regulating the ongoing participation in Ontario's capital markets of the payor and other market participants.

2.4 Registered individuals — The participation fee is paid at the firm level under the Rule. For example, a "registrant firm" is required to pay a participation fee, not an individual who is registered as a representative of the firm.

2.5 Activity fees — (1) Activity fees are generally charged where a document of a designated class is filed. Estimates of the direct cost of Commission resources expended in undertaking the activities listed in Appendix C of the Rule are considered in determining these fees (e.g., reviewing prospectuses, registration applications, and applications for discretionary relief). Generally, the activity fee charged for filing a document of a particular class is based on the average cost to the Commission of reviewing documents of the class.

(2) Under certain circumstances, Staff may consider reducing activity fees for applications made by or on behalf of two or more reporting issuers that are affiliates of each other, and who are applying for the same exemptive relief. In such circumstances, the activity fees will be reduced such that the activity fees paid on an application will be the same as if one reporting issuer filed the application.

2.6 Registrants under the *Securities Act* and the *Commodity Futures Act* — (1) The Rule imposes an obligation to pay a participation fee on registrant firms, defined in the Rule as a person or company registered under the *Act* as a dealer, adviser or investment fund manager. An entity so registered may also be registered as a dealer or adviser under the *Commodity Futures Act*. Given the definition of "capital markets activities" under the Rule, the revenue of such an entity from its *Commodity Futures Act* activities must be included in its calculation of revenues when determining its fee under the Rule. Section 2.1 of OSC Rule 13-503 *(Commodity Futures Act) Fees* exempts such an entity from paying a participation fee under that rule if it has paid its participation fees under the *Securities Act* Rule.

(2) Note that dealers and advisers registered under the *Commodity Futures Act* are subject to activity fees under OSC Rule 13-503 *(Commodity Futures Act) Fees* even if they are not required to pay participation fees under that rule.

2.7 Refunds — (1) The Rule provides the specific circumstances where the Commission is required to refund fees in subsections 2.5(3) and 3.2(3) of the Rule. These subsections allow for a refund where a reporting issuer, registrant firm or unregistered capital markets participant overpaid an estimated participation fee provided the request is made within the time the related form was required to be filed.

(2) A further refund mechanism is provided under subsection 4.3(4). This subsection deals with a refund mechanism used to effect a cap of Part 3 and Part 4 participation fees for alternative trading systems, in an attempt to align the participation fees to those charged to other specified regulated entities.

(3) Generally, a person or company that pays a fee under the Rule is not entitled to a refund of that fee unless they meet the conditions set out in the Rule and discussed in subsections (1) and (2) above. For example, there is no refund available for an activity fee paid in connection with an action that is subsequently abandoned by the payor of the fee. Also, there is no refund available for a participation fee paid by a reporting issuer, registrant firm or unregistered capital markets participant that loses that status later in the financial year in respect of which the fee was paid.

(4) While the Commission will also review requests for adjustments to fees paid in the case of incorrect calculations, unless there are exceptional circumstances, we will not generally issue a refund if a request is made more than 90 days after the fee was required to be paid.

2.8 Indirect avoidance of Rule — The Commission may examine arrangements or structures implemented by a person or company and their affiliates that raise the suspicion of being structured for the purpose of reducing the fees payable under the Rule. For example, the Commission will review circumstances in which revenues from registrable activities carried on by a corporate group are not treated as revenues of a registrant firm to assess whether the firm has artificially reduced the firm's specified Ontario revenues and, consequently, its participation fee. Similarly, registrant firms or unregistered capital markets participants that operate under a cost recovery model in which there are no recorded revenues on their financial statements would be expected to report a reasonable proxy of the firm's capital markets activities in Ontario, subject to the conditions of any exemptive relief granted under section 8.1 of the Rule. In all cases, the Commission expects registrant firms and unregistered capital markets participants to pay participation fees based on all revenues attributable to capital markets activities in Ontario, irrespective of how these revenues are recorded or structured.

PART 3 — CORPORATE FINANCE PARTICIPATION FEES

3.1 Application to investment funds — Part 2 of the Rule does not apply to an investment fund if the investment fund has an investment fund manager. The reason for this is that under Part 3 of the Rule an investment fund's manager must pay a capital markets participation fee in respect of revenues generated from managing the investment fund.

3.2 Late fees — Section 2.7 of the Rule requires a reporting issuer to pay an additional fee when it is late in paying its participation fee. Reporting issuers should be aware that the late payment of participation fees may lead to the reporting issuer being noted in default and included on the list of defaulting reporting issuers available on the Commission's website.

3.3 Exemption for subsidiary entities — Under section 2.4 of the Rule, an exemption from participation fees is available to a reporting issuer that is a subsidiary entity if, among other requirements, the parent of the subsidiary entity has paid a participation fee applicable to the parent under section 2.2(1) of the Rule determined with reference to the parent's capitalization for the parent's financial year. For greater certainty, this condition to the exemption is not satisfied in circumstances where the parent of a subsidiary entity has paid a participation fee in reliance on subsection 2.2(2) or (3) of the Rule.

3.4 Determination of market value — (1) Paragraph 2.8(1)(a) of the Rule requires the calculation of the capitalization of a reporting issuer to include the total market value of all of its equity securities listed or quoted on a marketplace. This includes, but is not limited to, any listed shares, warrants, subscription receipts and rights.

(2) Paragraph 2.8(1)(b) of the Rule requires the calculation of the capitalization of a reporting issuer to include the total fair value of its debt securities that are listed or quoted on a marketplace, trade over the counter or otherwise generally available for sale without regard to a statutory hold period. This paragraph is intended to include all capital market debt issued by the reporting issuer, whether distributed under a prospectus or prospectus exemption, and includes, but is not limited to, bonds, debentures (including the equity portion of convertible debentures), commercial paper, notes and any debt securities to which a credit rating is attached, but is not intended to include bank debt (such as term loans and revolving credit facilities) and mortgages.

(3) If the closing price of a security on a particular date is not ascertainable because there is no trade on that date or the marketplace does not generally provide closing prices, a reasonable alternative, such as the most recent closing price before that date, the average of the high and low trading prices for that date, or the average of the bid and ask prices on that date is acceptable.

3.5 Owners' equity and non-current borrowings — A Class 2 reporting issuer calculates its capitalization on the basis of certain items reflected in its audited statement of financial position. Two such items are "share capital or owners' equity" and "non-current borrowings, including the current portion". The Commission notes that "owners' equity" is designed to describe the equivalent of share capital for non-corporate issuers, such as partnerships or trusts. "Non-current borrowings" is designed to describe the equivalent of long term debt or any other borrowing of funds beyond a period of twelve months.

3.6 Identification of non-current liabilities — If a Class 2 reporting issuer does not present current and non-current liabilities as separate classifications on its statement of financial position, the reporting issuer will still need to classify these liabilities for purposes of its capitalization calculation. In these circumstances non-current liabilities means total liabilities minus current liabilities, using the meanings ascribed to those terms under the accounting standards pursuant to which the entity's financial statements are prepared under Ontario securities law.

PART 4 — CAPITAL MARKETS PARTICIPATION FEES

4.1 Liability for capital markets participation fees — Capital markets participation fees are payable annually by registrant firms and unregistered capital markets participants, as defined in section 1.1 of the Rule.

4.2 Filing forms under section 3.2 of the Rule — If the estimated participation fee paid under subsection 3.2(1) of the Rule by a registrant firm or an unregistered capital markets participant does not differ from its true participation fee determined under paragraph 3.2(2)(b) of the Rule, the registrant firm or unregistered capital markets participant is not required to file either a Form 13-502F4 or a Form 13-502F5 under paragraph 3.2(2)(c) of the Rule.

4.3 Late fees — Section 3.4 of the Rule prescribes an additional fee if a participation fee is paid late. The Commission and the Director will, in appropriate circumstances, consider tardiness in the payment of fees as a matter going to the fitness for registration of a registrant firm. The Commission may also consider measures in the case of late payment of fees by an unregistered capital markets participant, such as: in the case of an unregistered investment fund manager, prohibiting the manager from continuing to manage any investment fund or cease trading the investment funds managed by the manager; or, in the case of an unregistered exempt international firm, making an order pursuant to section 127 of the Act, that the corresponding exemptions from registration requirements under which the firm acts do not apply to the firm (either permanently or for such other period as specified in the order).

4.4 Form of payment of fees — Registrant firms pay through the National Registration Database. The filings and payments for unregistered capital markets participants should be sent via wire transfer or sent to the Ontario Securities Commission (Attention: Manager, Compliance and Registrant Regulation).

4.5 "Capital markets activities" — (1) A person or company must consider its capital markets activities when calculating its participation fee. The Commission is of the view that these activities include, without limitation, carrying on the business of trading in securities, carrying on the business of an investment fund manager, providing securities-related advice or portfolio management services. The Commission notes that corporate advisory services may not require registration or an exemption from registration and would therefore, in those contexts, not be capital markets activities.

(2) The Commission is of the view that these activities include, without limitation, trading in commodity futures contracts, carrying on the business of providing commodity futures contracts-related advice and portfolio management services involving commodity futures contracts.

4.6 Permitted deductions — Subsection 3.6 of the Rule permits certain deductions to be made for the purpose of calculating specified Ontario revenues for unregistered capital markets participants and registrant firms. The purpose of these deductions is to prevent the "double counting" of revenues that would otherwise occur.

4.7 Active solicitation — For the purposes of the definition of unregistered investment fund manager in section 1.1 of the Rule, "active solicitation" refers to intentional actions taken by the investment fund or the investment fund manager to encourage a purchase of the fund's securities, such as proactive, targeted actions or communications that are initiated by an investment fund manager for the purpose of soliciting an investment. Actions that are undertaken by an investment fund manager at the request of, or in response to, an existing or prospective investor who initiates contact with the investment fund manager would not constitute active solicitation.

4.8 Confidentiality of forms — The material filed under Part 3 of the Rule will be kept confidential. The Commission is of the view that the material contains intimate financial, commercial and technical information and that the interests of the filers in non-disclosure outweigh the desirability of the principle that the material be available for public inspection.

PART 5 — OTHER PARTICIPATION FEES

5.1 General — Participation fees are also payable annually by specified regulated entities and designated credit rating organizations under Parts 4 and 5 of the Rule.

5.2 Specified regulated entities — The calculation of participation fees under Part 4 of the Rule is generally determined with reference to described classes of entities. The classes, and their level of participation fees, are set out in Appendix B.1 of the Rule.

(1) To provide more equitable treatment among exchanges and alternative trading systems (ATS) for exchange-traded securities and to take into account Part 3 participation fees payable by an alternative trading system entity for exchange-traded securities, its participation fee is adjusted under section 4.3.

For example, assume that participation fees under Part 3 for an eligible ATS payable on December 31, 2015 is $74,000 and the ATS's Canadian trading share is under 5%. In this case, the ATS would pay $74,000 on December 31 when filing its form 13-502F4. Before April 30, 2016 when filing form 13-502F7, the fee payable will be shown as $17,000 (the lesser of (a) $30,000 from row A1 of Appendix B.1 and (b) $17,000). In this case, the ATS will be entitled to a refund of $57,000 ($74,000 paid on December 31 less $17,000 required to be paid under Part 4). A mechanism that is similar in principle applies to other ATS entities under subsections 4.2(2) and (3).

An ATS described in subsection 4.3(6) will pay an aggregate participation fee calculated based on the type of securities traded on each of its platforms. For example, an ATS that has a platform for trading equities and another one for trading fixed income securities would pay a participation fee for its equity platform calculated as described above and a participation fee for its fixed income platform as described in Appendix B.1 row C2.

(2) If a specified regulated entity is recognized during the specified period, it must pay to the Commission, immediately upon recognition, designation etc., a participation fee for the remaining specified period. The participation fee owed to the Commission will be pro-rated based on the number of remaining complete months to March 31 subsequent to it being recognized, designated, etc. For example, if an exchange was recognized on January 15, 2016, it will owe to the Commission a pro-rated participation fee in the amount of $5,000 for the two complete months remaining until March 31 (calculated as $30,000 x 2/12). A form 13-502F7 must be filed with the pro-rated payment.

Continuing with the example above, the recognized exchange will also need to calculate the participation fee due before April 30, 2016 and file a second Form 13-502F7 with this payment. For the purpose of calculating its Canadian trading share, the exchange should use the actual Canadian trading share for the months of February and March 2016 and zero for the months before it received recognition (i.e. April 2015 to January 2016).

PART 6 — ACTIVITY FEES

6.1 Technical reports — Item A2 of Appendix C requires fee payment of $2,500 for the filing of a technical report, including where a technical report is incorporated by reference into a prospectus. Staff consider that a technical report is incorporated by reference into a prospectus even if the incorporation is indirect; for example, the technical report is referenced in an annual information form that itself is included or incorporated in the prospectus.

6.2 Concurrent application by permitted individual — Item K4 of Appendix C imposes a fee of $100 for an individual seeking approval as a permitted individual. Item K5 imposes a fee of $200 for an individual changing his or her status to a representative of a registrant firm. If an individual makes a concurrent application for approval as a permitted individual and as a representative of a registrant firm, staff would expect a fee of $200 in the aggregate.

PART 7 — LATE FEES

7.1 Late fees relating to Form 33-109F5 — Paragraph (e) to item A of Appendix D to the Rule provides for a late fee of $100 per day to a maximum cap for each year. Form 33-109F5 is required to be filed for changes in registration information within the time periods specified in Parts 3 and 4 of NI 33-109. In some cases, registrants file the form merging a number of changes that have occurred and were required to be reported at different times. Staff will generally apply the late fee under paragraph (e) of Item A for each change reported on the F5 on the basis that a separate form was required to be filed in respect of each change.

7.2 Late fees under section 6.4 of the Rule for registrant firms — Appendix D to the Rule outlines additional fees payable by registrant firms for the late filing or delivery of certain forms or documents required under the Act. The Commission may consider the late filing or delivery of forms or documents when assessing the ongoing suitability for registration of a registrant firm.

7.3 Late filings for the purpose of amending Form 33-109F6 — For amendments to item 5.5 *Bonding or insurance details* on Form 33-109F6, registrant firms are expected to notify the regulator of any change to bonding or insurance details in accordance with section 12.2 of NI 31-103, including the renewal of an insurance policy. The Commission will not charge a late fee with respect to renewal of bonding or insurance policies. However, late notifications of any changes in insurer or coverage amounts are subject to the late fees outlined in the Rule.

Adoption: (2003) 26 O.S.C.B. 4365 and (2003) 26 O.S.C.B. 891; Request for Comments: (2002) 25 O.S.C.B. 4067; (2001) 14 O.S.C.B. 1971.

Amendments to Policy: (2003) 26 O.S.C.B. 7758 and (2003) 26 O.S.C.B. 6481; Request for Comments: (2003) 26 O.S.C.B. 3768.

Adoption of Revised Policy: (2006) 29 O.S.C.B. 2362 and 597; Request for Comments: (2005) 28 O.S.C.B. 6663.

Adoption of Revised Policy: (2009) 32 O.S.C.B. 4445 and 2207; Request for Comments: (2008) 31 O.S.C.B. 9553.

Adoption of Amendments to Policy: (2009) 32 O.S.C.B. (Supp. 4) 385 and 32 O.S.C.B. (Supp. 2) 1; Request for Comments: (2008) 31 O.S.C.B. 2279.

Adoption of Amendment to Policy: (2010) 33 O.S.C.B. 2851 and 721; Request for Comments: (2009) 32 O.S.C.B. 7831.

Adoption of Amendment to Policy: (2010) 33 O.S.C.B. (Supp. 5) 40 and (Supp. 3) 1.

Rules: Rule 13-501, 13-502.

OSC Rule 13-503 — (Commodity Futures Act) Fees

Date: November 29, 2003; replaced effective April 1, 2006; replaced effective June 1, 2009; amended effective September 28, 2009, April 5, 2010 and April 1, 2013; replaced April 6, 2015

26 O.S.C.B. 7788; 29 O.S.C.B. 2367; 32 O.S.C.B. 4479; 32 O.S.C.B. (Supp. 4) 386; 33 O.S.C.B. 2852; 36 O.S.C.B. 1275; 38 O.S.C.B. 1001

[Not reproduced; this rule deals with fees payable under the *Commodity Futures Act*]

Final Rule: (2003) 26 O.S.C.B. 7800; Approval by OSC: (2003) 26 O.S.C.B. 6497; Request for Comments: (2003) 26 O.S.C.B. 3712.

Revised Rule: (2006) 29 O.S.C.B. 2367; Approval by OSC: 29 O.S.C.B. 637; Request for Comments: 28 O.S.C.B. 6663.

Revised Rule: (2009) 32 O.S.C.B. 4479; Approval by OSC: (2009) 32 O.S.C.B. 2248; Request for Comments: (2008) 31 O.S.C.B. 9592.

Amendments to Rule: (2010) 33 O.S.C.B. 2852; Approval by OSC: (2010) 33 O.S.C.B. 776; Request for Comments: (2009) 33 O.S.C.B. 7872.

Amendments to Rule: (2013) 36 O.S.C.B. 1275; Approval by OSC: (2012) 35 O.S.C.B. 11655; Request for Comments: (2012) 35 O.S.C.B. 7861.

Adoption of Amendments to Policy: (2009) 32 O.S.C.B. (Supp. 4) 386 and 32 O.S.C.B. (Supp. 2) 1; Request for Comments: (2008) 31 O.S.C.B. 2279.

Adoption of Amendments to Policy: (2010) 33 O.S.C.B. 2860 and 776; Request for Comments: (2009) 33 O.S.C.B. 7872.

OSC Policy 13-601 — Public Availability of Material Filed Under the Securities Act

A. General

1.   Section 137 [140] of the *Securities Act* (Ontario) (the "Act") requires, in effect, that material filed pursuant to the Act or the regulations made under the Act (the "Regulation") be made available for public inspection during normal business hours except for any material or class of material as to which the Ontario Securities Commission is of the opinion that it "discloses intimate financial, personal or other information and that the desirability of avoiding disclosure thereof in the interests of any person or company affected outweighs the desirability of adhering to the principle that material filed with the Commission be available to the public for inspection." This Policy Statement sets out how the Commission believes that section 137 [140] should be construed and applied.

2.   Nothing in this Policy Statement limits the authority of the Commission to make a determination that any specific material filed with it should, or should not, be made publicly available.

B. Meaning of "Filed"

The word "filed" is one of precise meaning in the Act. This Policy Statement deals with all of the classes and types of material that the Act and Regulation require to be filed. That does not mean that all other material is to be kept confidential. For example, material with respect to rights offerings delivered to the Commission in compliance with sections 34(1)14 [s. 3.1 of NI 45-101] of the Act will be made public except where special circumstances indicate that the material should be confidential and except that internal memoranda and correspondence with other regulatory authorities will be treated as confidential. By contrast, applications for registration will be treated as confidential. From time to time, this Policy Statement will be supplemented as to public availability of other information that is not technically "filed", such as documents that are only required to be "delivered" to the Commission.

C. Availability of Filed Material

The following are the classes of material required to be filed under the Act. Material of each class will be made publicly available except to the extent and in the circumstances noted in any comment after the description of that class:

(a)   Codes or symbols used to identify persons, companies or salesmen in confirmations and filed under section 35 [36].

       Comment — to be made public.

(b) Prospecting syndicate agreements filed under section 50 [51].

Comment — will be made public after the issuance of a receipt by the Director of the Commission. Supporting material will also be made public, except that the Commission has assigned to the Director under section 6 the right to make a case-by-case decision as to confidentiality in the same manner as for material filed supplementary to prospectuses, dealt with under clause (c) of this Section C.

(c) Preliminary prospectus and prospectus filed under section 52 [53], amendment to either of them filed under section 56 [57]; renewal prospectus filed under section 61 [62]; short form preliminary prospectus and prospectus filed pursuant to section 62 [63].

Comment — each of these documents is to be made public after the issuance of a receipt by the Director. At the end of the filing process — i.e., when a final receipt is issued for a prospectus, or an amendment is filed under section 56(1) [57(1)], or a receipt is issued for an amendment under section 56(2) [57(2)], or a receipt is issued for a renewal prospectus under section 61 [62] — then a determination will be made as to the availability of supplementary material, including material filed under section 55(2) [56(2)] and any other material received in connection with the specific filing. Pursuant to section 6 of the Act, the Commission has assigned to the Director the right to make that determination. It should be in accordance with the following guidelines:

(i) deficiency letters and correspondence relating thereto, including correspondence with other jurisdictions as well as correspondence with those responsible for the filing, should not be made public unless special circumstances are present, since the prospect of public availability of this material would detract from freedom of communication during the filing process. In any event, correspondence with or involving another regulatory authority should not be made public without the consent of that authority;

(ii) supporting material required by the staff as further information in connection with the filing such as auditors' letters, legal opinions, geologists' reports and similar data (but not including material contracts) should be made public unless confidentiality is specifically requested or the Director determines confidentiality is desirable;

(iii) where confidentiality is specifically requested as to supporting material, the Director may nonetheless determine that it shall be placed on the public file after providing the party requesting confidentiality with an opportunity to make oral or written submissions.

If a prospectus or a renewal prospectus is withdrawn before a final receipt is issued, the originally filed preliminary prospectus or renewal prospectus will be kept on the public file, stamped as withdrawn, but supplementary materials should not be on the public file unless the Director so determines.

(d) Reports filed under sections 71(3) [72(3)], 71(4)(c) [72(4)(c)], 71(5)(b) [72(5)(b)], 71(7)(b)(i) [72(7)(b)(i)] or 71(7)(b)(ii) [72(7)(b)(i)] with respect to transactions exempt from the prospectus requirements.

Comment — All of the forms relating to transactions in securities of a class in which a public trading market exists shall be made public.

(e) Statements of material facts filed under section 72(1)(b) [73(1)(b)].

Comment — the comment with respect to prospectuses applies here, with necessary changes. The draft statement of material facts need not be made public until after it is accepted for filing.

(f) Application for exemption order under section 73(1) [74(1)].

Comment — It is in the public interest that a copy of an application for an exemption order should be placed in the public file upon the receipt by the Commission of the application unless the applicant specifically requests confidentiality and demonstrates that it is not contrary to the public interest.

(g) Timely disclosure reports under sections 74(1) [75(1)] and 74(2) [75(2)] and copies of reports to other regulatory agencies filed pursuant to the Regulation.

Comment — to be made public, except that reports to other regulatory agencies should be treated as confidential to the extent contemplated by the Regulation (see section 6(4) of the Regulation).

(h) Confidential timely disclosure reports under section 74(3) [75(3)] and ten day up-date reports under section 74(4) [75(4)].

Comment — to be treated as confidential. If the issuer fails to file a ten day up-date report or if the reasons for confidentiality are considered to be insufficient by the staff the matter will be brought to the attention of the Commission, but no release may be initiated without consent of the issuer except upon an order of the Commission. Except in extraordinary situations, the Commission will provide the issuer with an opportunity to be heard before making such an order.

(i) Interim financial statements under sections 76(1) [77(1)] and 76(2) [77(2)]; annual comparative financial statements under section 77(1) [78(1)] with accompanying auditors' report under section 77(2) [78(2)]; information circular or annual report under sections 80(1) [81(1)] or 80(2) [81(2)]; finance company reports filed pursuant to the Regulation.

Comment — to be made public.

(j) Take-over bid circulars, varied take-over bid circulars, issuer bid circulars, directors' circulars (filing requirements in the Regulation).

Comment — to be made public. In some cases, for example, in compliance with Policy Statement 9.1 [Rule 61-501], the Director and the staff of the Commission review material of this type prior to publication and receive supporting material in connection with that review. The procedure set out in clause (c) of this Section C with respect to supporting material on a prospectus filing also applies here.

(k) Initial and subsequent insider reports and amended reports under section 107, and insider reports of change of registered holder under section 108, except for information contained in reports filed with the Commission that the Commission has determined to hold in confidence under Companion Policy 55-102CP to National Instrument 55-102 System for Electronic Disclosure by Insiders (SEDI);

Part 1:
PROCEDURE

reports by nominee holders under section 109; reports by mutual fund management companies under section 117(1), or comparable reports from other jurisdictions under section 121.

D. Availability of Lists of Reporting Issuers, Issuers in Default and Issuers Against which a Cease Trading Order Has Been Issued

As set forth in Policy Statement 2.5, the following lists are available during normal business hours for inspection in the public office of the Commission, 17th floor, 20 Queen Street West, Toronto:

(a)   a list of issuers deemed to be reporting issuers. This list is updated monthly and indicates which companies have outstanding cease trade orders and which are in default as of the date of the list. The list also indicates whether the securities of these issuers trade on a Canadian exchange (and, if so, which exchanges) or over-the-counter;

(b)   a list indicating those issuers deemed to be in default in accordance with section 71(9) [72(9)] of the Act. This list is updated daily; and

(c)   a list indicating companies against which a cease trade order has been issued. This list is updated as necessary.

(Renumbered as 13-601: (2001) 24 O.S.C.B. 2404; previously OSC Policy 2.2: (1982) 4 O.S.C.B. 366E; Former Policy 3-40: First published (1979) O.S.C.B. 189. Former Policy 3-49: First published (1980) O.S.C.B. 461.)

Adoption of Amendment by OSC: (2001) 24 O.S.C.B. 4414. Adoption of Amendment by OSC: (2003) 26 O.S.C.B. 1645.

OSC Staff Notice 13-704 — Applications for Participation Fee Relief for Certain Small Registered Firms and Reporting Issuers

Date: February 20, 2014

Citation: 37 O.S.C.B. 1794

[Not reproduced]

OSC Staff Notice 13-705 — Reduced Late Fee for Certain Outside Business Activities Filings

Date: January 22, 2015

38 O.S.C.B. 563

[Not reproduced]

OSC Staff Notice 13-706 — Sedar Filer Manual Update

Date: December 17, 2015

38 O.S.C.B. 10485

Introduction

National Instrument 13-101 *System for Electronic Document Analysis and Retrieval (SEDAR)* incorporates by reference the SEDAR *Filer Manual* (the Manual). The Manual has been updated a number of times, most recently in 2014. Staff of the Ontario Securities Commission are issuing this Notice to inform users that a new version of the Manual is available on SEDAR.com.

Manual Version 8.054

The new version of the Manual provides updated and new guidance related to the filing of certain exempt market documents on SEDAR in CSA jurisdictions other than Ontario and British Columbia. In Ontario, these exempt market documents are *required to be* submitted electronically through the electronic filing portal on the OSC website at: https://www.osc.gov.on.ca/filings. For further information, please refer to the Multilateral CSA Notice of Amendments to National Instrument 13-101 *System for Electronic Document Analysis and Retrieval (SEDAR)* and Multilateral Instrument 13-102 *System Fees for SEDAR and NRD* issued December 3, 2015.

The version number of the Manual is 8.054, to correspond with the most current SEDAR release, SEDAR version 8.054, implemented on December 7, 2015.

For more information

Please contact the CSA Service Desk at 1-800-219-5381.

1.4 — Definitions

National Instrument 14-101 — Definitions

Date: April 4, 1997, as amended effective July 1, 1999, December 31, 2002, March 17, 2008, September 28, 2009, April 30, 2010, January 1, 2011 and May 6, 2011

20 O.S.C.B. 1727, 22 O.S.C.B. 4069, 25 O.S.C.B. 8461, 31 O.S.C.B. 3563, (Supp. 2) 169, 32 O.S.C.B. (Supp. 4) 375, 33 O.S.C.B. 3695, 33 O.S.C.B. (Supp. 5) 34 and 34 O.S.C.B. 5171

PART 1 — DEFINITIONS AND INTERPRETATION

1.1 Definitions and Interpretation — (1) Every term that is defined or interpreted in the statute of the local jurisdiction referred to in Appendix B, the definition or interpretation of which is not restricted to a specific portion of the statute, has, if used in a national instrument or multilateral instrument, the meaning ascribed to it in that statute unless the context otherwise requires.

(2) A provision or reference within a provision of a national instrument or multilateral instrument that specifically refers by name to one or more jurisdictions other than the local jurisdiction shall not have any effect in the local jurisdiction, unless otherwise stated in the national instrument or multilateral instrument.

(3) In a national instrument or multilateral instrument

"1933 Act" means the *Securities Act* of 1933 of the United States of America, as amended from time to time;

"1934 Act" means the *Securities Exchange Act of 1934* of the United States of America, as amended from time to time;

"adviser registration requirement"means the requirement in securities legislation that prohibits a person or company from acting as an adviser unless the person or company is registered in the appropriate category of registration under securities legislation;

"blanket rulings and orders" means rulings and orders issued under Canadian securities legislation in certain jurisdictions that are applicable to a class of persons, trades, intended trades, securities, exchange contracts or transactions;

"Canadian financial institution" means a bank, loan corporation, trust company, insurance company, treasury branch, credit union or caisse populaire that, in each case, is authorized to carry on business in Canada or a jurisdiction, or the Confédération des caisses populaires et d'économie Desjardins du Québec;

"Canadian GAAP" means generally accepted accounting principles determined with reference to the Handbook;

"Canadian GAAS" means generally accepted auditing standards determined with reference to the Handbook;

"Canadian securities directions" means the instruments listed in Appendix A;

"Canadian securities legislation" means the statutes and the other instruments listed in Appendix B;

"Canadian securities regulatory authorities" means the securities commissions and similar regulatory authorities listed in Appendix C;

"CIPF" means the Canadian Investor Protection Fund;

"CSA" means the Canadian Securities Administrators;

"dealer registration requirement" means:

    (a) in every jurisdiction except British Columbia, Manitoba and New Brunswick, the requirement in securities legislation that prohibits a person or company from acting as a dealer unless that person or company is registered in the appropriate category of registration under securities legislation, and

    (b) in British Columbia, Manitoba and New Brunswick, the requirement in securities legislation that prohibits a person or company from trading in a security unless that person or company is registered in the appropriate category of registration under securities legislation;

"equity security" has the meaning ascribed to that term in securities legislation;

"foreign jurisdiction" means a country other than Canada or a political subdivision of a country other than Canada;

"Handbook" means the Handbook of the Canadian Institute of Chartered Accountants, as amended from time to time;

"IFRS" means the standards and interpretations adopted by the International Accounting Standards Board, as amended from time to time;

"implementing law of a jurisdiction" means, for a local jurisdiction, a regulation, rule, ruling or order of the Canadian securities regulatory authority that implements a national instrument or multilateral instrument in the local jurisdiction;

"insider reporting requirement" means

    (a) a requirement to file insider reports under Parts 3 and 4 of National Instrument 55-104 *Insider Reporting Requirements and Exemptions*;

    (b) a requirement to file insider reports under any provisions of Canadian securities legislation substantially similar to Parts 3 and 4 of National Instrument 55-104 *Insider Reporting Requirements and Exemptions*; and

    (c) a requirement to file an insider profile under National Instrument 55-102 *System for Electronic Disclosure by Insiders (SEDI)*.

"International Standards on Auditing" means auditing standards set by the International Auditing and Assurance Standards Board, as amended from time to time;

"investment fund manager registration requirement" means the requirement in securities legislation that prohibits a person or company from acting as an investment fund manager unless the person or company is registered in the appropriate category of registration under securities legislation;

"issuer bid" has the meaning ascribed to that term in securities legislation;

"ITA" means the *Income Tax Act* (Canada);

"jurisdiction" or "jurisdiction of Canada" means a province or territory of Canada except when used in the term foreign jurisdiction;

"local jurisdiction" means, in a national instrument or multilateral instrument adopted or made by a Canadian securities regulatory authority, the jurisdiction in which the Canadian securities regulatory authority is situate;

"networking notice requirement" means the requirement in securities legislation that a registrant give written notice to the securities regulatory authority or regulator before entering into a networking arrangement;

"person or company", for the purpose of a national instrument or multilateral instrument, means,

    (a) in British Columbia, a "person" as defined in section 1(1) of the *Securities Act* (British Columbia);

    (b) in New Brunswick, a "person" as defined in section 1(1) of the *Securities Act* (New Brunswick);

    (c) in the Northwest Territories, a "person" as defined in section 1 of the *Securities Act* (Northwest Territories);

    (c.1) in Nunavut, a "person" as defined in section 1 of the *Securities Act* (Nunavut);

    (d) in Prince Edward Island, a "person" as defined in section 1 of the *Securities Act* (Prince Edward Island);

(e) in Québec, a "person" as defined in section 5.1 of the *Securities Act* (Québec); and

(f) in Yukon Territory, a "person" as defined in section 1 of the *Securities Act* (Yukon territory).

"prospectus requirement" means the requirement in securities legislation that prohibits a person or company from distributing a security unless a preliminary prospectus and prospectus for the security have been filed and the regulator has issued receipts for them;

"provincial and territorial securities directions" means the instruments listed in Appendix A;

"provincial and territorial securities legislation" means the statutes and the other instruments listed in Appendix B;

"provincial and territorial securities regulatory authorities" means the securities commissions and similar regulatory authorities listed in Appendix C;

"registration requirement" means all of the following:

(a) the adviser registration requirement,

(b) the dealer registration requirement,

(c) the investment fund manager registration requirement, and

(d) the underwriter registration requirement;

"regulator" means, for the local jurisdiction, the person referred to in Appendix D opposite the name of the local jurisdiction;

"SEC" means the Securities and Exchange Commission of the United States of America;

"securities directions" means, for the local jurisdiction, the instruments listed in Appendix A opposite the name of the local jurisdiction;

"securities legislation" means, for the local jurisdiction, the statute and other instruments listed in Appendix B opposite the name of the local jurisdiction;

"securities regulatory authority" means, for the local jurisdiction, the securities commission or similar regulatory authority listed in Appendix C opposite the name of the local jurisdiction;

"SRO" means a self-regulatory organization, a self-regulatory body or an exchange;

"take-over bid" has the meaning ascribed to that term in securities legislation;

"underwriter registration requirement" means the requirement in securities legislation that prohibits a person or company from acting as an underwriter unless the person or company is registered in the appropriate category of registration under securities legislation; and

"U.S. federal securities law" means the federal statutes of the United States of America concerning the regulation of securities markets and trading in securities and the regulations, rules, forms and schedules under those statutes, all as amended from time to time;

PART 2 — EFFECTIVE DATE

2.1 Effective Date — This National Instrument comes into force on April 1, 1997.

Appendix A — Provincial and Territorial Securities Directions/Canadian Securities Directions

LOCAL JURISDICTION	INSTRUMENTS
ALBERTA	The policy statements and the written interpretations issued by the securities regulatory authority.
BRITISH COLUMBIA	The policy statements and the written interpretations issued by the securities regulatory authority.
MANITOBA	The policy statements and the written interpretations issued by the securities regulatory authority.
NEW BRUNSWICK	The policy statements and the written interpretations issued by the securities regulatory authority.
NEWFOUNDLAND	The policy statements and the written interpretations issued by the securities regulatory authority.
NORTHWEST TERRITORIES	The policy statements and the written interpretations issued by the securities regulatory authority.
NOVA SCOTIA	The policy statements and the written interpretations issued by the securities regulatory authority.
NUNAVUT	The policy statements and the written interpretations issued by the securities regulatory authority.
ONTARIO	None.
PRINCE EDWARD ISLAND	The policy statements and the written interpretations issued by the securities regulatory authority.
QUEBEC	The policy statements and the written interpretations issued by the securities regulatory authority.
SASKATCHEWAN	The policy statements and the written interpretations issued by the securities regulatory authority.
YUKON TERRITORY	The policy statements and the written interpretations issued by the securities regulatory authority.

Appendix B — Provincial and Territorial Securities Legislation/Canadian Securities Legislation

LOCAL JURISDICTION	STATUTE AND OTHER INSTRUMENTS
ALBERTA	*Securities Act* and the regulations and rules under that Act and the blanket rulings and orders issued by the securities regulatory authority.
BRITISH COLUMBIA	*Securities Act* and the regulations, rules and forms under that Act and the blanket rulings and orders issued by the securities regulatory authority.
MANITOBA	*The Securities Act* and the regulations under that Act and the blanket rulings and orders issued by the securities regulatory authority.
NEW BRUNSWICK	*Securities Act* and the regulations under that Act and the orders issued by the securities regulatory authority.

LOCAL JURISDICTION	STATUTE AND OTHER INSTRUMENTS
NEWFOUNDLAND	*Securities Act* and the regulations under that Act and the blanket rulings and orders issued by the securities regulatory authority.
NORTHWEST TERRITORIES	*Securities Act* and the regulations under that Act and the blanket rulings and orders issued by the securities regulatory authority.
NOVA SCOTIA	*Securities Act* and the regulations under that Act and the blanket rulings and orders issued by the securities regulatory authority.
NUNAVUT	*Securities Act* and the regulations under that Act and the blanket rulings and orders issued by the securities regulatory authority.
ONTARIO	*Securities Act* and the regulations and rules under that Act.
PRINCE EDWARD ISLAND	*Securities Act* and the regulations under that Act and the blanket rulings and orders issued by the securities regulatory authority.
QUEBEC	*Securities Act, An Act respecting the Autorité des marchés financiers* (R.S.Q., c. A-33.2), *Derivatives Act* (S.Q. 2008, c. 24), the regulations under those Acts, and the blanket rulings and orders issued by the securities regulatory authority.
SASKATCHEWAN	*The Securities Act, 1988* and the regulations and rules under that Act and the blanket rulings and orders issued by the securities regulatory authority.
YUKON TERRITORY	*Securities Act* and the regulations under that Act and the blanket rulings and orders issued by the securities regulatory authority.

Appendix C — Provincial and Territorial Securities Regulatory Authorities/Canadian Securities Regulatory Authorities

LOCAL JURISDICTION	SECURITIES REGULATORY AUTHORITY
ALBERTA	Alberta Securities Commission
BRITISH COLUMBIA	British Columbia Securities Commission
MANITOBA	The Manitoba Securities Commission
NEW BRUNSWICK	New Brunswick Securities Commission
NEWFOUNDLAND	Securities Commission of Newfoundland
NORTHWEST TERRITORIES	Superintendent of Securities, Northwest Territories
NOVA SCOTIA	Nova Scotia Securities Commission
NUNAVUT	Registrar of Securities, Nunavut
ONTARIO	Ontario Securities Commission
PRINCE EDWARD ISLAND	Superintendent of Securities, Prince Edward Island
QUEBEC	Autorité des marchés financiers or, where applicable, the Bureau de décision et de révision en valeurs mobilières
SASKATCHEWAN	Saskatchewan Securities Commission
YUKON TERRITORY	Superintendent of Securities, Yukon Territory

Appendix D — Regulator

LOCAL JURISDICTION	REGULATOR
ALBERTA	Executive Director, as defined under section 1 of the *Securities Act* (Alberta).
BRITISH COLUMBIA	Executive Director, as defined under section 1 of the *Securities Act* (British Columbia).
MANITOBA	Director, as defined under subsection 1(1) of *The Securities Act* (Manitoba).
NEW BRUNSWICK	Executive Director as defined in section 1 of the *Securities Act* (New Brunswick).
NEWFOUNDLAND	Director of Securities, designated under section 7 of the *Securities Act* (Newfoundland).
NORTHWEST TERRITORIES	Superintendent, as defined under section 1 of the *Securities Act* (Northwest Territories).
NOVA SCOTIA	Director, as defined under section 1 of the *Securities Act* (Nova Scotia).
NUNAVUT	Registrar, as defined under section 1 of the *Securities Act* (Nunavut)
ONTARIO	Director, as defined under section 1 of the *Securities Act* (Ontario).
PRINCE EDWARD ISLAND	Superintendent, as defined in section 1 of the *Securities Act* (Prince Edward Island).
QUEBEC	Autorité des marchés financiers.
SASKATCHEWAN	Director, as defined in section 1 of *The Securities Act, 1988* (Saskatchewan).
YUKON TERRITORY	Superintendent, as defined in section 1 of the *Securities Act* (Yukon Territory).

Final Rule: (1997) 20 O.S.C.B. 1727; Approval by OSC: (1996) 19 O.S.C.B. 6927; Request for Comments: (1996) 19 O.S.C.B. 4253.

Amendment to Rule: (1999) 22 O.S.C.B. 4069; Approval by OSC: (1999) 22 O.S.C.B. 1895; Request for Comments: (1998) 21 O.S.C.B. 5811.

Part 1:
PROCEDURE

Amendment to Rule: (2002) 25 O.S.C.B. 8461; Approval by OSC: (2002) 25 O.S.C.B. 6839 (October 18, 2002); Request for Comments: (2001) 24 O.S.C.B. 5825.

Amendment to Rule: (2008) 31 O.S.C.B. (Supp. 2) 69; Approval by OSC: (2007) 30 O.S.C.B. (Supp. 7) 1 (Dec. 21, 2007); Request for Comments: 29 O.S.C.B. (Supp. 3) 1 (Dec. 22, 2006).

Amendment to Rule: (2008) 31 O.S.C.B. 3563; Approval by OSC: (2008) 31 O.S.C.B. 123.

Amendment to Rule: (2009) 32 O.S.C.B. (Supp. 4) 375; Approval by OSC: (2009) 32 O.S.C.B. (Supp. 2) 65; Request for Comments: (2008) 31 O.S.C.B. 2279.

Amendment to Rule: (2010) 33 O.S.C.B. 3695; Approval by OSC: (2010) 33 O.S.C.B. 645; Request for Comments: (2008) 31 O.S.C.B. 12117.

Amendment to Rule: (2010) 33 O.S.C.B. (Supp. 5) 34; Approval by OSC: (2010) 33 O.S.C.B. (Supp. 3) 1; Request for Comments: (2009) 32 O.S.C.B. 7581.

Amendment to Rule: CSAN 11-314.

OSC Rule 14-501 — Definitions

Date: **August 1, 1997, as amended effective February 19, 1999 and September 28, 2009**

(1997) 20 O.S.C.B. 4054, 22 O.S.C.B. 1173 and 32 O.S.C.B. (Supp. 4) 387

1.1 Definitions — (1) Every term used in a rule that is

(a) defined or interpreted in section 1 of the Act has the meaning ascribed to it in that section unless it is otherwise defined or interpreted in the rule or the context otherwise requires;

(b) defined in subsection 1(2) of the Regulation has the meaning ascribed to it in that subsection unless it is otherwise defined or interpreted in the rule or the context otherwise requires; and

(c) defined in subsection 1.1(3) of National Instrument 14-101 Definitions has the meaning ascribed to it in that subsection unless it is otherwise defined or interpreted in the rule or the context otherwise requires.

(2) In a rule, unless otherwise defined in the rule

"AIF" means an annual information form filed under Ontario securities law;

"broker" means a person or company that is registered under the Act in the category of broker;

"business day" means any day other than a Saturday, a Sunday or a statutory holiday;

"CFA" means the *Commodity Futures Act*;

"Chair" means the Chair of the Commission;

"clearing corporation" means an association or organization through which trades in options or futures contracts are cleared and settled;

"Commission member" means a member of the Commission;

"contractual right of action" means a right of action, for rescission or damages, that

(a) is against an issuer if it is selling securities,

(b) is against a selling securityholder,

(c) is against an issuer and selling securityholder if they are both selling securities,

(d) is available to an investor to whom an offering memorandum containing a misrepresentation is delivered by or on behalf of the seller of securities,

(e) is exercisable on notice against the person or company that granted the right of action not later than 180 days after payment is made for the securities or after the initial payment, if a payment subsequent to the initial payment is made under a contractual commitment assumed before, or at the same time as, the initial payment,

(f) reasonably corresponds to the rights provided in section 130 of the Act applicable to a prospectus and may be subject to any applicable defences or limitations available under that section, and

(g) includes a provision stating that the right is in addition to any other right or remedy available at law to the investor;

"control person distribution" means a trade described in clause (c) of the definition of "distribution" in subsection 1(1) of the Act;

"convertible security" means a security that, by its terms, is convertible into, or exercisable or exchangeable for, or that carries the right to purchase or cause the purchase of, another security;

"custodian" means a person or company that holds securities for the benefit of another under a custodial agreement or other custodial arrangement;

"executive officer" means an individual who is or at any time during the most recently completed financial year was (a) a chair of the issuer, if that individual performed the functions of the office on a full time basis, (b) a vice-chair of the issuer, if that individual performed the functions of the office on a full time basis, (c) the president of the issuer, (d) a vice-president of the issuer in charge of a principal business unit, division, or function such as sales, finance, or production, (e) an officer of the issuer or any of its subsidiaries who performed a policy-making function in respect of the issuer, or (f) any other person who performed a policy-making function in respect of the issuer;

"financial intermediary" means,

(a) a bank listed in Schedule I or II to the Bank Act (Canada),

(b) a loan corporation or trust corporation registered under the Loan and Trust Corporations Act,

(c) an insurance company licensed under the Insurance Act,

(d) a credit union or caisse populaire incorporated or registered under the Credit Unions and Caisses Populaires Act,

(e) a co-operative to which the Co-operative Corporations Act applies;

"investment dealer" means a person or company that is registered under the Act in the category of investment dealer;

"LSIF" means

   (a) a labour sponsored investment fund corporation as defined in the *Labour Sponsored Venture Capital Corporations Act, 1992*, or

   (b) a registered labour sponsored venture capital corporation as defined in the ITA;

"market intermediary" means a person or company that engages or holds himself, herself or itself out as engaging in Ontario in the business of trading in securities as principal or agent, other than trading in securities purchased by the person or company for his, her or its own account for investment only and not with a view to resale or distribution, and, without limiting the generality of the foregoing, includes a person or company that engages or holds himself, herself or itself out as engaging in the business of,

   (a) entering into agreements or arrangements with underwriters or issuers, in connection with distributions of securities, to purchase or sell such securities,

   (b) participating in distributions of securities as a selling group member,

   (c) making a market in securities, or

   (d) trading in securities with accounts fully managed by the person or company as agent or trustee,

whether or not the person or company engages in trading in securities purchased for investment only.

"MD&A" means management's discussion and analysis of financial condition and results of operations prepared in accordance with Ontario securities law;

"mutual fund dealer" means a person or company that is registered under the Act in the category of mutual fund dealer;

"offering memorandum" means a document purporting to describe the business and affairs of an issuer that has been prepared primarily for delivery to and review by a prospective purchaser so as to assist the prospective purchaser to make an investment decision for a security being sold in a distribution to which section 53 of the Act would apply but for the availability of one or more of the exemptions contained in Ontario securities law but does not include a document setting out current information about an issuer for the benefit of a prospective purchaser familiar with the issuer through prior investment or business contacts;

"Ontario financial institution" means a bank listed in Schedule I or II to the *Bank Act* (Canada), a loan corporation or trust corporation registered under the *Loan and Trust Corporations Act*, a credit union or league to which the *Credit Unions and Caisses Populaires Act, 1994* applies or an insurance company licensed under the *Insurance Act*;

"option" means an agreement that provides the holder with the right, but not the obligation, to do one or more of the following on terms or at a price established by or determinable by reference to the agreement at or by a time established by the agreement:

   1. Receive an amount of cash determinable by reference to a specified quantity of the underlying interest of the option.

   2. Purchase a specified quantity of the underlying interest of the option.

   3. Sell a specified quantity of the underlying interest of the option;

"principal shareholder", if used to indicate a relationship with a person or company, means a person or company that is the direct or indirect beneficial owner of or exercises control or direction over more than 10 percent of any class or series of voting securities of the person or company;

"Regulation" means Regulation 1015 of the Revised Regulations of Ontario, 1990, as amended;

"related mutual fund securities" means, for a registrant, securities issued by a dealer managed mutual fund if the registrant is or is an affiliate of the dealer manager of the mutual fund;

"RESP" has the meaning ascribed to "registered education savings plan" in the ITA;

"RRIF" has the meaning ascribed to "registered retirement income fund" in the ITA;

"RRSP" has the meaning ascribed to "registered retirement savings plan" in the ITA;

"scholarship plan dealer" means a person or company that is registered under the Act in the category of scholarship plan dealer;

"selling group member" means, in respect of a distribution, a person or company whose interest in the distribution is limited to receiving the usual and customary distributor's or seller's commission payable by an underwriter or issuer.

"special relationship", when used in reference to a person or company in a special relationship with a reporting issuer, shall be interpreted in accordance with subsection 76(5) of the Act;

"trust indenture" means a document by which an issuer issues securities and in which a trustee is appointed for the holders of the securities issued under the document;

"trustee" means a person or company named as trustee under a trust indenture;

"underlying interest" means, for a derivative, the security, commodity, financial instrument, currency, interest rate, foreign exchanges rate, economic indicator, index, basket, agreement or benchmark or any other financial reference, interest or variable, and, if applicable, the relationship between any of the foregoing, from, to or on which the market price, value, or any payment obligation of the derivative is derived, referenced or based; and

"Vice-Chair" means a Vice-Chair of the Commission.

(3) For the purposes of the Act, the regulations and the rules,

"derivative" means an instrument, agreement or security, the market price, value or payment obligations of which is derived from, referenced to, or based on an underlying interest, other than a contract as defined for the purposes of the *Commodity Futures Act*.

"future-oriented financial information" has the meaning ascribed to the term "FOFI" in National Instrument 52-101 Future-Oriented Financial Information; and

"non-redeemable investment fund" means an issuer

   (a) whose primary purpose is to invest money provided by its securityholders;

   (b) that does not invest for the purpose of exercising effective control, seeking to exercise effective control, or being actively involved in the management of the issuers in which it invests, other than other mutual funds or non-redeemable investment funds; and

   (c) that is not a mutual fund.

Final Rule: (1997) 20 O.S.C.B. 4054; Approval by OSC: (1997) 20 O.S.C.B. 2687; Request for Comments: (1996) 19 O.S.C.B. 4895.

Amendment to Rule: (1999) 22 O.S.C.B. 1173; Approval by OSC: (1998) 21 O.S.C.B. 7509; Request for Comments: (1998) 21 O.S.C.B. 2341.

Amendment to Rule: (2009) 32 O.S.C.B. (Supp. 4) 387; Approval by OSC: (2009) 32 O.S.C.B. (Supp. 2) 1.

Related Provisions: OSA 1(1.1).

OSC Rule 14-502 — (Commodity Futures Act) Designation of Additional Commodities

Date: May 16, 2005

28 O.S.C.B. 4403

[Not reproduced]

1.5 — Hearings and Enforcement

OSC Staff Consultation Paper 15-401 — Proposed Framework for an OSC Whistleblower Program

Date: February 5, 2015

38 O.S.C.B. 1003

[Not reproduced]

OSC Notice 15-701 — Meetings with a Commissioner Regarding a Prospectus or an Application for Exemption or Registration

Date: 1994/07/22

17 O.S.C.B. 3529, Assigned number: (2001) 24 O.S.C.B. 2405

The Commission has decided to implement a procedure which would enable Staff and an applicant, or an issuer or selling securityholder which has filed a preliminary prospectus, to meet with a Commissioner to attempt to resolve serious differences of opinion or interpretation which have arisen between Staff and the applicant, selling securityholder or issuer in the course of the review of an application for exemption, registration, or other decision, or a preliminary prospectus, or to narrow the issues in dispute. This procedure is not intended to derogate from any administrative review or appeal procedures available under the legislation.

The applicant for a ruling or order of the Commission should have provided Staff with all necessary information to enable Staff to ascertain the relevant facts and the legal, financial reporting or policy issues involved and formulate a recommendation to the Commission. Staff will advise the applicant of its proposed recommendation to the Commission. The applicant may request that Staff not make its recommendation to the Commission at that time and may seek a meeting with a Commissioner.

The issuer or selling securityholder of securities proposed to be distributed pursuant to a prospectus, or an applicant for registration or other decision, should provide Staff with all necessary information to enable Staff to ascertain the relevant facts and the legal, financial reporting or policy issues involved. The Executive Director will advise the issuer, selling securityholder or applicant of his or her proposed decision to issue or refuse a receipt for a prospectus, or grant or deny an application. The issuer, selling securityholder or applicant may request that the Executive Director not make a decision at that time and may seek a meeting with a Commissioner.

The issuer, selling securityholder or applicant should advise the Executive Director of its desire to meet with a Commissioner to attempt to resolve the differences of opinion or interpretation without a hearing, or narrow the issues in dispute. Alternatively, Staff may recommend to the applicant, issuer or selling securityholder that a meeting with a Commissioner may assist in resolving the matter. If both the Executive Director and the applicant, issuer or selling securityholder agree that a meeting may be helpful, the Executive Director will arrange a meeting among the applicant, selling securityholder or issuer, Staff and a Commissioner. The parties directly affected will be notified to enable them to participate in the meeting.

Any views expressed by the Commissioner at the meeting will not constitute a ruling, order or decision under the *Securities Act* (Ontario) or the *Commodity Futures Act* (Ontario) or the Regulations made thereunder and will not be binding on the Executive Director, the applicant, selling securityholder or issuer or the Commission.

If, following the meeting, the Executive Director makes a decision which is subsequently reviewed by the Commission, or the application proceeds to the Commission for a hearing, the Commissioner who participated in the meeting will not sit on the panel which hears the review or application, or communicate with the panel about the matter. Neither the fact of or the substance of the discussion at the meeting with the Commissioner may be raised at the hearing.

Reference: Executive Director

OSC Staff Notice 15-702 — Revised Credit for Cooperation Program

Date: March 11, 2014 (Original notice: June 28, 2002)

37 O.S.C.B. 2583, 25 O.S.C.B. 3949

Purpose of the Notice

1. This notice relates to the compliance policy of the Ontario Securities Commission ("Commission") that market participants and others participating in the capital markets (collectively, "persons") should be encouraged to self-police, self-report and self-correct matters that may involve breaches of Ontario securities law or other types of misconduct that would be considered contrary to the public interest.

2. The results of cooperation by a person with Staff of the Commission in accordance with the following guidelines may lead to Staff recommendations which:

(a) narrow the scope of the allegations set out by Staff in connection with the commencement of an enforcement proceeding against the person;

(b) reduce the sanctions recommended by Staff in connection with an enforcement proceeding against the person;

(c) propose the resolution of the matter on the basis of a settlement agreement including, in limited circumstances, a settlement agreement in which the respondent makes no admissions of fact or liability; and

(d) in limited circumstances, result in Staff agreeing to take no enforcement action against the person.

3. This notice sets out the particulars aimed at encouraging persons to cooperate with Staff.

Staff's Expectations of Market Participants

4. A market participant that identifies a problem in respect of its systems of internal control, the reporting of financial results, misleading or incomplete disclosure, illegal or improper trading or any other inappropriate activity that has affected (or may affect) investors or cast doubt on the integrity of Ontario's capital markets, should promptly and fully self-report to the appropriate regulatory or law enforcement agency.

5. Market participants should fully cooperate with Staff, or any other regulator, when they are asked to provide assistance or information and should promptly and fully respond to all production orders and summonses.

6. When a matter is reported to Staff, a market participant should provide all necessary books and records required to assess the matter and any reports or analyses prepared by experts retained by the market participant or its counsel.

7. When a matter has been reported to a regulator, a market participant and its employees, officers and directors should make themselves available for interviews to allow Staff to assess the situation.

8. When a market participant has identified a breakdown of its system of internal controls, the market participant should promptly investigate, take corrective action and implement new systems of control, as appropriate.

9. A market participant that is aware that an employee, officer or director may have acted in a manner that is contrary to Ontario securities law, should fully investigate the matter and, independently of whatever action a regulator may take, deal with the matter promptly and appropriately.

10. A market participant should provide compensation, as appropriate, to any investors that have been harmed by inappropriate conduct or by a failure of internal controls.

What is Not Viewed as Cooperation

11. In general, Staff will not give credit for cooperation to a market participant in situations where, during the course of an investigation, the market participant puts the interest of the firm or its officers, directors or employees ahead of its obligations to clients, shareholders or the integrity of Ontario's capital markets.

12. Specifically, no credit for cooperation will be given when market participants:

(a) fail to promptly and fully report serious breaches of Ontario securities law to Staff or to another regulator when the facts of the matter are known to them;

(b) withhold information that, in light of the circumstances, should be provided to Staff;

(c) arrange their affairs in such a manner as to delay reporting a matter that should be reported or to claim a privilege to avoid providing details of potential breaches of Ontario securities law;

(d) undertake to provide Staff with books, records or information and then fail to comply with the undertaking or fail to provide the required documents in a timely fashion;

(e) misrepresent the facts of a situation;

(f) destroy documents in an attempt to avoid production of the records;

(g) invoke legal advice as a defence, but refuse to disclose the advice;

(h) enter into settlement arrangements with employees, clients or shareholders that include an agreement not to disclose information to a regulator or an agreement to withdraw any existing complaints; and

(i) continue the inappropriate conduct or fail to correct internal control problems after the conduct or internal control problems have been identified to senior management and/or the board of directors.

Examples of Credit For Cooperation

13. In general, if a potential respondent acts in a responsible and cooperative manner during the course of an investigation and has self-policed, self-reported and self-corrected the matters under investigation, Staff may agree that it may be in the public interest to resolve the matter by:

(a) recommending that the matter not proceed by way of a quasi-criminal prosecution before the courts under section 122 of the *Securities Act* ("Act") and/or an application before the courts under section 128 of the Act;

(b) issuing a Notice of Hearing and Statement of Allegations in respect of an administrative proceeding before the Commission under section 127 of the Act that recognizes and gives credit for cooperation by narrowing the scope of the allegations;

(c) recommending the resolution of an enforcement proceeding before the Commission on the basis of a settlement agreement that recognizes and gives credit for cooperation by, for example, narrowing the description of underlying facts and including a joint recommendation respecting sanctions;

(d) not issuing a Notice of Hearing and Statement of Allegations in connection with an administrative proceeding before the Commission under section 127 of the Act but rather recommending that the matter be addressed by one or more of the following:

    (i) placing terms and conditions on a potential respondent's registration; or

    (ii) obtaining an undertaking from the person that, in the future, they will not violate Ontario securities law; or

(e) in appropriate circumstances, concluding the matter without taking any action against the potential respondent.

14. As a practical matter, greater cooperation during the course of an investigation will lead to reduced costs incurred by the Commission and Staff, and consequently, a reduction of the potential costs that might be assessed under section 127.1 of the Act.

15. During the course of the investigation, persons who have been less than cooperative up to a point in time, may decide thereafter to fully cooperate with Staff, and in these circumstances, such persons would normally receive partial credit for the cooperation.

Settlement Agreements without Admissions of Fact or Liability

16. In limited circumstances, having regard to the factors set out in paragraph 17 below, Staff may conclude that it is appropriate to recommend to a Commission hearing panel that an enforcement matter be resolved on the basis of a settlement agreement in which the respondent makes no admissions respecting facts or that it contravened Ontario securities law or acted contrary to the public interest, and which would include:

(a) facts declared by Staff to be true based on its investigation and which are not denied by the respondent;

(b) the respondent's acceptance of the settlement agreement as a basis for resolving the proceeding; and

(c) the agreed sanctions in light of the conduct described in the settlement agreement.

17. Factors that Staff may consider in evaluating whether it may be appropriate to recommend to a Commission hearing panel the resolution of an enforcement matter on the basis of a settlement agreement that does not include admissions of fact or liability by the respondent include:

(a) the extent to which the person provided prompt, detailed and candid cooperation during Staff's investigation;

(b) the degree and timeliness of the self-reporting undertaken by the person in light of the circumstances of the misconduct;

(c) the degree of investor harm caused by the person's conduct;

(d) the remedial steps taken by the person to address the misconduct;

(e) the agreement of the person to pay such amounts as may be appropriate in the circumstances including, where appropriate, a payment for the benefit of third parties (such as compensation to persons affected by the misconduct) and costs of the investigation;

(f) the agreement of the person to cease the underlying conduct and undertaking to refrain from re-offending in the future;

(g) the deterrent effect of the settlement agreement on the future conduct of the person and others in the capital market; and

(h) the agreement of the person to pay monetary amounts, if any, contemplated by the settlement agreement contemporaneously with the approval of the settlement agreement.

18. Staff emphasize that they will continue to hold persons appropriately accountable for their misconduct.

19. Staff note that the Commission's Rules of Procedure respecting the consideration and approval of settlement agreements apply equally to settlement agreements in which the respondent makes no admissions of fact or liability and, accordingly, any such proposed resolution of an enforcement matter will be subject to the adjudicative discretion of an independent Commission hearing panel whether to approve any such settlement.

20. Notwithstanding the foregoing, a no-contest settlement agreement would not be available in any of the following circumstances:

(a) the person has engaged in abusive, fraudulent or criminal conduct;

(b) the person's misconduct has resulted in investor harm which has not been addressed in a satisfactory manner; and

(c) the person has misled or obstructed Staff during its investigation.

No Enforcement Action Agreements

21. In limited circumstances Staff may, in the exercise of its prosecutorial discretion, conclude that it is appropriate to refrain from taking enforcement action against a person, including through entering into a no enforcement action agreement with the person. Factors informing the availability of this form of credit for cooperation include:

(a) proactive self-reporting, cooperation with Staff and self-remediation;

(b) misconduct that reflects an inadvertent technical and/or isolated breach of Ontario securities law;

(c) the degree of investor harm caused by the person's conduct and related remedial steps taken to address that harm;

(d) the cessation of the underlying conduct by the person and undertaking to refrain from re-offending in the future;

(e) the agreement of the person to pay such amounts as may be appropriate in the circumstances, including, where appropriate, a payment for the benefit of third parties (such as compensation to persons affected by the misconduct) and costs of the investigation;

(f) the deterrent effect on the future conduct of the person; and

(g) in circumstances involving multi-person misconduct, a commitment by the person to provide Staff with active and ongoing cooperation respecting Staff's investigation and prosecution of other persons.

How to Contact Staff to Self-report and Offer Cooperation

22. A person may contact Staff to self-report and/or offer his/her cooperation in a number of ways:

(a) persons are encouraged to directly contact Enforcement Staff as well as the OSC Contact Centre;

(b) market participants that are the subject of a compliance review by Staff are encouraged to directly provide their information to Compliance Staff; and

(c) persons may contact Staff indirectly through their legal counsel as a step toward providing information.

23. Staff will generally require a person that is self-reporting and/or offering to provide cooperation to disclose particulars about their conduct and the circumstances so that Staff may evaluate the information and the potential benefits of cooperation, including possible credit. For example:

(a) a fact witness can forward documentation to Staff and attend an interview with Staff to provide further particulars and respond to questions; or

(b) a person who has failed to comply with Ontario securities law or acted contrary to the public interest can contact Staff directly (or through his/her legal counsel) to propose a meeting during which the person can provide particulars about his/her misconduct and discuss the prospect of offering cooperation to Staff respecting an investigation into the conduct of other persons.

24. At the discretion of Staff, a meeting with a person who may have engaged in misconduct may be held on the understanding that statements made by the person to Staff during the meeting would not be used against the person in subsequent enforcement proceedings by the Commission; however, the Commission and Staff could use statements made during the meeting for other purposes, including:

(a) as a source of leads to discover additional evidence;

(b) for impeachment purposes if the person makes later statements that are inconsistent;

(c) in a prosecution for perjury, obstructing justice and/or the giving of contradictory evidence; and

(d) sharing the information with another securities, derivatives or financial regulatory authority or self-regulatory body or organization.

Disclosure of Credit Granted for Cooperation

25. For the assistance of persons that may be considering self-reporting and offering to cooperate with Staff, Staff will disclose examples of credit that have been granted for cooperation in actual cases. This enhanced transparency will include:

(a) ensuring that hearing panels when considering sanctions are informed about the cooperation provided by a respondent and the corresponding credit recommended by Staff;

(b) ensuring that settlement agreements and/or related news releases include particulars as to any credit that may have been granted for cooperation provided by the respondent; and

(c) periodically reporting, on a generic basis, describing circumstances in which Staff has determined not to initiate an enforcement action against persons.

OSC Staff Notice 15-703 — Guidelines for Staff Disclosure of Investigations

Date: October 15, 2004

27 O.S.C.B. 8520

[Not reproduced.]

OSC Staff Notice 15-704 — Request for Comments on Proposed Enforcement Initiatives

Date: October 21, 2011

34 O.S.C.B. 10720

[Not reproduced]

OSC Staff Notice 15-705 — Notice of Extension of Time for Public Comment on Proposed Enforcement Initiatives and Continuation of Public Consultation through a Policy Hearing

Date: December 20, 2011

35 O.S.C.B. 615

[Not reproduced]

OSC Staff Notice 15-706 — Update to OSC Staff Notice 15-704 on Proposed Enforcement Initiatives

Date: June 13, 2013

36 O.S.C.B. 5898

[Not reproduced]

OSC Notice 15-902 — Guidelines for the Approval by the Executive Director of Settlements of Enforcement Matters

Date: November 28, 2008

31 O.S.C.B. 11407; Assigned number: (2012) 35 O.S.C.B. 1668

The purposes of the *Ontario Securities Act* (the "Act") are set out in Section 1.1 of the Act as follows:

(a) to provide protection to investors from unfair, improper or fraudulent practices; and

(b) to foster fair and efficient capital markets and confidence in capital markets.

The role of the Executive Director's Settlements in the administration of the Act

To promote public confidence in the administration of the Act, securities regulation generally, and enforcement proceedings in particular, must be conducted in an open and transparent manner. In resolving enforcement matters, the Commission must balance the requirements for a fair, timely and efficient disposition of matters with the need to encourage compliance by sending effective messages of deterrence. For the fair and expeditious administration of the Commission's enforcement authority under the Act, it may be in the public interest to resolve a matter through settlement at an early stage rather than through formal proceedings (after the issue of a notice of hearing) before a Commission panel or in the courts.

The resolution of enforcement matters at an early stage through agreement between Staff and parties alleged to have acted contrary to the Act, can result in more effective and immediate protection of investors and more rapid restoration of confidence in the capital markets than would be achieved through a more protracted formal proceeding. The early resolution of enforcement matters through settlement can also: (i) avoid unnecessary and potentially harmful delays; (ii) avoid circumstances where a detailed but unproven statement of allegations has been publicly issued and remains outstanding for an extended period; (iii) allow for a more flexible approach that achieves the Commission's regulatory objectives; (iv) avoid uncertainty to market participants as to the terms of a possible settlement and as to whether a settlement will be approved; (v) avoid the incurrence of unnecessary costs by market participants and the Commission; and (vi) result in a more efficient use of the Commission's resources.

In certain circumstances it may be appropriate that Staff, with the consent of the Executive Director, exercise its discretion to resolve an enforcement matter prior to the formal commencement of proceedings by entering into a voluntary settlement agreement with a party (an "Executive Director's Settlement"). For this purpose, a proceeding is considered to have been formally commenced either (i) on the issuance of a Statement of Allegations and Notice of Hearing in respect of a proceeding; or (ii) on the consent of the Chair of the Commission to the commencement of a proceeding under Section 122 of the Act in respect of a court proceeding. The settlement of an administrative proceeding that has been formally commenced must be approved by a panel of Commissioners.

Although the Commission recognizes that the decision to enter into an Executive Director's Settlement is an appropriate exercise of Staff's discretion, the Commission, in the exercise of its oversight of the administration of the Act, may from time to time provide general guidance on (i) the nature of matters that may be resolved by an Executive Director's Settlement, and (ii) the factors the Executive Director should consider in approving such a settlement.

Nature of matters that can be resolved

While it is within the discretion of the Executive Director to resolve any matter prior to initiation of a formal Proceeding[1], the Executive Director should not approve an Executive Director's Settlement where, in her or his opinion,

(i) the matter or settlement raises an important or novel policy issue or could be viewed as a significant precedent, which would reasonably be expected to be addressed by the Commission;

(ii) the alleged conduct is egregious; or

(iii) the matter or settlement involves or imposes significant terms or obligations.

The Executive Director may approve a settlement agreement for an Executive Director's Settlement containing a provision for a voluntary payment only where the payment has been or is to be made:

(i) for the benefit of specific persons or classes of persons identified as having been harmed by any alleged misconduct;

(ii) for the benefit of unspecified third parties for subsequent allocation by the Commission in its discretion; or

(iii) to the Commission to reimburse costs incurred or to be incurred by the Commission.

Factors to be considered in approving an Executive Director's Settlement

In approving any Executive Director's Settlement, the Executive Director may consider such factors as the Executive Director determines are appropriate or relevant in the circumstances. These factors would generally include:

• The party's history of compliance with securities law requirements and any enforcement action taken in respect of the party in the past;

• The manner in which the misconduct arose and/or came to the party's attention, the steps taken by the party in response and, in particular, whether the party would qualify for credit under Ontario Securities Commission Staff Notice 15-702 — *Credit for Cooperation*;

---

[1]The Commission recognizes that the Executive Director has discretion prior to the commencement of a formal proceeding, to decide such matters as (i) whether particular circumstances will be investigated, (ii) whether an investigation will be closed and on what terms, and (iii) whether a formal proceeding will be commenced. Approval of Executive Director's Settlements is consistent with that discretion.

- The nature and seriousness of the misconduct and, in particular, whether the misconduct:

    (i) would be considered to be a technical breach of the Act, or a more serious violation deserving of the kind of regulatory consequences available only in proceedings either before the Commission or in the courts;

    (ii) was deliberate or reckless;

- The nature and extent of the harm caused by the misconduct and, in particular, the harm to investors; and

- The appropriateness and effectiveness of the settlement in achieving the regulatory and policy objectives of the Act.

The overriding consideration, in every case, will be the Executive Director's determination that entering into an Executive Director's Settlement is in the public interest.

The Executive Director may consult with, and seek the advice of, the Chair at any time in connection with the Executive Director's consideration of a proposed settlement. The Chair does not sit on any panels in any proceedings, including any proceedings to consider a proposed settlement.

Procedure for approval of a settlement by the Executive Director

The Director of Enforcement, or such other Staff member of the Enforcement Branch as the Director may designate, shall provide to the Executive Director at the time of requesting the Executive Director's approval of a settlement:

(i) a copy of the proposed settlement agreement to be approved;

(ii) a memorandum of the Director (or a joint memorandum of the Director and the settling parties) setting out the reasons why the Director (or the Director and the settling parties together) recommends the approval of the settlement and a statement of the Director that he or she believes the settlement can be entered into in accordance with these Guidelines; and

(iii) any other information the Director (or the Director and the settling parties) believes to be relevant to the Executive Director's determination or that the Executive Director requests.

The Executive Director may, in her or his discretion, adopt such procedures for the consideration and approval of Executive Director's Settlements as she or he deems appropriate consistent with these Guidelines.

Publication of Executive Director's Settlements

Every settlement approved by the Executive Director shall be published in the *OSC Bulletin* and posted on the Commission's website as soon as practicable following its approval.

Concurrently with the publication of an approved settlement, the Executive Director may issue a public statement with respect to the settlement if, in her or his discretion, the Executive Director deems it advisable to do so in the public interest.

Reporting to the Commission

The Executive Director shall on at least a quarterly basis prepare a written report to the Commission describing any Executive Director's Settlements approved in such period.

Guidelines only

These Guidelines reflect the Commission's policy approach to Executive Director's Settlements and are not intended as prescriptive rules or to affect the legal rights or obligations of any person or the legal validity of any settlement agreement.

Part 1:
PROCEDURE

PART II — CERTAIN CAPITAL MARKET PARTICIPANTS

2.1 — Stock Exchanges

See also BOR 2.1, 2.2.

National Instrument 21-101 — Marketplace Operation

Date: November 2, 2001, as amended effective January 3, 2004, December 29, 2006, September 12, 2008, January 28, 2010, January 1, 2011, July 1, 2012, May 31, 2013 (CP only), December 31, 2014 and October 1, 2015

24 O.S.C.B. 6591, 27 O.S.C.B. 456, 29 O.S.C.B. 10011, 31 O.S.C.B. 8572, 33 O.S.C.B. 787, 33 O.S.C.B. (Supp. 5) 35, 35 O.S.C.B. 5369, 36 O.S.C.B. 2619 (CP only), 37 O.S.C.B. 9582 and 38 O.S.C.B. (Supp. 2)

Table of Contents

Form 21-101F6 CESSATION OF OPERATIONS REPORT FOR INFORMATION PROCESSOR

PART 1 — DEFINITIONS AND INTERPRETATION

1.1 Definitions — In this Instrument

"accounting principles" means accounting principles as defined in National Instrument 52-107 *Acceptable Accounting Principles and Auditing Standards*;

"alternative trading system",

(a) in every jurisdiction other than Ontario, means a marketplace that

(i) is not a recognized quotation and trade reporting system or a recognized exchange, and

(ii) does not

(A) require an issuer to enter into an agreement to have its securities traded on the marketplace,

(B) provide, directly, or through one or more subscribers, a guarantee of a two-sided market for a security on a continuous or reasonably continuous basis,

(C) set requirements governing the conduct of subscribers, other than conduct in respect of the trading by those subscribers on the marketplace, and

(D) discipline subscribers other than by exclusion from participation in the marketplace, and

(b) in Ontario has the meaning set out in subsection 1(1) of the *Securities Act* (Ontario);

"ATS" means an alternative trading system;

"corporate debt security" means a debt security issued in Canada by a company or corporation that is not listed on a recognized exchange or quoted on a recognized quotation and trade reporting system or listed on an exchange or quoted on a quotation and trade reporting system that has been recognized for the purposes of this Instrument and NI 23-101, and does not include a government debt security;

"exchange-traded security" means a security that is listed on a recognized exchange or is quoted on a recognized quotation and trade reporting system or is listed on an exchange or quoted on a quotation and trade reporting system that is recognized for the purposes of this Instrument and NI 23-101;

"foreign exchange-traded security" means a security that is listed on an exchange, or quoted on a quotation and trade reporting system, outside of Canada that is regulated by an ordinary member of the International Organization of Securities Commissions and is not listed on an exchange or quoted on a quotation and trade reporting system in Canada;

"government debt security" means

(a) a debt security issued or guaranteed by the government of Canada, or any province or territory of Canada,

(b) a debt security issued or guaranteed by any municipal corporation or municipal body in Canada, or secured by or payable out of rates or taxes levied under the law of a jurisdiction of Canada on property in the jurisdiction and to be collected by or through the municipality in which the property is situated,

(c) a debt security issued or guaranteed by a crown corporation or public body in Canada,

(d) in Ontario, a debt security of any school board in Ontario or of a corporation established under section 248(1) of the *Education Act* (Ontario), or

(e) in Québec, a debt security of the Comité de gestion de la taxe scolaire de l'île de Montréal

that is not listed on a recognized exchange or quoted on a recognized quotation and trade reporting system or listed on an exchange or quoted on a quotation and trade reporting system that has been recognized for the purposes of this Instrument and NI 23-101.

"IIROC" means the Investment Industry Regulatory Organization of Canada

"information processor" means any person or company that receives and provides information under this Instrument and has filed Form 21-101F5 and, in Quebec, that is a recognized information processor;

"inter-dealer bond broker" means a person or company that is approved by the IIROC under IIROC Rule 36 Inter-Dealer Bond Brokerage Systems, as amended, and is subject to IIROC Rule 36 and IIROC Rule 2100 Inter-Dealer Bond Brokerage Systems, as amended;

"marketplace",

(a) in every jurisdiction other than Ontario, means

(i) an exchange,

(ii) a quotation and trade reporting system,

(iii) a person or company not included in clause (i) or (ii) that

(A) constitutes, maintains or provides a market or facility for bringing together buyers and sellers of securities,

(B) brings together the orders for securities of multiple buyers and sellers, and

(C) uses established, non-discretionary methods under which the orders interact with each other, and the buyers and sellers entering the orders agree to the terms of a trade, or

(iv) a dealer that executes a trade of an exchange-traded security outside of a marketplace, but does not include an inter-dealer bond broker, and

(b) in Ontario has the meaning set out in subsection 1(1) of the *Securities Act* (Ontario),

"marketplace participant" means a member of an exchange, a user of a quotation and trade reporting system, or a subscriber of an ATS;

"member" means, for a recognized exchange, a person of company

(a) holding at least one seat on the exchange, or

(b) that has been granted direct trading access rights by the exchange and is subject to regulatory oversight by the exchange,

and the person or company's representatives;

"NI 23-101" means National Instrument 23-101 *Trading Rules*;

"order" means a firm indication by a person or company, acting as either principal or agent, of a willingness to buy or sell a security;"

"participant dealer" means a participant dealer as defined in Part 1 of National Instrument 23-103 *Electronic Trading and Direct Electronic Access to Marketplaces*;

"private enterprise" means a private enterprise as defined in Part 3 of National Instrument 52-107 *Acceptable Accounting Principles and Auditing Standards*;

"publicly accountable enterprise" means a publicly accountable enterprise as defined in Part 3 of National Instrument 52-107 *Acceptable Accounting Principles and Auditing Standards*;

"recognized exchange" means

(a) in Ontario, a recognized exchange as defined in subsection 1(1) of the *Securities Act* (Ontario),

(b) in Québec, an exchange recognized by the securities regulatory authority under securities or derivatives legislation as an exchange or self-regulatory organization, and

(c) in every other jurisdiction, an exchange recognized by the securities regulatory authority as an exchange, self-regulatory organization or self-regulatory body;

"recognized quotation and trade reporting system" means

(a) in every jurisdiction other than British Columbia, Ontario and Québec, a quotation and trade reporting system recognized by the securities regulatory authority under securities legislation to carry on business as a quotation and trade reporting system,

(b) in British Columbia, a quotation and trade reporting system recognized by the securities regulatory authority under securities legislation as a quotation and trade reporting system or as an exchange,

(b.1) in Ontario, a recognized quotation and trade reporting system as defined in subsection 1(1) of the *Securities Act* (Ontario), and

(c) in Québec, a quotation and trade reporting system recognized by the securities regulatory authority under securities or derivatives legislation as an exchange or a self-regulatory organization;

"regulation services provider" means a person or company that provides regulation services and is

(a) a recognized exchange,

(b) a recognized quotation and trade reporting system, or

(c) a recognized self-regulatory entity;

"self-regulatory entity" means a self-regulatory body or self-regulatory organization that

(a) is not an exchange, and

(b) is recognized as a self-regulatory body or self-regulatory organization by the securities regulatory authority;

"subscriber" means, for an ATS, a person or company that has entered into a contractual agreement with the ATS to access the ATS for the purpose of effecting trades or submitting, disseminating or displaying orders on the ATS, and the person or company's representatives;

"trading fee" means the fee that a marketplace charges for execution of a trade on that marketplace;

"trading volume" means the number of securities traded;

"unlisted debt security" means a government debt security or corporate debt security; and

"user" means, for a recognized quotation and trade reporting system, a person or company that quotes orders or reports trades on the recognized quotation and trade reporting system, and the person or company's representatives.

1.2 Interpretation — Marketplace — For the purpose of the definition of "marketplace" in section 1.1, a person or company is not considered to constitute, maintain or provide a market or facilities for bringing together buyers and sellers of securities, solely because the person or company routes orders to a marketplace or a dealer for execution.

1.3 Interpretation — Affiliated Entity, Controlled Entity and Subsidiary Entity — (1) In this Instrument, a person or company is considered to be an affiliated entity of another person or company if one is a subsidiary entity of the other or if both are subsidiary entities of the same person or company, or if each of them is a controlled entity of the same person or company.

(2) In this Instrument, a person or company is considered to be controlled by a person or company if

(a) in the case of a person or company,

(i) voting securities of the first-mentioned person or company carrying more than 50 percent of the votes for the election of directors are held, otherwise than by way of security only, by or for the benefit of the other person or company, and

(ii) the votes carried by the securities are entitled, if exercised, to elect a majority of the directors of the first-mentioned person or company;

(b) in the case of a partnership that does not have directors, other than a limited partnership, the second-mentioned person or company holds more than 50 percent of the interests in the partnership; or

(c) in the case of a limited partnership, the general partner is the second-mentioned person or company.

(3) In this Instrument, a person or company is considered to be a subsidiary entity of another person or company if

(a) it is a controlled entity of,

(i) that other,

(ii) that other and one or more persons or companies each of which is a controlled entity of that other, or

(iii) two or more persons or companies, each of which is a controlled entity of that other; or

(b) it is a subsidiary entity of a person or company that is the other's subsidiary entity.

1.4 Interpretation — Security — (1) In British Columbia, the term "security", when used in this Instrument, includes an option that is an exchange contract but does not include a futures contract.

(2) In Ontario, the term "security", when used in this Instrument, does not include a commodity futures contract or a commodity futures option that is not traded on a commodity futures exchange registered with or recognized by the Commission under the *Commodity Futures Act* or the form of which is not accepted by the Director under the *Commodity Futures Act*.

(3) In Québec, the term "security", when used in this Instrument, includes a standardized derivative as this notion is defined in the *Derivatives Act*.

1.5 Interpretation — NI 23-101 — Terms defined or interpreted in NI 23-101 and used in this Instrument have the respective meanings ascribed to them in NI 23-101.

PART 2 — APPLICATION

2.1 Application — This Instrument does not apply to a marketplace that is a member of a recognized exchange or a member of an exchange that has been recognized for the purposes of this Instrument and NI 23-101.

PART 3 — MARKETPLACE INFORMATION

3.1 Initial Filing of Information — (1) A person or company must file as part of its application for recognition as an exchange or a quotation and trade reporting system Form 21-101F1.

(2) A person or company must not carry on business as an ATS unless it has filed Form 21-101F2 at least 45 days before the ATS begins to carry on business as an ATS.

3.2 Change in Information — (1) Subject to subsection (2), a marketplace must not implement a significant change to a matter set out in the applicable Form 21-101F1 or in Form 21-101F2 unless the marketplace has filed an amendment to the information provided in Form 21-101F1 or in Form 21-101F2 in the manner set out in the applicable form at least 45 days before implementing the change.

(1.1) A marketplace that has entered into an agreement with a regulation services provider under NI 23-101 must not implement a significant change to a matter set out in Exhibit E — Operation of the Marketplace of Form 21-101F1 or Exhibit E — Operation of the Marketplace of Form 21-101F2 as applicable, or Exhibit I — Securities of Form 21-101F1 or Exhibit I — Securities of Form 21-101F2 as applicable, unless the marketplace has provided the applicable exhibit to its regulation services provider at least 45 days before implementing the change.

(2) A marketplace must file an amendment to the information provided in Exhibit L — Fees of Form 21-101F1 or Exhibit L — Fees of Form 21-101F2, as applicable, at least seven business days before implementing a change to the information provided in Exhibit L — Fees.

(3) For any change involving a matter set out in Form 21-101 F1 or Form 21-101F2 other than a change referred to in subsection (1) or (2), a marketplace must file an amendment to the information provided in the applicable form by the earlier of

    (a) the close of business on the 10th day after the end of the month in which the change was made, and

    (b) if applicable, the time the marketplace discloses the change publicly.

(4) The chief executive officer of a marketplace, or an individual performing a similar function, must certify in writing, within 30 days after the end of each calendar year, that the information contained in the marketplace's current Form 21-101F1 or Form 21-101F2, as applicable, including the description of its operations, is true, correct, and complete and that the marketplace is operating as described in the applicable form.

(5) A marketplace must file an updated and consolidated Form 21-101F1 or Form 21-101F2, as applicable, within 30 days after the end of each calendar year.

3.3 Reporting Requirements — A marketplace must file Form 21-101F3 within 30 days after the end of each calendar quarter during any part of which the marketplace has carried on business.

3.4 Ceasing to Carry on Business as an ATS — (1) An ATS that intends to cease carrying on business as an ATS must file a report on Form 21-101F4 at least 30 days before ceasing to carry on that business.

(2) An ATS that involuntarily ceases to carry on business as an ATS must file a report on Form 21-101F4 as soon as practicable after it ceases to carry on that business.

3.5 Forms Filed in Electronic Form — A person or company that is required to file a form or exhibit under this Instrument must file that form or exhibit in electronic form.

PART 4 — MARKETPLACE FILING OF AUDITED FINANCIAL STATEMENTS

4.1 Filing of Initial Audited Financial Statements — (1) A person or company must file as part of its application for recognition as an exchange or a quotation and trade reporting system, together with Form 21-101F1, audited financial statements for its latest financial year that

    (a) are prepared in accordance with Canadian GAAP applicable to publicly accountable enterprises or IFRS,

    (b) include notes to the financial statements that identify the accounting principles used to prepare the financial statements, and

    (c) are audited in accordance with Canadian GAAS or International Standards on Auditing and are accompanied by an unmodified auditor's report.

(2) A person or company must not carry on business as an ATS unless it has filed, together with Form 21-101F2, audited financial statements for its latest financial year.

4.2 Filing of Annual Audited Financial Statements — (1) A recognized exchange and a recognized quotation and trade reporting system must file annual audited financial statements within 90 days after the end of its financial year in accordance with the requirements outlined in subsection 4.1(1).

(2) An ATS must file annual audited financial statements.

PART 5 — MARKETPLACE REQUIREMENTS

5.1 Access Requirements — (1) A marketplace must not unreasonably prohibit, condition or limit access by a person or company to services offered by it.

(2) A marketplace must

(a) establish written standards for granting access to each of its services, and

(b) keep records of

(i) each grant of access including the reasons for granting access to an applicant, and

(ii) each denial or limitation of access, including the reasons for denying or limiting access to an applicant.

(3) A marketplace must not

(a) permit unreasonable discrimination among clients, issuers and marketplace participants, or

(b) impose any burden on competition that is not reasonably necessary and appropriate.

5.2 No Restrictions on Trading on Another Marketplace — A marketplace must not prohibit, condition, or otherwise limit, directly or indirectly, a marketplace participant from effecting a transaction on any marketplace.

5.3 Public Interest Rules — Rules, policies and other similar instruments adopted by a recognized exchange or a recognized quotation and trade reporting system

(a) must not be contrary to the public interest; and

(b) must be designed to

(i) ensure compliance with securities legislation,

(ii) prevent fraudulent and manipulative acts and practices,

(iii) promote just and equitable principles of trade, and

(iv) foster co-operation and co-ordination with persons or companies engaged in regulating, clearing, settling, processing information with respect to, and facilitating, transactions in securities.

5.4 Compliance Rules — A recognized exchange or a recognized quotation and trade reporting system must have rules or other similar instruments that

(a) require compliance with securities legislation; and

(b) provide appropriate sanctions for violations of the rules or other similar instruments of the exchange or quotation and trade reporting system.

5.5 Filing of Rules — A recognized exchange or a recognized quotation and trade reporting system must file all rules, policies and other similar instruments, and all amendments thereto.

5.6 [repealed]

5.7 Fair and Orderly Markets — A marketplace must take all reasonable steps to ensure that its operations do not interfere with fair and orderly markets.

5.8 Discriminatory Terms — A marketplace must not impose terms that have the effect of discriminating between orders that are routed to the marketplace and orders that are entered on that marketplace for execution.

5.9 Risk Disclosure for Trades in Foreign Exchange-Traded Securities — (1) A marketplace that is trading foreign exchange-traded securities must provide each marketplace participant with disclosure in substantially the following words:

The securities traded by or through the marketplace are not listed on an exchange in Canada and may not be securities of a reporting issuer in Canada. As a result, there is no assurance that information concerning the issuer is available or, if the information is available, that it meets Canadian disclosure requirements.

(2) Before the first order for a foreign exchange-traded security is entered onto the marketplace by a marketplace participant, the marketplace must obtain an acknowledgement from the marketplace participant that the marketplace participant has received the disclosure required in subsection (1).

5.10 Confidential Treatment of Trading Information — (1) A marketplace must not release a marketplace participant's order or trade information to a person or company other than the marketplace participant, a securities regulatory authority or a regulation services provider unless

(a) the marketplace participant has consented in writing to the release of the information,

(b) the release of the information is required by this Instrument or under applicable law, or

(c) the information has been publicly disclosed by another person or company, and the disclosure was lawful.

(1.1) Despite subsection (1), a marketplace may release a marketplace participant's order or trade information to a person or company if the marketplace

(a) reasonably believes that the information will be used solely for the purpose of capital markets research,

(b) reasonably believes that if information identifying, directly or indirectly, a marketplace participant or a client of the marketplace participant is released,

(i) it is required for the purpose of the capital markets research, and

(ii) that the research is not intended for the purpose of

(A) identifying a particular marketplace participant or a client of the marketplace participant, or

(B) identifying a trading strategy, transactions, or market positions of a particular marketplace participant or a client of the marketplace participant,

(c) has entered into a written agreement with each person or company that will receive the order and trade information from the marketplace that provides that

(i) the person or company must

(A) not disclose to or share any information with any person or company if that information could, directly or indirectly, identify a marketplace participant or a client of the marketplace participant without the marketplace's consent, other than as provided under subparagraph (ii) below,

(B) not publish or otherwise disseminate data or information that discloses, directly or indirectly, a trading strategy, transactions, or market positions of a marketplace participant or a client of the marketplace participant,

(C) not use the order and trade information, or provide it to any other person or company, for any purpose other than capital markets research,

(D) keep the order and trade information securely stored at all times,

(E) keep the order and trade information for no longer than a reasonable period of time after the completion of the research and publication process, and

(F) immediately inform the marketplace of any breach or possible breach of the confidentiality of the information provided,

(ii) the person or company may disclose order or trade information used in connection with research submitted to a publication if

(A) the information to be disclosed will be used solely for the purposes of verification of the research carried out by the person or company,

(B) the person or company must notify the marketplace prior to disclosing the information for verification purposes, and

(C) the person or company must obtain written agreement from the publisher and any other person or company involved in the verification of the research that the publisher or the other person or company will

(I) maintain the confidentiality of the information,

(II) use the information only for the purposes of verifying the research,

(III) keep the information securely stored at all times,

(IV) keep the information for no longer than a reasonable period of time after the completion of the verification, and

(V) immediately inform the marketplace of any breach or possible breach of the agreement or of the confidentiality of the information provided, and

(iii) the marketplace has the right to take all reasonable steps necessary to prevent or address a breach or possible breach of the confidentiality of the information provided or of the agreement.

(1.2) A marketplace that releases a marketplace participant's order or trade information under subsection (1.1) must

(a) promptly inform the regulator or, in Québec, the securities regulatory authority, in the event the marketplace becomes aware of any breach or possible breach of the confidentiality of the information provided or of the agreement, and

(b) take all reasonable steps necessary to prevent or address a breach or possible breach of the confidentiality of the information provided or of the agreement.

(2) A marketplace must not carry on business unless it has implemented reasonable safeguards and procedures to protect a marketplace participant's order or trade information, including

(a) limiting access to order or trade information of marketplace participants to

(i) employees of the marketplace, or

(ii) persons or companies retained by the marketplace to operate the system or to be responsible for compliance by the marketplace with securities legislation, and

(b) implementing standards controlling trading by employees of the marketplace for their own accounts.

(3) A marketplace must not carry on business as a marketplace unless it has implemented adequate oversight procedures to ensure that the safeguards and procedures established under subsection (2) are followed.

5.11 Management of Conflicts of Interest — A marketplace must establish, maintain and ensure compliance with policies and procedures that identify and manage any conflicts of interest arising from the operation of the marketplace or the services it provides.

5.12 Outsourcing — If a marketplace outsources any of its key services or systems to a service provider, which includes affiliates or associates of the marketplace, the marketplace must

(a) establish and maintain policies and procedures for the selection of service providers to which key services and systems may be outsourced and for the evaluation and approval of such outsourcing arrangements,

(b) identify any conflicts of interest between the marketplace and the service provider to which key services and systems are outsourced, and establish and maintain policies and procedures to mitigate and manage such conflicts of interest,

(c) enter into a contract with the service provider to which key services and systems are outsourced that is appropriate for the materiality and nature of the outsourced activities and that provides for adequate termination procedures,

(d) maintain access to the books and records of the service providers relating to the outsourced activities,

(e) ensure that the securities regulatory authorities have access to all data, information and systems maintained by the service provider on behalf of the marketplace for the purposes of determining the marketplace's compliance with securities legislation,

(f) take appropriate measures to determine that service providers to which key services or systems are outsourced establish, maintain and periodically test an appropriate business continuity plan, including a disaster recovery plan,

(g) take appropriate measures to ensure that the service providers protect the marketplace participants' proprietary, order, trade or any other confidential information, and

(h) establish processes and procedures to regularly review the performance of the service provider under any such outsourcing arrangement.

5.13 Access Arrangements with a Service Provider — If a third party service provider provides a means of access to a marketplace, the marketplace must ensure the third party service provider complies with the written standards for access that the marketplace has established pursuant to paragraph 5.1(2)(a) when providing the access services.

PART 6 — REQUIREMENTS APPLICABLE ONLY TO ATSS

6.1 Registration — An ATS must not carry on business as an ATS unless

(a) it is registered as a dealer;

(b) it is a member of a self-regulatory entity; and

(c) it complies with the provisions of this Instrument and NI 23-101.

6.2 Registration Exemption Not Available — Except as provided in this Instrument, the registration exemptions applicable to dealers under securities legislation are not available to an ATS.

6.3 Securities Permitted to be Traded on an ATS — An ATS must not execute trades in securities other than

(a) exchange-traded securities;

(b) corporate debt securities;

(c) government debt securities; or

(d) foreign exchange-traded securities.

6.4–6.6 [repealed]

6.7 Notification of Threshold — (1) An ATS must notify the securities regulatory authority in writing if,

(a) during at least two of the preceding three months of operation, the total dollar value of the trading volume on the ATS for a month in any type of security is equal to or greater than 10 percent of the total dollar value of the trading volume for the month in that type of security on all marketplaces in Canada,

(b) during at least two of the preceding three months of operation, the total trading volume on the ATS for a month in any type of security is equal to or greater than 10 percent of the total trading volume for the month in that type of security on all marketplaces in Canada, or

(c) during at least two of the preceding three months of operation, the number of trades on the ATS for a month in any type of security is equal to or greater than 10 percent of the number of trades for the month in that type of security on all marketplaces in Canada.

(2) An ATS must provide the notice referred to in subsection (1) within 30 days after the threshold referred to in subsection (1) is met or exceeded.

6.8 [repealed]

6.9 Name — An ATS must not use in its name the word "exchange", the words "stock market", the word "bourse" or any derivations of those terms.

6.10 [repealed]

6.11 Risk Disclosure to Non-Registered Subscribers — (1) When opening an account for a subscriber that is not registered as a dealer under securities legislation, an ATS must provide that subscriber with disclosure in substantially the following words:

Although the ATS is registered as a dealer under securities legislation, it is a marketplace and therefore does not ensure best execution for its subscribers.

(2) Before the first order submitted by a subscriber that is not registered as a dealer under securities legislation is entered onto the ATS by the subscriber, the ATS must obtain an acknowledgement from that subscriber that the subscriber has received the disclosure required in subsection (1).

(3) A marketplace that is subject to subsection (1) must not make the information referred to in that subsection available to any person or company before it makes that information available to an information processor or, if there is no information processor, to an information vendor.

PART 7 — INFORMATION TRANSPARENCY REQUIREMENTS FOR MARKETPLACES DEALING IN EXCHANGE-TRADED SECURITIES AND FOREIGN EXCHANGE-TRADED SECURITIES

7.1 Pre-Trade Information Transparency — Exchange-Traded Securities — (1) A marketplace that displays orders of exchange-traded securities to a person or company must provide accurate and timely information regarding orders for the exchange-traded securities displayed by the marketplace to an information processor as required by the information processor or, if there is no information processor, to an information vendor that meets the standards set by a regulation services provider.

(2) Subsection (1) does not apply if the marketplace only displays orders to its employees or to persons or companies retained by the marketplace to assist in the operation of the marketplace and if the orders posted on the marketplace meet the size threshold set by a regulation services provider.

(3) A marketplace that is subject to subsection (1) must not make the information referred to in that subsection available to any person or company before it makes that information available to an information processor or, if there is no information processor, to an information vendor.

7.2 Post-Trade Information Transparency — Exchange-Traded Securities — (1) A marketplace must provide accurate and timely information regarding trades for exchange-traded securities executed on the marketplace to an information processor as required by the information processor or, if there is no information processor, to an information vendor that meets the standards set by a regulation services provider.

(2) A marketplace that is subject to subsection (1) must not make the information referred to in that subsection available to any person or company before it makes that information available to an information processor or, if there is no information processor, to an information vendor.

7.3 Pre-Trade Information Transparency — Foreign Exchange-Traded Securities

(1) A marketplace that displays orders of foreign exchange-traded securities to a person or company must provide accurate and timely information regarding orders for the foreign exchange-traded securities displayed by the marketplace to an information vendor.

(2) Subsection (1) does not apply if the marketplace only displays orders to its employees or to persons or companies retained by the marketplace to assist in the operation of the marketplace and if the orders posted on the marketplace meet the size threshold set by a regulation services provider.

7.4 Post-trade Information Transparency — Foreign Exchange-Traded Securities — A marketplace must provide accurate and timely information regarding trades for foreign exchange-traded securities executed on the marketplace to an information vendor.

7.5 Consolidated Feed — Exchange-Traded Securities — An information processor must produce an accurate consolidated feed in real-time showing the information provided to the information processor under sections 7.1 and 7.2.

7.6 Compliance with Requirements of an Information Processor — A marketplace that is subject to this Part must comply with the reasonable requirements of the information processor to which it is required to provide information under this Part.

PART 8 — INFORMATION TRANSPARENCY REQUIREMENTS FOR MARKETPLACES DEALING IN UNLISTED DEBT SECURITIES, INTER-DEALER BOND BROKERS AND DEALERS

8.1 Pre-Trade and Post-Trade Information Transparency Requirements — Government Debt Securities — (1) A marketplace that displays orders of government debt securities to a person or company must provide to an information processor accurate and timely information regarding orders for government debt securities displayed by the marketplace as required by the information processor.

(2) Subsection (1) does not apply if the marketplace only displays orders to its employees or to persons or companies retained by the marketplace to assist in the operation of the marketplace.

(3) A marketplace must provide to an information processor accurate and timely information regarding details of trades of government debt securities executed on the marketplace as required by the information processor.

(4) An inter-dealer bond broker must provide to an information processor accurate and timely information regarding orders for government debt securities executed through the inter-dealer bond broker as required by the information processor.

(5) An inter-dealer bond broker must provide to an information processor accurate and timely information regarding details of trades of government debt securities executed through the inter-dealer bond broker as required by the information processor.

8.2 Pre-Trade and Post-Trade Information Transparency Requirements — Corporate Debt Securities — (1) A marketplace that displays orders of corporate debt securities to a person or company must provide accurate and timely information regarding orders for designated corporate debt securities displayed by the marketplace to an information processor, as required by the information processor, or if there is no information processor, to an information vendor that meets the standards set by a regulation services provider, as required by the regulation services provider.

(2) Subsection (1) does not apply if the marketplace only displays orders to its employees or to persons or companies retained by the marketplace to assist in the operation of the marketplace.

(3) A marketplace must provide accurate and timely information regarding details of trades of designated corporate debt securities executed on the marketplace to an information processor, as required by the information processor, or if there is no information processor, to an information vendor that meets the standards set by a regulation services provider, as required by the regulation services provider.

(4) An inter-dealer bond broker must provide accurate and timely information regarding details of trades of designated corporate debt securities executed through the inter-dealer bond broker to an information processor, as required by the information processor, or if there is no information processor, to an information vendor that meets the standards set by a regulation services provider, as required by the regulation services provider.

(5) A dealer executing trades of corporate debt securities outside of a marketplace must provide accurate and timely information regarding details of trades of designated corporate debt securities traded by or through the dealer to an information processor, as required by the information processor, or if there is no information processor, to an information vendor that meets the standards set by a regulation services provider, as required by the regulation services provider.

8.3 Consolidated Feed — Unlisted Debt Securities — An information processor must produce an accurate consolidated feed in real-time showing the information provided to the information processor under sections 8.1 and 8.2.

8.4 Compliance with Requirements of an Information Processor — A marketplace, inter-dealer bond broker or dealer that is subject to this Part must comply with the reasonable requirements of the information processor to which it is required to provide information under this Part.

8.5 [repealed]

8.6 Exemption for Government Debt Securities — Section 8.1 does not apply until January 1, 2018.

PART 9 — [REPEALED]

PART 10 — TRANSPARENCY OF MARKETPLACE OPERATIONS

10.1 Disclosure by Marketplaces — A marketplace must publicly disclose, on its website, information reasonably necessary to enable a person or company to understand the marketplace's operations or services it provides, including, but not limited to, information related to

(a) all fees, including any listing, trading, data, co-location and routing fees charged by the marketplace, an affiliate or by a party to which services have directly or indirectly been outsourced or which directly or indirectly provides those services,

(b) how orders are entered, interact and execute,

(c) all order types,

(d) access requirements,

(e) the policies and procedures that identify and manage any conflicts of interest arising from the operation of the marketplace or the services it provides,

(f) any referral arrangements between the marketplace and service providers,

(g) where routing is offered, how routing decisions are made,

(h) when indications of interest are disseminated, the information disseminated and the types of recipients of such indications of interest,

(i) any access arrangements with a third party service provider, including the name of the third party service provider and the standards for access to be complied with by the third party service provider, and

(j) the hours of operation of any testing environments provided by the marketplace, a description of any differences between the testing environment and production environment of the marketplace and the potential impact of these differences on the effectiveness of testing, and any policies and procedures relating to a marketplace's use of uniform test symbols for purposes of testing in its production environment.

PART 11 — RECORDKEEPING REQUIREMENTS FOR MARKETPLACES

11.1 Business Records — A marketplace must keep such books, records and other documents as are reasonably necessary for the proper recording of its business in electronic form.

11.2 Other Records — (1) As part of the records required to be maintained under section 11.1, a marketplace must include the following information in electronic form:

(a) a record of all marketplace participants who have been granted access to trading in the marketplace;

(b) daily trading summaries for the marketplace including

(i) a list of securities traded,

(ii) transaction volumes

(A) for securities other than debt securities, expressed as the number of issues traded, number of trades, total unit volume and total dollar value of trades and, if the price of the securities traded is quoted in a currency other than Canadian dollars, the total value in that other currency, and

(B) for debt securities, expressed as the number of trades and total dollar value traded and, if the price of the securities traded is quoted in a currency other than Canadian dollars, the total value in that other currency,

(c) a record of each order which must include

(i) the order identifier assigned to the order by the marketplace,

(ii) the marketplace participant identifier assigned to the marketplace participant transmitting the order,

(iii) the identifier assigned to the marketplace where the order is received or originated,

(iv) each unique client identifier assigned to a client accessing the marketplace using direct electronic access,

(v) the type, issuer, class, series and symbol of the security,

(vi) the number of securities to which the order applies,

(vii) the strike date and strike price, if applicable,

(viii) whether the order is a buy or sell order,

(ix) whether the order is a short sale order, if applicable,

(x) whether the order is a market order, limit order or other type of order, and if the order is not a market order, the price at which the order is to trade,

(xi) the date and time the order is first originated or received by the marketplace,

(xii) whether the account is a retail, wholesale, employee, proprietary or any other type of account,

(xiii) the date and time the order expires,

(xiv) whether the order is an intentional cross,

(xv) whether the order is a jitney and if so, the identifier of the underlying broker,

(xvi) the currency of the order,

(xvii) whether the order is routed to another marketplace for execution, and the date, time and name of the marketplace to which the order was routed, and

(xviii) whether the order is a directed-action order, and whether the marketplace marked the order as a directed-action order or received the order marked as a directed-action order, and

(d) in addition to the record maintained in accordance with paragraph (c), all execution report details of orders, including

(i) the identifier assigned to the marketplace where the order was executed,

(ii) whether the order was fully or partially executed,

(iii) the number of securities bought or sold,

(iv) the date and time of the execution of the order,

(v) the price at which the order was executed,

(vi) the identifier assigned to the marketplace participant on each side of the trade,

(vii) whether the transaction was a cross,

(viii) time-sequenced records of all messages sent to or received from an information processor, an information vendor or a marketplace,

(ix) the marketplace trading fee for each trade, and

(x) each unique client identifier assigned to a client accessing the marketplace using direct electronic access.

11.2.1 Transmission in Electronic Form — A marketplace must transmit

(a) to a regulation services provider, if it has entered into an agreement with a regulation services provider in accordance with NI 23-101, the information required by the regulation services provider within ten business days, in electronic form, and in the manner requested by the regulation services provider, and

(b) to the securities regulatory authority the information required by the securities regulatory authority under securities legislation within ten business days, in electronic form and in the manner requested by the securities regulatory authority.

11.3 Record Preservation Requirements — (1) For a period of not less than seven years from the creation of a record referred to in this section, and for the first two years in a readily accessible location, a marketplace must keep

(a) all records required to be made under sections 11.1 and 11.2;

(b) at least one copy of its standards for granting access to trading, if any, all records relevant to its decision to grant, deny or limit access to a person or company and, if applicable, all other records made or received by the marketplace in the course of complying with section 5.1;

(c) at least one copy of all records made or received by the marketplace in the course of complying with sections 12.1 and 12.4, including all correspondence, memoranda, papers, books, notices, accounts, reports, test scripts, test results, and other similar records;

(d) all written notices provided by the marketplace to marketplace participants generally, including notices addressing hours of system operations, system malfunctions, changes to system procedures, maintenance of hardware and software, instructions pertaining to access to the marketplace and denials of, or limitation to, access to the marketplace;

(e) the acknowledgement obtained under subsection 5.9(2) or 6.11(2);

(f) a copy of the agreement referred to in section 8.4 of NI 23-101;

(g) a copy of any agreement referred to in subsections 13.1(2) and 13.1(3);

(h) a copy of any agreement referred to in section 5.10; and

(i) a copy of any agreement referred to in paragraph 5.12(c).

(2) During the period in which a marketplace is in existence, the marketplace must keep

(a) all organizational documents, minute books and stock certificate books;

(b) copies of all forms filed under Part 3; and

(c) in the case of an ATS, copies of all notices given under section 6.7.

11.4 [repealed]

11.5 Synchronization of Clocks — (1) A marketplace trading exchange-traded securities or foreign exchange-traded securities, an information processor receiving information about those securities, and a dealer trading those securities must synchronize the clocks used for recording or monitoring the time and date of any event that must be recorded under this Part and under NI 23-101 with the clock used by a regulation services provider monitoring the activities of marketplaces and marketplace participants trading those securities.

(2) A marketplace trading corporate debt securities or government debt securities, an information processor receiving information about those securities, a dealer trading those securities, and an inter-dealer bond broker trading those securities must synchronize the clocks used for recording or monitoring the time and date of any event that must be recorded under this Part and under NI 23-101 with the clock used by a regulation services provider monitoring the activities of marketplaces, inter-dealer bond brokers or dealers trading those securities.

PART 12 — MARKETPLACE SYSTEMS AND BUSINESS CONTINUITY PLANNING

12.1 System Requirements — For each system, operated by or on behalf of the marketplace, that supports order entry, order routing, execution, trade reporting, trade comparison, data feeds, market surveillance and trade clearing, a marketplace must

(a) develop and maintain

(i) an adequate system of internal control over those systems, and

(ii) adequate information technology general controls, including without limitation, controls relating to information systems operations, information security, change management, problem management, network support and system software support,

(b) in accordance with prudent business practice, on a reasonably frequent basis and, in any event, at least annually,

(i) make reasonable current and future capacity estimates,

(ii) conduct capacity stress tests to determine the ability of those systems to process transactions in an accurate, timely and efficient manner, and

(c) promptly notify the regulator or, in Québec, the securities regulatory authority and, if applicable, its regulation services provider, of any material systems failure, malfunction, delay or security breach and provide timely updates on the status of the failure, malfunction, delay or security breach, the resumption of service and the results of the marketplace's internal review of the failure, malfunction, delay or security breach.

12.1.1 Auxiliary Systems — For each system that shares network resources with one or more of the systems, operated by or on behalf of the marketplace, that supports order entry, order routing, execution, trade reporting, trade comparison, data feeds, market surveillance and trade clearing, that, if breached, would pose a security threat to one or more of the previously mentioned systems, a marketplace must

(a) develop and maintain an adequate system of information security controls that relate to the security threats posed to any system that supports order entry, order routing, execution, trade reporting, trade comparison, data feeds, market surveillance and trade clearing, and

(b) promptly notify the regulator, or in Québec, the securities regulatory authority and, if applicable, its regulation services provider, of any material security breach and provide timely updates on the status of the breach, the resumption of service, where applicable, and the results of the marketplace's internal review of the security breach.

12.2 System Reviews — (1) A marketplace must annually engage a qualified party to conduct an independent systems review and prepare a report in accordance with established audit standards to ensure that the marketplace is in compliance with

(a) paragraph 12.1(a),

(b) section 12.1.1, and

(c) section 12.4.

(2) A marketplace must provide the report resulting from the review conducted under subsection (1) to

(a) its board of directors, or audit committee, promptly upon the report's completion, and

(b) the regulator or, in Québec, the securities regulatory authority, by the earlier of the 30th day after providing the report to its board of directors or the audit committee or the 60th day after the calendar year end.

12.3 Availability of Technology Requirements and Testing Facilities — (1) A marketplace must make publicly available all technology requirements regarding interfacing with or accessing the marketplace in their final form,

(a) if operations have not begun, for at least three months immediately before operations begin; and

(b) if operations have begun, for at least three months before implementing a material change to its technology requirements.

(2) After complying with subsection (1), a marketplace must make available testing facilities for interfacing with or accessing the marketplace,

(a) if operations have not begun, for at least two months immediately before operations begin; and

(b) if operations have begun, for at least two months before implementing a material change to its technology requirements.

(3) A marketplace must not begin operations before

(a) it has complied with paragraphs (1)(a) and (2)(a),

(b) its regulation services provider, if applicable, has confirmed to the marketplace that trading may commence on the marketplace, and

(c) the chief information officer of the marketplace, or an individual performing a similar function, has certified in writing to the regulator, or in Québec, the securities regulatory authority, that all information technology systems used by the marketplace have been tested according to prudent business practices and are operating as designed.

(3.1) A marketplace must not implement a material change to the systems referred to in section 12.1 before

(a) it has complied with paragraphs (1)(b) and (2)(a), and

(b) the chief information officer of the marketplace, or an individual performing a similar function, has certified in writing to the regulator, or in Québec, the securities regulatory authority, that the change has been tested according to prudent business practices and is operating as designed.

(4) Subsection (3.1) does not apply to a marketplace if the change must be made immediately to address a failure, malfunction or material delay of its systems or equipment if

(a) the marketplace immediately notifies the regulator, or in Québec, the securities regulatory authority, and, if applicable, its regulation services provider of its intention to make the change; and

(b) the marketplace publishes the changed technology requirements as soon as practicable.

12.3.1 Uniform Test Symbols — A marketplace must use uniform test symbols, as set by a regulator, or in Québec, the securities regulatory authority, for the purpose of performing testing in its production environment.

12.4 Business Continuity Planning — (1) A marketplace must

(a) develop and maintain reasonable business continuity plans, including disaster recovery plans, and

(b) test its business continuity plans, including disaster recovery plans, according to prudent business practices on a reasonably frequent basis and, in any event, at least annually.

(2) A marketplace with a total trading volume in any type of security equal to or greater than 10% of the total dollar value of the trading volume in that type of security on all marketplaces in Canada during at least two of the preceding three months of operation must establish, implement, and maintain policies and procedures reasonably designed to ensure that each system, operated by or on behalf of the marketplace, that supports order entry, order routing, execution, trade reporting, trade comparison, data feeds, and trade clearing, can resume operations within two hours following the declaration of a disaster by the marketplace.

(3) A recognized exchange or quotation and trade reporting system, that directly monitors the conduct of its members or users and enforces requirements set under section 7.1(1) or 7.3(1) of NI 23-101, must establish, implement, and maintain policies and procedures reasonably designed to ensure that each system, operated by or on behalf of the marketplace, that is critical and supports real-time market surveillance, can resume operations within two hours following the declaration of a disaster at the primary site by the exchange or quotation and trade reporting system.

(4) A regulation services provider, that has entered into a written agreement with a marketplace to conduct market surveillance for the marketplace, must establish, implement, and maintain policies and procedures reasonably designed to ensure that each system, operated by or on behalf of the regulation services provider, that is critical and supports real-time market surveillance can resume operations within two hours following the declaration of a disaster at the primary site by the regulation services provider.

12.4.1 Industry-Wide Business Continuity Tests — A marketplace, recognized clearing agency, information processor, and participant dealer must participate in all industry-wide business continuity tests, as determined by a regulation services provider, regulator, or in QuÂbec, the securities regulatory authority.

PART 13 — CLEARING AND SETTLEMENT

13.1 Clearing and Settlement — (1) All trades executed on a marketplace must be reported to and settled through a clearing agency.

(2) For a trade executed through an ATS by a subscriber that is registered as a dealer under securities legislation, the ATS and its subscriber must enter into an agreement that specifies whether the trade must be reported to a clearing agency by

(a) the ATS;

(b) the subscriber; or

(c) an agent for the subscriber that is a clearing member of a clearing agency.

(3) For a trade executed through an ATS by a subscriber that is not registered as a dealer under securities legislation, an ATS and its subscriber must enter into an agreement that specifies whether the trade must be reported to a clearing agency by

(a) the ATS; or

(b) an agent for the subscriber that is a clearing member of a clearing agency.

13.2 Access to Clearing Agency of Choice — (1) A marketplace must report a trade in a security to a clearing agency designated by a marketplace participant.

(2) Subsection (1) does not apply to a trade in a security that is a standardized derivative or an exchange-traded security that is an option.

PART 14 — REQUIREMENTS FOR AN INFORMATION PROCESSOR

14.1 Filing Requirements for an Information Processor — A person or company that intends to carry on business as an information processor must file Form 21-101F5 at least 90 days before the information processor begins to carry on business as an information processor.

14.2 Change in Information — (1) At least 45 days before implementing a significant change involving a matter set out in Form 21-101F5, an information processor must file an amendment to the information provided in Form 21-101F5 in the manner set out in Form 21-101F5.

(2) If an information processor implements a change involving a matter set out in Form 21-101F5, other than a change referred to in subsection (1), the information processor must, within 30 days after the end of the calendar quarter in which the change takes place, file an amendment to the information provided in Form 21-101F5 in the manner set out in Form 21-101F5.

14.3 Ceasing to Carry on Business as an Information Processor — (1) If an information processor intends to cease carrying on business as an information processor, the information processor must file a report on Form 21-101F6 at least 30 days before ceasing to carry on that business.

(2) If an information processor involuntarily ceases to carry on business as an information processor, the information processor must file a report on Form 21-101F6 as soon as practicable after it ceases to carry on that business.

14.4 Requirements Applicable to an Information Processor — (1) An information processor must enter into an agreement with each marketplace, inter-dealer bond broker and dealer that is required to provide information to the information processor that the marketplace, inter-dealer bond broker or dealer will

    (a) provide information to the information processor in accordance with Part 7 or 8, as applicable; and

    (b) comply with any other reasonable requirements set by the information processor.

(2) An information processor must provide timely, accurate, reliable and fair collection, processing, distribution and publication of information for orders for, and trades in, securities.

(3) An information processor must keep such books, records and other documents as are reasonably necessary for the proper recording of its business.

(4) An information processor must establish in a timely manner an electronic connection or changes to an electronic connection to a marketplace, inter-dealer bond broker or dealer that is required to provide information to the information processor.

(5) An information processor must provide prompt and accurate order and trade information and must not unreasonably restrict fair access to such information.

(6) An information processor must file annual audited financial statements within 90 days after the end of its financial year that

    (a) are prepared in accordance with Canadian GAAP applicable to publicly accountable enterprises, Canadian GAAP applicable to private enterprises or IFRS,

    (b) include notes to the financial statements that identify the accounting principles used to prepare the financial statements, and

    (c) are audited in accordance with Canadian GAAS or International Standards on Auditing and are accompanied by an auditor's report.

(6.1) If an information processor is operated as a division or unit of a person or company, the person or company must file the income statement and the statement of cash flow of the information processor and any other information necessary to demonstrate the financial condition of the information processor within 90 days after the end of the financial year of the person or company.

(7) An information processor must file its financial budget within 30 days after the start of a financial year.

(7.1) If an information processor is operated as a division or unit of a person or company, the person or company must file the financial budget relating to the information processor within 30 days of the start of the financial year of the person or company.

(8) An information processor must file, within 30 days after the end of each calendar quarter, the process and criteria for the selection of government debt securities, as applicable, and designated corporate debt securities and the list of government debt securities, as applicable, and designated corporate debt securities.

(9) An information processor must file, within 30 days after the end of each calendar year, the process to communicate the designated securities to the marketplaces, inter-dealer bond brokers and dealers providing the information required by the Instrument, including where the list of designated securities can be found.

14.5 System Requirements — An information processor must

    (a) develop and maintain

        (i) an adequate system of internal controls over its critical systems, and

        (ii) adequate information technology general controls, including, without limitation, controls relating to information systems operations, information security, change management, problem management, network support, and system software support,

    (b) in accordance with prudent business practice, on a reasonably frequent basis and in any event, at least annually,

        (i) make reasonable current and future capacity estimates for each of its systems, and

        (ii) conduct capacity stress tests of its critical systems to determine the ability of those systems to process information in an accurate, timely and efficient manner,

    (c) annually engage a qualified party to conduct an independent systems review and prepare a report in accordance with established audit standards to ensure that it is in compliance with paragraph (a) and section 14.6,

    (d) provide the report resulting from the review conducted under paragraph (c) to

        (i) its board of directors or the audit committee promptly upon the report's completion, and

        (ii) the regulator or, in Québec, the securities regulatory authority, by the earlier of the 30th day after providing the report to its board of directors or the audit committee or the 60th day after the calendar year end, and

(e) promptly notify the following of any failure, malfunction or material delay of its systems or equipment

(i) the regulator or, in Québec, the securities regulatory authority, and

(ii) any regulation services provider, recognized exchange or recognized quotation and trade reporting system monitoring trading of the securities about which information is provided to the information processor.

14.6 Business Continuity Planning — An information processor must

(a) develop and maintain reasonable business continuity plans, including disaster recovery plans,

(b) test its business continuity plans, including disaster recovery plans, according to prudent business practices and on a reasonably frequent basis and, in any event, at least annually, and

(c) establish, implement, and maintain policies and procedures reasonably designed to ensure that its critical systems can resume operations within one hour following the declaration of a disaster by the information processor.

14.7 Confidential Treatment of Trading Information — An information processor must not release order and trade information to a person or company other than the marketplace, inter-dealer bond broker or dealer that provided this information in accordance with this Instrument or a securities regulatory authority, unless

(a) the release of that information is required by this Instrument or under applicable law, or

(b) the information processor received prior approval from the securities regulatory authority.

14.8 Transparency of Operations of an Information Processor — An information processor must publicly disclose on its website information reasonably necessary to enable a person or company to understand the information processor's operations or services it provides including, but not limited to

(a) all fees charged by the information processor for the consolidated data,

(b) a description of the process and criteria for the selection of government debt securities, as applicable, and designated corporate debt securities and the list of government debt securities, as applicable, and designated corporate debt securities,

(c) access requirements, and

(d) the policies and procedures to manage conflicts of interest that may arise in the operation of the information processor.

PART 15 — EXEMPTION

15.1 Exemption — (1) The regulator or the securities regulatory authority may grant an exemption from this Instrument, in whole or in part, subject to such conditions or restrictions as may be imposed in the exemption.

(2) Despite subsection (1), in Ontario, only the regulator may grant such an exemption.

PART 16 — EFFECTIVE DATE

16.1 Effective Date — This Instrument comes into force on December 1, 2001.

Final Rule: 24 O.S.C.B. 6591 (November 2, 2001); Approval by OSC: 24 O.S.C.B. (Supp.) 85 (August 17, 2001); Request for Comments: 23 O.S.C.B. (Supp.) 299 (July 28, 2000).

Amendments to Rule: (2004) 27 O.S.C.B. 456; Approval by OSC: (2003) 26 O.S.C.B. 7147; Request for Comments: (2003) 26 O.S.C.B. 4377.

Amendments to Rule: (2006) 29 O.S.C.B. 10011; Approval by OSC: (2006) 24 O.S.C.B. 9731; Request for Comments: (2006) 29 O.S.C.B. 5735.

Amendments to Rule: (2008) 31 O.S.C.B. 8572; Approval by OSC: (2008) 31 O.S.C.B. 6303; Request for Comments: (2007) 30 O.S.C.B. (Supp. 3) 1 (April 20, 2007).

Amendments to Rule: (2010) 33 O.S.C.B. 787; Approval by OSC: (2009) 32 O.S.C.B. 9403; Request for Comments: (2008) 31 O.S.C.B. 10136.

Amendments to Rule: (2010) 33 O.S.C.B. (Supp. 5) 35; Approval by OSC: (2010) 33 O.S.C.B. (Supp. 3) 1.

Amendments to Rule: (2012) 35 O.S.C.B. 5369; Approval by OSC: (2012) 35 O.S.C.B. (Supp. 1) 1; Request for Comments: (2011) 34 O.S.C.B. (Supp. 1) 1.

Amendments to Rule: (2015) 38 O.S.C.B. 8535; Approval by OSC: (2015) 38 O.S.C.B. (Supp. 2) 7; Request for Comments: (2014) 37 O.S.C.B. 4197.

Policies and Orders: BOR 2.2; CSAN 11-321, 21-304, 21-306, 21-309, 21-310, 23-308, 23-311; OSCN 11-764, 21-704, 21-705, 21-706.

Form 21-101F1 — Information Statement Exchange or Quotation and Trade Reporting System

Filer: ❑ **EXCHANGE** ❑ **QUOTATION AND TRADE REPORTING SYSTEM**

Type of Filing: ❑ **INITIAL** ❑ **AMENDMENT; AMENDMENT No.**

1. Full name of exchange or quotation and trade reporting system:

2. Name(s) under which business is conducted, or name of market or facility, if different from item 1:

3. If this filing makes a name change on behalf of the exchange or quotation and trade reporting system in respect of the name set out in item 1 or item 2, enter the previous name and the new name:

Previous name:

New name:

4. Head office

   Address:

   Telephone:

   Facsimile:

5. Mailing address (if different):

6. Other offices

   Address:

   Telephone:

   Facsimile:

7. Website address:

8. Contact employee

   Name and title:

   Telephone number:

   Facsimile:

   E-mail address:

9. Counsel:

   Firm name:

   Contact name:

   Telephone number:

   Facsimile:

   E-mail address:

10. Market Regulation is being conducted by:

   ❏ the exchange

   ❏ the quotation and trade reporting system

   ❏ regulation services provider other than the filer (see Exhibit M)

Exhibits

File all Exhibits with the Filing. For each Exhibit, include the name of the exchange or quotation and trade reporting system, the date of filing of the Exhibit and the date as of which the information is accurate (if different from the date of the filing). If any Exhibit required is inapplicable, a statement to that effect must be furnished instead of such Exhibit.

Except as provided below, if the filer, recognized exchange or recognized quotation and trade reporting system files an amendment to the information provided in its Filing and the information relates to an Exhibit filed with the Filing or a subsequent amendment, the filer, recognized exchange or recognized quotation and trade reporting system, must, in order to comply with subsections 3.2(1), 3.2(2) or 3.2(3) of National Instrument 21-101, provide a description of the change, the expected date of the implementation of the change, and file a complete and updated Exhibit. The filer must provide a clean and a blacklined version showing changes from the previous filing.

If the filer, recognized exchange or recognized quotation and trade reporting system has otherwise filed the information required by the previous paragraph pursuant to section 5.5 of National Instrument 21-101, it is not required to file the information again as an amendment to an Exhibit. However, if supplementary material relating to a filed rule is contained in an Exhibit, an amendment to the Exhibit must also be filed.

Exhibit A — Corporate Governance

1. Legal status:

   ❏ Corporation

   ❏ Partnership

   ❏ Sole Proprietorship

   ❏ Other (specify):

2. Except where the exchange or quotation and trade reporting system is a sole proprietorship, indicate the following:

   1. Date (DD/MM/YYYY) of formation.

   2. Place of formation.

   3. Statute under which exchange or quotation and trade reporting system was organized.

3. Provide a copy of the constating documents (including corporate by-laws), shareholder agreements, partnership agreements and other similar documents, and all subsequent amendments.

4. Provide the policies and procedures to address potential conflicts of interest arising from the operation of the marketplace or the services it provides, including those related to the commercial interest of the marketplace, the interests of its owners and its operators, the responsibilities and sound functioning of the marketplace, and those between the operations of the marketplace and its regulatory responsibilities.

Exhibit B — Ownership

A list of the registered or beneficial holders of securities of, partnership interests in, or other ownership interests in, the exchange or recognized quotation and trade reporting system. For each of the persons listed in the Exhibit, please provide the following:

1. Name.

2. Principal business or occupation and title.

3. Ownership interest.

4. Nature of the ownership interest, including a description of the type of security, partnership interest or other ownership interest.

5. Whether the person has control (as interpreted in subsection 1.3(2) of National Instrument 21-101 *Marketplace Operation*).

In the case of an exchange or quotation and trade reporting system that is publicly traded, if the exchange or quotation and trade reporting system is a corporation, please only provide a list of each shareholder that directly owns five percent or more of a class of a voting security of the exchange or quotation and trade reporting system.

Exhibit C — Organization

1. A list of partners, officers, governors, and members of the board of directors and any standing committees of the board, or persons performing similar functions, who presently hold or have held their offices or positions during the previous year, indicating the following for each:

1. Name.

2. Principal business or occupation and title.

3. Dates of commencement and expiry of present term of office or position.

4. Type of business in which each is primarily engaged and current employer.

5. Type of business in which each was primarily engaged in the preceding five years, if different from that set out in item 4.

6. Whether the person is considered to be an independent director.

2. A list of the committees of the board, including their mandates and the Board mandate.

Exhibit D — Affiliates

1. For each affiliated entity of the exchange or quotation and trade reporting system provide the name, head office address and describe the principal business of the affiliate.

2. For each affiliated entity of the exchange or quotation and trade reporting system

(i) to which the exchange or quotation and trade reporting system has outsourced any of its key services or systems affecting the market or facility described in Exhibit E — Operations of the Marketplace, including order entry, trading, execution, routing and data, or

(ii) with which the exchange or quotation and trade reporting system has any other material business relationship, including loans, cross-guarantees, etc.,

provide the following information:

1. Name and address of the affiliate.

2. The name and title of the directors and officers, or persons performing similar functions, of the affiliate.

3. A description of the nature and extent of the contractual and other agreements with the exchange and quotation and trade reporting system, and the roles and responsibilities of the affiliate under the arrangement.

4. A copy of each material contract relating to any outsourced functions or other material relationship.

5. Copies of constating documents (including corporate by-laws), shareholder agreements, partnership agreements and other similar documents.

6. For the latest financial year of the affiliated entity, financial statements, which may be unaudited, prepared in accordance with

a. Canadian GAAP applicable to publicly accountable enterprises or

b. Canadian GAAP applicable to private enterprises, or

c. IFRS.

Where the affiliated entity is incorporated or organized under the laws of a foreign jurisdiction, such financial statements may also be prepared in accordance with

a. U.S. GAAP or

b. accounting principles of a designated foreign jurisdiction as defined under National Instrument 52-107 *Acceptable Accounting Principles and Auditing Standards*.

Exhibit E — Operations of the Marketplace

Describe in detail the manner of operation of the market or facility and its associated functions. This must include, but is not limited to, a description of the following:

1. The structure of the market (e.g., call market, auction market, dealer market).

2. Means of access to the market or facility and services, including a description of any co-location arrangements.

3. The hours of operation.

4. A description of the services offered by the marketplace including, but not limited to, order entry, co-location, trading, execution, routing and data.

5. A list of the types of orders offered, including, but not limited to, a description of the features and characteristics of orders.

6. Procedures regarding the entry, display and execution of orders. If indications of interest are used, please describe the information they include and list the types of recipients.

7. A description of how orders interact, including, but not limited to, the priority of execution for all order types.

8. A description of order routing procedures.

9. A description of order and trade reporting procedures.

10. A description of procedures for clearance and settlement of transactions.

11. The safeguards and procedures of the marketplace to protect trading information of marketplace participants.

12. Training provided to participants and a copy of any materials provided both with respect to systems of the marketplace, the requirements of the marketplace, and the rules of the regulation services providers, if applicable.

13. Steps taken to ensure that marketplace participants have knowledge of and comply with the requirements of the marketplace.

The filer must provide all policies, procedures and trading manuals related to the operation of the marketplace and, if applicable, the order router.

The filer must provide all material contracts related to order routing, execution, trade reporting, trade comparison, data feeds, market surveillance and trade clearing.

Exhibit F — Outsourcing

Where the exchange or quotation and trade reporting system has outsourced the operation of key services or systems affecting the market or facility described in Exhibit E — Operations of the Marketplace to an arms-length third party, including any function associated with the routing, trading, execution, data, clearing and settlement and, if applicable, surveillance, provide the following information:

1. Name and address of person or company to which the function has been outsourced.

2. A description of the nature and extent of the contractual or other agreement with the exchange or quotation and trade reporting system and the roles and responsibilities of the arms-length party under the arrangement.

3. A copy of each material contract relating to any outsourced function.

4. A copy of the marketplace's policies and procedures for the selection of service providers to which key services and systems may be outsourced and for the evaluation and approval of such outsourcing arrangements that are established and maintained pursuant to paragraph 5.12(a) of National Instrument 21-101 *Marketplace Operation.*

5. A description of any conflicts of interest between the marketplace and the service provider to which key services and systems are outsourced and a copy of the policies and procedures to mitigate and manage such conflicts of interest that have been established pursuant to paragraph 5.12(b) of National Instrument 21-101 Marketplace Operation.

6. A description of the measures the marketplace has taken pursuant to paragraph 5.12(f) of National Instrument 21-101 Marketplace Operation to ensure that the service provider has established, maintains and periodically tests an appropriate business continuity plan, including a disaster recovery plan.

7. A description of the measures the marketplace has taken pursuant to paragraph 5.12(g) of National Instrument 21-101 Marketplace Operation to ensure that the service provider protects the proprietary, order, trade or any other confidential information of the participants of the marketplace.

8. A copy of the marketplace's processes and procedures to regularly review the performance of a service provider under an outsourcing arrangement that are established pursuant to paragraph 5.12(h) of National Instrument 21-101 Marketplace Operation.

Exhibit G — Systems and Contingency Planning

General

Provide:

1. A high level description of the marketplace's systems that support order entry, order routing, execution, trade reporting, trade comparison, data feeds, co-location and if applicable, market surveillance and trade clearing.

2. An organization chart of the marketplace's information technology group unless otherwise provided as part of the report required by subsection 12.2(1) of the Instrument.

Business Continuity Planning

Please provide a description of the marketplace's business continuity and disaster recovery plans that includes, but is not limited to, information regarding the following:

1. Where the primary processing site is located.

2. What the approximate percentage of hardware, software and network redundancy is at the primary site.

3. Any uninterruptible power source (UPS) at the primary site.

4. How frequently market data is stored off-site.

5. Any secondary processing site, the location of any such secondary processing site, and whether all of the marketplace's critical business data is accessible through the secondary processing site.

6. The creation, management, and oversight of the plans, including a description of responsibility for the development of the plans and their ongoing review and updating.

7. Escalation procedures, including event identification, impact analysis, and activation of the plans in the event of a disaster or disruption.

8. Procedures for internal and external communications, including the distribution of information internally, to the securities regulatory authority, and, if appropriate, to the public, together with the roles and responsibilities of marketplace staff for internal and external communications.

9. The scenarios that would trigger the activation of the plans.

10. How frequently the business continuity and disaster recovery plans are tested.

11. Procedures for record keeping in relation to the review and updating of the plans, including the logging of tests and deficiencies.

12. The targeted time to resume operations of critical information technology systems following the declaration of a disaster by the marketplace and the service level to which such systems are to be restored.

13. Any single points of failure faced by the marketplace.

Systems Capacity

Please provide information regarding:

1. How frequently future market activity is evaluated in order to adjust processing capacity.

2. The approximate excess capacity maintained over average daily transaction volumes.

3. How often or at what point stress testing is performed.

Systems

Please provide information regarding:

1. Whether the trading engine was developed in-house or by a commercial vendor.

2. Whether the trading engine is maintained in-house or by a commercial vendor and provide the name of the commercial vendor, if applicable.

3. The marketplace's networks. Please provide a copy of a high-level network diagram of the systems referred to in section 12.1 of the Instrument, as applicable, together with a description of the external points of contact for the marketplace's networks.

4. The message protocols supported by the marketplace's systems.

5. The transmission protocols used by the marketplace's systems.

IT Risk Assessment

Please describe the IT risk assessment framework, including:

1. How the probability and likelihood of IT threats are considered.

2. How the impact of risks are measured according to qualitative and quantitative criteria.

3. The documentation process for acceptable residual risks with related offsets.

4. The development of management's action plan to implement a risk response to a risk that has not been accepted.

Exhibit H — Custody of Assets

1. If the exchange or quotation and trade reporting system proposes to hold funds or securities of a marketplace participant on a regular basis, a description of the controls that will be implemented to ensure the safety of the funds or securities.

2. If any other person or company, other than the exchange or quotation and trade reporting system, will hold or safeguard funds or securities of a marketplace participant on a regular basis, provide the name of the person or company and a description of the controls that will be implemented to ensure the safety of the funds or securities.

Exhibit I — Securities

1. List the types of securities listed on the exchange or quoted on the quotation and trade reporting system. If this is an initial filing, list the types of securities the filer expects to list or quote.

2. List the types of any other securities that are traded on the marketplace or quoted on the quotation and trade reporting system, indicating the exchange(s) on which such securities are listed. If this is an initial filing, list the types of securities the filer expects to trade.

Part 2: MARKET PARTICIPANTS

Exhibit J — Access to Services

1. A complete set of all forms, agreements or other materials pertaining to access to the services of the marketplace described in Exhibit E item 4, including trading on the exchange or quotation and trade reporting system.

2. Describe the classes of marketplace participants.

3. Describe the exchange or quotation and trade reporting service's criteria for access to the services of the marketplace.

4. Describe any differences in access to the services offered by the marketplace to different groups or classes of marketplace participants.

5. Describe conditions under which marketplace participants may be subject to suspension or termination with regard to access to the services of the exchange or quotation and trade reporting system.

6. Describe any procedures that will be involved in the suspension or termination of a marketplace participant.

7. Describe the exchange or quotation and trade reporting system's arrangements for permitting clients of marketplace participants to have access to the marketplace. Provide a copy of any agreements or documentation relating to these arrangements.

Exhibit K — Marketplace Participants

Provide an alphabetical list of all marketplace participants, including the following information:

     1. Name.

     2. Date of becoming a marketplace participant.

     3. Describe the type of trading activities engaged in by the marketplace participant (*e.g.*, agency trading, proprietary trading, registered trading, market making).

     4. The class of participation or other access. Please identify if the marketplace participant accesses the marketplace through co-location.

     5. Provide a list of all persons or entities that were denied or limited access to the marketplace, indicating for each

         (i) whether they were denied or limited access,

         (ii) the date the marketplace took such action,

         (iii) the effective date of such action, and

         (iv) the nature and reason for any denial or limitation of access.

Exhibit L — Fees

A description of the fee model and all fees charged by the marketplace, or by a party to which services have been directly or indirectly outsourced, including, but not limited to, fees relating to connecting to the market or facility, access, data, regulation (if applicable), trading, routing, and co-location, how such fees are set, and any fee rebates or discounts and how the rebates and discounts are set.

Exhibit M — Regulation

Market Regulation is being conducted by:

❏ the exchange or QTRS

     1. Provide a description of the regulation performed by the exchange or QTRS, including the structure of the department performing regulation, how the department is funded, policies and procedures in place to ensure confidentiality and the management of conflicts of interest, and policies and procedures relating to conducting an investigation.

     2. If more than one entity is performing regulation services for a type of security and the filer is conducting market regulation for itself and its members, provide a copy of the contract between the filer and the regulation services provider providing for co-ordinated monitoring and enforcement under section 7.5 of National Instrument 23-101 *Trading Rules.*

❏ a regulation services provider other than the filer (provide a copy of the contract between the filer and the regulation services provider)

Exhibit N — Acknowledgement

The form of acknowledgement required by subsection 5.9(2) of National Instrument 21-101 *Marketplace Operation.*

Certificate of Exchange or Quotation and Trade Reporting System

The undersigned certifies that the information given in this report is true and correct.

DATED at .... this .... day of .... 20..........

.... (Name of exchange or quotation and trade reporting system)

.... (Name of director, officer or partner — please type or print)

.... (Signature of director, officer or partner)

.... (Official capacity — please type or print)

Form 21-101F2 — Information Statement Alternative Trading System

TYPE OF FILING:

❏ **INITIAL OPERATION REPORT** ❏ **AMENDMENT; AMENDMENT No.**

Identification:

1. Full name of alternative trading system

2. Name(s) under which business is conducted, if different from item 1:

3. If this filing makes a name change on behalf of the alternative trading system in respect of the name set out in Item 1 or Item 2, enter the previous name and the new name.

    Previous name:

    New name:

4. Head office

    Address:

    Telephone:

    Facsimile:

5. Mailing address (if different):

6. Other offices

    Address:

    Telephone:

    Facsimile:

7. Website address:

8. Contact employee

    Name and title:

    Telephone number:

    Facsimile:

    E-mail address:

9. Counsel:

    Firm name:

    Contact name:

    Telephone number:

    Facsimile:

    E-mail address:

10. The ATS is

    ❏ a member of .... (name of the recognized self-regulatory entity)

    ❏ a registered dealer

11. If this is an initial operation report, the date the alternative trading system expects to commence operation:

12. The ATS has contracted with [name of regulation services provider] to perform market regulation for the ATS and its subscribers.

Exhibits

File all Exhibits with the Initial Operation Report. For each Exhibit, include the name of the ATS, the date of filing of the Exhibit and the date as of which the information is accurate (if different from the date of the filing). If any Exhibit required is inapplicable, a statement to that effect must be furnished instead of such Exhibit.

If the ATS files an amendment to the information provided in its Initial Operation Report and the information relates to an Exhibit filed with the Initial Operation Report or a subsequent amendment, the ATS must, in order to comply with subsection 3.2(1), 3.2(2) or 3.2(3) of National Instrument 21-101, provide a description of the change, the expected date of the implementation of the change, and file a complete and updated Exhibit. The ATS must provide a clean and blacklined version showing changes from the previous filing.

Exhibit A — Corporate Governance

1. Legal status:

    ❏ Corporation

    ❏ Partnership

    ❏ Sole Proprietorship

    ❏ Other (specify):

Part 2: MARKET PARTICIPANTS

2. Except where the ATS is a sole proprietorship, indicate the following:

    1. Date (DD/MM/YYYY) of formation.

    2. Place of formation.

    3. Statute under which the ATS was organized.

3. Provide a copy of the constating documents (including corporate by-laws), shareholder agreements, partnership agreements and other similar documents, and all subsequent amendments.

4. Provide the policies and procedures to address conflicts of interest arising from the operation of the marketplace or the services it provides, including those related to the commercial interest of the marketplace, the interests of its owners and its operators, and the responsibilities and sound functioning of the marketplace.

Exhibit B — Ownership

A list of the registered or beneficial holders of securities of, partnership interests in, or other ownership interests in, the ATS. For each of the persons listed in the Exhibit, please provide the following:

    1. Name.

    2. Principal business or occupation and title.

    3. Ownership interest.

    4. Nature of the ownership interest, including a description of the type of security, partnership interest or other ownership interest.

    5. Whether the person has control (as interpreted in subsection 1.3(2) of National Instrument 21-101 *Marketplace Operation*).

In the case of an ATS that is publicly traded, if the ATS is a corporation, please only provide a list of each shareholder that directly owns five percent or more of a class of a voting security of the ATS.

Exhibit C — Organization

1. A list of partners, officers, governors, and members of the board of directors and any standing committees of the board, or persons performing similar functions, who presently hold or have held their offices or positions during the previous year, indicating the following for each:

    1. Name.

    2. Principal business or occupation and title.

    3. Dates of commencement and expiry of present term of office or position.

    4. Type of business in which each is primarily engaged and current employer.

    5. Type of business in which each was primarily engaged in the preceding five years, if different from that set out in item 4.

    6. Whether the person is considered to be an independent director.

2. A list of the committees of the board, including their mandates.

Exhibit D — Affiliates

1. For each affiliated entity of the ATS provide the name, head office address and describe the principal business of the affiliate.

2. For each affiliated entity of the ATS

    (i) to which the ATS has outsourced any of its key services or systems affecting the market or facility described in Exhibit E — Operations of the Marketplace, including order entry, trading, execution, routing and data, or

    (ii) with which the ATS has any other material business relationship, including loans, cross-guarantees, etc.

provide the following information:

    1. Name and address of the affiliate.

    2. The name and title of the directors and officers, or persons performing similar functions, of the affiliate.

    3. A description of the nature and extent of the contractual and other agreements with the ATS and the roles and responsibilities of the affiliate under the arrangement.

    4. A copy of each material contract relating to any outsourced functions or other material relationship.

    5. Copies of constating documents (including corporate by-laws), shareholder agreements, partnership agreements and other similar documents.

Exhibit E — Operations of the Marketplace

Describe in detail the manner of operation of the market and its associated functions. This must include, but is not limited to, a description of the following:

    1. The structure of the market (e.g., call market, auction market, dealer market).

    2. Means of access to the market or facility and services, including a description of any co-location arrangements.

    3. The hours of operation.

    4. A description of the services offered by the marketplace including, but not limited to, order entry, co-location, trading, execution, routing and data.

5. A list of the types of orders offered, including, but not limited to, a description of the features and characteristics of orders.

6. Procedures regarding the entry, display and execution of orders. If indications of interest are used, please describe the information they include and list the types of recipients.

7. A description of how orders interact, including, but not limited to, the priority of execution for all order types.

8. A description of order routing procedures.

9. A description of order and trade reporting procedures.

10. A description of procedures for clearance and settlement of transactions.

11. The safeguards and procedures of the marketplace to protect trading information of marketplace participants.

12. Training provided to participants and a copy of any materials provided both with respect to systems of the marketplace, the requirements of the marketplace, and the rules of the regulation services providers, if applicable.

13. Steps taken to ensure that marketplace participants have knowledge of and comply with the requirements of the marketplace.

The filer must provide all policies, procedures and trading manuals related to the operation of the marketplace and, if applicable, the order router.

The filer must provide all material contracts relating to order routing, execution, trade reporting, trade comparison, data feeds, market surveillance and trade clearing.

Exhibit F — Outsourcing

Where the ATS has outsourced the operation of key services or systems affecting the market or facility described in Exhibit E — Operations of the Marketplace to an arms-length third party, including any function associated with routing, trading, execution, clearing and settlement, data and co-location, provide the following information:

1. Name and address of person or company to which the function has been outsourced.

2. A description of the nature and extent of the contractual or other agreement with the ATS and the roles and responsibilities of the arms-length party under the arrangement.

3. A copy of each material contract relating to any outsourced function.

4. A copy of the marketplace's policies and procedures for the selection of service providers to which key services and systems may be outsourced and for the evaluation and approval of such outsourcing arrangements that are established and maintained pursuant to paragraph 5.12(a) of National Instrument 21-101 *Marketplace Operation*.

5. A description of any conflicts of interest between the marketplace and the service provider to which key services and systems are outsourced and a copy of the policies and procedures to mitigate and manage such conflicts of interest that have been established pursuant to paragraph 5.12(b) of National Instrument 21-101 *Marketplace Operation*.

6. A description of the measures the marketplace has taken pursuant to paragraph 5.12(f) of National Instrument 21-101 *Marketplace Operation* to ensure that the service provider has established, maintains and periodically tests an appropriate business continuity plan, including a disaster recovery plan.

7. A description of the measures the marketplace has taken pursuant to paragraph 5.12(g) of National Instrument 21-101 *Marketplace Operation* to ensure that the service provider protects the proprietary order, trade or any other confidential information of the participants of the marketplace.

8. A copy of the marketplace's processes and procedures to regularly review the performance of a service provider under an outsourcing arrangement that are established pursuant to paragraph 5.12(h) of National Instrument 21-101 *Marketplace Operation*.

Exhibit G — Systems and Contingency Planning

General

Provide:

1. A high level description of the marketplace's systems that support order entry, order routing, execution, trade reporting, trade comparison, data feeds, co-location and if applicable, market surveillance and trade clearing.

2. An organization chart of the marketplace's information technology group unless otherwise provided as part of the report required by subsection 12.2(1) of the Instrument.

Business Continuity Planning

Please provide a description of the marketplace's business continuity and disaster recovery plans that includes, but is not limited to, information regarding the following:

1. Where the primary processing site is located.

2. What the approximate percentage of hardware, software and network redundancy is at the primary site.

3. Any uninterruptible power source (UPS) at the primary site.

4. How frequently market data is stored off-site.

5. Any secondary processing site, the location of any such secondary processing site, and whether all of the marketplace's critical business data is accessible through the secondary processing site.

6. The creation, management, and oversight of the plans, including a description of responsibility for the development of the plans and their ongoing review and updating.

7. Escalation procedures, including event identification, impact analysis, and activation of the plans in the event of a disaster or disruption.

8. Procedures for internal and external communications, including the distribution of information internally, to the securities regulatory authority, and, if appropriate, to the public, together with the roles and responsibilities of marketplace staff for internal and external communications.

9. The scenarios that would trigger the activation of the plans.

10. How frequently the business continuity and disaster recovery plans are tested.

11. Procedures for record keeping in relation to the review and updating of the plans, including the logging of tests and deficiencies.

12. The targeted time to resume operations of critical information technology systems following the declaration of a disaster by the marketplace and the service level to which such systems are to be restored.

13. Any single points of failure faced by the marketplace.

Systems Capacity

Please provide information regarding:

1. How frequently future market activity is evaluated in order to adjust processing capacity.

2. The approximate excess capacity maintained over average daily transaction volumes.

3. How often or at what point stress testing is performed.

Systems

Please provide information regarding:

1. Whether the trading engine was developed in-house or by a commercial vendor.

2. Whether the trading engine is maintained in-house or by a commercial vendor and provide the name of the commercial vendor, if applicable.

3. The marketplace's networks. Please provide a copy of a high-level network diagram of the systems referred to in section 12.1 of the Instrument, as applicable, together with a description of the external points of contact for the marketplace's networks.

4. The message protocols supported by the marketplace's systems.

5. The transmission protocols used by the marketplace's systems.

IT Risk Assessment

Please describe the IT risk assessment framework, including:

1. How the probability and likelihood of IT threats are considered.

2. How the impact of risks are measured according to qualitative and quantitative criteria.

3. The documentation process for acceptable residual risks with related offsets.

4. The development of management's action plan to implement a risk response to a risk that has not been accepted.

Exhibit H — Custody of Assets

1. If the ATS proposes to hold funds or securities of a marketplace participant on a regular basis, a description of the controls that will be implemented to ensure the safety of the funds or securities.

2. If any other person or company, other than the ATS, will hold or safeguard funds or securities of a marketplace participant on a regular basis, provide the name of the person or company and a description of the controls that will be implemented to ensure the safety of the funds or securities.

Exhibit I — Securities

List the types of securities that are traded on the ATS, indicating the exchange(s) on which such securities are listed. If this is an initial filing, list the types of securities the ATS expects to trade.

Exhibit J — Access to Services

1. A complete set of all forms, agreements or other materials pertaining to access to the services of the marketplace described in Exhibit E item 4, including trading on the ATS.

2. Describe the classes of marketplace participants (i.e. dealer, institution or retail).

3. Describe the ATS's criteria for access to the services of the marketplace.

4. Describe any differences in access to the services offered by the marketplace to different groups or classes of marketplace participants. Please identify if the marketplace participant accesses the marketplace through co-location.

5. Describe conditions under which marketplace participants may be subject to suspension or termination with regard to access to the services of the ATS.

6. Describe any procedures that will be involved in the suspension or termination of a marketplace participant.

7. Describe the ATS's arrangements for permitting clients of marketplace participants to have access to the marketplace. Provide a copy of any agreements or documentation relating to these arrangements.

Exhibit K — Marketplace Participants

Provide an alphabetical list of all marketplace participants, including the following information:

1. Name.

2. Date of becoming a marketplace participant.

3. Describe the type of trading activities primarily engaged in by the marketplace participant (*e.g.*, agency trading, proprietary trading, registered trading, market making).

4. The class of participation or other access. Please identify if the marketplace participant accesses the marketplace through co-location.

5. Provide a list of all persons or entities that were denied or limited access to the marketplace, indicating for each

    (i) whether they were denied or limited access,

    (ii) the date the marketplace took such action,

    (iii) the effective date of such action, and

    (iv) the nature and reason for any denial or limitation of access.

Exhibit L — Fees

A description of the fee model and all fees charged by the marketplace, or by a party to which services have been directly or indirectly outsourced, including, but not limited to, fees relating to connecting to the market or facility, access, data, regulation (if applicable), trading, routing, and co-location, how such fees are set and any fee rebates or discounts and how the rebates and discounts are set.

Exhibit M — Regulation

The ATS has contracted with regulation services provider .... to perform market regulation for ATS and its subscribers. Provide a copy of the contract between the filer and the regulation services provider.

Exhibit N — Acknowledgement

The form of acknowledgement required by subsections 5.9(2) and 6.11(2) of National Instrument 21-101 *Marketplace Operation*.

Certificate of Alternative Trading System

The undersigned certifies that the information given in this report is true and correct.

DATED at .... this .... day of .... 20..........

.... (Name of alternative trading system)

.... (Name of director, officer or partner — please type or print)

.... (Signature of director, officer or partner)

.... (Official capacity — please type or print)

21-101F3 — Quarterly Report of Marketplace Activities

A. — General Marketplace Information

1. Marketplace Name:

2. Period covered by this report:

3. Identification

    A. Full name of marketplace (if sole proprietor, last, first and middle name):

    B. Name(s) under which business is conducted, if different from item A:

    C. Marketplace main street address:

4. A list of all amendments in the information in Form 21-101F1 or 21-101F2 that were filed with the Canadian securities regulatory authorities and implemented during the period covered by the report. The list must include a brief description of each amendment, the date filed and the date implemented.

5. A list of all amendments in the information in Form 21-101F1 or 21-101F2 that have been filed with the Canadian securities regulatory authorities but not implemented as of the end of the period covered by the report. The list must include a brief description of each amendment, the date filed and the reason why it was not implemented.

6. Systems — If any outages occurred at any time during the period for any system relating to trading activity, including trading, routing or data, provide the date, duration, reason for the outage and its resolution.

7. Systems Changes — A brief description of any significant changes to the systems and technology used by the marketplace that support order entry, order routing, execution, trade reporting, trade comparison, data feeds, co-location and if applicable, market surveillance and trade

clearing that were planned, under development, or implemented during the quarter. Please provide the current status of the changes that are under development.

B. — Marketplace Activity Information

Section 1 — Marketplaces Trading Exchange-Listed Securities

1. General trading activity — For each type of security traded on the marketplace, provide the details (where appropriate) requested in the form set out in **Chart 1**. The information must be provided for transactions executed at the opening of the market, during regular trading hours, and after hours during the quarter. Enter "None", "N/A", or "0" where appropriate.

Chart 1 — General trading activity for marketplaces trading exchange-listed securities

Category of Securities	Volume		Value		Number of Trades	
	Transparent	Non-transparent	Transparent	Non-transparent	Transparent	Non-transparent
Exchange-Traded Securities						
1. Equity (includes preferred shares)	....	....	....	....	....	....
2. Exchange-traded funds (ETFs)	....	....	....	....	....	....
3. Debt securities	....	....	....	....	....	....
4. Options	....	....	....	....	....	....
Foreign Exchange-Traded Securities						
1. Equity (includes preferred shares)	....	....	....	....	....	....
2. ETFs	....	....	....	....	....	....
3. Debt securities	....	....	....	....	....	....
4. Options	....	....	....	....	....	....

2. Crosses — Provide the details (where appropriate) requested in the form set out in **Chart 2** below for each type of cross executed on the marketplace for trades executed at the opening of the market, during regular trading and after hours during the quarter. Enter "None", "N/A", or "0" where appropriate.

Chart 2 — Crosses

Types of Crosses	Volume	Value	Number of Trades
1. Intentional Crosses[1]	....	....	....
2. Internal crosses	....	....	....
3. Other crosses	....	....	....

3. Order information — Provide the details (where appropriate) requested in the form set out in **Chart 3** below for each type of order in exchange traded securities executed on the marketplace for orders entered at the opening of the market, during regular trading and after hours during the quarter. Enter "none", "N/A" or "0" where appropriate.

Chart 3 — Order information

Types of Orders	Number of Orders	Orders Executed	Orders Cancelled[2]
1. Anonymous[3]	....	....	....
2. Fully transparent	....	....	....
3. Pegged Orders	....	....	....
4. Fully hidden	....	....	....
5. Separate dark facility of a transparent market	....	....	....
6. Partially hidden (reserve)	....	....	....
7. Total number of orders entered during the quarter	....	....	....

---

[1]See definition of an Internal and Intentional Cross in Section 1.1 of the Universal Market Integrity Rules.

[2]By cancellations, we mean "pure" cancellations, i.e. cancellations that do not result in a new and amended order.

[3]Orders executed under ID 001.

4. Trading by security — Provide the details requested in the form set out in **Chart 4** below for the 10 most traded securities on the marketplace (based on the volume of securities traded) for trades executed at the opening of the market, during regular trading and after hours during the quarter. Enter "None", "N/A", or "0" where appropriate.

Chart 4 — Most traded securities

Category of Securities	Volume	Value	Number of Trades
Exchange-Traded Securities			
1. Equity (includes preferred shares) [Name of Securities] 1. 2. 3. 4. 5. 6. 7. 8. 9. 10.			
2. ETFs [Name of Securities] 1. 2. 3. 4. 5. 6. 7. 8. 9. 10.			
3. Debt [Enter issuer, maturity and coupon] 1. 2. 3. 4. 5. 6. 7. 8. 9. 10.			
Foreign Exchange-Traded Securities			
1. Equity (includes preferred shares) [Name of Securities] 1. 2. 3. 4. 5. 6. 7. 8. 9.			

Category of Securities	Volume	Value	Number of Trades
10.			
2. ETFs [Name of Securities]			
1.			
2.			
3.			
4.			
5.			
6.			
7.			
8.			
9.			
10.			
3. Debt [Name of Securities]			
1.			
2.			
3.			
4.			
5.			
6.			
7.			
8.			
9.			
10.			

5. Trading by marketplace participant — Provide the details requested in the form set out in **Chart 5** below for the top 10 marketplace participants (based on the volume of securities traded). The information must be provided for the total trading volume, including for trades executed at the opening of the market, during regular trading and after hours during the quarter. Enter "None", "N/A", or "0" where appropriate. Where a marketplace's marketplace participants are dealers and non-dealers, the marketplace must complete a separate chart for each.

Chart 5 — Concentration of trading by marketplace participant

Marketplace Participant Name	Total Active Volume	Total Passive Volume
1.		
2.		
3.		
4.		
5.		
6.		
7.		
8.		
9.		
10.		

6. Routing activities — Indicate the percentage of marketplace participants that used marketplace-owned or third party or affiliated routing services during the reporting period. In addition, provide the information in **Chart 6** below.

Chart 6 — Routing of marketplace orders

Number of orders executed on the reporting marketplace	....
Number of orders routed to away marketplaces (list all marketplaces where orders were routed)	....
Number of orders that are marked Directed Action Orders (DAO)	....

Section 2 — Fixed Income Marketplaces

1. General trading activity — Provide the details (where appropriate) requested in the form set out in **Chart 7** below for each type of fixed income security traded on the marketplace for transactions executed during regular trading hours during the quarter. Enter "None", "N/A", or "0" where appropriate.

Chart 7 — Fixed income activity

Category of Securities	Value Traded	Number of Trades
Domestic Unlisted Debt Securities — Government		
1. Federal		
2. Federal Agency		
3. Provincial and Municipal		
Domestic Unlisted Debt Securities — Corporate		
Domestic Unlisted Debt Securities — Other		
Foreign Unlisted Debt Securities — Government		
Foreign Unlisted Debt Securities — Corporate		
Foreign Unlisted Debt Securities — Other		

2. Trading by security — Provide the details requested in the form set out in **Chart 8** below for each fixed income security traded on the marketplace for trades executed during regular trading hours during the quarter. Enter "None", "N/A", or "0" where appropriate.

Chart 8 — Most traded fixed income securities

Category of Securities	Value Traded	Number of Trades
Domestic Unlisted Debt Securities — **Government**		
1. Federal		
[Enter issuer, maturity, coupon]		
2. Federal Agency		
[Enter issuer, maturity, coupon]		
3. Provincial and Municipal		
[Enter issuer, maturity, coupon]		
Domestic Unlisted Debt Securities — **Corporate**		
[Enter issuer, maturity, coupon]		
Domestic Unlisted Debt Securities — **Other**		
[Enter issuer, maturity, coupon]		
Foreign Unlisted Debt Securities — **Government**		
[Enter issuer, maturity, coupon]		
Foreign Unlisted Debt Securities — **Corporate**		
[Enter issuer, maturity, coupon]		
Foreign Unlisted Debt Securities — **Other**		
[Enter issuer, maturity, coupon]		

3. Trading by marketplace participant — Provide the details requested in the form set out in **Chart 9** below for the top 10 marketplace participants for trades executed during regular trading hours during the quarter. Enter "None", "N/A", or "0" where appropriate. If marketplace participants are dealers and non-dealer institutions, the marketplace must complete a separate chart for each.

Chart 9 — Concentration of trading by marketplace participant

Marketplace Participant Name	Value Traded
1.	
2.	
3.	
4.	
5.	
6.	
7.	
8.	
9.	
10.	

Part 2: MARKET PARTICIPANTS

365

Section 3 — Securities Lending Marketplaces

1. General lending activity — Please provide details (where appropriate) requested in the form set out in **Chart 10** below for each type of securities loaned on the marketplace. Enter "None", "N/A" or "0" where appropriate.

Chart 10 — Lending activity

Category of Securities	Quantity of Securities Lent During the Quarter	Aggregate Value of Securities Lent During the Quarter
Domestic		
1. Corporate Equity Securities		
1.1. Common Shares		
1.2. Preferred Shares		
2. Non-Corporate Equity Securities (e.g. trust units, partnership units, etc.) (please specify)		
3. Government Debt Securities		
4. Corporate Debt Securities		
5. Other Fixed Income Securities (please specify)		
Foreign		
1. Corporate Equity Securities		
1.1. Common Shares		
1.2. Preferred Shares		
2. Non-Corporate Equity Securities (e.g. trust units, partnership units, etc.) (please specify)		
3. Government Debt Securities		
4. Corporate Debt Securities		
5. Other Fixed Income Securities (please specify)		

2. Trading by marketplace participant — Provide the details requested in the form set out in **Chart 11** and **Chart 12** below for the top 10 borrowers and lenders based on their aggregate value of securities borrowed or loaned, respectively, during the quarter.

Chart 11 — Concentration of activity by borrower

Borrower Name	Aggregate Value of Securities Borrowed During the Quarter
1.	
2.	
3.	
4.	
5.	
6.	
7.	
8.	
9.	
10.	

Chart 12 — Concentration of activity by lender

Lender Name	Aggregate Value of Securities Loaned During the Quarter
1.	
2.	
3.	
4.	
5.	
6.	
7.	
8.	
9.	
10.	

3. Lending activity by security — Provide the details requested in the form set out in **Chart 13** below for the 10 most loaned securities on the marketplace (based on the quantity of securities loaned during the quarter). Enter "None", "N/A" or "0" where appropriate.

Chart 13 — Most loaned securities

Category of Securities	Quantity of Securities Lent During the Quarter	Aggregate Value of Securities Lent During the Quarter
Domestic		
1. Common Shares [Name of Security] 1. 2. 3. 4. 5. 6. 7. 8. 9. 10.		
2. Preferred Shares [Name of Security] 1. 2. 3. 4. 5. 6. 7. 8. 9. 10.		
3. Non-Corporate Equity Securities [Name of Security] 1. 2. 3. 4. 5. 6. 7. 8. 9. 10.		
4. Government Debt Securities [Name of Security] 1. 2. 3. 4. 5. 6. 7. 8. 9.		

Category of Securities	Quantity of Securities Lent During the Quarter	Aggregate Value of Securities Lent During the Quarter
10.		
5. Corporate Debt Securities [Name of Security]		
1.		
2.		
3.		
4.		
5.		
6.		
7.		
8.		
9.		
10.		
6. Other Fixed Income Securities [Name of Security]		
1.		
2.		
3.		
4.		
5.		
6.		
7.		
8.		
9.		
10.		
Foreign		
1. Common Shares [Name of Security]		
1.		
2.		
3.		
4.		
5.		
6.		
7.		
8.		
9.		
10.		
2. Preferred Shares [Name of Security]		
1.		
2.		
3.		
4.		
5.		
6.		
7.		
8.		
9.		
10.		
3. Non-Corporate Equity Securities [Name of Security]		
1.		

Category of Securities	Quantity of Securities Lent During the Quarter	Aggregate Value of Securities Lent During the Quarter
2.		
3.		
4.		
5.		
6.		
7.		
8.		
9.		
10.		
4. Government Debt Securities [Name of Security]		
1.		
2.		
3.		
4.		
5.		
6.		
7.		
8.		
9.		
10.		
5. Corporate Debt Securities [Name of Security] [Name of Security]		
1.		
2.		
3.		
4.		
5.		
6.		
7.		
8.		
9.		
10.		
6. Other Fixed Income Securities [Name of Security]		
1.		
2.		
3.		
4.		
5.		
6.		
7.		
8.		
9.		
10.		

Section 4 — Derivatives Marketplaces in Quebec

1. General trading activity — For each category of product traded on the marketplace, provide the details (where appropriate) requested in the form set out in **Chart 14** below. For products other than options on ETFs and equity options, provide the details on a product-by-product basis in the appropriate category. Details for options on ETFs and equity options must be provided on an aggregate basis (one total for options on ETFs and one for options on equities). The information must be provided for transactions executed in the early session, during the regular session, and in the extended session during the quarter. Enter "None", "N/A", or "0" where appropriate.

Chart 14 — General trading activity

Category of Product	Volume	Number of Trades	Open Interest (Number/End of Quarter)
Futures Products			
1(a) Interest rate — short term			
1(b) Interest rate — long term			
2. Index			
3. ETF			
4. Equity			
5. Currency			
6. Energy			
7. Others, please specify			
Options Products			
1(a) Interest rate — short term			
1(b) Interest rate — long term			
2. Index			
3. ETF			
4. Equity			
5. Currency			
6. Energy			
7. Others, please specify			

2. Trades resulting from pre-negotiation discussions — Provide the details (where appropriate) requested in the form set out in **Chart 15** below by product and for each type of trade resulting from pre-negotiation discussions. For products other than options on ETFs and equity options, provide the details on a product-by-product basis in the appropriate category. Details for options on ETFs and equity options must be provided on an aggregate basis (one total for options on ETFs and one for options on equities). The information must be provided for trades executed in the early session, during the regular session and in the extended session during the quarter. Enter "None", "N/A", or "0" where appropriate.

Chart 15 — Trades resulting from pre-negotiation discussions

Type of Trade	Volume	Number of Trades
Futures Products		
A. Cross		
B. Pre-arranged		
C. Block		
D. Exchange for physical		
E. Exchange for risk		
F. Riskless basis cross		
G. Others, please specify		
Options Products		
A. Cross		
B. Pre-arranged		
C. Block		
D. Others, please specify		

3. Order information — Provide the details (where appropriate) requested in the form set out in **Chart 16** below by product and for each type of order in exchange traded contracts executed on the marketplace. For products other than options on ETFs and equity options, provide the details on a product-by-product basis in the appropriate category. Details for options on ETFs and equity options must be provided on an aggregate basis (one total for options on ETFs and one for options on equities). The information must be provided for orders entered in the early session, during the regular session and in the extended session during the quarter. Enter "none", "N/A" or "0" where appropriate.

Chart 16 — Order information

Type of Orders	Volume	Number of Trades
1. Anonymous		
2. Fully transparent		
3. Pegged orders		
4. Fully hidden		
5. Separate dark facility of a transparent market		
6. Partially hidden (reserve, for example, iceberg orders)		

4. Trading by product — Provide the details requested in the form set out in **Chart 17** below. For each product other than options on ETFs and equity options, list the most actively-traded contracts (by volume) on the marketplace that in the aggregate constitute at least 75% of the total volume for each product during the quarter. The list must include at least 3 contracts. For options on ETFs and equity options, list the 10 most actively traded classes by volume. Details for options on ETFs and equity options must be provided on an aggregate basis (one total for options on ETFs and one for options on equities). The information must be provided for trades executed in the early session, during the regular session and in the extended session during the quarter. Enter "None", "N/A", or "0" where appropriate.

Chart 17 — Most traded contracts

Category of Product	Volume	Number of Trades	Open Interest (Number/End of Quarter)
Futures Products			
1. Name of products — 3 most-traded contracts (or more as applicable)			
1.			
2.			
3.			
Options Products			
2. ETF [Classes]			
1.			
2.			
3.			
4.			
5.			
6.			
7.			
8.			
9.			
10.			
3. Equity [Classes]			
1.			
2.			
3.			
4.			
5.			
6.			
7.			
8.			
9.			
10.			
4. Other listed options (specify for each) — 3 most traded contracts (or more as applicable)			
1.			
2.			
3.			

5. Concentration of trading by marketplace participant — Provide the details requested in the form set out in **Chart 18** below. For each product other than options on ETFs and equity options, list the top marketplace participants whose aggregate trading (by volume) constituted at least 75% of the total volume traded. The list must include at least 3 marketplace participants. For options on ETFs and equity options, provide the top 10 most active marketplace participants (by volume). The information must be provided on an aggregate basis (one total for options on ETFs and one for options on equities). The information must be provided for trades executed in the early session, during the regular session and in the extended session during the quarter. Enter "None", "N/A", or "0" where appropriate.

Chart 18 — Concentration of trading by marketplace participant

Product Name	Marketplace Participant Name	Volume
Futures		
Product Name (specify for each)	1.	
	2.	
	3. (more if necessary)	
Options		
ETF	1.	
	2.	
	3.	
	4.	
	5.	
	6.	
	7.	
	8.	
	9.	
	10.	
Equity	1.	
	2.	
	3.	
	4.	
	5.	
	6.	
	7.	
	8.	
	8.	
	9.	
	10.	
Other options (specify for each)	1.	
	2.	
	3. (more if necessary)	

C. — Certificate of Marketplace

The undersigned certifies that the information given in this report relating to the marketplace is true and correct.

DATED at..........this..........day of..........20..........

.... (Name of Marketplace)

.... (Name of director, officer or partner — please type or print)

.... (Signature of director, officer or partner)

.... (Official capacity — please type or print)

Form 21-101F4 — Cessation of Operations Report for Alternative Trading System

1. Identification:

    A. Full name of alternative trading system (if sole proprietor, last, first and middle name):

        ....

    B. Name(s) under which business is conducted, if different from item 1A:

        ....

2. Date alternative trading system proposes to cease carrying on business as an ATS:

....

3. If cessation of business was involuntary, date alternative trading system has ceased to carry on business as an ATS:

....

4. Please check the appropriate box:

❑ the ATS intends to carry on business as an exchange and has filed Form 21-101F1.

❑ the ATS intends to cease to carry on business.

❑ the ATS intends to become a member of an exchange.

Exhibits

File all Exhibits with the Cessation of Operations Report. For each exhibit, include the name of the ATS, the date of filing of the exhibit and the date as of which the information is accurate (if different from the date of the filing). If any Exhibit required is inapplicable, a statement to that effect must be furnished instead of such Exhibit.

Exhibit A

The reasons for the alternative trading system ceasing to carry on business as an ATS.

Exhibit B

A list of each of the securities the alternative trading system trades.

Exhibit C

The amount of funds and securities, if any, held for subscribers by the alternative trading system, or another person or company retained by the alternative trading system to hold funds and securities for subscribers and the procedures in place to transfer or to return all funds and securities to subscribers.

Certificate of Alternative Trading System

The undersigned certifies that the information given in this report is true and correct.

DATED at .... this .... day of .... 20.........

.... (Name of alternative trading system)

.... (Name of director, officer or partner — please type or print)

.... (Signature of director, officer or partner)

.... (Official capacity — please type or print)

Form 21-101F5 — Information Statement Information Processor

TYPE OF FILING:

❑ INITIAL FORM ❑ AMENDMENT: AMENDMENT No.

General Information

1. Full name of information processor:

2. Name(s) under which business is conducted, if different from item 1:

3. If this filing makes a name change on behalf of the information processor in respect of the name set out in item 1 or item 2, enter the previous name and the new name:

Previous name:

New name:

4. Head office

Address:

Telephone:

Facsimile:

5. Mailing address (if different):

6. Other offices

Address:

Telephone:

Facsimile:

7. Website address:

8. Contact employee

    Name and title:

    Telephone number:

    Facsimile:

    E-mail address:

9. Counsel

    Firm name:

    Contact name:

    Telephone number:

    Facsimile:

    E-mail address:

10. List of all marketplaces, dealers or other parties for which the information processor is acting or for which it proposes to act as an information processor. For each marketplace, dealer or other party, provide a description of the function(s) which the information processor performs or proposes to perform.

11. List all types of securities for which information will be collected, processed, distributed or published by the information processor. For each such marketplace, dealer or other party, provide a list of all securities for which information with respect to quotations for, or transactions in, is or is proposed to be collected, processed, distributed or published.

Exhibits

File all Exhibits with the Initial Form. For each Exhibit, include the name of the information processor, the date of filing of the Exhibit and the date as of which the information is accurate (if different from the date of the filing). If any Exhibit required is inapplicable, a statement to that effect must be furnished instead of such Exhibit.

If the information processor files an amendment to the information provided in its Initial Form, and the information relates to an Exhibit filed with the Initial Form or a subsequent amendment, the information processor must, in order to comply with sections 14.1 and 14.2 of National Instrument 21-101, provide a description of the change, the expected date of the implementation of the change, and file a complete and updated Exhibit. The information processor must provide a clean and a blacklined version showing changes from the previous filing.

Exhibit A — Corporate Governance

1. Legal status:

    ❑ Corporation

    ❑ Sole Proprietorship

    ❑ Partnership

    ❑ Other (specify):

2. Except where the information processor is a sole proprietorship, indicate the date and place where the information processor obtained its legal status (e.g., place of incorporation, place where partnership agreement was filed or where information processor was formed):

    1. Date (DD/MM/YYYY) of formation.

    2. Place of formation.

    3. Statute under which the information processor was organized.

3. Provide a copy of the constating documents (including corporate by-laws), shareholder agreements, partnership agreements and other similar documents, and all subsequent documents.

4. Provide the policies and procedures which promote independence of the information processor from the marketplaces, inter-dealer bond brokers and dealers that provide data.

5. Provide the policies and procedures which address the potential conflicts of interest between the interests of the information processor and its owners, partners, directors and officers.

Exhibit B — Ownership

List any person or company who owns 10 percent or more of the information processor's outstanding shares or who, either directly or indirectly, through agreement or otherwise, in any other manner, may control or direct the management or policies of the information processor. Provide the full name and address of each such person and attach a copy of the agreement or, if there is none written, describe the agreement or basis through which such person exercises or may exercise such control or direction.

Exhibit C — Organization

1. A list of the partners, directors, governors, and members of the board of directors and any standing committees of the board, or persons performing similar functions who presently hold or have held their offices or positions during the previous year, identifying those individuals

with overall responsibility for the integrity and timeliness of data reported to and displayed by the system (the "System") of the information processor, indicating the following for each:

1. Name.

2. Principal business or occupation and title.

3. Dates of commencement and expiry of present term of office or position.

4. Type of business in which each is primarily engaged and current employer.

5. Type of business in which each was primarily engaged in the preceding five years, if different from that set out in item 4.

6. Whether the person is considered to be an independent director.

7. A list of the committees of the board, including their mandates.

8. A narrative or graphic description of the organizational structure of the information processor.

Exhibit D — Staffing

A description of the personnel qualifications for each category of professional, non-professional and supervisory employee employed by the information processor. Detail whether the personnel are employed by the information processor or a third party, identifying the employees responsible for monitoring the timeliness and integrity of data reported to and displayed by the System.

Exhibit E — Affiliates

For each affiliated entity of the information processor, and for any person or company with whom the information processor has a contractual or other agreement relating to the operations of the information processor, including loans or cross-guarantees, provide the following information:

1. Name and address of person or company.

2. Form of organization (e.g., association, corporation, partnership, etc.).

3. Name of location and statute citation under which organized.

4. Date of incorporation in present form.

5. Description of nature and extent of affiliation and/or contractual or other agreement with the information processor.

6. Description of business or functions of the affiliates.

7. If a person or company has ceased to be an affiliated entity of the information processor during the previous year or ceased to have a contractual or other agreement relating to the operation of the information processor during the previous year, provide a brief statement of the reasons for termination of the relationship.

Exhibit F — Services

A description in narrative form of each service or function performed by the information processor. Include a description of all procedures utilized for the collection, processing, distribution, validation and publication of information with respect to orders and trades in securities.

Exhibit G — System and Operations

1. Describe the manner of operation of the System of the information processor that collects, processes, distributes and publishes information in accordance with National Instruments 21-101 and 23-101. This description must include the following:

    1. The means of access to the System.

    2. Procedures governing entry and display of quotations and orders in the System including data validation processes.

    3. A description of any measures used to verify the timeliness and accuracy of information received and disseminated by the System, including the processes to resolve data integrity issues identified.

    4. The hours of operation of the System.

    5. A description of the training provided to users of the System and any materials provided to the users.

2. Include a list of all computer hardware utilized by the information processor to perform the services or functions listed in Exhibit F, indicating:

    1. Manufacturer, and manufacturer's equipment and identification number.

    2. Whether purchased or leased (if leased, duration of lease and any provisions for purchase or renewal).

    3. Where such equipment (exclusive of terminals and other access devices) is physically located.

3. Provide a description of the measures or procedures implemented by the information processor to provide for the security of any system employed to perform the functions of an information processor. This must include a general description of any physical and operational safeguards designed to prevent unauthorized access to the system.

4. Provide a description of all backup systems which are designed to prevent interruptions in the performance of any information providing functions as a result of technical malfunctions or otherwise in the system itself, in any permitted input or output system connection or as a result of any independent source.

5. Describe the business continuity and disaster recovery plans of the information processor, and provide any relevant documentation.

6. List each type of interruption which has lasted for more than two minutes and has occurred within the six (6) months preceding the date of the filing, including the date of each interruption, the cause and duration. Provide the total number of interruptions which have lasted two minutes or less.

7. Describe the procedures for reviewing system capacity, and indicate current and future capacity estimates.

8. Quantify in appropriate units of measure the limits on the information processor's capacity to receive, collect, process, store or display the data elements included within each function.

9. Identify the factors (mechanical, electronic or other) which account for the current limitations on the capacity to receive, collect, process, store or display the data elements included within each function described in section 8 above.

10. Describe the procedures for conducting stress tests.

Exhibit H — Outsourcing

Where the information processor has outsourced the operation of any aspect of the services listed in Exhibit F to an arms-length third party, including any function related to the collection, consolidation, and dissemination of data, provide the following information:

1. Name and address of person or company to whom the function has been outsourced.

2. A description of the nature and extent of the contractual or other agreement with the information processor, and the roles and responsibilities of the arms-length third party under the arrangement.

3. A copy of each material contract relating to any outsourced function.

Exhibit I — Financial Viability

1. Provide a business plan with pro forma financial statements and estimates of revenue.

2. Discuss the financial viability of the information processor in the context of having sufficient financial resources to properly perform its functions.

Exhibit J — Fees and Revenue Sharing

1. Provide a complete list of all fees and other charges imposed, or to be imposed, by or on behalf of the information processor for its information services. This would include all fees to provide data and fees to receive the data from the information processor.

2. Where arrangements exist to share revenue from the sale of data disseminated by the information processor with marketplaces, inter-dealer bond brokers and dealers that provide data to the information processor in accordance with National Instrument 21-101, provide a complete description of the arrangements and the basis for these arrangements.

Exhibit K — Reporting to the Information Processor

1. List all persons and entities that provide data to the information processor in accordance with the requirements of National Instrument 21-101.

2. Provide a complete set of all forms, agreements and other materials pertaining to the provision of data to the information processor.

3. A description of any specifications or criteria required of marketplaces, inter-dealer bond brokers or dealers that provide securities information to the information processor for collection, processing for distribution or publication. Identify those specifications or criteria which limit, are interpreted to limit or have the effect of limiting access to or use of any services provided by the information processor and state the reasons for imposing such specifications or criteria.

4. For each instance during the past year in which any person or entity has been prohibited or limited to provide data by the information processor, indicate the name of each such person or entity and the reason for the prohibition or limitation.

Exhibit L — Access to the Services of the Information Processor

1. A list of all persons and entities who presently subscribe or who have notified the information processor of their intention to subscribe to the services of the information processor.

2. The form of contract governing the terms by which persons may subscribe to the services of an information processor.

3. A description of any specifications or criteria which limit, are interpreted to limit or have the effect of limiting access to or use of any services provided by the information processor and state the reasons for imposing such specifications or criteria. This applies to limits relating to providing information to the information processor and the limits relating to accessing the consolidated feed distributed by the information processor.

4. For each instance during the past year in which any person has been prohibited or limited in respect of access to services offered by the information processor, indicate the name of each such person and the reason for the prohibition or limitation.

Exhibit M — Selection of Securities for which Information Must Be Reported to the Information Processor

Where the information processor is responsible for making a determination of the data which must be reported, including the securities for which information must be reported in accordance with National Instrument 21-101, describe the manner of selection and communication of these securities. This description must include the following:

1. The criteria used to determine the securities for which information must be reported and the data which must be reported to the information processor.

2. The process for selection of the securities, including a description of the parties consulted in the process and the frequency of the selection process.

3. The process to communicate the securities selected and data to be reported to the marketplaces, inter-dealer bond brokers and dealers providing the information as required by National Instrument 21-101. The description must include where this information is located.

Certificate of Information Processor

The undersigned certifies that the information given in this report is true and correct.

DATED at ....this .... day of .... 20..........

.... (Name of information processor)

.... (Name of director, officer or partner — please type or print)

.... (Signature of director, officer or partner)

.... (Official capacity — please type or print)

Form 21-101F6 — Cessation of Operations Report for Information Processor

1. Identification:

   A. Full name of information processor:

   ....

   B. Name(s) under which business is conducted, if different from item 1A:

   ....

2. Date information processor proposes to cease carrying on business:

   ....

3. If cessation of business was involuntary, date information processor ceased to carry on business:

   ....

Exhibits

File all Exhibits with the Cessation of Operations Report. For each Exhibit, include the name of the information processor, the date of filing of the Exhibit and the date as of which the information is accurate (if different from the date of the filing). If any Exhibit required is inapplicable, a statement to that effect must be furnished instead of such Exhibit.

Exhibit A

The reasons for the information processor ceasing to carry on business.

Exhibit B

A list of each of the securities the information processor displays.

Certificate of Information Processor

The undersigned certifies that the information given in this report is true and correct.

DATED at .... this .... day of .... 20..........

.... (Name of information processor)

.... (Name of director, officer or partner — please type or print)

.... (Signature of director, officer or partner)

.... (Official capacity — please type or print)

Companion Policy 21-101CP — To National Instrument 21-101 Marketplace Operation

Table of Contents

Part 2: MARKET PARTICIPANTS

16.4 Systems Requirements

PART 1 — INTRODUCTION

1.1 Introduction — Exchanges, quotation and trade reporting systems and ATSs are marketplaces that provide a market facility or venue on which securities can be traded. The areas of interest from a regulatory perspective are in many ways similar for each of these marketplaces since they may have similar trading activities. The regulatory regime for exchanges and quotation and trade reporting systems arises from the securities legislation of the various jurisdictions. Exchanges and quotation and trade reporting systems are recognized under orders from the Canadian securities regulatory authorities, with various terms and conditions of recognition. ATSs, which are not recognized as exchanges or quotation and trade reporting systems, are regulated under National Instrument 21-101 *Marketplace Operation* (the Instrument) and National Instrument 23-101 *Trading Rules* (NI 23-101). The Instrument and NI 23-101, which were adopted at a time when new types of markets were emerging, provide the regulatory framework that allows and regulates the operation of multiple marketplaces.

The purpose of this Companion Policy is to state the views of the Canadian securities regulatory authorities on various matters related to the Instrument, including:

(a) a discussion of the general approach taken by the Canadian securities regulatory authorities in, and the general regulatory purpose for, the Instrument; and

(b) the interpretation of various terms and provisions in the Instrument.

1.2 Definition of Exchange-Traded Security — Section 1.1 of the Instrument defines an "exchange-traded security" as a security that is listed on a recognized exchange or is quoted on a recognized quotation and trade reporting system or is listed on an exchange or quoted on a quotation and trade reporting system that is recognized for the purposes of the Instrument and NI 23-101.

If a security trades on a recognized exchange or recognized quotation and trade reporting system on a "when issued" basis, as defined in IIROC's Universal Market Integrity Rules, the security would be considered to be listed on that recognized exchange or quoted on that recognized quotation and trade reporting system and would therefore be an exchange-traded security.

If no "when issued" market has been posted by a recognized exchange or recognized quotation and trade reporting system for a security, an ATS may not allow this security to be traded on a "when issued" basis on its marketplace.

A security that is inter-listed would be considered to be an exchange-traded security. A security that is listed on a foreign exchange or quoted on a foreign quotation and trade reporting system, but is not listed or quoted on a domestic exchange or quotation and trade reporting system, falls within the definition of "foreign exchange-traded security".

1.3 Definition of Foreign Exchange-Traded Security — The definition of foreign exchange-traded security includes a reference to ordinary members of the International Organization of Securities Commissions (IOSCO). To determine the current list of ordinary members, reference should be made to the IOSCO website at www.iosco.org.

1.4 Definition of Regulation Services Provider — The definition of regulation services provider is meant to capture a third party provider that provides regulation services to marketplaces. A recognized exchange or recognized quotation and trade reporting system would not be a regulation services provider if it only conducts these regulatory services for its own marketplace or an affiliated marketplace.

PART 2 — MARKETPLACE

2.1 Marketplace — (1) The Instrument uses the term "marketplace" to encompass the different types of trading systems that match trades. A marketplace is an exchange, a quotation and trade reporting system or an ATS. Subparagraphs (a)(iii) and (a)(iv) of the definition of "marketplace" describe marketplaces that the Canadian securities regulatory authorities consider to be ATSs. A dealer that internalizes its orders for exchange-traded securities and does not execute and print the trades on an exchange or quotation and trade reporting system in accordance with the rules of the exchange or the quotation and trade reporting system (including an exemption from those rules) is considered to be a marketplace pursuant to paragraph (d) of the definition of "marketplace" and an ATS.

(2) Two of the characteristics of a "marketplace" are

(a) that it brings together orders for securities of multiple buyers and sellers; and

(b) that it uses established, non-discretionary methods under which the orders interact with each other.

(3) The Canadian securities regulatory authorities consider that a person or company brings together orders for securities if it

(a) displays, or otherwise represents to marketplace participants, trading interests entered on the system; or

(b) receives orders centrally for processing and execution (regardless of the level of automation used).

(4) The Canadian securities regulatory authorities are of the view that "established, non-discretionary methods" include any methods that dictate the terms of trading among the multiple buyers and sellers entering orders on the system. Such methods include providing a trading facility or setting rules governing trading among marketplace participants. Common examples include a traditional exchange and a computer system, whether comprised of software, hardware, protocols, or any combination thereof, through which orders interact, or any other trading mechanism that provides a means or location for the bringing together and execution of orders. Rules imposing execution priorities, such as time and price priority rules, would be "established, non-discretionary methods."

(5) The Canadian securities regulatory authorities do not consider the following systems to be marketplaces for purposes of the Instrument:

(a) A system operated by a person or company that only permits one seller to sell its securities, such as a system that permits issuers to sell their own securities to investors.

(b) A system that merely routes orders for execution to a facility where the orders are executed.

(c) A system that posts information about trading interests, without facilities for execution.

In the first two cases, the criteria of multiple buyers and sellers would not be met. In the last two cases, routing systems and bulletin boards do not establish non-discretionary methods under which parties entering orders interact with each other.

(6) A person or company operating any of the systems described in subsection (5) should consider whether the person or company is required to be registered as a dealer under securities legislation.

(7) Inter-dealer bond brokers that conduct traditional inter-dealer bond broker activity have a choice as to how to be regulated under the Instrument and NI 23-101. Each inter-dealer bond broker can choose to be subject to IIROC Rule 36 and IIROC Rule 2100, fall within the definition of inter-dealer bond broker in the Instrument and be subject to the transparency requirements of Part 8 of the Instrument. Alternatively, the inter-dealer bond broker can choose to be an ATS and comply with the provisions of the Instrument and NI 23-101 applicable to a marketplace and an ATS. An inter-dealer bond broker that chooses to be an ATS will not be subject to Rule 36 or IIROC Rule 2100, but will be subject to all other IIROC requirements applicable to a dealer.

(8) Section 1.2 of the Instrument contains an interpretation of the definition of "marketplace". The Canadian securities regulatory authorities do not consider a system that only routes unmatched orders to a marketplace for execution to be a marketplace. If a dealer uses a system to match buy and sell orders or pair orders with contra-side orders outside of a marketplace and route the matched or paired orders to a marketplace as a cross, the Canadian securities regulatory authorities may consider the dealer to be operating a marketplace under subparagraph (a)(iii) of the definition of "marketplace". The Canadian securities regulatory authorities encourage dealers that operate or plan to operate such a system to meet with the applicable securities regulatory authority to discuss the operation of the system and whether the dealer's system falls within the definition of "marketplace".

PART 3 — CHARACTERISTICS OF EXCHANGES, QUOTATION AND TRADE REPORTING SYSTEMS AND ATSS

3.1 Exchange — (1) Securities legislation of most jurisdictions does not define the term "exchange".

(2) The Canadian securities regulatory authorities generally consider a marketplace, other than a quotation and trade reporting system, to be an exchange for purposes of securities legislation, if the marketplace

(a) requires an issuer to enter into an agreement in order for the issuer's securities to trade on the marketplace, i.e., the marketplace provides a listing function;

(b) provides, directly, or through one or more marketplace participants, a guarantee of a two-sided market for a security on a continuous or reasonably continuous basis, i.e., the marketplace has one or more marketplace participants that guarantee that a bid and an ask will be posted for a security on a continuous or reasonably continuous basis. For example, this type of liquidity guarantee can be carried out on exchanges through traders acting as principal such as registered traders, specialists or market makers;

(c) sets requirements governing the conduct of marketplace participants, in addition to those requirements set by the marketplace in respect of the method of trading or algorithm used by those marketplace participants to execute trades on the system (see subsection (3)); or

(d) disciplines marketplace participants, in addition to discipline by exclusion from trading, i.e., the marketplace can levy fines or take enforcement action.

(3) An ATS that requires a subscriber to agree to comply with the requirements of a regulation services provider as part of its contract with that subscriber is not setting "requirements governing the conduct of subscribers". In addition, marketplaces are not precluded from imposing credit conditions on subscribers or requiring subscribers to submit financial information to the marketplace.

(4) The criteria in subsection 3.1(2) are not exclusive and there may be other instances in which the Canadian securities regulatory authorities will consider a marketplace to be an exchange.

3.2 Quotation and Trade Reporting System — (1) Securities legislation in certain jurisdictions contains the concept of a quotation and trade reporting system. A quotation and trade reporting system is defined under securities legislation in those jurisdictions as a person or company, other than an exchange or registered dealer, that operates facilities that permit the dissemination of price quotations for the purchase and sale of securities and reports of completed transactions in securities for the exclusive use of registered dealers. A person or company that carries on business as a vendor of market data or a bulletin board with no execution facilities would not normally be considered to be a quotation and trade reporting system.

(2) A quotation and trade reporting system is considered to have "quoted" a security if

(a) the security has been subject to a listing or quoting process, and

(b) the issuer issuing the security or the dealer trading the security has entered into an agreement with the quotation and trade reporting system to list or quote the security.

3.3 Definition of an ATS — (1) In order to be an ATS for the purposes of the Instrument, a marketplace cannot engage in certain activities or meet certain criteria such as

(a) requiring listing agreements,

(b) having one or more marketplace participants that guarantee that a two-sided market will be posted for a security on a continuous or reasonably continuous basis,

(c) setting requirements governing the conduct of subscribers, in addition to those requirements set by the marketplace in respect of the method of trading or algorithm used by those subscribers to execute trades on the system, and

(d) disciplining subscribers.

A marketplace, other than a quotation and trade reporting system, that engages in any of these activities or meets these criteria would, in the view of the Canadian securities regulatory authorities, be an exchange and would have to be recognized as such in order to carry on business, unless exempted from this requirement by the Canadian securities regulatory authorities.

(2) An ATS can establish trading algorithms that provide that a trade takes place if certain events occur. These algorithms are not considered to be "requirements governing the conduct of subscribers".

(3) A marketplace that would otherwise meet the definition of an ATS in the Instrument may apply to the Canadian securities regulatory authorities for recognition as an exchange.

3.4 Requirements Applicable to ATSs — (1) Part 6 of the Instrument applies only to an ATS that is not a recognized exchange or a member of a recognized exchange or an exchange recognized for the purposes of the Instrument and NI 23-101. If an ATS is recognized as an exchange, the provisions of the Instrument relating to marketplaces and recognized exchanges apply.

(2) If the ATS is a member of an exchange, the rules, policies and other similar instruments of the exchange apply to the ATS.

(3) Under paragraph 6.1(a) of the Instrument, an ATS that is not a member of a recognized exchange or an exchange recognized for the purposes of the Instrument and NI 23-101 must register as a dealer if it wishes to carry on business. Unless otherwise specified, an ATS registered as a dealer is subject

to all of the requirements applicable to dealers under securities legislation, including the requirements imposed by the Instrument and NI 23-101. An ATS will be carrying on business in a local jurisdiction if it provides direct access to subscribers located in that jurisdiction.

(4) If an ATS registered as a dealer in one jurisdiction in Canada provides access in another jurisdiction in Canada to subscribers who are not registered dealers under securities legislation, the ATS must be registered in that other jurisdiction. However, if all of the ATS's subscribers in the other jurisdiction are registered as dealers in that other jurisdiction, the securities regulatory authority in the other jurisdiction may consider granting the ATS an exemption from the requirement to register as a dealer under paragraph 6.1(a) and all other requirements in the Instrument and in NI 23-101 and from the registration requirements of securities legislation. In determining if the exemption is in the public interest, a securities regulatory authority will consider a number of factors, including whether the ATS is registered in another jurisdiction and whether the ATS deals only with registered dealers in that jurisdiction.

(5) Paragraph 6.1(b) of the Instrument prohibits an ATS to which the provisions of the Instrument apply from carrying on business unless it is a member of a self-regulatory entity. Membership in a self-regulatory entity is required for purposes of membership in the Canadian Investor Protection Fund, capital requirements and clearing and settlement procedures. At this time, the IIROC is the only entity that would come within the definition.

(6) Any registration exemptions that may otherwise be applicable to a dealer under securities legislation are not available to an ATS, even though it is registered as a dealer (except as provided in the Instrument), because of the fact that it is also a marketplace and different considerations apply.

(7) Subsection 6.7(1) of the Instrument requires an ATS to notify the securities regulatory authority if one of three thresholds is met or exceeded. Upon being informed that one of the thresholds is met or exceeded, the securities regulatory authority intends to review the ATS and its structure and operations in order to consider whether the person or company operating the ATS should be considered to be an exchange for purposes of securities legislation or if additional terms and conditions should be placed on the registration of the ATS. The securities regulatory authority intends to conduct this review because each of these thresholds may be indicative of an ATS having significant market presence in a type of security, such that it would be more appropriate that the ATS be regulated as an exchange. If more than one Canadian securities regulatory authority is conducting this review, the reviewing jurisdictions intend to coordinate their review. The volume thresholds referred to in subsection 6.7(1) of the Instrument are based on the type of security. The Canadian securities regulatory authorities consider a type of security to refer to a distinctive category of security such as equity securities, debt securities or options.

(8) Any marketplace that is required to provide notice under section 6.7 of the Instrument will determine the calculation based on publicly available information.

PART 4 — RECOGNITION AS AN EXCHANGE OR QUOTATION AND TRADE REPORTING SYSTEM

4.1 Recognition as an Exchange or Quotation and Trade Reporting System — (1) In determining whether to recognize an exchange or quotation and trade reporting system, the Canadian securities regulatory authorities must determine whether it is in the public interest to do so.

(2) In determining whether it is in the public interest to recognize an exchange or quotation and trade reporting system, the Canadian securities regulatory authorities will look at a number of factors, including

(a) the manner in which the exchange or quotation and trade reporting system proposes to comply with the Instrument;

(b) whether the exchange or quotation and trade reporting system has fair and meaningful representation on its governing body, in the context of the nature and structure of the exchange or quotation and trade reporting system;

(c) whether the exchange or quotation and trade reporting system has sufficient financial resources for the proper performance of its functions;

(d) whether the rules, policies and other similar instruments of the exchange or quotation and trade reporting system ensure that its business is conducted in an orderly manner so as to afford protection to investors;

(e) whether the exchange or quotation and trade reporting system has policies and procedures to effectively identify and manage conflicts of interest arising from its operation or the services it provides;

(f) whether the requirements of the exchange or quotation and trade reporting system relating to access to its services are fair and reasonable; and

(g) whether the exchange or quotation and trade reporting system's process for setting fees is fair, transparent and appropriate, and whether the fees are equitably allocated among the participants, issuers and other users of services, do not have the effect of creating barriers to access and at the same time ensure that the exchange or quotation and trade reporting system has sufficient financial resources for the proper performance of its functions.

4.2 Process — Although the basic requirements or criteria for recognition of an exchange or quotation and trade reporting system may be similar in various jurisdictions, the precise requirements and the process for seeking a recognition or an exemption from recognition in each jurisdiction is determined by that jurisdiction.

PART 5 — ORDERS

5.1 Orders — (1) The term "order" is defined in section 1.1 of the Instrument as a firm indication by a person or company, acting as either principal or agent, of a willingness to buy or sell a security. By virtue of this definition, a marketplace that displays good faith, non-firm indications of interest, including, but not limited to, indications of interest to buy or sell a particular security without either prices or quantities associated with those indications, is not displaying "orders". However, if those prices or quantities are implied and determinable, for example, by knowing the features of the marketplace, the indications of interest may be considered an order.

(2) The terminology used is not determinative of whether an indication of interest constitutes an order. Instead, whether or not an indication is "firm" will depend on what actually takes place between the buyer and seller. At a minimum, the Canadian securities regulatory authorities will consider an indication to be firm if it can be executed without further discussion between the person or company entering the indication and the counterparty (i.e. the indication is "actionable"). The Canadian securities regulatory authorities would consider an indication of interest to be actionable if it includes sufficient information to enable it to be executed without communicating with the marketplace participant that entered the order. Such information may include the symbol of the security, side (buy or sell), size, and price. The information may be explicitly stated, or it may be implicit and determinable based on the features of the marketplace. Even if the person or company must give its subsequent agreement to an execution, the Canadian securities regulatory authorities will still consider the indication to be firm if this subsequent agreement is always, or almost always, granted so that the agreement is largely a formality. For instance, an indication where there is a clear or prevailing presumption that a trade will take place at the indicated or an implied price, based on understandings or past dealings, will be viewed as an order.

Part 2: MARKET PARTICIPANTS

(3) A firm indication of a willingness to buy or sell a security includes bid or offer quotations, market orders, limit orders and any other priced orders. For the purpose of sections 7.1, 7.3, 8.1 and 8.2 of the Instrument, the Canadian securities regulatory authorities do not consider special terms orders that are not immediately executable or that trade in special terms books, such as all-or-none, minimum fill or cash or delayed delivery, to be orders that must be provided to an information processor or, if there is no information processor, to an information vendor for consolidation.

(4) The securities regulatory authority may consider granting an exemption from the pre-trade transparency requirements in sections 7.1, 7.3, 8.1 and/or 8.2 of the Instrument to a marketplace for orders that result from a request for quotes or facility that allows negotiation between two parties provided that

(a) order details are shown only to the negotiating parties,

(b) other than as provided by paragraph (a), no actionable indication of interest or order is displayed by either party or the marketplace, and

(c) each order entered on the marketplace meets the size threshold set by a regulation services provider as provided in subsection 7.1(2) of the Instrument.

(5) The determination of whether an order has been placed does not turn on the level of automation used. Orders can be given over the telephone, as well as electronically.

PART 6 — MARKETPLACE INFORMATION AND FINANCIAL STATEMENTS

6.1 Forms Filed by Marketplaces — (1) The definition of marketplace includes exchanges, quotation and trade reporting systems and ATSs. The legal entity that is recognized as an exchange or quotation and trade reporting system, or registered as a dealer in the case of an ATS, owns and operates the market or trading facility. In some cases, the entity may own and operate more than one trading facility. In such cases the marketplace may file separate forms in respect of each trading facility, or it may choose to file one form covering all of the different trading facilities. If the latter alternative is chosen, the marketplace must clearly identify the facility to which the information or changes apply.

(2) The forms filed by a marketplace under the Instrument will be kept confidential. The Canadian securities regulatory authorities are of the view that the forms contain proprietary financial, commercial and technical information and that the interests of the filers in non-disclosure outweigh the desirability of adhering to the principle that the forms be available for public inspection.

(3) While initial Forms 21-101F1 and 21-101F2 and amendments thereto are kept confidential, certain Canadian securities regulatory authorities may publish a summary of the information included in the forms filed by a marketplace, or information related to significant changes to the forms of a marketplace, where the Canadian securities regulatory authorities are of the view that a certain degree of transparency for certain aspects of a marketplace would allow investors and industry participants to be better informed as to how securities trade on the marketplace.

(4) Under subsection 3.2(1) of the Instrument, a marketplace is required to file an amendment to the information provided in Form 21-101F1 or Form 21-101F2, as applicable, at least 45 days prior to implementing a significant change. The Canadian securities regulatory authorities consider a significant change to be a change that could significantly impact a marketplace, its systems, its market structure, its marketplace participants or their systems, investors, issuers or the Canadian capital markets

A change would be considered to significantly impact the marketplace if it is likely to give rise to potential conflicts of interest, to limit access to the services of a marketplace, introduce changes to the structure of the marketplace or result in costs, such as implementation costs, to marketplace participants, investors or, if applicable, the regulation services provider.

The following types of changes are considered to be significant changes as they would always have a significant impact:

(a) changes in the structure of the marketplace, including procedures governing how orders are entered, displayed (if applicable), executed, how they interact, are cleared and settled;

(b) new or changes to order types, and

(c) changes in the fees and the fee model of the marketplace.

The following may be considered by the Canadian securities regulatory authorities as significant changes, depending on whether they have a significant impact:

(d) new or changes to the services provided by the marketplace, including the hours of operation;

(e) new or changes to the means of access to the market or facility and its services;

(f) new or changes to types of securities traded on the marketplace;

(g) new or changes to types of securities listed on exchanges or quoted on quotation and trade reporting systems;

(h) new or changes to types of marketplace participants;

(i) changes to the systems and technology used by the marketplace that support order entry, order routing, execution, trade reporting, trade comparison, data feeds, co-location and, if applicable, market surveillance and trade clearing, including those affecting capacity;

(j) changes to the corporate governance of the marketplace, including changes to the composition requirements for the board of directors or any board committees and changes to the mandates of the board of directors or any board committees;

(k) changes in control over marketplaces;

(l) changes in affiliates that provide services to or on behalf of the marketplace;

(m) new or changes in outsourcing arrangements for key marketplace services or systems; and

(n) new or changes in custody arrangements.

(5) Changes to information in Form 21-101F1 or Form 21-101F2 that

(a) do not have a significant impact on the marketplace, its market structure, marketplace participants, investors, issuers or the Canadian capital markets, or

(b) are housekeeping or administrative changes such as

(i) changes in the routine processes, policies, practices, or administration of the marketplace,

(ii) changes due to standardization of terminology,

(iii) corrections of spelling or typographical errors,

(iv) necessary changes to conform to applicable regulatory or other legal requirements,

(v) minor system or technology changes that would not significantly impact the system or its capacity, and

(vi) changes to the list of marketplace participants and the list of all persons or entities denied or limited access to the marketplace,

would be filed in accordance with the requirements outlined in subsection 3.2(3) of the Instrument.

(6) As indicated in subsection (4) above, the Canadian securities regulatory authorities consider a change in a marketplace's fees or fee model to be a significant change. However, the Canadian securities regulatory authorities recognize that in the current, competitive multiple marketplace environment, which may at times require that frequent changes be made to the fees or fee model of marketplaces, marketplaces may need to implement fee changes within tight timeframes. To facilitate this process, subsection 3.2(2) of the Instrument provides that marketplaces may provide information describing the change in fees or fee model in a shorter timeframe, at least seven business days before the expected implementation date of the change in fees or fee model.

(7) For the changes referred to in subsection 3.2(3) of the Instrument, the Canadian securities regulatory authorities may review these filings to ascertain the appropriateness of the categorization of such filings. The marketplace will be notified in writing if there is disagreement with respect to the categorization of the filing.

(8) The Canadian securities regulatory authorities will make best efforts to review amendments to Forms 21-101F1 and 21-101F2 within the timelines specified in subsections 3.2(1) and (2) of the Instrument. However, where the changes are complex, raise regulatory concerns, or when additional information is required, the period for review may exceed these timeframes. The Canadian securities regulatory authorities will review changes to the information in Forms 21-101F1 and 21-101F2 in accordance with staff practices in each jurisdiction.

(8.1) In order to ensure records regarding the information in a marketplace's Form 21-101F1 or Form 21-101F2 are kept up to date, subsection 3.2(4) of the Instrument requires the chief executive officer of a marketplace to certify, within 30 days after the end of each calendar year, that the information contained in the marketplace's Form 21-101F1 or Form 21-101F2 as applicable, is true, correct and complete and the marketplace is operating as described in the applicable form. This certification is required at the same time as the updated and consolidated Form 21-101F1 or Form 21-101F2, as applicable, is required to be filed pursuant to subsection 3.2(5) of the Instrument. The certification under subsection 3.2(4) is also separate and apart from the form of certification in Form 21-101F1 and Form 21-101F2.

(8.2) The Canadian securities regulatory authorities expect that the certifications provided pursuant to subsection 3.2(4) of the Instrument will be preserved by the marketplace as part of its books and records obligation under Part 11 of the Instrument.

(9) Section 3.3 of the Instrument requires a marketplace to file Form 21-101F3 by the following dates: April 30 (for the calendar quarter ending March 31), July 30 (for the calendar quarter ending June 30), October 30 (for the calendar quarter ending September 30) and January 30 (for the calendar quarter ending December 31).

6.2 Filing of Financial Statements — Part 4 of the Instrument sets out the financial reporting requirements applicable to marketplaces. Subsections 4.1(2) and 4.2(2) respectively require an ATS to file audited financial statements initially, together with Form 21-101F2, and on an annual basis thereafter. These financial statements may be in the same form as those filed with IIROC. The annual audited financial statements may be filed with the Canadian securities regulatory authorities at the same time as they are filed with IIROC.

PART 7 — MARKETPLACE REQUIREMENTS

7.1 Access Requirements — (1) Section 5.1 of the Instrument sets out access requirements that apply to a marketplace. The Canadian securities regulatory authorities note that the requirements regarding access for marketplace participants do not restrict the marketplace from maintaining reasonable standards for access. The purpose of these access requirements is to ensure that rules, policies, procedures, and fees, as applicable, of the marketplace do not unreasonably create barriers to access to the services provided by the marketplace.

(2) For the purposes of complying with the order protection requirements in Part 6 of NI 23-101, a marketplace should permit fair and efficient access to

(a) a marketplace participant that directly accesses the marketplace,

(b) a person or company that is indirectly accessing the marketplace through a marketplace participant, or

(c) another marketplace routing an order to the marketplace.

The reference to "a person or company" in paragraph (b) includes a system or facility that is operated by a person or company.

(3) The reference to "services" in section 5.1 of the Instrument means all services that may be offered to a person or company and includes all services relating to order entry, trading, execution, routing, data and includes co-location.

(4) Marketplaces that send indications of interest to a selected smart order router or other system should send the information to other smart order routers or system to meet the fair access requirements of the Instrument.

(5) Marketplaces are responsible for ensuring that the fees they set are in compliance with section 5.1 of the Instrument. In assessing whether its fees unreasonably condition or limit access to its services, a marketplace should consider a number of factors, including

(a) the value of the security traded,

(b) the amount of the fee relative to the value of the security traded,

(c) the amount of fees charged by other marketplaces to execute trades in the market,

(d) with respect to market data fees, the amount of market data fees charged relative to the market share of the marketplace, and,

(e) with respect to order execution terms, including fees, whether the outcome of their application is consistent with the policy goals of order protection.

The Canadian securities regulatory authorities will consider these factors, among others, in determining whether the fees charged by a marketplace unreasonably condition or limit access to its services. With respect to trading fees, it is the view of the Canadian securities regulatory authorities that a trading fee equal to or greater than the minimum trading increment as defined in IIROC's Universal Market Integrity Rules, as amended, would unreasonably condition or limit access to a marketplace's services as it would be inconsistent with the policy goals of order protection. Trading fees below the minimum trading increment may also unreasonably condition or limit access to a marketplace's services when taking into account factors including those listed above.

7.2 Public Interest Rules — Section 5.3 of the Instrument sets out the requirements applicable to the rules, policies and similar instruments adopted by recognized exchanges and recognized quotation and trade reporting systems. These requirements acknowledge that recognized exchanges and quotation and trade reporting systems perform regulatory functions. The Instrument does not require the application of these requirements to an ATS's trading requirements. This is because, unlike exchanges, ATSs are not permitted to perform regulatory functions, other than setting requirements regarding conduct in respect of the trading by subscribers on the marketplace, i.e. requirements related to the method of trading or algorithms used by their subscribers to execute trades in the system. However, it is the expectation of the Canadian securities regulatory authority that the requirement in section 5.7 of the Instrument that marketplaces take reasonable steps to ensure they operate in a manner that does not interfere with the maintenance of fair and orderly markets, applies to an ATS's requirements. Such requirements may include those that deal with subscriber qualification, access to the marketplace, how orders are entered, interact, execute, clear and settle.

7.3 Compliance Rules — Section 5.4 of the Instrument requires a recognized exchange and recognized quotation and trade reporting system to have appropriate procedures to deal with violations of rules, policies or other similar instruments of the exchange or quotation and trade reporting system. This section does not preclude enforcement action by any other person or company, including the Canadian securities regulatory authorities or the regulation services provider.

7.4 Filing of Rules — Section 5.5 of the Instrument requires a recognized exchange and recognized quotation and trade reporting system to file all rules, policies and other similar instruments and amendments as required by the securities regulatory authority. Initially, all rules, policies and other similar instruments will be reviewed before implementation by the exchange or quotation and trade reporting system. Subsequent to recognition, the securities regulatory authority may develop and implement a protocol that will set out the procedures to be followed with respect to the review and approval of rules, policies and other similar instruments and amendments.

7.5 Review of Rules — The Canadian securities regulatory authorities review the rules, policies and similar instruments of a recognized exchange or recognized quotation and trade reporting system in accordance with the recognition order and rule protocol issued by the jurisdiction in which the exchange or quotation and trade reporting system is recognized. The rules of recognized exchanges and quotation and trade reporting systems are included in their rulebooks, and the principles and requirements applicable to these rules are set out in section 5.3 of the Instrument. For an ATS, whose trading requirements, including any trading rules, policies or practices, are incorporated in Form 21-101F2, any changes would be filed in accordance with the filing requirements applicable to changes to information in Form 21-101F2 set out in subsections 3.2(1) and 3.2(3) of the Instrument and reviewed by the Canadian securities regulatory authorities in accordance with staff practices in each jurisdiction.

7.6 Fair and Orderly Markets — (1) Section 5.7 of the Instrument establishes the requirement that a marketplace take reasonable steps to ensure it operates in a way that does not interfere with the maintenance of fair and orderly markets. This applies both to the operation of the marketplace itself and to the impact of the marketplace's operations on the Canadian market as a whole.

(2) This section does not impose a responsibility on the marketplace to oversee the conduct of its marketplace participants, unless the marketplace is an exchange or quotation and trade reporting system that has assumed responsibility for monitoring the conduct of its marketplace participants directly rather than through a regulation services provider. However, marketplaces are expected in the normal course to monitor order entry and trading activity for compliance with the marketplace's own operational policies and procedures. They should also alert the regulation services provider if they become aware that disorderly or disruptive order entry or trading may be occurring, or of possible violations of applicable regulatory requirements.

(3) Part of taking reasonable steps to ensure that a marketplace's operations do not interfere with fair and orderly markets necessitates ensuring that its operations support compliance with regulatory requirements including applicable rules of a regulation services provider. This does not mean that a marketplace must system-enforce all regulatory requirements. However, it should not operate in a manner that to the best of its knowledge would cause marketplace participants to breach regulatory requirements when trading on the marketplace.

7.7 Confidential Treatment of Trading Information — (0.1) The Canadian securities regulatory authorities are of the view that it is in the public interest for capital markets research to be conducted. Since marketplace participants' order and trade information may be needed to conduct this research, subsection 5.10(1.1) of the Instrument allows a marketplace to release a marketplace participant's order or trade information without obtaining its written consent, provided this information is used solely for capital markets research and only if certain terms and conditions are met. Subsection 5.10(1.1) is not intended to impose any obligation on a marketplace to disclose information if requested by a researcher and the marketplace may choose to maintain its marketplace participants' order and trade information in confidence. However, if the marketplace decides to disclose this information, it must ensure that certain terms and conditions are met to ensure that the marketplace participant's information is not misused.

(0.2) In order for a marketplace to disclose a marketplace participant's order or trade information, subparagraphs 5.10(1.1)(a)-(b) of the Instrument require a marketplace to reasonably believe that the information will be used by the recipient solely for the purposes of capital markets research and to reasonably believe that if information identifying, directly or indirectly, a marketplace participant, or a client of the marketplace participant is released, the information is necessary for the research and that the purpose of the research is not intended to identify the marketplace participant or client or to identify a trading strategy, transactions, or market positions of the marketplace participant or client. The Canadian securities regulatory authorities expect that a marketplace will make sufficient inquiries of the recipient of the information in order for the marketplace to sustain a reasonable belief that the information will be used by the recipient only for capital markets research. Where the information to be released to the recipient could identify a marketplace participant or a client of a marketplace participant, the Canadian securities regulatory authorities also expect the marketplace to make sufficient inquiries of the recipient in order for the marketplace to sustain a reasonable belief that the information identifying, directly or indirectly, a marketplace participant or its client is required for purposes of the research and that the purpose of the research is not to identify a particular marketplace participant or a client of the marketplace participant or to identify a trading strategy, transactions, or market positions of a particular marketplace participant or a client of the marketplace participant.

(0.3) In considering releasing order or trade information, the Canadian securities regulatory authorities expect a marketplace to exercise caution regarding information that could disclose the identity of a marketplace participant or client of the marketplace participant. In particular, a marketplace may only release information in any order entry field that would identify the marketplace participant or client, using a broker number, trader ID, or DEA client identifier, if it reasonably believes that this information is required for the research.

(0.4) Subparagraph 5.10(1.1)(c) of the Instrument requires a marketplace that intends to provide its marketplace participants' order and trade information to a researcher to enter into a written agreement with each person or company that will receive such information. Subparagraph 5.10(1.1)(c)(i) of the Instrument requires the agreement to provide that the person or company agrees to use the order and trade information only for capital markets research purposes. In the view of the Canadian securities regulatory authorities, commercialization of the information by the recipient, for example by using the information for the purposes of trading, advising others to trade or for reverse engineering a trading strategy, would not constitute use of the information for capital markets research purposes.

(0.5) Subparagraph 5.10(1.1)(c)(i) of the Instrument provides that the agreement must also prohibit the recipient from sharing the marketplace participants' order and trade data with any other person or company, such as a research assistant, without the marketplace's consent. The marketplace will be responsible for determining what steps are necessary to ensure the other person or company receiving the marketplace participants' data is not misusing this data. For example, the marketplace may enter into a similar agreement with each individual or company that has access to the data.

(0.6) To protect the identity of particular marketplace participants or their customers, subparagraph 5.10(1.1)(c)(i) of the Instrument requires the agreement to provide that recipients will not publish or disseminate data or information that discloses, directly or indirectly, a trading strategy, transactions, or market positions of a marketplace participant or its clients. Also, to protect the confidentiality of the data, the agreement must require that the order and trade information is securely stored at all times and that the data is kept for no longer than a reasonable period of time following the completion of the research and publication process.

(0.7) The agreement must also require that the marketplace be notified of any breach or possible breach of the confidentiality of the information. Marketplaces are required to notify the appropriate securities regulatory authorities of the breach or possible breach and have the right to take all reasonable steps necessary to prevent or address a breach or possible breach of the agreement or of the confidentiality of the information provided. In the view of the Canadian securities regulatory authorities, reasonable steps in the event of an actual or apparent breach of the agreement or of the confidentiality of the information may include the marketplace seeking an injunction preventing any unauthorized use or disclosure of the information by a recipient.

(0.8) Subparagraph 5.10(1.1)(c)(ii) of the Instrument provides for a limited carve-out from the restraints on the use and disclosure of the information by a recipient for purposes of allowing those conducting peer reviews of the research to have access to the data to verify the research prior to the publication of the results of the research. In particular, clause 5.10(1.1)(c)(ii)(C) requires a marketplace to enter into a written agreement with a person or company receiving order or trade information from the marketplace that provides that the person or company may disclose information used in connection with research submitted to a publication so long as the person or company obtains a written agreement from the publisher and anyone involved in the verification of the research that provides for certain restrictions on the use and disclosure of the information by the publisher or the other person or company. A marketplace may consider requiring a person or company that proposes to disclose order or trade information pursuant to subparagraph 5.10(1.1)(c)(ii) to acknowledge that it has obtained the agreement required by clause 5.10(1.1)(c)(ii)(C) at the time that it notifies the marketplace prior to disclosing the information for verification purposes, as required by clause 5.10(1.1)(c)(ii)(B).

(1) Subsection 5.10(2) of the Instrument provides that a marketplace must not carry on business as a marketplace unless it has implemented reasonable safeguards and procedures to protect a marketplace participant's trading information. These include

> (a) limiting access to the trading information of marketplace participants, such as the identity of marketplace participants and their orders, to those employees of, or persons or companies retained by, the marketplace to operate the system or to be responsible for its compliance with securities legislation; and

> (b) having in place procedures to ensure that employees of the marketplace cannot use such information for trading in their own accounts.

(2) The procedures referred to in subsection (1) should be clear and unambiguous and presented to all employees and agents of the marketplace, whether or not they have direct responsibility for the operation of the marketplace.

(3) Nothing in section 5.10 of the Instrument prohibits a marketplace from complying with National Instrument 54-101 *Communication with Beneficial Owners of Securities of a Reporting Issuer*. This statement is necessary because an investment dealer that operates a marketplace may be an intermediary for the purposes of National Instrument 54-101, and may be required to disclose information under that Instrument.

7.8 Management of Conflicts of Interest — (1) Marketplaces are required under section 5.11 of the Instrument to maintain and ensure compliance with policies and procedures that identify and manage conflicts of interest arising from the operation of the marketplace or the services it provides. These may include conflicts, actual or perceived, related to the commercial interest of the marketplace, the interests of its owners or its operators, referral arrangements and the responsibilities and sound functioning of the marketplace. For an exchange and quotation and trade reporting system, they may also include potential conflicts between the operation of the marketplace and its regulatory responsibilities.

(2) The marketplace's policies should also take into account conflicts for owners that are marketplace participants. These may include inducements to send order flow to the marketplace to obtain a larger ownership position or to use the marketplace to trade against the clients' order flow. These policies should be disclosed as provided in paragraph 10.1(e) of the Instrument.

7.9 Outsourcing — Section 5.12 of the Instrument sets out the requirements that marketplaces that outsource any of their key services or systems to a service provider, which may include affiliates or associates of the marketplace, must meet. Generally, marketplaces are required to establish policies and procedures to evaluate and approve these outsourcing agreements. Such policies and procedures would include assessing the suitability of potential service providers and the ability of the marketplace to continue to comply with securities legislation in the event of the service provider's bankruptcy, insolvency or termination of business. Marketplaces are also required to monitor the ongoing performance of the service provider to which they outsourced key services, systems or facilities. The requirements under section 5.12 of the Instrument apply regardless of whether the outsourcing arrangements are with third-party service providers, or with affiliates of the marketplaces.

7.10 Access Arrangements with a Service Provider — If a third party service provider provides a means of access to a marketplace, section 5.13 of the Instrument requires the marketplace to ensure the third party service provider complies with the written standards for access the marketplace has established pursuant to paragraph 5.1(2)(a) of the Instrument when providing access services. A marketplace must establish written standards for granting access to each of its services under paragraph 5.1(2)(a) and the Canadian securities regulatory authorities are of the view that it is the responsibility of the marketplace to ensure that these written standards are complied with when access to its platform is provided by a third party.

PART 8 — RISK DISCLOSURE TO MARKETPLACE PARTICIPANTS

8.1 Risk disclosure to marketplace participants — Subsections 5.9(2) and 6.11(2) of the Instrument require a marketplace to obtain an acknowledgement from its marketplace participants. The acknowledgement may be obtained in a number of ways, including requesting the signature of the marketplace participant or requesting that the marketplace participant initial an initial box or check a check-off box. This may be done electronically. The acknowledgement must be specific to the information required to be disclosed under the relevant subsection and must confirm that the marketplace participant has received the required disclosure. The Canadian securities regulatory authorities are of the view that it is the responsibility of the marketplace to ensure that an acknowledgement is obtained from the marketplace participant in a timely manner.

PART 9 — INFORMATION TRANSPARENCY REQUIREMENTS FOR EXCHANGE-TRADED SECURITIES

9.1 Information Transparency Requirements for Exchange-Traded Securities — (1) Subsection 7.1(1) of the Instrument requires a marketplace that displays orders of exchange-traded securities to any person or company to provide accurate and timely information regarding those orders to an information processor as required by the information processor or, if there is no information processor, to an information vendor that meets the standards set by a regulation services provider. The Canadian securities regulatory authorities consider that a marketplace that sends information about orders of exchange-traded securities, including indications of interest that meet the definition of an order, to a smart order router is "displaying" that information. The marketplace would be subject to the transparency requirements of subsection 7.1(1) of the Instrument. The transparency requirements of subsection 7.1(1) of the Instrument do not apply to a marketplace that displays orders of exchange-traded securities to its employees or to persons or companies retained by the marketplace to assist in the operation of the marketplace, as long as these orders meet a minimum size threshold set by the regulation services provider. In other words, the only orders that are exempt from the transparency requirements are those meeting the minimum size threshold. Section 7.2 requires a marketplace to provide accurate and timely information regarding trades of exchange-traded securities that it executes to an information processor as required by the information processor or, if there is no information processor, to an information vendor that meets the standards set by a regulation services provider. Some marketplaces, such as exchanges, may be regulation services providers and will establish standards for the information vendors they use to display order and trade information to ensure that the information displayed by the information vendors is timely, accurate and promotes market integrity. If the marketplace has entered into a contract with a regulation services provider under NI 23-101, the marketplace must provide information to the regulation services provider and an information vendor that meets the standards set by that regulation services provider.

(2) In complying with sections 7.1 and 7.2 of the Instrument, any information provided by a marketplace to an information processor or information vendor must include identification of the marketplace and should contain all relevant information including details as to volume, symbol, price and time of the order or trade.

(2.1) Subsections 7.1(3) and 7.2(2) prohibit a marketplace from making available order and trade information to any person or company before it makes the information available to the information processor or, if there is no information processor, to an information vendor. The Canadian securities regulatory authorities acknowledge that there may be differences between the time at which a marketplace participant that takes in market data directly from a marketplace receives the order and trade information and the time at which a marketplace participant that takes in market data from the information processor receives the information. However, in complying with subsections 7.1(3) and 7.2(2) of the Instrument, the Canadian securities regulatory authorities expect that marketplaces will release order and trade information simultaneously to both the information processor and to persons or companies that may receive order and trade information directly from the marketplace.

(3)–(4) [Repealed]

(5) It is expected that if there are multiple regulation service providers, the standards of the various regulation service providers must be consistent. In order to maintain market integrity for securities trading in different marketplaces, the Canadian securities regulatory authorities will, through their oversight of the regulation service providers, review and monitor the standards established by all regulation service providers so that business content, service level standards, and other relevant standards are substantially similar for all regulation service providers.

PART 10 — INFORMATION TRANSPARENCY REQUIREMENTS FOR UNLISTED DEBT SECURITIES

10.1 Information Transparency Requirements for Unlisted Debt Securities — (1) The requirement to provide transparency of information regarding orders and trades of government debt securities in section 8.1 of the Instrument does not apply until January 1, 2018. The Canadian securities regulatory authorities will continue to review the transparency requirements, in order to determine if the transparency requirements summarized in subsections (2) and (3) below should be amended.

(2) The requirements of the information processor for government debt securities are as follows:

(a) Marketplaces trading government debt securities and inter-dealer bond brokers are required to provide in real time quotation information displayed on the marketplace for all bids and offers with respect to unlisted debt securities designated by the information processor, including details as to type, issuer, coupon and maturity of security, best bid price, best ask price and total disclosed volume at such prices; and

(b) Marketplaces trading government debt securities and inter-dealer bond brokers are required to provide in real time details of trades of all government debt securities designated by the information processor, including details as to the type, issuer, series, coupon and maturity, price and time of the trade and the volume traded.

(3) The requirements of the information processor for corporate debt securities are as follows:

(a) Marketplaces trading corporate debt securities, inter-dealer bond brokers and dealers trading corporate debt securities outside of a marketplace are required to provide details of trades of all corporate debt securities designated by the information processor, including details as to the type of counterparty, issuer, type of security, class, series, coupon and maturity, price and time of the trade and, subject to the caps set out below, the volume traded, no later than one hour from the time of the trade or such shorter period of time determined by the information processor. If the total par value of a trade of an investment grade corporate debt security is greater than $2 million, the trade details provided to the information processor are to be reported as "$2 million+". If the total par value of a trade of a non-investment grade corporate debt security is greater than $200,000, the trade details provided to the information processor are to be reported as "$200,000+".

(b) Although subsection 8.2(1) of the Instrument requires marketplaces to provide information regarding orders of corporate debt securities, the information processor has not required this information to be provided.

(c) A marketplace, an inter-dealer bond broker or a dealer will satisfy the requirements in subsections 8.2(1), 8.2(3), 8.2(4) and 8.2(5) of the Instrument by providing accurate and timely information to an information vendor that meets the standards set by the regulation services provider for the fixed income markets.

(4) The marketplace upon which the trade is executed will not be shown, unless the marketplace determines that it wants its name to be shown.

(5) The information processor is required to use transparent criteria and a transparent process to select government debt securities and designated corporate debt securities. The information processor is also required to make the criteria and the process publicly available.

(6) An "investment grade corporate debt security" is a corporate debt security that is rated by a designated rating organization, or its DRO affiliate, that is at or above one of the following rating categories or that is at or above a category that preceded or replaces one of the following rating categories:

Designated Rating Organization	Long Term Debt	Short Term Debt
DBRS Limited	BBB	R-2
Fitch, Inc.	BBB	F3
Moody's Canada Inc.	Baa	Prime-3
Standard & Poor's Ratings Services (Canada)	BBB	A-3

(7) A "non-investment grade corporate debt security" is a corporate debt security that is not an investment grade corporate debt security.

(8) The information processor will publish the list of designated government debt securities and designated corporate debt securities. The information processor will give reasonable notice of any change to the list.

(9) The information processor may request changes to the transparency requirements by filing an amendment to Form 21-101F5 with the Canadian securities regulatory authorities pursuant to subsection 14.2(1) of the Instrument. The Canadian securities regulatory authorities will review the amendment to Form 21-101F5 to determine whether the proposed changes are contrary to the public interest, to ensure fairness and to ensure that there is an appropriate balance between the standards of transparency and market quality (defined in terms of market liquidity and efficiency) in each area of the market. The proposed changes to the transparency requirements will also be subject to consultation with market participants.

10.2 Availability of Information — In complying with the requirements in sections 8.1 and 8.2 of the Instrument to provide accurate and timely order and trade information to an information processor or an information vendor that meets the standards set by a regulation services provider, a marketplace, an inter-dealer bond broker or dealer should not make the required order and trade information available to any other person or company on a more timely basis than it makes that information available to the information processor or information vendor.

10.3 Consolidated Feed — Section 8.3 of the Instrument requires the information processor to produce a consolidated feed in real-time showing the information provided to the information processor.

PART 11 — MARKET INTEGRATION

11.1–11.4 [Repealed]

11.5 Market Integration — Although the Canadian securities regulatory authorities have removed the concept of a market integrator, we continue to be of the view that market integration is important to our marketplaces. We expect to achieve market integration by focusing on compliance with fair access and best execution requirements. We will continue to monitor developments to ensure that the lack of a market integrator does not unduly affect the market.

PART 12 — TRANSPARENCY OF MARKETPLACE OPERATIONS

12.1 Transparency of Marketplace Operations — (1) Section 10.1 of the Instrument requires that marketplaces make publicly available certain information pertaining to their operations and services. While section 10.1 sets out the minimum disclosure requirements, marketplaces may wish to make publicly available other information, as appropriate. Where this information is included in a marketplace's rules, regulations, policies and procedures or practices that are publicly available, the marketplace need not duplicate this disclosure.

(2) Paragraph 10.1(a) requires marketplaces to disclose publicly all fees, including listing, trading, co-location, data and routing fees charged by the marketplace, an affiliate or by a third party to which services have been directly or indirectly outsourced or which directly or indirectly provides those services. This means that a marketplace is expected to publish and make readily available the schedule(s) of fees charged to any and all users of these services, including the basis for charging each fee (e.g., a per share basis for trading fees, a per subscriber basis for data fees, etc.) and would also include any fee rebate or discount and the basis for earning the rebate or discount. With respect to trading fees, it is not the intention of the Canadian securities regulatory authorities that a commission fee charged by a dealer for dealer services be disclosed in this context.

(3) Paragraph 10.1(b) requires marketplaces to disclose information on how orders are entered, interact and execute. This would include a description of the priority of execution for all order types and the types of crosses that may be executed on the marketplace. A marketplace should also disclose whether it sends information regarding indications of interest or order information to a smart order router.

(4) Paragraph 10.1(e) requires a marketplace to disclose its conflict of interest policies and procedures. For conflicts arising from the ownership of a marketplace by marketplace participants, the marketplace should include in its marketplace participant agreements a requirement that marketplace participants disclose that ownership to their clients at least quarterly. This is consistent with the marketplace participant's existing obligations to disclose conflicts of interest under National Instrument 31-103 *Registration Requirements, Exemptions and Ongoing Registrant Requirements*. A marketplace should disclose if a marketplace or affiliated entity of a marketplace intends to trade for its own account on the marketplace against or in competition with client orders.

(5) Paragraph 10.1(f) requires marketplaces to disclose a description of any arrangements where the marketplace refers its participants to the services of a third-party provider where the marketplace receives some benefit (fee rebate, payment, etc.) if the marketplace participant uses the services of the third-party service provider, and has a potential conflict of interest.

(6) Paragraph 10.1(g) requires marketplaces that offer routing services to disclose a description of how routing decisions are made. The subsection applies whether routing is done by a marketplace-owned smart order router, by an affiliate of a marketplace, or by a third-party to which routing was outsourced.

(7) Paragraph 10.1(h) applies to marketplaces that disseminate indications of interest or any information in order to attract order flow. The Instrument requires that these marketplaces make publicly available information regarding their practices regarding the dissemination of information. This would include a description of the type of information included in the indication of interest displayed, and the types of recipients of such information. For example, a marketplace would describe whether the recipients of an indication of interest are the general public, all of its subscribers, particular categories of subscribers or smart order routers operated by their subscribers or by third party vendors.

PART 13 — RECORDKEEPING REQUIREMENTS FOR MARKETPLACES

13.1 Recordkeeping Requirements for Marketplaces — Part 11 of the Instrument requires a marketplace to maintain certain records. Generally, under provisions of securities legislation, the securities regulatory authorities can require a marketplace to deliver to them any of the records required to be kept by them under securities legislation, including the records required to be maintained under Part 11.

13.2 Synchronization of Clocks — Subsections 11.5(1) and (2) of the Instrument require the synchronization of clocks with a regulation services provider that monitors the trading of the relevant securities on marketplaces, and by, as appropriate, inter-dealer bond brokers or dealers. The Canadian securities regulatory authorities are of the view that synchronization requires continual synchronization using an appropriate national time standard as chosen by a regulation services provider. Even if a marketplace has not retained a regulation services provider, its clocks should be synchronized with any regulation services provider monitoring trading in the particular securities traded on that marketplace. Each regulation services provider will monitor the information that it receives from all marketplaces, dealers and, if appropriate, inter-dealer bond brokers, to ensure that the clocks are appropriately synchronized. If there is more than one regulation services provider, in meeting their obligation to coordinate monitoring and enforcement under section 7.5 of NI 23-101, regulation services providers are required to agree on one standard against which synchronization will occur. In the event there is no regulation services provider, a recognized exchange or recognized quotation and trade reporting system are also required to coordinate with other recognized exchanges or recognized quotation and trade reporting systems regarding the synchronization of clocks.

PART 14 — MARKETPLACE SYSTEMS AND BUSINESS CONTINUITY PLANNING

14.1 Systems Requirements — This section applies to all the systems of a particular marketplace that are identified in the introduction to section 12.1 of the Instrument whether operating in-house or outsourced.

(1) Paragraph 12.1(a) of the Instrument requires the marketplace to develop and maintain an adequate system of internal control over the systems specified. As well, the marketplace is required to develop and maintain adequate general computer controls. These are the controls which are implemented to support information technology planning, acquisition, development and maintenance, computer operations, information systems support, and security. Recognized guides as to what constitutes adequate information technology controls include '*Information Technology Control Guidelines*' from The Canadian Institute of Chartered Accountants (CICA) and '*COBIT* ®*5 Management Guidelines*, from the IT Governance Institute, © 2012 ISACA, *IT Infrastructure Library (ITIL)* — *Service Delivery best practices, ISO/IEC27002:2005* — *Information technology* — *Code of practice for information security management.*

(2) Paragraph 12.1(b) of the Instrument requires a marketplace to meet certain systems capacity, performance and disaster recovery standards. These standards are consistent with prudent business practice. The activities and tests required in this paragraph are to be carried out at least once a year. In practice, continuing changes in technology, risk management requirements and competitive pressures will often result in these activities being carried out or tested more frequently.

(2.1) Paragraph 12.1(c) of the Instrument refers to a material security breach. A material security breach or systems intrusion is any unauthorized entry into any of the systems that support the functions listed in section 12.1 of the Instrument or any system that shares network resources with one or more of these systems. Virtually any security breach would be considered material and thus reportable to the regulator. The onus would be on the marketplace to document the reasons for any security breach it did not consider material. Marketplaces should also have documented criteria to guide the decision on when to publicly disclose a security breach. The criteria for public disclosure of a security breach should include, but not be limited to, any instance in which client data could be compromised. Public disclosure should include information on the types and number of participants affected.

(3) Subsection 12.2(1) of the Instrument requires a marketplace to engage a qualified party to conduct an annual independent assessment to ensure that the marketplace is in compliance with paragraph 12.1(a), section 12.1.1 and section 12.4 of the Instrument. The focus of the assessment of any systems that share network resources with trading-related systems required under subsection 12.2(1)(b) would be to address potential threats from a security breach that could negatively impact a trading-related system. A qualified party is a person or company or a group of persons or companies with relevant experience in both information technology and in the evaluation of related internal controls in a complex information technology environment, such as external auditors or third party information system consultants. Before engaging a qualified party, a marketplace should discuss its choice with the regulator or, in Québec, the securities regulatory authority.

(3.1) The Canadian securities regulatory authorities also note the critical importance of an appropriate system of cyber-security controls over the systems described in section 12.1 of the Instrument. We further note that, as a matter of best practices, marketplaces may also conduct a vulnerability assessment of these controls in addition to the independent systems review required by subsection 12.2(1) of the Instrument. To the extent that a marketplace carries out, or engages an independent party to carry out on its behalf, a vulnerability assessment and prepares a report of that assessment as part of the development and maintenance of the controls required by section 12.1 of the Instrument, we expect a marketplace to provide that report to the regulator or, in Québec, the securities regulatory authority in addition to the report required to be provided by subsection 12.2(2) of the Instrument.

(4) Paragraph 12.1(c) of the Instrument requires the marketplace to notify the regulator or, in Québec, the securities regulatory authority of any material systems failure. The Canadian securities regulatory authorities consider a failure, malfunction or delay to be "material" if the marketplace would in the normal course of operations escalate the matter to or inform its senior management ultimately accountable for technology. The Canadian securities regulatory authorities also expect that, as part of this notification, the marketplace will provide updates on the status of the failure, the resumption of service and the results of its internal review of the failure.

(5) Under section 15.1 of the Instrument, a regulator or the securities regulatory authority may consider granting a marketplace an exemption from the requirements to engage a qualified party to conduct an annual independent systems review and prepare a report under subsection 12.2(1) of the Instrument provided that the marketplace prepare a control self-assessment and file this self-assessment with the regulator or in Québec, the securities regulatory authority. The scope of the self-assessment would be similar to the scope that would have applied if the marketplace underwent an independent systems review. Reporting of the self-assessment results and the timeframe for reporting would be consistent with that established for an independent systems review.

In determining if the exemption is in the public interest and the length of the exemption, the regulator or securities regulatory authority may consider a number of factors including: the market share of the marketplace, the timing of the last independent systems review, changes to systems or staff of the marketplace and whether the marketplace has experienced material systems failures, malfunction or delays.

14.2 Availability of Technology Specifications and Testing Facilities — (1) Subsection 12.3(1) of the Instrument requires marketplaces to make their technology requirements regarding interfacing with or accessing the marketplace publicly available in their final form for at least three months. If there are material changes to these requirements after they are made publicly available and before operations begin, the revised requirements should be made publicly available for a new three month period prior to operations. The subsection also requires that an operating marketplace make its technology specifications publicly available for at least three months before implementing a material change to its technology requirements.

The Canadian securities regulatory authorities consider a material change to a marketplace's technology requirements to include a change that would require a person or company interfacing with or accessing the marketplace to incur a significant amount of systems-related development work or costs in order to accommodate the change or to fully interact with the marketplace as a result of the change. Such material changes could include changes to technology requirements that would significantly impact a marketplace participant's trading activities, such as the introduction of an order type, or significant changes to a regulatory feed that a regulation services provider takes in from the marketplace.

(2) Subsection 12.3(2) of the Instrument requires marketplaces to provide testing facilities for interfacing with or accessing the marketplace for at least two months immediately prior to operations once the technology requirements have been made publicly available. Should the marketplace make its specifications publicly available for longer than three months, it may make the testing available during that period or thereafter as long as it is at least two months prior to operations. If the marketplace, once it has begun operations, proposes material changes to its technology systems, it is required to make testing facilities publicly available for at least two months before implementing the material systems change.

(2.1) Paragraph 12.3(3)(c) of the Instrument prohibits a marketplace from beginning operations before the chief information officer of the marketplace, or an individual performing a similar function, has certified in writing that all information technology systems used by the marketplace have been tested according to prudent business practices and are operating as designed. This certification may be based on information provided to the chief information officer from marketplace staff knowledgeable about the information technology systems of the marketplace and the testing that was conducted.

(2.2) In order to help ensure that appropriate testing procedures for material changes to technology requirements are being followed by the marketplace, subsection 12.3(3.1) of the Instrument requires the chief information officer of the marketplace, or an individual performing a similar function, to certify to the regulator or securities regulatory authority, as applicable, that a material change has been tested according to prudent business practices and is operating as designed. This certification may be based on information provided to the chief information officer from marketplace staff knowledgeable about the information technology systems of the marketplace and the testing that was conducted.

(3) Subsection 12.3(4) of the Instrument provides that if a marketplace must make a change to its technology requirements regarding interfacing with or accessing the marketplace to immediately address a failure, malfunction or material delay of its systems or equipment, it must immediately notify the regulator or, in Québec, the securities regulatory authority, and, if applicable, its regulation services provider. We expect the amended technology requirements to be made publicly available as soon as practicable, either while the changes are being made or immediately after.

14.2.1 Uniform Test Symbols — (1) Section 12.3.1 of the Instrument requires a marketplace to use uniform test symbols for the purpose of performing testing in its production environment. In the view of the Canadian securities regulatory authorities, the use of uniform test symbols is in furtherance to a marketplace's obligations at section 5.7 of the Instrument to take all reasonable steps to ensure that its operations do not interfere with fair and orderly markets.

(2) The use of uniform test symbols is intended to facilitate the testing of functionality in a marketplace's production environment; it is not intended to enable stress testing by marketplace participants. The Canadian securities regulatory authorities are of the view that a marketplace may suspend access to a test symbol where its use in a particular circumstance reasonably represents undue risk to the operation or performance of the marketplace's production environment. The Canadian securities regulatory authorities also note that misuse of the test symbols by marketplace participants could amount to a breach of the fair and orderly markets provisions of National Instrument 23-103 *Electronic Trading and Direct Electronic Access to Marketplaces*.

14.3 Business Continuity Planning — (1) Section 12.4 of the Instrument requires that marketplaces develop and maintain reasonable business continuity plans, including disaster recovery plans. Business continuity planning should encompass all policies and procedures to ensure uninterrupted provision of key services regardless of the cause of potential disruption. In fulfilling the requirement to develop and maintain reasonable business continuity plans, the Canadian securities regulatory authorities expect that marketplaces are to remain current with best practices for business continuity planning and to adopt them to the extent that they address their critical business needs.

(2) Paragraph 12.4(1)(b) of the Instrument also requires a marketplace to test its business continuity plans, including disaster recovery plans, according to prudent business practices on a reasonably frequent basis and, in any event, at least annually.

(3) Section 12.4 of the Instrument also establishes requirements for marketplaces meeting a minimum threshold of total dollar value of trading volume, recognized exchanges or quotation and trade reporting systems that directly monitor the conduct of their members, and regulation services providers that have entered into a written agreement with a marketplace to conduct market surveillance to establish, implement, and maintain policies and procedures reasonably designed to ensure that critical systems can resume operation within certain time limits following the declaration of a disaster. In fulfilling the requirement to establish, implement and maintain the policies and procedures prescribed by section 12.4, the Canadian securities regulatory authorities expect that these policies and procedures will form part of the entity's business continuity and disaster recovery plans and that the entities subject to the requirements at subsections 12.4(2) to (4) of the Instrument will be guided by their own business continuity plans in terms of what constitutes a disaster for purposes of the requirements.

14.4 Industry-Wide Business Continuity Tests — Section 12.4.1 of the Instrument requires a marketplace, recognized clearing agency, information processor, and participant dealer to participate in all industry-wide business continuity tests, as determined by a regulation services provider, regulator, or in Québec, the securities regulatory authority. The Canadian securities regulatory authorities expect that marketplaces will make their production environments available for purposes of all industry-wide business continuity tests.

PART 15 — CLEARING AND SETTLEMENT

15.1 Clearing and Settlement — Subsection 13.1(1) of the Instrument requires all trades executed through a marketplace to be reported and settled through a clearing agency. Subsections 13.1(2) and (3) of the Instrument require that an ATS and its subscriber enter into an agreement that specifies which entity will report and settle the trades of securities. If the subscriber is registered as a dealer under securities legislation, the ATS, the subscriber or an agent for the subscriber that is a member of a clearing agency may report and settle trades. If the subscriber is not registered as a dealer under securities legislation, the ATS or an agent for the subscriber that is a clearing member of a clearing agency may report and settle trades. The ATS is responsible for ensuring that an agreement with the subscriber is in place before any trade is executed for the subscriber. If the agreement is not in place at the time of the execution of the trade, the ATS is responsible for clearing and settling that trade if a default occurs.

15.2 Access to Clearing Agency of Choice — As a general proposition, marketplace participants should have a choice as to the clearing agency that they would like to use for the clearing and settlement of their trades, provided that such clearing agency is appropriately regulated in Canada. Subsection 13.2(1) of the Instrument thus requires a marketplace to report a trade in a security to a clearing agency designated by a marketplace participant.

The Canadian securities regulatory authorities are of the view that where a clearing agency performs only clearing services (and not settlement or depository services) for equity or other cash-product marketplaces in Canada, it would need to have access to the existing securities settlement and depository infrastructure on non-discriminatory and reasonable commercial terms.

Part 2: MARKET PARTICIPANTS

Subsection 13.2(2) of the Instrument provides that subsection 13.2(1) does not apply to trades in standardized derivatives or exchange-traded securities that are options.

PART 16 — INFORMATION PROCESSOR

16.1 Information Processor — (1) The Canadian securities regulatory authorities believe that it is important for those who trade to have access to accurate information on the prices at which trades in particular securities are taking place (i.e., last sale reports) and the prices at which others have expressed their willingness to buy or sell (i.e., orders).

(2) An information processor is required under subsection 14.4(2) of the Instrument to provide timely, accurate, reliable and fair collection, processing, distribution and publication of information for orders for, and trades in, securities. The Canadian securities regulatory authorities expect that in meeting this requirement, an information processor will ensure that all marketplaces, inter-dealer bond brokers and dealers that are required to provide information are given access to the information processor on fair and reasonable terms. In addition, it is expected that an information processor will not give preference to the information of any marketplace, inter-dealer bond broker or dealer when collecting, processing, distributing or publishing that information.

(3) An information processor is required under subsection 14.4(5) of the Instrument to provide prompt and accurate order and trade information, and to not unreasonably restrict fair access to the information. As part of the obligation relating to fair access, an information processor is expected to make the disseminated and published information available on terms that are reasonable and not discriminatory. For example, an information processor will not provide order and trade information to any single person or company or group of persons or companies on a more timely basis than is afforded to others, and will not show preference to any single person or company or group of persons or companies in relation to pricing.

16.2 Selection of an Information Processor — (1) The Canadian securities regulatory authorities will review Form 21-101F5 to determine whether it is contrary to the public interest for the person or company who filed the form to act as an information processor. In Québec, a person or company may carry on the activity of an information processor only if it is recognized by the securities regulatory authority. The Canadian securities regulatory authorities will look at a number of factors when reviewing the form filed, including,

    (a) the performance capability, standards and procedures for the collection, processing, distribution, and publication of information with respect to orders for, and trades in, securities;

    (b) whether all marketplaces may obtain access to the information processor on fair and reasonable terms;

    (c) personnel qualifications;

    (d) whether the information processor has sufficient financial resources for the proper performance of its functions;

    (e) the existence of another entity performing the proposed function for the same type of security;

    (f) the systems report referred to in paragraph 14.5(c) of the Instrument.

(2) The Canadian securities regulatory authorities request that the forms and exhibits be filed in electronic format, where possible.

(3) The forms filed by an information processor under the Instrument will be kept confidential. The Canadian securities regulatory authorities are of the view that they contain intimate financial, commercial and technical information and that the interests of the filers in non-disclosure outweigh the desirability of adhering to the principle that all forms be available for public inspection.

16.3 Change in Information — Under subsection 14.2(1) of the Instrument, an information processor is required to file an amendment to the information provided in Form 21-101F5 at least 45 days before implementing a significant change involving a matter set out in Form 21-101F5, in the manner set out in Form 21-101F5. The Canadian securities regulatory authorities would consider significant changes to include:

    (a) changes to the governance of the information processor, including the structure of its board of directors and changes in the board committees and their mandates;

    (b) changes in control over the information processor;

    (c) changes affecting the independence of the information processor, including independence from the marketplaces, inter-dealer bond brokers and dealers that provide their data to meet the requirements of the Instrument;

    (d) changes to the services or functions performed by the information processor;

    (e) changes to the data products offered by the information processor;

    (f) changes to the fees and fee structure related to the services provided by the information processor;

    (g) changes to the revenue sharing model for revenues from fees related to services provided by the information processor;

    (h) changes to the systems and technology used by the information processor, including those affecting its capacity;

    (i) new arrangements or changes to arrangements to outsource the operation of any aspect of the services of the information processor;

    (j) changes to the means of access to the services of the information processor; and

    (k) where the information processor is responsible for making a determination of the data which must be reported, including the securities for which information must be reported in accordance with the Instrument, changes in the criteria and process for selection and communication of these securities.

These would not include housekeeping or administrative changes to the information included in Form 21-101F5, such as changes in the routine processes, practice or administration of the information processor, changes due to standardization of terminology, or minor system or technology changes that do not significantly impact the system of the information processor or its capacity. Such changes would be filed in accordance with the requirements outlined in subsection 14.2(2) of the Instrument.

16.3.1 Filing of Financial Statements — Subsection 14.4(6) of the Instrument requires an information processor to file annual audited financial statements within 90 days after the end of its financial year. However, where an information processor is operated as a division or unit of a person or company, which may be a marketplace, clearing agency, issuer or any other person or company, the person or company must file an income statement, a statement of cash flow and any other information necessary to demonstrate the financial condition of the information processor. In this case, the income statement, statement of cash flow and other necessary financial information pertaining to the operation of the information processor may be unaudited.

16.4 System Requirements — The guidance in section 14.1 of this Companion Policy applies to the systems requirements for an information processor.

Adoption by OSC: 24 O.S.C.B. 6624 (November 2, 2001) and 24 O.S.C.B. (Supp.) 85 (August 17, 2001); Request for Comments: 23 O.S.C.B. (Supp.) 299 (July 28, 2000).

Adoption of Amendments by OSC: (2004) 27 O.S.C.B. 459 and (2003) 26 O.S.C.B. 7147; Request for Comments: (2003) 26 O.S.C.B. 4377.

Adoption of Amendments by OSC: (2006) 29 O.S.C.B. 10017 and 9731; Request for Comments: (2006) 29 O.S.C.B. 5735.

Adoption of Amendments by OSC: (2008) 31 O.S.C.B. 8572 and 6303; Request for Comments: (2007) 30 O.S.C.B. (Supp. 3) 1 (April 20, 2007).

Adoption of Amendments by OSC: (2010) 33 O.S.C.B. 787 and (2009) 32 O.S.C.B. 9403; Request for Comments: (2008) 31 O.S.C.B. 10136.

Adoption of Amendments by OSC: (2012) 35 O.S.C.B. 5414 and (Supp. 1) 1; Request for Comments: (2011) 34 O.S.C.B. (Supp. 1) 1.

Adoption of Amendments by OSC: (2013) 36 O.S.C.B. 2619; Request for Comments: (2012) 35 O.S.C.B. 6889.

Adoption of Amendments by OSC: (2015) 38 O.S.C.B. 8535; Request for Comments: (2014) 37 O.S.C.B. 4197.

CSA Notice 21-304 — Request for Filing of Form 21-101F5 Initial Operation Report for Information Processor by Interested Information Processors

Date: July 14, 2006

29 O.S.C.B. 5757

I. — Background

National Instrument 21-101 — *Marketplace Operation* (NI 21-101) (which, together with National Instrument 23-101 — *Trading Rules* are hereafter referred to as the ATS Rules) sets out pre-trade and post-trade transparency requirements for marketplaces that trade exchange-traded securities, and for marketplaces, inter-dealer bond brokers (IDBs) and dealers that trade government and corporate debt securities.[1] For government debt securities, the requirements for marketplaces and IDBs to provide order and trade information have been postponed until December 31, 2006. On today's date, the Canadian Securities Administrators (CSA) have published a proposal to provide additional transparency for government debt securities.[2]

II. — Current Status of Information Processors for debt and equity

i. — Equity

As set out in the Notice of Proposed Amendments which is being published today, we made amendments in 2003 to the ATS Rules to require information on orders and trades for exchange-traded securities to be sent to an information processor, or if there is no information processor, then to an information vendor. Currently there is no information processor for the equity marketplaces.

We remain of the view that availability of pre-trade and post-trade information is essential to facilitate best execution and market integrity, especially with multiple marketplaces trading the same securities. Under current requirements, dealers and regulators need to take into consideration information from all marketplaces trading the same securities and take appropriate steps to access orders. We believe that an information processor would facilitate a central source of consolidated data that is consistent, easily accessible and meets the needs of both the regulators and the industry.

ii. — Debt

The 2003 ATS Rules retained transparency and data consolidation requirements for corporate debt securities. In 2003, CanPX was approved as the information processor for corporate fixed income securities. We note that CanPX's approval expires on December 31, 2006. To the extent that transparency of additional debt securities, including government debt securities is phased in, the importance of having a robust system increases. While we will be considering extending CanPX's approval, we invite other entities that are interested in being the information processor to apply.

III. — Filing to be an Information Processor and Timing for Review of Filing

We encourage any interested parties to apply as an information processor for the purpose of consolidating pre-trade and post-trade information for the equity and/or fixed income markets. Any party interested in being an information processor for equity and/or fixed income securities should file Form 21-101F5 — *Initial Operation Report for Information Processor* (Form 21-101F5) by August 31, 2006. For more information on the purpose of establishing an information processor and the functions expected of an information processor, please refer to NI 21-101, Part 14 and the Companion Policy to NI 21-101, Part 16. In evaluating the filing, the CSA will consider a number of factors, including, but not limited to:

(a) the performance capability, standards and procedures for the collection, processing, distribution, and publication of information with respect to orders for, and trades in, securities;

---

[1]NI 21-101, Parts 7 and 8.

[2]Notice published today (Notice of Proposed Amendments to NI 21-101 *Marketplace Operation*, Companion Policy 21-101CP, NI 23-101 *Trading Rules*, and Companion Policy 23-101CP) provides additional details and background on the requirements.

(b) whether all marketplaces may obtain access to the information processor on fair and reasonable terms which are not unreasonably discriminatory;

(c) personnel qualifications;

(d) whether the information processor has sufficient financial resources for the proper performance of its functions;

(e) the existence of another entity performing the proposed function for the same type of security; and

(f) the systems report referred to in subsection 14.5(b) of NI 21-101.

The CSA are currently proposing amendments to Form 21-101F5, and we encourage any parties interested in being an information processor to review the proposed changes to Form 21-101F5 and include the additional information set out as part of the proposed amendments in the application. The proposed amendments to Form 21-101F5 would require any interested parties to include additional information:

a. further explanation about corporate governance processes and procedures that would promote independence from the marketplaces, inter-dealer bond brokers and dealers that provide data;

b. more information about the procedures used to collect, process, distribute, validate and publish information with respect to orders and trades in securities;

c. a description of the process to verify the timeliness and accuracy of the information received and disseminated by the information processor, including the processes to resolve data integrity issues identified;

d. a description of the process and criteria used to select securities for which information must be reported to the information processor; and

e. how revenues will be shared among marketplaces, inter-dealer bond brokers and dealers that provide information to the information processor.

A Notice identifying who has applied and a summary of the application will be published by the CSA for comment in September, 2006. The CSA will make a decision by December 31, 2006 regarding whether any entity has been accepted as an information processor.

Policies and Orders: CSAN 21-306, 21-309, 21-310.

CSA Staff Notice 21-306 — Notice of Filing of Forms 21-101F5 Initial Operation Report for Information Processor

Date: April 20, 2007

30 O.S.C.B. (Supp. 3) 111

[Not reproduced]

CSA Staff Notice 21-309 — Information Processor For Exchange-Traded Securities other than Options

Date: June 5, 2009

32 O.S.C.B. 4585

The purpose of this notice is to inform the public that TSX Inc. (TSX) will act as an information processor for exchange-traded securities other than options[1] under National Instrument 21-101 *Marketplace Operation* (NI 21-101) for a period of five years from July 1, 2009 to June 30, 2014.

1. — Regulatory Requirements

NI 21-101 provides for the operation and regulation of an information processor. An information processor is defined as a person or company that receives and provides information under NI 21-101 and has filed Form 21-101F5 *Initial Operation Report for Information Processor* (Form 21-101F5).

Part 7 of NI 21-101 requires that marketplaces that display orders of exchange-traded securities provide information regarding these orders to an information processor if one exists. Marketplaces are also required to provide trade information related to exchange-traded securities to an information processor or, in its absence, to an information vendor. The information processor has some flexibility regarding the information to be reported to it by the marketplaces.

The regulatory requirements that apply to an information processor are set out in Part 14 of NI 21-101. They include:

- a requirement to provide prompt and accurate order and trade information and not unreasonably restrict fair access to such information;

- a requirement that the information processor provides timely, accurate, reliable and fair collection, processing, distribution and publication of information for orders for, and trades in, securities;

- an obligation to maintain reasonable books and records; and

- certain system requirements, including an annual independent systems review.

---

[1]In Québec, options are not "exchange-traded securities", but are derivatives under the *Derivatives Act* (Québec) and are therefore already excluded.

In addition, the information processor is required to establish, in a timely manner, an electronic connection to each marketplace that is required to provide information under NI 21-101, and also to enter into an agreement with each such marketplace. The agreement must set out that the marketplace will provide the information processor information in accordance with Part 7 of NI 21-101 and that it will comply with any other reasonable requirements set by the information processor.

The information processor is designated as a market participant under the *Securities Act* (Ontario) and has been recognized as an information processor under the *Securities Act* (Québec).

2. — The Need for a Consolidated Source of Data and an Information Processor

The need for an information processor is twofold: first, where there are multiple marketplaces trading the same exchange-traded security, an information processor will address information fragmentation and provide investors and market participants with at least one source of consolidated data. Second, an information processor will facilitate compliance by marketplace participants with relevant regulatory requirements in a multiple marketplace environment. It will ensure the availability of consolidated data that meets regulatory standards and which users, as well as regulators, could use to demonstrate or evaluate compliance with certain regulatory requirements like best execution, short selling and "best price" or trade-through obligations.

We recognize that there is a perception that regulatory requirements effectively mandate that marketplace participants connect to and subscribe to data from all marketplaces or to the information processor to be able to comply with their regulatory obligations. Some believe that this, in turn, may lead marketplaces to charge fees that do not reflect the value of their data, or their market share of orders and/or trades. Previous CSA notices[2] and Companion Policy 23-101CP specifically state that this is not the case.

Subsection 4.1(5) of the Companion Policy 23-101CP indicates that, in order to meet best execution obligations where securities trade on multiple marketplaces in Canada, dealers should consider information from all appropriate marketplaces, and not just those marketplaces where a dealer is a participant. However, considering information from all appropriate marketplaces "does not mean that a dealer must have access to real-time feeds from each marketplace. However, its policies and procedures for seeking best execution should include the process for taking into account order and/or trade information from all appropriate marketplaces and the requirement to evaluate whether taking steps to access orders is appropriate under the circumstances." Guidance published relating to the "best execution" requirements established by the Investment Industry Regulatory Organization of Canada in UMIR 5.1 *Best Execution of Client Orders* echo this view as does the policy related to UMIR 5.2 *Best Price Obligation*.[3]

We would also like to clarify that, while we believe that consolidated data from an information processor will facilitate compliance by marketplace participants with their regulatory requirements, this is not the only source from which data can be obtained. Market participants are not required to take real-time data from the information processor and they may rely on other data sources to obtain the marketplace data that they need, such as information vendors or direct data feeds from the marketplaces.

3. — Background and Process to Date

a. — Request for filings of Forms 21-101F5

In July 2006, we invited entities interested in being an information processor to file Form 21-101F5, and published a separate notice for this purpose.[4] Bourse de Montreal Inc. (MX), CDS Inc. (CDS) and TSX applied to be an information processor for exchange-traded securities.[5] We published a summary of the filings received in April 2007, in CSA Staff Notice 21-306.[6] Since the initial filing, MX and CDS have withdrawn their applications and TSX updated its initial application. A summary of the revised proposal, prepared based on information provided by TSX, is attached at Appendix A of this notice.[7]

b. — Factors and criteria considered in the review

Section 16.2 of Companion Policy to NI 21-101 states that the CSA will review Form 21-101F5 to determine whether it is contrary to the public interest for the filer to act as an information processor and also describes the factors used when evaluating the filings received. They include the performance capabilities, standards and procedures for the collection, processing, distribution and publication of order and trade information; whether all marketplaces may obtain access to the information processor on fair and reasonable terms; whether the entity applying for the role of an information processor has sufficient financial resources for the role; the qualification of its personnel; the existence of another entity performing the role of an information processor; and the independent systems review prepared as required by subsection 14.5(b) of NI 21-101.

[2]Notice of Amendments to NI 21-101 Marketplace Operation, Companion Policy 21-101CP, NI 23-101 Trading Rules and Companion Policy 23-101CP, published at (2006) 29 OSCB 9731 December 15, 2006 and CSA Staff Notice 21-306 Notice of Filing of Forms 21-101F5 — Initial Operation Report for Information Processor, published at (2007) 30 OSCB (Supp-3) (CSA Staff Notice 21-306).

[3]UMIR and its related guidance and policies require dealers to have policies and procedures in place to determine if orders from a marketplace should be initially considered. Part of this consideration of a marketplace for trading is whether there is a reasonable likelihood of liquidity on that marketplace.

[4]CSA Notice 21-304 Request for Filing of Form 21-101F5 Initial Operation Report for Information Processor by Interested Information Processor, published in Ontario on July 14, 2006 at (2006) 29 OSCB 5757.

[5]MX and CDS also applied to be an information processor for corporate debt securities.

[6]*See supra* note 2.

[7]Please note that a detailed description of the technology to be used, including in Form 21-101F5 filed by TSX, has not been published as it is our view that it is commercial and confidential information. This is consistent with our view, also expressed in subsection 16.2(3) of Companion Policy to NI 21-101, that the forms filed by an information processor under NI 21-101 contain intimate financial, commercial and technical information, and that the interests of the filers in non-disclosure outweigh the desirability of adhering to the principle that all forms be available for public inspection.

In CSA Staff Notice 21-306[8] we identified the following criteria to be used to evaluate applications to be an information processor: financial viability; governance requirements; the existence of processes to manage inherent conflicts of interest; system requirements; a commitment to receiving and disseminating data in order to meet the transparency requirements set out in NI 21-101; a competitive fee structure; and, where revenue is shared with contributors of data, a fair method of revenue allocation.

c. — Review of TSX Form 21-101F5

As indicated above, since the original filing of Form 21-101F5 by TSX published in summary on April 2007, TSX revised its proposal. The following changes were made:

- TSX will establish a Governance Committee with marketplace representation to make decisions with respect to significant areas of the operations of the information processor;

- TSX updated the description of the products offered;

- TSX removed the access fees that it initially intended to charge marketplaces to connect to the IP; and

- TSX engaged a third party technology vendor.

These revisions were made not only to update the original filing by TSX to reflect the existing products and technology used by the TSX to consolidate data, but also to address CSA staff concerns regarding the proposed governance structure and the potential conflicts of interest, real or perceived, associated with TSX, a competing marketplace, acting as an information processor. These concerns, as well as concerns about the technology, were also raised by industry participants including dealers and marketplaces.

4. — CSA Conclusion

a. — TSX as an information processor

We are of the view that TSX's revised proposal meets all our criteria for evaluation of a potential information processor. We note that the governance structure proposed by the TSX promotes the independence of the governance of the information processor from that of TSX's business operations, and also ensures representation from each of the marketplaces contributing the data. The technology solution provides no unfair advantage to TSX, and an undertaking to this effect has been provided by TSX.[9] In addition, we understand that most marketplaces are satisfied with the technology solution proposed by the TSX. We are also satisfied that the fee model preserves the status quo for market data fees by passing the existing marketplaces' data fees through to the subscribers of the information. The fee model — the pass-through of data fees plus a distribution fee charged and retained by TSX — meets our criterion that an information processor have some method to share data fee revenue with the contributors of data.

Based on our review of the updated Form 21-101F5 filed by TSX, we believe that it is not contrary to the public interest for TSX to be an information processor for exchange-traded securities other than options[10], for a period of five years beginning July 1, 2009 and ending June 30, 2014. In connection with Form 21-101F5 and the information represented within it, TSX agreed to a number of undertakings, listed at Appendix B of this notice.

The TSX IP will disseminate the following products:

- Consolidated Data Feed, which will provide access to pre- and post-trade market data from each contributing marketplace;

- Consolidated Last Sale, which will provide real-time last sale data from all contributing marketplaces; and

- Canadian Best Bid and Offer, which will provide a consolidated best bid and offer for all exchange-traded securities, other than options.

The inclusion of a consolidated depth-of-book product will depend on the outcome of the discussions relating to the proposed CSA Trade-Through Protection Rule.

b. — Obligations of the marketplaces

We remind the marketplaces of the requirement in Part 7 of NI 21-101 to provide their data to TSX, as an information processor. In order to comply with this requirement, the marketplaces must, if they have not done so already, work with TSX, as an information processor, to establish the necessary connections on a timely basis. Upon publication of this notice, we expect marketplaces to immediately begin working with the TSX to establish connections and facilitate testing of those connections and the incorporation of that data into the existing TSX products. We acknowledge that providing information to the information processor and incorporating it into the feeds may take a number of months.

c. — Review of marketplace data fees

Recently, concerns were raised regarding the existing levels of fees charged by marketplaces, and the potential for a pass-through model to lead to an increase of those fees. Some thought that an information processor could be used to set data fees and even control marketplace fees.

The CSA will be undertaking a review of market data fees. This may entail reviewing the regulatory requirements relating to data fees globally; looking at fee models used by data consolidators, vendors and marketplaces in Canada and in other jurisdictions; understanding what

---

[8]*See supra* note 2.

[9]See undertaking 2c in Appendix B.

[10]In Québec, options are not "exchange-traded securities", but are derivatives under the *Derivatives Act* (Québec) and are therefore already excluded.

steps other markets have taken to ensure that the cost (including data fees) and benefits of marketplace participation are aligned; and reviewing the options available to correct or mitigate potential abuses. Once this review is completed, we will consider what, if any, steps should be taken in this area. Such steps may include further regulation or other mechanisms to correct or mitigate any potential issues.

It is our view, however, that the critical need for consolidated data in a multiple marketplace environment, and the important fact that the TSX IP fee model maintains the status quo, both mean that we should proceed with the current information processor initiative before our review of market data fees is complete. We confirm our expectation that the distribution of a marketplace's data through an information processor will not lead that marketplace to charge unjustified or excessive fees for its data. We would like to remind marketplaces and marketplace participants that, currently, NI 21-101 provides us with a way to take action if the fees charged by marketplaces unreasonably prohibit, condition or limit access to the services of the marketplaces.[11] Such fees would include data fees charged through an information processor.

Appendix A — Summary of TSX's Proposal for an Information Processor for Exchange-Traded Securities Other Than Options

1. — Corporate Governance

TSX Inc. (TSX) is wholly-owned by TMX Group Inc. (TMX Group), which is a publicly held company. TSX operates the Toronto Stock Exchange, and wholly owns TSX Venture Exchange Inc. Pursuant to NI 21-101, Toronto Stock Exchange and TSX Venture Exchange are required to contribute data to an information processor, if one is in place.

The TSX Information Processor (TSX IP) will be operated by the TMX Datalinx division of TSX. TMX Datalinx is the market data division of TMX Group. TMX Datalinx currently distributes equity market data for most equity marketplaces in Canada who contribute their data on a voluntary commercial basis. TMX Datalinx also obtains other data from a variety of marketplaces and partners which it distributes to downstream clients.

Personnel that would be involved in the operations of the TSX IP include staff from various TMX Group divisions representing data product management, sales, administration, vendor and customer support services, technologies, as well as staff from support functions such as finance and legal. Staff from independent, third party technology providers will also contribute to the operations of the TSX IP in accordance with documented service standards that are set out in the agreements that TSX has entered into with these third party providers. TMX Datalinx staff in particular will oversee the TSX IP's business and product development and manage operational priorities as well as any new policies and procedures related to enhancements and operational support.

The TSX IP will have a Governance Committee (IP Governance Committee). The IP Governance Committee will contribute to the development of a clear information processor strategy that is open, transparent and accountable. The IP Governance Committee will promote fair and impartial treatment for members and stakeholders and evaluate, on an ongoing basis, the IP Governance Committee's effectiveness.

Each marketplace that contributes data to the TSX IP will be entitled to nominate one representative on the IP Governance Committee. In addition, an individual who is independent of all marketplaces and TMX Group will sit on the IP Governance Committee in a non-voting capacity and act as Committee Chair. Each marketplace will have one voting seat.

The IP Governance Committee will have decision making authority with respect to scope of service, operational priorities and enhancements, bandwidth and capacity planning, criteria and methods for monitoring performance. Within the scope of service, the IP Governance Committee will establish the means in which to ensure the data set and quality of the TSX IP services are maintained and evaluated. As referenced above, TSX will appoint an independent, non-voting, Committee Chair of the IP Governance Committee.

The TSX IP will also establish a sub-committee of the IP Governance Committee (IP Advisory Sub-Committee), which will include additional representation from at least one data vendor, and one market participant from each of a buy and sell side firm. The IP Advisory Sub-Committee will have input into, and be a forum for raising issues on, TSX IP matters, and will be advisory in nature and non-voting. The IP Governance Committee will help determine the composition, structure and meeting frequency of the IP Advisory Sub-Committee.

To further address any perceived conflicts of interest, the TSX IP will implement policies and procedures to ensure that TSX staff who are not involved in operating the TSX IP do not acquire knowledge of, or access to, competitor data or client information. As well, TSX will enter into a universal information processor agreement with each contributing marketplace which will include detailed service level terms and change management and operational procedures which will ensure, on a commercial basis, that data transmitted to the TSX IP will not be inappropriately manipulated by TSX. Perceived conflicts of interest will also be mitigated by the use of a third party technology solution, as is described below under "Systems and Operations".

2. — Systems and Operations

TMX Datalinx uses a range of in-house and independent, third party technologies to distribute Canadian equity, news, fixed income, derivatives, and foreign exchange decision support content to capital markets participants globally. In 2007, TMX Datalinx selected a global, market-leading independent technology provider to deploy and manage the TSX IP solution, the consolidated data feed (CDF) suite of products. The CDF solution is intended to offer an exchange independent solution by deploying third party technology and operational/technical support while leveraging existing TSX hosting infrastructure with connectivity to over 100 market data vendors, 7,000 clients, and over 153,000 subscriptions.

The CDF solution simultaneously distributes real-time consolidated data (running hot/hot) from two production environments in separate physical locations providing clients with flexible connectivity options (in terms of location) and redundancy. Either location can be accessed as

[11]Subsection 5.1(b) of NI 21-101 states that "[a] recognized exchange ... must not unreasonably prohibit, condition or limit access by a person or company to services offered by it". Similarly, subsection 6.13(b) of NI 21-101 states that "[a]n ATS must not unreasonably prohibit, condition or limit access by a person or company to services offered by it".

the primary site. Information from a contributing marketplace can be transmitted to the TSX IP in its native format and will be normalized and consolidated by the TSX IP, saving marketplaces the one time and ongoing costs of building and supporting a new format for the TSX IP.

The CDF solution has been designed to provide timestamps when the data first touches its platform and timestamps when the data exits the platform, so that each marketplace and customer can monitor latency in real time, on a continuous basis.

TSX and its third party providers have procedures in place to add capacity to the TSX IP as required. The current technology is scalable through additional infrastructure, which is commoditized servers and operating systems. The TSX IP benefits from this independence while leveraging TMX Group's exchange grade data centers. Independent third party providers monitor system performance, manage capacity, and provide managed services for the CDF software applications and physical infrastructure while TMX Group staff provides infrastructure management for the facilities, network, and environmentals.

The TSX IP's technology providers will provide real-time and ongoing development support and 24/7 monitoring of software, hardware and helpdesk support.

The TSX IP will also rely on TMX Group's business continuity planning and disaster recovery planning model, which includes infrastructure investments and a detailed framework for operating markets and recovery from disasters, detailed planning procedures and 24/7 support. The CDF uses the TMX Datalinx distribution network of data distributors. With the recent combination with the Bourse de Montréal Inc., TMX Group now has its own network connectivity and points of presence in London, New York and Chicago, in addition to its existing network of major telecommunications carriers. Through these and other established connections, delivery of the data feed products are accessible almost anywhere in the world.

In addition to these resources, TMX Datalinx has a Senior Product Manager, Consolidated Data Feeds and a Services Analyst to provide business development and business support for the TSX IP. Users and marketplaces will also have access to TMX Vendor Services front line support.

3. — Fees and Revenue Sharing

The TSX IP will operate a pass-through fee model, which TSX asserts is the global data feed standard used by most exchanges, specialist data services and data distributors. Under this model, contributing marketplaces enter into contractual agreements with data vendors and subscribers directly, allowing each marketplace's fees and policies to be passed along to the end users.

The TSX IP will not charge marketplaces any fees to connect or contribute to the TSX IP. The TSX IP will not charge end users any fees for the CDF, the Canadian Best Bid and Offer (CBBO) or the Consolidated Last Sale (CLS) (The CDF and CBBO are already in use by market participants.) The TSX IP will charge a nominal monthly IP distribution fee only applicable to data vendors and dealers that receive the CDF, CBBO and CLS data feeds for the purpose of redistributing the CDF, CBBO or CLS data. These monthly fees will be $500 per month for the CDF, $300 per month for the CBBO, and $300 per month for the CLS. Any significant changes to fees proposed by the TSX IP would be reviewed and approved by the Canadian Securities Administrators.

The TSX IP data feeds are designed to provide the full data sets required to meet regulatory trade through obligations while also lowering overall costs by economizing telecommunication, network and support expenditures.

4. — Access

TSX anticipates that a variety of data vendors and dealers will want to access and/or re-distribute the CDF, CBBO, and/or CLS. All interested parties who execute the requisite data distribution agreement or addendum with TSX (as the information processor) and with each marketplace will be permitted to access and/or re-distribute data from the TSX IP. Individual subscribers will need to contract directly with a contributing marketplace in order to receive that marketplace's data.

There are a variety of telecommunication options for industry constituents to access the TSX IP hosted facilities, and in the vast majority of cases, those constituents will be able to access the TSX IP system using their existing communications links. Marketplaces can report their data to the TSX IP in their existing format and the TSX IP will disseminate in a widely used and adopted data format.

5. — Selection of Securities Reported to the Information Processor and Services Provided by the Information Processor

The TSX IP will consolidate data for all exchange-traded securities other than options, as required under NI 21-101. As required, the TSX IP will work with the marketplaces and Canadian Securities Administrators to determine if there is a regulatory reason to expand the type or scope of securities. The TSX IP will use the Symbol Status message sent out daily in each of the CDF services to communicate all symbols in each service.

The scope of services to be offered by the TSX IP to permit market participants to address their regulatory trade through protection obligations are the CDF, CBBO and CLS. Details about each service are provided below.

a. — Consolidated Data Feed (CDF)

The CDF feed provides access to pre- and post-trade market data from each contributing marketplace, through existing telecommunications links to TSX. As a multicast feed of consolidated data, where each marketplace is a permissionable data stream, CDF allows for a scalable solution for end users to acquire market data from the TSX IP for one or more marketplaces.

The TSX IP receives, normalizes, captures, and publishes all business content from the marketplaces contributing to the TSX IP including all data fields, markers, and tags for pre-and post-trade content. Specifically, this collection, processing, validation and publication of information captures all trade, order, cancellations, business content, market state and stock state messages. All messages have a consolidation of timestamps added indicating the time the message was received and published, enabling market participants to measure CDF performance. Each CDF message will contain the following mandatory fields:

- Attributed marketplace (Source)
- Timestamp from Source
- Timestamp received by the CDF
- Timestamp published by the CDF
- Business Class (order, cancel, trade)
- Business Action (buy, sell, trade, cancel)
- Broker Number
- Order Number
- Trade Number
- Volume
- Price
- Symbol
- Special Terms Markers

b. — Canadian Best Bid and Offer (CBBO)

The CBBO feed provides real-time access to the consolidated Canadian best bid and offer for exchange-traded securities other than options, as required under NI 21-101. The TSX IP aggregates all business content from the marketplaces contributing to the TSX IP including all data fields, markers, and tags for pre-trade messages. This collection, processing, validation and publication of a consolidated best bid and best offer include the attributed marketplace(s), aggregated volume and price. Each CBBO message will contain the following mandatory fields:

- Attributed marketplace ("Source")
- Timestamp received by the CDF
- Timestamp published by the CDF
- Business Action (bid, ask)
- Aggregated Volume
- Price
- Symbol

c. — Consolidated Last Sale (CLS)

The CLS feed provides real-time last sale data from contributing marketplaces commingled in a normalized consolidated feed. Each CLS message will contain attributed data for each trade and trade cancellation message including the following mandatory fields:

- Attributed marketplace (Source)
- Timestamp from Source
- Timestamp received by the CDF
- Timestamp published by the CDF
- Business Action (trade, trade cancellation)
- Broker Number (buyer and seller)
- Order Number
- Trade Number
- Volume
- Price
- Symbol
- Crosstype (Basis, Contingency, VWAP, Cash, Delayed Delivery, etc.)

Part 2: MARKET PARTICIPANTS

d. — *Other service capabilities of the TSX IP*

The CDF includes a software application which consumes the normalized market data and can publish a single consolidated view of the order book. The CDF technology permits the inclusion of a consolidated depth of book product at such time that the requirements and guidelines for a product that allows market participants to meet their regulatory trade through protection obligation has been determined by the Canadian Securities Administrators.

Appendix B — Undertakings Provided by TSX

In connection with the updated Form 21-101F5 (F5) filed by TSX Inc. (TSX) on April 24, 2009 and revised on May 21, 2009 and its role as the information processor (TSX IP) for exchange-traded securities other than options[12] *TSX undertakes the following:*

1. — Changes to Form 21-101F5

a. As required by section 14.2 of National Instrument 21-101 *Marketplace Operation* (NI 21-101), TSX will file with the CSA amendments to the information provided in Form 21-101F5. The significant changes referred to in section 14.2(1) of NI 21-101 will be reviewed and approved by CSA staff prior to their implementation. These significant changes include:

- changes to the governance of the TSX IP, including the structure of its Governance Committee (IP Governance Committee) and the IP Advisory Sub-Committee,

- significant changes to the fees related to the services provided by the TSX IP, including subscriber access fees and distribution fees,

- changes to the fee structure and fee / revenue sharing model related to the services provided by the TSX IP,

- changes to the data products offered by the TSX IP,

- significant changes to the systems and technology used by the TSX IP, including those affecting capacity, or

- changes that would have the effect of increasing the TSX IP's level of dependence on TMX Group Inc. proprietary technology.

b. TSX IP will notify CSA staff of the representatives of the IP Governance Committee and the IP Advisory Sub-Committee, and will provide notice of any changes to those representatives.

2. — Governance and Conflicts of Interest

a. The Boards of Directors of TMX Group Inc. and TSX will not be involved in IP Governance Committee decisions relating to the scope of service, operational priorities, bandwidth, capacity planning, performance management, including service levels, and the fee and revenue sharing model related to the TSX IP.

b. By July 31, 2009, the TSX IP will establish policies and procedures to separate TSX's marketplace business operations from the TSX IP operations and manage inherent conflicts of interest and provide them to CSA staff for review and approval.

c. The technology used by the TSX IP will not give the Toronto Stock Exchange or TSX Venture Exchange an unfair advantage with respect to their data as compared to other marketplaces.

3. — IP Products

a. The TSX IP will only distribute the following products which are described in Form 21-101F5 (together, the Consolidated Data Products):

- the Consolidated Data Feed (CDF);

- the Canadian Best Bid and Offer (CBBO);

- the Consolidated Last Sale (CLS); and

- the Consolidated Depth of Book Feed.

b. The TSX IP will not distribute any additional products using the data provided to it under Part 7 of NI 21-101 unless it obtains prior approval from CSA staff.

c. TSX will submit the final specification related to the CLS and the Consolidated Depth of Book Feed products to CSA staff for review and approval prior to the launch of the CLS and Consolidated Depth of Book Feed.

d. The TSX IP will use reasonable efforts to launch[13] the CLS product within 3 months of the later of (i) July 1, 2009, and (ii) the date of receipt of the CSA approval as required in paragraphs 3c and 4b. The TSX IP will use reasonable efforts to launch the CLS product with data from those marketplaces that are not currently contributing their data within 4 months of the later of (i) July 1, 2009, and (ii) the date of receipt of the CSA approval as required in paragraphs 3c and 4b. For greater certainty, the TSX IP will not be responsible for delays to the launch of the CLS product that are attributable to factors outside of the reasonable control of the TSX IP, including the timely performance of necessary activities by marketplaces and other third parties.

e. The TSX IP will use reasonable efforts to launch the Consolidated Depth of Book Feed within 6 months of the later of (i) July 1, 2009, and (ii) the date of receipt of the CSA approval as required in paragraphs 3c and 4b. For greater certainty, the TSX IP will not be responsible for delays to the launch of the Consolidated Depth of Book Feed that are attributable to factors outside of the reasonable control of the TSX IP, including the timely performance of necessary activities by marketplaces and other third parties.

---

[12]In Québec, options are not "exchange-traded securities", but are derivatives under the *Derivatives Act* (Québec) and are therefore already excluded.

[13]For purposes of paragraphs 3(d) and 3(e), a "launch" is achieved when the respective Consolidated Data Product is available for beta testing by market participants.

f. As provided by the TSX IP, each data product comprising the Consolidated Data Products is permitted to be bundled for sale to Data Purchasers[14], but will also be made available as separately permissionable feeds.

g. If TSX, or any affiliate (as defined in the *Securities Act* (Ontario)), intends to create and distribute products, using the data provided to the TSX IP under Part 7 of NI 21-101, through its commercial distribution channels and not through the TSX IP:

  i. the data required to be provided to the TSX IP by Data Contributors[15] will not be used for such other products without the permission of the Data Contributors; and

  ii. the additional products will be made available for purchase separately from, and will not be bundled with, the Consolidated Data Products and any other products approved under paragraph 3b.

TSX will not provide an associate (as defined in the *Securities Act* (Ontario)) with the underlying data which is provided by the Data Contributors to the TSX IP for the purposes of creating the Consolidated Data Products without the permission of the Data Contributors.

h. The TSX IP will consolidate, update and provide in real-time the Consolidated Data Products during the hours of operation of any Canadian marketplace required to provide information to an information processor under NI 21-101, provided that the TSX IP can perform normal course recycle, batch and maintenance operations. TSX IP will provide customer support between the hours of 7:30–17:30 and 24/7 technical support of the TSX IP.

4. — Agreements with Data Contributors

a. The TSX IP will ensure that all Data Contributors are given access to the TSX IP on fair and reasonable terms.

b. The standard agreements or contracts to be entered into between TSX IP and Data Contributors in connection with the TSX IP services will be provided to CSA staff for review and approval prior to their execution. In addition, any proposed material changes to these standard agreements or contracts will be provided to CSA staff for review and approval.

5. — Fees / Fee structure / Revenue sharing

a. TSX will make the fee schedule for the Consolidated Data Products available on its website.

b. If any adjustment or modification is proposed to fees, fee structure, or the fee / revenue sharing model relating to the services of the TSX IP, the TSX IP will ask the IP Governance Committee to seek input from the IP Advisory Sub-Committee prior to approving such adjustments or modifications.

c. The TSX IP will report annually to CSA staff, in writing, whether TSX has fully recovered its costs (including cost of capital and cost associated with reporting requirements under subsections 14.4(2), (4), and (5) of NI 21-101) associated with offering the TSX IP services and will review and report on whether the profit margin received from the TSX IP services is in line with industry standards.

d. If there are excess revenues over costs plus a reasonable profit margin, and that excess is not allocated to operating and/or capacity expansion of the TSX IP, the TSX IP will examine its options for the use of that excess revenue and analyze and recommend an appropriate use to the IP Governance Committee. The TSX IP will ask the IP Governance Committee to review the analysis and recommendations and provide its views in writing to the TSX IP. The analysis, recommendations and the views of the IP Governance Committee will be provided to CSA staff within 30 days of the IP Governance Committee having received the analysis and recommendations.

e. As of July 1, 2012 (Review Initiation Date), the TSX IP will conduct a review of the 'pass-through' fee model. Such review will examine the fee models used by data consolidators in other jurisdictions and the cost of data in Canada. It will also consider reports or studies available at the time of the review. A report outlining the conclusions from the review and the basis for those conclusions, along with any recommendations, will be provided to the IP Governance Committee promptly upon completion. The TSX IP will ask the IP Governance Committee to review the report and provide its views in writing to the TSX IP. The report and the views of the IP Governance Committee will be provided to CSA staff within 90 days of the Review Initiation Date.

6. — Non-exclusivity

a. TSX acknowledges that the selection of an information processor does not grant that information processor exclusive rights to consolidating and disseminating order and trade data. The TSX IP will not seek exclusivity through the terms of any contract relating to the Consolidated Data Products, or involving the data underlying the Consolidated Data Products, with a Data Contributor or Data Purchaser.

7. — Self-assessment

a. In addition to arranging for an annual independent system review referred to in section 14.5 of NI 21-101, the TSX IP will conduct an annual self-assessment of its compliance with subsections 14.4(2), (4), and (5) of NI 21-101 and with its performance with respect to the undertakings provided to the CSA. A report on the self-assessment will be provided to the IP Governance Committee promptly upon its completion. The TSX IP will ask the IP Governance Committee to review the report and provide its views in writing. The report and the views of the IP Governance Committee will be provided to CSA staff within 90 days of the end of the TSX IP's fiscal year.

8. — Financial Viability

a. TSX will provide the TSX IP with sufficient financial and other resources to ensure its financial viability and the proper performance of its functions.

Part 2: MARKET PARTICIPANTS

---

[14]For the purposes of this reference and any subsequent reference, the term Data Purchaser includes subscribers, vendors, and any other party that purchases any data product offered by the TSX IP.

[15]For the purposes of this reference and any subsequent reference, the term Data Contributor includes marketplaces and any other party that provides data to the TSX IP under requirements in NI 21-101 to provide order and trade information to an information processor.

9. — Term and Notice

a. TSX will act as an information processor for exchange traded securities other than options[16] for a period of five years starting from July 1, 2009 (5-year term). TSX will provide CSA staff with at least one year notice should it determine that it does not wish to continue to act as an information processor upon the expiry of the 5-year term.

CSA Staff Notice 21-310 — Information Processor for Corporate Debt Securities

Date: June 26, 2009

32 O.S.C.B. 5159

The purpose of this notice is to inform the public that CanPX Inc. (CanPX) will act as an information processor for corporate debt securities under National Instrument 21-101 *Marketplace Operation* (NI 21-101) for a period of five years from July 1, 2009 to June 30, 2014.

1. — Regulatory Requirements

NI 21-101 provides for the operation and regulation of an information processor. An information processor is defined as a person or company that receives and provides information under NI 21-101 and has filed Form 21-101F5 *Initial Operation Report for Information Processor* (Form 21-101F5).

Part 8 of NI 21-101 requires that marketplaces that display orders of corporate debt securities provide information regarding orders for designated corporate debt securities to an information processor. Marketplaces, inter-dealer bond brokers (IDBs) and dealers are also required to provide trade information for corporate debt securities to an information processor, if one is in place, as required by the information processor.[1]

The obligations of an information processor are set out in Part 14 of NI 21-101. They include:

- a requirement to provide prompt and accurate order and trade information and not unreasonably restrict fair access to such information;
- a requirement that the information processor provides timely, accurate, reliable and fair collection, processing, distribution and publication of information for orders for, and trades in, securities;
- an obligation to maintain reasonable books and records; and
- certain system requirements, including an annual independent systems review.

In addition, an information processor is required to establish, in a timely manner, an electronic connection to a marketplace, IDB or dealer that is required to provide it with information. It is also required to enter into an agreement with each marketplace, IDB or dealer required to provide it with information. The agreement must set out that the entities will provide the information processor information in accordance with Part 8 of NI 21-101 and that they will comply with any other reasonable requirements set by the information processor.

2. — Status of the Information Processor for Corporate Debt Securities and Process to Date

CanPX has been an information processor for corporate debt securities since 2003. Its initial term expired on December 31, 2006. In July 2006, as we considered extending CanPX's term, we invited other entities interested in being an information processor for corporate debt securities to file Form 21-101F5, and published a separate notice for this purpose.[2] Bourse de Montréal Inc. (MX), CDS Inc., TSX Inc. in conjunction with Candeal.ca Inc. (CanDeal), and Gmarkets Inc. (Gmarkets) each filed a Form 21-101F5 to act as an information processor for corporate debt securities.[3] We published a summary of the filings received in April 2007.[4]

We have since extended CanPX's status as an information processor for corporate debt securities to give us time to review the filings and to work through the issues, and have informed the public of the extensions in a number of staff notices.[5] In CSA Staff Notice 21-308, we notified the public that CanPX informed us that it was discussing the possibility of a partnership with other participants in the fixed income market, and that such partnership could result in a revised application for an information processor for corporate debt securities. We advised existing applicants for the corporate debt information processor that they may also revise and update their applications, and to submit any revised filings by January 31, 2009. A number of applicants, including CanPX, provided updates to their original filings.

---

[16]In Québec, options are not "exchange-traded securities", but are derivatives under the *Derivatives Act* (Québec) and are therefore already excluded.

[1]For government debt securities, the requirements for marketplaces and IDBs to provide order and trade information have been postponed until January 1, 2012.

[2]CSA Notice 21-304 Request for Filing of Form 21-101F5 *Initial Operation Report for Information Processor by Interested Information Processors* (CSA Notice 21-304), published in Ontario on July 14, 2006 at (2006) 29 OSCB 5757.

[3]CanPX, MX, CDS and TSX Inc. (without CanDeal) also applied to be an information processor for exchange-traded securities.

[4]CSA Staff Notice 21-306 Notice of Filing of Forms 21-101F5 *Initial Operation Report for Information Processor* (CSA Staff Notice 21-306), published in Ontario on April 20, 2007 at (2007) 30 OSCB (Supp-3).

[5]CSA Staff Notice 21-305 *Extension of Approval of Information Processor for Corporate Fixed Income Securities*, published in Ontario at (2006) 29 OSCB 8364; CSA Staff Notice 21-307 *Extension of Approval of Information Processor for Corporate Fixed Income Securities* published in Ontario at (2007) 30 OSCB 9222; and CSA Staff Notice 21-308 *Update on Applications to Become an Information Processor* (CSA Staff Notice 21-308), published in Ontario at (2008) 31 OSCB 11533.

3. — Factors and Criteria Considered in the Review of Form 21-101F5

Section 16.2 of Companion Policy 21-101 to National Instrument 21-101 *Marketplace Operation* (21-101CP) states that the CSA will review Form 21-101F5 to determine whether it is contrary to the public interest for the filer to act as an information processor, and also describes the factors used when evaluating the filings received. These factors, which we also communicated in CSA Notice 21-304, include: the performance capabilities, standards and procedures for the collection, processing, distribution and publication of order and trade information; whether all marketplaces may obtain access to the information processor on fair and reasonable terms; whether the entity applying for the role of an information processor has sufficient financial resources for the role; the qualification of its personnel; the existence of another entity performing the role of an information processor; and the independent systems review prepared as required by subsection 14.5(b) of NI 21-101.

In CSA Staff Notice 21-306, we identified the criteria we would use to evaluate applications to be an information processor as follows: financial viability; governance requirements; the existence of processes to manage inherent conflicts of interest; system requirements; a commitment to receiving and disseminating data in order to meet the transparency requirements set out in NI 21-101; a competitive fee structure; and, where revenue is shared with contributors of data, a fair method of revenue allocation.

4. — Review of CanPX Revised Form 21-101F5

As indicated above, since the filing of Form 21-101F5 by CanPX published in summary on April 2007, CanPX revised its proposal. The changes were in the following areas:

- CanPX will establish an Advisory Committee with representation from fixed income industry participants whose mandate will include providing CanPX with views and recommendations on issues of concern to data contributors and data purchasers; this Committee will also be included as part of the process for designating corporate debt securities[6]; and

- CanPX will replace its existing technical facilitator, Reuters Canada Limited with CanDeal.

A summary of the revised proposal, prepared based on information provided by CanPX, is included at Appendix A of this notice.

5. — CSA Conclusion

a. — *CanPX as an information processor for corporate debt securities*

We believe that CanPX's revised proposal meets our criteria for evaluation of a potential information processor. The implementation of an Advisory Committee, with representation from contributors and purchasers of data, would help ensure that all stakeholders have the opportunity to provide their views. In addition, it ensures that issues of concern will be raised through the Advisory Committee and properly considered by CanPX. As well, CanPX has a model for sharing revenue with its shareholders that are also contributors of data and has agreed in its undertakings to review this model to compensate all contributors of corporate bond data, regardless of whether they are shareholders.[7]

In addition, we are of the view that the participation of industry participants such as dealers and IDBs in the governance of CanPX helps promote industry input in decisions regarding transparency in the fixed income markets. We acknowledge, however, that there are inherent conflicts of interest associated with the industry participants' involvement in transparency decisions that may potentially impact their business. We believe that such conflicts, real or perceived, should be properly managed and note the undertakings that have been provided by CanPX to establish proper policies and procedures in this regard. In addition, we note that in the course of conducting our regulatory oversight of CanPX, the effectiveness of these policies and procedures will be examined.

Consequently, based on our review of the updated Form 21-101F5 filed by CanPX and the undertakings provided by CanPX (attached at Appendix B), we believe that it is not contrary to the public interest for CanPX to continue to be an information processor for corporate debt securities, for a period of five years beginning July 1, 2009 and ending June 30, 2014.

As an information processor, CanPX is designated as a market participant under the *Securities Act* (Ontario) and it was recognized as an information processor under the *Securities Act* (Québec).

b. — *Obligations of the marketplaces, IDBs and dealers*

We remind the marketplaces, IDBs and dealers of the requirements in Part 8 of NI 21-101 to provide their data to CanPX, as an information processor, as required by CanPX and in accordance with the requirements set out in Part 10 of 21-101CP. In order to comply with this requirement, the marketplaces, IDBs and dealers required to report the corporate debt information must work with CanPX and CanDeal, as its technical facilitator, to establish the necessary connections in a timely manner.

Appendix A — Summary of CanPX's Proposal for an Information Processor for Corporate Debt Securities

1. — Corporate Governance

Overall governance responsibilities for CanPX rest with the CanPX board of directors. Moreover, CanPX's technical facilitator, under the oversight of the CanPX board, is required to adopt policies and procedures to permit CanPX to comply with the requirements of NI 21-101. Additionally, CanPX maintains an Operating Committee comprised of a subset of CanPX board members to address the day-to-day operations of CanPX including contract negotiations with vendors, capital expenditures, financial statement preparations; etc. CanPX also currently

---

[6]For a description of the current list of designated corporate bonds, the selection criteria and the process for their selection, see http://www.canpx.ca/selection-criteria.jsp.

[7]Currently, no marketplaces meet the existing threshold to contribute data to CanPX.

utilizes a Corporate Bond Working Group and is in the early stages of developing an Advisory Committee as part of its governance structure. An overview of these two groups is provided below.

a. — Corporate Bond Working Group

The mandate of the Corporate Bond Working Group is to regularly review, and on a quarterly basis recommend modifications to, CanPX's designated list of corporate bond securities to ensure that the list continually meets the established criteria as documented on the CanPX website: http://www.canpx.ca/selectioncriteria.jsp. In addition, at the direction of the CanPX board of directors, the working group has succeeded in expanding the level of market transparency by gradually increasing over time the number of designated corporate bond securities.

The working group is comprised of fixed-income professionals from IIROC member dealers who sit on the Investment Industry Association of Canada (IIAC) Debt Markets Committee.

b. — Advisory Committee

CanPX has initialized the process of finding suitable representatives to sit on the planned Advisory Committee. The final composition of the Committee is expected to include a cross-section of fixed income industry professionals from the buy-side and sell-side (to represent the views of data purchasers and suppliers) as well as marketplaces, data vendors, and other possible stakeholder representatives. It is expected that, in general, the mandate of the Committee will be to bring to CanPX's attention issues of concern to Data Contributors as well as Data Purchasers/Vendors, and to recommend necessary corrective action. Though CanPX understands that it is acting as an information processor for corporate debt securities, and that the transparency requirements set out in Part 8 of NI 21-101 currently apply only to those debt securities, the Advisory Committee would be of greatest value to CanPX and overall market transparency if the Committee were to include in its scope a review of information related to government debt securities. It is anticipated that the Advisory Committee will be included as part of the existing process the designation of corporate bonds, as well as in developing the necessary criteria for entities required to provide data into CanPX. The Advisory Committee would report directly to the CanPX board of directors, and, as required, contact the Director of the Market Regulation Branch of the Ontario Securities Commission and the Directrice de la supervision des Organismes d'autoreglementation (OAR) at the AMF with any concerns that it may have regarding the governance or operations of the information processor.

2. — Systems and Operations

a. — Sources of data

Two groups of participants currently supply securities information to CanPX for collection, processing, distribution or publication: 12 investment dealers, that provide CanPX with information related to corporate debt securities, in accordance with the requirements set out in Part 8 of NI 21-101 and Part 10 of the Companion Policy 21-101CP (the Consolidated Data); and 3 inter-dealer brokers (IDBs), which provide CanPX information for government fixed income securities (the Supplementary Data). All participants actively participate in domestic fixed income markets.

Investment dealer participants are all members in good standing with the Investment Industry Regulatory Organization of Canada (IIROC). IIROC membership ensures that a high standard has been met by these dealers in areas such as capital requirements, internal compliance and business continuity planning. Investment dealer participants are also active market-makers in short-term and long-term debt securities and are designated as either Primary Dealers of Government of Canada treasury bills or Primary Dealers of Canada bonds by the Bank of Canada. Investment dealer participants are also represented on the IIAC Debt Markets Committee.

Considerations will be made by the CanPX board on a case by case basis to ensure that all new sources of data meet certain minimum requirements in such areas as:

- Experience with data collection and management
- Ability and willingness to manage any potential conflicts with other CanPX participants
- Systems reliability/business continuity
- Physical and logical security

b. — Means of access to the system

CanDeal has been selected as CanPX's new technical facilitator and marketing agent/ wholesale distributor. CanDeal will make the CanPX Consolidated and Supplementary Data available through a variety of distribution channels. Specifically, CanPX data will be available through: (a) a fully described, logical, record-based real-time broadcast feed; and in the future, (b) an internet protocol, FTP, near real-time mechanism to ensure broadest possible market reach.

CanDeal will wholesale data through its distributors that are connected with all Canadian telecommunications providers as well as extranet providers such as Radianz, TNS, SPTI, Savvis, Global Alliance and Xasax.

CanDeal is well positioned in the market data supply chain to ensure the broadest possible reach for the CanPX Consolidated and Supplementary Data.

Currently, CanPX provides free daily quotes for yields on Canadian benchmark bonds on its website. Other information such as list of current data contributors and list of designated corporate bonds is also publicly available on the CanPX website: www.CanPX.ca. Additional content is expected to be made available on CanPX website after it transitions to its new technical facilitator.

It is expected that under the transition to CanPX's new technical facilitator, there will be little or no change in existing connectivity methods or costs for current contributors to the Consolidated Data. A secure private network to receive trade files from the dealer community is already in place at CanDeal and the existing CanPX trade file format will be duplicated to ensure a seamless transition to the new technical facilitator. CanPX and its technical facilitator will endeavor to work with new data contributors to establish a preferred connectivity method.

c. — Procedures governing entry and display of quotations and trades in the system including collection, processing, distributing, publishing, including data validation processes

CanPX's technical facilitator is required to ensure that systems are in place to ensure the integrity of the data reported to and disseminated by CanPX. As part of their current data management business, CanDeal maintains procedures designed to ensure data integrity. Filters are utilized to reject bad data such as negative values, blank values, invalid CUSIP, missing values, etc. Once data passes through these filters, a proprietary algorithm consolidates price and yield sources into a Best Bid/Best Offer. Additional filters are then applied to ensure the final consolidated price/yield is an accurate indication of where the marketplace is for each security. CanDeal's customer service desk monitors composite data as well as individual dealer contributions to ensure timeliness and accuracy of the prices.

To ensure the timeliness and accuracy of the information received and disseminated by the system, CanPX requires that its technical facilitator provide a weekly report to the CanPX secretariat that lists all corporate trades contributed into the system that were delayed more than 1 hour. The report also includes details on amended trades. The report includes the necessary raw data from which the CanPX secretariat can perform the necessary analysis to detect reoccurring material failures on the part of data contributors. Any issues identified are brought to the attention of the CanPX Operating Committee. When necessary, contributors may be contacted for further details surrounding the delayed reporting. Additionally, CanPX maintains a log of services outages experienced at the technical facilitator and addresses issues or areas of concern with the facilitator.

Similar procedures are expected to be followed in CanPX's transition to its new facilitator.

Additionally, IIROC staff also receives the weekly report of delayed trades identified above for use in conjunction with any business conduct compliance examination they may conduct at IIROC member firms who are also CanPX corporate bond data contributors.

d. — Data storage

The CanPX technical facilitator is expected to maintain historical data records on all transactions for each of the IDB source feeds, investment dealer FTP feeds, and the CanPX Consolidated Data. Each item and their associated fields will be recorded on a tick by tick basis to the CanPX Storage.

e. — The hours of operation of the system

CanDeal will make CanPX data available from *07:30 to 19:00* (Eastern Time) on regular close Canadian Bond trading days and from *07:30* to the relevant appropriate industry close time on early close Canadian Bond trading days.

f. — Description of the training provided to users of the system and any materials provided to the users

Training and materials would include:

- Inbound feed specification documentation and examples;

- Outbound feed specification documentation and examples;

- Generic language written in plain English describing the content and context of the provided data from the information processor translated into appropriate global languages, including French;

- Support time as required to parties contributing information to the information processor;

- Support time as required to parties receiving information from the information processor;

- As appropriate, online documentation and training materials to help explain the content of the data;

- Educational materials for the investing public and subscriber base.

3. — Fees and Revenue Sharing

CanPX currently distributes the Consolidated Data (as well as the Supplementary Data) to subscribers through two vendors. The current subscription price for the Consolidated Data is $25 per month. An additional charge is applied for subscribers also wishing to receive the Supplementary Data. In addition, vendors may charge subscribers with a connectivity fee. It is not expected that subscription costs for the Consolidated Data will vary to a great degree following CanPX's transition to its new technical facilitator.

CanPX has a revenue sharing model in place with its marketplace participant shareholders. These shareholders are also contributors of the CanPX data. Additionally, provisions in the CanPX formation documents permit new contributors, such as Alternative Trading Systems, to become shareholders as well. Revenue-sharing is as follows: CanPX would allocate "Net Corporation Sales Revenue", which is the excess of revenue over expenses, calculated as between its shareholders based on their relative trading shares in "Total Market Issues" (being "Designated Issues" plus "Corporate Bonds") through a two-step process. CanPX will determine the total trading volume in "Total Market Issues" and then identify the percentage of such volume attributable to each of three separate "markets", being the "IDB Market", the "Corporate Bond Market" and the "ATS Market".

No methodology currently exists to allocate the Consolidated Data revenues to the contributors to the Consolidated Data irrespective of the contributors' shareholder status. CanPX understands the need to have such a model in place and will look at developing an equitable framework for all contributors to the Consolidated Data regardless of their shareholder status. CanPX is of the view that an acceptable revenue model must also take into consideration the capital contributions already provided by existing shareholders.

Part 2: MARKET PARTICIPANTS

4. — Marketplaces, Dealers or Other Parties for which the Information Processor is Acting or for which It Proposes to Act as an Information Processor, and a Description of the Function(s) which the Information Processor Performs or Proposes to Perform

Since May 2004, marketplaces and dealers that have achieved a market share of 0.5% of total corporate bond trading have been required to provide trade details on designated corporate bond debt instruments to CanPX within one hour of the trade, subject to volume caps of $2 million for investment grade corporate debt securities and $200,000 for non-investment grade corporate debt securities. CanPX has submitted Form 21-101F5 to the Canadian Securities Administrators for the opportunity to continue to act as the information processor for dealers or marketplaces that achieves the 0.5% threshold for corporate bond trading.

The following twelve investment dealers, who collectively represent the vast majority of bond trading in Canada, currently contribute corporate trade information into CanPX for the Consolidated Data:

1. BMO Nesbitt Burns Inc.
2. Casgrain & Company Limited
3. CIBC World Markets Inc.
4. Desjardins Securities Inc.
5. Laurentian Bank Securities
6. National Bank Financial
7. HSBC (Canada) Securities
8. Merrill Lynch Canada Inc.
9. Canaccord Capital Corporation
10. RBC Capital Markets Inc.
11. Scotia Capital Inc.
12. TD Securities Inc.

The following data is transmitted by contributors into CanPX:

- Issuer
- Security type
- Class
- Series
- Type of counterparty
- Coupon
- Maturity
- Price
- Time of the trade
- Volume

The CanPX system also consolidates real-time and traded prices for Canadian fixed income and money market products, utilizing electronic feeds from Canadian IDBs. Securities currently covered in the Supplementary Data include Government of Canada treasury bills and bonds and provincial bonds. CanPX formation documents also permit alternative trading systems (ATSs) to contribute feeds into CanPX and become shareholders of CanPX.

The following three IDBs contribute to the Supplementary Data:

1. Freedom International Brokerage Company
2. Shorcan Brokers Limited
3. Tullet Prebon Canada Limited

Trade data from CanPX contributors (both the Consolidated and Supplementary Data) is aggregated by CanPX's technical facilitator and made available to market participants and investors through data vendors contracted by CanPX.

In 2008, the CanPX board of directors elected to pursue a new initiative to make CanPX part of a more robust transparency framework by having CanPX offered as part of a broader package of fixed-income market data.

CanPX has selected CanDeal as the optimal partner for this initiative. CanDeal will take on the role of CanPX's new technical facilitator and marketing agent/wholesale distributor as part of a signed agreement, and subject to CanPX continuing to act as an information processor. The CanPX board of directors will retain responsibility for the governance of CanPX.

5. — Selection of Securities Reported to the Information Processor and Services Provided by the Information Processor

a. — Corporate Bonds (Consolidated Data — as required under NI 21-101)

Currently, trade data for designated corporate bonds is transmitted by participating investment dealers (who comprise the vast majority of bond trading Canada) within one hour of the trade. Trade publication takes place at hourly intervals. The list of corporate bonds for which information is collected is updated on a quarterly basis following the selection process summarized below. CanPX has succeeded in gradually increasing the size of the corporate bond list over time — the current list is represented by approximately 100 corporate securities as compared to fewer than 25 when CanPX first began reporting corporate bond trade information. A recent list of corporate bonds for which trade information is collected and disseminated through CanPX is available at www.CanPX.ca.

The current selection criteria with respect to corporate bond securities include: trading volumes, whether bonds are included in domestic Canadian corporate bond indices and issue size (with a minimum issue size of Cdn $250 million). Other factors are considered to ensure that the list of corporate bonds includes bonds:

- issued by issuers among the major industrial groups of issuers;
- that are highly liquid (relative to comparables);
- that represent a majority of trade flow within the corporate bond markets;
- of short-term maturities, mid-term maturities and long-term bonds; and
- from each industry classification (with at least two from each classification).

The list of corporate bonds includes private sector issuers that are represented in a major corporate bond index and are relatively well-known credits to retail investors.

The following procedure is currently observed:

1. The list of corporate securities is reviewed quarterly by the CanPX Corporate Bond Working Group.
2. New issues are added to, and issues will be removed, from the list, according to the criteria above.
3. The list of corporate bonds should be increased over time, subject to the practical constraints of obtaining enough liquidity or updates to report.
4. The proposed revised list is circulated to the CanPX board for approval.
5. Upon CanPX board approval, the final list will then be sent to the technical facilitator for implementation.
6. The corporate bond list is made publicly available on the CanPX website.

b. — Government of Canada treasury bills and bonds (part of Supplementary Data)

Bid/offer prices, yields and trades for government of Canada Treasury Bills and Bonds transacted through the IDB market are collected into CanPX and disseminated via CanPX vendors. Bids, offers and trade prices are published in real-time along with accompanying fields for Bid/Ask size, yield and trade volume.

c. — Provincial government bonds (part of Supplementary Data)

Bid/offer prices, yields and trades for provincial bonds transacted through the IDB market are collected into CanPX and disseminated via CanPX vendors. Bids, offers and trade prices are published in real-time along with accompanying fields for Bid/Ask size, yield and trade volume.

Appendix B — Undertakings Provided by CanPX

In connection with the updated Form 21-101F5 (F5) filed by CanPX Inc. (CanPX) on February 6, 2009 and revised on March 18, 2009 and its role as the information processor for corporate debt securities, CanPX undertakes the following:

1. — Changes to Form 21-101F5

a. As required by section 14.2 of National Instrument 21-101 *Marketplace Operation* (NI 21-101), CanPX will file with the CSA amendments to the information provided in Form 21-101F5. The significant changes referred to in section 14.2(1) of NI 21-101 will be reviewed and approved by CSA staff prior to their implementation. These significant changes include the following:

- changes to the governance of CanPX, including the structure of the Advisory Committee referred to in paragraph 2b below,
- significant changes to the fees charged for corporate debt information distributed as the IP,
- changes to the fee structure and fee / revenue sharing model related to the services provided as the IP,
- changes to the data products offered as the IP,
- changes to the threshold for reporting trades in corporate debt securities,
- removal of marketplaces, dealers or inter-dealer bond brokers required to report trade data regarding corporate debt securities,
- changes to the selection criteria for the corporate debt securities reported to CanPX,
- any reduction in the number of corporate debt securities reported to CanPX,
- significant changes to the systems, technology or technology provider used by CanPX, including those affecting capacity, or

- changes affecting the independence of the IP from the contributors of corporate debt securities information (Data Contributors) or the business activities of its technology provider.

2. — Governance

a. CanPX's Board of Directors will meet at regular times, and no less than quarterly.

b. CanPX will establish an Advisory Committee that will include representation from Data Contributors, and from subscribers and vendors (Data Purchasers) by October 31, 2009. The Advisory Committee's mandate will include that the committee will provide CanPX with views and recommendations on issues of concern to the committee members, including issues related to: the fee structure or fees charged by CanPX as the IP; the method of revenue allocation between the IP, the Data Contributors and the technology provider; the quality and timeliness of data provided by the information processor; new products or changes to existing products offered by the IP; and any conflict of interest matters. The IP will consider the views and recommendations of the Advisory Committee and, where it rejects such views, will inform the committee of the reasons and keep adequate record of all discussions and decisions.

c. CanPX will notify CSA staff of the composition, and any changes to the composition, of the Advisory Committee.

d. The mandate of the Advisory Committee will make reference to the ability of the committee to contact the Director of the Market Regulation Branch of the Ontario Securities Commission and the Director, SRO Oversight at the Autorité des marchés financiers with any concerns that it may have regarding the governance or operations of the IP.

e. The Advisory Committee will maintain minutes of its meetings and these minutes will reflect the views and recommendations provided to CanPX's management; the minutes will be made available, upon request, to CSA staff.

3. — Conflicts of Interest

a. By July 31, 2009, CanPX will establish policies and procedures to address the conflicts of interest related to the business activities of its board members.

b. By July 31, 2009, CanPX will establish policies and procedures to address the potential conflicts of interest that arise due to the fact that its technology provider is also a marketplace and a distributor of data.

c. CanPX will provide the policies and procedures described in paragraphs 3a and 3b, and any subsequent changes to those policies and procedures, to CSA staff for review and approval.

4. — IP Products

a. CanPX will limit the products distributed as the IP to a consolidated feed (the Consolidated Data Product) that displays the information related to corporate debt securities provided to it in accordance with the requirements set out in Part 8 of NI 21-101 and Part 10 of the Companion Policy 21-101CP. CanPX will display this information no later than one hour from the time of the trade.

b. CanPX will not distribute, as the IP, any additional products using the data provided to it under Part 8 of NI 21-101unless it obtains prior approval from CSA staff.

c. If CanPX intends to create and distribute, other than as the IP, any products using the data provided to it under Part 8 of NI 21-101:

> i. the data required to be provided to the IP by Data Contributors will not be used for such other products without the permission of the Data Contributors; and

> ii. the additional products will be made available for purchase separately from, and will not be bundled with, the Consolidated Data Product and any other products approved under paragraph 4b.

5. — Data reported to and disseminated by CanPX

a. By October 31, 2009, CanPX will establish and document:

> i. policies and procedures to verify the timeliness and accuracy of information received and disseminated by the IP; and

> ii. processes to resolve on a timely basis any data integrity issues identified.

b. CanPX will provide the policies and procedures described in paragraph 5a, and any further changes to those policies and procedures, to CSA staff for review and approval.

c. CanPX will monitor the timeliness and accuracy of information received by and disseminated by the IP on an ongoing basis and take adequate measures to resolve any data integrity issues on a timely basis. CanPX will report to its Board of Directors within 30 days of the end of each calendar quarter on the timeliness and accuracy of the information received by and disseminated by the IP, along with significant data integrity issues and the measures to address them. This report will be provided to CSA staff within 15 days of providing it to the Board.

d. By October 31, 2009, CanPX will complete an assessment of the adequacy of the current process to randomize the corporate bond data displayed in accordance with the requirements of NI 21-101. Immediately upon completion, CanPX will report the results of the assessment, as well as its action plan to address any identified issues, to CSA staff.

e. CanPX will assess, on an annual basis, the continuing adequacy of the existing threshold for reporting of corporate debt securities and of the parties that qualify as Data Contributors and will report the results of the assessment to CSA staff. This assessment will be included as part of the self-assessment described in paragraph 7a below.

f. Within 90 days of the end of CanPX's fiscal year, CanPX will provide to CSA staff its plan to increase the number of corporate debt securities for which trade information will be reported to and disseminated by the IP on an annual basis.

6. — Resources

a. CanPX will maintain sufficient financial resources to ensure its financial viability.

b. CanPX will provide to CSA staff its audited financial statements, along with the report signed by an independent auditor within 90 days of the end of each fiscal year.

c. CanPX will ensure that it has an adequate number of staff dedicated to its systems and operations to ensure the proper performance of its functions, including staff directly responsible for monitoring of the corporate debt data reported to it in accordance with the requirements of NI 21-101.

7. — Self-assessment

a. In addition to arranging for an annual independent system review referred to in section 14.5 of NI 21-101, CanPX will conduct an annual self-assessment of its compliance with subsections 14.4(2), (4) and (5) of NI 21-101 and with its performance with respect to the undertakings provided to the CSA. A report on the self-assessment will be provided to CanPX's Advisory Committee promptly upon its completion. CanPX will ask the Advisory Committee to review the report and provide its views in writing. The report and the views of the Advisory Committee will be provided to CSA staff within 90 days of the end of CanPX's fiscal year.

8. — Agreements with Data Contributors

a. CanPX will ensure that all Data Contributors are given access to CanPX on fair and reasonable terms.

b. New standard agreements or contracts to be entered into between CanPX and Data Contributors in connection with the IP services will be provided to CSA staff for review and approval prior to their execution. In addition, any proposed material changes to these standard agreements or contracts will be provided to CSA staff for review and approval.

9. — Fees / Fee structure / Revenue sharing

a. CanPX will make available, on its website, the fee schedule for the Consolidated Data Product, and any additional products subsequently approved by CSA staff to be distributed by CanPX as an information processor.

b. CanPX will revise its revenue sharing model to allow for compensation to all the contributors of corporate debt data regardless of whether or not they are shareholders by December 31, 2009.

10. — Non-exclusivity

a. CanPX acknowledges that the selection as an IP does not grant that IP exclusive rights to consolidate and disseminate order and trade data. CanPX will not seek such exclusivity through the terms of any contract with a Data Contributor or Data Purchaser.

11. — Time to implementation and transition to new technical facilitator

a. CanPX will use best efforts to have the new CanDeal-based platform functional and ready for testing by October 31, 2009.

b. CanPX will use best efforts to complete the transition from its existing technology provider to CanDeal by December 31, 2009.

c. CanPX will provide the CSA with a detailed schedule setting out the timeline for transition from its existing to the new technology provider promptly after July 1, 2009. CanPX will provide a monthly update to CSA staff indicating its progress.

d. CanPX will promptly report to the CSA any expected transition delays, along with its steps to address such delays.

12. — Term and notice

a. CanPX will continue to act as an information processor for corporate debt securities for a period of five years starting from July 1, 2009. CanPX will use its best efforts to provide CSA staff with at least one year notice should it determine that it does not wish to continue as an information processor upon the expiry of the 5-year term.

CSA Staff Notice 21-312 — Update on Consultation Paper 21-401 Real Time Market Data Fees

Date: November 7, 2013

36 O.S.C.B. 10601

[Not reproduced]

CSA Staff Notice 21-313 — Information Processor for Exchange-Traded Securities other than Options

Date: June 27, 2014

37 O.S.C.B. 6233

1. — Introduction

Canadian Securities Adminstrators (CSA) staff (CSA staff or we) are publishing this notice to inform the public that TMX Information Processor (TMX IP) will continue to act as an information processor for exchange-traded securities other than options[1] under National Instrument 21-101 *Marketplace Operation* (NI 21-101) for a period of four years from July 1, 2014 to June 30, 2018.

2. — Regulatory Requirements and the Need for an Information Processor

In the current environment where multiple marketplaces trade the same exchange-traded securities, it is important to have a consolidated source of data to address issues related to the fragmentation of information that may occur as a result. An information processor collects, consolidates and disseminates the marketplaces' data and thus ensures that investors and market participants have at least one source of consolidated data. An information processor also facilitates compliance by marketplace participants with relevant regulatory requirements that apply in a multiple marketplace environment by ensuring the availability of consolidated data that meets regulatory standards and which users can use to demonstrate or evaluate compliance with these requirements.

---

[1] In Québec, options are not "exchange-traded securities", but are derivatives under the *Derivatives Act* (Québec) and are therefore already excluded.

NI 21-101 provides for the operation and regulation of an information processor. An information processor is defined as a person or company that receives and provides information under NI 21-101 and has filed Form 21-101F5 *Initial Operation Report for Information Processor* (Form 21-101F5).

Part 7 of NI 21-101 sets out the transparency requirements for marketplaces that trade exchange-traded securities. Subsection 7.1(1) of NI 21-101 requires a marketplace that displays orders of exchange-traded securities to a person or company to provide accurate and timely information regarding orders for the exchange-traded securities displayed by the marketplace to an information processor or, in its absence, to an information vendor. An exception is provided in subsection 7.1(2) for marketplaces that only display orders to their employees or to persons or companies retained by the marketplaces to assist in the operation of the marketplace, if the orders posted on the marketplaces meet the size threshold set by a regulation services provider.

Section 7.2 of NI 21-101 requires marketplaces to provide trade information related to exchange-traded securities to an information processor or, in its absence, to an information vendor. The information processor has some flexibility regarding the information to be reported to it by the marketplaces.

The regulatory requirements that apply to the information processor are set out in Part 14 of NI 21-101. They include:

- a requirement to provide prompt and accurate order and trade information and to not unreasonably restrict fair access to such information;

- a requirement to provide timely, accurate, reliable and fair collection, processing, distribution and publication of information for orders for, and trades in, securities;

- an obligation to maintain reasonable books and records; and

- certain system requirements, including an annual independent systems review.

In addition, the information processor is required to establish, in a timely manner, an electronic connection to each marketplace that is required to provide information under NI 21-101, and also to enter into an agreement with each such marketplace. The agreement must set out that the marketplace will provide the information processor information in accordance with Part 7 of NI 21-101 and that it will comply with any other reasonable requirements set by the information processor.

An information processor is designated as a market participant under the *Securities Act* (Ontario) and may be recognized as an information processor under the *Securities Act* (Québec).

3. — TMX IP

TMX IP has been an information processor for exchange-traded securities other than options since July 1, 2009. It is operated by a division of TMX Group Limited. As an information processor, it collects data from all the marketplaces that are required to provide it to meet the requirements set out in Part 14 of NI 21-101, and consolidates and disseminates this data.

TMX IP disseminates the following products (together, the Consolidated Products):

- Consolidated Data Feed, which provides access to order and trade market data from each marketplace that contributes its data to the TMX IP (contributing marketplace);

- Consolidated Last Sale, which provides real-time trading data from all contributing marketplaces;

- Canadian Best Bid and Offer, which provides a consolidated best bid and offer for all Canadian exchange-traded securities other than options; and

- Consolidated Depth of Book, which provides a single consolidated view of the order book from the contributing marketplaces.

The TMX IP has a "pass-through" fee model, where the contributing marketplaces enter into contractual agreements with data vendors and subscribers directly, allowing each marketplace's fees to be passed along to the end users. A monthly fee is charged by TMX IP for each of the Consolidated Products. The fees are published on the TMX IP's website.[2] The TMX IP has a Governance Committee (the IP Governance Committee) with representatives from each contributing marketplace. An individual who is independent of all marketplaces and the TMX sits on the IP Governance Committee in a non-voting capacity and acts as Committee Chair. Each marketplace has one voting seat. The IP Governance Committee has decision-making authority with respect to the scope of service, operational priorities and enhancements, bandwidth and capacity planning, criteria and methods for monitoring performance.

CSA Staff Notice 21-309 *Information Processor for Exchange-Traded Securities other than Options* (CSA Staff Notice 21-309)[3] was published in 2009 to inform the public that TMX IP would act as an information processor. CSA Staff Notice 21-309 also outlined a number of undertakings over and above the applicable requirements in Part 14 of NI 21-101 with which TMX IP agreed to comply. A high-level summary of these undertakings is included below:

- TMX IP agreed to establish policies and procedures to address conflicts of interest related to the operation of the information processor by the TMX;

- TMX IP agreed to only distribute the Consolidated Products under the information processor designation and to obtain approval from CSA staff to distribute additional products using the data provided to it by marketplaces;

---

[2]http://www.tmx.com/en/pdf/IP_InfomationSheet.pdf.

[3]http://www.osc.gov.on.ca/documents/en/Securities-Category2/csa_20090605_21-309_processor-exchange.pdf.

- TMX IP agreed to conduct an annual self-assessment of its compliance with subsections 14.4(2), (4) and (5) of NI 21-101 and with its performance with respect to the undertakings;

- TMX IP agreed to provide a report of the self-assessment to the IP Governance Committee and file the report and the views of the IP Governance Committee with the CSA;

- TMX IP acknowledged that it does not have exclusive rights to consolidating and disseminating order and trade data; and

- TMX IP agreed to ensure that all data contributors are given access to the IP on fair and reasonable terms.

4. — CSA Oversight over TMX IP

Since July 1, 2009, TMX IP has been subject to ongoing oversight of CSA staff, which consists of:

- Quarterly and ad-hoc meetings or calls with TMX IP staff to discuss issues;

- Staff reviews of changes to the information included in Form 21-101F5 that were filed in accordance with the requirements of NI 21-101;

- Review of the reports related to the independent systems reviews that TMX IP arranged to have completed in accordance with the applicable requirement in NI 21-101;

- Review of minutes of meetings of the IP Governance Committee to understand the issues discussed and how they were resolved;

- Reviews of the reports of self-assessment prepared by TMX IP and of the comments from the IP Governance Committee;

- Review of financial information provided by TMX IP in accordance with the requirements of NI 21-101;

- Review of incident reports, including how the incidents were resolved; and

- An on-site oversight review to look at areas that may not have been fully covered through ongoing oversight, such as conflicts of interest, interaction between the TMX IP and the IP Governance Committee and financial viability.

We found, through our ongoing oversight, that TMX IP was in compliance with the applicable provisions in NI 21-101 and with its undertakings and do not have concerns regarding its performance as an IP.

5. — Conclusion

Based on the results of our oversight of the TMX IP, CSA staff believe that it is not contrary to the public interest for TMX IP to continue to act as an information processor for exchange-traded securities other than options for a period of four years from July 1, 2014 to June 30, 2018.

CSA staff note that, on May 15, 2014, the CSA published for comment Proposed Amendments to National Instrument 23-101 *Trading Rules*.[4] A significant part of the Proposed Amendments deals with the order protection rule (OPR). Currently, OPR requires that all better-priced orders be executed before inferior-priced orders, regardless of the marketplace on which the order is displayed. Under the Proposed Amendments, orders would only be protected when displayed on a marketplace that has met certain criteria. The comment period for the Proposed OPR Amendments ends on September 19, 2014, and the CSA will consider whether the Proposed Amendments will proceed in their current form or whether further changes will be needed. In the event that OPR will be amended to require that orders only be protected when displayed on certain marketplaces, staff will discuss the issue with TMX IP and will determine what changes are necessary prior to the implementation of the amendments. The TMX IP Undertakings have been revised to reflect this fact, and also to acknowledge that some of the undertakings that TMX IP had agreed to meet in 2009 have been completed. The new undertakings are listed at Appendix A of this notice.

6. — Questions

Please refer your questions any of the following:

[Omitted.]

Appendix A — Undertakings Provided by TMX IP

In connection with the extension of its role as the information processor for exchange-traded securities other than options[1] , TMX IP undertakes the following:

1. — Changes to Form 21-101F5

a. As required by section 14.2 of National Instrument 21-101 *Marketplace Operation* (NI 21-101), TMX IP will file with the CSA amendments to the information provided in Form 21-101F5. The significant changes referred to in section 14.2(1) of NI 21-101 will be reviewed and

---

[4]See CSA Notice and Request for Comment Proposed Amendments to National Instrument 23-101 Trading Rules, available at (2014), 37 OSCB 4873.

[1]In Quebec, options are not "exchange-traded securities", but are derivatives under the *Derivatives Act* (Quebec) and are therefore already excluded.

approved by CSA staff prior to their implementation. Examples of significant changes are provided in subsection 16.3 of the Companion Policy to NI 21-101 and, for greater certainty, include

- changes to the governance of the TMX IP, including the structure and mandate of its Governance Committee (IP Governance Committee) and the IP Advisory Sub-Committee,

- significant changes to the fees related to the services provided by the TMX IP, including subscriber access fees and distribution fees,

- changes to the fee structure and fee / revenue sharing model related to the services provided by the TMX IP,

- changes to the data products offered by the TMX IP,

- significant changes to the systems and technology used by the TMX IP, including those affecting capacity, or

- changes in the technology provider and any changes that would have the effect of increasing the TMX IP's level of dependence on TMX Group Limited proprietary technology.

b. TMX IP will notify CSA staff of the representatives of the IP Governance Committee and the IP Advisory Sub-Committee, and will provide notice of any changes to those representatives.

2. — Governance and Conflicts of Interest

a. The Boards of Directors of TMX Group Limited, TMX Group Inc. and TSX will not be involved in IP Governance Committee decisions relating to the scope of service, operational priorities, bandwidth, capacity planning, performance management, including service levels, and the fee and revenue sharing model related to the TMX IP.

b. TMX IP will maintain and monitor compliance with policies and procedures to separate TSX's marketplace business operations from the TMX IP operations and manage inherent conflicts of interest and provide changes to these policies and procedures to CSA staff for review and approval.

c. The technology used by the TMX IP will not give the marketplaces affiliated (as defined in NI 21-101) with TMX Group Limited an unfair advantage with respect to their data as compared to other marketplaces.

3. — IP Products

a. TMX IP will only distribute the following products which are described in Form 21-101F5 (together, the Consolidated Data Products):

- the Consolidated Data Feed (CDF);

- the Canadian Best Bid and Offer (CBBO);

- the Consolidated Last Sale (CLS); and

- the Consolidated Depth of Book Feed.

b. TMX IP will review the Consolidated Data Products, and consider any new products or changes to the Consolidated Data Products that may be reasonably required in response to amendments to Part 6 of National Instrument 23-101 *Trading Rules* (Order Protection Rule), as such amendments may be adopted by the CSA during the term of this Undertaking.

c. TMX IP will not distribute any additional products using the data provided to it under Part 7 of NI 21-101 unless it obtains prior approval from CSA staff.

d. As provided by TMX IP, each data product comprising the Consolidated Data Products is permitted to be bundled for sale to Data Purchasers[2], but will also be made available as separately permissionable feeds.

e. If TMX Group Limited or any affiliated entity, (where an affiliated entity has the meaning ascribed to it in section 1.3 of NI 21-101), intends to create and distribute products using the data provided to TMX IP under Part 7 of NI 21-101, through its commercial distribution channels and not through TMX IP:

    i. the data required to be provided to the TMX IP by Data Contributors[3] will not be used for such other products without the permission of the Data Contributors; and

    ii. the additional products will be made available for purchase separately from, and will not be bundled with, the Consolidated Data Products and any other products approved under paragraph 3a and 3c.

TMX Group Limited will not provide an associate (where an associate has the meaning ascribed to it in subsection 1(1) of the *Securities Act* (Ontario)) with the underlying data which is provided by the Data Contributors to TMX IP for the purposes of creating the Consolidated Data Products without the permission of the Data Contributors.

    f. TMX IP will consolidate, update and provide in real-time the Consolidated Data Products during the hours of operation of any Canadian marketplace required to provide information to an information processor under NI 21-101, provided that TMX IP can perform normal course recycle, batch and maintenance operations. TMX IP will provide customer support between the hours of 7:30–17:30 and 24/7 technical support for TMX IP.

---

[2]For the purposes of this reference and any subsequent reference, the term Data Purchaser includes subscribers, vendors, and any other party that purchases any data product offered by the TMX IP.

[3]For the purposes of this reference and any subsequent reference, the term Data Contributor includes marketplaces and any other party that provides data to the TMX IP under requirements in NI 21-101 to provide order and trade information to an information processor.

4. — Agreements with Data Contributors

a. TMX IP will ensure that all Data Contributors are given access to the TMX IP on fair and reasonable terms.

b. The standard agreements or contracts to be entered into between TMX IP and Data Contributors in connection with the TMX IP services will be provided to CSA staff for review and approval prior to their execution. In addition, any proposed material changes to these standard agreements or contracts will be provided to CSA staff for review and approval.

5. — Fees / Fee structure / Revenue sharing

a. TMX IP will make the fee schedule for the Consolidated Data Products available on its website.

b. If any adjustment or modification is proposed to fees, fee structure, or the fee / revenue sharing model relating to the services of TMX IP, the TMX IP will ask the IP Governance Committee to seek input from the IP Advisory Sub-Committee prior to approving such adjustments or modifications.

c. TMX IP will report annually to CSA staff, in writing, whether it has fully recovered its costs (including cost of capital and cost to meet the requirements under subsections 14.4(2), (4), and (5) of NI 21-101) associated with offering the TMX IP services and will review and report on whether the profit margin received from the TMX IP services is in line with industry standards.

d. If there are excess revenues over costs plus a reasonable profit margin, and that excess is not allocated to operating and/or capacity expansion of the TMX IP, the TMX IP will examine its options for the use of that excess revenue and analyze and recommend an appropriate use to the IP Governance Committee. TMX IP will ask the IP Governance Committee to review the analysis and recommendations and provide its views in writing to TMX IP. The analysis, recommendations and the views of the IP Governance Committee will be provided to CSA staff within 30 days of the IP Governance Committee having received the analysis and recommendations.

e. TMX IP will conduct a review of the "pass-through" fee model upon request by CSA staff. Such review will examine the fee models used by data consolidators in other jurisdictions and the cost of data in Canada. It will also consider reports or studies available at the time of the review. A report outlining the conclusions from the review and the basis for those conclusions, along with any recommendations, will be provided to the IP Governance Committee promptly upon completion. TMX IP will ask the IP Governance Committee to review the report and provide its views in writing to the TMX IP. The report and the views of the IP Governance Committee will be provided to CSA staff within 90 days of the Review Initiation Date.

6. — Non-exclusivity

TMX IP acknowledges that the selection of an information processor does not grant the information processor exclusive rights to consolidating and disseminating order and trade data. TMX IP will not seek exclusivity through the terms of any contract relating to the Consolidated Data Products, or involving the data underlying the Consolidated Data Products, with a Data Contributor or Data Purchaser.

7. — Self-assessment

In addition to arranging for an annual independent system review referred to in section 14.5 of NI 21-101, TMX IP will conduct an annual self-assessment of its compliance with subsections 14.4(2), (4), and (5) of NI 21-101 and with its performance with respect to the undertakings provided to the CSA. A report on the self-assessment will be provided to the IP Governance Committee promptly upon its completion. TMX IP will ask the IP Governance Committee to review the report and provide its views in writing. The report and the views of the IP Governance Committee will be provided to CSA staff within 90 days of the end of the TMX IP's fiscal year.

8. — Financial Viability

TMX Group Limited will provide TMX IP with sufficient financial and other resources to ensure its financial viability and the proper performance of its functions.

9. — Term and Notice

TMX IP will continue to act as an information processor for exchange traded securities other than options for a period of four years starting from July 1, 2014 to June 30, 2018 subject to the right of the TMX IP to provide CSA staff with at least one year notice should it determine that it does not wish to continue to act as an information processor.

CSA Staff Notice 21-314 — Information Processor for Corporate Debt Securities

Date: June 27, 2014

37 O.S.C.B. 6240

1. — Introduction

Canadian Securities Administrators (CSA) staff (CSA staff or we) are publishing this notice to inform the public that CanPX Inc. (CanPX) will continue to act as an information processor for corporate debt securities under National Instrument 21-101 *Marketplace Operation* (NI 21-101) for a period of 18 months from July 1, 2014 to December 31, 2015.

2. — Regulatory Requirements

NI 21-101 provides for the operation and regulation of an information processor. An information processor is defined as a person or company that receives and provides information under NI 21-101 and has filed Form 21-101F5 *Initial Operation Report for Information Processor* (Form 21-101F5). An information processor is designated as a market participant under the *Securities Act* (Ontario) and may be recognized as an information processor under the *Securities Act* (Quebec).

Part 8 of NI 21-101 sets out the transparency requirements applicable to corporate debt securities. Specifically, marketplaces that display orders of corporate debt securities are required to provide information regarding orders for designated corporate debt securities to an information processor, if an information processor is in place. Marketplaces, inter-dealer bond brokers (IDBs) and dealers are also required to provide trade information for corporate debt securities to an information processor, if one is in place, as required by the information processor.[1] CanPX is the information processor for corporate debt securities.

The regulatory requirements that apply to the information processor are set out in Part 14 of NI 21-101. They include:

- a requirement to provide prompt and accurate order and trade information and not unreasonably restrict fair access to such information;

- a requirement to provide timely, accurate, reliable and fair collection, processing, distribution and publication of information for orders for, and trades in, securities;

- an obligation to maintain reasonable books and records; and

- certain system requirements, including an annual independent systems review.

3. — CanPX

CanPX has been an information processor for corporate debt securities since 2003. Its status as an information processor was most recently renewed in 2009, for a period of five years from July 1, 2009 to June 30, 2014.[2]

As the information processor for corporate debt securities, CanPX is responsible for designating the corporate debt securities for which it receives and disseminates post-trade information (the Designated Corporate Debt Securities).[3] It makes the selection in accordance with a set of selection criteria which are published on its website[4] and which include trading volumes, whether bonds are included in domestic Canadian corporate bond indices and issue size.[5] At this time, approximately 340 securities are included on the Designated Corporate Debt Securities list. The information disseminated is subject to volume caps and is disseminated one hour after the trade was reported to CanPX. The volume caps are $2 million for investment grade corporate debt securities and $200,000 for non-investment grade corporate debt securities. The trade data is aggregated by CanPX's technical facilitator and made available to market participants and investors through data vendors contracted by CanPX.

CanPX currently requires that only marketplaces and dealers that have achieved a market share of 0.5% of total corporate bond trading provide trade details regarding the Designated Corporate Debt Securities. Currently, this includes 12 investment dealers.

In addition to complying with the applicable requirements in NI 21-101, CanPX has agreed to comply with a number of undertakings that, among others, require CanPX to address conflicts of interest such as those related to the business activities of its board members, maintaining transparency for corporate debt securities and maintaining the integrity of corporate debt data it disseminates. These initial undertakings were published in CSA Staff Notice 21-310 *Information Processor for Corporate Debt Securities*.[6]

4. — CSA Oversight over CanPX

CanPX has been subject to ongoing oversight of CSA staff which includes:

- Quarterly and ad-hoc meetings or calls with CanPX board members to discuss issues;

- Staff reviews of changes to the information included in Form 21-101F5 that were filed in accordance with the requirements of NI 21-101;

- Review of the reports related to the independent systems reviews that CanPX arranged to have completed in accordance with the requirement in NI 21-101;

- Review of minutes of meetings of the Advisory Committee to understand the issues discussed and how they were resolved;

- Reviews of the self-assessments prepared by CanPX;

- Review of financial information provided by CanPX in accordance with the requirements of NI 21-101; and

- An on-site oversight review to look at areas that may not have been fully covered through ongoing oversight, such as processes to address conflict of interest, processes for maintaining and increasing transparency in the corporate debt market, fees and resources, and the processes for maintaining the integrity of data reported to and disseminated by CanPX.

---

[1]For government debt securities, the requirements for marketplaces and IDBs to provide order and trade information have been postponed until December 31, 2014. On April 24, 2014, the CSA published for comment proposed amendments to NI 21-101 that would, among others, extend the exemption from transparency requirements for government debt securities for an additional three year period.

[2]CSA staff announced the renewal of CanPX in CSA Staff Notice 21-310 *Information Processor for Corporate Debt Securities*, published in Ontario at (2009) 32 OSCB 5159.

[3]The CSA allowed CanPX to make the selection in order to promote an industry solution to corporate debt transparency, in response to significant industry pressure against a solution to fixed income transparency that is mandated by regulators.

[4]For a description of the criteria and process for selection, see http://www.canpxonline.ca/selectioncriteria.php.

[5]Currently, this is $250 million, however, CanPX has proposed to eliminate this threshold.

[6]Ibid 2, at page 5167.

Our ongoing oversight shows that CanPX generally met its undertakings and was in compliance with the applicable requirements of NI 21-101. As of June 4, 2014, the list of Designated Corporate Debt Securities was approximately 340 securities.

We are concerned, however, that the increase in the number of Designated Corporate Debt Securities has been slow and that CanPX's corporate bond trade data has not been made readily available to investors, and specifically, to retail investors. This calls into question whether CanPX's contribution to corporate fixed income transparency has been meaningful.

We note that fixed income transparency, including corporate debt transparency, is an important regulatory objective. In Ontario, regulation of fixed income securities has been identified as one of the priorities of the Ontario Securities Commission for both the fiscal year 2013-2014[7] and fiscal year 2014-2015.[8] We included these considerations in our decision whether to extend CanPX's status as an information processor and for how long it should be extended.

CanPX has committed to a number of measures to increase corporate debt transparency to retail and institutional investors. These measures include enhancing the process through which corporate bonds are designated by CanPX for inclusion on the Designated Corporate Debt Securities list, increasing CanPX's profile in the marketplace to ensure that the public is aware of the existence of this consolidated source of information, and providing greater access to CanPX's transparency products, particularly among retail investors. Despite this, it is our intention to conduct a review of transparency in the corporate debt market to assess whether the current approach is appropriate to achieve our goal. As part of this review, we will determine whether it is appropriate to continue with an industry-led solution to corporate debt transparency or whether additional regulatory intervention is required. We have extended CanPX for the interim period and will assess its role at the conclusion of our review.

5. — Conclusion

CSA staff believe that it is not contrary to the public interest for CanPX to continue to act as an information processor for corporate debt securities for the interim period of 18 months from July 1, 2014 to December 31, 2015. CanPX has agreed to comply with additional undertakings to reflect this commitment. The new undertakings are listed at Appendix A of this notice.

In the meantime, as described above, we will conduct a review of the framework for corporate debt transparency and will consider steps to increase corporate debt transparency in the coming year

6. — Questions

Please refer your questions to any of the following:

[Omitted.]

Appendix A — Undertakings Provided by CanPX

In connection its role as the information processor for corporate debt securities, CanPX undertakes the following:

1. — Changes to Form 21-101F5

a. As required by section 14.2 of National Instrument 21-101 *Marketplace Operation* (NI 21-101), CanPX will file with the CSA amendments to the information provided in Form 21-101F5. The significant changes referred to in section 14.2(1) of NI 21-101 will be reviewed and approved by CSA staff prior to their implementation. These significant changes include the following:

- changes to the governance of CanPX, including the structure of the Advisory Committee referred to in paragraph 2b below,

- significant changes to the fees charged for corporate debt information distributed as the IP,

- changes to the fee structure and fee / revenue sharing model related to the services provided as the IP,

- changes to the data products offered as the IP,

- changes to the threshold for reporting trades in corporate debt securities,

- removal of marketplaces, dealers or inter-dealer bond brokers required to report trade data regarding corporate debt securities,

- changes to the selection criteria for the corporate debt securities reported to CanPX,

- any reduction in the number of corporate debt securities reported to CanPX,

- significant changes to the systems, technology or technology provider used by CanPX, including those affecting capacity, or

- changes affecting the independence of the IP from the contributors of corporate debt securities information (Data Contributors) or the business activities of its technology provider.

---

[7]OSC Notice 11-768 — *Notice of Statement of Priorities for Financial Year to End March 31, 2014*, available at http://www.osc.gov.on.ca/en/SecuritiesLaw_sn_20130627_11-768_sop-fiscal-2013-2014.htm.

[8]OSC Notice 11-769 — *Statement of Priorities — Request for Comments Regarding the Statement of Priorities for Financial Year to End March 31, 2015*, available at http://www.osc.gov.on.ca/en/SecuritiesLaw_sn_20140403_11-769_rfc-sop-fiscal-2014-2015.htm.

Part 2: MARKET PARTICIPANTS

2. — Governance

a. CanPX's Board of Directors will meet at regular times, and no less than quarterly.

b. CanPX will maintain its Advisory Committee that includes representation from Data Contributors, and from subscribers and vendors (Data Purchasers) and will provide a report within 15 days after each of its meetings that describes the topics discussed and their resolution.

c. CanPX will notify CSA staff of any changes to the composition of the Advisory Committee and of any changes to its mandate within 15 days from making the change.

d. The mandate of the Advisory Committee will continue to make reference to the ability of the committee to contact the Director of the Market Regulation Branch of the Ontario Securities Commission and the Senior Director, Market Structures at the Autorité des marchés financiers with any concerns that it may have regarding the governance or operations of the IP.

e. The Advisory Committee will maintain minutes of its meetings and these minutes will reflect the views and recommendations provided to CanPX's management. The minutes will be made available, upon request, to CSA staff.

3. — Conflicts of Interest

a. CanPX will maintain and monitor compliance with policies and procedures to address the conflicts of interest related to the business activities of its board members.

b. CanPX will maintain and monitor compliance with policies and procedures to address the potential conflicts of interest that arise due to the fact that its technology provider is also a marketplace and a distributor of data.

c. CanPX will provide any changes to the policies and procedures referred to in paragraphs 3a and 3b to CSA staff for review and approval.

4. — IP Products

a. CanPX will limit the products distributed as the IP to a consolidated feed (the Consolidated Data Product) that displays the information related to corporate debt securities provided to it in accordance with the requirements set out in Part 8 of NI 21-101 and Part 10 of the Companion Policy 21-101CP (Designated Corporate Debt Securities). CanPX will display this information no later than one hour from the time of the trade.

b. CanPX will not distribute, as the IP, any additional products using the data provided to it under Part 8 of NI 21-101 unless it obtains prior approval from CSA staff.

c. If CanPX intends to create and distribute, other than as the IP, any products using the data provided to it under Part 8 of NI 21-101:

   i. the data required to be provided to the IP by Data Contributors will not be used for such other products without the permission of the Data Contributors; and

   ii. the additional products will be made available for purchase separately from, and will not be bundled with, the Consolidated Data Product and any other products approved under paragraph 4b.

5. — Data reported to and disseminated by CanPX

a. CanPX will maintain and monitor compliance with:

   i. policies and procedures to verify the timeliness and accuracy of information received and disseminated by the IP; and

   ii. processes to resolve on a timely basis any data integrity issues identified.

b. CanPX will provide any changes to the policies and procedures referred to in paragraph 5a to CSA staff for review and approval'

c. CanPX will monitor the timeliness and accuracy of information received by and disseminated by the IP on an ongoing basis and take adequate measures to resolve any data integrity issues on a timely basis. CanPX will report to its Board of Directors at each of their quarterly meeting on the timeliness and accuracy of the information received by and disseminated by the IP, along with significant data integrity issues, for the most recent quarter. Within 15 days following the board meeting, a report will be provided by CanPX to CSA staff outlining the issues identified, if any, and the measures CanPX will take to address them.

d. CanPX will provide to CSA staff updates to its plan to increase the number of Designated Corporate Debt Securities by December 31, 2014 and by June 30, 2015.

e. CanPX will conduct additional reviews of the adequacy of the list of Designated Corporate Debt Securities by December 31, 2014 and by June 30, 2015 and prepare a report outlining the results of these reviews and its analysis to CSA staff within 15 days of the completion of the reviews. The report must include an analysis showing the coverage of retail-sized bonds trades, coverage of corporate bonds traded and coverage of total bonds issued, as well as statistics indicating the types of bonds on the Designated Corporate Debt Securities and the frequency of trades for bonds not included on the list.

f. CanPX will provide reports of the corporate debt securities removed from the Designated Corporate Debt Securities within 15 days of their removal. Such reports will include a brief analysis supporting the reason for their removal from the list.

g. CanPX will introduce a web-based application displaying end-of-day pricing for the previous day for each Designated Corporate Debt Securities, including the high and low traded prices and yields, by July 31, 2014.

h. CanPX will provide updates to staff regarding developments on new or potential agreements with data distributors on a monthly basis.

i. CanPX will assess, on an annual basis, the continuing adequacy of the existing threshold for reporting of corporate debt securities and of the parties that qualify as Data Contributors and will report the results of the assessment to CSA staff. This assessment will be included as part of the self-assessment described in paragraph 7a below.

6. — Resources

a. CanPX will maintain sufficient financial resources to ensure its financial viability.

b. CanPX will provide to CSA staff its audited financial statements, along with the report signed by an independent auditor within 90 days of the end of each fiscal year.

c. CanPX will ensure that it has an adequate number of staff dedicated to its systems and operations to ensure the proper performance of its functions, including staff directly responsible for monitoring of the corporate debt data reported to it in accordance with the requirements of NI 21-101.

7. — Self-assessment

a. In addition to arranging from an annual independent system review referred to in section 14.5 of NI 21-101, CanPX will conduct an annual self-assessment of its compliance with subsections 14.4(2), (4) and (5) of NI 21-101 and with its performance with respect to the undertakings provided to the CSA. A report on the self-assessment will be provided to CanPX's Advisory Committee promptly upon its completion. CanPX will ask the Advisory Committee to review the report and provide its views in writing. The report and the views of the Advisory Committee will be provided to CSA staff within 90 days of the end of CanPX's fiscal year.

8. — Agreements with Data Contributors

a. CanPX will ensure that all Data Contributors are given access to CanPX on fair and reasonable terms.

b. New standard agreements or contracts to be entered into between CanPX and Data Contributors in connection with the IP services will be provided to CSA staff for review and approval prior to their execution. In addition, any proposed material changes to these standard agreements or contracts will be provided to CSA staff for review and approval.

9. — Fees / Fee structure / Revenue sharing

CanPX will make available, on its website, the fee schedule for the Consolidated Data Product, and any additional products subsequently approved by CSA staff to be distributed by CanPX as an information processor.

10. — Non-exclusivity

CanPX acknowledges that the selection as an IP does not grant that IP exclusive rights to consolidate and disseminate order and trade data. CanPX will not seek such exclusivity through the terms of any contract with a Data Contributor or Data Purchaser.

11. — Term and notice

a. CanPX will continue to act as an information processor for corporate debt securities for a period of 18 months starting from July 1, 2014. CanPX will use best efforts to provide CSA staff with at least one year notice should it determine that it does not wish to continue as an information processor upon the expiry of this 18 month term.

CSA Staff Notice 21-316 — Information Processor for Corporate Debt Securities

Date: December 29, 2015

39 O.S.C.B. 1

1. — Introduction

Canadian Securities Administrators (CSA) staff (CSA staff or we) are publishing this notice to inform the public that CanPX Inc. (CanPX) will continue to act as an information processor for corporate debt securities under National Instrument 21-101 *Marketplace Operation* (NI 21-101) for a period of six months from January 1, 2016 to June 30, 2016.

2. — Requirements regarding Transparency of Corporate Debt Securities

Transparency of trading in corporate debt securities has been an important goal of the CSA. Providing information regarding trades in corporate bonds facilitates informed decision making by investors and contributes to the price discovery process.

Part 8 of NI 21-101 sets out the transparency requirements applicable to corporate debt securities. It requires marketplaces that display orders of corporate debt securities to provide information regarding orders for designated corporate debt securities to an information processor, as required by the information processor. Marketplaces, inter-dealer bond brokers and dealers are also required to provide trade information for corporate debt securities to an information processor, if one is in place, as required by the information processor.[1]

NI 21-101 also provides for the operation and regulation of an information processor.[2]

The regulatory requirements applicable to the information processor are set out in Part 14 of NI 21-101 and include requirements to:

• provide prompt and accurate order and trade information;

---

[1]For government debt securities, the requirements for marketplaces and inter-dealer bond brokers to provide order and trade information have been postponed until January 1, 2018.

[2]An information processor is defined as a person or company that receives and provides information under NI 21-101 and has filed Form 21-101F5 *Information Statement — Information Processor* (Form 21-101F5).

Part 2: MARKET PARTICIPANTS

- not unreasonably restrict fair access to such information;
- provide timely, accurate, reliable and fair collection, processing, distribution and publication of information for orders for, and trades in, securities;
- maintain reasonable books and records; and
- maintain resilient systems, including an annual independent systems review.

3. — CanPX as the Information Processor for Corporate Debt Securities

CanPX has been an information processor for corporate debt securities since 2003. We have included a high-level description of CanPX's operations at Appendix A. Its status as an information processor was most recently renewed in 2014 for an 18 month period, until December 31, 2015.[3]

We have recently published a proposed plan to increase fixed income transparency by transitioning the role of the information processor to the Investment Industry Regulatory Organization of Canada (IIROC). CSA Staff Notice and Request for Comment 21-315 *Next Steps in Regulation and Transparency of the Fixed Income Market* (CSA Staff Notice 21-315), published on September 17, 2015, included a description of the plan. It described our goal to expand corporate bond transparency so that post-trade information is available for all corporate bonds, subject to a dissemination delay and to volume caps. Our intention is to leverage IIROC's fixed income reporting platform (the Market Trade Reporting System, or MTRS 2.0)[4] and publish a subset of the information reported to IIROC by its dealer members. We will also work with IIROC after implementation to analyze the data received on MTRS 2.0 and develop a plan to reduce the dissemination delay.

In response to the request for comment on the planned transparency plan, we received 14 comment letters and are currently reviewing them. It is our expectation that we will publish additional information about the timing of the dissemination of the posttrade information, as well as details regarding what this information would include, in the first quarter of 2016.

In order to accommodate the transition of the information processor to IIROC, and also to consider and address the comments received on CSA Staff Notice 21-315, it is necessary to extend CanPX's status as an information processor until June 30, 2016. CanPX has agreed to continue to comply with a number of undertakings, set out at Appendix B of this Notice.

4. — Questions

Please refer your questions to any of the following:

     [Names not reproduced]

Appendix A — Overview of CanPX's Functions

As the information processor for corporate debt securities, CanPX is responsible for designating the corporate debt securities for which it receives and disseminates post-trade information (the Designated Corporate Debt Securities).[5] It makes the selection in accordance with a set of selection criteria which are published on its website[6] and which include whether the bonds are highly liquid, whether they represent a majority of trade flow within the corporate bond markets, whether they include bonds with short-term, mid-term and long-term maturities, and whether they cover each industry classification. At this time, approximately 450 securities are included on the Designated Corporate Debt Securities list. The information disseminated is subject to volume caps and is disseminated every hour. There are volume caps of $2 million for investment grade corporate debt securities and $200,000 for non-investment grade corporate debt securities. These volume caps mask the true dollar size of large trades. The trade data is aggregated by CanPX's technical facilitator and is made available to market participants and investors through data vendors contracted by CanPX. In addition, CanPX makes available on its website, free of charge, end-of-day pricing information on the Designated Corporate Debt Securities.[7]

CanPX currently requires that only marketplaces and dealers that have achieved a market share of 0.5% of total corporate bond trading provide to it trade details regarding the Designated Corporate Debt Securities. Currently, this includes 12 investment dealers.

In addition to complying with the applicable requirements in NI 21-101, CanPX has agreed to comply with a number of undertakings that, among others, require CanPX to address conflicts of interest such as those related to the business activities of its board members, maintaining transparency for corporate debt securities, and maintaining the integrity of corporate debt data it disseminates.[8]

---

[3]CSA staff announced the renewal of CanPX in CSA Staff Notice 21-314 *Information Processor for Corporate Debt Securities*, published in Ontario at (2014) 37 OSCB 6240.

[4]MTRS 2.0 was developed to facilitate the implementation of IIROC Rule 2800C *Transaction Reporting for Debt Securities*. This rule is being implemented in two stages. In the first stage, effective November 1, 2015, dealers that are Government Securities Distributors (GSDs) and affiliates that are GSDs are required to report. All other dealers will be required to report their transactions in the second stage, effective November 1, 2016.

[5]The CSA allowed CanPX to make the selection in order to promote an industry solution to corporate debt transparency, in response to significant industry pressure against a solution to fixed income transparency that is mandated by regulators.

[6]For a description of the criteria and process for selection, see http://www.canpxonline.ca/selectioncriteria.php.

[7]http://www.canpxonline.ca/quotes.php

[8]The existing undertakings in place until December 31, 2015 can be found at (2014) 37 OSCB 6243.

Appendix B — Undertakings Provided by CanPX

In connection with its role as the information processor for corporate debt securities, CanPX undertakes the following:

1. — Changes to Form 21-101F5

a. As required by section 14.2 of National Instrument 21-101 *Marketplace Operation* (NI 21-101), CanPX will file with the CSA amendments to the information provided in Form 21-101F5. The significant changes referred to in section 14.2(1) of NI 21-101 will be reviewed and approved by CSA staff prior to their implementation. These significant changes include the following:

- changes to the governance of CanPX, including the structure of the Advisory Committee referred to in paragraph 2b below,

- significant changes to the fees charged for corporate debt information distributed as the IP,

- changes to the fee structure and fee / revenue sharing model related to the services provided as the IP,

- changes to the data products offered as the IP,

- changes to the threshold for reporting trades in corporate debt securities,

- removal of marketplaces, dealers or inter-dealer bond brokers required to report trade data regarding corporate debt securities,

- changes to the selection criteria for the corporate debt securities reported to CanPX,

- any reduction in the number of corporate debt securities reported to CanPX,

- significant changes to the systems, technology or technology provider used by CanPX, including those affecting capacity, or

- changes affecting the independence of the IP from the contributors of corporate debt securities information (Data Contributors) or the business activities of its technology provider.

2. — Governance

a. CanPX's Board of Directors will meet at regular times, and no less than quarterly.

b. CanPX will maintain its Advisory Committee that includes representation from Data Contributors, and from subscribers and vendors (Data Purchasers) and will provide a report within 15 days after each of its meetings that describes the topics discussed and their resolution.

c. CanPX will notify CSA staff of any changes to the composition of the Advisory Committee and of any changes to its mandate within 15 days from making the change.

d. The mandate of the Advisory Committee will continue to make reference to the ability of the committee to contact the Director of the Market Regulation Branch of the Ontario Securities Commission and the Senior Director, Market Structures at the Autorité des marchés financiers with any concerns that it may have regarding the governance or operations of the IP.

e. The Advisory Committee will maintain minutes of its meetings and these minutes will reflect the views and recommendations provided to CanPX's management. The minutes will be made available, upon request, to CSA staff.

3. — Conflicts of Interest

a. CanPX will maintain and monitor compliance with policies and procedures to address the conflicts of interest related to the business activities of its board members.

b. CanPX will maintain and monitor compliance with policies and procedures to address the potential conflicts of interest that arise due to the fact that its technology provider is also a marketplace and a distributor of data.

c. CanPX will provide any changes to the policies and procedures referred to in paragraphs 3a and 3b to CSA staff for review and approval.

4. — IP Products

a. CanPX will limit the products distributed as the IP to a consolidated feed (the Consolidated Data Product) that displays the information related to corporate debt securities provided to it in accordance with the requirements set out in Part 8 of NI 21-101 and Part 10 of the Companion Policy 21-101CP (Designated Corporate Debt Securities). CanPX will display this information no later than one hour from the time of the trade.

b. CanPX will not distribute, as the IP, any additional products using the data provided to it under Part 8 of NI 21-101 unless it obtains prior approval from CSA staff.

c. If CanPX intends to create and distribute, other than as the IP, any products using the data provided to it under Part 8 of NI 21-101:

  i. the data required to be provided to the IP by Data Contributors will not be used for such other products without the permission of the Data Contributors; and

  ii. the additional products will be made available for purchase separately from, and will not be bundled with, the Consolidated Data Product and any other products approved under paragraph 4b.

Part 2: MARKET PARTICIPANTS

5. — Data reported to and disseminated by CanPX

a. CanPX will maintain and monitor compliance with:

   i. policies and procedures to verify the timeliness and accuracy of information received and disseminated by the IP; and

   ii. processes to resolve on a timely basis any data integrity issues identified.

b. CanPX will provide any changes to the policies and procedures referred to in paragraph 5a to CSA staff for review and approval'

c. CanPX will monitor the timeliness and accuracy of information received by and disseminated by the IP on an ongoing basis and take adequate measures to resolve any data integrity issues on a timely basis. CanPX will report to its Board of Directors at each of their quarterly meeting on the timeliness and accuracy of the information received by and disseminated by the IP, along with significant data integrity issues, for the most recent quarter. Within 15 days following the board meeting, a report will be provided by CanPX to CSA staff outlining the issues identified, if any, and the measures CanPX will take to address them.

d. CanPX will provide to CSA staff updates to its plan to increase the number of Designated Corporate Debt Securities by January 31, 2016.

e. CanPX will conduct an additional review of the adequacy of the list of Designated Corporate Debt Securities by January 31, 2016 and prepare a report outlining the results of this review and its analysis to CSA staff within 15 days of the completion of the review. The report must include an analysis showing the coverage of retail-sized bonds trades, coverage of corporate bonds traded and coverage of total bonds issued, as well as statistics indicating the types of bonds on the Designated Corporate Debt Securities and the frequency of trades for bonds not included on the list.

f. CanPX will provide reports of the corporate debt securities removed from the Designated Corporate Debt Securities within 15 days of their removal. Such reports will include a brief analysis supporting the reason for their removal from the list.

g. CanPX will provide updates to staff regarding developments on new or potential agreements with data distributors on a monthly basis.

6. — Resources

a. CanPX will maintain sufficient financial resources to ensure its financial viability.

b. CanPX will ensure that it has an adequate number of staff dedicated to its systems and operations to ensure the proper performance of its functions, including staff directly responsible for monitoring of the corporate debt data reported to it in accordance with the requirements of NI 21-101.

7. — Agreements with Data Contributors

a. CanPX will ensure that all Data Contributors are given access to CanPX on fair and reasonable terms.

b. New standard agreements or contracts to be entered into between CanPX and Data Contributors in connection with the IP services will be provided to CSA staff for review and approval prior to their execution. In addition, any proposed material changes to these standard agreements or contracts will be provided to CSA staff for review and approval.

8. — Fees / Fee structure / Revenue sharing

CanPX will make available, on its website, the fee schedule for the Consolidated Data Product, and any additional products subsequently approved by CSA staff to be distributed by CanPX as an information processor.

9. — Non-exclusivity

CanPX acknowledges that the selection as an IP does not grant that IP exclusive rights to consolidate and disseminate order and trade data. CanPX will not seek such exclusivity through the terms of any contract with a Data Contributor or Data Purchaser.

10. — Term and notice

a. CanPX will continue to act as an information processor for corporate debt securities for a period of six months starting from January 1, 2016, ending on June 30, 2016.

CSA Staff Notice 21-317 — Next Steps in Implementation of a Plan to Enhance Regulation of the Fixed Income Market

Date: **April 21, 2016**

39 OSCB 3817

[Not reproduced]

OSC Rule 21-501 — Deferral of Transparency Requirements for Government Debt Securities in National Instrument 21-101 *Marketplace Operation*

Date: **December 31, 2011**

34 O.S.C.B. 12493

[Repealed: (2012) 35 O.S.C.B. 5413]

Final Rule: (2011) 34 O.S.C.B. 12493; Approval by OSC: (2011) 34 O.S.C.B. 10953; Request for Comments: (2011) 34 O.S.C.B. (Supp. 1) 14.

OSC Staff Notice 21-702 — Regulatory Approach for Foreign-Based Stock Exchanges

Date: **October 31, 2003**

26 O.S.C.B. 7096

I. — Introduction

Staff of the Ontario Securities Commission (Staff) have received a number of inquiries from foreign-based stock exchanges interested in operating in Ontario. In response to these inquiries, Staff are proposing an approach to regulation of foreign-based stock exchanges that is aimed at facilitating investor choice while maintaining high standards of investor protection and market integrity.

This notice sets out the approach that Staff will use when evaluating the requests and making recommendations to the Commission regarding the appropriate level of regulation for foreign-based stock exchanges that wish to provide Ontario residents direct access to their markets.

II. — The Regulatory Framework for Stock Exchanges

Section 21 of the *Securities Act* (Ontario) (the Act) provides that "no person or company must carry on business as a stock exchange in Ontario unless recognized by the Commission under this section."

A foreign-based stock exchange is an exchange that is operating outside of Canada and is subject to regulation by a government authority responsible for the oversight of the exchange (home regulator). A foreign-based stock exchange that seeks to provide direct access to Ontario residents will be considered to be carrying on business in Ontario and must either apply for recognition under section 21 of the Act or apply for an exemption from recognition under section 147 of the Act. With increasing reliance on technology systems, Staff believe that a "carrying on business" test that relies solely on a physical location does not address the realities of the global capital markets.

(a) — Recognition of Stock Exchanges

A foreign-based stock exchange that seeks to carry on business in Ontario may apply for recognition under section 21 of the Act. The application process for a foreign-based stock exchange is the same as the one used for the recognition of a domestic-based stock exchange.[9] An application for recognition should include a description of the operations of the exchange and how the exchange meets criteria that deal with the following:

- corporate governance
- fees
- access
- information sharing
- fitness of officers and directors
- listed company rules
- financial viability
- self-listing conditions, if applicable
- regulation of the exchange and its participants
- systems and technology
- purpose of rules of the exchange

The detailed criteria are attached to this notice as Schedule A. The criteria reflect the characteristics that the Commission considers that a stock exchange, foreign or domestic, must have in order to protect the public interest and Ontario investors.

A recognition order issued by the Commission under section 21 may be subject to terms and conditions that are determined based on how the applicant satisfies the criteria and any other factors relevant to the applicant. Generally, if an exchange is recognized it will be required to:

- file rules, policies and other similar instruments for approval by the Commission
- file financial statements
- file quarterly and annual reports containing information relating to its participants access, investigations, listings, exemptions granted, and other items
- comply with the Automation Review Program[10]

---

[9]For an example of an application for recognition, please see the Toronto Stock Exchange Inc. Recognition: dated April 3, 2000, 23 O.S.C.B. 2495; amended January 29, 2002, 25 O.S.C.B. 929 and September 3, 2002, 25 O.S.C.B. 6134.

[10]The Automation Review Program ("ARP") provides a mechanism for any specified market infrastructure entity to follow a formal methodology in identifying and managing information technology risk. For a copy of the ARP, please see (2002) 25 OSCB 6789 and http://www.osc.gov.on.ca/en/HotTopics/marketplace. html.

- submit to examinations and reviews conducted by Staff

- comply with the terms and conditions modeled on the criteria described above

Any breach of a term and condition of the recognition order is a contravention of Ontario securities law.

(b) — Exemption from Recognition

A foreign-based stock exchange that seeks to carry on business in Ontario may alternatively apply for an exemption from recognition under section 147 of the Act.

(i) — Rationale for Granting an Exemption

Staff acknowledge that most foreign-based stock exchanges are already subject to a regulatory regime in their country of origin (home jurisdiction). Full regulation, similar to that applied to domestic exchanges, may be duplicative and inefficient when imposed in addition to the regulation of the home or another jurisdiction. As well, orders entered onto and trades executed on the foreign-based stock exchange should be subject to the same market rules, no matter where the investor is located or the order is entered. However, the regulatory regime of the home jurisdiction may not have a similar level of investor protection as that in Ontario and, in addition to some basic requirements to ensure ongoing consistency, the Commission may consider it necessary to impose additional requirements.

In developing the approach for regulating foreign-based exchanges, Staff believe that investor protection must be balanced with efficient markets when facilitating access to foreign-based stock exchanges. Staff propose to achieve this balance by requesting that the foreign-based stock exchange establish at the time of application that it meets the same criteria that a domestic exchange must meet and that access must be through an Ontario registrant. The criteria may be slightly tailored to the specific structure of the foreign-based stock exchange, the products traded on the exchange, or its regulatory environment. The foreign-based stock exchange may meet the criteria either through its own rules or the laws of the home regulator. Investor protection is achieved through the criteria and the gatekeeping role of the Ontario registrant. (Please refer to Part III). Once the foreign-based stock exchange has met the criteria at the time of the application and has established that it is subject to an appropriate regulatory regime, Staff propose that the foreign-based exchange will not be subject to many of the ongoing requirements that are applied to domestic exchanges (e.g. approval of rules, policies or similar instruments and regular examinations).

Staff propose to recommend to the Commission to exempt the foreign-based stock exchange, rely upon the regulatory regime of the home regulator and impose appropriate terms and conditions. The specific terms and conditions applicable to the foreign-based stock exchange may vary depending on the operations of the foreign-based stock exchange, the methods of access for its participants, and the regulatory regime in its home jurisdiction. The purpose of these terms and conditions is to enable the Commission to have access to information on the operations of the foreign-based stock exchange and the trading activity of Ontario participants. The following terms and conditions will be considered:

- ongoing compliance with home jurisdiction and oversight

- prior notice of material changes to the application

- quarterly and annual reporting of information relating to operational activities

- access restrictions

- financial reporting

- disclosure to investors regarding the regulatory structure, the implications of the exemption and the legal rights of an investor

- information sharing

- home jurisdiction adherence to IOSCO standards

- submission to non-exclusive jurisdiction

Breaches of a term and condition in the exemption order by the foreign-based stock exchange would be a contravention of Ontario securities law.

III. — Access through Registered Intermediaries

Access to the foreign-based stock exchange will be subject to Ontario securities laws and, in particular, the Ontario registration regime. The foreign-based stock exchange may provide direct access, either through terminals, data feeds or third party provided interfaces, to only those persons that are duly registered or licensed under the laws of Ontario. If an Ontario participant in a foreign-based stock exchange breaches the rules of that exchange or breaches Ontario securities laws while trading on the foreign-based stock exchange, the Commission or the appropriate self-regulatory organization may take action against that participant.

IV. — Other Jurisdictions

Reliance on foreign country regulation has been adopted by a number of foreign regulators, including the Australian Securities and Investment Commission (ASIC) and the Commodity Futures Trading Commission (CFTC) in the United States. Both ASIC and the CFTC have recognized the home country regulation of foreign-based exchanges and have allowed foreign-based exchanges to operate within their jurisdictions by imposing certain terms and conditions. This approach eliminates duplicative regulation while ensuring that securities markets and foreign-based stock exchange participants are subject to a uniform standard of regulation.

V. — Application Process

The application process for both recognition and exemption from recognition as a stock exchange is the same. The foreign-based stock exchange must file an application, detailing for example, its history, business and regulatory structure and addressing how it meets the specific criteria as outlined in Appendix A. After receipt of the application, Staff will provide comments on its content and will work with the applicant to ensure that the application contains all of the requisite information and to develop a draft order. Once the application and order have been finalized, Staff will request that the Commission approve the publication of the application and the order for a 30 day comment period. Publication will occur in the OSC Bulletin and on the OSC website. Once all issues raised during the comment process are resolved, Staff will submit the order for approval to the Commission in the form of the published order, as amended in response to the comment process. Once issued, the order will be published in the OSC Bulletin and on the website.

VI. — The Commodity Futures Act

The *Commodity Futures Act* (Ontario) imposes a similar regime for commodity futures exchanges that carry on business in Ontario. Section 15 provides that no person or company may carry on business in Ontario unless registered by the Commission as a commodity futures exchange. We would consider following a similar regulatory approach to foreign-based commodity futures exchanges as we have outlined above for foreign-based stock exchanges.

Appendix A — Criteria for Recognition and Exemption from Recognition

Responses to all of the following criteria must address:

(i) how the Exchange meets each criterion;

(ii) what requirements, if any, are imposed by the applicable regulator in the Exchange's jurisdiction (the Foreign Regulator) in each area; and

(iii) how the oversight of the Exchange by the Foreign Regulator ensures ongoing compliance with the criterion.

Part 1 — Corporate Governance

1.1 — Fair Representation

The governance structure of the Exchange provides for:

(i) appropriate, fair and meaningful representation on its Board and any committee thereof, and

(ii) appropriate representation by independent directors on the Board and any committee thereof.

1.2 — Appropriate Provisions for Directors and Officers

The Exchange takes reasonable steps to ensure:

(i) appropriate qualifications, remuneration, limitation of liability and indemnity provisions for directors and officers; and

(ii) each officer and director is a fit and proper person.

1.3 — Conflicts of Interest

The Exchange has appropriate conflict of interest provisions for all directors, officers and employees.

Part 2 — Fees

2.1 — Fees

The Exchange's process for setting fees is fair, transparent and appropriate. Any and all fees imposed by the Exchange on its participants are equitably allocated, do not have the effect of creating barriers to access and are balanced with the criterion that the Exchange has sufficient revenues to satisfy its responsibilities.

Part 3 — Access

3.1 — Fair Access

The requirements of the Exchange relating to access to the facilities of the Exchange are fair, transparent and reasonable and include requirements in respect of notice, an opportunity to be heard or make representations, the keeping of records, the giving of reasons and the provisions for appeals.

3.2 — Details of Access Criteria

In particular, the Exchange:

(i) has written standards for granting access to trading on its facilities to ensure users have appropriate integrity and fitness;

(ii) has and enforces financial integrity standards for those persons who enter orders for execution on the system, including, but not limited to, credit or position limits and clearing membership;

(iii) does not unreasonably prohibit or limit access by a person or company to services offered by it;

(iv) keeps records of each grant and denial or limitation of access, including reasons for granting, denying or limiting access; and

(v) restricts access to adequately trained system users who have demonstrated competence in the functions that they perform.

3.3 — Access for Ontario Residents

The Exchange provides direct access, either through terminals, data feeds or third party provided interfaces, to only those persons who are duly registered or licensed under Ontario laws.

Part 4 — Regulation

4.1 — Jurisdiction

The Exchange, foreign self-regulatory organization (Foreign SRO) and/or the Foreign Regulator have the jurisdiction to perform member and market regulation, including the ability to set rules, conduct compliance reviews and perform surveillance and enforcement.

4.2 — Issuer/Product Regulation

The products traded on the Exchange and the listing rules are approved by the appropriate authority.

4.3 — Member Regulation

Sales practices are fair, properly supervised and not contrary to the public interest.

4.4 — Transparency

Adequate provision has been made to record and publish accurate and timely trade and quotation information. This information is provided to all participants on an equitable basis.

4.5 — Sufficient Systems and Resources

The Exchange, Foreign SRO and/or its Foreign Regulator maintain appropriate systems and resources for conducting member regulation and market regulation, for evaluating compliance with Exchange, Foreign SRO or legislative requirements and disciplining participants.

4.6 — Record Keeping

The Exchange, Foreign SRO and/or its Foreign Regulator maintain adequate provisions for keeping books and records, including operations of the exchange, audit trail information on all trades and compliance and/or violations of Exchange requirements and securities legislation.

4.7 — Availability of Information to Foreign Regulator

The Exchange and/or the Foreign SRO have mechanisms in place to ensure that the information necessary to conduct adequate surveillance of the system for supervisory and enforcement purposes is available to the relevant regulatory authorities on a timely basis.

Part 5 — Rulemaking

5.1 — Purpose of Rules

The Exchange and the Foreign SRO maintain rules, policies and other similar instruments designed to, in particular:

(i) ensure compliance with the rules of the Exchange and the Foreign SRO;

(ii) prevent fraudulent and manipulative acts and practices;

(iii) promote just and equitable principles of trade;

(iv) foster co-operation and co-ordination with persons or companies engaged in regulating, clearing, settling, processing information with respect to, and facilitating transactions in, the products traded on the Exchange;

(v) provide for appropriate discipline;

(vi) ensure a fair and orderly market;

(vii) ensure that the Exchange business is conducted in a manner so as to afford protection to investors; and

(viii) provide for appropriate dispute procedures.

5.2 — No Discrimination or Burden on Competition

The rules of the Exchange and the Foreign SRO do not:

(i) permit unreasonable discrimination among issuers or participants; or

(ii) impose any burden on competition that is not reasonably necessary or appropriate.

Part 6 — Systems and Technology

6.1 — System Capability/Scalability

For each of its systems that support order entry, order routing, execution, data feeds, trade reporting, trade comparison and system-enforced rules, the Exchange maintains a level of capacity that allows it to properly carry on its business and has in place processes to ensure the integrity of each system. This includes maintaining reasonable back-up, contingency and business continuity plans, disaster recovery plans and internal controls.

6.2 — Information Technology Risk Management Procedures

The Exchange has procedures in place that:

(i) handle trading errors, trading halts and circuit breakers;

(ii) ensure the competence, integrity and authority of system users; and

(iii) ensure that the system users are adequately supervised.

Part 7 — Financial Viability

7.1 — Financial Viability

The Exchange has sufficient financial resources for the proper performance of its functions.

Part 8 — Clearing and Settlement

8.1 — Relationship with Clearing Agency

The Exchange has a clearing relationship with an established clearing agency (Clearing Agency) and all transactions executed on the Exchange are cleared through the Clearing Agency.

8.2 — Regulation of the Clearing Agency

The Clearing Agency is subject to regulation by the Foreign Regulator that addresses risk and promotes transparency, fairness and investor protection.

8.3 — Authority of the Foreign Regulator

The Foreign Regulator has the appropriate authority and procedures for oversight of the Clearing Agency. This oversight includes regular, periodic regulatory examinations of the Clearing Agency by the Foreign Regulator.

8.4 — Clearing and Settlement Arrangements

The Exchange is satisfied that appropriate clearing and settlement arrangements are in place to provide reasonable assurance that all obligations arising out of transactions on the Exchange will be met.

8.5 — Restrictions on Access to a Foreign Member

Any restrictions on access to the clearing system by a foreign member are adequately disclosed and justified by the legislation of the home jurisdiction, are not anti-competitive and do not unreasonably impose barriers to access.

8.6 — Technology of Clearing Corporation

The Exchange has assured itself that the information technology used by the Clearing Agency has been adequately reviewed and tested and provides at least the same level of safeguards as required of the Exchange.

8.7 — Risk Management of Clearing Corporation

The Exchange has assured itself that the Clearing Agency has established appropriate risk management policies and procedures, contingency plans, default procedures and internal controls.

Part 9 — information Sharing and Oversight Arrangements

9.1 — Information Sharing and Oversight Agreement

Satisfactory information sharing and oversight agreements exist among the Commission, the Foreign Regulator and/or the Foreign SRO.

9.2 — Co-operation

The Exchange will co-operate by the sharing of information and otherwise with the Commission and its staff.

Part 10 — IOSCO Principles

10.1 — IOSCO Principles

Regulation and oversight of the Exchange is carried out in a manner consistent with IOSCO principles.

OSC Staff Notice 21-704 — Market Regulation Branch Annual Report — 2010

Date: October 29, 2010

33 O.S.C.B. 9957

Part 2: MARKET PARTICIPANTS

Table of Contents

1. — Introduction

This report summarizes the Market Regulation Branch's key policy activities and initiatives relating to market structure and clearing and settlement for the fiscal year ending March 31, 2010 (fiscal 2010). It also provides an update on these key initiatives for the subsequent period up to September 15, 2010.

1.1 — Role of the Market Regulation Branch

The Market Regulation Branch (or we) regulates key market infrastructure entities and develops and implements policies to address market structure, trading and post-trade clearing and settlement issues.

Market infrastructure entities include marketplaces (exchanges and alternative trading systems (ATSs)), self-regulatory organizations (SROs), clearing agencies, compensation funds, information processors and matching service utilities.

These entities are required to comply with requirements that are imposed through securities legislation, or imposed by the OSC as terms and conditions of recognition, approval or exemption. The objective of our regulation and oversight is to assess compliance by these entities with statutory and other requirements. We do this by reviewing and approving their rules, conducting reviews of their operations and reviewing their reporting. We also work closely with some of them, such as SROs and other entities that play a role in the regulation of our market participants, in an effort to harmonize regulatory requirements.

1.2 — Focus of the Market Regulation Branch

Over the past few years, numerous ATSs have started operating in Canada, creating a multiple marketplace environment. As part of the competitive landscape, different ATSs and exchanges now offer market participants choices with respect to facilities and trading strategies. In addition, technology plays a key role in how marketplaces offer services and how market participants conduct trading. The evolution of technology has led to an increasingly complex market. These recent developments in market structure have had an impact on retail and institutional investors, marketplaces and dealers.

At the same time, the recent financial crisis highlighted the role of other market infrastructure entities, in particular clearing agencies, in reducing the risks and uncertainties faced by market participants, and thus their systemic importance.

As the Canadian market is undergoing significant changes, a key focus for the Market Regulation Branch in fiscal 2010 included analyzing and monitoring these changes and addressing regulatory concerns. In particular, we focused on issues related to trading on multiple marketplaces and the role of technology.

As part of policy development, we frequently consult with marketplaces, dealers, vendors, investors and other market participants, and seek feedback through the public comment process. We would like to thank everyone who participated in consultations and responded to our requests for comments. We welcome further comments as we continue to work through various initiatives.

2. — Changes in Market Structure

The emergence of multiple marketplaces and new order types and advances in technology have increased the complexity of trading. They have had an impact on how dealers and investors trade and have highlighted the need for a greater understanding by all who trade in the market of the options available.

The Market Regulation Branch at the OSC, and in some cases together with other CSA jurisdictions and the Investment Industry Regulatory Organization of Canada (IIROC), have been monitoring changes to the Canadian market structure and have been analyzing whether these changes give rise to regulatory concerns.

In fiscal 2010, we focused on order protection, the regulation of ATSs and exchanges and market structure issues relating to dark liquidity[1] and electronic trading. We have taken and will continue to take a holistic approach when reviewing market structure issues because they cannot be examined in isolation.

2.1 — Multiple marketplaces

The number of equity marketplaces operating in Canada has increased from six in 2005 to 10 in 2010. We have been examining various issues relating to the emergence of multiple marketplaces, in particular:

- The need to prevent immediately accessible, visible, better-priced limit orders from being traded through; and

- The appropriateness of regulation of ATSs and exchanges.

A. — Order protection rule

On November 13, 2009, the Canadian Securities Administrators (CSA) introduced the Order Protection Rule (OPR) through amendments to National Instrument 21-101 *Marketplace Operation* (NI 21-101) and related Companion Policy 21-101CP, and National Instrument 23-101 *Trading Rules* and related Companion Policy 23-101CP. The OPR will come into effect on February 1, 2011.

Currently, the applicable provisions are found in IIROC's UMIR 5.2 *Best Price Obligation*, which only applies to dealers. The OPR will shift the obligation to marketplaces. It will require marketplaces to have policies and procedures reasonably designed to prevent trade-throughs, so that immediately accessible, visible, better-priced limit orders are executed before inferior-priced orders. CSA staff are currently working with the industry to address implementation issues.

Order protection is essential in maintaining investor confidence and fairness in the market. In a multiple marketplace environment, market participants, including retail investors, must be assured that no immediately accessible, visible, better-priced limit orders are being traded through, regardless of the marketplace where the order is entered, the sophistication of the participant or the size of the order.

For more information:

- *CSA Notice of Amendments to National Instrument 21-101 Marketplace Operation and National Instrument 23-101 Trading Rules, published on November 13, 2009*

- *CSA Staff Notice 23-307 Order Protection Rule — Implementation Milestones*

- *CSA Staff Notice 23-309 Frequently Asked Questions about the Order Protection Rule and Intentionally Locked or Crossed Markets — Part 6 of National Instrument 23-101 and Related Companion Policy*

- *UMIR 5.2 Best Price Obligation*

B. — Regulation of ATSs and exchanges

Market Regulation staff at the OSC, together with staff of the other CSA jurisdictions, continue to review the regulatory requirements for recognized exchanges and ATSs to determine if they are up to date and appropriate for the current competitive landscape.

OSC staff completed the first phase of the review, which focused on transparency of filings by exchanges and ATSs. In October 2009, OSC staff implemented a process that would make public, summary information about proposed changes to operations of all marketplaces. This process has since been expanded to also publish summary information about initial operations of new ATSs. The summary information, both regarding proposed changes and initial operations, will be published for a 30-day comment period. OSC staff have also indicated that marketplaces are expected to publish a detailed description on their websites of how their market or facility operates and the order types available and order features or characteristics. This enables dealers and investors alike to obtain information about the choices they face when trading in Canada's multiple marketplace environment.

The second phase of the review involves examining the requirements for exchanges and ATSs set out in NI 21-101. Because of the similarities of certain operations of exchanges and ATSs, we are considering whether any requirements should be aligned. The second phase is expected to be completed at the end of 2010 and any resulting amendments to NI 21-101 will be published for comment.

For more information:

- *OSC Staff Notice 21-703 Transparency of the Operations of Stock Exchanges and Alternative Trading Systems [Editor's note: replaced by OSCN 21-706.]*

2.2 — The emergence of non-transparent marketplaces and new order types

On October 2, 2009, the CSA and IIROC published Concept Paper 23-404 *Dark Pools, Dark Orders and Other Developments in Market Structure in Canada*. The paper sought feedback on a broad range of market structure issues, including dark pools, new dark order types,

---

[1] "Dark liquidity" is a term that refers generally to dark pools and dark orders. Dark pools are marketplaces that offer no pre-trade transparency. Dark orders are orders that have limited or no transparency.

market pegged orders[2] and smart order routers (SORs)[3]. Click *here* to read the concept paper and the comments that we received. In addition, the CSA and IIROC held a forum on March 23, 2010 for market participants to discuss the issues raised in the concept paper.

The key issues raised by market participants in response to the concept paper and at the forum include:

- whether dark pools should be required to offer price improvement;

- the practice of dark pools sending indications of interest to attract order flow;

- the fairness of a marketplace using a proprietary SOR that has access to information on that marketplace that is not otherwise available to other marketplace participants; and

- the practice of broker preferencing[4].

On May 28, 2010, the CSA and IIROC published *Joint Staff Notice 23-308 Update on Forum to Discuss CSA/IIROC Joint Consultation Paper 23-404 "Dark Pools, Dark Orders and Other Developments in Market Structure in Canada" and Next Steps*

The notice summarizes the issues that were discussed and provides an overview of the views expressed on those issues including a summary of comments.

OSC staff, along with IIROC and other CSA staff, are currently working on a draft position paper to be published in fall 2010. It will outline our position on some of the issues identified in the concept paper and the forum relating specifically to dark pools and dark orders.

2.3 — Use of technology in trading

Technology has increased the speed and complexity of trading. It has also led to easier access to marketplaces for non-dealers, either by subscribing to ATSs or by having "direct market access" (DMA) through their dealers.

Together with other CSA jurisdictions and IIROC, we continue to examine the risks associated with technology and electronic trading and, where appropriate, we will develop responses to address any regulatory concerns.

A. — Market Events of May 6

The market volatility on May 6, 2010 dominated the equity market headlines, with financial markets experiencing a brief but very severe drop in prices, followed by an equally rapid recovery. Although less dramatic declines were seen in Canadian markets than in the U.S. markets, some declines were significant. The CSA and IIROC are working closely on a number of initiatives in response to the events of May 6. IIROC has also completed its analysis of the events and has published a report on its findings.

For more information:

- *Joint CSA/IIROC News Release dated May 14, 2010*

- *IIROC's report Review of the Market Events of May 6, 2010*

B. — Electronic trading and direct market access

The CSA and IIROC have been examining issues relating to direct market access (DMA) and are developing a proposal that will address risks associated with electronic trading (such as market risk, and credit risk), DMA and other issues associated with technology. We are also examining issues related to high frequency trading, co-location and outsourcing.

For more information:

- *Joint CSA/Market Regulation Services Inc. Notice on Trade-Through Protection, Best Execution and Access to Marketplaces, dated April 20, 2007*

- *CSA/IIROC Joint Staff Notice 23-308 Update on Forum to Discuss CSA/IIROC Joint Consultation Paper 23-404 "Dark Pools, Dark Orders and Other Developments in Market Structure in Canada" and Next Steps*

3. — Clearing and Settlement

3.1 — Mandatory recognition of clearing agencies

As of March 1, 2011, amendments to section 21.2 of the *Securities Act* (Ontario) will prohibit clearing agencies from carrying on business in Ontario unless they are recognized as a clearing agency by the Commission. Clearing agencies operating in Ontario will, therefore, be required to apply to be recognized or exempted from the recognition requirement.

On March 19, 2010, we issued OSC Staff Notice 24-702 *Regulatory Approach to Recognition and Exemption from Recognition of Clearing Agencies*. The notice sets out the following:

- the criteria that a clearing agency is expected to meet in order to operate in Ontario,

---

[2]Market pegged orders are orders that are priced and re-priced to a reference price such as the national best bid (offer) or a marketplace's best bid (offer). They are also referred to as reference priced orders.

[3]A smart order router is a technological tool that connects to multiple marketplaces and consolidates and analyzes order information from these marketplaces. It then makes order routing decisions seeking to obtain best execution and/or best price, or facilitate the execution of the strategy determined by the user.

[4]Broker preferencing means a marketplace feature that allows orders from the same participant or subscriber to execute ahead of other orders posted at the same price in a central limit order book.

- the application process,

- how we handle applications for recognition or exemption from the recognition requirement, and

- our approach in making recommendations to the Commission with respect to the application.

The notice also describes some scenarios where we may be prepared to recommend to the Commission that a clearing agency be exempted from the recognition requirement.

We encourage all entities operating, or intending to operate, as a clearing agency in Ontario to familiarize themselves with the new statutory requirement and to contact staff listed on OSC Staff Notice 24-702 with any questions.

For more information:

- *OSC Staff Notice 24-702 Regulatory Approach to Recognition and Exemption from Recognition of Clearing Agencies*

3.2 — Institutional trade matching deadline

On April 16, 2010, the CSA published amendments to NI 24-101 *Institutional Trade Matching and Settlement* (NI 24-101). NI 24-101 requires dealers and advisers to establish, maintain and enforce policies and procedures to achieve matching of institutional trades by a specified deadline. The original deadline was set at midnight on the date that the trades occurred (i.e. trade date), and NI 24-101 provided for a transition period to meet this deadline. The amendments remove the original matching deadline, and maintain the current deadline of no later than noon on the business day following the trade date (i.e. trade date + 1). The amendments became effective on July 1, 2010.

NI 24-101 came into force on April 1, 2007. Since then, CSA staff have been monitoring the industry's progress in achieving the matching deadline for institutional trades of midnight on the trade date. It became apparent that industry participants required more time to adjust their middle and back office processes to meet this matching deadline. The industry has also commented that this matching deadline is not justified from a cost-benefit perspective without a clear indication that the standard trade date + 3 settlement cycle in the North American capital markets would be shortened.

We, together with other CSA staff, continue to monitor developments in this area. In the future, the CSA may consider re-introducing the matching deadline of midnight on trade date into NI 24-101 if circumstances were to change, for example, if the standard trade date + 3 settlement cycle in global markets is shortened.

We are currently reviewing CSA Staff Notice 24-305 *Frequently Asked Questions About National Instrument 24-101 — Institutional Trade Matching and Settlement and Related Companion Policy* and will make any consequential changes necessary to reflect the amendments to NI 24-101.

For more information:

- *CSA Notice of Amendments to National Instrument 24-101 Institutional Trade Matching and Settlement and Companion Policy 24-101CP Institutional Trade Matching and Settlement dated April 16, 2010*

- *CSA Notice and Request for Comments on Proposed Amendments to National Instrument 24-101 Institutional Trade Matching and Settlement and Companion Policy 24-101CP Institutional Trade Matching and Settlement dated October 30, 2009*

- *CSA Staff Notice 24-305 Frequently Asked Questions About National Instrument 24-101 — Institutional Trade Matching and Settlement and Related Companion Policy*

[**Market Regulation Branch Contact List**omitted]

OSC Staff Notice 21-705 — Process for Marketplace Filings and Proposed Rules of Exchanges

Date: March 18, 2011

34 O.S.C.B. 3175

Exchanges, quotation and trade reporting systems (QTRS) and alternative trading systems (ATS) have initial and ongoing reporting requirements that are set out in National Instrument 21-101 *Marketplace Operation* (NI 21-101).[1] NI 21-101 also requires exchanges to file all rules, policies and other similar instruments (collectively, Rules), as well as amendments to these Rules.[2] Today, the Canadian Securities Administrators (CSA) published for comment a number of materials, including proposed amendments to NI 21-101 (Proposed Amendments). One of the objective of the Proposed Amendments is to update and streamline the regulatory and reporting requirements applicable to all marketplaces.[3]

In addition to the requirements in NI 21-101, recognized exchanges are subject to the terms and conditions of their recognition orders. These include requirements relating to the types of Rules that an exchange must have. The recognition orders also require recognized exchanges to comply with protocols that outline the process for filing, publication and Commission review and approval for new Rules and Rule amendments.

---

[1]Sections 3.1, 4.1 and subsection 6.4(1) of NI 21-101 include the initial filing requirements for exchanges, QTRSs and ATSs, respectively. Sections 3.2, 4.2 and subsections 6.4(2), 6.4(3) and 6.4(4) include the ongoing filing requirements.

[2]See section 5.5 of NI 21-101.

[3]As part of the Proposed Amendments, we propose to: shorten the prior notification period for fee changes; revise the filing requirements for changes that do not constitute significant changes; require that all marketplaces file quarterly reports of their trading activities; and give guidance on what is considered to be a significant change.

OSC staff's existing process for reviewing the initial filings for exchanges and ATSs and changes to certain of the operations of recognized exchanges and ATSs is described in OSC Staff Notice 21-703 *Transparency of the Operations of Stock Exchanges and Alternative Trading Systems (Revised — Previously Published October 9, 2009).*[4] *[Editor's note: replaced by OSCN 21-706.]*The staff notice also describes the information relating to the operations of ATSs that is made public and the publication process.

On December 9, 2010, a number of legislative amendments came into force in Ontario that would support the creation of a formal approval of both the initial Form 21-101F2 filed by an ATS and of changes in an ATS's operations as outlined in this form.[5] As a result, OSC staff are currently developing protocols that will set out the process for filing, publication, review and approval of changes to all marketplaces' operations described in Form 21-101F1 or 21-101F2, as applicable. We are also reviewing the existing rule protocols applicable to exchanges to assess what, if any, changes are needed to increase consistency among the existing protocols and with the processes applicable to ATSs.

We plan to consult during the development process. We will also consider comments received in the public comment process for the Proposed Amendments[6] in finalizing these protocols.

OSC Staff Notice 21-706 — Marketplaces' Initial Operations and Material System Changes

Date: October 4, 2012

35 O.S.C.B. 8928

I. — Background

OSC Staff (Staff) have been examining the regulatory requirements for recognized exchanges (Exchanges) and alternative trading systems (ATSs) set out in National Instrument 21-101 *Marketplace Operation* (NI 21-101) and in National Instrument 23-101 *Trading Rules* (together, the Marketplace Rules). We have also been reviewing the practices set out around those requirements in various recognition orders, rule protocols and staff practices. The purpose of our review was to update and, where appropriate, to align the regulatory requirements and processes for review of new operations and changes to the operations of Exchanges and ATSs.

As a first step, we issued OSC Staff Notice 21-703 — *Transparency of the Operations of Stock Exchanges and Alternative Trading Systems* (OSC Staff Notice 21-703), where we described Staff's process for reviewing the initial filings for Exchanges and ATSs and changes to certain of their operations. In that notice, we also set out our expectation that Exchanges and ATSs maintain an appropriate degree of transparency for certain aspects of their operations to ensure that investors and market participants are better informed as to how securities trade on these marketplaces. We described the types of information that marketplaces should publish in order to obtain feedback from other market participants regarding certain proposed changes to marketplace operations, and to increase transparency of marketplace features and operations. We also described the process for publication and Staff review.

The next phase of our examination was a review of the regulatory requirements set out in the Marketplace Rules in order to streamline and update them and to increase consistency, where appropriate, between the requirements applicable to Exchanges and to ATSs. We made a number of revisions to the Marketplace Rules (the Amendments) that came into force on July 1, 2012. In addition to the objectives outlined above, the Amendments also aim to increase the transparency of the operations of marketplaces. For example, a marketplace must disclose on its website information regarding its operations including fees, a description of its order types and how these orders interact, and access requirements.

II. — Purpose of this notice

This notice sets out Staff's process to review the initial filings of entities applying to be recognized as Exchanges by the Commission and those applying to be registered as ATSs. The notice also sets out Staff's expectations regarding the timing of a marketplace's commencement of operations and the timing of the implementation of material systems changes. This notice incorporates and updates the content of OSC Staff Notice 21-703 and replaces that notice. The processes for filing, publication, review and approval of changes in marketplace operations, previously documented in OSC Staff Notice 21-703, have been set out in the Marketplace Rules and in each marketplace's protocol for reviewing rules or changes to the marketplace's operations (the Marketplace Protocols).

III. — Review of initial operations

(a) — Exchanges

An applicant that seeks to carry on business as an Exchange in Ontario must file an application for recognition under section 21 of the *Securities Act* (Ontario) (Application). The Application must include a description of the operations of the Exchange and how the Exchange would meet the provisions of NI 21-101 and certain recognition criteria such as governance, fees, access, regulation of products and participants, rulemaking, clearing and settlement, and systems and technology. The rules of the Exchange also form part of the Application and often describe the order types and structure of the Exchange. As part of the process, an applicant for recognition as an Exchange must also file Form 21-101F1 *Information Statement Exchange or Quotation and Trade Reporting System* (F1).[1] The F1 contains detailed information about many of the aspects described in the Application, and is confidential as it contains proprietary financial, commercial and technical information.

---

[4]Available at http://www.osc.gov.on.ca/en/28679.htm.

[5]Specifically, new section 21.0.1 of the Act added regulatory powers relating to decision-making authority with respect to ATSs; definitions of "ATS" and "marketplace" were added to the Act; and a reference was added to paragraph 12(i) under subsection 143(1) of the Act to mirror the Commission's existing rulemaking activity in relation to exchanges.

[6]The Proposed Amendments are published for a 90 day comment period that ends on June 16, 2011.

[1]The F1 contains information about the Exchange that describes, among other things, the governance of the Exchange, the manner of operation of its trading system, the means of access to the market and the Exchange's listing criteria, fees and regulation.

The Application, along with the Exchange's rules, policies and a draft recognition order are published for a 30-day comment period in the OSC Bulletin and on the OSC website. Once all the issues raised during the comment process and Staff's own review of the application materials and the F1 are resolved, the Commission may exercise its discretion to recognize the Exchange.[2] If recognized, Staff will publish a notice indicating the approval of the Exchange recognition (Notice of Approval of Exchange Recognition) and the final recognition order.

(b) — ATSs

Pursuant to section 6.1 of NI 21-101, an ATS cannot carry on business in Ontario unless it registers as a dealer and is a member of a self-regulatory entity. Currently, the Investment Industry Regulatory Organization of Canada (IIROC) is the only applicable self-regulatory entity. An ATS must also file Form 21-101F2 *Initial Operation Report Alternative Trading System* (F2) at least 45 days before it begins to carry on business.[3] The information in the F2 is similar to that provided in an Exchange's F1 and is also confidential for the same reasons.

An ATS is also expected to file a notice providing summary information regarding its operations, similar to that in an Exchange's Application, but modified accordingly to reflect the fact that an ATS does not perform regulation functions (Notice of Initial Operations). The information to be included in the Notice of Initial Operations is set out in the next section.

The ATS's Notice of Initial Operations is published and accompanied by a notice published by Staff for a 30-day comment period in the OSC Bulletin and on the OSC website. The review process by Staff is similar to the review process for an Exchange Application. Once all of the issues associated with the ATS's filing(s) are resolved, including any issues with the associated registration application, the registration as an investment dealer is issued and staff will publish a notice indicating that Staff's review is complete (Notice of Completion of Staff Review).

Where an existing registered investment dealer is proposing to operate an ATS, the same filing, publication and review processes apply.

IV. — Information regarding initial operations

As noted above, when a marketplace plans to start operations and files the applicable documents, certain information is made publicly available to ensure transparency regarding the proposed operations of the marketplace and to give market participants an opportunity to provide feedback.

This information must be sufficiently detailed to allow marketplace participants to understand and assess the marketplace's proposed operations, given that the F1 or F2 is not published. As described in the previous section, in the case of an Exchange, this information would be contained in the Application and in the rules and policies that are published along with the Application. In the case of an ATS, the information would be contained in the Notice of Initial Operations. At a minimum, the Application or Notice of Initial Operations should include a description of:

- the structure of the marketplace, including how orders are entered, displayed (if applicable), executed, how they interact, and how they are cleared and settled;
- the marketplace's fees and fee model, if known;
- the services provided by the marketplace, including the hours of operation;
- the means of access to the market or facility and its services;
- the order types it offers;
- other information disseminated by the marketplace and the recipients of that information, such as indications of interest disseminated by a marketplace that operates without pre-trade transparency;
- the types of securities listed, quoted or traded on the marketplace, as applicable; and
- the types of marketplace participants.

If applicable, the materials published may include additional information, such as a description of the marketplace's policies and procedures to manage conflicts of interest, referral, outsourcing or custody arrangements, or any other information relevant to the entity's operations.

After the commencement of operations, a marketplace is required to maintain information regarding its operations on its website, in accordance with the disclosure requirements applicable to all marketplaces set out in section 10.1 *Disclosure by Marketplaces* of NI 21-101. Information regarding changes to a marketplace's operations, as reflected in changes to its F1 or F2, as applicable, may also be published for comment. The information to be filed for changes to a marketplace's F1 or F2 and the criteria and process for publication are set out in the Marketplace Protocols.

V. — Systems and launch of operations

Before a marketplace commences operations or makes any material system change (including introducing a new market or trading facility), it must make publicly available the technology requirements to interface with or access the marketplace or trading facility, and must make testing facilities available. Specifically, NI 21-101 requires that a marketplace make all technology requirements publicly available at least three months before it begins operations or before it implements a material change to its technology requirements.[4] NI 21-101 also requires a

---

[2]Some of the factors that would be considered by the Commission are described in Part 4 of 21-101CP.

[3]See subsection 3.1(2) of NI 21-101.

[4]Subsection 12.3(1) of NI 21-101.

marketplace to make testing facilities available at least two months before beginning operations or before implementing a material change to its technology requirements.[5]

Marketplaces need to ensure that marketplace participants and service providers have a reasonable opportunity to make the necessary changes to their systems so that they can access the marketplace. This involves time to do technology work and to test the system. We believe that three months is a reasonable time to allow marketplace participants and third parties to do the necessary development work and testing. However, it has come to our attention that due to potential uncertainty in the timing and outcome of the regulatory review process, many marketplace participants and service providers will not begin the systems work and testing before the Notice of Approval of Exchange Recognition or Notice of Completion of Staff Review, as applicable, has been published. As a result, if a marketplace launches operations or implements material system changes shortly after publication of the applicable Notice, market participants and service providers may not have sufficient time to make necessary systems changes and to complete their system testing, notwithstanding the fact that the marketplace has made the technology requirements and testing facilities publicly available for the requisite time periods in compliance with NI 21-101.

When planning the launch of operations or the implementation of material system changes, we expect marketplaces to take into consideration the commercial reality that market participants and service providers may postpone systems work and testing until the Notice of Approval of Exchange Recognition or Notice of Completion of Staff Review, as applicable, has been published.

With respect to the launch of initial operations (or a new market or trading facility), marketplaces should consider postponing the launch for a period of at least three months from the date of the publication of the Notice of Approval of Exchange Recognition or the Notice of Completion of Staff Review (as the case may be), rather than from the date the marketplace makes the technology requirements publicly available. Experience has shown that a three-month period generally provides reasonable advance notice to ensure fair access to the marketplace, promote fair, efficient and orderly markets, and facilitate market participants' compliance with applicable rules, including the Order Protection Rule. However, in some cases a longer period may be required. We believe that allowing a reasonable delay of the launch fairly balances the needs of marketplace participants and service providers with the interests of the marketplace.

Once a marketplace has commenced operations, if it intends to make a material system change (other than introducing a new market or trading facility) that would require marketplace participants or service providers to do development work or testing, it is our expectation that the marketplace will conduct an assessment of the amount of time and effort required to do the necessary work. The marketplace should delay the implementation of the material change until marketplace participants and their service providers have had a reasonable amount of time to complete the necessary work and testing following the approval of the change. What constitutes a reasonable amount of time will depend on the materiality and complexity of the change and its impact on marketplace participants' ability to comply with applicable regulatory requirements. Normally, the impact on marketplace participants will be greater for markets that display details of orders (and are subject to the Order Protection Rule) than for marketplaces that do not provide pre-trade transparency of orders.

Policies and Orders: CSAN 23-308; 23-311; OSCN 21-705.

OSC Staff Notice 21-707 — Swap Execution Facilities — Exemption From Requirement To Be Recognized As An Exchange

Date: October 10, 2013

36 O.S.C.B. 9716

Swap execution facilities (SEFs) are a new type of marketplace for trading swaps in the United States. They are governed by the Dodd-Frank Act and rules of the United States Commodity Future Trading Commission.

Because SEFs have self-regulatory responsibilities, they are considered "exchanges" under Ontario securities law. If a SEF provides access to participants in Ontario, it is considered to be doing business in Ontario and must be recognized as an exchange or obtain an exemption from recognition.

The Commission has exempted certain SEFs from the requirement to be recognized as an exchange, subject to the terms and conditions set out in each order. Copies of the exemption orders are in Chapter 2 of this Bulletin and on the OSC website.

Related Provisions: OSA 74 21(1)

OSC Staff Notice 21-709 — Marketplace Operation and Forms 21-101F1 and 21-101F2

Date: September 10, 2015

38 O.S.C.B. 7675

The purpose of this notice is to remind marketplaces and their operators that they are only permitted to operate within the scope of the operations described in their existing F1 or F2. Should a marketplace wish to engage in activity outside the scope of its F1 or F2, the requisite regulatory approvals must be obtained. Specifically, a marketplace must file an F1 or F2 amendment in accordance with the applicable protocol for review and approval of rules and the information contained in the F1 or F2 (Protocol), and receive regulatory approval before it offers new functionality to its participants.

A complete and accurate F1 or F2, and compliance with the Protocol, are fundamentally important to the Commission's oversight of all marketplaces. The information in the F1 or F2 comprises the basis on which the Commission and Staff understand the operations of the marketplace and underpins our ability to assess the potential impact on its operations, on the marketplace as a whole and on investors. This ensures our markets remain fair, efficient and that investor confidence is maintained.

---

[5]Subsection 12.3(2) of NI 21-101.

In addition, Staff remind marketplaces that recent changes to section 3.2(4) of NI 21-101, published in the OSC Bulletin on June 25, 2015,[1] will require annual written certification by the chief executive officer of a marketplace, or an individual performing a similar function verifying "that the information contained in the marketplace's current form F1 or F2, as applicable, is true, correct, and complete and that the marketplace is operating as described in the applicable form". These changes will take effect on October 1, 2015.

Should a marketplace fail to comply with applicable regulatory requirements, including requirements with respect to its F1 or F2, Staff will take appropriate steps under the *Securities Act* (Ontario).

I. — Questions

Questions may be referred to any of:

Paul Romain

promain@osc.gov.on.ca

Louis-Philippe Pellegrini

lpellegrini@osc.gov.on.ca

Tracey Stern

tstern@osc.gov.on.ca

Recognition Order 21-901 — Stock Exchange Recognition Order

Recognition Order: dated February 25, 1997: (1997), 20 O.S.C.B. 1034, as amended August 29, 2000: (2000), 23 O.S.C.B. 6079, November 7, 2000: 23 O.S.C.B. 7810 and October 18, 2001: 24 O.S.C.B. 6427.

[Not reproduced, as no longer relevant]

2.2 — Other Markets

2.3 — Trading Rules

National Instrument 23-101 — Trading Rules

Date: **November 2, 2001, as amended effective January 3, 2004, September 12, 2008, January 28, 2010, July 1, 2012 and October 1, 2015**

24 O.S.C.B. 6635, 27 O.S.C.B. 463, 31 O.S.C.B. 8572, 33 O.S.C.B. 795, 35 O.S.C.B. 5425, 38 O.S.C.B. (Supp. 2) 29 and 39 O.S.C.B. 3237.

Table of Contents

[1](2015), 38 OSCB (Supp-2).

Part 2: MARKET PARTICIPANTS

PART 1 — DEFINITION AND INTERPRETATION

1.1 Definition — In this Instrument

"automated trading functionality" means the ability to

(a) immediately allow an incoming order that has been entered on the marketplace electronically to be marked as immediate-or-cancel;

(b) immediately and automatically execute an order marked as immediate-or-cancel against the displayed volume;

(c) immediately and automatically cancel any unexecuted portion of an order marked as immediate-or-cancel without routing the order elsewhere;

(d) immediately and automatically transmit a response to the sender of an order marked as immediate-or-cancel indicating the action taken with respect to the order; and

(e) immediately and automatically display information that updates the displayed orders on the marketplace to reflect any change to their material terms;

"best execution" means the most advantageous execution terms reasonably available under the circumstances;

"calculated-price order" means an order for the purchase or sale of an exchange-traded security, other than an option, that is entered on a marketplace and for which the price of the security

(a) is not known at the time of order entry; and

(b) is not based, directly or indirectly, on the quoted price of an exchange-traded security at the time the commitment to execute the order was made;

"closing-price order" means an order for the purchase or sale of an exchange-traded security, other than an option, that is

(a) entered on a marketplace on a trading day; and

(b) subject to the conditions that

(i) the order be executed at the closing sale price of that security on that marketplace for that trading day; and

(ii) the order be executed subsequent to the establishment of the closing price;

"directed-action order" means an order for the purchase or sale of an exchange-traded security, other than an option, that,

(a) when entered on or routed to a marketplace, is to be immediately

(i) executed against a displayed order with any remainder to be booked or cancelled; or

(ii) placed in an order book;

(b) is marked as a directed-action order; and

(c) is entered on or routed to a marketplace

(i) to execute against a best-priced displayed order, or

(ii) at the same time that another order is entered on or routed to a marketplace to execute against any protected order with a better price than the entered or routed order;

"NI 21-101" means National Instrument 21-101 Marketplace Operation;

"non-standard order" means an order for the purchase or sale of an exchange-traded security, other than an option, that is entered on a marketplace and is subject to non-standardized terms or conditions related to settlement that have not been set by the marketplace on which the security is listed or quoted; and

"protected bid" means a bid for an exchange-traded security, other than an option

(a) that is displayed on a marketplace that provides automated functionality; and

Proposed Amendment —

(a) that is displayed on a marketplace that provides automated trading functionality and

(i) the marketplace meets or exceeds the market share threshold as set for the purposes of this definition by the regulator, or in Quebec, the securities regulatory authority; or

(ii) if the marketplace is a recognized exchange, the bid is for a security listed by and traded on that recognized exchange; and

[To come into force October 1, 2016]

(b) about which information is required to be provided pursuant to Part 7 of NI 21-101 to an information processor or, if there is no information processor, to an information vendor that meets the standards set by a regulation services provider;

"protected offer" means an offer for an exchange-traded security, other than an option,

(a) that is displayed on a marketplace that provides automated functionality; and

Proposed Amendment —

(a) that is displayed on a marketplace that provides automated trading functionality and

(i) the marketplace meets or exceeds the market share threshold as set for the purposes of this definition by the regulator, or in Quebec, the securities regulatory authority; or

(ii) if the marketplace is a recognized exchange, the offer is for a security listed by and traded on that recognized exchange; and

[To come into force October 1, 2016]

(b) about which information is required to be provided pursuant to Part 7 of NI 21-101 to an information processor or, if there is no information processor, to an information vendor that meets the standards set by a regulation services provider; and

"protected order" means a protected bid or protected offer.

"trade-through" means the execution of an order at a price that is,

(a) in the case of a purchase, higher than any protected offer, or

(b) in the case of a sale, lower than any protected bid.

1.2 Interpretation — NI 21-101 — Terms defined or interpreted in NI 21-101 and used in this Instrument have the respective meanings ascribed to them in NI 21-101.

PART 2 — APPLICATION OF THIS INSTRUMENT

2.1 Application of this Instrument — A person or company is exempt from subsection 3.1(1) and Parts 4 and 5 if the person or company complies with similar requirements established by

(a) a recognized exchange that monitors and enforces the requirements set under subsection 7.1(1) directly;

(b) a recognized quotation and trade reporting system that monitors and enforces requirements set under subsection 7.3(1) directly; or

(c) a regulation services provider.

PART 3 — MANIPULATION AND FRAUD

3.1 Manipulation and Fraud — (1) A person or company must not, directly or indirectly, engage in, or participate in any transaction or series of transactions, or method of trading relating to a trade in or acquisition of a security or any act, practice or course of conduct, if the person or company knows, or ought reasonably to know, that the transaction or series of transactions, or method of trading or act, practice or course of conduct

(a) results in or contributes to a misleading appearance of trading activity in, or an artificial price for, a security or a derivative of that security; or

(b) perpetrates a fraud on any person or company.

(2) In Alberta, British Columbia, Ontario, Québec and Saskatchewan, instead of subsection (1), the provisions of the *Securities Act* (Alberta), the *Securities Act* (British Columbia), the *Securities Act* (Ontario), the *Securities Act* and the *Derivatives Act* (Québec) and *The Securities Act, 1988* (Saskatchewan), respectively, relating to manipulation and fraud apply.

PART 4 — BEST EXECUTION

4.1 Application of this Part — This Part does not apply to a dealer that is carrying on business as an ATS in compliance with section 6.1 of NI 21-101.

4.2 Best Execution — A dealer and an adviser must make reasonable efforts to achieve best execution when acting for a client.

4.3 Order and Trade Information — To satisfy the requirements in section 4.2, a dealer or adviser must make reasonable efforts to use facilities providing information regarding orders and trades.

PART 5 — REGULATORY HALTS

5.1 Regulatory Halts — If a regulation services provider, a recognized exchange, recognized quotation and trade reporting system or an exchange or quotation and trade reporting system that has been recognized for the purposes of this Instrument and NI 21-101 makes a decision to prohibit trading in a particular security for a regulatory purpose, a person or company must not execute a trade for the purchase or sale of that security during the period in which the prohibition is in place.

PART 6 — ORDER PROTECTION

6.1 Marketplace Requirements for Order Protection — (1) A marketplace must establish, maintain and ensure compliance with written policies and procedures that are reasonably designed

    (a) to prevent trade-throughs on that marketplace other than the trade-throughs referred to in section 6.2; and

    (b) to ensure that the marketplace, when executing a transaction that results in a trade-through referred to in section 6.2, is doing so in compliance with this Part.

(2) A marketplace must regularly review and monitor the effectiveness of the policies and procedures required under subsection (1) and must promptly remedy any deficiencies in those policies and procedures.

(3) At least 45 days before implementation, a marketplace must file with the securities regulatory authority and, if applicable, its regulation services provider the policies and procedures, and any significant changes to those policies and procedures, established under subsection (1).

6.2 List of Trade-throughs — For the purposes of paragraph 6.1(1)(a) the permitted trade-throughs are:

    (a) a trade-through that occurs when the marketplace has reasonably concluded that the marketplace displaying the protected order that was traded through was experiencing a failure, malfunction or material delay of its systems or equipment or ability to disseminate marketplace data;

    (b) the execution of a directed-action order;

    (c) a trade-through by a marketplace that simultaneously routes a directed-action order to execute against the total displayed volume of any protected order that is traded through;

    (d) a trade-though if, immediately before the trade-through, the marketplace displaying the protected order that is traded through displays as its best price a protected order with a price that is equal or inferior to the price of the trade-through;

    (e) a trade-through that results when executing

        (i) a non-standard order;

        (ii) a calculated-price order; or

        (iii) a closing-price order;

    (f) a trade-through that was executed at a time when the best protected bid for the security traded through was higher than the best protected offer.

6.3 Systems or Equipment Failure, Malfunction or Material Delay — (1) If a marketplace experiences a failure, malfunction or material delay of its systems, equipment or its ability to disseminate marketplace data, the marketplace must immediately notify

    (a) all other marketplaces;

    (b) all regulation services providers;

    (c) its marketplace participants; and

    (d) any information processor or, if there is no information processor, any information vendor that disseminates its data under Part 7 of NI 21-101.

(2) If executing a transaction described in paragraph 6.2(a), and a notification has not been sent under subsection (1), the marketplace that is executing the transaction or routing the order for execution must immediately notify the following of the failure, malfunction or material delay

    (a) the marketplace that it reasonably concluded is experiencing a failure, malfunction or material delay of its systems or equipment or its ability to disseminate marketplace data;

    (b) all regulation services providers;

    (c) its marketplace participants; and

    (d) any information processor disseminating information under Part 7 of NI 21-101.

(3) If a marketplace participant reasonably concludes that a marketplace displaying a protected order is experiencing a failure, malfunction or material delay of its systems or equipment or its ability to disseminate marketplace data, and routes an order to execute against a protected order on another marketplace displaying an inferior price, the marketplace participant must notify the following of the failure, malfunction or material delay

    (a) the marketplace that may be experiencing a failure, malfunction or material delay of its systems or equipment or its ability to disseminate marketplace data; and

    (b) all regulation services providers.

6.4 Marketplace Participant Requirements for Order Protection — (1) A marketplace participant must not enter a directed-action order unless the marketplace participant has established, and maintains and ensures compliance with, written policies and procedures that are reasonably designed

(a) to prevent trade-throughs other than the trade-throughs listed below:

(i) a trade-through that occurs when the marketplace participant has reasonably concluded that the marketplace displaying the protected order that was traded through was experiencing a failure, malfunction or material delay of its systems or equipment or ability to disseminate marketplace data;

(ii) a trade-through by a marketplace participant that simultaneously routes a directed-action order to execute against the total displayed volume of any protected order that is traded through;

(iii) a trade-through if, immediately before the trade-through, the marketplace displaying the protected order that is traded through displays as its best price a protected order with a price that is equal or inferior to the price of the trade-through transaction;

(iv) a trade-through that results when executing

(A) a non-standard order;

(B) a calculated-price order; or

(C) a closing-price order;

(v) a trade-through that was executed at a time when the best protected bid for the security traded through was higher than the best protected offer; and

(b) to ensure that when executing a trade-through listed in paragraphs (a)(i) to (a)(v), it is doing so in compliance with this Part.

(2) A marketplace participant that enters a directed-action order must regularly review and monitor the effectiveness of the policies and procedures required under subsection (1) and must promptly remedy any deficiencies in those policies and procedures.

6.5 Locked or Crossed Orders — A marketplace participant or a marketplace that routes or reprices orders must not intentionally enter a displayed order on a marketplace that is subject to section 7.1 of NI 21-101, at a price that,

(a) in the case of an order to purchase, is the same as or higher than the best protected offer, or

(b) in the case of an order to sell, is the same as or lower than the best protected bid.

6.6 Trading Hours — A marketplace must set the hours of trading to be observed by marketplace participants.

6.6.1 Trading Fees — (1) In this section, "exchange-traded fund" means a mutual fund,

(a) the units of which are listed securities or quoted securities, and

(b) that is in continuous distribution in accordance with applicable securities legislation.

(2) A marketplace that is subject to section 7.1 of NI 21-101 must not charge a fee for executing an order that was entered to execute against a displayed order on that marketplace greater than

(a) $0.0030 per security traded for an equity security, or per unit traded for an exchange-traded fund, if the execution price of each security or unit traded is greater than or equal to $1.00; or

(b) $0.0004 per security traded for an equity security, or per unit traded for an exchange-traded fund, if the execution price of each security or unit traded is less than $1.0.

6.7 Anti-Avoidance — A person or company must not send an order to an exchange, quotation and trade reporting system or alternative trading system that does not carry on business in Canada in order to avoid executing against better-priced protected orders.

6.8 Application of this Part — In Québec, this Part, except for paragraph 6.3(1)(c), does not apply to standardized derivatives.

PART 7 — MONITORING AND ENFORCEMENT OF REQUIREMENTS SET BY A RECOGNIZED EXCHANGE AND A RECOGNIZED QUOTATION AND TRADE REPORTING SYSTEM

7.1 Requirements for a Recognized Exchange — (1) A recognized exchange must set requirements governing the conduct of its members, including requirements that the members will conduct trading activities in compliance with this Instrument.

(2) A recognized exchange must monitor the conduct of its members and enforce the requirements set under subsection (1), either

(a) directly, or

(b) indirectly through a regulation services provider.

(3) If a recognized exchange has entered into a written agreement under section 7.2, the recognized exchange must adopt requirements, as determined necessary by the regulation services provider, that govern the recognized exchange and the conduct of the exchange's members, and that enable the regulation services provider to effectively monitor trading on the exchange and across marketplaces.

7.2 Agreement between a Recognized Exchange and a Regulation Services Provider — A recognized exchange that monitors the conduct of its members indirectly through a regulation services provider must enter into a written agreement with the regulation services provider which provides that the regulation services provider will:

(a) monitor the conduct of the members of the recognized exchange,

(b) monitor the compliance of the recognized exchange with the requirements set under subsection 7.1(3), and

(c) enforce the requirements set under subsection 7.1(1).

7.2.1 Obligations of a Recognized Exchange to a Regulation Services Provider — A recognized exchange that has entered into a written agreement with a regulation services provider must

(a) transmit to the regulation services provider the information required under Part 11 of NI 21-101 and any information reasonably required by the regulation services provider in the form and manner requested by the regulation services provider to effectively monitor:

(i) the conduct of and trading by marketplace participants on and across marketplaces, including the compliance of marketplace participants with the requirements set under subsection 7.1(1), and

(ii) the conduct of the recognized exchange, including the compliance of the recognized exchange with the requirements set under subsection 7.1(3); and

(b) comply with all orders or directions made by the regulation services provider.

7.3 Requirements for a Recognized Quotation and Trade Reporting System — (1) A recognized quotation and trade reporting system must set requirements governing the conduct of its users, including requirements that the users will conduct trading activities in compliance with this Instrument.

(2) A recognized quotation and trade reporting system must monitor the conduct of its users and enforce the requirements set under subsection (1) either

(a) directly; or

(b) indirectly through a regulation services provider.

(3) If a recognized exchange has entered into a written agreement under section 7.2, the recognized exchange must adopt requirements, as determined necessary by the regulation services provider, that govern the recognized exchange and the conduct of the exchange's members, and that enable the regulation services provider to effectively monitor trading on the exchange and across marketplaces.

7.4 Agreement between a Recognized Quotation and Trade Reporting System and a Regulation Services Provider — A recognized quotation and trade reporting system that monitors the conduct of its users indirectly through a regulation services provider must enter into a written agreement with the regulation services provider which provides that the regulation services provider will

(a) monitor the conduct of the users of the recognized quotation and trade reporting system,

(b) monitor the compliance of the recognized quotation and trade reporting system with the requirements set under subsection 7.3(3), and

(c) enforce the requirements set under subsection 7.3(1).

7.4.1 Obligations of a Quotation and Trade Reporting System to a Regulation Services Provider — A recognized quotation and trade reporting system that has entered into a written agreement with a regulation services provider must

(a) transmit to the regulation services provider the information required under Part 11 of NI 21-101 and any information reasonably required by the regulation services provider in the form and manner requested by the regulation services provider to effectively monitor:

(i) the conduct of and trading by marketplace participants on and across marketplaces, including the compliance of marketplace participants with the requirements set under subsection 7.3(1), and

(ii) the conduct of the recognized quotation and trade reporting system, including the compliance of the recognized quotation and trade reporting system with the requirements set under subsection 7.3(3); and

(b) comply with all orders or directions made by the regulation services provider.

7.5 Co-ordination of Monitoring and Enforcement — A regulation services provider, recognized exchange, or recognized quotation and trade reporting system must enter into a written agreement with all other regulation services providers, recognized exchanges, and recognized quotation and trade reporting systems to coordinate monitoring and enforcement of the requirements set under Parts 7 and 8.

PART 8 — MONITORING AND ENFORCEMENT REQUIREMENTS FOR AN ATS

8.1 Pre-condition to Trading on an ATS — An ATS must not execute a subscriber's order to buy or sell securities unless the ATS has executed and is subject to the written agreements required by sections 8.3 and 8.4.

8.2 Requirements Set by a Regulation Services Provider for an ATS — (1) A regulation services provider must set requirements governing an ATS and its subscribers, including requirements that the ATS and its subscribers will conduct trading activities in compliance with this Instrument.

(2) A regulation services provider must monitor the conduct of an ATS and its subscribers and must enforce the requirements set under subsection (1).

8.3 Agreement between an ATS and a Regulation Services Provider — An ATS and a regulation services provider must enter into a written agreement that provides

(a) that the ATS will conduct its trading activities in compliance with the requirements set under subsection 8.2(1);

(b) that the regulation services provider will monitor the conduct of the ATS and its subscribers;

(c) that the regulation services provider will enforce the requirements set under subsection 8.2(1);

(d) that the ATS will transmit to the regulation services provider the information required by Part 11 of NI 21-101 and any other information reasonably required to effectively monitor:

(i) the conduct of and trading by marketplace participants on and across marketplaces, and

(ii) the conduct of the ATS; and

(e) that the ATS will comply with all orders or directions made by the regulation services provider.

8.4 Agreement between an ATS and its Subscriber — An ATS and its subscriber must enter into a written agreement that provides

(a) that the subscriber will conduct its trading activities in compliance with the requirements set under subsection 8.2(1);

(b) that the subscriber acknowledges that the regulation services provider will monitor the conduct of the subscriber and enforce the requirements set under subsection 8.2(1);

(c) that the subscriber will comply with all orders or directions made by the regulation services provider in its capacity as a regulation services provider, including orders excluding the subscriber from trading on any marketplace.

PART 9 — MONITORING AND ENFORCEMENT REQUIREMENTS FOR AN INTER-DEALER BOND BROKER

9.1 Requirements Set by a Regulation Services Provider for an Inter-Dealer Bond Broker — (1) A regulation services provider must set requirements governing an inter-dealer bond broker, including requirements that the inter-dealer bond broker will conduct trading activities in compliance with this Instrument.

(2) A regulation services provider must monitor the conduct of an inter-dealer bond broker and must enforce the requirements set under subsection (1).

9.2 Agreement between an Inter-Dealer Bond Broker and a Regulation Services Provider — An inter-dealer bond broker and a regulation services provider must enter into a written agreement that provides

(a) that the inter-dealer bond broker will conduct its trading activities in compliance with the requirements set under subsection 9.1(1);

(b) that the regulation services provider will monitor the conduct of the inter-dealer bond broker;

(c) that the regulation services provider will enforce the requirements set under subsection 9.1(1); and

(d) that the inter-dealer bond broker will comply with all orders or directions made by the regulation services provider.

9.3 Exemption for an Inter-Dealer Bond Broker — (1) Sections 9.1 and 9.2 do not apply to an inter-dealer bond broker, if the inter-dealer bond broker complies with the requirements of IIROC Rule 2800 Code of Conduct for Corporation Dealer Member Firms Trading in Wholesale Domestic Debt Markets, as amended.

PART 10 — MONITORING AND ENFORCEMENT REQUIREMENTS FOR A DEALER EXECUTING TRADES OF UNLISTED DEBT SECURITIES OUTSIDE OF A MARKETPLACE

10.1 Requirements Set by a Regulation Services Provider for a Dealer Executing Trades of Unlisted Debt Securities Outside of a Marketplace — (1) A regulation services provider must set requirements governing a dealer executing trades of unlisted debt securities outside of a marketplace, including requirements that the dealer will conduct trading activities in compliance with this Instrument.

(2) A regulation services provider must monitor the conduct of a dealer executing trades of unlisted debt securities outside of a marketplace and must enforce the requirements set under subsection (1).

10.2 Agreement between a Dealer Executing Trades of Unlisted Debt Securities Outside of a Marketplace and a Regulation Services Provider — A dealer executing trades of unlisted debt securities outside of a marketplace must enter into a written agreement with a regulation services provider that provides

(a) that the dealer will conduct its trading activities in compliance with the requirements set under subsection 10.1(1);

(b) that the regulation services provider will monitor the conduct of the dealer;

(c) that the regulation services provider will enforce the requirements set under subsection 10.1(1); and

(d) that the dealer will comply with all orders or directions made by the regulation services provider.

PART 11 — AUDIT TRAIL REQUIREMENTS

11.1 Application of this Part — (1) This Part does not apply to a dealer that is carrying on business as an ATS in compliance with section 6.1 of NI 21-101.

(2) A dealer or inter-dealer bond broker is exempt from the requirements in section 11.2 if the dealer or inter-dealer bond broker complies with similar requirements, for any securities specified, established by a regulation services provider and approved by the applicable securities regulatory authority.

11.2 Audit Trail Requirements for Dealers and Inter-Dealer Bond Brokers — (1) Recording Requirements for Receipt or Origination of an Order — Immediately following the receipt or origination of an order for equity, fixed income and other securities identified by a regulation services provider, a dealer and inter-dealer bond broker must record in electronic form specific information relating to that order including,

(a) the order identifier;

(b) the dealer or inter-dealer bond broker identifier;

(c) the type, issuer, class, series and symbol of the security;

(d) the face amount or unit price of the order, if applicable;

(e) the number of securities to which the order applies;

(f) the strike date and strike price, if applicable;

(g) whether the order is a buy or sell order;

(h) whether the order is a short sale order, if applicable;

(i) whether the order is a market order, limit order or other type of order, and if the order is not a market order, the price at which the order is to trade;

(j) the date and time the order is first originated or received by the dealer or inter-dealer bond broker;

(k) whether the account is a retail, wholesale, employee, proprietary or any other type of account;

(l) the client account number or client identifier;

(m) the date and time that the order expires;

(n) whether the order is an intentional cross;

(o) whether the order is a jitney and if so, the underlying broker identifier;

437

(p) any client instructions or consents respecting the handling or trading of the order, if applicable;

(q) the currency of the order;

(r) an insider marker;

(s) any other markers required by a regulation services provider;

(t) each unique client identifier assigned to a client accessing the marketplace using direct electronic access; and

(u) whether the order is a directed-action order.

(2) Recording Requirements for Transmission of an Order — Immediately following the transmission of an order for securities to a dealer, inter-dealer bond broker or a marketplace, a dealer or inter-dealer bond broker transmitting the order must add to the record of the order maintained in accordance with this section specific information relating to that order including,

(a) the dealer or inter-dealer bond broker identifier assigned to the dealer or inter-dealer bond broker transmitting the order and the identifier assigned to the dealer, inter-dealer bond broker or marketplace to which the order is transmitted; and

(b) the date and time the order is transmitted.

(3) Recording Requirements for Variation, Correction or Cancellation of an Order — Immediately following the variation, correction or cancellation of an order for securities, a dealer or inter-dealer bond broker must add to the record of the order maintained in accordance with this section specific information relating to that order including,

(a) the date and time the variation, correction or cancellation was originated or received;

(b) whether the order was varied, corrected or cancelled on the instructions of the client, the dealer or the inter-dealer bond broker;

(c) in the case of variation or correction, any of the information required by subsection (1) which has been changed; and

(d) the date and time the variation, correction or cancellation of the order is entered.

(4) Recording Requirements for Execution of an Order — Immediately following the execution of an order for securities, the dealer or inter-dealer bond broker must add to the record maintained in accordance with this section specific information relating to that order including,

(a) the identifier of the marketplace where the order was executed or the identifier of the dealer or inter-dealer bond broker executing the order if the order was not executed on a marketplace;

(b) the date and time of the execution of the order;

(c) whether the order was fully or partially executed;

(d) the number of securities bought or sold;

(e) whether the transaction was a cross;

(f) whether the dealer has executed the order as principal;

(g) the commission charged and all other transaction fees; and

(h) the price at which the order was executed, including mark-up or mark-down.

(5) [Repealed]

(6) [Repealed]

(7) Record preservation requirements — A dealer and an inter-dealer bond broker must keep all records in electronic form for a period of not less than seven years from the creation of the record referred to in this section, and for the first two years in a readily accessible location.

11.3 Transmission in Electronic Form — A dealer and inter-dealer bond broker must transmit

(a) to a regulation services provider the information required by the regulation services provider, within ten business days, in electronic form; and

(b) to the securities regulatory authority the information required by the securities regulatory authority under securities legislation, within ten business days, in electronic form.

PART 12 — EXEMPTION

12.1 Exemption — (1) The regulator or the securities regulatory authority may grant an exemption from this Instrument, in whole or in part, subject to such conditions or restrictions as may be imposed in the exemption.

(2) Despite subsection (1), in Ontario, only the regulator may grant such an exemption.

PART 13 — EFFECTIVE DATE

13.1 Effective Date — This Instrument comes into force on December 1, 2001.

Final Rule: 24 O.S.C.B. 6635 (November 2, 2001); Approval by OSC: 24 O.S.C.B. (Supp.) 85 (August 17, 2001); Request for Comments: 23 O.S.C.B. (Supp.) 259 (July 28, 2001).

Amendments to Rule: (2004) 27 O.S.C.B. 463; Approval by OSC: (2003) 26 O.S.C.B. 7147; Request for Comments: (2003) 26 O.S.C.B. 4377.

Amendments to Rule: (2006) 29 O.S.C.B. 10011; Approval by OSC: (2006) 29 O.S.C.B. 9731; Request for Comments: (2006) 29 O.S.C.B. 5735.

Amendments to Rule: (2008) 31 O.S.C.B. 8572; Approval by OSC: (2008) 31 O.S.C.B. 6303; Request for Comments: (2007) 30 O.S.C.B. (Supp. 3) 1 (April 20, 2007).

Amendments to Rule: (2010) 33 O.S.C.B. 795; Approval by OSC: (2009) 32 O.S.C.B. 9403; Request for Comments: (2008) 31 O.S.C.B. 10136.

Amendments to Rule: (2012) 35 O.S.C.B. 5425; Approval by OSC: (2012) 35 O.S.C.B. (Supp. 1) 1; Request for Comments: (2011) 34 O.S.C.B. (Supp. 1) 1.

Amendments to Rule: (2015) 38 O.S.C.B. 8557; Approval by OSC (2015) 38 O.S.C.B. (Supp. 2) 30; Request for Comments: (2014) 37 O.S.C.B. 4873.

Amendments to Rule: (2016) 39 O.S.C.B. 3237; Approval by OSC: (2015) 38 O.S.C.B. 8437; Request for Comments: (2014) 37 O.S.C.B. 4197

Rules: NI 21-101.

Policies and Orders: BOR 2.2; CSAN 23-308, 23-309, 23-311; OSCN 33-734, s. 3.2.

Companion Policy 23-101CP — To National Instrument 23-101 Trading Rules

Table of Contents

PART 1 — INTRODUCTION

1.1 Introduction — The purpose of this Companion Policy is to state the views of the Canadian securities regulatory authorities on various matters related to National Instrument 23-101 Trading Rules (the "Instrument"), including

(a) a discussion of the general approach taken by the Canadian securities regulatory authorities in, and the general regulatory purpose for, the Instrument; and

(b) the interpretation of various terms and provisions in the Instrument.

1.2 Just and Equitable Principles of Trade — While the Instrument deals with specific trading practices, as a general matter, the Canadian securities regulatory authorities expect marketplace participants to transact business openly and fairly, and in accordance with just and equitable principles of trade.

PART 1.1 — DEFINITIONS

1.1.1 Definition of best execution — (1) In the Instrument, best execution is defined as the "most advantageous execution terms reasonably available under the circumstances". In seeking best execution, a dealer or adviser may consider a number of elements, including:

    a. price;

    b. speed of execution;

    c. certainty of execution; and

    d. the overall cost of the transaction.

These four broad elements encompass more specific considerations, such as order size, reliability of quotes, liquidity, market impact (i.e. the price movement that occurs when executing an order) and opportunity cost (i.e. the missed opportunity to obtain a better price when an order is not completed at the most advantageous time). The overall cost of the transaction is meant to include, where appropriate, all costs associated with accessing an order and/or executing a trade that are passed on to a client, including fees arising from trading on a particular marketplace, jitney fees (i.e. any fees charged by one dealer to another for providing trading access) and settlement costs. The commission fees charged by a dealer would also be a cost of the transaction.

(2) The elements to be considered in determining "the most advantageous execution terms reasonably available" (i.e. best execution) and the weight given to each will vary depending on the instructions and needs of the client, the particular security, the prevailing market conditions and whether the dealer or adviser is responsible for best execution under the circumstances. Please see a detailed discussion below in Part 4.

1.1.2 Definition of automated trading functionality — Section 1.1 of the Instrument includes a definition of "automated trading functionality" which is the ability to: (1) act on an incoming order; (2) respond to the sender of an order; and (3) update the order by disseminating information to an information processor or information vendor. Automated trading functionality allows for an incoming order to execute immediately and automatically up to the displayed size and for any unexecuted portion of such incoming order to be cancelled immediately and automatically without being booked or routed elsewhere. Automated trading functionality involves no human discretion in determining the action taken with respect to an order after the time the order is received. A marketplace with this functionality should have appropriate systems and policies and procedures relating to the handling of immediate-or-cancel orders.

1.1.2.1 Application to marketplaces implementing intentional order processing delays — (1) Paragraph (b) of the definition of "automated trading functionality" refers to the ability of a marketplace to "immediately and automatically execute an order marked as immediate-or-cancel against the displayed volume".

With respect to the application of sections 6.1 and 6.4, Canadian securities regulatory authorities are of the view that where a marketplace has introduced functionality that imposes an intentional order processing delay that is not applied in the same way to all orders, that marketplace does not provide the ability for an immediate execution against the displayed volume and therefore, does not offer "automated trading functionality". As a result, an order on that marketplace would not be a "protected order" as defined in the instrument.

Delays in the execution of an order on a particular marketplace might result from operational or technological decisions by a marketplace. The determination of whether the marketplace with a delay offers the ability to immediately execute an order would also be based on, among other factors, how the operational model of the marketplace itself is applied, and the impact of the model or delay as it relates to fair and orderly trading. Although these delays generally would be considered intentional, they could still result in "immediate" executions on that marketplace, despite the fact that executions could be achieved faster on marketplaces that make different decisions.

If a marketplace operates more than one market or facility and it implements an intentional delay in order processing on one or more of them, only the market or facility with an intentional processing delay is considered not to provide automated trading functionality.

(2) For a greater certainty, an order processing delay that is imposed solely to comply with securities legislation is not considered an intentional delay.

1.1.3 Definition of protected order — (1) A protected order is defined to be a "protected bid or protected offer". A "protected bid" or "protected offer" is an order to buy or sell an exchange-traded security, other than an option, that is displayed on a marketplace that provides automated functionality and about which information is provided to an information processor or an information vendor, as applicable, pursuant to Part 7 of NI 21-101.

(2) The regulator, or in Quebec, the securities regulatory authority, will apply the threshold on an established periodic basis to assess which marketplaces, including which markets or facilities of a marketplace , meet or exceed the market share threshold for the purposes of the definitions of "protected bid" and "protected offer". The market share threshold will be applied at the market or facility level where the marketplace is comprised of more than one visible continuous auction order book, and will not be calculated in aggregate across those different markets or facilities. A list of those that meet or exceed the market share threshold will be published on the websites of the Canadian securities regulatory authorities and the regulation services provider, so that marketplace participants can easily identify the marketplaces on which displayed orders will be considered to be protected orders in accordance with subparagraph (a)(i) of the definitions of "protected bid" and "protected offer". An updated list will be published after each periodic assessment of which marketplaces meet or exceed the market share threshold, and participants will be given an appropriate amount of time before the effective date of the published list to make any changes to operational processes that might be needed.

(3) In accordance with subsection (a)(ii) of the definitions of "protected bid" and "protected offer", a protected order is also an order displayed on a marketplace that has not met the market share threshold where that marketplace is a recognized exchange, and the order being displayed is for a security listed by and traded on the exchange. The published list will also identify any such recognized exchanges.

(4) The market share threshold criteria, including the specifics regarding the time periods covered by the calculation and the effective date and duration of the published lists, will also be made public. The application of these criteria will be monitored and reviewed, and modifications will be made if and where appropriate or necessary. Advance public notice will be made regarding any changes to the market share threshold criteria.

(5) The term "displayed on a marketplace" refers to the information about total disclosed volume on a marketplace. Volumes that are not disclosed or that are "reserve" or hidden volumes are not considered to be "displayed on a marketplace". The order must be provided in a way that enables other marketplaces and marketplace participants to readily access the information and integrate it into their systems or order routers.

(6) Subsection 5.1(3) of 21-101CP does not consider orders that are not immediately executable or that have special terms as "orders" that are required to be provided to an information processor or information vendor under Part 7 of NI 21-101. As a result, these orders are not considered to be "protected orders" under the definition in the Instrument and do not receive order protection. However, those executing against these types of orders are required to execute against all better-priced orders first. In addition, when entering a "special terms order" on a marketplace, if it can be executed against existing orders despite the special term, then the order protection obligation applies.

1.1.4 Definition of calculated-price order — The definition of "calculated-price order" refers to any order where the price is not known at the time of order entry and is not based, directly or indirectly, on the quoted price of an exchange-traded security at the time the commitment to executing the order was made. This includes the following orders:

(a) **a call market order** — where the price of a trade is calculated by the trading system of a marketplace at a time designated by the marketplace;

(b) **an opening order** — where each marketplace may establish its own formula for the determination of opening prices;

(c) **a closing order** — where execution occurs at the closing price on a particular marketplace, but at the time of order entry, the price is not known;

(d) **a volume-weighted average price order** — where the price of a trade is determined by a formula that measures average price on one or more marketplaces; and

(e) **a basis order** — where the price is based on prices achieved in one or more derivative transactions on a marketplace. To qualify as a basis order, this order must be approved by a regulation services provider or an exchange or quotation and trade reporting system that oversees the conduct of its members or users respectively.

1.1.5 Definition of directed-action order — (1) An order marked as a directed-action order informs the receiving marketplace that the marketplace can act immediately to carry out the action specified by either the marketplace or marketplace participant who has sent the order and that the order protection obligation is being met by the sender. Such an order may be marked "DAO" by a marketplace or a marketplace participant. Senders can specify actions by adding markers that instruct a marketplace to:

(a) execute the order and cancel the remainder using an immediate-or-cancel marker,

(b) execute the order and book the remainder,

(c) book the order as a passive order awaiting execution, and

(d) avoid interaction with hidden liquidity using a bypass marker, as defined in IIROC's Universal Market Integrity Rules.

The definition allows for the simultaneous routing of more than one directed-action order in order to execute against any better-priced protected orders. In addition, marketplaces or marketplace participants may send a single directed-action order to execute against the best protected bid or best protected offer. When it receives a directed-action order, a marketplace can carry out the sender's instructions without checking for better-priced protected orders displayed by the other marketplaces and implementing the marketplace's own policies and procedures to reasonably prevent trade-throughs.

(2) Regardless of whether the entry of a directed-action order is accompanied by the bypass marker, the sender must take out all better-priced visible protected orders before executing at an inferior price. For example, if a marketplace or marketplace participant combines a directed-action order with a bypass marker to avoid executing against hidden liquidity, the order has order protection obligations regarding the visible protected liquidity. If a directed-action order interacts with hidden liquidity, the requirement to take out all better-priced protected visible orders before executing at a price that is inferior to the best protected bid or best protected offer remains.

1.1.6 Definition of non-standard order — The definition of "non-standard order" refers to an order for the purchase or sale of a security that is subject to terms or conditions relating to settlement that have not been set by the marketplace on which the security is listed or quoted. A marketplace participant, however, may not add a special settlement term or condition to an order solely for the purpose that the order becomes a non-standard order under the definition.

1.1.7 Definition of trade-through — The definition of "trade-through" applies only to a trade executed at a price that is inferior to the best protected bid or best protected offer. It is a trade-through regardless of whether the trade occurs on a marketplace that displays protected orders, or one that does not display protected orders. For example, a trade-through would occur if executing against an order that is displayed on an ATS that does not meet the market share threshold and at a price that is inferior to the best-priced protected order. However, a trade-through would not occur if executing against a best-priced protected order despite there being a better-priced order displayed on an ATS that does not meet the market share threshold.

PART 2 — APPLICATION OF THE INSTRUMENT

2.1 Application of the Instrument — Section 2.1 of the Instrument provides an exemption from subsection 3.1(1) and Parts 4 and 5 if a person or company complies with similar requirements established by a recognized exchange that monitors and enforces the requirements set under subsection 7.1(1) of the Instrument directly, a recognized quotation and trade reporting system that monitors and enforces requirements set under subsection 7.3(1) of the Instrument directly or a regulation services provider. The requirements are filed by the recognized exchange, recognized quotation and trade reporting system or regulation services provider and approved by a securities regulatory authority. If a person or company is not in compliance with the requirements of the recognized exchange, recognized quotation and trade reporting system or the regulation services provider, then the exemption does not apply and that person or company is subject to subsection 3.1(1) and Parts 4 and 5 of the Instrument. The exemption from subsection 3.1(1) does not apply in Alberta, British Columbia, Ontario, Québec and Saskatchewan and the relevant provisions of securities legislation apply.

PART 3 — MANIPULATION AND FRAUD

3.1 Manipulation and Fraud — (1) Subsection 3.1(1) of the Instrument prohibits the practices of manipulation and deceptive trading, as these may create misleading price and trade activity, which are detrimental to investors and the integrity of the market.

(2) Subsection 3.1(2) of the Instrument provides that despite subsection 3.1(1) of the Instrument, the provisions of the *Securities Act* (Alberta), the *Securities Act* (British Columbia), the *Securities Act* (Ontario), the *Securities Act* (Québec) and *The Securities Act, 1988* (Saskatchewan), respectively, relating to manipulation and fraud apply in Alberta, British Columbia, Ontario, Québec and Saskatchewan. The jurisdictions listed have provisions in their legislation that deal with manipulation and fraud.

Part 2: MARKET PARTICIPANTS

(3) For the purposes of subsection 3.1(1) of the Instrument, and without limiting the generality of those provisions, the Canadian securities regulatory authorities, depending on the circumstances, would normally consider the following to result in, contribute to or create a misleading appearance of trading activity in, or an artificial price for, a security:

(a) Executing transactions in a security if the transactions do not involve a change in beneficial or economic ownership. This includes activities such as wash-trading.

(b) Effecting transactions that have the effect of artificially raising, lowering or maintaining the price of the security. For example, making purchases of or offers to purchase securities at successively higher prices or making sales of or offers to sell a security at successively lower prices or entering an order or orders for the purchase or sale of a security to:

(i) establish a predetermined price or quotation,

(ii) effect a high or low closing price or closing quotation, or

(iii) maintain the trading price, ask price or bid price within a predetermined range.

(c) Entering orders that could reasonably be expected to create an artificial appearance of investor participation in the market. For example, entering an order for the purchase or sale of a security with the knowledge that an order of substantially the same size, at substantially the same time, at substantially the same price for the sale or purchase, respectively, of that security has been or will be entered by or for the same or different persons.

(d) Executing prearranged transactions that have the effect of creating a misleading appearance of active public trading or that have the effect of improperly excluding other marketplace participants from the transaction.

(e) Effecting transactions if the purpose of the transactions is to defer payment for the securities traded.

(f) Entering orders to purchase or sell securities without the ability and the intention to

(i) make the payment necessary to properly settle the transaction, in the case of a purchase; or

(ii) deliver the securities necessary to properly settle the transaction, in the case of a sale.

This includes activities known as free-riding, kiting or debit kiting, in which a person or company avoids having to make payment or deliver securities to settle a trade.

(g) Engaging in any transaction, practice or scheme that unduly interferes with the normal forces of demand for or supply of a security or that artificially restricts or reduces the public float of a security in a way that could reasonably be expected to result in an artificial price for the security.

(h) Engaging in manipulative trading activity designed to increase the value of a derivative position.

(i) Entering a series of orders for a security that are not intended to be executed.

(4) The Canadian securities regulatory authorities do not consider market stabilization activities carried out in connection with a distribution to be activities in breach of subsection 3.1(1) of the Instrument, if the market stabilization activities are carried out in compliance with the rules of the marketplace on which the securities trade or with provisions of securities legislation that permit market stabilization by a person or company in connection with a distribution.

(5) Section 3.1 of the Instrument applies to transactions both on and off a marketplace. In determining whether a transaction results in, contributes to or creates a misleading appearance of trading activity in, or an artificial price for a security, it may be relevant whether the transaction takes place on or off a marketplace. For example, a transfer of securities to a holding company for *bona fide* purposes that takes place off a marketplace would not normally violate section 3.1 even though it is a transfer with no change in beneficial ownership.

(6) The Canadian securities regulatory authorities are of the view that section 3.1 of the Instrument does not create a private right of action.

(7) In the view of the Canadian securities regulatory authorities, section 3.1 includes attempting to create a misleading appearance of trading activity in or an artificial price for, a security or attempting to perpetrate a fraud.

PART 4 — BEST EXECUTION

4.1 Best Execution — (1) The best execution obligation in Part 4 of the Instrument does not apply to an ATS that is registered as a dealer provided that it is carrying on business as a marketplace and is not handling any client orders other than accepting them to allow them to execute on the system. However, the best execution obligation does otherwise apply to an ATS acting as an agent for a client.

(2) Section 4.2 of the Instrument requires a dealer or adviser to make reasonable efforts to achieve best execution (the most advantageous execution terms reasonably available under the circumstances) when acting for a client. The obligation applies to all securities.

(3) What constitutes "best execution" will vary depending on the particular circumstances, and is subject to a "reasonable efforts" test that does not require achieving best execution for each and every order. To meet the "reasonable efforts" test, a dealer or adviser should be able to demonstrate that it has, and has abided by, its policies and procedures that (i) require it to follow the client's instructions and the objectives set, and (ii) outline the process it has designed toward the objective of achieving best execution. The policies and procedures should describe how the dealer or adviser evaluates whether best execution was obtained and should be regularly and rigorously reviewed. The policies outlining the obligations of the dealer or adviser will be dependent on the role it is playing in an execution. For example, in making reasonable efforts to achieve best execution, the dealer should consider the client's instructions and a number of factors, including the client's investment objectives and the dealer's knowledge of markets and trading patterns. An adviser should consider a number of factors, including assessing a particular client's requirements or portfolio objectives, selecting appropriate dealers and marketplaces and monitoring the results on a regular basis. In addition, if an adviser is directly accessing a marketplace, the factors to be considered by dealers may also be applicable.

(4) Where securities listed on a Canadian exchange or quoted on a Canadian quotation and trade reporting system are inter-listed either within Canada or on a foreign exchange or quotation and trade reporting system, in making reasonable efforts to achieve best execution, the dealer should assess whether it is appropriate to consider all marketplaces upon which the security is listed or quoted and where the security is traded, both within and outside of Canada.

(5) In order to meet best execution obligations where securities trade on multiple marketplaces in Canada, a dealer should consider information from all appropriate marketplaces, and not just marketplaces where the dealer is a participant. This does not mean that a dealer must have access to real-time data feeds from each marketplace. However, its policies and procedures for seeking best execution should include the process for considering activity

on appropriate marketplaces and an evaluation of whether steps should be taken to to access orders on a marketplace to which it does not have access. The steps to access orders may include making arrangements with another dealer who is a participant of a particular marketplace.

(6) As part of the evaluation of whether steps should be taken to access orders on a marketplace to which it does not have access, a dealer should consider how the decision to access or not access orders on that marketplace will impact its ability to achieve best execution for its clients, taking into consideration those clients' objectives and needs. This applies in relation to decisions as to whether to access marketplaces that do not provide pre-trade transparency of orders, as well as those that do display orders that are not protected orders. We expect the documented best execution policies and procedures would include the rationale for accessing or not accessing orders on particular marketplaces, and that the rationale will be reviewed for continued reasonableness at least annually, and more frequently if needed because of changes to the trading environment and market structure. This review might require an analysis of historical data relating to the order and trade activity on marketplaces to which the dealer does not have access. We expect that the factors to be considered in such an analysis would generally include the frequency at which a better price is available, size and depth of quotes, traded volumes, potential market impact, and market share (considering the types and classes of securities traded by clients, generally).

(7) For foreign exchange-traded securities, if they are traded on a marketplace in Canada, dealers should include in their best execution policies and procedures a regular assessment of whether it is appropriate to consider the marketplace as well as the foreign markets upon which the securities trade.

(8) Section 4.2 of the Instrument applies to registered advisers as well as registered dealers that carry out advisory functions but are exempt from registration as advisers.

(9) Section 4.3 of the Instrument requires that a dealer or adviser make reasonable efforts to use facilities providing information regarding orders and trades. These reasonable efforts refer to the use of the information displayed by the information processor or, if there is no information processor, an information vendor.

PART 5 — REGULATORY HALTS

5.1 Regulatory Halts — Section 5.1 of the Instrument applies when a regulatory halt has been imposed by a regulation services provider, a recognized exchange or a recognized quotation and trade reporting system. A regulatory halt, as referred to in section 5.1 of the Instrument, is one that is imposed to maintain a fair and orderly market, including halts related to a timely disclosure policy, or because there has been a violation of regulatory requirements. In the view of the Canadian securities regulatory authorities, an order may trade on a marketplace despite the fact that trading of the security has been suspended because the issuer of the security has ceased to meet minimum listing or quotation requirements, or has failed to pay to the recognized exchange, the recognized quotation and trade reporting system or the exchange or quotation and trade reporting system recognized for the purposes of the Instrument and NI 21-101 any fees in respect of the listing or quotation of securities of the issuer. Similarly, an order may trade on a marketplace despite the fact that trading of the security has been delayed or halted because of technical problems affecting only the trading system of the recognized exchange, recognized quotation and trading system or exchange or quotation and trade reporting system recognized for the purposes of the Instrument and NI 21-101.

PART 6 — ORDER PROTECTION

6.1 Marketplace Requirements for Order Protection — (1) Subsection 6.1(1) of the Instrument requires a marketplace to establish, maintain and ensure compliance with written policies and procedures that are reasonably designed to prevent trade-throughs by orders entered on that marketplace regardless of whether the marketplace on which that order is entered displays orders that are protected orders. A marketplace may implement this requirement in various ways. For example, the policies and procedures of a marketplace may reasonably prevent trade-throughs via the design of the marketplace's trade execution algorithms (by not allowing a trade-through to occur), or by voluntarily establishing direct linkages to other marketplaces. Marketplaces are not able to avoid their obligations by establishing policies and procedures that instead require marketplace participants to take steps to reasonably prevent trade-throughs.

(2) It is the responsibility of marketplaces to regularly review and monitor the effectiveness of their policies and procedures and take prompt steps to remedy any deficiencies in reasonably preventing trade-throughs and complying with subsection 6.1(2) of the Instrument. In general, it is expected that marketplaces maintain relevant information so that the effectiveness of its policies and procedures can be adequately evaluated by regulatory authorities. Relevant information would include information that describes:

  (a) steps taken by the marketplace to evaluate its policies and procedures;

  (b) any breaches or deficiencies found; and

  (c) the steps taken to resolve the breaches or deficiencies.

(3) As part of the policies and procedures required in subsection 6.1(1) of the Instrument, a marketplace is expected to include a discussion of their automated trading functionality and how they will handle potential delayed responses as a result of an equipment or systems failure or malfunction experienced by any other marketplace displaying protected orders. In addition, marketplaces should include a discussion of how they treat a directed-action order when received and how it will be used.

(4) Order protection applies whenever two or more marketplaces that display orders subject to the pre-trade transparency requirements in Part 7 of NI 21-101 are open for trading, and the displayed orders of at least one of those marketplaces are protected order. Some marketplaces provide a trading session at a price established by that marketplace during its regular trading hours for marketplace participants who are required to benchmark to a certain closing price. In these circumstances, under subparagraph 6.2(e)(iii) of the Instrument, a marketplace that provides such sessions would not be required to take steps to reasonably prevent trade-throughs of protected orders on another marketplace.

6.2 Marketplace Participant Requirements for Order Protection — (1) For a marketplace participant that wants to use a directed-action order, section 6.4 of the Instrument requires a marketplace participant to establish, maintain and ensure compliance with written policies and procedures that are reasonably designed to prevent trade-throughs of protected orders, regardless of whether the marketplace on which it is entering the directed-action order displays orders that are protected orders. In general, it is expected that a marketplace participant that uses a directed-action order would maintain relevant information so that the effectiveness of its policies and procedures can be adequately evaluated by regulatory authorities. Relevant information would include information that describes:

  (a) steps taken by the marketplace participant to evaluate its policies and procedures;

  (b) any breaches or deficiencies found; and

  (c) the steps taken to resolve the breaches or deficiencies.

The policies and procedures should also outline when it is appropriate to use a directed-action order and how it will be used as set out in paragraph 6.4(1)(a) of the Instrument.

(2) Order protection applies whenever two or more marketplaces that display orders subject to the pre-trade transparency requirements in Part 7 of NI 21-101 are open for trading, and the displayed orders of at least one of those marketplaces are protected orders. Some marketplaces provide a trading session at a price established by that marketplace during its regular trading hours for marketplace participants who are required to benchmark to a certain closing price. In these circumstances, under paragraph 6.4(a)(iv)(C) of the Instrument, a marketplace participant would not be required to take steps to reasonably prevent trade-throughs of protected orders on other marketplaces that result from an execution of the closing-price order.

6.3 List of Trade-throughs — Section 6.2 and paragraphs 6.4(a)(i) to (a)(v) of the Instrument set forth a list of "permitted" trade-throughs that are primarily designed to achieve workable order protection and to facilitate certain trading strategies and order types that are useful to investors.

    (a)   (i) Paragraphs 6.2(a) and 6.4(1)(a)(i) of the Instrument would apply where a marketplace or marketplace participant, as applicable, has reasonably concluded that the marketplace displaying the protected order that has been traded through is experiencing a failure, malfunction or material delay of its systems, equipment or ability to disseminate marketplace data. A material delay occurs when a marketplace repeatedly fails to respond immediately after receipt of an order. This is intended to provide marketplaces and marketplace participants with flexibility when dealing with a marketplace that is experiencing systems problems (either of a temporary nature or a longer term systems issue).

          (ii) Under subsection 6.3(1) of the Instrument, a marketplace that is experiencing systems issues is responsible for informing all other marketplaces, its marketplace participants, any information processor, or if there is no information processor, an information vendor disseminating its information under Part 7 of NI 21-101 and regulation services providers when a failure, malfunction or material delay of its systems, equipment or ability to disseminate marketplace data occurs. This applies both to marketplaces that display orders that are protected orders and marketplaces that display orders that are not protected orders. However, if a marketplace that displays orders that are protected orders fails repeatedly to provide an immediate response to orders received and no notification has been issued by that marketplace that it is experiencing systems issues, the routing marketplace or a marketplace participant may, pursuant to subsections 6.3(2) and 6.3(3) of the Instrument respectively, reasonably conclude that the marketplace is having systems issues and may therefore rely on paragraph 6.2(a) or 6.4(1)(a)(i) of the Instrument respectively. This reliance must be done in accordance with policies and procedures that outline processes for dealing with potential delays in responses by a marketplace and documenting the basis of its conclusion. If, in response to the notification by the routing marketplace or a marketplace participant, the marketplace confirms that it is not actually experiencing systems issues, the routing marketplace or marketplace participant may no longer rely on paragraph 6.2(a) or paragraph 6.4(1)(a)(i) of the Instrument respectively.

(b) Paragraph 6.2(b) of the Instrument provides an exception from the obligation on marketplaces to use their policies and procedures to reasonably prevent trade-throughs when a directed-action order is received. Specifically, a marketplace that receives a directed-action order may immediately execute or book the order (or its remaining volume) and not implement the marketplace's policies and procedures to reasonably prevent trade-throughs. However, the marketplace will need to describe its treatment of a directed-action order in its policies and procedures. Paragraphs 6.2(c) and 6.4(1)(a)(iii) of the Instrument provide an exception where a marketplace or marketplace participant simultaneously routes directed-action orders to execute against the total displayed volume of any protected order traded through. This accounts for the possibility that orders that are routed simultaneously as directed-action orders are not executed simultaneously causing one or more trade-throughs to occur because an inferior-priced order is executed first.

(c) Paragraphs 6.2(d) and 6.4(1)(a)(ii) of the Instrument provide some relief due to moving or changing markets. Specifically, the exception allows for a trade-through to occur when immediately before executing the order that caused the trade-through, the marketplace on which the execution occurred had the best price but at the moment of execution, the market changes and another marketplace has the best price protected order. The "changing markets" exception allows for the execution of an order on a marketplace, within the best protected bid or best protected offer on that marketplace but outside the best bid or offer displayed across marketplaces in certain circumstances. This could occur for example:

          (i) where orders are entered on a marketplace but by the time they are executed, the best bid or offer displayed across marketplaces changed; and

          (ii) where a trade is agreed to off-marketplace and entered on a marketplace within the best bid and best offer across marketplaces, but by the time the order is executed on the marketplace (i.e. printed) the best bid or offer as displayed across marketplaces may have changed, thus causing a trade-through.

(d) The basis for the inclusion of calculated-price orders, non-standard orders and closing-price orders in paragraphs 6.2(e) and 6.4(1)(a)(iv) of the Instrument is that these orders have certain unique characteristics that distinguish them from other orders. The characteristics of the orders relate to price (calculated-price orders and closing-price orders) and non-standard settlement terms (non-standard orders) that are not set by an exchange or a quotation and trade reporting system.

(e) Paragraphs 6.2(f) and 6.4(1)(a)(v) of the Instrument include a transaction that occurred when there is a crossed market between protected orders in the exchange-traded security. Without this allowance, no marketplace could execute transactions where the best protected bid and best protected offer are crossed because it would constitute a trade-through. With order protection only applying to displayed protected orders or parts of orders, hidden or reserve orders may remain in the book after all displayed protected orders are executed. Consequently, crossed markets between protected orders may occur. Intentionally crossing the best protected bid or best protected offer to take advantage of paragraphs 6.2(f) and 6.4(1)(a)(v) of the Instrument would be a violation of section 6.5 of the Instrument.

6.4 Locked and Crossed Markets — (1) Section 6.5 of the Instrument provides that a marketplace participant or a marketplace that routes or reprices orders must not intentionally lock or cross a protected order by entering a displayed order on any marketplace to either buy a security at a price that is the same as or higher than the best protected offer or sell a security at a price that is the same as or lower than the best protected bid. The intention of section 6.5 of the Instrument is to prevent intentional locks and crosses of protected orders. This applies regardless of whether the locking or crossing order is entered on a marketplace that displays orders that are protected orders. This provision is not intended to prohibit the use of marketable limit orders. Paragraphs 6.2(f) and 6.4(1)(a)(v) of the Instrument allow for the resolution of crossed markets that occur unintentionally.

The Canadian securities regulatory authorities consider an order that is routed or repriced to be "entered" on a marketplace. The Canadian securities regulatory authorities do not consider the triggering of a previously-entered on-stop order to be an "entry" or "repricing" of that order.

(2) Section 6.5 of the Instrument does not restrict the ability for a marketplace participant or a marketplace that routes or reprices orders from routing or entering a displayed order that will lock or cross with another displayed order that is not a protected order.

If the entry of a protected order locks or crosses with a displayed order on another marketplace that is not a protected order, section 6.5 of the Instrument would restrict the ability for additional orders to be entered that would lock or cross with the protected order. This should help to minimize the duration of a locked or crossed markets in these circumstances.

A displayed order that is not a protected order that becomes locked or crossed with a subsequently entered protected order does not need to be repriced or cancelled. If, however, the marketplace subsequently reprices the non-protected displayed order, as might occur with a pegged order, it will be considered to be "entered upon repricing" and subject to the restrictions against locking or crossing with a protected order.

If a marketplace participant deliberately attempts to circumvent section 6.5 of the Instrument by first entering a displayed order on a marketplace that is not a protected order, followed by the entry of a protected order on another marketplace that locks or crosses with the first displayed non-protected order it entered, the Canadian securities regulatory authorities would consider this to be a violation of section 6.5.

(3) And intentional locking or crossing of a protected order could occur where a marketplace system is programmed to reprice orders without checking to see if the new price would lock a protected order or where the marketplace routes orders to another marketplace that results in a lock with a protected order. It could also occur where the intention of the marketplace participant was to lock or cross a protected order to avoid fees charged by a marketplace or to take advantage of rebates.

There are situations where a locked or cross of a protected order may occur unintentionally. For example:

(a) the locking or crossing order was displayed at a time when the marketplace displaying the locked or crossed protected order was experiencing a failure, malfunction or material delay of its systems, equipment or ability to disseminate marketplace data;

(b) the locking or crossing order was displayed at a time when a protected bid was higher than a protected offer;

(c) the locking or crossing order was posted after all displayed protected liquidity was executed and a reserve order generated a new visible protected bid above the displayed protected offer or new visible protected offer below the displayed protected bid;

(d) the locking or crossing order was entered on a particular marketplace in order to comply with securities legislation requirements such as Rule 904 of Regulation S of the *Securities Act of 1933* that requires securities subject to resale restrictions in the United States to be sold in Canada on a "designated offshore securities market";

(e) the locking or crossing order was displayed due to "race conditions" when competing orders, at least one of which is a protected order, are entered on marketplaces at essentially the same time with neither party having knowledge of the other order at the time of entry;

(f) the locking or crossing order was a result of the differences in processing times and latencies between the systems of the marketplace participant, marketplaces, information processor and information vendors;

(g) the locking or crossing order was a result of marketplaces having different mechanisms to "restart" trading following a halt in trading for either regulatory or business purposes; and

(h) the locking or crossing order was a result of the execution of an order during the opening or closing allocation process of one market, while trading is simultaneously occurring on a continuous basis on another market displaying protected orders.

If a marketplace participant using a directed-action order chooses to book the order or the remainder of the order not immediately executed, then it is responsible for ensuring that the booked portion of the directed-action order does not lock or cross a protected order. The Canadian securities regulatory authorities would consider a directed-action order or remainder of a directed-action order that is booked and that locks or crosses a protected order to be an intentional locking or crossing of a protected order and a violation of section 6.5 of the Instrument.

6.5 Anti-Avoidance Provision — Section 6.7 of the Instrument prohibits a person or company from sending an order to an exchange, quotation and trade reporting system or alternative trading system that does not carry on business in Canada in order to avoid executing against better-priced protected orders on a marketplace in Canada. The intention of this section is to prevent the routing of orders to foreign marketplaces only for the purpose of avoiding the order protection regime in Canada.

PART 7 — MONITORING AND ENFORCEMENT

7.1 Monitoring and Enforcement of Requirements Set By a Recognized Exchange or Recognized Quotation and Trade Reporting System — Under section 7.1 of the Instrument, a recognized exchange will set its own requirements governing the conduct of its members. Under section 7.3 of the Instrument, a recognized quotation and trade reporting system will set its own requirements governing the conduct of its users. The recognized exchange or recognized quotation and trade reporting system can monitor and enforce these requirements either directly or indirectly through a regulation services provider. A regulation services provider is a person or company that provides regulation services and is either a recognized exchange, recognized quotation and trade reporting system or a recognized self-regulatory entity.

If a recognized exchange or recognized quotation and trade reporting system has entered into a written agreement with a regulation services provider, it is expected that the requirements adopted by the recognized exchange or recognized quotation and trade reporting system under Part 7 of the Instrument will consist of all of the rules of the regulation services provider that relate to trading. For example, if a recognized exchange or recognized quotation and trade reporting system has entered into a written agreement with IIROC, the rules adopted by the recognized exchange or recognized quotation and trade reporting system are all of IIROC's Universal Market Integrity Rules. Clock synchronization, trade markers and trading halt requirements would be examples of these adopted rules that relate to the regulation services provider's monitoring of trading on the recognized exchange or recognized quotation and trade reporting system and across marketplaces.

We are of the view that all of the rules of the regulation services provider related to trading must be adopted by a recognized exchange or recognized quotation and trade reporting system that has entered into a written agreement with the regulation services provider given the importance of these rules in the context of effectively monitoring trading on and across marketplaces. We note that the regulation services provider is required to monitor the compliance of, and enforce, the adopted rules as against the members of the recognized exchange or users of the recognized quotation and trade reporting system. The regulation services provider is also required to monitor the compliance of the recognized exchange or recognized quotation and trade reporting system with the adopted rules but it is the applicable securities regulatory authority that will enforce these rules against the recognized exchange or recognized quotation and trade reporting system.

Sections 7.2 and 7.4 of the Instrument require the recognized exchange or recognized quotation and trade reporting system that chooses to have the monitoring and enforcement performed by the regulation services provider to enter into an agreement with the regulation services provider in which the regulation services provider agrees to enforce the requirements of the recognized exchange or recognized quotation and trade reporting system adopted under subsection 7.1(1) and 7.3(1).

Specifically, sections 7.2 and 7.4 require the written agreement between a recognized exchange or recognized quotation and trade reporting system and its regulation services provider to provide that the regulation services provider will monitor and enforce the requirements set under subsection 7.1(1) or 7.3(1) and monitor the requirements adopted under subsection 7.1(3) or 7.3(3).

Paragraph 7.2.1(a)(i) mandates that a recognized exchange must transmit information reasonably required by the regulation services provider to effectively monitor the conduct of and trading by marketplace participants on and across marketplaces. The reference to monitoring trading "across marketplaces" refers to the instance where particular securities are traded on multiple marketplaces. Where particular securities are only traded on one marketplace, the reference to "across marketplaces" may not apply in all circumstances.

Paragraph 7.2.1(a)(ii) requires that a recognized exchange must transmit information reasonably required by the regulation services provider to effectively monitor the compliance of the recognized exchange with the requirements adopted under subsection 7.1(3). As well, subsection 7.2.1(b) requires a recognized exchange to comply with all orders or directions of its regulation services provider that are in connection with the conduct and trading by the recognized exchange's members on the recognized exchange and with the regulation services provider's oversight of the compliance of the recognized exchange with the requirements adopted under 7.1(3).

7.2 Monitoring and Enforcement Requirements for an ATS — Section 8.2 of the Instrument requires the regulation services provider to set requirements that govern an ATS and its subscribers. Before executing a trade for a subscriber, the ATS must enter into an agreement with a regulation services provider and an agreement with each subscriber. These agreements form the basis upon which a regulation services provider will monitor the trading activities of the ATS and its subscribers and enforce its requirements. The requirements set by a regulation services provider must include requirements that the ATS and its subscribers will conduct trading activities in compliance with the Instrument. The ATS and its subscribers are considered to be in compliance with the Instrument and are exempt from the application of most of its provisions if the ATS and the subscriber are in compliance with the requirements set by a regulation services provider.

7.3 Monitoring and Enforcement Requirements for an Inter-Dealer Bond Broker — Section 9.1 of the Instrument requires that a regulation services provider set requirements governing the conduct of an inter-dealer bond broker. Under section 9.2 of the Instrument, the inter-dealer bond broker must enter into an agreement with the regulation services provider providing that the regulation services provider monitor the activities of the inter-dealer bond broker and enforce the requirements set by the regulation services provider. However, section 9.3 of the Instrument provides inter-dealer bond brokers with an exemption from sections 9.1 and 9.2 of the Instrument if the inter-dealer bond broker complies with the requirements of IIROC Rule 2800 Code of Conduct for Corporation Dealer Member Firms Trading in Wholesale Domestic Debt Markets, as amended, as if that policy was drafted to apply to the inter-dealer bond broker.

7.4 Monitoring and Enforcement Requirements for a Dealer Executing Trades of Unlisted Debt Securities Outside of a Marketplace — Section 10.1 of the Instrument requires that a regulation services provider set requirements governing the conduct of a dealer executing trades of unlisted debt securities outside of a marketplace. Under section 10.2 of the Instrument, the dealer must also enter into an agreement with the regulation services provider providing that the regulation services provider monitor the activities of the dealer and enforce the requirements set by the regulation services provider.

7.5 Agreement between a Marketplace and a Regulation Services Provider — The purpose of subsections 7.2(c) and 7.4(c) of the Instrument is to facilitate the monitoring of trading by marketplace participants on and across multiple marketplaces by a regulation services provider. These sections of the Instrument also facilitate monitoring of the conduct of a recognized exchange and recognized quotation and trade reporting system for particular purposes. This may result in regulation services providers monitoring marketplaces that have retained them and reporting to a recognized exchange, recognized quotation and trade reporting system or securities regulatory authority if a marketplace is not meeting regulatory requirements or the terms of its own rules or policies and procedures. While the scope of this monitoring may change as the market evolves, we expect it to include, at a minimum, monitoring clock synchronization, the inclusion of specific designations, symbols and identifiers, order protection requirements and audit trail requirements.

7.6 Coordination of Monitoring and Enforcement — (1) Section 7.5 of the Instrument requires regulation services providers, recognized exchanges and recognized quotation and trade reporting systems to enter into a written agreement whereby they coordinate the enforcement of the requirements set under Parts 7 and 8. This coordination is required in order to achieve cross-marketplace monitoring.

(2) If a recognized exchange or recognized quotation and trade reporting system has not retained a regulation services provider, it is still required to coordinate with any regulation services provider and other exchanges or quotation and trade reporting systems that trade the same securities in order to ensure effective cross-marketplace monitoring.

(3) Currently, only IIROC is the regulation services provider for both exchange-traded securities, other than options and in Québec, other than standardized derivatives, and unlisted debt securities. If more than one regulation services provider regulates marketplaces trading a particular type of security, these regulation services providers must coordinate monitoring and enforcement of the requirements set.

PART 8 — AUDIT TRAIL REQUIREMENTS

8.1 Audit Trail Requirements — Section 11.2 of the Instrument imposes obligations on dealers and inter-dealer bond brokers to record in electronic form and to report certain items of information with respect to orders and trades. Information to be recorded includes any markers required by a regulation services provider (such as a significant shareholder marker). The purpose of the obligations set out in Part 11 is to enable the entity performing the monitoring and surveillance functions to construct an audit trail of order, quotation and transaction data which will enhance its surveillance and examination capabilities.

8.2 Transmission of Information to a Regulation Services Provider — Section 11.3 of the Instrument requires that a dealer and an inter-dealer bond broker provide to the regulation services provider information required by the regulation services provider, within ten business days, in electronic form. This requirement is triggered only when the regulation services provider sets requirements to transmit information.

8.3 Electronic Form — Subsection 11.3 of the Instrument requires any information required to be transmitted to the regulation services provider and securities regulatory authority in electronic form. Dealers and inter-dealer bond brokers are required to provide information in a form that is accessible to the securities regulatory authorities and the regulation services provider (for example, in SELECTR format).

Adoption by OSC: 24 O.S.C.B. 6641 (November 2, 2001) and 24 O.S.C.B. (Supp.) 85 (August 17, 2001); Request for Comments: 23 O.S.C.B. (Supp.) 299 (July 28, 2000).

Adoption of Amendments by OSC: (2004) 27 O.S.C.B. 464 and (2003) 26 O.S.C.B. 7147; Request for Comments: (2003) 26 O.S.C.B. 4377.

Adoption of Amendments by OSC: (2006) 29 O.S.C.B. 10020 and 9731; Request for Comments: (2006) 29 O.S.C.B. 5735.

Adoption of Amendments by OSC: (2008) 31 O.S.C.B. 8572 and 6303; Request for Comments: (2007) 30 O.S.C.B. (Supp. 3) 1 (April 20, 2007).

Adoption of Amendments by OSC: (2010) 33 O.S.C.B. 8006 and (2009) 32 O.S.C.B. 9403; Request for Comments: (2008) 31 O.S.C.B. 10136.

Adoption of Amendments by OSC: (2012) 35 O.S.C.B. 5427 and (Supp. 1) 1; Request for Comments: (2011) 34 O.S.C.B. (Supp. 1) 1.

Adoption of Amendments by OSC: (2015) 38 O.S.C.B. (Supp. 2) 30; Request for Comments: (2014) 37 O.S.C.B. 4873.

Policies and Orders: CSAN 23-301.

National Instrument 23-102 — Use of Client Brokerage Commissions

Date: June 30, 2010 as amended January 11, 2015

32 O.S.C.B. 10861 and 38 O.S.C.B. 342.

Table of Contents

PART 1 — DEFINITIONS

1.1 **Definitions** — In this Instrument,

"affiliated entity" has the meaning ascribed to it in section 1.3 of National Instrument 21-101 *Marketplace Operation*;

"client brokerage commissions" means brokerage commissions paid for out of, or charged to, a client account or investment fund managed by the adviser;

"managed account" has the meaning ascribed to it in section 1.1 of National Instrument 31-103 *Registration Requirements, Exemptions and Ongoing Registrant Obligations*;

"order execution goods and services" means

    (a) order execution; and

    (b) goods or services to the extent that they are directly related to order execution;

"research goods and services" means

    (a) advice relating to the value of a security or the advisability of effecting a transaction in a security,

    (b) an analysis, or report, concerning a security, portfolio strategy, issuer, industry, or an economic or political factor or trend, and

    (c) a database, or software, to the extent that it supports goods or services referred to in paragraphs (a) and (b).

1.2 **Interpretation — Security** — For the purposes of this Instrument,

    (a) in Alberta, British Columbia, New Brunswick and Saskatchewan, "security" includes an exchange contract; and

    (b) in Québec, "security" includes a standardized derivative.

1.3 **Interpretation — Adviser** — For the purposes of this Instrument, "adviser" means

    (a) a registered adviser; or

    (b) a registered dealer that carries out advisory functions but is exempt from registration as an adviser.

PART 2 — APPLICATION

2.1 **Application** — This Instrument applies to an adviser or a registered dealer in relation to a trade in a security if brokerage commissions are charged by a dealer for an account, or portfolio, over which the adviser has discretion to make investment decisions without requiring the express consent of the client, including, for greater certainty,

    (a) an investment fund; and

(b) a managed account.

PART 3 — COMMISSIONS ON BROKERAGE TRANSACTIONS

3.1 Advisers — (1) An adviser must not direct any brokerage transactions involving client brokerage commissions to a dealer in return for the provision of goods or services by the dealer or a third party, other than any of the following:

(a) order execution goods and services;

(b) research goods and services.

(2) An adviser that directs any brokerage transactions involving client brokerage commissions to a dealer, in return for the provision of any order execution goods and services or research goods and services by the dealer or a third party, must ensure that:

(a) the goods or services are to be used to assist with investment or trading decisions, or with effecting securities transactions, on behalf of the client or clients; and

(b) a good faith determination is made that the client or clients receive reasonable benefit considering both the use of the goods or services and the amount of client brokerage commissions paid.

3.2 Registered Dealers — A registered dealer must not accept, or forward to a third party, client brokerage commissions, or any portion of those commissions, in return for the provision to an adviser of goods or services by the dealer or a third party, other than any of the following:

(a) order execution goods and services;

(b) research goods and services.

PART 4 — DISCLOSURE OBLIGATIONS

4.1 Disclosure — (1) An adviser must provide the following disclosure to a client if any brokerage transactions involving the client brokerage commissions of that client have been or might be directed to a dealer in return for the provision of any good or service by the dealer or a third party, other than order execution:

(a) before the adviser opens a client account or enters into a management contract or a similar agreement to advise an investment fund,

(i) a description of the process for, and factors considered in, selecting a dealer to effect securities transactions, including whether receiving goods or services in addition to order execution is a factor, and whether and how the process may differ for a dealer that is an affiliated entity;

(ii) a description of the nature of the arrangements under which order execution goods and services or research goods and services might be provided;

(iii) a list of each type of good or service, other than order execution, that might be provided; and

(iv) a description of the method by which the determination in paragraph 3.1(2)(b) is made; and

(b) at least annually,

(i) the information required to be disclosed under paragraph (a) other than subparagraph (a)(iii);

(ii) a list of each type of good or service, other than order execution, that has been provided;

(iii) the name of any affiliated entity that provided any good or service referred to in subparagraph (ii), separately identifying each affiliated entity and each type of good or service provided by each affiliated entity; and

(iv) a statement that the name of any other dealer or third party that provided a good or service referred to in subparagraph (ii), if that name was not disclosed under subparagraph (iii), will be provided to the client upon request.

(2) An adviser must maintain a record of the name of any dealer or third party that provided a good or service, other than order execution under section 3.1, and must provide that information to the client upon request.

PART 5 — EXEMPTION

5.1 Exemption — (1) The regulator or the securities regulatory authority may grant an exemption from this Instrument, in whole or in part, subject to such conditions or restrictions as may be imposed in the exemption.

(2) Despite subsection (1), in Ontario only the regulator may grant an exemption.

(3) Except in Ontario, an exemption referred to in subsection (1) is granted under the statute referred to in Appendix B of National Instrument 14-101 *Definitions* opposite the name of the local jurisdiction.

PART 6 — EFFECTIVE DATE AND TRANSITION

6.1 Effective Date — This Instrument comes into force on June 30, 2010.

6.2 Transition — On or before December 31, 2010, an adviser must provide to a client, if the client was a client on June 30, 2010, the disclosure required under paragraph 4.1(1)(a) or (b).

Final Rule: (2009) 32 O.S.C.B. 10861; Approval by OSC: (2009) 32 O.S.C.B. 8079; Request for Comments: (2008) 31 O.S.C.B. 489 and (2005) 28 O.S.C.B. 1362.

Amendment to Rule: (2015) 38 O.S.C.B. 342.

Companion Policy 23-102CP — Use of Client Brokerage Commissions

Table of Contents

PART 1 — INTRODUCTION

1.1 Introduction — The purpose of this Companion Policy is to provide guidance regarding the various requirements of National Instrument 23-102 Use of Client Brokerage Commissions (the "Instrument"), including:

    (a) a discussion of the general regulatory purposes for the Instrument;

    (b) the interpretation of various terms and provisions in the Instrument; and

    (c) guidance on compliance with the Instrument.

1.2 General — Registered dealers and advisers have a fundamental obligation to deal fairly, honestly, and in good faith with their clients. Registered dealers and advisers are also required to make reasonable efforts to achieve best execution when acting for clients, and have certain obligations to identify and respond to conflicts of interest. Directing brokerage transactions involving client brokerage commissions to a dealer in return for the provision of goods or services other than order execution should therefore also be evaluated in light of the duty to deal fairly, honestly, and in good faith with clients, the obligation to make reasonable efforts to achieve best execution, and any requirements pertaining to conflicts of interest. The Instrument is therefore intended to provide more specific parameters for obtaining such goods or services when client brokerage commissions are involved. The Instrument also sets out disclosure requirements for advisers. This Companion Policy provides guidance on (a) the characteristics of the types of goods and services that might be eligible, including some examples; (b) the obligations of advisers and registered dealers; and (c) the disclosure obligations.

PART 2 — APPLICATION OF THE INSTRUMENT

2.1 Application — (1) The Instrument applies to advisers and registered dealers. Section 1.3 of the Instrument indicates that for the purposes of the Instrument, adviser means a registered adviser or a registered dealer that carries out advisory functions but is exempt from registration as an adviser. The Instrument governs certain trades in securities where payment for the transaction is made with client brokerage commissions, as set out in section 2.1 of the Instrument. The reference to "client brokerage commissions" includes any brokerage commission or similar transaction-based fee charged for a trade where the amount paid for the security is clearly separate and identifiable (e.g., the security is exchange-traded, or there is some other independent pricing mechanism that enables the adviser to accurately and objectively determine the amount of commissions or fees charged).

(2) The limitation of the Instrument to trades for which a brokerage commission is charged is based on the practical difficulties in applying these requirements to transactions such as principal transactions where an embedded mark-up is charged. An adviser that obtains goods or services other than order execution in conjunction with such transactions is subject to its duty to deal fairly, honestly, and in good faith with clients, and its obligation to make reasonable efforts to achieve best execution when acting for clients. As a result, an adviser should consider the goods or services obtained in relation to its duty to deal fairly, honestly, and in good faith with its clients, and in its evaluation of best execution. In addition, an adviser should also consider any relevant conflict of interest provisions, given the incentives created for advisers to place their interests ahead of their clients when obtaining goods or services other than order execution in conjunction with such transactions.

PART 3 — ORDER EXECUTION GOODS AND SERVICES AND RESEARCH GOODS AND SERVICES

3.1 Definitions of Order Execution Goods and Services and Research Goods and Services — (1) Section 1.1 of the Instrument includes the definitions of order execution goods and services and research goods and services and provides the broad characteristics of both.

(2) The definitions do not specify what form (e.g., electronic or paper) the goods or services should take, as it is their substance that is relevant in assessing whether the definitions are met.

(3) An adviser's responsibilities include determining whether any particular good or service, or portion of a good or service, may be obtained through brokerage transactions involving client brokerage commissions. In making this determination, the adviser is required under Part 3 of the Instrument to

ensure both that the good or service meets the definition of order execution goods and services or research goods and services and that it is to be used to assist with investment or trading decisions or with effecting securities transactions on behalf of the client or clients.

3.2 Order Execution Goods and Services — (1) Section 1.1 of the Instrument defines "order execution goods and services" as including the actual execution of the order itself, as well as goods or services to the extent that they are directly related to order execution. For the purposes of the Instrument, the term "order execution", as opposed to "order execution goods and services", refers to the entry, handling or facilitation of an order whether by a dealer or by an adviser (for example, through direct market access or as a subscriber to an alternative trading system), but not other goods or services provided to aid in the execution of trades.

(2) To be considered directly related to order execution, goods or services should generally be integral to the arranging and conclusion of the transactions that generated the commissions. A temporal standard should be applied to ensure that only goods or services used by an adviser that are directly related to the execution process are considered order execution goods and services. As a result, we generally consider that goods or services directly related to the execution process would be provided or used between the point at which an adviser makes an investment or trading decision and the point at which the resulting securities transaction is concluded. The conclusion of the resulting securities transaction occurs at the point that settlement is clearly and irrevocably completed.

(3) For example, order execution goods and services may include order management systems (to the extent they help arrange or effect a securities transaction), algorithmic trading software and market data (to the extent they assist in the execution of orders), and custody, clearing and settlement services that are directly related to an executed order that generated commissions.

3.3 Research Goods and Services — (1) The Instrument defines research goods and services as including advice, analyses or reports regarding various subject matter relating to investments, as well as databases and software to the extent that they support these goods or services. In order to be eligible, research goods and services generally should reflect the expression of reasoning or knowledge and be related to the subject matter referred to in the definition (i.e., securities, portfolio strategy, etc.). We would also consider databases and software that are used by advisers in support of or as an alternative to the provision by dealers of advice, analyses and reports to be research goods and services to the extent they relate to the subject matter referred to in the definition. Additionally, a general characteristic of research goods and services is that, in order to link these to order execution, they should be provided or used before an adviser makes an investment or trading decision.

(2) For example, traditional research reports, publications marketed to a narrow audience and directed to readers with specialized interests, seminars and conferences (i.e., fees, but not incidental expenses such as travel, accommodations and entertainment costs), and trading advice, such as advice from a dealer as to how, when or where to trade an order (to the extent it is provided before an order is transmitted), would generally be considered research goods and services. Databases and software that could be eligible as research goods and services could include quantitative analytical software, market data from feeds or databases, post-trade analytics from prior transactions (to the extent they are used to aid in a subsequent investment or trading decision), and possibly order management systems (to the extent they provide research or assist with the research process).

3.4 Mixed-Use Items — (1) Mixed-use items are those goods or services that contain some elements that may meet the definitions of order execution goods and services or research goods and services, and other elements that either do not meet the definitions or that would not meet the requirements of Part 3 of the Instrument. Where mixed-use items are obtained by an adviser through brokerage transactions involving client brokerage commissions, the adviser should make a reasonable allocation of those commissions paid according to the use of the goods or services. For example, client brokerage commissions might be involved when paying for the portion of order management systems used in the order execution process, but an adviser should use its own funds to pay for any portion of the systems used for compliance, accounting or recordkeeping purposes.

(2) For purposes of making a reasonable allocation, an adviser should make a good faith estimate supported by a fact-based analysis of how the good or service is used, which may include inferring relative costs from relative benefits. Factors to consider might include the relative utility derived from, or the time for which the good or service is used, eligible and ineligible uses.

(3) Advisers are expected to keep adequate books and records concerning the allocations made.

3.5 Non-Permitted Goods and Services — We consider certain goods and services to be clearly outside the scope of the permitted goods and services under the Instrument because they are not sufficiently linked to the securities transactions that generated the commissions. Goods and services that relate to overhead associated with the operation of an adviser's business rather than to the provision of services to its clients would not meet the requirements of Part 3 of the Instrument. Examples of non-permitted goods and services include office furniture and equipment (including computer hardware), trading surveillance or compliance systems, costs associated with correcting error trades, portfolio valuation and performance measurement services, computer software that assists with administrative functions, legal and accounting services relating to the management of an adviser's own business or operations, memberships, marketing services, and services provided by the adviser's personnel (e.g. payment of salaries, including those of research staff).

PART 4 — OBLIGATIONS OF ADVISERS AND REGISTERED DEALERS

4.1 Obligations of Advisers — (1) Subsection 3.1(1) of the Instrument restricts an adviser from directing any brokerage transactions involving client brokerage commissions to a dealer in return for the provision of goods or services by the dealer or a third party, other than order execution goods and services or research goods and services, as defined in the Instrument. This applies when brokerage transactions involving client brokerage commissions are used to obtain order execution goods and services or research goods and services under both formal and informal arrangements, including informal arrangements for the receipt of these goods and services from a dealer offering proprietary, bundled services. This would also apply when brokerage transactions involving client brokerage commissions are directed to any dealer, including where the adviser has direct market access or is a subscriber to an alternative trading system.

(2) Subsection 3.1(2) of the Instrument requires an adviser that directs any brokerage transaction involving client brokerage commissions to a dealer, in return for the provision of order execution goods and services or research goods and services by the dealer or a third party, to ensure that certain criteria are met. The criteria included under paragraph 3.1(2)(a) requires the adviser to ensure that the goods or services acquired are to be used to assist with investment or trading decisions, or with effecting securities transactions, on behalf of the adviser's client or clients. The goods or services should therefore be used in a manner that provides appropriate assistance to the adviser in making these decisions, or in effecting such transactions. A good or service that meets the definition of order execution goods and services or research goods and services, but is not to be used to assist the adviser with investment or trading decisions, or with effecting securities transactions, should not be obtained through brokerage transactions involving client brokerage commissions. The adviser should be able to demonstrate how the goods or services obtained under the Instrument are used to provide appropriate assistance.

(3) Paragraph 3.1(2)(b) of the Instrument requires the adviser to ensure that a good faith determination is made that the client or clients receive reasonable benefit considering both the use of the goods or services and the amount of client brokerage commissions paid. Benefit to the client is generally derived from the use of the goods and services (i.e., the assistance provided in relation to investment or trading decisions made, or securities transactions effected, on behalf of the client or clients), and is generally relative to the amount of client brokerage commissions paid. The determination required under paragraph 3.1(2)(b) can be made either with respect to a particular transaction or the adviser's overall responsibilities for client accounts.

(4) Also for the purposes of subsection 3.1(2) of the Instrument, a specific order execution good or service or research good or service may be used to benefit more than one client, and may not always be used to directly benefit each particular client whose brokerage commissions paid for the brokerage transactions through which the particular good or service was obtained. However, the adviser should have adequate policies and procedures in place, and apply those policies and procedures, so that, over time, all clients whose brokerage commissions may have been involved with such transactions receive fair and reasonable benefit.

(5) An adviser that, by virtue of paying client brokerage commissions on brokerage transactions, is provided with access to or receives goods or services on an unsolicited basis should consider whether or how usage of those goods or services has affected its obligations under the Instrument as part of its process for assessing compliance with the Instrument. For example, if an adviser considers unsolicited goods or services as a factor when selecting dealers or allocating brokerage transactions to dealers, the adviser should include these goods or services when assessing compliance with the obligations of the Instrument, and should include these in its disclosure.

4.2 Obligations of Registered Dealers — Section 3.2 of the Instrument indicates that a registered dealer must not accept, or forward to a third party, client brokerage commissions, or any portion of those commissions, in return for the provision to an adviser of goods or services by the dealer or a third party, other than order execution goods and services and research goods and services. A dealer may forward to a third party, on the instructions of an adviser, any portion of those commissions in return for order execution goods and services or research goods and services provided to the adviser by that third party. In either situation, the dealer would need to make an assessment as to whether or not the goods or services being paid for meet the definitions of order execution goods and services or research goods and services, in order to be meeting its obligations.

PART 5 — DISCLOSURE OBLIGATIONS

5.1 Disclosure Recipient — Part 4 of the Instrument requires an adviser to provide certain disclosure to a client if any brokerage transactions involving the client brokerage commissions of that client have been or might be directed to a dealer in return for the provision of any goods or services by the dealer or a third party, other than order execution. The recipient of the disclosure should typically be the party with whom the contractual arrangement to provide advisory services exists. For example, for an adviser to an investment fund, the client would typically be considered the fund for purposes of the disclosure requirements.

5.2 Timing of Disclosure — Part 4 of the Instrument requires an adviser to make certain initial and periodic disclosure to its clients. Initial disclosure should be made before an adviser opens a client account or enters into a management contract or a similar agreement to advise an investment fund and then periodic disclosure should be made at least annually. The period of time chosen for the periodic disclosure should be consistent from period to period.

5.3 Adequate Disclosure — (1) For the purposes of the disclosure made under section 4.1 of the Instrument, the information disclosed by an adviser may be client-specific, based on firm-wide information, or based on some other level of customization, so long as the information disclosed relates to those clients to whom the disclosure is directed. In any case, the disclosure required to be made by the adviser under section 4.1 of the Instrument would also reflect information pertaining to the processes, practices, arrangements, types of goods and services, etc., associated with brokerage transactions involving client brokerage commissions that have been or might be directed to dealers by its sub-advisers in return for the provision of any goods and services other than order execution.

(2) Also for the purposes of the disclosure under section 4.1 of the Instrument the use of the phrase "might be" in the requirement to make disclosure in situations where brokerage transactions involving client brokerage commissions have been or might be directed relates primarily to the disclosure to be made on an initial basis under paragraph 4.1(1)(a) of the Instrument. It is intended to require that the initial disclosure be made if it is or becomes reasonably foreseeable that brokerage transactions involving a new client's brokerage commissions could be directed in such a manner — for example, if brokerage transactions involving other existing clients' brokerage commissions are directed in such a manner, and it is likely that trades to be made on behalf of the new client will be aggregated with those made on behalf of the other existing clients.

(3) For the purposes of subparagraph 4.1(1)(a)(ii) of the Instrument, disclosure of the nature of the arrangements under which order execution goods and services or research goods and services might be provided should include whether goods and services are provided directly by a dealer or by a third party, and a description of the general mechanics of how client brokerage commissions are charged and might translate into payment for order execution goods and services and research goods and services.

(4) For the purposes of subparagraphs 4.1(1)(a)(iii) and 4.1(1)(b)(ii) of the Instrument, disclosure of each type of good or service should be sufficient to provide adequate description of the goods or services received (e.g., algorithmic trading software, research reports, trading advice, etc.).

(5) For purposes of subparagraph 4.1(1)(a)(iv), to the extent that more than one method is used, the description should be of those methods.

5.4 Form of Disclosure — Part 4 of the Instrument does not specify the form of disclosure. The adviser may determine the form of disclosure based on the needs of its clients, but the disclosure should be provided in conjunction with other initial and periodic disclosure relating to the management and performance of the account or portfolio. For managed accounts and portfolios, the initial disclosure could be included as a supplement to the management contract or similar agreement or the account opening form, and the periodic disclosure could be provided as a supplement to a statement of portfolio.

Adoption by OSC: (2009) 32 O.S.C.B. 10861 and 8079; Request for Comments: (2008) 31 O.S.C.B. 489 and (2005) 28 O.S.C.B. 1362.

National Instrument 23-103 — Electronic Trading and Direct Access to Marketplaces

Date: **March 1, 2013**

35 O.S.C.B. 6061

Table of Contents

Part 2 Requirements Applicable to Marketplace Participants

Part 3 Requirements Applicable to Use of Automated Order Systems

Part 4 Requirements Applicable to Marketplaces

Part 5 Exemption and Effective Date

PART 1 — DEFINITIONS AND INTERPRETATION

1. Definitions — In this Instrument,

"automated order system" means a system used to automatically generate or electronically transmit orders on a pre-determined basis;

"DEA client" means a client that is granted direct electronic access by a participant dealer;

"DEA client identifier" means a unique client identifier assigned to a DEA client;

"direct electronic access" means the access provided by a person or company to a client, other than a client that is registered as an investment dealer with a securities regulatory authority or, in Québec, is a foreign approved participant as defined in the Rules of the Montréal Exchange Inc., that permits the client to electronically transmit an order relating to a security to a marketplace, using the person or company's marketplace participant identifier,

(a) through the person or company's systems for automatic onward transmission to a marketplace; or

(b) directly to a marketplace without being electronically transmitted through the person or company's systems;

"marketplace and regulatory requirements" means

(a) the rules, policies, requirements or other similar instruments set by a marketplace respecting the method of trading by marketplace participants, including those related to order entry, the use of automated order systems, order types and features and the execution of trades;

(b) the applicable requirements in securities legislation; and

(c) the applicable requirements set by a recognized exchange, a recognized quotation and trade reporting system or a regulation services provider under section 7.1, 7.3 or 8.2 of National Instrument 23-101 *Trading Rules*;

and

"marketplace participant identifier" means the unique identifier assigned to a marketplace participant to access a marketplace; and

"participant dealer" means

(a) a marketplace participant that is an investment dealer, or

(b) in Québec, a foreign approved participant as defined in the Rules of the Montréal Exchange Inc., as amended from time to time.

2. Interpretation — A term that is defined or interpreted in National Instrument 21-101 *Marketplace Operation,* or National Instrument 31-103 *Registration Requirements, Exemptions and Ongoing Registrant Obligations* has, if used in this Instrument, the meaning ascribed to it in National Instrument 21-101 or National Instrument 31-103.

PART 2 — REQUIREMENTS APPLICABLE TO MARKETPLACE PARTICIPANTS

3. Risk Management and Supervisory Controls, Policies and Procedures — (1) A marketplace participant must

(a) establish, maintain and ensure compliance with risk management and supervisory controls, policies and procedures that are reasonably designed to manage, in accordance with prudent business practices, the financial, regulatory and other risks associated with marketplace access or providing clients with access to a marketplace; and

(b) record the policies and procedures required under paragraph (a) and maintain a description of the marketplace participant's risk management and supervisory controls in written form.

(2) The risk management and supervisory controls, policies and procedures required under subsection (1) must be reasonably designed to ensure that all orders are monitored and for greater certainty, include

(a) automated pre-trade controls; and

(b) regular post-trade monitoring.

(3) The risk management and supervisory controls, policies and procedures required in subsection (1) must be reasonably designed to

(a) systematically limit the financial exposure of the marketplace participant, including, for greater certainty, preventing

(i) the entry of one or more orders that would result in exceeding pre-determined credit or capital thresholds for the marketplace participant and, if applicable, its client with marketplace access provided by the marketplace participant;

(ii) the entry of one or more orders that exceed pre-determined price or size parameters;

(b) ensure compliance with marketplace and regulatory requirements, including, for greater certainty,

(i) preventing the entry of orders that do not comply with marketplace and regulatory requirements that must be satisfied on a pre-order entry basis;

(ii) limiting the entry of orders to those securities that a marketplace participant or, if applicable, its client with marketplace access provided by the marketplace participant, is authorized to trade;

(iii) restricting access to trading on a marketplace to persons authorized by the marketplace participant; and

(iv) ensuring that the compliance staff of the marketplace participant receives immediate order and trade information, including, for greater certainty, execution reports, resulting from orders sent by the marketplace participant or, if applicable, its client with marketplace access provided by the marketplace participant;

(c) enable the marketplace participant to immediately stop or cancel one or more orders entered by the marketplace participant or, if applicable, its client with marketplace access provided by the marketplace participant;

(d) enable the marketplace participant to immediately suspend or terminate any access to a marketplace granted to a client with marketplace access provided by the marketplace participant; and

(e) ensure that the entry of orders does not interfere with fair and orderly markets.

(4) A third party that provides risk management and supervisory controls, policies or procedures to a marketplace participant must be independent from each client with marketplace access provided by the marketplace participant, except if the client is an affiliate of the marketplace participant.

(5) A marketplace participant must directly and exclusively set and adjust the risk management and supervisory controls, policies and procedures required under this section, including those provided by third parties.

(6) A marketplace participant must

(a) regularly assess and document the adequacy and effectiveness of its risk management and supervisory controls, policies and procedures; and

(b) document any deficiencies in the adequacy or effectiveness of a risk management or supervisory control, policy or procedure and promptly remedy the deficiency.

(7) If a marketplace participant uses the services of a third party to provide risk management or supervisory controls, policies and procedures, the marketplace participant must

(a) regularly assess and document the adequacy and effectiveness of the third party's relevant risk management and supervisory controls, policies and procedures; and

(b) document any deficiencies in the adequacy or effectiveness of a risk management or supervisory control, policy or procedure and ensure the deficiency is promptly remedied.

4. Authorization to Set or Adjust Risk Management and Supervisory Controls, Policies and Procedures — Despite subsection 3(5), a participant dealer may, on a reasonable basis, authorize an investment dealer to perform, on the participant dealer's behalf, the setting or adjusting of a specific risk management or supervisory control, policy or procedure required under subsection 3(1) if

(a) the participant dealer has a reasonable basis for determining that the investment dealer, based on the investment dealer's relationship with the ultimate client, has better access to information relating to the ultimate client than the participant dealer such that the investment dealer can more effectively set or adjust the control, policy or procedure;

(b) a description of the specific risk management or supervisory control, policy or procedure and the conditions under which the investment dealer is authorized to set or adjust the specific risk management or supervisory control, policy or procedure are set out in a written agreement between the participant dealer and the investment dealer;

(c) before authorizing the investment dealer to set or adjust a specific risk management or supervisory control, policy or procedure, the participant dealer assesses and documents the adequacy and effectiveness of the investment dealer's setting or adjusting of the risk management or supervisory control, policy or procedure;

(d) the participant dealer

(i) regularly assesses the adequacy and effectiveness of the setting or adjusting of the risk management or supervisory control, policy or procedure by the investment dealer, and

(ii) documents any deficiencies in the adequacy or effectiveness of the setting or adjusting of the risk management or supervisory control, policy or procedure and ensures that the deficiencies are promptly remedied, and

(e) the participant dealer provides the investment dealer with the immediate order and trade information of the ultimate client that the participant dealer receives under subparagraph 3(3)(b)(iv).

PART 2.1 — REQUIREMENTS APPLICABLE TO PARTICIPANT DEALERS PROVIDING DIRECT ELECTRONIC ACCESS

4.1 Application of this Part — This Part does not apply to a participant dealer if the participant dealer complies with similar requirements established by

(a) a regulation services provider;

(b) a recognized exchange that directly monitors the conduct of its members and enforces requirements set under subsection 7.1(1) of NI 23-101; or

(c) a recognized quotation and trade reporting system that directly monitors the conduct of its users and enforces requirements set under subsection 7.3(1) of NI 23-101.

4.2 Provision of Direct Electronic Access — (1) A person or company must not provide direct electronic access unless it is a participant dealer.

(2) A participant dealer must not provide direct electronic access to a client that is acting and registered as a dealer with a securities regulatory authority.

4.3 Standards for DEA Clients — (1) A participant dealer must not provide direct electronic access to a client unless the participant dealer

(a) has established, maintains and applies standards that are reasonably designed to manage, in accordance with prudent business practices, the participant dealer's risks associated with providing direct electronic access; and

(b) assesses and documents that the client meets the standards established by the participant dealer under paragraph (a).

(2) The standards established by the participant dealer under subsection (1) must include the following:

(a) a client must not have direct electronic access unless the client has sufficient resources to meet any financial obligations that may result from the use of direct electronic access by that client,

(b) a client must not have direct electronic access unless the client has reasonable arrangements in place to ensure that all individuals using direct electronic access on behalf of the client have reasonable knowledge of and proficiency in the use of the order entry system that facilitates the direct electronic access,

(c) a client must not have direct electronic access unless the client has reasonable knowledge of and the ability to comply with all applicable marketplace and regulatory requirements, and

(d) a client must not have direct electronic access unless the client has reasonable arrangements in place to monitor the entry of orders through direct electronic access.

(3) A participant dealer must assess, confirm and document, at least annually, that the DEA client continues to meet the standards established by the participant dealer, including for greater certainty, those set out in this section.

4.4 Written Agreement — A participant dealer must not provide direct electronic access to a client unless the client has entered into a written agreement with the participant dealer that provides that,

(a) in the client's capacity as a DEA client,

(i) the client's trading activity will comply with marketplace and regulatory requirements;

(ii) the client's trading activity will comply with the product limits and credit or other financial limits specified by the participant dealer;

(iii) the client will take all reasonable steps to prevent unauthorized access to the technology that facilitates direct electronic access and will not permit any person or company to use the direct electronic access provided by the participant dealer other than those named by the client under the provision of the agreement referred to in subparagraph (vii);

(iv) the client will fully cooperate with the participant dealer in connection with any investigation or proceeding by any marketplace or regulation services provider with respect to trading conducted pursuant to the direct electronic access provided, including, upon request by the participant dealer, providing the marketplace or regulation services provider with access to information that is necessary for the purposes of the investigation or proceeding;

(v) the client will immediately inform the participant dealer if the client fails or expects not to meet the standards set by the participant dealer;

(vi) when trading for the accounts of another person or company, under subsection 4.7(1), the client will ensure that the orders of the other person or company are transmitted through the systems of the client and will be subject to reasonable risk management and supervisory controls, policies and procedures established and maintained by the client;

(vii) the client will immediately provide to the participant dealer in writing,

(A) the names of all personnel acting on the client's behalf that the client has authorized to enter an order using direct electronic access; and

(B) details of any change to the information in clause (A),

(b) the participant dealer has the authority to, without prior notice

(i) reject any order;

(ii) vary or correct any order to comply with a marketplace or regulatory requirement;

(iii) cancel any order entered on a marketplace; and

(iv) discontinue accepting orders from the DEA client.

4.5 Training of DEA Clients — (1) A participant dealer must not allow a client to have, or continue to have, direct electronic access unless the participant dealer is satisfied that the client has reasonable knowledge of applicable marketplace and regulatory requirements and the standards established by the participant dealer under section 4.3.

(2) A participant dealer must ensure that a DEA client receives any relevant amendments to applicable marketplace and regulatory requirements or changes or updates to the standards established by the participant dealer under section 4.3.

4.6 DEA Client Identifier — (1) Upon providing direct electronic access to a DEA client, a participant dealer must ensure the client is assigned a DEA client identifier in the form and manner required by

(a) a regulation services provider;

(b) a recognized exchange that directly monitors the conduct of its members and enforces requirements set under subsection 7.1(1) of NI 23-101; or

(c) a recognized quotation and trade reporting system that directly monitors the conduct of its users and enforces requirements set under subsection 7.3(1) of NI 23-101.

(2) A participant dealer under subsection (1) must immediately provide the DEA client identifier to each marketplace to which the DEA client has direct electronic access through the participant dealer.

(3) A participant dealer under subsection (1) must immediately provide the DEA client's name and the client's associated DEA client identifier to

(a) all regulation services providers monitoring trading on a marketplace to which the DEA client has access through the participant dealer;

(b) any recognized exchange or recognized quotation and trade reporting system that directly monitors the conduct of its members or users and enforces requirements set under subsection 7.1(1) or 7.3(1) of NI 23-101 and to which the DEA client has access through the participant dealer; and

(c) any exchange or quotation and trade reporting system that is recognized for the purposes of this Instrument and that directly monitors the conduct of its members or users and enforces requirements set under subsection 7.1(1) or 7.3(1) of NI 23-101 and to which the DEA client has access through the participant dealer.

(4) A participant dealer must ensure that an order entered by a DEA client using direct electronic access provided by the participant dealer includes the appropriate DEA client identifier.

(5) If a client ceases to be a DEA client, the participant dealer must promptly inform

(a) all regulation services providers monitoring trading on a marketplace to which the DEA client had access through the participant dealer;

(b) any recognized exchange or recognized quotation and trade reporting system that directly monitors the conduct of its members or users and enforces requirements set under section 7.1(1) or 7.3(1) of NI 23-101 and to which the DEA client had access through the participant dealer; and

(c) any exchange or quotation and trade reporting system that is recognized for the purposes of this Instrument and that directly monitors the conduct of its members or users and enforces requirements set under subsection 7.1(1) or 7.3(1) of NI 23-101 and to which the DEA client had access through the participant dealer.

4.7 Trading by DEA Clients — (1) A participant dealer must not provide direct electronic access to a DEA client that is trading for the account of another person or company unless the DEA client is

(a) registered or exempted from registration as an adviser under securities legislation; or

(b) a person or company that

(i) carries on business in a foreign jurisdiction,

(ii) under the laws of the foreign jurisdiction, may trade for the account of another person or company using direct electronic access, and

(iii) is regulated in the foreign jurisdiction by a signatory to the International Organization of Securities Commissions' Multilateral Memorandum of Understanding.

(2) If a DEA client referred to in subsection (1) is using direct electronic access to trade for the account of another person or company, the DEA client must ensure that the orders of the other person or company are transmitted through the systems of the DEA client before being entered on a marketplace.

(3) A participant dealer must ensure that when a DEA client is trading for the account of another person or company using direct electronic access, the orders of the other person or company are subject to reasonable risk management and supervisory controls, policies and procedures established and maintained by the DEA client.

(4) A DEA client must not provide access to or pass on its direct electronic access to another person or company other than the personnel authorized under subparagraph 4.4(a)(vii).

PART 3 — REQUIREMENTS APPLICABLE TO USE OF AUTOMATED ORDER SYSTEMS

5. Use of Automated Order Systems — (1) A marketplace participant must take all reasonable steps to ensure that its use of an automated order system or the use of an automated order system by any client, does not interfere with fair and orderly markets.

(2) A client of a marketplace participant must take all reasonable steps to ensure that its use of an automated order system does not interfere with fair and orderly markets.

(3) For the purpose of the risk management and supervisory controls, policies and procedures required under subsection 3(1), a marketplace participant must

(a) have a level of knowledge and understanding of any automated order system used by the marketplace participant or any client that is sufficient to allow the marketplace participant to identify and manage the risks associated with the use of the automated order system,

(b) ensure that every automated order system used by the marketplace participant or any client is tested in accordance with prudent business practices initially before use and at least annually thereafter, and

(c) have controls in place to immediately

(i) disable an automated order system used by the marketplace participant, and

(ii) prevent orders generated by an automated order system used by the marketplace participant or any client from reaching a marketplace.

PART 4 — REQUIREMENTS APPLICABLE TO MARKETPLACES

6. Availability of Order and Trade Information — (1) A marketplace must provide a marketplace participant with access to its order and trade information, including execution reports, on an immediate basis to enable the marketplace participant to effectively implement the risk management and supervisory controls, policies and procedures required under section 3.

(2) A marketplace must provide a marketplace participant access to its order and trade information referenced in subsection (1) on reasonable terms.

7. Marketplace Controls Relating to Electronic Trading — (1) A marketplace must not provide access to a marketplace participant unless it has the ability and authority to terminate all or a portion of the access provided to the marketplace participant.

(2) A marketplace must

(a) regularly assess and document whether the marketplace requires any risk management and supervisory controls, policies and procedures relating to electronic trading, in addition to those controls that a marketplace participant is required to have under subsection 3(1), and ensure that such controls, policies and procedures are implemented in a timely manner;

(b) regularly assess and document the adequacy and effectiveness of any risk management and supervisory controls, policies and procedures implemented under paragraph (a); and

(c) document and promptly remedy any deficiencies in the adequacy or effectiveness of the controls, policies and procedures implemented under paragraph (a).

8. Marketplace Thresholds — (1) A marketplace must not permit the execution of orders for exchange-traded securities to exceed the price and volume thresholds set by

(a) its regulation services provider;

(b) the marketplace, if it is a recognized exchange that directly monitors the conduct of its members and enforces requirements set under subsection 7.1(1) of NI 23-101; or

(c) the marketplace, if it is a recognized quotation and trade reporting system that directly monitors the conduct of its users and enforces the requirements set under subsection 7.3(1) of NI 23-101.

(2) A recognized exchange, recognized quotation and trade reporting system or regulation services provider setting a price threshold for an exchange-traded security under subsection (1) must coordinate its price threshold with all other exchanges, quotation and trade reporting systems and regulation services providers setting a price threshold under subsection (1) for the exchange-traded security or a security underlying the exchange-traded security.

9. Clearly Erroneous Trades — (1) A marketplace must not provide access to a marketplace participant unless it has the ability to cancel, vary or correct a trade executed by the marketplace participant.

(2) If a marketplace has retained a regulation services provider, the marketplace must not cancel, vary or correct a trade executed on the marketplace unless

(a) instructed to do so by its regulation services provider;

(b) the cancellation, variation or correction is requested by a party to the trade, consent is provided by both parties to the trade and notification is provided to the marketplace's regulation services provider; or

(c) the cancellation, variation or correction is necessary to correct an error caused by a system or technological malfunction of the marketplace systems or equipment, or caused by an individual acting on behalf of the marketplace, and the consent to cancel, vary or correct has been obtained from the marketplace's regulation services provider.

(3) A marketplace must establish, maintain and ensure compliance with reasonable policies and procedures that clearly outline the processes and parameters associated with a cancellation, variation or correction and must make such policies and procedures publicly available.

9.1 Support Use of DEA Client Identifiers — A marketplace must not permit a marketplace participant to provide direct electronic access to a person or company unless the marketplace's systems support the use of DEA client identifiers.

PART 5 — EXEMPTION AND EFFECTIVE DATE

10. Exemption — (1) The regulator or the securities regulatory authority may grant an exemption from this Instrument, in whole or in part, subject to such conditions or restrictions as may be imposed in the exemption.

(2) Despite subsection (1), in Ontario, only the regulator may grant such an exemption.

(3) Except in Ontario, an exemption referred to in subsection (1) is granted under the statute referred to in Appendix B of National Instrument 14-101 *Definitions* opposite the name of the local jurisdiction.

11. Effective Date — This Instrument comes into force on March 1, 2013.

Final Rule: (2012) 35 O.S.C.B. 8599; Approval by OSC: (2012) 35 O.S.C.B. 6037; Request for Comments: (2011) 34 O.S.C.B. 4133.

Amendment to Rule: (2013) 36 O.S.C.B. 8833; Approval by OSC: (2013) 36 O.S.C.B. 6771; Request for Comments: (2012) 35 O.S.C.B. 9627.

Recognitions: s. 5.1: Toronto Stock Exchange, Candian Venture Exchange and Bourse de Montréal: (2001) 24 O.S.C.B. 6574; s. 4.6(3)(c) and S. 4.6(5)(c); Bourse de Montréal and TSX Venture Exchange Inc.: (2014), 37 O.S.C.B. 2357.

National Instrument 23-103CP — Electronic Trading and Direct Electronic Access to Marketplaces

Table of Contents

PART 1 — GENERAL COMMENTS

1.1 Introduction — (1) **Purpose of National Instrument 23-103** — The purpose of National Instrument 23-103 *Electronic Trading and Direct Electronic Access to Marketplaces* (NI 23-103 or the Instrument) is to address areas of concern and risks brought about by electronic trading and direct electronic access (DEA). The increased speed and automation of trading on marketplaces give rise to various risks, including credit risk and market integrity risk. To protect marketplace participants from harm and to ensure continuing market integrity, these risks need to be reasonably and effectively controlled and monitored.

In the view of the Canadian Securities Administrators (CSA or we), marketplace participants should bear primary responsibility for ensuring that these risks are reasonably and effectively controlled and monitored. This responsibility applies to orders that are entered electronically by the marketplace participant itself, as well as orders from clients using the participant dealer's marketplace participant identifier.

This responsibility includes both financial and regulatory obligations. This view is premised on the fact that it is the marketplace participant that makes the decision to engage in trading or provide marketplace access to a client. However, the marketplaces also have some responsibilities to manage risks to the market.

NI 23-103 is meant to address risks associated with electronic trading on a marketplace with a key focus on the gatekeeping function of the executing broker. However, a clearing broker also bears financial and regulatory risks associated with providing clearing services. Under National Instrument 31-103 *Registration Requirements, Exemptions and Ongoing Registrant Obligations* (NI 31-103) a dealer must manage the risks associated with its business in accordance with prudent business practices. As part of that obligation, we expect a clearing dealer to have in place effective systems and controls to properly manage its risks.

NI 23-103 also provides a minimum framework for the provision of DEA; however we note that each marketplace has the discretion to determine whether to allow DEA and to impose stricter standards regarding the provision of DEA.

(2) **Scope of NI 23-103** — NI 23-103 applies to the electronic trading of securities on marketplaces. In Alberta and British Columbia, the term "security" when used in NI 23-103 includes an option that is an exchange contract but does not include a futures contract. In Ontario, the term "security" when used in NI 23-103, does not include a commodity futures contract or a commodity futures option that is not traded on a commodity futures exchange registered with or recognized by the Commission under the *Commodity Futures Act* or the form of which is not accepted by the Director under the *Commodity Futures Act*. In Québec, the term "security" when used in NI 23-103, includes a standardized derivative as this notion is defined in the *Derivatives Act*.

(3) Purpose of Companion Policy — This Companion Policy sets out how the CSA interpret or apply the provisions of NI 23-103 and related securities legislation.

Except for Part 1, the numbering of Parts and sections in this Companion Policy correspond to the numbering in NI 23-103. Any general guidance for a Part appears immediately after the Part name. Any specific guidance on sections in NI 23-103 follows any general guidance. If there is no guidance for a Part or section, the numbering in this Companion Policy will skip to the next provision that does have guidance.

All references in this Companion Policy to Parts and sections are to NI 23-103, unless otherwise noted.

1.2 Definitions — Unless defined in NI 23-103, terms used in NI 23-103 and in this Companion Policy have the meaning given to them in the securities legislation of each jurisdiction, in National Instrument 14-101 *Definitions*, National Instrument 21-101 *Marketplace Operation* (NI 21-101), or NI 31-103.

(1) Automated order systems — Automated order systems encompass both hardware and software used to generate or electronically transmit orders on a pre-determined basis and would include smart order routers and trading algorithms that are used by marketplace participants, offered by marketplace participants to clients or developed or used by clients.

(2) Direct electronic access — Section 1 defines "direct electronic access" as the access provided by a person or company to a client, other than a client that is registered as an investment dealer with a securities regulatory authority, or in Québec, is a foreign approved participant as defined in the Rules of the Montréal Exchange Inc. (Montréal Exchange), that permits the client to electronically transmit an order relating to a security to a marketplace, using the person or company's marketplace participant identifier either through the person or company's systems for automatic onward transmission to a marketplace or directly to the marketplace without being electronically transmitted through the person or company's systems.

While the term "person or company" is used in the definition of DEA, under subsection 4.2(1), only a participant dealer may provide DEA.

The Instrument outlines a DEA framework for clients of a participant dealer. Investment dealers and, in Québec, foreign approved participants, are outside the definition of "DEA". The granting of access to marketplaces by participant dealers to investment dealers or foreign approved participants of the Montréal Exchange is governed by the rules of either a regulation services provider or an exchange doing its own regulation. Those regimes are expected to be substantially similar to the framework NI 23-103 imposes upon DEA clients that are not investment dealers or foreign approved participants by requiring minimum client standards, written agreements and training. Furthermore, a derivatives dealer in Québec, which is an approved participant of the Montréal Exchange, must be registered as an investment dealer.

The CSA view a DEA order as including an order that is generated by an automated order system used by a DEA client if the DEA client determines the specified marketplace to which the order is to be sent and if the order is transmitted using the participant dealer's marketplace participant identifier. We hold this view regardless of whether or not the DEA client is using an automated order system that is offered by the participant dealer. We note that a DEA client's routing decisions may be varied for regulatory purposes by a participant dealer when an order passes through the participant dealer's system, for example to comply with the order protection rule or with the risk management requirements of NI 23-103, but we still consider the order to be a DEA order.

This definition does not capture orders entered using an order execution service or other electronic access arrangements in which a client uses the website of a dealer to enter orders since these services and arrangements do not permit the client to enter orders using a participant dealer's marketplace participant identifier.

(3) DEA client identifier — NI 23-103 requires each DEA client to have a unique identifier in order to track orders originating from that DEA client. A participant dealer is responsible for ensuring that each DEA client is assigned a DEA client identifier under subsection 4.6(1) and for ensuring that every order entered by a DEA client using DEA includes the appropriate DEA client identifier under subsection 4.6(4). Following current industry practice, we expect the participant dealer will collaborate with the marketplace with respect to the assignment of the necessary identifiers.

(4) Marketplace participant identifier — A marketplace participant identifier is the unique identifier assigned to the marketplace participant for trading purposes. The assignment of this identifier is co-ordinated with a regulation services provider of the marketplace, where applicable. We expect a marketplace participant to use its marketplace participant identifier across all marketplaces of which it is a member, user or subscriber.

PART 2 — REQUIREMENTS APPLICABLE TO MARKETPLACE PARTICIPANTS

3. Risk management and supervisory controls, policies and procedures — (1) National Instrument 31-103 requirements — For marketplace participants that are registered firms, section 11.1 of NI 31-103 requires the registered firm to establish, maintain and apply policies and procedures that establish a system of controls and supervision sufficient to: (a) provide reasonable assurance that the registered firm and each individual acting on its behalf complies with securities legislation; and (b) manage the risks associated with its business in accordance with prudent business practices. Section 3 of NI 23-103 builds on the obligations outlined in section 11.1 of NI 31-103. The CSA have included requirements in NI 23-103 for all marketplace participants that conduct trading on a marketplace to have risk management and supervisory controls, policies and procedures that are reasonably designed to manage their risks in accordance with prudent business practices. A marketplace participant must apply its risk management and supervisory controls, policies and procedures to all trading conducted under its marketplace participant identifier including trading conducted by a DEA client.

These requirements provide greater specificity with respect to the expectations surrounding controls, policies and procedures relating to electronic trading. The requirements apply to all marketplace participants, not just those that are registered firms.

(2) Documentation of risk management and supervisory controls, policies and procedures — Paragraph 3(1)(b) requires a marketplace participant to record its policies and procedures and maintain a copy of its risk management and supervisory controls in written form. This includes a narrative description of any electronic controls implemented by the marketplace participant as well as their functions.

We note that the risk management and supervisory controls, policies and procedures related to the trading of unlisted, government and corporate debt may not be the same as those related to the trading of equity securities due to the differences in the nature of trading of these types of securities. Different marketplace models such as a request for quote, negotiation system, or continuous auction market may require different risk management and supervisory controls, policies and procedures in order to appropriately address the varying levels of diverse risks these different marketplace models can pose to our markets.

A registered firm's obligation to maintain its risk management and supervisory controls in written form under paragraph 3(1)(b) includes retaining these documents and builds on a registered firm's obligation in NI 31-103 to retain its books and records. We expect a non-registered marketplace participant to retain these documents as part of its obligation under paragraph 3(1)(b) to maintain a description of its risk management and supervisory controls in written form.

(3) Clients that also maintain risk management controls — We are aware that a client that is not a registered dealer may maintain its own risk management controls. However, part of the intent of NI 23-103's risk management and supervisory controls, policies and procedures is to require a

participant dealer to manage its risks associated with electronic trading and to protect the participant dealer under whose marketplace participant identifier an order is being entered. Consequently, a participant dealer must maintain reasonably designed risk management and supervisory controls, policies and procedures regardless of whether its clients maintain their own controls. It is not appropriate for a participant dealer to rely on a client's risk management controls, as the participant dealer would not be able to ensure the sufficiency of the client's controls, nor would the controls be tailored to the particular needs of the participant dealer.

(4) Minimum risk management and supervisory controls, policies and procedures — Subsection 3(2) sets out the minimum elements of the risk management and supervisory controls, policies and procedures that must be addressed and documented by each marketplace participant. Automated pre-trade controls include an examination of the order before it is entered on a marketplace and the monitoring of entered orders whether executed or not. The marketplace participant should assess, document and implement any additional risk management and supervisory controls, policies and procedures that it determines are necessary to manage the marketplace participant's financial exposure and to ensure compliance with applicable marketplace and regulatory requirements.

With respect to regular post-trade monitoring, it is expected that the regularity of this monitoring will be conducted commensurate with the marketplace participant's determination of the order flow it is handling. At a minimum, an end of day check is expected.

(5) Pre-determined credit or capital thresholds — A marketplace participant can establish pre-determined credit thresholds by setting lending limits for a client and establish pre-determined capital thresholds by setting limits on the financial exposure that can be created by orders entered or executed on a marketplace under its marketplace participant identifier. The pre-determined credit or capital thresholds referenced in paragraph 3(3)(a) may be set based on different criteria, such as per order, trade account or other criteria, including overall trading strategy, or using a combination of these factors as required in the circumstances.

For example, a participant dealer that sets a credit limit for a client with marketplace access provided by the participant dealer could impose that credit limit by setting sub-limits applied at each marketplace to which the participant dealer provides access that together equal the total credit limit. A participant dealer may also consider whether to establish credit or capital thresholds based on sector, security or other relevant factors. In order to address the financial exposure that might result from rapid order entry, a participant dealer may also consider measuring compliance with set credit or capital thresholds on the basis of orders entered rather than executions obtained.

We note that different thresholds may be set for the marketplace participant's own order flow (including both proprietary and client order flow) and that of a client with marketplace access provided by the marketplace participant, if appropriate.

(6) Compliance with applicable marketplace and regulatory requirements — The CSA expect marketplace participants to prevent the entry of orders that do not comply with all applicable marketplace and regulatory requirements that must be satisfied on a pre-trade basis where possible. Specifically, marketplace and regulatory requirements that must be satisfied on a pre-order entry basis are those requirements that can effectively be complied with only before an order is entered on a marketplace, including: (i) conditions that must be satisfied under National Instrument 23-101 *Trading Rules* (NI 23-101) before an order can be marked a "directed-action order", (ii) marketplace requirements applicable to particular order types and (iii) compliance with trading halts. This requirement does not impose new substantive regulatory requirements on the marketplace participant. Rather it establishes that marketplace participants must have appropriate mechanisms in place that are reasonably designed to effectively comply with their existing regulatory obligations on a pre-trade basis in an automated, high-speed trading environment.

(7) Order and trade information — Subparagraph 3(3)(b)(iv) requires the risk management and supervisory controls, policies and procedures to be reasonably designed to ensure that the compliance staff of the marketplace participant receives immediate order and trade information. This will require the marketplace participant to ensure that it has the capability to view trading information in real-time or to receive immediate order and trade information from the marketplace, such as through a drop copy.

This requirement will help the marketplace participant fulfill its obligations under subsection 3(1) with respect to establishing and implementing reasonably designed risk management and supervisory controls, policies and procedures that manage its risks associated with access to marketplaces.

This provision does not prescribe that a marketplace participant carry out compliance monitoring in real-time. There are instances however, when automated, real-time monitoring should be considered, such as when an automated order system is used to generate orders. It is up to the marketplace participant to determine, based on the risk that the order flow poses to the marketplace participant, the appropriate timing for compliance monitoring. However, our view is that it is important that a marketplace participant have the necessary tools in place to facilitate order and trade monitoring as part of the marketplace participant's risk management and supervisory controls, policies and procedures.

(8) Direct and exclusive control over setting and adjusting of risk management and supervisory controls, policies and procedures — Subsection 3(5) specifies that a marketplace participant must directly and exclusively set and adjust its risk management and supervisory controls, policies and procedures. With respect to exclusive control, we expect that no person or company, other than the marketplace participant, will be able to set and adjust the controls, policies and procedures. With respect to direct control, a marketplace participant must not rely on a third party in order to perform the actual setting and adjusting of its controls, policies and procedures.

A marketplace participant can use technology of third parties, including that of marketplaces, as long as the marketplace participant, whether a registered dealer or institutional investor, is able to directly and exclusively set and adjust its supervisory and risk management controls, policies and procedures.

Section 4 provides a limited exception to the requirement in subsection 3(5) in that a participant dealer may, on a reasonable basis, and subject to other requirements, authorize an investment dealer to set or adjust a specific risk management or supervisory control, policy or procedure on behalf of the participant dealer.

(9) Risk management and supervisory controls, policies and procedures provided by an independent third party — Under subsection 3(4), a third party providing risk management and supervisory controls, policies or procedures to a marketplace participant must be independent of any client of the marketplace participant. However, an entity affiliated with a participant dealer that is also a client of the participant dealer may provide supervisory and risk management controls to the participant dealer. In all instances, the participant dealer must directly and exclusively set and adjust its supervisory and risk management controls.

Paragraph 3(7)(a) requires that a marketplace participant must regularly assess and document whether the risk management and supervisory controls, policies and procedures of the third party are effective and otherwise consistent with the provisions of NI 23-103 before engaging such services. Reliance on representations of a third party provider is insufficient to meet this assessment requirement. The CSA expect registered firms to be responsible and accountable for all functions that they outsource to a service provider as set out in Part 11 of Companion Policy 31-103CP *Registration Requirements, Exemptions and Ongoing Registrant Obligations*.

(10) Regular assessment of risk management controls and supervisory policies and procedures — Subsection 3(6) requires a marketplace participant to regularly assess and document the adequacy and effectiveness of the controls, policies and procedures it is required to establish under

subsection 3(1). Under subsection 3(7), the same assessment requirement also applies if a marketplace participant uses the services of a third party to provide risk management or supervisory controls, policies and procedures. A "regular" assessment would constitute, at a minimum, an assessment conducted annually of the controls, policies and procedures and whenever a substantive change is made to the controls, policies and procedures. A marketplace participant should determine whether more frequent assessments are required, depending on the particular circumstances.

A marketplace participant that is a registered firm is expected to retain the documentation of each such assessment as part of its obligation to maintain books and records in NI 31-103.

4. Authorization to set or adjust risk management and supervisory controls, policies and procedures — Section 4 is intended to address introducing (originating) and carrying (executing) arrangements or jitney arrangements that involve multiple dealers. In such arrangements, there may be certain controls that are better directed by the originating dealer, since it is the originating dealer that has knowledge of its client and is responsible for suitability and other "know your client" obligations. We expect the "ultimate client" to be a third party to the originating investment dealer in all instances.

The executing dealer must also have reasonable controls in place to manage the risks it incurs by executing orders for other dealers.

Therefore, section 4 provides that a participant dealer may, on a reasonable basis, authorize an investment dealer to set or adjust a specific risk management or supervisory control, policy or procedure on the participant dealer's behalf by written contract and after a thorough assessment. Our view is that where the originating investment dealer with the direct relationship with the ultimate client has better access than the participant dealer to information relating to the ultimate client, the originating investment dealer may more effectively assess the ultimate client's financial resources and investment objectives.

We also expect that the participant dealer will maintain a written contract with the investment dealer that sets out a description of the specific risk management or supervisory control, policy or procedure and the conditions under which the investment dealer is authorized to set or adjust the control, policy or procedure as part of its books and records obligations set out in NI 31-103.

Paragraph 4(d) requires a participant dealer to regularly assess the adequacy and effectiveness of the investment dealer's setting or adjusting of the risk management and supervisory controls, policies and procedures that it performs on the participant dealer's behalf. We expect that this will include an assessment of the performance of the investment dealer under the written agreement prescribed in paragraph 4(b). A "regular" assessment would constitute, at a minimum, an assessment conducted annually of the controls, policies and procedures and whenever a substantive change is made to the controls, policies or procedures. A marketplace participant should determine whether more frequent assessments are required, depending on the particular circumstances.

Under paragraph 4(e), the participant dealer must provide the compliance staff of the originating investment dealer with immediate order and trade information of the ultimate client. This is to allow the originating investment dealer to monitor trading more effectively and efficiently.

Authorizing an investment dealer to set or adjust a risk management or supervisory control, policy or procedure does not relieve the participant dealer of its obligations under section 3, including the overall responsibility to establish, document, maintain and ensure compliance with risk management and supervisory controls, policies and procedures reasonably designed to manage, in accordance with prudent business practices, the financial, regulatory and other risks associated with marketplace access.

PART 2.1 — REQUIREMENTS APPLICABLE TO PARTICIPANT DEALERS PROVIDING DIRECT ELECTRONIC ACCESS

4.2 Provision of DEA — (1) Registration requirement — Only marketplace participants that meet the definition of "participant dealer" are permitted to provide DEA to clients. NI 23-103 defines a participant dealer as a marketplace participant that is an investment dealer or, in Québec, a foreign approved participant as defined in the Rules of the Montréal Exchange as amended from time to time.

(2) Persons or companies not eligible for DEA — Subsection 4.2(2) specifically prohibits a participant dealer from providing DEA to clients that are acting and registered as dealers. We think that dealers that are acting as and registered in dealer categories other than "investment dealer" should not have this type of electronic access to marketplaces through a participant dealer unless they themselves are investment dealers and subject to Investment Industry Regulatory Organization of Canada (IIROC) rules. We note that investment dealers and foreign approved participants are not included under this subsection because they are outside the definition of DEA, which is a form of marketplace access given to clients other than an investment dealer or a foreign approved participant.

Investment dealers that are members of IIROC may trade electronically using routing arrangements as regulated under its Universal Market Integrity Rules. A client is ineligible for DEA if it is both registered as a dealer with a securities regulatory authority and is acting in its capacity as a registered dealer. For example, a person or company that is registered as an adviser, such as a portfolio manager or restricted portfolio manager, and that is also registered as a dealer is eligible for DEA if it only uses DEA when acting in its capacity as an adviser and not in its capacity as a dealer. If a dually registered firm uses DEA to place trades through a participant dealer for its managed account clients, then it is using DEA in its capacity as an adviser. NI 31-103 defines a managed account to mean an account of a client for which a person or company makes the investment decisions if that person or company has discretion to trade in securities for the account without requiring the client's express consent to a transaction. As a further example, if a firm uses DEA to place trades through a participant dealer for accounts of clients that are accredited investors (as defined in National Instrument 45-106 *Prospectus and Registration Exemptions*) but are not managed accounts, then it is using DEA in its capacity as a dealer, and therefore must not be using DEA for this trading activity.

Similarly, a foreign dealer that is also registered as a dealer with a securities regulatory authority is eligible for DEA if it only uses DEA when acting in its capacity as a foreign dealer and not in its capacity as a dealer registered with a securities regulatory authority.

(3) Order execution services — The definition of DEA does not include order execution services as they are governed by IIROC rules.

It is our view that, in general, retail investors should not be using DEA and should be sending orders using order execution services. However, there are some circumstances in which individuals are sophisticated and have access to the necessary technology to use DEA (for example, former registered traders or floor brokers). In these circumstances, we expect that if a participant dealer chooses to offer DEA to an individual, the participant dealer will set standards high enough to ensure that the participant dealer is not exposed to undue risk. It may be appropriate for these standards to be higher than those set for institutional investors. All requirements relating to risk management and supervisory controls, policies and procedures would apply when providing DEA to an individual.

4.3 Standards for DEA clients — (1) Minimum standards — A participant dealer's due diligence with respect to its clients is a key method of managing risks associated with providing DEA and necessitates a thorough vetting of potential DEA clients. As a result, section 4.3 requires the participant dealer to establish, maintain and apply standards that are reasonably designed to manage, in accordance with prudent business practices, the participant dealer's risks associated with providing DEA and to assess and document that the prospective DEA client meets these standards before providing DEA. A participant dealer's establishment, maintenance and application of standards that are reasonably designed to manage the participant dealer's risks associated with providing DEA would include evaluating its risks in providing DEA to a specific client. The participant dealer must establish, maintain and apply these standards with respect to all DEA clients. Subsection 4.3(2) requires a participant dealer's standards to include that a DEA client has sufficient resources to meet any financial obligation that may result from its use of direct electronic access and has reasonable knowledge of both the use of the order entry system and all applicable marketplace and regulatory requirements.

Each participant dealer has a different risk profile and as a result, we have provided flexibility to participant dealers in determining the specific levels of the minimum standards. We view these standards to be the minimum required for the participant dealer to properly manage its risks. The participant dealer should assess and determine what additional standards are reasonable given the particular circumstances of the participant dealer and each prospective DEA client. For example, a participant dealer might need to modify certain standards that it applies to an institutional client when determining whether an individual is suitable for receiving DEA.

Some additional factors a participant dealer could consider when setting such standards for prospective DEA clients include prior sanctions for improper trading activity, evidence of a proven track record of responsible trading, supervisory oversight, and the proposed trading strategy and associated volumes of trading.

(2) Monitoring the entry of orders — The requirement in paragraph 4.3(2)(d) for the DEA client to monitor the entry of orders though DEA is expected to help ensure that orders comply with marketplace and regulatory requirements, meet minimum standards set for managing risk and do not interfere with fair and orderly markets.

(3) Annual confirmation — Subsection 4.3(3) requires a participant dealer to assess, confirm and document, at least annually, that each DEA client continues to meet the minimum standards established by the participant dealer. It is up to the participant dealer to choose the method of confirmation. Obtaining a written annual certification by the DEA client is one way to meet this requirement. If the participant dealer does not require a written annual certification, the participant dealer should record the steps it has taken to perform the annual confirmation in order to be able to demonstrate compliance with this requirement.

4.4 Written agreement — While section 4.4 sets out the provisions that must be included in a written agreement between a participant dealer and its DEA client, the participant dealer may choose to include additional provisions in the agreement as well.

Subparagraph 4.4(a)(iii) requires a DEA client to take all reasonable steps to prevent unauthorized access to the technology that facilitates direct electronic access and to not permit any person or company to use the direct electronic access provided by the participant dealer other than those named by the DEA client under the provision of the agreement referred to in subparagraph 4.4(a)(vii). The steps taken should be commensurate with the risks posed by the type of technology and systems that are being used.

Subparagraph 4.4(a)(iv) specifies that when a participant dealer requests information from its DEA client in connection with an investigation or proceeding by any marketplace or regulation services provider with respect to trading conducted pursuant to the DEA provided, the information is required to only be given to the marketplace or regulation services provider conducting the investigation or proceeding in order to protect the confidentiality of the information.

Subparagraph 4.4(a)(vii) specifies that a DEA client will immediately provide to the participant dealer, in writing, the names of all personnel acting on the DEA client's behalf that it has authorized to enter an order using DEA. This requires a DEA client to formally authorize its personnel who will be entering orders using DEA when trading for the DEA client.

In order to assist a participant dealer in managing its risks with providing DEA, subsection 4.4(b) requires that the written agreement between a participant dealer and its DEA client provide that a participant dealer is authorized to reject any order, cancel any order entered on a marketplace and discontinue accepting orders from the DEA client, without prior notice. It also requires that the participant dealer be authorized to, without prior notice, vary or correct any order to comply with a marketplace or regulatory requirement. For example, this may occur when an order is re-priced by a participant dealer to ensure the order does not lock or cross the market. We note that the authorization to vary or correct any order to comply with a marketplace or regulatory requirement is the minimum expected by the CSA and a participant dealer may require greater latitude in the agreement to vary or correct orders of a DEA client than is mandated under the Instrument.

4.5 Training of DEA clients — Pursuant to subsection 4.5(1), before providing DEA to a client, and as necessary after DEA is provided, a participant dealer must satisfy itself that the client has reasonable knowledge of applicable marketplace and regulatory requirements. What constitutes "reasonable knowledge" will depend on the particular client's trading activity and the associated risks presented by each specific client.

The participant dealer must assess the client's knowledge and determine what, if any, training is required in the particular circumstances. The training must, at a minimum, enable the DEA client to understand the applicable marketplace and regulatory requirements and how trading on the marketplace system occurs. For example, it may be appropriate for the participant dealer to require the client to have the same training required of an approved participant under UMIR.

After DEA has been provided, an assessment of the DEA client's knowledge of applicable marketplace and regulatory requirements would be considered necessary if significant changes to these requirements are made or if the participant dealer notices unusual trading activity by the DEA client. If the participant dealer finds the DEA client's knowledge to be deficient after such an assessment, the participant dealer should require additional training for the DEA client until the DEA client achieves the requisite level of knowledge or discontinue providing DEA to that DEA client.

4.6 DEA client identifier — **(1) Assignment of DEA client identifier** — The purpose of requiring a unique identifier for each DEA client is to identify orders of clients entered onto a marketplace by way of DEA. NI 23-103 requires a participant dealer, upon providing DEA to a client, to ensure that the DEA client has been assigned a DEA client identifier. Following current industry practice, we expect the participant dealer will collaborate with the marketplace with respect to determining the necessary identifiers. We note that a DEA client may be assigned one or more DEA client identifiers.

(2) Information to marketplaces — Subsection 4.6(2) requires a participant dealer to immediately provide the assigned DEA client identifier to each marketplace to which the DEA client has direct electronic access through that participant dealer. This provision is to ensure that marketplaces are aware of which trading channels contain DEA flow in order for marketplaces to properly manage their risks. The CSA do not expect that a DEA client's name will be disclosed to a marketplace. Instead, a participant dealer would only need to provide the assigned DEA client identifier to a marketplace to enable the marketplace to more readily identify DEA flow.

4.7 Trading by DEA clients — **Client orders passing through the systems of the DEA client** — The CSA are of the view that DEA clients should not provide their DEA to their clients or any other person or company. Subsection 4.7(2) requires that if a DEA client is using DEA and trading for the account of another person or company, the orders of the other person or company must be transmitted through the systems of the DEA client before being entered on a marketplace. We consider the systems of the DEA client to include the DEA client's own proprietary systems or systems that are provided to the DEA client by a third party. The orders of the other person or company must be transmitted through the DEA client's systems regardless of whether a DEA client sends orders directly or indirectly through a participant dealer

This is meant to allow for those arrangements that the CSA are comfortable with, such as a DEA client acting as a "hub" and aggregating the orders of its affiliates before sending the orders to the participant dealer. Requiring orders to be transmitted through the systems of the DEA client allows the DEA client to impose any controls it deems necessary or is required to impose under any requirements to manage its risks. Although the participant dealer is required to have controls to manage its risks that arise from providing DEA to clients, including automated pre-trade controls, it is the DEA client that has knowledge of the person or company it is trading for. As a result, the DEA client is likely in a better position to determine the appropriate controls and parameters of those controls that are specific to each person or company it is trading for. The participant dealer is responsible for ensuring that the DEA client has adequate controls in place to monitor the orders entering the DEA client's systems.

PART 3 — REQUIREMENTS APPLICABLE TO THE USE OF AUTOMATED ORDER SYSTEMS

5. Use of automated order systems — Section 5 stipulates that a marketplace participant or any client must take all reasonable steps to ensure that its use of automated order systems does not interfere with fair and orderly markets. A marketplace participant must also take all reasonable steps to ensure that the use of an automated order system by a client does not interfere with fair and orderly markets. This includes both the fair and orderly trading on a marketplace or the market as a whole and the proper functioning of a marketplace. For example, the sending of a continuous stream of orders that negatively impacts the price of a security or that overloads the systems of a marketplace may be considered as interfering with fair and orderly markets.

Paragraph 5(3)(a) requires a marketplace participant to have a level of knowledge and understanding of any automated order systems used by either the marketplace participant or the marketplace participant's clients that is sufficient to allow the marketplace participant to identify and manage the risks associated with the use of the automated order system. We understand that detailed information of automated order systems may be treated as proprietary information by some clients or third party service providers; however, the CSA expect that the marketplace participant will be able to obtain sufficient information in order to properly identify and manage its own risks.

Paragraph 5(3)(b) requires that each automated order system is tested in accordance with prudent business practices. A participating dealer does not necessarily have to conduct tests on each automated order system used by its clients but must satisfy itself that these automated order systems have been appropriately tested. Testing an automated order system in accordance with prudent business practices includes testing it before its initial use and at least annually thereafter. We would also expect that testing would also occur after any significant change to the automated order system is made.

PART 4 — REQUIREMENTS APPLICABLE TO MARKETPLACES

6. Availability of order and trade information — (1) **Reasonable access** — Subsection 6(1) is designed to ensure that a marketplace participant has immediate access to the marketplace participant's order and trade information when needed. Subsection 6(2) will help ensure that the marketplace does not have any rules, polices, procedures, fees or practices that would unreasonably create barriers to the marketplace participant in accessing this information.

This obligation is distinct from the requirement for marketplaces to disseminate order and trade information through an information processor under Parts 7 and 8 of NI 21-101. The information to be provided pursuant to section 6 would need to include the private information included on each order and trade in addition to the public information disseminated through an information processor.

(2) **Immediate order and trade information** — For the purposes of providing access to order and trade information on an immediate basis, we consider a marketplace's provision of this information by a drop copy to be acceptable.

7. Marketplace controls relating to electronic trading — (1) **Termination of marketplace access** — Subsection 7(1) requires a marketplace to have the ability and authority to terminate all or a portion of the access provided to a marketplace participant before providing access to that marketplace participant. This requirement also includes the authority of a marketplace to terminate access provided to a client that is using a participant dealer's marketplace participant identifier to access the marketplace. We expect a marketplace to act when it identifies trading behaviour that interferes with the fair and orderly functioning of its market.

(2) **Assessments to be conducted** — Paragraph 7(2)(a) requires a marketplace to regularly assess and document whether the marketplace requires any risk management and supervisory controls, policies and procedures relating to electronic trading, in addition to the risk management and supervisory controls, policies and procedures that marketplace participants are required to have under subsection 3(1), and ensure that such controls, policies and procedures are implemented in a timely manner. As well, a marketplace must regularly assess and document the adequacy and effectiveness of any risk management and supervisory controls, policies and procedures put in place under paragraph 7(2)(a). A marketplace is expected to document any conclusions reached as a result of its assessment and any deficiencies noted. It must also promptly remedy any identified deficiencies.

It is important that a marketplace take steps to ensure it does not engage in activity that interferes with fair and orderly markets. Part 12 of NI 21-101 requires marketplaces to establish systems-related risk management controls. It is therefore expected that a marketplace will be generally aware of the risk management and supervisory controls, policies and procedures of its marketplace participants and assess whether it needs to implement additional controls, policies and procedures to eliminate any risk management gaps and ensure the integrity of trading on its market.

(3) **Timing of assessments** — A "regular" assessment would constitute, at a minimum, an assessment conducted annually and whenever a substantive change is made to a marketplace's operations, rules, controls, policies or procedures that relate to methods of electronic trading. A marketplace should determine whether more frequent assessments are required depending on the particular circumstances of the marketplace, for example when the number of orders or trades is increasing very rapidly or when new types of clients or trading activities are identified. A marketplace should document and preserve a copy of each such assessment as part of its books and records obligation in NI 21-101.

(4) **Implementing controls, policies and procedures in a timely manner** — A "timely manner" will depend on the particular circumstances, including the degree of potential risk of financial harm to marketplace participants and their clients or harm to the integrity of the marketplace and to the market as a whole. The marketplace must ensure the timely implementation of any necessary risk management and supervisory controls, policies and procedures.

8. Marketplace thresholds — Section 8 requires that each marketplace must not permit the execution of orders of exchange-traded securities exceeding price and volume thresholds set by its regulation services provider, or by the marketplace if it is a recognized exchange or recognized quotation and trade reporting system that directly monitors the conduct of its members or users and enforces certain requirements set under NI 23-101.

These price and volume thresholds are expected to reduce erroneous orders and price volatility by preventing the execution of orders that could interfere with a fair and orderly market.

There are a variety of methods that may be used to prevent the execution of these orders. However, the setting of the price threshold is to be coordinated among all regulation services providers, recognized exchanges and recognized quotation and trade reporting systems that set the threshold under subsection 8(1).

The coordination requirement also applies when setting a price threshold for securities that have underlying interests in an exchange-traded security. We note that there may be differences in the actual price thresholds set for an exchange-traded security and a security that has underlying interests in that exchange-traded security.

9. Clearly erroneous trades — (1) Application of section 9 — Section 9 provides that a marketplace cannot provide access to a marketplace participant unless it has the ability to cancel, vary or correct a trade executed by that marketplace participant. This requirement would apply in the instance where the marketplace decides to cancel, vary or correct a trade or is instructed to do so by a regulation services provider.

Before cancelling, varying or correcting a trade, paragraph 9(2)(a) requires that a marketplace receive instructions from its regulation services provider, if it has retained one. We note that this would not apply in the case of a recognized exchange or recognized quotation and trade reporting system that directly monitors the conduct of its members or users and enforces requirements set pursuant to subsection 7.1(1) or 7.3(1) respectively of NI 23-101.

(2) Cancellation, variation or correction where necessary to correct a system or technological malfunction or error made by the marketplace systems or equipment — Under paragraph 9(2)(c) a marketplace may cancel, vary or correct a trade where necessary to correct an error caused by a system or technological malfunction of the marketplace's systems or equipment or an individual acting on behalf of the marketplace. If a marketplace has retained a regulation services provider, it must not cancel, vary or correct a trade unless it has obtained permission from its regulation services provider to do so.

Examples of errors caused by a system or technological malfunction include where the system executes a trade on terms that are inconsistent with the explicit conditions placed on the order by the marketplace participant, or allocates fills for orders at the same price level in a manner or sequence that is inconsistent with the stated manner or sequence in which such fills are to occur on the marketplace. Another example includes where the trade price was calculated by a marketplace's systems or equipment based on some stated reference price, but it was calculated incorrectly.

(3) Policies and procedures — For policies and procedures established by the marketplace in accordance with the requirements of subsection 9(3) to be "reasonable", they should be clear and understandable to all marketplace participants.

The policies and procedures should also provide for consistent application. For example, if a marketplace decides that it will consider requests for cancellation, variation or correction of trades in accordance with paragraph 9(2)(b), it should consider all requests received regardless of the identity of the counterparty. If a marketplace chooses to establish parameters only within which it might be willing to consider such requests, it should apply these parameters consistently to each request, and should not exercise its discretion to refuse a cancellation or amendment when the request falls within the stated parameters and the consent of the affected parties has been provided.

When establishing any policies and procedures in accordance with subsection 9(3), a marketplace should also consider what additional policies and procedures might be appropriate to address any conflicts of interest that might arise.

Adoption by OSC: (2012) 35 O.S.C.B. 8599 and 6037; Request for Comments: (2011) 34 O.S.C.B. 4133.

Adoption of Amendments by OSC: (2013) 36 O.S.C.B. 8842 and 6782; Request for Comments: (2012) 35 O.S.C.B. 9639.

Policies and Orders: CSAN 23-314; OSCN 23-701.

CSA Staff Notice 23-301 — Joint Notice of the Staff of the Canadian Securities Administrators, Market Regulation Services Inc., Bourse de Montréal Inc., and the Investment Dealers Association — Electronic Audit Trails

Date: **March 28, 2003**

26 O.S.C.B. 2461

[superseded by CSAN 23-302]

CSA Staff Notice 23-302 — Joint Regulatory Notice — Electronic Audit Trail Initiative (TREATS)

Date: **April 15, 2005**

28 O.S.C.B. 3561

[Not reproduced; see CSAN 23-306]

CSA Notice 23-303 — Update on Concept Paper 23-402 Best Execution and Soft Dollar Arrangements

Date: **December 16, 2005**

28 O.S.C.B. 10063

[Not reproduced]

Joint CSA/SRO Notice 23-304 — Status of the Transaction Reporting and Electronic Audit Trail System

Date: **March 17, 2006**

29 O.S.C.B. 2265

Not reproduced; see CSAN 23-306]

CSA Staff Notice 23-306 — Status of the Transaction Reporting and Electronic Audit Trail System (TREATS)

Date: **January 9, 2009**

32 O.S.C.B. 282

CSA Staff Notice 23-306
Joint Notice of the Staff of the Canadian Securities Administrators, Market Regulation Services Inc., Bourse de Montréal Inc., and the Investment Industry Regulatory Organization of Canada
Status of the Transaction Reporting and Electronic Audit Trail System (TREATS)

A. — Background

The electronic audit trail initiative was a project initiated and managed by the Canadian Securities Administrators (CSA) with the participation of the Bourse de Montréal Inc and the Investment Industry Regulatory Organization of Canada[1] (together, the Regulators) to investigate, design and implement a solution to facilitate compliance with Canadian securities electronic audit trail requirements introduced in National Instrument 23-101 *Trading Rules* (NI 23-101).

The last update on the status of the TREATS project was published in October 2006[2] (the October 2006 Notice). Since that notice, the Regulators performed an examination of certain models currently being used in other jurisdictions, and completed work on a Benefits Analysis with the assistance of external consultants.

In addition, amendments to NI 23-101 and Companion Policy 23-101CP were approved in December 2006[3] that had the effect, among other things, of extending the deadline for the implementation of an electronic audit trail by dealers and inter-dealer bond brokers until January 1, 2010.

Further amendments to the above-noted instrument and companion policy were also proposed by the CSA in April 2007[4] that would have had the intended effect, among other things, of clarifying the record keeping requirements associated with the electronic audit trail.

B. — Update on Status of TREATS Project

As a result of the work performed since the October 2006 Notice, the Regulators have decided not to proceed with the TREATS project. This decision was made after considering the size and complexity of the undertaking in relation to the relative uncertainty as to whether the initiative's overall policy objective of enhanced market integrity would be achieved.

Other work focusing on enhancing the electronic audit trail information, in a more simplified manner, may be pursued in the future as a new initiative. Accordingly, there will be no further updates regarding the status of the TREATS project.

Amendments to NI 23-101 have therefore been made to reflect this decision.[5]

CSA/IIROC Joint Staff Notice 23-308 — Update on Forum to Discuss CSA/IIROC Joint Consultation Paper 23-404 "Dark Pools, Dark Orders and Other Developments in Market Structure in Canada" and Next Steps

Date: **May 28, 2010**

33 O.S.C.B. 4747

I. — Background

On October 2, 2009, the Canadian Securities Administrators (CSA) and the Investment Industry Regulatory Organization of Canada (IIROC and together with the CSA, we) published the CSA/IIROC Joint Consultation Paper 23-404 *Dark Pools, Dark Orders, and Other Developments in Market Structure in Canada* (Consultation Paper), requesting comments on a number of market structure issues, particularly the impact of marketplaces that offer no pre-trade transparency (dark pools), the introduction of new non-transparent order types, and the introduction of smart order routers. We received 23 response letters from a range of respondents including marketplaces, buy side and sell side representatives, and industry associations. A summary of the comment letters received is included at Appendix A of this Notice and a list of commenters at Appendix B.

---

[1] Two original participants in the project, Market Regulation Services Inc. and the Investment Dealers Association of Canada have merged to form the Investment Industry Regulatory Organization of Canada.

[2] Published on October 20, 2006 in English in the Ontario Securities Commission Bulletin at (2006) 29 OSCB 8222 and in French in the *Bulletin de l'Autorité des marchés financiers*, Vol. 3, no 42.

[3] The notice relating to the amendments was published on December 15, 2006 in English in the Ontario Securities Commission Bulletin at (2006) 29 OSCB 9731 and in French in the *Bulletin de l'Autorité des marchés financiers*, Vol. 3, no 50.

[4] The notice relating to the proposed amendments was published on April 20, 2007 in English in the Ontario Securities Commission Bulletin at (2007) 30 OSCB (Supp-3) and in French in the *Bulletin de l'Autorité des marchés financiers*, Vol. 4, no 16.

[5] The notice relating to the amendments was published on September 5, 2008 in English in the Ontario Securities Commission Bulletin at (2008) 31 OSCB 8572 and in French in the *Bulletin de l'Autorité des marchés financiers*, Vol. 5, no 35.

On March 23, 2010, the CSA and IIROC also hosted a forum to discuss the issues raised in the Consultation Paper and comment letters and to give respondents a chance to elaborate on their views. The morning session consisted of 11 formal presentations and the afternoon consisted of a roundtable discussion. Representatives from marketplaces, dealers and buy-side investors took part in the morning session and addressed questions from a panel consisting of senior executives from both the CSA and IIROC.[1] The afternoon session involved a roundtable discussion among the presenters facilitated by Wendy Rudd, which touched on issues raised in the Consultation Paper and in morning presentations. In addition, there was a luncheon keynote speech by Larry Tabb, founder and CEO of Tabb Group, discussing similar market structure issues in the United States.

Edited recordings of each of the presentations and the roundtable discussion[2] are available on the IIROC website at www.iiroc.ca under the heading "Member Resources" and the subheadings "Member Events — Webcasts/Recorded Events".

We thank those who contributed to the process by both responding to our request for comments or by presenting and participating in the forum. In particular, we thank Ms. Wendy Rudd who facilitated the afternoon session. We have gathered a great deal of information from this process and will be using it to inform our policy-making going forward.

II. — Themes of the Forum

We identified a number of themes that emerged during the forum. Many reiterated issues that had been raised in response letters we received, while others went beyond the topics addressed in the Consultation Paper and touched on other market structure issues of interest.

Some of the themes directly related to the issues raised for discussion in the Consultation Paper included:

- the practice of broker preferencing[3] at the marketplace level and internalization of order flow;

- the practice of dark pools sending Indications of Interest (IOIs) to attract order flow;

- the fairness of a marketplace using a proprietary smart order router (SOR) that has access to information on that marketplace that is not otherwise available to other marketplace participants;

- the use of market pegged orders[4] and whether those orders "free-ride" off the visible market;

- whether dark pools should be required to offer price improvement; and

- the use of sub-penny pricing.

Issues related to the Canadian equity market structure that were not raised specifically in the Consultation Paper included:

- concerns about marketplace data fee increases with the emergence of multiple marketplaces;

- direct and sponsored access to marketplaces;

- the impact of high-frequency trading on the market; and

- the need for regulators to take a holistic view of the market when considering regulation instead of dealing with specific issues in isolation.

We have compiled a high-level overview of the views expressed both in writing and at the forum and also included below a discussion of ongoing initiatives and proposed next steps to address some of the issues.

a. — Broker Preferencing

There were many different views on this issue. Some participants supported the concept stating that in the absence of inter-market time priority that broker preferencing is essentially irrelevant. Others believed that broker preferencing is inherently unfair as earlier orders are bypassed and ignored. A common point of discussion was the concern that the removal of broker preferencing from the Canadian marketplaces might result in dark pools being established by dealers to internalize orders which would reduce transparency. Forum participants also indicated that due to the relatively small number of dealers that control a significant portion of the order flow, additional internalization of order flow at the dealers is a factor that should be considered when analyzing dark pools.

We acknowledge that broker preferencing is a unique feature of certain Canadian marketplaces and that it is a by-product of Rule 6.3 of the UMIR that requires dealers to immediately expose "small" orders on a transparent marketplace. This rule supports price discovery and increases the breadth and depth of the displayed market and provides direction to achieve best execution for these small orders. In other jurisdictions, these types of orders are often withheld from the market and matched internally by the dealer, therefore eliminating the need for broker preferencing. We agree that the impact of the internalization of order flow is an important consideration in our review of the issues raised at the forum, including broker preferencing.

CSA and IIROC staff intend to examine the issue of broker preferencing. We do believe that at the outset, more transparency is required so that market participants understand how all trading options offered by the marketplaces function. CSA staff are considering requiring that marketplaces provide specific disclosure on their websites on how orders entered on a marketplace interact with other orders on that market-

---

[1] The panel consisted of: Louis Morisset, Superintendent, Securities Markets, Autorité des marchés financiers; Susan Wolburgh Jenah, President and CEO, IIROC; David Wilson, Chair of the Ontario Securities Commision; and Sinan Akdeniz, OSC Commissioner.

[2] The presentation and roundtable discussions were edited for the purposes of publication by removing housekeeping and other matters.

[3] We define broker preferencing to mean a marketplace feature that allows orders from the same participant or subscriber to execute ahead of other orders posted at the same price in a central limit order book.

[4] Market pegged orders are orders which automatically and continuously re-price, according to changes in a reference bid or offer.

place throughout the day, including a detailed description of each order type. This proposal will be part of a package of amendments to National Instrument 21-101 *Marketplace Operation* (NI 21-101) and National Instrument 23-101 *Trading Rules* that will deal with updating the regulatory regime for alternative trading systems.[5] CSA staff anticipate that the amendments will be published for comment by the Fall of 2010.

b. — Dissemination of IOIs by Dark Pools

The main issues related to IOIs disseminated by dark pools in order to attract order flow were:

- the point at which an IOI becomes an order[6] and becomes subject to the transparency requirements set out in Part 7 of NI 21-101; and

- the fairness and transparency of marketplaces' practices with respect to IOI dissemination.

- CSA and IIROC staff will be monitoring the initiatives taken in the U.S. with respect to "actionable IOIs".[7] CSA staff believes that enhanced transparency of marketplaces' practices regarding the dissemination of information respecting orders and trades, including the provision of IOIs, will also address some of the concerns raised.

- CSA staff are also considering providing clarification on the definition of an order and what features would qualify an IOI as an order.

c. — Use of SORs by Marketplaces

This issue revolves around the concept of a marketplace-owned smart order router using information about hidden orders on that marketplace when making routing decisions. Although some felt that this practice was not a concern as this is a routing decision only, others thought that all visible orders at a given price should have priority over all hidden orders.

CSA staff are assessing whether the use of marketplace-owned SORs which take into account hidden liquidity available on their own book gives that marketplace an unfair advantage over other marketplaces and SORs. CSA staff are also considering the impact that this practice has on investors and will be examining whether marketplaces that provide information on hidden liquidity to their proprietary SORs should be required to provide the same information to other third-party SORs in order to meet the fair access provisions of NI 21-101.[8]

d. — Market-Pegged Orders

Some forum participants raised concerns over market-pegged orders, specifically whether market-pegged orders have a negative impact on price discovery because they are simply free-riding the quotes from other marketplaces or whether the unrestricted use of such orders created a disincentive to display liquidity. Others were of the view that many order types are variations of pegs, and that the concept was simply centralizing a process which could be, and is currently, done by dealer algorithms or manually, and thus would result in a reduction of message traffic between market participants. This was also consistent with the majority of the responses to the Consultation Paper, which did not raise concerns with pegged orders. We will continue to review proposed order types from marketplaces.

e. — Price Improvement and Sub-Penny Pricing[9]

Forum participants discussed the idea of price improvement in dark pools, as well as the concept of sub-penny pricing. Questions were raised whether dark pools should always be required to offer price improvement, how much price improvement is meaningful, and whether sub-penny price improvement is desired or even relevant. It was noted that sub-penny price improvement may only be meaningful for dark pools achieving block sized execution, but is of questionable benefit to the overall market or to the investors for small orders. Participants also discussed the fairness of allowing dark pools to offer sub-penny price improvement while transparent markets are not allowed to offer the same execution opportunities. Some participants felt that sub-penny quoting on visible exchanges would not be desirable, one reason being the impact of increased messaging due to sub-penny pricing and marketplaces' technology infrastructure costs.

We will examine the issue of sub-penny pricing with the goal of assessing how any changes in either printing or quoting in sub-pennies would impact both the market as a whole, and the individual participants. Additionally, we will consider both transparent and dark markets, and whether principles of fairness would allow both types of venues to offer sub-penny price improvement and printing or execution, or whether different market structure models necessitate different treatment.

---

[5] This project will be the second phase to related initiatives set out in OSC Staff Notice 21-703 *Transparency of the Operations of Stock Exchanges and Alternative Trading Systems. [Editor's note: replaced by OSCN 21-706.]*

[6] NI 21-101 defines an order as meaning a firm indication by a person or company, acting as either principal or agent, of a willingness to buy or sell a security.

[7] SEC Release No. 34-60997 (October 21, 2009). The SEC proposed that, if the practical context in which IOIs are transmitted renders them "actionable", for example if they include sufficient information (including symbol, side (buy or sell), size (minimum of a round lot of trading interest), and price (explicit or implicit) they be included in the definition of "bid" or "offer" in Rule 600(b)(8) of Regulation NMS and thus become subject to transparency requirements.

[8] Subsections 5.1(b) and 6.13(b) of NI 21-101 require exchanges and ATSs, respectively, to not unreasonably prohibit, condition or limit access by a person or company to services offered by them.

[9] Subsection 6.1(1) of the UMIR does not allow the entry of orders on a marketplace at a price that includes a fraction or a part of a cent, other than orders with prices of less than $0.50 which may be entered to trade at an increment of one-half of one cent. However, executions for certain specialty orders (such as basis, call market or volume-weighted average price orders) may occur at sub-penny increments and may be reported in that fashion if permitted by the information processor or by the information vendor used by the marketplace.

Part 2: MARKET PARTICIPANTS

f. — Market Data Fees

Participants expressed concern that marketplace data fees are too high, especially in today's multiple marketplace environment where dealers need to consider data from all appropriate marketplaces, and not just those where a dealer is a participant. Some believed that dealers are, in effect, "captive consumers" of marketplaces' data, and that current fees for such data may not be commensurate with the marketplaces' market share or value of their data.

The CSA are currently conducting a review of all fees charged by marketplaces, including data fees. CSA staff's goal is to ensure that the costs involved with accessing services provided by marketplaces, including data, trading and routing are compliant with the fair access provisions in NI 21-101.[10]

g. — Electronic Trading and Direct Market Access

Some participants indicated that the regulators should examine the issues surrounding direct market access.

In April 2007, the CSA and IIROC published proposals relating to direct market access. Since that time, the market has changed, technology has significantly advanced and regulatory regimes governing direct market access have changed in other jurisdictions. As a result, CSA and IIROC staff have embarked on a broad scope review of electronic trading in Canada, including direct market access practices, with a view to assess what requirements are needed to address credit risk, market risk and systemic risk to the Canadian market. The objectives of the review of electronic trading include assessing what controls, filters and other mechanisms marketplaces and market participants should have to prevent errors at the order-entry stage and, in general, to promote fair and orderly markets.

As a result of the market volatility experienced on May 6th, 2010, we have expanded the scope of the project to include the examination of other electronic trading issues, including the need to standardize the volatility parameters used by Canadian marketplaces in times of extreme volatility.[11]

h. — High Frequency Trading

It was suggested at the forum that regulators also review high frequency trading, particularly as its growth may have impacted time priority benefits and the ability of some market participants to achieve trade execution. We continue to monitor developments in this area, and particularly recent initiatives in the U.S. aimed at reviewing short-term trading strategies and their impact on the market. A review of issues associated with high frequency trading was also included in the scope of the project to examine electronic trading discussed above.

IIROC staff continue to monitor changes in patterns of trading on Canadian marketplaces, and the impact of "high frequency trading" is included in that monitoring. Changes in technology and the development of competitive multiple marketplaces have significantly increased message traffic and order to trade ratios. Future rates of growth in high frequency trading will be dependent upon decisions which may be made with respect to such issues as sub-penny pricing.

i. — Other

A few forum participants were concerned that the scope of the Consultation Paper and of the forum discussions was limited to issues related to dark pools and certain order types. They indicated that the CSA and IIROC should expand their review and take a holistic view of the markets rather than considering the issues separately.

We believe that we are accomplishing this through our review of the issues discussed above. These issues are not considered in isolation and are, in many cases, related. We believe that our approach also allows us to focus our consultation with market participants on specific issues and to elicit meaningful comments.

III. — Conclusion

In the last few years, we have experienced significant developments in the Canadian capital markets. Most notably, the introduction of multiple marketplaces, which have different features and business models, has given rise to new market structure issues. We have described a number of initiatives currently in place to address such new issues. As we are working through these initiatives, we welcome any input and perspective of market participants. If you have any comments or questions, please contact any of the CSA or IIROC staff listed below.

[contacts and Appendix A and Appendix B omitted]

Policies and Orders: CSAN 23-311; OSCN 21-704.

CSA Staff Notice 23-309 — Frequently Asked Questions about the Order Protection Rule and Intentionally Locked or Crossed Markets — Part 6 of National Instrument 23-101 and Related Companion Policy

Date: **June 25, 2010**

33 O.S.C.B. 5761

---

[10]NI 21-101 5.1 and 6.13 state that exchanges and ATSs must not unreasonably prohibit, condition, or limit access by a person or company to services offered by it. As indicated in Companion Policy 21-101CP, these includes services related to data.

[11]Currently, some marketplaces use "freeze parameters" on their trading engines that allow them to freeze trading in specific securities where a significant price change occurs. This allows them to determine if a sudden price movement is due to potential erroneous trades. Currently, the use of these parameters is not consistent across the marketplaces.

The purpose of this notice is to answer some of the frequently asked questions (FAQs) regarding the Order Protection Rule (OPR) and the prohibition against intentionally locking or crossing markets.

The list of FAQs below is not exhaustive, but it includes key issues and questions discussed by the Trade-through Implementation Committee[1] or raised by other stakeholders. Staff of the Canadian Securities Administrators (CSA or we) may update these FAQs from time to time as necessary.

Some terms we use in this notice are defined in National Instrument 21-101 *Marketplace Operation* (NI 21-101) or in National Instrument 23-101 *Trading Rules* (NI 23-101).

Effective on February 1, 2011, the OPR will require marketplaces as well as marketplace participants that send directed action orders (DAOs), to establish, maintain and ensure compliance with written policies and procedures that are reasonably designed to prevent trade-throughs. To assist marketplaces and marketplace participants in developing these policies and procedures and complying with the OPR, we have compiled some of the issues and questions related to the OPR in the form of FAQs, together with our responses to the questions.

This notice also contains some FAQs regarding the provision that prohibits marketplace participants from intentionally locking or crossing markets. This provision is found in Part 6 of NI 23-101 but is separate from the OPR and is currently in force.

A. — Compliance with OPR Requirements

A-1 Q: When an entity is routing a DAO through a dealer that is a marketplace participant[2], who will be responsible for the proper use of the DAO marker?

A: A DAO may be routed in a variety of ways. We describe a number of DAO routing scenarios below and identify where the responsibility for proper use of the DAO marker would lie in each instance.

A: **Scenario 1**

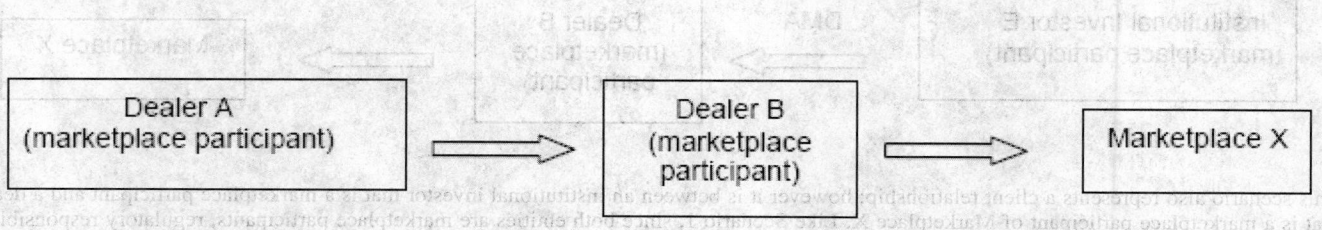

Dealer A is a marketplace participant but not a member or subscriber of Marketplace X. Dealer A's orders reach Marketplace X through Dealer B, which is a marketplace participant of Marketplace X. We consider this to be a jitney relationship between Dealer A and Dealer B. Under the OPR, regulatory responsibility for the proper use of a DAO marker rests with both Dealer A and Dealer B, since both are marketplace participants. However, they can agree about which of them will ensure proper use of the DAO marker. It is our view that reasonably designed written policies and procedures for Dealer A and Dealer B, respectively, include both clearly identifying which of them will ensure proper use of the DAO marker and requiring the other's acknowledgement.

Scenario 2

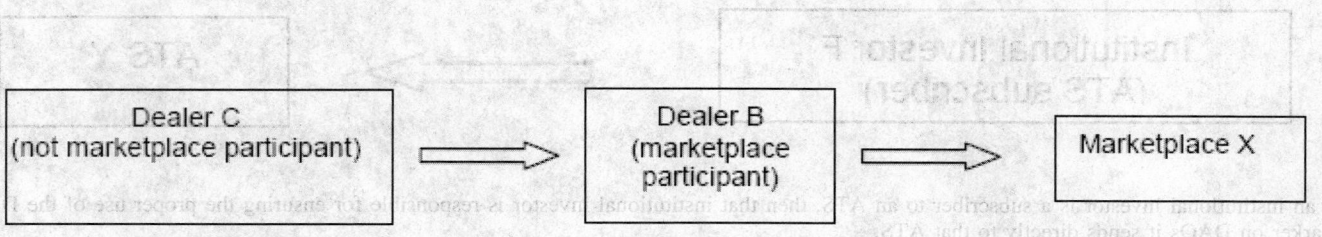

Dealer C is not a marketplace participant, therefore we consider this to be a client relationship between Dealer C and Dealer B. Dealer B is the only marketplace participant in this instance and therefore is responsible for proper usage of the DAO marker.

Scenario 3

The Trade-through Implementation Committee is an open membership committee comprised of representatives of dealers, marketplaces and vendors that has been meeting periodically since February 2009 to identify and resolve issues regarding the implementation of the OPR.

NI 21-101 defines a marketplace participant to mean a member of an exchange, a user of a quotation and trade reporting system, or a subscriber of an ATS.

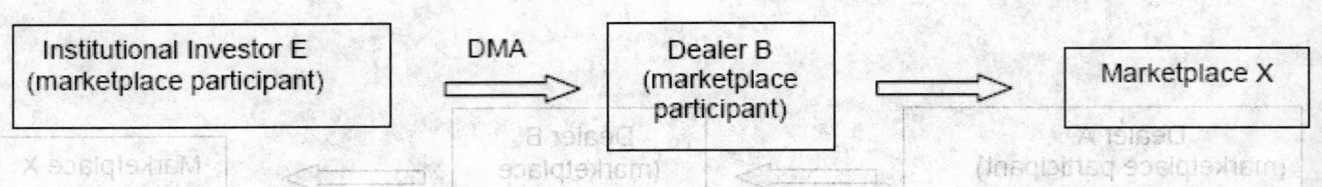

In this scenario, because Institutional Investor D is not a marketplace participant, we would consider this to be a client relationship between Institutional Investor D and Dealer B. Dealer B is the only marketplace participant in this scenario and therefore is responsible for proper usage of the DAO marker.

We note that it is up to a dealer to determine whether it will allow its clients to send DAOs to a marketplace via direct market access. In our view, reasonably designed written policies and procedures for a dealer offering this arrangement would include documenting this decision and the client's obligations.

Scenario 4

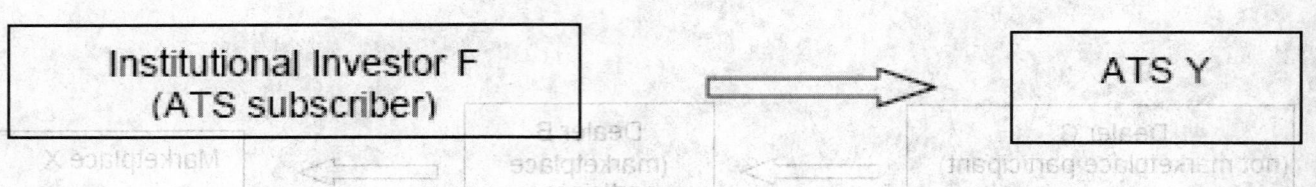

This scenario also represents a client relationship; however it is between an institutional investor that is a marketplace participant and a dealer that is a marketplace participant of Marketplace X. Like Scenario 1, since both entities are marketplace participants, regulatory responsibility for the proper use of a DAO marker rests with both the institutional investor and the dealer. However, they can agree about which of them will ensure proper use of the DAO marker. It is our view that reasonably designed written policies and procedures for the institutional investor and dealer, respectively, include both clearly identifying which of them will ensure proper use of the DAO marker and requiring the other's acknowledgement.

Scenario 5

Institutional Investor F
(ATS subscriber)   →   ATS Y

If an institutional investor is a subscriber to an ATS, then that institutional investor is responsible for ensuring the proper use of the DAO marker on DAOs it sends directly to that ATS.

A-2 Q: Who will enforce the OPR?

A: The OPR will be a CSA-level rule that will be enforced by the CSA. In addition, dealers will be subject to the Universal Market Integrity Rules (UMIR) of the Investment Industry Regulatory Organization of Canada (IIROC) related to the OPR and related policies, procedures and supervision. As all marketplaces have retained IIROC as a regulation services provider, IIROC will monitor compliance with UMIR and the OPR through its compliance reviews and surveillance of trading of its members (including ATSs) and access persons.[3] The CSA will also assess compliance of the OPR through their oversight reviews of exchanges.

A-3 Q: Sections 6.1(2) and 6.2(1) of Companion Policy 23-101CP (23-101 CP) will say that marketplaces or marketplace participants that use a DAO are expected to maintain relevant information so that the effectiveness of its policies and procedures can be adequately evaluated by regulatory authorities. What type of documentation needs to be kept in order to satisfy this expectation?

---

[3] "Access person" is defined in UMIR as "a person other than a Participant who is: (a) a subscriber; or (b) a user".

A: Each marketplace and marketplace participant that uses a DAO must regularly review its OPR policies and procedures. These reviews cover the effectiveness of the policies and procedures in place including the testing of any system used to facilitate OPR compliance. We recommend retaining documentation related to the reviews, any deficiencies found and any actions taken to address the deficiencies.

We also recommend that a marketplace or marketplace participant that uses a DAO keep or have access to a snapshot of what the market looked like at the time of making the routing decision and sending the DAO.

A-4 Q: Will the OPR require marketplaces to cancel any portion of a DAO that cannot be executed immediately?

A: No, the definition of a DAO will allow a marketplace to either book or cancel any unexecuted remainder of a DAO. Therefore, as part of its policies and procedures, a marketplace needs to clearly describe how it will treat unexecuted portions of DAOs and marketplace participants that send DAOs should verify the treatment of the DAO marker on that marketplace. To ensure the immediate cancellation of any remainder of a DAO that is not initially executed, marketplaces and marketplace participants sending a DAO should use the immediate-or-cancel (IOC) or fill-or-kill (FOK) designation if appropriate.

A-5 Q: Would the following scenario be compliant with the OPR: A marketplace participant that facilitates a manual block trade for a customer at a price that does not trade through a protected order at the time of the match, but when the trade is printed on a marketplace, the price is inferior to a protected order on another marketplace?

A: Yes, subsections 6.2(d) and 6.4(a)(iii) of NI 23-101 will provide some relief due to moving or changing markets.

Subsection 6.3(c) of 23-101CP (which discusses the "changing markets" exception in detail) states that the "changing markets" exception would allow for the execution of an order on a marketplace, within the best bid or offer on that marketplace but outside the best bid or offer displayed across marketplaces in the above circumstance.

A-6 Q: When a new marketplace launches, what OPR requirements must be met by: (i) the new marketplace, (ii) marketplaces in operation at that time and (iii) marketplace participants sending DAOs?

A: A new marketplace will have to establish, and be able to maintain and ensure compliance with, written policies and procedures that are reasonably designed to prevent trade-throughs prior to its launch.

A new marketplace is required under subsection 12.3(1) of NI 21-101 to publicly make available, for at least three months immediately before its operations begin, technology requirements regarding interfacing with or access to the marketplace in their final form. After publishing its technology requirements, subsection 12.3(2) of NI 21-101 requires a new marketplace to make testing facilities for interfacing with and accessing the marketplace publicly available for at least two months immediately before its operations begin.

A marketplace in operation at that time or a marketplace participant that sends DAOs should ensure it has appropriate access to the new marketplace in order to comply with its own OPR obligations.

B. — Systems Issues Requirements

B-1 Q: Will OPR requirements continue to apply when data is interrupted due to technical problems experienced by the information processor, an information vendor or an independent software vendor?

A: Yes, because the OPR will require that a marketplace or marketplace participant that sends DAOs establish, maintain and ensure compliance with written policies and procedures that are reasonably designed to prevent trade-throughs. Reasonably designed policies and procedures would include steps to address data interruptions.

We note that if a trade-through occurs due to a failure, malfunction or material delay of the systems, equipment or ability to disseminate marketplace data of the destination marketplace, the systems issues exception may be invoked.

B-2 Q: Subsection 6.3(1) of NI 23-101 will require that when a marketplace is aware it is experiencing a failure, malfunction or material delay of its systems, equipment or ability to disseminate marketplace data, it will inform all other marketplaces, its marketplace participants, any information processor, and any regulation services providers of the issue. What elements should be included in the policies and procedures of a marketplace with respect to this notification requirement?

A: In addition to notifying other marketplaces, marketplace participants, the information processor and the regulation services provider as will be required under subsection 6.3(1), marketplace policies and procedures should also address the requirement to promptly notify its regulator or, in Québec, the securities regulatory authority and, if applicable, its regulation services provider, of any material systems failure, malfunction or delay under subsection 12.1(c) of NI 21-101.

In addition, marketplaces have jointly created the "Canadian Marketplace Communication Protocol for Unplanned Service Interruptions", found at Schedule A of this Notice. This document sets out the elements and parameters around the notification procedures and protocols for the listed marketplaces which we recommend be included or referenced in the policies and procedures of all marketplaces.

B-3 Q: Subsections 6.3(2) and 6.3(3) of NI 23-101 will require that when a marketplace or marketplace participant suspects that a destination marketplace is experiencing a failure, malfunction or material delay of its systems, equipment or ability to disseminate marketplace data that it may bypass this marketplace (systems issues exception) subject to certain notification requirements. What should a marketplace or marketplace participant that sends DAOs include in its policies and procedures about invoking the systems issues exception?

A: We recommend that the policies and procedures of a marketplace participant that sends DAOs and a marketplace describe the following:

1. — Invoking and Ending the Use of the Systems Issues Exception

A marketplace's or marketplace participant's policies and procedures should include the circumstances in which it would invoke the systems issues exception. Such circumstances might include a destination marketplace repeatedly failing to provide an immediate response to orders received or material delays in the response time without notification by the destination marketplace that it may be experiencing systems issues.

The marketplaces, facilitated by the Investment Industry Association of Canada, created a "Marketplace Self-help Procedures" document, found at Appendix C to the Canadian Marketplace Communication Protocol for Unplanned Service Interruptions. This document lists the circumstances that will trigger individual marketplaces to rely on the systems issues exception. We recommend that marketplaces incorporate this element of the document into their OPR policies and procedures. We note that this document may be updated from time to time.

2. — Notification Process

The OPR will require in subsections 6.3(2) and 6.3(3) of NI 23-101 that a marketplace, and a marketplace participant sending DAOs, communicate their reliance on the systems issues exception. This notification may use various forms of technology, such as e-mail. We recommend incorporating how and when this notification will occur into the policies and procedures of marketplaces and marketplace participants that send DAOs.

We also recommend that marketplaces use a means of contact that is continuously monitored so that systems issues can be addressed promptly.

In addition to identifying the circumstances that will trigger the systems issues exception, the Marketplace Self-help Procedures document also outlines the communications steps each marketplace will take when it uses the systems exception against another marketplace. We recommend that this element of the document also be included in marketplace OPR policies and procedures.

3. — Systems Assessment

Subsection 6.3(a)(ii) of 23-101CP will explain that a marketplace, or marketplace participant sending DAOs, cannot invoke the systems issues exception against a marketplace unless it reasonably concludes that a particular marketplace is experiencing the problem. The systems issues exception is not available when the systems problem occurs at a vendor that provides services to a dealer.

Subsections 6.1(2) and 6.4(2) of NI 23-101 will require marketplaces and marketplace participants that use DAOs to regularly review and monitor the effectiveness of their OPR policies and procedures. As mentioned in question A-3 above, this includes the testing of any system used to facilitate OPR compliance. We view this as including the testing of:

- routing systems to ensure these systems are functioning properly; and

- the process to be conducted to ensure that the issue does not lie within the marketplace's, marketplace participant's or their vendor's own systems.

4. — Documentation of Reliance on Systems Exception

Subsection 6.1(3) of 23-101CP will provide guidance regarding marketplaces maintaining appropriate documentation when handling delayed responses. When relying on the systems issues exception, we recommend that marketplaces, and marketplace participants that use DAOs, maintain evidence of the problem, the notification provided and the systems assessment that was conducted.

C. — Locked or Crossed Markets[4]

C-1 Q: Is it permissible for a marketplace participant to join the bid or the offer if the market is already locked or crossed?

A: No, it is not permissible to simply join the bid or the offer when a market is locked or crossed.

Subsection 6.4(2)(c) of Companion Policy 23-101CP states that an example of a situation of where a locked or crossed market may occur unintentionally is when "the locking or crossing order was displayed at a time when a protected bid was higher than a protected offer". This is intended to include an order that is entered to uncross the market but not an order that simply joins the bid or the offer.

C-2 Q: What are some instances where a locked or crossed market may occur unintentionally?

A: Subsection 6.4(2) of Companion Policy 23-101CP outlines some situations where a locked or crossed market may occur unintentionally. There may be other situations where a locked or crossed market may also occur unintentionally including when securities legislation requires that the order be entered on or executed on a particular marketplace. For example, this might occur when securities being sold are subject to resale on a "designated offshore securities market" under Rule 904 of Regulation S of the *U.S. Securities Act* of 1933. Some other situations where a locked or crossed market may occur unintentionally include: (1) the execution of opening orders or market-on-close orders on a particular marketplace when trading is on-going or continues on at least one other marketplace and (2) the restarting of trading of a security on a marketplace following a halt for either regulatory or business purposes given that marketplaces may use different mechanisms to resume trading.

Schedule A — Canadian Marketplace Communication Protocol for Unplanned Service Interruptions

The objective of this Protocol document is to provide a clear framework detailing the minimum standards/benchmarks for communications when Canadian marketplaces experience an unplanned, material service interruption. The Protocol is a non-binding, best-practice guideline for industry-wide reference and adoption, intended to provide industry stakeholders with relevant information in a predictable and consistent manner when such interruptions occur. All Canadian markets as at the date of this document have agreed to use their best efforts to comply with the Protocol.

1. — Scope

The Protocol covers any unplanned material interruption to, or degradation of, a marketplace's service where the problem would cause the loss of integrity to the data stream; the loss of messages; stoppage or delay of updates; corruption of message formats or errors in content during normal operations; connectivity problems; stoppage or delay of order entry, order routing or other trading services (Material Service Interruption).

The scope of the Protocol is limited to notification schedules and communication processes, and includes the following elements:

- initial notice of the problem including what is affected and an estimate for restoring service;

---

[4]The prohibition on intentionally locking or crossing markets is set out in section 6.5 of NI 23-101.

- periodic follow-up until the problem is resolved;

- notice when service has been restored;

- preliminary and final description of the problem and how/when it will be / was fixed; and

- the requirement for contact names, numbers, points for escalation, and an open conference line that direct recipients can dial into wherever possible during actual events.

2. — Determination of Impact

It is in the discretion of each marketplace to determine if a problem is material in nature. In doing so, the following factors should be considered:

- number of participants unable to use the applicable marketplace service;

- degree of control the marketplace has over the service;

- impact on market liquidity and/or quality; and

- availability of other alternatives / workarounds.

Notification Guidelines	Preliminary Determination	Interim Updates	Service Restoration	Problem Resolution
Frequency	Upon becoming aware of a Material Service Interruption, the marketplace should notify all marketplace participants, service providers and/or stakeholders as appropriate (Recipients).	For longer outages, status updates should be provided whenever material information becomes known. Where no new information is available, marketplaces should communicate that fact to Recipients on at least an hourly basis.	The marketplace should provide notice that the service has been restored as soon as possible.	Within 24 hours after the problem has been resolved, the marketplace should provide a written (preliminary) assessment of the incident. If any further information comes to light, marketplaces should provide a final, written description of the incident within 1 week after this information becomes known.
Content	The initial notice should include, to the extent that the information is available: • a description of the problem; • what content and/or which systems are affected (particularly if the marketplace provides multiple feeds or services); • notice (or a reasonable projection) of when service will be restored or, if this is not possible, the next projected status update time; and	Interim updates should indicate progress toward resolution and an updated estimate of the resolution timeframe. The updates should also include any new information about the causes and impacts of the interruption.	The notice should: • provide times of when the incident began and when it was resolved • indicate whether restoration is partial or full • detail any elements of the service that may remain degraded	Marketplaces should provide a final, written description describing the problem, the permanent fix and any other steps, such as procedural, communications, hardware or software changes that have been or will be implemented to prevent a recurrence of the interruption. If the matter is still under investigation, this should be explained and further updates should be provided to fill in missing details.

Part 2: MARKET PARTICIPANTS

Notification Guidelines	Preliminary Determination	Interim Updates	Service Restoration	Problem Resolution
	• customer statements to Recipients (who can in turn pass on to their customers). If the outage is the result of a telecommunications problem, the marketplace should, when such information is known, provide details of the entity responsible for fixing the problem (e.g. the communications vendor, marketplace IT department or Recipient) and describe whether a restart of downstream devices or restart of an IP session is required. Timeliness of notification should supersede completeness of information when marketplaces are faced with such a trade-off.			If the fix is a temporary work-around with a permanent fix to come, this should be explained and target dates should be provided for the final resolution.

3. — Communication Channels

Notice should be disseminated via the appropriate electronic mechanisms, including telephone, e-mail, web site, pager, etc. Notice via logically formatted messages in the marketplace's data feed is the recommended method if the service itself is still available.

Follow-up updates may be provided in the same manner as the initial communication, or may be disseminated on a website accessible to Recipients, if the initial communication or any follow-up updates provide for such a procedure.

Where appropriate, marketplaces should also establish an open conference line that Recipients can dial into during a Material Service Interruption.

4. — Marketplace Resources and Contact Lists

Appendix A provides a list of contacts.

These contacts are responsible for initiating notices to recipients, and responding to any necessary inquiries from direct recipients; they should not also be responsible after recovery of the service, to ensure that there is no conflict with the requirement for customer notification and support. Attached is a list of the names and contact information. It is the obligation of each marketplace to inform the other marketplaces of any changes to this contact information.

5. — Marketplace Restart Procedures Following a Material Service Interruption

If a marketplace has suffered a Material Service Interruption, it will follow the procedures set out in Appendix B upon the restart of services.

6. — Marketplace Self-Help Procedures

If a marketplace declares self-help against another marketplace, it will follow the procedures set out in Appendix C.

Appendix A — Canadian Marketplace Contacts

Marketplace	Primary Contact	Phone	Email	Secondary Contact	Phone	Email	Open Conference Line
Alpha	General Client Services/ Operation Representative	647-259-0450	clientservices@alpha-trading-systems.ca	Lloyd Clarke, Manager, Trading Operations and Services Randee Pavalow, Head of Business Operations & Regulatory Matters	647-259-0460 647-259-0420	lloyd.clarke@ alphatradingsystems.ca Randee.pavalow@ alphatradingsystems.ca	
Chi-X	Chi-X Canada Operations	1-888-310-1560	operations@ chi-xcanada.com	Peter Trudeau, Director Subscriber and Vendor Services Dan Kessous, Chief Operating Officer	416-304-6373 416-304-6372	peter.trudeau@ chi-xcanada.com dan.kessous@ chi-xcanada.com	
Liquidnet		646-674-2100	memberservices@liquidnet.com				
Omega	Support	416-646-2428	support@omegaats.com	Raymond Tung Greg King	W: 416-646-2429 M: 416-660-6073 W: 416-646-2764 M:416-300-1585		
Pure Trading	CNSX Market Operations	416-306-0772	marketops@cnsx.ca	David Timpany	(b) 416-572-2000 ext 2290 (c) 416-917-1008	david.timpany@cnsx.ca	
TriAct-MATCH Now	Rob Durham — Trading Systems Administrator	416-861-1010 xO	support@triactcanada.com	Tom Doukas — Manager, Operations Heather Killian — Chief Operating Officer	416-861-1010 x0262	support@triactcanada.com hkillian@triactcanada.com	Distributed as required
TSX	Trading Services	416-947-4357 or TSX Vendor Services 416-947-4705	trading_services@tsx.com	Mark Jarrett — Director, Equity Operations John Washburn — Vice President, Business Operations	416-947-4693 416-947-4497	mark.jarrett@tsx .com john.washburn@tsx.com	Distributed as required

Appendix B — Canadian Marketplace Restart Procedures

Procedure	TSX/TSX-V	Alpha	Omega	Pure Trading	Chi-X	TriAct	Liquidnet
System outage however connection up	No new order flow/order modifications	No new orders/amends permitted until pre-open.	All orders are cancelled	All gateway connections are terminated	Status Orders	Cancel orders	Trading Halted. Negotiation cancelled
Notice to Members or Subscribers of Time of Restart	Yes	Yes	Yes	Yes	Yes	Yes	Yes
Type of Communication	Clients contacted through usual communication channels	Notice to Subscribers sent out via email.	E-mail to dealers and vendors	E-mail to CNSX Market Operations list and an admin msg over feed	E-mail to distribution list	E-mail to distribution list	E-mail to Members

Procedure	TSX/TSX-V	Alpha	Omega	Pure Trading	Chi-X	TriAct	Liquidnet
Pre-open rotation	Yes	Yes, during pre-open cancels and amends are allowed.	n/a	Yes		Yes	Not applicable
Typical time for Rotation	minimum of 30 minutes	Minimum of 30 minutes pre-open unless special circumstances. In each case notice of time period will be provided.	n/a	Depends		10 minutes+ 5 minutes/hour of outage	—
Post mortem e-mail		Yes, will be sent within 24 hours of service interruption	Sent to affected clients requesting a report		within 24 hours		Incident report created to document the event with root cause
Trading to not resume after a certain time		No				3:45 pm	Incident-by-Incident

Appendix C — Marketplace Self-help Procedures

Market Participants, including marketplaces, can declare self-help against a marketplace when a marketplace is having operational issues (failure, malfunction or material delay of its systems or equipment) which would make the routing of orders to that marketplace inappropriate. Notwithstanding any declaration of self-help by other marketplace participants, if a marketplace is aware of its own operational problems it should communicate in accordance with the principles set out in the Protocol document. Also, a marketplace participant cannot declare self-help against a marketplace when it is experiencing its own issues or is having problems with its vendor.

MARKETPLACE	REASONS FOR DECLARING SELF-HELP	COMMUNICATIONS AND ACTIONS REGARDING MARKETPLACE EXPERIENCING PROBLEMS
Alpha ATS	• Slow, Corrupted, or no Data from market-place • Connectivity to the marketplace is lost • Orders are not being received or processed	• Step 1 — Alpha contacts marketplace to report and inquire about issue. • Step 2 — Upon confirmation of the issue, self-help is declared with an email confirming the time and cause of the self-help declaration. A copy is sent to IIROC and OSC. • Step 3 — Notice to all marketplace participants of declaration of self help is issued. Receipt of data and routing to the marketplace is suspended. • Step 4 — Upon receipt from the marketplace of notification that the issue has been resolved, notice will be sent to marketplace, marketplace participants, and regulators that receipt of data and order routing will be resumed.
TriAct Canada Marketplace — MATCH Now	• Slow, Corrupted, or no Data from marketplace • Connectivity to the marketplace is lost	• Step 1 — TCM contacts marketplace to report and inquire about issue. • Step 2 — Upon confirmation of the issue, self-help is declared with an email confirming the time and cause of the self-help declaration. A copy is sent to IIROC. • Step 3 — Notice to all marketplace participants of declaration of self help is issued. Market data for the affected marketplace is removed from the NBBO calculation (used to determine MATCH Now pricing) • Step 4 — Upon receipt from the marketplace of notification that the issue has been resolved, TCM will confirm with market data vendor that feeds are stable and appear reliable. • Step 5 — Notice will be sent to marketplace, marketplace participants, and regulators revoking self-help and market data will be added back to the NBBO calculation
Chi-X	• Data issues or delays • Connectivity to the marketplace is lost • Orders are not being received or processed	• Step 1 — Chi-X contacts marketplace to report and inquire about issue. • Step 2 — Upon confirmation of the issue, self-help is declared with an email confirming the time and cause of the self-help declaration. A copy is sent to IIROC and OSC. • Step 3 — Self-help notice is sent to the trading community; Chi-X IOB and smart router remove target marketplace from consideration. • Step 4 — Upon written receipt from the marketplace that all outstanding issues have been resolved and stability can be confirmed, target marketplace will be reinstated for IOB and smart routing consideration.
Liquidnet ATS	• Self Help not applicable	Liquidnet ATS does not route
Omega ATS	• Self Help not applicable	Omega ATS does not route
TMX	• Material malfunction or interruption of order entry connectivity	• Step 1 — TSX Equity Operations will notify affected ATS by telephone, followed by an email, to inform the ATS that

MARKETPLACE	REASONS FOR DECLARING SELF-HELP	COMMUNICATIONS AND ACTIONS REGARDING MARKETPLACE EXPERIENCING PROBLEMS
	• Material malfunction or interruption of data connectivity/feeds • General system failure • Pattern of unreliable order execution	it intends or has begun to stop routing orders to ATS. The notice should include the time that problem was observed, the cause/basis of the concern, action taken by TMX and anticipated resolution criteria. • Step 2 — TSX Equity Operations will send a "Self-Help" notification to a TSX SOR e-mail distribution list which will include, but is not limited to, all TMX SOR subscribers and, IIROC. Should self-help status continue into subsequent trading day(s), Self Help Notification e-mail will be re-sent by 9:30AM of each day until resolved. • Step 3 — If the issue is resolved by TMX, TSX Equity Operations shall notify affected ATSs that the issue has been resolved and request that the cessation of routing services be revoked. • Step 4 — TMX Equity Operations will also send a Self-Help removal notification to a TSX SOR e-mail distribution list which will include, but is not limited to, all TMX SOR subscribers and IIROC.

Joint CSA/IIROC Staff Notice 23-311 — Regulatory Approach to Dark Liquidity in the Canadian Market

Date: July 29, 2011

34 O.S.C.B. 8219

I. — Introduction

The publication of this notice (Joint Notice) follows an extensive consultative process that started in 2009 regarding the use of dark liquidity on Canadian equity marketplaces. The Joint Notice describes the regulatory framework within which dark liquidity may be used in Canada and is being issued in conjunction with IIROC Notice 11-0225 (IIROC Notice) published today. The IIROC Notice seeks comment on proposed amendments to the Universal Market Integrity Rules (UMIR) respecting requirements governing dark liquidity on Canadian equity marketplaces (Proposed UMIR Amendments). The Proposed UMIR Amendments are being filed with the Canadian Securities Administrators (CSA) in accordance with the normal review process.

II. — Background

In late 2009, staff of the CSA and of the Investment Industry Regulatory Organization of Canada (IIROC) (together, we) published Joint CSA/IIROC Consultation Paper 23-404 *Dark Pools, Dark Orders, and Other Developments in Market Structure in Canada* (Consultation Paper).[1] The purpose of the Consultation Paper was to seek comment on a number of issues related to the impact of dark pools and dark orders[2] on various features of the Canadian market, including market liquidity, transparency, price discovery, fairness and integrity.

We received 23 response letters to the Consultation Paper and, on March 23, 2010, the CSA and IIROC hosted a forum (the Forum) to discuss further the issues raised in the Consultation Paper and the responses received. Themes discussed at the Forum included:

• Whether dark pools should be required to provide price improvement and if so, what is meaningful price improvement;

• The use of market pegged orders and whether those orders "free-ride" off the visible market;

• The use of sub-penny pricing;

• Broker preferencing at the marketplace level and dealer internalization of order flow;

• The use of indications of interest by dark pools to attract order flow; and

• The fairness of a marketplace offering smart order router services that use marketplace data that is not available to other market participants.

More details regarding the Forum are included in Joint CSA/IIROC Staff Notice 23-308 *Update on Forum to Discuss CSA/IIROC Joint Consultation Paper 23-404 "Dark Pools, Dark Orders and other Developments in Market Structure in Canada" and Next Steps*[3], published on May 28, 2010. That notice included a discussion of ongoing initiatives, proposed next steps, and a summary of the comments received in response to the Consultation Paper.

---

[1]Published at (2009) 32 OSCB, beginning at page 7877.

[2]In the Consultation Paper, dark pools were defined as marketplaces that provide no pre-trade transparency, and dark orders as orders with limited or no transparency.

[3]Published at (2010) 33 OSCB, beginning at page 4747.

On November 19, 2010, after considering the response letters and discussions with market participants on the topics discussed in the Consultation Paper and at the Forum, we published Joint CSA/IIROC Position Paper 23-405 *Dark Liquidity in the Canadian Market*[4] (Position Paper). The Position Paper outlined the preliminary responses of the CSA and IIROC to the following questions:

- Under which circumstances should dark pools or marketplaces that offer dark orders[5] be exempted from the pre-trade transparency requirements in National Instrument 21-101 *Marketplace Operation* (NI 21-101)?

- Should dark orders be required to provide meaningful price improvement over the national best bid or national best offer (NBBO) and under which circumstances?

- Should visible (lit) orders have priority over dark orders at the same price on the same marketplace?

- What is a meaningful level of price improvement?

The Position Paper did not address a number of issues discussed in the Consultation Paper and at the Forum, such as the use of indications of interest (IOIs) by dark pools to attract order flow, the fairness of a marketplace offering smart order routing (SOR) services that use marketplace data that is not available to other marketplace participants, and the practices of broker preferencing and internalization. Issues relating to the use of IOIs and SORs by certain marketplaces are being addressed in proposed amendments to NI 21-101 (Proposed NI 21-101 Amendments),[6] which were published for a 90 day comment period that ended on June 16, 2011. CSA staff are currently in the process of reviewing the comments received. The concept of broker preferencing and the internalization of order flow are also currently under review.

A summary of the recommendations in the Position Paper is set out below.

- **Recommendation 1** — The exemption to the pre-trade transparency requirements in NI 21-101 should only be available to an order that meets or exceeds a minimum size (the Dark Order Size Threshold); the Dark Order Size Threshold for posting passive dark orders would apply to all marketplaces, transparent or dark pools, regardless of the method of trade matching (including continuous auction, call or negotiation systems), and to all orders whether they are client, non-client or principal.

- **Recommendation 2** — Two dark orders meeting the Dark Order Size Threshold should be able to execute at the NBBO, and meaningful price improvement should be required in all other circumstances.

- **Recommendation 3** — On a marketplace, visible orders should execute before dark orders at the same price, but two dark orders meeting the Dark Order Size Threshold can be executed at that price ahead of visible orders.

- **Recommendation 4** — Meaningful price improvement should be one trading increment as defined in UMIR;[7] however, for securities with a difference between the best bid price and best ask price of one trading increment, one-half increment will be considered to be meaningful price improvement.

We received 20 comments to the Position Paper from buy and sell-side participants, marketplaces, and trade associations, and an independent consultant. We thank all the commenters. A summary of the comment letters received is included with this notice as well as a list of commenters.

III. — Regulatory Framework For Dark Liquidity

This Joint Notice describes and provides rationale for the steps being taken to implement the recommendations in the Position Paper, which is being effected through the Proposed NI 21-101 Amendments and the Proposed UMIR Amendments. The framework for dark liquidity in the Joint Notice and the Proposed UMIR Amendments are guided by the policy considerations outlined in the Position Paper to encourage the posting of orders on marketplaces' visible order books, while at the same time exposing as much liquidity as possible to the widest variety of market participants, including those using dark liquidity.

The Proposed NI 21-101 Amendments facilitate the implementation of Recommendation 1 by proposing a pre-trade transparency exemption that would require that a minimum size threshold be met. The Proposed UMIR Amendments would:

1. facilitate the implementation of Recommendation 1 by permitting IIROC to designate a minimum size for orders that are not displayed in a consolidated market display;

2. implement Recommendation 2 by providing that an order entered on a marketplace that trades with a dark order must receive meaningful price improvement, unless the former order exceeds a certain size threshold;

3. implement a variation of Recommendation 3 by providing that an order entered on a marketplace must trade with visible orders on that marketplace before trading with dark orders at the same price on that marketplace;[8]

4. implement Recommendation 4 by revising the definition of *better price* in section 1.1 of UMIR to be at least one trading increment as defined in UMIR or, for securities with a difference between the best bid and best ask price of one trading increment, of at least one-half of one trading increment.

---

[4]Published at (2010) 33 OSCB, beginning at page 10764.

[5]In the Position Paper, a dark pool referred to a marketplace that offers no pre-trade transparency on any orders, and a dark order referred to an order on any marketplace entered with no pre-trade transparency.

[6]Published at (2011) 34 OSCB (Supp-1).

[7]UMIR Rule 1.1 defines a "trading increment". UMIR Rule 6.1(1) states: "No order to purchase or sell a security shall be entered to trade on a marketplace at a price that includes a fraction or a part of a cent other than an increment of one-half of one cent in respect of an order with a price of less than $0.50."

[8]It should be noted that this is a variation from the recommendation in the Position Paper in that large dark orders would not be able to receive execution priority relative to visible orders at the same price. Further discussion regarding the rationale is included below.

In addition, the Proposed UMIR Amendments would include certain consequential amendments to other UMIR requirements, which are fully described in the IIROC Notice.

(a) — Definition of a dark order

As set out above, in the Position Paper, we referred to a dark order as an order on any marketplace that is entered with no pre-trade transparency and that is not required to be reported to an information processor or data vendor under the applicable rules. We indicated that a dark order does not include reserve or iceberg orders, as a portion of those orders is always displayed, and thus they contribute to the pre-trade price discovery process. We noted that dark orders can be entered on either a transparent marketplace or in a dark pool.

A few commenters to the Position Paper requested further clarification regarding the types of orders that would be considered dark orders, and specifically whether dark orders would include orders that are immediately filled or cancelled by marketplaces upon receipt (such as market, Immediate or Cancel and Fill or Kill orders). We confirm that immediately executable orders would not be considered dark orders for the purposes of our analysis, even though they do not have pre-trade transparency. Dark orders would also exclude specialty orders that may execute at a price outside the spread, such as orders entered on a matching facility of a marketplace during a separate opening or closing session of a marketplace.

The Proposed UMIR Amendments include a definition of a dark order that reflects these considerations.

(b) — Exemption from the pre-trade transparency requirements in NI 21-101

Part 7 of NI 21-101 sets out the information transparency requirements for marketplaces trading in exchange-traded securities. One of these requirements is that a marketplace that displays orders of exchange-traded securities must provide information regarding the orders displayed on that marketplace to an information processor.[9] An existing exemption from this requirement is available for orders that are only displayed to a marketplace's employees or those retained by the marketplace to assist in the operation of the marketplace.[10]

In the Position Paper, we recommended that the exemption from the pre-trade transparency requirements only apply to orders that meet the Dark Order Size Threshold. We requested feedback on what this minimum size should be. We also set out our expectation that marketplaces could not aggregate orders to meet the Dark Order Size Threshold and that, once posted, orders should not be changed to a quantity less than this threshold. In addition, where a dark order receives a partial fill which results in the remaining balance being less than the Dark Order Size Threshold, we indicated that the balance of the order could remain dark until fully executed or cancelled.

Approximately a third of the commenters were in favour of limiting the exemption from pre-trade transparency requirements to orders that meet a Dark Order Size Threshold for a number of reasons, including that this approach would help preserve the value and quality of the visible order book. The feedback received with respect to what would constitute an appropriate Dark Order Size Threshold varied, from 50 standard trading units[11] to suggestions that the threshold be based on a percentage of the average daily volume or a multiple of the average order size for a security.

The remainder of the respondents did not support establishing a Dark Order Size Threshold for a variety of reasons, including the small level of activity in dark pools and the lack of evidence of harm to market quality. In addition, some respondents indicated that dark pools allowed them to manage the impact costs of implementing trading strategies involving smaller order sizes.

We acknowledge that, to date, there has been limited activity in dark pools and no evidence that dark liquidity, including dark orders in visible marketplaces, has had a negative impact on the Canadian capital market. However, we are of the view that it is important and timely to establish a regulatory framework that can adapt to the changing market structure and developments, including an increasing number of dark pools and growth in the use of dark liquidity. In our view, this regulatory framework should include a requirement that orders meet a certain threshold in order to be entered without being subject to pre-trade transparency requirements. We continue to believe that transparency is a fundamental building block of a fair and efficient market. This has been our view since our consultation process began, and the framework will give regulators the ability to introduce a Dark Order Size Threshold to encourage transparency and to address risks to the quality of the price discovery process.

In order to implement this regulatory framework, the Proposed NI 21-101 Amendments included a requirement that orders meet a minimum size established by a regulation services provider in order to be exempt from the transparency requirements in NI 21-101.[12] No minimum order size was proposed.

In the Proposed UMIR Amendments published today, IIROC is proposing new UMIR Rule 6.5 that would permit IIROC to designate a minimum size for orders that are not displayed in a consolidated market display. The IIROC Notice also includes a description of the process to make a designation or change any designation and indicates that this process would involve consultation with both the public and the CSA. In addition, any size threshold proposed by IIROC would be subject to approval by the CSA. This would ensure that the process is transparent to the public, and that the public and the CSA have an opportunity to provide input.

---

[9] Subsection 7.1(1) of NI 21-101.

[10] Subsection 7.1(2) of NI 21-101. Rule 6.3 of UMIR also requires that a Participant immediately enter on a marketplace that displays orders in accordance with Part 7 of NI 21-101 a client order to purchase or sell 50 standard trading units or less of a security. This requirement is subject to certain exceptions, including when the client as specifically instructed the Participant to deal otherwise with the particular order (e.g. authorized the entry of the order on a dark pool).

[11] In respect to equity securities, UMIR defines a standard trading unit as being: (i) 1,000 units of a security trading at less than $0.10 per unit, (ii) 500 units of a security trading at $0.10 or more per unit and less than $1.00 per unit, and (iii) 100 units of a security trading at $1.00 or more per unit.

[12] See proposed amendments to sections 7.1 and 7.3 of NI 21-101.

At this time, neither the Proposed NI 21-101 Amendments nor the Proposed UMIR Amendments have included a specific Dark Order Size Threshold. However, in the coming months, we will examine the Canadian market and monitor market developments and regulatory approaches in other jurisdictions to determine the appropriate threshold.[13]

(c) — Price improvement by a dark order

Currently, orders posted in existing dark pools provide price improvement of at least 10% of the NBBO spread to all orders that execute against them. Dark orders entered on transparent marketplaces also provide price improvement, but have historically been permitted to trade at the NBBO, regardless of their size, as long as all visible orders and displayed portions of iceberg orders at the same price on that marketplace have been executed first.

In the Position Paper, we recommended that two dark orders should be allowed to trade at the NBBO only if both sides of the trade meet the Dark Order Size Threshold. We also recommended that meaningful price improvement should be provided by dark orders in all other circumstances. We indicated that both orders trading at the NBBO must be marked as "dark" to ensure that only those orders specifically utilizing the recommended minimum size exemption can do so, and not traditional liquidity-removing orders. Our position acknowledged that the execution of dark orders meeting the Dark Order Size Threshold contributes to the price discovery process through immediate post-trade transparency. In addition, it was our view that the size of the transaction may provide sufficient information to participants to stimulate further trading that might not otherwise have occurred in the absence of such a large-sized execution. These factors, in our view, justified allowing the execution of large dark orders without price improvement. We also discussed what would be considered to be meaningful price improvement.

The majority of the commenters supported the position that two dark orders meeting the Dark Order Size Threshold should be able to execute at the NBBO and that meaningful price improvement should be required in all other circumstances. A few, however, were not supportive, with one commenter being of the view that dark orders should be able to execute at the NBBO regardless of size.

We maintain our view that a dark order could execute at the NBBO in certain circumstances. The Proposed UMIR Amendments would require, subject to certain exceptions, that an order entered on a marketplace that trades with an order that has not been displayed in a consolidated market display either receive price improvement, or be for more than 50 standard trading units or have a value of more than $100,000. We are not requiring that such orders be marked "dark" in order to be able to trade with a passive dark order at the NBBO, as was recommended in the Position Paper. The requirement to mark these orders as "dark" was based on the fact that the Position Paper also recommended that two large dark orders meeting the Dark Order Size Threshold could execute at the NBBO ahead of visible orders at the same price. As will be discussed in the following section, we have revised our position with respect to the priority of order execution at the NBBO, and are of the view that visible orders on the same marketplace at the same price should always have priority. As such, it would be unnecessary to require a marketable order executing at the NBBO to be marked "dark", as it will be required to first displace any visible orders on that marketplace at the same price.

We acknowledge that requiring price improvement in specific cases may impact certain marketplaces' business models, as some transparent marketplaces offering dark order types currently allow marketable orders of any size to trade with a dark order at the NBBO. We are of the view, however, that any associated cost is justified for the reasons outlined above. As result, existing marketplaces that allow smaller orders to trade with dark orders at the NBBO would not be grandfathered from this requirement.

(d) — Execution priority of orders entered on the same marketplace at the same price

In the Position Paper, we expressed our view that visible orders on a marketplace should execute before dark orders at the same price on the same marketplace. We recommended an exception for two dark orders meeting the Dark Order Size Threshold to acknowledge the contribution such orders have to the price and size discovery process.

The majority of commenters were supportive of the above recommendation. A few supported the concept of visible orders executing before dark orders, but did not support an exception for two large dark orders.

We continue to be of the view that visible limit orders should execute before dark orders when they are on the same marketplace and at the same price. Proposed UMIR Rule 6.6, part of the Proposed UMIR Amendments, would introduce a formal requirement that visible orders receive execution priority relative to dark orders, when they are on the same marketplace and at the same price. This priority may not be circumvented by any dark orders, regardless of their size. This is a variation from our original recommendation in the Position Paper. After reviewing the comments received and the IOSCO Principles on Dark Liquidity,[14] we have reconsidered our position and are of the view that visible limit orders should always have priority over dark orders. This priority encourages visible liquidity in marketplaces and is fundamental to the protection of the price discovery process.

(e) — Meaningful price improvement

Currently, orders posted in existing dark pools provide price improvement to all orders that execute against them. Additionally, dark orders entered on transparent marketplaces may also trade against other orders at the NBBO, regardless of their size, as long as all visible and displayed portions of iceberg orders at the same price on that marketplace have been executed first. The amount or percentage of price improvement is at the discretion of the marketplace and may be as low as 10% over the NBBO.

---

[13]Notwithstanding that no Dark Order Size Threshold has been established, dealers that are Participants under UMIR will continue to be subject to the existing "Order Exposure Rule" that requires client orders for 50 standard trading units or less of a security to be immediately entered on a transparent marketplace. The rule is subject to a number of exceptions, including when the client has specifically instructed the Participant to deal otherwise with the particular order or the Participant executes the order upon receipt at a better price. IIROC accepts that a Participant may check a Dark Pool for a better price but any unexecuted portion of the order must then be entered on a marketplace that provides order transparency.

[14]Available at: http://www.iosco.org/library/pubdocs/pdf/IOSCOPD336.pdf.

Part 2: MARKET PARTICIPANTS

In the Position Paper, we discussed that one of the factors to be considered in determining what level of price improvement might be considered "meaningful" is examining whether there is a "tipping point" at which the individual benefit to an order receiving price improvement becomes outweighed by the risks to the overall quality of the market if increased numbers of orders are entered on marketplaces without pre-trade transparency. If small fractions of price improvement can facilitate an execution in front of a visible quote, the incentives to displaying a visible quote may be weakened. Our view, as expressed in the Position Paper, was that meaningful price improvement occurs when the price is improved over the NBBO by a minimum of one trading increment as defined in UMIR, except where the NBBO spread is already one trading increment. In that case, meaningful price improvement would be at least half of the applicable trading increment.

Comments received on the above recommendation were mixed. Many were in favour of the recommendation regarding price improvement. Some agreed that there should be meaningful price improvement, but did not support the CSA and IIROC's view regarding the amount. A few commenters did not agree with the notion of meaningful price improvement and indicated that any dark order should be allowed to execute at the NBBO.

After considering the comments received, we continue to be of the view that price improvement must be meaningful in order to avoid or minimize harm to the price discovery process through the increasing use of dark liquidity. One of the goals of our recommendation in the Position Paper was to limit the practice of providing increasingly smaller amounts of price improvement to achieve execution in front of visible orders and consequently decreasing the incentive to enter visible orders.

We do not believe that price improvement below one trading increment (except when the spread is at one trading increment) is meaningful to ensure that the benefit to investors from receiving price improvement outweighs the cost, whether quantified or unquantified,[15] of lost opportunities to trade because of dark orders offering minimal price improvement "jumping the queue".

As a result, we are moving forward with defining meaningful price improvement as proposed in the Position Paper. To implement this recommendation and the level of price improvement in the Position Paper, it is proposed that the definition of "better price" in UMIR be revised through the Proposed UMIR Amendments.

Dark orders on all marketplaces would have to provide this level of price improvement, including orders entered on dark pools and orders entered on transparent marketplaces offering dark order types. This requirement would also level the playing field between dark pools and transparent marketplaces, as they each could provide functionality allowing dark orders to trade at the NBBO in certain circumstances, and in all other circumstances provide price improvement of at least one half of the trading increment, which in some cases may be less than one penny.

IV. — International Developments

(a) — IOSCO Principles on Dark Liquidity

On May 20, 2011, the Technical Committee of the International Organization of Securities Commissions (IOSCO) published a final report, Principles on Dark Liquidity, containing principles to assist securities markets authorities in dealing with issues concerning dark liquidity.

We believe that, if implemented, the Proposed NI 21-101 Amendments and the Proposed UMIR Amendments would compliment the existing regulatory structure governing dark liquidity and increase consistency with the principles of the Technical Committee by:

- establishing a regulatory framework that would allow dark liquidity but manage its impact on price discovery, fairness and overall market quality; and

- mandating that transparent orders would have priority over dark orders at the same price within a marketplace, and thus promoting the use of transparent orders.

In this section, we have identified each IOSCO principle and have discussed the Canadian regulatory approach.

IOSCO Principle 1: The price and volume of firm orders should generally be transparent to the public. However, regulators may choose not to require pre-trade transparency for certain types of market structures and orders. In these circumstances, they should consider the impact of doing so on price discovery, fragmentation, fairness and overall market quality.

Canadian regulatory approach

In our view, the Canadian approach both currently in place and as proposed meets this principle. With respect to existing requirements, NI 21-101 requires that information relating to all orders be provided to and publicly disseminated by an information processor, unless that order is shown only to the employees of a marketplace, or a person or company retained to assist with its operation. As such, while pre-trade transparency is generally required, our existing regulatory framework, and specifically the exemption described above, permits the existence of dark pools and dark orders.

In addition, Rule 6.3 of the UMIR *Exposure of Client Orders* (the Order Exposure Rule) promotes transparency of small-sized orders, by requiring that a Participant immediately enter on a marketplace that displays orders a client order to purchase or sell 50 standard trading units or less unless, among other exceptions, the Participant provides price improvement to that order.

New requirements have been proposed only after extensive consideration of the impact of dark liquidity on price discovery, fairness and market quality. The CSA proposal to introduce a minimum size threshold in order to be exempt from the transparency requirements in NI 21-101, along with the Proposed UMIR Amendments that would permit IIROC to designate a minimum size for such orders, would establish a

---

[15]For example, an investor posting a non-marketable limit order may incur the unquantifiable loss of missing an execution if a dark order steps in front of their order and provides a minimal amount of price improvement to the contra-side marketable order that would have executed against the investor's order. To avoid this potential outcome, the investor could adjust the limit price of its order and pay the full spread, thus incurring a quantifiable loss.

new framework which seeks to balance the desire of participants to use dark liquidity and the potential negative impact on overall market quality.

IOSCO Principle 2: Information regarding trades, including those executed in dark pools or as a result of dark orders entered in transparent markets, should be transparent to the public. With respect to the specific information that should be made transparent, regulators should consider both the positive and negative impact of identifying a dark venue and/or the fact that the trade resulted from a dark order.

Canadian regulatory approach

NI 21-101 requires that information regarding all trades, including those executed on transparent marketplaces or dark pools, be disseminated to an information processor for inclusion in consolidated information in real time. Trade information is also disseminated by data vendors and includes all pertinent information including the identity of the marketplace, the security's symbol, quantity, price and time.

IOSCO Principle 3: In those jurisdictions where dark trading is generally permitted, regulators should take steps to support the use of transparent orders rather than dark orders executed on transparent markets or orders submitted into dark pools. Transparent orders should have priority over dark orders at the same price within a trading venue.

Canadian regulatory approach

In Canada, there are already a number of incentives to foster the use of transparent orders, such as the Order Exposure Rule discussed above, as well as the Order Protection Rule (OPR)[16] which requires marketplaces to have policies and procedures that are reasonably designed to prevent trade-throughs. Specifically, OPR ensures that immediately accessible, visible, better-priced limit orders are executed prior to inferior-priced limit orders.

We currently require and the Proposed UMIR Amendments would codify that visible orders must be given priority over dark orders at the same price on the same marketplace. Specifically, an order entered on a marketplace must trade with visible orders on that marketplace before trading with dark orders at the same price on that marketplace.

IOSCO Principle 4: Regulators should have a reporting regime and/or means of accessing information regarding orders and trade information in venues that offer trading in dark pools or dark orders.

Canadian regulatory approach

IIROC receives, in real-time, order and trade information from all marketplaces, including dark pools. In addition, alternative trading systems are currently required by NI 21-101 to provide to the CSA quarterly reports regarding trade information. In the Proposed NI 21-101 Amendments, the CSA proposed to enhance this reporting to include additional information regarding dark orders and trading activity to give us an overview of the activities of marketplaces.[17]

IOSCO Principle 5: Dark pools and transparent markets that offer dark orders should provide market participants with sufficient information so that they are able to understand the manner in which their orders are handled and executed.

Canadian regulatory approach

In the Proposed NI 21-101 Amendments, the CSA proposed that all marketplaces, including dark pools and transparent marketplaces that offer dark orders, disclose on their website information regarding their operations, including a description of how orders are entered, how they interact and execute, the order types they offer, and the marketplaces' access requirements.

IOSCO Principle 6: Regulators should periodically monitor the development of dark pools and dark orders in their jurisdictions to seek to ensure that such developments do not adversely affect the efficiency of the price formation process, and take appropriate action as needed.

Canadian regulatory approach

The CSA and IIROC monitor closely the trading activity on all marketplaces, including dark pools and transparent marketplaces offering dark order types. We review the operations of marketplaces that propose to operate in Canada, including dark pools, before they commence their operations. We also review changes to existing marketplace operations, which may include new order types or changes to order types. Our review allows us to understand the impact of dark pools and dark orders in the Canadian capital market, and to take appropriate action when there is a risk that such developments may have a negative impact on the quality of the Canadian capital market.

(b) — Other Relevant Current International Work

The proposed regulatory framework related to dark liquidity is also consistent with steps being considered or taken by other regulatory authorities. For example, the Australian Securities and Investments Commission (ASIC) released, on April 29, 2011, new market integrity rules for competition in exchange markets.[18] ASIC has introduced requirements with respect to pre-trade transparency, and has specifically introduced a framework which includes a minimum threshold for exemption from the pre-trade transparency requirements, initially set at zero. This will enable ASIC to respond quickly if there is a shift of liquidity from the pre-trade transparent market in the short term at a level that would affect the price formation process. ASIC intends to undertake further consultation in Q3 of this year taking account of the responses it received to its earlier consultation with the aim of adopting revised rules in early 2012.

[16]National Instrument 23-101 *Trading Rules*, Part 6.

[17]Proposed Form 21-101F3 *Quarterly Report of Marketplace Activities*, available at (2011) 34 OSCB (Supp-1), beginning at page 57.

[18]Available at http://www.asic.gov.au/asic/ASIC.NSF/byHeadline/Market%20integrity%20rules.

In Europe, Directive 2004/39/EC, promulgated under the Markets in Financial Instruments Directive (MiFID), is being reviewed by the European Commission and the European Securities and Markets Authority (ESMA). As part of its own review, ESMA published a consultation paper[19] on equity markets which includes, among other things, the examination of existing pre-trade transparency waivers provided under MiFID and policy options regarding crossing systems and processes operated by investment firms. In July 2010, EMSA published a report[20] in which it recommended, among others, that the existing exceptions to pre-trade transparency continue to be allowed under certain circumstances, and that the European Commission undertake or commission further analytical work regarding the existing thresholds.

On February 18, 2011, the Joint CFTC-SEC Advisory Committee on Emerging Regulatory Issues presented its summary report, containing 14 recommendations regarding regulatory responses to the market events of May 6, 2010.[21] The Committee's report included the following two recommendations:

> 11. The Committee recommends that the SEC conduct further analysis regarding the impact of a broker-dealer maintaining privileged execution access as a result of internalizing its customer's orders or through preferencing arrangements. The SEC's review should, at a minimum, consider whether to (i) adopt its rule proposal requiring that internalized or preferred orders only be executed at a price materially superior (e.g., 50 mils for most securities) to the quoted best bid or offer, and/or (ii) require firms internalizing customer order flow or executing preferenced order flow to be subject to market maker obligations that require them to execute some material portion of their order flow during volatile market periods.

> 12. The Committee recommends that the SEC study the costs and benefits of alternative routing requirements. In particular, we recommend that the SEC consider adopting a "trade at" routing regime. The Committee further recommends analysis of the current "top of book" protection protocol and the costs and benefits of its replacement with greater protection to limit orders placed off the current quote or increased disclosure of relative liquidity in each book.

To date, the SEC has not proposed any rules or regulations based on these two recommendations, and we will continue to monitor regulatory developments in the United States on these and other key issues.

V. — Conclusion

Market structure in Canada has experienced many new developments, including the increased use of dark liquidity, whether in dark pools or as dark orders on transparent marketplaces. Our regulatory objectives in undertaking a review of dark liquidity were to establish a framework which recognizes the need for dark liquidity, promotes innovation and accommodates different market models and marketplace features, while at the same time protecting the integrity of the price discovery process.

We believe that the Proposed NI 21-101 Amendments and the Proposed UMIR Amendments will establish this framework. We recognize the benefits of dark liquidity, and the fact that it is still a small component of the existing market structure. However, we continue to be of the view that it is critical to introduce a framework for our market that fosters fairness, efficiency and confidence. In our view, the framework being proposed will achieve this goal by protecting price discovery and market quality. It will:

- encourage the use of visible orders, by ensuring the priority of visible orders over dark orders at the same price on the same marketplace;

- acknowledge the contribution of dark orders to the post-trade price discovery process and their value to certain investors; and

- ensure meaningful price improvement and level the playing field between transparent marketplaces and dark pools.

[Contacts, Summary of Public Comments and List of Commenters omitted]

CSA/IIROC Joint Notice 23-312 — Transparency of Short Selling and Failed Trades

Date: March 2, 2012

35 O.S.C.B. 2099

[Not reproduced]

Multilateral CSA Staff Notice 23-313 — Blanket Orders Exempting Marketplace Participants from Certain Provisions of National Instrument 23-103 Electronic Trading and Related OSC Staff Position

Date: December 7, 2012

35 O.S.C.B. 11134

[Not reproduced]

---

[19]CESR consultation paper ref: CESR/10-394, CESR Technical Advice to the Commission in the Context of the MiFID Review — Secondary Markets, April 2010, available at http://www.esma.europa.eu.

[20]CESR Technical Advice to the European Commission in the Context of the MiFID Review and Responses to the European Commission Request for Additional Information, available at http://www.esma.europa.eu/index.php?page=document_details&from_title=Documents&id=7003.

[21]Published at: http://www.cftc.gov/ucm/groups/public/@aboutcftc/documents/file/jacreport_021811.pdf.

CSA Staff Notice 23-314 — Frequently Asked Questions about National Instrument 23-103 Electronic Trading

Date: December 20, 2012

35 O.S.C.B. 11460

The purpose of this notice is to answer some of the frequently asked questions (FAQs) regarding National Instrument 23-103 *Electronic Trading* (the rule or NI 23-103). NI 23-103 is effective on March 1, 2013 and sets out requirements that apply to marketplace participants, marketplaces and the use of automated order systems in order to address the risks of electronic trading.

The list of FAQs below is not exhaustive, but it includes key issues and questions market participants have posed to us. Staff of the Canadian Securities Administrators (CSA or we) may update these FAQs from time to time as necessary.

Some terms we use in this notice are defined in NI 23-103, National Instrument 21-101 *Marketplace Operation* (NI 21-101) or in National Instrument 23-101 *Trading Rules*.

A. — Scope of NI 23-103

A-1 Q: Does NI 23-103 apply to all securities trading activity on Canadian marketplaces, including debt and derivatives?

A: The scope of NI 23-103 is set out in subsection 1.1(2) of Companion Policy 23-103CP (CP). The rule applies to the electronic trading of securities, including debt securities, on marketplaces in Canada. NI 23-103 requires marketplace participants to ensure compliance with marketplace and regulatory requirements.

As set out in NI 21-101 and incorporated in NI 23-103, in Québec, standardized derivatives are considered to be securities and therefore the electronic trading of standardized derivatives on a marketplace in Québec would be subject to the requirements of NI 23-103. NI 23-103 and the CP also provide interpretations of "security" in Alberta, British Columbia and Ontario.

A-2 Q: Does NI 23-103 apply to all orders executed on a marketplace or only to orders generated by an automated order system?

A: The rule applies to the electronic trading of securities on marketplaces in Canada. Therefore, NI 23-103 applies to all orders sent electronically to a marketplace whether generated by an automated order system or not. This means that NI 23-103 applies to orders manually handled by a marketplace participant but sent electronically to a marketplace.

B. — Pre-Trade Risk Management and Supervisory Controls

B-1 Q: What, if any, automated pre-trade controls are required for orders intermediated by a marketplace participant?

A: Subsection 3(3) of NI 23-103 sets out the minimum requirements regarding pre-trade risk controls including those relating to capital, credit, price and volume. Subsection 3(4) of the CP provides further guidance on minimum risk management and supervisory controls, policies and procedures.

It is important to note that each marketplace participant must examine its own business model to manage its financial, regulatory and other risks associated with marketplace access or providing clients with access to a marketplace. This examination will drive the specific controls that the marketplace participant will have to establish.

B-2 Q: Do pre-trade credit checks apply to proprietary order flow?

A: The requirement under subparagraph 3(3)(a)(i) of NI 23-103 is that a marketplace participant's risk management and supervisory controls, policies and procedures must be reasonably designed to prevent the entry of one or more orders that would result in exceeding pre-determined credit or capital thresholds of the marketplace participant. Therefore, all order flow that is sent electronically by a marketplace participant to a marketplace, including proprietary order flow, would be subject to pre-trade capital or credit checks as applicable.

B-3 Q: Where should pre-trade risk controls be placed with respect to smart order routers?

A: NI 23-103 does not specify where the mandatory pre-trade risk controls should be placed with respect to a smart order router and therefore it is up to the marketplace participant to determine the optimal location of its pre-trade risk controls. Under section 3(2) of the rule, orders must pass through automated pre-trade risk filters that are under the control of the marketplace participant before being entered on a marketplace. Therefore, if orders do not pass through automated controls that have been set by the marketplace participant prior to entry to a smart order router, the automated controls would have to be placed at the smart order router level.

We also note that under subsection 5(1) of NI 23-103, a marketplace participant must take all reasonable steps to ensure that the use of an automated order system, including a smart order router, by itself or any client, does not interfere with fair and orderly markets. Therefore, a marketplace participant must have a way to monitor if a smart order router used by itself or any client malfunctions and erroneously sends orders to a marketplace.

B-4 Q: If a client is a DEA client and also sends orders to trading desks of the same firm, does the marketplace participant need to enforce an aggregated pre-trade capital limit on all of its client's trading with the firm, whether by DEA, telephone or orders sent to a sales trader?

A: If a marketplace participant does not enforce a pre-trade capital limit aggregated in real-time on all of its client's trading with the firm, a marketplace participant should establish separate limits for the various trading channels (both electronic and non-electronic) the DEA client uses at the firm. We emphasize that these limits need to be established in light of the marketplace participant's total financial exposure that can result from its client's order flow. A marketplace participant must first have a good understanding of its total exposure with respect to a specific client and then set pre-trade capital limits for each trading channel accordingly. The limits do not need to be electronically linked, but do need to consider the total exposure the marketplace participant faces with respect to its client.

B-5 Q: Is it acceptable for a marketplace participant to place separate pre-trade limits on each electronic marketplace access channel used by a client and continue to assess the aggregate risk posed by that client on a post-trade basis?

A: Yes. Pre-trade credit and capital limits may be applied to different electronic marketplace access channels separately but need to be determined in the aggregate as discussed in the answer to question B-4. We emphasize that it is important when setting limits in this manner that the limits be established in order to manage the total financial exposure of the marketplace participant that might result from its client.

B-6 Q: Must a marketplace participant's pre-trade risk controls take into account the threshold limits applicable to marketplaces established under section 8 of NI 23-103?

A: IIROC is currently consulting industry participants regarding the manner and levels at which the marketplace thresholds should be set. We note that the obligation in section 8 of NI 23-103 to not execute orders that exceed the price and volume thresholds as set by a regulation services provider or a marketplace that directly monitors the conduct of its participants rests with the marketplace, not the marketplace participant. Therefore, a marketplace participant is not obligated under NI 23-103 to specifically prevent sending orders that exceed a set marketplace threshold.[1]

B-7 Q: Are pre-determined capital or credit thresholds to be based on: (i) all outstanding open orders in the marketplace, (ii) all orders staged to go out to the marketplace, open on the marketplace, and executed or (iii) executed orders only?

A: Guidance regarding the setting of pre-determined credit or capital thresholds is found in subsection 3(5) of the CP. Specifically, the CP notes that pre-determined credit or capital thresholds may be set based on different criteria, such as per order, per trade account, trading strategies or using a combination of these factors. The CP also states that the marketplace participant may also consider measuring compliance with set credit or capital thresholds on the basis of orders entered rather than executions obtained. In general, it is up to the marketplace participant to determine the best method as to how to set the pre-determined capital or credit threshold in order to manage the risks associated with marketplace access or providing clients with access to a marketplace. Regardless of how the marketplace participant measures compliance with its thresholds, the marketplace participant should consider whether to take into account the existence of executed but unsettled trades, including those from previous days. We expect that this consideration would be driven by the marketplace participant's assessment of its business model's risks.

B-8 Q: Please clarify what aggregate margin and capital limits would be required.

A: We are of the view that a one-size-fits-all approach with respect to limits for capital thresholds would not best serve our markets and therefore there are no specific capital limits that are mandated under NI 23-103. The rule uses a principles based approach that provides a marketplace participant with flexibility in setting limits that are appropriate to its business model and risk tolerance. This approach is also in line with current global standards.

B-9 Q: Is a marketplace participant required to set risk controls to avoid price movements that trigger the single stock circuit breakers (i.e. reject orders that may impact price by greater than 10%)?

A: No. NI 23-103 does not require a marketplace participant to set risk controls that would prevent price movements that trigger the single stock circuit breakers; however, this would not preclude a marketplace participant from doing so if it thought important to manage its risks associated with marketplace access or providing clients with access to a marketplace.[2]

B-10 Q: As noted in the introduction of the CP, the intent of NI 23-103 is to focus on the gate-keeping functions of the executing broker. It is also noted that the clearing broker bears some responsibility in managing its risks under National Instrument 31-103 *Registration Requirements, Exemptions and Ongoing Registrant Obligations* **(NI 31-103). Are executing and clearing brokers required to share client information for the purposes of managing the pre-trade risk settings under NI 23-103?**

A: There is no requirement under NI 23-103 for executing and clearing brokers to share client information for the purposes of managing pre-trade risk thresholds; however, a clearing broker may choose to require this information before continuing to provide its clearing services in order to meet its requirement under NI 31-103 to manage the risks of its business in accordance with prudent business practices.

B-11 Q: Since each ATS is also registered as a dealer, will an ATS be responsible for assigning limits for its subscribers?

A: No. The marketplace participant is obligated under section 3(1) of NI 23-103 to establish, maintain and ensure compliance with risk management and supervisory controls, policies and procedures that are reasonably designed to manage the risks associated with marketplace access or providing clients with access to a marketplace.

Third parties, including marketplaces, may provide the automated pre-trade risk controls required under section 3(2); however, as set out in section 3(5) of NI 23-103, a marketplace participant must directly and exclusively set and adjust the risk management and supervisory controls, policies and procedures, including those provided by third parties.

B-12 Q: May a third-party vendor set or adjust pre-trade risk limits at the specific written request of a marketplace participant?

---

[1]However, if the trading of the marketplace participant is subject to the Universal Market Integrity Rules, IIROC will expect that the parameters be set to prevent an order exceeding the marketplace thresholds applicable to the marketplace on which the order is intended to be entered to the extent that such marketplace thresholds are publicly disclosed and readily ascertainable. See IIROC Notice 12-0364 — Rules Notice — Guidance Note — UMIR — *Guidance Respecting Electronic Trading* (December 7, 2012). At this time, IIROC has not established guidance on acceptable marketplace thresholds.

[2]However, if the trading of the marketplace participant is subject to the Universal Market Integrity Rules, IIROC will expect that the parameters be set to prevent an order exceeding the limits publicly disclosed by IIROC for the exercise of the power of a Market Integrity Official under Rule 10.9 of UMIR. See IIROC Notice 12-0364 — Rules Notice — Guidance Note — UMIR — *Guidance Respecting Electronic Trading* (December 7, 2012). For the limits on price movement before IIROC will consider regulatory intervention see IIROC Notice 12-0040 — Guidance Note — UMIR — *Guidance Respecting the Implementation of Single-Stock Circuit Breakers* (February 2, 2012) and IIROC Notice 12-0258 — Guidance Note — UMIR — *Guidance on Regulatory Intervention for the Variation or Cancellation of Trades* (August 20, 2012).

A: Yes. A third-party vendor would be able to effect the setting or adjusting of a specific risk management or supervisory control, policy or procedure for a marketplace participant but only if the marketplace participant solely determines the specific threshold for each pre-trade risk control. We note that a third-party vendor may especially need to perform the actual setting or adjusting of risk limits in the case when there are connectivity issues or other outages between the vendor's system and the marketplace participant's system.

C. — Monitoring of Trading Activity

C-1 Q: Does the requirement under subparagraph 3(3)(b)(iv) of NI 23-103 for compliance staff of a marketplace participant to receive immediate order and trade information refer to the compliance department of the firm or the business supervisors that have a compliance function?

A: The reference to "compliance staff" in subparagraph 3(3)(b)(iv) is meant to be interpreted broadly as the arrangements and set-up of compliance departments can widely vary among marketplace participants. The required order and trade information should go to the individual or group that has the main responsibility to review the compliance of those orders and trades with securities laws and IIROC requirements for the marketplace participant.

C-2 Q: What types of same-day reviews of order and trade information are required under NI 23-103 given that prescribed capital and other risk checks will be applied automatically in real time? Are there any specific criteria that should be reviewed same day?

A: Order and trade information is to be reviewed regularly, in part to ensure that the automated pre-trade risk checks are functioning appropriately and also to identify any anomalous trading behaviour that cannot be identified merely through automated pre-trade risk controls. No specific criteria have been listed in NI 23-103 or the CP as to what must be reviewed on a same-day basis; rather, it is left up to the marketplace participant's discretion to determine what the relevant criteria should be and how often these criteria should be reviewed in order to prudently manage the risks of its business.

C-3 Q: In circumstances where introducing brokers know their clients best and set pre-trade risk thresholds for their clients, must a carrying broker also set pre-trade limits notwithstanding the introducing broker's pre-trade risk limits?

A: Section 4 of the CP explains that a participant dealer may, on a reasonable basis, authorize an investment dealer to set or adjust a specific risk management or supervisory control, policy or procedure on the participant dealer's behalf by written contract and after a thorough assessment of the investment dealer's risk management or supervisory control, policy or procedure. However, the participant dealer that is the executing dealer must also have reasonable controls in place to manage the risks it incurs by executing orders for other dealers. While an executing dealer may not need to set the limits for specific risk management or supervisory controls, policies or procedures for the ultimate client because it has authorized the introducing broker to do so, the executing dealer will need to ensure it sets limits for the flow it receives from the introducing broker as a whole.

Authorizing an investment dealer to set or adjust a risk management or supervisory control, policy or procedure does not relieve the participant dealer of its obligations under section 3 of NI 23-103. We note that subsection 4(d) of NI 23-103 requires the participant dealer to regularly assess the adequacy and effectiveness of the setting or adjusting of the risk management or supervisory control, policy or procedure by the investment dealer.

D. — Automated Order Systems

D-1 Q: Section 5(1) of NI 23-103 provides that a marketplace participant must ensure that the use of an automated order system by any client does not interfere with fair and orderly markets. What does this entail? For example, does this require an average daily volume check on client orders since a large market order can freeze a symbol? Does this apply equally to equity as well as equity options and other asset classes?

A: The requirement for a marketplace participant to take all reasonable steps to ensure that the use of an automated order system by any client does not interfere with fair and orderly markets is an overarching principle that obliges a marketplace participant to monitor and manage the use of each automated order system by a client.[3] There is no requirement to conduct an average daily volume check under NI 23-103, but if a marketplace participant is of the view that this would be a useful tool to manage its risks and help ensure that the use of an automated order system by a client does not interfere with the fair and orderly functioning of the markets, the marketplace participant may choose to institute such a check.

The requirement under section 5(1) of the rule applies to each instance where a client uses an automated order system to trade a security, as that term is defined in each CSA jurisdiction. For the scope of NI 23-103, see our response to question A-1.

D-2 Q: Subsection 5(3)(b) of NI 23-103 requires that every automated order system used by a marketplace participant or any client is tested in accordance with prudent business practices. Can a marketplace participant rely on a third-party vendor for the testing of these systems and applications?

A: Section 5 of the CP outlines that a participating dealer does not necessarily have to conduct tests on each automated order system used by its clients itself but must be satisfied that these automated order systems have been appropriately tested.

A marketplace participant should consider how it documents the testing that has been conducted on an automated order system used by itself or any client.

---

[3]If the trading of the marketplace participant is subject to the Universal Market Integrity Rules, Rule 10.9 of UMIR allows IIROC to delay, halt or suspend trading in a security at any time and for such period of time as IIROC may consider appropriate in the interest of a fair and orderly market. IIROC has issued guidance on when trading activity may be considered to be interfering with a "fair and orderly market". In particular, see IIROC Notice 12-0040 — Guidance Notice — UMIR — *Guidance Respecting the Implementation of Single-Stock Circuit Breakers* (February 2, 2012) and IIROC Notice 12-0258 — Guidance Note — UMIR — *Guidance on Regulatory Intervention for the Variation or Cancellation of Trades* (August 20, 2012).

D-3 Q: Subparagraph 5(3)(c)(ii) of NI 23-103 requires a marketplace participant to have controls in place to immediately prevent orders generated by an automated order system used by the marketplace participant or any client from reaching a marketplace. Would a reasonable process involving human interaction be considered to "immediately" stop orders from an automated order system from being entered on a market? For example, would a process where a marketplace participant calls a vendor or marketplace in order to terminate access for a third-party smart order router be considered to meet that standard?

A: The overarching requirement of this provision is that a marketplace participant's risk management controls, policies and procedures are reasonably designed to manage, in accordance with prudent business practices, the financial, regulatory and other risks associated with marketplace access or providing clients with access to a marketplace. It is therefore up to the marketplace participant, based on its business model, the type of order flow that it handles, and the speed at which a malfunctioning automated order system can harm market integrity, to determine whether an automated function or manual process to stop orders from reaching a marketplace is appropriate.

Implementation of NI 23-103

Further to Multilateral CSA Staff Notice 23-313 *Blanket Orders Exempting Marketplace Participant from Certain Provisions of National Instrument 23-103 Electronic Trading and Related OSC Staff Position*[4], we note that New Brunswick has also issued a blanket order, effective March 1, 2013, that provides temporary relief from paragraph 3(3)(a) of NI 23-103 to marketplace participants that are testing the automated pre-trade risk controls required under paragraph 3(3)(a) of NI 23-103 by March 1, 2013. The blanket order grants relief until May 31, 2013.

CSA/IIROC Joint Notice 23-315 — Summary of Comments on CSA/IIROC Joint Notice 23-312 — Request for Comments — Transparency of Short Selling and Failed Trades

Date: February 28, 2013

36 O.S.C.B. 1978

[Not reproduced]

OSC Rule 23-501 — Designation as Market Participant

Date: November 2, 2001

24 O.S.C.B. 6645

1.1 *Alternative Trading System* — An alternative trading system is designated as a market participant for the purposes of the Act.

1.2 *Information Processor* — An information processor is designated as a market participant for the purposes of the Act.

Final Rule: 24 O.S.C.B. 6645 (November 2, 2001); Approval by OSC: 24 O.S.C.B. (Supp.) 85 (August 17, 2001); Request for Comments: 23 O.S.C.B. (Supp.) 299 (July 28, 2000).

Related Provisions: OSA 74 1(1) "market participant".

OSC Staff Notice 23-701 — Electronic Trading Risk Analysis

Date: November 15, 2012

35 O.S.C.B. 10231

National Instrument 23-103 *Electronic Trading* (NI 23-103) together with Companion Policy 23-103CP, which come into effect on March 1, 2013, establish the regulatory framework to help ensure that marketplace participants and marketplaces manage the risks associated with electronic trading. On October 25, 2012, the Canadian Securities Administrators (CSA) published proposed amendments to NI 23-103 to expand upon that framework that would, in part, impose additional requirements on participant dealers that provide direct electronic access (DEA).

We note that there has been increased focus on the adequacy of controls over electronic trading, and in particular whether the measures that regulators have introduced are sufficient to mitigate the risks of electronic trading. To examine this issue, OSC staff have retained a consultant to analyze the tools and controls that have been proposed and introduced in Canada, and to provide recommendations on any identified gaps that should be addressed. This analysis will not impact the timelines for the recently proposed amendments.

Part of the work to be performed by the consultant will include the gathering of information from market participants (e.g., dealers, institutional investors, DEA clients, marketplaces and vendors) regarding the risks posed by electronic trading and the provision of DEA, existing controls, and planned controls needed to comply with the implementation of NI 23-103 and the proposed amendments.

If you would like to participate in the information gathering exercise, please send an email to marketregulation@osc.gov.on.ca containing contact information where you can be contacted by OSC staff by November 29, 2012.

OSC Staff Notice 23-702 — Electronic Trading Risk Analysis Update

Date: December 12, 2013

36 O.S.C.B. 11767

---

[4](2012) 35 OSCB 11134.

I. — Introduction

This Notice is an update from staff (OSC Staff or we) of the Ontario Securities Commission (OSC or Commission) on our electronic trading risk analysis that included a review of National Instrument 23-103 *Electronic Trading* (NI 23-103), which establishes the regulatory framework for the oversight and management of the risks associated with the use of electronic trading on Canadian marketplaces. The regulatory requirements in this rule are intended to provide better protection for investors and support the integrity and efficiency of the capital markets of Canada. In order to ensure our regulatory framework is effective and robust, we have engaged in a review to assist us in:

- Analyzing the tools and controls on electronic trading in Canada;

- Assessing whether there are any gaps in NI 23-103; and

- Seeking recommendations on any identified gaps that should be addressed.

NI 23-103 and Companion Policy 23-103CP came into effect on March 1, 2013, and the Canadian Securities Administrators (CSA) have issued amendments to expand upon the framework to manage risks associated with direct electronic access (DEA).

The OSC regulates Ontario's capital markets in the context of rapid developments in market structure, technology, investment products and the global regulatory regime, among other things. As stated in its 2013-14 *Statement of Priorities*, the OSC has identified the evolution of market structure a key area of focus in 2013-2014: "The OSC will examine the issues associated with the evolution of the markets, including the impact of the order protection rule, algorithmic and other electronic trading and market data fees, to determine what regulatory responses may be required." It is in this context that we are, and have been, examining the issues surrounding electronic trading. These potential risks include those raised by high frequency trading strategies and use of sophisticated technology and algorithms. While this work does not measure the impact of the increased use of high frequency trading strategies on market quality, the Investment Industry Regulatory Organization of Canada (IIROC) has an initiative underway that will examine order and trade information and conduct an analysis of the impact of high frequency trading on the market.[1]

II. — The OSC and the Electronic Trading System Risk Analysis

As part of our review, the OSC retained an independent consultant, Fionnuala Martin and Associates (Consultant), to provide us with an assessment of the risks posed by electronic trading and whether any gaps exist in NI 23-103.[2] This assessment included interviews with market participants and other research regarding:

- Electronic trading practices, procedures and controls;

- The risks posed by electronic trading;

- The sufficiency of the current regulatory framework and whether any gaps exist in that framework; and

- How to best mitigate electronic trading risks.

The Consultant presented her report to the Commission. The report contains the Consultant's analysis, views and recommendations relating to electronic trading risks and is attached as Appendix A to this Notice. The report states that NI 23-103 provides comprehensive and adequate controls for the identified risks associated with electronic trading and that no gaps in NI 23-103 were identified. The language in NI 23-103 was considered by market participants to be clear, providing a good risk management framework for electronic trading. As a result of NI 23-103, according to the report, "The industry now has electronic trading rules and guidance on effective risk management through financial and supervisory controls for marketplace participants, regardless of the types of electronic trading they support."

In addition, the report includes several recommendations for possible improvements relating to industry testing, protocols and standards for marketplace operations. OSC Staff are reviewing the recommendations of the report carefully to consider any appropriate next steps. We recognize that as the speed, capacity and complexity of trading securities increase, the OSC must continue to consider the appropriate safeguards necessary to mitigate the risks of changing technologies and continue to gather information and examine whether regulatory requirements are complete, robust and effective. We also understand that electronic trading safeguards must continue to evolve as markets evolve and any requirements must be considered in the context of fair and efficient capital markets. This review and the Consultant's report is one example of this undertaking.

III. — Electronic Trading Risks and How Canadian Regulators Address Them

The increased use of complex trading technology and strategies, including high frequency trading strategies, has introduced additional risks to the markets that can impact dealers, marketplaces, and investor confidence. Three key electronic trading risks and the regulatory mechanisms in place to address them are described below. These risks and controls were also considered as part of the Consultant's analysis.

(i) — Credit Risk

Credit risk includes the risk that a dealer will be held financially responsible for trades that are beyond its financial capability. It also includes the broader systemic risk that may result if a dealer is unable to cover its financial liabilities and this failure spreads to the market as a whole. An additional risk exists where a dealer provides DEA in that the dealer is held financially responsible for the execution of all trades by its

---

[1]The HOT Study, Phases I and II of IIROC's Study of High Frequency Trading Activity on Canadian Equity Marketplaces, Trading Review and Analysis — Analytics Group, Investment Industry Regulatory Organization of Canada, 2013.

[2]Fionnuala Martin has over 30 years diverse experience in the Canadian markets providing trading technology related consulting services to a marketplace, a number of investment dealers, and a service vendor.

Part 2: MARKET PARTICIPANTS

DEA client. Without adequate controls, the speed at which orders are entered into the market by dealers or their DEA clients increases the possibility that executed trades surpass a dealer's financial capability.

In response, Canadian regulators have instituted a number of controls under NI 23-103 and the Universal Market Integrity Rules (UMIR) to mitigate this risk, including:

- Pre-trade risk control requirements;
- Requirements regarding the monitoring and cancellation of orders;
- Requirements related to the use of automated order systems;
- Marketplace thresholds;
- Circuit breakers; and
- Guidance on the regulatory treatment of erroneous and unreasonable trades.

1. — Pre-Trade Risk Controls

NI 23-103 and UMIR require dealers to have risk management and supervisory controls, including pre-trade risk controls, which limit the financial exposure of the dealer. Specifically, these controls prevent the entry of orders that exceed pre-determined credit or capital thresholds as well as pre-determined price or size parameters set by the dealer.

2. — Order Monitoring and Cancellation

The risk to a dealer's credit is exacerbated if a dealer cannot keep track of the orders that it or its DEA clients enter or if a dealer lacks proper controls to stop the execution of erroneous orders. To address this issue, NI 23-103 and UMIR require a dealer to have mechanisms in place to ensure that the dealer monitors all orders it enters as well as those entered by its DEA clients and that a dealer is able to immediately stop or cancel any of its orders or orders entered by its DEA clients. To further address the possibility that orders from a DEA client can pose a risk to a dealer's credit, NI 23-103 and UMIR mandate that a dealer must be able to immediately stop, when necessary, any direct electronic access it provides to a client.

3. — Use of Automated Order Systems

The use of automated order systems[3] is widespread. With the speed at which technology is employed in today's trading environment, an error in the programming or execution of an automated order system can quickly impact a dealer, or with the possibility of contagion, the market as a whole. This can affect investor confidence.

When an automated order system such as an algorithm is used, an error with respect to its output or its programming, such as the creation of a loop that sends erroneous orders into the market, can quickly make a dealer responsible for trades that are beyond its financial capability. This can have a negative impact on the market, especially if the erroneous orders impact a wide number of market participants or the price of a security or number of securities.

To mitigate this risk, we have imposed controls on the creation and use of automated order systems. NI 23-103 and UMIR require that dealers ensure that automated order systems are tested on a regular basis and that dealers have controls in place to immediately stop any automated order system and prevent the orders generated by an automated order system from reaching a marketplace if necessary. For example, this may include the use of a kill switch or other mechanism that will stop run away algorithms as soon as possible.

Because automated order systems can produce many orders in a very short period of time, understanding the type of order flow that will be generated by an automated order system is critical so that a dealer can better manage the risks to its business of electronic trading.

To address this risk, NI 23-103 and UMIR require a dealer to have an understanding of any automated order system that it or any of its clients use. Knowing the expected behaviour of an automated order system will not only help with setting pre-trade risk controls, but will also help the dealer to quickly determine if an automated order system is functioning abnormally and decide whether to shut off the automated order system or cut off a client's access.

4. — Marketplace Thresholds

NI 23-103 also prohibits a marketplace from executing orders that exceed set price and volume thresholds. Since orders over a certain size or value will not be able to be executed on a marketplace, the extent of volatility in trading that can occur on our markets and the risk to a dealer's credit is contained. The specific thresholds are to be determined by a regulation services provider such as IIROC or by a recognized exchange that directly monitors the conduct of its members, such as the Montréal Exchange. We note that IIROC is currently conducting consultations as to how best implement this requirement.

5. — Circuit Breakers

IIROC has implemented circuit breakers which are another mechanism to stop trading during unusually volatile trading periods to allow investors to reassess their trading positions and strategy. Single-stock and market-wide circuit breakers operate at multiple levels and the triggers for each level of market-wide circuit breaker is co-ordinated so that they work effectively to address unusual market volatility.

---

[3] An "automated order system" is defined in NI 23-103 as a system used to automatically generate or electronically transmit orders on a predetermined basis.

Single-stock circuit breakers are the first level of circuit breakers and halt the trading of a security for five minutes if the price of that security swings 10% or more within a five-minute period. This is helpful when a particular security is experiencing unusual trading volatility.

Market-wide circuit breakers constitute the second level of circuit breakers. These types of circuit breakers come into play when many securities experience large fluctuations in price. Market-wide circuit breakers pause trading on all securities after a decline of a predetermined size of the S&P 500 Index. These trigger levels and pause lengths are tied to those in the United States due to the interconnectedness between the two markets.

6. — Guidance on Regulatory Treatment of Erroneous and Unreasonable Trades

Despite the controls described above, all trading errors cannot be prevented. When these errors occur, IIROC has the ability to vary or cancel a trade to maintain fair and orderly markets. IIROC has published guidance to provide transparency to investors as to how erroneous or unreasonable trades will be dealt with by IIROC.

(ii) — Market Integrity Risk

Another risk of electronic trading is market integrity risk. Market integrity risk refers not only to the risk of non-compliance of a dealer with regulatory requirements but also the risk that the integrity of and confidence in the market is diminished if there is a lack of compliance.

With the ability to rapidly enter orders comes an increased risk of violations of regulatory requirements. To address this issue, the pre-trade risk controls mandated in NI 23-103 and UMIR must also be designed to prevent the entry of orders that do not comply with all applicable marketplace and regulatory requirements that must be satisfied on a pre-trade basis where possible. These regulatory requirements include compliance with the Order Protection Rule.

NI 23-103 and UMIR also require a dealer to be satisfied that a prospective DEA client has reasonable knowledge of regulatory requirements before providing DEA to that client. Once DEA is provided, NI 23-103 further requires a dealer to update its DEA clients about relevant changes to regulatory requirements to help ensure each DEA client maintains its reasonable knowledge of regulatory requirements. This is important to ensure that those that are sending orders directly to Canadian marketplaces understand the rules of trading and contribute to the maintenance of market integrity.

Market integrity risk is further mitigated through the NI 23-103 requirements for dealers to ensure each DEA client is assigned a unique identifier and that this identifier is included in each order sent by the DEA client. These identifiers will allow regulators, including IIROC, to identify DEA trading more readily and determine the specific client behind each trade more easily. This will improve the ability of regulators to investigate suspicious trading and market abuse.

In addition, the marketplace thresholds, circuit breakers, and guidance on erroneous trades described above also act as protections to ensure a fair and orderly market and therefore help to address market integrity risk as well.

(iii) — Technology or Systems Risk

Technology or systems risks relate to the possibility for failure of systems or technology and the impact of that failure. The potential problems may be due to systems failures, lack of capacity or programming errors in or by marketplaces, dealers, vendors or clients. These risks are exacerbated by the high degree of interconnectivity and rapid speed of communication among marketplace, dealer, and DEA client systems required by electronic trading resulting in potentially wide-reaching consequences should something go wrong in any one component. In addition, technology or systems failures that impact the ability of investors to trade or the prices that they receive for execution or the availability of those prices, introduce the possibility of cancellations or variations of trades. All of these could impact investor confidence in the market.

To mitigate these risks, requirements related to marketplace systems have been included in National Instrument 21-101 *Marketplace Operation* (NI 21-101). In addition, in Ontario, key market infrastructure entities are also required to comply with an Automation Review Program (ARP) as described below.

1. — NI 21-101 Systems Related Requirements

NI 21-101 imposes requirements on marketplaces to develop and maintain adequate systems of internal control and information technology general controls with respect to their systems, including order entry, order routing, execution, and data feed systems. To ensure this occurs, an independent systems review (ISR), must be conducted by marketplaces on an annual basis by a qualified third party.

To help ensure that marketplaces will be able to operate during periods of higher than normal trading volumes and during disasters, NI 21-101 also requires marketplaces to meet certain systems capacity, performance and disaster recovery standards which are consistent with prudent business practice.

2. — ARP Requirements

The ARP, as mandated by the OSC, applies to key market infrastructure entities, including recognized clearing agencies and exchanges. The ARP has three main components:

- A systems reporting procedure that requires entities to provide the OSC information on material system outages, other systems related issues, planned major production system changes and significant systems incidents on a timely basis;

- An annual ISR as described above; and

- Technology reviews which involve a review of the entity's systems and procedures with a focus on one or more particular systems related issues.

Part 2: MARKET PARTICIPANTS

The information obtained from the ARP components provides the Commission with relevant information to conduct its oversight of the systems of key entities while also helping to strengthen the key entities' own internal processes through responding to and implementing ISR recommendations.

IV. — Robust Regulation of Electronic Trading

In our view, the measures described above constitute a robust and effective response by the OSC, CSA and IIROC to help ensure that marketplaces and market participants appropriately manage the risks associated with electronic trading. Although the risks of technological failure or human error can never be completely eliminated, having a number of layers of controls substantially mitigates the risks of such occurrences and we expect them to minimize the impact in the event of an error or failure.

It is important for us to keep abreast of developments in trading technology and market structure and enhance our understanding of how innovations impact markets, market participants and investors. We will continue to be proactive in strengthening the oversight of marketplaces and trading in appropriate alignment with the regulatory principles for fostering fair and efficient markets and investor protection. This review and the Consultant's report is one example of this effort.

As we continue to examine the issues associated with electronic trading, the Consultant's recommendations, along with industry input beyond the anonymous feedback provided to the Consultant, and other pertinent information and factors will be considered. With respect to marketplace systems oversight, we are currently considering:

- Whether ARP requirements for key infrastructure entities, including recognized exchanges, require updating or supplementing; and

- The U.S. Securities and Exchange Commission's proposed Regulation Systems Compliance and Integrity (Regulation SCI) to assess if any of the proposed provisions would enhance our regulatory framework.[4]

Our examination to enhance the marketplace systems oversight framework may necessitate changes to NI 21-101. Any new requirements relating to electronic trading risks will be proposed and dealt with within the normal comment processes where required. We will also look for opportunities to further enhance the marketplace systems oversight framework through our ongoing oversight of marketplaces and market participant feedback.

Moreover, we will continue to work with the CSA and IIROC to identify and address electronic trading risks, where appropriate, through policy development and through consultations with market participants, investors and international regulators, in particular, the International Organization of Securities Commissions.

The OSC is working with other regulators and co-operating with market participants towards mitigating the risks to markets and investors in the context of rapidly evolving global capital markets. By implementing specific requirements for appropriate controls, policies and procedures relating to electronic trading, we endeavour to foster investor confidence in the integrity of our capital markets.

Appendix A

Electronic Trading System Risk Report [Not reproduced]

23-703 — Order Protection Rule — Industry Roundtable

Date: **July 3, 2014**

Citation: 37 O.S.C.B. 6251

[Not reproduced]

2.4 — Clearing and Settlement

National Instrument 24-101 — Institutional Trade Matching and Settlement

Date: April 1, 2007, as amended effective September 28, 2009, July 1, 2010, September 22, 2014 and January 11, 2015
30 O.S.C.B. 1649, 32 O.S.C.B. (Supp. 4) 376, O.S.C.B. 5589, 37 O.S.C.B. (Supp. 4) and 38 O.S.C.B. 342.

Table of Contents

PART 1 DEFINITIONS AND INTERPRETATION

PART 2 APPLICATION

PART 3 TRADE MATCHING REQUIREMENTS

PART 4 REPORTING BY REGISTERED FIRMS

PART 5 REPORTING REQUIREMENTS FOR CLEARING AGENCIES

PART 6 REQUIREMENTS FOR MATCHING SERVICE UTILITIES

PART 7 TRADE SETTLEMENT

PART 8 REQUIREMENTS OF SELF-REGULATORY ORGANIZATIONS AND OTHERS

---

[4]Regulation SCI would require certain market participants to have comprehensive policies and procedures in place for their technological systems.

PART 9 EXEMPTION

PART 10 EFFECTIVE DATES AND TRANSITION

Form 24-101F1 REGISTERED FIRM EXCEPTION REPORT OF DAP/RAP TRADE REPORTING AND MATCHING

Form 24-101F2 CLEARING AGENCY — QUARTERLY OPERATIONS REPORT OF INSTITUTIONAL TRADE REPORTING AND MATCHING

Form 24-101F3 MATCHING SERVICE UTILITY — NOTICE OF OPERATIONS

Form 24-101F4 MATCHING SERVICE UTILITY — NOTICE OF CESSATION OF OPERATIONS

Form 24-101F5 MATCHING SERVICE UTILITY — QUARTERLY OPERATIONS REPORT OF INSTITUTIONAL TRADE REPORTING AND MATCHING

PART 1 — DEFINITIONS AND INTERPRETATION

1.1 Definitions — In this Instrument,

"clearing agency" means,

(a) in Ontario, a clearing agency recognized by the securities regulatory authority under section 21.2 of the *Securities Act* (Ontario),

(b) in Quebec, a clearing house for securities recognized by the securities regulatory authority, and

(c) in every other jurisdiction, an entity that is carrying on business as a clearing agency in the jurisdiction;

"custodian" means a person or company that holds securities for the benefit of another under a custodial agreement or other custodial arrangement;

"DAP/RAP trade" means a trade

(a) executed for a client trading account that permits settlement on a delivery against payment or receipt against payment basis through the facilities of a clearing agency, and

(b) for which settlement is made on behalf of the client by a custodian other than the dealer that executed the trade;

"institutional investor" means a client of a dealer that has been granted DAP/RAP trading privileges by the dealer;

"marketplace" has the same meaning as in National Instrument 21-101 *Marketplace Operation*;

"matching service utility" means a person or company that provides centralized facilities for matching, but does not include a clearing agency;

"North American region" means Canada, the United States, Mexico, Bermuda and the countries of Central America and the Caribbean;

"registered firm" means a person or company registered under securities legislation as a dealer or adviser.

"trade-matching agreement" means, for trades executed with or on behalf of an institutional investor, a written agreement entered into among trade-matching parties setting out the roles and responsibilities of the trade-matching parties in matching those trades and including, without limitation, a term by which the trade-matching parties agree to establish, maintain and enforce policies and procedures designed to achieve matching as soon as practical after a trade is executed;

"trade-matching party" means, for a trade executed with or on behalf of an institutional investor,

(a) a registered adviser acting for the institutional investor in processing the trade,

(b) if a registered adviser is not acting for the institutional investor in processing the trade, the institutional investor unless the institutional investor is

(i) an individual, or

(ii) a person or company with total securities under administration or management not exceeding $10 million,

(c) a registered dealer executing or clearing the trade, or

(d) a custodian of the institutional investor settling the trade;

"trade-matching statement" means, for trades executed with or on behalf of an institutional investor, a signed written statement of a trade-matching party confirming that it has established, maintains and enforces policies and procedures designed to achieve matching as soon as practical after a trade is executed;

"T" means the day on which a trade is executed;

"T+1" means the next business day following T;

"T+2" means the second business day following T;

"T+3" means the third business day following T.

1.2 Interpretation — trade matching and Eastern Time — (1) In this Instrument, matching is the process by which

(a) the details and settlement instructions of an executed DAP/RAP trade are reported, verified, confirmed and affirmed or otherwise agreed to among the trade-matching parties, and

(b) unless the process is effected through the facilities of a clearing agency, the matched details and settlement instructions are reported to a clearing agency.

(2) Unless the context otherwise requires, a reference in this Instrument to

(a) a time is to Eastern Time, and

(b) a day is to a twenty-four hour day from midnight to midnight Eastern Time.

PART 2 — APPLICATION

2.1 This Instrument does not apply to

(a) a trade in a security of an issuer that has not been previously issued or for which a prospectus is required to be sent or delivered to the purchaser under securities legislation,

(b) a trade in a security to the issuer of the security,

(c) a trade made in connection with a take-over bid, issuer bid, amalgamation, merger, reorganization, arrangement or similar transaction,

(d) a trade made in accordance with the terms of conversion, exchange or exercise of a security previously issued by an issuer,

(e) a trade that is a securities lending, repurchase, reverse repurchase or similar financing transaction,

(f) a trade in a security of a mutual fund to which National Instrument 81-102 — *Investment Funds* applies,

(g) a trade to be settled outside Canada,

(h) a trade in an option, futures contract or similar derivative, or

(i) a trade in a negotiable promissory note, commercial paper or similar short-term debt obligation that, in the normal course, would settle in Canada on T.

PART 3 — TRADE MATCHING REQUIREMENTS

3.1 Matching deadlines for registered dealer — (1) A registered dealer shall not execute a DAP/RAP trade with or on behalf of an institutional investor unless the dealer has established, maintains and enforces policies and procedures designed to achieve matching as soon as practical after such a trade is executed and in any event no later than 12 p.m. (noon) on T+1.

(2) Despite subsection (1), the dealer may adapt its policies and procedures to permit matching to occur no later than 12 p.m. (noon) on T+2 for a DAP/RAP trade that results from an order to buy or sell securities received from an institutional investor whose investment decisions or settlement instructions are usually made in and communicated from a geographical region outside of the North American region.

3.2 Pre-DAP/RAP trade execution documentation requirement for dealers — A registered dealer shall not open an account to execute a DAP/RAP trade for an institutional investor or accept an order to execute a DAP/RAP trade for the account of an institutional investor unless its policies and procedures are designed to encourage each trade-matching party to

(a) enter into a trade-matching agreement with the dealer, or

(b) provide a trade-matching statement to the dealer.

3.3 Matching deadlines for registered adviser — (1) A registered adviser shall not give an order to a dealer to execute a DAP/RAP trade on behalf of an institutional investor unless the adviser has established, maintains and enforces policies and procedures designed to achieve matching as soon as practical after such a trade is executed and in any event no later than 12 p.m. (noon) on T+1.

(2) Despite subsection (1), the adviser may adapt its policies and procedures to permit matching to occur no later than 12 p.m. (noon) on T+2 for a DAP/RAP trade that results from an order to buy or sell securities received from an institutional investor whose investment decisions or settlement instructions are usually made in and communicated from a geographical region outside of the North American region.

3.4 Pre-DAP/RAP trade execution documentation requirement for advisers — A registered adviser shall not open an account to execute a DAP/RAP trade for an institutional investor or give an order to a dealer to execute a DAP/RAP trade for the account of an institutional investor unless its policies and procedures are designed to encourage each trade-matching party to

(a) enter into a trade-matching agreement with the adviser, or

(b) provide a trade-matching statement to the adviser.

PART 4 — REPORTING BY REGISTERED FIRMS

4.1 Exception reporting requirement — A registered firm shall deliver Form 24-101F1 to the securities regulatory authority no later than 45 days after the end of a calendar quarter if

(a) less than 90 per cent of the DAP/RAP trades executed by or for the registered firm during the quarter matched within the time required in Part 3, or

(b) the DAP/RAP trades executed by or for the registered firm during the quarter that matched within the time required in Part 3 represent less than 90 per cent of the aggregate value of the securities purchased and sold in those trades.

PART 5 — REPORTING REQUIREMENTS FOR CLEARING AGENCIES

5.1 A clearing agency through which trades governed by this Instrument are cleared and settled shall deliver Form 24-101F2 to the securities regulatory authority no later than 30 days after the end of a calendar quarter.

PART 6 — REQUIREMENTS FOR MATCHING SERVICE UTILITIES

6.1 Initial information reporting — (1) A person or company shall not carry on business as a matching service utility unless

(a) the person or company has delivered Form 24-101F3 to the securities regulatory authority, and

(b) at least 90 days have passed since the person or company delivered Form 24-101F3.

(2) During the 90 day period referred to in subsection (1), if there is a significant change to the information in the delivered Form 24-101F3, the person or company shall inform the securities regulatory authority in writing immediately of that significant change by delivering an amendment to Form 24-101F3 in the manner set out in Form 24-101F3.

6.2 Anticipated change to operations — At least 45 days before implementing a significant change to any item set out in Form 24-101F3, a matching service utility shall deliver an amendment to the information in the manner set out in Form 24-101F3.

6.3 Ceasing to carry on business as a matching service utility — (1) If a matching service utility intends to cease carrying on business as a matching service utility, it shall deliver a report on Form 24-101F4 to the securities regulatory authority at least 30 days before ceasing to carry on that business.

(2) If a matching service utility involuntarily ceases to carry on business as a matching service utility, it shall deliver a report on Form 24-101F4 as soon as practical after it ceases to carry on that business.

6.4 Ongoing information reporting and record keeping — (1) A matching service utility shall deliver Form 24-101F5 to the securities regulatory authority no later than 30 days after the end of a calendar quarter.

(2) A matching service utility shall keep such books, records and other documents as are reasonably necessary to properly record its business.

6.5 System requirements — For all of its core systems supporting trade matching, a matching service utility shall

(a) consistent with prudent business practice, on a reasonably frequent basis, and, in any event, at least annually,

(i) make reasonable current and future capacity estimates,

(ii) conduct capacity stress tests of those systems to determine the ability of the systems to process transactions in an accurate, timely and efficient manner,

(iii) implement reasonable procedures to review and keep current the testing methodology of those systems,

(iv) review the vulnerability of those systems and data centre computer operations to internal and external threats, including breaches of security, physical hazards and natural disasters, and

(v) maintain adequate contingency and business continuity plans;

(b) annually cause to be performed an independent review and written report, in accordance with generally accepted auditing standards, of the stated internal control objectives of those systems; and

(c) promptly notify the securities regulatory authority of a material failure of those systems.

PART 7 — TRADE SETTLEMENT

7.1 Trade settlement by registered dealer — (1) A registered dealer shall not execute a trade unless the dealer has established, maintains and enforces policies and procedures designed to facilitate settlement of the trade on a date that is no later than the standard settlement date for the type of security traded prescribed by an SRO or the marketplace on which the trade would be executed.

(2) Subsection (1) does not apply to a trade for which terms of settlement have been expressly agreed to by the counterparties to the trade at or before the trade was executed.

PART 8 — REQUIREMENTS OF SELF-REGULATORY ORGANIZATIONS AND OTHERS

8.1 A clearing agency or matching service utility shall have rules or other instruments or procedures that are consistent with the requirements of Parts 3 and 7.

8.2 A requirement of this Instrument does not apply to a member of an SRO if the member complies with a rule or other instrument of the SRO that deals with the same subject matter as the requirement and that has been approved, non-disapproved, or non-objected to by the securities regulatory authority and published by the SRO.

PART 9 — EXEMPTION

9.1 Exemption — (1) The regulator or the securities regulatory authority may grant an exemption from this Instrument, in whole or in part, subject to such conditions or restrictions as may be imposed in the exemption.

(2) Despite subsection (1), in Ontario, only the regulator may grant such an exemption.

(3) Except in Ontario, an exemption referred to in subsection (1) is granted under the statute referred to in Appendix B of National Instrument 14-101 *Definitions* opposite the name of the local jurisdiction.

PART 10 — EFFECTIVE DATES AND TRANSITION

10.1 Effective dates — (1) Except as provided in subsections (2) and (3), this Instrument comes into force on April 1, 2007.

(2) The following come into force on October 1, 2007:

(a) section 3.2;

(b) section 3.4;

(c) Part 4;

(d) Part 6.

(3) Despite paragraph (2)(d), Part 6 comes into force in Ontario on the later of

(a) October 1, 2007, and

(b) the day on which Rule 24-501 — *Designation as Market Participant* comes into force.

10.2 Transition — (1) A reference to "the end of T" in subsections 3.1(1) and 3.3(1) shall each be read as a reference to "12:00 p.m. (noon) on T+1" for trades executed before July 1, 2008.

(2) A reference to "the end of T+1" in subsections 3.1(2) and 3.3(2) shall each be read as a reference to "12:00 p.m. (noon) on T+2" for trades executed before July 1, 2008.

(3) A reference to "95 percent" in sections 4.1(a) and (b) shall each be read as a reference to:

(a) "80 percent", for trades executed after September 30, 2007, but before January 1, 2008;

(b) "90 percent", for trades executed after December 31, 2007, but before July 1, 2008;

(c) "70 percent", for trades executed after June 30, 2008, but before January 1, 2009;

(d) "80 percent", for trades executed after December 31, 2008, but before July 1, 2009; and

(e) "90 percent", for trades executed after June 30, 2009, but before January 1, 2010.

(4) A person or company need not comply with section 6.1 if that person or company

(a) is already carrying on business as a matching service utility on the date that Part 6 comes into force, and

(b) delivers Form 24-101F3 to the securities regulatory authority within 45 days after Part 6 comes into force.

Final Rule: (2007) 30 O.S.C.B. 2609; Approval by OSC: (2007) 30 O.S.C.B. 335; Request for Comments: (2006) 29 O.S.C.B. 1829.

Amendment to Rule: (2009) 32 O.S.C.B. (Supp. 4) 376; Approval by OSC: (2009) 32 O.S.C.B. (Supp. 2) 1.

Amendment to Rule: (2010) 33 O.S.C.B. 5589; Approval by OSC: (2010) 33 O.S.C.B. 3379; Request for Comments: (2009) 32 O.S.C.B. 9059.

Amendment to Rule: Approved by OSC: (2014) 37 O.S.C.B. (Supp 4) 28; Request for Comments: 36 O.S.C.B. (Supp 3).

Amendment to Rule: (2015) 38 O.S.C.B. 342.

Rules: Rule 24-501.

Policies and Orders: CSAN 24-304, 24-305, 24-306; OSCN 21-704.

Form 24-101F1 — Registered Firm Exception Report of DAP/RAP Trade Reporting and Matching

CALENDAR QUARTER PERIOD COVERED:

From: .... to: ....

REGISTERED FIRM IDENTIFICATION AND CONTACT INFORMATION:

1. Full name of registered firm (if sole proprietor, last, first and middle name):

2. Name(s) under which business is conducted, if different from item 1:

3a. Address of registered firm's principal place of business:

3b. Indicate below the jurisdiction of your principal regulator within the meaning of National Instrument 31-103 *Registration Requirements, Exemptions and Ongoing Registrant Obligations*:

  ❏ Alberta

  ❏ British Columbia

  ❏ Manitoba

  ❏ New Brunswick

  ❏ Newfoundland&Labrador

  ❏ Northwest Territories

  ❏ Nova Scotia

  ❏ Nunavut

  ❏ Ontario

  ❏ Prince Edward Island

  ❏ Québec

  ❏ Saskatchewan

  ❏ Yukon

3c. Indicate below all jurisdictions in which you are registered:

  ❏ Alberta

  ❏ British Columbia

  ❏ Manitoba

  ❏ New Brunswick

  ❏ Newfoundland&Labrador

  ❏ Northwest Territories

  ❏ Nova Scotia

  ❏ Nunavut

  ❏ Ontario

  ❏ Prince Edward Island

  ❏ Québec

  ❏ Saskatchewan

  ❏ Yukon

4. Mailing address, if different from business address:

5. Type of business:
  • Dealer
  • Adviser
6. Category of registration:
7. (a) Registered firm NRD number:

  (b) If the registered firm is a participant of a clearing agency, the registered firm's CUID number:

8. Contact employee name:

Telephone number:

E-mail address:

Instructions:

Deliver this form for both equity and debt DAP/RAP trades together with Exhibits A, B and C pursuant to section 4.1 of the Instrument, covering the calendar quarter indicated above, within 45 days of the end of the calendar quarter if

  (a) less than 90 per cent of the equity and/or debt DAP/RAP trades executed by or for you during the quarter matched within the time required in Part 3 of the Instrument, or

  (b) the equity and/or debt DAP/RAP trades executed by or for you during the quarter that matched within the time required in Part 3 of the Instrument represent less than 90 per cent of the aggregate value of the securities purchased and sold in those trades."

Exhibits:

Exhibit A — DAP/RAP trade statistics for the quarter

Complete Tables 1 and 2 below for each calendar quarter.

(1) — Equity DAP/RAP trades

Entered into CDS by deadline (to be completed by dealers only)				Matched by deadline			
# of Trades	%	$ Value of Trades	%	# of Trades	%	$ Value of Trades	%
....	.....	....	.....	....	.....	....	.....

(2) — Debt DAP/RAP trades

Entered into CDS by deadline (to be completed by dealers only)				Matched by deadline			
# of Trades	%	$ Value of Trades	%	# of Trades	%	$ Value of Trades	%
....	.....	....	.....	....	.....	....	.....

Exhibit B — Reasons for not meeting exception reporting thresholds

Describe the circumstances or underlying causes that resulted in or contributed to the failure to achieve the percentage target for matched equity and/or debt DAP/RAP trades within the maximum time prescribed by Part 3 of the Instrument. Reasons given could be one or more matters within your control or due to another trade-matching party or service provider. If you have insufficient information to determine the percentages, the reason for this should be provided. See also Companion Policy 24-101CP to the Instrument.

Exhibit C — Steps to address delays

Describe what specific steps you are taking to resolve delays in the equity and/or debt DAP/RAP trade reporting and matching process in the future. Indicate when each of these steps is expected to be implemented. The steps being taken could be internally focused, such as implementing a new system or procedure, or externally focused, such as meeting with a trade-matching party to determine what action should be taken by that party. If you have insufficient information to determine the percentages, the steps being taken to obtain this information should be provided. See also Companion Policy 24-101CP to the Instrument.

Certificate of Registered Firm

The undersigned certifies that the information given in this report on behalf of the registered firm is true and correct.

DATED at .... this .... day of .... 20..........

.... (Name of registered firm — type or print)

.... (Name of director, officer or partner — type or print)

.... (Signature of director, officer or partner)

.... (Official capacity — type or print)

Part 2: MARKET PARTICIPANTS

Form 24-101F2 — Clearing Agency Quarterly Operations Report of Institutional Trade Reporting and Matching

CALENDAR QUARTER PERIOD COVERED:

From: .... to: ....

Identification and Contact Information:

1. Full name of clearing agency:

2. Name(s) under which business is conducted, if different from item 1:

3. Address of clearing agency's principal place of business:

4. Mailing address, if different from business address:

5. Contact employee name:

Telephone number:

E-mail address:

Instructions:

Deliver this form together with all exhibits pursuant to section 5.1 of the Instrument, covering the calendar quarter indicated above, within 30 days of the end of the calendar quarter.

Exhibits shall be provided in an electronic file, in the following file format: "CSV" (Comma Separated Variable) (e.g., the format produced by Microsoft Excel).

Exhibits:

1. — Data Reporting

Exhibit A — Aggregate matched trade statistics

For client trades, provide the information to complete Tables 1 and 2 below for each month in the quarter. These two tables can be integrated into one report. Provide separate aggregate information for trades that have been reported or entered into your facilities as matched trades by a matching service utility.

Month/Year: .... (MMM/YYYY)

Table 1 — Equity trades:

	Entered into clearing agency by dealers				Matched in clearing agency by custodians			
	# of Trades	% Industry	$ Value of Trades	% Industry	# of Trades	% Industry	$ Value of Trades	% Industry
T	....	....	....	....	....	....	....	....
T+1 - noon	....	....	....	....	....	....	....	....
T+1	....	....	....	....	....	....	....	....
T+2	....	....	....	....	....	....	....	....
T+3	....	....	....	....	....	....	....	....
>T+3	....	....	....	....	....	....	....	....
Total	....	....	....	....	....	....	....	....

Table 2 — Debt trades:

	Entered into clearing agency by dealers				Matched in clearing agency by custodians			
	# of Trades	% Industry	$ Value of Trades	% Industry	# of Trades	% Industry	$ Value of Trades	% Industry
T	....	....	....	....	....	....	....	....
T+1 - noon	....	....	....	....	....	....	....	....
T+1	....	....	....	....	....	....	....	....
T+2	....	....	....	....	....	....	....	....
T+3	....	....	....	....	....	....	....	....
>T+3	....	....	....	....	....	....	....	....
Total	....	....	....	....	....	....	....	....

Legend

"# of Trades" is the total number of transactions in the month; and

"$ Value of Trades" is the total value of the transactions (purchases and sales) in the month.

Exhibit B — Individual matched trade statistics

Using the same format as Exhibit A above, provide the relevant information for each participant of the clearing agency in respect of client trades during the quarter that have been entered by the participant and matched within the timelines indicated in Exhibit A.

Certificate of Clearing Agency

The undersigned certifies that the information given in this report on behalf of the clearing agency is true and correct.

DATED at .... this .... day of .... 20..........

.... (Name of clearing agency — type or print)

.... (Name of director, officer or partner — type or print)

.... (Signature of director, officer or partner)

.... (Official capacity — type or print)

Form 24-101F3 — Matching Service Utility Notice of Operations

Date of Commencement Information:
Effective date of commencement of operations: .... (DD/MMM/YYYY)

Type of Information:
- INITIAL SUBMISSION
- AMENDMENT

Matching Service Utility Identification and Contact Information:
1. Full name of matching service utility:
2. Name(s) under which business is conducted, if different from item 1:
3. Address of matching service utility's principal place of business:
4. Mailing address, if different from business address:
5. Contact employee name:
Telephone number:
E-mail address:
6. Legal counsel:
Firm name:
Telephone number:
E-mail address:

General Information:
7. Website address:
8. Date of financial year-end: .... (DD/MMM/YYYY)

9. Indicate the form of your legal status (e.g., corporation, limited or general partnership), the date of formation, and the jurisdiction under which you were formed:

Legal status:

- CORPORATION

- OTHER (SPECIFY):

- PARTNERSHIP

      (a) Date of formation: .... (DD/MMM/YYYY)

      (b) Jurisdiction and manner of formation:

10. Specify the general types of securities for which information is being or will be received and processed by you for transmission of matched trades to a clearing agency (e.g. exchange-traded domestic equity and debt securities, exchange-traded foreign equity and debt securities, equity and debt securities traded over-the-counter).

Instructions:

Deliver this form together with all exhibits pursuant to section 6.1 or 10.2(4) of the Instrument.

For each exhibit, include your name, the date of delivery of the exhibit and the date as of which the information is accurate (if different from the date of the delivery). If any exhibit required is not applicable, a full statement describing why the exhibit is not applicable shall be furnished in lieu of the exhibit. To the extent information requested for an exhibit is identical to the information requested in another form that you have filed or delivered under National Instrument 21-101 *Marketplace Operation*, simply attach a copy of that other form and indicate in this form where such information can be found in that other form.

If you are delivering an amendment to Form 24-101F3 pursuant to section 6.1(2) or 6.2 of the Instrument, and the amended information relates to an exhibit that was delivered with such form, provide a description of the change and complete and deliver an updated exhibit. If you are delivering Form 24-101F3 pursuant to section 10.2(4) of the Instrument, simply indicate at the top of this form under "Date of Commencement Information" that you were already carrying on business as a matching service utility in the relevant jurisdiction on the date that Part 6 of the Instrument came into force.

Exhibits:

1. — Corporate Governance

Exhibit A — Constating documents

Provide a copy of your constating documents, including corporate by-laws and other similar documents, as amended from time to time.

Exhibit B — Ownership

List any person or company that owns 10 percent or more of your voting securities or that, either directly or indirectly, through agreement or otherwise, may control your management. Provide the full name and address of each person or company and attach a copy of the agreement or, if there is no written agreement, briefly describe the agreement or basis through which the person or company exercises or may exercise control or direction.

Exhibit C — Officials

Provide a list of the partners, officers, directors or persons performing similar functions who presently hold or have held their offices or positions during the current and previous calendar year, indicating the following for each:

    1. Name.

    2. Title.

    3. Dates of commencement and expiry of present term of office or position and length of time the office or position held.

    4. Type of business in which each is primarily engaged and current employer.

    5. Type of business in which each was primarily engaged in the preceding five years, if different from that set out in item 4.

    6. Whether the person is considered to be an independent director.

Exhibit D — Organizational structure

Provide a narrative or graphic description of your organizational structure.

Exhibit E — Affiliated entities

For each person or company affiliated to you, provide the following information:

    1. Name and address of affiliated entity.

    2. Form of organization (e.g., association, corporation, partnership).

    3. Name of jurisdiction and statute under which organized.

    4. Date of incorporation in present form.

5. Brief description of nature and extent of affiliation or contractual or other agreement with you.

6. Brief description of business services or functions.

7. If a person or company has ceased to be affiliated with you during the previous year or ceased to have a contractual or other agreement relating to your operations during the previous year, provide a brief statement of the reasons for termination of the relationship.

2. — Financial Viability

Exhibit F — Audited financial statements

Provide your audited financial statements for the latest financial year and a report prepared by an independent auditor.

3. — Fees

Exhibit G — Fee list, fee structure

Provide a complete list of all fees and other charges imposed, or to be imposed, by you for use of your services as a matching service utility, including the cost of establishing a connection to your systems.

4. — Access

Exhibit H — Users

Provide a list of all users or subscribers for which you provide or propose to provide the services of a matching service utility. Identify the type(s) of business of each user or subscriber (e.g., custodian, dealer, adviser or other party).

If applicable, for each instance during the past year in which any user or subscriber of your services has been prohibited or limited in respect of access to such services, indicate the name of each such user or subscriber and the reason for the prohibition or limitation.

Exhibit I — User contract

Provide a copy of each form of agreement governing the terms by which users or subscribers may subscribe to your services of a matching service utility.

5. — Systems and Operations

Exhibit J — System description

Describe the manner of operation of your systems for performing your services of a matching service utility (including, without limitation, systems that collect and process trade execution details and settlement instructions for matching of trades). This description should include the following:

1. The hours of operation of the systems, including communication with a clearing agency.

2. Locations of operations and systems (e.g., countries and cities where computers are operated, primary and backup).

3. A brief description in narrative form of each service or function performed by you.

6. — Systems Compliance

Exhibit K — Security

Provide a brief description of the processes and procedures implemented by you to provide for the security of any system used to perform your services of a matching service utility.

Exhibit L — Capacity planning and measurement

1. Provide a brief description of capacity planning/performance measurement techniques and system and stress testing methodologies.

2. Provide a brief description of testing methodologies with users or subscribers. For example, when are user/subscriber tests employed? How extensive are these tests?

Exhibit M — Business continuity

Provide a brief description of your contingency and business continuity plans in the event of a catastrophe.

Exhibit N — Material systems failures

Provide a brief description of policies and procedures in place for reporting to regulators material systems failures. Material systems failures include serious incidents that result in the interruption of the matching of trades for more than thirty minutes during normal business hours.

Exhibit O — Independent systems audit

1. Briefly describe your plans to provide an annual independent audit of your systems.

2. If applicable, provide a copy of the last external systems operations audit report.

7. — Interoperability

Exhibit P — Interoperability agreements

List all other matching service utilities for which you have entered into an *interoperability* agreement. Provide a copy of all such agreements.

8. — Outsourcing

Exhibit Q — Outsourcing firms

For each person or company (outsourcing firm) with whom or which you have an outsourcing agreement or arrangement relating to your services of a matching service utility, provide the following information:

    1. Name and address of the outsourcing firm.

    2. Brief description of business services or functions of the outsourcing firm.

    3. Brief description of the outsourcing firm's contingency and business continuity plans in the event of a catastrophe.

Certificate of Matching Service Utility

The undersigned certifies that the information given in this report on behalf of the matching service utility is true and correct.

DATED at .... this .... day of .... 20..........

.... (Name of matching service utility — type or print)

.... (Name of director, officer or partner — type or print)

.... (Signature of director, officer or partner)

.... (Official capacity — type or print)

Form 24-101F4 — Matching Service Utility Notice of Cessation of Operations

Date of Cessation Information:

Type of information:

- VOLUNTARY CESSATION

- INVOLUNTARY CESSATION

Effective date of operations cessation: .... (DD/MMM/YYYY)

Matching Service Utility Identification and Contact Information:

1. Full name of matching service utility:

2. Name(s) under which business is conducted, if different from item 1:

3. Address of matching service utility's principal place of business:

4. Mailing address, if different from business address:

5. Legal counsel:

Firm name:

Telephone number:

E-mail address:

Instructions:

Deliver this form together with all exhibits pursuant to section 6.3 of the Instrument.

For each exhibit, include your name, the date of delivery of the exhibit and the date as of which the information is accurate (if different from the date of the delivery). If any exhibit required is not applicable, a full statement describing why the exhibit is not applicable shall be furnished in lieu of the exhibit.

Exhibits:

Exhibit A

Provide the reasons for your cessation of business.

Exhibit B

Provide a list of all the users or subscribers for which you provided services during the last 30 days prior to you ceasing business. Identify the type(s) of business of each user or subscriber (e.g., custodian, dealer, adviser, or other party).

Exhibit C

List all other matching service utilities for which an *interoperability* agreement was in force immediately prior to cessation of business.

Certificate of Matching Service Utility

The undersigned certifies that the information given in this report on behalf of the matching service utility is true and correct.

DATED at .... this.......... day of .... 20..........

.... (Name of matching service utility — type or print)

.... (Name of director, officer or partner — type or print)

.... (Signature of director, officer or partner)

.... (Official capacity — type or print)

Form 24-101F5 — Matching Service Utility Quarterly Operations Report Of Institutional Trade Reporting And Matching

Calendar Quarter Period Covered:

From: .... to: ....

Matching Service Utility Identification and Contact Information:

1. Full name of matching service utility:

2. Name(s) under which business is conducted, if different from item 1:

3. Address of matching service utility's principal place of business:

4. Mailing address, if different from business address:

5. Contact employee name:

Telephone number:

E-mail address:

Instructions:

Deliver this form together with all exhibits pursuant to section 6.4 of the Instrument, covering the calendar quarter indicated above, within 30 days of the end of the calendar quarter.

Exhibits shall be reported in an electronic file, in the following format: "CSV" (Comma Separated Variable) (e.g., the format produced by Microsoft Excel).

If any information specified is not available, a full statement describing why the information is not available shall be separately furnished.

Exhibits

1. — Systems Reporting

Exhibit A — External systems audit

If an external audit report on your core systems was prepared during the quarter, provide a copy of the report.

Exhibit B — Material systems failures reporting

Provide a brief summary of all material systems failures that occurred during the quarter and for which you were required to notify the securities regulatory authority under section 6.5(c) of the Instrument.

2. — Data Reporting

Exhibit C — Aggregate matched trade statistics

Provide the information to complete Tables 1 and 2 below for each month in the quarter. These two tables can be integrated into one report.

Month/Year: .... (MMM/YYYY)

Table 1 — Equity trades:

	Entered into matching service utility by dealer-users/subscribers				Matched in matching service utility by other users/subscribers			
	# of Trades	% Industry	$ Value of Trades	% Industry	# of Trades	% Industry	$ Value of Trades	% Industry
T	....	....	....	....	....	....	....	....
T+1 - noon	....	....	....	....	....	....	....	....
T+1	....	....	....	....	....	....	....	....
T+2	....	....	....	....	....	....	....	....
T+3	....	....	....	....	....	....	....	....

	Entered into matching service utility by dealer-users/subscribers				Matched in matching service utility by other users/subscribers			
	# of Trades	% Industry	$ Value of Trades	% Industry	# of Trades	% Industry	$ Value of Trades	% Industry
>T+3	....	....	....	....	....	....	....	....
Total	....	....	....	....	....	....	....	....

Table 2 — Debt trades:

	Entered into matching service utility by dealer-users/subscribers				Matched in matching service utility by other users/subscribers			
	# of Trades	% Industry	$ Value of Trades	% Industry	# of Trades	% Industry	$ Value of Trades	% Industry
T	....	....	....	....	....	....	....	....
T+1 - noon	....	....	....	....	....	....	....	....
T+1	....	....	....	....	....	....	....	....
T+2	....	....	....	....	....	....	....	....
T+3	....	....	....	....	....	....	....	....
>T+3	....	....	....	....	....	....	....	....
Total	....	....	....	....	....	....	....	....

Legend

"# of Trades" is the total number of transactions in the month;

"$ Value of Trades" is the total value of the transactions (purchases and sales) in the month.

Exhibit D — Individual matched trade statistics

Using the same format as Exhibit C above, provide the relevant information for each user or subscriber in respect of trades during the quarter that have been entered by the user or subscriber and matched within the timelines indicated in Exhibit C.

Certificate of Matching Service Utility

The undersigned certifies that the information given in this report on behalf of the matching service utility is true and correct.

DATED at .... this .... day of .... 20..........

.... (Name of matching service utility — type or print)

.... (Name of director, officer or partner — type or print)

.... (Signature of director, officer or partner)

.... (Official capacity — type or print)

Companion Policy 24-101CP — To National Instrument 24-101 — Institutional Trade Matching and Settlement

Table of Contents

PART 1 — INTRODUCTION, PURPOSE AND DEFINITIONS[1]

1.1 Purpose of Instrument — National Instrument 24-101 — *Institutional Trade Matching and Settlement* (Instrument) provides a framework in provincial securities regulation for more efficient and timely trade settlement processing, particularly institutional trades. The increasing volumes and dollar values of securities traded in Canada and globally by institutional investors mean existing back-office systems and procedures of market partici-

---

[1]In this Companion Policy, the terms "CSA", "we", "our" or "us" are used interchangeably and generally mean the same thing as *Canadian securities regulatory authorities* defined in National Instrument 14-101 — *Definitions*.

pants are challenged to meet post-execution processing demands. New requirements are needed to address the increasing risks. The Instrument is part of a broader initiative in the Canadian securities markets to implement straight-through processing (STP).[2]

1.2 General explanation of matching, clearing and settlement — (1) Parties to institutional trade — A typical trade with or on behalf of an institutional investor might involve at least three parties:

- a registered adviser or other *buy-side* manager acting for an institutional investor in the trade — and often acting on behalf of more than one institutional investor in the trade (i.e., multiple underlying institutional client accounts) — who decides what securities to buy or sell and how the assets should be allocated among the client accounts;

- a registered dealer (including an Alternative Trading System registered as a dealer) responsible for executing or clearing the trade; and

- any financial institution or registered dealer (including under a *prime brokerage* arrangement) appointed to hold the institutional investor's assets and settle trades.

(2) Matching — A first step in settling a securities trade is to ensure that the buyer and the seller agree on the details of the transaction, a process referred to as trade confirmation and affirmation or trade *matching*.[3] A registered dealer who executes trades with or on behalf of others is required to report and confirm trade details, not only with the counterparty to the trade, but also with the client for whom it acted or the client with whom it traded (in which case, the client would be the counterparty). Similarly, a registered adviser or other buy-side manager is required to report trade details and provide settlement instructions to its custodian. The parties must agree on trade details — sometimes referred to as *trade data elements* — as soon as possible so that errors and discrepancies in the trades can be discovered early in the clearing and settlement process.

(3) Matching process — Verifying the trade data elements is necessary to *match* a trade executed on behalf of or with an institutional investor. Matching occurs when the relevant parties to the trade have, after verifying the trade data elements, reconciled or agreed to the details of the trade. Matching also requires that any custodian holding the institutional investor's assets be in a position to affirm the trade so that the trade can be ready for the clearing and settlement process through the facilities of the clearing agency. To illustrate, trade matching usually includes these following activities:

(a) The registered dealer notifies the buy-side manager that the trade was executed.

(b) The buy-side manager advises the dealer and any custodian(s) how the securities traded are to be allocated among the underlying institutional client accounts managed by the buy-side manager.[4] For so-called *block settlement trades*, the dealer sometimes receives allocation information from the buy-side manager based only on the number of custodians holding institutional investors' assets instead of on the actual underlying institutional client accounts managed by the buy-side manager.

(c) The dealer reports and confirms the trade details to the buy-side manager and clearing agency. The trade details required to be confirmed for matching, clearing and settlement purposes are generally similar to the information required in the customer trade confirmation delivered pursuant to securities legislation or self-regulatory organization (SRO) rules.[5]

(d) The custodian or custodians of the assets of the institutional investor verify the trade details and settlement instructions against available securities or funds held for the institutional investor. After trade details are agreed, the buy-side manager instructs the custodian(s) to release funds and/or securities to the dealer through the facilities of the clearing agency.

(4) Clearing and settlement — The clearing of a trade begins after the execution of the trade. After matching is completed, clearing will involve the calculation of the mutual obligations of participants for the exchange of securities and money — a process which generally occurs within the facilities of a clearing agency. The *settlement* of a trade is the moment when the securities are transferred finally and irrevocably from one participant to another in exchange for a corresponding transfer of money. In the context of settlement of a trade through the facilities of a clearing agency, often acting as central counterparty, settlement will be the discharge of obligations in respect of funds or securities, computed on a net basis, between and among the clearing agency and its participants. Through the operation of novation and set-off in law or by contract, the clearing agency becomes a counterparty to each trade so that the mutual obligation to settle the trade is between the clearing agency and each participant.

1.3 Section 1.1 — Definitions and scope — (1) Clearing agency — Today, the definition of *clearing agency* applies only to The Canadian Depository for Securities Limited (CDS). The definition takes into account the fact that securities regulatory authorities in Ontario and Quebec currently

---

[2]For a discussion of Canadian STP initiatives, see Canadian Securities Administrators' (CSA) Discussion Paper 24-401 on *Straight-through Processing* and Request for Comments, April 16, 2004 (2004) 27 OSCB 3971 to 4031 (Discussion Paper 24-401); and CSA Notice 24-301 — *Responses to Comments Received on Discussion Paper 24-401 on Straight-through Processing, Proposed National Instrument 24-101 Post-trade Matching and Settlement, and Proposed Companion Policy 24-101CP to National Instrument 24-101 Post-trade Matching and Settlement*, February 11, 2005 (2005) 28 OSCB 1509 to 1526.

[3]The processes and systems for matching of "non-institutional trades" in Canada have evolved over time and become automated, such as retail trades on an exchange, which are matched or *locked-in* automatically at the exchange, or direct non-exchange trades between two participants of a clearing agency, which are generally matched through the facilities of the clearing agency. Dealer to dealer trades are subject to Investment Industry Regulatory Organization of Canada (IIROC) Member Rule 800.49, which provides that trades in non-exchange traded securities (including government debt securities) among dealers must be entered or accepted or rejected through the facilities of an "Acceptable Trade Matching Utility" within one hour of the execution of the trade.

[4]We remind registered advisers of their obligations to ensure fairness in allocating investment opportunities among its clients. An adviser must establish, maintain and apply policies and procedures that provide reasonable assurance that the firm and each individual acting on its behalf fairly allocates investment opportunities among its clients. If the adviser allocates investment opportunities among its clients, the firm's fairness policies should, at a minimum, indicate the method used to allocate the following: (i) price and commission among client orders when trades are bunched or blocked; (ii) block trades and initial public offerings (IPOs) among client accounts, and (iii) block trades and IPOs among client orders that are partially filled, such as on a pro-rata basis. The fairness policies should also address any other situation where investment opportunities must be allocated.

A summary of the fairness policies must be delivered to each client at the time the adviser opens an account for the client, and in a timely manner if there is a significant change to the summary last delivered to the client.

See sections 14.3 and 14.10 of National Instrument 31-103 *Registration Requirements, Exemptions and Ongoing Registrant Obligations* (NI 31-103) and section 14.10 the Companion Policy to NI 31-103.

[5]See, for example, section 36 of the *Securities Act* (Ontario), The Toronto Stock Exchange (TSX) Rule 2-405 and IIROC Member Rule 200.1(h).

recognize or otherwise regulate clearing agencies in Canada under provincial securities legislation.[6] The functional meaning of *clearing agency* can be found in the securities legislation of certain jurisdictions.[7]

(2) Custodian — While investment assets are sometimes held directly by investors, most are held on behalf of the investor by or through securities accounts maintained with a financial institution or dealer. The definition of *custodian* includes both a financial institution (non-dealer custodian) and a dealer acting as custodian (dealer custodian). Most institutional investors, such as pension and mutual funds, hold their assets through custodians that are prudentially-regulated financial institutions. However, others (like hedge funds) often maintain their investment assets with dealers under so-called *prime-brokerage* arrangements. A financial institution or dealer in Canada need not necessarily have a direct contractual relationship with an institutional investor to be considered a custodian of portfolio assets of the institutional investor for the purposes of the Instrument if it is acting as sub-custodian to a global custodian or international central securities depository.

(3) Institutional investor — A client of a dealer that has been granted DAP/RAP trading privileges is an institutional investor. This will likely be the case whenever a client's investment assets are held by or through securities accounts maintained with a custodian instead of the client's dealer that executes its trades. While the expression "institutional trade" is not defined in the Instrument, we use the expression in this Companion Policy to mean broadly any DAP/RAP trade.

(4) DAP/RAP trade — The concepts *delivery against payment* and *receipt against payment* are generally understood by the industry. They are also defined terms in the Notes and Instructions (Schedule 4) to the *Joint Regulatory Financial Questionnaire and Report* of the Canadian SROs. All DAP/RAP trades, whether settled by a non-dealer custodian or a dealer custodian, are subject to the requirements of Part 3 of the Instrument. The definition of DAP/RAP trade excludes a trade for which settlement is made on behalf of a client by a custodian that is also the dealer that executed the trade.

(5) Trade-matching party — An institutional investor, whether Canadian or foreign-based, may be a trade-matching party. As such, it, or its adviser that is acting for it in processing a trade, should enter into a trade-matching agreement or provide a trade-matching statement under Part 3 of the Instrument. However, an institutional investor that is an individual or a person or company with total securities under administration or management not exceeding $10 million, is not a trade-matching party. A custodian that settles a trade on behalf of an institutional investor is also a trade-matching party and should enter into a trade-matching agreement or provide a trade-matching statement. However, a foreign global custodian or international central securities depository that holds Canadian portfolio assets through a local Canadian sub-custodian would not normally be considered a trade-matching party if it is not a clearing agency participant or otherwise directly involved in settling the trade in Canada.

(6) Application of Instrument — Part 2 of the Instrument enumerates certain types of trades that are not subject to the Instrument.

PART 2 — TRADE MATCHING REQUIREMENTS

2.1 Trade data elements — Trade data elements that must be verified and agreed to are those identified by the SROs or the best practices and standards for institutional trade processing established and generally adopted by the industry. See section 2.4 of this Companion Policy. To illustrate, trade data elements that should be transmitted, compared and agreed to may include the following:

(a) *Security identification*: standard numeric identifier, currency, issuer, type/class/series, market ID; and

(b) *Order and trade information*: dealer ID, account ID, account type, buy/sell indicator, order status, order type, unit price/face amount, number of securities/quantity, message date/time, trade transaction type, commission, accrued interest (fixed income), broker settlement location, block reference, net amount, settlement type, allocation sender reference, custodian, payment indicator, IM portfolio/account ID, quantity allocated, and settlement conditions.

2.2 Trade matching deadlines for registered firms — The obligation of a registered dealer or registered adviser to establish, maintain and enforce policies and procedures, pursuant to sections 3.1 and 3.3 of the Instrument, will require the dealer or adviser to take reasonable steps to achieve matching as soon as practical after the DAP/RAP trade is executed and in any event no later than 12 p.m. (noon) on T+1. If the trade results from an order to buy or sell securities received from an institutional investor whose investment decisions or settlement instructions are usually made in and communicated from a geographical region outside of the North American region, the deadline for matching is 12 p.m. (noon) on T+2 (subsections 3.1(2) and 3.3(2)). As defined, the North American region comprises Canada, the United States, Mexico, Bermuda and the countries of Central America and the Caribbean.

2.3 Choice of trade-matching agreement or trade-matching statement — (1) Establishing, maintaining and enforcing policies and procedures —

(a) Under sections 3.2 and 3.4, a registered dealer's or registered adviser's policies and procedures must be designed to encourage trade-matching parties to either (i) enter into a trade-matching agreement with the dealer or adviser or (ii) provide or make available a trade-matching statement to the dealer or adviser. The purpose of the trade-matching agreement or trade-matching statement is to ensure that all trade-matching parties have established, maintain, and enforce appropriate policies and procedures designed to achieve matching of a DAP/RAP trade as soon as practical after the trade is executed. If the dealer or adviser is unable to obtain a trade-matching agreement or statement from a trade-matching party, it should document its efforts in accordance with its policies and procedures.

(b) The parties described in paragraphs (a), (b), (c) and (d) of the definition "trade-matching party" in section 1.1 of the Instrument need not necessarily all be involved in a trade for the requirements of sections 3.2 and 3.4 of the Instrument to apply. There is no need for an adviser to be involved in the matching process of an institutional investor's trades for the requirement to apply. In this case, the trade-matching parties that should have appropriate policies and procedures in place would be the institutional investor, the dealer and the custodian.

(c) The Instrument does not provide the form of a trade-matching agreement or trade-matching statement other than it be in writing. Subsections (2) and (3) below provide some guidance on these documents. A trade-matching agreement or trade-matching statement should be signed by a senior executive officer of the entity to ensure its policies and procedures are given sufficient attention and priority within the entity's senior management. A senior executive officer would include any individual who is (a) the chair of the entity, if that individual performs the functions of the office on a full time basis, (b) a vice-chair of the entity, if that individual performs the functions of the office on a full time basis, (c) the president, chief executive officer or chief operating officer of the entity, and (d) a senior vice-president of the entity in charge of the entity's operations and back-office functions.

---

[6]CDS is also regulated by the Bank of Canada pursuant to the *Payment Clearing and Settlement Act* (Canada).

[7]See, for example, s. 1(1) of the *Securities Act* (Ontario).

(2) **Trade-matching agreement** —

(a) A registered dealer or registered adviser need only enter into one trade-matching agreement with the other trade-matching parties for new or existing DAP/RAP trading accounts of an institutional investor for all future trades in relation to such account. The trade-matching agreement may be a single multi-party agreement among the trade-matching parties, or a network of bilateral agreements. A single trade-matching agreement is also sufficient for the general and all sub-accounts of the registered adviser or buy-side manager. If the dealer or adviser uses a trade-matching agreement, the form of such agreement may be incorporated into the institutional account opening documentation and may be modified from time to time with the consent of the parties.

(b) The agreement must specify the roles and responsibilities of each of the trade-matching parties and should describe the minimum standards and best practices to be incorporated into the policies and procedures that each party has in place. This should include the timelines for accomplishing the various steps and tasks of each trade-matching party for timely matching. For example, the agreement may include, as applicable, provisions dealing with:

For the dealer executing and/or clearing the trade:

- how and when the notice of trade execution (NOE) is to be given to the institutional investor or its adviser, including the format and content of the NOE (e.g., electronic);
- how and when trade details are to be entered into the dealer's internal systems and the clearing agency's systems;
- how and when the dealer is to correct or adjust trade details entered into its internal systems or the clearing agency's systems as may be required to agree to trade details with the institutional investor or its adviser;
- general duties of the dealer to cooperate with other trade-matching parties in the investigation, adjustment, expedition and communication of trade details to ensure trades can be matched within prescribed timelines.

For the institutional investor or its adviser:

- how and when to review the NOE's trade details, including identifying any differences from its own records;
- how and when to notify the dealer of trade differences, if any, and resolve such differences;
- how and when to determine and communicate settlement details and account allocations to the dealer and/or custodian(s);
- general duties of the institutional investor or its adviser to cooperate with other trade-matching parties in the investigation, adjustment, expedition and communication of trade details to ensure trades can be matched within prescribed timelines.

For the custodian settling the trade at the clearing agency:

- how and when to receive trade details and settlement instructions from institutional investors or their advisers;
- how and when to review and monitor trade details submitted to the clearing agency on an ongoing basis for items entered and awaiting affirmation or challenge;
- how and when to report to institutional investors or their advisers on an ongoing basis changes to the status of a trade and the matching of a trade;
- general duties of the custodian to cooperate with other trade-matching parties in the investigation, adjustment, expedition and communication of trade details to ensure trades can be matched within prescribed timelines.

(3) **Trade-matching statement** — A single trade-matching statement is sufficient for the general and all sub-accounts of the registered adviser or buy-side manager. A registered dealer or registered adviser may accept a trade-matching statement signed by a senior executive officer of a trade-matching party without further investigation and may continue to rely upon the statement for all future trades in an account, unless the dealer or adviser has knowledge that any statements or facts set out in the statement are incorrect. Mass mailings or emails of a trade-matching statement, or the posting of a single uniform trade-matching statement on a Website, would be acceptable ways of providing the statement to other trade-matching parties. A registered firm may rely on a trade-matching party's representations that the trade-matching statement was provided to the other trade-matching parties without further investigation.

(4) **Monitoring and enforcement of undertakings in trade-matching documentation** — Registered dealers and advisers should use reasonable efforts to monitor compliance with the terms or undertakings set out in the trade-matching agreements or trade-matching statements in accordance with their policies and procedures.

Registered dealers and advisers should also take active steps to address problems if the policies and procedures of other trade-matching parties appear to be inadequate and are causing delays in the matching process. Such steps might include imposing monetary incentives (e.g. penalty fees) or requesting a third party review or assessment of the party's policies and procedures. This approach could enhance cooperation among the trade-matching parties leading to the identification of the root causes of failures to match trades on time.

2.4 Determination of appropriate policies and procedures — (1) **Best practices** — We are of the view that, when establishing appropriate policies and procedures, a party should consider the industry's generally adopted best practices and standards for institutional trade processing. It should also include those policies and procedures into its regulatory compliance and risk management programs.

(2) **Different policies and procedures** — We recognize that appropriate policies and procedures may not be the same for all registered dealers, registered advisers and other market participants because of the varying nature, scale and complexity of a market participant's business and risks in the trading process. For example, policies and procedures designed to achieve matching may differ among a registered dealer that acts as an "introducing broker" and one that acts as a "carrying broker".[8] In addition, if a dealer is not a clearing agency participant, the dealer's policies and procedures to expeditiously achieve matching should be integrated with the clearing arrangements that it has with any other dealer acting as carrying or clearing broker for the dealer. Establishing appropriate policies and procedures may require registered dealers, registered advisers and other market participants to upgrade their systems and enhance their interoperability with others.[9]

---

[8]See IIROC Member Rule No. 35 — *Introducing Broker / Carrying Broker Arrangements.*
[9]See Discussion Paper 24-401, at p. 3984, for a discussion of *interoperability.*

2.5 Use of matching service utility — The Instrument does not require the trade-matching parties to use the facilities or services of a matching service utility to accomplish matching of trades within the prescribed timelines. However, if such facilities or services are made available in Canada, the use of such facilities or services may help a trade-matching party's compliance with the Instrument's requirements.

PART 3 — INFORMATION REPORTING REQUIREMENTS

3.1 Exception reporting for registered firms —

(a) Part 4 of the Instrument requires a registered firm to complete and deliver to the securities regulatory authority Form 24-101F1 and related exhibits. Form 24-101F1 need only be delivered if less than a percentage target of the DAP/RAP trades executed by or for the registered firm in any given calendar quarter have matched within the time required by the Instrument. Tracking of a registered firm's trade-matching statistics may be outsourced to a third party service provider, including a clearing agency or custodian. However, despite the outsourcing arrangement, the registered firm retains full legal and regulatory liability and accountability to the Canadian securities regulatory authorities for its exception reporting requirements. If a registered firm has insufficient information to determine whether it has achieved the percentage target of matched DAP/RAP trades in any given calendar quarter, it must explain in Form 24-101F1 the reasons for this and the steps it is taking to obtain this information in the future.

(b) Form 24-101F1 requires registered firms to provide aggregate quantitative information on their equity and debt DAP/RAP trades. They must also provide qualitative information on the circumstances or underlying causes that resulted in or contributed to the failure to achieve the percentage target for matched equity and/or debt DAP/RAP trades within the maximum time prescribed by Part 3 of the Instrument and the specific steps they are taking to resolve delays in the trade reporting and matching process in the future. Registered firms should provide information that is relevant to their circumstances. For example, dealers should provide information demonstrating problems with NOEs or reporting of trade details to the clearing agency. Reasons given for the failure could be one or more matters within the registered firm's control or due to another trade-matching party or service provider.

(c) The steps being taken by a registered firm to resolve delays in the matching process could be internally focused, such as implementing a new system or procedure, or externally focused, such as meeting with a trade-matching party to determine what action should be taken by that party. Dealers should confirm what steps they have taken to inform and encourage their clients to comply with the requirements or undertakings of the trade-matching agreement and/or trade-matching statement. They should confirm what problems, if any, they have encountered with their clients, other trade-matching parties or service providers. They should identify the trade-matching party or service provider that appears to be consistently not meeting matching deadlines or to have no reasonable policies and procedures in place. Advisers should provide similar information, including information demonstrating problems with communicating allocations or with service providers or custodians.

3.2 Regulatory reviews of registered firm exception reports —

(a) We will review the completed Forms 24-101F1 on an ongoing basis to monitor and assess compliance by registered firms with the Instrument's matching requirements. We will identify problem areas in matching, including identifying trade-matching parties that have no or weak policies and procedures in place to ensure matching of trades is accomplished within the time prescribed by Part 3 of the Instrument. Monitoring and assessment of registered firm matching activities may be undertaken by the SROs in addition to, or in lieu of, reviews undertaken by us.

(b) Consistent inability to meet the matching percentage target will be considered as evidence by the Canadian securities regulatory authorities that either the policies and procedures of one or more of the trade matching parties have not been properly designed or, if properly designed, have been inadequately complied with. Consistently poor qualitative reporting will also be considered as evidence of poorly designed or implemented policies and procedures. See also section 2.3(4) of this Companion Policy for a further discussion of our approach to compliance and enforcement of the trade-matching requirements of the Instrument.

3.3 Other information reporting requirements — Clearing agencies and matching service utilities are required to include in Forms 24-101F2 and 24-101F5 certain trade-matching information in respect of their participants or users/subscribers. The purpose of this information is to facilitate monitoring and enforcement by the Canadian securities regulatory authorities or SROs of the Instrument's matching requirements.

3.4 Forms delivered in electronic form — Registered firms may complete their Form 24-101F1 online on the CSA's website at the following URL addresses:

In English: http://www.securities-administrators.ca/industry_resources.aspx?id=52
In French: http://www.autorites-valeurs-mobilieres.ca/ressources_professionnelles.aspx?id=52.

3.5 Confidentiality of information — The forms delivered to the securities regulatory authority by a registered firm, clearing agency and matching service utility under the Instrument will be treated as confidential by us, subject to the applicable provisions of the freedom of information and protection of privacy legislation adopted by each province and territory. We are of the view that the forms contain intimate financial, commercial and technical information and that the interests of the providers of the information in non-disclosure outweigh the desirability of making such information publicly available. However, we may share the information with SROs and may publicly release aggregate industry-wide matching statistics on equity and debt DAP/RAP trading in the Canadian markets.

PART 4 — REQUIREMENTS FOR MATCHING SERVICE UTILITIES

4.1 Matching service utility — (1) Part 6 of the Instrument sets out reporting, systems capacity, and other requirements of a matching service utility. The term *matching service utility* expressly excludes a clearing agency. A matching service utility would be any entity that provides the services of a post-execution centralized matching facility for trade-matching parties. It may use technology to match in real-time trade data elements throughout a trade's processing lifecycle. A matching service utility would not include a registered dealer who offers "local" matching services to its institutional investor-clients.

(2) A matching service utility would be viewed by us as an important infrastructure system involved in the clearing and settlement of securities transactions. We believe that, while a matching service utility operating in Canada would largely enhance operational efficiency in the capital markets, it would raise certain regulatory concerns. Comparing and matching trade data are complex processes that are inextricably linked to the clearance and settlement process. A matching service utility concentrates processing risk in the entity that performs matching instead of dispersing that risk more to the dealers and their institutional investor-clients. Accordingly, we believe that the breakdown of a matching service utility's ability to accurately verify and match trade information from multiple market participants involving large numbers of securities transactions and sums of money could have adverse consequences for the efficiency of the Canadian securities clearing and settlement system. The requirements of the Instrument applicable to a matching service utility are intended to address these risks.

4.2 Initial information reporting requirements for a matching service utility — Sections 6.1(1) and 10.2(4) of the Instrument require any person or company that carries on or intends to carry on business as a matching service utility to deliver Form 24-101F3 to the securities regulatory authority. We will review Form 24-101F3 to determine whether the person or company that delivered the form is an appropriate person or company to act as a matching service utility for the Canadian capital markets. We will consider a number of factors when reviewing the form, including:

(a) the performance capability, standards and procedures for the transmission, processing and distribution of details of trades executed on behalf of institutional investors;

(b) whether market participants generally may obtain access to the facilities and services of the matching service utility on fair and reasonable terms;

(c) personnel qualifications;

(d) whether the matching service utility has sufficient financial resources for the proper performance of its functions;

(e) the existence of, and interoperability arrangements with, another entity performing a similar function for the same type of security; and

(f) the systems report referred to in section 6.5(b) of the Instrument.

4.3 Change to significant information — Under section 6.2 of the Instrument, a matching service utility is required to deliver to the securities regulatory authority an amendment to the information provided in Form 24-101F3 at least 45 days before implementing a significant change involving a matter set out in Form 24-101F3. In our view, a significant change includes a change to the information contained in the General Information items 1–10 and Exhibits A, B, E, G, I, J, O, P and Q of Form 24-101F3.

4.4 Ongoing information reporting and other requirements applicable to a matching service utility — (1) Ongoing quarterly information reporting requirements will allow us to monitor a matching service utility's operational performance and management of risk, the progress of interoperability in the market, and any negative impact on access to the markets. A matching service utility will also provide trade matching data and other information to us so that we can monitor industry compliance.

(2) Completed forms delivered by a matching service utility will provide useful information on whether it is:

(a) developing fair and reasonable linkages between its systems and the systems of any other matching service utility in Canada that, at a minimum, allow parties to executed trades that are processed through the systems of both matching service utilities to communicate through appropriate, effective interfaces;

(b) negotiating with other matching service utilities in Canada fair and reasonable charges and terms of payment for the use of interface services with respect to the sharing of trade and account information; and

(c) not unreasonably charging more for use of its facilities and services when one or more counterparties to trades are customers of other matching service utilities than the matching service utility would normally charge its customers for use of its facilities and services.

4.5 Capacity, integrity and security system requirements — (1) The activities in section 6.5(a) of the Instrument must be carried out at least once a year. We would expect these activities to be carried out even more frequently if there is a significant change in trading volumes that necessitates that these functions be carried out more frequently in order to ensure that the matching service utility can appropriately service its clients.

(2) The independent review contemplated by section 6.5(b) of the Instrument should be performed by competent and independent audit personnel, in accordance with generally accepted auditing standards. Depending on the circumstances, we would consider accepting a review performed and written report delivered pursuant to similar requirements of a foreign regulator to satisfy the requirements of this section. A matching service utility that wants to advocate for that result must submit a request for discretionary relief.

(3) The notification of a material systems failure under section 6.5(c) of the Instrument should be provided promptly from the time the incident was identified as being material and should include the date, cause and duration of the interruption and its general impact on users or subscribers. We consider promptly to mean within one hour from the time the incident was identified as being material. Material systems failures include serious incidents that result in the interruption of the matching of trades for more than thirty minutes during normal business hours.

PART 5 — TRADE SETTLEMENT

5.1 Trade settlement by dealer — Section 7.1 of the Instrument is intended to support and strengthen the general settlement cycle rules of the SROs and marketplaces. Current SRO and marketplace rules mandate a standard T+3 settlement cycle period for most transactions in equity and long term debt securities.[10] If a dealer is not a participant of a clearing agency, the dealer's policies and procedures to facilitate the settlement of a trade should be combined with the clearing arrangements that it has with any other dealer acting as carrying or clearing broker for the dealer.

PART 6 — REQUIREMENTS OF SELF-REGULATORY ORGANIZATIONS AND OTHERS

6.1 Standardized documentation — Without limiting the generality of section 8.2 of the Instrument, an SRO may require its members to use, or recommend that they use, a standardized form of trade-matching agreement or trade-matching statement prepared or approved by the SRO, and may negotiate on behalf of its members with other trade-matching parties and industry associations to agree on the standardized form of trade-matching agreement or trade-matching statement to be used by all relevant sectors in the industry (dealers, buy-side managers and custodians).

Adoption by OSC: (2007) 30 O.S.C.B. 2631 and 335; Request for Comments: (2006) 29 O.S.C.B. 1829.

Adoption of Amendment by OSC: (2009) 32 O.S.C.B. (Supp. 4) 376 and 32 O.S.C.B. (Supp. 2) 1.

Adoption of Amendment by OSC: (2010) 33 O.S.C.B. 5609 and 3379; Request for Comments: (2009) 32 O.S.C.B. 9059.

Part 2: MARKET PARTICIPANTS

---

[10]See, for example, IIROC Member Rule 800.27 and TSX Rule 5-103(1).

National Instrument 24-102 — Clearing Agency Requirements

Date: December 3, 2015

38 O.S.C.B. (Supp. 5) 27

TABLE OF CONTENTS

NATIONAL INSTRUMENT 24-102 — CLEARING AGENCY REQUIREMENTS

PART 1 — DEFINITIONS, INTERPRETATION AND APPLICATION

1.1 Definitions — In this Instrument

"accounting principles" means accounting principles as defined in National Instrument 52-107 *Acceptable Accounting Principles and Auditing Standards*;

"auditing standards" means auditing standards as defined in National Instrument 52-107 *Acceptable Accounting Principles and Auditing Standards*;

"board of directors" means, in the case of a recognized clearing agency that does not have a board of directors, a group of individuals that acts for the clearing agency in a capacity similar to a board of directors;

"central counterparty" means a person or company that interposes itself between the counterparties to securities or derivatives transactions in one or more financial markets, acting functionally as the buyer to every seller and the seller to every buyer or the counterparty to every party;

"central securities depository" means a person or company that provides centralized facilities as a depository of securities, including securities accounts, central safekeeping services and asset services, which may include the administration of corporate actions and redemptions;

"exempt clearing agency" means a clearing agency that has been granted a decision of the securities regulatory authority pursuant to securities legislation exempting it from the requirement in such legislation to be recognized by the securities regulatory authority as a clearing agency;

"link" means, in relation to a clearing agency, contractual and operational arrangements that directly or indirectly through an intermediary connect the clearing agency and one or more other systems for the clearing, settlement or recording of securities or derivatives transactions;

"participant" means a person or company that has entered into an agreement with a clearing agency to access the services of the clearing agency and is bound by the clearing agency's rules and procedures;

"PFMI Disclosure Framework Document" means a disclosure document completed substantially in the form of *Annex A: FMI disclosure template* of the December 2012 report *Principles for financial market infrastructures: Disclosure framework and Assessment methodology* published by the Committee on Payments and Market Infrastructures and the International Organization of Securities Commissions, as amended, supplemented or superseded from time to time, or a similar disclosure document required to be completed regularly and disclosed publicly by a clearing agency in accordance with the regulatory requirements of a foreign jurisdiction in which the clearing agency is located;

"PFMI Principle" means a principle, including applicable key considerations, in the April 2012 report *Principles for financial market infrastructures* published by the Committee on Payments and Market Infrastructures and the International Organization of Securities Commissions, as amended from time to time;

"publicly accountable enterprise" means a publicly accountable enterprise as defined in Part 3 of National Instrument 52-107 Acceptable Accounting Principles and Auditing Standards;

"securities settlement system" means a system that enables securities to be transferred and settled by book entry according to a set of predetermined multilateral rules.

1.2 Interpretation — Affiliated Entity, Controlled Entity and Subsidiary Entity — (1) In this Instrument, a person or company is considered to be an affiliated entity of another person or company if one is a subsidiary entity of the other or if both are subsidiary entities of the same person or company, or if each of them is a controlled entity of the same person or company.

(2) In this Instrument, a person or company is considered to be controlled by a person or company if

    (a) in the case of a person or company,

        (i) voting securities of the first-mentioned person or company carrying more than fifty percent of the votes for the election of directors are held, otherwise than by way of security only, by or for the benefit of the other person or company, and

        (ii) the votes carried by the securities are entitled, if exercised, to elect a majority of the directors of the first-mentioned person or company;

(b) in the case of a partnership that does not have directors, other than a limited partnership, the second-mentioned person or company holds more than fifty percent of the interests in the partnership; or

(c) in the case of a limited partnership, the general partner is the second-mentioned person or company.

(3) In this Instrument, a person or company is considered to be a subsidiary entity of another person or company if

(a) it is a controlled entity of

(i) that other,

(ii) that other and one or more persons or companies, each of which is a controlled entity of that other, or

(iii) two or more persons or companies, each of which is a controlled entity of that other; or

(b) it is a subsidiary entity of a person or company that is the other's subsidiary entity.

1.3 Interpretation — Extended Meaning of Affiliated Entity — For the purposes of the PFMI Principles, a person or company is considered to be an affiliate of a participant, the person or company and the participant each being described in this section as a "party", where,

(a) a party holds, otherwise than by way of security only, voting securities of the other party carrying more than 20 percent of the votes for the election of directors, or

(b) in the event paragraph (a) is not applicable,

(i) a party holds, otherwise than by way of security only, an interest in the other party that allows it to direct the management or operations of the other party; or

(ii) financial information in respect of both parties is consolidated for financial reporting purposes.

1.4 Interpretation — Clearing Agency — For the purposes of this Instrument, in Québec, a clearing agency includes a clearing house, a central securities depository and a settlement system within the meaning of the Québec *Securities Act* and a clearing house and a settlement system within the meaning of the Québec *Derivatives Act*.

1.5 Application — (1) Part 3 applies to a recognized clearing agency that operates as any of the following:

(a) a central counterparty;

(b) a central securities depository;

(c) a securities settlement system.

(2) Unless the context otherwise indicates, Part 4 applies to a recognized clearing agency whether or not it operates as a central counterparty, central securities depository or securities settlement system.

(3) In Québec, if there is a conflict or an inconsistency between section 2.2 and the provisions of the Québec *Derivatives Act* governing the self-certification process with respect to a clearing agency implementing a significant change or a fee change, the provisions of the Québec *Derivatives Act* prevail.

(4) The requirements of section 2.2 or 2.5 apply only to the extent that the subject matters of the section are not otherwise governed by the terms and conditions of a decision of the securities regulatory authority that recognizes a clearing agency or that exempts a clearing agency from a recognition requirement.

PART 2 — CLEARING AGENCY RECOGNITION OR EXEMPTION FROM RECOGNITION

2.1 Application and initial filing of information — (1) An applicant for recognition as a clearing agency under securities legislation, or for exemption from the requirement to be recognized as a clearing agency under securities legislation, must include in its application all of the following:

(a) if applicable, the applicant's most recently completed PFMI Disclosure Framework Document;

(b) sufficient information to demonstrate that the applicant is in compliance with

(i) provincial and territorial securities legislation, or

(ii) the regulatory regime of a foreign jurisdiction in which the applicant's head office or principal place of business is located;

(c) any additional relevant information sufficient to demonstrate that it is in the public interest for the securities regulatory authority to recognize or exempt the applicant, as the case may be.

(2) In addition to the requirement set out in subsection (1), an applicant that has a head office or principal place of business located in a foreign jurisdiction must

(a) certify that it will assist the securities regulatory authority in accessing the applicant's books and records and in undertaking an onsite inspection and examination at the applicant's premises, and

(b) certify that it will provide the securities regulatory authority, if requested by such authority, with an opinion of legal counsel that the applicant has, as a matter of law, the power and authority to

(i) provide the securities regulatory authority with prompt access to its books and records, and

(ii) submit to onsite inspection and examination by the securities regulatory authority.

(3) In addition to the requirements set out in subsections (1) and (2), an applicant whose head office or principal place of business is located in a foreign jurisdiction must file a completed Form 24-102F1 *Submission to Jurisdiction and Appointment of Agent for Service*.

(4) An applicant must inform the securities regulatory authority in writing of any material change to the information provided in its application, or if any of the information becomes materially inaccurate for any reason, as soon as the change occurs or the applicant becomes aware of any inaccuracy.

2.2 Significant changes, fee changes and other changes in information — (1) In this section, for greater certainty, a "significant change" includes, in relation to a clearing agency,

(a) any change to the clearing agency's constating documents or by-laws;

(b) any change to the clearing agency's corporate governance or corporate structure, including any change of control of the clearing agency, whether direct or indirect;

(c) any material change to an agreement among the clearing agency and participants in connection with the clearing agency's operations and services, including those agreements to which the clearing agency is a party and those agreements among participants to which the clearing agency is not a party, but that are expressly referred to in the clearing agency's rules or procedures and are made available by participants to the clearing agency;

(d) any material change to the clearing agency's rules, operating procedures, user guides, manuals, or other documentation governing or establishing the rights, obligations and relationships among the clearing agency and participants in connection with the clearing agency's operations and services;

(e) any material change to the design, operation or functionality of any of the clearing agency's operations and services;

(f) the establishment or removal of a link or any material change to an existing link;

(g) commencing to engage in a new type of business activity or ceasing to engage in a business activity in which the clearing agency is then engaged;

(h) any other matter identified as a significant change in the recognition terms and conditions.

(2) Subject to subsection (4), a recognized clearing agency must not implement a significant change unless it has filed a written notice of the significant change with the securities regulatory authority at least 45 days before implementing the change.

(3) If a proposed significant change referred to in subsection (2) would affect the information set out in its PFMI Disclosure Framework Document filed with the securities regulatory authority, a recognized clearing agency must complete and file with the securities regulatory authority, concurrently with providing the written notice referred to in subsection (2), an appropriate amendment to its PFMI Disclosure Framework Document.

(4) If a recognized clearing agency proposes to modify a fee or introduce a new fee for any of its clearing, settlement or depository services, the clearing agency must notify in writing the securities regulatory authority of such fee change before implementing the fee change within a period stipulated by the terms and conditions of a decision of the securities regulatory authority that recognizes the clearing agency.

(5) An exempt clearing agency must notify in writing the securities regulatory authority of any material change to the information provided to the securities regulatory authority in its PFMI Disclosure Framework Document and related application materials, or if any of the information becomes materially inaccurate for any reason, as soon as the change occurs or the exempt clearing agency becomes aware of any inaccuracy.

2.3 Ceasing to carry on business — (1) A recognized clearing agency or exempt clearing agency that intends to cease carrying on business in the local jurisdiction as a clearing agency must file a report on Form 24-102F2 *Cessation of Operations Report for Clearing Agency* with the securities regulatory authority

(a) at least 180 days before ceasing to carry on business if a significant reason for ceasing to carry on business relates to the clearing agency's financial viability or any other matter that is preventing, or may potentially prevent, it from being able to provide its operations and services as a going concern, or

(b) at least 90 days before ceasing to carry on business for any other reason.

(2) A recognized clearing agency or exempt clearing agency that involuntarily ceases to carry on business in the local jurisdiction as a clearing agency must file a report on Form 24-102F2 *Cessation of Operations Report for Clearing Agency* with the securities regulatory authority as soon as practicable after it ceases to carry on that business.

2.4 Filing of initial audited financial statements — (1) An applicant must file audited financial statements for its most recently completed financial year with the securities regulatory authority as part of its application under section 2.1.

(2) The financial statements referred to in subsection (1) must

(a) be prepared in accordance with Canadian GAAP applicable to publicly accountable enterprises, IFRS or the generally accepted accounting principles of the foreign jurisdiction in which the person or company is incorporated, organized or located,

(b) identify in the notes to the financial statements the accounting principles used to prepare the financial statements,

(c) disclose the presentation currency, and

(d) be audited in accordance with Canadian GAAS, International Standards on Auditing or the generally accepted auditing standards of the foreign jurisdiction in which the person or company is incorporated, organized or located.

(3) The financial statements referred to in subsection (1) must be accompanied by an auditor's report that

(a) expresses an unmodified or unqualified opinion,

(b) identifies all financial periods presented for which the auditor's report applies,

(c) identifies the auditing standards used to conduct the audit,

(d) identifies the accounting principles used to prepare the financial statements,

(e) is prepared in accordance with the same auditing standards used to conduct the audit, and

(f) is prepared and signed by a person or company that is authorized to sign an auditor's report under the laws of a jurisdiction of Canada or a foreign jurisdiction, and that meets the professional standards of that jurisdiction.

2.5 Filing of annual audited and interim financial statements — (1) A recognized clearing agency or exempt clearing agency must file annual audited financial statements that comply with the requirements set out in subsections 2.4(2) and (3) with the securities regulatory authority no later than the 90th day after the end of the recognized clearing agency or exempt clearing agency's financial year.

(2) A recognized clearing agency or exempt clearing agency must file interim financial statements that comply with the requirements set out in paragraphs 2.4(2)(a) and (2)(b) with the securities regulatory authority no later than the 45th day after the end of each interim period.

PART 3 — PFMI PRINCIPLES APPLICABLE TO RECOGNIZED CLEARING AGENCIES

3.1 PFMI Principles — A recognized clearing agency must establish, implement and maintain rules, procedures, policies or operations designed to ensure that it meets or exceeds PFMI Principles 1 to 3, 10, 13, 15 to 19, 20 other than key consideration 9, 21 to 23 and the following:

(a) if the clearing agency operates as a central counterparty, PFMI Principles 4 to 9, 12 and 14;

(b) if the clearing agency operates as a securities settlement system, PFMI Principles 4, 5, 7 to 9 and12; and

(c) if the clearing agency operates as a central securities depository, PFMI Principle 11.

PART 4 — OTHER REQUIREMENTS OF RECOGNIZED CLEARING AGENCIES

DIVISION 1 — GOVERNANCE:

4.1 Board of directors — (1) A recognized clearing agency must have a board of directors.

(2) The board of directors must include appropriate representation by individuals who are

    (a) independent of the clearing agency, and

    (b) not employees or executive officers of a participant or their immediate family members.

(3) For the purposes of paragraph (2)(a), an individual is independent of a clearing agency if he or she has no direct or indirect material relationship with the clearing agency.

(4) For the purposes of subsection (3), a "material relationship" is a relationship that could, in the view of the clearing agency's board of directors, be reasonably expected to interfere with the exercise of a member's independent judgment.

4.2 Documented procedures regarding risk spill-overs — The board of directors and management of a recognized clearing agency must have documented procedures to manage possible risk spill over where the clearing agency provides services with a different risk profile than its depository, clearing and settlement services.

4.3 Chief Risk Officer and Chief Compliance Officer — (1) A recognized clearing agency must designate a chief risk officer and a chief compliance officer, who must report directly to the board of directors or, if determined by the board of directors, to the chief executive officer of the clearing agency.

(2) The chief risk officer must

    (a) have full responsibility and authority to maintain, implement and enforce the risk management framework established by the clearing agency,

    (b) make recommendations to the clearing agency's board of directors regarding the clearing agency's risk management framework,

    (c) monitor the effectiveness of the clearing agency's risk management framework, and

    (d) report to the clearing agency's board of directors on a timely basis upon becoming aware of any significant deficiency with the risk management framework.

(3) The chief compliance officer must

    (a) establish, implement, maintain and enforce written policies and procedures to identify and resolve conflicts of interest and ensure that the clearing agency complies with securities legislation,

    (b) monitor compliance with the policies and procedures described in paragraph (a),

    (c) report to the board of directors of the clearing agency as soon as practicable upon becoming aware of any circumstance indicating that the clearing agency, or any individual acting on its behalf, is not in compliance with securities legislation and one or more of the following apply:

        (i) the non-compliance creates a risk of harm to a participant,

        (ii) the non-compliance creates a risk of harm to the broader financial system,

        (iii) the non-compliance is part of a pattern of non-compliance, or

        (iv) the non-compliance may have an impact on the ability of the clearing agency to carry on business in compliance with securities legislation,

    (d) prepare and certify an annual report assessing compliance by the clearing agency, and individuals acting on its behalf, with securities legislation and submit the report to the board of directors,

    (e) report to the clearing agency's board of directors as soon as practicable upon becoming aware of a conflict of interest that creates a risk of harm to a participant or to the capital markets, and

    (f) concurrently with submitting a report under paragraphs (c), (d) or (e), file a copy of such report with the securities regulatory authority.

4.4 Board or advisory committees — (1) The board of directors of a recognized clearing agency must, at a minimum, establish and maintain committees on risk management, finance and audit.

(2) If a committee is a board committee, it must be chaired by a sufficiently knowledgeable individual who is independent of the clearing agency.

(3) Subject to subsection (4), a committee must have an appropriate representation by individuals who are independent of the clearing agency.

(4) An audit or risk committee must have an appropriate representation by individuals who are

    (a) independent of the clearing agency, and

    (b) not employees or executive officers of a participant or their immediate family members.

DIVISION 2 — DEFAULT MANAGEMENT:

4.5 Use of own capital — A recognized clearing agency that operates as a central counterparty must dedicate and use a reasonable portion of its own capital to cover losses resulting from one or more participant defaults.

DIVISION 3 — OPERATIONAL RISK:

4.6 Systems requirements — For each system operated by or on behalf of a recognized clearing agency that supports the clearing agency's clearing, settlement and depository functions, the clearing agency must

    (a) develop and maintain

        (i) an adequate system of internal controls over that system, and

Part 2: MARKET PARTICIPANTS

(ii) adequate information technology general controls, including, without limitation, controls relating to information systems operations, information security, change management, problem management, network support and system software support,

(b) in accordance with prudent business practice, on a reasonably frequent basis and, in any event, at least annually

(i) make reasonable current and future capacity estimates, and

(ii) conduct capacity stress tests to determine the ability of that system to process transactions in an accurate, timely and efficient manner, and

(c) promptly notify the regulator or, in Québec, the securities regulatory authority of any material systems failure, malfunction, delay or security breach, and provide timely updates on the status of the failure, malfunction, delay or security breach, the resumption of service, and the results of the clearing agency's internal review of the failure, malfunction, delay or security breach.

4.7 Systems reviews — (1) A recognized clearing agency must annually engage a qualified party to conduct an independent systems review and vulnerability assessment and prepare a report in accordance with established audit standards and best industry practices to ensure that the clearing agency is in compliance with paragraph 4.6(a) and section 4.9.

(2) The clearing agency must provide the report resulting from the review conducted under subsection (1) to

(a) its board of directors, or audit committee, promptly upon the report's completion, and

(b) the regulator or, in Québec, the securities regulatory authority, by the earlier of the 30th day after providing the report to its board of directors or the audit committee or the 60th day after the calendar year end.

4.8 Clearing agency technology requirements and testing facilities — (1) A recognized clearing agency must make available to participants, in their final form, all technology requirements regarding interfacing with or accessing the clearing agency

(a) if operations have not begun, sufficiently in advance of operations to allow a reasonable period for testing and system modification by participants, and

(b) if operations have begun, sufficiently in advance of implementing a material change to technology requirements to allow a reasonable period for testing and system modification by participants.

(2) After complying with subsection (1), the clearing agency must make available testing facilities for interfacing with or accessing the clearing agency

(a) if operations have not begun, sufficiently in advance of operations to allow a reasonable period for testing and system modification by participants, and

(b) if operations have begun, sufficiently in advance of implementing a material change to technology requirements to allow a reasonable period for testing and system modification by participants.

(3) The clearing agency must not begin operations before

(a) it has complied with paragraphs (1)(a) and (2)(a), and

(b) the chief information officer of the clearing agency, or an individual performing a similar function, has certified in writing to the regulator or, in Québec, the securities regulatory authority, that all information technology systems used by the clearing agency have been tested according to prudent business practices and are operating as designed.

(4) The clearing agency must not implement a material change to the systems referred to in section 4.6 before

(a) it has complied with paragraphs (1)(b) and (2)(b), and

(b) the chief information officer of the clearing agency, or an individual performing a similar function, has certified in writing to the regulator or, in Québec, the securities regulatory authority, that the change has been tested according to prudent business practices and is operating as designed.

(5) Subsection (4) does not apply to the clearing agency if the change must be made immediately to address a failure, malfunction or material delay of its systems or equipment and if

(a) the clearing agency immediately notifies the regulator or, in Québec, the securities regulatory authority, of its intention to make the change, and

(b) the clearing agency discloses to its participants the changed technology requirements as soon as practicable.

4.9 Testing of business continuity plans — A recognized clearing agency must

(a) develop and maintain reasonable business continuity plans, including disaster recovery plans, and

(b) test its business continuity plans, including its disaster recovery plans, according to prudent business practices and on a reasonably frequent basis and, in any event, at least annually.

4.10 Outsourcing — If a recognized clearing agency outsources a critical service or system to a service provider, including to an affiliated entity of the clearing agency, the clearing agency must do all of the following:

(a) establish, implement, maintain and enforce written policies and procedures to conduct suitable due diligence for selecting service providers to which a critical service and system may be outsourced and for the evaluation and approval of those outsourcing arrangements;

(b) identify any conflicts of interest between the clearing agency and the service provider to which a critical service and system is outsourced, and establish, implement, maintain and enforce written policies and procedures to mitigate and manage those conflicts of interest;

(c) enter into a written contract with the service provider to which a critical service or system is outsourced that

(i) is appropriate for the materiality and nature of the outsourced activities,

(ii) includes service level provisions, and

(iii) provides for adequate termination procedures;

(d) maintain access to the books and records of the service provider relating to the outsourced activities;

(e) ensure that the securities regulatory authority has the same access to all data, information and systems maintained by the service provider on behalf of the clearing agency that it would have absent the outsourcing arrangements;

(f) ensure that all persons conducting audits or independent reviews of the clearing agency under this Instrument have appropriate access to all data, information and systems maintained by the service provider on behalf of the clearing agency that such persons would have absent the outsourcing arrangements;

(g) take appropriate measures to determine that the service provider to which a critical service or system is outsourced establishes, maintains and periodically tests an appropriate business continuity plan, including a disaster recovery plan;

(h) take appropriate measures to ensure that the service provider protects the clearing agency's proprietary information and participants' confidential information, including taking measures to protect information from loss, thefts, vulnerabilities, threats, unauthorized access, copying, use and modification, and discloses it only in circumstances where legislation or an order of a court or tribunal of competent jurisdiction requires the disclosure of such information;

(i) establish, implement, maintain and enforce written policies and procedures to monitor the ongoing performance of the service provider's contractual obligations under the outsourcing arrangements.

DIVISION 4 — PARTICIPATION REQUIREMENTS:

4.11 Access requirements and due process — (1) A recognized clearing agency must not

(a) unreasonably prohibit, condition or limit access by a person or company to the services offered by the clearing agency,

(b) unreasonably discriminate among its participants or indirect participants,

(c) impose any burden on competition that is not reasonably necessary and appropriate,

(d) unreasonably require the use or purchase of another service for a person or company to utilize the clearing agency's services offered by it, and

(e) impose fees or other material costs on its participants that are unfairly or inequitably allocated among the participants.

(2) For any decision made by the clearing agency that terminates, suspends or restricts a participant's membership in the clearing agency or that declines entry to membership to an applicant that applies to become a participant, the clearing agency must ensure that

(a) the participant or applicant is given an opportunity to be heard or make representations, and

(b) it keeps records of, gives reasons for, and provides for reviews of its decisions, including, for each applicant, the reasons for granting access or for denying or limiting access to the applicant, as the case may be.

(3) Nothing in subsection (2) limits or prevents the clearing agency from taking timely action in accordance with its rules and procedures to manage the default of one or more participants or in connection with the clearing agency's recovery or orderly wind-down, whether or not such action adversely affects a participant.

PART 5 — BOOKS AND RECORDS AND LEGAL ENTITY IDENTIFIER

5.1 Books and records — (1) A recognized clearing agency or exempt clearing agency must keep books, records and other documents as are necessary to account for the conduct of its clearing, settlement and depository activities, business transactions and financial affairs and must keep those other books, records and documents as may otherwise be required under securities legislation.

(2) The clearing agency must retain the books and records maintained under this section

(a) for a period of seven years from the date the record was made or received, whichever is later,

(b) in a safe location and a durable form, and

(c) in a manner that permits them to be provided promptly to the securities regulatory authority.

5.2 Legal Entity Identifier — (1) In this section,

"Global Legal Entity Identifier System" means the system for unique identification of parties to financial transactions developed by the LEI Regulatory Oversight Committee, and

"LEI Regulatory Oversight Committee" means the international working group established by the Finance Ministers and the Central Bank Governors of the Group of Twenty nations and the Financial Stability Board, under the Charter of the Regulatory Oversight Committee for the Global Legal Entity Identifier System dated November 5, 2012.

(2) For the purposes of any recordkeeping and reporting requirements required under securities legislation, a recognized clearing agency or exempt clearing agency must identify itself by means of a single legal entity identifier assigned to the clearing agency in accordance with the standards set by the Global Legal Entity Identifier System.

(3) If the Global Legal Entity Identifier System is unavailable to the clearing agency, all of the following apply:

(a) the clearing agency must obtain a substitute legal entity identifier that complies with the standards established by the LEI Regulatory Oversight Committee for pre-legal entity identifiers;

(b) the clearing agency must use the substitute legal entity identifier until a legal entity identifier is assigned to the clearing agency in accordance with the standards set by the Global Legal Entity Identifier System;

(c) after the holder of a substitute legal entity identifier is assigned a legal entity identifier in accordance with the standards set by the Global Legal Entity Identifier System, the clearing agency must ensure that it is identified only by the assigned identifier.

PART 6 — EXEMPTIONS

6.1 Exemption — (1) The regulator or the securities regulatory authority may grant an exemption from the provisions of this Instrument, in whole or in part, subject to such conditions or restrictions as may be imposed in the exemption.

(2) Despite subsection (1), in Ontario, only the regulator may grant an exemption.

(3) Except in Ontario, an exemption referred to in subsection (1) is granted under the statute referred to in Appendix B of National Instrument 14-101 *Definitions* opposite the name of the local jurisdiction.

PART 7 — EFFECTIVE DATE AND TRANSITION

7.1 Effective date and transition — (1) This Instrument comes into force on February 17, 2016.

(2) Despite section 3.1, until December 31, 2016, a recognized clearing agency is not required to implement rules, procedures, policies or operations designed to ensure that a recognized clearing agency meets or exceeds the following:

(a) PFMI Principle 14;

(b) key consideration 4 of PFMI Principle 3 and key consideration 3 of PFMI Principle 15 with respect to a clearing agency's recovery and orderly wind-down plans; and

(c) PFMI Principle 19.

(3) In Saskatchewan, despite subsection (1), if these regulations are filed with the Registrar of Regulations after February 17, 2016, these regulations come into force on the day on which they are filed with the Registrar of Regulations.

Date: December 3, 2015 , (2015) 38 O.S.C.B. (Supp. 5) 27

Form 24-102F1 — Clearing Agency Submission to Jurisdiction and Appointment of Agent for Service of Process

1. Name of clearing agency (the "Clearing Agency"):

....

2. Jurisdiction of incorporation, or equivalent, of Clearing Agency:

....

3. Address of principal place of business of Clearing Agency:

....

4. Name of the agent for service of process (the "Agent") for the Clearing Agency:

....

5. Address of the Agent in .... [name of local jurisdiction]:

....

6. The .... [name of securities regulatory authority] ("securities regulatory authority") issued an order recognizing the Clearing Agency as a clearing agency pursuant to securities legislation, or the securities regulatory authority issued an order exempting the Clearing Agency from the requirement to be recognized as a clearing agency pursuant to such legislation, on ....

7. The Clearing Agency designates and appoints the Agent as its agent upon whom may be served a notice, pleading, subpoena, summons or other process in any action, investigation or administrative, criminal, quasi-criminal, penal or other proceeding arising out of or relating to or concerning the activities of the Clearing Agency in .... [province of local jurisdiction]. The Clearing Agency hereby irrevocably waives any right to challenge service upon its Agent as not binding upon the Clearing Agency.

8. The Clearing Agency agrees to unconditionally and irrevocably attorn to the non-exclusive jurisdiction of (i) the courts and administrative tribunals of .... [name of local jurisdiction] and (ii) any proceeding in any province or territory arising out of, related to, concerning or in any other manner connected with the regulation and oversight of the activities of the Clearing Agency in .... [name of local jurisdiction].

9. The Clearing Agency must file a new submission to jurisdiction and appointment of agent for service of process in this form at least 30 days before the Clearing Agency ceases to be recognized or exempted by the securities regulatory authority, to be in effect for six years from the date it ceases to be recognized or exempted unless otherwise amended in accordance with section 10.

10. Until six years after it has ceased to be a recognized or exempted by the securities regulatory authority, the Clearing Agency must file an amended submission to jurisdiction and appointment of agent for service of process at least 30 days before any change in the name or above address of the Agent.

11. The Clearing Agency agrees that this submission to jurisdiction and appointment of agent for service of process is to be governed by and construed in accordance with the laws of .... [name of local jurisdiction].

Dated: ....

....
Signature of the Clearing Agency

....
Print name and title of signing officer of the Clearing Agency

Agent — Consent to Act as Agent for Service

I, ... [name of Agent in full; if a corporation, full corporate name] of .... [business address], hereby accept the appointment as agent for service of process of .... [insert name of Clearing Agency] and hereby consent to act as agent for service pursuant to the terms of the appointment executed by .... [insert name of Clearing Agency] on .... [insert date].

Dated: ....

....
Signature of Agent

....
Print name of person signing and, if Agent is not an individual, the title of the person

Form 24-102F2 — Cessation of Operations Report for Clearing Agency

1. Identification:

   A. Full name of the recognized or exempted clearing agency:

   B. Name(s) under which business is conducted, if different from item 1A:

2. Date clearing agency proposes to cease carrying on business as a clearing agency:

3. If cessation of business was involuntary, date clearing agency has ceased to carry on business as a clearing agency:

Exhibits

File all exhibits with the Cessation of Operations Report. For each exhibit, include the name of the clearing agency, the date of filing of the exhibit and the date as as of which the information is accurate (if different from the date of the filing). If any exhibit required is inapplicable, a statement to that effect must be provided instead of the exhibit.

Exhibit A

The reasons for the clearing agency ceasing to carry on business as a clearing agency.

Exhibit B

A list of all participants in Canada during the last 30 days prior to ceasing business as a clearing agency.

Exhibit C

A description of the alternative arrangements available to participants in respect of the services offered by the clearing agency immediately before the cessation of business as a clearing agency.

Exhibit D

A description of all links the clearing agency had immediately before the cessation of business as a clearing agency with other clearing agencies or trade repositories.

Certificate of Clearing Agency

The undersigned certifies that the information given in this report is true and correct.

DATED at .... this .... day of .... 20..........

.... (Name of clearing agency)

.... (Name of director, officer or partner — please type or print)

.... (Signature of director, officer or partner)

.... (Official capacity — please type or print)

Companion Policy 24-102CP — To National Instrument 24-102 Clearing Agency Requirements

Date: December 3, 2015

(2015) 38 O.S.C.B. (Supp. 5)

TABLE OF CONTENTS

COMPANION POLICY 24-102CP — TO NATIONAL INSTRUMENT 24-102 CLEARING AGENCY REQUIREMENTS

PART I — GENERAL COMMENTS

1.1 Introduction — (1) This Companion Policy (CP) sets out how the Canadian Securities Administrators (the CSA or we) interpret or apply provisions of National Instrument 24-102 *Clearing Agency Requirements* (the Instrument) and related securities legislation.

(2) Except for this Part 1 of the CP, section 3.2 and 3.3 of Part 3 of this CP, and the *text boxes* in Annex I to this CP, the numbering of Parts, sections and subsections in this CP generally corresponds to the numbering in the Instrument. Any general guidance or introductory comments for a Part appears immediately after the Part's name. Specific guidance on a section or subsection in the Instrument follows any general guidance. If there is no guidance for a Part, section or subsection, the numbering in this CP will skip to the next provision that does have guidance.

(3) Unless otherwise stated, any reference in this CP to a Part, section, subsection, paragraph or defined term is a reference to the corresponding Part, section, subsection, paragraph or defined term of the Instrument. The CP also makes references to certain paragraphs in the April 2012 report *Principles for financial market infrastructures* (the PFMIs or PFMI Report, as the context requires) and the PFMI Principles set out therein. A reference to a PFMI Principle may include a reference to an applicable key consideration (see definition of "PFMI Principle" in section 1.1).

1.2 Background and overview — (1) Securities legislation in certain jurisdictions of Canada requires an entity seeking to carry on business as a clearing agency in the jurisdiction to be (i) recognized by the securities regulatory authority in that jurisdiction, or (ii) exempted from the recognition requirement.[1] Accordingly, Part 2 sets out certain requirements in connection with the application process for recognition as a clearing agency or exemption from the recognition requirement. Guidance on the CSA's regulatory approach to such an application is set out in this CP.

(2) Parts 3 and 4 set out on-going requirements applicable to a recognized clearing agency. Part 3 adopts the PFMI Principles generally but does restrict their application only to a clearing agency that operates as a central counterparty (CCP), securities settlement system (SSS) or central securities depository (CSD), as relevant. Part 4 applies to a clearing agency whether or not it operates as a CCP, SSS or CSD. The PFMI Principles were developed jointly by the Committee on Payments and Market Infrastructures (CPMI)[2] and the International Organization of Securities Commissions (IOSCO).[3] The PFMI Principles harmonize and strengthen previous international standards for financial market infrastructures (FMIs).[4]

(3) Annex I to this CP includes supplementary guidance in *text boxes* that applies to recognized domestic clearing agencies that are also overseen by the Bank of Canada (BOC). The supplementary guidance (Joint Supplementary Guidance) was prepared jointly by the CSA and BOC to provide additional clarity on certain aspects of the PFMI Principles within the Canadian context.

1.3 Definitions, interpretation and application — (1) Unless defined in the Instrument or this CP, defined terms used in the Instrument and this CP have the meaning given to them in the securities legislation of each jurisdiction or in National Instrument 14-101 *Definitions*.

(2) The terms "clearing agency" and "recognized clearing agency" are generally defined in securities legislation. For the purposes of the Instrument, a clearing agency includes, in Quebec, a clearing house, central securities depository and settlement system within the meaning of the Québec *Securities Act* and a clearing house and settlement system within the meaning of the Québec *Derivatives Act*. See section 1.4. The CSA notes that, while Part 3 applies only to a recognized clearing agency that operates as a CCP, CSD or SSS, the term "clearing agency" may incorporate certain other centralized post-trade functions that are not necessarily limited to those of a CCP, CSD or SSS, e.g., an entity that provides centralized facilities for comparing data respecting the terms of settlement of a trade or transaction may be considered a clearing agency, but would not be considered a CCP, CSD or SSS. Except in Québec, such an entity would be required to apply either for recognition as a clearing agency or an exemption from the requirement to be recognized.[5] The CSA considers that a recognized clearing agency, which is not a CCP, CSD or SSS, should not be subject to the application of Part 3. Such a clearing agency is, however, subject to provisions in Part 2 and all of Parts 4 and 5.

(3) A clearing agency may serve either or both the securities and derivatives markets. A clearing agency serving the securities markets can be a CCP, CSD or SSS. A clearing agency serving the derivatives markets is typically only a CCP.

(4) In this CP, FMI means a financial market infrastructure, which the PFMI Report describes as follows: payment systems, CSDs, SSSs, CCPs and trade repositories.

PART 2 — CLEARING AGENCY RECOGNITION OR EXEMPTION FROM RECOGNITION

2.0 Recognition and exemption — (1) An entity seeking to carry on business as a clearing agency in certain jurisdictions in Canada is required under the securities legislation of such jurisdictions to apply for recognition or an exemption from the recognition requirement. For greater clarity, a foreign-based clearing agency that provides, or will provide, its services or facilities to a person or company resident in a jurisdiction would be considered to be carrying on business in that jurisdiction.

---

[1] The entity is prohibited from carrying on business as a clearing agency unless recognized or exempted.

[2] Prior to September 1, 2014, CPMI was known as the Committee on Payment and Settlement Systems (CPSS).

[3] See the CPMI-IOSCO *Principles for Financial Market Infrastructures* Report, published in April 2012, available on the Bank for International Settlements' website (www.bis.org) and the IOSCO website (www.iosco.org).

[4] See (i) 2001 CPMI report *Core principles for systemically important payment systems*, (ii) 2001 CPMI-IOSCO report *Recommendations for securities settlement systems* (together with the 2002 CPMI-IOSCO report *Assessment methodology for Recommendations for securities settlement systems*); and (iii) 2004 CPMI-IOSCO report *Recommendations for central counterparties*. All of these reports are available on the Bank for International Settlements' website (www.bis.org). The CPMI-IOSCO reports are also available on IOSCO website (www.iosco.org).

[5] In Québec, an entity that provides such centralized facilities for comparing data would be required to apply either for recognition as a matching service utility or for an exemption from the recognition requirement, in application of the *Securities Act* or the *Derivatives Act*.

(2) — Recognition of a clearing agency — The CSA takes the view that a clearing agency that is systemically important to a jurisdiction's capital markets, or that is not subject to comparable regulation by another regulatory body, will generally be recognized by a securities regulatory authority.[6] A securities regulatory authority may consider the systemic importance of a clearing agency to its capital markets based on the following list of guiding factors: value and volume of transactions processed, cleared and settled by the clearing agency;[7] risk exposures (particularly credit and liquidity) of the clearing agency to its participants; complexity of the clearing agency;[8] and centrality of the clearing agency with respect to its role in the market, including its substitutability, relationships, interdependencies and interactions.[9] The list of guiding factors is non-exhaustive, and no single factor described above will be determinative in an assessment of systemic importance. A securities regulatory authority retains the ability to consider additional quantitative and qualitative factors as may be relevant and appropriate.[10]

(3) Because of the approach described in subsection 2.0(2) of this CP, a securities regulatory authority may require a foreign-based clearing agency to be recognized if the clearing agency's proposed business activities in the local jurisdiction are systemically important to the jurisdiction's capital markets, even if it is already subject to comparable regulation in its home jurisdiction. In such circumstances, the recognition decision would focus on key areas that pose material risks to the jurisdiction's market and rely, where appropriate, on the current regulatory requirements and processes to which the entity is already subject in its home jurisdiction. Terms and conditions of a recognition decision that require a foreign clearing agency to report information to a Canadian securities regulatory authority may vary among foreign clearing agencies. Among other factors, they will depend on whether Canadian securities regulatory authorities have entered into an agreement or memorandum of understanding with the home regulator for sharing information and cooperation.

(4) — Exemption from recognition — Depending on the circumstances, a clearing agency may be granted an exemption from recognition pursuant to securities legislation and subject to appropriate terms and conditions, where it is not considered systemically important or where it does not otherwise pose significant risk to the capital markets. For example, such an approach may be considered for an entity that provides limited services or facilities, thereby not warranting full regulation, such as a clearing agency that does not perform the functions of a CCP, CSD or SSS. However, in such cases, terms and conditions may be imposed. In addition, a foreign-based clearing agency that is already subject to a comparable regulatory regime in its home jurisdiction may be granted an exemption from the recognition requirement as full regulation may be duplicative and inefficient when imposed in addition to the regulation of the home jurisdiction. The exemption may be subject to certain terms and conditions, including reporting requirements and prior notification of certain material changes to information provided to the securities regulatory authority.

2.1 Application and initial filing of information — The application process for both recognition and exemption from recognition as a clearing agency is similar. The entity that applies will typically be the entity that operates the facility or performs the functions of a clearing agency. The application for recognition or exemption will require completion of appropriate documentation. This will include the items listed in subsection 2.1(1). Together, the application materials should present a detailed description of the history, regulatory structure, and business operations of the clearing agency. A clearing agency that operates as a CCP, CSD or SSS will need to describe how it meets or will meet the requirements of Parts 3 and 4. An applicant based in a foreign jurisdiction should also provide a detailed description of the regulatory regime of its home jurisdiction and the requirements imposed on the clearing agency, including how such requirements are similar to the requirements in Parts 3 and 4.

Where specific information items of the PFMI Disclosure Framework Document are not relevant to an applicant because of the nature or scope of its clearing agency activities, its structure, the products it clears or settles, or its regulatory environment, the application should explain in reasonable detail why the information items are not relevant.

The application filed by an applicant will generally be published for public comment for a 30-day period. Other materials filed with the application, which the applicant wishes to maintain confidential, will generally be kept confidential in accordance with securities and privacy legislation. However, the clearing agency will be required to publicly disclose its PFMI Disclosure Framework Document. See PFMI Principle 23, key consideration 5.

2.2 Significant changes, fee changes, and other changes in information — Section 2.2 is subject to the application provisions of subsections 1.5(3) and (4). For example, where the terms and conditions of a recognition decision made by a securities regulatory authority require a recognized clearing agency to obtain the approval of the authority before implementing a new fee for a service, the process to seek such approval set forth in the terms and conditions will apply instead of the prior notification requirement in subsection 2.2(4).

(2) The written notice should provide a reasonably detailed description of the significant change (as defined in subsection 2.2(1)) and the expected date of the implementation of the change. It should enclose or attach updated relevant documentation, including clean and blacklined versions of the documentation that show how the significant change will be implemented. If the notice is being filed by a foreign-based clearing agency, the notice should also describe the approval process or other involvement by the primary or home-jurisdiction regulator for implementing the significant change. The clearing agency is required to file concurrently with the notice any changes required to be made to the clearing agency's PFMI Disclosure Framework Document as a result of implementing the significant change, in accordance with subsection 2.2(3).

2.3 Ceasing to carry on business — A recognized or exempt clearing agency that ceases to carry on business in a local jurisdiction as a clearing agency, either voluntarily or involuntarily, must file a completed Form 24-102F2 *Cessation of Operations Report for Clearing Agency* within the appropriate timelines. In certain jurisdictions, the clearing agency intending to cease carrying on business must also make an application to voluntarily surrender its recognition to the securities regulatory authority pursuant to securities legislation. The securities regulatory authority may accept the voluntary surrender subject to terms and conditions.[11]

---

[6]We would consider comparable regulation by another regulatory body to be regulation that generally results in similar outcomes in substance to the requirements of Part 3 and 4.

[7]We would consider, for example, the current aggregate monetary values and volumes of such transactions, as well as the entity's potential for growth.

[8]We would look, for example, to the nature and complexity of the clearing agency, taking into account an analysis of the various products it processes, clears or settles.

[9]We would consider, for example, the centrality or importance of the clearing agency to the particular market or markets it serves, based on the degree to which it critically supports, or that its failure or disruption would affect, such markets or the entire Canadian financial infrastructure.

[10]Additional factors may be based on the characteristics of the clearing agency under review, such as the nature of its operations, its corporate structure, or its business model.

[11]See, for example, section 21.4 of the *Securities Act* (Ontario).

PART 3 — PFMI PRINCIPLES APPLICABLE TO RECOGNIZED CLEARING AGENCIES

3.0 Introduction — (1) Section 3.1 adopts the PFMI Principles generally but excludes the application of specific PFMI Principles for certain types of clearing agencies. We have adopted only those PFMI Principles that are relevant to clearing agencies operating as a CCP, CSD or SSS.[12]

(2) Part 3, together with the PFMI Principles, is intended to be consistent with a flexible and principles-based approach to regulation. In this regard, Part 3 anticipates that a clearing agency's rules, procedures, policies and operations will need to evolve over time so that it can adequately respond to changes in technology, legal requirements, the needs of its participants and their customers, trading volumes, trading practices, linkages between financial markets, and the financial instruments traded in the markets that a clearing agency serves.

3.1 PFMI Principles — The definition of PFMI Principles in the Instrument includes the applicable key considerations for each principle. Annex E to the PFMI Report provides additional guidance on how each key consideration will apply to the specified types of clearing agencies. In interpreting and implementing the PFMI Principles, regard is to be given to the explanatory notes in the PFMI Report, as appropriate, unless otherwise indicated in section 3.1 or this Part 3 of the CP.[13] As discussed in subsection 1.2(3) of this CP, the CSA and BOC have together developed Joint Supplementary Guidance to provide additional clarity on certain aspects of some PFMI Principles within the Canadian context. The Joint Supplementary Guidance is directed at recognized domestic clearing agencies that are also overseen by the BOC. The Joint Supplementary Guidance is included in separate *text boxes* in Annex I to this CP under the relevant headings of the PFMI Principles. Except as otherwise indicated in this Part 3 of the CP, other recognized domestic clearing agencies should assess the applicability of the Joint Supplementary Guidance to their respective entity as well.

3.2 PFMI Principle 5: Collateral — Notwithstanding section 3.1 of the CP and the Joint Supplementary Guidance relating to PFMI Principle 5: *Collateral* (see Box 5.1 in Annex I to this CP), we are of the view that letters of credit may be permitted as collateral by a recognized domestic clearing agency operating as a CCP serving derivatives markets that is not also overseen by the BOC, provided that the collateral and the clearing agency's collateral policies and procedures otherwise meet the requirements of PFMI Principle 5: *Collateral*. However, the recognized clearing agency must first obtain regulatory approval of its rules and procedures that govern the use of letters of credit as collateral before accepting letters of credit.

3.3 PFMI Principle 14: Segregation and portability for CCPs serving cash markets — PFMI Principle 14: *Segregation and portability* requires, pursuant to section 3.1, that a CCP have rules and procedures that enable the segregation and portability[14] of positions and related collateral of a CCP participant's customers, particularly to protect the customers from the default or insolvency of the participant. The explanatory notes in the PFMI Report offer an "alternate approach" to meeting PFMI Principle 14. The report notes that, in certain jurisdictions, cash market CCPs operate in legal regimes that facilitate segregation and portability to achieve the protection of customer assets by alternate means that offer the same degree of protection as the approach in PFMI Principle 14.[15] The features of the alternate approach are described in the PFMI Report.[16]

— **Customers of IIROC dealer members:** — Currently, most participants of domestic cash market CCPs that clear for customers are investment dealers.[17] They are required to be members of the Investment Industry Regulatory Organization of Canada (IIROC)[18] and to contribute to the Canadian Investor Protection Fund (CIPF).[19] The CSA is of the view that the customer asset protection regime applicable to investment dealers (IIROC-CIPF regime) is an appropriate alternative framework for customers of investment dealers that are direct participants of a cash-market CCP. The IIROC-CIPF regime meets the criteria for the alternate approach for CCPs serving certain domestic cash markets because:

- IIROC's requirements governing, among other things, an investment dealer's books and records, capital adequacy, internal controls, client account margining, and segregation of client securities and cash help ensure that customer positions and collateral can be identified timely,

- customers of an investment dealer are protected by CIPF, and

- through a combination of IIROC's member rules and oversight powers, CIPF's role in the administration of the bankruptcy of a dealer, and the overarching policy objectives of Part XII of the federal *Bankruptcy and Insolvency Act* (BIA) (discussed below), customer accounts can be moved from a failing dealer to another dealer in a timely manner and customers' assets can be restored.

Part XII of the BIA sets out a special bankruptcy regime for administering the insolvency of a securities firm. The regime generally provides for all cash and securities of a bankrupt securities firm, whether held for its own account and for its customers, to vest in the appointed trustee in bankruptcy. The trustee, in turn, is directed to pool such assets into a "customer pool fund" for the benefit of the customers, which are entitled to a pro rata share of the customer pool fund according to their respective "net equity" claims as a priority claim before the general creditors are paid. To the extent there is a shortfall in customer recovery from the customer pool fund and any remaining assets in the insolvent estate, the assets are allocated among the

---

[12] PFMI Principles that are relevant to payment systems and trade repositories, but not CCPs, SSSs and CSDs, are not adopted in Part 3.

[13] For example, the Instrument uses specialized terminology related to the clearing and settlement area. Not all such terminology is defined in the Instrument, but instead may be defined or explained in the PFMI Report. Regard should be given to the PFMI Report in understanding such terminology, as appropriate, including Annex H: *Glossary*.

[14] Portability refers to the operational aspects of the transfer of contractual positions, funds, or securities from one party to another party. See paragraph 3.14.3 of the PFMI Report.

[15] See paragraph 3.14.6 of the PFMI Report, at p. 83.

[16] Features of such regimes are that, if a participant fails, (a) the customer positions can be identified in a timely manner, (b) customers will be protected by an investor protection scheme designed to move customer accounts from the failed or failing participant to another participant in a timely manner, and (c) customer assets can be restored. As an example, the PFMIs suggest that domestic law may subject participants to explicit and comprehensive financial responsibility and customer protection requirements that obligate participants to make frequent determinations (for example, daily) that they maintain possession and control of all customers' fully paid and excess margin securities and to segregate their proprietary activities from those of their customers. Under these types of regimes, pending securities purchases do not belong to the customer; thus there is no customer trade or position entered into the CCP. As a result, participants who provide collateral to the CCP do not identify whether the collateral is provided on behalf of their customers regardless of whether they are acting on a principal or agent basis, and the CCP is not able to identify positions or the assets of its participants' customers.

[17] Investment dealers are firms registered in the category of "investment dealer" under provincial securities legislation. Investment dealers are required to be members of IIROC. See section 9.1 of National Instrument 31-103 *Registration Requirements, Exemptions and Ongoing Registrant Obligations*.

[18] IIROC is the national self-regulatory organization (SRO) which oversees all investment dealers and trading activity on debt and equity marketplaces in Canada. It is a recognized SRO in all 10 provinces in Canada and is subject to regulation and oversight by the CSA.

[19] CIPF is an investor compensation protection fund that is sponsored by IIROC and approved by the CSA.

customers on a pro rata basis. CIPF, which works in conjunction with IIROC and the bankruptcy trustee,[20] provides protection to eligible customers for losses up to $1 million per account.[21]

— Customers of other types of participants: — A recognized clearing agency operating as a cash market CCP for participants that are not IIROC investment dealers will need to have segregation and portability arrangements at the CCP level that meet PFMI Principle 14. Where the clearing agency is proposing to rely on an alternate approach for the purposes of protecting the customers of such participants, the clearing agency will need to demonstrate how the applicable legal or regulatory framework in which it operates achieves the same degree of protection and efficiency for such customers that would otherwise be achieved by segregation and portability arrangements at the CCP level described in PFMI Principle 14. See the PFMI Report, at paragraph 3.14.6.

PART 4 — OTHER REQUIREMENTS OF RECOGNIZED CLEARING AGENCIES

4.0 Introduction — As discussed in section 1.2(2) of this CP, the provisions of Part 4 are in addition to the requirements of Part 3, and apply to a clearing agency whether or not it operates as a CCP, SSS or CSD.

DIVISION 1 — GOVERNANCE:

4.1 Board of directors — (4) Consistent with the explanatory notes in the PFMI Report (see paragraph 3.2.10), we are of the view that the following individuals have a relationship with a clearing agency that would reasonably be expected to interfere with the exercise of the individual's independent judgment:

(a) an individual who is, or has been within the last year, an employee or executive officer of the clearing agency or any of its affiliated entities;

(b) an individual whose immediate family member is, or has been within the last year, an executive officer of the clearing agency or any of its affiliated entities;

(c) an individual who beneficially owns, directly or indirectly, voting securities carrying more than ten per cent of the voting rights attached to all voting securities of the clearing agency or any of its affiliated entities for the time being outstanding;

(d) an individual whose immediate family member beneficially owns, directly or indirectly, voting securities carrying more than ten per cent of the voting rights attached to all voting securities of the clearing agency or any of its affiliated entities for the time being outstanding;

(e) an individual who is, or has been within the last year, an executive officer of a person or company that beneficially owns, directly or indirectly, voting securities carrying more than ten per cent of the voting rights attached to all voting securities of the clearing agency or any of its affiliated entities for the time being outstanding; and

(f) an individual who accepts or who received within the last year, directly or indirectly, any audit, consulting, advisory or other compensatory fee from the clearing agency or any of its affiliated entities, other than as remuneration for acting in his or her capacity as a member of the board of directors or any board committee, or as a part-time chair or vice-chair of the board or any board committee.

For the purposes of paragraph (f) above, compensatory fees would not normally include the receipt of fixed amounts of compensation under a retirement plan (including deferred compensation) for prior service with the clearing agency if the compensation is not contingent in any way on continued service. Also, the indirect acceptance by an individual of any audit, consulting, advisory or other compensatory fee includes acceptance of a fee by (a) an individual's immediate family member; or (b) an entity in which such individual is a partner, a member, an officer such as a managing director occupying a comparable position or an executive officer, or occupies a similar position (except limited partners, non-managing members and those occupying similar positions who, in each case, have no active role in providing services to the entity) and which provides accounting, consulting, legal, investment banking or financial advisory services to the clearing agency or any of its affiliated entities.

In addition, an individual appointed to the board of directors or board committee of the clearing agency or any of its affiliated entities or of a person or company referred to in paragraph (e) above would not be considered to have a material relationship with the clearing agency solely because the individual acts, or has previously acted, as a chair or vice-chair of the board of directors or a board committee.

4.2 Documented procedures regarding risk spill-overs — For guidance on this provision, see the Joint Supplementary Guidance in Box 2.2 in Annex I of this CP.

4.3 Chief Risk Officer (CRO) and Chief Compliance Officer (CCO) — Section 4.3 is consistent with PFMI Principle 2, key consideration 5, which requires a clearing agency to have an experienced management with a mix of skills and the integrity necessary to discharge its operations and risk management responsibilities.

(3) The reference to "harm to the broader financial system" in subparagraph 4.3(3)(c)(ii) may be in relation to the domestic or international financial system. The CSA is of the view that the role of a CCO may, in certain circumstances, be performed by the Chief Legal Officer or General Counsel of the clearing agency, where the individual has sufficient time to properly carry out his or her duties and, provided that there are appropriate safeguards in place to avoid conflicts of interest.

4.4 Board or advisory committees — Section 4.4 is intended to reinforce the clearing agency's obligations to meet the PFMI Principles, particularly PFMI Principles 2 and 3. The CSA is of the view that the mandates of the committees should, at a minimum, include the following:

(a) providing advice and recommendations to the board of directors to assist it in fulfilling its risk management responsibilities, including reviewing and assessing the clearing agency's risk management policies and procedures, the adequacy of the implementation of appropriate procedures to mitigate and manage such risks, and the clearing agency's participation standards and collateral requirements;

(b) ensuring adequate processes and controls are in place over the models used to quantify, aggregate, and manage the clearing agency's risks;

(c) monitoring the financial performance of the clearing agency and providing financial management oversight and direction to the business and affairs of the clearing agency;

---

[20]CIPF is a "customer compensation body" for the purposes of Part XII of the BIA. Where the accounts of a securities firm are protected (in whole or in part) by CIPF, the trustee in bankruptcy is required to consult with CIPF on the administration of the bankruptcy, and CIPF may designate an inspector to act on its behalf. See section 264 of the BIA.

[21]The losses must be in respect of a claim for the failure of the dealer to return or account for securities, cash balances, commodities, futures contracts, segregated insurance funds or other property received, acquired or held by the dealer in an account for the customer.

(d) implementing policies and processes to identify, address, and manage potential conflicts of interest of board members; and

(e) regularly reviewing the board of directors' and senior management's performance and the performance of each individual member.

Section 4.4 is a minimum requirement. Consistent with the explanatory notes in the PFMI Principles (see paragraph 3.2.9), a recognized clearing agency should also consider forming other types of board committees, such as a compensation committee. All committees should have clearly assigned responsibilities and procedures. The clearing agency's internal audit function should have sufficient resources and independence from management to provide, among other activities, a rigorous and independent assessment of the effectiveness of its risk-management and control processes. See section 4.1 for the concept of independence. A board will typically establish an audit committee to oversee the internal audit function. In addition to reporting to senior management, the audit function should have regular access to the board through an additional reporting line.

DIVISION 2 — DEFAULT MANAGEMENT:

4.5 Use of own capital — The CSA is of the view that a CCP's own capital contribution should be used in the default waterfall, immediately after a defaulting participant's contributions to margin and default fund resources have been exhausted, and prior to non-defaulting participants' contributions. Such equity should be significant enough to attract senior management's attention, and separately retained and not form part of the CCP's resources for other purposes, such as to cover general business risk.

DIVISION 3 — OPERATIONAL RISK:

4.6 to 4.10 Sections 4.6 to 4.10 complement PFMI Principle 17, which requires a clearing agency to identify the plausible sources of operational risk, both internal and external, and mitigate their impact through the use of appropriate systems, policies, procedures, and controls. PFMI Principle 17 further requires that systems should be designed to ensure a high degree of security and operational reliability and should have adequate, scalable capacity, and business continuity management should aim for timely recovery of operations and fulfilment of the FMI's obligations, including in the event of a wide-scale or major disruption.

4.6 Systems requirements —

(a) The intent of these provisions is to ensure that controls are implemented to support information technology planning, acquisition, development and maintenance, computer operations, information systems support, and security. Recognized guides as to what constitutes adequate information technology controls include "Information Technology Control Guidelines" from the Canadian Institute of Chartered Accountants (CICA) and "COBIT" from the IT Governance Institute.

(b) Capacity management requires that the clearing agency monitor, review, and test (including stress test) the actual capacity and performance of the system on an ongoing basis. Accordingly, under subsection 4.6(b), the clearing agency is required to meet certain standards for its estimates and for testing. These standards are consistent with prudent business practice. The activities and tests required in this subsection are to be carried out at least once a year. In practice, continuing changes in technology, risk management requirements and competitive pressures will often result in these activities being carried out or tested more frequently.

(c) A failure, malfunction or delay or other incident is considered to be "material" if the clearing agency would, in the normal course of operations, escalate the matter to or inform its senior management ultimately accountable for technology. It is also expected that, as part of this notification, the clearing agency will provide updates on the status of the failure and the resumption of service. Further, the clearing agency should have comprehensive and well-documented procedures in place to record, report, analyze, and resolve all operational incidents. In this regard, the clearing agency should undertake a "post-incident" review to identify the causes and any required improvement to the normal operations or business continuity arrangements. Such reviews should, where relevant, include the clearing agency's participants. The results of such internal reviews are required to be communicated to the securities regulatory authority as soon as practicable. Subsection 4.6(c) also refers to a material security breach. A material security breach or systems intrusion is considered to be any unauthorized entry into any of the systems that support the functions of the clearing agency or any system that shares resources with one or more of these systems. Virtually any security breach would be considered material and thus reportable to the securities regulatory authority. The onus would be on the clearing agency to document the reasons for any security breach it did not consider material.

4.7 Systems reviews — (1) A qualified party is a person or company or a group of persons or companies with relevant experience in both information technology and in the evaluation of related internal systems or controls in a complex information technology environment. Qualified persons may include external auditors or third party information system consultants, as well as employees of the clearing agency or an affiliated entity of the clearing agency, but may not be persons responsible for the development or operation of the systems or capabilities being tested. Before engaging a qualified party, a clearing agency should discuss its choice with the regulator or, in Québec, the securities regulatory authority.

4.8 Clearing agency technology requirements and testing facilities — (1) The technology requirements required to be disclosed under subsection 4.8(1) do not include detailed proprietary information.

(5) We expect the amended technology requirements to be disclosed as soon as practicable, either while the changes are being made or immediately after.

4.9 Testing of business continuity plans — Business continuity management is a key component of a clearing agency's operational risk-management framework. A recognized clearing agency's business continuity plan and its associated arrangements should be subject to frequent review and testing. At a minimum, under section 4.9, such tests must be conducted annually. Tests should address various scenarios that simulate wide-scale disasters and inter-site switchovers. The clearing agency's employees should be thoroughly trained to execute the business continuity plan and participants, critical service providers, and linked clearing agencies should be regularly involved in the testing and be provided with a general summary of the testing results. The CSA expects that the clearing agency will also facilitate and participate in industry-wide testing of the business continuity plan (domestically-based recognized clearing agencies are required to participate in all industry-wide business continuity tests, as determined by a regulation services provider, regulator, or in Québec, the securities regulatory authority, pursuant to National Instrument 21-101 *Marketplace Operation*). The clearing agency should make appropriate adjustments to its business continuity plan and associated arrangements based on the results of the testing exercises.

4.10 Outsourcing — Where a recognized clearing agency relies upon or outsources some of its operations to a service provider, it should generally ensure that those operations meet the same requirements they would need to meet if they were provided internally. Under section 4.10, the clearing agency must meet various requirements in respect of the outsourcing of critical services or systems to a service provider. These requirements apply regardless of whether the outsourcing arrangements are with thirdparty service providers, or with affiliated entities of the clearing agency.

Generally, the clearing agency is required to establish, implement, maintain and enforce policies and procedures to evaluate and approve outsourcing agreements to critical service providers. Such policies and procedures should include assessing the suitability of potential service providers and the ability of the clearing agency to continue to comply with securities legislation in the event of the service provider's bankruptcy, insolvency or termination of business. The clearing agency is also required to monitor and evaluate the on-going performance and compliance of the service provider to which they outsourced critical services, systems or facilities. Accordingly, the clearing agency should define key performance indicators that will measure the service level. Further, the clearing agency should have robust arrangements for the substitution of such providers, timely access to all necessary information, and the proper controls and monitoring tools.

Under section 4.10, a contractual relationship should be in place between the clearing agency and the critical service provider allowing it and relevant authorities to have full access to necessary information. The contract should ensure that the clearing agency's approval is mandatory before the critical service provider can itself outsource material elements of the service provided to the clearing agency, and that in the event of such an arrangement, full access to the necessary information is preserved. Clear lines of communication should be established between the outsourcing clearing agency and the critical service provider to facilitate the flow of functions and information between parties in both ordinary and exceptional circumstances.

Where the clearing agency outsources operations to critical service providers, it should disclose the nature and scope of this dependency to its participants. It should also identify the risks from its outsourcing and take appropriate actions to manage these dependencies through appropriate contractual and organisational arrangements. The clearing agency should inform the securities regulatory authority about any such dependencies and the performance of these critical service providers. To that end, the clearing agency can contractually provide for direct contacts between the critical service provider and the securities regulatory authority, contractually ensure that the securities regulatory authority can obtain specific reports from the critical service provider, or the clearing agency may provide full information to the securities regulatory authority.

DIVISION 4 — PARTICIPATION REQUIREMENTS:

4.11 **Access requirements and due process** — Section 4.11 complements PFMI Principle 18, which requires a clearing agency to have objective, risk-based, and publicly disclosed criteria for participation, which permit fair and open access.

(1)

(b) We consider an indirect participant to be an entity that relies on the services provided by other entities (participants) to use a clearing agency's clearing and settlement facilities. As defined in the Instrument, a participant (sometimes also referred to as a "direct participant") is an entity that has entered into an agreement with a clearing agency to access the services of the clearing agency and is bound by the clearing agency's rules and procedures. While indirect participants are generally not bound by the rules of the clearing agency, their transactions are cleared and settled through the clearing agency in accordance with the clearing agency's rules and procedures. The concept of indirect participant is discussed in the PFMI Report, at paragraph 3.19.1.

(d) We are of the view that a requirement on participants of a clearing agency serving the derivatives markets to use a trade repository that is an affiliated entity to report derivatives trades would be unreasonable.

PART 5 — BOOKS AND RECORDS AND LEGAL ENTITY IDENTIFIER

5.2 **Legal Entity Identifiers** — (1) The Global Legal Entity Identifier System defined in subsection 5.2(1) and referred to in subsections 5.2(2) and 5.2(3) is a G20 endorsed system[22] that will serve as a public-good utility responsible for overseeing the issuance of legal entity identifiers (LEIs) globally to counterparties that enter into transactions in order to uniquely identify parties to transactions. It is currently being designed and implemented under the direction of the LEI Regulatory Oversight Committee (ROC), a governance body endorsed by the G20.

(3) If the Global LEI System is not available at the time a clearing agency is required to fulfill their recordkeeping or reporting requirements under securities legislation, they must use a substitute LEI. The substitute LEI must be in accordance with the standards established by the LEI ROC for pre-LEI identifiers. At the time the Global LEI System is operational, a clearing agency or its affiliated entities must cease using their substitute LEI and commence using their LEI. It is conceivable that the two identifiers could be identical.

PART 6 — EXEMPTIONS

6.1 **Exemptions** — As Part 3 adopts a principles-based approach to incorporating the PFMI Principles into the Instrument, the CSA has sought to minimize any substantive duplication or material inefficiency due to cross-border regulation. Where a recognized foreign-based clearing agency does face some conflict or inconsistency between the requirements of sections 2.2 and 2.5 and Part 4 and the requirements of the regulatory regime in its home jurisdiction, the clearing agency is expected to comply with the Instrument. However, where such a conflict or inconsistency causes a hardship for the clearing agency, and provided that the entity is subject to requirements in its home jurisdiction resulting in similar outcomes in substance to the requirements of sections 2.2 and 2.5 and Part 4, an exemption from a provision of the Instrument may be considered by a securities regulatory authority. The exemption may be subject to appropriate terms or conditions.

ANNEX I — TO COMPANION POLICY 24-102CP

Joint Supplementary Guidance Developed by the Bank of Canada and Canadian Securities Administrators

— **PFMI Principle 2: Governance**

Box 2.1: — Joint Supplementary Guidance — Financial Stability and Other Public Interest Considerations

Context

The PFMIs define governance as the set of relationships between an FMI's owners, board of directors (or equivalent), management, and other relevant parties, including participants, authorities, and other stakeholders (such as participants' customers, other interdependent FMIs, and the broader market). Governance provides the processes through which an organization sets its objectives, determines the means for achieving those objectives, and monitors performance against those objectives. This note provides supplementary regulatory guidance for Canadian FMIs on their governance arrangements as it relates to supporting relevant public interest considerations.

---

[22]See http://www.financialstabilityboard.org/list/fsb_publications/tid_156/index.htm for more information.

Public interest considerations in the context of the PFMIs

The PFMIs indicate that FMIs should "explicitly support financial stability and other relevant public interests." However, there may be circumstances where providing explicit support of relevant public interests conflict with other FMI objectives and therefore require appropriate prioritization and balancing. For example, addressing the potential trade-offs between protecting the participants and the FMI while ensuring the financial stability interests are upheld.

Guidance within the PFMIs

The following text has been extracted directly from the PFMIs. The pertinent information is in bold italics.

PFMI paragraph 3.2.2:

Given the importance of FMIs and the fact that their decisions can have widespread impact, affecting multiple financial institutions, markets, and jurisdictions, it is essential for each FMI to place a high priority on the safety and efficiency of its operations and explicitly support financial stability and other relevant public interests. Supporting the public interest is a broad concept that includes, for example, fostering fair and efficient markets. For example, in certain over the counter derivatives markets, industry standards and market protocols have been developed to increase certainty, transparency, and stability in the market. If a CCP in such markets were to diverge from these practices, it could, in some cases, undermine the market's efforts to develop common processes to help reduce uncertainty. An FMI's governance arrangements should also include appropriate consideration of the interests of participants, participants' customers, relevant authorities, and other stakeholders. (. . .) For all types of FMIs, governance arrangements should provide for fair and open access (see Principle 18 on access and participation requirements) and for effective implementation of recovery or wind-down plans, or resolution.

PFMI paragraph 3.2.8:

An FMI's board has multiple roles and responsibilities that should be clearly specified. These roles and responsibilities should include (a) establishing clear strategic aims for the entity; (b) ensuring effective monitoring of senior management (including selecting its senior managers, setting their objectives, evaluating their performance, and, where appropriate, removing them); (c) establishing appropriate compensation policies (which should be consistent with best practices and based on long-term achievements, in particular, the safety and efficiency of the FMI); (d) establishing and overseeing the risk-management function and material risk decisions; (e) overseeing internal control functions (including ensuring independence and adequate resources); (f) ensuring compliance with all supervisory and oversight requirements; *(g) ensuring consideration of financial stability and other relevant public interests*; and (h) providing accountability to the owners, participants, and other relevant stakeholders.

The CPMI-IOSCO PFMI Disclosure framework and Assessment methodology provides questions to guide the assessment of the FMI against the PFMIs. Questions related to public interest considerations are focused on ensuring that the FMI's objectives are clearly defined, giving a high priority to safety, financial stability and efficiency while also ensuring all other public interest considerations are identified and reflected in the FMI's objectives.

Supplementary Guidance for designated Canadian FMIs

By definition the PFMIs apply to systemically important FMIs, so safety and financial stability objectives should be given a high priority.

Efficiency is also a high priority that should contribute to (but not supersede) the safety and financial stability objectives.

Other public interest considerations such as competition and fair and open access should also be considered in the broader safety and financial stability context.

A framework (objectives, policies and procedures) should be in place for default and other emergency situations. The framework should articulate explicit principles to ensure financial stability and other relevant public interests are considered as part of the decision making process. For example, it should provide guidance on discretionary management decisions, consider the trade-offs between protecting the participants and the FMI while also ensuring the financial stability interests are upheld, and articulate a communication protocol with the board and regulators.

Practical questions/approaches to assessing the appropriateness of the framework include:

- Does the enabling legislation, articles of incorporation, corporate by-laws, corporate mission, vision statements, corporate risk statements/frameworks/methodology clearly articulate the objectives and are they appropriately aligned and communicated (transparent)?

- Do the objectives give appropriate priority to safety, financial stability, efficiency and other public interest considerations?

- Does the Board structure ensure the right mix of skills/experience and interests are in place to ensure the objectives are clear, appropriately prioritized, achieved and measured?

- What is the training provided to the Board and management to support the objectives?

- Do the service offerings and business plans support the objectives?

- Do the system design, rules, procedures support the objectives?

- Are the inter-dependencies and key dependencies considered and managed in the context of the broader financial stability objectives? For instance, do problem and default management policies and procedures appropriately provide for consideration of the broader financial stability interests and do they engage the key stakeholders and regulators?

- Are there procedures in place to get timely engagement of the Board to discuss emerging/current issues, consider scenarios, provide guidance and make decision?

- Does the framework ensure that the broader financial stability issues are considered in any actions relating to a participant suspension?

Box 2.2: — Joint Supplementary Guidance — Vertically and Horizontally Integrated FMIs

Context

Consolidation, or integration, of FMI services may bring about benefits for merging FMIs; however it may also create new governance challenges. The PFMIs contain some general guidance regarding how FMIs should manage governance issues that arise in integrated entities.

This note provides supplementary regulatory guidance for Canadian FMIs that either belong to an integrated entity or are considering consolidating with another entity to form one. The guidance applies to both vertically and horizontally integrated entities.

Vertical and horizontal integration in the context of FMIs

The PFMIs define a vertically integrated FMI group as one that brings together post-trade infrastructure providers under common ownership with providers of other parts of the value chain (for example, one entity owning and operating an exchange, CCP and SSS) and a horizontally integrated group as one that provides the same post-trade service offerings across a number of different products (for example, one entity offering CCP services for derivatives and cash markets).[23] Examples are shown in Figure 1.

Figure 1: Examples of FMI integration in the value chain

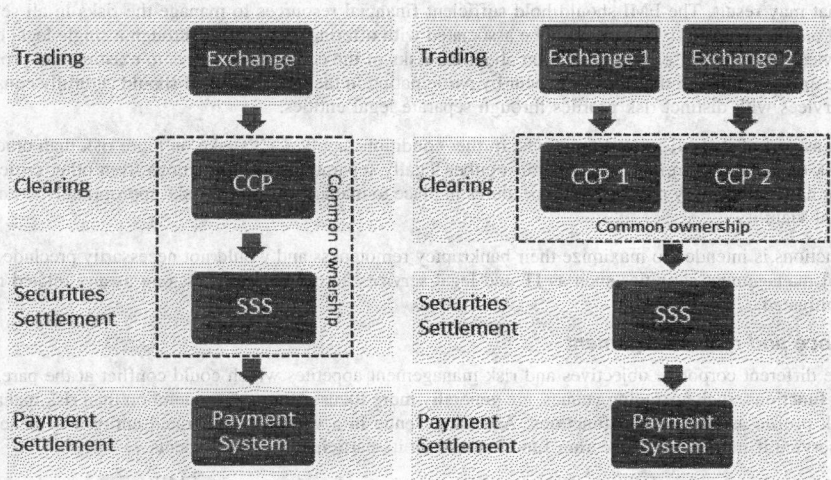

Guidance within the PFMIs

The following text has been extracted directly from the PFMIs. The pertinent information is in bold italics.

PFMI paragraph 3.2.5:

> *Depending on its ownership structure and organisational form, an FMI may need to focus particular attention on certain aspects of its governance arrangements. **An FMI that is part of a larger organisation, for example, should place particular emphasis on the clarity of its governance arrangements, including in relation to any conflicts of interests and outsourcing issues that may arise because of the parent or other affiliated organisation's structure. The FMI's governance arrangements should also be adequate to ensure that decisions of affiliated organisations are not detrimental to the FMI.**[24] **An FMI that is, or is part of, a for-profit entity may need to place particular emphasis on managing any conflicts between income generation and safety.***

PFMI paragraph 3.2.6:

> *An FMI may also need to focus particular attention on certain aspects of its risk-management arrangements as a result of its ownership structure or organisational form. **If an FMI provides services that present a distinct risk profile from, and potentially pose significant additional risks to, its payment, clearing, settlement, or recording function, the FMI needs to manage those additional risks adequately. This may include separating the additional services that the FMI provides from its payment, clearing, settlement, and recording function legally, or taking equivalent action.** The ownership structure and organisational form may also need to be considered in the preparation and implementation of the FMI's recovery or wind-down plans or in assessments of the FMI's resolvability.*

Supplementary guidance for designated Canadian FMIs

An FMI that is part of a larger entity faces additional risk considerations compared to stand-alone FMIs. While there are potential benefits from integrating services into one large entity, including potential risk reduction benefits, integrated entities could face additional risks such as a greater degree of general business risk. Examples of how this could occur include the following:

- losses in one function may spill-over to the entity's other functions;
- the consolidated entity may face high combined exposures across its functions; and
- the consolidated entity may face exposures to the same participants across its functions.

---

[23]CPMI-IOSCO 2010. "Market structure developments in the clearing industry: implications for financial stability." CPMI-IOSCO Paper No 92. Available at: http://www.bis.org/publ/cpss92.htm.

[24]If an FMI is wholly owned or controlled by another entity, authorities should also review the governance arrangements of that entity to see that they do not have adverse effects on the FMI's observance of this principle.

For a more extensive discussion of potentially heightened risks that integrated FMIs may face, see CPMI, "Market structure developments in the clearing industry: implications for financial stability" (2010).[25]

If an FMI belongs to a larger entity, or is considering consolidating with another entity, it should consider how its risk profile differs as part of the consolidated entity, and take appropriate measures to mitigate these risks.

In addition, FMIs that either belong to an integrated entity or are considering merging to form one should meet the following conditions.

1) — Measures to protect critical FMI functions

- FMIs may be part of a larger consolidated entity. These FMIs must either:

  - legally separate FMI-related functions[26] from non-FMI-related functions performed by the consolidated entity in order to maximize bankruptcy remoteness of the FMI-related functions; or

  - have satisfactory policies and procedures in place to manage additional risks resulting from the non-FMI-related functions appropriately to ensure the FMI's financial and operational viability.

- If an FMI performs multiple FMI-related functions with distinct risk profiles within the same entity, the operator should effectively manage the additional risks that may result. The FMI should hold sufficient financial resources to manage the risks in all services it offers, including the combined or compounded risks that would be associated with offering the services through a single legal entity. If the FMI provides multiple services, it should disclose information about the risks of the combined services to existing and prospective participants to give an accurate understanding of the risks they incur by participating in the FMI. The FMI should carefully consider the benefits of offering critical services with distinct risk profiles through separate legal entities.

- If an FMI offers CCP services as part of its FMI-related functions, further conditions apply. CCPs take on more risk than other FMIs, and are inherently at higher risk of failure. Therefore, the FMI must either legally separate its CCP functions from other critical (non-CCP) FMI-related functions, or have satisfactory policies and procedures in place to manage additional risks appropriately to ensure the FMI's financial and operational viability.

- Legal separation of critical functions is intended to maximize their bankruptcy remoteness and would not necessarily preclude integration of common organizational management activities such as IT and legal services across functions as long as any related risks are appropriately identified and mitigated.

2) — Independence of governance and risk management

- FMIs and non-FMIs may have different corporate objectives and risk management appetites which could conflict at the parent level. For example, non-FMI-related functions, such as trading venues, are generally more focused on profit generation than risk management and do not have the same risk profile as FMI-related functions. A trading venue in a vertically integrated entity may benefit from increased participation in its service if its associated clearing function lessens its participation requirements.

- To mitigate potential conflicts, in particular the ability of other functions to negatively influence the FMI's risk controls, each FMI subsidiary should have a governance structure and risk management decision-making process that is separate and independent from the other functions and should maintain an appropriate level of autonomy from the parent and other functions to ensure efficient decision making and effective management of any potential conflicts of interest. In addition, the consolidated entity's broad governance arrangements should be reviewed to ensure they do not impede the FMI-related function's observance of the CPMI-IOSCO principle on governance.

3) — Comprehensive management of risks

- Although risk management governance and decision-making should remain independent, it is nonetheless necessary that the consolidated entity is able to manage risk appropriately across the entity. At a consolidated level, the entity should have an appropriate risk management framework that considers the risks of each subsidiary and the additional risks related to their interdependencies.

- An FMI should identify and manage the risks it bears from and poses to other entities as a result of interdependencies. Consolidated FMIs should also identify and manage the risks they pose to one another as a result of their interdependencies. Consolidated FMIs may have exposures to the same participants, liquidity providers, and other critical service providers across products, markets and/or functions. This may increase the entity's dependence on these providers and may heighten the systemic risk associated with the consolidated entity compared to a stand-alone FMI. Where possible, the consolidated entity and its FMIs should consider ways to mitigate risks arising from shared dependencies. The consolidated entity and its FMIs should also consider conducting entity-wide operational risk testing related to identifying and mitigating these risks.

4) — Sufficient capital to cover potential losses

- Consolidated entities face the risk that a single participant defaults in more than one subsidiary simultaneously. This could result in substantial losses for the consolidated entity which will then also need to replenish resources for the FMIs to continue to operate. FMIs should consider such risks in developing their resource replenishment plan.

- Consolidated entities may face higher or lower business risk than individual FMIs depending on size, complexity and diversification across affiliates. Consolidated entities should consider these impacts in their general business risk profiles and in determining the appropriate level of liquid assets needed to cover their potential general business losses.[27]

---

[25] Available at http://www.bis.org/cpmi/publ/d92.pdf.

[26] FMI-related functions are CCP, SSS, and CSD functions, including other core aspects of clearing and settlement necessary to perform the CCP, SSS, and CDS functions (see the CPMI-IOSCO glossary definitions of "clearing" and "settlement", available at http://www.bis.org/cpmi/publ/d00b.pdf).

[27] Liquid assets held for general business losses must be funded by equity (such as common stock, disclosed reserves, or retained earnings) rather than debt.

— PFMI Principle 5: Collateral

Box 5.1: — Joint Supplementary Guidance — Collateral

Context

The PFMIs establish the form and attributes of collateral that an FMI holds to manage its own credit exposures or those of its participants. This note provides additional guidance for Canadian FMIs to meet the components of the collateral principle related to: (i) acceptance of collateral with low credit, liquidity and market risk; (ii) concentrated holdings of certain assets; and (iii) calculating haircuts. In certain circumstances, regulators may allow exceptions to the collateral policy on a case-by-case basis if the FMI demonstrates that the risks can be adequately managed.

(i) — Acceptable collateral

An FMI should conduct its own assessment of risks when determining collateral eligibility. In general, collateral held to manage the credit exposures of the FMI or those of its participants should have minimal credit, liquidity and market risk, even in stressed market conditions. However, asset categories with additional risk may be accepted when subject to conservative haircuts and adequate concentration limits.[28]

The following clarifies regulators' expectations on what is acceptable collateral by specifying:

1) minimum requirements for all assets that are acceptable as collateral;

2) the asset categories that are judged to have minimal credit, liquidity and market risk; and

3) additional asset categories that could be acceptable as collateral if subject to conservative haircuts and concentration limits.

1) An FMI should conduct its own internal assessment of the credit, liquidity and market risk of the assets eligible as collateral. The FMI should review its collateral policy at least annually, and whenever market factors justify a more frequent review. At a minimum, acceptable assets should:

> **i) be freely transferable without legal, regulatory, contractual or any other constraints that would impair liquidation in a default;**

> **ii) be marketable securities that have an active outright sale market even in stressed market conditions;**

> **iii) have reliable price data published on a regular basis;**

> **iv) be settled over a securities settlement system compliant with the Principles; and**

> **v) be denominated in the same currency as the credit exposures being managed, or in a currency that the FMI can demonstrate it has the ability to manage.**

An FMI should not rely only on external opinions to determine what acceptable collateral is. The FMI should conduct its own assessment of the riskiness of assets, including differences within a particular asset category, to determine whether the risks are acceptable. Since the primary purpose of accepting collateral is to manage the credit exposures of the FMI and its participants, it is paramount that assets eligible as collateral can be liquidated for fair value within a reasonable time frame to cover credit losses following a default. The annual review of the FMI's collateral policy provides an opportunity to assess whether risks continue to be adequately managed. Owing to the dynamic nature of capital markets, the FMI should monitor changes in the underlying risk of the specific assets accepted as collateral, and should adjust its collateral policy in the interim period between annual reviews, when required.

At a minimum, an asset should have certain characteristics in order to provide sufficient assurance that it can be liquidated for fair value within a reasonable time frame. These characteristics relate primarily to the FMI's ability to reliably sell the asset as required to manage its credit exposures. The asset should be unencumbered, that is, it must be free of legal, regulatory, contractual or other restrictions that would impede the FMI's ability to sell it. The challenges associated with selling or transferring non-marketable assets, or those without an active secondary market, preclude their acceptance as collateral.

2) Assets generally judged to have minimal credit, liquidity and market risk are the following:

> **i) cash;**

> **ii) securities issued or guaranteed by the Government of Canada;[29]**

> **iii) securities issued or guaranteed by a provincial government; and**

> **iv) securities issued by the U.S. Treasury.**

In general, the assets judged to have minimal risk are cash and debt securities issued by government entities with unique powers, such as the ability to raise taxes and set laws, and that have a low probability of default. Total Canadian debt outstanding is currently dominated by securities issued or guaranteed by the Government of Canada and by provincial governments. The relatively large supply of securities issued by these entities and their generally high creditworthiness contribute to the liquidity of these assets in the domestic capital market. Securities issued by the U.S. Treasury are also deemed to be of high quality for the same reasons. The overall riskiness of securities issued by the Government of Canada and the U.S. Treasury is further reduced by their previous record of maintaining value in stressed market conditions, when they tend to benefit from a "flight to safety."

It is essential that an FMI regularly assesses the riskiness of even the specific high-quality assets identified in this section to determine their adequacy as eligible collateral. In some cases, only certain assets within the more general asset category may be deemed acceptable.

3) An FMI should consider its own distinct arrangements for allocating credit losses and managing credit exposures when accepting a broader range of assets as collateral. The following asset classes may be acceptable as collateral if they are subject to conservative haircuts and concentration limits:

> **i) securities issued by a municipal government;**

---

[28]See PFMI Principle 5, key considerations 1 and 4.

[29]Guarantees include securities issued by federal and provincial Crown corporations or other entities with an explicit statement that debt issued by the entity represents the general obligations of the sovereign.

Part 2: MARKET PARTICIPANTS

ii) bankers' acceptances;

iii) commercial paper;

iv) corporate bonds;

v) asset-backed securities that meet the following criteria: (1) sponsored by a deposit-taking financial institution that is prudentially regulated at either the federal or provincial level, (2) part of a securitization program supported by a liquidity facility, and (3) backed by assets of an acceptable credit quality;

vi) equity securities traded on marketplaces regulated by a member of the CSA and the Investment Industry Regulatory Organization of Canada; and

vii) other securities issued or guaranteed by a government, central bank or supranational institution classified as Level 1 high-quality assets by the Basel Committee on Banking Supervision.

An FMI should take into account its specific risk profile when assessing whether accepting certain assets as collateral would be appropriate. The decision to broaden the range of acceptable collateral should also consider the size of collateral holdings to cover the credit exposures of the FMI relative to the size of asset markets. In cases where the total collateral required to cover credit exposures is small compared with the market for high-quality assets, there is less potential strain on participants to meet collateral requirements.

Accepting a broader range of collateral has certain advantages. Most importantly, it provides participants with more flexibility to meet the FMI's collateral requirements, which may be especially important in stressed market conditions. A broader range of collateral diversifies the risk exposures faced by the FMI, since it may be easier to liquidate diversified collateral holdings when liquidity unexpectedly dries up for a particular asset class. It also diversifies market risk by reducing potential exposure to idiosyncratic shocks. Accepting a broader range of assets recognizes the increased cost to market participants of posting only the highest-quality assets, as well as the increasing encumbrance of these assets in order to meet new regulatory standards.[30]

(ii) — Concentration Limits

An FMI should avoid concentrated holding of assets where this could potentially introduce credit, market and liquidity risk beyond acceptable levels. In addition, the FMI should mitigate specific wrong-way risk by limiting the acceptance of collateral that would likely lose value in the event of a participant default, and prevent participants from posting assets they or their affiliates have issued. The FMI should measure and monitor the collateral posted by participants on a regular basis, with more frequent analysis required when more flexible collateral policies have been implemented.[31]

The following points clarify regulators' expectations regarding the composition of collateral accepted by an FMI by specifying:

1) broad limits for riskier asset classes to mitigate concentration risk;

2) targeted limits for securities issued by financial sector entities to mitigate specific wrong-way risk; and

3) the level of monitoring required for collateral posted by participants.

1) An FMI should limit assets from the broader range of acceptable assets identified in section (i)3) to a maximum of 40 per cent of the total collateral posted from each participant. Within the broader range of acceptable assets, the FMI should consider implementing more specific concentration limits for different asset categories.

An FMI should limit securities issued by a single issuer from the broader range of acceptable assets to a maximum of 5 per cent of total collateral from each participant.

The guidance limits the acceptance of collateral from the broader range of assets to a maximum of 40 per cent because a higher proportion could potentially create unacceptable risks to FMIs and their participants. This limit is currently applied to the Bank's Standing Liquidity Facility and the Liquidity Coverage Ratio under Basel III. The benefits of expanding collateral — namely, providing participants with more flexibility and achieving greater diversification — are achieved within the limit of 40 per cent, with collateral in excess of this limit increasing the overall risk exposures with less benefit. In some circumstances, regulators may permit an FMI to accept more than 40 per cent of total collateral from the broader range of assets if the risk from a particular participant is low.

Employing a limit of 5 per cent of total collateral for securities issued by a single issuer is a prudent measure to limit exposures from idiosyncratic shocks. It also reduces the need for procyclical adjustments to collateral requirements following a decline in value.

An FMI should consider implementing more stringent concentration limits, as well as imposing limits on certain asset categories, depending on the FMI's specific arrangements for managing credit exposures. The considerations described in section (i) 3) for accepting a broader range of assets as collateral apply equally to the decision over whether more stringent concentration limits should be implemented.

2) An FMI should limit the collateral from financial sector issuers to a maximum of 10 per cent of total collateral pledged from each participant. The FMI should not allow participants to post their own securities or those of their affiliates as collateral.

An FMI is exposed to specific wrong-way risk when the collateral posted is highly likely to decrease in value following a participant default. It is highly likely that the value of debt and equity securities issued by companies in the financial sector would be adversely affected by the default of an FMI participant, introducing wrong-way risk. This is especially the case for interconnected FMI participants with activities that are concentrated in domestic financial markets. Implementing a limit on financial sector issuers mitigates potential risk exposures from specific wrong-way risk. More stringent limits should be implemented where appropriate.

3) In cases where only the highest-quality assets are accepted, an FMI is required to measure and monitor the collateral posted by participants during periodic evaluations of participant creditworthiness. The FMI should measure and monitor the correlation between a participant's creditworthiness and the collateral posted more frequently when a broader range of collateral is accepted. The FMI should have the ability to adjust the composition and to increase the collateral required from participants experiencing a reduction in creditworthiness.

---

[30]The encumbrance of high-quality assets is expected to increase through a number of regulatory reforms, including Basel III, over-the-counter derivatives reform and the Principles.

[31]See Principle 5, key considerations 1 and 4.

When only the highest-quality assets are accepted as collateral, there is less risk associated with the composition of collateral posted by a participant; hence, such risk does not need to be monitored as closely. The FMI should monitor the composition of collateral pledged by participants more frequently when riskier assets are eligible, since such assets are more likely to be correlated with the participant's creditworthiness. FMIs should also consider the general credit risk of their participants when deciding how frequently monitoring should be conducted. In all circumstances, the FMI should have the contractual and legal ability to unilaterally require more collateral and to request higher-quality collateral from a participant that is judged to present a greater risk.

(iii) — Haircuts

An FMI should establish stable and conservative haircuts that consider all aspects of the risks associated with the collateral. An FMI should evaluate the performance of haircuts by conducting backtesting and stress testing on a regular basis.[32]

The following points clarify regulators' expectations regarding the calculation and testing of haircuts by outlining:

    1) requirements for calculating haircuts; and

    2) requirements for testing the adequacy of haircuts and overall collateral accepted.

1) An FMI should apply stable and conservative haircuts that are calibrated against stressed market conditions. When the same haircut is applied to a group of securities, it should be sufficient to cover the riskiest security within the group. Haircuts should reflect both the specific risks of the collateral accepted and the general risks of an FMI's collateral policy.

Including periods of stressed market conditions in the calibration of haircuts should increase the haircut rate. In addition to representing a conservative approach, this helps to mitigate the risk of a procyclical increase in haircuts during a period of high volatility. Typically, FMIs group similar securities by shared characteristics for the purposes of calculating haircuts (e.g., Government of Canada bonds with similar maturities). An FMI should recognize the different risks associated with each individual security by ensuring that the haircut is sufficient to cover the security with the most risk within each group. Haircuts should always account for all of the specific risks associated with each asset accepted as collateral. However, the FMI should also consider the portfolio risk of the total collateral posted by a participant; the FMI may consider employing deeper haircuts for concentration and wrong-way risk above certain thresholds.

2) An FMI should perform backtesting of its collateral haircuts on at least a monthly basis, and conduct a more thorough review of haircuts quarterly. The FMI's stress tests should take into account the collateral posted by participants.

FMIs are expected to calculate stable and conservative haircuts by considering stressed market conditions. In general, including stressed market conditions in the calibration of haircuts should provide a high level of coverage that does not require continuous testing and verification. Nonetheless, backtesting on a monthly basis allow the adequacy of haircuts to be evaluated against observed outcomes. A quarterly review of haircuts balances the objective of stable haircuts with the need to adjust haircuts as required. Including changes to collateral values as part of stress testing provides a more accurate assessment of potential losses in a default scenario.

— PFMI Principle 7: Liquidity risk

Box 7.1: — Joint Supplementary Guidance — Liquidity Risk

Context

The PFMIs define liquidity risk as risk that arises when the FMI, its participants or other entities cannot settle their payment obligations when due as part of the clearing or settlement process. This note provides additional guidance for Canadian FMIs to meet the components of the liquidity-risk principle related to: (i) maintaining sufficient liquid resources and (ii) qualifying liquid resources.

(i) — Maintaining sufficient liquid resources

An FMI should maintain sufficient qualifying liquid resources to cover its liquidity exposures to participants with a high degree of confidence. An FMI should maintain additional liquid resources sufficient to cover a wide range of potential stress scenarios that should include, but not be limited to, the default of the participant and its affiliates that would generate the largest aggregate liquidity obligation for the FMI in extreme but plausible conditions. Liquidity stress testing should be performed on a daily basis. An FMI should verify that its liquid resources are sufficient through comprehensive stress testing conducted at least monthly.[33]

The information provided in this section clarifies regulators' expectations of sufficient qualifying liquid resources by specifying:

    1) the degree of confidence required to cover liquidity exposures;

    2) the total liquid resources that should be maintained; and

    3) how the FMI should verify that its liquid resources are sufficient and adjust liquid resources when necessary.

1) Qualifying liquid resources should meet an established single-tailed confidence level of at least 97 per cent with respect to the estimated distribution of potential liquidity exposures.[34] The FMI should have an appropriate method for estimating potential exposures that accounts for the design of the FMI and other relevant risk factors.

The guidance requires a high threshold for covering liquidity exposures with qualifying liquid resources, while also considering the expense associated with obtaining these resources. A 97 per cent degree of confidence is equivalent to less than one observation per month (on average) in which a liquidity exposure is greater than the FMI's qualifying liquid resources. However, if it is to meet the required threshold, the FMI should estimate its potential liquidity exposures accurately. The FMI should account for all relevant predictive factors when estimating potential exposures. While historical exposures are expected to form the basis of estimated potential exposures, the FMI should account for the impact of new products, additional participants, changes in the way transactions settle or other relevant market- risk factors.

Part 2: MARKET PARTICIPANTS

---

[32]See PFMI Principle 5, key considerations 2 and 3.

[33]See PFMI Principle 7, key considerations 3, 5, 6 and 9.

[34]A "potential liquidity exposure" is defined as the estimated maximum daily liquidity needs resulting from the market value of the FMI's payment obligations under normal business conditions. FMIs should consider potential liquidity exposures over a rolling one-year time frame.

2a) An FMI should maintain additional liquid resources that are sufficient to cover a wide range of potential stress scenarios. Total liquid resources should cover the FMI's largest potential exposure under a variety of extreme but plausible conditions. The FMI should have a liquidity plan that justifies the use of other liquid resources and provides the supporting rationale for the total liquid resources that it maintains.

The guidance requires that total liquid resources be determined by the largest potential exposure in extreme but plausible conditions. This implies maintaining total liquid resources sufficient to cover at least the FMI's largest observed liquidity exposures, but the liquidity resources would likely be larger, based on an assessment of potential liquidity exposures in extreme but plausible conditions. The FMI's liquidity plan should explain why the FMI's estimated largest potential exposure is an accurate assessment of the FMI's liquidity needs in extreme but plausible conditions, thereby demonstrating the adequacy of the FMI's total liquid resources.

It is permissible for an FMI to manage this risk in part with other liquid resources because it may be prohibitively expensive, or even impossible, for the FMI to obtain sufficient qualifying liquid resources. FMIs face increased risk from liquid resources that do not meet the strict definition of "qualifying," and thus an FMI should include in its liquidity plan a clear explanation of how these resources could be used to satisfy a liquidity obligation. This additional explanation is warranted in all cases, even when the FMI's dependence on other liquid resources is minimal.

2b) When applicable, the possibility that a defaulting participant is also a liquidity provider should be taken into account.

Generally, the liquidity providers for Canadian FMIs are also participants in the FMI. When a defaulting participant is also a liquidity provider, it is important that the FMI's liquidity facilities are arranged in such a way that it has sufficient liquidity. To do so, the FMI should either have additional liquid resources or negotiate a backup liquidity provider, so that the FMI has sufficient liquidity (as specified in this guidance) in the event that one of its liquidity providers defaults.

3) FMIs should perform liquidity stress testing on a daily basis to assess their liquidity needs. At least monthly, FMIs should conduct comprehensive stress tests to verify the adequacy of their total liquid resources and to serve as a tool for informing risk management. Stress-testing results should be reviewed by the FMI's risk-management committee and reported to regulators on a regular basis.

FMIs should have clear procedures to determine whether their liquid resources are sufficient and to adjust their available liquid resources when necessary. A full review and potential resizing of liquid resources should be completed at least annually.

The annual validation of an FMI's model for managing liquidity risk should determine whether its stress testing follows best practices and captures the potential risks faced by the FMI.

FMIs should assess their liquidity needs through stress testing that includes the measurement of the largest daily liquidity exposure that they face. FMIs should also conduct stress testing to verify whether their liquid resources are sufficient to cover potential liquidity exposures under a wide range of stress scenarios. An annual full review and potential resizing of liquid resources provides adequate time to negotiate with liquidity providers. While it may be impractical for FMIs to frequently obtain additional liquid resources, it is important that FMIs clearly define the circumstances requiring prompt adjustment of their available liquid resources, and have a reliable plan for doing so. Establishing clear procedures provides transparency regarding an FMI's decision-making process and prevents the FMI from delaying required increases in liquid resources beyond what is reasonably acceptable. The review of stress-testing results by the FMI's risk-management committee provides additional assurance that liquid resources are sufficient, and whether an interim resizing is necessary. Reporting results to regulators on a monthly basis allows for timely intervention if liquid resources have been deemed inadequate.

Comprehensive stress testing should also encompass a broad range of stress scenarios, not just to verify whether the FMI's liquid resources are sufficient, but also to identify potential risk factors. Reverse stress testing, more extreme stress scenarios, valuation of liquid assets and focusing on individual risk factors (e.g., available collateral) all help to inform the FMI of potential risks. The annual validation of the FMI's risk-management model enables it to fully assess the appropriateness of the stress scenarios conducted and the procedures for adjusting liquid resources.

(ii) — Qualifying liquid resources

Qualifying liquid resources should be highly reliable and have same-day availability. Liquid resources are reliable when the FMI has near certainty that the resources it expects will be available when required. Qualifying liquid resources should be available on the same day that they are needed by the FMI to meet any immediate liquidity obligation (e.g., a participant's default). Qualifying liquid resources that are denominated in the same currency as the FMI's exposures count toward its minimum liquid-resource requirement.[35]

The following section clarifies regulators' expectations as to what is considered a qualifying liquid resource by:

1) identifying the assets in the possession, custody or control of the FMI that are considered qualifying liquid resources; and

2) setting clear standards for liquidity facilities to be considered qualifying liquid resources, including more-stringent standards for uncommitted liquidity facilities.

1) Cash and treasury bills[36] in the possession, custody or control of an FMI are qualifying liquid resources for liquidity exposures denominated in the same currency.[37]

Cash held by an FMI does not fluctuate in value and can be used immediately to meet a liquidity obligation, thereby satisfying the criteria for liquid resources to be highly reliable and available on the same day.[38] Treasury bills issued by the Government of Canada or the U.S. Treasury also meet the definition of a qualifying liquid resource. By market convention, sales of treasury bills settle on the same day, allowing funds to be obtained immediately, whereas other bonds can settle as late as three days after the date of the trade.

---

[35] See PFMI Principle 7, key considerations 4, 5 and 6

[36] "Treasury bills" refers to bonds issued by the Government of Canada and the U.S. Treasury with a maturity of one year or less.

[37] This section refers to unencumbered assets free of legal, regulatory, contractual or other restrictions on the ability of the FMI to liquidate, sell, transfer or assign the asset.

[38] "Cash" refers to currency deposits held at the issuing central bank and at creditworthy commercial banks. "Value" in this context refers to the nominal value of the currency.

Treasury bills can also be transacted in larger sizes with less market impact than most other bonds. In addition, the shorter-term nature of treasury bills makes them more liquid than other securities during a crisis (i.e., they benefit from a "flight to liquidity"). Thus, there is a high degree of certainty that the FMI would obtain liquid resources in the amount expected following the sale of treasury bills.

2a) Committed liquidity facilities are qualifying liquid resources for liquidity exposures denominated in the same currency if the following criteria are met:

    i) facilities are pre-arranged and fully collateralized;

    ii) there is a minimum of three independent liquidity providers;[39] and

    iii) the FMI conducts a level of due diligence that is as stringent as the risk assessment completed for FMI participants.

For liquidity facilities to be considered reliable, an FMI should have near certainty that the liquidity provider will honour its obligation. Pre-arranged liquidity facilities provide clarity on terms and conditions, allowing greater certainty regarding the obligations and risks of the liquidity providers. Pre- arranged facilities also reduce complications associated with obtaining liquidity, when required. Furthermore, a liquidity provider is most likely to honour its obligations when lending is fully collateralized. Therefore, only the amount that is collateralized will be considered a qualifying liquid resource. A liquidity facility is more reliable when the risk of non-performance is not concentrated in a single institution. By having at least three independent liquidity providers, the FMI would continue to diversify its risks should even a single provider default. To monitor the continued reliability of a liquidity facility, the FMI should assess its liquidity providers on an ongoing basis. In this respect, an FMI's risk exposures to its liquidity providers are similar to the risks posed to it by its participants. Therefore, it is appropriate for the FMI to conduct comparable evaluations of the financial health of its liquidity providers to ensure that the providers have the capacity to perform as expected.

2b) Uncommitted liquidity facilities are considered qualifying liquid resources for liquidity exposures in Canadian dollars if they meet the following additional criteria:

    i) the liquidity provider has access to the Bank of Canada's Standing Liquidity Facility (SLF);

    ii) the facility is fully collateralized with SLF-eligible collateral; and

    iii) the facility is denominated in Canadian dollars.

More-stringent standards are warranted for uncommitted facilities because a liquidity provider's incentives to honour its obligations are weaker. However, the risk that the liquidity provider will be unwilling or unable to provide liquidity is reduced by the requirement that it needs to be a direct participant in the Large Value Transfer System and that the collateral be eligible for the Standing Liquidity Facility (SLF). This is because the collateral obtained from the FMI in exchange for liquidity can be pledged to the Bank of Canada under the SLF. This option significantly reduces the liquidity pressures faced by the liquidity provider that could interfere with its ability to perform on its obligations. A facility in a foreign currency would not qualify because the Bank does not lend in currencies other than the Canadian dollar. The increased reliability of liquidity providers with access to routine credit from the central bank is recognized explicitly within the PFMIs.

— PFMI Principle 15: General business risk

Box 15.1: — Joint Supplementary Guidance — General Business Risk

Context

The PFMIs define general business risk as any potential impairment of the financial condition (as a business concern) of an FMI owing to declines in its revenue or growth in its expenses, resulting in expenses exceeding revenues and a loss that must be charged against capital. These risks arise from an FMI's administration and operation as a business enterprise. They are not related to participant default and are not covered separately by financial resources under the Credit or Liquidity Risk Principles. To manage these risks, the PFMIs state that FMIs should identify, monitor and manage their general business risk and hold sufficient liquid net assets funded by equity to cover potential general business losses. This note provides additional guidance for Canadian FMIs to meet the components of the general business risk principle related to: (i) governing general business risk; (ii) determining sufficient liquid net assets; and (iii) identifying qualifying liquid net assets. It also establishes the associated timelines and disclosure requirements.

(i) — Governance of general business risk

Principle 15, key consideration 1 of the PFMIs states:

An FMI should have robust management and control systems to identify, monitor, and manage general business risk.

The following points clarify the authorities' expectations on how an FMI's governance arrangements should address general business risk.

An FMI's Board of Directors should be involved in the process of identifying and managing business risks.

Management of business risks should be integrated within an FMI's risk-management framework, and the Board of Directors should be responsible for determining risk tolerances related to business risk and for assigning responsibility for the identification and management of these risks. These risk tolerances and the process for the identification and management of business risk should be the foundation for the FMI's business risk-management policy. Based on the PFMIs, the policies and procedures governing the identification and management of business risk should meet the standards outlined below.

- The FMI's business risk-management policy should be approved by the Board of Directors and reviewed at least annually. The policy should be consistent with the Board's overall risk tolerance and risk-management strategy.

- The Board's Risk Committee should have a role in advising the Board on whether the business risk-management policy is consistent with the FMI's general risk-management strategy and risk tolerance.

- The business risk-management policy should provide clear responsibilities for decision making by the Board, and assign responsibility for the identification, management and reporting of business risks to management.

---

[39]The Liquidity providers should not be affiliates to be considered independent.

(ii) — Determining sufficient liquid net assets

Principle 15, key consideration 2 of the PFMIs states:

An FMI should hold liquid net assets funded by equity [. . .] so that it can continue operations and services as a going concern if it incurs general business losses. The amount of liquid net assets funded by equity an FMI should hold should be determined by its general business risk profile and the length of time required to achieve a recovery or orderly wind-down, as appropriate, of its critical operations and services if such action is taken.

Principle 15, key consideration 3 of the PFMIs states:

An FMI should maintain a viable recovery or orderly wind-down plan and should hold sufficient liquid net assets funded by equity to implement this plan. At a minimum, an FMI should hold liquid net assets funded by equity equal to at least six months of current operating expenses.

The following points clarify the authorities' expectations on how FMIs should calculate their sufficient liquid net assets:

Until guidance for recovery planning and for calculating the associated costs is completed, FMIs are required to hold liquid net assets to cover a minimum of six months of current operating expenses.

In calculating current operating expenses, FMIs will need to:

- **Assess and understand the various general business risks they face** to allow them to estimate as accurately as possible the required amount of liquid net assets. These estimates should be based on financial projections, which take into consideration, for example, past loss events, anticipated projects and increased operating expenses.

- **Restrict the calculation to ongoing expenses.** FMIs will need to adjust their operating costs such that any extraordinary expenses (i.e., unessential, infrequent or one-off costs) are excluded. Typically, operating costs include both fixed costs (e.g., premises, IT infrastructure, etc.) and variable costs (e.g., salaries, benefits, research and development, etc.).

- **Assess the portion of staff from each corporate department required to ensure the smooth functioning of the FMI during the six-month period.** The calculation of operating expenses would include some indirect costs. FMIs would require not only dedicated operational staff, but also various supporting staff. These could include (but are not limited to) staff from the FMI's Legal, IT and HR departments or staff required to ensure the continued functioning of other FMIs that could be necessary to support the FMI.

To fully observe Principle 15, FMIs must hold sufficient liquid assets to cover the greater of (i) funds required for FMIs to implement their recovery or wind-down; or (ii) six months of current operating expenses. In the interim, until recovery planning guidance is published, only the latter amount will apply.

The amount of liquid net assets required to implement an FMI's recovery or wind-down plans will depend on the scenarios or tools available to the FMI. The acceptable recovery and orderly wind-down plans for Canadian FMIs will be articulated by the authorities in forthcoming guidance. Once this guidance on recovery planning has been developed, the guidance on general business risk will be updated to provide FMIs with additional clarity on how to calculate the costs associated with these plans and determine the amount of liquid net assets required.

(iii) — Qualifying liquid net assets

Explanatory note 3.15.5 of the PFMIs states:

An FMI should hold liquid net assets funded by equity (such as common stock, disclosed reserves or other retained earnings) so that it can continue operations and services as a going concern if it incurs general business losses. Equity allows an FMI to absorb losses on an ongoing basis and should be permanently available for this purpose.

Principle 15, key consideration 4 of the PFMIs states:

Assets held to cover general business risk should be of high quality and sufficiently liquid to allow the FMI to meet its current and projected operating expenses under a range of scenarios, including in adverse market conditions.

Principle 15, key consideration 3 of the PFMIs states:

These assets are in addition to resources held to cover participant defaults or other risks covered under the financial resources principles.

The following points clarify the authorities' expectations on which assets qualify to be held against general business risk, and how these assets should be held to ensure that they are permanently available to absorb general business losses.

Assets held against general business risk should be of high quality and sufficiently liquid, such as cash, cash equivalents and liquid securities.

Authorities have developed regulatory guidance related to managing liquidity and investment risks, which provides additional clarity on the definition of cash equivalents and liquid securities, respectively.

- **Cash equivalents** — are considered to be treasury bills[40] issued by either the Canadian or U.S. federal governments. As noted in the liquidity guidance, by market convention, sales of treasuries settle on the same day, allowing funds to be obtained immediately, whereas other bonds can settle as late as three days after the trade date.

- **Liquid securities** — for the purposes of general business risk, liquid securities are defined by the financial instruments criteria listed in the guidance on the Investment Risk Principle. These criteria outline financial instruments considered to have minimal credit, market, and liquidity risk.

Liquid net assets must be held at the level of the FMI legal entity to ensure that they are unencumbered and can be accessed quickly. Liquid net assets may be pooled with assets held for other purposes, but must be clearly identified as held against general business risk.

---

[40]Treasury bills refer to short-term (i.e. maturity of one year or less) debt instruments issued by the Canadian or U.S. federal government.

FMIs may need to accumulate liquid net assets for purposes other than to meet the General Business Risk Principle. However, assets held against general business risk cannot be used to cover participant default risk or any other risks covered by the financial resources principles.

Liquid net assets can be pooled with assets held for other purposes, but must be clearly identified as held against general business risk in the FMI's reports to its regulators.

(iv) — Timelines for assessing and reporting the level of liquid net assets

Explanatory note 3.15.8 of the PFMIs states:

To ensure the adequacy of its own resources, an FMI should regularly assess and report its liquid net assets funded by equity relative to its potential business risks to its regulators.

The following clarifies the authorities' expectations of the frequency with which FMIs should assess and report their required level of liquid net assets.

FMIs should report to authorities the amount of liquid net assets held against business risk annually, at a minimum.

An FMI should report to the authorities the amount of liquid net assets funded by equity held exclusively against business risk and quantify its business risks as major developments arise, or at least on an annual basis. This report should include an explanation of the methodology used to assess the FMI's business risks and to calculate its requirements for liquid net assets.

FMIs should recalculate the required amount of liquid net assets annually, at a minimum.

Once FMI operators have established the amount of liquid net assets required to cover six months of operating expenses, FMIs should recalculate the required amount of liquid net assets as major developments occur, or annually, at a minimum. Once the authorities have provided further guidance on recovery and FMIs have developed recovery plans, FMIs should also evaluate the need to increase the amount of liquid net assets they should hold to meet the General Business Risk Principle.

To establish clear procedures that improve transparency regarding an FMI's decision-making process and to prevent the FMI from delaying required increases in liquid resources beyond what is reasonably acceptable, FMIs should maintain a viable capital plan for raising additional acceptable resources should these resources fall close to or below the amount needed. This plan should be approved by the Board of Directors and updated annually, or as major developments occur.

FMIs should review their methodology for calculating the required level of liquid net assets at least once every five years, or as major developments occur.[41]

The methodology for calculating the amount of required liquid net assets should be reviewed at least every five years to ensure that the calculation remains relevant over time.

— PFMI Principle 16: Custody and investment risks

Box 16.1: — Joint Supplementary Guidance — Custody and Investment Risks

Context

The PFMIs define investment risk as the risk faced by an FMI when it invests its own assets or those of its participants.

- An FMI holds assets for a variety of purposes, some of which are referred to specifically in the PFMIs: to cover its business risk (Principle 15), to cover credit losses (Principle 4) and to cover credit exposures (Principle 6) using the collateral pledged by participants.

- An FMI may also hold financial assets for purposes not directly related to the risk management issues addressed within the PFMIs (e.g., employee pensions, general investment assets).

An FMI's strategy for investing assets should be consistent with its overall risk-management strategy (Principle 16). The purpose of this note is to provide further guidance on regulators' expectations regarding the management of investment risk. This guidance helps to ensure that an FMI's investments are managed in a way that protects the financial soundness of the FMI and its participants.[42]

(i) — Governance

The PFMIs state that the Board of Directors is responsible for overseeing the risk-management function and approving material risk decisions. An FMI should develop an investment policy to manage the risk arising from the investment of its own assets and those of its participants.

- The FMI's investment policy should be approved by the Board and reviewed at least annually. The policy should be consistent with the Board's overall risk tolerance and considered part of the FMI's risk-management framework.

- The Risk Committee should advise the Board on whether the investment policy is consistent with the FMI's general risk-management strategy and risk tolerance.

- The Board should assess the advantages and disadvantages of managing assets internally or outsourcing them to an external manager. The FMI retains full responsibility for any actions taken by its external manager.

- The FMI should establish criteria for the selection of an external manager.[43]

---

[41]In the context of this specific guidance item, "major developments" refers to the major changes to operations, product and service offerings, or classes of participation.

[42]This guidance on investment risk is based on aspects of Principle 2 — Governance, Principle 3 — Comprehensive Framework for the Management of Risk, and Principle 16 — Custody and Investment Risk.

[43]At a minimum, external managers should have demonstrated past performance and expertise, as well as strong risk-management practices such as an internal audit function and processes to protect and segregate the FMI's assets.

The FMI's investment policy should clearly identify those who are accountable for investment performance. The investment policy should also:

- Provide a clear explanation of the Board's delegated responsibility for investment decision making.

- Specify clear responsibilities for monitoring investment performance (against established benchmarks) and risk exposures (against limits or constraints). Procedures should be established to ensure that appropriate actions are taken when breaches occur, including possible reporting to the Board.

- Investment performance and key risk metrics should be reported to the Board at least quarterly.[44]

(ii) — Investment strategy

The investment strategy chosen by an FMI should not allow the pursuit of profit to compromise its financial soundness. As outlined below, additional consideration should be given to the investment strategy governing assets held specifically for risk-management purposes (i.e. Principle 4–7 and Principle 15).

Investment objectives

The investment policy should include appropriate investment objectives for the various assets held for risk-management purposes. The stated expected return and risk tolerance of the investment objectives should reflect the:

- specific purpose of the assets;

- relative importance of the assets in the overall risk management of the FMI; and

- requirement within the PFMIs for FMIs to invest in instruments with minimal credit, market and liquidity risk (see the Appendix for the minimum standards of acceptable instruments).

The investment objectives should also help to determine the appropriate benchmarks for measuring investment performance.

Investment constraints

The importance of assets held for risk-management purposes warrants the use of investment constraints. It is paramount that an FMI have prompt access to these assets with minimal price impact to avoid interference with their primary use for risk management. Investment of these assets should, at a minimum, observe the following:

- To reduce concentration risk, no more than 20 per cent of total investments should be invested in municipal and private sector securities. Investment in a single private sector or municipal issuer should be no more than 5 per cent of total investments.

- To mitigate specific wrong-way risk, investments should, as much as possible, be inversely related to market events that increase the likelihood of those assets being required. Investment in financial sector securities should be no more than 10 per cent of total investments. An FMI should not invest assets in the securities of its own affiliates. An FMI is not permitted to reinvest participant assets in a participant's own securities or those of its affiliates, as specified in Principle 16.

- For investments that are subject to counterparty credit risk, an FMI should set clear criteria for choosing investment counterparties and setting exposure limits.

The investment constraints should be clearly stated in the investment policy in order to provide clear guidance for those responsible for investment decision making.[45]

Link to risk management

FMIs should account for the implications of investing assets on their broader risk-management practices. The following issues should be considered when investing assets held for risk management purposes:

- An FMI's process for determining whether sufficient assets are available for risk management should account for potential investment losses. For example, investing the assets available to a CCP to cover losses from a participant default could lose value in a default scenario, resulting in less credit-risk protection. An FMI should hold additional assets to cover potential losses from its investments held for risk-management purposes.

- An FMI should account for the implications of investing assets on its ability to effectively manage liquidity risk. In particular, identification of the FMI's available liquid resources should account for the investment of its own and participants' assets. For example, cash held at a creditworthy commercial bank would no longer be considered a qualifying liquid resource under Principle 7 if it were invested in the debt instrument of a private sector issuer.

- The investment of an FMI's own assets and those of its participants should not circumvent related risk management requirements. For example, the reinvestment of participants' collateral should still respect the FMI's collateral concentration limits applicable to those assets.

Appendix

For the purposes of Principle 16, financial instruments can be considered to have minimal credit, market and liquidity risk if they meet *each* of the following conditions:

1. Investments are debt instruments that are:

    a. securities issued by the Government of Canada;

---

[44]Investment performance may also be reported to a Board committee with special expertise to which the Board has delegated the authority to review investment performance (e.g., an Investment Committee).

[45]The use of investment vehicles where investments are held indirectly (e.g. mutual funds and exchange-traded funds) should not result in breaches to the investment constraints listed.

b. securities guaranteed by the Government of Canada;

c. marketable securities issued by the United States Treasury;

d. securities issued or guaranteed by a provincial government;

e. securities issued by a municipal government;

f. bankers' acceptances;

g. commercial paper;

h. corporate bonds; and

i. asset-backed securities that meet the following criteria: (1) sponsored by a deposit-taking financial institution that is prudentially regulated at either the federal or provincial level, (2) part of a securitization program supported by a liquidity facility, and (3) backed by assets of an acceptable credit quality.

2. The FMI employs a defined methodology to demonstrate that debt instruments have low credit risk. This methodology should involve more than just mechanistic reliance on credit-risk assessments by an external party.

3. The FMI employs limits on the average time-to-maturity of the portfolio based on relevant stress scenarios in order to mitigate interest rate risk exposures.

4. Instruments have an active market for outright sales or repurchase agreements, including in stressed conditions.

5. Reliable price data on debt instruments are available on a regular basis.

6. Instruments are freely transferable and settled over a securities settlement system compliant with the PFMIs.

— PFMI Principle 23: Disclosure of rules, key procedures, and market data

Box 23.1: — Joint Supplementary Guidance — Disclosure of Rules, Key Procedures and Market Data

Context

The PFMIs state that FMIs should provide sufficient information to their participants and prospective participants to enable them to clearly understand the risks and responsibilities of participating in the system. This note provides additional guidance for Canadian FMIs to meet the components of the disclosure principle related to: (i) public qualitative disclosure and (ii) public quantitative disclosure.

Requirements included in the PFMIs

Principle 23 outlines requirements for disclosure to participants as well as the general public. In addition, specific disclosure requirements are listed in the principles to which they pertain.

The following text has been extracted directly from the PFMIs, Principle 23, key consideration 5:

An FMI should complete regularly and disclose publicly responses to the CPMI-IOSCO Disclosure framework for financial market infrastructures. An FMI also should, at a minimum, disclose basic data on transaction volumes and values.

To supplement key consideration 5, CPMI-IOSCO published two documents: the Disclosure framework for financial market infrastructures (the Disclosure Framework),[46] and the Public quantitative disclosure standards for central counterparties (the Quantitative Disclosure Standards).[47] This note will refer to the disclosures that result from completing the templates provided in these documents as the Qualitative Disclosure and the Quantitative Disclosure, respectively.

Supplementary guidance for Canadian FMIs designated by the Bank of Canada

On its public website, an FMI should publish its Qualitative Disclosure and Quantitative Disclosure, as well as any other public disclosure requirements specified in Principle 23 or in other principles. Any public disclosure should be written for an audience with general knowledge of the financial sector.

(a) — Qualitative disclosure (Applies to all types of FMIs)

A Qualitative Disclosure should provide the public with a high-level understanding of an FMI's governance, operation and risk-management framework.

Summary narrative disclosure

In part four of the Disclosure Framework, FMIs are required to provide a summary narrative of their observance of the Principles. FMIs should provide these narratives at the principle level, and are not required to address key considerations or to provide answers to the detailed questions listed in Section 5 of the Disclosure Framework report. Instead, the narrative disclosure should focus on providing a broad audience with an understanding of how each Principle applies to the FMI, and what the FMI has done or plans to do to ensure its observance.

Timing

FMIs should update and publish their Qualitative Disclosures following significant changes[48] to the system or its environment, or at least every two years. Only the most current Qualitative Disclosure needs to be maintained on the FMI's website.

---

[46]The Disclosure Framework is part of a document published in December 2012, titled "Principles for financial market infrastructures: Disclosure framework and Assessment methodology", and is available at http://www.bis.org/press/p121214.htm.

[47]This document is available at http://www.bis.org/cpmi/publ/d125.pdf.

[48]Updated Qualitative Disclosures should be published subsequent to regulatory approval, and prior to the effective date of the significant change. Significant changes can include, but are not limited to: (i) any changes to the FMI's constating documents, bylaws, corporate governance or corporate structure; (ii) any material change to an agreement between the FMI and its participants or to the FMI's rules, operating procedures, user guides, or manuals or the design,

(b) — Quantitative disclosure (Applies only to CCPs)

Quantitative Disclosures specify the set of key quantitative information required in the Disclosure Framework. They should follow the format provided by CPMI-IOSCO, allowing stakeholders, including the general public, to easily evaluate and compare FMIs.

Currently, CPMI-IOSCO has developed public quantitative disclosure standards only for CCPs. The following guidance applies only to CCPs; Canadian authorities will provide further guidance on the quantitative disclosure requirements of FMIs other than CCPs when such standards have been developed.

Context

Where a general audience may need additional context to properly interpret the data, it should be provided in explanatory notes or addressed in the CCP's Qualitative Disclosure. CCPs are encouraged to provide charts, background information and additional documentation where it may aid the reader's understanding.

Comparability

Regulators recognize that, given the different structures and arrangements among CCPs, an overly homogenized presentation format could lead to inaccurate comparability. Subject to regulatory approval, a CCP may provide analogous data in place of a disclosure requirement that is not applicable to its business or representative of the risks it faces. The CCP must justify to authorities the necessity and selection of the alternative metric.[49] If granted approval, the CCP must provide the original data to authorities with the frequency specified in the Quantitative Disclosure Standards, and must explain in each public disclosure why an alternative metric was chosen.

Confidentiality

A CCP's public disclosure obligation does not release it from its confidentiality duties. Where a required disclosure item could reveal (or allow knowledgeable parties to deduce) commercially sensitive information about individual clearing members, clients, third-party contractors or other relevant stakeholders, or where disclosure may amount to a breach of laws or regulations for maintaining market integrity, the data must be omitted. In this case, the CCP must justify the omission to authorities.[50] If granted approval, the CCP must provide the confidential data to authorities with the frequency specified in the Quantitative Disclosure Standards, and must explain the reason for the omission in each public disclosure.

Timing

Quantitative Disclosures should be reported quarterly, and updated with the frequency specified in the Quantitative Disclosure Standards.[51] Even though some required data may already be publicly disclosed in other reports, or may not have changed from the previous quarter, the data should still be included in the disclosure matrix for completeness and consistency. Data should be publicly disclosed no later than 60 days after the end of each fiscal quarter, and should remain available on its website for at least three years so that trends can be examined.

CSA Notice 24-301 — Responses to Comments on Discussion Paper 24-401 on Straight-Through Processing, Proposed National Instrument 24-101 Post-Trade Matching and Settlement, and Proposed Companion Policy 24-101CP to National Instrument 24-101 Post-Trade Matching and Settlement

Date: February 11, 2005

28 O.S.C.B. 1509

[Not reproduced]

CSA Notice 24-302 — Entitlement Payments to CDS

Date: March 3, 2006

29 O.S.C.B. 1802

1. — Purpose of Notice

The *Canadian Securities Administrators* (CSA or we) are asking all issuers and offerors[1] that pay entitlements in Canadian dollars to CDS,[2] for distribution to CDS' participants, to make such payments using the Large Value Transfer System (LVTS) operated by the *Canadian*

---

operation or functionality of its operations and services; and (iii) the establishment of, or removal or material change to, a link, or commencing or ceasing to engage in a business activity.

[49]If the authorities are satisfied with the justification, the CCP need not resubmit the substitution unless the CCP's structure or arrangements change the applicability of the original disclosure requirement, or the CCP wishes to change its substituted metric. CCPs are responsible for informing authorities of any changes that could affect the applicability of the originally required or substituted data.

[50]If the authorities are satisfied with the justification, the CCP need not resubmit the omission unless the circumstances change the confidentiality of the disclosure. CCPs are responsible for informing the authorities of any changes that could affect the confidentiality of such data.

[51]According to the Quantitative Disclosure Standards, items under general business risk should be updated annually, and all other items should be updated on a quarterly basis.

[1]For the purposes of this Notice, an *offeror* is a person or company that acquires securities in exchange for funds, or for both funds and other securities, pursuant to an offer to acquire, take-over bid, issuer bid, plan of arrangement or other form of business reorganization.

[2]Or, alternatively, its nominee, CDS & Co.

Payments Association (CPA). While the rules of the CPA already effectively require issuers and offerors to make payments that exceed $25 million in LVTS funds, we encourage issuers and offerors (and their agents[3]) to arrange with their financial institutions to pay entitlements of $25 million or less in LVTS funds instead of cheques or other forms of payment that do not provide immediately final and irrevocable funds upon receipt.[4]

2. — What are entitlement payments

An entitlement payment is any money payment made in respect of issued and outstanding securities to holders of such securities. Entitlement payments include interest payments made on debt securities, cash dividend payments or other similar distributions made on equity securities, payments made upon redemptions, repurchases, or maturities of securities, and payments made in a transaction whereby securities are acquired in exchange for cash, or for both cash and other securities, under an offer to acquire, take-over bid, issuer bid, plan of arrangement or other form of business reorganization.

3. — What is the Large Value Transfer System (LVTS)

The LVTS, launched in 1999 by the CPA, is an electronic wire payment system that allows financial institutions and their customers to send large payments securely in real time. Through LVTS, funds can be transferred between participating financial institutions almost instantaneously, and the money can thus be credited to the recipient's account on a timely basis. All LVTS payments are immediately final and irrevocable. The recipient may withdraw the money, invest it or use it to make another payment. According to the CPA, more than $130 billion in payments daily, representing approximately 88 per cent of the total value flowing through Canada's payments system, are being settled through the LVTS.[5]

4. — What is CDS' role in processing entitlement payments

CDS is Canada's national securities depository, clearing and settlement organization that holds over $2.6 trillion of securities on deposit and handles over 65 million securities trades annually. Most publicly-traded Canadian equity, corporate and government debt and money market securities, and many U.S. securities owned by Canadian investors, are held through CDS. When making entitlement payments to its registered or bearer securities holders, an issuer in Canada will usually make, by far, the largest entitlement payment to CDS or its nominee. CDS then processes the entitlement payment it receives from the issuer and credits the funds to its participants' accounts. Participants in turn make payments to their customers.

CDS' records show that, during its fiscal year ended October 31, 2004, it processed the following entitlement payments:

- interest: $59.4 billion

- dividends: $22.4 billion

- corporate actions: $135 billion

- money market maturities: $2.1 trillion

Of the total number of entitlement payments paid directly to CDS, 65.12 per cent were made by cheque (representing 21.49 per cent of the total value of such payments).[6] In the United States, apparently 99.5 per cent of the value of entitlement payments to the U.S. central securities depository are made by means of FedWire, a real-time gross settlement payment system operated by the U.S. Federal Reserve Board.[7]

5. — Why is the ongoing use of cheques to pay entitlements to CDS a growing concern to regulators

Many issuers and offerors currently pay their entitlements by uncertified cheque or other forms of paper-based payment items. This method of payment of entitlements is inefficient, costly and poses certain risks to CDS and its participants. The main risk is that there is no finality of payment with paper-based items, as they can be reversed if there are insufficient funds in the account on which the cheque or other paper-based item is drawn. If an entitlement payment is reversed, participant recipients would be required to return such reversed payments to CDS. Risk is created where a participant is unable to return reversed payments. There is also the risk of loss or theft of such paper-based items. In addition, CDS is required to maintain costly manual processes to receive and handle large quantities of cheques, including data entry, reconciliation, safekeeping, and cheque conversion.[8]

International best practices and standards require payment arrangements that enable market participants to retransfer the proceeds of securities transactions as soon as possible — ideally intraday or at a minimum before the end of business on the same day — so as to limit their liquidity

---

[3]Generally, *transfer agents* act for issuers and *depositary agents* act for offerors.

[4]The CPA rule limits the use of cheques, bank drafts and other paper-based payment items that can be processed through the CPA's older Automated Clearing Settlement System (ACSS) to payments of $25 million or less. See Section 14 of CPA Rule A1 — *General Rules Pertaining to Items Acceptable for Exchange, for the Purpose of Clearing and Settlement*. The CPA's rules can be found on its web site at: http://www.cdnpay.ca/.

[5]For more information on the LVTS and the CPA, visit the CPA's web site at http://www.cdnpay.ca/ and the web site of the Bank of Canada at http://www.bank-banque-canada.ca/.

[6]Entitlement payments paid by means of a debit to a CDS participant's funds account are not included in these numbers.

[7]See letter of the Canadian Capital Markets Association (CCMA) dated May 12, 2003 — *Letter to CSA Responding to Questions on Mandating Use of LVTS for Entitlement Payments* — available on the CCMA's web site at: http://www.ccma-acmc.ca/ccmahome.nsf/Splash?OpenPage.

[8]*Ibid.*

risk and any credit risks associated with the assets used.[9] International benchmarking studies suggest that current entitlement management processes in the Canadian capital markets are likely adversely affecting our country's otherwise high standing in global custody service rankings.[10]

Led by the Canadian Capital Markets Association (CCMA), the securities industry in Canada has raised this issue as an impediment to the industry's move towards straight-through processing (STP) and eventual move to a standard T+1 settlement cycle. From an STP perspective, LVTS entitlement payments will eliminate the current reliance on manual intervention to process payments, thus reducing the potential for errors and delays associated with payments by cheque. According to the CCMA, these are features that investors, and in particular foreign investors, consider when selecting markets in which to invest.[11]

The CSA agree that this issue impacts the efficiency of our capital markets, and that the use of LVTS funds for all entitlement payments will improve market efficiency and reduce risk. The CSA share the industry's view that the payment of entitlements using LVTS funds will ensure that:

- all payments within the securities clearing and settlement system are final and irrevocable,

- beneficiaries receive entitlement payments that are immediately available to them on an unconditional basis,

- Canada is better prepared to achieve STP and an eventual standard T+1 settlement period.

6. — What are the potential costs to issuers and offerors in making LVTS entitlement payments to CDS

In a letter to the CSA dated May 12, 2003, the CCMA described the potential costs to issuers and offerors of making an LVTS payment. The costs will vary depending on the size of the issuer or offeror, the nature of its commercial relationship with its financial institution,[12] how the entitlement payments are funded and other factors. The CCMA suggested that, depending on the size of the overall financial-institution relationship, the explicit cost of a particular LVTS payment could be nil.[13]

The CSA are cognizant of concerns about higher fees and costs to change banking practices and convert cheque payments to LVTS payments. This Notice is asking issuers and offerors to voluntarily change their payment practices.

7. — What have the industry and CSA said about this issue in the past

Numerous industry submissions and white papers on the LVTS issue have been made since 2000.[14] For example, in a written submission dated July 17, 2002 to the CSA, the CCMA requested that we mandate as quickly as possible the use of LVTS funds when payment of corporate entitlements are made to recognized depositories. The industry provided various reasons for this request, including that, even without any move to a standard T+1 settlement cycle, "... requiring entitlement payments to be made by LVTS is still critical to improving the efficiency of Canadian capital markets."[15]

In November 2002, we published *CSA Notice 51-305* encouraging market participants to comment on a CCMA white paper that recommended, among other things, a requirement that entitlements to recognized depositories be paid in LVTS funds. We also published *CSA Discussion Paper 24-401 on Straight-through Processing* in April 2004 that contained a discussion and sought comment on the LVTS entitlement payments issue. Also in April 2004, a working group (LVTS working group) comprising staff from CDS, the Bank of Canada, CPA, Ontario Securities Commission, and Autorité des marchés financiers (Québec) was struck to find ways to encourage or require the use of the LVTS when making entitlement payments to CDS. Finally, in February 2005, we published *CSA Notice 24-301*,[16] which summarized the comments we received on Discussion Paper 24-401. Most comments on the LVTS entitlement payments issue suggested that the CSA should require issuers and offerors to use the LVTS, regardless of the value of the entitlement to be paid to CDS. Notice 24-301 also confirmed, among other things, our support of industry and regulatory initiatives to increase the use of LVTS by issuers.

---

[9]See par. 3.52 of *Recommendations for securities settlement systems* — November 2001 report of the joint Task Force on Securities Settlement Systems of the Committee on Payment and Settlement Systems (CPSS) of the central banks of the Group of Ten countries and the Technical Committee of the International Organization of Securities Commissions (IOSCO). The CPSS-IOSCO report is available at: http://www.iosco.org/pubdocs/pdf/IOSCOPD123-English.pdf, or http://www.bis.org/publ/cpss46.pdf.

[10]An October 22, 2002 CCMA White Paper — *Corporate Actions and Other Entitlements White Paper* — makes reference to a 1997–1999 *GSCS Benchmarks* annual survey, which suggested that Canada's "undisciplined" entitlement-management process contributes to lowering Canada's standing in world rankings, citing Canadian custody client criticisms regarding corporate action handling. The CCMA White Paper is available on the CCMA's web site at: http://www. ccma-acma.ca/ccmahome.nsf/Main-E?OpenFrameSet. The latest *Thomas Murray* capital market infrastructure risk assessment on Canada seems to echo these concerns. See *Thomas Murray Capital Markets Infrastructure Risk Ratings — Canada*, 2005 Report; Thomas Murray, London, U.K. The Thomas Murray web site is at www.thomasmurray.com.

[11]See May 12, 2003 CCMA letter to the CSA, *supra*, note 7.

[12]For example, fees may be bundled into the overall relationship package.

[13]The CCMA letter goes into more detail on the cost components of making an LVTS payment. See May 12, 2003 CCMA letter to the CSA, *supra*, note 7.

[14]See the CCMA's Website at www.ccma-acmc.ca for some of these submissions and white papers.

[15]This CCMA written submission dated July 17, 2002 — *CCMA Letter to the Canadian Securities Administrators (CSA) on the Large Value Transfer System (LVTS)* — is available on the CCMA's web site at: http://www.ccma-acmc.ca/ccmahome.nsf/Main-E?OpenFrameSet.

[16]See *CSA Notice 24-301 — Responses to Comments Received on Discussion Paper 24-401 on Straight-through Processing, Proposed National Instrument 24-101 Post-trade Matching and Settlement, and Proposed Companion Policy 24-101CP to National Instrument 24-101 Post-trade Matching and Settlement.*

8. — Conclusion

The industry and LVTS working group considered a range of mandatory and non-mandatory options to achieve greater use of the LVTS when making entitlement payments of $25 million or less to CDS. Instead of implementing a mandatory measure at this time, we have decided through this Notice to encourage the voluntary use of the LVTS. We ask all issuers and offerors (and their agents) that pay Canadian dollar entitlements to CDS or its nominee, for distribution to CDS' participants, to make such payment in LVTS funds to CDS' account at the Bank of Canada. We believe that the use of LVTS funds for all entitlement payments to CDS will contribute to market efficiency and reduce risk. We propose to assess in a year from now whether there has been any meaningful progress[17] towards the use of the LVTS by issuers and offerors (and their agents).

CSA Notice 24-303 — CSA SRO Oversight Project — Review of Oversight of Self-Regulatory Organizations and Market Infrastructure Entities — Report of the CSA SRO Oversight Project Committee — December 2006

Date: December 8, 2006

29 O.S.C.B. 9462

[Not reproduced]

CSA Staff Notice 24-304 — CSA-Industry Working Group on NI 24-101 — Institutional Trade Matching and Settlement

Date: July 6, 2007

30 O.S.C.B. 6014

A CSA-Industry working group (Working Group) consisting of industry representatives and staff of the Canadian Securities Administrators (CSA) has recently been established to act as an advisory group for the CSA in identifying and resolving issues in relation to National Instrument 24-101 — *Institutional Trade Matching and Settlement* (NI 24-101). The Working Group will meet periodically to discuss the issues.

Members of the Working Group

The Working Group includes representatives of the industry's sell-side, buy-side and custodian sectors and representatives of the Canadian Capital Markets Association (CCMA), Investment Industry Association of Canada (IIAC), Investment Dealers Association of Canada (IDA) and CDS Clearing and Depository Services Inc. (CDS).

The following is a list of the Working Group members:

Name and Firm	Email address	Sector or Industry Group Representation
Barbara Amsden (IIAC)	bamsden@iiac.ca	IIAC
Jerry Beniuk (TDBFG)	Jerry.Beniuk@td.com	Buy side/Sell side/Custodian
Brian Calvert (RBC Investments)	brian.calvert@rbcinvestments.com	Sell side
Richard Corner (IDA)	rcorner@ida.ca	IDA
Jane Davis (CCMA)	JDavis@cds.ca	CCMA
Aaron Ferguson (CDS)	AFerguson@cds.ca	CDS
Lynn Higgins (Canaccord)	Lynn_higgins@canaccord.com	Sell side
Heidi Johnston (Phillips Hager North)	hjohnston@phn.com	Buy side
Patricia Johnston (FirstEnergy Capital Corp.)	pmjohnston@firstenergy.com	Sell side
Glenn MacPherson (CCMA)	GMacPherson@cds.ca	CCMA
Fionnuala Martin (BMO Financial Group)	Fionnuala.martin@bmonb.com	Sell side
Chuck Murray (Mackenzie Financial Corporation)	cmurray@mackenziefinancial.com	Buy side
Wayne Ralph (Canadian Imperial Bank of Commerce)	Wayne.Ralph@CIBC.ca	Sell side
Answerd Ramcharan (IDA)	aramcharan@ida.ca	IDA
Randy Reid (CIBC Mellon)	randy_reid@cibcmellon.com	Custodian
Lorne Rintoul (Scotia Capital)	Lorne_rintoul@scotiacapital.com	Sell side
Jesus Sanchez (NBCN Inc.)	Jesus.sanchez@nbcn.ca	Sell side
Domenic Sgambelluri (Northern Trust Co., Canada)	DS124@ntrs.com	Custodian
Barry Stienstra (RBC Dexia Investor Services)	barry.stienstra@rbcdexia-is.com	Custodian

---

[17]As measured in terms of narrowing the gap between the use of electronic payments in Canada and in the United States.

Name and Firm	Email address	Sector or Industry Group Representation
Pierre Tremblay (Caisse Centrale Desjardins)	Pierre.tremblay@ccd.desjardins.com	Buy side
Jenny Tsouvalis (OMERS)	Jtsouvalis@omers.com	Buy side
Mark Weseluck (CDS)	mweseluck@cds.ca	CDS

CSA STP Committee Staff

Serge Boisvert	Serge.boisvert@lautorite.qc.ca	AMF
Shaun Fluker	Shaun.fluker@seccom.ab.ca	ASC
Nathalie Gallant	Nathalie.gallant@lautorite.qc.ca	AMF
John Kearns	jkearns@osc.gov.on.ca	OSC
Janice Leung	jleung@bcsc.bc.ca	BCSC
Maxime Paré	mpare@osc.gov.on.ca	OSC
Michael Sorbo	msorbo@bcsc.bc.ca	BCSC
Emily Sutlic	esutlic@osc.gov.on.ca	OSC

You are invited to raise issues or questions you may have regarding NI 24-101 with any member of the Working Group.

CSA staff propose to publish later this year a notice that will answer a number of key questions on NI 24-101.

CSA Staff Notice 24-305 (Revised) — Frequently Asked Questions About NI 24-101 — *Institutional Trade Matching and Settlement* and Related Companion Policy

Date: December 14, 2007 as revised effective May 6, 2011

30 O.S.C.B. 10202 and 34 O.S.C.B. 5179

To assist market participants in complying with National Instrument 24-101 — *Institutional Trade Matching and Settlement* (NI 24-101 or the Instrument), we have compiled some frequently asked questions (FAQs) with our responses. This list of FAQs is not exhaustive, but includes issues and questions raised by stakeholders.

Some terms we have used in these FAQs are defined in NI 24-101, in related Companion Policy 24-101CP (CP), or in National Instrument 14-101 *Definitions*.

We have divided the FAQs into the following categories:

    A. Definitions, interpretation and concepts

    B. Application

    C. Trade matching requirements — general policies and procedures

    D. Trade matching documentation (Sections 3.2 and 3.4 of the Instrument)

    E. Trade matching requirements specific to advisers

    F. Trade matching requirements — cross-border trade orders

    G. Reporting requirements for registered firms

    H. CSA contacts

A. — Definitions, interpretation and concepts

A-1 Q: What types of trades are typically considered as "DAP/RAP trades"?

A: DAP/RAP trades are trades for a delivery-against-payment or receipt-against-payment (or similarly named) account of an institutional investor that are generally settled through a separate custodian on the books of the clearing agency, CDS Clearing and Depository Services Inc. (CDS). The Instrument applies to all types of DAP/RAP trades except those described in section 2.1 of the Instrument.

A-2 Q: Who is an "institutional investor" under the Instrument?

A: An institutional investor is a client of a dealer that has been granted DAP/RAP trading privileges by the dealer, which typically include investment funds, pension plans, and financial institutions.

A-3 Q: GHI Mutual Fund is a client of Specialized Broker (SB), a dealer that provides specialized trade execution services. SB is not a participant of CDS and has a clearing arrangement with Clearing Broker (CB), a dealer that provides clearing, settlement and custody services for SB. GHI Mutual Fund has a direct custodial arrangement with the Custodian Trust Company, which holds GHI Mutual Fund's investments. Would trades executed by SB and cleared by CB for GHI Mutual Fund be DAP/RAP trades? If so, which dealer would be required to comply with Parts 3 and 4 of the Instrument for these trades, and who would be "trade-matching parties"?

A: Trades executed by SB and cleared by CB for GHI Mutual Fund would be DAP/RAP trades because these trades would be settled for the client on a delivery-against-payment or receipt-against-payment basis through the facilities of a clearing agency by Custodian Trust Company. SB would be required to comply with Parts 3 and 4 of the Instrument in this case. In addition to SB, each of CB, GHI Mutual Fund and Custodian Trust Company would be trade-matching parties under the Instrument. Trade matching parties are encouraged to enter into a trade-matching agreement with, or provide a trade-matching statement to, SB. See section 3.2 of the Instrument. The purpose of such agreements or statements is to promote among trade-matching parties policies and procedures designed to achieve matching as soon as practical after a trade is executed. See the definitions of "trade-matching agreement" and "trade-matching statement" in section 1.1 of the Instrument.

A-4 Q: DEF Hedge Fund is a client of ABC Broker, a full-service dealer that provides prime brokerage services for DEF Hedge Fund and other hedge funds, including custodial functions. DEF Hedge Fund uses ABC Broker to execute all of its trades. Do the matching requirements of NI 24-101 apply to these trades?

A: No. These are not DAP/RAP trades because ABC Broker is both executing and settling the trades on behalf of DEF Hedge Fund. A separate custodian is not involved in the trades.

A-5 Q: Assume the same facts as above (A-4), except that DEF Hedge Fund sometimes uses other dealers in addition to ABC Broker to execute its trades. Do the matching requirements of NI 24-101 apply to the trades executed by the other dealers for DEF Hedge Fund?

A: Yes. If another dealer (e.g., XYZ Broker) executes a trade for DEF Hedge Fund, this trade will likely fall within the Instrument's definition of a DAP/RAP trade. This trade is likely settled for DEF Hedge Fund on a delivery-against-payment or receipt-against-payment basis through CDS, involving the accounts of both ABC Broker (as the custodian) and XYZ Broker (as the executing dealer).[1]

A-6 Q: What if, in the above scenario (A-5), XYZ Broker "gives up" a trade executed for DEF Hedge Fund in favour of ABC Broker. Would such a trade still be a DAP/RAP trade?

A: We understand that in a trade "give up" the executing dealer places a trade on behalf of another dealer as if the latter had actually executed the trade itself. Sometimes an institutional client may ask the executing dealer to relinquish or assign the trade (a binding contract) to its prime broker. If the "give up" arrangement is in place prior to execution of the trade and does not involve a trade that is settled for the client on a delivery-against-payment or receipt-against-payment basis through the facilities of a clearing agency by a separate custodian, then we would not view such trades as DAP/RAP trades.

A-7 Q: How are partial fills (i.e., orders that are filled over several days) treated under the matching requirements of NI 24-101?

A: The answer depends on the terms of the agreement governing the trading relationship between the dealer and the investment manager. If the investment manager is contractually bound by a partial fill, thus triggering a notice of execution (NOE) from the dealer either intra-day or at the end of the trading day, that trade is subject to the matching requirements of NI 24-101. If, on the other hand, the investment manager is not bound by the order until it is complete and the NOE is triggered only when the dealer advises the investment manager of the fill, the matching requirements of NI 24-101 only come into effect when the complete order has been filled.[2]

A-8 Q: We are a mutual fund management group that uses a separate registered portfolio manager (PM) to process our trades on behalf of each of our mutual funds through various executing dealers. Are we a "trade-matching party"?

A: No, so long as a PM is acting for your mutual funds in processing their trades. See paragraphs (a) and (b) of the definition "trade-matching party" in section 1.1 of the Instrument.

A-9 Q: We are a mutual fund management group that uses separate domestic and foreign sub-advisers to process our trades on behalf of our mutual funds through various executing dealers. The sub-advisers are responsible for the trades, including the clearing and settlement process. Would all the sub-advisers be "trade-matching parties"?

A: If a sub-adviser is dealing with a registered dealer directly to process DAP/RAP trades on behalf of the mutual funds, the sub-adviser would meet the definition of a trade-matching party in section 1.1 of the Instrument. This applies to all sub-advisers regardless of whether they are based or registered in Canada.

As a trade-matching party, your sub-advisers are encouraged to either enter into a trade-matching agreement with the dealer, or provide a trade-matching statement to the dealer. You may need to work with your sub-advisers to identify your respective roles and responsibilities in the processing of the trades of your mutual funds.

In addition to being a trade-matching party, those sub-advisers that are registered firms are subject to sections 3.3, 3.4 and 4.1 of the Instrument.

A-10 Q: In the above scenario (A-9), some of our U.S.-based sub-advisers may be trading in the Canadian markets for our funds. They usually do not deal directly with a Canadian registered dealer for DAP/RAP trades in Canada, but instead give trade orders to a U.S. broker-dealer, who in turn deals directly with a Canadian registered dealer for DAP/RAP trades in Canada. Would these sub-advisers be "trade-matching parties"?

A: The U.S.-based sub-advisers would not be considered to be trade-matching parties in this case. However, the U.S. broker-dealer dealing directly with the Canadian registered dealer for executing DAP/RAP trades may be considered a trade-matching party under paragraph (b) of the definition of that term in section 1.1 of the Instrument. See Part F for more cross-border questions.

A-11 Q: Does "matching" under the Instrument mean when both sides of a trade report the same details of the trade into a system, and the system itself performs the matching?

A: The concept of matching for the purposes of the Instrument is broader. See section 1.2(1) of the Instrument. Conceptually, it is the *end result* of either a sequential confirmation and affirmation process or a "virtual matching" process among trade-matching parties. As a result, the Instrument contemplates, and is neutral towards, either matching approach, which is consistent with the industry's best practices and standards.

---

[1] If XYZ Broker is not a direct participant of CDS, then settlements would involve the accounts of ABC Broker (as custodian) and XYZ Broker's corresponding clearing broker maintained at CDS.

[2] This answer is consistent with industry best practices and standards for institutional trade processing. See section 2.4(1) of the CP.

B. — Application

B-1 Q: The Instrument does not apply to trades "to be settled outside Canada" (see section 2.1(g) of the Instrument). What do you mean by that?

A: Trades that are cleared and settled through the facilities of a clearing agency based outside of Canada would be trades settled outside of Canada.

B-2 Q: Are trades in investment products that normally do not settle through the facilities of a clearing agency subject to the Instrument (e.g., partnership units)?

A: The trade matching requirements of the Instrument (Parts 3 and 4) apply to DAP/RAP trades, which, by definition, are trades that settle on a delivery-against-payment or receipt-against-payment basis through the facilities of a clearing agency. Therefore, trades in investment products that do not settle through the facilities of a clearing agency would not be subject to such requirements. However, the trade settlement requirement of Part 7 of the Instrument may apply to these trades.

C. — Trade matching requirements — general policies and procedures

C-1 Q: The CP says that when establishing appropriate policies and procedures, a party should consider the industry's generally adopted best practices and standards for institutional trade processing. My PM firm has developed and designed specific policies and procedures that are unique to our own business structure and risk profile in the trading and investing of securities. While my firm's policies and procedures may differ from those of other firms, they are adequate to meet the requirements of NI 24-101. Is my firm complying with NI 24-101?

A: Yes, provided that your policies and procedures are reasonably designed to meet the requirements of NI 24-101. See section 2.4(1) of the CP. We recognize that market participants may have different policies and procedures for their unique business circumstances. See section 2.4(2) of the CP.

C-2 Q: A number of logistical issues are associated with compliance with NI 24-101, for example:

- What do we have to cover in our trade matching policies and procedures?
- What systems and processes do we have to change to comply with the Instrument?
- What are some of the systems or service providers available to help us comply?
- Are we going to have to retrain or hire additional staff?

A: NI 24-101 is generally a principles-based rule. It does not prescribe in detail what a market participant's policies and procedures should cover. However, the CP does provide some useful guidance on this question. See section 2.4 and 2.3(2)(b) of the CP. The industry has made suggestions to assist market participants in this area. Based on those suggestions, we recommend that trade-matching parties follow these basic steps:

1. Review your current systems capabilities and processes to identify what may prevent your firm from achieving the Instrument's requirements;

2. Develop policies and procedures to achieve the target set out in section 4.1 of the Instrument;

3. Identify what changes need to be made to the services provided by third party vendors, or whether third party service providers could assist you in complying with the Instrument;

4. Develop with your trade-matching parties a form of trade-matching statement or agreement;

5. Put in place monitoring processes to assess your own and other trade-matching parties' compliance with the Instrument including the required timelines;

6. Plan to meet the exception reporting target for each calendar quarter;

7. Make and test any systems and process changes needed; and

8. Enter into any agreements and/or receive any statements from other trade matching parties.

Some service providers will likely be matching service utilities (MSUs) operating in the Canadian institutional marketplace. These MSUs may facilitate the matching process for certain trade-matching parties. See section 2.5 of the CP. In the short term, you may need to retrain or hire additional back-office staff to comply with the matching requirements. If so, as you become more efficient, you may be able to re-allocate staff. In addition, you may need to upgrade your systems to enhance your *interoperability* with other trade matching parties. See section 2.4(2) of the CP.

C-3 Q: If I choose to, can I still match trades on a manual basis?

A: As noted, NI 24-101 is generally a principles-based rule and does not prescribe how you match trades. In assessing any trade matching process, you may want to consider how it fits into your firm's overall back-office processes and your trade-matching parties' systems in the long term.

D. — Trade matching documentation (sections 3.2 and 3.4 of the Instrument)

D-1 Q: Does the Instrument prescribe the form of a trade-matching statement or trade-matching agreement?

A: No, the Instrument does not prescribe the form of the trade-matching statement or agreement, other than that it be in writing.

The CP provides guidance on the use and delivery of a trade-matching statement. See section 2.3(3) of the CP. A model trade-matching statement is posted on the website of the Investment Industry Association of Canada at: http://www.iiac.ca

The CP also provides guidance on the types of matters that a trade-matching agreement could address, as well as guidance on the use of an agreement (including that an agreement may be incorporated into the institutional account opening documentation). See section 2.3(2) of the CP. The trade-matching agreement is an alternative to the trade-matching statement. Parties may prefer to use a trade-matching agreement instead of a statement if they have unique trade processing issues and wish to clarify their roles and responsibilities in the matching process.

D-2 Q: We are a dealer that has many foreign institutional clients trading in the Canadian markets. We have policies and procedures in place for timely institutional trade matching, and we are attempting to obtain trade-matching statements from all of our clients pursuant to section 3.2 of the Instrument. However, some clients are reluctant to provide a trade-matching statement that confirms their compliance with NI 24-101. How do we resolve this issue?

A: We note that a trade-matching statement need only confirm that your client has policies and procedures designed to achieve matching as soon as practical after a trade is executed. If a dealer or adviser is unable to obtain a trade-matching agreement or statement from a trade-matching party, it should document its efforts in accordance with its policies and procedures. See section 2.3(1)(a) of the CP.

E. — Trade matching requirements specific to advisers

E-1 Q: We are a PM firm that advises a number of mutual funds, hedge funds, and pension plans in managing their portfolio assets. Whom should we enter into a trade-matching agreement with? Alternatively, from whom should we ask for a trade-matching statement? And to whom should we give one?

A: If your PM firm is acting for an institutional investor in processing DAP/RAP trades, your policies and procedures must be designed to encourage the following trade-matching parties to (i) enter into a trade-matching agreement with your firm or (ii) provide to your firm a trade-matching statement:

- The dealer or dealers executing and clearing the DAP/RAP trades, and

- The custodian or custodians of the institutional investor that are settling the DAP/RAP trades.

E-2 Q: In the above situation (E-1), are the mutual funds, hedge funds, and pension plans trade-matching parties within the meaning of the Instrument that should enter into a trade-matching agreement or provide a trade-matching statement?

A: No. If the PM is acting for the funds or plans in processing the DAP/RAP trades, the funds or plans are not trade matching parties. An institutional investor is only a "trade-matching party" when an adviser *is not acting* for the institutional investor in processing DAP/RAP trades.

E-3 Q: When is a registered adviser "acting for the institutional investor in processing the trade" for the purposes of the definition "trade-matching party"?

A: A registered adviser will be acting for an institutional investor in processing a trade when it is involved in the post-trade execution functions of a trade on behalf of an institutional investor (e.g., the trade comparison, clearing, settlement and portfolio reconciliation functions of the institutional investor). A registered adviser that is merely providing advice to the institutional investor or placing a trade order to a dealer or through a marketplace for the institutional investor would not be a trade-matching party.

E-4 Q: How will a PM firm determine their record of trade matching performance by calendar quarter?

A: Registered advisers should maintain or obtain a record of their DAP/RAP trade matching performance to determine whether they will need to provide to the regulators an exception report on Form 24-101F1 for any given calendar quarter. As noted in section 3.1(b) of the CP, Form 24-101F1 requires registered advisers to provide, among other things, aggregate quantitative information on their equity and debt DAP/RAP trades. Tracking of a registered adviser's trade-matching statistics may be outsourced to another party, such as a custodian. See section 3.1(a) of the CP. Registered advisers may need to obtain from the custodians of their institutional investor clients the details of when each DAP/RAP trade is matched. We understand that custodians have developed standardized DAP/RAP trade matching performance reports for their clients.

F. — Trade matching requirements — cross-border trade orders

F-1 Q: We are a foreign dealer that gives orders from time to time to various Canadian-based registered dealers to execute trades in the Canadian markets on behalf of our foreign institutional clients. Do the requirements of registered dealers in Parts 3 and 4 of the Instrument apply to us?

A: No. You are not subject to the requirements of registered dealers in Parts 3 and 4 of the Instrument if a Canadian registered dealer is executing DAP/RAP trades for you. However, you may be considered a trade-matching party, in which case you are encouraged to enter into a trade-matching agreement with, or provide a trade-matching statement to, the Canadian dealer. See sections 3.2 of the Instrument and 1.3(5) of the CP.

F-2 Q: We are a mid-sized Canadian dealer that has a significant foreign client base. We receive orders from various foreign institutional investors. Most of our foreign institutional clients use a foreign global custodian to hold their portfolio assets, which in turn uses a local Canadian custodian to hold their Canadian portfolio investments and process their DAP/RAP trades settled in Canada. Would our foreign institutional investor clients that trade on a DAP/RAP account basis in Canada be considered "trade-matching parties" under the Instrument?

A: Yes. Where a registered adviser is not acting for the foreign institutional investor in processing DAP/RAP trades, the foreign institutional investor will be a "trade-matching party." See section 1.3(5) of the CP.

F-3 Q: In the above scenario (F-2), we often receive orders to trade securities on a Canadian marketplace directly from European institutional investors. Which other entities would be "trade-matching parties" to process the trade in this case and how is the matching deadline impacted?

A: In addition to the European institutional investor, you (the dealer) and the local Canadian custodian are trade-matching parties. See section 1.3(5) of the CP. Although the CP notes that a foreign global custodian would not normally be considered a trade-matching party in these circumstances, you, the foreign institutional investor or the local custodian may need to work with the global custodian in establishing, maintaining and enforcing your respective policies and procedures. If the European institutional investor's investment decisions or settlement instructions are usually made in and communicated from a geographical region outside of the North American region, the timeline is extended by a day to noon on T+2. See section 3.1(2) and the definition "North American region" in section 1.1 of the Instrument.

F-4 Q: We are a Canadian dealer that often receives orders to execute DAP/RAP trades from broker-dealers in the United States acting for various foreign institutional investors, but we do not always know who those foreign institutional investors are or where they are based (i.e., whether within or outside the North American region). Who are the "trade-matching parties" in these cases?

A: We would consider the U.S. broker-dealer as the "institutional investor" in the DAP/RAP trade in Canada for the purposes of the Instrument, not the underlying foreign institutional investor. Therefore, you (the dealer), the U.S. broker-dealer (in the capacity of institutional investor) and the local Canadian custodian would be considered the trade-matching parties.

F-5 Q: In the above scenario (F-4), to what extent are we required to match the details of the trades executed in Canada for the underlying foreign institutional investors?

A: You will likely match the details of the "Canadian component" of the trades in this scenario, which are the DAP/RAP trades placed by the U.S. broker-dealer with you and settled with the local Canadian custodian. You are not required to match the underlying "non-Canadian component" of the transactions among the U.S. broker-dealer, its foreign institutional investor clients, and their global custodian or custodians, if information required to match the underlying transactions (e.g., allocations to global custodian) is not needed to match the "Canadian component" of the transactions. We would view the non-Canadian component of the transactions as trades that are settled outside of Canada, to which the Instrument does not apply.

F-6 Q: In the above scenario (F-4), what is the timeline that applies?

A: Because we would likely consider the U.S. broker-dealer as an institutional investor whose investment decisions or settlement instructions are usually made in and communicated from the U.S., the North American region timeline will apply. However, if you need information about the non-Canadian component of the transactions to match and settle the Canadian component of the transactions, you may want to find out from the U.S. broker-dealer where the underlying foreign institutional investor is based, so that you can determine whether the North American region or non-North American region timeline applies.

F-7 Q: Will our firm be required to track trade matching statistics for two separate streams of investors for exception reporting purposes, i.e., one for North American region institutional investors and the other for non-North American region institutional investors?

A: You are not required to track your trade matching statistics separately for the two streams of investors. Sections 3.1(2) and 3.3(2) of the Instrument aim to give the trade-matching parties in the DAP/RAP trades of non-North American region institutional investors more flexibility, by providing an extra day to achieve matching.

If your trading business for foreign non-North American region investors is a small percentage of your overall trading business, it may not be useful or efficient for you to track these trades separately to avoid exception reporting. If trading for foreign non-North American region investors is an important part of your overall trading business, you may want to track such trades separately, including working with any foreign dealer or global custodian to track these trades separately.

G. — Reporting requirements for registered firms

G-1 Q: If my firm delivers Form 24-101F1 to the regulators for a calendar quarter, does that mean we have not complied with the trade matching requirements of NI 24-101 for that quarter?

A: No. A requirement to provide Form 24-101F1 for a calendar quarter will not necessarily mean that you have failed to establish, maintain and enforce policies and procedures designed to achieve timely matching of DAP/RAP trades. Because there are multiple trade-matching parties involved in a DAP/RAP trade, your firm may not be responsible for failing to meet the NI 24-101 exception reporting targets. For example, the failure may have been due to poor policies and procedures of another trade-matching party. Exhibit B of Form 24-101F1 asks for such reasons.

G-2 Q: When would the regulators consider that my firm does not have adequate trade-matching policies and procedures in place to ensure the timely matching of DAP/RAP trades?

A: We may consider a firm to have an inadequate compliance program for the firm's trade-matching processes if it consistently:

- Fails to meet the matching percentage targets and triggers the exception reporting, or

- Provides poor qualitative reporting.

These or other signs may show that either the policies and procedures of one or more of the trade-matching parties have not been properly designed or, if properly designed, have not been followed. See section 3.2(b) of the CP.

G-3 Q: If my firm is required to provide Form 24-101F1 to the regulators for a number of calendar quarters in a row, but it is apparent that the underlying causes for failing to achieve the percentage target for matched DAP/RAP trades within the timelines are poor policies and procedures of another trade-matching party or service provider that are involved in processing my DAP/RAP trades, what should my firm do?

A: The CP provides guidance in this area. See sections 2.3(4) and 3.1(c).

G-4 Q: Assuming we are required to complete Form 24-101F1, Exhibit A of the Form requires us to provide data for equity and debt DAP/RAP trades for each calendar quarter. Please explain what you require under the column headings "entered into CDS by deadline (to be completed by dealers only)" and "matched by deadline".

A: We seek aggregate information on the DAP/RAP trades executed by you (if you are a dealer) or for you (if you are an adviser) during the calendar quarter, and submitted to CDS. See section 3.1(b) of the CP.

Dealer Perspective:

A dealer needs the following information to complete Exhibit A of Form 24-101F1:

1. Number and value of DAP/RAP trades entered into CDS by noon on T+1 during the quarter;
2. Number and value of DAP/RAP trades entered into CDS during the quarter (whether entered by noon on T+1 or not);
3. Number and value of DAP/RAP trades matched at CDS by noon on T+1 during the quarter;
4. Number and value of DAP/RAP trades matched at CDS during the quarter (whether matched by noon on T+1 or not).

If you are a dealer, you should show under the column heading "entered into CDS by deadline (to be completed by dealers only)" the aggregate number of DAP/RAP trades and the aggregate value of DAP/RAP trades that were executed by you and entered into CDS' system within the deadline. The percentage columns should show the aggregate trade number or value entered into CDS by the deadline as a percentage of total number or value of trades entered into CDS' system during the calendar quarter, whether entered by the deadline or not.

If you are an introducing broker that executes DAP/RAP trades that are cleared through a corresponding clearing broker, you should obtain the relevant data from your corresponding clearing broker.

Under the column heading "matched by deadline", you should show the aggregate number and the aggregate value of trades executed by you that were matched by a dealer or custodian in CDS' system by the deadline. The percentage is determined by dividing such number or value by the total number or value of your trades that were matched during the calendar quarter by a dealer or custodian in CDS' system, whether on time or late.

Please see Appendix A for an example of the calculation to be performed by a dealer.

Adviser Perspective:

An adviser needs the following information to complete Exhibit A of Form 24-101F1:

1. Number and value of DAP/RAP trades matched at CDS by noon on T+1 during the quarter;
2. Number and value of DAP/RAP trades matched at CDS during the quarter (whether matched by noon on T+1 or not).

If you are an adviser you need only complete the column heading "matched by deadline". Information about the number and value of DAP/RAP trades matched at CDS during the quarter should be provided to you by your institutional client's custodian(s).

Under the column heading "matched by deadline", you should have the aggregate number and the aggregate value of trades executed for you that were matched by a custodian in CDS' system by the deadline. The percentage is determined by dividing such number or value by the total number or value of your trades that were matched during the calendar quarter by a custodian in CDS' system, whether on time or late.

Please see Appendix B for an example of the calculation to be performed by an adviser.

G-5 Q: Assuming we are required to complete Form 24-101F1, Exhibit B of the Form requires us to provide information explaining the reasons for the failure to achieve the percentage target for matched equity and/or debt DAP/RAP trades within the deadline for a calendar quarter. If a particular trade-matching party that we regularly deal with is consistently matching trades late, and such party is unable or unwilling to explain why this is happening, what information do we include in Exhibit B?

A: You should explain this situation in Exhibit B, and generally follow the guidance set out in question G-3 above.

G-6 Q. We are a registered dealer that provides a range of services for our institutional investor clients. For some clients, we may provide trade execution and clearing services only. For others, we may provide only custodial and DAP/RAP trade settlement agent services. Assuming we must report on Form 24-101F1 for the calendar quarter, should we combine our matching performance for DAP/RAP trades based on our dealer functions and custodial/settlement agent functions?

A. The roles of a dealer, adviser and custodian in DAP/RAP trading are quite different as they relate to NI 24-101. For a dealer, Form 24-101F1 is only required if the dealer did not achieve the target for the quarter for DAP/RAP trades for which it provided trade execution services. If this report is required, it should **not** include trades for which it provided only custodial and trade settlement agent services.

G-7 Q: How do we complete the exception reporting forms under the Instrument?

Registered firms may complete their Form 24-101F1 on-line in a secure manner that is accessible from the CSA's website at: http://www.securities-administrators.ca.

G-8 Q: As a registered dealer and direct participant of CDS, can we rely solely on the report of trade matching results provided to us by CDS?

A: In general, you should be able to rely on the trade matching report provided to you by CDS as your basis for determining whether you have achieved the trade matching target for a particular quarter. However, there are two important exceptions to this.

First, the CDS code trade for "client trades" captures slightly broader types of trades than the DAP/RAP trades defined in the Instrument. CDS will be able to identify some "client trades" that are excluded by the Instrument, such as same-day settled trades, and remove them from the data in CDS' Form 24-101F2 report. However, CDS will not be able to identify certain other types of trades, such as reorganizations and share conversions, that are coded as "client trades" but are excluded by the Instrument. For further information, see the joint IIROC (formerly IDA) and CDS notice MR0495 dated September 28, 2007 that sets out guidance on how dealers and other CDS participants should code their trades entered into CDS for the purposes of the Instrument and IIROC Member Regulation 800.49.

If you use any of these "excluded" trade types during a quarter, and if these trade types, taken together, make the difference between meeting the target and not meeting the target for that quarter, you should determine the number and value of these trades and report this on Form 24-101F1.

Second, to the extent that your trades are processed by an MSU and sent to CDS as matched trades, these will not be included in CDS' Form 24-101F2 report. As a result, you will need to combine your results from CDS with those of the MSU in order to determine whether or not you have achieved the trade matching target for the calendar quarter.

Appendix A

Dealer example of how to complete Exhibit A of Form NI 24-101F1

A dealer will need the following quarterly information:

Number of DAP/RAP trades entered into CDS	56,000
Number of DAP/RAP trades entered into CDS by deadline	50,000
Number of DAP/RAP trades matched at CDS	48,000
Number of DAP/RAP trades matched at CDS by deadline	35,000
Value of DAP/RAP trades entered into CDS	$4,100,000
Value of DAP/RAP trades entered into CDS by deadline	$3,700,000
Value of DAP/RAP trades matched at CDS	$3,200,000
Value of DAP/RAP trades matched at CDS by deadline	$2,900,000

Entered into CDS by Deadline:

Number of DAP/RAP trades entered into CDS by deadline: 50,000

Percentage of number of DAP/RAP trades entered into CDS by deadline:

$$=50,000/56,000\times100=89\%$$

Value of DAP/RAP trades entered into CDS by deadline: $3,700,000

Percentage of value of DAP/RAP trades entered into CDS by deadline:

$$=\$3,700,000/\$4,100,000\times100=90\%$$

Matched by Deadline:

Number of DAP/RAP trades matched at CDS by deadline: 35,000

Percentage of number of DAP/RAP trades matched at CDS by deadline:

$$=35,000/48,000\times100=73\%$$

Value of DAP/RAP trades matched at CDS by deadline: $2,900,000

Percentage of value of DAP/RAP trades matched at CDS by deadline:

$$=\$2,900,000/\$3,200,000\times100=91\%$$

Appendix B

Adviser example of how to complete Exhibit A of Form NI 24-101F1

An adviser will need the following quarterly information:

Number of DAP/RAP trades matched at CDS	55,000
Number of DAP/RAP trades matched at CDS by deadline	43,000
Value of DAP/RAP trades matched at CDS	$6,800,000
Value of DAP/RAP trades matched at CDS by deadline	$3,700,000

Matched by Deadline:

Number of DAP/RAP trades matched at CDS by deadline: 43,000

Percentage of number of DAP/RAP trades matched at CDS by deadline:

$$=43,000/55,000\times100=78\%$$

Value of DAP/RAP trades matched at CDS by deadline: $3,700,000

Percentage of value of DAP/RAP trades matched at CDS by deadline:

$$=\$3,700,000/\$6,800,000\times100=54\%$$

Policies and Orders: CSAN 24-306, 21-704.

CSA Staff Notice 24-306 — NI 24-101 Institutional Trade Matching and Settlement — Exception Reporting

Date:　February 1, 2008

31 O.S.C.B. 1231

Part 4 of National Instrument 24-101 — *Institutional Trade Matching and Settlement* (Instrument) requires registrants in certain circumstances to complete and deliver Form 24-101F1 *Registrant Exception Report of DAP/RAP Trade Reporting and Matching* (Form) to the applicable securities regulatory authority. The Form must be delivered *if less than* a percentage target of the DAP/RAP trades (measured by volume or value) executed by the registrant (if a dealer) or for the registrant (if an adviser) in any given calendar quarter have *matched* within the time required by the Instrument. Please see Part 10 of the Instrument or Part 7 of the related Companion Policy for transition dates, relevant timelines and percentages.

How to deliver the Form

On-line Electronic Delivery

A registrant can complete an electronic version of the Form and submit it to the applicable securities regulatory authority through the CSA website at *www.csa-acvm.ca.*

Manual Delivery

Alternatively, a registrant can print the Form from the link provided on the CSA website and deliver the completed Form to the applicable securities regulatory authority via mail, fax or email. Fax numbers and email addresses for the applicable securities regulatory authority are provided below.

Information on the Instrument, Companion Policy and CSA Staff Notice 24-305 Frequently Asked Questions about the Instrument is posted on the following websites:

- CSA Website: *www.csa-acvm.ca*

- AMF Website:

    http://www.lautorite.qc.ca/reglementation/valeurs-mobilieres/autres-reglements-textes-vigueur.fr.html

- ASC Website:

    http://albertasecurities.com/securitiesLaw/Pages/ViewDocument.aspx?ProjectId=b9440adf-71d1-4e2b-9d7a-87aae368f84b

- BCSC Website:

    http://www.bcsc.bc.ca/policy.aspx?id=5508&cat=2%20-%20Certain%20Capital%20Market%20Participants

- MSC Website:

    http://www.msc.gov.mb.ca/legal_docs/legislation/rules/24_101_msc_rule_2007_1.pdf

- OSC Website:

    http://www.osc.gov.on.ca/HotTopics/STP/stp_index.jsp

CSA Staff Notice 24-310 — Status Update on Proposed Local Rules 24-503 — Clearing Agency Requirements and Related Companies Policies

Date: July 17, 2014
37 O.S.C.B. 6677

[Not reproduced]

CSA Multilateral Staff Notice 24-311 — Qualifying Central Counterparties

Date: July 28, 2014
37 O.S.C.B. 7027

This notice is being jointly issued by the Bank of Canada (BoC), the Alberta Securities Commission (ASC), the Autorité des marchés financiers (AMF, Québec), the British Columbia Securities Commission (BCSC), the Manitoba Securities Commission (MSC) and the Ontario Securities Commission (OSC).

The purpose of this notice is to indicate that the Canadian-domiciled central counterparties (CCPs) listed in Table 1 can be considered qualifying central counterparties (QCCPs) under the standard on the capital treatment of certain bank exposures to central counterparties developed by the Basel Committee on Banking Supervision (BCBS).[1]

Table 1: Canadian-domiciled qualifying central counterparties

Legal entity (system)[a]	Designated or recognized by
CDS Clearing and Depository Services Inc.[b]	BoC
(CDSX)	AMF

---

[1]The BCBS issued interim rules for the Capital requirements for bank exposures to CCPs in July 2012. The final standard was published in April 2014 and will take effect on 1 January 2017. The interim requirements will continue to apply until that time. Both the interim requirements and the final standard include the same definition of a QCCP.

Part 2: MARKET PARTICIPANTS

Table 1: Canadian-domiciled qualifying central counterparties

Legal entity (system)[a]	Designated or recognized by
	BCSC
	OSC
Canadian Derivatives Clearing Corporation	BoC
(Canadian Derivatives Clearing Service)	AMF
	BCSC
	OSC
ICE Clear Canada, Inc.	MSC
Natural Gas Exchange Inc.	ASC

Notes:

a   The provincial securities regulators have recognized the respective legal entities operating the clearing systems as subject to their regulatory oversight, while the Bank of Canada has designated the respective systems providing central clearing services for its oversight.

b   The parent company, The Canadian Depository for Securities Limited, is also recognized by the AMF and OSC under their respective laws.

The BCBS standard distinguishes between CCPs on the basis of their regulatory status. Certain bank exposures to CCPs that are prudentially regulated according to standards consistent with the *Principles for Financial Market Infrastructures* (PFMIs) established by the Committee on Payment and Settlement Systems (CPSS) and the International Organization of Securities Commissions (IOSCO) are subject to lower capital requirements than other CCPs. More specifically, the BCBS standard defines a QCCP as:

> . . . an entity that is licensed to operate as a CCP (including a license granted by way of confirming an exemption), and is permitted by the appropriate regulator/overseer to operate as such with respect to the products offered. This is subject to the provision that the CCP is based and prudentially supervised in a jurisdiction where the relevant regulator/overseer has established, and publicly indicated that it applies to the CCP on an ongoing basis, domestic rules and regulations that are consistent with the CPSS-IOSCO Principles for Financial Market Infrastructures.

At the end of 2012, the BCBS published a set of *frequently asked questions* clarifying that "if a CCP regulator has provided a public statement on the status of a CCP (QCCP or nonqualifying), then banks will treat exposures to this CCP accordingly."

In Canada, the Office of the Superintendent of Financial Institutions (OSFI), which regulates and supervises all banks in Canada, adopted the BCBS definition of a QCCP in its Capital Adequacy Requirements Guideline. OSFI still reserves the right to require banks to hold additional capital against their exposures to such CCPs via *Pillar 2* of the BCBS regulatory framework for banks.

The Bank of Canada and provincial securities regulators have the authority to oversee or regulate CCPs in Canada. The relevant authorities have all adopted the CPSS-IOSCO PFMIs as their risk-management standard for CCPs. The Bank of Canada and provincial securities regulators are working in consultation to apply the PFMIs in a consistent manner.

- Under the *Payment Clearing and Settlement Act* (Canada), the Bank of Canada is responsible for the designation and regulatory oversight of clearing and settlement systems, with a view to controlling systemic risk. The objectives of the Bank of Canada in its oversight role are to ensure that designated financial market infrastructures (including CCPs) operate in such a manner that risk is properly controlled and to promote efficiency and stability in the Canadian financial system. The Canadian Derivatives Clearing Service and the CDSX (CDSX provides the CCP service known as Continuous Net Settlement) have been designated as systemically important systems and are prudentially overseen by the Bank of Canada. In 2012, the Bank of Canada adopted the CPSS-IOSCO PFMIs as its risk-management standards for designated financial market infrastructures.

- Under their respective laws and regulations, provincial securities regulators are responsible for protecting investors and ensuring fairness, efficiency and confidence in capital markets. Such provincial regulatory regimes for securities cover a wide range of matters, including the recognition, oversight and prudential supervision of financial market infrastructures that are "clearing agencies" (generally defined to include CCPs). The ASC, AMF, BCSC, MSC and OSC require the CCPs that they recognize to observe the CPSS-IOSCO PFMIs under their respective recognition orders. The terms and conditions of such recognition orders have the force of law over the recognized entities. Moreover, such authorities are developing rules governing clearing agencies, including CCPs, that will be consistent with the CPSS-IOSCO PFMIs, and have publicly indicated that such rules will apply to recognized CCPs on an ongoing basis. Four Canadian-domiciled CCPs have currently been recognized in at least one province: CDS Clearing and Depository Services Inc., the Canadian Derivatives Clearing Corporation, ICE Clear Canada Inc. and the Natural Gas Exchange Inc.

Together, the actions taken by the Bank of Canada and the provincial securities regulators allow the CCPs identified above to meet the definition of a QCCP adopted by the BCBS and OSFI. These QCCPs are licensed to operate as a CCP and are prudentially supervised by a regulator/overseer that has established, and publicly indicated that it applies to the CCP on an ongoing basis, domestic rules and regulations that are consistent with the CPSS-IOSCO PFMIs.

The status of a CCP may change. In the event that one of the CCPs listed above no longer qualifies as a QCCP, this notice will be updated accordingly.

Questions

Questions with respect to this Notice may be referred to:

[Omitted.]

CSA Staff Notice 24-312 — Preparing for the Implementation of T+2 Settlement

Date:　　　April 2, 2015
38 O.S.C.B. 2955

[Not reproduced]

Multilateral CSA Staff Notice 24-313 — CSA Staff's Review of Proposed Amendments to Fee Schedule of The Canadian depository for Securities Limited and CDS Clearing and Depository Services Inc.

Date:　　　May 14, 2015
38 O.S.C.B. 4456

[Not reproduced]

Multilateral CSA Staff Notice 24-314 — CSA Staff's Review of Proposed Amendments to Fee Schedule of The Canadian Depository for Securities Limited and CDS Clearing and Depository Services Inc.

Date:　　　May 14, 2015
38 O.S.C.B. 4456

[Not reproduced]

OSC Rule 24-501 — Designation as Market Participant

Date:　　　October 1, 2007
30 O.S.C.B. 7907

PART 1 — DEFINITIONS

1.1 Definitions — In this Rule,

"matching service utility" has the same meaning as in NI 24-101;

"NI 24-101" means National Instrument 24-101 *Institutional Trade Matching and Settlement*.

PART 2 — DESIGNATION AS MARKET PARTICIPANT

2.1 Matching Service Utility — A matching service utility that delivers Form 24-101F3 under NI 24-101 to the Commission is designated as a market participant for the purposes of the Act.

PART 3 — EFFECTIVE DATE

3.1 Effective Date — This Rule comes into force on October 1, 2007.

Final Rule: 30 O.S.C.B. 7907; Approval by OSC: 30 O.S.C.B. 6285; Request for Comments: 30 O.S.C.B. 395.

Definitions: OSA 74 1(1) "market participant".

OSC Rule 24-502 — Exemption from Transitional Rule: Extension of Transitional Phase-In Period in National Instrument 24-101 — Institutional Trade Matching and Settlement

Date:　　　June 30, 2008
31 O.S.C.B. 5751

[Revoked (2010) 33 O.S.C.B. 3451.]

Final Rule: (2008) 31 O.S.C.B. 5751; Approval by OSC: (2008) 31 O.S.C.B. 3819; Request for Comments: none.

Notice 24-702 — Regulatory Approach to Recognition and Exemption from Recognition of Clearing Agencies

Date:　　　March 19, 2010
33 O.S.C.B. 2323

Part 2: MARKET PARTICIPANTS

I — Introduction

Section 21.2[1] of the *Securities Act* (Ontario) (the Act) prohibits clearing agencies from carrying on business in Ontario unless they are recognized by the Commission as a clearing agency or are exempt from the requirement to be recognized by order of the Commission.[2] Staff of the Ontario Securities Commission (we or Staff) are publishing this notice to set out Staff's regulatory approach to an application for recognition as a clearing agency or exemption from the recognition requirement. We will use this approach when evaluating the requests and making recommendations to the Commission regarding whether to recognize or exempt an applicant and the appropriate regulation for entities desiring to carry on business as a clearing agency in Ontario.

II — The Regulatory Framework for Clearing Agencies

Subsection 21.2(0.1) of the Act provides that "no person or company shall carry on business in Ontario as a clearing agency unless the person or company is recognized by the Commission under this section as a clearing agency". The term "clearing agency" is defined in subsection 1(1) of the Act as follows:

"clearing agency" means a person or company that,

(a) acts as an intermediary in paying funds or delivering securities, or both, in connection with trades and other transactions in securities,

(b) provides centralized facilities for the clearing of trades and other transactions in securities, including facilities for comparing data respecting the terms of settlement of a trade or transaction, or

(c) provides centralized facilities as a depository of securities,

but does not include,

(d) the Canadian Payments Association or its successors,

(e) a stock exchange or a quotation and trade reporting system,

(f) a registered dealer, or

(g) a bank, trust company, loan corporation, insurance company, treasury branch, credit union or caisse populaire that, in the normal course of its authorized business in Canada, engages in an activity described in clause (a), but does not also engage in an activity described in clause (b) or (c);"[3]

A clearing agency that seeks to operate in Ontario will be required to either apply for recognition under subsection 21.2(0.1) of the Act or apply for an exemption under section 147 of the Act. Generally, we would recommend to the Commission that a clearing agency that performs certain key functions or provides certain facilities, such as central depository, central counter-party, multilateral netting and/or guarantor functions, be recognized and subject to the Commission's full clearing agency regulation and oversight discussed in Part II(a) of this notice (full regulation).

Depending on the circumstances, Staff may recommend to the Commission that a clearing agency be granted an exemption from recognition pursuant to section 147 of the Act. For example, we may consider this approach for an entity that provides limited services or facilities and does not present significant risks to the capital market. We may also consider this approach for a foreign-based clearing agency that intends to operate in Ontario if the clearing agency is subject to an appropriate regulatory and oversight regime in a foreign jurisdiction. A clearing agency that is granted an exemption would generally be subject to certain terms and conditions discussed in more detail in Part II(b) of this notice.[4]

(a) — Recognition of Clearing Agency

An application for recognition should include a detailed description of the business operations of the clearing agency and how the clearing agency meets specified criteria that deal with the following:

- Governance
- Fees
- Access
- Rules and rulemaking
- Due process
- Risk management
- Systems and technology
- Financial viability and reporting

---

[1]As amended in 2005 by section 2 of Schedule 20 — *Securities Act* — of the *Budget Measures Act*, 2005 (No. 2), S.O. 2005, c. 31 (Bill 18). The amendments were proclaimed on February 24, 2010 by Order in Council to be in force as of March 1, 2011. See *Ontario Gazette* of Saturday, March 6, 2010, Vol. 143-10, page 435.

[2]In this notice, we refer to this requirement as the "recognition requirement".

[3]The definition "clearing agency" in subsection 1(1) of the Act was amended in 2006 by section 144 of the *Securities Transfer Act*, 2006, S.O. 2006, c. 8 (Bill 41), which came into force on January 1, 2006.

[4]A Commission order, including any terms and conditions contained in the order, forms part of Ontario securities law. See definition "Ontario securities law" in subsection 1(1) of the Act.

- Operational reliability

- Protection of assets

- Outsourcing

- Information sharing and regulatory cooperation

The detailed criteria are attached to this notice as Appendix A. Staff consider the criteria to be characteristics that a clearing agency must have in order to carry on business in Ontario.

A recognition order issued by the Commission under section 21.2 will be subject to terms and conditions that are determined based on the criteria, the operations of the clearing agency, and other relevant factors. Generally, if a clearing agency is recognized it will be required to:

- file rules, procedures and other similar instruments for approval by the Commission

- file financial statements

- file annual reports containing information relating to its participants, risk controls and risk management, and other items

- comply with Staff's Automation Review Program[5]

- be subject to oversight reviews conducted by Staff

- comply with the terms and conditions.

(b) — Exemption from Recognition

A clearing agency may request an exemption from the recognition requirement pursuant to section 147 of the Act in certain circumstances. For example, an entity may perform limited activities which do not present significant risk to the Ontario capital markets, such that full regulation may not be warranted. Depending on the nature of the functions performed by the clearing agency and the risks arising from such functions, we may recommend that the exemption be subject to certain terms and conditions. The specific terms and conditions may vary depending on the operations of the clearing agency, its risk controls, the methods of access for its participants, and any regulatory regime to which it is already subject. Whether a clearing agency is recognized or is exempted from recognition, there will be terms and conditions to enable the Commission to have access to information on its operations and the trading and clearing activity of Ontario participants.

We discuss below two circumstances in which we may be prepared to recommend an exemption from recognition: foreign-based clearing agencies and matching service utilities. An application for an exemption should include a detailed description of the operations of the clearing agency and how the clearing agency meets the specified criteria in Appendix A.

(i) — Foreign-based clearing agencies

A foreign-based clearing agency that is carrying on business or intends to carry on business in Ontario would be required to apply either for recognition or for an exemption from recognition. A foreign-based clearing agency that offers to provide its services or facilities to a person or company resident in Ontario would be considered to be carrying on business in Ontario.[6] Depending on the circumstances, Staff may recommend to the Commission that a foreign-based clearing agency be granted an exemption from recognition pursuant to section 147 of the Act if the clearing agency does not pose significant risk to the Ontario capital markets and is subject to an appropriate regulatory and oversight regime in a foreign jurisdiction. We recognize that some foreign-based clearing agencies are already subject to a regulatory regime in their country of origin (home jurisdiction). Full regulation, similar to that applied to domestic clearing agencies, may be duplicative and inefficient when imposed in addition to the regulation of the home jurisdiction. However, where the regulatory regime of the home jurisdiction is not comparable to that of Ontario, the Commission may consider it necessary to impose additional requirements.

The foreign-based clearing agency should establish at the time of application that it meets the criteria in Appendix A. The application should explain how the clearing agency meets each criterion and provide a detailed description of the regulatory regime of the home jurisdiction and the regulatory requirements imposed on the clearing agency in its home jurisdiction.

The following terms and conditions may be considered:

- ongoing compliance with home jurisdiction regulation and oversight

- prior notice of material changes to the application

- periodic reporting of information relating to operational activities

- access restrictions

- financial reporting

- information sharing arrangements

---

[5]The Automation Review Program (ARP) provides a mechanism for any specified market infrastructure entity to follow a formal methodology in identifying and managing information technology risk. For a copy of the ARP, please see (2002) 25 OSCB 6789.

[6]We note that electronic access in Ontario to a clearing agency's systems and facilities will generally indicate that it is "carrying on business" in Ontario, even if the clearing agency has no physical presence in Ontario. This is similar to the approach used by Staff for foreign-based stock exchanges. See OSC Staff Notice 21-702 *Regulatory Approach for Foreign-Based Stock Exchanges*, dated October 31, 2003.

- home jurisdiction's adherence to CPSS-IOSCO standards for securities settlement systems and/or central counter-parties[7]

- submission to non-exclusive jurisdiction

(ii) — Matching service utilities

One type of entity that may be considered by Staff to have limited activities is a "matching service utility" (MSU) governed by National Instrument 24-101 — *Institutional Trade Matching and Settlement* (NI 24-101). An MSU is a provider of centralized automated services and facilities for the institutional trade matching process, i.e., it facilitates the clearing of trades executed by or on behalf of institutional investors, where multiple parties such as a dealer, investment manager and custodian are required to provide information to confirm and agree to the terms and settlement instructions of a trade. An MSU is subject to certain reporting and other requirements under NI 24-101. Depending on the circumstances, Staff may be prepared to recommend an exemption subject to terms and conditions.

IV — Application Process

The application process for both recognition and exemption from recognition as a clearing agency is similar. The clearing agency must file an application, detailing, for example, its history, business and regulatory structure (if any), and addressing how it meets the specific criteria as outlined in Appendix A. Where specific criteria in Appendix A may not be relevant to an applicant because of the nature or scope of its clearing agency activities, its specific structure, the products it clears or settles, or its regulatory environment, the application should explain in reasonable detail why the criteria are not relevant.

After discussing the application with the applicant, Staff will seek the Commission's approval to publish the application, together with a draft order, for a 30 day comment period. Publication will occur in the OSC Bulletin and on the OSC website. Once all issues raised during the comment process are resolved, Staff will submit the order for approval to the Commission in the form of the published order, as amended in response to the comment process.

Appendix A — Criteria for Recognition and Exemption from Recognition as a Clearing Agency

Responses to the criteria in this Appendix A must address, where applicable, the following:

(i) Describe how the clearing agency meets each criterion. Where a specific criterion may not be relevant because of the nature or scope of the clearing agency's activities, please explain in reasonable detail why it is not relevant.

(ii) Where an application for an exemption is being made by a foreign clearing agency, describe the requirements, if any, that are imposed by the applicable regulator in the clearing agency's jurisdiction (the foreign regulator) in each area.

(iii) Describe how the oversight of the foreign clearing agency by the foreign regulator ensures ongoing compliance with the criteria.

Part 1 — Governance

1.1 The governance structure and governance arrangements of the clearing agency ensures:

(a) effective oversight of the clearing agency;

(b) the clearing agency's activities are in keeping with its public interest mandate;

(c) fair, meaningful and diverse representation on the governing body (Board) and any committees of the Board, including a reasonable proportion of independent directors;

(d) a proper balance among the interests of the owners and the different entities seeking access (participants) to the clearing, settlement and depository services and facilities (settlement services) of the clearing agency;

(e) the clearing agency has policies and procedures to appropriately identify and manage conflicts of interest;

(f) each director or officer of the clearing agency, and each person or company that owns or controls, directly or indirectly, more than 10 percent of the clearing agency is a fit and proper person; and

(g) there are appropriate qualifications, limitation of liability and indemnity provisions for directors and officers of the clearing agency.

Part 2 — Fees

2.1 All fees imposed by the clearing agency are equitably allocated. The fees do not have the effect of creating unreasonable barriers to access.

2.2 The process for setting fees is fair and appropriate, and the fee model is transparent.

Part 3 — Access

3.1 The clearing agency has appropriate written standards for access to its services.

3.2 The access standards and the process for obtaining, limiting and denying access are fair and transparent. A clearing agency keeps records of

(a) each grant of access including, for each participant, the reasons for granting such access, and

---

[7]See *Recommendations for securities settlement systems — Report of the Committee on Payment and Settlement Systems and Technical Committee of the International Organization of Securities Commissions*, dated November 2001; and *Recommendations for Central Counterparties — Report of the Committee on Payment and Settlement Systems and Technical Committee of the International Organization of Securities Commissions*, dated November 2004.

(b) each denial or limitation of access, including the reasons for denying or limiting access to an applicant.

Part 4 — Rules and Rulemaking

4.1 The clearing agency's rules are designed to govern all aspects of the settlement services offered by the clearing agency, and

(a) are not inconsistent with securities legislation,

(b) do not permit unreasonable discrimination among participants, and

(c) do not impose any burden on competition that is not necessary or appropriate.

4.2 The clearing agency's rules and the process for adopting new rules or amending existing rules should be transparent to participants and the general public.

4.3 The clearing agency monitors participant activities to ensure compliance with the rules.

4.4 The rules set out appropriate sanctions in the event of non-compliance by participants.

Part 5 — Due Process

5.1 For any decision made by the clearing agency that affects an applicant or a participant, including a decision in relation to access, the clearing agency ensures that:

(a) an applicant or a participant is given an opportunity to be heard or make representations; and

(b) the clearing agency keeps a record of, gives reasons for, and provides for appeals or reviews of, its decisions.

Part 6 — Risk Management

6.1 The clearing agency's settlement services are designed to minimize systemic risk.

6.2 The clearing agency has appropriate risk management policies and procedures and internal controls in place.

6.3 Without limiting the generality of the foregoing, the clearing agency's services or functions are designed to achieve the following objectives:

1. Where the clearing agency acts as a central counterparty, it rigorously controls the risks it assumes.

2. The clearing agency minimizes principal risk by linking securities transfers to funds transfers in a way that achieves delivery versus payment.

3. Final settlement occurs no later than the end of the settlement day. Intraday or real-time finality is provided where necessary to reduce risks.

4. Where the clearing agency extends intraday credit to participants, including a clearing agency that operates net settlement systems, it institutes risk controls that, at a minimum, ensure timely settlement in the event that the participant with the largest payment obligation is unable to settle.

5. Assets used to settle the ultimate payment obligations arising from securities transactions carry little or no credit or liquidity risk. If central bank money is not used, steps are to be taken to protect participants in settlement services from potential losses and liquidity pressures arising from the failure of the cash settlement agent whose assets are used for that purpose.

6. If the clearing agency establishes links to settle cross-border trades, it designs and operates such links to reduce effectively the risks associated with cross-border settlements.

6.4 The clearing agency engaging in activities not related to settlement services carries on such activities in a manner that prevents the spillover of risk to the clearing agency that might affect its financial viability or negatively impact any of the participants in the settlement service.

Part 7 — Systems and Technology

7.1 For its settlement services systems, the clearing agency:

(a) develops and maintains,

(i) reasonable business continuity and disaster recovery plans,

(ii) an adequate system of internal control,

(iii) adequate information technology general controls, including controls relating to information systems operations, information security, change management, problem management, network support, and system software support;

(b) on a reasonably frequent basis, and in any event, at least annually, and in a manner that is consistent with prudent business practice,

(i) makes reasonable current and future capacity estimates,

(ii) conducts capacity stress tests to determine the ability of those systems to process transactions in an accurate, timely and efficient manner,

(iii) tests its business continuity and disaster recovery plans; and

(c) promptly notifies the regulator of any material systems failures.

7.2 The clearing agency annually engages a qualified party to conduct an independent systems review and prepare a report in accordance with established audit standards regarding its compliance with section 7.1(a).

Part 8 — Financial Viability and Reporting

8.1 The clearing agency has sufficient financial resources for the proper performance of its functions and to meet its responsibilities and allocates sufficient financial and staff resources to carry out its functions as a clearing agency in a manner that is consistent with any regulatory requirements.

Part 9 — Operational Reliability

9.1 The clearing agency has procedures and processes to ensure the provision of accurate and reliable settlement services to participants.

Part 10 — Protection of Assets

10.1 The clearing agency has established accounting practices, internal controls, and safekeeping and segregation procedures to protect the assets that are held by the clearing agency.

Part 11 — Outsourcing

11.1 Where the clearing agency has outsourced any of its key functions, it has appropriate and formal arrangements and processes in place that permit it to meet its obligations and that are in accordance with industry best practices. The outsourcing arrangement provides regulatory authorities with access to all data, information, and systems maintained by the third party service provider required for the purposes of regulatory oversight of the agency.

Part 12 — Information Sharing and Regulatory Cooperation

12.1 For regulatory purposes, the clearing agency cooperates by sharing information or otherwise with the Commission and its staff, self-regulatory organizations, exchanges, quotation and trade reporting systems, alternative trading systems, other clearing agencies, investor protection funds, and other appropriate regulatory bodies.

2.5 — Other Participants

National Instrument 25-101 — Designated Rating Organizations

Date: April 20, 2012, amended May 5, 2015

35 O.S.C.B. 2383 and 38 O.S.C.B. 4147

PART 1 — DEFINITIONS AND INTERPRETATION

1. Definitions — In this Instrument

"board of directors" means, in the case of a designated rating organization that does not have a board of directors, a group that acts in a capacity similar to a board of directors;

"code of conduct" means the code of conduct referred to in Part 4 of this Instrument and may include, for greater certainty, one or more codes;

"compliance officer" means the compliance officer referred to in section 12;

"designated rating organization" means a credit rating organization that has been designated under securities legislation;

"DRO affiliate" means an affiliate of a designated rating organization that issues credit ratings in a foreign jurisdiction and that has been designated as a DRO affiliate under the terms of the designated rating organizations' designation;

"DRO employee" means an individual, other than an employee or agent of a DRO affiliate, who is

    (a) employed by a designated rating organization, or

    (b) an agent who provides services directly to the designated rating organization and who is involved in determining, approving or monitoring a credit rating issued by the designated rating organization;

"Form NRSRO" means the annual certification on Form NRSRO, including exhibits, required to be filed by an NRSRO under the 1934 Act;

"NRSRO" means a nationally recognized statistical rating organization, as defined in the 1934 Act;

"rated entity" means a person or company that is issuing, or that has issued, securities that are the subject of a credit rating issued by a designated rating organization and includes a person or company that made a submission to a designated rating organization for the designated rating organization's initial review or for a preliminary rating but did not request a final rating;

"rated securities" means the securities issued by a rated entity that are the subject of a credit rating issued by a designated rating organization;

"ratings employee" means any DRO employee who participates in determining, approving or monitoring a credit rating issued by the designated rating organization;

"related entity" means in relation to an issuer of a structured finance product, an originator, arranger, underwriter, servicer or sponsor of the structured finance product or any person or company performing similar functions;

"structured finance product" means any of the following:

    (a) a security that entitles the security holder to receive payments that primarily depend on the cash flow from self-liquidating financial assets collateralizing the security, such as loans, leases, mortgages, and secured or unsecured receivables, including:

        (i) an asset-backed security;

        (ii) a collateralized mortgage obligation;

        (iii) a collateralized debt obligation;

        (iv) a collateralized bond obligation;

(v) a collateralized debt obligation of asset-backed securities;

(vi) a collateralized debt obligation of collateralized debt obligations;

(b) a security that entitles the security holder to receive payments that substantially reference or replicate the payments made on one or more securities of the type described in paragraph (a) but that do not primarily depend on the cash flow from self-liquidating financial assets that collateralize the security, including:

(i) a synthetic asset-backed security;

(ii) a synthetic collateralized mortgage obligation;

(iii) a synthetic collateralized debt obligation;

(iv) a synthetic collateralized bond obligation;

(v) a synthetic collateralized debt obligation of asset-backed securities;

(vi) a synthetic collateralized debt obligation of collateralized debt obligations.

2. Interpretation — Nothing in this Instrument is to be interpreted as regulating the content of a credit rating or the methodology a credit rating organization uses to determine a credit rating.

3. Affiliate — (1) In this Instrument, a person or company is an affiliate of another person or company if either of the following apply:

(a) one of them is the subsidiary of the other;

(b) each of them is controlled by the same person or company.

(2) For the purposes of paragraph (1)(b), a person or company (first person) is considered to control another person or company (second person) if any of the following apply:

(a) the first person beneficially owns, or controls or directs, directly or indirectly, securities of the second person carrying votes which, if exercised, would entitle the first person to elect a majority of the directors of the second person, unless that first person holds the voting securities only to secure an obligation;

(b) the second person is a partnership, other than a limited partnership, and the first person holds more than 50% of the interests of the partnership;

(c) the second person is a limited partnership and the general partner of the limited partnership is the first person.

4. Credit rating — In British Columbia, credit rating means an assessment that is publicly disclosed or distributed by subscription concerning the creditworthiness of an issuer,

(a) as an entity, or

(b) with respect to specific securities or a specific pool of securities or assets.

5. Market participant in Ontario — In Ontario, a DRO affiliate is deemed to be a market participant.

PART 2 — DESIGNATION OF RATING ORGANIZATIONS

6. Application for designation — (1) A credit rating organization that applies to be a designated rating organization must file a completed Form 25-101F1.

(2) Despite subsection (1), a credit rating organization that is an NRSRO may file its most recent Form NRSRO.

(3) A credit rating organization that applies to be a designated rating organization that is incorporated or organized under the laws of a foreign jurisdiction and does not have an office in Canada must file a completed Form 25-101F2.

(4) Any person or company that will be a DRO affiliate upon the designation of a credit rating agency that does not have an office in Canada must file a completed Form 25-101F2.

PART 3 — BOARD OF DIRECTORS

7. Board of directors — A designated rating organization must not issue a credit rating unless it, or a DRO affiliate that is a parent of the designated rating organization, has a board of directors.

8. Composition — (1) For the purposes of section 7, a board of directors of a designated rating organization, or the board of directors of the DRO affiliate that is a parent of the designated rating organization, as the case may be, must be composed of a minimum of three members.

(2) At least one-half, but not fewer than two, of the members of the board of directors must be independent of the organization and any DRO affiliate.

(3) For the purposes of subsection (2), a member of the board of directors is not considered independent if the director

(a) other than in his or her capacity as a member of the board of directors or a board committee, accepts any consulting, advisory or other compensatory fee from the designated rating organization or a DRO affiliate;

(b) is a DRO employee or an employee or agent of a DRO affiliate;

(c) has a relationship with the designated rating organization that could, in the opinion of the board of directors, be reasonably expected to interfere with the exercise of a director's independent judgment; or

(d) has served on the board of directors for more than five years in total.

(4) For the purposes of paragraph 3(c), in forming its opinion, the board of directors is not required to conclude that a member is not independent solely on the basis that the member is, or was, a user of the designated rating organization's rating services.

PART 4 — CODE OF CONDUCT

9. Code of conduct — (1) A designated rating organization must establish, maintain and comply with a code of conduct.

(2) A designated rating organization's code of conduct must incorporate each of the provisions set out in Appendix A.

10. **Filing and publication** — (1) A designated rating organization must file a copy of its code of conduct and post a copy of it prominently on its website promptly upon designation.

(2) Each time an amendment is made to a code of conduct by a designated rating organization, the amended code of conduct must be filed, and prominently posted on the organization's website, within five business days of the amendment coming into effect.

11. **Waivers** — A designated rating organization's code of conduct must specify that a designated rating organization must not waive provisions of its code of conduct.

PART 5 — COMPLIANCE OFFICER

12. **Compliance officer** — (1) A designated rating organization must not issue a credit rating unless it, or a DRO affiliate that is a parent of the designated rating organization, has a compliance officer that monitors and assesses compliance by the designated rating organization and its DRO employees with the organization's code of conduct and with securities legislation.

(2) The compliance officer must regularly report on his or her activities directly to the board of directors.

(3) The compliance officer must report to the board of directors as soon as reasonably possible if the compliance officer becomes aware of any circumstances indicating that the designated rating organization or its DRO employees may be in non-compliance with the organization's code of conduct or securities legislation and any of the following apply:

    (a) the non-compliance would reasonably be expected to create a significant risk of harm to a rated entity or the rated entity's investors;

    (b) the non-compliance would reasonably be expected to create a significant risk of harm to the capital markets;

    (c) the non-compliance is part of a pattern of non-compliance.

(4) The compliance officer must not, while serving in such capacity, participate in any of the following:

    (a) the development of credit ratings, methodologies or models;

    (b) the establishment of compensation levels, other than for DRO employees reporting directly to the compliance officer.

(5) The compensation of the compliance officer and of any DRO employee that reports directly to the compliance officer must not be linked to the financial performance of the designated rating organization or its DRO affiliates and must be determined in a manner that preserves the independence of the compliance officer's judgment.

PART 6 — BOOKS AND RECORDS

13. **Books and records** — (1) A designated rating organization must keep such books and records and other documents as are necessary to account for the conduct of its credit rating activities, its business transactions and financial affairs and must keep such other books, records and documents as may otherwise be required under securities legislation.

(2) A designated rating organization must retain the books and records maintained under this section

    (a) for a period of seven years from the date the record was made or received, whichever is later;

    (b) in a safe location and a durable form; and

    (c) in a manner that permits it to be provided promptly to the securities regulatory authority upon request.

PART 7 — FILING REQUIREMENTS

14. **Filing requirements** — (1) No later than 90 days after the end of its most recently completed financial year, each designated rating organization must file a completed Form 25-101F1.

(2) Upon any of the information in a Form 25-101F1 filed by a designated rating organization becoming materially inaccurate, the designated rating organization must promptly file an amendment to, or an amended and restated version of, its Form 25-101F1.

(3) Until six years after it has ceased to be a designated rating organization in any jurisdiction of Canada, a designated rating organization must file a completed amended Form 25-101F2 at least 30 days before

    (a) the termination date of Form 25-101F2, or

    (b) the effective date of any changes to Form 25-101F2.

(4) Until six years after it has ceased to be a DRO affiliate in any jurisdiction of Canada, a DRO affiliate must file a completed amended Form 25-101F2 at least 30 days before

    (a) the termination date of Form 25-101F2, or

    (b) the effective date of any changes to Form 25-101F2.

PART 8 — EXEMPTIONS AND EFFECTIVE DATE

15. **Exemptions** — (1) The regulator or the securities regulatory authority may grant an exemption from the provisions of this Instrument, in whole or in part, subject to such conditions or restrictions as may be imposed in the exemption.

(2) Despite subsection (1), in Ontario, only the regulator may grant an exemption.

(3) Except in Ontario, an exemption referred to in subsection (1) is granted under the statute referred to in Appendix B of National Instrument 14-101 *Definitions* opposite the name of the local jurisdiction.

16. **Effective date** — This Instrument comes into force on April 20, 2012.

APPENDIX A — PROVISIONS REQUIRED TO BE INCLUDED IN A DESIGNATED RATING ORGANIZATION'S CODE OF CONDUCT

1. — Interpretation

1.1 A term used in this code of conduct has the same meaning as in National Instrument 25-101 *Designated Rating Organizations* if used in that Instrument.

2. — Quality and Integrity of the Rating Process

A. — Quality of the rating process

I — General requirements

2.1 A designated rating organization must adopt, implement and enforce procedures in its code of conduct to ensure that the credit ratings it issues are based on a thorough analysis of all information known to the designated rating organization that is relevant to its analysis according to its rating methodologies.

2.2 A designated rating organization must include a provision in its code of conduct that it will use only rating methodologies that are rigorous, systematic, continuous and subject to validation based on experience, including back-testing.

II — Specific provisions

2.3 Each ratings employee involved in the preparation, review or issuance of a credit rating, action or report must use methodologies established by the designated rating organization. Each ratings employee must apply a given methodology in a consistent manner, as determined by the designated rating organization.

2.4 A credit rating must be assigned by the designated rating organization and not by an employee or agent of the designated rating organization.

2.5 A credit rating must reflect all information known, and believed to be relevant, to the designated rating organization, consistent with its published methodology. The designated rating organization will ensure that its ratings employees and agents have appropriate knowledge and experience for the duties assigned.

2.6 The designated rating organization, its ratings employees and its agents must take all reasonable steps to avoid issuing a credit rating, action or report that is false or misleading as to the general creditworthiness of a rated entity or rated securities.

2.7 The designated rating organization will ensure that it has and devotes sufficient resources to carry out high-quality credit assessments of all rated entities and rated securities. When deciding whether to rate or continue rating an entity or securities, the organization will assess whether it is able to devote sufficient personnel with sufficient skill sets to make a credible rating assessment, and whether its personnel are likely to have access to sufficient information needed in order make such an assessment. A designated rating organization will adopt all necessary measures so that the information it uses in assigning a rating is of sufficient quality to support a credible rating and is obtained from a source that a reasonable person would consider to be reliable.

2.8 The designated rating organization will appoint a senior manager, or establish a committee made up of one or more senior managers, with appropriate experience to review the feasibility of providing a credit rating for a structure that is significantly different from the structures the designated rating organization currently rates.

2.9 The designated rating organization will assess whether the methodologies and models used for determining credit ratings of a structured finance product are appropriate when the risk characteristics of the assets underlying the structured finance product change significantly. If the quality of the available information is not satisfactory or if the complexity of a new type of structure, instrument or security should reasonably raise concerns about whether the designated rating organization can provide a credible rating, the designated rating organization will not issue or maintain a credit rating.

2.10 The designated rating organization will ensure continuity and regularity, and avoid conflicts of interest, in the rating process.

B. — Monitoring and updating

2.11 The designated rating organization will establish a committee to be responsible for implementing a rigorous and formal process for reviewing, on at least an annual basis, and making changes to the methodologies, models and key ratings assumptions it uses. This review will include consideration of the appropriateness of the designated rating organization's methodologies, models and key ratings assumptions if they are used or intended to be applied to new types of structures, instruments or securities. This process will be conducted independently of the business lines that are responsible for credit rating activities. The committee will report to its board of directors or the board of directors of a DRO affiliate that is a parent of the designated rating organization.

2.12 If a methodology, model or key ratings assumption used in a credit rating activity is changed, the designated rating organization will do each of the following:

(a) promptly identify each credit rating likely to be affected if the credit rating were to be re-rated using the new methodology, model or key ratings assumption and, using the same means of communication the organization generally uses for the credit ratings, disclose the scope of credit ratings likely to be affected by the change in methodology, model or key ratings assumption;

(b) promptly place each credit rating identified under subsection (a) under surveillance;

(c) within six months of the change, review each credit rating identified under subsection (a) with respect to its accuracy;

(d) re-rate a credit rating if, following the review required in subsection (c), the change, alone or combined with all other changes, affects the accuracy of the credit rating.

2.13 The designated rating organization will ensure that adequate personnel and financial resources are allocated to monitoring and updating its credit ratings. Except for ratings that clearly indicate they do not entail ongoing monitoring, once a rating is published the designated rating organization will monitor the rated entity's creditworthiness on an ongoing basis and, at least annually, update the rating. In addition, the designated rating organization must initiate a review of the accuracy of a rating upon becoming aware of any information that might reasonably be expected to result in a rating action (including termination of a rating), consistent with the applicable rating methodology and must promptly update the rating, as appropriate, based on the results of such review.

Subsequent monitoring will incorporate all cumulative experience obtained.

2.14 If the designated rating organization uses separate analytical teams for determining initial ratings and for subsequent monitoring, the organization will ensure each team has the requisite level of expertise and resources to perform their respective functions competently and in a timely manner.

2.15 If the designated rating organization discloses a credit rating to the public and subsequently discontinues the rating, the designated rating organization will disclose that the rating has been discontinued using the same means of communication as was used for the disclosure of the rating. If the designated rating organization discloses a rating only to its subscribers, if it discontinues the rating, the designated rating organization will disclose to each subscriber of that rating that the rating has been discontinued. In both cases, a subsequent publication by the designated rating organization of the discontinued rating will indicate the date the rating was last updated and disclose that the rating is no longer being updated and the reasons for the decision to discontinue the rating.

C. — Integrity of the rating process

2.16 The designated rating organization, its ratings employees and agents will comply with all applicable laws and regulations governing its activities.

2.17 The designated rating organization, its ratings employees and agents must deal fairly, honestly and in good faith with rated entities, investors, other market participants, and the public.

2.18 The designated rating organization will hold its ratings employees and agents to a high standard of integrity, and the designated rating organization will not employ an individual which a reasonable person would consider to be lacking in or have compromised integrity.

2.19 The designated rating organization and its ratings employees and agents will not, either implicitly or explicitly, give any assurance or guarantee of a particular rating prior to a rating assessment. The designated rating organization may develop prospective assessments if the assessment is to be used in a structured finance product or similar transaction.

2.20 A person or company listed below must not make a recommendation to a rated entity about the corporate or legal structure, assets, liabilities, or activities of the rated entity:

    (a) a designated rating organization;

    (b) an affiliate or related entity of the designated rating organization;

    (c) the ratings employees of any of the above.

2.21 The designated rating organization will instruct its employees and agents that, upon becoming aware that the organization, another employee or an affiliate, or an employee of an affiliate of the designated rating organization, is or has engaged in conduct that is illegal, unethical or contrary to the designated rating organization's code of conduct, the employee or agent must report that information immediately to the compliance officer. Upon receiving the information, the compliance officer will take appropriate action, as determined by the laws and regulations of the jurisdiction and the rules and guidelines set forth by the designated rating organization. The designated rating organization will not take or allow retaliation against the employee or agent by employees, agents, the designated rating organization itself or its affiliates.

D. — Governance requirements

2.22 The designated rating organization will not issue a credit rating unless a majority of its board of directors, or the board of directors of a DRO affiliate that is a parent of the designated rating organization, including its independent directors, have, what a reasonable person would consider, sufficient expertise in financial services to fully understand and properly oversee the business activities of the designated rating organization. If the designated rating organization issues a credit rating for a structured finance product, at least one independent member and one other member must have, what a reasonable person would consider to be, in-depth knowledge and experience at a senior level, regarding the structured finance product.

2.23 The designated rating organization will not issue a credit rating if a member of its board of directors, or the board of directors of a DRO affiliate that is a parent of the designated rating organization, participated in any deliberation involving a specific rating in which the member has a financial interest in the outcome of the rating.

2.24 The designated rating organization will not compensate an independent member of its board of directors, or the board of directors of a DRO affiliate that is a parent of the designated rating organization, in a manner or in an amount that a reasonable person could conclude that the compensation is linked to the business performance of the designated rating organization or its affiliates. The organization will only compensate directors in a manner that preserves the independence of the director.

2.25 The board of directors of a designated rating organization or a DRO affiliate that is a parent of the designated rating organization must monitor the following:

    (a) the development of the credit rating policy and of the methodologies used by the designated rating organization in its credit rating activities;

    (b) the effectiveness of any internal quality control system of the designated rating organization in relation to credit rating activities;

    (c) the effectiveness of measures and procedures instituted to ensure that any conflicts of interest are identified and either eliminated or managed and disclosed, as appropriate;

    (d) the compliance and governance processes, including the performance of the committee identified in section 2.11.

2.26 The designated rating organization will design reasonable administrative and accounting procedures, internal control mechanisms, procedures for risk assessment, and control and safeguard arrangements for information processing systems. The designated rating organization will implement and maintain decision-making procedures and organizational structures that clearly, and in a documented manner, specify reporting lines and allocate functions and responsibilities.

2.27 The designated rating organization will monitor and evaluate the adequacy and effectiveness of its administrative and accounting procedures, internal control mechanisms, procedures for risk assessment, and control and safeguard arrangements for information processing systems, established in accordance with securities legislation and the designated rating organization's code of conduct, and take any measures necessary to address any deficiencies.

2.28 The designated rating organization will not outsource activities if doing so impairs materially the effectiveness of the designated rating organization's internal controls or the ability of the securities regulatory authority to conduct compliance reviews of the designated rating organization's compliance with securities legislation or its code of conduct. The designated rating organization will not outsource the functions or duties of the designated rating organization's compliance officer.

3. — Independence and Conflicts of Interest

A. — General

3.1 The designated rating organization will not refrain from taking a rating action based in whole or in part on the potential effect (economic or otherwise) of the action on the designated rating organization, a rated entity, an investor, or other market participant.

3.2 The designated rating organization and its employees will use care and professional judgment to remain independent and maintain the appearance of independence and objectivity.

3.3 The determination of a credit rating will be influenced only by factors relevant to the credit assessment.

3.4 The designated rating organization will not allow its decision to assign a credit rating to a rated entity or rated securities to be affected by the existence of, or potential for, a business relationship between the designated rating organization or its affiliates and any other person or company including, for greater certainty, the rated entity, its affiliates or related entities.

3.5 The designated rating organization and its affiliates will keep separate, operationally and legally, their credit rating business and their rating employees from any ancillary services (including the provision of consultancy or advisory services) that may present conflicts of interest with their credit rating activities and will ensure that the provision of such services does not present conflicts of interest with their credit rating activities. The designated rating organization will define and publicly disclose what it considers, and does not consider, to be an ancillary service and identify those that are ancillary services. The designated rating organization will disclose in each ratings report any ancillary services provided to a rated entity, its affiliates or related entities.

3.6 The designated rating organization will not rate a person or company that is an affiliate or associate of the organization or a ratings employee. The designated rating organization must not assign a credit rating to a person or company if a ratings employee is an officer or director of the person or company, its affiliates or related entities.

B. — Procedures and policies

3.7 The designated rating organization will identify and eliminate or manage and publicly disclose any actual or potential conflicts of interest that may influence the opinions and analyses of ratings employees.

3.8 The designated rating organization will disclose the actual or potential conflicts of interest it identifies under section 3.7 in a complete, timely, clear, concise, specific and prominent manner.

3.9 The designated rating organization will disclose the general nature of its compensation arrangements with rated entities.

(1) If the designated rating organization or an affiliate receives from a rated entity, an affiliate or a related entity compensation unrelated to its ratings service, such as compensation for ancillary services (as referred to in section 3.5), the designated rating organization will disclose the percentage that non-rating fees represent out of the total amount of fees received by the designated rating organization or its affiliate, as the case may be, from the rated entity, the affiliate or the related entity.

(2) If the designated rating organization or its affiliates receives directly or indirectly 10 percent or more of its annual revenue from a particular rated entity or subscriber, including revenue received from an affiliate or related entity of the rated entity or subscriber, the organization will disclose that fact and identify the particular rated entity or subscriber.

3.10 A designated rating organization and its DRO employees and their associates must not trade a security, derivative or exchange contract if the organization's employee's or associate's interests in the trade conflict with their interests relating to a credit rating.

3.11 If a designated rating organization is subject to the oversight of a rated entity, or an affiliate or related entity of the rated entity, the designated rating organization will use different DRO employees to conduct the rating actions in respect of that entity than those involved in the oversight.

C. — Employee independence

3.12 Reporting lines for a ratings employee or DRO employees and their compensation arrangements will be structured to eliminate or manage actual and potential conflicts of interest.

(1) The designated rating organization will not compensate or evaluate a ratings employee on the basis of the amount of revenue that the designated rating organization or its affiliates derives from rated entities that the ratings employee rates or with which the ratings employee regularly interacts.

(2) The designated rating organization will conduct reviews of compensation policies and practices for its DRO employees within reasonable regular time periods to ensure that these policies and practices do not compromise the objectivity of the designated rating organization's rating process.

3.13 The designated rating organization will take reasonable steps to ensure that its ratings employees, and any agent who has responsibility for developing or approving procedures or methodologies used for determining credit ratings, do not initiate, or participate in, discussions or negotiations regarding fees or payments with any rated entity or its affiliates or related entities.

3.14 The designated rating organization will not permit a ratings employee to participate in or otherwise influence the determination of a credit rating if the ratings employee

(a) owns directly or indirectly securities, derivatives or exchange contracts of the rated entity, other than holdings through an investment fund;

(b) owns directly or indirectly securities, derivatives or exchange contracts of a rated entity or its related entities, the ownership of which causes or may reasonably be perceived as causing a conflict of interest;

(c) has had a recent employment, business or other relationship with the rated entity, its affiliates or related entities that causes or may reasonably be perceived as causing a conflict of interest; or

(d) has an associate who currently works for the rated entity, its affiliates or related entities.

3.15 The designated rating organization will not permit a ratings employee or an associate of such ratings employee to buy or sell or engage in any transaction involving a security, a derivative or an exchange contract based on a security issued, guaranteed, or otherwise supported by any person or company within such ratings employee's area of primary analytical responsibility, other than holdings through an investment fund.

3.16 The designated rating organization will not permit a ratings employee or an associate of such ratings employee to accept gifts, including entertainment, from anyone with whom the designated rating organization does business, other than items provided in the normal course of business if the aggregate value of all gifts received is nominal.

3.17 If a DRO employee of a designated rating organization becomes involved in any personal relationship that creates any actual or potential conflict of interest, the DRO employee must disclose the relationship to the designated rating organization's compliance officer. The designated rating organization will not issue a credit rating if a DRO employee has an actual or potential conflict of interest with a rated entity. If the credit rating has been issued, the designated rating organization will publicly disclose in a timely manner that the credit rating may be affected.

Part 2: MARKET PARTICIPANTS

3.18 The designated rating organization will review the past work of any ratings employee that leaves the organization and joins a rated entity (or an affiliate or related entity of the rated entity) if

    (a) the ratings employee has, within the last year, been involved in rating the rated entity, or

    (b) the rated entity is a financial firm with which the ratings employee had, within the last year, significant dealings as part of his or her duties at the designated rating organization.

4. — Responsibilities to the Investing Public and Issuers

A. — Transparency and timeliness of ratings disclosure

4.1 The designated rating organization will distribute in a timely manner its ratings decisions regarding the entities and securities it rates.

4.2 The designated rating organization will publicly disclose its policies for distributing ratings, ratings reports and updates.

4.3 Except for a rating it discloses only to the rated entity, a designated rating organization will disclose to the public, on a non-selective basis and free of charge, any ratings decision regarding rated entities that are reporting issuers or the securities of such issuers, as well as any subsequent decisions to discontinue such a rating, if the rating decision is based in whole or in part on material non-public information.

4.4 In each of its ratings reports, a designated rating organization will disclose the following:

    (a) when the rating was first released and when it was last updated;

    (b) the principal methodology or methodology version that was used in determining the rating and where a description of that methodology can be found. If the rating is based on more than one methodology, or if a review of only the principal methodology might cause investors to overlook other important aspects of the rating, the designated rating organization must explain this fact in the ratings report, and include a discussion of how the different methodologies and other important aspects factored into the rating decision;

    (c) the meaning of each rating category and the definition of default or recovery, and the time horizon the designated rating organization used when making a rating decision;

    (d) any attributes and limitations of the credit rating. If the rating involves a type of financial product presenting limited historical data (such as an innovative financial vehicle), the designated rating organization will disclose, in a prominent place, the limitations of the rating;

    (e) all material sources, including the rated entity, its affiliates and related entities, that were used to prepare the credit rating and whether the credit rating has been disclosed to the rated entity or its related entities and amended following that disclosure before being issued.

4.5 In each of its ratings reports in respect of a structured finance product, a designated rating organization will disclose the following:

    (a) all information about loss and cash-flow analysis it has performed or is relying upon and an indication of any expected change in the credit rating. The designated rating organization will also disclose the degree to which it analyzes how sensitive a rating of a structured finance product is to changes in the designated rating organization's underlying rating assumptions;

    (b) the level of assessment the designated rating organization has performed concerning the due diligence processes carried out at the level of underlying financial instruments or other assets of structured finance products. The designated rating organization will also disclose whether it has undertaken any assessment of such due diligence processes or whether it has relied on a third-party assessment and how the outcome of such assessment impacts the credit rating.

4.6 If, to a reasonable person, the information required to be included in a ratings report under sections 4.4 and 4.5 would be disproportionate to the length of the ratings report, the designated rating organization will include a prominent reference to where such information can be easily accessed.

4.7 A designated rating organization will disclose on an ongoing basis information about all structured finance products submitted to it for its initial review or for a preliminary rating, including whether the issuer requested the designated rating organization to provide a final rating.

4.8 The designated rating organization will publicly disclose the methodologies, models and key rating assumptions (such as mathematical or correlation assumptions) it uses in its credit rating activities and any material modifications to such methodologies, models and key rating assumptions. This disclosure will include sufficient information about the designated rating organization's procedures, methodologies and assumptions (including financial statement adjustments that deviate materially from those contained in the issuer's published financial statements and a description of the rating committee process, if applicable) so that outside parties can understand how a rating was arrived at by the designated rating organization.

4.9 The designated rating organization will differentiate ratings of structured finance products from traditional corporate bond ratings through a different rating symbology. The designated rating organization will also disclose how this differentiation functions. The designated rating organization will clearly define a given rating symbol and apply it in a consistent manner for all types of securities to which that symbol is assigned.

4.10 The designated rating organization will assist investors in developing a greater understanding of what a credit rating is, and the limits to which credit ratings can be put to use in relation to a particular type of financial product that the designated rating organization rates. The designated rating organization will clearly indicate the attributes and limitations of each credit rating.

4.11 When issuing or revising a rating, the designated rating organization will provide in its press releases and public reports an explanation of the key elements underlying the rating opinion.

4.12 Before issuing or revising a rating, the designated rating organization will inform the issuer of the critical information and principal considerations upon which a rating will be based and afford the issuer an opportunity to clarify any likely factual misperceptions or other matters that the designated rating organization would wish to be made aware of in order to produce an accurate rating. The designated rating organization will duly evaluate the response.

4.13 Every year, the designated rating organization will publicly disclose data about the historical default rates of its rating categories and whether the default rates of these categories have changed over time. If the nature of the rating or other circumstances make a historical default rate inappropriate, statistically invalid, or otherwise likely to mislead the users of the rating, the designated rating organization will explain this. This information will include verifiable, quantifiable historical information about the performance of its rating opinions, organized and structured, and, where possible, standardized in such a way so as to assist investors in drawing performance comparisons between different designated rating organizations.

4.14 For each rating, the designated rating organization will disclose whether the rated entity and its related entities participated in the rating process and whether the designated rating organization had access to the accounts and other relevant internal documents of the rated entity or its related entities. Each rating not initiated at the request of the rated entity will be identified as such. The designated rating organization will also disclose its policies and procedures regarding unsolicited ratings.

4.15 The designated rating organization will fully and publicly disclose, in a timely fashion, any material modification to its methodologies, models, key ratings assumptions and significant systems, resources or procedures. Where a reasonable person would consider feasible and appropriate, disclosure of such material modifications will be made before they go into effect. The designated rating organization will carefully consider the various uses of credit ratings before modifying its methodologies, models, key ratings assumptions and significant systems, resources or procedures.

B. — The treatment of confidential information

4.16 The designated rating organization and its DRO employees will take all reasonable measures to protect the confidential nature of information shared with them by rated entities under the terms of a confidentiality agreement or otherwise under a mutual understanding that the information is shared confidentially. Unless otherwise permitted by the confidentiality agreement or required by applicable laws, regulations or court orders, the designated rating organization and its DRO employees will not disclose confidential information.

4.17 The designated rating organization and its DRO employees will not use confidential information for any purpose except for their rating activities or in accordance with applicable legislation or a confidentiality agreement with the rated entity to which the information relates.

4.18 The designated rating organization and its DRO employees will take all reasonable measures to protect all property and records relating to credit rating activities and belonging to or in possession of the designated rating organization from fraud, theft or misuse.

4.19 A designated rating organization will ensure that its DRO employees do not engage in transactions in securities, derivatives or exchange contracts when they possess confidential information concerning the issuer of such security or to which the derivative or the exchange contract relates.

4.20 A designated rating organization will cause its DRO employees to familiarize themselves with the internal securities trading policies maintained by the designated rating organization and certify their compliance with such policies within reasonable regular time periods.

4.21 The designated rating organization and its DRO employees will not selectively disclose any non-public information about ratings or possible future rating actions of the designated rating organization, except to the issuer or its designated agents.

4.22 The designated rating organization and its DRO employees will not share confidential information entrusted to the designated rating organization with employees of any affiliate that is not a designated rating organization or a DRO affiliate. The designated rating organization and its DRO employees will not share confidential information within the designated rating organization, except as necessary in connection with the designated rating organization's credit rating functions.

4.23 A designated rating organization will ensure that its DRO employees do not use or share confidential information for the purpose of buying or selling or engaging in any transaction in any security, derivative or exchange contract based on a security issued, guaranteed, or otherwise supported by any person or company, or for any other purpose except the conduct of the designated rating organization's business.

Final Rule: (2012) 35 O.S.C.B. 3294; Approval by OSC: (2012) 35 O.S.C.B. 2383 and 913; Request for Comments: (2011) 34 O.S.C.B. 3249 and (2010) 33 O.S.C.B. 6353.

Form 25-101F1 — Designated Rating Organization Application and Annual Filing

Instructions

(1) Terms used in this form but not defined in this form have the meaning given to them in the Instrument.

(2) Unless otherwise specified, the information in this form must be presented as at the last day of the applicant's most recently completed financial year. If necessary, the applicant must update the information provided so it is not misleading when it is filed. For information presented as at any date other than the last day of the applicant's most recently completed financial year, specify the relevant date in the form.

(3) Applicants are reminded that it is an offence under securities legislation to give false or misleading information on this form.

(4) Applicants may apply to the securities regulatory authority to hold in confidence portions of this form which disclose intimate financial, personal or other information. Securities regulatory authorities will consider the application and accord confidential treatment to those portions to the extent permitted by law.

(5) When this form is used for an annual filing, the term "applicant" means the designated rating organization.

Item 1 — Name of Applicant

State the name of the applicant.

Item 2 — Organization and Structure of Applicant

Describe the organizational structure of the applicant, including, as applicable, an organizational chart that identifies the ultimate and intermediate parent companies, subsidiaries, and material affiliates of the applicant (if any); an organizational chart showing the divisions, departments, and business units of the applicant; and an organizational chart showing the managerial structure of the applicant, including the compliance officer referred to in section 12 of the Instrument. Provide detailed information regarding the applicant's legal structure and ownership.

Item 3 — DRO Affiliates

Provide the name, address and governing jurisdiction of each affiliate that is (or, in the case of an applicant, proposes to be) a DRO affiliate.

Item 4 — Rating Distribution Model

Briefly describe how the applicant makes its credit ratings readily accessible for free or for a fee. If a person must pay a fee to obtain a credit rating made readily accessible by the applicant, provide a fee schedule or describe the price(s) charged.

Item 5 — Procedures and Methodologies

Briefly describe the procedures and methodologies used by the applicant to determine credit ratings, including unsolicited credit ratings. The description must be sufficiently detailed to provide an understanding of the processes employed by the applicant in determining credit ratings, including, as applicable:

- policies for determining whether to initiate a credit rating;

- the public and non-public sources of information used in determining credit ratings, including information and analysis provided by third-party vendors;

- whether and, if so, how information about verification performed on assets underlying or referenced by a security issued by an asset pool or as part of any asset-backed or mortgage-backed securities transaction is relied on in determining credit ratings;

- the quantitative and qualitative models and metrics used to determine credit ratings, including whether and, if so, how assessments of the quality of originators of assets underlying or referenced by a security issued by an asset pool or as part of any asset-backed or mortgage-backed securities transaction factor into the determination of credit ratings;

- the methodologies by which credit ratings of other credit rating agencies are treated to determine credit ratings for securities issued by an asset pool or as part of any asset-backed or mortgaged-backed securities transaction;

- the procedures for interacting with the management of a rated obligor or issuer of rated securities;

- the structure and voting process of committees that review or approve credit ratings;

- procedures for informing rated obligors or issuers of rated securities about credit rating decisions and for appeals of final or pending credit rating decisions; and

- procedures for monitoring, reviewing, and updating credit ratings, including how frequently credit ratings are reviewed, whether different models or criteria are used for ratings surveillance than for determining initial ratings, whether changes made to models and criteria for determining initial ratings are applied retroactively to existing ratings, and whether changes made to models and criteria for performing ratings surveillance are incorporated into the models and criteria for determining initial ratings; and procedures to withdraw, or suspend the maintenance of, a credit rating.

An applicant may provide the location on its website where additional information about the procedures and methodologies is located.

Item 6 — Code of Conduct

Unless previously provided, attach a copy of the applicant's code of conduct.

Item 7 — Policies and Procedures re Non-public Information

Unless previously provided, attach a copy of the most recent written policies and procedures established, maintained, and enforced by the applicant to prevent the misuse of material non-public information.

Item 8 — Policies and Procedures re Conflicts of Interest

Unless previously provided, attach a copy of the most recent written policies and procedures established with respect to conflicts of interest.

Item 9 — Policies and Procedures re Internal Controls

Describe the applicant's internal control mechanisms designed to ensure the quality of its credit rating activities.

Item 10 — Policies and Procedures re Books and Records

Describe the applicant's policies and procedures regarding record-keeping.

Item 11 — Ratings Employees

Disclose the following information about the applicant's ratings employees and the persons who supervise the ratings employees:

- The total number of ratings employees,

- The total number of ratings employees supervisors,

- A general description of the minimum qualifications required of the ratings employees, including education level and work experience (if applicable, distinguish between junior, mid, and senior level ratings employees), and

- A general description of the minimum qualifications required of the ratings employees supervisors, including education level and work experience.

Item 12 — Compliance Officer

Disclose the following information about the compliance officer of the applicant:

- Name,

- Employment history,

- Post secondary education, and
- Whether employed by the applicant full-time or part-time.

Item 13 — Specified Revenue

Disclose information, as applicable, regarding the applicant's aggregate revenue for the most recently completed financial year:

- Revenue from determining and maintaining credit ratings,
- Revenue from subscribers,
- Revenue from granting licenses or rights to publish credit ratings, and
- Revenue from all other services and products offered by the credit rating organization (include descriptions of any major sources of revenue).

Include financial information on the revenue of the applicant divided into fees from credit rating and non-credit rating activities, including a comprehensive description of each.

This information is not required to be audited.

Item 14 — Credit Rating Users

(a) Disclose a list of the largest users of credit rating services of the applicant by the amount of net revenue earned by the applicant attributable to the user during the most recently completed financial year. First, determine and list the 20 largest issuers and subscribers in terms of net revenue. Next, add to the list any obligor or underwriter that, in terms of net revenue during the financial year, equalled or exceeded the 20th largest issuer or subscriber. In making the list, rank the users in terms of net revenue from largest to smallest and include the net revenue amount for each person. For purposes of this Item:

- *"credit rating services"* means any of the following: rating an issuer's securities (regardless of whether the issuer, underwriter, or any other person or company paid for the credit rating) and providing credit ratings, credit ratings data, or credit ratings analysis to a subscriber; and
- *"net revenue"* means revenue earned by the applicant for any type of service or product provided to the person or company, regardless of whether related to credit rating services, and net of any rebates and allowances the applicant paid or owes to the person or company.

(b) Disclose a list of users of credit rating services whose contribution to the growth rate in the generation of revenue of the applicant in the previous fiscal year exceeded the growth rate in the applicant's total revenue in that year by a factor of more than 1.5 times. A user must be disclosed only if, in that year, the user accounted for more than 0.25% of the applicant's worldwide total revenue.

Item 15 — Financial Statements

Attach a copy of the audited financial statements of the applicant, which must include a statement of financial position, a statement of comprehensive income, and a statement of changes in equity, for each of the three most recently completed financial years. If the applicant is a division, unit, or subsidiary of a parent company, the applicant may provide audited consolidated financial statements of its parent company.

Item 16 — Verification Certificate

Include a certificate of the applicant in the following form:

The undersigned has executed this Form 25-101F1 on behalf of, and on the authority of, [the Applicant]. The undersigned, on behalf of the [Applicant], represents that the information and statements contained in this Form, including appendices and attachments, all of which are part of this Form, are true and correct.

....

(Date)   (Name of the Applicant/Designated Rating Organization)

By: ....

        (Print Name and Title)

        ....

        (Signature)

Form 25-101F2 — Submission to Jurisdiction and Appointment of Agent for Service of Process

1. Name of credit rating organization (the *CRO*):

2. Jurisdiction of incorporation, or equivalent, of CRO:

3. Address of principal place of business of CRO:

4. Name of agent for service of process (the *Agent*):

5. Address for service of process of Agent in Canada (the address may be anywhere in Canada):

6. The CRO designates and appoints the Agent at the address of the Agent stated in Item 5 as its agent upon whom may be served any notice, pleading, subpoena, summons or other process in any action, investigation or administrative, criminal, quasi-criminal, penal or other proceeding (the *Proceeding*) arising out of, relating to or concerning the issuance and maintenance of credit ratings or the obligations of the CRO as a

Part 2: MARKET PARTICIPANTS

designated rating organization, and irrevocably waives any right to raise as a defence in any such Proceeding any alleged lack of jurisdiction to bring such Proceeding.

7. The CRO irrevocably and unconditionally submits to the non-exclusive jurisdiction of

   (a) the judicial, quasi-judicial and administrative tribunals of each of the provinces and territories of Canada in which it is a designated rating organization; and

   (b) any administrative proceeding in any such province or territory,

in any Proceeding arising out of or related to or concerning the issuance or maintenance of credit ratings or the obligations of the CRO as a designated rating organization.

8. This submission to jurisdiction and appointment of agent for service of process is governed by and construed in accordance with the laws of [insert province or territory of above address of Agent].

....
Signature of Credit Rating Organization   Date

....
Print name and title of signing officer of Credit Rating Organization

Agent

The undersigned accepts the appointment as agent for service of process of [insert name of CRO] under the terms and conditions of the appointment of agent for service of process set out in this document.

....
Signature of Agent   Date

....
Print name of person signing and, if Agent is not an individual, the title of the person

National Policy 25-201 — Guidance for Proxy Advisory Firms

Date: **April 30, 2015**
38 O.S.C.B. 4130

PART 1 — PURPOSE AND APPLICATION

1.1 Purpose of this Policy — The Canadian Securities Administrators (CSA or we) recognize that proxy voting is an important method by which shareholders can effect governance and communicate preferences about an issuer's management and stewardship. Issuers rely on shareholder voting to elect directors and to approve other corporate governance matters or certain corporate transactions. Proxy voting is therefore fundamental to, and enhances the quality and integrity of, our public capital markets.

We acknowledge that proxy advisory firms play an important role in the proxy voting process by providing services that facilitate investor participation in the voting process such as analyzing proxy materials and providing vote recommendations. Some proxy advisory firms also provide other types of services to issuers, including consulting services on corporate governance matters.

The purpose of this Policy is to set out recommended practices for proxy advisory firms in relation to the services they provide to their clients and their activities. This Policy provides guidance to proxy advisory firms designed to

   (a) promote transparency in the processes leading to a vote recommendation and the development of proxy voting guidelines, and

   (b) foster understanding among market participants about the activities of proxy advisory firms.

The guidance addresses conflicts of interest, the determination of vote recommendations, the development of proxy voting guidelines and communications with clients, market participants, other stakeholders, the media and the public.

The guidance in this Policy is not intended to be prescriptive or exhaustive.

The CSA encourage proxy advisory firms to consider this guidance in developing and implementing practices that are tailored to their structure and activities.

1.2 Application — This Policy is designed to assist all firms that provide proxy advisory services. Proxy advisory services include any of the following:

   (a) analyzing the matters put to a vote at a shareholders' meeting;

   (b) making vote recommendations;

   (c) developing proxy voting guidelines.

Although some proxy advisory firms may provide other types of services, this Policy addresses processes that lead to vote recommendations and proxy voting guidelines determined or developed by proxy advisory firms.

PART 2 — GUIDANCE

2.1 Conflicts of interest — (1) Effective identification, management and mitigation of actual or potential conflicts of interest are essential in ensuring the ability of the proxy advisory firm to offer independent and objective services to a client.

(2) An actual or potential conflict of interest arises where the interests of a proxy advisory firm are or may be perceived to be inconsistent with, or diverge from, those of a client. An actual or potential conflict might also arise between the interests of one group of clients and another. By way of example, an actual or potential conflict of interest arises in any of the following circumstances:

(a) a proxy advisory firm provides vote recommendations to an investor client on corporate governance matters of an issuer to which the proxy advisory firm provided consulting services;

(b) an investor client of a proxy advisory firm submits a shareholder proposal to be put to a vote at a shareholders' meeting that could be the subject of a favourable vote recommendation by the proxy advisory firm;

(c) a proxy advisory firm is owned, in whole or in part, by an investor client who invests in issuers in relation to which the proxy advisory firm is or has been mandated to make vote recommendations.

(3) Proxy advisory firms may address actual or potential conflicts of interest by implementing appropriate practices. Proxy advisory firms may consider taking the following steps to address actual or potential conflicts of interest:

(a) establishing, maintaining and applying written policies and procedures designed to identify, manage and mitigate actual or potential conflicts of interest that could influence their research and analysis, vote recommendations or proxy voting guidelines;

(b) designing and implementing internal safeguards and controls designed to monitor the effectiveness of the policies and procedures, including organizational structures, lines of reporting and information barriers, to mitigate actual or potential conflicts of interest;

(c) establishing, maintaining and complying with a code of conduct that sets standards of behaviour and practices for the proxy advisory firm, including individuals acting on its behalf;

(d) obtaining affirmation of the code of conduct from all individuals acting on their behalf upon hiring and on an annual basis thereafter and providing related training on a regular basis;

(e) evaluating the effectiveness of their policies and procedures, internal safeguards and controls and code of conduct on a regular basis to ensure that they remain appropriate and effective.

(4) The board of directors of a proxy advisory firm or, if the proxy advisory firm does not have a board of directors, the executive management team or a designated committee of the proxy advisory firm, is generally expected to be responsible for overseeing:

(a) the development of written policies and procedures and a code of conduct designed to address actual or potential conflicts of interest;

(b) the implementation of internal safeguards and controls to identify, manage and mitigate actual or potential conflicts of interest;

(c) the effectiveness of the policies and procedures, code of conduct and internal safeguards and controls instituted to ensure that actual or potential conflicts of interest are identified, managed and mitigated, as appropriate.

(5) To assist with addressing actual or potential conflicts of interest, proxy advisory firms may wish to consider designating an appropriately qualified person (or a committee of appropriately qualified persons) who would be responsible for, among other things:

(a) monitoring and assessing compliance by the proxy advisory firm, and individuals acting on its behalf, with its policies and procedures and code of conduct;

(b) assessing the appropriateness of the internal safeguards and controls adopted by the proxy advisory firm and monitoring the identification, management and mitigation of conflicts of interest;

(c) periodically reporting on his or her activities to the board of directors of the proxy advisory firm or, if the proxy advisory firm does not have a board of directors, the executive management team or designated committee of the proxy advisory firm.

(6) We expect proxy advisory firms to disclose to their clients, in a timely manner, actual or potential conflicts of interest. We expect proxy advisory firms to provide sufficient information to enable clients to understand the nature and scope of the conflict so as to make an assessment about the independence and objectivity of the proxy advisory firms and the services, including any steps taken to address the conflict.

(7) Where possible and without compromising the proprietary or commercially sensitive nature of such information, we expect proxy advisory firms to post or describe on their websites their policies and procedures, internal safeguards and controls, code of conduct and compliance program respecting actual or potential conflicts of interest, including any related amendments.

2.2 (1) It is important for market participants to understand how proxy advisory firms arrive at a specific vote recommendation and to assess the quality of the research and analysis behind such a recommendation. Proxy advisory firms can facilitate this by ensuring that vote recommendations are determined in a transparent manner and that the information underlying those recommendations is accurate.

(2) We expect proxy advisory firms to ensure that:

(a) vote recommendations are determined in a consistent manner in accordance with the proxy voting guidelines of the proxy advisory firm or the proxy voting guidelines of the clients;

(b) vote recommendations are determined based on up-to-date publicly available information about the issuer;

(c) vote recommendations are prepared in accordance with approaches or methodologies aimed at, among other things, reducing the risk of factual errors or inaccuracies.

(3) Proxy advisory firms may consider taking the following steps when determining vote recommendations:

(a) establishing, maintaining and applying written policies and procedures describing the approaches or methodologies used to prepare vote recommendations, such as research, information and data gathering, benchmarks, sources of information from third parties, local market or regulatory conditions, criteria, analytical models and assumptions, and the relative weight of these elements in preparing vote recommendations;

(b) designing and implementing internal safeguards and controls to increase the accuracy and reliability of the information and data used in the preparation of vote recommendations. We encourage proxy advisory firms to have in place a quality assurance process to review vote recommendations before they are provided to clients, including verifying the accuracy of information and data used and reviewing the research and analysis performed by individuals acting on their behalf;

(c) evaluating the effectiveness of their policies and procedures as well as internal safeguards and controls on a regular basis to ensure that they remain appropriate and effective.

(4) We encourage proxy advisory firms to have the resources, knowledge and expertise required to prepare rigorous and credible vote recommendations. This includes hiring, training and retaining individuals that have the particular experience, competencies, skills and knowledge to perform their duties on behalf of the proxy advisory firm in the ordinary course of business.

(5) Where possible and without compromising the proprietary or commercially sensitive nature of such information, we expect proxy advisory firms to post or describe on their websites their policies and procedures and internal safeguards and controls applicable to the preparation of vote recommendations, including any related amendments. We also encourage proxy advisory firms to generally describe on their websites the practices adopted with respect to hiring, training and retaining individuals to ensure that they have the appropriate experience, competencies, skills and knowledge to prepare the vote recommendations.

2.3 (1) It is good practice for proxy advisory firms to ensure that their proxy voting guidelines, which may have an influence on corporate governance practices of issuers, are developed in a consultative and comprehensive manner. This promotes a clearer and more complete understanding of the proxy voting guidelines and their underlying rationale and enables market participants to evaluate the applicability of the proxy voting guidelines to the corporate governance practices of issuers.

(2) Proxy advisory firms may consider taking the following steps when developing proxy voting guidelines:

(a) establishing, maintaining and applying written policies and procedures describing the process followed in developing and updating proxy voting guidelines, such as identification of standards and practices, policy formulation and approval, implementation and evaluation of proxy voting guidelines;

(b) regularly consulting with and considering the preferences and views of their clients, market participants and other stakeholders on corporate governance issues and on their proxy voting guidelines;

(c) taking into account local market or regulatory conditions and other relevant characteristics of the issuers which may include, for example, size, industry and governance structure.

(3) We encourage proxy advisory firms to ensure that they have the resources, knowledge and expertise required to develop and update appropriate proxy voting guidelines. This includes hiring, training and retaining individuals that have the particular experience, competencies, skills and knowledge to perform their duties on behalf of the proxy advisory firm in the ordinary course of business.

(4) Without compromising the proprietary or commercially sensitive nature of such information, we expect proxy advisory firms to post on their websites their proxy voting guidelines and any updates to them. We encourage proxy advisory firms to explain the rationale for their proxy voting guidelines and to provide any other relevant information which could contribute to understanding the reasons behind the proxy voting guidelines and any updates to them.

(5) Where possible and without compromising the proprietary or commercially sensitive nature of such information, we expect proxy advisory firms to post or describe on their websites their policies and procedures and consultations applicable to the development and update of proxy voting guidelines, including any related amendments. We also encourage proxy advisory firms to generally describe on their websites the practices adopted with respect to hiring, training and retaining individuals to ensure that they have the appropriate experience, competencies, skills and knowledge to develop and update the proxy voting guidelines.

2.4 (1) It is good practice for proxy advisory firms to properly manage their communications with clients, market participants, other stakeholders, the media and the public to foster understanding of the activities of proxy advisory firms.

(2) When issuing their vote recommendations, we expect proxy advisory firms to communicate the following information to their clients in their reports:

(a) how the relevant approaches or methodologies were used or applied in determining the vote recommendations;

(b) the sources of information used in preparing the vote recommendations;

(c) a description of the extent to which proxy voting guidelines were used or applied when preparing vote recommendations and the reasons for any deviation from the proxy voting guidelines;

(d) where applicable, the nature and outcome of dialogue or contact with the issuer, shareholder proponents or other stakeholders in the preparation of the vote recommendations;

(e) the limitations or conditions in the research and analysis used to prepare the vote recommendations;

(f) a statement that the vote recommendations and the underlying research and analysis are intended solely as guidance to assist the clients in their decision making process.

(3) We expect proxy advisory firms to post or describe on their websites their policies and procedures regarding dialogue or contact with issuers, shareholder proponents and other stakeholders when they prepare vote recommendations, including whether they provide drafts of reports to issuers for review and comment before sending the final reports to their clients.

(4) We expect proxy advisory firms to correct any factual errors or inaccuracies found in a report and to duly inform their clients in a timely manner. We also encourage proxy advisory firms to duly inform their clients of any report updates or revisions to reflect new publicly available information about an issuer in a timely manner.

(5) We encourage proxy advisory firms to establish, maintain and apply written policies and procedures governing their communications with clients, market participants, other stakeholders, the media and the public, including in relation to the preparation or release of any vote recommendation.

(6) We encourage proxy advisory firms to establish a contact person to manage communications with clients, market participants, other stakeholders, the media and the public, including any questions, concerns or complaints that the proxy advisory firm may receive.

(7) Where possible and without compromising the proprietary or commercially sensitive nature of such information, we expect proxy advisory firms to post or describe on their websites their policies and procedures governing their communications, including any related amendments.

PART 3 — EFFECTIVE DATE

3.1 Effective date — This Policy comes into force on April 30, 2015.

CSA Staff Notice 25-301 — Update on CSA Consultation Paper 25-401 *Potential Regulation of Proxy Advisory Firms*

Date: September 19, 2013

Citation: 36 O.S.C.B. 9113

[Not reproduced]

PART III — REGISTRATION AND RELATED MATTERS

3.1 — Registration Requirements

See also OPS 4.3, NPS 11-204.

National Instrument 31-101 — National Registration System

Date: April 4, 2005, as amended effective August 1, 2006

28 O.S.C.B. 3073 and 29 O.S.C.B. 6489

[Repealed: (2009) 32 O.S.C.B. (Supp. 2) 424]

Final Rule: (2005) 28 O.S.C.B. 3073; Approval by OSC: (2005) 28 O.S.C.B. 87 and 1267; Request for Comments: (2004) 27 O.S.C.B. 618.

Amendment to Rule: (2006) 29 O.S.C.B. 6489; Approval by OSC: (2006) 29 O.S.C.B. 3555; Request for Comments: (2006) 29 O.S.C.B. 9527.

National Instrument 31-102 — National Registration Database

Date: January 31, 2003, as amended effective May 15, 2007, September 28, 2009 and October 12, 2013

26 O.S.C.B. 926, 30 O.S.C.B. 5494, 32 O.S.C.B. (Supp. 4) 225 and 36 O.S.C.B. 9608

Table of Contents

PART 1 — DEFINITIONS AND INTERPRETATION

1.1 Definitions — In this Instrument

"authorized firm representative" or "AFR" means, for a firm filer, an individual with his or her own NRD user ID and who is authorized by the firm filer to submit information in NRD format for that firm filer and individual filers with respect to whom the firm filer is the sponsoring firm;

"chief AFR" means, for a firm filer, an individual who is an AFR and has accepted an appointment as a chief AFR by the firm filer;

"firm filer" means a person or company that is required under securities legislation to make an NRD submission in accordance with this Instrument and that is registered as, or has applied for registration as, a dealer, adviser, or investment fund manager;

"individual filer" means an individual that is required under securities legislation to make an NRD submission in accordance with this Instrument;

"NI 33-109" means National Instrument 33-109 Registration Information;

"National Registration Database" or "NRD" means the online electronic database of registration information regarding NRD filers and includes the computer system providing for the transmission, receipt, review and dissemination of that registration information by electronic means;

"NRD account" means an account with a member of the Canadian Payments Association from which fees may be paid with respect to NRD by electronic pre-authorized debit;

"NRD administrator" means the Alberta Securities Commission or a successor appointed by the securities regulatory authority to operate NRD;

"NRD filer" means an individual filer or a firm filer;

"NRD format" means the electronic format for submitting information through the NRD website;

"NRD number" means the unique number first generated by NRD to identify an NRD filer or a business location;

"NRD submission" means information that is submitted under securities legislation or securities directions in NRD format, or the act of submitting information under securities legislation or securities directions in NRD format, as the context requires;

"NRD website" means the website operated by the NRD administrator for the NRD submissions;

1.2 Interpretation — Terms defined in NI 33-109 and used in this Instrument have the respective meanings ascribed to those terms in NI 33-109.

PART 2 — INFORMATION TO BE SUBMITTED IN NRD FORMAT

2.1 Registration Information — A person or company that is required to submit any of the following to the securities regulatory authority or regulator must make the submission in NRD format:

1. Form 33-109F1;

2. Form 33-109F2;

3. Form 33-109F3;

4. Form 33-109F4;

5. Form 33-109F5 to report a change to any information previously submitted in respect of Form 33-109F4;

6. Form 33-109F7.

PART 3 — MAKING NRD SUBMISSIONS

3.1 NRD Submissions — 1) An NRD filer that is required under securities legislation to submit information in NRD format must make that NRD submission

(a) through the NRD website,

(b) using the NRD number of the NRD filer or business location, and

(c) in accordance with this Instrument.

2) A requirement in securities legislation relating to the format in which a document or other information to be submitted must be printed, or specifying the number of copies of a document that must be submitted, does not apply to an NRD submission required to be made in accordance with this Instrument.

3) An NRD filer making an NRD submission must make the NRD submission through an AFR.

3.2 Ongoing Firm Filer Requirements — A firm filer must

(a) be enrolled with the NRD administrator to use NRD;

(b) have one and no more than one chief AFR enrolled with the NRD administrator;

(c) maintain one and no more than one NRD account;

(d) notify the NRD administrator of the appointment of a chief AFR within 7 days of the appointment;

(e) notify the NRD administrator of any change in the name of the firm's chief AFR within 7 days of the change;

(f) submit any change in the name of an AFR, other than the firm's chief AFR, in NRD format within 7 days of the change; and

(g) submit any change in the phone number, fax number or e-mail address of the chief AFR in NRD format within 7 days of the change.

PART 4 — PAYMENT OF FEES THROUGH NRD

4.1 Payment of Submission Fees — (1) If a fee is required with respect to an NRD submission, a firm filer must pay the required fee by electronic preauthorized debit through NRD.

(2) A payment under subsection (1) must be made from the firm filer's NRD account.

4.2 Payment of Annual Registration Fees — (1) If an NRD filer is required to pay an annual registration fee, the NRD filer must pay the required fee by electronic pre-authorized debit through NRD.

(2) A payment under subsection (1) must be made from the NRD filer's NRD account.

4.3 Payment of NRD User Fees — Annual — (1) If a firm filer is required to pay an annual NRD user fee, the firm filer must pay the required fee by electronic pre-authorized debit through NRD.

(2) A payment under subsection (1) must be made from the firm filer's NRD account.

4.4 Payment of Late Filing Fees — (1) If a firm filer is required to pay late filing fees because of an activity that creates or relates to an NRD submission, the firm filer must pay the required fee by electronic pre-authorized debit through NRD.

(2) A payment under subsection (1) must be made from the firm filer's NRD account.

4.5 Exemption for Registrants not Resident in Canada — Sections 3.2(c), 4.1, 4.2, 4.3 and 4.4 do not apply to a registered firm that

(a) has no business office in a jurisdiction of Canada,

(b) does not have an account with a member of the Canadian Payments Association,

(c) is not an affiliate of a registered firm resident in a jurisdiction of Canada,

(d) pays the fees referred to in sections 4.1, 4.2 and 4.4 within 14 days of the date the payment is due,

(e) pays the following fees within 14 days of the date the payment is due by submitting a cheque, payable to the Ontario Securities Commission in Canadian currency, to CSA Service Desk, Attn: NRD Administrator, 12 Millenium Blvd. Suite 210, Moncton, NB E1C 0M3

(i) NRD user fees required in respect of an NRD submission;

(ii) annual NRD user fees, and

(f) pays any fee referred to in sections 4.1, 4.2 and 4.4, other than an NRD user fee, by submitting a cheque in Canadian funds to the securities regulatory authority or regulator in the local jurisdiction within 14 days of the date the payment is due.

PART 5 — TEMPORARY HARDSHIP EXEMPTION

5.1 Temporary Hardship Exemption — (1) If unanticipated technical difficulties prevent an NRD filer from making an NRD submission within the time required under securities legislation, the NRD filer is exempt from the requirement to make the submission within the required time period, if the NRD filer makes the submission other than through the NRD website or in NRD format no later than 7 days after the day on which the information was required to be submitted.

(2) If unanticipated technical difficulties prevent an individual filer from submitting an application in NRD format, the individual filer may submit the application other than through the NRD website.

(3) For the purpose of subsections (1) and (2), the NRD filer may make a notification or application other than through the NRD website by submitting it to the principal regulator.

(4) Despite subsection (3), for the purpose of an application submitted under (2) which includes Ontario, the individual filer may make the application by submitting it to

(a) the principal regulator, if the principal jurisdiction is Ontario, or

(b) the principal regulator and the regulator in Ontario.

(5) If an NRD filer makes a submission other than through the NRD website under this section, the NRD filer must include the following legend in capital letters at the top of the first page of the submission:

IN ACCORDANCE WITH SECTION 5.1 OF NATIONAL INSTRUMENT 31-102 *NATIONAL REGISTRATION DATABASE* (NRD), THIS [SPECIFY DOCUMENT] IS BEING SUBMITTED OTHER THAN THROUGH THE NRD WEBSITE UNDER A TEMPORARY HARD-SHIP EXEMPTION.

(6) If an NRD filer makes a submission other than through the NRD website under this section, the NRD filer must resubmit the information in NRD format as soon as practicable and in any event within 14 days after the unanticipated technical difficulties have been resolved.

PART 6 — EXEMPTION

6.1 Exemption — (1) The regulator or the securities regulatory authority may grant an exemption from this Instrument, in whole or in part, subject to such conditions or restrictions as may be imposed in the exemption.

(2) Despite subsection (1), in Ontario only the regulator may grant such an exemption.

(3) Except in Ontario, an exemption referred to in subsection (1) is granted under the statute referred to in Appendix B of National Instrument 14-101 Definitions, opposite the name of the local jurisdiction.

Final Rule: (2003) 26 O.S.C.B. 926; Approval by OSC: (2002) 25 O.S.C.B. 7503; Request for Comments: (2002) 25 O.S.C.B. 3405 and (2001) 24 O.S.C.B. 7438.

Amendment to Rule: (2007) 30 O.S.C.B. 5494: Approval by OSC: (2007) 30 O.S.C.B. 1649; Request for Comments: (2006) 29 O.S.C.B. 3961.

Amendment to Rule: (2009) 32 O.S.C.B. (Supp. 4) 225; Approval by OSC: (2009) 32 O.S.C.B. (Supp. 2) 308; Request for Comments: (2008) 31 O.S.C.B. 2419.

Amendment to Rule: (2013) 36 O.S.C.B. 9608; Approval by OSC: (2013) O.S.C.B. 8569 (corrections) and 7217; Request for Comments: (2013) 36 O.S.C.B. 1081.

Rules: NI 13-102, 31-103, 33-109; Rule 13-502, App. C, Item E(2.1).

Policies and Orders: NPS 11-204, OSCN 31-710.

Companion Policy 31-102CP — To National Instrument 31-102 — National Registration Database

Part 1 — Purpose

The purpose of NI 31-102 is to establish requirements for the electronic submission of registration information through NRD. References in this policy to "we" mean the securities regulatory authority and regulator.

Part 2 — Production of NRD Filings

The securities legislation of several jurisdictions contains a requirement to produce or make available an original or certified copy of information filed under the securities legislation. We consider that it may satisfy such a requirement in the case of information filed in NRD format by providing a printed copy or other output of the information in readable form that contains or is accompanied by a certification by the securities regulatory authority or regulator that the printed copy or output is a copy of the information filed in NRD format.

Part 3 — Date of Filing

We think that information filed in NRD format is, for purposes of securities legislation, filed on the day that the transmission of the information to NRD is completed.

Part 4 — Official Copy of NRD Filings

For purposes of securities legislation, securities directions or any other related purpose, we think hat the official record of any information filed in NRD format by an NRD filer is the electronic information stored in NRD.

Part 5 — Authorized Firm Representative as Agent

We think that when making an NRD submission an AFR is an agent of the firm or individual to whom the filing relates.

Part 6 — Ongoing Firm Filer Requirements

We expect that firm filers will follow the processes set out in the NRD Use Guide to:

    (a) enrol with the NRD administrator;

    (b) keep their enrolment information current; and

    (c) keep their NRD account information current.

Part 7 — Commodity Futures Act Submissions

In Ontario and Manitoba, if a person or company is required to make a submission under both NI 31-102 and OSC Rule 31-509 (*Commodity Futures Act*), or in Manitoba, MSC Rule 2000-1 (*Commodity Futures Act*), with respect to the same information, the securities regulatory authority is of the view that a single filing on a form required under either rule satisfies both requirements.

Adoption by OSC: (2003) 26 O.S.C.B. 933 and (2002) 25 O.S.C.B. 7503; Request for Comments: (2002) 25 O.S.C.B. 3405 and (2001) 24 O.S.C.B. 7458.

Adoption of Amendment: (2007) 30 O.S.C.B. 1649; Request for Comments: (2006) 29 O.S.C.B. 3961.

Adoption of Replacement Policy: (2009) 32 O.S.C.B (Supp. 4) 227 and 32 O.S.C.B. (Supp. 2) 308 [correction: 32 O.S.C.B. 8637]; Request for Comments: (2008) 31 O.S.C.B. 2419.

Rules: NI 33-109.

National Instrument 31-103 — Registration Requirements, Exemptions and Ongoing Registrant Obligations

Date: September 28, 2009, as amended January 1, 2011, July 11, 2011, February 28, 2012, September 28, 2012 (CP only), May 31, 2013, July 15, 2013, May 1, 2014, September 22, 2014, January 11, 2015 and July 11, 2015

32 O.S.C.B. (Supp. 4) 1, 33 O.S.C.B. (Supp. 5) 107, 34 O.S.C.B. 7547, 35 O.S.C.B. 1440, 35 O.S.C.B. 8547, 36 O.S.C.B. 5723, 36 O.S.C.B. 5723, 37 O.S.C.B. 2369, 37 O.S.C.B. (Supp 4), 37 O.S.C.B. (Supp. 5) and 38 O.S.C.B. 299.

Table of Contents

Part 3: REGISTRATION

Part 3:
REGISTRATION

PART 1 — INTERPRETATION

1.1 Definitions of terms used throughout this Instrument — In this Instrument

"book cost" means the total amount paid to purchase a security, including any transaction charges related to the purchase, adjusted for reinvested distributions, returns of capital and corporate reorganizations;

"Canadian financial institution" has the same meaning as in section 1.1 of National Instrument 45-106 *Prospectus and Registration Exemptions*;

"connected issuer" has the same meaning as in section 1.1 of National Instrument 33-105 *Underwriting Conflicts*;

"debt security" has the same meaning as in section 1.1 of National Instrument 45-106 *Prospectus and Registration Exemptions*;

"designated rating" has the same meaning as in National Instrument 81-102 *Investment Funds*;

"designated rating organization" has the same meaning as in National Instrument 81-102 Investment Funds;

"DRO affiliate" means an affiliate of a designated rating organization that issues credit ratings in a foreign jurisdiction and that has been designated as such under the terms of the designated rating organization's designation;

"eligible client" means a client of a person or company if any of the following apply:

(a) the client is an individual and was a client of the person or company immediately before becoming resident in the local jurisdiction;

(b) the client is the spouse or a child of a client referred to in paragraph (a);

(c) except in Ontario, the client is a client of the person or company on September 27, 2009 pursuant to the person or company's reliance on an exemption from the registration requirement under Part 5 of Multilateral Instrument 11-101 *Principal Regulator System* on that date;

"exempt market dealer" means a person or company registered in the category of exempt market dealer;

"IIROC" means the Investment Industry Regulatory Organization of Canada;

"IIROC provision" means a by-law, rule, regulation or policy of IIROC named in Appendix G, as amended from time to time;

"investment dealer" means a person or company registered in the category of investment dealer;

"interim period" means a period commencing on the first day of the financial year and ending 9, 6 or 3 months before the end of the financial year;

"managed account" means an account of a client for which a person or company makes the investment decisions if that person or company has discretion to trade in securities for the account without requiring the client's express consent to a transaction;

"marketplace" has the same meaning as in section 1.1 of National Instrument 21-101 *Marketplace Operation*;

"MFDA" means the Mutual Fund Dealers Association of Canada;

"MFDA provision" means a by-law, rule, regulation or policy of the MFDA named in Appendix H, as amended from time to time;

"mutual fund dealer" means a person or company registered in the category of mutual fund dealer;

"operating charge" means any amount charged to a client by a registered firm in respect of the operation, transfer or termination of a client's account and includes any federal, provincial or territorial sales taxes paid on that amount;

"original cost" means the total amount paid to purchase a security, including any transaction charges related to the purchase;

"permitted client" means any of the following:

    (a) a Canadian financial institution or a Schedule III bank;

    (b) the Business Development Bank of Canada incorporated under the *Business Development Bank of Canada Act* (Canada);

    (c) a subsidiary of any person or company referred to in paragraph (a) or (b), if the person or company owns all of the voting securities of the subsidiary, except the voting securities required by law to be owned by directors of the subsidiary;

    (d) a person or company registered under the securities legislation of a jurisdiction of Canada as an adviser, investment dealer, mutual fund dealer or exempt market dealer;

    (e) a pension fund that is regulated by either the federal Office of the Superintendent of Financial Institutions or a pension commission or similar regulatory authority of a jurisdiction of Canada or a wholly-owned subsidiary of such a pension fund;

    (f) an entity organized in a foreign jurisdiction that is analogous to any of the entities referred to in paragraphs (a) to (e);

    (g) the Government of Canada or a jurisdiction of Canada, or any Crown corporation, agency or wholly-owned entity of the Government of Canada or a jurisdiction of Canada;

    (h) any national, federal, state, provincial, territorial or municipal government of or in any foreign jurisdiction, or any agency of that government;

    (i) a municipality, public board or commission in Canada and a metropolitan community, school board, the Comité de gestion de la taxe scolaire de l'île de Montréal or an intermunicipal management board in Québec;

    (j) a trust company or trust corporation registered or authorized to carry on business under the *Trust and Loan Companies Act* (Canada) or under comparable legislation in a jurisdiction of Canada or a foreign jurisdiction, acting on behalf of a managed account managed by the trust company or trust corporation, as the case may be;

    (k) a person or company acting on behalf of a managed account managed by the person or company, if the person or company is registered or authorized to carry on business as an adviser or the equivalent under the securities legislation of a jurisdiction of Canada or a foreign jurisdiction;

    (l) an investment fund if one or both of the following apply:

        (i) the fund is managed by a person or company registered as an investment fund manager under the securities legislation of a jurisdiction of Canada;

        (ii) the fund is advised by a person or company authorized to act as an adviser under the securities legislation of a jurisdiction of Canada;

    (m) in respect of a dealer, a registered charity under the *Income Tax Act* (Canada) that obtains advice on the securities to be traded from an eligibility adviser, as defined in section 1.1 of National Instrument 45-106 *Prospectus and Registration Exemptions*, or an adviser registered under the securities legislation of the jurisdiction of the registered charity;

    (n) in respect of an adviser, a registered charity under the *Income Tax Act* (Canada) that is advised by an eligibility adviser, as defined in section 1.1 of National Instrument 45-106 *Prospectus and Registration Exemptions*, or an adviser registered under the securities legislation of the jurisdiction of the registered charity;

    (o) an individual who beneficially owns financial assets, as defined in section 1.1 of National Instrument 45-106 *Prospectus and Registration Exemptions*, having an aggregate realizable value that, before taxes but net of any related liabilities, exceeds $5 million;

    (p) a person or company that is entirely owned by an individual or individuals referred to in paragraph (o), who holds the beneficial ownership interest in the person or company directly or through a trust, the trustee of which is a trust company or trust corporation registered or authorized to carry on business under the *Trust and Loan Companies Act* (Canada) or under comparable legislation in a jurisdiction of Canada or a foreign jurisdiction;

    (q) a person or company, other than an individual or an investment fund, that has net assets of at least $25 million as shown on its most recently prepared financial statements;

    (r) a person or company that distributes securities of its own issue in Canada only to persons or companies referred to in paragraphs (a) to (q);

"portfolio manager" means a person or company registered in the category of portfolio manager;

"principal jurisdiction" means

    (a) for a person or company other than an individual, the jurisdiction of Canada in which the person or company's head office is located, and

    (b) for an individual, the jurisdiction of Canada in which the individual's working office is located;

"principal regulator" has the same meaning as in section 4A.1 of Multilateral Instrument 11-102 *Passport System*;

"registered firm" means a registered dealer, a registered adviser, or a registered investment fund manager;

"registered individual" means an individual who is registered

    (a) in a category that authorizes the individual to act as a dealer or an adviser on behalf of a registered firm,

    (b) as ultimate designated person, or

    (c) as chief compliance officer;

"related issuer" has the same meaning as in section 1.1 of National Instrument 33-105 *Underwriting Conflicts*;

"restricted dealer" means a person or company registered in the category of restricted dealer;

"restricted portfolio manager" means a person or company registered in the category of restricted portfolio manager;

"Schedule III bank" means an authorized foreign bank named in Schedule III of the *Bank Act* (Canada);

"scholarship plan dealer" means a person or company registered in the category of scholarship plan dealer;

"sponsoring firm" means the registered firm on whose behalf an individual acts as a dealer, an underwriter, an adviser, a chief compliance officer or an ultimate designated person;

"sponsoring firm" means the firm registered in a jurisdiction of Canada on whose behalf an individual acts as a dealer, an underwriter, an adviser, a chief compliance officer or an ultimate designated person;

"sub-adviser" means an adviser to

(a) a registered adviser, or

(b) a registered dealer acting as a portfolio manager as permitted by section 8.24 [*IIROC members with discretionary authority*];

"subsidiary" has the same meaning as in section 1.1 of National Instrument 45-106 *Prospectus and Registration Exemptions*;

Proposed Addition —

"**total percentage return**" means the cumulative realized and unrealized capital gains and losses of an investment, plus income from the investment, over a specified period of time, expressed as a percentage;

[To come into force July 15, 2016.]

"trailing commission" means any payment related to a client's ownership of a security that is part of a continuing series of payments to a registered firm or registered individual by any party;

"transaction charge" means any amount charged to a client by a registered firm in respect of a purchase or sale of a security and includes any federal, provincial or territorial sales taxes paid on that amount;

"working office" means the office of the sponsoring firm where an individual does most of his or her business.

1.2 Interpretation of "securities" in Alberta, British Columbia, New Brunswick and Saskatchewan — In Alberta, British Columbia, New Brunswick and Saskatchewan, a reference to "securities" in this Instrument includes "exchange contracts", unless the context otherwise requires.

1.3 Information may be given to the principal regulator — (1) [Repealed.]

(2) For the purpose of a requirement in this Instrument to notify or to deliver or submit a document to the regulator or the securities regulatory authority, the person or company may notify or deliver or submit the document to the person or company's principal regulator.

(3) [Repealed.]

(4) Despite subsection (2), for the purpose of the notice and delivery requirements in section 11.9 [*registrant acquiring a registered firm's securities or assets*], if the principal regulator of the registrant and the principal regulator of the firm identified in paragraph 11.9(1)(a) or 11.9(1)(b), if registered in any jurisdiction of Canada, are not the same, the registrant must deliver the written notice to the following:

(a) the registrant's principal regulator; and

(b) the principal regulator of the firm identified in paragraph 11.9(1)(a) or 11.9(1)(b) as applicable, if registered in any jurisdiction of Canada identified in paragraph 11.9(1)(a) or 11.9(1)(b).

(5) Subsection (2) does not apply to

(a) section 8.18 [*international dealer*], and

(b) section 8.26 [*international adviser*].

PART 2 — CATEGORIES OF REGISTRATION FOR INDIVIDUALS

2.1 Individual categories — (1) The following are the categories of registration for an individual who is required, under securities legislation, to be registered to act on behalf of a registered firm:

(a) dealing representative;

(b) advising representative;

(c) associate advising representative;

(d) ultimate designated person;

(e) chief compliance officer.

(2) An individual registered in the category of

(a) dealing representative may act as a dealer or an underwriter in respect of a security that the individual's sponsoring firm is permitted to trade or underwrite,

(b) advising representative may act as an adviser in respect of a security that the individual's sponsoring firm is permitted to advise on,

(c) associate advising representative may act as an adviser in respect of a security that the individual's sponsoring firm is permitted to advise on if the advice has been approved under subsection 4.2(1) [*associate advising representatives — pre-approval of advice*],

(d) ultimate designated person must perform the functions set out in section 5.1 [*responsibilities of the ultimate designated person*], and

(e) chief compliance officer must perform the functions set out in section 5.2 [*responsibilities of the chief compliance officer*].

(3) Subsection (1) does not apply in Ontario.

Note: In Ontario, the same categories of registration for individuals as in subsection 2.1(1) are set out under section 25 of the *Securities Act* (Ontario).

2.2 Client mobility exemption — individuals — (1) The registration requirement does not apply to an individual if all of the following apply:

(a) the individual is registered as a dealing, advising or associate advising representative in the individual's principal jurisdiction;

(b) the individual's sponsoring firm is registered in the firm's principal jurisdiction;

(c) the individual does not act as a dealer, underwriter or adviser in the local jurisdiction other than as he or she is permitted to in his or her principal jurisdiction according to the individual's registration in that jurisdiction;

(d) the individual does not act as a dealer, underwriter or adviser in the local jurisdiction other than for 5 or fewer eligible clients;

(e) the individual complies with Part 13 *Dealing with clients — individuals and firms*

(f) the individual deals fairly, honestly and in good faith in the course of his or her dealings with an eligible client;

(g) before first acting as a dealer or adviser for an eligible client, the individual's sponsoring firm has disclosed to the client that the individual, and if the firm is relying on section 8.30 [*client mobility exemption — firms*], the firm,

(i) is exempt from registration in the local jurisdiction, and

(ii) is not subject to requirements otherwise applicable under local securities legislation.

(2) If an individual relies on the exemption in this section, the individual's sponsoring firm must submit a completed Form 31-103F3 *Use of Mobility Exemption* to the securities regulatory authority of the local jurisdiction as soon as possible after the individual first relies on this section.

2.3 Individuals acting for investment fund managers — The investment fund manager registration requirement does not apply to an individual acting on behalf of a registered investment fund manager.

PART 3 — REGISTRATION REQUIREMENTS — INDIVIDUALS
DIVISION 1 — GENERAL PROFICIENCY REQUIREMENTS

3.1 Definitions — In this Part

"Branch Manager Proficiency Exam" means the examination prepared and administered by the RESP Dealers Association of Canada and so named on the day this Instrument comes into force, and every examination that preceded that examination, or succeeded that examination, that does not have a significantly reduced scope and content when compared to the scope and content of the first-mentioned examination;

"Canadian Investment Funds Course Exam" means the examination prepared and administered by the IFSE Institute and so named on the day this Instrument comes into force, and every examination that preceded that examination, or succeeded that examination, that does not have a significantly reduced scope and content when compared to the scope and content of the first-mentioned examination;

"Canadian Investment Manager designation" means the designation earned through the Canadian investment manager program prepared and administered by CSI Global Education Inc. and so named on the day this Instrument comes into force, and every program that preceded that program, or succeeded that program, that does not have a significantly reduced scope and content when compared to the scope and content of the first-mentioned program;

"Canadian Securities Course Exam" means the examination prepared and administered by CSI Global Education Inc. and so named on the day this Instrument comes into force, and every examination that preceded that examination, or succeeded that examination, that does not have a significantly reduced scope and content when compared to the scope and content of the first-mentioned examination;

"Chief Compliance Officers Qualifying Exam" means the examination prepared and administered by CSI Global Education Inc. and so named on the day this Instrument comes into force, and every examination that preceded that examination, or succeeded that examination, that does not have a significantly reduced scope and content when compared to the scope and content of the first-mentioned examination;

"CFA Charter" means the charter earned through the Chartered Financial Analyst program prepared and administered by the CFA Institute and so named on the day this Instrument comes into force, and every program that preceded that program, or succeeded that program, that does not have a significantly reduced scope and content when compared to the scope and content of the first-mentioned program;

"Exempt Market Products Exam" means the examination prepared and administered by the IFSE Institute and so named on the day this Instrument comes into force, and every examination that preceded that examination, or succeeded that examination, that does not have a significantly reduced scope and content when compared to the scope and content of the first-mentioned examination;

"Investment Funds in Canada Course Exam" means the examination prepared and administered by CSI Global Education Inc. and so named on the day this Instrument comes into force, and every examination that preceded that examination, or succeeded that examination, that does not have a significantly reduced scope and content when compared to the scope and content of the first-mentioned examination;

"Mutual Fund Dealers Compliance Exam" means the examination prepared and administered by the IFSE Institute and so named on the day this Instrument comes into force, and every examination that preceded that examination, or succeeded that examination, that does not have a significantly reduced scope and content when compared to the scope and content of the first-mentioned examination;

"New Entrants Course Exam" means the examination prepared and administered by CSI Global Education Inc. and so named on the day this Instrument comes into force, and every examination that preceded that examination, or succeeded that examination, that does not have a significantly reduced scope and content when compared to the scope and content of the first-mentioned examination;

"PDO Exam" means

(a) the Officers', Partners' and Directors' Exam prepared and administered by the IFSE Institute and so named on the day this Instrument comes into force, and every examination that preceded that examination, or succeeded that examination, that does not have a significantly reduced scope and content when compared to the scope and content of the first-mentioned examination, or

(b) the Partners, Directors and Senior Officers Course Exam prepared and administered by CSI Global Education Inc. and so named on the day this Instrument comes into force, and every examination that preceded that examination, or succeeded that examination, that does not have a significantly reduced scope and content when compared to the scope and content of the first-mentioned examination;

"Sales Representative Proficiency Exam" means the examination prepared and administered by the RESP Dealers Association of Canada and so named on the day this Instrument comes into force, and every examination that preceded that examination, or succeeded that examination, that does not have a significantly reduced scope and content when compared to the scope and content of the first-mentioned examination;

"Series 7 Exam" means the examination prepared and administered by the Financial Industry Regulatory Authority in the United States of America and so named on the day this Instrument comes into force, and every examination that preceded that examination, or succeeded that examination, that does not have a significantly reduced scope and content when compared to the scope and content of the first-mentioned examination.

3.2 U.S. equivalency — In this Part, an individual is not required to have passed the Canadian Securities Course Exam if the individual has passed the Series 7 Exam and the New Entrants Course Exam.

3.3 Time limits on examination requirements — (1) For the purpose of this Part, an individual is deemed to have not passed an examination unless the individual passed the examination not more than 36 months before the date of his or her application for registration.

(2) Subsection (1) does not apply if the individual passed the examination more than 36 months before the date of his or her application and has met one of the following conditions:

(a) the individual was registered in the same category in any jurisdiction of Canada at any time during the 36-month period before the date of his or her application;

(b) the individual has gained 12 months of relevant securities industry experience during the 36-month period before the date of his or her application.

(3) For the purpose of paragraph (2)(a), an individual is not considered to have been registered during any period in which the individual's registration was suspended.

(4) Subsection (1) does not apply to the examination requirements in

(a) section 3.7 [*scholarship plan dealer — dealing representative*] if the individual was registered in a jurisdiction of Canada as a dealing representative of a scholarship plan dealer on and since September 28, 2009, and

(b) section 3.9 [*exempt market dealer — dealing representative*] if the individual was registered as a dealing representative of an exempt market dealer in Ontario or Newfoundland and Labrador on and since September 28, 2009.

DIVISION 2 — EDUCATION AND EXPERIENCE REQUIREMENTS

3.4 Proficiency — initial and ongoing — (1) An individual must not perform an activity that requires registration unless the individual has the education, training and experience that a reasonable person would consider necessary to perform the activity competently, including understanding the structure, features and risks of each security the individual recommends.

(2) A chief compliance officer must not perform an activity set out in section 5.2 [*responsibilities of the chief compliance officer*] unless the individual has the education, training and experience that a reasonable person would consider necessary to perform the activity competently.

3.5 Proficiency — initial and ongoing — A dealing representative of a mutual fund dealer must not act as a dealer in respect of the securities listed in paragraph 7.1(2)(b) unless any of the following apply:

(a) the individual has passed the Canadian Investment Funds Course Exam, the Canadian Securities Course Exam or the Investment Funds in Canada Course Exam;

(b) the individual has met the requirements of section 3.11 [*portfolio manager* — advising representative];

(c) the individual has earned a CFA Charter and has gained 12 months of relevant securities industry experience in the 36-month period before applying for registration;

(d) the individual is exempt from section 3.11 [*portfolio manager — advising representative*] because of subsection 16.10(1) [*proficiency for dealing and advising representatives*].

3.6 Mutual fund dealer — chief compliance officer — A mutual fund dealer must not designate an individual as its chief compliance officer under subsection 11.3(1) [*designating a chief compliance officer*] unless any of the following apply:

(a) the individual has

(i) passed the Canadian Investment Funds Course Exam, the Canadian Securities Course Exam or the Investment Funds in Canada Course Exam,

(ii) passed the PDO Exam, the Mutual Fund Dealers Compliance Exam or the Chief Compliance Officers Qualifying Exam, and

(iii) gained 12 months of relevant securities industry experience in the 36-month period before applying for registration;

(b) the individual has met the requirements of section 3.13 [*portfolio manager — chief compliance officer*].

(c) section 3.13 [*portfolio manager — chief compliance officer*] does not apply in respect of the individual because of subsection 16.9(2) [*registration of chief compliance officers*].

3.7 Scholarship plan dealer — dealing representative — A dealing representative of a scholarship plan dealer must not act as a dealer in respect of the securities listed in paragraph 7.1(2)(c) unless the individual has passed the Sales Representative Proficiency Exam.

3.8 Scholarship plan dealer — chief compliance officer — A scholarship plan dealer must not designate an individual as its chief compliance officer under subsection 11.3(1) [*designating a chief compliance officer*] unless the individual has

(a) passed the Sales Representative Proficiency Exam,

(b) passed the Branch Manager Proficiency Exam,

(c) passed the PDO Exam or the Chief Compliance Officers Qualifying Exam, and

(d) gained 12 months of relevant securities industry experience in the 36-month period before applying for registration.

3.9 Exempt market dealer — dealing representative — A dealing representative of an exempt market dealer must not perform an activity listed in paragraph 7.1(2)(d) unless any of the following apply:

(a) the individual has passed the Canadian Securities Course Exam;

(b) the individual has passed the Exempt Market Products Exam;

Part 3:
REGISTRATION

(c) the individual has earned a CFA Charter and has gained 12 months of relevant securities industry experience in the 36-month period before applying for registration;

(d) the individual satisfies the conditions set out in section 3.11 [*portfolio manager — advising representative*];

(e) the individual is exempt from section 3.11 [*portfolio manager — advising representative*] because of subsection 16.10(1) [*proficiency for dealing and advising representatives*].

3.10 Exempt market dealer — chief compliance officer — An exempt market dealer must not designate an individual as its chief compliance officer under subsection 11.3(1) [*designating a chief compliance officer*] unless any of the following apply:

    (a) the individual has

        (i) passed the Exempt Market Products Exam or the Canadian Securities Course Exam,

        (ii) passed the PDO Exam or the Chief Compliance Officers Qualifying Exam, and

        (iii) gained 12 months of relevant securities industry experience in the 36-month period before applying for registration;

    (b) the individual has met the requirements of section 3.13 [*portfolio manager — chief compliance officer*];

    (c) section 3.13 [*portfolio manager — chief compliance officer*] does not apply in respect of the individual because of subsection 16.9(2) [*registration of chief compliance officers*].

3.11 Portfolio manager — advising representative — An advising representative of a portfolio manager must not act as an adviser on behalf of the portfolio manager unless any of the following apply:

    (a) the individual has earned a CFA Charter and has gained 12 months of relevant investment management experience in the 36-month period before applying for registration;

    (b) the individual has received the Canadian Investment Manager designation and has gained 48 months of relevant investment management experience, 12 months of which was gained in the 36-month period before applying for registration.

3.12 Portfolio manager — associate advising representative — An associate advising representative of a portfolio manager must not act as an adviser on behalf of the portfolio manager unless any of the following apply:

    (a) the individual has completed Level 1 of the Chartered Financial Analyst program and has gained 24 months of relevant investment management experience;

    (b) the individual has received the Canadian Investment Manager designation and has gained 24 months of relevant investment management experience.

3.13 Portfolio manager — chief compliance officer — A portfolio manager must not designate an individual as its chief compliance officer under subsection 11.3(1) [*designating a chief compliance officer*] unless any of the following apply:

    (a) the individual has

        (i) earned a CFA Charter or a professional designation as a lawyer, Chartered Accountant, Certified General Accountant or Certified Management Accountant in a jurisdiction of Canada, a notary in Québec, or the equivalent in a foreign jurisdiction,

        (ii) passed the PDO Exam or the Chief Compliance Officers Qualifying Exam and, unless the individual has earned the CFA Charter, the Canadian Securities Course Exam, and;

        (iii) either

            A) gained 36 months of relevant securities experience while working at an investment dealer, a registered adviser or an investment fund manager, or

            B) provided professional services in the securities industry for 36 months and also worked at a registered dealer, a registered adviser or an investment fund manager for 12 months;

    (b) the individual has passed the Canadian Securities Course Exam and either the PDO Exam or the Chief Compliance Officers Qualifying Exam and any of the following apply:

        (i) the individual has worked at an investment dealer or a registered adviser for 5 years, including for 36 months in a compliance capacity;

        (ii) the individual has worked for 5 years at a Canadian financial institution in a compliance capacity relating to portfolio management and also worked at a registered dealer or a registered adviser for 12 months;

    (c) the individual has passed either the PDO Exam or the Chief Compliance Officers Qualifying Exam and has met the requirements of section 3.11 [*portfolio manager — advising representative*].

3.14 Investment fund manager — chief compliance officer — An investment fund manager must not designate an individual as its chief compliance officer under subsection 11.3(1) [*designating a chief compliance officer*] unless any of the following apply:

    (a) the individual has

        (i) earned a CFA Charter or a professional designation as a lawyer, Chartered Accountant, Certified General Accountant or Certified Management Accountant in a jurisdiction of Canada, a notary in Québec, or the equivalent in a foreign jurisdiction,

        (ii) passed the PDO Exam or the Chief Compliance Officers Qualifying Exam and, unless the individual has earned the CFA Charter, the Canadian Securities Course Exam, and,

        (iii) either

            A) gained 36 months of relevant securities experience while working at a registered dealer, a registered adviser or an investment fund manager, or

            B) provided professional services in the securities industry for 36 months and also worked in a relevant capacity at an investment fund manager for 12 months;

(b) the individual has

(i) passed the Canadian Investment Funds Course Exam, the Canadian Securities Course Exam, or the Investment Funds in Canada Course Exam,

(ii) passed the PDO Exam or the Chief Compliance Officers Qualifying Exam, and

(iii) gained 5 years of relevant securities experience while working at a registered dealer, registered adviser or an investment fund manager, including 36 months in a compliance capacity.

(c) the individual has met the requirements of section 3.13 [*portfolio manager — chief compliance officer*].

(d) section 3.13 [*portfolio manager — chief compliance officer*] does not apply in respect of the individual because of subsection 16.9(2) [*registration of chief compliance officers*].

DIVISION 3 — MEMBERSHIP IN A SELF-REGULATORY ORGANIZATION

3.15 Who must be approved by an SRO before registration — (1) A dealing representative of an investment dealer that is a member of IIROC must be an "approved person" as defined under the rules of IIROC.

(2) Except in Québec, a dealing representative of a mutual fund dealer that is a member of the MFDA must be an "approved person" as defined under the rules of the MFDA.

3.16 Exemptions from certain requirements for SRO-approved persons — (1) The following sections do not apply to a registered individual who is a dealing representative of a member of IIROC:

(a) subsection 13.2(3) [*know your client*];

(b) section 13.3 [*suitability*];

(c) section 13.13 [*disclosure when recommending the use of borrowed money*].

(1.1) Subsection (1) only applies to a registered individual who is a dealing representative of a member of IIROC in respect of a requirement specified in any of paragraphs (1)(a) to (c) if the registered individual complies with the corresponding IIROC provisions that are in effect.

(2) The following sections do not apply to a registered individual who is a dealing representative of a member of the MFDA:

(a) section 13.3 [*suitability*];

(b) section 13.13 [*disclosure when recommending the use of borrowed money*].

(2.1) Subsection (2) only applies to a registered individual who is a dealing representative of a member of the MFDA in respect of a requirement specified in paragraph (2)(a) or (b) if the registered individual complies with the corresponding MFDA provisions that are in effect.

(3) In Québec, the requirements listed in subsection (2) do not apply to a registered individual who is a dealing representative of a mutual fund dealer to the extent equivalent requirements to those listed in subsection (2) are applicable to the registered individual under the regulations in Québec.

PART 4 — RESTRICTIONS ON REGISTERED INDIVIDUALS

4.1 Restriction on acting for another registered firm — (1) A firm registered in any jurisdiction of Canada must not permit an individual to act as a dealing, advising or associate advising representative of the registered firm if either of the following apply:

(a) the individual acts as an officer, partner or director of another firm registered in any jurisdiction of Canada that is not an affiliate of the first-mentioned registered firm;

(b) the individual is registered as a dealing, advising or associate advising representative of another firm registered in any jurisdiction of Canada.

(2) Paragraph (1)(b) does not apply in respect of a representative whose registration as a dealing, advising or associate advising representative of more than one registered firm was granted before July 11, 2011.

4.2 Associate advising representatives — pre-approval of advice — (1) An associate advising representative of a registered adviser must not advise on securities unless, before giving the advice, the advice has been approved by an individual designated by the registered firm under subsection (2).

(2) A registered adviser must designate, for an associate advising representative, an advising representative to review the advice of the associate advising representative.

(3) No later than 7 days following the date of a designation under subsection (2), a registered adviser must provide the regulator or, in Québec, the securities regulatory authority with the names of the advising representative and the associate advising representative who are the subject of the designation.

PART 5 — ULTIMATE DESIGNATED PERSON AND CHIEF COMPLIANCE OFFICER

5.1 Responsibilities of the ultimate designated person — The ultimate designated person of a registered firm must do all of the following:

(a) supervise the activities of the firm that are directed towards ensuring compliance with securities legislation by the firm and each individual acting on the firm's behalf;

(b) promote compliance by the firm, and individuals acting on its behalf, with securities legislation.

5.2 Responsibilities of the chief compliance officer — The chief compliance officer of a registered firm must do all of the following:

(a) establish and maintain policies and procedures for assessing compliance by the firm, and individuals acting on its behalf, with securities legislation;

(b) monitor and assess compliance by the firm, and individuals acting on its behalf, with securities legislation;

(c) report to the ultimate designated person of the firm as soon as possible if the chief compliance officer becomes aware of any circumstances indicating that the firm, or any individual acting on its behalf, may be in non-compliance with securities legislation and any of the following apply:

(i) the non-compliance creates, in the opinion of a reasonable person, a risk of harm to a client;

(ii) the non-compliance creates, in the opinion of a reasonable person, a risk of harm to the capital markets;

(iii) the non-compliance is part of a pattern of non-compliance;

(d) submit an annual report to the firm's board of directors, or individuals acting in a similar capacity for the firm, for the purpose of assessing compliance by the firm, and individuals acting on its behalf, with securities legislation.

PART 6 — SUSPENSION AND REVOCATION OF REGISTRATION — INDIVIDUALS

6.1 If individual ceases to have authority to act for firm — If a registered individual ceases to have authority to act as a registered individual on behalf of his or her sponsoring firm because of the end of, or a change in, the individual's employment, partnership, or agency relationship with the firm, the individual's registration with the firm is suspended until reinstated or revoked under securities legislation.

6.2 If IIROC approval is revoked or suspended — If IIROC revokes or suspends a registered individual's approval in respect of an investment dealer, the individual's registration as a dealing representative of the investment dealer is suspended until reinstated or revoked under securities legislation.

6.3 If MFDA approval is revoked or suspended — Except in Québec, if the MFDA revokes or suspends a registered individual's approval in respect of a mutual fund dealer, the individual's registration as a dealing representative of the mutual fund dealer is suspended until reinstated or revoked under securities legislation.

6.4 If sponsoring firm is suspended — If a registered firm's registration in a category is suspended, the registration of each registered dealing, advising or associate advising representative acting on behalf of the firm in that category is suspended until reinstated or revoked under securities legislation.

6.5 Dealing and advising activities suspended — If an individual's registration in a category is suspended, the individual must not act as a dealer, an underwriter or an adviser, as the case may be, under that category.

6.6 Revocation of a suspended registration — individual — If a registration of an individual has been suspended under this Part and it has not been reinstated, the registration is revoked on the 2nd anniversary of the suspension.

6.7 Exception for individuals involved in a hearing or proceeding — Despite section 6.6, if a hearing or proceeding concerning a suspended individual is commenced under securities legislation or under the rules of an SRO, the individual's registration remains suspended.

6.8 Application of Part 6 in Ontario — Other than section 6.5 [*dealing and advising activities suspended*], this Part does not apply in Ontario.

Note: In Ontario, measures governing suspension in section 29 of the *Securities Act* (Ontario) are similar to those in Parts 6 and 10.

PART 7 — CATEGORIES OF REGISTRATION FOR FIRMS

7.1 Dealer categories — (1) The following are the categories of registration for a person or company that is required, under securities legislation, to be registered as a dealer:

(a) investment dealer;

(b) mutual fund dealer;

(c) scholarship plan dealer;

(d) exempt market dealer;

(e) restricted dealer.

(2) A person or company registered in the category of

(a) investment dealer may act as a dealer or an underwriter in respect of any security,

(b) mutual fund dealer may act as a dealer in respect of any security of

(i) a mutual fund, or

(ii) an investment fund that is a labour-sponsored investment fund corporation or labour-sponsored venture capital corporation under legislation of a jurisdiction of Canada,

(c) scholarship plan dealer may act as a dealer in respect of a security of a scholarship plan, an educational plan or an educational trust,

(d) exempt market dealer may

(i) act as a dealer by trading a security that is distributed under an exemption from the prospectus requirement, whether or not a prospectus was filed in respect of the distribution,

(ii) subject to subsection (5), act as a dealer by trading a security that, if the trade were a distribution, would be exempt from the prospectus requirement, or

(iii) [Repealed.]

(iv) act as an underwriter in respect of a distribution of securities that is made under an exemption from the prospectus requirement;

(e) restricted dealer may act as a dealer or an underwriter in accordance with the terms, conditions, restrictions or requirements applied to its registration.

(3) [repealed]

(4) Subsection (1) does not apply in Ontario.

(5) An exempt market dealer must not trade a security if

(a) the security is listed, quoted or traded on a marketplace, and

(b) the trade in the security does not require reliance on a further exemption from the prospectus requirement.

Note: In Ontario, the same categories of registration for firms acting as dealers as in subsection 7.1(1) are set out under subsection 26(2) of the *Securities Act* (Ontario).

7.2 Adviser categories — (1) The following are the categories of registration for a person or company that is required, under securities legislation, to be registered as an adviser:

    (a) portfolio manager;

    (b) restricted portfolio manager.

(2) A person or company registered in the category of

    (a) portfolio manager may act as an adviser in respect of any security, and

    (b) restricted portfolio manager may act as an adviser in respect of any security in accordance with the terms, conditions, restrictions or requirements applied to its registration.

(3) Subsection (1) does not apply in Ontario.

Note: In Ontario, the same categories of registration for firms acting as advisers as in subsection 7.2(1) are set out under subsection 26(6) of the *Securities Act* (Ontario).

7.3 Investment fund manager category — The category of registration for a person or company that is required, under securities legislation, to be registered as an investment fund manager is "investment fund manager".

PART 8 — EXEMPTIONS FROM THE REQUIREMENT TO REGISTER

DIVISION 1 — EXEMPTIONS FROM DEALER AND UNDERWRITER REGISTRATION

8.0.1 General condition to dealer registration requirement exemptions — The exemptions in this Division are not available to a person or company if the person or company is registered in the local jurisdiction and if their category of registration permits the person or company to act as a dealer or trade in a security for which the exemption is provided.

8.1 Interpretation of "trade" in Québec — In this Part, in Québec, "trade" refers to any of the following activities:

    (a) the activities described in the definition of "dealer" in section 5 of the *Securities Act* (R.S.Q., c. V-1.1), including the following activities:

        (i) the sale or disposition of a security by onerous title, whether the terms of payment are on margin, installment or otherwise, but does not include a transfer or the giving in guarantee of securities in connection with a debt or the purchase of a security, except as provided in paragraph (b);

        (ii) participation as a trader in any transaction in a security through the facilities of an exchange or a quotation and trade reporting system;

        (iii) the receipt by a registrant of an order to buy or sell a security;

    (b) a transfer or the giving in guarantee of securities of an issuer from the holdings of a control person in connection with a debt.

8.2 Definition of "securities" in Alberta, British Columbia, New Brunswick and Saskatchewan — Despite section 1.2, in Alberta, British Columbia, New Brunswick and Saskatchewan, a reference to "securities" in this Division excludes "exchange contracts".

8.3 Interpretation — exemption from underwriter registration requirement — In this Division, an exemption from the dealer registration requirement is an exemption from the underwriter registration requirement.

8.4 Person or company not in the business of trading in British Columbia, Manitoba and New Brunswick — (1) In British Columbia and New Brunswick, a person or company is exempt from the dealer registration requirement if the person or company

    (a) is not engaged in the business of trading in securities or exchange contracts as a principal or agent, and

    (b) does not hold himself, herself or itself out as engaging in the business of trading in securities or exchange contracts as a principal or agent.

(2) In Manitoba, a person or company is exempt from the dealer registration requirement if the person or company

    (a) is not engaged in the business of trading in securities as a principal or agent, and

    (b) does not hold himself, herself or itself out as engaging in the business of trading in securities as a principal or agent.

8.5 Trades through or to a registered dealer — The dealer registration requirement does not apply to a person or company in respect of a trade in a security if either of the following applies:

    (a) trade is made through a registered dealer, if the dealer is registered in a category that permits the trade unless, in furtherance of the trade, the person or company seeking the exemption solicits or contacts directly any purchaser or prospective purchaser in relation to the trade;

    (b) the trade is made to a registered dealer who is purchasing as principal, if the dealer is registered in a category that permits the trade.

8.5.1 Trades through a registered dealer by registered adviser — The dealer registration requirement does not apply to a registered adviser, or an advising representative or associate advising representative acting on behalf of the registered adviser, in respect of trading activities that are incidental to its providing advice to a client, if the trade is made through a dealer registered in a category that permits the trade or a dealer operating under an exemption from the dealer registration requirement.

8.6 Investment fund trades by adviser to managed account — (1) The dealer registration requirement does not apply to a registered adviser, or an adviser that is exempt from registration under section 8.26 [*international adviser*], in respect of a trade in a security of an investment fund if both of the following apply:

    (a) the adviser acts as the fund's adviser and investment fund manager;

    (b) the trade is to a managed account of a client of the adviser.

(2) The exemption in subsection (1) is not available if the managed account or investment fund was created or is used primarily for the purpose of qualifying for the exemption.

(3) An adviser that relies on subsection (1) must provide written notice to the regulator or, in Québec, the securities regulatory authority that it is relying on the exemption within 10 days of its first use of the exemption.

8.7 Investment fund reinvestment — (1) Subject to subsections (2), (3), (4) and (5), the dealer registration requirement does not apply to an investment fund, or the investment fund manager of the fund, in respect of a trade in a security with a security holder of the investment fund if the trade is permitted by a plan of the investment fund and is in a security of the investment fund's own issue and if any of the following apply:

(a) a dividend or distribution out of earnings, surplus, capital or other sources payable in respect of the investment fund's securities is applied to the purchase of the security that is of the same class or series as the securities to which the dividends or distributions are attributable;

(b) the security holder makes an optional cash payment to purchase the security of the investment fund and both of the following apply:

(i) the security is of the same class or series of securities described in paragraph (a) that trade on a marketplace;

(ii) the aggregate number of securities issued under the optional cash payment does not exceed, in the financial year of the investment fund during which the trade takes place, 2 per cent of the issued and outstanding securities of the class to which the plan relates as at the beginning of the financial year.

(2) The exemption in subsection (1) is not available unless the plan that permits the trade is available to every security holder in Canada to which the dividend or distribution is available.

(3) The exemption in subsection (1) is not available if a sales charge is payable on a trade described in the subsection.

(4) At the time of the trade, if the investment fund is a reporting issuer and in continuous distribution, the investment fund must have set out in the prospectus under which the distribution is made

(a) details of any deferred or contingent sales charge or redemption fee that is payable at the time of the redemption of the security, and

(b) any right that the security holder has to elect to receive cash instead of securities on the payment of a dividend or making of a distribution by the investment fund and instructions on how the right can be exercised.

(5) At the time of the trade, if the investment fund is a reporting issuer and is not in continuous distribution, the investment fund must provide the information required by subsection (4) in its prospectus, annual information form or a material change report.

8.8 Additional investment in investment funds — The dealer registration requirement does not apply to an investment fund, or the investment fund manager of the fund, in respect of a trade in a security of the investment fund's own issue with a security holder of the investment fund if all of the following apply:

(a) the security holder initially acquired securities of the investment fund as principal for an acquisition cost of not less than $150,000 paid in cash at the time of the acquisition;

(b) the trade is in respect of a security of the same class or series as the securities initially acquired, as described in paragraph (a);

(c) the security holder, as at the date of the trade, holds securities of the investment fund and one or both of the following apply:

(i) the acquisition cost of the securities being held was not less than $150,000;

(ii) the net asset value of the securities being held is not less than $150,000.

8.9 Additional investment in investment funds if initial purchase before September 14, 2005 — The dealer registration requirement does not apply in respect of a trade by an investment fund in a security of its own issue to a purchaser that initially acquired a security of the same class as principal before September 14, 2005 if all of the following apply:

(a) the security was initially acquired under any of the following provisions:

(i) in Alberta, section 86(e) and paragraph 131(1)(d) of the *Securities Act* (Alberta) as they existed prior to their repeal by sections 9(a) and 13 of the *Securities Amendment Act* (Alberta), 2003 SA c.32 and sections 66.2 and 122.2 of the *Alberta Securities Commission Rules* (General);

(ii) in British Columbia, sections 45(2) (5) and (22), and 74(2) (4) and (19) of the *Securities Act* (British Columbia);

(iii) in Manitoba, section 19(3) and paragraph 58(1)(a) of the *Securities Act* (Manitoba) and section 90 of the *Securities Regulation* MR 491/88R;

(iv) in New Brunswick, section 2.8 of Local Rule 45-501 *Prospectus and Registration Exemptions*;

(v) in Newfoundland and Labrador, section 36(1)(e) and paragraph 73(1)(d) of the *Securities Act* (Newfoundland and Labrador);

(vi) in Nova Scotia, paragraphs 41(1)(e) and 77(1)(d) of the *Securities Act* (Nova Scotia);

(vii) in Northwest Territories, sections 3(c) and (z) of Blanket Order No. 1;

(viii) in Nunavut, sections 3(c) and (z) of Blanket Order No. 1;

(ix) in Ontario, section 35(1)5 and paragraph 72(1)(d) of the *Securities Act* (Ontario) as they existed prior to their repeal by sections 5 and 11 of the *Securities Act* (Ontario) S.O. 2009, c. 18, Sch. 26 and section 2.12 of Ontario Securities Commission Rule 45-501 *Exempt Distributions* that came into force on January 12, 2004;

(x) in Prince Edward Island, paragraph 2(3)(d) of the former *Securities Act* (Prince Edward Island) and Prince Edward Island Local Rule 45-512 Exempt Distributions — *Exemption for Purchase of Mutual Fund Securities*;

(xi) in Québec, former section 51 and subsection 155.1(2) of the *Securities Act* (Québec);

(xii) in Saskatchewan, paragraphs 39(1)(e) and 81(1)(d) of *The Securities Act, 1988* (Saskatchewan);

(b) the trade is for a security of the same class or series as the initial trade;

(c) the security holder, as at the date of the trade, holds securities of the investment fund that have one or both of the following characteristics:

(i) an acquisition cost of not less than the minimum amount prescribed by securities legislation referred to in paragraph (a) under which the initial trade was conducted;

(ii) a net asset value of not less than the minimum amount prescribed by securities legislation referred to in paragraph (a) under which the initial trade was conducted.

8.10 **Private investment club** — The dealer registration requirement does not apply in respect of a trade in a security of an investment fund if all of the following apply:

(a) the fund has no more than 50 beneficial security holders;

(b) the fund does not seek and has never sought to borrow money from the public;

(c) the fund does not distribute and has never distributed its securities to the public;

(d) the fund does not pay or give any remuneration for investment management or administration advice in respect of trades in securities, except normal brokerage fees;

(e) the fund, for the purpose of financing its operations, requires security holders to make contributions in proportion to the value of the securities held by them.

8.11 **Private investment fund — loan and trust pools** — (1) The dealer registration requirement does not apply in respect of a trade in a security of an investment fund if all of the following apply:

(a) the fund is administered by a trust company or trust corporation that is registered or authorized by an enactment of Canada or a jurisdiction of Canada to carry on business in Canada or a jurisdiction of Canada;

(b) the fund has no promoter or investment fund manager other than the trust company or trust corporation referred to in paragraph (a);

(c) the fund commingles the money of different estates and trusts for the purpose of facilitating investment.

(2) Despite subsection (1), a trust company or trust corporation registered under the laws of Prince Edward Island that is not registered under the *Trust and Loan Companies Act* (Canada) or under comparable legislation in another jurisdiction of Canada is not a trust company or trust corporation for the purpose of paragraph (1)(a).

8.12 **Mortgages** — (1) In this section, "syndicated mortgage" means a mortgage in which two or more persons or companies participate, directly or indirectly, as lenders in the debt obligation that is secured by the mortgage.

(2) Subject to subsection (3), the dealer registration requirement does not apply in respect of a trade in a mortgage on real property in a jurisdiction of Canada by a person or company who is registered or licensed, or exempted from registration or licensing, under mortgage brokerage or mortgage dealer legislation of that jurisdiction.

(3) In Alberta, British Columbia, Manitoba, Québec and Saskatchewan, subsection (2) does not apply in respect of a trade in a syndicated mortgage.

(4) This section does not apply in Ontario.

Note: In Ontario a similar exemption from the dealer registration requirement is provided under subsection 35(4) of the *Securities Act* (Ontario).

8.13 **Personal property security legislation** — (1) The dealer registration requirement does not apply in respect of a trade to a person or company, other than an individual in a security evidencing indebtedness secured by or under a security agreement, secured in accordance with personal property security legislation of a jurisdiction of Canada that provides for the granting of security in personal property.

(2) This section does not apply in Ontario.

Note: In Ontario a similar exemption from the dealer registration requirement is provided under subsection 35(2) of the *Securities Act* (Ontario).

8.14 **Variable insurance contract** — (1) In this section

"contract", "group insurance", "insurance company", "life insurance" and "policy" have the respective meanings assigned to them in the legislation referenced opposite the name of the local jurisdiction in Appendix A of National Instrument 45-106 *Prospectus and Registration Exemptions*;

"variable insurance contract" means a contract of life insurance under which the interest of the purchaser is valued for purposes of conversion or surrender by reference to the value of a proportionate interest in a specified portfolio of assets.

(2) The dealer registration requirement does not apply in respect of a trade in a variable insurance contract by an insurance company if the variable insurance contract is

(a) a contract of group insurance,

(b) a whole life insurance contract providing for the payment at maturity of an amount not less than 75% of the premium paid up to age 75 years for a benefit payable at maturity,

(c) an arrangement for the investment of policy dividends and policy proceeds in a separate and distinct fund to which contributions are made only from policy dividends and policy proceeds, or

(d) a variable life annuity.

8.15 **Schedule III banks and cooperative associations — evidence of deposit** — (1) The dealer registration requirement does not apply in respect of a trade in an evidence of deposit issued by a Schedule III bank or an association governed by the *Cooperative Credit Associations Act* (Canada).

(2) This section does not apply in Ontario or Alberta.

Note: In Ontario, subsection 8.15(1) is not required because the security described in the exemption is excluded from the definition of "security" in subsection 1(1) of the *Securities Act* (Ontario).

8.16 **Plan administrator** — (1) In this section

"consultant" has the same meaning as in section 2.22 of National Instrument 45-106 *Prospectus and Registration Exemptions*;

"executive officer" has the same meaning as in section 1.1 of National Instrument 45-106 *Prospectus and Registration Exemptions*;

"permitted assign" has the same meaning as in section 2.22 of National Instrument 45-106 *Prospectus and Registration Exemptions*;

"plan" means a plan or program established or maintained by an issuer providing for the acquisition of securities of the issuer by employees, executive officers, directors or consultants of the issuer or of a related entity of the issuer;

Part 3: REGISTRATION

"plan administrator" means a trustee, custodian, or administrator, acting on behalf of, or for the benefit of, employees, executive officers, directors or consultants of an issuer or of a related entity of an issuer;

"related entity" has the same meaning as in section 2.22 of National Instrument 45-106 *Prospectus and Registration Exemptions.*

(2) The dealer registration requirement does not apply in respect of a trade made pursuant to a plan of the issuer in a security of an issuer, or an option to acquire a security of the issuer, made by the issuer, a control person of the issuer, a related entity of the issuer, or a plan administrator of the issuer with any of the following:

> (a) the issuer;

> (b) a current or former employee, executive officer, director or consultant of the issuer or a related entity of the issuer;

> (c) a permitted assign of a person or company referred to in paragraph (b).

(3) The dealer registration requirement does not apply in respect of a trade in a security of an issuer, or an option to acquire a security of the issuer, made by a plan administrator of the issuer if

> (a) the trade is pursuant to a plan of the issuer, and

> (b) the conditions in section 2.14 of National Instrument 45-102 *Resale of Securities* are satisfied.

8.17 Reinvestment plan — (1) Subject to subsections (3), (4) and (5), the dealer registration requirement does not apply in respect of the following trades by an issuer, or by a trustee, custodian or administrator acting for or on behalf of the issuer, to a security holder of the issuer if the trades are permitted by a plan of the issuer:

> (a) a trade in a security of the issuer's own issue if a dividend or distribution out of earnings, surplus, capital or other sources payable in respect of the issuer's securities is applied to the purchase of the security;

> (b) subject to subsection (2), a trade in a security of the issuer's own issue if the security holder makes an optional cash payment to purchase the security of the issuer that trades on a marketplace.

(2) The aggregate number of securities issued under the optional cash payment referred to in paragraph (1)(b) must not exceed, in any financial year of the issuer during which the trade takes place, 2% of the issued and outstanding securities of the class to which the plan relates as at the beginning of the financial year.

(3) A plan that permits the trades described in subsection (1) must be available to every security holder in Canada to which the dividend or distribution out of earnings, surplus, capital or other sources is available.

(4) This section is not available in respect of a trade in a security of an investment fund.

(5) Subject to section 8.4 [*transition — reinvestment plan*] of National Instrument 45-106 *Prospectus and Registration Exemptions*, if the security traded under a plan described in subsection (1) is of a different class or series than the class or series of the security to which the dividend or distribution is attributable, the issuer or the trustee, custodian or administrator must have provided to each participant that is eligible to receive a security under the plan either a description of the material attributes and characteristics of the security traded under the plan or notice of a source from which the participant can obtain the information without charge.

8.18 International dealer — (1) In this section

"foreign security" means

> (a) a security issued by an issuer incorporated, formed or created under the laws of a foreign jurisdiction, or

> (b) a security issued by a government of a foreign jurisdiction.

(2) Subject to subsections (3) and (4), the dealer registration requirement does not apply in respect of any of the following:

> (a) an activity, other than a sale of a security, that is reasonably necessary to facilitate a distribution of securities that are offered primarily in a foreign jurisdiction;

> (b) a trade in a debt security with a permitted client during the security's distribution, if the debt security is offered primarily in a foreign jurisdiction and a prospectus has not been filed with a Canadian securities regulatory authority for the distribution;

> (c) a trade in a debt security that is a foreign security with a permitted client, other than during the security's distribution;

> (d) a trade in a foreign security with a permitted client, unless the trade is made during the security's distribution under a prospectus that has been filed with a Canadian securities regulatory authority;

> (e) a trade in a foreign security with an investment dealer;

> (f) a trade in any security with an investment dealer that is purchasing as principal.

(3) The exemption under subsection (2) is not available to a person or company unless all of the following apply:

> (a) the head office or principal place of business of the person or company is in a foreign jurisdiction;

> (b) the person or company is registered under the securities legislation of the foreign jurisdiction in which its head office or principal place of business is located in a category of registration that permits it to carry on the activities in that jurisdiction that registration as a dealer would permit it to carry on in the local jurisdiction;

> (c) the person or company engages in the business of a dealer in the foreign jurisdiction in which its head office or principal place of business is located;

> (d) the person or company is trading as principal or agent for

>> (i) the issuer of the securities

>> (ii) a permitted client, or

>> (iii) a person or company that is not a resident of Canada;

> (e) the person or company has submitted to the securities regulatory authority a completed Form 31-103F2 *Submission to Jurisdiction and Appointment of Agent for Service.*

(4) The exemption under subsection (2) is not available to a person or company in respect of a trade with a permitted client unless one of the following applies:

(a) the permitted client is a person or company registered under the securities legislation of a jurisdiction of Canada as an adviser or dealer;

(b) the person or company has notified the permitted client of all of the following:

(i) the person or company is not registered in the local jurisdiction to make the trade;

(ii) the foreign jurisdiction in which the head office or principal place of business of the person or company is located;

(iii) all or substantially all of the assets of the person or company may be situated outside of Canada;

(iv) there may be difficulty enforcing legal rights against the person or company because of the above;

(v) the name and address of the agent for service of process of the person or company in the local jurisdiction.

(5) A person or company that relied on the exemption in subsection (2) during the 12-month period preceding December 1 of a year must notify the regulator or, in Québec, the securities regulatory authority of that fact by December 1 of that year.

(6) In Ontario, subsection (5) does not apply to a person or company that complies with the filing and fee payment requirements applicable to an unregistered exempt international firm under Ontario Securities Commission Rule 13-502 Fees.

(7) The adviser registration requirement does not apply to a person or company that is exempt from the dealer registration requirement under this section if the person or company provides advice to a client and the advice is

(a) in connection with an activity or trade described under subsection (2), and

(b) not in respect of a managed account of the client.

8.19 Self-directed registered education savings plan — (1) In this section

"self-directed RESP" means an educational savings plan registered under the *Income Tax Act* (Canada)

(a) that is structured so that contributions by a subscriber to the plan are deposited directly into an account in the name of the subscriber, and

(b) under which the subscriber maintains control and direction over the plan that enables the subscriber to direct how the assets of the plan are to be held, invested or reinvested subject to compliance with the *Income Tax Act* (Canada).

(2) The dealer registration requirement does not apply in respect of a trade in a self-directed RESP to a subscriber if both of the following apply:

(a) the trade is made by any of the following:

(i) a dealing representative of a mutual fund dealer who is acting on behalf of the mutual fund dealer in respect of securities listed in paragraph 7.1(2)(b);

(ii) a Canadian financial institution;

(iii) in Ontario, a financial intermediary;

(b) the self-directed RESP restricts its investments in securities to securities in which the person or company who trades the self-directed RESP is permitted to trade.

8.20 Exchange contract — Alberta, British Columbia, New Brunswick and Saskatchewan — (1) In Alberta, British Columbia, New Brunswick and Saskatchewan, the dealer registration requirement does not apply to a person or company in respect of a trade in an exchange contract by the person or company if one of the following applies:

(a) the trade is made through a registered dealer, if the dealer is registered in a category that permits the trade unless, in furtherance of the trade, the person or company seeking the exemption solicits or contacts directly any purchaser or prospective purchaser in relation to the trade;

(b) the trade is made to a registered dealer who is purchasing as principal, if the dealer is registered in a category that permits the trade.

8.20.1 Exchange contract trades through or to a registered dealer — Alberta, British Columbia, New Brunswick and Saskatchewan — The dealer registration requirement does not apply to a registered adviser, or an advising representative or associate advising representative acting on behalf of the registered adviser, in respect of trading activities related to exchange contracts that are incidental to its providing advice to a client, if the trade is made through a dealer registered in a category that permits the trade or a dealer operating under an exemption from the dealer registration requirement.

8.21 Specified debt — (1) In this section

"permitted supranational agency" means any of the following:

(a) the African Development Bank, established by the Agreement Establishing the African Development Bank which came into force on September 10, 1964, that Canada became a member of on December 30, 1982;

(b) the Asian Development Bank, established under a resolution adopted by the United Nations Economic and Social Commission for Asia and the Pacific in 1965;

(c) the Caribbean Development Bank, established by the Agreement Establishing the Caribbean Development Bank which came into force on January 26, 1970, as amended, that Canada is a founding member of;

(d) the European Bank for Reconstruction and Development, established by the Agreement Establishing the European Bank for Reconstruction and Development and approved by the *European Bank for Reconstruction and Development Agreement Act* (Canada), that Canada is a founding member of;

(e) the Inter-American Development Bank, established by the Agreement establishing the Inter-American Development Bank which became effective December 30, 1959, as amended from time to time, that Canada is a member of;

(f) the International Bank for Reconstruction and Development, established by the Agreement for an International Bank for Reconstruction and Development approved by the Bretton Woods and *Related Agreements Act* (Canada);

(g) the International Finance Corporation, established by Articles of Agreement approved by the *Bretton Woods and Related Agreements Act* (Canada).

(2) The dealer registration requirement does not apply in respect of a trade in any of the following:

(a) a debt security issued by or guaranteed by the Government of Canada or the government of a jurisdiction of Canada;

(b) a debt security issued by or guaranteed by a government of a foreign jurisdiction if the debt security has a designated rating from a designated rating organization or its DRO affiliate;

(c) a debt security issued by or guaranteed by a municipal corporation in Canada;

(d) a debt security secured by or payable out of rates or taxes levied under the law of a jurisdiction of Canada on property in the jurisdiction and collectible by or through the municipality in which the property is situated;

(e) a debt security issued by or guaranteed by a Canadian financial institution or a Schedule III bank, other than debt securities that are subordinate in right of payment to deposits held by the issuer or guarantor of those debt securities;

(f) a debt security issued by the Comité de gestion de la taxe scolaire de l'île de Montréal;

(g) a debt security issued by or guaranteed by a permitted supranational agency if the debt securities are payable in the currency of Canada or the United States of America.

(3) Paragraphs (2)(a), (c) and (d) do not apply in Ontario.

Note: In Ontario, exemptions from the dealer registration requirement similar to those in paragraphs 8.21(a), (c) and (d) are provided under paragraph 2 of subsection 35(1) of the *Securities Act* (Ontario).

8.22 Small security holder selling and purchase arrangements — (1) In this section

"exchange" means

(a) TSX Inc.,

(b) TSX Venture Exchange Inc., or

(c) an exchange that

(i) has a policy that is substantially similar to the policy of the TSX Inc., and

(ii) is designated by the securities regulatory authority for the purpose of this section;

"policy" means,

(a) in the case of TSX Inc., sections 638 and 639 [*Odd lot selling and purchase arrangements*] of the TSX Company Manual, as amended from time to time,

(b) in the case of the TSX Venture Exchange Inc., Policy 5.7 Small Shareholder Selling and Purchase Arrangements, as amended from time to time, or

(c) in the case of an exchange referred to in paragraph (c) of the definition of "exchange", the rule, policy or other similar instrument of the exchange on small shareholder selling and purchase arrangements.

(2) The dealer registration requirement does not apply in respect of a trade by an issuer or its agent, in securities of the issuer that are listed on an exchange, if all of the following apply:

(a) the trade is an act in furtherance of participation by the holders of the securities in an arrangement that is in accordance with the policy of that exchange;

(b) the issuer and its agent do not provide advice to a security holder about the security holder's participation in the arrangement referred to in paragraph (a), other than a description of the arrangement's operation, procedures for participation in the arrangement, or both;

(c) the trade is made in accordance with the policy of that exchange, without resort to an exemption from, or variation of, the significant subject matter of the policy;

(d) at the time of the trade after giving effect to a purchase under the arrangement, the market value of the maximum number of securities that a security holder is permitted to hold in order to be eligible to participate in the arrangement is not more than $25,000.

(3) For the purposes of paragraph (2)(c), an exemption from, or variation of, the maximum number of securities that a security holder is permitted to hold under a policy in order to be eligible to participate in the arrangement provided for in the policy is not an exemption from, or variation of, the significant subject matter of the policy.

8.22.1 Short-term debt — (1) In this section, "short-term debt instrument" means a negotiable promissory note or commercial paper maturing not more than one year from the date of issue.

(2) Except in Ontario, the dealer registration requirement does not apply to any of the following in respect of a trade in a short-term debt instrument with a permitted client:

(a) a bank listed in Schedule I, II or III to the *Bank Act* (Canada);

(b) an association to which the *Cooperative Credit Associations Act* (Canada) applies or a central cooperative credit society for which an order has been made under subsection 473 (1) of that Act;

(c) a loan corporation, trust company, trust corporation, insurance company, treasury branch, credit union, caisse populaire, financial services cooperative or credit union league or federation that is authorized by a statute of Canada or of a jurisdiction in Canada to carry on business in Canada or in any jurisdiction in Canada, as the case may be;

(d) the Business Development Bank of Canada;

(3) The exemption under subsection (2) is not available to a person or company if the short-term debt instrument is convertible or exchangeable into, or accompanied by a right to purchase, another security other than another short-term debt instrument.

[Note: In Ontario, an exemption from the dealer registration requirement similar to that in section 8.22.1 is provided under section 35.1 of the *Securities Act* (Ontario).]

DIVISION 2 — EXEMPTIONS FROM ADVISER REGISTRATION

8.22.2 General condition to adviser registration requirement exemptions — The exemptions in this Division are not available to a person or company if the person or company is registered in the local jurisdiction in a category of registration that permits the person or company to act as an adviser in respect of the activities for which the exemption is provided.

8.23 Dealer without discretionary authority — The adviser registration requirement does not apply to a registered dealer, or a dealing representative acting on behalf of the dealer, that provides advice to a client if the advice is

(a) in connection with a trade in a security that the dealer and the representative are permitted to make under his, her or its registration,

(b) provided by the representative, and

(c) not in respect of a managed account of the client.

8.24 IIROC members with discretionary authority — The adviser registration requirement does not apply to a registered dealer, or a dealing representative acting on behalf of the dealer, that acts as an adviser in respect of a client's managed account if the registered dealer is a member of IIROC and the advising activities are conducted in accordance with the rules of IIROC.

8.25 Advising generally — (1) For the purposes of subsections (3) and (4), "financial or other interest" includes the following:

(a) ownership, beneficial or otherwise, in the security or in another security issued by the same issuer;

(b) an option in respect of the security or another security issued by the same issuer;

(c) a commission or other compensation received, or expected to be received, from any person or company in connection with the trade in the security;

(d) a financial arrangement regarding the security with any person or company;

(e) a financial arrangement with any underwriter or other person or company who has any interest in the security.

(2) The adviser registration requirement does not apply to a person or company that acts as an adviser if the advice the person or company provides does not purport to be tailored to the needs of the person or company receiving the advice.

(3) If a person or company that is exempt under subsection (2) recommends buying, selling or holding a specified security, a class of securities or the securities of a class of issuers in which any of the following has a financial or other interest, the person or company must disclose the interest concurrently with providing the advice:

(a) the person or company;

(b) any partner, director or officer of the person or company;

(c) any other person or company that would be an insider of the first-mentioned person or company if the first-mentioned person or company were a reporting issuer.

(4) If the financial or other interest of the person or company includes an interest in an option described in paragraph (b) of the definition of "financial or other interest" in subsection (1), the disclosure required by subsection (3) must include a description of the terms of the option.

(5) This section does not apply in Ontario.

Note: In Ontario, measures similar to those in section 8.25 are in section 34 of the *Securities Act* (Ontario).

8.26 International adviser — (1) Despite section 1.2, in Alberta, British Columbia, New Brunswick and Saskatchewan, a reference to "securities" in this section excludes "exchange contracts".

(2) In this section

"aggregate consolidated gross revenue" does not include the gross revenue of an affiliate of the adviser if the affiliate is registered in a jurisdiction of Canada;

"foreign security" means

(a) a security issued by an issuer incorporated, formed or created under the laws of a foreign jurisdiction, and

(b) a security issued by a government of a foreign jurisdiction;

(3) The adviser registration requirement does not apply to a person or company in respect of its acting as an adviser to a permitted client, other than a permitted client that is a person or company registered under the securities legislation of a jurisdiction of Canada as an adviser or dealer, if the adviser does not advise that client on securities of Canadian issuers, unless providing that advice is incidental to its providing advice on a foreign security.

(4) The exemption under subsection (3) is not available unless all of the following apply:

(a) the adviser's head office or principal place of business is in a foreign jurisdiction;

(b) the adviser is registered in a category of registration, or operates under an exemption from registration, under the securities legislation of the foreign jurisdiction in which its head office or principal place of business is located, that permits it to carry on the activities in that jurisdiction that registration as an adviser would permit it to carry on in the local jurisdiction;

(c) the adviser engages in the business of an adviser in the foreign jurisdiction in which its head office or principal place of business is located;

(d) as at the end of its most recently completed financial year, not more than 10% of the aggregate consolidated gross revenue of the adviser, its affiliates and its affiliated partnerships was derived from the portfolio management activities of the adviser, its affiliates and its affiliated partnerships in Canada;

(e) before advising a client, the adviser notifies the client of all of the following:

(i) the adviser is not registered in the local jurisdiction to provide the advice described under subsection (3);

(ii) the foreign jurisdiction in which the adviser's head office or principal place of business is located;

(iii) all or substantially all of the adviser's assets may be situated outside of Canada;

(iv) there may be difficulty enforcing legal rights against the adviser because of the above;

(v) the name and address of the adviser's agent for service of process in the local jurisdiction;

(f) the adviser has submitted to the securities regulatory authority a completed Form 31-103F2 Submission to jurisdiction and appointment of agent for service.

(5) A person or company that relied on the exemption in subsection (3) during the 12 month period preceding December 1 of a year must notify the regulator or, in Québec, the securities regulatory authority of that fact by December 1 of that year.

(6) In Ontario, subsection (5) does not apply to a person or company that complies with the filing and fee payment requirements applicable to an unregistered exempt international firm under Ontario Securities Commission Rule 13-502 Fees.

8.26.1 International sub-adviser — (1) The adviser registration requirement does not apply to a sub-adviser if all of the following apply:

(a) the obligations and duties of the sub-adviser are set out in a written agreement with the registered adviser or registered dealer;

(b) the registered adviser or registered dealer has entered into a written agreement with its clients on whose behalf investment advice is or portfolio management services are to be provided, agreeing to be responsible for any loss that arises out of the failure of the sub-adviser

(i) to exercise the powers and discharge the duties of its office honestly, in good faith and in the best interests of the registrant and each client of the registrant for whose benefit the advice is or portfolio management services are to be provided, or

(ii) to exercise the degree of care, diligence and skill that a reasonably prudent person would exercise in the circumstances.

(2) The exemption under subsection (1) is not available unless all of the following apply:

(a) the sub-adviser's head office or principal place of business is in a foreign jurisdiction;

(b) the sub-adviser is registered in a category of registration, or operates under an exemption from registration, under the securities legislation of the foreign jurisdiction in which its head office or principal place of business is located, that permits it to carry on the activities in that jurisdiction that registration as an adviser would permit it to carry on in the local jurisdiction;

(c) the sub-adviser engages in the business of an adviser in the foreign jurisdiction in which its head office or principal place of business is located.

DIVISION 3 — EXEMPTIONS FROM INVESTMENT FUND MANAGER REGISTRATION

8.26.2 General condition to investment fund manager registration requirement exemptions — The exemptions in this Division are not available to a person or company if the person or company is registered in the local jurisdiction as an investment fund manager.

8.27 Private investment club — The investment fund manager registration requirement does not apply to a person or company in respect of its acting as an investment fund manager for an investment fund if all of the following apply:

(a) the fund has no more than 50 beneficial security holders;

(b) the fund does not seek and has never sought to borrow money from the public;

(c) the fund does not distribute and has never distributed its securities to the public;

(d) the fund does not pay or give any remuneration for investment management or administration advice in respect of trades in securities, except normal brokerage fees;

(e) the fund, for the purpose of financing its operations, requires security holders to make contributions in proportion to the value of the securities held by them.

8.28 Capital accumulation plan — (1) In this section

"capital accumulation plan" means a tax assisted investment or savings plan, including a defined contribution registered pension plan, a group registered retirement savings plan, a group registered education savings plan, or a deferred profit-sharing plan, that permits a plan member to make investment decisions among two or more investment options offered within the plan, and in Québec and Manitoba, includes a simplified pension plan;

"plan sponsor" means an employer, trustee, trade union or association or a combination of them that establishes a capital accumulation plan, and includes a plan service provider to the extent that the plan sponsor has delegated its responsibilities to the plan service provider; and

"plan member" means a person that has assets in a capital accumulation plan;

"plan service provider" means a person that provides services to a plan sponsor to design, establish, or operate a capital accumulation plan.

(2) The investment fund manager registration requirement does not apply to a plan sponsor or their plan service provider in respect of activities related to a capital accumulation plan.

8.29 Private investment fund — loan and trust pools — (1) The investment fund manager registration requirement does not apply to a trust company or trust corporation that administers an investment fund if all of the following apply:

(a) the trust company or trust corporation is registered or authorized by an enactment of Canada or a jurisdiction of Canada to carry on business in Canada or a jurisdiction of Canada;

(b) the fund has no promoter or investment fund manager other than the trust company or trust corporation;

(c) the fund commingles the money of different estates and trusts for the purpose of facilitating investment.

(2) The exemption in subsection (1) is not available to a trust company or trust corporation registered under the laws of Prince Edward Island unless it is also registered under the *Trust and Loan Companies Act* (Canada) or under comparable legislation in another jurisdiction of Canada.

(3) This section does not apply in Ontario.

Note: In Ontario, subsection 35.1 of the Securities Act (Ontario) provides a general exemption from the registration requirement for trust companies, trust corporations and other specified financial institutions.

DIVISION 4 — MOBILITY EXEMPTION — FIRMS

8.30 Client mobility exemption — firms — The dealer registration requirement and the adviser registration requirement do not apply to a person or company if all of the following apply:

(a) the person or company is registered as a dealer or adviser in its principal jurisdiction;

(b) the person or company does not act as a dealer, underwriter or adviser in the local jurisdiction other than as it is permitted to in its principal jurisdiction according to its registration;

(c) the person or company does not act as a dealer, underwriter or adviser in the local jurisdiction other than in respect of 10 or fewer eligible clients;

(d) the person or company complies with Parts 13 *Dealing with clients — individuals and firms* and 14 *Handling client accounts — firms*;

(e) the person or company deals fairly, honestly and in good faith in the course of its dealings with an eligible client.

PART 9 — MEMBERSHIP IN A SELF-REGULATORY ORGANIZATION

9.1 IIROC membership for investment dealers — An investment dealer must not act as a dealer unless the investment dealer is a "dealer member", as defined under the rules of IIROC.

9.2 MFDA membership for mutual fund dealers — Except in Québec, a mutual fund dealer must not act as a dealer unless the mutual fund dealer is a "member", as defined under the rules of the MFDA.

9.3 Exemptions from certain requirements for IIROC members — (1) Unless it is also registered as an investment fund manager, a registered firm that is a member of IIROC is exempt from the following requirements:

(a) section 12.1 [*capital requirements*];

(b) section 12.2 [*subordination agreement*];

(c) section 12.3 [*insurance — dealer*];

(d) section 12.6 [*global bonding or insurance*];

(e) section 12.7 [*notifying the regulator of a change, claim or cancellation*];

(f) section 12.10 [*annual financial statements*];

(g) section 12.11 [*interim financial information*];

(h) section 12.12 [*delivering financial information — dealer*];

(i) subsection 13.2(3) [*know your client*];

(j) section 13.3 [*suitability*];

(k) section 13.12 [*restriction on lending to clients*];

(l) section 13.13 [*disclosure when recommending the use of borrowed money*];

(l.1) section 13.15 [*handling complaints*];

(m) subsection 14.2(2) [*relationship disclosure information*];

(n) section 14.6 [*holding client assets in trust*];

(o) section 14.8 [*securities subject to a safekeeping agreement*];

(p) section 14.9 [*securities not subject to a safekeeping agreement*];

(q) section 14.12 [*content and delivery of trade confirmation*].

(1.1) Subsection (1) only applies to a registered firm in respect of a requirement specified in any of paragraphs (1)(a) to (q) if the registered firm complies with the corresponding IIROC provisions that are in effect.

(2) If a registered firm is a member of IIROC and is registered as an investment fund manager, the firm is exempt from the following requirements:

(a) section 12.3 [*insurance — dealer*];

(b) section 12.6 [*global bonding or insurance*];

(c) section 12.12 [*delivering financial information — dealer*];

(d) subsection 13.2(3) [*know your client*];

(e) section 13.3 [*suitability*];

(f) section 13.12 [*restriction on lending to clients*];

(g) section 13.13 [*disclosure when recommending the use of borrowed money*];

(h) section 13.15 [*handling complaints*];

(i) subsection 14.2(2) [*relationship disclosure information*];

(j) section 14.6 [*holding client assets in trust*];

(k) section 14.8 [*securities subject to a safekeeping agreement*];

(l) section 14.9 [*securities not subject to a safekeeping agreement*];

(m) section 14.12 [*content and delivery of trade confirmation*]., *and*

(2.1) Subsection (2) only applies to a registered firm in respect of a requirement specified in any of paragraphs (2)(a) to (m) if the registered firm complies with the corresponding IIROC provisions that are in effect.

9.4 Exemptions from certain requirements for MFDA members — (1) Unless it is also registered as an exempt market dealer, a scholarship plan dealer or an investment fund manager, a registered firm that is a member of the MFDA is exempt from the following requirements:

(a) section 12.1 [*capital requirements*];

(b) section 12.2 [*subordination agreement*];

(c) section 12.3 [*insurance — dealer*];

(d) section 12.6 [*global bonding or insurance*];

(e) section 12.7 [*notifying the regulator of a change, claim or cancellation*];

(f) section 12.10 [*annual financial statements*];

(g) section 12.11 [*interim financial information*];

(h) section 12.12 [*delivering financial information — dealer*];

     (i) section 13.3 [*suitability*];

     (j) section 13.12 [*restriction on lending to clients*];

     (k) section 13.13 [*disclosure when recommending the use of borrowed money*];

     (l) section 13.15 [*handling complaints*];

     (m) subsection 14.2(2) [*relationship disclosure information*];

     (n) section 14.6 [*holding client assets in trust*];

     (o) section 14.8 [*securities subject to a safekeeping agreement*];

     (p) section 14.9 [*securities not subject to a safekeeping agreement*];

     (q) section 14.12 [*content and delivery of trade confirmation*].

(1.1) Subsection (1) only applies to a registered firm in respect of a requirement specified in any of paragraphs (1)(a) to (q) if the registered firm complies with the corresponding MFDA provisions that are in effect.

(2) If a registered firm is a member of the MFDA and is registered as an exempt market dealer, scholarship plan dealer or investment fund manager, the firm is exempt from the following requirements:

     (a) section 12.3 [*insurance — dealer*];

     (b) section 12.6 [*global bonding or insurance*];

     (c) section 13.3 [*suitability*];

     (d) section 13.12 [*restriction on lending to clients*];

     (e) section 13.13 [*disclosure when recommending the use of borrowed money*];

     (f) section 13.15 [*handling complaints*];

     (g) subsection 14.2(2) [*relationship disclosure information*];

     (h) section 14.6 [*holding client assets in trust*];

     (i) section 14.8 [*securities subject to a safekeeping agreement*];

     (j) section 14.9 [*securities not subject to a safekeeping agreement*];

     (k) section 14.12 [*content and delivery of trade confirmation*].

(2.1) Subsection (2) only applies to a registered firm in respect of a requirement specified in any of paragraphs (2)(a) to (k) if the registered firm complies with the corresponding MFDA provisions that are in effect.

(3) Subsections (1) and (2) do not apply in Québec.

(4) In Québec, the requirements listed in subsection (1) do not apply to a mutual fund dealer to the extent equivalent requirements to those listed in subsection (1) are applicable to the mutual fund dealer under the regulations in Québec.

PART 10 — SUSPENSION AND REVOCATION OF REGISTRATION — FIRMS
DIVISION 1 — WHEN A FIRM'S REGISTRATION IS SUSPENDED

10.1 Failure to pay fees — (1) In this section, "annual fees" means

     (a) in Alberta, the fees required under section 2.1 of the Schedule — Fees in Alta. Reg. 115/95 — Securities Regulation,

     (b) in British Columbia, the annual fees required under section 22 of the Securities Regulation, B.C. Reg. 196/97,

     (c) in Manitoba, the fees required under paragraph 1.(2)(a) of the *Manitoba Fee Regulation*, M.R 491\88R,

     (d) in New Brunswick, the fees required under section 2.2(c) of Local Rule 11-501 *Fees*,

     (e) in Newfoundland and Labrador, the fees required under section 143 of the *Securities Act*,

     (f) in Nova Scotia, the fees required under Part XIV of the Regulations,

     (g) in Northwest Territories, the fees required under sections 1(c) and 1(e) of the Securities Fee regulations, R-066-2008,

     (h) in Nunavut, the fees required under section 1(a) of the Schedule to R-003-2003 to the Securities Fee regulation, R.R.N.W.T. 1990, c.20,

     (i) in Prince Edward Island, the fees required under section 175 of the *Securities Act* R.S.P.E.I., Cap. S-3.1,

     (j) in Québec, the fees required under section 271.5 of the Québec Securities Regulation,

     (k) in Saskatchewan, the annual registration fees required under section 176 of The Securities Regulations (Saskatchewan), and

     (l) in Yukon, the fees required under O.I.C. 2009\66, pursuant to section 168 of the *Securities Act*.

(2) If a registered firm has not paid the annual fees by the 30th day after the date the annual fees were due, the registration of the firm is suspended until reinstated or revoked under securities legislation.

10.2 If IIROC membership is revoked or suspended — If IIROC revokes or suspends a registered firm's membership, the firm's registration in the category of investment dealer is suspended until reinstated or revoked under securities legislation.

10.3 If MFDA membership is revoked or suspended — Except in Québec, if the MFDA revokes or suspends a registered firm's membership, the firm's registration in the category of mutual fund dealer is suspended until reinstated or revoked under securities legislation.

10.4 Activities not permitted while a firm's registration is suspended — If a registered firm's registration in a category is suspended, the firm must not act as a dealer, an underwriter, an adviser, or an investment fund manager, as the case may be, under that category.

DIVISION 2 — REVOKING A FIRM'S REGISTRATION

10.5 Revocation of a suspended registration — firm — If a registration has been suspended under this Part and it has not been reinstated, the registration is revoked on the 2nd anniversary of the suspension.

10.6 Exception for firms involved in a hearing or proceeding — Despite section 10.5, if a hearing or proceeding concerning a suspended registrant is commenced under securities legislation or under the rules of an SRO, the registrant's registration remains suspended.

10.7 Application of Part 10 in Ontario — Other than section 10.4 [*activities not permitted while a firm's registration is suspended*], this Part does not apply in Ontario.

Note: In Ontario, measures governing suspension in section 29 of the *Securities Act* (Ontario) are similar to those in Parts 6 and 10.

PART 11 — INTERNAL CONTROLS AND SYSTEMS

DIVISION 1 — COMPLIANCE

11.1 Compliance system — A registered firm must establish, maintain and apply policies and procedures that establish a system of controls and supervision sufficient to

(a) provide reasonable assurance that the firm and each individual acting on its behalf complies with securities legislation, and

(b) manage the risks associated with its business in accordance with prudent business practices.

11.2 Designating an ultimate designated person — (1) A registered firm must designate an individual who is registered under securities legislation in the category of ultimate designated person to perform the functions described in section 5.1 [*responsibilities of the ultimate designated person*].

(2) A registered firm must designate an individual under subsection (1) who is one of the following:

(a) the chief executive officer of the registered firm or, if the firm does not have a chief executive officer, an individual acting in a capacity similar to a chief executive officer;

(b) the sole proprietor of the registered firm;

(c) the officer in charge of a division of the registered firm, if the activity that requires the firm to register occurs only within the division and the firm has significant other business activities.

(3) If an individual who is registered as a registered firm's ultimate designated person ceases to meet any of the conditions listed in subsection (2), the registered firm must designate another individual to act as its ultimate designated person.

11.3 Designating a chief compliance officer — (1) A registered firm must designate an individual who is registered under securities legislation in the category of chief compliance officer to perform the functions described in section 5.2 [*responsibilities of the chief compliance officer*].

(2) A registered firm must not designate an individual to act as the firm's chief compliance officer unless the individual has satisfied the applicable conditions in Part 3 *Registration requirements — individuals* and the individual is one of the following:

(a) an officer or partner of the registered firm;

(b) the sole proprietor of the registered firm.

(3) If an individual who is registered as a registered firm's chief compliance officer ceases to meet any of the conditions listed in subsection (2), the registered firm must designate another individual to act as its chief compliance officer.

11.4 Providing access to the board of directors — A registered firm must permit its ultimate designated person and its chief compliance officer to directly access the firm's board of directors, or individuals acting in a similar capacity for the firm, at such times as the ultimate designated person or the chief compliance officer may consider necessary or advisable in view of his or her responsibilities.

DIVISION 2 — BOOKS AND RECORDS

11.5 General requirements for records — (1) A registered firm must maintain records to

(a) accurately record its business activities, financial affairs, and client transactions, and

(b) demonstrate the extent of the firm's compliance with applicable requirements of securities legislation.

(2) The records required under subsection (1) include, but are not limited to, records that do the following:

(a) permit timely creation and audit of financial statements and other financial information required to be filed or delivered to the securities regulatory authority;

(b) permit determination of the registered firm's capital position;

(c) demonstrate compliance with the registered firm's capital and insurance requirements;

(d) demonstrate compliance with internal control procedures;

(e) demonstrate compliance with the firm's policies and procedures;

(f) permit the identification and segregation of client cash, securities, and other property;

(g) identify all transactions conducted on behalf of the registered firm and each of its clients, including the parties to the transaction and the terms of the purchase or sale;

(h) provide an audit trail for

(i) client instructions and orders, and

(ii) each trade transmitted or executed for a client or by the registered firm on its own behalf;

(i) permit the generation of account activity reports for clients;

(j) provide securities pricing as may be required by securities legislation;

(k) document the opening of client accounts, including any agreements with clients;

(l) demonstrate compliance with sections 13.2 [*know your client*] and 13.3 [*suitability*];

(m) demonstrate compliance with complaint-handling requirements;

(n) document correspondence with clients;

(o) document compliance and supervision actions taken by the firm.

11.6 Form, accessibility and retention of records — (1) A registered firm must keep a record that it is required to keep under securities legislation

(a) for 7 years from the date the record is created,

(b) in a safe location and in a durable form, and

(c) in a manner that permits it to be provided to the regulator or, in Québec, the securities regulatory authority in a reasonable period of time,

(2) A record required to be provided to the regulator, or, in Québec, the securities regulatory authority must be provided in a format that is capable of being read by the regulator or the securities regulatory authority.

(3) Paragraph (1)(c) does not apply in Ontario.

Note: In Ontario, how quickly a registered firm is required to provide information to the regulator is addressed in subsection 19(3) of the *Securities Act* (Ontario).

DIVISION 3 — CERTAIN BUSINESS TRANSACTIONS

11.7 Tied settling of securities transactions — A registered firm must not require a person or company to settle that person's or company's transaction with the registered firm through that person's or company's account at a Canadian financial institution as a condition, or on terms that would appear to a reasonable person to be a condition, of supplying a product or service, unless this method of settlement would be, to a reasonable person, necessary to provide the specific product or service that the person or company has requested.

11.8 Tied selling — A dealer, adviser or investment fund manager must not require another person or company

(a) to buy, sell or hold a security as a condition, or on terms that would appear to a reasonable person to be a condition, of supplying or continuing to supply a product or service, or

(b) to buy, sell or use a product or service as a condition, or on terms that would appear to a reasonable person to be a condition, of buying or selling a security.

11.9 Registrant acquiring a registered firm's securities or assets — (1) A registrant must give the regulator or, in Québec, the securities regulatory authority written notice in accordance with subsection (2) if it proposes to acquire any of the following:

(a) for the first time, direct or indirect ownership, beneficial or otherwise, of 10% or more of the voting securities or other securities convertible into voting securities of

(i) a firm registered in any jurisdiction of Canada or any foreign jurisdiction, or

(ii) a person or company of which a firm registered in any jurisdiction of Canada or any foreign jurisdiction is a subsidiary;

(b) all or a substantial part of the assets of a firm registered in any jurisdiction of Canada or any foreign jurisdiction.

(2) The notice required under subsection (1) must be delivered to the regulator or, in Québec, the securities regulatory authority at least 30 days before the proposed acquisition and must include all relevant facts regarding the acquisition sufficient to enable the regulator or the securities regulatory authority to determine if the acquisition is

(a) likely to give rise to a conflict of interest,

(b) likely to hinder the registered firm in complying with securities legislation,

(c) inconsistent with an adequate level of investor protection, or

(d) otherwise prejudicial to the public interest.

(3) [Repealed.]

(4) Except in Ontario and British Columbia, if, within 30 days of the receipt of a notice under subsection (1), the regulator or, in Québec, the securities regulatory authority notifies the registrant making the acquisition that the regulator or, in Québec, the securities regulatory authority objects to the acquisition, the acquisition must not occur until the regulator or the securities regulatory authority approves it.

(5) In Ontario, if, within 30 days of the receipt of a notice under subparagraph (1)(a)(i) or paragraph (1)(b), the regulator notifies the registrant making the acquisition that the regulator objects to the acquisition, the acquisition must not occur until the regulator approves it.

(6) Following receipt of a notice of objection under subsection (4) or (5), the person or company who submitted the notice under subsection (1) may request an opportunity to be heard on the matter by the regulator or, in Québec, the securities regulatory authority objecting to the acquisition.

11.10 Registered firm whose securities are acquired — (1) A registered firm must give the regulator or, in Québec, the securities regulatory authority written notice in accordance with subsection (2) if it knows or has reason to believe that any person or company, alone or in combination with any other person or company, is about to acquire, or has acquired, for the first time, direct or indirect ownership, beneficial or otherwise, of 10% or more of the voting securities or other securities convertible into voting securities of any of the following:

(a) the registered firm;

(b) person or company of which the registered firm is a subsidiary.

(2) The notice required under subsection (1) must,

(a) be delivered to the regulator or, in Québec, the securities regulatory authority as soon as possible,

(b) include the name of each person or company involved in the acquisition, and

(c) include all facts that to the best of the registered firm's knowledge after reasonable inquiry regarding the acquisition are sufficient to enable the regulator or the securities regulatory authority to determine if the acquisition is

(i) likely to give rise to a conflict of interest,

(ii) likely to hinder the registered firm in complying with securities legislation,

(iii) inconsistent with an adequate level of investor protection, or

(iv) otherwise prejudicial to the public interest.

(3) [Repealed.]

(4) This section does not apply if notice of the acquisition was provided under section 11.9 [*registrant acquiring a registered firm's securities or assets*].

(5) Except in British Columbia and Ontario, if, within 30 days of the receipt of a notice under subsection (1), the regulator or the securities regulatory authority notifies the person or company making the acquisition that the regulator or, in Québec, the securities regulatory authority objects to the acquisition, the acquisition must not occur until the regulator or the securities regulatory authority approves it.

(6) In Ontario, if, within 30 days of the receipt of a notice under paragraph (1)(a), the regulator notifies the person or company making the acquisition that the regulator objects to the acquisition, the acquisition must not occur until the regulator approves it.

(7) Following receipt of a notice of objection under subsection (5) or (6), the person or company proposing to make the acquisition may request an opportunity to be heard on the matter by the regulator or, in Québec, the securities regulatory authority objecting to the acquisition.

PART 12 — FINANCIAL CONDITION

DIVISION 1 — WORKING CAPITAL

12.1 **Capital requirements** — (1) If, at any time, the excess working capital of a registered firm, as calculated in accordance with Form 31-103F1 *Calculation of Excess Working Capital*, is less than zero, the registered firm must notify the regulator or, in Québec, the securities regulatory authority as soon as possible.

(2) The excess working capital of a registered firm, as calculated in accordance with Form 31-103F1 *Calculation of Excess Working Capital*, must not be less than zero for 2 consecutive days.

(3) For the purpose of completing Form 31-103F1 *Calculation of Excess Working Capital*, the minimum capital is

(a) $25,000, for a registered adviser that is not also a registered dealer or a registered investment fund manager,

(b) $50,000, for a registered dealer that is not also a registered investment fund manager, and

(c) $100,000, for a registered investment fund manager.

(4) Paragraph (3)(c) does not apply to a registered investment fund manager that is exempt from the dealer registration requirement under section 8.6 [*investment fund trades by adviser to managed account*] in respect of all investment funds for which it acts as adviser.

(5) This section does not apply to a registered firm that is a member of IIROC and is registered as an investment fund manager if all of the following apply:

(a) the firm has a minimum capital of not less than $100,000 as calculated in accordance with IIROC Form 1 *Joint Regulatory Financial Questionnaire and Report*;

(b) the firm notifies the regulator or, in Québec, the securities regulatory authority as soon as possible if, at any time, the firm's risk adjusted capital, as calculated in accordance with IIROC Form 1 *Joint Regulatory Financial Questionnaire and Report* is less than zero;

(c) the risk adjusted capital of the firm, as calculated in accordance with IIROC Form 1 *Joint Regulatory Financial Questionnaire and Report*, is not less than zero for 2 consecutive days.

(6) This section does not apply to a mutual fund dealer that is a member of the MFDA if it is also registered as an exempt market dealer, a scholarship plan dealer or an investment fund manager and if all of the following apply:

(a) the firm has a minimum capital, as calculated in accordance with MFDA Form 1 *MFDA Financial Questionnaire and Report*, of not less than

(i) $50,000, if the firm is registered as an exempt market dealer or scholarship plan dealer,

(ii) $100,000, if the firm is registered as an investment fund manager;

(b) the firm notifies the regulator or, in Québec, the securities regulatory authority as soon as possible if, at any time, the firm's risk adjusted capital, as calculated in accordance with MFDA Form 1 *MFDA Financial Questionnaire and Report* is less than zero;

(c) the risk adjusted capital of the firm, as calculated in accordance with MFDA Form 1 *MFDA Financial Questionnaire and Report*, is not less than zero for 2 consecutive days.

12.2 **Subordination agreement** — If a registered firm has entered into a subordination agreement in the form set out in Appendix B, it may exclude the amount of non-current related party debt subordinated under that agreement from the calculation of its excess working capital on Form 31-103F1 *Calculation of Excess Working Capital*.

(2) The registered firm must deliver an executed copy of the subordination agreement referred to subsection (1) to the regulator or, in Québec, the securities regulatory authority on the earliest of the following dates:

(a) 10 days after the date on which the subordination agreement is executed;

(b) the date on which the amount of the subordinated debt is excluded from the registered firm's non-current related party debt as calculated on Form 31-103F1 *Calculation of Excess Working Capital*.

(3) The registered firm must notify the regulator or, in Québec, the securities regulatory authority 10 days before it

(a) repays the loan or any part of the loan, or

(b) terminates the agreement.

DIVISION 2 — INSURANCE

12.3 **Insurance — dealer** — (1) A registered dealer must maintain bonding or insurance

(a) that contains the clauses set out in Appendix A [*bonding and insurance clauses*], and

(b) that provides for a double aggregate limit or a full reinstatement of coverage.

(2) A registered dealer must maintain bonding or insurance in respect of each clause set out in Appendix A in the highest of the following amounts for each clause:

(a) $50,000 per employee, agent and dealing representative or $200,000, whichever is less;

(b) one per cent of the total client assets that the dealer holds or has access to, as calculated using the dealer's most recent financial records, or $25,000,000, whichever is less;

(c) one per cent of the dealer's total assets, as calculated using the dealer's most recent financial records, or $25,000,000, whichever is less;

(d) the amount determined to be appropriate by a resolution of the dealer's board of directors, or individuals acting in a similar capacity for the firm.

(3) In Québec, this section does not apply to a scholarship plan dealer or a mutual fund dealer registered only in Québec.

12.4 Insurance — adviser — (1) A registered adviser must maintain bonding or insurance

(a) that contains the clauses set out in Appendix A [*bonding and insurance clauses*], and

(b) that provides for a double aggregate limit or a full reinstatement of coverage.

(2) A registered adviser that does not hold or have access to client assets must maintain bonding or insurance in respect of each clause set out in Appendix A in the amount of $50,000 for each clause.

(3) A registered adviser that holds or has access to client assets must maintain bonding or insurance in respect of each clause set out in Appendix A in the highest of the following amounts for each clause:

(a) one per cent of assets under management that the adviser holds or has access to, as calculated using the adviser's most recent financial records, or $25,000,000, whichever is less;

(b) one per cent of the adviser's total assets, as calculated using the adviser's most recent financial records, or $25,000,000, whichever is less;

(c) $200,000;

(d) the amount determined to be appropriate by a resolution of the adviser's board of directors or individuals acting in a similar capacity for the firm.

12.5 Insurance — investment fund manager — (1) A registered investment fund manager must maintain bonding or insurance

(a) that contains the clauses set out in Appendix A [*bonding and insurance clauses*], and

(b) that provides for a double aggregate limit or a full reinstatement of coverage.

(2) A registered investment fund manager must maintain bonding or insurance in respect of each clause set out in Appendix A in the highest of the following amounts for each clause:

(a) one per cent of assets under management, as calculated using the investment fund manager's most recent financial records, or $25,000,000, whichever is less;

(b) one per cent of the investment fund manager's total assets, as calculated using the investment fund manager's most recent financial records, or $25,000,000, whichever is less;

(c) $200,000;

(d) the amount determined to be appropriate by a resolution of the investment fund manager's board of directors or individuals acting in a similar capacity for the firm.

12.6 Global bonding or insurance — A registered firm must not maintain bonding or insurance under this Division that benefits, or names as an insured, another person or company unless the bond provides, without regard to the claims, experience or any other factor referable to that other person or company, the following:

(a) the registered firm has the right to claim directly against the insurer in respect of losses, and any payment or satisfaction of those losses must be made directly to the registered firm;

(b) the individual or aggregate limits under the policy must only be affected by claims made by or on behalf of

(i) the registered firm, or

(ii) a subsidiary of the registered firm whose financial results are consolidated with those of the registered firm.

12.7 Notifying the regulator or the securities regulatory authority of a change, claim or cancellation — A registered firm must, as soon as possible, notify the regulator or, in Québec, the securities regulatory authority in writing of any change in, claim made under, or cancellation of any insurance policy required under this Division.

DIVISION 3 — AUDITS

12.8 Direction by the regulator or the securities regulatory authority to conduct an audit or review — A registered firm must direct its auditor in writing to conduct any audit or review required by the regulator or, in Québec, the securities regulatory authority during its registration and must deliver a copy of the direction to the regulator or the securities regulatory authority

(a) with its application for registration, and

(b) no later than the 10th day after the registered firm changes its auditor.

12.9 Co-operating with the auditor — A registrant must not withhold, destroy or conceal any information or documents or otherwise fail to cooperate with a reasonable request made by an auditor of the registered firm in the course of an audit.

DIVISION 4 — FINANCIAL REPORTING

12.10 Annual financial statements — (1) Annual financial statements delivered to the regulator or, in Québec, the securities regulatory authority under this Division for financial years beginning on or after January 1, 2011 must include the following:

(a) a statement of comprehensive income, a statement of changes in equity and a statement of cash flows, each prepared for the most recently completed financial year and the financial year immediately preceding the most recently completed financial year, if any;

(b) a statement of financial position, signed by at least one director of the registered firm, as at the end of the most recently completed financial year and the financial year immediately preceding the most recently completed financial year, if any;

(c) notes to the financial statements.

(2) The annual financial statements delivered to the regulator or, in Québec, the securities regulatory authority under this Division must be audited.

12.11 Interim financial information — (1) Interim financial information delivered to the regulator or, in Québec, the securities regulatory authority under this Division for interim periods relating to financial years beginning on or after January 1, 2011 may be limited to the following:

(a) a statement of comprehensive income for the 3-month period ending on the last day of the interim period and for the same period of the immediately preceding financial year, if any;

(b) a statement of financial position, signed by at least one director of the registered firm, as at the end of the interim period and as at the end of the same interim period of the immediately preceding financial year, if any.

(2) The interim financial information delivered to the regulator or, in Québec, the securities regulatory authority under this Division must be prepared using the same accounting principles that the registered firm uses to prepare its annual financial statements.

12.12 Delivering financial information — dealer — (1) A registered dealer must deliver the following to the regulator or, in Québec, the securities regulatory authority no later than the 90th day after the end of its financial year:

(a) its annual financial statements for the financial year;

(b) a completed Form 31-103F1 *Calculation of Excess Working Capital*, showing the calculation of the dealer's excess working capital as at the end of the financial year and as at the end of the immediately preceding financial year, if any.

(2) A registered dealer must deliver the following to the regulator or, in Québec, the securities regulatory authority no later than the 30th day after the end of the first, second and third interim period of its financial year:

(a) its interim financial information for the interim period;

(b) a completed Form 31-103F1 *Calculation of Excess Working Capital*, showing the calculation of the dealer's excess working capital as at the end of the interim period and as at the end of the immediately preceding quarter, if any.

(2.1) If a registered firm is a member of the MFDA and is registered as an exempt market dealer or scholarship plan dealer, the firm is exempt from paragraphs (1)(b) and (2)(b) if all of the following apply:

(a) the firm has a minimum capital of not less than $50,000 as calculated in accordance with MFDA Form 1 *MFDA Financial Questionnaire and Report*;

(b) the firm delivers to the regulator or, in Québec, the securities regulatory authority a completed MFDA Form 1 *MFDA Financial Questionnaire and Report*, no later than the 90th day after the end of its financial year, that shows the calculation of the firm's risk adjusted capital as at the end of the financial year and as at the end of the immediately preceding financial year, if any;

(c) the firm delivers to the regulator or, in Québec, the securities regulatory authority a completed MFDA Form 1 *MFDA Financial Questionnaire and Report*, no later than the 30th day after the end of the first, second and third interim period of its financial year, that shows the calculation of the firm's risk adjusted capital as at the end of the interim period and as at the end of the immediately preceding month, if any.

(3) Subsection (2) does not apply to an exempt market dealer unless it is also registered in another category, other than the portfolio manager or restricted portfolio manager category.

12.13 Delivering financial information — adviser — A registered adviser must deliver the following to the regulator or, in Québec, the securities regulatory authority no later than the 90th day after the end of its financial year:

(a) its annual financial statements for the financial year;

(b) a completed Form 31-103F1 *Calculation of Excess Working Capital*, showing the calculation of the adviser's excess working capital as at the end of the financial year and as at the end of the immediately preceding financial year, if any.

12.14 Delivering financial information — investment fund manager — (1) A registered investment fund manager must deliver the following to the regulator or, in Québec, the securities regulatory authority no later than the 90th day after the end of its financial year:

(a) its annual financial statements for the financial year;

(b) a completed Form 31-103F1 *Calculation of Excess Working Capital*, showing the calculation of the investment fund manager's excess working capital as at the end of the financial year and as at the end of the immediately preceding financial year, if any;

(c) a completed Form 31-103F4 *Net Asset Value Adjustments* if any net asset value adjustment has been made in respect of an investment fund managed by the investment fund manager during the financial year.

(2) A registered investment fund manager must deliver the following to the regulator or, in Québec, the securities regulatory authority no later than the 30th day after the end of the first, second and third interim period of its financial year:

(a) its interim financial information for the interim period;

(b) a completed Form 31-103F1 *Calculation of Excess Working Capital*, showing the calculation of the investment fund manager's excess working capital as at the end of the interim period and as at the end of the immediately preceding interim period, if any;

(c) a completed Form 31-103F4 *Net Asset Value Adjustments* if any net asset value adjustment has been made in respect of an investment fund managed by the investment fund manager during the interim period.

(3) [Repealed.]

(4) If a registered firm is a member of IIROC and is registered as an investment fund manager, the firm is exempt from paragraphs (1)(b) and (2)(b) if

    (a) the firm has a minimum capital of not less than $100,000, as calculated in accordance with IIROC Form 1 *Joint Regulatory Financial Questionnaire and Report*;

    (b) the firm delivers to the regulator or, in Québec, the securities regulatory authority a completed IIROC Form 1 *Joint Regulatory Financial Questionnaire and Report*, no later than the 90th day after the end of its financial year, that shows the calculation of the firm's risk adjusted capital as at the end of the financial year and as at the end of the immediately preceding financial year, if any, and

    (c) the firm delivers to the regulator or, in Québec, the securities regulatory authority a completed IIROC Form 1 *Joint Regulatory Financial Questionnaire and Report*, no later than the 30th day after the end of the first, second and third interim period of its financial year, that shows the calculation of the firm's risk adjusted capital as at the end of the interim period and as at the end of the immediately preceding month, if any.

(5) If a registered firm is a member of the MFDA and is registered as an investment fund manager, the firm is exempt from paragraphs (1)(b) and (2)(b) if

    (a) the firm has a minimum capital of not less than $100,000, as calculated in accordance with MFDA Form 1 *MFDA Financial Questionnaire and Report*,

    (b) the firm delivers to the regulator or, in Québec, the securities regulatory authority a completed MFDA Form 1 *MFDA Financial Questionnaire and Report*, no later than the 90th day after the end of its financial year, that shows the calculation of the firm's risk adjusted capital as at the end of the financial year and as at the end of the immediately preceding financial year, if any, and

    (c) the firm delivers to the regulator or, in Québec, the securities regulatory authority a completed MFDA Form 1 *MFDA Financial Questionnaire and Report*, no later than the 30th day after the end of the first, second and third interim period of its financial year, that shows the calculation of the firm's risk adjusted capital as at the end of the interim period and as at the end of the immediately preceding month, if any.

12.15 Exemptions for financial years beginning in 2011 — (1) Despite subsections 12.10(1), 12.11(1), 12.12(1) and (2), 12.13 and 12.14(1) and (2), the annual financial statements, the interim financial information, and the completed Form 31-103F1 *Calculation of Excess Working Capital*, for a financial year beginning in 2011 or for interim periods relating to a financial year beginning in 2011 may exclude comparative information for the preceding financial period.

(2) Despite subsection 12.12(2), the first interim financial information, and the first completed Form 31-103F1 *Calculation of Excess Working Capital*, required to be delivered in respect of an interim period beginning on or after January 1, 2011 must be delivered no later than the 45th day after the end of the interim period.

(3) Despite subsection 12.14(2), the first interim financial information, the first completed Form 31-103F1 *Calculation of Excess Working Capital*, and the description of any net asset value adjustment, required to be delivered in respect of an interim period beginning on or after January 1, 2011 must be delivered no later than the 45th day after the end of the interim period.

PART 13 — DEALING WITH CLIENTS — INDIVIDUALS AND FIRMS

DIVISION 1 — KNOW YOUR CLIENT AND SUITABILITY

13.1 Investment fund managers exempt from this Division — This Division does not apply to an investment fund manager in respect of its activities as an investment fund manager.

13.2 Know your client — (1) For the purpose of paragraph 2(b) in Ontario, Nova Scotia and New Brunswick, "insider" has the meaning ascribed to that term in the *Securities Act* except that "reporting issuer", as it appears in the definition of "insider", is to be read as "reporting issuer or any other issuer whose securities are publicly traded".

(2) A registrant must take reasonable steps to

    (a) establish the identity of a client and, if the registrant has cause for concern, make reasonable inquiries as to the reputation of the client,

    (b) establish whether the client is an insider of a reporting issuer or any other issuer whose securities are publicly traded,

    (c) ensure that it has sufficient information regarding all of the following to enable it to meet its obligations under section 13.3 [*suitability*] or, if applicable, the suitability requirement imposed by an SRO:

        (i) the client's investment needs and objectives;

        (ii) the client's financial circumstances;

        (iii) the client's risk tolerance, and

    (d) establish the creditworthiness of the client if the registered firm is financing the client's acquisition of a security.

(3) For the purpose of establishing the identity of a client that is a corporation, partnership or trust, the registrant must establish the following:

    (a) the nature of the client's business;

    (b) the identity of any individual who,

        (i) in the case of a corporation, is a beneficial owner of, or exercises direct or indirect control or direction over, more than 25% of the voting rights attached to the outstanding voting securities of the corporation, or

        (ii) in the case of a partnership or trust, exercises control over the affairs of the partnership or trust.

(4) A registrant must take reasonable steps to keep the information required under this section current.

(5) This section does not apply if the client is a registered firm, a Canadian financial institution or a Schedule III bank.

(6) Paragraph (2)(c) does not apply to a registrant in respect of a permitted client if

    (a) the permitted client has waived, in writing, the requirements under subsections 13.3(1) and (2), and

    (b) the registrant does not act as an adviser in respect of a managed account of the permitted client.

(7) Paragraph (2)(b) does not apply to a registrant in respect of a client for which the registrant only trades securities referred to in paragraphs 7.1(2)(b) and 7.1(2)(c).

13.3 Suitability — (1) A registrant must take reasonable steps to ensure that, before it makes a recommendation to or accepts an instruction from a client to buy or sell a security, or makes a purchase or sale of a security for a client's managed account, the purchase or sale is suitable for the client.

(2) If a client instructs a registrant to buy, sell or hold a security and in the registrant's reasonable opinion following the instruction would not be suitable for the client, the registrant must inform the client of the registrant's opinion and must not buy or sell the security unless the client instructs the registrant to proceed nonetheless.

(3) This section does not apply if the client is a registered firm, a Canadian financial institution or a Schedule III bank.

(4) This section does not apply to a registrant in respect of a permitted client if

(a) the permitted client has waived, in writing, the requirements under this section, and

(b) the registrant does not act as an adviser in respect of a managed account of the permitted client.

DIVISION 2 — CONFLICTS OF INTEREST

13.4 Identifying and responding to conflicts of interest — (1) A registered firm must take reasonable steps to identify existing material conflicts of interest, and material conflicts of interest that the registered firm in its reasonable opinion would expect to arise, between the firm, including each individual acting on the firm's behalf, and a client.

(2) A registered firm must respond to an existing or potential conflict of interest identified under subsection (1).

(3) If a reasonable investor would expect to be informed of a conflict of interest identified under subsection (1), the registered firm must disclose, in a timely manner, the nature and extent of the conflict of interest to the client whose interest conflicts with the interest identified.

(4) This section does not apply to an investment fund manager in respect of an investment fund that is subject to National Instrument 81-107 *Independent Review Committee for Investment Funds*.

13.5 Restrictions on certain managed account transactions — (1) In this section, "responsible person" means, for a registered adviser,

(a) the adviser,

(b) a partner, director or officer of the adviser, and

(c) each of the following who has access to, or participates in formulating, an investment decision made on behalf of a client of the adviser or advice to be given to a client of the adviser:

(i) an employee or agent of the adviser;

(ii) an affiliate of the adviser;

(iii) a partner, director, officer, employee or agent of an affiliate of the adviser.

(2) A registered adviser must not knowingly cause an investment portfolio managed by it, including an investment fund for which it acts as an adviser, to do any of the following:

(a) purchase a security of an issuer in which a responsible person or an associate of a responsible person is a partner, officer or director unless

(i) this fact is disclosed to the client, and

(ii) the written consent of the client to the purchase is obtained before the purchase;

(b) purchase or sell a security from or to the investment portfolio of any of the following:

(i) a responsible person;

(ii) an associate of a responsible person;

(iii) an investment fund for which a responsible person acts as an adviser;

(c) provide a guarantee or loan to a responsible person or an associate of a responsible person.

13.6 Disclosure when recommending related or connected securities — A registered firm must not make a recommendation in any medium of communication to buy, sell or hold a security issued by the registered firm, a security of a related issuer or, during the security's distribution, a security of a connected issuer of the registered firm, unless any of the following apply:

(a) the firm discloses, in the same medium of communication, the nature and extent of the relationship or connection between the firm and the issuer;

(b) the recommendation is in respect of a security of a mutual fund, a scholarship plan, an educational plan or an educational trust that is an affiliate of, or is managed by an affiliate of, the registered firm and the names of the registered firm and the fund, plan or trust, as the case may be, are sufficiently similar to indicate that they are affiliated.

DIVISION 3 — REFERRAL ARRANGEMENTS

13.7 Definitions — referral arrangements — In this Division

"client" includes a prospective client;

"referral arrangement" means any arrangement in which a registrant agrees to pay or receive a referral fee;

"referral fee" means any form of compensation, direct or indirect, paid for the referral of a client to or from a registrant.

13.8 Permitted referral arrangements — A registered firm, or a registered individual whose registration is sponsored by the registered firm, must not participate in a referral arrangement with another person or company unless,

(a) before a client is referred by or to the registrant, the terms of the referral arrangement are set out in a written agreement between the registered firm and the person or company;

(b) the registered firm records all referral fees, and

(c) the registrant ensures that the information prescribed by subsection 13.10(1) [*disclosing referral arrangements to clients*] is provided to the client in writing before the party receiving the referral either opens an account for the client or provides services to the client.

13.9 Verifying the qualifications of the person or company receiving the referral — A registered firm, or a registered individual whose registration is sponsored by the registered firm, must not refer a client to another person or company unless the firm first takes reasonable steps to satisfy itself that the person or company has the appropriate qualifications to provide the services, and if applicable, is registered to provide those services.

13.10 Disclosing referral arrangements to clients — (1) The written disclosure of the referral arrangement required by paragraph 13.8(c) [*permitted referral arrangements*] must include the following:

(a) the name of each party to the agreement referred to in paragraph 13.8(a);

(b) the purpose and material terms of the agreement, including the nature of the services to be provided by each party;

(c) any conflicts of interest resulting from the relationship between the parties to the agreement and from any other element of the referral arrangement;

(d) the method of calculating the referral fee and, to the extent possible, the amount of the fee;

(e) the category of registration of each registrant that is a party to the agreement with a description of the activities that the registrant is authorized to engage in under that category and, giving consideration to the nature of the referral, the activities that the registrant is not permitted to engage in;

(f) if a referral is made to a registrant, a statement that all activity requiring registration resulting from the referral arrangement will be provided by the registrant receiving the referral;

(g) any other information that a reasonable client would consider important in evaluating the referral arrangement.

(2) If there is a change to the information set out in subsection (1), the registrant must ensure that written disclosure of that change is provided to each client affected by the change as soon as possible and no later than the 30th day before the date on which a referral fee is next paid or received.

13.11 Referral arrangements before this Instrument came into force — (1) This Division applies to a referral arrangement entered into before this Instrument came into force if a referral fee is paid under the referral arrangement after this Instrument comes into force.

(2) Subsection (1) does not apply until 6 months after this Instrument comes into force.

DIVISION 4 — LOANS AND MARGIN

13.12 Restriction on lending to clients — (1) A registrant must not lend money, extend credit or provide margin to a client.

(2) Notwithstanding subsection (1), an investment fund manager may lend money on a short term basis to an investment fund it manages, if the loan is for the purpose of funding redemptions of its securities or meeting expenses incurred by the investment fund in the normal course of its business.

13.13 Disclosure when recommending the use of borrowed money — (1) If a registrant recommends that a client should use borrowed money to finance any part of a purchase of a security, the registrant must, before the purchase, provide the client with a written statement that is substantially similar to the following:

> *"Using borrowed money to finance the purchase of securities involves greater risk than a purchase using cash resources only. If you borrow money to purchase securities, your responsibility to repay the loan and pay interest as required by its terms remains the same even if the value of the securities purchased declines."*

(2) Subsection (1) does not apply if one of the following applies

(a) the registrant has provided the client with the statement described under subsection (1) no earlier than the 180th day before the date of the proposed purchase,

(b) [repealed]

(c) the client is a permitted client.

DIVISION 5 — COMPLAINTS

13.14 Application of this Division — (1) This Division does not apply to an investment fund manager in respect of its activities as an investment fund manager.

(2) In Québec, a registered firm is deemed to comply with this Division if it complies with sections 168.1.1 to 168.1.3 of the *Securities Act* (Québec).

13.15 Handling complaints — A registered firm must document and, in a manner that a reasonable investor would consider fair and effective, respond to each complaint made to the registered firm about any product or service offered by the firm or a representative of the firm.

13.16 Dispute resolution service — (1) In this section,

"complaint" means a complaint that

(a) relates to a trading or advising activity of a registered firm or a representative of the firm, and

(b) is received by the firm within 6 years of the day when the client first knew or reasonably ought to have known of an act or omission that is a cause of or contributed to the complaint;

"OBSI" means the Ombudsman for Banking Services and Investments.

(2) If a registered firm receives a complaint from a client, the firm must, as soon as possible, provide the client with a written acknowledgement of the complaint that includes the following:

(a) description of the firm's obligations under this section;

(b) the steps that the client must take in order for an independent dispute resolution or mediation service to be made available to the client under subsection (4);

(3) If a registered firm decides to reject a complaint or to make an offer to resolve a complaint, the firm must, as soon as possible, provide the client with written notice of the decision and include the information referred to in subsection (2).

(4) A registered firm must as soon as possible ensure that an independent dispute resolution or mediation service is made available to a client at the firm's expense with respect to a complaint if either of the following apply:

(a) after 90 days of the firm's receipt of the complaint, the firm has not given the client written notice of a decision under subsection (3), and the client has notified the independent dispute resolution or mediation service specified under paragraph (2)(c) that the client wishes to have the complaint considered by the service;

(b) within 180 days of the client's receipt of written notice of the firm's decision under subsection (3), the client has notified the independent dispute resolution or mediation service specified under paragraph (2)(c) that the client wishes to have the complaint considered by the service.

(5) Subsection (4) does not apply unless the client agrees that any amount the client will claim for the purpose of the independent dispute resolution or mediation service's consideration of the complaint will be no greater than $350,000.

(6) For the purposes of the requirement to make available an independent dispute resolution or mediation service under subsection (4), a registered firm must take reasonable steps to ensure that OBSI will be the service that is made available to the client.

(7) Subsection (6) does not apply in Québec.

(8) This section does not apply in respect of a complaint made by a permitted client that is not an individual.

[Note: Except in Quebec, section 13.16, as amended, will not apply to a dealer or advisor that that was first registered on or before August 1, 2014. Section 13.16, as amended, will not apply to a dealer or advisor first registered during the period commencing on September 29, 2009 and ending on April 30, 2014 for complaints received received on or before August 1, 2014.]

DIVISION 6 — REGISTERED SUB-ADVISERS

13.17 Exemption from certain requirements for registered sub-advisers — (1) A registered sub-adviser is exempt from the following requirements in respect of its activities as a sub-adviser:

(a) section 13.4 [*identifying and responding to conflicts of interest*];

(b) division 3 [*referral arrangements*] of Part 13;

(c) division 5 [*complaints*] of Part 13;

(d) section 14.3 [*disclosure to clients about the fair allocation of investment opportunities*];

(e) section 14.5 [*notice to clients by non-resident registrants*];

(f) section 14.14 [*account statements*].

(2) The exemption under subsection (1) is not available unless all of the following apply:

(a) the obligations and duties of the registered sub-adviser are set out in a written agreement with the sub-adviser's registered adviser or registered dealer;

(b) the registered adviser or registered dealer has entered into a written agreement with its clients on whose behalf investment advice is or portfolio management services are to be provided agreeing to be responsible for any loss that arises out of the failure of the registered sub-adviser

(i) to exercise the powers and discharge the duties of its office honestly, in good faith and in the best interests of the registrant and each client of the registrant for whose benefit the advice is or portfolio management services are to be provided, or

(ii) to exercise the degree of care, diligence and skill that a reasonably prudent person would exercise in the circumstances.

PART 14 — HANDLING CLIENT ACCOUNTS — FIRMS

DIVISION 1 — INVESTMENT FUND MANAGERS

14.1 Application of this Part to investment fund managers — Other than section 14.6, subsection 14.12(5) and section 14.15, this Part does not apply to an investment fund manager in respect of its activities as an investment fund manager.

Proposed Amendment —

14.1 Application of this Part to investment fund managers — Other than section 14.1.1, section 14.6, subsection 14.12(5) and section 14.15, this Part does not apply to an investment fund manager in respect of its activities as an investment fund manager.

[To come into force July 15, 2016.]

Proposed Addition —

14.1.1 Duty to provide information — A registered investment fund manager of an investment fund must, within a reasonable period of time, provide a registered dealer, or a registered adviser, who has a client that owns securities of the investment fund, with the information concerning deferred sales charges and any other charges deducted from the net asset value of securities, and the information concerning trailing commissions paid to the dealer or adviser, that is required by the dealer or adviser in order to comply with paragraphs 14.12(1)(c) and 14.17(1)(h).

[To come into force July 15, 2016.]

DIVISION 2 — DISCLOSURE TO CLIENTS

14.2 Relationship disclosure information — (1) A registered firm must deliver to a client all information that a reasonable investor would consider important about the client's relationship with the registrant.

(2) Without limiting subsection (1), the information delivered under that subsection must include the following:

(a) a description of the nature or type of the client's account;

(b) a general description of the products and services the registered firm offers to the client;

(c) a general description of the types of risks that a client should consider when making an investment decision;

(d) a description of the risks to a client of using borrowed money to finance a purchase of a security;

(e) a description of the conflicts of interest that the registered firm is required to disclose to a client under securities legislation;

(f) disclosure of the operating charges the client might be required to pay related to the client's account;

(g) a general description of the types of transaction charges the client might be required to pay;

(h) a general description of any compensation paid to the registered firm by any other party in relation to the different types of products that a client may purchase through the registered firm;

(i) a description of the content and frequency of reporting for each account or portfolio of a client;

(j) disclosure of the firm's obligations if a client has a complaint contemplated under section 13.16 [*dispute resolution service*] and the steps that the client must take in order for an independent dispute resolution or mediation service to be made available to the client at the firm's expense;

(k) a statement that the registered firm has an obligation to assess whether a purchase or sale of a security is suitable for a client prior to executing the transaction or at any other time;

(l) the information a registered firm must collect about the client under section 13.2 [*know your client*].

(m) a general explanation of how investment performance benchmarks might be used to assess the performance of a client's investments and any options for benchmark information that might be made available to clients by the registered firm;

(n) if the registered firm is a scholarship plan dealer, an explanation of any terms of the scholarship plan offered to the client by the registered firm that, if those terms are not met by the client or the client's designated beneficiary under the plan, might cause the client or the designated beneficiary to suffer a loss of contributions, earnings or government contributions in the plan.

(3) A registered firm must deliver the information in subsection (1), if applicable, and subsection (2) to the client in writing, except that the information in paragraph (2)(b) may be provided orally or in writing, before the firm first

(a) purchases or sells a security for the client, or

(b) advises the client to purchase, sell or hold a security.

(4) If there is a significant change in respect of the information delivered to a client under subsections (1) or (2), the registered firm must take reasonable steps to notify the client of the change in a timely manner and, if possible, before the firm next

(a) purchases or sells a security for the client; or

(b) advises the client to purchase, sell or hold a security.

(5) [repealed]

(5.1) A registered firm must not impose any new operating charge in respect of an account of a client, or increase the amount of any operating charge in respect of an account of a client, unless written notice of the new or increased operating charge is provided to the client at least 60 days before the date on which the imposition or increase becomes effective.

(6) This section does not apply to a registered firm in respect of a permitted client that is not an individual.

(7) Except for subsections (5.1), (6) and (8), this section does not apply to a registered dealer in respect of a client for whom the dealer purchases or sells securities only as directed by a registered adviser acting for the client.

(8) A registered dealer referred to in subsection (7) must deliver the information required under paragraphs (2)(a) and (e) to (j) to the client in writing, and the information in paragraph (2)(b) orally or in writing, before the dealer first purchases or sells a security for the client.

14.2.1 Pre-trade disclosure of charges — (1) Before a registered firm accepts an instruction from a client to purchase or sell a security in an account other than a managed account, the firm must disclose to the client

(a) the charges the client will be required to pay in respect of the purchase or sale, or a reasonable estimate if the actual amount of the charges is not known to the firm at the time of disclosure,

(b) in the case of a purchase to which deferred charges apply, that the client might be required to pay a deferred sales charge on the subsequent sale of the security and the fee schedule that will apply, and

(c) whether the firm will receive trailing commissions in respect of the security.

(2) This section does not apply to a registered firm in respect of a permitted client that is not an individual.

(3) This section does not apply to a dealer in respect of a client for whom the dealer purchases or sells securities only as directed by a registered adviser acting for the client.

14.3 Disclosure to clients about the fair allocation of investment opportunities — A registered adviser must deliver to a client a summary of the policies required under section 11.1 [*compliance system*] that provide reasonable assurance that the firm and each individual acting on its behalf complies with section 14.10 [*allocating investment opportunities fairly*] and that summary must be delivered

(a) when the adviser opens an account for the client, and

(b) if there is a significant change to the summary last delivered to the client, in a timely manner and, if possible, before the firm next

(i) purchases or sells a security for the client, or

(ii) advises the client to purchase, sell or hold a security.

14.4 When the firm has a relationship with a financial institution — (1) If a registered firm opens a client account to trade in securities, in an office or branch of a Canadian financial institution or a Schedule III bank, the registered firm must give the client a written notice stating that it is a separate legal entity from the Canadian financial institution or Schedule III bank and, unless otherwise advised by the registrant, securities purchased from or through the registrant

(a) are not insured by a government deposit insurer,

(b) are not guaranteed by the Canadian financial institution or Schedule III bank, and

(c) may fluctuate in value.

(2) A registered firm that is subject to subsection (1) must receive a written confirmation from the client that the client has read and understood the notice before the registered firm

    (a) purchases or sells a security for the client, or

    (b) advises the client to purchase, sell or hold a security.

(3) This section does not apply to a registered firm if the client is a permitted client.

14.5 Notice to clients by non-resident registrants — (1) A registered firm whose head office is not located in the local jurisdiction must provide a client in the local jurisdiction with a statement in writing disclosing the following:

    (a) the firm is not resident in the local jurisdiction;

    (b) the jurisdiction in Canada or the foreign jurisdiction in which the head office or the principal place of business of the firm is located;

    (c) all or substantially all of the assets of the firm may be situated outside the local jurisdiction;

    (d) there may be difficulty enforcing legal rights against the firm because of the above;

    (e) the name and address of the agent for service of process of the firm in the local jurisdiction.

(2) This section does not apply to a registered firm whose head office is in Canada if the firm is registered in the local jurisdiction.

DIVISION 3 — CLIENT ASSETS

14.6 Holding client assets in trust — A registered firm that holds client assets must hold the assets

    (a) separate and apart from its own property,

    (b) in trust for the client, and

    (c) in the case of cash, in a designated trust account at a Canadian financial institution, a Schedule III bank, or a member of IIROC.

14.7 Holding client assets — non-resident registrants — (1) A registered firm whose head office is not located in a jurisdiction of Canada must ensure that all client assets are held

    (a) in the client's name,

    (b) on behalf of the client by a custodian or sub-custodian that

        (i) meets the guidelines prescribed for acting as a sub-custodian of the portfolio securities of a mutual fund in Part 6 of National Instrument 81-102 *Investment Funds*, and

        (ii) is subject to the Bank for International Settlements' framework for international convergence of capital measurement and capital standards, or

    (c) on behalf of the client by a registered dealer that is a member of an SRO and that is a member of the Investor Protection Fund or other comparable compensation fund or contingency trust fund.

(2) Section 14.6 [*holding client assets in trust*] does not apply to a registered firm that is subject to subsection (1).

14.8 Securities subject to a safekeeping agreement — A registered firm that holds unencumbered securities for a client under a written safekeeping agreement must

    (a) segregate the securities from all other securities,

    (b) identify the securities as being held in safekeeping for the client in

        (i) the registrant's security position record,

        (ii) the client's ledger, and

        (iii) the client's statement of account, and

    (c) release the securities only on an instruction from the client.

14.9 Securities not subject to a safekeeping agreement — (1) A registered firm that holds unencumbered securities for a client other than under a written safekeeping agreement must

    (a) segregate and identify the securities as being held in trust for the client, and

    (b) describe the securities as being held in segregation on

        (i) the registrant's security position record,

        (ii) the client's ledger, and

        (iii) the client's statement of account.

(2) Securities described in subsection (1) may be segregated in bulk.

DIVISION 4 — CLIENT ACCOUNTS

14.10 Allocating investment opportunities fairly — A registered adviser must ensure fairness in allocating investment opportunities among its clients.

14.11 Selling or assigning client accounts — If a registered firm proposes to sell or assign a client's account in whole or in part to another registrant, the registered firm must, prior to the sale or assignment, give a written explanation of the proposal to the client and inform the client of the client's right to close the client's account.

DIVISION 5 — REPORTING TO CLIENTS

14.11.1 Determining market value — (1) For the purposes of this Division, the market value of a security

    (a) that is issued by an investment fund which is not listed on an exchange must be determined by reference to the net asset value provided by the investment fund manager of the fund on the relevant date,

(b) in any other case, is the amount that the registered firm reasonably believes to be the market value of the security

(i) after referring to a price quotation on a marketplace, if one is published for the security, using the last bid price in the case of a long security and the last ask price in the case of a short security, as shown on a consolidated pricing list or exchange quotation sheet as of the close of business on the relevant date or the last trading day before the relevant date, and after making any adjustments considered by the registered firm to be necessary to accurately reflect the market value,

(ii) if no reliable price for the security is quoted on a marketplace, after referring to a published market report or inter-dealer quotation sheet, on the relevant date or the last trading day before the relevant date, and after making any adjustments considered by the registered firm to be necessary to accurately reflect the market value,

(iii) if the market value for the security cannot be reasonably determined in accordance with subparagraph (i) or (ii), after applying the policy of the registered firm for determining market value, which must include procedures to assess the reliability of valuation inputs and assumptions and provide for

(A) the use of inputs that are observable, and

(B) the use of unobservable inputs and assumptions, if observable inputs are not reasonably available.

(2) If a registered firm determines the market value of a security in accordance with subparagraph (1)(b)(iii), when it refers to the market value in a statement under section 14.14 [*account statements*], 14.14.1 [*additional statements*], 14.14.2 [*position cost information*], 14.15 [*security holder statements*] or 14.16 [*scholarship plan dealer statements*], the registered firm must include the following notification or a notification that is substantially similar:

"There is no active market for this security so we have estimated its market value"

(3) If a registered firm reasonably believes that it cannot determine the market value of a security in accordance with subsection (1), the market value of the security must be reported in a statement delivered under section 14.14 [*account statements*], 14.14.1 [*additional statements*], 14.14.2 [*position cost information*], 14.15 [*security holder statements*] or 14.16 [*scholarship plan dealer statements*] as not determinable, and the market value of the security must be excluded from the calculations in paragraphs 14.14(5)(b), 14.14.1(2)(b) and 14.14.2(5)(a).

Proposed Amendment —

(3) If a registered firm reasonably believes that it cannot determine the market value of a security in accordance with subsection (1), the market value of the security must be reported in a statement delivered under section 14.14 [*account statements*], 14.14.1 [*additional statements*], 14.14.2 [*position cost information*], 14.15 [*security holder statements*] or 14.16 [*scholarship plan dealer statements*] and in an investment performance report delivered under section 14.18 [*investment performance report*] as not determinable, and the market value of the security must be excluded from the calculations in paragraphs 14.14(5)(b), 14.14.1(2)(b) and 14.14.2(5)(a) and subsection 14.19(1) [*content of investment performance report*].

[To come into force July 15, 2016.]

14.12 Content and delivery of trade confirmation — (1) A registered dealer that has acted on behalf of a client in connection with a purchase or sale of a security must promptly deliver to the client or, if the client consents in writing, to a registered adviser acting for the client, a written confirmation of the transaction, setting out the following:

(a) the quantity and description of the security purchased or sold;

(b) the price per security paid or received by the client;

(b.1) in the case of a purchase of a debt security, the security's annual yield;

(c) the commission, sales charge, service charge and any other amount charged in respect of the transaction;

Proposed Amendment —

(c) the amount of each transaction charge, deferred sales charge or other charge in respect of the transaction, and the total amount of all charges in respect of the transaction;

[To come into force July 15, 2016.]

(c.1) in the case of a purchase or sale of a debt security, either of the following:

(i) the total amount of any mark-up or mark-down, commission or other service charges the registered dealer applied to the transaction;

(ii) the total amount of any commission charged to the client by the registered dealer and, if the dealer applied a mark-up or mark-down or any service charge other than a commission, the following notification or a notification that is substantially similar:

"Dealer firm remuneration has been added to the price of this security (in the case of a purchase) or deducted from the price of this security (in the case of a sale). This amount was in addition to any commission this trade confirmation shows was charged to you".

(d) whether the registered dealer acted as principal or agent;

(e) the date and the name of the marketplace, if any, on which the transaction took place, or if applicable, a statement that the transaction took place on more than one marketplace or over more than one day;

(f) the name of the dealing representative, if any, involved in the transaction;

(g) the settlement date of the transaction;

(h) if applicable, that the security is a security issued by the registered dealer, a security issued by a related issuer of the registered dealer or, if the transaction occurred during the security's distribution, a security issued by a connected issuer of the registered dealer.

(2) If a transaction under subsection (1) involved more than one transaction or if the transaction took place on more than one marketplace the information referred to in subsection (1) may be set out in the aggregate if the confirmation also contains a statement that additional details concerning the transaction will be provided to the client upon request and without additional charge.

(3) Paragraph (1)(h) does not apply if all of the following apply:

(a) the security is a security of a mutual fund that is established and managed by the registered dealer or by an affiliate of the registered dealer, in its capacity as investment fund manager of the mutual fund;

(b) the names of the dealer and the mutual fund are sufficiently similar to indicate that they are affiliated or related., *and*

(4) For the purpose of paragraph (1)(f), a dealing representative may be identified by means of a code or symbol if the confirmation also contains a statement that the name of the dealing representative will be provided to the client on request of the client.

(5) A registered investment fund manager that has executed a redemption order received directly from a security holder must promptly deliver to the security holder a written confirmation of the redemption, setting out the following:

(a) the quantity and description of the security redeemed;

(b) the price per security received by the client;

(c) the commission, sales charge, service charge and any other amount charged in respect of the redemption;

(d) the settlement date of the redemption.

(6) Subsection 14.12(5) does not apply to trades in a security of an investment fund made on reliance on section 8.6 [*investment fund trades by adviser to managed account*].

14.13 Confirmations for certain automatic plans — The requirement under section 14.12 [*content and delivery of trade confirmation*] to deliver a confirmation promptly does not apply to a registered dealer in respect of a transaction if all of the following apply:

(a) the client gave the dealer prior written notice that the transaction is made pursuant to the client's participation in an automatic payment plan, including a dividend reinvestment plan, or an automatic withdrawal plan in which a transaction is made at least monthly;

(b) the registered dealer delivered a confirmation as required under section 14.12 [*content and delivery of trade confirmation*] for the first transaction made under the plan after receiving the notice referred to in paragraph (a);

(c) the transaction is in a security of a mutual fund, scholarship plan, educational plan or educational trust;

14.14 Account statements — (1) A registered dealer must deliver to a client a statement that includes the information referred to in subsections (4) and (5)

(a) at least once every 3 months, or

(b) if the client has requested to receive statements on a monthly basis, for each one-month period

(2) A registered dealer must deliver to a client a statement that includes the information referred to in subsections (4) and (5) after the end of any month in which a transaction was effected in securities held by the dealer in the client's account, other than a transaction made under an automatic withdrawal plan or an automatic payment plan, including a dividend reinvestment plan.

(2.1) Paragraph 1(b) and subsection (2) do not apply to a mutual fund dealer in connection with its activities as a dealer in respect of the securities listed in paragraph 7.1(2)(b) [*dealer categories*].

(3) A registered adviser must deliver to a client a statement that includes the information referred to in subsections (4) and (5) at least once every 3 months, except that if the client has requested to receive statements on a monthly basis, the adviser must deliver a statement to the client every month.

(3.1) [Repealed.]

(4) If a registered dealer or registered adviser made a transaction for a client during the period covered by a statement delivered under subsection (1), (2) or (3), the statement must include the following:

(a) the date of the transaction;

(b) whether the transaction was a purchase, sale or transfer;

(c) the name of the security;

(d) the number of securities;

(e) the price per security if the transaction was a purchase or sale;

(f) the total value of the transaction if it was a purchase or sale.

(5) If a registered dealer or registered adviser holds securities owned by a client in an account of the client, a statement delivered under subsection (1), (2) or (3) must indicate that the securities are held for the client by the registered firm and must include the following information about the client's account determined as at the end of the period for which the statement is made:

(a) the name and quantity of each security in the account;

(b) the market value of each security in the account and, if applicable, the notification in subsection 14.11.1(2) [*determining market value*] ;

(c) the total market value of each security position in the account;

(d) any cash balance in the account;

(e) the total market value of all cash and securities in the account, *and*

(f) whether the account is covered under an investor protection fund approved or recognized by the securities regulatory authority and, if it is, the name of the investor protection fund;

(g) which securities in the account might be subject to a deferred sales charge if they are sold.

(6) [Repealed.]

(7) For the purposes of this section, a security is considered to be held by a registered firm for a client if

(a) the firm is the registered owner of the security as nominee on behalf of the client, or

(b) the firm has physical possession of a certificate evidencing ownership of the security.

14.14.1 Additional statements — (1) A registered dealer or registered adviser must deliver a statement that includes the information referred to in subsection (2) to a client if any of the following apply in respect of a security owned by the client that is held or controlled by a party other than the dealer or adviser:

(a) the dealer or adviser has trading authority over the security or the client's account in which the security is held or was transacted;

(b) the dealer or adviser receives continuing payments related to the client's ownership of the security from the issuer of the security, the investment fund manager of the issuer or any other party;

(c) the security is issued by a scholarship plan, a mutual fund or an investment fund that is a labour-sponsored investment fund corporation, or labour-sponsored venture capital corporation, under legislation of a jurisdiction of Canada and the dealer or adviser is the dealer or adviser of record for the client on the records of the issuer of the security or the records of the issuer's investment fund manager.

(2) A statement delivered under subsection (1) must include the following in respect of the securities or the account referred to in subsection (1), determined as at the end of the period for which the statement is made:

(a) the name and quantity of each security;

(b) the market value of each security and, if applicable, the notification in subsection 14.11.1(2) [*determining market value*];

(c) the total market value of each security position;

(d) any cash balance in the account;

(e) the total market value of all of the cash and securities;

(f) the name of the party that holds or controls each security and a description of the way it is held;

(g) whether the securities are covered under an investor protection fund approved or recognized by the securities regulatory authority and, if they are, the name of the fund;

(h) which of the securities might be subject to a deferred sales charge if they are sold.

(3) If subsection (1) applies to a registered dealer or a registered adviser, the dealer or adviser must deliver a statement that includes the information in subsection (2) to a client at least once every 3 months, except that if a client has requested to receive statements on a monthly basis, the adviser must deliver a statement to the client every month.

(4) If subsection (1) applies to a registered dealer or a registered adviser that is also required to deliver a statement to a client under subsection 14.14(1) or (3), a statement delivered under subsection (1) must be delivered to the client in one of the following ways:

(a) combined with a statement delivered to the client under subsection 14.14(1) or (3) for the period ending on the same date;

(b) as a separate document accompanying a statement delivered to the client under subsection 14.14(1) or (3) for the period ending on the same date;

(c) as a separate document delivered within 10 days after the statement delivered to the client under subsection 14.14(1) or (3) for the period ending on the same date.

(5) For the purposes of this section, a security is considered to be held for a client by a party other than the registered firm if any of the following apply:

(a) the other party is the registered owner of the security as nominee on behalf of the client;

(b) ownership of the security is recorded on the books of its issuer in the client's name;

(c) the other party has physical possession of a certificate evidencing ownership of the security;

(d) the client has physical possession of a certificate evidencing ownership of the security.

(6) This section does not apply to a registered firm in respect of a permitted client that is not an individual.

14.14.2 Position cost information — (1) If a registered dealer or registered adviser is required to deliver a statement to a client that includes information required under subsection 14.14(5) [*account statements*] or 14.14.1(2) [*additional statements*], the dealer or adviser must deliver the information referred to in subsection (2) to a client at least once every 3 months.

(2) The information delivered under subsection (1) must disclose the following:

(a) for each security position in the statement opened on or after July 15, 2015,

(i) the cost of the position, determined as at the end of the period for which the information under subsection 14.14(5) or 14.14.1(2) is provided, presented on an average cost per unit or share basis or on an aggregate basis, or

(ii) if the security position was transferred from another registered firm, the information referred to in subparagraph (i) or the market value of the security position as at the date of the position's transfer if it is also disclosed in the statement that it is the market value as of the transfer date, not the cost of the security position, that is being disclosed;

(b) for each security position in the statement opened before July 15, 2015,

(i) the cost of the position, determined as at the end of the period for which the information under subsection 14.14(5) or 14.14.1(2) is provided, presented on an average cost per unit or share basis or on an aggregate basis, or

(ii) the market value of the security position as at July 15, 2015 or an earlier date, if the same date and value are used for all clients of the firm holding that security and it is also disclosed in the statement that it is the market value as of that date, not the cost of the security position, that is being disclosed;

(c) the total cost of all of the security positions in the statement, determined in accordance with paragraphs (a) and (b);

(d) for each security position for which the registered firm reasonably believes it cannot determine the cost in accordance with paragraphs (a) and (b), disclosure of that fact in the statement.

(3) The cost of security positions required to be disclosed under subsection (2) must be either the book cost or the original cost and must be accompanied by the definition of "book cost" [*definitions of terms used throughout this Instrument*] in section 1.1 or the definition of "original cost" in section 1.1, as applicable.

(4) The information delivered under subsection (1) must be delivered to the client in one of the following ways:

(a) combined with a statement delivered to the client that includes the information required under subsection 14.14(5) or 14.14.1(2) for the period ending on the same date;

(b) in a separate document accompanying a statement delivered to the client that includes information required under subsection 14.14(5) or 14.14.1(2) for the period ending on the same date;

(c) in a separate document delivered within 10 days after a statement delivered to the client that includes information required under subsection 14.14(5) or 14.14.1(2) for the period ending on the same date.

(5) If the information under subsection (1) is delivered to the client in a separate document in accordance with paragraph (4)(c), the separate document must also include the following:

(a) the market value of each security in the statement and, if applicable, the notification in subsection 14.11.1(2) [*determining market value*];

(b) the total market value of each security position in the statement;

(c) the total market value of all cash and securities in the statement.

(6) This section does not apply to a registered firm in respect of a permitted client that is not an individual.

14.15 Security holder statements — If there is no dealer or adviser of record for a security holder on the records of a registered investment fund manager, the investment fund manager must deliver to the security holder at least once every 12 months a statement that includes the following:

(a) the information required under subsection 14.14(4) [*account statements*] for each transaction that the registered investment fund manager made for the security holder during the period;

(b) the information required under subsection 14.14.1(2) [*additional statements*] for the securities of the security holder that are on the records of the registered investment fund manager;

(c) the information required under section 14.14.2 [*position cost information*].

14.16 Scholarship plan dealer statements — Sections 14.14 [*account statements*], 14.14.1 [*additional statements*] and 14.14.2 [*position cost information*] do not apply to a scholarship plan dealer if both of the following apply:

(a) the scholarship plan dealer is not registered in another dealer or adviser category;

(b) the scholarship plan dealer delivers to a client a statement at least once every 12 months that provides the information required under subsections 14.14(4) and 14.14.1(2).

Proposed Addition —

14.17 Report on charges and other compensation — **(1)** For each 12-month period, a registered firm must deliver to a client a report on charges and other compensation containing the following information, except that the first report delivered after a client has opened an account may cover a period of less than 12 months:

(a) the registered firm's current operating charges which might be applicable to the client's account;

(b) the total amount of each type of operating charge related to the client's account paid by the client during the period covered by the report, and the total amount of those charges;

(c) the total amount of each type of transaction charge related to the purchase or sale of securities paid by the client during the period covered by the report, and the total amount of those charges;

(d) the total amount of the operating charges reported under paragraph (b) and the transaction charges reported under paragraph (c);

(e) if the registered firm purchased or sold debt securities for the client during the period covered by the report, either of the following:

(i) the total amount of any mark-ups, mark-downs, commissions or other service charges the firm applied on the purchases or sales of debt securities;

(ii) the total amount of any commissions charged to the client by the firm on the purchases or sales of debt securities and, if the firm applied mark-ups, mark-downs or any service charges other than commissions on the purchases or sales of debt securities, the following notification or a notification that is substantially similar:

> *For debt securities purchased or sold for you during the period covered by this report, dealer firm remuneration was added to the price you paid (in the case of a purchase) or deducted from the price you received (in the case of a sale). This amount was in addition to any commissions you were charged.*

(f) if the registered firm is a scholarship plan dealer, the unpaid amount of any enrolment fee or other charge that is payable by the client;

(g) the total amount of each type of payment, other than a trailing commission, that is made to the registered firm or any of its registered individuals by a securities issuer or another registrant in relation to registerable services to the client during the period covered by the report, accompanied by an explanation of each type of payment;

(h) if the registered firm received trailing commissions related to securities owned by the client during the period covered by the report, the following notification or a notification that is substantially similar:

> *We received $[amount] in trailing commissions in respect of securities you owned during the 12-month period covered by this report.*
>
> *Investment funds pay investment fund managers a fee for managing their funds. The managers pay us ongoing trailing commissions for the services and advice we provide you. The amount of the trailing commission depends on the sales charge option you chose when you purchased the fund. You are not directly charged the trailing commission or the management fee. But, these fees affect you because they reduce the amount of the fund's return to you. Information about management fees and other charges to your investment funds is included in the prospectus or fund facts document for each fund.*

(2) For the purposes of this section, the information in respect of securities of a client required to be reported under subsection 14.14(5) [*account statements*] must be delivered in a separate report on charges and other compensation for each of the client's accounts.

(3) For the purposes of this section, the information in respect of securities of a client required to be reported under subsection 14.14.1(1) [*additional statements*] must be delivered in a report on charges and other compensation for the client's account through which the securities were transacted.

(4) Subsections (2) and (3) do not apply if the registered firm provides a report on charges and other compensation that consolidates, into a single report, the required information for more than one of a client's accounts and any securities of the client required to be reported under subsection 14.14(5) or 14.14.1(1) and if the following apply:

(a) the client has consented in writing to the form of disclosure referred to in this subsection;

(b) the consolidated report specifies the accounts and securities with respect to which information is required to be reported under subsection 14.14.1(1) [*additional statements*].

Part 3: REGISTRATION

(5) This section does not apply to a registered firm in respect of a permitted client that is not an individual.

14.18 Investment performance report — **(1)** A registered firm must deliver an investment performance report to a client every 12 months, except that the first report delivered after a registered firm first makes a trade for a client may be sent within 24 months after that trade.

(2) For the purposes of this section, the information in respect of securities of a client required to be reported under subsection 14.14(5) [*account statements*] must be delivered in a separate report for each of the client's accounts.

(3) For the purposes of this section, the information in respect of securities of a client required to be reported under subsection 14.14.1(1) [*additional statements*] must be delivered in the report for each of the client's accounts through which the securities were transacted.

Proposed Amendment —

(4) Subsections (2) and (3) do not apply if the registered firm provides a report that consolidates, into a single report, the required information for more than one of a client's accounts and any securities of the client required to be reported under subsection 14.14(5) or 14.14.1(1) and if the following apply:

(a) the client has consented in writing to the form of disclosure referred to in this subsection;

(b) the consolidated report specifies the accounts and securities with respect to which information is required to be reported under subsection 14.14.1(1) [*additional statements*].

(5) This section does not apply to

Proposed Amendment —

(1) An investment performance report required to be delivered under section 14.18 by a registered firm must include all of the following in respect of the securities referred to in a statement in respect of which subsection 14.14(1), (2) or (3) [*account statements*] or 14.14.1(1) [*additional statements*] apply:

(a) a client's account that has existed for less than a 12-month period;

(b) a registered dealer in respect of a client's account in which the dealer executes trades only as directed by a registered adviser acting for the client; and

(c) a registered firm in respect of a permitted client that is not an individual.

(6) If a registered firm reasonably believes there are no securities of a client with respect to which information is required to be reported under subsection 14.14(5) [*account statements*] or subsection 14.14.1(1) [*additional statements*] and for which a market value can be determined, the firm is not required to deliver a report to the client for the period.

14.19 Content of investment performance report — **(1)** An investment performance report required to be delivered under section 14.18 by a registered firm must include all of the following in respect of the securities referred to in a statement in respect of which subsection 14.14(1), (2) or (3) [*account statements*] or 14.14.1(1) [*additional statements*] apply:

(a) the market value of all cash and securities in the client's account as at the beginning of the 12-month period covered by the investment performance report;

(b) the market value of all cash and securities in the client's account as at the end of the 12-month period covered by the investment performance report;

(c) the market value of all deposits and transfers of cash and securities into the client's account, and the market value of all withdrawals and transfers of cash and securities out of the account, in the 12-month period covered by the investment performance report;

(d) subject to paragraph (e), the market value of all deposits and transfers of cash and securities into the client's account, and the market value of all withdrawals and transfers of cash and securities out of the account, since opening the account;

(e) if the client's account was opened before July 15, 2015 and the registered firm reasonably believes market values are not available for all deposits, withdrawals and transfers since the account was opened, the following:

(i) the market value of all cash and securities in the client's account as at July 15, 2015;

(ii) the market value of all deposits and transfers of cash and securities into the account, and the market value of all withdrawals and transfers of cash and securities out of the account, since July 15, 2015;

(f) the annual change in the market value of the client's account for the 12-month period covered by the investment performance report, determined using the following formula

$$A - B - C + D$$

where

A = the market value of all cash and securities in the account as at the end of the 12-month period covered by the investment performance report;

B = the market value of all cash and securities in the account at the beginning of that 12-month period;

C = the market value of all deposits and transfers of cash and securities into the account in that 12-month period; and

D = the market value of all withdrawals and transfers of cash and securities out of the account in that 12-month period;

(g) subject to paragraph (h), the cumulative change in the market value of the account since the account was opened, determined using the following formula

$$A - E + F$$

where

A   = the market value of all cash and securities in the account as at the end of the 12-month period covered by the investment performance report;

E   = the market value of all deposits and transfers of cash and securities into the account since account opening; and

F   = the market value of all withdrawals and transfers of cash and securities out of the account since account opening;

(h) if the registered firm reasonably believes the market value of all deposits and transfers of cash and securities into the account since the account was opened or the market value of all withdrawals and transfers of cash and securities out of the account since the account was opened required in paragraph (g) is not available to the registered firm, the cumulative change in the market value of the account determined using the following formula

$$A - G - H + I$$

where

A   = the market value of all cash and securities in the account as at the end of the 12-month period covered by the investment performance report;

G   = the market value of all cash and securities in the account as at July 15, 2015;

H   = the market value of all deposits and transfers of cash and securities into the account since July 15, 2015; and

I   = the market value of all withdrawals and transfers of cash and securities out of the account since July 15, 2015;

(i) the amount of the annualized total percentage return for the client's account calculated net of charges, using a money-weighted rate of return calculation method generally accepted in the securities industry;

(j) the definition of "total percentage return" in section 1.1 and a notification indicating the following:

    (i) that the total percentage return in the investment performance report was calculated net of charges;

    (ii) the calculation method used;

    (iii) a general explanation in plain language of what the calculation method takes into account.

(2) The information delivered for the purposes of paragraph (1)(i) must be provided for each of the following periods:

(a) the 12-month period covered by the investment performance report;

(b) the 3-year period preceding the end of the 12-month period covered by the report;

(c) the 5-year period preceding the end of the 12-month period covered by the report;

(d) the 10-year period preceding the end of the 12-month period covered by the report;

(e) the period since the client's account was opened if the account has been open for more than one year before the date of the report or, if the account was opened before July 15, 2015 and the registered firm reasonably believes the annualized total percentage return for the period before July 15, 2015 is not available, the period since July 15, 2015.

Proposed Amendment —

(3) Despite subsection (2), if any portion of a period referred to in paragraph (2)(b), (c) or (d) was before July 15, 2015, the registered firm is not required to report the annualized total percentage return for that period.

(4) Despite subsection (1), the information a scholarship plan dealer is required to deliver under section 14.18 [*investment performance report*] in respect of each scholarship plan in which a client has invested through the scholarship plan dealer is the following:

(a) the total amount that the client has invested in the plan as at the date of the investment performance report;

(b) the total amount that would be returned to the client if, as at the date of the investment performance report, the client ceased to make prescribed payments into the plan;

(c) a reasonable projection of future payments that the plan might pay to the client's designated beneficiary under the plan, or to the client, at the maturity of the client's investment in the plan;

(d) a summary of any terms of the plan that, if not met by the client or the client's designated beneficiary under the plan, might cause the client or the designated beneficiary to suffer a loss of contributions, earnings or government contributions in the plan.

(5) The information delivered under section 14.18 [*investment performance report*] must be presented using text, tables and charts, and must be accompanied by notes in the investment performance report explaining

(a) the content of the report and how a client can use the information to assess the performance of the client's investments; and

(b) the changing value of the client's investments as reflected in the information in the report.

(6) If a registered firm delivers information required under this section in a report to a client for a period of less than one year, the firm must not calculate the disclosed information on an annualized basis.

(7) If the registered firm reasonably believes the market value cannot be determined for a security position, the market value must be assigned a value of zero in the calculation of the information delivered under subsection 14.18(1) and the fact that its market value could not be determined must be disclosed to the client.

14.20 Delivery of report on charges and other compensation and investment performance report — **(1)** A report under section 14.17 [*report on charges and other compensation*] and a report under section 14.18 [*investment performance report*] must include information for the same 12-month period and the reports must be delivered together in one of the following ways:

(a) combined with a statement delivered to the client that includes information required under subsection 14.14(1), (2) or (3) [*account statements*], subsection 14.14.1(2) [*additional statements*] or section 14.16 [*scholarship plan dealer statements*];

(b) accompanying a statement delivered to the client that includes information required under subsection 14.14(1), (2) or (3) [*account statements*], subsection 14.14.1(2) [*additional statements*] or section 14.16 [*scholarship plan dealer statements*];

(c) within 10 days after a statement delivered to the client that includes information required under subsection 14.14(1), (2) or (3) [*account statements*], subsection 14.14.1(2) [*additional statements*] or section 14.16 [*scholarship plan dealer statements*].

(2) Subsection (1) does not apply in respect of the first report under section 14.17 [*report on charges and other compensation*] and the first report under section 14.18 [*investment performance report*] for a client.

[To come into force July 15, 2016.]

PART 15 — GRANTING AN EXEMPTION

15.1 Who can grant an exemption — (1) The regulator or the securities regulatory authority may grant an exemption from this Instrument, in whole or in part, subject to such conditions or restrictions as may be imposed in the exemption.

(2) Despite subsection (1), in Ontario only the regulator may grant such an exemption.

(3) Except in Ontario, an exemption referred to in subsection (1) is granted under the statute referred to in Appendix B of National Instrument 14-101 *Definitions* opposite the name of the local jurisdiction.

PART 16 — TRANSITION

16.1 Change of registration categories — individuals — On the day this Instrument comes into force, an individual registered in a category referred to in

(a) column 1 of Appendix C [*new category names — individuals*], opposite the name of the local jurisdiction, is registered as a dealing representative,

(b) column 2 of Appendix C [*new category names — individuals*], opposite the name of the local jurisdiction, is registered as an advising representative, and

(c) column 3 of Appendix C [*new category names — individuals*], opposite the name of the local jurisdiction, is registered as an associate advising representative.

16.2 Change of registration categories — firms — On the day this Instrument comes into force, a person or company registered in a category referred to in

(a) column 1 of Appendix D [*new category names — firms*], opposite the name of the local jurisdiction, is registered as an investment dealer,

(b) column 2 of Appendix D [*new category names — firms*], opposite the name of the local jurisdiction, is registered as a mutual fund dealer,

(c) column 3 of Appendix D [*new category names — firms*], opposite the name of the local jurisdiction, is registered as a scholarship plan dealer,

(d) column 4 of Appendix D [*new category names — firms*], opposite the name of the local jurisdiction, is registered as a restricted dealer,

(e) column 5 of Appendix D [*new category names — firms*], opposite the name of the local jurisdiction, is registered as a portfolio manager, and

(f) column 6 of Appendix D [*new category names — firms*], opposite the name of the local jurisdiction, is registered as a restricted portfolio manager.

16.3 Change of registration categories — limited market dealers — (1) This section applies in Ontario and Newfoundland and Labrador.

(2) On the day this Instrument comes into force, a person or company registered as a limited market dealer is registered as an exempt market dealer.

(3) On the day this Instrument comes into force, an individual registered to trade on behalf of a limited market dealer is registered as a dealing representative of the dealer.

(4) Sections 12.1 [*capital requirements*] and 12.2 [*notifying the regulator of a subordination agreement*] do not apply to a person or company registered as an exempt market dealer under subsection (2) until one year after this Instrument comes into force.

(5) Sections 12.3 [*insurance — dealer*] and 12.7 [*notifying the regulator of a change, claim or cancellation*] do not apply to a person or company registered as an exempt market dealer under subsection (2) until 6 months after this Instrument comes into force.

16.4 Registration for investment fund managers active when this Instrument comes into force — (1) The requirement to register as an investment fund manager does not apply to a person or company that is acting as an investment fund manager on the day this Instrument comes into force

(a) until one year after this Instrument comes into force, or

(b) if the person or company applies for registration as an investment fund manager within one year after this Instrument comes into force, until the regulator or, in Québec, the securities regulatory authority has accepted or refused the registration.

(2) Subsection (1) is repealed one year after this Instrument comes into force.

(3) Section 12.5 [*insurance — investment fund manager*] does not apply to a registered dealer or a registered adviser that is acting as an investment fund manager on the day this Instrument comes into force.

(4) Subsection (3) is repealed one year after this Instrument comes into force.

16.5 Temporary exemption for Canadian investment fund manager registered in its principal jurisdiction — (1) A person or company is not required to register in the local jurisdiction as an investment fund manager if it is registered, or has applied for registration, as an investment fund manager in the jurisdiction of Canada in which its head office is located.

(2) Subsection (1) is repealed on September 28, 2012. [*Editor's note: see CSAN 31-330.*]

16.6 Temporary exemption for foreign investment fund managers — (1) The investment fund manager registration requirement does not apply to a person or company that is acting as an investment fund manager if its head office is in not in a jurisdiction of Canada.

(2) Subsection (1) is repealed on September 28, 2012. [*Editor's note: see CSAN 31-330.*]

16.7 Registration of exempt market dealers — (1) This section does not apply in Ontario and Newfoundland and Labrador.

(2) In this section, "the exempt market" means those trading and underwriting activities listed in subparagraph 7.1(2)(d) [*dealer categories*].

(3) The requirement to register as an exempt market dealer does not apply to a person or company that acts as a dealer in the exempt market on the day this Instrument comes into force

(a) until one year after this Instrument comes into force, or

(b) if the person or company applies for registration as an exempt market dealer within one year after this Instrument comes into force, until the regulator or, in Québec, the securities regulatory authority has accepted or refused the registration.

(4) The requirement to register as a dealing representative of an exempt market dealer does not apply to an individual who acts as a dealer in the exempt market on the day this Instrument comes into force

(a) until one year after this Instrument comes into force, or

(b) if the individual applies to be registered as a dealing representative of an exempt market dealer within one year after this Instrument comes into force, until the regulator or, in Québec, the securities regulatory authority has accepted or refused the registration.

16.8 Registration of ultimate designated persons — If a person or company is a registered firm on the day this Instrument comes into force, section 11.2 [*designating an ultimate designated person*] does not apply to the firm

(a) until 3 months after this Instrument comes into force, or

(b) if an individual applies to be registered as the ultimate designated person of the firm within 3 months after this Instrument comes into force, until the regulator or, in Québec, the securities regulatory authority has accepted or refused the registration.

16.9 Registration of chief compliance officers — (1) If a person or company is a registered firm on the date this Instrument comes into force, section 11.3 [*designating a chief compliance officer*] does not apply to the firm

(a) until 3 months after this Instrument comes into force, or

(b) if an individual applies to be registered as the chief compliance officer of the firm within 3 monts after this Instrument comes into force, until the regulator or, in Québec, the securities regulatory authority has accepted or refused the registration.

(2) If an individual applies to be registered as the chief compliance officer compliance officer of a registered firm within 3 months after this Instrument comes into force and the individual was identified on the National Registration Database as the firm's compliance officer on the date this Instrument came into force, the following sections do not apply in respect of the individual so long as he or she remains registered as the firm's chief compliance officer:

(a) section 3.6 [*mutual fund dealer — chief compliance officer*], if the registered firm is a mutual fund dealer;

(b) section 3.8 [*scholarship plan dealer — chief compliance officer*], if the registered firm is a scholarship plan dealer;

(c) section 3.10 [*exempt market dealer — chief compliance officer*], if the registered firm is an exempt market dealer;

(d) section 3.13 [*portfolio manager — chief compliance officer*], if the registered firm is a portfolio manager.

(3) If an individual applies to be registered as the chief compliance officer of a registered firm within 3 months after this Instrument comes into force and the individual was not identified on the National Registration Database as the firm's compliance officer on the date this Instrument came into force, the following sections do not apply in respect of the individual until one year after this Instrument comes into force:

(a) section 3.6 [*mutual fund dealer — chief compliance officer*], if the registered firm is a mutual fund dealer;

(b) section 3.8 [*scholarship plan dealer — chief compliance officer*], if the registered firm is a scholarship plan dealer;

(c) section 3.10 [*exempt market dealer — chief compliance officer*], if the registered firm is an exempt market dealer;

(d) section 3.13 [*portfolio manager — chief compliance officer*], if the registered firm is a portfolio manager.

(4) In Ontario and Newfoundland and Labrador, despite paragraphs (2)(c) and (3)(c), if an individual applies to be registered as the chief compliance officer of an exempt market dealer within 3 months after this Instrument comes into force, section 3.10 [*exempt market dealer — chief compliance officer*] does not apply in respect of the individual until one year after this Instrument comes into force.

16.10 Proficiency for dealing and advising representatives — If an individual is registered in a jurisdiction of Canada as a dealing or advising representative in a category referred to in a section of Division 2 [*education and experience requirements*] of Part 3 on the day this Instrument comes into force, that section does not apply to the individual so long as the individual remains registered in the category.

16.11 Capital requirements — (1) A person or company that is a registered firm on the day this Instrument comes into force is exempt from sections 12.1 [*capital requirements*] and 12.2 [*notifying the regulator of a subordination agreement*] if it complies with each provision listed in Appendix E [*non-harmonized capital requirements*] across from the name of the firm's principal jurisdiction.

(2) Subsection (1) is repealed one year after this Instrument comes into force.

16.12 Continuation of existing discretionary relief — A person or company that was entitled to rely on an exemption, waiver or approval granted to it by a regulator or securities regulatory authority relating to a requirement under securities legislation or securities directions existing immediately before this Instrument came into force is exempt from any substantially similar provision of this Instrument to the same extent and on the same conditions, if any, as contained in the exemption, waiver or approval.

16.13 Insurance requirements — (1) A person or company that is a registered firm on the day this Instrument comes into force is exempt from sections 12.3 [*insurance — dealer*] to 12.7 [*notifying the regulator of a change, claim or cancellation*] if it complies with each provision listed in Appendix F [*non-harmonized insurance requirements*] across from the name of the firm's principal jurisdiction.

(2) In Québec, subsection (1), does not apply to a registered firm that is a mutual fund dealer or a scholarship plan dealer on the day this Instrument comes into force.

(3) Subsections (1) and (2) are repealed 6 months after this Instrument comes into force.

16.14 Relationship disclosure information — (1) Section 14.2 [*relationship disclosure information*] does not apply to a person or company that is a registrant on the day this Instrument comes into force.

(2) Subsection (1) is repealed one year after this Instrument comes into force.

Part 3:
REGISTRATION

16.15 Referral arrangements — (1) Division 3 [*referral arrangements*] of Part 13 does not apply to a person or company that is a registrant on the day this Instrument comes into force.

(2) Subsection (1) is repealed 6 months after this Instrument comes into force.

16.16 Complaint handling — (1) In each jurisdiction of Canada except Québec, section 13.16 [*dispute resolution service*] does not apply to a person or company that is a registered firm in a jurisdiction of Canada on the day this Instrument comes into force.

(2) Subsection (1) is repealed on September 28, 2012. [*Editor's note: see CSAN 31-330.*]

16.17 Account statements — mutual fund dealers — (1) Section 14.14 [*account statements*] does not apply to a person or company that was, on September 28, 2009, either of the following:

    (a) a member of the MFDA;

    (b) a mutual fund dealer in Québec, unless it was also a portfolio manager in Québec.

(2) Subsection (1) is repealed on September 28, 2011.

16.18 Transition to exemption — international dealers — (1) This section applies in Ontario and Newfoundland and Labrador.

(2) If a person or company is registered in the category of international dealer on the day this Instrument comes into force, its registration in that category is revoked.

(3) If a person or company is registered in the category of international dealer on the day this Instrument comes into force, paragraphs 8.18(3)(e) and 8.18(4)(b) [*international dealer*] do not apply to the person or company until one month after this Instrument comes into force.

16.19 Transition to exemption — international advisers — (1) This section applies in Ontario.

(2) If a person or company is registered in the category of international adviser on the day this Instrument comes into force, its registration in that category is revoked one year after this Instrument comes into force.

(3) If the registration of a person or company is revoked under subsection (2), the registration of each individual registered to act as an adviser on behalf of the person or company is revoked.

(4) If a person or company is registered in the category of international adviser on the day this Instrument comes into force, paragraphs (e) and (f) of subsection 8.26(4) [*international adviser*] do not apply to the person or company until one year after this Instrument comes into force.

16.20 Transition to exemption — portfolio manager and investment counsel (foreign) — (1) This section applies in Alberta.

(2) If a person or company is registered in the category of portfolio manager and investment counsel (foreign) on the day this Instrument comes into force, its registration in that category is revoked one year after this Instrument comes into force.

(3) If the registration of a person or company is revoked under subsection (2), the registration of each individual registered to act as an adviser on behalf of the person or company is revoked.

(4) If a person or company is registered in the category of portfolio manager and investment counsel (foreign) on the day this Instrument comes into force, paragraphs (e) and (f) of subsection 8.26(4) [*international adviser*] do not apply to the person or company until one year after this Instrument comes into force.

PART 17 — WHEN THIS INSTRUMENT COMES INTO FORCE

17.1 Effective date — (1) Except in Ontario, this Instrument comes into force on September 28, 2009.

(2) In Ontario, this Instrument comes into force on the later of the following:

    (a) September 28, 2009;

    (b) the day on which sections 4, 5 and subsections 20(1) to (11) of Schedule 26 of the *Budget Measures Act, 2009* are proclaimed in force.

Final Rule: (2009) 32 O.S.C.B. (Supp. 4) 1; Approval by OSC: (2009) 32 O.S.C.B. (Supp. 2) 1; Request for Comments: (2008) 31 O.S.C.B. 2279 and (2007) 30 O.S.C.B. 1606.

Amendment to Rule: (2010) 33 O.S.C.B. (Supp. 5) 107; Approval by OSC: (2010) 33 O.S.C.B. (Supp. 3) 203; Request for Comments: (2009) 32. O.S.C.B. 8721.

Amendment to Rule: (2011) 34 O.S.C.B. 7547; Approval by OSC: (2011) 34 O.S.C.B. (Supp. 3) 1; Request for Comments: (2010) 33 O.S.C.B. (Supp. 2) 1.

Amendment to Rule: (2012) 35 O.S.C.B. 1440; Approval by OSC: (2011) 34 O.S.C.B. 11819; Request for Comments: (2011) 34 O.S.C.B. 5517.

Amendment to Rule: (2013) 36 O.S.C.B. 5721; Approval by OSC: (2013) 36 O.S.C.B. 2619; Request for Comments: (2012) 35 O.S.C.B. 6887.

Amendment to Rule: (2013) 36 O.S.C.B. 5723; Approval by OSC: (2013) 36 O.S.C.B. 3173; Request for Comments: (2012) 35 O.S.C.B. 5429 and (2011) 34 O.S.C.B. 7087.

Amendment to Rule: (2014) 37 O.S.C.B. 2369; Approval by OSC: (2013) 36 O.S.C.B. 12173; Request for Comments: (2012) 35 O.S.C.B. 10349.

Amendment to Rule: Approval by OSC: (2014) 37 O.S.C.B. (Supp. 4) 128; Request for Comments: (2013) 36 O.S.C.B. (Supp. 3).

Amendment to Rule: Approval by OSC: (2014) 37 O.S.C.B. (Supp. 5); Request for Comments: (2013) 36 O.S.C.B. (Supp. 7).

Amendment to Rule: (2015) 38 O.S.C.B. 299.

Related Provisions: OSA Part XI.

Rules: NI 31-102, 33-109; Rule 35-502, 13-502, App. C., Item E(2.1) and (3) and H.

Policies and Orders: NPS 31-103CP, 33-109CP; CSAN 11-321, 31-313, 31-314, 31-317, 31-323, 31-324, 31-325, 31-326, 31-327, 31-329, 31-330, 31-331, 31-332, 31-333, 31-334, 31-335, 33-315, 45-304; OSCN 11-764, 33-733, 33-734, 33-735, 33-736, 33-738, 33-739, 33-740, 33-742.

Form 31-103F1 — Calculation of Excess Working Capital

.... Firm Name

Capital Calculation (as at .... with comparative figures as at ....)

	Component	Current period	Prior period
1.	Current assets		
2.	Less current assets not readily convertible into cash (e.g., prepaid expenses)		
3.	Adjusted current assets Line 1 minus line 2 =		
4.	Current liabilities		
5.	Add 100% of non-current related party debt unless the firm and the lender have executed a subordination agreement in the form set out in Appendix B of National Instrument 31-103 *Registration Requirements, Exemptions and Ongoing Registrant Obligations* and the firm has delivered a copy of the agreement to the regulator or, in Québec, the securities regulatory authority. See section 12.2 of National Instrument 31-103 *Registration Requirements, Exemptions and Ongoing Registrant Obligations*.		
6.	Adjusted current liabilities Line 4 plus line 5 =		
7.	Adjusted working capital Line 3 minus line 6 =		
8.	Less minimum capital		
9.	Less market risk		
10.	Less any deductible under the bonding or insurance policy required under Part 12 of National Instrument 31-103 *Registration Requirements, Exemptions and Ongoing Registrant Obligations*		
11.	Less Guarantees		
12.	Less unresolved differences		
13.	**Excess working capital**	.	

Notes:

Form 31-103F1 *Calculation of Excess Working Capital* must be prepared using the accounting principles that you use to prepare your financial statements in accordance with National Instrument 52-107 *Acceptable Accounting Principles and Auditing Standards*. Section 12.1 of Companion Policy 31-103CP *Registration Requirements, Exemptions and Ongoing Registrant Obligations* provides further guidance in respect of these accounting principles.

Line 5. Related-party debt Refer to the CICA Handbook for the definition of "related party" for publicly accountable enterprises. The firm is required to deliver a copy of the executed subordination agreement to the regulator or, in Québec, the securities regulatory authority on the earlier of a) 10 days after the date the agreement is executed or b) the date an amount subordinated by the agreement is excluded from its calculation of excess working capital on Form 31-103F1 *Calculation of Excess Working Capital*. **The firm must notify the regulator or, in Québec, the securities regulatory authority, 10 days before it repays the loan (in whole or in part), or terminates the subordination agreement.** See section 12.2 of National Instrument 31-103 *Registration Requirements, Exemptions and Ongoing Registrant Obligations*.

Line 8. Minimum Capital — The amount on this line must be not less than (a) $25,000 for an adviser and (b) $50,000 for a dealer. For an investment fund manager, the amount must be not less than $100,000 unless subsection 12.1(4) of National Instrument 31-103 *Registration Requirements, Exemptions and Ongoing Registrant Obligations* applies.

Line 9. Market Risk — The amount on this line must be calculated according to the instructions set out in Schedule 1 to Form 31-103F1 *Calculation of Excess Working Capital*. A schedule supporting the calculation of any amounts included in Line 9 as market risk should be provided to the regulator or, in Québec, the securities regulatory authority in conjunction with the submission of Form 31-103F1 *Calculation of Excess Working Capital*.

Line 11. Guarantees — If the registered firm is guaranteeing the liability of another party, the total amount of the guarantee must be included in the capital calculation. If the amount of a guarantee is included in the firm's statement of financial position as a current liability and is reflected in line 4, do not include the amount of the guarantee on line 11.

Line 12. Unresolved differences — Any unresolved differences that could result in a loss from either firm or client assets must be included in the capital calculation.

The examples below provide guidance as to how to calculate unresolved differences:

(i) If there is an unresolved difference relating to client securities, the amount to be reported on Line 12 will be equal to the fair value of the client securities that are short, plus the applicable margin rate for those securities.

(ii) If there is an unresolved difference relating to the registrant's investments, the amount to be reported on Line 12 will be equal to the fair value of the investments (securities) that are short.

(iii) If there is an unresolved difference relating to cash, the amount to be reported on Line 12 will be equal to the amount of the shortfall in cash.

Please refer to section 12.1 of Companion Policy 31-103CP *Registration Requirements, Exemptions and Ongoing Registrant Obligations* for further guidance on how to prepare and file Form 31-103 *Calculation of Excess Working Capital*.

Management Certification

Registered Firm Name: ....

We have examined the attached capital calculation and certify that the firm is in compliance with the capital requirements as at ....

	Name and Title	**Signature**	**Date**
1.	....		
	....		
2.	....	....
	....		

Schedule 1 — of Form 31-103F1 Calculation of Excess Working Capital (calculating line 9 [market risk])

For purposes of completing this form:

(1) "Fair value" means the value of a security determined in accordance with Canadian GAAP applicable to publicly accountable enterprises;

(2) For each security whose value is included in line 1, Current Assets, multiply the fair value of the security by the margin rate for that security set out below. Add up the resulting amounts for all of the securities you hold. The total is the "market risk" to be entered on line 9.

(a) Bonds, Debentures, Treasury Bills and Notes

(i) Bonds, debentures, treasury bills and other securities of or guaranteed by the Government of Canada, of the United Kingdom, of the United States of America and of any other national foreign government (provided such foreign government securities are currently rated Aaa or AAA by Moody's Canada Inc. or its DRO affiliate or Standard & Poor's Rating Services (Canada) or its DRO affiliate, respectively), maturing (or called for redemption):

within 1 year:	1% of fair value multiplied by the fraction determined by dividing the number of days to maturity by 365
over 1 year to 3 years:	1% of fair value
over 3 years to 7 years:	2% of fair value
over 7 years to 11 years:	4% of fair value
over 11 years:	4% of fair value

(ii) Bonds, debentures, treasury bills and other securities of or guaranteed by any jurisdiction of Canada and obligations of the International Bank for Reconstruction and Development, maturing (or called for redemption):

within 1 year:	2% of fair value multiplied by the fraction determined by dividing the number of days to maturity by 365
over 1 year to 3 years:	3% of fair value
over 3 years to 7 years:	4% of fair value
over 7 years to 11 years:	5% of fair value
over 11 years:	5% of fair value

(iii) Bonds, debentures or notes (not in default) of or guaranteed by any municipal corporation in Canada or the United Kingdom maturing:

within 1 year:	3% of fair value multiplied by the fraction determined by dividing the number of days to maturity by 365
over 1 year to 3 years:	5% of fair value
over 3 years to 7 years:	5% of fair value
over 7 years to 11 years:	5% of fair value
over 11 years:	5% of fair value

(iv) Other non-commercial bonds and debentures, (not in default): 10% of fair value

(v) Commercial and corporate bonds, debentures and notes (not in default) and non-negotiable and non-transferable trust company and mortgage loan company obligations registered in the registered firm's name maturing:

within 1 year:	3% of fair value
over 1 year to 3 years:	6% of fair value
over 3 years to 7 years:	7% of fair value
over 7 years to 11 years:	10% of fair value
over 11 years:	10% of fair value

(b) Bank Paper

Deposit certificates, promissory notes or debentures issued by a Canadian chartered bank (and of Canadian chartered bank acceptances) maturing:

within 1 year:	2% of fair value multiplied by the fraction determined by dividing the number of days to maturity by 365
over 1 year:	apply rates for commercial and corporate bonds, debentures and notes

(c) Acceptable foreign bank paper

Deposit certificates, promissory notes or debentures issued by a foreign bank, readily negotiable and transferable and maturing:

within 1 year:	2% of fair value multiplied by the fraction determined by dividing the number of days to maturity by 365
over 1 year:	apply rates for commercial and corporate bonds, debentures and notes

"Acceptable Foreign Bank Paper" consists of deposit certificates or promissory notes issued by a bank other than a Canadian chartered bank with a net worth (i.e., capital plus reserves) of not less than $200,000,000.

(d) Mutual Funds

Securities of mutual funds qualified by prospectus for sale in any jurisdiction of Canada:

(i) 5% of the net asset value per security as determined in accordance with National Instrument 81-106 Investment Fund Continuous Disclosure, where the fund is a money market mutual fund as defined in National Instrument 81-102 Investment Funds; or

(ii) the margin rate determined on the same basis as for listed stocks multiplied by the net asset value per security of the fund as determined in accordance with National Instrument 81-106 Investment Fund Continuous Disclosure.

Securities of mutual funds qualified by prospectus for sale in the United States of America: 5% of the net asset value per security if the fund is registered as an investment company under the *Investment Companies Act of 1940*, as amended from time to time, and complies with Rule 2a-7 thereof.

(e) Stocks

In this paragraph, "securities" includes rights and warrants and does not include bonds and debentures.

(i) On securities including investment fund securities, rights and warrants listed on any exchange in Canada or the United States of America:

Long Positions — Margin Required

Securities selling at $2.00 or more — 50% of fair value

Securities selling at $1.75 to $1.99 — 60% of fair value

Securities selling at $1.50 to $1.74 — 80% of fair value

Securities selling under $1.50 — 100% of fair value

Short Positions — Credit Required

Securities selling at $2.00 or more — 150% of fair value

Securities selling at $1.50 to $1.99 — $3.00 per share

Securities selling at $0.25 to $1.49 — 200% of fair value

Securities selling at less than $0.25 — fair value plus $0.25 per shares

(ii) For positions in securities that are constituent securities on a major broadly-based index of one of the following exchanges, 50% of the fair value:

(a) Australian Stock Exchange Limited

(b) Bolsa de Madrid

(c) Borsa Italiana

(d) Copenhagen Stock Exchange

(e) Euronext Amsterdam

(f) Euronext Brussels

(g) Euronext Paris S.A.

(h) Frankfurt Stock Exchange

(i) London Stock Exchange

Part 3: REGISTRATION

(j) New Zealand Exchange Limited

(k) Stockholm Stock Exchange

(l) SIX Swiss Exchange

(m) The Stock Exchange of Hong Kong Limited

(n) Tokyo Stock Exchange

(f) Mortgages

(i) For a firm registered in any jurisdiction of Canada except Ontario:

(a) Insured mortgages (not in default): 6% of fair value

(b) Mortgages which are not insured (not in default): 12% of fair value.

(ii) For a firm registered in Ontario:

(a) Mortgages insured under the *National Housing Act* (Canada) (not in default): 6% of fair value

(b) Conventional first mortgages (not in default): 12% of fair value.

If you are registered in Ontario regardless of whether you are also registered in another jurisdiction of Canada, you will need to apply the margin rates set forth in (ii) above.

(g) For all other securities — 100% of fair value.

Form 31-103F2 — Submission to Jurisdiction and Appointment of Agent for Service

(sections 8.18 [international dealer] and 8.26 [international adviser])

1. Name of person or company ("International Firm"):

2. If the International Firm was previously assigned an NRD number as a registered firm or an unregistered exempt international firm, provide the NRD number of the firm.

3. Jurisdiction of incorporation of the International Firm:

4. Head office address of the International Firm:

5. The name, e-mail address, phone number and fax number of the International Firm's chief compliance officer.

Name:

E-mail address:

Phone:

Fax:

6. Section of National Instrument 31-103 *Registration Requirements, Exceptions and Ongoing Registrant Obligations* the International Firm is relying on:

❑ Section 8.18 [*international dealer*]

❑ Section 8.26 [*international adviser*]

❑ Other

7. Name of agent for service of process (the "Agent for Service"):

8. Address for service of process on the Agent for Service:

9. The International Firm designates and appoints the Agent for Service at the address stated above as its agent upon whom may be served a notice, pleading, subpoena, summons or other process in any action, investigation or administrative, criminal, quasi-criminal or other proceeding (a "Proceeding") arising out of or relating to or concerning the International Firm's activities in the local jurisdiction and irrevocably waives any right to raise as a defence in any such proceeding any alleged lack of jurisdiction to bring such Proceeding.

10. The International Firm irrevocably and unconditionally submits to the non-exclusive jurisdiction of the judicial, quasi-judicial and administrative tribunals of the local jurisdiction in any Proceeding arising out of or related to or concerning the International Firm's activities in the local jurisdiction.

11. Until 6 years after the International Firm ceases to rely on section 8.18 [*international dealer*] or section 8.26 [*international adviser*], the International Firm must submit to the securities regulatory authority

a. a new Submission to Jurisdiction and Appointment of Agent for Service in this form no later than the 30th day before the date this Submission to Jurisdiction and Appointment of Agent for Service is terminated; and

b. an amended Submission to Jurisdiction and Appointment of Agent for Service no later than the 30th day before any change in the name or above address of the Agent for Service.

12. This Submission to Jurisdiction and Appointment of Agent for Service is governed by and construed in accordance with the laws of the local jurisdiction.

Dated: ....

.... (Signature of the International Firm or authorized signatory)

.... (Name and Title of authorized signatory)

Acceptance

The undersigned accepts the appointment as Agent for Service of (Insert name of International Firm) under the terms and conditions of the foregoing Submission to Jurisdiction and Appointment of Agent for Service.

Dated: ....

.... (Signature of Agent for Service or authorized signatory)

.... (Name and Title of authorized signatory)

Form 31-103F3 — Use of Mobility Exemption

(section 2.2 [client mobility exemption — individuals])

This is to notify the securities regulatory authority that the individual named in paragraph 1 is relying on the exemption in section 2.2 [*client mobility exemption — individuals*] of National Instrument 31-103 *Registration Requirements, Exemptions and Ongoing Registrant Obligations*.

1. — Individual information

Name of individual:..........

NRD number of individual:..........

The individual is relying on the client mobility exemption in each of the following jurisdictions of Canada:..........

2. — Firm information

Name of the individual's sponsoring firm:..........

NRD number of firm: ....

Dated: ....

.... (Signature of an authorized signatory of the individual's sponsoring firm)

.... (Name and title of authorized signatory)

Form 31-103F4 — Net Asset Value Adjustments

(Section 12.14 [delivering financial information — investment fund manager])

This is to notify the regulator or, in Québec, the securities regulatory authority, of a net asset value (NAV) adjustment made in respect of an investment fund managed by the investment fund manager in accordance with paragraph 12.14(1)(c) or paragraph 12.14(2)(c). All of the information requested should be provided on a fund by fund basis. Please attach a schedule if necessary.

1. Name of the investment fund manager:

2. Name of each of the investment funds for which a NAV adjustment occurred:

3. Date(s) the NAV error occurred:

4. Date the NAV error was discovered:

5. Date of the NAV adjustment:

6. Original total NAV on the date the NAV error first occurred:

7. Original NAV per unit on each date(s) the NAV error occurred:

8. Revised NAV per unit on each date(s) the NAV error occurred:

9. NAV error as percentage (%) of the original NAV on each date(s) the NAV error occurred:

10. Total dollar amount of the NAV adjustment:

11. Effect (if any) of the NAV adjustment per unit or share:

12. Total amount reimbursed to security holders, or any corrections made to purchase and redemption transactions affecting the security holders of each investment fund affected, if any:

13. Date of the NAV reimbursement or correction to security holder transactions, if any:

14. Total amount reimbursed to investment fund, if any:

15. Date of the reimbursement to investment fund, if any:

16. Description of the cause of the NAV error:

17. Was the NAV error discovered by the investment fund manager?

    Yes ❏ No ❏

18. If No, who discovered the NAV error?

19. Was the NAV adjustment a result of a material error under the investment fund manager's policies and procedures?

    Yes ❏ No ❏

Part 3:
REGISTRATION

20. Have the investment fund manager's policies and procedures been changed following the NAV adjustment?

    Yes ❑ No ❑

21. If Yes, describe the changes:

22. If No, explain why not:

23. Has the NAV adjustment been communicated to security holders of each of the investment funds affected?

    Yes ❑ No ❑

24. If Yes, describe the communications:

Notes:

Line 2. NAV adjustment — Refers to the correction made to make the investment fund's NAV accurate.

Line 3. NAV error — Refers to the error discovered on the Original NAV. Please refer to Section 12.14 of *Companion Policy 31-103CP Registration Requirements, Exemptions and Ongoing Registrant Obligations* for guidance on NAV error and causes of NAV errors.

Line 3. Date(s) the NAV error occurred — Means the date of the NAV error first occurred and the subsequent dates of the NAV error.

Line 8. Revised NAV per unit — Refers to the NAV per unit calculated after taking into account the NAV error.

Line 9. NAV error as a percentage (%) of the original NAV — Refers to the following calculation:

$$(\text{Revised NAV} / \text{Original NAV}) - 1 \times 100$$

Appendix A — Bonding and Insurance Clauses

(section 12.3 [insurance — dealer], section 12.4 [insurance — adviser] and section 12.5 [insurance — investment fund manager])

Clause	Name of Clause	Details
A	Fidelity	This clause insures against any loss through dishonest or fraudulent act of employees.
B	On Premises	This clause insures against any loss of money and securities or other property through robbery, burglary, theft, hold-up, or other fraudulent means, mysterious disappearance, damage or destruction while within any of the insured's offices, the offices of any banking institution or clearing house or within any recognized place of safe-deposit.
C	In Transit	This clause insures against any loss of money and securities or other property through robbery, burglary, theft, hold-up, misplacement, mysterious disappearance, damage or destruction, while in transit in the custody of any employee or any person acting as messenger except while in the mail or with a carrier for hire other than an armoured motor vehicle company.
D	Forgery or Alterations	This clause insures against any loss through forgery or alteration of any cheques, drafts, promissory notes or other written orders or directions to pay sums in money, excluding securities.
E	Securities	This clause insures against any loss through having purchased or acquired, sold or delivered, or extended any credit or acted upon securities or other written instruments which prove to have been forged, counterfeited, raised or altered, or lost or stolen, or through having guaranteed in writing or witnessed any signatures upon any transfers, assignments or other documents or written instruments.

Appendix B — Subordination Agreement

(Line 5 of Form 31-103F1 Calculation of excess working capital)

Subordination Agreement

THIS AGREEMENT is made as of the .... day of ...., 20.........

BETWEEN:

[insert name]

(the "**Lender**")

AND

[insert name]

(the "**Registered Firm**", which term shall include all successors and assigns of the Registered Firm)

(collectively, the "**Parties**")

This Agreement is entered into by the Parties under National Instrument 31-103 *Registration Requirements, Exemptions and Ongoing Registrant Obligations* ("NI 31-103") in connection with a loan made on the ....day of ...., 20.......... by the Lender to the Registered Firm in the amount of $ ....(the "**Loan**") for the purpose of allowing the Registered Firm to carry on its business.

For good and valuable consideration, the Parties agree as follows:

1. — Subordination

The repayment of the loan and all amounts owed thereunder are subordinate to the claims of the other creditors of the Registered Firm.

2. — Dissolution, winding-up, liquidation, insolvency or bankruptcy of the Registered Firm

In the event of the dissolution, winding-up, liquidation, insolvency or bankruptcy of the Registered Firm:

(a) the creditors of the Registered Firm shall be paid their existing claims in full in priority to the claims of the Lender;

(b) the Lender shall not be entitled to make any claim upon any property belonging or having belonged to the Registered Firm, including asserting the right to receive any payment in respect to the Loan, before the existing claims of the other creditors of the Registered Firm have been settled.

3. — Terms and conditions of the Loan

During the term of this Agreement:

(a) interest can be paid at the agreed upon rate and time, provided that the payment of such interest does not result in a capital deficiency under NI 31-103;

(b) any loan or advance or posting of security for a loan or advance by the Registered Firm to the Lender, shall be deemed to be a payment on account of the Loan.

4. — Notice to the Securities Regulatory Authority

The Registered Firm must notify the Securities Regulatory Authority 10 days before the full or partial repayment of the loan. Further documentation may be requested by the Securities Regulatory Authority after receiving the notice from the Registered Firm.

5. — Termination of this Agreement

This Agreement may only be terminated by the Lender once the notice required pursuant to Section 4 of this Agreement is received by the Securities Regulatory Authority.

The Parties have executed and delivered this Agreement as of the date set out above.

[Registered Firm]

.... Authorized signatory

.... Authorized signatory

[Lender]

.... Authorized signatory

.... Authorized signatory

Appendix C

[Lapsed.]

Appendix D

[Lapsed.]

Appendix E

[Lapsed.]

Appendix F

[Lapsed.]

Appendix G — Exemptions from Certain Requirements for IIROC Members

(Section 9.3 [exemptions from certain requirements for IIROC members])

NI 31-103 Provision	IIROC provision
section 12.1 *[capital requirements]*	1. Dealer Member Rule 17.1; and 2. Form 1 *Joint Regulatory Financial Questionnaire and Report* — Part I, Statement B, "Notes and Instructions"
section 12.2 *[subordination agreement]*	1. Dealer Member Rule 5.2; and 2. Dealer Member Rule 5.2A
section 12.3 *[insurance — dealer]*	1. Dealer Member Rule 400.2 *[Financial Institution Bond]*; 2. Dealer Member Rule 400.4 *[Amounts Required]*; and

	3.	Dealer Member Rule 400.5 *[Provisos with respect to Dealer Member Rules 400.2, 400.3 and 400.4]*
section 12.6 *[global bonding or insurance]*	1.	Dealer Member Rule 400.7 *[Global Financial Institution Bonds]*
section 12.7 *[notifying the regulator of a change, claim or cancellation]*	1.	Dealer Member Rule 17.6;
	2.	Dealer Member Rule 400.3 *[Notice of Termination]*; and
	3.	Dealer Member Rule 400.3B *[Termination or Cancellation]*
section 12.10 *[annual financial statements]*	1.	Dealer Member Rule 16.2 *[Dealer Member Filing Requirements]*; and
	2.	Form 1 *Joint Regulatory Financial Questionnaire and Report*
section 12.11 *[interim financial information]*	1.	Dealer Member Rule 16.2 *[Dealer Member Filing Requirements]*; and
	2.	Form 1 *Joint Regulatory Financial Questionnaire and Report*
section 12.12 *[delivering financial information — dealer]*	1.	Dealer Member Rule 16.2 *[Dealer Member Filing Requirements]*
subsection 13.2(3) *[know your client]*	1.	Dealer Member Rule 1300.1(a)–(n) *[Identity and Creditworthiness]*;
	2.	Dealer Member Rule 1300.2;
	3.	Dealer Member Rule 2500, Section II *[Opening New Accounts]*; and
	4.	Form 2 *New Client Application Form*
section 13.3 *[suitability]*	1.	Dealer Member Rule 1300.1(o) *[Business Conduct]*;
	2.	Dealer Member Rule 1300.1(p) *[Suitability Generally]*;
	3.	Dealer Member Rule 1300.1(q) *[Suitability Determination Required When Recommendation Provided]*;
	4.	Dealer Member Rule 1300.1(r) and Dealer Member Rule 1300.1(s) *[Suitability Determination Not Required]*;
	5.	Dealer Member Rule 1300.1(t) *[Corporation Approval]*;
	6.	Dealer Member Rule 2700, Section I *[Customer Suitability]*; and
	7.	Dealer Member Rule 3200 *[Minimum Requirements for Dealer Members Seeking Approval Under Rule 1300.1(t) for Suitability Relief for Trades not Recommended by the Member]*
section 13.12 *[restriction on lending to clients]*	1.	Dealer Member Rule 100 *[Margin Requirements]*
section 13.13 *[disclosure when recommending the use of borrowed money]*	1.	Dealer Member Rule 29.26
section 13.15 *[handling complaints]*	1.	Dealer Member Rule 2500B *[Client Complaint Handling]*; and
	2.	Dealer Member Rule 2500, Section VIII *[Client Complaints]*
subsection 14.2(2) *[relationship disclosure information]*	1.	Dealer Member Rules of IIROC that set out the requirements for relationship disclosure information similar to those contained in IIROC's Client Relationship Model proposal, published for comment on January 7, 2011;
	2.	Dealer Member Rule 29.8;
	3.	Dealer Member Rule 200.1(c);
	4.	Dealer Member Rule 200.1(h);
	5.	Dealer Member Rule 1300.1(p) *[Suitability Generally]*;
	6.	Dealer Member Rule 1300.1(q) *[Suitability Determination Required When Recommendation Provided]*;
	7.	Dealer Member Rule 1300.2; and
	8.	Dealer Member Rule 2500B, Part 4 *[Complaint procedures / standards]*
	9.	Dealer Member Rule 3500 *[Relationship Disclosure]*
section 14.6 *[holding client assets in trust]*	1.	Dealer Member Rule 17.3
section 14.8 *[securities subject to a safekeeping agreement]*	1.	Dealer Member Rule 17.2A
	2.	Dealer Member Rule 2600 — Internal Control Policy Statement 5 *[Safekeeping of Clients' Securities]*
section 14.9 *[securities not subject to a safekeeping agreement]*	1.	Dealer Member Rule 17.3;
	2.	Dealer Member Rule 17.3A; and
	3.	Dealer Member Rule 200.1(c)
section 14.12 *[content and delivery of trade confirmation]*	1.	Dealer Member Rule 200.1(h)

Appendix H — Exemptions from Certain Requirements for MFDA Members

(Section 9.4 [exemptions from certain requirements for MFDA members])

NI 31-103 Provision	MFDA provision
section 12.1 [capital requirements]	1. Rule 3.1.1 [Minimum Levels]; 2. Rule 3.1.2 [Notice]; 3. Rule 3.2.2 [Member Capital]; 4. Form 1 MFDA Financial Questionnaire and Report; and 5. Policy No. 4 [Internal Control Policy Statements — Policy Statement 2: Capital Adequacy]
section 12.2 [subordination agreement]	1. Form 1 MFDA Financial Questionnaire and Report, Statement F [Statement of Changes in Subordinated Loans]; and 2. Membership Application Package — Schedule I (Subordinated Loan Agreement)
section 12.3 [insurance — dealer]	1. Rule 4.1 [Financial Institution Bond]; 2. Rule 4.4 [Amounts Required]; 3. Rule 4.5 [Provisos]; and 4. Policy No. 4 [Internal Control Policy Statements — Policy Statement 3: Insurance]
section 12.6 [global bonding or insurance]	1. Rule 4.7 [Global Financial Institution Bonds]
section 12.7 [notifying the regulator of a change, claim or cancellation]	1. Rule 4.2 [Notice of Termination]; and 2. Rule 4.3 [Termination or Cancellation]
section 12.10 [annual financial statements]	1. Rule 3.5.1 [Monthly and Annual]; 2. Rule 3.5.2 [Combined Financial Statements]; and 3. Form 1 MFDA Financial Questionnaire and Report
section 12.11 [interim financial information]	1. Rule 3.5.1 [Monthly and Annual]; 2. Rule 3.5.2 [Combined Financial Statements]; and 3. Form 1 MFDA Financial Questionnaire and Report
section 12.12 [delivering financial information — dealer]	1. Rule 3.5.1 [Monthly and Annual]
section 13.3 [suitability]	1. Rule 2.2.1 ["Know-Your-Client"]; and 2. Policy No. 2 [Minimum Standards for Account Supervision]
section 13.12 [restriction on lending to clients]	1. Rule 3.2.1 [Client Lending and Margin]; and 2. Rule 3.2.3 [Advancing Mutual Fund Redemption Proceeds]
section 13.13 [disclosure when recommending the use of borrowed money]	1. Rule 2.6 [Borrowing for Securities Purchases]
section 13.15 [handling complaints]	1. Rule 2.11 [Complaints] 2. Policy No. 3 [Complaint Handling, Supervisory Investigations and Internal Discipline]; and 3. Policy No. 6 [Information Reporting Requirements]
subsection 14.2(2) [relationship disclosure information]	1. Rule 2.2.5 [Relationship Disclosure]
section 14.6 [holding client assets in trust]	1. Rule 3.3.1 [General]; 2. Rule 3.3.2 [Cash]; and 3. Policy No. 4 [Internal Control Policy Statements — Policy Statement 4: Cash and Securities, and Policy Statement 5: Segregation of Clients' Securities]
section 14.8 [securities subject to a safekeeping agreement]	1. Rule 3.3.3 [Securities]; and 2. Policy No. 4 [Internal Control Policy Statements — Policy Statement 4: Cash and Securities, and Policy Statement 5: Segregation of Clients' Securities]
section 14.9 [securities not subject to a safekeeping agreement]	1. Rule 3.3.3 [Securities]
section 14.12 [content and delivery of trade confirmation]	1. Rule 5.4.1 [Delivery of Confirmations]; 2. Rule 5.4.2 [Automatic Payment Plans]; and

Companion Policy 31-103CP — Registration Requirements, Exemptions and Ongoing Registrant Obligations

Table of Contents

Part 3:
REGISTRATION

Part 1 — Definitions and fundamental concepts

1.1 — Introduction

Purpose of this Companion Policy

This Companion Policy sets out how the Canadian Securities Administrators (the CSA or we) interpret or apply the provisions of National Instrument 31-103 *Registration Requirements, Exemptions and Ongoing Registrant Obligations* (NI 31-103) and related securities legislation.

Numbering system

Except for Part 1, the numbering of Parts, Divisions and sections in this Companion Policy corresponds to the numbering in NI 31-103. Any general guidance for a Part or a Division appears immediately after the Part or Division name. Any specific guidance on sections in NI 31-103 follows any general guidance. If there is no guidance for a Part, Division or section, the numbering in this Companion Policy will skip to the next provision that does have guidance.

All references in this Companion Policy to sections, Parts and Divisions are to NI 31-103, unless otherwise noted.

Additional requirements applicable to registrants

For additional requirements that may apply to them, registrants should refer to:

- National Instrument 31-102 *National Registration Database* (NI 31-102) and the Companion Policy to NI 31-102
- National Instrument 33-109 *Registration Information* (NI 33-109) and the Companion Policy to NI 33-109
- National Policy 11-204 *Process for Registration in Multiple Jurisdictions* (NP 11-204), and
- securities and derivatives legislation in their jurisdiction

Registrants that are members of a self-regulatory organization (SRO) must also comply with their SRO's requirements.

Disclosure and notices

Delivering disclosure and notices to the principal regulator

Under section 1.3, registrants must deliver all disclosure and notices required under NI 31-103 to the registrant's principal regulator. This does not apply to notices under sections 8.18 [*international dealer*] and 8.26 [*international adviser*]. Registrants must deliver these notices to the regulator in each jurisdiction where they are registered or relying on an exemption from registration.

Registrants must deliver these notices to the regulator in each jurisdiction where they are registered or relying on an exemption from registration.

Electronic delivery of documents

These documents may be delivered electronically. Registrants should refer to National Policy 11-201 *Electronic Delivery of Documents* (NP 11-202).

See Appendix A for contact information for each regulator.

Clear and meaningful disclosure to clients

We expect registrants to present disclosure information to clients in a clear and meaningful manner in order to ensure clients understand the information presented. Registrants should ensure that investors can readily understand the information. These requirements are consistent with the obligation to deal fairly, honestly and in good faith with clients.

1.2 — Definitions

Unless defined in NI 31-103, terms used in NI 31-103 and in this Companion Policy have the meaning given to them in the securities legislation of each jurisdiction or in National Instrument 14-101 *Definitions*. See Appendix B for a list of some terms that are not defined in NI 31-103 or this Companion Policy but are defined in other securities legislation.

In this Companion Policy "regulator" means the regulator or securities regulatory authority in a jurisdiction.

Permitted client

The following discussion provides guidance on the term "permitted client", which is defined in section 1.1.

"Permitted client" is used in the following sections:

- 8.18 [*international dealer*]
- 8.22.1 [*short-term debt*]
- 8.26 [*international adviser*]
- 13.2 [*know your client*]
- 13.3 [*suitability*]
- 13.13 [*disclosure when recommending the use of borrowed money*]
- 14.2 [*relationship disclosure information*]
- 14.2.1 [*pre-trade disclosure of charges*]
- 14.4 [*when the firm has a relationship with a financial institution*]
- 14.14.1 [*additional statements*]
- 14.14.2 [*position cost information*]
- 14.17 [*report on charges and other compensation*]
- 14.18 [*investment performance report*]

Exemptions from registration when dealing with permitted clients

Sections 8.18 and 8.26 exempt international dealers and international advisers from the registration requirement if they deal with certain permitted clients and meet certain other conditions.

Section 8.22.1 exempts certain financial institutions from the dealer registration requirement when dealing in a short-term debt instrument with permitted clients.

Exemptions from other requirements when dealing with permitted clients

Under section 13.3, permitted clients may waive their right to have a registrant determine that a trade is suitable. In order to rely on this exemption, the registrant must determine that a client is a permitted client at the time the client waives their right to suitability.

Under sections 13.13 and 14.4, registrants do not have to provide certain disclosures to permitted clients. In order to rely on these exemptions, registrants must determine that a client is a permitted client at the time the client opens an account.

Under sections 14.2, 14.2.1, 14.14.1, 14.14.2, 14.17 and 14.18, registrants do not have to provide certain disclosures or reports to a permitted client that is not an individual.

Determining assets

The definition of permitted client includes monetary thresholds based on the value of the client's assets. The monetary thresholds in paragraphs (o) and (q) of the definition are intended to create "bright-line" standards. Investors who do not satisfy these thresholds do not qualify as permitted clients under the applicable paragraph.

Paragraph (o) of the definition

Paragraph (o) refers to an individual who beneficially owns financial assets with an aggregate realizable value that exceeds $5 million, before taxes but net of any related liabilities.

In general, determining whether financial assets are beneficially owned by an individual should be straightforward. However, this determination may be more difficult if financial assets are held in a trust or in other types of investment vehicles for the benefit of an individual.

Factors indicating beneficial ownership of financial assets include:

- possession of evidence of ownership of the financial asset
- entitlement to receive any income generated by the financial asset
- risk of loss of the value of the financial asset, and
- the ability to dispose of the financial asset or otherwise deal with it as the individual sees fit

For example, securities held in a self-directed RRSP for the sole benefit of an individual are beneficially owned by that individual. Securities held in a group RRSP are not beneficially owned if the individual cannot acquire and deal with the securities directly.

"Financial assets" is defined in section 1.1 of National Instrument 45-106 *Prospectus and Registration Exemptions* (NI 45-106). Realizable value is typically the amount that would be received by selling an asset.

Paragraph (q) of the definition

Paragraph (q) refers to a person or company that has net assets of at least $25 million, as shown on its last financial statements. "Net assets" under this paragraph is total assets minus total liabilities.

1.3 — Fundamental concepts

This section describes the fundamental concepts that form the basis of the registration regime:

- requirement to register
- business trigger for trading and advising, and
- fitness for registration

A registered firm is responsible for the conduct of the individuals whose registration it sponsors. A registered firm

- must undertake due diligence before sponsoring an individual to be registered to act on its behalf (see further guidance in Part 4 *Due diligence by firms* of the Companion Policy to NI 33-109)
- has an ongoing obligation to monitor and supervise its registered individuals in an effective manner (see further guidance in section 11.1 of this Companion Policy)

Failure of a registered firm to take reasonable steps to discharge these responsibilities may be relevant to the firm's own continued fitness for registration.

Requirement to register

The requirement to register is found in securities legislation. Firms must register if they are:

- in the business of trading
- in the business of advising
- holding themselves out as being in the business of trading or advising
- acting as an underwriter, or

- acting as an investment fund manager

Individuals must register if they trade, underwrite or advise on behalf of a registered dealer or adviser, or act as the ultimate designated person (UDP) or chief compliance officer (CCO) of a registered firm. Except for the UDP and the CCO, individuals who act on behalf of a registered investment fund manager do not have to register.

However, all permitted individuals of any registrant must file Form 33-109F4 *Registration of Individuals and Review of Permitted Individuals* (Form 33-109F4).

There is no renewal requirement for registration, but fees must be paid every year to maintain registration.

Multiple categories

Registration in more than one category may be necessary. For example, an adviser that also manages an investment fund may have to register as a portfolio manager and an investment fund manager. An adviser that manages a portfolio and distributes units of an investment fund may have to register as a portfolio manager and as a dealer.

Registration exemptions

NI 31-103 provides exemptions from the registration requirement. There may be additional exemptions in securities legislation. Some exemptions do not need to be applied for if the conditions of the exemption are met. In other cases, on receipt of an application, the regulator has discretion to grant exemptions for specified dealers, advisers or investment fund managers, or activities carried out by them if registration is required but specific circumstances indicate that it is not otherwise necessary for investor protection or market integrity.

Business trigger for trading and advising

We refer to trading or advising in securities for a business purpose as the "business trigger" for registration.

We look at the type of activity and whether it is carried out for a business purpose to determine if an individual or firm must register. We consider the factors set out below, among others, to determine if the activity is for a business purpose. For the most part, these factors are from case law and regulatory decisions that have interpreted the business purpose test for securities matters.

Factors in determining business purpose

This section describes factors that we consider relevant in determining whether an individual or firm is trading or advising in securities for a business purpose and, therefore, subject to the dealer or adviser registration requirement.

This is not a complete list. We do not automatically assume that any one of these factors on its own will determine whether an individual or firm is in the business of trading or advising in securities.

(a) — Engaging in activities similar to a registrant

We usually consider an individual or firm engaging in activities similar to those of a registrant to be trading or advising for a business purpose. Examples include promoting securities or stating in any way that the individual or firm will buy or sell securities. If an individual or firm sets up a business to carry out any of these activities, we may consider them to be trading or advising for a business purpose.

(b) — Intermediating trades or acting as a market maker

In general, we consider intermediating a trade between a seller and a buyer of securities to be trading for a business purpose. This typically takes the form of the business commonly referred to as a broker. Making a market in securities is also generally considered to be trading for a business purpose.

(c) — Directly or indirectly carrying on the activity with repetition, regularity or continuity

Frequent or regular transactions are a common indicator that an individual or firm may be engaged in trading or advising for a business purpose. The activity does not have to be their sole or even primary endeavour for them to be in the business.

We consider regularly trading or advising in any way that produces, or is intended to produce, profits to be for a business purpose. We also consider any other sources of income and how much time an individual or firm spends on all activities associated with the trading or advising.

(d) — Being, or expecting to be, remunerated or compensated

Receiving, or expecting to receive, any form of compensation for carrying on the activity, including whether the compensation is transaction or value based, indicates a business purpose. It does not matter if the individual or firm actually receives compensation or in what form. Having the capacity or the ability to carry on the activity to produce profit is also a relevant factor.

(e) — Directly or indirectly soliciting

Contacting anyone to solicit securities transactions or to offer advice may reflect a business purpose. Solicitation includes contacting someone by any means, including advertising that proposes buying or selling securities or participating in a securities transaction, or that offers services or advice for these purposes.

Business trigger examples

This section explains how the business trigger might apply to some common situations.

(a) — Securities issuers

A securities issuer is an entity that issues or trades in its own securities. In general, securities issuers with an active non-securities business do not have to register as a dealer if they:

- do not hold themselves out as being in the business of trading in securities

- trade in securities infrequently

- are not, or do not expect to be, compensated for trading in securities

- do not act as intermediaries, and

- do not produce, or intend to produce, a profit from trading in securities

During the start-up stage, securities issuers may not yet be actively carrying on their intended business. We consider a start-up securities issuer to have an "active non-securities business" if the entity is raising capital to start a non-securities business. Although the entity does not need to be producing a product or delivering a service, we would expect it to have a bona fide business plan to do so, containing milestones and the time anticipated to reach those milestones. For example, technology companies may raise money with only a business plan for many years before they start producing a product or delivering a service. Similarly, junior exploration companies may raise money with only a business plan long before they find or extract any resources.

However, securities issuers may have to register as dealers if they are in the business of trading. Conduct that would indicate that security issuers are in the business includes frequently trading in securities. While frequent trading is a common indicator of being in the business of trading, we recognize that trading may be more frequent during the start-up stage, as an issuer needs to raise capital to launch and advance the business. If the trading is primarily for the purpose of advancing the issuer's business plan, then the frequency of the activities alone should not result in the issuer being in the business of trading in securities. If the capital raising and use of that capital are not advancing the business, the issuer may need to register as a dealer.

Securities issuers may also have to register as a dealer if they

- employ or contract individuals to perform activities on their behalf that are similar to those performed by a registrant (other than under-writing in the normal course of a distribution or trading for their own account)

- actively solicit investors, subject to the discussion below, or

- act as an intermediary by investing client money in securities

For example, an investment fund manager that carries on the activities described above may have to register as a dealer.

Many issuers actively solicit through officers, directors or other employees. If these individuals' activities are incidental to their primary roles with an issuer, they would likely not be in the business of trading. Factors that would suggest that the issuer and these individuals are in the business of trading are:

- the principal purpose of the individual's employment is raising capital through distributions of the issuer's securities;

- the individuals spend the majority of their time raising capital in this manner;

- the individuals' compensation or remuneration is based solely or primarily on the amount of capital they raise for the issuer.

Securities issuers that are distributing securities issuers are subject to the prospectus requirements in securities legislationunless an exemption is available. Regulators have the discretionary authority to require an underwriter for a prospectus distribution.

(b) — Venture capital and private equity

This guidance does not apply to labour sponsored or venture capital funds as defined in National Instrument 81-106 *Investment Fund Continuous Disclosure* (NI 81-106).

Venture capital and private equity investing are distinguished from other forms of investing by the role played by venture capital and private equity management companies (collectively, VCs). This type of investing includes a range of activities that may require registration.

VCs typically raise money under one of the prospectus exemptions in NI 45-106, including for trades to "accredited investors". The investors typically agree that their money will remain invested for a period of time. The VC uses this money to invest in securities of companies that are usually not publicly traded. The VC usually becomes actively involved in the management of the company, often over several years.

Examples of active management in a company include the VC having:

- representation on the board of directors

- direct involvement in the appointment of managers

- a say in material management decisions

The VC looks to realize on the investment either through a public offering of the company's securities, or a sale of the business. At this point, the investors' money can be returned to them, along with any profit.

Investors rely on the VC's expertise in selecting and managing the companies it invests in. In return, the VC receives a management fee or "carried interest" in the profits generated from these investments. They do not receive compensation for raising capital or trading in securities.

Applying the business trigger factors to the VC activities as described above, there would be no requirement for the VC to register as:

- a portfolio manager, if the advice provided in connection with the purchase and sale of companies is incidental to the VC's active management of these companies, or

- a dealer, if both the raising of money from investors and the investing of that money by the VC (in securities of companies that are usually not publicly traded) are occasional and uncompensated activities

If the VC is actively involved in the management of the companies it invests in, the investment portfolio would generally not be considered an investment fund. As a result, the VC would not need to register as an investment fund manager.

The business trigger factors and investment fund manager analysis may apply differently if the VC engages in activities other than those described above.

(c) — One-time activities

In general, we do not require registration for one-time trading or advising activities. This includes trading or advising that:

- is carried out by an individual or firm acting as a trustee, executor, administrator, personal or other legal representative, or
- relates to the sale of a business

(d) — Incidental activities

If trading or advising activity is incidental to a firm's primary business, we may not consider it to be for a business purpose.

For example, merger and acquisition specialists that advise the parties to a transaction between companies are not normally required to register as dealers or advisers in connection with that activity, even though the transaction may result in trades in securities and they will be compensated for the advice. If the transaction results in trades in the securities of the company to an acquirer, this is considered incidental to the acquisition transaction. However, if the merger and acquisition specialists also engage in capital raising from prospective investors (including private placements), they will need to consider whether such activity would be in the business of trading and require registration.

Another example is professionals, such as lawyers, accountants, engineers, geologists and teachers, who may provide advice on securities in the normal course of their professional activities. We do not consider them to be advising on securities for a business purpose. For the most part, any advice on securities will be incidental to their professional activities. This is because they:

- do not regularly advise on securities
- are not compensated separately for advising on securities
- do not solicit clients on the basis of their securities advice, and
- do not hold themselves out as being in the business of advising on securities

Registration trigger for investment fund managers

Investment fund managers are subject to a registration trigger. This means that if a firm carries on the activities of an investment fund manager, it must register. However, investment fund managers are not subject to the business trigger.

Fitness for registration

The regulator will only register an applicant if they appear to be fit for registration. Following registration, individuals and firms must maintain their fitness in order to remain registered. If the regulator determines that a registrant has become unfit for registration, the regulator may suspend or revoke the registration. See Part 6 of this Companion Policy for guidance on suspension and revocation of individual registration. See Part 10 of this Companion Policy for guidance on suspension and revocation of firm registration.

Terms and conditions

The regulator may impose terms and conditions on a registration at the time of registration or at any time after registration. Terms and conditions imposed at the time of registration are generally permanent, for example, in the case of a restricted dealer who is limited to specific activities. Terms and conditions imposed after registration are generally temporary. For example, if a registrant does not maintain the required capital, it may have to file monthly financial statements and capital calculations until the regulator's concerns are addressed.

Opportunity to be heard

Applicants and registrants have an opportunity to be heard by the regulator before their application for registration is denied. They also have an opportunity to be heard before the regulator imposes terms and conditions on their registration if they disagree with the terms and conditions.

Assessing fitness for registration — firms

We assess whether a firm is or remains fit for registration through the information it is required to provide on registration application forms and as a registrant, and through compliance reviews. Based on this information, we consider whether the firm is able to carry out its obligations under securities legislation. For example, registered firms must be financially viable. A firm that is insolvent or has a history of bankruptcy may not be fit for registration.

In addition, when determining whether a firm whose head office is outside Canada is, and remains, fit for registration, we will consider whether the firm maintains registration or regulatory organization membership in the foreign jurisdiction that is appropriate for the securities business it carries out there.

Part 3:
REGISTRATION

Assessing fitness for registration — individuals

We use three fundamental criteria to assess whether an individual is or remains fit for registration:

- proficiency
- integrity, and
- solvency

(a) — Proficiency

Individual applicants must meet the applicable education, training and experience requirements prescribed by securities legislation and demonstrate knowledge of securities legislation and the securities they recommend.

Registered individuals should continually update their knowledge and training to keep pace with new securities, services and developments in the industry that are relevant to their business. See Part 3 of this Companion Policy for more specific guidance on proficiency.

(b) — Integrity

Registered individuals must conduct themselves with integrity and have an honest character. The regulator will assess the integrity of individuals through the information they are required to provide on registration application forms and as registrants, and through compliance reviews. For example, applicants are required to disclose information about conflicts of interest, such as other employment or partnerships, service as a member of a board of directors, or relationships with affiliates, and about any regulatory or legal actions against them.

(c) — Solvency

The regulator will assess the overall financial condition of an individual applicant or registrant. An individual that is insolvent or has a history of bankruptcy may not be fit for registration. Depending on the circumstances, the regulator may consider the individual's contingent liabilities. The regulator may take into account an individual's bankruptcy or insolvency when assessing their continuing fitness for registration.

Part 2 — Categories of registration for individuals

2.1 — Individual categories

Multiple individual categories

Individuals who carry on more than one activity requiring registration on behalf of a registered firm must:

- register in all applicable categories, and
- meet the proficiency requirements of each category

For example, an advising representative of a portfolio manager who is also the firm's CCO must register in the categories of advising representative and CCO. They must meet the proficiency requirements of both of these categories.

Individual registered in a firm category

An individual can be registered in both a firm and individual category. For example, a sole proprietor who is registered in the firm category of portfolio manager must also be registered in the individual category of advising representative.

2.2 — Client mobility exemption — individuals

Conditions of the exemption

The mobility exemption in section 2.2 allows registered individuals to continue dealing with and advising clients who move to another jurisdiction, without registering in that other jurisdiction. Section 8.30 *Client mobility exemption — firms* contains a similar exemption for registered firms.

The exemption becomes available when the client (not the registrant) moves to another jurisdiction. An individual may deal with up to five "eligible" clients in each other jurisdiction. Each of the client, their spouse and any children are an eligible client.

An individual may only rely on the exemption if:

- they and their sponsoring firm are registered in their principal jurisdiction
- they and their sponsoring firm only act as a dealer, underwriter or adviser in the other jurisdiction as permitted under their registration in their principal jurisdiction
- they comply with Part 13 *Dealing with clients — individuals and firms*
- they act fairly, honestly and in good faith in their dealings with the eligible client, and
- their sponsoring firm has disclosed to the eligible client that the individual and if applicable, their sponsoring firm, are exempt from registration in the other jurisdiction and are not subject to the requirements of securities legislation in that jurisdiction

As soon as possible after an individual first relies on this exemption, their sponsoring firm must complete and file Form 31-103F3 *Use of mobility exemption* (Form 31-103F3) with the other jurisdiction.

Limits on the number of clients

Sections 2.2 and 8.30 are independent of each other: individuals may rely on the exemption from registration in section 2.2 even though their sponsoring firm is registered in the local jurisdiction (and is not relying on the exemption from registration in section 8.30). The limits in sections 2.2 and 8.30 are per jurisdiction.

For example a firm using the exemption in section 8.30 could have 10 clients in each of several local jurisdictions where it is not registered. An individual may also use the exemption in section 2.2 to have 5 clients in each of several jurisdictions where the individual is not registered.

The individual limits are per individual. For example several individuals working for the same firm could each have 5 clients in the same local jurisdiction and each individual could still rely on the exemption in section 2.2. However, the firm may not exceed its 10 client limit if it wants to rely on the exemption in section 8.30. If the firm exceeds the 10 client limit, the firm must be registered in the local jurisdiction.

Part 3 — Registration requirements — individuals

Division 1 — General proficiency requirements

Application of proficiency requirements

Part 3 sets out the initial and ongoing proficiency requirements for

- dealing representatives and chief compliance officers of mutual fund dealers, scholarship plan dealers and exempt-market dealers respectively
- advising representatives, associate advising representatives and chief compliance officers of portfolio managers
- chief compliance officers of investment fund managers

The regulator is required to determine the individual's fitness for registration and may exercise discretion in doing so.

Section 3.3 does not provide proficiency requirements for dealing representatives of investment dealers since the IIROC Rules provide those requirements for the individuals who are approved persons of IIROC member firms.

Exam based requirements

Individuals must pass exams — not courses — to meet the education requirements in Part 3. For example, an individual must pass the Canadian Securities Course Exam, but does not have to complete the Canadian Securities Course. Individuals are responsible for completing the necessary preparation to pass an exam and for proficiency in all areas covered by the exam.

3.3 — Time limits on examination requirements

Under section 3.3, there is a time limit on the validity of exams prescribed in Part 3. Individuals must pass an exam within 36 months before they apply for registration. However, this time limit does not apply if the individual:

- was registered in an active capacity (i.e., not suspended), in the same category in a jurisdiction of Canada at any time during the 36-month period before the date of their application; or
- has gained relevant securities industry experience for a total of 12 months during the 36-month period before the date of their application: these months do not have to be consecutive, or with the same firm or organization

These time limits do not apply to the CFA Charter or the CIM designation, since we do not expect the holders of these designations to have to retake the courses forming part of the requirements applicable to these designations. However, if the individual no longer has the right to use the CFA Charter or the CIM designation, by reason of revocation of the designation or otherwise, we may consider the reasons for such a revocation to be relevant in determining an individual's fitness for registration. Registered individuals are required to notify the regulator of any change in the status of their CFA Charter or the CIM designation within 10 days of the change, by submitting Form 33-109F5 *Change of Registration Information* in accordance with 31-102.

When assessing an individual's fitness for registration, the regulator may consider

- the date on which the relevant examination was passed, and
- the length of time between any suspension and reinstatement of registration during the 36-month period

See Part 6 of this Companion Policy for guidance on the meaning of "suspension" and "reinstatement".

Relevant securities industry experience

The securities industry experience under subsection 3.3(2)(b) should be relevant to the category applied for. It may include experience acquired:

- during employment at a registered dealer, a registered adviser or an investment fund manager
- in related investment fields, such as investment banking, securities trading on behalf of a financial institution, securities research, portfolio management, investment advisory services or supervision of those activities
- in legal, accounting or consulting practices related to the securities industry
- in other professional service fields that relate to the securities industry, or
- in a securities-related business in a foreign jurisdiction

Division 2 — Education and experience requirements

See Appendix C for a chart that sets out the proficiency requirements for each individual category of registration.

Granting exemptions

The regulator may grant an exemption from any of the education and experience requirements in Division 2 if it is satisfied that an individual has qualifications or relevant experience that is equivalent to, or more appropriate in the circumstances than, the prescribed requirements.

Proficiency for representatives of restricted dealers and restricted portfolio managers

The regulator will decide on a case-by-case basis what education and experience are required for registration as:

- a dealing representative or CCO of a restricted dealer, and

- an advising representative or CCO of a restricted portfolio manager

The regulator will determine these requirements when it assesses the individual's fitness for registration.

3.4 — Proficiency — initial and ongoing

Proficiency principle

Under section 3.4, registered individuals must not perform an activity that requires registration unless they have the education, training and experience that a reasonable person would consider necessary to perform the activity competently, including understanding the structure, features and risks of each security they recommend to a client (also referred to as know-your-product or KYP).

The requirement to understand the structure, features and risks of each security recommended to a client is a proficiency requirement. This requirement is in addition to the suitability obligation in section 13.3 and applies even where there is an exemption from the suitability obligation such as, for example, the exemption in subsection 13.3(4) in respect of permitted clients.

CCOs must also not perform an activity that requires registration unless they have the education, training and experience that a reasonable person would consider necessary to perform the activity competently. CCOs must have a good understanding of the regulatory requirements applicable to the firm and individuals acting on its behalf. CCOs must also have the knowledge and ability to design and implement an effective compliance system.

Responsibility of the firm

The responsibility of registered firms to oversee the compliance of registered individuals acting on their behalf extends to ensuring that they are proficient at all times. A registered firm must not permit an individual they sponsor to perform an activity if the proficiency requirements are not met.

Firms should perform their own analysis of all securities they recommend to clients and provide product training to ensure their registered representatives have a sufficient understanding of the securities and their risks to meet their suitability obligations under section 13.3. Similarly, registered individuals should have a thorough understanding of a security before they recommend it to a client (also referred to as know-your-product or KYP).

3.11 — Portfolio manager — advising representative

3.12 — Portfolio manager — associate advising representative

The 12 months of relevant investment management experience referred to in section 3.11 and 24 months of relevant investment management experience referred to in section 3.12 do not have to be consecutive, or with the same firm or organization.

For individuals with a CFA charter, the regulator will decide on a case-by-case basis whether the experience they gained to earn the charter qualifies as relevant investment management experience.

Relevant investment management experience

The relevant investment management experience requirement is in addition to the specific course or designation requirements for each category of registration. We will assess whether an individual has acquired relevant investment management experience on a case-by-case basis. This section describes factors we may consider in assessing certain types of experience.

Relevant investment management experience under sections 3.11 and 3.12 may vary according to the level of specialization of the individual. It may include:

- securities research and analysis experience, demonstrating an ability in, and understanding of, portfolio analysis or portfolio security selection, or

- management of investment portfolios on a discretionary basis, including investment decision making, rebalancing and evaluating performance

Advising representatives

An advising representative may have discretionary authority over investments of others. Accordingly, this category of registration involves the most onerous proficiency requirements. We expect an individual who seeks registration as an advising representative to demonstrate a high quality of experience that is clearly relevant to discretionary portfolio management. This section sets out specific examples of experience that may satisfy the relevant investment management experience requirement for advising representatives.

(a) — Discretionary portfolio management

We may consider experience performing discretionary portfolio management in a professional capacity to be sufficient to meet the relevant investment management experience requirement for registration as an advising representative. Such experience may include working at:

- an adviser registered or operating under an exemption from registration in a foreign jurisdiction
- an insurance company
- a pension fund
- a government, corporate, bank or trust company treasury
- an IIROC member firm

(b) — Assistant or associate portfolio management

We may consider experience supporting registered portfolio managers or other professional discretionary asset managers to be sufficient to meet the relevant investment management experience requirement for registration as an advising representative. This may include:

- working with portfolio managers to formulate, draft and implement written investment policy statements for clients, and
- researching and analysing individual securities for potential inclusion in investment portfolios

(c) — Research analyst with an IIROC member firm or registered adviser

We may consider experience performing research and analysis of individual securities with recommendations for the purpose of determining their suitability for inclusion in client investment portfolios to be sufficient to meet the relevant investment management experience requirement for registration as an advising representative.

Associate advising representatives

This category may be appropriate for individuals who meet the minimum education and experience requirements in section 3.12 but do not meet the more onerous requirements for registration as an advising representative under section 3.11. In evaluating the experience required to obtain registration as an associate advising representative, we take into account that the advice provided by an associate advising representative must be approved by an advising representative in accordance with section 4.2. Experience gained as an associate advising representative does not automatically qualify an individual to be registered as an advising representative.

We will assess on a case-by-case basis whether such experience meets the more stringent quality of experience required for registration as an advising representative. This section sets out specific examples of experience that may satisfy the relevant investment management experience requirement for associate advising representatives.

(a) — Client relationship management

We may consider client relationship management experience with a registered portfolio manager firm to be sufficient to meet the relevant investment management experience requirement for registration as an associate advising representative where the applicant has assisted portfolio managers in tailoring strategies for specific clients. This may include experience assisting the portfolio managers in assessing suitability, creating investment policy statements, determining asset allocation, monitoring client portfolios and performing research and analysis on the economy or asset classes generally.

We recognize that many individuals who perform client relationship management services may not provide specific advice and therefore may not trigger the registration requirement. For example, some client services representatives conduct activities such as marketing the services of the firm by providing general information about the registrant firm and its services that do not include a strategy tailored to any specific client. While some client service representatives may accompany advising representatives or associate advising representatives to meetings with clients and provide assistance with marketing and client development activities, without registration they may not themselves develop an investment policy statement for the client, provide specific information such as recommending a particular model portfolio for the client or explain the implications of discretionary portfolio decisions that were made by the client's advising representative.

(b) — Corporate finance

We may consider corporate finance experience involving valuing and analysing securities for initial public offerings, debt and equity financings, takeover bids and mergers to be sufficient to meet the relevant investment management experience requirement for registration as an associate advising representative where this experience demonstrates an ability in, and understanding of, portfolio analysis or portfolio securities selection.

Some types of experience remain highly case-specific

While the quality and nature of the experience discussed above may differ from individual to individual and we assess experience on a case-by-case basis, there are some types of experience that are even more highly case-specific. This section sets out specific examples of case specific experience that may satisfy the relevant investment management experience requirement for advising representatives and associate advising representatives.

(a) — IIROC registered representatives

Some registered representatives may offer a broad range of products involving security-specific research and analysis of their own, in addition to meeting with clients to review and discuss know-your-client and investment suitability. We may consider this to be sufficient experience to meet the relevant investment management experience requirement for registration as an advising representative. Other registered representatives may sell mostly or exclusively a limited number of model portfolios or "portfolio solutions" to clients based on their investment objectives, risk profile or other factors unique to the individual client. We may consider this sufficient experience to meet the relevant investment management experience requirement for registration as an associate advising representative.

However, where an individual is restricted to the sale of mutual funds, we may not consider such experience to be sufficient to meet the relevant investment management experience requirement for registration as an advising representative or associate advising representative.

(b) — Consultants

Consulting services relating to portfolio manager selection and monitoring may be highly specific to the individual or firm providing the services and may vary greatly among consultants in the sophistication of research and analysis and specificity of advice. Some may be responsible for hiring and ongoing monitoring of advisers or sub-advisers, while others may simply provide a desired asset allocation and list of recommended advisers based on the investment objectives of the client. We would generally expect to see a very high degree of sophistication and specificity in the analysis provided by the consultant and a high degree of investor reliance on the consultant in order for the individual to meet the relevant investment management experience requirement for registration as an advising representative.

Research and analysis to review and monitor the performance of registered portfolio managers, and referring clients for discretionary money management based on that review and monitoring, may meet the relevant investment management experience requirement for registration as an associate advising representative. We would not expect that general financial planning advice and referrals to portfolio managers alone would meet the threshold for relevant investment management experience required for registration as an advising representative or associate advising representative.

In some situations, the activities submitted as relevant investment management experience involve or may involve providing specific advice to clients and therefore may require registration. We also recognize that many individuals who provide portfolio manager selection and monitoring do not provide specific advice and therefore may not trigger the registration requirement. We may consider the following factors in determining whether a consultant is required to register:

- the client contracts directly with the consultant, rather than with the portfolio managers
- the consultant manages the hiring and evaluation of the portfolio managers
- there is reliance by the client on the consultant
- there are client expectations about the services to be provided by the consultant

Division 3 — Membership in a self-regulatory organization

3.16 — Exemptions from certain requirements for SRO-approved persons

Section 3.16 exempts registered individuals who are dealing representatives of IIROC or MFDA members from the requirements in NI 31-103 for suitability and disclosure when recommending the use of borrowed money. This is because IIROC and the MFDA have their own rules for these matters.

In Québec, these requirements do not apply to dealing representatives of a mutual fund dealer to the extent that equivalent requirements are applicable to those dealing representatives under regulations in Québec.

This section also exempts registered individuals who are dealing representatives of IIROC from the know your client obligations in section 13.2.

We expect registered individuals who are dealing representatives of IIROC or MFDA members to comply with the by-laws, rules, regulations and policies of IIROC or the MFDA, as applicable (SRO provisions). These individuals cannot rely on the exemptions in section 3.16 unless they are complying with the corresponding SRO provisions specified in NI 31-103. We regard compliance with IIROC or MFDA procedures, interpretations, notices, bulletins and practices as relevant to compliance with the applicable SRO provisions.

For these purposes, an individual that has an exemption from an SRO provision and complies with the terms of that exemption would be considered to have complied with that SRO provision.

Part 4 — Restrictions on registered individuals

4.1 — Restriction on acting for another registered firm

We will consider exemption applications on a case by case basis. When reviewing a registered firm's application for relief from this restriction, we will consider if:

- there are valid business reasons for the individual to be registered with both firms
- the individual will have sufficient time to adequately serve both firms
- the applicant's sponsoring firms have demonstrated that they have policies and procedures addressing any conflicts of interest that may arise as a result of the dual registration, and
- the sponsoring firms will be able to deal with these conflicts, including supervising how the individual will deal with these conflicts

In the case of paragraph 4.1(1)(b), namely a dealing, advising or associate advising representative acting for another registered firm, affiliation of the firms may be one of the factors that we would consider in respect of an exemption application.

We note that the prohibitions in section 4.1 are in addition to the conflicts of interest provisions set out in section 13.4 [*identifying and responding to conflicts of interest*]. See section 13.4 for further guidance on individuals who serve on boards of directors.

4.2 — Associate advising representatives — pre-approval of advice

The associate advising representative category allows an individual to work at a registered adviser while completing the proficiency requirements for an advising representative. For example, a previously registered advising representative could work in an advising capacity while acquiring the relevant work experience required for an advising representative under section 3.11.

Associate advising representatives are not required to subsequently register as a full advising representative since this category also accommodates individuals who provide specific advice to clients, but do not manage client portfolios without supervision.

As required by section 4.2, registered firms must designate an advising representative to approve the advice provided by an associate advising representative. The designated advising representative must approve the advice before the associate advising representative gives the advice. The appropriate processes for approving the advice will depend on the circumstances, including the associate advising representative's level of experience.

Registered firms that have associate advising representatives must:

- document their policies and procedures for meeting the supervision and approval obligations as required under section 11.1

- implement controls as required under section 11.1

- maintain records as required under section 11.5, and

- notify the regulator of the names of the advising representative and the associate advising representative whose advice they are approving no later than the seventh day after the advising representative is designated

Part 5 — Ultimate designated person and chief compliance officer

Sections 11.2 and 11.3 require registered firms to designate a UDP and a CCO. The UDP and CCO must be registered and perform the compliance functions set out in sections 5.1 and 5.2. While the UDP and CCO have specific compliance functions, they are not solely responsible for compliance — it is the responsibility of the firm as a whole.

The same person as UDP and CCO

The UDP and the CCO can be the same person if they meet the requirements for both registration categories. We prefer firms to separate these functions, but we recognize that it might not be practical for some registered firms.

UDP or CCO as advising or dealing representative

The UDP or CCO may also be registered in trading or advising categories. For example, a small registered firm might conclude that one individual can adequately function as UDP and CCO, while also carrying on advising and trading activities. We may have concerns about the ability of a UDP or CCO of a large firm to conduct these additional activities and carry out their UDP, CCO and advising responsibilities at the same time.

5.1 — Responsibilities of the ultimate designated person

The UDP is responsible for promoting a culture of compliance and overseeing the effectiveness of the firm's compliance system. They do not have to be involved in the day to day management of the compliance group. There are no specific education or experience requirements for the UDP. However, they are subject to the proficiency principle in section 3.4.

5.2 — Responsibilities of the chief compliance officer

The CCO is an operating officer who is responsible for the monitoring and oversight of the firm's compliance system. This includes:

- establishing or updating policies and procedures for the firm's compliance system, and

- managing the firm's compliance monitoring and reporting according to the policies and procedures

At the firm's discretion, the CCO may also have authority to take supervisory or other action to resolve compliance issues.

The CCO must meet the proficiency requirements set out in Part 3. No other compliance staff have to be registered unless they are also advising or trading. The CCO may set the knowledge and skills necessary or desirable for individuals who report to them.

If a firm is registered in multiple categories, the CCO must meet the most stringent of the proficiency requirements of the firm's categories of registration.

Firms must designate one CCO. However, in large firms, the scale and kind of activities carried out by different operating divisions may warrant the designation of more than one CCO. We will consider applications, on a case-by-case basis, for different individuals to act as the CCO of a firm's operating divisions.

We will not usually register the same person as CCO of more than one firm unless the firms are affiliated, and the scale and kind of activities carried out make it reasonable for the same person to act as CCO of more than one firm. We will consider applications, on a case-by-case basis, for the CCO of one registered firm to act as the CCO of another registered firm.

Paragraph 5.2(c) requires the CCO to report to the UDP any instances of non-compliance with securities legislation that:

- create a reasonable risk of harm to a client or to the market, or

- are part of a pattern of non-compliance

The CCO should report non-compliance to the UDP even if it has been corrected.

Paragraph 5.2(d) requires the CCO to submit an annual report to the board of directors.

Part 6 — Suspension and revocation of registration — individuals

The requirements for surrendering registration and additional requirements for suspending and revoking registration are found in the securities legislation of each jurisdiction. The guidance for Part 6 relates to requirements under both securities legislation and NI 31-103.

There is no renewal requirement for registration. A registered individual may carry on the activities for which they are registered until their registration is:

- suspended automatically under NI 31-103

- suspended by the regulator under certain circumstances, or

- surrendered by the individual

6.1 — If individual ceases to have authority to act for firm

Under section 6.1, if a registered individual ceases to have authority to act on behalf of their sponsoring firm because their working relationship with the firm ends or changes, the individual's registration with the registered firm is suspended until reinstated or revoked under securities legislation. This applies whether the individual or the firm ends the relationship.

If a registered firm terminates its working relationship with a registered individual for any reason, the firm must complete and file a notice of termination on Form 33-109F1 *Notice of Termination of Registered Individuals and Permitted Individuals* (Form 33-109F1) no later than ten days after the effective date of the individual's termination. This includes when an individual resigns, is dismissed or retires.

The firm must file additional information about the individual's termination prescribed in Part 5 of Form 33-109F1 (except where the individual is deceased), no later than 30 days after the date of termination. The regulator uses this information to determine if there are any concerns about the individual's conduct that may be relevant to their ongoing fitness for registration. Under NI 33-109, the firm must provide this information to the individual on request.

Suspension

An individual whose registration is suspended must not carry on the activity they are registered for. The individual otherwise remains a registrant and is subject to the jurisdiction of the regulator. A suspension remains in effect until the regulator reinstates or revokes the individual's registration.

If an individual who is registered in more than one category is suspended in one of the categories, the regulator will consider whether to suspend the individual's registration in other categories or to impose terms and conditions, subject to an opportunity to be heard.

Automatic suspension

An individual's registration will automatically be suspended if:

- they cease to have a working relationship with their sponsoring firm

- the registration of their sponsoring firm is suspended or revoked, or

- they cease to be an approved person of an SRO

An individual must have a sponsoring firm to be registered. If an individual leaves their sponsoring firm for any reason, their registration is automatically suspended. Automatic suspension is effective on the day that an individual no longer has authority to act on behalf of their sponsoring firm.

Individuals do not have an opportunity to be heard by the regulator in the case of any automatic suspension.

Suspension in the public interest

An individual's registration may be suspended if the regulator exercises its power under securities legislation and determines that it is no longer in the public interest for the individual to be registered. The regulator may do this if it has serious concerns about the ongoing fitness of the individual. For example, this may be the case if an individual is charged with a crime, in particular fraud or theft.

Reinstatement

"Reinstatement" means that a suspension on a registration has been lifted. Once reinstated, an individual may resume carrying on the activity they are registered for. If a suspended individual joins a new sponsoring firm, they will have to apply for reinstatement under the process set out in NI 33-109. In certain cases, the reinstatement or transfer to the new firm will be automatic.

Automatic transfers

Subject to certain conditions set out in NI 33-109, an individual's registration may be automatically reinstated if they:

- transfer directly from one sponsoring firm to another registered firm in the same jurisdiction
- join the new sponsoring firm within 90 days of leaving their former sponsoring firm
- seek registration in the same category as the one previously held, and
- complete and file Form 33-109F7 *Reinstatement of Registered Individuals and Permitted Individuals* (Form 33-109F7)

This allows individuals to engage in activities requiring registration from their first day with the new sponsoring firm.

Individuals are not eligible for an automatic reinstatement if they:

- have new information to disclose regarding regulatory, criminal, civil or financial matters as described in Item 9 of Form 33-109F7, or
- as a result of allegations of criminal activity, breach of securities legislation or breach of SRO rules:
  - were dismissed by their former sponsoring firm, or
  - were asked by their former sponsoring firm to resign

In these cases, the individual must apply to have their registration reinstated under NI 33-109 using Form 33-109F4.

6.2 — If IIROC approval is revoked or suspended

6.3 — If MFDA approval is revoked or suspended

Registered individuals acting on behalf of member firms of an SRO are required to be an approved person of the SRO.

If an SRO suspends or revokes its approval of an individual, the individual's registration in the category requiring SRO approval will be automatically suspended. This automatic suspension of individuals does not apply to mutual fund dealers registered only in Québec.

If an SRO suspends an individual for reasons that do not involve significant regulatory concerns and subsequently reinstates the individual's approval, the individual's registration will usually be reinstated by the regulator as soon as possible.

Revocation

6.6 — Revocation of a suspended registration — individual

If an individual's registration has been suspended under Part 6 but not reinstated, it will be automatically revoked on the second anniversary of the suspension.

"Revocation" means that the regulator has terminated the individual's registration. An individual whose registration has been revoked must submit a new application if they want to be registered again.

Surrender or termination of registration

If an individual wants to terminate their registration in one or more of the non-principal jurisdictions where the individual is registered, the individual may apply to surrender their registration at any time by completing Form 33-109F2 *Change or Surrender of Individual Categories* (Form 33-109F2) and having their sponsoring firm file it.

If an individual wants to terminate their registration in their principal jurisdiction, Form 33-109F1 must be filed by the individual's sponsoring firm. Once Form 33-109F1 is filed, the individual's termination of registration will be reflected in all jurisdictions.

Part 7 — Categories of registration for firms

The categories of registration for firms have two main purposes:

- to specify the type of business that the firm may conduct, and
- to provide a framework for the requirements the registrant must meet

Firms registered in more than one category

A firm may be required to register in more than one category. For example, a portfolio manager that manages an investment fund must register both as a portfolio manager and as an investment fund manager.

Individual registered in a firm category

An individual can be registered in both a firm and individual category. For example, a sole proprietor who is registered in the firm category of portfolio manager must also be registered in the individual category of advising representative.

7.1 — Dealer categories

Underwriting is a subset of dealing activity for specified categories. Investment dealers may underwrite any securities. Exempt market dealers may underwrite securities in limited circumstances. For example, exempt market dealers may participate in a private placement of securities. Exempt market dealers may not act as an underwriter in a prospectus offering without exemptive relief.

Exempt market dealer

Under paragraph 7.1(2)(d), exempt market dealers may only act as a dealer in the "exempt market". The permitted activities of an exempt market dealer are determined with reference to the prospectus exemptions in NI 45-106 and include trades to "accredited investors" and purchasers of at least $150,000 of a security and trades to anyone under the offering memorandum exemption.

Exempt market dealers are permitted to participate in

- a distribution of securities, including securities of investment funds or reporting issuers, made under an exemption from the prospectus requirement

- a resale of securities that are subject to resale restrictions

- a resale of securities that are freely tradeable, if the securities are not traded on a marketplace. For example, the securities are traded on an over-the-counter basis

These activities may be conducted with accredited investors or other investors who are eligible to purchase the securities on a prospectus-exempt basis.

Exempt market dealers are not permitted to

- participate as an underwriter in a distribution of securities offered under a prospectus

- directly or indirectly, participate in a resale of securities traded on a domestic or foreign marketplace whether the transaction is on-exchange or off-exchange, unless the transaction requires reliance on a further exemption from the prospectus requirement. This includes establishing an omnibus account with an investment dealer and trading securities for clients through that account.

These activities should be conducted by investment dealers.

Restricted dealer

The restricted dealer category in paragraph 7.1(2)(e) permits specialized dealers that may not qualify under another dealer category, to carry on a limited trading business. It is intended to be used only if there is a compelling case for the proposed trading to take place outside the other registration categories.

The regulator will impose terms and conditions that restrict the dealer's activities. The CSA will co-ordinate terms and conditions for restricted dealers.

7.2 — Adviser categories

The registration requirement in section 7.2 applies to advisers who give "specific advice". Advice is specific when it is tailored to the needs and circumstances of a client or potential client. For example, an adviser who recommends a security to a client is giving specific advice.

Restricted portfolio manager

The restricted portfolio manager category in subsection 7.2(2)(b) permits individuals or firms to advise in specific securities, classes of securities or securities of a class of issuers.

The regulator will impose terms and conditions on a restricted portfolio manager's registration that limit the manager's activities. For example, a restricted portfolio manager might be limited to advising in respect of a specific sector, such as securities of oil and gas issuers.

7.3 — Investment fund manager category

Investment fund managers direct the business, operations or affairs of an investment fund. They organize the fund and are responsible for its management and administration. If an entity is uncertain about whether it must register as an investment fund manager, it should consider whether the fund is an "investment fund" for the purposes of securities legislation. See section 1.2 of the Companion Policy to NI 81-106 for guidance on the general nature of investment funds.

For additional guidance on the investment fund manager registration requirement in Alberta, British Columbia, Manitoba, Nova Scotia, New Brunswick, Northwest Territories, Nunavut, Prince Edward Island, Saskatchewan and Yukon see Multilateral Policy 31-202 *Registration Requirement for Investment Fund Manager*. Newfoundland and Labrador, Ontario and Québec have adopted Multilateral Instrument 32-102 *Registration Exemptions for Non-Resident Investment Fund Managers* and Companion Policy 32-102CP *Registration Exemptions for Non-Resident Investment Fund Managers*, which provide limited exemptions from, and guidance on, the investment fund manager registration requirement for non-resident investment fund managers.

An investment fund manager may:

- advertise to the general public a fund it manages without being registered as an adviser, and

- promote the fund to registered dealers without being registered as a dealer

If an investment fund manager acts as portfolio manager for a fund it manages, it should consider whether it may have to be registered as an adviser. If it distributes units of the fund directly to investors, it should consider whether it may have to be registered as a dealer.

In most fund structures, the investment fund manager is a separate legal entity from the fund itself. However, in situations where the board of directors or the trustee(s) of an investment fund direct the business, operations or affairs of the investment fund, the fund itself may be required to register in the investment fund manager category. To address the investor protection concerns that may arise from the investment fund manager and the fund being the same legal entity, and the practical issues of applying the ongoing requirements of a registrant on the fund, terms and conditions may be imposed.

An investment fund manager may delegate or outsource certain functions to other service providers. However, the investment fund manager is responsible for these functions and must supervise the service provider. See Part 11 of this Companion Policy for more guidance on outsourcing.

Investment fund complexes or groups with more than one investment fund manager

Determining whether investment fund registration is necessary involves applying a functional test that examines the activities being carried out to determine whether an entity is directing the business, operations or affairs of an investment fund. Typically an investment fund has only one investment fund manager. However, there may be limited circumstances where investment fund complexes or groups may have more than one entity within the fund complex that is acting as an investment fund manager. Although the investment fund manager functions are often delegated to one entity within the fund complex, there may be more than one entity in the group subject to investment fund manager registration, absent an exemption from registration. We will consider exemption applications on a case-by-case basis to allow only one investment fund manager within the fund complex to be registered in appropriate circumstances.

Part 8 — Exemptions from the requirement to register

NI 31-103 provides several exemptions from the registration requirement. There may be additional exemptions in securities legislation. If a firm is exempt from registration, the individuals acting on its behalf are also exempt from registration. A person or company cannot rely on the exemptions in Divisions 1, 2 and 3 of this Part in a local jurisdiction if the person or company is registered to conduct the activities covered by the exemption in that jurisdiction. We expect registrants to conduct activities within a jurisdiction under their category of registration, in full compliance with securities legislation, including the requirements of NI 31-103.

Division 1 — Exemptions from dealer and underwriter registration

We provide no specific guidance for the following exemptions because there is guidance on them in the Companion Policy to NI 45-106:

- 8.12 [*mortgages*]
- 8.17 [*reinvestment plan*]
- 8.20 *Exchange contract — Alberta, British Columbia, New Brunswick and Saskatchewan*

8.5 — Trades through or to a registered dealer

No solicitation or contact

Section 8.5 provides an exemption from the dealer registration requirement for trades made

- through an appropriately registered dealer, or
- to an appropriately registered dealer that is purchasing for that dealer's account.

The exemption in paragraph 8.5(1)(a) for trades made through a registered dealer is not available if the person relying on it solicits or contacts purchasers of the securities directly. For example, if an individual acts in furtherance of a by soliciting or contacting potential purchasers of securities (sometimes referred to as a finder) and then the sale to the purchaser is executed through a registered dealer, the individual would not qualify for this exemption.

A person may utilize the exemption for acts in furtherance of a trade in relation to working with issuers or appropriately registered dealers, provided they do not directly solicit or contact purchasers.

Cross-border trades (jitneys)

Section 8.5 provides an exemption from the dealer registration requirement if the trade is made through a registered dealer, provided the person relying on the exemption has no direct contact with the purchaser of the security. On that basis, the execution of a trade through or to an appropriately registered dealer by a dealer located in another jurisdiction would qualify under this exemption.

However, if for example a dealer in the United States that is not registered in Alberta contacts a potential purchaser in Alberta to solicit the purchase of securities, this trade does not qualify for this exemption. The dealer in the United States must instead contact a dealer registered in Alberta, and have that dealer contact potential purchasers in Alberta.

Plan administrators

A plan administrator can rely on this exemption to place sell orders with dealers in respect of shares of issuers held by plan participants. Section 8.16 [*plan administrator*] covers the activity of the plan administrator receiving sell orders from plan participants.

8.5.1 — Trades through a registered dealer by registered adviser

Section 8.5.1 provides that the dealer registration requirement does not apply to a registered adviser for incidental trading activities. The exemption is only available if the trade is made through a registered dealer or a dealer exempt from registration. For example, a portfolio manager may not use the exemption to trade units of a pooled fund it manages, without involving a registered dealer or having another exemption available, including the exemption in section 8.6.

8.6 — Investment fund trades by adviser to managed account

Registered advisers often create and use investment funds as a way to efficiently invest their clients' money. In issuing units of those funds to managed account clients, they are in the business of trading in securities. Under the exemption in section 8.6, a registered adviser does not have to register as a dealer does for a trade in a security of an investment fund if they:

- act as the fund's adviser and investment fund manager, and

- distribute units of the fund only into their clients' managed accounts

The exemption is also available to those who qualify for the international adviser exemption under section 8.26.

Subsection 8.6(2) limits the availability of this exemption to legitimate managed accounts. We do not intend for the exemption to be used to distribute the adviser's investment funds on a retail basis.

8.18 — International dealer

General principle

This exemption allows international dealers to provide limited services without having to register in Canada. The term "permitted client" is defined in section 1.1. International dealers that seek wider access to Canadian investors must register in an appropriate category.

Notice requirement

If a firm is relying on the exemption in more than one jurisdiction, it must provide an initial notice by filing a Form 31-103F2 *Submission to Jurisdiction and Appointment of Agent for Service* (Form 31-103F2) with the regulator in each jurisdiction where it relies on the exemption. If there is any change to the information in the firm's Form 31-103F2, it must update it by filing a replacement Form 31-103F2 with them.

So long as the firm continues to rely on the exemption, it must file an annual notice with each regulator. Subsection 8.18(5) does not prescribe a form of annual notice. An email or letter will therefore be acceptable.

In Ontario, compliance with the filing and fee payment requirements applicable to an unregistered exempt international dealer under Ontario Securities Commission Rule 13-502 Fees satisfies the annual notification requirement in subsection (5).

8.19 — Self-directed registered education savings plan

We consider the creation of a self-directed registered education savings plan, as defined in section 8.19, to be a trade in a security, whether or not the assets held in the plan are securities. This is because the definition of "security" in securities legislation of most jurisdictions includes "any document constituting evidence of an interest in a scholarship or educational plan or trust".

Section 8.19 provides an exemption from the dealer registration requirement for the trade when the plan is created but only under the conditions described in subsection 8.19(2).

8.22.1 — Short-term debt

This exemption allows specified financial institutions to trade short-term debt instruments with permitted clients, without having to register. The exemption is available in all jurisdictions of Canada, except Ontario. In Ontario, there are alternate exemptions that may be available for trading in short-term debt instruments, including the exemptions in section 35.1 of the *Securities Act* (Ontario) and section 4.1 of the Ontario Securities Commission Rule 45-501 *Ontario Prospectus and Registration Exemptions*.

Division 2 — Exemptions from adviser registration

8.24 — IIROC members with discretionary authority

Section 8.24 contains an exemption from the requirement to register as an adviser for registered dealers that are members of IIROC and their dealing representatives. The exemption is available when they act as an adviser in respect of a client's managed account. The term "managed account" is defined in section 1.1 of NI 31-103. This exemption is available for all managed accounts, including where the client is a pooled fund or investment fund.

8.25 — Advising generally

Section 8.25 contains an exemption from the requirement to register as an adviser if the advice is not tailored to the needs of the recipient.

In general, we would not consider advice about specific securities to be tailored to the needs of the recipient if it:

- is a general discussion of the merits and risks of the security

- is delivered through investment newsletters, articles in general circulation newspapers or magazines, websites, e-mail, Internet chat rooms, bulletin boards, television or radio, and

- does not claim to be tailored to the needs and circumstances of any recipient

This type of general advice can also be given at conferences. However, if a purpose of the conference is to solicit the audience and generate specific trades in specific securities, we may consider the advice to be tailored or we may consider the individual or firm giving the advice to be engaged in trading activity.

Under subsection 8.25(3), if an individual or firm relying on the exemption has a financial or other interest in the securities they recommend, they must disclose the interest to the recipient when they make the recommendation.

8.26 — *International adviser*

This exemption allows international advisers to provide limited services to certain permitted clients without having to register in Canada. The term "permitted client" is defined in section 1.1 and, for the purposes of section 8.26, excludes registered dealers and advisers. International advisers that seek wider access to Canadian investors must register in an appropriate category.

Incidental advice on Canadian securities

An international adviser relying on the exemption in section 8.26 may advise in Canada on foreign securities without having to register. It may also advise in Canada on securities of Canadian issuers, but only to the extent that the advice is incidental to its acting as an adviser for foreign securities.

However, this is not an exception or a "carve-out" that allows some portion of a permitted client's portfolio to be made up of Canadian securities chosen by the international adviser without restriction. Any advice with respect to Canadian securities must be directly related to the activity of advising on foreign securities. Permissible incidental advice would include, for example:

- an international adviser, when advising on a portfolio with a particular investment objective, such as gold mining companies, could advise on securities of a Canadian gold mining company within that portfolio, provided that the portfolio is otherwise made up of foreign securities

- an international adviser, having a mandate to advise on equities traded on European exchanges could advise with respect to the securities of a Canadian corporation traded on a European exchange, to the extent the Canadian corporation forms part of the mandate

Revenue derived in Canada

An international adviser is only permitted to undertake a prescribed amount of business in Canada. In making the calculation required under paragraph 8.26(4)(d), it is necessary to include all revenues derived from portfolio management activities in Canada, which would include any sub-adviser arrangements. However, the calculation of aggregate consolidated gross revenue derived in Canada does not include the gross revenue of affiliates that are registered in a jurisdiction of Canada.

An international adviser is not required to monitor Canadian revenue on an ongoing basis. Eligibility for the exemption is assessed with reference to revenues as of the end of the adviser's last financial year. The 10% threshold in paragraph 8.26(4)(d) is determined by looking back at the revenue of the firm and its affiliates "during its most recently completed financial year".

Notice requirement

If a firm is relying on the exemption in more than one jurisdiction, it must provide an initial notice by filing a Form 31-103F2 with the regulator in each jurisdiction where it relies on the exemption. If there is any change to the information in the firm's Form 31-103F2, it must update it by filing a replacement Form 31-103F2 with them.

So long as the firm continues to rely on the exemption, it must file an annual notice with each regulator. Subsection 8.26(5) does not prescribe a form of annual notice. An email or letter will therefore be acceptable.

In Ontario, compliance with the filing and fee payment requirements applicable to an unregistered exempt international firm under Ontario Securities Commission Rule 13-502 *Fees* satisfies the annual notification requirement in subsection (5).

8.26.1 — International sub-adviser

This exemption permits a foreign sub-adviser to provide advice to certain registrants, without having to register as an adviser in Canada. In these arrangements, the registrant is the foreign sub-adviser's client, and it receives the advice, either for its own benefit or for the benefit of its clients. One of the conditions of this exemption is that the registrant has entered into an agreement with its client that it is responsible for losses that arise out of certain failures by the sub-adviser.

We expect that a registrant taking on this liability will conduct appropriate initial and ongoing due diligence on the sub-adviser and ensure the investments are suitable for the registrant's client. We also expect that the registrant will maintain records of the due diligence conducted. See Part 11 of this Companion Policy for more guidance.

Division 3 — *Exemptions from investment fund manager registration*

8.28 — *[Repealed.]*

Division 4 — *Mobility exemption — firms*

8.30 — *Client mobility exemption — firms*

The mobility exemption in section 8.30 allows registered firms to continue dealing with and advising clients who move to another jurisdiction, without registering in that other jurisdiction. Section 2.2 [*client mobility exemption — individuals*] contains a similar exemption for registered individuals.

The exemption becomes available when the client (not the registrant) moves to another jurisdiction. A registered firm may deal with up to 10 "eligible" clients in each other jurisdiction. Each of the client, their spouse and any children are an eligible client.

A firm may only rely on the exemption if:

- it is registered in its principal jurisdiction

- it only acts as a dealer, underwriter or adviser in the other jurisdiction as permitted under its registration in its principal jurisdiction

- the individual acting on its behalf is eligible for the exemption in section 2.2
- it complies with Parts 13 *Dealing with clients — individuals and firms* and 14 *Handling client accounts — firms*, and
- it acts fairly, honestly and in good faith in its dealings with the eligible client

Firm's responsibilities for individuals relying on the exemption

In order for a registered individual to rely on the exemption in section 2.2, their sponsoring firm must disclose to the eligible client that the individual and if applicable, the firm, are exempt from registration in the other jurisdiction and are not subject to the requirements of securities legislation in that jurisdiction.

As soon as possible after an individual first relies on the exemption in section 2.2, their sponsoring firm must complete and file Form 31-103F3 in the other jurisdiction.

The registered firm must have appropriate policies and procedures for supervising individuals who rely on a mobility exemption. Registered firms must also keep appropriate records to demonstrate they are complying with the conditions of the mobility exemption.

See the guidance in section 2.2 of this Companion Policy on the client mobility exemption available to individuals.

Part 9 — Membership in a self-regulatory organization

9.3 — Exemptions from certain requirements for IIROC members

9.4 — Exemptions from certain requirements for MFDA members

NI 31-103 has two distinct sections, sections 9.3 and 9.4, which distinguish the exemptions which are available on the basis of whether or not the member of IIROC or the MFDA is registered in another category. This clarifies our intent with respect to the exemptions for SRO members and recognizes that IIROC and the MFDA have rules in these areas.

Sections 9.3 and 9.4 contain exemptions from certain requirements for investment dealers that are IIROC members, for mutual fund dealers that are MFDA members and in Québec, for mutual fund dealers to the extent equivalent requirements are applicable under the regulations in Québec.

However, if an SRO member is registered in another category, these sections do not exempt them from their obligations as a registrant in that category. For example, if a firm is registered as an investment fund manager and as an investment dealer with IIROC, section 9.3 does not exempt them from their obligations as an investment fund manager under NI 31-103.

However SRO members that are registered in multiple categories may use the forms prescribed by the SROs, on certain conditions. See sections 12.1, 12.12 and 12.14 for requirements on calculating working capital and the delivery of working capital calculations for SRO members that are registered in multiple categories.

We expect registered firms that are members of IIROC or the MFDA to comply with the by-laws, rules, regulations and policies of IIROC or the MFDA, as applicable (SRO provisions). These firms cannot rely on the exemptions in Part 9 unless they are complying with the corresponding SRO provisions specified in NI 31-103. We regard compliance with IIROC or MFDA procedures, interpretations, notices, bulletins and practices as relevant to compliance with the applicable SRO provisions.

For these purposes, a firm that has an exemption from an SRO provision and complies with the terms of that exemption would be considered to have complied with that SRO provision.

Part 10 — Suspension and revocation of registration — firms

The requirements for surrendering registration and additional requirements for suspending and revoking registration are found in the securities legislation of each jurisdiction. The guidance for Part 10 relates to requirements under both securities legislation and NI 31-103.

There is no renewal requirement for registration but firms must pay fees every year to maintain their registration and the registration of individuals acting on their behalf. A registered firm may carry on the activities for which it is registered until its registration is:

- suspended automatically under NI 31-103
- suspended by the regulator under certain circumstances, or
- surrendered by the firm

Division 1 — When a firm's registration is suspended

Suspension

A firm whose registration has been suspended must not carry on the activity it is registered for. The firm otherwise remains a registrant and is subject to the jurisdiction of the regulator. A suspension remains in effect until the regulator reinstates or revokes the firm's registration.

If a firm that is registered in more than one category is suspended in one of the categories, the regulator will consider whether to suspend the firm's registration in other categories or to impose terms and conditions, subject to an opportunity to be heard.

Automatic suspension

A firm's registration will automatically be suspended if:

- it fails to pay its annual fees within 30 days of the due date

- it ceases to be a member of IIROC, or

- except in Québec, it ceases to be a member of the MFDA

Firms do not have an opportunity to be heard by the regulator in the case of any automatic suspension.

10.1 — Failure to pay fees

Under section 10.1, a firm's registration will be automatically suspended if it has not paid its annual fees within 30 days of the due date.

10.2 — If IIROC membership is revoked or suspended

Under section 10.2, if IIROC suspends or revokes a firm's membership, the firm's registration as an investment dealer is suspended until reinstated or revoked.

10.3 — If MFDA membership is revoked or suspended

Under section 10.3, if the MFDA suspends or revokes a firm's membership, the firm's registration as a mutual fund dealer is suspended until reinstated or revoked. Section 10.3 does not apply in Québec.

Suspension in the public interest

A firm's registration may be suspended if the regulator exercises its power under securities legislation and determines that it is no longer in the public interest for the firm to be registered. The regulator may do this if it has serious concerns about the ongoing fitness of the firm or any of its registered individuals. For example, this may be the case if a firm or one or more of its registered or permitted individuals is charged with a crime, in particular fraud or theft.

Reinstatement

"Reinstatement" means that a suspension on a registration has been lifted. Once reinstated, a firm may resume carrying on the activity it is registered for.

Division 2 — Revoking a firm's registration

Revocation

10.5 — Revocation of a suspended registration — firm

10.6 — Exception for firms involved in a hearing or proceeding

Under sections 10.5 and 10.6, if a firm's registration has been suspended under Part 10 and has not been reinstated, it is revoked on the second anniversary of the suspension, except if a hearing or proceeding concerning the suspended registrant has commenced. In this case the registration remains suspended.

"Revocation" means that the regulator has terminated the firm's registration. A firm whose registration has been revoked must submit a new application if it wants to be registered again.

Surrender

A firm may apply to surrender its registration in one or more categories at any time. There is no prescribed form for an application to surrender. A firm should file an application to surrender registration with its principal regulator. If Ontario is a non-principal jurisdiction, it should also file the application with the regulator in Ontario. See the Companion Policy to Multilateral Instrument 11-102 *Passport System* for more details on filing an application to surrender.

Before the regulator accepts a firm's application to surrender registration, the firm must provide the regulator with evidence that the firm's clients have been dealt with appropriately. This evidence does not have to be provided when a registered individual applies to surrender registration. This is because the sponsoring firm will continue to be responsible for meeting obligations to clients who may have been served by the individual.

The regulator does not have to accept a firm's application to surrender its registration. Instead, the regulator can act in the public interest by suspending, or imposing terms and conditions on, the firm's registration.

When considering a registered firm's application to surrender its registration, the regulator typically considers the firm's actions, the completeness of the application and the supporting documentation.

The firm's actions

The regulator may consider whether the firm:

- has stopped carrying on activity requiring registration

- proposes an effective date to stop carrying on activity requiring registration that is within six months of the date of the application to surrender, and

- has paid any outstanding fees and submitted any outstanding filings at the time of filing the application to surrender

Completeness of the application

Among other things, the regulator may look for:

- the firm's reasons for ceasing to carry on activity requiring registration

- satisfactory evidence that the firm has given all of its clients reasonable notice of its intention to stop carrying on activity requiring registration, including an explanation of how it will affect them in practical terms, and

- satisfactory evidence that the firm has given appropriate notice to the SRO, if applicable

Supporting documentation

The regulator may look for:

- evidence that the firm has resolved all outstanding client complaints, settled all litigation, satisfied all judgments or made reasonable arrangements to deal with and fund any payments relating to them, and any subsequent client complaints, settlements or liabilities

- confirmation that all money or securities owed to clients has been returned or transferred to another registrant, where possible, according to client instructions

- up-to-date audited financial statements with an auditor's comfort letter

- evidence that the firm has satisfied any SRO requirements for withdrawing membership, and

- an officer's or partner's certificate supporting these documents

Part 11 — Internal controls and systems

General business practices — outsourcing

Registered firms are responsible and accountable for all functions that they outsource to a service provider. Firms should have a written, legally binding contract that includes the expectations of the parties to the outsourcing arrangement.

Registered firms should follow prudent business practices and conduct a due diligence analysis of prospective third-party service providers. This includes third-party service providers that are affiliates of the firm. Due diligence should include an assessment of the service provider's reputation, financial stability, relevant internal controls and ability to deliver the services.

Firms should also:

- ensure that third-party service providers have adequate safeguards for keeping information confidential and, where appropriate, disaster recovery capabilities

- conduct ongoing reviews of the quality of outsourced services

- develop and test a business continuity plan to minimize disruption to the firm's business and its clients if the third-party service provider does not deliver its services satisfactorily, and

- note that other legal requirements, such as privacy laws, may apply when entering into outsourcing arrangements

The regulator, the registered firm and the firm's auditors should have the same access to the work product of a third-party service provider as they would if the firm itself performed the activities. Firms should ensure this access is provided and include a provision requiring it in the contract with the service provider, if necessary.

Division 1 — Compliance

11.1 — Compliance system

General principles

Section 11.1 requires registered firms to establish, maintain and apply policies and procedures that establish a system of controls and supervision (a compliance system) that:

- provides assurance that the firm and individuals acting on its behalf comply with securities legislation, and

- manages the risks associated with the firm's business in accordance with prudent business practices

Operating an effective compliance system is essential to a registered firm's continuing fitness for registration. It provides reasonable assurance that the firm is meeting, and will continue to meet, all requirements of applicable securities laws and SRO rules and is managing risk in accordance with prudent business practices. A compliance system should include internal controls and monitoring systems that are reasonably likely to identify non-compliance at an early stage and supervisory systems that allow the firm to correct non-compliant conduct in a timely manner.

The responsibilities of the UDP are set out in section 5.1 and those of the CCO in section 5.2. However, compliance is not only a responsibility of a specific individual or a compliance department of the firm, but rather is a firm-wide responsibility and an integral part of the firm's activities. Everyone in the firm should understand the standards of conduct for their role. This includes the board of directors, partners, management, employees and agents, whether or not they are registered.

Having a UDP and CCO, and in larger firms, a compliance group and other supervisory staff, does not relieve anyone else in the firm of the obligation to report and act on compliance issues. A compliance system should identify those who will act as alternates in the absence of the UDP or CCO.

Elements of an effective compliance system

While policies and procedures are essential, they do not make an acceptable compliance system on their own. An effective compliance system also includes internal controls, day to day and systemic monitoring, and supervision elements.

Internal controls

Internal controls are an important part of a firm's compliance system. They should mitigate risk and protect firm and client assets. They should be designed to assist firms in monitoring compliance with securities legislation and managing the risks that affect their business, including risks that may relate to:

- safeguarding of client and firm assets
- accuracy of books and records
- trading, including personal and proprietary trading
- conflicts of interest
- money laundering
- business interruption
- hedging strategies
- marketing and sales practices, and
- the firm's overall financial viability

Monitoring and supervision

Monitoring and supervision are essential elements of a firm's compliance system. They consist of day to day monitoring and supervision, and overall systemic monitoring.

(a) — Day to day monitoring and supervision

In our view, an effective monitoring and supervision system includes:

- monitoring to identify specific cases of non-compliance or internal control weaknesses that might lead to noncompliance
- referring non-compliance or internal control weaknesses to management or other individuals with authority to take supervisory action to correct them
- taking supervisory action to correct them, and
- minimizing the compliance risk in key areas of a firm's operations

In our view, effective day to day monitoring should include, among other things

- approving new account documents
- reviewing and, in some cases, approving transactions
- approving marketing materials, and
- preventing inappropriate use or disclosure of non-public information.

Firms can use a risk-based approach to monitoring, such as reviewing an appropriate sample of transactions.

The firm's management is responsible for the supervisory element of correcting non-compliance or internal control weaknesses. However, at a firm's discretion, its CCO may be given supervisory authority, but this is not a necessary component of the CCO's role.

Anyone who supervises registered individuals has a responsibility on behalf of the firm to take all reasonable measures to ensure that each of these individuals:

- deals fairly, honestly and in good faith with their clients
- complies with securities legislation
- complies with the firm's policies and procedures, and
- maintains an appropriate level of proficiency

(b) — Systemic monitoring

Systemic monitoring involves assessing, and advising and reporting on the effectiveness of the firm's compliance system. This includes ensuring that:

- the firm's day to day supervision is reasonably effective in identifying and promptly correcting cases of non-compliance and internal control weaknesses
- policies and procedures are enforced and kept up to date, and

- everyone at the firm generally understands and complies with the policies and procedures, and with securities legislation

Specific elements

More specific elements of an effective compliance system include:

(a) — Visible commitment

Senior management and the board of directors or partners should demonstrate a visible commitment to compliance.

(b) — Sufficient resources and training

The firm should have sufficient resources to operate an effective compliance system. Qualified individuals (including anyone acting as an alternate during absences) should have the responsibility and authority to monitor the firm's compliance, identify any instances of non-compliance and take supervisory action to correct them.

The firm should provide training to ensure that everyone at the firm understands the standards of conduct and their role in the compliance system, including ongoing communication and training on changes in regulatory requirements or the firm's policies and procedures.

(c) — Detailed policies and procedures

The firm should have detailed written policies and procedures that:

- identify the internal controls the firm will use to ensure compliance with legislation and manage risk

- set out the firm's standards of conduct for compliance with securities and other applicable legislation and the systems for monitoring and enforcing compliance with those standards

- clearly outline who is expected to do what, when and how

- are readily accessible by everyone who is expected to know and follow them

- are updated when regulatory requirements and the firm's business practices change, and

- take into consideration the firm's obligation under securities legislation to deal fairly, honestly and in good faith with its clients

(d) — Detailed records

The firm should keep records of activities conducted to identify compliance deficiencies and the action taken to correct them.

Setting up a compliance system

It is up to each registered firm to determine the most appropriate compliance system for its operations. Registered firms should consider the size and scope of their operations, including products, types of clients or counterparties, risks and compensating controls, and any other relevant factors.

For example, a large registered firm with diverse operations may require a large team of compliance professionals with several divisional heads of compliance reporting to a CCO dedicated entirely to a compliance role.

All firms must have policies, procedures and systems to demonstrate compliance. However, some of the elements noted above may be unnecessary or impractical for smaller registered firms.

We encourage firms to meet or exceed industry best practices in complying with regulatory requirements.

11.2 — Designating an ultimate designated person

Under subsection 11.2(1), registered firms must designate an individual to be the UDP. Firms should ensure that the individual understands and is able to perform the obligations of a UDP under section 5.1. The UDP must be:

- the chief executive officer (CEO) of the registered firm or the individual acting in a similar capacity, if the firm does not have a CEO. The person acting in a similar capacity to a CEO is the most senior decision maker in the firm, who might have the title of managing partner or president, for example

- the sole proprietor of the registered firm, or

- the officer in charge of a division of the firm that carries on all of the registerable activity if the firm also has significant other business activities, such as insurance, conducted in different divisions. This is not an option if the core business of the firm is trading or advising in securities and it only has some other minor operations conducted in other divisions. In this case, the UDP must be the CEO or equivalent.

To designate someone else as the UDP requires an exemptive relief order. Given that the intention of section 11.2 is to ensure that responsibility for its compliance system rests at the very top of a firm, we will only grant relief in rare cases.

We note that in larger organizations, the UDP is sometimes supported by an officer who has a compliance oversight role and title within the organization and who is more senior than the CCO. We have no objection to such arrangements, but it must be understood that they can in no way diminish the UDP's regulatory responsibilities.

If the person designated as the UDP no longer meets these requirements, and the registered firm is unable to designate another UDP, the firm should promptly advise the regulator of the actions it is taking to designate a new UDP who meets these requirements.

11.3 — Designating a chief compliance officer

Under subsection 11.3(1), registered firms must designate an individual to be the CCO. Firms should ensure that the individual understands and is able to perform the obligations of a CCO under section 5.2.

The CCO must meet the applicable proficiency requirements in Part 3 and be:

- an officer or partner of the registered firm, or
- the sole proprietor of the registered firm

If the CCO no longer meets any of the above conditions and the registered firm is unable to designate another CCO, the firm should promptly advise the regulator of the actions it is taking to designate an appropriate CCO.

Division 2 — Books and records

Under securities legislation, the regulator may access, examine and take copies of a registered firm's records. The regulator may also conduct regular and unscheduled compliance reviews of registered firms.

11.5 — General requirements for records

Under subsection 11.5(1), registered firms must maintain records to accurately record their business activities, financial affairs and client transactions, and demonstrate compliance with securities legislation.

The following discussion provides guidance for the various elements of the records described in subsection 11.5(2).

Financial affairs

The records required under paragraphs 11.5(2)(a), (b) and (c) are records firms must maintain to help ensure they are able to prepare and file financial information, determine their capital position, including the calculation of excess working capital, and generally demonstrate compliance with the capital and insurance requirements.

Client transactions

The records required under paragraphs 11.5(2)(g), (h), (i), (l) and (n) are records firms must maintain to accurately and fully document transactions entered into on behalf of a client. We expect firms to maintain notes of communications that could have an impact on the client's account or the client's relationship with the firm. These communications include

- oral communications
- all e-mail, regular mail, fax and other written communications

While we do not expect registered firms to save every voicemail or e-mail, or to record all telephone conversations with clients, we do expect that registered firms maintain records of all communications relating to orders received from their clients.

The records required under paragraph 11.5(2)(g) should document buy and sell transactions, referrals, margin transactions and any other activities relating to a client's account. They include records of all actions leading to trade execution, settlement and clearance, such as trades on exchanges, alternative trading systems, over-the-counter markets, debt markets, and distributions and trades in the prospectus-exempt market.

Examples of these records are:

- trade confirmation statements
- summary information about account activity
- communications between a registrant and its client about particular transactions, and
- records of transactions resulting from securities a client holds, such as dividends or interest paid, or dividend reinvestment program activity

Paragraph 11.5(2)(l) requires firms to maintain records that demonstrate compliance with the know your client obligations in section 13.2 and the suitability obligations in section 13.3. This includes records for unsuitable trades in subsection 13.3(2).

Client relationship

The records required under paragraphs 11.5(2)(k) and (m) should document information about a registered firm's relationship with its client and relationships that any representatives have with that client.

These records include:

- communication between the firm and its clients, such as disclosure provided to clients and agreements between the registrant and its clients
- account opening information
- change of status information provided by the client
- disclosure and other relationship information provided by the firm
- margin account agreements

- communications regarding a complaint made by the client
- actions taken by the firm regarding a complaint
- communications that do not relate to a particular transaction, and
- conflicts records

Each record required under paragraph 11.5(2)(k) should clearly indicate the name of the accountholder and the account the record refers to. A record should include information only about the accounts of the same accountholder or group. For example, registrants should have separate records for an individual's personal accounts and for accounts of a legal entity that the individual owns or jointly holds with another party.

Where applicable, the financial details should note whether the information is for an individual or a family. This includes spousal income and net worth. The financial details for accounts of a legal entity should note whether the information refers to the entity or to the owner(s) of the entity.

If the registered firm permits clients to complete new account forms themselves, the forms should use language that is clear and avoids terminology that may be unfamiliar to unsophisticated clients.

Internal controls

The records required under paragraphs 11.5(2)(d), (e), (f), (j) and (o) are records firms must maintain to support the internal controls and supervision components of their compliance system.

11.6 — Form, accessibility and retention of records

Third party access to records

Paragraph 11.6(1)(b) requires registered firms to keep their records in a safe location. This includes ensuring that no one has unauthorized access to information, particularly confidential client information. Registered firms should be particularly vigilant if they maintain books and records in a location that may be accessible by a third party. In this case, the firm should have a confidentiality agreement with the third party.

Division 3 — Certain business transactions

11.8 — Tied selling

Section 11.8 prohibits an individual or firm from engaging in abusive sales practices such as selling a security on the condition that the client purchase another product or service from the registrant or one of its affiliates. These types of practices are known as "tied selling". In our view, this section would be contravened if, for example, a financial institution agreed to lend money to a client only if the client acquired securities of mutual funds sponsored by the financial institution.

However, section 11.8 is not intended to prohibit relationship pricing or other beneficial selling arrangements similar to relationship pricing. Relationship pricing refers to the practice of industry participants offering financial incentives or advantages to certain clients.

11.9 — Registrant acquiring a registered firm's securities or assets

Notice requirement

Under section 11.9, registrants must give the regulator notice if they propose to acquire an ownership interest in voting securities (or securities convertible into voting securities) or assets of aanother registered firm or the parent of another registered firm. This notice must be delivered to the principal regulator of the registrant proposing to make the acquisition and to the principal regulator of the registered firm they propose to acquire, if that firm is registered in Canada. If the principal regulator of both firms is the same, only one notice is required.

Registrants acquiring securities or assets of another registered firm for a client in nominee name do not need to provide notice under section 11.9. For purposes of this section, a substantial part of the assets of the registered firm would include a registered firm's book of business, a business line or a division of the firm, among other things. This notice gives the regulator an opportunity to consider ownership issues that may affect a firm's fitness for registration.

Filing of the notice with the principal regulator

It is intended that the notice filed with the principal regulator(s) will be shared with other regulators with an interest in the proposed acquisition. Therefore, although only the principal regulator(s) will receive a notice, other jurisdictions may object to the proposed acquisition under subsections 11.9(4) and 11.9(5). The registrant will have an opportunity to be heard in any jurisdiction that has objected to the proposed acquisition. It is our intent, however, to coordinate the review of these notices and any decisions to object to these proposed acquisitions.

Subsection 11.9(4) does not apply in British Columbia. However, the regulator in British Columbia may exercise discretion under section 36 or 161 of the BC *Securities Act* (BCSA) to impose conditions, restrictions or requirements on the registrant's registration or to suspend or revoke the registration if it decides that an acquisition would affect the registrant's fitness for registration or be prejudicial to the public interest. In these circumstances, the registrant would be entitled to an opportunity to be heard, except if the regulator issues a temporary order under section 161 of the BCSA.

Content of the notice

When preparing the notice under section 11.9, registrants should consider including the following information to help the regulator assess the proposed transaction:

- the proposed closing date for the transaction
- the business reasons for the transaction
- the corporate structure, both before and after the closing of the proposed transaction, including all affiliated companies and subsidiaries of the acquirer and any registered firm involved in the proposed transaction whether interests in a company, partnership or trust are held directly or through a holding company, trust or other entity
- information on the operations and business plans of the acquirer and any registered firm involved in the proposed transaction, including any changes to Item 3.1 of Form 33-109F6 Firm Registration such as primary business activities, target market, and the products and services provided to clients of any registered firm involved in the proposed transaction
- any significant changes to the business operations of any registered firm involved in the proposed transaction, including changes to the CCO, the UDP, key management, directors, officers, permitted individuals or registered individuals
- whether the registered firms involved in the proposed transaction have written policies and procedures to address conflicts of interest that may arise following the transaction and information on how such conflicts of interest have been or will be addressed.
- whether the registered firms involved in the proposed transaction have adequate resources to ensure compliance with all applicable conditions of registration
- a confirmation that any registered firm involved in the proposed transaction will comply with section 4.1 following the transaction
- details of any client communications in connection with the transaction that have been made or are planned or an explanation of why no communications to clients are anticipated
- whether a press release will be issued in relation to the proposed transaction

11.10 — Registered firm whose securities are acquired

Notice requirement

Under section 11.10, registered firms must notify their principal regulator if they know or have reason to believe that any individual or firm is about to acquire 10% or more of the voting securities (or securities convertible into voting securities) of the firm or the firm's parent. This notice gives the regulator an opportunity to consider ownership issues that may affect a firm's fitness for registration. We expect this notice to be sent as soon as the registered firm knows or has reason to believe such an acquisition is going to take place.

Filing of the notice with the principal regulator

It is intended that the notice filed with the principal regulator(s) will be shared with other regulators with an interest in the proposed acquisition. Therefore, although only the principal regulator(s) will receive a notice, other jurisdictions may object to the proposed acquisition under subsections 11.10(5) and 11.10(6). The registered firm will have an opportunity to be heard in any jurisdiction that has objected to the proposed acquisition. It is our intent, however, to coordinate the review of these notices and any decisions to object to these proposed acquisitions.

Application for registration

We expect any individual or firm that acquires assets of a registered firm and is not already a registrant will have to apply for registration. We will assess their fitness for registration when they apply.

Subsection 11.10(5) does not apply in British Columbia. However, the regulator in British Columbia may exercise discretion under section 36 or 161 of the BCSA to impose conditions, restrictions or requirements on the registrant's registration or to suspend or revoke the registration if it decides that an acquisition would affect the registrant's fitness for registration or be prejudicial to the public interest. In these circumstances, the registrant would be entitled to an opportunity to be heard, except if the regulator issues a temporary order under section 161 of the BCSA.

Content of the notice

Refer to the guidance in section 11.9.

Part 12 — Financial condition

Division 1 — Working capital

12.1 — Capital requirements

Frequency of working capital calculations

Section 12.1 requires registered firms to notify the regulator as soon as possible if their excess working capital is less than zero.

Registered firms should know their working capital position at all times. This may require a firm to calculate its working capital every day. The frequency of working capital calculations depends on many factors, including the size of the firm, the nature of its business and the stability of the components of its working capital. For example, it may be sufficient for a sole proprietor firm with a dedicated and stable source of working capital to do the calculation on a monthly basis.

Form 31-103F1 Calculation of excess working capital

Application of NI 52-107 Acceptable Accounting Principles and Auditing Standards

Form 31-103F1 *Calculation of Excess Working Capital* (Form 31-103F1) must be prepared using the accounting principles used to prepare financial statements in accordance with National Instrument 52-107 *Acceptable Accounting Principles and Auditing Standards* (NI 52-107). Refer to section 12.10 of this Companion Policy and Companion Policy 52-107 *Acceptable Accounting Principles and Auditing Standards* (52-107CP) for further guidance on audited financial statements.

IIROC and MFDA member firms that are also registered in another category

IIROC and MFDA member firms that are also registered in a category that does not require SRO membership must still comply with the financial filing requirements in Part 12 *Financial condition*, even if they are relying on the exemptions in sections 9.3 and 9.4. Provided certain conditions are met, SRO members that are registered in other categories may be permitted to calculate their working capital in accordance with the SRO forms and file the SRO forms instead of Form 31-103F1.

For example, if the SRO firm is also an investment fund manager, it will need to report any net asset value (NAV) adjustments quarterly in order to comply with the investment fund manager requirements, notwithstanding that its SRO has no such requirements. However, they may be permitted to calculate their working capital in accordance with the SRO forms and file the SRO forms instead of Form 31-103F1. See sections 12.1, 12.12 and 12.14 for the requirements on delivery of working capital calculations for SRO members that are registered in multiple categories.

Working capital requirements are not cumulative

The working capital requirements for registered firms set out in section 12.1 are not cumulative. If a firm is registered in more than one category, it must meet the highest capital requirement of its categories of registration, except for those investment fund managers who are also registered as portfolio managers and meet the requirements of the exemption in section 8.6. These investment fund managers need only meet the lower capital requirement for portfolio managers.

If a registrant becomes insolvent or declares bankruptcy

The regulator will review the circumstances of a registrant's insolvency or bankruptcy on a case-by-case basis. If the regulator has concerns, it may impose terms and conditions on the registrant's registration, such as close supervision and delivering progress reports to the regulator, or it may suspend the registrant's registration.

12.2 — Subordination agreements

Long-term related party debt must be deducted from a firm's working capital on Form 31-103F1, unless the firm and the lender have executed a subordination agreement in the form set out in Appendix B of NI 31-103 and delivered a copy of that agreement with the regulator.

Non-current related party debt must be deducted from a firm's working capital on Form 31-103F1, unless the firm and the lender have executed a subordination agreement in the form set out in Appendix B of NI 31-103 and delivered a copy of that agreement to the regulator. A portion of the non-current loan becoming current would not impact the original subordination agreement; the firm would have to notify the regulator if the firm repays the loan or any part of the non-current portion of the loan. However, the current portion of the originally-intended non-current subordinated loan would have to be included in Line 4 of Form 31-103F1, and could not be included in Line 5 of Form 31-103F1. This may not be the total amount of the original loan as set out in the subordination agreement, and as such the amount in the subordination agreement would not agree to Line 5 of Form 31-103F1.

Related party debt due on demand or repayable by the firm at any time, including pursuant to a revolving line of credit, is an example of a current liability. These types of liabilities are not eligible to be subordinated for the purposes of calculating excess working capital. The amount of current related party debt must be included in line 4 — *Current liabilities* of Form 31-103F1.

Firms must deliver subordination agreements to the regulator on the earlier of 10 days after the execution of the agreement or the date on which the firm excludes the amount of the related party debt from its excess working capital calculation. A firm may not exclude the amount until the subordination agreement is executed and delivered to the regulator.

The firm's obligations under section 12.2 to notify the regulator 10 days before it repays the loan or terminates the subordination agreement apply regardless of the terms of any loan agreement. Firms should ensure the terms of their loan agreements do not conflict with their regulatory requirements.

If a subordinated related party debt is being increased and the incremental increase is to be subordinated, the subordination agreement submitted to the regulator should only report the incremental increase. Firms should not report the full balance of the related party debt, as noted on the statement of financial position, on the new subordination agreement unless the previous subordination agreement is terminated and notification of this termination is made in accordance with section 12.2.

In conjunction with the submission of a new subordination agreement, the regulator may request that the firm provide a schedule detailing the total outstanding subordinated debt.

The regulator may request that additional documentation be provided in conjunction with the firm's notice of repayment of a subordinated debt in order to assess whether the firm will have sufficient excess working capital following the repayment. This may include updated interim financial information and a completed Form 31-103F1.

At the time the firm submits a notice of repayment, the firm should provide an updated schedule to the regulator, detailing the total outstanding subordinated debt following the repayment.

Division 2 — Insurance

Insurance coverage limits

Registrants must maintain bonding or insurance that provides for a "double aggregate limit" or a "full reinstatement of coverage" (also known as "no aggregate limit"). The insurance provisions state that the registered firm must "maintain" bonding or insurance in the amounts specified. We do not expect that the calculation would differ materially from day to day. If there is a material change in a firm's circumstances, it should consider the potential impact on its ability to meet its insurance requirements.

Most insurers offer aggregate limit policies that contain limits based on a single loss and on the number or value of losses that occur during the coverage period.

Double aggregate limit policies have a specified limit for each claim. The total amount that may be claimed during the coverage period is twice that limit. For example, if an adviser maintains a financial institution bond of $50,000 for each clause with a double aggregate limit, the adviser's coverage is $50,000 for any one claim and $100,000 for all claims during the coverage period.

Full reinstatement of coverage policies and no aggregate limit policies have a specified limit for each claim but no limit on the number of claims or losses during the coverage period. For example, if an adviser maintains a financial institution bond of $50,000 for each clause with a full reinstatement of coverage provision, the adviser's maximum coverage is $50,000 for any one claim, but there is no limit on the total amount that can be claimed under the bond during the coverage period.

Insurance requirements are not cumulative

Insurance requirements are not cumulative. For example, a firm registered in the categories of portfolio manager and investment fund manager need only maintain insurance coverage for the higher of the amounts required for each registration category. Despite being registered as both a portfolio manager and an investment fund manager, when calculating the investment fund manager insurance requirement under subsection 12.5(2), an investment fund manager should only include the total assets under management of its own investment funds. It is only with respect to its own funds that the registrant is acting as an investment fund manager.

12.4 — Insurance — adviser

The insurance requirements for advisers depend in part on whether the adviser holds or has access to client assets.

An adviser will be considered to hold or have access to client assets if they do any of the following:

- hold client securities or cash for any period
- accept funds from clients, for example, a cheque made payable to the registrant
- accept client money from a custodian, for example, client money that is deposited in the registrant's bank or trust accounts before the registrant issues a cheque to the client
- have the ability to gain access to client assets
- have, in any capacity, legal ownership of, or access to, client funds or securities
- have the authority, such as under a power of attorney, to withdraw funds or securities from client accounts
- have authority to debit client accounts to pay bills other than investment management fees
- act as a trustee for clients, or
- act as fund manager or general partner for investment funds

12.6 — Global bonding or insurance

Registered firms may be covered under a global insurance policy. Under this type of policy, the firm is insured under a parent company's policy that covers the parent and its subsidiaries or affiliates. Firms should ensure that the claims of other entities covered under a global insurance policy do not affect the limits or coverage applicable to the firm.

Division 4 — Financial reporting

12.10 — Annual financial statements

12.11 — Interim financial information

Division

Accounting Principles

Registrants are required to deliver annual financial statements and interim financial information that comply with NI 52-107. Depending on the financial year, a registrant will look to different parts of NI 52-107 to determine which accounting principles and auditing standards apply:

- Part 3 of NI 52-107 applies for financial years beginning on or after January 1, 2011;
- Part 4 of NI 52-107 applies to financial years beginning before January 1, 2011.

Part 3 of NI 52-107 refers to Canadian GAAP applicable to publicly accountable enterprises, which is IFRS as incorporated into the Handbook. Under Part 3 of NI 52-107, annual financial statements and interim financial information delivered by a registrant must be prepared in accordance with Canadian GAAP applicable to publicly accountable enterprises except that any investments in subsidiaries, jointly controlled entities and associates must be accounted for as specified for separate financial statements in International Accounting Standard 27 Consolidated and Separate Financial Statements. Separate financial statements are sometimes referred to as non-consolidated financial statements.

Subsection 3.2(3) of NI 52-107 requires annual financial statements to include a statement and description about this required financial reporting framework. Section 2.7 of 52-107CP provides guidance on subsection 3.2(3). We remind registrants to refer to these provisions in NI 52-107 and 52-107CP in preparing their annual financial statements and interim financial information.

Part 4 of NI 52-107 refers to Canadian GAAP for public enterprises, which is Canadian GAAP as it existed before the mandatory effective date for the adoption of IFRS, included in the Handbook as Part V. Under Part 4 of NI 52-107, annual financial statements and interim financial information delivered by a registrant must be prepared in accordance with Canadian GAAP for public enterprises except that the financial statements and interim financial information must be prepared on a non-consolidated basis.

Changeover to International Financial Reporting Standards

When preparing annual financial statements, interim financial information or Form 31-103F1 for a financial year beginning in 2011 or for interim periods relating to a financial year beginning in 2011, registrants may rely on the exemption in subsection 12.15(1) and exclude comparative information for the preceding financial year. Section 3.2(4) of NI 52-107 provides a corresponding exemption for the accounting principles used by registrants. If a registrant relies on these exemptions, its date of transition to IFRS will be the first day of its financial year beginning in 2011. Section 2.7 of 52-107CP provides further guidance on this topic. We remind registrants to refer to the provisions in NI 52-107 and 52-107CP in preparing their financial statements and interim financial information for a financial period beginning in 2011.

12.14 — Delivering financial information — investment fund manager

NAV errors and adjustments

Section 12.14 requires investment fund managers to periodically deliver to the regulator, among other things, a completed Form 31-103F4 *Net Asset Value Adjustments* if any NAV adjustment has been made. A NAV adjustment is necessary when there has been a material error and the NAV per unit does not accurately reflect the actual NAV per unit at the time of computation.

Some examples of the causes of NAV errors are:

- mispricing of a security
- corporate action recorded incorrectly
- incorrect numbers used for issued and outstanding units
- incorrect expenses and income used or accrued
- incorrect foreign exchange rates used in the valuation, and
- human error, such as inputting an incorrect value

We expect investment fund managers to have policies that clearly define what constitutes a material error that requires an adjustment, including threshold levels, and how to correct material errors. If an investment fund manager does not have a threshold in place, it may wish to consider the threshold in IFIC Bulletin Number 22 *Correcting Portfolio NAV Errors* or adopt a more stringent policy.

Part 13 — Dealing with clients — individuals and firms

Division 1 — Know your client and suitability

13.2 — Know your client

General principles

Registrants act as gatekeepers of the integrity of the capital markets. They should not, by act or omission, facilitate conduct that brings the market into disrepute. As part of their gatekeeper role, registrants are required to establish the identity of, and conduct due diligence on, their clients under the know your client (KYC) obligation in section 13.2. Complying with the KYC obligation can help ensure that trades are completed in accordance with securities laws.

KYC information forms the basis for determining whether trades in securities are suitable for investors. This helps protect the client, the registrant and the integrity of the capital markets. The KYC obligation requires registrants to take reasonable steps to obtain and periodically update information about their clients.

Verifying a client's reputation

Paragraph 13.2(2)(a) requires registrants to make inquiries if they have cause for concern about a client's reputation. The registrant must make all reasonable inquiries necessary to resolve the concern. This includes making a reasonable effort to determine, for example, the nature of the client's business or the identity of beneficial owners where the client is a corporation, partnership or trust. See subsection 13.2(3) for additional guidance on identifying clients that are corporations, partnerships or trusts.

Identifying insiders

Under paragraph 13.2(2)(b), a registrant must take reasonable steps to establish whether the client is an insider of a reporting issuer or any other issuer whose securities are publicly traded.

We consider "reasonable steps" to include explaining to the client what an insider is and what it means for securities to be publicly traded.

For purposes of this paragraph, "reporting issuer" has the meaning given to it in securities legislation and "other issuer" means any issuer whose securities are traded in any public market. This includes domestic, foreign, exchange-listed and over-thecounter markets. This definition does not include issuers whose securities have been distributed through a private placement and are not freely tradeable.

A registrant need not ascertain whether the client is an insider if the only securities traded for the client are mutual fund securities and scholarship plan securities referred to in paragraphs 7.1(2)(b) and 7.1(2)(c). However, we encourage firms, when selling highly concentrated pooled funds, to enquire as to whether a client is an insider of the issuer of any securities held by the fund, notwithstanding the exemption provided in subsection 13.2(7). In addition, we remind registrants that they remain subject to the requirement in paragraph 13.2(2)(b) when they trade any other securities than those listed in paragraphs 7.1(2)(b) and 7.1(2)(c).

This exemption does not change an insider's reporting and conduct responsibilities.

Clients that are corporations, partnerships or trusts

Subsection 13.2(3) requires registrants to establish the identity of any person who owns or controls 25% or more of the shares of a client that is a corporation or exercises control over the affairs of a client that is a partnership or trust. We remind registrants that this is in addition to the requirement in paragraph 13.2(2)(a) which requires registrants to make inquiries if they have cause for concern about a client's reputation. If a registrant has cause for concern about a particular client that is a corporation, partnership or trust, they may need to identify all beneficial owners of such entity.

Keeping KYC information current

Under subsection 13.2(4), registrants are required to make reasonable efforts to keep their clients' KYC information current.

We consider information to be current if it is sufficiently up-to-date to support a suitability determination. For example, a portfolio manager with discretionary authority should update its clients' KYC information frequently. A dealer that only occasionally recommends trades to a client should ensure that the client's KYC information is up-to-date at the time a proposed trade or recommendation is made.

13.3 — Suitability

Suitability obligation

Subsection 13.3(1) requires registrants to take reasonable steps to ensure that a proposed trade is suitable for a client before making a recommendation or accepting instructions from the client. To meet this suitability obligation, registrants should have in-depth knowledge of all securities that they buy and sell for, or recommend to, their clients. This is often referred to as the "know your product" or KYP obligation.

Registrants should know each security well enough to understand and explain to their clients the security's risks, key features, and initial and ongoing costs and fees. Having the registered firm's approval for representatives to sell a product does not mean that the product will be suitable for all clients. Individual registrants must still determine the suitability of each transaction for every client.

Registrants should also be aware of, and act in compliance with, the terms of any exemption being relied on for the trade or distribution of the security.

In all cases, we expect registrants to be able to demonstrate a process for making suitability determinations that are appropriate in the circumstances.

Suitability obligations cannot be delegated

Registrants may not:

- delegate their suitability obligations to anyone else, or
- satisfy the suitability obligation by simply disclosing the risks involved with a trade

Only permitted clients may waive their right to a suitability determination. Registrants must make a suitability determination for all other clients. If a client instructs a registrant to make a trade that is unsuitable, the registrant may not allow the trade to be completed until they warn the client as required under subsection 13.3(2).

KYC information for suitability depends on circumstances

The extent of KYC information a registrant needs to determine suitability of a trade will depend on the:

- client's circumstances
- type of security
- client's relationship to the registrant, and
- registrant's business model

In some cases, the registrant will need extensive KYC information, for example, if the registrant is a portfolio manager with discretionary authority. In these cases, the registrant should have a comprehensive understanding of the client's:

- investment needs and objectives, including the client's time horizon for their investments

- overall financial circumstances, including net worth, income, current investment holdings and employment status, and

- risk tolerance for various types of securities and investment portfolios, taking into account the client's investment knowledge

In other cases, the registrant may need less KYC information, for example, if the registrant only occasionally deals with a client who makes small investments relative to their overall financial position.

If the registrant recommends securities traded under the prospectus exemption for accredited investors in NI 45-106, the registrant should determine whether the client qualifies as an accredited investor.

If a client is opening more than one account, the registrant should indicate whether the client's investment objectives and risk tolerance apply to a particular account or to the client's whole portfolio of accounts.

Registered firm and financial institution clients

Under subsection 13.3(3), there is no obligation to make a suitability determination for a client that is a registered firm, a Canadian financial institution or a Schedule III bank.

Permitted clients

Under subsection 13.3(4), registrants do not have to make a suitability determination for a permitted client if:

- the permitted client has waived their right to suitability in writing, and

- the registrant does not act as an adviser for a managed account of the permitted client

A permitted client may waive their right to suitability for all trades under a blanket waiver.

SRO exemptions

SRO rules may also provide conditional exemptions from the suitability obligation, for example, for dealers who offer order execution only services.

Division 2 — Conflicts of interest

13.4 — Identifying and responding to conflicts of interest

Section 13.4 covers a broad range of conflicts of interest. It requires registered firms to take reasonable steps to identify existing material conflicts of interest and material conflicts that the firm reasonably expects to arise between the firm and a client. As part of identifying these conflicts, a firm should collect information from the individuals acting on its behalf regarding the conflicts they expect to arise with their clients.

We consider a conflict of interest to be any circumstance where the interests of different parties, such as the interests of a client and those of a registrant, are inconsistent or divergent.

Responding to conflicts of interest

A registered firm's policies and procedures for managing conflicts should allow the firm and its staff to:

- identify conflicts of interest that should be avoided

- determine the level of risk that a conflict of interest raises, and

- respond appropriately to conflicts of interest

When responding to any conflict of interest, registrants should consider their standard of care for dealing with clients and apply consistent criteria to similar types of conflicts of interest.

In general, three methods are used to respond to conflicts of interest:

- avoidance

- control, and

- disclosure

If a registrant allows a serious conflict of interest to continue, there is a high risk of harm to clients or to the market. If the risk of harming a client or the integrity of the markets is too high, the conflict needs to be avoided. If a registered firm does not avoid a conflict of interest, it should take steps to control or disclose the conflict, or both. The firm should also consider what internal structures or policies and procedures it should use or have to reasonably respond to the conflict of interest.

Avoiding conflicts of interest

Registrants must avoid all conflicts of interest that are prohibited by law. If a conflict of interest is not prohibited by law, registrants should avoid the conflict if it is sufficiently contrary to the interests of a client that there can be no other reasonable response.

For example, some conflicts of interest are so contrary to another person's or company's interest that a registrant cannot use controls or disclosure to respond to them. In these cases, the registrant should avoid the conflict, stop providing the service or stop dealing with the client.

Controlling conflicts of interest

Registered firms should design their organizational structures, lines of reporting and physical locations to control conflicts of interest effectively. For example, the following situations would likely raise a conflict of interest:

- advisory staff reporting to marketing staff
- compliance or internal audit staff reporting to a business unit, and
- registered representatives and investment banking staff in the same physical location

Depending on the conflict of interest, registered firms may control the conflict by:

- assigning a different representative to provide a service to the particular client
- creating a group or committee to review, develop or approve responses
- monitoring trading activity, or
- using information barriers for certain internal communication

Disclosing conflicts of interest

(a) — When disclosure is appropriate

Registered firms should ensure that their clients are adequately informed about any conflicts of interest that may affect the services the firm provides to them. This is in addition to any other methods the registered firm may use to manage the conflict.

(b) — Timing of disclosure

Under subsection 13.4(3), if a reasonable investor would expect to be informed of a conflict, a registered firm must disclose the conflict in a timely manner. Registered firms and their representatives should disclose conflicts of interest to their clients before or at the time they recommend the transaction or provide the service that gives rise to the conflict. This is to give clients a reasonable amount of time to assess the conflict.

We note that where this disclosure is provided to a client before the transaction takes place, we expect the disclosure to be provided shortly before the transaction takes place. For example, if it was initially provided with the client's account opening documentation months or years previously we expect that a registered representative would also disclose this conflict to the client shortly before the transaction or at the time the transaction is recommended.

For example, if a registered individual recommends a security that they own, this may constitute a material conflict which should be disclosed to the client before or at the time of the recommendation.

(c) — When disclosure is not appropriate

Disclosure may not be appropriate if a conflict of interest involves confidential or commercially sensitive information, or the information amounts to "inside information" under insider trading provisions in securities legislation.

In these situations, registered firms will need to assess whether there are other methods to adequately respond to the conflict of interest. If not, the firm may have to decline to provide the service to avoid the conflict of interest.

Registered firms should also have specific procedures for responding to conflicts of interest that involve inside information and for complying with insider trading provisions.

(d) — How to disclose a conflict of interest

Registered firms should provide disclosure about material conflicts of interest to their clients if a reasonable investor would expect to be informed about them. When a registered firm provides this disclosure, it should:

- be prominent, specific, clear and meaningful to the client, and
- explain the conflict of interest and how it could affect the service the client is being offered

Registered firms should not:

- provide generic disclosure
- give partial disclosure that could mislead their clients, or
- obscure conflicts of interest in overly detailed disclosure

Examples of conflicts of interest

This section describes specific situations where a registrant could be in a conflict of interest and how to manage the conflict.

Relationships with related or connected issuers

When a registered firm trades in, or recommends securities of, a related or connected issuer, it should respond to the resulting conflict of interest by disclosing it to the client.

To provide disclosure about conflicts with related issuers, a registered firm may maintain a list of the related issuers for which it acts as a dealer or adviser. It may make the list available to clients by:

- posting the list on its website and keeping it updated

- providing the list to the client at the time of account opening, or

- explaining to the client at the time of account opening how to contact the firm to request a copy of the list free of charge

The list may include examples of the types of issuers that are related or connected and the nature of the firm's relationship with those issuers. For example, a firm could generally describe the nature of its relationship with an investment fund within a family of investment funds. This would mean that the firm may not have to update the list when a new fund is added to that fund family.

However, this type of disclosure may not meet the expectations of a reasonable investor when a specific conflict with a related or connected issuer arises, for example, when a registered individual recommends a trade in the securities of a related issuer. In these circumstances, a registered firm should provide the client with disclosure about the specific conflict with that issuer. This disclosure should include a description of the nature of the firm's relationship with the issuer.

Like all disclosure, information regarding a conflict with a related or connected issuer should be made available to clients before or at the time of the advice or trade giving rise to the conflict, so that clients have a reasonable amount of time to assess it. Registrants should use their judgment for the best way and time to inform clients about these conflicts. Previous disclosure may no longer be relevant to, or remembered by, a client, while disclosure of the same conflict more than once in a short time may be unnecessary and confusing.

Firms do not have to disclose to clients their relationship with a related or connected issuer that is a mutual fund managed by an affiliate of the firm if the names of the firm and the fund are similar enough that a reasonable person would conclude they are affiliated.

Relationships with other issuers

Firms should assess whether conflicts of interest may arise in relationships with issuers that do not fall within the definitions of related or connected issuers. Examples include non-corporate issuers such as a trust, partnership or special purpose entity or conduit issuing asset-backed commercial paper. This is especially important if a registered firm or its affiliates are involved in sponsoring, manufacturing, underwriting or distributing these securities.

The registered firm should disclose the relationship with these types of issuers if it may give rise to a conflict of interest that a reasonable client would expect to be informed about.

Competing interests of clients

If clients of a registered firm have competing interests, the firm should make reasonable efforts to be fair to all clients. Firms should have internal systems to evaluate the balance of these interests.

For example, a conflict of interest can arise between investment banking clients, who want the highest price, lowest interest rate or best terms in general for their issuances of securities, and retail clients who will buy the product. The firm should consider whether the product meets the needs of retail clients and is competitive with alternatives available in the market.

Individuals who serve on a board of directors

(a) — Board of directors of another registered firm

Under section 4.1, a registered individual must not act as a director of another registered firm that is not an affiliate of the individual's sponsoring firm.

(b) — Board of directors of non registered persons or companies

Section 4.1 does not apply to registered individuals who act as directors of unregistered firms. However, significant conflicts of interest can arise when a registered individual serves on a board of directors. Examples include conflicting fiduciary duties owed to the company and to a registered firm or client, possible receipt of inside information and conflicting demands on the representative's time.

Registered firms should consider controlling the conflict by:

- requiring their representatives to seek permission from the firm to serve on the board of directors of an issuer, and

- having policies for board participation that identify the circumstances where the activity would not be in the best interests of the firm or its clients

The regulator will take into account the potential conflicts of interest that may arise when an individual serves on a board of directors when assessing that individual's application for registration or continuing fitness for registration.

(c) — Board of directors of reporting issuers

A representative of a registrant acting as a director of or adviser to a reporting issuer raises concerns with respect to conflicts of interest, particularly in relation to issues of insider information, trading and timely disclosure. All registrants should be conscious of their responsibilities in these situations and weigh the burden of dealing in an ethical manner with the conflicts of interest against the advantages of acting as a director of a reporting issuer, many shareholders of which may be clients of the registrant.

Directors of a reporting issuer have an obligation not to reveal any confidential information about the issuer until there is full public disclosure of the information, particularly when the information might have a bearing on the market price or value of the securities of the issuer.

Any director of a reporting issuer who is a partner, director, officer, employee or agent of a registrant should recognize that the director's first responsibility with respect to confidential information is to the reporting issuer. A director should meticulously avoid any disclosure of inside information to partners, directors, officers, employees or agents of the registrant or to its clients.

If a partner, director, officer, employee or agent of a registrant is not a director but is acting in an advisory capacity to a reporting issuer and discussing confidential matters, the same care should be taken as if that person were a director. Should the matter require consultation with other personnel of the registrant, adequate measures should be taken to guard the confidential nature.

Individuals who have outside business activities

Conflicts can arise when registered individuals are involved in outside business activities, for example, because of the compensation they receive for these activities or because of the nature of the relationship between the individual and the outside entity. Before approving any of these activities, registered firms should consider potential conflicts of interest. If the firm cannot properly control a potential conflict of interest, it should not permit the outside activity.

Registrants must disclose all outside business activities in Form 33-109F4 (or Form 33-109F5 for changes in outside business activities after registration). Required disclosure includes the following, whether the registrant receives compensation or not:

- any employment and business activities outside the registrant's sponsoring firm
- all officer or director positions, and
- any other equivalent positions held, as well as positions of influence.

The following are examples of outside business activities that we would expect to be disclosed:

- paid or unpaid roles with charitable, social or religious organizations where the individual is in a position of power or influence and where the activity places the registered individual in contact with clients or potential clients, including positions where the registrant handles investments or monies of the organization
- being an owner of a holding company

The regulator will take into account the potential conflicts of interest that may arise as a result of an individual's outside business activities when assessing that individual's application for registration or continuing fitness for registration., including the following:

- whether the individual will have sufficient time to properly carry out their registerable activities, including remaining current on securities law and product knowledge
- whether the individual will be able to properly service clients
- what is the risk of client confusion and are there effective controls and supervision in place to manage the risk
- whether the outside business activity presents a conflict of interest for the individual, and whether that conflict of interest should be avoided or can be appropriately managed
- whether the outside business activity places the individual in a position of power or influence over clients or potential clients, in particular clients or potential clients that may be vulnerable
- whether the outside business activity provides the individual with access to privileged, confidential or insider information relevant to their registerable activities

A registered firm is responsible for monitoring and supervising the individuals whose registration it sponsors. In relation to outside business activities, this includes:

- having appropriate policies and procedures to deal with outside business activities, including ensuring outside business activities do not:
  - involve activities that are inconsistent with securities legislation, IIROC requirements or MFDA requirements; and
  - interfere with the individual's ability to remain current on securities law and product knowledge
- requiring individual registrants to disclose to their firm, and requiring the firm to review and approve, all outside business activities prior to the activities commencing
- ensuring the firm's chief compliance officer is able to properly supervise and monitor the outside business activities
- maintaining records documenting its supervision of outside business activities and ensuring these records are available for review by regulators
- ensuring that potential conflicts of interest are identified and appropriate steps are taken to manage such conflicts
- ensuring outside business activities do not impair the ability to provide adequate client service, including, where necessary, having an alternate representative available for the client
- ensuring the outside business activity is consistent with the registrant's duty to deal fairly, honestly and in good faith with its clients
- implementing risk management, including proper separation of the outside business activity and registerable activity
- preventing exposure of the firm to complaints and litigation
- assessing whether the firm's knowledge of the individual's lifestyle is commensurate with its knowledge of the individual's business activities and staying alert to other indicators of possible fraudulent activity. For example, if information comes to the firm's knowledge (including through a client complaint) that a registered individual's lifestyle is not commensurate with the individual's compensation by the firm, we would expect the registered firm to make further inquiries to assess the situation.

Failure to discharge these responsibilities may be relevant to the firm's continued fitness for registration.

Compensation practices

Registered firms should consider whether any particular benefits, compensation or remuneration practices are inconsistent with their obligations to clients, especially if the firm relies heavily on commission-based remuneration. For example, if there is a complex product that carries a high commission, the firm may decide that it is not appropriate to offer that product.

13.5 — Restrictions on certain managed account transactions

Section 13.5 prohibits a registered adviser from engaging in certain transactions in investment portfolios it manages for clients on a discretionary basis where the relationship may give rise to a conflict of interest or a perceived conflict of interest. The prohibited transactions include trades in securities in which a responsible person or an associate of a responsible person may have an interest or over which they may have influence or control.

Disclosure when responsible person is partner, director or officer of issuer

Paragraph 13.5(2)(a) prohibits a registered adviser from purchasing securities of an issuer in which a responsible person or an associate of a responsible person is a partner, officer or director for a client's managed account. The prohibition applies unless the conflict is disclosed to the client and the client's written consent is obtained prior to the purchase.

If the client is an investment fund, the disclosure should be provided to, and the consent obtained from, each security holder of the investment fund in order for it to be meaningful. This disclosure may be provided in the offering memorandum that is provided to security holders. Like all disclosure about conflicts, it should be prominent, specific, clear and meaningful to the client. Consent may be obtained in the investment management agreement signed by the clients of the adviser that are also security holders of the investment fund.

This approach may not be practical for prospectus qualified mutual funds. Investment fund managers and advisers of these funds should also consider the specific exemption from the prohibition under section 6.2 of National Instrument 81-107 *Independent Review Committee for Investment Funds* (NI 81-107) for prospectus-qualified investment funds.

Restrictions on trades with certain investment portfolios

Paragraph 13.5(2)(b) prohibits certain trades, including, for example, those between the managed account of a client and the managed account of:

- a spouse of the adviser
- a trust for which a responsible person is the trustee, or
- a corporation in which a responsible person beneficially owns 10% or more of the voting securities

It also prohibits inter-fund trades. An inter-fund trade occurs when the adviser for an investment fund knowingly directs a trade in portfolio securities to another investment fund that it acts for or instructs the dealer to execute the trade with the other investment fund. Investment fund managers and their advisers should also consider the exemption from the prohibition that exists for inter-fund trades by public investment funds under section 6.1 of NI 81-107.

Paragraph 13.5(2)(b) is not intended to prohibit a responsible person from purchasing units in the investment fund itself, nor is it intended to prohibit one investment fund from purchasing units of another fund in situations where they have the same adviser.

In instances where an IIROC dealer, who is also an adviser to a managed account, trades between its inventory account and the managed account, the dealer is expected to have policies and procedures that sufficiently mitigate the conflicts of interest inherent in such transactions. Generally, we expect these policies and procedures to ensure that:

- the trades achieve best execution as referenced in National Instrument 23-101 *Trading Rules*, while ensuring that the trades are consistent with the objectives of the managed account

- reasonable steps are taken to access information, including marketplace quotations or quotes provided by arms-length parties, to ensure that the trade is executed at a fair price

- there is appropriate oversight and a compliance mechanism to monitor this trading activity in order to ensure that it complies with applicable regulatory requirements, including the requirements referred to above.

13.6 — Disclosure when recommending related or connected securities

Section 13.6 restricts the ability of a registered firm to recommend a trade in a security of a related or connected issuer. The restrictions apply to recommendations made in any medium of communication. This includes recommendations in newsletters, articles in general circulation newspapers or magazines, websites, e-mail, Internet chat rooms, bulletin boards, television and radio.

It does not apply to oral recommendations made by registered individuals to their clients. These recommendations are subject to the requirements of section 13.4.

Division 3 — Referral arrangements

Division 3 sets out the requirements for permitted referral arrangements. Regulators want to ensure that under any referral arrangements:

- individuals and firms that engage in registerable activities are appropriately registered

- the roles and responsibilities of the parties to the written agreement are clear, including responsibility for compliance with securities legislation, and

- clients are provided with disclosure about the referral arrangement to help them evaluate the referral arrangement and the extent of any conflicts of interest

Registered firms have a responsibility to monitor and supervise all of their referral arrangements to ensure that they comply with the requirements of NI 31-103 and other applicable securities laws and continue to comply for so long as the arrangement remains in place.

Obligations to clients

A client who is referred to an individual or firm becomes the client of that individual or firm for the purposes of the services provided under the referral arrangement.

The registrant receiving a referral must meet all of its obligations as a registrant toward its referred clients, including know your client and suitability determinations.

Registrants involved in referral arrangements should manage any related conflicts of interest in accordance with the applicable provisions of Part 13 [*Dealing with clients — individuals and firms*]. For example, if the registered firm is not satisfied that the referral fee is reasonable, it should assess whether an unreasonably high fee may create a conflict that could motivate its representatives to act contrary to their duties toward their clients.

13.7 — Definitions — referral arrangements

Section 13.7 defines "referral arrangement" in broad terms. Referral arrangement means an arrangement in which a registrant agrees to pay or receive a referral fee. The definition is not limited to referrals for providing investment products, financial services or services requiring registration. It also includes receiving a referral fee for providing a client name and contact information to an individual or firm. "Referral fee" is also broadly defined. It includes sharing or splitting any commission resulting from the purchase or sale of a security.

In situations where there is no expectation of reward or compensation, we would not consider the receipt of an unexpected gift of appreciation to fall within the scope of a referral arrangement. One of the key elements of the referral arrangement is that the registrant agrees to pay or receive a referral fee for the referral of a client. This agreement or understanding is absent in the case of unexpected gifts.

13.8 — Permitted referral arrangements

Under section 13.8, parties to a referral arrangement are required to set out the terms of the arrangement in a written agreement. This is intended to ensure that each party's roles and responsibilities are made clear. This includes obligations for registered firms involved in referral arrangements to keep records of referral fees. Payments do not necessarily have to go through a registered firm, but a record of all payments related to a referral arrangement must be kept.

We expect referral agreements to include:

- the roles and responsibilities of each party
- limitations on any party that is not a registrant (to ensure that it is not engaging in any activities requiring registration)
- the disclosure to be provided to referred clients, and
- who provides the disclosure to referred clients

If the individual or firm receiving the referral is a registrant, they are responsible for:

- carrying out all activity requiring registration that results from the referral arrangement, and
- communicating with referred clients

Registrants may wish to refer their clients to other registrants for services that they are not authorized to perform under their category of registration. In making referrals, registrants should ensure that the referral does not itself constitute an activity that the registrant is not authorized to engage in under its category of registration.

We would generally not consider the referral by a registrant of a client to a registered dealer to constitute trading by the referring registrant if, in the referral:

- the referring registrant does not make any statement to the client about the merits of a specific security or trade,
- the referring registrant does not make any recommendation or otherwise represent to the client that a specific trade is suitable for that client or another person or company, and
- the referring registrant does not accept any instructions from the client in respect of trades to be made by the registered dealer.

13.9 — Verifying the qualifications of the person or company receiving the referral

Section 13.9 requires the registrant making a referral to satisfy itself that the party receiving the referral is appropriately qualified to perform the services, and if applicable, is appropriately registered. The registrant is responsible for determining the steps that are appropriate in the particular circumstances. For example, this may include an assessment of the types of clients that the referred services would be appropriate for.

13.10 — Disclosing referral arrangements to clients

The disclosure of information to clients required under section 13.10 is intended to help clients make an informed decision about the referral arrangement and to assess any conflicts of interest. The disclosure should be provided to clients before or at the time the referred services are provided. A registered firm, and any registered individuals who are directly participating in the referral arrangement, should take reasonable steps to ensure that clients understand:

- which entity they are dealing with
- what they can expect that entity to provide to them
- the registrant's key responsibilities to them
- the limitations of the registrant's registration category
- any relevant terms and conditions imposed on the registrant's registration
- the extent of the referrer's financial interest in the referral arrangement, and
- the nature of any potential or actual conflict of interest that may arise from the referral arrangement

Division 4 — Loans and margin

13.12 — Restriction on lending to clients

The purpose of section 13.12 is intended to limit the financial exposure of a registered firm. To the extent that products sold to clients are structured in a way that would result in the registrant becoming a lender to the clients, including the registrant extending margin to the client, we would consider the registrant to not be in compliance with section 13.12.

Section 13.12 prohibits registrants from lending money, extending credit or providing margin to clients as we consider that this activity creates a conflict of interest which cannot be easily managed.

We note that SROs are exempt from section 13.12 as they have their own rules or prohibitions on lending, extending credit and providing margin to clients. Direct lending to clients (margin) is reserved for IIROC members. The MFDA has its own rules prohibiting margining and, except in specific limited circumstances, lending.

Division 5 — Complaints

Registered firms in Québec must comply with sections 168.1.1 to 168.1.3 of the Québec *Securities Act*, which has provided a substantially similar regime since 2002. The guidance in Division 5 of this Companion Policy applies to firms registered in any jurisdiction, including Québec.

13.14 — Application of this Division

Investment fund managers are only subject to Division 5 if they also operate under a dealer or adviser registration, in which case the requirements in this Division apply in respect of the activities conducted under their dealer or adviser registration.

In Québec, a registered firm is deemed to comply with this Division if it complies with sections 168.1.1 to 168.1.3 of the Québec *Securities Act*, which provides a substantially similar regime for complaint handling.

The guidance in Division 5 of this Companion Policy applies to firms registered in any jurisdiction, including Québec.

However, section 168.1.3 of the Québec *Securities Act*, includes requirements with respect to dispute resolution or mediation services that are different than those set out in section 13.16 of NI 31-103. In Québec, registrants must inform each complainant, in writing and without delay, that if the complainant is dissatisfied with how the complaint is handled or with the outcome, they may request the registrant to forward a copy of the complaint file to the Autorité des marchés financiers. The registrant must forward a copy of the complaint file to the Autorité des marchés financiers, which will examine the complaint. The Autorité des marchés financiers may act as a mediator if it considers it appropriate to do so and the parties agree.

13.15 — Handling complaints

General duty to document and respond to complaints

Section 13.15 requires registered firms to document complaints, and to effectively and fairly respond to them. We are of the view that registered firms should document and respond to all complaints received from a client, a former client or a prospective client who has dealt with the registered firm (complainant).

Firms are reminded that they are required to maintain records which demonstrate compliance with complaint handling requirements under subsection 11.5(2)(m).

Complaint handling policies

An effective complaint system should deal with all formal and informal complaints or disputes in a timely and fair manner. To achieve the objective of handling complaints fairly, the firm's complaint system should include standards allowing for objective factual investigation and analysis of the matters specific to the complaint.

We take the view that registered firms should take a balanced approach to the gathering of facts that objectively considers the interests of

- the complainant
- the registered representative, and
- the firm

Registered firms should not limit their consideration and handling of complaints to those relating to possible violations of securities legislation.

Complaint monitoring

The firm's complaint handling policy should provide for specific procedures for reporting the complaints to superiors, in order to allow the detection of frequent and repetitive complaints made with respect to the same matter which may, on a cumulative basis, indicate a serious problem. Firms should take appropriate measures to deal with such problems as they arise.

Responding to complaints

Types of complaints

All complaints relating to one of the following matters should be responded to by the firm by providing an initial and substantive response, both in writing and within a reasonable time:

- a trading or advising activity

- a breach of client confidentiality

- theft, fraud, misappropriation or forgery

- misrepresentation

- an undisclosed or prohibited conflict of interest, or

- personal financial dealings with a client

Firms may determine that a complaint relating to matters other than the matters listed above is nevertheless of a sufficiently serious nature to be responded to in the manner described below. This determination should be made, in all cases, by considering if an investor, acting reasonably, would expect a written response to their complaint.

When complaints are not made in writing

We would not expect that complaints relating to matters other than those listed above, when made verbally and when not otherwise considered serious based on an investor's reasonable expectation, would need to be responded to in writing. However, we do expect that verbal complaints be given as much attention as written complaints. If a complaint is made verbally and is not clearly expressed, the firm may request the complainant to put the complaint in writing and we expect firms to offer reasonable assistance to do so.

Firms are entitled to expect the complainant to put unclear verbal issues into written format in order to try to resolve confusion about the nature of the issue. If the verbal complaint is clearly frivolous, we do not expect firms to offer assistance to put the complaint in writing. The firm may nonetheless ask the complainant to put the complaint in writing on his or her own.

Timeline for responding to complaints

Firms should

- promptly send an initial written response to a complainant: we consider that an initial response should be provided to the complainant within five business days of receipt of the complaint

- provide a substantive response to all complaints relating to the matters listed under "Types of complaints" above, indicating the firm's decision on the complaint

A firm may also wish to use its initial response to seek clarification or additional information from the client.

Requirements for providing information about the availability of dispute resolution or mediation services paid for by the firm are discussed below.

We encourage firms to resolve complaints relating to the matters listed above within 90 days.

13.16 — Dispute resolution service

Section 13.15 requires a registered firm to document and respond to each complaint made to it about any product or service that is offered by the firm or one of its representatives. Section 13.16 provides for recourse to an independent dispute resolution or mediation service at a registered firm's expense for specified complaints where the firm's internal complaint handling process has not produced a timely decision that is satisfactory to the client.

Registered firms may be required to make an independent dispute resolution or mediation service paid for by the firm available to a client in respect of a complaint that

- relates to a trading or advising activity of the firm or its representatives, and

- is raised within six years of the date when the client knew or reasonably ought to have known of the act or ommission that is a cause of or contributed to the complaint

As soon as possible after a client makes a complaint (for example, when sending its acknowledgment or initial response to the complaint), and again when the firm informs the client of its decision in respect of the complaint, a registered firm must provide a client with information about

- the firm's obligations under section 13.16,

- the steps the client must take for an independent dispute resolution or mediation service to be made available to the client at the firm's expense, and

- the name of the independent service that will be made available to the client (outside of Québec, this will normally be the Ombudsman for Banking Services and Investments (OBSI), as discussed below) and how to contact it

A client may escalate an eligible complaint to the independent dispute resolution or mediation service made available by the registered firm in two circumstances:

- If the firm fails to give the client notice of its decision within 90 days of receiving the complaint (telling the client that the firm plans to take more than 90 days to make its decision does not "stop the clock"). The client is then entitled to escalate the complaint to the independent service immediately or at any later date until the firm has notified the client of its decision.

- If the firm has given the client notice of its decision about the complaint (whether it does so within 90 days or after a longer period) and the client is not satisfied with the decision, the client then has 180 days in which escalate the complaint to the independent service.

In either instance, the client may escalate the complaint by directly contacting the independent service.

We think that it may sometimes be appropriate for the independent service, the firm and the client involved in a complaint to agree to longer notice periods than the prescribed 90 and 180 day periods as a matter of fairness. We recognize that where a client does not cooperate with reasonable requests for information relating to a complaint, a firm may have difficulty making a timely decision in respect of the complaint. We expect that this would be relevant to any subsequent determination or recommendation made by an independent service about that complaint.

The client must agree that the amount of any recommendation by the independent service for monetary compensation will not exceed $350,000. This limit applies only to the amount that can be recommended. Until it is escalated to the independent service, a complaint made to a registered firm may include a claim for a larger amount.

Except in Québec, a registered firm must take reasonable steps to ensure that the dispute resolution and mediation service that is made available to its clients for these purposes will be OBSI. The reasonable steps we expect a firm to take include maintaining ongoing membership in OBSI as a "Participating Firm" and, with respect to each complaint, participating in the dispute resolution process in a manner consistent with the firm's obligation to deal fairly, honestly and in good faith with its client. This would include entering into consent agreements with clients contemplated under OBSI's procedures.

Since section 13.16 does not apply in respect of a complaint made by a permitted client that is not an individual, we would not expect a firm that only has clients of that kind to maintain membership in OBSI.

A registered firm should not make an alternative independent dispute resolution or mediation service available to a client at the same time as it makes OBSI available. Such a parallel offering would not be consistent with the requirement to take reasonable steps to ensure that OBSI will be the independent service that is made available to the client. Except in Québec, we expect that alternative service providers will only be used for purposes of section 13.16 in exceptional circumstances.

We would regard it as a serious compliance issue if a firm misrepresented OBSI's services or exerted pressure on a client to refuse OBSI's services.

If a client declines to make use of OBSI in respect of a complaint, or if a client abandons a complaint that is under consideration by OBSI, the registered firm is not obligated to provide another service at the firm's expense. A firm is only required to make one dispute resolution or mediation service available at its expense for each complaint.

Nothing in section 13.16 affects a client's right to choose to seek other recourse, including through the courts.

Registrants that are members of an SRO, including those that are registered in Québec, must also comply with their SRO's requirements with respect to the provision of independent dispute resolution or mediation services.

Registrants who do business in other sectors

Some registrants are also registered or licensed to do business in other sectors, such as insurance. These registrants should inform their clients of the complaint mechanisms for each sector in which they do business and how to use them.

Division 3 — Registered sub-advisers

13.17 — Exemption from certain requirements for registered sub-advisers

Section 13.17 contains an exemption from certain client related requirements for registered sub-advisers. These requirements are not necessary because in a sub-adviser arrangement the sub-adviser's client is another registrant. We remind registrants that these exemptions do not apply if the client is not a registrant. One of the conditions of this exemption is that the other registrant has entered into an agreement with its client that it is responsible for losses that arise out of certain failures by the sub-adviser. We expect that a registrant taking on this liability will conduct appropriate initial and ongoing due diligence on the sub-adviser and before making recommendations or investment decisions based on the sub-adviser's advice, ensure the investment is suitable for the registrant's client.

We also expect that the other registrant and the sub-adviser will maintain records of their transactions and that the other registrant will maintain records of the due diligence conducted on the sub-adviser. See Part 11 of this Companion Policy for more guidance.

Part 14 — Handling client accounts — firms

If a client consents, documents required in this Part can be delivered in electronic form. For further guidance, see NP 11-201.

Division 1 — Investment fund managers

Section 14.1 sets out the limited application of Part 14 to investment fund managers that are not also registered in other categories, including section 14.1.1 [*duty to provide information*], section 14.6 [*holding client assets in trust*], subsection 14.12(5) [*content and delivery of trade confirmation*] and section 14.15 [*security holder statements*].

Section 14.1.1 requires investment fund managers to provide, within a reasonable period of time, information concerning deferred sales charges and any other charges deducted from the net asset value of the securities, and trailing commissions to dealers and advisers in order that they may comply with their obligations under paragraphs 14.12(1)(c) [*content and delivery of trade confirmation*] and 14.17(1)(h) [*report on charges and other compensation*]. This is a principles-based requirement. An investment fund manager must work with the dealers and advisers who distribute fund products to determine what information they need from the investment fund manager in order to satisfy their client reporting obligations. The information and arrangements for its delivery may vary, reflecting different operating models and information systems.

Division 2 — Disclosure to clients

14.2 — Relationship disclosure information

Registrants should ensure that clients understand who they are dealing with. They should carry on all registerable activities in their full legal or registered trade name. Contracts, confirmation and account statements, among other documents, should contain the registrant's full legal name.

Content of relationship disclosure information

There is no prescribed form for the relationship disclosure information required under section 14.2. A registered firm may provide this information in a single document, or in separate documents, which together give the client the prescribed information.

Relationship disclosure information should be communicated in a manner consistent with the guidance on client communications under section 1.1 of this Companion Policy. We encourage registrants to avoid the use of technical terms and acronyms when communicating with clients. To satisfy their obligations under section 14.2, registered individuals must spend sufficient time with clients as part of an in-person or telephone meeting, or other method that is consistent with their operations, to adequately explain the information that is delivered to them. We expect a firm to have policies and procedures requiring its registered individuals to demonstrate they have done so. What is considered "sufficient" will depend on the circumstances, including a client's understanding of the delivered documents.

Evidence of compliance with client disclosure requirements at account opening, prior to trades and at other times, can include detailed notes of meetings or discussions with clients, signed client acknowledgements and tape-recorded phone conversations.

Promoting client participation

Registered firms should help their clients understand the registrant-client relationship. They should encourage clients to actively participate in the relationship and provide them with clear, relevant and timely information and communications.

In particular, registered firms should help and encourage clients to:

- **Keep the firm up to date.** Clients should be encouraged to
  - provide full and accurate information to the firm and the registered individuals acting for the firm
  - promptly inform the firm of any change to their information that could result in a change to the types of investments appropriate for them, such as a change to their income, investment objectives, risk tolerance, time horizon or net worth

- **Be informed.** Clients should be
  - helped to understand the potential risks and returns on investments
  - encouraged to carefully review sales literature provided by the firm
  - encouraged to consult professionals, such as a lawyer or an accountant, for legal or tax advice where appropriate

- **Ask questions.** Clients should be encouraged to
  - request information from the firm to resolve concerns about their account, transactions or investments, or their relationship with the firm or a registered individual acting for the firm

- **Stay on top of their investments.** Clients should be encouraged to
  - review all account documentation provided by the firm
  - regularly review portfolio holdings and performance

Disclosure of charges and other compensation

Under paragraphs 14.2(2)(f), (g) and (h), registered firms must provide clients with information on the operating and transaction charges they might pay in making, holding and selling investments, and a general description of any compensation paid to the firm by any other party. We expect this disclosure to include all charges a client might pay during the course of holding a particular investment.

A registered firm's charges to a client and the compensation it may receive from third parties in respect of the client will vary depending on the type of relationship with the client and the nature of the services and investment products offered. At account opening, registered firms must provide clients with general information on the operating charges and transaction charges that the clients may be required to pay, as well as other compensation the firms may receive as a result of their business relationship. A firm is not expected to provide information on all the types of accounts that it offers and the fees related to these accounts if it is not relevant to the client's situation.

"Operating charge" is defined broadly in section 1.1 and examples include (but are not exclusive to) service charges, administration fees, safekeeping fees, management fees, transfer fees, account closing fees, annual registered plan fees and any other charges associated with maintaining and using an account that are paid to the registrant. For registered firms that charge an all-in fee for the operation of the account, such as a percentage of assets under management, that fee is the operating charge. We do not expect firms with an all-in operating charge to provide a breakdown of the items covered by the fee.

"Transaction charges" is also defined broadly in section 1.1 and examples include (but are not exclusive to) commissions, transaction fees, switch or change fees, performance fees, short-term trading fees, and sales charges or redemption fees that are paid to the registrant. Although we do not consider "foreign exchange spreads" to be a transaction charge, we encourage firms to include a general notification in trade confirmations and reports on charges and other compensation that the firm may have incurred a gain or loss from a foreign exchange transaction as a best practice.

Operating charges and transaction charges include only charges paid to the registered firm by the client. Third-party charges, such as custodian fees that are not paid to the registered firm, are not included in operating charges or transaction charges. Operating and transaction charges include any sales taxes that are paid on the amounts charged to the client. Registrants may wish to inform clients where a charge includes sales tax, or separately disclose the components of the charge. Withholding taxes would not be considered a charge.

Providing general information on charges is appropriate at the time of account opening. However, section 14.2.1 [*pre-trade disclosure of charges*] requires that, before a registered firm accepts an instruction from a client to purchase or sell a security, the firm must provide more specific information as to the nature and amount of the actual charges that will apply. Registrants are encouraged to explain charges to their clients.

For example, if a client will be investing in a mutual fund security, the description should briefly explain each of the following and how they may affect the investment:

- the management fee
- the sales charge or deferred sales charge option available to the client and an explanation as to how such charges work. This means registered firms should advise clients that mutual funds sold on a deferred sales charge basis are subject to charges upon redemption that are applied on a declining rate scale over a specified period of years, until such time as the charges decrease to zero. Any other redemption fees or short-term trading fees that may apply should also be discussed
- any trailing commission, or other embedded fees
- any options regarding front end loads
- any fees related to the client changing or switching investments ("switch or change fees")

Registrants may also wish to explain to clients that trailing commissions are included in the management fees that are charged to their investment funds and are not additional charges paid by the client to the registrant. "Trailing commission" is defined for purposes of NI 31-103 in section 1.1 in broad terms designed to ensure that payments similar to what are generally known as trailing commissions will be subject to similar reporting requirements under this instrument.

Registrants should advise clients with managed accounts whether the registrant will receive compensation from third parties, such as trailing commissions, on any securities purchased for the client and, if so, whether the fee paid by the client to the registrant will be affected by this. For example, the management fee paid by a client on the portion of a managed account related to mutual fund holdings may be lower than the overall fee on the rest of the portfolio.

Description of content and frequency of client reporting

Under paragraph 14.2(2)(i), a registered firm is required to provide a description of the content and frequency of reporting to the client. Reporting to clients includes, as applicable:

- trade confirmations under section 14.12
- account statements under section 14.14
- additional statements under section 14.14.1
- position cost information under section 14.14.2
- annual report on charges and other compensation under section 14.17
- investment performance reports under section 14.18

Guidance about registered firm's client reporting obligations is provided in Division 5 of this Part.

KYC information

Paragraph 14.2(2)(l) requires registrants to provide their clients with a copy of their KYC information at the time of account opening. We would expect registered firms to also provide a description to the client of the various terms which make up the KYC information, and explain how this information will be used in assessing the client's financial situation, investment objectives, investment knowledge and risk tolerance in determining investment suitability.

Benchmarks

Paragraph 14.2(2)(m) requires registered firms to provide clients with a general explanation of how investment performance benchmarks might be used to assess the performance of a client's investments and any options available to the client to obtain information about benchmarks from the registered firm. Other than this general discussion, there is no requirement for registered firms to provide benchmark information to clients. Nonetheless, we encourage firms to do so as a best practice. Guidance on the provision of benchmarks is set out in this Companion Policy at the end of the discussion of the content of investment performance reports under section 14.19.

Scholarship plan dealers

Paragraph 14.2(2)(n) requires an explanation of the important aspects of the scholarship plan that, if not fulfilled, would cause loss to the client. To be complete, this prescribed disclosure could include any options that would allow the investor to retain notional earnings in the event that they do not maintain prescribed payments under the plan and any fees associated with those options.

Order execution trading

Subsections 14.2(7) and (8) provide that only limited relationship disclosure information must be delivered by a dealer whose relationship with a client is limited to executing trades as directed by a registered adviser acting for the client. In a relationship of this kind, each registrant must explain to the client its role and responsibility to the client, and what services and reporting the client can expect of it.

14.2.1 — Pre-trade disclosure of charges

For non-managed accounts, section 14.2.1 requires disclosure to a client of charges specific to a transaction prior to the acceptance of a client's instruction. This disclosure is not required to be in writing. Oral disclosure of charges is sufficient for the purposes of disclosing charges at the time of a transaction. Specific charges must be reported in writing on the trade confirmation as required in section 14.12.

For a purchase of a security on a deferred sales charge basis, disclosure that a deferred sales charge might be triggered upon the redemption of the security, and the schedule that would apply if it is sold within the time period that a deferred sales charge would be applicable, must be presented. The actual amount of the deferred sales charge, if any, would need to be disclosed once the security is redeemed. For the purposes of disclosing trailing commissions, the dealing representative may draw attention to the information in the prospectus or the fund facts document if that document is provided at the point of sale.

With respect to a transaction involving a debt security, pre-trade disclosure should include a discussion of any commission the registered firm will receive on the trade. This discussion should include both the number of basis points that the charge represents as well as the corresponding dollar amount, or a reasonable estimate of the amount if the actual amount of the charges is not known to the firm at the time.

Switch or change transactions

Processing a switch or change transaction without client knowledge is contrary to a registrant's duty to act fairly, honestly and in good faith. In our view, compliance with this duty requires that clients are informed, before any switch or change transaction is processed, of charges associated with the transaction, dealers' incentives for such a transaction (including increased trailing commissions), and any tax or other implications of such a transaction. In each case, we expect dealers to explain why a proposed switch or change transaction is appropriate for the client. We consider that providing clients with clear and complete disclosure of the charges at the time of a transaction will help clients to be aware of the implications of proposed transactions and deter registrants from transacting for the purpose of generating commissions. Registrants are also reminded that their obligations in connection with suitability and conflicts of interest apply to such transactions, as well as their obligations under any applicable SRO requirements or guidance.

We expect all changes or switches to a client's investments to be accurately reported in trade confirmations by reporting each of the purchase and sale transactions making up the change or switch, as required in section 14.12, with a description of the associated charges.

14.4 — When the firm has a relationship with a financial institution

As part of their duty to clients, registrants who have a relationship with a financial institution should ensure that their clients understand which legal entity they are dealing with. In particular, clients may be confused if more than one financial services firm is carrying on business in the same location. Registrants may differentiate themselves through various methods, including signage and disclosure.

Division 3 — Client assets

14.6 — Holding client assets in trust

Section 14.6 requires a registered firm to segregate client assets and hold them in trust. We consider it prudent for registrants who are not members of an SRO to hold client assets in client name only. This is because the capital requirements for non-SRO members are not designed to reflect the added risk of holding client assets in nominee name.

Division 4 — Client accounts

14.10 — Allocating investment opportunities fairly

If the adviser allocates investment opportunities among its clients, the firm's fairness policy should, at a minimum, indicate the method used to allocate the following:

- price and commission among client orders when trades are bunched or blocked

- block trades and initial public offerings among client accounts

- block trades and initial public offerings among client orders that are partially filled, such as on a pro-rata basis

The fairness policy should also address any other situation where investment opportunities must be allocated.

Division 5 — Reporting to clients

Reporting to clients is on an account basis, except that

- securities that are not held in an account (i.e., securities reported under an additional statement) must be included in a report for the account through which they were traded, and

- subsection 14.18(4) permits performance reports for more than one account of a client and also securities not held in an account to be combined with the client's written consent.

Registered firms may choose how they meet their client reporting obligations within the framework set out in the Instrument. We encourage firms to combine client statements, position cost information and client reports into comprehensive documents or send them together. For example, an account statement and an additional statement for securities traded through (but not held) in an account might be combined, perhaps along with position cost information, each quarter. Once a year, an integrated statement such as this could be further combined with the report on charges and other compensation and the performance report, or delivered along with a separate document that combines the two reports.

We believe that integrating client reporting as much as possible within the limitations of firms' systems capabilities will better enable clients to make use of the information and that it is in the interests of registrants to have clients that are well informed about the services they provide. When client reporting information is combined or delivered together, we expect registered firms will give each element sufficient prominence among the others that a reasonable investor can readily locate it.

Consistent with the guidance on clear and meaningful disclosure to clients in section 1.1 of this Companion Policy, we expect registrants to present client statements and reports in an understandable manner and to explain, if applicable, what securities are included in different statements. Registered firms should encourage clients to contact their dealing or advising representative or the firm directly with questions about their statements and reports. We expect registered firms to ensure that clients know how their investments will be held (for example, by the firm or at an issuing fund company) and understand the different implications that this will have for them in such matters as client reporting, investor protection fund coverage and custody of their assets. If a registered firm trades in exempt market securities for a client, the firm should also explain the reasons why it is not always possible for the firm to determine a market value for products sold in the exempt market or whether the client still owns the security, and the implications that this may have for reporting on exempt-market securities.

It is the responsibility of the registered firm to produce these client statements and reports, not that of individual representatives. Registered firms should have policies and procedures in place to ensure that they are adequately supervising their registered representatives' communications with clients about the prescribed information.

The requirement to produce and deliver a trade confirmation under section 14.12, an account statement under section 14.14, an additional statement under section 14.14.1, position cost information under section 14.14.2, a security holder statement under section 14.15, a scholarship plan dealer statement under section 14.16 or client reports under sections 14.17 and 14.18 may be outsourced by a registered firm to a third-party service provider that acts as its agent. Third-party pricing providers may also be used to value securities for these purposes. Like all outsourcing arrangements, the registrant is ultimately responsible for the function and must supervise the service provider. See Part 11 of this Companion Policy for more guidance on outsourcing.

14.11.1 — Determining market value

Section 14.11.1 sets out the basis on which market value must be determined for client reporting purposes.

Paragraph 14.11.1(1)(a) requires the market value of a security that is issued by an investment fund not listed on an exchange to be determined by reference to the net asset value provided by the investment fund manager of the fund on the relevant date.

For other securities, a hierarchy of valuation methods that depend on the availability of relevant information is prescribed in paragraph 14.11.1(1)(b). Registrants are required to act reasonably in applying these methodologies and we understand that this process will often require a registrant to exercise professional judgement.

Where possible, market value should be determined by reference to a quoted value on a marketplace. The quoted value will be the last bid or ask price on the relevant date or the last trading day prior to the relevant date. Registered firms should ensure that any quoted values used to determine market value do not represent stale or old prices that are not reflective of current values. If no current value for a security is quoted on a marketplace, market value should be determined by reference to published market reports or inter-dealer quotes.

We recognize that it is not always possible to obtain a market value by these methods. In such cases, we will accept a valuation policy that is consistently applied and includes procedures that assess the reliability of any valuation inputs and assumptions. If available, valuation inputs and assumptions should be based on observable market data or inputs, such as market prices or yield rates for comparable securities and quoted interest rates. If observable inputs are not available, valuation can be based on unobservable inputs and assumptions. In some cases, it may be reasonable and appropriate to value at cost, where there has been no material subsequent event affecting value (e.g. a market event or new capital raising by the issuer). "Observable" and "unobservable" inputs are concepts under International Financial Reporting Standards (IFRS), and we expect them to be applied consistent with IFRS.

Subsection 14.11.1(3) provides that where the registered firm reasonably believes that it cannot determine the market value of a security, the firm must report that no value can be determined and the security must not be included in the calculation of the total market value of cash and securities in the client's account or in calculations for the investment performance report (see also subsection 14.19(7)).

If the market value for a security subsequently becomes determinable, a registered firm must begin to report it in client statements and add that value to the opening market values or deposits included in the calculations in subsection 14.19(1). This would be expected if the firm had previously assigned the security a value of zero in the calculation of opening market values or deposits because it could not determine the security's market value, as required by subsection 14.19(7). This would reduce the risk of presenting a misleading improvement in the performance of the investment by only adding the value of the security to the other calculations required under section 14.19. If the deposits used to purchase the security were already included in the calculation of opening market values or deposits, the registered firm would not need to adjust these figures.

We encourage firms to disclose the foreign exchange rate used in calculating the market value of non-Canadian dollar denominated securities as a best practice.

14.12 — Content and delivery of trade confirmation

Section 14.12 requires registered dealers to deliver trade confirmations.

Under paragraph 14.12(1)(b.1), registered dealers must provide the yield on a purchase of a debt security in a trade confirmation. For non-callable debt securities, the yield to maturity would be appropriate. For callable securities, the yield to call may be more useful.

Under paragraph 14.12(1)(c.1), registrants may disclose the total dollar amount of compensation (which may consist of any mark-up or mark-down, commission or other service charge) or, alternatively, the total dollar amount of commission, if any, and if the registrant applied a mark-up or mark-down or any service charge other than a commission, a prescribed general notification. The notification is a minimum requirement and a firm may elect to provide more information in its trade confirmations.

Each trade should be reported in the currency in which it was executed. If a trade is executed in a foreign currency through a Canadian dollar account, the exchange rate should be reported to the client.

14.14 — Account statements

Section 14.14 requires registered dealers and advisers to deliver statements to clients at least once every three months. There is no prescribed form for these statements but they must contain the information referred to in subsections 14.14(4) and (5). The types of transactions that must be disclosed in an account statement include any purchase, sale or transfer of securities, dividend or interest payment received or reinvested, any fee or charge, and any other account activity. A firm must deliver an account statement with the information referred to in subsection (4) if any transaction was made for the client in the reporting period. Effective July 15, 2015, a firm is only required to provide the account balance information referred to in subsection (5) if it holds securities owned by a client in an account of the client.

14.14.1 — Additional statements

A firm is required to deliver additional statements if the circumstances described in subsection 14.14.1(1) apply. The additional statements must be delivered once every three months, except that an adviser must deliver the statements on a monthly basis if requested by the client as provided in subsection 14.14.1(3). The requirements set out for the frequency of delivering account statements and additional statements are minimum standards. Firms may choose to provide the statements more frequently.

Firms may choose to include securities that must be reported under the additional statement requirement in a document that it refers to as an account statement, consistent with their clients' expectations that their accounts are not limited to securities held by the firm, provided it satisfies the requirements for content of statements set out in sections 14.14 and 14.14.1.

14.14.2 — Position cost information

Section 14.14.2 requires the delivery on a quarterly basis of position cost information for securities reported in account statements and additional statements. Position cost may be either the book cost or the original cost, as defined in section 1.1. Position cost information provides investors with a comparison to the market value of each security position they have open.

Where securities were transferred from another registrant firm and the information required to calculate position cost is unavailable, a registrant may elect to use market value information as at the date of the transfer as the position cost going forward.

Firms must include the definition of book cost or original cost in client statements. Firms can comply with that requirement by making reference to the definition in a footnote.

Position cost information must be delivered at least quarterly, within 10 days after an account statement or additional statement. A firm may combine position cost information with the statement(s) for the period, or it may send it separately. If it chooses to send position cost information separately, the firm must also include the market value information from the statement(s) for the period in order that the client will be able to readily compare the information. Although a firm may deliver statements under section 14.14 or section 14.14.1 more frequently than quarterly, it is not required to provide position cost information except on a quarterly basis.

14.15 — Security holder statements

Section 14.15 sets out the client reporting requirements applicable to a registered investment fund manager where there is no dealer or adviser of record for a security holder on the records of the investment fund manager.

14.16 — Scholarship plan dealer statements

Section 14.16 provides that sections 14.14 [*account statements*], 14.14.1 [*additional statements*] and 14.14.2 [*position cost information*] do not apply to a scholarship plan dealer that delivers prescribed information to a client at least once every 12 months. Subsection 14.19(4) sets out performance reporting requirements for scholarship plans.

Proposed Amendment —

14.17 — Report on charges and other compensation

Registered firms must provide clients with an annual report on the firm's charges and other compensation received by the firm in connection with their investments. Examples of operating charges and transaction charges are provided in the discussion of the disclosure of charges and other compensation in section 14.2 of this Companion Policy.

The discussion of debt security disclosure requirements in section 14.12 of this Companion Policy is also relevant with respect to paragraph 14.17(1)(e).

Scholarship plans often have enrolment fees payable in instalments in the first few years of a client's investment in the plan. Paragraph 14.17(1)(f) requires that scholarship plan dealers include a reminder of the unpaid amount of any such fees in their annual reports on charges and other compensation.

Payments that a registered firm or its registered representatives receive from issuers of securities or other registrants in relation to registerable services to a client must be reported under paragraph 14.17(1)(g). Examples of payments that would be included in this part of the report on charges and other compensation include some referral fees, success fees on the completion of a transaction or finder's fees. This part of the report does not include trailing commissions, as they are specifically addressed in paragraph 14.17(1)(h).

Registered firms must disclose the amount of trailing commissions they received related to a client's holdings. The disclosure of trailing commissions received in respect of a client's investments must be included with a notification prescribed in paragraph 14.17(1)(h). The notification must be in *substantially* the form prescribed, so a registered firm may modify it to be consistent with the actual arrangements. For example, a firm that receives a payment that falls within the definition of "trailing commission" in section 1.1 in respect of securities that are not investment funds can modify the notification accordingly. The notification set out is the required minimum and firms can provide further explanation if they believe it will be helpful to their clients.

Registered firms may want to organize the annual report on charges and other compensation with separate sections showing the charges paid by the client to the firm, and the other compensation received by the firm in respect of the client's account.

Appendix D of this Companion Policy includes a sample Report on Charges and Other Compensation, which registered firms are encouraged to use as guidance.

14.18 — Investment performance report

Where more than one registrant provides services pertaining to a client's account, responsibility for performance reporting rests with the registered firm with the client-facing relationship. For example, if a registered adviser has trading authority over a client's account at a registered dealer, the adviser must provide the client with an annual investment performance report; this is not an obligation of the dealer that only executes adviser-directed trades or provides custodial services in respect of the client's account.

Performance reporting to clients is required to be provided separately for each account. Securities of a client required to be reported in an additional statement under section 14.14.1, if any, must be covered in a performance report that also includes any other securities in the account through which they were transacted. However, subsection 14.18(4) provides that with client consent, a registrant may provide consolidated performance reporting for that client. A registrant may also provide a consolidated performance report for multiple clients, such as a family group, but only as a supplemental report, in addition to reports required under section 14.18.

14.19 — Content of investment performance report

Subsection 14.19(5) requires the use of each of text, tables and charts in the presentation of investment performance reports. Explanatory notes and the definition of "total percentage return" must also be included. The purpose of these requirements is to make the information as understandable to investors as possible.

To help investors get the most out of their investment performance reports and encourage informed discussion with their registered dealing representative or advising representative, we encourage registered firms to consider including:

- additional definitions of the various performance measures used by the registrant
- additional disclosure that enhances the performance presentation
- a discussion with clients about what the information means to them

Registrants should not mislead a client by presenting a return of the client's capital in a manner that suggests it forms part of the client's return on an investment.

Registered representatives are also encouraged to meet with clients, as part of an in-person or telephone meeting, to help ensure they understand their investment performance reports and how the information relates to the client's investment objectives and risk tolerance.

Appendix E of this Companion Policy includes a sample Investment Performance Report which registered firms are encouraged to use as guidance.

Opening market value, deposits and withdrawals

As part of paragraphs 14.19(1)(a) and (b), registered firms must disclose the market value of cash and securities in the client's account as at the beginning and the end of the 12-month period covered by the investment performance report. The market value of cash and securities at account opening is assumed to be zero.

Under paragraphs 14.19(1)(c) and (d), registered firms must also disclose the market value of all deposits and transfers of cash and securities into the account, and the market value of all withdrawals and transfers of cash and securities out of the account, for the 12-month period covered by the performance report, as well as since account opening. Deposits and transfers into the account (which do not include reinvested distributions or interest income) should be shown separately from withdrawals and transfers out of the account. Where an account was opened before July 15, 2015 and market values are not available for all deposits, withdrawals and transfers since account opening, under paragraph 14.19(1)(e) registered firms must present the market value of all cash and securities in the client's account as at July 15, 2015, and the market value of all deposits, withdrawals and transfers of cash and securities since July 15, 2015.

Subsection 14.19(7) requires a registered firm that cannot determine the market value for a security position to assign the security a value of zero for the performance reporting purposes and the reason for doing so must be disclosed to the client. The explanation may be included as a note in the performance report. As described in section 14.11.1 of this Companion Policy, if a registered firm is subsequently able to value that security it may need to adjust the calculation of the market values or deposits to avoid presenting a misleading improvement in the performance of the account.

Change in market value

The opening market value, plus deposits and transfers in, less withdrawals and transfers out, should be compared to the market value of the account as at the end of the 12-month period for which the performance reporting is provided and also since inception in order to provide clients, in dollar terms, with the performance of their account.

The change in the market value of the account since inception is the difference between the closing market value of the account and total of opening market value plus deposits less withdrawals since inception. The change in the value of the account for the 12-month period is the difference between the closing market value of the account and total of opening market value plus deposits less withdrawals during the period. Where market values since inception are not available, registered firms are required to disclose the change in value of a client's account since July 15, 2015.

The change in market value includes components such as income (dividends, interest) and distributions, including reinvested income or distributions, realized and unrealized capital gains or losses in the account, and the effect of operating charges and transaction charges if these are deducted directly from the account. Rather than show the change in value as a single amount, registered firms may opt to break this out into its components to provide more detail to clients.

Percentage return calculation method

Paragraph 14.19(1)(i) requires firms to provide the annualized total percentage return using a money-weighted rate of return calculation method. No specific formula is prescribed, but the method used by a firm must be one that is generally accepted in the securities industry. A registered firm may, if it so chooses, provide percentage returns calculated using both money-weighted and time-weighted methods. In such cases, the firm should explain in plain language the difference between the two sets of performance returns.

Paragraph 14.19(1)(j) requires that performance reports provide specified information about how the client's percentage return was calculated. This includes an explanation in general terms of what the calculation method takes into account. For example, a firm could explain that under a money weighted method, decisions a client made about deposits and withdrawals to and from the client's account have affected the returns calculated in the report. A firm that also uses a time weighted method could explain that the returns calculated under this method may not be the same as the actual returns in the client's account because they do not necessarily show the effect of deposits and withdrawals to and from the account. We do not expect firms to include a formula or an exhaustive list. We expect firms to use this notification to help clients understand the most important implications of the calculation methodology.

Performance reporting periods

Subsection 14.19(2) outlines the minimum reporting periods of 1, 3, 5 and 10 years and the period since the inception of the account. Registered firms may opt to provide more frequent performance reporting. However performance returns for periods of less than one year can be misleading and therefore, must not be presented on an annualized basis, consistent with subsection 14.19(6).

Scholarship plans

Under paragraph 14.19(4)(c), for scholarship plans, the information required to be delivered in the investment performance report includes a reasonable projection of future scholarship payments that the plan may pay to the client or the client's designated beneficiary upon the maturity of the client's investment in the plan.

A scholarship plan dealer is also required under paragraph 14.19(4)(d) to provide a summary of any terms of the plan, which if not met by the client or the client's designated beneficiary under the plan, may cause the client or the designated beneficiary to suffer a loss of contributions, earnings or government contributions in the plan. The disclosure here is not intended to be as detailed as the disclosure at account opening. It is intended to remind the client of the unique risks of the plan and the ways in which the client's scholarship plan may be seriously impaired. This disclosure must be consistent with other disclosures required to be delivered to clients under applicable securities legislation.

To the extent that a scholarship plan dealer and the plan itself are not the same legal entity but are affiliates of one another, the dealer may meet obligations to deliver annual investment performance reports by drawing attention to the plan's direct mailing of reports to a client by the plan's administrator.

Benchmarks and investment performance reporting

The use of benchmarks for investment performance reporting is optional. There is no requirement to provide benchmarks to clients in any of the reports required under NI 31-103.

However, we encourage registrants to use benchmarks that are relevant to a client's investments as a useful way for a client to assess the performance of their portfolio. Benchmarks need to be explained to clients in terms they will understand, including factors that should be considered by the client when comparing their investment returns to benchmark returns. For example, a registrant could discuss the differences

**Part 3:
REGISTRATION**

between the composition of a client's portfolio that reflects the investment strategy they have agreed upon and the composition of an index benchmark, so that a comparison between them is fair and not misleading. A discussion of the impact of operating charges and transaction charges as well as other expenses related to the client's investments would also be helpful to clients, since benchmarks generally do not factor in the costs of investing.

If a registered firm chooses to present benchmark information, the firm should ensure that it is not misleading. We expect registrants to use benchmarks that are

- discussed with clients to ensure they understand the purpose of comparing the performance of their portfolio to the chosen benchmarks and determine if their information needs will be met
- reasonably reflective of the composition of the client's portfolio so as to ensure that a relevant comparison of performance is presented
- relevant in terms of the investing time horizon of the client
- based on widely recognized and available indices that are credible and not manufactured by the registrant or any of its affiliates using proprietary data
- broad-based securities market indices which can be linked to the major asset classes into which the client's portfolio is divided. The determination of a major asset class should be based on the firm's own policies and procedures and the client's portfolio composition. An asset class for benchmarking purposes may be based on the type of security and geographical region. We do not expect an asset class to be determined by industry sector
- presented for the same reporting periods as the client's annualized total percentage returns
- clearly named
- applied consistently from one reporting period to the next for comparability reasons, unless there has been a change to the pre-determined asset classes. In this case, the change in the benchmark(s) presented should be discussed with the client and included in the explanatory notes, along with the reasons for the change

Examples of acceptable benchmarks would include, but are not limited to, the S&/TSX Composite index for Canadian equities, the S&P 500 index for U.S. equities, and the MSCI EAFE index as a measure of the equity markets outside of North America.

14.20 — Delivery of report on charges and other compensation and investment performance report

Registered firms must deliver the annual report on charges and other compensation under section 14.17 and the investment performance report under section 14.18 for a client together. These client reports may be combined with or accompany an account statement or additional statement for a client, or must be sent within 10 days after an account statement or additional statement for the client.

[To come into force July 15, 2016]

Appendix A — Contact information

Jurisdiction	E-mail	Fax	Address
Alberta	registration@asc.ca	(403) 297-4113	Alberta Securities Commission, Suite 600, 250-5th St. SW Calgary, AB T2P 0R4 Attention: Registration
British Columbia	registration@bcsc.bc.ca	(604) 899-6506	British Columbia Securities Commission P.O. Box 10142, Pacific Centre 701 West Georgia Street Vancouver, BC V7Y 1L2 Attention: Registration
Manitoba	registrationmsc@gov.mb.ca	(204) 945-0330	The Manitoba Securities Commission 500-400 St. Mary Avenue Winnipeg, MB R3C 4K5 Attention: Registrations
New Brunswick	nrs@nbsc-cvmnb.ca	(506) 658-3059	Financial and Consumer Services Commission of New Brunswick / Commission des services financiers du Nouveau Brunswick Suite 300, 85 Charlotte Street Saint John, NB E2L 2J2 Attention: Registration Officer
Newfoundland & Labrador	scon@gov.nl.ca	(709) 729-6187	Superintendent of Securities, Service NL P.O. Box 8700, 2nd Floor, West Block Confederation Building

Jurisdiction	E-mail	Fax	Address
			St. John's, NL A1B 4J6 Attention: Manager of Registrations
Northwest Territories	SecuritiesRegistry@gov.nt.ca	(867) 873-0243	Government of the Northwest Territories P.O. Box 1320 Yellowknife, NWT X1A 2L9 Attention: Deputy Superintendent of Securities
Nova Scotia	nrs@novascotia.ca	(902) 424-4625	Nova Scotia Securities Commission Suite 400, 5251 Duke Street P.O. Box 458 Halifax, NS B3J 2P8 Attention: Deputy Director, Capital Markets
Nunavut	CorporateRegistrations@gov.nu.ca	(867) 975-6590 (Faxing to NU is unreliable. The preferred method is e-mail.)	Legal Registries Division Department of Justice Government of Nunavut P.O. Box 1000 Station 570 Iqaluit, NU X0A 0H0 Attention: Deputy Registrar
Ontario	registration@osc.gov.on.ca	(416) 593-8283	Ontario Securities Commission 22nd Floor 20 Queen Street West Toronto, ON M5H 3S8 Attention: Compliance and Registrant Regulation
Prince Edward Island	ccis@gov.pe.ca	(902) 368-6288	Consumer and Corporate Services Division, Office of the Attorney General P.O. Box 2000, 95 Rochford Street Charlottetown, PE C1A 7N8 Attention: Superintendent of Securities
Québec	inscription@lautorite.qc.ca	(514) 873-3090	Autorité des marchés financiers Direction de l'encadrement des intermédiaires 800 square Victoria, 22e étage C.P 246, Tour de la Bourse Montréal (Québec) H4Z 1G3
Saskatchewan	registrationsfsc@gov.sk.ca	(306) 787-5899	Financial and Consumer Affairs Authority of Saskatchewan Suite 601 1919 Saskatchewan Drive Regina, SK S4P 4H2 Attention: Registration
Yukon	corporateaffairs@gov.yk.ca	(867) 393-6251	Department of Community Services Yukon Yukon Securities Office P.O. Box 2703 C-6 Whitehorse, YT Y1A 2C6 Attention: Superintendent of Securities

Appendix B — Terms not defined in NI 31-103 or this Companion Policy

Terms defined in National Instrument 14-101 *Definitions*:

- adviser registration requirement
- Canadian securities regulatory authority
- dealer registration requirement
- foreign jurisdiction

Part 3:
REGISTRATION

- jurisdiction or jurisdiction of Canada
- local jurisdiction
- investment fund manager registration requirement
- prospectus requirement
- registration requirement
- regulator
- securities directions
- securities legislation
- securities regulatory authority
- SRO
- underwriter registration requirement

Terms defined in National Instrument 45-106 *Prospectus and Registration Exemptions:*

- accredited investor
- eligibility adviser
- financial assets

Terms defined in National Instrument 81-102 *Investment Funds:*

- money market fund

Terms defined in the Securities Act of most jurisdictions:

- adviser
- associate
- company
- control person
- dealer
- director
- distribution
- exchange contract (BC, AB, SK and NB only)
- insider
- individual
- investment fund
- investment fund manager
- issuer
- mutual fund
- officer
- person
- promoter
- records
- registrant
- reporting issuer
- security
- trade
- underwriter

Appendix C — Proficiency requirements for individuals acting on behalf of a registered firm

The tables in this Appendix set out the education and experience requirements, by firm registration category, for individuals who are applying for registration under securities legislation.

An individual must not perform an activity that requires registration unless the individual has the education, training and experience that a reasonable person would consider necessary to perform the activity competently, including, in the case of registered representatives, understanding the structure, features and risks of each security the individual recommends.

CCOs must also not perform an activity set out in section 5.2 unless they have the education, training and experience that a reasonable person would consider necessary to perform the activity competently.

Acronyms used in the tables

BMP:	Branch Manager Proficiency Exam
CA:	Chartered Accountant
CCO:	Chief Compliance Officer
CCOQ:	Chief Compliance Officers Qualifying Exam
CFA:	CFA Charter
CGA:	Certified General Accountant Exam/Partners, Directors
CMA:	Certified Management Accountant
CIF:	Canadian Investment Funds Course Exam
CIM:	Canadian Investment Manager designation
CSC:	Canadian Securities Course Exam
EMP:	Exempt Market Products Exam
IFIC:	Investment Funds in Canada Course
MFDC:	Mutual Funds Dealer Compliance Exam
PDO:	Officers', Partners' and Directors' and Senior Officers Course Exam
SRP:	Sales Representative Proficiency Exam

Investment dealer

Dealing representative	CCO
Proficiency requirements set by IIROC	Proficiency requirements set by IIROC

Mutual fund dealer

Dealing representative	CCO
One of these five options: 1. CIF 2. CSC 3. IFIC 4. CFA Charter and 12 months of relevant securities industry experience in the 36-month period before applying for registration 5. Advising representative requirements — portfolio manager or exempt from these under section 16.10(1)	One of these two options: 1. CIF, CSC or IFIC; and PDO, MFDC or CCOQ and 12 months of relevant securities industry experience in the 36-month period before applying for registration 2. CCO requirements — portfolio manager or exempt from these under section 16.9(2)

Exempt market dealer

Dealing representative	CCO
One of these four options: 1. CSC 2. EMP 3. CFA Charter and 12 months of relevant securities industries experience in the 36-months before applying for registration 4. Advising representative requirements — portfolio manager or exempt from these under section 16.10(1)	One of these two options: 1. PDO or CCOQ and EMP or CSC 2. CCO requirements — portfolio manager or exempt from these under section 16.9(2) 3. CCO requirements — portfolio manager

Scholarship plan dealer

Dealing representative	CCO

SRP	SRP, BMP, and PDO or CCOQ

Restricted dealer	
Dealing representative	**CCO**
Regulator to determine on a case-by-case basis	Regulator to determine on a case-by-case basis

Portfolio manager		
Advising representative	**Associate advising representative**	**CCO**
One of these two options:	One of these two options:	One of these three options:
1. CFA and 12 months of relevant investment management experience in the 36-month period before applying for registration	1. Level 1 of the CFA and 24 months of relevant investment management experience	1. CSC except if the individual has the CFA or CIM designation, PDO or CCOQ, and CFA or a professional designation as a lawyer, CA, CGA, CMA, notary in Québec or the equivalent in a foreign jurisdiction, and:
2. CIM and 48 months of relevant investment management experience (12 months gained in the 36-month period before applying for registration)	2. CIM and 24 months of relevant investment management experience	• 36 months of relevant securities experience working at an investment dealer, registered adviser or investment fund manager, or
		• 36 months providing professional services to the securities industry and 12 months working at a registered dealer, registered adviser or investment fund manager, for a total of 48 months
		2. CSC except if the individual has the CFA or CIM designation, PDO or CCOQ and five years working at:
		• an investment dealer or a registered adviser (including 36 months in a compliance capacity), or
		• a Canadian financial institution in a compliance capacity relating to portfolio management and 12 months at a registered dealer or registered adviser, for a total of six years
		3. PDO or CCOQ and advising representative requirements — portfolio manager

Restricted portfolio manager		
Advising representative	**Associate advising representative**	**CCO**
Regulator to determine on case-by-case basis	Regulator to determine on a case-by-case basis	Regulator to determine on a case-by-case basis

Investment fund manager		
CCO		
One of these three options:		
1.	CSC except if the individual has the CFA or CIM designation, PDO or CCOQ, and CFA or a professional designation as a lawyer, CA, CGA, CMA, notary in Quebec or the equivalent in a foreign jurisdiction, and:	
	•	36 months of relevant securities experience working at a registered dealer, registered adviser or investment fund manager, or
	•	36 months providing professional services in the securities industry and 12 months working in a relevant capacity at an investment fund manager, for a total of 48 months
2.	CIF, CSC or IFIC; PDO or CCOQ and five years of relevant securities experience working at a registered dealer, registered adviser or an investment fund manager (including 36 months in a compliance capacity)	
3.	CCO requirements for portfolio manager or exempt from these requirements under section 16.9(2)	

Appendix D

[Name of Firm]
Annual Charges and Compensation Report

Client name   Your Account Number: 123456
Address line 1
Address line 2
Address line 3

This report summarizes the compensation that we received directly and indirectly in 20XX. Our compensation comes from two sources:

> **1. What we charge you directly. Some of these charges are associated with the operation of your account. Other charges are associated with purchases, sales and other transactions you make in the account.**

> **2. What we receive through third parties.**

Charges are important because they reduce your profit or increase your loss from investing. If you need an explanation of the charges described in this report, your representative can help you.

Charges you paid directly to us		
RSP administration fee	$100	
Total charges associated with the operation of your account		**$100**
Commissions on purchases of mutual funds with a sales charge	$101	
Switch fees	$45	
Total charges associated with transactions we executed for you		**$146**
Total charges you paid directly to us		**$246**
Compensation we received through third parties		
Commissions from mutual fund managers on purchases of mutual funds (see note 1)		$503
Trailing commissions from mutual fund managers (see note 2)		$286
Total compensation we received through third parties		**$789**
Total charges and compensation we received in 20XX		**$1,035**

Notes::

1. When you purchased units of mutual funds on a deferred sales charge basis, we received a commission from the investment fund manager. During the year, these commissions amounted to $503.

2. We received $286 in trailing commissions in respect of securities you owned during the 12-month period covered by this report.

   Investment funds pay investment fund managers a fee for managing their funds. The managers pay us ongoing trailing commissions for the services and advice we provide you. The amount of the trailing commission depends on the sales charge option you chose when you purchased the fund. You are not directly charged the trailing commission or the management fee. But, these fees affect you because they reduce the amount of the fund's return to you. Information about management fees and other charges to your investment funds is included in the prospectus or fund facts document for each fund.

Our current schedule of operating charges

[As part of the annual report of charges and compensation, registrants are required to provide their current operating charges that may be applicable to their clients' accounts. For the purposes of this sample document, we are not providing such a list.]

Appendix E

Your investment performance report   **For the period ending December 31, 2030**

Investment account 123456789

Client name
Address line 1
Address line 2
Address line 3

This report tells you how your account has performed to December 31, 2030. It can help you assess your progress toward meeting your investment goals.

Speak to your representative if you have questions about this report. It is important that you tell your representative if your personal or financial circumstances have changed. Your representative can recommend adjustments to your investments to keep you on track to meeting your goals.

Amount invested means opening market value plus deposits including:

the market value of all deposits and transfers of securities and cash into your account, not including interest or dividends reinvested.

Less withdrawals including:

the market value of all withdrawals and transfers out of your account.

Total value summary

Your investments have increased by $36,492.34 since you opened the account

Your investments have increased by $2,928.85 during the past year

Amount invested since you opened
your account on January 1, 2015 $ 16,300.00
Market value of your account on December 31, 2030 $ 52,792.34

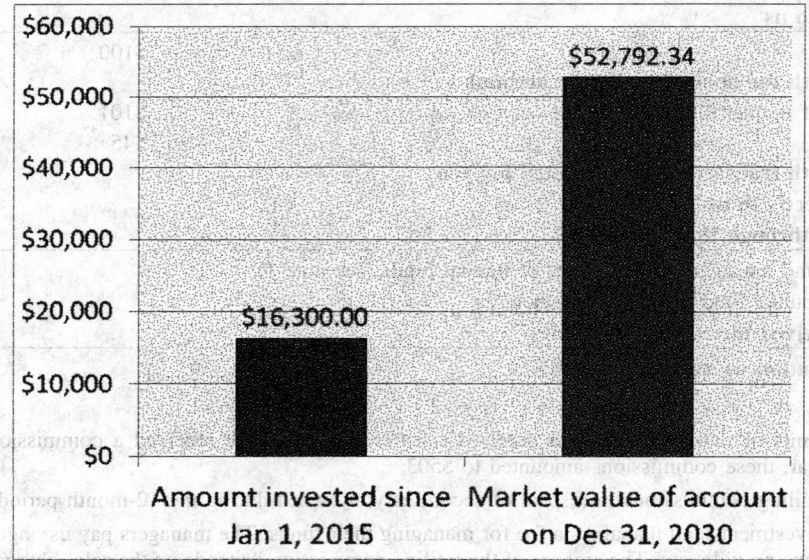

Change in the value of your account

This table is a summary of the activity in your account. It shows how the value of your account has changed based on the type of activity.

	Past year	Since you opened your account
Opening market value	$51,063.49	$0.00
Deposits	$4,000.00	$21,500.00
Withdrawals	$(5,200.00)	$(5,200.00)
Change in the market value of your account	$2,928.85	$36,492.34
Closing market value	**$52,792.34**	**$52,792.34**

What is a total percentage return?

This represents gains and losses of an investment over a specified period of time, including realized and unrealized capital gains and losses plus income, expressed as a percentage.

For example, an annual total percentage return of 5% for the past three years means that the investment effectively grew by 5% a year in each of the three years.

Your personal rates of return

The table below shows the total percentage return of your account for periods ending December 31, 2030. Returns are calculated after charges have been deducted. These include charges you pay for advice, transaction charges and account-related charges, but not income tax.

Keep in mind your returns reflect the mix of investments and risk level of your account. When assessing your returns, consider your investment goals, the amount of risk you're comfortable with, and the value of the advice and services you receive.

	Past year	Past 3 years	Past 5 years	Past 10 years	Since you opened your account
Your account	5.51%	10.92%	12.07%	12.90%	13.09%

Calculation method

We use a money weighted method to calculate rates of return. Contact your representative if you want more information about this calculation.

The returns in this table are your personal rates of return. Your returns are affected by changes in the value of the securities you have invested in, dividends and interest that they paid, and also deposits and withdrawals to and from your account.

If you have a personal financial plan, it will contain a target rate of return, which is the return required to achieve your investment objectives. By comparing the rates of return you actually achieved (shown in the table) with your target rate of return, you can see whether you are on track to meet your investment objectives.

Contact your representative to discuss your rate of return and investment objectives.

Adoption of Policy: (2009) 32 O.S.C.B. (Supp. 4) 69; 32 O.S.C.B. (Supp. 2) 1; Request for Comments: (2008) 31 O.S.C.B. 2279 and (2007) 30 O.S.C.B. 1606.

Adoption of Amendment to Policy: (2010) 33 O.S.C.B. (Supp. 5) 109 and (Supp. 3) 203; Request for Comments: (2009) 32 O.S.C.B. 8721.

Adoption of Revised Policy: (2011) 34 O.S.C.B. (Supp. 3) 1; Request for Comments: (2010) 33 O.S.C.B. (Supp. 2) 1.

Adoption of Amendment to Policy: (2011) 34 O.S.C.B. 11819; Request for Comments: (2011) 34 O.S.C.B. 5517.

Adoption of Amendment to Policy: (2012) 35 O.S.C.B. 8547 and 6303; Request for Comments: (2012) 35 O.S.C.B. 1445.

Adoption of Amendment to Policy: (2013) 36 O.S.C.B. 5723 and 3173; Request for Comments: (2012) 35 O.S.C.B. 5429 and (2011) 34 O.S.C.B. 7087.

Adoption of Amendment to Policy: (2014) 37 O.S.C.B. (Supp 4) 130; Request for Comments: (2013) 36 O.S.C.B. (Supp 3)

OSC Staff Notice 31-175 — Mystery Shopping for Investment Advice: Insight into advisory practices and the investor experience in Ontario

Date: September 17, 2015

38 O.S.C.B. 7995

[Not reproduced]

National Policy 31-201 — National Registration System

Date: April 4, 2005, as amended effective August 1, 2006

28 O.S.C.B. 3082 [Corrections 28 O.S.C.B. 7365] and 29 O.S.C.B. 6490

[Rescinded: (2009) 32 O.S.C.B. (Supp. 2) 424]

Adoption by OSC: (2005) O.S.C.B. 3082, 1267 and 87; Request for Comments: (2004) 27 O.S.C.B. 618.

Adoption of amendments by OSC: (2006) 29 O.S.C.B. 6490 and 3555; Request for Comments: (2005) 28 O.S.C.B. 9527.

Part 3:
REGISTRATION

CSA Staff Notice 31-313 — NI 31-103 Registration Requirements and Exemptions and Related Instruments — Frequently Asked Questions as of December 18, 2009

Date: **December 18, 2009**

32 O.S.C.B. 10427

Background

On September 28, 2009, new National Instrument 31-103 *Registration Requirements and Exemptions* and amendments to related instruments including NI 33-109 *Registration Information* came into force. We have compiled this list of frequently asked questions (FAQs) from the enquiries we have received concerning NI 31-103 and NI 33-109 in order to assist those working with these instruments.

NI 31-103 *Registration Requirements and Exemptions*

NI 31-103 SECTION		QUESTION	ANSWER
PART 1	**INTERPRETATION**		
1.1	**Definitions of terms used throughout this Instrument**	**How will accounting terms in NI 31-103 work with International Financial Reporting Standards (IFRS) Amendments?**	Proposed amendments to NI 31-103 necessary to accommodate IFRS were published for comment on October 23, 2009, except in Québec and New Brunswick where the proposed amendments will be published in early 2010. The comment period will end on January 21, 2010, including in Québec and New Brunswick which have issued a staff notice on January 21, 2010.
PART 2	**CATEGORIES OF REGISTRATION FOR INDIVIDUALS**		
2.2	**Client mobility exemption — individuals**	**Are sections 2.2 [Client mobility exemption — individuals] and 8.30 [Client mobility exemption — firms] independent of each other? How do the firm and individual limits work together?**	Sections 2.2 [*Client mobility exemption — individuals*] and 8.30 [*Client mobility exemption — firms*] are independent of each other: individuals may rely on section 2.2 in circumstances where they are not registered in the local jurisdiction even though their firm does not rely on section 8.30 because the firm is registered in the local jurisdiction.

The limits are per jurisdiction. For example a firm using the exemption could have 10 clients in each of several local jurisdictions where it is not registered. An individual could also be using the exemption to have 5 clients in each of several jurisdictions where the individual is not registered.

The individual limits are per individual. For example several individuals working for a firm could each have 5 clients in the same local jurisdiction, if their firm was registered in the jurisdiction. Even

if a firm is registered in a local jurisdiction and has more than 10 clients served by registered individuals it can have unregistered individuals using the exemption in the jurisdiction.

If a firm is not registered in a jurisdiction, the firm may not exceed its 10 client limit, shared among its representatives.

NI 31-103 SECTION	QUESTION	ANSWER
2.3 **Individuals acting for investment fund managers**	**Do permitted individuals of an investment fund manager (IFM) need to file Form 33-109F4** *Registration of Individuals and Review of Permitted Individuals***?**	Although individuals acting on behalf of a registered IFM are not required to register pursuant to section 2.3 of NI 31-103, permitted individuals of an IFM must nonetheless file Form 33-109F4 *Registration of Individuals and Review of Permitted Individuals.*

"Permitted individual" is defined in section 1.1 of National Instrument 33-109 *Registration Information.*

PART 3   REGISTRATION REQUIREMENTS — INDIVIDUALS

Division 1   *General proficiency requirements*

NI 31-103 SECTION	QUESTION	ANSWER
3.4 **Proficiency — initial and ongoing**	**Has the CSA published any additional guidance relating to the proficiency requirement in section 3.4?**	CSA Staff Notice 33-315 *Suitability Obligation and Know Your Product* was published on September 2, 2009. It discusses the requirement for registered individuals to "know your product", which forms part of the ongoing proficiency obligation.
3.6 **Mutual fund dealer — chief compliance officer**	**How do proficiency time limits apply to chief compliance officers (CCO) in Québec?**	The CCO category is new in Québec. Prior to September 28, 2009, an individual could act in Québec in a similar capacity, with activities normally performed by a CCO but without however being identified on NRD in this category. Prior to September 28, 2009, the CCO or compliance officer categories existed only in Ontario, British Columbia and New Brunswick (the CCO jurisdictions).
3.8 **Scholarship plan dealer — chief compliance officer**		
3.10 **Exempt market dealer — chief compliance officer**		
3.13 **Portfolio manager — chief compliance officer**		In Québec individuals acting as *personne responsable (ou chef) de la conformité* prior to the coming into force of NI 31-103 must register before December 28, 2009 pursuant to subsection 16.9(1) of NI 31-103 and have until September 2010 pursuant to subsection 16.9(3) to meet the proficiency requirements set out in sections 3.6, 3.8, 3.10 and 3.13 as the case may be, for the following reasons:

Subsection 16.9(2), when referring to "the individual identified on the National Registration Database as the firm's compliance officer", refers to such compliance officers as were identified prior to September 28, 2009. This section can only apply in the CCO jurisdictions. In these jurisdictions, proficiency requirements applied to the compliance officer.

In Québec therefore subsection 16.9(2) of NI 31-103 does not constitute a "grandfathering" clause for individuals *acting as personne responsable (ou chef) de la conformité* prior to September 28, 2009.

As a result, there are in Québec the following 2 options:

NI 31-103 SECTION	QUESTION	ANSWER
		1. If the individual acting as *personne responsable (ou chef) de la conformité* in Québec prior to September 28, 2009 was identified as compliance officer or CCO in one of the CCO jurisdictions, the "grandfathering" clause in subsection 16.9(2) applies to this individual. The individual is therefore not required to meet the proficiency requirements of NI 31-103, so long as the individual remains registered as the firm's CCO.
		2. If the individual acting as *personne responsable (ou chef) de la conformité* in Québec prior to September 28, 2009 was not identified as compliance officer or CCO in one of the CCO jurisdictions, subsection 16.9(3) applies: the individual is required to meet the proficiency requirements of NI 31-103, but has 12 months to do so.
3.6	Mutual fund dealer — chief compliance officer	Can the chief compliance officer (CCO) of a portfolio manager (PM) whose proficiency is grandfathered	Although PM CCO proficiency set out in section 3.13 is available as an alternative to other proficiency requirements for CCOs of MFDs, EMDs and IFMs in sections 3.6, 3.10 and 3.14, respectively, there is no corresponding provision that would accommodate a PM CCO whose proficiency is grandfathered under subsection 16.9(2) on the basis of different qualifications than are prescribed in section 3.13.
3.10	Exempt market dealer — chief compliance officer	under subsection 16.9(2) continue to be its CCO if the firm is registered as a mutual fund dealer	
3.13	Portfolio manager — chief compliance officer	(MFD), exempt market dealer (EMD) or investment fund manager (IFM)?	This was not our intention, and we will be issuing an order providing an exemption from proficiency requirements for the CCO of an MFD, EMD or IFM where the firm was registered as a PM on the date NI 31-103 came into force and the individual was on that date designated as the CCO of the firm, for so long as they remain registered as the firm's CCO.
3.14	Investment fund manager — chief compliance officer		
3.9	Exempt market dealer — dealing representative	Will exemptions from the proficiency requirements for exempt market dealer (EMD) dealing representatives in section 3.9 be available?	We will always consider applications for exemptive relief. However, proficiency is one of the fundamental fitness criteria for individual registrants, so we anticipate granting exemptions from the EMD dealing representative proficiency requirements set out in section 3.9 only in rare cases.
PART 4	RESTRICTIONS ON REGISTERED INDIVIDUALS		

NI 31-103 SECTION	QUESTION	ANSWER
4.2 **Associate advising representatives — pre-approval of advice**	**If a firm has previously designated an adviser to review the advice of an associate advising representative (AAR), does it need to re-designate an adviser to review the AAR's advice under subsection 4.2(2)?**	No. If a firm has previously designated an adviser, it does not need to re-designate under NI 31-103 unless: • the firm has hired new AARs subsequent to the original designation, or • the designated advising representative changes This also applies in those jurisdictions that did not have the category of associate advising representative but imposed supervision on "junior" advisers through terms and conditions, if an adviser was designated to review the advice.

PART 7 CATEGORIES OF REGISTRATION FOR FIRMS

7.1 **Dealer categories**	**A. Can an exempt market dealer (EMD) trade prospectus qualified securities to clients such as accredited investors or those making a minimum purchase in an amount sufficient to qualify for prospectus-exempt distribution?** **B. If so, can the EMD provide the investor with a copy of the prospectus?**	A. Yes. As set out in clause 7.1(2)(d)(ii), an EMD can trade a prospectus-qualified security in circumstances where an exemption from the prospectus requirement would be available. B. Yes, the EMD may provide the investor with a copy of the prospectus.
	Can an exempt market dealer (EMD) underwrite a distribution that is not exempt from the prospectus requirement?	No. As set out in clause 7.1(2)(d)(iv), an EMD may only underwrite a distribution of securities that is made under an exemption from the prospectus requirement.
	Can an exempt market dealer (EMD) underwrite a prospectus-qualified distribution if it only distributes securities to accredited investors or other clients who may purchase securities offered under a prospectus exemption?	No. Although clause 7.1(2)(d)(ii) would permit an EMD to trade in such circumstances, clause 7.1(2)(d)(iv) restricts an EMD to underwriting permitted distributions that are, in fact, made under a prospectus exemption.
	When will the jurisdictions that are participating in the "alternative approach to regulating certain intermediaries in the exempt market" described in Appendix D to the CSA Notice of NI 31-103 (published on July 17, 2009) issue their exemptions from exempt market dealer (EMD) registration?	The jurisdictions that have agreed to this alternative approach will issue local blanket orders to exempt certain intermediaries from EMD registration shortly before the registration exemptions in NI 45-106 *Prospectus and Registration Exemptions* expire (March 27, 2010).

Part 3: REGISTRATION

NI 31-103 SECTION	QUESTION	ANSWER
	Must a mutual fund dealer in Québec or Manitoba also have to register as an EMD in Québec in order to sell principal protected notes (PPNs)?	PPNs include the instruments commonly described as market-linked GICs (market-linked GICs) and linked notes (market-linked notes). Market-linked GICs are described as term deposits that guarantee principal through a CDIC-insured (or equivalent) deposit-taking institution, with a return linked to a number of underlying investments, including stock market indices, mutual funds or hedge funds. Market-linked notes are described as debt instruments that provide a principal guarantee through the credit-worthiness of the issuer, with returns linked to a variety of underlying investments, including stock market indices, mutual funds, and hedge funds.

If certain conditions are met in connection with the type of PPN being sold, registration in the EMD category is not required for a mutual fund dealer in Québec.

The treatment of PPNs in Québec varies according to whether the PPN is a market-linked GIC or a market-linked note:

- market-linked GICs are term deposits to which the *Securities Act* (Québec) applies. Paragraph 9º of section 3 of the Act provides that the dealer registration requirement set out in section 148 of the Act does not apply to term deposits. The sale of market-linked GICs does not therefore require registration

- market-linked notes are debt securities to which the *Securities Act* (Québec) applies. Paragraph 14º of section 3 of the Act provides that the dealer registration requirement set out in section 148 of the Act does not apply to debt securities issued or guaranteed by a bank or an authorized foreign bank listed in Schedule I, II or III to the *Bank Act*, except a debt security conferring a right of payment ranking lower than a deposit contemplated in paragraph 9º of section 3 and entrusted to the issuer or the guarantor of the debt security

PPNs which meet the conditions of these exemptions may be sold in Québec by mutual fund dealers not also registered as EMDs.

In Manitoba, market-linked GICs and market-linked notes are securities. The Manitoba Securities Commission has issued relief which will permit registered mutual fund dealers to trade these products without registration as an EMD.

NI 31-103 SECTION	QUESTION	ANSWER
7.3 Investment fund manager category	**When is investment fund manager (IFM) registration required?** **Examples:** **A.** I manage a real estate investment trust (REIT). Do I need to register as an IFM? **B.** I manage a fund that does not invest in securities. Do I need to register as an IFM?	All managers of investment funds must register as IFMs unless an applicable exemption is available. The threshold question is whether a collective investment vehicle is an "investment fund". The next step is to identify who is the "investment fund manager" for the investment fund. Both terms are defined in local jurisdictions' securities legislation. There is also guidance in section 7.3 of the Companion Policy and in the Companion Policy to NI 81-106 *Investment Fund Continuous Disclosure* (81-106 Companion Policy). Examples: A. No. Subsection 1.2(2), of the 81-106 Companion Policy provides that business income trusts, REITs and royalty trusts are not investment funds. B. If the fund falls within the definition of investment fund, you must register unless otherwise exempt. The definition of investment fund is not restricted to funds that invest in securities. There are, for example, funds that invest in uranium or gold bullion. Note that sections 16.5 and 16.6 provide temporary exemptions for a Canadian investment fund manager registered in its principal jurisdiction and for foreign investment fund managers, respectively.
	Must an otherwise unregistered firm that is temporarily exempt from registration as an investment fund manager (IFM) under section 16.4 comply with the requirements in NI 31-103 if it seeks registration before the temporary exemption expires?	Yes. While section 16.4 provides a one-year exemption from registration, a firm that chooses to register before the end of that period must comply with NI 31-103 as soon as it becomes registered. The transition provisions that provide temporary exemptions from certain IFM requirements (sections 16.8 [*Registration of ultimate designated persons*], 16.9 [*Registration of chief compliance officers*], 16.11 [*Capital requirements*] and 16.13 [*Insurance requirements*]) only apply to firms that were already registered when NI 31-103 came into force.
	If a firm was already registered when NI 31-103 was implemented, will it lose the benefit of the transitional exemptions set out in Part 16 if it adds registration in another category?	No. A firm would not lose the benefit of the transitional exemptions provided in Part 16 for firms that are registered on the day NI 31-103 came into force (sections 16.8 [*Registration of ultimate designated persons*], 16.9 [*Registration of chief compliance officers*], 16.11 [*Capital requirements*] and 16.13 [*Insurance requirements*]) if it adds another registration category to what it had on the day when NI 31-103 came into force.

Part 3:
REGISTRATION

NI 31-103 SECTION	QUESTION	ANSWER
		Note also that subsection 16.4(3) provides a one-year transitional exemption from the investment fund manager (IFM) insurance requirement for a registered dealer or adviser that was acting as an IFM when NI 31-103 came into force.
PART 8 EXEMPTIONS FROM THE REQUIREMENT TO REGISTER		
Division 1 Exemptions from dealer and underwriter registration		
8.5 Trades through or to a registered dealer	**Can a foreign dealer rely on the exemption in section 8.5 for trades through or to a registered dealer?**	Yes. The exemption requires only that all trading activity that occurs within the local jurisdiction is done through or to a local registered dealer.

On that basis, we would regard the "jitney" of a trade through or to an appropriately registered dealer in a local Canadian jurisdiction by an unregistered dealer who is located in a foreign jurisdiction as a trade solely through a registered dealer in the local jurisdiction, consistent with the exemption in section 8.5. The fact that the transaction is executed through an agency arrangement involving intermediation by a dealer in another jurisdiction does not in itself mean that the "trade" in the local jurisdiction ceases to be made "solely" through a registered dealer.

However, if the dealer in the other jurisdiction is engaged in other trading activities in the local jurisdiction in connection with the transaction, it would no longer be a trade solely through a registered dealer and the exemption would not be available. It is important to bear in mind that a "trade" includes acts in furtherance of a trade.

For example, the trade would not be solely through a registered dealer if the foreign dealer or its client interacted directly with the (prospective) purchaser in the local jurisdiction. One way this could occur would be if the foreign dealer or its foreign client contacted the potential purchaser in the local jurisdiction and directly solicited the purchase of securities. The unregistered foreign dealer should instead solicit the purchase by contacting the registered dealer in the local jurisdiction, leaving it to the local registered dealer to contact potential purchasers in the local jurisdiction. |
| | **Is this exemption only available to issuers selling their own shares?** | No, the exemption is not limited to issuers or sales of one's own shares. |

NI 31-103 SECTION	QUESTION	ANSWER
	Can a plan administrator rely on the exemption in section 8.5 in connection with its activity of placing sell orders with brokers in respect of shares of issuers held by plan participants?	Yes, a plan administrator can rely on the exemption in section 8.5 in connection with its activity of placing sell orders with dealers in respect of shares of issuers held by plan participants. The Companion Policy discussion of section 8.5 is not meant to suggest that the exemption is only available in respect of trades in a person or company's own securities.
		Section 8.16 [*Plan administrator*] covers the activity of the plan administrator receiving sell orders from plan participants.
8.18　　International dealer	**Must a foreign dealer use the international dealer exemption in section 8.18 to trade through or to a registered dealer?**	No. If a foreign dealer's trading activities fall within the exemption in section 8.5 [*Trades through or to a registered dealer*], it does not need to rely on any other exemption from registration.
	A.　Can a registered firm also rely on the international dealer exemption?	A.　The exemption in section 8.18 is available to a firm that is registered in a jurisdiction in Canada.
	B.　If so, what notice should it provide to clients?	B.　A registered firm that is relying on the exemption may meet the client notification requirement in clause 8.18(4)(b)(i) by notifying the client that it is not registered in the jurisdiction in respect of the activities for which the exemption is being relied upon.
	If a firm is relying on the exemption in section 8.18 in more than one jurisdiction, must it file a Form 31-103F2 Submission to Jurisdiction and Appointment of Agent for Service (as required by subsection 8.18(5)) with each regulator or can it use the passport system?	If a firm is relying on the exemption in more than one jurisdiction, it must file a Form 31-103F2 *Submission to Jurisdiction and Appointment of Agent for Service* with the regulator in each jurisdiction where it relies on the exemption — see subsection 1.3(2).
	Subsection 8.18(5) requires a firm to notify the regulator each year that it continues to rely on the exemption. Does that mean a firm has to file Form 31-103F2 Submission to Jurisdiction and Appointment of Agent for Service every year?	No. Subsection 8.18(5) does not prescribe the form of annual notice to the regulator, so an email or letter will be acceptable.
	What must an international dealer in Ontario do to rely on subsection 8.18(6)?	To comply with subsection 8.18(6) in Ontario, a firm must pay participation fees under Part 3 of OSC Rule 13-502 *Fees*. By December 1 of each year, the firm must file a completed Form 13-502F4 *Capital Markets Participation Fee Calculation*. The firm must pay its participation fee by cheque, draft, money order or other acceptable means no later than December 31 each year. The filings and payments should be sent to the Ontario Securities Commission (Attention: Manager, Registrant Regulation).

Part 3: REGISTRATION

NI 31-103 SECTION	QUESTION	ANSWER
8.22 **Small security holder selling and purchase arrangements**	How should "market value" be determined?	Where possible, market value should be determined by reference to a quoted value on a recognized exchange or marketplace. If market value is not quoted on an exchange (e.g. bonds) market value may be determined by reference to quotes that are available through brokers. We recognize that it is not always possible to obtain a market value by these methods. In such cases, we will accept a valuation policy that is consistently applied and is based on measures considered reasonable in the industry, such as value at cost where there has been no material subsequent event (e.g. a market event or new capital raising by the issuer).

Division 2   *Exemptions from adviser registration*

8.26 **International adviser**	How does a foreign adviser act as a sub-adviser to a registered adviser if dealers and advisers are not "permitted clients" for the purposes of the international adviser exemption?	Foreign sub-advisers may continue to rely on the sub-adviser exemption that remains in section 7.3 of OSC Rule 35-502 *Non Resident Advisers*, and apply for discretionary relief in other jurisdictions.

In Québec, a general exemption has been granted on December 18, 2009 on the same terms and conditions as the exemptive relief available in the other jurisdictions. This general exemption will take effect on December 28, 2009 since the exemption available under section 5 of the Regulation to amend the Securities Regulation (former 194.2 of the Securities Regulation) remains in force only until that date. |
	A. Can a registered firm also rely on the international adviser exemption?	A. The exemption in section 8.26 is available to a firm that is registered in the local jurisdiction or elsewhere in Canada.
	B. If so, what notice should it provide to clients?	B. A registered firm that is relying on the exemption may meet the client notification requirement in clause 8.26(4)(e)(i) by notifying the client that it is not registered in the jurisdiction in respect of the activities for which the exemption is being relied upon.
	If a firm is relying on the exemption in section 8.26 in more than one jurisdiction, must it file a Form 31-103F2 Submission to Jurisdiction and Appointment of Agent for Service (as required by subsection 8.26(5)) with each regulator or can it use the passport system?	If a firm is relying on the exemption in more than one jurisdiction, it must file a Form 31-103F2 *Submission to Jurisdiction and Appointment of Agent for Service* with the regulator in each jurisdiction where it relies on the exemption — see subsection 1.3(2).

NI 31-103 SECTION	QUESTION	ANSWER
	Subsection 8.26(5) requires a firm to notify the regulator each year that it continues to rely on the exemption. Does that mean a firm has to file Form 31-103F2 Submission to Jurisdiction and Appointment of Agent for Service every year?	No. Subsection 8.26(5) does not prescribe the form of annual notice to the regulator, so an email or letter will be acceptable.
	What must an international adviser in Ontario do to rely on subsection 8.26(6)?	To comply with subsection 8.26(6) in Ontario, a firm must pay participation fees under Part 3 of OSC Rule 13-502 *Fees*. By December 1 of each year, the firm must file a completed Form 13-502F4 *Capital Markets Participation Fee Calculation*. The firm must pay its participation fee by cheque, draft, money order or other acceptable means no later December 31 each year. The filings and payments should be sent to the Ontario Securities Commission (Attention: Manager, Registrant Regulation).
	Do revenues derived from "portfolio management activities" under paragraph 8.26(4)(d) include revenues from sub-advisory activities?	Yes, in making the calculation required under paragraph 8.26(4)(d), it is necessary to include all revenues derived from portfolio management activities in Canada, which would include any sub-adviser arrangements.

Division 4   Mobility exemption — firms

8.30 Client mobility exemption — firms	**Are sections 2.2 [Client mobility exemption — individuals] and 8.30 [Client mobility exemption — firms] independent of each other? How do the firm and individual limits work together?**	Sections 2.2 [*Client mobility exemption — individuals*] and 8.30 [*Client mobility exemption — firms*] are independent of each other: individuals may rely on section 2.2 in circumstances where they are not registered in the local jurisdiction even though their firm does not rely on section 8.30 because the firm is registered in the local jurisdiction.

The limits are per jurisdiction. For example a firm using the exemption could have 10 clients in each of several local jurisdictions where it is not registered. An individual could also be using the exemption to have 5 clients in each of several jurisdictions where the individual is not registered.

The individual limits are per individual. For example several individuals working for a firm could each have 5 clients in the same local jurisdiction, if their firm was registered in the jurisdiction. Even if a firm is registered in a local jurisdiction and has more than 10 clients served by registered individuals it can have unregistered individuals using the exemption in the jurisdiction.

If a firm is not registered in a jurisdiction, the firm may not exceed its 10 client limit, shared among its representatives.

NI 31-103 SECTION	QUESTION	ANSWER
	Can a person or company that is not registered in any jurisdiction in Canada rely on the client mobility exemption?	No. The client mobility exemption is only available to a person or company that is registered in a jurisdiction of Canada.

PART 11   INTERNAL CONTROLS AND SYSTEMS

Division 1   Compliance

| **11.2** | **Designating an ultimate designated person** | **When can someone be designated for registration as a firm's ultimate designated person (UDP) on the basis that they are acting in a capacity similar to that of the chief executive officer (CEO) or sole proprietor?** | The primary purpose of paragraph 11.2(2)(c) is to address the situation where a firm does not have a CEO or sole proprietor (for example, because it is organized as a partnership).

It is not normally possible to act in a capacity similar to a CEO or sole proprietor when someone else is the actual CEO or sole proprietor. Consequently, designation pursuant to paragraph 11.2(2)(c) is not available when the firm has a CEO or sole proprietor. If a firm has a CEO or sole proprietor, that person must be designated for registration as its UDP, unless another person qualifies under paragraph 11.2(2)(b).

To designate someone else in these circumstances would require an exemptive relief order. Given that the intention of section 11.2 is to ensure responsibility for its compliance system rests at the very top of a firm, we would only anticipate granting relief in rare cases.

If a firm does not have a CEO and is not a sole proprietorship, and no other person qualifies under paragraph 11.2(2)(b), the most senior decision maker in the firm is the individual who would be most likely to be acting in a similar capacity to a CEO or sole proprietor. They might have the title of managing partner or president, for example, and would be the individual we would expect to see designated as UDP under paragraph 11.2(2)(c).

We note that in larger organizations, the UDP is sometimes supported by an officer who has a compliance oversight role and title within the organization that is more senior than the chief compliance officer. This is an acceptable arrangement, so long as it is understood that it in no way diminishes the UDP's regulatory responsibilities. |

Division 3   Certain business transactions

NI 31-103 SECTION	QUESTION	ANSWER
11.9 Registrant acquiring a registered firm's securities or assets	**Does the exemption in subsection 11.9(3) extend to the situation of a parent company registrant that proposes to acquire all of the assets of its wholly-owned registered subsidiary and then cause it to be wound up and dissolved?**	A wind-up and dissolution is not an amalgamation, merger, arrangement or treasury issue and does not qualify as a reorganization. The exemption in subsection 11.9(3) would therefore not be available.
11.9 Registrant acquiring a registered firm's securities or assets **11.10** Registered firm whose securities are acquired	**Are sections 11.9 and 11.10 intended to capture minor purchases by individual registrants of securities of their registered employer?**	No. Paragraph 11.9(3)(b) and subsection 11.10(1) both include 10% thresholds that may apply to the purchase of securities of the firm by its registered individuals.
	If the firm is registered in more than one jurisdiction, can the notices required under sections 11.9 and 11.10 be delivered to the principal regulator alone?	No. If a firm is required to give notice, it must be filed with *each* regulator — see subsection 1.3(2).

PART 12 FINANCIAL CONDITION

Division 1 Working capital

12.1 Capital requirements	**If a firm is registered in a category that requires membership in the Investment Industry Regulatory Organization of Canada (IIROC) or the Mutual Fund Dealers Association of Canada (the MFDA), and also in another category that does not require membership in either self-regulatory organization (SRO), will the firm still need to file Form 31-103F1 Calculation of Excess Working Capital with the regulator?** **Example: A firm that is registered as an investment fund manager and a mutual fund dealer and is a member of the MFDA.**	Yes. The exemptions for IIROC and MFDA member firms in section 9.3 do not include an exemption from the requirement to file Form 31-103F1 *Calculation of Excess Working Capital* with the regulator if a firm is also registered in a category that does not require SRO membership.

Division 2 Insurance

12.3 Insurance — dealer **12.4** Insurance — adviser **12.5** Insurance — investment fund manager	**How do I make the calculations required in sections** **12.3, 12.4 and 12.5?**	The calculation required in paragraphs 12.3(2)(b) and (c), 12.4(3)(a) and (b) and 12.5(a)and (b) is based on the lesser of 1% of assets or $25 million (and not 1% of $25 million). The word "and" following "Appendix A" in subsections 12.3(2), 12.4(2) and (3), and 12.5(2) should be ignored. We will remove it in amendments in order to clarify the meaning of these provisions.

Part 3: REGISTRATION

QUESTION

ANSWER

What is the timing of the calculation of insurance requirements — when must a firm adjust its insurance?

The insurance provisions say that the registered firm must "maintain" bonding or insurance in the amounts specified. We do not expect that the calculation would differ materially from day-to-day. If there is a material change in a firm's circumstances, it should consider the potential impact on its ability to meet its insurance requirements.

What are the "assets under management" that must be included in the insurance calculations of a firm registered in the categories of portfolio manager (PM) and investment fund manager (IFM)?

Insurance requirements are *not* cumulative. So, for a firm registered in the categories of PM and IFM, insurance coverage must be in the higher amount of the calculations with respect to its IFM or PM registration.

Despite being registered as both a PM and an IFM, when calculating the IFM insurance requirement under subsection 12.5(2), an IFM should only include the total assets under management of its own investment funds. It is only with respect to its own funds that the registrant is acting as an IFM.

To calculate the PM insurance requirement look to section 12.4. The required level of insurance will depend on whether the PM holds or has access to client assets. See section 12.4 of the Companion Policy for what we consider to be holding or having access to client assets.

Division 4   Financial reporting

How will accounting terms in NI 31-103 work with International Financial Reporting Standards (IFRS) Amendments?

Proposed amendments to NI 31-103 necessary to accommodate IFRS were published for comment on October 23, 2009, except in Québec and New Brunswick where the proposed amendments will be published in early 2010. The comment period will end on January 21, 2010.

12.12   Delivering financial information — dealer

12.13   Delivering financial information — adviser

12.14   Delivering financial information — investment fund manager

Is there a transition provision applicable to the requirement to deliver Form 31-103F1 Calculation of Excess Working Capital?

There is no transition provision applicable to the requirement to use Form 31-103F1 *Calculation of Excess Working Capital*. Registered firms are required to deliver Form 31-103F1 *Calculation of Excess Working Capital*. However, we recognize that there may be some discrepancies where firms rely on the transitional relief from section 12.1 [*Capital requirements*] that is provided under section 16.11 for firms that continue to comply with former non-harmonized capital requirements. If a firm relies on section 16.11 it must also deliver the capital calculations required under former requirements, if any.

In Ontario, we do not expect a firm that calculates its working capital based on consolidated financial statements in reliance on the transitional relief in section 16.11 to deliver a Form 31-103F1 *Calculation of Excess Working Capital*.

NI 31-103 SECTION	QUESTION	ANSWER
	If a firm has multiple registrations, is it required to deliver multiple capital calculations using Form 31-103F1 Calculation of Excess Working Capital?	No. If a firm has multiple registrations, it only needs to file only one Form 31-103F1 *Calculation of Excess Working Capital* to the regulators, but must include all required information. For example,
		• if the firm is a portfolio manager (PM) and investment fund manager (IFM), it will need to file Form 31-103F1 *Calculation of Excess Working Capital* quarterly and report any net asset value (NAV) adjustments quarterly (to comply with IFM requirements, notwithstanding that a PM has no such requirements)
		• if the firm is a mutual fund dealer registered in Québec which is also registered as an exempt market dealer in Québec, it will need to file Form 31-103F1 *Calculation of Excess Working Capital* quarterly as well as the bi-monthly net free capital calculation as set out in Appendix I of the *Regulation respecting the trust accounts and financial resources of securities firms.*
		A firm that is a member of a self-regulatory organization (SRO) may also have capital calculation delivery requirements under the SRO's rules.
12.12	**Delivering financial information — dealer**	
	Is there a transition period for former limited market dealers in respect of the requirements to deliver audited annual financial statements and Form 31-103F1 Calculation of Excess Working Capital?	Yes. For former limited market dealers in Ontario and Newfoundland and Labrador "mapped-over" to exempt market dealers (EMDs) under section 16.3, a transitional relief order was issued on September 28, 2009, exempting them from the requirements in subsection 12.12(1) to deliver audited annual financial statements and prescribed capital calculations for a period of one year, consistent with the other solvency-related transitional relief provided in section 16.3. The relief is only available to the extent a mapped-over EMD is not registered in another category that requires delivery of financial statements or client statements during the applicable transition period.

PART 13   DEALING WITH CLIENTS — INDIVIDUALS AND FIRMS

Division 1   *Know your client and suitability*

13.3	**Suitability**	
	Has the CSA published any additional guidance on section 13.3?	Yes. CSA Staff Notice 33-315 *Suitability Obligation and Know Your Product* was published on September 2, 2009.

Part 3: REGISTRATION

NI 31-103 SECTION		QUESTION	ANSWER
Division 2	*Conflicts of interest*	**Are registrants still required to provide a specified statement of policies disclosure as was previously required in some jurisdictions (e.g. in Ontario, section 223 of the Regulations)?**	No. There is no prescribed form of disclosure required in the conflicts of interest provisions of NI 31-103. The Companion Policy provides additional guidance in regards to disclosure about relationships with related or connected issuers.
Division 3	*Referral Arrangements*		
13.7	**Definitions — referral arrangements**	**Does "referral fee" include non-monetary compensation?**	Yes. "Referral fee" is defined in section 13.7 as *any* form of compensation. For example, gift certificates would be included.
PART 14	**HANDLING CLIENT ACCOUNTS — FIRMS**		
Division 2	*Disclosure to clients*		
14.2	**Relationship disclosure information**	**Does section 14.2 apply to clients who opened accounts before NI 31-103 came into effect?**	Yes. Section 14.2 applies to all clients, including those clients who opened accounts prior to September 28, 2009. Section 16.14 provides a one-year transition period from the requirements in section 14.2.
14.4	**When the firm has a relationship with a financial institution**	**Does section 14.4 apply to accounts opened before NI 31-103 came into effect?**	No. Section 14.4 applies only to new accounts opened after September 28, 2009.
14.5	**Notice to clients by non-resident registrants**	**Does the non-resident notice provision in section 14.5 apply to a Canadian registrant whose head office is located in another Canadian jurisdiction?**	Yes. However, it was not our intention to include registrants based in Canada if they have a physical place of business in the jurisdiction. We anticipate issuing an order that provides relief from section 14.5 for registered firms that have their head office in a Canadian jurisdiction and a physical place of business in the local jurisdiction.
Division 3	*Client Assets*		
14.6	**Holding client assets in trust**	**Is there an exemption for a Canadian manager of an offshore fund that may have difficulty satisfying the requirement of paragraph 14.6(c) that cash be held effectively in Canada?**	No. NI 31-103 does not provide an exemption from the requirement in paragraph 14.6(c). However, we recognize that it may be difficult to comply in the circumstances described. We will consider granting discretionary relief on terms consistent with section 14.7.
Division 5	*Account activity reporting*		
14.12	**Content and delivery of trade confirmation**	**Must all of the information required in subsection 14.12(1) be provided to the client in a single document?**	There is no prescribed confirmation document that must be delivered to the client separately from any other documentation related to the transaction. The requirement for a written confirmation of a transaction can be satisfied by promptly delivering to the client a subscription agreement or other document or combination of documents which, taken together, provide all of the information listed in subsection 14.12(1).

NI 31-103 SECTION		QUESTION	ANSWER
14.12	Content and delivery of trade confirmation	Can confirmations and client statements be delivered electronically?	Yes. Confirmations and client statements can be delivered electronically (i.e., internet, fax or other "written" form) if the client agrees. See NP 11-201 *Delivery of Documents by Electronic Means*.
14.13	Semi-annual confirmations for certain automatic plans		
14.14	Client statements		
14.14	Client statements	Must a registrant provide a monthly statement if there is no activity in the account?	Only if the firm is a registered dealer and a client has asked for monthly statements, unless the registrant is a mutual fund dealer. Otherwise, statements may be sent on a quarterly basis, except in the case of scholarship plan dealers, who must provide an annual statement.
		If my firm was not subject to client statement requirements before NI 31-103 came into force, do I have to send out client statements that include transactions that took place before then?	No. If a firm was not subject to client statement requirements before NI 31-103 came into force, only transactions that took place after that date are required to be included in the firm's first monthly or quarterly client statements.
		How should "market value" for the purposes of subsection 14.14(5) be determined?	Where possible, market value should be determined by reference to a quoted value on a recognized exchange or marketplace. If market value is not quoted on an exchange (e.g. bonds) market value may be determined by reference to quotes that are available through brokers. We recognize that it is not always possible to obtain a market value by these methods. In such cases, we will accept a valuation policy that is consistently applied and is based on measures considered reasonable in the industry, such as value at cost where there has been no material subsequent event (e.g. a market event or new capital raising by the issuer).
		Does a former limited market dealer "mapped-over" to exempt market dealer (EMD) under section 16.3 have transitional relief from the requirement to deliver client statements?	Yes. For former limited market dealers in Ontario and Newfoundland and Labrador "mapped-over" to EMDs under section 16.3, a transitional relief order was issued on September 28, 2009, exempting them from the requirements in section 14.14 to deliver client statements for a period of two years, consistent with the transitional relief provided for mutual fund dealers (MFDs) in section 16.17. The relief is not available to a mapped-over EMD that is also registered in a category other than MFD or investment fund manager (IFM).
PART 16	TRANSITION		
		Are the transition periods flexible?	We will always consider applications for exemptive relief. However, we anticipate granting extensions of the transition periods only in rare circumstances.

NI 31-103 SECTION	QUESTION	ANSWER
	What if a registrant does not meet an applicable requirement under NI 31-103 before the end of the applicable transition period?	The registrant should immediately contact the regulator. A registrant in that situation might be required to cease to conduct registerable activities until they comply with the requirement, or a temporary exemption might be granted subject to terms and conditions, depending on the circumstances.
16.3 Change of registration categories — limited market dealers **16.7** Registration of exempt market dealers	**What is the passport procedure for registration of a former limited market dealer that has been "mapped-over" to exempt market dealer (EMD) in Ontario or Newfoundland and Labrador, but has its principal regulator (PR) in another jurisdiction?**	The mapped-over EMD should file a complete Form 33-109F6 *Firm Registration* with its PR. The application should be filed before the expiry of the transition period in section 16.7.
	Given the different transition periods in section 8.5 of NI 45-106 Prospectus and Registration Exemptions (expiry of registration exemptions on March 27, 2010) and section 16.7 of NI 31-103, when must a person or company register as an exempt market dealer (EMD) if it is in the business of trading in exempt market securities and unable to rely on the "alternative approach to regulating certain intermediaries in the exempt market" described in Appendix D to the CSA Notice of NI 31-103 (published on July 17, 2009)?	If the person or company was in the business of trading in exempt market securities in a jurisdiction when NI 31-103 came into effect, they may rely on the transition period in section 16.7 of NI 31-103 in that jurisdiction. They must apply for registration by September 28, 2010. If the person or company did not start operating in the exempt market until after September 28, 2009, they must register by March 28, 2010, which is when the registration exemptions in NI 45-106 *Prospectus and Registration Exemptions* expire. The person or company should apply for registration well in advance of March 28, 2010 to ensure that registration is granted by that date.
	When will the jurisdictions that are participating in the "alternative approach to regulating certain intermediaries in the exempt market" described in Appendix D to the CSA Notice of NI 31-103 (published on July 17, 2009) issue their exemptions from exempt market dealer (EMD) registration?	The jurisdictions that have agreed to this alternative approach will issue local blanket orders to exempt certain intermediaries from EMD registration shortly before the registration exemptions in NI 45-106 *Prospectus and Registration Exemptions* expire (March 27, 2010).
16.11 Capital requirements **16.13** Insurance requirements	**If a firm was already registered when NI 31-103 was implemented, will it lose the benefit of the transitional exemptions set out in Part 16 if it adds registration in another category?**	No. A firm would not lose the benefit of the transitional exemptions provided in Part 16 for firms that are registered on the day NI 31-103 came into force (sections 16.8 [*Registration of ultimate designated persons*], 16.9 [*Registration of chief compliance officers*], 16.11 [*Capital requirements*] and 16.13 [*Insurance requirements*]) if it adds another registration category to what it had on the day when NI 31-103 came into force. Note also that subsection 16.4(3) provides a one-year transitional exemption from the investment fund manager (IFM) insurance requirement for a registered dealer or adviser that was acting as an IFM when NI 31-103 came into force.

NI 31-103 SECTION	QUESTION	ANSWER

FORMS

FORM 31-103F1 *CALCULATION OF EX-CESS WORKING CAPITAL*

How is "market value" determined?

Where possible, market value is determined by reference to a quoted value on a recognized exchange or marketplace. If market value is not quoted on an exchange (e.g. bonds) market value may be determined by reference to quotes that are available through brokers. We recognize that it is not always possible to obtain a market value by these methods. In such cases, we will accept a valuation policy that is consistently applied and is based on measures considered reasonable in the industry, such as value at cost where there has been no material subsequent event (e.g. a market event or new capital raising by the issuer).

What margin rate applies to securities (other than bonds and debentures) listed on exchanges in Canada or the United States?

The Canadian and United States exchanges listed in clause (e)(ii) of Schedule 1 (50% margin) should not have been included there. Clause (e)(i) sets out the appropriate rates.

Who should sign the management certification at the end of Form 31-103F1 Calculation of Excess Working Capital?

The most senior decision maker at the firm, who will typically have a title such as chief executive officer, president or managing partner, should be one of the signatories. The firm's chief financial officer or functional equivalent, if there is one, should also sign. If your firm has only one officer, then only one signature is necessary.

FORM 31-103F2 *SUBMISSION TO JURIS-DICTION AND APPOINTMENT OF AGENT FOR SERVICE*

If I am relying on the international adviser or international dealer exemptions in sections 8.18 and 8.26, respectively, how can I ensure my firm receives communications from the regulator in a timely manner?

When submitting your firm's Form 31-103F2 *Submission to Jurisdiction and Appointment of Agent for Service*, include the name of the chief compliance officer or equivalent, their email address, and their telephone and fax numbers, as well as the firm's National Registration Database number, if it has one.

NI 33-109 *Registration Information*

NI 33-109 SECTION	QUESTION	ANSWER

2.3   Reinstatement

How can a permitted individual be reinstated on the National Registration Database (NRD) if their position at the new sponsoring firm is not identical to their position at the old sponsoring firm?

For permitted individuals, NRD will not allow the individual to be reinstated with a sponsoring firm unless the position at the new sponsoring firm is identical to the position at the old sponsoring firm. So, if, for example, an officer wished to transfer to another sponsoring firm as an officer and director, the sponsoring firm would have to use one of two options:

1.   Make a reactivation submission using Form 33-109F4 *Registration of Individuals and Review of Permitted Individuals*; or

NI 33-109 SECTION	QUESTION	ANSWER
		2. Submit Form 33-109F7 *Reinstatement of Registered Individuals and Permitted Individuals* to reinstate the individual for the officer position and Form 33-109F2 *Change or Surrender of Individual Categories* to add the director position.
6.1 All registered firms to file Form 33-109F6 — September 30, 2010	**What supporting documents must registered firms submit with their Form 33-109F6 Firm Registration within one year of implementation to their principal regulator (PR)? Must audited financial statements as per question 5.13 be included?**	If submitting Form 33-109F6 *Firm Registration* pursuant to this section, do not check off any of the boxes for question 1.3 as the reason for submitting the form. Simply make a note in your cover letter or email that you are submitting the form further to section 6.1 of NI 33-109. No supporting documents or audited financial statements are required.
FORM 33-109F4 *REGISTRATION OF INDIVIDUALS AND REVIEW OF PERMITTED INDIVIDUALS*	**Is there a requirement for individuals to update their Form 33-109F4 Registration of Individuals and Review of Permitted Individuals, since there are updated questions in the form?**	An individual is only required to update the questions in items 12 to 17 if there is a change to the response previously provided.
	Do permitted individuals of investment fund managers (IFM) need to submit Form 33-109F4 Registration of Individuals and Review of Permitted Individuals?	Although individuals acting on behalf of a registered IFM are not required to register pursuant to section 2.3 of NI 31-103, permitted individuals of an IFM must nonetheless file Form 33-109F4 *Registration of Individuals and Review of Permitted Individuals*. "Permitted individual" is defined in section 1.1 of National Instrument 33-109 *Registration Information*.
	When completing Schedule C of Form 33-109F4 Registration of Individuals and Review of Permitted Individuals, must a chief compliance officer (CCO) check off the "Officer — specify title" box, or only the CCO box?	If an individual's only officer title is CCO, then only the CCO box should be checked-off. However, if they also have an officer title that is listed in the definition of "permitted individual" in section 1.1 of NI 33-109 (CEO, CFO, COO or functional equivalent), then they should also check the "Officer" box and specify their title.
	In Québec, when should an authorized firm representative (AFR) submit a professional liability insurance policy and payment of fees payable to the Chambre de la sécurité financière (CSF)?	When an individual is seeking registration in Québec as a dealing representative of a mutual fund dealer or of a scholarship plan dealer who is not already registered in one of these categories.
FORM 33-109F6 *FIRM REGISTRATION*	**If I am a new applicant filing a Form 33-109F6 Firm Registration (not a current registrant updating my information), when do I submit payment?**	After Form 33-109F6 *Firm Registration* is received, we will contact you and provide you with a submission number in order that you are able to make payment through the National Registration Database.

NI 33-109 SECTION	QUESTION	ANSWER
	What supporting documents must registered firms submit with their Form 33-109F6 Firm Registration if registering in an additional jurisdiction or adding a registration category, such as investment fund manager (IFM)? Must audited financial statements as per question 5.13 be included?	Item 1.3 specifies the questions that must be responded to if adding a jurisdiction or category. As question 5.13 is not specified, audited financial statements are not required.

However, we will require exempt market dealers (EMDs) registering for the first time (i.e., not already registered in another category in any jurisdiction) and former limited market dealers "mapped-over" to EMD in Ontario and Newfoundland and Labrador under section 16.3 of NI 31-103 to provide audited financial statements, since we will not already have them. |
| | If my firm has audited annual financial statements prepared for its most recent year end, but those audited statements are more than 90 days old as of the date of our application for registration, must we have new audited financial statements prepared? | In appropriate cases, where an applicant files audited annual financial statements prepared for its most recent year end, but those audited statements are more than 90 days old, we will accept unaudited financial statements for the period from the financial year end to the month end prior to application.

Since these filings would be made as part of the initial application process, as attachments to the Form 33-109F6 *Firm Registration*, you may request the exemption at that time. No separate exemptive relief application need be filed in respect of this exercise of the Director's discretion. |
	Must a firm that has its head office outside of Canada be registered in the foreign jurisdiction where it is based?	Foreign firms applying for registration are normally expected to be registered in a relevant category in their home jurisdiction. This is part of the fit and proper assessment to be registered in Canadian jurisdictions and is also relevant to our compliance oversight capabilities.
FORM 33-109F7 *REINSTATEMENT OF REGISTERED INDIVIDUALS AND PERMITTED INDIVIDUALS*	My firm recently hired an individual that had terms and conditions imposed on his/her registration. What does this mean for our firm?	By signing Form 33-109F7 *Reinstatement of Registered Individuals and Permitted Individuals*, the authorized partner or officer of the new sponsoring firm certifies that the individual's terms and conditions remain in effect and agrees to assume any ongoing obligations that apply to the sponsoring firm in respect of the individual.
Registration-related fees	Where can I get information on the fees payable to the regulators in different jurisdictions?	There is a link to each of the CSA jurisdiction's fee schedules on the National Registration Database information website at *www.nrd-info.ca*. The schedules are located under the left-hand navigation bar labelled "Regulatory fees".

Policies and Orders: CSAN 31-314.

CSA Staff Notice 31-314 — NI 31-103 Registration Requirements and Exemptions and Related Instruments — Frequently Asked Questions as of February 5, 2010

Date: February 5, 2010

33 O.S.C.B. 1157

Background

This notice supplements CSA Staff Notice 31-313 — NI 31-103 *Registration Requirements and Exemptions* and Related Instruments — Frequently Asked Questions as of December 18, 2009. The questions addressed in this notice all relate to financial reporting requirements during the first year under the new registration regime that was introduced on September 28, 2009.

NI 31-103 *Registration Requirements and Exemptions*

NI 31-103 SECTION	QUESTION	ANSWER
PART 12 **FINANCIAL CONDITION**		

Division 4   Financial reporting

12.10(3) **Annual financial statements**	Some registrants were previously required by the securities legislation of some provinces to deliver annual audited consolidated financial statements. Subsection 12.10(3) of NI 31-103 requires registrants to deliver financial statements prepared in accordance with National Instrument 52-107 *Acceptable Accounting Principles, Auditing Standards and Reporting Currency* (NI 52-107) except that the statements must be prepared on a non-consolidated basis. Interim financial information delivered under subsection 12.11(2) of NI 31-103 must also be delivered on a non-consolidated basis.	For annual audited financial statements for financial years ended on or between September 30, 2009 to August 31, 2010 (and for interim periods within that period), staff will accept financial statements prepared under one of the following two options, even though these do not comply with NI 52-107: 1) non-consolidated financial statements and interim financial information with no comparative figures, or 2) non-consolidated financial statements and interim financial information with non-consolidated comparative figures.
	For registrants that previously delivered audited consolidated financial statements, what comparative figures do regulators expect to be delivered in the first year after the effective date of NI 31-103 (i.e. for financial years ended on or between September 30, 2009 to August 31, 2010)?	CSA staff have concluded that, if a registrant delivers annual non-consolidated financial statements and interim financial information using one of the options above, it would not be appropriate or in the public interest for staff to impose terms and conditions on the registrant. CSA staff have concluded that it would not be appropriate for a registrant to deliver financial statements or interim financial information that includes a current period that is non-consolidated and a comparative period that is presented using a different basis of accounting (e.g. consolidated comparative information).
	Subsection 12.10(3) of NI 31-103 requires a registrant to prepare annual financial statements in accordance with National Instrument 52-107 *Acceptable Accounting Principles, Auditing Standards and Reporting Currency*, except that the statements must be prepared on a non-consolidated basis. The annual financial statements must be audited. What form of audit report should the auditor be using when auditing financial statements of registrants that are prepared on a non-consolidated basis for regulatory purposes?	Since the annual non-consolidated financial statements are prepared in accordance with a basis of accounting other than generally accepted accounting principles, they must be accompanied by an auditor's report prepared in accordance with CICA Handbook Section 5600 *Auditor's Report on Financial Statements Prepared Using a Basis of Accounting other than Generally Accepted Auditing Principles* that does not contain a reservation.

NI 31-103 SECTION	QUESTION	ANSWER
	What is the basis of accounting and acceptable assurance requirements for audited non-consolidated financial statements that exclude comparative figures for entities registering with one or more of the securities regulators for the first time during the period prior to September 28, 2010?	The non-consolidated financial statements for the current period must be prepared in accordance with Canadian generally accepted accounting principles for public enterprises, except that they have been prepared on a non-consolidated basis and exclude comparative information. The financial statements must include a note describing this basis of accounting, and may not include any other material differences from Canadian generally accepted accounting principles for public enterprises.
		Since the annual non-consolidated financial statements are prepared in accordance with a basis of accounting other than generally accepted accounting principles, they must be accompanied by an auditor's report prepared in accordance with CICA Handbook Section 5600 *Auditor's Report on Financial Statements Prepared Using a Basis of Accounting other than Generally Accepted Auditing Principles* that does not contain a reservation.
	What is the basis of accounting and acceptable assurance requirements for non-consolidated comparative figures included in annual audited financial statements for entities registering with one or more of the securities regulators for the first time during the period prior to September 28, 2010?	The non-consolidated financial statements for the current period must be prepared in accordance with Canadian generally accepted accounting principles for public enterprises, except that they have been prepared on a non-consolidated basis. The financial statements must include a note describing this basis of accounting, and may not include any other material differences from Canadian generally accepted accounting principles for public enterprises.
		Since the annual non-consolidated financial statements are prepared in accordance with a basis of accounting other than generally accepted accounting principles, it must be accompanied by an auditor's report prepared in accordance with CICA Handbook Section 5600 *Auditor's Report on Financial Statements Prepared Using a Basis of Accounting other than Generally Accepted Auditing Principles* that does not contain a reservation.
	Will an application for registration delivered prior to September 28, 2010 be rejected if the audited non-consolidated financial statements delivered by the applicant do not include audited non-consolidated comparative figures?	No. An application will not be rejected solely on the basis of failure to provide audited non-consolidated comparative figures. However, we encourage such applicants to include non-consolidated comparative figures where possible, even if they are not available in audited form.
12.11(2)	**Interim financial information** Some registrants were previously required by the securities legislation of some provinces to deliver annual audited consolidated financial statements. Subsection 12.10(3) of NI 31-103 requires registrants to deliver financial statements prepared in accordance with National Instrument 52-107 *Acceptable Accounting Principles, Auditing*	For annual audited financial statements for financial years ended on or between September 30, 2009 to August 31, 2010 (and for interim periods within that period), staff will accept financial statements prepared under one of the following two options, even though these do not comply with NI 52-107:

NI 31-103 SECTION	QUESTION	ANSWER
	Standards and Reporting Currency (NI 52-107) except that the statements must be prepared on a non-consolidated basis. Interim financial information delivered under subsection 12.11(2) of NI 31-103 must also be delivered on a non-consolidated basis.	1) non-consolidated financial statements and interim financial information with no comparative figures, or 2) non-consolidated financial statements and interim financial information with non-consolidated comparative figures.
	For registrants that previously delivered audited consolidated financial statements, what comparative figures do regulators expect to be delivered in the first year after the effective date of NI 31-103 (i.e. for financial years ended on or between September 30, 2009 to August 31, 2010)?	CSA staff have concluded that, if a registrant delivers annual non-consolidated financial statements and interim financial information using one of the options above, it would not be appropriate or in the public interest for staff to impose terms and conditions on the registrant. CSA staff have concluded that it would not be appropriate for a registrant to deliver financial statements or interim financial information that includes a current period that is non-consolidated and a comparative period that is presented using a different basis of accounting (e.g. consolidated comparative information).
	What is the basis of accounting for interim financial information delivered by registrants?	The interim financial information must be prepared and presented on a similar basis as the annual non-consolidated financial statements (see discussion above with respect to subsection 12.10(3)).

NI 33-109 *Registration Information*

NI 33-109 SECTION	QUESTION	ANSWER
FORM 33-109F6 FIRM REGISTRATION	Will an application for registration delivered prior to September 28, 2010 be rejected if the audited non-consolidated financial statements delivered by the applicant do not include audited non-consolidated comparative figures?	No. An application will not be rejected solely on the basis of failure to provide audited non-consolidated comparative figures. However, we encourage such applicants to include non-consolidated comparative figures where possible, even if they are not available in audited form.

CSA Staff Notice 31-315 — Omnibus / Blanket Orders Exempting Registrants from Certain Provisions of NI 31-103 Registration Requirements and Exemptions

Date: February 26, 2010

33 O.S.C.B. 1737

[Not reproduced]

CSA Staff Notice 31-317 (Revised) — Reporting Obligations Related to Terrorist Financing

Date: April 16, 2010 as revised effective July 30, 2010

33 O.S.C.B. 3285 and 33 O.S.C.B. 6821

Since the Canadian Securities Administrators (CSA) published CSA Staff Notice 31-317 Reporting Obligations Related to Terrorist Financing for Registrants, Exempt International Dealers, and Exempt International Advisers on April 16, 2010 (the Notice), CSA staff have been receiving questions as to whether federal monthly reporting and other requirements relating to terrorist financing and United Nations sanctions apply to entities in the business of dealing or advising in securities who avail themselves of registration exemptions other than exempt international dealers and exempt international advisers. Under sections 8.18 and 8.26 of National Instrument 31-103 Registration Requirements and Exemptions (NI 31-103), international dealers and international advisers (as defined in NI 31-103) transitioned in certain CSA jurisdictions from registered firms to firms doing business pursuant to registration exemptions. In the Notice, the CSA made clear its expectation that newly exempted international dealers and international advisers would continue to comply with any applicable federal provisions relating to terrorist financing and United Nations sanctions. The Notice also sets out CSA staff's view on the mechanics of complying with the reporting requirements contemplated by the specified federal law.

The reporting obligations set out in section 83.11 of the Criminal Code *of Canada (the* **Criminal Code***) apply to entities "authorized under provincial legislation to engage in the business of dealing in securities, or to provide portfolio management or investment counselling services." The language in the* Criminal Code *does not limit the scope of these federal provisions to registered firms.*

Accordingly, the Notice and the corresponding consolidated CSA reporting form have been revised to clarify that the CSA expects exempt dealers and exempt advisers, provided that they engage in the business of "dealing in securities" or "providing portfolio management or investment counselling services" in any CSA jurisdiction, to comply with any applicable federal provisions relating to terrorist financing and United Nations sanctions.

The Canadian Securities Administrators (**CSA**) are issuing this Staff Notice regarding monthly reporting and other requirements relating to terrorist financing and United Nations Act sanctions on certain countries under the:

- *Criminal Code of Canada (**Criminal Code**)*
- *Regulations Implementing the United Nations Resolutions on the Suppression of Terrorism*
- *United Nations Al-Qaida and Taliban Regulations*
- *Regulations Implementing the United Nations Resolution on the Democratic People's Republic of Korea*
- *Regulations Implementing the United Nations Resolution on Iran*

While this Staff Notice reflects CSA staff views on the application of this federal law, those potentially affected by the federal law are advised to seek legal advice on the matters dealt with by this Notice.

The CSA are issuing this Notice for the following purposes:

- to provide registrants, entities engaging in the business of "dealing in securities" pursuant to exemptions from the dealer registration requirement (**exempt dealers**) and entities engaging in the business of providing "portfolio management or investment counselling services" pursuant to exemptions from the adviser registration requirement (**exempt advisers**) with information on the new consolidated reporting form that will be used by each principal regulator,

- to provide information regarding the submission of monthly reports and advise registrants, exempt dealers and exempt advisers that the report may be filed with the principal regulator by e-mail, and

- to provide summary information on the laws which impose the monthly reporting requirements on registrants, exempt dealers and exempt advisers.

In a number of cases, the federal law requires reports to be made to a "principal agency or body" supervising a person or entity. In the case of a registrant, CSA staff consider that this reference corresponds to a "principal regulator" for securities purposes. While the federal law is not specific on this point, for convenience CSA staff advise exempt dealers and exempt advisers to make these reports to the jurisdiction in Canada where most of their clients reside. In this Staff Notice, such a regulator is also referred to as a "principal regulator".

Note: This notice provides summary information only and reflects information as of the date set out above. Please refer to the text of the laws set out above for a complete description of your obligations.

Types of reporting

Registrants, exempt dealers and exempt advisers have certain obligations under federal laws. These include requirements for "persons and entities authorized under provincial legislation to engage in the business of dealing in securities, or to provide portfolio management or investment advising services" to provide specified monthly reports to the principal agency or body that supervises or regulates the registrant, exempt dealer or exempt adviser under federal or provincial law. The regulator, in turn, forwards information derived from these reports to the Office of the Superintendent of Financial Institutions (**OSFI**). Further information on these laws and the reporting obligations can be found on the OSFI website at: http://www.osfi-bsif.gc.ca.

There are two types of reporting to their principal regulator required of registrants, exempt dealers and exempt advisers:

- reporting against names listed under federal laws relating to terrorist financing

- reporting against names listed under federal laws relating to United Nations sanctions.

These were previously addressed by several CSA jurisdictions in two separate reporting forms. We have now consolidated these two types of reports into a single form that can be used for reporting by e-mail to the appropriate CSA member (i.e., the principal regulator).

Overview of the applicable laws

Terrorist financing

Registrants, exempt dealers and exempt advisers are subject to requirements under federal laws that, among other things, address the financing of terrorism and permit the listing of persons and entities in respect of which registrants, exempt dealers and exempt advisers (and others) must report dealings. Canada now has three mechanisms for designating individuals and entities as terrorists or terrorist organizations:

- *Criminal Code*

Part 3:
REGISTRATION

- *Regulations Implementing the United Nations Resolutions on the Suppression of Terrorism*, SOR/2001-360 (**UN SupTerror**) (formerly, the *United Nations Suppression of Terrorism Regulations*) (**Old UN SupTerror**)

- *United Nations Al-Qaida and Taliban Regulations*, SOR/99-444 (**UN Al-Qaida**) (formerly, the *United Nations Afghanistan Regulations*) (**Old UN Al-Qaida**)

In 2006, the federal government amended the regulations referred to above to ensure, among other things, that they correspond more closely to each other and to the requirements in the *Criminal Code*. This is set out in more detail in the regulatory impact analysis statement that accompanied the publication of the amendments in the *Canada Gazette* on July 12, 2006. For further details, please refer to the *Canada Gazette* website at http://www.gazette.gc.ca for July 12, 2006.

Generally, these amendments did not materially change the specific names and entities that were previously designated under the *Criminal Code* and the Old UN SupTerror and Old UN Al-Qaida. Names subject to the regulations made under the *Criminal Code* and those names subject to the UN SupTerror and the UN Al-Qaida have been combined into the lists currently posted on the OSFI website at http://www.osfi-bsif.gc.ca.

United Nations Act sanctions

In addition to the regulations referred to above, the government has enacted the:

- *Regulations Implementing the United Nations Resolution on the Democratic People's Republic of Korea* (**UN NKorea**), SOR/2006-287 (November 9, 2006)

- *Regulations Implementing the United Nations Resolution on Iran* (**UN Iran**), SOR/2007-44 (February 22, 2007)

The UN NKorea were published in Part II of the Canada Gazette on November 29, 2006 and the UN Iran were published in Part II of the Canada Gazette on March 7, 2007: http://www.gazette.gc.ca

Among other things, the UN NKorea and the UN Iran impose similar prohibitions, searching obligations and monthly reporting requirements with respect to designated persons, as are contained in the *Criminal Code*, the UN SupTerror and the UN Al-Qaida. For more information, please refer to the November 29, 2006 and the February 27, 2007 supervisory advisory letters from OSFI at: http://www.osfi-bsif.gc.ca

Please note that the lists of designated persons for the UN Iran and the UN NKorea are available on the OSFI website at: http://www.osfi-bsif.gc.ca. The lists can also be found at the annex to United Nations Security Council Resolution 1737 (2006), which is at: http://www.un.org

Overview of certain duties

The duties imposed under the laws referred to above may include the following:

Duty to review and make filings

Under section 83.11 of the *Criminal Code*, section 7 of the UN SupTerror, section 5.1 of the UN Al-Qaida, section 11 of the UN Iran and section 11 of the UN NKorea:

- you must review your records on a continuing basis to determine whether you are in possession or control of property owned or controlled by or on behalf of a designated person and report your findings on a monthly basis

- if you determine that none of your clients are designated persons you are still required to report to your principal regulator that you have a *Nil* response. The term "designated person" in this Notice includes listed entities under the *Criminal Code*, listed persons under the UN SupTerror and those persons and entities covered by the UN Al-Qaida, the UN Iran and the UN NKorea.)

Reports are to be provided on the 14th day of each month, to your principal regulator. A senior officer of the firm, preferably the Chief Compliance Officer, should sign the monthly report.

As noted above, the OSFI website contains updated consolidated lists of designated persons for purposes of the *Criminal Code*, the UN SupTerror and the UN Al-Qaida. OSFI has also made available a listing of designated persons under the UN Iran and the UN NKorea. These lists are available in downloadable and printable formats.

Please refer to the updated lists on the OSFI website prior to completing each report. Please also note that OSFI amends its lists from time to time, as a result of corrections made by the United Nations Security Council (**UNSC**) to the list of designated persons, even though such changes have not been specifically highlighted by the UNSC. Because of the nature of these amendments, it is not practical for OSFI to identify them in detail.

Therefore, it is important that registrants, exempt dealers and exempt advisers download the consolidated lists periodically; OSFI recommends that this be done on a monthly basis.

Freezing property

Under section 83.08 of the *Criminal Code*, section 4 of the UN SupTerror, sections 4 and 4.1 of the UN Al-Qaida, section 9 of the UN Iran and section 9 of the UN NKorea, no person in Canada and no Canadian outside Canada shall knowingly:

- deal, directly or indirectly, with property of a designated person

- enter into or facilitate, directly or indirectly, any transaction in respect of such property

- provide any financial or other services in respect of such property.

In addition, section 4 of the UN SupTerror, sections 4 and 4.1 of the UN Al-Qaida, section 9 of the UN Iran and section 9 of the UN NKorea prohibit making any property or any other financial or other related service available to or for the benefit of a designated person. Consequently, any property held directly or indirectly on behalf of a designated person must be held or be frozen.

We note that OSFI has indicated that these prohibitions extend to the debiting of service charges and crediting of interest and/or if the frozen property is a securities portfolio, the crediting of interest, dividends or other entitlements and the charging of custodial fees, transaction fees or any other debits or credits to the account: see the "Special Comments" in OSFI's November 30, 2006 reminder letter re monthly reporting, which can be found on the OSFI website at the link set out above.

Duty to disclose

Under section 83.1 of the *Criminal Code*, section 8 of the UN SupTerror, section 5.2 of the UN Al-Qaida, section 12 of the UN Iran and section 12 of the UN NKorea, every person in Canada and every Canadian outside Canada must forthwith report to both the RCMP and CSIS any property held for any designated person and any information about transactions or proposed transactions with respect to that property. Information may be provided to these organizations as follows:

- **RCMP**

  Anti-terrorist Financing Group

  Unclassified fax: (613) 993-9474

- **CSIS Financing Unit**

  Unclassified fax: (613) 231-0266

In addition, under section 7.1 of the *Proceeds of Crime (Money Laundering) and Terrorist Financing Act*, persons and entities reporting to the RCMP and CSIS that are also reporting entities under that section are required to submit a terrorist property report to the Financial Transactions and Reports Analysis Centre of Canada (**FINTRAC**).

For instructions relating to the preparation and submission of this report, reporting entities should visit the FINTRAC website at: http://www.fintrac-canafe.gc.ca

New consolidated reporting form

The CSA regulators have revised their previous reporting forms to create a new CSA consolidated form. In addition, in order to keep reporting requirements to the principal regulator as streamlined as possible we have also changed the reporting process to allow for the new form to be submitted to the principal regulator by e-mail. Members of the Investment Industry Regulatory Organization of Canada (**IIROC**) are requested to use the appropriate reporting forms issued by, and file those forms with, IIROC.

Registrants, exempt dealers and exempt advisers should file only one monthly consolidated report in respect of the laws relating to both terrorist financing and United Nations Act sanctions, even though names may be listed under several or all of the laws referred to above.

Registrants, exempt dealers and exempt advisers should use the new reporting form and submit their report to their principal regulator by e-mail.

The new consolidated CSA reporting form for registrants, exempt dealers and exempt advisers to use in complying with their monthly reporting obligations under the *Criminal Code*, UN SupTerror, the UN Al-Qaida, the UN NKorea and the UN Iran is available on the websites of the CSA regulators.

Please refer to the attached Appendix A for the website address of your principal regulator (please complete the form, print it, and have it signed by the appropriate individual before you scan it for e-mailing to your principal regulator).

The e-mail address for submitting your report to your principal regulator is listed in the attached Appendix A. If you have any questions about these requirements, you can contact your principal regulator at the telephone number or e-mail address listed in the Appendix A.

Note: This Notice provides summary information only. Please refer to the text of the laws set out above for a complete description of your obligations. Some of the laws referred to above also contain certain additional prohibitions and obligations regarding dealings with persons in certain countries. You should read the laws carefully for a complete description of the applicable obligations.

In addition, there are other federal regulations that may be applicable to registrants, exempt dealers and exempt advisers that include searching, monitoring, asset freezing and reporting obligations with respect to designated persons (as defined in the respective regulations). In the case of reporting obligations under some of these other regulations, you must report to the RCMP, rather than to your principal regulator.

Registrants, exempt dealers and exempt advisers should continue to monitor the notices from OSFI for any new regulations that may come into effect regarding similar obligations, or updates to existing obligations to search, monitor and report. You may want to visit the OSFI website http://www.osfi-bsif.gc.ca for the purpose of familiarizing yourself with the reporting requirements and any other obligations. In addition, we encourage you to subscribe to the notification service on the OSFI website http://www.osfi-bsif.gc.ca in order to receive new updating e-mail notices and reminders concerning new developments and reporting requirements.

Appendix A — List of CSA Regulators E-mail Addresses, Websites, and inquiry details for Monthly Reporting (Please send the reports to the e-mail address of your principal regulator only — Attention: UN Reports)

Alberta

Alberta Securities Commission

Web: www.albertasecurities.com

Questions: registration@asc.ca

E-mail to: unreports@asc.ca

British Columbia

British Columbia Securities Commission

Web: www.bcsc.bc.ca

Questions: 604 899-6667

E-mail to: mstreport@bcsc.bc.ca

Manitoba

The Manitoba Securities Commission

Web: www.msc.gov.mb.ca

Questions: 204-945-5195 or

paula.white@gov.mb.ca

e-mail to: unreports@gov.mb.ca

New Brunswick

New Brunswick Securities Commission

Web: www.nbsc-cvmnb.ca

Questions: 506 658 3060

E-mail to: nrs@nbsc-cvmnb.ca

Newfoundland and Labrador

Securities NL

Financial Services Regulation Division

Department of Government Services

Web: www.gs.gov.nl.ca

Questions: 709 729-0959

Email to: scon@gov.nl.ca

Nova Scotia

Nova Scotia Securities Commission

Web: www.gov.ns.ca/nssc/

Questions: 902 424-4592

E-Mail to: MURPHYBW@gov.ns.ca

Northwest Territories

Government of the Northwest Territories

Office of Superintendent of Securities

Department of Justice

Web: www.justice.gov.nt.ca/SecuritiesRegistry

Questions: 867 920- 3318

E-Mail to: SecuritiesRegistries@gov.nt.ca

Nunavut

Government of Nunavut

Office of Superintendent of Securities

Department of Justice

Web: www.justice.gov.nu.ca

Questions: 867 975-6590

E-mail to: theffernan@gov.nu.ca

or CorporateRegistrations@gov.nu.ca

Ontario

Ontario Securities Commission

Web: www.osc.gov.on.ca

Questions: 416 593-8314 or 1-877-785-1555

E-mail to: UNReports@osc.gov.on.ca

Prince Edward Island

Superintendent of Securities

Office of the Attorney General

Web: www.gov.pe.ca/securities

Questions: 902 368-4542

E-mail to: kptummon@gov.pe.ca

Québec

Autorité des marchés financiers

Web: www.lautorite.qc.ca

Questions: 1 877 525-0337 Ext 4755

E-mail to: rapportsterrorisme@lautorite.qc.ca

Saskatchewan

Saskatchewan Financial Services Commission

Web: www.sfsc.gov.sk.ca

Questions: 306 787-9397

E-mail to: registrationsfsc@gov.sk.ca

Yukon

Department of Community Services Yukon

Corporate Affairs (C-6)

Superintendent of Securities

Web:www.community.gov.yk.ca/corp/secureinvest.html

Questions: 867 667-5225

E-mail to: corporateaffairs@gov.yk.ca

CSA/ACVM   **Autorités canadiennes en valeurs mobilières**

Canadian Securities Administrators

Confidential when completed

Revised July 30, 2010

Monthly Suppression of Terrorism and UN Sanctions Report

Suppression of Terrorism — Report under section 83.11 of the Criminal Code of Canada (Criminal Code) and section 7 of the Regulations Implementing the United Nations Resolutions on the Suppression of Terrorism (UN SupTerror) and section 5.1 of the United Nations Al-Qaida and Taliban Regulations (UN Al-Qaida)

    and

UN Sanctions — Report under subsection 11(2) of the Regulations Implementing the United Nations Resolution on Iran (UN Iran) or subsection 11(2) of the Regulations Implementing the United Nations Resolution on the Democratic People's Republic of Korea (UN NKorea)

**Name of Registrant/Exempt
Dealer/Exempt Adviser:**

         Date of filing of this report: ..../.........

                                                              (dd/ (mm)/ yy)

Address:

         Monthly period covered in this report: ..../........../.........

         (see Note 2)   (dd/ (mm)/ yy)

                                                    to   ..../........../.........

                                                                (dd/ (mm)/ yy)

Type of Registration or Exempt Dealer/Exempt Adviser:
(check all applicable categories):

                                                 ❏   Exempt Adviser

                                                 ❏   Exempt Dealer

                                                 ❏   Exempt Market Dealer (Registered)

                                                 ❏   Investment Dealer

**Part 3:
REGISTRATION**

❑ Investment Fund Manager"
❑ Mutual Fund Dealer
❑ Portfolio Manager
❑ Restricted Dealer
❑ Restricted Portfolio Manager
❑ Scholarship Plan Dealer
❑ Other ....

"only required to file if also in the business of dealing and/or advising in securities

If you have a POSITIVE REPORT to file, check "YES", then fill out page three of this form, sign the certificate section at page 4 and file this report.

If you have a NIL REPORT to file, check "NO", then sign the certificate section below and file this report.

Yes ❑ The above Registrant/Exempt Dealer/Exempt Adviser has accounts in the name of a Designated Person*, or has contracts with a Designated Person, or possesses or controls property that is owned or controlled by or on behalf of a Designated Person.

No ❑ The above Registrant/Exempt Dealer/Exempt Adviser does not have an account in the name of a Designated Person*, or have a contract with a Designated Person, or possess or control property that is owned or controlled by or on behalf of a Designated Person. • Please refer to the definitions at page 3 for the definition of "Designated Person".

* Please refer to the definitions at page 3 for the definition of "Designated Person".

* Please refer to the definitions at page 3 for the definition of "Designated Person".

Certificate

The Undersigned certifies that, to the best of his/her knowledge, and after having made reasonable enquires, the information contained in this report is correct.

Name	Signature	Title	Telephone	Date (dd/mm/yyyy):
....	....	....	....	

If you have checked the "Yes" box above, please complete the table below and the certificate at the end of this form.

Definitions:

- "Number of Accounts" means the number of accounts, policies or contracts associated with a Designated Person.

- "Designated Person", for purposes of the Suppression of Terrorism report, refers to the persons and entities listed as of the end of the month prior to the date of the report. The listing consists of the names of listed entities under the Criminal Code, listed persons under the UN SupTerror and those persons and entities covered by the UN Al-Qaida which have been combined into the list currently posted on the Office of the Superintendent of Financial Institutions (OSFI) website: http://www.osfi-bsif.gc.ca. For purposes of the UN Sanctions report, "Designated Person" has the meaning assigned to it under section 1 of the UN Iran (see list of Designated Persons under the UN Iran, on the OSFI website) or section 1 of the UN NKorea (see list of Designated Persons under the UN NKorea on the OSFI website)

- "Property" has the meaning assigned to it under the Criminal Code, the UN SupTerror and the UN Al-Qaida, and under section 1 of the UN Iran and section 1 of UN NKorea and includes assets under administration (both discretionary and non-discretionary).

SUMMARY OF PROPERTY (see Note 3)

Type of Property	Number of Accounts (see Note 2)		Property Value (Canadian $) (see Note 3)	
	Suppression of Terrorism (combined list for Criminal Code, UN SupTerror and UN Al-Qaida)	UN Sanctions (list $ for UN Iran and UN NKorea)	Suppression of Terrorism (combined list for Criminal Code, UN SupTerror and UN Al-Qaida)	UN Sanctions (list $ for UN Iran and UN NKorea)
Cash, cash equivalents, demand and term deposits	....	....	....	....

SUMMARY OF PROPERTY (see Note 3)

Type of Property	Number of Accounts (see Note 2)		Property Value (Canadian $) (see Note 3)	
	Suppression of Terrorism (combined list for Criminal Code, UN SupTerror and UN Al-Qaida)	UN Sanctions (list $ for UN Iran and UN NKorea)	Suppression of Terrorism (combined list for Criminal Code, UN SupTerror and UN Al-Qaida)	UN Sanctions (list $ for UN Iran and UN NKorea)
Securities (bonds, debentures, commercial paper, treasury bills, mutual fund units, scholarship plan units, common and preferred shares and derivatives).	....	....	....	....
Loans (including, mortgages, overdrafts, credit card balances, term loans, lines of credit and other indebtedness)	....	....	....	....
Annuities (cash surrender value/monthly income)	....	....	....	....
Life insurance policies	....	....	....	....
Property & casualty insurance policies (policy limit)	....	....	....	....
Other property, including real estate	....	....	....	....
Total	0	0	$0.00	$0.00

Certificate

The Undersigned certifies that, to the best of his/her knowledge, and after having made reasonable enquires, the information contained in this report is correct and, if applicable, any property summarized has been frozen and the relevant account details have been reported to the Royal Canadian Mounted Police and the Canadian Security Intelligence Service and, if applicable, the Financial Transactions and Reports Analysis Centre of Canada, and in respect of any foreign operations, to foreign law enforcement officials, as appropriate.

Name	Signature	Title	Telephone	Date (dd/mm/yyyy)
....	....	....	....	....

Instructions:

This report must be filed by every entity that is authorized under provincial legislation to engage in the business of dealing in securities, or to provide portfolio management or investment counselling services ("Registrants/Exempt Dealers/Exempt Advisers") (see Note 1). The report must be sent to the e-mail address that has been set up to receive these reports of your principal regulator no later than the fourteenth (14th) day of each calendar month. Please see Appendix A of this form for the e-mail address designated by each of the CSA regulators for this purpose. If such day falls on Saturday, Sunday or statutory holiday, the report is due on the next business day. The reporting month is the month on which the report is based (e.g. for the report due on December 14, the reporting month would be November). You must review your records on a continuing basis for any dealing with Designated Persons. You must consult the updated combined list of names for UN SupTerror and the list of names under the UN Iran and UN NKorea, posted on the OSFI website http://www.osfi-bsif.gc.ca before filing the report.

Notes:

Part 3: REGISTRATION

These Notes are provided as general information only. They do not constitute legal advice, and are not intended to replace the laws referred to in this report. You should refer to these laws for full details regarding your obligations.

1. The information required in this report is required pursuant to section 83.11 of the *Criminal Code*, section 7 of the UN SupTerror, section 5.1 of the UN Al-Qaida, and subsection 11(2) of the UN Iran and subsection 11(2) of the UN NKorea. Reports must be filed by all entities authorized under provincial legislation to engage in the business of dealing in securities or to provide portfolio management or investment counselling services. Members of the Investment Industry Regulatory Organization of Canada (IIROC) are requested to use the appropriate reporting forms issued by, and file those forms with, IIROC.

2. All reports must cover continuous dates and there must be no gaps in the reporting periods starting with the first day of each month and ending with the last day. The report is cumulative; therefore, you must continue to include information reported in a previous report, provided that the information remains unchanged.

3. All amounts must be stated in Canadian dollars. NOTE: If the original amount of the property frozen is denominated in a currency other than Canadian dollars, then the Canadian dollar equivalent should be reported using the same rate of exchange that was in effect on the date that the property was originally frozen and reported to law enforcement.

4. You must include information from any branches located outside Canada.

5. This is an aggregate report of dealings that Registrants/Exempt Dealers/Exempt Advisers have with Designated Persons. Do not append personal information or account or policy information. Such information must be directed, if applicable, to the Royal Canadian Mounted Police, the Canadian Security Intelligence Service, and if applicable, the Financial Transactions and Reports Analysis Centre of Canada (FINTRAC) and, in respect of any foreign operations, to foreign law enforcement officials.

6. If there are no assets frozen, you may file a NIL report by checking the "No" box on page 2 to confirm this. This includes situations where you may be seeking clarification from the authorities about whether an account holder is in fact a Designated Person; in other words you may file a NIL report where you have not made a determination that you are dealing with a Designated Person. There is no need to report numbers of accounts where you are still seeking clarification from the authorities.

Reminder: Section 83.1 of the Criminal Code, section 8 of the UN SupTerror, section 5.2 of the UN Al-Qaida, section 12 of the UN Iran and section 12 of the UN NKorea require every person in Canada and every Canadian outside of Canada to disclose forthwith to the Commissioner of the Royal Canadian Mounted Police and the Director of the Canadian Security Intelligence Service (a) the existence of property in their possession or control that they know or have reason to believe is owned or controlled by or on behalf of a Designated Person, and (b) information about a transaction or proposed transaction in respect of a property in their possession or control that they know or have reason to believe is owned or controlled by or on behalf of a Designated Person. In addition, under the Proceeds of Crime (Money Laundering) and Terrorist Financing Act, persons subject to Part 1 of that Act are also required to report to the FINTRAC.

Appendix A — List of CSA Regulators E-mail Addresses, Websites, and inquiry details for Monthly Reporting (Please send the reports to the e-mail address of your principal regulator only- Attention: UN Reports)

Alberta

Alberta Securities Commission

Web: www.albertasecurities.com

Questions: registration@asc.ca

E-mail to: unreports@asc.ca

British Columbia

British Columbia Securities Commission

Web: www.bcsc.bc.ca

Questions: 604 899-6667

E-mail to: mstreport@bcsc.bc.ca

Manitoba

The Manitoba Securities Commission

Web: www.msc.gov.mb.ca

Questions: 204-945-5195 or

paula.white@gov.mb.ca

e-mail to: unreports@gov.mb.ca

New Brunswick

New Brunswick Securities Commission

Web: www.nbsc-cvmnb.ca

Questions: 506 658 3060

E-mail to: nrs@nbsc-cvmnb.ca

Newfoundland and Labrador

Securities NL

Financial Services Regulation Division

Department of Government Services

Web: www.gs.gov.nl.ca

Questions: 709 729-0959

Email to: scon@gov.nl.ca

Northwest Territories

Government of the Northwest Territories

Office of Superintendent of Securities

Department of Justice

Web: www.justice.gov.nt.ca/SecuritiesRegistry

Questions: 867 920- 3318

E-Mail to: SecuritiesRegistries@gov.nt.ca

Nova Scotia

Nova Scotia Securities Commission

Web: www.gov.ns.ca/nssc/

Questions: 902 424-4592

E-Mail to: MURPHYBW@gov.ns.ca

Nunavut

Government of Nunavut

Office of Superintendent of Securities

Department of Justice

Web: www.justice.gov.nu.ca

Questions: 867 975-6590

E-mail to: theffernan@gov.nu.ca

or CorporateRegistrations@gov.nu.ca

Ontario

Ontario Securities Commission

Web: www.osc.gov.on.ca

Questions: 416 593-8314 or 1-877-785-1555

E-mail to: UNReports@osc.gov.on.ca

Prince Edward Island

Superintendent of Securities

Office of the Attorney General

Web: www.gov.pe.ca/securities

Questions: 902 368-4542

E-mail to: kptummon@gov.pe.ca

Québec

Autorité des marchés financiers

Web: www.lautorite.qc.ca

Questions: 1 877 525-0337 Ext 4755

E-mail to: rapportsterrorisme@lautorite.qc.ca

Saskatchewan

Saskatchewan Financial Services Commission

Web: www.sfsc.gov.sk.ca

Questions: 306 787-9397

E-mail to: registrationsfsc@gov.sk.ca

Yukon

Department of Community Services Yukon

Corporate Affairs (C-6)

Superintendent of Securities

Web: www.community.gov.yk.ca/corp/secureinvest.html

Questions: 867 667-5225

E-mail to: corporateaffairs@gov.yk.ca

CSA Notice 31-320 — Additional Request for Comment on Proposed Exemptions from Investment Fund Manager Registration Requirement for International and Certain Domestic Investment Fund Managers

Date: October 15, 2010

33 O.S.C.B. 9637

[Not reproduced]

CSA Staff Notice 31-323 — Guidance Relating to the Registration Obligations of Mortgage Investment Entities

Date: February 25, 2011

34 O.S.C.B. 2248

On August 20, 2010, each of the members of the Canadian Securities Administrators (the CSA or we) issued parallel orders providing exemptive relief for mortgage investment entities (MIEs) from the investment fund manager registration requirement and the adviser registration requirement under securities legislation until December 31, 2010. This relief was granted to allow each of the CSA members to review the requirement for MIEs to register as investment fund managers and advisers.

On December 3, 2010, all jurisdictions except British Columbia extended the relief until March 31, 2011. British Columbia extended the relief until June 30, 2011.

This Notice is to clarify the registration requirements that apply to MIEs in each of the CSA jurisdictions pursuant to the requirements of National Instrument *31-103 Registration Requirements and Exemptions (NI 31-103)*.

Definition of MIE

In this guidance, the term MIE refers to a person or company whose purpose is to directly or indirectly invest substantially all of its assets in debts owing to it that are secured by mortgages, hypothecs or in any other manner on real property (collectively, "mortgages" for purposes of this guidance), and whose other assets are limited to:

- deposits with a bank or other financial institution

- cash

- debt securities referenced in section 8.21 *[Specified debt]* of NI 31-103

- real property which is directly or indirectly held on a temporary basis as a result of action taken to enforce its rights as a secured lender

- instruments intended solely to hedge specific risks relating to the debts owing to it that are secured by mortgages, hypothecs or in any other manner on real property

Mortgage syndications

A MIE holding an interest in a single mortgage will not typically be subject to the investment fund manager registration requirement where that MIE or a related entity had a role in the creation or syndication of that mortgage (such MIEs are commonly referred to as "mortgage syndications").

Pooled MIEs

Investment Fund Manager registration

The applicability of the investment fund manager registration requirement to a MIE managing a portfolio of mortgages (Pooled MIE) varies in different CSA jurisdictions. Pooled MIEs commonly include "mortgage investment corporations" as defined in the *Income Tax Act* (Canada).

(a) — In jurisdictions other than Alberta

In all CSA jurisdictions other than Alberta, a Pooled MIE may or may not be subject to the investment fund manager registration requirement based on the criteria below.

A Pooled MIE will be considered to be an *investment fund* if its primary activity is managing an investment portfolio that includes mortgages. Factors that we would consider relevant to this determination include:

- the Pooled MIE does not take an active role in originating the mortgages that become part of the investment portfolio, and

- the Pooled MIE buys or sells mortgages in accordance with a stated portfolio investment strategy.

A Pooled MIE that is an investment fund must ensure that the person or company that directs its business, operations or affairs is registered as an investment fund manager.

A Pooled MIE will not be considered to be an *investment fund* if its primary activity is mortgage lending, that is, by operating a business that creates and manages mortgages. Factors that we would consider relevant to this determination include:

- the Pooled MIE originates the mortgages in the name of the Pooled MIE directly or through an agent retained by the Pooled MIE and acting on its behalf

- the Pooled MIE funds the mortgages

- the Pooled MIE enters into the mortgage agreements as the mortgagee, and

- the Pooled MIE administers the mortgages, either directly or through an agent acting on its behalf

The investment fund manager registration requirement will not typically apply in respect of a Pooled MIE that is not an investment fund.

(b) — In Alberta

For a Pooled MIE whose principal jurisdiction is Alberta, the above stated analysis with respect to determining whether a Pooled MIE is subject to the investment fund registration requirement does not apply. Instead, a Pooled MIE that has the power to direct and exercises the responsibility of directing the affairs of an "investment fund" as defined in the *Securities Act* (Alberta) will be required to register as an investment fund manager. A Pooled MIE that does not have the power to direct and does not exercise the responsibility of directing the affairs of an investment fund will not be subject to the investment fund manager registration requirement.

If an entity is uncertain about whether it is subject to the investment fund manager registration requirement, it should consider whether the Pooled MIE is an "investment fund" for the purposes of securities legislation. Sections 7.3 of Companion Policy 31-103CP *Registration Requirements and Exemptions* (31-103CP) and 1.2 of Companion Policy 81-106CP *Investment Fund Continuous Disclosure* provide guidance on the general nature of investment funds.

Adviser registration

A person or company that advises a Pooled MIE that is an investment fund about investing in or buying or selling mortgages or other securities will be subject to the adviser registration requirement if it is in the business of advising in securities. A person or company that advises a Pooled MIE that is not an investment fund should consider whether it is in the business of advising in securities as outlined in the guidance in section 1.3 of 31-103CP and, on that basis, required to register.

We will consider applications from advisers to Pooled MIEs for discretionary exemptions from the prescribed portfolio manager proficiencies. If exempted, an adviser will typically be registered as a restricted portfolio manager, with terms and conditions limiting its registration to advising in respect of the Pooled MIE's activities.

In jurisdictions where mortgage broker legislation prescribes proficiency requirements for MIEs, we may consider those to be acceptable alternatives to the proficiency requirements in securities legislation. Such exemptions from the proficiency requirements will also be considered in jurisdictions that do not have mortgage broker legislation that prescribes proficiency requirements applicable to MIEs.

Dealer registration

In all CSA jurisdictions except British Columbia, a MIE or any other person or company trading its securities will be subject to the dealer registration requirement if it is in the business of trading in securities. If a MIE or any other person or company trading its securities is uncertain about whether it must register as a dealer, it should consider whether it is in the business of trading in securities as outlined in the guidance in section 1.3 of 31-103CP.

In British Columbia, a MIE will not be subject to dealer registration until BC Instrument 32-517 in British Columbia expires on June 30, 2011. The British Columbia Securities Commission will issue further guidance about the dealer registration requirement for MIEs in B.C. prior to June 30, 2011.

Ongoing Monitoring

The Ontario Securities Commission intends to monitor the application of registration requirements to MIEs operating in Ontario under different business models and structures and may review its position if investor protection concerns are identified.

CSA Staff Notice 31-324 — Exempt Market Dealers and Account Statement Requirements in National Instrument 31-103 Registration Requirements and Exemptions

Date: June 22, 2011

34 O.S.C.B. 6970

Exempt Market Dealer (**EMD**) is a new registration category introduced with National Instrument 31-103 *Registration Requirements and Exemptions* (**NI 31-103**). This Staff Notice:

- sets out our expectations for EMDs' compliance with the account statement requirements in NI 31-103

- notes that we will focus attention on EMDs distributing securities of related or connected issuers

- draws attention to guidance we have published on the valuation of securities

Part 3: REGISTRATION

Account statement requirements

As registered firms, EMDs are required to deliver client statements, also referred to as "account statements". EMDs must deliver account statements to their clients at least once every three months (**quarterly account statements**) and may also be required to deliver a monthly account statement if a transaction is effected in the account during that month, other than transactions made under an automatic withdrawal/payment plan (**end-of-month account statements**).

Account statements have two main components:

- **transaction information** relating to transactions the registered firm has effected for its client during the reporting period, and

- **account balance information** relating to cash and all securities that are in the client's account as at the end of the reporting period

The account statement requirements are found in section 14.14 of NI 31-103. The requirement for quarterly account statements of a registered dealer is found in subsection 14.14(1). The requirement for end-of-month account statements of a registered dealer is found in paragraph 14.14(2)(b). Transaction information is prescribed in subsection 14.14 (4). Account balance information for cash and securities that are in the client's account is prescribed in subsection 14.14(5).

The requirement to deliver quarterly account statements applies to all registered firms. These statements must include transaction information for all transactions made for the client during the period. However, the requirements to send an end-of-month account statement and provide account balance information are connected to transactions, cash or securities that are "in the account" of the client.

NI 31-103 does not specify what securities the Canadian Securities Administrators (the **CSA** or **we**) consider to be in the account and, so far, we have not published guidance on how we would interpret those words. As firms registered in a new category, EMDs have no established industry practice in this regard, unlike advisers or dealers registered in other categories.

Securities of a client which a registered firm holds or controls are in the client's account, and the established practice of registered dealers and advisers is to provide account balance information on securities they hold or control. In many cases, they also provide account balance information on securities that they have sold to clients, but do not hold or control. Examples of securities of a client not held or controlled by their dealer or adviser include those registered in a client's name on a third-party issuer's books ("client name" securities), or securities issued in certificate form that are kept in the possession of the client. For firms that are members of the *Investment Industry Regulatory Organization of Canada* (**IIROC**) or the *Mutual Fund Dealers Association of Canada* (**MFDA**), what securities must be included in account statements is set out in rules of their self-regulatory organization (**SRO**).

Staff expectations for contents of account statements

We acknowledge that it may be difficult for EMDs to develop systems to provide their clients with account balance information without having a requirement or guidance specifying which securities of a client should be considered to be in the account for those purposes.

CSA staff are currently developing proposals for further requirements or guidance on the content of account statements. In the meantime, until we publish new guidance, or new requirements come into effect, we will *not* expect an EMD to:

- deliver end-of-month account statements, or

- include account balance information in quarterly account statements,

in connection with securities of a client that are not held or controlled by the EMD.

We *will* expect an EMD to deliver quarterly account statements containing:

- transaction information covering each transaction it made for a client during the quarter, and

- account balance information for all cash and securities of the client that it holds or controls

If an EMD does not hold or control any cash or securities of a client, and it makes no transactions for the client during a quarter, we will not expect the EMD to send an account statement for that quarter to the client.

Where an EMD is also registered in another dealer category or as an adviser, we will expect it to provide all of its clients with account statements that are consistent with its practices under the other category of registration. An EMD that is also registered in a category that requires membership in IIROC or the MFDA must comply with applicable SRO rules.

We encourage EMDs that have adopted the practice of delivering account statements that include account balance information about securities that they do not hold and control to continue to do so.

Transitional relief in Ontario and Newfoundland and Labrador

In Ontario and Newfoundland and Labrador, there is transitional relief from the account statement requirement (i.e., section 14.14) for EMDs that had been registered under the former registration category of limited market dealer (referred to as "mapped-over" EMDs). This transitional relief remains available until its scheduled expiry on September 28, 2011. After that date, mapped-over EMDs will be expected to deliver account statements that are, at a minimum, consistent with the guidance in this Notice.

Securities of related or connected issuers

We have identified a disproportionate rate of compliance deficiencies among EMDs that distribute the securities of related or connected issuers where the same individuals form the management of both the EMD and the issuer. Specific instances include failure to adequately discharge the EMD's know-your-client obligation and obligation to make a determination that an investment is suitable for its client. We have also found cases of such EMDs failing to deal fairly, honestly and in good faith with their clients by using investor proceeds raised by them for their related or connected issuers for purposes other than those disclosed and marketed to investors.

Staff will focus compliance attention in this area, including monitoring client reporting by such EMDs. We will take enforcement action or other regulatory action where they are found to be acting contrary to securities law.

For guidance on when we will consider an issuer to be related or connected to an EMD, see the definitions in National Instrument 33-105 *Underwriting Conflicts* and its Companion Policy.

Valuation of securities

With respect to the requirement to include market valuations of clients' securities in account balance information, we draw attention to the guidance on the market value of securities in our proposed amendments to the companion policy to NI 31-103 that were published today as part of our proposals for cost disclosure and performance reporting by registrants. This guidance is consistent with what we previously published in the NI 31-103 "frequently asked questions" (**FAQ**). The proposed amendments and FAQ are available on CSA websites, including:

> www.albertasecurities.com
>
> www.lautorite.qc.ca
>
> www.bcsc.bc.ca
>
> www.msc.gov.mb.ca
>
> www.gov.ns.ca/nssc
>
> www.nbsc-cvmnb.ca
>
> www.osc.gov.on.ca

CSA Staff Notice 31-325 — Marketing Practices of Portfolio Managers

Date: July 5, 2011

34 O.S.C.B. 7436

Purpose

Staff in various provinces from the Canadian Securities Administrators (CSA staff or we) conducted a focused compliance review (the review) of the marketing practices of firms registered as portfolio managers (PMs). This notice summarizes our findings from the review and provides guidance to portfolio managers on suggested practices in the preparation, review and use of marketing materials. We will also use this notice to assess the marketing practices of other registered firms, where appropriate.

Background

The marketing practices of PMs are an ongoing area of concern for the CSA because the materials PMs use when marketing their firm's services, skills and experience influence investors.

We continue to see a number of issues in the marketing practices of PMs, including those that advise and market non-prospectus qualified investment funds, such as pooled funds and hedge funds.

As a result, the CSA Compliance Committee (the Committee) decided to conduct the review as part of our goal to better understand the marketing practices used by PMs and to harmonize compliance oversight approaches across Canada.

For Ontario PMs

In the fiscal year 2006/07, the Ontario Securities Commission (OSC) completed a focused review of the marketing practices of Investment Counsel/Portfolio Managers (now PMs). The concerns identified, as well as suggested practices, were outlined in OSC Staff Notice 33-729 — *Marketing Practices of Investment Counsel/Portfolio Managers* (Ontario Notice). The findings in this notice are generally consistent with the Ontario Notice published in November 2007. However, this notice includes issues and guidance in new areas and includes updates in certain areas previously identified in the Ontario Notice.

The discussion of items 1, 3 and 8 below have been updated from the Ontario Notice based on new guidance. Items 6 and 7 are new issues not previously discussed in the Ontario Notice. All remaining items provide guidance consistent with the Ontario Notice.

This notice also updates the Ontario Notice on the use of hypothetical performance data as a result of further information gathered by the OSC and other CSA staff from ongoing compliance reviews and from industry consultations.

Objectives of the Review

The main objectives of the review were to:

- assess PMs' compliance with applicable securities laws
- broaden our understanding of the types and content of marketing materials PMs use
- develop a consistent compliance approach when reviewing a firm's marketing practices

Scope and Methodology

The Committee gathered preliminary information on the PM firms' marketing activities through a survey. The Committee then used a risk-based approach to select a representative sample of 56 PMs for a review of their marketing practices. We also reviewed other aspects of the PMs' operations.

The sample included PMs of:

- non-prospectus qualified investment funds (i.e. pooled funds and hedge funds)
- large institutional investors
- retail and private clients

These PMs, in many instances, were also registered in other categories of registration including investment fund manager and exempt market dealer. We did not focus on mutual fund sales communications that are governed under National Instrument 81-102 — *Investment Funds* as this was beyond the scope of our review.

Outcome

We sent a compliance deficiency report to each of the PMs selected for a review. We required each PM to submit a written response to the deficiencies we identified, including the proposed corrective actions they would take.

CSA staff will work with these PMs to ensure they address and resolve the marketing, and any other, deficiencies within a reasonable time frame. Where we continue to have concerns with a firm's actions in resolving deficiencies, we may consider other appropriate regulatory action.

We also sent follow up letters to those PMs that we surveyed, but did not review, where we identified specific breaches of securities laws in the marketing materials the PMs submitted. In these letters, we identified the breaches and required the firms to remedy the deficiencies in a timely manner.

Rules

When reviewing marketing materials for compliance with securities law, we rely on specific rules and instruments, both prescriptive and principles based. These rules require PMs to deal fairly, honestly and in good faith with their clients[1]. They also prohibit any person or company from making statements that are untrue or omitting information that is necessary to prevent the statement from being false or misleading.

While the relevant securities legislation is generally principles based, we intend the guidance in this notice to provide direction to PMs regarding how to meet these obligations. There may be other ways to meet these obligations. The suggested practices will serve as guidelines that the CSA will apply when assessing and determining compliance with securities law.

Summary of Issues

We identified a number of deficiencies in the preparation, review and use of marketing materials by the PMs we reviewed. Generally, the deficiencies were grouped into one of the following areas:

1. Preparation and use of hypothetical performance data
2. Exaggerated and unsubstantiated claims
3. Policies, procedures and internal controls
4. Use of benchmarks
5. Performance composites
6. Holding out and use of names
7. Other performance return issues
8. Disclosure related issues

Summary of Guidance

Based on the results of the review, we identify below suggested practices to assist PMs in meeting their obligations under securities law, including the obligation to deal fairly, honestly and in good faith with their clients and to ensure that statements provided to investors are fair and not misleading. We expect and encourage PMs to refer to the suggested practices when preparing their marketing materials.

The following is a summary of the suggested practices we discuss in this notice:

1. presenting actual client performance returns and not hypothetical performance data with its inherent risks and limitations except in limited circumstances when appropriate
2. being able to substantiate all claims made in marketing materials
3. developing and implementing written policies and procedures that govern firms' marketing activities
4. using benchmarks that are relevant and comparable to a PM's investment strategy
5. including all portfolios that meet the criteria of a composite in the composite

---

[1]In the participating CSA jurisdictions, this requirement is found in section 2.1 of Ontario Securities Commission Rule 31-505 *Conditions of Registration*, section 14 of the Securities Rules (British Columbia), section 75.2 of the *Securities Act* (Alberta), subsection 33.1(1) of the *Securities Act* (Saskatchewan), subsection 154.2(2) of the *Securities Act* (Manitoba), section 160 of the *Securities Act* (Quebec), subsection 54(1) of the *Securities Act* (New Brunswick) and section 39A of the *Securities Act* (Nova Scotia).

6. firms and registered individuals using registered trade names and business titles that are not misleading

7. reporting performance returns from a previous firm or a firm's proprietary account only in limited circumstances where it is appropriate

8. ensuring marketing materials contain disclosure that is accurate, meaningful and up-to-date

Use of Social Media Web Sites

Before we discuss the specific issues and guidance from the review, we want to discuss a recent trend of using social media for marketing. In the review, we found that generally PMs are not currently making use of social media web sites to market the firm's advisory services. However, since there has been a steady increase in the general use of social media web sites such as Facebook, Twitter, LinkedIn and various chat rooms and blogs, we anticipate that firms and their registered individuals may begin to use these methods of communication to market their business activities and communicate with clients. We expect that firms and their registered individuals will comply with applicable regulatory requirements and securities legislation in their use of social media web sites.

Potential concerns

There are compliance and supervisory challenges that we expect registered firms to consider when using social media web sites as a means of communicating with clients and the general public for business purposes. Under subsection 11.5(1) of National Instrument 31-103 — *Registration Requirements and Exemptions* (NI 31-103) registrants are required to maintain records of their business activities, financial affairs and client transactions. There is increased risk that registrants may not be retaining adequate records of their business activities and client communications when using social media web sites. This is the result of interactive social media web sites that include the posting of both real time and static content. Registrants need to consider designing systems that will allow for compliant record retention as well as retrieval capability.

The use of social media web sites poses challenges from a supervisory perspective as firms need to consider the type of supervision that would be appropriate. Registered firms must determine the level or extent of supervision necessary as they have an obligation to protect clients from the use of misleading and false statements. This may include the use of a risk-based approach to determine the extent to which a firm's review of electronic communications is appropriate to meet its supervisory obligations.

Guidance

Registered firms should consider the following when determining whether to use social media web sites for business purposes:

- establishing policies and procedures for the review, supervision, retention and retrieval of materials on social media web sites

- designating an appropriate individual to be responsible for the supervision or approval of communications

- reviewing the adequacy of systems and programs to ensure compliant record retention and retrieval capability

Specific Issues and Guidance

The following is a more detailed discussion of the issues we identified in the review and suggested practices. We encourage registrants to use this notice as a self-assessment tool and to determine the areas where they can improve their marketing practices.

1. — Preparation and use of hypothetical performance data

Hypothetical performance data is performance data that is not the performance of actual client portfolios. It is sometimes referred to as "simulated" or "theoretical" performance data and typically consists of either:

- back-tested performance data (i.e. past period), or

- model performance data (i.e. real time or future periods)

Hypothetical performance data also includes statistics such as standard deviation and Sharpe ratios, which are measures of volatility. Some of the PMs we reviewed presented the hypothetical performance data for the primary purpose of attracting new clients.

Back-tested performance data

Back-tested performance data refers to performance results created by applying a particular investment strategy to historical data over a period of time. PMs may create the data by using quantitative methods or formulas that may use historical index data, historical information about individual securities or historical performance data from existing investment funds the PMs manage.

For example, we identified a few PMs that presented back-tested performance data for fund of funds based on performance of existing funds or the performance of a particular index.

Model performance data

Model performance data refers to simulated investment results of a notional portfolio of securities that are presented over a period of time. In some cases, no actual client accounts follow the model. Generally, model portfolios are forward looking and are presented by the PM on an ongoing basis. They may also include portfolio returns that attempt to illustrate expected future returns.

PMs sometimes present model portfolios to illustrate their primary investment strategy for client portfolios. A PM will typically have clients whose managed account portfolios follow the same investment strategy and hold the same securities as the model. However, there may be variations in the percentage of each security held, the timing of security purchases and sales, and the price of a particular security.

Concerns

Approximately 20% of the PMs we reviewed had deficiencies with the hypothetical performance data they presented to investors. We identified the following general concerns related to the use of hypothetical performance data:

- many investors may not have sophisticated investment knowledge sufficient to fully understand the inherent risks and limitations of this data

- any outcome may be achieved as the performance data is produced with the benefit of hindsight and is subject to potential manipulation

- the data is often combined or linked with actual client performance data, which may give the appearance of a longer track record and that the information is based entirely on actual client performance

- there is inadequate disclosure regarding the methodology and assumptions used by the PM in calculating the data

- PMs can take increased risks with the creation of hypothetical portfolios as they do not have to manage these portfolios in real market conditions

- it is difficult to verify the calculation of hypothetical performance data

- PMs do not always deduct trading and other costs from the performance data (e.g. commissions and custodial fees). If they do, the amounts they deduct are estimates and not actual trading costs

PMs must comply with their obligations to deal fairly, honestly and in good faith with clients in the preparation and presentation of hypothetical performance data. This includes ensuring that the use of hypothetical performance data is fair and not misleading.

Factors we consider

We expect PMs to present actual performance returns for clients of the firm. However, in limited circumstances it may be appropriate to present hypothetical performance data in marketing materials. We consider all of the following factors when determining if the use of hypothetical performance data is fair and not misleading:

- Does the client receiving the information have sophisticated investment knowledge sufficient to fully understand the risks and limitations of the hypothetical performance data?

- Is the performance data calculated on a reasonable basis?

- Is the information provided in a manner that is not widely disseminated (e.g. provided to clients as part of a one-on-one presentation)?

- Is there clear and meaningful disclosure that the data is hypothetical and not actual, as well as the underlying assumptions used, the calculation methodology, the risks and limitations of the hypothetical performance data and other relevant factors?

Guidance

We expect PMs to market their actual client performance results. However, if a PM presents hypothetical performance data, considering the factors described above, we typically expect the following practices to be applied:

- ascertaining an investor's level of investment knowledge sophistication, as part of the PM's obligation to obtain KYC information and assess suitability, prior to the presentation of hypothetical performance data

- restricting the presentation to investors known to have sophisticated investment knowledge (i.e. not widely disseminating the presentation on a website or in an advertisement)

- labelling the presentation as "hypothetical" in a clear and prominent manner

- not linking the hypothetical performance data with actual performance returns of the PM. We expect hypothetical performance data to be presented separately from actual client performance data

- including clear and meaningful disclosure regarding the methodology and assumptions used to calculate the performance data, and any other relevant factors, and

- disclosing clearly a description of the inherent risks and limitations of the hypothetical performance data

2. — *Exaggerated and unsubstantiated claims*

Exaggerated and unsubstantiated claims are statements made by PMs in marketing materials distributed without evidence to verify these claims. Generally, these claims relate to the PMs' performance, skills, proficiency, education, investment experience and client service.

This was the most common deficiency we identified, with approximately 60% of PMs deficient in this area. For example, we identified:

- claims of "superior track record" that were not substantiated or where the actual performance presented was lower than the returns of a relevant benchmark

- claims that individual PMs were "experts" in particular areas of portfolio management without sufficient evidence to support these claims

Concerns

Exaggerated and unsubstantiated claims to existing and prospective clients do not adequately reflect the PM's actual performance, skills, experience and education. Furthermore, prospective investors may place undue reliance on these types of claims when deciding whether or not to contract the services of a PM.

PMs must comply with their obligations to deal fairly, honestly and in good faith with clients in the preparation and review of their marketing materials. This includes avoiding making claims that are exaggerated or unsubstantiated. Certain CSA jurisdictions also have specific securities legislation prohibiting a registrant from making misleading representations. Registrants should not make a statement that a reasonable investor would consider relevant when deciding to enter into an advisory relationship with that PM if the statement is untrue or omits information necessary to prevent the statement from being false or misleading.

Guidance

PMs should be able to substantiate all claims they make in their marketing materials. We expect to see adequate references to the information supporting their claims so that investors can easily assess the merits of these claims. If a PM cannot verify a particular claim, it may be inappropriate to use.

3. — Policies, procedures and internal controls

Approximately 33% of the PMs we reviewed had deficiencies relating to at least one of the following areas:

- no or inadequate written policies and procedures governing the preparation, use and approval of marketing activities

- lack of review of marketing materials by compliance or independent personnel

- no or inadequate books and records to properly record marketing activities conducted

Concerns

There is a risk that misleading statements will be communicated to investors, unless procedures are in place to ensure that this does not occur, such as, procedures to conduct an adequate review and obtain approval for marketing materials. The most common deficiency we identified was inadequate written policies and procedures for marketing activities or policies that did not reflect the actual marketing practices of the firm. For some of the PMs we reviewed, there were inadequate controls in place to ensure that marketing materials were adequately reviewed and approved by an independent individual, other than the preparer, prior to the dissemination of the marketing materials.

Registrants must establish, maintain and apply policies and procedures that establish a system of controls and supervision to ensure compliance with securities legislation and manage the risks associated with the registrant's business in accordance with prudent business practices. This requirement includes having processes in place to ensure that a firm regularly updates its written policies and procedures to reflect changes in the firm's business practices or to securities legislation. See section 11.1 of NI 31-103.

In addition, firms must maintain appropriate books and records to record and demonstrate compliance with their policies and procedures, as well as applicable requirements of securities legislation, as required under subsection 11.5(2) of NI 31-103.

Guidance

PMs should establish, maintain and apply written policies and procedures that are tailored to their marketing activities. At a minimum, we would expect compliant written policies and procedures to include guidance on:

- preparation, review and approval of marketing materials to prevent false and misleading statements

- ensuring compliance with applicable securities legislation, including prohibitions on holding out a non-registered individual as a registrant and misrepresentations

- independent review and approval of marketing materials by individuals with appropriate authority and proficiency (e.g. Chief Compliance Officer (CCO))

- construction, presentation and disclosure of performance composites, hypothetical performance data or any other performance data

- selection and presentation of benchmarks, including blended benchmarks

4. — Use of benchmarks

A benchmark is a standard against which the performance of the PMs' investment strategy can be objectively compared and measured. PMs typically use benchmarks to assess the relative performance of their investment strategies, as they select benchmarks to represent the characteristics of the investment strategy.

Approximately 23% of the PMs we reviewed were deficient in the presentation and use of benchmarks in marketing materials.

We identified the use of benchmarks that were not:

- comparable to the PMs' investment strategy

- disclosed with the full name of the benchmark

- presented in the same currency or on the same basis as the investment strategy or investment fund (e.g. total return or return without reinvested dividends)

In some instances, PMs did not maintain adequate books and records to support their calculations of the blended benchmarks or inadequately disclosed the composition of blended benchmarks they used in their marketing materials.

Concerns

Presenting inappropriate benchmarks does not provide a meaningful and relevant comparison to the PM's investment strategy or performance. As a result, investors or clients could draw, or infer, incorrect conclusions from the comparison. Inappropriate benchmarks may also result in the appearance that an investment fund or strategy is performing better than it actually is. PMs must comply with their obligation to deal fairly, honestly and in good faith with their clients when presenting benchmarks in their marketing materials.

Guidance

PMs should compare their performance returns against relevant benchmarks. In most cases, this means that there should be a significant degree of comparability and similarity between the investment strategy and the benchmark used.

In limited instances, it may be appropriate for a PM to compare its performance returns against a benchmark that has a different composition to that of its investment strategy. For example, a PM may compare its investment strategy to the S&P/TSX Composite Index or the S&P 500 Index, which are widely known and followed indices. In these cases, we would typically expect adequate disclosure to be made to explain the relevance of the benchmark in order to make the comparison fair and meaningful to clients. As applicable, we also expect a PM to include a discussion of the differences between the benchmark and the PM's investment strategy as well as the reason for using the benchmark.

5. — Performance composites

A performance composite is an aggregation or grouping of the performance of one or more client portfolios that represent a similar investment objective or strategy. Often, PMs use performance composites when reporting performance to prospective clients. In our review, PMs typically presented composites to institutional and high net worth clients.

Approximately 30% of the PMs we reviewed were deficient in the construction, presentation and disclosure of performance composites. These deficiencies included:

- inappropriate grouping of client portfolios into a particular composite (i.e. PMs grouped client portfolios with dissimilar investment mandates and strategies into the same composite)

- composites that did not include all relevant client portfolios

- terminated portfolios not retained in the performance history of the composite up to the last full measurement period

- inappropriate claims of compliance with the CFA Institute's Global Investment Performance Standards (GIPS) when all the requirements of GIPS were not met

- inadequate policies and procedures for constructing, presenting and disclosing performance composites

Concerns

Inadequate construction, presentation and disclosure of performance composites results in inaccurate and unfair presentation of performance data to prospective clients. This is misleading to clients and considered contrary to a PM's requirement to deal fairly, honestly and in good faith with clients.

When PMs do not include all client portfolios with a similar investment strategy or mandate in a performance composite, there is a risk that the PM will "cherry pick" the portfolios with the best performance returns in order to present better than actual results. In some instances, we identified PMs that used one client's performance to represent the investment strategy of the firm instead of presenting the returns for a composite. We also identified PMs that included some, but not all, relevant client portfolios that followed the same investment strategy or objective in a composite.

As stated above, PMs must deal fairly, honestly and in good faith with their clients. NI 31-103 also requires PMs to establish, maintain and apply policies and procedures that establish a system of controls and supervision to, among other things, manage the risks associated with their business in accordance with prudent business practices. These rules apply to the use of performance composites.

Guidance

The inappropriate omission or inclusion of client portfolios in a composite will generally result in performance returns that do not reflect the actual performance of the PMs investment strategy. To avoid presenting misleading information, we expect PMs to include all portfolios that meet the criteria of a composite in the composite. In addition, we generally expect PMs to calculate composite returns by asset-weighting the individual portfolio returns.

When presenting performance composites in marketing materials, PMs should provide adequate disclosure to ensure the composite presentation is meaningful and not misleading. For example, we would expect the disclosure to:

- clearly outline the investment strategy that is reflected in the composite

- state whether the composite returns are net of fees, or gross of portfolio management fees and/or other expenses

- include any other key information about the composite including minimum asset levels for inclusion of accounts in the composite, if any, or other information such as the use of sub-advisers and currency used to express performance

PMs should also establish written policies and procedures for the construction, presentation and disclosure of composites. Where appropriate, we expect these to include requirements for composite construction, calculation methodology, and the types of disclosure that must accompany a presentation of composites.

6. — Holding out and use of names

Approximately 27% of PMs, including their registered individuals, had deficiencies in at least one of the following areas:

- unregistered individuals using business titles that implied that they were registered

- inappropriate use of business or trade names

- use of names of other registered firms without prior consent

For example, we identified some PMs who used a trade name, instead of their full legal name without notifying the applicable regulator. In other instances, individuals used titles on business cards that were misleading as they implied that the individuals were registered in some capacity when they were not. In some cases, PMs used the name of another registrant on its website without the consent of that firm.

Concerns

The use of inappropriate trade names or titles is misleading and confusing to investors as they might not understand which entity they are dealing with or the experience and proficiency of an individual they are dealing with. Subsection 14.2(1) of NI 31-103 requires a firm to deliver to clients all information that a reasonable investor would consider important about its relationship with the firm. Part 14 of Companion Policy 31-103CP — *Registration Requirements and Exemptions* (NI 31-103CP) clarifies that this includes ensuring that the firm's clients understand with whom they are dealing and carrying on all registrable activities in either the PM's full legal name or its registered trade name.

Where a registered firm uses a business or trade name, the firm is required to notify the applicable regulator of its use and must register that trade name under applicable corporate legislation, where required. The securities legislation of certain CSA jurisdictions prohibits firms and individuals from making false representations about their registration. Where a PM uses or makes reference to another registered firm's name, the PM must, where required, obtain written consent prior to the use of this name in their marketing materials.

Guidance

Firms should use their full legal name or registered trade name when marketing their activities. Individuals acting on behalf of a registered firm should use job titles that adequately reflect the nature of their duties or category of registration. Individuals should not use titles that imply they are registered when they are not. For example, an individual registered as an associate advising representative should not hold out their job title as a portfolio manager.

PMs should also ensure adequate policies and procedures are put in place to review and approve the use of trade names of the firm and of job titles by individuals.

7. — Other performance return issues

We identified issues with the use of the following in marketing materials:

- performance returns from an individual's previous firm

- proprietary firm and individual PM's performance returns

Concerns

It may be misleading for PMs to market the performance returns their advising representatives achieved while employed at another firm as well as returns achieved by a firm's proprietary account or an advising representative's personal trading account. Generally, PMs with limited or no track record of their own marketed these types of returns.

In some cases we reviewed, PMs marketed the performance returns from a previous firm when:

- the advising representative was not responsible for generating the presented returns

- the investment strategy at the previous firm was different from that of the new firm

In these cases, it was misleading and not relevant to market the performance results from a previous firm.

We have also seen examples where PMs marketed their proprietary or advising representative's personal performance returns when:

- the advising representative was not employed by the registered firm or registered as an advising representative for the periods presented

- the returns were presented for periods prior to the firm's registration as a PM

- the investment strategy of a newly created investment fund was implemented in a firm's proprietary or individual's personal trading account prior to its launch, and was held out as the performance of the investment fund

It is generally misleading and not relevant to market the returns of a firm's proprietary account or an advising representative's personal trading account. We have concerns where individual PMs market the performance returns of their personal trading accounts since they are not accounts of the registered firm. In addition, PMs can employ different strategies and take greater risks when managing their own investments. We also have concerns if the performance returns are for periods prior to the individual's registration as an advising representative, when the individual was not subject to proficiency or supervision requirements. In such cases, the personal account returns may be difficult to verify.

PMs have an obligation to deal fairly, honestly and in good faith with their clients when presenting performance returns, including returns from a previous firm or from the firm's proprietary account. This includes avoiding the presentation of performance returns that are misleading and not relevant.

Guidance

We expect PMs to present only the performance returns of the firms' actual performance composites or investment funds since the firms have been registered.

There are limited circumstances where it may be appropriate to market the performance from a previous firm. We consider all of the following when determining whether the circumstances are appropriate:

- the key investment decision maker at the previous firm is now employed with the new firm
- the investment strategy at the previous firm is substantially similar to that of the new firm
- the new firm has books and records that adequately support the historical data presented from the previous firm
- there is adequate disclosure that the performance presented is from a previous firm, and of any other relevant facts

There are also limited circumstances where the marketing of a firm's proprietary account may be appropriate. We consider all of the following when determining whether the circumstances are appropriate:

- the PM launches a new investment strategy in the firm's proprietary account prior to its use in a client portfolio
- proprietary returns are for periods since the firm's registration as a PM
- the PM provides adequate disclosure that the performance presented relates to the firm's proprietary account only
- the PM maintains adequate books and records to support the proprietary performance returns

Where a PM uses a substantially similar investment strategy in its proprietary and client accounts, we expect PMs not to present or report proprietary account performance data at all. Instead, we expect the PM to use and present performance composites which include all relevant client portfolios. Also, where applicable, we expect PMs not to link proprietary returns in the same table or graph with the performance returns of an investment fund because doing so would be misleading.

8. — Disclosure related issues

Approximately 57% of the PMs we reviewed were deficient in this area. The disclosure related issues included:

- marketing materials that contained outdated information
- no disclosure of the source of third party information (other than data from recognized financial and statistical reporting services)
- inadequate or inconsistent disclosure in offering memoranda and other offering documents of non-prospectus qualified investment funds
- inadequate, or lack of, performance return related disclosures (i.e. performance return data that was not dated, no disclosure of whether returns were net or gross of fees and no disclaimers regarding past performance)

Concerns

Marketing materials that do not contain adequate disclosure relating to a PM's advisory activities, performance, services and product offerings may be misleading to investors, who place significant reliance on and may be influenced by these types of marketing materials. PMs must comply with their obligation to deal fairly, honestly and in good faith with clients in the preparation and review of their marketing materials. This includes ensuring that their marketing materials are not misleading.

Guidance

PMs should ensure that their marketing materials disclose information that is accurate, meaningful and up-to-date. As described above, we expect this to include implementing a process where the CCO and/or other designated individual is involved in the review and approval of marketing materials to ensure adherence to internal policies and obligations under securities legislation.

When presenting performance return data we expect firms to date the period presented and provide adequate disclaimers regarding past performance as appropriate. Where a firm presents third party information, it should disclose the source of the information if it is not obtained from recognized financial and statistical reporting services.

Next Steps

CSA staff will continue to review the marketing practices of PMs through the compliance review process. While the specific securities legislation used is generally principles based, the suggested practices identified in this notice are intended to provide guidance on how the CSA expects registrants to interpret the specific legislation. The suggested practices will serve as a guideline that compliance staff of the CSA will apply when assessing and determining compliance with securities law.

Policies and Orders: OSCN 33-729.

CSA Staff Notice 31-326 — Outside Business Activities

Date: July 15, 2011

34 O.S.C.B. 7760

This notice reminds registrants of their obligation to ensure outside business activities do not impair or impede the performance of their regulatory obligations, including compliance with the conflicts of interest provisions under National Instrument 31-103 *Registration Requirements, Exemptions and Ongoing Registrant Obligations*.

Registrants that are members of the Investment Industry Regulatory Organization of Canada (IIROC) or the Mutual Fund Dealers Association of Canada (MFDA) are reminded that the firm and the individuals they employ are also subject to IIROC and MFDA requirements that relate to outside business activities.

National Instrument 33-109 *Registration Information* requires disclosure of all outside business activities. Staff of the Canadian Securities Administrators (CSA) will take into account issues that may arise in relation to an individual registrant's outside business activities when assessing their initial application for registration, when there is a change in their registration and in considering continuing fitness for registration. In this evaluation, CSA staff consider a number of matters, including:

- whether the individual will have sufficient time to properly carry out their registerable activities, including remaining current on securities law and product knowledge
- whether the individual will be able to properly service clients
- what is the risk of client confusion and are there effective controls and supervision in place to manage the risk
- whether the outside business activity presents a conflict of interest for the individual, and whether that conflict of interest should be avoided or can be appropriately managed
- whether the outside business activity places the individual in a position of power or influence over clients or potential clients, in particular clients or potential clients that may be vulnerable
- whether the outside business activity provides the individual with access to privileged, confidential or insider information relevant to their registerable activities

A registered firm is responsible for monitoring and supervising the individuals whose registration it sponsors. In relation to outside business activities, this includes:

- having appropriate policies and procedures to deal with outside business activities, including ensuring outside business activities do not:
  - involve activities that are inconsistent with securities legislation and IIROC and MFDA requirements; and
  - interfere with the individual's ability to remain current on securities law and product knowledge
- requiring individual registrants to disclose to their firm, and requiring the firm to review and approve, all outside business activities prior to the activities commencing
- ensuring the firm's chief compliance officer is able to properly supervise and monitor the outside business activities
- maintaining records documenting its supervision of outside business activities and ensuring these records are available for review by regulators
- ensuring that potential conflicts of interest are identified and appropriate steps are taken to manage such conflicts (See section 13.4 of Companion Policy 31-103CP for further guidance.)
- ensuring outside business activities do not impair the ability to provide adequate client service, including, where necessary, having an alternate representative available for the client
- ensuring the outside business activity is consistent with the registrant's duty to deal fairly, honestly and in good faith with its clients
- implementing risk management, including proper separation of the outside business activity and registerable activity
- preventing exposure of the firm to complaints and litigation
- assessing whether the individual's lifestyle is commensurate with the firm's knowledge of the individual's business activities and staying alert to other indicators of possible fraudulent activity

Failure to discharge these responsibilities may be relevant to the firm's continued fitness for registration.

CSA Staff Notice 31-327 — Broker-Dealer Registration in the Exempt Market Dealer Category

Date: September 2, 2011

34 O.S.C.B. 9073

Purpose

Staff of the Canadian Securities Administrators (**CSA** or **we**) have recently learned that there are a number of firms registered as exempt market dealers (**EMD**) that are carrying out brokerage activities (trading securities listed on an exchange in foreign or Canadian markets) for accredited investors. We understand that these are primarily broker-dealer firms registered in the United States that are members of the

Financial Industry Regulatory Authority (**FINRA**). CSA staff have also received applications from firms seeking registration in the EMD category for the same purpose.

CSA staff do not believe that the EMD category of registration was intended for firms that conduct brokerage activities. This raises serious policy issues that regulators and the industry need to consider. The purpose of this Notice is to outline our concerns and our interim response to this problem and to advise that we will be examining these activities in a wider consultation and review process.

Background — the EMD Category

National Instrument 31-103 *Registration Requirements, Exemptions and Ongoing Registrant Obligations* (**NI 31-103**) became effective September 28, 2009 and introduced the EMD category of registration, which was a new category to most CSA jurisdictions and represented a significant change to the pre-existing limited market dealer category in Ontario and Newfoundland and Labrador.

The EMD category was designed to allow increased oversight and regulation of market participants in the exempt market. The category permits trading in securities distributed under prospectus exemptions. We did not envision that EMDs would be involved in brokerage activities, including trading securities on an exchange, or entering into arrangements similar to introducing-carrying broker activities.

Firms providing brokerage activities have historically been categorized as investment dealers, which are subject to the Investment Industry Regulatory Organization of Canada (**IIROC**) requirements and supervision.

Applications by Firms Seeking Registration in the EMD Category

The current applicants seek to rely on section 7.1(2)(d) of NI 31-103 combined with the prospectus exemption provided in section 2.3 of National Instrument 45-106 *Prospectus and Registration Exemptions* that exempts distributions to accredited investors. Some of the applicants also seek an exemption from section 13.12 of NI 31-103 to allow lending or providing margin to clients. Therefore, an EMD could technically trade in any securities for an accredited investor, including securities listed on an exchange.

Issues

We have concerns with firms applying for registration in the EMD category and with firms already registered in the category because we do not think the EMD category was intended to allow firms to engage in brokerage activities.

IIROC monitors brokerage activities and it has developed rules and an oversight infrastructure to supervise this activity. If EMDs are conducting brokerage activities which would otherwise be carried out by Canadian investment dealers who are members of IIROC, similar activities would be regulated within Canada differently, resulting in differences in regulatory oversight depending on whether the activity is carried out by an EMD or an IIROC member.

Interim Action

In view of these regulatory concerns, we will consider registering these broker-dealers in the restricted dealer category with terms and conditions. One condition is that these broker-dealers only deal with permitted clients. The registration will be limited in time. This interim registration will allow applicants to engage in limited activities while we engage in a consultation process.

Consultation

We will be examining these issues in a consultation and review process to allow all interested stakeholders an opportunity to comment. Our goal is to ensure appropriate regulatory requirements apply to all firms that engage in brokerage activities in Canada. The securities industry should be aware that the outcome of these consultations is likely to result in changes to our rules.

Policies and Orders: CSAN 31-331, 31-333.

CSA Staff Notice 31-328 — Revocation of Omnibus/Blanket Orders Exempting Registrants from Certain Provisions of NI 31-103 Registration Requirements, Exemptions and Ongoing Registrant Obligations

Date: September 16, 2011

34 O.S.C.B. 9530

[Not reproduced]

CSA Staff Notice 31-329 — Omnibus/Blanket Orders Exempting Registrants from Certain Provisions of NI 31-103 Registration Requirements, Exemptions and Ongoing Registrant Obligations and Related Staff Positions

Date: September 28, 2011

34 O.S.C.B. 9960

Purpose

Since the coming into effect of National Instrument 31-103 *Registration Requirements, Exemptions and Ongoing Registrant Obligations* (NI 31-103), the Canadian Securities Administrators (the CSA or we) have received applications for exemptive relief, comments and inquiries in respect of certain provisions of NI 31-103. CSA members have issued a number of parallel orders (the "orders") or related staff positions, as described in this notice and relating to:

    1. the requirement to register when trading in short-term debt instruments;

    2. the restrictions on the registration exemptions for international dealers and international advisers in sections 8.18 [*international dealer*] and 8.26 [*international adviser*]; and

    3. the requirement in section 14.2(1) to provide relationship disclosure information.

This Notice summarizes the orders and related staff positions.

1. — Interim relief exempting certain persons and companies from the requirement to register when trading in short-term debt instruments

Background

All CSA members except Ontario issued parallel orders of general application, effective March 27, 2010 (the "2010 orders"), that provided that the dealer registration requirement does not apply to

    (i) a bank listed in Schedule I, II or III to the *Bank Act* (Canada);

    (ii) an association to which the *Cooperative Credit Associations Act* (Canada) applies or a central cooperative credit society for which an order has been made under subsection 473(1) of that Act;

    (iii) a loan corporation, trust company, trust corporation, insurance company, treasury branch, credit union, caisse populaire, financial services cooperative or credit union league or federation that is authorized by a statute of Canada or of a jurisdiction in Canada to carry on business in Canada or in any jurisdiction in Canada, as the case may be; and

    (iv) the Business Development Bank of Canada;

in respect of a trade in a negotiable promissory note or commercial paper maturing not more than one year from the date of issue, if the note or commercial paper traded

    (a) is not convertible or exchangeable into or accompanied by a right to purchase another security other than a security described in the order, and

    (b) has an approved credit rating as specified in the order.

Ontario

In Ontario there are alternate exemptions from the dealer registration requirement that may be available for trading in short-term debt, such as the exemption in section 8.5 [*trades through or to a registered dealer*] of NI 31-103 and, in the case of financial institutions, the exemptions in section 35.1 of the *Securities Act* (Ontario) and section 4.1 of the Ontario Securities Commission ("OSC") Rule 45-501 *Ontario Prospectus and Registration Exemptions*.

New orders

The 2010 orders expire on September 28, 2011. CSA members, other than the OSC (for the reasons indicated above), have issued parallel orders that continue to provide interim relief exempting certain persons and companies from the requirement to register when trading in short-term debt instruments, on the same terms and conditions as the 2010 orders. These new orders will expire on September 28, 2014.

Ongoing work

We are continuing our work in this area and may publish proposed amendments to NI 31-103 for comment in the future.

2. — Interim relief from the new restrictions on registration exemptions for international dealers and international advisers in sections 8.18 and 8.26 of NI 31-103

Background

Effective July 11, 2011, amendments to NI 31-103 came into effect. The amendments incorporated new restrictions in the registration exemptions in sections 8.18 [*international dealer*] and 8.26 [*international adviser*] of NI 31-103. These sections now contemplate an international dealer or adviser dealing with a "Canadian permitted client" instead of a "permitted client". After we published the amendments, it was brought to CSA staff's attention that the new definition may be more restrictive than we intended.

As we indicated in our June 25, 2010 notice[1], the purpose of these amendments was to clarify our intent that the exemptions may not be relied upon to trade with (or advise) foreign clients. Instead, as we had previously indicated in our response to comments on the first publication of NI 31-103, the intention of these exemptions was to allow Canadian investors access to foreign securities offerings and foreign expertise.[2]

---

[1]Notice and Request for Comments on Proposed Amendments to National Instrument 31-103 and National Instrument 33-109, published on June 25, 2010.
[2]See page 18 of "Summary of Comments received by June 30, 2007", published on February 29, 2008.

Relief being provided (other than by the OSC)

As a result, all CSA members, other than the OSC, have issued parallel orders that provide interim relief from the new restrictions. This relief allows a person or company to rely on the exemptions in section 8.18 (the "international dealer exemption") or section 8.26 (the "international adviser exemption") of NI 31-103, as if the term "Canadian permitted client" is read as "permitted client".

OSC staff position

The OSC will not be issuing an order of this nature given that orders of general application are not authorized under Ontario securities law. However, OSC staff are of the view that, while work in this area is ongoing, there is no public interest in recommending or pursuing an enforcement action against a person or company for failure to comply with the applicable dealer or adviser registration requirement in circumstances where the person or company:

(a) would satisfy the requirements of the corresponding international dealer exemption or international adviser exemption, if the definition of "Canadian permitted client" in these sections instead referred to a "permitted client" (as now defined in section 1.1 [*definitions of terms used throughout this Instrument*] of NI 31-103 but excluding, in the case of the international adviser exemption, a dealer or adviser registered under the securities legislation of a jurisdiction of Canada);

(b) complies with the other provisions of Ontario securities law applying to those who rely on the international dealer exemption or international adviser exemption, including OSC Rule 13-502 Fees; and

(c) identifies on the Form 31-103F2 *Submission to Jurisdiction and Appointment of Agent for Service* required to be filed under section 8.18(3)(e) or section 8.26(4)(f) that, in addition to the corresponding international dealer exemption or international adviser exemption, the person or company is also relying on this notice (by checking, in paragraph 6, the applicable exemption and also checking the "other" box with a notation stating that "*CSA Staff Notice 31-329 is being relied on*").

The above position of OSC staff may be withdrawn after further consideration of this matter. OSC staff expect that this position will be withdrawn on the coming into effect of any amendments to NI 31-103 dealing with the definition of "Canadian permitted client".

Ongoing work

We are continuing our work in this area and expect to publish proposed amendments to NI 31-103 for comment in the future.

3. — Interim relief from the requirement in section 14.2(1) of NI 31-103 to provide relationship disclosure information for SRO members and for mutual fund dealers in Québec

Background

Section 14.2(1) of NI 31-103 sets out the principle that a registered firm must deliver to a client all information that a reasonable investor would consider important about the client's relationship with the registrant. All CSA members have issued parallel orders that extend previously issued temporary relief from the requirement to provide relationship disclosure information in compliance with section 14.2(1) of NI 31-103:

- for firms that are members of the Investment Industry Regulatory Organization of Canada (IIROC);

- for members of the Mutual Fund Dealers Association of Canada (the MFDA); and

- for mutual fund dealers in Québec.

Relief from the requirement to provide the relationship disclosure information prescribed by section 14.2(1) of NI 31-103 for IIROC member firms

IIROC is currently finalizing its proposal on relationship disclosure information (the IIROC RDI proposal). The purpose of the IIROC RDI proposal is to set out detailed requirements to assist IIROC member firms to comply with the general principle in section 14.2(1) of NI 31-103.

It is anticipated that the IIROC RDI proposal will be finalized and new IIROC member rules reflecting the IIROC RDI proposal (the IIROC RDI rules) will be approved before the end of 2011, with provisions for their implementation in phases over a two-year transition period.

All CSA members have issued parallel orders that exempt a dealer that is a member of IIROC from the application of the requirements of section 14.2(1) of NI 31-103 provided that after the IIROC RDI Rules are approved, the IIROC member complies with them, subject to applicable transition periods. The orders will expire on December 31, 2013, by which time the IIROC RDI rules are expected to be fully implemented.

Relief from the requirement to provide the relationship disclosure information prescribed by section 14.2(1) of NI 31-103 for mutual fund dealers

(a) — MFDA members

The MFDA has adopted new member rules for relationship disclosure information (the MFDA RDI rules). The purpose of the MFDA RDI rules is to set out detailed requirements to assist MFDA member firms to comply with the general principle in section 14.2(1) of NI 31-103. The MFDA RDI rules will be implemented in phases, starting on September 28, 2011 and ending December 3, 2013.

All CSA members except Québec have issued parallel orders that exempt a dealer that is a member of the MFDA from the application of the requirements of section 14.2(1) of NI 31-103 provided it complies with the MFDA RDI rules, subject to applicable transition periods.

The orders will expire on December 31, 2013, by which time the MFDA RDI rules are expected to be fully implemented.

This relief applies to MFDA members notwithstanding their registration in other categories.

(b) — Mutual fund dealers registered in Québec

In Québec, the Autorité des marchés financiers issued an order on September 1, 2010 exempting mutual fund dealers in Québec from the requirement, in section 14.2(1) of NI 31-103, to provide relationship disclosure information until the earlier of September 28, 2011 or the coming into effect of new regulations for mutual fund dealers in Québec.

There is currently no equivalent requirement, under the regulations in Québec, relating to relationship disclosure information. This renders the exemption provided in section 9.4(4) of NI 31-103, in respect of the application of section 14.2(2) of NI 31-103, unavailable to mutual fund dealers in Québec.

Beginning on September 28, 2011, the requirement to provide relationship disclosure information, as provided in section 14.2 of NI 31-103, will apply to mutual fund dealers in Québec. However, the Autorité des marchés financiers has issued a new order exempting mutual fund dealers in Québec from the application of the requirements of section 14.2(1) of NI 31-103, but in respect of existing clients only.

This order will expire on December 31, 2013.

This relief applies to mutual fund dealers in Québec notwithstanding their registration in other categories.

We are publishing the orders with this Notice. The orders are also available on websites of CSA members, including:

> www.lautorite.qc.ca
>
> www.albertasecurities.com
>
> www.bcsc.bc.ca
>
> www.msc.gov.mb.ca
>
> www.gov.ns.ca/nssc
>
> www.nbsc-cvmnb.ca
>
> www.osc.gov.on.ca
>
> www.sfsc.gov.sk.ca

CSA Staff Notice 31-330 — Omnibus/Blanket Orders Extending Certain Transition Provisions Relating to the Investment Fund Manager Registration Requirement and the Obligation to Provide Dispute Resolution Services

Date: July 5, 2012

35 O.S.C.B. 6260

Introduction

This Notice announces the issuance by members of the Canadian Securities Administrators (the **CSA**, or **we**) of parallel orders (the "**orders**") to extend the transition provisions in the following sections of Part 16 of National Instrument 31-103 *Registration Requirements, Exemptions and Ongoing Registrant Obligations* (**NI 31-103**):

- Section 16.5 [*Temporary exemption for Canadian investment fund manager registered in its principal jurisdiction*]

- Section 16.6 [*Temporary exemption for foreign investment fund manager*]

- Section 16.16 [*Complaint handling*]

Purpose

The purpose of the orders is to extend certain transition provisions that are available in Part 16 of NI 31-103.

Background and Summary of Orders

Transitional Relief from the Requirement to Register as an Investment Fund Manager

On July 5, 2012:

- securities regulators in British Columbia, Alberta, Saskatchewan, Manitoba, Prince Edward Island, Nova Scotia, New Brunswick, Northwest Territories, Yukon and Nunavut published Multilateral Policy 31-202 *Registration Requirement for Investment Fund Managers* (**MP 31-202**)

- securities regulators in Ontario, Quebec and Newfoundland and Labrador, published Multilateral Instrument 32-102 *Registration Exemptions for Non-Resident Investment Fund Managers* (**MI 32-102**) and Companion Policy 32-102CP *Registration Exemptions for Non-Resident Investment Fund Managers*

- securities regulators in all CSA jurisdictions published amendments to Companion Policy 31-103CP *Registration Requirements, Exemptions and Ongoing Registrant Obligations*

These new and amended instruments and policies relating to the registration of investment fund managers come into effect on September 28, 2012, subject in certain jurisdictions to necessary approvals. You can find more information about each of these policies and instruments in the Notices accompanying the publication of MP 31-202 and MI 32-102.

Sections 16.5 and 16.6 of NI 31-103 provide temporary exemptions for certain investment fund managers from the investment fund manager registration requirement that expire on September 28, 2012. These exemptions are available to investment fund managers that are registered, or have applied for registration, in the jurisdiction of Canada in which their head office is located and investment fund managers that do not have a head office in Canada. In order to provide additional time for affected investment fund managers to comply with these new and amended instruments and policies relating to the registration requirements described above, the CSA is extending the duration of these temporary exemptions.

As a result of these extensions, investment fund managers registered in the jurisdiction of Canada in which their head office is located and investment fund managers that do not have a head office in Canada now have until December 31, 2012 to apply for registration.

Transitional Relief from the Requirement to Provide Dispute Resolution Services Prescribed by Section 13.16 of NI 31-103

The CSA is currently reviewing the dispute resolution provisions in NI 31-103 and may publish proposed amendments for comment in the future.

Section 16.16 of NI 31-103 provides a temporary exemption for registrants from the requirements of section 13.16 of NI 31-103 that require registered firms to make independent dispute resolution or mediation services available to clients. The temporary exemption in section 16.16, which does not apply in Quebec by reason of the existing regime in that jurisdiction, expires on September 28, 2012. Since we are considering publishing proposed amendments to the dispute resolution provisions in section 13.16 of NI 31-103 for comment, CSA members are extending this temporary exemption until the earlier of September 28, 2014 or the coming into effect of amendments to section 13.16 of NI 31-103. This order will not apply in Quebec.

CSA Staff Notice 31-331 — Follow-up to Broker Dealer Registration in the Exempt Market Dealer Category

Date: July 12, 2012
35 O.S.C.B. 6425

Introduction

On September 2, 2011, Canadian Securities Administrators (**CSA** or we) published CSA Staff Notice 31-327 *Broker-Dealer Registration in the Exempt Market Dealer Category* (**CSA Staff Notice 31-327**). This notice is a follow-up to the CSA Staff Notice 31-327.

Substance and Purpose

The purpose of this notice is to introduce an Investment Industry Regulatory Organization of Canada (**IIROC**) Concept Paper published as IIROC Notice 12-0217 (the **IIROC proposal**).

Background

CSA Staff Notice 31-327 raised concerns with firms applying for registration, or registered, in the exempt market dealer (**EMD**) category that are conducting brokerage activities (trading securities listed on an exchange in foreign or Canadian markets) (**brokerage activities**). It stated that we would be examining this issue to ensure that appropriate regulatory requirements apply to all firms conducting brokerage activities.

Consultation

We conducted a survey of all EMD firms to determine the extent of these activities. We determined that it is primarily broker-dealer firms registered in the United States that are members of the Financial Industry Regulatory Authority (**FINRA**) that are conducting brokerage activities. We are of the view that IIROC should oversee these firms because IIROC rules and supervision govern exchange trading practices and address the risks associated with brokerage activities. Accordingly, we have been working with IIROC and have asked IIROC to consider a framework for the oversight of these firms.

IIROC Proposal

The IIROC proposal introduces a new class of IIROC Member, called a "Restricted Dealer Member", which is intended to migrate firms currently registered as EMDs or restricted dealers carrying out brokerage activities to IIROC membership. Based on this proposal, firms would surrender their EMD or restricted dealer registration and apply for investment dealer registration as well as seek IIROC membership.

Next Steps

We look forward to reviewing any comments on the IIROC proposal. At the conclusion of the consultation period, IIROC may make changes to its by-laws and rules. We may also propose changes to National Instrument 31-103 *Registration Requirements, Exemptions and Ongoing Registrant Obligations* to expressly limit the types of activities that EMDs can conduct.
Policies and Orders: CSAN 31-333.

CSA Staff Notice 31-332 — Relevant Investment Management Experience for Advising Representatives and Associate Advising Representatives of Portfolio Managers

Date: January 17, 2013
36 O.S.C.B. 758

Introduction

Since September 28, 2009, when National Instrument 31-103 — *Registration Requirements, Exemptions and Ongoing Registrant Obligations* (NI 31-103) came into effect, staff from the various provinces from the Canadian Securities Administrators (CSA staff or we) have reviewed over 2500 applications for registration as Advising Representatives (ARs) or Associate Advising Representatives (AARs).

Substance and Purpose

This notice provides applicants for AR and AAR registration with a summary of decisions about *relevant investment management experience*. We expect prospective applicants to consider the information in this notice when deciding whether to apply for AR or AAR registration, and when preparing an application.

Applicants need to meet both the educational and *relevant investment management experience* requirements in sections 3.11 and 3.12 of NI 31-103. Companion Policy 31-103CP — *Registration Requirements, Exemptions and Ongoing Registrant Obligations* (the CP) provides some guidance on relevant investment management experience.

Scope

In all cases in this notice, the applicant's educational qualifications met NI 31-103 requirements and the only question was whether the applicant had relevant investment management experience.

Staff retains discretion to consider each application on its own facts

This notice does not constrain staff's ability to assess each application on its facts. Nonetheless, staff strive to make consistent decisions.

AAR registration does not automatically qualify an applicant for AR registration

CSA staff consider whether experience gained while registered as an AAR is relevant investment management experience on a case-by-case basis. For example, many client relationship managers may not gain sufficient experience as an AAR to qualify as an AR.

Client relationship management experience unlikely to qualify an applicant for AR registration

We have often registered AR applicants who have client relationship management experience in a portfolio management context as AARs instead. Client relationship management experience, even when performed by AARs, may not provide sufficient experience performing securities research and analysis to qualify an individual for registration as an AR.

Client Relationship Manager not approved as AR but approved as AAR

The applicant possessed a number of years of industry experience, including 5 years assisting a registered AR at a registered Portfolio Manager (PM) firm. The applicant's experience assisting the AR in assessing suitability, creating investment policy statements, determining asset allocation, monitoring client portfolios and producing macroeconomic reports for the AR and for clients of the PM firm was considered valuable. However, the applicant had not demonstrated experience performing research or analysis of individual securities.

Client relationship management may not trigger the registration requirement

We recognize that many individuals who perform client relationship management services may not provide specific advice and therefore may not trigger the registration requirement.

For example, some client services representatives conduct activities such as marketing the services of the firm by providing general information about the registrant firm and its services that do not include a strategy tailored to any specific client. While some client service representatives may accompany an AR or AAR to meetings with clients and provide assistance with the completion of KYC forms, they might not themselves develop an investment policy statement for the client, provide specific information such as recommending a particular model portfolio for the client or explain the implications of discretionary portfolio decisions that were made by the client's AR.

Corporate finance experience may not qualify an applicant for AR registration

We have declined to register a number of individuals who have corporate finance experience as ARs and instead registered them as AARs. While corporate finance experience may involve the valuation and analysis of companies and securities, the applicants' experience did not demonstrate an ability in, and understanding of, portfolio analysis or portfolio securities selection nor were the applicants able to demonstrate alternative experience managing investments on a discretionary basis.

Investment Banker not approved as AR but approved as AAR

The applicant possessed more than 4 years of experience working in the corporate finance division of a registered investment dealer. The applicant's experience valuing securities for initial public offerings, debt and equity financings, take-over bids and mergers and acquisitions was considered valuable. However, the applicant had not demonstrated any experience performing portfolio analysis or selecting securities for a portfolio of investments, such as KYC or suitability analysis or analysing correlation of securities. The applicant had also not demonstrated any experience managing investment portfolios on a discretionary basis.

Experience at an IIROC dealer may not qualify an Applicant for AR registration

For example, some registered representatives sell mostly or exclusively a limited number of model portfolios or "portfolio solutions" to clients based on their investment objectives, risk profile or other factors unique to the individual client. In these instances, we have generally registered the individual as an AAR.

IIROC dealing representative not approved as AR but approved as AAR

The applicant had been employed for more than 4 years with an IIROC member firm as a registered representative. The applicant met with clients to review and discuss KYC information and establish risk tolerance, objectives and time horizon. The applicant would make specific investment recommendations to achieve this asset mix recommendation and construct the portfolio by selecting the appropriate investment solutions and fixed income securities in accordance with the firm's model portfolios. The applicant discussed specific investment returns with the client and compared them to industry benchmarks and kept up-to-date on market and world events.

Other registered representatives may offer a much broader range of products involving significant security-specific research and analysis of their own. In some of these cases, depending on the specific facts provided, we registered the individuals as ARs.

IIROC dealing representative approved as AR

The applicant had been employed for more than 4 years with an IIROC member firm as a registered representative. The applicant met with clients to review and discuss KYC information and establish risk tolerance, objectives and time horizon. The applicant performed detailed research and analysis of investment funds, fixed income securities, structured investment products and single stocks. The applicant obtained data from various sources including issuer prospectuses, offering memorandums and other source documents. The application described the registered representative's process for performing detailed analysis with this data for different types of securities, the analysis of each individual security for the client and the analysis of the portfolio as a whole for the client.

Consulting experience with portfolio manager selection and monitoring may not qualify an applicant for AR registration

We have received applications from individuals who have experience as consultants, providing advice to individuals and corporations on asset allocation and the selection and ongoing performance of their investment portfolios or investment managers. We have found that the degree of specific advice and securities analysis, if any, performed by the individuals can vary extensively among firms and individuals and whether the individual has been approved as an AR, AAR or not approved at all is very case-specific.

Consultant not approved as AR, AAR recommended based in part on other experience[1]

The applicant carried on business providing general financial planning advice. The applicant did not specifically research individual securities in this capacity. The applicant would provide guidelines for investment policy and asset allocation. The applicant would perform research and analysis to review the performance of various registered portfolio managers and would refer clients for discretionary money management based on the research and analysis. The applicant also monitored the registered PMs based upon certain described criteria. While the applicant was not able to demonstrate any specific securities research and analysis or securities selection in this role, the applicant was able to demonstrate some experience analysing the merits of specific securities in a different role.

In some situations, the activities submitted as relevant investment management experience involve or may involve providing specific advice to clients and therefore may require registration. We also recognize that many individuals who provide portfolio manager selection and monitoring do not provide specific advice and therefore may not trigger the registration requirement. Among the factors we have taken into account are:

- whether the client contracts with the portfolio manager(s) or the consultant
- whether the consultant manages the hiring and evaluation of the portfolio managers
- the degree of reliance by the client on the consultant
- the client's expectations as set out in the contract with the consultant.

Mutual fund sales experience unlikely to qualify applicant as AAR or AR

We have received applications from individuals employed by IIROC firms or mutual fund dealer firms who have primarily or exclusively sold mutual funds to clients based on the investment objectives, risk profile and other factors unique to the individual client. We have not generally registered individuals whose experience has been limited to mutual fund sales as ARs or AARs because they were not able to demonstrate sufficient experience analysing individual securities or managing investments on a discretionary basis.

Mutual Fund dealing representative not approved as AR or AAR

The applicant possessed over 10 years of experience as a mutual fund dealing representative. The applicant met with clients to review and discuss KYC information and establish risk tolerance, objectives and time horizon and recommended a combination of proprietary mutual funds based on this assessment. The applicant possessed an additional year of experience taking orders for the purchase and sale of securities as a registered investment representative at a discount brokerage firm. The applicant was not able to demonstrate any significant experience performing individual securities analysis or selection or any experience working in a discretionary investment management environment.

CSA Staff Notice 31-333 — Follow-up to Broker-Dealer Registration in the Exempt Market Dealer Category

Date: February 7, 2013

36 O.S.C.B. 1409

---

[1]The application was withdrawn.

Introduction

On September 2, 2011, the Canadian Securities Administrators (**CSA** or **we**) published CSA Staff Notice 31-327 *Broker-Dealer Registration in the Exempt Market Dealer Category* (**CSA Staff Notice 31-327**). On July 12, 2012, we published CSA Staff Notice 31-331 *Follow-Up to Broker-Dealer Registration in the Exempt Market Dealer Category* (**CSA Staff Notice 31-331**). CSA Staff Notice 31-331 introduced IIROC Notice 12-0217 *IIROC Concept Proposal — Restricted Dealer Member Proposal* (the **Restricted Dealer Member Proposal**). This notice provides a further update on broker-dealer registration in the exempt market dealer (**EMD**) category.

Substance and Purpose

The purpose of this notice is to inform FINRA firms currently conducting brokerage activities while registered in the EMD category or in the restricted dealer category that the Investment Industry Regulatory Organization of Canada (**IIROC**) does not intend to proceed with the Restricted Dealer Member Proposal, as detailed in IIROC Notice 13-0042 dated February 7, 2013 (the **IIROC Notice**). In the future, firms will need to conduct all brokerage activities through a full IIROC member firm.

Background

CSA Staff Notice 31-327 outlines our concerns about firms using the EMD category to conduct brokerage activities (trading securities listed on an exchange in foreign or Canadian markets) (**brokerage activities**). We also stated that we would examine the issue to ensure that appropriate regulatory requirements applied to all firms that were engaging in brokerage activities in Canada.

We are of the view that IIROC should regulate these firms because IIROC has rules that address the risks associated with brokerage activities. Therefore, on July 12, 2012 we published CSA Staff Notice 31-331 in tandem with the Restricted Dealer Member Proposal. The Restricted Dealer Member Proposal introduced a new class of IIROC Member, called a "Restricted Dealer Member", which was intended to migrate firms currently registered as EMDs or restricted dealers carrying out brokerage activities to IIROC membership.

Now that the 90-day comment period has concluded, IIROC is publishing the IIROC Notice. The IIROC Notice summarizes the comments received on the Restricted Dealer Member Proposal and discusses IIROC's intention not to proceed with the proposal.

We remain of the view that IIROC should regulate firms that conduct brokerage activities. Therefore, we intend to publish proposed amendments to National Instrument 31-103 *Registration Requirements, Exemptions and Ongoing Registrant Obligations* (**NI 31-103**) later in 2013 in order to prohibit EMDs from conducting brokerage activities (the **NI 31-103 Amendments**).

Next Steps

Based on the above, impacted firms need to consider the following:

- EMDs that are conducting brokerage activities may continue to conduct these activities until the NI 31-103 Amendments come into force, but they will thereafter be required to restrict their activities to those permitted by the EMD category after the NI 31-103 Amendments are effective; and

- restricted dealers that are conducting brokerage activities in accordance with the terms and conditions of their registration will have their registration and any related exemptive relief extended to the date the NI 31-103 Amendments are effective.

Impacted firms may wish to consider how they will conduct brokerage activities in the future. Options include transferring their brokerage activities to a Canadian incorporated IIROC firm, tailoring their activities to fit solely within the EMD category, or relying upon the international dealer exemption in section 8.18 of NI 31-103.

CSA Staff Notice 31-334 — CSA Review of Relationship Disclosure Practices

Date: **July 18, 2013**
36 O.S.C.B. 7120

Introduction

Staff from the Canadian Securities Administrators in various provinces (CSA staff or we) reviewed the relationship disclosure practices of registered portfolio managers (PMs) and exempt market dealers (EMDs) (the review). This notice summarizes our findings from the review and provides staff guidance on relationship disclosure information (RDI) practices. We will apply the guidance in this notice when assessing the relationship disclosure practices of registered firms, where appropriate. We also encourage registered firms to use this notice as a self-assessment tool to determine how they can improve their relationship disclosure practices.

Background

Section 14.2 of National Instrument 31-103 *Registration Requirements, Exemptions and Ongoing Registrant Obligations* (NI 31-103) requires PMs and EMDs to provide clients with RDI. Companion Policy 31-103CP *Registration Requirements, Exemptions and Ongoing Registrant Obligations* (31-103CP) provides guidance on relationship disclosure requirements.

Objectives of the Review

The main objectives of the review were to:

- assess compliance by PMs and EMDs with relationship disclosure requirements and related securities legislation

- broaden our understanding of the current practices surrounding relationship disclosure (i.e. preparing, reviewing, delivering and revising disclosure documents)

- develop a harmonized compliance approach across Canada when reviewing a firm's relationship disclosure practices

Scope and Methodology

In November 2011, we sent a questionnaire to a representative sample of 124 registered firms across Canada. The sample included:

- 46 firms registered only as PMs

- 26 firms registered only as EMDs

- 52 firms registered in multiple categories, such as PM, EMD and investment fund manager (IFM)

The firms sampled primarily provided products and services to retail, private and institutional clients. The questionnaire asked the firms to provide information about how they meet the relationship disclosure requirements. We assessed the firms' responses against the requirements in applicable securities legislation, including subsections 14.2(1) and 14.2(2) of NI 31-103.

Outcome

Where we identified deficiencies, we sent a compliance deficiency report to the firm. Most CSA jurisdictions required firms to submit a written response to the deficiencies and any revised RDI documents. CSA staff reviewed these responses to ensure that each firm addressed any RDI deficiencies. Firms in certain CSA jurisdictions were notified that we would review the identified deficiencies on the next scheduled compliance examination. Where we continue to have concerns with a firm's actions in resolving the deficiencies, we may consider appropriate regulatory action.

Regulatory Requirements

When assessing the responses to our questionnaire, we primarily considered the requirements in NI 31-103. Subsection 14.2(1) of NI 31-103 requires a registered firm to deliver to a client all information that a reasonable investor would consider important about the client's relationship with the registrant. Given this, it is not our intention to prescribe all of the RDI that a registered firm may provide to their clients. Registered firms should consider what other RDI should be provided to their clients to meet the requirements of subsection 14.2(1).

Our intention is to provide guidance on subsection 14.2(2) which requires a registered firm to deliver specific information to a client, and subsections 14.2(3) and (4) which prescribes when the registered firm must deliver and revise RDI to clients. We also considered the requirement that a registrant deal fairly, honestly and in good faith with clients[1].

Since the review, the relationship disclosure requirements in NI 31-103 have been amended, with the implementation of the new amendments under Phase 2 of the Client Relationship Model Project starting on July 15, 2013 (the CRM2 Amendments). 31-103CP has also been amended with expanded discussion of the RDI requirements, as well as with the addition of guidance corresponding to the new requirements in the CRM2 Amendments. For more information, please refer to the CSA Notice of Amendments to National Instrument 31-103 *Registration Requirements, Exemptions and Ongoing Registrant Obligations* and to Companion Policy 31-103CP *Registration Requirements, Exemptions and Ongoing Registrant Obligations* (Cost Disclosure, Performance Reporting and Client Statements) published on March 28, 2013 (CRM2 Notice)[2].

This staff notice identifies the relationship disclosure requirements at the time of the review, and we also draw attention to clarifications and changes that are effective as of July 15, 2013. Note that there are other new requirements in the CRM2 Amendments that will come into effect starting on July 15 in each of 2013, 2014, 2015 and 2016. Registrants should refer to the CRM2 Notice for more detail about all of the CRM2 Amendments. Firms are expected to identify and implement all necessary steps to ensure their compliance with these amendments.

Concerns with Deficient Client Relationship Disclosure Information

Clients may rely on and make decisions based on a registered firm's RDI. As a result, the RDI should be fulsome and provide meaningful information. If the RDI is deficient, clients may:

- misunderstand the type of services and investment products the registered firm offers and is authorized and able to provide

- incorrectly gauge the level of risk of an investment product or strategy

- not be aware of the fees and costs associated with an investment product or account

- not be aware of conflicts of interest between the registered firm and the client

---

[1]In the participating jurisdictions, this requirement is in section 75.2 of the Securities Act (Alberta), section 14 of the Securities Rules (British Columbia), subsection 154.2(2) of the Securities Act (Manitoba), subsection 54(1) of the Securities Act (New Brunswick), section 39A of the Securities Act (Nova Scotia), section 2.1 of Ontario Securities Commission Rule 31-505 Conditions of Registration, section 160 of the Securities Act (Quebec), section 26.2 of the Securities Act (Newfoundland and Labrador), and subsection 33.1(1) of the Securities Act (Saskatchewan). In Manitoba, subsection 154.2(2) further requires registered firms with discretionary authority to act in the client's best interests.

[2]CRM2 Notice is available on websites of CSA jurisdictions.

Preparing, reviewing, delivering and revising relationship disclosure information

Practices

As part of the review, we asked registered firms how they prepared, reviewed, delivered and revised RDI. We found the following acceptable practices:

- firms provided RDI in separate documents, such as the Investment Management Agreement (IMA), Advisory Agreement, Investment Policy Statement (IPS), Know Your Client (KYC) forms and offering documents, which together gave the client the required information

- firms typically provided RDI to clients at the time of account opening, and at the very least, before making or advising the client to make an investment

- firms personally delivered RDI to the client, and if that was not possible, sent it to the client by mail, electronically or by fax

- firms required clients to acknowledge receipt of the disclosure documents

- firms kept signed copies of all relationship disclosure documents either in hard copy or electronic format

- firms advised clients in a timely manner if there was a significant change to the RDI by letter, phone or email, and required clients to acknowledge the change

While most registered firms had a process for reviewing the disclosures provided to clients, some did not have policies and procedures specifically designed to address the requirements under section 14.2 of NI 31-103. This practice is not consistent with the requirements in section 11.1 of NI 31-103 (compliance system).

Guidance

We intend the following guidance to assist registered firms with preparing, reviewing, delivering and revising RDI:

- Under section 11.1 of NI 31-103, registered firms must have policies and procedures that establish a system of controls and supervision sufficient to provide reasonable assurance that the firm and each individual acting on its behalf complies with securities legislation. This extends to the relationship disclosure requirements. Written policies and procedures should reflect the registered firm's practices when preparing, reviewing, delivering and revising relationship disclosure documents.

- RDI should contain accurate, complete and up-to-date information. We suggest that registered firms review their RDI annually or more frequently, as necessary. Subsection 14.2(4) requires registered firms to take reasonable steps to notify clients, in a timely manner, of significant changes in respect of the RDI delivered to a client.

- The RDI that registered firms provide to clients should contain meaningful, understandable information that enables clients to make informed investment decisions.

- Registered firms should ensure that the RDI clearly explains the products and services the firm offers, contains adequate description of the fees and costs associated with those products and services, and provides sufficient explanations of the risks a client should consider when making investment decisions.

In addition to the foregoing, please note that as of July 15, 2013:

- Subsection 14.2(3) of NI 31-103 prescribes when RDI is to be delivered to the client. As of July 15, 2013, it specifies that registered firms must deliver the information referred to in subsection 14.2(1), if applicable, and subsection 14.2(2) to the client in writing. However, the firm may provide the information in paragraph 14.2(2)(b) orally or in writing. If firm choose to provide the information in paragraph 14.2(2)(b) orally, they should maintain evidence of the discussion[3].

- The language of certain requirements in section 14.2 is amended to clarify where a general description of RDI is sufficient.

- The guidance about RDI communication in 31-103CP is expanded.

- New subsection 14.2(5.1) prohibits registered firms from imposing any new or increased operating charge in respect of a client's account unless 60 days prior written notice is provided.

- The cost disclosure requirements are now more specific, and firms are now required to separately disclose applicable information about "operating charges" and "transaction charges" (paragraphs 14.2(2)(f) and (g)). These terms are defined in section 1.1 of NI 31-103 and there is guidance on their meanings in section 14.2 of 31-103CP. The term "costs" in section 14.2 of NI 31-103 is replaced with the term "charges" to avoid confusing the charges associated with the operation of an account or executing transactions with the purchase cost of a security.

Summary of Results

We identified a number of deficiencies in the RDI that registered firms must deliver to clients under subsection 14.2(2) of NI 31-103. The following is a list of these requirements ranked in order of most to least identified deficiencies:

- Description of the risks of using borrowed money to finance a purchase of a security — paragraph 14.2(2)(d)

- Information a firm must collect about the client (Know Your Client) — paragraph 14.2(2)(l)

---

[3]The CRM2 Amendments include guidance in section 14.2 of 31-103CP about keeping evidence of compliance with client disclosure requirements.

- Statement that the firm has an obligation to assess suitability prior to executing a transaction — paragraph 14.2(2)(k)

- Description of the content and frequency of reporting for each account or portfolio of a client — paragraph 14.2(2)(i)

- Description of the types of risks that a client should consider when making investment decisions — paragraph 14.2(2)(c)

- Description of the nature or type of client account — paragraph 14.2(2)(a)

- Description of the conflicts of interest the firm is required to disclose to a client — paragraph 14.2(2)(e)

- Disclosure of all costs to a client for the operation of an account, and description of the costs clients will pay in making, holding and selling investments — paragraphs 14.2(2)(f) and 14.2(2)(g)

- Discussion that identifies the products or services offered by the firm — paragraph 14.2(2)(b)

- Description of the compensation paid to the firm in relation to different types of products that a client may purchase — paragraph 14.2(2)(h)

Specific Issues and Guidance

The following section discusses the requirements under subsection 14.2(2) in the order they are stated in that subsection, and provides details about the findings, as well as guidance to registered firms in order to meet their obligations.

1. — Describe the Nature or Type of the Client's Account

Under paragraph 14.2(2)(a), a registered firm must provide clients with a description of the nature or type of account that the client has with the firm. In particular, the registered firm should provide the client with sufficient information to enable the client to understand the type of accounts they hold, how the accounts will operate, and the services associated with the accounts.

22% of registered firms sampled were deficient in this area.

We found the following deficiencies:

- Firms did not disclose the type or nature of account that they managed for the client, or the disclosure was unclear.

- The disclosure did not discuss in what capacity the firm was acting on behalf of the client, for example, if the PM had discretion over the account or if the firm was acting as an EMD for the client.

- Some EMDs did not think they were required to disclose this information since their relationship with the client existed only on a transactional basis.

Guidance

PMs

RDI should disclose that the registered firm acts as a PM for the client and indicate whether the client has a discretionary or non-discretionary account. While there is no need to specify the type of account that the client holds (for example, registered, cash, etc.), PMs should describe the type of services that they will provide to the client and disclose where the client assets are held (for example, if they are held at a custodian).

EMDs

RDI should disclose that the firm acts as an EMD for the client. EMDs should describe how they will operate client accounts and outline the services that they will provide to their clients. EMDs should disclose where and how assets are held, for example, that they will be held in client name with the issuer of the exempt securities.

2. — Identify the Products or Services the Registered Firm Offers

Paragraph 14.2(2)(b) requires a registered firm to include a discussion that identifies the products or services the registered firm offers to clients[4]. The registered firm should provide and disclose:

- sufficient information to identify the types of products or services the firm is registered to provide

- what parameters the firm will use to select investments

- information about all registerable activities or types of business involving the registered firm 11% of registered firms sampled were deficient in this area.

We found the following deficiencies:

- PMs provided information about their investment mandate, but did not specifically discuss the types of securities that they invest in to fulfill that mandate.

- Registered firms did not explain to clients that the description of products or services was located elsewhere than in the RDI (i.e., in their engagement letter, on their website or in a related offering document).

---

[4]Paragraph 14.2(2)(b) changed as follows since the review: a general description of the products and services the registered firm offers to the client.

- Firms registered in multiple categories provided disclosure relating to one segment of their business, but not for other activities they are registered to provide.

- Registered firms identified the products that they offered, but did not discuss the services.

Guidance

PMs

PMs should disclose that they will advise in securities for the client, for example, in accordance with an IPS.

EMDs

EMDs should indicate that they sell third party or proprietary prospectus-exempt products. EMDs may refer clients to another entity's offering documents (typically prepared by an issuer) provided the disclosure is adequately fulfilling the dealer's disclosure obligations. EMDs should also indicate that products are not offered by prospectus, rather than just indicating that they sell "exempt products".

3. — Describe the Types of Risks that a Client Should Consider

Paragraph 14.2(2)(c) requires registered firms to provide clients with a description of the types of risks a client should consider when making investment decisions[5].

32% of registered firms sampled were deficient in this area.

We found the following deficiencies:

- Registered firms provided only a generic list of the risks, but did not describe the risk implications on the client's investment decisions.

- Registered firms verbally discussed the risks with the client (i.e., during the KYC and IPS development process), but did not provide anything to the client in writing or maintain evidence of the discussion.

- Where a registered firm undertook a particular investment strategy for a client, the firm did not discuss or document the potential risks of participating in that strategy.

- Descriptions of risk were vague and did not provide sufficient detail for clients.

- Some EMDs did not provide risk disclosure or refer clients to the risks discussed in the issuer's offering documents.

Guidance[6]

PMs

A PM should either provide an explanation of the risks associated with making investment decisions to the client (i.e., currency, interest rate, margin, leverage, liquidity, etc.) or refer to the risks discussed in the IPS. The risks described should be relevant to the PM's business environment, the investments offered, and the investment strategies recommended for the client.

EMDs

An EMD should either explain the specific risks of each product clearly in the relationship disclosure document or refer to the risk disclosure contained in the Offering Memorandum or other offering documents, provided that the EMD is satisfied that the disclosure is adequate. EMDs should ensure that the RDI provided to clients also includes a discussion of the risks of investing in the exempt market in general.

4. — Describe the Risks to a Client of Using Borrowed Money

Paragraph 14.2(2)(d) requires registered firms to provide a description of the risks of using borrowed money to finance a purchase of a security.

41% of registered firms sampled were deficient in this area.

We found the following deficiencies:

- Registered firms thought this requirement did not apply to them because they:

  - did not purchase investments on margin, recommend leverage strategies to clients, or provide service to or accept clients who borrow to invest

  - only dealt with accredited investors who are aware of the risks of investing using borrowed money

- Registered firms did not provide this disclosure and instead relied on disclosure provided by other entities (such as the issuer or the custodian).

- Registered firms noted they discussed the risks associated with leverage verbally with clients, but did not include this information in their written disclosure or maintain evidence of the discussion.

---

[5]As of July 15, 2013, paragraph 14.2(2)(c) is amended as follows: a general description of the types of risks that a client should consider when making an investment decision.

[6]As of July 15, 2013, subsection 14.2(3) requires a registered firm to deliver the information in paragraph 14.2(2)(c) in writing.

Guidance[7]

PMs and EMDs

PMs and EMDs must disclose the risks of using borrowed money to invest to all clients, regardless of whether or not the client uses leverage or the firm recommends the use of borrowed money to purchase investments. This disclosure is important, as the firm may not be aware that the client is making an investment with borrowed funds.

In circumstances where a firm recommends the use of borrowed money to finance any part of a purchase of a security, the following disclosure found in section 13.13 of NI 31-103 must be included, or disclosure that is substantially similar:

> *Using borrowed money to finance the purchase of securities involves greater risk than a purchase using cash resources only. If you borrow money to purchase securities, your responsibility to repay the loan and pay interest as required by its terms remains the same even if the value of the securities purchased declines.*

5. — Describe the Conflicts of Interest

Under paragraph 14.2(2)(e), registered firms must provide a description of the conflicts of interest that the registered firm is required to disclose to a client under securities legislation. One such requirement is in section 13.4 of NI 31-103, which provides that a registered firm must take reasonable steps to identify and then respond to existing and potential material conflicts of interest between the firm and the client. 31-103CP provides guidance on the conflict of interest requirements under section 13.4 and includes examples of situations where registered firms can be in a conflict of interest and how to manage the conflict.

Registered firms should provide clients with information about relationships with related or connected issuers, competing interests of clients, compensation practices, fair allocation, soft dollar arrangements, etc. If a firm has determined it has no conflicts that they are required to disclose, the firm should maintain written documentation to evidence that they have considered the issue.
21% of registered firms sampled were deficient in this area.
We found the following deficiencies:

- Registered firms considered themselves to operate independently, and assumed that they did not have relationships that could potentially present a conflict of interest requiring disclosure, but this was not the case.

- Registered firms indicated that their policies and procedures manual or other internal policies described their conflicts, but acknowledged that they did not disclose these conflicts to clients.

- EMDs indicated that the issuer's offering documents adequately described the conflicts of interest, but this was not the case.

- Registered firms disclosed that they had conflicts, but they did not describe the conflicts or explain how they were addressing them.

- Registered firms provided an insufficient or unclear explanation about their conflicts and did not discuss the potential impact on clients.

- Registered firms disclosed the conflicts of interest at the individual dealing or advising level, but did not consider and disclose conflicts of interest at the firm level.

Guidance

PMs

PMs must identify and respond to conflicts of interest. Most PMs will have some conflicts that require disclosure, such as soft dollar arrangements, fair allocation and personal trading. PMs should disclose and describe all potential or existing material conflicts in detail. If PMs determine that they have no conflicts that they are required to disclose, they should maintain written documentation to evidence that they have considered this issue.

EMDs

EMDs must identify and respond to conflicts of interest. Most EMDs will have some conflicts that require disclosure, such as compensation received from issuers or an affiliation with an issuer. Similar to risk disclosure, an EMD may refer a client to an offering memorandum when disclosing conflicts, if the EMD is satisfied that the disclosure is adequately fulfilling the dealer's disclosure obligations. EMDs should consider whether the disclosure in the offering memorandum relates to the issuer's conflicts, which are not necessarily reflective of the conflicts of interest of the registered firm. In particular, EMDs must also consider the conflicts of interest that exist when selling securities of related or connected issuers. Where EMDs can address the conflict by disclosure, they should ensure that they adequately disclose the nature and extent of the conflict to clients. If EMDs determine that they have no conflicts that they are required to disclose, they should maintain written documentation to evidence that they have considered this issue.

---

[7]As of July 15, 2013, subsection 14.2(3) requires a registered firm to deliver the information in paragraph 14.2(2)(d) in writing.

6. — Disclose all Costs to Clients

Under paragraph 14.2(2)(f), registered firms must provide disclosure of all costs to clients for the operation of an account.[8] Under paragraph 14.2(2)(g), they must provide a description of the costs a client will pay in making, holding and selling an investment.[9] These two requirements ensure that clients receive all relevant information to evaluate all of the costs associated with the products and services they receive from a registered firm.

16% of registered firms sampled were deficient in this area.

We found the following deficiencies:

- Registered firms only referred to costs and fees generally rather than providing specific and meaningful information.

- PMs disclosed details about the management fees they charge in their advisory agreement, but did not discuss that there may be third party costs associated with the operation of the account, such as custodial or brokerage fees.

- Registered firms disclosed information about costs and fees verbally at the time of account opening, but did not maintain evidence in writing that they had verbally provided the client with the disclosure.

- Registered firms indicated in their disclosure that they could change fees without notice to the client. However, under subsection 14.2(4), if there is a significant change to the information delivered to a client under subsection (1), the registered firm must take reasonable steps to notify the client of the change in a timely manner.

- Some EMDs did not disclose fees that they directly charged to the client. Instead, the only disclosure about fees associated with the investment was in the issuer's offering documents.

- Some EMDs did not clearly state the details of compensation or explain that the offering memorandum or subscription agreement may also disclose the amount of compensation.

- Some EMDs' disclosure did not clearly state that the client would be paying fees on a transactional basis, and that costs could differ depending on the investment purchased.

Guidance[10]

PMs

PMs should provide clients with a clear description, and calculation method where applicable, of any fees that the PM charges. We would also expect that if a firm facilitates a clients' entering into third party service arrangements for custody or brokerage, disclosure of the details of any costs associated with these services would be provided at the time the client account is opened. If the PM has negotiated fixed fees for clients (i.e., bundled fees, flat rate for custodial or brokerage charges), the PM should disclose this to clients.

EMDs

EMDs should clearly disclose all trading costs for a client. This includes direct compensation that the EMD or dealing representative receives, and any embedded compensation as disclosed in the offering memorandum. If EMD clients will incur custodial fees, EMDs should provide a description of these fees. If EMDs disclose information in separate documents, they should provide a list of these documents to clients and set out where they can find them. EMDs should disclose all transaction costs incurred by a client when buying or selling the investment, as well as any holding costs associated with the investment (for example, the cost of holding an exempt product in a registered account). EMDs should clearly state whether they charge a fee to operate an account (for example, if any fees are required to open, maintain, close or transfer an account).

7. — Describe Compensation Paid for Different Types of Products

Paragraph 14.2(2)(h) requires that registered firms provide clients with a description of the compensation paid to the firm in relation to the different types of products that a client may purchase through the firm[11]. This requirement clarifies the compensation that a registered firm receives, particularly when a firm:

- receives varying levels of compensation for providing the same service or product, or

- provides a varied range of investment services and products to their clients.

6% of registered firms sampled were deficient in this area.

We found the following deficiencies:

- Some EMDs did not explain the compensation that they receive. For example, the issuer may pay an EMD to maintain a product on the firm's shelf, sales incentive bonuses, or to perform due diligence activities relating to their products.

---

[8]As of July 15, 2013, paragraph 14.2(2)(f) is amended as follows: (f) disclosure of the operating charges the client might be required to pay related to the account.

[9]As of July 15, 2013, paragraph 14.2(2)(g) is amended as follows: (g) a general description of the types of transaction charges the client might be required to pay

[10]As of July 15, 2013, subsection 14.2(3) requires a registered firm to deliver the information in paragraphs 14.2(2)(f) and (g) in writing.

[11]As of July 15, 2013, this paragraph is amended as follows: (h) a general description of any compensation paid to the registered firm by any other party in relation to the different types of products that a client may purchase through the registered firm.

- Some EMDs did not disclose and explain the commissions that they and the dealing representative receive. Rather, EMDs referred the client to the offering document, which in some cases contained insufficient information.

Guidance

EMDs and PMs

While this deficiency was found in 23% of the EMD samples, it is important for both EMDs and PMs to provide clear and meaningful disclosure about the compensation that they receive from any other parties. For example, EMDs should disclose any commission, sales bonuses, and trailer fees they receive from issuers. When providing such disclosure, EMDs may refer a client to an offering document, if the EMD is satisfied that the disclosure is clear and fulsome and adequately fulfills the dealer's disclosure obligations. If the disclosure in the offering document is vague (i.e., "the fee on this purchase is up to 10%"), the EMD should provide more specific disclosure information.

Registrants should also refer to the guidance on the requirements in paragraphs 14.2(2)(f), (g) and (h) that is provided under subsection 14.2 of 31-103CP as amended as of July 15, 2013.

8. — Describe the Content and Frequency of Reporting

Under paragraph 14.2(2)(i), registered firms must provide a description of the content and frequency of reporting for each account or portfolio of a client. Subsections 14.14(1) and (3) of NI 31-103 require registered dealers and advisers to deliver account statements to clients at least once every three months.[12] Although there is no prescribed form for these statements, they must contain the information set out in subsections 14.14(4) and 14.14(5) of NI 31-103.

33% of registered firms sampled were deficient in this area.

We found the following deficiencies:

- The registered firm's RDI discussed the frequency of the reporting, but not the content.

- The description of the content of the quarterly reporting was insufficient and did not encompass everything required under subsections 14.14(4) and 14.14(5).

- Registered firms stated in the disclosure information that the custodian would provide the reporting, without explaining the frequency or the content.

- EMDs thought that quarterly account reporting was not required on the basis that they did not have client "accounts" but rather offered a transactional service only.

Guidance

PMs and EMDs

PMs and EMDs RDI must include a description of the content of the statement and the correct reporting frequency in accordance with section 14.14. Under subsections 14.14(1) and (3), a registered firm must deliver an account statement to a client at least once every three months, or monthly, if the client requests it. Registered firms can increase the frequency of account statement delivery to more than every three months.

CSA Staff Notice 31-324 *Exempt Market Dealers and Account Statement Requirements* in National Instrument 31-103 *Registration Requirements and Exemptions* sets out expectations for EMDs' compliance with the account statement delivery requirements. The CRM2 Amendments introduce new requirements for account statements and additional statements that will be applicable to PMs and EMDs, effective July 15, 2015. Until then, EMDs should continue to refer to Staff Notice 31-324 which, among other guidance, states that

> *We will expect an EMD to deliver quarterly account statements containing:*
>
> - *transaction information [i.e., information required under subsection 14.14(4)] covering each transaction it made for a client during the quarter, and*
>
> - *account balance information [i.e., information required under subsection 14.14(5)] for all cash and securities of the client that it holds or controls*
>
> *If an EMD does not hold or control any cash or securities of a client, and it makes no transactions for the client during a quarter, we will not expect the EMD to send an account statement for that quarter to the client.*

9. — Disclose that Independent Dispute Resolution or Mediation is Available

Under paragraph 14.2(2)(j), if section 13.16 of NI 31-103 (dispute resolution service) applies, registered firms must disclose that independent dispute resolution or mediation services are available at the firm's expense to resolve any dispute that might arise between the client and the firm about any trading or advising activity of the firm or one of its representatives.[13]

---

[12]As of July 15, 2013, subsection (3) is amended as follows: A registered adviser must deliver a statement to a client at least once every 3 months, except that if the client has requested to receive statements on a monthly basis, the adviser must deliver a statement to the client every month. On July 15, 2015, section 14.14 is further amended and new sections 14.14.1, 14.14.2, 14.15 and 14.16 are added. For further information, see CRM2 Notice.

[13]In Québec, a registered firm is deemed to comply with section 13.16 if it complies with sections 168.1.1 to 168.1.3 of the *Securities Act* (Québec). These provisions set out a complaint handling regime whereby the Autorité des marchés financiers (the AMF) may act as amediator (the Québec regime).

Section 13.16 requires that registered firms make available an independent dispute resolution or mediation service to clients, at the firms' expense. At the time of the review, section 13.16 did not apply to firms which were registered when NI 31-103 came into force.[14] As the requirement did not apply to most of the firms we sampled, we do not have information to report on this aspect of relationship disclosure requirements.

10. — State the Obligation to Assess Whether a Purchase or Sale of a Security is Suitable for a Client

Under paragraph 14.2(2)(k), registered firms are required to deliver a statement to clients that the firm has an obligation to assess whether a purchase or sale of a security is suitable for a client prior to executing the transaction or at any other time. This requirement is straightforward, and directly relates to the obligation of a registered firm to meet their suitability obligations under sections 13.2 and 13.3 of NI 31-103.

35% of registered firms sampled were deficient in this area.

We found the following deficiencies:

- The registered firm's disclosure information did not include the specific statement required under paragraph 14.2(2)(k). Some firms thought it was sufficient to:

    - Have policies and procedures in place for assessing suitability

    - Manage client accounts consistent with the KYC information and investment objectives for each client but not provide the statement

    - Include language other than what is required in paragraph14.2(2)(k) or no statement at all

Guidance

PMs and EMDs

PMs and EMDs must include the specific statement required in paragraph 14.2(2)(k) in their RDI.[15]

11. — Disclose the Information that must be collected About Clients

Under paragraph 14.2(2)(l), a registered firm is required to disclose the information that they must collect about their clients as required by section 13.2 of NI 31-103 (know your client). Section 13.2 sets out the information a registrant must obtain and document to establish the identity of a client, determine if the client is an insider, and assess the suitability of proposed investments.

39% of registered firms sampled were deficient in this area.

We found the following deficiencies:

- Registered firms routinely collected adequate KYC information and provided a copy of the completed KYC form to clients, but did not explain in their RDI the terms in the KYC form or state that the firm uses this information to assess suitability.

- Registered firms indicated that they only dealt with accredited investors, and therefore this requirement was not applicable.

- Registered firms did not set out the KYC information that it is required to collect under section 13.2.

Guidance

PMs and EMDs

Registered firms should provide clients with a statement that lists and describes the information that they must collect, and an explanation of how the firm uses this information to assess the suitability of investments for clients.

Registrants should also refer to the guidance on the requirements in paragraphs 14.2(2)(l) that is provided under subsection 14.2 of 31-103CP as amended as of July 15, 2013.

New Requirements

We draw your attention to the new RDI requirements in paragraphs 14.2(2)(m) and (n) that come into force on July 15, 2014. Specifically, paragraph 14.2(2)(m) requires firms to provide each client with a general explanation of benchmarks and whether the firm offers any options for benchmark reporting to clients. Guidance on the new requirements is provided in the amended 31-103CP. See the CRM2 Notice for further information.

Next Steps

We will review the relationship disclosure practices of registered firms during our ongoing compliance reviews and will apply the guidance in this notice when assessing whether a firm is complying with relationship disclosure requirements, and the guidance in the amended 31-103CP.

---

[14]On July 5, 2012, the CSA published parallel orders further extending the temporary relief from Section 13.16 until the earlier of: (i) the coming into force of amendments to section 13.16, and (ii) September 28, 2014. The temporary relief does not apply in Quebec. On November 15, 2012, the CSA published proposed amendments to NI 31-103 about the dispute resolution service. The comment period ended February 15, 2013.

[15]As of July 15, 2013, subsection 14.2(3) requires a registered firm to deliver the information in paragraph 14.2(2)(l) in writing.

CSA Staff Notice 31-335 — Extension of Interim Relief for Members of the Investment Industry Regulatory Organization of Canada from the Requirement in section 14.2(1) of National Instrument 31-103 — Registration Requirements, Exemptions and Ongoing Registrant Obligations in Respect of the Provision of Relation Disclosure Information to Existing Clients

Date: October 3, 2013

36 O.S.C.B. 9503

Introduction

All Canadian Securities Administrators (**CSA**) members have issued parallel orders that provide a limited extension of previously issued interim relief from the requirement to provide relationship disclosure information (**RDI**) prescribed by section 14.2(1) of National Instrument 31-103 *Registration Requirements, Exemptions and Ongoing Registrant Obligations* (**NI 31-103**) for firms that are members of the Investment Industry Regulatory Organization of Canada (**IIROC**). The relief has been extended to March 26, 2014 in respect of the provision of RDI to existing clients only (i.e. clients that were clients of the firm before March 26, 2013).

Relief

Section 14.2(1) of NI 31-103 sets out the principle that a registered firm must deliver to a client all information that a reasonable investor would consider important about the client's relationship with the registrant.

As announced in CSA Staff Notice 31-329 issued on September 28, 2011, all CSA members issued parallel orders that exempted firms that are members of IIROC from the application of the requirement of section 14.2(1) of NI 31-103, provided that after the IIROC RDI rules are approved, the IIROC member complies with them, subject to applicable transition periods. The orders were set to expire on December 31, 2013, by which time the IIROC RDI rules were expected to be fully implemented.

On March 26, 2012, IIROC announced in IIROC Notice 12-0107 *Client Relationship Model — Implementation* the implementation of, among other things, new IIROC Dealer Member Rule 3500 — *Relationship disclosure* (the **IIROC RDI Rule**). The IIROC RDI Rule sets out detailed requirements to assist registered firms who are IIROC members to comply with the general principle in section 14.2(1) of NI 31-103.

The implementation schedule for the IIROC RDI Rule provided that the provision of RDI to: (i) new clients be given a one year transition period, with an effective implementation date of March 26, 2013, and (ii) existing clients be given a two year transition period, with an implementation date of March 26, 2014.

Since the IIROC RDI Rule will not come into effect until March 26, 2014 in respect of the provision of RDI to existing clients, all CSA members have issued parallel orders that exempt registered firms that are members of IIROC from the application of the requirements of section 14.2(1) of NI 31-103 in respect of the provision of RDI to their clients that were clients of the firm before March 26, 2013. The orders will come into effect on December 31, 2013 and will expire on March 26, 2014, by which time the IIROC RDI Rule will be fully implemented.

We are publishing the orders with this Notice. The orders are also available on websites of CSA members, including:

www.lautorite.qc.ca
www.albertasecurities.com
www.bcsc.bc.ca
www.msc.gov.mb.ca
www.qov.ns.ca/nssc
www.nbsc-cvmnb.ca
www.osc.gov.on.ca
www.sfsc.gov.sk.ca

CSA Staff Notice 31-336 — Guidance for Portfolio Managers, Exempt Market Dealers and Other Registrants on the Know-Your-Client, Know-Your-Product and Suitability Obligations

Date: January 9, 2014

37 O.S.C.B. 401

Purpose of this Notice

The know-your-client (**KYC**), know-your-product (**KYP**) and suitability obligations are among the most fundamental obligations owed by registrants to their clients and are cornerstones of our investor protection regime. Staff from the Canadian Securities Administrators (**CSA staff** or **we**) assess registrants' compliance with these important regulatory requirements as part of our compliance oversight reviews. For example, in 2012, staff of the Ontario Securities Commission conducted a targeted review (**Sweep**) of 87 portfolio managers (**PMs**) and exempt market dealers (**EMDs**) to assess their compliance with the KYC, KYP and suitability obligations. The findings of the Sweep are summarized in OSC Staff Notice 33-740 *Report on the results of the 2012 targeted review of portfolio managers and exempt market dealers to assess compliance with the know-your-client, know-your-product and suitability obligations*.

As a result of our compliance oversight reviews, CSA staff have concluded that additional guidance (including CSA staff's views as to practices that may be considered to be "best practices" and practices that we consider to be "unacceptable practices") in the areas of KYC, KYP, and suitability obligations is required to assist registrants, such as PMs, EMDs, and other registrants who are not members of a self-regulatory organization (**SRO**) in meeting their regulatory obligations.

We strongly encourage registrants to use this Notice to improve their understanding of, and compliance with, the very important KYC, KYP, and suitability obligations. We also suggest that registrants use this report as a self-assessment tool to strengthen their compliance with securities laws. Going forward, CSA staff will continue to closely monitor registrants' compliance in these areas and will take appropriate regulatory action to ensure compliance with securities laws.

Top line highlights of the Notice

- **KYC, KYP and suitability obligations are among the most fundamental obligations owed by registrants to their clients, and are cornerstones of our investor protection regime.** The CSA has repeatedly recognised that these requirements are basic obligations of a registrant, and a course of conduct by a registrant involving a failure to comply with them is an extremely serious matter.

- **We expect registrants to comply not only with the letter of the securities law requirements themselves, but also with the spirit of the requirements.** We expect market participants to conduct themselves in a manner that is consistent with the principles of securities regulation. This requires market participants to respect not just the letter of the law, but also the spirit of the law.

- **KYC, KYP and suitability obligations are extensions of each registrant's general duty to deal fairly, honestly and in good faith with its clients.** In Quebec, this duty is framed as the registrant's duty to deal fairly, honestly, loyally and in good faith with its clients.

- **A meaningful suitability assessment is required.** Assessing suitability is more than a mechanical fact-finding or "tick the box" exercise. It requires meaningful dialogue with the client to obtain a solid understanding of the client's investment needs and objectives, and to explain how a proposed investment strategy is suitable for the client in light of the client's investment needs and objectives.

- **Failure to adequately know your client may lead to a distribution of securities by an issuer or dealer in breach of a prospectus exemption which is a serious breach of securities law.** An illegal distribution may also provide an investor with a continuing right of action for rescission or damages against the issuer or dealer for non-delivery of a prospectus.

- **Adequate documentation of the suitability process (including KYC) is critical to ensuring that a registrant is meeting its securities law obligations.**

What's in the Notice?

In addition to providing guidance, this Notice briefly summarises the applicable securities law requirements relating to KYC, KYP, and suitability for registrants. It also sets out selected requirements and guidance for KYC, KYP, and suitability requirements for dealer members of the Investment Industry Regulatory Organization of Canada (**IIROC**) and the Mutual Fund Dealers Association of Canada (**MFDA**). Although these requirements are not applicable to registrants who are not members of an SRO, they may provide helpful guidance to registrants in their determination of how to meet their KYC, KYP, and suitability obligations under securities law.

In this Notice, we will generally refer to registrants who are under the direct oversight of the CSA as registrants. Unless the context otherwise requires, a reference to registrants includes both registered firms and their registered individuals.

The guidance provided represents our expectations of registrants. While the best practices set out in this report are intended to present acceptable methods registrants can use to meet their KYC, KYP, and suitability obligations, they are not the only acceptable methods. Registrants may use alternative methods, provided those methods adequately demonstrate that registrants have met their KYC, KYP and suitability obligations.

Outline of this Notice

The following is an outline of this Notice:

- Purpose of this Notice

- Importance of the KYC, KYP, and suitability obligations

- The KYC obligation
  - What is the basic KYC obligation?
  - What KYC information is required?
  - When does the KYC obligation apply?

- KYC guidance
  - How often should registrants update KYC information?
  - Signing and dating of KYC information by clients and registrants
  - What processes should registrants use to determine whether investors are Accredited Investors (**AIs**)?
  - How should registrants collect and document KYC information?

- What is the basic KYP obligation?

- KYP guidance
  - What are the key areas to consider in assessing KYP?
  - Additional areas to consider when dealing with prospectus-exempt securities

- Reliance on third-party analysis and reports
- CSA Staff Notice 33-315 *Suitability Obligations and Know-Your-Product*
- What is the basic suitability obligation?
- Suitability guidance
  - Why is the suitability analysis so important?
  - How should a registrant demonstrate compliance with the suitability assessment?
  - How is the client-directed trade instruction appropriately used?

Importance of the KYC, KYP, and suitability obligations

Securities laws impose a general duty on registrants to deal fairly, honestly and in good faith with clients. Part 13 of National Instrument 31-103 *Registration Requirements, Exemptions and Ongoing Registrant Obligations* (**NI 31-103**) sets out the principal KYC, KYP, and suitability obligations for registrants. These obligations work together. The KYC, KYP and suitability obligations are an extension of the duty to deal fairly. In turn, the suitability obligation requires a registrant to *know* the client, *know* the product that is the subject of the proposed recommendation or client order, and to form an opinion as to whether the product is suitable in light of the client's investment needs and objectives.

Certain KYC and suitability obligations in NI 31-103 do not apply to firms that are members of a SRO and their representatives if they comply with corresponding SRO requirements. However, a failure to comply with SRO requirements by SRO dealer members may also be a breach of securities law.

CSA staff is committed to taking appropriate regulatory action where we identify significant compliance issues in these areas and the following are examples of some recent decisions which highlight the importance of a registrant's KYC, KYP and suitability obligations:

- Recent Court decisions (including *Sawh v. Ontario Securities Commission*, 2013 ONSC 4018 and *Ridel v. Cassin*, 2013 ONSC 2279),
- Recent decisions of the Ontario Securities Commission (including *Re Trapeze Asset Management Inc.* (2012), 35 O.S.C.B. 4322, and *Re Sawh and Trkulja*, 34 O.S.C.B. 1059 (Director), 35 O.S.C.B. 7431 at 164 (Commission)),
- Recent decision of the Bureau de décision et de révision (Autorité des marchés financiers c. Solutions monétaires Monarc inc. et Karina Stevens et Paul Hauck, 2012-046-001), and the withdrawal of their rights (news release of l'Autorité des marchés financiers on October 17, 2013),
- Recent decisions of, and reviews by, IIROC and the MFDA focusing on their members' compliance with KYC, KYP, and suitability obligations,

As a result of the importance of these obligations, we will continue to focus compliance reviews on issues relating to KYC, KYP, and suitability.

The KYC obligation

What is the basic KYC obligation?

NI 31-103

Section 13.2 of NI 31-103, among other things, requires registrants (including dealer members of IIROC and the MFDA) to take reasonable steps to establish the identity of a client, and to ensure that they have sufficient information to meet their suitability obligation.

Section 13.2 of the Companion Policy to NI 31-103 (**CP 31-103**) explains why securities law imposes a KYC obligation on registrants:

> Registrants act as gatekeepers of the integrity of the capital markets. They should not, by act or omission, facilitate conduct that brings the market into disrepute. As part of their gatekeeper role, registrants are required to establish the identity of, and conduct due diligence on, their clients under the [KYC] obligation . . . KYC information forms the basis for determining whether trades in securities are suitable for investors. This helps protect the client, the registrant and the integrity of the capital markets. The KYC obligation requires registrants to take reasonable steps to obtain and periodically update information about their clients.

SRO rules

The KYC requirements in NI 31-103 also apply to SRO dealer members. Supplemental KYC requirements for SRO dealer members are set out in:

- IIROC Rule 1300 *Supervision of Accounts* (**IIROC Rule 1300**),
- IIROC Rules Notice Guidance Note 12-0109 *Know your client and suitability — Guidance* dated March 26, 2012 (**IIROC Notice 12-0109**),
- Section 2.2.1 of MFDA Rules,
- MFDA Policy No. 2 *Minimum Standards for Account Supervision* (**MFDA Policy No. 2**), and
- MFDA Staff Notice 0069 *Suitability* (**MFDA Notice 0069**).

IIROC Notice 12-0109 says the following about the suitability requirements:

> Dealer Members and Registered Representatives are reminded that compliance with the suitability requirements is fundamental to compliance with general business conduct standards and is essential to good business practice. The suitability requirement is also complementary to the fundamental obligation under securities legislation for all Dealer Members and their representatives to deal fairly, honestly and in good faith with clients.

What KYC information is required?

NI 31-103

To meet their suitability obligation, registrants (including dealer members of IIROC and the MFDA) must take reasonable steps to ensure that they have sufficient information about their client's:

- investment needs and objectives (including the client's time horizon for their investments),

- financial circumstances (including net worth, income, current investment holdings, and employment status), and

- risk tolerance for various types of securities and investment portfolios (taking into account the client's investment knowledge) (collectively, **investment needs and objectives**).

The extent of KYC information a registrant needs to determine suitability of a trade will depend on the:

- client's circumstances,

- type of security,

- client's relationship to the registrant, and

- registrant's business model.

Accredited Investors and Permitted Clients

If a registrant proposes to make a trade in reliance on the prospectus exemption for AIs in National Instrument 45-106 *Prospectus and Registration Requirements* (**NI 45-106**), the registrant must determine whether the client is an AI. For additional guidance in this area, see the Companion Policy to NI 45-106.

A person distributing or trading securities in reliance on a prospectus exemption is responsible for determining whether the exemption is available. A person may rely on factual representations by a purchaser, provided that the person has no reasonable grounds to believe the representations are false. A registrant's obligation to determine that a prospectus exemption is available is supplemented and informed by the registrant's obligation to "know" the client. Accordingly, the obligation to determine whether (and how) a client satisfies the AI definition will generally be higher on registrants than an issuer or other sellers that are not in the business of trading securities. Factual representations, such as a representation in a subscription agreement that the client is an AI, will generally not, by themselves, in CSA staff's view, be sufficient for a registrant to satisfy its KYC obligation. Similarly, if a registrant is relying on subsections 13.2(6) and 13.3(4) of NI 31-103 which allow a permitted client to waive certain KYC and suitability requirements, the registrant must collect adequate information to determine that the client is a permitted client. It is not sufficient to simply rely on the client's initialling or checking off the box in the permitted client certificate/attestation form.

SRO rules

IIROC recently amended its suitability requirements to require each Dealer Member, when making a recommendation to a client or accepting an order from a client (and also where certain other triggering events occur) to use due diligence to ensure that the suitability assessment is made considering the overall account portfolio. See IIROC Rule 1300 and MFDA Policy No. 2 (which is similar).

Although the SRO rules in some cases use additional terms, such as "time horizon" or "portfolio composition" that are not explicitly used in NI 31-103, we take the view that these factors are subsumed within the broader terms used in subsection 13.2 of NI 31-103. For example, a registrant cannot meaningfully determine a client's investment needs and objectives, financial circumstances, or risk tolerance without understanding the client's time horizon or current investment portfolio composition.

IIROC Notice 12-0109 set out a useful discussion on a registrant's assessment of a client's investment objectives versus a client's risk tolerance. The notice states:

> . . . the client's investment objectives and risk tolerance are two separate but related factors; each factor must be assessed based on the clients' financial and personal circumstances and must be reasonable in light of those circumstances . . . For example, designating an 80% high risk tolerance for an elderly client may be unreasonable if the client has a modest net worth and has opened the account to invest a substantial portion of her net worth. On the other hand, the 80% high risk tolerance may not be unreasonable if the elderly client has a substantial net worth and opens an account to invest a small fraction of her net worth.

MFDA Notice 0069 provides guidance to its dealer members on how to establish a suitability framework to ensure compliance with their obligations. The notice also provides guidance on KYC information and how to maintain accurate and complete KYC information.

When does the KYC obligation apply?

NI 31-103

A registrant must have current KYC information whenever a suitability determination is required. A registrant (other than a dealer member of IIROC or the MFDA, which is subject to the requirements set out in the next section) is required in section 13.3 of NI 31-103 to make a suitability determination before a registrant

- makes a recommendation to or accepts an instruction from a client to buy or sell a security, or

- purchases or sells a security for a client's managed account.

In addition, registrants are required in subsection 13.2(4) to make reasonable efforts to keep their clients' KYC information current. We consider information to be current if it is sufficiently up-to-date to support a suitability determination.

SRO rules

Under SRO rules, a suitability determination is generally required when:

- accepting an order from a client,

- recommending to the client the purchase, sale, exchange, or holding of a security,

- securities are received into the client's account by way of deposit or transfer,

- there is a change in the registered representative or portfolio manager responsible for the account, or

- there is a material change in the client's life circumstances or objectives that has resulted in revisions to the client's KYC information as maintained by the dealer member.

KYC guidance

1. — How often should registrants update KYC information?

A registrant is required to obtain current KYC information about a client's investment needs and objectives whenever a suitability determination is required. Some registrants ask their clients to advise them when their KYC information changes. However, we expect registrants to be proactive in ensuring that KYC information is kept up-to-date. We expect PMs (and EMDs that have an ongoing relationship with their clients — see below for further information) to update KYC information at least annually and more often if there is a material change in a client's circumstances (for example, marriage, divorce, birth of a child, loss or change in employment), or investment needs or objectives. Without adequate and timely KYC information, registrants cannot meet their suitability obligation to clients.

EMDs

An EMD may have a transactional relationship or an ongoing relationship with a client depending on the particular facts and circumstances. An example of a transactional relationship is a situation where the EMD's relationship with the client is limited to a specific private placement transaction, neither the EMD nor a related issuer of the EMD holds (directly or indirectly) client assets or securities, the EMD is not paid a trailer fee or similar ongoing compensation in relation to the client's ownership of a security, and there is no expectation on the part of the client that the EMD will continue to provide services to the client after the completion of the transaction. In contrast, if any of these factors are present, or if the EMD is also registered in another category of registration such as PM, the EMD may be viewed as having an ongoing relationship with the client. Similarly, if an EMD acts for a client in a series of transactions, we would consider that the EMD has an ongoing relationship with the client. In the case of an EMD or other registrant that is not an SRO member with an ongoing relationship with a client, we recommend that they implement policies and procedures that reflect the SRO concept of "trigger events" as a best practice.

PMs

We think that a PM's suitability obligation in the context of a managed account is a continuing obligation to ensure that the investment strategy determined by the PM remains suitable for the client. Accordingly, we think that it would be prudent business practice for a PM with discretionary trading authority over a client's account to follow the SRO criteria relating to KYC "trigger events" (set out briefly below) in order to ensure that the investment strategy determined by the PM remains suitable for the client.

SRO rules

Both IIROC Rule 2500 *Minimum Standards for Retail Customer Account Supervision* and MFDA Rule 2.2.4 *Updating Client Information* have similar requirements that their dealer members must update KYC information when there is a material change in client information, such as a change in investment objectives, financial situation or risk tolerance. In addition, MFDA Rule 2.2.4 requires dealer members to (a) send a written request at least annually to each client asking the client to notify the dealer member if there are any material changes to the client's circumstances, and (b) update the client information accordingly.

As well, IIROC Notice 12-0109 provides that account information must be updated any time there is a material change in a client's circumstances such as marriage, divorce, birth of a child, loss of or change in employment, etc. The notice states that this requirement can be met by periodically asking each client about material changes in their circumstances, asking about material changes when meeting with the client to review his/her portfolio, otherwise corresponding with the client to discuss account related matters, or by annually contacting the client to verify the accuracy of account information.

2. — Signing and dating of KYC information by clients and registrants

Although NI 31-103 does not expressly require the signing and dating of KYC information by clients and registrants, we recommend that registrants implement policies and procedures to ensure that both the client and the registrant that reviewed the KYC information with the client sign and date the information. Both the client and registrant should also sign and date amendments to KYC information, whether done as addendums to the original information, or as "fresh" KYC information. Signing and dating KYC information:

- assists with demonstrating compliance with securities law requirements,

- assists with providing evidence that the client confirmed that the information provided was accurate and that the information was discussed with the registrant, and

- may protect the registrant in the event a client later claims that an investment was unsuitable.

3. — What processes should registrants use to determine whether investors are AIs?

NI 45-106 requires all registrants selling securities under an exemption to ensure that adequate processes are in place to determine whether the exemption is available. If a registrant is relying on the AI exemption, the registrant must ensure that the client meets the criteria in the AI definition.

In our compliance reviews, we identified some EMDs that had sold exempt securities to non-AIs without adequate processes in place to assess whether the investors were AIs, or whether other prospectus exemptions were available. In *Sawh and Trkulja* (*Re Sawh and Trkulja* (2012), 35 O.S.C.B. 7431, at 7454, para. 183, ; affirmed 2013 ONSC 4018 (Div. Ct.)), the Ontario Securities Commission said:

> The fact that an investor declared himself to be an accredited investor does not absolve a registrant of the responsibility to take adequate steps in the circumstances to ascertain that the investor meets the criteria to be accredited based on his or her financial circumstances.

As well, some KYC forms used by these EMDs were not designed to allow the EMD to determine whether the client met the AI definition. In addition, some of the information contained in the so-called "AI certificate" was inconsistent with the client's KYC form.

If a client does not satisfy the definition of AI or fall within another exemption, the distribution is a serious breach of securities law. It is also important to note that EMDs are limited to dealing with clients who are eligible to purchase securities under a prospectus exemption. Accordingly, if the client does not meet the requirements of the prospectus exemptions, then the EMD is acting outside of its registration category contrary to securities law.

Suggested practices for registrants that distribute securities in reliance on a prospectus exemption

Registrants should ensure that they have adequate policies and procedures in place to ensure compliance with the conditions of the exemption. Registrants should:

- **Develop a KYC form that has sufficient information about the client to allow the registrant to determine if the client meets the requirement of the prospectus exemptions.** Thresholds used in the KYC form should be consistent with the minimum income and asset thresholds in the AI or eligible investor definition contained in NI 45-106.

- **Tailor or develop a separate KYC form for clients that are corporations, partnerships, trusts or other entities, and not individuals, to support reliance on the exemption.** For example, if the registrant is relying on paragraph (t) of the AI definition in NI 45-106 *[an entity that is owned by persons who are AIs]*, the registrant must collect and document adequate information about the *owners* of the entity to support reliance on the exemption.

- **Understand the different categories of investor that make up the definition of AI or eligible investor and the conditions contained in these categories.** Registrants should pay specific attention to the differences between the definitions of "assets" and "financial assets" (which *exclude* an investor's personal residence or other real estate) and the requirement that financial assets be *net* of any related liabilities.

- **Obtain a breakdown of financial assets and net assets of the client** to ensure that the information collected accurately reflects the client's financial circumstances and to assist the registrant in assessing the availability of the prospectus exemptions and the suitability of any investment made.

- **Make further inquiries about the client's financial circumstances** in situations where there is a reasonable doubt about the accuracy of information given by the client or the validity of the client's claim to be an AI or eligible investor. Document the inquiries in the client's file.

- **Establish policies and procedures and provide training to dealing and advising representatives** to ensure they fully understand the prospectus exemptions and that exempt securities may only be distributed to investors who meet the requirement of the prospectus exemptions.

Unacceptable practices

Registrants should not:

- **Rely** *solely* **on the investor's representation in an AI certificate, Resident Exemption Form or Eligible Investor Questionnaire without obtaining KYC information from clients to independently assess reliance on the exemption.** Also, it is not appropriate to rely on inferences based on the registrant's knowledge of a client (example, job title, type of car, or location of residence) to assess whether a client is able to rely on an exemption.

Part 3:
REGISTRATION

- **Assume that another person (whether another registrant that has previously dealt with a client or another individual within a registrant firm that is dealing with a client) has complied with the KYC obligation or the obligation to determine that the client is eligible to purchase securities on a prospectus-exempt basis.** Each registrant dealing with a client has an obligation to comply with these obligations or to confirm that the registrant firm has properly conducted and documented this determination.

- **Process prospectus-exempt trades without complete and adequate KYC information to support reliance on the exemption.**

4. — How should registrants collect and document KYC information?

In our compliance reviews, we continue to identify issues related to inadequate collection and documentation of KYC information. Registrants did not ensure that KYC forms were fully completed for all clients. As well, many registrants did not have a process in place to update KYC forms.

In order to meet the KYC and suitability obligations, registrants must take reasonable steps to ensure they have sufficient current information regarding a client's investment needs and objectives. Collecting and documenting KYC information is more than just a fact-finding or "tick the box" exercise. Registrants should make all necessary enquiries to obtain a solid understanding of a client's investment needs and objectives. They should engage in a meaningful dialogue with their clients and explain to them why the KYC information is required.

The MFDA and IIROC have issued similar KYC guidance to their member firms. For more details please refer to:

- IIROC Notice 12-0109,

- IIROC Notice 12-0108 *Client Relationship Model — Guidance*, and

- MFDA Staff Notice 0069.

Suggested practices for collecting and documenting KYC information

Registrants should:

- **Engage in meaningful KYC discussions with clients** and consider the use of a questionnaire to facilitate the collection and documentation of KYC information. If possible, meet with clients face to face and ask detailed questions to assist in their understanding of the clients' investment needs and objectives. If it is not possible to meet with a client face to face, a registrant should carefully document the additional steps taken to demonstrate compliance with KYC and suitability obligations.

- **Collect and document sufficient minimum KYC information** including name, age, investment objectives, annual income, net financial assets, net assets, liquidity needs, time horizon, risk tolerance, and portfolio composition. This should include registrant representatives' notes of discussions with clients. Registrants should also obtain a breakdown of financial assets (deposits and type of securities such as mutual funds, listed stocks, exempt securities etc.) and net worth (types of assets and liabilities).

- **Collect relevant information from each client so as to establish their identity.** Maintain a record of the identification document (for example, passport or driver's licence number and place of issue).

- **Develop an "investor-friendly" KYC form** by ensuring all terms used in the KYC form such as investment objectives, investment knowledge, and risk are clearly explained in plain language.

- **Consider a client's** *willingness* **to accept risk and** *ability* **to accept risk when assessing a client's risk tolerance.** A client may be willing to accept risk; however, this does not necessarily mean that a client has the ability to financially withstand a downturn in the market or other partial or total loss of their investment. Alternatively, a client may have the financial means to absorb losses, but may not be willing to do so.

- **Review the completed KYC form with the client for accuracy** to ensure that the information collected reflects the client's investment needs and objectives. The KYC form should also be signed, dated and reviewed by the registrant and the client should receive a signed copy of the KYC form for their records.

- **Update KYC information at least annually** (for PMs, and for EMDs that have an ongoing relationship with their clients), if there is a significant change in a client's life circumstances, or a significant change in market conditions. Any changes in KYC information (or a confirmation that there are no changes) should be signed, dated and reviewed by the registrant and the client should receive a signed copy of the revised KYC form for their records.

- **PMs should develop a tailored investment policy statement (IPS) for each managed account.** The IPS should document the client's investment needs and objectives and set out a planned asset allocation. PMs should provide a signed (and dated) copy of the IPS to each client at the time the IPS is first signed and when it is updated.

- **Establish policies and procedures for collecting, documenting and reviewing sufficient KYC information for each client.**

- **Provide adequate training to their staff** to ensure they fully understand the importance of collecting, reviewing and maintaining adequate and up-to-date KYC information.

Unacceptable practices

Registrants should not:

- **Collect KYC information solely by asking clients to tick a box that best describes their investment objectives or risk tolerance.** This mechanical "tick box" approach is not sufficient to fulfill a registrant's suitability obligation.

- **Rely only on a KYC form or other document to know the client.** This "form based" approach is not sufficient to fulfill a registrant's suitability obligation.

- **Process a trade (other than a liquidating transaction upon a client's request) if there is any missing or conflicting KYC information** that may affect their ability to assess the availability of the prospectus exemption or the suitability of the investment.

- **Delegate the KYC or suitability obligation to an unregistered individual** (for example, an administrative assistant or a referrer) to collect KYC information, complete the KYC form for the client, or explain products to a client. Although a registrant may rely on an unregistered individual to assist in incidental administrative tasks related to the collection of KYC information, the registrant has the obligation to "know" the client and the client's investment needs and objectives. If an unregistered individual or firm purports to collect KYC information or explain products to clients, these activities may be considered to be registerable dealing or advising activities (since these activities may themselves constitute acts in furtherance of a trade).

- **Use outdated KYC information or an outdated KYC form to assess the suitability of a client's investment.**

- **Use a KYC form or other document that contains disclaimer language** which purports to limit liability for all losses, including losses resulting from a breach of the registrant's obligations under securities law.

What is the basic KYP obligation?

NI 31-103

As explained in section 3.4 of CP 31-103 [*Proficiency — initial and ongoing*], registered individuals must understand the structure, features, and risks of each product they recommend as part of their initial and ongoing proficiency obligations. Section 3.4 of NI 31-103 sets out that an individual "must not perform an activity that requires registration unless the individual has the education, training and experience . . . including understanding the structure, features and risks of each security the individual recommends". These requirements are applicable to all registrants, including SRO members. This proficiency requirement (also referred to as **know-your-product** or **KYP**) is in addition to the suitability obligation in section 13.3 and applies even when there is an exemption from the suitability obligation (such as, for example, the exemption for permitted clients).

The KYP obligation is also a necessary element of the KYC and suitability determination. Section 13.3 of NI 31-103 requires registrants to take reasonable steps to ensure that a proposed trade is suitable for a client before making a recommendation or accepting instructions from a client. To meet this obligation, registrants should have an in-depth knowledge of all securities that they buy and sell for, or recommend to, their clients.

Although the KYP obligation is triggered when a registrant "recommends" a product to a client, a registrant may expressly or implicitly recommend a product through conduct such as placing a product on the registrant's "shelf" and making it available to a client, by advertising or promoting the product, or by distributing marketing material about the product to a client.

SRO rules

IIROC Notice 12-0109 sets out similar requirements for their dealer members. In addition, IIROC Guidance Note 09-0087 *Best practices for product due diligence* revised on March 25, 2009 sets out IIROC's expectations regarding procedures and criteria that dealer members should consider when assessing and introducing products that they approve or recommend for sale. Lastly, IIROC recently published Guidance Note 13-0039 *Recommendations and best practices for distribution of non-arm's length investment products* which provides guidance on distributions of non-arm's length investment products.

MFDA Staff Notice MSN-0048 *Know Your Product* dated October 31, 2005 (**MSN-0048**) clarifies the obligations of MFDA dealer members and approved persons with respect to the approval and sale of investment products by dealer members. The notice requires dealer members to perform a reasonable level of due diligence on products prior to their approval for sale by Approved Persons.

In addition, as part of the KYP obligation, CSA staff expects a registrant to assess the suitability of leveraged trades or leveraging strategies for those clients that borrow funds to trade in securities. The MFDA recently amended their KYC rule and Policy No. 2 (see MFDA Rule 2.2.1 and Policy No. 2) to clarify the obligation of their dealer members to assess the suitability of orders involving the use of borrowed funds. The rule clarifies that dealer members must assess suitability of leveraging strategies in light of the client's investment knowledge, risk tolerance, and investment objectives. The MFDA also published a leveraging supervision guide which provides further guidance to its dealer members on how to maintain appropriate documentation of leverage recommendations and supervision, and addressing unsuitable leveraging.

KYP guidance

1. — What are the key areas to consider in assessing KYP?

Registrants must conduct their own product due diligence and be able to explain to their clients the security's risks, key features, and initial and ongoing costs and fees. As part of their product due diligence, registrants should review and assess the information contained within the offering memorandum (**OM**) or other documentation provided by the issuer. If the information is not sufficient to allow the registrant to conduct a meaningful KYP assessment of the issuer and the product, the registrant will need to conduct further due diligence on the issuer and the product or refrain from dealing with that product. Registrants must be able to evidence their own product due diligence.

A registrant should only place a product on its approved product list after they have concluded that the product has a reasonable prospect of meeting its investment objectives and that the product has a reasonable prospect of being a suitable investment for some clients. The product assessment requires a critical analysis of the features inherent in the product, and how those features affect the investment's potential risk and reward. Registrants should assess what factors may affect the success of the product, and should proceed only on the basis of some reasoned assessment of the product's actual potential.

Having the registered firm's approval for representatives to sell a product does not mean that the product will be suitable for all clients. Individual registrants should understand the structure, features, risks, fees and costs of each product they recommend to their clients to determine the suitability of each transaction.

CSA staff take the view that the KYP obligation is triggered not only by the particular attributes of a security, viewed in isolation, but also by the proposed *quantum of the investment amount* or the proposed *trading strategy* involving the security.

For example, an investment in a high-risk security may be suitable for a client where the proposed investment would represent a small portion of the client's investment portfolio. However, an investment in the same security may not be suitable for the client where the proposed investment would represent a substantial portion of the client's portfolio or where the proposed investment strategy involves leverage. If registrants choose to categorize products using broad categories such as "low risk", "medium risk" and "high risk", registrants should ensure that the categorizations are reasonable, and consistent with industry standards and client expectations. Registrants should carefully explain the meaning of these terms to the client in plain language terms and should document this process.

As well, registrants that choose to categorize investment objectives or trading strategies using terms such as "balanced" should ensure that these categorizations are reasonable, and consistent with industry standards and client expectations. Registrants should also carefully explain the meaning of these terms to the client in plain language terms and document this process.

2. — *Additional areas to consider when dealing with prospectus-exempt securities*

The sale of prospectus-exempt securities poses a special KYP challenge for registrants. In *Sawh and Trkulja*, the Ontario Securities Commission reviewed the KYP obligation described in MSN-0048 and NI 31-103, and found that the registrants had failed to properly discharge their KYP obligation in the context of the sale of securities sold pursuant to prospectus exemptions. The Ontario Securities Commission was critical of the registrants' simple reliance on representations made in the offering memorandum and other documents provided to them by the issuer. The Ontario Securities Commission went on to add:

> In our view, the Applicants' due diligence process was particularly inadequate in light of the fact that [the securities in question] were sold pursuant to exemptions under applicable securities legislation. Limited partnership units sold under an exemption from securities law do not benefit from the same transparency and liquidity characteristics or regulatory oversight as other products. For example, securities sold under an exemption will not be liquid investments. Offering memoranda are not prospectuses and are not subject to regulatory review. Given the absence of such safeguards, we find that the Applicants failed to conduct an adequate review of the Exempt Products.

In assessing products sold on a prospectus-exempt basis, registrants should also consider additional risks associated with:

- Liquidity risk, reflecting the fact that any resale of such securities may be subject to resale restrictions or indefinite hold periods and the fact that there will generally be no market for such resale,

- Valuation risk, reflecting the fact that the securities may be more difficult to value due to the lack of prospectus and continuous disclosure about the issuer, and

- Conflict of interest risk, reflecting the fact that the securities may be issued by a related party.

A failure to properly categorize a product may result in significant legal and regulatory risk to a registrant. See *Re Trapeze Asset Management Inc.* (2012), 35 O.S.C.B. 4322.

3. — *Reliance on third-party analysis and reports*

We have recently identified a number of situations where issuers and registrants have distributed securities on the basis of marketing materials that include so-called "independent" analyses or reports prepared by unregistered third parties.

We have also seen cases where a registrant may choose to rely on a report prepared by a third-party as part of its own due diligence process; however, this does not relieve the registrant of its obligation to "know-the-product" and to conduct its own KYP and suitability analysis. Registrants should be particularly careful when relying on disclosure prepared by an issuer or a so-called "independent" report prepared by a third-party and commissioned by the issuer.

Where a registrant distributes a security on the basis of a third-party report that purports to "rate" a security, compare a security with other securities of other issuers, or describes an exempt market security as "investment grade", the registrant should perform its own product assessment to ensure that the report is fair, balanced and not misleading.

4. — *CSA Staff Notice 33-315 Suitability Obligation and Know-Your-Product*

CSA Staff Notice 33-315 *Suitability Obligations and Know-Your*-Product dated September 2, 2009 reminds registrants of their duty under securities law to satisfy their suitability obligations, including the requirement to fully understand the products recommended to clients. In particular, the notice contains guidance on a firm's product review process, including procedures for identifying, reviewing and approving (or rejecting) new products, and for monitoring existing products for significant changes to those products.

Suggested practices to satisfy the KYP obligation

Registrants should:

- **Have an in-depth understanding of each of the items listed below before recommending a product to clients:**
  - general features and structure — including return, use of leverage, conflicts of interest, time horizon, overall complexity of the product.
  - risks — including the possibility that clients may lose some or all of the principal invested, liquidity risk, redemption risk, risks from underlying derivatives or structured product, conflicts of interest risk.

- costs — including fees paid to registrants or other parties (commissions, sales charges, trailer fees, management fees, incentive fees, referral fees, embedded fees, executive compensation)

- parties involved — including issuer's financial position and history, qualifications, reputation and track record of the parties involved in key aspects of the product, and

- legal and regulatory framework — including frequency, completeness and accuracy of the issuer's disclosure.

- **Establish policies and procedures for reviewing and approving new products and existing products whose structure or features have significantly changed.** The extent of the product review process will vary depending on the structure and features of the product. For example, complex investment products (including those that are novel, not transparent in structure, involve leverage, options, other derivatives, or have limited disclosure) may require a more extensive review than more straightforward products.

- **Carefully review offering documents or other documentation prepared by the issuer or other third parties and ask questions where appropriate.** Products that are sold under a prospectus exemption may require a more extensive review because of the limited disclosure available about them. As part of their product due diligence, registrants should review and assess the information contained within the offering documents or other documentation prepared by the issuer or other third parties. If the information contained within does not contain sufficient information to allow the registrant to conduct a meaningful KYP assessment of the issuer and the product, the registrant will need to conduct further due diligence on the issuer and the product or refrain from dealing with that product.

- **Consider competitive products that may be less risky or less costly to clients.** If competitive products are less risky or less costly, registrants should maintain adequate documentation to demonstrate the suitability of the product recommended.

- **Perform a conflict of interest assessment**, particularly if a registrant is planning to distribute a product of a related issuer or connected issuer, where often the same individuals form the management of both the registrant and the issuer. Assess and determine whether the conflicts of interest can be adequately managed through disclosure or control. If not, a registrant should not distribute the product.

- **Assess suitability of leveraging strategies** in light of the client's investment knowledge, risk tolerance, and investment objectives.

- **Provide training sessions** to ensure that dealing representatives and advising representatives fully understand and are able to explain clearly the product features and risks to clients.

Unacceptable practices

Registrants should not:

- **Fail to fully understand the structure and features of the products** and recommend a product solely based on:

  - information from issuers or other third parties, including related parties, about the product's suitability, risk profile or expected return,

  - similarities with other products, or

  - recommendations made by other market participants to their clients or by unregistered persons providing general advice.

- **Rely solely on a product being on the firm's "approved product list" rather than conducting a product analysis or understanding a product themselves.**

What is the basic suitability obligation?

NI 31-103

Section 13.3 of NI 31-103 requires a registrant to take reasonable steps to ensure that, before it makes a recommendation to, or accepts an instruction from, a client to buy or sell a security, or makes a purchase or sale of a security for a client's managed account, the purchase or sale is suitable for the client.

As explained in CP 31-103, suitability obligations cannot be:

- delegated to a third party,

- satisfied simply by disclosing the risks of the trade, or

- waived (except by investors that are "permitted clients" as defined in NI 31-103).

Some EMDs may have a relationship with the issuer (or other sellers of the securities). In some cases, these EMDs failed to recognize that the persons purchasing securities from these issuers or sellers were the EMD's clients and that the EMDs have obligations, including suitability obligations, to these purchasers. CSA staff reminds EMDs that it is a breach of their obligations, including their fair dealing obligations to prefer an issuer, seller or their own interests over an investor's interests.

Similarly, even if a registrant has determined that a prospectus exemption is available to the client this does not necessarily mean that the investment will be suitable for the client. The obligation to determine that a prospectus exemption is available is entirely separate and distinct from the obligation to determine that a proposed recommendation or client order is suitable for the client. A proposed trade or recommendation may be wholly unsuitable for a client in light of the client's time horizon, risk tolerance, existing portfolio composition, or other factors within the client's investment needs and objectives, notwithstanding the fact that the client is eligible to make the investment on a prospectus-exempt basis.

Part 3: REGISTRATION

SRO rules

IIROC's suitability requirement is set out in IIROC Rule 1300.1, which requires dealer members to use due diligence to ensure that recommendations to clients regarding the purchase, sale, exchange, or holding or any security is suitable for the client based on factors including investment objectives, time horizon, risk tolerance and the account's current investment portfolio composition and risk level. IIROC Notice 12-0109 expands the suitability obligation and requires dealer members to ensure that the order type, trading strategy and method of financing the trade recommended are also suitable for the client.

Suitability guidance

1. — Why is the suitability analysis so important?

As set out in this Notice, KYC, KYP, and suitability obligations are among the most fundamental obligations owed by registrants to their clients. These obligations are also cornerstones of our investor protection regime. Thus it is critical for registrants to fully comply with these obligations — not only the securities law requirements themselves, but also with the spirit of the requirements. CSA staff will take appropriate regulatory action to ensure compliance.

We expect registrants to perform a meaningful suitability assessment and to appropriately document that assessment. The suitability assessment should be more than a mechanical fact-finding or "tick the box" exercise. It requires a meaningful dialogue with the client to obtain a solid understanding of the client's investment needs and objectives, and to explain how a proposed investment is suitable for the client in light of the clients' investment needs and objectives.

Suggested practices to satisfy the suitability obligation

Registrants should:

- **Consider all relevant KYC information (including, investment objectives, time horizon and risk tolerance) when assessing the suitability of an investment.** For example, a client may have a high risk tolerance but also have a short term time horizon and therefore a high risk investment with redemption restrictions may not be suitable for that client.

- **Review each trade independently to ensure it is suitable**. A registrant should not process a trade unless it is reviewed and approved. In addition, PMs should have an adequate process in place to monitor clients' portfolio holdings in accordance with their investment mandate.

- **Develop a system or process to identify and reject trades that are inconsistent with a client's investment needs and objectives.** The firm should also monitor trends or patterns (for example, number of rejected trades by the Chief Compliance Officer for a particular dealing representative) that may indicate potential areas for training or revisions to processes to ensure compliance.

- **Provide adequate training to registered individuals** to ensure they fully understand the suitability obligation and the firm's process for assessing suitability of investments.

Unacceptable practices

Registrants should not:

- **Assume that all products that are set out on the firm's approved product list are suitable for every client.**

- **Rely on out-of-date KYC or KYP information.**

2. — How should a registrant demonstrate compliance with the suitability assessment?

In our compliance reviews, we found a number of instances where it was not clear that the registrant had conducted an appropriate KYC, KYP, or suitability determination due to inadequate, incomplete, or (in some cases) completely missing documentation. These instances constitute a breach of securities law requirements as sections 11.1 and 11.5 of NI 31-103 require registrants to establish, maintain and apply policies and procedures that establish a system of internal controls and supervision, and to maintain books and records that demonstrate the extent of the registrant's compliance with applicable securities law requirements. As well, a failure to document the KYC, KYP, and suitability process also significantly raises the risk of adverse legal and regulatory consequences to the registrant in the event a client's investment ultimately proves to be unsuitable. Therefore, it is critical that registrants establish policies and procedures and maintain adequate documentation to support their suitability analysis.

EMDs and PMs are specifically reminded to take extra care in complying with their KYC, KYP, and suitability obligations when dealing with clients who are seniors, on a fixed income, or who otherwise may be in a position of vulnerability. A loss from a registrant's failure to comply with these obligations may have particularly devastating consequences for these clients. CSA staff will take regulatory action, including enforcement action, in circumstances where registrants do not appropriately address the special needs of these clients.

SROs

Both IIROC and the MFDA have provided suitability guidance to their member firms on how to comply with their suitability assessment requirements including when to perform a suitability assessment and how to deal with unsuitable investments. For details, please refer to IIROC Notice 12-0109, IIROC Notice 12-0108 *Client Relationship Model — Guidance* and MFDA Notice 69.

Suggested practices to demonstrate compliance with the suitability obligation

Registrants should:

- **Establish policies and procedures for assessing suitability of an investment** (including the criteria used to assess suitability and when to perform a suitability assessment) and ensure that it is consistently applied across the firm. Some examples of criteria include risk tolerance, investment objectives, time horizon, concentration risk, and conflicts of interest. There should also be adequate controls and oversight in place to identify and respond to any conflicts of interest with any investment recommendation.

- **Maintain adequate documentation of the suitability analysis for each trade.** A registrant should be able to demonstrate how each proposed trade was assessed for suitability.

- **Establish a process to periodically review a sample of client files to ensure that the suitability process is consistently applied throughout the firm.** Results of the suitability review should be documented and independently reviewed by someone senior in the firm (like the CCO). Areas of non-compliance should be discussed with staff in a timely manner and highlighted in training sessions. If the review identifies significant compliance issues, they should be escalated to the UDP to ensure that corrective action is taken in a timely manner to resolve the issues.

3. — How is the client-directed trade instruction appropriately used?

Section 13.3(2) of NI 31-103 provides that, if a client instructs a registrant to buy, sell or hold a security and in the registrant's reasonable opinion following the instruction would not be suitable for the client, the registrant should inform the client of the registrant's opinion and should not buy or sell the security unless the client instructs the registrant to proceed nonetheless (**client-directed trade instruction**).

The client-directed trade instruction is not meant to be an alternative to assessing client suitability in circumstances where clients have no other available exemptions, or where the trades likely would not be suitable for them. A registrant cannot actively promote a security (and thereby recommend the security) and then rely on boiler plate language to claim that the trade was a client-directed trade and is not recommended by the registrant.

During compliance reviews, we noticed that some registrants recommended that clients purchase securities of a single exempt market issuer (that in many cases was a related or connected issuer to the registrant) in an amount that accounted for a large portion (in some cases over 30%) of their net financial assets. Although there may be circumstances for a registrant to proceed with a client-directed trade, we identified that some EMDs may be inappropriately using the client-directed trade instruction in an attempt to circumvent the suitability obligation.

For example, we identified one EMD who distributed products of a related issuer that relied extensively on the use of a purported "client-directed trade instruction" in situations where there were strong grounds for concluding that the trades were unsuitable for their clients. Most of the clients signed KYC forms that indicated that they were non-AIs and that they were relying on the $150,000 minimum purchase exemption to purchase the securities. In many cases, the KYC form had the client-directed trade instruction "buried" at the end of the KYC form, and when asked by staff of the Ontario Securities Commission, the clients did not recall being asked to sign the instruction or any discussion over suitability with the EMD. As well, we have concerns about whether clients were fully aware of the impact of concentration risk in their portfolios which resulted from these clientdirected trades.

In our view, this practice is not acceptable, nor is it consistent with the client-directed trade instruction, or the obligation to deal honestly, fairly and good faith in securities laws. In future reviews, we will consider further regulatory action in these circumstances.

Suitability and concentration of investments

Registrants should recognize that diversification is an important factor to consider when assessing suitability of investments. The lack of diversification may expose the clients to significant investment risks. For example, in selling securities of mortgage investment corporations, real estate investment trusts, or similar real estate linked products, the EMD should consider and discuss with the client whether the client's portfolio may be subject to undue concentration risk through over-concentration in:

- Securities of a single issuer, or group of related issuers, as compared to a broadly based portfolio of issuers,

- Securities of illiquid exempt market securities as compared to publicly traded securities, and

- Securities of an issuer, or group of related issuers, that provides exposure to a single industry or asset class (for example, real estate) as compared with a broadly based portfolio of issuers that provide exposure to diversified industries or asset classes.

Most CSA staff will consider investments (either individually or taken together with prior investments) in securities of a single issuer or group of related issuers that represent more than 10% of the investor's net financial assets as potentially raising suitability concerns due to concentration.

With respect to real estate-linked products, we expect that registrants (as part of meeting their KYC obligation) will discuss the potential risks associated with the product and the issuer, including risks that may arise from a downturn in the real estate market or other adverse changes in market conditions. For example, if the performance of a product is sensitive to a change in the residential or commercial market values or to the ability of the sub-prime borrower to meet their mortgage repayment obligations, the registrant should ensure that the client is aware of the potential impact on the performance of the product if market values were to fall.

Suggested Practices for client-directed trades

Registrants should:

- **Analyze whether the investment is suitable for an investor in light of the investor's investment needs, objectives, time horizon and/or concentration and form an opinion based on this analysis.**

- **Inform the investor of their opinion that the proposed trade would not be suitable for the investor** in light of the investor's investment needs, objectives, time horizon and/or concentration and provide the client with a written explanation of the basis for the registrant's opinion.

- **Maintain adequate documentation of the suitability analysis which demonstrates the documentation reviewed and the suitability analysis completed.**

- **Maintain the investor's written instructions to proceed with the trade** (assuming that the client still directs the registrant to purchase the investment).

- **Develop a separate disclosure document for the client-directed trade instruction** and explain to the client how the client-trade instruction is used.

- **Assess the suitability of the client-directed trade considering the client's entire portfolio holdings within the same account for PMs accepting a client-directed trade.**

- **Establish policies and procedures** for ensuring that the client-directed trade instruction is appropriately used.

- **Provide adequate training to registered individuals** to ensure they understand when a client-directed trade instruction can be used.

Suggested practices relating to concentration of investments in client portfolios

Registrants should:

- **Consider and document reasonable concentration thresholds** to ensure that a client's total investment in a particular stock (e.g. securities in a single issuer or related group of issuers), sector or industry does not exceed thresholds which would result in the investment being unsuitable. Registrants should consider a number of factors when determining the thresholds, for example the type of security, market conditions, and redemption restrictions. Generally, the higher the concentration in a particular investment in a stock sector or industry, the more steps the registrant should take (and appropriately document) to demonstrate that the investment was suitable for the client.

- **Establish written procedures to monitor and manage concentration risks in a client's portfolio.** These procedures should be consistently applied to all client accounts.

- **Explain the concentration risk to the client and how it affects the overall account position if the proposed investment recommendation could result in a concentrated position.** If the registrant determines that an investment is unsuitable for a client in light of the concentration risk and the client's investment needs and objectives, the registrant is required to inform the client that the proposed trade is unsuitable. If the client still wishes to invest in the security, see *How is the client-directed trade instruction appropriately used?*

Unacceptable practices

Use of client-directed trade instruction

Registrants should not:

- **Promote a security actively (and thereby recommend the security) and then rely on boiler plate language to claim that the trade was a client-directed trade and was not recommended by the registrant.**

- **Determine that an exempt security is suitable for an investor solely because the investor qualifies for the prospectus exemption.**

- **"Hide" or "bury" the client-directed trade instruction in the KYC form or other client documentation.**

Suitability and concentration of investments

Registrants should not:

- **Fail to consider diversification as an important factor in their suitability determination.**

- **Fail to have adequate procedures in place to monitor the concentration level of a client's investments or evaluate whether the portfolios are appropriately diversified in light of client's KYC information.**

CSA Staff Notice 31-337 — Cost Disclosure, Performance Reporting and Client Statements — Frequently Asked Questions and Additional Guidance as of February 27, 2014

Date: February 27, 2014

37 O.S.C.B. 2055

Background

Amendments to National Instrument 31-103 *Registration Requirements, Exemptions and Ongoing Registrant Obligations* (**NI 31-103**) and Companion Policy 31-103CP *Registration Requirements, Exemptions and Ongoing Registrant Obligations* (**31-103CP** or the **CP**) implementing phase 2 of the client relationship model came into force on July 15, 2013 (the **CRM2 Amendments**). Staff from the Canadian Securities Administrators (**CSA staff** or **we**) have compiled this list of frequently asked questions we have received to date and provide our response and additional guidance (**FAQs**). In this document, we refer to exempt market dealers as "**EMDs**", portfolio managers as "**PMs**" and investment fund managers as "**IFMs**".

Implementation planning

The CRM2 Amendments are implemented in stages, with new requirements coming into effect on July 15 in each of 2014, 2015 and 2016. We encourage registrants to plan now so that they can be ready to be in compliance with the new requirements. Here are some things firms should consider including in their CRM2 Amendments implementation planning:

- scheduling, developing, testing and implementing systems changes

- updating policies and procedures

- training staff

- updating compliance oversight practices, and

- communicating with clients about the new information that they will be getting

Firms will also need to compile the information that will form the basis for the new reports on investment performance.

FAQs

	NI 31-103 SECTION	QUESTION	ANSWER
1.	GENERAL QUESTIONS	When does someone cease to be a client, such that a registrant is no longer required to provide the statements and reports contemplated in the CRM2 Amendments?	It is not possible to provide a bright line test for determining when a client relationship has ended that will apply in all cases. We expect firms to exercise reasonable professional judgement, erring in favour of providing client reporting where there is doubt as to whether there is still a client relationship. Some principles that apply to the exercise of that judgement are: • A person remains a client of a registered dealer or adviser for so long as the dealer or adviser holds securities owned by the person, or the circumstances described in subsection 14.14.1(1) [*additional statements*] apply. • A firm should consider the totality of its dealings with a client and the client's expectations of ongoing services from the firm. • Whether a client relationship is ongoing or not depends on the particular facts and circumstances of the relationship. Note that a registered dealer or adviser may not avoid the client reporting requirements in NI 31-103 by selectively choosing to cease to be the dealer of record for some of a client's securities. For example, a dealer may not tell the IFM of a client's mutual funds that it is no longer the dealer of record for some of the client's securities (unless those securities have been transferred to an account of the client at another dealer or an adviser), and at the same time, keep an account for the client. See also the guidance in cell 21 [re s.14.15 security holder statements], below.

	NI 31-103 SECTION	QUESTION	ANSWER
2.		Do EMDs have the same client statement and annual report requirements under the CRM2 Amendments as advisers and other dealers?	Most of the CRM2 Amendments do not distinguish between categories of registered advisers and dealers. All firms must review the requirements in section 14.14 [*account statements*] and section 14.14.1 [*additional statements*] to determine if they are required to deliver account and/or additional statements. Firms also need to consider the totality of their dealings with a client and the client's expectation of ongoing services of the firm.
			An EMD, that does not hold a client's securities, and where the circumstances of subsection 14.14.1(1) do not apply to those securities, should consider the totality of its relationship with the client:
			• Is it doing only one exempt market transaction or does it plan to do other transactions with the client?
			• Is the client expecting that the firm will continue to provide services?
			• Is the firm also engaged with the client in a different capacity, for example, as a registered adviser managing the client's other investments?
			These factors are not exhaustive. There may be other relevant factors. We expect the EMD to exercise its reasonable professional judgement.
			Where there is only one transaction and the factors suggest there is no ongoing relationship with the client, the EMD would be required to deliver:
			• one account statement with transactional information under subsection 14.14(4) (see further guidance in cell 16 [re s.14.14 account statements], below);
			• no annual report on charges and other compensation; and
			• no annual investment performance report.
3.		Do disclosure and reporting requirements in CRM2 Amendments apply to other investments that may not be securities, such as segregated funds?	The jurisdiction of the Canadian Securities Administrators (**CSA**) limits the CRM2 Amendments to securities (including exchange contracts in Alberta, British Columbia, New Brunswick and Saskatchewan). If an investment is not a security or an exchange contract in Alberta, British Columbia, New Brunswick and Saskatchewan within the meaning of those terms in securities legislation, a registered firm will not be subject to any requirement in NI 31-103 for reporting on that investment.

NI 31-103 SECTION	QUESTION	ANSWER
		Nonetheless, we encourage registrants to provide their clients with information that meets the standards set in the CRM2 Amendments in respect of all of their investments. This will enable investors to better understand the relative costs of different investments and their performance.
		Note that requirements imposed by self-regulatory organizations may extend to such investments.
4.	Where should switch fees and short-term trading fees be reported?	Switch fees charged by a registered dealer or adviser are considered a transaction charge (see the discussion of the definition of "transaction charge" in the CP. They must be disclosed before the trade (s. 14.2.1), in a trade confirmation (s.14.12(1)(c)) and in the annual report on charges and other compensation (s.14.17(1)(c)). Short-term trading fees paid to an investment fund must be disclosed in a trade confirmation (s.14.12(1)(c)) but are not included in the requirements for the annual report on charges and other compensation.
Division 1 *Investment fund managers*		
14.1 **Application of this Part to investment fund managers**	—	—
5.	**14.1.1** **Duty to provide information**	The requirement in section 14.1.1 for investment fund managers to provide a dealer/adviser with the information on trailing commissions that is required by the dealer/adviser in order to comply with 14.17(1)(h) comes into effect on July 15, 2016. Do the CSA expect investment fund managers to be ready on July 15, 2016 to deliver information for the preceding year?	Dealers and advisers may have various reporting cycles, on a calendar basis or otherwise. We expect investment fund managers to work with dealers and advisers, so that the new required information about charges will be included in clients' reports on charges and other compensation for the period that includes July 15, 2016. For greater certainty, this encompasses reports for the periods January 1, 2016 to December 31, 2016 and July 16, 2015 to July 15, 2016. The latest possible 12-month period will be July 15, 2016 to July 14, 2017. These are the first reports for different year-ends:

First day of reporting period	Last day of reporting period (year-end)
August 1, 2015	July 31, 2016
September 1, 2015	August 31, 2016
October 1, 2015	September 30, 2016
November 1, 2015	October 31, 2016
December 1, 2015	November 30, 2016
January 1, 2016	December 31, 2016
February 1, 2016	January 31, 2017

	NI 31-103 SECTION	QUESTION	ANSWER	
			March 1, 2016	February 28, 2017
			April 1, 2016	March 31, 2017
			May 1, 2016	April 30, 2017
			June 1, 2016	May 31, 2017
			July 1, 2016	June 30, 2017
	Division 2 *Disclosure to clients*			
6.	**14.2** **Relationship disclosure information**	Before July 15, 2013, there was an exemption in former subsection 14.2(6) from section 14.2 in respect of a permitted client if (a) the client had waived it in writing, and (b) the registrant did not act as an adviser in respect of a managed account of the client. Under the CRM2 Amendments, the exemption was changed to a permitted client that is not an individual. Is the registrant now required to deliver relationship disclosure information to an individual permitted client who had previously waived the section?	Yes. If the individual permitted client had previously waived relationship disclosure information, in light of the CRM2 Amendments, a registered firm must deliver relationship disclosure to all individuals, whether or not they are permitted clients. We expect registered firms to act reasonably as to when they next deliver the relationship disclosure information. If there is a significant change in respect of the relationship disclosure information, then the registered firm should act right away. Otherwise, we would expect the relationship disclosure information to be updated the next time the firm is updating client information (for advisers) or before doing a transaction (for dealers).	
7.		If an individual permitted client has waived the suitability requirement under subsection 13.3(4), how will a firm meet the requirement in paragraph 14.2(2)(k) to deliver a statement that the firm has an obligation to assess whether a purchase or sale of a security is suitable for a client prior to executing the transaction or at any other time?	When there is no obligation to make a suitability determination because of the application of subsection 13.3(4), the firm will have met the requirement in paragraph 14.2(2)(k) by simply informing the client that the firm has no suitability obligation because the client has waived the requirement.	
8.		If a firm is exempt from certain know your client (KYC) obligations under subsection 13.2(6), how will it meet the requirement in paragraph 14.2(2)(l) to deliver the information a registered firm must collect about the client under section 13.2?	The firm will meet the requirement in paragraph 14.2(2)(l) by delivering the information collected under the KYC obligation in section 13.2. If a firm is exempted from collecting certain KYC information, then the firm is not obligated to deliver that information under paragraph 14.2(2)(l).	
9.		Will the CSA be providing additional guidance on benchmarks? Are benchmarks optional? If a firm decides to provide benchmarks, what is the expected frequency?	Other than a general discussion as part of the relationship disclosure information requirement in paragraph 14.2(2)(m), there is no requirement for registered firms to provide benchmark information to clients and for greater certainty, we have provided guidance under sections 14.2 [*relationship disclosure information*] and 14.19 [*content of investment performance report*] of the CP.	

	NI 31-103 SECTION	QUESTION	ANSWER
			Since benchmarks are optional, we did not prescribe any periods or other specifications for provision of benchmark information. However, we have provided guidance on the provision of benchmarks in section 14.19 of the CP, including, importantly, that benchmark information be not misleading. We are not providing specific guidance on benchmarks beyond that already set out in the CP. We expect firms to use their professional judgement when determining which benchmarks are relevant to a client's investments and explain to clients the use of benchmarks in terms they will understand.
10.		When does the guidance on the use of benchmarks set out under section 14.19 [*content of investment performance report*] in the CP come into effect?	The guidance in section 14.19 of the CP is relevant to the use of benchmarks today and is consistent with previously published guidance.
11.	**14.2.1** **Pre-trade disclosure of charges**	Can registrants use the Fund Facts document to satisfy the requirements in section 14.2.1 [*pre-trade disclosure of charges*]? The question arises because 31-103CP suggests a mutual fund's management fee should be discussed in the pre-trade disclosure of charges, but the Fund Facts document is not required to include the management fee in all cases (only in the case of a new fund for which the management expense ratio (**MER**) is not available).	If a registrant delivers the Fund Facts document at the point of sale and explains the specific costs of the transaction to the client, then the registrant may use it further to satisfy the requirements of section 14.2.1 for the disclosure of charges related to the transaction. Since the management fee generally constitutes most of the MER of a mutual fund, we think this would be in line with the guidance in the CP.
	Division 5 *Reporting to clients*		
12.	**14.11.1** **Determining market value**	Why use last bid/ask price instead of closing price? Is it not misleading sometimes; for example, when there are large bid-ask deviations?	We chose last bid/ask price because not all securities are actively traded on a market and there have been consistent problems with firms using stale data based on old closing prices. That said, we recognize that no one measure will always work best, so the requirement is for the firm to report the amount it reasonably believes to be the market value, after making any adjustments it considers necessary to accurately reflect the market value.
13.		What if the net asset value (**NAV**) of an investment fund which is not listed on an exchange is not available on a daily basis?	The most recent NAV provided by the investment fund manager should be used. If a registered dealer or adviser reasonably believes the NAV for an investment fund is stale or otherwise inaccurate, it may include an explanatory note to that effect in the statement provided to its client.
14.	**14.12** **Content and delivery of trade confirmation**	The prescribed notification under subparagraph 14.12(1)(c.1)(ii) says remuneration "has" been added or deducted from the price of the security. Can "has been" be replaced with "may have been" where the firm will have difficulty determining which trades had dealer firm remuneration added and which did not?	Yes. Since the requirement is to provide a notification that is "substantially" in the form prescribed, a firm can modify the prescribed text to use "may have" instead of "has been", provided the firm has made reasonable efforts to determine whether it can make the more definitive statement to the client.

	NI 31-103 SECTION	QUESTION	ANSWER
15.	**14.14** **Account statements**	Is there any additional guidance on providing electronic statements?	National Policy 11-201 *Electronic Delivery of Documents* provides guidance to securities industry participants who want to use electronic delivery to fulfill delivery requirements in securities legislation. Monthly and/or quarterly statements, as applicable can be delivered electronically. All of the content required under section 14.14 and, where applicable, section 14.14.1 must be provided at the required intervals. However, if a firm chooses to provide electronic access to account information on a more frequent basis than required in sections 14.14 and 14.14.1, that supplemental access does not have to conform with the requirements of those sections.
16.		How do the account statement and additional statement requirements in sections 14.14 and 14.14.1 apply where a registered firm does not (a) hold or control a client's securities in nominee name, nor (b) meet criteria set out in subsection 14.14.1(1)?	Under subsection 14.14(4), the registrant will be required to provide the client with an account statement that sets out transaction information for the reporting period in which a transaction occurred. The account balance information required under subsection 14.14(5) will not be required. There will be no requirement to provide an additional statement under section 14.14.1.
17.		If securities are transferred to a managed account for passive holding, is the PM responsible for reporting on these "legacy" securities?	Yes, if securities are in an account managed by a PM, that PM is responsible for reporting on them. See also cell 18, immediately below, concerning statements sent by a custodian.
18.	**14.14.1 Additional statements**	Are statements sent by a custodian acceptable to meet the additional statement requirement?	The requirement to deliver additional statements comes into effect on July 15, 2015. The CSA is considering guidance on PMs' client statement delivery responsibilities where a custodian also provides statements to the same client.
19.	**14.14.2** **Position cost information**	How should short positions be reported?	If using book cost, a short security position should be reported as the total amount received for the security, net of any transaction charges related to the sale, adjusted for any distributions, returns of capital and corporate reorganizations. If using original cost, a short security position should be reported as the total amount received for the security, net of any transaction charges related to the sale.
20.	**14.14.2** **Position cost information**	Does "within 10 days after" in paragraph 14.14.2(4)(c) mean within 10 business days or 10 calendar days?	References to "days" in the CRM2 Amendments are to calendar days.
21.	**14.15** **Security holder statements**	Is there any guidance regarding the requirement to send a statement for "orphaned accounts"?	The requirement for an IFM to send a security holder statement to an account without a dealer of record — an orphaned account — is not new. It is an accommodation of the temporary and very limited circumstance that arises where there ceases to be a registered dealer or adviser serving the client. See also the guidance in cell 1 [re ceasing to be a client], above.

	NI 31-103 SECTION	QUESTION	ANSWER
			The CRM2 Amendments in section 14.15 expand the existing requirements for the information that IFMs must send to security holders to include some of the information registered dealers and advisers will be required to deliver to their clients, such as position cost information.
	14.16 **Scholarship plan dealer statements**	—	—
22.	**14.17** **Report on charges and other compensation**	The requirement to provide an annual report on charges and other compensation comes into effect on July 15, 2016. For what period will the first annual report be required?	Firms may have various reporting cycles, on a calendar year basis or otherwise. If July 15, 2016 falls within the start and end dates of a 12-month period, an annual report will be required for that period. So if a firm reports or wishes to report on a calendar year basis, the first annual report will be required for a period from January 1, 2016 to December 31, 2016. If a firm reports or wishes to report for a period ending July 15, then the first annual reports will be required for the period beginning July 16, 2015.
23.		If there are no charges or other compensation to be disclosed, is a nil report still required to be delivered?	No, nil reports on charges and other compensation are not required.
24.		Are the charges levied within an investment fund held by an investor (e.g. management fees) included in operating charges? Do PMs who manage their clients' money through pooled funds have to "look through" to those fees?	No. We would expect this information to be disclosed as part of the relationship disclosure information delivered at account opening or when the investment is made. But, a firm is not required to include the fund management fee in its annual report on charges and other compensation. The definition of operating charge is specific to the account and is not a product related fee. Operating charges (and transaction charges) include only charges paid to the registered firm by the client. Nonetheless, if such fees are a significant part of the portfolio manager's compensation model — say if a portfolio manager used in-house funds as the primary investment vehicle for its clients and took much of its compensation in fund management fees instead of the traditional fee based on clients' assets under management — we would expect that the firm would communicate to its clients about the way it is being compensated, consistent with the duty of fairness, honesty and good faith.
25.		If a client leaves the firm and transfers out in the middle of the year, does the firm have an obligation to send an annual report on charges and other compensation?	Once the client relationship has ended, there is no longer an obligation to send an annual report on charges and other compensation. We do, however, encourage firms to provide departing clients with information on charges and other compensation received during the year-to-date.
26.		Does the requirement to disclose the dollar amount of trailing commissions mean separate disclosures for the amount paid to the firm and the amount paid to the registered representative?	The report on charges and other compensation is at the firm level. This means the dollar amount of trailing commissions disclosed in the report is the total amount received in respect of the client's holdings. That amount is not broken down to show how much the firm retained and how much it passed on to the client's dealing or advising representative. The intention is that the client will see the aggregate amount of trailing commission that was generated by their account.

	NI 31-103 SECTION	QUESTION	ANSWER
27.		How should typical mutual fund related charges other than trailing commissions be reported in the annual report on charges and other compensation?	If there is an up-front commission charged to the client by the registered dealer or adviser when the securities are purchased, it would be included in the amount reported under paragraph 14.17(1) (c). In the sample annual report in the CP, this appears under "Charges you paid directly to us ... Commissions on purchases of mutual funds with a sales charge".
			If there is a commission or other payment from the IFM or another party other than the client to the registered dealer or adviser when the securities are purchased, that payment is reported under paragraph 14.17(1) (g). In the sample annual report in Appendix D of the CP, this appears under "Compensation we received through third parties ... Commissions from mutual fund managers on purchases of mutual funds (see Note 1)".
			If, when the securities are sold by the client (i.e., redeemed back to the issuer), a deferred sales charge is triggered but no commission or other payment goes to the registered dealer or adviser, there is no requirement to include it in the annual report.
			If, when securities are sold by the client a commission or other payment was received by the registered dealer or adviser, it would be reported under paragraphs 14.17(1)(c) or (g), depending whether it was paid by the client or another party. See also the guidance in cell 4 [re switch fees and short-term trading fees].
			If a registered dealer or adviser is concerned that clients might assume trailing commissions are charged directly to the client, we would have no objection to the firm including in its annual reports a clear explanation of the charges. For example, note 1 in the sample Report on Charges and Other Compensation in Appendix D of the CP could be expanded along the lines of the second paragraph in note 2.
28.		If a registered dealer or adviser receives referral fees in relation to registerable services to the client during a reporting period and the client has two or more accounts with the firm, how should the firm disclose the referral fees in the annual reports for the client's accounts?	If the referral fees relate only to one of the client's accounts, they would be included in the annual report for that account alone. If the referral fees relate to more than one of the client's accounts, we expect the firm to present disclosure information in a clear and meaningful manner. For example, the firm could report the full amount in the annual report for each account, or report a pro-rated amount in the annual report for each account, but in either case the firm should include an explanatory note so that the client will not be confused as to the total amount of the referral fees received by the firm during the period.

	NI 31-103 SECTION	QUESTION	ANSWER
29.	**14.18** **Investment performance report**	The requirement to provide an annual investment performance report comes into effect on July 15, 2016. For what period will the first annual report be required?	Firms may have various reporting cycles, on a calendar year basis or otherwise. If July 15, 2016 falls within the start and end dates of a 12-month period, an annual report will be required for that period. So if a firm reports or wishes to report on a calendar year basis, the first annual reports will be required for a period from January 1, 2016 to December 31, 2016. If a firm reports or wishes to report for a period ending July 15, then the first annual reports will be required for the 12-month period beginning July 16, 2015.
30.	**14.19** **Content of investment performance report**	Can a registered firm send performance reports to its clients more frequently than once per year? If so, must all of its performance reports include all of the content prescribed for annual reports and be formatted in accordance with subsection 14.19(5)?	So long as a performance report that includes the prescribed content is delivered annually, firms are free to send more frequent reports. Such supplemental reports need not include the prescribed content and need not be formatted in accordance with subsection 14.19(5).
31.		If a firm chooses to provide percentage returns calculated using both money-weighted rate of return (MWRR) and time-weighted rate of return (TWRR) methods, what are the requirements for using TWRR?	The CRM2 Amendments do not prescribe periods, accounts or other specifications for the provision of additional percentage return information using TWRR. A firm may show returns using TWRR, as long as the firm also provides the return using MWRR in accordance with the requirements in section 14.19. In such cases, in addition to the general explanation in plain language of what the MWRR calculation method takes into account required under paragraph 14.19(1)(j), the firm should similarly explain the TWRR calculation method in plain language and help clients understand the difference between two sets of performance returns.
32.		Will the CSA publish an approved formula to calculate MWRR?	No. There are different ways of calculating MWRR and the requirement is that firms use a method that is generally accepted in the securities industry. The CSA does not prescribe any method in particular because standards evolve over time. Approximation methods such as Modified Dietz are not acceptable. Approximations can produce misleading results compared to MWRR and advances in computing power make it unnecessary to use them.
33.		Is the XIRR function in Microsoft Excel acceptable for MWRR calculations?	Yes. A registered firm may provide performance reports calculated with the XIRR function of Microsoft Excel. Firms should be aware that some versions of this software may have defects that affect these calculations.
34.		Where a client account predates the requirement to collect client information for performance reporting and the firm has legacy data available only manually, can the firm choose a date that is later than the account opening date as the baseline date for an account's investment performance reports?	The baseline date for an account's investment performance reports must be either (a) the account opening date or (b), if the firm reasonably believes it does not have available all of the information that it would need in order to produce performance reports that cover the whole of the period since the account was opened, July 15, 2015.

	NI 31-103 SECTION	QUESTION	ANSWER
35.	14.20 **Delivery of report on charges and other compensation and investment performance report**	Does "within 10 days after" in paragraph 14.20(1)(c) mean within 10 business days or 10 calendar days?	References to "days" in the CRM2 Amendments are to calendar days.

CSA Staff Notice 31-338 — Guidance on Dispute Resolution Services — Client Disclosure for Registered Dealers and Advisers that are not Members of a Self-Regulatory Organization

Date: May 1, 2014

37 O.S.C.B. 4430

Introduction

The Canadian Securities Administrators (the CSA or we) are implementing amendments to National Instrument 31-103 *Registration Requirements, Exemptions and Ongoing Registrant Obligations* (NI 31-103) as well as Companion Policy 31-103CP *Registration Requirements, Exemptions and Ongoing Registrant Obligations* (31-103CP) relating to the provision of independent dispute resolution or mediation services to clients of all registered dealers and registered advisers (collectively, the Amendments). The Amendments provide that, outside Québec, a firm must take reasonable steps to ensure that the Ombudsman for Banking Services and Investments (OBSI) will be the independent dispute resolution or mediation service that is made available to a client that has an eligible complaint. The Amendments also include the requirement to inform clients in writing about the firm's obligation and to set out the steps a client must take in order to be able to make use of OBSI's services.

In Québec, the Autorité des marchés financiers (the AMF) already provides a mediation service to clients residing in Québec of all registered dealers and registered advisers. The Québec regime will remain unchanged and firms registered in Québec should continue to inform clients residing in Québec of the availability of the AMF mediation services. In this Notice, all references to OBSI are made by CSA members excluding the AMF.

Purpose

Our purpose in requiring the use of OBSI as the dispute resolution service is to provide investors with the following benefits:

- access to a free, independent, consistent dispute resolution service,

- uniform handling of investor complaints, and

- clarity on who investors should contact if complaints are not resolved.

Registered firms that are members of a self-regulatory organization (SRO), including those that are registered in Québec, should continue to comply with their SRO's requirements with respect to the provision of independent dispute resolution or mediation services.

For the purposes of this notice, a registered firm refers to registered dealers and registered advisers that are not members of an SRO and does not include a registered investment fund manager.

Substance

At three points in time, a registered firm must provide its clients with information about the availability of independent dispute resolution or mediation services and the steps the client must take in order to make use of those services at account opening, as soon as possible after a client makes a complaint (for example, when a firm sends its acknowledgement), and again when the registered firm informs the client of its decision in respect of the complaint.

This staff notice is intended to provide guidance to registered firms in preparing and delivering client disclosure that meets their obligations under section 13.16 and paragraph 14.2(2)(j) of NI 31-103. To assist registered firms with establishing clear and meaningful client disclosure, we have provided a sample client disclosure in Appendix A. While the sample client disclosure document is intended to serve as an example of an acceptable method for registered firms to meet their disclosure obligations, it is not the only acceptable method. Registered firms may use alternative methods, provided those methods adequately demonstrate that the firm has met its disclosure obligations. We encourage registered firms to use this Notice to improve their understanding of, and compliance with their client disclosure obligations.

This staff notice also provides sample text and best practices for how a firm might meet their requirement regarding internal complaint handling procedures.

When do you have to provide client disclosure?

(1) — At Account Opening

Under paragraph 14.2(2)(j) of NI 31-103, registered firms must disclose to their client the firm's obligations if a client has a complaint contemplated under section 13.16 and the steps that the client must take in order for an independent dispute resolution or mediation service to be made available to the client at the firm's expense. A registered firm may provide this information in a single document (together with other required relationship disclosure information) or in a separate document. This disclosure must be provided in writing to the client and should be communicated in a manner consistent with the guidance on client communications under section 1.1 of 31-103CP. We encourage registered firms to avoid the use of technical terms and acronyms when communicating with clients.

The sample client disclosure in Appendix A is designed to provide an example of clear and meaningful disclosure to a client about the firm's obligations with respect to independent dispute resolution services, including the requirement that a client must first file their complaint with the registered firm. While many registered firms already have in place a method of communicating to a client about their internal complaint handling processes, the sample client disclosure provides additional guidance and best practices in this area.

(2) — At the time of the Complaint

Under subsection 13.16(2), if a registered firm receives a complaint from a client, the firm must, as soon as possible, provide the client with a written acknowledgement of the complaint that includes the following:

(a) a description of the firm's obligations under section 13.16;

(b) the steps that the client must take in order for an independent dispute resolution or mediation service to be made available to the client under subsection 13.16(4);

(c) the name of the independent dispute resolution or mediation service that will be made available to the client under subsection 13.16(4) and contact information for the service.

The registered firm must send a written acknowledgement letter to the client as soon as possible, typically within 5 business days of receipt of a complaint. The following is a list of the types of information the firm should include in the acknowledgement letter:

- information about the firm's complaint process, including timelines for responding to client complaints,
- when and how to take their complaint to an independent dispute resolution or mediation service,
- contact information for the independent dispute resolution or mediation service, and
- any other options available to the client to resolve their complaint.

Registered firms may refer to the sample client disclosure to assist with the content of the acknowledgment letter.

Registered firms may also want to consider including a request for any information reasonably required to investigate the complaint, if such information can be identified within the 5 business days of receipt of the complaint. Where possible, such as with less complex complaints, it may be possible to also provide the firm's decision at the same time as acknowledging the complaint.

(3) — At the time of the Decision

If a registered firm decides to reject a complaint or to make an offer to resolve a complaint, the firm must, as soon as possible, provide the client with written notice of the decision including:

- the decision on the complaint, and
- information about dispute resolution services, including the timelines applicable for use of the dispute resolution services, the monetary limits associated with the dispute resolution services and the contact information for those services.

As a best practice, a firm may consider including the following in their written notice to the client:

- a summary of the complaint, and
- the reasons for the firm's decision.

A registered firm is expected to provide a decision to the client complaint within 90 days of receipt of the complaint. At the time of the decision, a registered firm may opt to provide information about independent dispute resolution services to clients in a separate document, or insert the information in the firm's written decision to the client.

We recommend including the disclosure in the body of the firm's decision letter, or referencing that it is being included, as this would:

- assist with providing evidence that the client received the required information, and
- may protect the registered firm in the event a client later claims they did not receive information about independent dispute resolution services.

When do you need to offer OBSI?

Subsection 13.16(4) requires a registered firm to ensure that independent dispute resolution or mediation service is available to a client if either of the following apply:

- after 90 days of the firm's receipt of the complaint, the firm has not given the client written notice of a decision, and the client has notified the independent dispute resolution or mediation service that it wants to use the service;
- within 180 days of the client's receipt of written notice of the firm's decision, the client has notified the independent dispute resolution or mediation services that it wants to use the service.

Subsection 13.16(6) requires the firm to take reasonable steps to ensure that OBSI will be the independent dispute resolution and mediation service made available to clients.

When do you need to update Relationship Disclosure Information?

Under subsection 14.2(4) of NI 31-103 registered firms are required to take reasonable steps to notify clients, in a timely manner, of significant changes in respect of the relationship disclosure information delivered to a client. The Amendments include an amendment to paragraph 14.2(2) (j) with respect to the availability of independent dispute resolution services. As the amendment to paragraph 14.2(2) (j) is considered

Part 3: REGISTRATION

a significant change to the relationship disclosure information, registered firms will be expected to take reasonable steps to notify clients, in a timely manner of the change to the relationship disclosure information. Sending it separately or including it with an upcoming client communication, such as their next monthly or quarterly statement, or before doing a transaction, would satisfy this obligation.

Membership in OBSI

We expect firms to maintain ongoing membership in OBSI as a "Participating Firm" and participate in OBSI's services in a manner consistent with the firm's obligation to deal fairly, honestly and in good faith with its clients.

Coming into force and transition

The Amendments subject to necessary approvals in each CSA jurisdiction come into force May 1, 2014. The Amendments provide for a transition period for firms registered by May 1, 2014 of 3 months after the Amendments come into effect with the exception of Québec, by reason of the existing regime in that jurisdiction. The transition period will end on August 1, 2014. Please refer to the Amendments for specific terms associated with the transition period.

For more information on how to register as a Participating Firm, visit www.obsi.ca.

Questions

Please refer your questions to any of the following:

[Omitted.]

Appendix A — [Name of firm]

What to do if you have a complaint

Our complaint process

Filing a complaint with us

If you have a complaint about our services or a product, contact us at:

[Firm contact information]

You may want to consider using a method other than email for sensitive information.

Tell us:

- what went wrong
- when it happened
- what you expect, for example, money back, an apology, account correction

We will acknowledge your complaint

We will acknowledge your complaint in writing, as soon as possible, typically within 5 business days of receiving your complaint. We may ask you to provide clarification or more information to help us resolve your complaint.

Help us resolve your complaint sooner

- Make your complaint as soon as possible.
- Reply promptly if we ask you for more information.
- Keep copies of all relevant documents, such as letters, emails and notes of conversations with us.

We will provide our decision

We normally provide our decision in writing, within 90 days of receiving a complaint. It will include:

- a summary of the complaint
- the results of our investigation
- our decision to make an offer to resolve the complaint or deny it, and an explanation of our decision

If our decision is delayed

If we cannot provide you with our decision within 90 days, we will:

- inform you of the delay
- explain why our decision is delayed, and
- give you a new date for our decision

You may be eligible for the independent dispute resolution service offered by the Ombudsman for Banking Services and Investments (OBSI).

A word about legal advice

You always have the right to go to a lawyer or seek other ways of resolving your dispute at any time. A lawyer can advise you of your options. There are time limits for taking legal action. Delays could limit your options and legal rights later on.

If you are not satisfied with our decision

You may be eligible for OBSI's dispute resolution service.

If you are a Québec resident

You may consider the free mediation service offered by the Autorité des marchés financiers.

Taking your complaint to OBSI

You may be eligible for OBSI's free and independent dispute resolution service if:

- we do not provide our decision within 90 days after you made your complaint, or
- you are not satisfied with our decision

OBSI can recommend compensation of up to $350,000.

OBSI's service is available to clients of our firm. This does not restrict your ability to take a complaint to a dispute resolution service of your choosing at your own expense, or to bring an action in court. Keep in mind there are time limits for taking legal action.

Who can use OBSI

You have the right to use OBSI's service if:

- your complaint relates to a trading or advising activity of our firm or by one of our representatives
- you brought your complaint to us within 6 years from the time that you first knew, or ought to have known, about the event that caused the complaint, and
- you file your complaint with OBSI according to its time limits below

Time limits apply

- If we do not provide you with our decision within 90 days, you can take your complaint to OBSI any time after the 90-day period has ended.
- If you are not satisfied with our decision, you have up to 180 days after we provide you with our decision to take your complaint to OBSI.

Filing a complaint with OBSI

Contact OBSI

Email: ombudsman@obsi.ca

Telephone: 1-888-451-4519 or 416-287-2877 in Toronto

OBSI will investigate

OBSI works confidentially and in an informal manner. It is not like going to court, and you do not need a lawyer.

During its investigation, OBSI may interview you and representatives of our firm. We are required to cooperate in OBSI's investigations.

Information OBSI needs to help you

OBSI can help you best if you promptly provide all relevant information, including:

- your name and contact information
- our firm's name and contact information
- the names and contact information of any of our representatives who have been involved in your complaint
- details of your complaint
- all relevant documents, including any correspondence and notes of discussions with us

OBSI will provide its recommendations

Once OBSI has completed its investigation, it will provide its recommendations to you and us. OBSI's recommendations are not binding on you or us.

OBSI can recommend compensation of up to $350,000. If your claim is higher, you will have to agree to that limit on any compensation you seek through OBSI. If you want to recover more than $350,000, you may want to consider another option, such as legal action, to resolve your complaint.

For more information about OBSI, visit www.obsi.ca

CSA Staff Notice 31-339 — Omnibus/Blanket Orders Exempting IIROC and MFDA Registrants from Certain Provisions of National Instrument 31-103 Registration Requirements, Exemptions and Ongoing Registrant Obligations

Date: May 29, 2014
37 O.S.C.B. 5245

Introduction

All CSA members have issued parallel orders that provide Investment Industry Regulatory Organization of Canada (**IIROC**) member firms with relief from certain provisions of National Instrument 31-103 *Registration Requirements, Exemptions and Ongoing Registrant Obligations* (**NI 31-103**), which form part of the Client Relationship Model Phase 2 (**CRM2**). All CSA members except Québec have issued parallel orders that provide Mutual Fund Dealers Association of Canada (**MFDA**) member firms with relief from certain CRM2 provisions of NI 31-103. Those CRM2 provisions of NI 31-103 do not apply to IIROC and MFDA member firms, provided they comply with the corresponding requirements of IIROC and the MFDA, respectively.

Background

On July 15, 2014, the following provisions of NI 31-103, which form part of CRM2, will come into effect:

(a) paragraph 14.2(2)(m) [*relationship disclosure information*];

(b) section 14.2.1 [*pre-trade disclosure of charges*]; and

(c) paragraphs 14.12(1)(b.1) and (c.1) [*content and delivery of trade confirmation*].

IIROC and the MFDA (together, these self-regulatory organizations are referred to as the **SROs**) have published amendments to their respective member rules that will have materially the same effect as the amendments to NI 31-103 and will also come into effect on July 15, 2014.

Relief

All CSA members have issued parallel orders that provide IIROC member firms with relief from the relevant provisions of NI 31-103, provided they comply with the corresponding requirements of IIROC.

All CSA members except Québec have issued parallel orders that provide MFDA member firms with relief from the relevant provisions of NI 31-103, provided they comply with the corresponding requirements of the MFDA.

The orders will expire on the date on which amendments to Part 9 of NI 31-103 and Appendices G and H of NI 31-103 come into force providing equivalent exemptions for IIROC and MFDA members. We will take the appropriate steps to make the necessary amendments to Part 9 of NI 31-103 in due course.

Questions

If you have questions regarding this Notice, please refer them to any of the following:

[Omitted.]

CSA Staff Notice 31-340 — OBSI Joint Regulators Committee Annual Report for 2014

Date: March 19, 2015
38 O.S.C.B. 2551

[Not reproduced]

CSA Staff Notice 31-341 — Omnibus/Blanket Orders Exempting Registrants from Certain CRM2 Provisions of National Instrument 31-103 Registration Requirements, Exemptions and Ongoing Registrant Obligations

Date: May 21, 2015
38 O.S.C.B. 4659

Introduction

All members of the Canadian Securities Administrators (the **CSA** or "we") have issued parallel orders providing relief from certain provisions of National Instrument 31-103 *Registration Requirements, Exemptions and Ongoing Registrant Obligations* (**NI 31-103**) related to the Client Relationship Model Phase 2 amendments to NI 31-103 which come into effect in stages in 2015 and 2016 (the *2015/2016 CRM2 Amendments*).

Background

The Investment Industry Regulatory Organization of Canada (**IIROC**) and the Mutual Fund Dealers Association of Canada (**MFDA**) (together, these self-regulatory organizations are referred to as the **SROs**) have adopted amendments to their respective member rules that are materially harmonized with the 2015/2016 CRM2 Amendments.

Some registered firms have indicated they may experience difficulty implementing the 2015/2016 CRM2 Amendments or corresponding SRO provisions by their effective dates.

Certain technical issues have also been identified relating to the delivery of information prescribed in the 2015/2016 CRM2 Amendments or corresponding SRO provisions.

Summary of Relief

To address these matters, CSA members (except the Autorité des marchés financiers with respect to relief specific to MFDA member firms) have issued parallel orders to the following effect:

1. Non-SRO members: More time to implement certain provisions; additional relief addressing technical issues. For non-SRO members, conditional relief from specified 2015/2016 CRM2 Amendments to the following effect:

- The new requirements relating to market value, position cost, account statements, additional statements, scholarship plan dealer statements and security holder statements that come into effect on July 15, 2015 may be met starting with statements delivered for the period ending December 31, 2015, instead of the period that includes July 15, 2015.

- Where a firm uses market value instead of position cost as contemplated in the position cost information provisions,
  - for security positions transferred from another registered firm, it may meet the requirement to disclose in the statement that the market value, not the cost of the security position, is being disclosed without having to specify that it is the market value as of the transfer date;
  - for existing accounts, it may use a date as at December 31, 2015 or a date earlier than December 31, 2015 chosen by the firm that is the same for all "similar clients" of the firm holding the security, rather than for all clients of the firm holding the security;

  "similar clients" for purposes of the order means any of the following:

  (a) clients whose accounts or security positions were transferred together,

  (b) clients on the same reporting system if a registered firm has more than one reporting system,

  (c) other clients whose accounts or security positions would appear to a reasonable person to be similar in a way that relates to the recording or calculation of market value or position cost.

- The requirement to identify securities that may be covered under an investor protection fund in their additional statements does not have to be met (we plan to publish a proposal to amend this requirement at a later date). IIROC's existing investor protection fund disclosure requirements remain in effect. The MFDA has introduced equivalent requirements that will come into effect as of December 31, 2015.

- The requirements that investment performance reports must include market value information as at and since July 15, 2015 may be met instead,
  - where the firm has decided to report on a calendar year basis (i.e., its first reports will cover the period January 1, 2016 to December 31, 2016), by including market value information as at and since January 1, 2016 (the firm is not required to provide the information for any earlier period), or a date earlier than January 1, 2016 chosen by the firm that is the same for all similar clients;
  - where the firm has decided not to report on a calendar year basis (e.g., its first reports will cover the period from July 15, 2016 to July 14, 2017), by including market value information as at and since July 15, 2015 or a date earlier than July 15, 2015 chosen by the firm that is the same for all similar clients.

- The requirements that investment performance reports must include annualized total percentage return information since inception or for the period since July 15, 2015 may be met as follows,
  - where the firm has decided to report on a calendar year basis, by providing the information for the 12-month period ending December 31, 2016 (the firm is not required to provide the information for any earlier period or in any subsequent performance reports that cover the 12-month periods ending December 31, 2017 and each calendar year thereafter);
  - where the firm has decided not to report on a calendar year basis, by providing the information:

    (A) for the period since the account was opened, if the account has been opened for at least a year before the date of the report, or

    (B) for the period since July 15, 2015 *or an earlier date chosen by the firm that is the same for all "similar clients"*, if the account was opened before July 15, 2015 (the firm is not required to conclude that it believes information since inception is not available; it should have a reasonable basis for its choice of date).

2. SRO Members: Member rules instead of 2015/2016 CRM2 Amendments. For SRO members, relief from the 2015/2016 CRM2 Amendments, if they comply with the corresponding SRO provisions applicable to them instead.

> Note that an SRO member seeking discretionary relief from any provisions other than those relating to investment fund manager or scholarship plan dealer activities should apply only to their SRO — there is no need to also apply to the CSA for relief from the corresponding provision in NI 31-103.

The CSA members plan to publish proposals to amend NI 31-103 to revise certain of the 2015/2016 CRM2 Amendments permanently. The SROs plan to make housekeeping amendments to conform their member rules with certain of the relief described in paragraph 1 of this Notice.

Relief Order

The order will take effect on July 15, 2015.

For the specific provisions of the relief summarized above, see the applicable orders available on websites of CSA members including here:

www.lautorite.qc.ca

www.albertasecurities.com

www.bcsc.bc.ca

www.msc.gov.mb.ca

www.gov.ns.ca/nssc

www.nbsc-cvmnb.ca

www.osc.gov.on.ca/en/Dealersomnibusorders.htm

www.fcaa.gov.sk.ca

Questions

Please refer your questions to any of the following:

[Omitted.]

CSA Staff Notice 31-342 — Guidance for Portfolio Managers Regarding Online Advice

Date: September 24, 2015

38 O.S.C.B. 8197

[Not reproduced]

CSA Staff Notice 31-343 — Conflicts of interest in distributing securities of related or connected issuers

Date: November 26, 2015

38 O.S.C.B. 9828

Purpose

Staff of the Canadian Securities Administrators (**CSA staff** or **we**) consider the identification of, and response to, conflicts of interest to be fundamental regulatory obligations. A registrant must manage conflicts that arise whenever it trades in or advises on securities issued by *related or connected issuers* (as defined in National Instrument 33-105 *Underwriting Conflicts*). Firms registered solely as exempt market dealers, that distribute securities of related or connected issuers with common mind and management (captive dealers) raise serious concerns in terms of how they respond to these conflicts of interest.

We consider a conflict of interest to be any circumstance where the interests of different parties, such as the interests of a client and those of a registrant, are inconsistent, competing or divergent. The inherent conflict of interest in the captive dealer business model may affect a registrant's ability to meet its know-your-client (**KYC**), know-your-product (**KYP**) and suitability obligations, and its duty to act fairly, honestly and in good faith with clients (**fair dealing duty**). National Instrument 31-103 *Registration Requirements, Exemptions and Ongoing Registrant Obligations* (**NI 31-103**) and its companion policy (**Companion Policy**) provide a principles-based framework that requires registrants to identify and respond to material conflicts of interest.

We think additional guidance (including "acceptable practices" and "unacceptable practices") will help captive dealers meet their regulatory obligations. Although we intend this notice (**Notice**) to provide guidance to captive dealers, it may be useful to other registrants too. In this Notice, unless the context otherwise requires, a reference to registrants includes both firms and their registered individuals.

We intend this Notice to:

- set out our concerns with the conflicts of interest that arise from the captive dealer business model to help captive dealers decide how to respond to conflicts of interest by avoiding, or controlling and disclosing them
- suggest acceptable practices and unacceptable practices for addressing conflicts of interest
- outline what firms proposing to be captive dealers can expect when applying for registration
- outline what captive dealers can expect when CSA staff perform compliance reviews

Registrant obligations

Conflicts of interest

Registrants must comply with Part 13, Division 2 Conflicts of Interest of NI 31-103, which requires them to take reasonable steps to:

- identify existing material conflicts of interest and those that the firm reasonably expects to arise between the firm and a client, and
- respond appropriately to existing or potential conflicts of interest

The Companion Policy outlines three methods to respond to conflicts of interest: avoidance, control and disclosure. It also describes specific examples of conflicts of interest and gives guidance on how registrants can avoid, control and/or disclose them.

KYC, KYP and suitability

Many prospectus exemptions allow issuers to raise capital from persons who can assess the merits of the investment without a prospectus. Certain of these investments are higher risk and often illiquid, and the information available to investors at the time of investment — and, in many cases, after investment — will be more limited. Any offering document used will not undergo prior review by the regulators, and the extensive continuous disclosure obligations on reporting issuers may not apply. Registrants play a critical role in ensuring that investors understand the risks associated with their investments and that the investments are suitable.

The KYC, KYP and suitability obligations and the fair dealing duty apply to all registered dealers and advisers, and apply to trades made under prospectus exemptions. CSA Staff Notice 31-336 *Guidance for Portfolio Managers, Exempt Market Dealers and Other Registrants on the Know-Your-Client, Know-Your-Product and Suitability Obligations* gives additional guidance on the applicable securities legislation requirements relating to KYC, KYP and suitability.

Concerns with captive dealers

The captive dealer business model creates a material conflict of interest between the captive dealer's financial incentive to sell its related or connected issuer's securities, and its regulatory obligations, including KYC, KYP, suitability, and its fair dealing duty.

We have identified captive dealers who did not recognize that investors were their clients, instead treating them as clients of their related or connected issuers. A registrant's primary obligation is to ensure that the securities it recommends to investors are suitable for them.

The material conflict of interest inherent in the captive dealer business model gives rise to inconsistent, competing or divergent interests, which make it difficult for a captive dealer to fulfil its duties to investors objectively. We have identified the following problems among captive dealers:

- failing in their suitability obligations to investors because the registrant has poor product knowledge
- failing to disclose or providing inadequate disclosure to investors about related or connected issuers in cases where there is negative information (for example, where the issuer is experiencing financial difficulty), resulting in investors taking on more risk than they could bear or more risk than they wish to bear
- relying on related or connected issuers' product reviews and assessments to satisfy their KYP obligation, instead of providing a review or assessment independent of the related or connected issuer
- financial dependence on related or connected issuers, creating an incentive to distribute unsuitable products
- inadequate disclosure of significant fees and charges paid to related or connected issuers, in some instances for little or no apparent services performed, resulting in investors not understanding the costs associated with their investment
- related or connected issuers using the proceeds raised from their distributions for purposes other than those stated in their offering or marketing materials

CSA staff have identified the inability of captive dealers to identify and address conflicts of interest and the delegation of the suitability obligation as significant compliance deficiencies. We have taken regulatory action against registrants and issuers as needed, including suspension and referrals to enforcement.

Responding to conflicts of interest

Captive dealers should avoid material conflicts of interest that they cannot address through controls and/or disclosure. Avoidance includes ceasing to provide a service, or dealing with a client, or not trading in a particular product or products. Captive dealers that solely or primarily trade in related or connected issuer securities are most at risk of being unable to address conflicts of interest through controls and/or disclosure. In this Notice, we provide suggestions to address conflicts of interest.

When we review captive dealer businesses, we will assess each business in relation to its related or connected issuers and their investment products, to assess the nature and severity of the existing conflicts of interest. In compliance reviews, we have seen instances where captive dealers could not demonstrate that they had met their conflicts of interest obligations under Part 13 of NI 31-103, because they did not:

- understand when, as a result of material negative changes to their business (for example, significant financial losses of a related issuer), they could no longer manage their conflicts of interest, and therefore should respond by avoiding them
- identify and document that they identified and responded to conflicts of interest, and why their response was appropriate
- assess each related or connected issuer product they sell in relation to each trade; instead they assumed that the suitability of one related or connected issuer product makes all of their related or connected issuer products suitable for an investor
- consider the concentration of related or connected issuer products in an investor's investment portfolio

We encourage captive dealers to:

- separate decision-making roles in related or connected issuer and dealer businesses
- establish policies and procedures that require an ongoing assessment of their captive dealer business models and the products they trade
- establish an independent review committee to conduct product due diligence and to consider on an ongoing basis whether to avoid, control, or disclose conflicts of interest
- consider offering securities of third-party issuers in addition to those of related or connected issuers, and ensure that dealing representatives are aware and understand that the firm offers a diversified product shelf
- provide balanced product training to sales staff by someone other than the issuer
- provide balanced training to sales staff outlining their responsibility to meet their KYP, KYC and suitability obligations

Captive dealers' registrant obligations

Captive dealers that do not avoid conflicts of interest should demonstrate instead that they are controlling and/or disclosing them appropriately.

In our experience, captive dealers that do not appropriately control and/or disclose material conflicts of interest that result from their relationships with related or connected issuers will also fail to conduct KYC, KYP and suitability assessments properly.

Below are some effective practices for controlling and/or disclosing conflicts of interest. In our compliance reviews, we will focus closely on whether captive dealers have implemented any of these practices. We will expect captive dealers that have not done so to explain what alternative or additional methods they have in place.

Acceptable practices[1]

- Develop policies and procedures that describe how you will identify and respond to conflicts of interest.
- Document your independent KYP assessment, for instance by keeping a due diligence checklist and documents that demonstrate your review of key documents such as offering documents, business plans and financial statements.
- Have an independent review committee:
  - review policies and procedures to ensure they address conflicts of interest, KYC, KYP, suitability, and the fair dealing duty
  - conduct initial due diligence on related or connected issuer products, including an assessment of the accuracy and reliability of materials provided by the related or connected issuers
  - identify those products that pose too severe a conflict of interest to be distributed generally and consider whether trades in such products should be restricted to certain investors or classes of investors only

The independent review committee's review and approval of any product for distribution does not relieve the captive dealer of its obligation to ensure the product is suitable for each client.

- Provide clients with meaningful disclosure, including:
  - the issuer's audited financial statements
  - a simplified document, similar to a mutual fund fact sheet, with appropriate highlights and risk disclosures about the investment, including clear disclosure of the conflicts of interest and the concerns it raises
  - other relevant information, in plain language
- Assign a responsible individual (such as the chief compliance officer or ultimate designated person), who has not been directly involved in any way with the trade in question, to ensure that investors understand:
  - the relationship between the captive dealer and the related or connected issuer
  - the key features of the investment (e.g. that the security is sold under a prospectus exemption and therefore may be illiquid, the risks of the investment and the compensation received by the captive dealer for the trade)
  - the concentration risks associated with investing in a limited number of related or connected issuers
- Provide training to ensure that registered individuals and other relevant staff understand the nature of the material conflicts of interest inherent in the business model and the importance of avoiding, managing and/or disclosing them.
- Have unrelated dealers distribute the securities of your related or connected issuers, demonstrating to CSA staff that a third party has reviewed the products and found them suitable for distribution.
- Sell products other than those of related or connected issuers; product diversification is an important factor to help reduce financial dependence of the dealer on an issuer.

Unacceptable practices

- Fail to identify and document your assessment and response to the conflicts of interest inherent in your captive dealer structure.
- Assume that disclosing a conflict of interest alone is sufficient to respond to it.
- Inadequate policies and procedures to identify, determine the risk of, and respond appropriately to conflicts of interest.

---

[1]This is not an exhaustive list, and the adoption of one or more of these suggestions will not ensure compliance.

- Assume that the related or connected issuer has complied with KYC, KYP or suitability requirements. Each captive dealer has an independent obligation to comply with these requirements and to keep compliance records. You cannot delegate the KYC, KYP and suitability processes.

- Present conflicts of interest disclosure in an obscure or confusing manner, such as in lengthy and complex documents. This disclosure should be in plain language, and easily understood by a reasonable person.

- Ask a client to waive conflicts of interest disclosure and/or a suitability assessment. Permitted clients may waive their right to a suitability review in writing.

Registration applications from firms proposing to be captive dealers

In assessing new registration applications, CSA staff will consider applications by captive dealers on a case-by-case basis. The likelihood of harm to investors and to the capital markets will be the main factors in our determination. For example, we may not grant registration where the applicant proposes to distribute securities of a related or connected issuer whose financial statements raise concerns about its financial viability. We would be concerned in this circumstance, since the captive dealer may be financially dependent on the issuer and would therefore have an added incentive to distribute unsuitable securities in an attempt to improve the issuer's financial condition.

Our review of registration applications will include an assessment of the captive dealer's business plan, both in the short term and in the longer term. We will also assess the firm's policies and procedures manual to test if it has an adequate compliance system in place to control and/or disclose conflicts of interest. Depending on our assessment, we may advise the applicant that without changes, we may recommend a refusal of registration. We expect captive dealer applicants to be forthright in disclosing conflicts of interest to CSA staff reviewing the registration application. Failure to disclose conflicts of interest to CSA staff may result in a recommendation of refusal of registration.

Compliance reviews of captive dealers

During our compliance reviews of captive dealers, we will, among other things, discuss with them why they did or did not adopt some or all of the effective practices in this Notice and assess whether the practices they have adopted are sufficient to address conflicts of interest in the captive dealer business model.

If we encounter conflicts of interest that captive dealers did not appropriately resolve, resulting in unsuitable sales, we will consider both the failure to resolve the conflict of interest and the suitability failure as significant deficiencies. Staff will closely monitor registrants' compliance with conflicts of interest, KYC, KYP and suitability requirements, and will take appropriate regulatory action to ensure compliance with securities legislation.

Reminder about changes in business models

We expect all registrants to report changes in business models using Form 33-109F5 *Change of Registration Information* (**Form F5**). Changes in business models can significantly affect the compliance risk of a firm, for instance by introducing material conflicts of interest. Registrants must file a Form F5, if they change their business structure to a captive dealer business model. Firms should assess their business models on an ongoing basis to comply with their obligations under securities legislation.

Questions

If you have questions regarding this Notice, please refer them to any of the following:

[Omitted.]

CSA Staff Notice 31-344 — OBSI Joint Regulators Committee Annual Report for 2015

Date: April 7, 2016

39 O.S.C.B. 3091

[Not reproduced]

CSA Staff Notice 31-345 — Cost Disclosure, Performance Reporting and Client Statements — Frequently Asked Questions and Additional Guidance

Date: April 14, 2016

39 O.S.C.B. 3569

Background

Amendments to National Instrument 31-103 *Registration Requirements, Exemptions and Ongoing Registrant Obligations* (**NI 31-103**) and Companion Policy 31-103CP *Registration Requirements, Exemptions and Ongoing Registrant Obligations* (**31-103CP** or the **CP**) implementing phase 2 of the Client Relationship Model (**CRM2**) came into force on July 15, 2013 (the **CRM2 Amendments**). Staff of the Canadian Securities Administrators (**CSA staff** or **we**) have compiled these frequently asked questions and our responses as well as further guidance (**FAQs**) in addition to that which we published in CSA Staff Notice 31-337 *Cost Disclosure, Performance Reporting and Client Statements — Frequently Asked Questions and Additional Guidance as of February 27, 2014* (**CSA SN 31-337**). FAQs from CSA SN 31-337 have been consolidated with the further FAQs in this notice. For that reason, CSA SN 31-337 is hereby withdrawn. Some of the earlier FAQs have been superseded in part by the further FAQs or left out of this consolidation because they are no longer necessary. Among other things, this notice includes a section on the applicability of the CRM2 Amendments to exempt market dealers. Some parts of this guidance were previously published in CSA Staff Notice 31-324 *Exempt Market Dealers and Account Statement Requirements in National Instrument 31-103 Registra-*

Part 3: REGISTRATION

tion Requirements and Exemptions dated June 22, 2011 (**CSA SN 31-324**). With the publication of the updated guidance in this notice, CSA SN 31-324 is also hereby withdrawn.

In this notice, "**registered firm**" or "**firm**" includes both registered dealers and registered advisers unless otherwise specified, and we refer to mutual fund dealers as "**MFDs**", exempt market dealers as "**EMDs**", portfolio managers as "**PMs**" and investment fund managers as "**IFMs**".

All references in this notice to sections, subsections, paragraphs and subparagraphs are to NI 31-103, unless otherwise noted.

CRM2 Transition

These FAQs concern ongoing CRM2 Amendments. The CRM2 Amendments are being phased-in over a three-year transition period from 2013 through 2016. Certain transitional relief has been published in the form of blanket or omnibus orders issued by all Canadian Securities Administrators (**CSA**) members and in housekeeping amendments to member rules of the self-regulatory organizations (**SROs**), the Investment Industry Regulatory Organization of Canada (**IIROC**) and the Mutual Fund Dealers Association of Canada (**MFDA**). The CSA and the SROs have also published CRM2 implementation planning tips documents. Registrants should refer to these publications for information that may be relevant to their transition planning.

CRM2 Amendments and EMDs

With the exception of a few provisions specific to IFMs and a few provisions relating to scholarship plans that will have unique implications for scholarship plan dealers, the CRM2 Amendments do not differentiate between categories of registrant. Any differences in the application of the CRM2 Amendments between different registered dealers or registered advisers will be the result of their different operating models, which may bring different CRM2 Amendments into play for them.

The CRM2 Amendments include exemptions with respect to permitted clients that are not individuals and there are corresponding exemptions in IIROC member rules. Consequently, firms that focus exclusively on institutional investors may not be significantly affected by the introduction of the CRM2 Amendments.

Questions about how the CRM2 Amendments will apply to a category of registrant are most often asked with regard to EMDs that are not also registered as advisers or in another category of dealer (**sole EMDs**). The guidance below discusses how the CRM2 Amendments may affect a sole EMD. It in no way supersedes the provisions in NI 31-103.

Overview:

Holding client assets and other specified criteria

The applicability of some of the CRM2 Amendments depends on whether a registered firm holds client assets (account statements) or, if it does not, whether certain other specific criteria apply (additional statements). Other CRM2 Amendments may or may not apply depending on whether a registered firm has a "client" at the relevant point in time (annual report on charges and other compensation, and annual report on investment performance).

Sole EMDs do not normally hold client assets and where that is the case, they can disregard provisions that only apply where client assets are held by a registered firm. In circumstances where a sole EMD holds client assets (as may be the case with mortgage syndications), it must deliver account statements with the information required under subsections 14.14(4) and 14.14(5) along with position cost information under section 14.14.2. Furthermore, since holding client assets is a clear indication of an ongoing client relationship, a sole EMD is also subject to the requirement to deliver an annual report on charges and other compensation under section 14.17 and an annual investment performance report under section 14.18.

Transactional vs ongoing client relationship

Some sole EMDs have only limited, transactional relationships with their clients — as opposed to the ongoing client relationships that are typical of most other registrants' operating models. An example of a transactional relationship would be where an EMD's relationship with a client is limited to a specific private placement transaction and does not involve

- a security specified in paragraph 14.14.1(1)(c)

- any trailer fee or similar ongoing compensation in relation to the client's ownership of a security

- the EMD holding client assets

- any expectation on the part of the EMD that there may be further transactions with the client or services provided to the client. For example, if an EMD regularly contacts the client regarding any securities offered by the EMD, this will be considered an ongoing relationship.

CRM2 Amendments and EMDs

- any expectation on the part of the client that the EMD will continue to provide services to the client after the completion of the transaction. The example described above applies in this case as well.

In this example, the EMD would be required to deliver one account statement with transactional information under subsection 14.14(4), but would not be required to deliver any

- further account statements under section 14.14

- additional statements under section 14.14.1

- position cost information under section 14.14.2

- annual report on charges and other compensation under section 14.17

- annual investment performance report under section 14.18

A sole EMD should consider carefully whether it is in an ongoing client relationship before concluding that any of the CRM2 Amendments does not apply to it.

Section-by-section analysis:

Relationship disclosure information, pre-trade disclosure of charges and trade confirmation

A sole EMD always has a client at the time of the transaction and will be subject to CRM2 Amendments (and other NI 31-103 requirements) relating to the relationship disclosure (section 14.2), pre-trade disclosure of charges (section 14.2.1) and trade confirmations (section 14.12). However, if it has no other dealings with the investor, the EMD might conclude that it is no longer in a client relationship at the point in time when it would otherwise be required to prepare further client statements and reports, as discussed below.

Account statements

An account statement has two principal elements: transactional information and account position information. Transactional information is specific to the securities involved and is required in almost all circumstances where there has been a transaction. Account position information is a snap-shot of the whole account and is required only where the firm holds client assets.

Subsection 14.14(1) requires an EMD to deliver transactional information prescribed under subsection 14.14(4) to clients on a quarterly basis or, if so requested, each month. This requirement applies regardless of whether the firm holds client assets. For EMDs that hold client assets, account position information under subsection 14.14(5) is also required. Note that subsection 14.14(2) requires an EMD to deliver an account statement with transactional information under subsection 14.14(4) "after the end of *any month* in which a transaction was effected in securities *held* by the dealer in the client's account" [emphasis added].

The effect of these requirements is that, if one or more transactions occurred in the reporting period, a sole EMD must provide the client with an account statement with transactional information (but not account position information if no clients assets are held) either

- at the end of the month, if requested by a client, or

- at the end of the quarter, by default.

This applies even where an EMD does not have an ongoing client relationship.

Additional statements

An "additional statement" (registered firms subject to the requirements in section 14.14.1 are not required to call it this in client communications — "account statement" would do for those purposes) is the way clients get the equivalent of account position information where the registered firm does not hold their assets. It only applies in certain circumstances. More specifically, subsection 14.14.1(1) requires a registered dealer or adviser that does not hold client assets to provide an additional statement with account position information under subsection 14.14.1(2) on a quarterly basis if

Part 3:
REGISTRATION

CRM2 Amendments and EMDs

- it has trading authority over the client's account in which the securities are held or were transacted (not, of course, applicable to a sole EMD),

- it receives certain continuing payments in respect of securities it traded for a client (e.g., trailing commission), or

- it is the dealer of record for a client's securities issued by a mutual fund or certain labour-sponsored investment vehicles (EMDs trading securities of an investment fund should be aware of the definition of "mutual fund" under securities legislation).

In effect, a registered firm is deemed to have an ongoing client relationship in these circumstances. If none of these circumstances apply, there is no requirement for a sole EMD to provide clients with an additional statement.

Position cost information

Subsection 14.14.2(1) requires quarterly delivery of position cost information under criteria which effectively mean that if a sole EMD has to provide account position information to a client, either in an account statement or an additional statement, it also has to provide position cost information to the client.

Annual report on charges and other compensation

Subsection 14.17(1) requires delivery of a report on charges and other compensation to a client every 12 months. This is an instance where a sole EMD must decide whether it has an ongoing client relationship, as discussed above. It certainly does if it is subject to the requirement to provide account position information to a client, either in an account statement or an additional statement.

However, even if the requirement in subsection 14.17(1) is triggered, the EMD would not be required to send a "nil" report if none of the specified charges or other compensation were received by it during the 12-month period.

Annual investment performance report

Subsection 14.18(1) requires annual delivery of an investment performance report to a client. The considerations discussed above will also apply when determining whether an EMD has an ongoing client relationship that would require it to provide an investor with this report.

Note that the elements of the performance report set out in section 14.19 will depend on market values that are contained in the account position information provided in the account statements and additional statements sent under sections 14.14 and 14.14.1, respectively. There is no requirement to deliver a performance report if none of a client's securities can be valued.

CRM2 Amendments and SRO Members

The CSA have approved member rules of the SROs that are harmonized with the CRM2 Amendments. Provided that they are in compliance with applicable rules of their SRO, dealers that are members of IIROC and the MFDA are exempt from the corresponding requirements of NI 31-103. Although the CRM2 requirements in SRO rules and NI 31-103 are harmonized to a high degree, there are a few differences and SRO members should look first to guidance from their SRO if they have questions about the interpretation of CRM2 requirements, turning to CSA guidance (including these FAQs) only if a question is not addressed in guidance from their SRO.

Note that IIROC and MFDA members who are also registered in categories that do not require SRO membership may be required to comply with NI 31-103 in respect of activities carried on under that other registration. For example, if a firm is registered as an IFM and is also registered as a MFD and a member of the MFDA, it will be subject to the requirements in Part 14 of NI 31-103 that apply to IFMs, but it will be able to rely on exemptions set out in Part 9 of NI 31-103 in respect of its MFD activities, so long as it complies with the corresponding requirements in MFDA member rules.

Applicability of SROs' CRM2 Guidance to non-SRO Members

In these FAQs, we have incorporated some SRO guidance concerning questions that have also been asked of CSA staff by non-members. We also endorse more generally the CRM2 guidance that the SROs have published for their members. Although some of the SRO guidance is specific to the operating models of member firms or may relate to aspects of member rules that differ in detail from the corresponding requirements in NI 31-103, much of it can be instructive for non-members who have questions that have not been specifically addressed in CSA guidance.

FREQUENTLY ASKED QUESTIONS

QUESTION	ANSWER
General Questions	
1. When does someone cease to be a client, such that a registrant is no longer required to provide the statements and reports contemplated in the CRM2 Amendments?	It is not possible to provide a bright line test for determining when a client relationship has ended that will apply in all cases. We expect firms to exercise reasonable professional judgement, erring in favour of providing client reporting where there is doubt as to whether there is still a client relationship. Some principles that apply to the exercise of that judgement are: • A person remains a client of a registered dealer or adviser for so long as the dealer or adviser holds securities owned by the person, or the circumstances described in subsection 14.14.1(1) [*additional statements*] apply. • A firm should consider the totality of its dealings with a client and the client's expectations of ongoing services from the firm. • Whether a client relationship is ongoing or not depends on the particular facts and circumstances of the relationship. Note that a registered dealer or adviser may not avoid the client reporting requirements in NI 31-103 by selectively choosing to cease to be the dealer of record for some of a client's securities. For example, a dealer may not tell the IFM of a client's mutual funds that it is no longer the dealer of record for some of the client's securities (unless those securities have been transferred to an account of the client at another dealer or an adviser), and at the same time, keep an account for the client. See also the guidance in question 35 regarding section 14.15 [*security holder statements*].
2. Do disclosure and reporting requirements in CRM2 Amendments apply to other investments that may not be securities, such as segregated funds?	The jurisdiction of the CSA limits the CRM2 Amendments to securities (including derivatives or exchange contracts, as applicable, in certain jurisdictions pursuant to the requirements of section 1.2 of NI 31-103). Nonetheless, we encourage registrants to provide their clients with information that meets the standards set in the CRM2 Amendments in respect of all of their investments. This will enable investors to better understand the relative costs of different investments and their performance. Note that requirements imposed by SROs may extend to such investments.
3. Where should switch fees and short-term trading fees be reported?	Switch fees charged by a registered dealer or adviser are considered a transaction charge (see the discussion of the definition of "transaction charge" in section 14.2 of the CP). They must be disclosed before the trade (section 14.2.1), in a trade confirmation (paragraph 14.12(1)(c)) and in the annual report on charges and other compensation (paragraph 14.17(1)(c)). Short-term trading fees paid to an investment fund must be disclosed in a trade confirmation but are not included in the requirements for the annual report on charges and other compensation.
14.2 Relationship disclosure information	
4. Before July 15, 2013, there was an exemption in former subsection 14.2(6) from section 14.2 in respect of a permitted client if (a) the client had waived it in writing, and (b) the registrant did not act as an adviser in respect of a managed account of the client. Under the CRM2 Amendments, the exemption was changed to a permitted client that is not an individual. Is the registrant now required to deliver relationship disclosure information to an individual permitted client who had previously waived the section?	Yes. If the individual permitted client had previously waived relationship disclosure information, in light of the CRM2 Amendments, a registered firm must deliver relationship disclosure to all individuals, whether or not they are permitted clients. We expect registered firms to act reasonably as to when they next deliver the relationship disclosure information. If there is a significant change in respect of the relationship disclosure information, then the registered firm should act right away. Otherwise, we would expect the relationship disclosure information to be updated the next time a firm purchases or sells a security for a client or advises a client to purchase, sell or hold a security.

FREQUENTLY ASKED QUESTIONS

	QUESTION	ANSWER
5.	If an individual permitted client has waived the suitability requirement under subsection 13.3(4), how will a firm meet the requirement in paragraph 14.2(2)(k) to deliver a statement that the firm has an obligation to assess whether a purchase or sale of a security is suitable for a client prior to executing the transaction or at any other time?	When there is no obligation to make a suitability determination because of the application of subsection 13.3(4), the firm will have met the requirement in paragraph 14.2(2)(k) by simply informing the client that the firm has no suitability obligation because the client has waived the requirement.
6.	If a firm is exempt from certain know your client (**KYC**) obligations under subsection 13.2(6), how will it meet the requirement in paragraph 14.2(2)(l) to deliver the information a registered firm must collect about the client under section 13.2?	The firm will meet the requirement in paragraph 14.2(2)(l) by delivering the information collected under the KYC obligation in section 13.2. If a firm is exempted from collecting certain KYC information, then the firm is not obligated to deliver that information under paragraph 14.2(2)(l).
7.	Will the CSA be providing additional guidance on benchmarks? Are benchmarks optional? If a firm decides to provide benchmarks, what is the expected frequency?	Other than a general discussion as part of the relationship disclosure information requirement in paragraph 14.2(2)(m), there is no requirement for registered firms to provide benchmark information to clients and for greater certainty, we have provided guidance under sections 14.2 [*relationship disclosure information*] and 14.19 [*content of investment performance report*] of the CP. Since benchmarks are optional, we did not prescribe any periods or other specifications for provision of benchmark information. However, we have provided guidance on the provision of benchmarks in section 14.19 of the CP, including, importantly, that benchmark information not be misleading. We are not providing specific guidance on benchmarks beyond that already set out in the CP. We expect firms to use their professional judgement when determining which benchmarks are relevant to a client's investments and explain to clients the use of benchmarks in terms they will understand.
8.	When does the guidance on the use of benchmarks set out under section 14.19 [*content of investment performance report*] in the CP come into effect?	The guidance in section 14.19 of the CP is relevant to the use of benchmarks today and is consistent with previously published guidance.

14.2.1 Pre-trade disclosure of charges

	QUESTION	ANSWER
9.	Can registrants use the Fund Facts document to satisfy the requirements in section 14.2.1 [*pre-trade disclosure of charges*]? The question arises because 31-103CP suggests a mutual fund's management fee should be discussed in the pretrade disclosure of charges, but the Fund Facts document is not required to include the management fee in all cases (only in the case of a new fund for which the management expense ratio (**MER**) is not available).	If a registrant delivers the Fund Facts document at the point of sale and explains the specific costs of the transaction to the client, then the registrant may use it further to satisfy the requirements of section 14.2.1 for the disclosure of charges related to the transaction. Since the management fee generally constitutes most of the MER of a mutual fund, we think this would be in line with the guidance in the CP.
10.	Must charges associated with a transfer of securities be disclosed before the transfer is effected?	A transfer is a transaction, so the client must receive pre-trade disclosure of charges. Whether it is the delivering registered firm or the receiving registered firm that provides a client with information about charges associated with a transfer (or both of them) will depend on which of them has the relevant information.
11.	Must pre-trade disclosure be provided where standard charges apply?	Yes. But, in the case of a client who is a frequent trader, where the firm has good reason to believe applicable charges are well understood, a brief confirmation that the usual charges will apply would be acceptable.

14.11.1 Determining market value

FREQUENTLY ASKED QUESTIONS

	QUESTION	ANSWER
12.	What if the net asset value (**NAV**) of an investment fund which is not listed on an exchange is not available on a daily basis?	The most recent NAV provided by the IFM should be used. If a registered dealer or adviser reasonably believes the NAV for an investment fund is stale or otherwise inaccurate, it may include an explanatory note to that effect in the statement provided to its client.
13.	Can a registered firm rely on a valuation provided by the issuer of securities when the firm is determining market value under section 14.11.1?	A registered firm that is required to provide market value information determined under section 14.11.1, is responsible for the information reported to its clients. The firm may not simply take valuation information from an issuer and pass it on to clients as the market value for purposes of the firm's reporting obligations. The firm must exercise its professional judgement as to the reliability of information provided by an issuer as an input to the firm's determination of market value. It should retain a record of the reasons for its decision.
14.	Why use last bid/ask price instead of closing price? Is it not misleading sometimes; for example, when there are large bid-ask deviations?	We chose last bid/ask price because not all securities are actively traded on a marketplace and there have been consistent problems with firms using stale data based on old closing prices. That said, we recognize that no one measure will always work best, so the requirement is for the firm to report the amount it reasonably believes to be the market value, after making any adjustments it considers necessary to accurately reflect the market value.
15.	Where there is an active market for a security, can a firm use the closing price in determining market value?	In the case of a liquid security for which a reliable price is quoted on a marketplace, if it can be demonstrated through use of a periodic assessment that a "last traded price" valuation approach results in security market values that are materially the same as under the "last bid and ask prices" valuation approach, it may be acceptable to use this current "last traded price" valuation approach.
16.	In the case of illiquid securities, when should a registered firm indicate that the market value is not determinable or is zero?	The prescribed methodology for determining market value must be applied where the value cannot be readily determined by reference to an active market. A firm may not simply default to stating that market value is not determinable or is zero. If, having applied the prescribed methodology, the firm reasonably believes it cannot determine the market value of a security, it must then report its value as "not determinable" in client statements and exclude it from the calculations in client statements and reports, as prescribed in subsection 14.11.1(3). This is not the same as determining that the market value of a security is zero for purposes of client statement reporting. However, we would expect that if the market value of a security cannot be determined for a prolonged period of time, that may be an indication that the market value of the security should now be determined to be zero.
		The following considerations can be used in determining when the market value for a particular security is "not determinable":
		• the security is illiquid
		• there is little or no issuer and issuer-related financial data available, or the data is stale
		• there is little or no financial data available for comparable issuers or for the issuer's business sector
		• there is not enough data to use the International Financial Reporting Standards (**IFRS**) based valuation methodologies prescribed in paragraph 14.11.1(1)(b) and/or the results of the various IFRS methodologies used have been determined to be unreliable because of the use of unreliable data or the results indicate a wide range in possible values
		• the acquisition cost of the security is no longer a good estimate of the security's market value as the cost is outside the range of possible values for the security

Part 3: REGISTRATION

FREQUENTLY ASKED QUESTIONS

	QUESTION	ANSWER
		Important to applying these considerations is establishing and maintaining a firm policy as to how many days beyond which the last data available is considered to be stale. Similarly, key to determining which securities are assigned a market value of zero is establishing and maintaining a firm policy as to how many days a security can have a "non determinable" value beyond which the market value of the security is considered to be zero.
		Firms are reminded that for calculations required to prepare investment performance reports, subsection 14.19(7) prescribes a deemed market value of zero for a security whenever a firm believes it cannot determine its market value.

14.12 Content and delivery of trade confirmation

	QUESTION	ANSWER
17.	The prescribed notification under sub-paragraph 14.12(1)(c.1)(ii) says remuneration "has been" added or deducted from the price of the security. Can "has been" be replaced with "may have been" where the firm will have difficulty determining which trades had dealer firm remuneration added and which did not?	Yes. Since the requirement is to provide a notification that is "substantially" in the form prescribed, a firm can modify the prescribed text to use "may have been" instead of "has been", provided the firm has made reasonable efforts to determine whether it can make the more definitive statement to the client.

14.14 Account statements and 14.14 1 additional statements

	QUESTION	ANSWER
18.	Is there any additional guidance on providing electronic statements?	National Policy 11-201 *Electronic Delivery of Documents* provides guidance to securities industry participants who want to use electronic delivery to satisfy any applicable delivery requirements in securities legislation.
		Monthly and/or quarterly statements, as applicable can be delivered electronically. All of the content required under section 14.14 and, where applicable, section 14.14.1 must be provided at the required intervals.
		However, if a firm chooses to provide electronic access to account information on a more frequent basis than required in sections 14.14 and 14.14.1, that supplementary access does not have to conform with the requirements of those sections.
19.	How do the account statement and additional statement requirements in sections 14.14 and 14.14.1 apply where a registered firm does not (a) hold or control a client's securities, nor (b) meet criteria set out in subsection 14.14.1(1)?	Under subsection 14.14(4), the registrant will be required to provide the client with an account statement that sets out transaction information for the reporting period in which a transaction occurred. The account position information required under subsection 14.14(5) will not be required. There will be no requirement to provide an additional statement under section 14.14.1.
20.	If securities are transferred to a managed account for passive holding, is the PM responsible for reporting on these "legacy" securities?	Yes, if securities are in an account managed by a PM, that PM is responsible for reporting on them.
21.	If a security is redeemable at a discount to market value (e.g., "95% of net asset value if sold within 2 years"), should this security be shown as subject to a deferred sales charge under paragraphs 14.14(5)(g) and 14.14.1(2)(h)?	Yes. It is a deferred sales charge in substance: a contingent cost that the client should be reminded to bear in mind before making a decision to sell the position.
22.	Can an account statement or additional statement cover more than one account?	No. There is no provision for consolidated statements in section 14.14 or 14.14.1. A registered dealer or registered adviser must provide every client with an applicable statement for each of their accounts.

FREQUENTLY ASKED QUESTIONS

	QUESTION	ANSWER
		Registered firms may provide supplementary reporting that they think their client might find useful. For example, a firm might provide a consolidated year-end statement where a client has requested a consolidated performance report under subsection 14.18(4).
23.	If a client's assets are held at a third party custodian, must account statements or additional statements that a registered firm delivers to the client include cash that is held for the client by the custodian?	Yes. The requirements in sections 14.14 and 14.14.1 apply in respect of cash and securities that are in the client's account with a registered firm or traded through the account. The use of a third party custodian has no effect in this regard.
24.	What should be disclosed in an additional statement about the party that holds the securities?	The disclosure must provide sufficient information for the client to be able to identify the party that holds their securities. A custodian must be named (e.g., "X is the custodian that holds these securities as nominee for you"). A more general statement concerning securities held in the client's name at an issuer is acceptable, since the name of an issuer is evident (e.g., "These securities are registered in your name at the fund company / the company that issued them.")

14.14.2 Position cost information

	QUESTION	ANSWER
25.	How should short positions be reported?	If using book cost, a short security position should be reported as the total amount received for the security, net of any transaction charges related to the sale, adjusted for any distributions (other than dividends), returns of capital and corporate reorganizations. If using original cost, a short security position should be reported as the total amount received for the security, net of any transaction charges related to the sale.
26.	Does "within 10 days after" in paragraph 14.14.2(4)(c) mean within 10 business days or 10 calendar days?	References to "days" in the CRM2 Amendments are to calendar days.
27.	Can a firm adjust position cost to align it with tax cost or otherwise provide a value that reflects tax cost instead of position cost?	No. A firm must provide position cost using either original cost or book cost as defined in section 1.1. If a firm also wishes to provide tax cost information in addition to position cost, it may do so, so long as the differences are made clear to the client.
28.	Can the position cost of flow-through shares be reduced down to zero following the allocation of gains and losses for tax purposes (assuming book cost is used, rather than original cost)?	No. Book cost for CRM2 reporting is as defined in section 1.1 and is not intended to be tax cost. Therefore, the allocation of gains and losses in a flow-through (as vs. actual distributions) is not factored into the book cost of a position.
29.	In determining position cost for transferred securities, can a registered firm rely on position cost information provided by the transferring firm?	Yes, if • the transferring-out firm is also subject to the requirement to provide individual position cost information to clients, and • the transferring-in firm has no reason to believe the information is not reliable.
30.	Can a firm use one of book or original cost for some positions, and market value for other positions on the same statement?	Yes. You must identify which method is used for each security position. Subparagraphs 14.14.2(2)(a)(ii) and (b)(ii) set out the circumstances in which it is acceptable to use market value instead of using original or book cost.
31.	How should position cost be determined if a security position is built up with successive purchases, and original or book cost is available for some purchases but market value has also been used?	An average can be used to determine the cost of the position. The average may include cost information based on either or both of (a) the book cost or original cost determined in accordance with the definitions of those terms in section 1.1, and (b) market value used where section 14.14.2 contemplates it (where a security position was opened before the transition to CRM2 or was transferred into the account).

Part 3:
REGISTRATION

FREQUENTLY ASKED QUESTIONS

	QUESTION	ANSWER
		The disclosure applicable where market value is used should be modified as may be necessary. For example: "The cost of this security position has been determined using an average of market value as of the date on which some securities were transferred into your account when it was opened, and the book cost of securities that we subsequently purchased for your account."
		It is also permissible to differentiate between positions in the same security, reporting (a) and (b) above separately, instead of averaging them into a single number. This alternative approach has the potential to confuse clients. Clear explanatory notations should be provided if it is used.
32.	Is it necessary to indicate which security positions have been valued using market value rather than original cost or book cost, or is it acceptable to provide blanket disclosure along the lines of "where book/original was unavailable, we used ..."?	Reporting is per security position and so you do need to indicate what method was used to determine its cost. A client statement might have an asterisk that indicates each position that was valued at book, and another flag that indicates other positions where "because book cost information was unavailable, we have used market value information as of the transfer date as the position cost" or similar disclosure. When an average of book or original cost and market value is used to determine the cost of a position, the disclosure should be modified as may be necessary.
33.	If client moves from one series of a fund that is organized as a trust to another series of the same fund (e.g., a deferred sales charge schedule is up and the investor is moved to a different series with either the same or a lower management fee), will the position cost change?	Position cost will not change unless there is a fee associated with the switch because the client is still invested in the same fund with the same portfolio of underlying investments.
34.	If a client moves from one fund to another fund within a "corporate class" fund structure (e.g., to execute a change in investment strategy), will the position cost change?	Yes, the position cost will change because the client is now invested in a different fund, with a different portfolio of underlying investments. The fact that there may not be a disposition for tax purposes is not relevant to this determination. See subsection 1.3(1) in both NI 81-102 *Investment Funds* and NI 81-106 *Investment Fund Continuous Disclosure*: "Each section, part, class or series of a class of securities of an investment fund that is referable to a separate portfolio of assets is considered to be a separate investment fund for purposes of this Instrument." The same analysis is applicable with respect to section 14.14.2.

14.15 Security holder statements

35.	Is there any guidance regarding the requirement to send a statement for "orphaned accounts"?	The requirement for an IFM to send a security holder statement to an account without a dealer of record — an orphaned account — is not new. This is an accommodation of the temporary and very limited circumstance that arises where there ceases to be a registered dealer or adviser serving the client. See also the guidance in question 1 regarding when a client relationship has ended.
		The CRM2 Amendments in section 14.15 expand the existing requirements for the information that IFMs must send to security holders to include some of the information registered dealers and advisers will be required to deliver to their clients, such as position cost information.

14.17 Report on charges and other compensation

36.	The requirement to provide an annual report on charges and other compensation comes into effect on July 15, 2016. For what period will the first annual report be required?	Firms may have various reporting cycles, on a calendar year basis or otherwise. If July 15, 2016 falls within the start and end dates of a 12-month period, an annual report will be required for that period. So if a firm reports or wishes to report on a calendar year basis, the first annual report will be required for a period from January 1, 2016 to December 31, 2016. If a firm reports or wishes to report for a period ending July 15, then the first annual reports will be required for the period beginning July 16, 2015.
37.	If there are no charges or other compensation to be disclosed, is a nil report still required to be delivered?	No, nil reports on charges and other compensation are not required.

FREQUENTLY ASKED QUESTIONS

	QUESTION	ANSWER
38.	Are the charges levied within an investment fund held by an investor (e.g., management fees) included in operating charges? Do PMs who manage their clients' money through pooled funds have to "look through" to those fees?	No. We would expect this information to be disclosed as part of the relationship disclosure information delivered at account opening or when the investment is made. However, a firm is not required to include the fund management fee in its annual report on charges and other compensation. The definition of operating charge is specific to the account and is not a product related fee. Operating charges (and transaction charges) include only charges paid to the registered firm by the client. Nonetheless, if such fees are a significant part of the PM's compensation model — say if a PM used in-house funds as the primary investment vehicle for its clients and took much of its compensation in fund management fees instead of the traditional fee based on clients' assets under management — we would expect that the firm would communicate to its clients about the way it is being compensated, consistent with the duty to deal fairly, honestly and in good faith with clients.
39.	If a client leaves the firm and transfers out in the middle of the year, does the firm have an obligation to send an annual report on charges and other compensation?	Once the client relationship has ended, there is no longer an obligation to send an annual report on charges and other compensation. We do, however, encourage firms to provide departing clients with information on charges and other compensation received during the year-to-date.
40.	Does the requirement to disclose the dollar amount of trailing commissions mean separate disclosures for the amount paid to the firm and the amount paid to the registered representative?	The report on charges and other compensation is at the firm level. This means the dollar amount of trailing commissions disclosed in the report is the total amount received in respect of the client's holdings. That amount is not broken down to show how much the firm retained and how much it passed on to the client's dealing or advising representative. The intention is that the client will see the aggregate amount of trailing commission that was generated by their account.
41.	How should typical mutual fund related charges other than trailing commissions be reported in the annual report on charges and other compensation?	If there is an up-front commission charged to the client by the registered dealer or adviser when the securities are purchased, it would be included in the amount reported under paragraph 14.17(1)(c). In the sample annual report in Appendix D of the CP, this appears under "Charges you paid directly to us ... Commissions on purchases of mutual funds with a sales charge". If there is a commission or other payment from the IFM or another party other than the client to the registered dealer or adviser when the securities are purchased, that payment is reported under paragraph 14.17(1)(g). In the sample annual report in Appendix D of the CP, this appears under "Compensation we received through third parties ... Commissions from mutual fund managers on purchases of mutual funds (see Note 1)". If, when the securities are sold by the client (i.e., redeemed back to the issuer), a deferred sales charge is triggered but no commission or other payment goes to the registered dealer or adviser, there is no requirement to include it in the annual report. If, when securities are sold by the client, a commission or other payment was received by the registered dealer or adviser, it would be reported under paragraph 14.17(1)(c) or (g), depending on whether it was paid by the client or another party. See also the guidance in question 3 regarding switch fees and short-term trading fees. If a registered dealer or adviser is concerned that clients might assume trailing commissions are charged directly to the client, we would have no objection to the firm including in its annual reports a clear explanation of the charges. For example, note 1 in the sample Report on Charges and Other Compensation in Appendix D of the CP could be expanded along the lines of the second paragraph in note 2.

FREQUENTLY ASKED QUESTIONS

	QUESTION	ANSWER
42.	If a registered dealer or adviser receives referral fees in relation to registerable services to the client during a reporting period and the client has two or more accounts with the firm, how should the firm disclose the referral fees in the annual reports for the client's accounts?	If the referral fees relate only to one of the client's accounts, they would be included in the annual report for that account alone. If the referral fees relate to more than one of the client's accounts, we expect the firm to present disclosure information in a clear and meaningful manner. For example, the firm could report the full amount in the annual report for each account, or report a pro-rated amount in the annual report for each account, but in either case the firm should include an explanatory note so that the client will not be confused as to the total amount of the referral fees received by the firm during the period.
43.	How should rebated fees be reported?	The requirement is to report the full (i.e., gross) amount the client was charged by the registrant, rather than a reduced amount (i.e., the charge net of fees). However, a firm may choose to provide the net amount along with the gross amount, so long as it also includes an explanatory note. Firms paying rebates in respect of mutual fund-related charges should also refer to NI 81-105 *Mutual Fund Sales Practices*, section 7.1.
44.	What reporting is required if a firm receives payment from an issuer, IFM or PM of a fund based on a "high water mark" performance of a security it has traded to a client's account?	Regardless of what they are called and regardless of whether they are paid directly to the registered firm or as a shared portion of compensation paid to a PM of the fund, such payments are compensation for trading securities to investors and must therefore be included in the annual report on charges and other compensation pursuant to paragraph 14.17(1)(g).
45.	Does the requirement in paragraph 14.17(1)(a) to deliver a registered firm's current operating charges that might be applicable to the client's account mean that the firm must include the fees for every service the firm offers?	No. A firm may only include the fees for those of its services that it would reasonably expect the particular client to utilize in the coming 12-month period.

14.18 Investment performance report

46.	The requirement to provide an annual investment performance report comes into effect on July 15, 2016. For what period will the first annual report be required?	Firms may have various reporting cycles, on a calendar year basis or otherwise. If July 15, 2016 falls within the start and end dates of a 12-month period, an annual report will be required for that period. So if a firm reports or wishes to report on a calendar year basis, the first annual reports will be required for a period from January 1, 2016 to December 31, 2016. If a firm reports or wishes to report for a period ending July 15, then the first annual reports will be required for the 12-month period beginning July 16, 2015.

14.19 Content of investment performance report

47.	Can a registered firm send performance reports to its clients more frequently than once per year? If so, must all of its performance reports include all of the content prescribed for annual reports and be formatted in accordance with subsection 14.19(5)?	So long as a performance report that includes the prescribed content is delivered annually, firms are free to send more frequent reports. Such supplementary reports need not include the prescribed content and need not be formatted in accordance with subsection 14.19(5).
48.	If a firm chooses to provide percentage returns calculated using both money-weighted rate of return (MWRR) and time-weighted rate of return (TWRR) methods, what are the requirements for using TWRR?	The CRM2 Amendments do not prescribe periods, accounts or other specifications for the provision of additional percentage return information using TWRR. A firm may show returns using TWRR, as long as the firm also provides the return using MWRR in accordance with the requirements in section 14.19. In such cases, in addition to the general explanation in plain language of what the MWRR calculation method takes into account required under paragraph 14.19(1)(j), the firm should similarly explain the TWRR calculation method in plain language and help clients understand the difference between the two sets of performance returns.
49.	Will the CSA publish an approved formula to calculate MWRR?	No. There are different ways of calculating MWRR and the requirement is that firms use a method that is generally accepted in the securities industry. The CSA does not prescribe any method in particular because standards evolve over time. Approximation methods such as Modified Dietz are not acceptable. Approximations can produce misleading results compared to MWRR and advances in computing capability make it unnecessary to use them.

FREQUENTLY ASKED QUESTIONS

QUESTION		ANSWER
50.	Is the XIRR function in Microsoft Excel acceptable for MWRR calculations?	Yes. A registered firm may provide performance reports calculated with the XIRR function of Microsoft Excel. Firms should be aware that some versions of this software may have defects that affect these calculations. It is the responsibility of the firm to ensure that the calculation by the XIRR function of Microsoft Excel is being performed correctly.
14.20 Delivery of report on charges and other compensation and investment performance report		
51.	Does "within 10 days after" in paragraph 14.20(1)(c) mean within 10 business days or 10 calendar days?	References to "days" in the CRM2 Amendments are to calendar days.

Questions

If you have questions regarding this notice, please refer them to any of the following:

[Names not reproduced]

OSC Rule 31-501 — Registrant Relationships

Date: June 27, 1997 as amended effective March 31, 2003

20 O.S.C.B. 3354 and 26 O.S.C.B. 1434

[Revoked upon NI 31-103 coming into force.]

Final Rule: (1997) 20 O.S.C.B. 4633; Approval by OSC: (1997) 20 O.S.C.B. 3554; Request for Comments: (1996) 19 O.S.C.B. 4748; Replaces former OLP 4.4.

Amendment to Rule: (2003) 26 O.S.C.B. 1434; Approval by OSC: (2002) 25 O.S.C.B. 8007.

Companion Policy 31-501CP — Registrant Relationships

[Rescinded upon NI 31-103 coming into force.]

Adoption by OSC: (1997) 20 O.S.C.B. 3354; Request for Comments: (1996) 4748.

OSC Rule 31-502 — Proficiency Requirements for Registrants

Date: August 18, 2000, as amended effective November 5, 2003, May 21, 2007 and October 24, 2008

23 O.S.C.B. 5658, 26 O.S.C.B. 7170, 30 O.S.C.B. 5683 and 32 O.S.C.B 9163

[Revoked upon NI 31-103 coming into force.]

Final Rule: (2000) 23 O.S.C.B. 5658; Approval by OSC: (2000) 23 O.S.C.B. 4381; Request for Comments: (1999) 22 O.S.C.B. 5739, (1998) 21 O.S.C.B. 5306, (1998) 21 O.S.C.B. 466 and (1996) 19 O.S.C.B. 4751. A version of this Rule was approved by the OSC, (1998) O.S.C.B. 6581, but returned by the Minister for further consideration, (1998) 21 O.S.C.B. 7709.

Amendment to Rule: (2003) 26 O.S.C.B. 7170; Approval by OSC: (2003) 26 O.S.C.B. 6149; Request for Comments: (2002) 25 O.S.C.B. 8463.

Amendment to Rule: (2007) 30 O.S.C.B. 5683; Approval by OSC: (2007) 30 O.S.C.B. 2097; Request for Comments: (2006) 29 O.S.C.B. 1671.

Amendment to Rule: (2008) 31 O.S.C.B. 9163; Approval by OSC: (2008) 31 O.S.C.B. 7631; Request for Comments: (2007) 30 O.S.C.B. 2101.

Companion Policy 31-502CP — Proficiency Requirements for Registrants

[Rescinded upon NI 31-103 coming into force.]

Adoption by OSC: (2000) 23 O.S.C.B. 4381 and 5664; Request for Comments: (1999) 22 O.S.C.B. 5739, (1998) 21 O.S.C.B. 5306, (1998) 21 O.S.C.B. 466 and (1996) 19 O.S.C.B. 4751.

OSC Rule 31-503 — Limited Market Dealers

Date: January 30, 1998, as amended effective September 14, 2005

21 O.S.C.B. 613 and 28 O.S.C.B. (Supp-4) 140

[Revoked upon NI 31-103 coming into force.]

Final Rule: (1998) 21 O.S.C.B. 2316; Approval by OSC: (1998) 21 O.S.C.B. 611; Request for Comments: (1997) 20 O.S.C.B. 4763.

Amendment to Rule: (2005) 28 O.S.C.B. (Supp-4) 140; Approval by OSC: (2005) 28 O.S.C.B. (Supp-3) 222; Request for Comments: (2004) 27 O.S.C.B. (Supp-3) 1.

Part 3: REGISTRATION

OSC Rule 31-504 — Dealer and Adviser Applications for Registration

Date: September 12, 1997, amended effective February 21, 2003

20 O.S.C.B. 4634, 26 O.S.C.B. 1435

[Revoked upon NI 31-103 coming into force.]

Final Rule: (1997) 20 O.S.C.B. 4634; Approval by OSC: (1997) 20 O.S.C.B. 3357; Request for Comments: (1996) 19 O.S.C.B. 4766.

Amendment to Rule: (2003) 26 O.S.C.B. 1435; Approval by OSC: (2002) 25 O.S.C.B. 8010.

OSC Rule 31-505 — Conditions of Registration

Date: January 29, 1999, as amended effective November 5, 2003 and September 28, 2009

22 O.S.C.B. 731, 26 O.S.C.B. 7170 and 32 O.S.C.B. (Supp. 4) 81

Table of Contents

PART 1 — [REPEALED]

PART 2 — GENERAL DUTIES

2.1 General Duties — (1) A registered dealer or adviser shall deal fairly, honestly and in good faith with its clients.

(2) A representative of a registered dealer or a registered adviser shall deal fairly, honestly and in good faith with his or her clients.

PART 3 — [REPEALED]

PART 4 — EXEMPTION

4.1 Exemption — The Director may grant an exemption to this Rule, in whole or in part, subject to such conditions or restrictions as may be imposed in the exemption.

Final Rule: (1999) 22 O.S.C.B. 731; Approval by OSC: (1998) 21 O.S.C.B. 6591; Request for Comments: (1998) 21 O.S.C.B. 5317 and (1998) 21 O.S.C.B. 475.

Amendment to Rule: (2003) 26 O.S.C.B. 7170; Approval by OSC: (2003) 26 O.S.C.B. 6149; Request for Comments: (2002) 25 O.S.C.B. 8463.

Amendment to Rule: (2009) 32 O.S.C.B. (Supp. 4) 388; Approval by OSC: (2009) 32 O.S.C.B. (Supp. 2) 81; Request for Comments: (2008) 31 O.S.C.B. 2279.

Policies and Orders: OSCN 81-704; 33-734, ss. 3.2 and 3.4.

OSC Rule 31-506 — SRO Membership — Mutual Fund Dealers

Date: April 13, 2001

24 O.S.C.B. 2333

[Revoked upon NI 31-103 coming into force.]

Final Rule: 24 O.S.C.B. 2333 (April 13, 2001); Approved by OSC: 24 O.S.C.B. (Supp.) 1 (February 16, 2001); Request for Comments: 23 O.S.C.B. (Supp.) 163 (June 16, 2000), 21 O.S.C.B. 3875 (June 19, 1998) and 20 O.S.C.B. 5051 (October 3, 1997). The Rule was approved by the OSC at 23 O.S.C.B. 6985 (October 13, 2000) but returned by the Minister of Finance for further consideration 23 O.S.C.B. 8466 (December 22, 2000). The effective date was April 23, 2001.

OSC Rule 31-507 — SRO Membership — Securities Dealers and Brokers

Date: August 18, 2000

23 O.S.C.B. 5657

[Revoked upon NI 31-103 coming into force.]

Final Rule: (2000) 23 O.S.C.B. 5657; Approved by OSC: (2000) 23 O.S.C.B. 4565; Request for Comments: (2000) 22 O.S.C.B. 2755, (1998) 21 O.S.C.B. 3878 and (1997) 20 O.S.C.B. 5053.

OSC Rule 31-509 — National Registration Database (Commodity Futures Act)

Date: January 31, 2003, amended effective September 28, 2009 and October 12, 2013

26 O.S.C.B. 934, 32 O.S.C.B. (Supp. 4) 335 and 36 O.S.C.B. 9611

[Not reproduced; this rule relates to registration under the Commodity Futures Act and is substantially the same as NI 31-102.]

Final Rule: (2003) 26 O.S.C.B. 934; Approval by OSC: (2002) 25 O.S.C.B. 7517; Request for Comments: (2002) 25 O.S.C.B. 3443 and (2001) 24 O.S.C.B. 7459.

Amendments to Rule: (2009) 32 O.S.C.B. (Supp. 4) 335; Approval by OSC: (2009) 32 O.S.C.B. (Supp. 2) 1; Request for Comments: (2008) 31 O.S.C.B. 2279.

Amendments to Rule: (2013) 36 O.S.C.B. 9611; Approval by OSC: (2013) 36 O.S.C.B. 8569 (corrections) and 7217; Request for Comments: (2013) 36 O.S.C.B. 1081.

Companion Policy 31-509CP — National Registration Database (Commodity Futures Act)

Date: January 31, 2003, amended effective September 28, 2009

26 O.S.C.B. 940 and 32 O.S.C.B. (Supp. 4) 337

[Not reproduced]

Adoption by OSC: (2003) 26 O.S.C.B. 940 and (2002) 25 O.S.C.B. 7517; Request for Comments: (2002) 25 O.S.C.B. 3443 and (2001) 24 O.S.C.B. 7459.

Adoption of Amendments to Policy: (2009) 32 O.S.C.B. (Supp. 4) 337 and (2009) 32 O.S.C.B. (Supp. 2) 1; Request for Comments: (2008) 31 O.S.C.B. 2279.

OSC Staff Notice 31-712 — Mutual Fund Dealers Business Arrangements

Date: June 11, 2004; replaced November 19, 2004

27 O.S.C.B. 5623; 27 O.S.C.B. 9291

Introduction

This Staff Notice amends and replaces the OSC Staff Notice 31-712 published on June 11, 2004.

The Ontario Securities Commission (OSC) has reviewed certain business arrangements between mutual fund dealers and investment dealers that have evolved to enable clients of mutual fund dealers to have a broad range of security holdings in their accounts, including securities in which the mutual fund dealers are not registered to trade (Prohibited Securities). Accommodating clients' needs to hold all their securities in one account poses problems for mutual fund dealers since their registration limits the types of investments in which they can trade and for which they can provide advice. Our registration system recognizes that there are differing regulatory requirements that are applicable to restricted categories of registration. For example, the proficiency requirements for salespersons that are restricted to the sale of mutual fund products are lower than those required of a full service dealer; and the minimum capital requirements are generally lower for a mutual fund dealer. The following two business arrangements are not in compliance with current regulatory requirements and raise investor protection concerns:

   1. Omnibus account arrangements — under these arrangements, a mutual fund dealer maintains an omnibus account in its name at an investment dealer to hold Prohibited Securities for its clients; and

   2. Joint service arrangements — under these arrangements, a mutual fund dealer and an investment dealer jointly service a client who maintains an account at the investment dealer.

At the request of the OSC, the Mutual Fund Dealers Association of Canada (MFDA) and the Investment Dealers Association of Canada (IDA) issued a Joint Notice in June 2004 instructing their members not to enter into any new joint service or omnibus account arrangements, and not to accept new clients utilizing any existing arrangements. The OSC also considered requiring mutual fund dealers and investment dealers to unwind these arrangements. Since this could have a significant impact on clients, as well as industry participants, we were prepared to consider alternate solutions, if any, that would effectively address the regulatory and investor protection concerns that are raised by these arrangements. To achieve this result through the most appropriate course of action, the OSC engaged the industry in a consultation process in the summer of 2004. As part of the consultation process, the OSC invited members of the MFDA and the IDA to comment on the Issues Paper *Mutual Fund Dealers Business Arrangements* published in June 2004, to propose solutions to address the concerns, and to attend a roundtable meeting with a panel of Commissioners. A copy of the Issues Paper was also published for information purposes.

Industry Consultation

Over 20 comment letters were received from the industry, including MFDA members, IDA members, the Investment Funds Institute of Canada (IFIC), and the MFDA. Over 10 dealers, IFIC and the joint MFDA-IDA industry working group participated in the roundtable meeting. The written submissions and the oral submissions at the roundtable meeting were largely consistent. Copies of the comment letters and the Issues Paper are available on the OSC website at www.osc.gov.on.ca. The OSC would like to express its appreciation to the industry for their input in this matter.

Industry Trends

A number of comments were received regarding the industry trends, including:

(a) Some commenters noted that clients do not have a preference for one-stop financial shopping nor do they need to consolidate all their financial assets into one account; they, however, prefer to have one individual overseeing their overall financial needs;

(b) Other commenters noted that omnibus account arrangements were established to accommodate clients' needs to consolidate all their assets, including Prohibited Securities, at the mutual fund dealer;

(c) The MFDA noted that only a limited number of its members are party to omnibus account arrangements and joint service arrangements;

(d) Some commenters believe that joint service arrangements, in the form of a mutual fund dealer and investment dealer introducing/carrying arrangement, should be allowed if they are subject to certain controls or restrictions;

(e) A number of commenters indicated that omnibus account arrangements and joint service arrangements should be prohibited; and

(f) The mutual fund dealer registration category continues to be appropriate at this time, and addresses the needs of certain clients.

Proposed Solutions

The following solutions were proposed by the industry:

(a) Referral arrangements;

(b) MFDA/IDA introducing/carrying arrangements;

(c) Back office servicing arrangements;

(d) Trust company/financial intermediary model;

(e) Restricted sales representatives at full-service firms; and

(f) Enforcement of current requirements.

A number of dealers noted that they have chosen not to enter into omnibus account arrangements and joint service arrangements to ensure compliance with current regulatory requirements. These dealers found alternative solutions that are in compliance with current regulatory requirements to respond to their clients' needs. Two alternative solutions are as follows:

Referral Arrangements

Many commenters acknowledged that referral arrangements have been established by mutual fund dealers to address clients' needs to access different types of products and services. When clients of a mutual fund dealer want to purchase or otherwise trade in Prohibited Securities or other services that the mutual fund dealer cannot offer, the mutual fund dealer will refer the clients to other dealer(s) that have the appropriate expertise and proficiency. The requirement to maintain different accounts with different dealers also ensures that the responsibilities and liability of each dealer are separate and clear. It also ensures that clients will have the benefits of the applicable investor protection fund coverage should the need arise due to the failure of the dealer.

Existing Trust Company/Financial Intermediary Model

Under this model, responsibilities to service a client are clearly divided among a trust company, a mutual fund dealer and an investment dealer. The trust company acts as a trustee for the client's registered plan, and provides statements for the registered plan to the client. The mutual fund dealer and the investment dealer are each responsible for executing trades for and providing advice to the client in relation to those securities in which they are registered to trade. They are also responsible for issuing statements of account to the client on those transactions for which they are responsible. The trust company or the investment dealer is responsible for holding the securities in the registered plan.

Other Solutions

During the consultation process, many industry participants supported the mutual fund dealer and investment dealer introducing/carrying arrangement. However, this arrangement cannot be implemented until the MFDA becomes a sponsoring self-regulatory organization of the Canadian Investor Protection Fund, which will not be in the foreseeable future. Therefore, this is not a viable solution at this time.

Other solutions were also raised. The MFDA and IDA suggested back office servicing arrangements, which will allow mutual fund dealers to outsource their back office functions to affiliated investment dealers. The OSC understands that this solution only resolves the systems issues relating to joint service arrangements, and will only be available to affiliated dealers. Another alternative suggested during the consultation is to allow full-service investment dealers to hire restricted sales representatives. The OSC notes that this alternative might necessitate changes to existing registration provisions and will consider this as part of the Registration Project.

Next Steps

Based on the comments received and discussions with the industry, we have noted that a number of mutual fund dealers have chosen not to enter into omnibus account arrangements and joint service arrangements and are able to continue to service their clients using other business arrangements. For example, referral arrangements and the trust company/financial intermediary model can be utilized to address client needs without dealers being offside current regulatory requirements. The other proposed solutions cannot be implemented immediately and do not address all the investor protection concerns, e.g. pressure to act beyond the scope of registration, client confusion, unclear supervisory responsibilities and liability, and lack of protection fund coverage. In addition, only a limited number of mutual fund dealers utilize omnibus account and joint service arrangements.

As a result, the OSC has directed the MFDA and the IDA to enforce current regulatory requirements, i.e. mutual fund dealers and investment dealers must unwind existing omnibus account arrangements and joint service arrangements. Mutual fund dealers should not trade in, provide advice on or act in furtherance of trades in Prohibited Securities. Dealers should notify their clients of changes to the omnibus account and joint service arrangements, impact to their clients, and options available to minimize or eliminate any potential adverse consequences to their clients. In order to allow dealers time to implement these changes and to ensure that client interests are placed first, a transition period expiring October 31, 2005 will be provided. The OSC has also directed the MFDA and the IDA to monitor the progress of their members in unwinding these arrangements.

OSC Staff Notice 31-714 — OSC Staff Supplement to CSAN 31-328 Revocation of Omnibus/Blanket Orders Exempting Registrants from Certain Provisions of NI 31-103 Registration Requirements, Exemptions and Ongoing Registrant Obligations

Date: September 16, 2011

34 O.S.C.B. 9533

[Not reproduced]

3.2 — Registration Exemptions

National Instrument 32-101 — Small Securityholder Selling and Purchase Arrangements

[Repealed upon the coming into force of NI 45-106]

Final Rule: (1997) 20 O.S.C.B. 5435; Approval by the OSC: (1997) 20 O.S.C.B. 4349; Request for Comments: (1997) 20 O.S.C.B. 245; Replaced two rules which were originally blanket rulings, (1987) 10 O.S.C.B. 1455 and (1987) 10 O.S.C.B. 4938, which were deemed to be rules under s. 143.1(1) of the Act and remade into rules entitled *In the Matter of a Policy of the Toronto Stock Exchange on Small Securityholder Selling and Purchase Arrangements* (1997) 20 O.S.C.B. 1217 and *In the Matter of a Policy of The Montreal Exchange on Small Securityholder Selling and Purchase Arrangements* (1997) 20 O.S.C.B. 1217.

Repeal: (2005) 28 O.S.C.B. (Supp-4) 117; Approval by OSC: (2005) 28 O.S.C.B. (Supp-3) 83; Request for Comments: (2004) 27 O.S.C.B. (Supp-3) 1.

Multilateral Instrument 32-102 — Registration Exemptions for Non-Resident Investment Fund Managers

Date: September 28, 2012

35 O.S.C.B. 8547

[*Editor's note: MI 31-102 has been adopted in Ontario, Quebec, and Newfoundland and Labrador.*]

PART 1 — DEFINITIONS AND APPLICATION

1. Definitions — In this Instrument, "permitted client" has the same meaning as in section 1.1 of National Instrument 31-103 *Registration Requirements, Exemptions and Ongoing Registrant Obligations*, except that it excludes paragraph (m) and (n) and includes a registered charity under the *Income Tax Act* (Canada) that obtains advice on the securities to be traded from an eligibility adviser, as defined in section 1.1 of NI 45-106 *Prospectus and Registration Exemptions*, or an adviser registered under the securities legislation of the jurisdiction of the registered charity.

2. Application of this Instrument — This Instrument applies in Ontario, Québec and Newfoundland and Labrador.

PART 2 — EXEMPTIONS FROM INVESTMENT FUND MANAGER REGISTRATION

3. No security holders or active solicitation in the local jurisdiction — The investment fund manager registration requirement does not apply to a person or company acting as an investment fund manager of one or more investment funds if it does not have a place of business in the local jurisdiction and if one or more of the following apply:

(a) none of the investment funds has security holders resident in the local jurisdiction;

(b) the person or company and those investment funds have not, at any time after September 27, 2012, actively solicited residents in the local jurisdiction to purchase securities of the fund.

4. Permitted clients — (1) The investment fund manager registration requirement does not apply to a person or company acting as an investment fund manager of one or more investment funds if all securities of the investment funds distributed in the local jurisdiction were distributed under an exemption from the prospectus requirement to a permitted client.

(2) The exemption in subsection (1) is not available unless all of the following apply:

(a) the investment fund manager does not have its head office or its principal place of business in Canada;

(b) the investment fund manager is incorporated, formed or created under the laws of a foreign jurisdiction;

(c) none of the investment funds is a reporting issuer in any jurisdiction of Canada;

(d) the investment fund manager has submitted to the securities regulatory authority in the local jurisdiction a completed Form 32-102F1 *Submission to Jurisdiction and Appointment of Agent for Service for International Investment Fund Manager*;

(e) the investment fund manager has notified the permitted client in writing of all of the following:

(i) the investment fund manager is not registered in the local jurisdiction to act as an investment fund manager;

(ii) the foreign jurisdiction in which the head office or principal place of business of the investment fund manager is located;

(iii) all or substantially all of the assets of the investment fund manager may be situated outside of Canada;

(iv) there may be difficulty enforcing legal rights against the investment fund manager because of the above;

(v) the name and address of the agent for service of process of the investment fund manager in the local jurisdiction.

(3) A person or company that relied on the exemption in subsection (1) during the 12 month period preceding December 1 of a year must notify the securities regulatory authority in the local jurisdiction, by December 1 of that year, of the following:

(a) the fact that it relied upon the exemption in subsection (1);

(b) for all investment funds for which it acts as an investment fund manager, the total assets under management expressed in Canadian dollars, attributable to securities beneficially owned by residents of the local jurisdiction as at the most recently completed month.

(4) A person or company relying on the exemption in subsection (1) must file with the securities regulatory authority in the local jurisdiction, a completed Form 32-102F2 *Notice of Regulatory Action* within 10 days of the date on which that person or company began relying on that exemption.

(5) A person or company must notify the securities regulatory authority in the local jurisdiction, of any change to the information previously submitted in Form 32-102F2 *Notice of Regulatory Action* under subsection (4) within 10 days of the change.

PART 3 — NOTICE TO INVESTORS BY INTERNATIONAL INVESTMENT FUND MANAGERS

5. Contents of the notice — A registered investment fund manager whose head office or principal place of business is not located in Canada must provide or cause to be provided, to security holders with an address of record in the local jurisdiction on the records of each investment fund in respect of which the investment fund manager acts as an investment fund manager, a statement in writing disclosing the following:

(a) the investment fund manager is not resident in the local jurisdiction;

(b) the foreign jurisdiction in which the head office or the principal place of business of the investment fund manager is located;

(c) all or substantially all of the assets of the investment fund manager may be situated outside of Canada;

(d) there may be difficulty enforcing legal rights against the investment fund manager because of the above;

(e) the name and address of the agent for service of process of the investment fund manager in the local jurisdiction.

PART 4 — GRANTING AN EXEMPTION

6. Who can grant an exemption — (1) The regulator, except in Québec, or the securities regulatory authority may grant an exemption from this Instrument, in whole or in part, subject to such conditions or restrictions as may be imposed in the exemption.

(2) Despite subsection (1), in Ontario, only the regulator may grant such an exemption.

(3) Except in Ontario, an exemption referred to in subsection (1) is granted under the statute referred to in Appendix B of National Instrument 14-101 *Definitions* opposite the name of the jurisdiction.

PART 5 — WHEN THIS INSTRUMENT COMES INTO FORCE

7. Effective date — (1) Except as set out in subsection (2), this Instrument comes into force on September 28, 2012.

(2) Section 5 comes into force on March 31, 2013.

Final Rule: (2012) 35 O.S.C.B. 8547; Approval by OSC: (2012) 35 O.S.C.B. 6303; Request for Comments: (2012) 35 O.S.C.B. 1445.

Form 32-102F1 — Submission to Jurisdiction And Appointment Of Agent For Service For International Investment Fund Manager

(section 4 [permitted clients])

1. Name of person or company ("International Firm"):

2. If the International Firm was previously assigned an NRD number as a registered investment fund manager or an unregistered exempt international firm, provide the NRD number of the firm.

3. Jurisdiction of incorporation of the International Firm:

4. Address of head office or principal place of business of the International Firm:

5. The name, e-mail address, phone number and fax number of the International Firm's chief compliance officer.

Name:

E-mail address:

Phone:

Fax:

6. Name of agent for service of process (the "Agent for Service"):

7. Address for service of process on the Agent for Service:

8. The International Firm designates and appoints the Agent for Service at the address stated above as its agent upon whom may be served a notice, pleading, subpoena, summons or other process in any action, investigation or administrative, criminal, quasi-criminal or other proceeding (a "Proceeding") arising out of or relating to or concerning the International Firm's activities in the local jurisdiction and irrevocably waives any right to raise as a defence in any such proceeding any alleged lack of jurisdiction to bring such Proceeding.

9. The International Firm irrevocably and unconditionally submits to the non-exclusive jurisdiction of the judicial, quasi-judicial and administrative tribunals of the local jurisdiction in any Proceeding arising out of or related to or concerning the International Firm's activities in the local jurisdiction.

10. Until 6 years after the International Firm ceases to rely on section 4 [*permitted clients*], the International Firm must submit to the securities regulatory authority

    a. a new *Submission to Jurisdiction and Appointment of Agent for Service for International Investment Fund Manager* in this form no later than the 30th day before the date this Submission to Jurisdiction and Appointment of Agent for Service*for International Investment Fund Manager* is terminated; and

    b. an amended *Submission to Jurisdiction and Appointment of Agent for Service for International Investment Fund Manager* no later than the 30th day before any change in the name or above address of the Agent for Service.

11. This Submission to *Jurisdiction and Appointment of Agent for Service for International Investment Fund Manager* is governed by and construed in accordance with the laws of the local jurisdiction.

Dated: ....

.... (Signature of the International Firm or authorized signatory)

.... (Name and Title of authorized signatory)

Acceptance

The undersigned accepts the appointment as Agent for Service of (Insert name of International Firm) under the terms and conditions of the foregoing *Submission to Jurisdiction and Appointment of Agent for Service for International Investment Fund Manager*.

Dated: ....

.... (Signature of Agent for Service or authorized signatory)

.... (Name and Title of authorized signatory)

Form 32-102F2 — Notice of Regulatory Action

(section 4 [permitted clients])

Definitions

Parent — a person or company that directly or indirectly has significant control of another person or company.

Significant control — a person or company has significant control of another person or company if the person or company:

- directly or indirectly holds voting securities representing more than 20 per cent of the outstanding voting rights attached to all outstanding voting securities of the other person or company, or

- directly or indirectly is able to elect or appoint a majority of the directors (or individuals performing similar functions or occupying similar positions) of the other person or company.

Specified affiliate — a person or company that is a parent of a firm, a specified subsidiary of a firm, or a specified subsidiary of a firm's parent.

Specified subsidiary — a person or company of which another person or company has significant control.

All of the questions below apply to any jurisdiction and any foreign jurisdiction. The information must be provided in respect of the last 7 years.

1. Has the firm, or any predecessors or specified affiliates of the firm entered into a settlement agreement with any financial services regulator, securities or derivatives exchange, self-regulatory organization (SRO) or similar agreement with any financial services regulator, securities or derivatives exchange, SRO or similar organization?

    Yes .... No ....

If yes, provide the following information for each settlement agreement:

Name of entity
Regulator/organization
Date of settlement (yyyy/mm/dd)
Details of settlement
Jurisdiction

2. Has any financial services regulator, securities or derivatives exchange, SRO or similar organization:

	Yes	No
(a) Determined that the firm, or any predecessors or specified affiliates of the firm violated any securities regulations or any rules of a securities or derivatives exchange, SRO or similar organization?		
(b) Determined that the firm, or any predecessors or specified affiliates of the firm made a false statement or omission?		
(c) Issued a warning or requested an undertaking by the firm, or any predecessors or specified affiliates of the firm?		
(d) Suspended or terminated any registration, licensing or membership of the firm, or any predecessors or specified affiliates of the firm?		
(e) Imposed terms or conditions on any registration or membership of the firm, or predecessors or specified affiliates of the firm?		
(f) Conducted a proceeding or investigation involving the firm, or any predecessors or specified affiliates of the firm?		
(g) Issued an order (other than en exemption order) or a sanction to the firm, or any predecessors or specified affiliates of the firm for securities or derivatives-related activity (e.g. cease trade order)?		

If yes, provide the following information for each action:

Name of Entity	
Type of Action	
Regulator/organization	
Date of action (yyyy/mm/dd)	Reason for action
Jurisdiction	

3. Is the firm aware of any ongoing investigation of which the firm or any of its specified affiliates is the subject?

        Yes .... No ....

If yes, provide the following information for each investigation:

Name of entity	
Reason or purpose of investigation	
Regulator/organization	
Date investigation commenced (yyyy/mm/dd)	
Jurisdiction	
Name of firm	
Name of firm's authorized signing officer or partner	
Title of firm's authorized signing officer or partner	
Signature	
Date (yyyy/mm/dd)	

Witness

The witness must be a lawyer, notary public or commissioner of oaths.

Name of witness	
Title of witness	
Signature	
Date (yyyy/mm/dd)	

Companion Policy 32-102CP — Registration Exemptions for Non-Resident Investment Fund Managers

Part 1 — Fundamental concepts

Introduction

Part Purpose of this Companion Policy

This Companion Policy sets out how the Ontario Securities Commission, the Autorité des marchés financiers and the Financial Services Regulation Division, Service NL, Government of Newfoundland and Labrador (collectively, we) interpret or apply the provisions of Multilateral Instrument 32-102 *Registration Exemptions for Non-Resident Investment Managers* (MI 32-102) and related securities legislation.

MI 32-102 applies in Ontario, Québec and Newfoundland and Labrador.

Appendix A contains a chart illustrating the requirement to register as an investment fund manager for those investment fund managers who are non-residents, as well as the availability of the exemptions provided in MI 32-102.

Part Numbering system

Except for Part 1, the numbering of Parts and sections in this Companion Policy correspond to the numbering in MI 32-102. Any general guidance for a Part appears immediately after the name of the Part. Any specific guidance on sections in MI 32-102 follows any general guidance. If there is no guidance for a Part or section, the numbering in this Companion Policy will skip to the next provision that does have guidance.

All references in this Companion Policy to sections and Parts are to MI 32-102, unless otherwise noted.

Part Definitions

Unless defined in MI 32-102, terms used in MI 32-102 and in this Companion Policy have the meaning given to them in the securities legislation of each jurisdiction or in National Instrument 14-101 *Definitions*.

In this Companion Policy "regulator" means the regulator or securities regulatory authority in a jurisdiction.

This guidance applies to investment fund managers

- that do not have their head office or their principal place of business in a jurisdiction of Canada (international investment fund managers); and

- that are domestic investment fund managers which do not have a place of business in the local jurisdiction (domestic non-resident investment fund managers).

We refer to international and domestic non-resident investment fund managers, collectively, as non-resident investment fund managers.

Part Requirement to register as an investment fund manager

An investment fund manager is required to register if it directs or manages the business, operations or affairs of one or more investment funds. Some of the functions and activities that an investment fund manager directs, manages or performs include:

- establishing a distribution channel for the fund
- marketing the fund
- establishing and overseeing the fund's compliance and risk management programs
- overseeing the day-to-day administration of the fund
- retaining and liaising with the portfolio manager, the custodian, the dealers and other service providers of the fund
- overseeing advisers' compliance with investment objectives and overall performance of the fund
- preparing the fund's prospectus or other offering documents
- preparing and delivering security holder reports
- identifying, addressing and disclosing conflicts of interest
- calculating the net asset value (NAV) of the fund and the NAV per share or unit
- calculating, confirming and arranging payment of subscriptions and redemptions, and arranging for the payment of dividends or other distributions, if required

Part Where to register as an investment fund manager

(a) — Investment fund managers with a place of business in the local jurisdiction

An investment fund manager is required to register in the local jurisdiction if it directs or manages the business, operations or affairs of one or more investment funds from a place of business in that jurisdiction.

(b) — Non-resident investment fund managers

Triggering registration in the case of non-resident investment fund managers in a local jurisdiction depends on whether

   (i) the person or company acts as an investment fund manager; and

   (ii) that manager is managing one or more investment funds that distribute or have distributed securities to residents of the local jurisdiction

To the extent the person or company is acting as an investment fund manager, the next question is whether the non-resident investment fund manager is managing one or more investment funds that have distributed securities to residents in the local jurisdiction.

If one or more of the investment funds managed by the investment fund manager have security holders in the local jurisdiction, this gives rise to investment fund management activities in such jurisdiction, including activities reflecting the relationship between the fund, the investment fund manager (who is responsible for directing those activities), and the security holders. Such activities include the delivery of financial statements and other periodic reporting, calculating net asset values and fulfilling redemption and dividend payment obligations.

Whether or not the distribution process is continuous, by way of a prospectus or under a prospectus exemption, is not relevant to this connecting factor, since the investment fund is an issuer over which the regulator in the local jurisdiction has authority. The actual distribution of the investment fund's securities is subject to dealer registration and prospectus requirements.

It is the fact that there has been a distribution to holders in the local jurisdiction, and not how the distribution was carried out, that connects the non-resident investment fund manager to the jurisdiction in the regulatory perspective of investor protection. Investors in investment funds managed by non-resident investment fund managers face the same risks as those who invest in local investment funds.

Part 2 — Exemptions from investment fund manager registration

3. — No security holders or active solicitation

Part General

Generally, a non-resident investment fund manager will not be required to register if:

- the investment fund no longer has security holders in the local jurisdiction, notwithstanding a distribution of securities in the past;
- the investment fund has security holders in the local jurisdiction but has not actively solicited residents in the local jurisdiction after the coming into the force of MI 32-102;
- the security holders are permitted clients.

Part Conditions of the exemption

An investment fund manager that does not have a place of business in the local jurisdiction is exempt from the investment fund manager registration requirement if there are no security holders of any of the investment funds managed by it who are resident in that jurisdiction or there is no active solicitation by the investment fund manager or any of the investment funds in that jurisdiction.

Part Active solicitation

One of the conditions of this exemption is that the investment fund manager and the investment funds it manages have not, after September 27, 2012, actively solicited the purchase of the funds' securities by residents in the local jurisdiction. Active solicitation refers to intentional actions taken by the investment fund or the investment fund manager to encourage a purchase of the fund's securities, such as pro-active, targeted actions or communications that are initiated by an investment fund manager for the purpose of soliciting an investment.

Actions that are undertaken by an investment fund manager at the request of, or in response to, an existing or prospective investor who initiates contact with the investment fund manager would not constitute active solicitation.

Examples of active solicitation include:

- direct communication with residents of the local jurisdiction to encourage their purchases of the investment fund's securities

- advertising in Canadian or international publications or media (including the Internet), if the advertising is intended to encourage the purchase of the investment fund's securities by residents of the local jurisdiction (either directly from the fund or in the secondary/resale market)

- purchase recommendations being made by a third party to residents of the local jurisdiction, if that party is entitled to be compensated by the investment fund or the investment fund manager, for the recommendation itself, or for a subsequent purchase of fund securities by residents of the local jurisdiction in response to the recommendation.

Active solicitation would not include:

- advertising in Canadian or international publications or media (including the Internet) only to promote the image or general perception of an investment fund

- responding to unsolicited enquiries from prospective investors in the local jurisdiction

- the solicitation of a prospective investor that is only temporarily in the local jurisdiction, such as in the case where a resident from another jurisdiction is vacationing in the local jurisdiction.

4. — Permitted clients

An investment fund manager that does not have its head office or its principal place of business in Canada is exempt from the investment fund manager registration requirement if the outstanding securities of its investment funds have been distributed in the local jurisdiction to permitted clients only and certain other conditions set out in subsection 4(2) are satisfied.

If an investment fund manager is relying on the exemption, it must provide an initial notice by filing a Form 32-102F1 *Submission to Jurisdiction and Appointment of Agent for Service for International Investment Fund Manager* (Form 32-102F1) with the regulator in the local jurisdiction. If there is any change to the information in the investment fund manager's Form 32-102F1, the investment fund manager must update it by filing a replacement Form 32-102F1 with the regulator in the local jurisdiction. So long as the investment fund manager continues to rely on the exemption, it must file an annual notice with the regulator in the local jurisdiction. Subsection 4(3) does not prescribe a form of annual notice. An e-mail or letter will therefore be acceptable.

Appendix A — chart illustrating the non-resident investment fund manager registration requirement and the availability of exemptions

The following chart illustrates the requirement to register as an investment fund manager for those investment fund managers who are non-residents, as well as the availability of the exemptions provided in MI 32-102.

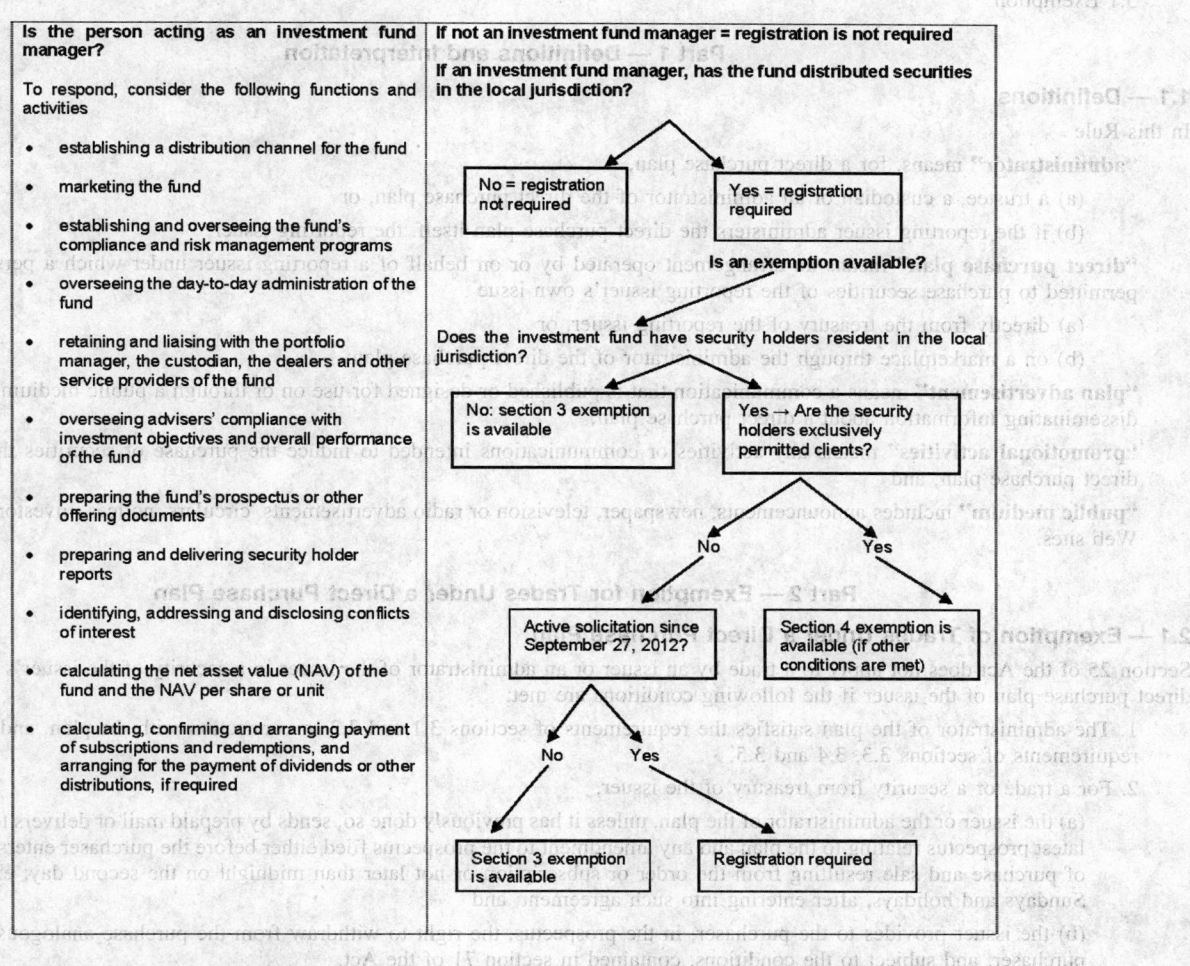

Is the person acting as an investment fund manager?

To respond, consider the following functions and activities

- establishing a distribution channel for the fund
- marketing the fund
- establishing and overseeing the fund's compliance and risk management programs
- overseeing the day-to-day administration of the fund
- retaining and liaising with the portfolio manager, the custodian, the dealers and other service providers of the fund
- overseeing advisers' compliance with investment objectives and overall performance of the fund
- preparing the fund's prospectus or other offering documents
- preparing and delivering security holder reports
- identifying, addressing and disclosing conflicts of interest
- calculating the net asset value (NAV) of the fund and the NAV per share or unit
- calculating, confirming and arranging payment of subscriptions and redemptions, and arranging for the payment of dividends or other distributions, if required

If not an investment fund manager = registration is not required

If an investment fund manager, has the fund distributed securities in the local jurisdiction?

No = registration not required

Yes = registration required

Is an exemption available?

Does the investment fund have security holders resident in the local jurisdiction?

No: section 3 exemption is available

Yes → Are the security holders exclusively permitted clients?

No

Yes

Active solicitation since September 27, 2012?

Section 4 exemption is available (if other conditions are met)

No

Yes

Section 3 exemption is available

Registration required

Adoption of Policy: (2012) 35 O.S.C.B. 8388 and 6303; Request for Comments: (2012) 35 O.S.C.B. 1445.

OSC Rule 32-501 — Direct Purchase Plans

Date: October 5, 2001

24 O.S.C.B. 5919

Table of Contents

Part 3:
REGISTRATION

PART 5 EXEMPTION

5.1 Exemption

Part 1 — Definitions and Interpretation

1.1 — Definitions

In this Rule

"**administrator**" means, for a direct purchase plan,

(a) a trustee, a custodian or an administrator of the direct purchase plan, or

(b) if the reporting issuer administers the direct purchase plan itself, the reporting issuer;

"**direct purchase plan**" means an arrangement operated by or on behalf of a reporting issuer under which a person or company is permitted to purchase securities of the reporting issuer's own issue

(a) directly from the treasury of the reporting issuer, or

(b) on a marketplace through the administrator of the direct purchase plan;

"**plan advertisement**" means a communication that is published or designed for use on or through a public medium for the purpose of disseminating information about a direct purchase plan;

"**promotional activities**" means any activities or communications intended to induce the purchase of securities through a particular direct purchase plan; and

"**public medium**" includes announcements, newspaper, television or radio advertisements, circulars, notices, investor fairs, and Internet Web sites.

Part 2 — Exemption for Trades Under a Direct Purchase Plan

2.1 — Exemption of Trades Under a Direct Purchase Plan

Section 25 of the Act does not apply to a trade by an issuer or an administrator of the issuer in a security of the issuer's own issue under a direct purchase plan of the issuer if the following conditions are met:

1. The administrator of the plan satisfies the requirements of sections 3.1 and 3.2 in connection with the plan, and, if applicable, the requirements of sections 3.3, 3.4 and 3.5.

2. For a trade of a security from treasury of the issuer,

(a) the issuer or the administrator of the plan, unless it has previously done so, sends by prepaid mail or delivers to the purchaser the latest prospectus relating to the plan and any amendment to the prospectus filed either before the purchaser enters into an agreement of purchase and sale resulting from the order or subscription or not later than midnight on the second day, excluding Saturday, Sundays and holidays, after entering into such agreement; and

(b) the issuer provides to the purchaser, in the prospectus, the right to withdraw from the purchase analogous to the rights of a purchaser, and subject to the conditions, contained in section 71 of the Act.

3. An investor disclosure statement containing the information described in section 4.2 has been provided to the purchaser of the security in accordance with subsection 4.2(2).

Part 3 — Operational Safeguards

3.1 — Segregation of Funds

All funds received by the administrator for investment through the direct purchase plan shall be deposited promptly into a segregated bank account with a Canadian financial institution, and used only to purchase securities under the direct purchase plan or to pay fees associated with the direct purchase plan.

3.2 — Segregation of Securities

(1) All securities issued under a direct purchase plan held on behalf of purchasers by the administrator shall be

(a) maintained in a separate account directly in the names of the purchasers, or in the name of the administrator, and allocated to each purchaser on a register maintained by the administrator; and

(b) kept separate from any other securities held by the administrator.

(2) For securities deposited with a depository or clearing agency that operates a book-based system, the administrator shall ensure that the applicable participantes in the book-based system or the administrator contain a designation sufficient to show that the beneficial ownership of the securities is vested in the purchasers under the direct purchase plan.

3.3 — Bonding and Insurance

An administrator of a direct purchase plan shall maintain bonding or insurance, by means of a broker's blanket bond, in an amount of not less than $25,000.

3.4 — Record Keeping

An administrator of a direct purchase plan shall maintain books and records necessary to record properly all transactions involving the direct purchase plan, and in doing so shall keep the records referred to in subsection 113(3) of the Regulation.

3.5 — Statements of Account

The administrator of a direct purchase plan shall send to each investor in the direct purchase plan the statements of account referred to in subsections 123(1) to (4) of the Regulation.

3.6 — Exemption for Regulated Institutions

Sections 3.3, 3.4 and 3.5 do not apply to an administrator of a direct purchase plan that is an institution that is subject to requirements under its governing legislation that are substantially similar to those contained in sections 3.3, 3.4 and 3.5.

Part 4 — Advertising and Disclosure Requirements

4.1 — Advertising Requirements

(1) No person or company may engage in promotional activities concerning a direct purchase plan, except as permitted in subsections (2) or (3).

(2) A person or company may place or distribute plan advertisements relating to a direct purchase plan that describe only

   (a) the existence and availability of the direct purchase plan;

   (b) the name of the reporting issuer whose securities are distributed under the direct purchase plan, and a brief description of the business carried on by the reporting issuer;

   (c) the securities to be issued under the direct purchase plan;

   (d) a description of how the direct purchase plan operates; and

   (e) information about how a person or company may obtain a copy of the prospectus for the direct purchase plan.

(3) No person or company, other than a person or company that is registered under the Act, shall provide any investment advice or recommendations in connection with the purchase of securities under a direct purchase plan.

4.2 — Disclosure Statement

(1) An issuer or plan administrator shall provide to any person or company purchasing securities through a direct purchase plan the following disclosure:

Securities sold through the [name of issuer] direct purchase plan are sold under a rule of the Ontario Securities Commission that permits these sales without the involvement of a registered broker or dealer. A person or company making such a purchase therefore receives no investment advice concerning the purchase, does not have the benefit of the assistance of a broker or dealer and is solely responsible for assessing the appropriateness of the investment for himself, herself or itself. A person or company that wishes to receive investment advice in connection with the direct purchase plan should contact his, her or its broker or dealer.

(2) The disclosure required by subsection (1) shall be contained in a separate document given to the purchaser before he, she or it enters into a binding agreement of purchase and sale for securities under a direct purchase plan.

Part 5 — Exemption

5.1 — Exemption

The Director may grant an exemption to this Rule, in whole or in part, subject to such conditions or restrictions as may be imposed in the exemption.

Final Rule: 24 O.S.C.B. 5919 (October 12, 2001); Approval by OSC: 24 O.S.C.B. 4743 (August 3, 2001); Request for Comments: 23 O.S.C.B. 7867 (November 17, 2000).

OSC Rule 32-502 — Registration Exemption for Certain Trades by Financial Intermediaries

[Revoked by Rule 45-802 and replaced by s. 4.1 of Rule 45-501]

Final Rule: (1997) 20 O.S.C.B. 699 and (1996) 19 O.S.C.B. 6923; Approval by OSC: (1996) 19 O.S.C.B. 6462.

Amendment to Rule: (1998) 21 O.S.C.B. 2315; Approval by OSC: (1998) 21 O.S.C.B. 955; Reqest for Comments: (1997) 20 O.S.C.B. 5753.

History: This continues a series of orders commencing with a ruling dated July 7, 1987: (1987) 10 O.S.C.B. 412 which provided the exemption until January 31, 1988, and followed by rulings dated January 22, 1988: (1988) 11 O.S.C.B. 274 extending the exemption to May 1, 1988, but excluding mutual funds from the exemption; dated April 28, 1988: (1988), 11 O.S.C.B. 1862 extending the exemption to December 31, 1988; dated December 22, 1988: (1988) 11 O.S.C.B. 5141 extending the exemption to June 30, 1989; dated June 29, 1989: (1989) 12 O.S.C.B. 2818 extending the exemption to December 31, 1989; dated December 20, 1989: (1989) 12 O.S.C.B. 4871 extending the exemptions to June 30, 1990; dated June 28, 1990: (1990) 13 O.S.C.B. 2685 extending the exemptions to December 31, 1990 and adding an exemption from the requirement to register as an underwriter; dated December 21, 1990: (1991) 14 O.S.C.B. 9 extending the exemptions to June 30, 1991; dated June 27, 1991: (1991) 14 O.S.C.B. 3335 extending the exemptions to June 30, 1992; dated June 24, 1992: (1992) 15 O.S.C.B. 3055 extending the exemptions to December 31, 1992; dated December 8, 1992: (1992) 15 O.S.C.B. 6063 extending the exemptions to June 30, 1993; dated June 8, 1993: (1993) 16 O.S.C.B. 2831 extending the exemptions to December 31, 1993; dated December 14, 1993: (1994) 17 O.S.C.B. 502 extending the exemptions to September 30, 1994; dated August 30, 1994: (1994) 17 O.S.C.B. 4308 extending the exemptions to December 31, 1994; dated November 8, 1994: (1994) 17 O.S.C.B. 5516 extending the exemptions to December 31, 1996.

OSC Rule 32-503 — Registration and Prospectus Exemption for Trades by Financial Intermediaries in Mutual Fund Securities to Corporate Sponsored Plans

[Revoked by Rule 45-802 and replaced by s. 3.2 of Rule 45-501]

Final Rule: (1997) 20 O.S.C.B. 700 and (1996) 19 O.S.C.B. 6923; Approval by OSC: (1996) 19 O.S.C.B. 6462.

Amendment to Rule: (1998) 21 O.S.C.B. 2316; Approval by OSC: (1998) 21 O.S.C.B. 956; Request for Comments: (1997) 20 O.S.C.B. 5755.

History: This continues a series of orders commencing with a ruling dated September 17, 1987: (1987) 10 O.S.C.B. 5447 which provided registration and prospectus exemptions for certain private mutual funds and corporate sponsored pooled funds until December 31, 1987, and followed by rulings: dated December 31, 1987: (1988) 11 O.S.C.B. 11 which extended the exemptions to March 31, 1988; dated January 22, 1988: (1988) 11 O.S.C.B. 276 which amended the foregoing ruling by extending the prospectus exemption for certain corporate sponsored plans; dated March 30, 1988: (1988), 11 O.S.C.B. 1941 which amended the December 31, 1987 ruling by extending the prospectus exemption for private mutual funds to May 31, 1988; dated June 26, 1988: (1988) 11 O.S.C.B. 2773 which amended the December 31, 1987 ruling by extending the prospectus exemption for corporate sponsored plans (but not private mutual funds) to December 31, 1988; dated December 22, 1988: (1988) 11 O.S.C.B. 5141 extending the exemption to June 30, 1989; dated June 29, 1989: (1989) 12 O.S.C.B. 2818 extending the exemption to December 31, 1989; dated December 20, 1989: (1989) 12 O.S.C.B. 4871 extending the exemptions to June 30, 1990; dated June 28, 1990: (1990) 13 O.S.C.B. 2685 extending the exemptions to December 31, 1990 and adding an exemption from the requirement to register as an underwriter; dated December 21, 1990: (1991) 14 O.S.C.B. 9 extending the exemptions to June 30, 1991; dated June 27, 1991: (1991) 14 O.S.C.B. 3335 extending the exemptions to June 30, 1992; dated June 24, 1992: (1992) 15 O.S.C.B. 3055 extending the exemptions to December 31, 1992; dated December 8, 1992: (1992) 15 O.S.C.B. 6064 extending the exemptions to December 31, 1993; dated December 14, 1993: (1994) 17 O.S.C.B. 503 extending the exemptions to December 31, 1994; dated November 8, 1994: (1994) 17 O.S.C.B. 5517 extending the exemptions to December 31, 1996.

OSC Rule 32-504 — (Under the Commodity Futures Act) Advisory Registration Exemption

Date: September 14, 2005

28 O.S.C.B. (Supp-4) 143

[Not reproduced as this rule deals with the *Commodity Futures Act*]

Final Rule: (2005) 28 O.S.C.B. (Supp-4) 143; Approval by OSC: (2005) 28 O.S.C.B. (Supp-3) 225; Request for Comments: (2004) 27 O.S.C.B. (Supp-3) 1.

OSC Staff Notice 32-505 — Conditional Exemption from Registration for United States Broker-Dealers and Advisers Servicing U.S. Clients from Ontario

Date: April 23, 2015

38 O.S.C.B. 3904

Introduction

The Ontario Securities Commission (the **Commission**) is publishing proposed OSC Rule 32-505 *Conditional Exemption from Registration for United States Broker-Dealers and Advisers Servicing U.S. Clients from Ontario* (the **Rule**). The Commission is relying on paragraph 143.2(5)(b) of the *Securities Act* (Ontario) (the Act) to make an expedited rule, and for this reason, the Rule is not being published for comment.

The Rule provides exemptions from the relevant dealer and adviser registration requirements under the Act, subject to certain conditions, for broker-dealers (**U.S. broker-dealers**) and advisers (**U.S. advisers**) that are trading to, with, or on behalf of, clients that are resident in the USA (**U.S. clients**), or acting as advisers to U.S. clients, but that trigger the requirement to register as a dealer or adviser in Ontario because they have offices or employees in Ontario. The exemptions in the Rule are not available to U.S. broker-dealers that trade to, with, or on behalf of, persons or companies that are resident in Ontario (**Ontario residents**), or U.S. advisers that act as advisers to Ontario residents.

Contents of this notice

This notice gives an overview of the Rule and its Companion Policy (defined below) and contains the following annexes:

- Annex A — OSC Rule 32-505 *Conditional Exemption from Registration for United States Broker-Dealers and Advisers Servicing U.S. Clients from Ontario*
- Annex B — Companion Policy 32-505CP *Conditional Exemption from Registration for United States Broker-Dealers and Advisers Servicing U.S. Clients from Ontario* (the **Companion Policy**)

Adoption of the Amendments

Under section 143.3 of the Act, the Rule and other required materials were delivered to the Minister of Finance on April 23, 2015. The Rule grants an exemption that is not likely to have a substantial effect on the interests of persons or companies other than those who benefit under it. Accordingly, the Commission is relying on paragraph 143.2(5)(b) of the Act to make an expedited rule. An expedited rule does not require publication for comment before it is approved.

The Rule requires the approval of the Minister of Finance. Unless the Minister rejects the Rule or returns it to the Commission for further consideration, it will come into force no later than July 7, 2015. The Companion Policy will come into effect on the same date.

Background and Purpose

The Commission is aware that U.S. broker-dealers and U.S. advisers, subject to federal securities law in the USA, are not registered, or relying on an exemption, in Ontario, but have offices or employees in Ontario and are (i) trading to, with, or on behalf, of U.S. clients, or (ii) acting as an adviser to U.S. clients. The U.S. broker-dealer firms do not trade to, with, or on behalf of, Ontario residents, and the U.S. adviser firms do not act as advisers to Ontario residents. These firms may be subsidiaries of, affiliates to, or have arrangements with registered firms in Ontario.

Registration as an adviser or a dealer, or an exemption from such registration requirement, is required for a firm and its representatives who act as an adviser or a dealer, as applicable, in Ontario, even if the firm's clients are not resident in Ontario; therefore, U.S. broker-dealers and U.S. advisers may be acting off side Ontario securities law by not being registered or relying on an exemption from the requirement to register.

Over the last decade, the Commission has, subject to certain conditions, exempted U.S. broker-dealers and U.S. advisers, with offices in Ontario, from the requirement to register, on the basis that they:

- trade to, with, or on behalf of, only U.S. clients or act as an adviser only to U.S. clients
- are appropriately registered (or exempt from registration) in the USA
- are subject to the oversight of an acceptable securities regulator in the USA

On March 26, 2015, members of the Canadian Securities Administrators (the **CSA**), except Ontario, issued parallel orders of general application (the **Blanket Orders**) granting exemptions from the requirement to register as a dealer to U.S. broker-dealers and their representatives operating from the applicable local jurisdiction and an exemption from the requirement to register as an adviser to U.S. advisers and their representatives operating from the applicable local jurisdiction, if they comply with the conditions in the Blanket Orders.

Orders of general application are not authorized under Ontario securities law. In order to harmonize with the action taken by the CSA, the Commission is making an expedited rule that will grant an exemption from the dealer and adviser registration requirements, as applicable, under the Act, on substantially the same conditions as the Blanket Orders.

In CSA Staff Notice 32-301 *Omnibus/Blanket Orders Exempting Certain U.S. Broker-Dealers and U.S. Advisers from the Requirement to Register in Respect of Trades and Advice for U.S. Resident Clients* (the **CSA Notice**), also published on March 26, 2015, Commission staff stated that they would consider recommending that the Commission grant exemptive relief to a U.S. broker-dealer or a U.S. adviser on substantially the same terms as the Blanket Orders, if an application for relief was filed. Instead, the Commission is codifying the prior line of exemptive relief orders (referenced above) by making this Rule. An expedited rule is also the most efficient way to harmonize with the CSA while imposing minimal costs and regulatory burden on firms affected by this Rule, and it allows the Commission to have regulatory oversight over the firms that rely on the exemptions in the Rule as these firms will be subject to the provisions in the Act applicable to a "market participant", including those set out in Part VII (record-keeping and compliance reviews). In addition, the form submitted to the Commission under the Rule will identify the firms, and individuals acting on their behalf, who are operating out of Ontario, and whether these firms are affiliated with any Canadian registrants.

The CSA expects firms relying on certain exemptions from the dealer or adviser registration requirements to comply with any applicable Canadian federal laws relating to terrorist financing and United Nations sanctions. For more information see CSA Staff Notice 31-317 (Revised) *Reporting Obligations Related to Terrorist Financing*.

Summary of the Rule

If approved, the Rule will provide exemptions from the relevant dealer and adviser registration requirements under the Act, subject to certain conditions. There may be additional exemptions in securities legislation. If the U.S. adviser or U.S. broker-dealer is exempt from registration, the individuals acting on its behalf are also exempt from registration.

Registration as an adviser or a dealer, or an exemption from such registration, is required for a firm and its representatives who act as an adviser or a dealer, as applicable, in Ontario even if the firm's clients are not resident in Ontario. The exemptions in this Rule will only be effective as of the date that they are relied on. Reliance on the exemptions in this Rule will not cure any prior non-compliance with Ontario securities law.

To undertake the activities contemplated in the Rule, a firm and its representatives must be either appropriately registered under U.S. securities law or have available to them an exemption from the applicable registration requirement. We understand that the U.S. broker-dealers are members of the Financial Industry Regulatory Authority (**FINRA**) and the U.S. advisers are subject to registration with the United States Securities and Exchange Commission (**SEC**) or are operating under an exemption from registration with the SEC. The Commission has a supervisory memorandum of understanding (**MOU**) in place with FINRA and the SEC for mutual cooperation and information sharing, including oversight of the relevant U.S. broker-dealer or U.S. adviser.

If a U.S. adviser or U.S. broker-dealer with offices or employees in Ontario is not able to comply with the conditions of the relevant exemption from adviser or dealer registration in the Rule, it must register as an adviser or dealer in Ontario, rely on another applicable exemption, apply for exemptive relief, or cease operations in Ontario.

Part 3:
REGISTRATION

Authority for the proposed amendments

The rule making authority for the Rule is in paragraph 8 of subsection 143(1) of the Act. Paragraph 143.2(5)(b) of the Act, as discussed above, permits the Commission to make the Rule without publishing the Rule for comment.

Where to find more information

The Rule and the Companion Policy are available at: www.osc.gov.on.ca

Questions

Please refer your questions to the following Commission staff:

[Contact omitted]

OSC Rule 32-505 — Conditional Exemption from Registration for United States Broker-Dealers and Advisers Servicing U.S. Clients from Ontario

Date: **June 5, 2015**

38 O.S.C.B. 3907

PART 1 — DEFINITIONS

1. Definitions — In this Rule,

"*Ontario resident*" means, for a U.S. adviser or U.S. broker-dealer, a person or company that is resident in Ontario;

"*representative*" means, for a U.S. adviser or U.S. broker-dealer, an individual that acts on behalf of the U.S. adviser or U.S. broker-dealer;

"*U.S. adviser*" means a person or company that is

(a) registered as an adviser under U.S. federal securities law, or

(b) exempt from registration as an adviser under U.S. federal securities law;

"*U.S. broker-dealer*" means a person or company registered as a "broker-dealer" under U.S. federal securities law; and

"*U.S. client*" means, for a U.S. adviser or U.S. broker-dealer, a client that is resident in the United States of America, its territories and possessions, any State of the United States of America and the District of Columbia.

PART 2 — REGISTRATION EXEMPTIONS

2. Dealer registration exemption — (1) The dealer registration requirement does not apply to a U.S. broker-dealer in respect of a trade in securities made by the U.S. broker-dealer to, with, or on behalf of, a U.S. client, if at the time of the trade, all of the following apply:

(a) under U.S. federal securities law, the U.S. broker-dealer is permitted to trade to, with, or on behalf of, the U.S. client;

(b) any representative of the U.S. broker-dealer that trades to, with, or on behalf of, the U.S. client is registered under U.S. federal securities law;

(c) in connection with the trade, the U.S. broker-dealer and any representative of the U.S. broker-dealer do not trade securities to, with, or on behalf of, an Ontario resident, or act as an adviser to an Ontario resident, unless the U.S. broker-dealer and the representative

(i) are registered under the Act in the appropriate category of registration, or

(ii) rely on an exemption from the applicable dealer registration requirement or adviser registration requirement;

(d) the U.S. broker-dealer has submitted a completed Form 32-505F1 *Information Report for United States Broker-Dealers and Advisers Servicing U.S. Clients from Ontario* to the Commission.

(2) The exemption from registration in this Rule is not an applicable exemption for purposes of subparagraph (1)(c)(ii).

(3) A U.S. broker-dealer must notify the Commission of any change in the information previously submitted under paragraph (1)(d) or this subsection within 10 days of the change.

3. Adviser registration exemption — (1) The adviser registration requirement does not apply to a U.S. adviser in respect of it acting as an adviser in respect of securities to a U.S. client, if at, or prior to, the time of providing the advice, both of the following apply:

(a) under U.S. federal securities law, the U.S. adviser is permitted to act as an adviser to the U.S. client;

(b) the U.S. adviser has submitted a completed Form 32-505F1 *Information Report for United States Broker-Dealers and Advisers Servicing U.S. Clients from Ontario* to the Commission.

(2) A U.S. adviser must notify the Commission of any change in the information previously submitted under paragraph (1)(b) or this subsection within 10 days of the change.

Approval of Rule: 38 O.S.C.B. 4890

Form 32-505F1 — Information Report for United States Broker-Dealers and Advisers Servicing U.S. Clients From Ontario

Complete the applicable sections.

Indicate if you intend to rely on any of the following:

[ ] the dealer registration exemption in Part 2 of the Rule.

[ ] the adviser registration exemption in Part 3 of the Rule.

Indicate the jurisdiction(s) in which:

    (i) the U.S. broker-dealer has representatives that trade to, with, or on behalf of, U.S. clients, or

    (ii) the U.S. adviser has representatives who are acting as advisers to U.S. clients.

....

[Name of U.S. broker-dealer or U.S. adviser]

....

[Address]

....

[Telephone number]

....

[NRD number, if applicable]

....

[Name of registered firm in a jurisdiction of Canada with which the U.S. broker-dealer or U.S. adviser is affiliated, has a business arrangement, or shares employees or offices]

....

[NRD number of above noted registered firm]

....

[Name of individual responsible for ensuring conditions to use this exemption are met]

....

[Telephone number for responsible individual]

....

[E-mail address for responsible individual]

....

[Names of representatives who are acting in Ontario as advisers to U.S. clients, or that, in Ontario, trade to, with, or on behalf of, U.S. clients. Use separate sheet if necessary]

....

[Date]

Companion Policy 32-505CP — Conditional Exemption from Registration for United States Broker-Dealers and Advisers Servicing U.S. Clients from Ontario

This Companion Policy sets out how we interpret or apply OSC Rule 32-505 *Conditional Exemption from Registration for United States Broker-Dealers and Advisers Servicing U.S. Clients from Ontario* (the **Rule**).

Unless defined in the Rule, terms used in the Rule and in this Companion Policy have the meaning given to them in OSC Rule 14-501 *Definitions* which includes certain terms that are defined in the *Securities Act* (Ontario) (the **Act**), the Regulation and National Instrument 14-101 *Definitions*.

Registration as an adviser or a dealer, or an exemption from such registration, is required for a firm and its representatives who act as an adviser or a dealer, as applicable, in Ontario even if the firm's clients are not resident in Ontario. The Rule provides exemptions from the relevant dealer and adviser registration requirements under the Act, subject to certain conditions. There may be additional exemptions in securities legislation. If the U.S. adviser or U.S. broker-dealer is exempt from registration, the individuals acting on its behalf are also exempt from registration.

The exemptions under the Rule are not available where trading or advising involves Ontario residents, whether directly or indirectly. In considering the availability of the exemptions under this Rule, we will look to the substance of trades or advice in reliance on this Rule. For example, a U.S. broker-dealer relying on the exemption in this Rule from the dealer registration requirement must not trade, directly or *indirectly* to, with, or on behalf of, an Ontario resident unless the U.S. broker-dealer is appropriately registered in Ontario to trade with the Ontario resident or has an available exemption, such as the exemption from the dealer registration requirement for trades with a permitted client in section 8.18 of National Instrument 31-103 *Registration Requirements, Exemptions and Ongoing Registrant Obligations*.

Where a trade is in respect of a security that is listed, quoted or traded on a Canadian marketplace, access requirements of Canadian marketplaces trading these exchange-traded securities require that the execution of the trade in this security on the Canadian marketplace must be made by the U.S. broker-dealer through an investment dealer that is registered in a jurisdiction of Canada and a member of the Investment Industry Regulatory Organization of Canada.

By relying on the exemption from the dealer or adviser registration requirement in the Rule, the U.S. broker-dealer or U.S. adviser, as applicable, will become a "market participant" as defined under subsection 1(1) of the Act. Market participants are subject to the provisions in the Act applicable to a "market participant", including those set out in Part VII (Record-Keeping and Compliance Reviews). Among other requirements, as a "market participant", the U.S. broker-dealer or U.S. adviser, as applicable, is required to comply with the record keeping and provision of information requirements in section 19 of the Act, which includes a requirement that the firm keep such books, records and other documents as are necessary for the proper recording of its business transactions and financial affairs and to deliver such records to the Commission if required. In addition, as a "market participant" the U.S. broker-dealer or U.S. adviser, as applicable, may be subject to a compliance review under section 20 of the Act.

Part 3:
REGISTRATION

OSC Staff Notice 32-701 and 33-712 — Processing of Equity and Fixed Income Trades by Financial Institutions and Mutual Fund Dealers

Date: November 12, 1999

22 O.S.C.B. 7091

Staff has become aware that certain financial institutions have been facilitating equity and fixed income trades in a manner that may be contrary to the exemptions for financial institutions under the *Securities Act* (Ontario) (the "Act") and the Regulation made under the Act (the "Regulation") and may result in the financial institution carrrying on registerable activity. Through the processing of equity and fixed income trades, the financial institution may promote activity in related mutual fund dealers that is contrary to terms of the dealer's registration and may lead to client confusion. Equity and fixed income trades for clients of these mutual fund dealers are being processed using the exemptions under s. 35(1)11 of the Act and s. 209(1)(i) of the Regulation which permit a financial institution to accept and process unsolicited equity trades without registration provided the trades are executed through a registered dealer. Some financial institutions in these cases have pre-printed equity and fixed income trade tickets which are distributed to mutual fund dealers for use by their clients. The tickets are pre-printed to indicate that the trade is unsolicited. In some cases, the representative of the mutual fund dealer signs the trade ticket using a power of attorney granted by the client. Some dealers have advertised the ability to process trades through the financial institution to both registered representatives and clients

Many, if not all, of these "unsolicited" equity and fixed income trades take place in the self-directed RRSP accounts offered by the mutual fund dealer. Further, mutual fund dealers have also acted as administrators for these self-directed RRSP accounts on behalf of the financial institution. As administrator under one of these bare trustee arrangements, the mutual fund dealer is responsible for keeping all records and acting as custodian of all assets, other than cash, held in the RRSP accounts. Should these accounts hold equity and fixed income securities, staff is of the view that the mutual fund dealer is carrying on activities not in compliance with the limitations of its registration.

Staff concerned that financial institution are using these trade exemptions to allow the mutual fund dealer to carry on an extensive business in processing client trades that a mutual fund dealer is not entitled to make under its registration. Staff is further concerned that these trades are not truly unsolicited since there is a high volume of such trades, the practice has been advertised and pre-printed, mass produced trade tickets are being provided to clients. This would suggest the financial institution is also carrying on improper trading activities.

In the course of processing these trades, mutual fund salespersons may be acting in furtherance of trades in these equities or fixed income products, which would be outside of their proficiency and registration. Mutual fund dealers engaged in this practice are holding accounts with equity and fixed income securities, keeping records of those accounts and providing confirmations and statements of the accounts. These activities may mean that the mutual fund dealer may be carrying on activities it is not entitled to do under its registration.

In staff's view, the use of the exemptions in s.35(1)11 and s.209(1)(i) should be limited to exceptional and one-time trades and should not be used on a systematic basis by either a client or a financial institution. the preparation and distribution of trade tickets/order forms to mutual fund dealers to facilitate equity and fixed income trade suggests that the resulting trade is solicited.

In staff's view, compliance with securities legislation necessitates that financial institutions and mutual fund dealers who have employed a structure described above advise clients that they are not permitted by securities law to handle trades in equity and fixed income securities and take immediate action to remedy any non-compliance with the Act and Regulations.

Staff considers the following as acceptable alternatives to effect compliance with the Act and Regulation for those accounts containing equity and fixed income securities currently being held on the books and records of the mutual fund dealer: the dealer could give clients the option of (1) transferring their accounts to an appropriately registered dealer; (2) splitting out the equity and fixed income portion of the account and transferring that portion to an appropriately registered dealer; or (3) opening a delivery-against-payment account at a securities or investment dealer for each client to facilitate equity and fixed income transactions and transferring all positions in the account to the trust company who will act as custodian of all assets in the account and will provide statements and confirmations to the client. Under Option 3, clients would have to direct all equity and fixed income trades directly to the securities or investment dealer.

Staff intends to devote field examination resources to further address these issues.

3.3 — Ongoing Requirements Affecting Registrants

See also OPS 1.9, 4.3.

National Instrument 33-102 — Regulation of Certain Registrant Activities

Date: July 20, 2001

24 O.S.C.B. 4409

[Revoked upon NI 31-103 coming into force.]
Final Rule: 24 O.S.C.B. 4409 (July 20, 2001); Approval by OSC: 24 O.S.C.B. 3030 (May 11, 2001); Request for Comments: 23 O.S.C.B. 4983 (July 21, 2000) and 20 O.S.C.B. 6274 (November 28, 1997). Replaced the Principles of Regulation.

Companion Policy 33-102CP — Regulation of Certain Registrant Activities

Date: July 20, 2001

24 O.S.C.B. 4411

[Rescinded upon NI 31-103 coming into force.]

Adoption by OSC: 24 O.S.C.B. 4409 (July 20, 2001) and 24 O.S.C.B. 3030 (May 11, 2001); Request for Comments: 23 O.S.C.B. 4983 (July 21, 2000) and 20 O.S.C.B. 6274 (November 28, 1997).

National Instrument 33-105 — Underwriting Conflicts

Date: December 21, 2001, as amended effective September 14, 2005, September 28, 2009 and September 8, 2015

24 O.S.C.B. 7684, 28 O.S.C.B. (Supp-4) 118 and 32 O.S.C.B. (Supp. 4) 376, (Supp. 5) 158 and 38 O.S.C.B. 5777

Table of Contents

PART 1 — DEFINITIONS, INTERPRETATION AND APPLICATION

1.1 Definitions — In this Instrument

"associated party" means, if used to indicate a relationship with a person or company

  (a) a trust or estate in which

    (i) that person or company has a substantial beneficial interest, unless that trust or estate is managed under discretionary authority by a person or company that is not a member of any professional group of which the first mentioned person or company is a member, or

    (ii) that person or company serves as trustee or in a similar capacity,

  (b) an issuer in respect of which that person or company beneficially owns or controls, directly or indirectly, voting securities carrying more than 10 percent of the voting rights attached to all outstanding voting securities of the issuer, or

  (c) a relative, including the spouse, of that person, or a relative of that person's spouse, if

    (i) the relative has the same home as that person, and

    (ii) the person has discretionary authority over the securities held by the relative;

"connected issuer" means, for a specified firm registrant,

  (a) an issuer distributing securities, if the issuer or a related issuer of the issuer has a relationship with any of the following persons or companies that may lead a reasonable prospective purchaser of the securities to question if the specified firm registrant and the issuer are independent of each other for the distribution:

    (i) the specified firm registrant,

    (ii) a related issuer of the specified firm registrant,

    (iii) a director, officer or partner of the specified firm registrant,

    (iv) a director, officer or partner of a related issuer of the specified firm registrant, or

(b) a selling securityholder distributing securities, if the selling securityholder or a related issuer of the selling securityholder has a relationship with any of the following persons or companies that may lead a reasonable prospective purchaser of the securities to question if the specified firm registrant and the selling securityholder are independent of each other for the distribution:

    (i) the specified firm registrant,

    (ii) a related issuer of the specified firm registrant,

    (iii) a director, officer or partner of the specified firm registrant,

    (iv) a director, officer or partner of a related issuer of the specified firm registrant;

"direct underwriter" means, for a distribution,

(a) an underwriter that is in a contractual relationship with the issuer or selling securityholder to distribute the securities that are being offered in the distribution, or

(b) a dealer manager, if the distribution is a rights offering;

"foreign issuer" has the meaning ascribed to that term in National Instrument 71-101 The Multijurisdictional Disclosure System;

"independent underwriter" means, for a distribution, a direct underwriter that is not the issuer or the selling securityholder in the distribution and in respect of which neither the issuer nor the selling securityholder is a connected issuer or a related issuer;

"influential securityholder" means, in relation to an issuer,

(a) a person or company or professional group that

    (i) holds, has the power to direct the voting of, or has direct or indirect beneficial ownership of, voting securities entitling the person or company or professional group to cast more than 20 percent of the votes for the election or removal of directors of the issuer,

    (ii) holds, has the power to direct the voting of, or has direct or indirect beneficial ownership of, equity securities entitling the person or company or professional group to receive more than 20 percent of the dividends or distributions to the holders of the equity securities of the issuer, or more than 20 percent of the amount to be distributed to the holders of equity securities of the issuer on the liquidation or winding up of the issuer,

    (iii) controls or is a partner of the issuer if the issuer is a general partnership, or

    (iv) controls or is a general partner of the issuer if the issuer is a limited partnership,

(b) a person or company or professional group that

    (i) holds, has the power to direct the voting of, or has direct or indirect beneficial ownership of,

        (A) voting securities entitling the person or company or professional group to cast more than 10 percent of the votes for the election or removal of directors of the issuer, or

        (B) equity securities entitling the person or company or professional group to receive more than 10 percent of the dividends or distributions to the holders of the equity securities of the issuer, or more than 10 percent of the amount to be distributed to the holders of equity securities of the issuer on the liquidation or winding up of the issuer, and

    (ii) either

        (A) together with its related issuers

            (I) is entitled to nominate at least 20 percent of the directors of the issuer or of a related issuer of the issuer, or

            (II) has officers, directors or employees who are also directors of the issuer or a related issuer of the issuer, constituting at least 20 percent of the directors of the issuer or of the related issuer, or

        (B) is a person or company of which the issuer, together with its related issuers,

            (I) is entitled to nominate at least 20 percent of the directors of the person or company or at least 20 percent of the directors of a related issuer of the person or company, or

            (II) has officers, directors or employees who are also directors of the person or company or a related issuer of the person or company, constituting at least 20 percent of the directors of the person or company or of the related issuer of the person or company, or

(c) a person or company

    (i) of which the issuer holds, has the power to direct the voting of, or has direct or indirect beneficial ownership of,

        (A) voting securities entitling the issuer to cast more than 10 percent of the votes for the election or removal of directors of the person or company, or

        (B) equity securities entitling the issuer to receive more than 10 percent of the dividends or distributions to the holders of the equity securities of the person or company, or more than 10 percent of the amount to be distributed to the holders of equity securities of the person or company on the liquidation or winding up of the person or company, and

    (ii) either

        (A) that, together with its related issuers

            (I) is entitled to nominate at least 20 percent of the directors of the issuer or of a related issuer of the issuer, or

            (II) has officers, directors or employees who are also directors of the issuer or a related issuer of the issuer, constituting at least 20 percent of the directors of the issuer or of the related issuer, or

        (B) of which the issuer, together with its related issuers

            (I) is entitled to nominate at least 20 percent of the directors of the person or company or at least 20 percent of the directors of a related issuer of the person or company, or

(II) has officers, directors or employees who are also directors of the person or company or a related issuer of the person or company, constituting at least 20 percent of the directors of the person or company or of the related issuer of the person or company, or

(d) if a professional group is within paragraph (a) or (b), the specified firm registrant of the professional group;

"professional group" means a group comprised of a specified firm registrant and all of the following persons or companies:

(a) any employee of the specified firm registrant,

(b) any partner, officer or director of the specified firm registrant,

(c) any affiliate of the specified firm registrant,

(d) any associated party of any person or company described in paragraphs (a) through (c) or of the specified firm registrant;

"related issuer" means a party described in subsection 1.2(2);

"special warrant" means a security that, by its terms or the terms of an accompanying contractual obligation, entitles or requires the holder to acquire another security without payment of material additional consideration and obliges the issuer of the special warrant or the other security to undertake efforts to file a prospectus to qualify the distribution of the other security; and

"specified firm registrant" means a person or company registered, or required to be registered, under securities legislation as a registered dealer, registered adviser or registered investment fund manager.

1.2 Interpretation — (1) For the purposes of calculating a percentage of securities that are owned, held or under the direction of a person or company in the definition of "influential securityholder"

(a) the determination shall be made

(i) first, by including in the calculation only voting securities or equity securities that are outstanding, and

(ii) second, if the person or company is not an influential securityholder by reason of a calculation under subparagraph (i), by including all voting securities or equity securities that would be outstanding if all outstanding securities that are convertible or exchangeable into voting securities or equity securities, and all outstanding rights to acquire securities that are convertible into, exchangeable for, or carry the right to acquire, voting securities or equity securities, are considered to have been converted, exchanged or exercised, as the case may be, and

(b) securities held by a specified firm registrant in its capacity as an underwriter in the course of a distribution are considered not to be securities that the specified firm registrant holds, has the power to direct the voting of, or has direct or indirect beneficial ownership of.

(2) A person or company is a "related issuer" of another person or company if

(a) the person or company is an influential securityholder of the other person or company,

(b) the other person or company is an influential securityholder of the person or company, or

(c) each of them is a related issuer of the same third person or company.

(3) Calculations of time required to be made in this Instrument in relation to a "distribution" shall be made in relation to the date on which the underwriting or agency agreement for the distribution is signed.

1.3 Application of Instrument — This Instrument does not apply to a distribution of

(a) securities described in the provisions of securities legislation listed in Appendix A; or

(b) mutual fund securities.

PART 2 — RESTRICTIONS ON UNDERWRITING

2.1 Restrictions on Underwriting — (1) No specified firm registrant shall act as an underwriter in a distribution of securities in which it is the issuer or selling securityholder, or as a direct underwriter in a distribution of securities of or by a connected issuer or a related issuer of the specified firm registrant, unless the distribution is made under a prospectus or another document that, in either case, contains the information specified in Appendix C.

(2) For a distribution of special warrants or a distribution made under a prospectus no specified firm registrant shall act

(a) as an underwriter if the specified firm registrant is the issuer or selling securityholder in the distribution; or

(b) as a direct underwriter if a related issuer of the specified firm registrant is the issuer or selling securityholder in the distribution.

(3) Subsection (2) does not apply to a distribution

(a) in which

(i) at least one specified firm registrant acting as direct underwriter acts as principal, so long as an independent underwriter underwrites not less than the lesser of

(A) 20 percent of the dollar value of the distribution, and

(B) the largest portion of the distribution underwritten by a specified firm registrant that is not an independent underwriter, or

(ii) each specified firm registrant acting as direct underwriter acts as agent and is not obligated to act as principal, so long as an independent underwriter receives a portion of the total agents' fees equal to an amount not less than the lesser of

(A) 20 percent of the total agents' fees for the distribution, and

(B) the largest portion of the agents' fees paid or payable to a specified firm registrant that is not an independent underwriter; and

(b) the identity of the independent underwriter and disclosure of the role of the independent underwriter in the structuring and pricing of the distribution and in the due diligence activities performed by the underwriters for the distribution is contained in

(i) a document relating to the special warrants that is delivered to the purchaser of the special warrants before that purchaser enters into a binding agreement of purchase and sale for the special warrants, for a distribution of special warrants, or

(ii) the prospectus, for a distribution made under a prospectus.

2.2 Calculation Rules — The following rules shall be followed in calculating the size of a distribution and the amount of independent underwriter involvement required for purposes of subsection 2.1(3):

(a) For a distribution that is made entirely in Canada, the calculation shall be based on the aggregate dollar value of securities distributed in Canada or the aggregate agents' fees relating to the distribution in Canada, and the aggregate dollar value of the distribution underwritten, or aggregate dollar value of agents' fees received, by the independent underwriter in Canada.

(b) For a distribution that is made partly in Canada of securities of an issuer that is not a foreign issuer, the calculation shall be based on the aggregate dollar value of securities distributed in Canada and outside of Canada or the aggregate agents' fees relating to the distribution in Canada and outside of Canada, and the aggregate dollar value of the distribution underwritten, or aggregate dollar value of agents' fees received, by the independent underwriter in Canada and outside of Canada.

(c) For a distribution that is made partly in Canada by a foreign issuer and that is not exempt from the requirements of subsection 2.1(2) by subsection 2.1(3) or by section 3.2, the calculation shall be based on the dollar value of securities distributed in Canada or the agents' fees relating to the distribution paid or payable in Canada, and the dollar value of the distribution underwritten, or aggregate dollar value of agents' fees received, by the independent underwriter in Canada.

PART 3 — NON-DISCRETIONARY EXEMPTIONS

3.1 Exemption from Disclosure Requirement — Subsection 2.1(1) does not apply to a distribution that

(a) is made under a document other than a prospectus if each of the purchasers of the securities

(i) is a related issuer of the specified firm registrant,

(ii) purchases as principal, and

(iii) does not purchase as underwriter; or

(b) is made under section 2.8 of National Instrument 45-102 *Resale of Securities*.

3.2 Exemption from Independent Underwriter Requirement — Subsection 2.1(2) does not apply to a distribution of securities of a foreign issuer if more than 85 percent of the aggregate dollar value of the distribution is made outside of Canada or if more than 85 percent of the agents' fees relating to the distribution are paid or payable outside of Canada.

PART 3A — NON-DISCRETIONARY EXEMPTIONS — ELIGIBLE FOREIGN SECURITIES

3A.1 Definitions — In this Part,

"eligible foreign security" means a security offered primarily in a foreign jurisdiction as part of a distribution of securities in either of the following circumstances:

(a) the security is issued by an issuer

(i) that is incorporated, formed or created under the laws of a foreign jurisdiction,

(ii) that is not a reporting issuer in a jurisdiction of Canada,

(iii) that has its head office outside of Canada, and

(iv) that has a majority of the executive officers and a majority of the directors ordinarily resident outside of Canada;

(b) the security is issued or guaranteed by the government of a foreign jurisdiction;

"executive officer" means, for an issuer, an individual who

(a) is a chair, vice-chair or president,

(b) is a chief executive officer or chief financial officer,

(c) is a vice-president in charge of a principal business unit, division or function including sales, finance or production, or

(d) performs a policy-making function in respect of the issuer;

"exempt offering document" means:

(a) in New Brunswick, Nova Scotia, Ontario and Saskatchewan, an offering memorandum as defined under the securities legislation of that jurisdiction, and

(b) in all other jurisdictions, a document including any amendments to the document, that

(i) describes the business and affairs of an issuer, and

(ii) has been prepared primarily for delivery to and review by a prospective purchaser to assist the prospective purchaser in making an investment decision in respect of securities being distributed pursuant to an exemption from the prospectus requirement;

"FINRA" means the self regulatory organization in the United States of America known as the Financial Industry Regulatory Authority;

"permitted client" has the same meaning as in section 1.1 of National Instrument 31-103 *Registration Requirements, Exemptions and Ongoing Registrant Obligations*.

3A.2 Application — This Part does not apply to a distribution if a prospectus has been filed with a Canadian securities regulatory authority for the distribution.

3A.3 Exemption based on U.S. disclosure — Subsection 2.1(1) does not apply to a distribution of a security described in paragraph (a) of the definition of eligible foreign security if all of the following apply:

(a) the distribution is made to a permitted client through a registered dealer or international dealer;

(b) the registered dealer or international dealer delivers a written notice to the permitted client before or during the distribution of the eligible foreign security that specifies the exemption relied on and a reference to this section;

(c) an exempt offering document prepared with respect to the distribution is delivered to the permitted client;

(d) a concurrent distribution of the security is made by the issuer to investors in the U.S.;

(e) the exempt offering document contains the same disclosure as that provided to investors in the U.S.;

(f) if applicable, the disclosure provided in the exempt offering document for a distribution referred to in paragraph (d) is made in compliance with FINRA rule 5121, as amended from time to time;

(g) the distribution referred to in paragraph (d) is made in compliance with applicable U.S. federal securities law.

3A.4 Exemption for foreign government securities — Subsection 2.1(1) does not apply to a distribution of a security described in paragraph (b) of the definition of eligible foreign security if:

(a) the distribution is made to a permitted client through a registered dealer or international dealer, and

(b) the registered dealer or international dealer delivers a written notice to the permitted client, before or during the distribution of the eligible foreign security that specifies the exemption relied on and a reference to this section.

3A.5 Manner of notice — For greater certainty, a notice required under paragraphs 3A.3(b) and 3A.4(b) may be incorporated into the exempt offering document delivered to the permitted client.

3A.6 Alternative compliance with notice requirement — A notice will be considered to have been delivered to a permitted client in compliance with paragraph 3A.3(b) or 3A.4(b), if

(a) the registered dealer or international dealer has previously delivered a notice to the permitted client in compliance with paragraph 3A.3(b) or 3A.4(b), and

(b) the notice stated that the registered dealer or international dealer intends to rely on the exemption in paragraph 3A.3(b) or 3A.4(b), as applicable, for any distribution in the future of an eligible foreign security to the permitted client.

PART 4 — VALUATION REQUIREMENT

4.1 Valuation Requirement — A purchaser of securities offered in a distribution for which information is required to be given under subsection 2.1(1) shall be given a document that contains a summary of a valuation of the issuer by a member of the Canadian Institute of Chartered Business Valuators, a chartered accountant or by a registered dealer of which the issuer is not a related issuer, and that specifies a reasonable time and place at which the valuation may be inspected during the distribution, if

(a) the issuer in the distribution

(i) is not a reporting issuer,

(ii) is a registered dealer, or an issuer all or substantially all of whose assets are securities of a registered dealer,

(iii) is issuing voting securities or equity securities, and

(iv) is effecting the distribution other than under a prospectus; and

(b) there is no independent underwriter that satisfies subsection 2.1(3).

PART 5 — EXEMPTION

5.1 Exemption — (1) The regulator or securities regulatory authority may grant an exemption from this Instrument, in whole or in part, subject to such conditions or restrictions as may be imposed in the exemption.

(2) Despite subsection (1), in Ontario only the regulator may grant such an exemption.

5.2 Evidence of Exemption — Without limiting the manner in which an exemption under section 5.1 may be evidenced, the issuance by the regulator of a receipt for a prospectus or an amendment to a prospectus is evidence of the granting of the exemption if

(a) the person or company that sought the exemption has delivered to the regulator, on or before the date that the preliminary prospectus or an amendment to the preliminary prospectus was filed, a letter or memorandum describing the matters relating to the exemption and indicating why consideration should be given to the granting of the exemption; and

(b) the regulator has not sent written notice to the contrary to the person or company that sought the exemption before, or concurrent with, the issuance of the receipt.

PART 6 — EFFECTIVE DATE

6.1 Effective Date — This National Instrument comes into force on January 3, 2002.

APPENDIX A — EXEMPT SECURITIES

Jurisdiction	Section Legislation Reference
All	Sections 2.20, 2.21, 2.35, 2.38 and 2.39 of National Instrument 45-106 *Prospectus and Registration Exemptions*
All except Ontario	Sections 2.34, 2.36 and 2.37 of National Instrument 45-106 *Prospectus and Registration Exemptions*
Alberta	Section 87(h), (h.1) and (h.2) of the *Securities Act* (Alberta)
Manitoba	Subsection 19(2)(g) and (h) of the *Securities Act* (Manitoba)
Newfoundland and Labrador	Subsections 36(2)(h) and (i) of the *Securities Act* (Newfoundland and Labrador)
Nova Scotia	Clause 41(2)(i) of the *Securities Act* (Nova Scotia)

Part 3: REGISTRATION

Jurisdiction	Section Legislation Reference
Ontario	Paragraphs 73(1)(a) and (b)of the *Securities Act* (Ontario)
	Sections 2.4 to 2.6 of OSC Rule 45-501
	Paragraphs 2.34(2)(b), (d.1), (e) and (f) of National Instrument 45-106 *Prospectus and Registration Exemptions*
Prince Edward Island	Subsection 2(4)(f) and (g) of the *Securities Act* (Prince Edward Island)
Quebec	Section 41 of the *Securities Act* (Québec)
Saskatchewan	Subsection 39(2)(i) and (j) of *The Securities Act, 1988* (Saskatchewan)

APPENDIX B

[Repealed]

APPENDIX C — REQUIRED INFORMATION

Required Information for the Front Page of the Prospectus or Other Document

1. A statement in bold type, naming the relevant specified firm registrant or specified firm registrants, that the issuer or the selling securityholder is a connected issuer or a related issuer of a specified firm registrant or specified firm registrants in connection with the distribution.

2. A summary, naming the relevant specified firm registrant or specified firm registrants, of the basis on which the issuer or selling securityholder is a connected issuer or a related issuer of the specified firm registrant or specified firm registrants.

3. A cross-reference to the applicable section in the body of the prospectus or other document where further information concerning the relationship between the issuer or selling securityholder and specified firm registrant or specified firm registrants is provided.

Required Information for the Body of the Prospectus or Other Document

4. A statement, naming the relevant specified firm registrant or specified firm registrants, that the issuer or the selling securityholder is a connected issuer or a related issuer of a specified firm registrant or specified firm registrants for the distribution.

5. The basis on which the issuer or selling securityholder is a connected issuer or a related issuer for each specified firm registrant referred to in paragraph 4, including

(a) if the issuer or selling securityholder is a related issuer of the specified firm registrant, the details of the holding, power to direct voting, or direct or indirect beneficial ownership of, securities that cause the issuer or selling securityholder to be a related issuer;

(b) if the issuer or selling securityholder is a connected issuer of the specified firm registrant because of indebtedness, the disclosure required by paragraph 6 of this Appendix; and

(c) if the issuer or selling securityholder is a connected issuer of the specified firm registrant because of a relationship other than indebtedness, the details of that relationship.

6. If the issuer or selling securityholder is a connected issuer of the specified firm registrant because of indebtedness,

(a) the amount of the indebtedness;

(b) the extent to which the issuer or selling securityholder is in compliance with the terms of the agreement governing the indebtedness,

(c) the extent to which a related issuer has waived a breach of the agreement since its execution;

(d) the nature of any security for the indebtedness; and

(e) the extent to which the financial position of the issuer or selling securityholder or the value of the security has changed since the indebtedness was incurred.

7. The involvement of each specified firm registrant referred to in paragraph 4 and of each related issuer of the specified firm registrant in the decision to distribute the securities being offered and the determination of the terms of the distribution, including disclosure concerning whether the issue was required, suggested or consented to by the specified firm registrant or a related issuer of the specified firm registrant and, if so, on what basis.

8. The effect of the issue on each specified firm registrant referred to in paragraph 4 and each related issuer of that specified firm registrant, including

(a) information about the extent to which the proceeds of the issue will be applied, directly or indirectly, for the benefit of the specified firm registrant or a related issuer of the specified firm registrant, or

(b) if the proceeds will not be applied for the benefit of the specified firm registrant or a related issuer of the specified firm registrant, a statement to that effect.

9. If a portion of the proceeds of the distribution is to be directly or indirectly applied to or towards

(a) the payment of indebtedness or interest owed by the issuer, an associate or related issuer of the issuer, a person or company of which the issuer is an associate, the selling securityholder, an associate or related issuer of the selling securityholder, a person or company of which the selling securityholder is an associate, to the specified firm registrant or a related issuer of the specified firm registrant, or

(b) the redemption, purchase for cancellation or for treasury, or other retirement of shares other than equity securities of the issuer, an associate or related issuer of the issuer, a person or company of which the issuer is an associate, the selling securityholder, an associate or related issuer of the selling securityholder, or of a person or company of which the selling securityholder is an associate, held by the specified firm registrant or a related issuer of the specified firm registrant

particulars of the indebtedness or shares in respect of which the payment is to be made and of the payment proposed to be made.

10. Any other material facts with respect to the relationship or connection between each specified firm registrant referred to in paragraph 4, a related issuer of each specified firm registrant and the issuer that are not required to be described by the foregoing.

Specified Firm Registrant as Issuer or Selling Securityholder

11. If the specified firm registrant is the issuer or selling securityholder in the distribution, then the information required by this Appendix shall be provided to the extent applicable.

Final Rule: 24 O.S.C.B. 7687 (December 21, 2001); Approval by OSC: 24 O.S.C.B. 6443 (October 26, 2001); Request for Comments: 24 O.S.C.B. 3805 (June 22, 2001) and 21 O.S.C.B. 781 (February 6, 1998).

Amendment to Rule: (2005) 28 O.S.C.B. (Supp-4) 118; Approval by OSC: (2005) 28 O.S.C.B. (Supp-3) 84; Request for Comments: (2004) 27 O.S.C.B. (Supp-3) 1.

Amendment to Rule: (2009) 32 O.S.C.B. (Supp. 4) 376; Approval by OSC: (2009) 32 O.S.C.B. (Supp. 2) 1; Request for Comments: (2008) 31 O.S.C.B. 2279.

Amendment to Rule: (2009) 32 O.S.C.B. (Supp. 5) 158; Approval by OSC: (2009) 32 O.S.C.B. (Supp. 3) 1; Request for Comments: (2008) 32 O.S.C.B. 4233 and (2008) 31 O.S.C.B. (Supp. 1) 1.

Amendment to Rule: (2015) 38 O.S.C.B. 5777.

Companion Policy 33-105CP — To National Instrument 33-105 Underwriting Conflicts

Date: December 21, 2001, as amended effective September 28, 2009

24 O.S.C.B. 7695 and 32 O.S.C.B. (Supp. 4) 377

Table of Contents

PART 1 — INTRODUCTION

1.1 **Purpose** — The purpose of this Policy is to state the views of the Canadian Securities Administrators (the "CSA") on various matters relating to National Instrument 33-105 Underwriting Conflicts (the "Instrument"), and to provide market participants with guidance in understanding the operation of the Instrument and the policy concerns that lie behind some of the provisions of the Instrument. This Policy includes, as Appendix A, a series of flow charts designed to illustrate the analysis required to be made in determining whether a party falls under certain of the defined terms of the Instrument and whether the requirements of the Instrument apply to a given distribution. The flow charts are for illustrative purposes only and, in all cases, reference should be made to the precise language of the Instrument.

1.2 **General Policy Rationale for the Instrument** — (1) Two of the basic objectives of securities legislation are to ensure that investors purchasing securities in the course of a distribution purchase those securities at a price determined through a process unaffected by conflicts of interest, and receive full, true and plain disclosure of all material facts regarding the issuer and the securities offered. The Instrument is based upon the premise that those objectives are best achieved if the issuer and the underwriters deal with each other as independent parties, free of any relationship that might negatively affect the performance of their respective roles.

(2) The Instrument seeks to protect the integrity of the underwriting process in circumstances in which there is a direct or indirect relationship between the issuer or selling securityholder and the underwriter that might give rise to a perception that they are not independent of each other in connection with a distribution. The Instrument imposes two basic requirements in those circumstances. First, full disclosure of the relationships giving rise to the potential conflict of interest is required to be given to investors, and second, an independent underwriter is required in certain circumstances to participate in the transaction.

Part 3: REGISTRATION

PART 2 — GENERAL STRUCTURE OF THE INSTRUMENT

2.1 Relationships of Concern — (1) The Instrument identifies three types of relationships between a specified firm registrant acting as underwriter on a distribution and the issuer or selling securityholder of securities in the distribution that give rise to concerns over conflicts of interest; each of these relationships may be subject to the requirements of the Instrument.

(a) The specified firm registrant as issuer or selling securityholder. This relationship represents the relationship with the highest degree of conflict of the three recognized by the Instrument.

(b) An issuer or selling securityholder that is a "related issuer" of the specified firm registrant. This relationship is created primarily as the result of cross-ownership between an issuer or selling securityholder and the specified firm registrant. Subsection 1.2(2) of the Instrument provides that an entity is a related issuer to another entity if one of them is an "influential securityholder" of the other, or each of them is a related issuer of the same third party.

(c) An issuer or selling securityholder that is not a related issuer of the specified firm registrant, but that has some other relationship with the specified firm registrant that would cause a reasonable prospective purchaser of the securities being offered to question if the specified firm registrant and the issuer or selling securityholder are independent of each other for the distribution. This type of issuer is a "connected issuer" of the relevant specified firm registrant.

(2) The Instrument recognizes the relative degrees of relationships and the resulting potential for conflict by imposing additional requirements for distributions by specified firm registrants and their related issuers than for distributions by connected issuers.

(3) The term "independent underwriter" is defined in the Instrument to mean a specified firm registrant acting as direct underwriter in a distribution if the specified firm registrant does not have one of the relationships with the issuer or selling securityholder described in this section. The term "non-independent underwriter" is used in this Policy to describe a specified firm registrant acting as direct underwriter that does have one of those relationships.

2.2 General Requirements of the Instrument — The general requirements of the Instrument, contained in section 2.1, provide, in effect, that a specified firm registrant that would be a non-independent underwriter on a distribution may not act as a direct underwriter in the distribution, unless certain requirements are satisfied or an exemption is available. The requirements are the disclosure obligation, required by subsection 2.1(1) of the Instrument and discussed in section 2.3 of this Policy, and, in the case of related issuer distributions, the independent underwriter obligation, required by the combination of subsections 2.1(2) and (3) of the Instrument and discussed in section 2.4 of this Policy. An exemption from the independent underwriter obligation is contained in Part 3 of the Instrument and discussed in Part 3 of this Policy.

2.3 Disclosure Obligation — (1) The disclosure obligation applicable to a distribution in which a non-independent underwriter participates, contained in subsection 2.1(1) of the Instrument, requires that the distribution be made under a prospectus or other document that contains the information described in Appendix C of the Instrument. This requirement is applicable both to transactions made under a prospectus and to those done by way of a private placement without a prospectus. Appendix C is designed to require full disclosure of the relationship between the underwriter and issuer or selling securityholder.

(2) Market participants are reminded that section 10.1 of National Instrument 71-101 The Multijurisdictional Disclosure System exempts distributions under that National Instrument from the disclosure requirements of the Instrument.

2.4 Requirement for Independent Underwriter Involvement — (1) Subsection 2.1(2) of the Instrument provides that, in the case of a distribution of special warrants or a distribution made under a prospectus, a specified firm registrant may not act

(a) as an underwriter if the specified firm registrant is the issuer or selling securityholder in the distribution; or

(b) as a direct underwriter if a related issuer of the specified firm registrant is the issuer or selling securityholder in the distribution.

(2) Subsection 2.1(3) of the Instrument provides that subsection 2.1(2) of the Instrument does not apply to a distribution otherwise caught by that subsection if there is an independent underwriter and if certain disclosure is made in a disclosure document or prospectus. The requirement for independent underwriter involvement is satisfied if at least one independent underwriter participates in the offering to the extent specified in subsection 2.1(3). Subsection 2.1(3) provides alternate threshold criteria for such involvement, depending upon whether the distribution is a "firm commitment" underwriting or a "best efforts agency" offering.

In the case of a firm commitment underwriting, an independent underwriter is required to underwrite not less than the lesser of

(a) 20 percent of the dollar value of the distribution, and

(b) the largest portion of the distribution underwritten by a specified firm registrant that is not an independent underwriter.

In the case of a best efforts agency offering, an independent underwriter must receive a portion of the total agents' fees equal to an amount not less than the lesser of

(a) 20 percent of the total agents' fees for the distribution, and

(b) the largest portion of the agents' fees paid or payable to a specified firm registrant that is not an independent underwriter.

(3) Subsection 2.1(3) of the Instrument requires the relevant disclosure document to disclose what role the independent underwriter played in the structuring, pricing and due diligence activities of the distribution. The Instrument does not specify what functions the independent underwriter must fulfil, because it is recognized that the appropriate role will vary according to the nature of the distribution and the issuer or selling securityholder, and because it is expected that the requirement to disclose the role actually played will impose a measure of market discipline on the process. Subsection 2.1(3) of the Instrument also requires the name of the independent underwriter to be disclosed.

(4) Section 2.2 of the Instrument sets out the rules for calculating the size of a distribution and the requirements for independent underwriter involvement. These rules deal with issues that may arise when distributions occur in more than one jurisdiction, or only partly in Canada.

(5) Market participants are directed to National Instrument 44-102 Shelf Distributions for applicable provisions on how the requirements of the Instrument are satisfied for shelf distributions.

PART 3 — EXEMPTION FROM INDEPENDENT UNDERWRITER REQUIREMENT

3.1 Exemption from Independent Underwriter Requirement — Section 3.2 of the Instrument provides an exemption from the independent underwriter requirement for distributions of securities of a foreign issuer if more than 85 percent of the dollar value of the distribution is effected outside of

Canada or if more than 85 percent of the agents' fees relating to the distribution are paid or payable outside of Canada. This exemption is expected to be primarily used in the context of international offerings of major issuers.

PART 4 — COMMENTARY ON RELATIONSHIPS DESCRIBED IN THE INSTRUMENT

4.1 Related Issuers — (1) Common ownership is the traditional measure of a non-arm's length relationship in which a conflict of interest is seen to arise. The definition of "related issuer", together with the definitions of "influential securityholder" and "professional group", contain the test used in the Instrument for these non-arm's length relationships.

(2) The Instrument provides that two persons or companies are related issuers of each other if one of them is an influential securityholder of the other, or if each of them are related issuers to a third person or company.

(3) The term "influential securityholder" is defined to include relationships between an issuer and another person or company or, in some cases, a professional group, that involve specified thresholds of share ownership or rights to elect directors, as summarized in subsection (4).

(4) Briefly stated, a person or company or professional group ("A") is an influential securityholder of an issuer ("I") under the definition of "influential securityholder" in the following circumstances.

(a) A owns or controls 20 percent of the voting or equity securities of I (paragraph (a) of the definition), or controls or is a general partner of the issuer, if the issuer is either a general partnership or a limited partnership.

(b) A owns or controls 10 percent of the voting or equity securities of I and either

(i) A is entitled to nominate 20 percent of the directors of I or has officers, directors or shareholders that constitute 20 percent of the directors of I; or

(ii) I is entitled to nominate 20 percent of the directors of A or has officers, directors or shareholders that constitute 20 percent of the directors of A (paragraph (b) of the definition).

(c) I owns or controls 10 percent of the voting or equity securities of A (other than a professional group) and either

(i) A is entitled to nominate 20 percent of the directors of I or has officers, directors or shareholders that constitute 20 percent of the directors of I; or

(ii) I is entitled to nominate 20 percent of the directors of A or has officers, directors or shareholders that constitute 20 percent of the directors of A (paragraph (c) of the definition).

Paragraph (c) of the definition contains no reference to professional groups in recognition of the fact that it is not possible to hold a voting or equity interest in such an entity nor does such an entity have a board of directors.

(d) If a professional group is an influential securityholder of I within paragraphs (a) or (b) of the definition, then the specified firm registrant that is part of that professional group will also be an influential securityholder of I (paragraph (d) of the definition).

(5) It is noted that under subsection 1.2(2) of the Instrument only a person or company can be a related issuer of another person or company; therefore, a professional group cannot be a related issuer of a person or company even if it is an influential securityholder of that person or company. Professional groups have been included in the definition of "influential securityholder" in order to allow paragraph (d) of the definition of "influential securityholder" to operate; this ensures that the specified firm registrant that is part of a professional group that is an influential securityholder of a person or company is itself an influential securityholder, and therefore a related issuer, of that person or company.

(6) The CSA note the following matters relating to the "influential securityholder" tests:

(a) The definition of "influential securityholder" requires an aggregation of all securities held, directly or indirectly beneficially owned and ones over which the holder has the right to direct the voting.

(b) Paragraphs 1.2(2)(a) and (b) provide that A is a related issuer of B if A is an influential securityholder of B or if B is an influential securityholder of A. Paragraph 1.2(2)(c) of the Instrument ties together all related issuers by providing that two persons or companies that are related issuers of a third person or company are related issuers of each other. The following examples illustrate the operation of paragraph 1.2(2)(c).

(i) If A is an influential securityholder of B, meaning that A is a related issuer of B under paragraph 1.2(2)(a), and B is an influential securityholder of C, meaning that C is a related issuer of B under paragraph 1.2(2)(b), then A is a related issuer of C, since both A and C are related issuers of the same person, B.

(ii) If D is an influential securityholder of both E and F, meaning that D is a related issuer of both E and F, then E and F are related issuers of each other.

(c) There is no provision in the Instrument for "diluting" indirect ownership interests in making calculations. Therefore, if A owns 45 percent of the voting shares of B that in turn owns 22 percent of the voting shares of C, all three of A, B, and C are related issuers of each other.

(d) The operation of paragraph 1.2(1)(a) of the Instrument requires, in effect, the calculation of a person or company's percentage ownership in another person or company to be done twice; first, only the outstanding voting or equity securities held would be counted, and, second, if the 10 percent or 20 percent ownership level is not reached, the calculation should be repeated on a fully diluted basis, assuming all convertible or exchangeable securities of the relevant class issued and outstanding were converted or exchanged.

4.2 Connected Issuers — (1) One relationship described in section 2.1 of this Policy as being of concern in connection with conflict matters is that of an issuer that is a connected issuer, but not a related issuer, to a specified firm registrant in a distribution. This relationship historically has led to some difficulties of interpretation under analogous provisions of securities legislation. The definition of "connected issuer" in the Instrument provides that the test for whether an issuer/selling securityholder and specified firm registrant are "connected" is whether the relationship between the issuer or selling securityholder (or their related issuers) and a specified firm registrant (or its related issuers) may lead a reasonable prospective purchaser of the securities to question the independence of such parties for purposes of the distribution.

(2) The test contained in the definition requires that the question of independence, or lack of independence, of a specified firm registrant be determined with reference to the activities of concern in a distribution and from the viewpoint of a reasonable prospective purchaser. The key issues in making that assessment are

(a) whether the investor would perceive that the relationship would interfere with the ability or inclination of the specified firm registrant to do proper due diligence, or to ensure complete disclosure of all material facts related to the issuer or affect the price placed on the securities being distributed; and

Part 3:
REGISTRATION

(b) whether the investor would perceive that the relationship would make the issuer or selling securityholder more subject to influence in the disclosure, due diligence or pricing process from the underwriter or its related issuer.

In either case, would the result be that some party's interests are perceived to be favoured to the detriment of those of investors?

(3) As in the case of related issuers, a relationship of concern may arise directly between the issuer or selling securityholder and the specified firm registrant or indirectly through one or more related issuers of either the issuer or selling securityholder or the specified firm registrant or any of them.

4.3 Issues Relating to "Connected Issuer" Relationships — (1) The definition of "connected issuer" is designed to catch relationships of concern between the issuer/selling securityholder and the specified firm registrant that are not related issuer relationships. For example, if a significant shareholder of the specified firm registrant is the chairman of the board of directors of the issuer and another related issuer of the specified firm registrant owns a large number of preferred shares that are to be repaid out of the proceeds of a distribution, the issuer may be a connected issuer of the specified firm registrant for the purposes of the distribution. In each case, the issuer, specified firm registrant and their advisers will have to weigh the totality of the relationships between the issuer and the specified firm registrant against whether a prospective purchaser might question the independence of the issuer and dealer to determine if there is a connected issuer relationship.

(2) The mere existence of a debtor/creditor relationship between the issuer and the specified firm registrant, or any of their respective related issuers, does not necessarily give rise to a connected issuer relationship. The test is whether in the circumstances the relationships among the parties might, in the view of a reasonable prospective purchaser, affect their independence from one another. Factors that may be relevant in reaching the conclusion in cases in which the relationship is debtor/creditor may include the size of the debt, the materiality of the amount of the debt to both the creditor and debtor, the terms of the debt, whether the lending arrangement is in good standing, and whether the proceeds of the issue are being used for repayment of the debt.

(3) Preference shares are not presently treated by Canadian GAAP as liabilities on the balance sheet of issuers, although they may be held by investors as an alternative to making loans or holding securities more conventionally thought of as debt. If there is cross-ownership of a material number of preference shares, there may be a relationship of concern between the issuer or selling securityholder and the specified firm registrant. Factors to be considered include the terms of the preference shares (whether the shares are term preferred shares, redeemable at the option of the holder, or represent relatively permanent capital of the issuer or selling securityholder) and the materiality of the shareholding to the issuer or selling securityholder or to the preference shareholder.

(4) Most relationships of concern are likely to arise through debtor/creditor relationships or cross-ownership. However, in some circumstances there may be other relationships between the issuer or selling securityholder and the underwriter that raise concerns. These other business relationships would have to be material to the issuer, selling securityholder, underwriter or one or more of their related entities and give rise to some special interest in the continued viability of the other entity or the success of the distribution over and above that of other entities with a similar relationship with that company. The following relationships, among others, could be material in this context.

(a) A relationship in which an issuer was a joint venture partner with a person that owed money to a related party of a specified firm registrant could raise conflict issues. In circumstances in which the joint venture party needed funds to be able to satisfy its obligations to the related party of the specified firm registrant, and those funds would be provided by the issuer following a distribution, there is the possibility that the specified firm registrant might be motivated in an underwriting for the issuer by interests other than those of an independent underwriter.

(b) A relationship in which an issuer's supplier was a related party of a specified firm registrant could also raise conflict issues, particularly if the financial condition of the issuer could put the supply arrangements in jeopardy. The specified firm registrant could be motivated to act inappropriately in raising equity for the issuer.

(c) Franchise relationships could also raise conflict issues. An issuer that is a franchisor might need to raise funds to support its franchisees or to keep the entire franchise arrangement in place. If the specified firm registrant was a related party of creditors of the franchisees that were dependent upon a successful offering to raise such funds, the independence of the specified firm registrant might be compromised.

PART 5 — CONTROL MEASURES

5.1 Control Measures — The CSA encourage specified firm registrants to adopt written internal control measures to ensure that, in connection with the distribution of securities of a "related issuer" or a "connected issuer", they deal with the issuer as an independent party, as if acting at arm's length. Although this recommendation is not intended to be prescriptive, specified firm registrants should note that they may be asked, in the normal course of inspections, whether such control measures have been adopted and a copy thereof may be requested in the course of such inspections.

PART 6 — APPENDICES

6.1 Appendices — To illustrate the analysis required to be made in determining the application of the Instrument to a distribution, Appendices A-1, A-2, A-3 and A-4 have been included in this Policy. Appendices A-1 and A-2 assist in determining whether parties are related issuers. Appendix A-3 assists in determining whether parties are connected issuers to specified firm registrants. Appendix A-4 provides a general analysis of whether, or how, the Instrument applies to a given distribution.

Appendix A-1
Related Issuer

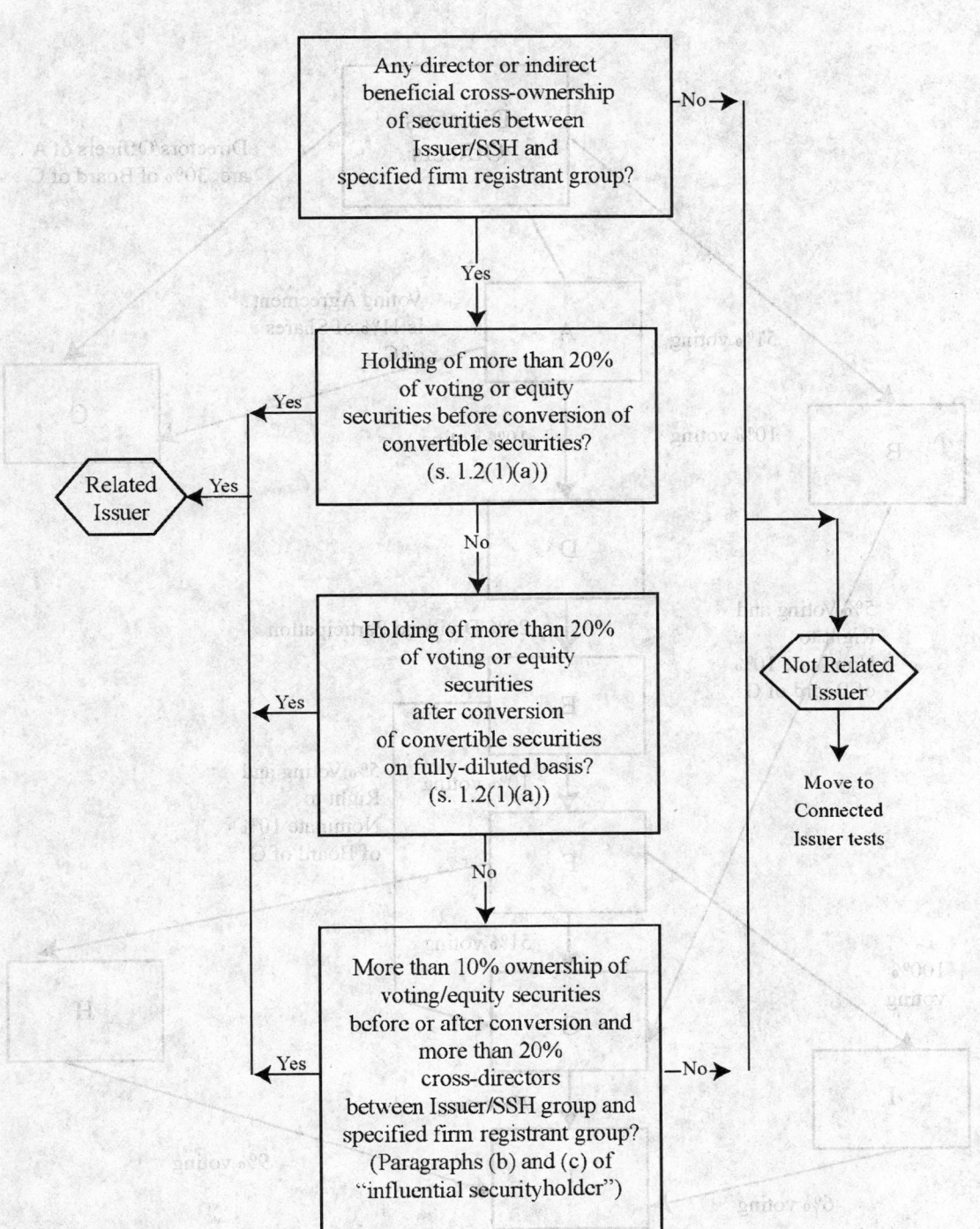

Any director or indirect beneficial cross-ownership of securities between Issuer/SSH and specified firm registrant group?

No →

Yes

Holding of more than 20% of voting or equity securities before conversion of convertible securities? (s. 1.2(1)(a))

Yes

Related Issuer

Yes

No

Holding of more than 20% of voting or equity securities after conversion of convertible securities on fully-diluted basis? (s. 1.2(1)(a))

Yes

No

More than 10% ownership of voting/equity securities before or after conversion and more than 20% cross-directors between Issuer/SSH group and specified firm registrant group? (Paragraphs (b) and (c) of "influential securityholder")

Yes

No →

Not Related Issuer

Move to Connected Issuer tests

Part 3:
REGISTRATION

Appendix A-2
Related Issuer
Influential Securityholder

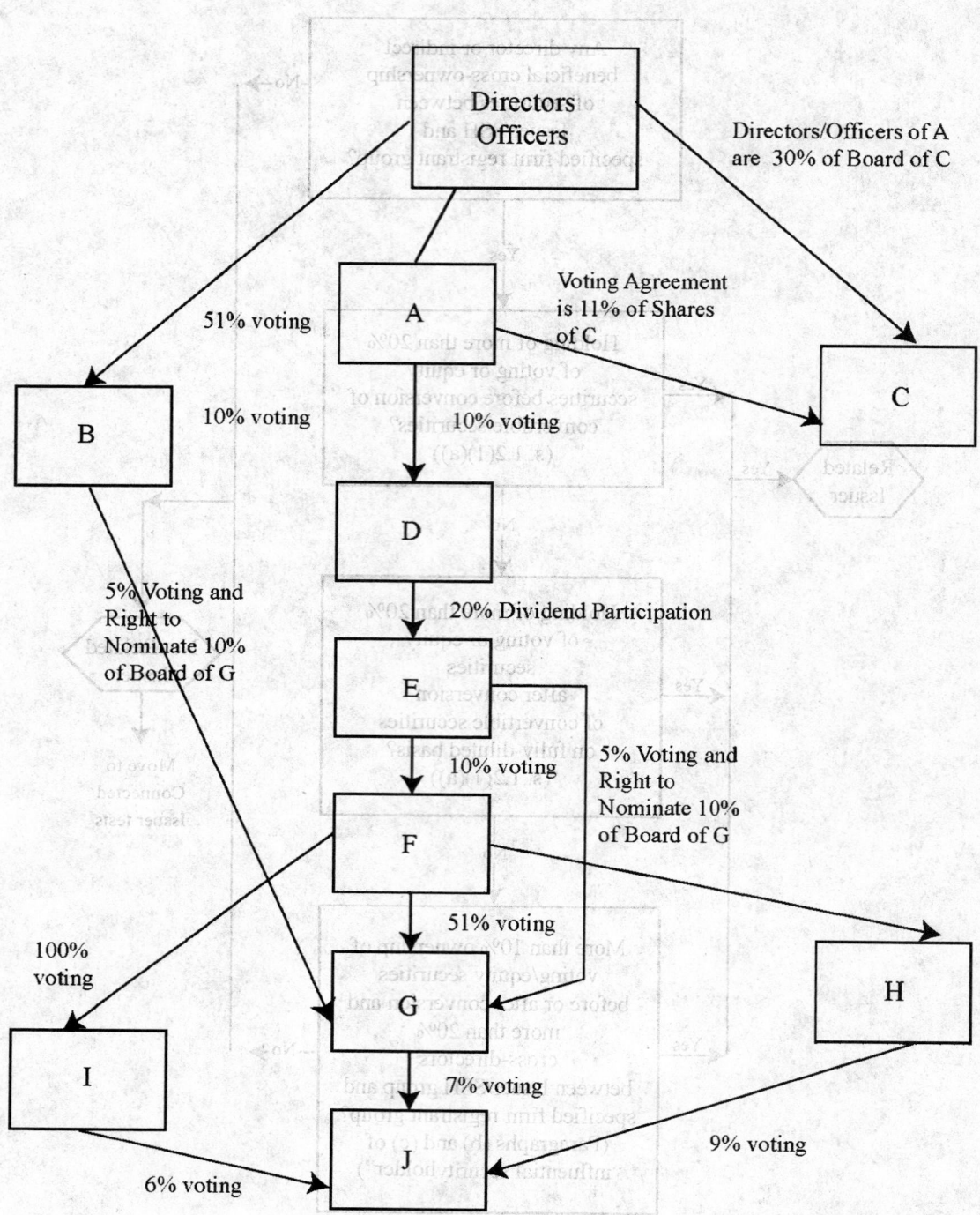

Directors/Officers of A
are 30% of Board of C

Voting Agreement
is 11% of Shares
of C

51% voting

10% voting

10% voting

5% Voting and
Right to
Nominate 10%
of Board of G

20% Dividend Participation

5% Voting and
Right to
Nominate 10%
of Board of G

10% voting

51% voting

100%
voting

7% voting

6% voting

9% voting

Appendix A-3
Connected/Related Issuer

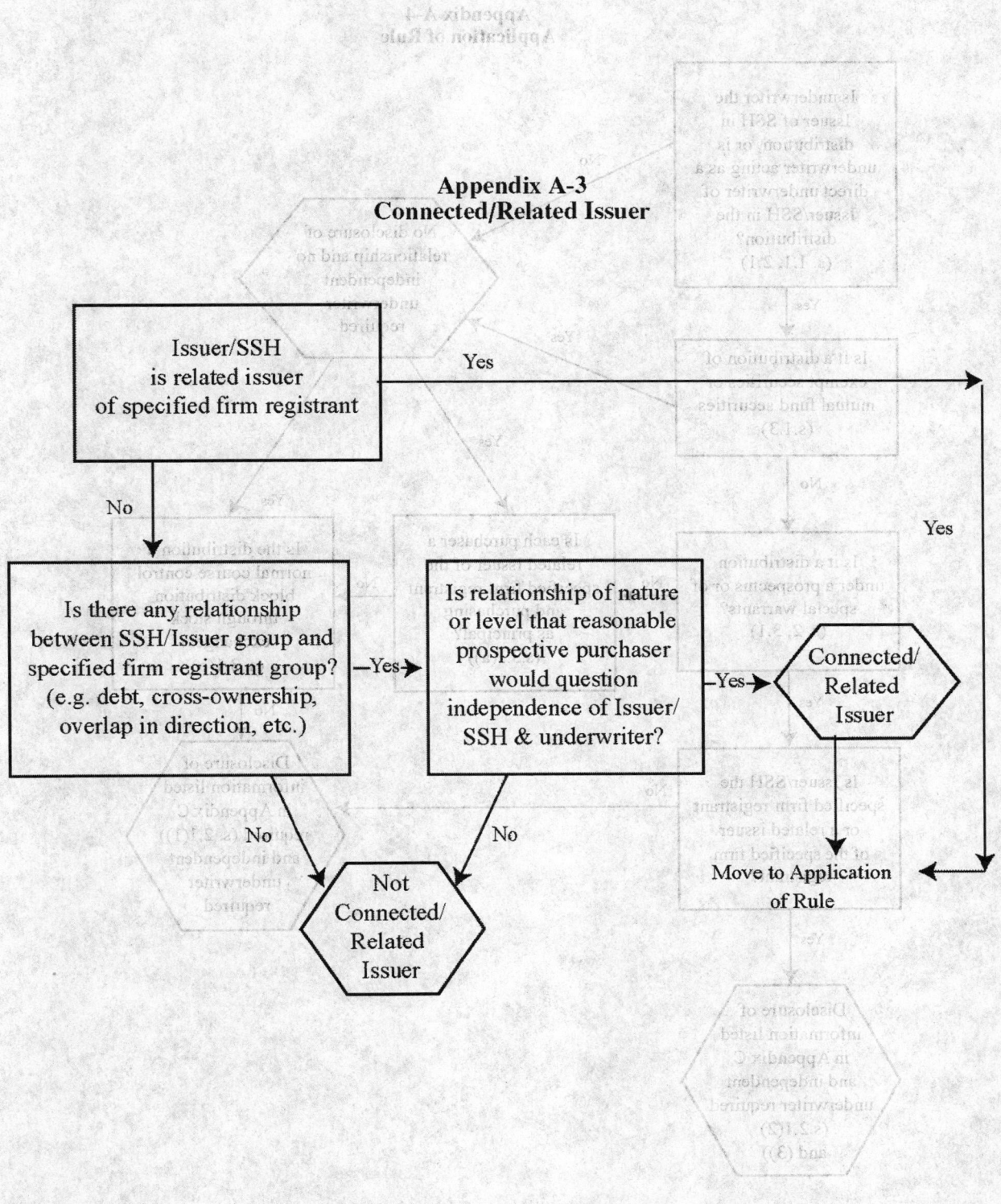

Issuer/SSH
is related issuer
of specified firm registrant

— Yes →

No

Is there any relationship
between SSH/Issuer group and
specified firm registrant group?
(e.g. debt, cross-ownership,
overlap in direction, etc.)

—Yes→

Is relationship of nature
or level that reasonable
prospective purchaser
would question
independence of Issuer/
SSH & underwriter?

—Yes→

Connected/
Related
Issuer

Yes

No

No

Not
Connected/
Related
Issuer

Move to Application
of Rule

Appendix A-4
Application of Rule

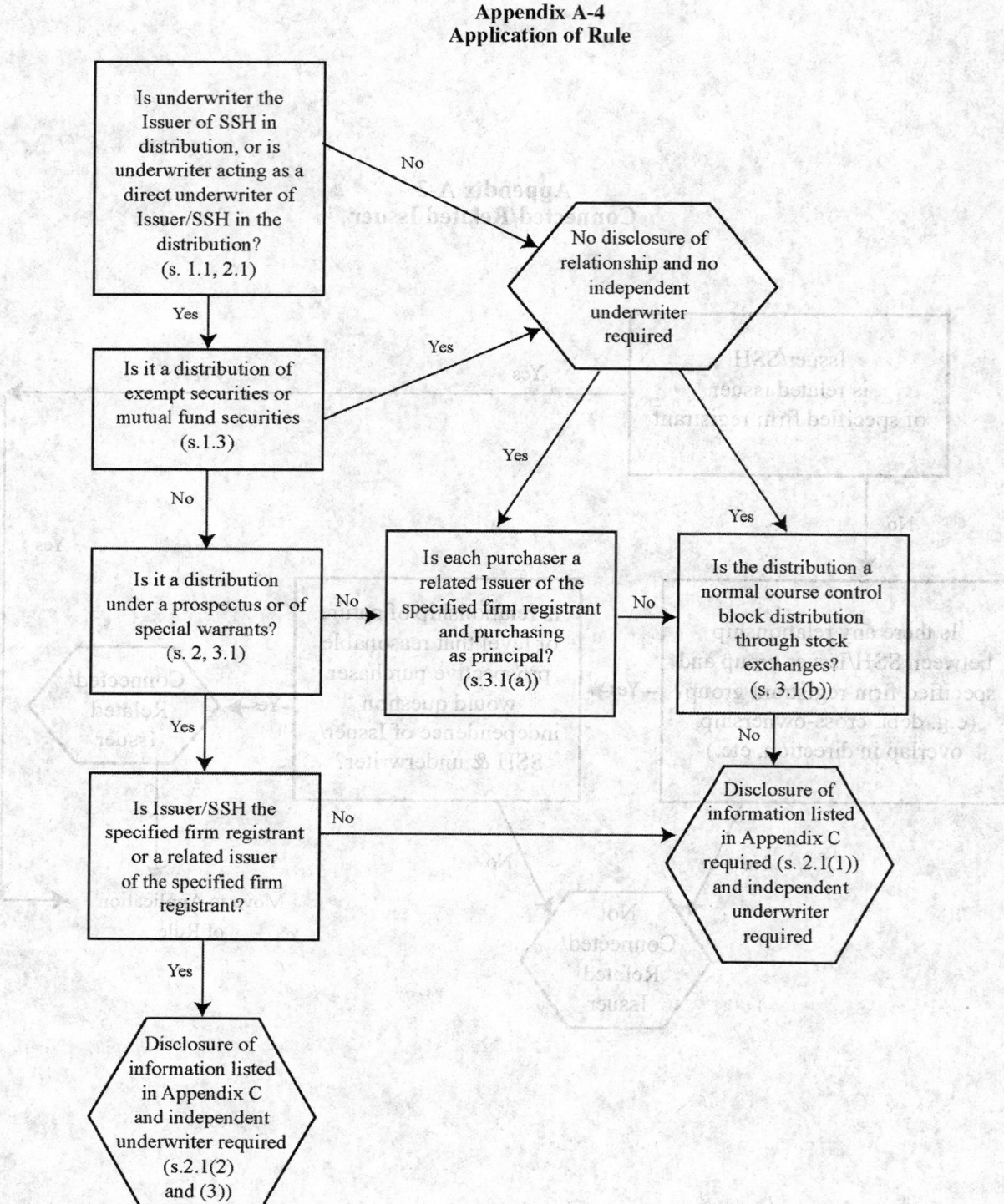

Adoption by OSC: 24 O.S.C.B. 7687 (December 21, 2001) and 24 O.S.C.B. 6443 (October 26, 2001); Request for Comments: 24 O.S.C.B. 3805 (June 27, 2001) and 21 O.S.C.B. 781 (February 6, 1998).

Adoption of Amendment by OSC: (2009) 32 O.S.C.B. (Supp. 4) 377 and 32 O.S.C.B. (Supp. 2) 1; Request for Comments: (2008) 31 O.S.C.B. 2279.

National Instrument 33-109 — Registration Information

Date: February 14, 2003, amended effective May 15, 2007; replaced effective September 28, 2009, as amended effective January 1, 2011, July 11, 2011, May 31, 2013, September 22, 2014 and January 11, 2015

26 O.S.C.B. 1313, 30 O.S.C.B. 5477, 32 O.S.C.B. (Supp. 4) 115, 33 O.S.C.B. (Supp. 5) 110, 34 O.S.C.B. 7572, 36 O.S.C.B. 2619, 37 O.S.C.B. (Supp 4) and 37 O.S.C.B. (Supp. 5)

Table of Contents

PART 1 — DEFINITIONS AND INTERPRETATION

1.1 Definitions — In this Instrument

"business location" means a location where the firm carries out an activity that requires registration, and includes a residence if regular and ongoing activity that requires registration is carried out from the residence or if records relating to an activity that requires registration are kept at the residence;

"cessation date" means the last day on which an individual had authority to act as a registered individual on behalf of their sponsoring firm or was a permitted individual of their sponsoring firm, because of the end of, or a change in, the individual's employment, partnership, or agency relationship with the firm;

"firm" means a person or company that is registered, or is seeking registration, as a dealer, adviser or investment fund manager;

"Form 33-109F1" means Form 33-109F1 *Notice of Termination of Registered Individuals and Permitted Individuals*;

"Form 33-109F2" means Form 33-109F2 *Change or Surrender of Individual Categories*;

"Form 33-109F3" means Form 33-109F3 *Business Locations other than Head Office*;

"Form 33-109F4" means Form 33-109F4 *Registration of Individuals and Review of Permitted Individuals*;

"Form 33-109F5" means Form 33-109F5 *Change of Registration Information*;

"Form 33-109F6" means Form 33-109F6 *Firm Registration*;

"Form 33-109F7" means Form 33-109F7 *Reinstatement of Registered Individuals and Permitted Individuals*;

"former sponsoring firm" means the registered firm for which an individual most recently acted as a registered individual or permitted individual;

"NRD submission number" means the unique number generated by NRD to identify each NRD submission;

"permitted individual" means

(a) a director, chief executive officer, chief financial officer, or chief operating officer of a firm, or a functional equivalent of any of those positions,

(b) an individual who has beneficial ownership of, or direct or indirect control or direction over, 10 percent or more of the voting securities of a firm, or

(c) a trustee, executor, administrator, or other personal or legal representative, that has direct or indirect control or direction over 10 percent or more of the voting securities of a firm;

"principal jurisdiction" means,

(a) for a firm, whose head office is in Canada, the jurisdiction of Canada in which the firm's head office is located,

(b) for an individual whose working office is in Canada, the jurisdiction of Canada in which the individual's working office is located,

(c) for a firm whose head office is outside Canada, the jurisdiction of the firm's principal regulator, as identified by the firm on its most recently submitted Form 33-109F5 or Form 33-109F6, and

(d) for an individual whose working office is outside Canada, the principal jurisdiction of the individual's sponsoring firm;

"principal regulator" means, for a person or company, the securities regulatory authority or regulator of the person or company's principal jurisdiction;

"registered firm" means a registered dealer, registered adviser or registered investment fund manager;

"registered individual" means an individual who is registered under securities legislation to do any of the following on behalf of a registered firm:

(a) act as a dealer, underwriter or adviser;

(b) act as a chief compliance officer;

(c) act as an ultimate designated person;

"sponsoring firm" means,

(a) for a registered individual, the registered firm on whose behalf the individual acts,

(b) for an individual applying for registration, the firm on whose behalf the individual will act if the individual's application is approved,

(c) for a permitted individual of a registered firm, the registered firm, and

(d) for a permitted individual of a firm that is applying for registration, the applicant firm.

1.2 Interpretation — Terms used in this Instrument and that are defined in National Instrument 31-102 *National Registration Database* have the same meanings as in National Instrument 31-102 *National Registration Database*.

PART 2 — APPLICATION FOR REGISTRATION AND REVIEW OF PERMITTED INDIVIDUALS

2.1 Firm Registration — A firm that applies for registration as a dealer, adviser or investment fund manager must submit each of the following to the regulator:

(a) a completed Form 33-109F6;

(b) for each business location of the applicant in the local jurisdiction other than the applicant's head office, a completed Form 33-109F3 in accordance with National Instrument 31-102 *National Registration Database*.

2.2 Individual Registration — (1) Subject to subsection (2) and sections 2.4 and 2.6, an individual who applies for registration under securities legislation must submit a completed Form 33-109F4 to the regulator in accordance with National Instrument 31-102 *National Registration Database*.

(2) A permitted individual of a registered firm who applies to become a registered individual with the firm must submit a completed Form 33-109F2 to the regulator in accordance with National Instrument 31-102 *National Registration Database*.

2.3 Reinstatement — (1) An individual who applies for reinstatement of registration under securities legislation must submit a completed Form 33-109F4 to the regulator in accordance with National Instrument 31-102 *National Registration Database*, unless the individual submits a completed Form 33-109F7 in accordance with subsection (2).

(2) The registration of an individual suspended under section 6.1 [*If an individual ceases to have authority to act for firm*] of National Instrument 31-103 *Registration Requirements, Exemptions and Ongoing Registrant Obligations* is reinstated on the date the individual submits a completed Form 33-109F7 to the regulator in accordance with National Instrument 31-102 *National Registration Database* if all of the following apply:

(a) the Form 33-109F7 is submitted on or before the 90th day after the cessation date;

(b) the individual's employment, partnership or agency relationship with the former sponsoring firm did not end because the individual was asked by the firm to resign, resigned voluntarily, or was dismissed, following an allegation against the individual of any of the following:

(i) criminal activity;

(ii) a breach of securities legislation;

(iii) a breach of a rule of an SRO;

(c) after the cessation date there have been no changes to the information previously submitted in respect of any of the following items of the individual's Form 33-109F4:

(i) item 13 [*Regulatory disclosure*] (other than Item 13.3(c));

(ii) item 14 [*Criminal disclosure*];

(iii) item 15 [*Civil disclosure*];

(iv) item 16 [*Financial disclosure*];

(d) the individual is seeking reinstatement with a sponsoring firm in one or more of the same categories of registration in which the individual was registered on the cessation date;

(e) the new sponsoring firm is registered in the same category of registration in which the individual's former sponsoring firm was registered.

2.4 **Application to Change or Surrender Individual Registration Categories** — A registered individual who applies for registration in an additional category, or to surrender a registration category, must make the application by submitting a completed Form 33-109F2 to the regulator in accordance with National Instrument 31-102 *National Registration Database*.

2.5 **Permitted Individuals** — (1) A permitted individual must submit a completed Form 33-109F4 to the regulator, in accordance with National Instrument 31-102 *National Registration Database*, no more than 10 days after becoming a permitted individual, unless the individual submits a Form 33-109F7 in accordance with subsection (2).

(2) An individual who has ceased to be a permitted individual of a former sponsoring firm and becomes a permitted individual of a new sponsoring firm may submit a completed Form 33-109F7 to the regulator if all of the following apply:

    (a) the Form 33-109F7 is submitted in accordance with National Instrument 31-102 *National Registration Database*

        (i) no more than 10 days after becoming a permitted individual of the new sponsoring firm, and

        (ii) no more than 90 days after the cessation date;

    (b) the individual holds the same permitted individual status with the new sponsoring firm that they held with the former sponsoring firm;

    (c) the conditions described in paragraphs (b) and (c) of subsection 2.3(2) are met.

2.6 *Commodity Futures Act* **Registrants** — (1) In Manitoba and Ontario, despite paragraph 2.1(b), if a firm applies for registration under section 2.1 and is registered under the *Commodity Futures Act*, the applicant is not required to submit a completed Form 33-109F3 under section 3.2 for any business location of the applicant that is recorded on NRD.

(2) In Manitoba and Ontario, despite subsection 2.2(1), if an individual applies for registration under securities legislation and is recorded on NRD with his or her sponsoring firm as registered under the *Commodity Futures Act*, the individual must make the application by submitting a completed Form 33-109F2 to the regulator in accordance with National Instrument 31-102 *National Registration Database*.

PART 3 — CHANGES TO REGISTERED FIRM INFORMATION

3.1 **Notice of Change to a Firm's Information** — (1) Subject to subsection (3) or (4), a registered firm must notify the regulator of a change to any information previously submitted in Form 33-109F6 or under this subsection, as follows:

    (a) for a change previously submitted in relation to part 3 of Form 33-109F6, within 30 days of the change;

    (b) for a change previously submitted in relation to any other part of Form 33-109F6, within 10 days of the change.

(2) A notice of change referred to in subsection (1) must be made by submitting a completed Form 33-109F5.

(3) A notice of change is not required under subsection (1) if the change relates to any of the following:

    (a) a business location other than the head office of the firm if the firm submits a completed Form 33-109F3 under section 3.2;

    (b) a termination, or a change, of a registered firm's employment, partnership or agency relationship with an officer, partner or director of the registered firm if the firm submits a completed Form 33-109F1 under subsection 4.2(1);

    (c) the addition of an officer, partner, or director to the registered firm if that individual submits either of the following:

        (i) a completed Form 33-109F4 under subsection 2.2(1) or 2.5(1);

        (ii) a completed Form 33-109F7 under subsection 2.3(2) or 2.5(2);

    (d) the information in the supporting documents referred to in any of the following items of Form 33-109F6:

        (i) item 3.3 [*Business documents*];

        (ii) item 5.1 [*Calculation of excess working capital*];

        (iii) item 5.7 [*Directors' resolution for insurance*];

        (iv) item 5.13 [*Audited financial statements*];

        (v) item 5.14 [*Letter of direction to auditors*].

(4) A person or company that submitted a completed Schedule B [*Submission to jurisdiction and appointment of agent for service*] to Form 33-109F6 must notify the regulator of a change to the information previously submitted in item 3 [*Name of agent for service of process*] or item 4 [*Address for service of process on the agent for service*] of that schedule, by submitting a completed Schedule B no more than 10 days after the change;

(5) Subsection (4) does not apply to a person or company after they have ceased to be registered for a period of 6 years or more.

(6) For the purpose of subsections (2) and (4), the person or company may give the notice by submitting it to the principal regulator.

3.2 **Changes to Business Locations** — A registered firm must notify the regulator of the opening of a business location, other than a new head office, or of a change to any information previously submitted in Form 33-109F3, by submitting a completed Form 33-109F3 to the regulator in accordance with National Instrument 31-102 *National Registration Database*, within 10 days of the opening of the business location or change.

PART 4 — CHANGES TO REGISTERED INDIVIDUAL AND PERMITTED INDIVIDUAL INFORMATION

4.1 **Notice of Change to an Individual's Information** — (1) Subject to subsection (2), a registered individual or permitted individual must notify the regulator of a change to any information previously submitted in respect of the individual's Form 33-109F4 as follows:

    (a) for a change of information previously submitted in items 4 [*Citizenship*] and 11 [*Previous employment*] of Form 33-109F4, within 30 days of the change;

    (b) for a change of information previously submitted in any other items of Form 33-109F4, within 10 days of the change.

(2) A notice of change is not required under subsection (1) if the change relates to information previously submitted in item 3 [*Personal information*] of Form 33-109F4.

(3) A notice of change under subsection (1) must be made by submitting a completed Form 33-109F5 to the regulator in accordance with National Instrument 31-102 *National Registration Database*.

(4) Despite subsection (3), a notice of change referred to in subsection (1) must be made by submitting a completed Form 33-109F2 to the regulator in accordance with National Instrument 31-102 *National Registration Database*, if the change relates to:

    (a) an individual's status as a permitted individual of the sponsoring firm,

    (b) the removal or the addition of a category of registration,

    (c) the surrender of registration in one or more non-principal jurisdictions, or

    (d) any information on Schedule C of Form 33-109F4.

4.2 Termination of Employment, Partnership or Agency Relationship — (1) A registered firm must notify the regulator of the end of, or a change in, a sponsored individual's employment, partnership, or agency relationship with the firm if the individual ceases to have authority to act on behalf of the firm as a registered individual or permitted individual by submitting a Form 33-109F1 to the regulator in accordance with National Instrument 31-102 *National Registration Database* with

    (a) items 1 through 4 completed, and

    (b) item 5 completed unless the reason for termination under item 4 was death of the individual.

(2) A registered firm must submit to the regulator the information required under

    (a) paragraph (1)(a), within 10 days of the cessation date, and

    (b) paragraph (1)(b), within 30 days of the cessation date.

(3) A registered firm must, within 10 days of a request from an individual for whom the registered firm was the former sponsoring firm, provide to the individual a copy of the Form 33-109F1 that the registered firm submitted under subsection (1) in respect of that individual.

(4) If a registered firm completed and submitted the information in item 5 of a Form 33-109F1 in respect of an individual who made a request under subsection (3) and that information was not included in the initial copy provided to the individual, the registered firm must provide to that individual a further copy of the completed Form 33-109F1, including the information in item 5, within the later of

    (a) 10 days after the request by the individual under subsection (3), and

    (b) 10 days after the submission pursuant to paragraph (2)(b).

PART 5 — DUE DILIGENCE AND RECORD-KEEPING

5.1 Sponsoring Firm Obligations — (1) A sponsoring firm must make reasonable efforts to ensure the truth and completeness of information that is submitted in accordance with this Instrument for any individual.

(2) A sponsoring firm must obtain from each individual who is registered to act on behalf of the firm, or who is a permitted individual of the firm, a copy of the Form 33-109F1 most recently submitted by the individual's former sponsoring firm in respect of that individual, if any, within 60 days of the firm becoming the individual's sponsoring firm.

(3) A sponsoring firm must retain all documents used by the firm to satisfy its obligation under subsection (1) as follows:

    (a) in the case of a registered individual, for no less than 7 years after the individual ceases to be registered to act on behalf of the firm;

    (b) in the case of an individual who applied for registration but whose registration was refused by the regulator, for no less than 7 years after the individual applied for registration; or

    (c) in the case of a permitted individual, for no less than 7 years after the individual ceases to be a permitted individual with the firm.

(4) Without limiting subsection (3), if a registered individual, an individual applying for registration, or a permitted individual appoints an agent for service, the sponsoring firm must keep the original Appointment of Agent for Service executed by the individual for the period of time set out in paragraph (3)(b).

(5) A sponsoring firm that retains a document under subsection (3) or (4) in respect of an NRD submission must record the NRD submission number on the first page of the document.

PART 6 — TRANSITION

6.1 All Registered Firms to File Form 33-109F6 — September 30, 2010 — A registered firm that was registered before September 28, 2009 must submit a completed Form 33-109F6 to the regulator on or before September 30, 2010.

6.2 Notice of Change for Firms Registered before September 28, 2009 — (1) In this section, "Form 3" means the form that a firm submitted before this Instrument came into force to apply for registration as a dealer, adviser or underwriter in the jurisdiction that, at the time the application was made, would have been the firm's principal jurisdiction under this Instrument.

(2) Subject to subsection (5), a registered firm that was first registered in a jurisdiction of Canada before this Instrument came into force and that has not submitted a completed Form 33-109F6 to the regulator, must notify the regulator of a change to any information previously submitted

    (a) in a notice of agent and address for service, by submitting to the regulator a completed Schedule B to Form 33-109F6, no more than 10 days after the change;

    (b) in Form 3 or in any notice of change to information in that form submitted to the regulator, as follows:

        (i) for a change of information equivalent to the information referred to in part 3 of Form 33-109F6, within 30 days of the change;

        (ii) for a change of information equivalent to the information referred to in any other part of Form 33-109F6, within 10 days of the change.

(3) A registered firm referred to in subsection (2) must notify the regulator of a change in its auditor or financial year-end within 10 days of the change.

(4) For the purpose of subsections (2) and (3) the firm may give the notice by submitting it to the principal regulator.

(5) A notice of change is not required under subsection (2) if the change relates to any of the following:

    (a) the addition of an officer, partner, or director to the registered firm if that individual

        (i) submits a completed Form 33-109F4 under subsection 2.2(1) or 2.5(1), or

        (ii) submits a completed Form 33-109F7 under subsection 2.3(2) or 2.5(2);

(b) a termination, or a change, of a registered firm's employment, partnership or agency relationship with an officer, partner or director of the registered firm if the firm submits a completed Form 33-109F1 under subsection 4.2(1);

(c) a business location other than the head office of the firm if the firm submits a completed Form 33-109F3 under section 3.2;

(d) information equivalent to the information referred to in section 3.1(3)(d).

6.3 National Registration Database Transition Period — (1) In this section, "NRD access date" means the first day following September 25, 2009 that an NRD filer has access to NRD to make NRD submissions.

(2) A notice submitted by an NRD filer before September 25, 2009, and not accepted or denied by the regulator by that date, must be resubmitted, as if the time required for the submission had fallen within the period commencing on September 25, 2009 and ending on the day before the NRD access date, in accordance with subsections (3), (4) and (6) as applicable.

(3) Except in the case of a notice referred to in subsection (4), if the time required for making either of the following submissions falls within the period commencing on September 25, 2009 and ending on the day before the NRD access date, the time for making the submission is extended to the 45th day following the NRD access date:

(a) a notice that is required to be submitted in NRD format;

(b) a Form 33-109F4 that is required to be submitted under subsection 2.5(1).

(4) If the time required for making either of the following submissions falls within the period commencing on September 25, 2009 and ending on the day before the NRD access date, the submission must be made other than through the NRD website:

(a) a notice referred to in subsection 4.1(1) if the change relates to previously submitted information about any of the following items of the individual's Form 33-109F4:

(i) item 14 [*Criminal disclosure*];

(ii) item 15 [*Civil disclosure*];

(iii) item 16 [*Financial disclosure*];

(b) a notice of termination referred to in subsection 4.2(1) from a former sponsoring firm, within the time required under subsection 4.2(2), if the individual's employment, partnership or agency relationship with the firm ended because the individual resigned or was dismissed for cause.

(5) From September 28, 2009 to the day before the NRD access date, an individual may submit any of the following to the regulator other than through the NRD website:

(a) Form 33-109F7;

(b) Form 33-109F2;

(c) Form 33-109F4 other than under subsection 2.5(1).

(6) If an NRD filer makes a submission other than through the NRD website under subsection (4) or (5), the NRD filer must resubmit the information in NRD format to the regulator as follows:

(a) for a Form 33-109F7 submitted under paragraph (5)(a),

(i) if the cessation date was on or after September 28, 2009, by submitting a completed Form 33-109F7 no later than 30 days after the NRD access date;

(ii) if the cessation date was before September 28, 2009, by submitting a completed Form 33-109F4 no later than 30 days after the NRD access date;

(b) for any other submission no later than 30 days after the NRD access date.

6.4 Transition — Reinstatement under Subsections 2.3(2) and 2.5(2) — (1) Despite subsection 2.3(2), from the NRD access date to December 28, 2009 an individual who seeks reinstatement of registration under subsection 2.3(2) must submit a completed Form 33-109F4 to the regulator in accordance with National Instrument 31-102 *National Registration Database*, if the cessation date occurred before September 28, 2009.

(2) For greater certainty, the registration of an individual who makes a submission under subsection (1) is reinstated in accordance with subsection 2.3(2) only if all of the conditions in paragraphs (a) through (e) of subsection 2.3(2) are met.

(3) Subsection 2.5(2) does not apply to a permitted individual whose cessation date occurred before September 28, 2009.

PART 7 — EXEMPTION

7.1 Exemption — (1) The regulator or the securities regulatory authority may grant an exemption from this Instrument, in whole or in part, subject to such conditions or restrictions as may be imposed in the exemption.

(2) Despite subsection (1), in Ontario, only the regulator may grant such an exemption.

(3) Except in Ontario, an exemption referred to in subsection (1) is granted under the statute referred to in Appendix B of National Instrument 14-101 *Definitions*, opposite the name of the local jurisdiction.

PART 8 — REPEAL AND EFFECTIVE DATE

8.1 Repeal — National Instrument 33-109 *Registration Information*, which came into force on February 14, 2003, is repealed.

8.2 Effective Date — This Instrument comes into force on the day National Instrument 31-103 *Registration Requirements and Exemptions* comes into force.

Final Rule: (2003) 26 O.S.C.B. 1313; Approval by OSC: (2002) 25 O.S.C.B. 7526; Request for Comments: (2002) 25 O.S.C.B. 3463 and (2001) 24 O.S.C.B. 7480.

Amendment to Rule: (2007) 30 O.S.C.B. 5477; Approval by OSC: (2007) 30 O.S.C.B. 1649; Request for Comments: (2006) 29 O.S.C.B. 3961.

Replacement Rule: (2009) 32 O.S.C.B. (Supp. 4) 115; Approval by OSC: (2009) 32 O.S.C.B. (Supp. 2) 1; Request for Comments: (2008) 31 O.S.C.B. 2419.

Amendment to Rule: (2010) 33 O.S.C.B. (Supp. 5) 110; Approval by OSC: (2010) 33 O.S.C.B. (Supp. 3) 203.

Amendment to Rule: (2011) 34 O.S.C.B. 7572; Approval by OSC: (2011) 34 O.S.C.B. (Supp. 3) 1; Request for Comments: (2010) 33 O.S.C.B. (Supp. 2) 1.

Amendment to Rule: Approval by OSC: (2014) 37 O.S.C.B. (Supp 4); Request for Comments: (2013) 36 O.S.C.B. (Supp 3).

Amendment to Rule: (2015) 38 O.S.C.B. 312.

Amendment to Form 33-109F6: Approved by OSC: (2013) 36 O.S.C.B. 2619; Request for Comments: (2012) 35 O.S.C.B. 6887.

Rules: NI 31-102, 31-103; Rule 13-502.

Policies and Orders: CSAN 31-313, 31-314; OSCN 33-734.

Form 33-109F1 — Notice of Termination of Registered Individuals and Permitted Individuals

(section 4.2)

General Instructions

Complete and submit this form to notify the relevant regulator(s) or, in Québec, the securities regulatory authority, or self-regulatory organization (SRO) that a registered individual or permitted individual has left their sponsoring firm or has ceased to act in a registerable activity or as a permitted individual.

Terms

In this form, "cessation date" (or "effective date of termination") means the last day on which an individual had authority to act as a registered individual on behalf of their sponsoring firm or the last day on which an individual was a permitted individual of their sponsoring firm, because of the end of, or a change in, the individual's employment, partnership, or agency relationship with the firm.

How to submit the form

Submit this form at the National Registration Database (NRD) website in NRD format at www.nrd.ca.

If you are relying on the temporary hardship exemption in section 5.1 of National Instrument 31-102 *National Registration Database*, you may submit this form in a format other than NRD format.

When to submit the form

You must submit the responses to Item 1, Item 2, Item 3 and Item 4 within 10 days of the effective date of termination.

If you are required to complete Item 5, you must submit those responses within 30 days of the cessation date. If you are submitting the responses to Item 5, in NRD format, after Items 1 to 4 have been submitted at NRD, use the NRD submission type called "Update/Correct Termination Information" to complete Item 5 of this form.

Item 1 — Terminating firm

1. Name ....

2. NRD number ....

Item 2 — Terminated individual

1. Name ....

2. NRD number ....

Item 3 — Business location of the terminated individual

1. Business location address ....

2. NRD number ....

Item 4 — Date and reason for termination

1. Cessation date / Effective date of termination .... (YYYY/MM/DD)

This is the last day that the individual had authority to act in a registerable capacity on behalf of the firm, or the last day that the individual was a permitted individual.

2. Reason for termination / cessation (check one):

     Resigned — voluntary ❑

     Resigned — at the firm's request ❑

     Dismissed in good standing ❑

     Dismissed for cause ❑

     Completed temporary employment contract ❑

     Retired ❑

Deceased ❏

Other ❏

If "Other", explain: ....

Item 5 — Details about the termination

Complete Item 5 except where the individual is deceased. In the space below:

- state the reason(s) for the cessation / termination and

- provide details if the answer to any of the following questions is "Yes".

[For NRD Format only:]

❏ This information will be disclosed within 30 days of the effective date of termination

❏ Not applicable: individual is deceased

Answer the following questions to the best of the firm's knowledge.

Item

In the past 12 months:

		Yes	No
1.	Was the individual charged with any criminal offence?	❏	❏
2.	Was the individual the subject of any investigation by any securities or financial industry regulator?	❏	❏
3.	Was the individual subject to any significant internal disciplinary measures at the firm or at any affiliate of the firm related to the individual's activity as a registrant?	❏	❏
4.	Were there any written complaints, civil claims and/or arbitration notices filed against the individual or against the firm about the individual's securities-related activities that occurred while the individual was registered or a permitted individual authorized to act on behalf of the firm?	❏	❏
5.	Does the individual have any undischarged financial obligations to clients of the firm?	❏	❏
6.	Has the firm or any affiliate of the firm suffered significant monetary loss or harm to its reputation as a result of the individual's actions?	❏	❏
7.	Did the firm or any affiliate of the firm investigate the individual relating to possible material violations of fiduciary duties, regulatory requirements or the compliance policies and procedures of the firm or any affiliate of the firm? Examples include making unsuitable trades or investment recommendations, stealing or borrowing client money or securities, hiding losses from clients, forging client signatures, money laundering, deliberately making false representations and engaging in undisclosed outside business activity.	❏	❏
8.	Did the individual repeatedly or materially fail to follow compliance policies and procedures of the firm or any affiliate of the firm?	❏	❏
9.	Did the individual engage in discretionary management of client accounts or otherwise engage in register-able activity without appropriate registration or without the firm's authorization?	❏	❏

Reasons/Details: ....

Item 6

[repealed]

Item 7 — Warning

It is an offence under securities legislation and derivatives legislation, including commodity futures legislation, to give false or misleading information on this form.

Item 8 — Certification

Certification-NRD format:

❏ I am making this submission as agent for the firm. By checking this box, I certify that the firm provided me with all of the information on this form.

Certification-Format other than NRD format:

By signing below I certify to the regulator or, in Québec, the securities regulatory authority, in each jurisdiction where I am submitting this form for the firm, either directly or through the principal regulator, that:

- I have read this form and understand the questions, and

- all of the information provided on this form is true and complete.

Name of firm ....

Name of authorized signing officer or partner ....

Title of authorized signing officer or partner ....

Signature of authorized signing officer or partner ....

Date signed .... (YYYY/MM/DD)

Form 33-109F2 — Change or Surrender of Individual Categories

(section 2.2(2), 2.4, 2.6(2) or 4.1(4))

General Instructions

Complete and submit this form to notify the relevant regulator(s) or, in Québec, the securities regulatory authority, or self-regulatory organization (SRO) that a registered individual or permitted individual seeks to add and/or remove individual registration categories or permitted activities or provide notice of other changes to the information on Schedule C of Form 33-109F4.

Terms

In this form, "you", "your" and "individual" mean the registered individual or permitted individual who is seeking to add and/or remove registration categories or permitted activities.

How to submit this form

Submit this form at the National Registration Database (NRD) website in NRD format at www.nrd.ca.

If you are relying on the temporary hardship exemption in section 5.1 of National Instrument 31-102 *National Registration Database*, you may submit this form in a format other than NRD format.

Item 1 — Individual

Name of individual ....

NRD number of individual ....

Item 2 — Registration jurisdictions

1. Are you filing this form under the passport system / interface for registration?

Choose "No" if you are registered in

   (a) only one jurisdiction in Canada

   (b) more than one jurisdiction of Canada and you are requesting a surrender in a non-principal jurisdiction or jurisdictions, but not in your principal jurisdiction, or

   (c) more than one jurisdiction of Canada and you are requesting a change only in your principal jurisdiction.

   Yes ❏ No ❏

2. Check each jurisdiction where you are seeking the change or surrender.

   ❏ Alberta
   ❏ British Columbia
   ❏ Manitoba
   ❏ New Brunswick
   ❏ Newfoundland and Labrador
   ❏ Northwest Territories
   ❏ Nova Scotia
   ❏ Nunavut
   ❏ Ontario
   ❏ Prince Edward Island
   ❏ Québec
   ❏ Saskatchewan
   ❏ Yukon

Item 3 — Removing categories

What categories are you seeking to remove?

....

Item 4 — Adding categories

1. — Categories

What categories are you seeking to add? ....

2. — Professional liability insurance (Québec mutual fund dealers and Québec scholarship plan dealers)

If you are seeking registration as a representative of a mutual fund dealer or of a scholarship plan dealer in Québec, are you covered by your sponsoring firm's professional liability insurance?

Yes ❑ No ❑

If "No", state:

The name of your insurer ....

Your policy number ....

3. — Relevant securities industry experience

If you have not been registered in the last 36 months and you passed the required examination more than 36 months ago, do you consider that you have gained 12 months of relevant securities industry experience during the 36-month period?

Yes ❑ No ❑

If you are an individual applying for IIROC approval, select N/A.

If "Yes", complete Schedule A.

Item 5 — Reason for surrender

If you are seeking to remove a registration category or permitted activity, state the reason for the surrender in the local jurisdiction.

. . .

Item 6 — Notice of collection and use of personal information

The personal information required under this form is collected on behalf of, and used by, the securities regulatory authorities in the jurisdictions set out in Schedule B to administer and enforce certain provisions of their securities legislation or derivatives legislation or both.

The personal information required under this form is also collected by and used by the SRO set out in Schedule B to administer and enforce its by-laws, regulations, rules, rulings and policies.

By submitting this form, the individual consents to the collection by the securities regulatory authorities or applicable SRO of this personal information, and any police records, records from other government or non-governmental regulators or SROs, credit records and employment records about the individual that the securities regulatory authorities or applicable SRO may need to complete their review of the information submitted in this form relating to the individual's continued fitness for registration or approval, if applicable, in accordance with the legal authority of the securities regulatory authorities while the individual is registered with or approved by it. Securities regulatory authorities or SROs may contact government and private bodies or agencies, individuals, corporations and other organizations for information about the individual.

If you have any questions about the collection and use of this information, contact the securities regulatory authorities or applicable SRO in any jurisdiction in which the required information is submitted. See Schedule B for details. In Québec, you can also contact the Commission d'accès à l'information at 1-888-528-7741 or visit its website at www.cai.gouv.qc.ca.

Item 7 — Warning

It is an offence under securities legislation and derivatives legislation, including commodity futures legislation, to give false or misleading information on this form.

Item 8 — Certification

Certification-NRD format:

I confirm I have discussed the questions in this form with an officer, branch manager or supervisor of my sponsoring firm. To the best of my knowledge and belief, the officer, branch manager or supervisor was satisfied that I fully understood the questions. I will limit my activities to those permitted by my category of registration.

❑ I am making this submission as agent for the individual identified in this form. By checking this box, I certify that the individual provided me with all of the information on this form.

Certification-Format other than NRD format:

By signing below:

    1. I certify to the regulator or, in Québec, the securities regulatory authority, in each jurisdiction where I am submitting this form, either directly or through the principal regulator, that:

      • I have read this form and understand the questions, and

- all of the information provided on this form is true, and complete.

2. I confirm I have discussed the questions in this form with an officer, branch manager or supervisor of my sponsoring firm. To the best of my knowledge and belief, the officer, branch manager or supervisor was satisfied that I fully understood the questions. I will limit my activities to those permitted by my category of registration.

Signature of individual ....

Date signed .... (YYYY/MM/DD)

By signing below, I certify to the regulator or, in Québec, the securities regulatory authority, in each jurisdiction where I am submitting this form for the individual, either directly or through the principal regulator, that:

1. the individual identified in this form will be engaged by the firm as a registered individual, or a non registered individual, and

2. I have, or a branch manager or supervisor or another officer or partner has, discussed the questions set out in this form with the individual. To the best of my knowledge and belief, the individual fully understands the questions.

Name of firm ....

Name of authorized signing officer or partner ....

Title of authorized signing officer or partner ....

Signature of authorized signing officer or partner ....

Date signed .... (YYYY/MM/DD)

Schedule A — Relevant securities industry experience (Item 4)

Describe your responsibilities in areas relating to the category you are applying for, including the title(s) you have held, as well as start and end dates:

....

What is the percentage of your time devoted to these activities?

..........%

Indicate the continuing education activities in which you have participated during the last 36 months and that are relevant to the category of registration you are applying for:, and

Schedule B — Contact information for Notice of collection and use of personal information

Alberta

Alberta Securities Commission

Suite 600, 250-5th St. SW

Calgary, AB T2P 0R4

Attention: Information Officer

Telephone: (403) 297-6454

British Columbia

British Columbia Securities Commission

P.O. Box 10142, Pacific Centre

701 West Georgia Street

Vancouver, BC V7Y 1L2

Attention: Freedom of Information Officer

Telephone: (604) 899-6500 or (800) 373-6393 (in Canada)

Manitoba

The Manitoba Securities Commission

500 - 400 St. Mary Avenue

Winnipeg, MB R3C 4K5

Attention: Director of Registrations

Telephone: (204) 945-2548

Fax (204) 945-0330

New Brunswick

Financial and Consumer Services Commission of New Brunswick / Commission des services financiers et des services aux consommateurs du Nouveau-Brunswick

Suite 300, 85 Charlotte Street

Saint John, NB E2L 2J2

Attention: Director of Securities

Telephone: (506) 658-3060

Newfoundland and Labrador

Superintendent of Securities, Service NL

Government of Newfoundland and Labrador

P.O. Box 8700

2nd Floor, West Block

Confederation Building

St. John's, NL A1B 4J6

Attention: Manager of Registrations

Telephone: (709) 729-5661

Nova Scotia

Nova Scotia Securities Commission

Suite 400, 5251 Duke Street

Halifax, NS B3J 1P3

Attention: Deputy Director, Capital Markets

Telephone: (902) 424-7768

Northwest Territories

Government of the Northwest Territories

Department of Justice

1st Floor Stuart M. Hodgson Building

5009 - 49th Street

Yellowknife, NWT X1A 2L9

Attention: Deputy Superintendent of Securities

Telephone: (867) 920-8984

Nunavut

Government of Nunavut

Department of Justice

P.O. Box 1000 Station 570

Iqaluit, NU X0A 0H0

Attention: Deputy Registrar of Securities

Telephone: (867) 975-6590

Ontario

Ontario Securities Commission

22nd Floor

20 Queen Street West

Toronto, ON M5H 3S8

Attention: Compliance and Registrant Regulation

Telephone: (416) 593-8314

e-mail: registration@osc.gov.on.ca

Prince Edward Island

Securities Office

Department of Community Affairs and Attorney General

P.O. Box 2000

Charlottetown, PE C1A 7N8

Attention: Deputy Registrar of Securities

Telephone: (902) 368-6288

Québec

Autorité des marchés financiers

800, square Victoria, 22e étage

C.P. 246, tour de la Bourse

Montréal (Québec) H4Z 1G3

Attention: Responsable de l'accès à l'information

Telephone: (514) 395-0337 or (877) 525-0337

Saskatchewan

Financial and Consumer Affairs Authority of Saskatchewan

Suite 601, 1919 Saskatchewan Drive

Regina, SK S4P 4H2

Attention: Deputy Director, Capital Markets

Telephone: (306) 787-5871

Yukon

Government of Yukon

Superintendent of Securities

Department of Community Services

P.O. Box 2703 C-6

Whitehorse, YT Y1A 2C6

Attention: Superintendent of Securities

Telephone: (867) 667-5314

Self-regulatory organization

Investment Industry Regulatory Organization of Canada

121 King Street West, Suite 2000

Toronto, Ontario M5H 3T9

Attention: Privacy Officer

Telephone: (416) 364-6133

E-mail: PrivacyOfficer@iiroc.ca

Form 33-109F3 — Business Locations other than Head Office

(section 3.2)

General Instructions

Complete and submit this form to notify the relevant regulator(s) or, in Québec, the securities regulatory authority, or self-regulatory organization (SRO) that a business location has opened or closed, or information about a business location has changed.

Check one of the following and complete the entire form:

> ❏ Opening this business location

> ❏ Closing this business location

> ❏ Change to the information previously submitted about this business location. Clearly specify the information that has changed.

How to submit this form

Submit this form at the National Registration Database (NRD) website in NRD format at www.nrd.ca

If you are relying on the temporary hardship exemption in section 5.1 of National Instrument 31-102 *National Registration Database*, you may complete and submit this form in a format other than NRD format.

Item 1 — Type of business location

Branch or Business Location ❏

Sub-branch (Mutual Fund Dealers Association of Canada members only) ❏

Item 2 — Supervisor or branch manager

Name of designated supervisor or branch manager ....

NRD number of the designated supervisor or branch manager ....

Item 3 — Business location information

Business location address .... (a post office box is not a valid business location address)

Mailing address (if different from business location address)..................................

Telephone number (..........) ....

Fax number (..........) ....

E-mail address ....

Item 4 — Notice of collection and use of personal information

The personal information required under this form is collected on behalf of, and used by, the securities regulatory authorities in the jurisdictions set out in Schedule A to administer and enforce certain provisions of their securities legislation or derivatives legislation or both.

The personal information required under this form is also collected by and used by the SRO set out in Schedule A to administer and enforce its by-laws, regulations, rules, rulings and policies.

By submitting this form, the individual consents to the collection by the securities regulatory authorities or applicable SRO of this personal information, and any police records, records from other government or non-governmental regulators or SROs, credit records and employment records about the individual that the securities regulatory authorities or applicable SRO may need to complete their review of the information submitted in this form relating to the individual's continued fitness for registration or approval, if applicable, in accordance with the legal authority of the securities regulatory authorities while the individual is registered with or approved by it. Securities regulatory authorities or SROs may contact government and private bodies or agencies, individuals, corporations and other organizations for information about the individual.

If you have any questions about the collection and use of this information, contact the securities regulatory authorities or applicable SRO in any jurisdiction in which the required information is submitted. See Schedule A for details. In Québec, you can also contact the Commission d'accès à l'information at 1-888-528-7741 or visit its website at www.cai.gouv.qc.ca.

Item 5 — Warning

It is an offence under securities legislation and derivatives legislation, including commodity futures legislation, to give false or misleading information on this form.

Item 6 — Certification

Certification-NRD format:

❑ I am making this submission as agent for the firm. By checking this box, I certify that the firm provided me with all of the information on this form.

❑ If the business location is a residence, the individual conducting business from that business location has completed a Form 33-109F4 *Registration of Individuals and Review of Permitted Individuals* certifying that they give their consent for the regulator or, in Québec, the securities regulatory authority to enter the residence for the administration of securities legislation and derivatives legislation, including commodity futures legislation.

Certification-Format other than NRD format:

By signing below, I certify to the securities regulator or, in Québec, the securities regulatory authority, in each jurisdiction where I am submitting this form for the firm, either directly or through the principal regulator, that:

- I have read this form and understand the questions,

- all of the information provided on this form is true, and complete, and

- if the business location specified in this form is a residence, the individual conducting business from that business location has completed a Form 33-109F4 *Registration of Individuals and Review of Permitted Individuals* certifying that they give their consent for the regulator or, in Québec, the securities regulatory authority to enter the residence for the administration of securities legislation and derivatives legislation, including commodity futures legislation.

Name of firm ....

Name of authorized signing officer or partner ....

Title of authorized signing officer or partner ....

Signature of authorized signing officer or partner ....

Date signed .... (YYYY/MM/DD)

Schedule A — Contact information for Notice of collection and use of personal information

Alberta

Alberta Securities Commission

Suite 600, 250-5th St. SW

Calgary, AB T2P 0R4

Attention: Information Officer

Telephone: (403) 297-6454

British Columbia

British Columbia Securities Commission

P.O. Box 10142, Pacific Centre

701 West Georgia Street

Vancouver, BC V7Y 1L2

Attention: Freedom of Information Officer

Telephone: (604) 899-6500 or (800) 373-6393 (in Canada)

Manitoba

The Manitoba Securities Commission

500 - 400 St. Mary Avenue

Winnipeg, MB R3C 4K5

Attention: Director of Registrations

Telephone: (204) 945-2548

Fax (204) 945-0330

New Brunswick

Financial and Consumer Services Commission of New Brunswick / Commission des services financiers et des services aux consommateurs du Nouveau-Brunswick

Suite 300, 85 Charlotte Street

Saint John, NB E2L 2J2

Attention: Director of Securities

Telephone: (506) 658-3060

Newfoundland and Labrador

Superintendent of Securities, Service NL

Government of Newfoundland and Labrador

P.O. Box 8700

2nd Floor, West Block

Confederation Building

St. John's, NL A1B 4J6

Attention: Manager of Registrations

Telephone: (709) 729-5661

Nova Scotia

Nova Scotia Securities Commission

Suite 400, 5251 Duke Street

Halifax, NS B3J 1P3

Attention: Deputy Director, Capital Markets

Telephone: (902) 424-7768

Northwest Territories

Government of the Northwest Territories

Department of Justice

1st Floor Stuart M. Hodgson Building

5009 - 49th Street

Yellowknife, NWT X1A 2L9

Attention: Deputy Superintendent of Securities

Telephone: (867) 920-8984

Nunavut

Government of Nunavut

Department of Justice

P.O. Box 1000 Station 570

Iqaluit, NU X0A 0H0

Attention: Deputy Registrar of Securities

Telephone: (867) 975-6590

Ontario

Ontario Securities Commission

22nd Floor

20 Queen Street West

Toronto, ON M5H 3S8

Attention: Compliance and Registrant Regulation

Telephone: (416) 593-8314

e-mail: registration@osc.gov.on.ca

Prince Edward Island

Securities Office

Department of Community Affairs and Attorney General

P.O. Box 2000

Charlottetown, PE C1A 7N8

Attention: Deputy Registrar of Securities

Telephone: (902) 368-6288

Québec

Autorité des marchés financiers

800, square Victoria, 22e étage

C.P. 246, tour de la Bourse

Montréal (Québec) H4Z 1G3

Attention: Responsable de l'accès à l'information

Telephone: (514) 395-0337 or (877) 525-0337

Saskatchewan

Financial and Consumer Affairs Authority of Saskatchewan

Suite 601, 1919 Saskatchewan Drive

Regina, SK S4P 4H2

Attention: Deputy Director, Capital Markets

Telephone: (306) 787-5871

Yukon

Government of Yukon

Superintendent of Securities

Department of Community Services

P.O. Box 2703 C-6

Whitehorse, YT Y1A 2C6

Attention: Superintendent of Securities

Telephone: (867) 667-5314

Self-regulatory organization

Investment Industry Regulatory Organization of Canada

121 King Street West, Suite 2000

Toronto, Ontario M5H 3T9

Attention: Privacy Officer

Telephone: (416) 364-6133

E-mail: PrivacyOfficer@iiroc.ca

Form 33-109F4 — Registration of Individuals and Review of Permitted Individuals

(section 2.2)

General Instructions

Complete and submit this form to the relevant regulator(s) or in Québec, the securities regulatory authority, or self-regulatory organization (SRO) if an individual is seeking

- registration in individual categories,
- to be reviewed as a permitted individual.

You are only required to submit one form even if you are applying to be registered in several categories. This form is also used if you are seeking to be reviewed as a permitted individual. A post office box is not acceptable as a valid business location address.

Terms

In this form:

"Approved person" means, in respect of a member (Member) of the Investment Industry Regulatory Organization of Canada (IIROC), an individual who is a partner, director, officer, employee or agent of a Member who is approved by IIROC or another Canadian SRO to perform any function required under any IIROC or other Canadian SRO by-law, rule, or policy;

"Canadian Investment Manager designation" means the designation earned through the Canadian investment manager program prepared and administered by CSI Global Education Inc. and so named on the day this Instrument comes into force, and every program that preceded that program, or succeeded that program, that does not have a significantly reduced scope and content when compared to the scope and content of the first-mentioned program;

"CFA Charter" means the charter earned through the Chartered Financial Analyst program prepared and administered by the CFA Institute and so named on the day this Instrument comes into force, and every program that preceded that program, or succeeded that program, that does not have a significantly reduced scope and content when compared to the scope and content of the first-mentioned program;

"Derivatives" means financial instruments, such as futures contracts (including exchange traded contracts), futures options and swaps whose market price, value or payment obligations are derived from, or based on, one or more underlying interests. Derivatives can be in the form of instruments, agreements or securities;

"Major shareholder" and "shareholder" mean a shareholder who, in total, directly or indirectly owns voting securities carrying 10 per cent or more of the votes carried by all outstanding voting securities;

"Sponsoring firm" means the registered firm where you will carry out your duties as a registered or permitted individual; and

"You", "your" and "individual" mean the individual who is seeking registration or the individual who is filing this form as a permitted individual under securities legislation or derivatives legislation or both.

How to submit this form

NRD format

Submit this form at the National Registration Database (NRD) website in NRD format at www.nrd.ca. If you have any questions, contact the compliance, registration or legal department of the sponsoring firm or a legal adviser with securities law experience, or visit the NRD information website at www.nrd-info.ca.

Format, other than NRD format

If you are relying on the temporary hardship exemption in section 5.1 of National Instrument 31-102 National Registration Database, you may submit this form in a format other than NRD format.

If you need more space, use a separate sheet of paper. Clearly identify the item and question number. Complete and sign the form, and send it to the relevant regulator(s) or, in Québec, the securities regulatory authority, SRO (s) or similar authority. The number of originally signed copies of the form you are required to submit depends on the province or territory, and on the regulator, the securities regulatory authority or SRO.

To avoid delays in processing this form, be sure to answer all of the questions that apply to you. If you have questions, contact the compliance, registration or legal department of the sponsoring firm or a legal adviser with securities law experience, or visit the NRD information website at www.nrd-info.ca.

Item 1 — Name

1. — Legal name

.... Last name First name Second name (N/A ❑) Third name (N/A ❑)

NRD number (if applicable) ....

2. — Other personal names

Are you currently, or have you ever been, known by any names other than your full legal name above, for example, nicknames or names due to marriage?

Yes ❑ No ❑

If "Yes", complete Schedule A.

3. — Use of other names

Are you currently, or have you ever used, operated under, or carried on business under any name other than the name(s) mentioned above, for example, trade names for sole proprietorships or team names?

Yes ❑ No ❑

If "Yes", complete Schedule A.

Item 2 — Residential address

Provide all of your residential addresses, including any foreign residential addresses, for the past 10 years.

1. — Current and previous residential addresses

.... (number, street, city, province, territory or state, country, postal code)

Telephone number ....

Lived at this address since (YYYY/MM) ....

If you have lived at this address for less than 10 years, complete Schedule B.

2. — Mailing address

❑ Check here if your mailing address is the same as your current residential address provided above. Otherwise, complete the following:

.... (number, street, city, province, territory or state, country, postal code)

3. — Business e-mail address

....

Item 3 — Personal information

1. Date of birth .... (YYYY/MM/DD)
2. Place of birth .... (city, province, territory or state, country)
3. Gender Female ❑ Male ❑
4. Eye colour ....
5. Hair colour ....
6. Height .... ❑ in. or ....❑ cm.
7. Weight .... ❑ lbs. or .... ❑ kg.

Item 4 — Citizenship

1. Citizenship information

What is your country of citizenship?

❑ Canada

❑ Other, specify: ....

2. If you are a citizen of a country other than Canada, complete the following for that citizenship.

❑ Check here if you do not have a valid passport. Otherwise, provide:

Passport number: ....

Date of issue: .... (YYYY/MM/DD)

Place of issue: .... (city, province, territory or state, country)

Item 5 — Registration jurisdictions

1. Are you filing this form under the passport system / interface for registration?

    Only choose "No" if:

        (a) you are seeking registration only in your principal jurisdiction,

        (b) you are seeking review as a permitted individual

    and you are not currently registered under securities legislation in any jurisdiction of Canada.

Yes ❏ No ❏

2. Check each jurisdiction where you are seeking registration or review as a permitted individual:

❏ All jurisdictions
❏ Alberta
❏ British Columbia
❏ Manitoba
❏ New Brunswick
❏ Newfoundland and Labrador
❏ Northwest Territories
❏ Nova Scotia
❏ Nunavut
❏ Ontario
❏ Prince Edward Island
❏ Québec
❏ Saskatchewan
❏ Yukon

Item 6 — Individual categories

1. On Schedule C, check each category for which you are seeking registration as an individual or review as a permitted individual. If you are seeking review as a permitted individual, check each category that describes your position with your sponsoring firm.

2. If you are seeking registration as a representative of a mutual fund dealer or of a scholarship plan dealer in Québec, are you covered by your sponsoring firm's professional liability insurance?

Yes ❏ No ❏

If "No", state:

The name of your insurer ....

Your policy number ....

Item 7 — Address and agent for service

1. — Address for service

You must have one address for service in each province or territory where you are submitting this form. A residential address or a business address is acceptable. A post office box is not an acceptable address for service. Complete Schedule D for each additional address for service you are providing.

Address for service: .... (number, street, city, province or territory, postal code)

Telephone number ....

Fax number, if applicable ....

Business e-mail address..........

2. — Agent for service

If you have appointed an agent for service, provide the following information for the agent in each province or territory where you have an agent for service. The address of your agent for service must be the same as the address for service above. If your agent for service is not an individual, provide the name of your contact person.

Name of agent for service: ....

Contact person: .... Last name, First name

Item 8 — Proficiency

1. — Course, examination or designation information and other education

Complete Schedule E to indicate each course, examination and designation that is required for registration or approval and that you have successfully completed or have been exempted from.

❏ Check here if you are not required under securities legislation or derivatives legislation or both, or the rules of an SRO to satisfy any course, examination or designation requirements.

2. — Student numbers

If you have a student number for a course that you successfully completed with one of the following organizations, provide it below:

CSI Global Education:...................................

IFSE Institute:....................................

Institute of Canadian Bankers (ICB):.....................................

CFA Institute:....................................

Advocis:....................................

RESP Dealers Association of Canada: ....

Other: ....

3. — Exemption refusal

Has any securities regulator, derivatives regulator or SRO refused to grant you an exemption from a course, examination, designation or experience requirement?

Yes ❑ No ❑

If "Yes", complete Schedule F.

4. — Relevant securities industry experience

If you are an individual applying for IIROC approval, select "N/A".

If you have not been registered in the last 36 months and you passed the required examination more than 36 months ago, do you consider that you have gained 12 months of relevant securities industry experience during the 36-month period?

Yes ❑ No ❑ N/A ❑

If "Yes", complete Schedule F.

Item 9 — Location of employment

1. Provide the following information for your new sponsoring firm. If you will be working out of more than one business location, provide the following information for the business location out of which you will be doing most of your business. If you are only filing this form because you are a permitted individual and you are not employed by, or acting as agent for, the sponsoring firm, select "N/A".

NRD location number: ....

Unique Identification Number (optional): ....

Business location address: .... (number, street, city, province, territory or state, country, postal code)

Telephone number: (..........) ....

Fax number: (..........) ....

N/A ❑

2. If the firm has a foreign head office, and/or you are not a resident of Canada, provide the address for the business location in which you will be conducting most of your business. If you are only filing this form because you are a permitted individual and you are not employed by, or acting as agent for, the sponsoring firm, select "N/A".

Business location address: .... (number, street, city, province, territory or state, country, postal code)

Telephone number: (..........) ....

Fax number: (..........) ....

N/A ❑

[The following under #3 "Type of business location", #4 and #5 is for a Format other than NRD format only]

3. Type of business location:

  ❑ Head office

  ❑ Branch or business location

  ❑ Sub-branch (members of the Mutual Fund Dealers Association of Canada only)

4. Name of supervisor or branch manager:

5. ❑ Check here if the mailing address of the business location is the same as the business location address provided above. Otherwise, complete the following:

Mailing address: .... (number, street, city, province, territory or state, country, postal code)

Item 10 — Current employment, other business activities, officer positions held and directorships

Complete a separate Schedule G for each of your current business and employment activities, including employment and business activities with your sponsoring firm and any employment and business activities outside your sponsoring firm. Also include all officer or director positions and any other equivalent positions held, as well as positions of influence. The information must be provided

  • whether or not you receive compensation for such services, and

  • whether or not any such position is business related.

Item 11 — Previous employment and other activities

On Schedule H, complete your history of employment and other activities for the past 10 years.

Item 12 — Resignations and terminations

Have you ever resigned, been terminated or been dismissed for cause by an employer from a position following allegations that you:

   1. Violated any statutes, regulations, rules or standards of conduct?

   Yes ❑ No ❑

   If "Yes", complete Schedule I, Item 12.1.

   2. Failed to appropriately supervise compliance with any statutes, regulations, rules or standards of conduct?

   Yes ❑ No ❑

   If "Yes", complete Schedule I, Item 12.2.

   3. Committed fraud or the wrongful taking of property, including theft?

   Yes ❑ No ❑

   If "Yes", complete Schedule I, Item 12.3.

Item 13 — Regulatory disclosure

1. — Securities and derivatives regulation

The questions below relate to any jurisdiction of Canada and any foreign jurisdiction.

   a) Other than a registration or permitted individual status that has been recorded under this NRD number, are you now, or have you ever been, registered or licensed with any securities regulator or derivatives regulator or both to trade in or advise on securities or derivatives or both?

   Yes ❑ No ❑

   If "Yes", complete Schedule J, Item 13.1(a).

   b) Have you ever been refused registration or a licence to trade in or advise on securities or derivatives or both?

   Yes ❑ No ❑

   If "Yes", complete Schedule J, Item 13.1(b).

   c) Have you ever been denied the benefit of any exemption from registration provided in any securities or derivatives or both legislation or rules, other than what was disclosed in Item 8.3 of this form?

   Yes ❑ No ❑

   If "Yes", complete Schedule J, Item 13.1(c).

   d) Are you now, or have you ever been subject to any disciplinary proceedings or any order resulting from disciplinary proceedings under any securities legislation or derivatives legislation or both?

   Yes ❑ No ❑

   If "Yes", complete Schedule J, Item 13.1(d).

2. — SRO regulation

a) Other than an approval that has been recorded under this NRD number, are you now, or have you ever been, an approved person of an SRO or similar organization in any province, territory, state or country?

Yes ❑ No ❑

If "Yes", complete Schedule J, Item13.2(a).

b) Have you ever been refused approved person status by an SRO or similar organization in any province, territory, state or country?

Yes ❑ No ❑

If "Yes", complete Schedule J, Item 13.2(b).

c) Are you now, or have you ever been, subject to any disciplinary proceedings conducted by any SRO or similar organization in any province, territory, state or country?

Yes ❑ No ❑

If "Yes", complete Schedule J, Item 13.2(c).

3. — Non-securities regulation

a) Are you now, or have you ever been, registered or licensed under any legislation which requires registration or licensing to deal with the public in any capacity other than to trade in or advise on securities or derivatives or both in any province, territory, state or country (e.g. insurance, real estate, accountant, lawyer, teacher)?

Yes ❑ No ❑

If "Yes", complete Schedule J, Item 13.3(a).

b) Have you ever been refused registration or a licence under any legislation relating to your professional activities unrelated to securities or derivatives in any province, territory, state or country?

Yes ❑ No ❑

If "Yes", complete Schedule J, Item 13.3(b).

c) Are you now, or have you ever been, a subject of any disciplinary actions conducted under any legislation relating to your professional activities unrelated to securities or derivatives in any province, territory, state or country?

Yes ❑ No ❑

If "Yes", complete Schedule J, Item 13.3(c).

Item 14 — Criminal disclosure

Offences you must disclose

The questions below apply to offences committed in any jurisdiction of Canada and any foreign jurisdiction.

You must disclose all offences, including:

- a criminal offence under federal statutes such as the *Criminal Code* (Canada), *Income Tax Act* (Canada), *the Competition Act* (Canada), *Immigration and Refugee Protection Act* (Canada) and the *Controlled Drugs and Substances Act* (Canada), even if
  - a record suspension has been ordered under the *Criminal Records Act* (Canada)
  - you have been granted an absolute or conditional discharge under the *Criminal Code* (Canada), and
- a criminal offence, with respect to questions 14.2 and 14.4, of which you or your firm has been found guilty or for which you or your firm have participated in the alternative measures program within the previous three years, even if a record suspension has been ordered under the *Criminal Records Act* (Canada)

You are not required to disclose:

- charges for summary conviction offences that have been stayed for six months or more,
- charges for indictable offences that have been stayed for a year or more,
- offences under the *Youth Criminal Justice Act* (Canada), and
- speeding or parking violations.

Subject to the exceptions above:

1. Are there any outstanding or stayed charges against you alleging a criminal offence that was committed?

Yes ❑ No ❑

If "Yes", complete Schedule K, Item 14.1.

2. Have you ever been found guilty, pleaded no contest to, or been granted an absolute or conditional discharge from any criminal offence that was committed?

Yes ❑ No ❑

If "Yes", complete Schedule K, Item 14.2.

3. To the best of your knowledge, are there any outstanding or stayed charges against any firm of which you were, at the time the criminal offence was alleged to have taken place, a partner, director, officer or major shareholder?

Yes ❑ No ❑

If "Yes", complete Schedule K, Item 14.3.

4. To the best of your knowledge, has any firm, when you were a partner, officer, director or major shareholder, ever been found guilty, pleaded no contest to or been granted an absolute or conditional discharge from a criminal offence that was committed?

Yes ❑ No ❑

If "Yes", complete Schedule K, Item 14.4.

Offences you do not have to disclose

The appropriate response is "No" if any of the following circumstances apply.

You are not required to disclose:

- crimes for which you received an absolute or conditional discharge if the crime has been purged from the criminal records in accordance with the *Criminal Records Act* (Canada)
- speeding, parking violations or any offence for which a pardon has been granted under the *Criminal Records Act* (Canada) and the pardon has not been revoked
- stayed charges for summary conviction offences that have been stayed for six months or more
- stayed charges for indictable offences that have been stayed for a year or more, and
- offences under the former *Young Offenders Act* (Canada)*or the Youth Criminal Justice Act* (Canada)

Part 3:
REGISTRATION

With respect to questions 14.2 and 14.4, you are not required to disclose an offence for which you or your firm was found guilty if you or the firm participated in the Alternative Measures Program more than three years ago for that offence.

    1. Are there any outstanding or stayed charges against you alleging a criminal offence that was committed in any province, territory, state or country?

    Yes ❏ No ❏

    If "Yes", complete Schedule K, Item 14.1.

    2. Have you ever been found guilty, pleaded no contest to, or granted an absolute or conditional discharge from any criminal offence that was committed in any province, territory, state or country?

    Yes ❏ No ❏

    If "Yes", complete Schedule K, Item 14.2.

    3. To the best of your knowledge, are there any outstanding charges against any firm of which you were, at the time the criminal offence was alleged to have taken place in any province, territory, state or country, a partner, director, officer or major shareholder?

    Yes ❏ No ❏

    If "Yes", complete Schedule K, Item 14.3.

    4. To the best of your knowledge, has any firm, when you were a partner, officer, director or major shareholder, ever been found guilty, pleaded no contest to or granted an absolute or conditional discharge from a criminal offence that was committed in any province, territory, state or country?

    Yes ❏ No ❏

    If "Yes", complete Schedule K, Item 14.4.

Item 15 — Civil disclosure

The questions below relate to any jurisdiction of Canada and any foreign jurisdiction.

1. Are there currently any outstanding civil actions alleging fraud, theft, deceit, misrepresentation or similar misconduct against you or a firm where you are or were a partner, director, officer or major shareholder?

Yes ❏ No ❏

If "Yes", complete Schedule L, Item 15.1.

2. Have you or a firm where you are or were a partner, director, officer or major shareholder ever been a defendant or respondent in any civil proceeding in which fraud, theft, deceit, misrepresentation or similar misconduct is, or was, successfully established in a judgment?

Yes ❏ No ❏

If "Yes", complete Schedule L, Item 15.2.

Item 16 — Financial disclosure

1. — Bankruptcy

Under the laws of any applicable jurisdiction, have you or has any firm when you were a partner, director, officer or major shareholder of that firm:

    a) Had a petition in bankruptcy issued or made a voluntary assignment in bankruptcy or any similar proceeding?

    Yes ❏ No ❏

    If "Yes", complete Schedule M, Item 16.1(a).

    b) Made a proposal under any legislation relating to bankruptcy or insolvency or any similar proceeding?

    Yes ❏ No ❏

    If "Yes", complete Schedule M, Item 16.1(b).

    c) Been subject to proceedings under any legislation relating to the winding up or dissolution of the firm, or under the *Companies' Creditors Arrangement Act* (Canada)?

    Yes ❏ No ❏

    If "Yes", complete Schedule M, Item 16.1(c).

    d) Been subject to or initiated any proceedings, arrangement or compromise with creditors? This includes having a receiver, receiver-manager, administrator or trustee appointed by or at the request of creditors, privately, through court process or by order of a regulatory authority, to hold your assets.

    Yes ❏ No ❏

    If "Yes", complete Schedule M, Item 16.1(d).

2. — Debt obligations

Over the past 10 years, have you failed to meet a financial obligation of $10,000 or more as it came due or, to the best of your knowledge, has any firm, while you were a partner, director, officer or major shareholder of that firm, failed to meet any financial obligation of $10,000 or more as it came due?

Yes ❑ No ❑

If "Yes", complete Schedule M, Item 16.2.

3. — Surety bond or fidelity bond

Have you ever been refused for a surety or fidelity bond?

Yes ❑ No ❑

If "Yes", complete Schedule M, Item 16.3.

4. — Garnishments, unsatisfied judgments or directions to pay

Has any federal, provincial, territorial, state authority or court ever issued any of the following against you regarding your indebtedness or, to the best of your knowledge, the indebtedness of a firm where you are or were a partner, director, officer or major shareholder:

	Yes	**No**
Garnishment	❑	❑
Unsatisfied judgment	❑	❑
Direction to pay	❑	❑

If "Yes", complete Schedule M, Item 16.4.

Item 17 — Ownership of securities and derivatives firms

Are you now, or have you ever been, a partner or major shareholder of any firm (including your sponsoring firm) whose business is trading in or advising on securities or derivatives or both?

Yes ❑ No ❑

If "Yes", complete Schedule N.

Item 18 — Agent for service

By submitting this form, you certify that in each jurisdiction of Canada where you have appointed an agent for service, you have completed the appointment of agent for service required in that jurisdiction.

Item 19 — Submission to jurisdiction

By submitting this form, you agree to be subject to the securities legislation or derivatives legislation or both of each jurisdiction of Canada, and to the by-laws, regulations, rules, rulings and policies (collectively referred to as "rules" in this form) of the SROs to which you have submitted this form. This includes the jurisdiction of any tribunals or any proceedings that relate to your activities as a registrant or a partner, director or officer of a registrant under that securities legislation or derivatives legislation or both or as an Approved Person under SRO rules.

Item 20 — Notice of collection and use of personal information

The personal information required under this form is collected on behalf of, and used by, the securities regulatory authorities in the jurisdictions set out in Schedule O to administer and enforce certain provisions of their securities legislation or derivatives legislation or both.

By submitting this form, the individual consents to the collection by the securities regulatory authorities of this personal information, and any police records, records from other government or non-governmental regulators or SROs, credit records and employment records about the individual that the securities regulatory authorities may need to complete their review of the information submitted in this form relating to the individual's continued fitness for registration or approval, if applicable, in accordance with the legal authority of the securities regulatory authorities while the individual is registered with or approved by it. Securities regulatory authorities may contact government and private bodies or agencies, individuals, corporations and other organizations for information about the individual.

If you have any questions about the collection and use of this information, contact the securities regulatory authority in any jurisdiction in which the required information is submitted. See Schedule O for details. In Québec, you can also contact the Commission d'accès à l'information at 1-888-528-7741 or visit its website at www.cai.gouv.qc.ca.

SROs

The principal purpose for the collection of personal information is to assess your suitability for registration or approval and to assess your continued fitness for registration or approval in accordance with the applicable securities legislation and the rules of the SROs.

By submitting this form, you authorize the SROs to which this form is submitted to collect any information from any source whatsoever. This includes, but is not limited to, personal confidential information about you that is otherwise protected by law such as police, credit, employment, education and proficiency course completion records, and records from other government or non-governmental regulatory authorities, securities commissions, stock exchanges, or other SROs, private bodies, agencies, individuals or corporations, as may be necessary for the SROs to complete their review of your form or continued fitness for registration or approval in accordance with their rules for the duration of the period you remain so registered or approved. You further consent to and authorize the transfer of confidential information between SROs, securities commissions or stock exchanges from whom you now, or may in the future, seek registration or approval, or with which you are currently registered or approved for the purpose of determining fitness or continued fitness for registration or approval or in connection with the performance of an investigation or other exercise of regulatory authority, whether or not you are registered with or approved by them.

Part 3: REGISTRATION

By submitting this form, you certify that you understand the rules of the applicable SROs of which you are seeking registration or approval or of which your sponsoring firm is a member or participating organization. You also undertake to become conversant with the rules of any SROs of which you or your sponsoring firm becomes a member or participating organization. You agree to be bound by, observe and comply with these rules as they are from time to time amended or supplemented, and you agree to keep yourself fully informed about them as they are amended and supplemented. You submit to the jurisdiction of the SROs from whom you are seeking registration or approval, or of which your sponsoring firm is now or in the future becomes a member or participating organization and, wherever applicable, their Governors, Directors and Committees. You agree that any registration or approval granted pursuant to this form may be revoked, terminated or suspended at any time in accordance with the then applicable rules of the respective SROs. In the event of any such revocation or termination, you must terminate all activities which require registration or approval and, thereafter, not perform services that require registration or approval for any member of the SROs or any approved affiliated company or other affiliate of such member without obtaining the approval of or registration with the SROs, in accordance with their rules.

By submitting this form, you undertake to notify the SROs from whom you are seeking registration or approval or with which you are currently or may in the future be registered or approved of any material change to the information herein provided in accordance with their respective rules. You agree to the transfer of this form, without amendment, to other SROs in the event that at some time in the future you seek registration or approval from such other SROs.

You certify that you have discussed the questions in this form, together with this Agreement, with an Officer, Supervisor or Branch Manager of your sponsoring member firm and, to your knowledge and belief, the authorized Officer, Supervisor or Branch Manager was satisfied that you fully understood the questions and the terms of this Agreement. You further certify that your business activities that are subject to securities rules and derivatives rules or both will be limited strictly to those permitted by the category of your registration or approval.

Item 21 — Warning

It is an offence under securities legislation and derivatives legislation, including commodity futures legislation, to give false or misleading information on this form.

Item 22 — Certification

1. — Certification — NRD format

I confirm I have discussed the questions in this form with an officer, branch manager or supervisor of my sponsoring firm. To the best of my knowledge, the officer, branch manager or supervisor was satisfied that I fully understood the questions. I will limit my activities to those permitted by my category of registration.

If the business location specified in this form is a residence, I hereby give my consent for the regulator or, in Québec, the securities regulatory authority to enter that residence for the administration of securities legislation and derivatives legislation, including commodity futures legislation.

❑ I am making this submission as agent for the individual identified in this form. By checking this box, I certify that the individual provided me with all of the information on this form and the certification above.

2. — Certification — Format other than NRD format

Individual

By signing below, I certify to the regulator, or in Québec the securities regulatory authority, in each jurisdiction where I am filing or submitting this form, either directly or through the principal regulator, that:

- I have read this form and understand the questions,

- all of the information provided on this form is true, and complete, and

- if the business location specified in this form is a residence, I hereby give my consent for the regulator or, in Québec, the securities regulatory authority to enter that residence for the administration of securities legislation and derivatives legislation, including commodity futures legislation.

Signature of individual .... Date ....

Authorized partner or officer of the firm

By signing below, I certify to the regulator, or in Québec the securities regulatory authority, in each jurisdiction where I am submitting this form, either directly or through the principal regulator, for the individual that:

- the individual identified in this form will be engaged by the sponsoring firm as a registered individual or a permitted individual, and

- I have, or a branch manager, or supervisor, or another officer or partner has, discussed the questions set out in this form with the individual and, to the best of my knowledge, the individual fully understands the questions.

Name of firm ....

Name of authorized signing officer or partner ....

Title of authorized signing officer or partner ....

Signature of authorized signing officer or partner ....

Date signed .... (YYYY/MM/DD)

Schedule A — Names (Item 1)

Item 1.2 — Other personal names

Name 1:

....

Last name First name Second name (N/A ❑) Third name (N/A ❑)

Provide the reasons for the use of this name (for example, marriage, divorce, court order, commonly used name or nickname).

....

When did you use this name? From: To:

....

(YYYY/MM) (YYYY/MM)

Name 2:

....

Last name First name Second name (N/A ❑) Third name (N/A ❑)

Provide the reasons for the use of this name (for example, marriage, divorce, court order, commonly used name or nickname).

....

When did you use this name? From: To:

....

(YYYY/MM) (YYYY/MM)

Name 3:

....

Last name First name Second name (N/A ❑) Third name (N/A ❑)

Provide the reasons for the use of this name (for example, marriage, divorce, court order, commonly used name or nickname).

....

When did you use this name? From: To:

....

(YYYY/MM) (YYYY/MM)

Item 1.3 — Use of other names

Name 1:

Name: ....

Provide the reasons for the use of this other name (for example, trade name or team name): ....

If this other name is or was used in connection with any sponsoring firm, did the sponsoring firm approve the use of the name?

Yes ❑ No ❑ N/A ❑

When did you use this name? From: To:

....

(YYYY/MM) (YYYY/MM)

Name 2:

Name: ....

Provide the reasons for the use of this other name (for example, trade name or team name):

If this other name is or was used in connection with any sponsoring firm, did the sponsoring firm approve the use of the name?

Yes ❑ No ❑ N/A ❑

When did you use this name? From: To:

....

(YYYY/MM) (YYYY/MM)

Name 3:

Name: ....

Provide the reasons for the use of this other name (for example, trade name or team name):

If this other name is or was used in connection with any sponsoring firm, did the sponsoring firm approve the use of the name?

Yes ❑ No ❑ N/A ❑

When did you use this name? From: To:

....

Part 3:
REGISTRATION

(YYYY/MM) (YYYY/MM)

When did you use this name?   From: To:

....

(YYYY/MM)   (YYYY/MM)

Name 2:

Name: ....

Provide the reasons for the use of this other name (for example, trade name or team name):

If this other name is or was used in connection with any sponsoring firm, did the sponsoring firm approve the use of the name?

Yes ❑ No ❑

When did you use this name?   From: To:

....

(YYYY/MM)   (YYYY/MM)

Name 3:

Name: ....

Provide the reasons for the use of this other name (for example, trade name or team name):

If this other name is or was used in connection with any sponsoring firm, did the sponsoring firm approve the use of the name?

Yes ❑ No ❑

When did you use this name?   From: To:

....

(YYYY/MM)   (YYYY/MM)

Schedule B — Residential address (Item 2)

Item 2.1 — Current and previous residential addresses

If you have lived at your current address for less than 10 years, list all previous addresses for the past 10 years.

You do not have to include a postal code or ZIP code, or a telephone number for any previous address.

Address 1:

Residential address: ....

(number, street, city, province, territory or state, country)

When did you live at this address?   From: To:

....

(YYYY/MM)   (YYYY/MM)

Address 2:

Residential address: ....

(number, street, city, province, territory or state, country)

When did you live at this address?   From: To:

....

(YYYY/MM)   (YYYY/MM)

Address 3:

Residential address: ....

(number, street, city, province, territory or state, country)

When did you live at this address?   From: To:

....

(YYYY/MM)   (YYYY/MM)

Schedule C — Individual Categories (Item 6)

Check each category for which you are seeking registration, approval or review as a permitted individual.

Categories common to all jurisdictions under securities legislation

Firm categories [Format other than NRD format only]

❑ Investment Dealer

❑ Mutual Fund Dealer

❑ Scholarship Plan Dealer
❑ Exempt Market Dealer
❑ Restricted Dealer
❑ Portfolio Manager
❑ Restricted Portfolio Manager
❑ Investment Fund Manager

Individual categories and permitted activities

❑ Dealing Representative
❑ Advising Representative
❑ Associate Advising Representative
❑ Ultimate Designated Person
❑ Chief Compliance Officer
 Permitted Individual
❑ Officer — Specify title:
❑ Director
❑ Partner
❑ Shareholder
❑ Branch Manager (MFDA members only)
❑ IIROC approval only

IIROC

Approval categories

❑ Executive
❑ Director (Industry)
❑ Director (Non-Industry)
❑ Supervisor
❑ Investor
❑ Registered Representative
❑ Investment Representative
❑ Trader

Additional approval categories

❑ Chief Compliance Officer
❑ Chief Financial Officer
❑ Ultimate Designated Person

Products

❑ Non-Trading
❑ Securities
❑ Options
❑ Futures Contracts and Futures Contract Options
❑ Mutual Funds only

Customer type

❑ Retail
❑ Institutional
❑ Not Applicable

Portfolio management

❑ Portfolio Management

Categories under local commodity futures and derivatives legislation

Ontario

Firm categories

❏ Commodity Trading Adviser
❏ Commodity Trading Counsel
❏ Commodity Trading Manager
❏ Futures Commission Merchant

Individual categories and permitted activities

❏ Advising Representative
❏ Salesperson
❏ Branch Manager
❏ Officer — Specify title:
❏ Director
❏ Partner
❏ Shareholder
❏ IIROC approval only

Manitoba

Firm categories

❏ Dealer (Merchant)
❏ Dealer (Futures Commission Merchant)
❏ Dealer (Floor Broker)
❏ Adviser
❏ Local

Individual categories and permitted activities

❏ Floor Broker
❏ Salesperson
❏ Branch Manager
❏ Adviser
❏ Officer — Specify title:
❏ Director
❏ Partner
❏ Futures Contracts Portfolio Manager
❏ Associate Futures Contracts Portfolio Manager
❏ IIROC approval only
❏ Local

Québec

Firm categories

[ ] Derivatives Dealer
[ ] Derivatives Portfolio Manager

Individual categories and permitted activities

[ ] Derivatives Dealing Representative
[ ] Derivatives Advising Representative
[ ] Derivatives Associate Advising Representative

Schedule D — Address and agent for service (Item 7)

Item 7.1 — Address for service

You must have one address for service in each province or territory in which you are now, or are seeking to become, a registered individual or permitted individual. A post office box is not an acceptable address for service.

Address for service: ....

(number, street, city, province or territory, postal code)

Telephone number: (........) .... Fax number: (........) ....

Business e-mail address ....

Item 7.2 — Agent for service

If you have appointed an agent for service, provide the following information about the agent. The address for service provided above must be the address of the agent named below.

Name of agent for service: .... *(if applicable)*

Contact person: ....

Last name, First name

Schedule E — Proficiency (Item 8)

Item 8.1 — Course, examination or designation information and other education

Course, examination, designation or other education	Date completed (YYYY/MM/DD)	Date exempted (YYYY/MM/DD)	Regulator/securities regulatory authority granting the exemption

If you have listed the CFA Charter in Item 8.1, please indicate by checking "Yes" below if you are a current member of the CFA Institute permitted to use this charter.

Yes ❑ No ❑

If "No", please explain why you no longer hold this designation:

....

If you have listed the Canadian Investment Manager Designation in Item 8.1, please indicate by checking "Yes" below if you are currently permitted to use this designation.

Yes ❑ No ❑

If "No", please explain why you no longer hold this designation:

....

Schedule F — Proficiency (Items 8.3 and 8.4)

Item 8.3 — Exemption refusal

Complete the following for each exemption that was refused.

1. Which securities regulator, derivatives regulator or SRO refused to grant the exemption?

....

State the name of the course, examination, designation or experience requirement:

....

State the reason given for not being granted the exemption:

....

Date exemption refused: .... (YYYY/MM/DD)

2. Which securities regulator, derivatives regulator or SRO refused to grant the exemption?

....

State the name of the course, examination, designation or experience requirement:

....

State the reason given for not being granted the exemption:

....

Date exemption refused: .... (YYYY/MM/DD)

3. Which securities regulator, derivatives regulator or SRO refused to grant the exemption?

....

State the name of the course, examination, designation or experience requirement:

....

State the reason given for not being granted the exemption:

....

Date exemption refused: .... (YYYY/MM/DD)

Item 8.4 — Relevant securities industry experience

Describe your responsibilities in areas relating to the category you are applying for, including the title(s) you have held, as well as the start and end dates:

....

What is the percentage of your time devoted to these activities?

..........%

Indicate the continuing education activities in which you have participated during the last 36 months and that are relevant to the category of registration you are applying for:

....

Schedule G — Current employment, other business activities, officer positions held and directorships (Item 10)

Complete a separate Schedule G for each of your current business and employment activities, including employment and business activities with your sponsoring firm and any employment and business activities outside your sponsoring firm. Also include all officer or director positions and any other equivalent positions held, as well as positions of influence. The information must be provided

- whether or not you receive compensation for such services, and

- whether or not any such position is business related.

1. — Start date .... (YYYY/MM/DD)

2. — Firm information

❏ Check here if this activity is employment with your sponsoring firm.

If the activity is with your sponsoring firm, you are not required to indicate the firm name and address information below:

Name of business or employer: ....

Address of business or employer: .... (number, street, city, province, territory or state, country)

Name and title of your immediate supervisor: ....

3. — Description of duties

Describe all employment and business activities related to this employer. Include the nature of the business and your duties, title or relationship with the business. If you are seeking registration that requires specific experience, include details such as level of responsibility, value of accounts under direct supervision, number of years of experience, and percentage of time spent on each activity.

....

4. — Number of work hours per week

How many hours per week do you devote to this business or employment? ....

If this activity is employment with your sponsoring firm and you work less than 30 hours per week, explain why.

....

5. — Conflicts of interest

If you have more than one employer or are engaged in business related activities:

A. Disclose any potential for confusion by clients and any potential for conflicts of interest arising from your multiple employment or business related activities or proposed business related activities.

....

B. Indicate whether or not any of your employers or organizations where you engage in business related activities are listed on an exchange.

....

C. Confirm whether the firm has procedures for minimizing potential conflicts of interest and if so, confirm that you are aware of these procedures.

....

D. State the name of the person at your sponsoring firm who has reviewed and approved your multiple employment or business related activities or proposed business related activities.

....

E. If you do not perceive any conflicts of interest arising from this employment, explain why.

....

Schedule H — Previous employment and other activities
(Item 11)

Provide the following information for each of your employment and other activities in the past 10-years. Account for all of your time, including full-time and part-time employment, self-employment or military service. Include your status for each, such as unemployed, full-time student, or other similar statuses. Do not include short-term employment of four months or less while a student, unless it was in the securities, derivatives or financial industry.

In addition to the information required in the paragraph above, if you were employed or had business activities in the securities or derivatives industry or both during and before the 10-year period, disclose all your securities and derivatives or both employment or business activities (both before and during the 10-year period).

❏ Unemployed

❏ Full-time student

❏ Employed or self-employed

From: .... (YYYY/MM)

To: .... (YYYY/MM)

Complete the following only if you are, or were, employed or self-employed during this period.

Name of business or employer:

....

Address of business or employer:

.... (number, street, city, province, territory or state, country)

Name and title of immediate supervisor, if applicable:

....

Describe the firm's business, your position, duties and your relationship to the firm. If you are seeking registration in a category of registration that requires specific experience, include details of that experience. Examples include level of responsibility, value of accounts under direct supervision, number of years of that experience and research experience, and percentage of time spent on each activity.

Reason why you left the firm:

....

Schedule I — Resignations and terminations (Item 12)

Item 12.1

For each allegation of violation of any statutes, regulations, rules or internal/external standards of conduct, state below (1) the name of the firm from which you resigned, were terminated or dismissed for cause, (2) whether you resigned, were terminated or dismissed for cause, (3) the date you resigned, were terminated or dismissed for cause, and (4) the circumstances relating to your resignation, termination or dismissal for cause.

....

Item 12.2

For each allegation of failure to supervise compliance with any statutes, regulations, rules or standards of conduct, state below, (1) the name of the firm from which you resigned, were terminated or dismissed for cause, (2) whether you resigned, were terminated or dismissed for cause, (3) the date you resigned, were terminated or dismissed for cause, and (4) the circumstances relating to your resignation, termination or dismissal for cause.

....

Item 12.3

For each allegation of fraud or the wrongful taking of property, including theft, state below (1) the name of the firm from which you resigned, were terminated or dismissed for cause, (2) whether you resigned, were terminated or dismissed for cause, (3) the date you resigned, were terminated or dismissed for cause, and (4) the circumstances relating to your resignation, termination or dismissal for cause.

Part 3:
REGISTRATION

Schedule J — Regulatory disclosure (Item 13)

Item 13.1 — Securities and derivatives regulation

a) For each registration or licence, state below (1) the name of the firm, (2) the securities or derivatives regulator with which you are, or were, registered or licensed, (3) the type or category of registration or licence, and (4) the period that you held the registration or licence.

....

b) For each registration or licence refused, state below (1) the name of the firm, (2) the securities or derivatives regulator that refused the registration or licence, (3) the type or category of registration or licence refused, (4) the date of the refusal, and (5) the reasons for the refusal.

....

c) For each exemption from registration denied or licence refused, *other than what was disclosed in Item 8.3 of this form*, state below (1) the party that was refused the exemption from registration or licence, (2) the securities or derivatives regulator that refused the exemption from registration or licence, (3) the type or category of registration or licence refused, (4) the date of the refusal, and (5) the reasons for the refusal.

....

d) For each order or disciplinary proceeding, state below (1) the name of the firm, (2) the securities or derivatives regulator that issued the order or is conducting or conducted the proceeding, (3) the date any notice of proceeding was issued, (4) the date any order or settlement was made, (5) a summary of any notice, order or settlement (including any sanctions imposed), (6) whether you are or were a partner, director, officer or major shareholder of the firm and named individually in the order or disciplinary proceeding, and (7) any other relevant details.

....

Item 13.2 — SRO regulation

a) For each approval, state below (1) the name of the firm, (2) the SRO with which you are or were an approved person, (3) the categories of approval, and (4) the period that you held the approval.

....

b) For each approval refused, state below (1) the name of the firm, (2) the SRO that refused the approval, (3) the category of approval refused, (4) the date of the refusal, and (5) the reasons for the refusal.

....

c) For each order or disciplinary proceeding, state below (1) the name of the firm, (2) the SRO that issued the order or that is, or was, conducting the proceeding, (3) the date any notice of proceeding was issued, (4) the date any order or settlement was made, (5) a summary of any notice, order or settlement (including any sanctions imposed), (6) whether you are or were a partner, director, officer or major shareholder of the firm and named individually in the order or disciplinary proceeding, and (7) any other information that you think is relevant or that the regulator or, in Québec, the securities regulatory authority may request.

....

Item 13.3 — Non-securities regulation

a) For each registration or licence, state below (1) the party who is, or was, registered or licensed (if insurance licensed, also indicate the name of the insurance agency), (2) with which regulatory authority, or under what legislation, the party is, or was, registered or licensed, (3) the type or category of registration or licence, and (4) the period that the party held the registration or licence.

....

b) For each registration or licence refused, state below (1) the party that was refused registration or licensing (if insurance licensed, also indicate the name of the insurance agency), (2) with which regulatory authority, or under what legislation, the registration or licence was refused, (3) the type or category of registration or licence refused, (4) the date of the refusal, and (5) the reasons for the refusal.

....

c) For each order or disciplinary proceeding, indicate below (1) the party against whom the order was made or the proceeding taken (if insurance licensed, indicate the name of the insurance agency), (2) the regulatory authority that made the order or that is, or was, conducting the proceeding, or under what legislation the order was made or the proceeding is being, or was conducted, (3) the date any notice of proceeding was issued, (4) the date any order or settlement was made, (5) a summary of any notice, order or settlement (including any sanctions imposed), (6) whether you are or were a partner, director, officer or major shareholder of the firm and named individually in the order or disciplinary proceeding and (7) any other information that you think is relevant or that the regulatory authority may request.

....

Schedule K — Criminal disclosure (Item 14)

Item 14.1

For each charge, state below (1) the type of charge, (2) the date of the charge, (3) any trial or appeal dates, and (4) the court location.

....

Item 14.2

For each finding of guilty, pleading no contest to, or granting of an absolute or conditional discharge from a criminal offence, state below (1) the offence, (2) the date found guilty, and (3) the disposition (any penalty or fine and the date any fine was paid).

....

Item 14.3

For each charge, state below (1) the name of the firm, (2) the type of charge, (3) the date of the charge, (4) any trial or appeal dates, and (5) the court location.

....

Item 14.4

For each finding of guilty, pleading no contest to, or granting of an absolute or conditional discharge from a criminal offence, state below (1) the name of the firm, (2) the offence, (3) the date of the conviction, and (4) the disposition (any penalty or fine and the date any fine was paid).

....

Schedule L — Civil disclosure (Item 15)

Item 15.1

For each outstanding civil proceeding, state below (1) the dates the statement of claim and statement of defence were issued, (2) the name of the plaintiff(s) in the proceeding, (3) whether the proceeding is pending or on appeal, (4) whether the proceeding was against a firm where you are, or were, a partner, director, officer or major shareholder and whether you have been named individually in the allegations, and (5) the jurisdiction where the action is being pursued.

....

Item 15.2

For each civil proceeding, state below (1) the dates the statement of claim and statement of defence were issued, (2) each plaintiff in the proceeding, (3) the jurisdiction where the action was pursued, (4) whether the proceeding was about a firm where you are, or were, a partner, director, officer or major shareholder and whether you have been named individually in the allegations and (5) a summary of any disposition or any settlement over $10,000. You must disclose any actions settled without admission of liability.

....

Schedule M — Financial Disclosure (Item 16)

Item 16.1 — Bankruptcy

(a) For each event, state below (1) the date of the petition or voluntary assignment, (2) the person or firm about whom this disclosure is being made, (3) any amounts currently owing, (4) the creditors, (5) the status of the matter, (6) a summary of any disposition or settlement, (7) date of discharge or release, if applicable, and (8) any other information that you think is relevant or that the regulator or, in Québec, the securities regulatory authority may request.

....

(b) For each event, state below (1) the date of the proposal, (2) the person or firm about whom this disclosure is being made, (3) any amounts currently owing, (4) the creditors, (5) the status of the matter, (6) a summary of any disposition or settlement, and (7) any other information that you think is relevant or that the regulator or, in Québec, the securities regulatory authority may request.

....

(c) For each event, state below (1) the date of the proceeding, (2) the person or firm about whom this disclosure is being made, (3) any amounts currently owing, (4) the creditors, (5) the status of the matter, (6) a summary of any disposition or settlement, and (7) any other information that you think is relevant or that the regulator or, in Québec, the securities regulatory authority may request.

....

(d) For each proceeding, arrangement or compromise with creditors, state below (1) the date of proceeding, (2) the person or firm about whom this disclosure is being made, (3) any amounts currently owing, (4) the creditors, (5) the status of the matter, (6) a summary of any disposition or settlement, and (7) any other information that you think is relevant or that the regulator or, in Québec, the securities regulatory authority may request.

....

Item 16.2 — Debt obligation

For each event, state below (1) the person or firm that failed to meet its financial obligation, (2) the amount that was owing at the time the person or firm failed to meet its financial obligation, (3) the person or firm to whom the amount is, or was, owing, (4) any relevant dates (for example, when payments are due or when final payment was made), (5) any amounts currently owing, and (6) any other information that you think is relevant or that the regulator or, in Québec, the securities regulatory authority may request, including why the obligation has not been met/satisfied.

Part 3: REGISTRATION

....

Item 16.3 — Surety bond or fidelity bond

For each bond refused, state below (1) the name of the bonding company, (2) the address of the bonding company, (3) the date of the refusal, and (4) the reasons for the refusal.

....

Item 16.4 — Garnishments, unsatisfied judgments or directions to pay

For each garnishment, unsatisfied judgment or direction to pay regarding your indebtedness, indicate below (1) the amount that was owing at the time the garnishment, judgment or direction to pay was rendered, (2) the person or firm to whom the amount is, or was, owing, (3) any relevant dates (for example, when payments are due or when final payment was made), (4) the percentage of earnings to be garnished or the amount to be paid, (5) any amounts currently owing, and (6) any other information that you think is relevant or that the regulator or, in Québec, the securities regulatory authority may request.

....

Schedule N — Ownership of securities and derivatives firms (Item 17)

Name of firm (whose business is trading in or advising on securities or derivatives, or both):

....

What is your relationship to the firm? Partner ❏ Major shareholder ❏
What is the period of this relationship?

From: To: *(if applicable)*

....
(YYYY/MM)   (YYYY/MM)

Provide the following information:

a) State the number, value, class and percentage of securities, or the amount of partnership interest you own or propose to acquire when you are registered or approved as a result of the review of this form. If acquiring shares when you are so approved or registered, state the source (for example, treasury shares, or if upon transfer, state name of transferor).

....

b) State the market value (approximate, if necessary) of any subordinated debentures or bonds of the firm to be held by you or any other subordinated loan to be made by you to the firm:

....

c) If another person or firm has provided you with funds to invest in the firm, provide the name of the person or firm and state the relationship between you and that person or firm:

....

d) Are the funds to be invested (or proposed to be invested) guaranteed directly or indirectly by any person or firm?

Yes ❏ No ❏

If "Yes", provide the name of the person or firm and state the relationship between you and that person or firm:

....

e) Have you directly or indirectly given up any rights relating to these securities or this partnership interest, or do you, when you are registered or approved as a result of the review of this form, intend to give up any of these rights (including by hypothecation, pledging or depositing as collateral the securities or partnership interest with any firm or person)?

Yes ❏ No ❏

If "Yes", provide the name of the person or firm, state the relationship between you and that person or firm and describe the rights that have been or will be given up: ....

f) Is a person other than you the beneficial owner of the shares, bonds, debentures, partnership units or notes held by you?

Yes ❏ No ❏

If "Yes", complete (g), (h) and (i).

g) Name of beneficial owner:

....	....	....	....
Last name	First name	Second name	Third name
		(N/A ❏)	(N/A ❏)

h) Residential address:

.... (number, street, city, province, territory or state, country, postal code)

i) Occupation:

....

Schedule O — Contact information for Notice of collection and use of personal information

Alberta

Alberta Securities Commission

Suite 600, 250-5th St. SW

Calgary, AB T2P 0R4

Attention: Information Officer

Telephone: (403) 297-6454

British Columbia

British Columbia Securities Commission

P.O. Box 10142, Pacific Centre

701 West Georgia Street

Vancouver, BC V7Y 1L2

Attention: Freedom of Information Officer

Telephone: (604) 899-6500 or (800) 373-6393 (in Canada)

Manitoba

The Manitoba Securities Commission

500 - 400 St. Mary Avenue

Winnipeg, MB R3C 4K5

Attention: Director of Registrations

Telephone: (204) 945-2548

Fax (204) 945-0330

New Brunswick

Financial and Consumer Services Commission of New Brunswick / Commission des services financiers et des services aux consommateurs du Nouveau-Brunswick

Suite 300, 85 Charlotte Street

Saint John, NB E2L 2J2

Attention: Director of Securities

Telephone: (506) 658-3060

Newfoundland and Labrador

Superintendent of Securities, Service NL

Government of Newfoundland and Labrador

P.O. Box 8700

2nd Floor, West Block

Confederation Building

St. John's, NL A1B 4J6

Attention: Manager of Registrations

Telephone: (709) 729-5661

Nova Scotia

Nova Scotia Securities Commission

Suite 400, 5251 Duke Street

Halifax, NS B3J 1P3

Attention: Deputy Director, Capital Markets

Telephone: (902) 424-7768

Northwest Territories

Government of the Northwest Territories

Department of Justice

1st Floor Stuart M. Hodgson Building

5009 - 49th Street

Yellowknife, NWT X1A 2L9

Attention: Deputy Superintendent of Securities
Telephone: (867) 920-8984

Nunavut
Government of Nunavut
Department of Justice
P.O. Box 1000 Station 570
Iqaluit, NU X0A 0H0
Attention: Deputy Registrar of Securities
Telephone: (867) 975-6590

Ontario
Ontario Securities Commission
22nd Floor
20 Queen Street West
Toronto, ON M5H 3S8
Attention: Compliance and Registrant Regulation
Telephone: (416) 593-8314
e-mail: registration@osc.gov.on.ca

Prince Edward Island
Securities Office
Department of Community Affairs and Attorney General
P.O. Box 2000
Charlottetown, PE C1A 7N8
Attention: Deputy Registrar of Securities
Telephone: (902) 368-6288

Québec
Autorité des marchés financiers
800, square Victoria, 22e étage
C.P. 246, tour de la Bourse
Montréal (Québec) H4Z 1G3
Attention: Responsable de l'accès à l'information
Telephone: (514) 395-0337 or (877) 525-0337

Saskatchewan
Financial and Consumer Affairs Authority of Saskatchewan
Suite 601, 1919 Saskatchewan Drive
Regina, SK S4P 4H2
Attention: Deputy Director, Capital Markets
Telephone: (306) 787-5871

Yukon
Government of Yukon
Superintendent of Securities
Department of Community Services
P.O. Box 2703 C-6
Whitehorse, YT Y1A 2C6
Attention: Superintendent of Securities
Telephone: (867) 667-5314

Self-regulatory organization
Investment Industry Regulatory Organization of Canada
121 King Street West, Suite 2000
Toronto, Ontario M5H 3T9
Attention: Privacy Officer
Telephone: (416) 364-6133

Form 33-109F5 — Change of Registration Information

(sections 3.1 and 4.1)

General Instructions

Complete and submit this form to notify the relevant regulator(s) or, in Québec, the securities regulatory authority, or self-regulatory organization (SRO) of changes to information in the following forms:

- Form 33-109F6, except for the changes set out in section 3.1 of National Instrument 33-109, or

- Form 33-109F4.

Name of firm ....

Registration categories ....

NRD number (firm) ....

How to submit this form

To report changes to information in a Form 33-109F4, submit this form at the National Registration Database website in NRD format at www.nrd.ca.

Submit this form in a format other than NRD format to report changes to information in a:

a) Form 33-109F6, or

b) Form 33-109F4, if the individual is relying on the temporary hardship exemption in section 5.1 of National Instrument 31-102 *National Registration Database*.

Item 1 — Type of form

Check the form that is being updated:

❏ Form 33-109F6

If submitting changes to Form 33-109F6, please attach a blackline of the amended sections of the form.;

❏ Form 33-109F4 Name of individual ....

Item 2 — Details of change

Provide the item number and details for each change to the form selected above:

Item number .... Details ....

Effective date of change .... (YYYY/MM/DD)

Item 3 — Notice of collection and use of personal information

The personal information required under this form is collected on behalf of, and used by, the securities regulatory authorities in the jurisdictions set out in Schedule A to administer and enforce certain provisions of their securities legislation or derivatives legislation or both.

The personal information required under this form is also collected by and used by the SRO set out in Schedule A to administer and enforce its by-laws, regulations, rules, rulings and policies.

By submitting this form, the individual consents to the collection by the securities regulatory authorities or applicable SRO of this personal information, and any police records, records from other government or non-governmental regulators or SROs, credit records and employment records about the individual that the securities regulatory authorities or applicable SRO may need to complete their review of the information submitted in this form relating to the individual's continued fitness for registration or approval, if applicable, in accordance with the legal authority of the securities regulatory authorities while the individual is registered with or approved by it. Securities regulatory authorities or SROs may contact government and private bodies or agencies, individuals, corporations and other organizations for information about the individual.

If you have any questions about the collection and use of this information, contact the securities regulatory authorities or applicable SRO in any jurisdiction in which the required information is submitted. See Schedule A for details. In Québec, you can also contact the Commission d'accès à l'information at 1-888-528-7741 or visit its website at www.cai.gouv.qc.ca.

Item 4 — Warning

It is an offence under securities legislation and derivatives legislation, including commodity futures legislation, to give false or misleading information on this form.

Item 5 — Certification

1. Use the following certification when submitting this form in NRD format when making changes to Form 33-109F4

I confirm I have discussed the questions in this form with an officer, branch manager or supervisor of my sponsoring firm. To the best of my knowledge and belief, the officer, branch manager or supervisor was satisfied that I fully understood the questions. I will limit my activities to those permitted by my category of registration.

[ ] I am making this submission as agent for the individual identified in this form. By checking this box, I certify that the individual provided me with all of the information on this form.

2. Use the following certification when submitting this form in a format other than NRD format when making changes to Form 33-109F6

By signing below I certify to each regulator or, in Québec, the securities regulatory authority, in each jurisdiction where I am submitting this form, either directly or through the principal regulator, that:

- I have read this form and understand the questions, and

- all of the information provided on this form is true, and complete.

Name of authorized signing officer or partner ....

Title of authorized signing officer or partner ....

Signature of authorized signing officer or partner ....

Date signed .... (YYYY/MM/DD)

3. Use the following certification when submitting this form in a format other than NRD format under the temporary hardship exemption in section 5.1 of NI 31-102 *National Registration Database* **when making change to Form 33-109F4**

By signing below, I certify to the regulator or, in Québec, the securities regulatory authority, in each jurisdiction where I am submitting this form, either directly or through the principal regulator, that:

- I have read this form and understand the questions; and

- all of the information provided on this form is true and complete.

Signature of individual ....

Date signed .... (YYYY/MM/DD)

Schedule A — Contact information for Notice of collection and use of personal information

Alberta

Alberta Securities Commission

Suite 600, 250-5th St. SW

Calgary, AB T2P 0R4

Attention: Information Officer

Telephone: (403) 297-6454

British Columbia

British Columbia Securities Commission

P.O. Box 10142, Pacific Centre

701 West Georgia Street

Vancouver, BC V7Y 1L2

Attention: Freedom of Information Officer

Telephone: (604) 899-6500 or (800) 373-6393 (in Canada)

Manitoba

The Manitoba Securities Commission

500 - 400 St. Mary Avenue

Winnipeg, MB R3C 4K5

Attention: Director of Registrations

Telephone: (204) 945-2548

Fax (204) 945-0330

New Brunswick

Financial and Consumer Services Commission of New Brunswick / Commission des services financiers et des services aux consommateurs du Nouveau-Brunswick

Suite 300, 85 Charlotte Street

Saint John, NB E2L 2J2

Attention: Director of Securities

Telephone: (506) 658-3060

Newfoundland and Labrador

Superintendent of Securities, Service NL

Government of Newfoundland and Labrador

P.O. Box 8700

2nd Floor, West Block

Confederation Building

St. John's, NL A1B 4J6

Attention: Manager of Registrations

Telephone: (709) 729-5661

Nova Scotia

Nova Scotia Securities Commission

Suite 400, 5251 Duke Street

Halifax, NS B3J 1P3

Attention: Deputy Director, Capital Markets

Telephone: (902) 424-7768

Northwest Territories

Government of the Northwest Territories

Department of Justice

1st Floor Stuart M. Hodgson Building

5009 - 49th Street

Yellowknife, NWT X1A 2L9

Attention: Deputy Superintendent of Securities

Telephone: (867) 920-8984

Nunavut

Government of Nunavut

Department of Justice

P.O. Box 1000 Station 570

Iqaluit, NU X0A 0H0

Attention: Deputy Registrar of Securities

Telephone: (867) 975-6590

Ontario

Ontario Securities Commission

22nd Floor

20 Queen Street West

Toronto, ON M5H 3S8

Attention: Compliance and Registrant Regulation

Telephone: (416) 593-8314

e-mail: registration@osc.gov.on.ca

Prince Edward Island

Securities Office

Department of Community Affairs and Attorney General

P.O. Box 2000

Charlottetown, PE C1A 7N8

Attention: Deputy Registrar of Securities

Telephone: (902) 368-6288

Québec

Autorité des marchés financiers

800, square Victoria, 22e étage

C.P. 246, tour de la Bourse

Montréal (Québec) H4Z 1G3

Attention: Responsable de l'accès à l'information

Telephone: (514) 395-0337 or (877) 525-0337

Saskatchewan

Financial and Consumer Affairs Authority of Saskatchewan

Suite 601, 1919 Saskatchewan Drive

Regina, SK S4P 4H2

Attention: Deputy Director, Capital Markets

Telephone: (306) 787-5871

Yukon

Government of Yukon

Superintendent of Securities

Department of Community Services

P.O. Box 2703 C-6

Whitehorse, YT Y1A 2C6

Attention: Superintendent of Securities

Telephone: (867) 667-5314

Self-regulatory organization

Investment Industry Regulatory Organization of Canada

121 King Street West, Suite 2000

Toronto, Ontario M5H 3T9

Attention: Privacy Officer

Telephone: (416) 364-6133

E-mail: PrivacyOfficer@iiroc.ca

Form 33-109F6 — Firm Registration

Who should complete this form?

This form is for firms seeking registration under securities legislation, derivatives legislation or both.

Complete and submit this form to seek initial registration as a dealer, adviser or investment fund manager, or to add one or more jurisdiction of Canada or categories to a firm's registration.

Definitions

In this form:

Chief compliance officer — see section 2.1 of NI 31-103.

Derivatives — financial instruments, such as futures contracts (including exchange traded contracts), futures options and swaps whose market price, value or payment obligations are derived from or based on one or more underlying interests. Derivatives can be in the form of instruments, agreements or securities.

Firm — the person or company seeking registration.

Foreign jurisdiction — see National Instrument 14-101 *Definitions*.

Form — Form 33-109F6 *Firm registration*.

NI 31-103 — National Instrument 31-103 *Registration Requirements, Exemptions and Ongoing Registrant Obligations*.

Jurisdiction or jurisdiction of Canada — see National Instrument 14-101 *Definitions*.

NI 33-109 — National Instrument 33-109 *Registration Information*.

NI 52-107 — National Instrument 52-107 *Acceptable Accounting Principles and Auditing Standards*.

NRD — National Registration Database. For more information, visit www.nrd-info.ca.

Parent — a person or company that directly or indirectly has significant control of another person or company.

Permitted individual — see NI 33-109.

Predecessor — any entity listed in question 3.6 of this form.

Principal regulator — see NI 33-109.

Significant control — a person or company has significant control of another person or company if the person or company:

- directly or indirectly holds voting securities representing more than 20 per cent of the outstanding voting rights attached to all outstanding voting securities of the other person or company, or

- directly or indirectly is able to elect or appoint a majority of the directors (or individuals performing similar functions or occupying similar positions) of the other person or company.

Specified affiliate — a person or company that is a parent of the firm, a specified subsidiary of the firm, or a specified subsidiary of the firm's parent.

Specified subsidiary — a person or company of which another person or company has significant control.

SRO — see National Instrument 14-101 *Definitions*.

Ultimate designated person — see section 2.1 of NI 31-103.

You — the individual who completes, submits, files and/or signs the form on behalf of the firm.

We and the regulator — the securities regulatory authority or regulator in the jurisdiction(s) of Canada where the firm is seeking registration.

Contents of the form

This form consists of the following:

Part 1 — Registration details

Part 2 — Contact information

Part 3 — Business history and structure

Part 4 — Registration history

Part 5 — Financial condition

Part 6 — Client relationships

Part 7 — Regulatory action

Part 8 — Legal action

Part 9 — Certification

Schedule A — Contact information for notice of collection and use of personal information

Schedule B — Submission to jurisdiction and appointment of agent for service

Schedule C — Form 31-103F1 *Calculation of excess working capital*

You are also required to submit the following supporting documents with your completed form:

1. Schedule B — Submission to jurisdiction and appointment of agent for service for each jurisdiction where the firm is seeking registration (question 2.4)

2. Business plan, policies and procedures manual, and client agreements (except in Ontario) (question 3.3)

3. Constating documents (question 3.7)

4. Organization chart (question 3.11)

5. Ownership chart (question 3.12)

6. Calculation of excess working capital (question 5.1)

7. Directors' resolution approving insurance (question 5.7)

8. Audited financial statements (question 5.13)

9. Letter of direction to auditors (question 5.14)

How to complete and submit the form

The firm is required to pay a registration fee in each jurisdiction of Canada where it is submitting and filing this form. Refer to the prescribed fees of the applicable jurisdiction for details.

All dollar values are in Canadian dollars. If a question does not apply to the firm, write "n/a" in the space for the answer.

If the firm is seeking registration in more than one jurisdiction of Canada or category, other than in the category of restricted dealer, you only need to complete and submit one form. If the firm is seeking registration as a restricted dealer, submit and file the form with each jurisdiction of Canada where the firm is seeking that registration.

You can complete this form:

• on paper and deliver it to the principal regulator or relevant SRO

• on paper, scan it and e-mail it to the principal regulator or SRO

If the firm is seeking registration in Ontario, and Ontario is not the firm's principal regulator, you must also file a copy of this form, without supporting documents, with the Ontario Securities Commission.

You can find contact information for submitting and filing the form in Appendix B of Companion Policy 33-109CP *Registration Information*.

We may accept the form in other formats. Please check with the regulator before you complete, submit and file the form. If you are completing the form on paper and need more space to answer a question, use a separate sheet of paper and attach it to this form. Clearly identify the question number.

You must include all supporting documents with your submission. We may ask you to provide other information and documents to help determine whether the firm is suitable for registration.

In most of this form, answers are required to questions that apply only to Canadian provinces and territories; you will find that the questions are referenced to "jurisdictions" or "jurisdiction of Canada". These refer to all provinces and territories of Canada. However, the questions in Part 4 — *Registration History* and Part 7 — *Regulatory Action* are to be answered in respect of any jurisdiction in the world.

It is an offence under securities legislation and derivatives legislation, including commodity futures legislation, to give false or misleading information on this form.

Updating the information on the form

See Part 3 of NI 33-109.

The firm is required to notify the regulator, within specified times, of any changes to the information on this form by submitting and filing Form 33-109F5 *Change of Registration Information*.

Collection and use of personal information

We and the SROs (if applicable) require personal information about the people referred to in this form as part of our review to determine whether the firm is suitable for registration. If the firm is approved, we also require this information to assess whether the firm continues to meet the registration requirements.

We may only:

- collect the personal information under the requirements in securities legislation or derivatives legislation or both
- use this information to administer and enforce provisions of the securities legislation or derivatives legislation or both

We may collect personal information from police records, records of other regulators or SROs, credit records, employment records, government and private bodies or agencies, individuals, corporations, and other organizations. We may also collect personal information indirectly.

We may provide personal information about the individuals referred to in this form to other regulators, securities or derivatives exchanges, SROs or similar organizations, if required for an investigation or other regulatory issue.

If anyone referred to in this form has any questions about the collection and use of their personal information, they can contact the regulator or SRO, if applicable, in the relevant jurisdiction of Canada. See Schedule A for details. In Québec, they can also contact the Commission d'accès à l'information du Québec at 1-888-528-7741 or visit its website at www.cai.gouv.qc.ca.

Part 1 — Registration details

1.1 — Firm's full legal name

Provide the full legal name of the firm as it appears on the firm's constating documents required under question 3.7. If the firm is a sole proprietorship, provide your first, last and any middle names.

If the firm's legal name is in English and French, provide both versions.

1.2 Firm's NRD number

For more information, visit www.nrd-info.ca.

1.3 — Why are you submitting this form?

Complete:

❑   To seek initial registration as a firm in one or more jurisdictions of Canada   The entire form

❑   To add one or more jurisdictions of Canada   Questions 1.1, 1.2, 1.4, 1.5, 2.4, 3.9, 5.4, 5.6*, and Part 9

❑   To add one or more categories to the firm's registration   Questions 1.1, 1.2, 1.4, 1.5, 3.1, 5.1, 5.4, 5.5, 5.6*, 5.7, 5.8, Part 6 and Part 9

* If the firm is adding Québec as a jurisdiction for registration in the category of mutual fund dealer or scholarship plan dealer, complete question 5.6.

1.4 — In what category and jurisdiction is the firm seeking registration? Check all that apply

(a) Categories under securities legislation

Jurisdiction

Abbreviations	Category	AB	BC	MB	NB	NL	NS	NT	NU	ON	PE	QC	SK	YT
Alberta (AB) British Columbia (BC)	Investment dealer	❑	❑	❑	❑	❑	❑	❑	❑	❑	❑	❑	❑	❑

Jurisdiction

Abbreviations	Category	AB	BC	MB	NB	NL	NS	NT	NU	ON	PE	QC	SK	YT
Manitoba (MB) New Brunswick (NB)	Mutual fund dealer	❑	❑	❑	❑	❑	❑	❑	❑	❑	❑	❑	❑	❑
Newfoundland and Labrador (NL)	Scholarship plan dealer	❑	❑	❑	❑	❑	❑	❑	❑	❑	❑	❑	❑	❑
Northwest Territories (NT) Nova Scotia (NS)	Exempt market dealer	❑	❑	❑	❑	❑	❑	❑	❑	❑	❑	❑	❑	❑
Nunavut (NU) Ontario (ON)	Restricted dealer Investment	❑	❑	❑	❑	❑	❑	❑	❑	❑	❑	❑	❑	❑
Prince Edward Island (PE) Québec (QC)	fund manager Portfolio	❑	❑	❑	❑	❑	❑	❑	❑	❑	❑	❑	❑	❑
Saskatchewan (SK) Yukon (YT)	manager Restricted portfolio manager	❑	❑	❑	❑	❑	❑	❑	❑	❑	❑	❑	❑	❑

(b) Categories under derivatives legislation (Manitoba and Ontario only)

Category	Manitoba
Dealer (merchant)	❑
Dealer (futures commission merchant)	❑
Dealer (floor broker)	❑
Local	❑
Adviser	❑
	Ontario
Commodity trading adviser	❑
Commodity trading counsel	❑
Commodity trading manager	❑
Futures commission merchant	❑

(c) Investment dealers and portfolio managers (Québec only)

If the firm is seeking registration in Québec as an investment dealer or a portfolio manager, will the firm also act as a:

Derivatives dealer	Yes ❑	No ❑
Derivatives portfolio manager	Yes ❑	No ❑

1.5 — Exemptions

Is the firm applying for any exemptions under securities or derivatives legislation?

Yes ❑ No ❑

If yes, provide the following information for each exemption:

Type of exemption

Legislation

Jurisdiction(s) where the firm has applied for the exemption

AB	BC	MB	NB	NL	NS	NT	NU	ON	PE	QC	SK	YT
❑	❑	❑	❑	❑	❑	❑	❑	❑	❑	❑	❑	❑

Part 2 — Contact information

Addresses

2.1 — Head office address

A post office box on its own is not acceptable for a head office address.

Address line 1

Address line 2

City	Province/territory/state

Country	Postal/zip code

Telephone number	Fax number
Website	

If the firm's head office is in Canada, go to question 2.3.

If the firm's head office is not in Canada, go to question 2.2.

2.2 — Firms whose head office is not in Canada

(a) Does the firm have any business location addresses in Canada?

Yes ❑ No ❑

If yes, provide the firm's primary Canadian business location address:

Address line 1	
Address line 2	
City	Province/territory/state
Postal code	

The securities regulatory authority in this jurisdiction of Canada is the firm's principal regulator in Canada.

(b) If a firm is not registered in a jurisdiction of Canada, indicate the jurisdiction of Canada in which the firm expects to conduct most of its activities that require registration as at the end of its current financial year or conducted most of its activities that require registration as at the end of its most recently completed financial year.

AB	BC	MB	NB	NL	NS	NT	NU	ON	PE	QC	SK	YT
❑	❑	❑	❑	❑	❑	❑	❑	❑	❑	❑	❑	❑

2.3 — Mailing address

A post office box is acceptable for a mailing address.

❑ Same as the head office address

Address line 1	
Address line 2	
City	Province/territory/state
Country	Postal/zip code

2.4 — Address for service and agent for service

If the firm does not have an office in a jurisdiction of Canada where it is seeking registration, it must appoint an agent for service in that jurisdiction of Canada.

Attach a completed Schedule B *Submission to jurisdiction and appointment of agent for service* for each jurisdiction of Canada where the firm is seeking registration and does not have an office.

Contact names

2.5 — Ultimate designated person

A registered firm must have an individual registered in the category of ultimate designated person.

Legal name	
Officer title	
Telephone number	
E-mail address	

NRD number, if available	

Address	
❏ Same as firm head office address	

Address line 1	

Address line 2	

City	Province/territory/state

Country	Postal/zip code

2.6 — Chief compliance officer

❏ Same as ultimate designated person

A registered firm must have an individual registered in the category of chief compliance officer.

Legal name	

Officer title	

Telephone number	

E-mail address	

NRD number, if available	

Address	
❏ Same as firm head office address	

Address line 1	

Address line 2	

City	Province/territory/state

Country	Postal/zip code

Part 3 — Business history and structure

Business activities

3.1 — The firm's business

Provide a description of the firm's proposed business, including its primary business activities, target market, and the products and services it will provide to clients.

3.2 — Other names

In addition to the firm's legal name in question 1.1, does the firm use any other names, such as a trade name?

Yes ❏ No ❏

If yes, list all other names and indicate if each name has been registered:

3.3 — Business documents

Does the firm have the following documents to support its business activities?

		Yes	No
(a)	Business plan for at least the next three years		
(b)	Policies and procedures manual, including account opening procedures and the firm's policy on fairness in allocation of investment opportunities, if applicable		

If no, explain why the firm does not have the document:

Attach the firm's business plan, policies and procedures manual and client agreements, including any investment policy statements and investment management agreements, except if the regulator in Ontario is the principal regulator of the firm seeking registration, unless the regulator in Ontario has requested they be provided.

History of the firm

3.4 — When was the firm created?

yyyy/mm/dd

3.5 — How was the firm created?

New start-up	❑	Go to question 3.7.
Merger or amalgamation	❑	Go to question 3.6.
Reorganization	❑	Go to question 3.6.
Other statutory arrangement	❑	Please specify below and go to question 3.6.

3.6 — Predecessors

List the entities that were merged, amalgamated, reorganized or otherwise arranged to create the firm.

3.7 — Constating documents

Attach the legal documents that established the firm as an entity, for example, the firm's articles and certificate of incorporation, any articles of amendments, partnership agreement or declaration of trust. If the firm is a sole proprietorship, provide a copy of the registration of trade name.

As part of their constating documents, firms whose head office is outside Canada may be required to provide proof of extra-provincial registration.

Business structure and ownership

3.8 — Type of legal structure

Sole proprietorship	❑	
Partnership	❑	
Limited partnership	❑	Name of general partner ....
Corporation	❑	
Other	❑	Please specify ....

3.9 — Business registration number, if applicable

This is the firm's corporate registration number or Québec enterprise number (NEQ).

List the firm's business registration number for each jurisdiction of Canada where the firm is seeking registration.

Business registration number	Jurisdiction of Canada

3.10 — Permitted individuals

List all permitted individuals of the firm.

Name	Title	NRD number, if applicable

3.11 — Organization chart

Attach an organization chart showing the firm's reporting structure. Include all permitted individuals, the ultimate designated person and the chief compliance officer.

3.12 — Ownership chart

Attach a chart showing the firm's structure and ownership. At a minimum, include all parents, specified affiliates and specified subsidiaries. Include the name of the person or company, and class, type, amount and voting percentage of ownership of the firm's securities.

Part 4 — Registration history

The questions in Part 4 apply to any jurisdiction and any foreign jurisdiction.

4.1 — Securities registration

In the last seven years, has the firm, or any predecessors or specified affiliates of the firm been registered or licensed to trade or advise in securities or derivatives?

Yes ❑ No ❑

If yes, provide the following information for each registration:

Name of entity

Registration category

Regulator/organization

Date registered or licensed (yyyy/mm/dd)	Expiry date, if applicable (yyyy/mm/dd)

Jurisdiction

4.2 — Exemption from securities registration

Is the firm currently relying on any exemptions from registration or licensing to trade or advise in securities or derivatives?

Yes ❑ No ❑

If yes, provide the following information for each exemption:

Type of exemption

Regulator/organization

Date of exemption (yyyy/mm/dd)

Jurisdiction

4.3 — Membership in an exchange or SRO

In the last seven years, has the firm, or any predecessors or specified affiliates of the firm been a member of a securities or derivatives exchange, SRO or similar organization?

Yes ❑ No ❑

If yes, provide the following information for each membership:

Name of entity

Organization	
Date of membership (yyyy/mm/dd)	Expiry date, if applicable (yyyy/mm/dd)
Jurisdiction	

4.4 — Exemption from membership in an exchange or SRO

Is the firm currently relying on any exemptions from membership with a securities or derivatives exchange, SRO or similar organization?

Yes ❑ No ❑

If yes, provide the following information for each exemption:

Type of exemption
Organization
Date of exemption (yyyy/mm/dd)
Jurisdiction

4.5 — Refusal of registration, licensing or membership

Has the firm, or any predecessors or specified affiliates of the firm been refused registration, licensing or membership with a financial services regulator, securities or derivatives exchange, SRO or similar organization?

Yes ❑ No ❑

If yes, provide the following information for each refusal:

Name of entity
Reason for refusal
Regulator/organization
Date of refusal (yyyy/mm/dd)
Jurisdiction

4.6 — Registration for other financial products

Examples of other financial products include financial planning, life insurance and mortgages.

In the last seven years, has the firm, or any predecessors or specified affiliates of the firm been registered or licensed under legislation that requires registration or licensing to sell or advise in a financial product other than securities or derivatives?

Yes ❑ No ❑

If yes, provide the following information for each registration or licence:

Name of entity	
Type of licence or registration	
Regulator/organization	
Date of registration (yyyy/mm/dd)	Expiry date, if applicable (yyyy/mm/dd)
Jurisdiction	

Part 5 — Financial condition

Capital requirements

5.1 — Calculation of excess working capital

Attach the firm's calculation of excess working capital.

- Investment dealers must use the capital calculation form required by the Investment Industry Regulatory Organization of Canada (IIROC).

- Mutual fund dealers must use the capital calculation form required by the Mutual Fund Dealers Association of Canada (MFDA), except for mutual fund dealers registered in Québec only.

- Firms that are not members of either IIROC or the MFDA must use Form 31-103F1 *Calculation of Excess Working Capital*. See Schedule C.

5.2 — Sources of capital

List all cash, cash equivalents, debt and equity sources of the firm's capital.

Name of person or entity providing the capital	Type of capital	Amount ($)

5.3 — Guarantors

See Schedule C Form 31-103F1 *Calculation of Excess Working Capital*.

In relation to its business, does the firm:

		Yes	No
(a)	Have any guarantors?		
(b)	Act as a guarantor for any party?		

If yes, provide the following information for each guarantee:

Name of party to the guarantee	
NRD number, if applicable	
Relationship to the firm	Amount of guarantee ($)
Details of the guarantee	

Bonding and insurance

Questions 5.4 to 5.8 apply to the firm's bonding or insurance coverage or proposed bonding or insurance coverage for securities and derivatives activities only. This in accordance with Part 12, Division 2 of NI 31-103.

5.4 — Jurisdictions covered

This information is on the financial institution bond.

Where does the firm have bonding or insurance coverage?

AB ❑
BC ❑
MB ❑
NB ❑
NL ❑
NS ❑
NT ❑
NU ❑
ON ❑
PE ❑
QC ❑
SK ❑
YT ❑

Part 3:
REGISTRATION

If the firm's bonding or insurance does not cover all jurisdictions of Canada where it is seeking registration, explain why.

5.5 — Bonding or insurance details

This information is on the binder of insurance or on the financial institution bond.

Name of insurer	
Bond or policy number	
Specific insuring agreements and clauses	
Coverage for each claim ($)	Annual aggregate coverage ($)
Total coverage ($)	
Amount of the deductible ($)	Expiry date (yyyy/mm/dd)

If the firm's insurance or proposed insurance is not in the form of a financial institution bond, explain how it provides equivalent coverage to the bond.

5.6 — Professional liability insurance (Québec only)

If the firm is seeking registration in Québec as a mutual fund dealer or a scholarship plan dealer, provide the following information about the firm's professional liability insurance:

Name of insurer	
Policy number	
Specific insuring agreements and clauses	
Coverage for each claim ($)	Annual aggregate coverage ($)
Total coverage ($)	
Amount of the deductible ($)	Renewal date (yyyy/mm/dd)

Jurisdictions covered:

AB	BC	MB	NB	NL	NS	NT	NU	ON	PE	QC	SK	YT
❏	❏	❏	❏	❏	❏	❏	❏	❏	❏	❏	❏	❏

Which insurance policy applies to your representatives?

Firm's policy ❏   Individual's policy ❏   Both ❏

This information is required only if the firm is applying for registration in Québec as a mutual fund dealer or as a scholarship plan dealer.

5.7 — Directors' resolution approving insurance

Attach a directors' resolution confirming that the firm has sufficient insurance coverage for its securities or derivatives-related activities.

5.8 — Bonding or insurance claims

In the last seven years, has the firm made any claims against a bond or on its insurance?

Yes ❏ No ❏

If yes, provide the following information for each claim:

Type of bond or insurance	
Date of claim (yyyy/mm/dd)	Amount ($)
Reason for claim	

Date resolved (yyyy/mm/dd)	Result

Jurisdiction	

Solvency

5.9 — Bankruptcy

In the last seven years, has the firm or any of its specified affiliates declared bankruptcy, made an assignment or proposal in bankruptcy, or been the subject of a petition in bankruptcy, or the equivalent in any jurisdiction?

Yes ❑ No ❑

If yes, provide the following information for each bankruptcy or assignment in bankruptcy:

Name of entity	

Reason for bankruptcy or assignment	

Date of bankruptcy, assignment or petition (yyyy/mm/dd)	Date discharge granted, if applicable (yyyy/mm/dd)

Name of trustee	

Jurisdiction	

If applicable, attach a copy of any discharge, release or equivalent document.

5.10 — Appointment of receiver

In the last seven years, has the firm or any of its specified affiliates appointed a receiver or receiver manager, or had one appointed, or the equivalent in any jurisdiction?

Yes ❑ No ❑

If yes, provide the following information for each appointment of receiver:

Name of entity	

Date of appointment (yyyy/mm/dd)	Reason for appointment

Date appointment ended (yyyy/mm/dd)	Reason appointment ended

Name of receiver or receiver manager	

Jurisdiction	

Financial reporting

5.11 — Financial year-end

(mm/dd)

If the firm has not established its financial year-end, explain why.

5.12 — Auditor

Provide the name of the individual auditing the financial statements and the name of the firm, if applicable.

Name of auditor and accounting firm

5.13 — Audited financial statements

(a) Attach, for your most recently completed year, either

    (i) non-consolidated audited financial statements; or

    (ii) audited financial statements prepared in accordance with section 3.2(3) of NI 52-107.

Part 3:
REGISTRATION

(b) If the audited financial statements attached for item (a) were prepared for a period ending more than 90 days before the date of this application, also attach an interim financial report for a period of not more than 90 days before the date of this application.

If the firm is a start-up company, you can attach an audited opening statement of financial position instead.

5.14 — Letter of direction to auditors

We may request an audit of the firm at any time while the firm is registered.

Attach a letter of direction from the firm authorizing the auditor to conduct any audit or review of the firm that the regulator may request.

Part 6 — Client relationships

6.1 — Client assets

See Part 14, Division 3 of NI 31-103 and Companion Policy 31-103CP.

Will the firm hold or have access to client assets?

Yes ❑ No ❑

If yes, provide the following information for each financial institution where the trust accounts for client assets are held.

For guidance regarding whether a firm will hold or have access to client assets see section 12.4 of Companion Policy 31-103CP.

Name of financial institution	
Address line 1	
Address line 2	
City	Province/territory
Postal code	Telephone number

6.2 — Conflicts of interest

Does the firm have or expect to have any relationships that could reasonably result in any significant conflicts of interest in carrying out its registerable activities in accordance with securities or derivatives legislation?

Yes ❑ No ❑

If yes, complete the following questions:

    (a) Provide details about each conflict:

    (b) Does the firm have policies and procedures to identify and respond to its conflicts of interest?

    Yes ❑ No ❑

    If no, explain why:

Part 7 — Regulatory action

The questions in Part 7 apply to any jurisdiction and any foreign jurisdiction. The information must be provided in respect of the last 7 years.

7.1 — Settlement agreements

Has the firm, or any predecessors or specified affiliates of the firm entered into a settlement agreement with any financial services regulator, securities or derivatives exchange, SRO or similar organization?

Yes ❑ No ❑

If yes, provide the following information for each settlement agreement:

Name of entity
Regulator/organization
Date of settlement (yyyy/mm/dd)
Details of settlement
Jurisdiction

7.2 — Disciplinary history

Has any financial services regulator, securities or derivatives exchange, SRO or similar organization:

		Yes	No
(a)	Determined that the firm, or any predecessors or specified affiliates of the firm violated any securities regulations or any rules of a securities or derivatives exchange, SRO or similar organization?		
(b)	Determined that the firm, or any predecessors or specified affiliates of the firm made a false statement or omission?		
(c)	Issued a warning or requested an undertaking by the firm, or any predecessors or specified affiliates of the firm?		
(d)	Suspended or terminated any registration, licensing or membership of the firm, or any predecessors or specified affiliates of the firm?		
(e)	Imposed terms or conditions on any registration or membership of the firm, or predecessors or specified affiliates of the firm?		
(f)	Conducted a proceeding or investigation involving the firm, or any predecessors or specified affiliates of the firm?		
(g)	Issued an order (other than an exemption order) or a sanction to the firm, or any predecessors or specified affiliates of the firm for securities or derivatives-related activity (e.g. cease trade order)?		

If yes, provide the following information for each action:

Name of entity	
Type of action	
Regulator/organization	
Date of action (yyyy/mm/dd)	Reason for action
Jurisdiction	

7.3 — Ongoing investigations

Is the firm aware of any ongoing investigations of which the firm or any of its specified affiliates is the subject?

Yes ❑ No ❑

If yes, provide the following information for each investigation:

Name of entity
Reason or purpose of investigation
Regulator/organization
Date investigation commenced (yyyy/mm/dd)
Jurisdiction

Part 8 — Legal action

The firm must disclose offences or legal actions under any statute governing the firm and its business activities in any jurisdiction. The information must be provided in respect of the last 7 years.

8.1 — Criminal convictions

Has the firm, or any predecessors or specified affiliates of the firm been convicted of any criminal or quasi-criminal offence?

Yes ❑ No ❑

If yes, provide the following information for each conviction:

Name of entity	
Type of offence	
Case name	Case number, if applicable
Date of conviction (yyyy/mm/dd)	
Jurisdiction	

8.2 — Outstanding criminal charges

Is the firm or any of its specified affiliates currently the subject of any outstanding criminal or quasi-criminal charges?

Yes ❏ No ❏

If yes, provide the following information for each charge:

Name of entity
Type of offence
Date of charge (yyyy/mm/dd)
Jurisdiction

8.3 — Outstanding legal actions

		Yes	No
(a)	Is the firm currently a defendant or respondent (or the equivalent in any jurisdiction) in any outstanding legal action?		
(b)	Are any of the firm's specified affiliates currently a defendant or respondent (or the equivalent in any jurisdiction) in any outstanding legal action that involves fraud, theft or securities-related activities, or that could significantly affect the firm's business?		

If yes, provide the following information for each legal action:

Name of entity
Type of legal action
Date of legal action (yyyy/mm/dd)
Current stage of litigation
Remedies requested by plaintiff or appellant
Jurisdiction

8.4 — Judgments

		Yes	No
(a)	Has any judgment been rendered against the firm or is any judgment outstanding in any civil court for damages or other relief relating to fraud, theft or securities-related activities?		
(b)	Are any of the firm's specified affiliates currently the subject of any judgments that involve fraud, theft or securities-related activities, or that could significantly affect the firm's business?		

If yes, provide the following information for each judgment:

Name of entity
Type of judgment

Date of judgment (yyyy/mm/dd)	
Current stage of litigation, if applicable	
Remedies requested by plaintiffs	

Part 9 — Certification

It is an offence under securities legislation and derivatives legislation, including commodity futures legislation, to give false or misleading information on this form.

By signing below, you:

1. Certify to the regulator in each jurisdiction of Canada where the firm is submitting and filing this form, either directly or through the principal regulator, that:

- you have read this form, and

- to the best of your knowledge and after reasonable inquiry, all of the information provided on this form is true and complete.

2. Certify to each regulator in a non-principal jurisdiction of Canada where the firm is submitting and filing this form, either directly or through the principal regulator, that at the date of this submission:

- the firm has submitted and filed all information required to be submitted and filed under the securities legislation or derivatives legislation or both of the principal jurisdiction of Canada in relation to the firm's registration in that jurisdiction, and

- this information is true and complete.

3. Authorize the principal regulator to give each non-principal regulator access to any information the firm has submitted or filed with the principal regulator under securities legislation or derivatives legislation or both of the principal jurisdiction of Canada in relation to the firm's registration in that jurisdiction.

4. Acknowledge that the regulator may collect and provide personal information about the individuals referred to in this form under *Collection and use of personal information.*

5. Confirm that the individuals referred to in this form have been notified that their personal information is disclosed on this form, the legal reason for doing so, how it will be used and who to contact for more information.

Name of firm	
Name of firm's authorized signing officer or partner	
Title of firm's authorized signing officer or partner	
Signature	
Date (yyyy/mm/dd)	

Witness

The witness must be a lawyer, notary public or commissioner of oaths.

Name of witness	
Title of witness	
Signature	
Date (yyyy/mm/dd)	

Schedule A — Contact information for Notice of collection and use of personal information

Alberta

Alberta Securities Commission

Suite 600, 250-5th St. SW

Calgary, AB T2P 0R4

Attention: Information Officer

Telephone: (403) 297-6454

British Columbia

Part 3:
REGISTRATION

British Columbia Securities Commission

P.O. Box 10142, Pacific Centre

701 West Georgia Street

Vancouver, BC V7Y 1L2

Attention: Freedom of Information Officer

Telephone: (604) 899-6500 or (800) 373-6393 (in Canada)

Manitoba

The Manitoba Securities Commission

500 - 400 St. Mary Avenue

Winnipeg, MB R3C 4K5

Attention: Director of Registrations

Telephone: (204) 945-2548

Fax (204) 945-0330

New Brunswick

Financial and Consumer Services Commission of New Brunswick / Commission des services financiers et des services aux consommateurs du Nouveau-Brunswick

Suite 300, 85 Charlotte Street

Saint John, NB E2L 2J2

Attention: Director of Securities

Telephone: (506) 658-3060

Newfoundland and Labrador

Superintendent of Securities, Service NL

Government of Newfoundland and Labrador

P.O. Box 8700

2nd Floor, West Block

Confederation Building

St. John's, NL A1B 4J6

Attention: Manager of Registrations

Telephone: (709) 729-5661

Nova Scotia

Nova Scotia Securities Commission

Suite 400, 5251 Duke Street

Halifax, NS B3J 1P3

Attention: Deputy Director, Capital Markets

Telephone: (902) 424-7768

Northwest Territories

Government of the Northwest Territories

Department of Justice

1st Floor Stuart M. Hodgson Building

5009 - 49th Street

Yellowknife, NWT X1A 2L9

Attention: Deputy Superintendent of Securities

Telephone: (867) 920-8984

Nunavut

Government of Nunavut

Department of Justice

P.O. Box 1000 Station 570

Iqaluit, NU X0A 0H0

Attention: Deputy Registrar of Securities

Telephone: (867) 975-6590

Ontario

Ontario Securities Commission

22nd Floor

20 Queen Street West

Toronto, ON M5H 3S8

Attention: Compliance and Registrant Regulation

Telephone: (416) 593-8314

e-mail: registration@osc.gov.on.ca

Prince Edward Island

Securities Office

Department of Community Affairs and Attorney General

P.O. Box 2000

Charlottetown, PE C1A 7N8

Attention: Deputy Registrar of Securities

Telephone: (902) 368-6288

Québec

Autorité des marchés financiers

800, square Victoria, 22e étage

C.P. 246, tour de la Bourse

Montréal (Québec) H4Z 1G3

Attention: Responsable de l'accès à l'information

Telephone: (514) 395-0337 or (877) 525-0337

Saskatchewan

Financial and Consumer Affairs Authority of Saskatchewan

Suite 601, 1919 Saskatchewan Drive

Regina, SK S4P 4H2

Attention: Deputy Director, Capital Markets

Telephone: (306) 787-5871

Yukon

Government of Yukon

Superintendent of Securities

Department of Community Services

P.O. Box 2703 C-6

Whitehorse, YT Y1A 2C6

Attention: Superintendent of Securities

Telephone: (867) 667-5314

Self-regulatory organization

Investment Industry Regulatory Organization of Canada

121 King Street West, Suite 2000

Toronto, Ontario M5H 3T9

Attention: Privacy Officer

Telephone: (416) 364-6133

E-mail: PrivacyOfficer@iiroc.ca

Schedule B — Submission to jurisdiction and appointment of agent for service

1. Name of person or company (the "Firm"):

2. Jurisdiction of incorporation of the person or company:

3. Name of agent for service of process (the "Agent for Service"):

4. Address for service of process on the Agent for Service:

Phone number of the Agent for Service: ....

5. The Firm designates and appoints the Agent for Service at the address stated above as its agent upon whom may be served a notice, pleading, subpoena, summons or other process in any action, investigation or administrative, criminal, quasi-criminal or other proceeding (a

Part 3: REGISTRATION

"Proceeding") arising out of or relating to or concerning the Firm's activities in the local jurisdiction and irrevocably waives any right to raise as a defense in any such proceeding any alleged lack of jurisdiction to bring such Proceeding.

6. The Firm irrevocably and unconditionally submits to the non-exclusive jurisdiction of the judicial, quasi-judicial and administrative tribunals of the local jurisdiction and any administrative proceeding in the local jurisdiction, in any proceeding arising out of or related to or concerning the Firm's activities in the local jurisdiction.

7. Until six years after the Firm ceases to be registered, the Firm must file

    a. a new Submission to jurisdiction and appointment of agent for service in this form no later than the 10th day after the date this Submission to jurisdiction and appointment of agent for service is terminated; and

    b. an amended Submission to jurisdiction and appointment of agent for service no later than the 10th day after any change in the name or above address of the Agent for Service.

8. This Submission to jurisdiction and appointment of agent for service is governed by and construed in accordance with the laws of the local jurisdiction.

Dated: ....

.... (Signature of the Firm or authorized signatory)

.... (Name and Title of authorized signatory)

Acceptance

The undersigned accepts the appointment as Agent for Service of (Insert name of the Firm) under the terms and conditions of the foregoing Submission to jurisdiction and appointment of agent for service.

Dated: ....

.... (Signature of Agent for Service or authorized signatory)

.... (Name and Title of authorized signatory)

Schedule C — Form 31-103F1 Calculation of excess working capital

.... Firm Name

Capital Calculation (as at .... with comparative figures as at ....)

	Component	Current period	Prior period
1.	Current assets	....	....
2.	Less current assets not readily convertible into cash (e.g., prepaid expenses)	....	....
3.	Adjusted current assets Line 1 minus line 2 =	....	....
4.	Current liabilities	....	....
5.	Add 100% of long-term related party debt unless the firm and the lender have executed a subordination agreement in the form set out in Appendix B and the firm has delivered a copy of the agreement to the regulator or, in Québec, the securities regulatory authority	....	....
6.	Adjusted current liabilities Line 4 plus line 5 =	....	....
7.	Adjusted working capital Line 3 minus line 6 =	....	....
8.	Less minimum capital	....	....
9.	Less market risk	....	....
10.	Less any deductible under the bonding or insurance policy required under Part 12 of National Instrument 31-103, *Registration Requirements, Exemptions and Ongoing Registrant Obligations*	....	....
11.	Less Guarantees	....	....
12.	Less unresolved differences		

Component	Current period	Prior period
13. **Excess working capital**	....	....

Notes:

This form must be prepared using the accounting principles that you use to prepare your financial statements in accordance with National Instrument 52-107 *Acceptable Accounting Principles and Auditing Standards*. Section 12.1 of Companion Policy 31-103CP *Registration Requirements, Exemptions and Ongoing Registrant Obligations* provides further guidance in respect of these accounting principles.

Line 5. Related-party debt — Refer to the CICA Handbook for the definition of "related party" for publicly accountable enterprises.

Line 8. Minimum Capital — The amount on this line must be not less than (a) $25,000 for an adviser and (b) $50,000 for a dealer. For an investment fund manager, the amount must be not less than $100,000 unless subsection 12.1(4) applies.

Line 9. Market Risk — The amount on this line must be calculated according to the instructions set out in Schedule 1 to this Form.

Line 11. Guarantees — If the registered firm is guaranteeing the liability of another party, the total amount of the guarantee must be included in the capital calculation. If the amount of a guarantee is included in the firm's balance sheet as a current liability and is reflected in line 4, do not include the amount of the guarantee on line 11.

Line 12. Unresolved differences — Any unresolved differences that could result in a loss from either firm or client assets must be included in the capital calculation.

The examples below are intended to provide guidance as to how to calculate unresolved differences:

(i) If there is an unresolved difference relating to client securities, the amount to be reported on Line 12 will be equal to the market value of the client securities that are short, plus the applicable margin rate for those securities.

(ii) If there is an unresolved difference relating to the registrant's investments, the amount to be reported on Line 12 will be equal to the market value of the investments (securities) that are short.

(iii) If there is an unresolved difference relating to cash, the amount to be reported on Line 12 will be equal to the amount of the shortfall in cash.

Please refer to section 12.1 of Companion Policy 31-103CP *Registration Requirements, Exemptions and Ongoing Registrant Obligations* for further guidance on how to prepare and file this form.

Schedule C — Form 31-103F1 Calculation of Excess Working Capital

.... Firm Name

Capital Calculation (as at .... with comparative figures as at ....)

	Component	Current period	Prior period
1.	Current assets		
2.	Less current assets not readily convertible into cash (e.g., prepaid expenses)		
3.	Adjusted current assets Line 1 minus line 2 =		
4.	Current liabilities		
5.	Add 100% of non-current related party debt unless the firm and the lender have executed a subordination agreement in the form set out in Appendix B of National Instrument 31-103 *Registration Requirements, Exemptions and Ongoing Registrant Obligations* and the firm has delivered a copy of the agreement to the regulator or, in Québec, the securities regulatory authority. See section 12.2 of National Instrument 31-103 *Registration Requirements, Exemptions and Ongoing Registrant Obligations*.		

Part 3: REGISTRATION

	Component	Current period	Prior period
6.	Adjusted current liabilities Line 4 plus line 5 =		
7.	Adjusted working capital Line 3 minus line 6 =		
8.	Less minimum capital		
9.	Less market risk		
10.	Less any deductible under the bonding or insurance policy required under Part 12 of National Instrument 31-103 *Registration Requirements, Exemptions and Ongoing Registrant Obligations*		
11.	Less Guarantees		
12.	Less unresolved differences		
13.	Excess working capital		

Notes:

Form 31-103F1 *Calculation of Excess Working Capital* must be prepared using the accounting principles that you use to prepare your financial statements in accordance with National Instrument 52-107 *Acceptable Accounting Principles and Auditing Standards*. Section 12.1 of Companion Policy 31-103CP *Registration Requirements, Exemptions and Ongoing Registrant Obligations* provides further guidance in respect of these accounting principles.

Line 5. Related-party debt — Refer to the CICA Handbook for the definition of "related party" for publicly accountable enterprises. The firm is required to deliver a copy of the executed subordination agreement to the regulator or, in Québec, the securities regulatory authority on the earlier of a) 10 days after the date the agreement is executed or b) the date an amount subordinated by the agreement is excluded from its calculation of excess working capital on Form 31-103F1 *Calculation of Excess Working Capital*. **The firm must notify the regulator or, in Québec, the securities regulatory authority, 10 days before it repays the loan (in whole or in part), or terminates the subordination agreement.** See section 12.2 of National Instrument 31-103 *Registration Requirements, Exemptions and Ongoing Registrant Obligations*.

Line 8. Minimum Capital — The amount on this line must be not less than (a) $25,000 for an adviser and (b) $50,000 for a dealer. For an investment fund manager, the amount must be not less than $100,000 unless subsection 12.1(4) of National Instrument 31-103 *Registration Requirements, Exemptions and Ongoing Registrant Obligations* applies.

Line 9. Market Risk — The amount on this line must be calculated according to the instructions set out in Schedule 1 to Form 31-103F1 *Calculation of Excess Working Capital*. A schedule supporting the calculation of any amounts included in Line 9 as market risk should be provided to the regulator or, in Québec, the securities regulatory authority in conjunction with the submission of Form 31-103F1 *Calculation of Excess Working Capital*.

Line 11. Guarantees — If the registered firm is guaranteeing the liability of another party, the total amount of the guarantee must be included in the capital calculation. If the amount of a guarantee is included in the firm's statement of financial position as a current liability and is reflected in line 4, do not include the amount of the guarantee on line 11.

Line 12. Unresolved differences — Any unresolved differences that could result in a loss from either firm or client assets must be included in the capital calculation. The examples below provide guidance as to how to calculate unresolved differences:

(i) If there is an unresolved difference relating to client securities, the amount to be reported on Line 12 will be equal to the fair value of the client securities that are short, plus the applicable margin rate for those securities.

(ii) If there is an unresolved difference relating to the registrant's investments, the amount to be reported on Line 12 will be equal to the fair value of the investments (securities) that are short.

(iii) If there is an unresolved difference relating to cash, the amount to be reported on Line 12 will be equal to the amount of the shortfall in cash.

Please refer to section 12.1 of Companion Policy 31-103CP *Registration Requirements, Exemptions and Ongoing Registrant Obligations* for further guidance on how to prepare and file Form 31-103F1 *Calculation of Excess Working Capital*.

Management Certification

Registered Firm Name: ....

We have examined the attached capital calculation and certify that the firm is in compliance with the capital requirements as at ....

Name and Title	Signature	Date
1.	....	....
....		
2.	....	....
....		

Schedule 1 — of Form 31-103F1 Calculation of Excess Working Capital
(calculating line 9 [market risk])

For purposes of completing this form:

(1) "Fair value" means the value of a security determined in accordance with Canadian GAAP applicable to publicly accountable enterprises.

(2) For each security whose value is included in line 1, Current Assets, multiply the fair value of the security by the margin rate for that security set out below. Add up the resulting amounts for all of the securities you hold. The total is the "market risk" to be entered on line 9.

(a) Bonds, Debentures, Treasury Bills and Notes

(i) Bonds, debentures, treasury bills and other securities of or guaranteed by the Government of Canada, of the United Kingdom, of the United States of America and of any other national foreign government (provided such foreign government securities are currently rated Aaa or AAA by Moody's Canada Inc. or its DRO affiliate, or Standard & Poor's Rating Services (Canada) or its DRO affiliate, respectively), maturing (or called for redemption):

within 1 year:	1% of fair value multiplied by the fraction determined by dividing the number of days to maturity by 365
over 1 year to 3 years:	1 % of fair value
over 3 years to 7 years:	2% of fair value
over 7 years to 11 years:	4% of fair value
over 11 years:	4% of fair value

(ii) Bonds, debentures, treasury bills and other securities of or guaranteed by any jurisdiction of Canada and obligations of the International Bank for Reconstruction and Development, maturing (or called for redemption):

within 1 year:	2% of fair value multiplied by the fraction determined by dividing the number of days to maturity by 365
over 1 year to 3 years:	3 % of fair value
over 3 years to 7 years:	4% of fair value
over 7 years to 11 years:	5% of fair value
over 11 years:	5% of fair value

(iii) Bonds, debentures or notes (not in default) of or guaranteed by any municipal corporation in Canada or the United Kingdom maturing:

within 1 year:	3% of fair value multiplied by the fraction determined by dividing the number of days to maturity by 365
over 1 year to 3 years:	5 % of fair value
over 3 years to 7 years:	5% of fair value
over 7 years to 11 years:	5% of fair value
over 11 years:	5% of fair value

(iv) Other non-commercial bonds and debentures (not in default): 10% of fair value

(v) Commercial and corporate bonds, debentures and notes (not in default) and non-negotiable and non-transferable trust company and mortgage loan company obligations registered in the registered firm's name maturing:

within 1 year:	3% of fair value
over 1 year to 3 years:	6 % of fair value
over 3 years to 7 years:	7% of fair value
over 7 years to 11 years:	10% of fair value
over 11 years:	10% of fair value

(b) Bank Paper

Deposit certificates, promissory notes or debentures issued by a Canadian chartered bank (and of Canadian chartered bank acceptances) maturing:

within 1 year:	2% of fair value multiplied by the fraction determined by dividing the number of days to maturity by 365
over 1 year:	apply rates for commercial and corporate bonds, debentures and notes

(c) Acceptable foreign bank paper

Deposit certificates, promissory notes or debentures issued by a foreign bank, readily negotiable and transferable and maturing:

within 1 year:	2% of fair value multiplied by the fraction determined by dividing the number of days to maturity by 365
over 1 year:	apply rates for commercial and corporate bonds, debentures and notes

"Acceptable Foreign Bank Paper" consists of deposit certificates or promissory notes issued by a bank other than a Canadian chartered bank with a net worth (i.e., capital plus reserves) of not less than $200,000,000.

(d) Mutual Funds

Securities of mutual funds qualified by prospectus for sale in any jurisdiction of Canada:

(i) 5% of the net asset value per security as determined in accordance with National Instrument 81-106 *Investment Fund Continuous Disclosure*, where the fund is a money market mutual fund as defined in National Instrument 81-102 *Investment Funds*; or

(ii) the margin rate determined on the same basis as for listed stocks multiplied by the net asset value per security of the fund as determined in accordance with National Instrument 81-106 *Investment Fund Continuous Disclosure*.

Securities of mutual funds qualified by prospectus for sale in the United States of America: 5% of the net asset value per security if the fund is registered as an investment company under the *Investment Companies Act of 1940*, as amended from time totime, and complies with Rule 2a-7 thereof.

(e) Stocks

In this paragraph, "securities" includes rights and warrants and does not include bonds and debes.

(i) On securities including investment fund securities, rights and warrants, listed on any exchange in Canada or the United States of America:

    Long Positions — Margin Required

        Securities selling at $2.00 or more — 50% of fair value

        Securities selling at $1.75 to $1.99 — 60% of fair value

        Securities selling at $1.50 to $1.74 — 80% of fair value

        Securities selling under $1.50 — 100% of fair value

    Short Positions — Credit Required

        Securities selling at $2.00 or more — 150% of fair value

        Securities selling at $1.50 to $1.99 — $3.00 per share

        Securities selling at $0.25 to $1.49 — 200% of fair value

        Securities selling at less than $0.25 — fair value plus $0.25 per share

(ii) For positions in securities that are constituent securities on a major broadly-based index of one of the following exchanges, 50% of the fair value:

    (a) Australian Stock Exchange Limited

    (b) Bolsa de Madrid

    (c) Borsa Italiana

    (d) Copenhagen Stock Exchange

    (e) Euronext Amsterdam

    (f) Euronext Brussels

    (g) Euronext Paris S.A.

    (h) Frankfurt Stock Exchange

    (i) London Stock Exchange

(j) New Zealand Exchange Limited

(k) Stockholm Stock Exchange

(l) SIX Swiss Exchange

(m) The Stock Exchange of Hong Kong Limited

(n) Tokyo Stock Exchange

(f) Mortgages

(i) For a firm registered in any jurisdiction of Canada except Ontario:

(a) Insured mortgages (not in default): 6% of fair value

(b) Mortgages which are not insured (not in default): 12% of fair value.

(ii) For a firm registered in Ontario:

(a) Mortgages insured under the *National Housing Act* (Canada) (not in default): 6% of fair value

(b) Conventional first mortgages (not in default): 12% of fair value.

> If you are registered in Ontario regardless of whether you are also registered in another jurisdiction of Canada, you will need to apply the margin rates set forth in (ii) above.

(g) For all other securities — 100% of fair value.

Form 33-109F7 — Reinstatement of Registered Individuals and Permitted Individuals

(sections 2.3 and 2.5(2))

General Instructions

Complete and submit this form to the relevant regulator(s) or in Québec, the securities regulatory authority, or self-regulatory organization (SRO) if an individual has left a sponsoring firm and is seeking to reinstate their registration in one or more of the same categories or reinstate their same status of permitted individual as before with a sponsoring firm.

1. this form is submitted on or before the 90th day after the cessation date of the individual's employment, partnership or agency relationship with the individual's former sponsoring firm,

2. there have been no changes to the information previously submitted in respect of Items 13 (Regulatory Disclosure) other than changes to Item 13.3(c), 14 (Criminal Disclosure), 15 (Civil Disclosure) and 16 (Financial Disclosure) of the individual's Form 33-109F4 since the individual left their former sponsoring firm, and

3. the individual's employment, partnership or agency relationship with their former sponsoring firm did not end because the individual was asked by the firm to resign, resigned voluntarily or was dismissed following an allegation against the individual of criminal activity, a breach of securities legislation, or a breach of the rules of an SRO.

If you do not meet all of the above conditions then you must apply for reinstatement by completing on NRD a Form 33-109F4 by making the NRD submission entitled 'Reactivation of Registration'.

Terms

In this form, "you", "your" and "individual" means the individual who is seeking to reinstate their registration or their statues as permitted individual.

"former sponsoring firm" means the registered firm where you most recently carried out duties as a registered or permitted individual.

"major shareholder" and "shareholder" mean a shareholder who, in total, directly or indirectly owns voting securities carrying 10 per cent or more of the votes carried by all outstanding voting securities.

"new sponsoring firm" means the registered firm where you will begin carrying out duties as a registered or permitted individual when your registration or permitted individual status is reinstated.

Several terms used in this form are defined in the Form 33-109F4 *Registration of Individuals and Review of Permitted Individuals* that you submitted when you first became registered.

How to submit this form

NRD format

Submit this form at the National Registration Database (NRD) website in NRD format at www.nrd.ca. If you have any questions, contact the compliance, registration or legal department of the new sponsoring firm or a legal adviser with securities law experience, or visit the NRD information website at www.nrdinfo.ca.

Format, other than NRD format

If you are relying on the temporary hardship exemption in section 5.1 of National Instrument 31-102 *National Registration Database*, you may submit this form in a format other than NRD format.

If you need more space, use a separate sheet of paper. Clearly identify the Item and question number. Complete and sign the form, and send it to the relevant regulator(s) or, in Québec, the securities regulatory authority, SRO (s) or similar authority. The number of originally signed copies of the form you are required to submit depends on the province or territory, and on the regulator, the securities regulatory authority or SRO.

To avoid delays in processing this form, be sure to answer all of the items that apply to you. If you have questions, contact the compliance, registration or legal department of the new sponsoring firm or a legal adviser with securities law experience, or visit the National Registration Database information website at www.nrd-info.ca.

Item 1 — Name

1. NRD number:..............

2. Legal name:

....

Last name First name Second name (N/A ❑) Third name (N/A ❑)

3. Date of birth (YYYY/MM/DD): ....

4. Use of other names

Are you currently using, or have you ever used, operated under, or carried on business under, a name other than the name(s) mentioned above (for example, trade names for sole proprietorships or team names)?

Yes ❑ No ❑

If "Yes", complete Schedule A.

Item 2 — Number of jurisdictions

1. Are you seeking to reinstate your registration or permitted individual status in more than one jurisdiction of Canada?

Yes ❑ No ❑

2. Check each province or territory in which you are seeking reinstatement of registration or reinstatement as a permitted individual:

- ❑ All jurisdictions
- ❑ Alberta
- ❑ British Columbia
- ❑ Manitoba
- ❑ New Brunswick
- ❑ Newfoundland and Labrador
- ❑ Northwest Territories
- ❑ Nova Scotia
- ❑ Nunavut
- ❑ Ontario
- ❑ Prince Edward Island
- ❑ Québec
- ❑ Saskatchewan
- ❑ Yukon

Item 3 — Individual categories

1. On Schedule B, check each category for which you are seeking to reinstate your registration or permitted individual status. If you are seeking reinstatement of status as a permitted individual, check each category that describes your position with your new sponsoring firm.

2. If you are seeking reinstatement as a representative of a mutual fund dealer or of a scholarship plan dealer in Québec, are you covered by your new sponsoring firm's professional liability insurance?

Yes ❑ No ❑

If "No", state:

The name of your insurer ....

Your policy number ....

Item 4 — Address and agent for service

1. — Address for service

You must have one address for service in each province or territory where you are submitting this form. A residential or business address is acceptable. A post office box is not acceptable. Complete Schedule C for each additional address for service you are providing.

Address for service:

.... (number, street, city, province or territory, postal code)

Telephone number .... Fax number, if applicable ....

Business e-mail address ....

2. — Agent for service

If you have appointed an agent for service, provide the following information for the agent in each province or territory where you have an agent for service. The address of your agent for service must be the same as the address for service above. If your agent for service is not an individual, provide the name of your contact person.

Name of agent for service:

....

Contact person:

.... Last name, First name

Item 5 — Location of employment

1. Provide the following information for your new sponsoring firm. If you will be working out of more than one business location, provide the following information for the business location out of which you will be doing most of your business. If you are only filing this form because you are a permitted individual and are not employed by, or acting as agent for, the sponsoring firm, select "N/A".

Unique Identification Number (optional): ....

NRD location number: ....

Business location address:................................ (number, street, city, province, territory or state, country, postal code)

Telephone number: (..........) .... Fax number: (..........) ....

N/A ❑

2. If the new sponsoring firm has a foreign head office, and/or you are not a resident of Canada, provide the address for the business location in which you will be conducting most of your business. If you are only filing this form because you are a permitted individual and are not employed by, or acting as agent for, the sponsoring firm, select "N/A".

Business location address:................................ (number, street, city, province, territory or state, country, postal code)

Telephone number: (..........).......... Fax number: (..........)..........

N/A ❑

[The following under #3 "Type of business location", #4 and #5 is for a Format other than NRD format only]

3. Type of business location:

❑ Head office

❑ Branch or business location

❑ Sub-branch (Mutual Fund Dealers Association of Canada members only)

4. Name of supervisor or branch manager: ....

5. ❑ **Check here if the mailing address of the business location is the same as the business location address provided above. Otherwise, complete the following:**

Mailing address:................................ (number, street, city, province, territory or state, country, postal code)

Item 6 — Previous employment

Provide the following information for your former sponsoring firm.

Name: ....

Date on which you were no longer authorized to act on behalf of your former sponsoring firm as a registered individual or permitted individual: .... (YYYY/MM/DD)

The reason why you left your former sponsoring firm: ....

Item 7 — Current employment, other business activities, officer positions held and directorships

Name of your new sponsoring firm: ....

Complete a separate Schedule D for each of your current business and employment activities, including employment and business activities with your new sponsoring firm and any employment and business activities outside your new sponsoring firm. Also include all officer or director positions and any other equivalent positions held, as well as positions of influence. The information must be provided

- whether or not you receive compensation for such services, and

- whether or not any such position is business related.

Item 8 — Ownership of securities in new sponsoring firm

Are you a partner or major shareholder of your new sponsoring firm?

Yes ❑ No ❑

If "Yes", complete Schedule E.

Part 3:
REGISTRATION

Item 9 — Confirm permanent record

1. Check the appropriate box to indicate that, since leaving your former sponsoring firm, there has been a change to any information previously submitted for the items of your Form 33-109F4 that are listed below.

❏ Regulatory disclosure (Item 13), other than changes to Item 13.3(c)

❏ Criminal disclosure (Item 14)

❏ Civil disclosure (Item 15)

❏ Financial disclosure (Item 16)

2. Check the box below — *I am eligible to file this Form 33-109F7, only* if you satisfy both of the following conditions:

(a) there are no changes to any of the disclosure items under Item 9.1 above, and

(b) your employment, partnership or agency relationship with your former sponsoring firm did not end because you were asked by the firm to resign or resigned voluntarily, or were dismissed, following an allegation against you of

- criminal activity,

- a breach of securities legislation, or

- a breach of the rules of an SRO.

If you do not meet the above conditions for selecting the box "I am eligible to file this Form 33-109F7", then you must apply for reinstatement by completing on NRD a Form 33-109F4 by making the NRD submission entitled "Reactivation of Registration". If you are submitting a Form 33-109F4 in a format other than NRD format you must complete the entire form.

❏ I am eligible to file this Form 33-109F7.

Item 10 — Acknowledgements, submission to jurisdiction and notice of collection and use of personal information

By submitting this form, you:

- acknowledge that the submission to jurisdiction, consent to collection and use of personal information, and authorization in respect of SROs (to the extent applicable) that you provided in your Form 33-109F4 remain in effect and extend to this form

- consent to the collection and disclosure of your personal information by regulators and by your sponsoring firm, in each case, for registration and other related regulatory purposes.

If you have any questions about the collection and use of your personal information, contact the securities regulatory authority or applicable SRO in the relevant jurisdiction. See Schedule F for details. In Québec, you can also contact the Commission d'accès à l'information at 1-888-528-7741 or visit its website at www.cai.gouv.qc.ca.

You acknowledge and agree that if you are seeking reinstatement of your registration and it was subject to any undischarged terms and conditions when you left your former sponsoring firm, those terms and conditions will remain in effect at your new sponsoring firm.

Item 11 — Warning

It is an offence under securities legislation and derivatives legislation, including commodity futures legislation, to give false or misleading information on this form.

Item 12 — Certification

1. — Certification — NRD format:

I confirm I have discussed the questions in this form with an officer, branch manager or supervisor of my sponsoring firm. To the best of my knowledge, the officer, branch manager or supervisor was satisfied that I fully understood the questions. I will limit my activities to those permitted by my category of registration. If the business location specified in this form is a residence, I hereby give my consent for the regulator or, in Québec, the securities regulatory authority to enter that residence for the administration of securities legislation and derivatives legislation, including commodity futures legislation.

❏ I am making this submission as agent for the individual. By checking this box, I certify that the individual provided me with all of the information on this form and the certification above.

2. — Certification — Format other than NRD format:

Individual

By signing below, I certify to the regulator, or in Québec the securities regulatory authority, in each jurisdiction where I am submitting this form, either directly or through the principal regulator that:

- I have read the form and understand the questions,

- all of the information provided on this form is true, and complete, and

- if the business location specified in this form is a residence, I hereby give my consent for the regulator or, in Québec, the securities regulatory authority to enter that residence for the administration of securities legislation and derivatives legislation, including commodity futures legislation.

Signature of individual .... Date signed.......... (YYYY/MM/DD)

Authorized partner or officer of the new sponsoring firm

By signing below, I certify to the regulator, or in Québec the securities regulatory authority, in each jurisdiction where I am submitting this form for the individual that:

- the individual will be engaged by the new sponsoring firm as a registered individual or a permitted individual

- I have, or a branch manager or another officer or supervisor has, discussed the questions set out in this form with the individual and, to the best of my knowledge, the individual fully understands the questions, and

- the new sponsoring firm understands that if the individual's reinstatement of registration was subject to any undischarged terms and conditions when the individual left their former sponsoring firm, those terms and conditions remain in effect and agrees to assume any ongoing obligations that apply to the sponsoring firm in respect of the individual under those terms and conditions.

Name of firm ....

Name of authorized signing officer or partner ....

Title of authorized signing officer or partner ....

Signature of authorized signing officer or partner ....

Date signed .... (YYYY/MM/DD)

Schedule A — Use of other names (Item 1.4)

Item 1.4 — Use of other names

Name 1:

Name: ....

Provide the reasons for the use of this other name (for example, trade name or team name)?: ....

If this other name is or was used in connection with any sponsoring firm, did the sponsoring firm approve the use of the name?

Yes ❑ No ❑

When did you use this name?

From:	To:
....	....
(YYYY/MM)	**(YYYY/MM)**

Name 2:

Name: ....

Provide the reasons for the use of this other name (for example, trade name or team name):

If this other name is or was used in connection with any sponsoring firm, did the sponsoring firm approve the use of the name?

Yes ❑ No ❑

When did you use this name?

From:	To:
....	....
(YYYY/MM)	**(YYYY/MM)**

Name 3:

Name: ....

Provide the reasons for the use of this other name (for example, trade name or team name):

If this other name is or was used in connection with any sponsoring firm, did the sponsoring firm approve the use of the name?

Yes ❑ No ❑

When did you use this name?

From:	To:
....	....
(YYYY/MM)	**(YYYY/MM)**

Schedule B — Individual Categories (Item 3)

Check each category for which you are seeking reinstatement of registration, approval or permitted individual status

Categories Common to all jurisdictions under securities legislation

Firm categories [Format other than NRD format only]

❑ Investment Dealer

❑ Mutual Fund Dealer

❑ Scholarship Plan Dealer

- ❏ Exempt Market Dealer
- ❏ Restricted Dealer
- ❏ Portfolio Manager
- ❏ Restricted Portfolio Manager
- ❏ Investment Fund Manager

Individual categories and permitted activities

- ❏ Dealing Representative
- ❏ Advising Representative
- ❏ Associate Advising Representative
- ❏ Ultimate Designated Person
- ❏ Chief Compliance Officer
- ❏ Permitted Individual
- ❏ Officer — Specify title:
- ❏ Director
- ❏ Partner
- ❏ Shareholder
- ❏ Branch Manager (MFDA members only)
- ❏ IIROC approval only

IIROC

Approval categories

- ❏ Executive
- ❏ Director (Industry)
- ❏ Director (Non-Industry)
- ❏ Supervisor
- ❏ Investor
- ❏ Registered Representative
- ❏ Investment Representative
- ❏ Trader

Additional approval categories

- ❏ Chief Compliance Officer
- ❏ Chief Financial Officer
- ❏ Ultimate Designated Person

Products

- ❏ Non-Trading
- ❏ Securities
- ❏ Options
- ❏ Futures Contracts and Futures Contract Options
- ❏ Mutual Funds only

Customer type

- ❏ Retail
- ❏ Institutional
- ❏ Not Applicable

Portfolio management

- ❏ Portfolio Management

Categories under local commodity futures and derivatives legislation

Ontario

Firm categories

❑ Commodity Trading Adviser

❑ Commodity Trading Counsel

❑ Commodity Trading Manager

❑ Futures Commission Merchant

Individual categories and permitted activities

❑ Advising Representative

❑ Salesperson

❑ Branch Manager

❑ Officer — Specify title:

❑ Director

❑ Partner

❑ Shareholder

❑ IIROC approval only

Manitoba

Firm categories

❑ Dealer (Merchant)

❑ Dealer (Futures Commission Merchant)

❑ Dealer (Floor Broker)

❑ Adviser

❑ Local

Individual categories and permitted activities

❑ Floor Broker

❑ Salesperson

❑ Branch Manager

❑ Adviser

❑ Officer — Specify title

❑ Director

❑ Partner

❑ Futures Contracts Portfolio Manager

❑ Associate Futures Contracts Portfolio Manager

❑ IIROC approval only

❑ Local

Québec — activities relating to derivatives

Firm categories

❑ Derivatives Dealers

❑ Derivatives Portfolio Manager

Individual categories and permitted activities

❑ Derivatives Dealing Representative

❑ Derivatives Advising Representative

❑ Derivatives Associate Advising Representative

Schedule C — Address and agent for service (Item 4)

Item 4.1 — Address for service

You must have one address for service in each province or territory in which you are now, or are seeking to become, a registered individual or permitted individual. A post office box is not an acceptable address for service.

Address for service: .... (number, street, city, province or territory, postal code)

Telephone number: (........) .... Fax number: (........) ....

Business e-mail address ....

Item 4.2 — Agent for service

If you have appointed an agent for service, provide the following information for the agent. The address for service provided above must be the address of the agent named below.

Name of agent for service: .... *(if applicable)*

Contact person: .... Last name, First name

Schedule D — Current employment, other business activities, officer positions held and directorships (Item 7)

Complete a separate Schedule D for each of your current business and employment activities, including employment and business activities with your new sponsoring firm and any employment and business activities outside your new sponsoring firm. Also include all officer or director positions and any other equivalent positions held, as well as positions of influence. The information must be provided

- whether or not you receive compensation for such services, and

- whether or not any such position is business related.

1. — Start date

.... (YYYY/MM/DD)

2. — Firm information

❏ Check here if this activity is employment with your sponsoring firm.

If the activity is with your sponsoring firm, you are not required to indicate the firm name and address information below:

Name of business or employer: ....

Address of business or employer: .... (number, street, city, province, territory or state, country)

Name and title of your immediate supervisor: ....

3. — Description of duties

Describe all employment and business activities related to this employer. Include the nature of the business and your duties, title or relationship with the business. If you are seeking registration that requires specific experience, include details such as level of responsibility, value of accounts under direct supervision, number of years of experience, and percentage of time spent on each activity.

4. — Number of work hours per week

How many hours per week do you devote to this business or employment? ....

If this activity is employment with your sponsoring firm and you work less than 30 hours per week, explain why.

....

5. — Conflict of Interest

If you have more than one employer or are engaged in businss related activities:

A: Disclose any potential for confusion by clients and any potential for conflicts of interest arising from your multiple employment or business related activities or proposed business related activities.

....

B. Indicate whether or not any of your employers or organizations where you engage in business related activities are listed on an exchange.

....

C. Confirm whether the firm has procedures for minimizing potential conflicts of interest and, if so, confirm that you are aware of these procedures.

....

D. State the name of the person at your sponsoring firm who has reviewed and approved your multiple employment or business related activities or proposed business related activities.

....

....

....

E. If you do not perceive any conflicts of interest arising from this employment, explain why.

. . .

Schedule E — Ownership of Securities in New Sponsoring Firm (Item 8)

Firm name (whose business is trading in or advising on securities or derivatives, or both): ....

What is your relationship to the firm? Partner ❑ Major shareholder ❑

What is the period of this relationship?

From: To: *(if applicable)*

.... (YYYY/MM) .... (YYYY/MM)

Provide the following information:

a) State the number, value, class and percentage of securities, or the amount of partnership interest you own or propose to acquire when you are reinstated or approved as a result of the review of this form. If acquiring shares when you are so approved or registered, state the source (for example, treasury shares, or if upon transfer, state name of transferor).

....

b) State the market value (approximate, if necessary) of any subordinated debentures or bonds of the firm to be held by you or any other subordinated loan to be made by you to the firm:

....

c) If another person or firm has provided you with funds to invest in the firm, provide the name of the person or firm and state the relationship between you and that person or firm:

....

d) Are the funds to be invested (or proposed to be invested) guaranteed directly or indirectly by any person or firm?

Yes ❑ No ❑

If "Yes", provide the name of the person or firm and state the relationship between you and that person or firm:

....

e) Have you directly or indirectly given up any rights relating to these securities or this partnership interest, or do you, when you are registered or approved as a result of the review of this form, intend to give up any of these rights (including by hypothecation, pledging or depositing as collateral the securities or partnership interest with any firm or person)?

Yes ❑ No ❑

If "Yes", provide the name of the person or firm, state the relationship between you and that person or firm and describe the rights that have been or will be given up: ....

f) Is a person other than you the beneficial owner of the shares, bonds, debentures, partnership units or notes held by you?

Yes ❑ No ❑

If "Yes", complete (g), (h) and (i).

g) Name of beneficial owner:

....	....	....	....
Last name	First name	Second name (N/A ❑)	Third name (N/A ❑)

h) Residential address:

.... (number, street, city, province, territory or state, country, postal code)

i) Occupation: ....

Schedule F — Contact information for Notice of collection and use of personal information

Alberta

Alberta Securities Commission

Suite 600, 250-5th St. SW

Calgary, AB T2P 0R4

Attention: Information Officer

Part 3:
REGISTRATION

Telephone: (403) 297-6454

British Columbia

British Columbia Securities Commission

P.O. Box 10142, Pacific Centre

701 West Georgia Street

Vancouver, BC V7Y 1L2

Attention: Freedom of Information Officer

Telephone: (604) 899-6500 or (800) 373-6393 (in Canada)

Manitoba

The Manitoba Securities Commission

500 - 400 St. Mary Avenue

Winnipeg, MB R3C 4K5

Attention: Director of Registrations

Telephone: (204) 945-2548

Fax (204) 945-0330

New Brunswick

Financial and Consumer Services Commission of New Brunswick / Commission des services financiers et des services aux consommateurs du Nouveau-Brunswick

Suite 300, 85 Charlotte Street

Saint John, NB E2L 2J2

Attention: Director of Securities

Telephone: (506) 658-3060

Newfoundland and Labrador

Superintendent of Securities, Service NL

Government of Newfoundland and Labrador

P.O. Box 8700

2nd Floor, West Block

Confederation Building

St. John's, NL A1B 4J6

Attention: Manager of Registrations

Telephone: (709) 729-5661

Nova Scotia

Nova Scotia Securities Commission

Suite 400, 5251 Duke Street

Halifax, NS B3J 1P3

Attention: Deputy Director, Capital Markets

Telephone: (902) 424-7768

Northwest Territories

Government of the Northwest Territories

Department of Justice

1st Floor Stuart M. Hodgson Building

5009 - 49th Street

Yellowknife, NWT X1A 2L9

Attention: Deputy Superintendent of Securities

Telephone: (867) 920-8984

Nunavut

Government of Nunavut

Department of Justice

P.O. Box 1000 Station 570

Iqaluit, NU X0A 0H0

Attention: Deputy Registrar of Securities

Telephone: (867) 975-6590

Ontario

Ontario Securities Commission

22nd Floor

20 Queen Street West

Toronto, ON M5H 3S8

Attention: Compliance and Registrant Regulation

Telephone: (416) 593-8314

e-mail: registration@osc.gov.on.ca

Prince Edward Island

Securities Office

Department of Community Affairs and Attorney General

P.O. Box 2000

Charlottetown, PE C1A 7N8

Attention: Deputy Registrar of Securities

Telephone: (902) 368-6288

Québec

Autorité des marchés financiers

800, square Victoria, 22e étage

C.P. 246, tour de la Bourse

Montréal (Québec) H4Z 1G3

Attention: Responsable de l'accès à l'information

Telephone: (514) 395-0337 or (877) 525-0337

Saskatchewan

Financial and Consumer Affairs Authority of Saskatchewan

Suite 601, 1919 Saskatchewan Drive

Regina, SK S4P 4H2

Attention: Deputy Director, Capital Markets

Telephone: (306) 787-5871

Yukon

Government of Yukon

Superintendent of Securities

Department of Community Services

P.O. Box 2703 C-6

Whitehorse, YT Y1A 2C6

Attention: Superintendent of Securities

Telephone: (867) 667-5314

Self-regulatory organization

Investment Industry Regulatory Organization of Canada

121 King Street West, Suite 2000

Toronto, Ontario M5H 3T9

Attention: Privacy Officer

Telephone: (416) 364-6133

E-mail: PrivacyOfficer@iiroc.ca

Companion Policy 33-109CP — To National Instrument 33-109 Registration Information

Table of Contents

PART 1 GENERAL

Part 1 — General

1.1 — Purpose

This Companion Policy sets out how the Canadian Securities Administrators interpret or apply National Instrument 33-109 *Registration Information* (the Rule).

1.2 — Definition of permitted individuals

Section 1.1 of the Rule defines a permitted individual as an individual who meets the criteria set forth in paragraph (a) of the definition. A permitted individual may or may not be a registered individual. For example, the chief executive officer of a registered firm is registered as the firm's ultimate designated person and is also a permitted individual. The definition of permitted individual allows the Rule to separate out the filing requirements which are applicable only to permitted individuals from those which are applicable to registered individuals.

1.3 — Overview of the forms

The following forms are for firms:

- Form 33-109F3 *Business Locations other than Head Office* — to disclose each business location of the firm and any change of business location

- Form 33-109F6 *Firm Registration* — to apply for registration as a dealer, adviser or investment fund manager

The following forms are for individuals and are submitted in NRD format:

- Form 33-109F1 *Notice of Termination of Registered Individuals and Permitted Individuals* — to notify the regulator that a registered or permitted individual has ceased to have authority to act on behalf of the firm

- Form 33-109F2 *Change or Surrender of Individual Categories* — to apply for registration or review in an additional category or to surrender a category

- Form 33-109F4 Registration of Individuals and Review of Permitted Individuals — to apply for registration or review as a permitted individual

- Form 33-109F7 *Reinstatement of Registered Individuals and Permitted Individuals* — to reinstate an individual's registration or a permitted individual status

1.4 — Notice requirements

Form 33-109F5 *Change of Registration Information* is used by firms and individuals to notify regulators of any change to their registration information. Under sections 3.1 and 4.1 of the Rule a registrant and a permitted individual must keep their registration information current on an ongoing basis by filing notices of change of information within the required time.

Appendix A summarizes the notice requirements, time periods and the forms under the Rule to notify regulators of a change to a firm's or individual's registration information.

1.5 — Contact information

When a firm submits a Form 33-109F6, supporting documents or a Form 33-109F5, it can make the submission using e-mail, fax or mail. Appendix B attached to this policy sets out the contact information for the regulator in each jurisdiction of Canada and for the Investment Industry Regulatory

Organization of Canada (**IIROC**) in those jurisdictions where the securities regulatory authority has delegated, assigned or authorized IIROC to perform registration functions.

Part 2 — Forms Used by Individuals

2.1 — National Registration Database (NRD)

The NRD is the database containing information about all registrants and permitted individuals under securities or commodity futures legislation in each jurisdiction of Canada. The requirement for firms to enrol, and to make certain submissions, on NRD are set out in National Instrument 31-102 *National Registration Database*. Detailed information about the NRD and the enrolment process is available in the NRD User Guide published at *www.nrd-info.ca*.

2.2 — Form 33-109F4

Types of submissions using Form 33-109F4

The NRD format for submitting a completed Form 33-109F4 under subsection 2.2(1) or 2.5(1) of the Rule include four distinct NRD submission types that are made in the following circumstances:

- Initial *Registration*, when an individual is seeking registration, or review as a permitted individual, through NRD for the first time

- *Registration in an Additional Jurisdiction*, when an individual is registered or is a permitted individual in a jurisdiction of Canada and is seeking registration, or review as a permitted individual, in an additional jurisdiction

- *Registration with an Additional Sponsoring Firm*, when an individual is registered, or is a permitted individual, on behalf of one sponsoring firm and applies for registration, or seeks review as a permitted individual, to act on behalf of an additional sponsoring firm

- *Reactivation of Registration*, when an individual who has an NRD record is applying for registration, reinstatement of registration or is seeking review as a permitted individual and is not eligible under subsection 2.3(2) or 2.5(2) of the Rule to submit a Form 33-109F7

Submissions by permitted individuals

Under subsection 2.5(1) of the Rule, within 10 days of becoming a permitted individual, the individual must submit a Form 33-109F4 for review by the regulator. An individual whose registration is suspended may apply to reinstate the registration by submitting a completed Form 33-109F4 to the regulator. This is done with the *Reactivation of registration* submission on NRD. After making this submission the individual may not conduct activities requiring registration unless and until the regulator has approved the application. However, an application for reinstatement or review is not required if the individual meets all of the conditions for automatic reinstatement in subsection 2.3(2) or 2.5(2) of the Rule, which include submitting a completed Form 33-109F7 to the regulator as described in section 2.5 below.

Agent for service

Item 18 *Agent for service* of Form 33-109F4 is a certification clause by the individual that he or she has completed the appointment for service required in each relevant jurisdiction. There is no distinct form under NI 33-109 for the appointment of an agent for service for use by individuals. Please refer to the form used by the registered firm. This format is acceptable to the regulator.

2.3 — Form 33-109F2

This form is used by individuals to apply to add or to surrender a registration category to seek review of a change in their permitted individual category or to change any information on Schedule C of a previously submitted Form 33-109F4. If an individual has ceased to have authority to act on behalf of their sponsoring firm as a registered or permitted individual in the last jurisdiction of Canada where they were so acting, they cannot submit a Form 33-109F2. Instead, the individual's sponsoring firm submits a Form 33-109F1 to notify the regulator of the termination or cessation of authority to act on behalf of the firm.

2.4 — Form 33-109F5 for individuals

When an individual submits a Form 33-109F5 to update their registration information NRD will transmit the information to the regulator in each jurisdiction in which the individual is registered or is a permitted individual. However, only the principal regulator processes the submission to update the individual's registration information on NRD, or if necessary to deny or withdraw the submission.

Form 33-109F5 should not be used by an individual applying to add or surrender a registration category or to seek review of a change in his/her permitted individual category. In this case, Form 33-109F2 is used. It should also be noted that Form 33-109F5 is not used by an individual that is registered or is a permitted individual in a jurisdiction of Canada and is seeking registration, or review as a permitted individual, in an additional jurisdiction. In this case, a Form 33-109F4 is used and is identified on NRD as *Registration in an Additional Jurisdiction*. This also applies to an individual adding a sponsoring firm; Form 33-109F4 is used and is identified on NRD as *Registration with an Additional Sponsoring Firm*.

2.5 — Form 33-109F7 for reinstatement

When an individual leaves a sponsoring firm and joins a new registered firm, they may submit a Form 33-109F7 to have their registration or permitted individual status automatically reinstated in one or more of the same categories and jurisdictions as before, subject to all of the conditions set out in subsection 2.3(2) or 2.5(2) of the Rule. An individual who meets all of the applicable conditions will be able to transfer directly from one sponsoring firm to another and start engaging in activities requiring registration from the first day that they submit the Form 33-109F7.

2.6 — Business locations (Form 33-109F4 and Form 33-109F7)

The term "business location" is defined in section 1.1 of the Rule. If the business location specified in Item 9 of Form 33-109F4 or Item 5 of NI 33-109F7 is a residence, the individual must certify in both these forms that they give their consent for the regulator or, in Québec, the securities regulatory authority to enter the residence for the administration of securities legislation.

2.7 — Ongoing fitness for registration

Every registrant must maintain their fitness for registration on an ongoing basis. Under securities legislation, the regulator has discretionary authority to suspend or revoke an individual's registration or to restrict it with terms and conditions at any time. The regulator may do this, for example, if it receives information through a notice of termination from an individual's former sponsoring firm or any other source that raises concerns about the individual's continued fitness for registration. Individuals will be given an opportunity to be heard before a decision is made to suspend or revoke registration or to impose terms and conditions.

Part 3: REGISTRATION

Part 3 — Forms Used by Firms

3.1 — Form 33-109F6

When a firm submits a Form 33-109F6 to apply for registration, it may pay the regulatory fees to the applicable regulators by cheque or by using the NRD function called *Resubmit Fee Payment*. A firm that applies in multiple jurisdictions should submit its application to the regulator in the principal jurisdiction or, if Ontario is a non-principal jurisdiction, to the regulators in the principal jurisdiction and in Ontario. For more details refer to National Policy 11-204 *Process for Registration in Multiple Jurisdictions*.

Under section 4A.1 of Multilateral Instrument 11-102 *Passport System*, the principal regulator for a foreign firm is the securities regulatory authority or regulator identified in Item 2.2(b) of the firms most recent Form 33-109F6 or Form 33-109F5 *Change of Registration Information* if the change noted in that form relates to Item 2.2(b) of Form 33-109F6. For firms without a head office in Canada or not already registered in a jurisdiction of Canada, Item 2.2(b) of Form 33-109F6 specifies that the principal regulator is the jurisdiction of Canada in which the firm expects to conduct most of its activities that require registration as at the end of its current financial year or conducted most of its activities that require registration as at the end of its most recently completed financial year. Firms should determine whether to base the selection on where they expect to conduct most of their activities or where they conducted most of their activities the previous year based on which they feel is most appropriate.

The factors a firm should consider in identifying the principal regulator are:

- the jurisdiction in which the firm has a business location

- when applying for dealer registration or adviser registration, the jurisdiction in which the firm expects to have most of its clients as at the end of its current financial year or the jurisdiction in which most of the firm's clients were located at the end of its most recently completed financial year

- when applying for investment fund manager registration, the jurisdiction in which the firm expects to conduct most of its investment fund manager activities as at the end of its current financial year or the jurisdiction in which most of the firm's investment fund manager activities were conducted at the end of its most recently completed financial year

- when applying for investment fund manager registration and another category of registration, the jurisdiction in which firm expects to conduct most of the activities that require registration as at the end of its current financial year or conducted most of the activities that require registration as at the end of its most recently completed financial year based on the foregoing

Under section 4A.2 of Multilateral Instrument 11-102 *Passport System*, a securities regulatory authority or regulator has the discretion to change the principal regulator for the firm.

3.2 — Form 33-109F5

A firm that is registered in multiple jurisdictions may submit a Form 33-109F5 to its principal regulator only to notify regulators of a change to the firm's registration information, in accordance with subsection 3.1(6) of the Rule.

3.3 — Form 33-109F3

A firm must notify the regulator of each business location in the jurisdiction. The term "business location" is defined in section 1.1 of the Rule and may include a residence where a firm's registered individuals are based for the purpose of carrying out activities that require registration.

Firms certify in Item 22 of Form 33-109F4 that if the business location is a residence, the individual conducting business from that business location has completed a Form 33-109F4 certifying that they give their consent for the regulator or, in Québec, the securities regulatory authority to enter the residence for the administration of securities legislation.

Firms submit this form through the NRD website.

3.4 — Discretionary exemption for bulk transfers

Regulators will consider an application for an exemption from certain requirements in the Rule to facilitate a reorganization or combination of firms which would otherwise require a large number of submissions to change business locations and transfer individuals. The information required, and the conditions to obtain, this type of exemption application are described in the attached Appendix C.

3.5 — Form 33-109F1

Under section 4.2 of the Rule, a registered firm must notify the regulator no more than 10 days after an individual ceased to have authority to act on behalf of the firm, as a registered or permitted individual. Typically, this occurs due to the termination of the individual's employment, partnership or agency relationship with the firm. However, it also occurs when an individual is reassigned to a different position at the firm that does not require registration or is not a permitted individual category. Form 33-109F1 is submitted through the NRD website to give notice of the cessation date and the reason for the termination or cessation.

Under paragraph 4.2(1)(b) of the Rule, the information in item 5 [*Details about the termination*] of a Form 33-109F1 must be submitted unless the cessation of authority to act on behalf of the firm was caused by the death of the individual. A firm can submit the information in item 5 either at the time of the making the initial submission on NRD, if the information is available within that 10 day period, or within 30 days of the cessation date, by making an NRD submission entitled *Update / Correct Termination Information*.

Part 4 — Due Diligence by Firms

4.1 — Obligations of former sponsoring firm

After submitting a Form 33-109F1 with regard to a former sponsored individual a firm should promptly send the individual a copy of the completed Form 33-109F1. Under subsections 4.2(3) and (4) of the Rule, within 10 days of a request by a former sponsored individual, a firm must provide the individual with a copy of the Form 33-109F1 that was submitted, and if necessary, a further copy that includes the information in item 5 of the Form 33-109F1, within 10 days of submitting that information.

4.2 — Obligations of new sponsoring firm

(1) In fulfilling its obligations under subsection 5.1(1) of the Rule, a firm should make reasonable efforts to do all of the following:

- establish written policies and procedures to verify an individual's information prior to submitting a Form 33-109F4 or Form 33-109F7 on behalf of the individual

- document the firm's review of an individual's information in accordance with the firm's policies and procedures

- regularly remind registered and permitted individuals about their disclosure obligations under the Rule, such as notifying the regulator about changes to their registration information

Under subsection 5.1(2) of the Rule, within 60 days of hiring a sponsored individual a firm must obtain a copy of the most recent Form 33-109F1, if any, for the individual. If a sponsoring firm cannot obtain it from the sponsored individual, as a last resort the individual should request it from the regulator.

The information referred to above will assist the firm in meeting its obligations under subsection 5.1(1) of the Rule and should inform the firm's hiring decisions. If an individual is hired before a completed Form 33-109F1 is available and if the firm discovers an inconsistency in the individual's disclosure to the firm or the regulator, then the firm should take appropriate action. All of the required information should be available within 60 days of hiring the individual, which will often fall within the individual's probation period under their employment or agency contract.

Part 5 — *Commodity Futures Act* Submissions

5.1 — Ontario

In Ontario, if a person or company is required to make a submission under both the Rule and OSC Rule 33-506 (*Commodity Futures Act*) *Registration Information* with respect to the same information, the securities regulatory authority is of the view that a single filing on a form required under either rule satisfies both requirements.

5.2 — Manitoba

In Manitoba, the Rule is a rule under each of the *Securities Act* and the *Commodity Futures Act*. A single submission with respect to the same information will satisfy the requirements of both statutes.

APPENDIX A — SUMMARY OF NOTICE REQUIREMENTS IN NATIONAL INSTRUMENT 33-109

Description of Change	Notice Period	Section	Form submitted
Firms — Form 33-109F6 information			**by e-mail, fax or mail**
Part 1 — Registration details	10 days		
Part 2 — Contact information, including head office address (except 2.4)	10 days	3.1(1)(b)	Form 33-109F5
Item 2.4 — Agent and Address for service [items 3 and 4 of Schedule B to Form 33-109F6]	10 days	3.1(4)	Schedule B to Form 33-109F6 *Submission to jurisdiction*
Part 3 — Business history & structure	30 days	3.1(1)(a)	
Part 4 — Registration history	10 days		
Part 5 — Financial condition	10 days		
Part 6 — Client relationships	10 days	3.1(1)(b)	Form 33-109F5
Part 7 — Regulatory action	10 days		
Part 8 — Legal action	10 days		
Firms — other notice requirements			**in NRD format**
Open/change of business location (other than head office)	10 days	3.2	Form 33-109F3
Termination/Cessation of Authority of a registered or permitted individual — items 1–4	10 days	4.2(2)(a)	Form 33-109F1
item 5	30 days	4.2(2)(b)	
Individuals — Form F4 information			**in NRD format**
Item 1 — Name	10 days		
Item 2 — Address	10 days	4.1(1)(b)	
Item 3 — Personal information	No update required	4.1(2)	
Item 4 — Citizenship	30 days	4.1(1)(a)	
Item 5 — Registration jurisdictions	10 days		
Item 6 — Individual categories	10 days		
Item 7 — Address for service	10 days	4.1(1)(b)	
Item 8 — Proficiency	10 days		
Item 9 — Location of employment	10 days		Form 33-109F5
Item 10 — Current employment	10 days		
Item 11 — Previous employment	30 days	4.1(1)(a)	
Item 12 — Terminations	10 days		
Item 13 — Regulatory disclosure	10 days		
Item 14 — Criminal disclosure	10 days	4.1(1)(b)	
Item 15 — Civil disclosure	10 days		

Part 3:
REGISTRATION

Item 16 — Financial disclosure	10 days		
Item 17 — Ownership of securities	10 days		
Change of F4: registrant position or relationship with sponsoring firm / permitted status	10 days	4.1(4)	Form 33-109F2
Review of a Permitted individual	10 days after appointment	2.5	Form 33-109F4 or 33-109F7, subject to conditions
Automatic reinstatement of registration subject to conditions	within 90 days of cessation date	2.3(2)	Form 33-109F7

APPENDIX B — CONTACT INFORMATION FOR THE REGULATORS AND IIROC

- Part 1 provides the regulators' contact information for registrants in all categories, except for those in the jurisdictions and categories listed in Part 2

- Part 2 below, provides IIROC's contact information in the jurisdictions where IIROC performs registration functions for representatives of investment dealers and, in some cases, for investment dealer firms

Part 1 — Regulators' Contact Information

Alberta

e-mail: registration@asc.ca

fax: (403) 297-4113

Alberta Securities Commission,

Suite 600, 250-5th St. SW

Calgary, AB T2P 0R4 Registration department

British Columbia

e-mail: registration@bcsc.bc.ca

fax: (604) 899-6506

British Columbia Securities Commission

P.O. Box 10142, Pacific Centre

701 West Georgia Street

Vancouver, BC V7Y 1L2

Attention: Registration

Manitoba

e-mail: registrationmsc@gov.mb.ca

fax: (204) 945-0330

The Manitoba Securities Commission

500-400 St. Mary Avenue

Winnipeg, MB R3C 4K5

Attention: Registrations

New Brunswick

e-mail: nrs@fcnb.ca

fax:(506) 658-3059

Financial and Consumer Services Commission of New Brunswick / Commission des services financiers et des services aux consommateurs du Nouveau-Brunswick

Suite 300, 85 Charlotte Street

Saint John, NB E2L 2J2

Attention: Registration Officer

Newfoundland and Labrador

e-mail: scon@gov.nl.ca

fax: (709) 729-6187

Superintendent of Securities, Service NL

Government of Newfoundland and Labrador

P.O. Box 8700, 2nd Floor, West Block

Confederation Building

St. John's, NL A1B 4J6

Attention: Registration Section

Northwest Territories

e-mail: SecuritiesRegistry@gov.nt.ca

fax: (867) 873-0243

Government of the Northwest Territories

Department of Justice

P.O. Box 1320

Yellowknife, NWT X1A 2L9

Attention: Exemption Review Staff

Nova Scotia

e-mail: nrs@novascotia.ca

fax: (902) 424-4625

Nova Scotia Securities Commission

Suite 400, 5251 Duke Street

Halifax, NS B3J 1P3

Attention: Registration

Nunavut

e-mail: CorporateRegistrations@gov.nu.ca

fax: (867) 975-6594

Government of Nunavut

Department of Justice

P.O. Box 1000 Station 570

Iqaluit, NU X0A 0H0

Attention: Deputy Registrar

Ontario

Telephone: (416) 593-8314

e-mail: registration@osc.gov.on.ca

Ontario Securities Commission

22nd Floor

20 Queen Street West

Toronto, ON M5H 3S8

Attention: Compliance and Registrant Regulation

Prince Edward Island

e-mail: ccis@gov.pe.ca

fax: (902) 368-5283

Securities Office

Department of Community Affairs and Attorney General

P.O. Box 2000, 95 Rochford Street

Charlottetown, PE C1A 7N8

Attention: Superintendent of Securities

Québec

e-mail: inscription@lautorite.qc.ca

fax: (514) 873-3090

Autorité des marchés financiers

Direction de l'encadrement des intermédiaires

800 square Victoria, 22e étage

C.P 246, Tour de la Bourse

Montréal (Québec) H4Z 1G3

Saskatchewan

e-mail: registrationsfsc@gov.sk.ca

fax: (306) 787-5871

Financial and Consumer Affairs Authority of Saskatchewan

Suite 601

1919 Saskatchewan Drive

Regina, SK S4P 4H2

Attention: Registration

Yukon

e-mail: corporateaffairs@gov.yk.ca

fax: (867) 393-6251

Government of Yukon

Superintendent of Securities

P.O. Box 2703

Whitehorse, YT Y1A 2C6

Attention: Superintendent of Securities

Part 2 — Investment Industry Regulatory Organization of Canada Contact Information

** registration of investment dealer firms and their representatives **

* registration of investment dealer representatives *

** Alberta — IIROC **

British Columbia — IIROC

e-mail: « registration@iiroc.ca »

fax: 604-683-3491

1055 West Georgia Street

Suite 2800 - Royal Centre

Vancouver, BC V6E 3R5

Attention: Registration department

** Saskatchewan — IIROC **

e-mail: « registration@iiroc.ca »

fax: (403) 265-4603

#2300, 355- 4th Avenue SW,

Calgary, AB T2P 0J1

Attention: Registration department

** Newfoundland and Labrador — IIROC **

* Ontario — IIROC *

e-mail: « registration@iiroc.ca »

fax: (416) 364-9177

Suite 1600,

121 King Street West

Toronto, ON M5H 3T9

Attention: Registration department

* Québec — IIROC *

e-mail: « registration@iiroc.ca »

fax: (514) 878-0797

Organisme canadien de réglementation du commerce des valeurs mobilières

5 Place Ville Marie

Bureau 1550

Montréal (Québec) H3B 2G2

Attention: Service des inscriptions

APPENDIX C — DISCRETIONARY EXEMPTION FOR BULK TRANSFERS OF LOCATIONS AND INDIVIDUALS

(1) If a registered firm is acquiring a large number of business locations (for example, as a result of an amalgamation or asset purchase) from one or more other registered firms that are located in the same jurisdiction(s) and registered in the same categories as the acquiring firm, and if a significant number of individuals are associated on NRD with the business locations, the regulator will consider granting an exemption from any or all of the following requirements:

(a) to submit a notice regarding the termination of each employment, partner, or agency relationship under section 4.2 of the Rule;

(b) to submit a registration application or a reinstatement notice for each individual seeking be a registered individual under section 2.2 or 2.3 of the Rule;

(c) to submit a Form 33-109F4 or Form 33-109F7 for each permitted individual under section 2.5 of the Rule;

(d) to notify the regulator of a change to the business location information in Form 33-109F3 under section 3.2 of the Rule.

(2) The exemption application should be submitted by the registered firm that will acquire control of the business locations at the closing of the transaction and should be submitted well in advance of the date (**transfer date**) on which the business locations will be transferred. It would typically be sufficient if a firm submits the application at least 30 days before the transfer date. An application for this type of exemption should include the following information:

(a) the name and NRD number of the registered firm that will acquire control of the business locations;

(b) for each registered firm that is transferring control of the business locations;

    (i) the name and NRD number of the registered firm,

    (ii) the address and NRD number of each business location that is being transferred from the registered firm named in (b)(i) to the registered firm named in (a),

    (iii) the date that the business locations and individuals will be transferred to the registered firm named in (a).

(3) If the exemption is granted, as soon as practicable after the transfer date, the regulator will instruct the NRD administrator to record on NRD the transfer of the business locations, registered individuals and permitted individuals.

(4) Bulk transfers involving firms that are registered in different categories or different jurisdictions may need to take additional steps. Firms involved in such a transaction should contact their principal regulator to discuss what steps are required for the firm to be eligible for a bulk transfer exemption as described above.

(5) A firm applying for this type of exemption in more than one jurisdiction should refer to National Policy 11-203 *Process for Exemption Applications in Multiple Jurisdictions* for guidance on the form of application and the information required. The firm may set out the information referred to in (2) as follows:

A) « Registered firm that will acquire the business locations »

Name:

Firm NRD number:

B) « Registered firm transferring the business locations »

Name:

Firm NRD number:

« Business locations that will be transferred »

Address of business location:

NRD number of business location:

Address of business location:

NRD number of business location:

(Repeat for each business location as necessary)

C) Date that business locations will be transferred:

Adoption by OSC: (2003) 26 O.S.C.B. 1362 and (2002) 25 O.S.C.B. 7526; Request for Comments: (2002) 25 O.S.C.B. 3463 and (2001) 25 O.S.C.B. 7480.

Adoption of Amendment by OSC: (2007) 30 O.S.C.B. 1649; Request for Comments: (2006) 29 O.S.C.B. 3961.

Adoption of Replacement Policy by OSC: (2009) 32 O.S.C.B. (Supp. 4) 215 and 32 O.S.C.B. (Supp. 2) 312; Request for Comments: (2008) 31 O.S.C.B. 2419.

Adoption of Replacement Policy by OSC: (2011) 34 O.S.C.B. (Supp. 3) 1; Request for Comments: (2010) 33 O.S.C.B. (Supp. 2) 1.

CSA Staff Notice 33-305 — Sale of Insurance Products by Dually Employed Salespersons

Date: **January 7, 2000**

23 O.S.C.B. 8

On August 27, 1999, the CSA Distribution Structures Position Paper (the "Paper") was published setting out the CSA position with respect to commercial structures employed by dealer registrants. One of the issues addressed in the Paper is that of dually employed salespersons. The Paper takes the position that dual employment should be allowed provided the salesperson's other employment does not interfere with his/her duties and responsibilities as a salesperson and the dealer is responsible for all financial activities of the salesperson that are not subject to another regulatory regime. The Paper includes insurance product sales and deposit taking activities as examples of activities that are subject to another regulatory regime.

Staff has become aware that some dealers and salespersons have interpreted the Paper to mean that *all* activities of the salesperson must be the responsibility of the dealer, including the sale of insurance products.

Staff would like to emphasize that the Paper does not require salespersons to offer the sale of insurance products through a dealer. However, if insurance products are being offered through or by the dealer, the dealer would be responsible for the sale of those products by the salesperson.

CSA Notice 33-310 — Joint Forum Releases Summary of Comments and Responses on Principles and Practices for the Sale of Products and Services in the Financial Sector

Date: **February 13, 2004**

27 O.S.C.B. 1832

The Joint Forum of Financial Market Regulators (the "Joint Forum") is releasing a summary of comments and responses on its consultation package entitled *Principles and Practices for the Sale of Products and Services in the Financial Sector*. The Canadian Securities Administrators are a constituent member of the Joint Forum together with the Canadian Council of Insurance Regulators and the Canadian Association of Pension Supervisory Authorities.

Part 3: REGISTRATION

The Joint Forum released the consultation package on March 6, 2003. The comment period closed on May 29, 2003 and 17 submissions were received. The full text of all the comment letters can be viewed on the following web sites:

- Ontario Securities Commission — www.osc.gov.on.ca

- Canadian Council of Insurance Regulators — www.ccir-ccra.org.

The Joint Forum's objective in undertaking this project was to develop standards of professionalism and fair conduct that Canadian consumers should be able to expect in their financial transactions, regardless of the product or service being sold, or the regulatory regime that applies. The Joint Forum hopes to obtain the endorsement of these principles and practices by key industry participants across the financial services sector.

The proposed practice standards will be introduced as voluntary guidelines, not legal requirements. However, we expect most industry associations and individual firms to adopt the guidelines. This will benefit consumers of financial products and services by setting a minimum standard of conduct that they can expect from all participating firms, without imposing burdensome requirements on the industry.

The Joint Forum Sub-committee on Practice Standards is currently overseeing the next steps in this project and will be working on the implementation issues.

On behalf of the Joint Forum, the CSA would like to thank all parties that submitted comments. We appreciate the time and effort they took in responding to the consultation package.

Contacts

[omitted]

About the Joint Forum

The Joint Forum was founded in 1999 by the Canadian Council of Insurance Regulators, the Canadian Association of Pension Supervisory Authorities and the Canadian Securities Administrators, and also includes a representative from the Canadian Insurance Services Regulatory Organizations. The mandate of the Joint Forum is to pro-actively facilitate and coordinate the development of harmonized, cross-sectoral and cross-jurisdictional solutions to financial services regulatory issues.

[Summary of comments not reproduced]

CSA Staff Notice 33-315 — Suitability Obligation and Know Your Product

Date: September 4, 2009

32 O.S.C.B. 6890

Purpose

This notice reminds registrants of their duty under securities law to satisfy their suitability obligations to clients, including the requirement to fully understand the products recommended to clients. It also provides guidance to registrants on how to meet their obligations.

Suitability obligation

Securities law requires registrants to determine whether a proposed purchase or sale of a security[1] for a client is suitable.[2]

There are two key requirements for determining suitability. Registrants must understand:

1. the general investment needs and objectives of their client and any other factors necessary for them to be able to determine whether a proposed purchase or sale is suitable (know your client or KYC), and

2. the attributes and associated risks of the products they are recommending to clients (commonly referred to as know your product or KYP)

Registrants must meet the KYC and KYP requirements in order to make the suitability determination required by law. This notice focuses on the KYP requirement.

Know your product

Registrants must understand the structure and features of each investment product they recommend. This includes costs, risks and eligibility requirements. The KYP requirement applies to both the firm and the individual.

We expect firms to have a process for reviewing and approving new products and existing products whose structure or features have significantly changed. However, if a product is on the firm's "approved list", it does not mean that it will be suitable for all clients. Individual registrants must still determine suitability of each proposed transaction for each client.

KYP applies to all investment products whether or not they are sold under a prospectus. The extent of the product review process will depend on the structure and features of the product.

---

[1]In Alberta, British Columbia, Saskatchewan and as of September 28, 2009, New Brunswick, a reference to "security" in this notice includes "exchange contract".

[2]The requirement to assess whether the purchase or sale of securities is suitable for a client is in section 13.3 of National Instrument 31-103 — *Registration Requirements and Exemptions* (NI 31-103). Before NI 31-103, provincial securities laws imposed similar suitability requirements.

For example, complex investment products (including those that are novel or not transparent in structure) may require a more extensive review than more straightforward products. Products that are sold under a prospectus exemption may require a more extensive review because of the limited disclosure available about them.

Individual registrants

The firm's approval of an investment product alone does not satisfy KYP. Individual registrants must thoroughly understand a product before they can determine whether it is suitable to recommend the product to a client. Firms may want to provide product training to ensure that their representatives can conduct their suitability review with an appropriate understanding of the products and their risks.

Although firms may set out general investor profiles describing the type of investor for whom a product may be suitable, individual registrants must still determine suitability on each transaction for a client. Individual registrants should also explain the risks of products they are recommending to their clients.

Unless a registrant can rely on a specific exemption from its suitability obligation, a registrant has a suitability obligation to all clients, including accredited investors and investors who buy a product under a prospectus exemption. Individual registrants may not delegate their suitability obligations to their client, another registrant or anyone else.

Product review process

The firm's product review process should include procedures for identifying, reviewing and approving (or rejecting) new products and for monitoring existing products for significant changes to those products.

Registered firms must have the appropriate skills and experience to perform their own analysis of all products they recommend to clients. They cannot recommend a product based solely on:

- information from issuers or other third parties, including related parties, about the product's suitability or risk profile

- similarities with other products, or

- recommendations made by other market participants to their clients

Registrants should consider factors such as product features and structure, including risks, costs, management and financial strength of the issuer. They should also determine whether expected returns are realistic. Registrants will also need to re-evaluate an existing product if a change to a key feature causes significant changes to the risk and return profile of the product.

Listed below are some factors that registrants should consider when assessing investment products.

General features and structure

- basis of security's return (e.g. minimum return, dividends, interest rate)

- use of leverage

- conflicts of interest arising from the compensation structure or other factors

- overall complexity, transparency and uniqueness of features of the product's structure

Risks

- the possibility that a client may lose some or all of the principal amount invested

- risks relating to the product, such as liquidity risk (including redemption rights and any features that lock in the principal and/or returns for a specified period), price volatility, default risk, and exposure to counterparty risk

- risks related to assets underlying derivatives or structured products

Costs

- fees paid to registrants or other parties, such as commissions, sales charges, trailer fees, management fees, incentive fees, referral fees and early redemption fees

- embedded costs, such as bid-ask spreads or other expenses

Parties involved

- the issuer's financial position and history

- qualifications, reputation and track record of the parties involved in key aspects of the product, for example, the fund manager, portfolio manager, product manufacturer or sponsor, any guarantors and significant counterparties

Legal and regulatory framework

- any laws or rules of self-regulatory organizations that apply to the registrant

- if distributed under an exemption, whether the product meets the requirements of that exemption

- legal characteristics of derivatives and structured products (e.g. jurisdiction of special purpose vehicles, bankruptcy protection and RSP eligibility)

- frequency, completeness and quality of the issuer's disclosure

Policies and procedures

Registrants should establish and enforce written policies and procedures to ensure that they satisfy their KYC and suitability obligations, including KYP. These policies and procedures should include the steps the registered firm and registered individuals should follow to identify investment products requiring review, the process to review these products, and how to assess the suitability of a product for each client. All firms should have these written policies and procedures, regardless of the firm's size. Firms should monitor and assess compliance by the firm and its individual registrants.

Guidance from self-regulatory organizations

The Investment Industry Regulatory Organization of Canada (IIROC) and the Mutual Fund Dealers Association of Canada (MFDA) have issued the following notices addressing their members' know your product and suitability obligations:

- IIROC Notice 09-0087 *Best practices for product due diligence* dated March 23, 2009

- MFDA Member Regulation Notice MR-0048 *Know-Your-Product* dated October 31, 2005, and

- MFDA Member Regulation Notice MR-0069 *Suitability Guidelines* dated April 14, 2008

CSA Staff Notice 33-316 — Status Report on Consultation under CSA Constulation Paper 33-403

Date: Decemebr 17, 2013

Citation: 37 O.S.C.B. 401

[Not reproduced]

CSA Staff Notice 33-317 — Next Steps in the CSA's Work to Enhance the Obligations of Advisers, Dealers and Representatives Toward Their Clients

Date: April 7, 2016

39 OSCB 3110

[Not reproduced]

OSC Rule 33-501 — Surrender of Registration

Date: April 10, 1998

21 O.S.C.B. 2317

[Revoked upon NI 31-103 coming into force.]

Final Rule: (1998) 21 O.S.C.B. 2317; Approval by O.S.C.: (1998) 21 O.S.C.B. 614; Request for Comments: (1997) 20 O.S.C.B. 3376.

OSC Rule 33-502 — Exceptions to Conflict Rules in The Sale of Mutual Fund Securities

Date: October 9, 1998

21 O.S.C.B. 6429

[Revoked upon NI 31-103 coming into force.]

Final Rule: (1998) 21 O.S.C.B. 6429; Approval by OSC: (1998) 21 O.S.C.B. 4787; Request for Comments: (1998) 21 O.S.C.B. 1701. Replaced a rule which was originally a blanket order (1991) 14 O.S.C.B. 3763 which was deemed to be a rule under s. 143.1(1) of the Act and remade into a rule entitled *In the Matter of Mutual Fund Securities* (1997) 20 O.S.C.B. 3763 and amended by (1998) 21 O.S.C.B. 3361.

OSC Rule 33-504 — Compliance with Section 42

Date: April 10, 1998

21 O.S.C.B. 2318

[As section 42 of the OSA has been revoked, this Rule is not reproduced]

Final Rule: (1998) 21 O.S.C.B. 2318; Approval by OSC: (1998) 21 O.S.C.B. 616; Request for Comments: (1997) 20 O.S.C.B. 3377.

OSC Rule 33-506 — (Commodity Futures Act) Registration Information

Date: February 14, 2003 as replaced effective September 28, 2009, as amended July 1, 2011 and January 11, 2015

26 O.S.C.B. 1374, 32 O.S.C.B. (Supp. 4) 229, 34 O.S.C.B. 7594 and 37 O.S.C.B. (Supp. 5)

[Not reproduced; this rule relates to registrations under the *Commodity Futures Act*.]

Final Rule: (2003) 26 O.S.C.B. 1374; Approval by OSC: (2003) 26 O.S.C.B. 7582; Request for Comments: (2002) 25 O.S.C.B. 2463 and (2001) 24 O.S.C.B. 7480.

Replacement Rule: (2009) 32 O.S.C.B. (Supp. 4) 229; Approval by OSC: (2009) 32 O.S.C.B. (Supp. 2) 1; Request for Comments: (2008) 31 O.S.C.B. 2513.

Amendment to Rule: (2011) 34 O.S.C.B. 7594; Approval by OSC: (2011) 34 O.S.C.B. (Supp. 2) 309; Request for Comments: (2010) 33 O.S.C.B. (Supp. 2) 1.

Amendment to Rule: (2014) 37 O.S.C.B. (Supp. 5) 400.

Companion Policy 33-506CP — (Commodity Futures Act) Registration Information

[Not reproduced]

Adoption by OSC: (2003) 26 O.S.C.B. 1422 and (2002) 25 O.S.C.B. 7582; Request for Comments: (2002) 25 O.S.C.B. 2463 and (2001) 24 O.S.C.B. 7480.

Adoption of Replacement Policy by OSC: (2009) 32 O.S.C.B. (Supp. 4) 328 and 32 O.S.C.B. (Supp. 2) 1; Request for Comments: (2008) 31 O.S.C.B. 2513.

Adoption of Amendments: (2011) 34 O.S.C.B. 7616 and (Supp. 2) 309; Request for Comments: (2010) 33 O.S.C.B. (Supp. 2) 1.

Adoption of Amendments: (2014) 37 O.S.C.B. (Supp. 5) 537.

OSC Policy 33-601 — Guidelines for Policies and Procedures Concerning Inside Information

Date: January 30, 1998

21 O.S.C.B. 617

PART 1 — DEFINITIONS AND INTERPRETATION

1.1 Definitions — In this Policy

"employees" includes employees, directors, officers, partners, independent contractors and agents;

"grey list" means a highly confidential list, compiled by a registrant, of issuers about which the registrant has inside information;

"inside information" means a material fact or a material change with respect to a reporting issuer that has not been generally disclosed; and

"restricted list" means a list, compiled by a registrant, of issuers about which the registrant may have inside information.

1.2 Purpose — This Policy provides general guidelines that registrants may wish to consider in satisfying the requirements of the exemption contained in subsection 175(1) of the Regulation. Subsection 175(1) of the Regulation provides an exemption from the insider trading provisions of subsection 76(1) of the Act. These guidelines are not exhaustive, nor would following them necessarily result in the registrant having implemented and maintained reasonable policies and procedures necessary to sustain the burden of proof required by the exemption in subsection 175(1) of the Regulation. Registrants should consider which practices and procedures would be appropriate for their business.

PART 2 — POLICIES AND PROCEDURES

2.1 General — (1) While the selection and implementation of policies and procedures by a registrant to prevent contravention of subsection 76(1) of the Act must be determined by the registrant having regard to its business activities, a registrant should consider establishing written policies and procedures in the following areas

    (a) education of employees;

    (b) containment of inside information;

    (c) restriction of transactions; and

    (d) compliance.

(2) In the view of the Commission, the board of directors and senior officers of a registrant should be responsible for ensuring that appropriate policies and procedures for the business activities of the registrant are adopted, maintained and enforced.

2.2 Education of Employees — To educate employees about insider trading and ethical standards, a registrant should consider advising employees as to

    (a) what constitutes inside information and the legal restrictions on its transmission and use;

    (b) the legal consequences to the registrant and its employees for breaches of the restrictions on the transmission and use of inside information, including civil and quasi-criminal liability, self-regulatory organization and securities commission disciplinary proceedings and internal disciplinary action, including dismissal, by the registrant against its offending employees; and

    (c) their ethical responsibilities as members of the securities industry and, if applicable, as registrants under the Act.

2.3 Policies and Procedures to Contain Inside Information — To limit the unauthorized transmission of inside information, a registrant should consider

    (a) restricting access to those areas of the registrant that typically are in receipt of inside information, including the corporate finance and mergers and acquisitions departments, by

        (i) designating departments as sensitive areas and separating those departments from others within the registrant, or

        (ii) if restricting access to departments is impractical or impossible, as in the case of a smaller registrant, treating all of its departments as being "behind the wall" so that if the registrant is in receipt of inside information, all trading and advisory activities of the registrant are subject to any restrictions imposed; and

    (b) assuring the security of confidential information within the registrant by, among other things,

        (i) assuring the security of confidential information within the registrant by, among other things,

        (ii) using code names in place of the names of issuers for confidential projects being worked on,

        (iii) keeping information in sensitive areas secured when not immediately supervised by persons working on the project, and

        (iv) ensuring electronic transmission of inside information takes place only when there are adequate controls for sending and receiving the transmissions.

2.4 Policies and Procedures to Restrict Transactions — (1) When the registrant is, or may be, in receipt of inside information about an issuer a registrant should consider whether to monitor, restrict or discontinue certain activities of the registrant and its employees related to securities of that issuer, including trading, advising and dissemination of research material.

(2) Policies and procedures commonly used by a registrant to restrict transactions include the use of grey lists and restricted lists.

2.5 Use of Grey Lists — (1) A registrant should normally place an issuer on the grey list when it has received inside information about the issuer; for example, when the registrant has been invited to manage or participate in a possible offering or to act concerning a possible merger or acquisition or other corporate assignment.

(2) A registrant should normally disseminate grey lists only to those employees who require the list to monitor unusual principal or agent trading in the securities by the registrant or its employees and, if necessary, to inquire about or restrict trading.

(3) A registrant should seek legal or other advice before new research materials and opinions concerning securities on the grey list are published or disseminated by it or its employees.

(4) A registrant should normally remove an issuer's name from the grey list when the registrant no longer has inside information regarding the issuer.

2.6 Use of Restricted Lists — (1) A registrant should normally move an issuer's name from the registrant's grey list to the registrant's restricted list when the registrant has agreed to act as an underwriter, or banking group member, or to represent the issuer in a merger or acquisition and the transaction in which the registrant is acting has been generally disclosed but the registrant is still in possession of or may gain access to inside information during the course of the transaction.

(2) Trading by the registrant as principal, except for normal market-making or other permitted activities, should cease and the dissemination of research materials should be restricted or stopped for securities of issuers on the restricted list.

(3) A registrant should normally remove an issuer's name from the restricted list when the registrant is no longer in possession of inside information, for example, when that information has been disclosed following completion of a distribution or a merger or acquisition.

2.7 Compliance Policies and Procedures — (1) To promote compliance with requirements related to insider trading under securities laws, self-regulatory organizations' regulations and the registrant's policies and procedures, a registrant should consider

    (a) developing, implementing, maintaining and enforcing written policies and procedures, approved by the registrant's board, appropriate to the type of business being carried on by the registrant;

    (b) monitoring and reviewing trading for the registrant's account;

    (c) monitoring and/or restricting trading in securities of issuers about which the registrant or the registrant's employees possess or may possess inside information;

    (d) monitoring, reviewing and/or restricting trading of all employees and, in particular, employees who in the normal course might be in receipt of inside information; for example senior management, merger and acquisition employees, corporate finance employees and professional traders;

    (e) unless a recognized self-regulatory organization or stock exchange has provided otherwise in a by-law, rule, regulation or policy that has been approved by the Commission, requiring all employees and associates to maintain accounts with the employer-registrant only;

    (f) requiring a senior officer of the registrant to be responsible for the implementation and enforcement of the policies and procedures; and

    (g) instituting a periodic review of the adequacy of its policies and procedures, including a written report on their effectiveness to senior officers or the board of directors of the registrant, which report should normally be kept on file.

Adoption by OSC: (1998) 21 O.S.C.B. 617; Request for Comments: (1997) 20 O.S.C.B. 3379. Replaced OPS 10.2.

OSC Staff Notice 33-704 — List of Non-Complying Ontario Registered Firms Under National Instrument 33-106

Date: **February 26, 1999**

22 O.S.C.B. 1309

[Not reproduced]

OSC Staff Notice 33-712 — Processing of Equity and Fixed Income Trades by Financial Institutions and Mutual Fund Dealers

[See OSCN 32-701]

OSC Staff Notice 33-713 — Registrant Regulatory Filings

Date: May 19, 2000

23 O.S.C.B. 3512

Staff of the Ontario Securities Commission ("Staff") remind registrants of the regulatory filing requirements imposed on them pursuant to both the *Securities Act* (Ontario) (the "Act") and the Regulation made under the Act (the "Regulation"). For example, pursuant to section 21.10 of the Act and section 139 of the Regulation most non-SRO members must file annual audited financial statements and other regulatory filings prescribed by the regulations within ninety days after the end of their financial year. Most registrants must also maintain certain minimum capital and other regulatory requirements, as prescribed by sections 107 to 112 of the Regulation.

Staff have noted that non-SRO registrants are at times deficient in meeting their regulatory filing requirements. These deficiencies include failure to file audited financial statements, late filings of audited financial statements or filings with a qualified audit opinion or a capital deficiency reported.

Staff stress the importance of non-SRO registrants meeting their regulatory filing requirements on a timely and complete basis. Staff are treating regulatory filing deficiencies as a significant issue to be addressed as part of the Commission's objective to strengthen the Compliance-Enforcement continuum.

Consequences of deficient regulatory filings could include the imposition of terms and conditions on a non-SRO registrant or the suspension of registration. Some examples of possible terms and conditions that might be imposed on a non-SRO registrant are:

1. A requirement to file unaudited interim financial statements and capital calculation on a monthly basis.

2. An increase in the required minimum free capital to be maintained at all times.

3. A prohibition on the opening of any new branch/sub-branch offices, hiring/registering any new salespeople, opening of any new customer accounts or changing in any material respect the inventory positions of the registrant.

OSC Staff Notice 33-721 — CSA/OSC STP Readiness Assessment Survey

Date: February 21, 2003

26 O.S.C.B. 1568

Industry Initiative

The Canadian Capital Markets Association (CCMA), an organization founded in 2000 by participants in the Canadian financial services industries to indentify and recommend ways to meet the challenges and opportunities faced by our capital markets, is promoting straight-through processing (STP) strategies among market participants. The CCMA's STP milestones show interim goals in 2004, with the final milestone being the acheivement of STP by mid-2005. STP implies electronic rather than manual interfaces between participants, competitors and providers. To be STP compliant, all registrants and other market participants will need to examine their systems and processes and remove the entire life cycle of a securities transaction.

Regulators' Monitoring

The Canadian Securities Administrators' (CSA) believe that STP is an extremely important initiative. The continuing success of our capital markets depends on the ability of our markets to compete with global markets, particularly the U.S. markets. The CCMA are spearheading this initiative.

Because the OSC has a responsibility to foster confidence in the capital markets in Ontario, it is monitoring the industry's move to STP. The OSC, together with other CSA jurisdictions, will be providing a servey to business registrants to assess the preparedness of the industry in Canada for STP.

As a first step, the OSC recently wrote to approximately 850 business registrants in Ontario in January, 2003 informing them of the survey and requesting that they provide the name of the most senior individual that has direct responsibility for the STP project within their organization. We will forward a further letter via email in early March to that individual, providing instructions on how to access our web-base survey.

For more information on the STP initiative, please visit the OSC website at www.osc.gov.on.ca and the CCMA website at www.ccma-acmc.ca.

OSC Staff Notice 33-723 — Fair Allocation of Investment Opportunities — Compliance Team Desk Review

Date: September 23, 2005

28 O.S.C.B. 7769

What we did and why

Staff of the Compliance team of the Ontario Securities Commission (OSC) recently completed a desk review of the fairness policies and related business practices of approximately 40 investment counsel/portfolio managers (ICPMs).

Regulation 115 of the *Securities Act* (Ontario) requires ICPMs to treat clients fairly in allocating investment opportunities and to file a copy of their current fairness policy with the OSC.

The OSC has received comments from the public regarding the use of "generic" fairness policies by ICPMs. The generic policies do not clearly set out how ICPMs allocate investment opportunities for the types of activities carried on. The Compliance annual reports for fiscal 2002/2003 and 2003/2004 indicate that a significant number of ICPMs examined during the periods had deficiencies in their fairness policies.

How we did it

The Compliance team of the OSC conducted a desk review of the fairness policies and related business processes of approximately 40 ICPMs. A desk review is a review completed at OSC offices by OSC staff of information provided by a group of selected market participants. No on site field review is performed and our follow up on the information provided is limited to written and verbal requests for additional information or clarification of information already provided.

Each ICPM was asked to complete a questionnaire and provide a copy of its most recent fairness policy. No review of actual trades was completed. The questionnaire included questions regarding preparation, filing and amendments to the fairness policy and questions regarding specific policies to ensure fair allocation of investment opportunities, such as:

- whether the ICPM uses block trades and, if so, how fills are allocated and the method used to allocate fills

- whether the ICPM includes proprietary, employee and/or personal accounts with block trades for clients

- whether the ICPM participates in initial public offerings (IPOs) and, if so, how fills are allocated and the method used to allocate fills

What we found

The following disclosure or filing deficiencies were noted:

- 74% of the fairness policies were missing one or more of the disclosures set out below under "What should be in an ICPM's fairness policy?"

- 26% of the fairness policies currently in use had not been filed with the OSC. Since the filing of a fairness policy is required prior to registration being granted, all registrants surveyed should have filed at least one previous fairness policy with the OSC.

- 26% of the fairness policies currently in use had not been provided to clients.

- 15% of the fairness policies were "generic" policies. Some of the fairness policies filed appeared to be identical (other than the name of the registrant). As a result, it wasn't clear to staff whether the "generic" policies reflected the actual practice of the ICPM in allocating investment opportunities for the types of activities carried on in its business.

All of the ICPMs with disclosure or filing deficiencies have rectified their deficiencies. Staff ensured that any "generic" policies filed accurately reflected the actual practice of the ICPM.

As well, 9% of the ICPMs included proprietary, employee and/or personal accounts in block trades and allocated a pro-rata share of partially filled blocked trades or IPOs to proprietary, employee and/or personal accounts. All of these ICPMs have now amended, or will be amending, their fairness policies and their practices so that proprietary, employee and/or personal accounts are not allocated a pro-rata share of partially filled blocked trades or IPOs before clients trades are completely filled.

Finally, where an ICPM has contracted advisory services to a subadvisor, the ICPM should monitor the subadvisers' compliance with the ICPM's fairness policy. No issues were noted regarding subadvisers' compliance with ICPMs' fairness policies.

What should be in an ICPM's fairness policy?

The following disclosures should be included in an ICPM's fairness policy, where applicable to its investment processes.

- method used to allocate price and commission among clients when trades are bunched or blocked.

- method used to allocate block trades and IPOs among client accounts.

- method used to allocate block trades and IPOs among clients that are partially filled (e.g. prorata).

What we'll do in the future and what we expect in the future

Staff will continue to monitor compliance by ICPMs with Regulation 115 as part of our regular compliance field reviews.

Staff expects ICPMs to enhance their compliance with Regulation 115 and that fewer deficiencies will be found in future compliance field reviews in this area. Staff will take seriously any deficiencies found in future compliance field reviews.

Staff also expects that improved documentation of policies and procedures will result in increased fairness in the allocation of investment opportunities to clients by ICPMs.

For more information, please contact:

Marianne Bridge, Manager, Compliance

(416) 595-8907

mbridge@osc.gov.on.ca

Scott Laskey, Accountant, Compliance

(416) 204-8981

slaskey@osc.gov.on.ca

September 23, 2005

OSC Notice 33-724 (2002) — OSC Compliance Team, Capital Markets Branch, Annual Report

Date: September 6, 2002

25 O.S.C.B. 5921; assigned number (2005) 28 O.S.C.B. 10298

[Not reproduced]

OSC Notice 33-724 (2003) — OSC Compliance Team, Capital Markets Branch, Annual Report

Date: July 11, 2003

26 O.S.C.B. 5230; assigned number (2005) 28 O.S.C.B. 10298

[Not reproduced]

OSC Notice 33-724 (2004) — OSC Compliance Team, Capital Markets Branch, Annual Report

Date: July 9, 2004

27 O.S.C.B. 6249; assigned number (2005) 28 O.S.C.B. 10298

[Not reproduced]

OSC Notice 33-724 (2006) — OSC Compliance Team, Capital Markets Branch, Annual Report

Date: September 15, 2006

29 O.S.C.B. 7354

[Not reproduced]

OSC Notice 33-725 — Industry Report on Scholarship Plan Dealers

Date: July 16, 2004

27 O.S.C.B. 6464; assigned number (2005) 28 O.S.C.B. 10298

Scholarship Plan Dealers — Industry Report

Executive Summary

The Canadian Securities Administrators performed a National Compliance Review (NCR) of scholarship plan dealers in 2003. The purpose of the NCR was to assess the compliance of scholarship plan dealers with applicable provincial securities legislation and to enhance information sharing of regulatory issues among the provincial regulators.

The Compliance team of the Capital Markets branch of the Ontario Securities Commission (Commission) has prepared this report to provide guidance to scholarship plan dealers in complying with Ontario securities law. Although the report focuses on staff's findings, we feel they are also representative of those found during the NCR by the other participating jurisdictions. Due to the numerous and varying findings across the different dealers, we have focused our report on the deficiencies that were most commonly identified and those that were considered to be the most serious.

Participating Provinces

The NCR was conducted by the securities regulators in British Columbia, Manitoba, New Brunswick, Nova Scotia, Ontario and Prince Edward Island. The Bureau des Services Financiers in Quebec also participated in the review since it is responsible for the oversight of dealers in that province. Each participating jurisdiction reviewed certain branch operations in their province while Ontario also reviewed the head office operations. In total, five scholarship plan dealers were reviewed as part of the 2003 NCR.

Scope of the Review

The scope of the review included the following areas:

- Capital Requirements
- Contractual Agreements and other Business Arrangements
- Compliance and Supervision
- Opening of New Accounts and Maintenance of Know Your Client (KYC) Information
- Scholarship Plan Enrolment Process
- Books and Records
- Sales Practices
- Sales Representative Interviews

Part 3:
REGISTRATION

Within each of the above areas, we performed testing to evaluate compliance with applicable securities legislation and to identify weaknesses in the practices of the dealers. Compliance examination reports outlining the deficiencies noted were forwarded to each dealer for a written response. Each jurisdiction is dealing separately with their respective reports and will determine what further action, if any, will be required to ensure that the deficiencies are adequately addressed and rectified. Ongoing Commission initiatives are described in the next section of this report.

Overall Comments

Numerous deficiencies were identified as a result of the NCR. In many cases, we identified issues which had been previously brought to the attention of the dealers by other securities regulators. For example, the Alberta Securities Commission conducted both initial and follow-up reviews of scholarship plan dealers and issued an industry report on common deficiencies in October 2002. Many of the deficiencies outlined in that report were still prevalent during the 2003 NCR indicating that the industry did not take appropriate action to remedy these concerns.

Commission Initiatives

The short term priority of staff is to deal immediately with the responses received from the dealers on the deficiencies noted during the NCR and determine whether appropriate action has been taken to ensure resolution of the issues identified and discussed in this report. We require the dealers to make the necessary changes to their operations to address these deficiencies and to establish adequate policies and procedures for ongoing compliance. We conducted focused follow-up compliance reviews in March and April 2004 after giving the dealers adequate time to make the changes that were represented in their responses. We compared the findings from the follow-up review to the initial findings to assess whether adequate measures had been taken in the intervening period. We noted some improvements in all of the dealers reviewed, however, numerous deficiencies continued to be outstanding. Due to the repeated non-compliance, more stringent measures are being taken and varying terms and conditions have been imposed on the registration of these dealers. The Compliance team will monitor the progression of each dealer in adequately addressing all deficiencies found in both the initial and follow-up reviews before these terms and conditions are removed.

As more of a medium term initiative, Commission staff resources have been dedicated to rulemaking in respect of scholarship plan dealers. While it is too early to determine specifically the nature and breadth of such rules and to describe them in this report, it is clear from the nature and the volume of the deficiencies noted during both the NCR and the focused follow-up reviews that more specific rules are required. In the interim, each dealer should review this report and use it as a self-assessment tool for enhanced compliance with Ontario securities law.

Major Findings

Outlined below are the major findings from staff's review of scholarship plan dealers. These findings are presented on an aggregate basis and in some cases, include examples that support the findings. The examples provided have been consolidated based on our findings across all the dealer firms and do not all necessarily apply to each dealer. We have also provided suggested practices to assist scholarship plan dealers in improving their existing practices and in strengthening their compliance environment. The suggested practices encompass both requirements under existing legislation and recommended best practices but are not meant to be an exhaustive list of the practices and procedures that could be incorporated by the dealers to mitigate the existence of the weaknesses identified.

1.0 — Compliance and Supervision

1.1 — Role of the Compliance Officer

Subsection 1.3(1) of OSC Rule 31-505 requires every registered dealer to designate a registered partner or officer as the compliance officer who is responsible for discharging the obligations of the registered dealer under Ontario securities law. We noted a number of instances where the designated compliance officers did not ensure that the dealers discharged their obligations under Ontario securities law as follows:

- The compliance officer is responsible for supervising the branch manager's conduct over the review of new accounts and the supervision of client trades and advice. However, there is no review of the branch manager's activities by the compliance officer to ensure that these functions are being carried out adequately. (see Role of the Branch Manager in Point 1.2)

- There is no formal reporting requirement from the branch managers to the compliance officer and limited contact, if any, between the parties.

- The compliance officer does not periodically visit or perform supervisory reviews of the branches or sub-branches to ensure that both Ontario securities law and internal policies and procedures are being adhered to.

- The compliance officer does not review the enrolment applications and transaction orders initiated by the branch managers.

Many of the deficiencies identified during the NCR and reported on throughout this report are directly linked to the weaknesses in the compliance structure and the role of the compliance officer. These deficiencies will be dealt with separately in other areas of the report.

Suggested Practices

- The compliance officer should develop a formal branch review program and perform branch reviews on a regular basis. All of the issues identified should be communicated to the branch manager and be followed-up and resolved in a timely manner.

- A sample of transactions and enrolment applications from each branch should be reviewed to ensure that all sign offs and reviews have taken place at the branch level.

- The compliance officer should be responsible for reviewing the branch managers' activities, including trades processed for their clients.

- Internal policies and procedures should be communicated to branch managers and sales representatives on a regular basis to ensure that they are understood and are being followed.

1.2 — Role of the Branch Manager

Subsection 1.4(1) of OSC Rule 31-505 states that if a registered dealer operates a branch office, the dealer must designate a registered salesperson, officer or partner as the branch manager for the branch. Subsection 1.4(2) of OSC Rule 31-505 further states that the branch manager is responsible for functions such as opening new accounts, supervising trades made for or with each client and supervising advice provided to each client. In addition, the branch manager shall report directly to the compliance officer.

We noted a number of instances where the branch managers did not adequately or effectively supervise their sales representatives:

- Some branch managers are supervising a large group of sales representatives that render the supervision inadequate and ineffective.
- There was a lack of review of trade transactions at the branch level (see Point 1.3).
- Some branch managers allowed enrolment applications and transaction forms to be submitted to head office for processing without any branch manager review or to be reviewed by administrative personnel at the branch location.
- There was inadequate collection and documentation of KYC and suitability information and review thereof (see Point 2.1).
- Several branch managers told us that they did not have a direct supervisor.
- There is limited interaction between the sales representatives and the branch manager, and the branch manager and the compliance officer.
- A limited number of sales representatives indicated that they act without the advice of their branch manager in dealing with client complaints.

Suggested Practices

- Limit the number of sales representatives to be supervised by one branch manager to a manageable and reasonable number, taking into account the other responsibilities of the branch manager, the geographic location of the representatives that are being supervised and whether the sales representatives can be visited on a periodic basis to evaluate their sales practices and their dealings with clients.
- Branch managers should review all new enrolment applications and should ensure that trade transactions are reviewed prior to processing at head office. If these duties are delegated to another individual at the branch, that individual should have adequate proficiency and the branch manager is responsible for the oversight of such duties.
- Client files should be reviewed regularly to ensure there is adequate and current KYC information on file.
- Branch managers should communicate regularly with the sales representatives at the branch and reiterate that they should be notified of client complaints and any other issues requiring branch manager review and approval, such as marketing and other sales endeavors.

1.3 — Trade Suitability Review

The branch manager is responsible for opening new accounts, supervising trades made for each client and supervising advice provided to each client as per subsection 1.4(2) of OSC Rule 31-505. We noted significant weaknesses in the review for trade suitability as follows:

- Most sales representatives had no branch manager reviewing their trades and enrolment application forms before submitting them to head office for processing.
- There was no evidence of review of the enrolment forms at the head office level in the absence of branch level review.
- In some cases, the forms were reviewed by administrative personnel for completeness. These individuals lack the proficiency and knowledge to assess suitability of the trade for clients.
- There was no evidence that the branch managers' trades were reviewed or that branch managers themselves were reviewing sales representatives' trades for suitability.
- Some sales representatives indicated that the overall financial situation of clients was not always considered when assessing suitability or affordability of the plan. In other cases, sales representatives indicated that irrelevant criteria such as home surroundings were used to assess suitability.
- There were suitability concerns on a sample of enrolment applications that we reviewed relating to the value of the monthly deposit relative to the clients' income and KYC information provided.
- Certain plans had a high number of terminations or cancellations indicating that these plans were potentially unsuitable for clients at the onset. However, there is no review of the terminations by the compliance officer to determine the reasons.

Suggested Practices

- All trades and enrolment applications must be reviewed by the branch manager at the branch, prior to submitting the forms to head office.

- There should be evidence of the review by the branch manager in the form of initials and the date of the review. Similarly, there should be an individual responsible for reviewing the branch managers' activities and there should be evidence of review and approval of their trades.

- Guidelines should be developed and communicated to sales representatives on the affordability of plans, taking into consideration the income of the household and the proposed monthly contribution. Any deviations from the guidelines should be approved by the branch manager.

- The branch manager and/or the compliance officer should conduct reviews on a regular basis to identify unfavorable trends. For example, sales representatives with a high number of terminations or with a high volume of leveraged clients should be questioned about the suitability of the plan for their clients.

2.0 — Opening of New Accounts and Maintenance of KYC Information

2.1 — Collection and Update of KYC and Suitability Information

Section 1.5 of OSC Rule 31-505 requires registrants to make enquiries about each of their clients as are appropriate to ascertain the general investment needs and objectives of the client and the suitability of a proposed purchase of a security for the client.

We noted the following deficiencies with respect to the collection, documentation and review of KYC and suitability information:

- We noted that a large portion of the enrolment applications that we sampled contained incomplete or missing KYC information, thereby impeding the ability of the dealers to assess whether a plan is affordable and suitable for a client.

- There was no evidence of review and approval of the new account opening forms.

- There is no process in place to update KYC information to reflect any material changes to clients' circumstances.

- In one instance, training materials and sales representative proficiency exams did not adequately address KYC and suitability rules.

- Enrolment applications did not require all the appropriate KYC information, such as the number of dependents of the subscribers and whether leveraging is being used to purchase units in scholarship plans.

Suggested Practices

- Complete KYC information must be collected for all clients prior to any trade execution, including such information as the client's identity, age, credit worthiness, occupation, annual income, net worth, investment objectives, investment knowledge, investment time frame, risk tolerance and source of funds.

- KYC information should be periodically updated.

- Clients must sign the KYC information form.

- The enrolment application form must be reviewed and approved by the branch manager.

- If possible, KYC information should be maintained in an electronic format which can be used to generate exception reports.

- Maintain a pending file when a KYC form is incomplete.

- The pending file should be cleared on a timely basis.

2.2 — Inadequate Disclosure

There are many fees associated with the purchase of scholarship plan units, however, we noted a lack of disclosure and clarity to clients on the nature of these fees and their implications on the plans' returns. Section 1.2 of OSC Rule 31-505 requires every dealer to establish and enforce written procedures for dealing with clients that conform to prudent business practice and enable the dealer to serve its clients adequately. Furthermore, adequate disclosure ensures that the registrant is dealing fairly, honestly and in good faith with its clients as required under section 2.1 of OSC Rule 31-505.

The following weaknesses were noted with respect to the disclosure provided to clients:

- Sales representatives lacked adequate knowledge of the product being sold to clients, and its associated costs (see Point 8.1).

- Enrolment fees were misrepresented in some cases, leading clients to believe that the potential for loss was nil.

- Enrolment fees and the related consequences of terminations were not always discussed with clients.

- The 60 day grace period was not always explained to clients.

- In some cases, there was no mention of other types of fees incurred by the plans.

Suggested Practices

- Ensure that sales representatives have sufficient knowledge of the product, including all fees, prior to the commencement of selling units to clients.

- A copy of the most recent prospectus should be provided to all clients and sales representatives should indicate where the fees are disclosed therein.

- The implications of terminations or plan cancellations, both within 60 days and thereafter, should be discussed with clients.

- Guidelines, such as a checklist, could be developed and incorporated into the account opening procedures. The checklist would outline each type of fee and the client could initial each one after it has been discussed and understood.

3.0 — Registration Requirements

3.1 — Unregistered Activities

The assets of the scholarship plan must be managed by a registered adviser who has the adequate proficiency to perform this function. Paragraph 25(1)(c) of the Act states that no person shall act as an adviser unless the person is registered as an adviser. We noted two instances where plan assets were being managed, in part, by non-registered individuals as follows:

- Investment decisions were being made and all trade activities were being approved by these non-registered individuals.

- The individuals were responsible for reviewing the portfolios to ensure conformance with the strategy.

- The individuals provided analysis and outlook for the investment market and were designated as the key persons to communicate with their investment dealers in facilitating trade execution.

All dealers should ensure that the persons or companies that are acting as advisers over their plan assets are properly registered and have the proficiency to manage the portfolios as required. In addition, the plans' advisers should be disclosed in the prospectus to ensure that full, true and plain disclosure of all material facts is included therein.

3.2 — Registration of Branches and Sub-branches

Each dealer operates a number of branches and sub-branches where sales representatives meet with clients to conduct business and maintain client files. We did not have any record of these branches and sub-branches being registered with the Commission or a list of the individuals designated to be the branch manager at these locations as required under section 3.2 of Multilateral Instrument 33-109.

Every registered dealer must notify the Commission within five business days of the opening or closing of any branch office in Ontario and, in the case of the opening of any branch office in Ontario, the name and address of the person in charge of that office.

3.3 — Statement of Policies

Section 223 of the Regulation requires scholarship plan dealers to prepare and file a statement of policies with the Commission as well as provide a copy to their clients. This statement should outline the activities of the dealer in respect of related or connected issuers. The scholarship plans distributed by the dealers are considered to be related and/or connected issuers and must be disclosed in their statement of policies.

We noted that a statement of policies was not prepared and a copy was not filed with the Commission or provided to clients.

Suggested practices

- A current statement of policies must be prepared and filed with the Commission.

- If a significant change occurs, a revised statement of policies must be filed with the Commission and distributed to all clients.

- A copy of the statement of policies must be provided to all clients.

- The statement of policies must include a complete listing of related issuers along with a concise description of the nature of the relationship with each of the related issuers.

- The statement must include the disclosure required in Regulation 223(1)(d).

Many dealers were opposed to preparing a statement of policies as some of the information required therein is already contained in the prospectus. However, unless an exemption from this requirement is obtained under section 233 of the Regulation, these dealers must comply with the requirements of Regulation 223.

4.0 — Sales Practices

4.1 — Holding Out

It is the dealer's responsibility to ensure that clients understand with which legal entity they are dealing. Furthermore, a clear distinction must be drawn between the foundation, which is the sponsor of the plan, and the dealer who is distributing it as required under National Policy Statement 15. Staff noted the following issues related to holding out:

- Some sales representatives indicated to clients that they work for the foundation, a not-for-profit entity, rather than for the dealer which is a for-profit organization.

- Training manuals and other reference tools used by the sales representatives encourage them to hold themselves out as working for the foundation and to inform clients that they are not selling anything.

Suggested Practices

- All clients must be informed that the sales representatives are acting on behalf of a dealer and will be compensated for the sale of units of scholarship plans.

- Training materials and client scripts should exclude misleading representations.

- The full legal name of the dealer must be used on all correspondence with clients, on business cards and in marketing materials to make it clear to clients with which entity they are dealing.

- The dealer name and the foundation name should not be so similar as to cause confusion among clients.

4.2 — Business Cards, Branch Signage and Telephone Greetings

The use of names other than the full legal name of the dealer may be misleading to clients. In addition, paragraph 25(1)(a) of the Act states that no person or company may act as a dealer unless registered. We reviewed a sample of business cards, branch signage and telephone greetings and noted the following deficiencies which may cause confusion for clients:

- A number of sales representatives were using outdated business cards.

- Some business cards did not include the name of the dealer or contained the names of the sales representatives' non-registered companies, rather than that of the dealer.

- Branches did not display the registered dealer name on their premises or use it in their telephone greetings.

- Business cards contained inappropriate and misleading titles.

- Business cards had the name of the foundation, not the dealer.

Suggested Practices

- Business card orders should be handled centrally by head office to ensure all business cards are consistent, contain the full legal name of the dealer only and do not contain misleading or inappropriate titles.

- All branches should display the legal name of the dealer.

4.3 — Misleading Marketing

Section 2.1 of OSC Rule 31-505 states that all dealers must deal fairly, honestly, and in good faith with their clients. Accordingly, all marketing materials should contain information that is accurate and should not make representations that are misleading to clients.

We noted misleading information in materials prepared by both head office and sales representatives as follows:

- Outdated information was used in pamphlets and brochures, such as the value of assets under management and the total amount returned to subscribers since inception.

- Actual rates of return provided in the marketing materials did not contain adequate disclosure regarding the assumptions used and whether the returns are gross or net of fees.

- Within the same dealer firm, there was no consistent methodology for calculating rates of return. For example, rates of return were calculated using creative calculations to make the returns appear higher, or were based on selected returns for only some periods, or were grossed up from net returns using estimates of fees paid rather than actual fees paid by clients.

- Projected rates of return were not reflective of recent performance of the plan, or were based on inflated percentages for assumed interest rates.

- Marketing materials claimed "superior returns", "excellent rate of return", "earns the highest income" and "exceptional returns" without any support to substantiate these claims.

- The full legal name of the dealer was not always used in marketing materials or was not used with the same prominence as the foundation name, which may cause client confusion about the entity with which they are dealing.

- The products were represented as "risk-free", "guaranteed", "government insured", "safest funding methods", "fully protected" and overall, as bearing no risk to clients.

- Some materials indicated that the dealer was a not-for-profit organization.

- Materials indicated that the security regulators had endorsed the product. Others included letters from government agencies and Commission registration letters which may mislead clients to believe that they are government or Commission endorsed.

- Inconsistent information was contained within the prospectus and the marketing materials.

- Materials claimed that only guaranteed securities were invested in by the plan, however, other types of non-guaranteed securities were also purchased for the plan.

- The government's Canada Education Savings Grant program has a limit of $400 per year, however, materials represented that the government would add 20% to the plan each year. No mention of the dollar limit was included.

Overall, many more instances of misleading information were noted in the materials we reviewed than those mentioned above.

Suggested Practices

- Establish and enforce procedures with respect to the preparation, review and approval of marketing materials.

- All marketing materials should be reviewed and approved by someone independent of their preparation.

- Establish guidelines on the preparation of performance data and apply them consistently from period to period.

- Rates of return should be accompanied by adequate disclosure which is clear and easily understood by clients. At a minimum, this would include the assumptions used, the effects of enhancement factors due to plan forfeitures and other non-market related conditions, and the methodology used.

- Materials should not imply that Commission staff has in any way passed upon the financial standing, fitness or conduct of the dealer or upon the merits of the product being offered.

- Marketing materials should be regularly updated to ensure all information is complete and accurate and not misleading to clients.

- All claims made within the marketing materials should be adequately supported.

5.0 — Contractual Agreements and Business Arrangements

5.1 — Sales Representative Agreements

Subsection 1(1) of the Act defines a salesperson as an individual who is employed by a dealer for the purpose of making trades in securities on behalf of the dealer. Sales representatives are acting on behalf of a dealer and this should be reflected in their contracts with their respective dealer. Overall, we felt that the agreements signed by sales representatives of the dealers did not adequately reflect the responsibilities of the sales representatives or their relationship with the dealers. The following weaknesses were noted as a result of our review of these agreements:

- Agreements were between the sales representative and the branch, or the sales representative and the branch manager and not between the sales representative and the dealer.

- The agreements indicated that sales representatives were acting on behalf of the branch manager.

- The agreements did not define the responsibilities of each party to clients.

- The agreements did not outline which party has supervisory responsibilities.

- The agreements limited the liability of the dealers for the misrepresentations of their sales representatives.

Suggested Practices

- Agreements must be between the sales representative and the dealer.

- The agreements should clearly indicate that the securities related business is that of the dealer, and not the sales representative or the branch manager.

- The agreements should clearly outline the responsibilities of both the dealer and the sales representative, including those over the supervisory functions.

- The agreements should make it clear that the dealer is liable for the actions of its sales representatives.

5.2 — Branch Manager Agreements

We noted similar issues as those indicated above when we reviewed the branch managers' agreements with the dealers. Specifically, we noted the following deficiencies:

- There was inadequate detail regarding the branch manager's responsibility to supervise the activities of the sales representatives at the branch.

- Responsibilities were assigned to the branch manager that we think are the primary responsibility of the dealer. For example, the payment of commissions, the registration of sales representatives and the recruitment and training of sales representatives were allocated to the branch manager by the dealer.

- The agreements limited the liability of the dealers for the misrepresentations of their branch managers.

Suggested Practices

- The agreements should include the responsibilities of the branch manager to approve the opening of new accounts, to supervise trades made for or with each client, and to supervise the advice provided to each client.

- The relationship between the branch manager and the dealer must be structured as that of an agent or employee of the dealer.

- The agreements should reflect that the securities related business is that of the dealer, not the branch manager. Accordingly, the branch manager may assist the dealer with certain functions, however, the dealer is ultimately responsible for the registration, training and compensation of its sales representatives.

- The agreements should not limit the liability of the dealer for the actions or misrepresentations of its branch managers.

Part 3: REGISTRATION

5.3 — Business Arrangements

Section 1.2 of OSC Rule 31-505 requires that every registered dealer establish and enforce written procedures that conform to prudent business practice. Accordingly, business arrangements with other entities should be approved by an individual with adequate authority and should be properly documented. We discussed business arrangements with both the dealers and their sales representatives and noted the following issues:

- Some sales representatives entered into arrangements with other entities without the knowledge of the dealer or the branch manager.

- Arrangements were entered into with individuals or companies that are not registered to trade in securities of scholarship plans, however, the arrangements indicated that these individuals or companies would be performing acts in the furtherance of a trade.

- Commissions were paid by sales representatives to the other parties in their business arrangements who are not registered.

- The terms of the business arrangements were not always in writing.

- The dealer's letterhead was used on client's statements for units sold by the other party dealer in the business arrangement.

- Commissions were paid to the other parties' sales representatives directly, rather than to the firm itself. As such, commissions were recorded off the books of the other entities.

Suggested Practices

- All business arrangements should be approved in writing by head office.

- If arrangements with other parties include acts in the furtherance of a trade, the other entities should be properly registered for those types of trades.

- Commissions should be paid by head office directly to the other party, not to its sales representatives.

- The terms of the business arrangement should be clearly documented.

- The other entities' branch managers or compliance officers should review the trades of their sales representatives and ensure that these trades are properly recorded in their books and records. Similarly, the sales commissions should be recorded on the books of the other parties.

- The dealer's letterhead should only be used on client statements of its own clients.

6.0 — Capital Requirements

6.1 — Capital Calculations

Subsection 113(3), paragraph 10 of the Regulation requires that each registrant prepare a monthly calculation of minimum free capital, adjusted liabilities and capital required (capital calculation) within a reasonable period of time after each month end. The capital calculation is to be prepared based on monthly financial statements prepared in accordance with generally accepted accounting principles. All market participants are required to inform the Commission immediately should they be become capital deficient and are required to rectify the capital deficiency within 48 hours.

During our reviews, we observed the following:

- Capital calculations were not always prepared or were not prepared on a timely basis and, therefore, monitoring of the firm's capital was not done.

- There was no evidence that a review of the calculation was performed by someone other than the preparer.

- The calculation of adjusted liabilities was incorrect.

Suggested practices

- Capital calculations must be performed on a monthly basis and within a reasonable period of time after month end.

- Copies of the capital calculations should be maintained for purposes of an audit trail.

- A person other than the preparer should review the capital calculations to ensure that they are accurate.

- Evidence of the review should be documented.

- The Commission should be informed immediately should the dealer's capital position become deficient.

7.0 — Books and Records

7.1 — Inadequate Books and Records

Section 113 of the Regulation requires that registered dealers maintain books and records necessary to properly record their business transactions and financial affairs.

During our reviews, we observed the following:

- The dealer did not maintain a trade blotter or the blotter maintained was incomplete.

- Client statements of account were not delivered to clients on a monthly basis.

- Client statements of account did not include all necessary information such as the price per unit or units purchased to date.

- Client statements of account contained misleading information.

- The dealer did not send trade confirmations to its clients, rather it relied on the foundation to do so.

- The trade confirmation was incomplete.

Suggested practices

A list of books and records that dealers are required to maintain is contained in subsection 113(3) of the Regulation. In the absence of any exemptive relief, client statements of account should be delivered to clients on a monthly basis.

7.2 — Policies and Procedures

Section 1.2 of OSC Rule 31-505 states that every dealer should develop and enforce written procedures for dealing with clients that conform to prudent business practice and enable it to serve its clients adequately. The policies and procedures should be in sufficient detail, be updated on a periodic basis and be made available to all relevant staff. In addition, the relevant regulatory requirements should be outlined in the policies and procedures. We feel that written policies and procedures contribute to an effective compliance environment.

During our reviews, we observed the following:

- The dealer did not have a documented policies and procedures manual.

- The policies and procedures were not sufficiently detailed and/or did not contain procedures covering all major areas of the business.

- The actual practices of the dealer were not consistent with the documented procedures.

- The documented procedures were not being adhered to by the dealer's sales representatives and were not adequately enforced by the dealer.

Suggested practices

Each dealer should establish and enforce a written policies and procedures manual that is sufficiently detailed, up to date, and which covers all relevant areas of its business. At a minimum, the following list of topics should be considered for inclusion in the documented policies and procedures:

Trading

- Monitoring and resolving cancelled and/or rejected trade orders, including the individuals responsible for such activities.

- Guidelines on trade suitability review.

- Procedures over the preparation and delivery of trade confirmations, including procedures to ensure accuracy and completeness of information prior to delivery.

New Accounts, KYC and Suitability Information

- Collection, documentation and timely updating of KYC and suitability information for clients.

- Guidelines on how account application forms are to be completed, reviewed and approved.

- Specify the individual who is responsible for approving new client accounts.

- List the criteria to be used for approving new accounts.

- Specify the timing for approving new accounts.

- Guidelines on when transfers-in are suitable for clients.

- Requirement to obtain information regarding whether a client is using leverage to purchase the securities.

- Requirement to provide leverage disclosure document to clients and obtain their signature.

Administration

- Handling of client complaints and maintenance of a log of complaints.

- Procedures over the preparation and delivery of client statements of account, including procedures to ensure accuracy and completeness of information prior to delivery.

Marketing

- Ensuring adequate disclosure and adherence to applicable legislative requirements.

- Ensuring the exclusion of false or misleading information.

Part 3:
REGISTRATION

- Procedures over the review and approval of marketing material, including websites.
- Guidelines over the preparation and presentation of performance results.
- Procedures over the use of draw boxes.
- Procedures over the distribution of marketing materials.

Other Employment

- Guidelines over what is acceptable as other employment and monitoring of conflicts of interest.

Financial Condition

- Preparation, review and monitoring of monthly capital calculations.

Referral and Other Business Arrangements

- Procedures over the review, acceptance and monitoring of arrangements with other parties.

Money Laundering Prevention

- Definition of "money laundering" and examples of suspicious transactions.
- Handling of prescribed and suspicious transactions.
- Procedures to report prescribed and suspicious transactions to the Financial Transactions and Reports Analysis Centre of Canada.
- Documenting the records which should be maintained under the *Proceeds of Crime (Money Laundering) and Terrorist Financing Act and Regulations.*
- Establishing a compliance regime and employee training at the Registrant to ensure it meets its obligations under the *Proceeds of Crime (Money Laundering) and Terrorist Financing Act and Regulations.*
- Requirements to maintain a large cash transaction record.

8.0 — Sales Representatives

8.1 — Training of Sales Representatives

The training provided to sales representatives varied greatly between dealers and also, between different branches of the same dealer. In many instances, the training of sales representatives was carried out by the branch manager or another sales representative, with little or no involvement by head office. This is consistent with the inappropriate structure adopted by many dealers where the branches are acting as autonomous business units with inadequate supervision by head office.

A strong training program for sales representatives, both at the onset of registration and on an ongoing basis, contributes greatly to a more effective compliance environment. Every dealer is responsible for the supervision of its sales representatives, partners and officers, including ensuring that they are properly trained.

The following weaknesses were noted regarding the training of sales representatives:

- The current proficiency exams do not adequately address compliance issues such as KYC and suitability rules.
- Sales representatives were allowed to complete the proficiency exams with the assistance of others.
- Sales representatives who transferred from another dealer were not required to write the proficiency exam at their new dealer, even though the exam contains materials specific to the new dealer's product.
- Mandatory training was not being completed by all sales representatives and its completion was not being enforced by the dealer.
- Sales representatives were not aware of training courses being offered.
- Training materials were inadequate in areas dealing with regulatory requirements.
- Training materials encouraged high-pressure sales tactics.
- Training materials indicated that the products were approved by the Commission, which is misleading since no approval has been made by the Commission.

Suggested practices

- Head office should develop detailed training procedures and materials and ensure that they are distributed to all branches and used in the training of all sales representatives.
- Attendance at training should be monitored to ensure all sales representatives have attended mandatory sessions.
- Proficiency exams should be completed by all sales representatives prior to any dealings with clients.
- The administration of the proficiency exams and the passing requirements should be rigorous and consistent among all branches.

- The proficiency exam should be challenging and also address regulatory requirements, not just questions on product knowledge and sales techniques.

- Training should be provided on an ongoing basis to remind sales representatives of their duties and responsibilities.

RESP Dealers Association

The RESP Dealers Association of Canada ("Association") was formed in 1999 to represent the group plan distributors of registered education savings plans. Members of the Association have taken steps to create standards and uniformity in the industry. For example, a code of sales practices was developed and the Association is also working towards the development of a more in-depth proficiency exam.

We consider these to be positive steps towards streamlining the practices of the scholarship plan dealers in Ontario. However, further measures need to be taken by the dealers to increase the awareness of its sales representatives and branch managers in regards to the Association and its initiatives for enhanced compliance.

OSC Staff Notice 33-728 — 2007 Annual Report — Compliance Team

Date: August 24, 2007

30 O.S.C.B. 7303

[Not reproduced]

OSC Staff Notice 33-729 — Marketing Practices of Investment Counsel/Portfolio Managers

Date: November 9, 2007

30 O.S.C.B. 9213

Purpose of Notice

Staff of the Compliance team of the Ontario Securities Commission (OSC) conducted a focused review of the marketing practices of firms registered as investment counsel/portfolio managers (ICPMs). This report summarizes our findings and provides guidance to market participants on best practices in the preparation and use of marketing materials.

Background

Marketing practices have increasingly become an area of concern. During our field reviews in recent years, we have identified an increasing number of deficiencies in this area. Marketing was the number one significant deficiency identified by the Compliance team in its 2006 and 2007 annual reports.

In particular, we have seen a rise in the number of issues in the marketing practices of ICPMs for non-prospectus qualified securities, such as pooled funds and hedge funds. We have also seen claims that are more aggressive and a greater complexity in the types of performance data in marketing materials.

We are concerned about marketing materials because investors are influenced by these types of documents. Naturally, ICPMs are motivated to present their performance, skills and services in a favourable light in these materials as a way to attract new clients and to retain existing ones. However, we have seen a number of instances where the materials were prepared in a way that highlights or exaggerates favourable points while omitting or failing to disclose facts that may be less favourable to the ICPM.

As a result, we decided to conduct a focused review of the preparation and use of marketing materials by ICPMs.

Reviews

Objectives

The main objectives of the reviews were to:

- broaden our understanding of the type and content of marketing materials used by ICPMs

- assess ICPMs' compliance with Ontario securities law

- identify any regulatory gaps

Scope

The Compliance team gathered preliminary information from about 50 ICPMs that we had not recently reviewed and that were actively carrying on marketing activities. We applied a risk-based approach to select 21 ICPMs for an in-depth review of their marketing practices. The sample included ICPMs that were portfolio managers of non-prospectus qualified investment funds, ICPMs that catered to large institutional investors and ICPMs with a variety of clients, including private clients.

Our review did not focus on ICPMs that act as fund managers solely for prospectus-qualified mutual funds. The marketing materials for these funds are subject to requirements under specific legislation, such as National Instrument 81-102 — *Mutual Funds* (NI 81-102).

Compliance staff reviewed a variety of marketing documents, including brochures, offering documents for products managed by the ICPM, newspaper and magazine advertisements, one-on-one presentations made by ICPMs to clients, websites and market commentaries.

OSC Rules

When reviewing marketing materials for compliance with Ontario securities law, we look to section 2.1 of OSC Rule 31-505 — *Conditions of Registration* (OSC Rule 31-505). This rule requires registrants to deal fairly, honestly and in good faith with their clients. This provision is a broad principle that applies to registrants generally and we expect registrants to apply it to all areas of their activities, including marketing practices and marketing materials.

We also look to the mutual fund rules for sales communications and prohibited representations for guidance on what constitutes misleading performance advertising in marketing materials. These rules, which are in Part 15 of NI 81-102 and Part 13 of its Companion Policy, contain guidance on specific issues, such as the use of benchmarks.

Although NI 81-102 applies to prospectus-qualified mutual funds, it provides principles that are appropriate and consistent with a registrant's obligation to deal fairly, honestly and in good faith with its clients. As such, these rules provide a best-practices standard that can be applied to the marketing materials of other types of investment funds and investment strategies.

Summary of suggested practices

As a result of the review, we have several key suggested practices. These suggested practices are intended to assist registrants in meeting their obligation to deal fairly, honestly and in good faith with their clients. We expect that market participants will look to these practices when preparing marketing materials. Failure to follow these practices may result in inaccurate and unfair marketing materials, which we consider misleading to clients.

The suggested practices include the following:

- ICPMs should present performance data that is based on their actual client performance returns, not on hypothetical returns which have a number of inherent risks and are difficult to verify.

- Performance composites should be constructed to include all portfolios with a similar investment strategy.

- Performance data should be calculated using a consistent methodology so that any comparisons are not misleading.

- Benchmarks should be relevant to the ICPM's investment strategy. There should be adequate disclosure to make the comparison fair and meaningful for clients.

- ICPMs should be able to support the claims made in their marketing materials.

These suggested practices are discussed in further detail in this notice.

Summary of the results

We identified a number of deficiencies in the preparation and use of marketing materials in the ICPMs we reviewed.

Most of the deficiencies fall into one of the following areas:

1. preparation and use of hypothetical performance data
2. linking actual performance of the ICPM's investment fund or investment strategy with the performance of another fund or investment strategy
3. construction and marketing of performance composites
4. construction and use of benchmarks in marketing materials
5. use of exaggerated and unsubstantiated claims in marketing materials

The following is a discussion of the issues in each of these areas and suggested practices.

1. Hypothetical performance data

Hypothetical performance data refers to performance data that is not the performance of actual client portfolios. It is also sometimes referred to as "simulated performance data".

There are different types of hypothetical performance data, including back-tested performance data and model performance data, which are discussed below.

Almost all of the ICPMs that presented hypothetical performance data in marketing materials used it in ways that were misleading or provided inadequate disclosure. Most of these deficiencies related to the marketing of non-prospectus qualified investment funds.

The following are some of the issues that we identified:

- ICPMs presented:
  - hypothetical performance data in a way that may mislead clients to believe that it is the actual performance returns of their investment fund or investment strategy
  - the returns of an index or indexes as returns of the ICPM's own fund or investment strategy
  - model performance data for a strategy that no actual clients were following
  - model performance data instead of the returns of actual client accounts

- There was a lack of disclosure accompanying hypothetical performance data. For example, there was no disclosure of the fact that the performance data was hypothetical, how the hypothetical performance data was calculated and the underlying assumptions on which the hypothetical performance data was based.

- Disclosure accompanying the hypothetical performance data was not clear and prominent.

General concerns

There are a number of general concerns related to the use of hypothetical performance data. For example:

- Any outcome can be achieved. The returns are generally always positive; otherwise, ICPMs would not present them to prospective clients.

- Hypothetical performance data is often combined with, or confused with, actual performance.

- ICPMs do not disclose the assumptions used to derive hypothetical performance data.

- It is difficult to verify the calculation of hypothetical performance data.

- ICPMs can take bigger risks with hypothetical portfolios and act differently than they otherwise would with actual client portfolios.

a) Back-tested performance data

Back-tested performance data refers to hypothetical performance data created by applying a particular investment strategy to historical data over a period of time. The data may be created using quantitative methods or formulas. We also saw the term "back-tested performance data" used to refer to hypothetical performance constructed from the historical performance of existing funds.

Back-tested results aim to show investment returns that theoretically would have been achieved if the strategy had been used during a past time period. ICPMs often use back-tested performance data to attract clients when the ICPM has no track record or has a short track record of less than five years.

An example of back-tested performance data that we saw involved ICPMs managing funds-of-funds that constructed hypothetical performance data from the historical performance of existing funds. This hypothetical performance data was based on assumptions made by the ICPM on what the fund-of-funds would have invested in if it had existed at that time, and used the historical performance data of the underlying funds.

We identified several instances where ICPMs presented performance data for periods that were much longer than the life of the firm's non-prospectus qualified investment fund. In some instances, the back-tested performance data for the period prior to the fund's inception was based on purely hypothetical performance data, such as the performance of an index. In other instances, the back-tested performance data for the period prior to the fund's inception was based on the performance of other existing funds or the underlying funds for a fund-of-funds structure.

In addition, we identified many cases where there was inadequate disclosure about the back-tested performance data, including the underlying assumptions, calculation methodology, and the risks and limitations of the back-tested performance data.

In a number of instances, the disclosure accompanying the back-tested performance data was not prominent and clear. For example, the disclosure was in very small print in a footnote at the end of a marketing piece.

Concerns

In addition to the general concerns with the use of hypothetical performance data outlined above, the following are specific concerns we have about the use of back-tested performance data:

- ICPMs have the benefit of hindsight and do not have to manage in real market conditions.

- ICPMs can alter their strategy to fit the historical data.

Suggested practices

ICPMs should only market their actual performance. They should not use back-tested performance data because it is subject to manipulation and has many limitations. As such, back-tested performance data may be misleading and inappropriate. In addition, there is no way to verify whether the returns would have been achieved.

However, we recognize that there are limited circumstances where back-tested performance data may not be misleading or the risks relating to its use may be mitigated with appropriate disclosure. ICPMs may use back-tested performance data if it is based on actual fund performance (either in a fund-of-funds situation or where a newly created fund follows the same investment strategy of an existing fund) and the following conditions are met:

- *For a newly created fund that follows the same investment strategy of an existing fund.* The actual performance and name of the existing fund is shown separately from the newly created fund's performance, and the newly created fund has the same ICPM as the existing fund.

- *For newly created fund-of-funds or a newly created fund that is based on the investment strategy of more than one existing fund.* Disclose the details about the underlying funds that it invests in and upon which the back-tested performance data is based. This includes the name of each underlying fund and the percentage of the portfolio allocated to each of these funds, provided that the percentage that is invested in each of the existing funds does not change over time.

- *For both situations:*

  - The presentation of the back-tested performance data clearly discloses that the performance data is that of the existing or underlying fund(s) and not the performance of the newly created fund.

  - The actual performance data for the existing or underlying fund(s) that the back-tested performance data is based on is presented for appropriate periods (e.g. 1, 3, 5 and 10 years or since inception). Each of these funds must be in existence for the entire periods presented.

  - Any differences in fees between the newly created fund and the existing or underlying fund(s) are adjusted for and disclosed.

If the back-tested performance data meets the criteria outlined above, the disclosure should be clear and prominent and provide enough detail about the methodology and assumptions used to calculate the back-tested performance data. These are critical in calculating the returns. Failing to disclose them would be omitting information that is integral to making the presentation fair and not misleading. Failure to include this information is contrary to section 2.1 of OSC Rule 31-505.

In addition, the disclosure should clearly state that the performance returns are hypothetical and describe the limitations of the back-tested performance data. For example, ICPMs should disclose that back-tested performance data is hypothetical performance, it is not actual performance returns for the fund and that it was calculated with the benefit of hindsight.

Lastly, the back-tested performance data that satisfies the criteria outlined above should be presented separately from actual performance data. See "Linking performance" below.

b) Model performance data

Model performance data refers to the investment results of a "model" portfolio or "imaginary" portfolio of securities that are presented over a period of time. Most model portfolios are forward-looking in that they use an investment strategy from a point in time going forward and are managed on an ongoing basis (as opposed to applying an investment strategy to historical data).

A model portfolio is often presented as the ideal balance of securities for a particular client's portfolio. ICPMs usually have clients whose portfolios follow the same investment strategy and hold the same securities as the model, but will vary in the percentage held in each security, the timing of purchases and sales, and price per security.

We identified situations where ICPMs presented performance data of a model portfolio instead of the actual performance data for clients. One ICPM presented performance data of a model portfolio but did not have any clients who were following that investment strategy. The ICPM presented the hypothetical performance data of the model portfolio to attract new clients.

Concerns

Our concerns about hypothetical performance also apply to model performance data. In addition, a significant concern with using model performance data is that it is difficult to assess whether it represents actual performance results of existing clients.

Actual performance data may differ from model performance data because:

- Trading costs may not be deducted in the model. If they are deducted, they are estimates and not actual trading costs.

- The trading prices for securities in the model may differ from trading prices in clients' portfolios. The ICPM may not have actually been able to trade at the price used for a given security in the model portfolio, especially for thinly traded securities.

- Model portfolios tend to be fully invested in securities, while actual client accounts typically maintain cash for liquidity. Therefore, the model may have better results than actual results in rising markets and poorer results in falling markets.

Suggested practices

ICPMs should present actual performance data for an investment strategy instead of model performance data. Actual results are more accurate and better reflect the investment strategy's true performance.

In particular, ICPMs should not present the performance data of a model portfolio if no clients are following that investment strategy. If they do, it is misleading because the model performance cannot be verified. For example, there is no way to ensure that the ICPM would have made the same investment decisions in the past or that the securities selected in the model would actually have been traded on a given date at a given quantity and price. This is consistent with an ICPM's obligation under section 2.1 of OSC Rule 31-505 to deal fairly, honestly and in good faith with its clients.

2. Linking performance

ICPMs sometimes link the actual performance data of their investment fund or investment strategy with the performance data of another fund or investment strategy. For example, back-tested performance data of another existing investment fund with a longer track record is presented as the actual performance data of the ICPM's fund, even though the ICPM's fund did not exist for the entire period presented.

In many instances, the performance data of the other existing fund or investment strategy is linked to the actual performance data of the investment strategy or fund in the same table or graph. This may also include performance metrics or risk analysis, such as standard deviation and the Sharpe ratio.

Concerns

Linking these separate sets of performance data in the same table or graph or mathematically is misleading because:

- clients may be misled to believe that the performance data is the actual performance of the fund or investment strategy

- it appears that the fund or investment strategy has a longer track record than it really has

- the performance may not be comparable across time periods, or

- the same method of calculating performance may not have been used for each set of data

Suggested practices

The actual performance data of an ICPM's fund or investment strategy should be presented separately from the back-tested performance data of the other existing fund(s) or investment strategy. It should not be mathematically linked or presented in the same table or graph with the actual performance data of the fund or investment strategy managed by the ICPM. Each graph or chart should be clearly labelled. This will distinguish the actual performance data of the fund or investment strategy from that of the other existing fund(s) or investment strategy.

3. Performance composites

A performance composite is an aggregation or grouping of the performance of one or more client portfolios that represent a similar investment mandate, objective or strategy. ICPMs often use performance composites in reporting performance to prospective clients.

More than half of the ICPMs adopted unsatisfactory practices in the construction and/or presentation of their composites. We identified the following:

- A composite did not include all relevant client portfolios.

- Client portfolios were not consistently included in a composite over time. For example, the historical performance of terminated portfolios was excluded from the composite.

- An inconsistent or inappropriate methodology was used to calculate the performance of a composite. For example, average returns were used instead of asset-weighted returns.

- ICPMs did not have adequate policies and procedures for constructing and presenting composites.

- There was a lack of adequate disclosure about the performance returns of composites. For example, ICPMs did not disclose whether the returns were net of fees, or gross of portfolio management fees and/or other expenses.

- The disclosure claimed that the ICPM complied with the Global Investment Performance Standards (GIPS) of the CFA Institute when it did not.

- Inadequate books and records were maintained to support performance composite data.

Concerns

Each of the issues noted above results in an inaccurate and unfair presentation of performance data. We consider this misleading to clients. If the composite does not include all client portfolios with a similar investment strategy, there is a risk that the ICPM will "cherry-pick" the portfolios with the best performance returns in order to present the most favourable results. In some instances, we found that ICPMs used one client's performance to represent the investment strategy instead of presenting the performance returns for a composite.

Also, without a proper process in place over composite construction, composites may be prepared inconsistently or inappropriately. This results in performance data that is not comparable from period to period and is misleading.

Suggested practices

All portfolios that meet the criteria of the composite should be included in the composite. Inappropriately including or excluding portfolios in a composite results in performance returns that do not truly reflect the actual performance of the ICPM's investment strategy. This improper practice is misleading to clients and contrary to section 2.1 of OSC Rule 31-505.

In addition, composite returns should be calculated by asset-weighting the individual portfolios' returns.

ICPMs should provide adequate disclosure in their marketing document that explains all the factors that are necessary to make the composite presentation meaningful. For example, the disclosure should:

- clearly outline the investment strategy that is reflected in the composite

- state whether the composite returns are net of fees, or gross of portfolio management fees and/or other expenses, and

- include any other key information about the client portfolios included in the composite, such as:
  - minimum asset level, if any
  - use of a sub-adviser, and
  - currency used to express performance

Section 1.2 of OSC Rule 31-505 requires ICPMs to establish and enforce written procedures for dealing with clients that conform to prudent business practice and enable the ICPM to serve its clients adequately.

Prudent business practice requires ICPMs to establish policies and procedures for the construction of composites to ensure that they are constructed appropriately and consistently. These policies and procedures should cover how to treat terminated portfolios, new portfolios and portfolios that have changed strategies and switched composites.

4. Benchmarks

A benchmark is a standard against which the performance of an investment strategy managed by an ICPM can be compared or measured. In general, benchmarks are chosen to represent the characteristics of the investment strategy and help to measure its degree of success.

More than half of the ICPMs we reviewed were deficient in the presentation and use of benchmarks. We identified the following:

- Benchmarks were not:
  - comparable to the fund or investment strategy
  - widely recognized and/or available
  - presented in the same currency or on the same basis as the fund or investment strategy (e.g. total return vs. return without reinvested dividends).

- There was inadequate disclosure about the use of a benchmark. For example, there was no disclosure of the name of the benchmark or inadequate disclosure regarding the composition of a blended benchmark.

- Inadequate books and records were maintained to support benchmark data. For example, there was no evidence to support calculations in the case of a blended benchmark.

Concerns

Presenting an inappropriate benchmark does not result in a meaningful comparison. As a result, the wrong conclusions could be drawn or implied by it. For example, compared to the benchmark, the performance of a fund or investment strategy may appear better than it really is.

Suggested practices

ICPMs should compare their performance returns against a relevant benchmark. That is, there should be a connection between the investment strategy and the benchmark used.

The benchmark's full name should be disclosed and the components of a blended benchmark should be clearly disclosed (e.g. 40% S&P/TSX Composite Index and 60% S&P 500 Index).

However, in limited instances, an ICPM may want to compare performance returns against a benchmark that has a different composition than its investment strategy. For example, an ICPM may compare its investment strategy to the S&P/TSX Composite Index because the index is widely known and followed.

If the ICPM's investment strategy is not similar to that of the benchmark and the benchmark is widely known and followed, adequate disclosure is necessary to explain the relevance of the use of this benchmark. This should include a discussion of the differences between the benchmark and the investment strategy of the ICPM. This disclosure would make the comparison fair and meaningful for clients.

In addition, as a best practice, paragraph 15.3(1)(a) of NI 81-102 provides that a sales communication shall not compare the performance of a mutual fund with the performance of a benchmark unless it includes all facts, that if disclosed, would be likely to alter materially the conclusions reasonably drawn or implied by the comparison. Paragraph 15.3(1)(c) of NI 81-102 provides that the sales communication must explain any factors necessary to make the comparison fair and not misleading.

5. Exaggerated and unsubstantiated claims

Exaggerated and unsubstantiated claims are statements and claims made by ICPMs in marketing materials without evidence to support these claims. These claims often relate to the ICPM's performance, skills, education, portfolio management experience or services.

For example, we identified claims of "superior performance" that were unsubstantiated or where the actual performance of the fund or investment strategy was lower than the returns of a comparable benchmark. We also found claims that the ICPM was a "leading expert" in a particular area without sufficient evidence to support this claim.

Two-thirds of the ICPMs reviewed used these types of claims.

Concerns

Exaggerated claims are misleading to clients because they do not accurately reflect the ICPM's actual performance, skills, education, experience or services. In addition, investors may base their decision to contract the services of an ICPM on inaccurate information.

Suggested practices

ICPMs should be able to substantiate all claims made in their marketing materials. They should reference the information supporting the claim where the claim is made in the marketing material so that clients can easily assess it. ICPMs should ensure that all claims accurately reflect their performance, skills, education, portfolio management experience and services. This is consistent with their obligation under section 2.1 of OSC Rule 31-505.

In addition, there are provisions in the Securities Act (Ontario) (the Act) that deal with specific types of claims made by a registrant. ICPMs should also follow these provisions in the preparation of marketing materials. For example, subsection 38(2) of the Act states that no person or company, with the intention of effecting a trade in a security, shall give any undertaking relating to the future value or price of the security. Section 45 of the Act provides that an unregistered person or company cannot hold himself/herself or itself out as being registered.

Other marketing-related deficiencies

We identified other deficiencies in the preparation and use of marketing materials, including:

Lack of appropriate policies and procedures

One-third of the ICPMs did not have appropriate policies and procedures dealing with marketing activities or had policies and procedures that did not reflect their actual marketing practices. The majority of these ICPMs had an inadequate process for reviewing and approving their marketing materials.

Section 1.2 of OSC Rule 31-505 requires registrants to develop and enforce written procedures for dealing with clients that conform to prudent business practice and enable them to serve clients adequately. These policies and procedures should be in sufficient detail and cover all aspects of the ICPM's marketing activities, from preparing the materials to reviewing and approving them.

Suggested practices

ICPMs should develop and enforce written policies and procedures that are tailored to their specific marketing activities. At a minimum, the policies and procedures should include guidelines on:

- preparing and reviewing marketing materials to prevent false or misleading statements and to ensure compliance with securities legislation

- having marketing materials approved by an appropriate person

- preparing performance data to be used in marketing materials

- constructing and presenting performance composites, including:
  - composite definitions
  - calculation methodologies
  - valuation policies
  - treatment of new and terminated portfolios
  - treatment of large cash flows

- selecting and presenting benchmarks

Outdated or incorrect information

More than one-third of ICPMs were deficient in this area. In some instances, the marketing materials contained outdated information (e.g. firm's website contained outdated performance returns or information about the ICPM itself). In other instances, marketing materials contained errors (e.g. errors in performance returns presented).

As described above, section 1.2 of OSC Rule 31-505 requires registrants to develop and enforce written procedures for dealing with clients that conform to prudent business practice and enable them to serve clients adequately.

Suggested practices

ICPMs should ensure that their marketing materials contain accurate and up-to-date information. As described above, implementing a process for independent review and approval of marketing materials can help eliminate errors in marketing materials. In addition, regular review of an ICPM's website can help to ensure that the content is up-to-date.

Our response

We sent compliance deficiency reports to each of the ICPMs we reviewed. Each ICPM was required to provide a written response to the deficiencies identified in our report within 30 days.

We are working directly with these ICPMs to help them understand our concerns with the issues identified with their marketing practices. We will continue to proactively work with them to ensure that deficiencies are resolved appropriately within a reasonable time frame. If they do not resolve their deficiencies, we may take further action, such as imposing terms and conditions on their registration, conducting follow-up reviews or referring the matter to the OSC's Enforcement Branch.

Next steps

We will continue to review the marketing practices of market participants during our regular field reviews. While the provisions in Ontario securities law dealing with marketing practices are broad in nature, the suggested practices described in this notice are intended to provide guidance to market participants on how we expect them to apply these provisions. The suggested practices are the guidelines that Compliance staff will apply in assessing and monitoring the compliance of marketing practices with Ontario securities law.

We encourage market participants to use this notice to help them enhance their marketing practices. In the meantime, we will continue to gather more information and consider whether any further guidance to the industry in this area is necessary.

Policies and Orders: CSAN 33-325; OSCN 33-734, s. 3.2.

OSC Staff Notice 33-730 — Capital Calculations for Investment Counsel/Portfolio Managers

Date: June 10, 2008

31 O.S.C.B. 5869

Overview

The Compliance team of the Ontario Securities Commission (OSC) has noticed a slight increase in the number of investment counsel/portfolio managers (portfolio managers) that are deficient in meeting the minimum capital requirements under the *Securities Act* (Ontario) (the Act) based on their year end audited financial statements. While the vast majority of portfolio managers do maintain adequate capital, this notice is to remind all portfolio managers of the capital requirements under the Act and also describes the terms and conditions that are recommended by staff when a portfolio manager is capital deficient.

All portfolio managers are required to prepare monthly capital calculations within a reasonable period of time after each month end. Capital calculations must be based on monthly financial statements prepared in accordance with generally accepted accounting principles (GAAP).

Proposed changes to Ontario securities law will change the capital requirements of portfolio managers and will also capture other market participants who are not currently required to prepare capital calculations, such as investment fund managers and certain exempt market dealers. Therefore, this notice also reminds all market participants, including portfolio managers, to be watchful of future changes to the amount and scope of capital requirements as a result of proposed National Instrument 31-103 *Registration Requirements* (NI 31-103).

Minimum free capital requirement

Regulation 107(3) under the Act requires every portfolio manager to maintain minimum free capital of the maximum amount, if any, that is deductible under any clause of the bonding or insurance policy required under Regulation 108(3) plus $5,000 of working capital calculated in accordance with GAAP. Portfolio managers who have access to or take possession of client funds or securities are required to maintain minimum free capital of the maximum insurance deductible plus $25,000 of working capital calculated in accordance with GAAP.

In addition, portfolio managers are required under Regulation 113(3)(10) to maintain a record of a reasonable calculation of required capital for each month within a reasonable time after the month.

Registrants who do not meet the prescribed capital requirement for any given month should inform the OSC immediately of the deficiency and take corrective measures within 48 hours.

Historically, issues concerning capital calculations have been among the most common deficiencies encountered during compliance reviews. Registrants should refer to OSC Staff Notice 33-728 *2007 Annual Report — Compliance Team* for our observations and suggested practices for dealing with capital calculations which may be found on the OSC website at www.osc.gov.on.ca.

Terms and conditions

Staff recommends imposing terms and conditions on a registrant's registration in all circumstances where the OSC becomes aware of a capital deficiency. The terms and conditions are generally imposed for a six month period and include requirements to:

- File year-to-date unaudited financial statements with the OSC every month, including a balance sheet and income statement, prepared in accordance with GAAP;

- File a capital calculation for each month end;

- Review their policies and procedures for compliance with Ontario securities law and file a compliance report that includes:

    (a) the reasons for the registrant's failure to meet the capital requirement as required under Ontario securities law;

    (b) a certification from its compliance officer to the effect that the registrant has reviewed its system for on-going compliance with Ontario securities law and rectified the problem(s) that led to its failure to satisfy the capital requirement; and

    (c) details of the specific measures that will be taken to ensure that the capital requirement will be satisfied at all times in the future.

We impose similar terms and conditions on registrants who do not meet their regulatory filing requirements. See OSC Staff Notice 33-713 *Registrant Regulatory Filings* for more information.

Under section 26(3) of the Act, registrants may oppose the imposition of recommended terms and conditions on registration and request an opportunity to be heard.

Proposed NI 31-103

On February 28, 2008, the Canadian Securities Administrators published for second comment proposed NI 31-103. Changes under proposed NI 31-103 will affect the minimum capital requirements for registered firms who are not members of a self regulatory organization (SRO), including portfolio managers. The proposed changes are meant to more closely link the minimum capital with the associated risks of a particular category of registration.

Key changes to the proposed capital requirements, some of which may impact portfolio managers, include:

- an increase in the minimum capital requirement for most non-SRO members;

- an increase in the frequency of filings for most non-SRO members; and

- an enhanced capital calculation formula to better reflect the firm's business model.

Market participants should refer to proposed NI 31-103 to familiarize themselves with the proposed preparation and reporting requirements and the proposed changes to their capital requirements.

OSC Staff Notice 33-731 — 2008 Compliance Team Annual Report

Date: September 5, 2008

31 O.S.C.B. 8503

[Not reproduced]

OSC Staff Notice 33-732 — 2009 Compliance Team Annual Report

Date: September 25, 2009

32 O.S.C.B. 7549

Contents

Introduction

This report is a summary of the Compliance team's activities for the 2009 fiscal year (April 1, 2008 to March 31, 2009). During this period, the capital markets in Ontario experienced an unprecedented period of financial and market turmoil. No doubt this was a challenging year for securities regulators, as well as market participants, around the world.

The Compliance team, as part of the Compliance and Registrant Regulation Branch at the Ontario Securities Commission (OSC), played an important role in responding to the current market turmoil by conducting a series of proactive reviews of Ontario-based investment fund managers (IFMs) covering major segments of the investment funds industry.

In this report, we discuss how the Compliance team responded to the market turmoil, our key areas of focus, and the outcome of these reviews. As in our previous reports, we also discuss the three most commonly occurring significant deficiencies from reviews of portfolio managers (PMs) and limited market dealers (LMDs).

We encourage market participants[1] to use this report as a self-assessment tool to strengthen their compliance with Ontario securities law and to improve their systems of internal controls and supervision.

This report is divided into seven sections:

1. Our role. This section describes our role and how we continue to work to strengthen the compliance-enforcement continuum.

2. Response to recent market turmoil. This section summarizes the work the Compliance team conducted in response to the market turmoil.

3. General compliance initiatives. This section describes the 2009 new registrant sweeps, the desk review of mutual fund dealers, and the development of the LMD risk assessment questionnaire. It also discusses the initiatives we have planned for the 2010 fiscal year.

4. Significant deficiencies among market participants. This section summarizes the three most commonly occurring significant deficiencies found in our 2009 reviews of PMs and LMDs. We also include suggested best practices to help market participants improve existing procedures and establish policies in areas where they are lacking, and to give general guidance on improving overall compliance.

5. Outcomes of our reviews. This section describes the various outcomes of our reviews.

6. National Instrument 31-103 — *Registration Requirements and Exemptions* (NI 31-103). This section provides an update on the registration reform project.

7. International Financial Reporting Standards (IFRS). This section provides an update to market participants on IFRS and how the move to IFRS may affect them in preparing financial statements for delivery to the OSC.

Part 3:
REGISTRATION

---

[1]Market participants include investment fund managers, LMDs, portfolio managers and scholarship plan dealers.

1. — Our role

1.1 — Compliance team

The Compliance team is part of the OSC's Compliance and Registrant Regulation Branch. Our team has 32 staff including 28 chartered accountants and lawyers. Our role is to enhance investor protection and enhance confidence in the capital markets by:

- overseeing market participants that are not members of a recognized self-regulatory organization (SRO) including PMs, IFMs, LMDs and scholarship plan dealers (SPDs)

- promoting compliance by market participants with Ontario securities law by conducting compliance oversight reviews

- recommending and taking remedial action against market participants that do not comply with Ontario securities law. This may include the issuance of a deficiency report, imposing terms and conditions, or referral to the Enforcement branch

- determining whether additional standards or rules are needed for market participants

- participating in the development of these standards or rules

- creating awareness of new or proposed rules

- fostering a culture of compliance

- coordinating with other branches of the OSC to promote effective oversight of market participants and strengthen the compliance-enforcement continuum, and

- providing guidance and information to the industry on significant issues identified during our reviews. For example, we publish staff notices, and participate in seminars and conferences.

1.2 — Who we oversee

At March 31, 2009, we had oversight responsibility over approximately 1,600 market participants[2]. The following chart shows the number of market participants by type.

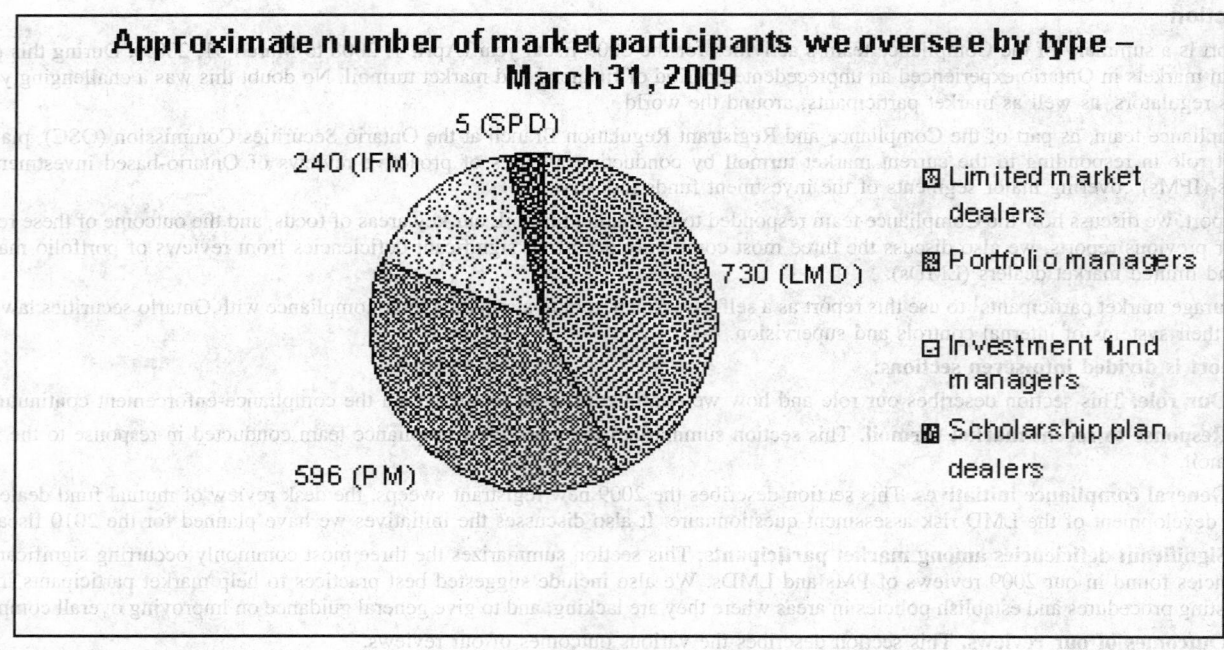

1.3 — Compliance review process

As set out in our previous annual reports, we have developed risk-assessment models to select market participants for compliance oversight reviews. The risk assessment models enable us to allocate resources more effectively and efficiently by targeting those market participants with higher risk profiles.

---

[2]If a market participant is operating in more than one capacity, for example, as a portfolio manager and as an investment fund manager, it is considered to be two market participants for oversight purposes.

1.4 — Compliance-Enforcement continuum

The Compliance team coordinates and works actively with other branches at the OSC, in particular, the Enforcement Branch. When we identify any serious violation of securities law, we discuss the findings with the Enforcement Branch and together staff determines an appropriate course of action. As well, Enforcement staff may have concerns about compliance issues at a market participant and Compliance staff will provide expert advice as required. There is ongoing information sharing between the two branches of the OSC, with Compliance (whose main focus is on prevention and remediation) on one end of the spectrum, and Enforcement (whose main focus is on protection and deterrence) on the other end.

The flowchart illustrates our role and how we interact with our market participants, industry and other branches at the OSC.

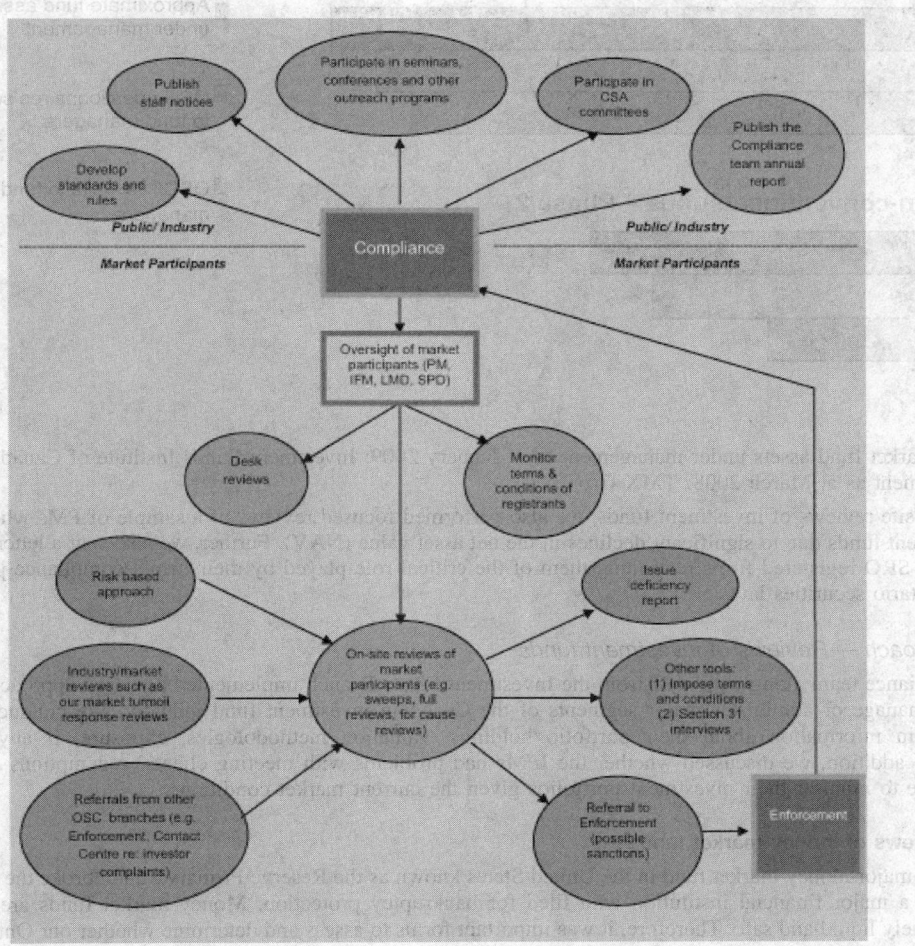

2. — Response to recent market turmoil

The global financial services industry has experienced an unprecedented period of turmoil. In response to the concerns emerging about the current market conditions, Compliance staff (along with staff from the Investment Funds Branch on some reviews) initiated a series of on-site reviews to identify any issues at market participants that the OSC oversees that posed an increased risk to investors.

These on-site reviews were executed in phases and included IFMs and PMs that manage various major segments of our investment fund industry including money market funds, non-conventional funds and hedge funds.

The chart below shows the approximate total assets under management, the share of the respective marketplace that was targeted in our reviews, and the share that was covered by our on-site visits of IFMs.

Part 3:
REGISTRATION

Response to recent market turmoil - reviews of investment funds

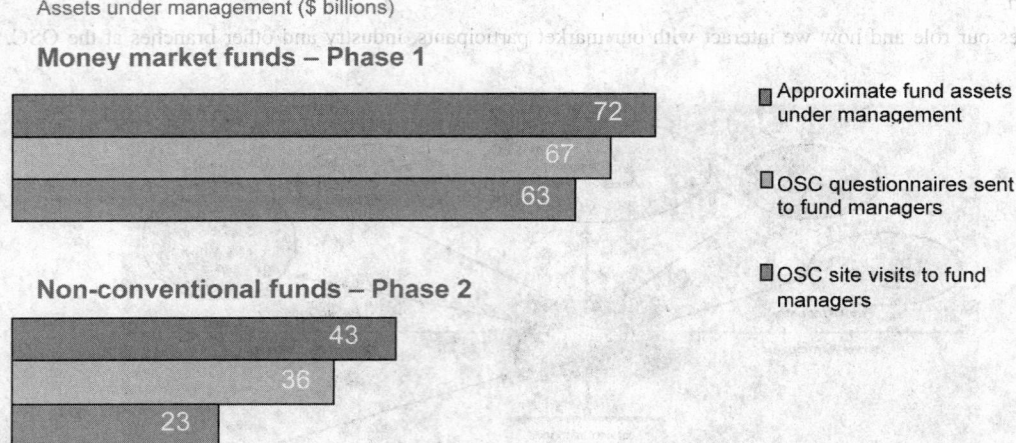

Assets under management ($ billions)

Money market funds – Phase 1

72

67

63

■ Approximate fund assets under management

□ OSC questionnaires sent to fund managers

■ OSC site visits to fund managers

Non-conventional funds – Phase 2

43

36

23

Sources — Money market fund assets under management as at January 2009: Investment Funds Institute of Canada. Non-conventional fund assets under management as at March 2008: TMX Group.

In addition to the on-site reviews of investment funds, we also performed focused reviews of a sample of PMs who had suspended redemptions of their investment funds due to significant declines in the net asset value (NAV). Further, we also sent a letter to the Chief Compliance Officers of OSC non-SRO registered firms reminding them of the critical role played by their firm's compliance programs in meeting their obligations under Ontario securities law.

2.1 — Phased approach — Reviews of investment funds

Staff from the Compliance team along with staff from the Investment Funds Branch implemented a phased approach for assessing the operations of IFMs who manage or administer major segments of the Canadian investment fund industry. We conducted meetings with senior management to obtain information about their portfolio holdings, valuation methodologies, exposure, if any, to illiquid assets, and counterparty risks. In addition, we discussed whether the IFMs had problems with meeting clients' redemptions and what procedures and controls were in place to monitor their investment portfolios given the current market conditions.

(i) — Phase 1 — Reviews of money market funds

In September 2008, a major money market fund in the United States known as the Reserve Primary Fund "broke the buck" due to its exposure to Lehman Brothers, a major financial institution who filed for bankruptcy protection. Money market funds are generally considered by investors to be extremely liquid and safe. Therefore, it was important for us to assess and determine whether our Ontario-based money market funds faced similar issues as those in the United States relating to exposure to financial institutions, illiquid securities and redemption levels.

Review process

In September 2008, we initiated a fact finding review of Ontario-based money market funds by sending a questionnaire to 50 Ontario money market fund managers.

The questionnaire focused on a number of key areas covering:

• portfolio holdings

• valuation of portfolio securities (with a focus on illiquid securities), and

• sales and redemptions levels.

We reviewed and risk-ranked the fund manager responses. We then selected a representative sample of IFMs for on-site reviews.

This sample included money market assets under management of approximately $63 billion, representing 90% of the money market fund assets of the 50 IFMs (see our response to the market turmoil chart above).

Focus on key risk areas

The on-site reviews focused on various key risk areas relating to:

• financial sector exposure

- concentration levels
- counterparty exposure
- levels of redemptions, and
- valuation of securities in these investment funds.

We met with senior management and performed substantive testing of the funds' portfolios to assess whether IFMs were using appropriate valuation methodologies, monitoring counterparty exposure, managing concentration risks, and levels of redemptions.

Outcomes of our reviews

Based on our on-site reviews: we found that:

- the portfolios were generally invested in a manner consistent with a conservative investment strategy (i.e. in a combination of t-bills, bankers acceptances, deposit notes etc.)
- IFMs were generally able to meet redemptions
- valuation methodologies were generally appropriate
- we did not identify any IFMs with any material exposure to the U.S. companies experiencing financial difficulties, and
- IFMs were generally maintaining a more liquid portfolio than previously, with shorter terms to maturity.

In general, we found that the IFMs that we reviewed had adequate procedures in place to ensure compliance with their regulatory requirements. Some IFMs had automated exception reporting systems allowing them to monitor and assess compliance with regulatory requirements. If the administrative functions of a fund were outsourced to a service provider, the IFMs reviewed generally had adequate oversight procedures in place. In addition, we also noted that some IFMs had put a number of mechanisms in place to monitor investors' redemptions.

(ii) — Phase 2 — Reviews of non-conventional funds

The second phase of our response to the market turmoil was led by the Investment Funds Branch with participation from the Compliance Team. We conducted on-site reviews of selected non-conventional funds. These non-conventional funds included closed-end funds and exchange-traded funds which generally invest in a broader array of asset classes and employ higher risk investment strategies than conventional mutual funds.

Review process

Our review process was similar to that used for money market funds. We sent a questionnaire to 27 fund managers whose non-conventional funds are listed on the Toronto Stock Exchange. We reviewed and risk-ranked their responses. We then selected a representative sample of non-conventional fund managers for on-site reviews.

This sample represented assets under management of approximately $23 billion, representing 54% of the non-conventional assets under management in Ontario (see our response to the market turmoil chart above).

Focus on key risk areas

Our on-site reviews focused on various key risk areas relating to:

- high risk investment strategies
- going concern
- financial sector exposure
- concentration levels
- counterparty exposure
- redemptions, and
- valuation of securities in these investment funds.

Outcomes of our reviews

Based on the results of our on-site reviews, we found that these funds had generally experienced losses and depletion of assets. In some cases, the market turmoil had an impact on the fund's ability to make distributions or to offer an annual redemption right at net asset value. These funds followed their previously disclosed policies with respect to such events, including appropriate public disclosure and disclosure to unit holders.

(iii) — Phase 3 — Reviews of hedge funds

In general, the hedge fund industry has also been affected by the global markets crisis. For example, some hedge funds experienced deterioration in their NAV and also faced significant pressure in meeting investor redemptions. In the face of increased redemptions from investors and shrinking asset bases, some hedge fund managers have decided to either wind down their funds or temporarily suspend redemptions.

Part 3: REGISTRATION

In February 2009, Compliance staff commenced a review of hedge fund managers based in Ontario to assess whether they posed any significant risks to investors, given the prevailing market conditions. All IFMs are market participants. However, the majority of the hedge fund managers we reviewed are either registered as PMs or LMDs. NI 31-103 will generally require registration of IFMs which includes hedge fund managers.

Review process

We sent a hedge fund questionnaire to 90 hedge fund managers and asked them questions on a range of topics including:

- investment fund strategy
- number of unitholders
- composition of clients (i.e. retail versus institutional clients)
- portfolio holdings, and
- service providers.

We reviewed and risk-ranked the responses. We then selected a representative sample of hedge fund managers for on-site reviews.

Focus on key risk areas

Our on-site reviews focused on various key risk areas relating to:

- custody of investors' assets
- levels of redemptions
- going concern
- concentration levels
- counterparty exposure
- valuation of portfolio securities, and
- oversight of service providers.

Outcomes of our reviews

On-site reviews are still ongoing. Once the reviews are completed, we will assess whether there are any industry issues that need to be addressed.

2.2 — Focused meetings with IFMs who had suspended redemptions of their investment funds

Compliance staff also conducted focused meetings with senior management of selected IFMs who had suspended redemptions in their investment funds due to a significant decline in the investment funds' NAV. The objective of these focused meetings was to gain a better understanding as to why these investment funds declined in value and to assess whether senior management were taking appropriate action to protect the interests and assets of all investors.

We monitored the actions of these IFMs closely through the periodic update reports we asked them to provide. Where necessary, we referred the matter to the Enforcement Branch for further review.

We will continue to conduct focused meetings where necessary, in order to assess whether investors' interests and assets are protected.

2.3 — Letter to Chief Compliance Officers

Some registrants may have decided to downsize their compliance departments in an effort to reduce costs during the economic downturn. However, it is important that this decision fully consider the impact it will have on the firm's ability to meet its obligations under Ontario securities law.

The compliance program plays a critical role in a firm and serves as a control function to ensure clients' interests and assets are adequately protected and helps to detect and prevent misconduct. Therefore, ensuring that a firm's compliance program is adequately funded and staffed and that it is supported and monitored by senior management of the firm is integral to ensuring its effectiveness.

On March 23, 2009, the Compliance team sent a letter to the Chief Compliance Officers of all OSC non-SRO registered firms reminding them of their continuing obligations to ensure compliance with securities law and that clients' assets are protected. It reiterated that registrants must ensure that they have adequate policies and procedures to ensure compliance. Examples include:

(1) providing appropriate disclosure about the impact of the market conditions on their portfolio investments

(2) updating "Know Your Client" (KYC) information for all investors

(3) for registered individuals, understanding the products they are recommending to investors, commonly known as "Know Your Product" (KYP)

(4) using appropriate valuation methodologies for valuing investments including hard to value investments

3. — *General compliance initiatives*

This section describes the new registrant sweeps of PMs and LMDs we conducted in 2009, the LMD risk assessment questionnaire, the desk reviews of mutual fund dealers who are not members of the Mutual Fund Dealers Association of Canada (MFDA), and the initiatives we plan to conduct in fiscal 2010.

3.1 — *New registrant sweeps*

Since 2008, the Compliance team has conducted sweeps of a sample of registrants including PMs and LMDs that are newly registered with the OSC within the past year and a half. A sweep is a review of a sample of market participants focused on an issue or issues.

A sweep of newly registered PMs was conducted in the fall of 2008, and a sweep of newly registered LMDs was conducted in early 2009.

The sweeps were jointly conducted by staff from the Compliance team and the Registrant Regulation team. Our objectives were to enhance investor protection and prevent market abuse by:

- obtaining a better understanding of the new registrants business operations

- confirming whether their current business activities are consistent with representations in their registration applications

- assessing their compliance with Ontario securities law, and

- providing guidance and information to new registrants to assist them in complying with Ontario securities law.

The sweeps also provided an opportunity for the members of our registration team to meet, in person, our registrants with whom they have continuous and frequent dealings. Reviews of new registrants now form part of our compliance oversight program.

Summary of the Results

PMs

The following are examples of areas in which we noted commonly occurring deficiencies during our review of newly registered PMs:

- marketing

- capital calculations

- individual registration issues

- policies and procedures manual, and

- business continuity plan.

Deficiencies in each of these areas are among the 10 most commonly occurring deficiencies of PMs. Last year, we published a separate summary of the 10 most commonly occurring deficiencies of PMs and suggested best practices. For additional guidance, please refer to this summary which is available on the OSC website at *www.osc.gov.on.ca*. See also section 4.1 for a discussion of the most commonly occurring significant deficiencies found during compliance reviews of PMs this year.

LMDs

The following are examples of commonly occurring deficiency areas that we noted during our review of newly registered LMDs:

- understanding the investment products they are recommending (KYP) and understanding their clients' circumstances (KYC) in order to make the suitability determination required by law

- individual registration issues

- policies and procedures manual

- maintenance of adequate books and records

- marketing, and

- business continuity plan.

For suggested best practices on some of these deficiencies, please refer to section 4.2 of this report.

3.2 — *LMD risk assessment questionnaire*

In 2009, we developed a risk assessment model for LMDs. A risk assessment questionnaire will be sent to the LMDs in the near future. Data from the model will be used to assist us in prioritizing and planning LMD reviews going forward.

3.3 — *Desk reviews of Mutual Fund Dealers who are not members of the MFDA*

OSC Rule 31-506 *SRO Membership — Mutual Fund Dealers* requires all registrants registered as a mutual fund dealer to become a member of the MFDA after July 2, 2002. Registrants whose mutual fund dealer activities were limited at the time of the rule could apply for an exemption from becoming a member of the MFDA.

As the exemptions were granted approximately 6 years ago, staff from the Compliance team conducted a desk review to determine if exempted registrants were still relying on and complying with the terms and conditions of their exemption. A questionnaire was sent to all registrants exempted from becoming a member of the MFDA that are currently registered as mutual fund dealers. Overall, staff did not find any mutual fund dealers that were inappropriately relying on the exemptions provided to them.

3.4 — Future initiatives

Impact reviews

We have further enhanced our oversight strategy for market participants. Going forward, we will perform "impact reviews" on larger market participants over a defined cycle.

In general, our compliance oversight reviews to date indicate that larger market participants tend to have adequate policies and procedures and controls in place. However, irrespective of other risk factors, a breakdown of internal controls at a larger market participant may have a significant impact on the capital markets given the larger number of clients and dollar amounts involved. As a result, we intend to focus some of our compliance oversight resources on larger market participants over a defined number of years. The impact reviews will most often be in the form of sweep reviews.

Market turmoil initiatives

We will continue to closely monitor the prevailing market conditions and will conduct special reviews or sweeps to address any significant issues which may arise.

Fiscal 2010 Sweeps

In the past few years, we have shifted towards performing more sweep type reviews than regular or full field reviews. We think that sweeps are a better oversight tool as they allow us to focus on a particular topic of interest and cover a large sample of market participants within a short period of time.

Our plan is to conduct at least one sweep each year on each of IFMs, PMs and LMDs. After we complete a sweep, we normally share our findings with the public by issuing a staff notice or an industry report. Issuing public reports helps us meet our Compliance team's role of enhancing investor protection and preventing market abuse.

4. — Significant deficiencies among market participants

If we find significant deficiencies in a market participant's operations, we identify them in the deficiency report to enable senior management to focus on the key issues identified. The identification of significant deficiencies also helps to highlight areas of regulatory concern so that appropriate action can be taken by the market participant to improve compliance. Increased regulatory compliance by market participants helps ensure that investors are protected and that market abuse is prevented.

We have established various criteria to assess whether a deficiency is significant, including:

- risk to client assets

- conflicts of interest

- misleading information to clients

- ineffective compliance structure

We also take into account other factors, including:

- current issues, such as best execution and marketing practices

- the frequency of findings

- the impact of the deficiency on the market participant's operations

The following sections summarize the three most commonly occurring significant deficiencies for fiscal 2009 of PMs and LMDs. We did not include information on the most commonly occurring significant deficiencies for IFMs in this section as significant resources were allocated to the market turmoil reviews during this fiscal period. As a result, we are not in a position to make general comments on significant deficiencies for IFMs. Please see section 2 of the report.

Some of the most commonly occurring significant deficiencies for PMs and LMDs remain the same every year, for example, marketing materials, capital calculations and KYC. We review different firms each year and we target higher risk market participants for review. For firms reviewed, we expect them to continue to review their procedures to ensure compliance. Our expectation is that firms not yet reviewed will use this report as a self-assessment tool to improve their overall compliance. Over time, staff expect to see increased compliance in these areas and we plan on conducting sweeps in the future to verify continued compliance.

4.1 — PMs

Our normal field reviews of PMs in the 2009 fiscal year resulted in an average of 15 deficiencies per firm reviewed. An average of six or 40% of these deficiencies were significant. The chart below shows the three most commonly occurring areas in which we found significant deficiencies among PMs, compared with the 2008 fiscal year. One of the three most commonly occurring significant deficiencies in fiscal 2009 (registration issues) is different from those identified in 2008.[3] See the discussion below with respect to the specific deficiencies that we identified in these areas.

We will continue to focus on these areas of significant deficiencies as part of our compliance oversight process. We expect PMs to take appropriate action in these areas to improve their compliance.

Significant deficiencies among portfolio managers - fiscal years 2009 and 2008

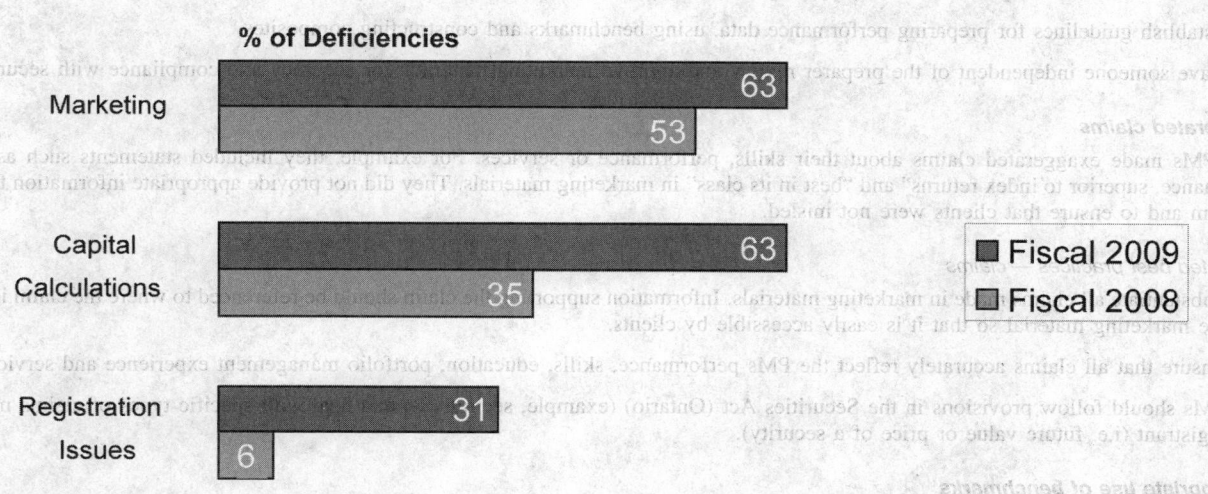

Note: The percentage of deficiencies represents the percentage of PMs that were deficient in this area in the reviews performed in the 2009 fiscal year.

1. — Marketing

Marketing remains the most commonly occurring significant deficiency. About 63% of the PMs reviewed had significant deficiencies in this area. The percentage of deficiencies in this area increased by 10% in the 2009 fiscal year. We believe this increase may be partly due to a larger number of smaller PMs being reviewed, as compared to the 2008 fiscal year.

In general, smaller PMs tend to have less developed processes and procedures for preparing, reviewing and approving marketing materials prior to use. We intend to conduct another sweep review of the marketing practices of PMs in the near future. We expect to see increased compliance with Section 2.1 of OSC Rule 31-505 — *Conditions of Registration* (OSC Rule 31-505) and OSC Staff Notice 33-729 — *Marketing Practices of Investment Counsel/ Portfolio Managers* (OSC Staff Notice 33-729). As well, we will consider taking appropriate action, up to and including enforcement action, when we identify serious deficiencies in a PM's marketing materials.

Section 2.1 of OSC Rule 31-505 requires registrants to deal fairly, honestly and in good faith with their clients. This provision is a broad principle that applies to registrants generally. We expect registrants to apply it to all areas of their activities, including marketing practices and marketing materials.

For additional guidance, please refer to OSC Staff Notice 33-729. This notice provides guidance to market participants on complying with applicable legislation and best practices in the preparation and use of marketing materials. OSC Staff Notice 33-729 is available on the OSC website at *www.osc.gov.on.ca*.

We found the following marketing-related issues:

Inadequate disclosure relating to performance data

As in the previous fiscal period, some PMs did not disclose whether performance returns were gross or net of fees, or the names of the composites or pooled funds that the performance returns related to. Others provided inadequate disclosure of the differences between client account returns and the benchmarks to which they are compared.

---

[3]The three most commonly occurring significant deficiencies in the 2008 fiscal year were marketing, capital calculations and personal trading.

Suggested best practices — performance data

- Provide clear and adequate disclosure in marketing materials to ensure that performance data is meaningful and comparisons are fair and not misleading. This includes providing:

  - a description of the investment strategy that is reflected in the performance data

  - a statement about whether returns are net or gross of portfolio management fees and/or other expenses

  - key information about client portfolios in the composite, such as minimum asset level.

- Update marketing materials regularly to ensure all information is complete, accurate and not misleading to clients.

- Establish and enforce procedures for preparing, reviewing and approving marketing materials.

- Establish guidelines for preparing performance data, using benchmarks and constructing composites.

- Have someone independent of the preparer review and approve marketing materials for accuracy and compliance with securities law.

Exaggerated claims

Some PMs made exaggerated claims about their skills, performance or services. For example, they included statements such as "proven performance, superior to index returns" and "best in its class" in marketing materials. They did not provide appropriate information to support the claim and to ensure that clients were not misled.

Suggested best practices — claims

- Substantiate all claims made in marketing materials. Information supporting the claim should be referenced to where the claim is made in the marketing material so that it is easily accessible by clients.

- Ensure that all claims accurately reflect the PMs performance, skills, education, portfolio management experience and services.

- PMs should follow provisions in the Securities Act (Ontario) (example, section 38) that deal with specific types of claims made by a registrant (i.e. future value or price of a security).

Inappropriate use of benchmarks

Some PMs compared the return of their funds or accounts to benchmarks that, in staff's view, were inappropriate or misleading to clients. Also, there was inadequate disclosure provided for some of the benchmarks used. For example, there was no disclosure of the name of the benchmark or inadequate disclosure regarding the components of a blended benchmark.

Suggested best practices — benchmarks

- Use benchmarks that are relevant to the investment strategy employed.

- The benchmark's full name should be disclosed. Where a blended/customized benchmark is used, disclose the components and names of the benchmarks used.

- If a widely known and followed benchmark is not similar to that of the investment strategy, adequate disclosure should be provided to explain the relevance of use, including a discussion of the differences between the benchmark and investment strategy of the portfolio manager.

2. — Capital calculations

PMs are required to prepare monthly calculations of regulatory capital (capital calculations) within a reasonable period of time after each month end (Regulation 113(3)). Capital calculations must be based on monthly financial statements prepared in accordance with Canadian GAAP. If a PM has inadequate regulatory capital (i.e. it is capital deficient), the PM should inform the OSC immediately and to correct the capital deficiency within 48 hours. As well, higher levels of regulatory capital and insurance are required if a PM takes possession of client assets.

About 63% of the PMs reviewed had significant deficiencies in this area. Overall deficiencies in capital calculations increased by 28% from the previous fiscal year. This significant increase may be partly due to additional reviews conducted on smaller firms in fiscal 2009. In addition, some PMs took possession of clients' assets, however, they were not aware of the higher capital and insurance requirements. We noted a number of PMs with inadequate insurance coverage and capital deficiencies as a result of incorrectly using the lower insurance and capital requirements.

We found the following issues relating to capital calculations:

- Capital calculations were prepared using:

  - financial statements that were not in accordance with Canadian GAAP

  - an incorrect minimum capital or insurance deductible

- Capital calculations were not prepared on a monthly basis or were not prepared at all.

- There was a lack of evidence that someone independent of the preparer reviewed the capital calculations.

- Higher capital and insurance requirements were not maintained for PMs who had the ability to take possession of clients' assets.

To enhance investor protection, if a registrant files annual financial statements that indicate that it was capital deficient at its year end or if we identify a registrant during the course of an on-site review that was capital deficient during the review period, staff generally recommends that terms and conditions be imposed on its registration. The recommended terms and conditions include providing us with unaudited financial statements and capital calculations each month for a minimum six-month period. Also, a registrant must review its compliance procedures and file a report with the OSC. The report must describe the measures that will be taken to prevent capital deficiencies in the future. The registrant must also certify that it has reviewed its compliance system and has rectified the problems that led to the capital deficiency.

With the implementation of NI 31-103, PMs will be required to maintain a minimum capital of $25,000 regardless of whether they hold or have access to clients' assets.

For additional guidance on capital calculations, please refer to OSC Staff Notice 33-730 — *Capital Calculations for Investment Counsel/Portfolio Managers.*

Suggested best practices — capital calculations

- Prepare capital calculations on a monthly basis

- Prepare capital calculations using financial statements prepared in accordance with Canadian GAAP.

- Maintain copies of the capital calculations.

- Have someone independent of the preparer review the capital calculations for accuracy on a timely basis.

- Keep a record of the review.

- Inform the OSC immediately if a capital deficiency occurs.

- Inform the OSC immediately if you take custody or have the ability to take possession of clients assets. For example, if a PM is a signatory of a client account or acts as a general partner for a limited partnership advised by the firm.

3. — Registration issues

There was a significant increase in registration related deficiencies from 6% to 31% in the 2009 fiscal year. This significant increase was mainly due to senior officers of the firm performing advising activities without being registered. We will take appropriate action, up to and including enforcement action, when we identify individuals performing registerable activity without registration.

We found the following issues relating to registration:

- Individuals at PMs were advising without registration.

- directors and officers of PMs were not approved or registered.

- the OSC was not notified of specific changes to registered firm and individual information.

Paragraph (1)(c) of section 25 of the Act states that no person or company shall act as an adviser unless the person or company is registered as an adviser, or is registered as a representative or as a partner or as an officer of a registered adviser and is acting on behalf of the adviser. PMs are responsible for ensuring that they maintain appropriate registration for the activities conducted.

PMs are required to notify the OSC of any change in the status of directors and/or officers within five business days. PMs are also required to notify the OSC of the opening of any office or branch, and of any changes in the status of the compliance officer, PMs and representatives. National Instrument 33-109 — *Registration Information* sets out the requirements for notification of changes to registered firm and individual information.

Suggested best practices — registration matters

- Ensure that individuals who provide advice to others are appropriately registered as PMs.

- Promptly notify the OSC of all changes to registration.

- Promptly register branch office locations.

- Notify the OSC when trade names are used.

4.2 — LMDs

The field reviews of LMDs we conducted in the 2009 fiscal year resulted in an average of five deficiencies per firm reviewed. An average of two or 40% of these deficiencies were significant. Please note that we review different LMDs each year.

The following chart shows the three most commonly occurring significant deficiencies we found among LMDs, compared with the 2008 fiscal year.[4] We will continue to focus on these areas of significant deficiencies as part of our compliance oversight process. We expect LMDs to take appropriate action in these areas to improve their compliance.

---

[4]The three most commonly occurring significant deficiencies in 2008 fiscal year were suitability and KYC information, use of prospectus and registration exemptions and disclosure in offering memorandums.

Significant deficiencies among LMDs
Fiscal years 2009 and 2008

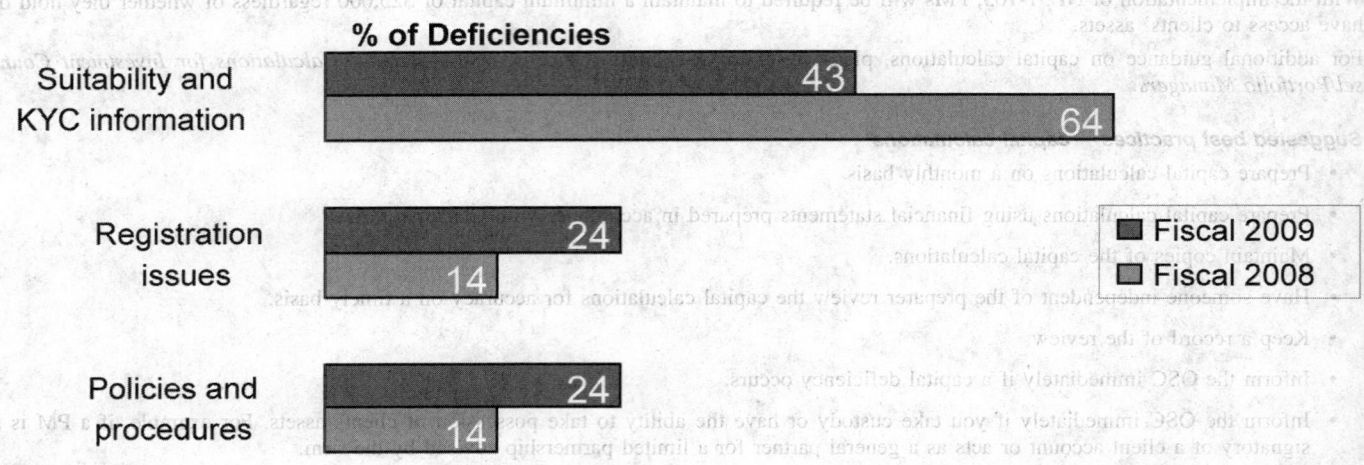

% of Deficiencies

	Fiscal 2009	Fiscal 2008
Suitability and KYC information	43	64
Registration issues	24	14
Policies and procedures	24	14

Note: The percentage of deficiencies represents the percentage of LMDs that were deficient in this area in the reviews performed in the 2009 fiscal year.

1. — Suitability: KYC and KYP

Dealers are required under section 1.5 of OSC Rule 31-505 — *Conditions of Registration* to collect and document sufficient and appropriate KYC information to ensure that trades are suitable for clients. This requirement applies to both trades in securities under a prospectus exemption and trades in prospectus-qualified securities.

Improperly collecting and documenting KYC information remains the most commonly occurring significant deficiency for LMDs. About 43% of the LMDs reviewed in the 2009 fiscal year had significant deficiencies in this area, an improvement from 64% noted in 2008. LMDs, in general, are more aware of the requirements to collect and document KYC information. However, some still did not have a formal process in place and others did not collect KYC information for certain types of clients.

To ensure that trades are suitable for their clients, LMDs must have a thorough understanding of the investment products they are recommending (KYP) and an understanding of their clients' circumstances (KYC). LMDs have a suitability obligation to all investors. LMDs may not contract out of or delegate their duty to ensure that trades are suitable for clients.

For additional guidance, please refer to Canadian Securities Administrators Staff Notice 33-315 *Suitability and know your product*. The CSA staff notice is available on the OSC website at *www.osc.gov.on.ca*.

We identified the following issues relating to KYC information and the suitability determination:

- Risks associated with an investment were not adequately explained to clients.

- Some LMDs did not collect or document KYC information.

- KYC information was, in part, inadequate or incomplete.

- KYC information was not collected for certain clients, e.g. clients who subscribed to private placements, foreign clients or corporate clients.

- There was no evidence of an independent review of trades for suitability.

- There was no process in place to verify if clients were able to rely on a valid prospectus exemption, such as the accredited investor exemption.

- Some LMDs did not always maintain documentation to support whether clients qualify either as accredited investors or under another prospectus exemption.

- Some LMDs tried to contract out of their duty to collect KYC information and to ensure that trades are suitable for their clients.

Suggested best practices — suitability obligation

- LMDs have a suitability obligation to all clients, including accredited investors, corporations and partnerships. LMDs should collect and document KYC information for each of their clients for the suitability determination. This includes the client's investment needs and objectives, investment restrictions, investment time frame, risk tolerance, investment knowledge, and financial circumstances (such as annual income and net worth).

- Clients should sign and date their KYC information.

- The salesperson and the compliance officer should review and approve the client's KYC documentation to ensure that KYC information collected from the client is sufficient for the LMD to make the suitability determination and is appropriate for the types of securities being traded.

- LMDs should review and maintain the subscription agreements and accredited investor certificates completed by investors.

- LMDs and their salespeople should understand the attributes and associated risks of the securities being traded or recommended in order to make an appropriate suitability determination. This includes understanding the general features and structure of the product, product risks including the risk/return profile and risks such as liquidity risks, management and financial strength of the issuer, costs, and any eligibility requirements of each product.

2. — Registration issues

About 24% of the LMDs reviewed had significant deficiencies in this area, an increase from 14% noted in 2008. The LMDs selected for our review this year are larger in size and some have multiple business lines. It is important for LMDs to ensure that individuals, the firms or affiliated entities are appropriately registered with the OSC prior to conducting registerable activities.

Paragraph 25(1)(a) of the Act states that no person or company shall trade in a security unless the person or company is registered as a dealer or as a salesperson, a partner or an officer of a registered dealer and is acting on behalf of the dealer. Meeting with current and prospective investors to provide information on an investment product is engaging in activities that require registration.

Paragraph (1)(c) of section 25 of the Act states that no person or company shall act as an adviser unless the person or company is registered as an adviser, or is registered as a representative or as a partner or as an officer of a registered adviser and is acting on behalf of the adviser. Section 99 of R.R.O. 1990, Regulation 1015 (the Regulation) sets out the categories of registration, and requires an entity to be registered as an ICPM in order to carry out the business of advising and managing the portfolio of others.

We identified the following issues relating to registration:

- Individuals who were not registered in any capacity were engaged in trading activities of the LMDs.

- LMDs or their affiliates were advising and making investment decisions for investment products distributed by the LMDs; however, they were not registered as PMs.

Suggested best practices — registration issues

- LMDs should ensure that individuals or entities that conduct registerable activities are registered with the OSC in the appropriate categories of registration.

- Policies and procedures should be developed and enforced by LMDs to assist them in ensuring that individuals or affiliated entities are appropriately registered if they are carrying out registerable activities.

3. — Written policies and procedures

Section 1.2 of OSC Rule 31-505 requires LMDs to develop and enforce written policies and procedures for dealing with clients that conform to prudent business practice and enable LMDs to serve their clients adequately. LMDs should develop policies and procedures that cover all areas of their businesses, including all relevant regulatory requirements.

We identified the following issues relating to written policies and procedures:

- Some LMDs did not have any written policies and procedures.

- Written policies and procedures were inadequate and did not cover all business areas.

- Policies and procedures were not enforced.

- There were no policies and procedures on employees' personal trading, particularly policies to prevent insider trading even though LMDs could have access to material non-public information. Also, there was no review and approval of personal trades.

Suggested best practices — policies and procedures

Policies and procedures that are clearly documented and enforced contribute to a strong compliance environment in a firm and thereby enhance investor protection and prevent market abuse. LMDs should develop and enforce policies and procedures that are sufficiently detailed and cover areas relevant to their business operations and allow them to serve their clients adequately. LMDs should also regularly review, assess and update their policies and procedures for changes in securities legislation and industry practices. Adequate training should be provided to all employees of the LMDs to ensure employees understand the established policies and procedures and understand how to incorporate them in their daily business activities.

The policies and procedures should address, at a minimum, the following areas:

Compliance
- duties and responsibilities of the compliance officer.

KYC and suitability information

- collection, documentation and timely update of KYC and suitability information.

- review and approval of KYC and accredited investor information.

- new product review process.

- performance of sufficient research and due diligence to support recommendations to clients.

For additional guidance, please refer to Canadian Securities Administrators Staff Notice 33-315 *Suitability and know your product.* The CSA staff notice is available on the OSC website at *www.osc.gov.on.ca.*

Disclosure in offering documents

- guidelines to ensure appropriate and adequate disclosure on general features and structure of the product, risks, fees, management and financial strength of the issuer, and any eligibility requirements of each product.

- review and approval of offering documents prior to distribution to investors.

Marketing

- guidelines on the preparation, review, approval and regular updates of marketing materials and website content.

- guidelines on the preparation, review and approval of performance data.

- ensuring compliance with securities legislation, including prohibitions on holding out a non-registered person as being registered, advertising the LMDs' registration, and representations that the OSC has passed upon the financial standing, fitness or conduct of the LMDs, or upon the merits of any security or issuer.

Personal trading and conflicts of interest

- procedures for approving and reviewing personal trades, including written pre-approval.

- definition of material non-public information and policies and procedures to restrict the dissemination of any non-public information.

Books and records

- the time period for the maintenance of books and records.

- maintenance of business agreements.

- disclosure to clients regarding conflicts of interest and fees arrangements.

Referral arrangements

- criteria used to set up referral arrangements and requirements for referral arrangements.

- review and approval by senior management prior to signing referral agreements.

- guidelines to ensure appropriate and adequate disclosure is provided to clients.

- review and approval of the disclosure given to clients.

Client complaints

- handling of client complaints.

- identification, monitoring and resolution of client complaints.

5. — Outcomes of our reviews

After we complete a review, we normally send a report to the market participant outlining the deficiencies that we found. A market participant normally has 30 days to respond in writing to the report. The response should set out the steps that the market participant will take, or has taken, to address the deficiencies.

However, if we find a large number of significant deficiencies at a market participant, we may not issue a deficiency report and may instead refer the file to the Enforcement Branch for further review.

Listed below are the possible outcomes from our reviews. In most cases, the OSC staff deficiency report to the market participant is sufficient to cause the market participant to resolve the identified compliance deficiencies. In other cases, we may have to take further action to assist us in obtaining compliance by market participants.

- **Enhanced compliance.** At the end of each review, we generally issue a deficiency report to the market participant identifying areas of non-compliance with securities law. We work with the market participant to ensure that all deficiencies are resolved to our satisfaction. Our compliance reviews generally have the effect of enhancing overall compliance of these market participants.

- **Monitoring of market participants with greater than 30% significant deficiencies.** We monitor a market participant when 30% or more of the deficiencies found in its review are significant. We may conduct a follow-up review, if necessary. We may also monitor market participants with less than 30% significant deficiencies if we think that further follow up is appropriate.

- **Terms and conditions.** We may impose terms and conditions to further assist in monitoring how a registrant is complying with Ontario securities law. Registrants have an opportunity to be heard before terms and conditions are imposed by the Director. Terms and conditions are posted on the OSC website.

- **Referral to the Enforcement Branch.** If we identify a serious breach of Ontario securities law, we discuss our findings with the Enforcement Branch of the OSC. The Enforcement Branch together with our staff will assess the case and determine an appropriate course of action.

The following chart shows the outcomes of our reviews of market participants (PMs, LMDs and IFMs) during the 2009 fiscal year:

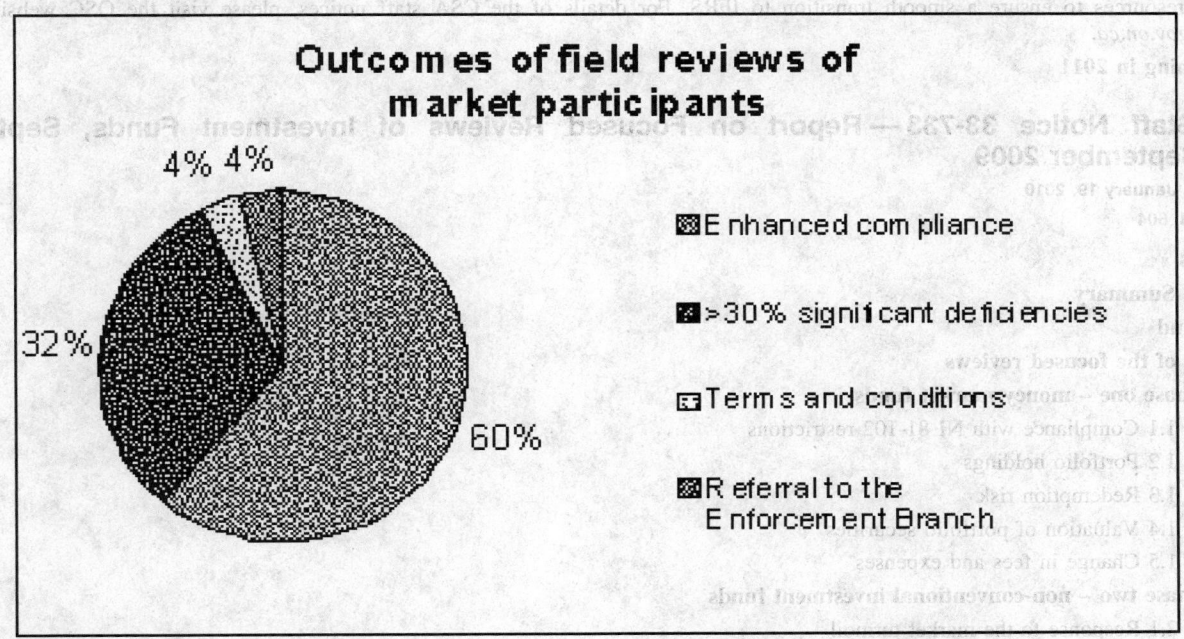

6. — National Instrument 31-103 — Registration Requirements and Exemptions

On July 17, 2009, the Canadian Securities Administrators (CSA) published NI 31-103. The purpose of NI 31-103 is to harmonize, streamline and modernize the registration regime across Canada for firms and individuals who deal in securities, provide investment advice or manage investment funds.

The new rules recognize that the registration regime must accommodate a wide variety of business models, scales of operation, clients and products. The new regime is more flexible and easier to use, enhances investor protection and benefits industry by bringing increased efficiencies to the registration system.

The new regime has higher proficiency standards for some registrants, and enhanced rules for consumer disclosure, referral arrangements, handling investor complaints, and disclosing and addressing conflicts of interest. It also introduces a registration requirement for IFMs, exempt market dealers and senior officers responsible for compliance.

NI 31-103 and related rules and amendments is expected to come into force on September 28, 2009. It is important that market participants come to fully understand the new regime and how it impacts their operations and develop appropriate procedures to ensure a smooth transition. For details of the Instrument, please visit the OSC website site at *www.osc.gov.on.ca*.

NI 31-103 — effective September 28, 2009

7. — International Financial Reporting Standards (IFRS)

In February 2008, the Canadian Accounting Standards Board (AcSB) confirmed that all publicly accountable enterprises will be required to report their financial results under IFRS for fiscal periods beginning on or after January 1, 2011.

IFRS will replace current Canadian standards and interpretations as Canadian generally accepted accounting principles. Non-publicly accountable enterprises are permitted, but not required, to adopt IFRS in 2011.

At present, all registrants (except LMDs) who are not members of a self-regulatory organization (SRO) are required to deliver financial statements to the CSA.

On September 12, 2008, the CSA issued CSA Staff Notice 33-313 *International Financial Reporting Standards and Registrants* which set out its view that all non-SRO registrants[5] who hold or have access to clients' assets would be required to prepare and deliver IFRS financial statements to the CSA.

On July 10, 2009, the CSA issued CSA Staff Notice 33-314 *International Financial Reporting Standards and Registrants*. In this notice, the CSA set out its view that all non-SRO registrants would be required to deliver IFRS financial statements to the CSA in 2011.

The CSA is currently in the process of preparing proposed amendments to National Instrument 52-107 — *Acceptable Accounting Principles, Auditing Standards and Reporting Currency* reflecting the proposed requirement, as well as other amendments necessary to the rule and other rules as a result of Canada's changeover to IFRS. These amendments are expected to be published for public comment later this year.

Non-SRO registrants should review and assess the impact on them of converting to IFRS. It is important that non-SRO registrants have adequate resources to ensure a smooth transition to IFRS. For details of the CSA staff notices, please visit the OSC website site at *www.osc.gov.on.ca*.

IFRS coming in 2011

OSC Staff Notice 33-733 — Report on Focused Reviews of Investment Funds, September 2008–September 2009

Date: January 19, 2010

33 O.S.C.B. 604

Contents

Executive Summary

Background

Overview of the focused reviews

Executive Summary

This report summarizes the compliance review work conducted by staff of the Compliance and Registrant Regulation Branch (Compliance Team) and the Investment Funds Branch of the Ontario Securities Commission (OSC) in response to concerns emerging from the market

---

[5]Non-SRO registrants include portfolio managers, scholarship plan dealers and limited market dealers. National Instrument 31-103 *Registration Requirements* includes new registration categories, including exempt market dealers and investment fund managers.

turmoil experienced by the global financial services industry. Beginning in September 2008, the Compliance Team and the Investment Funds Branch conducted extensive reviews through a three-phased approach, focusing on major segments of the Canadian investment fund industry, namely money market funds, non-conventional investment funds and hedge funds.

Our primary focus in all three phases was to assess fund managers' compliance with Ontario securities laws. We did not assess the merits of the investment products covered by our reviews. We gathered information about the funds' portfolio holdings, exposure to distressed and/or illiquid assets, valuation methodologies, and how the managers managed the risk of large redemptions during the market downturn.

This report summarizes the findings from our questionnaire responses and the observations from our on-site visits, and includes further reporting on our review of money market funds and non-conventional investment funds in more detail than was previously provided in OSC Staff Notice 33-732 *2009 Compliance Team Annual Report*. It also includes some suggested practices. We encourage fund managers to use this report as a self-assessment tool to strengthen their compliance with Ontario securities laws and to improve their systems of internal controls and supervision.

In phase one, the review of money market funds, our focus was to determine if Canadian money market funds faced issues similar to those faced by U.S. money market funds relating to exposure to financial institutions having financial difficulties, illiquid securities or redemption risk. We observed that during the review period all funds were able to meet redemption requests, no investments held by the funds defaulted or were written down, and most funds were in compliance with the securities laws regulating money market funds.

In phase two, we reviewed non-conventional investment funds which include open-end and closed-end funds listed and traded on the Toronto Stock Exchange (TSX). We observed that some of these funds adopted more protective investment strategies as a result of the market turmoil and maintained higher levels of cash. Some fund managers reorganized some of their funds. Fund managers monitored redemption levels closely and provided additional disclosure to their investors on the impact of the market turmoil.

In phase three, we reviewed hedge funds which are sold primarily to high-net-worth individuals and institutional investors by way of an offering memorandum. We observed that hedge fund assets were held with independent custodians, fund portfolios were fairly liquid, well-diversified and securities were valued appropriately.

Despite the overall market downturn and its impact on the returns of many of these products during our review period, we did not observe any industry-wide compliance issues. We noted some instances of non-compliance during our on-site visits which we addressed separately with each individual fund manager.

Background

The global financial markets have experienced a period of market turmoil. The subprime mortgage crisis in the U.S., which began in the summer of 2007, is generally viewed as the triggering event. Due to a significant increase in the default and foreclosure rates for subprime mortgages, structured-finance products (such as mortgage-backed securities, asset-backed commercial paper (ABCP) and collateralized debt obligations (CDOs)) performed poorly. Investor confidence weakened, causing the resale market for some of these products to collapse and liquidity to evaporate. The weakening of the market for these products also led to valuation problems for those holding these products.

In Canada, the market turmoil led to the freezing of the then $35 billion market for non-bank sponsored ABCP in August 2007. Some retail mutual funds were invested in non-bank sponsored ABCP when it froze. Mutual fund managers or other related entities of these mutual funds voluntarily bought all of the frozen ABCP from the funds at par plus accrued interest. This ensured that retail mutual fund investors would not incur losses from these investments.[1]

The market turmoil continued into 2008 creating significant liquidity challenges. Balance sheets were under pressure as a result of the near shutdown of the securitization markets. Lending between banks came to a halt, essentially freezing the credit markets. With the near failure of Bear Stearns in the spring of 2008 and the collapse of Lehman Brothers in September of that year, broker-dealers became less willing to extend credit to their counterparties, including hedge funds. Also, in September 2008 a money market fund in the U.S. known as the Reserve Primary Fund "broke the buck". Some hedge funds were also put under redemption pressure and were forced to liquidate assets as financing terms tightened. As a group, beginning in late summer 2008, their performance deteriorated sharply which led to further investor redemptions.

In response to the concerns emerging from these market events, the OSC executed a three-phased review initiative to assess the impact of the market turmoil in major segments of the Canadian investment fund industry. The three phases focused on fund managers that manage (1) money market funds; (2) non-conventional investment funds; and (3) hedge funds.

Given the events affecting the money market fund industry in the U.S. and liquidity concerns over the short-term debt market, we initiated a focused review of Ontario-based money market funds in September 2008. Our focus, in phase one, was to determine if our money market funds faced issues similar to those faced by U.S. money market funds relating to exposure to financial institutions having financial difficulties, illiquid securities or redemption risk.

In phase two, we extended our work to non-conventional investment funds. Our initial concerns were liquidity, credit risk and counterparty risk stemming from the credit crisis.

In phase three, we focused on hedge funds. The hedge fund industry has become an increasingly important component of Ontario's capital markets. Hedge funds offer flexibility in investment style and diversification benefits to investors. These benefits may also bring challenges and risks which were magnified when the global markets came under tremendous pressure in the second half of 2008.

[1]The impact of market turmoil on non-bank sponsored ABCP and mutual funds was discussed in the CSA Consultation Paper — *Securities Regulatory Proposals Stemming from the 2007-08 Credit Market Turmoil and its Effect on the ABCP Market in Canada* dated October 2008.

Overview of the focused reviews

The Compliance Team and the Investment Funds Branch began the market turmoil focused reviews in September 2008 and completed them in September 2009. We executed our work in a three-phased approach. In all three phases, we focused on funds that were offered to Ontario investors and managed by fund managers based in Ontario. Over the course of the year, we sent out approximately 200 questionnaires, conducted meetings with senior management of selected fund managers and executed 56 on-site visits. Appendix A summarizes information relating to the fund managers that completed the questionnaires and those that received a site visit.

The comments in this report relate only to our observations of those fund managers that completed our questionnaires and those that were subject to an on-site visit. These observations are also limited to the scope of our reviews.

Phase one – money market funds

Investors generally view money market funds as safe and liquid investment vehicles. Portfolios held by these funds are generally more liquid because money market funds in Canada are subject to a number of investment restrictions in National Instrument 81-102 *Mutual Funds* (NI 81-102). A common feature of money market funds in Canada is that they strive to maintain a constant net asset value (NAV) of $10. However, there is no guarantee that the NAV will remain at $10.

Phase one, the review of money market funds, began in September 2008. We sent a questionnaire to 50 fund managers offering open-ended mutual funds in Ontario. These 50 managers had money market fund assets under management of approximately $67 billion, representing approximately 93% of the total money market fund assets[2]. We risk-ranked the questionnaires and selected 18 fund managers that would receive an on-site visit. The period reviewed was from August 1, 2007 to September 19, 2008.

We also completed further follow-up work on the money market funds subsequent to the on-site visits. We sent a follow-up questionnaire in May 2009 to the same fund managers of money market funds to assess whether any material changes had occurred since our review in September 2008.

Phase two – non-conventional investment funds

The focus of phase two was non-conventional investment funds listed and traded on the TSX. These include split share companies[3], actively managed funds, index tracking funds and structured products based on credit related derivatives[4]. Non-conventional investment funds have some of the following characteristics:

- *Product complexity.* Because non-conventional investment funds are generally subject to fewer regulatory investment restrictions than conventional mutual funds, they are able to employ more complex investment strategies and use leverage.

- *Illiquid assets.* Some non-conventional investment funds may have significant exposure to illiquid assets, which can lead to valuation issues.

- *Market risk.* Volatile markets can affect exchange-traded investment funds by lowering the value of their portfolio holdings. The trading value of the investment fund's own units or shares can also be negatively affected.

- *Sector exposure.* Some funds may have significant exposure to the foreign financial sector, senior loan markets and mortgage-backed securities.

- *Redemption risk.* Most non-conventional investment funds allow an annual (or more frequent) redemption at NAV. The risk of arbitrage for these funds can be increased if the discount between NAV and the listed price of the securities widens.

Phase two, the review of non-conventional investment funds, began in October 2008. We sent questionnaires to 27 Ontario-based managers of non-conventional investment funds. These managers had assets under management of approximately $36 billion, representing 84% of the industry total[5]. Based on the information reported in the questionnaires, staff selected six fund managers that would receive an on-site visit. The period reviewed was from August 1, 2007 to September 30, 2008.

Our review of non-conventional investment funds also included continuous disclosure reviews of certain investment fund issuers that received our questionnaire but were not selected for an on-site visit. We also performed a review of disclosure provided by linked note issuers and monitored information provided in the media by non-conventional investment funds. This included reviewing press releases relating to non-conventional investment funds. We focused on announcements of any suspension of redemptions, deferrals of or reductions to expected distributions, re-organizations or credit rating downgrades.

Phase three – hedge funds

Hedge funds in Ontario are typically pooled funds that are sold primarily to sophisticated or high-net-worth investors by way of an offering memorandum. They are not subject to certain securities laws and are generally required to provide less disclosure to potential investors. They are also subject to fewer investment restrictions as compared to traditional mutual funds. Hedge fund managers, however, are subject to

---

[2]Money market fund assets under management was $72 billion as at January 2009: Investment Funds Institute of Canada.

[3]A split share company, for the purposes of our review, is an investment fund that acquires a fixed portfolio of securities and issues two classes of shares (preferred shares and capital shares) to investors.

[4]Structured products based on credit related derivatives, for the purposes of our review, are funds that invest in credit default securities or derivatives whose performance is based on credit events of specified issuers.

[5]Non-conventional fund assets under management, measured by market capitalization, was $43 billion as at March 2008: TMX Group.

Ontario securities laws which require investment fund managers to exercise their duties honestly, in good faith and in the best interests of their investment funds and the investors who have invested their money in their funds.

Issues affecting hedge funds include:

- *Valuation.* Many hedge funds hold complex, over-the-counter or illiquid financial instruments. The valuation of these instruments can be difficult as they may not have a verifiable market value.

- *Leverage.* While hedge funds employ leverage with the objective of magnifying potential returns, the use of leverage also magnifies losses suffered by investors and lenders in the event that the hedge fund incurs losses. In addition, leverage magnifies fluctuations in securities prices.

- *Liquidity.* Some hedge funds may experience redemption pressure because of illiquid markets and limited credit.

- *Transparency.* Many hedge fund managers are reluctant to disclose their investment holdings for competitive reasons. This lack of transparency creates concerns as to whether investors have adequate information to assess the investment risks of a particular hedge fund.

The review of hedge funds began in February 2009. We sent a questionnaire to approximately 90 hedge fund managers in Ontario. After risk ranking the responses, we selected 32 fund managers for an on-site visit. The period reviewed was from July 1, 2007 to December 31, 2008. These fund managers managed 192 funds, totalling $16 billion in assets under management as at December 31, 2008. Of these funds, 93 funds, totalling $8.9 billion, were funds of hedge funds, and 99 funds, totalling $7.1 billion, were standalone funds.

1. — Phase one – money market funds

Our review of money market funds focused on the following areas:

1.1 Compliance with NI 81-102 restrictions

1.2 Portfolio holdings

1.3 Redemption risk

1.4 Valuation of portfolio securities

1.5 Change in fees and expenses

1.1 — Compliance with NI 81-102 restrictions

Securities laws require money market funds to restrict their investments to a diversified portfolio of short- term debt instruments of a specific credit quality.

Observations

- Most money market funds complied with the investment restrictions under section 1.1 of NI 81-102[6] and with the concentration restrictions under section 2.1 of NI 81-102[7]. Fund managers had adequate monitoring procedures to ensure compliance with these restrictions.

- Where fund managers outsourced their fund administrative functions to an external service provider, they generally had good oversight procedures over the service provider.

- We noted some instances of non-compliance with the dollar-weighted average term to maturity requirement and with the 10% concentration restriction under NI 81-102. The instances of non-compliance were not material and were addressed with each individual fund manager.

Suggested practices

- Perform daily monitoring of compliance with the investment restrictions and concentration restrictions under NI 81-102 as money market funds are bought and sold daily.

- Include bankers' acceptances and bearer deposit notes in monitoring concentration restrictions under NI 81-102.

- Develop appropriate procedures to identify non-compliance with the investment restrictions and concentration restrictions under NI 81-102.

- Fund managers should ensure that the portfolio managers:

  - are familiar with all applicable regulatory requirements

  - monitor compliance on a frequent basis

---

[6]Money market funds are required to comply with the investment restrictions under section 1.1 of NI 81-102, including (i) all of the assets must be invested in cash, cash equivalents, debt with a term to maturity of no more than 365 days and/or floating rate debt; (ii) dollar-weighted average term to maturity should not exceed 90 days; (iii) not less than 95% of the assets must be invested in the currency in which the NAV of the fund is calculated; and (iv) not less than 95% of the assets must be invested in cash, cash equivalents or evidence of indebtedness of issuers, provided that the commercial paper of the issuer has an approved credit rating.

[7]Under section 2.1 of NI 81-102, a mutual fund is prohibited from purchasing securities of an issuer if, after the purchase, more than 10% of its net assets would be invested in any one issuer.

- report any instances of non-compliance immediately to the fund manager
- rectify any non-compliance immediately

1.2. — Portfolio holdings

Observations

- Fund managers generally performed adequate and regular reviews of fund portfolios to ensure compliance with securities laws and with the funds' investment mandates.

- Chart 1 below shows the top five categories of portfolio holdings held by money market funds as at September 19, 2008 and April 30, 2009. The portfolio holdings are shown as a percentage of total portfolio holdings held by money market funds that completed our questionnaire. The top five categories of portfolio holdings as at April 30, 2009, based on responses from the follow-up questionnaire, did not change.

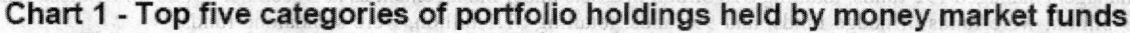

Chart 1 - Top five categories of portfolio holdings held by money market funds

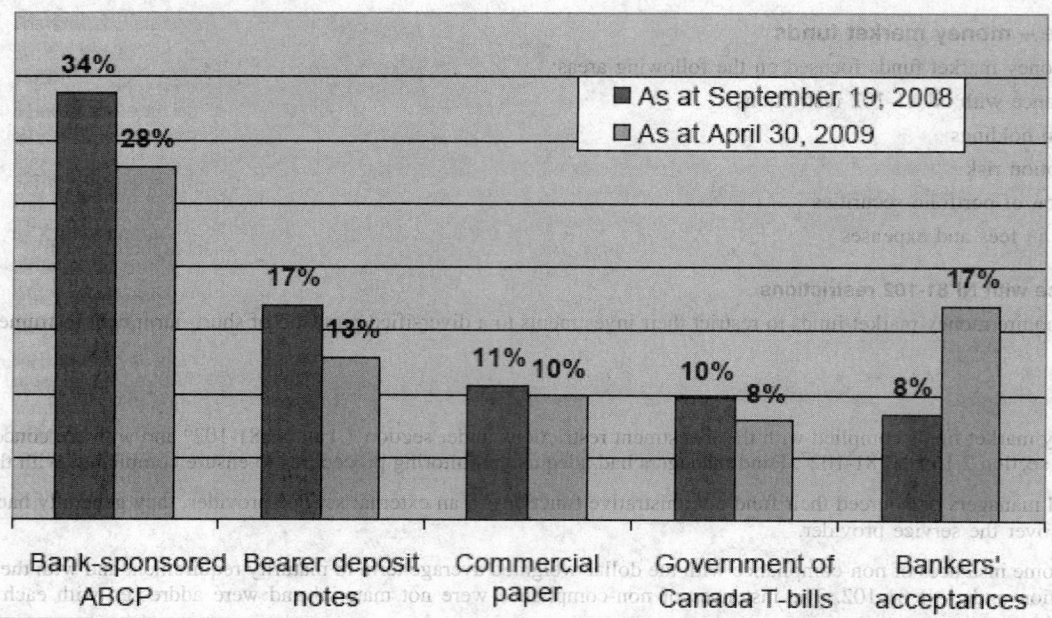

- Most funds were only exposed to Canadian issuers of money market securities. A small number of funds were also exposed to issuers in the U.S. and in Europe.

- None of the funds had exposure to illiquid assets.

- None of the fund managers wrote down any securities.

- The level of cash held in funds increased as a means to meet an increase in redemptions. In many cases, the term to maturity of the portfolios became shorter.

- ABCP held by the funds was bank-sponsored and had global-style liquidity support. Where the fund manager was also the portfolio manager, the fund manager performed adequate due diligence prior to investing in ABCP, and monitored the quality of the holdings on a continuous basis.

Suggested practices

- Monitor concentration risk by:
  - calculating and monitoring exposure to a single issuer at least on a daily basis
  - calculating exposure to a single issuer by including bank deposits with securities issued by that issuer
  - aggregating and monitoring exposure to an issuer and its related issuers
- Document procedures for monitoring credit quality of issuers, including:
  - frequency of review of credit ratings

- procedures to deal with situations where inappropriate credit risk in a security or issuer is identified
- ongoing credit monitoring procedures
- record keeping (i.e. retain information to document the monitoring of credit risk)

1.3 — Redemption risk

Observations

- Fund managers did not have issues in meeting redemption requests by fund investors. In addition, they did not foresee issues in meeting future redemption requests given the high level of liquidity of their portfolios.

- Fund managers put a number of mechanisms in place to manage redemption requests. We noted that:
  - fund managers generally maintained a more liquid portfolio and decreased the weighted average term to maturity of the fund portfolios
  - some fund managers monitored the holdings of individual unitholders so as to monitor the risk of having a single large unitholder redeem
  - some fund managers used a large unitholder agreement to restrict further purchases, to require a minimum holding period, or to require a longer notice period for a large redemption

Suggested practices

- Review daily sales and redemptions reports along with investments by maturity to manage cashflows effectively

- Monitor the holdings of individual unitholders to monitor the risk of having a single large unitholder redeem

1.4 — Valuation of portfolio securities

Observations

- All fund managers valued their money market instruments in their money market funds at amortized cost, i.e. at cost plus accrued interest, based on their conclusion that amortized cost approximated fair market value.

- A number of fund managers also calculated the market value of their fund's portfolio which they compared to the amortized cost of the portfolio to confirm that amortized cost remained a valid approximation of fair market value.

Suggested practices

- Where amortized cost is used, ensure compliance with National *Instrument 81-106 Investment Fund Continuous Disclosure* (NI 81-106) which requires that the fund's portfolio be valued at market. The valuation of the fund's portfolio should be performed as often as the NAV of the fund is calculated.

1.5 — Change in fees and expenses

Observations

- In light of the current low interest rate environment, nearly all of the fund managers reviewed had reduced or waived management fees and certain expenses to ensure that their money market funds continued to have a positive yield.

- Some managers chose to reduce trailer fees paid to dealers on money market funds held in the dealers' client accounts.

- Many fund managers disclosed the fee changes to their investors by issuing a press release, providing the information on the fund manager's website or filing an amendment to the fund's simplified prospectus.

Suggested practices

- Fund managers should ensure that information regarding fee changes is disclosed to their investors on a timely basis.

- Any waivers or absorptions of fees are required to be disclosed in the fund's financial statements and management reports of fund performance.

2. — Phase two – non-conventional investment funds

Our review of non-conventional investment funds focused on the following areas:

  2.1 Response to the market turmoil
  2.2 Counterparty, credit and financial sector exposure
  2.3 Level and valuation of illiquid assets
  2.4 Investor communication and continuous disclosure

2.1 — Response to the market turmoil

Observations

- Fund managers monitored market conditions and assessed the impact on their funds on a continual basis. They worked with portfolio managers, dealers and other stakeholders in devising action plans aimed at protecting their funds, within the parameters of the constating documents of each fund. These plans included suspension of redemptions, decreases in distributions, equity offerings, rights offerings, changes to investment objectives and strategies, and fund mergers.

- Within the limits of each fund's investment restrictions, funds adopted more protective strategies, such as holding a higher proportion of the fund's portfolio in cash, or writing covered call options.

- Fund mergers were used to consolidate assets of non-conventional investment funds in order to provide unitholders with better liquidity and economies of scale. Some fund managers had different policies for mergers of non-conventional funds than for mergers of conventional funds that they also manage.

- Where an investment fund has a fund manager, administrator, portfolio manager, sub-advisors and valuation agent, the division of duties and obligations between them may overlap. In responding to the market turmoil, some fund managers needed additional time to determine which of the other service providers should be involved in particular decisions and to collect relevant information from them.

Suggested practices

- The investment restrictions followed by the fund are material information that investors use when making their investment decisions. Changes to the investment restrictions should be publicly disclosed in a timely manner.

- Fund managers should bear the cost of merging their non-conventional investment funds. While a fund merger may benefit unitholders, fund managers also benefit from mergers by maintaining assets under management. The policy rationale underlying the rules applicable to conventional mutual fund mergers applies equally, in staff's view, to mergers of non-conventional investment funds.

- When functions are delegated to third-party service providers, fund managers should maintain appropriate oversight and have the ability to review the accuracy and quality of the services provided in a timely manner. Even if delegating to service providers, fund managers maintain the ultimate responsibility for the operations of the fund. Fund managers should always be aware of the issues affecting their funds, such as potential counterparty risks or the valuation of illiquid assets.

2.2 — Counterparty, credit and financial sector exposure

Observations

- Some non-conventional investment funds were exposed to the foreign financial sector, certain debt markets (that were under stress) and complex credit derivatives, but this exposure was limited in comparison to the overall number and size of all non-conventional investment funds in the industry.

- Many structured products offered leverage exposure to the financial sector that was not expected to be volatile. The downturn in the financial sector had a severe impact on some of these structured products, which triggered protection events in favour of the debt holders, so that equity investors would be unable to participate in any future market recovery.

- Most of the non-conventional investment funds we reviewed were exposed to Canadian counterparties, which did not result in elevated counterparty risk. A small number of non-conventional investment funds were using foreign counterparties, but the level of exposure to the foreign entity was relatively small.

Suggested practices

- In addition to complying with the existing continuous disclosure requirements, managers of sector or specialized investment funds should provide updated and timely information to investors so that investors can understand and assess the impact of the market conditions to their fund. For example, for a complex investment structure, a sensitivity analysis may be helpful.

2.3 — Level and valuation of illiquid assets

Observations

- Some funds invested a substantial portion of their assets in illiquid investments, creating liquidity issues and valuation issues. These funds were generally trading at a significant discount to their NAV, as investors made their own assessment of the value of the illiquid assets.

- Fund managers incorporated the market developments into their valuation methodology for illiquid assets, but not always to the same degree. For some illiquid securities, the changes in valuation did not fully reflect the overall change in value in the particular sector. In some cases, fund managers remained more optimistic about the future value of certain portfolio holdings.

- Some fund managers provided additional disclosure to investors regarding the level and valuation of illiquid assets in their fund.

- In at least one case, previous fund mergers resulted in the continuing fund facing challenges with respect to the combined level of illiquid assets.

Suggested practices

- The valuation of illiquid assets is inherently difficult and subject to numerous variables. Each NAV calculation should take into consideration all available information at the time the calculation is being made to properly reflect the fund's current value, not the manager's anticipation of the fund's value at a future point in time.

2.4 — Investor communication and continuous disclosure

Observations — continuous disclosure reviews

- Fund managers were active in communicating with investors during the market turmoil. In most cases, the impact of the market turmoil was discussed in the funds' management report of fund performance.

- In addition to required regulatory filings, fund managers used their websites to update investors regarding the funds' investment exposure. One fund manager managing credit linked investment products used sensitivity analyses to show what the impact would be if certain credit events materialized.

- Investment funds based on credit related derivatives were generally structured as passive vehicles employing limited discretionary portfolio management. When these investment funds were under stress, fund managers responded differently. Most managers did not intervene to modify the fund's strategy. However, one fund manager actively implemented a defensive strategy by securitizing distribution payments in return for the ability of the fund to absorb further unfavourable credit events.

Observations — linked notes

- Linked notes had become increasingly popular and available to retail investors. However, these investments are usually complex and the exposure they offer can have features similar to certain embedded derivatives.

- Linked note issuers provided necessary information during the pre-clearance process.[8] However, as linked notes are not investment funds, they do not file financial statements and management reports of fund performance (they are included in the issuer's own disclosure filings). The primary source of continuous disclosure information specific to the linked note is the issuer's website.

- The impact of the market turmoil on the current value of the linked notes appeared to be in line with our expectations based on the underlying assets the notes were linked to.

- Linked notes have many key terms and conditions, including mitigating control features based on market disruption events. During the period of market turmoil, the interpretation of certain key terms was subject to additional scrutiny, raising questions of how certain linked note features should operate (for example, determining if a "market disruption event" had occurred which would trigger the need for an independent valuation agent).

Observations — media surveillance

- There was an increase in the number of press releases and filings during the period we examined.

- Many non-conventional investment funds announced that they were deferring or suspending scheduled distribution payments in order to preserve their net asset value. Some also gave advance notice that they would not be accepting redemption requests if they were close to an upcoming redemption date.

- Many non-conventional investment funds announced restructurings, including mergers, and capital raising initiatives (such as rights offerings). In addition to regulatory filings, fund managers were actively issuing press releases to clarify issues, including exposure to ABCP, specific investment exposure, as well as more details regarding material holdings of illiquid assets.

Suggested practices

- Information should be provided to investors in a manner designed to help them understand the impact of unusual market events on their investment. Fund managers should use their websites as effectively as possible to provide timely information to investors.

- The interpretation and applicability of key terms and conditions of linked notes, such as the market disruption clause, knock-out and knock-in events, should be stated in a clear and easily understood manner so that investors can better understand when certain events will trigger each of them.

3. — Phase three – hedge funds

Our review of hedge funds focused on the following areas:

    3.1 Custody

    3.2 Portfolio holdings

    3.3 Leverage usage and monitoring

    3.4 Prime broker / counterparty exposure

    3.5 Monitoring of funds of hedge funds

Part 3:
REGISTRATION

---

[8]See CSA Staff Notice 44-304 *Linked Notes Distributed Under Shelf Prospectus System* for a description of linked notes and the pre-clearance process.

3.6 Liquidity or viability issues

3.7 Fund valuation

3.8 Use of service providers

3.9 Offering document disclosure

3.10 Other regulatory compliance matters

3.11 Comparison of fund manager practices to best practices suggested by Alternative Investment Management Association (AIMA)

3.1 — Custody

Observations

- Fund portfolio assets were segregated and held with independent, reputable custodians. We verified the existence of fund assets by reviewing custodial statements on a sample basis and did not note any issues.

- Most fund managers performed reconciliations to the custodian's reported holdings on a regular basis.

- A few managers used the same bank account to process investors' transactions and corporate activities.

Suggested practices

- Maintain separate banking accounts to process investors' transactions and corporate activities. Effective September 28, 2009, section 14.6 of National Instrument 31-103 — *Registration Requirements and Exemptions* requires all registered firms to segregate and hold in trust client assets.

- Reconcile securities positions to the custodian's reported holdings on a regular basis. Follow up any discrepancies in a timely manner.

Other statistics

- 93% of the fund managers used a third-party custodian; 7% of the fund managers used an affiliate as the custodian.

- 95% of the fund managers used a member firm of Investment Industry Regulatory Organization of Canada for prime brokerage and custodial services.

- 75% of the fund managers used affiliates of Canadian Schedule 1 banks for prime brokerage and custodial services.

- The top four prime brokers and custodians used by the fund managers were affiliates of Canadian Schedule 1 banks.

3.2 — Portfolio holdings

Observations

- The majority (83% based on assets under management) of the standalone hedge funds held a diversified portfolio (i.e. not more than 10% of the fund's net assets invested in any single holding).

- Hedge funds managed in Ontario had fairly liquid portfolios. The majority (91% based on assets under management) of the funds held less than 10% of the fund's net assets in private or illiquid holdings.

- Fund managers performed adequate and regular reviews of fund portfolios to ensure compliance with the funds' investment objectives, and to monitor portfolio risk and the liquidity level of each of their funds. A few large fund managers/portfolio managers also had an independent committee, separate from the portfolio management team, to oversee and manage portfolio risk and liquidity risk of the funds.

- Five hedge funds in our sample did not comply with the prohibited investment restrictions under subsection 111(2)(b) of the Act[9], which prohibits a mutual fund from making an investment in a company in which it is a substantial security holder. This subsection applies to hedge funds that meet the definition of a mutual fund under the *Securities Act* (Ontario).

- Six hedge fund managers, who were also the portfolio manager for their funds, did not comply with subsections 118(2)(a) and 118(2)(b) of the Act[10].

- Five hedge fund managers were providing investment advice without registration as a Portfolio Manager with the OSC.

- In each case of non-compliance with securities laws, we addressed the specific issues with the individual fund managers.

---

[9]Subsection 111(2)(b) of the Act prohibits a mutual fund from making an investment in any person or company in which the mutual fund, alone or together with one or more related mutual funds, is a substantial security holder, i.e. owning more than 20% of the voting securities.

[10]Subsection 118(2)(a) of the Act prohibited a portfolio manager from investing in an issuer in which a responsible person is an officer or director. Subsection 118(2)(b) of the Act prohibited a portfolio manager from cross trading between two accounts. With the implementation of National Instrument 31-103 — *Registration Requirements and Exemptions* (NI 31-103), section 118 of the Act was repealed. Section 13.5 of NI 31-103 contains prohibitions on certain managed account transactions and captures the same type of transactions that were prohibited under section 118 of the Act.

Suggested practices

- Have a strong and independent compliance function appropriate to the size and complexity of the operations. The individual(s) responsible for the compliance function should possess adequate regulatory knowledge and industry experience to establish and maintain a strong compliance system and to ensure compliance with securities laws.

- Develop policies and procedures to prevent and detect conflicts of interest. Such policies and procedures should include, but are not limited to:
    - review ownership percentage in each investment held by a hedge fund on a regular basis
    - monitor outside business activities of responsible persons and their associates and create a list of related issuers that the funds cannot invest in
    - prohibit cross trading between accounts of a responsible person, an associate of a responsible person or the portfolio manager
    - have officers and directors sign an undertaking to report their holdings

Other statistics

- The majority (81%) of the hedge fund managers (or their affiliates) were also the portfolio manager to their funds.

- The majority (75%) of the hedge fund managers (or their affiliates) were also the distributor of their funds.

- Funds of hedge funds represented about 42% of total hedge fund assets.

- Two funds had a combined exposure of $8 million to Madoff, which was a large ponzi scheme uncovered in the U.S.

- Equity long/short strategy dominated our marketplace. Chart 2 below shows a breakdown by strategy of the standalone hedge fund assets as at December 31, 2008.

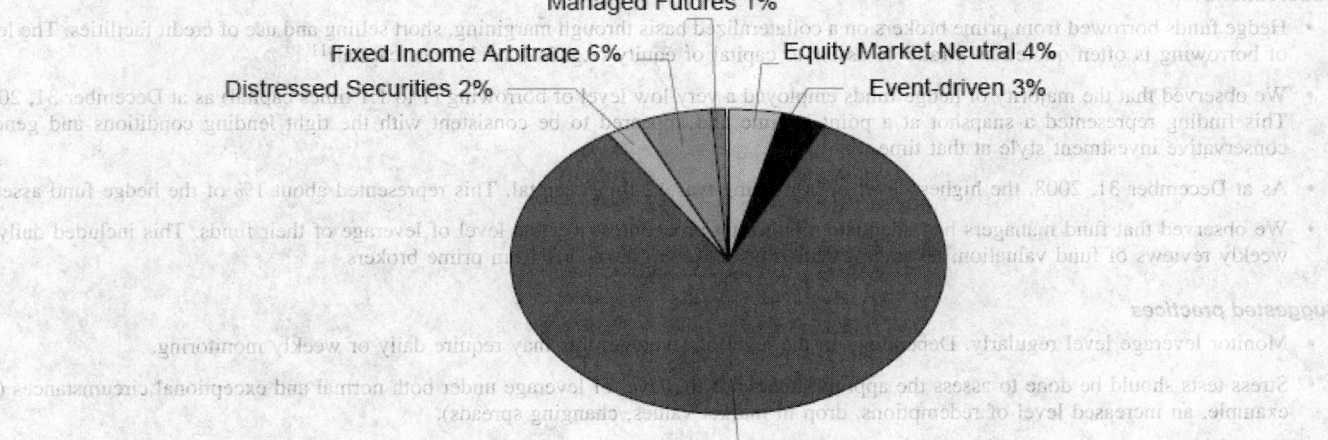

Chart 2 - Breakdown of hedge fund assets by strategy

Managed Futures 1%
Fixed Income Arbitrage 6%   Equity Market Neutral 4%
Distressed Securities 2%   Event-driven 3%
Equity Long/Short 84%

- Chart 3 illustrates the percentage of the funds' net assets invested in private or illiquid holdings as at December 31, 2008. For example, 3% of the funds reviewed (based on net assets) held between 31% to 50% of their net assets in private or illiquid holdings.

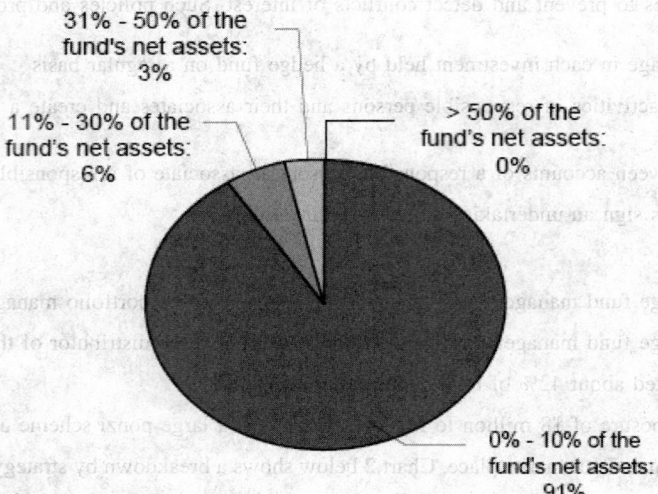

Chart 3 - Percentage of private/illiquid holdings held by standalone hedge funds

31% - 50% of the fund's net assets: 3%

11% - 30% of the fund's net assets: 6%

> 50% of the fund's net assets: 0%

0% - 10% of the fund's net assets: 91%

3.3 — Leverage usage and monitoring

As with the other statistics in this report, we reviewed the use of leverage at a specific point in time (December 31, 2008). We did not collect data on leverage embedded in derivatives or underlying investments held by hedge funds.

Observations

- Hedge funds borrowed from prime brokers on a collateralized basis through margining, short selling and use of credit facilities. The level of borrowing is often quoted as a ratio of assets to capital or equity (e.g. 3: 1 or 3 times capital)[11].

- We observed that the majority of hedge funds employed a very low level of borrowing (1 to 1.1 times capital) as at December 31, 2008. This finding represented a snapshot at a point in time and appeared to be consistent with the tight lending conditions and general conservative investment style at that time.

- As at December 31, 2008, the highest level of borrowing was 12 times capital. This represented about 1% of the hedge fund assets.

- We observed that fund managers had adequate monitoring procedures over the level of leverage of their funds. This included daily or weekly reviews of fund valuation, leverage calculations and margin reports from prime brokers.

Suggested practices

- Monitor leverage level regularly. Depending on the level of leverage, this may require daily or weekly monitoring.

- Stress tests should be done to assess the appropriateness of the level of leverage under both normal and exceptional circumstances (for example, an increased level of redemptions, drop in market values, changing spreads).

3.4 — Prime broker / counterparty exposure

Observations

- The majority of the fund managers used prime brokers that are affiliates of Canadian Schedule 1 banks.

- The majority of the hedge fund managers used counterparties that are major banks in Canada or the U.S.

- Most fund managers monitored the creditworthiness of their counterparties informally. Some fund managers had formal procedures in place to monitor their counterparty exposure. Procedures included setting a minimum credit rating requirement, monitoring the credit rating of counterparties on a regular basis, and reviewing aggregate exposure to each counterparty.

---

[11]There are several ways borrowing is measured in the industry. Some common measures are:
- gross market exposure, measured by the total of long and short positions, divided by capital
- net market exposure, measured by long positions less short positions, divided by capital

The majority of the fund managers quoted borrowing on a gross market exposure basis.

Suggested practices

- Monitor, on a regular basis, the financial stability and credit risk of all counterparties including prime brokers by assessing the fund's aggregate exposure to each counterparty regularly, checking the credit rating of counterparties regularly, and maintaining regular contact with the counterparties.

- Diversify counterparty risk, where possible.

3.5 — Monitoring of funds of hedge funds

This section relates only to those fund managers who were also acting as the portfolio manager.

Observations

- The majority of the fund of hedge fund managers performed adequate due diligence before making an investment in an underlying hedge fund. We observed fund managers having well-documented and traceable procedures for selecting underlying hedge funds based on both qualitative and quantitative characteristics of the funds and the fund manager.

- The majority of the fund managers received an in-person meeting with the underlying fund manager. They reviewed the most recent audited financial statements of the underlying fund and made appropriate enquiries in considering whether the liquidity level of the underlying fund was appropriate and sufficient for the fund of hedge funds to meet its redemption obligations.

- Some fund managers would only invest in an underlying hedge fund if an external fund administrator performed the valuation function.

- The majority of the fund of hedge fund managers had regular communication (usually weekly) with the underlying fund managers to evaluate fund performance, portfolio composition and the financial condition of the underlying funds.

- Some fund of hedge fund managers did not have full transparency of the underlying fund holdings at any time. Some managers only had full transparency on an infrequent basis.

Suggested practices

- Before making an investment decision, a fund of hedge fund manager should make reasonable enquiries to ensure that:
  - the underlying portfolio manager possesses adequate expertise, experience and qualifications
  - assets of the underlying fund are held by an independent, reputable custodian
  - the underlying fund is audited by an independent, reputable auditor at least annually
  - the underlying fund manager has well-established systems and controls in place to administer their funds. If any functions are outsourced to a service provider, assess that there is adequate oversight of the service provider
  - the valuation function is performed independently
  - the underlying fund manager will provide adequate information on the fund's activities on a regular basis; this information should include information on fund holdings, leverage level, financial results, and significant events
  - the liquidity level of the underlying fund is appropriate and sufficient for the fund of hedge funds to meet its redemption obligations
  - it has considered the liquidity of the types of instruments held by the underlying fund and is aware of any limitations on redemption privileges that can be imposed by the underlying fund manager
- Document due diligence performed when selecting the underlying hedge funds.
- Obtain and review the most recent audited financial statements of the underlying funds prior to investing. Subsequent to that, obtain and review the audited financial statements at least annually.
- Have full transparency of the underlying fund holdings at all times in order to manage the fund portfolio and assess risks at the aggregate fund level.
- Collect leverage information from each underlying fund and assess overall leverage at the portfolio level.

3.6 — Liquidity or viability issues

Observations

- Most fund managers increased cash balances during the market turmoil in anticipation of heavier than normal redemptions. This, along with the low percentage in private or illiquid holdings in general (as noted under Portfolio Holdings section above), enabled most fund managers to not have to exercise their right to suspend redemptions.

- Redemption restrictions imposed by the fund managers in our sample were carried out as permitted by the funds' offering documents. We did not note any incidences where preferential treatment was given to some unitholders allowing them to redeem their holdings prior to the fund manager deciding to suspend or restrict redemptions of a fund.

- Fund managers took appropriate steps to distribute assets of funds that were in the process of winding up in an equitable manner.

Part 3:
REGISTRATION

Suggested practices

- Monitor unitholder activities and liquidity requirements on a regular basis

- Communicate major events to investors in a timely manner

- Consider the interests of all unitholders when dealing with redemption requests

Other statistics

- 21 (0.9% based on assets under management) hedge funds had been wound up or were in the process of winding up, primarily as a result of market conditions.

- 16 (0.7% based on assets under management) hedge funds suspended redemptions during our review period. 12 (0.5% based on assets under management) of those that suspended redemptions were in the process of winding up during our review period.

3.7 — Fund valuation

Observations

- The majority of fund managers used an independent third-party service provider to perform the valuation function.

- We observed fund managers using appropriate valuation methodologies to value portfolio securities. They applied their valuation methodologies consistently, and maintained adequate documentation to support any manually-priced securities and write-downs.

- Fund managers reviewed pricing of hard-to-value securities frequently (usually weekly) to determine if a revaluation was warranted. Some fund managers had individuals who were independent of the portfolio management function (for example, an independent valuation committee or a compliance officer) review and approve securities revaluation.

- Some fund managers valued restricted stocks at the market value of the freely traded underlying stock price and failed to apply a discount to reflect the illiquidity of these investments.

- Some fund managers valued warrants at the intrinsic value rather than the fair value. These fund managers did not have a process in place to ensure that the intrinsic value and the fair value were not materially different.

- Some fund managers did not have adequate written policies and procedures in the following areas:

  - valuation methodologies and processes to be followed for private, illiquid or restricted securities

  - processes for making manual price adjustments

  - review and approval processes for NAV calculations

  - processes to rectify NAV errors

Suggested practices

- Develop and implement written policies and procedures that include, at a minimum, the following:

  - valuation methodologies for all types of securities held in the funds' portfolios

  - valuation processes for securities that do not have readily available market prices

  - procedures to review and approve each NAV calculation, and to detect non-compliance with internal guidelines

  - procedures to investigate price variances over a pre-determined tolerance level

  - procedures for the identification, rectification and accounting treatment for NAV errors

- Disclose valuation policies and procedures, the role of third parties, and procedures for mitigating potential conflicts of interest during valuation.

- Apply valuation policies and procedures consistently.

- For hard-to-value securities, the fund manager may be involved in pricing the securities. The fund manager should provide the external fund administrator with sufficient supporting documentation.

- Ensure that responsibilities between the portfolio management function and the valuation function are segregated.

- Where it is necessary to use estimates in a fund of hedge fund structure to calculate NAV, develop appropriate procedures to review and adjust the NAV for any differences between the actual and the estimated NAV of the underlying funds.

3.8 — Use of service providers

Observations

- The majority of the fund managers used a third-party fund administrator to perform administrative functions, including fund valuation. These fund managers maintained adequate controls over key functions, and adequate oversight over their service providers. They reviewed NAV calculations, fee calculations and reconciliations prepared by their service provider, and reconciled their own records with those of the service provider.

- Some fund managers did not maintain adequate books and records evidencing their oversight of the service provider. They did not maintain evidence of review or approval of NAV calculations, fee calculations and reconciliations prepared by the service provider.

- Three fund managers delegated their fund administration responsibility to a service provider but did not enter into a written service level agreement outlining the roles and responsibilities of the service provider in administering their funds.

Suggested practices

- Fund managers should maintain appropriate oversight and have the ability to review the accuracy and quality of the services provided in a timely manner. Even if delegating to service providers, fund managers maintain the ultimate responsibility for the operations of the fund.

- Enter into agreements that clearly outline the service providers' roles and responsibilities.

- Review service providers' processes, information flows, NAV and fee calculations, and ensure that adequate operational controls are maintained by the service providers.

- When the valuation of certain instruments can only be done by the manager, it is important that the external fund administrator also maintains documentation supporting the valuation.

- Assess service quality of all service providers at least annually, considering issues encountered and errors made by the service providers.

- Establish guidelines on how to monitor each outsourced function. This would include the types and frequency of reports to be provided by service providers, the types of issues that should be escalated to the fund manager; maintain evidence of the reviews of the outsourced functions.

- Maintain effective internal controls, checks and balances and segregation of duties. For example, require dual signatures to approve significant transactions, and reconcile cash and securities positions to the service provider's records regularly.

3.9 — Offering document disclosure

Hedge funds are sold primarily to high-net-worth individuals and institutional investors by way of an offering memorandum.

Observations

- Overall, hedge fund managers in our sample provided adequate and clear disclosure in their funds' offering documents in most areas, except as noted below:
  - six fund managers did not adequately disclose risk factors associated with investing in their funds, including:
    - counterparty risk
    - credit risk
    - interest rate risk
    - risk of using derivatives
    - risk of using leverage
  - five fund managers did not fully disclose the fees and expenses incurred by their funds, including:
    - personnel and office space expenses
    - administrative fees
    - legal, audit and custodian fees
  - five fund managers did not disclose the material contracts they entered into on behalf of their funds, including with service providers
  - seven fund managers provided inconsistent, incorrect or outdated information in the offering documents of their funds

Suggested practices

- Fund managers should disclose all material information consistently and accurately in the fund's offering document. Such information should include, at a minimum, the following:
  - investment objectives, strategies and restrictions, including the use of leverage and derivatives
  - material risk factors
  - valuation policies and procedures
  - types of fees and expenses incurred by the fund
  - material contracts, including the use of service providers
  - conflicts of interest and procedures to identify and address them

Part 3:
REGISTRATION

- subscription and redemption policies

- Fund managers should provide investors with adequate information throughout the life of their investment to allow them to monitor the investment over time. Such information should include, at a minimum, the following:

  - semi-annual and annual financial statements

  - periodic performance information

  - regular investor communication, reporting on significant events, any changes in the fund's risk profile, etc.

3.10 — Other regulatory compliance matters

- Four fund managers distributed units of their hedge funds without being registered as an Exempt Market Dealer (formally Limited Market Dealer) with the OSC. Firms that are in the business of distributing hedge fund securities pursuant to a prospectus exemption must be registered as an Exempt Market Dealer.

- If the hedge fund meets the definition of a mutual fund, NI 81-106, which contains continuous disclosure requirements, applies. Sections 2.1 and 2.3 of NI 81-106 describe the filing requirements, and section 2.11 exempts certain funds from these filing requirements if certain criteria are met. One of these criteria requires the delivery of the fund's financial statements to unitholders within a specified time period. Six hedge fund managers did not deliver the annual and semi-annual financial statements of their funds to their unitholders within 90 days after the year-end and within 60 days after the end of a semi-annual period. These instances of non-compliance were addressed with each individual fund manager.

3.11 — Comparison of fund manager practices to best practices suggested by Alternative Investment Management Association (AIMA)

AIMA published *Guide to Sound Practices for Hedge Fund Administrators* in September 2009. We compared the practices of the fund managers visited against some of the key suggested best practices by AIMA. The results are shown in Appendix B.

Appendix A — Statistics on fund managers who completed our questionnaire and who received a site visit

	Information gathering stage	Site visit stage	% visited
Money market funds			
No. of fund managers	36[12]	18	50%
Total net assets[13]	$67 billion	$63 billion	94%
No. of money market funds	89	61	69%
Non-conventional investment funds			
No. of fund managers	27	6	22%
Total market capitalization[14]	$36 billion	$23 billion	64%
No. of non-conventional investment funds	265	99	37%
Hedge funds			
No. of fund managers	88	32	36%
Total net assets[15]	$26 billion	$16 billion	62%
Total net assets with Ontario investors[16]	$8.4 billion	$6 billion	71%
No. of hedge funds[17]	312	192	62%
No. of hedge funds with Ontario investors[18]	233	132	57%

---

[12] 50 fund managers received our questionnaire, but only 36 of them managed money market fund(s).

[13] As at September 19, 2008.

[14] Total market capitalization as at March 2008: TMX Group.

[15] This represents the total net assets of the hedge funds managed by the hedge fund managers as at December 31, 2008, which includes fund assets held by Canadians and non-Canadians.

[16] This represents the portion of total net assets held by Ontario investors as at December 31, 2008.

[17] This represents the total number of hedge funds managed by the hedge fund managers as at December 31, 2008, which includes funds offered to Canadians and non-Canadians.

[18] This represents the number of hedge funds with investors residing in Ontario.

Appendix B — Hedge fund managers' practices against AIMA's suggested best practices[19]

> *Legend*
> o performed by more than 70% of hedge fund managers
> • performed by 50–70% of hedge fund managers
> ❑ performed by less than 50% of hedge fund managers

AIMA's key suggested best practices	Hedge fund managers visited
Have an independent valuation function, or have adequate segregation of duties between the valuation function and the investment management function.	o
Have a detailed valuation policy document, approved by the governing body, which is usually the board of directors, or the general partner.	•
Apply the valuation policy consistently. Any deviations from the policy should be approved by the governing body.	o
Use multiple price sources to verify the valuation of a fund's portfolio.	•
Any pricing models used by the fund manager should be independently tested and verified.	❑
Accrue fund expenses accurately and on a timely basis in order to strike an accurate NAV.	o
Reconcile cash and securities positions to prime broker or custodian statements.	o
Set out clearly the roles and responsibilities of the fund administrator in an administration agreement and/or a service level agreement.	o
Choose a fund administrator that can offer the necessary technology and staff expertise to support the fund's operating model.	o
Ensure that all fund offering documents are accurate and disclose all relevant information, including the role of the administrator, valuation provisions and subscription/redemption procedures.	•
Disclose the party who performs the NAV calculation function.	•

Policies and Orders: OSCN 33-733.

OSC Staff Notice 33-734 — 2010 Compliance and Registrant Regulation Branch Annual Report

Date: October 15, 2010
33 O.S.C.B. 9426

Contents

Introduction

Part 3:
REGISTRATION

---

[19]Alternative Investment Management Association, Guide to Sound Practices for Hedge Fund Administrators, September 2009.

Introduction

This report is a summary of the Compliance and Registrant Regulation (CRR) Branch's key activities and initiatives for the 2010 fiscal year (April 1, 2009 to March 31, 2010). The CRR Branch's mission is to protect investors by registering and overseeing approximately 1,400 firms and 65,000 individuals in Ontario that trade or advise in securities or commodity futures, or act as an investment fund manager. This includes direct oversight of firms and individuals registered in the categories of portfolio manager, investment fund manager, commodity trading manager, exempt market dealer and scholarship plan dealer. We also register firms and individuals in the category of mutual fund dealer and firms in the category of investment dealer that are directly overseen by their self-regulatory organizations, the Mutual Fund Dealers Association of Canada (MFDA) and the Investment Industry Regulatory Organization of Canada (IIROC), respectively.

In previous years, the Compliance team of the CRR Branch published annual reports that summarized the findings from compliance oversight reviews of registrants, together with our suggested practices. This year's report continues this, but also covers our branch's other activities such as:

- the introduction of the new registration regime

- the reorganization of our branch in March 2010, and

- the common deficiencies found in our reviews of registration applications and actions to address them.

This report is primarily targeted to registered firms and individuals, and people that support them such as their legal counsel and compliance consultants. We encourage existing and potential registrants to use this report to improve their understanding of:

- their initial and on-going registration and compliance requirements

- our expectations of registrants and our interpretations of regulatory requirements, and

- new and proposed rules and other regulatory initiatives.

This report can also serve as a self-assessment tool to strengthen registrants' compliance with Ontario securities law, and to improve their systems of internal controls and supervision.[1]

1. — Registration Reform

1.1 — New Registration Regime

After years of work, we developed and implemented a new registration regime that came into force on September 28, 2009. We developed the new regime with other members of the Canadian Securities Administrators (CSA), with an objective to harmonize, streamline and modernize the registration requirements across Canada. In Ontario, these reforms were introduced through National Instrument 31-103 *Registration Requirements and Exemptions* (NI 31-103) and amendments to the *Securities Act* (Ontario) and to related rules. These reforms replaced a patchwork of rules across Canada that imposed different requirements in each jurisdiction, and are intended to strike an appropriate balance between providing an efficient system for registrants and protecting investors.

The reforms introduce new requirements for the registration of individuals and firms, along with new ongoing requirements for their business operations and client relationships.

Key changes to the requirements for individual and firm registration include:

- requiring firms and individuals to register as a dealer when they are in the business of trading in securities (which is a business trigger) instead of when they trade in a security (which is a trade trigger)

- the introduction of the investment fund manager category of registration for firms that direct the business, operations and affairs of investment funds

- the introduction of the exempt market dealer category of registration, which replaces the former limited market dealer category and adds more robust requirements (including new proficiency, working capital and insurance requirements), and

- the introduction of registration requirements for chief compliance officers and ultimate designated persons for all registered firms.

---

[1]The content of this report is provided as guidance for information purposes and not as advice. We recommend that you seek advice from a qualified professional adviser before acting on any information in this report, or on any web site to which this report is linked.

Key changes to the on-going requirements for the business operations and client relationships of registered firms include:

- more robust and risk-based working capital and insurance requirements

- a requirement to identify and respond to conflicts of interest

- a requirement to fairly and effectively deal with client complaints, and

- new requirements for referral arrangements, including written disclosure to clients.

Changes were also made to the National Registration Database to convert firms and individuals that were already registered to their new categories of registration. We also updated our compliance oversight programs to reflect the new requirements.

Since we've harmonized on-going requirements for registrants, it is important to continue to harmonize our registrant oversight. We are working with other members of the CSA to harmonize the compliance oversight programs for registrants across Canada.

To help make market participants aware of the new requirements, we have

- responded to questions from stakeholders (together with the OSC's Inquiries and Contact Centre)

- published responses to frequently asked questions (FAQs) on NI 31-103 (see CSA Staff Notices 31-313 and 31-314)

- issued relief orders to deal with some transitional issues (see CSA Staff Notice 31-315), and

- communicated changes to the industry through speaking engagements and e-mail blasts to registrants.

We will continue to keep our stakeholders informed of key developments.

On June 25, 2010, the CSA published for comment a package of proposed amendments to NI 31-103. If the amendments are implemented in their current form, they would primarily address practical issues identified during the implementation stage. They would also:

- expand the circumstances in which registered firms are required to ensure that independent dispute resolution or mediation services are made available to their clients to resolve complaints to include, for example, cases of misrepresentation, theft, fraud, misappropriation or forgery

- codify, as part of the proficiency requirements, an obligation for registered individuals to understand the structure, features and risks of each security they recommend (referred to as "know your product")

- address the impact of the coming introduction of International Financial Reporting Standards on the valuation of securities, such as for account reporting to clients, and

- obligate investment fund managers to deliver trade confirmations and account statements to investors who deal with them directly, rather than through a dealer.

The CSA also requested feedback to questions on potentially amending NI 31-103 to require periodic account statements to include reporting of client name securities. For more information, see Notice of and Request for Comment on Proposed Amendments to NI 31-103.

1.2 — Reorganization of CRR Branch

This section describes the changes we made to our branch to better serve our stakeholders under the new registration regime.

The new registration regime introduced a significant number of new on-going requirements, many of which are principles-based. To deal with these changes, and to improve the effectiveness and efficiency of our branch and ultimately improve investor protection, we reorganized the branch effective March 2010.

Former Branch Structure

Previously, our branch was organized into three groups:

- the registration group, which consisted of registration officers who reviewed and processed firm and individual registration applications

- the compliance group, which primarily consisted of accountants who performed oversight reviews of registrants to assess compliance with regulatory requirements, and

- the registrant legal services group, which consisted of lawyers who developed policy affecting registrants and handled exemptions from registration requirements.

New Branch Structure

As part of the reorganization, the previous groups were replaced with three integrated teams of lawyers, registration officers, and accountants. Each team focuses on registration, oversight, policy changes, and exemption applications for a particular category of registrant. One team focuses on portfolio managers, the second on investment fund managers, and the third on dealers (including exempt market dealers and scholarship plan dealers). Each team has developed depth of knowledge of their particular registration category and can draw on the experience of team members trained in different disciplines.

A fourth team was created to focus on registrant conduct and risk analysis. This team supports the other three teams in cases of potential registrant misconduct and on risk assessment matters. For example, it handles opportunity to be heard hearings before the Director, and is involved in suspensions of registration, applying terms and conditions on registration and referrals of certain suspected registrant misconduct to the Enforcement Branch. This team will also lead in the development of a risk-based approach for assessing applications for initial registration.

It is anticipated that the reorganization will further enhance our ability to:

- protect investors
- promote high standards of registrant conduct
- treat registrants fairly and consistently
- understand the products and business of registrants and the issues they face
- use risk-based approaches to pursue the higher-risk issues, and
- be proactive and strive for practical, timely and valued added outcomes.

1.3 — New CRR Branch Organization Chart

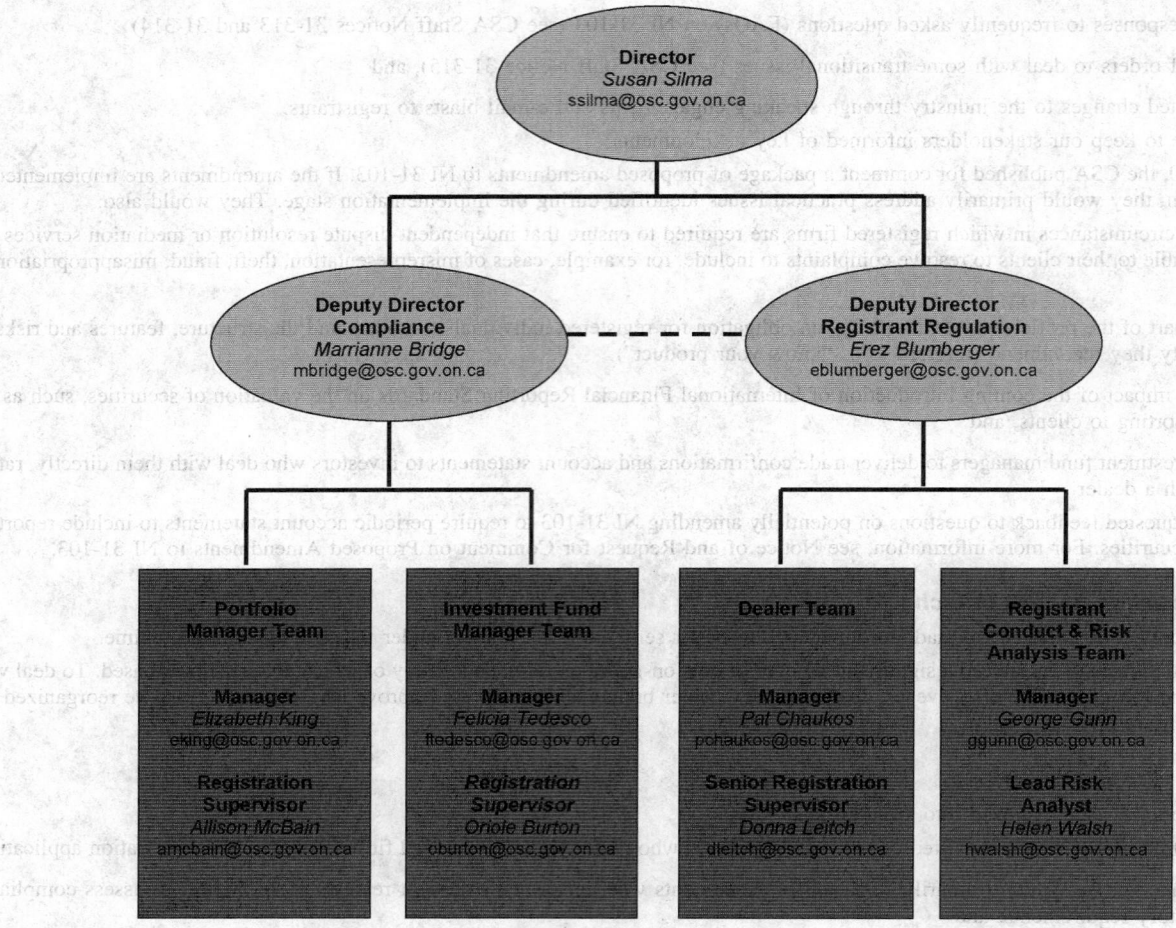

See Appendix for the organization charts for each of the CRR Branch's teams.

2. — Information for New Applicants for Registration

2.1 — Applying for Registration

This section provides information for firms and individuals applying for registration for the first time.

The CRR Branch reviews firm and individual applications for registration as an adviser, dealer or investment fund manager under securities law and commodity futures law in Ontario. Firms and individuals must complete prescribed forms to register. For example, Form 33-109F6 *Firm Registration* and Form 33-109F4 *Registration of Individuals and Review of Permitted Individuals* must be completed by firms and individuals applying for registration under the *Securities Act*. For more information about the registration process, see the Information for Dealers, Advisers and Investment Fund Managers section of the OSC's website.

An applicant may apply for registration in more than one province or territory as part of its application. If the OSC is the principal regulator, the application is processed under the passport system. We conduct a review of the application and our decision will be effective in the other jurisdictions. If the OSC is not the principal regulator, the application is processed under the interface system. Generally, this means that the applicant only deals with the principal regulator who reviews the application. We decide whether to opt in (with or without local terms and conditions) or opt out of the principal regulator's decision. If we are unable to resolve opt out issues, the applicant will need to deal with us directly to resolve them. For more information about registering in more than one jurisdiction, see National Policy 11-204 *Process for Registration in Multiple Jurisdictions*.

2.2 — Risk-Based Approach to Registration Reviews

We intend to rate an applicant's risk of not meeting registration requirements by establishing a risk model that will allow us to focus more attention on higher risk applicants. We plan to develop a risk assessment process for reviewing both firm and individual registration applications. In the short term, we will be focusing our attention on investment fund manager registration applications (which were due by September 28, 2010). A risk assessment process for other registration categories will be developed in the longer term. Our risk model may include the following criteria:

- previous sanctions or warning letters issued to an applicant

- if the applicant is the subject of an investigation

- criminal record

- solvency, and

- firm record.

Other factors may also impact our risk assessment.

2.3 — Common Deficiencies from Registration Applications

Sometimes, the registration review process is longer because the information provided to us in a registration application form is incomplete or lacks sufficient detail for us to adequately assess the information. To address this, we created a list of the most common deficiencies from our reviews of individual and firm registration applications. To address each deficiency, we provide actions to be taken by applicants when completing their registration applications. To expedite the application and review process, we encourage applicants for registration to review these common deficiencies and to follow the provided actions before submitting their registration applications to us.

The deficiencies and actions to be taken are listed in the same order as the information is requested on the applicable registration application forms. References to item numbers and schedules are to specific sections of the firm or individual registration application forms.

Firm Applications — Form 33-109F6

Deficiency noted	Action to be taken
The firm's National Registration Database (NRD) number is not provided. (Item 1.2)	Include the firm's NRD number. To obtain an NRD number, firms must enroll on NRD. For more information, visit www.nrd-info.ca
Agent and address for service information is not completed, when applicable. (Item 2.4/Schedule B)	Include the agent's name, full address and contact details (telephone, fax number and e-mail address) when the firm does not have an office in a jurisdiction of Canada where it is seeking registration.
Insufficient information is provided regarding the firm's proposed business activities. (Item 3.1)	Provide detailed information about the firm's proposed activities, target market, and products and services to be offered. Section 26 of the *Securities Act* should be kept in mind when completing this item.
The firm's business registration number(s) is not provided, when applicable. (Item 3.9)	Provide the firm's business registration number(s) for each jurisdiction of Canada where the firm is seeking registration, when a business registration number is required under the local laws of the jurisdiction.
The firm's ownership chart is incomplete or does not provide the requested information. (Item 3.12)	Include a complete ownership chart that includes the owner's name(s), and the class, type, amount and voting percentage of ownership of the firm's securities.
The firm's subordination agreement(s) is not provided, when applicable. (Item 5.1/Line 5 of Schedule C)	Provide a copy of all subordination agreements (in the form set out in Appendix B to NI 31-103) that the firm has executed with its lenders to exclude an amount from its long-term related party debt as calculated on Form 31-103F1 *Calculation of Excess Working Capital*.
Bonding or insurance details are incomplete. (Item 5.5)	Include all requested bonding or insurance details, including name of insurer, policy number, coverage details, amount of deductible, and renewal date. We will accept a binder of insurance with the initial application. Confirmation that the insurance is in effect must be provided prior to registration being granted.

Part 3: REGISTRATION

Individual Applications — Form 33-109F4

Deficiency noted	Action to be taken
Proficiency information is not provided or updated. (Item 8)	Include information on all required and otherwise relevant courses and examinations, along with student numbers where requested.
Incomplete information is provided on current employment, other business activities, and officer and director positions held. For example, some activities are missing or the description of the activities is missing or inadequate. (Item 10, Schedule G) Also, activities outside of the sponsoring firm are not approved by the sponsoring firm, and the potential conflicts of interest from these outside activities is not addressed by the sponsoring firm.	Individuals must provide information on all current employment and other business activities for which they receive compensation, as well as any officer or director positions held (whether or not compensation is received). This includes, for example, positions as directors of charitable organizations. Individuals should provide a detailed description of their duties for each activity. This helps us to assess if any of these activities (especially those that are securities related) are a conflict of interest with the individual's activities as a registrant. The sponsoring firm must approve activities outside of the sponsoring firm, and potential conflicts of interest must be addressed. See section 13.4 of the Companion Policy to NI 31-103 for guidance on conflicts of interest.
Incomplete information is provided for: • resignations and terminations • regulatory disclosure • criminal disclosure • civil disclosure, and • financial disclosure. (Items 12 to 16 inclusive)	It is the responsibility of the firm to conduct its own due diligence on an individual it intends to sponsor. Firms should ensure that resignations and terminations, and regulatory, criminal, civil and financial disclosure are complete and accurate. Incomplete or misleading information may lead to the individual's registration being delayed or refused or to other regulatory action.
Information on the ownership of securities and derivatives firms is missing or incomplete. (Item 17)	Information on the ownership of any securities or derivatives firms should be provided and be complete and accurate.

Other Common Deficiencies Applicable to Both Firm and Individual Applications

Deficiency noted	Action to be taken
Updating the Form 33-109F6 (F6) and Form 33-109F4 (F4): Changes to the information previously filed on these forms are often not made within deadlines prescribed under securities law.	Use Form 33-109F5 (F5) to update changes in information on the F6 and F4. The F5 must generally be filed within seven days of most changes to the information provided in the forms. National Instrument 33-109 *Registration Information* outlines the changes that require notification to the regulator and the filing deadlines. Making these filings on time will prevent the firm being assessed a late fee of $100 per business day, as well as, in some cases, the imposition of terms and conditions.
Exemption applications: Applications for exemption from the proficiency requirements are received without sufficient detail to determine if exemptive relief is appropriate.	Provide complete and relevant details on the nature of the relief sought, and the reasons why the relief should be granted. For example, explain how the applicant's education or experience is equivalent to the education or experience requirements under securities law. Exemption applications should be provided with, or shortly following, the submission of an application for registration. If this is not done, the application for registration may be delayed.
Trade names: We are often not properly notified of the use of trade names. Trade names are registered to, and used by, (a) one or more representatives, or (b) a firm. We often incorrectly receive an F5 from a firm requesting that an individual's trade name be added as the firm's trade name.	If one or more representatives are using a trade name, this information must be added under Item 1(3) of each individual's F4. If a firm is using a firm-wide trade name, this information must be added by filing an F5. All trade names must be registered, where required, under the business names legislation that applies to the firm (for example, the *Business Names Act* (Ontario)).
Certification: Required forms are often certified as true and complete, when some applicable questions are not completed, or supporting documents are not included.	Ensure that all required documents and attachments are submitted and questions are answered with an appropriate level of detail before certifying the information in the form. Incomplete applications will not be treated as filed and will not be added to the queue for review.

3. — Information for Advisers, Investment Fund Managers and Dealers

The information in this section includes the key findings from our normal course reviews of all registrants[2] we regulate, and also our focused reviews (sweep) of investment fund managers conducted as a result of the market turmoil, our sweep of large portfolio managers, and our sweep of newly registered portfolio managers. We highlight deficiencies from our oversight reviews of registrants and provide suggested practices to address the deficiencies. The suggested practices are intended to give guidance to registrants to help them comply with their regulatory obligations, as they provide our interpretations of the legal requirements and our expectations of registrants. We also discuss new or proposed rules and initiatives impacting registrants.

This part of the report is divided into four main sections. The first section contains general information that is relevant for all registrants. The other three sections contain information and trends specific to portfolio managers, investment fund managers and exempt market dealers, respectively. We recommend that registrants review all sections in this part, as some of the deficiencies noted in the past year for one type of registrant could be relevant in future years to other registrants.

3.1 — All Registrants

This section includes a general discussion of our compliance review process and its outcomes. It also includes new or proposed rules and initiatives impacting registrants.

A. — Compliance Review Process and Its Outcomes

On an on-going basis, the CRR Branch conducts compliance reviews of selected registered firms using a risk-based approach. However, we occasionally select firms for review on a random basis, for example, to help us evaluate the effectiveness of our risk-based approach. We usually conduct compliance reviews on-site at a registrant's premises, but may also perform reviews from our offices (known as desk reviews). Most reviews are routine in nature, but we also perform reviews on a for-cause basis where we are aware of a potential compliance issue, for example, from a referral or complaint. We also conduct sweeps, which are reviews of a sample of registered firms on a specific topic or industry sector over a short period of time. Sweeps allow us to respond quickly to industry-wide concerns or issues, such as the recent market turmoil.

The purpose of compliance reviews is to assess compliance with securities laws. Any deficiencies noted are raised with the registered firm we reviewed so that appropriate corrective action is taken. During our compliance reviews, we also stay alert to any signs of potential fraud, and will take appropriate steps if we identify these signs.

We monitor the outcomes from our reviews of registrants to assess overall compliance and to identify areas of focus for future reviews. Compliance reviews often lead to enhanced compliance at registrants, but may also result in regulatory actions such as terms and conditions being imposed on a registrant's registration, or referrals to our Enforcement Branch. Also, as part of the new registration regime, amendments were made to the *Securities Act* that provide the Director with the power to revoke or suspend a registrant's registration.[3] The four outcomes of our compliance reviews in fiscal 2010, with comparables for 2009, are presented in the following table, and are listed in their increasing order of seriousness. The percentages in the table are based on the registered firms we reviewed during the year, and not the population of registered firms.

Outcomes of compliance reviews (all registration categories)[4]	Fiscal 2010	Fiscal 2009
Enhanced compliance	37%	60%
Significantly enhanced compliance[5]	50%	32%
Terms and conditions on registration	3%	4%
Referral to the Enforcement Branch	10%	4%

Each of the outcomes is explained below. In some cases, there may be more than one outcome from a review. In these cases, the review is counted only under its most serious outcome. We also provide an explanation for the changes in outcomes from last year.

- *Enhanced compliance*: At the end of a review, in almost all cases, we issue a report to the registered firm identifying areas of non-compliance that require corrective action. We work with these firms to facilitate the appropriate resolution of these deficiencies. Compliance reviews result in enhanced compliance, as registrants' actions to address the identified deficiencies improve their compliance systems. In fiscal 2010, 37% of reviews resulted in enhanced compliance by the registrant. The decrease from 60% in fiscal 2009 is offset by the increase in the significantly enhanced compliance outcome, as explained below.

- *Significantly enhanced compliance*: Where warranted by the seriousness of the deficiencies identified during a review, in addition to the steps taken in the enhanced compliance outcome, we also increase our monitoring of the registrant. For example, we may conduct a follow-up review of a registrant or require the registrant to provide additional evidence, to assess if they have appropriately addressed the identified deficiencies. The increased monitoring and the registrant's response generally results in significantly enhanced compliance. In fiscal 2010, 50% of field reviews resulted in significantly enhanced compliance. This outcome increased from last year's 32% primarily as a result of us focusing our attention on areas that we considered to be problematic during the recent market turmoil.

---

[2]In this report, registrants includes investment fund managers as the new registration regime requires these firms to register, subject to transition provisions.

[3]See section 28 of the *Securities Act* (Ontario)

[4]Includes portfolio managers, exempt market dealers (formerly limited market dealers) and investment fund managers (before the new registration regime an investment fund manager was a market participant but not a registrant).

[5]In previous years, we referred to this outcome as >30% significant deficiencies.

- *Terms and conditions on registration*: We may impose terms and conditions on a firm's registration to more closely monitor a registrant's compliance with securities law. We may also impose terms and conditions to require a registered firm to take a specific action or to restrict their business activities. For example, terms and conditions may require the firm to submit information (such as financial statements and capital calculations) to the OSC more frequently, retain a consultant to improve its compliance systems, or prohibit the registrant from opening new client accounts. In fiscal 2010, 3% of field reviews resulted in the imposition of terms and conditions on registration, which is consistent with last year's result of 4%.

- *Referral to the Enforcement Branch*: If we identify a serious breach of securities law, we will discuss our findings with the Enforcement Branch, and together determine an appropriate course of action. In fiscal 2010, 10% of field reviews resulted in referrals to the Enforcement Branch, compared to 4% in fiscal 2009. The increase from the prior year is a result of performing more for-cause reviews, and continued enhancements to our risk-based approach to selecting registered firms for review.

B. — New and Proposed Rules and Initiatives Impacting All Registrants

In addition to the new registration regime, we actively participated with other members of the CSA in the development and implementation of new and proposed rules and other initiatives. We also worked with other OSC branches on policy initiatives that impact registrants. The key rules and initiatives that generally impact all registrants are described below.

"Know Your Product" (KYP) Obligation

CSA Staff Notice 33-315 *Suitability Obligation and Know Your Product* (CSA Staff Notice 33-315) was published on September 4, 2009. This notice reminds registrants of their requirement to satisfy their suitability obligations to clients, including the duty to fully understand the structure, features and risks of products they recommend to clients. It also provides guidance to registrants on how to meet these obligations. For more information, see CSA Staff Notice 33-315. Proposed amendments to NI 31-103 would codify the KYP obligation as part of the proficiency requirements for registered individuals.

Client Relationship Model (CRM)

Together with the CSA, IIROC and the MFDA, we are continuing to work on improving and harmonizing requirements in a number of areas related to a client's relationship with a registrant. We addressed some elements of the CRM in NI 31-103 by requiring disclosure of relationship information to clients (including disclosure of costs for the operation of their account) and requiring registrants to identify and respond to conflicts of interest.

We have now started phase 2 of CRM, in which we anticipate proposing the introduction of the following additional CRM principles and requirements for registered firms in NI 31-103:

- additional disclosure to clients of all costs associated with the products and services they receive, and

- meaningful reporting to clients on how their investments perform.

Improvements to Reporting Process on Terrorist Financing

Working with the CSA, we have improved the process for reporting terrorist financing information by introducing a consolidated reporting form. The reporting requirements apply to registered dealers and advisers, and exempt dealers and advisers who are in the business of dealing in securities or providing portfolio management or investment counselling services in any CSA jurisdiction. The reporting requirements do not apply to investment fund managers unless they are also in the business of trading or advising in securities.

To facilitate reporting and explain the changes, we have published guidance for firms on their monthly reporting and other requirements relating to terrorist financing and *United Nations Act* sanctions on certain countries. The guidance provides information on the new consolidated reporting form that will be used by each principal regulator, describes the new process for sending the monthly reports by e-mail to the principal regulator, and provides summary information on the relevant laws. For more information, see CSA Staff Notice 31-317 (Revised) *Reporting Obligations Related to Terrorist Financing*.

International Financial Reporting Standards (IFRS)

Canada's public companies and registrants are moving to adopt IFRS for financial reporting. This move reflects an increasing international acceptance of a single, harmonized set of accounting standards. For financial years beginning on or after January 1, 2011, Canadian registered firms will be required to present their financial statements using IFRS. The OSC and the CSA have released regulatory proposals and guidance to assist registrants as they prepare for the changeover. For more information, see Notice of IFRS-Related Amendments to Registration Materials.

Contracts for Difference

In October 2009, OSC staff issued OSC Staff Notice 91-702 *Offerings of Contracts for Difference and Foreign Exchange Contracts to Investors in Ontario* (OSC Staff Notice 91-702) to provide general guidance to market participants about offerings of Contracts for Difference (CFDs), foreign exchange (forex) contracts and similar over-the-counter (OTC) derivatives to investors in Ontario. The notice also highlights our investor protection concerns, particularly when these products are offered to retail investors by unregistered, offshore entities through the internet.

OSC staff concluded that CFDs are "securities" when they are offered to Ontario investors. As such, in staff's view, engaging in or holding oneself out as engaging in the business of trading or advising in CFDs triggers the dealer and adviser registration requirements under the *Securities Act*. The notice states that since CFDs use margin, the appropriate registration category for a dealer who trades in CFDs is investment dealer (which requires IIROC membership), regardless of whether the trades are made to retail investors or accredited investors. For more information, see OSC Staff Notice 91-702.

Alternative Exam Providers

Proficiency requirements for registered individuals are prescribed by NI 31-103 and generally include industry experience and completion of specific examinations. As the investment industry changes and new investment products emerge, it is important for us to be flexible in deciding which exams are required for proficiency in the future. As such, we are participants in a CSA committee which will review proposals from exam providers to consider alternatives to the proficiency exams prescribed in NI 31-103. This may allow for the development of specialized courses and exams, instead of generalist ones, and for a wider variety of exam providers.

3.2 — Portfolio Managers

This section contains information specific to portfolio managers. It includes trends in deficiencies and suggested practices from our normal course compliance reviews of portfolio managers, along with deficiencies and suggested practices from our focused reviews of large portfolio managers and our sweep of newly registered portfolio managers. We also discuss our in-progress sweep on marketing practices and new or proposed rules that will impact portfolio managers.

A. — Trends in Deficiencies from Compliance Reviews and Suggested Practices

This section discusses some new trends in the deficiencies identified from our normal course compliance reviews of portfolio managers, along with suggested practices to prevent their recurrence.

Delegating Know Your Client (KYC) and Suitability Obligations to Other Parties

Some portfolio managers enter into referral arrangements with mutual fund dealers and their salespersons, or with financial planners, for the referral of clients to the portfolio manager for a managed account, in return for an on-going referral fee. In some of these cases, the portfolio managers do not meet with their clients to understand their investment needs and objectives, financial circumstances and risk tolerance. Instead, they rely on the mutual fund salesperson or financial planner to perform these duties, assist the client in completing the portfolio manager's managed account agreement, and updating KYC information. This practice is contrary to securities law, as registrants may not delegate their KYC and suitability obligations to other parties. If portfolio managers do not have complete and accurate KYC information for their clients, they cannot adequately perform their suitability obligations.

Portfolio managers are required by sections 13.2 and 13.3 of NI 31-103 to establish the identity of each of their clients and to ensure they have sufficient and current KYC information for each client (including the client's investment needs and objectives, financial circumstances, and risk tolerance) so that they can assess the suitability of each trade made for their clients. Further, mutual fund salespersons and financial planners do not have the proficiency or registration required to perform these activities for a managed account. Referral arrangements must not allow an individual or firm to perform registerable activities unless the individual or firm is appropriately registered.

Suggested Practices

A registered portfolio manager should:

- meet with each client to understand their KYC information before managing their portfolio

- explain the firm's investment process and strategy and other relationship information to the client

- assist the client in completing and signing necessary forms and agreements, such as an investment policy statement and managed account agreement

- regularly communicate the investment holdings and performance of the managed account to the client, and

- keep each client's KYC information up-to-date by:
  - immediately contacting the client when they know that their circumstances have changed, and
  - periodically contacting the client (at least annually) to assess if their circumstances have changed.

Also, registered firms should review referral arrangements to ensure that all activity requiring registration is performed by appropriately registered firms and individuals.

Marketing Performance Returns from a Previous Firm

We have concerns with portfolio managers who market the performance returns achieved by their advising representatives when they were employed at another firm. This is often done by newly registered portfolio managers with no (or a limited) performance track record of their own.

We have seen cases where portfolio managers were marketing the performance returns from another firm when:

- the advising representative was not responsible for generating the presented returns, or
- the investment strategy at the previous firm was different from that of the new firm.

In our view, it is misleading and not relevant to market the returns from a previous firm in these cases.

Misleading statements are prohibited by section 2.1 of OSC Rule 31-505 *Conditions of Registration* (OSC Rule 31-505) which requires registrants to deal fairly, honestly and in good faith with clients. Also, section 44(2) of the *Securities Act* prohibits making statements to an investor who is deciding to enter into or maintain an advising relationship, if the statement is untrue or omits information necessary to prevent it from being misleading.

However, there are limited cases where, in our view, it may not be misleading to market the performance returns from a previous firm, as explained below.

Suggested Practices

Portfolio managers should present the returns of the firm's actual performance composite(s) or investment fund(s) since the firm has been registered.

There are some limited circumstances where it may be relevant and not misleading to market the performance of a previous firm, such as when:

- the key investment decision maker(s) at the previous firm are now employed at the new firm
- the investment strategy at the previous firm is substantially similar to that of the new firm
- the new firm has books and records that adequately support the historical data presented from the previous firm, and
- there is adequate disclosure that the performance presented is from a previous firm, and of any other relevant facts.

Best Execution Obligations

Some portfolio managers use only one dealer (which is generally the clients' custodian) to execute all of their clients' trades. We are concerned that this practice may result in the portfolio manager not meeting its best execution obligations to its clients. If portfolio managers use one dealer to execute all clients' trades, they need to have adequate support to demonstrate that they are meeting their best execution obligations.

Section 4.2 of National Instrument 23-101 *Trading Rules* (NI 23-101) requires portfolio managers to make reasonable efforts to achieve best execution when acting for a client. Section 4.3 of NI 23-101 states that, to satisfy the above requirement, portfolio managers should make reasonable efforts to use facilities providing information regarding orders and trades.

Best execution is defined in section 1.1 of NI 23-101 as the most advantageous execution terms reasonably available under the circumstances. See Part 4 of the Companion Policy to NI 23-101 for additional guidance on best execution.

Suggested Practices

- Maintain and apply written policies and procedures which outline a process designed to achieve best execution
- The policies should describe how the portfolio manager evaluates whether best execution was obtained and should be regularly reviewed
- Consider a number of factors to achieve best execution, including assessing a particular client's requirements or portfolio objectives, selecting appropriate dealers and marketplaces and monitoring the results on a regular basis, and
- Disclose the portfolio manager's trading practices to clients in writing, including selection and use of dealers, especially if only one dealer is used to execute clients' trades.

Risk Management

All registered firms, regardless of size, should have adequate risk management processes to mitigate risk and protect firm and client assets. Some portfolio managers do not have an adequate system of controls to identify and manage their firm's key business risks. These include for example, the firm's operational, financial, regulatory and legal risks, and also investment risks in client portfolios. The risk management processes should reflect the firm's size, business activities, and clients' investments.

An example of a business risk is failing to resume services to clients on a timely basis after a business interruption or disaster. This risk can be managed through developing and testing a business continuity plan. An example of an investment risk in client portfolios is foreign currency risk. This risk can be managed through currency hedging.

Internal controls are an important element of a registrant's compliance system. Section 32(2) of the *Securities Act* requires registrants to establish and maintain systems of control and supervision in accordance with the regulations for controlling their activities and supervising their representatives. Section 11.1 of NI 31-103 requires registered firms to establish a system of controls and supervision by establishing, maintaining and applying policies and procedures which are sufficient to provide reasonable assurance of compliance with securities legislation and that manage the firm's business risks in accordance with prudent business practices.

For further guidance on internal controls and risk management, see Part 11 of the Companion Policy to NI 31-103, under the heading "Internal controls."

Suggested Practices

All registered firms should:

- appoint a senior individual or committee to be responsible for risk management that reports to senior management or the board of directors
- establish and apply written policies and procedures which demonstrate how the firm identifies and manages or controls the firm's business risks

- on a regular basis, identify, understand, evaluate and monitor the firm's key business risks and how each risk is managed or controlled, and

- document, and periodically review and update, the identified key risks and how each risk is managed or controlled.

B. — Deficiencies from Focused Reviews of Large Portfolio Managers and Suggested Practices

We conducted reviews of a sample of large portfolio managers (based on client assets under management). We focused on the firms' portfolio management and risk management processes, and on their marketing practices. These reviews were performed to allocate some of our compliance oversight resources on larger firms since a breakdown in their compliance systems may have a significant impact on investors and the capital markets.

The key deficiencies we identified from these focused reviews are discussed in the following table, along with suggested practices (or where to get more information).

Deficiency noted	Suggested practices
Marketing practices. Some firms had marketing materials that included: (a) exaggerated or unsubstantiated claims regarding the firm's products, services or skills (b) improper claims of compliance with the CFA Institute's Global Investment Performance Standards (GIPS) (c) inadequate disclosure when comparing the firm's performance against a benchmark, and (d) improper statements indicating that the OSC had approved the financial standing, fitness or conduct of a registrant.	(a) See OSC Staff Notice 33-729 *Marketing Practices of Investment Counsel/Portfolio Managers* for a discussion and suggested practices on exaggerated and unsubstantiated claims (b) It is misleading to claim compliance with the GIPS standards, such as compliance with the composite calculation methodology, unless all requirements of the GIPS standards are met. Firms should refer to the GIPS standards when making any reference to these standards in marketing materials (c) See OSC Staff Notice 33-729 for a discussion and suggested practices on the use of benchmarks, and (d) Section 46 of the *Securities Act* prohibits representing that the OSC has approved the financial standing, fitness or conduct of a registrant. As a result, registrants should not state, for example, that an OSC compliance review resulted in no material findings.
Risk management. Some firms had inadequate written policies and procedures to demonstrate how they identify and prudently manage their business risks (including investment risks in client portfolios). Although the firms generally had an adequate risk management process, the overall processes followed by the firms were not documented in writing.	Each firm should have written policies and procedures to demonstrate how it identifies and manages its business risks. See section 3.2 of this report for a discussion on risk management and suggested practices.
Know your product. Some firms had inadequate written policies and procedures to demonstrate how they review the structure, features and risks of investment products they purchase for clients (referred to as "know your product"). Although the firms generally had an adequate know your product process, the processes followed were not documented in writing.	Each firm should have written policies and procedures to: • identify investment products which require review • review these products' structure, features and risks, and • assess the suitability of these products for each client. See CSA Staff Notice 33-315 for further guidance on suitability obligations and know your product.

C. — Deficiencies from Compliance Reviews of Newly Registered Portfolio Managers and Suggested Practices

We continued our practice of conducting sweeps of newly registered firms to assess their compliance with Ontario securities law and to provide guidance and information to them on their key regulatory requirements (including NI 31-103). In the fall of 2009, we used a risk-based approach to select a sample of newly registered portfolio managers. We then conducted an on-site review of each selected firm to gain an understanding of its business, products and services, and clients. As part of these reviews, we assessed each firm's portfolio management process, trading practices, compliance systems, marketing practices and financial condition.

The common deficiencies we identified from these reviews are discussed in the following table, along with suggested practices (or where to get more information).

Deficiency noted	Suggested practices
Inadequate marketing practices, including: (a) marketing materials that disclosed exaggerated or unsubstantiated information regarding the firm's products, services or skills (b) inappropriate use of benchmarks (c) improper use of back-tested performance data, and (d) improper marketing of performance returns from a previous firm.	See OSC Staff Notice 33-729 for a discussion and suggested practices on marketing practices, including exaggerated and unsubstantiated claims, benchmarks, and hypothetical performance data (including back-tested performance data). See section 3.2 of this report for a discussion and suggested practices on marketing performance returns from a previous firm.
Inadequate written policies and procedures relating to key business areas such as portfolio management, trading and brokerage, and marketing, or non-compliance with existing written policies and procedures.	See our report titled 10 Most Common Deficiencies Among Portfolio Managers for topics and guidelines that should be included in a standard policies and procedures manual for a portfolio manager. Firms should provide a copy of, and training on, their written policies and procedures to their staff, and monitor for compliance on an on-going basis.
Lack of or inadequate business continuity plan (BCP) to allow the firm to mitigate, respond to, and recover from a disaster or disruption that may impact its ability to provide services to clients.	See our report titled 10 Most Common Deficiencies Among Portfolio Managers for suggested practices on what a firm's BCP should cover.
Inadequate disclosure to clients regarding fairness in allocation of investment opportunities amongst clients (fairness policy), or on conflicts of interest such as advising in securities of related or connected issuers.	For guidance on the content of a fairness policy and disclosing conflicts of interest to clients, see sections 14.10 and 13.4 respectively, of the Companion Policy (CP) to NI 31-103.

We also noted capital calculation deficiencies, including using an insufficient amount of minimum capital, failing to deduct the deductible under the firm's bonding or insurance policy, and not preparing capital calculations on at least a monthly basis. For capital calculation requirements under NI 31-103 (which apply to all registrants as of September 28, 2010), please see section 12.1 of NI 31-103 and its CP, and Form 31-103F1 *Calculation of Excess Working Capital*.

D. — Sweep of Marketing Practices in 2010

Since we continue to find deficiencies in the marketing practices of portfolio managers during compliance reviews, we decided to conduct a second sweep of their marketing practices as part of a CSA initiative.

This sweep will help us to assess if investors are being provided with fair and accurate information when they decide to enter into, or maintain, an advising relationship with a portfolio manager. We started the marketing sweep in the summer of 2010 by sending a sample of portfolio managers a survey that requested information about their marketing practices and copies of their marketing materials. A sub-set of the portfolio managers who received the survey have been selected for on-site reviews, which are in-progress. At the end of the sweep, we plan on publishing our findings in a CSA Staff Notice.

E. — New and Proposed Rules Impacting Portfolio Managers

This section discusses new and proposed rules that impact portfolio managers.

Use of Client Brokerage Commissions

National Instrument 23-102 *Use of Client Brokerage Commissions* (NI 23-102) was published on October 9, 2009 and became effective on June 30, 2010, at which time OSC Policy 1.9 was rescinded. NI 23-102 sets out new requirements for trades in securities involving brokerage commissions charged to clients that are directed by a portfolio manager to a dealer in return for the provision of order execution goods and services or research goods and services. It also requires portfolio managers to disclose certain information to their clients on their use of client brokerage commissions by the end of 2010. For more information see NI 23-102.

Institutional Trade Matching

Final amendments to National Instrument 24-101 *Institutional Trade Matching and Settlement* (NI 24-101) came into force on July 1, 2010, at which time the transitional requirements in OSC Rule 24-502 were revoked. The revised NI 24-101 requires registered advisers and dealers to match delivery against payment/receipt against payment (DAP/RAP) trades by no later than noon on the business day following the trade date, and no longer has an ultimate requirement to match DAP/RAP trades by the end of the trade date. For more information see revised NI 24-101.

Sub-Adviser Registration Exemption

Together with the CSA, we are considering adding a sub-adviser registration exemption in NI 31-103 that would apply across Canada that is similar to the existing Ontario exemption in section 7.3 of OSC Rule 35-502 *Non Resident Advisers*. Most other Canadian jurisdictions currently grant discretionary relief with similar terms in exemption orders, but there are different CSA views on how to interpret the terms. As part of this work, we will review how the industry uses the existing exemptions.

3.3 — Investment Fund Managers

This section contains information specific to investment fund managers, including the findings and suggested practices from compliance reviews, an update on our focused reviews of investment funds as a result of the market turmoil, and proposals for the registration of non-resident investment fund managers.

A. — Deficiencies from Compliance Reviews of Investment Fund Managers and Suggested Practices

Use of Side Letters

We have concerns with investment fund managers that give preferential treatment to one or more investors in the same class of units of an investment fund, as they disadvantage the other investors. Some investment fund managers of non-prospectus investment funds have entered into agreements (or "side letters") with one or more investors in their funds that give those investors preferential rights and terms compared to those given to other investors in the same class of units of the fund. Examples include preferential portfolio transparency, redemption rights, fund reporting, and management and performance fees.

Side letters that give preferential rights to one or more investors can harm the fund and its other investors. For example, if some investors have portfolio transparency and more frequent redemption rights, they can use their knowledge of the portfolio and their right to redeem their units before others, to their benefit and to the disadvantage of the fund and its other investors.

Section 116 of the *Securities Act* imposes a standard of care on investment fund managers for the investment funds they manage. In our view, investment fund managers do not meet their standard of care by giving preferential rights and terms to one or more investors, but not all investors, in the same class of units of an investment fund.

Also, sections 13.4(1) and (2) of NI 31-103 require registered firms to identify and respond to all existing or potential material conflicts of interest between their firm, including the individuals acting on its behalf, and its clients. In our view, it is a material conflict of interest to provide preferential rights and terms to an investor in the same class of units as other investors in an investment fund.

Suggested Practices

- Avoid entering into arrangements (including "side letters") that give preferential rights and terms to one or more investors in the same class of units of an investment fund

- If investors in the same investment fund are provided with different rights and terms:
  - create separate classes of units for the fund, and
  - disclose the rights and terms of each class of units in the fund's offering documents.

Responsibility for Valuation and Error Correction

Some investment fund managers appear to be contracting out of their duties and obligations under securities law to properly value their funds' investments and correct any net asset value (NAV) calculation errors. We noted a small number of cases where non-prospectus funds' offering documents state or imply that when there is a valuation error, the investment fund manager will not adjust the NAV of the fund retroactively.

In our view, for investment fund managers to meet their standard of care under section 116 of the *Securities Act*, they should ensure that the NAV of each fund under their management is accurately calculated, and that they correct any of their fund's material NAV errors (including making retroactive adjustments). Investment fund managers may not avoid their legal duties or obligations through disclosure in an investment fund's offering documents.

Suggested Practices

- Maintain and apply written policies and procedures to ensure that the fund's investments are properly valued and that the NAV is accurately calculated

- Maintain and apply written policies and procedures to identify and correct any NAV calculation errors, including policies and procedures that:
  - establish a reasonable materiality threshold for NAV error corrections
  - rectify NAV calculation errors, and
  - make the fund and its unitholders whole as appropriate where the NAV has been materially overstated or understated

- Make adjustments to the fund's NAV (including retroactive adjustments) to make the fund and its unitholders whole as appropriate when there is a material NAV calculation error, and

- Ensure that disclosure in the fund's offering documents and the fund manager's policies are consistent with the fund manager's standard of care to make the fund and its investors whole when there has been a material NAV calculation error.

Prohibited Investments for Investment Funds

Some investment funds make investments that are prohibited under securities law. We found cases where investment funds' portfolios held securities:

- of companies that were related to the fund or its investment fund manager, portfolio manager, or principal distributor, or to any of their shareholders, directors or officers

- in the form of loans from the investment fund to its related parties (including the fund's portfolio manager and investment fund manager), and

- in companies and other investment funds, which represented an ownership of more than 20% of the outstanding voting securities of those companies or other investment funds.

In most cases, these investments were held in portfolios of non-prospectus qualified investment funds.

Investment funds that meet the definition of a mutual fund in Ontario[6] have specific prohibitions against investments (including loans) in securities of their related parties, unless an exemption applies. Section 111 of the *Securities Act* outlines the investments that are prohibited for mutual funds in Ontario. One of the prohibitions disallows making or holding an investment in any person or company (including another investment fund) in which the mutual fund, alone or together with its related mutual funds, owns more than 20% of the outstanding voting securities.

In addition, section 13.5 of NI 31-103 prohibits a portfolio manager from causing an investment portfolio managed by it, including an investment fund, from providing a guarantee or loan to a responsible person or associate of a responsible person (which includes the portfolio manager).

For investment funds sold by simplified prospectus, further investment restrictions may apply. For example, see Parts 2 and 4 on Investments and Conflicts of Interest respectively, in National Instrument 81-102 *Mutual Funds*. In some cases, investment funds that are reporting issuers with an independent review committee (IRC) may be permitted to make investments in securities of related parties if they are in the best interests of the fund and are approved by the IRC, and if the other conditions in National Instrument 81-107 *Independent Review Committee for Investment Funds* are met.

There are also general requirements that apply to all investment funds. For example, section 116 of the *Securities Act* imposes a standard of care on investment fund managers, requiring them, among other things, to act in the best interests of their investment funds. In our view, this obliges them to ensure that any investments (including loans) in securities of related parties held by their investment funds are in the best interests of the fund. Compliance with this obligation may prevent investment funds from making certain investments, even if they are not specifically prohibited by securities law.

Suggested Practices

- Prior to making an investment (including a loan) for an investment fund in securities of its related parties, assess if it complies with all relevant investment restrictions under applicable securities legislation and is in the best interests of the fund, and document the results of the assessment

- Maintain records of the investments held by all mutual funds under common management to monitor if any mutual fund (alone or together with its related mutual funds) approaches or exceeds ownership of more than 20% of the outstanding voting securities of those investments (including investments in other investment funds)

- Review any existing investments (including loans) by an investment fund in securities of its related parties, and any concentrated positions in securities, to determine if the investment complies with all relevant securities legislation, and is in the best interests of the fund, and

- Take appropriate action to address any instances of non-compliance.

B. — Focused Reviews of Investment Funds in Response to Market Turmoil

We responded to the turmoil in the financial markets in 2008 and 2009 by using a risk-based approach to conduct focused reviews of investment funds. We performed on-site compliance reviews of samples of Ontario-based money market funds, non-conventional investment funds and hedge funds. We have now completed our focused reviews, and despite the market downturn, we did not identify any industry-wide compliance issues during the period reviewed. Instances of non-compliance identified during our on-site reviews were addressed separately with each individual fund manager.

A summary of our initiative was published on January 19, 2010 as OSC Staff Notice 33-733 *Report on Focused Reviews of Investment Funds*. This report summarizes our findings based on the industry's responses to our questionnaires, as well as our observations and suggested practices from all three phases of our on-site reviews.

Going forward, we will continue to monitor market conditions and will conduct focused reviews or sweeps to address any significant market issues which may arise.

C. — Registration of Non-Resident Investment Fund Managers

The new registration regime introduces the investment fund manager category of registration for firms that direct the business, operations and affairs of investment funds. We are working with the other members of the CSA to determine how this registration requirement applies to non-resident investment fund managers. Specifically, we are examining the following:

- the circumstances under which investment fund managers resident outside of Canada would need to register, and

- in what provinces and territories an investment fund manager with a head office in Canada would need to register in addition to the province or territory where its head office is located.

---

[6]See definition for mutual fund in Ontario in section 1(1) of the *Securities Act*.

In the fall of 2010, we expect to publish for comment proposed changes to NI 31-103 with respect to the registration of non-resident investment fund managers.

3.4 — Exempt Market Dealers

A. — Risk Assessment Questionnaire for Exempt Market Dealers

We developed and sent out a risk assessment questionnaire (RAQ) to all exempt market dealers (formerly limited market dealers) registered in Ontario to help us determine which firms would be selected for a compliance review and what areas of their business to focus on. We reviewed the responses to the RAQs to get a general understanding of each firm and its business activities. Based on the information provided to us, we selected a smaller group of firms from which to obtain additional information on the firm's business activities, KYC and accredited investor information, products and services, and marketing and disclosure practices. We are reviewing this additional information, and may ask further questions or conduct on-site reviews of these firms.

B. — Deficiencies from Compliance Reviews of Exempt Market Dealers and Suggested Practices

During the course of our compliance reviews, we reviewed a number of exempt market dealers (EMDs) that were distributing high-yield investment products. Our reviews identified significant deficiencies, including the failure to adequately meet know your client (KYC) and suitability obligations (including know your product), inadequate disclosure to clients, and inadequate compliance systems. We generally raised these and other deficiencies with each EMD reviewed so that they could take appropriate corrective action to address the concerns. However, where appropriate, we referred the case to our Enforcement Branch or took action to suspend the firm's registration.

As part of our on-going reviews of EMDs, we will continue to focus our attention on the areas that we found deficiencies from prior reviews, and will take appropriate regulatory action if we identify significant deficiencies.

The key deficiencies from our reviews are discussed below, accompanied by suggested practices.

KYC and Suitability Obligations (Including Know Your Product (KYP))

Significant KYC and suitability deficiencies noted during field reviews conducted in fiscal 2008 and 2009 continue to exist. For example, we noted that:

- the majority of EMDs reviewed did not adequately collect and document KYC information for clients

- some EMDs that collected KYC information were not using it appropriately in their suitability assessment

- when assessing suitability, many EMDs did not have adequate knowledge of the investment product being recommended (referred to as KYP), and

- many EMDs did not perform sufficient product due diligence prior to recommending a product to investors.

Many EMDs did not collect and document their clients' investment needs and objectives, risk tolerance, and financial circumstances. In some cases, EMDs that collected this KYC information recommended a security to the client that was not suitable.

Many EMDs (both the firm and its registered individuals) did not adequately understand the structure, features and risks of the investment products that they recommended. In addition, there was a lack of ongoing due diligence, as they were unaware of changes to the investment product's key features and risks, and to the issuer's financial condition — all of which could impact investors' decisions and future returns.

Many of the EMDs that distributed products of a third-party issuer had only a basic understanding of the investment product. EMDs generally relied on the information provided by the issuer and did not perform sufficient due diligence before accepting the product for distribution and had limited or no information regarding the issuer's financial condition.

EMDs distributing products of a related issuer did not disclose the issuer's financial condition to their clients, even though they had knowledge of this information. As a result, some EMDs were misrepresenting the product to their investors, and investors may have been misled regarding the financial viability and risks of the product.

Section 13.2 of NI 31-103 requires registrants to take reasonable steps to ensure they have sufficient and current KYC information for clients including the clients' investment needs and objectives, financial circumstances and risk tolerance. Section 13.3 of NI 31-103 requires registrants to take reasonable steps to ensure that all securities recommended to clients are suitable. See sections 13.2 and 13.3 of the Companion Policy to NI 31-103 and CSA Staff Notice 33-315 for guidance on KYC, suitability and KYP requirements.

Suggested Practices

EMDs and their registered individuals should ensure that they:
- have a process in place to collect and document sufficient KYC information for each client (for example by using a standard KYC form) so they can properly assess the suitability of investment products they recommend

- have an in-depth understanding of:
  - the general features and structure of the product
  - the product risks including the risk/return profile and liquidity risks
  - the management and financial strength of the issuer
  - costs, and
  - any eligibility requirements for each product

before recommending it to clients

- perform an independent analysis of the product rather than recommending a product solely based on information from issuers, similarities with other products, or suggestions from other parties, and

- perform ongoing due diligence of the issuer and products to assess changes to their structure or features and determine the impact on their clients' investments.

Inadequate Disclosure to Clients

We identified a number of areas where clients did not receive sufficient disclosure to properly assess the relevant attributes and associated risks of the investment products recommended by EMDs. For example, we noted:

- inadequate disclosure of investor rights, costs, risks, and eligibility requirements of recommended products

- inadequate disclosure of the use of investor money

- inadequate disclosure of conflicts of interest, and

- misleading disclosure in marketing materials.

Section 2.1 of OSC Rule 31-505 requires EMDs to deal fairly, honestly and in good faith with their clients. In our view, this includes ensuring that information contained in offering documents and marketing materials is complete, accurate, and not misleading.

Also, section 13.4(3) of NI 31-103 requires EMDs to provide timely disclosure to its clients on the nature and extent of existing or potential material conflicts of interest between the EMD (including each individual acting on its behalf), and the client. In our view, this includes disclosing to clients any conflicts of interest that could impact a client's decision to purchase an investment product. The disclosure should be provided when a reasonable investor would expect to be informed of the conflict. In our view, this is before or at the time an EMD recommends a security transaction that gives rise to the conflict. For additional guidance on conflicts of interest, see section 13.4 of the Companion Policy to NI 31-103.

Suggested Practices

Disclosure in Offering Documents

- Guidelines should be set by the firm to ensure appropriate disclosure on the general features and structure of the product, risks, fees, management and financial strength of the issuer, and any eligibility requirements of each product, and

- All offering documents should be reviewed and approved by the EMD prior to distribution to investors.

Disclosure of the Use of Investor Money

- There should be complete and accurate disclosure to clients on the issuer's use of investor proceeds, and

- Funds lent to related parties should be disclosed, including the nature of the loan and relevant terms such as the risks associated with the loan, whether investor funds are secured against assets, repayment terms, and interest rates.

Disclosure of Conflicts of Interest

- Guidelines should be set by the firm to ensure conflicts of interests that are relevant to a client's investment decision are disclosed in a timely manner. Specifically, relationships with affiliates and other related parties should be disclosed. The disclosure should be prominent, specific, clear and meaningful to the client, and explain the conflict of interest and how it could impact the client.

Disclosure in Marketing Materials

- Marketing materials must be free of misleading or inaccurate information. As such, comparisons to alternative investments should be restricted to products with similar features and risks, and relevant differences should also be disclosed to enable the investor to adequately assess the risks and rewards of each investment product.

Inadequate Compliance System

A number of EMDs reviewed did not have an adequate compliance system to ensure that the firm and its individuals complied with securities legislation, as evidenced by the following findings:

- inadequate collection, review and approval of KYC and suitability information for clients prior to an investment being made

- inadequate review of accredited investor information to assess whether the accredited investor exemption relied on was consistent with the information obtained in the KYC process

- inadequate review and approval of offering documents and marketing materials, resulting in misleading or inaccurate information being provided to clients and inadequate disclosure of product risks

- written policies and procedures were inadequate and did not cover all business areas, and

- existing policies and procedures were not enforced.

Section 11.1 of NI 31-103 requires EMDs to establish a system of controls and supervision by establishing, maintaining and applying policies and procedures that ensure compliance with securities legislation and manage their business risks. See section 11.1 of the Companion Policy to NI 31-103 for guidance on compliance systems.

Suggested Practices

- Clients' KYC information documented by the EMD's dealing representatives should be reviewed for completeness and be approved by the EMD's compliance officer

- Investments recommended to clients by the EMD's dealing representatives should also be assessed for suitability by the EMD's compliance officer using each client's KYC information

- Accredited investor information should be compared to completed KYC forms to assess whether the use of the accredited investor exemption is reasonable. Where KYC information is not sufficient to make this assessment, evidence of follow-up supporting the appropriateness of the firm's reliance on the exemption should be included in the client's file

- EMDs should review offering documents and marketing materials to ensure they present information to clients in a clear, accurate and complete manner, and

- Written policies and procedures should be tailored to a firm's business operations, be up-to-date with Ontario securities law, and be enforced.

4. — Additional Resources

This section discusses how registrants can get more information about their obligations.

A part of our branch's mandate is to foster a culture of compliance through outreach and other initiatives. Although as a regulatory body we cannot provide legal or financial advice, we try to assist registrants in meeting their regulatory requirements in a number of ways. Some special stakeholder initiatives this past year are discussed below.

We updated the CRR Branch's section of the OSC's website (www.osc.gov.on.ca) in May 2010. The "Information for Dealers, Advisers and Investment Fund Managers" section of the website provides firms and individuals with comprehensive information about the registration process and their ongoing obligations under the new registration regime. The new section features an expanded navigation and layout which makes it easier to understand the initial registration process and the ongoing obligations of a registrant. It also includes information about compliance reviews and suggested practices. The section also provides quick links to forms, FAQs relating to the new registration rules and various guides.

Also, we hosted a forum for chief compliance officers (CCOs) of portfolio managers in February 2010. The objective of the forum was to heighten CCOs' awareness of their responsibility for compliance and the importance of a strong and effective compliance regime. Topics discussed included:

- Importance of a compliance regime

- OSC's compliance oversight approach

- Portfolio manager common deficiencies

- NI 31-103

- *Proceeds of Crime (Money Laundering) and Terrorist Financing Act*

- Soft dollars

- IFRS

Until February 1, 2011, you may access an audio recording of this forum by going to the following web page and following the on-screen instructions: http://events.startcast.com/events6/413/C0001/Default.aspx

[Appendix omitted]

OSC Staff Notice 33-735 — Sale of Exempt Securities to Non-Accredited Investors

Date: May 13, 2011

34 O.S.C.B. 5424

Purpose of this Notice

Staff of the Ontario Securities Commission (staff or we) are concerned that some issuers (including companies and investment funds) and dealers are selling exempt securities in reliance on the accredited investor exemption (AI exemption) to individual investors who do not meet the definition of an Accredited Investor (as set out below). This Notice provides our view on the Accredited Investor definition and the AI exemption contained in National Instrument 45-106 *Prospectus and Registration Exemptions* (NI 45-106) and our expectations of issuers and dealers who sell exempt securities to Accredited Investors.

In Ontario, issuers and registered dealers are permitted to sell exempt securities without a prospectus if they sell to individual investors who meet minimum asset or income thresholds, referred to as Accredited Investors. However, we have found that many dealers do not collect adequate know-your-client (KYC) information to reasonably determine whether the investor is in fact an Accredited Investor. This raises significant investor protection concerns. Issuers and dealers should review their current practices for selling exempt securities to Accredited Investors.

We will continue to closely monitor the activities of issuers and dealers that sell exempt securities, including conducting compliance reviews of those firms. We will take enforcement proceedings or other regulatory action where issuers and dealers are acting contrary to securities law by selling exempt securities under the AI exemption to investors who are not Accredited Investors.

Accredited Investor

Generally, a security sold to an investor in Ontario must be issued pursuant to a prospectus. A prospectus is a comprehensive disclosure document that sets out detailed information about the company or investment fund, describing the securities being issued and the risk associated with purchasing those securities. However, in recognition of the relative sophistication of certain investors and their ability to withstand financial loss, securities laws permit the sale of securities to Accredited Investors without a prospectus. Securities that are exempt from the prospectus requirement are referred to as exempt securities. A sale of exempt securities to an Accredited Investor is referred to as a sale under the AI exemption. The definition of an Accredited Investor is set out in section 1.1 of NI 45-106. Issuers and dealers should refer to that section before selling a security to Accredited Investors.

Section 1.1 of NI 45-106 enumerates the specific circumstances in which an investor will be considered an Accredited Investor, some of which apply to corporations, and others of which apply to individuals. Dealers and issuers frequently rely on that portion of the Accredited Investor definition relating to an individual investor's income, financial assets, or net assets when determining if that individual investor meets the definition. Section 1.1 of NI 45-106 defines an Accredited Investor as:

- An individual who, either alone or with a spouse, beneficially owns *financial assets* having an aggregate realizable value before taxes, but net of any related liabilities, that exceeds $1,000,000;

- An individual whose *net income* before taxes exceeded $200,000 in each of the two most recent calendar years or whose net income before taxes combined with that of a spouse exceeded $300,000 in each of the two most recent calendar years *and* who, in either case, reasonably expects to exceed that net income level in the current calendar year; or

- A individual who, either alone or with a spouse, has *net assets* of at least $5,000,000.

Financial Assets versus Net Assets

As stated above, staff is concerned that some issuers and dealers are selling exempt securities in reliance on the AI exemption to individual investors who do not meet the Accredited Investor definition. A frequent misunderstanding of the Accredited Investor definition relates to the respective meanings of "financial assets" and "net assets". The two concepts are different and should not be confused with each other.

Financial assets include (i) cash, (ii) securities, or (iii) a contract of insurance, deposit or an evidence of a deposit that is not a security for the purposes of securities legislation. The value of an investor's personal residence or other real estate is *not* included in the calculation of financial assets. By comparison, *net assets* includes all of the investor's assets, minus all of his or her liabilities, and so could include an investor's personal residence and other real estate. For more guidance, please refer to section 3.5 of the Companion Policy to NI 45-106.

It has come to our attention that in assessing whether their clients meet the Accredited Investor definition, some dealers are not making it clear to their clients that the client's personal residence or other real estate cannot be included in their financial assets. As a result, these issuers and dealers may be selling exempt securities in reliance on the AI exemption to investors who do not, in fact, meet the definition of an Accredited Investor, contrary to securities laws.

Our Expectations for Issuers and Dealers Selling Securities to Accredited Investors

The issuer and dealer selling a security are responsible for determining whether an investor meets the definition of Accredited Investor and is therefore eligible to purchase exempt securities. Pursuant to NI 45-106, an issuer has an obligation to ensure that exempt securities are only distributed under the AI exemption to investors who meet the definition of an Accredited Investor. Generally, an issuer will engage a dealer to distribute its exempt securities to investors. It is important that an issuer ensure that the distribution of its securities through the dealer will be made in compliance with securities law.

The following is a non-exhaustive list of steps that dealers should take in order to meet their obligations under securities laws when selling exempt securities to an Accredited Investor:

- *Read and understand the definition of Accredited Investor:* Compliance with securities law begins with understanding securities law. Pursuant to Part 11 of NI 31-103 *Registration Requirements and Exemptions* (NI 31-103), we expect registered firms to provide adequate training to their chief compliance officers and dealing representatives to ensure that they understand the definition of an Accredited Investor and how to determine whether a client meets the definition. Dealers should pay specific attention to the difference between financial assets and net assets.

- *Develop an accurate form for collecting KYC information:* Section 13.2 of NI 31-103 requires registrants to collect KYC information, which includes the client's financial circumstances, their investment objective, and risk tolerance. Information collected on a KYC form should help to determine whether the client meets the definition of an Accredited Investor. Dealers should also review and update the KYC form to ensure that the dollar thresholds used for net assets and net financial assets are correct.

- *Explain the Accredited Investor definition to clients and ensure that their KYC forms are properly completed:* Dealers should explain the Accredited Investor definition to clients before they complete their KYC form. Many clients may not initially understand the distinction between financial assets and net assets, and are likely to include the value of their personal residence or other real estate in both cases. Dealers should explain to clients what a financial asset is, and should also make it clear to them that the value of their personal residence or other real estate is not to be included in calculating their financial assets.

- *Do not sell an exempt security if you do not have sufficient information to determine whether the client qualifies as an Accredited Investor:* Subscription agreements for exempt securities usually contain a statement (commonly referred to as the accredited investor certificate) that the investor is purchasing the security as an Accredited Investor, and investors are asked to initial or place a check mark in a box to indicate that the statement applies to them. It is not sufficient for issuers and their dealers to simply rely on the client's initialling or checking off of this box; the information contained in the client's completed KYC form or other documentation (see below) must also demonstrate that they meet the definition of an Accredited Investor.

- *Ensure the exempt security is suitable for the client:* Section 13.3 of NI 31-103 requires a registrant to take reasonable steps to ensure that a particular investment is suitable for a client. Even if a client qualifies as an Accredited Investor, a registrant must still assess whether the exempt security in question is suitable for the investor. As described in CSA Staff Notice 33-315 *Suitability Obligation and Know Your Product*, there are two key requirements for determining suitability in order to comply with NI 31-103. Registrants must understand (i) the general investment needs and objectives of their clients and any other factors necessary for them to be able to determine whether a proposed purchase or sale is suitable (KYC information), and (ii) the attributes and associated risks of the securities they are recommending to clients (commonly referred to as the know-your-product).

- *Review the KYC form:* The Chief Compliance Officer (CCO) of the dealer should review the completed KYC form to ensure that the information collected is complete and consistent with that portion of the Accredited Investor definition to be relied on and that the trade is suitable for the client. Where conflicting information exists between the accredited investor certificate and the KYC form, the dealer must take appropriate follow-up steps to ensure that the investor is in fact an Accredited Investor. Evidence of follow-up procedures should be documented in client files and reviewed by the CCO.

- *Retain documentation:* Dealers should maintain records to support the reliance on the Accredited Investor definition, including KYC forms and the dealing representative's notes. We do not consider a verbal representation from the investor that they are accredited as sufficient support that they meet the Accredited Investor definition.

- *Establish policies and procedures:* Dealers should establish policies and procedures to ensure that exempt securities are only distributed under the AI exemption to investors who meet the Accredited Investor definition.

- *Report the sale of exempt securities to the OSC:* Issuers must ensure that sales of exempt securities made in reliance on the AI exemption are reported to the OSC by filing a Form 45-106F1 (as required by NI 45-106), and that full purchaser details are included in the completed form.

The content of this notice is to assist you in understanding the Accredited Investor definition and the AI exemption contained in NI 45-106. We also describe procedures that we expect a dealer to undertake in order to meet its obligations when selling exempt securities to an Accredited Investor. We encourage you to seek legal advice where further clarification is required.

OSC Staff Notice 33-736 — 2011 Annual Summary Report for Dealers, Advisers and Investment Fund Managers

Date: September 23, 2011

34 O.S.C.B. 9750

[Not reproduced]

OSC Staff Notice 33-737 — Enhanced Transparency of Communications with Registrants

Date: June 28, 2012

35 O.S.C.B. 5935

Background

The mandate of the Ontario Securities Commission (the **OSC**) is to protect investors from unfair, improper and fraudulent practices, and to foster fair and efficient capital markets and confidence in capital markets. Staff of the OSC is committed to increasing the transparency with which it interacts with its stakeholders, including firms registered under the *Securities Act* (Ontario) (the **Act**), as part of an ongoing effort to further its mandate.

Under Part XI of the Act, the Director is responsible for making decisions concerning the registration status of individuals and firms who are required to be registered under the Act or who are seeking registration under the Act (**registrants**). The Director is an administrative official, and is defined in subsection 1(1) of the Act as the Executive Director of the Commission, a Director or Deputy Director of the Commission, or a person employed by the Commission in a position designated by the Executive Director as a Director.

When staff recommends that the Director refuse, amend, or suspend an individual's registration, or impose terms and conditions on an individual's registration, staff will send the registrant a letter providing written notice of its recommendation and brief reasons for it (the **Letter of Brief Reasons**). Section 31 of the Act then gives the registrant the right to be heard by the Director before a decision is made concerning staff's recommendation.

Historically, the OSC would send the Letter of Brief Reasons only to the individual registrant. The OSC would send a brief written notice to the registrant's sponsoring firm indicating staff's recommendation and advising the firm of the individual's right to be heard. In these notices, staff did not include any of the reasons underlying its recommendation, noting only that reasons had been communicated to the individual registrant.

What's New

Registrants are advised that, effective immediately, staff will now also be sending a copy of the Letter of Brief Reasons to the sponsoring firm. This copy will be sent to the sponsoring firm at the same time that the Letter of Brief Reasons is sent to the registrant.

Reason for Change in Process

In staff's view, providing registered firms with the Letter of Brief Reasons will promote the accuracy and completeness of information provided in respect of individuals they sponsor, thereby assisting firms in fulfilling their obligations under s. 5.1 of National Instrument 33-109 *Registration Information*.

Staff is of the view that investor protection will be enhanced by communicating important information about individual registrants and applicants to the registered firms responsible under Ontario securities law for supervising these individuals.

OSC Staff Notice 33-738 — 2012 OSC Annual Summary Report for Dealers, Advisers and Investment Fund Managers

Date: November 22, 2012

35 O.S.C.B. 10473

Contents

Introduction

This report provides information for dealers that are directly regulated by the OSC (primarily exempt market dealers (EMDs) and scholarship plan dealers (SPDs)), advisers (portfolio managers or PMs) and investment fund managers (IFMs) (collectively, registrants). The main purpose of this report is to assist registrants in complying with their regulatory obligations under Ontario securities law. It was prepared by the OSC's Compliance and Registrant Regulation (CRR) Branch, which registers and oversees approximately 1,300 firms and 66,000 individuals in Ontario that trade or advise in securities or commodity futures, or act as IFMs. Although the OSC registers firms and individuals in the category of mutual fund dealer (MFD) and firms in the category of investment dealer, these firms and individuals are directly overseen by their self-regulatory organizations (SROs), the Mutual Fund Dealers Association of Canada (MFDA) and the Investment Industry Regulatory Organization of Canada (IIROC), respectively.

This report summarizes new and proposed rules and initiatives impacting registrants, current trends in deficiencies from compliance reviews of registrants (and suggested practices to address them), and current trends in registration issues. We also focus on know-your-client (KYC), know-your-product (KYP) and suitability obligations to clients for dealers and PMs, and what we are doing to assess compliance with these obligations.

This report also provides a summary of some key registrant misconduct cases, provides guidance on preparing for an OSC compliance review, explains how registrants can get more information about their obligations, and provides OSC contact information.

We strongly encourage registrants to use this report to improve their understanding of

- initial and ongoing registration and compliance requirements,

- OSC staff expectations of registrants and our interpretation of regulatory requirements, and

- new and proposed rules and other regulatory initiatives.

We also suggest registrants use this report as a self-assessment tool to strengthen their compliance with Ontario securities law, and to improve their systems of internal controls and supervision.[1]

1. — Key policy initiatives impacting registrants

1.1 — Cost disclosure, performance reporting and client statements

The Canadian Securities Administrators (the CSA), along with IIROC and the MFDA, have been working to develop requirements in a number of areas related to a client's relationship with a registrant. This initiative was previously referred to as the Client Relationship Model project, which, as part of the new regime for registrants, developed requirements on relationship disclosure information delivered to clients at account opening, and comprehensive requirements for managing conflicts of interest.

On June 14, 2012, we published for a second round of public comment proposed amendments on cost disclosure, performance reporting and client statements (Client Relationship Model Phase 2 or CRM2). We regard this as an important investor protection initiative. If adopted, CRM2 will introduce performance reporting requirements and enhance existing cost disclosure requirements in *National Instrument 31-103 Registration Requirements, Exemptions and Ongoing Registrant Obligations* (NI 31-103).

We conducted investor research during the second half of 2011 and consulted with four industry organizations in the early part of 2012. The reports on the investor research are available on the OSC's website at *Investor Research Reports and Document Testing*. We have amended the proposals in response to public comments after the first publication, investor research and industry consultation.

CRM2 includes, among other things, requirements for dealers and advisers to provide their clients with annual reports that show them

- in dollars, what the dealer or adviser was paid for the products and services it provided; and

- in dollars and percentages, how the client's investments performed during that year and over longer periods.

The purpose of the cost disclosure requirements is for investors to be made aware of all the costs, and dealer and adviser compensation, associated with the products and services they receive from registrants.

The purpose of the performance-reporting requirements is for investors to get clear and meaningful information that will enable them to evaluate how well their investments are doing. To that end, dealers and advisers would be required to provide clients with annual performance reports that cover

- deposits into, and withdrawals from, the client's account;

- the change in value of the account; and

- the percentage returns for the previous year; the previous three, five and ten years; and for the period since the account was opened.

CRM2 contains a model performance report to provide guidance to registrants.

---

[1]The content of this report is provided as guidance for information purposes and not as advice. We recommend that you seek advice from a qualified professional advisor before acting on any information in this report, or on any website to which this report is linked.

CRM2 also includes proposals for

- the disclosure of some fixed income commissions to provide more clarity about embedded costs;

- an expanded "client statement", replacing the existing account statement, that includes reporting on securities whether they are held in nominee name or client name;

- a new hierarchy of steps for determining the market value of securities; and

- new disclosure requirements for SPDs that are tailored to the unique risks associated with investments in scholarship plans.

IIROC and the MFDA have worked with the CSA on the CRM2 project. If adopted, CRM2 would apply in all CSA jurisdictions. We would expect the requirements for members of IIROC and the MFDA to be materially harmonized.

For more information, see *Proposed Amendments to NI 31-103 on Cost Disclosure, Performance Reporting and Client Statements*. Also, see section 5.5.1 of this report on *Inappropriate expenses charged to funds* for staff's views on IFMs charging CRM2 costs to their investment funds.

1.2 — Potential best interest standard for dealers and advisers

We are re-evaluating the advisor-client relationship by considering whether an explicit statutory fiduciary or best interest standard should apply to dealers and advisers in Ontario and on what terms. A fiduciary duty is essentially a duty to act in a client's best interest.

In Ontario, section 116 of the *Securities Act* (the Act) applies a best interest standard to IFMs in their dealings with the investment funds they manage. However, there is no equivalent provision under the Act that explicitly applies a best interest standard to dealers and advisers in their dealings with their clients (but there is a requirement to deal fairly, honestly and in good faith with their clients[2]). Although there is no statutory fiduciary duty for dealers and advisers in Ontario, Canadian courts can find that a given dealer or adviser owes a fiduciary duty to his or her client depending on the nature of their relationship. This may be the case, for example, if:

(a) the client is vulnerable and places significant trust and reliance on the dealer or adviser and the dealer or adviser accepts this responsibility, and

(b) where the dealer or adviser has explicit (as in the case of a managed account) or implicit (as in the case of a non-managed account where the client essentially always follows the advice provided) discretion or power over the client.

Recently, there have been important international developments on the issue of a best interest standard. In the United States, staff of the Securities and Exchange Commission recommended introducing a common statutory best interest standard for investment advisers and broker-dealers when they are providing personalized advice to retail customers. They are currently conducting extensive cost-benefit analysis on this recommendation as a prelude to publishing a draft rule for comment. In Australia, the government recently passed legislation that will make advisers subject to a best interest duty when providing personal advice to retail clients. In the United Kingdom and the European Union (EU), firms are already required to act honestly, fairly and professionally in accordance with the best interests of their clients.

In accordance with the OSC's *2012-2013 Statement of Priorities*, we participated in the publication on October 25, 2012 of *CSA Consultation Paper 33-403 The Standard of Conduct for Advisers and Dealers: Exploring the Appropriateness of Introducing a Statutory Best Interest Duty When Advice is Provided to Retail Clients*, and encourage interested stakeholders to participate in this consultation process. We are also continuing to monitor the fiduciary duty debate internationally, as well as related policy developments in the US, Australia, the UK and the EU.

1.3 — OTC derivatives regulation

Working with the CSA, we are continuing to develop proposals for the regulation of over-the-counter (OTC) derivatives to meet Canada's G20 commitments made following the recent global financial crisis. The proposals cover the regulation of derivatives market participants, trading, clearing, margin, capital and collateral, and trade reporting to a trade repository. The OSC, led by our Derivatives Branch, has been a key participant in developing these proposals.

Since the CSA published its high-level consultation paper on *OTC Derivatives Regulation in Canada* in late 2010, the CSA has also published the following consultation papers on these specific areas:

- reporting trades to a trade repository

- surveillance and enforcement of trades

- segregation and portability of collateral in OTC derivatives clearing

- exemptions from the regulatory requirements (the end-user exemption), and

- central counterparty clearing.

See the *Derivatives section* on our website to view these consultation papers.

Over the next few months, the CSA plans to publish three additional consultation papers for comment. These papers will address

- the registration and regulation of derivatives market participants,

- exchange and platform trading, and

---

[2]Section 2.1 of OSC Rule 31-505 Conditions of Registration.

- capital and collateral.

Dealers and advisers in OTC derivatives should particularly monitor the proposals for the registration and regulation of derivatives market participants.

The CSA will consider the feedback from the consultation process when it develops rules for OTC derivatives regulation in Canada.

1.4 — Review of prospectus exemptions

We recognize that the exempt market in Canada has become increasingly important for investors and issuers. Accordingly, as part of a CSA policy review, we continue to assess whether the existing minimum amount and accredited investor prospectus exemptions remain appropriate or whether changes should be made. OSC Staff has also broadened the scope of this review to consider

- the exempt market regulatory regime more generally, and

- whether we should introduce other prospectus exemptions to facilitate capital raising for business enterprises.

For example, we are looking at the experience of other CSA jurisdictions with prospectus exemptions not currently available in Ontario and relevant developments in other jurisdictions.

We intend to publish a second consultation note (to follow November 2011's *CSA Consultation Note 45-401 Review of Minimum Amount and Accredited Investor Exemptions*) about the proposed introduction of any new prospectus exemptions and, if so, under what circumstances or terms. We will also hold public consultation sessions and reach out to investors and other stakeholders to obtain their feedback. We also established an Exempt Market Advisory Committee to provide advice on these issues. Although this initiative is being led at the OSC by our Corporate Finance Branch, the CRR Branch is also involved since this initiative may have important implications for EMDs and other registrants.

For more information, see *OSC Staff Notice 45-707 OSC Broadening Scope of Review of Prospectus Exemptions*.

2. — Focusing on KYC and suitability assessments by registrants

One of the cardinal rules under securities law is for dealers and advisers to know their clients and to recommend suitable investments for them. We continue to identify significant deficiencies in compliance by some registrants with their KYC and suitability obligations and unsuitable investments are a common subject of investor complaints. Accordingly, we continue to focus our resources on assessing whether registrants are meeting their KYC and suitability obligations.

2.1 — Highlights of recent enforcement case on KYC and suitability of recommendations

In April 2012, the OSC approved a settlement agreement between Staff and Trapeze Asset Management Inc. (Trapeze), a firm registered as a PM and EMD, and two of its advising representatives, for breaching KYC and suitability obligations owed to clients between September 2006 and August 2010.

At certain points in time over the period, many clients experienced substantial declines in the market values of their accounts at Trapeze. Trapeze admitted in the settlement that, in some cases, they did not adequately ascertain the client's investment needs and objectives and risk tolerance. Further, Trapeze admitted that they inaccurately assessed the risk associated with many of the investments purchased on behalf of clients in managed accounts resulting in a failure to ensure that investments Trapeze made on behalf of clients were suitable for all clients. The settlement required Trapeze to hire an independent consultant to review its practices and procedures regarding its KYC and suitability obligations (including for determining risk levels of individual securities and portfolios of securities), to conduct client account reviews for all clients in accordance with those new practices and procedures, and to ensure that the investments in each clients' accounts are suitable. Trapeze also agreed to an administrative penalty of $1 million and to pay $250,000 towards investigation costs.

This is an important case that demonstrates the serious implications for registrants that fail to comply with their KYC and suitability requirements. We encourage PMs and dealers to review the details of this settlement, and to ensure that their KYC and suitability processes and practices are in compliance with Ontario securities law.

For more information, see *Trapeze settlement*.

2.2 — Suitability sweep and new initiative to contact investors

In addition to Trapeze, our compliance reviews continue to identify significant deficiencies with respect to some dealers' and PMs' compliance with their KYC, KYP, and suitability obligations to clients. For example, KYC information such as the client's investment needs and objectives, financial circumstances and risk tolerance is not always collected and documented, or the information is not kept current. Further, at some dealers there is inadequate product knowledge among dealing representatives that recommend products to clients. For both dealers and PMs, we found that some investments were not suitable for clients based on the KYC information that was collected and documented. We also found some PMs that did not adhere to the clients' asset mix or investment instructions for their investment portfolios.

We have also found cases where registrants were improperly relying on the accredited investor exemption for the distribution of prospectus-exempt securities to clients. A registrant is required to determine, before a client purchases prospectus-exempt securities, that the client qualifies as an accredited investor or that the client can rely on another prospectus exemption. This is a key part of the registrant's KYC and suitability obligations. It is also important for registrants who recommend that their clients borrow money to purchase securities to determine that the use of leverage is suitable for the clients.

To address these concerns, in June 2012 we started a targeted review (sweep) of over 85 EMDs and PMs to assess their compliance with their KYC, KYP and suitability obligations under sections 13.2 and 13.3 of NI 31-103.

This sweep introduced our new approach of contacting a sample of a dealer's or adviser's clients as part of our normal course compliance reviews. Although we've contacted investors in the past as part of for-cause reviews, this was the first time we contacted investors as a routine part of our compliance review process. Clients who are contacted may be asked a number of questions about their registrant firm and dealing or advising representative, including the completeness and accuracy of their KYC information obtained by the firm and the investment recommendations and advice provided to them. Clients' participation in this process is voluntary. We've found that investor contact is a valuable method to assess if their registrant is complying with Ontario securities law. Our new approach of contacting investors will be used for our ongoing reviews of dealers and advisers. For more information, see *OSC new review procedure of calling investors*.

Although our suitability sweep is ongoing, at this time, we have identified the following preliminary findings:

Findings for both EMDs and PMs:
- some registrants inadequately collect and/or document KYC information which is required to confirm a client's identity, ascertain if the client is an insider of a reporting issuer and to assess the suitability of proposed investments
- some registrants made unsuitable investments for clients. For example, a PM invested in the securities of only three companies for its smaller managed accounts resulting in a non-diversified and higher risk portfolio that was unsuitable based on the clients' KYC information
- some registrants have inadequate or no written policies and procedures on their KYC, KYP and/or suitability obligations
- some registrants did not meet the relationship disclosure information obligations (in section 14.2(2)(k) of NI 31-103) because the document provided to clients did not state that the firm has an obligation to assess whether a purchase or sale of a security is suitable for a client prior to executing the transaction or at any other time.

Findings for EMDs:
- some EMDs improperly relied on the accredited investor exemption when distributing prospectus-exempt securities to investors. For example, some EMDs documented in their client files that investors were accredited investors. However, our review indicated that the information collected about the investors' net income or net financial assets was not consistent with the test for their status as accredited investors
- some EMDs did not collect specific KYC information to demonstrate compliance with their use of the accredited investor exemption. For example, the EMD's KYC form collects information on the client's "net worth" rather than their "net financial assets", when the "greater than $1 million in net financial assets" test was used to determine the client's status as an accredited investor

We encourage EMDs to review section 5.2.1 of this report for suggested practices on KYC, KYP and suitability obligations, and on the use of the accredited investor exemption.

Findings for PMs:
- ssome PMs did not update KYC information at least annually, or met with their clients at least annually to update KYC information but did not maintain any record of the meeting or document any KYC updates
- some PMs improperly delegated their KYC and suitability responsibilities to another party. See discussion of this deficiency in section 5.2A of *OSC Staff Notice 33-736 2011 Annual Summary Report for Dealers, Advisers and Investment Fund Managers* (OSC Staff Notice 33-736)

We also noted some best practices during our reviews of PMs, which we encourage all PMs to consider:

Best practices for PMs:
- An advising representative has meaningful discussions with a prospective client at a number of in-person meetings to fully understand the client and their circumstances and to explain to them the PM's investment philosophy and strategies. To assist in this process, the advising representative uses a financial planning questionnaire.
- The advising representative uses the information obtained from the in-person meetings and questionnaire to develop a tailored investment policy statement (IPS) for each client which is used as a plan to manage the client's portfolio. The IPS documents the client's investment needs and objectives, risk tolerance, financial circumstances, time horizon, liquidity requirements, tax considerations, and any legal, regulatory or other requirements or information. The IPS also sets out a planned asset allocation. Each client signs and receives a copy of his or her completed questionnaire and IPS to ensure it is complete and accurate.
- At least annually, the advising representative meets with the client to discuss the IPS and their portfolio, or as soon as possible after their circumstances change. If the advising representative revises the IPS, the client signs and receives a copy. If there is no change to the IPS, the client confirms in writing that their IPS remains current and valid.

If we identify significant deficiencies in compliance by dealers or advisers with their KYC, KYP and suitability obligations (such as unsuitable investments), we will take appropriate regulatory action, including referrals to our Enforcement Branch. Once our sweep is completed, we will review the results to assess if further guidance is needed about KYC, KYP and suitability obligations. In the meantime, we strongly encourage firms to review the above findings and perform their own self-assessment for compliance with the KYC, KYP and suitability obligations.

2.3 — "Online" delivery platforms: KYC and suitability obligations

From time to time, we are presented with new business models developed by industry participants. Recently, an investment dealer sought relief for a novel business model: a full service brokerage service including suitability recommendations delivered through an online security trading platform with involvement by registered representatives.

In August 2012, the OSC granted relief to this investment dealer from the obligation to register as an adviser in order to provide suitability advice (i.e., investment recommendations to clients) in the ordinary course of its dealer business. Providing suitability advice via a hybrid online platform is novel but this model otherwise fits within the existing regulatory framework. Section 8.23 of NI 31-103 allows a registered dealer to provide suitability recommendations without also having to register as an adviser, so long as the client does not have a managed account. As an IIROC member, this investment dealer also required and obtained relief from certain IIROC rules.

This relief relates to the ability of an IIROC member to provide investment dealer services through an online platform with registered representative involvement. This business model is not a new type of service outside of existing registration categories, nor does it represent a lowering of the suitability standards (it is not, for example, "discount brokerage plus advice", "discount advice" or "advice-lite"). The element of suitability advice here is consistent with the suitability advice that a traditional individual registered representative, without having to be registered as a PM, is expected and obliged to provide in his relationship with a client.

We continue to support innovative business models developed by industry that can benefit investors. For more information, see the decision *In the matter of BMO InvestorLine Inc.*, dated August 1, 2012.

3. — Acting on registrant misconduct

3.1 — Registrant misconduct cases of interest

We stay alert for signs of potential registrant misconduct or fraud and when we find evidence of this we take appropriate steps. The CRR Branch works together with the Enforcement Branch to maintain an effective compliance-enforcement continuum for registrants, and to take appropriate regulatory actions when justified. These include sanctions such as the suspension or termination of the registration of a registered firm and/or its registered individuals, administrative penalties, and disgorgement of monies.

In addition to the Trapeze case, some notable registrant misconduct cases from the past year are summarized below. Please note that some cases are still ongoing. To get more information on a particular case, click on the respondent's name. Documents related to OSC proceedings before the Commission and before the Courts are available on our website under *OSC Proceedings*. Further, *Director's Decisions* from the CRR Branch are also available under the Information for Dealers, Advisers and IFMs section of our website.

Roger Rowan, Watt Carmichael Inc., Harry Carmichael, and Michael McKenney v. Ontario Securities Commission (March 29, 2012). Mr. Rowan was a director of Biovail Corporation (Biovail), and a registered representative with Watt Carmichael Inc., an investment dealer with discretionary trading authority over a number of trust accounts that held securities of Biovail. The trust accounts were set up by Eugene Melnyk, the former chairman of Biovail. The Commission had previously found that Mr. Rowan had traded millions of Biovail shares, generating over $2.3 million in commissions for Watt Carmichael Inc. over a two-year period, and that he breached Ontario securities law by failing to file insider reports in respect of these trades. The Commission also found Watt Carmichael Inc., Mr. Carmichael (the firm's ultimate designated person), and Mr. McKenney (the firm's chief compliance officer) had failed to adequately supervise Mr. Rowan's trading activities in Biovail shares. The Commission assessed administrative monetary penalties against the registrants under section 127(1)9 of the Act. In addition, the Commission rejected the registrants' challenge to the constitutionality of section 127(1)9. The registrants appealed the Commission's decision before the Divisional Court, which upheld the Commission's decision, and then to the Court of Appeal for Ontario, which upheld the provision. The Court rejected the arguments by the firm, Mr. Carmichael and Mr. McKenney that the Commission's finding that they had failed to adequately supervise Mr. Rowan was unreasonable.

Re Daniel Sternberg, Parkwood GP Inc., and Philco Consulting Inc. (April 26, 2012). Mr. Sternberg, who was not registered, was the principal of the general partner of a limited partnership which operated as an investment fund. The fund had retained a registered PM, but Mr. Sternberg provided advisory services to this PM in respect of the fund, and the PM remitted most of the management fees it received from the fund to Mr. Sternberg. Mr. Sternberg also acted in furtherance of trades in units of the fund. When we discovered what Mr. Sternberg was doing, he undertook in writing to cease performing registrable activities, but he failed to do so and continued to perform registrable activities. The Commission subsequently approved a settlement agreement between Staff and Mr. Sternberg to settle proceedings brought by the Enforcement Branch. The terms of the settlement agreement included a prohibition on Mr. Sternberg becoming a registrant for a period of one year.

Re Swift Trade Inc., Peter Beck, and others (June 21, 2012). Swift Trade Inc. was registered as an EMD until it dissolved in December 2010. Swift Trade Inc. and the other respondents were involved in a large-volume day-trading business. The operation involved several thousand traders located in Ontario and around the world, none of whom were registered in Ontario, placing orders on marketplaces in Canada, the US, the UK and elsewhere. In March 2009, the CRR Branch conducted a compliance review of Swift Trade Inc. that identified conduct which, in its view, constituted breaches of Ontario securities law, including failing to establish proper supervisory processes, not properly recording business transactions, employing compliance personnel with an insufficient understanding of Swift Trade Inc.'s complicated business structure, failing to detect questionable trading, and trading being conducted through unregistered entities. On June 21, 2012, a hearing panel of the Commission approved a settlement agreement between staff of the Commission, Swift Trade Inc., Peter Beck, and the other respondents in which the respondents agreed, among other things, to a statement of facts relating to their conduct, to pay an administrative monetary penalty, costs, and also to prohibitions, specific to each respondent, pertaining to trading securities, and becoming registrants for varying lengths of time.

Re M.H. (January 5, 2012), *Re Pyasetsky* (February 28, 2012), and *Re Couto* (April 20, 2012). Each of these cases involved an applicant for registration as a mutual fund dealing representative who omitted to disclose a material fact on their application; or who otherwise made misleading statements to Staff during the course of the application process. In each case, the Director refused the application for registration after offering the applicant an opportunity to be heard. Ms. Pyasetsky is currently seeking a review of the decision of her case by a Panel of the Commission.

Re Blueport and Hare (December 13, 2011, with written reasons issued January 12, 2012) and *Re Morgan Dragon Development Corp., John Cheong, and Herman Tse* (January 27, 2012, with written reasons issued February 10, 2012). Each of these cases involved an EMD in respect of which serious deficiencies were identified following a compliance review, including the inappropriate use of investor money. In both cases the firm and its registered individuals were suspended by the Director after an opportunity to be heard. Because the Director considered the registrants' ongoing registration to be a significant risk to investors, the registrants were suspended at the conclusion of the opportunity to be heard, with written reasons being issued a short time later. The registrants in *Morgan Dragon* were also referred to the Enforcement Branch, and a Statement of Allegations was issued on March 22, 2012. A hearing before the Commission into the allegations contained in the Statement of Allegations has not yet occurred.

David Phillips and John Wilson. On June 4, 2012, the Enforcement Branch issued a Statement of Allegations against David Phillips and John Wilson arising out of their involvement with First Leaside Securities Inc., an investment dealer, and F.L. Securities Inc., an EMD. Both companies are members of the First Leaside Group, and in February 2012 both companies had their registration suspended and also obtained protection from creditors under the *Companies Creditors Arrangement Act*. The Statement of Allegations alleges that Phillips and Wilson directed and oversaw the sale of First Leaside Group equity and debt offerings which raised approximately $19 million from investors. The Statement of Allegations also alleges that Phillips and Wilson did not properly disclose the fact that an independent accounting firm had recently issued a report commenting negatively on the financial status of the First Leaside Group. A hearing before the Commission into the allegations contained in the Statement of Allegations has not yet occurred.

Gentree Asset Management Inc. Gentree Asset Management Inc. was registered as a PM and EMD. A compliance review of this firm identified serious issues, including that the firm planned to correct a large working capital deficiency by selling securities of itself. The matter was referred to the Enforcement Branch, and the firm had its registration suspended by way of temporary orders dated August 17, 2011 and September 26, 2011. On March 27, 2012, a Statement of Allegations was issued alleging that the firm sold securities on a prospectus-exempt basis to individuals who did not qualify for an exemption, that some investor proceeds were used in a manner not disclosed in the offering memorandum, that the firm failed to meet the minimum working capital requirements of NI 31-103, and that the firm did not maintain proper books and records. A hearing before the Commission into the allegations contained in the Statement of Allegations has not yet occurred.

Colby Cooper Capital Inc. Colby Cooper Capital Inc. (Colby Cooper) was a registered EMD until its registration was suspended by the Director on January 31, 2012 because it did not have a properly qualified chief compliance officer. Following a compliance review, on March 27, 2012, the Enforcement Branch issued a Statement of Allegations against Colby Cooper, several related companies and their directing mind, Lee Mason. The Statement of Allegations alleges that Colby Cooper engaged unregistered individuals to conduct a high-pressure telephone sales campaign selling securities of a related issuer which falsely represented that it would use investor funds to develop oil and gas properties in Alberta and Texas, when in fact the funds were put to other uses, including financing Mr. Mason's lifestyle. A hearing before the Commission into the allegations contained in the Statement of Allegations has not yet occurred.

Re Sextant Capital Management Inc., Otto Spork, and others (June 1, 2012). In May 2011, a hearing Panel of the Commission found that Sextant Capital Management Inc., formerly a PM and EMD, had engaged in fraud by falsely inflating the value of its investment fund, and receiving performance fees and management fees based on those inflated values. This matter had been referred to the Enforcement Branch as a result of the concerns identified from a compliance review of this firm in the fall of 2008. On June 1, 2012, the Commission released its decision on sanctions, which included, among other things, suspensions of corporate and individual registrations, and orders for the payment of administrative monetary penalties, disgorgement, and costs. The Commission's decision is being appealed.

Re New Solutions Capital Inc., Ron Ovenden, and others. New Solutions Capital Inc. was formerly registered as an EMD, and Ron Ovenden was its ultimate designated person. As a result of the findings from a compliance review of this firm, the matter was referred to the Enforcement Branch, which obtained a temporary order on April 11, 2012 ceasing all trading by New Solutions Capital Inc. in a number of related issuers. (This order was subsequently extended.) The basis for the temporary order was that it appeared to the Commission that New Solutions Capital Inc. may have failed to deal fairly, honestly, and in good faith with its clients, may have made misrepresentations to clients, and may have contravened the anti-fraud provisions of the Act. On April 12, 2012, we notified the registrants that we had recommended to the Director that their registrations be suspended, and on April 13, 2012, the firm's chief compliance officer resigned. On April 26, 2012, the Director suspended the registrants on the basis that their ongoing registration would be objectionable in light of the temporary order against it, and on the basis that the firm did not have a chief compliance officer.

Re Sawh and Trkulja. (August 1, 2012). Sawh and Trkulja were formerly dealing representatives in the categories of MFD and EMD, and were the principals of a dealer named The Investment House of Canada. In 2009, Sawh and Trkulja settled disciplinary proceedings brought against them by the MFDA on terms that included their firm's resignation from membership in the MFDA, which also resulted in the suspension of their individual registration under the Act. In the settlement agreement with the MFDA, Sawh and Trkulja admitted to misconduct pertaining to the sale of certain prospectus-exempt securities. After entering into the settlement agreement, Sawh and Trkulja applied for a reinstatement of their registration as mutual fund and exempt market dealing representatives. On November 2, 2010, an opportunity to be heard was held, following which the Director issued a written decision refusing to grant either individual's application. Sawh and Trkulja then applied to the Commission for a hearing and review of the Director's decision under section 8 of the Act. In comprehensive reasons issued August 1, 2012, the Commission reviewed the general legal principles relating to suitability for registration under the Act, as well as the duties imposed on registrants by Ontario securities law relating to their dealings with clients. The Commission explained how Sawh and Trkulja failed to properly discharge their duties with regards to KYC and suitability, reliance on the accredited investor exemption, KYP requirements, and conflict of interest disclosure. As a result, the Commission dismissed the application for hearing and review, and refused to register either applicant. Sawh and Trkulja have appealed the Commission's decision to the Divisional Court.

4. — Registration of firms and individuals

The registration requirements under securities law helps to protect investors from unfair, improper or fraudulent practices by participants in the securities markets. The information required to support a registration allows us to assess a firm's and individual's fitness for registration, including whether a firm is able to carry out its obligations under securities law and an individual's proficiency, integrity and solvency. These fitness requirements are the cornerstones of the registration requirements.

4.1 — New registration requirements

4.1.1 — Registration of non-resident IFMs

The new regime for registrants introduced a registration requirement for every firm that directs the business, operations or affairs of an investment fund. All IFMs operating in Canada prior to September 28, 2009 were required to apply for registration in the jurisdiction where their head office is located by September 28, 2010.

On July 5, 2012, we published Multilateral Instrument 32-102 *Registration Exemptions for Non-Resident Investment Fund Managers* (MI 32-102) on the registration requirements that apply in Ontario, Quebec and Newfoundland and Labrador to non-resident IFMs, which includes

- international IFMs who carry out investment fund management activities outside of Canada, and

- domestic IFMs who do not have a place of business in the province.

Under MI 32-102, we require registration of all non-resident IFMs that have a significant connecting factor to Ontario unless they can rely on one of the available exemptions. This initiative will enhance our regulatory oversight of IFMs and provide greater protection to Ontario investors from the ongoing operational risks associated with investment funds regardless of where the IFM is located.

Non-resident IFMs will not be required to register in Ontario if

- there are no Ontario security holders in an investment fund that is managed by the non-resident IFM,

- the non-resident IFM does not actively solicit Ontario residents after September 27, 2012, or

- an investment fund managed by the non-resident IFM only has "permitted clients" and other conditions are met (only for international IFMs).

MI 32-102 and the exemptions came into force on September 28, 2012. If a non-resident IFM does not intend to rely on one of the exemptions, then it must apply for registration by December 31, 2012.

For more information, see *MI 32-102*.

4.1.2 — Registration and oversight of foreign broker-dealers

Since publishing *CSA Staff Notice 31-327 Broker-Dealer Registration in the Exempt Market Dealer Category* on September 2, 2011, we have undertaken a consultation process with stakeholders. We distributed a survey to all EMDs to determine which firms are engaging in brokerage activities (trading securities listed on an exchange in foreign or Canadian markets). We met with stakeholders including IIROC member firms and Financial Industry Regulatory Authority (FINRA) member firms. The results of the survey showed that this issue is specific to US broker-dealer firms who are FINRA members. We worked collaboratively with IIROC and involved FINRA.

On July 12, 2012 we published CSA Staff Notice 31-331 *Follow-Up to Broker-Dealer Registration in the Exempt Market Dealer Category* (CSA Staff Notice 31-331). The notice introduced an IIROC concept paper developed in response to the CSA's and IIROC's concerns. The IIROC concept paper, also published on July 12 as IIROC Notice 12-0217, proposes a framework for the oversight of these firms under a new class of IIROC member called a "Restricted Dealer Member". Based on the proposal, firms would surrender their EMD or restricted dealer registration and apply for investment dealer registration as well as seek IIROC membership.

As next steps, we will review any comments received on the IIROC proposal. At the conclusion of the consultation period, IIROC may make changes to its by-laws and rules. We may also propose changes to NI 31-103 to expressly limit the types of activities that EMDs can conduct.

For more information, see *CSA Staff Notice 31-331*.

4.2 — Current trends in registration issues

Internet platforms and other unregistered entities engaged in registrable activities

Over the last year, we have considered a number of situations involving market participants that, although not dealers or advisers in the traditional sense, appear to be engaged in registrable trading or advising activities. In these cases, we have assessed whether these entities should be considered "in the business" of trading or advising and therefore subject to the dealer or adviser registration requirement under the Act.

To assist these entities in determining their status, we will generally refer them to the guidance in section 1.3 of Companion Policy 31-103CP *Registration Requirements, Exemptions and Ongoing Registrant Obligations* (31-103CP). We also remind these entities that the definition of "trade" is very broad and includes "any act, advertisement, solicitation, conduct or negotiation directly or indirectly in furtherance of" a trade.

The question of whether these entities satisfy the "business trigger" will generally be fact-specific and may not apply to all entities engaged in such activities. Some examples of entities that we consider to be in the business of trading or advising include

- an internet platform that seeks to showcase investment opportunities to investors in return for fees from issuers and dealers that advertise on the platform;

- an angel investor organization or investment club that identifies investment opportunities for members, assists with due diligence on investments, and provides updates on the performance of investments in return for membership fees and, in some cases, fees and/or broker warrants granted as compensation on investments (collectively broker-type compensation);

- an issuer that filed a final prospectus that indicated that an offering would be made through an agent but subsequently marketed the offering through active client solicitation and sold 87% of the offering itself; and

- "finders" and "investor relations" entities who participate in private placements and prospectus offerings in return for broker-type compensation.

We continue to support innovative business models developed by industry that can benefit investors. In the case of entities that seek to advertise investment opportunities to investors through the internet, depending on the business model, we are open to considering exemptive relief from certain dealer requirements if these requirements are not appropriate for this type of entity, and if investor protection concerns can otherwise be adequately addressed.

Mortgage investment entities (MIEs)

In February 2011, we issued guidance on the registration requirements that apply to MIEs in each CSA jurisdiction in CSA Staff Notice 31-323 *Guidance Relating to the Registration Obligations of Mortgage Investment Entities* (CSA Staff Notice 31-323). However, we have identified a number of MIEs doing business in Ontario that have not applied for registration. We have sent these MIEs a letter requesting a response to our registration questions and concerns, and are assessing their responses. We are also considering additional measures for these identified MIEs and any other firms that are performing registrable activities in Ontario without registration, which may involve regulatory action. Therefore, MIEs, or firms which provide services to MIEs, which are carrying out registrable activities in Ontario should review and act on the information in *CSA Staff Notice 31-323*.

Designating a chief compliance officer (CCO)

From time to time, we receive a notification from a registered firm that their CCO has left unexpectedly, and that they do not currently employ an individual who meets the proficiency requirements for registration as a CCO.

We remind registered firms of the requirement under section 11.3 of NI 31-103 to designate an individual as CCO who meets the conditions for registration, including the required proficiency. Registered firms should therefore consider how they would be able to fulfill this requirement if their registered CCO were to suddenly resign or be unable to execute his or her responsibilities. For example, a firm may wish to ensure that it has one or more individuals who have the required proficiency and are familiar with the firm's compliance system so that the individual may step in as the CCO on a temporary or ongoing basis if the need arises.

If firms are not able to register a replacement CCO within a reasonable period of time, we may recommend regulatory action such as the imposition of terms and conditions or suspension of the firm's registration.

Outside business activities

We have noted that some CCOs and dealing representatives of EMDs, MFDs and SPDs have employment or other business activities outside the registrant. In a number of cases, we have found that these outside business activities (OBAs) create a potential conflict of interest or place the registrant in a position of power or influence.

For example, we have seen situations where

- lawyers who are employed with law firms apply as CCOs or dealing representatives of registered firms or seek to register their own EMD or PM firms and register themselves as Ultimate Designated Persons (UDPs), CCOs, and in some cases, dealing or advising representatives of the firm, and

- dealing representatives sponsored by MFDs and SPDs who are also employed as teachers or healthcare workers, who are involved with organizations that have a religious affiliation, or who are employed by or affiliated with childcare providers.

To address these situations, in some cases, we have imposed terms and conditions on a firm's or a representative's registration, including restricting them from dealing with individuals over whom they have power or influence. For example, lawyers would be restricted from dealing in securities with clients of their law firm, and teachers would be restricted from dealing with their students and their students' close family members.

We have also noted a trend with small firms that are registered or seeking registration as EMDs, hiring a CCO that has other full-time or part-time employment. Many of these individuals appear to be a CCO "in name only" and are being offered the CCO position mainly because they meet the proficiency requirements under NI 31-103. Sometimes, such individuals may not truly be part of the registrant's compliance function and organizational structure. For example, we have found that some of these CCOs are not physically located at the office of the EMD and only work a few hours per week in their role at the EMD. Sometimes, these individual applicants act as consultants to other registrants. All successful CCO applicants must demonstrate that they can effectively maintain and oversee the registrant's compliance system. This means that CCO applicants must have the appropriate amount of involvement, time and resources to fulfill their regulatory obligations, and must be able to manage any conflict of interest issues that may exist in a dual employment situation.

We remind registered firms of their obligation to ensure the OBAs of the individuals they sponsor do not impair or impede the performance of their regulatory obligations. See *CSA Staff Notice 31-326 Outside Business Activities* for issues to consider when reviewing the circumstances of an individual's OBAs.

We also wish to remind registrants that all OBAs must be disclosed in Form 33-109F4 (or Form 33-109F5 for changes in OBAs after registration). Required disclosure includes

- having a paid or unpaid role with a charitable or religious organization,

- serving as an officer or director, and

- being a significant owner of a holding company.

Misrepresentations in registration applications

We have been conducting a more in-depth review of applications for registration from firms and individuals involved or proposing to be involved in higher-risk activities (e.g., firms that intend to deal in securities of related or connected issuers, and individuals that are officers or directors of a reporting issuer). We find that some applicants appear to be making material misrepresentations in their applications, including

- not disclosing full-time employment outside the registrant;

- not disclosing the failure to meet a financial obligation of $5,000 or more as it came due; or

- in cases where the firm does not have a Chief Executive Officer, the designated UDP is not the most senior decision-maker in the firm.

We also noted omissions after registration has been granted, such as new shareholders, officers or directors not filing the required application form as a permitted individual.

We remind firms of their obligations under section 5.1 of National Instrument 33-109 *Registration Information* (*NI 33-109*) to ensure applications include truthful and complete information and that the information is updated as required under sections 3.1 and 4.1 of NI 33-109.

Late filings

We have also seen a trend in registrants incurring late fees for failing to meet the filing deadlines set out in NI 33-109. For example, registered and permitted individuals do not disclose their OBAs or information related to criminal, civil or financial disclosure. This non-disclosure may occur either at the initial application stage or after a change takes place after they have been registered and we are not notified on a timely basis. For example, on October 1, 2012, a firm files a late Form 33-109F5 which updates information on a Form 33-109F4. That firm must pay a late fee within 30 days (by October 31, 2012) or be automatically suspended.

Also, many registered firms incur late fees because they fail to file their Form 13-502F4 *Capital Markets Participation Fee Calculation* by December 1 of each calendar year.

We remind registrants that when late fees remain unpaid for more than 30 days after they are due, the firm's registration is automatically suspended in accordance with section 29(1) of the Act.

Common deficiencies from registration applications

In last year's report, we outlined common deficiencies from our review of firms' and individuals' registration applications, along with actions to be taken to avoid the deficiencies. From our review of this year's common deficiencies, we found many similar deficiencies, and as such do not repeat them here. To access last year's guidance (which continues to apply), see section 4.3 of *OSC Staff Notice 33-736*.

4.3 — Common deficiencies from notices on proposed ownership changes or asset acquisitions of a registrant and suggested practices

Under sections 11.9 and 11.10 of NI 31-103, an acquirer and/or a registered firm must give notice in the case of certain acquisitions of a registered firm's assets or securities. If we notify the registered firm or person making the acquisition that we object to the acquisition within 30 days of the receipt of such notice, then the acquisition must not occur until the objection is withdrawn.

To decide whether or not to object, we examine whether the acquisition is:

- likely to give rise to a conflict of interest,

- likely to hinder the registered firm in complying with securities legislation,

- inconsistent with an adequate level of investor protection, or

- otherwise prejudicial to the public interest.

We often find that the notice filed does not provide sufficient information for us to make this determination. Accordingly, we have to request additional information, which may result in further delays before we can make a final decision.

The following are suggested practices to prepare a section 11.9 or 11.10 notice. We acknowledge that some of these suggested practices may not be relevant depending on the type of transaction or specific facts.

Suggested practices

- Provide details about the business reasons for the transaction.

- Set out details about the registered firm's operations and business plan after closing. The information regarding any changes to business operations should include details required in Item 3.1 of the Form 33-109F6 *Firm Registration* (i.e., primary business activities, target market, and the products and services it provides to clients).

- Include any significant changes to business operations and any changes to the CCO, the UDP, key management, directors, officers, permitted individuals or registered individuals. If no changes are contemplated, confirm this is the case.

- Discuss whether the registered firm has written policies and procedures in place to address any conflicts of interest that may arise.

- If there is a potential conflict of interest because of the transaction, explain how this conflict of interest has been addressed.

- Discuss whether the parties to the transaction have adequate resources to ensure compliance with all applicable conditions of registration.

- Discuss whether directors, officers, partners, advising representatives and dealing representatives of the registered firm, if applicable, will be in compliance with section 4.1 of NI 31-103 (restrictions on acting for another registered firm).

- Provide details of any client communications in connection with the transaction that have been made or are planned. If you do not propose to communicate with clients about the transaction, advise us and explain why.

- Provide a copy of the press release announcing the transaction. If you do not plan to issue a press release, advise us and explain why.

- Confirm the proposed closing date.

- Provide corporate charts (before and after the closing of the transaction) that include all affiliated companies and subsidiaries of the registered firm.

Part 3: REGISTRATION

- On the charts provided, identify any companies or affiliates which are registered under the Act and/or the *Commodity Futures Act* and specify their category of registration.
- Where any individuals are shown on the corporate charts as holding an interest in a company, partnership or trust, confirm whether the individual holds that interest directly or through a holding company, trust or other entity (a Holdco). If ownership is through a Holdco, provide the name of the Holdco and its ownership structure.

Acting on the above suggested practices will help us to assess a proposed transaction while minimizing the exchange of correspondence that can sometimes cause additional delays.

4.4 — New initiatives

Enhanced transparency of communications with registrants

In the past, when we recommended that an individual's registration be refused or be subject to terms and conditions or amendment, a letter that provided written notice of the recommendation and brief reasons for it was provided only to the individual (and not also to their sponsoring firm). The sponsoring firm was sent a written notice outlining our recommendation and informing them of the individual's right to be heard and that the reasons were provided to the individual. As a result, the sponsoring firm was not always aware of the reasons for the recommendation.

We now also provide the individual's sponsoring firm with the reasons underlying the recommendation. This will improve the transparency of our communications with registrants and will assist sponsoring firms in ensuring the accuracy and completeness of information that they provide to us for individuals that they sponsor. For more information, see *OSC Staff Notice 33-737 Enhanced Transparency of Communications with Registrants.*

5. — Information for dealers, advisers and investment fund managers

The information in this section includes the key findings and outcomes from our ongoing compliance reviews of the registrants we directly regulate. We highlight deficiencies from our reviews and provide suggested practices to address those deficiencies. The suggested practices are intended to give guidance to registrants to help them comply with their regulatory obligations, as they provide our interpretations of the legal requirements and our expectations of registrants. We also discuss new or proposed rules and initiatives impacting registrants.

This part of the report is divided into five main sections. The first section contains general information that is relevant for all registrants. The other sections contain information specific to EMDs, SPDs, PMs and IFMs, respectively. This report is organized to allow a registrant to focus on reading the section for all registrants and the sections that apply to their registration categories. However, we recommend that registrants review all sections in this part, as some of the information presented for one type of registrant may be relevant to other registrants.

5.1 — All registrants

This section outlines our compliance review process and its outcomes, current trends in deficiencies and suggested practices to address them, and details new and proposed rules and initiatives impacting all registrants.

5.1.1 — Compliance review process and its outcomes

We conduct compliance reviews of selected registered firms on a continuous basis. Generally, we select registrants for review using a risk-based approach. However, we occasionally select firms for review on a random basis to help us evaluate the effectiveness of our risk-based approach. Compliance reviews of registered firms generally focus on their conduct, practices, operations and capital adequacy. The risk-based approach is intended to identify those registrants that are most likely to have material issues, including risk of harm to investors. We normally conduct compliance reviews on-site at a registrant's premises, but may also perform reviews from our offices, which are known as desk reviews. The majority of reviews are proactive in nature, but we also perform reviews on a for-cause basis where we are aware of a potential compliance issue, for example, from a complaint or a referral from another OSC branch, an SRO or another regulator. We also conduct sweeps, which are compliance reviews of a sample of registered firms on a specific topic or in an industry sector over a short period of time. Sweeps allow us to respond on a timely basis to industry-wide concerns or issues.

The purpose of compliance reviews is to assess compliance with Ontario securities law. In most cases, the deficiencies noted are raised with the firm reviewed so that appropriate corrective action can be taken. However, we stay alert to any signs of potential registrant misconduct or fraud and will take appropriate steps if we identify these signs. In fiscal 2012, 18% of our compliance reviews resulted in a combination of the following: terms and conditions placed on the firms' registration, referrals to OSC Enforcement for further regulatory action, or the suspension of the firms' registration.

The outcomes of our compliance reviews in fiscal 2012, with comparables for 2011, are presented in the following table and are listed in their increasing order of seriousness. The percentages in the table are based on the registered firms we reviewed during the year and not the population of all registered firms.

Outcomes of compliance reviews (all registration categories)	Fiscal 2012	Fiscal 2011[3]
Enhanced compliance	34%	31%
Significantly enhanced compliance	47%	55%

---

[3]Percentages for 2011 have been revised to conform to our new reporting method for 2012.

Outcomes of compliance reviews (all registration categories)	Fiscal 2012	Fiscal 2011[3]
Terms and conditions on registration	8%	3%
Surrender of registration	1%	1%
Referral to the Enforcement Branch	6%	7%
Suspension of registration	4%	3%

Each outcome is explained in Appendix A. In some cases, there may be more than one outcome from a review. In these cases, the review is counted only under its most serious outcome.

Sweep of higher risk registrants

In June 2011, we sent out an updated and integrated risk assessment questionnaire (RAQ) to all PMs, IFMs and EMDs registered in Ontario. The RAQ included questions on various areas of a firm's operations such as their business activities, financial condition, custody, fee arrangements, marketing practices, and compliance systems. The registrant's responses to each question generated a risk score that was used to rank similarly registered firms. For example, firms registered as IFMs and PMs were ranked against other firms registered as IFMs and PMs. We used the risk scores to help us allocate our resources to higher risk registrants and higher risk activity. Starting in late 2011, we began conducting on-site compliance reviews of firms that had higher risk scores compared to their peers. Our reviews focused on the higher-risk activities of the selected firms. Most reviews resulted in a report issued to the registrant that outlined the deficiencies we found, and that required corrective action by the registrant. Registrants were required to respond to us in writing on how they addressed deficiencies identified as significant, such as an inadequate compliance system. We then assessed whether each registrant had addressed all significant deficiencies. Although our sweep of the higher risk registrants is complete, we continue to use the information we collected on the RAQ to help us decide which firms to review in the future, which areas of their business to focus on, and to identify compliance trends.

What to expect from, and how to prepare for, an OSC compliance review

When a registered firm is selected for an on-site compliance review, we contact the firm's CCO to make arrangements. We explain the focus or scope of the review and the time period that the review will cover. We normally give several business days advance notice before starting a review. However, when appropriate, we may give a shorter or longer advance notice period. We will not defer the start of a review unless there are exceptional circumstances and there is no known risk of harm to investors.

We next send the CCO a list of the registered firm's books and records that we would like to be compiled or made accessible for the start of the review. See *Lists of Books and Records* for examples. Our books and records requests are often customized based on the type and nature of the review. We prefer that registrants provide us with copies of their documents, and when appropriate, that they be made available in an electronic format (e.g., for a record of all trades in securities for clients over the past year). We also request additional books and records after we start the review (e.g., samples of client files).

When we attend a registered firm's offices, we present the CCO with a written designation under section 20 of the Act authorizing us to enter the firm's business premises and inquire into, examine, and copy the firm's books and records. At the start of the review, we usually have a two-to-three hour meeting with senior management of the registrant to obtain a high-level understanding of the firm. We normally expect the UDP, CCO and other senior management to attend this meeting. In general, at least two accountants and sometimes a lawyer will attend all or part of the review for the OSC. The length of time that we are on-site varies depending on the scope and nature of the review, the issues we find, and other factors (including size and complexity of the firm), but is generally between one day and three weeks.

Unless our review is a sweep that is targeting a specific topic only, we generally assess the adequacy of each registrant's compliance system, its internal controls and systems, marketing and sales practices, financial condition, dealing with clients and handling of client accounts. For dealers and advisers, we also generally focus on how they meet their KYC and suitability obligations, including how they research and make investment recommendations for clients. For IFMs, we also generally focus on their fund accounting, transfer agency and trust accounting functions, and oversight of any service providers if these functions are outsourced. We also examine other ongoing obligations of registrants. At the end of each review, we normally communicate any deficiencies with Ontario securities law that require corrective action by the registrant in a report to the CCO. The registered firm is expected to address all matters identified in the report on a timely basis, but must respond to us in writing within 30 days on their actions to address all deficiencies identified as significant. When all significant deficiencies have been satisfactorily addressed, we normally send the CCO a letter stating that our review is closed. However, this letter does not necessarily mean that the registrant is in compliance with all aspects of Ontario securities law. For example, reviews are often focused on a particular area of a firm's business and are therefore not comprehensive, and our reviews test for compliance on a sample basis, and using a risk-based approach.

The best way to prepare for an OSC compliance review is by having an effective compliance system that is appropriate to the registered firm's business. An effective compliance system enables registrants to understand their regulatory obligations, to assess if they are complying with them, and to take corrective action when necessary. In most reviews we aim to help registrants improve their understanding and compliance with Ontario securities law. However, it is not acceptable for registrants to rely on us to inform them of their legal responsibilities and to identify non-compliance. We expect registrants to know and to comply with the law.

For more information, see the *compliance review section* on the OSC website.

The following are suggested practices to prepare for an OSC compliance review.

Suggested practices

- Periodically perform a self-assessment of your firm's compliance with Ontario securities law, or engage a compliance consultant to perform a mock regulatory review, and take corrective action in any areas that are deficient.

- Set out details about the registered firm's operations and business plan after closing. The information regarding any changes to business operations should include details required in Item 3.1 of the Form 33-109F6 *Firm Registration* (i.e., primary business activities, target market, and the products and services it provides to clients).

- If applicable, review your firm's most recent OSC RAQ, and any past compliance review deficiency reports and your responses.

- Be prepared to explain your firm's business, including, but not limited to, your corporate and organizational structure, products, services, types of clients, compliance and risk management systems, investment process (including KYC, KYP, and suitability), marketing practices and financial condition.

- Inform relevant persons that the OSC is conducting a compliance review, and that they may need to be available for interviews during the review.

- Appoint a contact person (e.g., the CCO) to answer our questions, schedule meetings, and request and collect additional documents.

- Provide us with use of a private meeting room or office to review the books and records and conduct meetings with your staff.

- Maintain an ongoing dialogue with field review staff so that you are aware of the status and progress of the review.

5.1.2 — Current trends in deficiencies and suggested practices

Inadequate compliance systems and CCOs not adequately performing responsibilities

Our compliance reviews have identified a number of registered firms that do not have an adequate compliance system in place and CCOs who are not adequately performing their responsibilities.[4] For example, we found that some CCOs lacked knowledge of key requirements in NI 31-103 and had limited involvement in the compliance function.

When we find deficiencies of this nature, we consider this a serious matter and will take appropriate regulatory action. This may include

- requiring registered firms to self-correct their deficiencies through a concerted effort to review and apply securities law to their operations;

- requiring firms to hire an external compliance consultant to correct the deficiencies; or

- being subject to strict regulatory action, including suspension of their registration where warranted.

In May 2012, we communicated our concerns to all CCOs and UDPs of registered firms that we directly regulate. We also provided examples of inadequate compliance systems and CCOs not adequately performing their responsibilities, and outlined our regulatory approach when we identify concerns in this area. We also clarified our expectations and made suggestions on how a CCO or UDP can improve a firm's compliance systems.

Registered firms are required to register a CCO who meets the education and experience requirements in Part 3 of NI 31-103. Although the CCO's responsibilities are to be fulfilled on an ongoing basis, we recognize that many CCOs of small and mid-sized firms may also have other duties and responsibilities. A CCO must have the appropriate amount of involvement, time and resources to fulfill his or her responsibility to monitor and assess compliance with regulatory requirements. In performing his or her duties and responsibilities as CCO, the CCO must have a good understanding of the regulatory requirements applicable to the firm and individuals acting on its behalf. On an ongoing basis, the CCO must demonstrate that he or she can effectively maintain and oversee the compliance system of the registrant firm. It is also important that firms allocate adequate staff and resources to the compliance function, by taking into account the size, nature, complexity and risk of their business. For example, at larger, higher risk or more complex firms, it is generally appropriate for the firm's CCO to dedicate most of their time to compliance responsibilities and for the firm to have other staff employed in a compliance role.

Registered firms and their CCOs should also perform ongoing self-assessments of their compliance with Ontario securities law and take action to improve their internal controls, monitoring, supervision and policies and procedures when necessary. Where appropriate, firms should consider engaging external legal counsel or a compliance consultant to provide advice, including making recommendations to improve the firm's compliance system. When we require a registered firm to engage a compliance consultant to improve its compliance system through terms and conditions of registration, we consider the following factors when assessing the acceptability of the consultant:

- their knowledge, resources and staff

- their experience with the type of registrant that the engagement relates to, and

- any conflicts of interest.

We may also consider factors in addition to those listed above. We also encourage CCOs to attend compliance-focused seminars and participate in compliance officer associations. For more information, see *OSC Message to CCOs and UDPs on Inadequate Compliance Systems*, which includes guidance from us and the SROs that may also be applicable to non-SRO registrants.

Inadequate relationship disclosure information

In November 2011, we participated in a desk review (sweep) with several other CSA members to assess the type of relationship disclosure information (RDI) dealers and advisers provide to clients to meet the requirements under section 14.2 of NI 31-103.

---

[4]Since we use a risk-based approach to select a sample of registered firms for compliance reviews over the year, we expect to find more issues at firms we review than are likely to be present in our overall population of registered firms.

The RDI requirements were established to provide clients with increased transparency and a better understanding of the registrant-client relationship. The information that is required to be disclosed includes

- the nature and type of the client's account

- the products or services the firm offers to clients

- the types of risks a client should consider in making investment decisions

- costs to a client for the operation of an account

- costs the client will pay in making, holding and selling investments

- the content and frequency of reporting to clients.

We reviewed and assessed the RDI for 40 firms in Ontario, out of a total of 120 firms that were selected across the participating CSA jurisdictions. Our sample included firms that were registered as sole PMs, sole EMDs, or registered in multiple categories of registration. Our purpose was to review and understand how registrants were meeting the RDI requirements.

We have completed our review of the 40 Ontario firms. Deficiency letters were delivered to registrants who failed to adequately meet the RDI requirements. The most common deficiencies identified related to inadequate disclosure of

- the types of risks a client should consider when making investment decisions

- the information a registered firm must collect about the client under section 13.2 of NI 31-103 (KYC)

- the risks to a client of using borrowed money to invest, or

- the content and frequency of reporting for each account or portfolio of a client.

We anticipate that the CSA will provide registrants with further guidance on compliance with the RDI requirements.

Inaccurate calculations of excess working capital

We continue to identify instances where registered firms are not accurately calculating their excess working capital on Form 31-103F1. Inaccurate reporting on Form 31-103F1 may result in a firm failing to meet the capital requirements set out in section 12.1 of NI 31-103.

To address this, we have listed in the table below the significant deficiencies identified from our reviews of Form 31-103F1s over the last year. The deficiencies have been separated out by each line item on Form 31-103F1. In order to reduce errors when calculating their excess working capital, registered firms should avoid these deficiencies and follow the actions to be taken when preparing their Form 31-103F1s.

Form 31-103F1 Calculation of Excess Working Capital

Deficiency noted	Action to be taken
Line 1 *Current assets*	
(a) Inclusion of accounts receivables, especially from related parties, that are not readily convertible to cash.	(a) Any receivables that are included on Line 1 and that cannot be converted into cash in a prompt and timely manner should be deducted on Line 2 *Less current assets not readily convertible into cash (e.g., prepaid expenses)*. Firms should be able to provide evidence to us that if the related party receivable was called upon by the firm, the amount could be promptly received. Evidence may include, among other items, a copy of the most recent audited financial statements of the related party or a bank statement supporting the amount of cash available.
(b) Inclusion of cash that is committed to serve a specific purpose (e.g., for collateral or as a security deposit).	(b) Any cash that is not readily available for use by the registrant for its current business purposes or to settle its current liabilities is considered to be restricted cash and should be deducted on Line 2.
Line 5 *Add long-term related party debt*	
(a) Failure to add back 100% of long-term related party debt.	(a) All long-term related party debt is required to be added back on Line 5 unless the firm and the lender have executed a subordination agreement in the form set out in Appendix B to NI 31-103 and the firm has delivered a copy of the agreement to its principal regulator. Preferred shares issued to related parties and classified as a financial liability are considered to be long-term related party debt.

Deficiency noted	Action to be taken
(b) Failure to deliver a copy of the subordination agreement to the regulator when subordination agreements have been executed.	(b) Firms are required to deliver a copy of all subordination agreements to their principal regulator.
	Refer to *Appendix B of NI 31-103* for a copy of a subordination agreement template.
	Only subordination agreements executed in the format outlined in Appendix B comply with the requirements of Line 5. Related party debt subordinated in any other format is not considered to be subordinated for the purposes of determining excess working capital.
(c) Repayment of subordinated debt is made without prior notice to the regulator.	(c) As indicated on Clause 4 of the subordination agreement template in Appendix B of NI 31-103, firms must notify their principal regulator 10 days before the full or partial repayment of the loan. Further documentation may be requested by the principal regulator after receiving the notice from the firm.
	Firms are also required to provide an updated subordination agreement or a schedule indicating the outstanding balance after a partial repayment of the loan.

Line 9 *Less market risk*

(a) The market risk calculation is omitted.	(a) For all securities whose values are included in Line 1 current assets, the market risk for each security must be determined based on its fair value and the applicable margin rates set out in Schedule 1 of Form 31-103F1.
	Refer to section 1(1) of the Act for the definition of the term "security".
	See Schedule 1 of Form 31-103F1 for instructions on calculating market risk.
	Firms may be asked to provide evidence of the market risk calculation.
(b) In determining market risk for US-registered money market funds, 1% or 5% margin rates are being applied to the value of these securities.	(b) A margin rate of 100% must be applied to the value of US-registered money market funds as these securities meet the criteria outlined in Schedule 1(g) of Form 31-103F1. For all other securities.
	Any securities that do not meet the exact criteria outlined in Schedule 1 clauses (a) to (f) require a 100% margin rate to be applied to their fair value.

Line 11 *Less guarantees*

Failure to include the amount of a liability of another party that is guaranteed by the registered firm.	If the registered firm is guaranteeing the liability of another party, regardless of whether there are other guarantors to the liability, the total amount of the guarantee must be included on Line 11 (unless the amount of the guarantee is already included on Line 4 Current liabilities).

Inappropriate sale of registrants' securities to their clients

We have concerns when a registered firm sells securities in itself to its clients. We have noted a number of cases recently where a registered firm was directly selling securities (such as notes, common or preferred shares) of the registered firm itself to its clients. In these cases, the investors were not taking control or direction over the firm, were not sophisticated investors, and were arm's-length from the registrant and its principals. Where this occurs, we have identified a number of serious issues, including

- registrants raising money from investors to fund their operations when the registrant was in financial difficulty, or had negative cash flow. Investors were not adequately informed of the financial difficulty of the registrant, and its associated risks, and were not provided with current and ongoing financial statements of the firm. Rather, the interest rate or dividend yield of the security was emphasized;

- the securities that were sold to investors were not suitable based on their investment needs and objectives, risk tolerance and financial circumstances, and the securities comprised a large percentage of the investor's financial assets;

- the securities were sold by improperly relying on a prospectus exemption. For example, the registrant relied upon the accredited investor exemption when the investor did not meet any of the definitions for an accredited investor;

- the money raised by the security offering was not used for the purposes told to investors or outlined in offering documents;

- the risks of the investments were not disclosed or they were inaccurate or understated, or other misrepresentations were made to the investors.

In each of these cases, the matters were referred to our Enforcement Branch for appropriate action.

It is a material conflict of interest when a registered firm sells securities in itself to clients. Section 13.4 of NI 31-103 requires registrants to identify and respond to existing or potential material conflicts of interest between the registered firm (including each individual that acts on its behalf) and a client.

Section 13.4 of 31-103CP identifies three ways to respond to conflicts of interest:

- avoidance
- control, and
- disclosure.

If the risk of harming investors or the markets is high, the conflict needs to be avoided. If a registered firm does not avoid a conflict of interest, it should take steps to control or disclose the conflict, or both.

Further, section 2.1 of OSC Rule 31-505 *Conditions of Registration* (OSC Rule 31-505) obligates dealers and advisers to deal fairly, honestly and in good faith with their clients. This fair dealing obligation must be met when a registrant sells securities in itself to clients, and may be difficult to meet given the fundamental conflict of interest from this practice.

Suggested practices

- Given the fundamental conflict of interest, registrants should avoid selling securities in themselves to clients.
- Registrants who think they are able to address the conflict of interest through control and disclosure should first obtain legal advice before engaging in this practice.
- Registrants that need to raise working capital should obtain it from the firm's existing owners, financial institutions or sophisticated investors, or engage independent dealers to raise the money for them.

Failure by CCO to submit an annual compliance report

In last year's report, we discussed how we often found no evidence that a registered firm's CCO submitted an annual report to the firm's board of directors (or its equivalent) to assess the firm's, and its registered individuals', compliance with securities law. Since we continued to see this deficiency during many of this year's reviews, we emphasize it again.

Section 5.2 of NI 31-103 outlines the responsibilities of a registered firm's CCO. These include submitting an annual report to the firm's board of directors, or individuals acting in a similar capacity for the firm, for the purposes of assessing compliance by the firm, and individuals acting on its behalf, with securities legislation.

When the CCO has not submitted an annual compliance report to the registrant's board, this raises questions about the adequacy of the registrant's compliance system, and whether the CCO is adequately performing his or her responsibilities. See the *Inadequate compliance systems and CCOs not adequately performing responsibilities* section of this report.

Suggested practices

- A CCO should prepare and maintain a *written* annual report that the CCO provides and presents to the firm's board of directors. The report should outline the CCO's assessment of the firm's and its registered individuals' compliance with securities law for the period of the report.
- Where appropriate, a CCO should provide and present a report more frequently than annually. This may be appropriate:
  - at larger firms
  - when there are external members on the firm's board of directors, or
  - when there are significant compliance deficiencies at the firm.
- The CCO should describe in the report the steps that were taken to perform the assessment, the results of the assessment (including any significant instances of non-compliance such as those that create a risk of harm to a client or the capital markets), and what has been done or will be done to address the non-compliance.
- The CCO may also want to discuss in the report:
  - the status and effectiveness of the firm's internal controls, monitoring and supervision; the firm's commitment to compliance, resources and training; and changes to the firm's policies and procedures;
  - any deficiencies identified in the firm's or its individuals' compliance with securities law;
  - the status and outcome of any regulatory reviews, internal audits, inquiries or investigations involving the firm or its individuals;
  - complaints or lawsuits against the firm or its individuals where there is potential non-compliance with securities law;
  - proposed changes to securities law that materially impact the firm;

> - key compliance risks facing the firm and how they are being addressed; and
> - an overall assessment of the firm's and its individuals' compliance with securities law.
> - In cases where the CCO has decided not to prepare a written report, but instead provides an oral presentation of his or her report to the firm's board of directors, the minutes to the board meeting should document the discussion, and describe the same information as outlined in the suggested practices for a written report above. An oral presentation without a written report may be appropriate, for example, in the case of a small firm with limited business lines that did not have any significant instances of non-compliance.
>
> These suggested practices apply to all registered firms, including one-person firms and when the CCO is the sole member of the registered firm's board of directors.

Acting on the above suggested practices will help us to assess if a CCO has fulfilled his or her responsibilities under section 5.2 of NI 31-103.

5.1.3 — New and proposed rules and initiatives impacting all registrants

Update on independent dispute resolution services for registrants

We have extended the transition period (except in Québec) for certain registered firms to make available to their clients independent dispute resolution or mediation services to September 28, 2014 (unless we implement amendments before this date). If a firm was registered for the first time after September 28, 2009, then this extension does not apply and we expect the firm to comply with the independent dispute resolution requirements.

On November 15, 2012 we proposed amendments to NI 31-103 to require all registered dealers and advisers to utilize the services of the Ombudsman for Banking Services and Investments for their dispute resolution or mediation services obligations (except in Québec). For more information, see *Proposed Amendments to NI 31-103 on Dispute Resolution Service*.

We remind registrants that we expect them to have internal complaint handling policies to ensure that any client complaints are addressed.

On-line submission process for Form 31-103F1, financial statements and other information

We are currently developing, and plan on implementing, an on-line submission process that requires all registered firms whose principal regulator is the OSC to electronically complete and submit Form 31-103F1 *Calculation of Excess Working Capital* (Form 31-103F1).

Firms would also be required to attach and submit audited financial statements, interim financial information and other information that is relevant to the financial condition of the firm.

The implementation of an electronic submission process is in line with the Commission's priorities to modernize our regulatory systems and approaches.

Registered firms would benefit from the convenience of filing through a centralized submission point, receiving instant filing receipt information, as well as assisting in reducing the environmental impact of printing.

Upcoming desk review on accuracy of Form 31-103F1 filings

We will be conducting a targeted desk review of a sample of registered firms to assess the accuracy of Form 31-103F1 filings.

This desk review will complement our on-going reviews of Form 31-103F1s, audited financial statements and other financial information that are required to be filed with us.

The desk review will focus on the line-by-line calculation of Form 31-103F1. We plan to commence the desk review this fall. The purpose of the desk review is to assess compliance with the capital requirements in section 12.1 of NI 31-103 and to assess whether further guidance in this area is needed.

5.2 — Exempt market dealers

This section contains information specific to EMDs, including current trends in deficiencies and suggested practices to address them, and new and proposed rules impacting EMDs.

5.2.1 — Current trends in deficiencies and suggested practices

Our EMD reviews focused on areas that we found to be problematic in recent years, including

- inadequate compliance systems and supervision
- inadequate collection and documentation of KYC information
- failure to assess the suitability of trades and selling unsuitable investments
- insufficient product due diligence (KYP)
- failure to identify and respond to conflicts of interest, and
- improper reliance on the accredited investor exemption.

We will continue to focus our compliance resources on these areas.

In addition to the matters discussed at section 5.1.2 of this report on *Inadequate compliance systems and CCOs not adequately performing responsibilities*, the following are trends in deficiencies identified during this year's reviews of EMDs. Where relevant, we also highlight some recent regulatory proceedings brought against EMDs to demonstrate our response when we identify registrant misconduct and the consequences when EMDs fail to comply with securities law.

Conflicts of interest when selling securities of related or connected issuers

EMDs that distribute the securities of related or connected issuers[5] continue to be an area of focus and concern for us due to the disproportionate rate of compliance deficiencies found in many of these firms.

In particular, some EMDs failed to identify and respond appropriately to the conflicts of interests that arise from these relationships. There are significant potential conflicts of interest when the mind and management of the issuer and the EMD are the same. These potential conflicts of interest include the EMD sponsoring dealing representatives that are also employees of, or related to, various issuers whose securities the EMD distributes. These include, for example, dealing representatives that:

- perform investor relations services for the issuers
- perform consulting services for the issuers, or
- act as officers or directors (or in an equivalent position) for an issuer.

Among our concerns is that dealing representatives may put their personal interests or the interests of the issuers ahead of their investor clients. *In the Matter of Staff's Recommendation to Suspend the Registration of Carter Securities Inc.* is a recent Director's Decision involving the suspension of an EMD based on a repeated failure to disclose material conflicts of interest to its clients. This EMD failed to inform investors that it directed investor funds into a related party loan from the related issuer it was distributing. The firm's failure to disclose the conflict demonstrated a lack of the integrity required of registered firms.

As previously discussed, section 13.4 of NI 31-103 requires EMDs to identify and respond to existing or potential material conflicts of interest between the EMD (including each individual that acts on its behalf) and a client. Section 13.4 of 31-103CP identifies three ways to respond to conflicts of interest:

- avoidance
- control, and
- disclosure.

If the risk of harming investors or the markets is high, the conflict needs to be avoided. If a registered firm does not avoid a conflict of interest, it should take steps to control or disclose the conflict, or both. For example, the registered firm could require an independent audit of the issuer's financial statements to mitigate the potential conflicts.

EMDs who are making prospectus-exempt distributions of related or connected issuers must also meet their disclosure obligations of the relationship as required under National Instrument 33-105 *Underwriting Conflicts* (*NI 33-105*). In particular, section 2.1(1) of NI 33-105 imposes a disclosure obligation applicable to a distribution in which a non-independent underwriter participates. This obligation is designed to require full disclosure of the relationship and specifies the disclosure requirements in Appendix C to NI 33-105.

Suggested practices

EMDs should

- have a process in place to identify and respond to any conflicts of interest that could impact clients' decisions to purchase an investment product, such as providing examples of material conflicts of interest to their dealing representatives and requiring them to timely inform the CCO if any actual or potential conflicts of interest arise;
- avoid the conflict if the risk of harm to clients is high;
- have a process in place to provide prominent, specific and clear disclosure to clients that explains any conflicts of interest, how the firm is dealing with the conflict, and how conflicts of interest could affect clients; and
- have a process in place to inform investors of a conflict before or at the time they recommend a security transaction that gives rise to the conflict, and what controls are in place to deal with the conflict.

Misuse of the accredited investor exemption

Some EMDs continue to misuse the accredited investor exemption. These EMDs are selling prospectus-exempt securities to investors without ensuring that investors qualify as accredited investors within the meaning of *National Instrument 45-106 Prospectus and Registration Exemptions* (NI 45-106). For example, some EMDs simply rely on a statement from the investor stating that he or she meets the accredited investor definition without collecting any other information to support this statement. As we explained in *OSC Staff Notice 33-735 Sale of Exempt Securities to Non-Accredited Investors* (OSC Staff Notice 33-735), we are concerned that individuals who are purchasing securities as "accredited investors" do not meet the required minimum income or asset thresholds. Many EMDs continue to incorrectly interpret the definition of "financial assets" by including non-financial assets such as precious metals, the investor's primary residence, and other real estate as "financial assets" for purposes of determining if an investor satisfies the financial assets test in paragraph (j) of the accredited investor definition in section 1.1 of NI 45-106.

As set out in section 7.1(2)(d) of NI 31-103, an EMD can trade a security only where the trade is exempt from the prospectus requirement. Section 1.9 of the Companion Policy to NI 45-106 states that it is the responsibility of the person distributing or trading securities to determine whether an exemption is available. EMDs must ensure the information collected from investors supports the use of the accredited investor exemption. If the client is not an accredited investor (and another prospectus exemption is not available), a prospectus is required, and the EMD is acting outside of its registration category.

---

[5]See definition of related and connected issuer in section 1.1 of NI 33-105 Underwriting Conflicts.

Recent decisions that illustrate some of the potential consequences of an EMD's failure to comply with this requirement include *Re Morgan Dragon Development Corp., John Cheong, Herman Tse,* and *Re Blueport and Hare.* See section 3.1 of this report for more information.

Suggested practices

EMDs and their registered individuals should confirm that they

- have a process in place to collect and document sufficient information for each prospective investor to determine whether the product can be sold pursuant to the accredited investor exemption; and
- understand the criteria that must be met to qualify under the accredited investor definition.

EMDs should also refer to OSC Staff Notice 33-735 for additional guidance.

Unsuitable investments and failure to meet KYC, KYP and suitability obligations

We continue to identify issues in the areas of KYC information, assessment of suitability, and knowledge of products recommended to clients. We are now performing targeted reviews of EMDs to further assess compliance with their KYC, KYP and suitability obligations. See section 2.2 of this report for more information.

During this year's reviews, we noted

- inadequate collection and documentation of KYC information for clients necessary to assess the suitability of trades and to ascertain investors' eligibility for securities traded under a prospectus exemption;
- some products sold to investors were unsuitable based on the clients' risk tolerance, financial situation and other client information;
- inadequate assessment of suitability of investment for clients; and
- insufficient due diligence and knowledge of an investment product prior to recommending it to investors. Many EMDs did not have a process in place to understand (or were unable to demonstrate) the structures and key features, including risks, of their product offerings. Some EMDs relied solely on the information provided by the issuer to satisfy their KYP obligations without further assessing the product, including the financial viability of the issuer and the use of investor proceeds.

We remind EMDs of their obligations under section 13.2 of NI 31-103 to take reasonable steps to ensure they have sufficient and current KYC information for clients, including their investment needs and objectives, financial circumstances and risk tolerance. Also, EMDs are required under section 13.3 of NI 31-103 to take reasonable steps to ensure that all securities recommended to clients are suitable. To meet this suitability obligation, EMDs should also understand the structure and features of each investment product they recommend, including features such as costs, risks and eligibility requirements.

The KYC and suitability requirements are a critical element in protecting investors. An EMD's failure to comply with these requirements is taken very seriously. Two recent examples of regulatory proceedings that illustrate the potential consequences of an EMD's failure to comply with these requirements include *Re Blueport and Hare* and *Re Morgan Dragon Development Corp, John Cheong, and Herman Tse.*

Suggested practices

EMDs and their registered individuals should

- have a process in place to collect and document sufficient KYC information for each client (for example by using a standard KYC form) so they can properly assess the suitability of investment products they recommend;
- have clients sign-off on their completed KYC forms;
- have an in-depth understanding of
  - the general features and structure of the product,
  - the product risks including the risk/return profile and liquidity risks,
  - the management and financial condition of the issuer,
  - the intended use of investor proceeds,
  - costs, and
  - any eligibility requirements for each product
  before recommending a product to clients;
- perform adequate due diligence of products before recommending them to clients;
- perform ongoing due diligence of the issuers and products to assess changes to their structure or features and determine the impact on their clients' investments;
  - develop and use documented criteria and guidelines for assessing the suitability of investment recommendations to clients; and
- have a trade review process in place that includes having a proficient individual in a supervisory capacity to review and approve the suitability assessments made by dealing representatives that recommend investment products to clients.

EMDs should also refer to *CSA Staff Notice 33-315 Suitability Obligation and Know Your Product* for additional guidance.

Inappropriate use of investor monies

We continue to be concerned about EMDs using investor proceeds for their related or connected issuers for purposes other than those set out in the offering documents provided to investors. We will take regulatory action when we identify evidence of inappropriate use of investor monies. See, for example, the Statement of Allegations for *Re Colby Cooper Capital Inc.*

Section 2.1 of OSC Rule 31-505 requires EMDs to deal fairly, honestly and in good faith with their clients. We expect EMDs to apply this principle to all areas of their activities, including handling of client monies in accordance with the use of proceeds disclosed to investors.

Suggested practices
EMDs should:
- provide clear and adequate disclosure to investors regarding the use of investor proceeds,
- have policies in place to ensure investor monies are used in accordance with the stated investment objectives, and

disclose any related parties and appropriately deal with existing or potential conflicts of interest, including fees and payments to related parties.

Inadequate supervision of dealing representatives

We continue to see that some EMDs are not adequately supervising their dealing representatives, especially when representatives are working in different locations from their supervisor. Among our concerns are that dealing representatives, who are the primary contact for investors, are not being adequately trained in relevant securities law obligations, on their sponsoring firm's policies and procedures, and on the investment products that they are recommending. Further, we have concerns that some EMDs are sponsoring dealing representatives solely for the purpose of distributing securities of a particular issuer and are "renting out" their firms' registration, rather than providing the necessary training and required supervision.

We remind EMDs of their ongoing obligation to monitor and supervise their registered individuals in an effective manner. Supervision of dealing representatives should be performed by an individual who has adequate training, knowledge and authority. EMDs should establish and maintain procedures for supervising their dealing representatives, and maintain evidence of their supervisory reviews.

Section 32(2) of the Act requires registrants to establish and maintain systems of control and supervision for controlling their activities and supervising their representatives. Also, section 11.1 of 31-103CP, under the heading "Day-to-day supervision", states that anyone who supervises registered individuals has a responsibility on behalf of the firm to take all reasonable measures to ensure that each of these individuals

- deals fairly, honestly and in good faith with their clients,
- complies with securities legislation,
- complies with the firm's policies and procedures, and
- maintains an appropriate level of proficiency.

Section 3.4 of NI 31-103 requires that a registered individual must not perform an activity that requires registration unless the individual has the education, training and experience that a reasonable person would consider necessary to perform the activity competently, including understanding the structure, features and risks of each security the individual recommends.

Suggested practices

EMDs should provide ongoing training for their dealing representatives so that they
- are aware of the securities law requirements impacting their activities,
- have policies in place to ensure investor monies are used in accordance with the stated investment objectives, and
- understand and comply with their sponsoring firm's policies and procedures,
- have an in-depth understanding of the products they recommend to clients, and
- are informed of any changes to the above on a timely basis.

EMDs should develop written policies and procedures to supervise the activities of their dealing representatives, including
- the activities to be supervised and by whom,
- the frequency of supervision, and

how the supervision will be evidenced and enforced by the firm.

Not disclosing outside business activities

We continue to note that many EMDs do not disclose to clients, or provide notice to the Commission, of their OBAs. These include

- acting as an officer, director or in an equivalent position for a company other than their registered firm, and
- employment with a company other than their registered firm.

EMDs must disclose existing and potential material conflicts of interest to investors in accordance with section 13.4(3) of NI 31-103.

EMDs must also notify the Commission of OBAs. Section 4.1(1)(b) of NI 33-109 requires a registered or permitted individual to notify the Commission of changes to information previously submitted in a Form 33-109F4 *Registration of Individuals and Review of Permitted Individuals* (Form 33-109F4), within 10 days of the change, including the information in item 10 of Form 33-109F4. Item 10 requires a list and description of all current business and employment activities, including all business-related officer or director or equivalent positions.

For additional guidance on a registrant's obligation to disclose all OBAs, see *CSA Staff Notice 31-326 Outside Business Activities*. Failure to comply can result in the firm incurring significant late fees for failing to meet the filing deadlines set out in NI 33-109. See section 4.2 of the report for more information on late filings.

Suggested practices

EMDs and their registered individuals should confirm that they:
- have policies and procedures in place that requires all registered individuals to disclose new OBAs to the OSC and deal with any potential conflicts of interest, and

provide clients with clear, adequate and timely disclosure of OBAs.

5.2.2 — New and proposed rules impacting EMDs

Review of prospectus exemptions

See section 1.4 of this report for a discussion on the review of prospectus exemptions.

Broker-dealer registration in the EMD category

See section 4.1.2 of this report for a discussion on registration and oversight of foreign broker-dealers registered as EMDs.

Electronic report of exempt distribution on Form 45-106F1

On June 21, 2012, we published *OSC Staff Notice 45-708 Introduction of Electronic Report of Exempt Distribution on Form 45-106F1* to notify issuers, underwriters and their professional advisers that an electronic version (the E-form) of Form 45-106F1 *Report of Exempt Distribution* is being made available on the OSC's website. Issuers and underwriters are required to prepare and file a report of exempt distribution in connection with certain prospectus exemptions (including the accredited investor exemption under NI 45-106) on Form 45-106F1 (the Report). Filers may prepare and file the Report using the E-form, instead of in a paper format.

At this time, filing the Report electronically is voluntary, although we anticipate moving towards mandatory electronic filings in the future. Until this time, filers may continue to prepare and file the paper version of the Report. However, we encourage filers to use the E-form whenever possible, as we anticipate that it will be faster and more efficient.

To provide guidance for preparing and filing the Report, the CSA published *CSA Staff Notice 45-308 Guidance for Preparing and Filing Reports of Exempt Distribution*. We also separately published *OSC Staff Notice 45-709 Tips for Filing Reports of Exempt Distribution* which provides tips to help filers avoid common deficiencies in completing and filing the Report.

5.3 — Scholarship plan dealers

This section contains information specific to SPDs, including the results of our review of SPDs, and new and proposed rules impacting SPDs.

5.3.1 — Review of SPDs

We recently conducted compliance reviews of all five firms registered solely as SPDs. SPDs may act as a dealer in securities of scholarship plans, education plans or educational trusts (collectively referred to as education savings plan products or ESP products in this section). We have performed several reviews of SPDs in past years, both on our own and jointly with other CSA members. During past years' reviews, we identified a number of significant deficiencies at certain firms, including failings with respect to their

- compliance structure
- KYC and suitability of investments
- dealing representatives' knowledge of ESP products sold to investors
- supervision of branch locations and dealing representatives
- marketing and sales practices, and
- conflicts of interest.

As part of this year's reviews, we performed an on-site review at each SPD's head office, visited a sample of 25 branch offices in Ontario, and interviewed over 70 dealing representatives.

We found that some of the issues identified in previous reviews continued to be a problem. In many instances, we identified issues which had been brought to the attention of SPDs in previous reviews. Key areas of concern from our recent reviews included

- CCO and UDP not adequately performing their responsibilities;
- failure to meet KYC and suitability requirements;
- failure to meet KYP obligations;
- use of misleading marketing materials;
- use of high-pressure sales tactics to enroll investors in an ESP product; and
- inadequate oversight of branches and dealing representatives, including
  - inadequate trade review of enrolment applications for ESP products,
  - inconsistent or inadequate training of dealing representatives, and
  - failure to identify and rectify compliance issues at the branch level.

Outcome of recent SPD compliance reviews

We referred four SPD firms to our Enforcement Branch after identifying serious concerns with sales practices during the compliance reviews of these firms. To address investor protection concerns and, in particular, concerns on the suitability of specific ESP products recommended to investors, interim terms and conditions were imposed on consent on the registrations of these four SPDs. The terms and conditions vary, but require each of these SPDs to

- retain an OSC-approved independent consultant to develop and implement a compliance enhancement plan (Compliance Plan);

- retain an OSC-approved independent monitor to review new clients, including calling certain clients to confirm accuracy of their KYC information, confirm that the ESP product is suitable and affordable, confirm that the investor understands the ESP product's fees, and unwind any unsuitable investments, until the Compliance Plan has been approved;

- require the monitor to provide regular reports and have an ongoing role during the implementation of the Compliance Plan; and

- not open any new branch locations or hire any new dealing representatives (unless replacing an existing dealing representative and certain conditions are met) until the Compliance Plan has been fully implemented.

For more information, see the interim orders for *Children's Education Funds Inc.*, *Global RESP Corporation.*, *Heritage Education Funds Inc.*, and *Knowledge First Financial Inc.*

5.3.2 — New and proposed rules impacting SPDs

Cost disclosure, performance reporting and client statements

As discussed in section 1.1 of this report, the CSA has recently published proposed rules on cost disclosure, performance reporting and client statements. The proposals will apply to SPDs, and have been tailored to recognize the unique features of ESP products that merit different disclosure and reporting requirements.

The proposals aim to provide investors with information relevant to investments in ESP products, including a specific discussion at the account-opening stage of the consequences to the client of (i) the client failing to maintain prescribed plan payments, or (ii) a beneficiary not participating in or completing a qualifying educational program.

Further, the proposal will require that an annual report be sent to clients that provides information on charges and other compensation, including information about any outstanding front-loaded fees.

Lastly, the proposal will require an investment performance report to be provided to clients that provides relevant information on their ESP product including

- how much has been invested,

- how much would be returned if the client stopped paying into the plan, and

- a reasonable projection of the income the client should expect to see if they stay invested to maturity and their designated beneficiary attends a designated educational institution.

For more information, see *Proposed Amendments to NI 31-103 on Cost Disclosure, Performance Reporting and Client Statements*.

5.4 — Advisers (portfolio managers)

This section contains information specific to PMs, including current trends in deficiencies and suggested practices to address them. We also discuss our desk review of the client account statement practices of PMs, and new and proposed rules impacting PMs.

5.4.1 — Current trends in deficiencies and suggested practices

Unfair allocation of investment opportunities

In a small number of cases, PMs are not fairly allocating investment opportunities to their clients. When a PM places an investment order to a dealer for more than one of its clients (a bunched or blocked trade), and the order is partially filled (such as for a new issue or illiquid security), some PMs allocate these securities to clients with a smaller portfolio size, or to clients whose portfolios are underperforming. We do not consider these to be fair allocation practices, as they favour certain clients based on their asset size or performance, to the disadvantage of others. Examples of other unfair allocation practices include allocations (i) based on compensation arrangements, such as favouring clients that pay performance fees, (ii) based on client types, such as favouring investment funds over private clients, (iii) to newer accounts over older accounts or vice versa, (iv) based on client relationships or to obtain future business, and (v) to proprietary, employee or personal accounts over third-party accounts.

Since it may not be possible to treat clients equally for every investment opportunity, we acknowledge that there may be trades where one client or group of clients is allocated investments and not others. But over time, PMs should allocate suitable investment opportunities to their clients using a systematic and fair process, and not consistently favour one client or group of clients over others. Further, PMs do not meet their obligations to fairly allocate investment opportunities to clients through disclosure of an unfair allocation practice.

Section 14.10 of NI 31-103 requires advisers to ensure fairness in allocating investment opportunities among their clients. Section 11.1 of NI 31-103 requires advisers to establish, maintain and apply policies and procedures that establish a system of controls and supervision sufficient to provide reasonable assurance that they comply with securities legislation, including a policy to ensure fairness in allocating investment opportunities (Fairness Policy). Section 14.3 of NI 31-103 requires advisers to deliver a summary of the Fairness Policy to their clients when they open an account for the client and when there has been a significant change to the summary previously delivered.

Suggested practices

- An adviser's Fairness Policy should, at a minimum, disclose the method used to allocate the following:
  - price and commission among client orders when trades are bunched or blocked (such as average price per share and average commission rate per share),
  - block trades and initial public offerings (IPOs) among client accounts, and
  - block trades and IPOs among client orders that are partially filled, such as on a pro-rata basis. (A pro-rata allocation is when clients are allocated an amount of securities in proportion to their account size or the original trade order.)

Part 3: REGISTRATION

- A Fairness Policy should also address any other situation where investment opportunities must be allocated (such as how private placements will be handled).
- A Fairness Policy should be sufficiently objective and specific to permit independent verification of the fairness of the allocation. A Fairness Policy that states that an adviser "uses judgment" to allocate investments does not meet this test.
- Advisers should use the pro-rata allocation method for partially filled trades. When this method is not practical (for example, if it would result in clients being allocated a very small number of shares), use another pre-determined formula that is fair and objective, such as a rotational allocation (when the adviser regularly changes the sequence in which orders are allocated to clients) or a statistically random allocation (when each client is given an equal chance to participate).
- Advisers should not allocate partially filled trades to proprietary, employee or personal accounts until all other accounts are completely filled.

Any exceptions to the firm's Fairness Policy should be approved by the adviser's CCO and reasons for the exception should be documented.

Not reflecting all revenue for capital market activities

Some PMs are not reflecting all of the revenue earned from their portfolio management services on their firm's financial statements and on the form that is used to calculate their Ontario capital markets participation fees (Form 13-502F4) to the OSC. We are concerned that these firms' financial statements may not be accurate since revenues are not fully reflected and that they may not be paying the full amount of their fees.

We found that an Ontario-based PM earned performance fees from an associated investment fund that was attributable to its portfolio management services, but did not reflect these performance fees as revenue on its financial statements or as revenue on its Form 13-502F4. Further, another Ontario-based PM entered into an arrangement with its parent company so that all of the portfolio management fees earned by the PM firm were reflected as revenue on the financial statements of the parent company, rather than the PM firm. As part of the arrangement, the PM firm was then attributed revenue by the parent company that was based on recovery of costs plus a mark-up. The PM firm reflected this attributed amount as its revenue on its financial statements and as revenue on its Form 13-502F4.

Section 3.1 of OSC Rule 13-502 *Fees* (OSC Rule 13-502) requires PMs and other registered firms, unregistered IFMs, and unregistered exempt international firms to pay capital markets participation fees (as outlined in Appendix B of OSC Rule 13-502) to the OSC each year based on their specified Ontario revenues calculated in accordance with sections 3.3, 3.4 or 3.5 of OSC Rule 13-502.

The specified Ontario revenues must include all actual revenues from the firm's capital markets activities in Ontario, subject to certain deductions permitted on Form 13-502F4. Capital markets activities are activities for which registration under the Act or an exemption from registration is required. These include providing securities-related advice or portfolio management services.

Firms that have not appropriately reflected and paid their capital markets participation fees are subject to payment of the overdue fees along with late fees, and may also be subject to other regulatory action.

Further, market participants (which include registrants) must properly reflect all of their revenues on their financial statements in order to comply with their record-keeping obligations under section 19(1) of the Act.

This deficiency applies not only to PMs, but also to other registered firms, unregistered IFMs and unregistered exempt international firms.

Suggested practices

Registered firms, unregistered IFMs, and unregistered exempt international firms should
- assess which revenues of the firm are derived from Ontario capital markets activities, and

have a process in place to ensure that all the firm's revenues from their Ontario capital markets activities are reflected on its financial statements and Form 13-502F4.

Use of consolidated account statements

Some PMs provide clients with "consolidated" account statements which combine the security holdings and/or transaction information for more than one account they manage for a client in a single summary statement. These PMs generally consolidate different types of accounts managed for one client (for example, taxable and tax-deferred accounts), along with accounts managed for client relationships, such as family accounts (for example, spouses and dependants) or accounts of affiliated parties.

We have concerns when PMs provide consolidated statements to clients, especially when the PM does not also provide them with a statement for each account that they manage for the client. Clients may not understand the information they are receiving, the grouping of accounts may be inappropriate or cause privacy concerns, and it may be difficult for clients to compare information from the PM with information on statements from their custodian (which is presented on an account-by-account basis).

PMs must deliver a statement for each account that they manage for their client to meet their account statement requirements in section 14.14(3) of NI 31-103. It may be appropriate for PMs to provide consolidated statements to a client when it is provided as supplementary information to the client's statements for each account managed by the PM. We recognize that consolidated statements can provide added value for clients by presenting a complete, summarized picture of a client's portfolio. If a PM provides clients with a consolidated statement as supplementary information, whether initiated by the PM or upon request of the client, they should consider the suggested practices below.

Suggested practices

A PM should only deliver a consolidated account statement to a client when
- it helps clients to better understand their overall investment portfolios managed by the PM;

- the accounts that are included in the consolidation are for an appropriate client relationship (which may be one or more persons) and have similar investment goals and objectives. For example, it may be appropriate to group accounts for spouses whose goals and objectives are saving for retirement, and exclude an account whose objective is to fund their child's education; and
- the client consents to, or requests, the delivery of a consolidated statement.

If the above criteria are met, the PM should provide adequate disclosure on the consolidated statement, such as

- a prominent heading on the statement noting that it is a "consolidated" statement (or another appropriate term, such as "summary" or "combined" statement), and then explain the term used and what information is being presented;
- the account numbers and the beneficial owner(s) for the accounts that were included in the "consolidated" statement;
- which entity holds the assets in the client's accounts; and
- a statement that clients should refer to their "account-by-account" statements to see their holdings and transactions for each account.

Lack of awareness of trade-matching requirements

A number of PMs were not aware of the institutional trade-matching (ITM) requirements in *National Instrument 24-101 Institutional Trade Matching and Settlement* (NI 24-101). As a result, they were not meeting the rule's ITM requirements. The ITM requirements apply to a PM who places a DAP/RAP trade (defined below) in an equity or debt security with a dealer for one or more of its clients with DAP/RAP trading privileges. Clients with DAP/RAP trading privileges typically include institutional clients such as investment funds and pension plans, but may also include clients that are individuals.

Under NI 24-101, a DAP/RAP trade is a trade that is:

(a) executed for a client trading account that permits settlement on a delivery against payment or receipt against payment basis through the facilities of a clearing agency (such as CDS), and

(b) for which settlement is made on behalf of the client by a custodian other than the dealer that executed the trade.[6]

Section 3.3(1) of NI 24-101 prohibits an adviser from giving an order to a dealer to execute a DAP/RAP trade on behalf of an institutional investor[7] unless they first establish, maintain and enforce policies and procedures designed to achieve matching as soon as practical after the trade is executed, but by no later than noon (Eastern Time) on the next business day following the trade date (T+1).

Section 3.4 of NI 24-101 requires advisers to have ITM policies and procedures in place to encourage each of their trade-matching parties (i.e., the dealers and custodians involved in processing trades executed with or on behalf of institutional investors) to enter into a *trade-matching agreement* with, or provide a *trade-matching statement* to, the adviser. This must generally be done before the adviser opens an account to execute a DAP/RAP trade for the account of an institutional investor or gives an order to a dealer to execute a DAP/RAP trade for the account of an institutional investor. Dealers have similar ITM requirements in section 3.2 of NI 24-101, so will also request trade-matching agreements or statements from PMs that are their trade-matching parties.

Section 4.1 of NI 24-101 is an exception reporting requirement. Advisers are required to deliver Form 24-101F1 *Registered Firm Exception Report of DAP/RAP Trade Reporting and Matching* to their principal regulator (via an on-line reporting tool on the CSA's website) no later than 45 days after each calendar quarter-end if less than 90% of the equity or debt DAP/RAP trades executed for the adviser during the quarter are not matched by noon on T+1. The 90% test is determined both by number of trades and the aggregate dollar value of the securities purchased and sold in those trades. The percentage is also determined for transactions in equity and debt securities separately. On the exception report, advisers must provide a brief explanation as to why they did not meet the thresholds, and discuss their steps to address the delays.

Suggested practices

Determine if NI 24-101 applies to your firm by assessing if you give orders to a dealer to execute a DAP/RAP trade on behalf of an institutional investor.

If NI 24-101 applies, then

- Develop written ITM policies and procedures to ensure trades are matched as soon as practical after trades are executed (but by no later than noon on T+1). See the guidance on trade-matching policies and procedures in section 2.4 of the Companion Policy to NI 24-101 and section C of CSA Staff Notice 24-305 *Frequently Asked Questions About NI 24-101,*
- Determine who your trade-matching parties are (in order to exchange trade-matching statements or enter into trade-matching agreements),
- If you are unable to obtain a trade-matching agreement or statement from a trade-matching party, document your efforts to obtain this documentation in accordance with your policies and procedures (see section D of CSA Staff Notice 24-305), and
- At least quarterly, monitor your firm's trade-matching statistics to assess if your ITM policies and procedures are effective and to determine if you have to file an exception report. Where useful, you should be able to obtain trade-matching performance reports from your clients' custodians.

For more guidance, see the *Companion Policy to NI 24-101* and *CSA Staff Notice 24-305* for answers to frequently asked questions about NI 24-101. For guidance on filing an exception report on the CSA's website, see *CSA Staff Notice 24-306.*

5.4.2 — PM client account statement practices

---

[6]See the definition "DAP/RAP trade" in section 1.1 of NI 24-101.

[7]Section 1.1 of NI 24-101 defines an institutional investor to mean a client of a dealer that has been granted DAP/RAP trading privileges by the dealer.

In last year's report, we discussed our in-progress desk review of the client account statement practices of a sample of Ontario-based PMs. The purpose of the review was to better understand their practices and to assess if further guidance was needed to help firms comply with their requirements. We have now completed our desk review, and this is what we found:

- About 33% of the PMs in our sample did not deliver account statements to their clients. Many of these firms do not send a statement because the clients' custodian sends a statement with the required information at the required times.

- Of the PMs that deliver quarterly account statements to their clients, about 30% do not disclose information on security transactions made for clients.

These findings indicate that many PMs are not in compliance with their client account statement obligations. Section 14.14(3) of NI 31-103 states that "Except if the client has otherwise directed, a registered adviser must deliver a statement to a client at least once every 3 months." Further, sections 14.14(4) and (5) require that the statements must include prescribed information on transactions made for each client during the period and prescribed information on security holdings in the client's account.

We also found that there are different views amongst PMs on what the term "Except if the client has otherwise directed" in section 14.14(3) of NI 31-103 means. Staff's view is that the client may request statements more frequently than once every 3 months. It does not mean that the client can consent to not receiving a statement at all from their adviser. To clarify this, proposed changes to section 14.14(3) have been made as part of the CRM2 proposals discussed in section 1.1 of this report. The proposed text clarifies that an adviser must deliver an account statement at least once every 3 months, unless the client requests monthly statements. For more information on potential changes to client account statement requirements as part of the CRM2 proposals, see *Proposed Amendments to NI 31-103 on Cost Disclosure, Performance Reporting and Client Statements*.

We are currently discussing with the CSA the client account statement obligations of PMs. This may result in us providing further guidance on these obligations in the future.

For information and suggested practices on the use of consolidated account statements, see section 5.4.1 of this report.

5.4.3 — New and proposed rules impacting PMs

Update on direct electronic access (DEA)

In last year's report, we discussed proposed National Instrument 23-103 (then titled *Electronic Trading and Direct Electronic Access to Marketplaces*), which was relevant for PMs and EMDs who used DEA to directly send trade orders to marketplaces. The proposed rule permitted PMs to use DEA when it was provided by a participant dealer[8] for trading in their own accounts or the accounts of their clients. It was further proposed that the participant dealers that provided DEA to PMs would be subject to additional requirements including

- standards to be applied before granting DEA to a PM,

- specific elements to be included in a written agreement with the PM,

- training the PM, and

- assigning a unique identifier to each PM for each of their orders.

Since then, in June 2012, the CSA announced that the rules governing electronic trading in NI 23-103 (since re-titled as *Electronic Trading*) would be adopted[9] other than the requirements on the provision of DEA (as described above). The CSA decided that other forms of marketplace access, such as order execution service accounts and dealer-to-dealer routing, raise similar risks to DEA, and should be subject to similar requirements. To address these issues, the CSA published for comment on October 25, 2012 new proposed rules to provide a framework for the provision of DEA.

For more information, see *Proposed Amendments to NI 23-103 Electronic Trading*.

Potential regulation of proxy advisory firms

Most PMs have been authorized by their clients to vote proxies for securities held in their managed accounts. When PMs have this authority, we generally expect them to vote the proxies using guidelines that form part of their written policies and procedures, and to be able to justify the manner in which all proxies are voted.

PMs are increasingly engaging proxy advisory firms to analyze client proxies and to make recommendations on how to vote them, which they use to help formulate their voting decisions for clients.

The increased use of and reliance on proxy advisory firms' recommendations by institutional investors (including PMs) has raised concerns, including a lack of transparency on how proxy advisory firms reach their voting recommendations, and how they address any conflicts of interest. As such, in June 2012, the CSA published for comment a consultation paper on the potential regulation of proxy advisory firms. The purpose of regulation would be to increase the accountability of proxy advisory firms and to make the process leading to vote recommendations more transparent.

For more information, see *CSA Consultation Paper 25-401 Potential Regulation of Proxy Advisory Firms*.

---

[8]A participant dealer is a marketplace participant that is a registered investment dealer and an IIROC member.

[9]This rule sets out a regulatory framework to help ensure that marketplace participants and marketplaces manage the risks associated with electronic trading.

5.5 — Investment fund managers

This section contains information specific to registered IFMs, including current trends in deficiencies and suggested practices to address them, new and proposed rules and initiatives, and IFM resources.

5.5.1 — Current trends in deficiencies and suggested practices

Insufficient oversight of outsourced functions and service providers

Many IFMs choose to outsource aspects of their IFM operations (such as fund accounting and unitholder recordkeeping) to third-party service providers. Some IFMs rely solely on the third-party service provider and do not perform any oversight to ensure that these service providers are fulfilling their duties and responsibilities. As a result, these IFMs are not satisfactorily discharging their obligations to comply with applicable securities legislation.

Section 11.1 of NI 31-103 requires IFMs to establish a system of controls and supervision to ensure compliance with securities legislation and to manage their business risks in accordance with prudent business practices. Part 11 of 31-103CP, under the heading "General business practices — outsourcing", states that registrants that outsource aspects of their business operations to third-party service providers are responsible and accountable for all functions that have been outsourced. An IFM is required to oversee its service providers in order to meet its obligation of being responsible and accountable for the work performed by the service providers.

Suggested practices

IFMs should

- establish and implement policies and procedures to actively monitor the work of service providers,
- review the work performed by service providers; for example, by reviewing reports for the calculation of net asset value,
- conduct oversight of service providers on a frequent and as appropriate basis, taking into account the IFM's business operations, and
- ensure the monitoring of service providers is adequately documented.

Improper valuation of restricted securities

A number of investment funds invest in securities that are restricted from resale for a specified period of time. Some IFMs have been valuing these restricted securities using a quote from an active market for publicly listed securities of the same issuer that do not have a resale restriction.

An investment fund is required by section 2.6 of National Instrument 81-106 *Investment Fund Continuous Disclosure* (NI 81-106) to prepare its financial statements using generally accepted accounting principles which requires all securities to be valued using a fair value. Further, section 14.2 of NI 81-106 requires the net asset value of an investment fund that is a reporting issuer to be calculated using the fair value of the investment fund's assets and liabilities. A quoted price in an active market does not reflect the fact that a restricted security is illiquid for a specific period of time.

Suggested practices

IFMs should

- develop a valuation policy to determine the fair value of a restricted security, and
- if a quote from an active market is used to value a restricted security, the valuation policy should consider applying a discount to the value of the security to reflect the illiquid nature of the security during the restricted time period.

Inappropriate expenses charged to funds

In last year's report, we highlighted our concern that some IFMs are charging inappropriate expenses to the investment funds that they manage. Since we continued to identify this practice during this year's reviews, we emphasize this deficiency again. When this issue is identified, we require the IFM to reimburse the applicable fund(s) for the inappropriate expenses, and depending on the nature of the inappropriate expenses, we may take further action.

IFMs should only charge expenses to their investment funds that are related to the operation of the investment funds. Some IFMs are allocating to their investment funds expenses that are related to the operation of the IFMs' business and not the investment funds. Some examples of such inappropriately allocated expenses, which we identified when conducting compliance reviews, include capital market participation fees, premiums on their bonding or insurance, expenses relating to the wholesaling activities of the IFM, and expenses relating to social events and holiday parties.

If proposed requirements discussed at section 1.1 *Cost disclosure, performance reporting and client statements* are implemented, they would require IFMs to provide information to dealers and advisers of the dollar amount of the trailing commissions paid to dealers and advisers in respect of their client's investment. Consistent with the principle above, we would expect that compliance with this new requirement would be a business expense of the IFM relating to its choice of distribution method, and not an expense attributable to the operation of the investment funds.

Section 116 of the Act imposes a standard of care on IFMs for the investment funds they manage. In our view, to meet this standard of care, IFMs should ensure that the investment funds they manage are only paying for expenses that are related to the operation of the investment funds. The expenses listed above are related to the operation of the IFM. We consider these expenses to be the cost of running a fund management business and should therefore be borne by the IFM, and not their investment funds.

Suggested practices

An IFM should

- establish policies and procedures and a system of controls to ensure that its investment funds are only paying for expenses that are related to the operation of the investment funds, and
- review expense allocations on a regular basis to ensure that only appropriate expenses are charged to and paid by its investment funds.

Inadequate insurance coverage

Some IFMs are not maintaining adequate insurance when their assets under management increase during the year. Furthermore, some IFMs did not maintain insurance that provides for a "double aggregate limit" or "full reinstatement of coverage".

IFMs must maintain adequate levels of bonding or insurance as required under section 12.5 of NI 31-103. The amount of insurance required is based on calculations that take into account various factors, including assets under management. IFMs should take into account likely increases in their assets under management when assessing the level of insurance coverage they require.

IFMs should also ensure that their bonding or insurance provides for a "double aggregate limit" or a "full reinstatement of coverage" as explained under Division 2 — Insurance of Part 12 of 31-103CP.

Suggested practices

To ensure adequate insurance coverage, IFMs should

- factor in any likely increase in their assets under management, and
- regularly review the adequacy of their insurance coverage, especially when there is a material change in their business or circumstances.

Misleading marketing practices

Many IFMs are preparing marketing materials for investors with information about their investment funds that is outdated, misleading, or contain unsubstantiated claims. For example, some IFMs use terms such as "best", "exceptional" or "leading" to describe their services or the performance of their investment funds without also including disclosure containing evidence to support using these claims. Some IFMs are also comparing an investment fund's performance against the returns of benchmarks that are not comparable to the fund's investment strategy, without any explanation on why the comparison is relevant.

Section 116 of the Act imposes a standard of care on IFMs for the investment funds they manage. In our view, to meet this standard of care, IFMs should ensure that the marketing materials for their investment funds are fair and not misleading. Also, part 15 of National Instrument 81-102 *Mutual Funds* provides requirements on sales communications for mutual funds.

CSA Staff Notice 31-325 Marketing Practices of Portfolio Managers provides guidance to PMs to help them comply with securities legislation and best practices in the preparation and use of marketing materials. This guidance is applicable to other registrants, including IFMs.

Suggested practices

- provide clear and adequate disclosure in marketing materials to ensure that the information is complete, accurate and meaningful;
- substantiate all claims made in marketing materials (adequate references to the information supporting the claim should be provided where the claim is made in the marketing material so that investors can easily assess the merits of the claim);
- review and update marketing materials regularly to ensure all information is complete, accurate and current;
- use benchmarks that are relevant and comparable to an investment fund's investment strategy; and
- if a non-comparable benchmark is used but is relevant since it is widely known and followed, disclose the relevance of the benchmark and the differences between the benchmark and the fund's investment strategy.

5.5.2 — New and proposed rules and initiatives impacting IFMs
Registration of non-resident IFMs

For information on the new registration requirements for non-resident IFMs, see section 4.1.1 of this report.

Information on International Financial Reporting Standards (IFRS)

In March 2012, the CSA updated IFMs on the deferral of the mandatory changeover date to IFRS for investment funds in Canada to January 1, 2014. For more information, see *CSA Staff Notice 81-320 (Revised) Update on International Financial Reporting Standards for Investment Funds.*

Investment fund initiatives

The OSC, led by staff from the Investment Funds Branch, is working on a number of initiatives with the CSA that are applicable to IFMs. Some of the key initiatives are described below.

Investment funds modernization project

The purpose of this project is to modernize the product regulation of publicly offered investment funds.

Phase 1 of the modernization project was completed with the publication of final amendments to NI 81-102 on February 9, 2012. For more information, see *Notice of Amendments to NI 81-102 Mutual Funds and Companion Policy 81-102CP.*

As part of phase 2 of this project, the CSA is now working on amendments to NI 81-102 that would implement certain key restrictions and operational requirements for non-redeemable investment funds (also referred to as "closed-end funds"), consistent with similar requirements for mutual funds. For more information, see *CSA Staff Notice 81-322 Status Report on the Implementation of the Modernization of Investment Fund Product Regulation Project.*

Point of sale disclosure

On June 21, 2012, the CSA published for second comment changes to the proposed amendments to National Instrument 81-101 *Mutual Fund Prospectus Disclosure* aimed at implementing stage 2 of the point of sale initiative, to allow for the delivery of the Fund Facts document to satisfy the legislative requirement to deliver a prospectus within two days of buying a mutual fund. The proposed changes focus primarily on the presentation of risk in the Fund Facts document. The comment period ended on September 6, 2012.

For more information, see *Implementation of Stage 2 of Point of Sale Disclosure for Mutual Funds.*

New prospectus form for scholarship plans

Amendments to National Instrument 41-101 *General Prospectus Requirements* have been proposed to create a new, tailored prospectus form for scholarship plans. The proposed amendments were republished for a second comment period in late 2011 and reflect changes made as a result of comments received by the CSA after the initial publication in 2010.

For more information, see *New Prospectus Form for Scholarship Plans.*

5.5.3 — Investment fund manager resources

Published guidance for IFMs

Various organizations publish industry guidance as suggested "best practices" for IFMs. These organizations include the Investment Funds Institute of Canada, the Alternative Investment Management Association and the Hedge Fund Standards Board. We encourage IFMs to review the guidance prepared by these organizations and assess the applicability of this guidance to the operations of their investment funds.

The Investment Funds Practitioner

The Practitioner is an ongoing publication prepared by the OSC's Investment Funds Branch that provides an overview of operational issues arising from applications for discretionary relief, prospectuses, and continuous disclosure documents that are filed with the OSC. It is intended to assist IFMs and their staff or advisers who regularly prepare public disclosure documents and applications for exemptive relief on behalf of investment funds.

The Practitioner is also intended to make IFMs more broadly aware of some of the issues the Investment Funds Branch has raised in connection with their review of documents filed with them and how these issues have been resolved. The Practitioner is intended to serve as a useful resource when preparing applications and disclosure documents.

Past editions of The Practitioner can be accessed on our website under *Information for: Investment Funds.*

Disclosure of portfolio holdings

The Investment Funds Branch published in August 2012 a staff notice outlining its findings and recommendations from its targeted review of the disclosure of portfolio holdings in financial statements, Management Reports of Fund Performance, and Fund Facts documents of investment funds.

For more information, see *OSC Staff Notice 81-717 Report on Staff's Continuous Disclosure Review of Portfolio Holdings by Investment Funds.*

More information for IFMs

In addition to the initiatives and resources summarized in this report, the Investment Funds Branch has also published a number of documents as guidance for IFMs. For a complete listing of available information, see the *Information for: Investment Funds* section of the OSC's website.

6. — Additional resources

This section discusses how registrants can get more information about their obligations.

The CRR Branch works to foster a culture of compliance through outreach and other initiatives. We try to assist registrants in meeting their regulatory requirements in a number of ways.

We encourage registrants to visit the OSC's website at www.osc.gov.on.ca for more information regarding their obligations. The *Information for Dealers, Advisers and Investment Fund Managers* section provides firms and individuals with detailed information about the registration process and their ongoing obligations. It also includes information about compliance reviews and suggested practices, provides quick links to forms, rules and past reports and email blasts to registrants.

Registrants may also contact us. Please see Appendix B to this report for the CRR Branch's contact information. The CRR Branch's portfolio manager, investment fund manager and dealer teams focus on registration, oversight, policy changes, and exemption applications for their respective registration categories. The Registrant Conduct and Risk Analysis team supports the other teams in cases of potential registrant misconduct and reviews registrant submissions regarding financial reporting.

We also have an *Investors section* on our website that provides information to help investors. For example, investors can learn more about investing (such as the risks of borrowing to invest), help protect themselves against fraud and use tools and resources (such as checking the registration status of a person or company).

Part 3:
REGISTRATION

Appendix A — Explanation of compliance review outcomes

- **Enhanced compliance**: At the end of a review, we usually issue a report to the firm identifying areas of non-compliance that require corrective action. We work with the firm to facilitate the appropriate resolution of deficiencies. Compliance field reviews generally result in enhanced compliance at these firms following their actions to address the identified matters and to improve their compliance systems, internal controls, or policies and procedures.

- **Significantly enhanced compliance**: When the seriousness of the deficiencies identified during a review warrants it, in addition to the steps taken in the enhanced compliance outcome, we increase our monitoring of the registrant. For example, we may conduct a follow-up review of a registrant or require the registrant to provide additional evidence to assess whether it has appropriately addressed the identified deficiencies. The increased monitoring and the registrant's actions generally result in significantly enhanced compliance by the firm.

- **Terms and conditions on registration**: We may impose terms and conditions on a firm's registration to more actively monitor how a registrant is complying with securities law. We may also impose terms and conditions requiring a registered firm to take a specific action or to restrict its business activities. For example, terms and conditions may require the firm to submit information (such as financial statements and excess working capital calculations) to us more frequently, retain a consultant to improve its compliance systems, or prohibit the registrant from opening new client accounts.

- **Surrender of registration**: In some cases, a registered firm may decide to surrender its registration during or after a compliance review. However, we will not consent to the firm's surrender of registration unless our compliance review is completed and any significant deficiencies identified from the review (for example, those impacting the firm's clients) have been appropriately addressed.

- **Referral to the Enforcement Branch**: If we identify a serious breach of securities law, we discuss the findings with the Enforcement Branch, and together determine an appropriate course of action.

- **Suspension of registration**. If we identify a serious breach of securities law that causes us to conclude that a registrant's continued fitness for registration is no longer appropriate, CRR Branch staff will recommend to the Director that the firm's registration be suspended. The Director will decide to accept or reject staff's recommendations based on staff's submissions, and the registrant's submissions (when provided) at an opportunity to be heard.

Appendix B — Contact Information for Registrants

Compliance and Registrant Regulation Branch

[omitted]

OSC Staff Notice 33-739 — Termination of the Ontario Contingency Trust Fund

Date: December 6, 2012

35 O.S.C.B. 10873

Substance and Purpose

The trustee (**Trustee**) of the Ontario Contingency Trust Fund (the **Fund** or **Plan**) has proposed that the Fund be wound up in accordance with advice and direction that the Trustee will seek from the court. The Commission has advised the Trustee that it does not object to the Trustee pursuing such a wind-up of the Plan.

This Notice outlines why the Trustee has proposed such a wind-up. It also sets out a simplified procedure (with templates) for existing participants in the OCTF that are currently required by Ontario securities law to participate in the Plan to apply for an exemption from this requirement on the terms set out in this Notice and without any application fee.

Background

Subsection 110(1) of Ontario Regulation 1015[1] requires every dealer that is registered under the *Securities Act* (Ontario)(the **Act**), other than an exempt market dealer, to participate in a compensation fund or contingency trust fund that has been approved by the Commission and satisfies certain other requirements set out in that subsection (the **compensation fund participation requirement**).

Overview of the OCTF

The OCTF is a contingency trust fund that has been approved by the Commission. It came into being in the early 1970s, and has been the fund for dealers that are not members of a self-regulatory organization.

Twenty-nine registered dealers that are not members of either the Investment Industry Regulatory Organization of Canada (**IIROC**) or the Mutual Fund Dealers Association of Canada (the **MFDA**) participate in the OCTF to comply with the compensation fund participation requirement.

---

[1] R.R.O. 1990, as amended, made under the Act.

The terms of the Plan are set out in a form of trust agreement (the **Trust Agreement**) that has been entered into by each participant with the Trustee of the Plan.[2]

The OCTF provides for very limited compensation to clients of a participating dealer in the event the dealer is not able to return funds or securities belonging to a client that were held on behalf of the client at the participating dealer. The Plan has a coverage limit of $5,000 on eligible claims.

Since it was established, the OCTF has been called upon to respond to claims arising as a result of the insolvency of three "securities dealers", including most recently *Buckingham Securities Corporation*.[3] As part of registration reform, "securities dealer" was eliminated as a category of registration; and dealers that were previously registered as "securities dealer" are now required to be registered as an "investment dealer" (and as such, are members of IIROC) to carry out the same trading activities.

Current Status of OCTF

As at September 30, 2012, the capital in the OCTF was approximately $2.5 million.

There are currently 451 participants in the OCTF. Of this number, 422 are no longer required by Ontario securities law to participate in the Plan because they now participate in another approved compensation fund or they are no longer registered.

The Trust Agreement restricts participants from withdrawing from the Plan if there are potential claims against the Plan. Currently, the Trustee is not permitting any participants to withdraw from the Plan because the Trustee has not yet made a final call for claims in respect of Buckingham. The Trustee expects to soon make such a final call, and then be in a position to resume the return of capital to those 422 participants that would be eligible to withdraw from the Plan.[4] This would, however, result in the Plan's remaining capital falling well below the critical mass necessary to sustain its continued operation; and if all of these 422 participants were to withdraw their capital, the remaining capital in the Plan would be essentially depleted.

Wind-up of OCTF

The Trustee has therefore proposed that the OCTF be wound up in accordance with advice and direction that the Trustee will seek from the court.

The Commission has advised the Trustee that it does not object to the Trustee pursuing such a wind-up of the Plan.

Exemptions from Requirement to Participate in a Compensation Fund

Action will need to be taken by Participants in the OCTF that remain registered and are not members of IIROC or the MFDA to continue to be in compliance with the compensation fund participation requirement. They may wish to apply to the Commission for an exemption from this requirement on the terms set out in Exhibit 1.

Staff will recommend that the Commission issue an exemption on the terms set out in Exhibit 1.

Staff will also recommend that the Director grant an exemption from the requirement to pay the corresponding application fee on the terms set out in Exhibit 1, if the application is received before January 31, 2013.

Simplified Procedure for Obtaining an Exemption

Applications for these exemptions need not be formal in nature and may be made by way of an e-mail from the applicant (or its authorized agent).

The e-mail should refer to "OSC Notice 33-739" and identify the full legal name of the applicant in the subject line of the e-mail, and in the body of the e-mail state that:

- The above-referenced registered dealer hereby applies to be included as a Filer for the exemptions set out in Exhibit 1 to OSC Staff Notice 33-739

- As a Filer, the applicant makes the representations to the Commission and Director which are identified as being made by a Filer, in paragraphs a, b, c, d, e and f of Exhibit 1 under the heading "Representations of each Filer"

The e-mail should identify the individual applying on behalf of the applicant (with their full name, position, e-mail address, and telephone number) and be sent before January 31, 2013 to the following address:

applications@osc.gov.on.ca

---

[2]The form of agreement incorporates terms and conditions that were prescribed in Ontario Regulation 208/70, as amended.

[3]The other dealers were *E. A. Manning Limited* (in 1995) and *Marchment & Mackay Limited* (in 1999).

[4]Each participant was required to make an initial capital contribution of $10,000.

Exhibit 1

**In the Matter of
the *Securities Act*,
R.S.O. 1990, c. S.5, as Amended (the "Act"),
Regulation 1015
R.R.O. 1990, as Amended, Made under the Act (the "Regulation")**

and

Ontario Securities Commission Rule 13-502 Fees (the "Fee Rule")

and

**In the Matter of
Ontario Securities Commission Staff Notice 33-739
Termination of the Ontario Contingency Trust Fund**

and

Certain Registered Dealers

**Commission Order
(Section 147 of the Act)**

**Director Exemption Decision
(Section 6.1 of the Fee Rule)**

Background

1. Subsection 110(1) of the Regulation requires every registered dealer, other than an exempt market dealer as defined in National Instrument 31-103 *Registration Requirements and Exemptions* (**NI 31-103**), to participate in a compensation fund or contingency trust fund that has been approved by the Commission and satisfies certain other requirements set out in that subsection (the **compensation fund participation requirement**).

2. The Ontario Contingency Trust Fund (the **OCTF** or **Plan**) is one of three compensation funds or contingency trust funds that have been approved by the Commission for the purposes of subsection 110(1) of the Regulation.

3. The terms of the OCTF are set out in a form of trust agreement (the Trust Agreement) that has been entered into by each participant in the Plan with the trustee (the **Trustee**) of the Plan.

4. Twenty-nine registered dealers (**OCTF Dealers**) that are not members of the Investment Industry Regulatory Organization of Canada (**IIROC**) or the Mutual Fund Dealers Association of Canada (**MFDA**) participate in the OCTF, and as such do not participate in the corresponding approved compensation fund for members of these self-regulatory organizations.

5. OCTF Dealers comprise scholarship plan dealers and mutual fund dealers that obtained an exemption from the requirement in Ontario securities law to be a member of the MFDA.

6. As indicated in Ontario Securities Commission Staff Notice 33-739 *Termination of the Ontario Contingency Trust Fund* (the **Notice**), the continued operation of the Plan is not financially sustainable. The Trustee has proposed that the OCTF be wound up in accordance with advice and direction from the court and the Commission has advised the Trustee that it does not object to the Trustee pursuing such a wind-up.

Applications

Each of the OCTF Dealers (each, a **Filer**) listed in the attached Appendix has applied to the Commission for an order, under section 147 of the Act, exempting the Filer from the compensation fund participation requirement on the terms set out in this Order.

Each Filer has also applied to the Director, under section 6.1 of the Fee Rule, for an exemption from the requirement in section 4.1 to pay a fee for its filing of these exemption applications.

Representations of each Filer

Each Filer has represented to the Commission and the Director that:

    a. The Filer is not a member of either IIROC or the MFDA, and the Filer is not required by Ontario securities law to be a member of either of these self-regulatory organizations.

    b. The Filer does not now hold for its clients any funds, securities or other property (**Client Assets**).

    c. So long as the Filer relies upon the exemption from the compensation fund participation requirement set out in this Order, the Filer will not hold any Client Assets.

d. Before any person or company that is not a client of the Filer on the Effective Date (defined below) becomes a client of the Filer, the Filer will provide to that person or company prominent written notice of the following:

The Filer has obtained an exemption from the requirement in Ontario securities law to participate in an approved compensation fund or contingency trust fund. These funds provide for certain compensation to eligible clients of a participating dealer who suffer a financial loss as a result of the dealer becoming insolvent and not being able to return assets which it was holding on behalf of clients.

It is a condition of the exemption that the Filer not hold any client assets.

e. On the Effective Date, the Filer will have provided to any person or company that is an existing client of the Filer prominent written notice of the following:

The Filer has obtained an exemption from the requirement in Ontario securities law to participate in an approved compensation fund or contingency trust fund. These funds provide for certain compensation to eligible clients of a participating dealer who suffer a financial loss as a result of the dealer becoming insolvent and not being able to return assets which it was holding on behalf of clients.

It is a condition of the exemption that the Filer not hold any client assets.

The Filer was a participant in the Ontario Contingency Trust Fund at the time it applied for this exemption. It applied for this exemption in response to the proposed wind-up of that fund, as discussed in Ontario Securities Commission Staff Notice 33-739 Termination of the Ontario Contingency Trust Fund.

f. The Filer will not rely upon the passport provisions of Canadian securities legislation to passport this Ontario Order into any other jurisdiction of Canada without the prior written consent of that other jurisdiction.

Commission Order

In the opinion of the Commission it is not prejudicial to the public interest to make this Order.

It is ordered by the Commission pursuant to section 147 of the Act that:

(i) beginning on the Effective Date (as defined below), each of the Filers is exempt from subsection 110(1) of the Act, but only so long as, in the case of that Filer:

A. the Filer is not required by Ontario securities law to be a member of either IIROC or the MFDA;

B. the Filer does not hold any Client Assets; and

C. the Filer provides the disclosure to its clients referred to in paragraph (d) above and has provided the disclosure to its clients referred to in the paragraph (e) above; and

(ii) this Order shall be effective on the day that is 30 calendar days after the date hereof (the "**Effective Date**").

DATED at Toronto, Ontario this .... day of ...., 2012.

....

Commissioner
Ontario Securities Commission

....

Commissioner
Ontario Securities Commission

Director Exemption Decision

The Director is satisfied that to grant this Exemption would not be prejudicial to the public interest.

It is the decision of the Director, pursuant to section 6.1 of the Fee Rule, that each Filer is exempt from the requirement in section 4.1 of the Fee Rule to pay an activity fee for the filing by the Filer of the above-referenced applications.

DATED at Toronto, Ontario this .... day of ...., 2012.

....

Deputy Director
Compliance and Registrant Regulation
Ontario Securities Commission

Appendix

[to be completed following the submission of applications]

OSC Staff Notice 33-740 — Report on the Results of the 2012 Targeted Review of Portfolio Managers and Exempt Market Dealers to Assess Compliance with the Know-Your-Client, Know-Your-Product and Suitability Obligations

Date: June 6, 2013

36 O.S.C.B. 5647

[Not reproduced]

OSC Staff Notice 33-741 — Report on the Results of the Reviews of Capital Markets Participation Fees

Part 3:
REGISTRATION

Date: July 18, 2013
36 O.S.C.B. 7115

Purpose of this Notice

Staff of the Compliance and Registrant Regulation Branch (**Staff or we**) of the Ontario Securities Commission (**OSC**) conducted a review of the capital markets participation fees (**participation fees**) that are required to be submitted annually under OSC Rule 13-502 *Fees* (**OSC Rule 13-502**). This Notice summarizes our findings and provides guidance on suggested practices in the calculation of capital markets participation fees. We will also use this Notice and the guidance provided in our ongoing reviews of participation fees.

Background

On an annual basis, registrant firms and unregistered capital markets participants (i.e. unregistered investment fund managers or unregistered exempt international firms) (collectively referred to as **firms**) are required to pay participation fees based on the firms' revenues attributable to their capital markets activities in Ontario. The participation fees are calculated using Form 13-502F4 *Capital Markets Participation Fee Calculation* (**Form 13-502F4**). The participation fees are due on December 31 of each year for registrant firms and unregistered exempt international firms or due no later than 90 days after the end of their fiscal year for unregistered investment fund managers.

In 2012, we identified a number of issues in the calculation of participation fees. As a result, we decided to review a sample of Form 13-502F4s submitted by firms in 2012.

Objectives of the review

The main objectives of the review were to:

- assess the accuracy and completeness of participation fees submitted to the OSC for 2012,

- identify common errors when calculating participation fees,

- broaden our understanding of firms' interpretation of OSC Rule 13-502 and Form 13-502F4, and

- develop guidance for firms to follow when calculating their participation fees.

Scope and methodology

We gathered information on firms' participation fees through a review of the Form 13-502F4s submitted to the OSC for 2012 and then selected samples of firms to review. The types of firms reviewed included:

- Investment Industry Regulatory Organization of Canada (**IIROC**) member firms,

- Mutual Fund Dealers Association of Canada (**MFDA**) member firms,

- unregistered investment fund managers,

- investment fund managers (**IFMs**),

- portfolio managers,

- other dealers (other than IIROC and MFDA members, including exempt market dealers, scholarship plan

- dealers and mutual fund dealers that are not members of the MFDA),

- firms relying on the international dealer exemption in section 8.18 of National Instrument 31-103 *Registration*

- *Requirements, Exemptions and Ongoing Registrant Obligations* (**NI 31-103**) or the international adviser

- exemption in section 8.26 of NI 31-103, and

- commodity trading managers.

We selected three samples of firms to review between January and April, 2013 as follows:

- 100 firms were selected based on a risk based review of Form 13-502F4s filed by all firms,

- 98 firms were selected for review on a random basis, and

- 291 IFMs with fiscal year ends in September, October, November and December, which had estimated their gross revenues in determining the participation fee for 2012, were selected for review.

For the first two samples, we requested supporting documentation for each line item on Form 13-502F4. For the last sample, we asked firms to confirm that a recalculation of their participation fees was done using the revenues reported on their audited annual financial statements and confirm whether the correct participation fees had been paid.

Summary of issues identified

We identified a number of issues in the calculation of participation fees. The issues fell into the following categories:

- incorrect reporting of revenue,

- incorrect deductions taken,

- incorrect calculation of the Ontario percentage used to determine the specified Ontario revenues subject to
- participation fees, and
- other.

Specific issues and guidance

The following is a more detailed discussion of the issues we identified along with guidance on how these issues should be addressed.

1. — Incorrect reporting of revenue

The issues noted in this category relate to line 1 of Part III of Form 13-502F4 "Gross revenue for relevant fiscal year".

a) — Gross revenue did not tie into revenue reported on the firm's audited annual financial statements

A number of firms reported gross revenue attributable to Ontario activities on line 1 of Form 13-502F4, instead of revenue as reported on their annual audited financial statements. As set out in note 1 under this part of the form, the gross revenue on line 1 of Form 13-502F4 is the sum of all revenues reported on the audited annual financial statements, except where unaudited financial statements are permitted in accordance with subsection 3.4(4) or (5) of OSC Rule 13-502. Therefore, the gross revenues on line 1 of Form 13-502F4 should include the gross global revenue reported on a firm's audited annual financial statements, unless as noted above.

b) — No Gross revenue reported based on a "cost recovery model" of operations

In some instances, firms did not report any gross revenue on the basis that they operated using a "cost recovery model" of operations (i.e. the firm was paid a fee that was equal to the costs or expenses of the firm's operations). In these cases, the firms did not report the fees received to cover their expenses as gross revenue.

Staff's view is that fees received to cover the cost of a firm's operations are gross revenue for the purpose of calculating participation fees. As a result, these fees should be reported on line 1 of Form 13-502F4 as gross revenue.

2. — Incorrect deductions taken

Incorrect deductions were identified with respect to two sections of Part III of Form 13-502F4 — line 2 (revenue not attributable to capital markets activities), and lines 3 to 6 (redemption fee revenue, administration fee revenue, advisory or sub-advisory fees paid to registrant firms or exempt international firms, and trailer fees paid to registrant firms).

a) — Deductions for revenue not attributable to capital markets activities

"Capital markets activities" is defined in section 1.1 of OSC Rule 13-502 to include:

  i. Activities for which registration under the *Securities Act* (Ontario) or an exemption from registration is required,

  ii. Acting as an investment fund manager, or

  iii. Activities for which registration under the *Commodity Futures Act*, or an exemption from registration under the *Commodity Futures Act*, is required.

Firms deducted capital markets revenue earned outside of Ontario on line 2 of Form 13-502F4. The purpose of line 2 is to deduct revenue that is not generated through capital markets activities, such as consulting or interest income. Therefore, on line 2 of Form 13-502F4, firms are required to deduct revenue that is not earned in relation to their global capital markets activities.

b) — Other deductions taken were attributed to Ontario activities only

The deductions taken should relate to a firm's global activities for that particular line of Form 13-502F4 and not only to its Ontario activities.

3. — Incorrect calculation of the Ontario percentage used to determine the specified Ontario revenues subject to participation fees

The issues noted in this category relate to the calculation of the Ontario percentage for the relevant fiscal year.

a) — Firms that recorded only Ontario gross revenues on line 1 of Form 13-502F4 applied 100% as the Ontario percentage

Many firms applied an Ontario percentage of 100% since they only recorded Ontario gross revenues on the participation fee calculation. As a result, 100% of the revenue recorded was subject to participation fees.

As noted in issue 1 above, gross revenue should include revenue attributable to the firm's global operations as reported on the firm's audited annual financial statements. The Ontario percentage should then be determined to reflect the portion of gross revenue attributed to Ontario capital markets activities.

b) — Firms based their Ontario percentage on a factor other than their revenues or taxable income

Some firms used the number of clients in Ontario relative to the total number of global clients in determining the Ontario percentage for the relevant fiscal year.

The definition of "Ontario percentage" is set out in section 1.1 of OSC Rule 13-502.

Part 3: REGISTRATION

For firms with a permanent establishment in Ontario in the fiscal year, the firm's Ontario allocation factor (**OAF**) expressed as a percentage should be used in determining the Ontario percentage. The OAF, as defined in the *Taxation Act, 2007*, refers to a firm's Ontario taxable income in comparison to the firm's total taxable income.

In any other case, firms should use the percentage of the revenues earned from their Ontario clients relative to the revenue earned from all of their global clients in the fiscal year to determine the Ontario percentage.

c) — Incorrect Ontario percentage where firms had the same fiscal year and taxation year

In some instances where a firm had a permanent establishment in Ontario (required to file an Ontario corporate tax return) and the same fiscal and taxation year, the Ontario percentage derived from a firm's corporate income tax return varied substantially from the Ontario percentage used to calculate participation fees.

If a firm's corporate tax year is the same as its fiscal year, we expect that the Ontario percentage used to calculate participation fees would be the same as the Ontario percentage derived from the firm's corporate tax return.

If a firm's corporate tax year and its fiscal year are not the same, we expect that a firm would apply the same method used to determine the Ontario percentage on the assumption that the firm had the same corporate tax year as its fiscal year.

4. — Other

a) — Management certification

A number of firms certified the information reported on Form 13-502F4 with one member of senior management in Part IV of Form 13-502F4 when the firms had more than one member of senior management.

General Instruction 11 to Form 13-502F4 requires the information reported on Form 13-502F4 to be certified by two members of senior management to attest its completeness and accuracy. However, it is acceptable to provide certification by only one member of senior management for firms with only one officer and director.

We consider the review and sign off of participation fees by the Ultimate Designated Person (**UDP**) and the Chief Financial Officer (**CFO**) or other similar position, to be an integral aspect of an adequate compliance system. As part of an adequate compliance system, we also expect the Chief Compliance Officer (**CCO**) to understand the process involved in completing the Form 13-502F4 prior to the submission of participation fees to the OSC.

Additional guidance for future filings

We expect firms to take these items into account when completing and submitting the participation fee calculation.

a) — Books and records

Each firm should maintain a signed copy of the Form 13-502F4 submitted to the OSC. In addition, each firm should maintain adequate books and records to support each figure included on Form 13-502F4, including evidence to support the review and approval by the UDP and the CCO, or senior management in cases where the firm is not registered with the OSC. The books and records should be readily available if requested by Staff.

The requirement to maintain books and records is outlined in section 19(1) of the *Securities Act* (Ontario) in respect of market participants and section 11.5 of NI 31-103 in respect of registered firms.

b) — Reference fiscal year

OSC Rule 13-502 was amended effective April 1, 2013. One of the amendments involved the inclusion of a reference fiscal year to calculate participation fees. Please ensure that you are aware of the parameters of when to use a reference fiscal year.

"Reference fiscal year" is defined in section 1.1 of OSC Rule 13-502.

A firm's "reference fiscal year" is its last fiscal year ending before May 1, 2012, assuming it was a registrant firm, unregistered investment fund manager or an unregistered exempt international firm at the end of that fiscal year.

Subparagraph (a)(ii) of this definition only applies where a participant becomes a reporting issuer in that fiscal year as a result of receiving a prospectus receipt.

Next steps

We will continue to review participation fee calculations on an on-going basis. Firms should use this Notice as a self-assessment tool to ensure that participation fees are calculated correctly.

OSC Staff Notice 33-742 — 2013 OSC Annual Summary Report for Dealers, Advisers and Investment Fund Managers

Issue: November 7, 2013

36 O.S.C.B. 10599

Introduction

This report provides information for registered firms and individuals (registrants) that are directly regulated by the Ontario Securities Commission (OSC). These registrants primarily include:

- exempt market dealers (EMDs)
- scholarship plan dealers (SPDs)
- advisers (portfolio managers or PMs), and
- investment fund managers (IFMs).

It was prepared by the OSC's Compliance and Registrant Regulation (CRR) Branch, which registers and oversees approximately 1,300 firms and 66,000 individuals in Ontario that trade or advise in securities or commodity futures, or act as IFMs. Although the OSC registers firms and individuals in the category of mutual fund dealer and firms in the category of investment dealer, these firms and individuals are directly overseen by their self-regulatory organizations (SROs), the Mutual Fund Dealers Association of Canada (MFDA) and the Investment Industry Regulatory Organization of Canada (IIROC), respectively.

In this report, we summarize new and proposed rules and initiatives impacting registrants, current trends in deficiencies from compliance reviews of registrants (and suggested practices to address them), and current trends in registration issues. We discuss our new registrant outreach program that will help strengthen our communication with registrants on compliance practices. We also provide a summary of some key registrant misconduct cases, explain where registrants can get more information about their obligations, and provide OSC contact information.

This report is a key part of our outreach to registrants. We strongly encourage registrants to thoroughly read and use this report to enhance their understanding of:

- initial and ongoing registration and compliance requirements,
- OSC staff expectations of registrants and our interpretation of regulatory requirements, and
- new and proposed rules and other regulatory initiatives.

We also recommend registrants pro-actively use this report as a self-assessment tool to strengthen their compliance with Ontario securities law, and as appropriate, to make changes to enhance their systems of compliance, internal controls and supervision.[1]

1. — Key policy initiatives impacting registrants

1.1 — Cost disclosure, performance reporting and client statements

Effective July 15, 2013, the Canadian Securities Administrators (CSA) amended National Instrument (NI 31-103 *Registration Requirements, Exemptions and Ongoing Registrant Obligations* (NI 31-103), as well as its Companion Policy (31-103CP), implementing new requirements to ensure all investors receive essential information about the costs and performance of their investments. The amendments are relevant to all categories of registered dealer and registered adviser, with some application to IFMs. The amendments are commonly referred to as the "Client Relationship Model — Phase 2" or "CRM2".

The amendments will be phased-in over three years. Beginning this July, minor clarifications to NI 31-103 took effect, such as enhancements to relationship disclosure information.

Beginning July 15, 2014, registered firms will need to:

- provide pre-trade disclosure of charges; and
- report on compensation from debt securities transactions

Beginning July 15, 2015, the new account statement /additional statement requirements take effect. These include requirements to provide position cost information and to determine market values using a prescribed methodology.

Beginning July 15, 2016, registered firms will need to:

- provide an annual report on charges and other compensation that shows, in dollars, what the dealer or adviser was paid for the products and services it provided; and
- provide an annual investment performance report that covers
  - deposits into, and withdrawals from, the client's account;
  - the change in value of the account; and
  - the percentage returns for the previous year; and the previous three, five and ten years.

Additional guidance about implementing the CRM2 requirements can be found in *CSA Staff Notice 31-334 CSA Review of Relationship Disclosure Practices* (CSA Staff Notice 31-334) and in an "FAQ" that we expect to publish this fall.

The CSA expects the IIROC and MFDA member rules to be materially harmonized with the CSA's CRM2 requirements and to be implemented on substantially the same schedule.

---

[1]The content of this report is provided as guidance for information purposes and not as advice. We encourage firms to seek advice from a professional advisor as they conduct their self-assessment and/or implement any changes to address issues raised in the report.

For more information, see *CSA Notice of Amendments to NI 31-103 and to 31-103CP (Cost Disclosure, Performance Reporting and Client Statements)*.

1.2 — Potential statutory best interest standard for dealers and advisers

We are re-evaluating the advisor-client relationship by considering whether an explicit statutory fiduciary or best interest standard should apply to dealers and advisers and on what terms. A fiduciary duty is essentially a duty to act in a client's best interest.

In Ontario, section 116 of the *Securities Act (Ontario)* (Act) applies a best interest standard to IFMs in their dealings with the investment funds they manage. There is no equivalent provision under the Act that explicitly applies a best interest standard to dealers and advisers in their dealings with their clients, although section 2.1 of *OSC Rule 31-505 Conditions of Registration* (OSC Rule 31-505) requires dealers and advisers to deal fairly, honestly and in good faith with their clients. While there is no statutory best interest duty for dealers and advisers in Ontario, Canadian courts can find that a given dealer or adviser owes a best interest duty to his or her client depending on the nature of their relationship.

CSA Consultation Paper 33-403 The Standard of Conduct for Advisers and Dealers: Exploring the Appropriateness of Introducing a Statutory Best Interest Duty When Advice is Provided to Retail Clients was published on October 25, 2012. With the CSA, we are reviewing over ninety comment letters and conducted three roundtable sessions to engage stakeholders on the issues raised in the paper.

Working with the CSA, we plan to publish an update on the consultation findings this fall.

1.3 — Independent dispute resolution services for registrants

In November 2012, the CSA proposed rule amendments to NI 31-103 that would require all registered dealers and advisers, outside of Québec, to use the Ombudsman for Banking Services and Investments (OBSI) as the common dispute-resolution service for the securities industry. OBSI is an independent, not-for-profit organization with significant experience as a dispute-resolution service. The CSA has reviewed stakeholder comments on the proposal and is considering appropriate next steps.

Except in Québec, the transition period for dealers and advisers that were registered as of September 28, 2009 to make available to their clients independent dispute resolution or mediation services has been extended to the earlier of September 28, 2014 or the implementation of amendments to the requirement. If a firm became registered after September 28, 2009, then this extension does not apply and we expect the firm to immediately comply with the independent dispute resolution requirements.

For more information, see *Proposed Amendments to NI 31-103 on Dispute Resolution Service.*

We remind all dealers and advisers of their existing requirements in section 13.15 of NI 31-103 to have internal complaint handling policies to ensure that all client complaints are addressed appropriately.

1.4 — Registration of OTC derivatives market participants

As part of the CSA's ongoing development of proposals for the regulation of over-the-counter (OTC) derivatives in Canada, the CSA's Derivatives Committee published on April 18, 2013 a consultation paper on the registration and regulation of derivatives market participants.

CSA Consultation Paper 91-407 Derivatives: Registration (CSA CP 91-407) proposes three categories of registration as follows:

- Derivatives dealer for persons carrying on the business of trading in derivatives (or holding themselves out as doing so),
- Derivatives adviser for persons carrying on the business of advising others in derivatives (or holding themselves out as doing so), and
- Large derivatives participant for entities (other than derivatives dealers) that have a substantial aggregate derivatives exposure.

The paper recommends that all derivatives registrants be subject to requirements on:

- Proficiency,
- Financial condition and solvency,
- Compliance systems and internal business conduct,
- Honest dealing, and
- Holding of client and counterparty assets.

In addition, the paper also recommends that derivatives dealers and advisers be subject to:

- Gatekeeper obligations (to ensure market integrity and to assess counterparty risks), and
- Business conduct requirements, including know your client (KYC) and suitability obligations, addressing conflicts of interest, and fair dealing obligations.

The paper also proposes exemptions from regulatory requirements (but not registration) for persons subject to equivalent requirements, and also exemptions from registration (such as for derivatives dealers that provide incidental advice from also having to also register as derivatives advisers).

The CSA is reviewing over 40 comment letters it received on the consultation paper (comments closed on June 17, 2013), which will be considered when it develops rules for an OTC derivatives regulatory framework.

For more information, see *CSA CP 91-407.*

1.5 — Review of prospectus exemptions

The OSC is actively involved in exempt market initiatives including the CSA policy review of the existing minimum amount and accredited investor prospectus exemptions and the OSC's expanded review of potential new prospectus exemptions. These initiatives will have important implications for EMDs and other registrants selling exempt market products.

We are evaluating whether any changes should be made to the existing accredited investor and minimum amount exemptions. The feedback from industry highlighted the need for greater access to the exempt market for issuers, particularly start-ups and small and medium sized enterprises. As a result of that feedback, on December 14, 2012, we published *OSC Staff Consultation Paper 45-710 Considerations for New Capital Raising Prospectus Exemptions*, which sets out four concept ideas for new prospectus exemptions in Ontario. The comment period closed on March 8, 2013 and we received over 100 comment letters. We also held several town hall sessions and consulted with numerous stakeholders including SROs, foreign regulators, investor advocates, industry associations, portals, and academics.

To assist us in our review of potential new prospectus exemptions, we established the OSC's Exempt Market Advisory Committee to advise us on possible regulatory approaches to the exempt market. In addition, we considered the experience of other CSA jurisdictions with prospectus exemptions not currently available in Ontario, as well as international developments relevant to capital raising in the exempt market.

On August 28, 2013, we published OSC Notice 45-712 *Progress Report on Review of Prospectus Exemptions to Facilitate Capital Raising* (OSC Notice 45-712), which sets out the next steps in the OSC's exempt market review and consideration of the following prospectus exemptions:

- a crowdfunding exemption,

- a family, friends and business associates exemption,

- an offering memorandum exemption,

- a streamlined version of the existing rights offering exemption currently available across Canada, and

- amending the accredited investor exemption in Ontario to allow fully managed accounts to purchase investment fund securities.

This work is a priority for the OSC and any resulting proposals will be brought to the public for comment before making any final decisions. For more information, see *OSC Notice 45-712*.

1.6 — Ongoing amendments to registration requirements, exemptions and ongoing registrant obligations

Since the implementation of *NI 31-103* in September 2009, and amendments which came into force in July 2011, we have monitored this new regulatory regime for registrants and engaged in discussions with stakeholders about questions and concerns regarding their practical experience working with the regime. With the CSA, we have developed additional technical and substantive amendments to NI 31-103 and NI 33-109 *Registration Information* (NI 33-109) arising from this ongoing process.

This fall, we expect to publish for comment these proposed amendments to codify current exemption orders, refine certain exemptions, and provide guidance and clarifications that will enhance investor protection and improve the day-to-day operation of the registration regime for industry participants and regulators. In addition, we believe that the proposed amendments will further clarify our legislative intent.

2. — Outreach to registrants

2.1 — New outreach program

In July 2013, the CRR Branch launched its new outreach program to registrants. The new program will strengthen our communications with Ontario registrants we directly regulate and other industry participants (such as lawyers and compliance consultants), and is intended to promote stronger compliance practices and enhance investor protection.

Our new outreach program is interactive and will enhance dialogue with registrants. It has the following features:

Registrant Outreach web page

We have set up a *Registrant Outreach web page* on the OSC's website, which has been designed to enhance awareness of topical compliance issues. Registrants are encouraged to check the web page on a regular basis for updates on regulatory issues impacting Ontario registrants.

Educational seminars

Beginning September 2013, we began hosting a series of targeted seminars to provide registrants with practical knowledge on compliance related matters, such as calculating regulatory capital, understanding KYC, know your product (KYP), and suitability obligations, and getting through an OSC compliance review. Interested registrants can find the seminar calendar, course descriptions, and how to register on the *Registrant Outreach web page*.

Registrant Outreach Community

Registrants are also encouraged to join our Registrant Outreach Community to receive regular email updates on OSC policies and initiatives impacting registrants, as well as the latest publications and guidance on our expectations regarding compliance. To join, visit the *Registrant Outreach web page*.

Registrant Resources

Our Registrant Outreach web page has a Registrant Resources section to provide registrants and other industry participants with easy, centralized access to recent compliance materials.

If you have questions related directly to the Registrant Outreach program or have suggestions for seminar topics, please send an email to RegistrantOutreach@osc.gov.on.ca.

2.2 — Registrant advisory committee

The CRR Branch has formed a new committee to help us to consult with our stakeholders and to assist registrants in meeting their regulatory obligations. In December 2012, we established the Registrant Advisory Committee (RAC) to serve as a forum to discuss issues and challenges faced by registrants in interpreting and complying with Ontario securities law, including registration and compliance related matters. The committee's mandate is to assess these issues, discuss possible resolutions, consider the implication of each feasible option, and help to ensure that solutions are applied consistently across registrants. The committee also plays a consultative role by providing feedback to the CRR Branch on the development and implementation of policy and rule making initiatives that promote investor protection and fair and efficient capital markets.

The RAC is chaired by the CRR Branch's Director and consists of members representing the different registration categories and registrant business models, industry advisory groups and SROs. The RAC meets approximately four to six times per year, in addition to ad hoc meetings as required, with members serving two-year terms.

3. — Registration of firms and individuals

The registration requirements under securities law help to protect investors from unfair, improper or fraudulent practices by participants in the securities markets. The information required to support a registration application allows us to assess a firm's and individual's fitness for registration. When assessing a firm's fitness for registration we consider whether it is able to carry out its obligations under securities law. For example, registered firms must be financially viable. We use three fundamental criteria to assess an individual's fitness; their proficiency, integrity and solvency. These fitness requirements are the cornerstones of the registration regime.

In this section, we discuss foreign broker-dealers registered as EMDs, current trends in registration issues, novel business activities potentially requiring registration, relevant investment management experience for advising representatives, and amendments to the fees rule.

3.1 — Registration and oversight of foreign broker-dealers

Following a public consultation process, the CSA and IIROC have concluded that IIROC should regulate all firms that conduct brokerage activities (trading securities listed on an exchange in foreign or Canadian markets), and that firms using the EMD registration category should not be permitted to conduct brokerage activities with accredited investors. We intend to publish proposed amendments to NI 31-103 later in 2013 as part of the ongoing amendments to that rule in order to prohibit EMDs from conducting brokerage activities. In our most recent notice, we suggest that impacted firms may wish to consider how they will conduct brokerage activities in the future, including transferring their brokerage activities to a Canadian incorporated IIROC firm, tailoring their activities to fit solely within the EMD registration category, or relying upon the international dealer exemption in section 8.18 of NI 31-103.

For more information, see the most recent notices published by the CSA and IIROC on February 7, 2013:

- *CSA Staff Notice 31-333 Follow-up to Broker-Dealer Registration in the Exempt Market Dealer Category*

- *IIROC Notice 13-0042 IIROC Concept Proposal Restricted Dealer Member Proposal — Summary of Comments*

3.2 — Current trends in registration issues

Outside business activities

Registrants sometimes have business activities in addition to those with their sponsoring firm. Registrants must ensure that these outside business activities (OBAs) do not impair or impede the performance of their regulatory obligations, including with the conflicts of interest provision in NI 31-103. We remind registrants that all OBAs must be disclosed in Item 10 of *From 33-109F4* (Form F4), or *Form 33-109F5* for changes in OBAs after registration.

Below, we list some of the inquiries we received on which OBAs must be disclosed and our interpretation of the requirements.

What does "business related" mean in Form F4?

Any activity that places the registered individual in regular contact with clients or potential clients can be considered "business related".

What does "officer or director positions and . . . any other equivalent positions" mean in Form F4?

Equivalent positions to an officer or director include roles where the individual is in a position of power or influence over clients or potential clients. This may include non-leadership and/or unpaid roles. For example, some of the activities that we have required to be disclosed include:

- roles handling investments or monies of an organization, such as being on a charity's investment or finance committee, as these roles are similar to activities performed by registrants,

- acting as a pastor, as this role places the individual in a position of influence over his or her congregation, and

- mentoring youth through an organization, as it places the individual in a position of influence over potential clients, including family members of the youth.

Does being an owner of a holding company require disclosure?

Yes. Having ownership in a holding company is a "business" activity that requires disclosure. This is because owning a holding company allows a person to perform, control or influence a business activity indirectly. However, where the ownership is at a negligible level of 1% or 2%, we generally do not require disclosure.

Does an OBA have to be "material" in order to merit disclosure?

No. Whether an activity is material is subjective. An OBA that falls under Form F4 must be disclosed, even if it is "immaterial" from the perspective of the firm or the registered individual. Once the activity has been disclosed, we will review the activity and take into account the potential conflicts of interest that may arise as a result of that activity.

Return of (or requests to withdraw) incomplete or delayed applications

In some instances, we receive applications for registration that are substantially incomplete. For example, required provincial business name registrations have not been obtained, audited financial statements have not been prepared, an auditor has not been appointed, or firms are not prepared to file the individual registration applications on the National Registration Database (NRD). In these instances, we may return the applications without review for completion.

As well, in other cases when we review applications, applicants provide inadequate, incomplete or no responses to deficiencies we raise or to our requests for further information, despite multiple follow-ups. Also, applications for exemptive relief from certain registration requirements (such as proficiency) provided with registration applications are also sometimes deficient in the information they include or filers are slow to respond to questions. These deficiencies cause delays in the time to process these applications. In these instances, we may require the applicant to withdraw the application.

Applicants should be aware that when we return an application or require the withdrawal of an application, when the application is re-filed, we may require the filing fees to be paid again.

As such, to avoid processing delays and paying additional filing fees, applicants should ensure that applications are complete and contain all required information when they are filed and that they have the resources to respond to our deficiencies and questions within a reasonable time-frame.

Late filings

We continue to see a trend in registrants incurring late fees for failing to meet deadlines to notify us of changes in registration information. In particular, we see numerous late filings relating to terminations, OBAs, and criminal, civil and financial disclosure. *NI 33-109* sets out the deadlines for these and other filings.

Also, many registered firms and exempt international firms fail to file their *Form 13-502F4 Capital Markets Participation Fee Calculation* by December 1, or in the case of unregistered investment fund managers, within 90 days of their fiscal year ends. Also, some registrants are filing late notices under section 11.9 of NI 31-103 (see section 4.1.2 on *Failure to provide notice of ownership changes or asset acquisitions*). We will charge late fees in applicable circumstances. The fees for late filings are outlined in Appendix D to *OSC Rule 13-502 Fees* (OSC Rule 13-502).

When late fees remain unpaid for more than 30 days after they are due, the firm's registration is automatically suspended pursuant to section 29(1) of the Act.

We remind firms that they are expected to have policies and procedures in place to ensure that required filings are made within the deadlines established under securities laws. Maintaining these policies and procedures will also help firms avoid incurring late fees. In addition, repeated late filings may impact our assessment of a firm's suitability for registration.

3.3 — Novel business activities potentially requiring registration

Over the last year, we reviewed a number of cases involving persons and companies engaging in (or proposing to engage in) novel business activities that appeared to be registrable trading or advising activities. In these cases, we assessed whether these entities would be "in the business" of trading or advising and therefore subject to the dealer or adviser registration requirements under the Act.

To assist entities in determining whether their activities require registration, we generally refer them to the guidance in section 1.3 of *31-103CP* under *Business trigger for trading and advising*. The definition of "trade" is very broad and includes "any act, advertisement, solicitation, conduct or negotiation directly or indirectly in furtherance of" a trade. The question of whether entities satisfy the "business trigger" will generally be fact-specific and may not apply to all entities engaged in similar activities.

Some recent examples of entities that we have found to be in the business of trading or advising include:

- an online platform that aims to bring together accredited investors and issuers,

- entities that offer "auto-trading", "mirror investing" and "trade copying" services to clients,

- promoters and distributors of certain tax shelter products, particularly products that involve leveraged donations of property to charities in the expectation that clients will receive tax credits,

- finders, referral agents and investor relations entities who regularly participate in private placements and prospectus offerings in return for fees and/or warrants granted as compensation,

- an online portfolio management system for investors to use to build investment portfolios based on their investment needs and objectives, and

- unregistered firms in Ontario that were trading or advising in securities with investors located outside of Ontario.

Some of these examples are discussed in more detail below.

1) — Online platform to facilitate investing

We recently granted restricted dealer registration to a not-for-profit online platform (the Filer) that aims to facilitate "impact investing" by bringing together accredited investors in Ontario (and potentially elsewhere) and issuers that aim to solve social or environmental challenges in Ontario.

The Filer also obtained exemptive relief from certain KYC and suitability requirements (Client-Specific KYC and Suitability Requirements) in NI 31-103.

The decision states that, subject to certain investment limits and other terms and conditions, the Filer is exempt from the obligation to determine that sales of securities by issuers to accredited investors who are matched to the issuers through the Filer's platform are suitable for the investors in light of the investor's investment needs and objectives, financial circumstances and risk tolerance. The Filer continues to be required to comply with customary gatekeeper KYC requirements, such as establishing the identity of a client, confirming that the client is an accredited investor and complying with anti-money laundering requirements. The Filer may not issue securities or have related or connected issuers and no transactions may be executed, settled or cleared through the Filer's platform.

The time-limited relief from the Client-Specific KYC and Suitability Requirements for the Filer's platform is based on the particular facts and circumstances of the application and on very specific, rigorous conditions relating to processes such as the criteria for selecting issuers and background checks. There is no assurance that a similar exemption from KYC and suitability requirements would be granted to others, including crowdfunding portals.

For more information, see the June 17, 2013 decision *In the Matter of MaRS VX*.

2) — Auto-trading, mirror investing and trade copying services

We have considered a number of situations involving "auto-trading", "mirror investing" and "trade copying" services.

In one case, we considered a firm based in Ontario that provides auto-trading services to clients for a fee. The firm operates a website that allows investors to subscribe to one or more non-affiliated investment newsletter services that provide buy and sell recommendations for the trading of shares and options. The firm provides an automated trading service whereby the firm will, through the use of software and a power of attorney arrangement over the client's brokerage account, match newsletter recommendations with client instructions to create a trade order for each of its relevant clients which the firm electronically delivers to the client's investment dealer. Based on the nature of the services provided by the firm and the terms of the agreement between the firm and its clients, we concluded that the firm was in the business of advising in securities in Ontario.

We have also received enquiries from a number of individuals who proposed to set up "mirror investing" or "trade copying" arrangements for a fee. In one case, an individual claimed that he was an experienced trader who had developed a personal trading strategy that yielded consistent and positive returns. The individual wished to offer a service whereby other investors could benefit from his trading strategy by using "trade copying" software that would copy trades from his personal trading account to their trading accounts in exchange for a share of the profits. We asked this individual to seek appropriate legal advice before proceeding as we would likely take the view that these activities would be registrable advising activity.

3) — Promoters and distributors of tax shelter products

We have recently reviewed a number of cases that involved promoters and distributors of tax shelter products. Based upon our review of the products and how they were promoted, and the relevant caselaw, including the recent Synergy Group decision,[2] we concluded that the entities were engaged in registrable activity and were required to register as a dealer.

4) — Online portfolio management system

An unregistered firm located in Ontario developed a web-based personal portfolio management system that investors could subscribe to, for a monthly fee, to enable them to build, design and manage an investment portfolio with securities using portfolio management tools and approaches. After investors input their portfolio needs, asset allocation and risk and reward preferences to the system, the firm's software (using algorithms) would provide them with a customized short-list of securities that the investor could consider for purchase through their on-line brokerage account at a registered investment dealer. The firm claimed that its system provided a research tool for self-directed investors and did not provide advice. We disagreed with this claim. Our view was that it would be in the business of providing tailored securities advice to investors based on their investment needs and objectives, and that the firm would need to register as an adviser if it launched its system in Ontario.

5) — Trading or advising in Ontario with non-Ontario investors

We have recently seen a number of cases in which individuals and firms located in Ontario were engaged in registrable trading or advising activities with investors outside of Ontario without being registered in Ontario.

We remind market participants that registration in Ontario is generally required (unless a registration exemption is otherwise available) where registrable activities are provided to investors resident in Ontario or where registrable activities are conducted within Ontario, regardless of the location of the clients. If the trading or advising activity is taking place within Ontario, then to comply with section 25 of the Act the individual or firm is generally required to be registered as a dealer or adviser (as applicable) in Ontario, or rely on a registration exemption. Individuals and firms that conduct these activities may not avoid registration by informing prospective clients that they do not offer or provide their services to Ontario investors.

---

[2]See decision of the Alberta Court of Appeal in *Synergy Group (2000) Inc. v. Alberta (Securities Commission)*, 2011 ABCA 194.

In the recent *Crowe* decision,[3] the Ontario Superior Court of Justice (Divisional Court) reaffirmed that provincial securities legislation is not limited to protecting the interests of investors located within the province from unfair, improper or fraudulent activities. Provincial securities legislation regulates individuals and firms within the province in order to protect investors both within and outside the province from unfair, improper or fraudulent activities. Where a trade has an extra-provincial character, the Commission's jurisdiction over the trade is not determined by the location of the investors; rather, the Commission will have jurisdiction over a trade where there is a sufficient connection between Ontario and the impugned activities and the entities involved.

The Commission has recently granted relief from the dealer and adviser registration requirements in a number of cases[4] where registrable services were being conducted in Ontario but were provided to clients resident in the US or another foreign jurisdiction and the firm was appropriately registered to provide such services in the US or other foreign jurisdiction. While staff would not necessarily consider these cases to be precedents, we will consider recommending exemptive relief by analogy to the principles reflected in these cases in appropriate circumstances.

3.4 — Relevant investment management experience for advising representatives

An individual applying to register as an advising representative or associate advising representative with a PM needs to meet the "relevant investment management experience" and educational requirements to qualify for registration.

We receive many inquiries about the factors we consider in assessing what constitutes "relevant investment management experience." In response, on January 17, 2013 we published CSA Staff Notice 31-332 *Relevant Investment Management Experience for Advising Representatives and Associate Advising Representatives of Portfolio Managers* (CSA Staff Notice 31-332). While we assess each application on its facts, we expect prospective applicants to consider the information in this notice when deciding whether to apply for registration as an advising representative or associate advising representative.

The notice discusses decisions on experience relating to:

- client relationship management

- corporate finance/investment banking

- dealing representative with IIROC member

- consulting on portfolio manager selection and monitoring, and

- mutual fund sales

For more information, see *CSA Staff Notice 31-332*.

3.5 — Amendments to calculation of capital markets participation fees

On April 1, 2013, amendments to OSC Rule 13-502 on fees came into force.[5] In the past, registrants and unregistered capital markets participants were required to calculate information on Form 13-502F4 *Capital Markets Participation Fee Calculation* (Form 13-502F4) based on their most recently completed fiscal year. However, as a result of the amendments to the fees rule, registered firms, exempt international firms relying on sections 8.18 [international dealer] and 8.26 [international adviser] of NI 31-103 and unregistered IFMs[6] will complete Form 13-502F4 for the required filings for 2013, 2014 and 2015 based on information from their financial statements for their "reference year".

For most firms, the "reference year" will be their last fiscal year ending before May 1, 2012. Therefore, the specified Ontario revenues reported on most firms' Form 13-502F4 should be the same in each of 2013, 2014 and 2015. However, in cases where a firm was not a registrant firm, exempt international firm or unregistered IFM at the end of its last fiscal year ending before May 1, 2012, the firm's "reference year" will not be static. In these cases, registrant firms and exempt international firms will use their financial statements for their last fiscal year ending in the calendar year (or, in the case of unregistered investment fund managers, their last fiscal year) when completing Form 13-502F4. Therefore, the specified Ontario revenues reported on these firms' Form 13-502F4 will likely be different in each of 2013, 2014 and 2015. This scenario might apply where a firm became registered in Ontario for the first time on or after May 1, 2012 or became registered for the first time before May 1, 2012 but had not yet experienced a full fiscal year before May 1, 2012.

For more information, see *OSC Rule 13-502*. Also, see section 4.1.2 of this report on *Incorrect calculation of capital markets participation fees*.

---

[3]See *Crowe v. OSC* (2012) 108 O.R. (3d) 410 (Aitken J., Pardu J., Swinton J.) (December 5, 2011); leave to appeal to the Court of Appeal dismissed July, 2012.

[4]See, e.g., the following adviser registration cases: *Re Macquarie Private Wealth Inc. and Macquarie Private Wealth Corp.* dated October 19, 2012; *Re BMO Nesbitt Burns Securities Ltd.* dated April 11, 2012; *Re Manulife Asset Management (North America) Limited* dated October 28, 2011; *Re Goodman & Company N.Y. Ltd. and Goodman & Company, Investment Counsel Ltd.* dated October 25, 2011; and *Re Gavin Management Group, Inc.* dated June 3, 2011; and the following dealer registration cases: *Re NCP Northland Capital Partners Inc. and NCP Northland Capital Partners (USA) Inc.* dated March 11, 2011; *Re Stonecap Securities Inc. and SCS (USA) Inc.* dated February 18, 2011; and *Re Thomas Weisel Partners Canada Inc. and Thomas Weisel Partners (USA) Inc.* dated October 7, 2008. All cases are available on the OSC's website.

[5]On April 1, 2013, amendments to OSC Rule 13-503 (*Commodity Futures Act*) Fees also came into force. This rule covers fees for persons or companies registered as dealers or advisers under the *Commodity Futures Act* (Ontario).

[6]See section 1.1 of OSC Rule 13-502 for the definition of an "unregistered investment fund manager."

Part 3:
REGISTRATION

4. — Information for dealers, advisers and investment fund managers

The information in this section includes the key findings and outcomes from our ongoing compliance reviews of the registrants we directly regulate. We highlight current trends in deficiencies from our reviews and provide suggested practices to address the deficiencies. We also discuss new or proposed rules and initiatives impacting registrants.

This part of the report is divided into four main sections. The first section contains general information that is relevant for all registrants. The other sections contain information specific to dealers (EMDs and SPDs), advisers (PMs) and IFMs, respectively. This report is organized to allow a registrant to focus on reading the section for all registrants and the sections that apply to their registration categories. *However, we recommend that registrants review all sections in this part, as some of the information presented for one type of registrant may be relevant to other registrants.*

4.1 — All registrants

This section discusses our compliance review process, current trends in deficiencies and suggested practices to address them, and new and proposed rules and initiatives impacting all registrants.

4.1.1 — Compliance review process

We conduct compliance reviews of registered firms on a continuous basis. The purpose of compliance reviews is primarily to assess compliance with Ontario securities law; but they also help registrants to improve their understanding of regulatory requirements and our expectations, and help us to learn about a specific industry topic or practice we may have concerns with.

Risk-based approach

Firms are generally selected for review using a risk-based approach. This approach is intended to identify firms that are most likely to have material compliance issues (including risk of harm to investors) or a significant impact to the capital markets if there is a compliance breach. To determine which firms should be reviewed, we consider a number of factors, including firms' responses to the most recent OSC risk assessment questionnaire, their compliance review history, complaints or tips from external parties and referrals from another OSC branch, an SRO or another regulator.

We frequently conduct compliance reviews on-site at a registrant's premises, but also perform reviews from our offices, which are known as desk reviews. For information on "What to expect from, and how to prepare for, an OSC compliance review" see section 5.1.1 of *OSC Staff Notice 33-738 2012 OSC Annual Summary Report for Dealers, Advisers and Investment Fund Managers* (OSC Staff Notice 33-738).

As part of our risk-based approach to reviews, we also assess which areas of a registered firm's business and operations to review and focus on. This means that on any given review, we may not review all aspects of a firm's business, but may focus on certain functions or risks. For example, we may decide to review a PM firm's portfolio management and trading practices, but not to review their marketing practices. But we always perform certain review steps for on-site reviews, including interviewing senior management of the registrant to obtain an understanding of their business, reviewing the firm's most recent financial statements and excess working capital calculations, reviewing regulatory reports (such as the annual compliance report to the board of directors), and assessing the firm's overall compliance and supervision structure.

Sweep reviews

In addition to reviewing individual firms, we conduct sweeps which are compliance reviews of a sample of registered firms on a specific topic or in an industry sector. Sweeps allow us to respond on a timely basis to industry-wide concerns or issues. We regularly perform sweeps of newly registered firms to assess if they are off to a good start and to help them to understand their requirements and our expectations. We also regularly review large or "impact" firms to help ensure we allocate sufficient compliance oversight resources to firms that would have a material impact to investors and the Ontario capital markets if there was a significant failure in their systems of control and supervision.

Some of the sweep reviews we performed this year are high-lighted below:

- We reviewed a sample of newly registered PMs. See section 4.3.2 for a summary of this sweep and its findings.

- We started an on-site sweep review of a sample of "impact" PMs, IFMs and EMDs. We assessed a PM or IFM to be an "impact" firm if it had a high value of assets under administration or management and a high number of clients compared to other firms. We assessed an EMD to be an "impact" firm if it had a high number of dealing representatives compared to other firms.

- We performed a desk review of the custody practices of a sample of EMDs, PMs and IFMs that had custody of their client's assets. See section 4.1.3 *Review of custody requirements for non-SRO registrants* for a summary of this sweep and its findings.

- We performed a desk review sweep of a sample of firms' excess working capital calculations for periods during their financial year. This sweep complemented our ongoing reviews of firms' financial statements and other financial information that firms deliver to us for their financial year-ends. See section 4.1.2 on *Inaccurate calculations of excess working capital* for deficiencies identified from this sweep (and actions to be taken).

- We performed a desk review of a sample of firms' 2012 capital markets participation fees to the OSC. See section 4.1.2 on *Incorrect calculation of capital markets participation fees* for this sweep's findings and guidance.

Outcomes of compliance reviews

In most cases, the deficiencies found in a compliance review are set out in a written report to the firm so that they can take appropriate corrective action. After a firm addresses its deficiencies, the expected outcome is that they have enhanced their compliance. If a firm had many significant deficiencies, once it addresses these, the expected outcome is that they have significantly enhanced their compliance.

In addition to issuing compliance deficiency reports, we take additional regulatory action when warranted (including when we identify signs of potential registrant misconduct or fraud).

The outcomes of our compliance reviews in fiscal 2013, with comparables for 2012, are presented in the following table and are listed in their increasing order of seriousness. The percentages in the table are based on the registered firms we reviewed during the year and not the population of all registered firms.

Outcomes of compliance reviews (all registration categories)	Fiscal 2013	Fiscal 2012
Enhanced compliance	38%	34%
Significantly enhanced compliance	52%	47%
Terms and conditions on registration	3%	8%
Surrender of registration	1%	1%
Referral to the Enforcement Branch	2%	6%
Suspension of registration	4%	4%

For an explanation of each outcome, see Appendix A in *OSC Staff Notice 33-738*. In some cases, there may be more than one outcome from a review. In these cases, the review is counted only under its most serious outcome.

Non-significant deficiencies

In August 2011, we changed our approach to compliance deficiency reports issued to registrants upon the completion of a review. Previously, we required that registrants respond to us explaining how they will address all deficiencies included in the report. With our new approach, we require registrants to only respond in writing to deficiencies that we have identified as being "significant." This helps us to better allocate our resources and focus on higher-risk activities. However, we still expect registrants to address the non-significant deficiencies, even though there is no requirement for them to respond to us in writing. We informed registrants that on a sample basis we would follow up with them to assess that they have adequately addressed the non-significant deficiencies.

In November 2012 we conducted a desk review of a sample of EMDs, PMs and IFMs to assess if they had taken corrective actions regarding non-significant deficiencies identified from previous reviews. We required the selected registrants to provide us with the appropriate documentation to evidence that the non-significant deficiencies were addressed. Overall, we were satisfied with the corrective action taken for the non-significant deficiencies. Based on this sample, we believe that our new approach is effective and will therefore continue.

Contacting investors as part of compliance reviews

As part of our ongoing, normal course reviews of dealers and advisers, we contact a sample of their clients by telephone. Clients who are contacted may be asked a number of questions about their registrant firm and dealing or advising representative, including the completeness and accuracy of their KYC information obtained by the firm and the investment recommendations and advice provided to them. Clients' participation in this process is voluntary. We've found that investor contact is a valuable method to assess if registrants are complying with Ontario securities law. For more information, see *OSC New Review Procedure of Calling Investors* and *Frequently Asked Questions on Receiving Calls from the OSC* on the OSC's website.

Protection of registrant and investor information

As part of our on-site compliance reviews, we examine the books, records and other documents maintained by registrants, including personal information concerning their clients. This is normally done at the registrant's offices. However, we may make copies of this information and take it back to our offices. We also obtain information from registrants and applicants for other purposes, such as reviewing registration applications and notices of the sale of a registrant's securities or assets.

The OSC is subject to the provisions of the *Freedom of Information and Protection of Privacy Act* (Ontario), which imposes obligations on how we collect, use, disclose, retain, secure and destroy personal information. In addition, OSC staff are also subject to the OSC's Code of Conduct which requires us to use and protect confidential information appropriately. For example, access to registrant and client information obtained from a compliance review is limited to OSC staff participating in the review or others who may be involved in performing their duties because of issues raised by the review.

We have a responsibility to protect the information we obtain from our stakeholders, and will take all necessary steps in the event of a security breach.

4.1.2 — Current trends in deficiencies and suggested practices

In this section, we summarize key trends in deficiencies from recent compliance reviews of EMDs, PMs, and IFMs. For each deficiency, we summarize the applicable requirements under Ontario securities law which must be followed. In addition, where applicable, we provide suggested practices. *The suggested practices throughout this report are intended to give guidance to help registrants address the deficiencies, and provide our expectations of registrants.*

Part 3:
REGISTRATION

We strongly recommend registrants review the deficiencies and suggested practices in this report that apply to their registration categories and operations to assess and, as needed, implement enhancements to their firm's systems of compliance and internal controls.

Non-compliance with KYC, KYP and suitability requirements and accredited investor requirements

We continue to have concerns that some dealers and advisers are not adequately meeting their KYC, KYP and suitability obligations. We also remain concerned that some EMDs are selling securities to investors that do not qualify under a prospectus exemption (such as the accredited investor exemption).

In 2012, we conducted a targeted review (Suitability Sweep) of 87 firms registered in the categories of EMD and PM. Our Suitability Sweep identified a number of significant suitability compliance issues at the registrants we reviewed, which we think is unacceptable. On May 30, 2013, we published OSC Staff Notice 33-740 *Report on the results of the 2012 targeted review of portfolio managers and exempt market dealers to assess compliance with the know-your-client, know-your-product and suitability obligations* (OSC Staff Notice 33-740) which summarized the Suitability Sweep's findings. Some of the major findings are highlighted below.

Findings from reviews of EMDs

- Selling exempt securities to non-accredited investors

- Inadequate suitability assessment, including due to over-concentration in one investment and due to inadequate documentation to satisfy how a suitability determination was made

- Inadequate process for collection, documentation and maintenance of KYC information

Findings from reviews of PMs

- Inadequate relationship disclosure information

- Inadequate process on collection, documentation and maintenance of KYC information

For more information, see *OSC Staff Notice 33-740*. For guidance to dealers on complying with the accredited investor exemption, see *OSC Staff Notice 33-735 Sale of Exempt Securities to Non-Accredited Investors* (OSC Staff Notice 33-735).

Later this year, we plan on issuing guidance (including suggested practices) in the areas of KYC, KYP and suitability to assist registrants in meeting their obligations. We will continue to focus on assessing if EMDs and PMs are meeting their KYC, KYP and suitability obligations, and if EMDs are selling exempt securities to non-accredited investors. Where we identify significant compliance issues in these areas, we will take appropriate regulatory action. As well, we intend to pay particular attention to registrants relying on purported "client-directed trade instructions", or selling investments using the $150,000 minimum amount exemption when the investment represents more than 10% of the client's net financial assets.

Inadequate compliance systems and UDPs and CCOs not meeting their responsibilities

In a limited number of cases, we find that registered firms have an inadequate compliance system and that their Ultimate Designated Person (UDP) and Chief Compliance Officer (CCO) are not meeting their responsibilities. For example, we identified some firms with significant compliance issues, such as selling exempt securities to retail investors, dealing or advising in securities of related and connected issuers when it was not suitable or appropriate for clients, or having unregistered persons engage in dealing or advising activities on the firm's behalf. We assessed these firms as having inadequate compliance systems and that their UDP and CCO (who in some cases were the same individual) were not meeting their responsibilities.

There are serious consequences when firms have deficiencies of this nature. In addition to requiring the firm to correct their deficiencies through a concerted effort to review and apply securities law to their operations, we may take further regulatory action including:

- requiring the firm to hire an external compliance consultant to correct the deficiencies and to strengthen the firm's compliance system,

- requiring the firm to replace its CCO with a better suited individual, and

- referring the matter to the Enforcement Branch or suspending the firm's registration.

Registered firms are required to maintain a control and supervisory system sufficient to ensure compliance with securities law and to manage business risks (see section 32(2) of the Act and section 11.1 of NI 31-103). A firm's UDP and CCO have extremely important compliance roles. They are ultimately responsible for ensuring that a compliance system is in place to ensure that the firm, and its representatives, comply with securities law. It is critical that they understand and fulfill their required responsibilities and roles under sections 5.1 and 5.2 of NI 31-103.

The UDP is responsible to supervise the firm's compliance activities and to promote compliance.

The CCO is responsible to establish and maintain policies for assessing compliance by the firm, and individuals acting on its behalf, with securities legislation. The CCO must also monitor and assess compliance by the firm, and individuals acting on its behalf, with securities legislation.

An effective compliance system is essential to a registered firm's continued fitness for registration. Elements include day-to-day monitoring and supervision, overall systemic monitoring, identifying non-compliance at an early stage, and allowing for correction of non-compliant conduct in a timely manner. Although the firm's UDP and CCO serve important roles, compliance is a responsibility that extends to everyone in the firm, whether they are registered or not.

Suggested practices

- UDPs should ensure that adequate staff and resources are allocated to their firm's compliance function, taking into account the size, nature, complexity and risk of their business.

- UDPs should communicate and reinforce to all staff that compliance with securities law is a firm-wide responsibility.

- CCOs should ensure that they have an appropriate amount of involvement, time and resources to fulfill their responsibility to monitor and assess compliance with regulatory requirements.

- Firms and their CCOs should perform ongoing self-assessments of their compliance with Ontario securities law and take action to improve their internal controls, monitoring, supervision and policies and procedures when necessary.

- Firms should provide regular training to their staff so that they understand the firm's policies and procedures and applicable regulatory requirements.

- Firms should consider engaging external legal counsel or a compliance consultant to provide advice on compliance, including making recommendations to improve the firm's compliance system.

- CCOs should continuously educate themselves on compliance and regulatory topics, such as by attending compliance-focused seminars and participating in compliance officer associations.

- Firms should appoint individuals to act as alternates in the brief absence of the CCO or UDP (such as during vacations).

- Firms should keep detailed records of activities they conduct to identify compliance deficiencies and the actions taken to correct them.

For more guidance, see section 11.1 of 31-103CP and our May 2012 *OSC Message to CCOs and UDPs on Inadequate Compliance Systems*.

Inadequate or no annual compliance report

We continue to find cases where a registered firm's CCO does not provide an annual report to the firm's board of directors that assesses the firm's, and its registered individuals', compliance with securities law. In addition, we also find cases where a CCO submits a perfunctory report that concludes that the firm has complied with securities law, but does not provide any support for how the CCO made his or her assessment.

One of the CCO's responsibilities is to submit an annual report to the firm's board of directors, or individuals acting in a similar capacity for the firm, for the purpose of assessing compliance by the firm, and individuals acting on its behalf, with securities legislation (see section 5.2 of NI 31-103).

When the CCO has not submitted an annual compliance report, or submits a perfunctory report, this raises questions about the adequacy of the registrant's compliance system, and whether the CCO is adequately performing his or her responsibilities.

We review firm's annual reports during all on-site compliance reviews and use it as a factor to assess the adequacy of the reviewed firm's compliance system and if the CCO is performing his or her responsibilities.

For suggested practices on the CCO's annual compliance report, see section 5.1.2 of *OSC Staff Notice 33-738* under the heading *Failure by CCO to submit an annual compliance report*.

Failure to provide notice of ownership changes or asset acquisitions

Some registrants do not provide us with the required notice under sections 11.9 or 11.10 of NI 31-103 of proposed ownership changes in, or asset acquisitions of, registered firms. We have found a number of cases where:

- registered firms or registered individuals (including the UDP, CCO, advising representative, or dealing representative of the firm) have acquired 10% or more of the securities of another registered firm, or their sponsoring firm, without first providing us with the required notice

- registered firms or registered individuals have acquired a security or securities in addition to the 10% or more securities that they already own without first providing us with the required notice; or

- registered firms have not provided us with the required notice as soon as the registered firm knew, or had reason to believe, that 10% or more of its voting securities were going to be acquired by a non-registrant, including an officer, director, permitted individual or employee of the firm (barring exceptional circumstances, we expect to receive notice of these transactions at least 30 days prior to the transaction taking place).

We have also found that some IIROC or MFDA member firms did not file the required 11.9 or 11.10 notices based on the view that their SRO notice process was sufficient. This is not the case. The notice obligations apply to all registrants, including member firms of IIROC and the MFDA, and arise from the OSC's responsibility to register, among others, dealer firms.

If we notify the registered firm or person making the proposed acquisition that we object to the transaction (within 30 days of receipt of the notice), then the acquisition must not take place until our objection is withdrawn.

In the cases where registrants did not provide us with the required notice for their completed acquisitions, we required them to file the notice, pay the applicable filing fees and be subjected to our notice review process. So far, we have not objected to any of these transactions, but instead have issued a written letter to each firm warning them of the seriousness of their failure to provide notice. However, if we were to object to a completed transaction in the future, we would take regulatory action, including potentially having the transaction unwound. In the future, registrants that do not give us the required notice may also be charged late filing fees.

In last year's report, we provided guidance to assist firms in providing sufficient information to us on their section 11.9 or 11.10 notices. See section 4.3 *Common deficiencies from notices on proposed ownership changes or asset acquisitions of a registrant and suggested practices* in *OSC Staff Notice 33-738*.

Inaccurate calculations of excess working capital

Registered firms must meet their capital requirements in section 12.1 of NI 31-103 to maintain their registration in good standing. Despite the importance of the capital requirements, our ongoing desk and field reviews continue to identify cases where firms are incorrectly calculating their excess working capital on *Form 31-103F1 Calculation of Excess Working Capital* (Form 31-103F1). An inaccurate calculation on Form 31-103F1 may result in a firm failing to meet its capital requirements once corrections are made.

To assist firms in correctly preparing their capital calculations, we have listed in the table below the common deficiencies identified from our reviews of Form 31-103F1s over the last year. Where applicable, the deficiencies have been separated out by each line item on Form 31-103F1. In order to reduce errors in calculating their capital, registered firms should avoid these deficiencies and follow the identified actions to be taken when preparing their Form 31-103F1s.

Deficiency noted	Action to be taken
Line 1 Current assets and Line 2 Current liabilities	
The amounts for current assets and current liabilities are accounted for on a cash-basis and not an accrual basis.	Form 31-103F1 must be prepared using the accounting principles used to prepare the firm's financial statements in accordance with NI 52-107 *Acceptable Accounting Principles and Auditing Standards*. These accounting principles include using an accrual basis of accounting.
Line 1 *Current assets*	
(a) Inclusion of accounts receivables, especially from related parties, that are not readily convertible to cash.	(a) Any receivables that are included on Line 1 and that cannot be converted into cash in a prompt and timely manner should be deducted on Line 2 *Less current assets not readily convertible into cash (e.g., prepaid expenses)*.
	Firms should maintain evidence that if the related party receivable was called upon by the firm, the amount could be promptly received. Evidence may include, among other items, the most recent audited financial statements of the related party or a bank statement supporting the amount of cash available.
(b) Inclusion of cash that is committed to serve a specific purpose (e.g., for collateral or as a security deposit).	(b) Any cash that is not readily available for use by the registrant for its current business purposes or to settle its current liabilities is considered to be restricted cash and should be deducted on Line 2.
Line 5 *Add long-term related party debt*	
(a) Failure to add back 100% of long-term related party debt.	(a) All long-term related party debt is required to be added back on Line 5 unless the firm and the lender have executed a subordination agreement in the form and content prescribed in Appendix B to NI 31-103 <<and>> the firm has delivered a copy of the agreement to its principal regulator.
(b) Failure to deliver a copy of the subordination agreement to the regulator when subordination agreements have been executed.	(b) Firms are required to deliver a copy of all subordination agreements to their principal regulator.
	Long-term related party debt is only considered to be subordinated when the executed agreement is delivered to the principal regulator.
(c) Subordinated debt is repaid without prior notice to the regulator.	(c) Firms are required to notify their principal regulator 10 days before the full or partial repayment of a subordinated loan or the termination of the agreement (see section 12.2 of NI 31-103). We may request further supporting documentation, such as updated interim financial information and Form 31-103F1, to assess whether the firm will have sufficient excess working capital following the loan repayment.
	After a partial repayment of a loan, the firm should provide an updated schedule to its principal regulator indicating the updated outstanding subordinated loan balance.
Line 9 *Less market risk*	

Deficiency noted	**Action to be taken**
A market risk deduction has not been made when the value of securities are included on Line 1.	For all securities whose values are included in Line 1 current assets, the market risk for each security must be determined based on its fair value and the applicable margin rates set out in Schedule 1 of Form 31-103F1.
	See Schedule 1 of Form 31-103F1 for instructions on calculating market risk. Firms should provide documentation to support the market risk calculation as part of its annual and/or interim financial statement filing.
Form 31-103F1 is not prepared at least monthly.	Registered firms should know their capital position at all times. This may require a firm to calculate its excess working capital every day. The frequency of capital calculations depends on many factors, including the size of the firm, the nature of its business and the stability of the components of its working capital. However, firms should prepare their excess working capital calculation at least monthly.

Insufficient working capital and failure to report capital deficiency

Some registered firms do not always maintain sufficient working capital. Section 12.1(2) of NI 31-103 requires that a registered firm's excess working capital using Form 31-103F1 must not be less than zero for 2 consecutive days. We treat any failures to meet the capital requirements seriously. We expect firms to resolve any capital deficiencies in a timely basis, usually within 48 hours. This may be done in a number of ways, including injection of new capital into the firm or by subordinating any long-term related party debt. If a firm does not resolve a capital deficiency in a reasonable period of time, we may take regulatory action such as recommending terms and conditions be placed on the firm's registration to restrict their business activities (such as no securities dealings until the deficiency is rectified and notification to existing clients of the terms and conditions imposed) or recommending that the firm's registration be suspended.

In addition, some firms do not notify us when their excess working capital is less than zero. These capital deficiencies were later detected during compliance reviews. Firms are required under section 12.1(1) of NI 31-103 to notify their principal regulator as soon as possible of any capital deficiency.

After a firm resolves its capital deficiency, it is our practice to either recommend terms and conditions be placed on the firm's registration requiring it to send to us copies of its Form 31-103F1 and financial statements each month for a period of time, or warn the firm in writing of the seriousness of the deficiency and that if a capital deficiency recurs, we will recommend terms and conditions. When deciding on whether to recommend terms and conditions or issue a warning letter, we consider a number of factors including whether the firm notified us of its capital deficiency on a timely basis.

Suggested practices

When a firm notifies us of a capital deficiency, they should contact one of the financial analysts in the Compliance, Strategy and Risk team of the CRR Branch (see Appendix A), and:

- Explain the details and nature of the deficiency

- Provide a copy of the firm's Form 31-103F1 and supporting records (such as financial statements and market risk calculation) for the date(s) of the capital deficiency

- Explain what they have done, or will do, to resolve the capital deficiency, and once resolved, what steps were taken to prevent the recurrence of the deficiency

- Once the deficiency is resolved, provide a copy of the firm's Form 31-103F1 and supporting records (as above) that demonstrate that the firm is meeting the capital requirements

- Provide evidence of how the deficiency was resolved (such as a copy of a deposit slip or bank statement to support additional cash injected into the firm or a copy of the executed subordination agreement if long-term related party debt was subordinated).

Financial statements not prepared in accordance with NI 52-107

Some firms prepare their annual financial statements and interim financial information in accordance with International Financial Reporting Standards (IFRS) without accounting for, or disclosing, the adjustments to IFRS as required by NI 52-107 *Acceptable Accounting Principles and Auditing Standards* (NI 52-107).

Section 3.2(3)(a) of NI 52-107 requires a registered firm's financial statements and interim financial information to be prepared in accordance with Canadian Generally Accepted Accounting Principles applicable to publicly accountable enterprises (i.e. IFRS), except that any investments in subsidiaries, jointly controlled entities and associates must be accounted for as specified for separate financial statements in International Accounting Standard 27 *Separate Financial Statements* (IAS 27). Separate financial statements are sometimes referred to as non-consolidated financial statements.

Section 3.2(3)(b) of NI 52-107 also requires a registered firm's annual financial statements to include the following:

- a sentence indicating that the financial statements are prepared in accordance with the financial reporting framework specified in section 3.2(3)(a) or, for foreign firms, section 3.15 of NI 52-107, and

- a description of the financial reporting framework used to prepare the financial statements.

The additional sentence should be outlined in the independent auditor's report. The description of the financial reporting framework used to prepare the financial statements should be disclosed in the notes and refer to the requirement to account for any investments in subsidiaries,

Part 3:
REGISTRATION

jointly controlled entities and associates as specified for separate financial statements in IAS 27, even if the registered firm does not have these types of investments.

Requirements for annual financial statements and interim financial information for foreign registered firms are set out in section 3.15 of NI 52-107.

Inadequate relationship disclosure information

Dealers and advisers regularly do not provide their clients with adequate information on their relationship with clients, as required by section 14.2 of NI 31-103.

In July 2013, we published CSA Staff Notice 31-334 to summarize the findings of the CSA's 2012 sweep of the relationship disclosure information (RDI) practices of over 120 PMs and EMDs. The notice provides guidance on RDI practices, and considers the recent RDI changes made as part of the CRM2 amendments (see section 1.1 of this report).

The notice sets out suggested practices, including on the disclosure of:

- Risks of using borrowed money to finance the purchase of a security,

- The obligation to assess suitability prior to executing a transaction,

- Content and frequency of reporting for each account of a client,

- Types of risks that a client should consider,

- Conflicts of interest,

- All costs to a client for the operation of an account, and

- Compensation paid to the firm.

For more information, see *CSA Staff Notice 31-334*.

Incorrect calculation of capital markets participation fees

Each year, registered firms and unregistered capital markets participants are required to pay participation fees to the OSC based on the firm's revenues attributable to their capital markets activities in Ontario. Some firms are incorrectly calculating these fees. We recently conducted a review of the 2012 capital markets participation fees that were required to be submitted to the OSC under OSC Rule 13-502, using Form 13-502F4. During the review, we identified a number of errors in some firms' calculations of their capital markets participation fees on Form 13-502F4.

On July 18, 2013 we published OSC Staff Notice 33-741 *Report on the Results of the Reviews of Capital Markets Participation Fees* (OSC Staff Notice 33-741) to summarize the review's findings and provide guidance on the calculation of capital markets participation fees. The review's findings include:

- incorrect reporting of revenue

- incorrect deductions taken from gross revenue

- attributing an incorrect percentage to revenues earned in Ontario, and

- misinterpretation of OSC Rule 13-502.

We will continue to review capital markets participation fees on an ongoing basis.

For more information, see *OSC Staff Notice 33-741*. Also, see section 3.5 of this report on *Amendments to calculation of capital markets participation fees*.

4.1.3 — New and proposed rules and initiatives impacting all registrants

Review of custody requirements for non-SRO registrants

Although Ontario securities law does not prohibit registrants from holding client assets, most of the registered firms we directly regulate do not have custody of their clients' assets (securities and cash). Instead, the assets are held at banks, trust companies or dealers that are members of IIROC (Custodian Firms). However, we are aware of a small number of firms that have custody of their clients' assets. By "custody" we mean holding client assets (e.g. by registering securities in nominee name or taking physical possession) or by having "deemed" custody over client assets (e.g. by acting as trustee for clients or having a power of attorney over some clients' assets.)

This year, we conducted a desk review of the custody practices of 70 firms in Ontario registered as EMDs, PMs, or IFMs. We identified these firms as potentially having actual custody of clients' assets from analyzing responses to our most recent risk assessment questionnaires. The purpose of the desk review was to:

- confirm and better understand these firms' custodial practices including the types of controls that are in place to safeguard client assets, and

- identify risks and investor protection concerns that are not addressed by the existing custody requirements for non-SRO registrants in NI 31-103.

We identified 21 firms in our review that had actual custody of their clients' assets and were not members of an SRO. The nature of the custody arrangements vary, but include:

- PMs that maintain "omnibus" accounts in their firm's name at a Custodian Firm to hold their clients' assets on an aggregate basis, and

- PMs, EMDs and IFMs that hold clients' share certificates in private companies at their offices.

In addition, we found that a number of registrants have "deemed" custody over clients' assets, for example, by acting as a trustee for a client or having the authority to withdraw funds from a client's account at a Custodial Firm through a power of attorney.

We have concerns with these arrangements. It is a risk to investors when registrants have actual or deemed custody of their clients' assets. The existing custody requirements for EMDs, PMs and IFMs in sections 14.6 to 14.9 of NI 31-103 focus primarily on maintaining clients' assets separate and apart from the registrants' assets and do not have specific requirements for who can act as a custodian for client's securities. Further, when an EMD, PM or IFM has custody of client assets, there is no requirement for them to hold those assets in each client's name.

Dealers that are members of IIROC and the MFDA commonly hold clients' assets in nominee name on behalf of their clients. To address the risks related to holding client assets in nominee name, IIROC and the MFDA have prescriptive rules governing capital, insurance, custody and segregation requirements for their members, and they both have investor protection funds for dealer insolvencies. There are also prescriptive requirements for custody of the assets of investment funds sold by prospectus in NI 81-102 *Mutual Funds* (NI 81-102) and NI 41-101 *General Prospectus Requirements* (NI 41-101), including that the fund's assets must be held at a qualified custodian.

Together with the CSA, we are reviewing the existing custody requirements in NI 31-103 for non-SRO registrants to assess if they adequately protect client assets. When this review is complete, the CSA may propose enhancements to the custody requirements. We will also continue to review custody practices of registered firms as part of our compliance field reviews.

Electronic delivery of documents to the OSC

On October 31, 2013, we published a rule that will make electronic filing mandatory for a number of documents that are currently filed with the OSC in paper format. The documents generally include the forms, notices and other materials required under Ontario's securities rules that are not covered already by SEDAR, SEDI[7] and NRD, the CSA's national electronic filing systems. The rule is expected to come into force on February 19, 2014.

Electronic filing is a convenience to filers and will allow for the efficient collection and use of information by the OSC. Under the rule, each required document must be transmitted to the OSC electronically in accordance with system instructions on the OSC's website.

The documents that are to be delivered electronically that affect registered firms include:

- Form 31-103F1 together with audited annual financial statements and other financial information,

- Notice of repayment or termination of a subordination agreement,

- Notice of change, claim or cancellation of an insurance policy,

- Capital markets participation fee calculations,

- Notices of proposed ownership changes or asset acquisitions of registrants,

- Reporting obligations related to terrorist financing,

- Firm registrations and changes in registration information,

- Reports of exempt distributions and delivery of an offering memorandum, and

- Registered Firm Exception Report of DAP/RAP Trade Reporting and Matching (Form 24-101F1).

Initially, it is anticipated that many of the required documents will be filed using PDF. However, at the time the rule comes into force, we expect the following forms to be available only as online web-based forms:

- Form 24-101F1,

- Form 31-103F1,

- Form 45-106F1 and 45-501F1 *Report of Exempt Distribution*, and

- Applications for exemptive relief and pre files.

These forms are currently available on the OSC website either to the general public on a voluntary basis, or to select market participants on a 'pilot' testing basis. We anticipate that the online filing portal will be available on a voluntary basis for all users by January 10, 2014 with electronic filing becoming mandatory on February 19, 2014.

For more information, see *Notice of Commission Approval of OSC Rule 11-501 Electronic Delivery of Documents to the Ontario Securities Commission*.

Planned research on suitability of advice

In the *OSC's Statement of Priorities for 2013-14*, we proposed to conduct a "mystery shop" research sweep of dealers and advisers this fiscal year to gauge the suitability of advice currently being provided and identify areas of concern and assist in targeting future OSC suitability

[7]System for Electronic Document Analysis and Retrieval (SEDAR) and System for Electronic Disclosure by Insiders (SEDI).

sweeps. Mystery shopping is a tool that can be used to measure quality of service or compliance with regulation. The mystery consumer's specific identity and purpose is generally not known by the entity being evaluated. In this case, individuals will pose as investors seeking investment advice and provide detailed reports or feedback about their experiences. Once this research is completed, we expect to publish the findings.

4.2 — Dealers (exempt market dealers and scholarship plan dealers)

This section contains information that is specific to EMDs and SPDs, including current trends in deficiencies from compliance reviews of EMDs (and suggested practices to address them), an update on the results of our SPD reviews, and our new initiative to address concerns with EMDs that distribute related party products.

4.2.1 — Current trends in deficiencies of EMDs and suggested practices

This year's compliance reviews of EMDs focused on areas that we found to be problematic in recent years, including:

- inadequate compliance systems and supervision of dealing representatives,

- failure to assess the suitability of trades and the sale of unsuitable investments, especially when there is a high investment concentration in related or connected issuers,

- insufficient product due diligence (KYP),

- failure to identify and respond to conflicts of interest,

- improper reliance on the accredited investor exemption, and

- inadequate collection and documentation of KYC information.

We will continue to focus on these areas of concern in future reviews of EMDs.

In addition to the deficiencies from the Suitability Sweep as outlined in *OSC Staff Notice 33-740* and in section 4.1.2 of this report, the following are deficiencies that we identified during this year's compliance reviews of EMDs.

Conflicts of interest when selling securities of related or connected issuers

We continue to have significant concerns with EMDs that distribute the securities of related or connected issuers, particularly EMDs that solely distribute these types of securities.[8] The significant deficiencies that we identified include:

- misappropriation of investor funds,

- concealment of poor financial condition of the related or connected issuer,

- sale of unsuitable, high-risk investments to investors, and

- high investment concentration in the securities of a related or connected issuer.

These deficiencies are in large part attributable to the lack of separation between the mind and management of the EMDs and their related or connected issuers, which gives rise to significant conflicts of interest. Investor proceeds are not being used in accordance with what has been disclosed to investors and in some instances are used to pay for the personal expenses of officers or directors or to satisfy obligations to existing investors. Also, we identified the sale of unsuitable, high-risk investments, which form a high concentration of investors' portfolios. These deficiencies suggest that the interests of the EMD and its related or connected issuers take precedence over those of investors and, therefore, that the EMD is not dealing fairly, honestly and in good faith with its clients as required by section 2.1 of OSC Rule 31-505.

EMDs are required to take reasonable steps to identify existing material conflicts of interest, and material conflicts that the firm reasonably expects to arise between the EMD and a client (see section 13.4 of NI 31-103). A conflict of interest is any circumstance where the interests of different parties, for instance those of an EMD and its client, are inconsistent or divergent. If the risk of harming a client or the integrity of the markets is too high, then the conflict of interest in question needs to be avoided. If the conflict of interest is not avoided, then the EMD should take steps to control or disclose it, as appropriate. See *Inadequate disclosure of conflicts of interest* directly below for additional information, including suggested practices, on the disclosure of conflicts of interest.

Suggested practices

EMDs should:

- collect information from the individuals acting on their behalf regarding the conflicts they expect to arise with clients,

- avoid conflicts of interest that are contrary to the interests of clients and where controls or disclosure are not appropriate responses to these conflicts, and

- ensure their organizational structures, lines of reporting and physical locations will enable the firm to control these risks and conflicts of interest effectively.

Inadequate disclosure of conflicts of interest

Some EMDs are not meeting their disclosure obligations in *NI 33-105 Underwriting Conflicts* (NI 33-105). In particular, section 2.1(1) of NI 33-105 imposes a disclosure obligation for distributions where there is a direct or indirect relationship between the issuer or selling securi-

---

[8]See definitions of "connected issuer" and "related issuer" in section 1.1 of NI 33-105 *Underwriting Conflicts*.

tyholder and the underwriter. An offering document must contain the information specified in Appendix C of NI 33-105, which includes a statement on the front page of the offering document that summarizes the basis on which the issuer is a related or connected issuer of the EMD, as well as a cross reference to the applicable section in the body of the offering document where further information concerning this relationship is provided.

An EMD that trades in, or recommends the securities of, a related or connected issuer must provide specific disclosure about the issuer. An EMD may, for instance, maintain and post on its website a list of related or connected issuers for whom its acts as a dealer. This disclosure may not meet the expectations of a reasonable investor when a registered individual recommends a trade in the securities of the related or connected issuer. In these circumstances, the EMD should provide the client with disclosure about the specific conflict of interest with the related or connected issuer, including a description of the nature of the relationship between the two entities, including why the issuer is considered "related" or "connected" (e.g., common ownership) and information on the extent to which the proceeds of a sale of securities will be applied for the benefit of the EMD or a related or connected issuer of the EMD. The EMD must disclose this information in a timely manner, in order to give clients a reasonable amount of time to assess the conflict.

Suggested practices

EMDs should:

- draft prominent, specific, clear and meaningful disclosure about material conflicts of interest and explain how the conflict of interest could affect the service being offered,

- avoid providing generic disclosure, giving partial disclosure that could mislead clients, or obscuring conflicts of interest in overly detailed or complex disclosure,

- disclose conflicts of interest to clients before or at the time they recommend the transaction in question and keep evidence of this disclosure, and

- refresh disclosure to clients about conflicts of interest, since previous disclosure may no longer be relevant to (or remembered by) the client.

Inadequate risk disclosure information

Some EMDs do not deliver adequate, or any, risk disclosure information to clients before acting for them. Section 14.2 of NI 31-103 requires EMDs to deliver to clients all information that a reasonable investor would consider important about their relationship with the clients. This includes a description of the risks of using borrowed money to finance the purchase of a security and a description of the types of risks that clients should consider when making investment decisions. For more guidance on the risk disclosure requirements in section 14.2 of NI 31-103, see *CSA Staff Notice 31-334.*

Section 2.1 of OSC Rule 31-505 requires EMDs to deal fairly, honestly and in good faith with their clients. The person purchasing the investment product is the client of the EMD. EMDs' disclosure to clients should accurately reflect the risks of the specific products recommended; and EMDs should ensure that their clients understand the risk features prior to making a purchase in a security. Registered individuals should spend sufficient time with clients to adequately explain the risk disclosure information that is delivered to them.

Suggested practices

EMDs should:

- present risk disclosure information in a clear and meaningful manner,

- have policies and procedures in place that require their registered individuals to demonstrate that they have satisfied their obligations to adequately explain the risk disclosure to clients,

- keep evidence of compliance with client disclosure requirements at account opening, prior to trades and at other required times (e.g., through detailed notes and signed client acknowledgements),

- review relevant documents (e.g., KYC forms, term sheets and offering memoranda) regularly to ensure that they contain the required risk disclosure information, and

- promote client participation, for instance by helping clients understand investment risks and encouraging them to review the sales literature and to consult with necessary professionals, including lawyers and accountants, where appropriate.

4.2.2 — Update on results of scholarship plan dealer reviews

In the prior year, we conducted compliance reviews of all five firms registered solely as SPDs in Ontario. An SPD acts as a dealer in securities of scholarship plans, education plans or educational trusts. We referred four SPDs to our Enforcement Branch after identifying serious concerns with the compliance systems and sales practices of these SPDs. See section 5.3.1 of *OSC Staff Notice 33-738* for more information about the key areas of concern from these compliance reviews.

Regulatory proceedings were brought against the four SPDs in response to significant non-compliance by the firms. In order to address our investor protection concerns, interim terms and conditions on their registration were imposed by the Commission on consent of each of Children's Education Funds Inc. (CEFI), Global RESP Corporation (Global RESP), Heritage Education Funds Inc. (HEFI), and Knowledge First Financial Inc. (KFFI). The terms and conditions that were imposed by temporary orders on the four SPDs required them to:

- retain an OSC-approved independent consultant (the Consultant) to develop and implement a plan to strengthen the firm's compliance system (Compliance Plan), and to provide progress reports as to the implementation of the Compliance Plan,

- retain an OSC-approved independent monitor (the Monitor) to review new client applications, call certain clients to confirm accuracy of their KYC information, confirm that the product is suitable and affordable, confirm that the investor understands the applicable fees, and unwind any unsuitable investments, and provide regular reports to us, and

- not open any new branch locations or hire any new dealing representatives (except to replace an existing dealing representative provided that the Consultant is satisfied that the new dealing representative is adequately trained and supervised) until the Compliance Plan has been fully implemented.

Each Compliance Plan was to include recommendations to strengthen the firm's compliance system and to rectify the deficiencies identified in the compliance reviews including:

- documenting and collecting clients' KYC information,

- ensuring that all trades are suitable for its clients,

- training and supervising dealing representatives,

- overseeing branch location, and

- preparing and distributing marketing materials.

For more information, see the temporary orders for *CEFI, Global RESP*, and *HEFI*. The temporary orders have been extended and in certain cases have been varied from the original terms and conditions set out above. On October 23, 2013, *KFFI's temporary order was revoked* and its remaining terms and conditions were deleted. All public information about the proceedings against the SPDs is available on the OSC's website under *All Commission Proceedings*.

We are of the view that the imposed terms and conditions were necessary to deal with SPDs that failed to comply with their regulatory obligations. Once the proceedings against the SPDs are concluded, we will publish a report including a summary of the deficiencies and suggested practices to provide guidance to new firms that plan to register as SPDs on how to meet their regulatory obligations.

4.2.3 — EMDs that distribute related party products

We have seen a number of cases of commingling of assets and inappropriate use of investor proceeds by the EMD and/or its related party issuer (see section 4.2.1 on *Conflicts of interest when selling securities of related or connected issuers*) when EMDs sell related party investments. We have also found that conflicts of interest matters respecting related parties that were not properly managed. This has resulted in regulatory action being taken on many firms (e.g. suspension of firms, or enforcement proceedings and sanctions).

In light of the significant issues we continue to find, we started an initiative to consider how to address these concerns. Our policy objective is to increase investor protection and deter misuse of investor funds by EMDs and their related parties.

4.3 — Advisers (portfolio managers)

This section contains information specific to PMs, including current trends in deficiencies and suggested practices to address them. We also discuss our sweep of newly registered PMs, PM client account statement practices, and the new framework for direct electronic access.

4.3.1 — Current trends in deficiencies and suggested practices

Inadequate personal trading policies

Some PMs have inadequate policies and procedures for the personal trading of their advising representatives, research analysts, traders and other persons who have access to their clients' trading and investment information (Access Persons).

We found cases where PM firms did not:

- maintain personal trading policies and procedures,

- enforce the firm's established personal trading policies,

- require written pre-approval for personal trades of Access Persons,

- review and maintain the personal trading records of Access Persons to ensure they complied with the firm's personal trading policies, or

- have complete information on the personal trading accounts of all Access Persons.

There is a risk of investor harm when Access Persons trade for their personal accounts since they may put their personal interests ahead of their clients' interests or otherwise abuse their position of trust. Policies and procedures create a framework to monitor and supervise Access Persons' personal trading practices. Without policies and procedures, registered firms are unable to detect inappropriate personal trading practices, which is unacceptable.

Registered firms are required to maintain a control and supervisory system sufficient to ensure compliance with securities law and to manage business risks (see section 32(2) of the Act and section 11.1 of NI 31-103).

Section 119 of the Act prohibits a person with access to information concerning an investment portfolio managed under discretionary authority from making securities transactions for their own account where the client's investment portfolio holds the same security and the person has used the information for their direct benefit.

PMs should establish, maintain and apply written personal trading policies and procedures for their Access Persons. This will help to ensure compliance with section 119 of the Act and prevent and detect self-dealing and other abusive practices.

Suggested practices

- A PM's personal trading policies should, at a minimum:
    - include an annual acknowledgement in writing from all Access Persons that they understand and will comply with the firm's personal trading policies,

- appoint a qualified person, such as the CCO, to be responsible for monitoring the firm's personal trading policies,

- define who is an Access Person,

- clarify the application of policies to spouses of Access Persons and accounts that Access Persons have control over,

- maintain a restricted securities list,

- establish blackout periods,

- require written pre-approval of Access Persons' personal trades by a qualified person, such as the CCO,

- require direct receipt of Access Persons' personal trading records (such as account statements),

- require the review and timely reconciliation of Access Person's pre-approved trades to their personal trading records, and

- set out details of repercussions for non-compliance with the policies, and reporting of non-compliance to senior management.

- PMs should maintain records of personal trade pre-approvals and personal trading records of Access Persons.

- PMs should assess compliance with the personal trading policies as part of the CCO's annual compliance report to the board.

Inadequate investment management agreements

Some PMs do not have adequate investment management agreements (IMAs) with their clients. We found cases where:

- The IMA did not state that the PM must manage the client's assets in accordance with their KYC and suitability information or that the PM is responsible for proxy voting.

- The IMA did not clearly state the type of investment authority the PM has over its client's assets. For example, the IMA states that the client grants the PM authorization to make investment decisions in their accounts without stating that the PM has discretionary trading authorization.

- PMs did not sign an IMA with all clients, or could not locate copies of IMAs we requested.

- IMAs were not current. For example, the fee arrangements had changed from what was outlined in the IMA, but the IMA was not updated to reflect the change.

- A PM inappropriately attempted in the IMA to limit the extent of their legal obligation to obtain KYC and suitability information from the client. The IMA stated that the client had sole responsibility for their KYC and suitability information.

There is a risk of harm to investors when they do not have an IMA with their PM, or do not have an adequate IMA. PMs have a significant amount of authority and responsibility over their clients' assets. A well-drafted and up-to-date IMA helps investors to adequately protect their assets and ensure that the PM manages their assets in accordance with their KYC and suitability information and instructions.

Section 11.5(1) of NI 31-103 requires PMs to maintain records to accurately record their business activities, financial affairs and client transactions. Section 11.5(2)(k) of NI 31-103 states that this includes records that document the opening of client accounts, including any agreements with clients.

PMs are responsible for collecting KYC information from clients and keeping the information current to support their suitability determinations; it is not the sole responsibility of the PM's clients. PMs may not use client agreements to limit their KYC or suitability obligations or mislead clients as to their obligation to know their clients and make suitability determinations.

Suggested practices

- PMs need to have a written IMA with each client that sets out the services to be provided, the roles and responsibilities of each party, and addresses all aspects of the investment advisory process.

- Since the IMA is a legal document, PMs should consult with legal counsel on its terms and keep it current.

- Each completed IMA should be reviewed, approved and signed and dated by senior management of the PM and the client, with a copy provided to the client.

- The terms of an IMA should include, but not be limited to:

  - the type of authority the PM has over the client's assets (such as discretionary or non-discretionary trading authority),

  - how the client's assets managed by the PM will be held (such as in the client's name at a third-party custodian),

  - any client instructions or restrictions,

  - who is responsible for proxy voting and insider reporting obligations,

  - how any conflicts of interests that impact the advisory services to be provided are addressed,

  - fee arrangements with clients, including how and when investment management fees (including performance fees) are calculated and charged, and

  - the notice period for terminating the agreement.

- IMAs should state that the PM is required to manage the client's assets in accordance with the client's investment needs and objectives, risk tolerance, financial circumstances and any client instructions or restrictions.

**Part 3:
REGISTRATION**

Inadequate supervision of advising representatives and research analysts

We noted several cases where a PM firm did not adequately supervise its advising representatives (AR), associate advising representatives (AAR), or research analysts.

In one case, a PM firm failed to supervise a number of ARs that the firm sponsored. The ARs operated under the PM firm's name, but effectively carried out their advising activities independent of, and without adequate oversight by, the PM firm. For example:

- the ARs did not follow, and lacked knowledge of, the firm's policies and procedures for meeting with clients and documenting their advising activities,

- clients did not sign a standard IMA with the firm; instead, each AR had a different agreement that their clients signed,

- the firm did not have an established process for collecting, documenting and updating KYC and suitability information from clients; instead each AR had their own process that was often inadequate,

- some of the ARs conducted their advising activities from their home office that was not a registered office of the firm, and that was not subject to adequate oversight by the firm,

- the ARs had their own distinct marketing materials and referral arrangements that often were not reviewed and approved by the firm, and

- some of the AR's books and records were not accessible to the firm.

In another case, an unregistered research analyst employed by a PM firm appeared to be making investment decisions for several managed account clients of the firm as part of a specific investment strategy. The firm's UDP, CCO and sole AR told us that he authorized the analyst's trades before they were placed with a dealer. But we had concerns that this individual did not fully understand the trades made by the analyst, did not adequately document his authorization of the trades, did not adequately monitor the investment strategy in question, and did not adequately supervise the research analyst.

We also noted some cases where a designated AR at a PM firm was not adequately supervising the advice of an AAR that he or she was responsible for (as required by section 25(3) of the Act). Specifically, there was no evidence that the designated AR had pre-approved investment decisions that the AAR had made for clients' managed accounts.

In each of the above cases, we took appropriate steps to ensure the firms took corrective action to adequately supervise their staff and meet other requirements under securities law. In one case, terms and conditions were placed on the firm's registration requiring the retention of a compliance consultant.

PMs are required to maintain a control and supervisory system sufficient to ensure compliance with securities law and to manage business risks (see section 32(2) of the Act and section 11.1 of NI 31-103).

PMs should have written policies and procedures on how they supervise their ARs, AARs, and research analysts, and how designated ARs are to supervise their AARs. A PM's system of control and supervision, and policies and procedures, should apply to all of the firm's ARs, AARs, and research analysts, and should take into account if these individuals work at locations other than the firm's head office. It is unacceptable for PM firms to sponsor individuals as their ARs or AARs when they are permitted to act independently of the firm's system of control and supervision, and policies and procedures.

For PMs to meet their suitability requirements in section 13.3(1) of NI 31-103, an AR (or AAR under the supervision of their designated AR) must fully understand the structure, features and risks of each trade before it is placed with a dealer, and monitor the client's managed account portfolio on an ongoing basis.

Section 4.2 of NI 31-103 requires PMs to designate an AR to approve the advice provided by an AAR. The designated AR must approve the advice before the AAR gives it to a client or makes an investment decision for a client's managed account.

Suggested practices

- All trades conducted on behalf of a PM's clients should be authorized, in writing, by an AR (or AAR under the supervision of an AR), before the trades are placed with dealers.

- An AR designated to supervise the advice of an AAR should document his or her pre-approval of the advice made by the AAR to clients.

- PMs should train their investment staff on the advising activities they are permitted to perform under their AR or AAR category of registration (if registered) or not permitted to perform (if not registered).

- PMs should refer to *CSA Staff Notice 33-315 Suitability Obligation and Know Your Product* for guidance on meeting their suitability and KYP obligations.

- PMs should assess whether a change in an individual's role, responsibilities or activities within the firm requires them to be registered.

Delegating KYC and suitability obligations to referral agents

We continue to be concerned about the practice by some PMs of delegating their KYC and suitability obligations to referral agents such as mutual fund dealing representatives and financial planners. We detailed our concerns in previous annual reports and set out a list of suggested practices for PMs. Despite this, some PMs are still delegating their KYC and suitability obligations to referral agents. In the future, we intend to respond to this type of conduct more aggressively, for example, by recommending a suspension of registration or by referring the matter to our Enforcement Branch.

This year, we reviewed a case where a referral agent, an individual who had formerly been registered with an MFDA member firm, but was no longer registered in any capacity, had referred a large number of clients to a PM, and where no AR of the PM had spoken with those clients before trades were made on their behalf. The referral agent also met with the clients on an ongoing basis to review their investment portfolios, and discussed with the PM the selection of specific securities for inclusion in, or removal from, the clients' portfolios. Many of the activities performed by the referral agent required registration, and should have been carried out by an appropriately registered individual acting on behalf of the PM.

PMs must comply with the referral arrangement requirements in sections 13.8 to 13.10 of NI 31-103 (also, see the guidance in Part 13 of 31-103CP). A client who is referred to a PM becomes the client of that PM for the purposes of the services provided under the referral arrangement. The PM receiving a referral must meet all of its obligations as a registrant towards its referred clients, including KYC and suitability determinations. PMs may not use a referral arrangement to assign, contract out of or otherwise avoid their regulatory obligations.

PMs that use referral agents should carefully review their practices to ensure that only appropriately registered individuals are performing registrable activities. Registrable activities include meeting with investors to ascertain their investment needs and objectives, risk tolerance and financial circumstances, discussing and recommending investment opportunities, and performing ongoing portfolio reviews. We also encourage PMs to review the guidance in section 5.2A of *OSC Staff Notice 33-736 2011 Annual Summary Report for Dealers, Advisers and Investment Fund Managers* under the heading *Delegating know your client and suitability obligations*.

4.3.2 — Sweep of newly registered PMs

This year we conducted a sweep review of a sample of newly registered PMs in Ontario to gain an understanding of each firm's business, assess their compliance with Ontario securities law, and provide guidance on key regulatory requirements. We selected 23 firms to review using risk-based criteria. Our reviews focused on each firm's compliance system, financial condition and processes for portfolio management, trading, and marketing.

Of the 23 PM firms we reviewed, 18 (78%) were issued a report that required them to take corrective action on deficiencies we identified. A total of 8 firms had experienced an excess working capital deficiency (34%) within the last 12 months that had not been previously reported to the OSC. Each of these 8 firms had already corrected their capital deficiency at the time of our review, or did so after our review on a timely basis. Each of the 8 firms were informed of the seriousness of not meeting their capital requirements (and the requirement to report capital deficiencies to the OSC on a timely basis) either through a warning letter or by placing terms and conditions on the firm's registration requiring them to send to us monthly capital calculations and financial information. We also identified it as a significant deficiency when we reported to the firm on the review's findings.

The common deficiencies we identified from the sweep are listed below, along with where to get more information on the requirements and guidance to address the deficiencies.

1. Excess working capital deficiency. See section 4.1.2 of this report under *Insufficient working capital and failure to report capital deficiency* and *Inaccurate calculations of excess working capital*.

2. Inadequate relationship disclosure information to clients. See section 4.1.2 of this report under *Inadequate relationship disclosure information*.

3. Misleading marketing practices. See *CSA Staff Notice 31-325 Marketing Practices of Portfolio Managers*.

4. Inadequate trade matching policies. See *Lack of awareness of trade-matching requirements* in section 5.4.1 of *OSC Staff Notice 33-738*.

5. Inadequate personal trading policies. See section 4.3.1 of this report on *Inadequate personal trading policies*.

We believe that this sweep was effective in helping the reviewed firms to better understand their key regulatory requirements, and in enhancing their compliance through the corrective actions they took to address identified deficiencies. It also developed a relationship for the reviewed firms with staff from the CRR Branch. We will continue to perform sweep reviews of newly registered firms on an ongoing basis and will use the information we obtain to enhance our outreach to registrants.

4.3.3 — PM client account statement practices

In last year's report, we outlined our concern that some PMs are not meeting their obligations to deliver an account statement to each of their clients as required under section 14.14 of NI 31-103. These PMs are not delivering account statements because their clients' custodians deliver account statements to them for accounts over which the PMs have discretionary trading authority. Some of these PMs told us that they outsourced their account statement delivery to their clients' custodians; however, in many cases these PMs do not appear to be responsible or accountable for the custodians' delivery of the account statements. We also found that some PMs that deliver account statements do not list the transactions that they have made in their clients' accounts, as they only disclose investment holdings.

We expect PMs to deliver an account statement in their firm's name to each of their clients at least quarterly for each account that they manage for the client (unless monthly statements are requested). The statements must contain transaction and holding information, and should not contain disclaimers on the completeness or accuracy of the reported information. A consolidated account statement may be provided when appropriate accounts are grouped and they contain adequate disclosure, and the consolidated statement is delivered in addition to statements for each account managed by the PM (see guidance on *Use of consolidated account statements* in section 5.4.1 of *OSC Staff Notice 33-738*).

PMs do not meet their statement delivery obligation by solely relying on the fact that their clients' custodians deliver account statements to them. PMs may outsource statement delivery to a service provider if they meet the guidance in 31-103CP for outsourcing arrangements which includes that they:

- are responsible and accountable for all functions that they outsource to a service provider,

- supervise the service provider, and

- have a written, legally binding contract with the service provider that includes the expectations of the parties to the outsourcing arrangement.

See Parts 11 and 14 of *31-103CP* for the CSA's complete expectations when registered firms enter into outsourcing arrangements.

We believe that clients of most PM firms receive account statements from their PM and separate statements from the clients' custodian. The PM statement reports on the trades and investments that the PM has authorized and made for them as being suitable to meet the client's investment objectives and frequently also provides performance and cost reporting. The custodian statement reports the assets that an IIROC dealer member or financial institution holds and protects for a client, and that are obligations of the custodian to the client.

We think that investors are better protected and served when they receive statements from both their PM and custodian. However, given certain firms' practices where only one statement is provided, we are considering whether and in what circumstances investors will be equally protected by this practice. We are working with the CSA to review service arrangements between PMs and their clients' custodians, including for account statement delivery, and to determine if any changes to the custody requirements impact account statement delivery requirements (see section 4.1.3 *Review of custody requirements for non-SRO registrants*). In addition, as part of the CRM2 amendments that begin on July 15, 2015, PMs will be required to provide to their clients "additional statements" about the investments over which they have trading authority. This requirement will be a factor for us to consider as we review the practices of certain firms who provide only one statement.

Until this work is completed, we consider the following when assessing if a PM is meeting its statement delivery obligations to its clients when only the client's custodian delivers a statement to the client:

- if all of the client's assets managed by the PM are held at the custodian (and not the PM or another party);

- if the PM ensures that an account statement is delivered to each of the PM's clients directly by the custodian at the frequency, and with the content, required by NI 31-103 (such as by receiving a copy of the statement or testing the delivery practices of the custodian); and

- if the PM takes reasonable steps to ensure the content of the custodian's statement to its clients is complete and accurate (such as by regularly reconciling its records against the custodian's records).

4.3.4 — New framework for direct electronic access

The CSA and IIROC have established a new regulatory framework for managing the risks associated with direct electronic access (DEA) to marketplaces. On July 4, 2013, the CSA published amendments to NI 23-103 *Electronic Trading* (NI 23-103) and IIROC published related amendments to the Universal Market Integrity Rules and their Dealer Member Rules (see *IIROC Notice 13-0184*). The new DEA framework builds on the existing framework to address risks in Canadian markets arising from the speed and automation of electronic trading, and is expected to come into force on March 1, 2014.

The rule changes are relevant for entities that offer or use DEA to send orders to marketplaces. The amendments allow only a participant dealer[9] to offer DEA to others. Participant dealers may not offer DEA to registered dealers including EMDs, as these dealers are not subject to the same standards as investment dealers. We note that the use of DEA by investment dealers is covered under the IIROC amendments rather than under NI 23-103. A PM may use DEA when it is provided by a participant dealer for trading in its own accounts or the accounts of its advisory clients, subject to additional requirements.

For more information, see *Amendments to NI 23-103*, which is to be retitled as *Electronic Trading and Direct Electronic Access to Marketplaces*.

4.4 — Investment fund managers

This section contains information specific to IFMs, including current trends in deficiencies and suggested practices to address them, and new and proposed rules and initiatives.

4.4.1 — Current trends in deficiencies and suggested practices

Inappropriate expenses charged to funds

We continue to find that some IFMs are charging inappropriate expenses to the investment funds they manage. This negatively impacts the fund's investors, as it inappropriately reduces the fund's net assets and returns. Although we have highlighted this deficiency in previous years, we emphasize it once again given its importance. When we identify this deficiency, we require the IFM to reimburse the applicable fund(s) for the inappropriate expenses, and depending on the facts and circumstances, we may take further regulatory actions, such as imposing terms and conditions or recommending suspension of registration.

IFMs should only charge expenses to their investment funds that are related to the operation of the investment funds. Some IFMs are charging their investment funds expenses that are related to the operation of the IFMs' business and not the investment funds. Some examples of inappropriate expenses noted in our compliance reviews include fees for the audit of the IFM (as opposed to audit fees for the funds), and insurance premiums, professional dues and recruiting expenses of the IFM. We consider these expenses to be the cost of running a fund management business and should therefore be borne by the IFM, and not its investment funds.

We also find that a number of IFMs do not properly allocate the appropriate amount of expenses between the operation of the IFM and the operation of the funds. This occurs because often there are expenses common to the operation of the IFM business and the management of the funds. This often results in an over-allocation of expenses to some of the investment funds. For example, some IFMs use a single allocation rate to allocate different types of overhead expenses to their investment funds without considering whether each type of expense relates to the operation of each of the funds, and whether the single allocation rate is the appropriate rate for all types of expenses. Also, some IFMs do not have procedures to review the expense allocation methodology on a regular basis to ensure that it remains fair and reasonable to all funds.

---

[9]A participant dealer is a marketplace participant that is an investment dealer or in Quebec, a foreign approved participant.

Section 116 of the Act imposes a standard of care on IFMs for the investment funds they manage. In our view, to meet this standard of care, IFMs should ensure that the investment funds they manage are only paying for expenses that are related to the operation of the investment funds. They should also ensure that expenses are allocated fairly and appropriately to all funds.

Suggested practices

IFMs should:

- establish policies and procedures to ensure that their investment funds are only paying for expenses that are related to the operation of those funds. The policies and procedures should, at a minimum:
  - address the types of expenses that are eligible to be paid by the funds,
  - ensure that expense invoices are reviewed and approved by an authorized person before they are processed for payment, and
  - ensure that expenses charged to the funds are only for types of expenses that are disclosed in the funds' offering documents as being permitted expenses.
- review their expense allocation methodology for their funds on a regular basis and maintain evidence of the review. The review should cover, at a minimum:
  - how each type of expense relates to the operations of the funds, and
  - the factors used to determine the allocation rate for each type of expense.
- provide clear and specific disclosure in the funds' offering documents regarding the types of expenses that will be charged to the funds.

Inadequate disclosure in offering memoranda

We reviewed a number of IFMs that manage investment funds offered through offering memoranda (instead of prospectus or simplified prospectus). We noted some instances where the offering memoranda contained inadequate and/or misleading disclosure, particularly in the following areas:

- conflict of interest matters,
- types of expenses that are paid by the investment funds, and
- the method of calculating performance fees; in particular, how any hurdle rate is to be applied in the event that a fund's performance exceeds any high water mark part-way through the year.

We also noted some cases where the IFMs, who were also the distributors of the investment funds, did not recognize that certain promotional documents (such as term sheets and confidential information memoranda) provided to potential investors met the definition of an "offering memorandum" under section 1(1) of the Act. In these cases, there was no disclosure of the purchaser's right of action for damages and right of rescission under section 130.1 of the Act, and the documents were not delivered to the OSC as required under section 5.4 of *OSC Rule 45-501 Ontario Prospectus and Registration Exemptions* (OSC Rule 45-501).

Under the standard of care requirement in section 116 of the Act, IFMs should ensure that all information contained in the offering memorandum of an investment fund managed by them is factual, accurate and not misleading. Section 5.3 of OSC Rule 45-501 requires an offering memorandum to disclose a purchaser's right of action for damages and right of rescission in the event of a misrepresentation (as outlined in section 130.1 of the Act) for many distributions under a prospectus exemption (see section 5.1 of OSC Rule 45-501), including the accredited investor and minimum amount investment exemptions. Furthermore, the offering memorandum needs to be delivered to the OSC within 10 days of the distribution.

Suggested practices

IFMs should review the offering memoranda of their investment funds to ensure that they adequately and accurately disclose all material facts relating to the investment funds, including:

- the types of expenses that are to be paid by the funds in clear and specific terms,
- conflict of interest matters, such as fees paid to related parties, and
- details on how any performance fees are calculated, including how any hurdle rate is to be applied if the fund's performance exceeds any high water mark part-way through the year.

Inadequate oversight of outsourced functions and service providers

We continue to identify situations where IFMs inadequately oversee their funds' service providers. Many IFMs outsource certain aspects of their IFM operations (such as fund accounting, trust accounting and transfer agency) to third-party service providers. Some IFMs rely solely on third-party service providers and do not perform any oversight to ensure that these service providers are fulfilling their duties and responsibilities. As a result, these IFMs are not satisfactorily discharging their obligations to comply with applicable securities legislation.

Section 11.1 of NI 31-103 requires IFMs to establish a system of controls and supervision to ensure compliance with securities legislation and to manage their business risks in accordance with prudent business practices. Part 11 of 31-103CP, under the heading *General business practices — outsourcing*, states that registrants that outsource aspects of their business operations to third-party service providers are responsible and accountable for all functions that have been outsourced. An IFM is required to oversee its service providers in order to meet its obligation of being responsible and accountable for the work performed by the service providers.

Suggested practices

IFMs should:

- establish and implement policies and procedures to actively monitor the work of service providers,

- on an ongoing basis, review the quality of work performed by service providers, including:

  - the calculation of net asset value,

  - reports on income and expenses of the funds,

  - valuation of hard-to-value securities,

  - reconciliation of total number of units outstanding between fund accounting records and transfer agent records,

  - security position reconciliations between fund accounting records and the fund's custodian records, and

  - trust account reconciliations,

- review exception reports and follow-up on variances,

- adequately document their monitoring of service providers,

- ensure that service providers have adequate safeguards for keeping information confidential, and

- develop and test a business continuity plan to minimize disruption to the IFM if the service providers do not deliver their services satisfactorily.

Non-delivery of net asset value adjustments

A number of IFMs did not provide us with a description of net asset value (NAV) adjustments for investment funds that they manage as part of their annual or interim financial reporting.

Section 12.14 of NI 31-103 requires an IFM to deliver to its principal regulator a description of any NAV adjustment made in respect of an investment fund it manages during the year or interim period (as applicable), within 90 days after the end of the IFM's financial year and no later than 30 days after the end of the first, second and third interim period of the IFM's financial year (as applicable). The description of a NAV adjustment must include:

- the name of the fund,

- assets under administration of the fund,

- the cause of the adjustment,

- the dollar amount of the adjustment, and

- the effect of the adjustment on NAV per unit or share and any corrections made to the purchase and sale transactions affecting either the investment fund or security holders of the investment fund.

We expect IFMs to have policies and procedures in place to ensure that descriptions of any NAV adjustments made to their investment funds are delivered to their principal regulator within the required timeframe.

Suggested practices

We encourage IFMs to also provide the following details as part of the description submitted for a NAV adjustment:

- date(s) of the NAV error

- date of the NAV adjustment

- total dollar amount of the NAV adjustment for each investment fund affected by the NAV adjustment

- percentage change in NAV for each of the investment funds affected due to the NAV adjustment

- if the NAV adjustment was the result of a material error under the IFM's policies and procedures

- date of the reimbursement

- total amount reimbursed to each of the investment funds, if any

- total amount reimbursed to the security holders of each of the investment funds, if any

- description and date of any corrections made to purchase and redemption transactions affecting either the investment funds or security holders of each of the investment funds

- how long before the NAV error was discovered

- how long after the NAV error was discovered that the NAV adjustment was made

- if the NAV error was discovered by the IFM or by another person

- if the policies and procedures of the IFM were changed following the NAV adjustment and if so, a description of the changes, and

- if the NAV adjustment was communicated to security holders of each of the investment funds affected and if so, a description of the communications

4.4.2 — New and proposed rules and initiatives impacting IFMs

Our Investment Funds Branch has worked on a number of new and proposed rules with the CSA on the regulation of investment funds, and other initiatives, which impact IFMs. A summary of some of this work follows.

Investment funds modernization project

On March 27, 2013, the CSA published for comment (now closed) proposed amendments to NI 81-102 to introduce core operational requirements for publicly offered non-redeemable investment funds. The CSA also sought input on an alternative fund framework, to be effected through amendments to NI 81-104 *Commodity Pools*. This framework would operate in conjunction with the proposed NI 81-102 amendments and would govern investment funds that invest in assets, or use investment strategies, that would not be permitted under the proposed NI 81-102 amendments.

These proposals are the first stage of Phase 2 of the CSA's investment funds modernization project. The objective is to identify and address any market efficiency, investor protection or fairness issues from the differing regulatory regimes that apply to different types of publicly offered investment funds.

The CSA will next review the investment restrictions applicable to mutual funds to assess if any changes should be made in light of market and product developments. For more information, see *Amendments to NI 81-102 and Companion Policy 81-102CP*.

Point of sale disclosure

On June 13, 2013, the CSA published the final amendments to NI 81-101 *Mutual Fund Prospectus Disclosure* which (i) include amendments to the Fund Facts form requirements, and (ii) require delivery of the Fund Facts instead of the prospectus to satisfy the requirement to deliver a prospectus within two days of buying a mutual fund. The amendments will take effect June 13, 2014.

The CSA continues to encourage early adoption of the delivery of the Fund Facts instead of the prospectus, in order to assist investors in their decision-making process and in discussions with their financial advisors.

For more information, see *CSA Implementation of Stage 2 of Point of Sale Disclosure for Mutual Funds — Delivery of Fund Facts*.

New prospectus form for scholarship plans

The CSA amended the prospectus requirements for scholarship plans by introducing a prospectus form tailored to reflect the unique features of scholarship plans. This is an important investor-focused initiative. New Form 41-101F3 *Information Required in a Scholarship Plan Prospectus* will require scholarship plans to provide investors with key information in a simple, accessible and comparable format to assist them in making more informed investment decisions. Central to the new prospectus form is the Plan Summary document. It is written in plain language, will generally be no more than four pages, and highlights the potential benefits, risks and the costs of investing in a scholarship plan. It will form part of the prospectus, but will be bound separately.

The amendments came into force on May 31, 2013. For more information, see the *CSA's notice on Implementation of a New Prospectus Form for Scholarship Plans* as part of amendments to NI 41-101.

Mutual fund fees

The CSA is examining the mutual fund fee structure in Canada to see if there are investor protection or fairness issues, and to determine whether any regulatory responses are needed. The CSA published *CSA Discussion Paper and Request for Comment 81-407 Mutual Fund Fees* in late 2012, and held a consultation roundtable in June 2013 to engage various stakeholders in the discussion of the issues raised in the paper. At the same time, the CSA continues to monitor and assess the effects of related regulatory reforms in Canada and globally.

Continuous disclosure review of sales communications

Our Investment Funds Branch recently conducted a targeted review of sales communications from a sample of publicly offered investment funds. *OSC Staff Notice 81-720 Report on Staff's Continuous Disclosure Review of Sales Communications by Investment Funds* summarizes the findings and provides guidance to address the findings.

5. — Acting on registrant misconduct

5.1 — Registrant misconduct cases of interest

We stay alert for signs of potential registrant misconduct or fraud and when we find evidence of either we take appropriate regulatory action. The CRR Branch works together with the Enforcement Branch to maintain an effective compliance-enforcement continuum for registrants, and to take appropriate regulatory action when justified. These include sanctions such as the suspension or termination of the registration of a registered firm and/or its registered individuals, administrative penalties, and disgorgement of monies.

In addition to the four SPD cases discussed in section 4.2.2 of this report, some notable registrant misconduct cases from the past year are summarized below. Please note that some cases are still ongoing. To get more information on a particular case, click on the respondent's name. Documents related to OSC proceedings before the Commission and before the Courts are available on the OSC's website under *All Commission Proceedings*. Further, *Director's Decisions* from the CRR Branch are also available on our website.

In 2012, we performed a Suitability Sweep of almost 90 PMs and EMDs (see *OSC Staff Notice 33-740*). To date, this sweep has resulted in the suspension of one firm and two individuals:

- In *Re Investment Allocation International Inc. and Miller* (June 4, 2013), the registrants were a PM and its UDP, CCO, and sole advising representative. During the Suitability Sweep, we found, among other things, that the firm did not have sufficient working capital, and the individual had raised money for his small internet start-up company by selling securities of the company to most of his clients whose portfolios he managed on a discretionary basis. We alleged that the registrants had not properly addressed the conflicts of interest in the sale of these securities, and that certain management fees were not properly disclosed to investors. We recommended to the Director that the registrants be suspended, and the registrants requested an opportunity to be heard (an OTBH) in relation to that recommendation. Ultimately, staff and the registrants settled the matter on terms that included a permanent suspension of the firm and the individual as a UDP and CCO, and a temporary suspension of the individual's registration as an advising representative.

- In *Re Gbalajobi* (July 26, 2013), the registrant was the CCO and dealing representative of an EMD. During the Suitability Sweep, we found, among other things, that the registrant had traded in securities while his firm was suspended, that he did not properly record KYC information for a number of clients, and that he could not demonstrate to staff that he had assessed the suitability of an investment for another client. We recommended to the Director that the individual be suspended, and after an OTBH was requested, the matter was settled on the basis that the individual's registration as a CCO would be suspended for three years, and his registration as a dealing representative would be suspended for nine months.

Although staff has made use of settlement agreements as part of the OTBH process, such arrangements are not appropriate in all cases, and we remain committed to pursuing regulatory action through contested OTBH proceedings when necessary. For example:

- In *Re Trinity Wood Securities Ltd. and Browning* (October 31, 2012), the Director refused a firm's application for registration as an IFM and EMD, and the individual's application to be its UDP, CCO, and dealing representative. The individual applicant, and companies related to him, had incurred outstanding liabilities of approximately $2.6 million during his previous tenure as the owner of a registered dealer. The Director was not persuaded by the applicant's submissions during the OTBH that his significant financial difficulties were irrelevant to his application because the corporate applicant was not legally responsible for his outstanding liabilities.

- In *Re White Capital Corporation and White* (April 26, 2013), the Director suspended an EMD and its UDP, CCO, and dealing representative. This decision was made following an OTBH in which the Director found, among other things, that the registrants had not properly addressed a conflict of interest arising out of the firm's receipt of funds from a company related to one of the issuers it was selling, and that their books and records were not sufficient to satisfy its KYC and suitability obligations to clients.

Two earlier OTBH decisions of the Director were the subject of review proceedings decided in 2013:

- In *Re Pyasetsky* (March 28, 2013), the Commission reviewed the decision of the Director to refuse the applicant's application for registration as a dealing representative in the category of mutual fund dealer. The applicant had failed to disclose in her application for registration that she had been employed by a "boiler room", and the Director concluded that this, and other statements by her, indicated that she lacked the requisite integrity for registration. Following a hearing and review under section 8 of the Act, a panel of the Commission also concluded that the applicant did not have the integrity required for registration, and refused her application.

- In *Sawh v. Ontario Securities Commission* (June 12, 2013), the Divisional Court dismissed an appeal brought by two applicants in respect of a decision of the Commission to refuse their applications for registration as dealing representatives in the category of mutual fund dealer. In 2011, the Director determined that the applicants lacked the requisite integrity for registration on the basis of, among other things, their conduct in selling prospectus-exempt securities to clients that did not qualify for any prospectus exemptions, and for whom the investments were unsuitable. In 2012, the Commission reviewed the Director's decision pursuant to section 8 of the Act, and reached the same conclusion. Before the Divisional Court, the applicants argued that the Commission ought to have showed deference to a settlement agreement the applicants entered into with the MFDA regarding the conduct in question. That settlement did not impose a ban on the applicants becoming dealing representatives. The Divisional Court rejected this argument, and confirmed that the Commission, and not the MFDA, has the jurisdiction over the registration of dealing representatives in the category of mutual fund dealer.

This year has also seen a number of registrant-related enforcement matters before the Commission:

- In *Re Morgan Dragon Development Corp.* (April 10, 2013), the Commission imposed monetary penalties and trading and registration bans against a registered firm and its UDP and CCO, who admitted that they had engaged unregistered individuals to act as commissioned securities salespeople, and had traded in prospectus-exempt securities with individuals who did not qualify for prospectus exemptions.

- In *Re Juniper Fund Management Corp.* (April 11, 2013), the Commission found that a fund manager and its president, with respect to its investment funds, (i) failed to maintain proper books and records, (ii) failed to provide full, true and plain disclosure of all material facts, and (iii) breached their statutory duty of care. The Commission also found that one of the Juniper funds provided prohibited loans and held prohibited investments contrary to sections 111 and 112 of the Act. A sanctions and costs hearing started on October 25, 2013 and is ongoing.

- In *Re Crown Hill Capital Corp.* (August 23, 2013), the Commission found that an IFM and its directing mind breached their fiduciary duty in connection with several transactions made for their investment funds. The decision states that an IFM's fiduciary duty under section 116 of the Act requires it to:
  - act with utmost good faith and in the best interests of the investment fund and put the interests of the fund and its unitholders ahead of its own,
  - generally avoid material conflicts of interest and transactions that give rise to material conflicts of interest on the part of the IFM, including self-interested and related party transactions,
  - where a conflict of interest cannot be avoided, or where a material self-interested or related party transaction is proposed, ensure that the conflict of interest or transaction is appropriately addressed as a matter of good governance and in compliance with NI 81-107 *Independent Review Committee for Investment Funds*,
  - make full disclosure to the board of directors, the independent review committee and unitholders, as the circumstances may dictate, in respect of all of the circumstances surrounding a material conflict of interest or self-interested or related party transaction,

- obtain the informed consent of unitholders where a conflict of interest or self-interested or related party transaction is sufficiently material to warrant obtaining such consent, and

- ensure compliance in all material respects with the terms of the declaration of trust governing the relationship between the IFM and the investment fund.

A sanctions and costs hearing has not yet occurred.

- In *Re Quadrexx Asset Management Inc.* (ongoing), the Commission suspended the registration of an IFM, PM, and EMD, and issued a cease trade order in respect of certain investment products managed by the firm, after the firm reported a large capital deficiency that it was unable to rectify. The firm's portfolio management clients have been transferred out, and a receiver has been appointed to manage the wind-up of the firm. This matter remains ongoing.

- In *Re Pro-Financial Asset Management Inc.* (ongoing), the Commission suspended the EMD registration of a firm and placed its PM registration on terms and conditions pending the proposed sale of the firm's portfolio management and investment fund management business. The firm's auditor confirmed a large capital deficiency, and the firm also informed us of a shortfall in the proceeds necessary to honour redemption requests of certain series of principal protected notes. This matter remains ongoing.

6. — Additional resources

This section discusses how registrants can get more information about their obligations.

The CRR Branch works to foster a culture of compliance through outreach and other initiatives. We try to assist registrants in meeting their regulatory requirements in a number of ways.

We developed a new outreach program to registrants (see section 2.1 of this report) to help them understand and comply with their obligations. We encourage registrants to visit our *Registrant Outreach web page* on the OSC's website.

Also, the *Information for: Dealers, Advisers and IFMs* section on the OSC website provides detailed information about the registration process and registrants' ongoing obligations. It includes information about compliance reviews and suggested practices, provides quick links to forms, rules and past reports and email blasts to registrants. It also contains links to previous years' versions of our annual summary reports to registrants.

The *Information for: Investment Funds* section on our website also contains useful information for IFMs, including past editions of The Investment Funds Practitioner published by our Investment Funds Branch.

Registrants may also contact us. Please see Appendix A to this report for the CRR Branch's contact information. The CRR Branch's PM, IFM and dealer teams focus on registration, oversight, policy changes, and exemption applications for their respective registration categories. The Registrant Conduct team supports the PM, IFM and dealer teams in cases of potential registrant misconduct. The financial analysts on the Compliance, Strategy and Risk team review registrant submissions for financial reporting (such as audited annual financial statements, calculations of excess working capital and subordination agreements).

Appendix A — Contact Information for Registrants Compliance and Registrant Regulation Branch

[Not reproduced]

OSC Staff Notice 33-743 — Guidance on Sales Practices, Expense Allocation and Other Relevant Areas Developed from the Results of the Targeted Review of Large Investment Fund Managers

Date: June 19, 2014
37 O.S.C.B. 5377

Purpose of this Notice

Staff of the Compliance and Registrant Regulation Branch (**Staff** or **we**) of the Ontario Securities Commission (**OSC**) recently conducted a targeted review or sweep of a sample of large investment fund managers (**IFMs**), based on assets under management. The reviews focused on the IFMs' compliance with Ontario securities law in key operational areas. This Notice provides a summary of our findings and related guidance.

We strongly encourage IFMs to use this Notice to improve their understanding of, and compliance with, applicable regulatory requirements. We also suggest that IFMs use this Notice as a self-assessment tool to strengthen their compliance with Ontario securities law and as appropriate, to make changes to enhance their systems of compliance, internal controls and supervision.

Background

In May 2013, we commenced targeted, on-site reviews of a sample of large IFMs to assess their compliance with securities law. The IFMs collectively had over $500 billion in assets under management at the time and manage a wide range of investment funds, including traditional mutual funds, pooled funds, exchange traded funds and closed end funds. As part of these reviews, we focused on key operational areas of the IFMs, such as:

- minimum working capital requirements and custody

- securityholder reporting/transfer agency

- trust accounting

- fund accounting
- oversight of service providers
- conflicts of interest
- sales practices
- overall compliance structure

In cases where the IFMs were dually registered or had an affiliated portfolio manager, we also performed testing of the portfolio management and trading activities in conjunction with the targeted review of large advisers being done at the same time.

Purposes of the sweep

The purposes of the sweep were to:

- use our oversight role to focus on IFMs who manage a significant portion of investment funds as a breakdown in their compliance structure or key operations could put investors and the capital markets at risk

- assess compliance of large IFMs with regulatory requirements and the adequacy of controls related to the key operations of their investment funds

- identify areas where additional guidance is needed

Major findings

Aside from the issuance of deficiency reports, the sweep did not result in further regulatory action on any of the IFMs reviewed. However, we identified areas where deficiencies were more prevalent and additional guidance is needed. These areas are discussed in dedicated parts below and include:

    I. sales practices

    II. allocation of expenses to investment funds

    III. mutual fund borrowings

    IV. prohibited cross trades

    V. outsourcing and oversight of service providers

The guidance in large part is meant to assist IFMs in meeting their duty to act honestly, in good faith and in the best interests of their funds as required by section 116 of the *Securities Act* (Ontario). Many of the concepts related to some of the above topics, such as primary purpose and cost reasonableness, require judgment and can be interpreted differently within the existing legislation. We have tried to establish parameters around these concepts which best correlate with an IFM's standard of care.

We coordinated our review with staff in the Investment Funds branch to ensure consistent approaches in interpreting and applying the legislation.

We would also like to remind IFMs to review OSC Staff Notice 33-742 *2013 Annual Summary Report for Dealers, Advisers and Investment Fund Managers* and OSC Staff Notice 81-723 *Summary Report for Investment Fund Issuers 2013* which contain information and guidance in other areas relevant to IFMs.

Part I — Sales practices

Background

The purpose of Part 5 of National Instrument 81-105 *Mutual Fund Sales Practices* (**NI 81-105**) is to regulate the sales practices of industry participants in connection with the distribution of publicly offered securities of mutual funds to safeguard the interests of investors. As a result, NI 81-105 establishes a minimum standard of conduct to ensure that any compensation or benefits provided to participating dealers and their respective representatives are not in any way "excessive" or "extravagant" so as to improperly influence the selection of mutual funds for distribution by a representative to its clients.

In addition to the information contained in this Notice, IFMs should also refer to the guidance contained in OSC Staff Notice 11-760 *Report on Mutual Fund Sales Practices Under Part 5 of National Instrument 81-105* (**Staff Notice 11-760**) which was based on the findings of a 2006 targeted review of sales practices and which continues to be relevant.

Scope and key findings

For the purposes of this sweep, we focused on the following areas of Part 5 of NI 81-105:

i) — Section 5.1 — Cooperative marketing practices

Section 5.1 permits IFMs to pay a portion of the costs of a sales communication, investor conference or investor seminar (collectively, **cooperative marketing practices**) that participating dealers organize and present to investors.

The major findings in this area, shown along with their incidence rate, were:

- cooperative marketing practices did not meet the primary purpose of promoting or providing educational information concerning a mutual fund, a mutual fund family or mutual funds generally in order to be eligible for support (25%)

- inadequate disclosure on cooperative marketing materials to indicate that the IFM paid for a portion of the costs of the cooperative marketing practice (25%)

- inconsistent application of the IFM's methodology to calculate primary purpose across all cooperative marketing practice requests (13%)

ii) — Section 5.2 — Mutual fund sponsored conferences

Section 5.2 outlines the conditions under which IFMs may provide a non-monetary benefit to a sales representative of a participating dealer to attend a conference or seminar organized and presented by the IFM.

The major findings in this area, shown along with their incidence rate, were:

- IFMs paid for expenses of the sales representatives, such as travel and accommodation, not permitted under section 5.2 (50%)
- the non-monetary benefits relating to the mutual fund sponsored conference, such as meals and entertainment, were excessive having regard to the purpose of the conference (25%)

iii) — Section 5.5 — Participating dealer sponsored events

Section 5.5 permits IFMs to pay a portion of the costs of conferences and seminars organized and presented by dealers (that are not investor conferences or seminars referred to in section 5.1), within certain parameters.

The major findings in this area, shown along with their incidence rate, were:

- IFMs provided support for dealer organized conferences which included amounts related to meals and entertainment that were excessive having regard to the purpose of the conference (25%)
- IFMs provided support for dealer organized conferences in excess of the 10% reimbursement limit of direct costs incurred by the dealer relating to the conference (25%)

iv) — Policies and procedures related to sales practices

We also noted the following weaknesses with respect to IFMs' policies and procedures in this area:

- IFMs did not have adequate policies and procedures regarding sales practices (38%)
- IFMs did not adhere to their documented policies and procedures relating to sales practices (25%)

Guidance

Based on the above-noted findings, assessing primary purpose and the reasonability of costs associated with mutual fund sales practices are areas where IFMs can benefit from further guidance to encourage a more consistent application among industry participants to these otherwise subjective areas of Part 5 of NI 81-105.

Please refer to Appendix A which provides a decision tree to assist in evaluating primary purpose and the reasonability of costs. These are also discussed separately in the sections below.

Assessing primary purpose

IFMs had challenges meeting the primary purpose test which is essential for deciding whether to accept or reject a cooperative marketing request, organize a mutual fund sponsored conference or provide monetary support for a dealer sponsored conference. Primary purpose also determines whether an IFM can pay for the cost of a sales representative to attend an industry association sponsored event or a third party sponsored educational event.

The main challenges for assessing primary purpose relate to the following:

- *Content:* The primary purpose test is based on specific topical content and is more restrictive in section 5.1 of NI 81-105 as compared to sections 5.2 to 5.5, which permit the primary purpose to include educational information on the broader topics of financial planning or investing in securities
- *Time:* NI 81-105 does not provide a prescribed percentage or bright line test to determine what amount of time must be allocated to appropriate content to meet primary purpose

Content and time are codependent in determining primary purpose as the content has to be evaluated not only on whether it is based on the provision of educational information, but also on the amount of time spent overall on appropriate content. Each is discussed in more detail below.

i) — Content

The primary purpose of the sales practices in sections 5.1 to 5.5 must be the provision of educational information as set out in the table below (collectively, **permitted topics**):

Section of NI 81-105	Permitted topics
5.1 — Cooperative marketing practices	To promote or provide educational information concerning a mutual fund, a mutual fund family or mutual funds generally
5.2 — IFM sponsored conferences	To provide educational information about financial planning, investing in securities, mutual
5.5 — Dealer sponsored events	fund industry matters, a mutual fund, a mutual fund family or mutual funds generally

Section of NI 81-105	Permitted topics
5.3 — Third party sponsored events	To provide educational information about financial planning, investing in securities, mutual
5.4 — Industry association sponsored events	fund industry matters, or mutual funds generally

Since 2008, the OSC has granted relief, subject to several conditions, to IFMs who have made formal applications to expand the permitted topics set out in section 5.1 of NI 81-105. Initially, the relief permitted IFMs to sponsor the costs of cooperative marketing practices whose primary purpose is to provide educational information concerning tax and estate planning. More recently however, the OSC granted relief that further expanded the permitted topics to include the broader topic of financial planning.

To ensure compliance with the permitted topics and if applicable, any relief granted by the OSC, IFMs should review materials related to cooperative marketing practices, or other conferences and seminars for which their support is being sought under Part 5. This would include the final version of a sales communication and for conferences or seminars, the final agenda or program description and presentation materials. This will assist IFMs in ensuring that the content of the sales practice is consistent, in whole or in part, with the permitted topics.

The content of most sales communications under section 5.1 can likely be assessed for primary purpose from a quick visual review of the document breakdown. For seminars or conferences which also include non-permitted topics and recreational activities, an IFM should evaluate the amount of time spent on non-permitted topics and activities in relation to the event as a whole to determine whether the primary purpose test can still be met. This will be discussed in section ii) below.

Examples of non-permitted topics include, but are not limited to:

- business practice management sessions (selling mutual funds effectively, building/increasing book of business)

- motivational speakers

- award ceremonies

- sessions on general business operations

- time spent on recreational activities, such as golf, fishing or attending sporting events

ii) — Time

We expect the time spent on permitted topics to be proportionate or exceed the amount of time spent on non-permitted topics and recreational activities. We encourage the use of a detailed and mathematical approach which objectively assesses the time spent on permitted topics in relation to the event as a whole because it can be applied consistently and is a verifiable method to determine whether the primary purpose test is met.

Although we recommend IFMs follow a mathematical approach, we acknowledge there are some areas in the time assessment where judgment is required, for example:

- Breakfasts, lunches and breaks during the conference may be excluded from the time assessment. However, if these are unusually long (i.e. a 3 hour lunch) or are incorporated as part of a wider non-permitted topic or recreational activity, these likely should be included as a non-permitted topic in the time assessment.

- The evaluation of time to determine primary purpose should focus on activities taking place during regular business hours. However, the totality of the event, including activities taking place after business hours, must still be considered when assessing the reasonableness of costs which is discussed in the next section.

Regardless of these guidelines, IFMs must still be mindful that if the dinner events or other forms of entertainment appear excessive in relation to the duration of the educational portion of the conference or seminar (for example, an entire day of golf during a two day event), or if the costs associated with these are excessive and unreasonable, this would not be consistent with meeting the primary purpose test.

For investor conferences or seminars under section 5.1 organized by a dealer for which an IFM is providing support, IFMs must confirm that the event is truly for educational purposes based on the amount of time spent on permitted topics. It may be difficult for IFMs to determine whether or not an investor seminar or conference crosses the line into a client appreciation event, which is not eligible for support, without obtaining adequate documentation from the dealer. IFMs must ensure that they receive sufficient information in order to evaluate whether the primary purpose test is met based on the amount of time spent on permitted topics.

Events which consist of only a short presentation related to mutual funds followed by a lengthy entertainment program would likely fall under the client appreciation category. Similarly, for IFM sponsored events under section 5.2, the overall objective of the event may be viewed as business promotion if the educational content is overshadowed by excessive recreational activities and free time.

Q&A

Q: A representative has requested cooperative marketing support for an investor conference. The details of the agenda submitted to the IFM include the following:

- 1 hour presentation by a portfolio manager on mutual funds

- Following the presentation, a sporting activity estimated to last a couple of hours where the portfolio manager will be available to speak with the dealing representatives on an informal basis.

Would this investor conference meet the primary purpose of providing educational information about mutual funds?

A: No. The duration of the recreational activity exceeds the one hour presentation provided by the portfolio manager. The portfolio manager's mere presence at the sporting event is not sufficient to conclude that the purpose of the entire event is for the provision of educational information. As a result, the time spent on non-permitted topics and activities exceeds the time spent on permitted topics. This event would be considered a client appreciation event which is not eligible for support under section 5.1 of NI 81-105.

Staff Notice 11-760 provides in-depth guidance on issues related to sales practices. The following guidance is meant to complement that notice based on the issues we identified during this sweep for evaluating whether an event contemplated in Part 5 of NI 81-105 meets the primary purpose test:

Suggested practices

We expect:

- IFMs to develop guidelines and internal percentage thresholds that are **consistent** and **verifiable** when evaluating the content of a sales communication, seminar, conference or other event to assess if it meets the primary purpose of providing educational information on the permitted topics prescribed in sections 5.1 to 5.5 of NI 81-105, as applicable

- IFMs to request sufficient and appropriate documentation to confirm that any sales communication, conference or seminar is sufficiently focused on permitted topics based on the allotted time and their internal guidelines and percentage thresholds. This should include:

  - a copy of the final version of the sales communication or the final agenda for the investor conference or seminar (section 5.1)

  - the agendas or program descriptions for events sponsored by third parties, industry associations or participating dealers (sections 5.3 to 5.5, respectively)

- For cooperative marketing practices, IFMs must ensure their full legal name appears in the sales communication or conference/seminar agenda and that clear language indicates that the IFM has paid for a portion of the cooperative marketing practice

- Documentation related to determining primary purpose must be maintained, with sufficient evidence of review and approval prior to the support being granted

- IFMs, at a minimum, to develop written policies and procedures which include

  - the definition of primary purpose for each type of sales practice

  - guidelines and internal thresholds that have been established

  - procedures to review the costs, time and content of an event or sales communication prior to granting approval to determine if the primary purpose test is met, including the types of documentation that must be obtained for the review, the individuals that will provide approval and the type of evidence that should be maintained

(refer also to Appendix A of Staff Notice 11-760 for a more detailed listing of policies and procedures)

Reasonability of costs

The main issues identified during the sweep in this area related to:

- inadequate processes to ensure that the non-monetary benefits provided to investors or sales representatives attending a seminar or conference, whether organized by the IFM or a participating dealer, were not extravagant and were consistent with the spirit of NI 81-105

- the payment of prohibited expenses, such as travel and accommodation, of representatives attending an IFM sponsored event

Each of these issues will be discussed in sections i) and ii) which follow below.

The financial limitations of Part 5 of NI 81-105 are set out in the table below and serve as a starting point in assessing what costs are permitted and reasonable:

Section of NI 81-105	Financial limitation
5.1 — Cooperative marketing practices	All IFMs, in aggregate, cannot pay more than 50% of the total direct costs incurred by the dealer (for sales communication, investor conference/seminar)
5.2 — IFM sponsored conferences	IFMs cannot pay any travel, accommodation or personal incidental expenses for the attendee; *and* the costs must be reasonable having regard to the purpose of the conference
5.3 — Third party sponsored events	IFMs can pay the registration fees for attendees
5.4 — Industry association sponsored events	The IFMs in a mutual fund family in aggregate cannot pay more than 10% of the total direct costs incurred by the prescribed industry associations or their affiliates
5.5 — Dealer sponsored events	The IFMs in a mutual fund family in aggregate cannot pay more than 10% of the total direct costs incurred by the dealer; *and* All IFMs, in aggregate, cannot pay more than 66% of the total direct costs incurred by the dealer

Direct costs (as defined in section 1.1 of NI 81-105) may include:

- *reasonable* food and beverage costs
- *reasonable* entertainment costs
- conference room rental fees
- conference or seminar materials
- audio visual equipment costs
- printing costs
- advertising costs of the seminar or conference
- speaker fees and expenses
- event planning fees

but do not include costs such as:

- salary and overhead of the dealer
- travel, accommodation or personal incidental expenses of the dealer's sales representatives
- prizes or gifts, unless they are of nominal value

i) — Reasonability of costs

Assessing the reasonableness of costs requires judgment. NI 81-105 does not provide a range or measure for firms to assess the reasonability of costs "having regard to the purpose of the conference or seminar." During our reviews, we looked at the totality of the costs associated with conferences or seminars and noted that the majority of the costs related to meals and entertainment and in particular, to costs that occurred after regular business hours. While this practice is not contrary to NI 81-105, staff was concerned that some IFMs lacked guidelines in terms of what an acceptable expenditure amount would be in these areas, particularly since this is where the majority of the money is being spent. Further, we found the costs of these meals and entertainment to be extravagant in some cases. For example, the cost per day for dinner and entertainment that we calculated in our sample of conferences and seminars ranged from less than $100 to well over $700 per person. While the latter seems completely extravagant and the former seems reasonable, we acknowledge that finding a balance is challenging.

IFMs must develop internal guidelines to assess and review whether the costs of meals and entertainment provided at conferences or seminars sponsored by them are reasonable having regard to the purpose of these events. Similarly, IFMs must also develop guidelines to use when reviewing the costs incurred by a participating dealer to organize an event under section 5.5 in which their monetary support is provided.

In developing these guidelines, IFMs need to look at these expenditures objectively and consider whether:

- the expenditures are necessary to achieve the objective of the conference or seminar,
- an outsider or an independent party such as the Independent Review Committee (**IRC**) of the funds would consider these costs excessive based on the venue selected or the type of entertainment being offered,
- there are alternatives that would be more reasonable and achieve the same purpose and outcome,

- investors would perceive the meals and entertainment or other non-monetary benefits being offered as excessive and not in line with the educational purpose of the event.

With respect to specific expenditures, the following should be considered by IFMs in establishing their internal guidelines on reasonability:

Food and beverages

- Develop an acceptable upper limit or range for
  - the cost per meal per attending representative
  - the daily average meal cost per representative
  - the total food and beverage cost over the duration of the conference or seminar, as a percentage of the total event costs
- Criteria for the selection of venue that are consistent with cost reasonability
- The reasonableness of ancillary costs, such as decorations and table linens, associated with providing the meal above and beyond the cost of the food and beverages (**Note:** ancillary costs such as decorations and flowers must be included when assessing the cost of food and beverages)

Entertainment and promotional activities

- Develop an acceptable upper limit or range for
  - the cost of the activity or entertainment per attending representative
  - the cost of an activity in total for all representatives participating over the duration of the conference or seminar
  - the total cost for all entertainment and activities over the duration of the conference or seminar, as a percentage of the total event costs
- Criteria to assess alternatives for entertainment and activities to ensure costs are reasonable and in line with the educational purpose of the event, taking into account factors such as the perception of excessiveness, the location of the activities and the ease of access to these events. For example, hiring a local performer rather than a well-known celebrity or providing tickets to a regular season sporting event rather than a play-off game would be valid alternatives that can be evaluated based on established criteria.

Gifts

- Dollar limit on the value of a gift per representative and the amount that may be spent on a representative on an annual basis
- Is the limit consistent with the gift being of nominal value and promotional in nature?
- Is the gift required for the effective and efficient execution of the conference or seminar?

Q&A

Q: As a door prize at our IFM sponsored conference, we would like to offer prepaid Visa gift cards of a nominal value. Would this be contrary to NI 81-105?

A: Although the value is nominal, these prepaid cards are not promotional in nature and are in substance, a cash gift to the recipient which is inconsistent with the requirement that the items be non-monetary in nature. Other gifts that are equivalent to a cash gift should also not be offered to sales representatives, such as other types of gift certificates and casino chips.

If these prizes are offered as part of an investor conference or seminar of a participating dealer, IFMs must scrutinize the expenses submitted by the participating dealer to ensure such costs are not included as part of the direct costs of the seminar or conference for which support is being sought.

We would also like to highlight the guidance found in subsection 7.3(1) of Companion Policy 81-105CP *Mutual Fund Sales Practices* (**81-105CP**) in relation to the provision of entertainment and gifts to representatives during IFM sponsored conferences which states:

> *The term "reasonable" costs would not include gifts or entertainment provided to attendees other than as permitted by section 5.6 of the Instrument.*

IFMs can provide gifts and entertainment to representatives attending IFM sponsored conferences provided that the value of the gifts and entertainment are in compliance with section 5.6 of NI 81-105. As a result, the provision of gifts and entertainment must not be so extensive so as to cause a reasonable person to question whether the provision of the gifts and entertainment would improperly influence the advice provided by the representative to its clients.

A number of IFM firms set a limit per representative that can be spent on gifts and entertainment on an annual basis under section 5.6 of NI 81-105.

Q&A

Q: As an IFM, we have an annual limit of $1,500 per representative to be spent on promotional items and business promotion activities. We would like to take a group of representatives to a play-off sporting event. Based on the cost, the entire limit per representative would be spent on this one time sporting event for the cost of the ticket and a limousine ride to the arena. Would this be contrary to NI 81-105?

A: Yes, the spending of the entire limit on a representative at one time would be considered excessive and therefore unreasonable under section 5.6 of NI 81-105. You should establish dollar limits per year, and per event, that may be spent on promotional items and business promotion activities for dealing representatives. Furthermore, the provision of a limousine ride to the event is considered to be a travel expense that is strictly prohibited under paragraph (b) of section 5.6 of NI 81-105.

The following guidance is suggested for assessing the reasonability of direct costs:

Suggested practices

We expect:

- IFMs to develop internal policies and procedures to determine the reasonability of the cost of food, beverages, gifts, entertainment and promotional activities provided to representatives during mutual fund sponsored conferences, or to be paid to dealers for conferences or seminars which they sponsor and for which support is being sought. The policies and procedures should include, at a minimum:

  - Internal parameters on what is considered a reasonable amount for each type of non-monetary benefit

  - Factors to consider when determining reasonability, such as the location of the event, whether it's a specialty event or a routine event or time of year the event is held and how these factors should be addressed

  - The type of documentation required to assess reasonability, including detailed invoices, receipts and budgets

  - The individual(s) responsible for assessing reasonability and providing documented approval of expenses

  - The involvement of the IRC in evaluating sales practices for reasonability

- IFMs to maintain evidence of their reasonability assessment and the review and approval of the non-monetary benefit, including how the choice to provide one non-monetary benefit over another was determined

- Prior to providing monetary support, IFMs to exercise reasonable diligence to confirm that costs indicated on invoices or receipts received from participating dealers represent direct costs that are reasonable under the circumstances

ii) — Prohibited expenses

Section 5.2 of NI 81-105 explicitly prohibits an IFM to pay any travel, accommodation or personal incidental expenses for sales representatives attending its sponsored conferences. Furthermore, an IFM cannot indirectly pay for prohibited expenses by subsidizing a portion of these costs and/or applying savings in a permissible area to cover a prohibited expense. For example, an IFM cannot pay for bus transportation from the airport to the hotel and then charge the attending representatives a reduced rate on that transportation. Similarly, an IFM cannot pay the hotel for room upgrades for each attending representative and then recover the cost through a discount offered on hotel catering services.

Further guidance on prohibited expenses is provided in subsection 7.1(1) of 81-105CP and these expenses are also outlined below. We noted that some IFMs were paying prohibited expenses on behalf of attending sales representatives.

Travel

The following expenses are *not* acceptable for the IFM to pay:

- Airfare or the payment of any other form of transportation

- Transportation to and from the airport to the hotel

- The payment of a car rental fee, parking expenses, gas, or mileage in relation to a car used by a representative during the conference

- Transportation from the location of the conference and/or the representative's hotel (if not the same location as the conference) to dinners during the conference

Q&A

Q: As an IFM, our conference will include a dinner where there will be alcoholic drinks available with dinner. Can we cover the travel expenses of the sales representatives of participating dealers incurred to travel from dinner back to the hotel and remain in compliance with NI 81-105?

A: Yes. Although the payment of costs associated with travel to dinner is **not** permissible, the payment of travel from dinner back to the hotel is allowed in light of the risk associated with the consumption of alcohol. While it would be prudent for a concerned IFM to mitigate these risks by serving limited or no alcohol, or advising those dealing representatives that they must pay out of pocket for alcohol, we acknowledge that IFMs may be exposed to a potential liability as a result of sponsoring an event where alcohol is permitted and no mode of transportation is offered to ensure safe arrival back at their hotel or home. As a result, we consider this travel cost to be permissible, as long as the cost is reasonable. For example, providing a multi-passenger vehicle or taxi chits to attendees would be considered reasonable while the use of a luxury limousine would be excessive.

Accommodation

The accommodation costs of a representative attending an IFM sponsored conference are not an expense that can be paid for by an IFM. This includes hotel expenses of the attending representative and any guests of the attending representative during the conference. In addition, an IFM cannot pay for an upgrade for the accommodation of the representatives. Any upgrade must be paid for by the representative directly or the representative's participating dealer.

Personal incidental expenses

The payment of personal incidental expenses incurred by a representative during the course of a conference is not allowed to be covered by the IFM. Examples of personal incidental expenses include:

- Car rental

- Parking fees, including valet parking

- Costs related to room service charges or other hotel services

- Costs incurred by a guest accompanying an attending representative related to any of the above

Suggested practices

For events that are sponsored by a dealer under section 5.1 or section 5.5, the IFM should, prior to providing monetary support:

- Obtain invoices with sufficient detail of the costs for which reimbursement has been requested and assess if the actual expenses represent direct costs as defined in section 1.1 of NI 81-105, rather than prohibited costs listed in subsection 7.1(1) of the 81-105CP

- A dealer requesting financial support for a sales practice under NI 81-105 must provide an IFM with enough information to enable the IFM to determine eligibility and compliance with NI 81-105

For all types of events contemplated under Part 5, we expect the IFM to

- Develop internal guidelines as part of the IFM's policies and procedures manual that outline permissible costs and develop a list of expenses that cannot be covered for sales representatives under any circumstance

Part II — Allocation of expenses to investment funds

Our review of fund expenses during the sweep did not indicate any significant issues in this area. However, some IFMs expressed that additional guidance in this area would be helpful to assist them in enhancing their fund expense allocation methodology. IFMs have a duty to act honestly, in good faith, and in the best interest of the investment funds. IFMs should be able to demonstrate that the allocation of expenses is not inconsistent with their duty of care and that they are not putting their own interests ahead of those of the fund and its securityholders. The amount of the expenses charged to the funds has a direct impact on the management expense ratio (**MER**). IFMs monitor the funds' MERs closely to ensure the funds remain competitive.

There is an inherent conflict of interest in fund expense allocation. IFMs must bring conflicts of interest matters to the IRC. Materials provided to the IRC should contain sufficient details for the IRC to review and assess the matters thoroughly prior to making any recommendation. With respect to the fund expense allocation policy, an IFM should provide the IRC with a detailed list that itemizes all types of expenses to be allocated to its investment funds. In the discussion with the IRC, IFMs should also highlight expense items that are considered contentious in relation to their necessity for the daily operation of the funds, that are payable to a related party service provider or are unique to their business operations. Ultimately, any expenses allocated to the funds should relate to the daily operation of the funds and be reasonable and justifiable.

Allocation models

Accumulating the appropriate expenses and allocating them to the investment funds using a sound methodology is a time consuming and challenging task depending on the expense model that is chosen by the IFMs. Some expense models are relatively easy to apply, for example, the fixed rate administration fee[1] or the operating expense subject to a cap[2] model. Other models require the IFMs to exercise judgment to determine:

- the appropriate types of expenses that may be eligible for allocation

- the appropriate method to equitably allocate these expenses to the investment funds, ensuring that the amount of expenses allocated to each fund is in proportion to the services provided to the fund

Types of expenses

i) — Expenses of an IFM

Expenses related to the operations and conduct of an IFM should be borne by the IFM and should not be allocated to the funds. An IFM directs the business, operations or affairs of an investment fund. Its major roles and responsibilities include:

- maintaining proper registration for the firm, the ultimate designated person (**UDP**) and the chief compliance officer (**CCO**)

- developing a system of compliance and controls, along with on-going monitoring and supervision, that covers all relevant areas of the IFM's business operations whether the functions are done in-house or by third-party service providers

- ensuring compliance with securities law and meeting all regulatory obligations

- establishing the firm's infrastructure and hiring qualified personnel

- entering into agreements with portfolio managers, custodians or third-party service providers

- establishing a distribution network for the investment funds by entering into distribution agreements with registered dealers and providing them with adequate and appropriate information

- promoting the investment funds

Expenses incurred by the IFM to fulfill its roles and responsibilities and to ensure the proper conduct of the firm and the investment funds with regulatory obligations should be paid for by the IFM. Further, the IFM earns a management fee paid by the investment funds to carry out its roles and responsibilities. The purpose of the management fee is to cover expenses related to the IFM's business activities.

Please refer to Appendix B of this Notice for a decision tree that assists in determining whether an expense item should be paid for by the IFM or allocated to its investment fund(s).

Q&A

Q: As an IFM, I will need to make system changes to produce the information required under CRM2 Amendments by July 15, 2016. How should I treat the costs incurred to make these system changes?

A: Providing the necessary information to registered dealers who distribute your investment funds is an obligation of the IFM. You should account for the costs associated with the system changes as part of your operating expenses and you should not allocate these expenses to the funds.

Q&A

Q: Our firm is currently going through the process of hiring an employee for our fund accounting group. We have engaged a search firm to assist us in this process. Can we charge the hiring expenses associated with this employee to the funds that we manage?

A: No. IFMs have a responsibility to establish the infrastructure for the daily operation of their funds to ensure compliance with securities law, including the hiring of staff. As a result, any expenses incurred for the hiring of this employee, such as the use of a recruiting firm, should be borne by the IFM and not the funds. Until this employee has commenced work at the IFM, there is no involvement with the daily operation of the funds.

However, a fund can be allocated salary and benefit costs that are part of a reasonable compensation package for employees whose jobs are directly related to the daily operation of the fund.

---

[1] The IFM is responsible for most of the expenses of the fund in return for an annual administration fee calculated by applying a fixed percentage to the fund's assets under management. The rate is disclosed in the fund's offering documents.

[2] The IFM applies a fixed basis point rate, a cap, to cover the fund's actual operating expenses instead of accumulating and allocating the expenses to the fund. It is called a cap because the rate is typically lower than what the IFM would have charged if actual operating expenses were allocated. IFMs should review and assess the cap periodically to ensure the cap rate is not higher than the actual expenses. The cap is done at the discretion of the IFM, who has no obligation to cap the operating expenses of the funds.

Q&A

Q: How do we treat the costs associated with our compliance department? While the compliance personnel ensure our IFM business is compliant with the requirements under securities laws, including NI 31-103, they also spend time on product-related compliance, such as dealing with certain requirements in NI 81-102. It would seem appropriate that some of these compliance costs be allocated to the investment funds.

A: The wide range of expenses incurred in managing investment funds, as well as the lack of specific disclosure regarding expense allocation provisions in the funds' offering documents, often result in varying interpretations by IFMs on which types of expenses should be allocated to the funds. IFMs should consider all expense allocation decisions in conjunction with their duty to act in the best interests of their funds and any excessive or unreasonable allocations to their funds may constitute a breach of this duty.

With that principle in mind, costs associated with ensuring compliance with securities law and meeting regulatory obligations, such as the salaries of dedicated compliance staff and any overhead allocated to that department, should *generally* be considered an expense of the IFM. We acknowledge that the compliance structures at IFMs vary greatly in size and nature, may include multiple layers and that there may be overlap across other departments in performing compliance-related duties. Accordingly, IFMs should consider their contractual agreements with the funds, the advice of the IRC and its disclosure in the offering documents if considering the allocation of certain compliance costs to their funds.

Compliance costs related to NI 31-103 clearly belong with the IFM. NI 31-103 deals primarily with firm conduct and a firm's regulatory roles and responsibilities and these are obligations that can only be met by the IFM. NI 31-103 requires each registrant to establish a system of compliance and controls, along with on-going monitoring and supervision, over all relevant areas of its business operations. This would include its fund operations and the related compliance costs of complying with product-specific legislation. The investment funds are already paying a management fee to the IFM that arguably covers these compliance and oversight expenses.

Using NI 81-102 as an example, many of the compliance-related costs are already linked to the management fee being paid by the fund. The revenue of an IFM is dependent on the proper operation of its mutual funds in compliance with applicable product regulation. Failure to do so would result in the inability to offer the product to the public. Mutual fund sales communications that are effective and compliant with legislation assist in growing the funds' assets under management which in turn, impact management fee revenues. Also, the product-related investment restrictions in NI 81-102 are managed by the portfolio manager (**PM**) who is being compensated out of the management fee to ensure that the funds are managed in accordance with their stated investment objectives and regulatory restrictions. A PM firm would not invoice an advisory client an additional amount for ensuring compliance with its PM mandate and the same logic would apply to an IFM in relation to its investment fund product. In addition, where the IFM and PM are not the same entity, the IFM has an obligation to oversee the PM as part of its oversight of service providers and should bear this cost.

ii) — Expenses of an investment fund

Only expenses that are related to the daily operations of the investment funds should be allocated to the investment funds. Expenses that investment funds incur on a daily basis can be grouped into three main categories as follows:

Direct expenses

We consider direct expenses to be expenses that can be directly linked to the investment funds. Examples of direct expenses may include expenses related to prospectus or other continuous disclosure filings, audit, legal, securityholder reporting, trading and brokerage, IRC and custodial fees. In most cases, these expenses are supported by invoices that provide a breakdown of the expenses on a fund-by-fund basis.

Fees paid to service providers for outsourced functions

IFMs may outsource certain functions to third-party or related service providers, such as the net asset value calculation or securityholder record keeping. These functions pertain to the daily operations of the investment funds and may be paid for by the investment funds. Unlike direct expenses, invoices submitted by third-party service providers may not include a breakdown of the fees associated with each fund. Accordingly, the IFM will need to allocate these costs to the funds using an appropriate cost driver — see discussion on *Allocation of fund expenses.*

Expenses incurred for functions performed in-house

IFMs that choose to administer the key business activities of their investment funds internally must develop a method to determine how to allocate the correct amount of these expenses to their funds. Some IFMs establish departments or cost centres for each function to clearly identify the expenses that are associated with the employees who are fully or partially dedicated to providing services to the funds. Similarly, the portion of expenses such as rent, office supplies, photocopier fees and telephone and internet charges that can be allocated to that department must be determined.

IFMs must critically assess and determine which expense items from the department should be included in the pool of expenses for allocation to the various funds. The expenses allocated must be directly related to the operations of the fund.

Part 3:
REGISTRATION

IFMs are responsible for ensuring that they obtain the best commercially available prices for the services used by their funds. If the provision of certain fund functions in-house is more cost favorable to a fund than outsourcing these functions, the difference in cost cannot be charged to the fund and retained by the IFM in addition to the management fees charged. This type of practice is contrary to an IFM's duty and responsibilities.

Q&A

Q: Our firm currently performs the fund accounting, trust accounting and securityholder recordkeeping internally. As a result, we have saved our funds a total of $100,000 which would have been the additional cost to the funds to hire a third party service provider to provide these services. What amount should we charge the funds for these services? The internal cost or the cost that we would have paid the service provider and then retain the difference as another fee paid to us as the IFM of our funds?

A: As the IFM of the funds, you have a responsibility to act in the best interest of the funds and secure the best commercially viable arrangements for the funds you manage. You determined that the best arrangement for your funds was to provide these services in-house and chose to do so. Therefore, the cost charged to the funds should be the cost of providing these services internally. It would be contrary to your duty as an IFM to charge your funds the third party rate and keep the difference as an extra fee for your services.

Furthermore, allocating and charging the funds for the costs associated with providing these services in-house is a conflict of interest matter that needs to be referred to the IRC.

Q&A

Q: We organized a party for an employee in the fund accounting department. Would it be appropriate to include this cost as part of the fund accounting department expenses that are allocated to the funds?

A: No, these expenses are to be paid for by the IFM, not the funds. As a guideline, expenses that do not in any way impact the operation of the funds, such as the social event described above, costs related to landscaping, design or general maintenance of the office and gifts to staff need to be paid for by the IFM and not be allocated to the funds.

Q&A

Q: Our firm is both the IFM and the PM of our investment funds. We subscribe to a number of research materials to assist us in our research and analysis which is part of the investment decision making process. Can we charge the subscription fees to the investment funds?

A: No. A PM manages the investment portfolios of the funds in return for an advisory fee as specified in the advisory agreement. Expenses incurred for the PM's research and analysis, or other costs associated with managing the funds' investment portfolios, are paid for by the PM because they are part of the costs of operating the PM's business. The answer may be less obvious when the firm has more than one role, i.e. being the IFM and PM. An IFM should consider whether it would pay for the subscription fees if the PM was a separate, unrelated entity. Since the PM is already compensated through its advisory fee which in turn, is paid out of the management fee collected from the funds, the IFM would not pay for the subscription fees.

Q&A

Q: Our firm is solely registered as an IFM and manages investment funds on a daily basis. The key operating activities for the funds, including fund accounting, trust accounting and securityholder recordkeeping, are performed in house. Can we charge the entire amount of the office rent expense and telephone and internet charges to the investment funds that we manage?

A: No, it would not be appropriate to charge 100% of the rent, telephone and internet charges or other common expenses to the funds that the firm manages. In addition to managing the funds on a daily basis, the IFM also conducts other duties that are not necessarily related to running the funds on a daily basis. For example, staff from the wholesale and compliance teams of the IFM also occupy office space and use the shared services such as the telephone and internet on a daily basis. As a result, the IFM should be charging a portion of the rent and telephone and internet charges to the funds and the IFM, respectively, based on a reasonable allocation methodology that appropriately reflects the usage of these shared costs.

Q&A

Q: We have a number of employees who divide their time between the IFM business and the investment funds as follows:

1) UDP — reviews financial statements and management reports of fund performance of the investment funds; meets with the CCO regarding compliance updates and compliance issues; sits on the Board of Directors of the IFM.

2) Controller — responsible for entries and the review of the general ledger and the preparation of the financial statements of both the investment funds and the IFM.

3) Financial analyst — responsible for calculating management fees and MERs of the funds; aids the controller in compiling the financial statements of the funds and the IFM.

Can we charge the entire salaries and bonuses for these individuals to our funds?

A: No. If you would like to charge a portion of these salaries to the funds, you need to make an assessment of how much time is spent by these individuals on performing tasks related to the funds as compared to time spent on IFM matters, and allocate the salaries accordingly.

Time that is spent on the business of the IFM and ensuring its investment funds comply with applicable legislation is more appropriately allocated to the IFM. In the examples noted above, this would include the UDP's time spent on compliance matters and sitting on the Board. Similarly, the amount of time spent by the controller and the financial analyst on the financial statements and general ledger of the IFM can be charged to the IFM.

Where the duties of these employees are related to calculating management fees and MERs of the funds and preparing the funds' continuous disclosure documents, these costs may appropriately be charged to the funds.

Allocation of fund expenses

Once it is determined which expenses are attributable to the daily operation of the funds, an IFM must establish a process to determine the allocation of these expenses to the various funds. The allocation is straightforward when invoices provide a breakdown of the expenses on a fund-by-fund basis. Expenses that relate to multiple funds that cannot be directly linked to a particular fund based on an invoice should be accumulated and allocated to funds using relevant and appropriate factors. We have noted that IFMs use one or more factors to determine the expense allocation, including but not limited to:

- assets under management
- the number of securityholders
- the fund's mandate
- the number of classes/series in a fund

The decision on how to allocate an expense to a fund should be linked to how the expense is being charged (i.e. the cost driver), which in most cases will have a direct relationship with the time and effort spent on each fund by the external party providing the service or by the in-house department. IFMs should inquire of the service provider how the fees are being determined when negotiating the agreement with them. For in-house departments, IFMs generally keep track of the number of hours or the percentage of time spent on the funds per department, or use one of the above factors as a proxy to divide the time spent among the various funds. The allocation of the departmental expenses to each fund is then based mainly on the level of usage by the fund of that department's services.

Q&A

Q: Our firm is considering streamlining our fund expense allocation methodology to use only one factor to allocate all types of expenses to our funds instead of our current approach of using different factors. Is this change appropriate?

A: No. While it may be easier to allocate expenses to the funds using only one allocation factor, it is unlikely that this is an appropriate method to allocate fund expenses. There are many types of fund expenses that can be allocated to the funds and they usually do not correlate with one common factor. For example, securityholder reporting expenses tie closely with the number of securityholders, whereas the costs of calculating the net asset values (**NAV**) of the funds would have no direct relationship with the number of securityholders. As such, it is not appropriate to allocate both securityholder reporting expenses and expenses relating to the NAV calculation by using the number of securityholders as a common factor. Ultimately, your firm must determine the appropriate allocation factor(s) based on your knowledge of the cost driver of each expense item.

Disclosure in offering documents

Disclosure made in the funds' offering documents on fees and expenses should be clear and contain an appropriate level of detail to allow securityholders to fully understand the types of fees and expenses that are charged to the investment funds. IFMs should avoid using general or collective terms such as "administration costs" or "operating costs" to describe a group of expenses. The disclosure could be enhanced by providing a further breakdown to indicate what these expenses are, resulting in better and more meaningful disclosure.

For further guidance on disclosure, please refer to OSC Staff Notice 81-724 *Report on Staff's Continuous Disclosure Review of the Fees and Expenses Disclosure by Investment Funds* issued by the Investment Funds branch.

Documentation and periodic assessment

IFMs must maintain adequate documentation to demonstrate their rationale and the analysis performed in the development of their fund expense allocation policy. The documentation needs to support the methodology chosen, and demonstrate that the expenses allocated to the funds are reasonable, fair, and in the best interests of the funds. The policy should be reviewed at least on an annual basis or more frequently whenever there are changes in the IFMs' business activities or operations.

Suggested practices

We expect IFMs to establish and enforce written policies and procedures that include, at a minimum, the following:

- procedures to develop internal criteria and processes to identify and assess which expense items are related to the daily operations of the funds

- procedures to independently review expenses charged to the funds for appropriateness and accuracy, keeping in mind the internal criteria

- procedures to ensure that adequate controls are in place to review and approve invoices before they are processed for payment

- procedures to ensure that only those expenses disclosed in the offering documents are charged to the funds

- procedures to ensure that policies on fund expenses are up-to-date and where established, approved by the funds' IRC

IFMs should also develop and document procedures used to budget and accrue for expenses in the funds, for example:

- procedures to prepare and approve the funds' budgets at the beginning of each fiscal year to ensure that only reasonable and appropriate expenses will be charged to the funds

- procedures to monitor accrued amounts versus actual amounts on a periodic basis and guidelines on when an adjustment to the accruals should be made

When allocating expenses to the funds, we expect IFMs to:

- document the method used and maintain documentation on the rationale and analysis performed to support the chosen method

- determine the appropriate factors to be used for the allocation and how they are applied for each type of expense

- confirm the allocation method is fair and reasonable to all funds

---

Part III — Mutual fund borrowings

Sub-paragraph 2.6(a)(i) of National Instrument 81-102 *Mutual Funds* (**NI 81-102**) states that a mutual fund shall not borrow cash or provide a security interest over any of its portfolio assets unless the transaction is a temporary measure to meet redemption requests, or to permit the mutual fund to settle portfolio transactions, and the outstanding amount of *all borrowings* of the mutual fund does not exceed five percent of its NAV at the time of the borrowing.

We noted two issues in this area:

i) — Interpretation of the term "all borrowings"

During our reviews, we noted that some IFMs were calculating "all borrowings" in a mutual fund as the total of all its borrowings netted against its available cash balances for all the bank accounts of the mutual fund, rather than the sum of all borrowings of the mutual fund.

Under NI 81-102, mutual funds are not allowed to borrow except under the very limited circumstances outlined in the instrument. Consequently a strict and plain meaning interpretation to the borrowing provision should be applied. Accordingly, in the absence of any reference to "net borrowings" in NI 81-102, it is inappropriate to use excess cash in the bank accounts of the mutual fund to offset the total amount of a mutual fund's borrowing in account(s) where there is a balance owing. Until borrowed monies are actually repaid, those amounts are still outstanding and must factor into the "outstanding amount of all borrowings" as described in NI 81-102. Accordingly, the absolute sum of all borrowings of the mutual fund must be used when monitoring compliance with the borrowing provision.

ii) — Mutual funds borrowed in excess of 5% of their NAV

We identified IFMs with overdraft positions in their mutual funds' bank accounts in excess of the prescribed 5% of NAV limit in NI 81-102. This was also noted in some IFMs that were incorrectly netting the borrowings in the accounts of a mutual fund against cash balances in other bank accounts of the mutual fund which in effect, reduced the amount of the borrowings that should have been used to monitor the 5% limit.

Q&A

Q: One of our funds had a series of net redemptions this month which rendered the fund's bank account in an overdraft position for the entire month. Each overdraft was temporary in nature and it was corrected either in the following day or the day after. A new overdraft occurred due to redemption requests received in the following day. Are we in compliance with sub-paragraph 2.6(a)(i) of NI 81-102?

A: No. Sub-paragraph 2.6(a)(i) of NI 81-102 states that a mutual fund shall not borrow cash unless the transaction is a temporary measure to meet redemption requests. It is not a temporary measure when the fund was in a continuous overdraft position over a prolonged period of time. The IFM, together with the PM of the fund, should review and re-evaluate the cash position of the fund to ensure that it is adequate to meet redemption requests going forward.

Suggested practices

- IFMs need to establish an appropriate cash management process, including:

  - procedures over the settlement of securityholder trades to ensure that these are communicated to portfolio managers in a timely manner

  - procedures to sell investments in the fund's portfolio in the most favorable manner and minimize the likelihood of the fund going into an overdraft position

- IFMs must regularly monitor their mutual funds to ensure there is no overdraft position and to make certain that overdrafts, if they occur, are temporary and quickly resolved

- Overdraft positions should be reported to senior management, including the CCO, along with a description of the cause of the overdraft, impact of the overdraft (e.g. interest expense) and corrective actions to be taken to prevent an overdraft from recurring

Part IV — Prohibited cross trades

As part of our IFM reviews, we do not typically review trading activities relating to the funds' investment portfolios. However, during this sweep, if the IFM or one of its affiliates was also a registered adviser, we reviewed certain trading activities.

During our reviews, we noted that prohibited trades occurred between the investment funds advised by the firm ("inter-fund trades") or between investment funds and other managed accounts of the firm, collectively referred to as cross trades.

Clause 13.5(2)(b)(iii) of National Instrument 31-103 *Registration Requirements, Exemptions and Ongoing Registrant Obligations* (**NI 31-103**) prohibits an adviser from knowingly causing any investment portfolio it manages, including an investment fund, to purchase or sell a security from or to the investment portfolio of another investment fund for which a responsible person acts as an adviser.

Section 6.1 of National Instrument 81-107 *Independent Review Committee for Investment Funds* (**NI 81-107**) permits inter-fund trades that would otherwise be prohibited under NI 31-103 if certain conditions are met, including the approval or standing instruction by the funds' IRC. In the cases noted during our reviews, the inter-fund trades were not permissible under either NI 81-107 or NI 31-103.

Suggested practices

We expect IFMs to

- be aware of conflict of interest matters and refer them to the IRC where the funds are reporting issuers

- perform oversight of the funds' trading activities, whether performed in-house or outsourced

- confirm all inter-fund trades are permitted under NI 81-107 and have met all the conditions in section 6.1

Part 3:
REGISTRATION

- seek regulatory exemptive relief to permit the execution of cross trades between investment funds that are otherwise prohibited

IFMs should also refer to section 13.5 of the Companion Policy 31-103CP *Registration Requirements, Exemptions and Ongoing Registrant Obligations* (**31-103CP**), under the heading "Restrictions on trades with certain investment portfolios", for guidance on prohibited inter-fund trades.

Part V — Outsourcing and oversight of service providers

During our reviews, some IFMs expressed that additional guidance in the area of outsourcing would be helpful to assist them in enhancing their oversight procedures. Many IFMs outsource certain aspects of their IFM operations (such as fund accounting, trust accounting and transfer agency) to service providers.

During the reviews, we noted that the service provider typically used by an IFM is either a third party service provider or a related legal entity within the IFM's overall corporate group. It is our expectation that at least the same level of oversight should be performed on a related service provider by the IFM as that performed on a third party service provider. The IFM should also compare the fees charged by a related service provider to those charged by a third party to ensure the selection of a service provider is in the best interests of the funds, with referral of the matter to the IRC for consideration.

In addition, some firms which operate globally centralize certain functions of their IFM operations in order to achieve cost effectiveness and efficiency. Although we do not have issues with this business practice, we do expect that the Canadian compliance department of the IFM oversees the centralized function, as it would any service provider, and confirms that there is a robust process in place to obtain assurance that all requirements under Canadian securities laws are being adhered to.

Section 11.1 of NI 31-103 requires IFMs to establish a system of controls and supervision to ensure compliance with securities legislation and to manage their business risks in accordance with prudent business practices. Part 11 of 31-103CP, under the heading *General business practices — outsourcing*, states that registrants that outsource aspects of their business operations to third-party service providers are responsible and accountable for all functions that have been outsourced. An IFM is required to oversee its service providers in order to meet its obligation of being responsible and accountable for the work performed by the service providers.

Please refer to the suggested practices that were included in OSC Staff Notice 33-742 *2013 Annual summary Report for Dealers, Advisers and Investment Fund Managers* to provide IFMs with additional guidance regarding the monitoring of service providers.

Conclusion

This sweep enabled staff to focus on IFMs who are responsible for directing the business, operations and affairs of a significant segment of the industry's investment funds. This was an important step in evaluating the compliance systems of registrants who have a major impact on the capital markets. In addition, the results of the sweep highlighted areas where further guidance is needed. We hope that the guidance in this Notice, as well as other guidance referred to in this Notice, are helpful to registrants in meeting their regulatory obligations. Registrants should use this Notice as a self-assessment tool to assess their practices in the highlighted areas and to determine if changes are required.

Questions

If you have any questions regarding the content of this Notice, please refer them to any of the following:

[Omitted.]

Appendix A — Decision Tree — Part 5 of NI 81-105[3]

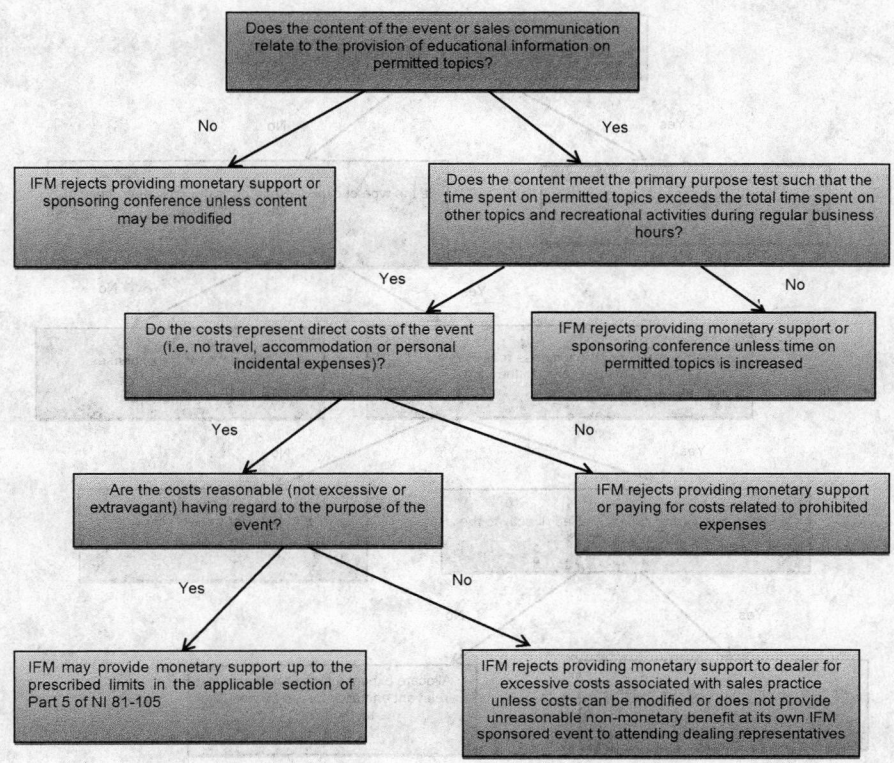

---

[3]The decision tree applies to parts 5.1 (cooperative marketing practices), 5.2 (IFM sponsored conferences) and 5.5 (dealer sponsored conferences) of NI 81-105 as these areas were the scope of our review.

Appendix B — Decision Tree — Expense allocation

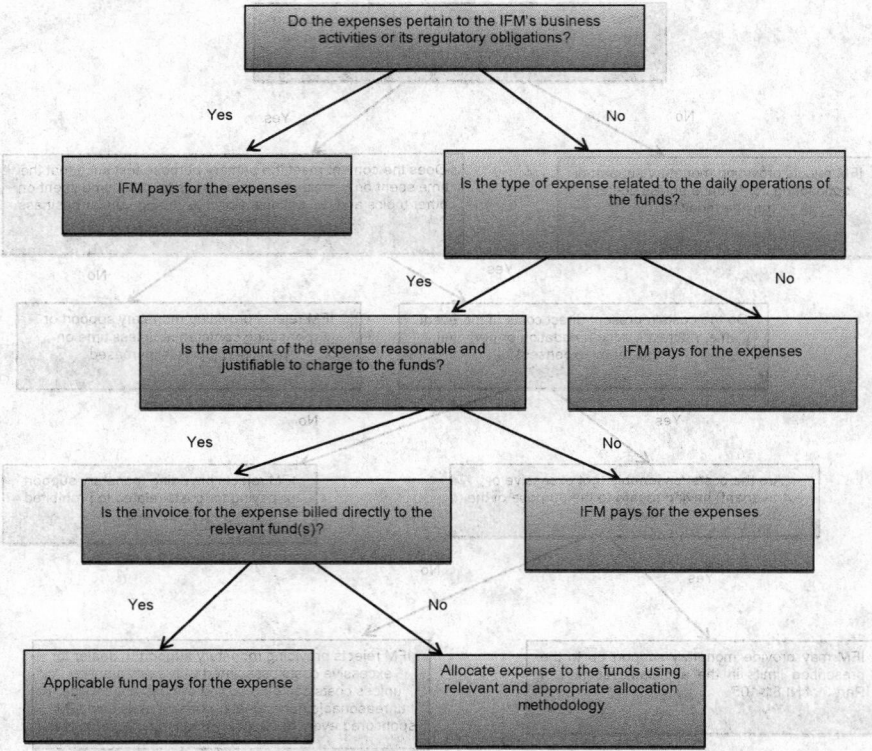

OSC Staff Notice 33-744 — Availability of Registration Exemptions to Foreign Dealers in Connection with Trades in Options and Futures Contracts Under the *Commodity Futures Act* (Ontario)

Date: September 18, 2014

Citation: 37 O.S.C.B. 8466

Purpose of this Notice

Staff of the Ontario Securities Commission (**staff** or **we**) have issued this notice (the **Notice**) to assist foreign dealers and other market participants in determining whether certain exemptions from the dealer registration requirement under the *Commodity Futures Act*, R.S.O. 1990, c. 20 (the **CFA**) are available to them.

Specifically, this Notice describes staff's view of the following:

- the circumstances in which the "unsolicited trade" exemption (as described below) is available, and activities that we consider inconsistent with the parameters of this exemption;

- the circumstances in which the "hedger" exemption (as described below) is available, and a market participant's obligations when relying on this exemption;

- the fee payment obligations of unregistered market participants that seek to trade with Ontario residents; and

- our expectations on foreign dealers and other unregistered market participants that intend to rely on exemptions from the registration requirement and actions that we may take where these expectations are not satisfied.

In this Notice, a reference to a "dealer" or "other market participant" includes both:

- a dealer or other market participant that is registered under the CFA, and

- an unregistered dealer or other market participant that is situate outside of Ontario but deals with customers in Ontario in reliance on an exemption from the registration requirement under the CFA.

We remind dealers and other market participants that there may be important differences in the regulatory treatment of exchange-traded futures and options across Canada and that market participants should review the specific requirements of securities, commodity futures and/or derivatives legislation in these jurisdictions prior to trading with customers in these jurisdictions.

Staff expect that this Notice will assist foreign dealers and other market participants in complying with the requirements of Ontario law until such time as the Canadian Securities Administrators (the CSA) develop a harmonized CSA approach to the regulation of exchange-traded options and futures contracts.

Background

Overview of regulatory regime in Ontario

In Ontario, exchange-traded futures and options are regulated as "commodity futures contracts" and "commodity futures options" under the CFA, and also, in some circumstances, as securities under the *Securities Act*, R.S.O. 1990, c. S.5 (the **OSA**).

Under the CFA, no person may trade [10] in a commodity futures contract or a commodity futures option (collectively, a **contract**) unless the person is registered as a dealer [*Futures Commission Merchant*], or as a representative of the dealer, or an exemption from the registration requirement is available.

Under the CFA, a "trade" is defined to include [11]

(a) entering into contracts, whether as principal or agent,

(b) acting as a floor trader,

(c) any receipt by a registrant of an order to effect a transaction in a contract,

(d) any assignment or other disposition of rights under a contract except a disposition arising from the death of an individual enjoying rights under a contract, and

(e) any act, advertisement, solicitation, conduct or negotiation directly or indirectly in furtherance of the foregoing.

Accordingly, under the CFA, a person who wishes to trade a contract is required to register as a dealer unless a registration exemption is available for the trade.

Registered dealers are required to be members of the Investment Industry Regulatory Organization of Canada (**IIROC**)[12] and to comply with IIROC rules. The most commonly used registration exemptions are considered below.

The "unsolicited trade" exemption

The CFA includes an exemption[13] from the registration requirement for a trade in a contract that is "unsolicited" and that meets certain other conditions (the **unsolicited trade exemption**). In order for a trade to meet the conditions of the unsolicited trade exemption, the trade must

- be executed on an exchange situate outside Ontario; and
- result from an order that
- is placed with a dealer who does not carry on business in Ontario; and
- did not involve any solicitation by or on behalf of the dealer.

Indicia of activities we consider to be "carrying on business" in Ontario

We consider each of the following to be indicia of a person "carrying on business" in Ontario:

- the establishment of an office or place of business in Ontario;
- the establishment of a relationship with an affiliated entity or third party in Ontario to conduct marketing or other activities that are in furtherance of a trade with a customer in Ontario;
- payment of commissions, fees or similar compensation to "introducing brokers", "finders", "referral agents" or other persons in connection with the trade with a customer in Ontario;
- trading with regularity with customers in Ontario, whether in reliance on the unsolicited trade exemption and/or in reliance on other exemptions, including exemptions contained in a discretionary exemptive relief order granted by the Commission under the CFA or the OSA.

Staff are of the view that the unsolicited trade exemption in the CFA was intended to apply to occasional, isolated trades by customers in Ontario that are not solicited by or on behalf of the foreign dealer. We do not believe that the exemption is available to permit the operation of unsolicited order-execution-only accounts by non-registered foreign dealers with customers in Ontario as we believe this would constitute trading with regularity with customers in Ontario and therefore carrying on business in Ontario.

Staff are generally prepared to recommend exemptive relief under the CFA to unregistered foreign dealers on terms and conditions that are similar to the terms and conditions contained in the international dealer exemption (the **international dealer exemption**) in section 8.18 of National Instrument 31-103 *Registration Requirements, Exemptions and Ongoing Registrant Obligations* (**NI 31-103**).

However, if a foreign dealer has obtained an order under the CFA exempting the foreign dealer from the requirement to be registered under the CFA by analogy to the international dealer exemption in NI 31-103, and the foreign dealer relies on that order to trade with regularity with

---

[10]See s. 22 of the CFA.

[11]See s. 1(1) of the CFA.

[12]See s. 10 of the General Regulation under the CFA, R.R.O. 1990, Reg. 90 (the **CFA Regulation**).

[13]See s. 32 of the CFA.

customers in Ontario, staff take the view that the foreign dealer is carrying on business in Ontario and is therefore unable to also rely on the unsolicited trade exemption in Ontario.

Indicia of activities we consider to be a "solicitation" in a jurisdiction

We consider each of the following to be indicia of activities that may be considered a "solicitation" in Ontario:

- any advertising or promotional activities that are directed to persons in Canada during the six months preceding the trade, including attendance at industry group conferences in Canada to promote the foreign dealer's products and services to Canadians;
- website disclosure that is addressed to Canadians or that provides information, including tax information, which is tailored to Canadians; and
- payment of commissions, fees or similar compensation to "introducing brokers", "finders", "referral agents" or other persons, whether situate in Ontario or not, in connection with a trade with a customer in Ontario.

- If an unregistered foreign dealer undertakes any of these activities, staff take the view that the foreign dealer has solicited the trade, and is therefore unable to rely on the unsolicited trade exemption for that trade.

The "hedger" exemption

In Ontario, if a customer meets the definition of a "hedger" for the purposes of a trade, the customer may trade in a contract without registration if the trade is made through a dealer,[14] including an unregistered foreign dealer.

The term "hedger" is defined in the CFA as follows:

> "hedger" means a person or company who carries on agricultural, mining, forestry, processing, manufacturing or other commercial activities and, as a necessary part of these activities, becomes exposed from time to time to a risk attendant upon fluctuations in the price of a commodity and offsets that risk through trading in contracts for the commodity or related commodities whether or not any particular trade is effected for that purpose, but a person or company is a hedger only as to trades in contracts for such commodity or related commodities;

The hedger exemption in subsection 32(a) of the CFA is an exemption for "a trade . . . by a hedger through a dealer". By its terms, the hedger exemption is only available to a customer who meets the definition of hedger for the purposes of that trade.

Staff are of the view that the hedger exemption is not available to an unregistered foreign dealer that wishes to trade with the hedger. An unregistered foreign dealer may trade with a customer in reliance on another exemption, such as the unsolicited trade exemption, the exemption for a trade made through a registered dealer[15] or an exemption in an exemptive relief order, provided the foreign dealer complies with the terms of such exemption.

Obligation to determine that a customer is a bona fide hedger for the trade

Where a dealer seeks to trade with a customer on the basis that the customer is a hedger, we expect the dealer to take reasonable steps to confirm that the customer is a *bona fide* hedger for such trading activities.

We generally would not consider it sufficient for a dealer to simply rely on the customer's self-certification in account-opening documentation. Collecting and documenting this information is more than just a "tick the box" exercise. Instead, we would expect the dealer to review with the customer the nature and extent of the risk that is sought to be hedged through trading in contracts, and to confirm that the trading is primarily for hedging purposes and not also for speculative or investment purposes.

We would also recommend that the dealer include in customer documentation appropriate representations that the customer:

(a) is a hedger;

(b) acknowledges that this representation is deemed to be repeated by the customer each time it enters an order for a contract and that the customer must be a hedger for the purposes of each trade resulting from such an order;

(c) agrees to notify the dealer if it ceases to be a hedger;

(d) represents that it will only enter orders for its own account.

We expect the dealer to periodically verify that the customer's trading activities are consistent with the terms of the hedger exemption and the above recommended representations.

Books and records obligations of an unregistered foreign dealer

We consider a foreign dealer or other market participant that seeks to trade with customers in Ontario in reliance on a registration exemption to be a "market participant" for the purposes of the CFA and OSA. Accordingly, we expect these entities

- to provide appropriate risk disclosure to a customer that explains, among other things, the structure, features and risks of the products being offered and the regulatory protections that are provided, or not provided, to the client, including whether client assets are protected under the Canadian Investor Protection Fund (**CIPF**), the U.S. Securities Investor Protection Corporation, or equivalent protections, or if there are no equivalent protections, a clear statement in plain language to this effect;
- to keep such books, records and other documents as are necessary for the proper recording of their business transactions and financial affairs, and the transactions that they execute on behalf of others; and

---

[14]See section 32(a) of the CFA.

[15]See section 32(b) of the CFA.

- to keep such books, records and documents as may otherwise be required by the laws of their home jurisdiction in connection with the trade.

We expect these books and records to include books and records that demonstrate the extent of the firms' compliance with applicable requirements of all applicable legislation and identify all transactions conducted on behalf of the entity and each of their clients, including the name and address of all parties to the transaction and its terms. For example, if a foreign dealer seeks to trade with a customer on the basis that the customer is a "hedger", we expect the entity to keep books and records that demonstrate how the entity determined the customer was a hedger for the purposes of that transaction.

Staff may, from time to time, conduct a compliance review of a foreign dealer or other unregistered entity to determine whether the firm is in compliance with the terms of any exemptions being relied upon and/or may contact the firm's home jurisdiction regulator for assistance.

Forms and Fees

A foreign dealer or other unregistered market participant that applies for exemptive relief in Ontario in order to trade with a customer in Ontario will generally be required, as a condition of the relief, to file a completed Form 31-103F2 *Submission to Jurisdiction and Appointment of Agent for Service* and to pay a participation fee under OSC Rule 13-502 *Fees*.

The participation fees under OSC Rule 13-502 *Fees* are for "capital market activities" which includes "activities for which registration under the *Commodity Futures Act*, or an exemption from registration under the *Commodity Futures Act*, is required". Accordingly, a firm is required to pay participation fees in respect of activities under both the OSA and the CFA.

Questions

If you have questions regarding this Notice, please refer them to any of the following:

[Omitted.]

OSC Staff Notice 33-745 — Compliance and Registrant Regulation — Annual Summary Report for Dealers, Advisers and Investment Fund Managers

Date: September 25, 2014

37 O.S.C.B. 8835

Director's Message

The Ontario Securities Commission (OSC) expects strong compliance by registrants and articulates its expectations through its oversight, guidance and outreach. Registrants have an obligation to deal fairly, honestly and in good faith with their clients so they can invest with confidence, which is essential to the integrity of the capital markets of Ontario.

To assist registrants with meeting their regulatory obligations, the OSC's Compliance and Registrant Regulation Branch (CRR) has focused its efforts on enhancing communication with registrants and providing tools to assist them with maintaining effective compliance systems. We launched a new Registrant Outreach Program in September, 2013 with the objective of opening the lines of communication between registrants and CRR and creating a central repository of tools and information that will assist registrants in maintaining effective compliance systems. Since the launch of the program, more than 2,000 people have attended educational seminars either in-person or via webinar and the feedback has been overwhelmingly positive. As we continue to add more resources to the Registrant Outreach Program, we encourage registrants to check the *program's* webpage frequently for updates.

In addition to this report, CRR staff has published topic-specific guidance to assist registrants with meeting their regulatory obligations. For example, we published guidance to help registrants meet their Know Your Client (KYC), Know Your Product (KYP) and suitability obligations as well as guidance to help investment fund managers avoid common issues when managing their investment funds. KYC, KYP and suitability obligations are among the most fundamental obligations owed by registrants to their clients, and we continue to see issues with the way registrants fulfill these obligations, so this will remain a focus for CRR.

We also use the traditional tools of on-site compliance reviews and sweeps to identify compliance deficiencies, where appropriate, at each firm we review. The remediation of these deficiencies through dialogue with CRR staff provides an opportunity to enhance compliance systems. Also, the data collected from the 2014 Risk Assessment Questionnaire will help us to focus our resources on higher-risk issues and registrants. CRR staff will commence on-site reviews based on this new data by the end of the year.

To better serve the registrant community, we created a new registration team within CRR and added the position of Manager, Registration. By pooling our registration resources under this one team, we will gain efficiencies and enhance internal practices. Also, registration is an important gatekeeper function and the team is enhancing the registration process by developing a new initiative that will move the initial registration for firms closer to a "first compliance review." This initiative is under development, but firms that seek registration for the first time can expect that we will request additional information and potentially an in-person meeting as part of the registration process. This will allow us to focus on the firm's fitness for registration, enhancing the firm's understanding of regulatory obligations prior to registration and establishing positive communications with the registrant. Registrants and CRR staff will benefit from open communications about current regulatory obligations and practices.

Increasing our engagement with registrants was one of CRR's goals which aligned with the expansion of the OSC's direct outreach to market participants in 2013-14. Open communication with registrants gives CRR staff valuable insights into how registrants are adapting to the changes in the market environment and investor expectations. We are delighted with the participation and feedback we have received regarding our efforts to engage with our registrant community. It has been a constructive dialogue about strengthening the culture of compliance with

Ontario securities law in the shared interest of protecting investors and fostering fair and efficient capital markets. We look forward to continuing the dialogue with our registrant community.

Debra Foubert

Director, Compliance and Registrant Regulation Branch

Introduction

Introduction

The regulatory framework for Ontario's capital markets is designed to provide protection to investors while fostering fair and efficient capital markets.

Ontario Securities Commission Notice 11-769 — Statement of Priorities

This annual summary report prepared by the CRR Branch (the annual report) provides information for registered firms and individuals (collectively, registrants) that are directly regulated by the OSC. These registrants primarily include:

- exempt market dealers (EMDs)

- scholarship plan dealers (SPDs)

- advisers (portfolio managers or PMs) and

- investment fund managers (IFMs).

The OSC's CRR Branch registers and oversees firms and individuals in Ontario that trade or advise in securities or act as IFMs.

Individuals	Firms		
66,210	1,056[1]		
	PMs	**EMDs**	**SPDs**	**IFMs**
	310[2]	261[2]	3[2]	482[3]

Notes:

1   This number excludes firms solely registered in the category of investment dealer, mutual fund dealer, commodity trading manager, futures commission merchant, restricted PM, and restricted dealer.

2   This number includes firms solely registered in this category.

3   This number includes sole IFMs and IFMs registered in multiple categories.

(i) — Registrants overseen by the OSC

Although the OSC registers firms and individuals in the category of mutual fund dealer and firms in the category of investment dealer, these firms and individuals are directly overseen by their self-regulatory organizations (SROs), the Mutual Fund Dealers Association of Canada (MFDA) and the Investment Industry Regulatory Organization of Canada (IIROC), respectively. This report focusses primarily on registered firms and individuals directly overseen by the OSC.

In this report, we summarize new and proposed rules and initiatives impacting registrants, current trends in deficiencies from compliance reviews of registrants (including acceptable practices to address them and unacceptable practices to prevent them), and current trends in registration. We provide an update on our Registrant Outreach program that helps strengthen our communication with registrants on compliance practices. We also provide a summary of some key registrant misconduct cases, explain where registrants can get more information about their obligations, and provide CRR contact information.

This report is a key component of our outreach to registrants. We strongly encourage registrants to thoroughly read and use this report to enhance their understanding of:

- initial and ongoing registration and compliance requirements,

- OSC staff expectations of registrants and our interpretation of regulatory requirements, and

- new and proposed rules and other regulatory initiatives.

As a means of promoting pro-active compliance, we recommend registrants use this report as a self-assessment tool to strengthen their compliance with Ontario securities law, and as appropriate, to make changes to enhance their systems of compliance, internal controls and supervision.[16]

---

[16] The content of this report is provided as guidance for information purposes and not as advice. We encourage firms to seek advice from a professional advisor as they conduct their self-assessment and/or implement any changes to address issues raised in the report.

Key Policy Initiatives Impacting Registrants

1 — Key policy initiatives impacting registrants

"There is a sea of change occurring in today's financial markets ..... This requires regulation that promotes confidence in our capital markets, is responsive to changes in the economic and business environment, and reflects the reality of today's global, competitive capital markets.

March 27, 2014 Speech by Howard Wetston, Chair, OSC to the Toronto Region Board of Trade

1.1 — Ongoing amendments to registration requirements, exemptions and ongoing registrant obligations

Since the implementation of *National Instrument 31-103 Registration Requirements, Exemptions and Ongoing Registrant Obligations* (NI 31-103) in September 2009, and the amendments which came into force in July 2011, we have monitored this relatively new regulatory regime for registrants and engaged in discussions with stakeholders about their practical experiences working with the regime. With the Canadian Securities Administrators (CSA), we developed additional technical and substantive amendments to NI 31-103 and NI 33-109 *Registration Information* (NI 33-109) arising from this ongoing consultation.

On December 5, 2013, the CSA published for comment *Proposed Amendments to NI 31-103, NI 33-109, NI 52-107, OSC Rule 33-506 and OSC Rule 35-502 and Related Forms* (NI 31-103 Proposed Amendments). The purpose of the NI 31-103 Proposed Amendments are to:

- codify current exemption orders,

- refine certain exemptions,

- provide guidance and clarification that will enhance investor protection and improve the day-to-day operation of the registration regime for industry participants and regulators,

- implement consequential amendments to other national instruments and rules as a result of the NI 31-103 Proposed Amendments (consequential amendments to NI 33-109, NI 52-107, OSC Rule 33-406 and OSC Rule 35-502), and

- further clarify the legislative intent of NI 31-103.

The NI 31-103 Proposed Amendments comment period is closed. The CSA has reviewed comments submitted by various stakeholders and is considering these comments in relation to the future NI 31-103 amendments.

For your ease of reference, the majority of the NI 31-103 Proposed Amendments are summarized in relevant sections throughout this report. For more information, see the published *NI 31-103 Proposed Amendments* on the OSC website.

1.2 — Exempt market review

EXEMPT MARKET REVIEW[5]

$104 BILLION	90%	74%
Ontario capital exemption distributions	Capital raised through accredited investor exemption	Capital raised through debt-related securities

Notes:

5   Source: OSC Filings — based on reports of exempt distributions filed with the OSC in 2012

As part of our continued work to enhance and expand the exempt market, we published proposals for both the CSA policy review of the existing minimum amount and accredited investor prospectus exemptions (accredited investor exemption) and the OSC's expanded review of potential new prospectus exemptions. These initiatives, discussed briefly below, will impact investors, issuers, EMDs and other registrants distributing exempt market products.

On February 27, 2014, the CSA published proposed amendments relating to the accredited investor exemption and the minimum amount investment prospectus exemption (MA exemption) in *National Instrument 45-106 Prospectus and Registration Exemptions* (NI 45-106).

The amendments include:

- a new risk acknowledgement form for individual accredited investors that describes, in plain language, the individual accredited investor categories and the protections an investor will not receive by purchasing under the accredited investor exemption,

- restricting the MA exemption to distributions involving non-individual investors, and

- amending the definition of accredited investor in Ontario to allow fully managed accounts to purchase investment fund securities using the managed account category of the accredited investor exemption, as is permitted in other Canadian jurisdictions.

For more information, see *Proposed Amendments to Accredited Investor and Minimum Amount Investment Prospectus Exemptions.*

On March 20, 2014, the OSC published a proposal setting out four new prospectus exemptions. The publication of these proposals follows a comprehensive review of the exempt market. As part of that review, we considered the written comments received on earlier proposals. We also conducted extensive consultations with a broad range of stakeholders through a series of one-on-one meetings and town hall meetings, and an online survey designed to gauge the views of retail investors on investing in start-ups and small and medium-sized enterprises.

The OSC also published for comment two new reports of exempt distribution: a report for investment funds and a report for all other issuers. For additional information on these reports and the proposed exemptions, see *Introduction of Proposed Prospectus Exemptions and Proposed Report of Exempt Distribution in Ontario.*

1.3 — Best interest standard

We are re-evaluating the advisor-client relationship by considering whether an explicit statutory fiduciary (or "best interest") standard should apply to dealers and advisers and on what terms. A fiduciary duty is essentially a duty to act in a client's best interest.

In Ontario, *section 116 of the Securities Act (Ontario)* (Act) applies a best interest standard to IFMs in their dealings with the investment funds they manage. There is no equivalent provision under the Act that explicitly applies a best interest standard to dealers and advisers in their dealings with their clients, although section 2.1 of OSC Rule 31-505 *Conditions of Registration* requires dealers and advisers to deal fairly, honestly and in good faith with their clients. While there is no statutory best interest duty for dealers and advisers in Ontario, Canadian courts can find that a given dealer or adviser owes a best interest duty to his or her client depending on the nature of their relationship.

CSA Consultation Paper 33-403 The Standard of Conduct for Advisers and Dealers: Exploring the Appropriateness of Introducing a Statutory Best Interest Duty When Advice is Provided to Retail Clients was published on October 25, 2012. We received numerous comment letters on the consultation paper and conducted three roundtables in June and July 2013 (all comment letters and the transcripts from the roundtables are available on the *OSC website*). On December 17, 2013, we published *CSA Staff Notice 33-316 — Status Report on Consultation under CSA Consultation Paper 33-403: The Standard of Conduct for Advisers and Dealers: Exploring the Appropriateness of Introducing a Statutory Best Interest Duty When Advice is Provided to Retail Clients*, which summarized the consultation work conducted to date in respect of the best interest consultation initiative, and identified the key themes that emerged from the best interest consultation process.

We continue to work with our CSA colleagues on this project. The continued work required will depend in part on the outcome of the research we conduct this year. Once this research and analysis has been completed, we will publish the results and our decision on how we plan to move forward with the best interest duty initiative, including timing.

1.4 — Cost disclosure, performance reporting and client statements

On July 15, 2013, the Client Relationship Model — Phase 2 (CRM2) amendments to NI 31-103 came into effect. They are being phased-in over a three-year period. The amendments introduce new requirements for reporting to clients about the costs and performance of their investments, and the content of the investments in their accounts. The requirements apply to dealers and PMs in all categories of registration, with some application to IFMs as well. For more information about these amendments, see *CSA Notice of Amendments to NI 31-103 and to Companion Policy 31-103CP (Cost Disclosure, Performance Reporting and Client Statements)*.

As of July 15, 2013, minor clarifications to NI 31-103 took effect, such as enhancements to relationship disclosure information. Beginning July 15, 2014, dealers and PMs were required to:

- provide pre-trade disclosure of charges, and

- report on compensation from debt securities transactions.

IIROC and MFDA member rules are harmonized with the CSA's CRM2 requirements and will be implemented on the same schedule. SRO members who comply with equivalent member rules will be exempted from the CRM2 requirements in NI 31-103.

To help industry implement the changes, on March 7, 2014 we sent an *email blast on CRM2 planning tips* directly to the chief compliance officers (CCOs) of all registered dealers and PMs. We have also initiated a CRM2 discussion forum with industry associations and regulators, including IIROC and the MFDA.

Beginning July 15, 2015, expanded account statement requirements will be implemented. These include requirements to provide position cost information and to determine market values using a prescribed methodology for most securities owned by clients, including those held in client name.

For additional information on future requirements, see section 1.1 of *OSC Staff Notice 33-742 — 2013 OSC Annual Summary Report for Dealers, Advisers and Investment Fund Managers* (OSC Staff Notice 33-742) and the frequently asked questions and additional guidance in *CSA Staff Notice 31-337 Cost Disclosure, Performance Reporting and Client Statements — Frequently Asked Questions and Additional Guidance as of February 27, 2014*.

1.5 — Independent dispute resolution services for registrants

On May 1, 2014, NI 31-103 was amended to make the Ombudsman for Banking Services and Investments (OBSI) the common dispute-resolution service for the securities industry in Canada except in Québec.

The transition period for existing registrants expired on August 1, 2014. All dealers and PMs registered in Ontario were required as of August 2, 2014 to be OBSI "Participating Firms" requiring registrants to take reasonable steps to make OBSI's services available to clients who have "eligible complaints" (as defined in section 13.16). There are also new related client disclosure requirements. For more information about these amendments, see *CSA Notice of Amendments to NI 31-103 and to 31-103CP (Dispute Resolution Services)*.

We remind all dealers and PMs of their existing requirements in section 13.15 of NI 31-103 to have internal complaint handling policies in place to ensure that all client complaints are addressed appropriately.

On May 1, 2014, the CSA published *CSA Staff Notice 31-338 Guidance on Dispute Resolution Services Client Disclosure for Registered Dealers and Advisers that are not members of a Self-Regulatory Organization*. This Notice provides guidance regarding the disclosure firms must provide to their clients about the availability of OBSI's services and internal complaint handling procedures that meet the requirements of the rule. The notice also provides a sample client disclosure document.

The participating CSA jurisdictions have entered into a *Memorandum of Understanding (MOU) with OBSI* concerning its oversight of this initiative. For additional information please refer to the MOU.

1.6 — PM — IIROC dealer service arrangements

Working together, CSA and IIROC staff are reviewing service arrangements between CSA-regulated PMs and investment dealers that are members of IIROC to assess if rules and/or guidance is needed.

Typically under these arrangements, an IIROC dealer provides trading and custody services to a PM and its clients, but may also provide recordkeeping, client account statements, and margin services. These arrangements are similar to introducing broker-carrying broker arrangements between IIROC dealers that are governed under *IIROC Dealer Member Rule 35*, but are not subject to any specific rules or guidance.

We identified a number of issues with PM-IIROC dealer service arrangements, including:

- agreement between the PM and the dealer,

- disclosure to the PM's clients, and

- in some cases, the PM relying on the dealer's books and records, and account statement delivery to the PM's clients, to meet its own obligations without being responsible and accountable for the services, and without adequate supervision.

The CSA is working with IIROC to address these issues. The working group is also considering whether PM clients need to continue to receive dual account statements separately from their respective PM and custodian, and if instead the delivery of one account statement (such as a joint account statement from the PM and custodian) is a viable option, keeping in mind investor protection and other regulatory concerns.

Until this work is complete, PMs are to comply with their existing account statement delivery obligations in section 14.14 of *NI 31-103*, and prepare for the new additional statement requirements in section 14.14.1 of NI 31-103 which come into force on July 15, 2015.

See section 4.3.3 of *OSC Staff Notice 33-742* for more information on OSC staff's current expectations and interim guidance on PM client account statement delivery practices.

1.7 — Derivatives regulation

In December 2010, the Act was amended to establish a framework for derivatives regulation in Ontario. However, certain amendments relating to derivatives regulation have not yet been proclaimed into force as the necessary supporting rules are not yet in place.

We are consulting with the OSC Derivatives Branch in developing a number of rules relating to the regulation of derivatives, including a rule for determining whether products should be regulated as securities, derivatives, or exempt from regulation (the Product Determination Rule), and a rule that will set out the principal registration requirements and exemptions for derivatives' market participants, including derivatives dealers, derivatives advisers and large derivatives' market participants (the Derivatives Registration Rule).

In April 2013, the CSA Derivatives Committee published for comment *CSA Consultation Paper 91-407 — Derivatives: Registration*. We are reviewing the comments received on the consultation paper and developing the proposed Derivatives Registration Rule.

On January 3, 2014, the OSC published a Notice of Ministerial Approval in connection with the Product Determination Rule, *OSC Rule 91-506 Derivatives: Product Determination*, and *OSC Rule 91-507 Trade Repositories and Derivatives Data Reporting* (the Trade Repositories Rule). The rules were effective December 31, 2013.

Although the Product Determination Rule only currently applies to the related Trade Repositories Rule, it is anticipated that, once the remaining rules relating to the new derivatives regulatory framework are in place, the Product Determination rule will be extended to apply generally.

As a result of amendments to the Trade Repositories Rule made in April 2014, the trade reporting requirements will take effect on October 31, 2014. We encourage registrants to review their policies and procedures in relation to the reporting of over the counter derivatives transactions. We are working with the OSC Derivatives Branch in developing an oversight program for testing registrant compliance with these new requirements.

Outreach to Registrants

2.1 Registrant Outreach program
- a) **Registrant outreach web page**
- b) **Educational seminars**
- c) **Registrant outreach community**
- d) **Registrant resources**

2.2 Registrant Advisory Committee

2.3 Communication tools for registrants

2.4 Impact of "Heartbleed" vulnerability on registrants

2 — Outreach to registrants

"We want to provide registrants with tools to build proactive compliance systems."

April 9, 2013 speech by Debra Foubert, Director, Compliance and Registrant Regulation at the Strategy Institute: Annual Registrant Regulation, Conduct & Compliance Summit

We continued to interact with our stakeholders through our outreach program to registrants which was launched in 2013. The objectives of our Registrant Outreach program are to strengthen our communication with Ontario registrants that we directly regulate and other industry participants (such as lawyers and compliance consultants), promote stronger compliance practices and, enhance investor protection.

Part 3: REGISTRATION

2.1 — Registrant Outreach program

REGISTRANT OUTREACH STATISTICS

16	2000	Key features
• In-person & webinar seminars provided to June 30, 2014	• Individuals attended outreach sessions to June 30, 2014	• dedicated web page • educational seminars • registrant outreach community • registrant resources

The Registrant Outreach program continues to provide Ontario registrants with practical knowledge on compliance-related matters and gives them the opportunity to hear first-hand from OSC Staff about the latest issues impacting them. Since the launch of the program in July 2013, approximately 2,000 individuals have attended registrant outreach sessions, either in-person or via webinar. The feedback from these participants has been very positive.

The outreach program is interactive and has the following features to enhance the dialogue with registrants:

a) — Registrant outreach web page

We set up a *Registrant Outreach* page on the OSC's website at www.osc.gov.on.ca, which was designed to enhance awareness of topical compliance issues and policy initiatives. Registrants are encouraged to check the web page on a regular basis for updates on regulatory issues impacting them.

b) — Educational seminars

Anyone interested in attending an event can go to the *Calendar of Events* section of the Registrant Outreach page of the OSC website, for seminar descriptions and registration.

c) — Registrant outreach community

Registrants are also encouraged to join our *Registrant Outreach Community* to receive regular e-mail updates on OSC policies and initiatives impacting registrants, as well as the latest publications and guidance on our expectations regarding compliance.

d) — Registrant resources

The registrant resources section of the web page provides registrants and other industry participants with easy, centralized access to recent compliance materials. If you have questions related directly to the Registrant Outreach program or have suggestions for seminar topics, please send an email to RegistrantOutreach@osc.gov.on.ca.

2.2 — Registrant Advisory Committee

The OSC's Registration Advisory Committee (RAC) was established in January 2013. The RAC, which is currently comprised of 11 external members, advises OSC staff on issues and challenges faced by registrants in interpreting and complying with Ontario securities law, including registration and compliance related matters. The RAC also acts as a source of feedback to OSC staff on the development and implementation of policy and rule making initiatives that promote investor protection and fair and efficient capital markets. The RAC meets quarterly and members serve a two year term. The initial two year term will expire in December 2014 and a call for new members will be made in the fall of 2014. You can find a *list of current RAC members* on the OSC website.

Topics of discussion with the RAC this year have included the proposed mutual fund risk classification methodology for use in the Fund Facts, the proposed exemptions included as part of the exempt market review process (discussed briefly above), current topics related to PMs and IFMs, the electronic delivery of documents to the OSC, the new proposed OSC derivatives rules (discussed briefly above), and proposed changes to the *OSC Rule 13-502 Fees* (the Fees Rule).

2.3 — Communication tools for registrants

We use a number of tools to communicate initiatives that we work on and the findings of those initiatives to our registrants, including OSC Compliance annual reports, Staff Notices (OSC and CSA) and e-mail blasts. The information provided to registrants via e-mail blasts is discussed in various sections of this report. The table below provides a listing of recent e-mail blasts sent to registrants.

Date of email blast	E-mail blast topic and additional information
June 19, 2014	**OSC Staff Notice 33-743** — *Guidance on sales practices, expense allocation and other relevant areas developed from the results of the targeted review of large investment fund managers* (OSC Staff Notice 33-743) See section 4.4 b) of this report.
June 10, 2014	**Risk Assessment Questionnaire (RAQ)** See section 4.1 a) (ii) of this report.
May 1, 2014	**Requirement to make OBSI available to clients** See section 1.5 of this report.

Date of email blast	E-mail blast topic and additional information
March 12, 2014	**Requirement to make OBSI available to clients** See section 1.5 of this report.
March 7, 2014	**CRM2 FAQ published; planning tips** See section 1.4 of this report.
February 11, 2014	**Requirement to deliver documents electronically to the Ontario Securities Commission (Effective February 19, 2014)** See section 4.1 d) (ii) of this report.
January 9, 2014	**CSA Staff Notice 31-336** — *Guidance for Portfolio Managers, Exempt Market Dealers and Other Registrants on the Know-Your-Client, Know-Your-Product and Suitability Obligations* See section 4.1 c) (i) of this report.
November 20, 2013	**Guidance for changes in calculating capital markets participation fees by registrant firms, unregistered exempt international firms and unregistered IFMs effective April 1, 2013** See section 4.1 e) of this report.
September 9, 2013	**Calculation of excess working capital and the use of subordination agreements** See section 4.1 c) (iv) 3) of this report.

For more information, see *OSC E-mail blasts*.

2.4 — Impact of "Heartbleed" vulnerability on registrants

On April 17, 2014, we sent a survey to registrants with head offices in Ontario in response to the "Heartbleed" bug. The "Heartbleed" bug presented a vulnerability to Internet services that allowed an attacker/hacker to read encrypted information which could expose sensitive data such as passwords and bank account information. The purpose of the survey was to gauge the degree to which the "Heartbleed" bug impacted our registrants.

The survey results indicated that 66% of registrants transacted with or for their clients or others through web sites, social media, file transfers or remote connections. This indicates that a large number of survey respondents not only use the Internet, but do so in such a way that sensitive information is likely exchanged over the web either with clients or service providers.

Strong and tailored cyber security measures are an important element of a registrant's controls in promoting reliability of their operations and the protection of confidential information. To manage the risks of a cyber threat, registrants and regulated entities should be aware of the challenges of cybercrime and should take the appropriate protective measures necessary to safeguard themselves and their clients and stakeholders.

For additional information on guidance to strengthen cyber security, refer to *CSA Staff Notice 11-326 Cyber Security* published on September 26, 2013.

Registration of Firms and Individuals

3 — Registration of firms and individuals

"Participation as a registrant in Ontario's capital markets is a privilege that comes with significant responsibilities to investors and the public at large"

June 13, 2012 speech by Mary Condon, Vice-Chair, Compliance & Risk Management Strategies Summit for Portfolio Managers and Fund Managers

The registration requirements under securities law help to protect investors from unfair, improper or fraudulent practices by market participants. The information required to support a registration application allows us to assess a firm's and an individual's fitness for registration. When assessing a firm's fitness for registration we consider whether it is able to carry out its obligations under securities law. We use three fundamental criteria to assess an individual's fitness: proficiency, integrity and solvency. These fitness requirements are the cornerstones of the registration regime.

In this section, we discuss current trends in registration, discuss novel business activities potentially requiring registration, provide an update on supervisory terms and conditions (T&Cs), outline a new pre-registration process recently implemented and provide a snapshot of the NI 31-103 Proposed Amendments that will impact registration requirements.

3.1 — New rules and initiatives for registrants

a) — Pre-registration reviews

We commenced pre-registration reviews by incorporating compliance review procedures as part of the registration process. We are referring to this process as "Registration as the first Compliance Review". The procedures include reviewing a firm's financial condition, business plan and at a high level the policies and procedures manual. Additional procedures may also be conducted with a focus on proposed operations, compliance systems, and proficiency of the firms' individuals. Information is gathered by OSC staff through written inquires, requests for documentation and/or interviews of a firm's key representatives.

The purpose of the pre-registration review is to assess compliance with Ontario securities law at the time of registration. Noted deficiencies are raised with firms and corrective action of all issues is required prior to firm registration. The pre-registration review will enhance firms' awareness of their obligations to establish an adequate compliance system.

Suggested practices to prepare for an OSC pre-registration review:

Firms must:

- Establish an effective compliance system prior to commencing registerable activities.

- Ensure that written policies and procedures adequately address all aspects of business operations.

- Be prepared to answer detailed questions (in writing or in person) regarding the firm's business plan and compliance systems including:

    - products and services that will be offered,

    - business growth plans,

    - details on referral arrangements, if any,

    - supervisory structure within the context of the firm's growth objectives,

    - marketing plans,

    - material business contracts, and

    - oversight for outsourced business arrangements.

- Be prepared to provide

    - the firm's application or membership in OBSI, if applicable,

    - details regarding planned custodial arrangements,

    - copies of business plans and policies and procedures manual, and

    - copies of other information such as offering documents, referral agreements, KYC documents, and disclosure documents.

Firms are encouraged to:

- Compile records requested on a timely basis.

- Perform an initial self-assessment to determine compliance with Ontario securities law, or engage a compliance consultant to perform the assessment prior to registration, and rectify all deficient areas prior to applying for registration.

Unacceptable practices

Firms are encouraged to avoid the following practices:

- Conduct the following after submission of a registration application:

    - draft the written policies and procedures manual, and

    - search for possible service providers.

- Provide documents related to the registration process in stages; complete documentation relating to the registration application should be provided at the time of registration including audited financial statements.

b) — NI 31-103 Proposed Amendments to registration requirements

The following chart provides a high level overview of the NI 31-103 Proposed Amendments to registration requirements that will impact registrants.

Proposed amendment[6]	Topic	Purpose
Section 3.3 of NI 31-103	Proficiency: review of time-limits used to stale date exams	Technical amendment to codify blanket/omnibus relief dated February 26, 2010 currently being relied on related to examinations and programs for dealing representatives of EMDs and SPDs.
Section 4.1 of NI 31-103	Prohibition in s. 4.1(1)(b) regarding dually registered individuals	To clarify that the dual registration prohibition applies to a firm registered in any jurisdiction of Canada.
Section 13.4 of the Companion Policy to National Instrument 31-103 (31-103CP)	Identifying and responding to conflicts of interest	To add guidance relating to conflicts of interest in relation to registered representatives that serve on the boards of reporting issuers or have outside business activities (OBAs).
NI 33-109	Amendments to NI 33-109 forms	To update and enhance certain NRD forms.

Notes:

6   Subject to change and final approval

For additional information see sections 1.1 and 3.3 of this report.

c) — Registration service commitment

In May 2014, we issued the *OSC service commitment* in which our service standards are set out in detail. The following standards, conditions and timelines pertain to registrants and registration-related filings where the OSC is the principal regulator.

Service Commitment Summary	
Item	**Service commitment**

New business submissions	• A registration officer will:
	     • contact your representative and provide instructions on fee payment and provide notification that the system is ready to accept applications from the "mind and management" of your business within **5 working days** upon receipt of your application
	     • best efforts target: **95%** of the filings.
	 • Aim to provide a decision to your application within **90 working days** where the following conditions are met:
	     • you are a non-SRO applicant,
	     • all questions are answered with sufficient detail,
	     • all regulatory obligations are met,
	     • there are no concerns with your fitness for registration, and
	     • you respond to our request for information in a timely manner
	     • best efforts target: **80%** or more of these filings.

Dealing representatives — new applications and reactivations	• Aim to review, analyze, and provide a decision to your application with **5 working days** where the following conditions are met:
	     • your application is complete,
	     • your application is not associated with a new business application, and
	     • here are no concerns with your fitness for registration
	     • best efforts target: **80%** or more of these filings.

Advising representatives (ARs), associate advising representatives (AARs) and CCOs — new applications and reactivations	• Aim to apply a decision to your application within **20 working days** where the following conditions are met:
	     • your application is complete,
	     • your application is not associated with a new business application, and
	     • there are no concerns with your fitness for registration
	     • best efforts target: **80%** or more of these filings.

Notices of termination (where individuals leave former firm in good standing)	• Aim to complete a notice of termination within **5 working days**. • best efforts target: **95%** or more of these filings

In relation to the service commitments summarized above, if we do not receive a response within three weeks of making a request relating to a registration filing, we will generally consider the file to be dormant and will take steps to close it. Prior to closing the file, we will send the filer another notification asking for a status update and informing them of the imminent files closure within two weeks unless we receive a response to our notification. In cases where a re-activation of the file is requested, an additional fee may be required.

3.2 — Trends in registration

a) — Registration of not for profit issuers

We became aware of a number of not for profit issuers that are distributing their own securities. *NI 45-106* provides an exemption from the prospectus requirement in section 2.38 for certain not for profit issuers distributing their own securities provided they comply with certain conditions. However, as of March 27, 2010, the registration exemption previously available under section 3.38 of NI 45-106 is no longer available. A not for profit issuer is required to consider whether it is engaged in the business of trading in securities (please refer to the *31-103CP* section 1.3 *Factors in determining business purpose*). If an issuer is in the business of trading its securities, then registration as a dealer is required.

b) — Tax shelter products

We remind registrants that tax shelter products, including ones that involve leveraged donations of property (for instance, artwork and medical supplies) to charities and ones that are marketed to investors on the basis of tax credits or deductions that are claimed to be available, are typically considered "securities" and require registration. See section 4.2 b) of this report for further information.

**Part 3:
REGISTRATION**

c) — Desk review of supervisory T&Cs

We conducted a desk review of non-SRO registrant firms whose sponsored individuals have been or are currently subject to supervisory T&Cs. The types of T&Cs reviewed included strict supervision, close supervision, OBAs, and requirement to deliver disclosure documents to clients. The objective of the review was to ensure adequate supervision by the firm over these T&Cs. We also compared the T&Cs to the original activities that led to their imposition and concluded that the T&Cs were fitting for the types of activities reported. The review concluded that most firms were adhering to the T&Cs imposed on their individual registrants and were conducting adequate supervision. One firm was identified as not fulfilling their supervisory obligations. We are following up with this firm.

d) — Registration of online portals

We have seen a number of firms applying to register as EMDs that plan to operate accredited investor only internet portals. EMDs can operate portals to facilitate distributions of securities in reliance on prospectus exemptions (e.g. the accredited investor exemption) provided they comply with all normal requirements applicable to the EMD category, including KYC and suitability.

In contrast, *Multilateral Instrument 45-108 Crowdfunding*, the proposed crowdfunding rule, contemplates that funding portals will register in the restricted dealer category. The crowdfunding prospectus exemption is aimed at allowing retail investors to participate in the capital raising of businesses in Canada. The crowdfunding portal is subject to important conditions (e.g. it can only distribute securities in reliance on the new crowdfunding prospectus exemption, which includes investment limits of $2,500 per investment/$10,000 per annum) and will not be able to distribute securities in reliance on other exemptions, e.g. the accredited investor exemption.

e) — Registration of online advisory businesses

We have seen increasing interest in advisers providing advice through online platforms. We have recently registered a small number of PM firms that will operate online and expect to see others enter the market. The online advice model that we have considered to be acceptable involves an interactive website used to collect KYC information, which will be reviewed by a registered AR. The AR will communicate with the client by telephone, video link, email or internet chats. The AR must ensure that sufficient KYC information has been gathered to support the PM firm's obligation to make suitability determinations for the client.

Each of the firms that we have registered to provide online advice operates on a discretionary managed account basis, using portfolios of unleveraged exchange traded funds (ETFs) or low cost mutual funds. In most cases, these are model portfolios which are selected for a client based on a profile generated by the KYC collection process. An AR will review and approve the suitability of the portfolio for the client. The client's account is periodically rebalanced to the parameters set for their portfolio.

This is not the so-called "robo-advice" model seen in the United States, where online advice has seen rapid growth in the last few years. The online advisers operating in Ontario are offering hybrid services that utilize an online platform for the efficiencies it offers, while ARs remain actively involved in decision making.

We do not think that an entirely automated decision making process would be acceptable at this stage. The KYC and suitability obligations of PMs that provide their services through online platforms remain the same as for any other PM. A PMs obligations under securities law does not change as a result of the delivery method of providing the services to a client. We expect firms that are interested in implementing an online advice operating model in Ontario to submit their proposed online KYC questionnaire and related processes for a due diligence review by CRR staff. This review in no way diminishes the firm's ongoing responsibilities under applicable securities law.

f) — Fees for late document filings

We continue to see late regulatory filings related to registration documents including, but not limited to:

- financial and civil disclosures,
- other business activities,
- ownership of securities and derivatives firms, and
- acquisition notices under sections 11.9 and 11.10 of NI 31-103 (see section 4.1 b) in this report for additional information).

Most registration updates must be filed within 10 days of a change to a registered firm's information in *Form 33-109F6 — Firm Registration Form* or *Form 33-109F4 — Individual Registration Form*.

When required documents are filed late, late fees will apply and be charged. The applicable fee is $100 per business day, subject to a maximum aggregate fee of $5,000 for all documents required to be filed within a calendar year. Please see the full list found in Appendix D — Additional Fees for Late Document Filings in the Fees Rule.

We remind firms that they are expected to have an effective compliance system in place to minimize late filings.

g) — Registration related conflicts of interest

The CSA provided clarification and guidance regarding OBAs in the NI 31-103 Proposed Amendments dated December 5, 2013. Disclosure is and will continue to be required for all officer or director positions and any other equivalent positions held as well as positions of influence per Item 10 — Current employment, other business activities, officer positions held and directorships in Form 33-109F4 (the F4). Guidance has also been added in the 31-103CP which clarifies that disclosure is required for certain paid or unpaid roles with charitable, social or religious organizations and/or for owners of a holding company.

We continue to place restricted client T&Cs on individuals with a position of influence (particularly over potentially vulnerable clients). These T&Cs restrict the individual from trading or advising clients met through the OBA (and close family members of those clients). For example, this year restricted client T&Cs were placed on:

- teachers (elementary, secondary and college),

- registered nurses (hospital and nursing home),

- early childhood educators (daycare and school),

- a volunteer minister, and

- support workers (work with clients with mental health issues, abused women or the elderly).

Suggested practices to adequately address OBA

Registrants Must:

- Assess OBAs to identify conflicts of interest, determine the level of risk, and respond appropriately (for example, approve each new OBA before it begins).

- Promote compliance with OBA requirements through an annual attestation and questionnaire, ongoing monitoring, and education.

- When onboarding a new registered or permitted individual:

  - review and discuss all pre-existing OBAs,

  - review and vet responses to all conflict of interest questions in Schedule G (Item 10 of the F4),

  - ensure OBA disclosure on NRD is complete and correct, and

  - remind the individuals that any change to this disclosure must be reported to the firm and filed on NRD within 10 days of the change.

Unacceptable practices

Registrants must not:

- Permit an OBA if it cannot properly control the potential conflict of interest.

- State in the F4 disclosure — Item 10 that there is no actual or potential conflicts of interest and client confusion when that is not true (e.g., individual holds an elected office or provides free investment management services to a social organization).

- Sponsor an individual with an OBA until the firm is ready to discuss what additional supervisory/oversight policies and procedures they are willing to perform to ensure compliance with the restricted client T&Cs.

3.3 — Proposed amendments to NI 31-103[17]

a) — Proficiency of registrants

Experience for CCOs of Dealers

In the course of compliance reviews, we identified a number of dealer firms that have CCOs who are not adequately performing their responsibilities. This deficiency is often associated with a finding that the CCO does not have relevant experience. As a result, we proposed amendments to add a requirement that CCOs of mutual fund dealers, SPDs and EMDs have 12 months of relevant securities industry experience in the 36-month period prior to applying for registration. These new requirements will apply to new firm applications only.

Proficiency Principle — CCOs of dealers, advisers and IFMs

The experience requirement being proposed for dealer CCOs is consistent with the proficiency principle in section 3.4 of NI 31-103 which states that a CCO must not perform an activity that requires registration unless the individual has the education, training and experience that a reasonable person would consider necessary to perform the activity competently. We have further elaborated on this principle in 31-103CP to clarify that this must include a good understanding of the regulatory requirements applicable to the firm (and individuals acting on its behalf) as well as the knowledge and ability to design and implement an effective compliance system.

Experience for ARs and AARs

We provided further guidance in 31-103CP clarifying what we may consider relevant investment management experience for AR and AARs. This guidance incorporates content from *CSA Staff Notice 31-332 Relevant Investment Management Experience for Advising Representatives and Associate Advising Representatives of Portfolio Managers* (CSA Staff Notice 31-332) published on January 17, 2013. Firms should continue to refer to the CSA Staff Notice 31-332 for specific examples. We expect firms and individuals to consider CSA Staff Notice 31-332 and 31-103CP as guidance at appropriate times, such as during the job application, hiring process and submission of applications for registration.

---

[17]Subject to change and final approval.

3.4 — Trends in applications for PM registration

We are receiving a number of registration applications for small and one person PM firms (which may also include the categories of IFM and EMD) where none of the applicants have been previously registered as an AR, employed at a registered PM firm or been employed in a compliance capacity.

In order for these individuals (and firms) to be registered, they must provide evidence that they have the required courses and relevant investment management experience to qualify as an AR or CCO, as is the case for all new CCO and AR applicants. The individuals must also demonstrate how they meet the requirements of the proficiency principle in section 3.4 of NI 31-103 to competently perform the activities requiring registration.

Suggested practices to adequately prepare individual registration applications

Applicants must:

- Send evidence of course completion.

- Provide information on experience that is clear, accurate and relevant. For example, the information should:
    - provide details of relevant past duties and responsibilities, including the dates and employers where the experience was obtained,
    - provide an estimate of the percentage of time spent on the more relevant activities,
    - focus on the experience of the individual; where it is helpful or necessary to include information about the individual's team or firm to put the information in context, ensure that the duties and responsibilities of the particular individual are clear, and
    - ensure that past experience is distinguished from proposed activities that the individual will conduct upon registration.

- Be prepared to provide evidence of the experience being described upon request (for example, a letter from a former supervisor confirming and describing the experience).

- Be prepared to answer questions about their understanding of the regulatory requirements for the category of registration applied for.

- For CCO applicants, provide information on how their past experience has provided them with the knowledge and ability to design and implement an effective compliance system.

Unacceptable practices

Applicants must not:

- Provide information that has not been reviewed for accuracy. By filing the application, the individual is certifying that the information is true and complete. It is also the firm's obligation under Part 5 of NI 33-109 to make reasonable efforts to ensure the truth and completeness of the information submitted.

- Expect that the discretionary management of the individual's own investment portfolio will qualify as relevant investment management experience or be sufficient to demonstrate the experience or competencies required for registration as a CCO.

- Rely solely on third parties such as legal counsel and compliance consultants to meet proficiency and other regulatory requirements. While we encourage registrants to make use of external supports, such as legal counsel and compliance consultants, the obligations set out in Part 5.2 of NI 31-103 are those of the registrant.

Information for Dealers, Advisers and Investment Fund Managers

4 — Information for dealers, advisers and investment fund managers

"Our job as a regulator is to create the framework and set the rules of the game to make Ontario's capital markets fairer and more efficient, and provide an appropriate level of investor protection."

May 2, 2013 speech by Howard Wetston, Chair, OSC to the 2013 EMDA Exempt Market

The information in this section includes the key findings and outcomes from our ongoing compliance reviews of the registrants we directly regulate. We highlight current trends in deficiencies from our reviews and provide suggested practices to address the deficiencies. We also discuss new or proposed rules and initiatives impacting registrants.

This part of the report is divided into four main sections. The first section contains general information that is relevant for all registrants. The other sections contain information specific to dealers (EMDs and SPDs), advisers (PMs) and IFMs, respectively. This report is organized to allow a registrant to focus on reading the section for all registrants and the sections that apply to their registration categories. *However, we recommend that registrants review all sections in this part, as some of the information presented for one type of registrant may be relevant to other registrants.*

4.1 — All registrants

This section discusses our compliance review process, current trends in deficiencies and suggested practices to address them, and new and proposed rules and initiatives impacting all registrants.

a) — Compliance review process

We conduct compliance reviews of registered firms on a continuous basis. The purpose of compliance reviews is primarily to assess compliance with Ontario securities law; but they also help registrants to improve their understanding of regulatory requirements and our expectations, and help us to learn about a specific industry topic or practice we may have concerns with. We frequently conduct compliance reviews on-site at a registrant's premises, but also perform desk reviews from our offices. For information on "What to expect from, and how to prepare for an OSC compliance review" see the slides from the Registrant Outreach session provided on October 22, 2013 on "*Start to finish: Getting through an OSC compliance review*".

(i) — Risk-based approach

Firms are generally selected for review using a risk-based approach. This approach is intended to identify firms that are most likely to have material compliance issues (including risk of harm to investors) or significant impact to the capital markets if there are compliance breaches. To determine which firms should be reviewed, we consider a number of factors, including firms' responses to the most recent RAQ, their compliance history, complaints or tips from external parties, and referrals from another OSC branch, an SRO or another regulator.

(ii) — Risk Assessment Questionnaire

"This process is essential for gathering data from the firms we regulate, which in turn, informs our approach to compliance . . . We use this data to make evidence-based decisions about which firms require further attention and oversight."

June 10, 2014 press release re Ontario Securities Commission Issues 2014 Risk Assessment Questionnaire

We issue a comprehensive RAQ periodically to collect information about our registrants' business operations. The *2014 RAQ* was sent on June 10, 2014 to firms that were registered with the OSC in the categories of PM, restricted PM, IFM, EMD, and/or restricted dealer. Firms had approximately 40 days to complete and submit the RAQ online.

The RAQ supports our risk based approach to select firms for on-site compliance reviews or targeted reviews. Based on the responses to this year's RAQ, we will select higher risk firms for on-site compliance reviews.

(iii) — Sweep reviews

In addition to reviewing firms based on risk selection, we also conduct sweeps which are compliance reviews on a specific topic on firms in an industry sector. Sweeps allow us to respond on a timely basis to industry-wide concerns or issues. We regularly perform sweeps of newly registered firms to assess if they are off to a good start and to help them to understand their requirements and our expectations. We also regularly review large or "impact" firms as discussed in (i) above.

Some of the sweep reviews we performed this year are highlighted below:

- We completed the reviews of a sample of "impact" PMs, IFMs and EMDs. The results of this sweep produced staff guidance in relation to IFMs only. See section 4.4 b) on *Sweep of large "impact" IFMs* for a summary of this sweep's findings and the guidance issued.

- We started on-site reviews of a sample of newly registered IFMs. We included IFMs in the sample that were registered during a specified time period and that had not previously been reviewed. See section 4.4 c) on *Sweep of newly registered IFMs* for additional information.

- We performed a desk review of the 2013 capital markets participation fees provided to the OSC for 123 registrants. See section 4.1 e) on *Ongoing review of capital markets participation fees* for additional information.

- We performed a desk review of supervisory T&Cs. See section 3.2 c) on *Desk review of supervisory T&Cs* for this sweep's findings.

(iv) — Outcomes of compliance reviews

In most cases, the deficiencies found in a compliance review are set out in a written report to the firm so that they can take appropriate corrective action. After a firm addresses its deficiencies, the expected outcome is that they have enhanced their compliance. If a firm had many significant deficiencies, once it addresses these, the expected outcome is that they have significantly enhanced their compliance.

In addition to issuing compliance deficiency reports, we take additional regulatory action when warranted (including when we identify potential registrant misconduct or fraud).

The outcomes of our compliance reviews in fiscal 2014, with comparables for 2013, are presented in the following table and are listed in their increasing order of seriousness. Firms are shown under the most serious outcome obtained for a particular review. The percentages in the table are based on the registered firms we reviewed during the year and not the population of all registered firms.

Outcomes of compliance reviews (all registration categories)	Fiscal 2014	Fiscal 2013
Enhanced compliance	53%	38%
Significantly enhanced compliance	28%	52%
Terms and conditions on registration	10%	3%
Surrender of registration	3%	1%
Referral to the Enforcement Branch	5%	2%
Suspension of registration[8]	9%	4%

Notes:

8   This percentage includes registrants suspended in the period reported on as a result of compliance reviews occurring in the reporting period and registrants suspended in the reporting period based on compliance reviews that occurred prior to the reporting period.

For an explanation of each outcome, see Appendix A in *OSC Staff Notice 33-738 — 2012 OSC Annual Summary Report for Dealers, Advisers and Investment Fund Managers* (OSC Staff Notice 33-738).

(v) — Contacting investors as part of compliance reviews

We continue to contact investors as part of our ongoing, normal course reviews of dealers and advisers. For additional information, see the section titled "Contacting investors as part of compliance reviews" in *OSC Staff Notice 33-742*.

b) — Failure to provide notice of ownership changes or asset acquisitions

We continue to have significant concerns with some registrants not providing us with the required notice under sections 11.9 or 11.10 of NI 31-103 of proposed ownership changes in, or asset acquisitions of, registered firms. For example, we continue to find a number of cases where:

- Registrants (including the Ultimate Designated Person (UDP), CCO, AR, or dealing representative of the firm) acquired 10% or more of the securities of another registered firm, or their sponsoring firm, without first providing us with the required notice.

- Registered firms have not provided us with the required notice as soon as the registered firm knew, or had reason to believe, that 10% or more of its voting securities were going to be acquired by a non-registrant, including an officer, director, permitted individual or employee of the firm (barring exceptional circumstances, we expect to receive notice of these transactions at least 30 days prior to the transaction taking place).

- Registrants acquired all or a substantial part of the assets of another registered firm without first providing us with the required notice. Examples of scenarios where we would expect to receive (and have, in fact, received) a section 11.9 or 11.10 notice in this context include:

  - the acquisition (whether structured as a "purchase" for compensation or not) of another registered firm's book of business, including where the other registered firm is a one-person firm

  - the acquisition of a business line or division of another, large registered firm, and

  - the acquisition of all of the investment fund management contracts of another registered firm that is an IFM.

We also found that some IIROC or MFDA member firms did not file the required notices under sections 11.9 or 11.10 based on the view that their SRO notice process was sufficient. This is not the case. The notice obligations apply to all registrants, including member firms of IIROC and the MFDA, and arise from the OSC's responsibility to register, among others, dealer firms.

In the cases where registrants did not provide us with the required notice for their completed acquisitions, we required them to file the notice materials for review and pay the applicable filing fees. Although in all of these cases to date we issued a letter to each firm warning them of the seriousness of their failure to provide notice, we may in appropriate circumstances also take other regulatory action. As we mentioned in last year's report, registrants that do not give us the required notice (or provide the notice after the specified deadline) will most likely also be charged late fees for the late notice, as well as applicable late fees for each related securities regulatory filing that is also filed late. For a further discussion regarding late fees generally, see section 3.2(f) of this report.

In addition to filing notices under sections 11.9 or 11.10 of NI 31-103, a change in share ownership of a registered firm, or an acquisition of its assets, typically triggers additional securities regulatory filings. In addition to any SRO filings (discussed above), these additional filings could include:

- filings under NI 33-109 (including, in particular, filings of *Form 33-109F5 Change of Registration Information*), and

- change of manager approval requests under section 5.5 of *National Instrument 81-102 Mutual Funds*.

Registrants must take care to ensure that all applicable securities regulatory filings are filed in accordance with their specified timelines in the event of a change in share ownership of a registered firm, or an acquisition of its assets.

Finally, NI 31-103 Proposed Amendments include proposed amendments that will streamline and clarify the filing requirements for notices under sections 11.9 and 11.10 of NI 31-103. For further information about these amendments, see sections 1.1 and 4.1 d) (i) of this report.

c) — Current trends in deficiencies and acceptable practices

In this section, we summarize key trends in deficiencies from recent compliance reviews of EMDs, PMs, and IFMs. For each deficiency, we summarize the applicable requirements under Ontario securities law which must be followed. In addition, where applicable, we provide acceptable and unacceptable practices relating to the deficiency discussed. *The acceptable and unacceptable practices throughout this report are intended to give guidance to help registrants address the deficiencies, and provide our expectations of registrants. While the best practices set out in this report are intended to present acceptable methods registrants can use to prevent or rectify a deficiency, they are not the only acceptable methods. Registrants may use alternative methods, provided those methods adequately demonstrate that registrants have met their responsibility under the spirit and letter of securities law.*

We strongly recommend registrants review the deficiencies and suggested practices in this report that apply to their registration categories and operations to assess and, as needed, implement enhancements to their compliance systems and internal controls.

(i) — Non-compliance with KYC, KYP and suitability requirements and accredited investor requirements

We continue to have concerns that some dealers and advisers are not adequately meeting their KYC, KYP and suitability obligations. We also remain concerned that some EMDs are selling securities to investors that do not qualify under a prospectus exemption (such as the accredited investor exemption).

On January 9, 2014, we published *CSA Staff Notice 31-336 — Guidance for Portfolio Managers, Exempt Market Dealers and Other Registrants on the Know-Your-Client, Know-Your-Product and Suitability Obligations* (CSA Staff Notice 31-336).

The notice provides additional guidance to registrants in the areas of KYC, KYP and suitability obligations and sets out our expectations of registrants on how to comply with these important regulatory requirements. In particular, we expect registrants to take extra care in complying with their KYC, KYP and suitability obligations when dealing with clients who are seniors or those who may be in a position of vulnerability. Some of the suggested practices and unacceptable practices are highlighted below:

Suggested practices to adequately address KYC, KYP, suitability and accredited investor requirements
Registrants must:

- Engage in a meaningful discussion with clients to obtain a solid understanding of the client's personal and financial circumstances.

- Update KYC information at least annually or more often if there is a significant change to the client's life circumstances or a significant change in market conditions.

- Conduct product due diligence and be able to explain clearly to clients a security's risks, key features, any conflicts of interest and initial and ongoing costs and fees.

- Maintain adequate documentation to support the suitability analysis of each trade and be able to explain to clients how the proposed investment strategy is suitable for the client and how it aligns with their investment needs and objectives.

Unacceptable practices
Registrants must not:

- Delegate KYC and the suitability obligation to an unregistered individual.

- Solely ask the clients to "tick a box" that best describes their investment objectives or risk tolerance without engaging in a discussion with the clients about their personal and financial circumstances.

- Fail to fully understand the structure and features of products before recommending them to clients.

We strongly encourage our registrants to use CSA Staff Notice 31-336 as a self-assessment tool to strengthen their compliance and to improve their systems of internal control and supervision.

(ii) — Written policies and procedures are not tailored to a registrant's operations

During our reviews of newly registered IFM firms (see section 4.4 c)) for additional information), we noted instances where some firms did not have a written policies and procedures manual that was tailored to their operations and did not adequately cover the processes and procedures that a firm should have in place to establish an adequate compliance system.

To meet the requirements of section 11.1 of NI 31-103, we expect firms to establish, maintain and apply policies and procedures that are tailored to their respective business operations in order to establish a system of controls and supervision to ensure compliance with securities law and to manage the risks associated with their business in accordance with prudent business practices.

Part 11 of 31-103CP provides guidance on the content and maintenance of written policies and procedures. We also expect firms to have a process in place to ensure that written policies and procedures are regularly updated for changes in the firm's business operations, industry practice and securities law.

Suggested practices to adequately tailor written policies and procedures to a registrant's operations
Registrants must:

- Develop and enforce policies and procedures that are applicable to their firm's business operations.
- Develop policies and procedures that are sufficiently detailed and cover areas relevant to a firm's business operations.

- Provide adequate training to all employees to ensure that employees understand the established policies and procedures and understand how to incorporate them in their daily business activities.

- Review the written policies and procedures on a frequent basis to confirm that the policies and procedures are current and adequately reflect the firm's business operations, industry practice and securities law.

- Remove sections from a policies and procedures manual that are not applicable to the firm's operations.

- Add sections to a policies and procedures manual that are specific to the firm's operations.

Unacceptable practices

Registrants must not:

- Use a template of written policies and procedures provided by another firm or a consultant without reviewing and tailoring the template to the firm's operations and security law obligations.

Section 11.1 of NI 31-103 requires you to establish, maintain and apply policies and procedures that establish a system of controls and supervision to ensure compliance with securities law and manage the risks associated with your business in accordance with prudent business practices. You must also have processes in place to ensure that your written policies and procedures are regularly updated, such as for changes in your business practice, industry practice or securities law.

Please refer to Part 11 of 31-103CP, under the heading "Detailed policies and procedures", for guidance on the content, accessibility and maintenance of written policies and procedures.

(iii) — Inadequate insurance coverage

Some IFMs that were part of the newly registered IFM reviews (discussed in section 4.4 b) of this report) did not maintain an adequate financial institution bond (FIB). In these cases, the FIB provided insurance coverage for the benefit plan of the firm's employees under the same insurance rider maintained by the firm to meet its obligations under section 12.6 of NI 31-103. Although this coverage is not offside securities law, the FIB did not include specific provisions to ensure that the claims made by and paid in relation to the employee benefit plan would not affect the limits or coverage applicable to the firm under the FIB.

We also noted that the firms that had this type of insurance coverage in place were not aware of the affect that the coverage could have on the limits available to the firm under the FIB.

Section 12.6 of NI 31-103 prohibits a firm from maintaining bonding or insurance that benefits, or names as an insured, another person or company unless certain conditions are met. One of these conditions is that the individual or aggregate limits under the FIB may only be affected by claims made by or on behalf of the firm or the firm's subsidiary whose financial results are consolidated with the firm's. Additional guidance related to this issue is also found in section 12.6 of 31-103CP.

There is a risk of harm to investors when a firm is not adequately meeting its insurance requirements. The requirement to maintain insurance exists to protect investors in the case of adverse circumstances.

Suggested practices to maintain adequate insurance coverage

Registrants must:

- Carefully read all sections of the insurance policy and understand the firm's insurance coverage.

- Fully understand the implications of insuring additional entities under the FIB on the limits available to the firm.

- Verify by reviewing the insurance policy that the limits available to the firm will not be affected by also insuring other entities and confirm this with the insurance provider.

- Confirm that the insurance coverage in place meets securities law requirements at all times.

- Have written policies and procedures in place to make sure that the insurance policy is regularly reviewed and approved for all of the above and for compliance with securities law.

Unacceptable practices

Registrants must not:

- Solely rely on their insurance provider to use a template insurance policy and FIB to meet the insurance requirements under Division 2 of NI 31-103.

- Sign off on an insurance policy without carefully reading the policy and understanding all of the implications to the firm's coverage by providing coverage to other entities.

(iv) — Repeat common deficiencies

The following includes the deficiencies that we continue to find in reviews of our registrants that have been reported on in previous annual reports and prior guidance. We encourage you to review the information sources provided as the previously published guidance is still applicable to these issues.

Repeat common deficiency	Information source
1) Inadequate compliance system and UDP and CCO not meeting their responsibilities	• Section 4.1.2 in *OSC Staff Notice 33-742* under the heading *Inadequate compliance systems and UDPs and CCOs not meeting their requirements* • Section 11.1 of 31-103CP • *May 2012 OSC e-mail blast to CCOs and UDPs on Inadequate Compliance Systems*
2) Inadequate or no annual compliance report	• Section 4.1.2 in *OSC Staff Notice 33-742* under the heading *Inadequate or no annual compliance report*

Repeat common deficiency	Information source
	• Section 5.1.2 in *OSC Staff Notice 33-738* under the heading *Failure by CCO to submit an annual compliance report*
3) Inaccurate calculations of excess working capital	• Section 4.1.2 in *OSC Staff Notice 33-742* under the heading *Inaccurate calculations of excess working capital*
4) Insufficient working capital and failure to report capital deficiency	• Section 4.1.2 in *OSC Staff Notice 33-742* under the heading *Insufficient working capital and failure to report capital deficiency*
5) Inadequate relationship disclosure information	• Section 4.1.2 in *OSC Staff Notice 33-742* under the heading *Inadequate relationship disclosure information* • *CSA Staff Notice 31-334 — CSA Review of Relationship Disclosure Practices*
6) Incorrect calculation of capital markets participation fees	• Section 4.1.2 in *OSC Staff Notice 33-742* under the heading *Incorrect calculation of capital markets participation fees* • Section 3.5 of *OSC Staff Notice 33-742* under the heading *Amendments to calculation of capital markets participation fees* • *OSC Staff Notice 33-741 — Report on the Results of the Reviews of Capital Markets Participation Fees*

d) — Proposed rules and initiatives impacting all registrants

(i) — NI 31-103 Proposed Amendments

The following chart provides a high level overview of the NI 31-103 Proposed Amendments to requirements that impact all registrants.

Proposed amendment[9]	Topic	Purpose
Sub-sections 8.0, 8.22.2 and 8.26.2 of NI 31-103	Availability of exemptions to registered firms ["prohibition on concurrent reliance"]	To ensure that registration exemptions are applied in a harmonized fashion across the CSA by ensuring that all activities undertaken by a registered firm are conducted by the firm pursuant to its registration, and not in reliance on an exemption available in Part 8 of NI 31-103.
Section 12.2 of NI 31-103	Subordination agreement	To clarify registered firms' obligations in deducting non-current related party debt from their working capital and delivery obligations regarding subordination agreements.
Form 31-103F1 — *Calculation of excess working capital*	Margin rate applicable to US money market funds when calculating a registered firm's working capital	To codify discretionary exemptive relief granted to certain US based registered firms.
Sections 1.3, 11.9 and 11.10 of NI 31-103	Clarify sections 11.9 and 11.10 (acquisitions of a registered firm's securities or assets)	To provide increased clarity to industry regarding when notices must be filed and to streamline the filing process.
Section 1.3 of 31-103CP	Securities issuers guidance in 31-103CP	To incorporate internal guidance on the application of the business trigger for issuers at the start-up stage.

Notes:

9 Subject to change and final approval

For additional information refer to section 1.1 in this report.

(ii) — Mandatory electronic delivery of documents to the OSC

Effective February 19, 2014, *OSC Rule 11-501 Electronic Delivery of Documents to the Ontario Securities Commission and Consequential Policy Amendments* (OSC Rule 11-501) required certain documents identified under Ontario's securities law, that were previously filed with the Commission in paper format, to be delivered electronically through the OSC's filing portal page. The new requirements include documents associated with forms, notices and other materials required under Ontario's securities law that are not already filed through the National Registration Database (NRD).

Each required document must be delivered to the OSC electronically in accordance with instructions on the OSC's website. For registered firms and exempt international firms, a list of these documents and submission methods can be found on the *OSC's website*.

For certain filings where a fee is due with the filing, payment may be made via NRD, cheque or submitted electronically (e.g. debit/credit/wire transfer). See further instructions on *paying registrant-related fees*.

For further filing instructions in Ontario, see *OSC's electronic filing portal*. For more information see OSC Rule 11-501.

e) — Fees

(i) — Capital markets participation fees

Each year, registered firms, exempt international firms and unregistered IFMs are required to pay participation fees to the OSC based on the firm's revenues attributable to their capital markets activities in Ontario.

The *Fees Rule* requires registered firms, exempt international firms relying on sections 8.18 [international dealer] and 8.26 [international adviser] of NI 31-103 and unregistered IFMs to complete *Form 13-502F4 Capital Markets Participation Fees* (Form 13-502F4) based on information from their financial statements for their "reference fiscal year".

Ongoing review of capital markets participation fees

We conducted a review of the 2013 capital markets participation fees for one hundred and twenty-three firms that were submitted to the OSC under the Fees Rule using Form 13-502F4. In addition, we identified over seven hundred firms that calculated the participation fees using the incorrect "reference fiscal year".

If the firm was registered or relying on an exemption from registration under the Act at the end of its last fiscal year ending before May 1, 2012, the "reference fiscal year" used to calculate participation fees is the firm's last fiscal year ending before May 1, 2012. Most firms will fit in this category.

For all other firms, the "reference fiscal year" used to calculate participation fees is their last fiscal year ending in the calendar year. For specific examples of how to apply the "reference fiscal year" concept, see the *e-mail sent to all firms on November 30, 2013*.

Also refer to section 4.1 c) (iv) 6) on *Incorrect calculation of capital markets participation fees* in this report for additional information.

We will continue to review capital markets participation fees on an ongoing basis.

2014 Capital Markets Participation Fees

Firms are required to continue using the "reference fiscal year" concept to complete Form 13-502F4 due no later than December 1, 2014 (i.e. same fiscal reference year as that used for their 2013 calculation). For unregistered IFMs only, Form 13-502F4, along with the participation fee, are due no later than 90 days after the end of their fiscal year.

All firms are required to complete the participation fee calculation electronically through the OSC website. The participation fee calculation can be accessed through the *OSC's website*.

Capital markets participation fee relief

On February 20, 2014, the OSC published *OSC Staff Notice 13-704 Applications for Participation Fee Relief for Certain Small Registered Firms and Reporting Issuers* (the Fee Relief Notice).

A total of twenty-one registered firms that applied by the deadline and met the criteria outlined in the Fee Relief Notice, were granted a one-time 50% refund (or reduction) of their participation fee, subject to payment of the minimum participation fee of $800.

For more information, see *OSC Staff Notice 13-704*.

For additional information on fees, see the *Fees Rule*.

(ii) — Amendments to capital markets participation fees

Amendments are currently being made to the Fees Rule. These amendments were published for comment on September 18, 2014 and can be found under *Proposed Amendments to OSC Rule 13-502 Fees and Companion Policy 13-502CP Fees*. The amendments do not apply to the calculation and payment of the 2014 capital markets participation fees.

f) — Conflicts of interest

A registered firm is responsible for having a compliance system that promotes compliance by the firm and its individuals with securities law. Registrants often encounter conflict of interest situations during their daily operational activities. A conflict of interest is any circumstance where the interests of different parties, such as the interests of a client and those of a registrant, are inconsistent or divergent. Registered firms are responsible for identifying and appropriately responding to any conflicts of interest under Part 13 of NI 31-103. In this section, we highlight common conflict of interest situations noted for each registration category and provide suggestions on how to address these conflict of interest issues.

(i) — EMD related conflicts of interest:

We continue to have significant concerns with EMDs that trade in, or recommend, the products of related and/or connected issuers (often referred to as "related party products"), particularly those EMDs that trade *solely* in these products[18]. Material conflicts of interest arise with these relationships, in large part due to the lack of separation between the mind and management of the EMD and the issuer.

Simply disclosing this conflict of interest to investors (e.g., providing the information required by *National Instrument 33-105 Underwriting Conflicts* (NI 33-105) is not acceptable. The conflict of interest may need to be (1) avoided because the risk of harming a client or the integrity of the markets is too high or (2) controlled, for instance through the establishment of an independent review committee (IRC) and the provision of the issuer's audited financial statements.

EMDs that trade in, or recommend, related party products are not exempt from registrant obligations, including those relating to KYC, KYP and suitability (refer to section 4.1 c)(i) and section 4.2 a)(ii) in this report for a discussion of an EMDs' KYC, KYP and suitability obligations). We continue to take corrective action, including suspension or sanctions or referrals to the Enforcement Branch, against EMDs that do not comply with applicable securities law requirements.

We continue to work toward our policy objective of increasing investor protection and deterring the misuse of investor funds by registrants and their related and/or connected issuers. In the interim, we have issued the Questionnaire (see section 4.1 a) (ii) of this report) that includes questions to aid us in identifying EMDs with significant conflicts in their business models.

Acceptable practices to deal with conflicts of interest

EMDs are encouraged to:

- Avoid conflicts of interest that are contrary to the interests of investors. In some situations, controls and/or disclosure are not appropriate responses to these conflicts.

- Ensure organizational structures, lines of reporting and physical locations will enable the firm to control these risks and conflicts of interest effectively.

- Provide specific and clear disclosure to investors about the relationships that raise potential conflicts so that investors can assess the conflict and ask appropriate questions if needed. Refer to *OSC Staff Notice 33-742* under the sections titled "Conflicts of interest when selling securities of related or connected issuers" and "Inadequate disclosure of conflicts of interest" for more detailed guidance.

Unacceptable practices

EMDs must not:

- Assume that disclosure of the conflict of interest is sufficient, without avoiding or controlling the conflict as needed.

- Assume that the firm is exempt from registrant obligations by virtue of its related and/or connected issuer relationship.

- When disclosing the conflict of interest, provide generic, partial or overly detailed or complex disclosure, or rely on previous disclosure that may not be up to date or timely.

(ii) — IFM related conflicts of interest:

We generally see two types of conflicts that arise in the operation of an investment fund:

- *Operational conflicts* — those relating to the operation by the fund manager of its investment funds that are not specifically regulated under securities law, except through the standard of care imposed on the fund manager under section 116 of the Act and the general conflict of interest requirements in Part 13 of NI 31-103

- *Structural conflicts* — those resulting from proposed transactions by the IFM with related entities of the IFM, investment fund or PM currently prohibited or restricted by securities law.

For investment funds that are reporting issuers, IFMs are required to comply with the requirements of *National Instrument 81-107 Independent Review Committee for Investment Funds* (NI 81-107). The conflict of interest provisions provided in NI 31-103 do not apply to investment funds that are subject to NI 81-107. The type of conflicts of interest that arise with investment funds that are reporting issuers can also apply to private investment funds that are not reporting issuers since public and private investment funds have similar operational areas and functions. As a result, we often turn to the conflicts of interest addressed by NI 81-107 and the methods used to deal with these conflicts as a guide on managing conflicts of interest for private investment funds as well.

Some of the operational conflicts of interest that arise with IFMs and the investment funds they manage, include, but are not limited to the following:

- *Fund Valuation* — if an IFM receives a performance fee that is based on the assets under management of the fund it manages, there is a conflict of interest if the IFM is also solely responsible for valuing the assets of the fund

- *Net Asset Value (NAV)/Error Correction* — conflicts of interest can arisse through an IFMs obligation to monitor NAV errors and reimburse investment funds that are affected by a NAV error.

---

[18]Significant deficiencies that we have continued to identify include misappropriation of investor funds; concealment of poor financial condition of related and/or connected issuer; sale of unsuitable, high-risk investments to investors; and high investment concentration in related party products.

An example of a structural conflict of interest that may arise with IFMs and the investment funds they manage, include, but are not limited to the following:

- *Fund on Fund Arrangements* — if a registered firm acts in the capacity of IFM for both a top and bottom fund in a fund of fund arrangement, there is a potential conflict of interest in the IFM meeting its best interest standard under section 116 of the Act for both investment funds in ensuring that the best interests of both funds are not compromised by the IFMs actions for one fund versus another.

A comprehensive, but not an exhaustive list of the type of conflict of interest situations that may arise can be found in section 2.3 of *OSC Staff Notice 81-713 Focussed Disclosure Review — National Instrument 81-107 Independent Review Committee for Investment Funds*.

Suggested practices to address conflicts of interest
IFMs must:

- Assess the IFMs operations and daily interaction with the investment funds to identify conflicts of interest that may arise.

- Establish written policies and procedures to identify and respond to material conflicts of interest between the IFM and the investment funds managed.

- Adequately respond to each conflict of interest that arises by either:

  - avoiding the conflict,

  - controlling the conflict, and

  - disclosing the conflict.

- Disclose, in a timely manner, the nature and extent of a conflict of interest to fund investors to allow them to make an informed investment decision.

- Establish standing instructions reviewed and approved by the IRC.

- Review standing instructions on a regular basis and update the IRC as required.

- Consult the IRC in situations where a standing instruction does not exist and even in variations to a situation where a standing instruction does exist.

IFMs are encouraged to:

- Consult the IRC (if the IFM has an IRC) for conflict of interest matters that arise in investment funds that are not reporting issuers; many IFMs have an IRC established for their reporting issuer investment funds, and also use the IRC for conflict of interest matters that arise with the private investment funds managed.

Unacceptable practices
IFMs must not:

- Enter into conflict of interest situations that result in a benefit to the IFM at the expense of the fund and its investors. In these circumstances, the IFM must avoid the conflict entirely. Disclosure and control of a conflict of interest situation that is detrimental to a fund and its unitholders is not an acceptable method to deal with a detrimental conflict of interest.

(iii) — PM related conflicts of interest:

We generally see two types of conflicts of interest that arise for PMs when dealing with their clients:

- *Competing PM and client interests* — where the interests of the PM are not aligned with the interests of its clients

- *Competing client interests* — where the interests of a client of the PM are not aligned with the interests of another client of the PM.

PM/client conflicts

Some transactions that cause conflicts of interest between PMs and their clients are prohibited. Subsection 13.5(2)(b) of NI 31-103 provides further details, however examples include:

- *Restricted Trades* — A PM must not knowingly cause a managed account of a client[19] to purchase or sell a security from or to another managed account, of the PM or an officer of the PM

- *Personal trading* — employees or other individuals at PMs that have access to clients' trading and investment information (Access Persons) must not use the information for their personal gain.

Some activities that create conflicts of interest between PMs and their clients are permitted, provided that the PM responds appropriately to the conflict of interest. Appropriate responses include control and/or disclosure of the conflicts of interest. Such activities include, but are not limited to:

- *Use of client brokerage commissions* — PMs direct trades involving clients' brokerage commissions to a dealer and receive goods and services (e.g. research reports) from the dealer or a third party.

---

[19]Including investment funds for which the PM acts as an adviser.

A PM using client brokerage commissions has to comply with *National Instrument 23-102 Use of Client Brokerage Commissions* (NI 23-102), which states that PMs must:

- only direct trades involving clients' brokerage commissions to a dealer in return for order execution and research goods and services provided by the dealer or a third party,

- ensure that the goods or services are used to assist with investment or trading decisions, or with effecting securities transactions, on behalf of clients,

- make a good faith determination that clients receive a reasonable benefit considering the use of the goods or services and the amount of client brokerage commissions paid, and

- disclose specific information[20] to a client on their use of client brokerage commissions of that client that have been or might be directed to a dealer in return for goods or services.

Suggested practices to address conflicts of interest related to PM and client services

PMs must:

- Make a reasonable allocation for using client brokerage commissions to pay for "mixed-use" items according to the use of the goods or services.

- Maintain records of the analysis conducted to determine the allocation for using client brokerage commissions to pay for "mixed use" items.

- Establish, maintain and apply written personal trading policies and procedures for their Access Persons[21].

- Maintain records of personal trade pre-approvals and personal trading records of Access Persons.

- Assess compliance with the personal trading policies as part of the CCO's annual compliance report to the board.

Unacceptable practices

PMs must not:

- Use client brokerage commissions to pay for goods and services that relate to the overhead associated with the operation of the PM's business. Examples of non-permitted goods and services that should not be paid with client brokerage commissions include office furniture and equipment, and trading surveillance or compliance systems.

- Receive Access Persons' personal trading records from the Access Persons. PMs should require direct receipt of Access Persons' personal trading records (such as account statements) from the Access Persons' brokers.

Competing interests of clients

PMs need to manage conflicts of interest where the interests of a client of the PM are not aligned with the interests of another client. Examples include:

- *Allocation of investment opportunities* — an investment opportunity may be suitable for a number of clients of a PM, but may be of limited supply, forcing the PM to allocate the trade among client accounts. A PM must deliver a summary of its policy to ensure fairness in allocating investment opportunities (Fairness Policy)[22] to its clients when it opens an account for the client and when there has been a significant change to the summary previously delivered

- *Trades between client accounts* — the sale of a security from one client's account to another client's account may not be in the best interest of both clients involved.

Suggested practices to manage competing interests of clients

PMs must:

- Allocate suitable investment opportunities to their clients using a systematic and fair process, for example using a pro-rata, rotational or statistically random allocation methodology.

- Establish policies and procedures for executing trades between client accounts, including the review and approval, pricing, execution cost, and execution through a dealer of trades between client accounts.

Unacceptable practices

PMs should not:

- Consistently allocate investment opportunities in favor of one client or group of clients over others, for example, allocation to clients with a smaller portfolio size, or to clients whose portfolios are underperforming.

---

[20]See section 4.1 of NI 23-102, Part 5 of the Companion Policy to NI 23-102 and section 5.2 of OSC Staff Notice 33-736 — 2011 Annual Summary Report for Dealers, Advisers and Investment Fund Managers for more details of disclosure obligations to clients.

[21]See section 4.3.1 of OSC Staff Notice 33-742 for more details of what to include in a PM's personal trading policy.

[22]See section 14.10 of 31-103CP and OSC Staff Notice 33-738 for more details of what to include in a PM's Fairness Policy.

- Justify unfair allocation of investment opportunities by disclosing the practice to clients.

- State in their fairness policy that judgment is used to allocate investments. A fairness policy should be sufficiently objective and specific to permit independent verification of the fairness of the allocation.

- Knowingly direct a trade in portfolio securities from one investment fund to another investment fund (inter-fund trades) unless these trades are approved by the investment funds' IRC and the trades comply with other prescribed conditions under section 6.1 of NI 81-107[23]. PMs should take particular care when directing trades for investment funds for the same portfolio security, but in opposing directions (i.e. buy and sell) at the same time and to the same broker, to ensure they are not knowingly causing inter-fund trades.

4.2 — Dealers (EMDs and SPDs)

This section contains information specific to EMDs and SPDs, including current trends in deficiencies from compliance reviews of EMDs (and acceptable practices to address them), an update on the results of the SPD reviews, and new and proposed rules and initiatives.

a) — *Current trends in deficiencies and acceptable practices*

Our EMD reviews continued to focus on areas that we found to be problematic in recent years, and also focused on large EMD firms with branches and sales representatives across the country. The areas of focus included:

- maintaining adequate compliance and supervision systems, including the UDP and CCO performing their responsibilities,

- identifying and responding to conflicts of interest,

- adequate collection and documentation of KYC information and assessing the suitability of trades,

- sufficient product review process and knowledge of products recommended, by both the firm and the individual dealing representatives (KYP), and

- fair sales and marketing practices, including how referral arrangements are used in the sales process.

We will continue to focus our compliance resources on these areas.

In addition to the deficiencies included in *CSA Staff Notice 31-336* (see section 4.1 c)(i)) the following are trends in deficiencies and other areas of concern identified during this year's reviews of EMDs. Where applicable, we also highlight recent regulatory proceedings brought against EMDs to demonstrate our response when we identify registrant misconduct and the consequences to EMDs that fail to comply with securities law.

(i) — *Ineffective compliance systems*

We continue to find firms that do not maintain an adequate compliance system and firms where the UDP and CCO are not meeting their responsibilities. This is most evident amongst EMDs that distribute related party products (e.g. securities of related or connected issuers), where the same individuals form the management of both the EMD and the issuer. We found significant compliance issues across many areas including:

- failure to address and respond to material conflicts of interests, particularly with respect to handling of conflicts of interest between the firm and the related party products being sold,

- allowing non-registered entities and individuals to trade on the firm's behalf without appropriate registration,

- selling of securities of related party products when they were not suitable and permitting high investment concentration in related issuers, and

- insufficient product review process by the dealer prior to distribution, including relying on an issuer's own analysis.

There were serious consequences to firms who had deficiencies of this nature and we took appropriate regulatory action including recommendations for suspension of the firm's registration or referrals to Enforcement. See section 5.1 of this report in relation to registrant misconduct cases.

Registrants are required to maintain internal controls and a sufficient supervisory system to ensure compliance with securities law and to manage business risks (see section 32(2) of the Act and section 11.1 of NI 31-103). A firm's UDP and CCO have extremely important compliance roles. They are ultimately responsible for ensuring that a compliance system is in place to ensure that the firm, and its representatives, comply with securities law. It is critical that they understand and fulfill their required responsibilities and roles under sections 5.1 and 5.2 of NI 31-103.

See section 4.1 c) (iv)(1) of this report for more information.

(ii) — *Failure to conduct sufficient and/or independent assessment of products*

We continue to identify a number of firms that are not performing a sufficient assessment of the issuers/products they are distributing. We noted deficiencies in the following areas:

- failure to perform sufficient due diligence on the issuer being distributed, including failure to obtain financial statements or other financial information related to the issuer and failing to understand the key features of the issuer (e.g. risks, redemption features),

---

[23]Also, see section 13.5 of 31-103CP, under the heading "Restrictions on trades with certain investment portfolios", for further guidance.

- failure to perform background checks on the issuer, its principals and where applicable the underlying business operations of the issuer,

- performing due diligence on the issuer only after distributing units of the issuer to clients of the firm, and

- relying solely on a third party due diligence assessment of the issuer (e.g. without independently reviewing the facts or the assumptions built into the assessment).

Registered firms are required to ensure that, before they make a recommendation or accept a client's instruction to buy or sell a security, the purchase or sale is suitable for the client (see section 13.3(1) of NI 31-103). To meet this suitability obligation, registrants should have an in-depth knowledge of all products they sell or recommend to clients and be able to explain to their clients the product's risks, key features, initial and ongoing costs and fees and other relevant information. Registrants are required to have conducted sufficient due diligence on the issuer prior to soliciting any clients or distributing securities of the issuer.

For further guidance on meeting KYP and suitability obligations, please refer to *CSA Staff Notice 31-336* and *CSA Staff Notice 33-315 — Suitability Obligation and Know Your Product.*

Acceptable practices to conduct a KYP assessment
EMDs must:

- Perform sufficient due diligence on an issuer prior to recommending the security to clients.

- Understand the key features, financial information, and product risks of the security and be able to explain them to their clients.

- Analyze and review any third party assessment of the issuer for completeness, reasonableness and accuracy.

Unacceptable practices
EMDs must not:

- Wait to perform due diligence of an issuer after beginning to distribute its securities to clients.

- Rely solely on the issuer's information or third parties to fulfill their KYP obligation, e.g. information in the offering memorandum.

- Recommend or sell a product without understanding the product's risk and key features.

(iii) — Referral arrangements and finders

Referral arrangements[24] entered into by EMDs must comply with securities law requirements, including those in Part 13, Division 3 of NI 31-103. These requirements include:

- that referral arrangements must be set out in a written agreement,

- all referral fees[25] must be recorded,

- clients must receive specified written disclosure, and

- an EMD must not refer a client to a person or company unless it first takes reasonable steps to ensure that the person or company is appropriately qualified and/or registered.

Firms must monitor and supervise all referral arrangements. Although dealing representatives can be parties to referral agreements, the registered firm itself must be a party, since it must be aware of the agreement in order to ensure compliance with applicable requirements. The obligation to monitor and supervise compliance continues for as long as the referral arrangement is in place.

A client that is referred to an EMD becomes that EMD's client for the purposes of the services provided under the referral arrangement. As a result the EMD must meet all of its registrant obligations, including those relating to KYC, KYP and suitability. Refer to section 4.1 c) (i) and section 4.2 a) (ii) of this report for a discussion on an EMD's KYC, KYP and suitability obligations. An EMD must also address conflicts of interest arising from the referral arrangement.

We understand that some finders inappropriately rely on section 8.5 of NI 31-103, which provides an exemption from the dealer registration requirement if a trade is made solely through a registered dealer. If a finder is "in the business of trading", as a result of it frequently or regularly contacting prospective investors, it cannot rely on this exemption and must be appropriately registered.

Acceptable practices to adequately address referral arrangements
EMDs must:

- Ensure that all parties to referral arrangements are registered, if required, including finders.

- Ensure that the roles and responsibilities of the parties to the written agreement are clear.

- Provide clients with disclosure about the referral arrangement to help them evaluate the arrangement, including any potential conflicts of interest. This disclosure must be provided before or at the time the referred services are provided.

- Manage conflicts of interest that arise from the referral arrangement in accordance with Part 13, Division 2 of NI 31-103.

---

[24]Any arrangement in which a registrant agrees to pay or receive a referral fee.

[25]Any form of direct or indirect compensation for the referral of a client to or from a registrant.

Unacceptable practices

EMDs must not:

- Interpret "referral arrangement" and "referral fee" narrowly, since NI 31-103 defines these terms broadly.

- Overlook unreasonably high referral fees that could motivate dealing representatives to act contrary to their duties towards clients.

- Use a referral arrangement to assign, contract out of or otherwise avoid its regulatory obligations (e.g. by using an unregistered finder to contact potential investors, instead of a properly registered dealing representative).

- Assume that registrant obligations can be reduced by contracting with unregistered individuals or firms through a referral arrangement.

b) — Charitable donation/taxable donation tax schemes

We remind market participants that tax shelter products, including ones that involve leveraged donations of property (for instance, artwork and medical supplies) to charities and ones that are marketed to investors on the basis of tax credits or deductions that are claimed to be available, are typically considered "securities" as defined in subsection 1(1) of the Act.

Consistent with the recent decision of the Alberta Court of Appeal *Re Synergy Group*[26], these arrangements typically constitute securities on one or more grounds, including that they are "investment contracts". Accordingly, we expect promoters and distributors of these products to comply with the necessary registration, disclosure and other Ontario securities law requirements.

When we review these products, to determine whether they are (1) securities and (2) suitable investments for investors, we will consider factors that include:

- Clients' objectives in participating. For example, in the case of a leveraged donation of property, is the client genuinely seeking to contribute to the charity or is the client seeking a financial return (and, therefore, making an investment decision)?

- If tax credits or deductions are being marketed to clients, what is the basis for doing so? For example, is there a legal opinion — and, if so, is it addressed to the clients or to the promoter/distributor? How is the quantum of these tax credits or deductions valued?

- Does the product have a tax shelter number for identification by the Canada Revenue Agency (CRA)?

- Has the CRA previously challenged the claims or deductions of clients in similar tax shelter arrangements or tax shelter arrangements facilitated by the same promoter/distributor of the current arrangement?

- Has the promoter/distributor been involved in any regulatory and/or legal proceedings involving the tax status of a similar arrangement?

We remind registrants to carefully consider their KYC, KYP and suitability obligations when promoting and selling tax shelter products. Refer to section 4.1 c) (i) and section 4.2 a) (ii) of this report for a discussion on an EMD's KYC, KYP and suitability obligations.

A number of promoters and distributors have marketed tax shelter products to investors using misleading claims, for instance regarding the availability of financial returns, while at the same time disclaiming responsibility for such claims. The CRA has recently challenged claims for tax credits or deductions by investors in these tax shelter products and we understand that the Royal Canadian Mounted Police has issued warnings stating that certain tax shelter products appear to be fraudulent.

We will continue to conduct reviews, including onsite compliance reviews, of entities promoting and/or distributing tax shelter products. Where necessary, we will take corrective action, including suspension, sanctions and referrals to the Enforcement Branch.

c) — Update on results of SPD reviews

As noted in section 5.3.1 of *OSC Staff Notice 33-738* and section 4.2.2 of *OSC Staff Notice 33-742* we conducted compliance reviews in 2011 of the five firms solely registered in the category of SPD. We referred four of these SPDs to our Enforcement Branch after identifying serious concerns with their compliance systems and sales practices.

Regulatory proceedings were brought against the four SPDs in response to significant non-compliance by the firms. In order to address our investor protection concerns, interim T&Cs on their registration were imposed by the Commission on consent of each of Children's Education Funds Inc., Global RESP Corporation, Heritage Education Funds Inc. and Knowledge First Financial Inc. Please see Section 4.2.2 of *OSC Staff Notice 33-742* for more information about the key T&Cs that were imposed by temporary orders on these registrants.

The proceedings against the SPDs have been concluded and all four of the temporary orders have been revoked. In addition, separate settlement agreements were reached with each of the four SPDs in which they acknowledged that changes were required to strengthen their respective compliance systems so as to better serve the public interest. All public information involving the SPDs is available on the OSC's website under *All Commission Proceedings*.

d) — New and proposed rules and initiatives impacting dealers

(i) — NI 31-103 Proposed Amendments for dealers

The following chart provides a high level overview of the NI 31-103 Proposed Amendments to requirements that impact dealers.

---

[26]*Synergy Group (2000) Inc. v. Alberta (Securities Commission)* (June 28, 2011), 2011 ABCA 194.

Proposed amendment[19]	Topic	Purpose
Sections 3.6, 3.8 and 3.10 of NI 31-103	Dealers CCO proficiency in NI 31-103 and 31-103CP	To introduce an experience requirement for dealer CCOs.
Section 7.1 of NI 31-103 and 31-103CP	"Foreign Broker Dealer" project	To prohibit EMDs from executing trades of securities on or off a marketplace or giving instructions to execute trades of securities on a marketplace (including by establishing omnibus accounts with investment dealers and trading for their clients through that account). To clarify that EMDs may only underwrite securities in limited circumstances.
Section 8.5 of NI 31-103	Trades through or to a registered dealer	To achieve a harmonized interpretation of section 8.5 and to clarify that this exemption is not available if the person relying on the exemption solicits or contacts any person or company that is a purchaser in relation to the trade.
Subsection 8.5.1 of NI 31-103	Trades through a registered dealer by registered adviser	To add an exemption from the dealer registration requirement for registered advisers in order to clarify that incidental trading activities by advisers do not require registration as a dealer, provided the trades are executed through a registered dealer.
Section 8.18 of NI 31-103	International dealer exemption	To revert back to the less restrictive "permitted client" conditions in this exemption that were in force prior to July 11, 2011.

Notes:

19   Subject to change and final approval

For additional information, refer to section 1.1 in this report.

e) — EMDs and direct electronic access

We remind EMDs that they are prohibited from using direct electronic access (DEA) under National Instrument 23-103 *Electronic Trading* (NI 23-103), which came into effect on March 1, 2013[27]. For additional information, refer to *the unofficial consolidation of National Instrument 23-103 and its companion policy* published on March 1, 2014. The CSA continue to be of the view that only dealers that are members of IIROC and subject to the Universal Market Integrity Rules (UMIR) are permitted to use DEA. However, a firm registered as both an EMD and a PM is permitted to use DEA, provided that it is only using DEA in its capacity as a PM for its managed account clients.

Please refer to section 5.2 (e) in *OSC Staff Notice 33-736 — 2011 Annual Summary Report for Dealers, Advisers and Investment Fund Managers* (OSC Staff Notice 33-736) under the heading *New and proposed rules impacting portfolio managers — Direct electronic access* and section 5.4(c) under the heading *New and proposed rules impacting exempt market dealers — Direct electronic access (DEA)* for a previous discussion on this topic. Please also refer to *IIROC Dealer Member Rules* and *UMIR* for additional information.

f) — Review of prospectus exemptions

See section 1.2 of this report for a discussion on the review of prospectus exemptions.

g) — Permitted activities in EMD category

See sections 1.1 and 4.2 d)(i) of this report for a discussion of the proposed amendments relating to the permitted activities for EMDs as outlined in Section 7.1(d) of NI 31-103 and Section 7.1 of 31-103CP.

h) — Proposed amendments to NI 33-105

In November 2013, the CSA published for comment (now closed) *proposed amendments to NI 33-105*. The amendments would, if adopted, provide exemptions from certain disclosure requirements in NI 33-105 that would otherwise apply to certain private placements of foreign securities to permitted clients (generally institutional investors) in Canada.

The purpose of the proposed amendments is to eliminate the need to prepare a "wrapper" when a foreign issuer offers securities in Canada to permitted clients under a prospectus exemption. A wrapper contains prescribed Canadian disclosure and other optional disclosure that is attached to the face of the foreign offering document. The proposed amendments are intended to streamline the process for offering foreign securities to institutional investors in Canada, and are intended to codify for all market participants certain exemptive relief that was granted to certain international dealers in the decision *Re Barclays Capital Inc.* dated April 23, 2014.

The comment period for the request for comments expired in February 2014. OSC staff in consultation with staff in the other CSA jurisdictions are currently considering the comments received.

---

[27]Amendments to NI 23-103 came into effect on March 1, 2014.

Part 3:
REGISTRATION

4.3 — Advisers (PMs)

This section contains information specific to PMs, including current trends in deficiencies from compliance reviews of PMs (and acceptable practices to address them) and new and proposed rules and initiatives.

a) — *Current trends in deficiencies and acceptable practices*

(i) — *Repeat common deficiencies*

The following includes the deficiencies that we continue to find in reviews of PMs that have been reported on in previous annual reports and prior guidance. We encourage you to review the information sources provided as the previously published guidance is still applicable to these issues.

Repeat common deficiency	Information source
1) Delegating KYC and suitability obligations to referral agents	• Section 4.3.1 under the heading *Delegating KYC and suitability obligations to referral agents* in *OSC Staff Notice 33-742* • Section 5.2A under the heading *Delegating know your client and suitability obligations* in *OSC Staff Notice 33-736* • Section 13.3 of *31-103CP*
2) Inadequate supervision of ARs and research analysts	• Section 4.3.1 of *OSC Staff Notice 33-742* under the heading *Inadequate supervision of advising representatives and research analysts* • Sections 32(2) of *the Act*, 11.1 of *NI 31-103* and 11.1 of *31-103CP*
3) Inadequate investment management agreements	• Section 4.3.1 of *OSC Staff Notice 33-742* under the heading *Inadequate investment management agreements* • Sections 11.5(1) and 11.5(2)(k) of *NI 31-103*
4) Account statement practices	• Section 1.6 of this report on *PM — IIROC dealer service arrangements* • Section 4.3.3 of *OSC Staff Notice 33-742* under the heading *PM client account statement practices* • Section 14.14 of *NI 31-103*
5) Lack of awareness of trade-matching requirements	• Section 5.4.1 of *OSC Staff Notice 33-738* under the heading *Lack of awareness of trade-matching requirements* • *National Instrument 24-101 Institutional Trade Matching and Settlement (NI 24-101)* and Companion Policy to NI 24-101 • *CSA Staff Notice 24-305 Frequently Asked Questions About National Instrument 24-101 — Institutional Trade Matching and Settlement and Related Companion Policy*

b) — *New and proposed rules and inititiaves impacting PMs*

(i) — *On-going amendments to NI 31-103*

The following chart provides a high level overview of the NI 31-103 Proposed Amendments to requirements that impact PMs.

Proposed amendment21[21]	Topic	Purpose
Sections 3.11 and 3.12 of 31-103CP	Proficiency: "relevant investment management experience" guidance	To provide increased clarity for industry regarding who qualifies for PM registration.
Section 8.26 of NI 31-103	International adviser exemption	To revert back to the less restrictive "permitted client" conditions in this exemption that were in force prior to July 11, 2011.
Subsection 8.26.1 of NI 31-103	Adding a sub-adviser exemption (not available outside of ON and QC otherwise)	To make the non-resident sub-adviser exemption available across Canada via NI 31-103 (currently available in Ontario and Quebec, exemptive relief application required in other provinces).
Section 13.17 of NI 31-103	Exemption from certain requirements for registered sub-advisers	To provide relief from certain requirements in NI 31-103, where a registered adviser acts as a sub-adviser for another registrant.

Notes:

21   Subject to change and final approval

For additional information, refer to section 1.1 in this report.

4.4 — Investment fund managers

This section contains information specific to IFMs, including current trends in deficiencies from compliance reviews of IFMs (and acceptable practices to address them), a discussion on our sweep of high impact IFMs, and new and proposed rules and initiatives.

a) — Current trends in deficiencies and acceptable practices

In this section, we summarize key trends in deficiencies from recent compliance reviews of IFMs.

(i) — Repeat common deficiencies

The following includes the deficiencies that we continue to find in reviews of our registrants that have been reported on in previous annual reports and prior guidance. We encourage you to review the information sources provided as the previously published guidance is still applicable to these issues.

Repeat common deficiency	Information source
1) Sales practices	• Part I of *OSC Staff Notice 33-743* • *OSC Staff Notice 11-760 Report on Mutual Fund Sales Practices Under Part 5 of National Instrument 81-105 — Mutual Fund Sales Practices* (OSC Staff Notice 11-760)
2) Inappropriate expenses charged to investment funds	• Section 4.4.1 under the heading *Inappropriate expenses charged to funds* in *OSC Staff Notice 33-742* • Part II of *OSC Staff Notice 33-743*
3) Inadequate oversight of outsourced functions and service providers	• Part V of *OSC Staff Notice 33-743* • Section 4.4.1 of *OSC Staff Notice 33-742* under the heading *Inadequate oversight of outsourced functions and service providers* • Section 11.1 of *NI 31-103* and 11.1 of *31-103CP*
4) Non-delivery of net asset value adjustments	• Section 4.4.1 of *OSC Staff Notice 33-742* under the heading *Non-delivery of net asset value adjustments* • Section 4.4 d) (i) of this report re Ongoing Amendments to NI 31-103

(ii) — Inadequate sales practices involving promotional items and business promotion activities

We reviewed a number of IFMs that manage mutual funds and engage in sales practice activities under section 5.6 of *National Instrument 81-105 Mutual Fund Sales Practices* (NI 81-105). We noted some instances where the promotional items and business promotion activities provided by IFMs to sales representatives were excessive and extravagant and not in keeping with section 5.6 of NI 81-105, particularly as follows:

- the amount spent on one promotional item or business promotion activity equated to the entire annual dollar limit set by an IFM for these types of activities per representative,

- the value of a promotional item or business promotion activity provided during one event exceeded the internal maximum that can be provided to each sales representative as set by the IFM,

- the value of all promotional items and business promotion activities provided to sales representatives over several events exceeded the internal maximum set by the IFM, and

- IFMs covered the cost of travel and personal incidental expenses incurred by sales representatives attending business promotion activities. For example, IFMs paid for expenses of sales representatives related to beverages and food outside of the meals and beverages already organized by the IFM and arranged for travel to and from the business promotion activity. The provision of travel and personal incidental expenses is strictly prohibited by section 5.6 of NI 81-105.

Section 5.6 of NI 81-105 provides specific parameters regarding the provision of promotional items and business promotion activities to sales representatives. IFMs must confirm that the provision of promotional items and business promotion activities fall within these set parameters.

Suggested practices to provide adequate sales practices under section 5.6 of NI 81-105

IFMs must:

- Develop internal policies and procedures to determine the reasonability of the cost of the promotional item and business promotion activity provided to sales representatives. IFMs are encouraged to consider the following in developing policies and procedures:
  - an annual limit per representative on these type of sales practices,
  - internal parameters on what is considered a reasonable amount for promotional items and business promotion activities,

Part 3:
REGISTRATION

- factors that should be considered when determining cost reasonability,
- the individual(s) responsible for assessing reasonability and providing documented approval of expenses,
- the type of documentation required to assess reasonability, and
- the involvement of the IRC in evaluating sales practices for reasonability.
- Maintain evidence of their reasonability assessment and the review and approval of the promotional item and business promotion activity.

Unacceptable practices

IFMs must not:

- Spend the entire annual limit set for promotional items and business promotion activities on any one item or event provided to a sales representative. This practice would be considered excessive and extravagant and not in keeping with the spirit of Part 5 of NI 81-105.
- Pay for travel expenses related to the provision of a promotional item or business promotion activity.
- Pay for any expenses, such as personal incidental expenses, above and beyond what was organized by the IFM for the business promotion activity.
- Provide promotional items or business promotion activities that would cost more in a location outside of where the IFMs head office is located (i.e. Toronto, Ontario).

For more information, see Part I of *OSC Staff Notice 33-743* under section i) *reasonability of costs*, section 5.6 of *NI 81-105* and paragraph 7.6 (2) of the *Companion Policy of NI 81-105*.

(iii) — Inappropriate IFM organizational structure

We noted issues with IFMs that were part of larger organizational structures regarding the registration of the correct entity as an IFM and the payment of capital market participation fees.

In the cases that we reviewed, we noted that the investment funds managed by the IFM were paying a management fee to either the parent company or an affiliate of the IFM. In turn, the IFM would receive only a portion of the management fee from the parent company or affiliate for its services as a PM and not also as an IFM. The remaining management fee would be retained by the parent company or the affiliated entity, an unregistered entity.

Two key implications result from this type of organizational structure as follows:

- Registration issues: Section 7.3 of 31-103CP states that an IFM directs the business, operations or affairs of an investment fund. The management fee is being paid to an unregistered entity that may be directing the business, operations or affairs of the investment fund, which is the responsibility of the registered IFM. We would question if the firm receiving a portion of the management fee is conducting registerable activity and required to be registered as an IFM with the OSC.
- Participation fee issues: The result of paying the management fee to an unregistered entity is the calculation and payment of incorrect participation fees per Form 13-502F4 since the entire management fee is not captured in the registered IFMs revenue per its annual audited financial statements.

In each of the cases identified, we took appropriate steps to verify that the firms remitted additional participation fees to us, if necessary, based on the entire management fee paid by the investment funds and that all firms were appropriately registered with the OSC.

Suggested practices to implement an adequate IFM operational structure

IFMs must:

- Register entities that direct the business, operations or affairs of investment funds.
- Record the entire amount of management fees paid by the investment funds on the financial statements of the entity registered as an IFM.
- Include the entire amount of management fees paid by investment funds when calculating the participation fees for the IFM per Form 13-502F4.
- Confirm that the entity performing the IFM responsibilities is registered with the OSC in the category of IFM.

Unacceptable practices

IFMs must not:

- Avoid paying participation fees under OSC Rule 13-502 by diverting revenue paid by an investment fund to unregistered entities.

b) — Sweep of large "impact" IFMs

In May 2013, we commenced targeted, on-site reviews of a sample of large IFMs to assess their compliance with securities law. These IFMs had over $500 billion in assets under management and they managed a wide range of investment funds, including traditional mutual funds, pooled funds, ETFs and closed end funds. As part of these reviews, we focused on key operational areas of the IFMs, such as:

- minimum working capital requirements and custody,

* securityholder reporting/transfer agency,

* trust accounting,

* fund accounting,

* oversight of service providers,

* conflicts of interest,

* sales practices, and

* overall compliance structure.

In cases where the IFMs were dually registered or had an affiliated PM, we also performed testing of the portfolio management and trading activities in conjunction with the targeted review of large advisers being done at the same time.

On June 19, 2014, we published *OSC Staff Notice 33-743* to summarize the findings of the large "impact" IFM sweep reviews.

The notice summarizes our findings and sets out suggested guidance on the following areas:

* sales practices,

* allocation of expenses to investment funds,

* mutual fund borrowings,

* prohibited cross trades, and

* outsourcing and oversight of service providers.

For more information, see *OSC Staff Notice 33-743*.

c) — Sweep of newly registered IFMs

This year we commenced reviews of a sample of newly registered IFMs in Ontario to gain an understanding of each firm's business, assess their compliance with Ontario securities law, and provide guidance on key regulatory requirements. We selected 40 firms in Ontario and are considering expanding the scope of the reviews to outside of Canada for firms for which we act as principal regulator. The firms were chosen based on their date of registration and other risk-based criteria. Our reviews focused on each firm's compliance system, financial condition and key IFM operational areas as well as key operational areas where the IFM was also registered in other categories such as a PM and/or EMD, as well as a KYC and suitability review. We have completed the 40 reviews. The objective of the sweep is to help newly registered IFM firms better understand their key regulatory requirements and help to enhance their compliance by identifying deficiencies in their compliance system. The common deficiencies we identified from the sweep are listed below, along with where to get more information on the requirements and guidance to address the deficiencies:

* Inadequate oversight of service providers — see section 4.4 a)(i)(3) in this report on *Current trends in deficiencies and acceptable practices and Repeat common deficiencies.*

* Inadequate insurance coverage — see section 4.1 c)(iii) in this report on *Current trends in deficiencies and acceptable practices* under *Inadequate insurance coverage.*

* Inadequate written policies and procedures — see section 4.1 c)(ii) in this report on *Current trends in deficiencies and acceptable practices* under *Written policies and procedures are not tailored to registrant's operations.*

* Inadequate collection, maintenance and documentation of KYC information — see section 4.1 c)(i) of this report on *Current trends in deficiencies and acceptable practices* under *Non-compliance with KYC, KYP and suitability requirements and accredited investor requirements.*

* Not determining proper reliance on accredited investor exemption — see section 4.1 c)(i) of this report on *Current trends in deficiencies and acceptable practices* under *Non-compliance with KYC, KYP and suitability requirements and accredited investor requirements.*

* Inadequate relationship disclosure information — see section 4.1 c)(iv)(5) in this report on *Current trends in deficiencies and acceptable practices* under *Repeat common deficiencies* and *Inadequate relationship disclosure information.*

We perform sweep reviews of newly registered firms on an ongoing basis and in addition to enhancing a firm's compliance system we also use the information we obtain to enhance our outreach to registrants.

d) — New and proposed rules and initiatives impacting IFMs

(i) — Ongoing Amendments to NI 31-103

The following chart provides a high level overview of the NI 31-103 Proposed Amendments to requirements that impact IFMs.

Part 3:
REGISTRATION

Proposed amendment[22]	Topic	Purpose
Section 8.28 of NI 31-103	Capital accumulation plan	To make this exemption permanent and to clarify that this exemption is only available to plan sponsors and plan service providers in respect of activities relating to a capital accumulation plan.
Section 12.14 of NI 31-103	Form 31-103F4 *Net Asset Value Adjustments* (Form 31-103F4)	New Form 31-103F4 Net Asset Value Adjustments on which an IFM will report NAV adjustments as required by section 12.14 of NI 31-103 in order to harmonize and streamline the information provided by IFMs about NAV errors and adjustments by specifying which items of disclosure must be covered and the level of detail to be provided to regulators.

Notes:

22   Subject to change and final approval

For additional information, refer to section 1.1 in this report

As discussed in section 1.1 of this report, the CSA is working on NI 31-103 Proposed Amendments. A new form to report NAV adjustments in respect of investment funds managed by an IFM is being proposed as part of the NI 31-103 Proposed Amendments referred to as Form 31-103F4.

IFMs are required under section 12.14 of NI 31-103 to deliver a quarterly report describing any NAV adjustments in respect of an investment fund managed by the IFM during the period being reported on. The CSA has noted that the NAV reporting received since the implementation of NI 31-103 has been sparse and minimal and at times CSA regulators need to follow up with the IFM directly to discuss the issue, potential cause and solution of the NAV error originally reported.

As a result, as part of the NI 31-103 Proposed Amendments, CSA staff proposed Form 31-103F4 relating to reporting NAV errors. The purpose of the form is to provide additional details on NAV errors. More fulsome information will allow the regulator to detect whether or not the IFM should have more adequate policies and procedures in place to detect, prevent and correct NAV errors and will also limit the back and forth between the regulator and the IFM to obtain additional information once the NAV error is reported.

(ii) — Changes to the Act

Part XXI of the Act, *Insider Trading and Self-Dealing* (Part XXI of the Act), contains conflict of interest investment restrictions which, until July 24, 2014, only applied to mutual funds. Part XXI of the Act has been amended to extend the conflict of interest investment restrictions to all investment funds, so that they apply to non-redeemable investment funds and mutual funds. Refer to the *Act* for additional information.

(iii) — Investment Funds and Structured Products Branch

Our Investment Funds and Structured Products Branch has worked on a number of new and proposed rules with the CSA on the regulation of investment funds, and other initiatives, which impact IFMs. A number of these initiatives represent a continuation of projects previously discussed in detail in section 4.4.2 of OSC Staff Notice 33-742. A summary of some of this work and the relevant information sources can be found in the following chart:

Project	Information source
1) Mutual fund fees	• Section 4.4.2 under the heading *New and Proposed Rules and Initiatives impacting IFMs* in *OSC Staff Notice 33-742* • On December 17, 2013 the CSA published *CSA Staff Notice 81-323 Status Report on Consultation under CSA Discussion Paper and Request for Comment 81-407 Mutual Fund Fees Section* which provides additional information on this initiative.
2) Mutual fund risk classification	• On December 12, 2013 the CSA published *CSA Staff Notice 81-324 Proposed CSA Mutual Fund Risk Classification Methodology for Use in Fund Facts* which provides additional information on this initiative.
3) Point of sale disclosure	• On March 26, 2014, the CSA published for second comment (now closed) changes to proposed amendments to National Instrument 81-101 *Mutual Fund Prospectus Disclosure* (the Rule or NI 81-101) and Companion Policy 81-101CP to National Instrument 81-101 *Mutual Fund Prospectus Disclosure* (the Companion Policy). See *CSA Notice and Request for Comment: Implementation of Stage 3 of Point of Sale Disclosure for Mutual Funds — Point of Sale Delivery of Fund Facts*.

	• See section 4.4.2 under the heading *New and Proposed Rules and Initiatives impacting IFMs* in *OSC Staff Notice 33-742*
4) Review of fees and expenses disclosure by investment funds	• Our Investment Funds and Structured Products Branch recently conducted a targeted review of the fees and expenses disclosure practices of investment funds. *OSC Staff Notice 81-724 Report on Staff's Continuous Disclosure Review of the Fees and Expenses Disclosure by Investment Funds,* summarizes the findings and provides guidance to address the findings.
5) Review of high management expense ratios	• Our Investment Funds and Structured Products Branch recently completed a review of investment funds with high management expense ratios. The *July 2014 Investment Funds Practitioner* provides a summary on the results of this initiative.
IFM Resources	**Information source**
1) Annual Summary Report	• Our Investment Funds and Structured Products Branch publishes an annual Summary Report for Investment Fund Issuers. Refer to the fourth annual Summary Report in *OSC Staff Notice 81-723 Summary Report for Investment Fund Issuers 2013*.
2) Investment Funds Practitioner	• *The Practitioner* is an ongoing publication prepared by the OSC's Investment Funds and Structured Products Branch that provides an overview of operational issues arising from applications for discretionary relief, prospectuses, and continuous disclosure documents that are filed with the OSC.

Acting on Registrant Misconduct

5 — Acting on registrant misconduct

"The OSC has a responsibility to deliver strong investor protection: it's at the core of everything we do.

April 9, 2013 speech by Debra Foubert, Director, Compliance and Registrant Regulation at Strategy Institute: Annual Registrant Regulation, Conduct & Compliance Summit

We are alert to potential misconduct by registrants and when we find evidence of this we take appropriate, timely and effective regulatory action. Our regulatory responses cover the compliance-enforcement continuum, and include remedies imposed by the Director (such as T&Cs or suspensions of registration) as well as referrals to our Enforcement Branch.

HIGHLIGHTS OF MISCONDUCT CASES	
"In my view, [the registrant's] ongoing compliance issues, . . ., are very serious and raise concerns about whether the business of the firm . . . may be carried on with integrity and in the best interests of [the] securityholders and in a way that would foster confidence in the capital markets"[23]	"Registration is a privilege, not a right, and it places significant obligations on registrants when they deal with members of the public who are potential investors or who are already clients. The public should not be exposed to the risk of a registrant that is under court protection from its creditors because it cannot meet its obligations as they become due . . . Instead it is reasonable for clients of a registered firm to expect that the firm is financially viable and not committing acts of bankruptcy. It is not in the public interest for [registrants] to continue in the business of trading in securities because it is not in a position to meet the many responsibilities that registrant firms must meet so that investors are protected."[24]

Notes:

23   Director's Decision — February 28, 2014 — Pro-Financial Asset Management Inc.

24   Director's Decision — November 11, 2013 — League Investment Services Inc.

Some notable registrant misconduct cases from the past year are summarized below. Please note that some cases are still ongoing. Documents related to OSC proceedings before the Commission and before the Courts are available on the OSC's website under *All Commission Proceedings*. Further, *Director's Decisions* from the CRR Branch are also available on the OSC's website.

Part 3:
REGISTRATION

a) — Regulatory action following compliance reviews

Registrant	Date of Director's Decision	Description
Sterling Grace & Co. Ltd. and Graziana Casale	November 18, 2013	During a compliance review of this EMD, we found that the firm was selling securities of an issuer under circumstances that gave rise to a serious undisclosed conflict of interest, and that the firm had failed to properly discharge its KYC and suitability obligations. Following a contested opportunity to be heard, the firm and its sole individual registrant were suspended by the Director. The Director's decision was stayed pending a hearing and review by a panel of the Commission pursuant to section 8 of the Act. The hearing and review was held in February and March, 2014. In September 2014, the panel released its reasons for the decision in which the panel agreed with the Director's findings on most issues, and suspended both the firm and the individual registrant.
League Investment Services Inc.	November 11, 2013	During a compliance review of this EMD, the firm and a number of its related party issuers filed for protection under the *Companies' Creditors Arrangement Act*. Staff of both the British Columbia Securities Commission (the **BCSC**) and the OSC sought to suspend the EMD's registration on solvency grounds, which the firm contested. The Executive Director of the BCSC found that the EMD was not suitable for registration because it was not in a position to meet its many responsibilities as a registered firm. After the BCSC suspension, the EMD withdrew its opposition to Staff's recommendation, and the Director suspended the EMD in Ontario as well.
FCPF Corporation (formerly Redev Corporation) and Richard Crenian	October 1, 2013	During a compliance review of this EMD, we found that the firm had employed an unregistered individual to trade in securities with clients and that it had traded in securities with some clients who did not qualify for prospectus exemptions. The registration of the firm and its UDP were suspended pursuant to a settlement agreement that was approved by the Director.
Kingsmont Investment Management Inc. and Paget Warner	September 24, 2013	During a compliance review of this PM and EMD, we found that the firm had failed to adequately discharge its KYC, KYP and suitability obligations. To address these concerns, the principal of the firm agreed to sell a majority share in the firm and surrender his UDP and CCO registrations, as well as the firm's EMD registration. Following a contested opportunity to be heard, the Director additionally suspended the principal's registration as an AR for six months for making misleading statements to OSC staff about a client complaint, and for requiring clients to sign an inappropriate risk disclaimer when investing in a particular issuer.
Takota Asset Management Inc.	July 29, 2013	T&Cs were imposed on the registration of this IFM, PM, and EMD requiring that it submit monthly financial reports to the OSC. The T&Cs were imposed due to the firm's failure to meet the excess working capital requirements and failure to notify the OSC of its capital deficiency, which had been identified by OSC staff during a compliance review.

Registrant	Date of Director's Decision	Description
Adewale Gbalajobi	July 26, 2013	A compliance review found that an EMD (FCPF Corporation) had used an unregistered individual to trade in securities with clients, some of whom did not qualify for prospectus exemptions. The firm was subsequently suspended by the Director. Mr. Gbalajobi was the CCO of the firm, and separately settled proceedings with the OSC that include a suspension of his registration.
Investment Allocation International Inc. and Marshall Miller	June 4, 2013	A compliance review of this one-man PM found that the registrant was selling securities of a related issuer to clients for whom the registrant provided discretionary management services. The investments were solicited by the registrant and made with the knowledge and consent of the client. The registrant did not fully disclose to its clients that a part of the investment proceeds would be used by the issuer to pay a management fee to the registrant. The registrant also had excess working capital of less than zero. The corporate and individual registrants were both suspended in accordance with a settlement agreement approved by the Director.

b) — Regulatory action following an application for registration

Registrant	Date of Director's Decision	Description
Anu Bala Jain	August 29, 2013	This individual was an approved person of a mutual fund dealer. In March 2012, the MFDA approved of a settlement agreement under which Ms. Jain was suspended as an approved person for a period of one year after she engaged in "stealth advising" (*i.e.*, signing paperwork for investments actually sold to clients by an unregistered individual), and in an attempt to cover up her actions, misled her sponsoring firm and the MFDA during their investigation into the matter. Ms. Jain completed her suspension and the other terms required by her MFDA settlement agreement, and applied to reactivate her registration. T&Cs were imposed on Ms. Jain's registration requiring that she be strictly supervised by her sponsoring firm for a period of one year.

Part 3:
REGISTRATION

c) — Matters referred to the Enforcement Branch

Registrant	Date of Decision	Description
Pro-Financial Asset Management Inc.	Ongoing	The Commission suspended the EMD registration of the firm, and placed T&Cs on the firm's PM registration prohibiting it from taking on new clients. The firm reported a large capital deficiency that it was not able to rectify, and also reported a discrepancy between the amount payable in respect of certain principal protected notes and the amount available to make those payments. Certain investment products managed by the firm are now subject to a cease trade order. Although the Director objected to a proposal to sell the firm's business to a purchaser, the Commission approved the transaction in July 2014 subject to T&Cs and after significant change was made to the transaction. The Enforcement Branch continues to investigate the firm's principal protected notes discrepancy.
Quadrexx Asset Management Inc.	Ongoing	As reported in section 5.1 of *OSC Staff Notice 33-742*, the Commission suspended the registration of this IFM, PM, and EMD, and issued a cease trade order in respect of certain investment products managed by the firm, after the firm reported a large capital deficiency that it was unable to rectify. Since then, the firm's business activities have been wound up, and a Statement of Allegations has been issued against the firm's principals and various related companies alleging, among other things, securities fraud. A hearing regarding the matters alleged in the Statement of Allegations has not yet occurred, and those allegations have not been proven.

Additional Resources

6 — Additional resources

This section discusses how registrants can get more information about their obligations.

The CRR Branch works to foster a culture of compliance through outreach and other initiatives. We try to assist registrants in meeting their regulatory requirements in a number of ways.

We developed a new outreach program to registrants (see section 2.1 of this report) to help them understand and comply with their obligations. We encourage registrants to visit our *Registrant Outreach web page* on the OSC's website.

Also, the *Information for: Dealers, Advisers and IFMs* section on the OSC website provides detailed information about the registration process and registrants' ongoing obligations. It includes information about compliance reviews and suggested practices, provides quick links to forms, rules and past reports and e-mail blasts to registrants. It also contains links to previous years' versions of our annual summary reports to registrants.

The *Information for: Investment Funds* section on our website also contains useful information for IFMs, including past editions of The Investment Funds Practitioner published by our Investment Funds and Structured Products Branch.

Registrants may also contact us. Please see Appendix A to this report for the CRR Branch's contact information. The CRR Branch's PM, IFM and dealer teams focus on oversight, policy changes, and exemption applications for their respective registration categories. The Registrant Conduct team supports the PM, IFM, dealer, registration and financial analyst teams in cases of potential registrant misconduct. The financial analysts on the Compliance, Strategy and Risk Analysis team review registrant submissions for financial reporting (such as audited annual financial statements, calculations of excess working capital and subordination agreements). The Registration team focuses on registration and registration-related matters for the PM, IFM and dealer registration categories, among others.

Appendix A — Compliance and Registrant Regulation Branch and contact information for Registrants

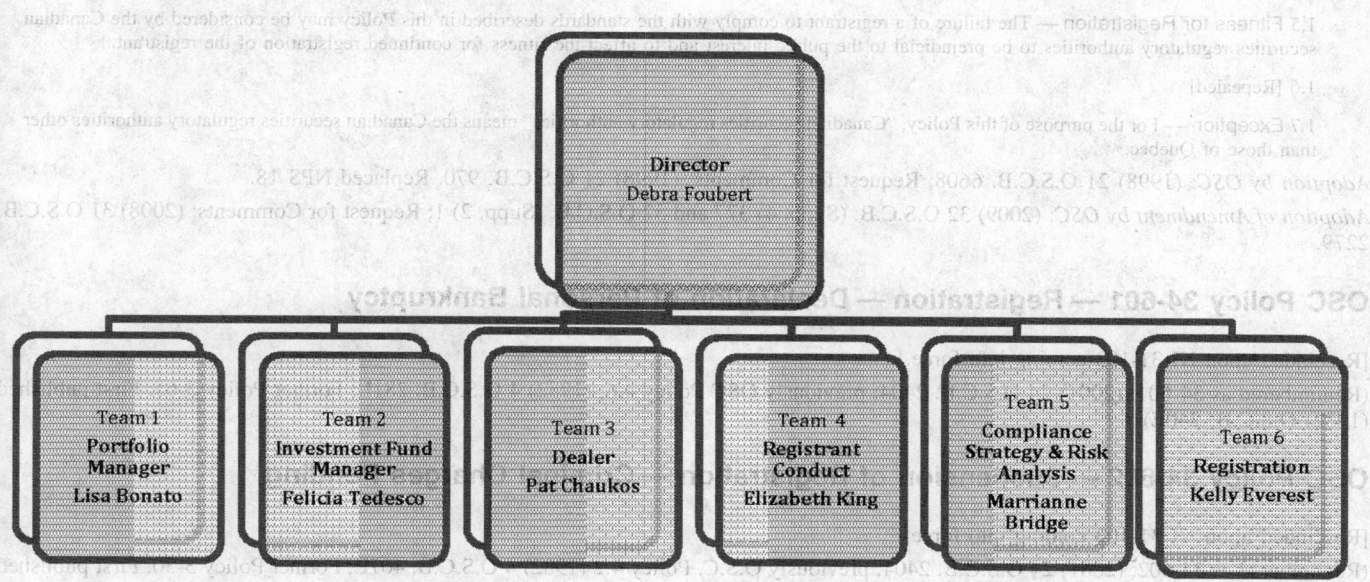

OSC Staff Notice 33-746 — Annual Summary Report for Dealers, Advisers and Investment Fund Managers

Date: September 24, 2015

38 O.S.C.B. 8202

[Not reproduced]

3.4 — Fitness for Registration

National Policy 34-201 — Breach of Requirements of Other Jurisdictions

Date: October 16, 1998

[Rescinded upon NI 31-103 coming into force.]

Adoption by the OSC: (1998) 21 O.S.C.B. 6607; Request for Comments: (1998) 21 O.S.C.B. 968. Replaced NPS 17.

Multilateral Policy 34-202 — Registrants Acting as Corporate Directors

Date: October 16, 1998 as amended effective September 28, 2009

Editor's Note: MPS 34-202 has been adopted in all jurisdictions except Quebec.

1.1 Introduction — The position of a representative of a registrant acting as a director of or adviser to a reporting issuer is one that is fraught with the possibility of a conflict of interest. This arises more particularly in regard to questions of insider information and trading, and timely disclosure.

1.2 Conflicts of Interest — The Canadian securities regulatory authorities emphasize that all registrants should be most conscious of their responsibilities in these situations and weigh the burden of dealing in an ethical manner with the conflicts of interest against the advantages of acting as a director of a reporting issuer, many shareholders of which may be clients of the registrant.

1.3 Disclosure of Information — Every director of a reporting issuer has a fiduciary obligation not to reveal any confidential information to anyone not authorized to receive it. Not until there is full public disclosure of the information, including compliance with applicable Canadian securities legislation, particularly when the information might have a bearing on the market price or value of the securities of the issuer, is a director released from the necessity of keeping information of this character confidential. Any director of a reporting issuer who is a partner, director, officer, employee or agent of a registrant should, in the view of the Canadian securities regulatory authorities, recognize that the director's first responsibility in this area is to the reporting issuer on whose board the director serves. A director should meticulously avoid any disclosure of inside information to partners, directors, officers, employees or agents of the registrant or to its clients.

Part 3:
REGISTRATION

1.4 Acting in Advisory Capacity — If a partner, director, officer, employee or agent of a registrant is not a director but is acting in an advisory capacity to a reporting issuer and discussing confidential matters, the Canadian securities regulatory authorities believe that the same care should be taken as if that person were a director. Should the matter require consultation with other personnel of the registrant, adequate measures should, in the view of the Canadian securities regulatory authorities, be taken to guard the confidential nature of the information to prevent its misuse within or outside the registrant.

1.5 Fitness for Registration — The failure of a registrant to comply with the standards described in this Policy may be considered by the Canadian securities regulatory authorities to be prejudicial to the public interest and to affect the fitness for continued registration of the registrant.

1.6 [Repealed]

1.7 Exception — For the purpose of this Policy, "Canadian securities regulatory authorities" means the Canadian securities regulatory authorities other than those of Quebec.

Adoption by OSC: (1998) 21 O.S.C.B. 6608; Request for Comments: (1998) 21 O.S.C.B. 970. Replaced NPS 18.

Adoption of Amendment by OSC: (2009) 32 O.S.C.B. (Supp. 4) 377 and 32 O.S.C.B. (Supp. 2) 1; Request for Comments: (2008) 31 O.S.C.B. 2279.

OSC Policy 34-601 — Registration — Declaration of Personal Bankruptcy

[Rescinded upon NI 31-103 coming into force.]

(Renumbered as 34-601: (2001) 24 O.S.C.B. 2404; previously OSC Policy 4.6: (1982) 4 O.S.C.B. 281E; Former Policy 3-65: First published (1982) O.S.C.B. 240E)

OSC Policy 34-602 — Suspension of Registration — Criminal Charges Pending

[Rescinded upon NI 31-103 coming into force.]

(Renumbered as 34-602: (2001) 24 O.S.C.B. 2404; previously O.S.C. Policy 4.2 (1982) 4 O.S.C.B. 407E; Former Policy 3-30: First published (1975) O.S.C.B. 1)

OSC Staff Notice 34-701 — Publication of Decisions of the Director on Registration Matters under Part XI of the *Securities Act* (Ontario) ("Opportunities to be Heard")

Date: May 20, 2011

34 O.S.C.B. 5782

The mandate of the Ontario Securities Commission (the **OSC**) is to protect investors from unfair, improper and fraudulent practices, and to foster fair and efficient capital markets and confidence in capital markets. Staff of the OSC is committed to dealing with its stakeholders, including investors, issuers, and securities professionals, in a transparent manner as an effective means of furthering its mandate.

Under Part XI of the *Securities Act* (Ontario) (the **Act**), the Director is responsible for making decisions concerning the registration status of individuals and firms who are required to be registered under the Act (**registrants**). The Director is an administrative official, and is defined in subsection 1(1) of the Act as the Executive Director of the Commission, a Director or Deputy Director of the Commission, or a person employed by the Commission in a position designated by the Executive Director as a Director.

If staff has recommended to the Director that certain regulatory actions be taken with regards to the registration status of a registrant (for example, a suspension of their registration or the imposition of terms and conditions), staff will send the registrant written notice setting out its recommendation. Section 31 of the Act then gives the registrant the right to be heard by the Director before a decision is made concerning staff's recommendation. When a registrant exercises this right, the resulting administrative proceeding is referred to as an "opportunity to be heard", or an "OTBH".

An OTBH may take the form of an exchange of written submissions, or an in-person appearance before the Director. During the OTBH process, whether in writing or in person, staff makes submissions to the Director to support its recommendation, and the registrant has the opportunity to challenge that recommendation by making their own submissions.

The result of an OTBH is a written decision of the Director setting out the facts of the case, the applicable law, the Director's decision, and the reasons for the decision. Director's decisions are published on the OSC's website and in the OSC Bulletin.

The OSC historically only published Director decisions for contested OTBHs. Registrants should be advised that staff will now also publish the following types of Director decisions:

- decisions approving joint recommendations to settle an OTBH where the recommendation is that the registrant be suspended;

- decisions approving joint recommendations to settle an OTBH where the recommendation is that terms and conditions requiring strict supervision be imposed;

- decisions to suspend a registrant where an OTBH has not been requested; and

- decisions to impose terms and conditions requiring strict supervision where an OTBH has not been requested.

Strict supervision requires a registrant's sponsoring firm to pre-approve trades for suitability and to file monthly reports regarding the registrant's business activities with the OSC.

In staff's view, the increased transparency resulting from the publication of decisions of the Director as described above will provide enhanced investor protection since important information regarding registrant conduct will be communicated to the public in a timely manner.

3.5 — Non-Resident Registrants

National Instrument 35-101 — Conditional Exemption from Registration for United States Broker-Dealers and Agents

Date: December 22, 2000

23 O.S.C.B. 8511

Table of Contents

PART 1 — DEFINITIONS

1.1 Definitions — In this Instrument,

"agent" means a partner, officer, director or salesperson of a broker-dealer who is acting on behalf of a broker-dealer in effecting trades of securities;

"broker-dealer" means a "broker" or "dealer", as those terms are defined in the 1934 Act, that has its principal place of business in the United States of America;

"foreign security" means a security

    (a) that is listed for trading or quoted on an exchange or market outside of Canada; or

    (b) of an issuer that is not incorporated, continued or organized under the laws of Canada or a jurisdiction of Canada; and

"NASD" means the National Association of Securities Dealers in the United States of America.

PART 2 — BROKER-DEALER EXEMPTION

2.1 Exemption from Dealer Registration Requirement — The dealer registration requirement does not apply to a broker-dealer if

    (a) the broker-dealer has no office or other physical presence in any jurisdiction in Canada;

    (b) the broker-dealer is trading in a foreign security;

    (c) the trading is with or for

        (i) an individual ordinarily resident in the United States of America who is temporarily resident in the local jurisdiction and with whom the broker-dealer had a broker-dealer client relationship before the individual became temporarily resident in the local jurisdiction; or

        (ii) an individual if the trade is for the individual's tax-advantaged retirement savings plan or with the individual's tax-advantaged retirement savings plan, and

            (i) the plan is located in the United States of America,

            (ii) the individual is a holder of or contributor to the plan, and

            (iii) the individual was previously resident in the United States of America;

    (d) the broker-dealer has not advertised for or solicited new clients in the local jurisdiction;

    (e) the broker-dealer is a member of the NASD;

    (f) the broker-dealer has delivered, or immediately after the broker-dealer first relies on this section delivers, to the securities regulatory authority

        (i) a notice that the broker-dealer is relying on an exemption from the registration requirement provided under this Instrument;

        (ii) a statement of the broker-dealer certifying that the broker-dealer is registered in the state of the United States of America where the broker-dealer was located when the broker-dealer first relied on this section; and

        (iii) an executed Form 35-101F1 Submission to Jurisdiction and Appointment of Agent for Service of Process;

    (g) the broker-dealer has delivered a notice to the securities regulatory authority describing any criminal or quasi-criminal proceeding brought against the broker-dealer or its agents in any jurisdiction or foreign jurisdiction, or of any decision, order, ruling, or other requirement made with respect to or imposed on the broker-dealer or its agents in a jurisdiction or foreign jurisdiction as a result of any administrative, self-regulatory or regulatory action, hearing or proceeding involving fraud, theft, deceit, misrepresentation or similar conduct;

    (h) the broker-dealer has disclosed to the client that the broker-dealer and its agents are not subject to the full regulatory requirements otherwise applicable under local securities legislation; and

    (i) the broker-dealer, in the course of its dealings with clients, acts fairly, honestly and in good faith.

2.2 Termination Notice — A broker-dealer shall immediately notify the securities regulatory authority if the broker-dealer will no longer engage in trading or advising activities under section 2.1.

2.3 Exemption from Adviser Registration Requirement — The adviser registration requirement does not apply to advising activities of the broker-dealer if those activities are solely incidental to trading activities of the broker-dealer under section 2.1.

PART 3 — AGENTS EXEMPTION

3.1 Agents Exemption — The dealer registration requirement does not apply to an agent if

    (a) the trading is on behalf of a broker-dealer that has notified the agent of its intent to rely on the exemption under section 2.1;

    (b) the agent has no office or other physical presence in any jurisdiction in Canada;

    (c) the agent is trading in a foreign security;

    (d) the trading is with or for

        (i) an individual ordinarily resident in the United States of America who is temporarily resident in the local jurisdiction and with whom the broker-dealer on whose behalf the agent is trading had a broker-dealer client relationship before the individual became temporarily resident in the local jurisdiction; or

        (ii) an individual if the trade is for the individual's tax-advantaged retirement savings plan or with the individual's tax-advantaged retirement savings plan, and

            (i) the plan is located in the United States of America,

            (ii) the individual is a holder of or contributor to the plan, and

            (iii) the individual was previously resident in the United States of America;

    (e) the agent has not advertised for or solicited new clients in the local jurisdiction;

    (f) the agent has delivered, or immediately after the agent first relied on this section delivers, to the securities regulatory authority

        (i) a notice that the agent is relying on this Instrument for an exemption from the registration requirement;

        (ii) a statement of the agent certifying that the agent is registered in the state in the United States of America where the agent was located when the agent first relied on this section; and

        (iii) an executed Form 35-101F2 Submission to Jurisdiction and Appointment of Agent for Service of Process;

    (g) the agent has delivered a notice to the securities regulatory authority describing any criminal or quasi-criminal proceeding brought against the agent in any jurisdiction or foreign jurisdiction, or of any decision, order, ruling, or other requirement made with respect to or imposed on the agent in a jurisdiction or foreign jurisdiction as a result of any administrative, self-regulatory or regulatory action, hearing or proceeding involving fraud, theft, deceit, misrepresentation or similar conduct;

    (h) the agent, in the course of its dealings with the broker-dealer's clients, acts fairly, honestly and in good faith.

3.2 Termination Notice — An agent shall immediately notify the securities regulatory authority if the agent will no longer engage in trading or advising activities under section 3.1.

3.3 Exemption from Adviser Registration Requirement — The adviser registration requirement does not apply to advising activities of the agent if those activities are solely incidental to trading activities of the agent under section 3.1.

PART 4 — EXEMPTION FROM PROSPECTUS AND UNDERWRITER REQUIREMENTS

4.1 Exemption from Prospectus and Underwriter Requirements — The prospectus requirement and underwriter registration requirement do not apply to a distribution of foreign securities if that distribution

    (a) is made by a broker-dealer or agent that is exempt from the adviser registration requirement and the dealer registration requirement under section 2.1 or 3.1; and

    (b) is made in compliance with all applicable

        (i) U.S. federal securities laws, and

        (ii) state securities legislation in the United States of America.

PART 5 — EFFECTIVE DATE

5.1 Effective Date — This Instrument comes into force on January 1, 2001.

Final Rule: (2000) 23 O.S.C.B. 8511; Approval by OSC: (2000) 23 O.S.C.B. 7855; Request for Comments: (1997) 20 O.S.C.B. 5325.

Policies and Orders: NPS 35-101CP.

Form 35-101F1 — Form of Submission to Jurisdiction and Appointment of Agent for Service of Process by Broker-Dealer

Instructions: Complete this form for each of the jurisdictions in which the broker-dealer seeks the conditional exemption from registration in National Instrument 35-101 (the "exemption"). Insert the name of the jurisdiction at each "".*

1. Name of broker-dealer (the "Broker-Dealer");

2. Jurisdiction of incorporation of the Broker-Dealer;

3. Name of agent for service of process (the "Agent for Service");

4. Address for service of process on the Agent for Service in *;

5. The Broker-Dealer designates and appoints the Agent for Service at the address stated above as its agent upon whom may be served a notice, pleading, subpoena, summons or other process in any action, investigation or administrative, criminal, quasi-criminal or other proceeding (a "Proceeding") arising out of or relating to or concerning the Broker-Dealer's activities in * under the exemption, and irrevocably waives any right to raise as defence in any such proceeding any alleged lack of jurisdiction to bring such Proceeding.

6. The Broker-Dealer irrevocably and unconditionally submits to the non-exclusive jurisdiction of the judicial, quasi-judicial and administrative tribunals of * and any administrative proceeding in *, in any Proceeding arising out of or related to or concerning the Broker-Dealer's activities in * under the exemption.

7. Until six years after the Broker-Dealer ceases to use the exemption, the Broker-Dealer shall file:

   a. a new Submission to Jurisdiction and Appointment of Agent for Service of Process in this form at least 30 days before termination for any reason of this Submission to Jurisdiction and Appointment of Agent for Service of Process; and

   b. An amended Submission to Jurisdiction and Appointment of Agent for Service of Process at least 30 days before any change in the name or above address of the Agent for Service.

8. This submission to Jurisdiction and Appointment of Agent for Service of Process is governed by and construed in accordance with the laws of *.

Dated: ....

.... (Signature of Broker-Dealer or authorized signatory)

.... (Name and Title of Authorized Signatory)

Acceptance

The undersigned accepts the appointment as agent for service of process on *(Insert name of Broker-Dealer)* under the terms and conditions of the foregoing Submission to Jurisdiction and Appointment of Agent for Service of Process.

Dated: ....

.... (Signature of Agent for Service or authorized signatory)

.... (Name and Title of Authorized Signatory)

Form 35-101F2 — Form of Submission to Jurisdiction and Appointment of Agent for Service of Process by Agents of the Broker-Dealer

Instructions: Complete this form for each of the jurisdictions in which agents of the broker-dealer seek the conditional exemption from registration in National Instrument 35-101 (the "exemption"). Insert the name of the jurisdiction at each "".*

1. Name of the broker-dealer (the "Broker-Dealer");

2. Jurisdiction of incorporation of the Broker-Dealer;

3. Name(s) and address(es) of agent(s) of the Broker-Dealer filing this form (the "Broker-Dealer Agents");

4. Name of agent for service of process (the "Agent for Service");

5. Address for service of process on the Agent for Service in *;

6. Each Broker-Dealer Agent designates and appoints the Agent for Service at the address of the Agent for Service stated above as its agent upon whom may be served a notice, pleading, subpoena, summons or other process in any action, investigation or administrative, criminal, quasi-criminal or other proceeding (a "Proceeding") arising out of or relating to or concerning the Broker-Dealer Agent's activities in * under the exemption, and irrevocably waives any right to raise as a defence in any such proceeding any alleged lack of jurisdiction to bring such Proceeding.

7. Each Broker-Dealer Agent irrevocably and unconditionally submits to the non-exclusive jurisdiction of the judicial, quasi-judicial and administrative tribunals of * and any administrative proceeding in *, in any Proceeding arising out of or related to or concerning the Broker-Dealer Agent's activities in * under the exemption.

8. Until the earlier of (i) the termination of a Broker-Dealer Agent's position as an agent of the Broker-Dealer and six years after the Broker-Dealer ceases to use the exemption, the Broker-Dealer Agent shall file:

   a. new Submission to Jurisdiction and Appointment of Agent for Service of Process in this form at least 30 days prior to termination for any reason of this Submission to Jurisdiction and Appointment of Agent for Service of Process; and

   b. an amended Submission to Jurisdiction and Appointment of Agent for Service of Process at least 30 days before any change in the name or above address of the Agent for Service.

9. This Submission to Jurisdiction and Appointment of Agent for Service of Process is governed by and construed in accordance with the laws of *.

Part 3:
REGISTRATION

Dated: ....

Signature of Broker-Dealer Agent)

Dated: ....

(Signature of Broker-Dealer Agent)

Dated: ....

(Signature of Broker-Dealer Agent)

Dated: ....

(Signature of Broker-Dealer Agent)

Acceptance

The undersigned accepts the appointment as agent for service of process on *(Insert name(s) of Broker-Dealer Agent(s))* pursuant to the terms and conditions of the foregoing Submission to Jurisdiction and Appointment of Agent for Service of Process.

Dated: ....

(Signature of Agent for Service or authorized signatory)

.... (Name and Title of Authorized Signatory)

Companion Policy 35-101CP — Conditional Exemption from Registration for United States Broker-dealers and Agents

Table of Contents

PART 1 — INTRODUCTION

1.1 Introduction — Cross-border trading activities between Canada and the United States of America often take place because of the movement of residents between the two countries. In order to facilitate certain cross-border trading activities that may arise between United States broker-dealers and their existing clients who are now located in Canada, the Canadian securities regulatory authorities have adopted National Instrument 35-101 Conditional Exemption From Registration for United States Broker-Dealers and Agents (the "Instrument") which provides certain broker-dealers, and their agents, resident in the United States of America with a conditional exemption from the applicable registration requirements and the prospectus requirement. This approach is consistent with the Instrument's underlying policy that investors will be relying primarily upon the regulation by securities regulators and statutory liability imposed by legislation in the broker-dealer's or agent's home jurisdiction for protection.

PART 2 — GENERAL PRINCIPLES

2.1 General — The Instrument provides that a United States broker-dealer and its agents may engage in two specific types of cross-border trading activities in foreign securities with an individual who was previously resident in the United States of America, and is now located in Canada, regardless of nationality. In Quebec, the term foreign securities includes futures.

2.2 Temporarily Resident — The first category of activity provided for under clause 2.1(c)(i) and clause 3.1(d)(i) of the Instrument permits brokers-dealers and their agents to deal in foreign securities with an individual ordinarily resident in the United States of America who is temporarily resident in a Canadian jurisdiction and with whom the broker-dealer had a broker-dealer client relationship before the individual became temporarily resident in the Canadian jurisdiction. This aspect of the Instrument is intended to allow persons from the United States who are on a temporary work assignment in Canada, or who may be in Canada on vacation or for other reasons, to trade with their home broker-dealer and agent in the United States of America. The concept of "temporarily" as it appears in the National Instrument is based upon SEC Rule 15a-6 which exempts certain non-United States broker-dealers from registering under the 1934 Act.

The Canadian Securities Administrators are of the view that a person that ceases to be "ordinarily resident" in the United States of America would not retain status as a United States resident "temporarily resident" in Canada under the Instrument.

2.3 Tax-Advantaged Plans — The second category of activity provided for under clause 2.1(c)(ii) and clause 3.1(d)(ii) of the Instrument permits broker-dealers and their agents to deal in foreign securities with an individual who was previously resident in the United States of America and who is resident in a Canadian jurisdiction for trades for and with the individual's tax-advantaged retirement savings plan (for example, an Individual Retirement Account), if the plan is located in the United States and the individual is either a holder of, or contributor to, the plan. Under laws of the United States of America, tax-advantaged retirement savings plans must be located in the United States of America and result in adverse tax consequences for United States individuals if collapsed. For these reasons, individuals are permitted by the Instrument to continue this type of trading activity with a broker-dealer and its agent in the United States of America whether or not there was a pre-existing relationship with the broker-dealer or agent while the individual was in the United States of America.

2.4 Prospectus and Underwriter Exemption — Part 4 of the Instrument exempts a distribution of foreign securities by United States broker-dealers and their agents under the registration exemptions provided for in the Instrument from the prospectus requirement and the underwriter registration requirement. However, the distribution of foreign securities must comply with applicable United States federal securities law and state law requirements in the United States of America, which include securities registration and prospectus delivery.

PART 3 — OPERATION OF EXEMPTIVE RELIEF

3.1 Affiliates — Section 2.1 of the Instrument requires that the broker-dealer have "no office or physical presence in any jurisdiction". A broker-dealer that has a Canadian affiliate in any jurisdiction is still able to take advantage of the exemptions provided for under the Instrument. The Canadian affiliate, however, is not able to take advantage of the exemptions.

3.2 Limitation of Exemptions — Any activity beyond the scope of the exemptions will constitute unregistered activity and will be subject to the applicable enforcement provisions provided for under Canadian securities legislation.

3.3 Retention of Authority — Under Canadian securities legislation, each of the Canadian securities regulatory authorities retains the authority to revoke the exemptions as they apply to a broker-dealer or agent if the broker-dealer's or agent's conduct is considered to be contrary to the public interest.

3.4 Receipt of Documentation — The Canadian securities regulatory authorities will acknowledge receipt of material sent by broker-dealers and agents under the Instrument.

3.5 Fees — No fees will be imposed on broker-dealers or agents by the Canadian securities regulatory authorities under the exemptions provided for under the Instrument.

PART 4 — INQUIRIES REGARDING PAST ACTIVITIES

4.1 Restricted Activities — A Canadian securities regulatory authority will not make inquiries about any possible failure by broker-dealers or their agents to register that rely on the exemption from registration for their

(a) trading activities and related incidental advising activities that may have been conducted with an individual from the United States of America that take place before the date which is 120 days after the coming into effect of the Instrument in the jurisdiction in which the Canadian securities regulatory authority is situate, if the individual

(i) was temporarily resident in the jurisdiction and the broker-dealer or agent had a broker-dealer client relationship with the individual before the individual became temporarily resident in the jurisdiction, or

(ii) if the trades were for or with a tax-advantaged retirement savings plan located in the United States of America and the individual was either the holder of, or contributor to, the plan; and

(b) any other trading and related incidental advising activities that may have been conducted in the jurisdiction before September 1, 1996.

4.2 Other Activities — A Canadian securities regulatory authority may make inquiries if it comes to its attention that a broker-dealer or its agent may have been engaged in improper activities in the jurisdiction in which the Canadian securities regulatory authority is situate beyond failing to register.

Adoption by OSC: (2000) 23 O.S.C.B. 8511 and (2000) 23 O.S.C.B. 7855; Request for Comments: (1997) 20 O.S.C.B. 5325.

OSC Rule 35-502 — Non-Resident Advisers

Date: November 24, 2000, amended effective February 21, 2003, November 5, 2003, September 28, 2009 and January 11, 2015

23 O.S.C.B. 7989; 26 O.S.C.B. 1436; 26 O.S.C.B. 7170; 32 O.S.C.B. (Supp. 4) 389 and 37 O.S.C.B. (Supp. 5)

Table of Contents

Part 3: REGISTRATION

7.11 Disclosure in Offering Documents

PART 8–PART 9 [Repealed]

PART 10 EXEMPTION

    10.1 Exemption

APPENDIX A [Repealed]

APPENDIX B [Repealed]

PART 1 — DEFINITIONS AND INTERPRETATION

1.1 Definitions — In this Rule

"fund" means a mutual fund or a non-redeemable investment fund;

"manager" means the person or company the [sic] directs the business, operations or affairs of a fund;

"NI 31-103" means National Instrument 31-103 Registration Requirements, Exemptions and Ongoing Registrant Obligations;

"portfolio adviser" means a person or company that provides investment advice or portfolio management services under a contract with a fund or with the manager of the fund; and

PARTS 2–6 — [REPEALED]

PART 7 — EXEMPTIONS FROM REGISTRATION

7.1 [Repealed]

7.2 Commodity Pool Programs — The adviser registration requirement does not apply to a person or company, not ordinarily resident in Ontario, that is registered under the *Commodity Futures Act,* in connection with that person or company acting as a portfolio adviser to a mutual fund that is subject to National Instrument 81-104 Commodity Pools or to a non-redeemable investment fund that would be subject to that National Instrument if it were a mutual fund.

7.3 — [Repealed.]

7.4, 7.5 [Repealed]

7.6 Advising Pension Funds of Affiliates — The adviser registration requirement does not apply to a person or company, not ordinarily resident in Ontario, in connection with that person or company acting as an adviser for a pension fund sponsored by an affiliate of the person or company for the benefit of the employees of the affiliate or affiliates of the affiliate.

7.7–7.10 [Repealed]

7.11 Disclosure in Offering Documents — A prospectus filed in Ontario for a fund whose portfolio adviser is relying upon an exemption from the adviser registration requirements provided by this Part or by section 8.26.1 of NI 31-103, or whose portfolio adviser receives investment advice or portfolio management services from a person or company that relies upon an exemption from the adviser registration requirements provided by this Part or by section 8.26.1 of NI 31-103, shall include disclosure that

    (a) if the person or company is advising a registrant in reliance on the exemption in section 8.26.1 of NI 31-103, the registrant or portfolio adviser has responsibility for the investment advice given or portfolio management services provided by the person or company; and

    (b) to the extent applicable, there may be difficulty in enforcing any legal rights against the person or company because it is resident outside Canada and all or a substantial portion of its assets are situated outside Canada.

PARTS 8–9 — [REPEALED]

PART 10 — EXEMPTION

10.1 Exemption — The Director may grant an exemption to this Rule, in whole or in part, subject to such conditions or restrictions as may be imposed in the exemption.

APPENDIX A — [REPEALED]

APPENDIX B — [REPEALED]

Final Rule: (2000) 23 O.S.C.B. 7989; Approval by OSC: (2000) 23 O.S.C.B. 6541; Request for Comments: (2000) 23 O.S.C.B. 4393 and (1998) 21 O.S.C.B. 6258. Replaced ON LPS 4.8.

Amendment to Rule: (2003) O.S.C.B. 1436; Approval by OSC: (2002) O.S.C.B. 8010.

Amendment to Rule: (2003) 26 O.S.C.B. 7170; Approval by OSC: (2003) 26 O.S.C.B. 6149; Request for Comments: (2003) 26 O.S.C.B. 8463.

Amendment to Rule: (2009) 32 O.S.C.B. (Supp. 4) 389; Approval by OSC: (2009) 32 O.S.C.B. (Supp. 2) 1; Request for Comments: (2008) 31 O.S.C.B. 2279.

Amendment to Rule: (2014) 37 O.S.C.B. (Supp. 5) 546

Related Provisions: OSA 19(3), 21.10, 147.

Rules: NI 33-109, 31-103, s. 8.26.

OSC Rule 35-503 — Trades by Certain Members of The Toronto Stock Exchange

Date: September 12, 1997

20 O.S.C.B. 4636

PART 1 — DEFINITIONS

1.1 Definitions — In this Rule

"extra-provincial member" means a person or company that is a member of the TSE and that does not have an office in Ontario;

"remote access trade" means a trade in a security in Ontario executed on the TSE by using a computer terminal that provides access to the trading systems of the TSE from outside of Ontario; and

"TSE" means The Toronto Stock Exchange

PART 2 — REGISTRATION EXEMPTION

2.1 Registration Exemption — Section 25 of the Act does not apply to a remote access trade by an extra-provincial member or by a partner, officer or employee of an extra-provincial member if at the time of the remote access trade

(a) the extra-provincial member is registered with a Canadian securities regulatory authority other than the Commission;

(b) the extra-provincial member has delivered to the Canadian securities regulatory authorities with which the extra-provincial member is registered the financial statements that they then require the extra-provincial member to have delivered;

(c) the extra-provincial member has filed with the SROs of which the extra-provincial member is a member the financial statements that they then require the extra-provincial member to have filed;

(d) the membership of the extra-provincial member in the TSE is not suspended and the extra-provincial member is not being deprived of any of the rights and privileges of membership by the TSE;

(e) the partner, officer or employee of the extra-provincial member effecfing the trade is registered with a Canadian securities regulatory authority with which the extra-provincial member is then registered; and

(f) the only residents of Ontario with whom the extra-provincial member and the partners, officers or employees of the extra-provincial member trade are partners, officers or employees of members of the TSE who are registered under the Act.

Final Rule: (1997) 20 O.S.C.B. 4636; Approval by OSC: (1997) 20 O.S.C.B. 3361; Request for Comments: (1996) 19 O.S.C.B. 4775; Replaced a rule which was originally a blanket ruling (1987) 10 O.S.C.B. 5936 which was deemed to be a rule under s. 143.1(1) of the Act and remade into a rule entitled *In the Matter of Certain Members of the Toronto Stock Exchange* (1997) 20 O.S.C.B. 1220.

OSC Policy 35-601 — Registration of Non-Resident Salesmen, Partners or Officers of Registered Dealers

[Rescinded upon NI 31-103 coming into force.]

(Renumbered as 35-601: (2003) 26 O.S.C.B. 2318; previously OSC Policy 4.7: (1982) 4 O.S.C.B. 417E (Former Policy 3-66: First published (1982) 4 O.S.C.B. 281E))

OSC Notice 35-704 — (Commodity Futures Act) — Non-Resident Advisers

Date: July 5, 2012

35 O.S.C.B. 6263

[Not reproduced]

PART IV — DISTRIBUTION REQUIREMENTS

4.1 — Prospectus Contents — Non-Financial Matters

National Instrument 41-101 — General Prospectus Requirements

Date: December 15, 2000; replaced effective March 17, 2008 and amended effective September 8, 2008, June 30, 2010, December 30, 2010, January 1, 2011, May 6, 2011, April 20, 2012, April 30, 2012, May 14, 2013, May 31, 2013 August 13, 2013, January 1, 2014 (Form 41-101F2 only), September 22, 2014, September 30, 2014, June 30, 2015, November 17, 2015 and December 8, 2015.

23 O.S.C.B. 761; 31 O.S.C.B. (Supp. 2) 1, 31 O.S.C.B. 8571, 33 O.S.C.B. 5587, 33 O.S.C.B. 9503, 33 O.S.C.B. (Supp. 5) 81, 34 O.S.C.B. 5171, 35 O.S.C.B. 2383, 35 O.S.C.B. 3431, 36 O.S.C.B. 4884, 36 O.S.C.B. 4817, 36 O.S.C.B. 2619, 36 O.S.C.B. 7977, 36 O.S.C.B. 9612, 37 O.S.C.B. (Supp. 4), 37 O.S.C.B. 6753, 38 O.S.C.B. 3379, 38 O.S.C.B. 7551, 38 O.S.C.B. 8314 and 38 O.S.C.B. 9327.

Table of Contents

Part 4:
DISTRIBUTIONS

PART 1 — DEFINITIONS AND INTERPRETATIONS

1.1 Definitions — In this Instrument:

"accredited investor" has the same meaning as in section 1.1 of NI 45-106

"acquisition" has the same meaning as in Part 8 of NI 51-102;

"acquisition date" has the same meaning as in section 1.1 of NI 51-102;

"acquisition of related businesses" has the same meaning as in Part 8 of NI 51-102;

"Aequitas personal information form" means a personal information form for an individual prepared pursuant to Aequitas NEO Exchange Inc. Form 3, as amended from time to time;

"alternative credit support" has the same meaning as in section 13.4 of NI 51-102;

"asset-backed security" has the same meaning as in section 1.1 of NI 51-102;

"base offering" means the number or principal amount of the securities distributed under a prospectus by an issuer or selling securityholder, excluding

    (a) any over-allotment option granted in connection with the distribution, or the securities issuable on the exercise of any such over-allotment option, and

    (b) securities issued or paid as compensation to a person or company for acting as an underwriter in respect of securities that are distributed under the prospectus, on an "as-if-converted" basis if these securities include securities that are convertible or exchangeable securities;

"board of directors" has the same meaning as in section 1.1 of NI 51-102;

"business acquisition report" has the same meaning as in section 1.1 of NI 51-102;

"business day" means any day other than a Saturday, a Sunday or a statutory holiday;

"class" has the same meaning as in section 1.1 of NI 51-102;

"credit supporter" has the same meaning as in section 13.4 of NI 51-102;

"custodian" means the institution appointed by an investment fund to act as custodian of the portfolio assets of the investment fund;

"date of transition to IFRS" has the same meaning as in section 1.1 of NI 51-102;

"derivative" means an instrument, agreement or security, the market price, value or payment obligation of which is derived from, referenced to, or based on an underlying interest;

"designated foreign jurisdiction" has the same meaning as in section 1.1 of NI 52-107;

"designated rating organization" has the same meaning as in section 1.1 of NI 51-102;

"DRO affiliate" has the same meaning as in section 1 of NI 25-101;

"equity investee" has the same meaning as in section 1.1 of NI 51-102;

"equity security" means a security of an issuer that carries a residual right to participate in the earnings of the issuer and, on the liquidation or winding up of the issuer, in its assets;

"executive officer" means, for an issuer or an investment fund manager, an individual who is

    (a) a chair, vice-chair or president,

    (a.1) a chief executive officer or chief financial officer,

    (b) a vice-president in charge of a principal business unit, division or function including sales, finance or production, or

    (c) performing a policy-making function in respect of the issuer or investment fund manager;

"final prospectus notice" means,

    (a) in British Columbia, New Brunswick, Newfoundland and Labrador, Nova Scotia, Ontario and Saskatchewan, a written communication relating to a final prospectus if that communication is permitted by a provision in securities legislation listed opposite the jurisdiction in Appendix E, or

    (b) in every other jurisdiction of Canada, a written communication relating to a final prospectus that only

        (i) identifies the security proposed to be issued,

        (ii) states the price of the security, and

        (iii) states the name and address of a person or company from whom purchases of the security may be made and from whom a final prospectus may be obtained;

"financial statements" includes interim financial reports;

"first IFRS financial statements" has the same meaning as in section 1.1 of NI 51-102;

"foreign disclosure requirements" has the same meaning as in section 1.1 of NI 52-107;

"Form 41-101F1" means Form 41-101F1 *Information Required in a Prospectus* of this Instrument;

"Form 41-101F2" means Form 41-101F2 *Information Required in an Investment Fund Prospectus* of this Instrument;

"Form 41-101F3" means Form 41-101F3 *Information Required in a Scholarship Plan Prospectus* of this Instrument;

"Form 44-101F1" means Form 44-101F1 *Short Form Prospectus* of NI 44-101;

"Form 51-101F1" means Form 51-101F1 *Statement of Reserves Data and Other Oil and Gas Information* of NI 51-101;

"Form 51-101F2" means Form 51-101F2 *Report on Reserves Data by Independent Qualified Reserves Evaluator or Auditor* of NI 51-101;

"Form 51-101F3" means Form 51-101F3 *Report of Management and Directors on Oil and Gas Disclosure* of NI 51-101;

"Form 51-102F1" means Form 51-102F1 *Management's Discussion & Analysis* of NI 51-102;

"Form 51-102F2" means Form 51-102F2 *Annual Information Form* of NI 51-102;

"Form 51-102F4" means Form 51-102F4 *Business Acquisition Report* of NI 51-102;

"Form 51-102F5" means Form 51-102F5 *Information Circular* of NI 51-102;

"Form 51-102F6" means Form 51-102F6 *Statement of Executive Compensation* of NI 51-102;

"Form 51-102F6V" means Form 51-102F6V *Statement of Executive Compensation – Venture Issuers* of NI 51-102;

"Form 52-110F1" means Form 52-110F1 *Audit Committee Information Required in an AIF* of NI 52-110;

"Form 52-110F2" means Form 52-110F2 *Disclosure by Venture Issuers* of NI 52-110;

"Form 58-101F1" means Form 58-101F1 *Corporate Governance Disclosure* of NI 58-101;

"Form 58-101F2" means Form 58-101F2 *Corporate Governance Disclosure (Venture Issuers)* of NI 58-101;

"full and unconditional credit support" means

    (a) alternative credit support that

        (i) entitles the holder of the securities to receive payment from the credit supporter, or enables the holder to receive payment from the issuer, within 15 days of any failure by the issuer to make a payment, and

        (ii) results in the securities receiving the same credit rating as, or a higher credit rating than, the credit rating they would have received if payment had been fully and unconditionally guaranteed by the credit supporter, or would result in the securities receiving such a rating if they were rated, or

    (b) a full and unconditional guarantee of the payments to be made, as interpreted in section 1.5, by the issuer of securities, as stipulated in the terms of the securities or in an agreement governing rights of holders of the securities, that results in the holder of such securities being entitled to receive payment from the credit supporter within 15 days of any failure by the issuer to make a payment;

"independent review committee" means an independent review committee under NI 81-107;

"information circular" has the same meaning as in section 1.1 of NI 51-102;

"interim period" has the same meaning as in

    (a) section 1.1 of NI 51-102 for an issuer other than an investment fund, or

    (b) section 1.1 of NI 81-106 for an investment fund;

"investment dealer" has the same meaning as in section 1.1 of National Instrument 31-103 *Registration Requirements, Exemptions and Ongoing Registrant Obligations*;

"IPO venture issuer" means an issuer that

    (a) files a long form prospectus,

    (b) is not a reporting issuer in any jurisdiction immediately before the date of the final long form prospectus, and

    (c) at the date of the long form prospectus, does not have any of its securities listed or quoted, has not applied to list or quote any of its securities, and does not intend to apply to list or quote any of its securities, on

        (i) the Toronto Stock Exchange,

        (i.1) Aequitas NEO Exchange Inc.,

        (ii) a U.S. marketplace, or

        (iii) a marketplace outside of Canada and the United States of America, other than the Alternative Investment Market of the London Stock Exchange or the PLUS markets operated by PLUS Markets Group plc;

"issuer's GAAP" has the same meaning as in section 1.1 of NI 52-107;

"junior issuer" means an issuer

    (a) that files a preliminary prospectus,

    (b) that is not a reporting issuer in any jurisdiction,

    (c) whose total consolidated assets as at the date of the most recent statement of financial position of the issuer included in the preliminary prospectus are less than $10,000,000,

    (d) whose consolidated revenue as shown in the most recent annual statement of comprehensive income of the issuer included in the preliminary prospectus is less than $10,000,000, and

    (e) whose equity as at the date of the most recent statement of financial position of the issuer included in the preliminary prospectus is less than $10,000,000,

taking into account all adjustments to asset, revenue and equity calculations necessary to reflect each significant proposed acquisition of a business or related business by an issuer that has progressed to a state where a reasonable person would believe that the likelihood of the issuer completing the acquisition is high, and each completed significant acquisition of a business or related business that was completed,

    (f) for paragraphs (c) and (e), before the date of the preliminary prospectus and after the date of the issuer's most recent statement of financial position included in the preliminary prospectus as if each acquisition had taken place as at the date of the issuer's most recent statement of financial position included in the preliminary prospectus, and

    (g) for paragraph (d), after the last day of the most recent annual statement of comprehensive income of the issuer included in the preliminary prospectus as if each acquisition had taken place at the beginning of the issuer's most recently completed financial year for which a statement of comprehensive income is included in the preliminary prospectus;

"labour sponsored or venture capital fund" has the same meaning as in section 1.1 of NI 81-106;

"lead underwriter" means, in respect of a syndicate of underwriters,

    (a) the underwriter designated under the underwriting agreement to act as the manager of the syndicate, or

    (b) if more than one underwriter is designated under the underwriting agreement to act as a manager of the syndicate, the underwriter designated under the agreement to have primary decision-making authority;

"limited-use version" means a template version in which the spaces for information have been completed in accordance with any of the following:

    (a) subsection 13.7(2) or 13.8(2);

    (b) subsection 7.6(2) of NI 44-101;

    (c) subsection 9A.3(2) of NI 44-102;

    (d) subsection 4A.3(3) of NI 44-103;

"long form prospectus" means a prospectus filed in the form of Form 41-101F1, Form 41-101F2 or Form 41-101F3;

"marketing materials" means a written communication intended for potential investors regarding a distribution of securities under a prospectus that contains material facts relating to an issuer, securities or an offering but does not include the following:

    (a) a prospectus or any amendment;

    (b) a standard term sheet;

    (c) a preliminary prospectus notice;

    (d) a final prospectus notice;

"marketplace" has the same meaning as in section 1.1 of NI 51-102;

"material contract" means any contract that an issuer or any of its subsidiaries is a party to, that is material to the issuer;

"mineral project" has the same meaning as in section 1.1 of NI 43-101;

"NI 14-101" means National Instrument 14-101 *Definitions*;

"NI 25-101" means National Instrument 25-101 *Designated Rating Organizations*;

"NI 33-105" means National Instrument 33-105 *Underwriting Conflicts*;

"NI 43-101" means National Instrument 43-101 *Standards of Disclosure for Mineral Projects*;

"NI 44-101" means National Instrument 44-101 *Short Form Prospectus Distributions*;

"NI 44-102" means National Instrument 44-102 *Shelf Distributions*;

"NI 44-103" means National Instrument 44-103 *Post-Receipt Pricing*;

"NI 45-106" means National Instrument 45-106 *Prospectus Exemptions*;

"NI 51-101" means National Instrument 51-101 *Standards of Disclosure for Oil and Gas Activities*;

"NI 51-102" means National Instrument 51-102 *Continuous Disclosure Obligations*;

"NI 52-107" means National Instrument 52-107 *Acceptable Accounting Principles and Auditing Standards*;

"NI 52-110" means National Instrument 52-110 *Audit Committees*;

"NI 58-101" means National Instrument 58-101 *Disclosure of Corporate Governance Practices*;

"NI 81-101" means National Instrument 81-101 *Mutual Fund Prospectus Disclosure*;

"NI 81-102" means National Instrument 81-102 *Investment Funds*;

"NI 81-106" means National Instrument 81-106 *Investment Fund Continuous Disclosure*;

"NI 81-107" means National Instrument 81-107 *Independent Review Committee for Investment Funds*;

"non-voting security" means a restricted security that does not carry the right to vote generally, except for a right to vote that is mandated, in special circumstances, by law;

"old financial year" means the financial year of an issuer that immediately precedes a transition year;

"over-allocation position" means the amount, determined as at the closing of a distribution, by which the aggregate number or principal amount of securities that are sold by one or more underwriters of the distribution exceeds the base offering;

"over-allotment option" means a right granted to one or more underwriters by an issuer or a selling securityholder of the issuer in connection with the distribution of securities under a prospectus to acquire, for the purposes of covering the underwriter's over-allocation position, a security of an issuer that has the same designation and attributes as a security that is distributed under such prospectus, and which

    (a) expires not later than the 60th day after the date of the closing of the distribution, and

    (b) is exercisable for a number or principal amount of securities that is limited to the lesser of

        (i) the over-allocation position, and

        (ii) 15% of the base offering;

"personal information form" means,

    (a) a completed Schedule 1 of Appendix A, or

    (b) a completed TSX/TSXV personal information form submitted by an individual to the Toronto Stock Exchange or to the TSX Venture Exchange to which is attached a completed certificate and consent in the form set out in Schedule 1 — Part B of Appendix A;

    (c) a completed Aequitas personal information form submitted by an individual to Aequitas NEO Exchange Inc., to which is attached a completed certificate and consent in the form set out in Schedule 1 – Part B of Appendix A;

"plan summary" means a document prepared in accordance with the requirements of Part A of Form 41-101F3;

"predecessor personal information form" means,

    (a) a completed Schedule 1 of Appendix A in the form that was in effect from March 17, 2008 until May 14, 2013, or

    (b) a completed TSX/TSXV personal information form to which is attached a completed certificate and consent in the form that was in effect from March 17, 2008 until May 14, 2013;

"preliminary prospectus notice" means,

    (a) in a jurisdiction other than Québec, a communication relating to a preliminary prospectus if that communication is permitted by a provision in securities legislation listed opposite the jurisdiction in Appendix D, or

    (b) in Québec, a written communication relating to a preliminary prospectus that only

        (i) identifies the security proposed to be issued,

        (ii) states the price of the security, if determined, and

        (iii) states the name and address of a person or company from whom purchases of the security may be made and from whom a preliminary prospectus may be obtained;

"principal securityholder" means a person or company who beneficially owns, or controls or directs, directly or indirectly, voting securities carrying 10% or more of the voting rights attached to any class of voting securities of the issuer;

"private issuer" has the same meaning as in section 2.4 of NI 45-106;

"profit or loss attributable to owners of the parent" has the same meaning as in Canadian GAAP applicable to publicly accountable enterprises;

"profit or loss from continuing operations attributable to owners of the parent" has the same meaning as in Canadian GAAP applicable to publicly accountable enterprises;

"publicly accountable enterprise" has the same meaning as in Part 3 of NI 52-107;

"related credit supporter" of an issuer means a credit supporter of the issuer that is an affiliate of the issuer;

"restricted security" means an equity security that is not a preferred security of an issuer if any of the following apply:

    (a) there is another class of securities of the issuer that carries a greater number of votes per security relative to the equity security,

    (b) the conditions attached to the class of equity securities, the conditions attached to another class of securities of the issuer, or the issuer's constating documents have provisions that nullify or significantly restrict the voting rights of the equity securities,

    (c) the issuer has issued another class of equity securities that entitle the owners of securities of that other class to participate in the earnings or assets of the issuer to a greater extent, on a per security basis, than the owners of the first class of equity securities, or

(d) except in Ontario and British Columbia, the regulator determines that the equity security is a restricted security;

"restricted security reorganization" means any event resulting in the creation of restricted securities, directly or through the creation of subject securities or securities that are, directly or indirectly, convertible, or exercisable or exchangeable for, restricted securities or subject securities or any change in the rights attaching to restricted securities, subject securities or securities that are, directly or indirectly, convertible into, or exercisable or exchangeable for, restricted securities or subject securities, including

    (a) any

        (i) amendment to an issuer's constating documents,

        (ii) resolution of the board of directors of an issuer setting the terms of a series of securities of the issuer, or

        (iii) restructuring, recapitalization, reclassification, arrangement, amalgamation or merger, or

    (b) if the issuer has one or more classes of restricted securities outstanding, an amendment to an issuer's constating documents to increase

        (i) the per security voting rights attached to any class of securities without at the same time making a proportionate increase in the per security voting rights attached to any other securities of the issuer, or

        (ii) the number of a class of securities authorized, other than a restricted security;

"restricted security term" means each of the terms "non-voting security", "subordinate voting security", and "restricted voting security";

"restricted voting security" means a restricted security that carries a right to vote subject to a restriction on the number or percentage of securities that may be voted or owned by one or more persons or companies, unless the restriction is

    (a) permitted or prescribed by statute or regulation, and

    (b) is applicable only to persons or companies that are not citizens or residents of Canada or that are otherwise considered as a result of any law applicable to the issuer to be non-Canadians;

"restructuring transaction" has the same meaning as in section 1.1 of NI 51-102;

"retrospective" has the same meaning as in section 1.1 of NI 51-102;

"retrospectively" has the same meaning as in section 1.1 of NI 51-102;

"reverse takeover" has the same meaning as in section 1.1 of NI 51-102;

"reverse takeover acquirer" has the same meaning as in section 1.1 of NI 51-102;

"road show" means a presentation to potential investors, regarding a distribution of securities under a prospectus, conducted by one or more investment dealers on behalf of an issuer in which one or more executive officers, or other representatives, of the issuer participate;

"SEC issuer" has the same meaning as in section 1.1 of NI 52-107;

"short form prospectus" means a prospectus filed in the form of Form 44-101F1;

"special warrant" means a security that, by its terms or the terms of an accompanying contractual obligation,

    (a) entitles or requires the holder to acquire another security without payment of material additional consideration and obliges the issuer of either security to undertake efforts to file a prospectus to qualify the distribution of the other security, or

    (b) entitles or requires the holder to acquire another security without payment of material additional consideration and the issuer files a prospectus to qualify the distribution of the other security;

"standard term sheet" means a written communication intended for potential investors regarding a distribution of securities under a prospectus that contains no information other than that referred to in subsections 13.5(2) and (3), subsections 13.6(2) and (3), subsections 7.5(2) and (3) of NI 44-101, subsections 9A.2(2) and (3) of NI 44-102 or subsections 4A.2(2) and (3) of NI 44-103, relating to an issuer, securities or an offering, but does not include the following:

    (a) a preliminary prospectus notice;

    (b) a final prospectus notice;

"subject security" means a security that results, or would result if and when issued, in an existing class of securities being considered restricted securities;

"subordinate voting security" means a restricted security that carries a right to vote, if there are securities of another class outstanding that carry a greater right to vote on a per security basis;

"template version" means a version of a document with spaces for information to be added in accordance with any of the following:

    (a) subsection 13.7(2) or 13.8(2);

    (b) subsection 7.6(2) of NI 44-101;

    (c) subsection 9A.3(2) of NI 44-102;

    (d) subsection 4A.3(3) of NI 44-103;

"transition year" means the financial year of an issuer or business in which the issuer or business changes its financial year-end;

"TSX/TSXV personal information form" means a personal information form for an individual pursuant to Toronto Stock Exchange Form 4 or TSX Venture Exchange Form 2A, each as amended from time to time;

"U.S. AICPA GAAS" has the same meaning as in section 1.1 of NI 52-107;

"U.S. GAAP" has the same meaning as in section 1.1 of NI 52-107;

"U.S. marketplace" has the same meaning as in section 1.1 of NI 51-102;

"U.S. PCAOB GAAS" has the same meaning as in section 1.1 of NI 52-107;

"venture issuer" has the same meaning as in section 1.1 of NI 51-102 except the "applicable time" is the date the prospectus is filed;

"waiting period" means the period of time between the issuance of a receipt by the regulator for a preliminary prospectus and the issuance of a receipt by the regulator for a final prospectus.

1.2 Interpretation of "prospectus", "preliminary prospectus", "final prospectus", "long form prospectus", and "short form prospectus" — (1) In this Instrument, a reference to a "prospectus" includes a preliminary long form prospectus, a final long form prospectus, a preliminary short form prospectus, and a final short form prospectus.

(2) In this Instrument, a reference to a "preliminary prospectus" includes a preliminary long form prospectus and a preliminary short form prospectus.

(3) In this Instrument, a reference to a "final prospectus" includes a final long form prospectus and a final short form prospectus.

(4) In this Instrument, a reference to a "long form prospectus" includes a preliminary long form prospectus and a final long form prospectus.

(5) In this Instrument, a reference to a "short form prospectus" includes a preliminary short form prospectus and a final short form prospectus.

(6) Despite subsections (1), (2), and (3), in Form 41-101F1, Form 41-101F2 and Form 41-101F3,

    (a) a reference to a "prospectus" only includes a preliminary long form prospectus and a final long form prospectus,

    (b) a reference to a "preliminary prospectus" only includes a preliminary long form prospectus, and

    (c) a reference to a "final prospectus" only includes a final long form prospectus.

1.3 Interpretation of "business" — In this Instrument, unless otherwise stated, a reference to a business includes an interest in an oil and gas property to which reserves, as defined in NI 51-101, have been specifically attributed.

1.4 Interpretation of "affiliate" — In this Instrument, an issuer is an affiliate of another issuer if the issuer would be an affiliate of the other issuer under subsection 1.1(2) of NI 51-102.

1.5 Interpretation of "payments to be made" — For the purposes of the definition of "full and unconditional credit support", payments to be made by an issuer of securities as stipulated in the terms of the securities include

    (a) any amounts to be paid as dividends in accordance with, and on the dividend payment dates stipulated in, the provisions of the securities, whether or not the dividends have been declared, and

    (b) any discretionary dividends, provided that the terms of the securities or an agreement governing rights of holders of the securities expressly provides that the holder of the securities will be entitled, once the discretionary dividend is declared, to receive payment from the credit supporter within 15 days of any failure by the issuer to pay the declared dividend.

PART 2 — REQUIREMENTS FOR ALL PROSPECTUS DISTRIBUTIONS

2.1 Application of the Instrument — (1) Subject to subsection (2), this Instrument applies to a prospectus filed under securities legislation and a distribution of securities subject to the prospectus requirement.

(2) This Instrument does not apply to a prospectus filed under NI 81-101 or a distribution of securities under such a prospectus.

2.2 Language — (1) An issuer must file a prospectus and any other document required to be filed under this Instrument or NI 44-101 in French or in English.

(2) In Québec, a prospectus and any document required to be incorporated by reference into a prospectus must be in French or in French and English.

(3) Despite subsection (1), if an issuer files a document only in French or only in English but delivers to an investor or prospective investor a version of the document in the other language, the issuer must file that other version not later than when it is first delivered to the investor or prospective investor.

(4) If an issuer files a document under this Instrument that is a translation of a document prepared in a language other than French or English, the issuer must

    (a) attach a certificate as to the accuracy of the translation to the filed document, and

    (b) make a copy of the document in the original language available on request.

2.3 General requirements — (1) An issuer must not file its first amendment to a preliminary prospectus more than 90 days after the date of the receipt for the preliminary prospectus that relates to the final prospectus.

(1.1) An issuer must not file a final prospectus more than 90 days after the date of the receipt for the preliminary prospectus or an amendment to the preliminary prospectus which relates to the final prospectus.

(1.2) If an issuer files an amendment to a preliminary prospectus, the final prospectus must be filed within 180 days from the date of the receipt of the preliminary prospectus.

(2) An issuer must not file

    (a) a prospectus more than three business days after the date of the prospectus, and

    (b) an amendment to a prospectus more than three business days after the date of the amendment to the prospectus.

2.4 Special warrants — (1) An issuer must not file a prospectus or an amendment to a prospectus to qualify the distribution of securities issued upon the exercise of special warrants or other securities acquired on a prospectus-exempt basis unless holders of the special warrants or other securities have been provided with a contractual right of rescission.

(2) A contractual right of rescission under subsection (1) must provide that, if a holder of a special warrant who acquires another security of the issuer on exercise of the special warrant as provided for in the prospectus is, or becomes, entitled under the securities legislation of a jurisdiction to the remedy of rescission because of the prospectus or an amendment to the prospectus containing a misrepresentation,

    (a) the holder is entitled to rescission of both the holder's exercise of its special warrant and the private placement transaction under which the special warrant was initially acquired,

    (b) the holder is entitled in connection with the rescission to a full refund of all consideration paid to the underwriter or issuer, as the case may be, on the acquisition of the special warrant, and

    (c) if the holder is a permitted assignee of the interest of the original special warrant subscriber, the holder is entitled to exercise the rights of rescission and refund as if the holder was the original subscriber.

PART 3 — FORM OF PROSPECTUS

3.1 Form of prospectus — (1) Subject to subsection (2), (2.1) and (3), an issuer filing a prospectus must file the prospectus in the form of Form 41-101F1.

(2) An issuer that is an investment fund, other than a scholarship plan, filing a prospectus must file the prospectus in the form of Form 41-101F2.

(2.1) An issuer that is a scholarship plan filing a prospectus must file the prospectus in the form of Form 41-101F3.

(3) An issuer that is qualified to file a short form prospectus may file a short form prospectus.

PART 3A — SCHOLARSHIP PLAN PROSPECTUS REQUIREMENTS

3A.1 Plain language and presentation — (1) A scholarship plan prospectus must be prepared using plain language and in a format that assists in readability and comprehension.

(2) A scholarship plan prospectus must

    (a) present all information briefly and concisely,

    (b) present the items listed in Parts A to D of Form 41-101F3 in the order set out in those parts,

    (c) use only the headings and sub-headings prescribed by Form 41-101F3 unless stated otherwise,

    (d) contain only information that is specifically mandated or permitted by Form 41-101F3, and

    (e) not incorporate by reference into the scholarship plan prospectus, information that is required to be included in a scholarship plan prospectus.

(3) A plan summary must

    (a) be prepared for each scholarship plan offered under a scholarship plan prospectus or multiple scholarship plan prospectus, and

    (b) not exceed 4 pages in length.

3A.2 Combinations of documents — (1) Subject to subsection (2), a scholarship plan prospectus may be consolidated with one or more scholarship plan prospectuses to a form a multiple scholarship plan prospectus.

(2) A scholarship plan prospectus must not be consolidated with one or more scholarship plan prospectuses to form a multiple scholarship plan prospectus unless the portions of each scholarship plan prospectus prepared in accordance with the requirements of Parts B and D of Form 41-101F3 are substantially similar.

3A.3 Order of contents of bound documents — If documents are attached to, or bound with, a scholarship plan prospectus or multiple scholarship plan prospectus

    (a) the scholarship plan prospectus or multiple scholarship plan prospectus must be the first document contained in the package, and

    (b) no pages must come before the scholarship plan prospectus or multiple scholarship plan prospectus other than, at the option of the scholarship plan, a general front cover and table of contents pertaining to the entire package.

3A.4 Plan summary — (1) Despite section 3A.3, a plan summary must not be attached to, or bound with, any other part of a scholarship plan prospectus, or to any other document, except as provided in this section.

(2) A plan summary of a scholarship plan may be attached to or bound with one or more plan summaries of other scholarship plans if the binding, to a reasonable person, would help present the information in a simple, accessible and comparable format.

3A.5 Documents to be delivered or sent upon request — (1) On request by a person or company, a scholarship plan must deliver or send a copy of one or more the following documents free of charge to the person or company:

    (a) the scholarship plan prospectus or multiple scholarship plan prospectus;

    (b) any document incorporated by reference into the scholarship plan prospectus;

    (c) any portion of a document described in paragraph (a) or (b).

(2) A document requested under subsection (1) must be delivered or sent within 3 business days of receipt of the request.

PART 4 — FINANCIAL STATEMENTS AND RELATED DOCUMENTS IN A LONG FORM PROSPECTUS

4.1 Application — (1) An issuer, other than an investment fund, that files a long form prospectus must include in the long form prospectus the financial statements and the management's discussion and analysis required by this Instrument.

(2) Subject to Part 15, an investment fund that files a long form prospectus must include in the long form prospectus the financial statements and the management reports of fund performance required by this Instrument.

(3) For the purposes of this Part, "*financial statements*" do not include pro forma financial statements.

4.2 Audit of financial statements — (1) Any financial statements included in a long form prospectus filed in the form of Form 41-101F1 must be audited in accordance with NI 52-107 unless an exception in section 32.5 or subsection 35.1(3) of Form 41-101F1 applies.

(2) Any financial statements, other than an interim financial report, included in or incorporated by reference into a long form prospectus of an investment fund filed in the form of Form of 41-101F2 or Form 41-101F3 must meet the audit requirements of Part 2 of NI 81-106.

4.3 Review of unaudited financial statements — (1) Subject to subsection (2) and (3), any unaudited financial statements included in, or incorporated by reference into, a long form prospectus must have been reviewed in accordance with the relevant standards set out in the Handbook for a review of financial statements by the person or company's auditor or a review of financial statements by a public accountant.

(2) Subsection (1) does not apply to an investment fund's unaudited financial statements filed after the date of filing of the prospectus that are incorporated by reference into the prospectus under Part 15.

(3) If NI 52-107 permits the financial statements of the person or company in subsection (1) to be audited in accordance with

(a) U.S. AICPA GAAS, the unaudited financial statements may be reviewed in accordance with the review standards issued by the American Institute of Certified Public Accountants,

(a.1) U.S. PCAOB GAAS, the unaudited financial statements may be reviewed in accordance with the review standards issued by the Public Company Accounting Oversight Board (United States of America),

(b) International Standards on Auditing, the unaudited financial statements may be reviewed in accordance with International Standards on Review Engagement issued by the International Auditing and Assurance Standards Board, or

(c) auditing standards that meet the foreign disclosure requirements of the designated foreign jurisdiction to which the person or company is subject, the unaudited financial statements

(i) may be reviewed in accordance with review standards that meet the foreign disclosure requirements of the designated foreign jurisdiction, or

(ii) do not have to be reviewed if

(A) the designated foreign jurisdiction does not have review standards for unaudited financial statements, and

(B) the long form prospectus includes disclosure that the unaudited financial statements have not been reviewed.

4.4 Approval of financial statements and related documents — (1) An issuer must not file a long form prospectus unless each financial statement, each management's discussion and analysis, and each management report of fund performance, as applicable, of a person or company included in, or incorporated by reference into, the long form prospectus has been approved by the board of directors of the person or company.

(2) An investment fund that is a trust must not file a long form prospectus unless each financial statement and each management report of fund performance of the investment fund included in, or incorporated by reference into, the long form prospectus has been approved by the trustee or trustees of the investment fund or another person or company authorized to do so by the constating documents of the investment fund.

PART 5 — CERTIFICATES

5.1 Interpretation — For the purposes of this Part,

(a) "issuer certificate form" means a certificate in the form set out in

(i) section 37.2 of Form 41-101F1,

(ii) section 39.1 of Form 41-101F2,

(ii.1) section 9.1 of Part D of Form 41-101F3,

(iii) section 21.2 of Form 44-101F1,

(iv) NI 44-102 in

(A) section 1.1 of Appendix A,

(B) section 2.1 of Appendix A,

(C) section 1.1 of Appendix B, or

(D) section 2.1 of Appendix B, or

(v) NI 44-103 in

(A) paragraph 7 of subsection 3.2(1), or

(B) paragraph 3 of subsection 4.5(2), and

(b) "underwriter certificate form" means a certificate in the form set out in

(i) section 37.3 of Form 41-101F1,

(ii) section 39.3 of Form 41-101F2,

(ii.1) section 9.3 of Part D of Form 41-101F3,

(iii) section 21.3 of Form 44-101F1,

(iv) NI 44-102 in

(A) section 1.2 of Appendix A,

(B) section 2.2 of Appendix A,

(C) section 1.2 of Appendix B, or

(D) section 2.2 of Appendix B, or

(v) NI 44-103 in

(A) paragraph 8 of subsection 3.2(1), or

(B) paragraph 4 of subsection 4.5(2).

5.2 Date of certificates — The date of the certificates in a prospectus or an amendment to a prospectus must be the same as the date of the prospectus or the amendment to the prospectus, as applicable.

5.3 Certificate of issuer — (1) Except in Ontario, a prospectus must contain a certificate signed by the issuer.

[Note: In Ontario, section 58 of the Securities Act *(Ontario) imposes a similar requirement that a prospectus contain a certificate of the issuer.]*[1]

(2) A prospectus certificate that is required to be signed by the issuer under this Instrument or other securities legislation must be in the applicable issuer certificate form.

5.4 Corporate issuer — (1) Except in Ontario, if the issuer is a company, a prospectus certificate that is required to be signed by the issuer under this Instrument or other securities legislation must be signed

    (a) by the chief executive officer and the chief financial officer of the issuer, and

    (b) on behalf of the board of directors, by

        (i) any two directors of the issuer, other than the persons referred to in paragraph (a) above, or

        (ii) if the issuer has only three directors, two of whom are the persons referred to in paragraph (a), all of the directors of the issuer.

(2) Except in Ontario, if the regulator is satisfied that either or both of the chief executive officer or chief financial officer cannot sign a certificate in a prospectus, the regulator may accept a certificate signed by another officer.

[Note: In Ontario, section 58 of the Securities Act *(Ontario) imposes similar requirements regarding who must sign the issuer certificate.]*

5.5 Trust issuer — (1) If the issuer is a trust, a prospectus certificate that is required to be signed by the issuer under this Instrument or other securities legislation must be signed by

    (a) the individuals who perform functions for the issuer similar to those performed by the chief executive officer and the chief financial officer of a company, and

    (b) two trustees of the issuer, on behalf of the trustees of the issuer.

(2) If a trustee that is signing the certificate of the issuer is

    (a) an individual, the individual must sign the certificate,

    (b) a company, the certificate must be signed

        (i) by the chief executive officer and the chief financial officer of the trustee, and

        (ii) on behalf of the board of directors of the trustee, by

            (A) any two directors of the trustee, other than the persons referred to in subparagraph (i), or

            (B) if the trustee has only three directors, two of whom are the persons referred to in subparagraph (i), all of the directors of the trustee,

    (c) a limited partnership, the certificate must be signed by each general partner of the limited partnership as described in subsection 5.6(2) in relation to an issuer that is a limited partnership, or

    (d) not referred to in paragraphs (a), (b) or (c), the certificate may be signed by any person or company with authority to bind the trustee.

(3) Despite subsections (1) and (2), if the issuer is an investment fund and the declaration of trust, trust indenture or trust agreement establishing the investment fund delegates the authority to do so, or otherwise authorizes an individual or company to do so, the certificate may be signed by the individual or company to whom the authority is delegated or that is authorized to sign the certificate.

(4) Despite subsections (1) and (2), if the trustees of an issuer, other than an investment fund, do not perform functions for the issuer similar to those performed by the directors of a company, the trustees are not required to sign the prospectus certificate of the issuer provided that at least two individuals who do perform functions for the issuer similar to those performed by the directors of a company sign the certificate.

(5) If the regulator is satisfied that an individual who performs functions for the issuer similar to those performed by either the chief executive officer or the chief financial officer of a company cannot sign a certificate in a prospectus, the regulator may accept a certificate signed by another individual.

5.6 Limited partnership issuer — (1) If the issuer is a limited partnership, a prospectus certificate that is required to be signed by the issuer under this Instrument or other securities legislation must be signed by

    (a) the individuals who perform functions for the issuer similar to those performed by the chief executive officer and the chief financial officer of a company, and

    (b) each general partner of the issuer.

(2) If a general partner of the issuer is

    (a) an individual, the individual must sign the certificate,

    (b) a company, the certificate must be signed

        (i) by the chief executive officer and the chief financial officer of the general partner, and

        (ii) on behalf of the board of directors of the general partner, by

            (A) any two directors of the general partner, other than the persons referred to in subparagraph (i), or

            (B) if the general partner has only three directors, two of whom are the persons referred to in subparagraph (i), all of the directors of the general partner,

    (c) a limited partnership, the certificate must be signed by each general partner of the limited partnership and, for greater certainty, this subsection applies to each general partner required to sign,

---

[1]In Ontario, a number of prospectus related requirements in this Instrument are either set out in the *Securities Act* (Ontario) or does not have a similar requirement. We have identified carve-outs from the Instrument where a similar requirement is set out in the Securities Act (Ontario). Where no corresponding statutory provision has been identified for an Ontario carve-out, Ontario has generally not adopted a similar requirement. Notes included in this Instrument have been inserted for convenience of reference only and do not form part of this Instrument or have any force or effect as a rule or policy.

(d) a trust, the certificate must be signed by the trustees of the general partner as described in subsection 5.5(2) in relation to an issuer that is a trust, or

(e) not referred to in paragraphs (a) to (d), the certificate may be signed by any person or company with authority to bind the general partner.

(3) If the regulator is satisfied that an individual who performs functions for the issuer similar to those performed by either the chief executive officer or the chief financial officer of a company cannot sign a certificate in a prospectus, the regulator may accept a certificate signed by another individual.

5.7 Other issuer — If an issuer is not a company, trust or limited partnership, a prospectus certificate that is required to be signed by the issuer under this Instrument or other securities legislation must be signed by the persons or companies that, in relation to the issuer, are in a similar position or perform a similar function to the persons or companies required to sign under sections 5.4, 5.5 and 5.6.

5.8 Reverse takeovers — Except in Ontario, if an issuer is involved in a proposed reverse takeover that has progressed to a state where a reasonable person would believe that the likelihood of the reverse takeover being completed is high, a prospectus must contain a certificate, in the applicable issuer certificate form, signed

(a) by the chief executive officer and the chief financial officer of the reverse takeover acquirer, and

(b) on behalf of the board of directors of the reverse takeover acquirer, by

(i) any two directors of the reverse takeover acquirer, other than the persons referred to in paragraph (a) above, or

(ii) if the reverse takeover acquirer has only three directors, two of whom are the persons referred to in paragraph (a), all of the directors of the reverse takeover acquirer.

5.9 Certificate of underwriter — (1) Except in Ontario, a prospectus must contain a certificate signed by each underwriter who, with respect to the securities offered by the prospectus, is in a contractual relationship with the issuer or a securityholder whose securities are being offered by the prospectus.

[Note: *In Ontario, subsection 59(1) of the* Securities Act *(Ontario) imposes a similar requirement that a prospectus contain a certificate signed by each underwriter in a contractual relationship with the issuer.*]

(2) A prospectus certificate that is required to be signed by an underwriter under this Instrument or other securities legislation must be in the applicable underwriter certificate form.

(3) Except in Ontario, with the consent of the regulator, a certificate in a prospectus may be signed by the underwriter's agent duly authorized in writing by the underwriter.

[Note: *In Ontario, subsection 59(2) of the* Securities Act *(Ontario) provides a similar discretion to the Director to permit the certificate to be signed by an underwriter's agent.*]

5.10 Certificate of investment fund manager — (1) If the issuer has an investment fund manager, a prospectus must contain a certificate, in the applicable issuer certificate form, signed by the investment fund manager.

(2) If the investment fund manager is a company, the certificate must be signed

(a) by the chief executive officer and the chief financial officer of the investment fund manager, and

(b) on behalf of the board of directors, by

(i) any two directors of the investment fund manager, other than the persons referred to in paragraph (a) above, or

(ii) if the investment fund manager has only three directors, two of whom are the persons referred to in paragraph (a), all of the directors of the investment fund manager.

(3) If the investment fund manager is a limited partnership, the certificate must be signed by the general partner of such limited partnership as described in subsection 5.6(2) in relation to an issuer that is a limited partnership.

5.10.1 Certificate of principal distributor — (1) If the issuer is an investment fund that has a principal distributor, a prospectus must contain a certificate, in the applicable underwriter certificate form, signed by the principal distributor.

(2) The certificate to be signed by the principal distributor must be signed by an officer or director of the principal distributor who is authorized to sign.

5.11 Certificate of promoter — (1) Except in Ontario, a prospectus must contain a certificate signed by each promoter of the issuer.

[Note: *In Ontario, subsection 58(1) of the* Securities Act *(Ontario) imposes a similar requirement that a prospectus shall contain a certificate signed by each promoter of the issuer.*]

(2) A prospectus certificate required to be signed by a promoter under this Instrument or other securities legislation must be in the applicable issuer certificate form.

(3) Except in Ontario, the regulator may require any person or company who was a promoter of the issuer within the two preceding years to sign a certificate to the prospectus, in the applicable issuer certificate form.

[Note: *In Ontario, subsection 58(6) of the* Securities Act *(Ontario) provides the Director with similar discretion to require a person or company who was a promoter of the issuer within the two preceding years to sign a prospectus certificate, subject to such conditions as the Director considers proper.*]

(4) Despite subsection (3), in British Columbia, the powers of the regulator with respect to the matters described in subsection (3) are set out in the *Securities Act* (British Columbia).

(5) Except in Ontario, with the consent of the regulator, a certificate of a promoter in a prospectus may be signed by an agent duly authorized in writing by the person or company required to sign the certificate.

[Note: *In Ontario, subsection 58(7) of the* Securities Act *(Ontario) provides the Director with similar discretion to permit a certificate in a prospectus to be signed by an agent of a promoter.*]

5.12 Certificate of credit supporter — (1) If there is a related credit supporter of the issuer or a subsidiary of the issuer, a prospectus must contain a certificate of the related credit supporter, in the applicable issuer certificate form, signed

    (a) by the chief executive officer and the chief financial officer of the credit supporter, and

    (b) on behalf of the board of directors of the credit supporter, by

        (i) any two directors of the credit supporter, other than the persons referred to in paragraph (a) above, or

        (ii) if the credit supporter has only three directors, two of whom are the persons referred to in paragraph (a), all of the directors of the credit supporter.

(2) With the consent of the regulator, a certificate in a prospectus may be signed by the credit supporter's agent duly authorized in writing by the credit supporter.

(3) Except in Ontario, the regulator may require any other person or company that is a credit supporter of either the issuer or a subsidiary of the issuer to sign a certificate to the prospectus, in the applicable issuer certificate form.

[Note: *In Ontario, subsection 58(6) of the* Securities Act *(Ontario) provides the Director with similar discretion to require a person or company who is a guarantor of the securities being distributed to sign a prospectus certificate, subject to such conditions as the Director considers proper.*]

(4) Despite subsection (3), in British Columbia, the powers of the regulator with respect to the matters described in subsection (3) are set out in the *Securities Act* (British Columbia).

5.13 Certificate of selling securityholders — (1) Except in Ontario, the regulator may require any person or company that is a selling securityholder to sign a certificate to the prospectus, in the applicable issuer certificate form.

(2) Despite subsection (1), in British Columbia, the powers of the regulator with respect to the matters described in subsection (1) are set out in the *Securities Act* (British Columbia).

5.14 Certificate of operating entity — (1) For the purposes of this section, the term "operating entity" means, in relation to an issuer, a person or company through which the business of the issuer, or a material part of the business of the issuer, is conducted and for which the issuer is required under securities legislation, or has undertaken, to provide to its securityholders separate financial statements of the person or company if the issuer's financial statements do not include consolidated information concerning the person or company.

(2) A prospectus of an issuer that is a trust must contain a certificate, in the applicable issuer certificate form, signed

    (a) by the chief executive officer and the chief financial officer of the operating entity, and

    (b) on behalf of the board of directors of the operating entity, by

        (i) any two directors of the operating entity, other than the persons referred to in paragraph (a) above, or

        (ii) if the operating entity has only three directors, two of whom are the persons referred to in paragraph (a), all of the directors of the operating entity.

5.15 Certificate of other persons — (1) Except in Ontario, the regulator may, in its discretion, require any person or company to sign a certificate to the prospectus, in the form that the regulator considers appropriate.

(2) Despite subsection (1), in British Columbia, the powers of the regulator with respect to the matters described in subsection (1) are set out in the *Securities Act* (British Columbia).

PART 6 — AMENDMENTS

6.1 Form of amendment — (1) An amendment to a prospectus must be either

    (a) an amendment that does not fully restate the text of the prospectus, or

    (b) an amended and restated prospectus.

(2) An amendment to a prospectus must be identified as follows:

    (a) for an amendment that does not restate the text of the prospectus:

        Amendment no. [insert amendment number] dated [insert date of amendment] to [identify prospectus] dated [insert date of prospectus being amended].; or

    (b) for an amended and restated prospectus:

        Amended and restated [identify prospectus] dated [insert date of amendment], amending and restating [identify prospectus] dated [insert date of prospectus being amended].

(3) Despite subsections (1) and (2), an amendment to a plan summary must be prepared in accordance with Part A of Form 41-101F3 without any further identification, and dated as of the date the plan summary is being amended.

6.2 Required documents for filing an amendment — An issuer that files an amendment to a prospectus must

    (a) file a signed copy of the amendment,

    (b) deliver to the regulator a copy of the prospectus blacklined to show the changes made by the amendment, if the amendment is also a restatement of the prospectus,

    (c) file or deliver any supporting documents required under this Instrument or other securities legislation to be filed or delivered with a prospectus, unless the documents originally filed or delivered with the prospectus are correct as of the date the amendment is filed, and

    (d) in case of an amendment to a final prospectus, file any consent letter required to be filed with a final prospectus, dated as of the date of the amendment.

6.3 Auditor's comfort letter — An issuer must deliver a new auditor's comfort letter, if an amendment to

    (a) a preliminary long form prospectus materially affects, or relates to, an auditor's comfort letter delivered under subparagraph 9.1(b)(iii),

(b) a preliminary short form prospectus materially affects, or relates to, an auditor's comfort letter delivered under subparagraph 4.1(b)(ii) of NI 44-101.

6.4 Delivery of amendments — Except in Ontario, an issuer must deliver an amendment to a preliminary prospectus as soon as practicable to each recipient of the preliminary prospectus according to the record of recipients required to be maintained under securities legislation.

[Note: In Ontario, subsection 57(3) of the Securities Act (Ontario) imposes a similar requirement regarding the delivery of amendments to a preliminary prospectus.]

6.5 Amendment to a preliminary prospectus — (1) Except in Ontario, if, after a receipt for a preliminary prospectus is issued but before a receipt for the final prospectus is issued, a material adverse change occurs, an amendment to the preliminary prospectus must be filed as soon as practicable, but in any event within 10 days after the day the change occurs.

[Note: In Ontario, subsection 57(1) of the Securities Act (Ontario) imposes a similar requirement to file an amendment to a preliminary prospectus where there has been a material adverse change.]

(2) The regulator must issue a receipt for an amendment to a preliminary prospectus as soon as practicable after the amendment is filed.

6.6 Amendment to a final prospectus — (1) Except in Ontario, if, after a receipt for a final prospectus is issued but before the completion of the distribution under the final prospectus, a material change occurs, an issuer must file an amendment to the final prospectus as soon as practicable, but in any event within 10 days after the day the change occurs.

[Note: In Ontario, subsection 57(1) of the Securities Act (Ontario) imposes a similar requirement to file an amendment to a final prospectus where there has been a material change.]

(2) Except in Ontario, if, after a receipt for a final prospectus or an amendment to the final prospectus is issued but before the completion of the distribution under the final prospectus or the amendment to the final prospectus, securities in addition to the securities previously disclosed in the final prospectus or the amendment to the final prospectus are to be distributed, an amendment to the final prospectus disclosing the additional securities must be filed, as soon as practicable, but in any event within 10 days after the decision to increase the number of securities offered.

[Note: In Ontario, subsection 57(2) of the Securities Act (Ontario) imposes a similar requirement to file an amendment to a prospectus any time there is a proposed distribution of securities in addition to that disclosed under the prospectus.]

(3) Except in Ontario, the regulator must issue a receipt for an amendment to a final prospectus filed under this section unless the regulator considers that there are grounds set out in securities legislation that would cause the regulator not to issue the receipt for a prospectus.

[Note: In Ontario, subsection 57(2.1) of the Securities Act (Ontario) imposes a similar obligation for the Director to issue a receipt for an amendment to a prospectus unless there are proper grounds for refusing the receipt.]

(4) Except in Ontario, the regulator must not refuse to issue a receipt under subsection (3) without giving the issuer who filed the prospectus an opportunity to be heard.

[Note: In Ontario, subsections 57(2.1) and 61(3) of the Securities Act (Ontario) impose a similar restriction on the Director to refuse to issue a receipt for a prospectus without first giving an issuer an opportunity to be heard.]

(5) Except in Ontario, an issuer must not proceed with a distribution or additional distribution if an amendment to a final prospectus is required to be filed until a receipt for the amendment to the final prospectus is issued by the regulator.

[Note: In Ontario, subsection 57(2.2) of the Securities Act (Ontario) imposes a similar restriction in respect of a distribution or additional distribution before a receipt is issued for an amendment to the final prospectus.]

(6) Subsection (5) does not apply to an investment fund in continuous distribution.

[Note: In Ontario, section 2.2 of OSC Rule 41-801 Implementing National Instrument 41-101 General Prospectus Requirements and Consequential Amendments provides a similar exemption for an investment fund in continuous distribution from the requirement to obtain a receipt prior to making a distribution or additional distribution under an amendment to a final prospectus.]

PART 7 — NON-FIXED PRICE OFFERINGS AND REDUCTION OF OFFERING PRICE UNDER A FINAL PROSPECTUS

7.1 Application — This Part does not apply to an investment fund in continuous distribution.

7.2 Non-fixed price offerings and reduction of offering price — (1) A person or company distributing a security under a prospectus must do so at a fixed price.

(2) Despite subsection (1), securities may be distributed for cash at non-fixed prices under a prospectus if the securities have received a rating, on a provisional or final basis, from at least one designated rating organization or its DRO affiliate at the time of

(a) the filing of the preliminary short form prospectus, if the issuer is filing a prospectus in the form of a short form prospectus under NI 44-101, or

(b) the filing of the long form prospectus.

(3) Despite subsection (1), if securities are distributed for cash under a prospectus, the price of the securities may be decreased from the initial offering price disclosed in the prospectus and, after such a decrease, changed from time to time to an amount not greater than the initial offering price, without filing an amendment to the prospectus to reflect the change, if

(a) the securities are distributed through one or more underwriters that have agreed to purchase all of the securities at a specified price,

(b) the proceeds to be received by the issuer or selling securityholders are disclosed in the prospectus as being fixed, and

(c) the underwriters have made a reasonable effort to sell all of the securities distributed under the prospectus at the initial offering price disclosed in the final prospectus.

(4) Despite subsections (2) and (3), the price at which securities may be acquired on exercise of rights must be fixed.

PART 8 — BEST EFFORTS DISTRIBUTIONS

8.1 Application — This Part does not apply to an investment fund in continuous distribution.

8.2 Distribution period — (1) Unless an amendment to the final prospectus is filed and the regulator has issued a receipt for the amendment, if securities are being distributed on a best efforts basis, the distribution must cease within 90 days after the date of the receipt for the final prospectus.

(2) Unless a further amendment to the final prospectus is filed and the regulator has issued a receipt for the further amendment, if an amendment to a final prospectus is filed and the regulator has issued a receipt for the amendment under subsection (1), the distribution must cease within 90 days after the date of the receipt for the amendment to the final prospectus.

(3) The total period of the distribution under subsections (1) and (2) must not end more than 180 days from the date of receipt for the final prospectus.

8.3 Minimum amount of funds — If securities are being distributed on a best efforts basis, other than an offering of securities to be distributed continuously, and the prospectus discloses that a minimum amount of funds must be raised,

    (a) the issuer must appoint a registered dealer authorized to make the distribution, a Canadian financial institution, or a lawyer who is a practicing member in good standing with a law society of a jurisdiction in which the securities are being distributed, or a notary in Québec, to hold in trust all funds received from subscriptions until the minimum amount of funds stipulated in the final prospectus has been raised, and

    (b) if the minimum amount of funds is not raised within the appropriate period of the distribution prescribed by section 8.2, the person or company holding the funds in trust referred to in paragraph (a) must return the funds to the subscribers without any deductions.

PART 8A — RIGHTS OFFERINGS

8A.1 Application and definitions — (1) This Part applies to an issuer that files a preliminary or final prospectus to distribute rights.

(2) In this Part,

"additional subscription privilege" means a privilege, granted to a holder of a right, to subscribe for a security not subscribed for by any holder under a basic subscription privilege;

"basic subscription privilege" means a privilege to subscribe for the number or amount of securities set out in a rights certificate held by the holder of the rights certificate;

"managing dealer" means a person or company that has entered into an agreement with an issuer under which the person or company has agreed to organize and participate in the solicitation of the exercise of the rights issued by the issuer;

"market price" means, for securities of a class for which there is a published market,

    (a) except as provided in paragraph (b),

        (i) if the published market provides a closing price, the simple average of the closing price of securities of that class on the published market for each of the trading days on which there was a closing price falling not more than 20 trading days immediately before the day as of which the market price is being determined, or

        (ii) if the published market does not provide a closing price, but provides only the highest and lowest prices of securities of the class traded, the average of the simple averages of the highest and lowest prices of securities of the class on the published market for each of the trading days on which there were highest and lowest prices falling not more than 20 trading days immediately before the day as of which the market price is being determined, or

    (b) if trading of securities of the class on the published market has occurred on fewer than 10 of the immediately preceding 20 trading days, the average of the following amounts established for each of the 20 trading days immediately before the day as of which the market price is being determined:

        (i) the average of the closing bid and closing ask prices for each day on which there was no trading, and

        (ii) if the published market

            (A) provides a closing price of securities of the class for each day that there was trading, the closing price, or

            (B) provides only the highest and lowest prices, the average of the highest and lowest prices of securities of that class for each day that there was trading;

"published market" means, for a class of securities, a marketplace on which the securities are traded, if the prices at which they have been traded on that marketplace are regularly

    (a) disseminated electronically, or

    (b) published in a newspaper or business or financial publication of general and regular paid circulation;

"soliciting dealer" means a person or company whose interest in a distribution of rights is limited to soliciting the exercise of the rights by holders of those rights;

"stand-by commitment" means an agreement by a person or company to acquire the securities of an issuer not subscribed for under the basic subscription privilege or the additional subscription privilege.

(3) For the purpose of the definition of "market price", if there is more than one published market for a security and

    (a) only one of the published markets is in Canada, the market price is determined solely by reference to that market,

    (b) more than one of the published markets is in Canada, the market price is determined solely by reference to the published market in Canada on which the greatest volume of trading in the particular class of securities occurred during the 20 trading days immediately before the date as of which the market price is being determined, and

    (c) none of the published markets are in Canada, the market price is determined solely by reference to the published market on which the greatest volume of trading in the particular class of securities occurred during the 20 trading days immediately before the date as of which the market price is being determined.

8A.2 Filing of prospectus for a rights offering — (1) An issuer must not file a prospectus for a distribution of rights unless all of the following apply:

(a) in addition to qualifying the distribution of the rights, the prospectus qualifies the distribution of the securities issuable upon the exercise of the rights;

(b) if there is a managing dealer, the managing dealer complies with section 5.9 as if the dealer were an underwriter;

(c) the exercise period for the rights is at least 21 days after the date on which the prospectus is sent to security holders;

(d) the subscription price for a security to be issued upon the exercise of a right is,

(i) if there is a published market for the security, lower than the market price of the security on the date of the final prospectus, or

(ii) if there is no published market for the security, lower than the fair value of the security on the date of the final prospectus unless the issuer restricts all of its insiders from increasing their proportionate interest in the issuer through the exercise of the rights distributed under the prospectus or through a stand-by commitment.

(2) If subparagraph (1)(d)(ii) applies, the issuer must deliver to the regulator or, in Québec, the securities regulatory authority independent evidence of fair value.

8A.3 Additional subscription privilege — (1) An issuer must not grant an additional subscription privilege to a holder of a right unless all of the following apply:

(a) the issuer grants the additional subscription privilege to all holders of a right;

(b) each holder of a right is entitled to receive, upon the exercise of the additional subscription privilege, the number or amount of securities equal to the lesser of

(i) the number or amount of securities subscribed for by the holder under the additional subscription privilege, and

(ii) the number calculated in accordance with the following formula:

$x(y/z)$ where

x = the aggregate number or amount of securities available through unexercised rights after giving effect to the basic subscription privilege;

y = the number of rights exercised by the holder under the basic subscription privilege;

z the aggregate number of rights exercised under the basic subscription privilege by holders of the rights that have subscribed for securities under the additional subscription privilege;

(c) all unexercised rights have been allocated on a pro rata basis to holders who subscribed for additional securities under the additional subscription privilege;

(d) the subscription price for the additional subscription privilege is the same as the subscription price for the basic subscription privilege.

8A.4 Stand-by commitments — If an issuer enters into a stand-by commitment for a distribution of rights, all of the following apply:

(a) the issuer must grant an additional subscription privilege to all holders of a right;

(b) the issuer must deliver to the regulator or, in Québec, the securities regulatory authority evidence that the person or company providing the stand-by commitment has the financial ability to carry out the stand-by commitment;

(c) the subscription price under the stand-by commitment must be the same as the subscription price under the basic subscription privilege.

8A.5 Appointment of depository — If an issuer has stated in a prospectus that no security will be issued upon the exercise of a right unless a stand-by commitment is provided, or unless proceeds of no less than the stated minimum amount are received by the issuer, all of the following apply:

(a) the issuer must appoint a depository to hold all money received upon the exercise of the rights until either the stand-by commitment is provided or the stated minimum amount is received and the depository is one of the following:

(i) a Canadian financial institution;

(ii) a registrant in the jurisdiction in which the funds are proposed to be held that is acting as managing dealer for the distribution of the rights, or, if there is no managing dealer for the distribution of the rights, that is acting as a soliciting dealer;

(b) the issuer and the depository must enter into an agreement, the terms of which require the depository to return the money referred to in paragraph (a) in full to the holders of rights that have subscribed for securities under the distribution of the rights if the stand-by commitment is not provided or if the stated minimum amount is not received by the depository during the exercise period for the rights.

8A.6 If an issuer has filed a final prospectus for a distribution of rights, the issuer must not change the terms of the distribution.

PART 9 — REQUIREMENTS FOR FILING A LONG FORM PROSPECTUS

9.1 Required documents for filing a preliminary or pro forma long form prospectus — (1) An issuer that files a preliminary or pro forma long form prospectus must

(a) file the following with the preliminary or pro forma long form prospectus

(i) Signed Copy — in the case of a preliminary long form prospectus, a signed copy of the preliminary long form prospectus;

(ii) Documents Affecting the Rights of Securityholders — a copy of the following documents, and any amendments to the following documents, that have not previously been filed:

(A) articles of incorporation, amalgamation, continuation or any other constating or establishing documents of the issuer, unless the constating or establishing document is a statutory or regulatory instrument,

(B) by-laws or other corresponding instruments currently in effect,

(C) any securityholder or voting trust agreement that the issuer has access to and that can reasonably be regarded as material to an investor in securities of the issuer,

(D) any securityholders' rights plans or other similar plans, and

(E) any other contract of the issuer or a subsidiary of the issuer that creates or can reasonably be regarded as materially affecting the rights or obligations of the issuer's securityholders generally;

(iii) **Material Contracts** — a copy of any material contract required to be filed under section 9.3;

(iv) **Investment Fund Documents** — if the issuer is an investment fund, the documents filed under subparagraphs (ii) and (iii) must include a copy of

(A) any declaration of trust or trust agreement of the investment fund, limited partnership agreement, or any other constating or establishing documents of the investment fund,

(B) any agreement of the investment fund or the trustee with the manager of the investment fund,

(C) any agreement of the investment fund, the manager or trustee with the portfolio advisers of the investment fund,

(D) any agreement of the investment fund, the manager or trustee with the custodian of the investment fund, and

(E) any agreement of the investment fund, the manager or trustee with the principal distributor of the investment fund;

(iv.1) if the issuer is a scholarship plan, in addition to the documents filed under subparagraph (iv), a copy of the scholarship plan contract for the scholarship plan under the prospectus;

(v) **Mining Reports** — if the issuer has a mineral project, the technical reports required to be filed with a preliminary long form prospectus under NI 43-101;

(vi) **Reports and Valuations** — a copy of each report or valuation referred to in the preliminary long form prospectus for which a consent is required to be filed under section 10.1 and that has not previously been filed, other than a technical report that

(A) deals with a mineral project or oil and gas activities, and

(B) is not otherwise required to be filed under subparagraph (v); and

(vii) **Marketing Materials** — a copy of any template version of the marketing materials required to be filed under paragraph 13.7(1)(e); an

(b) deliver to the regulator, concurrently with the filing of the preliminary or pro forma long form prospectus, the following:

(i) **Blacklined Copy** — in the case of a pro forma prospectus, a copy of the pro forma prospectus blacklined to show changes and the text of deletions from the latest prospectus previously filed;

(ii) **Personal Information Form and Authorization to Collect, Use and Disclose Personal Information** — a completed personal information form for,

(A) each director and executive officer of an issuer,

(B) if the issuer is an investment fund, each director and executive officer of the manager of the issuer,

(C) each promoter of the issuer, and

(D) if the promoter is not an individual, each director and executive officer of the promoter; and

(iii) **Auditor's Comfort Letter regarding Audited Financial Statements** — if a financial statement of an issuer or a business included in, or incorporated by reference into, a preliminary or pro forma long form prospectus is accompanied by an unsigned auditor's report, a signed letter addressed to the regulator from the auditor of the issuer or of the business, as applicable, prepared in accordance with the form suggested for this circumstance in the Handbook; and

(iv) **Marketing Materials** — a copy of any template version of the marketing materials required to be delivered under paragraph 13.7(4)(c) or 13.12(2)(c).

(2) Despite subparagraph (1)(b)(ii), an issuer is not required to deliver to the regulator a personal information form for an individual if the issuer, another issuer or, if the issuer is an investment fund, the manager of the investment fund issuer or another investment fund issuer, previously delivered a personal information form for the individual and all of the following are satisfied:

(a) the certificate and consent included in or attached to the personal information form was executed by the individual within three years preceding the date of filing of the preliminary or pro-forma long form prospectus;

(b) the responses given by the individual to questions 6 through 10 of the individual's personal information form are correct as at a date that is within 30 days of the filing of the preliminary or pro-forma long form prospectus;

(c) if the personal information form was previously delivered to the regulator by another issuer, the issuer delivers to the regulator, concurrently with the filing of the preliminary or pro forma long form prospectus, a copy of the previously delivered personal information form or alternative information that is satisfactory to the regulator.

(3) Until May 14, 2016, subparagraph (1)(b)(ii) does not apply to an issuer in respect of the delivery of a personal information form for an individual if the issuer or, if the issuer is an investment fund, the manager of the investment fund issuer, previously delivered to the regulator a predecessor personal information form for the individual and all of the following are satisfied:

(a) the certificate and consent included in or attached to the predecessor personal information form was executed by the individual within three years preceding the date of filing of the preliminary or pro-forma long form prospectus;

(b) the responses given by the individual to questions 4(B) and (C) and questions 6 through 9 or, in the case of a TSX/TSXV personal information form in effect after September 8, 2011, questions 6 through 10, of the individual's predecessor personal information form are correct as at a date that is within 30 days of the filing of the preliminary or pro-forma long form prospectus.

9.2 Required documents for filing a final long form prospectus — An issuer that files a final long form prospectus must

(a) file the following with the final long form prospectus:

(i) **Signed Copy** — a signed copy of the final long form prospectus;

(ii) **Documents Affecting the Rights of Securityholders** — a copy of any document described under subparagraph 9.1(a)(ii) that has not previously been filed;

(iii) **Material Contracts** — a copy of each material contract required to be filed under section 9.3 that has not previously been filed under subparagraph 9.1(a)(iii);

(iv) **Investment Fund Documents** — a copy of any document described under subparagraph 9.1(a)(iv) or (iv.1) that has not previously been filed;

(v) **Other Reports and Valuations** — a copy of any report or valuation referred to in the final long form prospectus, for which a consent is required to be filed under section 10.1 and that has not previously been filed, other than a technical report that

(A) deals with a mineral project or oil and gas activities of the issuer, and

(B) is not otherwise required to be filed under subparagraph 9.1(a)(v) or 9.1(a)(vi);

(vi) **Issuer's Submission to Jurisdiction** — a submission to jurisdiction and appointment of agent for service of process of the issuer in the form set out in Appendix B, if an issuer is incorporated or organized in a foreign jurisdiction and does not have an office in Canada;

(vii) **Non-Issuer's Submission to Jurisdiction** — a submission to jurisdiction and appointment of agent for service of process of

(A) each selling securityholder,

(A.1) each director of the issuer, and

(B) any other person or company that provides or signs a certificate under Part 5 or other securities legislation, other than an issuer,

in the form set out in Appendix C, if the person or company is incorporated or organized in a foreign jurisdiction and does not have an office in Canada or is an individual who resides outside of Canada;

(viii) **Expert's Consents** — the consents required to be filed under section 10.1;

(ix) **Credit Supporter's Consent** — the written consent of the credit supporter to the inclusion of its financial statements in the final long form prospectus, if financial statements of a credit supporter are required under Item 33 of Form 41-101F1 to be included in a final long form prospectus and a certificate of the credit supporter is not required under section 5.12 to be included in the final long form prospectus;

(x) **Undertaking in Respect of Credit Supporter Disclosure** — an undertaking of the issuer to file the periodic and timely disclosure of a credit supporter similar to the disclosure provided under section 12.1 of Form 44-101F1, so long as the securities being distributed are issued and outstanding;

(xi) **Undertaking in Respect of Continuous Disclosure** — An undertaking of the issuer to provide to its securityholders separate financial statements for an operating entity that investors need to make an informed decision about investing in the issuer's securities if

(A) the issuer is an income trust that is formed as a mutual fund trust as that term is used in the *Income Tax Act* (Canada), other than an "investment fund" as defined in section 1.1 of NI 81-106,

(B) the underlying business or income producing assets of the operating entity generate net cash flow available for distribution to the issuer's securityholders, and

(C) the issuer's performance and prospects depend primarily on the performance and operations of the operating entity;

(xii) **Undertaking to File Agreements, Contracts and Material Contracts** — if an agreement, contract or declaration of trust under subparagraph (ii) or (iv) or a material contract under subparagraph (iii) has not been executed before the filing of the final long form prospectus but will be executed on or before the completion of the distribution, the issuer must file with the securities regulatory authority, no later than the time of filing of the final long form prospectus, an undertaking of the issuer to the securities regulatory authority to file the agreement, contract, declaration of trust or material contract promptly and in any event no later than seven days after execution of the agreement, contract, declaration of trust or material contract;

(xii.1) **Undertaking to File Unexecuted Documents** — if a document referred to in subparagraph (ii) does not need to be executed in order to become effective and has not become effective before the filing of the final long form prospectus, but will become effective on or before the completion of the distribution, the issuer must file with the securities regulatory authority, no later than the time of filing of the final long form prospectus, an undertaking of the issuer to the securities regulatory authority to file the document promptly and in any event no later than seven days after the document becomes effective;

(xiii) **Undertaking in Respect of Restricted Securities** — for distributions of non-voting securities, an undertaking of the issuer to give notice to holders of non-voting securities of a meeting of securityholders if a notice of such a meeting is given to its registered holders of voting securities; and

(xiv) **Marketing Materials** — a copy of any template version of the marketing materials required to be filed under paragraph 13.7(1)(e), 13.7(7)(a), 13.8(1)(e) or 13.8(7)(b) that has not previously been filed; and,

(b) deliver to the regulator, no later than the filing of the final long form prospectus

(i) **Blackline Copy** — a copy of the final long form prospectus blacklined to show changes from the preliminary or pro forma long form prospectus;

(ii) **Communication with Exchange** — if the issuer has made an application to list the securities being distributed on an exchange in Canada, a copy of a communication in writing from the exchange stating that the application for listing has been made and has been accepted subject to the issuer meeting the requirements for listing of the exchange;

(iii) **Marketing Materials** — a copy of any template version of the marketing materials required to be delivered under paragraph 13.7(4)(c), 13.8(4)(c) or 13.12(2)(c) that has not previously been delivered,

(iv) **Evidence of financial ability** — the evidence of financial ability required to be delivered under section 8A.4 if it has not previously been delivered; and

(v) **Evidence of fair value** — the evidence of fair value required to be delivered under subsection 8A.2(2) if it has not previously been delivered.

9.3 Material contracts — (1) Unless previously filed, an issuer that files a long form prospectus must file a material contract entered into

(a) since the beginning of the last financial year ending before the date of the prospectus, or

(b) before the beginning of the last financial year ending before the date of the prospectus if that material contract is still in effect.

(2) Despite subsection (1), an issuer is not required to file a material contract entered into in the ordinary course of business unless the material contract is

(a) a contract to which directors, officers, promoters, selling securityholders or underwriters are parties, other than a contract of employment,

Part 4: DISTRIBUTIONS

(b) a continuing contract to sell the majority of the issuer's products or services or to purchase the majority of the issuer's requirements of goods, services, or raw materials,

(c) a franchise or licence or other agreement to use a patent, formula, trade secret, process or trade name,

(d) a financing or credit agreement with terms that have a direct correlation with anticipated cash distributions,

(e) an external management or external administration agreement, or

(f) a contract on which the issuer's business is substantially dependent.

(3) A provision in a material contract filed pursuant to subsections (1) or (2) may be omitted or marked to be unreadable if an executive officer of the issuer reasonably believes that disclosure of that provision would be seriously prejudicial to the interests of the issuer or would violate confidentiality provisions.

(4) Subsection (3) does not apply if the provision relates to

(a) debt covenants and ratios in financing or credit agreements,

(b) events of default or other terms relating to the termination of the material contract, or

(c) other terms necessary for understanding the impact of the material contract on the business of the issuer.

(5) If a provision is omitted or marked to be unreadable under subsection (3), the issuer must include a description of the type of information that has been omitted or marked to be unreadable immediately after the provision in the copy of the material contract filed by the issuer.

(6) Despite subsections (1) and (2), an issuer is not required to file a material contract entered into before January 1, 2002 if the issuer is a reporting issuer in at least one jurisdiction immediately before filing the prospectus.

PART 10 — CONSENTS AND LICENCES, REGISTRATIONS AND APPROVALS

10.1 Consents of experts — (1) Subject to subsection (1.1), an issuer must file the written consent of

(a) any solicitor, auditor, accountant, engineer, or appraiser,

(b) any notary in Québec, and

(c) any person or company whose profession or business gives authority to a statement made by that person or company.

(1.1) Subsection (1) does not apply unless the person or company is named in a prospectus or an amendment to a prospectus directly or, if applicable, in a document incorporated by reference into the prospectus or amendment,

(a) as having prepared or certified any part of the prospectus or the amendment,

(b) as having opined on financial statements from which selected information included in the prospectus has been derived and which audit opinion is referred to in the prospectus directly or in a document incorporated by reference, or

(c) as having prepared or certified a report, valuation, statement or opinion referred to in the prospectus or the amendment directly or in a document incorporated by reference.

(2) A consent referred to in subsection (1) must

(a) be filed no later than the time the final prospectus or the amendment to the final prospectus is filed or, for the purposes of future financial statements that have been incorporated by reference in a prospectus under subsection 15.2(3), no later than the date that those financial statements are filed,

(b) state that the person or company being named consents

(i) to being named, and

(ii) to the use of that person or company's report, valuation, statement or opinion,

(c) refer to the report, valuation, statement or opinion stating the date of the report, valuation, statement or opinion, and

(d) contain a statement that the person or company referred to in subsection (1)

(i) has read the prospectus, and

(ii) has no reason to believe that there are any misrepresentations in the information contained in it that are

(A) derived from the report, valuation, statement or opinion, or

(B) within the knowledge of the person or company as a result of the services performed by the person or company in connection with the report, financial statements, valuation, statement or opinion.

(3) In addition to any other requirement of this section, the consent of an auditor or accountant must also state

(a) the dates of the financial statements on which the report of the person or company is made, and

(b) that the person or company has no reason to believe that there are any misrepresentations in the information contained in the prospectus that are

(i) derived from the financial statements on which the person or company has reported, or

(ii) within the knowledge of the person or company as a result of the audit of the financial statements.

(4) Subsection (1) does not apply to a designated rating organization or its DRO affiliate that issues a rating to the securities being distributed under the prospectus.

10.2 Licences, registrations and approvals — If the proceeds of the distribution will be used to substantially fund a material undertaking that would constitute a material departure from the business or operations of the issuer and the issuer has not obtained all material licences, registrations and approvals necessary for the stated principal use of proceeds,

(a) the issuer must appoint a registered dealer authorized to make the distribution, a Canadian financial institution, or a lawyer who is a practicing member in good standing with a law society of a jurisdiction in which the securities are being distributed, or a notary in Québec, to hold in trust all funds received from subscriptions until all material licences, registrations and approvals necessary for the stated principal use of proceeds have been obtained, and

(b) if all material licences, registrations and approvals necessary for the operation of the stated principal use of proceeds have not been obtained within 90 days from the date of receipt of the final prospectus, the trustee must return the funds to subscribers.

PART 11 — OVER-ALLOCATION AND UNDERWRITERS

11.1 Over-allocation — Securities that are sold to create the over-allocation position in connection with a distribution under a prospectus must be distributed under the prospectus.

11.2 Distribution of securities under a prospectus to an underwriter — Except as required under section 11.3, no person or company may distribute securities under a prospectus to any person or company acting as an underwriter in connection with the distribution of securities under the prospectus, other than

(a) an over-allotment option granted to one or more persons or companies for acting as an underwriter in connection with the distribution or any security issuable or transferable on the exercise of such an over-allotment option; or

(b) securities issued or paid as compensation to one or more persons or companies for acting as an underwriter in respect of other securities that are distributed under the prospectus, where the number or principal amount of the securities issued as compensation, on an as-if-converted basis, does not in the aggregate exceed 10% of the total of the base offering on an as-if converted basis plus any securities that would be acquired upon the exercise of an over-allotment option.

11.3 Take-up by underwriter — If an underwriter has agreed to purchase a specified number or principal amount of the securities at a specified price, the underwriter must take up the securities, if at all, within 42 days after the date of the receipt for the final prospectus.

PART 12 — RESTRICTED SECURITIES

12.1 Application — This Part does not apply to

(a) securities of mutual funds,

(b) securities that carry a right to vote subject to a restriction on the number or percentage of securities that may be voted or owned by persons or companies that are not citizens or residents of Canada or that are otherwise considered as a result of any law applicable to the issuer to be non-Canadians, but only to the extent of the restriction, and

(c) securities that are subject to a restriction, imposed by any law governing the issuer, on the level of ownership of the securities by a person, company or combination of persons or companies, but only to the extent of the restriction.

12.2 Use of restricted security term — (1) An issuer must not refer to a security in a prospectus by a term or a defined term that includes the word "common" unless the security is an equity security to which are attached voting rights exercisable in all circumstances, irrespective of the number or percentage of securities owned, that are not less, per security, than the voting rights attached to any other outstanding security of the issuer.

(2) An issuer must not refer in a prospectus to a term or defined term that includes the word "preference" or "preferred", unless the security is a security, other than an equity security, to which is attached a preference or right over any class of equity security of the issuer.

(3) If restricted securities are referred to in the constating documents of the issuer by a term that is different from the appropriate restricted security term, the restricted securities may be described, in one place only in the prospectus, by the term used in the constating documents of the issuer; provided that, the description is not on the front page of the prospectus and is in the same type face and type size as that used generally in the body of the prospectus.

(4) A class of securities that is or may become restricted securities must be referred to in a prospectus using a term or a defined term that includes the appropriate restricted security term.

12.3 Prospectus filing eligibility — (1) Subject to subsection (3), an issuer must not file a prospectus under which restricted securities, subject securities or securities that are, directly or indirectly, convertible into, or exercisable or exchangeable for, restricted securities or subject securities, are distributed unless

(a) the distribution has received prior majority approval of the securityholders of the issuer in accordance with applicable law, including approval on a class basis if required and excluding any votes attaching at the time to securities held, directly or indirectly, by affiliates of the issuer or control persons of the issuer, or

(b) at the time of any restricted security reorganization related to the securities to be distributed

(i) the restricted security reorganization received prior majority approval of the securityholders of the issuer in accordance with applicable law, including approval on a class basis if required and excluding any votes attaching at the time to securities held, directly or indirectly, by affiliates of the issuer or control persons of the issuer,

(ii) the issuer was a reporting issuer in at least one jurisdiction, and

(iii) no purposes or business reasons for the creation of restricted securities were disclosed that are inconsistent with the purpose of the distribution.

(2) Subject to subsection (3), for each approval referred to in subsection (1), the issuer must have provided prior written disclosure in an information circular or notice to its securityholders that included

(a) the name of each affiliate of the issuer that was a beneficial owner of securities of the issuer and the number of securities beneficially owned, directly or indirectly, by the affiliate as of the date of the information circular or notice to the extent known to the issuer after reasonable inquiry,

(b) the name of each control person and the number of securities beneficially owned, directly or indirectly, by the control person as of the date of the information circular or notice, to the extent known to the issuer after reasonable inquiry,

(c) a statement of the number of votes attaching to the securities that were excluded for the purpose of the approval to the extent known to the issuer after reasonable inquiry, and

(d) the purpose and business reasons for the creation of restricted securities.

(3) Subsections (1) and (2) do not apply if

(a) the securities offered by the prospectus are of an existing class of restricted securities that were created before December 21, 1984,

(b) the issuer was a private issuer immediately before filing the prospectus,

(c) the securities offered by the prospectus are of the same class as securities distributed under a previous prospectus that was filed by an issuer that was, at the time of filing the previous prospectus, a private issuer,

(d) the securities offered by the prospectus are previously unissued restricted securities distributed by way of stock dividend in the ordinary course to securityholders instead of a cash dividend if at the time of distribution there is a published market for the restricted securities,

(e) the securities offered by the prospectus are distributed as a stock split that takes the form of a distribution of previously unissued restricted securities by way of stock dividend to holders of the same class of restricted securities if at the time of distribution there is a published market for the restricted securities and the distribution is part of a concurrent distribution by way of stock dividend to holders of all equity securities under which all outstanding equity securities of the issuer are increased in the same proportion, or

(f) as of a date not more than seven days before the date of the prospectus, the issuer expects that in each local jurisdiction in which the prospectus will be filed the number of securities of each class of equity securities held by registered holders whose last address as shown on the books of the issuer is in the local jurisdiction, or beneficially owned by persons or companies in the local jurisdiction, will be less than two percent of the outstanding number of securities of the class after giving effect to the proposed distribution.

PART 13 — ADVERTISING AND MARKETING IN CONNECTION WITH PROSPECTUS OFFERINGS OF ISSUERS OTHER THAN INVESTMENT FUNDS

13.0 Application — (1) This Part applies to issuers other than investment funds filing a prospectus in the form of Form 41-101F2 or Form 41-101F3.

(2) In this Part,

"comparables" means information that compares an issuer to other issuers;

"convertible security" has the same meaning as in section 1.1 of National Instrument 45-102 *Resale of Securities*;

"exchangeable security" has the same meaning as in section 1.1 of National Instrument 45-102 *Resale of Securities*;

"underlying security" has the same meaning as in section 1.1 of National Instrument 45-102 *Resale of Securities*;

"U.S. cross-border initial public offering" means an initial public offering of securities of an issuer being made contemporaneously in the United States of America and Canada by way of a prospectus filed with a securities regulatory authority in a jurisdiction of Canada and a U.S. prospectus filed with the SEC;

"U.S. cross-border offering" means an offering of securities of an issuer being made contemporaneously in the United States of America and Canada by way of a prospectus filed with a securities regulatory authority in a jurisdiction of Canada and a U.S. prospectus filed with the SEC, and includes a U.S. cross-border initial public offering;

"U.S. prospectus" means a prospectus that has been prepared in accordance with the disclosure and other requirements of U.S. federal securities law for an offering of securities registered under the 1933 Act.

(3) In this Part, for greater certainty, a reference to "provides" includes showing a document to a person without allowing the person to retain or make a copy of the document.

13.1 Legend for communications during the waiting period — (1) A preliminary prospectus notice or other communication used in connection with a prospectus offering during the waiting period must contain the following legend or words to the same effect:

> A preliminary prospectus containing important information relating to these securities has been filed with securities commissions or similar authorities in certain jurisdictions of Canada. The preliminary prospectus is still subject to completion or amendment. Copies of the preliminary prospectus may be obtained from [insert name and contact information for dealer or other relevant person or entity.] There will not be any sale or any acceptance of an offer to buy the securities until a receipt for the final prospectus has been issued.

(2) If the preliminary prospectus notice or other communication is in writing, include the wording required under subsection (1) in bold type that is at least as large as that used generally in the body of the text., *and*

(3) Subsection (1) does not apply to standard term sheets and marketing materials.

13.2 Legend for communications following receipt for the final prospectus — (1) A final prospectus notice or other communication used in connection with a prospectus offering following the issuance of a receipt for the final prospectus must contain the following legend or words to the same effect:

> This offering is only made by prospectus. The prospectus contains important detailed information about the securities being offered. Copies of the prospectus may be obtained from [insert name and contact information for dealer or other relevant person or entity.] Investors should read the prospectus before making an investment decision.

(2) If the final prospectus notice or other communication is in writing, include the wording required under subsection (1) in bold type that is at least as large as that used generally in the body of the text., *and*

(3) Subsection (1) does not apply to standard term sheets and marketing materials.

13.4 Testing of the waters exemption — IPO issuers — (1) In this section, "public issuer" means an issuer that

(a) is a reporting issuer in a jurisdiction of Canada;

(b) is an SEC issuer;

(c) has a class of securities that has been assigned a ticker symbol by the Financial Industry Regulatory Authority in the United States of America for use on any of the over-the-counter markets in the United States of America;

(d) has a class of securities that have been traded on an over-the-counter market with respect to which trade data is publicly reported; or

(e) has any of its securities listed, quoted or traded on a marketplace outside of Canada or any other facility outside of Canada for bringing together buyers and sellers of securities and with respect to which trade data is publicly reported.

(2) Subject to subsections (3) to (7), the prospectus requirement does not apply to a solicitation of an expression of interest in order to ascertain if there would be sufficient interest in an initial public offering of securities by an issuer pursuant to a long form prospectus if

(a) the issuer has a reasonable expectation of filing a preliminary long form prospectus in respect of an initial public offering in at least one jurisdiction of Canada;

(b) the issuer is not a public issuer before the date of the preliminary long form prospectus;

(c) an investment dealer makes the solicitation on behalf of the issuer;

(d) the issuer provided written authorization to the investment dealer to act on its behalf before the investment dealer made the solicitation;

(e) the solicitation is made to an accredited investor; and

(f) subject to subsection (3), the issuer and the investment dealer keep all information about the proposed offering confidential until the earlier of

(i) the information being generally disclosed in a preliminary long form prospectus or otherwise, or

(ii) the issuer confirming in writing that it will not be pursuing the potential offering.

(3) An investment dealer must not solicit an expression of interest from an accredited investor pursuant to subsection (2) unless

(a) all written material provided to the accredited investor

(i) is approved in writing by the issuer before it is provided,

(ii) is marked confidential, and

(iii) contains a legend stating that the material does not provide full disclosure of all material facts relating to the issuer, the securities or the offering and is not subject to liability for misrepresentations under applicable securities legislation; and

(b) before providing the investor with any information about the issuer, the securities or the offering, the investment dealer obtains confirmation in writing from the investor that the investor will keep information about the proposed offering confidential, and will not use the information for any purpose other than assessing the investor's interest in the offering, until the earlier of

(i) the information being generally disclosed in a preliminary long form prospectus or otherwise, or

(ii) the issuer confirming in writing that it will not be pursuing the potential offering.

(4) If any investment dealer solicits an expression of interest pursuant to subsection (2), the issuer must not file a preliminary long form prospectus in respect of an initial public offering until the date which is at least 15 days after the date on which any investment dealer last solicited an expression of interest from an accredited investor pursuant to that subsection.

(5) An issuer relying on the exemption in subsection (2) must keep

(a) a written record of any investment dealer that it authorized to act on its behalf in making solicitations in reliance on the exemption; and

(b) a copy of any written authorizations referred to in paragraph (2)(d).

(6) If an investment dealer solicits an expression of interest pursuant to subsection (2), the investment dealer must keep

(a) a written record of any accredited investor that it solicited in reliance on the exemption;

(b) a copy of any written material and written approval referred to in subparagraph (3)(a)(i); and

(c) any written confirmations referred to in paragraph (3)(b).

(7) Subsection (2) does not apply if

(a) any of the issuer's securities are held by a control person that is a public issuer; and

(b) the initial public offering of the issuer would be a material fact or material change with respect to the control person.

13.5 Standard term sheets during the waiting period — (1) An investment dealer that provides a standard term sheet to a potential investor during the waiting period is exempt from the prospectus requirement with respect to providing the standard term sheet if

(a) the standard term sheet complies with subsections (2) and (3);

(b) other than contact information for the investment dealer or underwriters, all information in the standard term sheet concerning the issuer, the securities or the offering is disclosed in, or derived from, the preliminary prospectus or any amendment; and

(c) a receipt for the preliminary prospectus has been issued in the local jurisdiction.

(2) A standard term sheet provided under subsection (1) must be dated and include the following legend, or words to the same effect, on the first page:

A preliminary prospectus containing important information relating to the securities described in this document has been filed with the securities regulatory authorit[y/ies] in [each of/certain of the provinces/provinces and territories of Canada].

The preliminary prospectus is still subject to completion. Copies of the preliminary prospectus may be obtained from *[insert contact information for the investment dealer or underwriters]*. There will not be any sale or any acceptance of an offer to buy the securities until a receipt for the final prospectus has been issued.

This document does not provide full disclosure of all material facts relating to the securities offered. Investors should read the preliminary prospectus, the final prospectus and any amendment for disclosure of those facts, especially risk factors relating to the securities offered, before making an investment decision.

(3) A standard term sheet provided under subsection (1) may contain only the information referred to in subsection (2) and the following information in respect of the issuer, the securities or the offering:

(a) the name of the issuer;

(b) the jurisdiction or foreign jurisdiction in which the issuer's head office is located;

(c) the statute under which the issuer is incorporated, continued or organized or, if the issuer is an unincorporated entity, the laws of the jurisdiction or foreign jurisdiction under which it is established and exists;

(d) a brief description of the business of the issuer;

(e) a brief description of the securities;

(f) the price or price range of the securities;

(g) the total number or dollar amount of the securities, or range of the total number or dollar amount of the securities;

(h) the terms of any over-allotment option;

(i) the names of the underwriters;

(j) whether the offering is on a firm commitment or best efforts basis;

(k) the amount of the underwriting commission, fee or discount;

(l) the proposed or expected closing date of the offering;

(m) a brief description of the use of proceeds;

(n) the exchange on which the securities are proposed to be listed, provided that the standard term sheet complies with the requirements of securities legislation for listing representations;

(o) in the case of debt securities, the maturity date of the debt securities and a brief description of any interest payable on the debt securities;

(p) in the case of preferred shares, a brief description of any dividends payable on the securities;

(q) in the case of convertible securities, a brief description of the underlying securities into which the convertible securities are convertible;

(r) in the case of exchangeable securities, a brief description of the underlying securities into which the exchangeable securities are exchangeable;

(s) in the case of restricted securities, a brief description of the restriction;

(t) in the case of securities for which a credit supporter has provided a guarantee or alternative credit support, a brief description of the credit supporter and the guarantee or alternative credit support provided;

(u) whether the securities are redeemable or retractable;

(v) a statement that the securities are eligible, or are expected to be eligible, for investment in registered retirement savings plans, tax-free savings accounts or other registered plans, if the issuer has received, or reasonably expects to receive, a legal opinion that the securities are so eligible;

(w) contact information for the investment dealer or underwriters.

(4) For the purposes of subsection (3), "brief description" means a description consisting of no more than three lines of text in type that is at least as large as that used generally in the body of the standard term sheet.

13.6 Standard term sheets after a receipt for a final prospectus — (1) An investment dealer must not provide a standard term sheet to a potential investor after a receipt for a final prospectus or any amendment is issued unless

(a) the standard term sheet complies with subsections (2) and (3);

(b) other than contact information for the investment dealer or underwriters, all information in the standard term sheet concerning the issuer, the securities or the offering is disclosed in, or derived from, the final prospectus or any amendment; and

(c) a receipt for the final prospectus has been issued in the local jurisdiction.

(2) A standard term sheet provided under subsection (1) must be dated and include the following legend, or words to the same effect, on the first page:

A final prospectus containing important information relating to the securities described in this document has been filed with the securities regulatory authorit[y/ies] in [each of/certain of the provinces/provinces and territories of Canada].

Copies of the final prospectus may be obtained from *[insert contact information for the investment dealer or underwriters]*.

This document does not provide full disclosure of all material facts relating to the securities offered. Investors should read the final prospectus, and any amendment, for disclosure of those facts, especially risk factors relating to the securities offered, before making an investment decision.

(3) A standard term sheet provided under subsection (1) may contain only the information referred to in subsection (2) and the information referred to in subsection 13.5(3).

13.7 Marketing materials during the waiting period — (1) An investment dealer that provides marketing materials to a potential investor during the waiting period is exempt from the prospectus requirement with respect to providing the marketing materials if

(a) the marketing materials comply with subsections (2) to (8);

(b) other than contact information for the investment dealer or underwriters and any comparables, all information in the marketing materials concerning the issuer, the securities or the offering is disclosed in, or derived from, the preliminary prospectus or any amendment;

(c) other than prescribed language, the marketing materials contain the same cautionary language in bold type as contained on the cover page, and in the summary, of the preliminary prospectus;

(d) a template version of the marketing materials is approved in writing by the issuer and the lead underwriter before the marketing materials are provided;

(e) a template version of the marketing materials is filed on or before the day that the marketing materials are first provided;

(f) a receipt for the preliminary prospectus has been issued in the local jurisdiction; and

(g) the investment dealer provides a copy of the preliminary prospectus and any amendment with the marketing materials.

(2) If a template version of the marketing materials is approved in writing by the issuer and lead underwriter under paragraph (1)(d) and filed under paragraph (1)(e), an investment dealer may provide a limited-use version of the marketing materials that

(a) has a date that is different than the template version;

(b) contains a cover page referring to the investment dealer or underwriters or a particular investor or group of investors;

(c) contains contact information for the investment dealer or underwriters; or

(d) has text in a format, including the type's font, colour or size, that is different than the template version.

(3) If a template version of the marketing materials is divided into separate sections for separate subjects and is approved in writing by the issuer and lead underwriter under paragraph (1)(d), and that template version is filed under paragraph (1)(e), an investment dealer may provide a limited-use version of the marketing materials that includes only one or more of those separate sections.

(4) The issuer may remove any comparables, and any disclosure relating to those comparables, from the template version of the marketing materials before filing it under paragraph (1)(e) or (7)(a) if

(a) the comparables, and any disclosure relating to the comparables, are in a separate section of the template version of the marketing materials;

(b) the template version of the marketing materials that is filed contains a note advising that the comparables, and any disclosure relating to the comparables, were removed in accordance with this subsection, provided that the note appears immediately after where the removed comparables and related disclosure would have been;

(c) if the prospectus is filed in the local jurisdiction, a complete template version of the marketing materials containing the comparables, and any disclosure relating to the comparables, is delivered to the securities regulatory authority; and

(d) the complete template version of the marketing materials contains disclosure proximate to the comparables which

(i) explains what comparables are;

(ii) explains the basis on which the other issuers were included in the comparables and why the other issuers are considered to be an appropriate basis for comparison with the issuer;

(iii) explains the basis on which the compared attributes were included;

(iv) states that the information about the other issuers was obtained from public sources and has not been verified by the issuer or the underwriters;

(v) discloses any risks relating to the comparables, including risks in making an investment decision based on the comparables; and

(vi) states that if the comparables contain a misrepresentation, the investor does not have a remedy under securities legislation.

(5) Marketing materials provided under subsection (1) must be dated and include the following legend, or words to the same effect, on the first page:

A preliminary prospectus containing important information relating to the securities described in this document has been filed with the securities regulatory authorit[y/ies] in [each of/certain of the provinces/provinces and territories of Canada]. A copy of the preliminary prospectus, and any amendment, is required to be delivered with this document.

The preliminary prospectus is still subject to completion. There will not be any sale or any acceptance of an offer to buy the securities until a receipt for the final prospectus has been issued.

This document does not provide full disclosure of all material facts relating to the securities offered. Investors should read the preliminary prospectus, the final prospectus and any amendment for disclosure of those facts, especially risk factors relating to the securities offered, before making an investment decision.

(6) If marketing materials are provided during the waiting period under subsection (1), the issuer must include the template version of the marketing materials filed under paragraph 1(e) in its final prospectus, or incorporate by reference the template version of the marketing materials filed under paragraph 1(e) into its final prospectus, in the manner described in subsection 36A.1(1) of Form 41-101F1 or subsection 11.6(1) of Form 44-101F1, as applicable.

(7) If the final prospectus or any amendment modifies a statement of a material fact that appeared in marketing materials provided during the waiting period under subsection (1), the issuer must

(a) prepare and file, at the time the issuer files the final prospectus or any amendment, a revised template version of the marketing materials that is blacklined to show the modified statement, and

(b) include in the final prospectus, or any amendment, the disclosure required by subsection 36A.1(3) of Form 41-101F1 or subsection 11.6(3) of Form 44-101F1, as applicable.

(8) A revised template version of the marketing materials filed under subsection (7) must comply with section 13.8.

(9) If marketing materials are provided during the waiting period under subsection (1) but the issuer does not comply with subsection (6), the marketing materials are deemed for purposes of securities legislation to be incorporated into the issuer's final prospectus as of the date of the final prospectus to the extent not otherwise expressly modified or superseded by a statement contained in the final prospectus.

13.8 Marketing materials after a receipt for a final prospectus — (1) An investment dealer must not provide marketing materials to a potential investor after a receipt for a final prospectus or any amendment is issued unless

(a) the marketing materials comply with subsections (2) to (8);

(b) other than contact information for the investment dealer or underwriters and any comparables, all information in the marketing materials concerning the issuer, the securities or the offering is disclosed in, or derived from, the final prospectus and any amendment;

(c) other than prescribed language, the marketing materials contain the same cautionary language in bold type as contained on the cover page, and in the summary, of the final prospectus;

(d) a template version of the marketing materials is approved in writing by the issuer and the lead underwriter before the marketing materials are provided;

(e) a template version of the marketing materials is filed on or before the day that the marketing materials are first provided;

(f) a receipt for the final prospectus has been issued in the local jurisdiction; and

(g) the investment dealer provides a copy of the final prospectus, and any amendment, with the marketing materials.

(2) If a template version of the marketing materials is approved in writing by the issuer and lead underwriter under paragraph (1)(d) and filed under paragraph (1)(e), an investment dealer may provide a limited-use version of the marketing materials that

(a) has a date that is different than the template version;

(b) contains a cover page referring to the investment dealer or underwriters or a particular investor or group of investors;

(c) contains contact information for the investment dealer or underwriters; or

(d) has text in a format, including the type's font, colour or size, that is different than the template version.

(3) If a template version of the marketing materials is divided into separate sections for separate subjects and is approved in writing by the issuer and lead underwriter under paragraph (1)(d), and that template version is filed under paragraph (1)(e), an investment dealer may provide a limited-use version of the marketing materials that includes only one or more of those separate sections.

(4) The issuer may remove any comparables, and any disclosure relating to those comparables, from the template version of the marketing materials before filing it under paragraph (1)(e) or (7)(b) if

(a) the comparables, and any disclosure relating to the comparables, are in a separate section of the template version of the marketing materials;

(b) the template version of the marketing materials that is filed contains a note advising that the comparables, and any disclosure relating to the comparables, were removed in accordance with this subsection, provided that the note appears immediately after where the removed comparables and related disclosure would have been;

(c) if the prospectus is filed in the local jurisdiction, a complete template version of the marketing materials containing the comparables, and any disclosure relating to the comparables, is delivered to the securities regulatory authority; and

(d) the complete template version of the marketing materials contains the disclosure referred to in paragraph 13.7(4)(d).

(5) Marketing materials provided under subsection (1) must be dated and include the following legend, or words to the same effect, on the first page:

A final prospectus containing important information relating to the securities described in this document has been filed with the securities regulatory authorit[y/ies] in [each of/certain of the provinces/provinces and territories of Canada]. A copy of the final prospectus, and any amendment, is required to be delivered with this document.

This document does not provide full disclosure of all material facts relating to the securities offered. Investors should read the final prospectus, and any amendment, for disclosure of those facts, especially risk factors relating to the securities offered, before making an investment decision.

(6) An investment dealer must not provide marketing materials under subsection (1) unless the issuer

(a) has included the template version of the marketing materials filed under paragraph 1(e) in its final prospectus, and any amendment, or incorporated by reference the template version of the marketing materials filed under paragraph 1(e) into its final prospectus, and any amendment, in the manner described in subsection 36A.1(1) of Form 41-101F1 or subsection 11.6(1) of Form 44-101F1, as applicable, or

(b) has included in its final prospectus, and any amendment, the statement described in subsection 36A.1(4) of Form 41-101F1 or subsection 11.6(4) of Form 44-101F1, as applicable.

(7) If an amendment to a final prospectus modifies a statement of material fact that appeared in marketing materials provided under subsection (1), the issuer must

(a) indicate in the amendment to the final prospectus that the marketing materials are not part of the final prospectus, as amended, to the extent that the contents of the marketing materials have been modified or superseded by a statement contained in the amendment;

(b) prepare and file, at the time the issuer files the amendment to the final prospectus, a revised template version of the marketing materials that is blacklined to show the modified statement; and

(c) include in the amendment to the final prospectus the disclosure required by subsection 36A.1(3) of Form 41-101F1 or subsection 11.6(3) of Form 44-101F1, as applicable.

(8) Any revised template version of the marketing materials filed under subsection (7) must comply with this section.

(9) If marketing materials are provided under subsection (1) but the issuer did not comply with subsection (6), the marketing materials are deemed for purposes of securities legislation to be incorporated into the issuer's final prospectus as of the date of the final prospectus to the extent not otherwise expressly modified or superseded by a statement contained in the final prospectus.

13.9 Road shows during the waiting period — (1) An investment dealer that conducts a road show for potential investors during the waiting period is exempt from the prospectus requirement with respect to that road show if

(a) the road show complies with subsections (2) to (4); and

(b) a receipt for the preliminary prospectus has been issued in the local jurisdiction.

(2) Subject to section 13.12, an investment dealer must not provide marketing materials to an investor attending a road show conducted under subsection (1) unless the marketing materials are provided in accordance with section 13.7.

(3) If an investment dealer conducts a road show, the investment dealer must establish and follow reasonable procedures to

(a) ask any investor attending the road show in person, by telephone conference call, on the internet or by other electronic means to provide their name and contact information;

(b) keep a record of any information provided by the investor; and

(c) provide the investor with a copy of the preliminary prospectus and any amendment.

(4) If an investment dealer permits an investor, other than an accredited investor, to attend a road show, the investment dealer must commence the road show with the oral reading of the following statement or a statement to the same effect:

This presentation does not provide full disclosure of all material facts relating to the securities offered. Investors should read the preliminary prospectus, the final prospectus and any amendment for disclosure of those facts, especially risk factors relating to the securities offered, before making an investment decision.

13.10 Road shows after a receipt for a final prospectus — (1) An investment dealer must not conduct a road show for potential investors after a receipt for a final prospectus or any amendment is issued unless

(a) the road show complies with subsections (2) to (4); and

(b) a receipt for the final prospectus has been issued in the local jurisdiction.

(2) Subject to section 13.12, an investment dealer must not provide marketing materials to an investor attending a road show conducted under subsection (1) unless the marketing materials are provided in accordance with section 13.8.

(3) If an investment dealer conducts a road show, the investment dealer must establish and follow reasonable procedures to

(a) ask any investor attending the road show in person, by telephone conference call, on the internet or by other electronic means to provide their name and contact information;

(b) keep a record of any information provided by the investor; and

(c) provide the investor with a copy of the final prospectus and any amendment.

(4) If an investment dealer permits an investor, other than an accredited investor, to attend a road show, the investment dealer must commence the road show with the oral reading of the following statement or a statement to the same effect:

This presentation does not provide full disclosure of all material facts relating to the securities offered. Investors should read the final prospectus and any amendment for disclosure of those facts, especially risk factors relating to the securities offered, before making an investment decision.

13.11 Exception from procedures for road shows for certain U.S. cross-border initial public offerings — (1) Subject to subsection (2), the following provisions do not apply to an investment dealer that conducts a road show in connection with a U.S. cross-border initial public offering:

(a) paragraphs 13.9(3)(a) and (b);

(b) paragraphs 13.10(3)(a) and (b).

(2) Subsection (1) does not apply unless

(a) the issuer is relying on the exemption from United States filing requirements in Rule 433(d)(8)(ii) under the 1933 Act in respect of the road show; and

(b) the investment dealer establishes and follows reasonable procedures to

(i) ask any investor attending the road show in person, by telephone conference call, on the internet or by other electronic means to voluntarily provide their name and contact information; and

(ii) keep a record of any information voluntarily provided by the investor.

13.12 Exception from filing and incorporation requirements for road shows for certain U.S. cross-border offerings — (1) Subject to subsections (2) to (4), if an investment dealer provides marketing materials to a potential investor in connection with a road show for a U.S. cross-border offering, the following provisions do not apply to the template version of the marketing materials relating to the road show:

(a) paragraphs 13.7(1)(e) and 13.8(1)(e);

(b) subsections 13.7(6) to (9);

(c) subsections 13.8(6) to (9);

(d) paragraphs 36A.1(1)(b) and (c), paragraph 36A.1(3)(b), subsection 36A.1(4) and section 37.6 of Form 41-101F1;

(e) paragraphs 11.6(1)(b) and (c), paragraph 11.6(3)(b) and subsection 11.6(4) of Form 44-101F1.

(2) Subsection (1) does not apply unless

(a) the underwriters have a reasonable expectation that the securities offered under the U.S. cross-border offering will be sold primarily in the United States of America;

(b) the issuer and the underwriters who sign the prospectus filed in the local jurisdiction provide a contractual right containing the language set out in subsection 36A.1(5) of Form 41-101F1, or words to the same effect, except that the language may specify that the contractual right does not apply to any comparables provided in accordance with subsection (3); and

(c) if the prospectus is filed in the local jurisdiction, the template version of the marketing materials relating to the road show is delivered to the securities regulatory authority.

(3) If the template version of the marketing materials relating to the road show contains comparables, the template version of the marketing materials must contain the disclosure referred to in paragraph 13.7(4)(d).

(4) For greater certainty, subsection (1) does not apply to marketing materials other than the marketing materials provided in connection with the road show.

PART 13A — ADVERTISING AND MARKETING IN CONNECTION WITH PROSPECTUS OFFERINGS OF INVESTMENT FUNDS

13A.1 Application — This Part applies to investment funds filing a prospectus in the form of Form 41-101F2 or Form 41-101F3.

13A.2 Legend for communications during the waiting period — (1) A preliminary prospectus notice or other communication used in connection with a prospectus offering during the waiting period must contain the following legend, or words to the same effect:

A preliminary prospectus containing important information relating to these securities has been filed with securities commissions or similar authorities in certain jurisdictions of Canada. The preliminary prospectus is still subject to completion or amendment. Copies of the preliminary prospectus may be obtained from *[insert name and contact information for dealer or other relevant person or company]*. There will not be any sale or acceptance of an offer to buy the securities until a receipt for the final prospectus has been issued.

(2) If the preliminary prospectus notice or other communication is in writing, include the wording required under subsection (1) in bold type that is at least as large as that used generally in the body of the text.

13A.3 Legend for communications following receipt for the final prospectus — (1) A final prospectus notice or other communication used in connection with a prospectus offering following the issuance of a receipt for the final prospectus must contain the following legend, or words to the same effect:

This offering is made only by prospectus. The prospectus contains important detailed information about the securities being offered. Copies of the prospectus may be obtained from *[insert name and contact information for dealer or other relevant person or company]*. Investors should read the prospectus before making an investment decision.

(2) If the final prospectus notice or other communication is in writing, include the wording required under subsection (1) in bold type that is at least as large as that used generally in the body of the text.

13A.4 Advertising during the waiting period — If the issuer is an investment fund, an advertisement used in connection with a prospectus offering during the waiting period may state only the following information:

(a) whether the security represents a share in an incorporated entity or an interest in an unincorporated entity;

(b) the name of the issuer;

(c) the price of the security;

(d) the fundamental investment objectives of the investment fund;

(e) the name of the manager of the investment fund;

(f) the name of the portfolio manager of the investment fund;

(g) the name and address of a person or company from whom a preliminary prospectus may be obtained and purchases of securities may be made;

(h) how many securities will be made available;

(i) whether the security is or will be a qualified investment for a registered retirement savings plan, registered retirement income fund, registered education savings plan or tax free savings account qualifies, or will qualify, the holder for special tax treatment.

PART 14 — CUSTODIANSHIP OF PORTFOLIO ASSETS OF AN INVESTMENT FUND

14.1 General — (1) This Part applies to an investment fund that prepares a prospectus in accordance with this Instrument, other than an investment fund subject to NI 81-102.

(2) Subject to sections 14.8 and 14.9, all portfolio assets of an investment fund must be held under the custodianship of one custodian that satisfies the requirements of section 14.2.

(3) No manager of an investment fund may act as a custodian or sub-custodian of the investment fund.

14.2 Who may act as custodian or sub-custodian — (1) If portfolio assets are held in Canada by a custodian or sub-custodian, the custodian or sub-custodian must be one of the following:

(a) a bank listed in Schedule I, II or III of the *Bank Act* (Canada);

(b) a trust company that

(i) is incorporated and licenced or registered under the laws of Canada or a jurisdiction, and

(ii) has equity, as reported in its most recent audited financial statement, of not less than $10,000,000;

(c) a company that is incorporated under the laws of Canada or a jurisdiction and is an affiliate of a bank or trust company referred to in paragraph (a) or (b), if

(i) the company has equity, as reported in its most recent audited financial statements that have been made public, of not less than $10,000,000, or

(ii) the bank or trust company has assumed responsibility for all of the custodial obligations of the company for that investment fund.

(2) If portfolio assets are held outside of Canada by a sub-custodian, the sub-custodian must be one of the following:

(a) an entity referred to in subsection (1);

(b) an entity that

(i) is incorporated or organized under the law of a country, or a political subdivision of a country, other than Canada,

(ii) is regulated as a banking institution or trust company by the government, or an agency of the government of the country or political subdivision of the country under whose laws it is incorporated or organized, and

(iii) has equity, as reported in its most recent audited financial statements of not less than the equivalent of $100,000,000;

(c) an affiliate of an entity referred to in paragraph (a) or (b) if

(i) the affiliate has equity, as reported in its most recent audited financial statements that have been made public, of not less than the equivalent of $100,000,000, or

(ii) the entity referred to in paragraphs (a) or (b) has assumed responsibility for all of the custodial obligations of the affiliate for that investment fund.

14.3 Standard of care — (1) The custodian and each sub-custodian of an investment fund, in carrying out their duties concerning the safekeeping of, and dealing with, the portfolio assets of the investment fund, must exercise

(a) the degree of care, diligence and skill that a reasonably prudent person would exercise in the circumstances, or

(b) at least the same degree of care as they exercise with respect to their own property of a similar kind, if this is a higher degree of care than the degree of care referred to in paragraph (a).

(2) No investment fund may relieve the custodian or a sub-custodian of the investment fund from liability to the investment fund or to a securityholder of the investment fund for loss that arises out of the failure of the custodian or sub-custodian to exercise the standard of care imposed by subsection (1).

(3) An investment fund may indemnify a custodian or sub-custodian against legal fees, judgments and amounts paid in settlement, actually and reasonably incurred by that entity in connection with custodial or sub-custodial services provided by that entity to the investment fund, if those fees, judgments and amounts were not incurred as a result of a breach of the standard of care described in subsection (1).

(4) No investment fund may incur the cost of any portion of liability insurance that insures a custodian or sub-custodian for a liability, except to the extent that the custodian or sub-custodian may be indemnified for that liability under this section.

14.4 Appointment of sub-custodian — (1) The custodian or a sub-custodian of an investment fund may appoint one or more sub-custodians to hold portfolio assets of the investment fund if,

(a) in the case where the appointment is by the custodian, the investment fund gives written consent to each appointment,

(b) in the case where the appointment is by a sub-custodian, the investment fund and the custodian of the investment fund give written consent to each appointment,

(c) the sub-custodian is an entity described in subsection 14.2(1) or (2), as applicable,

(d) the arrangements under which a sub-custodian is appointed are such that the investment fund may enforce rights directly, or require the custodian or a sub-custodian to enforce rights on behalf of the investment fund, to the portfolio assets held by the appointed sub-custodian, and

(e) the appointment is otherwise in compliance with this Instrument.

(2) Despite paragraphs (1)(a) and (b), a general consent to the appointment of persons or companies that are part of an international network of sub-custodians within the organization of the custodian appointed by the investment fund or the sub-custodian appointed by the custodian is sufficient if that general consent is part of an agreement governing the relationship between the investment fund and the appointed custodian or the custodian and the appointed sub-custodian.

(3) A custodian or sub-custodian must provide to the investment fund a list of each person or company that is appointed sub-custodian under a general consent referred to in subsection (2).

14.5 Content of agreements — (1) All custodian agreements and sub-custodian agreements of an investment fund must provide for

(a) the location of portfolio assets,

(b) the appointment of a sub-custodian, if any,

(c) the provision of lists of sub-custodians,

(d) the method of holding portfolio assets,

(e) the standard of care and responsibility for loss,

(f) review and compliance reports, and

(g) the safekeeping of portfolio assets on terms consistent with the agreement between the investment fund and the custodian, for an agreement between a custodian and a sub-custodian.

(2) The provisions of an agreement referred to under subsection (1) must comply with the requirements of this Part.

(3) A custodian agreement or sub-custodian agreement respecting the portfolio assets of an investment fund must not

(a) provide for the creation of any security interest on the portfolio assets except for a good faith claim for payment of the fees and expenses of the custodian or sub-custodian for acting in that capacity or to secure the obligations of the investment fund to repay borrowings by the investment fund from a custodian or sub-custodian for the purpose of settling portfolio transactions, or

(b) contain a provision that would require the payment of a fee to the custodian or sub-custodian for the transfer of the beneficial ownership of portfolio assets, other than for safekeeping and administrative services in connection with acting as custodian or sub-custodian.

14.6 Review and compliance reports — (1) The custodian of an investment fund must, on a periodic basis and at least annually,

(a) review the agreements referred to in section 14.5 to determine if those agreements are in compliance with this Part,

(b) make reasonable enquiries to ensure that each sub-custodian is an entity referred to in subsection 14.2(1) or (2), as applicable, and

(c) make or cause to be made any changes that may be necessary to ensure that

(i) the agreements are in compliance with this Part, and

(ii) each sub-custodian is an entity referred to in subsection 14.2(1) or (2), as applicable.

(2) The custodian of an investment fund must, within 60 days after the end of each financial year of the investment fund, advise the investment fund in writing

(a) of the names and addresses of all sub-custodians of the investment fund,

(b) if the agreements are in compliance with this Part, and

(c) if, to the best of the knowledge and belief of the custodian, each sub-custodian is an entity that satisfies the requirements of subsection 14.2(1) or (2), as applicable.

(3) A copy of the report referred to in subsection (2) must be delivered by or on behalf of the investment fund to the securities regulatory authority within 30 days after the filing of the annual financial statements of the investment fund.

14.7 Holding of portfolio assets and payment of fees — (1) Except as provided in subsections (2) and (3) and sections 14.8 and 14.9, portfolio assets not registered in the name of the investment fund must be registered in the name of the custodian or a sub-custodian of the investment fund or any of their respective nominees with an account number or other designation in the records of the custodian sufficient to show that the beneficial ownership of the portfolio assets is vested in the investment fund.

(2) The custodian or a sub-custodian of the investment fund or the applicable nominee must segregate portfolio assets issued in bearer form to show that the beneficial ownership of the property is vested in the investment fund.

(3) A custodian or sub-custodian of an investment fund may deposit portfolio assets with a depository or a clearing agency that operates a book-based system.

(4) The custodian or sub-custodian of an investment fund arranging for the deposit of portfolio assets with, and their delivery to, a depository, or clearing agency, that operates a book-based system must ensure that the records of any of the applicable participants in that book-based system or the custodian contain an account number or other designation sufficient to show that the beneficial ownership of the portfolio assets is vested in the investment fund.

(5) No investment fund may pay a fee to a custodian or sub-custodian for the transfer of beneficial ownership of portfolio assets other than for safekeeping and administrative services in connection with acting as custodian or sub-custodian.

**Part 4:
DISTRIBUTIONS**

14.8 Custodial provisions relating to derivatives and securities lending, repurchases and reverse repurchase agreements — (1) For the purposes of subsection (4), "specified derivative" has the same meaning as in NI 81-102.

(2) An investment fund may deposit portfolio assets as margin for transactions in Canada involving clearing corporation options, options on futures or standardized futures with a dealer that is a member of an SRO that is a participating member of CIPF if the amount of margin deposited does not, when aggregated with the amount of margin already held by the dealer on behalf of the investment fund, exceed 10% of the net assets of the investment fund, taken at market value as at the time of deposit.

(3) An investment fund may deposit portfolio assets with a dealer as margin for transactions outside Canada involving clearing corporation options, options on futures or standardized futures if

    (a) in the case of standardized futures and options on futures, the dealer is a member of a futures exchange or, in the case of clearing corporation options, is a member of a stock exchange, and, as a result in either case, is subject to a regulatory audit,

    (b) the dealer has a net worth, determined from its most recent audited financial statements that have been made public, in excess of the equivalent of $50 million, and

    (c) the amount of margin deposited does not, when aggregated with the amount of margin already held by the dealer on behalf of the investment fund, exceed 10% of the net assets of the investment fund, taken at market value as at the time of deposit.

(4) An investment fund may deposit with its counterparty portfolio assets over which it has granted a security interest in connection with a particular specified derivatives transaction.

(5) The agreement by which portfolio assets are deposited in accordance with subsection (2), (3) or (4) must require the person or company holding the portfolio assets to ensure that its records show that the investment fund is the beneficial owner of the portfolio assets.

(6) An investment fund may deliver portfolio assets to a person or company in satisfaction of its obligations under a securities lending, repurchase or reverse purchase agreement if the collateral, cash proceeds or purchased securities that are delivered to the investment fund in connection with the transaction are held under the custodianship of the custodian or a sub-custodian of the investment fund in compliance with this Part.

14.8.1 Custodial provisions relating to short sales — (1) For the purposes of subsection (2), "borrowing agent" has the same meaning as in NI 81-102.

(2) Except where the borrowing agent is the investment fund's custodian or sub-custodian, if an investment fund deposits portfolio assets with a borrowing agent as security in connection with a short sale of securities, the market value of portfolio assets deposited with the borrowing agent must not, when aggregated with the market value of portfolio assets already held by the borrowing agent as security for outstanding short sales of securities by the investment fund, exceed 10% of the net asset value of the investment fund at the time of deposit.

(3) An investment fund must not deposit portfolio assets as security in connection with a short sale of securities with a dealer in Canada unless that dealer is a registered dealer and is a member of the Investment Industry Regulatory Organization of Canada.

(4) An investment fund must not deposit portfolio assets as security in connection with a short sale of securities with a dealer outside Canada unless that dealer

    (a) is a member of a stock exchange and is subject to a regulatory audit, and

    (b) has a net worth, determined from its most recent audited financial statements that have been made public, in excess of the equivalent of $50 million.

14.9 Separate account for paying expenses — An investment fund may deposit cash in Canada with an entity referred to in paragraph (a) or (b) of subsection 14.2(1) to facilitate the payment of regular operating expenses of the investment fund.

PART 15 — DOCUMENTS INCORPORATED BY REFERENCE BY INVESTMENT FUNDS

15.1 Application — This Part applies only to an investment fund in continuous distribution.

15.2 Incorporation by reference — (1) An investment fund must incorporate by reference into its long form prospectus, by means of a statement to that effect, the filed documents listed in

    (a) section 37.1 of Form 41-101F2 for investment funds other than scholarship plans, and

    (b) subsection 4.1(1) of Part B of Form 41-101F3 for scholarship plans.

(2) If an investment fund does not incorporate by reference into its long form prospectus a document referred to in subsection (1), the document is deemed, for the purposes of securities legislation, to be incorporated by reference in the investment fund's long form prospectus as of the date of the long form prospectus.

(3) An investment fund must incorporate by reference in its long form prospectus, by means of a statement to that effect, the subsequently filed documents referred to in

    (a) section 37.2 of Form 41-101F2 for investment funds other than scholarship plans, and

    (b) subsection 4.1(2) of Part B of Form 41-101F3 for scholarship plans.

(4) If an investment fund does not incorporate by reference into its long form prospectus a document referred to in subsection (3), the document is deemed, for the purposes of securities legislation, to be incorporated by reference in the investment fund's long form prospectus as of the date the investment fund filed the document.

PART 16 — DISTRIBUTION OF PRELIMINARY PROSPECTUS AND DISTRIBUTION LIST

16.1 Distribution of preliminary prospectus and distribution list — Except in Ontario, any dealer distributing a security during the waiting period must

    (a) send a copy of the preliminary prospectus to each prospective purchaser who indicates an interest in purchasing the security and requests a copy of such preliminary prospectus, and

    (b) maintain a record of the names and addresses of all persons and companies to whom the preliminary prospectus has been forwarded.

[Note: *In Ontario, sections 66 and 67 of the* Securities Act *(Ontario) impose similar requirements regarding the distribution of a preliminary prospectus and maintaining a distribution list.*]

PART 17 — LAPSE DATE

17.1 **Pro forma prospectus** — (1) In this Part, "pro forma prospectus" means a long form prospectus that complies with the requirements described in subsection (2).

(2) A pro forma prospectus must be prepared in the form of a long form prospectus in accordance with Form 41-101F1, Form 41-101F2 or Form 41-101F3, as applicable, and other securities legislation, except that a pro forma prospectus is not required to contain prospectus certificates or to comply with sections 4.2, 4.3 and 4.4 of this Instrument.

(3) This Part does not apply to a prospectus filed in accordance with NI 44-101, NI 44-102 or NI 44-103.

17.2 **Refiling of prospectus** — (1) This section does not apply in Ontario.

(2) In this section, "lapse date" means, with reference to the distribution of a security that has been qualified under a prospectus, the date that is 12 months after the date of the most recent final prospectus relating to the security.

(3) An issuer must not continue the distribution of a security to which the prospectus requirement applies after the lapse date unless the issuer files a new prospectus that complies with securities legislation and a receipt for that new prospectus is issued by the regulator.

(4) Despite subsection (3), a distribution may be continued for a further 12 months after a lapse date if,

    (a) the issuer delivers a pro forma prospectus not less than 30 days before the lapse date of the previous prospectus;

    (b) the issuer files a new final prospectus not less than 10 days after the lapse date of the previous prospectus; and

    (c) a receipt for the new final prospectus is issued by the regulator within 20 days after the lapse date of the previous prospectus.

(5) The continued distribution of securities after the lapse date does not contravene subsection (3) unless and until any of the conditions of subsection (4) are not complied with.

(6) Subject to any extension granted under subsection (7), if a condition in subsection (4) is not complied with, a purchaser may cancel a purchase made in a distribution after the lapse date in reliance on subsection (4) within 90 days after the purchaser first became aware of the failure to comply with the condition.

(7) The regulator may, on an application of a reporting issuer, extend, subject to such terms and conditions as it may impose, the times provided by subsection (4) where in its opinion it would not be prejudicial to the public interest to do so.

[Note: *In Ontario, section 62 of the* Securities Act *(Ontario) imposes similar requirements and procedures regarding refiling of prospectuses.*]

PART 18 — STATEMENT OF RIGHTS

18.1 **Statement of rights** — Except in Ontario, a prospectus must contain a statement of the rights given to a purchaser under securities legislation in case of a failure to deliver the prospectus or in case of a misrepresentation in a prospectus.

[Note: *In Ontario, section 60 of the* Securities Act *(Ontario) imposes a similar requirement for the inclusion of a statement of rights in a prospectus.*]

PART 19 — EXEMPTION

19.1 **Exemption** — (1) The regulator or the securities regulatory authority may grant an exemption from the provisions of this Instrument, in whole or in part, subject to such conditions or restrictions as may be imposed in the exemption.

(2) Despite subsection (1), in Ontario, only the regulator may grant such an exemption.

(3) Except in Ontario, an exemption referred to in subsection (1) is granted under the statute referred to in Appendix B of NI 14-101 opposite the name of the local jurisdiction.

19.2 **Application for exemption** — An application made to the securities regulatory authority or regulator for an exemption from the provisions of this Instrument must include a letter or memorandum describing the matters relating to the exemption, and indicating why consideration should be given to the granting of the exemption.

19.3 **Evidence of exemption** — (1) Subject to subsection (2) and without limiting the manner in which an exemption under this Part may be evidenced, the granting under this Part of an exemption, other than an exemption from subsection 2.2(2), may be evidenced by the issuance of a receipt for a final prospectus or an amendment to a final prospectus.

(2) The issuance of a receipt for a final prospectus or an amendment to a final prospectus is not evidence that the exemption has been granted unless

    (a) the person or company that sought the exemption sent to the regulator

        (i) the letter or memorandum referred to in section 19.2 on or before the date of the filing of the pro forma or preliminary prospectus, or

        (ii) the letter or memorandum referred to in section 19.2 after the date of the filing of the pro forma or preliminary prospectus and received a written acknowledgement from the regulator that the exemption may be evidenced in the manner set out in subsection (1), and

    (b) the regulator has not before, or concurrently with, the issuance of the receipt sent notice to the person or company that sought the exemption, that the exemption sought may not be evidenced in the manner set out in subsection (1).

PART 20 — TRANSITION, EFFECTIVE DATE, AND REPEAL

20.1 [repealed]

20.2 **Effective date** — This Instrument comes into force on March 17, 2008.

20.3 **Repeal** — National Instrument 41-101 *Prospectus Disclosure Requirements*, which came into force on December 31, 2000, is repealed.

Part 4: DISTRIBUTIONS

Appendix A

Schedule 1, Part A — Personal Information Form and Authorization of Indirect Collection, Use and Disclosure of Personal Information

This Personal Information Form and Authorization of Indirect Collection, Use and Disclosure of Personal Information (the "Form") is to be completed by every individual who, in connection with an issuer filing a prospectus (the "Issuer"), is required to do so under Part 9 of National Instrument 41-101 *General Prospectus Requirements* or Part 4 of National Instrument 44-101 Short Form Prospectus Distributions or Part 2 of National Instrument 81-101 *Mutual Fund Prospectus Disclosure.*

The securities regulatory authorities do not make any of the information provided in this Form public.

General Instructions:

All Questions	*All questions must have a response.* The response of "N/A" or "Not Applicable" will not be accepted for any questions, *except* Questions 1(B), 2(iii) and 5.
	For the purposes of answering the questions in this Form, the term "issuer" includes an investment fund manager.
Questions 6 to 10	Please place a checkmark (✓) in the appropriate space provided. If your answer to any of questions 6 to 10 is "YES", you *must*, in an attachment, provide complete details, including the circumstances, relevant dates, names of the parties involved and final disposition, if known. *Any attachment must be initialled by the person completing this Form.* Responses must consider all time periods.
Delivery	*The issuer should deliver completed Forms electronically via the System for Electronic Document Analysis and Retrieval (SEDAR) under the document type "Personal Information Form and Authorization". Access to this document type is not available to the public.*

Caution

An individual who makes a false statement commits an offence under securities legislation. Steps may be taken to verify the answers you have given in this Form, including verification of information relating to any previous criminal record.

Definitions

"Offence" An offence *includes*:

    (a) a summary conviction or indictable offence under the *Criminal Code* (Canada);

    (b) a quasi-criminal offence (for example under the *Income Tax Act* (Canada), the *Immigration Act* (Canada) or the tax, immigration, drugs, firearms, money laundering or securities legislation of any Canadian or foreign jurisdiction);

    (c) a misdemeanour or felony under the criminal legislation of the United States of America, or any state or territory therein; or

    (d) an offence under the criminal legislation of any other foreign jurisdiction;

GUIDANCE: *If you have received a pardon under the* Criminal Records Act *(Canada) for an Offence that relates to fraud (including any type of fraudulent activity), misappropriation of money or other property, theft, forgery, falsification of books or documents or similar Offences, you must disclose the pardoned Offence in this Form. In such circumstances:*

    (a) the appropriate written response would be "Yes, pardon granted on (date)"; and

    (b) you must provide complete details in an attachment to this Form.

"Proceedings" means:

    (a) a civil or criminal proceeding or inquiry which is currently before a court;

    (b) a proceeding before an arbitrator or umpire or a person or group of persons authorized by law to make an inquiry and take evidence under oath in the matter;

    (c) a proceeding before a tribunal in the exercise of a statutory power of decision making where the tribunal is required by law to hold or afford the parties to the proceeding an opportunity for a hearing before making a decision; or

    (d) a proceeding before a self-regulatory entity authorized by law to regulate the operations and the standards of practice and business conduct of its members (including where applicable, issuers listed on a stock exchange) and individuals associated with those members and issuers, in which the self-regulatory entity is required under its by-laws, rules or policies to hold or afford the parties the opportunity to be heard before making a decision, but does not apply to a proceeding in which one or more persons are required to make an investigation and to make a report, with or without recommendations, if the report is for the information or advice of the person to whom it is made and does not in any way bind or limit that person in any decision the person may have the power to make;

"securities regulatory authority" or *"SRA"* means a body created by statute in any Canadian or foreign jurisdiction to administer securities law, regulation and policy (e.g. securities commission), but does not include an exchange or other self regulatory entity;

"self regulatory entity" or *"SRE"* means:

    (a) a stock, derivatives, commodities, futures or options exchange;

    (b) an association of investment, securities, mutual fund, commodities, or future dealers;

    (c) an association of investment counsel or portfolio managers;

    (d) an association of other professionals (e.g. legal, accounting, engineering); and

    (e) any other group, institution or self-regulatory organization, recognized by a securities regulatory authority, that is responsible for the enforcement of rules, policies, disciplines or codes under any applicable legislation, or considered an SRE in another country.

1. A. IDENTIFICATION OF INDIVIDUAL COMPLETING FORM

LAST NAME(S)   *FIRST NAME(S)*   *FULL MIDDLE NAME(S) (No initials. If none, please state)*

NAME(S) MOST COMMONLY KNOWN BY:

NAME OF ISSUER

PRESENT or PROPOSED POSITION(S) WITH THE ISSUER — check (✓) all positions below that are applicable.		**IF DIRECTOR / OFFICER DISCLOSE THE DATE ELECTED / APPOINTED**			**IF OFFICER — PROVIDE TITLE IF OTHER — PROVIDE DETAILS**
	(✓)	**Month**	**Day**	**Year**	
Director	....	....	....	....	....
Officer	....	....	....	....	
Other	....	....	....	....	

B.   Other than the name given in Question 1A above, provide any legal names, assumed names or nicknames under which you have carried on business or have otherwise been known, including information regarding any name change(s) resulting from marriage, divorce, court order or any other process. Use an attachment if necessary.

FROM		**TO**	
MM	**YY**	**MM**	**YY**
....	....	....	....
....	....	....	....

C.

	GENDER	**DATE OF BIRTH**			**PLACE OF BIRTH**		
		Month	**Day**	**Year**	**City**	**Province/State**	**Country**
Male	....	....	....	....	....	....	....
Female	....	....	....	....	....	....	....

D.   **MARITAL STATUS**   **FULL NAME OF SPOUSE — include common-law**   **OCCUPATION OF SPOUSE**

E. TELEPHONE AND FACSIMILE NUMBERS AND E-MAIL ADDRESS

RESIDENTIAL   (..........)   *FACSIMILE*   (..........)

BUSINESS   (..........)   *E-MAIL**

Provide an email address that the regulator may use to contact you regarding this personal information form. This email address may be used to exchange personal information relating to you.

F. RESIDENTIAL HISTORY — *Provide all residential addresses for the past 10 YEARS starting with your current principal residential address. If you are unable to recall the complete residential address for a period, which is beyond five years from the date of completion of this Form, the municipality and province or state and country must be identified. The regulator reserves the right to require the full address.*

STREET ADDRESS, CITY, PROVINCE/STATE, COUNTRY & POSTAL/ZIP CODE	**FROM**		**TO**	
	MM	**YY**	**MM**	**YY**
	....	....	....	....
	....	....	....	....
	....	....	....	....
	....	....	....	....

2. CITIZENSHIP

			YES	**NO**
(i)	Are you a Canadian citizen?		....	....
(ii)	Are you a person lawfully in Canada as an immigrant but are not yet a Canadian citizen?		....	....
(iii)	If "Yes" to Question 2(ii), the number of years of continuous residence in Canada:		....	....
(iv)	Do you hold citizenship in any country other than Canada?		....	....
(v)	If "Yes" to Question 2(iv), the name of the country(ies):		....	

3. EMPLOYMENT HISTORY

Provide your complete employment history for the *5 YEARS* immediately prior to the date of this Form starting with your current employment. Use an attachment if necessary. If you were unemployed during this period of time, state this and identify the period of unemployment.

EMPLOYER NAME	EMPLOYER ADDRESS	POSITION HELD	FROM		TO	
			MM	YY	MM	YY
			....	....	....	....
			....	....	....	....
			....	....	....	....

4. POSITIONS WITH OTHER ISSUERS

	YES	NO

A.   Are you or have you during the last 10 years ever been a director, officer, promoter, insider or control person for any .... reporting issuer?

B.   If "YES" to 4A above, provide the names of each reporting issuer. State the position(s) held and the period(s) during which you held the position(s). Use an attachment if necessary.

NAME OF REPORTING ISSUER	POSITION(S) HELD	MARKET TRADED ON	FROM			TO
			MM	YY	MM	YY
....	....	....	....	....		....
....	....	....	....	....		....
....	....	....	....	....		....
....	....	....	....	....		....

C.   While you were a director, officer or insider of an issuer, did any exchange or other self-regulatory entity ever refuse .... approval for listing or quotation of the issuer, including (i) a listing resulting from a business combination, reverse takeover or similar transaction involving the issuer that is regulated by an SRE or SRA, (ii) a backdoor listing or qualifying acquisition involving the issuer (as those terms are defined in the TSX Company Manual as amended from time to time) or (iii) a qualifying transaction, reverse takeover or change of business involving the issuer (as those terms are defined in the TSX Venture Corporate Finance Manual as amended from time to time)? If yes, attach full particulars.

5. EDUCATIONAL HISTORY

A.   **PROFESSIONAL DESIGNATION(S) — Identify any professional designation held and professional associations to which you belong, for example, Barrister & Solicitor, C.A., C.M.A., C.G.A., P.Eng., P.Geol., CFA, etc. and indicate which organization and the date the designations were granted.**

PROFESSIONAL DESIGNATION and MEMBERSHIP NUMBER	GRANTOR OF DESIGNATION and CANADIAN or FOREIGN JURISDICTION	DATE GRANTED	
		MM	YY
....	....		
....	....		
....	....		

Describe the current status of any designation and/or association (e.g. active, retired, non-practicing, suspended)

B. *Provide your post-secondary educational history starting with the most recent.*

SCHOOL	LOCATION	DEGREE OR DIPLOMA	DATE OBTAINED		
			MM	DD	YY
			....	....	....
			....	....	....

6. OFFENCES — If you answer "YES" to any item in Question 6, you *must* provide complete details in an attachment. **If you have received a pardon under the *Criminal Records Act* (Canada) for an Offence that relates to fraud (including any type of fraudulent activity), misappropriation of money or other property, theft, forgery, falsification of books or documents or similar Offences, you must disclose the pardoned Offence in this Form.**

	YES	NO

A.   Have you ever, in any Canadian or foreign jurisdiction, pled guilty to or been found guilty of an Offence? ....

B.   Are you the subject of any current charge, indictment or proceeding for an Offence, in any Canadian or foreign jurisdiction? ....

	YES	NO

C. To the best of your knowledge, are you currently or have you **ever** been a director, officer, promoter, insider, or control person of an issuer, in any Canadian or foreign jurisdiction, at the time of events that resulted in the issuer:

(i) pleading guilty to or being found guilty of an Offence? ....

(ii) now being the subject of any charge, indictment or proceeding for an alleged Offence? ....

7. BANKRUPTCY — If you answer "YES" to any item in Question 7, you *must* provide complete details in an attachment and attach a copy of any discharge, release or other applicable document. You must answer "YES" or "NO" for EACH of (A), (B) and (C) below.

	YES	NO

A. Have you, in any Canadian or foreign jurisdiction, within the past « *10 years* » had a petition in bankruptcy issued against you, made a voluntary assignment in bankruptcy, made a proposal under any bankruptcy or insolvency legislation, been subject to any proceeding, arrangement or compromise with creditors, or had a receiver, receiver-manager or trustee appointed to manage your assets? ....

B. Are you now an undischarged bankrupt? ....

C. To the best of your knowledge, are you currently or have you **ever** been a director, officer, promoter, insider, or control person of an issuer, in any Canadian or foreign jurisdiction, at the time of events, or for a period of 12 months preceding the time of events, where the issuer: ....

(i) has made a petition in bankruptcy, a voluntary assignment in bankruptcy, a proposal under any bankruptcy or insolvency legislation, been subject to any proceeding, arrangement or compromise with creditors or had a receiver, receiver-manager or trustee appointed to manage the issuer's assets? ....

(ii) is now an undischarged bankrupt? ....

8. PROCEEDINGS — If you answer "YES" to any item in Question 8, you must provide complete details in an attachment.

	YES	NO

A. **CURRENT PROCEEDINGS BY SECURITIES REGULATORY AUTHORITY OR SELF REGU-LATORY ENTITY. Are you now, in any Canadian or foreign jurisdiction, the subject of:**

(i) a notice of hearing or similar notice issued by an SRA or SRE? ....

(ii) a proceeding of or, to your knowledge, an investigation by, an SRA or SRE? ....

(iii) settlement discussions or negotiations for settlement of any nature or kind whatsoever with an SRA or SRE? ....

	YES	NO

B. **PRIOR PROCEEDINGS BY SECURITIES REGULATORY AUTHORITY OR SELF REGULATO-RY ENTITY. Have you ever:**

(i) been reprimanded, suspended, fined, been the subject of an administrative penalty, or been the subject of any proceedings of any kind whatsoever, in any Canadian or foreign jurisdiction, by an SRA or SRE? ....

(ii) had a registration or licence for the trading of securities, exchange or commodity futures contracts, real estate, insurance or mutual fund products cancelled, refused, restricted or suspended by an SRA or SRE? ....

(iii) been prohibited or disqualified by an SRA or SRE under securities, corporate or any other legislation from acting as a director or officer of a reporting issuer or been prohibited or restricted by an SRA or SRE from acting as a director, officer or employee of, or an agent or consultant to, a reporting issuer? ....

(iv) had a cease trading or similar order issued against you or an order issued against you by an SRA or SRE that denied you the right to use any statutory prospectus or registration exemption? ....

YES   NO

(v) had any other proceeding of any kind taken against you by an SRA or SRE?.

YES   NO

C.   SETTLEMENT AGREEMENT(S)

Have you ever entered into a settlement agreement with an SRA, SRE, attorney general or comparable official or body, in any Canadian or foreign jurisdiction, in a matter that involved actual or alleged fraud, theft, deceit, misrepresentation, conspiracy, breach of trust, breach of fiduciary duty, insider trading, unregistered trading in securities or exchange or commodity futures contracts, illegal distributions, failure to disclose material facts or changes or similar conduct, or any other settlement agreement with respect to any other violation of securities legislation in a Canadian or foreign jurisdiction or the rules, by-laws or policies of any SRE?

YES   NO

D.   *To the best of your knowledge, are you now or have you ever been a director, officer, promoter, insider, or control person of an issuer at the time of such event, in any Canadian or foreign jurisdiction, for which a securities regulatory authority or self regulatory entity has:*

(i) refused, restricted, suspended or cancelled the registration or licensing of an issuer to trade securities, exchange or commodity futures contracts, or to sell or trade real estate, insurance or mutual fund products?

(ii) issued a cease trade or similar order or imposed an administrative penalty of any nature or kind whatsoever against the issuer, other than an order for failure to file financial statements that was revoked within 30 days of its issuance?

(iii) refused a receipt for a prospectus or other offering document, denied any application for listing or quotation or any other similar application, or issued an order that denied the issuer the right to use any statutory prospectus or registration exemptions?

(iv) issued a notice of hearing, notice as to a proceeding or similar notice against the issuer?

(v) commenced any other proceeding of any kind against the issuer, including a trading halt, suspension or delisting of the issuer, in connection with an alleged or actual contravention of an SRA's or SRE's rules, regulations, policies or other requirements, but excluding halts imposed (i) in the normal course for proper dissemination of information, or (ii) pursuant to a business combination, reverse takeover or similar transaction involving the issuer that is regulated by an SRE or SRA, including a qualifying transaction, reverse takeover or change of business involving the issuer (as those terms are defined in the TSX Venture Corporate Finance Manual as amended from time to time)?

(vi) entered into a settlement agreement with the issuer in a matter that involved actual or alleged fraud, theft, deceit, misrepresentation, conspiracy, breach of trust, breach of fiduciary duty, insider trading, unregistered trading in securities or exchange or commodity futures contracts, illegal distributions, failure to disclose material facts or changes or similar conduct by the issuer, or any other violation of securities legislation or the rules, by-laws or policies of an SRE?

9. CIVIL PROCEEDINGS — If you answer "YES" to any item in Question 9, you *must* provide complete details in an attachment.

YES   NO

A.   JUDGMENT, GARNISHMENT AND INJUNCTIONS *Has a court in any Canadian or foreign jurisdiction:*

(i) rendered a judgment, ordered garnishment or issued an injunction or similar ban (whether by consent or otherwise) against « you » in a claim based in whole or in part on fraud, theft, deceit, misrepresentation, conspiracy, breach of trust, breach of fiduciary duty, insider trading, unregistered trading, illegal distributions, failure to disclose material facts or changes, or allegations of similar conduct?

(ii) rendered a judgment, ordered garnishment or issued an injunction or similar ban (whether by consent or otherwise) against « an issuer », of which you are currently or have ever been a director, officer, promoter, insider or control person in a claim based in whole or in part on fraud, theft, deceit, misrepresentation, conspiracy, breach of trust, breach of fiduciary duty, insider trading, unregistered trading, illegal distributions, failure to disclose material facts or changes, or allegations of similar conduct?

B.   CURRENT CLAIMS

		YES	NO

(i) Are « you » now subject, in any Canadian or foreign jurisdiction, to a claim that is based in whole or in part on actual or alleged fraud, theft, deceit, misrepresentation, conspiracy, breach of trust, breach of fiduciary duty, insider trading, unregistered trading, illegal distributions, failure to disclose material facts or changes, or allegations of similar conduct?

(ii) To the best of your knowledge, are you currently or have you ever been a director, officer, promoter, insider or control person of « an issuer » that is now subject, in any Canadian or foreign jurisdiction, to a claim that is based in whole or in part on actual or alleged fraud, theft, deceit, misrepresentation, conspiracy, breach of trust, breach of fiduciary duty, insider trading, unregistered trading, illegal distributions, failure to disclose material facts or changes, or allegations of similar conduct?

C. SETTLEMENT AGREEMENT

(i) Have « you » ever entered into a settlement agreement, in any Canadian or foreign jurisdiction, in a civil action that involved actual or alleged fraud, theft, deceit, misrepresentation, conspiracy, breach of trust, insider trading, unregistered trading, illegal distributions, failure to disclose material facts or changes, or allegations of similar conduct?

(ii) To the best of your knowledge, are you currently or have you ever been a director, officer, promoter, insider or control person of « an » issuer that has entered into a settlement agreement, in any Canadian or foreign jurisdiction, in a civil action that involved actual or alleged fraud, theft, deceit, misrepresentation, conspiracy, breach of trust, breach of fiduciary duty, insider trading, unregistered trading, illegal distributions, failure to disclose material facts or changes, or allegations of similar conduct?

10. INVOLVEMENT WITH OTHER ENTITIES

		YES	NO

A. Has your employment in a sales, investment or advisory capacity with any employer engaged in the sale of real estate, insurance or mutual funds ever been suspended or terminated for cause? If yes, attach full particulars.

B. Has your employment with a firm or company registered under the securities laws of any Canadian or foreign jurisdiction as a securities dealer, broker, investment advisor or underwriter, ever been suspended or terminated for cause? If yes, attach full particulars.

C. Has your employment as an officer of an issuer ever been suspended or terminated for cause? If yes, attach full particulars.

Schedule 1, Part B — Certificate and Consent

I, ... (Please Print — Name of Individual) hereby certify that:

(a) I have read and understand the questions, cautions, acknowledgement and consent in the personal information form to which this certificate and consent is attached or of which this certificate and consent forms a part (the "**Form**"), and the answers I have given to the questions in the Form and in any attachments to it are correct, except where stated to be answered to the best of my knowledge, in which case I believe the answers to be correct;

(b) I have been provided with and have read and understand the Personal Information Collection Policy (the "**Personal Information Collection Policy**") in Schedule 2 of Appendix A to National Instrument 41-101 *General Prospectus Requirements* ("**NI 41-101**");

(c) I consent to the collection, use and disclosure by a regulator or a securities regulatory authority listed in Schedule 3 of Appendix A to NI 41-101 (collectively the "**regulators**") of the information in the Form and to the collection, use and disclosure by the regulators of further personal information in accordance with the Personal Information Collection Policy including the collection, use and disclosure by the regulators of the information in the Form in respect of the prospectus filings of the Issuer and the prospectus filings of any other issuer in a situation where I am or will be:

(i) a director, executive officer or promoter of the other issuer,

(ii) a director or executive officer of a promoter of the other issuer, if the promoter is not an individual, or

(iii) where the other issuer is an investment fund, a director or executive officer of the investment fund manager; and

(d) I am aware that I am providing the Form to the regulators and I understand that I am under the jurisdiction of the regulators to which I submit the Form, and that it is a breach of securities legislation to provide false or misleading information to the regulators, whenever the Form is provided in respect of the prospectus filings of the Issuer or the prospectus filings of any other issuer of which I am or will be a director, executive officer or promoter.

Date [within 30 days of the date of the preliminary prospectus]

.... **Signature of Person Completing this Form**

Schedule 2 — Personal Information Collection Policy

The regulators and securities regulatory authorities (the "**regulators**") listed in Schedule 3 of Appendix A to National Instrument 41-101 *General Prospectus Requirements* ("**NI 41-101**"), collect the personal information in the personal information form as this term is defined in NI 41-101 (the

"Personal Information Form"), under the authority granted to them under provincial and territorial securities legislation. Under securities legislation, the regulators do not make any of the information provided in the Personal Information Form public.

The regulators collect the personal information in the Personal Information Form for the purpose of enabling the regulators to administer and enforce provincial and territorial securities legislation, including those provisions that require or permit the regulators to refuse to issue a receipt for a prospectus if it appears to the regulators that the past conduct of management or promoters of the Issuer affords reasonable grounds for belief that the business of the Issuer will not be conducted with integrity and in the best interests of its securityholders.

You understand that by signing the certificate and consent in the Personal Information Form, you are consenting to the Issuer submitting your personal information in Personal Information Form (the "Information") to the regulators and to the collection and use by the regulators of the Information, as well as any other information that may be necessary to administer and enforce provincial and territorial securities legislation. This may include the collection of information from law enforcement agencies, other government or non-governmental regulatory authorities, self-regulatory organizations, exchanges, and quotation and trade reporting systems in order to conduct background checks, verify the Information and perform investigations and conduct enforcement proceedings as required to ensure compliance with provincial and territorial securities legislation. Your consent also extends to the collection, use and disclosure of the Information as described above in respect of other prospectus filings of the Issuer and the prospectus filings of any other issuer in a situation where you are or will be:

    (a) a director, executive officer or promoter of the other issuer,

    (b) a director or executive officer of a promoter of the other issuer, if the promoter is not an individual, or

    (c) where the other issuer is an investment fund, a director or executive officer of the investment fund manager.

You understand that the Issuer is required to deliver the Information to the regulators because the Issuer has filed a prospectus under provincial and territorial securities legislation. You also understand that you have a right to be informed of the existence of personal information about you that is kept by regulators, that you have the right to request access to that information, and that you have the right to request that such information be corrected, subject to the applicable provisions of the freedom of information and protection of privacy legislation adopted by each province and territory.

You also understand and agree that the Information the regulators collect about you may also be disclosed, as permitted by law, where its use and disclosure is for the purposes described above. The regulators may also use a third party to process the Information, but when this happens, the third party will be carefully selected and obligated to comply with the limited use restrictions described above and with provincial and federal privacy legislation.

Warning: It is an offence to submit information that, in a material respect and at the time and in the light of the circumstances in which it is submitted, is misleading or untrue.

Questions

If you have any questions about the collection, use, and disclosure of the information you provide to the regulators, you may contact the regulator in the jurisdiction in which the required information is filed, at the address or telephone number listed in Schedule 3.

Schedule 3 — Regulators and Securities Regulatory Authorities

Local Jurisdiction	Regulator
Alberta	Securities Review Officer Alberta Securities Commission Suite 600, 250 — 5th Street S.W. Calgary, Alberta T2P 0R4 Telephone: (403) 297-6454 E-mail: inquiries@seccom.ab.ca www.albertasecurities.com
British Columbia	Review Officer British Columbia Securities Commission P.O. Box 10142 Pacific Centre 701 West Georgia Street Vancouver, British Columbia V7Y 1L2 Telephone: (604) 899-6854 Toll Free within British Columbia and Alberta: (800) 373-6393 E-mail: inquiries@bcsc.bc.ca www.bcsc.bc.ca
Manitoba	Director, Corporate Finance The Manitoba Securities Commission 500-400 St. Mary Avenue Winnipeg, Manitoba R3C 4K5 Telephone: (204) 945-2548 E-mail: securities@gov.mb.ca www.msc.gov.mb.ca
New Brunswick	Director Corporate Finance and Chief Financial Officer New Brunswick Securities Commission 85 Charlotte Street, Suite 300

Local Jurisdiction	Regulator
	Saint John, New Brunswick E2L 2J2
	Telephone: (506) 658-3060
	Fax: (506) 658-3059
	E-mail: information@nbsc-cvmnb.ca
Newfoundland and Labrador	Director of Securities
	Department of Government Services and Lands
	P.O. Box 8700
	West Block, 2nd Floor, Confederation Building
	St. John's, Newfoundland A1B 4J6
	Telephone: (709) 729-4189
	www.gov.nf.ca/gsl/cca/s
Northwest Territories	Superintendent of Securities
	Department of Justice
	Government of the Northwest Territories
	P.O. Box 1320,
	Yellowknife, Northwest Territories X1A 2L9
	Telephone: (867) 873- 7490
	www.justice.gov.nt.ca/SecuritiesRegistry
Nova Scotia	Deputy Director
	Compliance and Enforcement Division
	Nova Scotia Securities Commission
	P.O. Box 458
	Halifax, Nova Scotia B3J 2P8
	Telephone: (902) 424-5354
	www.gov.ns.ca/nssc
Nunavut	Superintendent of Securities
	Government of Nunavut
	Legal Registries Division
	P.O. Box 1000 — Station 570
	Iqaluit, Nunavut X0A 0H0
	Telephone: (867) 975-6590
Ontario	Administrative Assistant to the Director of Corporate Finance
	Ontario Securities Commission
	19th Floor, 20 Queen Street West
	Toronto, Ontario M5H 2S8
	Telephone: (416) 597-0681
	E-mail: Inquiries@osc.gov.on.ca
	www.osc.gov.on.ca
Prince Edward Island	Superintendent of Securities
	Government of Prince Edward Island
	95 Rochford Street, P.O. Box 2000, 4th Floor
	Charlottetown, Prince Edward Island C1A 7N8
	Telephone: (902) 368-4550
	www.gov.pe.ca/securities
Québec	Autorité des marchés financiers
	Stock Exchange Tower
	P.O. Box 246, 22nd Floor
	800 Victoria Square
	Montréal, Québec H4Z 1G3
	Attention: Responsable de l'accès à l'information
	Telephone: (514) 395-0337
	Toll Free in Québec: (877) 525-0337
	www.lautorite.qc.ca

Local Jurisdiction	Regulator
Saskatchewan	Director
	Financial and Consumer Affairs Authority of Saskatchewan
	Suite 601, 1919 Saskatchewan Drive
	Regina, Saskatchewan S4P 4H2
	Telephone: (306) 787-5842
	www.fcaa.gov.sk.ca
Yukon	Superintendent of Securities
	Office of the Yukon Superintendent of Securities
	Department of Community Services
	307 Black Street, Whitehorse, Yukon, Y1A 2N1
	Phone: 867-667-5466, Fax 867-393-6251

Appendix B — Issuer Form of Submission to Jurisdiction and Appointment of Agent for Service of Process

1. Name of issuer (the "Issuer"):

....

2. Jurisdiction of incorporation, or equivalent, of Issuer:

....

3. Address of principal place of business of Issuer:

....

4. Description of securities (the "Securities"):

....

5. Date of the prospectus (the "Prospectus") under which the Securities are offered:

....

6. Name of agent for service of process (the "Agent"):

....

7. Address for service of process of Agent in Canada (the address may be anywhere in Canada):

....

8. The Issuer designates and appoints the Agent at the address of the Agent stated above as its agent upon whom may be served any notice, pleading, subpoena, summons or other process in any action, investigation or administrative, criminal, quasi-criminal, penal or other proceeding (the "Proceeding") arising out of, relating to or concerning the distribution of the Securities made or purported to be made under the Prospectus or the obligations of the Issuer as a reporting issuer, and irrevocably waives any right to raise as a defence in any such Proceeding any alleged lack of jurisdiction to bring such Proceeding.

9. The Issuer irrevocably and unconditionally submits to the non-exclusive jurisdiction of

(a) the judicial, quasi-judicial and administrative tribunals of each of the provinces [and territories] of Canada in which the securities are distributed under the Prospectus; and

(b) any administrative proceeding in any such province [or territory],

in any Proceeding arising out of or related to or concerning the distribution of the Securities made or purported to be made under the Prospectus or the obligations of the issuer as a reporting issuer.

10. Until six years after it has ceased to be a reporting issuer in any Canadian province or territory, the Issuer shall file a new submission to jurisdiction and appointment of agent for service of process in this form at least 30 days before termination of this submission to jurisdiction and appointment of agent for service of process.

11. Until six years after it has ceased to be a reporting issuer in any Canadian province or territory, the Issuer shall file an amended submission to jurisdiction and appointment of agent for service of process at least 30 days before any change in the name or above address of the Agent.

12. This submission to jurisdiction and appointment of agent for service of process shall be governed by and construed in accordance with the laws of [insert province or territory of above address of Agent].

Dated: ....

.... Signature of Issuer

.... Print name and title of signing officer of Issuer

Agent

The undersigned accepts the appointment as agent for service of process of [insert name of Issuer] under the terms and conditions of the appointment of agent for service of process stated above.

Dated: ....

.... Signature of Agent

.... Print name of person signing and, if Agent is not an individual, the title of the person

Appendix C — Non-Issuer Form of Submission to Jurisdiction and Appointment of Agent for Service of Process

1. Name of issuer (the "Issuer"):

....

2. Jurisdiction of incorporation, or equivalent, of Issuer:

....

3. Address of principal place of business of Issuer:

....

4. Description of securities (the "Securities"):

....

5. Date of the prospectus (the "Prospectus") under which the Securities are offered:

....

6. Name of person filing this form (the "Filing Person"):

....

7. Filing Person's relationship to Issuer:

....

8. Jurisdiction of incorporation, or equivalent, of Filing Person, if applicable, or jurisdiction of residence of Filing Person:

....

9. Address of principal place of business of Filing Person:

....

10. Name of agent for service of process (the "Agent"):

....

11. Address for service of process of Agent in Canada (the address may be anywhere in Canada):

....

12. The Filing Person designates and appoints the Agent at the address of the Agent stated above as its agent upon whom may be served any notice, pleading, subpoena, summons or other process in any action, investigation or administrative, criminal, quasi-criminal, penal or other proceeding (the "Proceeding") arising out of, relating to or concerning the distribution of the Securities made or purported to be made under the Prospectus, and irrevocably waives any right to raise as a defence in any such Proceeding any alleged lack of jurisdiction to bring the Proceeding.

13. The Filing Person irrevocably and unconditionally submits to the non-exclusive jurisdiction of

    (a) the judicial, quasi-judicial and administrative tribunals of each of the provinces [and territories] of Canada in which the securities are distributed under the Prospectus; and

    (b) any administrative proceeding in any such province [or territory],

in any Proceeding arising out of or related to or concerning the distribution of the Securities made or purported to be made under the Prospectus.

14. Until six years after completion of the distribution of the Securities made under the Prospectus, the Filing Person shall file a new submission to jurisdiction and appointment of agent for service of process in this form at least 30 days before termination of this submission to jurisdiction and appointment of agent for service of process.

15. Until six years after completion of the distribution of the Securities under the Prospectus, the Filing Person shall file an amended submission to jurisdiction and appointment of agent for service of process at least 30 days before a change in the name or above address of the Agent.

16. This submission to jurisdiction and appointment of agent for service of process shall be governed by and construed in accordance with the laws of [insert province or territory of above address of Agent].

Dated: ....

.... Signature of Filing Person

.... Print name of person signing and, if the Filing Person is not an individual, the title of the person

Agent

The undersigned accepts the appointment as agent for service of process of [insert name of Filing Person] under the terms and conditions of the appointment of agent for service of process stated above.

Dated: ....

.... Signature of Agent

.... Print name of person signing and, if Agent is not an individual, the title of the person

Appendix D — Preliminary Prospectus Notice Provisions

Jurisdiction	Securities Legislation Reference
Alberta	Paragraph 123(a) of the *Securities Act* (Alberta)
British Columbia	Paragraph 78(2)(a) of the *Securities Act* (British Columbia)
Manitoba	Paragraph 38(b) of the *Securities Act* (Manitoba)

Jurisdiction	Securities Legislation Reference
New Brunswick	Paragraph 82(2)(a) of the *Securities Act* (New Brunswick)
Newfoundland and Labrador	Paragraph 66(2)(a) of the *Securities Act* (Newfoundland and Labrador)
Northwest Territories	Paragraph 97(a) of the *Securities Act* (Northwest Territories)
Nova Scotia	Paragraph 70(2)(a) of the *Securities Act* (Nova Scotia)
Nunavut	Paragraph 97(a) of the *Securities Act* (Nunavut)
Ontario	Paragraph 65(2)(a) of the *Securities Act* (Ontario)
Prince Edward Island	Paragraph 97(a) of the *Securities Act* (Prince Edward Island)
Saskatchewan	Paragraph 73(2)(a) of *The Securities Act, 1988* (Saskatchewan)
Yukon	Paragraph 97(a) of the *Securities Act* (Yukon)

Appendix E — Final Prospectus Notice Provisions

Jurisdiction	Securities Legislation Reference
British Columbia	Paragraph 82(c) of the *Securities Act* (British Columbia)
New Brunswick	Section 86 of the *Securities Act* (New Brunswick), but only in respect of a communication described in paragraph 82(2)(a) of that Act
Newfoundland and Labrador	Section 70 of the *Securities Act* (Newfoundland and Labrador), but only in respect of a communication described in paragraph 66(2)(a) of that Act
Nova Scotia	Section 74 of the *Securities Act* (Nova Scotia), but only in respect of a communication described in paragraph 70(2)(a) of that Act
Ontario	Section 69 of the *Securities Act* (Ontario), but only in respect of a communication described in clause 65(2)(a) of that Act
Saskatchewan	Paragraph 77(c) of *The Securities Act, 1988* (Saskatchewan).

Final Rule: (December 15, 2000) 23 O.S.C.B. (Supp) 764; Approval by OSC: (October 13, 2000) 23 O.S.C.B. (Supp) 619; Request for Comments: (1997) 20 O.S.C.B. 2561. Replaced NPS 12, 13, 32 and 35 and ON Reg. 1015, ss. 50 and 51.

Replacement Rule: (2008) 31 O.S.C.B. (Supp. 2) 1; Approval by OSC: (2008) 30 O.S.C.B. (Supp. 7) 1 (Dec. 21, 2007); Request for Comments: (2006) 29 O.S.C.B. (Supp. 3) 1 (Dec. 22, 2006).; NI 44-101, 33-105, 81-101; Rule 41-801.

Amendment to Rule: (2008) 31 O.S.C.B. 8571; Approval by OSC: (2008) 31 O.S.C.B. 6275; Request for Comments: (2007) 30 O.S.C.B. 4965.

Amendment to Rule: Approval by OSC: (2010) 33 O.S.C.B. 9503; Request for Comments: (2009) 32 O.S.C.B. 10523.

Amendment to Rule: (2010) 33 O.S.C.B. (Supp. 5) 81; Approval by OSC: (2010) 33 O.S.C.B. (Supp. 3) 161; Request for Comments: (2009) 32 O.S.C.B. (Supp. 6) 201.

Amendment to Rule: CSAN 11-314.

Amendment to Rule: (2012) 35 O.S.C.B. 3294; Approval by OSC: (2012) 35 O.S.C.B. 2383 and 913; Request for Comments: (2011) 34 O.S.C.B. 3249 and (2010) 33 O.S.C.B. 6353.

Amendment to Rule: (2012) 35 O.S.C.B. 3431; Approval by OSC: (2012) 35 O.S.C.B. 1375; Request for Comments: (2010) 33 O.S.C.B. 5833.

Amendment to Rule: (2013) 36 O.S.C.B. 4884; Approval by OSC: (2013) 36 O.S.C.B. (Supp. 2) 1; Request for Comments: (2011) 34 O.S.C.B. (Supp. 4) 1.

Amendment to Rule: (2013) 36 O.S.C.B. 4817; Approval by OSC: (2013) 36 O.S.C.B. (Supp. 1) 1; Request for Comments: (2011) 34 O.S.C.B. (Supp. 6) 1 and (2010) 33 O.S.C.B. (Supp. 1) 1.

Amendment to Rule: Approval by OSC: (2013) 36 O.S.C.B. 2619; Request for Comments: (2012) 35 O.S.C.B. 6887.

Amendment to Rule: (2013) 36 O.S.C.B. 7977; Approval by OSC: (2013) 36 O.S.C.B. (Supp. 4) 1; Request for Comments: (2011) 34 O.S.C.B. 11829

Amendment to Rule: Approval by OSC: (2014) 37 O.S.C.B. (Supp 4); Request for Comments: 36 O.S.C.B. (Supp 3)

Amendment to Rule: Approval by OSC: (2014) 37 O.S.C.B. 6753; Request for Comments: (2013) 36 O.S.C.B. 10147

Amendment to Rule: Approval by OSC: (2015) 38 O.S.C.B. 7551.

Amendment to Rule: (2015) 38 OSCB 9255; Approval by OSC: (2015) O.S.C.B. 3429

Amendments to Form 41-101F1: (2015) 38 O.S.C.B. 3429

Amendments to Form 41-101F2: Approval by OSC: (2013) 36 O.S.C.B. 9612; Request for Comments: (2009) 32 O.S.C.B. 8381

Rules: Rule 13-502, App. C, Item A.

Policies and Orders: OPS 41-201, NPS 41-101CP, 11-102, 46-201; CSAN 41-305, 41-307, 51-336; OSCN 41-702, 41-703, 51-720, 81-711, 81-714, 81-722.

Form 41-101F1 — Information Required in a Prospectus

GENERAL INSTRUCTIONS

ITEM 1 Cover Page Disclosure

   1.1 Required statement

   1.2 Preliminary prospectus disclosure

   1.3 Basic disclosure about the distribution

   1.4 Distribution

   1.5 Offering price in currency other than Canadian dollar

   1.6 Non-fixed price distributions

   1.7 Pricing disclosure

   1.8 Reduced price distributions

   1.9 Market for securities

   1.10 Risk factors

   1.11 Underwriter(s)

   1.12 Enforcement of judgment against foreign persons or companies

   1.13 Restricted securities

   1.14 Earnings coverage

ITEM 2 Table of Contents

   2.1 Table of contents

ITEM 3 Summary of Prospectus

   3.1 General

   3.2 Cautionary language

ITEM 4 Corporate Structure

   4.1 Name, address and incorporation

   4.2 Intercorporate relationships

ITEM 5 Describe the Business

   5.1 Describe the business

   5.2 History

   5.3 Issuers with asset-backed securities outstanding

   5.4 Issuers with mineral projects

   5.5 Issuers with oil and gas operations

ITEM 6 Use of Proceeds

   6.1 Proceeds

   6.2 Junior issuers

   6.3 Principal purposes — generally

   6.4 Principal purposes — indebtedness

   6.5 Principal purposes — asset acquisition

   6.6 Principal purposes — insiders, etc.

   6.7 Principal purposes — research and development

   6.8 Business objectives and milestones

   6.9 Unallocated funds in trust or escrow

Part 4:
DISTRIBUTIONS

Part 4:
DISTRIBUTIONS

GENERAL INSTRUCTIONS

(1) The objective of the prospectus is to provide information concerning the issuer that an investor needs in order to make an informed investment decision. This Form sets out specific disclosure requirements that are in addition to the general requirement under securities legislation to provide full, true and plain disclosure of all material facts relating to the securities to be distributed. Certain rules of specific application impose prospectus disclosure obligations in addition to those described in this Form.

(2) Terms used and not defined in this Form that are defined or interpreted in the Instrument bear that definition or interpretation. Other definitions are set out in NI 14-101.

(3) In determining the degree of detail required, a standard of materiality must be applied. Materiality is a matter of judgment in the particular circumstance, and is determined in relation to an item's significance to investors, analysts and other users of the information. An item of information, or an aggregate of items, is considered material if it is probable that its omission or misstatement would influence or change an investment decision with respect to the issuer's securities. In determining whether information is material, take into account both quantitative and qualitative factors. The potential significance of items must be considered individually rather than on a net basis, if the items have an offsetting effect.

(4) Unless an item specifically requires disclosure only in the preliminary prospectus, the disclosure requirements set out in this Form apply to both the preliminary prospectus and the prospectus. Details concerning the price and other matters dependent upon or relating to price, such as the number of securities being distributed, may be left out of the preliminary prospectus, along with specifics concerning the plan of distribution, to the extent that these matters have not been decided.

(5) The disclosure must be understandable to readers and presented in an easy-to-read format. The presentation of information should comply with the plain language principles listed in section 4.1 of Companion Policy 41-101CP General Prospectus Requirements. If technical terms are required, clear and concise explanations should be included.

(6) No reference need be made to inapplicable items and, unless otherwise required in this Form, negative answers to items may be omitted.

(7) Where the term "issuer" is used, it may be necessary, in order to meet the requirement for full, true and plain disclosure of all material facts, to also include disclosure with respect to persons or companies that the issuer is required, under the issuer's GAAP, to consolidate, proportionately consolidate or account for using the equity method (for example, including "subsidiaries" as that term is used in Canadian GAAP applicable to publicly accountable enterprises). If it is more likely than not that a person or company will become an entity that the issuer will be required, under the issuer's GAAP, to consolidate, proportionately consolidate or account for using the equity method, it may be necessary to also include disclosure with respect to the person or company.

(8) An issuer that is a special purpose entity may have to modify the disclosure items to reflect the special purpose nature of its business.

(9) If disclosure is required as of a specific date and there has been a material change or change that is otherwise significant in the required information subsequent to that date, present the information as of the date of the change or a date subsequent to the change instead.

(10) If an issuer discloses financial information in a preliminary prospectus or prospectus in a currency other than the Canadian dollar, prominently display the presentation currency.

(11) Except as otherwise required or permitted, include information in a narrative form. The issuer may include graphs, photographs, maps, artwork or other forms of illustration, if relevant to the business of the issuer or the distribution and not misleading. Include descriptive headings. Except for information that appears in a summary, information required under more than one Item need not be repeated.

(12) Certain requirements in this Form make reference to requirements in another instrument or form. Unless this Form states otherwise, issuers must also follow the instruction or requirement in the other instrument or form. These references include references to Form 51-102F2. Venture issuers must include such disclosure in a preliminary prospectus or prospectus even if they are not otherwise required to file an annual information form under NI 51-102.

(13) Wherever this Form uses the word "subsidiary", the term includes companies and other types of business organizations such as partnerships, trusts and other unincorporated business entities.

(14) Where requirements in this Form make reference to, or are substantially similar to, requirements in Form 51-102F2, issuers may apply the general provision in subpart 1(d) of Form 51-102F2. However, issuers must supplement this disclosure if the supplemented disclosure is necessary to ensure that the prospectus provides full, true and plain disclosure of all material facts related to the securities to be distributed as required under Item 29 of this Form.

(15) Forward-looking information, as defined in NI 51-102, included in a prospectus must comply with section 4A.2 of NI 51-102 and must include the disclosure described in section 4A.3 of NI 51-102. In addition to the foregoing, FOFI or a financial outlook, each as defined in NI 51-102, included in a prospectus must comply with Part 4B of NI 51-102. If the forward-looking information relates to an issuer or other entity that is not a reporting issuer in any jurisdiction, section 4A.2, section 4A.3 and Part 4B of NI 51-102 apply as if the issuer or other entity were a reporting issuer in at least one jurisdiction.

(16) Marketing materials prepared in accordance with subsections 13.7(1) or 13.8(1) of the Instrument are the only documents that can be incorporated by reference into a long form prospectus.

Item 1 — Cover Page Disclosure

Required statement

1.1 State in italics at the top of the cover page the following:

No securities regulatory authority has expressed an opinion about these securities and it is an offence to claim otherwise.

Preliminary prospectus disclosure

1.2 Every preliminary prospectus must have printed in red ink and in italics at the top of the cover page immediately above the disclosure required under section 1.1 the following, with the bracketed information completed:

A copy of this preliminary prospectus has been filed with the securities regulatory authority(ies) in [each of/certain of the provinces/provinces and territories of Canada] but has not yet become final for the purpose of the sale of securities. Information contained in this preliminary prospectus may not be complete and may have to be amended. The securities may not be sold until a receipt for the prospectus is obtained from the securities regulatory authority(ies).

INSTRUCTION

Issuers must complete the bracketed information by

(a) inserting the names of each jurisdiction in which the issuer intends to offer securities under the prospectus,

(b) stating that the filing has been made in each of the provinces of Canada or each of the provinces and territories of Canada, or

(c) identifying the filing jurisdictions by exception (i.e., every province of Canada or every province and territory of Canada, except [excluded jurisdictions]).

Basic disclosure about the distribution

1.3 State the following immediately below the disclosure required under sections 1.1 and 1.2 with the bracketed information completed:

[PRELIMINARY] PROSPECTUS

[INITIAL PUBLIC OFFERING OR NEW ISSUE AND/OR SECONDARY OFFERING]

[(Date)]

[Name of Issuer]

[number and type of securities qualified for distribution under the prospectus, including any options or warrants, and the price per security]

Distribution

1.4 (1) If the securities are being distributed for cash, provide the information called for below, in substantially the following tabular form or in a note to the table:

	Price to public (a)	Underwriting discounts or commission (b)	Proceeds to issuer or selling securityholders (c)
Per Security	....	....	....
Total	....	....	....

(2) Describe the terms of any over-allotment option or any option to increase the size of the distribution before closing.

(2.1) If there may be an over-allocation position provide the following disclosure:

A purchaser who acquires [*insert type of securities qualified for distribution under the prospectus*] forming part of the underwriters' over-allocation position acquires those securities under this prospectus, regardless of whether the over-allocation position is ultimately filled through the exercise of the over-allotment option or secondary market purchases.

(3) If the distribution of the securities is to be on a best efforts basis, and a minimum offering amount

    (a) is required for the issuer to achieve one or more of the purposes of the offering, provide totals for both the minimum and maximum offering amount, or

    (b) is not required for the issuer to achieve any of the purposes of the offering,

state the following in boldface type:

    No minimum amount of funds must be raised under this offering. This means that the issuer could complete this offering after raising only a small proportion of the offering amount set out above.

(4) If a minimum subscription amount is required from each subscriber, provide details of the minimum subscription requirements in the table required under subsection (1).

(5) If debt securities are being distributed at a premium or a discount, state in boldface type the effective yield if held to maturity.

(6) Disclose separately those securities that are underwritten, those under option and those to be sold on a best efforts basis, and, in the case of a best efforts distribution, the latest date that the distribution is to remain open.

(7) In column (b) of the table, disclose only commissions paid or payable in cash by the issuer or selling securityholder and discounts granted. Set out in a note to the table

    (a) commissions or other consideration paid or payable by persons or companies other than the issuer or selling securityholder,

    (b) consideration other than discounts granted and cash paid or payable by the issuer or selling securityholder, including warrants and options, and

    (c) any finder's fees or similar required payment.

(8) If a security is being distributed for the account of a selling securityholder, state the name of the securityholder and a cross-reference to the applicable section in the prospectus where further information about the selling securityholder is provided. State the portion of the expenses of the distribution to be borne by the selling securityholder and, if none of the expenses of the distribution are being borne by the selling securityholder, include a statement to that effect and discuss the reason why this is the case.

INSTRUCTIONS

    (1) Estimate amounts, if necessary. For non-fixed price distributions that are being made on a best efforts basis, disclosure of the information called for by the table may be set forth as a percentage or a range of percentages and need not be set forth in tabular form.

    (2) If debt securities are being distributed, also express the information in the table as a percentage.

Offering price in currency other than Canadian dollar

1.5 If the offering price of the securities being distributed is disclosed in a currency other than the Canadian dollar, disclose in boldface type the currency.

Non-fixed price distributions

1.6 If the securities are being distributed at non-fixed prices, disclose

    (a) the discount allowed or commission payable to the underwriter,

(b) any other compensation payable to the underwriter and, if applicable, that the underwriter's compensation will be increased or decreased by the amount by which the aggregate price paid for the securities by the purchasers exceeds or is less than the gross proceeds paid by the underwriter to the issuer or selling securityholder,

(c) that the securities to be distributed under the prospectus will be distributed, as applicable, at

(i) prices determined by reference to the prevailing price of a specified security in a specified market,

(ii) market prices prevailing at the time of sale, or

(iii) prices to be negotiated with purchasers,

(d) that prices may vary from purchaser to purchaser and during the period of distribution,

(e) if the price of the securities is to be determined by reference to the prevailing price of a specified security in a specified market, the price of the specified security in the specified market at the latest practicable date,

(f) if the price of the securities will be the market price prevailing at the time of the sale, the market price at the latest practicable date, and

(g) the net proceeds or, if the distribution is to be made on a best efforts basis, the minimum amount of net proceeds, if any, to be received by the issuer or selling securityholder.

Pricing disclosure

1.7 If the offering price or the number of securities being distributed, or an estimate of the range of the offering price or of the number of securities being distributed, has been publicly disclosed in a jurisdiction or a foreign jurisdiction as of the date of the preliminary prospectus, include this information in the preliminary prospectus.

Reduced price distributions

1.8 If an underwriter wishes to be able to decrease the price at which securities are distributed for cash from the initial offering price fixed in the prospectus, include in boldface type a cross-reference to the section in the prospectus where disclosure concerning the possible price decrease is provided.

Market for securities

1.9 (1) Identify the exchange(s) and quotation system(s), if any, on which securities of the issuer of the same class or series as the securities being distributed are traded or quoted and the market price of those securities as of the latest practicable date.

(2) Disclose any intention to stabilize the market. Provide a cross-reference to the section in the prospectus where further information about market stabilization is provided.

(3) If no market for the securities being distributed under the prospectus exists or is expected to exist upon completion of the distribution, state the following in boldface type:

> *There is no market through which these securities may be sold and purchasers may not be able to resell securities purchased under this prospectus. This may affect the pricing of the securities in the secondary market, the transparency and availability of trading prices, the liquidity of the securities, and the extent of issuer regulation. See 'Risk Factors'.*

(4) If the issuer has complied with the requirements of the Instrument as an IPO venture issuer, include a statement, in substantially the following form, with bracketed information completed:

> As at the date of this prospectus, [name of issuer] does not have any of its securities listed or quoted, has not applied to list or quote any of its securities, and does not intend to apply to list or quote any of its securities, on the Toronto Stock Exchange, Aequitas NEO Exchange Inc., a U.S. marketplace, or a marketplace outside Canada and the United States of America ("other than the Alternative Investment Market of the London Stock Exchange or the PLUS markets operated by PLUS Markets Group plc.")

Risk factors

1.10 Include a cross-reference to sections in the prospectus where information about the risks of an investment in the securities being distributed is provided.

Underwriter(s)

1.11 (1) State the name of each underwriter.

(2) If applicable, comply with the requirements of NI 33-105 for front page prospectus disclosure.

(3) If an underwriter has agreed to purchase all of the securities being distributed at a specified price and the underwriter's obligations are subject to conditions, state the following, with bracketed information completed:

> We, as principals, conditionally offer these securities, subject to prior sale, if, as and when issued by [name of issuer] and accepted by us in accordance with the conditions contained in the underwriting agreement referred to under Plan of Distribution.

(4) If an underwriter has agreed to purchase a specified number or principal amount of the securities at a specified price, state that the securities are to be taken up by the underwriter, if at all, on or before a date not later than 42 days after the date of the receipt for the final prospectus.

(5) If there is no underwriter involved in the distribution, provide a statement in boldface type to the effect that no underwriter has been involved in the preparation of the prospectus or performed any review or independent due diligence of the contents of the prospectus.

Part 4:
DISTRIBUTIONS

(6) Provide the following tabular information

Underwriter's Position	Maximum size or number of securities available	Exercise period or Acquisition date	Exercise price or average acquisition price
Over-allotment option	....	....	
Compensation option	....	....	
Any other option granted by issuer or insider of issuer to underwriter	....	....	....
Total securities under option issuable to underwriter	....	....	....
Other compensation securities issuable to underwriter	....	....	....

INSTRUCTION

If the underwriter has been granted compensation securities, state, in a footnote, whether the prospectus qualifies the grant of all or part of the compensation securities and provide a cross-reference to the applicable section in the prospectus where further information about the compensation securities is provided.

Enforcement of judgments against foreign persons or companies

1.12 If the issuer, a director of the issuer, a selling securityholder, or any other person or company that is signing or providing a certificate under Part 5 of the Instrument or other securities legislation, or any person or company for whom the issuer is required to file a consent under Part 10 of the Instrument, is incorporated, continued, or otherwise organized under the laws of a foreign jurisdiction or resides outside of Canada, state the following on the cover page or under a separate heading elsewhere in the prospectus, with the bracketed information completed:

> "The [issuer, director of the issuer, selling securityholder, or other person or company] is incorporated, continued or otherwise organized under the laws of a foreign jurisdiction or resides outside of Canada.
>
> [the person or company named below] has appointed the following agent(s) for service of process:

Name of Person or Company	Name and Address of Agent

> Purchasers are advised that it may not be possible for investors to enforce judgments obtained in Canada against any person or company that is incorporated, continued or otherwise organized under the laws of a foreign jurisdiction or resides outside of Canada, even if the party has appointed an agent for service of process."

Restricted securities

1.13 (1) Describe the number and class or classes of restricted securities being distributed using the appropriate restricted security terms in the same type face and type size as the rest of the description.

(2) If the securities being distributed are restricted securities and the holders of the securities do not have the right to participate in a takeover bid made for other equity securities of the issuer, disclose that fact.

Earnings coverage

1.14 If any of the earnings coverage ratios required to be disclosed under Item 9 is less than one-to-one, disclose this fact in boldface type.

Item 2 — Table of Contents

Table of contents

2.1 Include a table of contents.

Item 3 — Summary of Prospectus

General

3.1 (1) Briefly summarize, near the beginning of the prospectus, information appearing elsewhere in the prospectus that, in the opinion of the issuer or selling securityholder, would be most likely to influence the investor's decision to purchase the securities being distributed, including a description of

    (a) the principal business of the issuer and its subsidiaries,

    (b) the securities to be distributed, including the offering price and expected net proceeds,

(c) use of proceeds,

(d) risk factors,

(e) financial information, and

(f) if restricted securities, subject securities or securities that are directly or indirectly convertible into or exercisable or exchangeable for restricted securities or subject securities, are to be distributed under the prospectus

    (i) include a summary of the information required by section 10.6, and

    (ii) include, in boldface type, a statement of the rights the holders of restricted securities do not have, if the holders do not have all of the rights referred to in section 10.6.

(2) For the financial information provided under paragraph (1)(e),

    (a) describe the type of information appearing elsewhere in the prospectus on which the financial information is based,

    (b) disclose whether the information appearing elsewhere in the prospectus on which the financial information is based has been audited,

    (c) disclose whether the financial information has been audited, and

    (d) if neither the information appearing elsewhere in the prospectus on which the financial information is based nor the financial information has been audited, prominently disclose that fact.

(3) For each item summarized under subsection (1), provide a cross-reference to the information in the prospectus.

Cautionary language

3.2 At the beginning of the summary, include a statement in italics in substantially the following form:

The following is a summary of the principal features of this distribution and should be read together with the more detailed information and financial data and statements contained elsewhere in this prospectus.

Item 4 — Corporate Structure

Name, address and incorporation

4.1 (1) State the issuer's full corporate name or, if the issuer is an unincorporated entity, the full name under which it exists and carries on business, and the address(es) of the issuer's head and registered office.

(2) State the statute under which the issuer is incorporated, continued or organized or, if the issuer is an unincorporated entity, the laws of the jurisdiction or foreign jurisdiction under which it is established and exists.

(3) Describe the substance of any material amendments to the articles or other constating or establishing documents of the issuer.

Intercorporate relationships

4.2 (1) Describe, by way of a diagram or otherwise, the intercorporate relationships among the issuer and its subsidiaries.

(2) For each subsidiary described in subsection (1), state

    (a) the percentage of votes attaching to all voting securities of the subsidiary beneficially owned, or controlled or directed, directly or indirectly, by the issuer,

    (b) the percentage of each class of restricted securities of the subsidiary beneficially owned, or controlled or directed, directly or indirectly, by the issuer, and

    (c) where the subsidiary was incorporated, continued, formed or organized.

(3) If the securities distributed under the prospectus are being issued in connection with a restructuring transaction, describe by way of a diagram or otherwise these intercorporate relationships both before and after the completion of the proposed transaction.

(4) A particular subsidiary may be omitted from the disclosure required by this section if, at the most recent financial year end of the issuer

    (a) the total assets of the subsidiary do not exceed 10% of the consolidated assets of the issuer,

    (b) the revenue of the subsidiary does not exceed 10% of the consolidated revenue of the issuer, and

    (c) the conditions in paragraphs (a) and (b) would be satisfied if

        (i) the subsidiaries that may be omitted under paragraphs (a) and (b) were considered in the aggregate, and

        (ii) the reference to 10% in those paragraphs was changed to 20%.

Item 5 — Describe the Business

Describe the business

5.1 (1) Describe the business of the issuer and its operating segments that are reportable segments as those terms are described in the issuer's GAAP. Disclose information for each reportable segment of the issuer in accordance with subsection 5.1(1) of Form 51-102F2.

(2) Disclose the nature and results of any bankruptcy, receivership or similar proceedings against the issuer or any of its subsidiaries, or any voluntary bankruptcy, receivership or similar proceedings by the issuer or any of its subsidiaries, within the three most recently completed financial years or, if the issuer is a venture issuer or an IPO venture issuer, the two most recently completed financial years, or completed during or proposed for the current financial year.

(3) Disclose the nature and results of any material restructuring transaction of the issuer or any of its subsidiaries within the three most recently completed financial years or, if the issuer is a venture issuer or an IPO venture issuer, the two most recently completed financial years, or completed during or proposed for the current financial year.

(4) If the issuer has implemented social or environmental policies that are fundamental to the issuer's operations, such as policies regarding the issuer's relationship with the environment or with the communities in which the issuer does business, or human rights policies, describe them and the steps the issuer has taken to implement them.

History

5.2 (1) Describe how the issuer's business has developed over the last three completed financial years or, if the issuer is a venture issuer or an IPO venture issuer, the last two completed financial years, and any subsequent period to the date of the prospectus, including only events, such as acquisitions or dispositions, or conditions that have influenced the general development of the business.

(2) If the issuer produces or distributes more than one product or provides more than one kind of service, describe the products or services.

(3) Discuss changes in the issuer's business that the issuer expects will occur during the current financial year.

Issuers with asset-backed securities outstanding

5.3 If the issuer has asset-backed securities outstanding that were distributed under a prospectus, disclose information in accordance with section 5.3 of Form 51-102F2.

Issuers with mineral projects

5.4 If the issuer has a mineral project, disclose information for the issuer in accordance with section 5.4 of Form 51-102F2. For the purposes of this section, the alternative disclosure permitted in Instruction (ii) to section 5.4 of Form 51-102F2 does not apply.

Issuers with oil and gas operations

5.5 (1) If the issuer is engaged in oil and gas activities as defined in NI 51-101, disclose information in accordance with Form 51-101F1

    (a) as at the end of, and for, the most recent financial year for which the prospectus includes an audited statement of financial position of the issuer, or

    (b) in the absence of a completed financial year referred to in paragraph (a), as at the most recent date for which the prospectus includes an audited statement of financial position of the issuer, and for the most recent financial period for which the prospectus includes an audited statement of comprehensive income of the issuer.

(2) Include with the disclosure under subsection (1) a report in the form of Form 51-101F2, on the reserves data included in the disclosure required under subsection (1).

(3) Include with the disclosure under subsection (1) a report in the form of Form 51-101F3 that refers to the information disclosed under subsection (1).

(4) To the extent not reflected in the information disclosed in response to subsection (1), disclose the information contemplated by Part 6 of NI 51-101 in respect of material changes that occurred after the applicable statement of financial position referred to in subsection (1).

INSTRUCTION

Disclosure in a prospectus must be consistent with NI 51-101 if the issuer is engaged in oil and gas activities as defined in NI 51-101.

Item 6 — Use of Proceeds

Proceeds

6.1 (1) State the estimated net proceeds to be received by the issuer or selling securityholder or, in the case of a non-fixed price distribution or a distribution to be made on a best efforts basis, the minimum amount, if any, of net proceeds to be received by the issuer or selling securityholder from the sale of the securities distributed.

(2) State the particulars of any provisions or arrangements made for holding any part of the net proceeds of the distribution in trust or escrow subject to the fulfillment of conditions.

(3) If the prospectus is used for a special warrant or similar transaction, state the amount that has been received by the issuer of the special warrants or similar securities on the sale of the special warrants or similar securities.

Junior issuers

6.2 A junior issuer must disclose

    (a) the total funds available, and

    (b) the following breakdown of those funds:

        (i) the estimated net proceeds from the sale of the securities offered under the prospectus;

        (ii) the estimated consolidated working capital (deficiency) as at the most recent month end before filing the prospectus;

        (iii) the total other funds available to be used to achieve the principal purposes identified by the junior issuer pursuant to this Item.

Principal purposes — generally

6.3 (1) Describe in reasonable detail and, if appropriate, using tabular form, each of the principal purposes, with approximate amounts, for which

    (a) the net proceeds will be used by the issuer, or

    (b) the funds available as required under section 6.2 will be used by a junior issuer.

(2) If the closing of the distribution is subject to a minimum offering amount, provide disclosure of the use of proceeds for the minimum and maximum offering amounts.

(3) If the following apply, disclose how the proceeds will be used by the issuer, with reference to various potential thresholds of proceeds raised, in the event that the issuer raises less than the maximum offering amount:

    (a) the closing of the distribution is not subject to a minimum offering amount;

    (b) the distribution is to be on a best efforts basis;

    (c) the issuer has significant short-term non-discretionary expenditures including those for general corporate purposes, or significant short-term capital or contractual commitments, and may not have other readily accessible resources to satisfy those expenditures or commitments.

(4) If the issuer is required to provide disclosure under subsection (3), the issuer must discuss, in respect of each threshold, the impact, if any, of raising each threshold amount on its liquidity, operations, capital resources and solvency.

INSTRUCTIONS

If the issuer is required to disclose the use of proceeds at various thresholds under subsections 6.3(3) and (4), include as an example a threshold that reflects the receipt of 15% of the offering or less.

Principal purposes — indebtedness

6.4 (1) If more than 10% of the net proceeds will be used to reduce or retire indebtedness and the indebtedness was incurred within the two preceding years, describe the principal purposes for which the proceeds of the indebtedness were used.

(2) If the creditor is an insider, associate or affiliate of the issuer, identify the creditor and the nature of the relationship to the issuer, and disclose the outstanding amount owed.

Principal purposes — asset acquisition

6.5 (1) If more than 10% of the net proceeds are to be used to acquire assets, describe the assets.

(2) If known, disclose the particulars of the purchase price being paid for or being allocated to the assets or categories of assets, including intangible assets.

(3) If the vendor of the assets is an insider, associate or affiliate of the issuer, identify the vendor and the nature of the relationship to the issuer, and disclose the method used in determining the purchase price.

(4) Describe the nature of the title to or interest in the assets to be acquired by the issuer.

(5) If part of the consideration for the acquisition of the assets consists of securities of the issuer, give brief particulars of the class, number or amount, voting rights, if any, and other appropriate information relating to the securities, including particulars of the issuance of securities of the same class within the two preceding years.

Principal purposes — insiders, etc.

6.6 If an insider, associate or affiliate of the issuer will receive more than 10% of the net proceeds, identify the insider, associate or affiliate and the nature of the relationship to the issuer, and disclose the amount of net proceeds to be received.

Principal purposes — research and development

6.7 If more than 10% of the net proceeds from the distribution will be used for research and development of products or services, describe

    (a) the timing and stage of research and development programs that management anticipates will be reached using such proceeds,

    (b) the major components of the proposed programs that will be funded using the proceeds from the distribution, including an estimate of anticipated costs,

    (c) if the issuer is conducting its own research and development, is subcontracting out the research and development or is using a combination of those methods, and

    (d) the additional steps required to reach commercial production and an estimate of costs and timing.

Business objectives and milestones

6.8 (1) State the business objectives that the issuer expects to accomplish using the net proceeds of the distribution under section 6.1, or in the case of a junior issuer, using the funds available described under section 6.2.

(2) Describe each significant event that must occur for the business objectives described under subsection (1) to be accomplished and state the specific time period in which each event is expected to occur and the costs related to each event.

Unallocated funds in trust or escrow

6.9 (1) Disclose that unallocated funds will be placed in a trust or escrow account, invested or added to the working capital of the issuer.

(2) Give details of the arrangements made for, and the persons or companies responsible for,

(a) the supervision of the trust or escrow account or the investment of unallocated funds, and

(b) the investment policy to be followed.

Other sources of funding

6.10 If any material amounts of other funds are to be used in conjunction with the proceeds, state the amounts and sources of the other funds.

Financing by special warrants, etc.

6.11 (1) If the prospectus is used to qualify the distribution of securities issued upon the exercise of special warrants or the exercise of other securities acquired on a prospectus-exempt basis, describe the principal purposes for which the proceeds of the prospectus-exempt financing were used or are to be used.

(2) If all or a portion of the funds have been spent, explain how the funds were spent.

Item 7 — Dividends or Distributions

Dividends or distributions

7.1 (1) Disclose the amount of cash dividends or distributions declared per security for each class of the issuer's securities for each of the three most recently completed financial years and its current financial year.

(2) Describe any restrictions that could prevent the issuer from paying dividends or distributions.

(3) Disclose the issuer's dividend or distribution policy and any intended change in dividend or distribution policy.

Item 8 — Management's Discussion and Analysis

Interpretation

8.1 (1) For the purposes of this Item, MD&A means a completed Form 51-102F1 or, in the case of an SEC issuer, a completed Form 51-102F1 or management's discussion and analysis prepared in accordance with Item 303 of Regulation S-K under the 1934 Act.

(2) For MD&A in the form of Form 51-102F1, the issuer

(a) must read the references to a "venture issuer" in Form 51-102F1 to include an IPO venture issuer,

(b) must disregard

(i) the Instruction to section 1.11 of Form 51-102F1, and

(ii) section 1.15 of Form 51-102F1, and

(c) must include the disclosure required by section 1.10 of Form 51-102F1 in the prospectus.

INSTRUCTION

For the purposes of paragraph (2)(c), an issuer cannot satisfy the requirement in section 1.10 of Form 51-102F1 by incorporating by reference its fourth quarter MD&A into the prospectus.

MD&A

8.2 (1) Provide MD&A for

(a) the most recent annual financial statements of the issuer included in the prospectus under Item 32, and

(b) the most recent interim financial report of the issuer included in the prospectus under Item 32.

(2) If the prospectus includes the issuer's annual statements of comprehensive income, statements of changes in equity, and statements of cash flow for three financial years under Item 32, provide MD&A for the second most recent annual financial statements of the issuer included in the prospectus under Item 32.

(3) Despite subsection (2), MD&A for the second most recent annual financial statements of the issuer included in the prospectus under Item 32 may omit disclosure regarding statement of financial position items.

GUIDANCE

Under section 2.2.1 of Form 51-102F1, for financial years beginning on or after July 1, 2015, venture issuers, or IPO venture issuers, have the option of meeting the requirement to provide interim MD&A section 2.2 of Form 51-102F1 by providing quarterly highlights disclosure..

8.3 [repealed]

Disclosure of outstanding security data

8.4 (1) Disclose the designation and number or principal amount of

(a) each class and series of voting or equity securities of the issuer for which there are securities outstanding,

(b) each class and series of securities of the issuer for which there are securities outstanding if the securities are convertible into, or exercisable or exchangeable for, voting or equity securities of the issuer, and

(c) subject to subsection (2), each class and series of voting or equity securities of the issuer that are issuable on the conversion, exercise or exchange of outstanding securities of the issuer.

(2) If the exact number or principal amount of voting or equity securities of the issuer that are issuable on the conversion, exercise or exchange of outstanding securities of the issuer is not determinable, the issuer must disclose the maximum number or principal amount of each class and series of voting or equity securities that are issuable on the conversion, exercise or exchange of outstanding securities of the issuer and, if that maximum number or principal amount is not determinable, the issuer must describe the exchange or conversion features and the manner in which the number or principal amount of voting or equity securities will be determined.

(3) The disclosure under subsections (1) and (2) must be prepared as of the latest practicable date.

More recent financial information

8.5 If the issuer is required to include more recent historical financial information in the prospectus under subsection 32.6(2), the issuer is not required to update the MD&A already included in the prospectus under this Item.

Additional disclosure for venture issuers or IPO venture issuers without significant revenue

8.6 (1) If the issuer is a venture issuer or an IPO venture issuer that has not had significant revenue from operations in either of its last two financial years, disclose a breakdown of material components of

(a) exploration and evaluation assets or expenditures,

(b) expensed research and development costs,

(c) intangible assets arising from development,

(d) general and administrative expenses, and

(e) any material costs, whether expensed or recognized as assets, not referred to in paragraphs (a) through (d).

(2) Present the analysis of exploration and evaluation assets or expenditures required by subsection (1) on a property-by-property basis, if the issuer's business primarily involves mining exploration and development.

(3) Provide the disclosure in subsection (1) for the following periods:

(a) the two most recently completed financial years; and

(b) if the issuer is not providing disclosure in accordance with section 2.2.1 of Form 51-102F1, the most recent year-to-date interim period and the comparative year-to-date period presented in the interim financial report included in the prospectus, if any.

(4) Subsection (1) does not apply if the information required under that subsection has been disclosed in the financial statements included in the prospectus.

Additional disclosure for junior issuers

8.7 For a junior issuer that had negative cash flow from operating activities in its most recently completed financial year for which financial statements have been included in the prospectus, disclose

(a) the period of time the proceeds raised under the prospectus are expected to fund operations,

(b) the estimated total operating costs necessary for the issuer to achieve its stated business objectives during that period of time, and

(c) the estimated amount of other material capital expenditures during that period of time.

In determining cash flow from operating activities, the issuer must include cash payments related to dividends and borrowing costs.

Additional disclosure for issuers with significant equity investees

8.8 (1) An issuer that has a significant equity investee must disclose

(a) summarized financial information of the equity investee, including the aggregated amounts of assets, liabilities, revenue and profit or loss, and

(b) the issuer's proportionate interest in the equity investee and any contingent issuance of securities by the equity investee that might significantly affect the issuer's share of profit or loss.

(2) Provide the disclosure in subsection (1) for the following periods:

(a) the two most recently completed financial years;

(b) if the issuer is not providing disclosure in accordance with section 2.2.1 of Form 51-102F1, the most recent year-to-date interim period and the comparative year-to-date period presented in the interim financial report included in the prospectus, if any.

(3) Subsection (1) does not apply if

(a) the information required under that subsection has been disclosed in the financial statements included in the prospectus, or

(b) the issuer includes in the prospectus separate financial statements of the equity investee for the periods referred to in subsection (2).

Item 9 — Earnings Coverage Ratios

Earnings coverage ratios

9.1 (1) If the securities being distributed are debt securities having a term to maturity in excess of one year or are preferred shares, disclose the following earnings coverage ratios adjusted in accordance with subsection (2):

(a) the earnings coverage ratio based on the most recent 12-month period included in the issuer's annual financial statements included in the prospectus,

(b) if there has been a change in year end and the issuer's most recent financial year is less than nine months in length, the earnings coverage calculation for its old financial year, and

(c) the earnings coverage ratio based on the 12-month period ended on the last day of the most recently completed period for which an interim financial report of the issuer has been included in the prospectus.

(2) Adjust the ratios referred to in subsection (1) to reflect

(a) the issuance of the securities being distributed under the prospectus, based on the price at which these securities are expected to be distributed,

(b) in the case of a distribution of preferred shares,

(i) the issuance of all preferred shares since the date of the annual financial statements or interim financial report, and

(ii) the repurchase, redemption or other retirement of all preferred shares repurchased, redeemed, or otherwise retired since the date of the annual financial statements or interim financial report and of all preferred shares to be repurchased, redeemed, or otherwise retired from the proceeds to be realized from the sale of securities under the prospectus,

(c) the issuance of all financial liabilities, as defined in accordance with the issuer's GAAP, since the date of the annual financial statements or interim financial report, and

(d) the repayment, redemption or other retirement of all financial liabilities, as defined in accordance with the issuer's GAAP, since the date of the annual financial statements or interim financial report and all financial liabilities to be repaid or redeemed from the proceeds to be realized from the sale of securities distributed under the prospectus.

(3) [repealed]

(4) If the earnings coverage ratio is less than one-to-one, disclose in the prospectus the dollar amount of the numerator required to achieve a ratio of one-to-one.

(5) If the prospectus includes a pro forma income statement, calculate the pro forma earnings coverage ratios for the periods of the pro forma income statement, and disclose them in the prospectus.

INSTRUCTIONS

(1) Cash flow coverage may be disclosed but only as a supplement to earnings coverage and only if the method of calculation is fully disclosed.

(2) Earnings coverage is calculated by dividing an entity's profit or loss attributable to owners of the parent (the numerator) by its borrowing costs and dividend obligations (the denominator).

(3) For the earnings coverage calculation

(a) the numerator should be calculated using consolidated profit or loss attributable to owners of the parent before borrowing costs and income taxes;

(b) imputed interest income from the proceeds of a distribution should not be added to the numerator;

(c) [repealed]

(d) for distributions of debt securities, the appropriate denominator is borrowing costs, after giving effect to the new debt securities issue and any retirement of obligations, plus the borrowing costs that have been capitalized during the period;

(e) for distributions of preferred shares

(i) the appropriate denominator is dividends declared during the period, together with undeclared dividends on cumulative preferred shares, after giving effect to the new preferred share issue, plus the issuer's annual borrowing cost requirements, including the borrowing costs that have been capitalized during the period, less any retirement of obligations, and

(ii) dividends should be grossed-up to a before-tax equivalent using the issuer's effective income tax rate; and

(f) for distributions of both debt securities and preferred shares, the appropriate denominator is the same as for a preferred share issue, except that the denominator should also reflect the effect of the debt securities being offered pursuant to the prospectus.

(4) The denominator represents a pro forma calculation of the aggregate of an issuer's borrowing cost obligations on all financial liabilities and dividend obligations (including both dividends declared and undeclared dividends on cumulative preferred shares) with respect to all outstanding preferred shares, as adjusted to reflect

(a) the issuance of all financial liabilities and, in addition in the case of an issuance of preferred shares, all preferred shares issued, since the date of the annual financial statements or interim financial report;

(b) the issuance of the securities that are to be distributed under the prospectus, based on a reasonable estimate of the price at which these securities will be distributed; and

(c) the repayment or redemption of all financial liabilities since the date of the annual financial statements or interim financial report, all financial liabilities to be repaid or redeemed from the proceeds to be realized from the sale of securities under the

prospectus and, in addition, in the case of an issuance of preferred shares, all preferred shares repaid or redeemed since the date of the annual financial statements or interim financial report and all preferred shares to be repaid or redeemed from the proceeds to be realized from the sale of securities under the prospectus.

(5) [repealed]

(6) For debt securities, disclosure of earnings coverage shall include language similar to the following, with the bracketed and bulleted information completed:

> *[Name of the issuer]'s borrowing cost requirements, after giving effect to the issue of [the debt securities to be distributed under the prospectus], amounted to $• for the 12 months ended •. [Name of the issuer]'s profit or loss attributable to owners of the parent before borrowing costs and income tax for the 12 months then ended was $•, which is • times [name of the issuer]'s borrowing cost requirements for this period.*

(7) For preferred share issues, disclosure of earnings coverage shall include language similar to the following, with the bracketed and bulleted information completed:

> *[Name of the issuer]'s dividend requirements on all of its preferred shares, after giving effect to the issue of [the preferred shares to be distributed under the prospectus], and adjusted to a before-tax equivalent using an effective income tax rate of •%, amounted to $• for the 12 months ended •. [Name of the issuer]'s borrowing cost requirements for the 12 months then ended amounted to $•. [Name of the issuer]'s profit or loss attributable to owners of the parent before borrowing costs and income tax for the 12 months ended • was $•, which is • times [name of the issuer]'s aggregate dividend and borrowing cost requirements for this period.*

(8) Other earnings coverage calculations may be included as supplementary disclosure to the required earnings coverage calculations outlined above as long as their derivation is disclosed and they are not given greater prominence than the required earnings coverage calculations.

Item 10 — Description of the Securities Distributed

Equity securities

10.1 If equity securities are being distributed, state the description or the designation of the class of the equity securities and describe all material attributes and characteristics, including

(a) dividend rights,

(b) voting rights,

(c) rights upon dissolution or winding-up,

(d) pre-emptive rights,

(e) conversion or exchange rights,

(f) redemption, retraction, purchase for cancellation or surrender provisions,

(g) sinking or purchase fund provisions,

(h) provisions permitting or restricting the issuance of additional securities and any other material restrictions, and

(i) provisions requiring a securityholder to contribute additional capital.

Debt securities

10.2 If debt securities are being distributed, describe all material attributes and characteristics of the indebtedness and the security, if any, for the debt, including

(a) provisions for interest rate, maturity and premium, if any,

(b) conversion or exchange rights,

(c) redemption, retraction, purchase for cancellation or surrender provisions,

(d) sinking or purchase fund provisions,

(e) the nature and priority of any security for the debt securities, briefly identifying the principal properties subject to lien or charge,

(f) provisions permitting or restricting the issuance of additional securities, the incurring of additional indebtedness and other material negative covenants, including restrictions against payment of dividends and restrictions against giving security on the assets of the issuer or its subsidiaries, and provisions as to the release or substitution of assets securing the debt securities,

(g) the name of the trustee under any indenture relating to the debt securities and the nature of any material relationship between the trustee or any of its affiliates and the issuer or any of its affiliates, and

(h) any financial arrangements between the issuer and any of its affiliates or among its affiliates that could affect the security for the indebtedness.

Asset-backed securities

10.3 (1) This section applies only if any asset-backed securities are being distributed under the prospectus.

(2) Describe the material attributes and characteristics of the asset-backed securities, including

(a) the rate of interest or stipulated yield and any premium,

(b) the date for repayment of principal or return of capital and any circumstances in which payments of principal or capital may be made before such date, including any redemption or pre-payment obligations or privileges of the issuer and any events that may trigger early liquidation or amortization of the underlying pool of financial assets,

(c) provisions for the accumulation of cash flows to provide for the repayment of principal or return of capital,

(d) provisions permitting or restricting the issuance of additional securities and any other material negative covenants applicable to the issuer,

(e) the nature, order and priority of the entitlements of holders of asset-backed securities and any other entitled persons or companies to receive cash flows generated from the underlying pool of financial assets, and

(f) any events, covenants, standards or preconditions that may reasonably be expected to affect the timing or amount of payments or distributions to be made under the asset-backed securities, including those that are dependent or based on the economic performance of the underlying pool of financial assets.

(3) Provide financial disclosure that describes the underlying pool of financial assets for

    (a) the three most recently completed financial years ended more than

        (i) 90 days before the date of the prospectus, or

        (ii) 120 days before the date of the prospectus, if the issuer is a venture issuer,

    (b) if the issuer has not had asset-backed securities outstanding for three financial years, each completed financial year ended more than

        (i) 90 days before the date of the prospectus, or

        (ii) 120 days before the date of the prospectus, if the issuer is a venture issuer,

    (c) a period from the date the issuer had asset-backed securities outstanding to a date not more than 90 days before the date of the prospectus if the issuer has not had asset-backed securities outstanding for at least one financial year.

(4) For the purposes of the financial disclosure required by subsection (3), if an issuer changed its financial year end during any of the financial years referred to in subsection (3) and the transition year is less than nine months, the transition year is not a financial year.

(5) Despite subsection (4), all financial disclosure that describes the underlying pool of financial assets of the issuer for a transition year must be included in the prospectus for the most recent interim period, if any, ended

    (a) subsequent to the most recent financial year refer to in paragraphs (3)(a) and (3)(b) in respect of which financial disclosure on the underlying pool of financial assets is included in the prospectus, and

    (b) more than

        (i) 45 days before the date of the prospectus, or

        (ii) 60 days before the date of the prospectus if the issuer is a venture issuer.

(6) If the issuer files financial disclosure that describes the underlying pool of financial assets for a more recent period than required under subsection (3) or (5) before the prospectus is filed, the issuer must include that more recent financial disclosure that describes the underlying pool of financial assets in the prospectus.

(7) If financial disclosure that describes the underlying pool of financial assets of the issuer is publicly disseminated by, or on behalf of, the issuer through news release or otherwise for a more recent period than required under subsection (3) or (5), the issuer must include the content of the news release or public communication in the prospectus.

(8) The disclosure in subsections (3) and (5) must include a discussion and analysis of

    (a) the composition of the pool as at the end of the period,

    (b) profit and losses from the pool for the period presented on at least an annual basis or such shorter period as is reasonable given the nature of the underlying pool of assets,

    (c) the payment, prepayment and collection experience of the pool for the period on at least an annual basis or such shorter period as is reasonable given the nature of the underlying pool of assets,

    (d) servicing and other administrative fees, and

    (e) any significant variances experienced in the matters referred to in paragraphs (a) through (d).

(9) Describe the type of financial assets, the manner in which the financial assets originated or will originate and, if applicable, the mechanism and terms of the agreement governing the transfer of the financial assets comprising the underlying pool to or through the issuer, including the consideration paid for the financial assets.

(10) Describe any person or company who

    (a) originated, sold or deposited a material portion of the financial assets comprising the pool, or has agreed to do so,

    (b) acts, or has agreed to act, as a trustee, custodian, bailee or agent of the issuer or any holder of the asset-backed securities, or in a similar capacity,

    (c) administers or services a material portion of the financial assets comprising the pool or provides administrative or managerial services to the issuer, or has agreed to do so, on a conditional basis or otherwise, if

        (i) finding a replacement provider of the services at a cost comparable to the cost of the current provider is not reasonably likely,

        (ii) a replacement provider of the services is likely to achieve materially worse results than the current provider,

        (iii) the current provider of the services is likely to default in its service obligations because of its current financial condition, or

        (iv) the disclosure is otherwise material,

    (d) provides a guarantee, alternative credit support or other credit enhancement to support the obligations of the issuer under the asset-backed securities or the performance of some or all of the financial assets in the pool, or has agreed to do so, or

(e) lends to the issuer in order to facilitate the timely payment or repayment of amounts payable under the asset-backed securities, or has agreed to do so.

(11) Describe the general business activities and material responsibilities under the asset-backed securities of a person or company referred to in subsection (10).

(12) Describe the terms of any material relationships between

(a) any of the persons or companies referred to in subsection (10) or any of their respective affiliates, and

(b) the issuer.

(13) Describe any provisions relating to termination of services or responsibilities of any of the persons or companies referred to in subsection (10) and the terms on which a replacement may be appointed.

(14) Describe any risk factors associated with the asset-backed securities, including disclosure of material risks associated with changes in interest rates or prepayment levels, and any circumstances where payments on the asset-backed securities could be impaired or disrupted as a result of any reasonably foreseeable event that may delay, divert or disrupt the cash flows dedicated to service the asset-backed securities.

INSTRUCTIONS

(1) Present the information required under subsections (3) through (8) in a manner that will enable a reader to easily determine whether, and the extent to which, the events, covenants, standards and preconditions referred to in paragraph (2)(f) have occurred, are being satisfied or may be satisfied.

(2) If the information required under subsections (3) through (8) is not compiled specifically from the underlying pool of financial assets, but is compiled from a larger pool of the same assets from which the securitized assets are randomly selected so that the performance of the larger pool is representative of the performance of the pool of securitized assets, then an issuer may comply with subsections (3) through (8) by providing the financial disclosure required based on the larger pool and disclosing that it has done so.

(3) Issuers are required to summarize contractual arrangements in plain language and may not merely restate the text of the contracts referred to. The use of diagrams to illustrate the roles of, and the relationship among, the persons and companies referred to in subsection (10), and the contractual arrangements underlying the asset-backed securities is encouraged.

Derivatives

10.4 If derivatives are being distributed, describe fully the material attributes and characteristics of the derivatives, including

(a) the calculation of the value or payment obligations under the derivatives,

(b) the exercise of the derivatives,

(c) settlements that are the result of the exercise of the derivatives,

(d) the underlying interest of the derivatives,

(e) the role of a calculation expert in connection with the derivatives,

(f) the role of any credit supporter of the derivatives, and

(g) the risk factors associated with the derivatives.

Special warrants, etc.

10.5 If the prospectus is used to qualify the distribution of securities issued upon the exercise of special warrants or other securities acquired on a prospectus-exempt basis, provide the following disclosure in the prospectus to indicate that holders of such securities have been provided with a contractual right of rescission:

The issuer has granted to each holder of a special warrant a contractual right of rescission of the prospectus-exempt transaction under which the special warrant was initially acquired. The contractual right of rescission provides that if a holder of a special warrant who acquires another security of the issuer on exercise of the special warrant as provided for in the prospectus is, or becomes, entitled under the securities legislation of a jurisdiction to the remedy of rescission because of the prospectus or an amendment to the prospectus containing a misrepresentation,

(a) the holder is entitled to rescission of both the holder's exercise of its special warrant and the private placement transaction under which the special warrant was initially acquired,

(b) the holder is entitled in connection with the rescission to a full refund of all consideration paid to the underwriter or issuer, as the case may be, on the acquisition of the special warrant, and

(c) if the holder is a permitted assignee of the interest of the original special warrant subscriber, the holder is entitled to exercise the rights of rescission and refund as if the holder was the original subscriber.

INSTRUCTION

If the prospectus is qualifying the distribution of securities issued upon the exercise of securities other than special warrants, replace the term "special warrant" with the type of the security being distributed.

Part 4:
DISTRIBUTIONS

Restricted securities

10.6 (1) If the issuer has outstanding, or proposes to distribute under a prospectus restricted securities, subject securities or securities that are, directly or indirectly, convertible into or exercisable or exchangeable for restricted securities or subject securities, provide a detailed description of

(a) the voting rights attached to the restricted securities that are the subject of the distribution or that will result from the distribution, either directly or following a conversion, exchange or exercise, and the voting rights, if any, attached to the securities of any other class of securities of the issuer that are the same as or greater than, on a per security basis, those attached to the restricted securities,

(b) any significant provisions under applicable corporate and securities law that do not apply to the holders of the restricted securities that are the subject of the distribution or that will result from the distribution, either directly or following a conversion, exchange or exercise, but do apply to the holders of another class of equity securities, and the extent of any rights provided in the constating documents or otherwise for the protection of holders of the restricted securities,

(c) any rights under applicable corporate law, in the constating documents or otherwise, of holders of restricted securities that are the subject of the distribution or that will result from the distribution, either directly or following a conversion, exchange or exercise, to attend, in person or by proxy, meetings of holders of equity securities of the issuer and to speak at the meetings to the same extent that holders of equity securities are entitled, and

(d) how the issuer complied with, or the basis upon which it was exempt from, the requirements of Part 12 of the Instrument.

(2) If holders of restricted securities do not have all of the rights referred to in subsection (1) the detailed description referred to in that subsection must include, in boldface type, a statement of the rights the holders do not have.

(3) If the issuer is required to include the disclosure referred to in subsection (1), state the percentage of the aggregate voting rights attached to the issuer's securities that will be represented by restricted securities after effect has been given to the issuance of the securities being offered.

Other securities

10.7 If securities other than equity securities, debt securities, asset-backed securities or derivatives are being distributed, describe fully the material attributes and characteristics of those securities.

Modification of terms

10.8 (1) Describe provisions about the modification, amendment or variation of any rights attached to the securities being distributed.

(2) If the rights of holders of securities may be modified otherwise than in accordance with the provisions attached to the securities or the provisions of the governing statute relating to the securities, explain briefly.

Ratings

10.9 (1) If the issuer has asked for and received a credit rating, or if the issuer is aware that it has received any other kind of rating, including a stability rating or a provisional rating, from one or more credit rating organizations for securities of the issuer that are outstanding, or will be outstanding, and the rating or ratings continue in effect, disclose

(a) each rating received from a credit rating organization;

(b) for each rating disclosed under paragraph (a), the name of the credit rating organization that has assigned the rating;

(c) a definition or description of the category in which each credit rating organization rated the securities and the relative rank of each rating within the organization's overall classification system;

(d) an explanation of what the rating addresses and what attributes, if any, of the securities are not addressed by the rating;

(e) any factors or considerations identified by the credit rating organization as giving rise to unusual risks associated with the securities;

(f) a statement that a credit rating or a stability rating is not a recommendation to buy, sell or hold securities and may be subject to revision or withdrawal at any time by the credit rating organization; and

(g) any announcement made by, or any proposed announcement known to the issuer that is to be made by, a credit rating organization to the effect that the organization is reviewing or intends to revise or withdraw a rating previously assigned and required to be disclosed under this section.

(2) If payments were, or reasonably will be, made to a credit rating organization that provided a rating described in subsection (1), state that fact and state whether any payments were made to the credit rating organization in respect of any other service provided to the issuer by the credit rating organization during the last two years.

INSTRUCTIONS

There may be factors relating to a security that are not addressed by a credit rating organization when they give a rating. For example, in the case of cash settled derivative instruments, factors in addition to the creditworthiness of the issuer, such as the continued subsistence of the underlying interest or the volatility of the price, value or level of the underlying interest may be reflected in the rating analysis. Rather than being addressed in the rating itself, these factors may be described by a credit rating organization by way of a superscript or other notation to a rating. Any such attributes must be discussed in the disclosure under this section.

A provisional rating received before the issuer's most recently completed financial year is not required to be disclosed under this section.

Other attributes

10.10 (1) If the rights attaching to the securities being distributed are materially limited or qualified by the rights of any other class of securities, or if any other class of securities ranks ahead of or equally with the securities being distributed, include information about the other securities that will enable investors to understand the rights attaching to the securities being distributed.

(2) If securities of the class being distributed may be partially redeemed or repurchased, state the manner of selecting the securities to be redeemed or repurchased.

INSTRUCTION

This section requires only a brief summary of the provisions that are material from an investment standpoint. The provisions attaching to the securities being distributed or any other class of securities do not need to be set out in full. They may, in the issuer's discretion, be attached as a schedule to the prospectus.

Item 11 — Consolidated Capitalization

Consolidated capitalization

11.1 Describe any material change in, and the effect of the material change on, the share and loan capital of the issuer, on a consolidated basis, since the date of the issuer's financial statements for its most recently completed financial period included in the prospectus, including any material change that will result from the issuance of the securities being distributed under the prospectus.

Item 12 — Options to Purchase Securities

Options to purchase securities

12.1 (1) For an issuer that is not a reporting issuer in any jurisdiction immediately before filing the prospectus, state, in tabular form, as at a specified date within 30 days before the date of the prospectus, information about options to purchase securities of the issuer, or a subsidiary of the issuer, that are held or will be held upon completion of the distribution by

(a) all executive officers and past executive officers of the issuer, as a group, and all directors and past directors of the issuer who are not also executive officers, as a group, indicating the aggregate number of executive officers and the aggregate number of directors to whom the information applies,

(b) all executive officers and past executive officers of all subsidiaries of the issuer, as a group, and all directors and past directors of those subsidiaries who are not also executive officers of the subsidiary, as a group, excluding, in each case, individuals referred to in paragraph (a), indicating the aggregate number of executive officers and the aggregate number of directors to whom the information applies,

(c) all other employees and past employees of the issuer as a group,

(d) all other employees and past employees of subsidiaries of the issuer as a group,

(e) all consultants of the issuer as a group, and

(f) any other person or company, other than the underwriter(s), naming each person or company.

(2) Describe any material change to the information required to be included in the prospectus under subsection (1) to the date of the prospectus.

INSTRUCTIONS

(1) Describe the options, warrants, or other similar securities stating the material provisions of each class or type of option, including:

(a) the designation and number of the securities under option;

(b) the purchase price of the securities under option or the formula by which the purchase price will be determined, and the expiration dates of the options;

(c) if reasonably ascertainable, the market value of the securities under option on the date of grant;

(d) if reasonably ascertainable, the market value of the securities under option on the specified date; and

(e) with respect to options referred to in paragraph (1)(f), the particulars of the grant including the consideration for the grant.

(2) For the purposes of paragraph (1)(f), provide the information required for all options except warrants and special warrants.

Item 13 — Prior Sales

Prior sales

13.1 For each class or series of securities of the issuer distributed under the prospectus and for securities that are convertible or exchangeable into those classes or series of securities, state, for the 12-month period before the date of the prospectus,

(a) the price at which the securities have been issued or are to be issued by the issuer or sold by the selling securityholder,

(b) the number of securities issued or sold at that price, and

(c) the date on which the securities were issued or sold.

Trading price and volume

13.2 (1) For the following securities of the issuer that are traded or quoted on a Canadian marketplace, identify the marketplace and the price ranges and volume traded or quoted on the Canadian marketplace on which the greatest volume of trading or quotation for the securities generally occurs;

(a) each class or series of securities of the issuer distributed under the prospectus;

(b) securities of the issuer into which those classes or series of securities are convertible or exchangeable.

(2) For the following securities of the issuer that are not traded or quoted on a Canadian marketplace but are traded or quoted on a foreign marketplace, identify the foreign marketplace and the price ranges and volume traded or quoted on the foreign marketplace on which the greatest volume or quotation for the securities generally occurs:

(a) each class or series of securities of the issuer distributed under the prospectus;

(b) securities of the issuer into which those classes or series of securities are convertible or exchangeable.

(3) Provide the information required under subsections (1) and (2) on a monthly basis for each month or, if applicable, partial months of the 12-month period before the date of the prospectus.

Item 14 — Escrowed Securities and Securities Subject to Contractual Restriction on Transfer

Escrowed securities and securities subject to contractual restriction on transfer

14.1 (1) State as of a specified date within 30 days before the date of the prospectus, in substantially the following tabular form, the number of securities of each class of securities of the issuer held, to the knowledge of the issuer, in escrow or that are subject to a contractual restriction on transfer and the percentage that number represents of the outstanding securities of that class.

Escrowed Securities and Securities Subject to Contractual Restriction on Transfer

Designation of class	Number of securities held in escrow or that are subject to a contractual restriction on transfer	Percentage of class
....	....	....

(2) In a note to the table disclose the name of the depository, if any, and the date of and conditions governing the release of the securities from escrow or the date the contractual restriction on transfer ends, as applicable.

(3) Describe any material change to the information required to be included in the prospectus under subsection (1) to the date of the prospectus.

INSTRUCTIONS

(1) For purposes of this section, escrow includes securities subject to a pooling agreement.

(2) For the purposes of this section, securities subject to contractual restrictions on transfer as a result of pledges made to lenders are not required to be disclosed.

Item 15 — Principal Securityholders and Selling Securityholders

Principal securityholders and selling securityholders

15.1 (1) Provide the following information for each principal securityholder of the issuer and, if any securities are being distributed for the account of a securityholder, for each selling securityholder:

(a) the name;

(b) the number or amount of securities owned, controlled or directed of the class being distributed;

(c) the number or amount of securities of the class being distributed for the account of the securityholder;

(d) the number or amount of securities of the issuer of any class to be owned, controlled or directed after the distribution, and the percentage that number or amount represents of the total outstanding;

(e) whether the securities referred to in paragraph (b), (c) or (d) are owned both of record and beneficially, of record only, or beneficially only.

(2) If securities are being distributed in connection with a restructuring transaction, indicate, to the extent known, the holdings of each person or company described in paragraph (1)(a) that will exist after effect has been given to the transaction.

(3) If any of the securities being distributed are being distributed for the account of a securityholder and those securities were purchased by the selling securityholder within the two years preceding the date of the prospectus, state the date the selling securityholder acquired the securities and, if the securities were acquired in the 12 months preceding the date of the prospectus, the cost to the securityholder in the aggregate and on an average cost-per-security basis.

(4) If, to the knowledge of the issuer or the underwriter of the securities being distributed, more than 10% of any class of voting securities of the issuer is held, or is to be held, subject to any voting trust or other similar agreement, disclose, to the extent known, the designation of the securities, the number or amount of the securities held or to be held subject to the agreement and the duration of the agreement. State the names and addresses of the voting trustees and outline briefly their voting rights and other powers under the agreement.

(5) If, to the knowledge of the issuer or the underwriter of the securities being distributed, any principal securityholder or selling securityholder is an associate or affiliate of another person or company named as a principal securityholder, disclose, to the extent known, the

material facts of the relationship, including any basis for influence over the issuer held by the person or company other than the holding of voting securities of the issuer.

(6) In addition to the above, include in a footnote to the table the required calculation(s) on a fully-diluted basis.

(7) Describe any material change to the information required to be included in the prospectus under subsection (1) to the date of the prospectus.

INSTRUCTION

If a company, partnership, trust or other unincorporated entity is a principal securityholder of an issuer, disclose, to the extent known, the name of each individual who, through ownership of or control or direction over the securities of that company, trust or other unincorporated entity, or membership in the partnership, as the case may be, is a principal securityholder of that entity.

Item 16 — Directors and Executive Officers

Name, occupation and security holding

16.1 (1) Provide information for directors and executive officers of the issuer in accordance with section 10.1 of Form 51-102F2 as at the date of the prospectus.

(2) If information similar to the information required under subsection (1) is provided for any director or executive officer, who is not serving in such capacity as at the date of the prospectus, clearly indicate this fact and explain whether the issuer believes that this director or executive officer is liable under the prospectus.

Cease trade orders, bankruptcies, penalties or sanctions

16.2 Provide information for directors and executive officers of the issuer in accordance with section 10.2 of Form 51-102F2 as if the references in that section to "date of the AIF" read "date of the prospectus".

Conflicts of interest

16.3 Disclose particulars of existing or potential material conflicts of interest between the issuer or a subsidiary of the issuer and a director or officer of the issuer or of a subsidiary of the issuer.

Management of junior issuers

16.4 A junior issuer must provide the following information for each member of management:

    (a) state the individual's name, age, position and responsibilities with the issuer and relevant educational background;

    (b) state whether the individual works full time for the issuer or what proportion of the individual's time will be devoted to the issuer;

    (c) state whether the individual is an employee or independent contractor of the issuer;

    (d) state the individual's principal occupations or employment during the five years before the date of the prospectus, disclosing with respect to each organization as of the time such occupation or employment was carried on:

        (i) its name and principal business;

        (ii) if applicable, that the organization was an affiliate of the issuer;

        (iii) positions held by the individual; and

        (iv) whether it is still carrying on business, if known to the individual;

    (e) describe the individual's experience in the issuer's industry;

    (f) state whether the individual has entered into a non-competition or non-disclosure agreement with the issuer.

INSTRUCTION

For purposes of this section, "management" means all directors, officers, employees and contractors whose expertise is critical to the issuer, its subsidiaries and proposed subsidiaries in providing the issuer with a reasonable opportunity to achieve its stated business objectives.

Item 17 — Executive Compensation

Disclosure

17.1 Include in the prospectus a Statement of Executive Compensation prepared in accordance with Form 51-102F6 or, if the issuer is a venture issuer or an IPO venture issuer, in accordance with Form 51-102F6 or Form 51-102F6V and describe any intention to make any material changes to that compensation.

Item 18 — Indebtedness of Directors and Executive Officers

Aggregate indebtedness

18.1 Provide information for the issuer in accordance with section 10.1 of Form 51-102F5 as if the reference in that section to "date of the information circular" read "date of the prospectus".

Indebtedness of directors and executive officers under securities purchase and other programs

18.2 (1) Provide information for the issuer in accordance with section 10.2 of Form 51-102F5 as if the reference in this section to "date of the information circular" read "date of the prospectus".

(2) Do not disclose the information required under subsection (1) for

> (a) any indebtedness that has been entirely repaid on or before the date of the prospectus, or

> (b) routine indebtedness (as defined in paragraph 10.3(c) of Form 51-102F5 as if reference in this paragraph to "the company" read "the issuer").

Item 19 — Audit Committees and Corporate Governance

Audit committees

19.1 (1) Include in the prospectus the disclosure for the issuer in accordance with Form 52-110F1, as applicable, if the issuer is neither a venture issuer nor an IPO venture issuer.

(2) Include in the prospectus the disclosure for the issuer in accordance with Form 52-110F2, as applicable, if the issuer is a venture issuer or an IPO venture issuer.

Corporate governance

19.2 (1) Include in the prospectus the disclosure in accordance with Form 58-101F1, as applicable, if the issuer is neither a venture issuer nor an IPO venture issuer.

(2) Include in the prospectus the disclosure in accordance with Form 58-101F2, as applicable, if the issuer is a venture issuer or an IPO venture issuer.

Item 20 — Plan of Distribution

Name of underwriters

20.1 (1) If the securities are being distributed by an underwriter, state the name of the underwriter and describe briefly the nature of the underwriter's obligation to take up and pay for the securities.

(2) Disclose the date by which the underwriter is obligated to purchase the securities.

Disclosure of conditions to underwriters' obligations

20.2 If securities are distributed by an underwriter that has agreed to purchase all of the securities at a specified price and the underwriter's obligations are subject to conditions,

> (a) include a statement in substantially the following form, with the bracketed information completed and with modifications necessary to reflect the terms of the distribution:

>> Under an agreement dated [insert date of agreement] between [insert name of issuer or selling securityholder] and [insert name(s) of underwriter(s)], as underwriter[s], [insert name of issuer or selling security shareholder] has agreed to sell and the underwriter[s] [has/have] agreed to purchase on [insert closing date] the securities at a price of [insert offering price], payable in cash to [insert name of issuer or selling securityholder] against delivery. The obligations of the underwriter[s] under the agreement may be terminated at [its/their] discretion on the basis of [describe any "market out", "disaster out", "material change out" or similar provision] and may also be terminated upon the occurrence of certain stated events. The underwriter[s] [is/are], however, obligated to take up and pay for all of the securities if any of the securities are purchased under the agreement., and

> (b) describe any other conditions and indicate any information known that is relevant to whether such conditions will be satisfied.

Best efforts offering

20.3 Outline briefly the plan of distribution of any securities being distributed other than on the basis described in section 20.2.

Minimum distribution

20.4 If securities are being distributed on a best efforts basis and minimum funds are to be raised, state

> (a) the minimum funds to be raised,

> (b) that the issuer must appoint a registered dealer authorized to make the distribution, a Canadian financial institution, or a lawyer who is a practicing member in good standing with a law society of a jurisdiction in which the securities are being distributed, or a notary in Québec, to hold in trust all funds received from subscriptions until the minimum amount of funds stipulated in paragraph (a) has been raised, and

> (c) that if the minimum amount of funds is not raised within the distribution period, the trustee must return the funds to the subscribers without any deductions.

Determination of price

20.5 Disclose the method by which the distribution price has been or will be determined and, if estimates have been provided, explain the process of determining the estimates.

Stabilization

20.6 If the issuer, a selling securityholder or an underwriter knows or has reason to believe that there is an intention to over-allot or that the price of any security may be stabilized to facilitate the distribution of the securities, describe the nature of these transactions, including the anticipated size of any over-allocation position, and explain how the transactions are expected to affect the price of the securities.

Approvals

20.7 If the proceeds of the distribution will be used to substantially fund a material undertaking that would constitute a material departure from the business or operations of the issuer and the issuer has not obtained all material licences, registrations and approvals necessary for the stated principal use of proceeds, include a statement that

(a) the issuer will appoint a registered dealer authorized to make the distribution, a Canadian financial institution, or a lawyer who is a practicing member in good standing with a law society of a jurisdiction in which the securities are being distributed, or a notary in Québec, to hold in trust all funds received from subscriptions until all material licences, registrations and approvals necessary for the stated principal use of proceeds have been obtained, and

(b) if all material licences, registrations and approvals necessary for the operation of the material undertaking have not been obtained within 90 days from the date of receipt of the final prospectus, the trustee will return the funds to subscribers.

Reduced price distributions

20.8 If the underwriter may decrease the offering price after the underwriter has made a reasonable effort to sell all of the securities at the initial offering price disclosed in the prospectus in accordance with the procedures permitted by the Instrument, disclose this fact and that the compensation realised by the underwriter will be decreased by the amount that the aggregate price paid by purchasers for the securities is less than the gross proceeds paid by the underwriter to the issuer or selling securityholder.

Listing application

20.9 If application has been made to list or quote the securities being distributed, include a statement, in substantially the following form, with bracketed information completed:

The issuer has applied to [list/quote] the securities distributed under this prospectus on [name of exchange or other market]. [Listing/Quotation] will be subject to the issuer fulfilling all the listing requirements of [name of exchange or other market].

Conditional listing approval

20.10 If application has been made to list or quote the securities being distributed on an exchange or marketplace and conditional listing approval has been received, include a statement, in substantially the following form, with the bracketed information completed:

[name of exchange or marketplace] has conditionally approved the [listing/quotation] of these securities. [Listing/Quotation] is subject to the [name of issuer]'s fulfilling all of the requirements of the [name of exchange or marketplace] on or before [date], [including distribution of these securities to a minimum number of public securityholders].

IPO venture issuers

20.11 If the issuer has complied with the requirements of the Instrument as an IPO venture issuer, include a statement, in substantially the following form, with bracketed information completed:

As at the date of the prospectus, [name of issuer] does not have any of its securities listed or quoted, has not applied to list or quote any of its securities, and does not intend to apply to list or quote any of its securities, on the Toronto Stock Exchange, Aequitas NEO Exchange Inc., a U.S. marketplace, or a marketplace outside of Canada and the United States of America "("other than the Alternative Investment Market of the London Stock Exchange or the PLUS markets operated by PLUS Markets Group plc.")"

Constraints

20.12 If there are constraints imposed on the ownership of securities of the issuer to ensure that the issuer has a required level of Canadian ownership, describe the mechanism, if any, by which the level of Canadian ownership of the securities of the issuer will be monitored and maintained.

Special warrants acquired by underwriters or agents

20.13 Disclose the number and dollar value of any special warrants acquired by any underwriter or agent and the percentage of the distribution represented by those special warrants.

Item 21 — Risk Factors

Risk factors

21.1 (1) Disclose risk factors relating to the issuer and its business, such as cash flow and liquidity problems, if any, experience of management, the general risks inherent in the business carried on by the issuer, environmental and health risks, reliance on key personnel, regulatory constraints, economic or political conditions and financial history and any other matter that would be likely to influence an investor's decision to purchase securities of the issuer.

(2) If there is a risk that securityholders of the issuer may become liable to make an additional contribution beyond the price of the security, disclose that risk.

(3) Describe any risk factors material to the issuer that a reasonable investor would consider relevant to an investment in the securities being distributed and that are not otherwise described under subsection (1) or (2).

INSTRUCTIONS

(1) Disclose risks in the order of seriousness from the most serious to the least serious.

(2) A risk factor must not be de-emphasized by including excessive caveats or conditions.

Item 22 — Promoters

Promoters

22.1 *(1)* For a person or company that is, or has been within the two years immediately preceding the date of the prospectus, a promoter of the issuer or subsidiary of the issuer, state

(a) the person or company's name,

(b) the number and percentage of each class of voting securities and equity securities of the issuer or any of its subsidiaries beneficially owned, or controlled or directed, directly or indirectly, by the person or company,

(c) the nature and amount of anything of value, including money, property, contracts, options or rights of any kind received or to be received by the promoter directly or indirectly from the issuer or from a subsidiary of the issuer, and the nature and amount of any assets, services or other consideration received or to be received by the issuer or a subsidiary of the issuer in return, and

(d) for an asset acquired within the two years before the date of the preliminary prospectus, or to be acquired, by the issuer or by a subsidiary of the issuer from a promoter,

(i) the consideration paid or to be paid for the asset and the method by which the consideration has been or will be determined,

(ii) the person or company making the determination referred to in subparagraph (i) and the person or company's relationship with the issuer or the promoter, or an affiliate of the issuer or the promoter, and

(iii) the date that the asset was acquired by the promoter and the cost of the asset to the promoter.

(2) If a promoter referred to in subsection (1) is, as at the date of the preliminary prospectus, or was within 10 years before the date of the preliminary prospectus, a director, chief executive officer, or chief financial officer of any person or company, that

(a) was subject to an order that was issued while the promoter was acting in the capacity as director, chief executive officer or chief financial officer, or

(b) was subject to an order that was issued after the promoter ceased to be a director, chief executive officer or chief financial officer and which resulted from an event that occurred while the promoter was acting in the capacity as director, chief executive officer or chief financial officer,

state the fact and describe the basis on which the order was made and whether the order is still in effect.

(3) For the purposes of subsection (2), "order" means:

(a) a cease trade order,

(b) an order similar to a cease trade order, or

(c) an order that denied the relevant person or company access to any exemption under securities legislation,

that was in effect for a period of more than 30 consecutive days.

(4) If a promoter referred to in subsection (1)

(a) is, as at the date of the preliminary prospectus, or has been within the 10 years before the date of the preliminary prospectus, a director or executive officer of any person or company that, while the promoter was acting in that capacity, or within a year of that person ceasing to act in that capacity, became bankrupt, made a proposal under any legislation relating to bankruptcy or insolvency or was subject to or instituted any proceedings, arrangement or compromise with creditors or had a receiver, receiver manager or trustee appointed to hold its assets, state the fact, or

(b) has, within the 10 years before the date of the preliminary prospectus, become bankrupt, made a proposal under any legislation relating to bankruptcy or insolvency, or become subject to or instituted any proceedings, arrangement or compromise with creditors, or had a receiver, receiver manager or trustee appointed to hold the assets of the promoter, state the fact.

(5) Describe the penalties or sanctions imposed and the grounds on which they were imposed or the terms of the settlement agreement and the circumstances that gave rise to the settlement agreement, if a promoter referred to in subsection (1) has been subject to

(a) any penalties or sanctions imposed by a court relating to provincial and territorial securities legislation or by a provincial and territorial securities regulatory authority or has entered into a settlement agreement with a provincial and territorial securities regulatory authority, or

(b) any other penalties or sanctions imposed by a court or regulatory body that would be likely to be considered important to a reasonable investor in making an investment decision.

(6) Despite subsection (5), no disclosure is required of a settlement agreement entered into before December 31, 2000 unless the disclosure would likely be considered important to a reasonable investor in making an investment decision.

INSTRUCTIONS

(1) The disclosure required by subsections (2), (4) and (5) also applies to any personal holding companies of any of the persons referred to in subsections (2), (4), and (5).

(2) A management cease trade order which applies to a promoter referred to in subsection (1) is an "order" for the purposes of paragraph (2)(a) and must be disclosed, whether or not the director, chief executive officer or chief financial officer was named in the order.

(3) For the purposes of this section, a late filing fee, such as a filing fee that applies to the late filing of an insider report, is not a "penalty or sanction".

(4) The disclosure in paragraph (2)(a) only applies if the promoter was a director, chief executive officer or chief financial officer when the order was issued against the person or company. The issuer does not have to provide disclosure if the promoter became a director, chief executive officer or chief financial officer after the order was issued.

Item 23 — Legal Proceedings and Regulatory Actions

Legal proceedings

23.1 (1) Describe any legal proceedings the issuer is or was a party to, or that any of its property is or was the subject of, since the beginning of the most recently completed financial year for which financial statements of the issuer are included in the prospectus.

(2) Describe any such legal proceedings the issuer knows to be contemplated.

(3) For each proceeding described in subsections (1) and (2), include the name of the court or agency, the date instituted, the principal parties to the proceeding, the nature of the claim, the amount claimed, if any, whether the proceeding is being contested, and the present status of the proceeding.

INSTRUCTION

Information with respect to any proceeding that involves a claim for damages if the amount involved, exclusive of interest and costs, does not exceed 10% of the current assets of the issuer may be omitted. However, if any proceeding presents in large degree the same legal and factual issues as other proceedings pending or known to be contemplated, include the amount involved in the other proceedings in computing the percentage.

Regulatory actions

23.2 Describe any

(a) penalties or sanctions imposed against the issuer by a court relating to provincial and territorial securities legislation or by a securities regulatory authority within the three years immediately preceding the date of the prospectus,

(b) any other penalties or sanctions imposed by a court or regulatory body against the issuer necessary for the prospectus to contain full, true and plain disclosure of all material facts relating to the securities being distributed, and

(c) settlement agreements the issuer entered into before a court relating to provincial and territorial securities legislation or with a securities regulatory authority within the three years immediately preceding the date of the prospectus.

Item 24 — Interests of Management and Others in Material Transactions

Interests of management and others in material transactions

24.1 Provide information for the issuer for this section in accordance with section 13.1 of Form 51-102F2 as if the reference in that section to "within the three most recently completed financial years or during the current financial year that has materially affected or is reasonably expected to materially affect your company" read "within the three years before the date of the prospectus that has materially affected or is reasonably expected to materially affect the issuer or a subsidiary of the issuer".

Underwriting discounts

24.2 Disclose any material underwriting discounts or commissions upon the sale of securities by the issuer if any of the persons or companies listed in section 13.1 of Form 51-102F2 were or are to be an underwriter or are associates, affiliates or partners of a person or company that was or is to be an underwriter.

Item 25 — Relationship Between Issuer or Selling Securityholder and Underwriter

Relationship between issuer or selling securityholder and underwriter

25.1 (1) If the issuer or selling securityholder is a connected issuer or related issuer of an underwriter of the distribution, or if the issuer or selling securityholder is also an underwriter of the distribution, comply with the requirements of NI 33-105.

(2) For the purposes of subsection (1), "connected issuer" and "related issuer" have the same meanings as in NI 33-105.

Item 26 — Auditors, Transfer Agents and Registrars

Auditors

26.1 State the name and address of the auditor of the issuer.

Auditor that was not a participating audit firm

26.1.1(1) If the auditor referred to in section 26.1 was not a participating audit firm, as defined in NI 52-108, as at the date of the most recent auditor's report on financial statements included in the prospectus, include a statement in substantially the following form:

"[*Audit Firm A*] audited the financial statements of [*Entity B*] for the year ended [*state the period of the most recent financial statements included in the prospectus*] and issued an auditor's report dated [*state the date of the auditor's report for the relevant financial statements*]. As at [*state the date of the auditor's report for the relevant financial statements*], [*Audit Firm A*] was not required by securities legislation to enter, and had not entered, into a participation agreement with the Canadian Public Accountability Board. An audit firm that enters into a participation agreement is subject to the oversight program of the Canadian Public Accountability Board."

(2) If an auditor of the financial statements required by Item 32 was not a participating audit firm, as defined in NI 52-108, as at the date of the most recent auditor's report issued by that auditor on financial statements included in the prospectus, include a statement in substantially the following form:

"[*Audit Firm C*] audited the financial statements of [*Entity D*] for the year ended [*state the period of the most recent financial statements, if any, included in the prospectus under Item 32*] and issued an auditor's report dated [*state the date of the auditor's report for the relevant financial statements*]. As at [*state the date of the auditor's report for the relevant financial statements*], [*Audit Firm C*] was not required by securities legislation to enter, and had not entered, into a participation agreement with the Canadian Public Accountability Board. An audit firm that enters into a participation agreement is subject to the oversight program of the Canadian Public Accountability Board.

Transfer agents, registrars, trustees or other agents

26.2 For each class of securities, state the name of any transfer agent, registrar, trustee, or other agent appointed by the issuer to maintain the securities register and the register of transfers for such securities and indicate the location (by municipality) of each of the offices of the issuer or transfer agent, registrar, trustee or other agent where the securities register and register of transfers are maintained or transfers of securities are recorded.

Item 27 — Material Contracts

Material contracts

27.1 Give particulars of any material contract

(a) required to be filed under section 9.3 of the Instrument, or

(b) that would be required to be filed under section 9.3 of the Instrument but for the fact that it was previously filed.

INSTRUCTIONS

(1) Set out a complete list of all contracts for which particulars must be given under this section, indicating those that are disclosed elsewhere in the prospectus. Particulars need only be provided for those contracts that do not have the particulars given elsewhere in the prospectus.

(2) Particulars of contracts must include the dates of, parties to, consideration provided for in, and general nature and key terms of, the contracts.

Item 28 — Experts

Names of experts

28.1 Name each person or company

(a) who is named as having prepared or certified a report, valuation, statement or opinion in the prospectus or an amendment to the prospectus, and

(b) whose profession or business gives authority to the report, valuation, statement or opinion made by the person or company.

Interest of experts

28.2 For each person or company referred to in section 28.1, provide the disclosure in accordance with section 16.2 of Form 51-102F2, as of the date of the prospectus, as if that person or company were a person or company referred to in section 16.1 of Form 51-102F2.

Item 29 — Other Material Facts

Other material facts

29.1 Give particulars of any material facts about the securities being distributed that are not disclosed under any other Items and are necessary in order for the prospectus to contain full, true and plain disclosure of all material facts relating to the securities to be distributed.

Item 30 — Rights of Withdrawal and Rescission

General

30.1 Include a statement in substantially the following form, with the bracketed information completed:

Securities legislation in [certain of the provinces [and territories] of Canada/the Province of [insert name of local jurisdiction, if applicable]] provides purchasers with the right to withdraw from an agreement to purchase securities. This right may be exercised within two business days after receipt or deemed receipt of a prospectus and any amendment. [In several of the provinces/provinces and territories,] [T/t]he securities legislation further provides a purchaser with remedies for rescission [or[, in some jurisdictions,] revisions of the price or damages] if the prospectus and any amendment contains a misrepresentation or is not delivered to the purchaser, provided that the remedies for rescission[, revisions of the price or damages] are exercised by the purchaser within the time limit prescribed by the securities legislation of the purchaser's province [or territory]. The purchaser should refer to any applicable provisions of the securities legislation of the purchaser's province [or territory] for the particulars of these rights or consult with a legal adviser.

Non-fixed price offerings

30.2 In the case of a non-fixed price offering, replace, if applicable in the jurisdiction in which the prospectus is filed, the second sentence in the legend in section 30.1 with a statement in substantially the following form:

This right may only be exercised within two business days after receipt or deemed receipt of a prospectus and any amendment, irrespective of the determination at a later date of the purchase price of the securities distributed.

Convertible, exchangeable or exercisable securities

30.3 In the case of an offering of convertible, exchangeable or exercisable securities in which additional amounts are payable or may become payable upon conversion, exchange or exercise, provide a statement in the following form:

In an offering of [state name of convertible, exchangeable or exercisable securities], investors are cautioned that the statutory right of action for damages for a misrepresentation contained in the prospectus is limited, in certain provincial [and territorial] securities legislation, to the price at which the [state name of convertible, exchangeable or exercisable securities] is offered to the public under the prospectus offering. This means that, under the securities legislation of certain provinces [and territories], if the purchaser pays additional amounts upon [conversion, exchange or exercise] of the security, those amounts may not be recoverable under the statutory right of action for damages that applies in those provinces [and territories]. The purchaser should refer to any applicable provisions of the securities legislation of the purchaser's province [or territory] for the particulars of this right of action for damages or consult with a legal adviser.

Item 31 — List of Exemptions from Instrument

List of exemptions from Instrument

31.1 List all exemptions from the provisions of the Instrument, including this Form, granted to the issuer applicable to the distribution or the prospectus, including all exemptions to be evidenced by the issuance of a receipt for the prospectus pursuant to section 19.3 of the Instrument.

Item 32 — Financial Statement Disclosure for Issuers

Interpretation of "issuer"

32.1(1) Subject to subsection (2), the financial statements of an issuer required under this Item to be included in a prospectus must include

(a) the financial statements of any predecessor entity that formed, or will form, the basis of the business of the issuer, even though the predecessor entity is, or may have been, a different legal entity, if the issuer has not existed for three years,

(b) the financial statements of a business or businesses acquired by the issuer within three years before the date of the prospectus or proposed to be acquired, if a reasonable investor reading the prospectus would regard the primary business of the issuer to be the business or businesses acquired, or proposed to be acquired, by the issuer, and

(c) the restated combined financial statements of the issuer and any other entity with which the issuer completed a transaction within three years before the date of the prospectus or proposes to complete a transaction, if the issuer accounted for or will account for the transaction as a combination in which all of the combining entities or businesses ultimately are controlled by the same party or parties both before and after the combination, and that control is not temporary.

(2) An issuer is not required to include the financial statements for an acquisition to which paragraph (1)(a) or (b) applies if

(a) the issuer was a reporting issuer in any jurisdiction of Canada

    (i) on the date of the acquisition, in the case of a completed acquisition; or

    (ii) immediately before the filing of the prospectus, in the case of a proposed acquisition;

(b) the issuer's principal asset before the acquisition is not cash, cash equivalents, or its exchange listing; and

(c) the issuer provides disclosure in respect of the proposed or completed acquisition in accordance with Item 35.

Annual financial statements

32.2(1) Subject to section 32.4, include annual financial statements of the issuer consisting of

(a) a statement of comprehensive income, a statement of changes in equity, and a statement of cash flows for each of the three most recently completed financial years ended more than

    (i) 90 days before the date of the prospectus, or

    (ii) 120 days before the date of the prospectus, if the issuer is a venture issuer,

(b) a statement of financial position as at the end of the two most recently completed financial years described in paragraph (a),

(c) a statement of financial position as at the beginning of the earliest comparative period for which financial statements that are included in the prospectus comply with IFRS in the case of an issuer that

    (i) discloses in its annual financial statements an unreserved statement of compliance with IFRS, and

(ii) does any of the following

(A) applies an accounting policy retrospectively in its annual financial statements,

(B) makes a retrospective restatement of items in its annual financial statements, or

(C) reclassifies items in its annual financial statements,

(d) in the case of an issuer's first IFRS financial statements, the opening IFRS statement of financial position at the date of transition to IFRS, and

(e) notes to the annual financial statements.

(1.1) If an issuer presents the components of profit or loss in a separate income statement, the separate income statement must be displayed immediately before the statement of comprehensive income filed under subsection (1).

(2) If the issuer has not completed three financial years, include the financial statements described under subsection (1) for each completed financial year ended more than

(a) 90 days before the date of the prospectus, or

(b) 120 days before the date of the prospectus, if the issuer is a venture issuer.

(3) If the issuer has not included in the prospectus financial statements for a completed financial year, include the financial statements described under subsection (1) or (2) for a period from the date the issuer was formed to a date not more than 90 days before the date of the prospectus.

(4) If an issuer changed its financial year end during any of the financial years referred to in this section and the transition year is less than nine months, the transition year is deemed not to be a financial year for the purposes of the requirement to provide financial statements for a specified number of financial years in this section.

(5) Despite subsection (4), all financial statements of the issuer for a transition year referred to in subsection (4) must be included in the prospectus.

(6) Subject to section 32.4, if financial statements of any predecessor entity, business or businesses acquired by the issuer, or of any other entity are required under this section, then include

(a) statements of comprehensive income, statements of changes in equity, and statements of cash flow for the entities or businesses for as many periods before the acquisition as may be necessary so that when these periods are added to the periods for which the issuer's statements of comprehensive income, statements of changes in equity, and statements of cash flow are included in the prospectus, the results of the entities or businesses, either separately or on a consolidated basis, total three years,

(b) statements of financial position for the entities or businesses for as many periods before the acquisition as may be necessary so that when these periods are added to the periods for which the issuer's statements of financial position are included in the prospectus, the financial position of the entities or businesses, either separately or on a consolidated basis, total two years,

(c) if the entities or businesses have not completed three financial years, the financial statements described under paragraphs (a) and (b) for each completed financial year of the entities or businesses for which the issuer's financial statements in the prospectus do not include the financial statements of the entities or businesses, either separately or on a consolidated basis, and ended more than

(i) 90 days before the date of the prospectus, or

(ii) 120 days before the date of the prospectus, if the issuer is a venture issuer,

(d) if an entity's or business's first IFRS financial statements are included under paragraphs (a), (b) or (c), the opening IFRS statement of financial position at the date of transition to IFRS, and

(e) a statement of financial position as at the beginning of the earliest comparative period for which financial statements that are included in the prospectus comply with IFRS in the case of an issuer that

(i) discloses in its annual financial statements an unreserved statement of compliance with IFRS, and

(ii) does any of the following

(A) applies an accounting policy retrospectively in its financial statements,

(B) makes a retrospective restatement of items in its financial statements, or

(C) reclassifies items in its financial statements.

Interim financial report

32.3(1) Include a comparative interim financial report of the issuer for the most recent interim period, if any, ended

(a) subsequent to the most recent financial year in respect of which annual financial statements of the issuer are included in the prospectus, and

(b) more than

(i) 45 days before the date of the prospectus, or

(ii) 60 days before the date of the prospectus if the issuer is a venture issuer.

(2) The interim financial report referred to in subsection (1) must include

(a) a statement of financial position as at the end of the interim period and a statement of financial position as at the end of the immediately preceding financial year, if any,

(b) a statement of comprehensive income, a statement of changes in equity, and a statement of cash flows, all for the year-to-date interim period, and comparative financial information for the corresponding interim period in the immediately preceding financial year, if any,

(c) for interim periods other than the first interim period in an issuer's financial year, a statement of comprehensive income for the three month period ending on the last day of the interim period and comparative financial information for the corresponding period in the immediately preceding financial year, if any,

(d) a statement of financial position as at the beginning of the earliest comparative period for which financial statements that are included in the prospectus comply with IFRS in the case of an issuer that

(i) discloses in its interim financial report an unreserved statement of compliance with International Accounting Standard 34 *Interim Financial Reporting*, and

(ii) does any of the following

(A) applies an accounting policy retrospectively in its interim financial report,

(B) makes a retrospective restatement of items in its interim financial report, or

(C) reclassifies items in its interim financial report,

(e) in the case of the first interim financial report required to be filed in the year of adopting IFRS, the opening IFRS statement of financial position at the date of transition to IFRS, and

(f) notes to the interim financial report.

(3) If an issuer presents the components of profit or loss in a separate income statement, the separate income statement must be displayed immediately before the statement of comprehensive income filed under subsection (2).

(4) If the issuer is required to include under subsection 32.3(1), a comparative interim financial report of the issuer for the second or third interim period in the year of adopting IFRS, include

(a) the issuer's first interim financial report in the year of adopting IFRS, or

(b) both

(i) the opening IFRS statement of financial position at the date of transition to IFRS, and

(ii) the annual and date of transition to IFRS reconciliations required by IFRS 1 *First-time Adoption of International Financial Reporting Standards* to explain how the transition from previous GAAP to IFRS affected the issuer's reported financial position, financial performance and cash flows.

(5) Subsection (4) does not apply to an issuer that was a reporting issuer in at least one jurisdiction immediately before filing the prospectus.

Exceptions to financial statement requirements

32.4(1) Despite section 32.2, an issuer is not required to include the following financial statements in a prospectus

(a) the statement of comprehensive income, the statement of changes in equity, and the statement of cash flows for the third most recently completed financial year, if the issuer is

(i) an IPO venture issuer, or

(ii) a reporting issuer in at least one jurisdiction immediately before filing the prospectus,

(b) the statement of comprehensive income, the statement of changes in equity, and the statement of cash flows for the third most recently completed financial year, and the financial statements for the second most recently completed financial year, if

(i) the issuer is a reporting issuer in at least one jurisdiction immediately before filing the prospectus, and

(ii) the issuer includes financial statements for a financial year ended less than

(A) 90 days before the date of the prospectus, or

(B) 120 days before the date of the prospectus, if the issuer is a venture issuer,

(c) the statement of comprehensive income, the statement of changes in equity, and the statement of cash flows for the third most recently completed financial year, and the statement of financial position for the second most recently completed financial year, if the issuer includes financial statements for a financial year ended less than 90 days before the date of the prospectus,

(d) the statement of comprehensive income, the statement of changes in equity, and the statement of cash flows for the third most recently completed financial year, and the financial statements for the second most recently completed financial year, if

(i) the issuer is a reporting issuer in at least one jurisdiction immediately before filing the prospectus,

(ii) the issuer includes audited financial statements for a period of at least nine months commencing the day after the most recently completed financial year for which financial statements are required under section 32.2,

(iii) the business of the issuer is not seasonal, and

(iv) none of the financial statements required under section 32.2 are for a financial year that is less than nine months,

(e) the statement of comprehensive income, the statement of changes in equity, and the statement of cash flows for the third most recently completed financial year, and the statement of financial position for the second most recently completed financial year, if

(i) the issuer includes audited financial statements for a period of at least nine months commencing the day after the most recently completed financial year for which financial statements are required under section 32.2,

(ii) the business of the issuer is not seasonal, and

(iii) none of the financial statements required under section 32.2 are for a financial year that is less than nine months, or

(f) the separate financial statements of the issuer and the other entity for periods prior to the date of the transaction, if the restated combined financial statements of the issuer and the other entity are included in the prospectus under paragraph 32.1(c).

(2) Paragraphs (1)(a), (b) and (d) do not apply to an issuer

(a) whose principal asset is cash, cash equivalents or its exchange listing; or

(b) in respect of financial statements of a reverse takeover acquirer for a completed or proposed transaction by the issuer that was or will be accounted for as a reverse takeover.

Exceptions to audit requirement

32.5 The audit requirement in section 4.2 of the Instrument does not apply to the following financial statements

(a) any financial statements for the second and third most recently completed financial years required under section 32.2, if

(i) those financial statements were previously included in a final prospectus without an auditor's report pursuant to an exemption under applicable securities legislation, and

(ii) an auditor has not issued an auditor's report on those financial statements,

(b) any financial statements for the second and third most recently completed financial years required under section 32.2, if

(i) the issuer is a junior issuer,

(i.1) an auditor has not issued an auditor's report on those financial statements, and

(ii) the financial statements for the most recently completed financial year required under section 32.2 is not less than 12 months in length, or

(c) any interim financial report required under section 32.3.

Additional financial statements or financial information filed or released

32.6 (1) If the issuer files financial statements for a more recent period than required under section 32.2 or 32.3 before the prospectus is filed, the issuer must include in the prospectus those more recent financial statements.

(2) If historical financial information about the issuer is publicly disseminated by, or on behalf of, the issuer through news release or otherwise for a more recent period than required under section 32.2, the issuer must include the content of the news release or public communication in the prospectus.

Pro forma financial statements for an acquisition

32.7(1) An issuer must include in the prospectus the pro forma financial information set out in subsection (2) if

(a) the issuer has completed or proposes an acquisition of a business for which financial statement disclosure is required under section 32.1;

(b) less than nine months of the acquired business operations have been reflected in the issuer's most recent audited financial statements included in the prospectus; and

(c) the inclusion of the pro forma financial statements is necessary for the prospectus to contain full, true and plain disclosure of all material facts relating to the securities to be distributed.

(2) For the purposes of subsection (1), include the following:

(a) a pro forma statement of financial position of the issuer, as at the date of the issuer's most recent statement of financial position included in the prospectus, that gives effect, as if it had taken place as at the date of the pro forma statement of financial position, to the acquisition that has been completed, or is expected to be completed, but is not reflected in the issuer's most recent statement of financial position for an annual or interim period;

(b) a pro forma income statement of the issuer that gives effect to the acquisition completed, or expected to be completed, since the beginning of the issuer's most recently completed financial year for which it has included financial statements in its prospectus, as if it had taken place at the beginning of that financial year, for each of the following periods:

(i) the most recently completed financial year for which the issuer has included financial statements in its prospectus; and

(ii) the interim period for which the issuer has included an interim financial report in its prospectus, that started after the financial year referred to in subparagraph (i) and ended

(A) in the case of a completed acquisition, immediately before the acquisition date or, in the issuer's discretion, after the acquisition date;

(B) in the case of a proposed acquisition, immediately before the date of the filing of the prospectus, as if the acquisition had been completed before the filing of the prospectus and the acquisition date were the date of the prospectus; and

(c) pro forma earnings per share based on the pro forma financial statements referred to in paragraph (b).

(3) If an issuer is required to include pro forma financial statements in its prospectus under subsection (1),

(a) in the case where the pro forma financial statements give effect to more than one acquisition, the issuer must identify in the pro forma financial statements each acquisition,

(b) the issuer must include in the pro forma financial statements

(i) adjustments attributable to the acquisition for which there are firm commitments and for which the complete financial effects are objectively determinable;

(ii) adjustments to conform amounts for the business to the issuer's accounting policies; and

(iii) a description of the underlying assumptions on which the pro forma financial statements are prepared, cross-referenced to each related pro forma adjustment;

(c) in the case where the financial year-end of the business differs from the issuer's year-end by more than 93 days, for the purpose of preparing the pro forma income statement of the issuer's most recently completed financial year, the issuer must construct an income statement of the business for a period of 12 consecutive months ending no more than 93 days before or after the issuer's year-end, by adding the results for a subsequent interim period to a completed financial year of the business and deducting the comparable interim results for the immediately preceding year;

(d) in the case where a constructed income statement is required under paragraph (c), the pro forma financial statements must disclose the period covered by the constructed income statement on the face of the pro forma financial statements and must include a note stating that the financial statements of the business used to prepare the pro forma financial statements were prepared for the purpose of the pro forma financial statements and do not conform with the financial statements for the business included elsewhere in the prospectus;

(e) in the case where an issuer is required to prepare a pro forma income statement for an interim period required by paragraph (2)(b), and the pro forma income statement for the most recently completed financial year includes results of the business which are also included in the pro forma income statement for the interim period, the issuer must disclose in a note to the pro forma financial statements the revenue, expenses, and profit or loss from continuing operations included in each pro forma income statement for the overlapping period; and

(f) a constructed period referred to in paragraph (c) does not have to be audited.

Pro forma financial statements for multiple acquisitions

32.8 Despite subsection 32.7(1), an issuer is not required to include in its prospectus the pro forma financial statements otherwise required for each acquisition if the issuer includes in its prospectus one set of pro forma financial statements that

(a) reflects the results of each acquisition since the beginning of the issuer's most recently completed financial year for which financial statements of the issuer are included in the prospectus, and

(b) is prepared as if each acquisition had occurred at the beginning of the most recently completed financial year of the issuer for which financial statements of the issuer are included in the prospectus.

Exemption from financial statement disclosure for oil & gas acquisitions

32.9(1) In the case where sections 32.2, 32.3 and 32.7 apply to a completed or proposed acquisition by operation of section 32.1, those sections do not apply if

(a) the acquisition is an acquisition of a business which is an interest in an oil and gas property;

(b) the acquisition is not an acquisition of securities of another issuer, unless the vendor transferred the business referenced in paragraph (1)(a) to the other issuer and that other issuer

(i) was created for the sole purpose of facilitating the acquisition; and

(ii) other than assets or operations relating to the transferred business, has no

(A) substantial assets; or

(B) operating history;

(c) the issuer is unable to provide the financial statements in respect of the acquisition otherwise required under sections 32.2 and 32.3 because those financial statements do not exist or because the issuer does not have access to those financial statements;

(d) the acquisition does not constitute a reverse takeover;

(e) subject to subsections (2) and (3), in respect of the business for each of the financial periods for which financial statements would, but for this section, be required under sections 32.2 and 32.3, the prospectus includes

(i) an operating statement for the business prepared in accordance with section 3.17 of National Instrument 52-107 *Acceptable Accounting Principles and Auditing Standards*;

(ii) a pro forma operating statement of the issuer that gives effect to the acquisition completed or to be completed since the beginning of the issuer's most recently completed financial year for which financial statements are required to be included in the prospectus, as if the acquisition had taken place at the beginning of that financial year, for each of the financial periods referred to in paragraph 32.7(2)(b), unless

(A) more than nine months of the acquired business operations have been reflected in the issuer's most recent audited financial statements included in the prospectus; or

(B) the inclusion of the pro forma financial statements is not necessary for the prospectus to contain full, true and plain disclosure of all material facts relating to the securities to be distributed;

(iii) a description of the property or properties and the interest acquired by the issuer; and

(iv) disclosure of the annual oil and gas production volumes from the business;

(f) the operating statement for the three most recently completed financial years has been audited;

(g) the prospectus discloses

(i) the estimated reserves and related future net revenue attributable to the business, the material assumptions used in preparing the estimates and the identity and relationship to the issuer or to the vendor of the person who prepared the estimates; and

(ii) the estimated oil and gas production volumes from the business for the first year reflected in the estimated disclosure under subparagraph (i).

(2) Subparagraphs (1)(e)(i), (ii) and (iv) do not apply if production, gross sales, royalties, production costs and operating income were nil, or are reasonably expected to be nil for the business for each financial period and the prospectus discloses that fact.

(3) Paragraphs (1)(e) and (f) do not apply in respect of the third most recently completed financial year if the issuer has completed the acquisition and has included in the prospectus the following:

(a) information in accordance with Form 51-101F1 as at a date commencing on or after the acquisition date and within 6 months of the date of the preliminary prospectus;

(b) a report in the form of Form 51-101F2 on the reserves data included in the disclosure required under paragraph (a);

(c) a report in the form of Form 51-101F3 that refers to the information disclosed under paragraph (a).

Item 33 — Credit Supporter Disclosure, Including Financial Statements

Credit supporter disclosure, including financial statements

33.1 If a credit supporter has provided a guarantee or alternative credit support for all or substantially all of the payments to be made under the securities being distributed, include statements by the credit supporter providing disclosure about the credit supporter that would be required under Items 4, 5, 8, 9, 16, 21, 23, 25, 26, and 32 if the credit supporter were the issuer of the securities to be distributed and such other information about the credit supporter as is necessary to provide full, true and plain disclosure of all material facts relating to the securities to be distributed.

Item 34 — Exemptions for Certain Issues of Guaranteed Securities

Definitions and interpretation

34.1 (1) In this Item

(a) the impact of subsidiaries, on a combined basis, on the financial statements of the parent entity is "minor" if each item of the summary financial information of the subsidiaries, on a combined basis, represents less than three percent of the total consolidated amounts,

(b) a parent entity has "limited independent operations" if each item of its summary financial information represents less than three percent of the total consolidated amounts,

(c) a subsidiary is a "finance subsidiary" if it has minimal assets, operations, revenue or cash flows other than those related to the issuance, administration and repayment of the security being distributed and any other securities guaranteed by its parent entity,

(d) "parent credit supporter" means a credit supporter of which the issuer is a subsidiary,

(e) "parent entity" means a parent credit supporter for the purposes of sections 34.2 and 34.3 and an issuer for the purpose of section 34.4,

(f) "subsidiary credit supporter" means a credit supporter that is a subsidiary of the parent credit supporter, and

(g) "summary financial information" includes the following line items:

(i) revenue;

(ii) profit or loss from continuing operations attributable to owners of the parent;

(iii) profit or loss attributable to owners of the parent; and

(iv) unless the accounting principles used to prepare the financial statements of the entity permits the preparation of the entity's statement of financial position without classifying assets and liabilities between current and non-current and the entity provides alternative meaningful financial information which is more appropriate to the industry,

(A) current assets;

(B) non-current assets;

(C) current liabilities; and

(D) non-current liabilities.

INSTRUCTION

See section 1.1 of the Instrument for the definitions of "profit or loss attributable to owners of the parent" and "profit or loss from continuing operations attributable to owners of the parent".

(2) For the purposes of this Item, consolidating summary financial information must be prepared on the following basis

(a) an entity's annual or interim summary financial information must be derived from the entity's financial information underlying the corresponding consolidated financial statements of the parent entity included in the prospectus,

(b) the parent entity column must account for investments in all subsidiaries under the equity method, and

(c) all subsidiary entity columns must account for investments in non-credit supporter subsidiaries under the equity method.

Issuer is wholly-owned subsidiary of parent credit supporter

34.2 An issuer is not required to include the issuer disclosure required by Items 4, 5, 8, 9, 21, 23, 25, 26, and 32, if

(a) a parent credit supporter has provided full and unconditional credit support for the securities being distributed,

(b) the securities being distributed are non-convertible debt securities, non-convertible preferred shares, or convertible debt securities or convertible preferred shares that are convertible, in each case, into non-convertible securities of the parent credit supporter,

(c) the parent credit supporter is the beneficial owner of all the issued and outstanding voting securities of the issuer,

(d) no other subsidiary of the parent credit supporter has provided a guarantee or alternative credit support for all or substantially all of the payments to be made under the securities being distributed, and

(e) the issuer includes in the prospectus

(i) a statement that the financial results of the issuer are included in the consolidated financial results of the parent credit supporter, if

(A) the issuer is a finance subsidiary, and

(B) the impact of any subsidiaries of the parent credit supporter on a combined basis, excluding the issuer, on the consolidated financial statements of the parent credit supporter is minor, or

(ii) for the periods covered by the parent credit supporter's consolidated interim financial report and consolidated annual financial statements included in the prospectus under Item 33, consolidating summary financial information for the parent credit supporter presented with a separate column for each of the following:

(A) the parent credit supporter;

(B) the issuer;

(C) any other subsidiaries of the parent credit supporter on a combined basis;

(D) consolidating adjustments;

(E) the total consolidated amounts.

Issuer is wholly-owned subsidiary of, and one or more subsidiary credit supporters controlled by, parent credit supporter

34.3 (1) An issuer is not required to include the issuer disclosure required by Items 4, 5, 8, 9, 21, 23, 25, 26, and 32, or the credit supporter disclosure of one or more subsidiary credit supporters required by Item 33, if

(a) a parent credit supporter and one or more subsidiary credit supporters have each provided full and unconditional credit support for the securities being distributed,

(b) the guarantees or alternative credit supports are joint and several,

(c) the securities being distributed are non-convertible debt securities, non-convertible preferred shares, or convertible debt securities or convertible preferred shares that are convertible, in each case, into non-convertible securities of the parent credit supporter,

(d) the parent credit supporter is the beneficial owner of all the issued and outstanding voting securities of the issuer,

(e) the parent credit supporter controls each subsidiary credit supporter and the parent credit support has consolidated the financial statements of each subsidiary credit supporter into the parent credit supporter's financial statements that are included in the prospectus, and

(f) the issuer includes in the prospectus, for the periods covered by the parent credit supporter's financial statements included in the prospectus under Item 33, consolidating summary financial information for the parent credit supporter presented with a separate column for each of the following:

(i) the parent credit supporter;

(ii) the issuer;

(iii) each subsidiary credit supporter on a combined basis;

(iv) any other subsidiaries of the parent credit supporter on a combined basis;

(v) consolidating adjustments;

(vi) the total consolidated amounts.

(2) Despite paragraph (1)(f), the information set out in a column in accordance with

(a) subparagraph (1)(f)(iv) may be combined with the information set out in accordance with any of the other columns in paragraph (1)(f) if the impact of any subsidiaries of the parent credit supporter on a combined basis, excluding the issuer and all subsidiary credit supporters, on the consolidated financial statements of the parent credit supporter is minor, and

(b) subparagraph (1)(f)(ii), may be combined with the information set out in accordance with any of the other columns in paragraph (1)(f) if the issuer is a finance subsidiary.

Part 4:
DISTRIBUTIONS

One or more credit supporters controlled by issuer

34.4 An issuer is not required to include the credit supporter disclosure for one or more credit supporters required by Item 33, if

(a) one or more credit supporters have each provided full and unconditional credit support for the securities being distributed,

(b) there is more than one credit supporter, the guarantee or alternative credit supports are joint and several,

(c) the securities being distributed are non-convertible debt securities, non-convertible preferred shares, or convertible debt securities or convertible preferred shares that are convertible, in each case, into non-convertible securities of the issuer;

(d) the issuer controls each credit supporter and the issuer has consolidated the financial statements of each credit supporter into the issuer's financial statements that are included in the prospectus, and

(e) the issuer includes in the prospectus

(i) a statement that the financial results of the credit supporter(s) are included in the consolidated financial results of the issuer, if

(A) the issuer has limited independent operations, and

(B) the impact of any subsidiaries of the issuer on a combined basis, excluding the credit supporter(s) but including any subsidiaries of the credit supporter(s) that are not themselves credit supporters, on the consolidated financial statements of the issuer is minor, or

(ii) for the periods covered by the issuer's financial statements included in the prospectus under Item 32, consolidating summary financial information for the issuer, presented with a separate column for each of the following:

(A) the issuer;

(B) the credit supporters on a combined basis;

(C) any other subsidiaries of the issuer on a combined basis;

(D) consolidating adjustments;

(E) the total consolidated amounts.

Item 35 — Significant Acquisitions

Application and definitions

35.1 (1) This Item does not apply to

(a) a completed or proposed transaction by the issuer that was or will be a reverse takeover or a transaction that is a proposed reverse takeover that has progressed to a state where a reasonable person would believe that the likelihood of the reverse takeover being completed is high; or

(b) a completed or proposed acquisition

(i) by the issuer if

(A) the issuer's principal asset before the acquisition is cash, cash equivalents or its exchange listing; or

(B) the issuer was not a reporting issuer in any jurisdiction

(I) on the acquisition date, in the case of a completed acquisition; and

(II) immediately before filing the prospectus, in the case of a proposed acquisition; and

(ii) to which Item 32 applies by operation of section 32.1.

(2) [repealed]

(3) The audit requirement in section 4.2 of the Instrument does not apply to any financial statements or other information included in the prospectus under this Item, other than the financial statements or other information for the most recently completed financial year of a business or related businesses acquired, or proposed to be acquired, by the issuer.

(4) In this Item, *"significant acquisition"* means an acquisition of a business or related businesses that,

(a) if the issuer was a reporting issuer in at least one jurisdiction on the acquisition date, is determined to be a significant acquisition under section 8.3 of NI 51-102, or

(b) if the issuer was not a reporting issuer in any jurisdiction on the acquisition date, would be determined to be a significant acquisition under section 8.3 of NI 51-102, as if

(i) the issuer was a reporting issuer on the acquisition date,

(ii) the references to a "venture issuer" were read as an "IPO venture issuer" if the issuer is an IPO venture issuer,

(iii) for the purposes of the optional tests, the issuer used its financial statements for the most recently completed interim period or financial year that is included in the prospectus,

(iv) for the purposes of the optional profit or loss test, the most recently completed financial year of the business or related businesses were the financial year of the business ended before the date of the prospectus, and the 12 months ended on the last day of the most recently completed interim period of the business or related businesses were the 12 months ended on the last day of the most recently completed interim period before the date of the prospectus,

(v) subsection 8.3(11.1) of NI 51-102 did not apply,

(vi) references to "audited annual statements filed" meant "audited annual financial statements included in the long form prospectus", and

(vii) in subsection 8.3(15) of NI 51-102, the reference to "been required to file, and has not filed," meant "been required to include, and has not included, in the long form prospectus".

Completed acquisitions for which issuer has filed business acquisition report

35.2 If an issuer completed an acquisition of a business or related businesses since the beginning of its most recently completed financial year for which financial statements are included in the prospectus, and it has filed a business acquisition report under Part 8 of NI 51-102 for the acquisition, include all of the disclosure included in, or incorporated by reference into, that business acquisition report.

Completed acquisitions for which issuer has not filed business acquisition report because issuer was not reporting issuer on acquisition date

35.3 (1) An issuer must include the disclosure required under subsection (2), if

(a) the issuer completed an acquisition of a business or related businesses since the beginning of the issuer's most recently completed financial year for which financial statements of the issuer are included in the prospectus,

(b) the issuer was not a reporting issuer in any jurisdiction on the acquisition date,

(c) the acquisition is a significant acquisition, and

(d) the acquisition date was more than

(i) 90 days before the date of the prospectus, if the financial year of the acquired business ended 45 days or less before the acquisition, or

(ii) 75 days before the date of the prospectus.

(2) For an acquisition to which subsection (1) applies, include all the disclosure that would be required to be included in, or incorporated by reference into, a business acquisition report filed under Part 8 of NI 51-102, as if

(a) the issuer was a reporting issuer in at least one jurisdiction on the acquisition date,

(b) the business acquisition report was filed as at the date of the prospectus,

(c) the issuer was a venture issuer at the acquisition date, if the issuer is an IPO venture issuer,

(d) subsections 8.4(4) and 8.4(6) of NI 51-102 did not apply, and

(e) references to financial statements filed or required to be filed meant financial statements included in the prospectus.

Financial performance consolidated in financial statements of issuer

35.4 Despite section 35.2 and subsection 35.3(1), an issuer may omit the financial statements or other information of a business required to be included in the prospectus, if at least nine months of the acquired business or related businesses financial performance have been reflected in the issuer's most recent audited financial statements included in the prospectus.

Recently completed acquisitions

35.5 (1) Include the information required under subsection (2) for any significant acquisition completed by the issuer

(a) since the beginning of the issuer's most recently completed financial year for which financial statements of the issuer are included in the prospectus, and

(b) for which the issuer has not included any disclosure under section 35.2 or subsection 35.3(2).

(2) For a significant acquisition to which subsection (1) applies, include the following

(a) the information required by sections 2.1 through 2.6 of Form 51-102F4, and

(b) the financial statements of or other information about the acquisition under subsection (3) for the acquired business or related businesses, if

(i) the issuer was not a reporting issuer in any jurisdiction immediately before filing the prospectus, or

(ii) the issuer was a reporting issuer in at least one jurisdiction immediately before filing the prospectus, and the inclusion of the financial statements or other information is necessary for the prospectus to contain full, true and plain disclosure of all material facts relating to the securities to be distributed.

(3) The requirement to include financial statements or other information under paragraph (2)(b) must be satisfied by including

(a) if the issuer was a reporting issuer in at least one jurisdiction on the acquisition date, the financial statements or other information that will be required to be included in, or incorporated by reference into, a business acquisition report filed under Part 8 of NI 51-102,

(b) if the issuer was not a reporting issuer in any jurisdiction on the acquisition date, the financial statements or other information that would be required by subsection 35.3(2), or

(c) satisfactory alternative financial statements or other information.

Probable acquisitions

35.6 (1) Include the information required under subsection (2) for any proposed acquisition of a business or related businesses by an issuer that has progressed to a state where a reasonable person would believe that the likelihood of the issuer completing the acquisition is high, and that, if completed by the issuer at the date of the prospectus, would be a significant acquisition.

(2) For a proposed acquisition of a business or related businesses by the issuer that has progressed to a state where a reasonable person would believe that the likelihood of the issuer completing the acquisition is high and to which subsection (1) applies, include

   (a) the information required by sections 2.1 through 2.6 of Form 51-102F4, modified as necessary to convey that the acquisition has not been completed, and

   (b) the financial statements or other information of the probable acquisition under subsection (3) for the acquired business or related businesses, if

      (i) the issuer was not a reporting issuer in any jurisdiction immediately before filing the prospectus, or

      (ii) the issuer was a reporting issuer in at least one jurisdiction immediately before filing the prospectus, and the inclusion of the financial statements or other information is necessary for the prospectus to contain full, true and plain disclosure of all material facts relating to the securities to be distributed.

(3) For a proposed acquisition of a business or related businesses by the issuer that has progressed to a state where a reasonable person would believe that the likelihood of the issuer completing the acquisition is high and to which subsection (2) applies, the requirement to include financial statements or other information under subsection (2)(b) must be satisfied by including

   (a) if the issuer was a reporting issuer in at least one jurisdiction immediately before filing the prospectus, the financial statements or other information that would be required to be included in, or incorporated by reference into, a business acquisition report filed under Part 8 of NI 51-102, as if the acquisition date were the date of the prospectus,

   (b) if the issuer was not a reporting issuer in any jurisdiction immediately before filing the prospectus, the financial statements or other information that would be required to be included by subsection 35.3(2), as if the acquisition had been completed before the filing of the prospectus and the acquisition date were the date of the prospectus, or

   (c) satisfactory alternative financial statements or other information.

Pro forma financial statements for multiple acquisitions

35.7 Despite sections 35.2, 35.3, 35.5 and 35.6, an issuer is not required to include in its prospectus the pro forma financial statements otherwise required for each acquisition, if the issuer includes in its prospectus one set of pro forma financial statements that

   (a) reflects the results of each acquisition since the beginning of the issuer's most recently completed financial year for which financial statements of the issuer are included in the prospectus,

   (b) is prepared as if each acquisition had occurred at the beginning of the most recently completed financial year of the issuer for which financial statements of the issuer are included in the prospectus, and

   (c) is prepared in accordance with

      (i) if no disclosure is otherwise required for a probable acquisition under section 35.6, the section in this Item that applies to the most recently completed acquisition, or

      (ii) section 35.6.

Additional financial statements or financial information of business filed or released

35.8 (1) An issuer must include in its prospectus annual financial statements and an interim financial report of a business or related businesses for a financial period that ended before the acquisition date and is more recent than the periods for which financial statements are required under section 35.5 or 35.6 if, before the prospectus is filed, the financial statements of the business for the more recent period have been filed.

(2) If, before the prospectus is filed, historical financial information of a business or related businesses for a period more recent than the period for which financial statements are required under section 35.5 or 35.6, is publicly disseminated by news release or otherwise by or on behalf of the issuer, the issuer shall include in the prospectus the content of the news release or public communication.

Item 36 — Probable Reverse Takeovers

Probable reverse takeovers

36.1 If the issuer is involved in a proposed reverse takeover that has progressed to a state where a reasonable person would believe that the likelihood of the reverse takeover being completed is high, include statements by the reverse takeover acquirer providing disclosure about the reverse takeover acquirer that would be required under this Form, as applicable, if the reverse takeover acquirer were the issuer of the securities to be distributed, and such other information about the reverse takeover acquirer as is necessary to provide full, true and plain disclosure of all material facts relating to the securities to be distributed, including the disclosure required by Items 4, 5,7, 8, 9, 11, 12, 13, 14, 15, 16, 17, 18, 19, 21, 22, 23, 24, 25, 27, 28, and 32.

Marketing materials

36A.1 (1) If marketing materials were provided under subsection 13.7(1) or 13.8(1) of the Instrument, the issuer must

   (a) include a section, under the heading "Marketing Materials", proximate to the beginning of the prospectus that contains the disclosure required by this Item,

   (b) subject to subsection (2), include the template version of the marketing materials filed under the Instrument in the final prospectus, or incorporate by reference the template version of the marketing materials filed under the Instrument into the final prospectus, and

   (c) indicate that the template version of the marketing materials is not part of the final prospectus to the extent that the contents of the template version of the marketing materials have been modified or superseded by a statement contained in the final prospectus.

(2) An issuer may comply with paragraph (1)(b) by including the template version of the marketing materials filed under the Instrument in the section of the prospectus under the heading "Marketing Materials" or in an appendix to the prospectus that is referred to in that section.

(3) If the prospectus or any amendment modifies a statement of material fact that appeared in marketing materials provided earlier,

(a) provide details of how the statement in the marketing materials has been modified, and

(b) disclose that, pursuant to subsection 13.7(7) or 13.8(7) of the Instrument,

(i) the issuer has prepared a revised template version of the marketing materials which has been blacklined to show the modified statement, and

(ii) the revised template version of the marketing materials can be viewed under the issuer's profile on www.sedar.com.

(4) State that any template version of the marketing materials filed under the Instrument after the date of the final prospectus and before the termination of the distribution is deemed to be incorporated into the final prospectus.

(5) If the issuer relies on the exception in subsection 13.12(1) of the Instrument, include the following statement, or words to the same effect:

Before the filing of the final prospectus, the issuer and underwriters held road shows on *[insert dates and brief description of road shows for U.S. cross-border offering eligible for the exception in subsection 13.12(1) of the Instrument or other prospectus rule]* to which potential investors in *[insert the jurisdictions of Canada where the prospectus was filed]* were able to attend. The issuer and the underwriters provided marketing materials to those potential investors in connection with those road shows.

In doing so, the issuer and the underwriters relied on a provision in applicable securities legislation that allows issuers in certain U.S. cross-border offerings to not have to file marketing materials relating to those road shows on SEDAR or include or incorporate those marketing materials in the final prospectus. The issuer and the underwriters can only do that if they give a contractual right to investors in the event the marketing materials contain a misrepresentation.

Pursuant to that provision, the issuer and the underwriters signing the certificate contained in this prospectus have agreed that in the event the marketing materials relating to those road shows contain a misrepresentation (as defined in securities legislation in *[insert the jurisdictions of Canada where the prospectus was filed]*), a purchaser resident in *[insert the jurisdictions of Canada where the prospectus was filed]* who was provided with those marketing materials in connection with the road shows and who purchases the securities offered by this prospectus during the period of distribution shall have, without regard to whether the purchaser relied on the misrepresentation, rights against the issuer and each underwriter with respect to the misrepresentation which are equivalent to the rights under the securities legislation of the jurisdiction in Canada where the purchaser is resident, subject to the defences, limitations and other terms of that legislation, as if the misrepresentation was contained in this prospectus.

However, this contractual right does not apply to the extent that the contents of the marketing materials relating to the road shows have been modified or superseded by a statement in this prospectus. In particular, *[insert a description of how any statement in the marketing materials has been modified or superseded by a statement in the prospectus]*.

GUIDANCE

Marketing materials do not, as a matter of law, amend a preliminary prospectus, a final prospectus or any amendment.

Item 37 — Certificates

Certificates

37.1 Include the certificates required by Part 5 of the Instrument or by securities legislation.

Issuer certificate form

37.2 An issuer certificate form must state:

This prospectus constitutes full, true and plain disclosure of all material facts relating to the securities offered by this prospectus as required by the securities legislation of [insert the jurisdictions in which qualified].

Underwriter certificate form

37.3 An underwriter certificate form must state:

To the best of our knowledge, information and belief, this prospectus constitutes full, true and plain disclosure of all material facts relating to the securities offered by this prospectus as required by the securities legislation of [insert the jurisdictions in which qualified].

Amendments

37.4 *(1)* For an amendment to a prospectus that does not restate the prospectus, change "prospectus" to "prospectus dated [insert date] as amended by this amendment" wherever it appears in the statements in sections 37.2 and 37.3.

(2) For an amended and restated prospectus, change "prospectus" to "amended and restated prospectus" wherever it appears in the statements in sections 37.2 and 37.3.

Non-offering prospectuses

37.5 For a non-offering prospectus, change "securities offered by this prospectus" to "securities previously issued by the issuer" wherever it appears in the statements in sections 37.2 and 37.3.

37.6 If an issuer filed a template version of marketing materials under paragraph 13.7(1)(e) of the Instrument or intends to file a template version of marketing materials under paragraph 13.8(1)(e) of the Instrument, change "prospectus" to "prospectus (which includes the marketing materials included or incorporated by reference)" where it first appears in the statements in sections 37.2 and 37.3.

<h3 style="text-align:center">Item 38 — Transition</h3>

Interim financial report

38.1(1) Despite subsection 32.3(1), an issuer may include a comparative interim financial report of the issuer for the most recent interim period, if any, ended

    (a) subsequent to the most recent financial year in respect of which annual financial statements of the issuer are included in the prospectus, and

    (b) more than

        (i) 75 days before the date of the prospectus, or

        (ii) 90 days before the date of the prospectus if the issuer is a venture issuer.

(2) Subsection (1) does not apply unless

    (a) the comparative interim financial report is the first interim financial report required to be filed in the year of adopting IFRS in respect of an interim period beginning on or after January 1, 2011,

    (b) the issuer

        (i) is disclosing, for the first time, a statement of compliance with International Accounting Standard 34 *Interim Financial Reporting*, and

        (ii) did not previously file financial statements that disclosed compliance with IFRS,

    (c) the issuer is a reporting issuer in any jurisdiction immediately before the date of the final long form prospectus, and

    (d) the final long form prospectus is filed before July 5, 2012.

Asset-backed securities

38.2(1) Despite subsection 10.3(5), all financial disclosure that describes the underlying pool of financial assets of the issuer for a transition year must be included in the prospectus for the most recent interim period, if any, ended

    (a) subsequent to the most recent financial year referred to in paragraphs 10.3(3)(a) and 10.3(3)(b) in respect of which financial disclosure on the underlying pool of financial assets is included in the prospectus, and

    (b) more than

        (i) 75 days before the date of the prospectus, or

        (ii) 90 days before the date of the prospectus if the issuer is a venture issuer.

(2) Subsection (1) does not apply unless

    (a) the financial disclosure in respect of the interim period is the first interim financial report required to be filed in the year of adopting IFRS in respect of an interim period beginning on or after January 1, 2011,

    (b) the issuer

        (i) is disclosing, for the first time, a statement of compliance with International Accounting Standard 34 *Interim Financial Reporting*, and

        (ii) did not previously file financial statements that disclosed compliance with IFRS,

    (c) the issuer is a reporting issuer in any jurisdiction immediately before the date of the final long form prospectus, and

    (d) the final long form prospectus is filed before July 5, 2012.

Form 41-101F2 — Information Required in an Investment Fund Prospectus

General Instructions

Item 1: Cover Page Disclosure

    1.1 Preliminary Prospectus Disclosure

    1.2 Required Statement

    1.3 Basic Disclosure about the Distribution

    1.4 Distribution

    1.5 Offering Price in Currency Other than Canadian Dollar

    1.6 Non-fixed Price Distributions

    1.7 Pricing Disclosure

    1.8 Reduced Price Distributions

    1.9 Market for Securities

Part 4:
DISTRIBUTIONS

General Instructions

(1) The objective of the prospectus is to provide information concerning the investment fund that an investor needs in order to make an informed investment decision. This Form sets out specific disclosure requirements that are in addition to the general requirement under securities legislation to provide full, true and plain disclosure of all material facts relating to the securities to be distributed. This Form does not prohibit including information beyond what the Form requires. Further, certain rules of specific application impose prospectus disclosure obligations in addition to those described in this Form.

(2) Terms used and not defined in this Form that are defined or interpreted in the Instrument must bear that definition or interpretation. Other definitions are set out in NI 14-101 Definitions.

(3) In determining the degree of detail required, a standard of materiality must be applied. Materiality is a matter of judgment in the particular circumstance, and is determined in relation to an item's significance to investors, analysts and other users of the information. An item of information, or an aggregate of items, is considered material if it is probable that its omission or misstatement would influence or change an investment decision with respect to the investment fund's securities. In determining whether information is material, take into account both quantitative and qualitative factors. The potential significance of items must be considered individually rather than on a net basis, if the items have an offsetting effect.

(4) Unless an item specifically requires disclosure only in the preliminary prospectus, the disclosure requirements set out in this Form apply to both the preliminary prospectus and the prospectus. Details concerning the price and other matters dependent upon or relating to price, such as the number of securities being distributed, may be left out of the preliminary prospectus, along with specifics concerning the plan of distribution, to the extent that these matters have not been decided.

(5) The disclosure must be understandable to readers and presented in an easy-to-read format. The presentation of information should comply with the plain language principles listed in section 4.1 of Companion Policy 41-101CP General Prospectus Requirements. If technical terms are required, clear and concise explanations should be included.

(6) No reference need be made to inapplicable items and, unless otherwise required in this Form, negative answers to items may be omitted.

(7) The disclosure required in this Form must be presented in the order and using the headings specified in the Form. If no sub-heading for an Item is stipulated in this Form, an investment fund may include sub-headings under the required headings.

(8) Where the term "investment fund" is used, it may be necessary, in order to meet the requirement for full, true and plain disclosure of all material facts, to also include disclosure with respect to the investment fund's investees. If it is more likely than not that a person or company will become an investee, it may be necessary to also include disclosure with respect to the person or company. For this purpose, investees include entities that are consolidated, proportionately consolidated, or accounted for using the equity method.

(9) If disclosure is required as of a specific date and there has been a material change or change that is otherwise significant in the required information subsequent to that date, present the information as of the date of the change or a date subsequent to the change instead.

(10) If the term "class" is used in any item to describe securities, the term includes a series.

(11) Where performance data is presented in the prospectus, annual compound returns must be presented for standard applicable performance periods of 1, 3, 5 and 10 year periods and the period since inception unless otherwise specified by the requirements of this Form. Performance data for periods of less than one year must not be presented. Hypothetical or back-tested performance data must not be presented.

(12) An investment fund that has more than one class or series that are referable to the same portfolio may treat each class or series as a separate investment fund for the purposes of this Form, or may combine disclosure of one or more of the classes or series in one prospectus. If disclosure pertaining to more than one class or series is combined in one prospectus, separate disclosure in response to each item in this Form must be provided for each class or series unless the responses would be identical for each class or series.

(13) A section, part, class or series of a class of securities of an investment fund that is referable to a separate portfolio is considered to be a separate investment fund for the purposes of this Form. An investment fund that has more than one class or series of securities referable to separate portfolios may combine disclosure of one or more of the classes or series in one prospectus if each class or series is managed by the same manager. If disclosure pertaining to more than one class or series is combined in one prospectus, separate disclosure in response to each item in this Form must be provided for each class or series unless the responses would be identical for each class or series.

PROSPECTUS FORM

Item 1 — Cover Page Disclosure

1.1 — Preliminary Prospectus Disclosure

Every preliminary prospectus must have printed in red ink and in italics at the top of the cover page immediately above the disclosure required in section 1.2 the following, with the bracketed information completed:

> *"A copy of this preliminary prospectus has been filed with the securities regulatory authority(ies) in [each of/certain of the provinces/provinces and territories of Canada] but has not yet become final for the purpose of the sale of securities. Information contained in this preliminary prospectus may not be complete and may have to be amended. The securities may not be sold until a receipt for the prospectus is obtained from the securities regulatory authority(ies)."*

INSTRUCTION

Investment funds must complete the bracketed information by

> *(a) inserting the names of each jurisdiction in which the investment fund intends to offer securities under the prospectus;*

> *(b) stating that the filing has been made in each of the provinces of Canada or each of the provinces and territories of Canada; or*

> *(c) identifying the filing jurisdictions by exception (i.e., every province of Canada or every province and territory of Canada, except [excluded jurisdictions].*

1.2 — Required Statement

State in italics at the top of the cover page the following:

No securities regulatory authority has expressed an opinion about these securities and it is an offence to claim otherwise.

1.3 — Basic Disclosure about the Distribution

(1) State the following immediately below the disclosure required under sections 1.1 and 1.2 with the bracketed information completed:

"[PRELIMINARY OR PRO FORMA] PROSPECTUS

[INITIAL PUBLIC OFFERING OR NEW ISSUE AND/OR

SECONDARY OFFERING OR CONTINUOUS OFFERING]

[Date]

[Name of investment fund]

[number and type of securities qualified for distribution under the prospectus and the price per security]

[type of fund — state the following: "This investment fund is a [labour sponsored or venture capital fund, commodity pool, non-redeemable investment fund or exchange-traded mutual fund, or, if the issuer is another type of investment fund, state the type of fund]."

If securities of the investment fund are intended to be listed or quoted on an exchange or marketplace and conditional listing approval has been received, state the following: "[Name of exchange or marketplace] has conditionally approved the [listing/quotation] of the [type of securities qualified for distribution under the prospectus and to be listed/quoted], subject to the [name of investment fund] fulfilling all of the requirements of the [name of exchange or marketplace] on or before [date]."]"

(2) Briefly describe the investment objectives of the investment fund and provide a cross-reference to sections in the prospectus where information about the investment objectives is provided.

(3) State the name of the manager and portfolio adviser of the investment fund and provide a cross-reference to sections in the prospectus where information about the manager and portfolio adviser is provided.

1.4 — Distribution

(1) Subsections (2)–(8) do not apply to an investment fund in continuous distribution.

(2) If the securities are being distributed for cash, provide the information called for below, in substantially the following tabular form or in a note to the table:

	Price to public (a)	Underwriting discounts or commission (b)	Proceeds to issuer or selling securityholders (c)
Per Security	....	....	....
Total	....	....	....

(3) Describe the terms of any over-allotment option or any option to increase the size of the distribution before closing.

(3.1) If there may be an over-allocation position provide the following disclosure:

A purchaser who acquires [*insert type of securities qualified for distribution under the prospectus*] forming part of the underwriters' over-allocation position acquires those securities under this prospectus, regardless of whether the over-allocation position is ultimately filled through the exercise of the over-allotment option or secondary market purchases.

(4) If the distribution of the securities is to be on a best efforts basis, and a minimum offering amount,

(a) is required for the issuer to achieve one or more of the purposes of the offering, provide totals for both the minimum and maximum offering amount, or

(b) is not required for the issuer to achieve any of the purposes of the offering, state the following in boldface type:

There is no minimum amount of funds that must be raised under this offering. This means that the issuer could complete this offering after raising only a small proportion of the offering amount set out above.

(5) If debt securities are being distributed at a premium or a discount, state in boldface type the effective yield if held to maturity.

(6) Disclose separately those securities that are underwritten, those under option and those to be sold on a best efforts basis, and, in the case of a best efforts distribution, the latest date that the distribution is to remain open.

(7) In column (b) of the table, disclose only commissions paid or payable in cash by the investment fund or selling securityholder and discounts granted. Set out in a note to the table

(a) commissions or other consideration paid or payable by persons or companies other than the investment fund or selling securityholder,

(b) consideration other than discounts granted and cash paid or payable by the investment fund or selling securityholder, including warrants and options, and

(c) any finder's fees or similar required payment.

(8) If a security is being distributed for the account of a selling securityholder, state the name of the securityholder and a cross-reference to the applicable section in the prospectus where further information about the selling securityholder is provided. State the portion of the expenses of the distribution to be borne by the selling securityholder and, if none of the expenses of the distribution are being borne by the selling securityholder, include a statement to that effect and discuss the reason why this is the case.

(9) If a minimum subscription amount is required from each subscriber, provide details of the minimum subscription requirements.

INSTRUCTIONS

(1) Estimate amounts, if necessary. For non-fixed price distributions that are being made on a best efforts basis, disclosure of the information called for by the table may be set forth as a percentage or a range of percentages and need not be set forth in tabular form.

(2) If debt securities are being distributed, also express the information in the table as a percentage.

1.5 — Offering Price in Currency Other than Canadian Dollar

If the offering price of the securities being distributed is disclosed in a currency other than the Canadian dollar, disclose in boldface type the currency.

1.6 — Non-fixed Price Distributions

If the securities are being distributed at non-fixed prices, disclose

(a) the discount allowed or commission payable to the underwriter,

(b) any other compensation payable to the underwriter and, if applicable, that the underwriter's compensation will be increased or decreased by the amount by which the aggregate price paid for the securities by the purchasers exceeds or is less than the gross proceeds paid by the underwriter to the investment fund or selling securityholder,

(c) that the securities to be distributed under the prospectus will be distributed, as applicable, at

    (i) prices determined by reference to the prevailing price of a specified security in a specified market,

    (ii) market prices prevailing at the time of sale,

    (iii) prices to be negotiated with purchasers, or

    (iv) the net asset value of a security,

(d) that prices may vary from purchaser to purchaser and during the period of distribution,

(e) if the price of the securities is to be determined by reference to the prevailing price of a specified security in a specified market, the price of the specified security in the specified market at the latest practicable date,

(f) if the price of the securities will be the market price prevailing at the time of the sale, the market price at the latest practicable date, and

(g) the net proceeds or, if the distribution is to be made on a best efforts basis, the minimum amount of net proceeds, if any, to be received by the investment fund or selling securityholder.

1.7 — Pricing Disclosure

If the offering price or the number of securities being distributed, or an estimate of the range of the offering price or the number of securities being distributed, has been publicly disclosed in a jurisdiction or a foreign jurisdiction as of the date of the preliminary prospectus, include this information in the preliminary prospectus.

1.8 — Reduced Price Distributions

If an underwriter wishes to be able to decrease the price at which securities are distributed for cash from the initial offering price fixed in the prospectus, include in boldface type a cross-reference to the section in the prospectus where disclosure concerning the possible price decrease is provided.

1.9 — Market for Securities

(1) Identify the exchange(s) and quotation system(s), if any, on which securities of the investment fund of the same class as the securities being distributed are traded or quoted and the market price of those securities as of the latest practicable date.

(2) Disclose any intention to stabilize the market. Provide a cross-reference to the section in the prospectus where further information about market stabilization is provided.

(3) If no market for the securities being distributed under the prospectus exists or is expected to exist upon completion of the distribution, state the following in boldface type:

    "There is no market through which these securities may be sold and purchasers may not be able to resell securities purchased under this prospectus. This may affect the pricing of the securities in the secondary market, the transparency and availability of trading prices, the liquidity of the securities, and the extent of issuer regulation. See 'Risk Factors'."

(4) Subsection (3) does not apply to an investment fund in continuous distribution.

1.10 — Risk Factors

Include a cross-reference to sections in the prospectus where information about the risks of an investment in the securities being distributed is provided. State any significant risks including leverage.

1.11 — Underwriter(s)

(1) State the name of each underwriter.

(2) If applicable, comply with the requirements of NI 33-105 for front page prospectus disclosure.

(3) Other than a labour sponsored or venture capital fund or commodity pool, if there is no underwriter involved in the distribution, provide a statement in boldface type to the effect that no underwriter has been involved in the preparation of the prospectus or performed any review or independent due diligence of the contents of the prospectus.

1.12 — Commodity Pool

(1) For a commodity pool, state in substantially the following words:

"You should carefully consider whether your financial condition permits you to participate in this investment. The securities of this commodity pool are highly speculative and involve a high degree of risk. You may lose a substantial portion or even all of the money you place in the commodity pool.

The risk of loss in trading [nature of instruments to be traded by the commodity pool] can be substantial. In considering whether to participate in the [commodity pool], you should be aware that trading [nature of instruments] can quickly lead to large losses as well as gains. Such trading losses can sharply reduce the net asset value of the [commodity pool] and consequently the value of your interest in the [commodity pool]. Also, market conditions may make it difficult or impossible for the [commodity pool] to liquidate a position.

The [commodity pool] is subject to certain conflicts of interest. The [commodity pool] will be subject to the charges payable by it as described in this prospectus that must be offset by revenues and trading gains before an investor is entitled to a return on his or her investment. It may be necessary for the [commodity pool] to make substantial trading profits to avoid depletion or exhaustion of its assets before an investor is entitled to a return on his or her investment."

(2) For the initial prospectus, state in substantially the following words:

"The [commodity pool] is newly organized. The success of the [commodity pool] will depend upon a number of conditions that are beyond the control of the [commodity pool]. There is substantial risk that the goals of the [commodity pool] will not be met."

(3) If the promoter, manager, or a portfolio adviser of the commodity pool has not had a similar involvement with any other publicly offered commodity pool, state in substantially the following words:

"The [promoter], [manager] [and/or] [portfolio adviser] of the [commodity pool] has not previously operated any other publicly offered commodity pools [or traded other accounts]."

(4) If the commodity pool will execute trades outside Canada, state in substantially the following words:

"Participation in transactions in [nature of instrument to be traded by the commodity pool] involves the execution and clearing of trades on or subject to the rules of a foreign market.

None of the Canadian securities regulatory authorities or Canadian exchanges regulates activities of any foreign markets, including the execution, delivery and clearing of transactions, or has the power to compel enforcement of the rule of a foreign market or any applicable foreign law. Generally, any foreign transaction will be governed by applicable foreign laws. This is true even if the foreign market is formally linked to a Canadian market so that a position taken on a market may be liquidated by a transaction on another market. Moreover, such laws or regulations will vary depending on the foreign country in which the transaction occurs.

For these reasons, entities such as the commodity pool that trade [nature of instrument to be traded by the commodity pool] may not be afforded certain of the protective measures provided by Canadian legislation and the rules of Canadian exchanges. In particular, funds received from customers for transactions may not be provided the same protection as funds received in respect of transactions on Canadian exchanges."

(5) State that the commodity pool is a mutual fund but that certain provisions of securities legislation designed to protect investors who purchase securities of mutual funds do not apply.

(6) Immediately after the statements required by subsections (1)–(5), state in substantially the following words:

"These brief statements do not disclose all the risks and other significant aspects of investing in the [commodity pool]. You should therefore carefully study this prospectus, including a description of the principal risk factors at page [page number], before you decide to invest in the [commodity pool]."

1.13 — Restricted Securities

Describe the number and class or classes of restricted securities being distributed using the appropriate restricted security terms in the same type face and type size as the rest of the description.

1.14 — Enforcement of Judgements Against Foreign Persons or Companies

If the investment fund, investment fund manager or any other person or company that is signing or providing a certificate under Part 5 of the Instrument or other securities legislation, or any person or company for whom the issuer is required to file a consent under Part 10 of the Instrument, is incorporated, continued, or otherwise organized under the laws of a foreign jurisdiction or resides outside of Canada, state the following on the cover page or under a separate heading elsewhere in the prospectus, with the bracketed information completed:

The [investment fund, investment fund manager or any other person or company] is incorporated, continued or otherwise organized under the laws of a foreign jurisdiction or resides outside of Canada.

[the person or company named below] has appointed the following agent(s) for service of process:

Name of Person or Company	Name and Address of Agent

Purchasers are advised that it may not be possible for investors to enforce judgments obtained in Canada against any person or company that is incorporated, continued or otherwise organized under the laws of a foreign jurisdiction or resides outside of Canada, even if the party has appointed an agent for service of process.

1.15 — Documents Incorporated by Reference

For an investment fund in continuous distribution, state in substantially the following words:

"Additional information about the Fund is available in the following documents:

- the most recently filed annual financial statements;

- any interim financial report filed after those annual financial statements;

- the most recently filed annual management report of fund performance;

- any interim management report of fund performance filed after that annual management report of fund performance.

These documents are incorporated by reference into this prospectus which means that they legally form part of this prospectus. Please see the "Documents Incorporated by Reference" section for further details."

Item 2 — Table of Contents

2.1 — Table of Contents

Include a table of contents.

Item 3 — Summary of Prospectus

3.1 — Prospectus Summary

Under the heading "Prospectus Summary" include the information listed in sections 3.2 to 3.6.

3.2 — Cautionary Language

At the beginning of the summary, include a statement in italics in substantially the following form:

"The following is a summary of the principal features of this distribution and should be read together with the more detailed information and financial data and statements contained elsewhere in this prospectus [[if applicable] or incorporated by reference in the prospectus]."

3.3 — General

(1) Briefly summarize information appearing elsewhere in the prospectus that, in the opinion of the investment fund or selling securityholder, would be most likely to influence the investor's decision to purchase the securities being distributed. Include a description of

(a) how the investment fund has been organized (corporation, trust, etc.),

(b) the securities to be distributed, including the offering price and expected net proceeds,

(c) the investment objectives,

(d) the investment strategies,

(e) the use of leverage, including the following:

(i) if leverage is created through borrowing or the issuance of preferred securities, disclose any restrictions on the leverage used or to be used and whether the investment fund will borrow a minimum amount. Disclose the maximum amount of leverage the investment fund may use as a ratio calculated by dividing the maximum total assets of the investment fund by the net asset value of the investment fund, and

(ii) if leverage is created through the use of specified derivatives or by other means not disclosed in subparagraph (i), disclose any restrictions on the leverage used or to be used by the investment fund and whether the investment fund will use a minimum amount of leverage. Disclose the maximum amount of leverage the fund may use as a multiple of net assets. Provide a brief explanation of how the investment fund defines the term "leverage" and the significance of the maximum and minimum amounts of leverage to the investment fund,

(f) the use of proceeds,

(g) risk factors,

(h) income tax considerations,

(i) all available purchase options and state, if applicable, that the choice of different purchase options requires the investor to pay different fees and expenses and if applicable, that the choice of different purchase options affects the amount of compensation paid to a dealer,

(j) the redemption features,

(k) the distribution policy,

(l) the termination provisions,

(m) if restricted securities, subject securities or securities directly or indirectly convertible into or exercisable or exchangeable for restricted securities or subject securities are to be distributed under the prospectus,

(i) include a summary of the information required by section 21.6, and

(ii) include, in boldface type, a statement of the rights the holders of restricted securities do not have if the holders do not have all of the rights referred to in section 21.6, and

(n) whether the investment fund is eligible as an investment for registered retirement savings plans, registered retirement income plans, registered education savings plans or deferred profit sharing plans.

(2) For each item summarized under subsection (1), provide a cross-reference to the information in the prospectus.

INSTRUCTIONS

(1) For the purposes of Item 3.3(1)(e)(i), a fund must calculate its maximum total assets by aggregating the maximum value of its long positions, short positions and the maximum amount that may be borrowed.

(2) For the purposes of the disclosure required by Item 3.3(1)(e)(ii), the term "specified derivative" has the same meaning as in NI 81-102. The description of an investment fund's use of leverage under Item 3.3(1)(e)(ii) must provide investors with sufficient information to understand the magnitude of the market exposure of the investment fund as compared to the amount of money raised by the investment fund from investors.

3.4 — Organization and Management of the Investment Fund

(1) Provide, under the sub-heading "Organization and Management of the [name of investment fund]", information about the manager, trustee, portfolio adviser, promoter, custodian, registrar and transfer agent, auditor, principal distributor and securities lending agent of the investment fund in the form of a diagram or table.

(2) For each entity listed in the diagram or table, briefly describe the services provided by that entity and the relationship of that entity to the manager.

(3) For each entity listed in the diagram or table, other than the manager of the investment fund, provide the municipality and the province or country where it principally provides its services to the investment fund. Provide the complete municipal address for the manager of the investment fund.

INSTRUCTIONS:

(1) The information required to be disclosed in this section must be presented prominently, using enough space so that it is easy to read.

(2) Briefly describe the services provided by the listed entities. For instance, the manager may be described as "manages the overall business and operations of the fund", and a portfolio adviser may be described as "provides investment advice to the manager about the investment portfolio of the fund" or "manages the investment portfolio of the fund".

3.5 — Underwriter(s)

(1) Under the sub-heading "Underwriters" or "Agents", as applicable, state the name of each underwriter or agent.

(2) If an underwriter has agreed to purchase all of the securities being distributed at a specified price and the underwriter's obligations are subject to conditions, state the following, with the bracketed information completed:

"We, as principals, conditionally offer these securities, subject to prior sale, if, as and when issued by [name of investment fund] and accepted by us in accordance with the conditions contained in the underwriting agreement referred to under "Plan of Distribution"."

(3) If an underwriter has agreed to purchase a specified number or principal amount of the securities at a specified price, state that the securities are to be taken up by the underwriter, if at all, on or before a date not later than 42 days after the date of the receipt for the final prospectus.

(4) Provide the following tabular information:

Underwriter's Position	Maximum size or number of securities available	Exercise period/Acquisition date	Exercise price or average acquisition price
Over-allotment option	....	....	....
Compensation option	....	....	....
Any other option granted by investment fund or insider of investment fund to underwriter	....	....	....
Total securities under option issuable to underwriter	....	....	....
Other compensation securities issuable to underwriter	....	....	....

INSTRUCTION

If the underwriter has been granted compensation securities, state, in a footnote, whether the prospectus qualifies the grant of all or part of the compensation securities and provide a cross-reference to the applicable section in the prospectus where further information about the compensation securities is provided.

3.6 — Fees, Expenses and Returns

(1) Set out information about the fees and expenses payable by the investment fund and by investors in the investment fund under the sub-heading "Summary of Fees and Expenses".

(2) The information required by this section must be a summary of the fees, charges and expenses of the investment fund and investors presented in the form of the following table, appropriately completed, and introduced using substantially the following words:

> This table lists the fees and expenses that you may have to pay if you invest in the [insert the name of the investment fund]. You may have to pay some of these fees and expenses directly. The Fund may have to pay some of these fees and expenses, which will therefore reduce the value of your investment in the Fund.

Fees and Expenses Payable by the Fund

Type of Fee	Amount and Description

Fees and Expenses Payable Directly by You

Type of Fee	Amount and Description

(3) Describe the following fees and expenses in the table referred to in subsection (2):

Fees and Expenses Payable by the Fund

    (a) Fees payable to the Underwriters for Selling the Securities

    (b) Expenses of the Issue

    (c) Management Fees [*See Instruction (1)*]

    (d) Incentive or Performance Fees

    (e) Portfolio Adviser Fees

    (f) Counterparty Fees (if any)

    (g) Operating Expenses [*See Instructions (2) and (3)*]

    (h) Other Fees and Expenses [*specify type*] [*specify amount*]

Fees and Expenses Payable Directly by You

    (i) Sales Charges [*specify percentage, as a percentage of ....*]

    (j) Service Fees [*specify percentage, as a percentage of ....*]

    (k) Redemption Fees [*specify percentage, as a percentage of ...., or specify amount*]

    (l) Registered Tax Plan Fees [*include this disclosure and specify the type of fees if the registered tax plan is sponsored by the investment fund and is described in the prospectus*][*specify amount*]

    (m) Other Fees and Expenses [*specify type*] [*specify amount*].

(4) Under the sub-heading "Annual Returns, Management Expense Ratio and Trading Expense Ratio", provide, in the following table, returns for each of the past five years, the management expense ratio for each of the past five years and the trading expense ratio for each of the past five years as disclosed in the most recently filed annual management report of fund performance of the investment fund:

	[specify year]	[specify year]	[specify year]	[specify year]	[specify year]
Annual Returns	....	....	....	....	....
MER	....	....	....	....	....
TER	....	....	....	....	....

"MER" means management expense ratio based on management fees and operating expenses (excluding commissions and other portfolio transaction costs) expressed as an annualized percentage of daily average net asset value.

"TER" means trading expense ratio and represents total commissions and other portfolio transaction costs expressed as an annualized percentage of daily average net asset value .

INSTRUCTIONS:

(1) List the amount of the management fee, including any performance or incentive fee, for each investment fund separately.

(2) Under "Operating Expenses", state whether the investment fund pays all of its operating expenses and list the main components of those expenses. If the investment fund pays only certain operating expenses and is not responsible for payment of all such expenses, adjust the statement in the table to reflect the proper contractual responsibility of the investment fund and indicate who is responsible for the payment of these expenses.

(3) Show all fees or expenses payable by the investment fund (e.g. brokerage) and investors in the investment fund. The description of fees must also include sales and trailing commissions paid either by the investment fund or the investor.

Item 4 — Overview of the Structure of the Investment Fund

4.1 — Legal Structure

(1) Under the heading "Overview of the Legal Structure of the Fund", state the full corporate name of the investment fund or, if the investment fund is an unincorporated entity, the full name under which it exists and carries on business and the address(es) of the investment fund's head and registered office.

(2) State the statute under which the investment fund is incorporated or continued or organized or, if the investment fund is an unincorporated entity, the laws of the jurisdiction or foreign jurisdiction under which the investment fund is established and exists. Describe the substance of any material amendments to the articles or other constating or establishing documents of the investment fund.

(3) State whether the investment fund would be considered a mutual fund under securities legislation.

Item 5 — Investment Objectives

5.1 — Investment Objectives

(1) Set out under the heading "Investment Objectives" the fundamental investment objectives of the investment fund, including information that describes the fundamental nature of the investment fund, or the fundamental features of the investment fund, that distinguish it from other investment funds.

(2) If the investment fund purports to arrange a guarantee or insurance in order to protect all or some of the principal amount of an investment in the investment fund, include this fact as a fundamental investment objective of the investment fund and

    (a) identify the person or company providing the guarantee or insurance,

    (b) provide the material terms of the guarantee or insurance, including the maturity date of the guarantee or insurance,

    (c) if applicable, state that the guarantee or insurance does not apply to the amount of any redemptions before the maturity date of the guarantee or before the death of the securityholder and that redemptions before that date would be based on the net asset value of the investment fund at the time, and

    (d) modify any other disclosure required by this section appropriately.

INSTRUCTIONS:

    (1) State the type or types of securities, such as money market instruments, bonds or equity securities, in which the investment fund will primarily invest under normal market conditions.

    (2) If the investment fund primarily invests, or intends to primarily invest, or if its name implies that it will primarily invest

        (a) in a particular type of issuer, such as foreign issuers, small capitalization issuers or issuers located in emerging market countries,

        (b) in a particular geographic location or industry segment, or

        (c) in portfolio assets other than securities, the investment fund's fundamental investment objectives must so indicate.

    (3) If a particular investment strategy is an essential aspect of the investment fund, as evidenced by the name of the investment fund or the manner in which the investment fund is marketed, disclose this strategy as an investment objective. This instruction would be applicable, for example, to an investment fund that described itself as an "investment fund that invests primarily through the use of derivatives".

Item 6 — Investment Strategies

6.1 — Investment Strategies

(1) Describe under the heading "Investment Strategies"

    (a) the principal investment strategies that the investment fund intends to use in achieving its investment objectives,

    (b) the use of leverage, including the following:

        (i) if leverage is created through borrowing or the issuance of preferred securities, disclose any restrictions on the leverage used or to be used and whether the investment fund will borrow a minimum amount. Disclose the maximum amount of leverage the investment fund may use as a ratio calculated by dividing the maximum total assets of the investment fund by the net asset value of the investment fund, and

        (ii) if leverage is created through the use of specified derivatives or by other means not disclosed in subparagraph (i), disclose any restrictions on the leverage used or to be used by the investment fund and whether the investment fund will use a minimum amount of leverage. Disclose the maximum amount of leverage the fund may use as a multiple of net assets. Provide a brief explanation of how the investment fund defines the term "leverage" and the significance of the maximum and minimum amounts of leverage to the investment fund, and

    (c) the process by which the investment fund's portfolio adviser selects securities for the fund's portfolio, including any investment approach, philosophy, practices or techniques used by the portfolio adviser or any particular style of portfolio management that the portfolio adviser intends to follow.

(2) Indicate what types of securities, other than those held by the investment fund in accordance with its fundamental investment objectives, may form part of the investment fund's portfolio assets under normal market conditions.

Part 4: DISTRIBUTIONS

(3) If the investment fund intends to use derivatives

    (a) for hedging purposes only, state that the investment fund may use derivatives for hedging purposes only, or

    (b) for non-hedging purposes, or for hedging and non-hedging purposes, briefly describe

        (i) how derivatives are or will be used in conjunction with other securities to achieve the investment fund's investment objectives,

        (ii) the types of derivatives expected to be used and give a brief description of the nature of each type, and

        (iii) the limits of the investment fund's use of derivatives.

(4) If the investment fund may depart temporarily from its fundamental investment objectives as a result of adverse market, economic, political or other considerations, disclose any temporary defensive tactics the investment fund's portfolio adviser may use or intends to use in response to such conditions.

(5) If the investment fund intends to enter into securities lending, repurchase or reverse repurchase transactions, briefly describe

    (a) how those transactions are or will be entered into in conjunction with other strategies and investments of the investment fund to achieve the investment fund's investment objectives,

    (b) the types of those transactions to be entered into and give a brief description of the nature of each type, and

    (c) the limits of the investment fund's entering into those transactions.

(6) If the investment fund intends to sell securities short

    (a) state that the investment fund may sell securities short; and

    (b) briefly describe

        (i) the short selling process, and

        (ii) how short sales of securities are or will be entered into in conjunction with other strategies and investments of the investment fund to achieve the investment fund's investment objectives.

INSTRUCTIONS:

(1) For the purposes of Item 6.1(1)(b)(i), a fund must calculate its maximum total assets by aggregating the maximum value of its long positions, short positions and the maximum amount that may be borrowed.

(2) For the purposes of the disclosure required by Item 6.1(1)(b)(ii), the term "specified derivative" has the same meaning as in NI 81-102. The description of an investment fund's use of leverage under Item 6.1(1)(b)(ii) must provide investors with sufficient information to understand the magnitude of the market exposure of the investment fund as compared to the amount of money raised by the investment fund from investors.

6.2 — Overview of the Investment Structure

(1) Under the sub-heading, "Overview of the Investment Structure", describe, including a diagram for complex structures, the overall structure of the underlying investment or investments made or to be made by the investment fund, including any direct or indirect investment exposure. Include in the description and the diagram any counterparties under a forward or swap agreement entered into with the investment fund or its manager, the nature of the portfolio of securities being purchased by the investment fund, any indirect investment exposure that is related to the return of the investment fund and any collateral or guarantees given as part of the overall structure of the underlying investment or investments made by the investment fund.

(2) If the securities distributed under the prospectus are being issued in connection with a restructuring transaction, describe by way of a diagram or otherwise the intercorporate relationships both before and after the completion of the proposed transaction.

Item 7 — Overview of the Sector(s) that the Fund Invests in

7.1 — Sector(s) that the Fund Invests in

(1) Under the heading "Overview of the Sector[(s)] that the Fund Invests in", if the investment fund invests or intends to invest in a specific sector(s), briefly describe the sector(s) that the investment fund has been or will be investing in.

(2) Include in the description known material trends, events or uncertainties in the sector(s) that the investment fund invests or intends to invests in that might reasonably be expected to affect the investment fund.

7.2 — Significant Holdings in Other Entities

For a labour sponsored or venture capital fund, include in substantially the tabular form below, the following information as at a date within 30 days of the date of the prospectus with respect to each entity, 5 percent or more of whose securities of any class are beneficially owned directly or indirectly by the fund.

Significant Holdings of the [name of the labour sponsored or venture capital fund]

Name and Address of Entity	Nature of Entities' Principal Business	Percentage of Securities of each Class Owned by Fund

Item 8 — Investment Restrictions

8.1 — Investment Restrictions

(1) Under the heading "Investment Restrictions", describe any restrictions on investments adopted by the investment fund, beyond what is required under securities legislation.

(2) If the investment fund has received the approval of the securities regulatory authorities to vary any of the investment restrictions and practices contained in securities legislation, provide details of the permitted variations.

(3) Describe the nature of any securityholder or other approval that may be required in order to change the fundamental investment objectives and any of the material investment strategies to be used to achieve the investment objectives.

Item 9 — Management Discussion of Fund Performance

9.1 — Management Discussion of Fund Performance

Unless the investment fund's most recently filed management report of fund performance is incorporated by reference under Item 37 or attached to the prospectus under Item 38, provide, under the heading "Management Discussion of Fund Performance", management's discussion of fund performance in accordance with sections 2.3, 2.4, 2.5, 3, 4, 5 and 6 of Part B of Form 81-106F1 for the period covered by the financial statements required under Item 38.

Item 10 — Fees and Expenses

10.1 — Fees and Expenses

Under the heading "Fees and Expenses", set out information about all of the fees and expenses payable by the investment fund and by investors in the investment fund.

INSTRUCTION:

Describe each fee paid by the investment fund and by the investor in this section separately. The description of fees must also include sales and trailing commissions paid either by the investment fund or the investor.

Item 11 — Annual Returns and Management Expense Ratio

11.1 — Annual Returns, Management Expense Ratio and Trading Expense Ratio

Under the heading "Annual Returns, Management Expense Ratio and Trading Expense Ratio", provide, in the following table, returns for each of the past five years, the management expense ratio for each of the past five years and the trading expense ratio for each of the past five years as disclosed in the most recently filed annual management report of fund performance of the investment fund:

	[specify year]	[specify year]	[specify year]	[specify year]	[specify year]
Annual Returns	....	....	....	....	....
MER	....	....	....	....	....
TER	....	....	....	....	....

"MER" means management expense ratio based on management fees and operating expenses (excluding commissions and other portfolio transaction costs) expressed as an annualized percentage of daily average net asset value.

"TER" means trading expense ratio and represents total commissions and other portfolio transaction costs expressed as an annualized percentage of daily average net asset value.

Item 12 — Risk Factors

12.1 — Risk Factors

(1) Under the heading "Risk Factors", describe the risk factors material to the investment fund that a reasonable investor would consider relevant to an investment in the securities being distributed, such as the risks associated with any particular aspect of the fundamental investment objectives and investment strategies.

(2) Include a discussion of general market, political, market sector, liquidity, interest rate, foreign currency, diversification, leverage, credit, legal and operational risks, as appropriate.

(3) Include a brief discussion of general investment risks applicable to the investment fund, such as specific company developments, stock market conditions and general economic and financial conditions in those countries where the investments of the investment fund are listed for trading.

(4) As applicable, describe the risks associated with the investment fund entering into

    (a) derivative transactions for non-hedging purposes,

    (b) securities lending, repurchase or reverse repurchase transactions; and

    (c) short sales of securities.

(5) If there is a risk that purchasers of the securities distributed may become liable to make an additional contribution beyond the price of the security, disclose the risk.

INSTRUCTIONS:

(1) Describe risks in the order of seriousness from the most serious to the least serious.

(2) A risk factor must not be de-emphasized by including excessive caveats or conditions.

Item 13 — Distribution Policy

13.1 — Distribution Policy

Under the heading "Distribution Policy", describe the distribution policy, including

    (a) whether distributions are made by the investment fund in cash or reinvested in securities of the investment fund,

    (b) the targeted amount of any distributions,

    (c) whether the distributions are guaranteed or not, and

    (d) when the distributions are made.

Item 14 — Purchases of Securities

14.1 — Purchases of Securities

(1) Under the heading "Purchases of Securities", describe the procedure followed or to be followed by investors who desire to purchase securities of the investment fund or switch them for securities of other investment funds.

(2) Describe how the issue price of the securities of the investment fund is determined.

(3) Describe how the securities of the investment fund are distributed. If sales are effected through a principal distributor, give brief details of any arrangements with the principal distributor.

(4) Describe all available purchase options and state, if applicable, that the choice of different purchase options requires the investor to pay different fees and expenses and if applicable, that the choice of different purchase options affects the amount of compensation paid to a dealer.

(5) If applicable, disclose that a dealer may make provision in arrangements that it has with an investor that will require the investor to compensate the dealer for any losses suffered by the dealer in connection with a failed settlement of a purchase of securities of the investment fund caused by the investor.

(6) If applicable, for an investment fund that is being sold on a best efforts basis, state whether the issue price will be fixed during the initial distribution period, and state when the investment fund will begin issuing securities at the net asset value of a security of the investment fund.

Item 15 — Redemption of Securities

15.1 — Redemption of Securities

(1) Under the heading "Redemption of Securities", describe how investors may redeem securities of the investment fund, including

    (a) the procedures followed, or to be followed, by an investor who desires to redeem securities of the investment fund and specifying the procedures to be followed and the documents to be delivered before a redemption order pertaining to securities of the investment fund will be accepted by the investment fund for processing and before payment of the proceeds of redemption will be made by the investment fund,

    (a.1) the dates on which securities of the investment fund will be redeemed,

    (a.2) the dates on which payment of the proceeds of redemption will be made by the investment fund,

    (b) how the redemption price of the securities is determined and, if applicable, state that the redemption price of the securities is based on the net asset value of a security of that class, or series of a class, next determined after the receipt by the investment fund of the redemption order, and

    (c) the circumstances under which the investment fund may suspend redemptions of the securities of the investment fund.

(2) If the proceeds of redemption are computed by reference to the net asset value per security and amounts may be deducted from the net asset value per security, describe each amount that may be deducted and the entity to which each amount is paid. If there is a maximum amount or percentage that may be deducted from the net asset value per security, disclose that amount or percentage.

15.2 — Short-term Trading

For an investment fund in continuous distribution, under the sub-heading "Short-Term Trading",

    (a) describe the adverse effects, if any, that short-term trades in securities of the investment fund by an investor may have on other investors in the investment fund,

    (b) describe the restrictions, if any, that may be imposed by the investment fund to deter short-term trades, including the circumstances, if any, under which such restrictions may not apply,

    (c) where the investment fund does not impose restrictions on short-term trades, state the specific basis for the view of the manager that it is appropriate for the investment fund not to do so, and

    (d) describe any arrangements, whether formal or informal, with any person or company, to permit short-term trades in securities of the investment fund, including the name of such person or company and the terms of such arrangements, including any restrictions imposed on the short-term trades and any compensation or other consideration received by the manager, the investment fund or any other party pursuant to such arrangements.

INSTRUCTION

For the disclosure required by section 15.2, include a brief description of the short-term trading activities in the investment fund that are considered by the manager to be inappropriate or excessive. If the manager imposes a short-term trading fee, include a cross-reference to the disclosure provided under Item 10 of this Form.

Item 16 — Consolidated Capitalization

16.1 — Consolidated Capitalization

(1) This section does not apply to an investment fund in continuous distribution.

(2) Under the heading "Consolidated Capitalization", describe any material change in, and the effect of the material change on, the share and loan capital of the investment fund, on a consolidated basis, since the date of the investment fund's financial statements for its most recently completed financial period included in the prospectus, including any material change that will result from the issuance of the securities being distributed under the prospectus.

Item 17 — Prior Sales

17.1 — Prior Sales

(1) Subsection (2) does not apply to an investment fund in continuous distribution.

(2) Under the heading "Prior Sales", for each class of securities of the investment fund distributed under the prospectus and for securities that are convertible into those classes of securities, state, for the 12-month period before the date of the prospectus,

   (a) the price at which the securities have been issued or are to be issued by the investment fund or sold by the selling securityholder,

   (b) the number of securities issued or sold at that price, and

   (c) the date on which the securities were issued or sold.

17.2 — Trading Price and Volume

(1) For each class of securities of the investment fund that is traded or quoted on a Canadian marketplace, identify the marketplace and the price ranges and volume traded or quoted on the Canadian marketplace on which the greatest volume of trading or quotation generally occurs.

(2) If a class of securities of the investment fund is not traded or quoted on a Canadian marketplace but is traded or quoted on a foreign marketplace, identify the foreign marketplace and the price ranges and volume traded or quoted on the foreign marketplace on which the greatest volume or quotation generally occurs.

(3) Provide the information required under subsections (1) and (2) on a monthly basis for each month or, if applicable, partial months of the 12-month period before the date of the prospectus.

Item 18 — Income Tax Considerations

18.1 — Status of the Investment Fund

Under the heading "Income Tax Considerations" and under the sub-heading "Status of the Investment Fund", briefly describe the status of the investment fund for income tax purposes. Also disclose whether the investment fund is eligible as an investment for registered retirement savings plans, registered retirement income plans, registered education savings plans or deferred profit sharing plans.

18.2 — Taxation of the Investment Fund

Under the sub-heading "Taxation of the Investment Fund", state in general terms the bases upon which the income and capital receipts of the investment fund are taxed.

18.3 — Taxation of Securityholders

Under the sub-heading "Taxation of Securityholders", state in general terms the income tax consequences to the holders of the securities offered of

   (a) any distribution to the securityholders in the form of income, capital, dividends or otherwise, including amounts reinvested in securities of the investment fund,

   (b) the redemption of securities, and

   (c) the issue of securities.

18.4 — Taxation of Registered Plans

Under the sub-heading "Taxation of Registered Plans", explain the tax treatment applicable to securities of the investment fund held in a registered tax plan.

18.5 — Tax Implications of the Investment Fund's Distribution Policy

Under the sub-heading "Tax Implications of the Investment Fund's Distribution Policy", describe the impact of the investment fund's distribution policy on a taxable investor who acquires securities of the investment fund late in a calendar year.

Item 19 — Organization and Management Details of the Investment Fund

19.1 — Management of the Investment Fund

(1) Under the heading "Organization and Management Details of the Investment Fund" and under the sub-heading "Officers and Directors of the Investment Fund",

(a) list the name and municipality of residence of each director and executive officer of the investment fund and indicate their respective positions and offices held with the investment fund and their respective principal occupations during the five preceding years,

(b) state the period or periods during which each director has served as a director and when his or her term of office will expire,

(c) [repealed]

(d) disclose the board committees of the investment fund and identify the members of each committee,

(e) if the principal occupation of a director or executive officer of the investment fund is acting as an executive officer of a person or company other than the investment fund, disclose that fact and state the principal business of the person or company, and

(f) for an investment fund that is a limited partnership, provide the information required by this subsection for the general partner of the investment fund, modified as appropriate.

(2) Under the sub-heading "Cease Trade Orders and Bankruptcies", if a director or executive officer of the investment fund is, as at the date of the prospectus or pro forma prospectus, as applicable, or was within 10 years before the date of the prospectus or pro forma prospectus, as applicable, a director, chief executive officer or chief financial officer of any other issuer, that:

(a) was subject to an order that was issued while the director or executive officer was acting in the capacity as director, chief executive officer or chief financial officer, or

(b) was subject to an order that was issued after the director or executive officer ceased to be a director, chief executive officer or chief financial officer and which resulted from an event that occurred while that person was acting in the capacity as director, chief executive officer or chief financial officer,

state the fact and describe the basis on which the order was made and whether the order is still in effect.

(3) For the purposes of subsection (2), "order" means

(a) a cease trade order,

(b) an order similar to a cease trade order, or

(c) an order that denied the relevant investment fund access to any exemption under securities legislation,

that was in effect for a period of more than 30 consecutive days.

(4) If a director or executive officer of the investment fund

(a) is, as at the date of the prospectus or pro forma prospectus, as applicable, or has been within the 10 years before the date of the prospectus or pro forma prospectus, as applicable, a director or executive officer of any issuer that, while that person was acting in that capacity, or within a year of that person ceasing to act in that capacity, became bankrupt, made a proposal under any legislation relating to bankruptcy or insolvency or was subject to or instituted any proceedings, arrangement or compromise with creditors or had a receiver, receiver manager or trustee appointed to hold its assets, state the fact, or

(b) has, within the 10 years before the date of the prospectus or pro forma prospectus, as applicable, become bankrupt, made a proposal under any legislation relating to bankruptcy or insolvency, or become subject to or instituted any proceedings, arrangement or compromise with creditors, or had a receiver, receiver manager or trustee appointed to hold the assets of the director or executive officer, state the fact.

(5) Under the heading "Organization and Management Details of the Investment Fund" and under the sub-heading "Manager of the Investment Fund", provide the complete municipal address of the manager and details of the manager of the investment fund, including the history and background of the manager and any overall investment strategy or approach used by the manager in connection with the investment fund.

(6) Under the sub-heading "Duties and Services to be Provided by the Manager", provide a description of the duties and services that the manager will be providing to the investment fund.

(7) Under the sub-heading "Details of the Management Agreement", provide a brief description of the essential details of any management agreement that the manager has entered into or will be entering into with the investment fund, including any termination rights.

(8) Under the sub-heading "Officers and Directors of the Manager of the Investment Fund",

(a) list the name and municipality of residence of each partner, director and executive officer of the manager of the investment fund and indicate their respective positions and offices held with the manager and their respective principal occupations within the five preceding years,

(b) if a partner, director or executive officer of the manager has held more than one office with the manager within the past five years, state only the current office held, and

(c) if the principal occupation of a partner, director or executive officer of the manager is with an organization other than the manager of the investment fund, state the principal business in which the organization is engaged.

(9) Under the sub-heading "Cease Trade Orders and Bankruptcies of the Manager", provide the information required under subsections (2) and (4) for the directors and executive officers of the manager of the investment fund, modified as appropriate.

(10) Under the heading "Ownership of Securities of the Investment Fund and of the Manager" disclose

    (a) the percentage of securities of each class or series of voting or equity securities owned of record or beneficially, in aggregate, by all the directors and executive officers of the investment fund

        (i) in the investment fund if the aggregate level of ownership exceeds 10 percent,

        (ii) in the manager, or

        (iii) in any person or company that provides services to the investment fund or the manager; and

    (b) the percentage of securities of each class or series of voting or equity securities owned of record or beneficially, in aggregate, by all the directors and executive officers of the manager of the investment fund

        (i) in the investment fund if the aggregate level of ownership exceeds 10 percent,

        (ii) in the manager, or

        (iii) in any person or company that provides services to the investment fund or the manager; and

    (c) the percentage of securities of each class or series of voting or equity securities owned of record or beneficially, in aggregate, by all the independent review committee members of the investment fund

        (i) in the investment fund if the aggregate level of ownership exceeds 10 percent,

        (ii) in the manager, or

        (iii) in any person or company that provides services to the investment fund or the manager.

(11) If the management functions of the investment fund are carried out by employees of the investment fund, disclose in respect of those employees the disclosure concerning executive compensation that is required to be provided for executive officers of an issuer under securities legislation.

(12) Describe any arrangements under which compensation was paid or payable by the investment fund during the most recently completed financial year of the investment fund, for the services of directors of the investment fund, members of an independent board of governors or advisory board of the investment fund and members of the independent review committee of the investment fund, including the amounts paid, the name of the individual and any expenses reimbursed by the investment fund to the individual

    (a) in that capacity, including any additional amounts payable for committee participation or special assignments; and

    (b) as a consultant or expert.

(13) For an investment fund that is a trust, describe the arrangements, including the amounts paid and expenses reimbursed, under which compensation was paid or payable by the investment fund during the most recently completed financial year of the investment fund for the services of the trustee or trustees of the investment fund.

INSTRUCTIONS

(1) The disclosure required by subsections (2) and (4) also applies to any personal holding companies of any of the persons referred to in subsections (2) and (4).

(2) A management cease trade order which applies to directors and executive officers of the investment fund is an "order" for the purposes of paragraph (2)(a) and must be disclosed, whether or not the director, chief executive officer or chief financial officer was named in the order.

(3) For the purposes of this section, a late filing fee, such as a filing fee that applies to the late filing of an insider report, is not a "penalty or sanction".

(4) The disclosure in paragraph (2)(a) only applies if the director or executive officer of the investment fund was a director, chief executive officer or chief financial officer when the order was issued against the relevant investment fund. The investment fund does not have to provide disclosure if the director or executive officer became a director, chief executive officer or chief financial officer after the order was issued.

(5) The disclosure required under Item 19.1(11) regarding executive compensation for management functions carried out by employees of an investment fund must be made in accordance with the disclosure requirements of Form 51-102F6.

19.2 — Portfolio Adviser

(1) Under the sub-heading "Portfolio Adviser"

    (a) state the municipality and the province or country where the portfolio adviser principally provides its services to the investment fund and give details of the portfolio adviser of the investment fund, including the history and background of the portfolio adviser,

    (b) state the extent to which investment decisions are made by certain individuals employed by the portfolio adviser and whether those decisions are subject to the oversight, approval or ratification of a committee, and

    (c) state the name, title, and length of time of service of the person or persons employed by or associated with the portfolio adviser of the investment fund who is or are principally responsible for the day-to-day management of a material portion of the portfolio of the investment fund, implementing a particular material strategy or managing a particular segment of the portfolio of the investment fund, and each person's business experience in the last five years.

(2) Under the sub-heading "Details of the Portfolio Advisory Agreement", provide a brief description of the essential details of any portfolio advisory agreement that the portfolio adviser has entered into or will be entering into with the investment fund or the manager of the investment fund, including any termination rights.

Part 4:
DISTRIBUTIONS

19.2.1 — Brokerage Arrangements

Under the sub-heading "Brokerage Arrangements",

a) If any brokerage transactions involving the client brokerage commissions of the investment fund have been or might be directed to a dealer in return for the provision of any good or service, by the dealer or a third party, other than order execution, state

(i) the process for, and factors considered in, selecting a dealer to effect securities transactions for the investment fund, including whether receiving goods or services in addition to order execution is a factor, and whether and how the process may differ for a dealer that is an affiliated entity;

(ii) the nature of the arrangements under which order execution goods and services or research goods and services might be provided;

(iii) each type of good or service, other than order execution, that might be provided; and

(iv) the method by which the portfolio adviser makes a good faith determination that the investment fund, on whose behalf the portfolio adviser directs any brokerage transactions involving client brokerage commissions to a dealer in return for the provision of any order execution goods and services or research goods and services, by the dealer or a third party, receives reasonable benefit considering both the use of the goods or services and the amount of client brokerage commissions paid;

(b) If any brokerage transactions involving the client brokerage commissions of the investment fund have been or might be directed to a dealer in return for the provision of any good or service, by the dealer or a third party, other than order execution, since the date of the investment fund's last prospectus or last annual information form, whichever one is the most recent, state

(i) each type of good or service, other than order execution, that has been provided to the manager or the portfolio adviser of the investment fund; and

(ii) the name of any affiliated entity that provided any good or service referred to in subparagraph (i), separately identifying each affiliated entity and each type of good or service provided by each affiliated entity; and

(c) If any brokerage transactions involving the client brokerage commissions of the investment fund have been or might be directed to a dealer in return for the provision of any good or service, by the dealer or a third party, other than order execution, state that the name of any other dealer or third party that provided a good or service referred to in paragraph (b)(i), that was not disclosed under paragraph (b)(ii), will be provided upon request by contacting the investment fund or investment fund family at [insert telephone number] or at [insert investment fund or investment fund family e-mail address].

INSTRUCTIONS:

Terms defined in NI 23-102 — Use of Client Brokerage Commissions have the same meaning where used in this Item.

19.3 — Conflicts of Interest

Under the sub-heading "Conflicts of Interest", disclose particulars of existing or potential material conflicts of interest between

(1) the investment fund and a director or executive officer of the investment fund,

(2) the investment fund and the manager or any director or executive officer of the manager of the investment fund, and

(3) the investment fund and the portfolio adviser or any director or executive officer of the portfolio adviser of the investment fund.

19.4 — Independent Review Committee

Under the sub-heading "Independent Review Committee", provide a description of the independent review committee of the investment fund, including

(a) the mandate and responsibilities of the independent review committee,

(b) the composition of the independent review committee (including the names of its members), and the reasons for any change in its composition since the date of the most recently filed annual information form or prospectus of the investment fund, as applicable,

(c) that the independent review committee prepares a report at least annually of its activities for securityholders which is available on the [investment fund's/investment fund family's] Internet site at [insert investment fund's Internet site address], or at the securityholder's request at no cost, by contacting the [investment fund/investment fund family] at [investment fund's/investment fund family's email address], and

(d) the amount of fees and expenses payable in connection with the independent review committee by the investment fund, including any amounts payable for committee participation or special assignments, and state whether the investment fund pays all of the fees payable to the independent review committee.

19.5 — Trustee

Under the sub-heading "Trustee", provide details of the trustee of the investment fund, including the municipality and the province or country where the trustee principally provides its services to the investment fund.

19.6 — Custodian

(1) Under the sub-heading "Custodian", state the name, municipality of the principal or head office, and nature of business of the custodian and any principal sub-custodian of the investment fund.

(2) Describe generally the sub-custodial arrangements of the investment fund.

INSTRUCTION:

A "principal sub-custodian" is a sub-custodian to whom custodial authority has been delegated in respect of a material portion or segment of the portfolio assets of the investment fund.

19.7 — Auditor

Under the sub-heading "Auditor", state the name and address of the auditor of the investment fund.

19.8 — Transfer Agent and Registrar

Under the sub-heading, "Transfer Agent and Registrar", for each class of securities, state the name of the investment fund's transfer agent(s), registrar(s), trustee, or other agent appointed by the investment fund to maintain the securities register and the register of transfers for such securities and indicate the location (by municipalities) of each of the offices of the investment fund or transfer agent, registrar, trustee or other agent where the securities, register and register of transfers are maintained or transfers of securities are recorded.

19.9 — Promoters

(1) For a person or company that is, or has been within the two years immediately preceding the date of the prospectus or pro forma prospectus, a promoter of the investment fund, state under the sub-heading "Promoter"

(a) the person or company's name and municipality and the province or country of residence,

(b) the number and percentage of each class of voting securities and equity securities of the investment fund beneficially owned, or controlled or directed, directly or indirectly, by the person or company,

(c) the nature and amount of anything of value, including money, property, contracts, options or rights of any kind received or to be received by the promoter directly or indirectly from the investment fund, and the nature and amount of any assets, services or other consideration received or to be received by the investment fund in return, and

(d) for an asset acquired within the two years before the date of the preliminary prospectus or pro forma prospectus, or to be acquired, by the investment fund from a promoter,

(i) the consideration paid or to be paid for the asset and the method by which the consideration has been or will be determined,

(ii) the person or company making the determination referred to in subparagraph (i) and the person or company's relationship with the investment fund, the promoter, or an affiliate of the investment fund or of the promoter, and

(iii) the date that the asset was acquired by the promoter and the cost of the asset to the promoter.

(2) If a promoter referred to in subsection (1) is, as at the date of the prospectus or pro forma prospectus, as applicable, or was within 10 years before the date of the prospectus or pro forma prospectus, as applicable, a director, chief executive officer or chief financial officer of any person or company, that

(a) was subject to an order that was issued while the promoter was acting in the capacity as director, chief executive officer or chief financial officer, or

(b) was subject to an order that was issued after the promoter ceased to be a director, chief executive officer or chief financial officer and which resulted from an event that occurred while the promoter was acting in the capacity as director, chief executive officer or chief financial officer,

state the fact and describe the basis on which the order was made and whether the order is still in effect.

(3) For the purposes of subsection (2), "order" means:

(a) a cease trade order,

(b) an order similar to a cease trade order, or

(c) an order that denied the relevant person or company access to any exemption under securities legislation

that was in effect for a period of more than 30 consecutive days.

(4) If a promoter referred to in subsection (1)

(a) is, as at the date of the prospectus or pro forma prospectus, as applicable, or has been within the 10 years before the date of the prospectus or pro forma prospectus, as applicable, a director or executive officer of any person or company that, while the promoter was acting in that capacity, or within a year of that person ceasing to act in that capacity, became bankrupt, made a proposal under any legislation relating to bankruptcy or insolvency or was subject to or instituted any proceedings, arrangement or compromise with creditors or had a receiver, receiver manager or trustee appointed to hold its assets, state the fact, or

(b) has, within the 10 years before the date of the prospectus or pro forma prospectus, as applicable, become bankrupt, made a proposal under any legislation relating to bankruptcy or insolvency, or become subject to or instituted any proceedings, arrangement or compromise with creditors, or had a receiver, receiver manager or trustee appointed to hold the assets of the promoter, state the fact.

(5) Describe the penalties or sanctions imposed and the grounds on which they were imposed or the terms of the settlement agreement and the circumstances that gave rise to the settlement agreement, if a promoter referred to in subsection (1) has been subject to

(a) any penalties or sanctions imposed by a court relating to provincial and territorial securities legislation or by a provincial and territorial securities regulatory authority or has entered into a settlement agreement with a provincial and territorial securities regulatory authority, or

(b) any other penalties or sanctions imposed by a court or regulatory body that would be likely to be considered important to a reasonable investor in making an investment decision.

Part 4:
DISTRIBUTIONS

(6) Despite subsection (5), no disclosure is required of a settlement agreement entered into before December 31, 2000 unless the disclosure would likely be considered to be important to a reasonable investor in making an investment decision.

INSTRUCTIONS

(1) The disclosure required by subsections (2), (4) and (5) also applies to any personal holding companies of any of the persons referred to in subsections (2), (4), and (5).

(2) A management cease trade order which applies to a promoter referred to in subsection (1) is an "order" for the purposes of paragraph (2)(a) and must be disclosed, whether or not the director, chief executive officer or chief financial officer was named in the order.

(3) For the purposes of this section, a late filing fee, such as a filing fee that applies to the late filing of an insider report, is not a "penalty or sanction".

(4) The disclosure in paragraph (2)(a) only applies if the promoter was a director, chief executive officer or chief financial officer when the order was issued against the person or company. The investment fund does not have to provide disclosure if the promoter became a director, chief executive officer or chief financial officer after the order was issued.

19.10 — Principal Distributor

(1) If applicable, state the name and address of the principal distributor of the investment fund.

(2) Describe the circumstances under which any agreement with the principal distributor of the investment fund may be terminated and include a brief description of the essential terms of this agreement.

19.11 — Securities Lending Agent

(1) Under the sub-heading "Securities Lending Agent", state the name of each securities lending agent of the investment fund and the municipality of each securities lending agent's principal or head office.

(2) State whether any securities lending agent of the investment fund is an affiliate or associate of the manager of the investment fund.

(3) Briefly describe the essential terms of each agreement with each securities lending agent. Include the amount of collateral required to be delivered in connection with a securities lending transaction as a percentage of the market value of the loaned securities, and briefly describe any indemnities provided in, and the termination provisions of, each such agreement.

Item 20 — Calculation of Net Asset Value

20.1 — Calculation of Net Asset Value

Under the heading "Calculation of Net Asset Value",

(a) describe how the net asset value of the investment fund is calculated, and

(b) state the frequency at which the net asset value is calculated and the date and time of day at which it is calculated.

20.2 — Valuation Policies and Procedures

Under the sub-heading "Valuation Policies and Procedures of the Investment Fund",

(a) describe the methods used to value the various types or classes of assets of the investment fund and its liabilities for the purpose of calculating net asset value,

(a.1) If the valuation principles and practices established by the manager differ from Canadian GAAP, describe the differences, and

(b) if the manager has discretion to deviate from the investment fund's valuation practices described in paragraph (a), disclose when and to what extent that discretion may be exercised and, if it has been exercised in the past three years, provide an example of how it has been exercised or, if it has not been exercised in the past three years, so state.

20.3 — Reporting of Net Asset Value

Under the sub-heading "Reporting of Net Asset Value", describe

(a) how the net asset value and net asset value per security of the investment fund will be made available at no cost (e.g. website, toll-free telephone line, etc.), and

(b) the frequency at which the net asset value and net asset value per security is disclosed.

Item 21 — Description of the Securities Distributed

21.1 — Equity Securities

If equity securities of the investment fund are being distributed, under the heading "Attributes of the Securities" and under the sub-heading "Description of the Securities Distributed" state the description or the designation of the class of equity securities distributed and describe all material attributes and characteristics, including

(a) dividend or distribution rights,

(b) voting rights,

(c) rights upon dissolution, termination or winding-up,

(d) pre-emptive rights,

(e) conversion or exchange rights,

(f) redemption, retraction, purchase for cancellation or surrender provisions,

(g) sinking or purchase fund provisions,

(h) provisions permitting or restricting the issuance of additional securities and any other material restrictions, and

(i) provisions requiring a securityholder to contribute additional capital.

21.2 — Debt Securities

If debt securities are being distributed, under the heading "Attributes of the Securities" and under the sub-heading "Description of the Securities Distributed", describe all material attributes and characteristics of the indebtedness and the security, if any, for the debt, including

(a) provisions for interest rate, maturity and premium, if any,

(b) conversion or exchange rights,

(c) redemption, retraction, purchase for cancellation or surrender provisions,

(d) sinking or purchase fund provisions,

(e) the nature and priority of any security for the debt securities, briefly identifying the principal properties subject to lien or charge,

(f) provisions permitting or restricting the issuance of additional securities, the incurring of additional indebtedness and other material negative covenants, including restrictions against payment of distributions and restrictions against giving security on the assets of the investment fund, and provisions as to the release or substitution of assets securing the debt securities,

(g) the name of the trustee under any indenture relating to the debt securities and the nature of any material relationship between the trustee or any of its affiliates and the investment fund or any of its affiliates, and

(h) any financial arrangements between the investment fund and any of its affiliates or among its affiliates that could affect the security for the indebtedness.

21.3 — Derivatives

[Repealed]

21.4 — Other Securities

If securities other than the securities mentioned above are being distributed, under the heading "Attributes of the Securities" and under the sub-heading "Description of the Securities Distributed", describe fully the material attributes and characteristics of those securities.

21.5 — Special Warrants

If the prospectus is used to qualify the distribution of securities issued upon the exercise of special warrants or other securities acquired on a prospectus-exempt basis, disclose that holders of such securities have been provided with a contractual right of rescission and provide the following disclosure in the prospectus, with the bracketed information completed:

"The issuer has granted to each holder of a special warrant a contractual right of rescission of the prospectus-exempt transaction under which the special warrant was initially acquired. The contractual right of rescission provides that if a holder of a special warrant who acquires another security of the issuer on exercise of the special warrant as provided for in the prospectus is, or becomes, entitled under the securities legislation of a jurisdiction to the remedy of rescission because of the prospectus or an amendment to the prospectus containing a misrepresentation,

(a) the holder is entitled to rescission of both the holder's exercise of its special warrant and the private placement transaction under which the special warrant was initially acquired,

(b) the holder is entitled in connection with the rescission to a full refund of all consideration paid to the underwriter or issuer, as the case may be, on the acquisition of the special warrant, and

(c) if the holder is a permitted assignee of the interest of the original special warrant subscriber, the holder is entitled to exercise the rights of rescission and refund as if the holder was the original subscriber."

INSTRUCTION

If the prospectus is qualifying the distribution of securities issued upon the exercise of securities other than special warrants, replace the term "special warrant" with the type of the security being distributed.

21.6 — Restricted Securities

(1) If the investment fund has outstanding, or proposes to distribute under a prospectus, restricted securities, subject securities or securities that are, directly or indirectly, convertible into or exercisable or exchangeable for restricted securities or subject securities, provide a detailed description of

(a) the voting rights attached to the restricted securities that are the subject of the distribution or that will result from the distribution, either directly or following a conversion, exchange or exercise, and the voting rights, if any, attached to the securities of any other class of securities of the investment fund that are the same as or greater than, on a per security basis, those attached to the restricted securities,

(b) any significant provisions under applicable corporate and securities law that do not apply to the holders of the restricted securities that are the subject of the distribution or that will result from the distribution, either directly or following a conversion, exchange or exercise, but do apply to the holders of another class of equity securities, and the extent of any rights provided in the constating documents or otherwise for the protection of holders of the restricted securities,

(c) any rights under applicable corporate law, in the constating documents or otherwise, of holders of restricted securities that are the subject of the distribution or that will result from the distribution, either directly or following a conversion, exchange or exercise, to attend, in person or by proxy, meetings of holders of equity securities of the investment fund and to speak at the meetings to the same extent that holders of equity securities are entitled, and

(d) how the investment fund complied with, or the basis upon which it was exempt from, the requirements of Part 12 of the Instrument.

(2) If holders of restricted securities do not have all of the rights referred to in subsection (1), the detailed description referred to in that subsection must include, in boldface type, a statement of the rights the holders do not have.

(3) If the investment fund is required to include the disclosure referred to in subsection (1), state the percentage of the aggregate voting rights attached to the investment fund's securities that will be represented by restricted securities after effect has been given to the issuance of the securities being offered.

21.7 — Modification of Terms

(1) Describe provisions about the modification, amendment or variation of any rights attached to the securities being distributed.

(2) If the rights of holders of securities may be modified otherwise than in accordance with the provisions attached to the securities or the provisions of the governing statute relating to the securities, explain briefly.

21.8 — Ratings

(1) If the investment fund has asked for and received a credit rating, or if the investment fund is aware that it has received any other kind of rating, including a stability rating or a provisional rating, from one or more credit rating organizations for securities of the investment fund that are outstanding, or will be outstanding, and the rating or ratings continue in effect, disclose

(a) each rating received from a credit rating organization;

(b) for each rating disclosed under paragraph (a), the name of the credit rating organization that has assigned the rating;

(c) a definition or description of the category in which each credit rating organization rated the securities and the relative rank of each rating within the organization's overall classification system;

(d) an explanation of what the rating addresses and what attributes, if any, of the securities are not addressed by the rating;

(e) any factors or considerations identified by the credit rating organization as giving rise to unusual risks associated with the securities;

(f) a statement that a credit rating or a stability rating is not a recommendation to buy, sell or hold securities and may be subject to revision or withdrawal at any time by the credit rating organization; and

(g) any announcement made by, or any proposed announcement known to the investment fund that is to be made by, a credit rating organization to the effect that the organization is reviewing or intends to revise or withdraw a rating previously assigned and required to be disclosed under this section.

(2) If payments were, or reasonably will be, made to a credit rating organization that provided a rating described in subsection (1), state that fact and state whether any payments were made to the credit rating organization in respect of any other service provided to the investment fund by the credit rating organization during the last two years.

INSTRUCTIONS

There may be factors relating to a security that are not addressed by a credit rating organization when they give a rating. For example, in the case of cash settled derivative instruments, factors in addition to the creditworthiness of the issuer, such as the continued subsistence of the underlying interest or the volatility of the price, value or level of the underlying interest may be reflected in the rating analysis. Rather than being addressed in the rating itself, these factors may be described by a credit rating organization by way of a superscript or other notation to a rating. Any such attributes must be discussed in the disclosure under this section.

A provisional rating received before the investment funds's most recently completed financial year is not required to be disclosed under this section.

21.9 — Other Attributes

(1) If the rights attaching to the securities being distributed are materially limited or qualified by the rights of any other class of securities, or if any other class of securities ranks ahead of or equally with the securities being distributed, include information about the other securities that will enable investors to understand the rights attaching to the securities being distributed.

(2) If securities of the class being distributed may be partially redeemed or repurchased, state the manner of selecting the securities to be redeemed or repurchased.

INSTRUCTION

This section requires only a brief summary of the provisions that are material from an investment standpoint. The provisions attaching to the securities being distributed or any other class of securities do not need to be set out in full. They may, in the investment fund's discretion, be attached as a schedule to the prospectus.

Item 22 — Securityholder Matters

22.1 — Meetings of Securityholders

Under the heading "Securityholder Matters" and under the sub-heading "Meetings of Securityholders", describe the circumstances, processes and procedures for holding any securityholder meeting and for any extraordinary resolution.

22.2 — Matters Requiring Securityholder Approval

Under the sub-heading "Matters Requiring Securityholder Approval", describe the matters that require securityholder approval.

22.3 — Amendments to Declaration of Trust

For an investment fund established pursuant to a declaration of trust, under the sub-heading "Amendments to the Declaration of Trust", describe the circumstances, processes and procedures required to amend the declaration of trust.

22.4 — Reporting to Securityholders

Under the sub-heading "Reporting to Securityholders" describe the information or reports that will be delivered or made available to securityholders and the frequency with which such information or reports will be delivered or made available to securityholders, including any requirements under securities legislation.

Item 23 — Termination of the Fund

23.1 — Termination of the Fund

Under the heading "Termination of the Fund", describe the circumstances in which the investment fund will be terminated, including:

(a) the date of termination,

(b) how the value of the securities of the investment fund at termination will be determined,

(c) whether securityholders will receive cash or any other type of payment upon termination,

(d) the details of any rollover transaction, if securityholders will receive securities of another investment fund as part of a rollover transaction upon termination,

(e) how the assets of the investment fund will be distributed upon termination, and

(f) if the investment fund is a commodity pool, disclose whether the investment fund will be wound up without the approval of securityholders if the net asset value per security falls below a certain predetermined level, and, if so, the net asset value per security at which this will occur.

Item 24 — Use of Proceeds

24.1 — Application

This Item does not apply to an investment fund in continuous distribution.

24.2 — Proceeds

(1) Under the heading "Use of Proceeds", state the estimated net proceeds to be received by the investment fund or selling securityholder or, in the case of a non-fixed price distribution or a distribution to be made on a best efforts basis, the minimum amount, if any, of net proceeds to be received by the investment fund or selling securityholder from the sale of the securities distributed.

(2) Describe in reasonable detail and, if appropriate, using tabular form, each of the principal purposes, with approximate amounts, for which the net proceeds will be used by the investment fund.

(3) If the prospectus is used for a special warrant or similar transaction, state the amount that has been received by the issuer of the special warrants or similar securities on the sale of the special warrants or similar securities.

24.3 — Other Sources of Funding

If any material amounts of other funds are to be used in conjunction with the proceeds, state the amounts and sources of the other funds.

24.4 — Financing by Special Warrants, etc.

(1) If the prospectus is used to qualify the distribution of securities issued upon the exercise of special warrants or the exercise of other securities acquired on a prospectus-exempt basis, describe the principal purposes for which the proceeds of the prospectus-exempt financing were used or are to be used.

(2) If all or a portion of the funds have been spent, explain how the funds were spent.

Item 25 — Plan of Distribution

25.1 — Plan of Distribution

Under the heading "Plan of Distribution", briefly describe the plan of distribution.

25.2 — Name of Underwriters

(1) If the securities are being distributed by an underwriter, state the name of the underwriter and describe briefly the nature of the underwriter's obligation to take up and pay for the securities.

(2) Disclose the date by which the underwriter is obligated to purchase the securities.

25.3 — Disclosure of Conditions to Underwriters' Obligations

If securities are distributed by an underwriter that has agreed to purchase all of the securities at a specified price and the underwriter's obligations are subject to conditions,

(a) include a statement in substantially the following form, with the bracketed information completed and with modifications necessary to reflect the terms of the distribution:

"Under an agreement dated [insert date of agreement] between [insert name of investment fund or selling securityholder] and [insert name(s) of underwriter(s)], as underwriter[s], [insert name of investment fund or selling securityholder] has agreed to sell and the underwriter[s] [has/have] agreed to purchase on [insert closing date] the securities at a price of [insert offering price], payable in cash to [insert name of investment fund or selling securityholder] against delivery. The obligations of the underwriter[s] under the agreement may be terminated at [its/their] discretion on the basis of [its/their] assessment of the state of the financial markets and may also be terminated upon the occurrence of certain stated events. The underwriter[s] [is/are], however, obligated to take up and pay for all of the securities if any of the securities are purchased under the agreement.", and

(b) describe any other conditions and indicate any information known that is relevant to whether such conditions will be satisfied.

25.4 — Best Efforts Offering

Outline briefly the plan of distribution of any securities being distributed other than on the basis described in section 25.3.

25.5 — Minimum Distribution

If securities are being distributed on a best efforts basis and minimum funds are to be raised, state

(a) the minimum funds to be raised,

(b) that the investment fund must appoint a registered dealer authorized to make the distribution, a Canadian financial institution, or a lawyer who is a practising member in good standing with a law society of a jurisdiction in which the securities are being distributed, or a notary in Québec, to hold in trust all funds received from subscriptions until the minimum amount of funds stipulated in paragraph (a) has been raised, and

(c) that if the minimum amount of funds is not raised within the distribution period, the trustee must return the funds to the subscribers without any deductions.

25.6 — Determination of Price

Disclose the method by which the distribution price has been or will be determined and, if estimates have been provided, explain the process of determining the estimates.

25.7 — Stabilization

If the investment fund, a selling securityholder or an underwriter knows or has reason to believe that there is an intention to over-allot or that the price of any security may be stabilized to facilitate the distribution of the securities, describe the nature of these transactions, including the anticipated size of any over-allocation position, and explain how the transactions are expected to affect the price of the securities.

25.8 — Reduced Price Distributions

If the underwriter may decrease the offering price after the underwriter has made a reasonable effort to sell all of the securities at the initial offering price disclosed in the prospectus in accordance with the procedures permitted by the Instrument and NI 81-102, disclose this fact and that the compensation realised by the underwriter will be decreased by the amount that the aggregate price paid by purchasers for the securities is less than the gross proceeds paid by the underwriter to the investment fund or selling securityholder.

25.9 — Listing Application

If application has been made to list or quote the securities being distributed, include a statement, in substantially the following form, with the bracketed information completed:

"The investment fund has applied to [list/quote] the securities distributed under this prospectus on [name of exchange or other market]. [Listing/Quotation] will be subject to the investment fund fulfilling all the listing requirements of [name of exchange or other market]."

25.10 — Conditional Listing Approval

If application has been made to list or quote the securities being distributed on an exchange or marketplace and conditional listing approval has been received, include a statement, in substantially the following form, with the bracketed information completed:

"[name of exchange or marketplace] has conditionally approved the [listing/quotation] of these securities. [Listing/Quotation] is subject to the [name of investment fund]'s fulfilling all of the requirements of the [name of exchange or marketplace] on or before [date], [including distribution of these securities to a minimum number of public securityholders]."

25.11 — Constraints

If there are constraints imposed on the ownership of securities of the investment fund to ensure that the investment fund has a required level of Canadian ownership, describe the mechanism, if any, by which the level of Canadian ownership of the securities of the investment fund will be monitored and maintained.

25.12 — Special Warrants Acquired by Underwriters or Agents

Disclose the number and dollar value of any special warrants acquired by any underwriter or agent and the percentage of the distribution represented by those special warrants.

Item 26 — Relationship Between Investment Fund or Selling Securityholder and Underwriter

26.1 — Relationship Between Investment Fund or Selling Securityholder and Underwriter

(1) Under the heading "Relationship between Investment Fund [or Selling Securityholder] and Underwriter", if the investment fund or selling securityholder is a connected issuer or related issuer of an underwriter of the distribution, or if the selling securityholder is also an underwriter, comply with the requirements of NI 33-105.

(2) For the purposes of subsection (1), "connected issuer" and "related issuer" have the same meanings as in NI 33-105.

26.1.1 — Auditor that was not a participating audit firm

(1) If the auditor referred to in section 26.1 was not a participating audit firm, as defined in NI 52-108, as at the date of the most recent auditor's report on financial statements included in the prospectus, include a statement in substantially the following form:

> "[*Audit Firm A*] audited the financial statements of [*Entity B*] for the year ended [*state the period of the most recent financial statements included in the prospectus*] and issued an auditor's report dated [*state the date of the auditor's report for the relevant financial statements*]. As at [*state the date of the auditor's report for the relevant financial statements*], [*Audit Firm A*] was not required by securities legislation to enter, and had not entered, into a participation agreement with the Canadian Public Accountability Board. An audit firm that enters into a participation agreement is subject to the oversight program of the Canadian Public Accountability Board."

(2) If an auditor of the financial statements required by Item 32 was not a participating audit firm, as defined in NI 52-108, as at the date of the most recent auditor's report issued by that auditor on financial statements included in the prospectus, include a statement in substantially the following form:

> "[*Audit Firm C*] audited the financial statements of [*Entity D*] for the year ended [*state the period of the most recent financial statements, if any, included in the prospectus under Item 32*] and issued an auditor's report dated [*state the date of the auditor's report for the relevant financial statements*]. As at [*state the date of the auditor's report for the relevant financial statements*], [*Audit Firm C*] was not required by securities legislation to enter, and had not entered, into a participation agreement with the Canadian Public Accountability Board. An audit firm that enters into a participation agreement is subject to the oversight program of the Canadian Public Accountability Board."

Item 27 — Options to Purchase Securities

27.1 — Options to Purchase Securities

[Repealed]

Item 28 — Principal Holders of Securities of the Investment Fund and Selling Securityholders

28.1 — Principal Holders of Securities of the Investment Fund and Selling Securityholders

(1) Under the heading "Principal Holders of Securities of the Investment Fund [and Selling Securityholders]", provide the following information for each principal securityholder of the investment fund, if known or if ought to be known by the investment fund or the manager and, if any securities are being distributed for the account of a securityholder, for each selling securityholder, as of a specified date not more than 30 days before the date of the prospectus or pro forma prospectus, as applicable:

(a) the name,

(b) the number or amount of securities owned, controlled or directed of the class being distributed,

(c) the number or amount of securities of the class being distributed for the account of the securityholder,

(d) the number or amount of securities of the investment fund of any class to be owned, controlled or directed after the distribution, and the percentage that number or amount represents of the total outstanding, and

(e) whether the securities referred to in paragraphs (b), (c) or (d) are owned both of record and beneficially, of record only, or beneficially only.

(2) If securities are being distributed in connection with a restructuring transaction, indicate, to the extent known, the holdings of each person or company described in paragraph (1)(a) that will exist after effect has been given to the transaction.

(3) If any of the securities being distributed are being distributed for the account of a securityholder and those securities were purchased by the selling securityholder within the two years preceding the date of the prospectus or pro forma prospectus, as applicable, state the date the selling securityholder acquired the securities and, if the securities were acquired in the 12 months preceding the date of the prospectus or pro forma prospectus, as applicable, the cost to the securityholder in the aggregate and on an average cost-per-security basis.

(4) If, to the knowledge of the investment fund or the underwriter of the securities being distributed, more than 10 percent of any class of voting securities of the investment fund is held, or is to be held, subject to any voting trust or other similar agreement, disclose, to the extent known, the designation of the securities, the number or amount of the securities held or to be held subject to the agreement and the duration of the agreement. State the names and addresses of the voting trustees and outline briefly their voting rights and other powers under the agreement.

(5) If, to the knowledge of the investment fund or the underwriter of the securities being distributed, any principal securityholder or selling securityholder is an associate or affiliate of another person or company named as a principal securityholder, disclose, to the extent known, the

material facts of the relationship, including any basis for influence over the investment fund held by the person or company other than the holding of voting securities of the investment fund.

(6) In addition to the above, include in a footnote to the table the required calculation(s) on a fully-diluted basis.

(7) Describe any material change to the information required to be included in the prospectus under subsection (1) to the date of the prospectus.

INSTRUCTION

If a company, partnership, trust or other unincorporated entity is a principal securityholder of an investment fund, disclose, to the extent known, the name of each individual who, through ownership of or control or direction over the securities of the company, trust or other unincorporated entity, or membership in the partnership, as the case may be, is a principal securityholder of that entity.

Item 29 — Interests of Management and Others in Material Transactions

29.1 — Interests of Management and Others in Material Transactions

Under the heading "Interests of Management and Others in Material Transactions", describe, and state the approximate amount of, any material interest, direct or indirect, of any of the following persons or companies in any transaction within the three years before the date of the prospectus or pro forma prospectus that has materially affected or is reasonably expected to materially affect the investment fund:

(a) a director or executive officer of the investment fund or the investment fund manager,

(b) a person or company that beneficially owns, or controls or directs, directly or indirectly, more than 10 percent of any class or series of the outstanding voting securities of the investment fund or the investment fund manager, and

(c) an associate or affiliate of any of the persons or companies referred to in paragraphs (a) or (b).

29.2 — Underwriting Discounts

Disclose any material underwriting discounts or commissions upon the sale of securities by the investment fund if any of the persons or companies listed under section 29.1 were or are to be an underwriter or are associates, affiliates or partners of a person or company that was or is to be an underwriter.

INSTRUCTIONS

(1) The materiality of an interest is to be determined on the basis of the significance of the information to investors in light of all the circumstances of the particular case. The importance of the interest to the person having the interest, the relationship of the parties to the transaction with each other and the amount involved are among the factors to be considered in determining the significance of the information to investors.

(2) Give a brief description of the material transaction. Include the name of each person or company whose interest in any transaction is described and the nature of the relationship to the investment fund.

(3) For any transaction involving the purchase by or sale of assets to the investment fund, state the cost of the assets to the purchaser, and the cost of the assets to the seller if acquired by the seller within three years before the transaction.

(4) This Item does not apply to any interest arising from the ownership of securities of the investment fund if the securityholder receives no extra or special benefit or advantage not shared on an equal basis by all other holders of the same class of securities or all other holders of the same class of securities who are resident in Canada.

(5) No information need be given under this Item for a transaction if

(a) the rates or charges involved in the transaction are fixed by law or determined by competitive bids,

(b) the interest of a specified person or company in the transaction is solely that of a director of another company that is a party to the transaction,

(c) the transaction involves services as a bank or other depository of funds, a transfer agent, registrar, trustee under a trust indenture or other similar services, or

(d) the transaction does not involve remuneration for services and the interest of the specified person or company arose from the beneficial ownership, direct or indirect, of less than ten percent of any class of equity securities of another company that is party to the transaction and the transaction is in the ordinary course of business of the investment fund.

(6) Describe all transactions not excluded above that involve remuneration (including an issuance of securities), directly or indirectly, to any of the specified persons or companies for services in any capacity unless the interest of the person or company arises solely from the beneficial ownership, direct or indirect, of less than ten percent of any class of equity securities of another company furnishing the services to the investment fund.

Item 30 — Proxy Voting Disclosure

30.1 — Proxy Voting Disclosure for Portfolio Securities Held

Under the heading "Proxy Voting Disclosure for Portfolio Securities Held", include the disclosure required by subsection 10.2(3) of NI 81-106.

Item 31 — Material Contracts

31.1 — Material Contracts

Under the heading "Material Contracts", list and provide particulars of

(a) the articles of incorporation, the declaration of trust or trust agreement of the investment fund or any other constating document, if any,

(b) any agreement of the investment fund or trustee with the manager of the investment fund,

(c) any agreement of the investment fund, the manager or trustee with the portfolio adviser of the investment fund,

(d) any agreement of the investment fund, the manager or trustee with the custodian of the investment fund,

(e) any agreement of the investment fund, the manager or trustee with the underwriters or agents of the investment fund,

(f) any swap or forward agreement of the investment fund, the manager or trustee with a counterparty that is material to the investment fund fulfilling its investment objectives,

(g) any agreement of the investment fund, the manager or trustee with the principal distributor of the investment fund, and

(h) any other contract or agreement that can reasonably be regarded as material to an investor in the securities of the investment fund.

INSTRUCTIONS

(1) Set out a complete list of all contracts for which particulars must be given under this section, indicating those that are disclosed elsewhere in the prospectus. Particulars need only be provided for those contracts that do not have the particulars given elsewhere in the prospectus.

(2) Particulars of contracts must include the dates of, parties to, consideration provided for in, termination provisions, general nature and key terms of, the contracts.

Item 32 — Legal and Administrative Proceedings

32.1 — Legal and Administrative Proceedings

Under the heading "Legal and Administrative Proceedings", describe briefly any ongoing legal and administrative proceedings material to the investment fund, to which the investment fund, its manager or principal distributor is a party.

32.2 — Particulars of the Proceedings

(1) For all matters disclosed under section 32.1, disclose

(a) the name of the court or agency having jurisdiction,

(b) the date on which the proceeding was instituted,

(c) the principal parties to the proceeding,

(d) the nature of the proceeding and, if applicable, the amount claimed, and

(e) whether the proceeding is being contested and the present status of the proceeding.

(2) Provide similar disclosure about any proceedings known to be contemplated.

32.3 — Penalties and Sanctions

Describe the penalties or sanctions imposed and the grounds on which they were imposed or the terms of any settlement agreement and the circumstances that gave rise to the settlement agreement, if, within the 10 years before the date of the prospectus or pro forma prospectus, the manager of the investment fund, a director or executive officer of the investment fund or a partner, director or executive officer of the manager of the investment fund has

(a) been subject to any penalties or sanctions imposed by a court or a securities regulatory authority relating to Canadian securities legislation, promotion or management of an investment fund, theft or fraud or has entered into a settlement agreement before a court or with a regulatory body in relation to any of these matters, or

(b) been subject to any other penalties or sanctions imposed by a court or regulatory body or has entered into any other settlement agreement before a court or with a regulatory body that would likely be considered important to a reasonable investor in determining whether to purchase securities of the investment fund.

Item 33 — Experts

33.1 — Names of Experts

Under the heading "Experts", name each person or company

(a) who is named as having prepared or certified a report, valuation, statement or opinion in the prospectus or an amendment to the prospectus, and

(b) whose profession or business gives authority to the report, valuation, statement or opinion made by the person or company.

33.2 — Interests of Experts

(1) Disclose all registered or beneficial interests, direct or indirect, in any securities or other property of the investment fund or of an associate or affiliate of the investment fund received or to be received by a person or company whose profession or business gives authority to a

statement made by the person or company and who is named as having prepared or certified a part of the prospectus or prepared or certified a report or valuation described or included in the prospectus.

(2) For the purpose of subsection (1), if the ownership is less than one percent, a general statement to that effect is sufficient.

(3) If a person, or a director, officer or employee of a person or company referred to in subsection (1) is or is expected to be elected, appointed or employed as a director, officer or employee of the investment fund or of any associate or affiliate of the investment fund, disclose the fact or expectation.

(4) Despite subsection (1), an auditor who is independent in accordance with the auditor's rules of professional conduct in a jurisdiction of Canada or has performed an audit in accordance with US GAAS is not required to provide the disclosure in subsection (1) if there is disclosure that the auditor is independent in accordance with the auditor's rules of professional conduct in a jurisdiction of Canada or that the auditor has complied with the SEC's rules on auditor independence.

INSTRUCTIONS

(1) Section 33.2 does not apply to the investment fund's predecessor auditors, if any, for those periods when they were not the investment fund's auditor.

(2) Section 33.2 does not apply to registered or beneficial interests, direct or indirect, held through mutual funds.

Item 34 — Exemptions and Approvals

34.1 — Exemptions and Approvals

Under the heading "Exemptions and Approvals", describe all exemptions from or approvals under securities legislation obtained by the investment fund or the manager of the investment fund that continue to be relied upon by the investment fund or the manager, including all exemptions to be evidenced by the issuance of a receipt for the prospectus pursuant to section 19.3 of the Instrument.

Item 35 — Other Material Facts

35.1 — Other Material Facts

Under the heading "Other Material Facts", using sub-headings as appropriate, give particulars of any material facts about the securities being distributed that are not disclosed under any other section and are necessary in order for the prospectus to contain full, true and plain disclosure of all material facts relating to the securities to be distributed.

Item 36 — Purchasers' Statutory Rights of Withdrawal and Rescission

36.1 — General

For investment funds other than mutual funds, under the heading "Purchasers' Statutory Rights of Withdrawal and Rescission" include a statement in substantially the following form, with bracketed information completed:

> "Securities legislation in [certain of the provinces [and territories] of Canada/the Province of [insert name of local jurisdiction, if applicable]] provides purchasers with the right to withdraw from an agreement to purchase securities. This right may be exercised within two business days after receipt or deemed receipt of a prospectus and any amendment. [In several of the provinces/provinces and territories], [T/t]he securities legislation further provides a purchaser with remedies for rescission [or [, in some jurisdictions,] revisions of the price or damages] if the prospectus and any amendment contains a misrepresentation or is not delivered to the purchaser, provided that the remedies for rescission [, revisions of the price or damages] are exercised by the purchaser within the time limit prescribed by the securities legislation of the purchaser's province [or territory]. The purchaser should refer to any applicable provisions of the securities legislation of the purchaser's province [or territory] for the particulars of these rights or consult with a legal adviser."

36.2 — Mutual Funds

If the investment fund is a mutual fund, under the heading "Purchasers' Statutory Rights of Withdrawal and Rescission" include a statement in substantially the following form:

> "Securities legislation in [certain of the provinces [and territories] of Canada/the Province of [insert name of local jurisdiction, if applicable]] provides purchasers with the right to withdraw from an agreement to purchase mutual fund securities within two business days after receipt of a prospectus and any amendment or within 48 hours after the receipt of a confirmation of a purchase of such securities. If the agreement is to purchase such securities under a contractual plan, the time period during which withdrawal may be made may be longer. [In several of the provinces/provinces and territories], [T/t]he securities legislation further provides a purchaser with remedies for rescission [or [, in some jurisdictions,] revisions of the price or damages] if the prospectus and any amendment contains a misrepresentation or is not delivered to the purchaser, provided that the remedies for rescission [, revisions of the price or damages] are exercised by the purchaser within the time limit prescribed by the securities legislation of the purchaser's province [or territory]. The purchaser should refer to the applicable provisions of the securities legislation of the province [or territory] for the particulars of these rights or should consult with a legal adviser."

36.3 — Non-fixed Price Offerings

In the case of a non-fixed price offering, if applicable in the jurisdiction in which the prospectus is filed, replace the second sentence in the disclosure in section 36.1 with a statement in substantially the following form:

> "This right may only be exercised within two business days after receipt or deemed receipt of a prospectus and any amendment, irrespective of the determination at a later date of the purchase price of the securities distributed."

Item 37 — Documents Incorporated by Reference

37.1 — Mandatory Incorporation by Reference

If the investment fund is in continuous distribution, incorporate by reference the following documents in the prospectus, by means of the following statement in substantially the following words under the heading "Documents Incorporated by Reference":

"Additional information about the Fund is available in the following documents:

    1. The most recently filed comparative annual financial statements of the investment fund, together with the accompanying report of the auditor.

    2. Any interim financial report of the investment fund filed after those annual financial statements.

    3. The most recently filed annual management report of fund performance of the investment fund.

    4. Any interim management report of fund performance of the investment fund filed after that annual management report of fund performance.

These documents are incorporated by reference into the prospectus, which means that they legally form part of this document just as if they were printed as part of this document. You can get a copy of these documents, at your request, and at no cost, by calling [toll-free/collect] [insert the toll-free telephone number or telephone number where collect calls are accepted] or from your dealer.

[If applicable] These documents are available on the [investment fund's/investment fund family's] Internet site at [insert investment fund's Internet site address], or by contacting the [investment fund/investment fund family] at [insert investment fund's /investment fund family's email address].

These documents and other information about the Fund are available on the Internet at www.sedar.com."

37.2 — Mandatory Incorporation by Reference of Future Documents

If the investment fund is in continuous distribution, state that any documents, of the type described in section 37.1, if filed by the investment fund after the date of the prospectus and before the termination of the distribution, are deemed to be incorporated by reference in the prospectus.

Item 38 — Financial Disclosure

38.1 — Financial Statements

(1) Unless incorporated by reference under Item 37, include in the prospectus the comparative annual financial statements and the auditor's report prepared in accordance with NI 81-106 for the investment fund's most recently completed financial year.

(2) If an investment fund's most recent financial year ended within 90 days of the date of the prospectus referred to in subsection (1), the investment fund may treat the previous year as the most recently completed financial year under subsection (1).

(3) If the investment fund has not completed its first financial year, the fund must include in the prospectus audited financial statements and the auditor's report prepared in accordance with NI 81-106 for the period from the date of the fund's formation to a date not more than 90 days before the date of the prospectus and as at a date not more than 90 days before the date of the prospectus, as applicable.

(4) Despite subsections (1) and (3), if the investment fund is a newly established fund, include in the prospectus the opening statement of financial position of the investment fund, accompanied by the auditor's report prepared in accordance with NI 81-106.

38.2 — Interim Financial Reports

Unless incorporated by reference under Item 37, include in the prospectus financial statements for the investment fund prepared in accordance with NI 81-106 for the interim period that began immediately after the financial year to which the annual financial statements required to be included in the prospectus under section 38.1 relate, if the prospectus is filed 60 days or more after the end of that interim period.

38.3 — Management Reports of Fund Performance

Unless incorporated by reference under Item 37, include in the prospectus the most recently filed interim management report of fund performance, if filed after the most recently filed annual management report of fund performance and include the most recently filed annual management report of fund performance.

Item 39 — Certificates

39.1 — Certificate of the Investment Fund

Include a certificate of the investment fund in the following form:

"This prospectus [,together with the documents incorporated herein by reference,] constitutes full, true and plain disclosure of all material facts relating to the securities offered by this prospectus as required by the securities legislation of [insert the jurisdictions in which qualified]."

39.2 — Certificate of the Manager

Include a certificate of the manager of the investment fund in the same form as the certificate of the investment fund.

39.3 — Certificate of the Underwriter

Where a person or company is required to provide a certificate in the underwriter certificate form, the certificate must state:

"To the best of our knowledge, information and belief, this prospectus [,together with the documents incorporated herein by reference,] constitutes full, true and plain disclosure of all material facts relating to the securities offered by this prospectus as required by the securities legislation of [insert the jurisdictions in which qualified]."

39.4 — Certificate of the Promoter

If there is a promoter of the investment fund, include a certificate in the same form as the certificate of the investment fund.

39.5 — Amendments

(1) For an amendment to a prospectus that does not restate the prospectus, change "prospectus" to "prospectus dated [insert date] as amended by this amendment" wherever it appears in the statements in sections 39.1 to 39.4.

(2) For an amended and restated prospectus, change "prospectus" to "amended and restated prospectus" wherever it appears in the statements in sections 39.1 to 39.4.

39.6 — Non-offering Prospectus

For a non-offering prospectus, change "securities offered by this prospectus" to "securities previously issued by the investment fund" wherever it appears in the statements in sections 39.1 to 39.4.

Form 41-101F3 — Information Required in a Scholarship Plan Prospectus

Table of Contents

Part 4:
DISTRIBUTIONS

Part D - Detailed Plan Disclosure - Information about the Organization

General Instructions

(1) This Form describes the disclosure required in a scholarship plan prospectus. Each Item of this Form outlines disclosure requirements. Instructions as to how to complete this Form are printed in italic type.

(2) The objective of the scholarship plan prospectus is to provide information about the scholarship plan that an investor needs in order to make an informed investment decision. This Form sets out specific disclosure requirements that are in addition to the general requirement under securities legislation to provide full, true and plain disclosure of all material facts relating to the securities to be distributed.

(3) Terms defined in National Instrument 14-101 Definitions, *National Instrument 41-101* General Prospectus Requirements, *National Instrument 81-105* Mutual Fund Sales Practices, *National Instrument 81-106* Investment Fund Continuous Disclosure *or National Instrument 81-107* Independent Review Committee for Investment Funds *and used in this Form have the same meanings that they have in those national instruments except that references in those instruments to "mutual fund" must be read as references to "investment fund" or "scholarship plan" as the context requires.*

(4) A scholarship plan prospectus must contain only the information that is mandated or permitted under this Form.

(5) A scholarship plan prospectus must present the information in each Part of this Form briefly and concisely, in the order provided for by this Form, and use only the headings and sub-headings stipulated in this Form except that sub-headings not required by this Form may be used where permitted under an Item in this Form.

(6) Specific instructions are sometimes provided in this Form for a single prospectus and a multiple prospectus. Portions of Part B and Part D of this Form generally refer to disclosure required for "a scholarship plan" in a "prospectus". This disclosure must be modified as appropriate to reflect multiple scholarship plans covered by a multiple prospectus.

(7) National Instrument 41-101 requires that a prospectus be prepared using plain language and in a format that assists in readability and comprehension. For additional guidance, see the plain language principles listed in section 4.1 of Companion Policy 41-101 CP General Prospectus Requirements. If the use of technical terms is required, clear and concise explanations of those terms must be included.

(8) Respond as simply and directly to the requirements of this Form as is reasonably possible.

(9) No reference need be made to inapplicable items and, unless otherwise required in this Form, negative answers to items may be omitted.

(10) Certain Items in this Form require that a prospectus include wording that is the same or substantially the same as set out in those Items. A scholarship plan may modify the prescribed wording to more accurately reflect its features if the wording does not apply to the plan.

(11) Unless otherwise stated, this Form does not mandate the use of a specific font size or style but the font used must be legible. If the prospectus is made available online, information must be presented in a way that is both readable online and can be printed in a readable format.

(12) A prospectus may contain photographs and artwork only if they are relevant to the business of the scholarship plan or members of the organization of the scholarship plan and are not misleading.

(13) A prospectus must not contain design elements (e.g., graphics, photos, artwork) that would, to a reasonable person, detract from the information disclosed in the document.

(14) If disclosure is required as of a specific date and there has been a material change or a change that is otherwise significant to a reasonable investor to the required information subsequent to that date, present the information as of the date of the change or a date subsequent to the change.

Contents of a Scholarship Plan Prospectus

(15) This Form permits two formats: a prospectus for a single scholarship plan and a multiple prospectus for multiple scholarship plans.

(16) A scholarship plan prospectus must consist of four parts as set out below. Part A is the Plan Summary. Parts B, C and D are collectively the Detailed Plan Disclosure. The Plan Summary and the Detailed Plan Disclosure together form the scholarship plan prospectus. The four parts may be further described as follows:

(a) Part A contains the responses to the Items in Part A of this Form. The information in this Part contains a summary of key information about investing in a scholarship plan.

(b) Part B contains the responses to the Items in Part B of this Form and contains introductory information about the scholarship plan and general information about the scholarship plan family.

(c) Part C contains the responses to the Items in Part C of the Form and contains plan-specific information about the scholarship plan(s) offered in the prospectus.

(d) Part D contains the responses to the Items in Part D of this Form and contains information about the scholarship plan organization, the persons and entities involved in running the scholarship plan, and the prospectus certificates.

Consolidation of Scholarship Plan Prospectuses into a Multiple Prospectus

(17) Section 3A.2 of National Instrument 41-101 requires that a scholarship plan prospectus must not be consolidated with one or more scholarship plan prospectuses to form a multiple prospectus unless the disclosure in each of the Part B and Part D sections of this Form is substantially similar for each scholarship plan. This provision permits a scholarship plan organization to create a document that contains the disclosure for a number of scholarship plans in the same family.

(18) Similar to a single prospectus, a multiple prospectus must consist of four segments:

(a) The first segment consists of a number of Part A sections of this Form. Each Part A section must contain the information required under Part A of this Form about a single scholarship plan. The information required by the Part A section must be disclosed separately for each scholarship plan in the multiple prospectus. Each Part A section in a multiple prospectus must start on a new page.

(b) The second segment contains the information required under Part B of this Form for the scholarship plans described in the document. There must not be more than one Part B section for all of the scholarship plans in the prospectus.

(c) The third segment consists of a number of Part C sections of this Form. Each Part C section must contain the information required under Part C of this Form about a single scholarship plan. The information required by the Part C section must be disclosed separately for each scholarship plan in the multiple prospectus. Each Part C section in a multiple prospectus must start on a new page.

(d) The fourth segment contains the information required under Part D of the Form for the scholarship plans described in the document. There must not be more than one Part D section for all of the scholarship plans in the prospectus.

Part A — Plan Summary for a Scholarship Plan

Item 1 — Information about the Plan

Include at the top of a new page a heading consisting of

(a) the title "Plan Summary",

(b) the name of the scholarship plan to which the Plan Summary pertains and, if the scholarship plan has more than one class or series of securities, the name of the class or series of securities covered in the Plan Summary,

(c) the type of scholarship plan,

(d) the name of the investment fund manager of the scholarship plan, and

(e) the date of the Plan Summary.

INSTRUCTIONS

(1) The title "Plan Summary" and the name of the scholarship plan must be in bold type using a substantially larger font size than the other headings and text in the Plan Summary.

(2) The "type of scholarship plan" refers to whether the scholarship plan is a group scholarship plan, individual or family scholarship plan.

(3) The date for a Plan Summary that is filed as part of a preliminary scholarship plan prospectus or scholarship plan prospectus must be the date of the certificate of the scholarship plan required under Part D of this Form.

Item 2 — Withdrawal and Cancellation Rights

Immediately following the disclosure in Item 1, state the following using the same or substantially similar wording, with the last two sentences in bold type:

This summary tells you some key things about investing in the plan. You should read this Plan Summary and the Detailed Plan Disclosure carefully before you decide to invest.

If you change your mind

You have up to 60 days after signing your contract to withdraw from your plan and get back all of your money.

If you (or we) cancel your plan after 60 days, you'll get back your contributions, less sales charges and fees. You will lose the earnings on your money. Your government grants will be returned to the government. **Keep in mind that you pay sales charges up front. If you cancel your plan in the first few years, you could end up with much less than you put in.**

INSTRUCTION

The prescribed wording in this Item must be presented using a substantially larger font size relative to the rest of the text of the Plan Summary.

Item 3 — Description of the Scholarship Plan

(1) Under the heading "What is the [*insert type of scholarship plan*] scholarship plan?", state the following using the same or substantially similar wording:

The [*insert name of plan*] is a [*insert type of plan*] scholarship plan designed to help you save for a child's post-secondary education. When you open your [*insert name of plan*], we will apply to the Canada Revenue Agency to register the plan as a Registered Education Savings Plan (RESP). This allows your savings to grow tax-free until the child named as the beneficiary of the plan enrols in their studies. The Government of Canada and some provincial governments offer government grants to help you save even more. To register your plan as an RESP, we need social insurance numbers for yourself and the child you name in the plan as the beneficiary.

In a [*insert type of plan*] scholarship plan, you are part of a group of investors. Everyone's contributions are invested together. When the plan matures, each child in the group shares in the earnings on that money. Your share of those earnings plus your government grant money is paid to your child as educational assistance payments (EAPs).

There are two main exceptions. Your child will not receive EAPs, and you could lose your earnings, government grants and grant contribution room, if:

- your child does not enrol in a school or program that qualifies under this plan, or

- you leave the plan before it matures.

(2) For a group scholarship plan, state the following using the same or substantially similar wording, in bold type:

If you leave the plan, your earnings go to the remaining members of the group. However, if you stay in the plan until it matures, you might share in the earnings of those who left early.

INSTRUCTION

If the scholarship plan allows a subscriber to name more than one beneficiary at a time, amend the wording in section (1) to refer to multiple children or beneficiaries.

Item 4 — Suitability

(1) For a group scholarship plan, under the heading "Who is this plan for?", state the following using the same or substantially similar wording:

> A group scholarship plan can be a long-term commitment. It is for investors planning to save for a child's post-secondary education and who are fairly sure that:
>
> - they can make all their contributions on time
> - they will stay in the plan until it matures
> - their child will attend a qualifying school and program under the plan
>
> [Insert, for plan providers that also offer an individual or family scholarship plan — If this doesn't describe you, you should consider another type of plan. For example, an individual or family plan has fewer restrictions. See the Plan Summar[y/ies] for our [insert as applicable — individual plan/family plan/ individual and family plans] or pages [insert applicable page references] in the Detailed Plan Disclosure for more information.]

(2) For an individual or family scholarship plan, under the heading "Who is this plan for?", state the following using the same or substantially similar wording:

> [Insert, as applicable — An individual/ A family] scholarship plan is for investors planning to save for a child's post-secondary education and who are fairly sure that:
>
> - [Insert, for family plans only — they want to save for more than one child at a time]
> - they want more flexibility over when and how much to contribute to their plan
> - [Insert, for individual plans only — their child will attend a qualifying school and program under the plan
> - [Insert, for family plans only — one or more of their children will attend a qualifying school or program under the plan]
>
> [Insert, for plan providers that also offer a group scholarship plan — The [insert name of plan] generally has fewer restrictions and is more flexible than our group scholarship plan.]

Item 5 — The Plan's Investments

Under the heading "What does the plan invest in?", state the following using the same or substantially similar wording:

> The plan invests mainly in [specify the plan's primary investments]. The plan's investments have some risk. Returns will vary from year to year.

INSTRUCTION

The disclosure must state the type or types of securities, such as mortgages, bonds, government treasury bills, or equity securities, as applicable, in which the plan will be primarily invested under normal market conditions.

Item 6 — Contributions

(1) For a group scholarship plan, under the heading "How do I make contributions?", state the following using the same or substantially similar wording:

> With your contributions, you buy one or more "units" of the plan. These units represent your share of the plan. You may pay for them all at once, or you may make [state the most common contribution frequency options] contributions.
>
> You may change the amount of your contribution as long as you make the minimum contribution permitted under the plan. You may also change your contribution schedule after you've opened your plan. [Insert if applicable — A fee applies.]All of the different contribution options for the plan are described in the Detailed Plan Disclosure, or you can ask your sales representative for more information.

(2) For an individual or family scholarship plan, under the heading "How do I make contributions?", briefly describe how a subscriber can make contributions to their scholarship plan.

(3) State (i) the minimum total investment and (ii) the minimum amount per contribution, permitted under the scholarship plan's rules.

INSTRUCTIONS

(1) The disclosure regarding contribution frequency options in the first paragraph of subsection (1) of Item 6 must make reference only to the most commonly selected contribution options, and not to each contribution option that is available to a subscriber.

(2) If the individual or family scholarship plan uses the concept of "units" or has prescribed schedules for making contributions, this fact must be described in the required disclosure for subsection (2) of Item 6, using wording that is similar to the wording in subsection (1) of Item 6.

(3) For the purposes of the disclosure required under subsection (3) of Item 6, the "minimum total investment permitted under the scholarship plan's rules" must be stated as (i) a dollar amount or (ii) a quantity of units or securities of the scholarship plan (if applicable), and the "minimum amount per contribution under the plan's rules" must be stated as a dollar amount.

Item 7 — Payments

(1) Under the heading "What can I expect to receive from the plan?", state the following using the same or substantially similar wording:

> In your child's first year of college or university, you'll get back your contributions, less fees. You can have this money paid to you or directly to your child.

(2) For a group scholarship plan, state the following using the same or substantially similar wording:

> Your child will be eligible to receive EAPs in their [state, as applicable — first, second, third and fourth] year[s] of post-secondary education. [See instruction (1)] For each year, your child must show proof they are enrolled in a school and program that qualifies under this plan to get an EAP.

(3) For an individual or family scholarship plan, briefly describe when EAPs can be paid to a beneficiary, and whether EAPs can be paid in one year or must be paid in instalments for each year of eligible studies.

(4) State the following, in a separate paragraph:

EAPs are taxed in the child's hands.

INSTRUCTIONS

(1) If the group scholarship plan has multiple options for paying EAPs, disclose the other options in the disclosure in subsection (2) of Item 7, using a similar format.

(2) For the disclosure in subsection (3) of Item 7, the format set out for the disclosure in section (2) must be used.

Item 8 — Risks

(1) Under the heading "What are the risks?", state the following using the same or substantially similar wording:

If you do not meet the terms of the plan, you could lose some or all of your investment. Your child may not receive their EAPs.

(2) For a group scholarship plan, state the following using the same or substantially similar wording:

You should be aware of five things that could result in a loss:

1. You leave the plan before the maturity date. People leave the plan for many reasons. For example, if their financial situation changes and they can't afford their contributions. If your plan is cancelled more than 60 days from signing your contract, you'll lose part of your contributions to sales charges and fees. You'll also lose the earnings on your investment and your government grants will be returned to the government.

2. You miss contributions. If you want to stay in the plan, you'll have to make up the contributions you missed. You'll also have to make up what the contributions would have earned if you had made them on time. This could be costly.

If you have difficulty making contributions, you have options. You can reduce or suspend your contributions, transfer to another of our plans or to an RESP offered by a different provider, or cancel your plan. Restrictions and fees apply. Some options will result in a loss of earnings and government grants. [*Insert if applicable* — If you miss a contribution and don't take any action within [*insert the number of months*] months, we may cancel your plan].

3. You miss or your child misses a deadline. This can limit your options later on. You could also lose the earnings on your investment. Two of the key deadlines for this plan are:

- **Maturity date — the deadline for making changes to your plan**

  You have until the maturity date to make changes to your plan. This includes switching the plan to a different child, changing the maturity date if your child wants to start their program sooner or later than expected, and transferring to another RESP. Restrictions and fees apply.

- **[*Insert date*] — the EAP application deadline**

  If your child qualifies for an EAP, he or she must apply by [*insert date*] before each year of eligible studies to receive a payment for that year. Otherwise, your child may lose this money.

4. Your child doesn't go to a qualifying school or program. For example, [*State the types of programs or institutions that generally do not qualify for EAPs under the plan*] don't qualify for EAPs under this plan. [*Insert, if applicable* -Under this plan, fewer programs will qualify for an EAP than would otherwise qualify under the government's rules for RESPs. See the Detailed Plan Disclosure for more information.] If your child will not be going to a qualifying school or program under this plan, you have the option to name another child as beneficiary, transfer to another of our plans or to an RESP offered by a different provider, or cancel your plan. Restrictions and fees apply. Some options can result in a loss of earnings and government grants.

5. Your child doesn't complete their program. Your child may lose some or all of their EAPs if he or she takes time off from their studies, does not complete all required courses in a year or changes programs. [*Insert if applicable* — In some cases, your child may be able to defer an EAP for up to [*insert number of years*] year[s]]. [*Insert, if applicable* — Deferrals are at our discretion.]

(3) For an individual or family scholarship plan, list no more than 5 situations that could result in a loss of earnings in the scholarship plan for subscribers or EAPs for the beneficiary. Briefly describe the losses that could result in these outcomes as well as some options to mitigate this loss.

(4) State the following, in bold type:

If any of these situations arise with your plan, contact us or speak with your sales representative to better understand your options to reduce your risk of loss.

INSTRUCTIONS

(1) For an individual or family scholarship plan, the disclosure required in subsection (3) of Item 8 must include the following situations: a subscriber leaving a scholarship plan before it matures, a beneficiary failing to enrol in a qualifying school or program, and the subscriber or beneficiary failing to meet the scholarship plan's key deadlines.

(2) If the individual or family scholarship plan uses the concept of units paid for under a fixed contribution schedule, or otherwise requires subscribers to follow a prescribed schedule for making contributions to the scholarship plan, the disclosure required in subsection (3) of Item 8 must also include a situation in which a subscriber misses one or more contributions.

(3) The disclosure in subsection (3) of Item 8 must use a similar format and structure as the disclosure required for group scholarship plans in section (2).

Item 9 — Cancellation Rate

For a group scholarship plan, using the margin of the page, add a sidebar under the heading "What are the risks?", and state the following using the same or substantially similar wording with the title of the sidebar in bold type:

Cancellation Rate

Of the last five beneficiary groups of the [insert name of group scholarship plan] plan to reach maturity, an average of [see the Instructions]% of the plans in each group were cancelled before their maturity date.

INSTRUCTIONS

(1) To calculate the average percentage as required under Item 9, do the following:

(a) for each of the last five beneficiary groups in the group scholarship plan to reach maturity, calculate the percentage of scholarship plans in the beneficiary group that were cancelled before their maturity date, and

(b) calculate the simple average of the five percentages calculated pursuant to Instruction 1(a).

(2) For a beneficiary group referred to in Instruction (1)(a), calculate the percentage of the scholarship plans in each beneficiary group that were cancelled before their maturity date by dividing x by y, where

x   = *the number of scholarship plans with the same maturity date that were cancelled before maturity, and*

y   = *the total number of scholarship plans with the same maturity date, including plans with the same maturity date that were cancelled before maturity.*

(3) For the purposes of the disclosure required under Item 9, a "plan that was cancelled before maturity" is a scholarship plan that is not eligible to receive a share of the EAP account as at the maturity date because the total contributions required by the subscriber's contract have not been made by the maturity date. The number of scholarship plans with the same maturity date that did not reach maturity will be the difference between the total number of scholarship plans with the same maturity date and the number of scholarship plans that matured.

(4) Subject to Instruction (6), the number of scholarship plans with the same maturity date consists of every scholarship plan sold to subscribers who selected the same maturity date, including scholarship plans that were cancelled or transferred before maturity.

(5) For the purposes of calculating the percentage of scholarship plans in a beneficiary group that were cancelled before maturity, a scholarship plan whose subscriber changed the maturity date to an earlier date is considered to have the earlier maturity date and must be included in the calculations for the beneficiary group with the earlier maturity date. Similarly, a scholarship plan whose subscriber changed the maturity date to a later date is considered to have the later maturity date and must be included in the calculations for the beneficiary group with the later maturity date.

(6) Do not include a plan in the calculation of x or y under Instruction (2) if the subscriber withdrew from their scholarship plan within 60 days of the signing the contract to open the scholarship plan and received back all of their contributions and fees paid.

Item 10 — Costs

(1) Under the heading "How much does it cost?", provide information, in the form of the following tables, about the fees and expenses of the scholarship plan. Introduce the tables using the following wording or wording that is the same or substantially similar:

There are costs for joining and participating in the plan. The following tables show the fees and expenses of the plan. [*Insert, if applicable* — The fees and expenses of this plan are different than the other plans we offer.]

Fees you pay

These fees are deducted from the money you put in the plan. They reduce the amount that gets invested in your plan, which will reduce the amount available for EAPs.

Fee	What you pay	What the fee is for	Who the fee is paid to
Sales charge	[*Specify amount*]	This is the commission for selling your plan	[*Insert name of entity*]
Account maintenance fee	[*Specify amount*]	[*Specify the purpose of the fee*]	[*Insert name of entity*]
[*Insert if applicable* — Insurance Premium]	[*Specify amount*]	This is for insurance that makes sure your contributions continue if you die or become totally disabled.	[*Insert name of entity*]

Fees the plan pays

You don't pay these fees directly. They're paid from the plan's earnings. These fees affect you because they reduce the plan's returns, which reduces the amount available for EAPs.

Fee	What the plan pays	What the fee is for	Who the fee is paid to
Administrative fee	[*Specify amount*]	This is for operating your plan.	[*insert name of entity*]
Portfolio management fee	[*Specify amount*]	This is for managing the plan's investments.	[*insert name of entity*]
Custodian fee	[*Specify amount*]	This is for holding the plan's investments in trust.	[*Insert name of entity*]
Independent review committee	[*Specify amount*]	This is for the services of the plan's independent review committee. The committee reviews conflict of interest matters between the investment fund manager and the plan.	[*Insert name of entity*]

(2) If the sales charge listed in the "Fees you pay" table required by subsection (1) is deducted from contributions at a higher rate in the early period of participating in the scholarship plan, add a sidebar under the heading "How much does it cost", using the margin of the page adjacent to the table titled "Fees you pay", and state the following using the same or substantially similar wording with the title of the sidebar in bold type:

Paying off the sales charge

If, for example, you buy one unit of the plan on behalf of your newborn child, and you commit to paying for that unit by making monthly contributions until your plan's maturity date, then, based on how the sales charge is deducted from your contributions, it will take [*insert number of months*] months to pay off the sales charge. During this time, [*insert percentage*]% of your contributions will be invested in the plan.

(3) Using the margin of the page adjacent to the table titled "Fees the plan pays", add a sidebar under the heading "How much does it cost?", and state the following using the same or substantially similar wording with the title of the sidebar in bold:

Other fees

Other fees apply if you make changes to your plan. See page [*specify page number*] in the Detailed Plan Disclosure for details.

INSTRUCTIONS

(1) The tables must only summarize the most common fees that (i) all subscribers to the scholarship plan are required to pay or (ii) the scholarship plan is required to pay, as applicable. Do not include the entire list of fees required to be disclosed under Items 14.2 and 14.3 of Part C of the Form, or any of the fees required to be disclosed under Item 14.4 and 14.5 of Part C of the Form. Each fee must be listed in a separate row of the applicable table.

(2) If there are certain types of fees listed in the tables required under Item 10 above that are not payable, either by subscribers or the scholarship plan, in respect of the scholarship plan described in the Plan Summary, amend the tables as is necessary to reflect that fact.

(3) If certain fees listed in the tables required under Item 10 above are normally combined into a single fee payable by either the subscriber or the scholarship plan as applicable, the tables may be amended as is necessary to accurately reflect that fact.

(4) State the amount of each fee listed in the tables. In the table titled "Fees you pay" state the amount(s) in the column titled "What you pay". In the table titled "Fees the plan pays" state the amount(s) in the column titled "What the plan pays". The amount of each fee must be disclosed based on how the fee is calculated. For example, if a particular fee is calculated as a fixed dollar amount per unit, or a fixed amount per year, it must be stated as such. Similarly, if a fee is calculated as a percentage of the scholarship plan's assets, that percentage must be stated. A statement or note that a fee is subject to applicable taxes, such as goods and services taxes or harmonized sales taxes, is permitted, if applicable.

(5) For a group scholarship plan or other type of scholarship plan that normally calculates the sales charge payable as a fixed dollar amount linked to the amount of contribution by a subscriber (i.e. x.x x$ per unit), in addition to stating the fixed amount of sales charge per unit as required under Instruction (3), the disclosure of the amount of the sales charge in the table titled "Fees you pay" in the column titled "What you pay" must also be expressed as a percentage of the cost of a unit of the scholarship plan. If the total cost of a unit of the scholarship plan varies depending on the contribution option or frequency selected, the percentage sales charge must be expressed as a range, between the lowest and the highest percentage of the unit cost the sales charge can represent, based on the different contribution options available to subscribers under the scholarship plan. This must be calculated as follows: (i) divide the sales charge per unit by the contribution option that has the highest total cost per unit, and (ii) divide the sales charge per unit by the contribution option that has the lowest total cost per unit. For example, if a scholarship plan calculates its sales charge as $200/unit, and the total cost per unit for a subscriber can range from $1000 to $5000 (based on the different options available to subscribers), the percentage range of the sales charge disclosed in the table would be 4% (200/5000) to 20% (200/1000). The disclosure in the table must also state that the exact percentage of the sales charge per unit for a subscriber will depend on the contribution option selected for contributing to the scholarship plan and how old their beneficiary is at the time they open the scholarship plan.

(6) For the table titled "Fees you pay", in the column titled ""What you pay" describe how the fee is deducted from contributions if the amount deducted from each contribution is not the same. For example, if deductions for sales charges are not made from each contribution at a constant rate for the duration of a subscriber's investment in the scholarship plan or the duration for which contributions are required to be made if it is less than the scholarship plan's duration, describe the amounts from contributions that are deducted for sales charges.

(7) In both tables, in the column titled "What the fee is for" provide a concise explanation of what the fee is used for, using the same or substantially similar wording provided above in the tables.

(8) In both tables, in the column titled "Who the fee is paid to", state the name of the entity to which the fee is paid, e.g. the investment fund manager, the portfolio manager, the principal distributor or dealer, the foundation, etc.

(9) For the table titled "Fees the plan pays", the independent review committee fee must be disclosed as the total dollar amount paid in connection with the independent review committee for the most recently completed financial year of the scholarship plan.

(10) Disclosure of insurance premiums in the "Fees you pay" table is permitted only if the scholarship plan requires a subscriber to purchase insurance coverage in a jurisdiction in which the scholarship plan's securities are being distributed. If the scholarship plan's rules only require insurance coverage to be purchased by subscribers in some, but not all jurisdictions in which the scholarship plan's securities are distributed, then include disclosure stating the jurisdictions in which the scholarship plan requires subscribers to purchase insurance, under the heading titled "What the fee is for" in that table.

(11) The disclosure required under subsection (2) of Item 10 must be based on the following assumptions: (i) the beneficiary is a newborn, (ii) the subscriber is purchasing one unit of the scholarship plan, (iii) the subscriber has agreed to a monthly contribution schedule with contributions payable until the scholarship plan's maturity date, and (iv) all of the mandatory fees that are normally deducted from a subscriber's contributions are deducted during the relevant period.

(12)For the disclosure required in subsection (2) of Item 10, if the scholarship plan does not offer units but uses a similar method for deducting sales charges as is described under subsection (2) of Item 10, the wording may be amended as is necessary to properly reflect the scholarship plan's features.

(13) The "Other fees" sidebar required under subsection (3) of Item 10 refers to fees for specific transactions, such as changing a beneficiary, that are described in the table titled "Transaction Fees" in Item 14.4 of Part C of the Form.

Item 11 — Guarantees

Under the heading "Are there any guarantees?", state the following using the same or substantially similar wording:

> We cannot tell you in advance if your child will qualify to receive any payments from the plan or how much your child will receive. We do not guarantee the amount of any payments or that the payments will cover the full cost of your child's post-secondary education.

> Unlike bank accounts or GICs, investments in scholarship plans are not covered by the Canada Deposit Insurance Corporation or any other government insurer.

Item 12 — For More Information

(1) Under the sub-heading "For more information", state the following using the same or substantially similar wording:

> The Detailed Plan Disclosure delivered with this Plan Summary contains further details about this plan, and we recommend you read it. You may also contact [*insert name of investment fund manager*] or your sales representative for more information about this plan.

(2) State the name, address and toll-free telephone number of the investment fund manager of the plan and, if applicable, state the e-mail address and website of the investment fund manager of the plan.

Part B — Detailed Plan Disclosure — General Information

Item 1 — Cover Page Disclosure

1.1 — Preliminary Prospectus Disclosure

A preliminary prospectus must have printed in red ink and in italics at the top of the cover page of the Detailed Plan Disclosure immediately above the disclosure required in section 1.2 the following:

> *A copy of this preliminary prospectus has been filed with the securities regulatory authorit[y/ies] in [insert, as applicable the names of the provinces and territories of Canada] but has not yet become final for the purpose of the sale of securities. Information contained in this preliminary prospectus may not be complete and may have to be amended. The securities may not be sold until a receipt for the prospectus is obtained from the securities regulatory authorit[y/ies].*

INSTRUCTION

A scholarship plan must complete the bracketed information by:

> *(a) inserting the names of each jurisdiction in which the scholarship plan intends to offer securities under the prospectus,*

> *(b) stating that the filing has been made in each of the provinces of Canada or each of the provinces and territories of Canada, or*

> *(c) identifying the filing jurisdictions by exception (i.e., every province of Canada or every province and territory of Canada, except [insert excluded jurisdictions]).*

1.2 — Required Statement

State in italics at the top of the cover page the following:

> *No securities regulatory authority has expressed an opinion about these securities and it is an offence to claim otherwise.*

1.3 — Basic Disclosure about the Distribution

(1) State the following immediately below the disclosure required under sections 1.1 and 1.2:

[*Insert as applicable* — PRELIMINARY/ PRO FORMA] PROSPECTUS

CONTINUOUS OFFERING

DETAILED PLAN DISCLOSURE

[*Insert Date*]

[*Insert Name of Scholarship Plan(s)*]

[*State the type of securities qualified for distribution under the prospectus, and the price per security or minimum subscription amount*]

(2) State the following:

> [*Insert, as applicable* — This/These] investment fund[s] [*insert, as applicable* — is a/are] scholarship plan[s] that [*Insert, as applicable* — is/are] managed by [*state the name of the investment fund manager of the scholarship plan*].

INSTRUCTION

Write the date in full with the name of the month in words. A pro forma prospectus does not have to be dated, but may reflect the anticipated date of the prospectus.

Item 2 — Inside Cover Page

2.1 — Introduction

Starting on a new page on the inside cover page under the heading "Important information to know before you invest", include an introduction to the information provided in response to sections 2.2, 2.3, and 2.4 of this Part using the following wording:

> The following is important information you should know if you are considering an investment in a scholarship plan.

2.2 — No Social Insurance Number

Under the sub-heading "No social insurance number = No government grants, no tax benefits", state the following using the same or substantially similar wording with the last paragraph in bold type:

We need social insurance numbers for you and each child named as a beneficiary under the plan before we can register your plan as a Registered Education Savings Plan (RESP). The *Income Tax Act* (Canada) won't allow us to register your plan as an RESP without these social insurance numbers. Your plan must be registered before it can:

- qualify for the tax benefits of an RESP, and

- receive any government grants.

You can provide the beneficiary's social insurance number after the plan is open. If you don't provide the beneficiary's social insurance number when you sign your contract with us, we'll put your contributions into an unregistered education savings account. During the time your contributions are held in this account, we will deduct sales charges and fees from your contributions as described under "Costs of investing in this plan" in the prospectus. You will be taxed on any income earned in this account.

If we receive the beneficiary's social insurance number within [*insert the number of months — see Instruction (1)*] months of your application date, we'll transfer your contributions and the income they earned to your registered plan.

If we do not receive the social insurance numbers within [*insert number of months — see Instruction (1)*] months of your application date, we'll cancel your plan. You'll get back your contributions and the income earned, less sales charges and fees. Since you pay sales charges up front, you could end up with much less than you put in.

If you don't expect to get the social insurance number for your beneficiary within [*insert number of months — see Instruction (1)*] months of your application date, you should not enrol or make contributions to the plan.

INSTRUCTIONS

(1) State the maximum number of months after the application date of a subscriber's plan the following which the investment fund manager will cancel the scholarship plan for failure to provide the social insurance numbers required for registering the scholarship plan as an RESP.

(2) If the scholarship plan's rules do not permit a subscriber to open the plan or accept contributions without the beneficiary's social insurance number, amend the disclosure in this section to reflect that fact.

2.3 — Payments Not Guaranteed

(1) Following the disclosure required under section 2.2, state the following, on the inside cover page under the sub-heading "Payments not guaranteed", using the same or substantially similar wording:

We cannot tell you in advance if your beneficiary will qualify to receive any educational assistance payments (EAPs) [*insert, if applicable — or any discretionary payments*] from the plan or how much your beneficiary will receive. We do not guarantee the amount of any payments or that they will cover the full cost of your beneficiary's post-secondary education.

(2) For a group scholarship plan, under the sub-heading "Payments from group plans depend on several factors", state the following using the same or substantially similar wording:

The amount of the EAPs from a group plan will depend on how much the plan earns and the number of beneficiaries in the group who do not qualify for payments.

(3) If the scholarship plan provides for any discretionary payments, immediately following the disclosure required under subsection 2.3(1) or 2.3(2), as applicable, list the discretionary payments that may be provided and state the following using the same or substantially similar wording with the first sentence in bold type:

Discretionary payments are not guaranteed. You must not count on receiving a discretionary payment. The [*insert the name of the entity funding the discretionary payment*] decides if it will make a payment in any year and how much the payment will be. If the [*insert the name of the entity funding the discretionary payment*] makes a payment, you may get less than what has been paid in the past.

(4) Under the sub-heading "Understand the risks", state the following using the same or substantially similar wording in bold type:

If you withdraw your contributions early or do not meet the terms of the plan, you could lose some or all of your money. Make sure you understand the risks before you invest. Carefully read the information found under "Risks of investing in a scholarship plan" and "Risks of investing in this plan" in this Detailed Plan Disclosure.

2.4 — Withdrawal and Cancellation Rights

Under the sub-heading "If you change your mind", state the following using the same or substantially similar wording with the last two sentences in bold type:

You have up to 60 days after signing your contract to withdraw from your plan and get back all of your money.

If you (or we) cancel your plan after 60 days, you'll get back your contributions, less sales charges and fees. You will lose the earnings on your money. Your government grants will be returned to the government. **Keep in mind that you pay sales charges up front. If you cancel your plan in the first few years, you could end up with much less than you put in.**

Item 3 — Table of Contents

3.1 — Table of Contents

(1) Include a table of contents.

(2) Begin the table of contents on a new page.

Part 4:
DISTRIBUTIONS

(3) Include in the table of contents, under the heading "Specific information about our plan[s]", a list of all of the scholarship plans offered under the prospectus, with a reference to the page numbers where the plan-specific information about each scholarship plan required to be provided under Part C of this Form can be found.

Item 4 — *Introduction and Glossary*

4.1 — Introduction and Documents Incorporated by Reference

(1) On a new page or immediately after the table of contents, under the heading "Introduction", incorporate by reference the following documents in the prospectus by using the following wording or wording that is substantially similar:

> This Detailed Plan Disclosure contains information to help you make an informed decision about investing in our scholarship plan[s] and to understand your rights as an investor. It describes the plan[s] and how [it/they] work[s], including the fees you pay, the risks of investing in a plan and how to make changes to your plan. It also contains information about our organization. The prospectus is comprised of both this Detailed Plan Disclosure and each Plan Summary that was delivered with it.
>
> You can find additional information about the plan[s] in the following documents:
>
> - the plan's most recently filed annual financial statements,
> - any interim financial reports filed after the annual financial statements, and
> - the most recently filed annual management report of fund performance.
>
> These documents are incorporated by reference into the prospectus. That means they legally form part of this document just as if they were printed as part of this document.
>
> You can get a copy of these documents at no cost by calling us at [*insert the toll-free telephone number or telephone number where collect calls are accepted*] or by contacting us at [*insert the scholarship plan's e-mail address*].
>
> [*Insert if applicable* — You'll also find these documents on our website at [*insert the scholarship plan's website address*]].
>
> These documents and other information about the plan[s] are also available at www.sedar.com.

(2) State that any documents of the type described in subsection 4.1(1) above, if filed by the scholarship plan after the date of the prospectus and before the termination of the distribution, are deemed to be incorporated by reference in the prospectus.

(3) Include a description of each of the documents referred to in subsection 4.1(1) above and briefly explain the importance each document.

4.2 — Terms Used in the Prospectus

Under the heading "Terms used in this prospectus", provide the following list of defined terms using the same or substantially similar wording:

> In this document, "we", "us" and "our" refer to [*name of entities involved in the administration and distribution of scholarship plan securities*]. "You" refers to potential investors, subscribers and beneficiaries.
>
> The following are definitions of some key terms you will find in this prospectus:
>
> **Accumulated income payment (AIP)**: the earnings on your contributions and/or government grants that you may get from your plan if your beneficiary does not pursue post-secondary education and you meet certain conditions set by the federal government or by the plan.
>
> **AIP**: see Accumulated income payment.
>
> **Application date**: the date you opened your plan with us, which is the date you sign your contract.
>
> **Attrition**: under a group plan, a reduction in the number of beneficiaries who qualify for EAPs in a beneficiary group. See also pre-maturity attrition and post-maturity attrition.
>
> **Beneficiary**: the person you name to receive EAPs under the plan.
>
> **Beneficiary group**: beneficiaries in a group plan who have the same year of eligibility. They are typically born in the same year.
>
> **Contract**: the agreement you enter into with us when you open your education savings plan.
>
> **Contribution**: the amount you pay into a plan. Sales charges and other fees are deducted from your contributions and the remaining amount is invested in your plan.
>
> **Discretionary payment**: a payment, other than a fee refund, that beneficiaries may receive in addition to their EAPs, as determined by [*insert name of entity funding the discretionary payment*] in its discretion.
>
> **Discretionary payment account**: any account that holds money used to fund discretionary payments to beneficiaries.
>
> **EAP**: see Educational Assistance Payment.
>
> **EAP account**: for group plans, an account that holds the income earned on contributions made by subscribers. There is a separate EAP account for each beneficiary group. An EAP account includes the income earned on contributions of subscribers who have cancelled their plan or whose plan was cancelled by us. The money in this account is distributed to the remaining beneficiaries in the beneficiary group as part of their EAPs.
>
> **Earnings**: any money earned on your (i) contributions and (ii) government grants, such as interest and capital gains. For group plans, it does not include any income earned in the discretionary payment account, such as interest earned on income after the maturity date.
>
> **Educational assistance payment (EAP)**: In general, an EAP is a payment made to your beneficiary after the maturity date for eligible studies. An EAP consists of your earnings and your government grants. [*Insert, if the prospectus includes a group scholarship plan* — For a group plan, an EAP consists of your government grants, earnings on your government grants and your beneficiary's share of the EAP account.] EAPs do not include discretionary payments or fee refunds.
>
> **Eligible studies**: a post-secondary educational program that meets the plan's requirements for a beneficiary to receive EAPs.
>
> **Government Grant**: any financial grant, bond or incentive offered by the federal government, (such as the Canada Education Savings Grant, or the Canada Learning Bond), or by a provincial government, to assist with saving for post-secondary education in an RESP.

Grant contribution room: the amount of government grant you are eligible for under a federal or provincial government grant program.

Income: has the same meaning as Earnings.

Maturity date: the date on which the plan matures. In general, it is in the year your beneficiary is expected to enrol in their first year of post-secondary education.

Plan: means [*list the name(s) of each of scholarship plan sold under this prospectus*], [*insert for a multiple prospectus* — each] a scholarship plan that provides funding for a beneficiary's post-secondary education.

Post-maturity attrition: under a group plan, a reduction in the number of beneficiaries who qualify for EAPs in a beneficiary group after the maturity date. See also **Attrition**.

Pre-maturity attrition: under a group plan, a reduction in the number of beneficiaries who qualify for EAPs in a beneficiary group before the maturity date. See also Attrition.

Subscriber: the person who enters into a contract with [*insert legal name of entity entering into contract with subscribers*] to make contributions to a plan.

Unit: under a group plan, a unit represents your beneficiary's proportionate share of the EAP account. The terms of the contract you sign determine the value of the unit.

Year of eligibility: the year in which a beneficiary is first eligible to receive EAPs under a plan. For a group plan, it is typically the year the beneficiary will enter his or her [*insert as applicable* — first or second] academic year of eligible studies. In general, the year of eligibility is [*insert as applicable* — one year after/ the same year as] the maturity date. For other types of plans, the year of eligibility can be any time after the maturity date.

INSTRUCTIONS

(1) The list of defined terms must not contain material information not found elsewhere in the prospectus. The glossary must be limited to the terms provided.

(2) Use the terms set out in section 4.2 in the prospectus to facilitate comparability between scholarship plans.

(3) Include only the terms that are applicable to a scholarship plan included in the prospectus. For example, a prospectus that does not include a group scholarship plan must not include those terms that would be applicable only to a group scholarship plan.

Item 5 — Overview of Scholarship Plans

5.1 — Introductory Heading

Provide, at the top of a new page, the heading "Overview of our scholarship plan[s]".

5.2 — Description of Scholarship Plans

Under the heading "What is a scholarship plan?", state the following using the same or substantially similar wording:

A scholarship plan is a type of investment fund that is designed to help you save for a beneficiary's post-secondary education. Your plan must be registered as a Registered Education Savings Plan (RESP) in order to qualify for government grants and tax benefits. To do this, we need social insurance numbers for you and the person you name in the plan as your beneficiary.

You sign a contract when you open a plan with us. You make contributions under the plan. We invest your contributions for you, after deducting applicable fees. You will get back your contributions, less fees, whether or not your beneficiary goes on to post-secondary education. Your beneficiary will receive educational assistance payments (EAPs) from us if they enrol in eligible studies and all the terms of the contract are met.

Please read your contract carefully and make sure you understand it before you sign. If you or your beneficiary does not meet the terms of your contract, it could result in a loss and your beneficiary could lose some or all of their EAPs.

5.3 — List of Scholarship Plans Offered

(1) If the investment fund manager offers more than one type of scholarship plan, under the heading "Types of plans we offer", list the scholarship plans offered.

(2) State, as applicable, that there are differences in the enrolment criteria, contribution requirements, fees, eligible studies, payments to beneficiaries, options for receiving EAPs and options if the beneficiary does not pursue eligible studies among the scholarship plans offered. For a multiple prospectus, include a cross-reference to the plan-specific disclosure for each scholarship plan provided under Part C of this Form.

INSTRUCTION

For each scholarship plan listed under subsection 5.3(1), state the name of the issuer of the securities.

Item 6 — General Information about Scholarship Plan Life Cycle

6.1 — Overview of Scholarship Plan Life Cycle

(1) Using the heading "How our plan[s] work[s]", provide a brief description of the life cycle of the plan(s) offered under the prospectus, from enrolment in the plan(s) to EAPs being paid to the beneficiary.

(2) Using the margin of the page, add a sidebar under the heading "How our plan[s] work[s]", and state the following using the same or substantially similar wording with the title of the sidebar in bold type:

Make sure your contact information is up to date

It is important that you keep your address and contact information up to date. We will need to communicate important information to you throughout the life of your plan. We will also need to find you and the beneficiary when the plan matures so we can return your contributions and make payments to the beneficiary.

INSTRUCTIONS

(1) The disclosure provided under section 6.1 must not exceed one page in length, and may be provided by means of a table or diagram.

(2) In providing the disclosure required under section 6.1, briefly describe the life cycle of the scholarship plan(s) offered under the prospectus, including significant stages such as enrolling and registering the scholarship plan as an RESP under the Income Tax Act (Canada), making contributions and paying fees from contributions, investing contributions and government grants, ceasing investments in accordance with the scholarship plan's investment objectives and strategies upon plan maturity, returning contributions to subscribers at maturity and paying EAPs to beneficiaries for eligible studies.

(3) Do not provide a separate life cycle description for each scholarship plan offered under a multiple prospectus. Provide one life cycle description containing the elements that are common to the life cycle of each of the scholarship plans offered under the prospectus.

6.2 — Enrolling in a Scholarship Plan

(1) Under the sub-heading "Enrolling in a plan", describe the enrolment process for the scholarship plan(s) offered under the prospectus, including the requirement that the subscriber provide a social insurance number at the time of enrolment to register the plan as an RESP under the *Income Tax Act* (Canada).

(2) Describe the requirements for designation of a beneficiary of the scholarship plan, including Canadian residency and social insurance number requirements.

6.3 — Unregistered Accounts

(1) Under the sub-sub-heading "If your beneficiary does not have a social insurance number", list the options available to a subscriber whose beneficiary does not yet have a social insurance number, including the option to wait until the beneficiary has a social insurance number to purchase a scholarship plan that is eligible to be held in an RESP.

(2) If the scholarship plan provider offers an unregistered education savings account, describe

    (a) the features of the unregistered education savings account, including what happens to contributions made to the account,

    (b) whether the account is eligible to receive government grants, and

    (c) the tax treatment of the account.

(3) State the deadline for providing the beneficiary's social insurance number after which the investment fund manager will close the account.

INSTRUCTION

Any plan or account offered by the scholarship plan provider that is not eligible for registration by the federal government as an RESP or is not held in a registered education savings account must be referred to and described as an "unregistered education savings account".

6.4 — Government Grants

(1) Under the sub-heading "Government grants", list the government grants that the investment fund manager will apply for on a beneficiary's behalf. For each government grant program, provide

    (a) a brief description of the program,

    (b) the maximum amount that may be granted under the program annually and over the duration of an RESP,

    (c) if applicable, the annual contribution amount that would attract the maximum annual government grant, and

    (d) any requirement to repay government grants.

(2) Describe what happens to the government grants received by the investment fund manager on behalf of a beneficiary, including

    (a) the legal ownership of the money throughout the life span of an investment in the scholarship plan,

    (b) whether the money is pooled with the government grants of other beneficiaries,

    (c) whether the money is invested together with subscriber contributions or separately from contributions, and

    (d) how the money is allocated on distribution to a qualified beneficiary.

(3) State that a subscriber may contact their sales representative or the investment fund manager about the applications that the investment fund manager will make on behalf of the subscriber and disclose where a subscriber can obtain more information about available government grants.

INSTRUCTION

The disclosure provided under section 6.4 must not exceed two pages. The disclosure may be provided in the form of a table.

6.5 — Contribution Limits

(1) Under the sub-heading "Contribution limits", disclose whether the scholarship plan imposes a cumulative limit for contributions and indicate whether this is exclusive of any government grants.

(2) Disclose whether a subscriber can make contributions annually beyond the amount(s) that would result in the receipt of the maximum annual amount in government grants.

(3) If a subscriber is permitted to make additional contributions as described in subsection (2), disclose that the additional contributions are not eligible to attract further government grants and disclose how the additional contributions are invested.

(4) Disclose the maximum amount that may be contributed to an RESP under the *Income Tax Act* (Canada), and provide a cross-reference to the tax consequences of contributions beyond the limit set by the *Income Tax Act* (Canada) as disclosed under section 11.3 of this Part of this Form.

6.6 — Additional Services

If applicable, under the sub-heading "Additional services", describe additional services relating to an investment in the scholarship plan that are available to subscribers from the investment fund manager or the principal distributor.

INSTRUCTION

If insurance for contributions is offered for purchase by the principal distributor, provide a brief description of the insurance coverage, including the name of the insurer and whether the insurance is mandatory or optional for the subscriber. Include a cross-reference to the disclosure provided under section 14.5 of Part C of this Form.

6.7 — Fees and Expenses

(1) Under the sub-heading "Fees and expenses", state the following using the same or substantially similar wording:

There are costs for joining and participating in our plan[s]. You pay some of these fees and expenses directly from your contributions. The plan[s] pay[s] some of the fees and expenses, which are deducted from the [plan's/plans'] earnings. See "Costs of investing in this plan" in this Detailed Plan Disclosure for a description of the fees and expenses of [each of] our plan[s]. Fees and expenses reduce the plan's returns which reduces the amount available for EAPs.

(2) If the investment fund manager offers more than one type of scholarship plan, state, if applicable, that each scholarship plan offered requires the subscriber to pay different fees and expenses and, if applicable, that the choice of scholarship plan affects the amount of compensation paid to the dealer by a member of the organization of the scholarship plan or a subscriber.

6.8 — Eligible Studies

Under the sub-heading "Eligible studies", state the following using the same or substantially similar wording:

EAPs will be paid to your beneficiary only if he or she enrols in eligible studies. For a summary of the educational programs that qualify for EAPs under our plan[s], see "Summary of eligible studies" in this Detailed Plan Disclosure. [Insert if applicable -The plans offered under the prospectus each have their own criteria for what post-secondary programs qualify as eligible studies for receiving EAPs. We recommend that you carefully read the "Specific information about the plan" sections for each plan in this Detailed Plan Disclosure to better understand the differences among the plans.]

6.9 — Payments from the Scholarship Plan

(1) Under the sub-heading "Payments from the plan" with the sub-sub-heading "Return of contributions", state the following using the same or substantially similar wording:

We always return your contributions less fees to you or to your beneficiary. Earnings from the plan will generally go to your beneficiary. If your beneficiary does not qualify to receive the earnings from your plan, you may be eligible to get back some of those earnings as an "accumulated income payment (AIP)". See the "Accumulated income payments" section(s) in this Detailed Plan Disclosure for more information about AIPs.

(2) Under the sub-sub-heading "Educational assistance payments", state the following using the same or substantially similar wording:

We will pay EAPs to your beneficiary if you meet the terms of your plan, and your beneficiary qualifies for the payments under the plan. The amount of each EAP depends on the type of plan you have, how much you contributed to it, the government grants in your plan and the performance of the plan's investments.

You should be aware that the *Income Tax Act* (Canada) has restrictions on the amount of EAP that can be paid out of an RESP at a time. [*See Instruction*].

INSTRUCTION

For the disclosure under subsection (2), briefly describe the restrictions under the Income Tax Act (Canada) on the amount of EAPs that can be paid at a time.

6.10 — Unclaimed Accounts

(1) Under the sub-heading "Unclaimed accounts", briefly describe what an unclaimed account is.

(2) Describe the steps that the investment fund manager will take to contact the subscriber and the beneficiary with respect to an unclaimed account.

(3) Describe what will happen to any unclaimed contributions, unclaimed earnings on contributions, government grants and earnings on government grants if the investment fund manager is unable to locate the subscriber or the beneficiary.

(4) Describe how a subscriber or beneficiary can obtain payments of any unclaimed money.

Item 7 — Scholarship Plans with Same Investment Objectives (Multiple Prospectus)

7.1 — Investment Objectives

(1) This section applies to a multiple prospectus for scholarship plans that have the same investment objectives, investment strategies and investment restrictions.

(2) Set out, under the heading "How we invest your money" with the sub-heading "Investment objectives", the fundamental investment objectives of the scholarship plans, including any information that describes the fundamental nature of the scholarship plans or the fundamental features of the scholarship plans that distinguish them from other types of scholarship plans.

(3) Describe the nature of any securityholder or other approval that may be required to change the investment objectives of the scholarship plans.

(4) Describe any of the material investment strategies to be used to achieve those investment objectives.

(5) If each scholarship plan purports to arrange a guarantee or insurance in order to protect all or some of the principal amount of the investments made by subscribers, include this fact as a fundamental investment objective of the scholarship plans and

> (a) identify the person or company providing the guarantee or insurance,

> (b) provide the material terms of the guarantee or insurance, including the maturity date of the guarantee or insurance, and

> (c) provide the reasons for which the guarantor or insurer, as applicable, could limit or avoid execution of the guarantee or insurance policy.

INSTRUCTIONS

(1) State the type or types of securities, such as money market instruments, first mortgages and bonds, in which the scholarship plans will be primarily invested under normal market conditions.

(2) If a particular investment strategy is an essential aspect of the scholarship plans, as evidenced by the manner in which the scholarship plans are marketed, disclose this strategy as an investment objective.

Item 8 — Scholarship Plans with Same Investment Strategies (Multiple Prospectus)

8.1 — Investment Strategies

(1) This section applies to a multiple prospectus for scholarship plans that have the same investment objectives, investment strategies and investment restrictions.

(2) Describe under the sub-heading "Investment strategies" the following:

> (a) the principal investment strategies that the scholarship plans intend to use in achieving the investment objectives, and

> (b) the process by which the scholarship plans' portfolio adviser selects investments for the portfolios of the scholarship plans, including any investment approach, philosophy, practices or techniques used by the portfolio adviser or any particular style of portfolio management that the portfolio adviser intends to follow.

(3) Indicate the types of investments, other than those held by the scholarship plans in accordance with their fundamental investment objectives, which may form part of the portfolio assets of the scholarship plans under normal market conditions.

(4) If the scholarship plans may depart temporarily from their fundamental investment objectives as a result of adverse market, economic, political or other considerations, disclose any temporary defensive tactics the portfolio adviser may use or intends to use in response to such conditions.

INSTRUCTION

Scholarship plans may, in responding to subsection 8.1(2), provide a discussion of the general investment approach or philosophy followed by the portfolio adviser of the scholarship plan.

Item 9 — Scholarship Plans with Same Investment Restrictions (Multiple Prospectus)

9.1 — Investment Restrictions

(1) This section applies to a multiple prospectus for scholarship plans that have the same investment objectives, investment strategies and investment restrictions.

(2) Under the sub-heading "Investment restrictions", describe any restrictions on investments adopted by the scholarship plans, beyond what is required under securities legislation.

(3) If the scholarship plans have received the approval of the securities regulatory authorities to vary any of the investment restrictions and practices contained in securities legislation, provide details of the permitted variations.

(4) Describe the nature of any securityholder or other approval that may be required in order to change the investment restrictions of the scholarship plans.

Item 10 — *Risks of Investing in a Scholarship Plan*

10.1 — *Risks of Investing in a Scholarship Plan*

(1) Under the heading "Risks of investing in a scholarship plan", include an introduction using the following wording or wording that is substantially similar:

> If you or your beneficiary does not meet the terms of your contract, it could result in a loss and your beneficiary could lose some or all of their EAPs. Please read the description of the plan-specific risks under "Risks of investing in this plan" in this Detailed Plan Disclosure.

(2) Under the sub-heading "Investment risks", include an introduction using the following wording or wording that is substantially similar:

> The prices of the investments held by the scholarship plan[s] can go up or down. [*State, as applicable* — [Refer to "Risks of investing in this plan" in this Detailed Plan Disclosure for a description of/Below are [some of]] the risks that can cause the value of the scholarship plan ['s/s'] investments to change, which will affect the amount of EAPs available to beneficiaries.] Unlike bank accounts or guaranteed investment certificates, your investment in a scholarship plan is not covered by the Canada Deposit Insurance Corporation or any other government deposit insurer.

(3) For a multiple prospectus, list and describe the investment risks applicable to each of the scholarship plans offered under the prospectus.

(4) For a multiple prospectus that contains the disclosure required by section 7.1 of this Part of the Form, if, at any time during the 12-month period immediately preceding the date of the prospectus, more than 10% of the net assets of a scholarship plan were invested in the securities of an issuer other than a government security, disclose

   (a) the name of the issuer and the securities,

   (b) the highest percentage of the net assets of the scholarship plan that securities of that issuer represented during the 12-month period, and

   (c) the risks associated with the investments, including the possible or actual effect on the liquidity and diversification of the scholarship plan.

INSTRUCTIONS

(1) Each risk factor listed must be described under a separate sub-sub-heading.

(2) Describe the risks in the order of the most serious to the least serious.

(3) Do not de-emphasize a risk factor by including excessive caveats or conditions.

(4) Include a discussion of general market, political, market sector, liquidity, interest rate, foreign currency, diversification and credit risks that apply to the portfolio of the scholarship plan, as appropriate.

(5) The term "government security" has the same meaning as in National Instrument 81-102 Investment Funds.

Item 11 — *Income Tax Considerations*

11.1 — *Status of the Scholarship Plan*

Under the heading "How taxes affect your plan", briefly describe the status of the scholarship plan for income tax purposes.

11.2 — *Taxation of the Scholarship Plan*

Under the sub-heading "How the plan is taxed", state in general terms the basis upon which the income and capital received by the scholarship plan are taxed.

11.3 — *Taxation of the Subscriber*

(1) Under the sub-heading "How you are taxed", state in general terms how the subscriber will be taxed. State in general terms, as applicable to the scholarship plan(s) offered under the prospectus, using sub-sub-headings, the income tax consequences of

   (a) a return of contributions at the maturity date,

   (b) a withdrawal of contributions before the maturity date,

   (c) a refund of sales charges or other fees,

   (d) any other distributions to the subscriber in the form of income, capital or otherwise,

   (e) a cancellation of units prior to the maturity date,

   (f) a purchase of additional units,

   (g) a transfer between scholarship plans,

   (h) an additional contribution made to address backdating of a plan,

   (i) an additional contribution made to cure defaults under the scholarship plan, and

   (j) a contribution beyond the limit set by the *Income Tax Act* (Canada).

(2) Under the sub-sub-heading "If you receive an Accumulated income payment (AIP)",

   (a) state the tax consequences of receiving an AIP,

   (b) describe how an AIP may be transferred to a registered retirement savings plan, and

   (c) describe the tax consequences of a transfer of an AIP to a registered retirement savings plan.

11.4 — Taxation of the Beneficiary

Under the sub-heading "How your beneficiary is taxed", state in general terms the income tax consequences to a beneficiary of a payment made to the beneficiary under the scholarship plan, including, as applicable, an EAP, a discretionary payment and a fee refund.

Item 12 — Organization and Management Details of the Scholarship Plan

12.1 — Organization and Management Details

(1) Provide in a diagram or table, under the heading "Who is involved in running the plan[s]", information about the entities involved in operating the scholarship plan, including the investment fund manager, foundation, trustee, portfolio adviser, principal distributor, independent review committee, custodian, registrar and auditor of the scholarship plan.

(2) For each entity listed in the diagram or table, briefly describe the services provided by that entity, and the relationship of that entity to the investment fund manager. Include a description of how each of the following aspects of the operations of the scholarship plan is administered and who administers those functions:

(a) the management and administration of the scholarship plan, including valuation services, fund accounting and securityholder records, other than the management of the portfolio assets;

(b) the management of the portfolio assets, including the provision of investment analysis or investment recommendations and the making of investment decisions;

(c) the purchase and sale of portfolio assets by the scholarship plan and the making of brokerage arrangements relating to the portfolio assets;

(d) the distribution of the securities of the scholarship plan;

(e) if the scholarship plan is a trust, the trusteeship of the scholarship plan;

(f) if the scholarship plan is a corporation, the oversight of the affairs of the scholarship plan by the directors of the corporation;

(g) the custodianship of the assets of the scholarship plan;

(h) the oversight of the investment fund manager of the scholarship plan by the independent review committee;

(i) the oversight of the scholarship plan by any other body.

(3) For each entity listed in the diagram or table, other than the investment fund manager, provide, if applicable, the municipality and the province or country where it principally provides its services to the scholarship plan. Provide the complete municipal address for the investment fund manager of the scholarship plan.

INSTRUCTION

The "foundation" refers to the not-for-profit entity that is the sponsor of the scholarship plan.

Item 13 — Statement of Rights

13.1 — Statement of Rights

Under the heading "Your rights as an investor", state the following using the same or substantially similar wording:

You have the right to withdraw from an agreement to buy scholarship plan securities and get back all of your money (including any fees or expenses paid), within 60 days of signing the agreement. If the plan is cancelled after 60 days, you will only get back your contributions, less fees and expenses.

Any government grants you've received will be returned to the government.

In several provinces and territories, securities legislation also gives you the right to withdraw from a purchase and get back all of your money, or to claim damages, if the prospectus and any amendment contain a misrepresentation or are not delivered to you. You must act within the time limit set by the securities legislation in your province [*insert if the scholarship plan(s) is/are distributed in one or more territories of Canada* — or territory].

You can find out more about these rights by referring to the securities legislation of your province [*insert if the scholarship plan(s) is/are distributed in one or more territories of Canada* — or territory] or by consulting a lawyer.

Item 14 — Other Material Information

14.1 — Other Material Information

(1) Under the heading "Other important information", state any other material facts relating to the securities being offered that are not disclosed under any other item in this Form and are necessary for the prospectus to contain full, true and plain disclosure of all material facts about the securities to be distributed.

(2) Provide any specific disclosure required to be disclosed in a prospectus under securities legislation that is not otherwise required to be disclosed by this Form.

(3) Subsection (2) does not apply to requirements of securities legislation that are form requirements for a prospectus.

INSTRUCTIONS

(1) Sub-headings that are not mandated by this Form may be used in this Item.

(2) For a single prospectus, provide this disclosure either under this Item or under Item 23 of Part C of this Form, whichever is more appropriate.

(3) For a multiple prospectus, provide this disclosure under this Item if the disclosure pertains to all of the scholarship plans described in the document. If the disclosure does not pertain to all of the scholarship plans, provide the disclosure under Item 23 of Part C of this Form.

Item 15 — Back Cover

15.1 — Back Cover

(1) State on the back cover of the Detailed Plan Disclosure the name of the scholarship plan(s) offered under the prospectus, and the name, address and telephone number of the investment fund manager of the scholarship plan(s).

(2) State the following using the same or substantially similar wording:

You can find additional information about the plan[s] in the following documents:

- the plan's most recently filed annual financial statements,

- any interim financial reports filed after the annual financial statements, and

- the most recently filed annual management report of fund performance.

These documents are incorporated by reference into this prospectus. That means they legally form part of this document just as if they were printed as part of this document.

You can get a copy of these documents at no cost by calling us at [*insert the toll-free telephone number or telephone number where collect calls are accepted*] or by contacting us at [*insert the scholarship plan's e-mail address*].

[*Insert if applicable* — You'll also find these documents on our website at [*insert the scholarship plan's website address*]].

These documents and other information about the plan[s] are also available at www.sedar.com.

Part C — Detailed Plan Disclosure — Plan-Specific Information

Item 1 — General

The Items in this Part apply to each type of scholarship plan unless otherwise stated.

Item 2 — Introductory Disclosure

2.1 — For a Single Prospectus

Include at the top of the first page of the Part C section of the prospectus the heading "Specific information about the [*insert the name of the scholarship plan*]".

2.2 — For a Multiple Prospectus

Include,

(a) at the top of the first page of the first Part C section of the prospectus, the heading "Specific information about our plans", and

(b) at the top of each page of a Part C section of the prospectus, a heading consisting of the name of the scholarship plan described on that page.

Item 3 — Plan Description

3.1 — Plan Description

Under the heading "Type of plan", disclose in the form of a table

(a) the type of scholarship plan, and

(b) the date on which the scholarship plan was started.

INSTRUCTION

In disclosing the date on which the scholarship plan was started, use the date on which the securities of the scholarship plan first became available for offer to the public, which will be on or about the date of the issuance of the first receipt for a prospectus of the scholarship plan.

Item 4 — Eligibility and Suitability

4.1 — Eligibility and Suitability

(1) Under the heading "Who this plan is for", list the eligibility requirements for enrolment in the scholarship plan.

(2) Provide a brief statement of the suitability of the scholarship plan for particular investors, describing the characteristics of the subscriber and beneficiary for whom the scholarship plan may be an appropriate investment and for whom it may not be an appropriate investment.

INSTRUCTION

The disclosure provided under subsection 4.1(2) must be consistent with the disclosure provided under Item 4 of Part A of this Form. Discuss whether the scholarship plan is particularly suitable for certain types of investors. Conversely, if the scholarship plan is particularly unsuitable for certain types of investors, emphasize this aspect of the plan and disclose the types of investors who should not invest in the scholarship plan, on both a short- and long-term basis.

Item 5 — Beneficiary Group

5.1 — Beneficiary Group

(1) This Item applies to a group scholarship plan.

(2) Under the sub-heading "Your beneficiary group", describe

    (a) what a beneficiary group is and the significance of belonging to a beneficiary group, and

    (b) how the maturity date and year of eligibility are determined and the significance of the dates.

(3) Include the table below, introduced using the following wording or wording that is substantially similar:

The table below can help you determine your beneficiary group. In general, the beneficiary group is determined by the age of the beneficiary when you sign your contract.

Age of beneficiary when the plan is purchased	Beneficiary group
[Insert age of oldest beneficiary eligible to join the group scholarship plan] years old	*[Insert year of eligibility for oldest beneficiary]*
[Insert age corresponding to next year of eligibility in descending order] years old	*[Insert year of eligibility for next oldest beneficiary]*
...	
0 years old	*[Insert year of eligibility for youngest beneficiary]*

INSTRUCTIONS

(1) In responding to subsection 5.1(2), provide disclosure regarding the sharing of earnings on contributions based on the number of beneficiaries in a beneficiary group, including the sharing of earnings on contributions where there is pre-maturity and post-maturity attrition.

(2) The table required under subsection 5.1(3) is used to demonstrate how the year of eligibility relates to the age of the beneficiary on the application date. The disclosure in the column of this table titled "Age of beneficiary when the scholarship plan is purchased" must present the ages of the beneficiaries for whom subscribers may purchase a group scholarship plan, starting from the oldest to the youngest. For example, if a beneficiary cannot join the group scholarship plan after age 12, then that must be the age disclosed in the top row of that column. The ages disclosed in the subsequent row must follow in descending order.

(3) For the column titled "Beneficiary Group" in the table required under subsection 5.1(3), the "year of eligibility" disclosed in each row must be based on the year of eligibility that would typically correspond to a beneficiary of the age described in adjacent column of that table titled "Typical age of beneficiary when the scholarship plan is purchased" as of the date of the prospectus. For example, if the age of the beneficiary listed in the table is 12, the disclosure under "Beneficiary Group" must show the typical year of eligibility for a 12 year old beneficiary joining the scholarship plan as of the date of the prospectus.

Item 6 — Eligible Studies

6.1 — Summary of Eligible Studies

Under the heading "Summary of eligible studies", state the following using the same or substantially similar wording:

The following is a description of the post-secondary programs that are eligible studies and qualify for EAPs under the [insert name of the scholarship plan].

Contact us or your sales representative to find out if the educational programs your beneficiary is interested in are eligible studies. We can provide you with a current list of qualifying institutions and programs on request. This list is also available on the plan's website.

For more information about receiving EAPs, see "Educational assistance payments" on page [*insert page reference to the disclosure provided under section 19.2 of Part C of this Form*] of this Detailed Plan Disclosure.

6.2 — Description of Eligible Programs

Under the sub-heading "What's eligible", briefly describe the types of programs that qualify for EAPs under the scholarship plan.

6.3 — Description of Ineligible Programs

(1) Under the sub-heading "What's not eligible", briefly describe the types of programs that do not qualify for EAPs under the scholarship plan.

(2) If any post-secondary program that would qualify for an EAP under the *Income Tax Act* (Canada) would be considered eligible studies under the scholarship plan, state this fact. If there are differences between the types of programs eligible for payment of an EAP under the *Income Tax Act* (Canada) and programs recognized as eligible studies under the scholarship plan, state this fact and describe how the scholarship plan's requirements are different than the *Income Tax Act* (Canada) requirements.

(3) State, if applicable, that beneficiaries who do not enrol in eligible studies under the requirements of the scholarship plan will also not receive payments of government grants.

(4) If the scholarship plan does not recognize all of the same post-secondary programs that would qualify for an EAP under the *Income Tax Act* (Canada), then state the following using the same or substantially similar wording:

> If you are interested in a post-secondary program that doesn't qualify for EAPs under the [*insert the name of the scholarship plan*] but would qualify for an EAP under the *Income Tax Act* (Canada), you should consider another type of plan. [*Insert if applicable* — For example, in our [*insert, as applicable the name of the scholarship plan(s)*], any post-secondary program that would qualify for an EAP under the *Income Tax Act* (Canada) is considered eligible studies for receiving an EAP under the plan.]

INSTRUCTIONS

(1) The list of institutions and programs that are "eligible studies" under the scholarship plan and are referred to in section 6.1 must be provided in a format that facilitates comprehension by the investor. The list must also be available on the plan's website in a location that does not have restricted access, i.e., it does not require a password or login account.

(2) The disclosure required by sections 6.2 and 6.3 may be provided in the form of a table to assist readability.

(3) Describe the programs required to be disclosed under sections 6.2 and 6.3 based on characteristics such as the type of educational institutions offering the programs, the duration of the programs and the location of the educational institutions.

Item 7 — Investment Objectives

7.1 — Investment Objectives

(1) This section does not apply to a scholarship plan that is required to provide the disclosure under section 7.1 of Part B of this Form.

(2) Under the heading "How we invest your money" with the sub-heading "Investment objectives", state the fundamental investment objectives of the scholarship plan, including any information that describes the fundamental nature of the scholarship plan or the fundamental features of the scholarship plan that distinguish it from other types of scholarship plans.

(3) Describe the nature of any securityholder or other approval that may be required to change the investment objectives of the scholarship plan.

(4) Describe any of the material investment strategies to be used to achieve the scholarship plan's investment objectives.

(5) If the scholarship plan purports to arrange a guarantee or insurance in order to protect all or some of the principal amount of the investments made by subscribers, include this fact as a fundamental investment objective of the scholarship plan and

    (a) identify the person or company providing the guarantee or insurance,

    (b) provide the material terms of the guarantee or insurance, including the maturity date of the guarantee or insurance, and

    (c) provide the reasons for which the guarantor or insurer could limit or avoid execution of the guarantee or insurance policy.

INSTRUCTION

In providing the disclosure required by this Item, follow the Instructions that apply to section 7.1 of Part B of this Form.

Item 8 — Investment Strategies

8.1 — Investment Strategies

(1) This section does not apply to a scholarship plan that is required to provide the disclosure under section 8.1 of Part B of this Form.

(2) Describe under the sub-heading "Investment strategies" the following:

    (a) the principal investment strategies that the scholarship plan intends to use in achieving its investment objectives, and

    (b) the process by which the scholarship plan's portfolio adviser selects investments for the scholarship plan's portfolio, including any investment approach, philosophy, practices or techniques used by the portfolio adviser or any particular style of portfolio management that the portfolio adviser intends to follow.

(3) Indicate the types of investments, other than those held by the scholarship plan in accordance with its fundamental investment objectives, which may form part of the scholarship plan's portfolio assets under normal market conditions.

(4) If the scholarship plan may depart temporarily from its fundamental investment objectives as a result of adverse market, economic, political or other considerations, disclose any temporary defensive tactics the scholarship plan's portfolio adviser may use or intends to use in response to such conditions.

INSTRUCTION

A scholarship plan may, in responding to subsection 8.1(2), provide a discussion of the general investment approach or philosophy followed by the portfolio adviser of the scholarship plan.

Item 9 — Investment Restrictions

9.1 — Investment Restrictions

(1) This section does not apply to a scholarship plan that is required to provide the disclosure specified under section 9.1 of Part B of this Form.

(2) Under the sub-heading "Investment restrictions", describe any restrictions on investments adopted by the scholarship plan, beyond what is required under securities legislation.

(3) If the scholarship plan has received the approval of the securities regulatory authorities to vary any of the investment restrictions and practices contained in securities legislation, provide details of the permitted variations.

(4) Describe the nature of any securityholder or other approval that may be required in order to change the investment restrictions of the scholarship plan.

Item 10 — Plan-Specific Risks

10.1 — Plan Risks

(1) Under the heading "Risks of investing in this plan" with the sub-heading "Plan risks", include an introduction using the following wording or wording that is substantially similar:

> You sign a contract when you open a plan with us. Read the terms of the contract carefully and make sure you understand the contract before you sign. If you or your beneficiary does not meet the terms of your contract, it could result in a loss and your beneficiary could lose some or all of his or her EAPs.

> Keep in mind that payments from the plan are not guaranteed. We cannot tell you in advance if your beneficiary will qualify to receive any EAPs from the plan or how much your beneficiary will receive. We do not guarantee the amount of any payments or that the payments will cover the full cost of your beneficiary's post-secondary education.

> In addition to the investment risks described under "Investment risks" on page(s) [*insert a page reference to the investment risks disclosed under section 10.1(3) of Part B of this Form or section 10.2 of this Part of the Form, as applicable*] of the prospectus, the following is a description of the risks of participating in this plan:

(2) List and describe any material risks associated with an investment in the scholarship plan, other than the investment risks associated with the portfolio held by the scholarship plan that are disclosed under section 10.1 of Part B of this Form or section 10.2 of this Part, including, as applicable to the scholarship plan,

   (a) the risk of a change in attrition rates affecting the amount of EAPs available to beneficiaries,

   (b) the risk of a decision not to provide a discretionary payment affecting the amount of money available to beneficiaries who enrol in eligible studies,

   (c) the risk that the current sources of funding for discretionary payments may not be available at plan maturity,

   (d) if there is no guarantee for any refunds of sales charges or other fees, the risk that the current sources of funding for the refunds may not be available at or after the maturity date of the subscriber's scholarship plan, and

   (e) if the scholarship plan has more than one class or series of securities, the risk that the investment performance, expenses or liabilities of one class or series may affect the value of the securities of another class or series.

INSTRUCTION

In responding to section 10.2, follow Instructions (1) — (3) to section 10.1 of Part B of this Form.

10.2 — Investment Risks

(1) Subsections (2) to (5) do not apply to a scholarship plan that is required to provide the disclosure under section 7.1 of Part B of this Form.

(2) Under the heading "Risks of investing in this plan" with the sub-heading "Investment risks", include an introduction using the following wording or wording that is substantially similar:

> The prices of the investments held by the scholarship plan can go up or down. Below are the risks that can cause the value of the plan's investments to change, which will affect the amount of EAPs available to beneficiaries.

(3) List and describe the investment risks applicable to the scholarship plan, other than those risks previously discussed under subsection 10.1(3) of Part B of this Form.

(4) Include specific cross-references to the risks described in response to subsection 10.1(3) of Part B of this Form that are applicable to the scholarship plan.

(5) If, at any time during the 12-month period immediately preceding the date of the prospectus, more than 10% of the net assets of a scholarship plan were invested in the securities of an issuer other than a government security, disclose

   (a) the name of the issuer and the securities,

   (b) the maximum percentage of the net assets of the scholarship plan that securities of that issuer represented during the 12-month period, and

   (c) the risks associated with the investment in the securities, including the possible or actual effect on the liquidity and diversification of the scholarship plan.

(6) If the scholarship plan is required to provide the disclosure under section 7.1 of Part B of this Form, under the heading "Risks of investing in this plan" with the sub-heading "Investment risks", state the following using the same or substantially similar wording:

> The prices of the investments held by the scholarship plan can go up or down. You can find a list of risks that can cause the value of the plan's investments to change under "Investment risks" on page [*insert page reference to the risks disclosed under section 10.1(3) of Part B of this Form*].

INSTRUCTION

In providing disclosure under this section, follow the Instructions to section 10.1 of Part B of this Form.

Item 11 — Annual Returns

11.1 — Annual Returns

Under the heading "How the plan has performed", provide, in the form of the following table, the annual return of the scholarship plan for each of the past five years (or for a scholarship plan that has existed for less than five years, for each year the scholarship plan has been in existence) as disclosed in the most recently filed annual management report of fund performance of the scholarship plan, introduced using the following wording or wording that is substantially similar:

> The table below shows how the investments in [insert name of the scholarship plan] performed in each of the past five financial years ending on [insert date of end of financial year for the scholarship plan]. Returns are after expenses have been deducted. These expenses reduce the returns you get on your investment.
>
> It's important to note that this doesn't tell you how the plan's investments will perform in the future.

	[Insert most recently completed Financial Year]	[Insert most recently completed Financial Year minus 1]	[Insert most recently completed Financial Year minus 2]	[Insert most recently completed Financial Year minus 3]	[Insert most recently completed Financial Year minus 4]
Annual Return	[Specify annual return]%	[Specify annual return]%	[Specify annual return]%	[Specify annual return]%	[Specify annual return]%

Item 12 — Contributions

12.1 — Making Contributions

(1) Under the heading "Making contributions", state the minimum investment in the scholarship plan permitted under the prospectus and the maximum length of time a subscriber can make contributions under the plan.

(2) If the scholarship plan uses units, under the sub-heading "What is a unit?", describe the unit and state why the scholarship plan uses units. State if the value of a unit is based only on the value of the portfolio assets held by the scholarship plan and, if not, state what other factors the value of a unit is based on.

(3) Under the sub-heading "Your contribution options", describe all available contribution options.

(4) If the scholarship plan requires subscribers to make contributions to the plan in accordance with a contribution schedule, under the sub-heading "Contribution schedule", include an introduction to the contribution schedule using the following wording or wording that is substantially similar:

> The contribution schedule below shows how much you have to contribute to buy a unit. The price you pay depends on your beneficiary group and whether you pay for your units all at once or make periodic contributions to pay for your units. [For a group scholarship plan, state — The prices are calculated so that the contributions of each subscriber for a beneficiary group will generate the same earnings per unit.]
>
> Certain fees and expenses are deducted from your contributions. For more information, please see "Fees you pay" on page [insert page reference to the disclosure provided under section 14.2 of Part C of this Form].
>
> The contribution schedule was prepared by [indicate name of entity/entities that prepared the contribution schedule] in [specify year the contribution schedule was prepared].

(5) Include the contribution schedule of the scholarship plan in the form of the following table, together with the following examples to explain how to use the contribution schedule to determine the contributions required to pay for each unit. Introduce the table using the following wording or wording that is substantially similar with the title "How to use this table" in bold type:

How to use this table:

For example, let's assume your beneficiary is a newborn. If you want to make monthly contributions until maturity, it will cost $[insert amount payable monthly for this option] each month for each unit you buy. You would have to make [insert total number of payments for this option] contributions over the life of your plan, for a total investment of $[insert total amount payable for this option].

If your child is five years old and you want to make annual contributions until maturity, it will cost $[insert amount payable annually for this option] each year for each unit you buy. You would have to make [insert total number of payments for this option] contributions over the life of your plan, for a total investment of $[insert total amount payable for this option].

Contribution schedule				
Contribution options [See Instruction (2)]	[Insert youngest beneficiary by age][See Instruction (3)]	[Insert next youngest beneficiary by age]	...	[Insert oldest beneficiary by age]
Monthly contribution Contribution amount Total number of contributions Total amount of contributions	[See Instruction (4)]			
Annual contribution Contribution amount Total number of contributions Total amount of contributions				
...				
Lump sum contribution Contribution amount				

(6) State the assumptions on which the contribution schedule is based and confirm that the assumptions are still reflective of current conditions and circumstances.

INSTRUCTIONS

(1) The contribution schedule must outline all available contribution options, including the lump sum contribution option.

(2) List the contribution options in the order based on the total number of contributions, from the largest number of contributions to the smallest number of contributions. For example, if the scholarship plan permits monthly, annual and lump sum contributions, list the contribution options in that order.

(3) The contribution schedule must be presented in the order based on the age of the beneficiaries, from the youngest to oldest.

(4) For each contribution option, set out the amount of each contribution, the total number of contributions, and the total amount payable for one unit.

(5) If the scholarship plan permits a subscriber to date their plan as at a date that is earlier than the application date, disclose the conditions or requirements that must be met to backdate a plan, including the maximum number of months that a plan may be backdated and the basis of calculation of any amount(s) payable by the subscriber in addition to the contributions required under the contribution schedule. Include a cross-reference to the disclosure provided under paragraph 11.3(1)(h) of Part B of this Form.

(6) The contribution amounts in the contribution schedule must not include fees for insurance.

12.2 — Missing Contributions

(1) Under the sub-heading "If you have difficulty making contributions", state the following using the same or substantially similar wording:

> If you miss one or more contributions, you may be in default of your plan. To stay in the plan, you'll have to make up the contributions you missed. [*State if applicable* — You'll also have to make up what the contributions would have earned if you had made them on time]. This can be costly.

> For information about the steps you have to take to stay in the plan after missing contributions, see "Default, withdrawal or cancellation" on page [*insert page reference to the disclosure provided under Item 17 of Part C of this Form*].

(2) Under the sub-sub-heading "Your options", describe the options available to subscribers having difficulty making contributions, including reducing the amount of contributions, suspending contributions, transferring to another RESP and cancelling their scholarship plan.

(3) Describe any restrictions on the availability of the options referred to in subsection (2).

(4) For each option set out under subsection (2), disclose the fee payable for the option and the losses that may be incurred by the subscriber as a result of the option.

(5) Describe what will happen if a subscriber has difficulty making contributions and does not select any of the options set out under subsection (2).

INSTRUCTIONS

(1) A scholarship plan that does not require subscribers to make regular contributions to keep their plan in good standing must modify the disclosure under subsection 12.2(1) accordingly.

(2) If the cost of putting a plan in good standing after a voluntary suspension of the plan includes the payment of an amount equal to the interest that would have been earned on the missing contributions, disclose the current interest rate used as an annualized rate of interest and disclose how the interest is calculated.

(3) In disclosing any losses that may be incurred by a subscriber under subsection (4), state whether the subscriber may incur any loss of earnings, government grants, grant contribution room, amounts paid for sales charges and fees or loss of any other amount.

(4) If the disclosure for an option required by subsections (3) and (4) is provided elsewhere in Part C of the prospectus, a cross-reference to the disclosure for the option may be provided in response to subsections (3) and (4). For example, if transferring to another scholarship plan managed by the investment fund manager is an option available to the subscriber, a scholarship plan may refer investors to details of this type of transfer by providing a cross-reference to the disclosure provided under section 16.1 of Part C of this Form.

Item 13 — Withdrawing Contributions

13.1 — Withdrawing Contributions

(1) Under the heading "Withdrawing your contributions", describe a subscriber's entitlement to a return of contributions made, less fees, at any time before the maturity date of their scholarship plan.

(2) Describe the steps a subscriber must take to withdraw some or all of their contributions before the maturity date of their scholarship plan.

(3) Disclose the fee for a withdrawal from their scholarship plan and describe the losses that may be incurred by a subscriber upon a withdrawal.

(4) Disclose whether a subscriber's plan will be cancelled if the subscriber withdraws all the contributions made to their plan. If so, provide a cross-reference to the disclosure provided under section 17.3 of Part C of this Form.

INSTRUCTION

In describing any losses that may be incurred by a subscriber under subsection (3), disclose whether the subscriber may incur any loss of earnings, government grants, grant contribution room, amounts paid for sales charges and fees or loss of any other amount.

Item 14 — Fees and Expenses

14.1 — Costs of Investing in the Scholarship Plan

Under the heading "Costs of investing in this plan", state the following using the same or substantially similar wording:

> There are costs for joining and participating in the [*insert name of scholarship plan*]. The following tables list the fees and expenses of this plan. You pay some of these fees and expenses directly from your contributions. The plan pays some of the fees and expenses, which are deducted from the plan's earnings.

14.2 — Fees Payable by Subscriber from Contributions

(1) Under the sub-heading "Fees you pay", provide a list of the fees and expenses that are deducted from contributions and that are not required to be provided in the table under section 14.4 of Part C of this Form in the form of the following table. Introduce the table using the following wording:

> These fees are deducted from your contributions. They reduce the amount that gets invested in your plan, which will reduce the amount available for EAPs.

Fee	What you pay	What the fee is for	Who the fee is paid to
Sales charge	[*Specify amount*]	[*Specify the purpose*]	[*Insert name of entity*]
Account Maintenance Fee	[*Specify amount*]	[*Specify the purpose*]	[*Insert name of entity*]
[*Specify other fees and expenses*]	[*Specify amount*]	[*Specify the purpose*]	[*Insert name of entity*]

(2) If the sales charge listed in the table required by subsection (1) is deducted from contributions at a higher rate in the early period of participating in the scholarship plan, add a sidebar under the sub-heading "Fees you pay", using the margin of the page and state the following using the same or substantially similar wording with the title of the sidebar in bold type:

Paying off the sales charges

> For example, assume that you buy one unit of the [*Insert name of scholarship plan*] on behalf of newborn child, and you commit to making monthly contributions until the maturity date to pay for that unit. [All/[*specify lower percentage, if applicable*]] of your first [*insert number of contributions*] contributions go toward the sales charge until [half/[*specify other percentage if applicable*]] of the sales charge is paid off. [*State, as applicable —* [Half/[*specify other percentage if applicable*]] of your next [*insert number of contributions*] contributions go toward the sales charge until it's fully paid off.] Altogether, it will take you [*insert number of months*] months to pay off the sales charge. During this time, [*insert percentage*] of your contributions will be used to pay the sales charge and [*insert percentage*] of your contributions will be invested in your plan.

(3) State whether any of the fees listed in the table in subsection (1) may be increased without subscriber approval.

INSTRUCTIONS

(1) In the table required under subsection 14.2(1), list the fees payable by subscribers' contributions. Each fee must be listed on a separate row in the table.

(2) In the table required under subsection 14.2(1) in the column titled "What you pay" state the amount of each fee. The amount of each fee must be disclosed based on how the fee is calculated. For example, if a particular fee is calculated as a fixed dollar amount per unit, or a fixed amount per year, it must be stated as such. Similarly, if a fee is calculated as a percentage of plan assets, that percentage must be stated. A statement or note that a fee is subject to applicable taxes, such as goods and services taxes or harmonized sales taxes, is permitted, if applicable.

(3) For a group scholarship plan or other type of scholarship plan that normally calculates the sales charge payable as a fixed dollar amount linked to the amount of contribution by a subscriber (i.e. $x.xx per unit), in addition to stating the fixed amount of sales charge per unit as required under Instruction (2), the disclosure of the amount of sales charge in the table required under subsection 14.2(1) in the column titled "What you pay" must also be expressed as a percentage of the cost of a unit of the scholarship plan. If the total cost of a unit of the scholarship plan varies depending on the contribution option or frequency selected, the percentage sales charge must be expressed as a range, between the lowest and the highest percentage of the unit cost the sales charge can represent, based on the different contribution options available to subscribers under the scholarship plan. This must be calculated as follows: (i) divide the sales charge per unit by the contribution option that has the highest total cost per unit, and (ii) divide the sales charge per unit by the contribution option that has the lowest total cost per unit. For example, if a scholarship plan calculates its sales charge as $200/unit, and the total cost per unit for a subscriber can range from $1000 to $5000 (based on the different options available to subscribers), the percentage range of the sales charge disclosed in the table would be 4% (200/5000) to 20% (200/1000). The disclosure in the table must also state that the exact percentage of the sales charge per unit for a subscriber will depend on the contribution option selected for contributing to the scholarship plan and how old their beneficiary is at the time they open the scholarship plan.

(4) In the table required under subsection 14.2(1) in the column titled "What you pay" describe how the fee is deducted from contributions if the fee amount deducted from each contribution is not the same. For example, if deductions for sales charges are not made from each contribution at a constant rate for the duration of the plan or for the period for which contributions are required to be made under the scholarship plan if it is less than the scholarship plan's duration, describe the amounts from contributions that are deducted to pay sales charges.

(5) In the table required under subsection 14.2(1) in the column titled "What the fee is for" provide a concise explanation of what the fee is used for.

(6) In the table required under subsection 14.2(1) in the column titled "Who the fee is paid to", state the name of the entity to which the fee is paid, such as the investment fund manager, the portfolio manager, the dealer, the foundation, etc.

(7) The disclosure required under subsection 14.2(2) must be based on the following assumptions: (i) the beneficiary is a newborn, (ii) the subscriber is purchasing one unit of the scholarship plan, (iii) the subscriber has agreed to a monthly contribution schedule with contributions payable until the scholarship plan's maturity date, and (iv) all of the mandatory fees that are normally deducted from a subscriber's contributions are deducted during the relevant period. The disclosure provided under subsection 14.2(2) must be consistent with the disclosure provided under subsection (2) of Item 10 of Part A of the form.

(8) The disclosure required in subsection 14.2(2) may alternatively be provided in a text box below the table required under subsection 14.2(1).

(9) For the disclosure required in subsection 14.2(2), if the scholarship plan does not offer units but uses a similar method for deducting sales charges as is described under subsection 14.2(2), the wording may be amended as is necessary to properly reflect the scholarship plan's features.

14.3 — Fees Payable by the Scholarship Plan

(1) Under the sub-heading "Fees the plan pays", provide a list of the fees and expenses that are payable by the scholarship plan in the form of the following table and introduced using the following wording:

> The following fees are payable from the plan's earnings. You don't pay these fees directly. These fees affect you because they reduce the plan's returns which reduces the amount available for EAPs.

Fee	What the plan pays	What the fee is for	Who the fee is paid to
Administrative fee	*[Specify amount]*	*[Specify purpose]*	*[Insert name of entity]*
Portfolio management fee	*[Specify amount]*	*[Specify purpose]*	*[Insert name of entity]*
Custodian fee	*[Specify amount]*	*[Specify purpose]*	*[Insert name of entity]*
Independent review committee fee	*[Specify amount]*	*[Specify purpose]*	*[Insert name of entity]*
[Specify other fees and expenses]	*[Specify amount]*	*[Specify purpose]*	*[Insert name of entity]*

(2) State whether any of the fees or expenses listed in the table in subsection (1) may be increased without subscriber approval.

INSTRUCTIONS

(1) In the table, show all fees and expenses payable by the scholarship plan, even if it is expected that the investment fund manager or other member of the organization of the scholarship plan will waive or absorb some or all of those fees and expenses. Each fee must be listed in a separate row in the table.

(2) If one or more fees listed or required to be listed in the table are normally combined into an "all-inclusive fee" payable by the scholarship plan, the table may be amended as is necessary to reflect this fact.

(3) In the column titled "What the plan pays" state the amount of each fee listed in the table. The amount of fee stated must be disclosed based on how the fee is calculated. For example, if a fee is calculated based on a percentage of the scholarship plan's assets, it must be stated as such. For the "independent review committee fee", state the amount of any retainer payable to each member of the committee and any additional fees payable for meeting attendance and indicate if committee members expenses are reimbursed, and disclose the total dollar amount paid in connection with the independent review committee for the most recently completed financial year of the scholarship plan. A statement or note that a fee is subject to applicable taxes, such as goods and services taxes or harmonized sales taxes, is permitted, if applicable.

(4) In the column titled "What the fee is for" provide a concise explanation of what the fee is used for. If a fee is charged to the scholarship plan for on-going fund expenses, list the main components of those expenses covered by the fee.

(5) In the column titled "Who the fee is paid to", state the name of the entity to which the fee is paid, such as the investment fund manager, the portfolio manager, the dealer, the foundation, etc.

14.4 — Transaction Fees

Under the sub-heading "Transaction fees", provide a list of the transaction fees in the form of the following table introduced using the following wording:

> We will charge the following fees for the transactions listed below.

Fee	Amount	How the fee is paid	Who the fee is paid to
[Insert type of fee]	$*[Specify amount]*	*[Insert how the fee is charged]*	*[Insert name of entity]*

INSTRUCTIONS

(1) In the column titled "fee" describe the type of transaction for which the fee is charged; for example, replacing a cheque, changing the contribution schedule, changing the beneficiary, changing the maturity date, transferring a plan and a late application for EAPs. Each fee must be listed on a separate row in the table.

(2) In the column titled "Amount" specify the amount of each fee. The amount must be disclosed based on how the fee is calculated. For example if the fee is calculated as a fixed dollar amount or a percentage it must be disclosed as such.

(3) In the column titled "How the fee is paid" state how the fee for each transaction is charged, for example, if the fee is payable directly by the subscriber or beneficiary, or if it is deducted from the earnings of the scholarship plan.

(4) In the column titled "Who the fee is paid to" specify the entity to which the fee is paid, such as the scholarship plan dealer, the investment fund manager, the Foundation, etc.

14.5 — Fees for Additional Services

If applicable, under the sub-heading "Fees for additional services", provide a list of the fees payable for the additional services disclosed under section 6.6 of Part B of this Form in the form of the following table and introduced using the following wording:

The following fees are payable for the additional services listed below:

Fee	What you pay	How the fee is paid	Who the fee is paid to
[Specify type of fee]	$*[Specify amount]*	*[Specify how the fee is charged]*	*[Insert name of entity]*

INSTRUCTIONS

(1) In the column titled "Fee", describe the type of service for which the fee is charged (for example, insurance services). Each fee must be listed in a separate row in the table.

(2) Under the column titled "What you pay" specify the amount of each fee. The fee must be disclosed based on how it is calculated. A statement or note that a fee is subject to applicable taxes, such as goods and services taxes or harmonized sales taxes, is permitted, if applicable.

(3) If insurance services are provided, under the column "What you pay", disclose the fee for insurance and disclose the portion of the fee that is paid by the insurer to the principal distributor, the investment fund manager, or an affiliate.

(4) If the fee payable for an additional service varies so that specific disclosure of the amount of the fee cannot be provided in the prospectus, provide the range of fees payable under the column titled "What you pay".

(5) In the column titled "How the fee is paid" state how the fee for each service is charged, for example, if the fee is an amount payable by the subscriber on a monthly basis in addition to contributions made under the contribution schedule.

(6) In the column titled "Who the fee is paid to" state the name of the entity to which the fee is paid, such as the scholarship plan dealer, the investment fund manager, the Foundation, etc. If insurance services are provided, the name of the insurer must be disclosed.

14.6 — Refund of Sales Charges and Other Fees

(1) Under the sub-heading "Refund of sales charges [and other fees]", disclose the details of all arrangements for the refunding of sales charges and any other fee paid by subscribers.

(2) In the disclosure required by subsection (1), for each fee that may be refunded, describe

    (a) who pays the fee refund,

    (b) who funds the fee refund and the sources of funding for the fee refund,

    (c) whether the refund is guaranteed or not and what that means,

    (d) the conditions or requirements that must be met to receive the fee refund,

    (e) when the refund will be paid,

    (f) whether the amount refunded will include interest,

    (g) whether the refund is paid in cash to the subscriber or is credited to their plan,

    (h) if applicable, whether the amount refunded will be considered a contribution to the scholarship plan for tax purposes, and

    (i) whether the amount refunded is taxable to the subscriber or beneficiary.

(3) Describe the circumstances that may affect the ability of the current sources of funding for the fee refunds to continue to fund such payments.

(4) State whether the investment fund manager or any other entity has put any mechanism in place to continue to make fee refunds if any of the circumstances referred to in subsection (3) occurs.

(5) If a fee refund is payable on a discretionary basis, state the following wording with the first sentence in bold type:

    Discretionary refunds are not guaranteed. You should not count on receiving a discretionary refund. *[Specify entity]* decides if it will provide a fee refund in any year.

INSTRUCTIONS

(1) A return of an enrolment fee is considered to be a refund of sales charges for the purposes of disclosure under this section.

(2) If a fee refund is paid in instalments, disclose each payment date and the amount or proportion of the refund payable at each date.

Item 15 — Making Changes to a Subscriber's Plan

15.1 — Changing Contributions

(1) Under the heading "Making changes to your plan" and the sub-heading "Changing your contributions", disclose whether or not a subscriber can change the contributions under a scholarship plan.

(2) If a subscriber can change the contributions under a scholarship plan, disclose

    (a) the steps the subscriber must take to make the change,

    (b) the conditions or requirements that must be met to make the change,

    (c) the fee for making the change, and

    (d) the losses that may be incurred by the subscriber or the beneficiary if the change is made.

15.2 — Changing Maturity Date

(1) Under the sub-heading "Changing the maturity date", disclose whether or not a subscriber can change the maturity date of their plan.

(2) If a subscriber can change the maturity date, disclose

 (a) the steps the subscriber must take to make the change,

 (b) the conditions or requirements that must be met to make the change,

 (c) the fee for making the change, and

 (d) the losses that may be incurred by the subscriber or the beneficiary if the change is made.

15.3 — Changing Year of Eligibility

(1) Under the sub-heading "Changing your beneficiary's year of eligibility", disclose whether or not a subscriber can change the year of eligibility of a beneficiary.

(2) If a subscriber can change the year of eligibility, disclose

 (a) the steps the subscriber must take to make the change,

 (b) the conditions or requirements that must be met to make the change,

 (c) the fee for making the change, and

 (d) the losses that may be incurred by the subscriber or the beneficiary if the change is made.

15.4 — Changing Subscriber

(1) Under the sub-heading "Changing the subscriber", disclose whether the contract permits the subscriber to be changed at any time during the life of a scholarship plan.

(2) If the subscriber may be changed, disclose

 (a) the steps that are required to make the change,

 (b) the conditions or requirements that must be met to make the change,

 (c) the fee for making the change, and

 (d) the losses that may be incurred by the subscriber or the beneficiary if the change is made.

15.5 — Changing Beneficiary

(1) Under the sub-heading "Changing your beneficiary", disclose whether or not a subscriber can change the beneficiary of a scholarship plan.

(2) If the beneficiary may be changed, disclose

 (a) the steps the subscriber must take to make the change,

 (b) the conditions or requirements that must be met to make the change,

 (c) the fee for making the change, and

 (d) the losses that may be incurred by the subscriber or the beneficiary if the change is made.

15.6 — Death or Disability of Beneficiary

(1) Under the sub-heading "Death or disability of the beneficiary", disclose the options available to a subscriber in the event of the death or disability of the beneficiary of the scholarship plan.

(2) The disclosure under this item must include

 (a) how a disability is defined,

 (b) how each option may be initiated and the conditions or requirements that must be met for each option,

 (c) the fee for each option, and

 (d) the losses that may be incurred by the subscriber or the beneficiary if the option is selected.

INSTRUCTIONS

(1) In discussing a change in contributions under a scholarship plan in response to section 15.1, state if the change in contributions may be made as a result of changing the contribution frequency or the number of units for which contributions are made.

(2) The disclosure of the conditions or requirements for making a change to the subscriber's plan required under this Item must include a description of any amounts required to be paid to make the change and the deadline for making the change.

(3) In disclosing the losses that may be incurred by a subscriber or a beneficiary in response to this Item, state if the subscriber or the beneficiary might incur any loss of earnings, government grants, grant contribution room, amounts paid for sales charges and fees or loss of any other amount.

Item 16 — Transfer of Scholarship Plan

16.1 — Transferring to another plan managed by the investment fund manager

(1) Under the heading "Transferring your plan" with the sub-heading "Transferring to [*name the other scholarship plans managed by the investment fund manager of the scholarship plan*]", state whether or not the scholarship plan allows a subscriber to transfer from the current plan to any of the other plans offered by the investment fund manager.

(2) Disclose

    (a) the steps a subscriber must take to effect the transfer,

    (b) the conditions or requirements that must be met to effect the transfer,

    (c) the fee for the transfer,

    (d) the losses that may be incurred by the subscriber or the beneficiary if the transfer is made, and

    (e) for a group scholarship plan, whether or not a subscriber who has transferred out of a group plan may transfer back to the group plan.

16.2 — Transferring to another RESP Provider

(1) Under the sub-heading "Transferring to another RESP provider", state whether or not the scholarship plan allows a subscriber to transfer to an RESP provider unrelated to the investment fund manager.

(2) Disclose

    (a) the steps a subscriber must take to effect the transfer,

    (b) the conditions or requirements that must be met to effect the transfer,

    (c) the fee for the transfer, and

    (d) the losses that may be incurred by the subscriber or the beneficiary if the transfer is made.

16.3 — Transferring from another RESP Provider to the Scholarship Plan

(1) Under the sub-heading "Transferring to this plan from another RESP provider", state whether or not the scholarship plan allows a subscriber to transfer from an RESP provider unrelated to the investment fund manager to the scholarship plan.

(2) Disclose

    (a) the steps a subscriber must take to effect the transfer,

    (b) the conditions or requirements that must be met to effect the transfer, and

    (c) the fee for the transfer.

INSTRUCTIONS

(1) The disclosure of the conditions or requirements that must be met to effect a transfer of a plan described under this Item must include a description of any amounts required to be paid to effect the transfer and the deadline for effecting the transfer.

(2) In disclosing the losses that may be incurred by a subscriber or a beneficiary in response to this Item, state if the subscriber or the beneficiary might incur any loss of earnings, government grants, grant contribution room, amounts paid for sales charges and fees or loss of any other amount.

Item 17 — Default, Withdrawal or Cancellation

17.1 — Withdrawal or Cancellation by Subscriber

(1) Under the heading "Default, withdrawal or cancellation" with the sub-heading "If you withdraw from or cancel your plan", describe how a subscriber can withdraw from or cancel a scholarship plan.

(2) Describe the amounts a subscriber is entitled to receive if the subscriber withdraws from a scholarship plan up to 60 days after signing a contract.

(3) Describe the amounts a subscriber is entitled to receive if the subscriber cancels a scholarship plan more than 60 days after signing a contract.

(4) Disclose the charges payable by a subscriber for a cancellation or withdrawal.

(5) Disclose the losses that may be incurred by the subscriber or the beneficiary if the subscriber cancels or withdraws from their scholarship plan.

17.2 — Subscriber Default

(1) Under the sub-heading "If your plan goes into default", describe the circumstances in which a subscriber may be noted in default under the scholarship plan.

(2) Disclose the steps the investment fund manager will take to notify the subscriber when a default described in subsection (1) occurs.

(3) Disclose the steps a subscriber can take to remedy a default and disclose the costs associated with remedying the default, including any amounts payable by the subscriber. For a default due to missed contributions, describe how any amount payable by a subscriber as a result of missed contributions is calculated.

Part 4:
DISTRIBUTIONS

(4) For each default, disclose whether remedying the default will qualify a subscriber and a beneficiary for the same payments under the scholarship plan as if the default had not occurred.

(5) Disclose whether a default results in the cancellation of a subscriber's plan by the investment fund manager if the default is not remedied. If an unremedied default does not result in the cancellation of the subscriber's plan, disclose the losses that may be incurred by the subscriber or the beneficiary due to the default.

17.3 — Cancellation by Investment Fund Manager

(1) Under the sub-heading "If we cancel your plan", describe any circumstances other than a subscriber's default in which the investment fund manager of the scholarship plan may cancel a subscriber's plan.

(2) Describe the amounts a subscriber is entitled to receive if the subscriber's scholarship plan is cancelled by the investment fund manager.

(3) Disclose the costs payable by a subscriber in connection with a cancellation by the investment fund manager.

(4) Disclose the losses that may be incurred by the subscriber or the beneficiary if the investment fund manager cancels the subscriber's scholarship plan.

17.4 — Re-activation of Subscriber's Plan

(1) If applicable, under the sub-heading "Re-activating your plan", describe the circumstances in which a subscriber may re-activate a plan after cancellation of the scholarship plan, and specify the costs associated with re-activation and who bears the costs.

(2) Disclose whether re-activating a plan will qualify a subscriber and a beneficiary for the same payments under the scholarship plan as if the cancellation had not occurred.

17.5 — Plan Expiration

Under the sub-heading, "If your plan expires", discuss the maximum duration of a subscriber's scholarship plan before it must be collapsed and what happens to the money from a collapsed scholarship plan.

INSTRUCTIONS

(1) In disclosing the losses that may be incurred by a subscriber or a beneficiary in response to Item 17, state whether the subscriber or the beneficiary may incur any loss of earnings, government grants, grant contribution room, amounts paid for sales charges and fees or loss of any other amount.

(2) If the costs of putting a scholarship plan in good standing after missing contributions or re-activating a scholarship plan after cancellation include the payment of an amount equal to the interest that would have been earned on contributions required by the scholarship plan, disclose the rate as an annualized rate of interest and disclose how the rate is calculated.

(3) If an AIP may be received upon cancellation of a scholarship plan, include a cross-reference to the disclosure provided under Item 20 of Part C of this Form.

Item 18 — Plan Maturity

18.1 — Description of Plan Maturity

(1) Under the heading "What happens when your plan matures", briefly explain what happens to a subscriber's scholarship plan at the maturity date.

(2) State whether the investment fund manager will notify the subscriber about the maturity date of their scholarship plan and how the notice is provided.

INSTRUCTION

In responding to section 18.1, briefly explain what happens to the contributions, government grants and earnings at the maturity date, such as the earnings for a beneficiary group being transferred into an EAP account for distribution to qualified beneficiaries.

18.2 — If the Beneficiary Does Not Enrol in Eligible Studies

(1) Under the sub-heading "If your beneficiary does not enrol in eligible studies", state that a beneficiary who does not enrol in eligible studies will not receive EAPs from the scholarship plan.

(2) Describe the options for a subscriber whose beneficiary does not enrol in eligible studies and disclose the losses that may be incurred by the subscriber under each option.

(3) State whether a subscriber may be eligible to receive an AIP. If an AIP may be payable, provide a cross-reference to the disclosure provided under Item 20 of Part C of this Form.

INSTRUCTIONS

(1) In responding to section 18.2, describe options including naming another beneficiary before the maturity date, transferring to another RESP or cancelling the scholarship plan.

(2) In describing the losses that may be incurred by the subscriber in response to subsection 18.2(2), cross-references to the disclosure provided under Items 15 to 17 of Part C of this Form may be provided, as applicable.

Item 19 — Payments from the Scholarship Plan

19.1 — Return of Contributions

(1) Under the heading "Receiving payments from the plan" with the sub-heading "Return of contributions", describe when and how contributions are returned to the subscriber. State whether the amount returned is net of sales charges and fees deducted from contributions.

(2) If all or a part of a subscriber's contributions are returned, state what happens to the government grants. State whether it is possible for government grants to remain in the name of the beneficiary and if so, state the conditions or requirements that must be met to do so.

19.2 — Payments to Beneficiaries

(1) Under the sub-heading "Educational assistance payments", disclose the conditions and requirements necessary for a beneficiary to receive EAPs under the scholarship plan, including the deadline for applying for EAPs, and state what happens if the beneficiary misses the deadline.

(2) Describe each option for paying EAPs to beneficiaries. For each option, disclose

> (a) the number of payments,

> (b) when each payment is made, and

> (c) for a group scholarship plan, the percentage of the maximum total amount of EAPs payable at each payment date.

(3) For a group scholarship plan, if the total amount of EAPs payable to beneficiaries differs based on the number of years of eligible studies, disclose the number of years of eligible studies that qualifies for the payment of the maximum total amount of EAPs and briefly describe the eligible studies with that duration.

(4) For a group scholarship plan that does not offer EAP payment options tailored to reduced programs, state, if applicable, that beneficiaries who enrol in eligible studies of a shorter duration than the full period will not qualify for the maximum number of EAPs and will receive a lower total amount of EAPs over the duration of their eligible studies than beneficiaries who enrol in eligible studies for the full period.

(5) For a group scholarship plan that offers EAP payment options tailored to reduced programs, if the total amount of EAPs payable under an EAP payment option tailored to reduced programs is less than the maximum total amount of EAPs, state the total amount of EAPs payable under the EAP payment option as a percentage of the maximum total amount of EAPs.

INSTRUCTIONS

(1) In providing the disclosure under subsection 19.2(1), do not repeat the type of studies that qualify for EAPs. Instead, include a cross-reference to the disclosure provided under section 6.2 of Part C of this Form.

(2) The disclosure under subsection 19.2(1) must include a discussion of any requirements for a beneficiary to remain eligible for EAPs under the scholarship plan for each successive year of study.

(3) The "maximum total amount of EAPs" is the total amount of EAPs that can be received by a beneficiary who meets the requirements of the scholarship plan for receiving the maximum number and amount of EAPs.

(4) In providing the disclosure under subsection 19.2(3), describe generally the types of programs for which a beneficiary will receive the maximum total amount of EAPs (for example, four years of eligible studies that may consist of a 4-year program or two 2-year programs).

(5) The "full period" is the number of years of eligible studies that qualifies for the payment of the maximum total number and amount of EAPs.

(6) An "EAP payment option tailored to reduced programs" is an EAP payment option that pays approximately same total amount of EAPs for eligible studies with a shorter duration as the EAPs payable under the scholarship plan for eligible studies of longer duration. For example, an EAP payment option that makes two payments for a 2-year post-secondary program, where each payment is twice the amount of each of the four payments that would be made for a 4-year post-secondary program, is an EAP payment option tailored to reduced programs.

(7) A scholarship plan may use a table to illustrate the schedule of payments and the amount paid in each year of eligible studies for each EAP payment option offered.

19.3 — Amount of EAPs

(1) Under sub-sub-heading, "How we determine EAP amounts", state the components of EAPs paid under the scholarship plan.

(2) Describe how the value of EAPs is determined for each year of eligible study. State whether or not any oversight of the calculation of EAPs is provided by an entity other than the investment fund manager.

(3) Describe any restrictions, under the *Income Tax Act* (Canada) or the scholarship plan's rules, on the amount of EAP that can be paid for each year of eligible studies.

(4) Describe, as applicable to the type of scholarship plan,

> (a) how unrealized capital gains or losses on investments in the scholarship plan are allocated;

> (b) how earnings attributable to units or plans cancelled before the maturity date are allocated;

> (c) how earnings attributable to units or plans cancelled after the maturity date are allocated;

> (d) how the difference between the maximum total amount of EAPs and the lower amount collected by beneficiaries who enrol in eligible studies that do not qualify for the maximum total amount of EAPs is allocated;

> (e) how the government grants accrued in the scholarship plan and the earnings from government grants are allocated.

INSTRUCTION

The amount for which disclosure is required under paragraph 19.3(4)(d) is the amount that is not collected by beneficiaries in a beneficiary group because they do not enrol in eligible studies of sufficient duration to qualify for the maximum total amount of EAPs.

19.4 — Payments from the EAP Account

(1) This section applies to a group scholarship plan.

(2) Under the sub-sub-heading "Payments from the EAP account", provide information in the form of the following table about the funding of the EAP account. Introduce the table using the following wording or wording that is substantially similar with the title of the table "Past breakdown of income in the EAP account" in bold type:

> A portion of each EAP consists of a beneficiary's share of the EAP account. The rest of an EAP is made up of the beneficiary's government grants and the earnings on those government grants.

> The EAP account holds the income earned on contributions made by subscribers. This includes the income earned on contributions of subscribers who have cancelled their plan or whose plan was cancelled by us. There is a separate EAP account for each beneficiary group.

Past breakdown of income in the EAP account

> The table below shows the breakdown of income in the EAP account at the maturity date for the five beneficiary groups that most recently reached their year of eligibility.

> The breakdown of income can vary by beneficiary group. The amount of income earned on contributions depends on the performance of the plan's investments. The amount of income from cancelled plans depends on how many plans were cancelled, as well as the investment performance of that money.

	Beneficiary group				
	[Most recent year]	**[Most recent year minus 1]**	**[Most recent year minus 2]**	**[Most recent year minus 3]**	**[Most recent year minus 4]**
Income earned on contributions	*[Specify as percentage of total EAP account]*	*[Specify as percentage of total EAP account]*	*[Specify as percentage of total EAP account]*	*[Specify as percentage of total EAP account]*	*[Specify as percentage of total EAP account]*
Income from cancelled plans	*[Specify as percentage of total EAP account]*	*[Specify as percentage of total EAP account]*	*[Specify as percentage of total EAP account]*	*[Specify as percentage of total EAP account]*	*[Specify as percentage of total EAP account]*
EAP account Total	**100%**	**100%**	**100%**	**100%**	**100%**

(3) Provide information in the form of the following table about the historical payment of amounts from the EAP account. Introduce the table using the following wording or wording that is substantially similar with the title of the table "Past payments from the EAP account" in bold type:

Past payments from the EAP account

> The table below shows how much was paid from the EAP account per unit for the five beneficiary groups that most recently reached their year of eligibility. [*For a scholarship plan that offers EAP payment options tailored to reduced programs, state* — This table shows only the amount paid per unit for beneficiaries who selected the [*specify EAP payment option for the full period*]. We also offer [a] payment option[s] that pay[s] EAPs tailored to shorter programs].

> Keep in mind that scholarship plans are generally long-term investments. The payments shown largely reflect investments made years ago. It's important to note that this doesn't tell you how much a beneficiary will receive in the future.

Year of studies	Payments from EAP account by beneficiary group				
	[Most recent year]	**[Most recent year minus 1]**	**[Most recent year minus 2]**	**[Most recent year minus 3]**	**[Most recent year minus 4]**
First year *[if applicable][See Instruction (2)]*	$*[Specify amount]* per unit	$*[Specify amount]* per unit	$*[Specify amount]* per unit	$*[Specify amount]* per unit	$*[Specify amount]* per unit
Second year	See note 1	$*[Specify amount]* per unit	$*[Specify amount]* per unit	$*[Specify amount]* per unit	$*[Specify amount]* per unit
Third year	See note 1	See note 1	$*[Specify amount]* per unit	$*[Specify amount]* per unit	$*[Specify amount]* per unit
Fourth year	See note 1	See note 1	See note 1	$*[Specify amount]* per unit	$*[Specify amount]* per unit

> Note 1: The amount is not shown because the beneficiaries in this beneficiary group are not yet enrolled in that year of studies.

INSTRUCTION

The tables required in section 19.4 must list the five beneficiary groups that most recently reached their year of eligibility as at the date of the prospectus.

19.5 — If Beneficiary Does Not Complete or Advance in Eligible Studies

(1) For a group scholarship plan, immediately under the sub-heading "If your beneficiary does not complete or advance in eligible studies", state the following using the same or substantially similar wording:

> If your beneficiary does not complete or advance in their program, they may lose one or more EAPs. This can happen if your beneficiary does not complete all the courses required to advance to the next year of the program, decides to enrol in another program that is not considered an advancement from prior study, or drops out of school before completing their program.

> [*state, if applicable* — Your beneficiary may be able to defer a payment if they go back to a qualifying program. Deferrals are at our discretion.]

(2) Under the sub-heading "If your beneficiary does not complete or advance in eligible studies", disclose available options if the beneficiary does not complete or advance in their program.

(3) Disclose what happens to the earnings of the subscriber's scholarship plan if the beneficiary does not complete or advance in their program. For a group scholarship plan, also provide a cross-reference to the disclosure provided under section 22.3 of Part C of this Form.

INSTRUCTIONS

(1) If the scholarship plan provides the option for a beneficiary to defer the payment of an EAP, state the period of time that an EAP may be deferred and the conditions and requirements that must be met to receive a deferred payment after the disclosure in the second paragraph of subsection 19.5(1).

(2) If the details of an option provided under subsection 19.5(2) have been disclosed elsewhere in the prospectus, provide a cross-reference to the disclosure contained in the prospectus. For example, if a subscriber may cancel their scholarship plan and receive an AIP, provide a cross-reference to the disclosure provided under Item 17 and Item 20 of Part C of this Form..

Item 20 — Accumulated Income Payments

20.1 — Accumulated Income Payments

(1) Under the sub-heading "Accumulated income payments", disclose

    (a) the conditions or requirements necessary to receive an AIP,

    (b) the components of an AIP,

    (c) the option for a subscriber who has received an AIP to transfer the payment to a registered retirement savings plan, and

    (d) any costs or other losses that the subscriber or the beneficiary could incur in receiving an AIP.

(2) State whether there may be tax consequences as a result of receiving an AIP and provide a cross-reference to the disclosure provided under subsection 11.3(2) of Part B of this Form.

Item 21 — Discretionary Payments to Beneficiaries

21.1 — Discretionary Payments to Beneficiaries

(1) Under the sub-heading "Discretionary payments", if discretionary payments may be made to beneficiaries, state that beneficiaries may receive a discretionary payment in addition to their EAPs.

(2) Disclose when discretionary payments are made.

(3) State who decides whether a discretionary payment will be made and state the requirements or conditions that must be met in order to be eligible to receive a discretionary payment.

(4) Disclose how the amount of discretionary payments is determined and the sources of funding for the discretionary payments.

(5) Describe the circumstances that may affect the ability of the current sources of funding for the discretionary payments to continue to fund the discretionary payments.

(6) State whether the investment fund manager or any other entity has put any mechanism in place to continue to make discretionary payments if any of the circumstances referred to in subsection (5) occur.

(7) State whether the investment fund manager has established a funding and investment policy intended to ensure sufficient money is available to continue to fund discretionary payments at the historical levels reported in section 21.2 of Part C of this Form. Provide details of any funding policy and the current value of any fund. If no funding policy exists, state that fact and state the consequences of not having a policy.

(8) State the following using the same or substantially similar wording with the first sentence in bold type:

> **Discretionary payments are not guaranteed.** You must not count on receiving a discretionary payment. The [insert *name of the entity funding the discretionary payment*] decides if it will make a payment in any year and how much the payment will be. If the [insert *name of the entity funding the discretionary payment*] makes a payment, you may get less than what has been paid in the past. You may also get less than what is paid to beneficiaries in other beneficiary groups.

21.2 — Historical Amount of Discretionary Payments

Provide information in the form of the following table about the historical discretionary payments made. Introduce the table using the following wording or wording that is substantially similar with the title of the table "Past discretionary payments" in bold:

Past discretionary payments

> The table below shows the amount of discretionary payments paid per unit for the five beneficiary groups that most recently reached their year of eligibility.

It's important to note that this doesn't tell you if a beneficiary will receive a payment or how much they will receive. We may decide not to make these payments in future years. If we do make payments, they could be less than what we've paid in the past.

Year of studies	Discretionary payments by beneficiary group				
	[Most recent year]	[Most recent year minus 2]	[Most recent year minus 3]	[Most recent year minus 4]	[Most recent year minus 5]
First year *[if applicable]*	$[Specify amount] per unit	$[Specify amount] per unit	$[Specify amount] per unit	$[Specify amount] per unit	$[Specify amount] per unit
Second year	See note 1	$[Specify amount] per unit	$[Specify amount] per unit	$[Specify amount] per unit	$[Specify amount] per unit
Third year	See note 1	See note 1	$[Specify amount] per unit	$[Specify amount] per unit	$[Specify amount] per unit
Fourth year	See note 1	See note 1	See note 1	$[Specify amount] per unit	$[Specify amount] per unit

Note 1: The amount is not shown because the beneficiaries in this beneficiary group are not yet enrolled in that year of studies.

INSTRUCTIONS

(1) If the scholarship plan offers an EAP payment option tailored to reduced programs and the amount of discretionary payment per unit is the same for each EAP payment option, state, if applicable, that beneficiaries who select the EAP payment option tailored to reduced programs may receive a lesser total amount of discretionary payments than beneficiaries who receive the largest number of EAPs.

(2) If the amount of discretionary payment per unit is not the same for each EAP payment option, provide information, substantially in the form of the table required in section 21.2, for the historical discretionary payments per unit for each EAP payment option tailored to reduced programs.

Item 22 — Attrition

This Item applies to a group scholarship plan.

22.1 — Attrition

(1) Under the heading "Attrition", state the following using the same or substantially similar wording:

> You and your beneficiary must meet the terms of the plan in order for your beneficiary to qualify for all of the EAPs under the plan. If beneficiaries fail to qualify for some or all of their EAPs, there will be fewer beneficiaries remaining in the beneficiary group to share the amount of money available for paying EAPs. This is known as "attrition".
>
> Your beneficiary may not qualify for some or all of their EAPs if:
> - before the maturity date of the plan, you cancel your plan or transfer your plan to another RESP, or we cancel your plan because you failed to make contributions on schedule and did not take action to keep your plan in good standing. This is known as "pre-maturity attrition"; or
> - after the maturity date of the plan, your beneficiary decides not to pursue a post-secondary education, does not attend a qualifying education program, or does not attend a qualifying education institution for the maximum period provided for in the plan. This is known as "post-maturity attrition".

22.2 — Pre-Maturity Attrition

(1) Under the sub-heading "Pre-maturity attrition", state the following using the same or substantially similar wording:

> If you leave the plan before it matures, you will get back your contributions less fees. You will not get back any earnings. The earnings on your contributions up to the time your plan is cancelled will go to the EAP account and be paid to the remaining beneficiaries in your beneficiary group as part of their EAPs.

(2) If the group scholarship plan permits a subscriber to receive an AIP on the earnings from government grants, state the following using the same or substantially similar wording:

> You may, however, be eligible to receive an AIP on the earnings from the government grants in your plan. See "Accumulated income payments" for information on how to determine if you are eligible for an AIP from the plan.

(3) Provide information in the form of the following table about the income from cancelled units for each beneficiary group as at the scholarship plan's most recent financial year end. Introduce the table using the following wording or wording that is substantially similar with the title of the table "Income from cancelled units" in bold type:

Income from cancelled units

> The table below shows the current value of the income from cancelled units by beneficiary group. The amount of income from cancelled plans available to beneficiaries after the maturity date will depend on how many subscribers cancel their plan, how many beneficiaries qualify for EAPs and the investment performance of the scholarship plan.

Beneficiary group	Percentage of units that have been cancelled	Total income from cancelled units available to remaining units	Income from cancelled units available to each remaining unit
[Specify year of eligibility of oldest beneficiary group available for enrolment under the prospectus]	*[Specify as percentage of total number of units purchased for beneficiary group]*	$*[Specify amount]*	$*[Specify amount]* per unit
[Specify year of eligibility of next oldest beneficiary group available for enrolment under the prospectus]	*[Specify as percentage of total number of units purchased for beneficiary group]*	$*[Specify amount]*	$*[Specify amount]* per unit
...			
[Specify year of eligibility of youngest beneficiary group available for enrolment under the prospectus]	*[Specify as percentage of total number of units purchased for beneficiary group]*	$*[Specify amount]*	$*[Specify amount]* per unit

(4) Provide information in the form of the following table about the pre-maturity attrition rate for the scholarship plan. Introduce the table using the following wording or wording that is substantially similar with the title of the table "Plans that did not reach maturity" in bold type:

Plans that did not reach maturity:

The table below shows the percentage of plans that did not reach maturity for each of the five beneficiary groups shown below. The most common reasons why plans did not reach maturity were because the subscriber cancelled their plan, we cancelled their plan due to a default, the subscriber transferred to another type of plan we offer, or the subscriber transferred to another RESP provider.

Of the last five beneficiary groups of the *[insert name of group scholarship plan]*, an average of *[see Instruction (1)]*% of the plans in each group were cancelled before their maturity dates.

Maturity date of beneficiary group	Percentage of plans that did not reach maturity
[Most recent maturity date by year]	*[See Instruction (2)]*%
[Most recent maturity date by year minus 1]	*[See Instruction (2)]*%
[Most recent maturity date by year minus 2]	*[See Instruction (2)]*%
[Most recent maturity date by year minus 3]	*[See Instruction (2)]*%
[Most recent maturity date by year minus 4]	*[See Instruction (2)]*%
Average	*[See Instruction (1)]*%

INSTRUCTIONS

(1) Disclose the average rate required under subsection 22.2(3) using the same calculation set out in the Instructions that apply to Item 9 of Part A of this Form.

(2) For each beneficiary group that had a maturity date in the five most recent years, calculate the percentage of plans that did not reach maturity by following Instructions (2) to (5) that apply to Item 9 of Part A of this Form.

22.3 — Post-Maturity Attrition

(1) Under the sub-heading "Post-maturity attrition", state the following using the same or substantially similar wording:

If your beneficiary does not pursue or complete eligible studies, you will get back your contributions, less fees. You will not get back any earnings. *[Insert if applicable — A beneficiary may lose one or more EAPs if they do not enrol in four years of eligible studies.]*

(2) Provide information in the form of the following table about the EAP payment rates of the scholarship plan after maturity. Introduce the table using the following wording or wording that is substantially similar with the title of the table "Past payments of EAPs" in bold:

Past payments of EAPs *[state if the scholarship plan offers an EAP payment option tailored to reduced programs — four years of eligible studies]*

The table below shows the percentage of beneficiaries who received the maximum of *[insert maximum number of EAPs payable under the scholarship plan]* EAPs under the plan and those who received some or no EAPs, for each of the five beneficiary groups that would have most recently completed their eligible studies.

	Beneficiary group [See Instruction (1)]				
	[Most recent year]	**[Most recent year minus 1]**	**[Most recent year minus 2]**	**[Most recent year minus 3]**	**[Most recent year minus 4]**
Beneficiaries who received all [3 or 4] EAPs	*[Specify percentage]*% *[See Instructions (2) and (3)]*	*[Specify percentage]*%	*[Specify percentage]*%	*[Specify percentage]*%	*[Specify percentage]*%
Beneficiaries who received only 3 out of 4 EAPs [as applicable]	*[Specify percentage]*%	*[Specify percentage]*%	*[Specify percentage]*%	*[Specify percentage]*%	*[Specify percentage]*%
Beneficiaries who received only 2 out of [3 or 4] EAPs	*[Specify percentage]*%	*[Specify percentage]*%	*[Specify percentage]*%	*[Specify percentage]*%	*[Specify percentage]*%

	Beneficiary group [See Instruction (1)]				
	[Most recent year]	**[Most recent year minus 1]**	**[Most recent year minus 2]**	**[Most recent year minus 3]**	**[Most recent year minus 4]**
Beneficiaries who received only 1 out of [3 or 4] EAPs	[*Specify percentage*]%	[*Specify percentage*]%	[*Specify percentage*]%	[*Specify percentage*]%	[*Specify percentage*]%
Beneficiaries who received no EAPs	[*Specify percentage*]%	[*Specify percentage*]%	[*Specify percentage*]%	[*Specify percentage*]%	[*Specify percentage*]%
Total	**100%**	**100%**	**100%**	**100%**	**100%**

(3) If the scholarship plan offers an EAP payment option tailored to reduced programs, provide information in the form of the following table about the EAP payment rates of the scholarship plan after maturity. Introduce the table using the following wording or wording that is substantially similar with the title of the table "Past payments of EAPs [- [specify reduced number of years]-year program]" in bold:

Past payments of EAPs [- [specify reduced number of years]-year program]

For EAP payment options tailored to eligible studies of [*specify reduced number of years*] years, the table[s] below show[s] the number of beneficiaries who received all of their EAPs and the number who received some or none of their EAPs, for each of the five beneficiary groups that would have most recently completed their eligible studies.

	Beneficiary group [See Instruction (1)]				
	[Most recent year]	**[Most recent year minus 1]**	**[Most recent year minus 2]**	**[Most recent year minus 3]**	**[Most recent year minus 4]**
Beneficiaries who received [all] [1, 2, or 3] EAP[s]	[*Specify percentage*]% [*See Instructions (2)–(4)*]	[*Specify percentage*]%	[*Specify percentage*]%	[*Specify percentage*]%	[*Specify percentage*]%
Beneficiaries who received only 2 out of 3 EAPs [as applicable]	[*Specify percentage*]%	[*Specify percentage*]%	[*Specify percentage*]%	[*Specify percentage*]%	[*Specify percentage*]%
Beneficiaries who received only 1 out of [2 or 3] EAPs [as applicable]	[*Specify percentage*]%	[*Specify percentage*]%	[*Specify percentage*]%	[*Specify percentage*]%	[*Specify percentage*]%
Beneficiaries who received no EAPs	[*Specify percentage*]%	[*Specify percentage*]%	[*Specify percentage*]%	[*Specify percentage*]%	[*Specify percentage*]%
Total	**100%**	**100%**	**100%**	**100%**	**100%**

(4) Disclose in a footnote to the tables required under subsections (2) and (3) any change to the EAP payout option available to beneficiaries, if a change occurred in the past five years.

INSTRUCTIONS

(1) In the tables required under subsections 22.3(2) and (3), present the five most recent beneficiary groups by year of eligibility for which the maximum number of EAPs under the EAP payment option has been paid as at the most recent financial year end of the scholarship plan and beneficiaries in the beneficiary group have no further opportunity to collect EAPs. For example, do not include a beneficiary group that has been eligible to be paid only one EAP if the maximum number of EAPs payable is four.

(2) For a group scholarship plan that does not offer EAP payment options tailored to reduced programs, calculate each percentage as a percentage of the total number of beneficiaries in the beneficiary group at the maturity date.

For a group scholarship plan that offers EAP payment options tailored to reduced programs, calculate each percentage as a percentage of the total number of beneficiaries in the beneficiary group at the maturity date who selected the relevant payment option.

(3) Present the percentages as at the financial year end referred to in Instruction (1).

(4) For a group scholarship plan that offers EAP payment options tailored to reduced programs, in response to subsection 22.3(3), prepare a table for each payout option, modifying the number of rows in the table as applicable. For example, for a scholarship plan that provides the option to elect payment of two EAPs for a 3-year program, present a table containing rows to show the number of beneficiaries who received two out of two EAPs, the number of beneficiaries who received only one out of two EAPs and the number of beneficiaries who received no EAPs.

Item 23 — Other Material Information

23.1 — Other Material Information

(1) Under the heading "Other important information", state any other material facts relating to the securities being offered that are not disclosed under any other item in this Form and are necessary for the prospectus to contain full, true and plain disclosure of all material facts about the securities to be distributed.

(2) Provide any specific disclosure required to be disclosed in a prospectus under securities legislation that is not otherwise required to be disclosed by this Form.

(3) Subsection (2) does not apply to requirements of securities legislation that are form requirements for a prospectus.

INSTRUCTIONS

(1) Sub-headings that are not mandated by this Form may be used in this Item.

(2) For a single prospectus, provide this disclosure either under this Item or under Item 14 of Part B of this Form, whichever is more appropriate.

(3) For a multiple prospectus, provide this disclosure under this Item if the disclosure does not pertain to all of the scholarship plans described in the document. If the disclosure pertains to all of the scholarship plans described in the Detailed Plan Disclosure, provide the disclosure under Item 14 of Part B of this Form.

Part D — Detailed Plan Disclosure — Information about the Organization

Item 1 — Legal Structure of the Scholarship Plan

1.1 — Legal Structure

(1) At the top of the first page of the Part D section of the prospectus, under the heading "About [*insert name of the scholarship plan provider*]" with the sub-heading "An overview of the structure of our plan[s]", state the full corporate name of the scholarship plan or, if the scholarship plan is an unincorporated entity, the full name under which it carries on business, and the address of its head or registered office.

(2) State the names of the scholarship plan's directors, officers, trustees and partners, as applicable.

(3) State the laws under which the scholarship plan was formed or, if the scholarship plan is an unincorporated entity, the laws under which it carries on business, and the date and manner of its formation.

(4) Identify the constating documents of the scholarship plan and, if any material amendments have occurred in the last 10 years, state that the constating documents have been amended in the last 10 years and describe the amendments.

(5) If the scholarship plan's name has changed in the last 10 years, state the scholarship plan's former name and the date(s) on which it was changed.

INSTRUCTION

The information required for this Item may be presented in the form of a table.

Item 2 — Organization and Management Details

2.1 — Directors and Officers of the Plan

(1) Under the sub-heading "Directors and officers of the Plan", list the names, the municipality of residence or postal address, and the principal occupations at, or within the five years preceding the date of the prospectus, of all directors or executive officers of the scholarship plan.

(2) If the principal occupation of a director or executive officer of the scholarship plan is that of a partner, director or officer of a company other than the scholarship plan, state the business in which the company is engaged.

(3) If a director or executive officer of a scholarship plan has held more than one position in the scholarship plan, state only the first and last positions held.

2.2 — Investment Fund Manager

(1) Under the sub-heading "Manager of the scholarship plan", state the name, address, telephone number, e-mail address and, if applicable, website address of the investment fund manager of the scholarship plan.

(2) Provide particulars of the investment fund manager, including the legal structure of the investment fund manager, the history and background of the investment fund manager.

(3) Under the sub-sub-heading "Duties and services to be provided by the manager", describe the duties and services provided by the investment fund manager of the scholarship plan.

(4) Under the sub-sub-heading "Details of the management agreement", provide a brief description of the essential terms of any agreement with the investment fund manager entered into or to be entered into with the scholarship plan, including any termination rights.

(5) Under the sub-sub-heading "Officers and directors of the manager", state

    (a) the name and municipality of residence of each partner, director and executive officer of the investment fund manager and indicate the respective positions held with the investment fund manager and their respective principal occupations within the five preceding years,

    (b) if a partner, director or executive officer of the investment fund manager has held more than one office with the investment fund manager within the past five years, state only the current office held, and

    (c) if the principal occupation of a partner, director or executive officer of the investment fund manager is with an organization other than the investment fund manager, state the principal business in which the organization is engaged.

(6) Under the sub-sub-heading "Cease trade orders and bankruptcies",

    (a) if applicable, state if a partner, director or executive officer of the investment fund manager, the scholarship plan, the foundation or any other entity responsible for the day-to-day administration of the scholarship plan is, as at the date of the prospectus or pro forma prospectus, as applicable, or was within 10 years before the date of the prospectus or pro forma prospectus, as applicable, a director, chief executive officer or chief financial officer of any other issuer, that was

        (i) subject to an order that was issued while the partner, director or executive officer was acting in the capacity of director, chief executive officer or chief financial officer, or

(ii) was subject to an order that was issued after the partner, director or executive officer ceased to be a director, chief executive officer or chief financial officer and which resulted from an event that occurred while that person was acting in the capacity of director, chief executive officer or chief financial officer, and

(b) if a statement is required by paragraph (a), describe the basis on which the order was made and whether the order is still in effect.

(7) For the purposes of subsection (6), "order" means any of the following, if in effect for a period of more than 30 consecutive days:

(a) a cease trade order;

(b) an order similar to a cease trade order;

(c) an order that denied the relevant issuer access to any exemption under securities legislation.

(8) If applicable, state if a partner, director or executive officer of the investment fund manager, the scholarship plan, the foundation or any other entity responsible for the day-to-day administration of the scholarship plan

(a) is, as at the date of the prospectus or pro forma prospectus, or has been within the 10 years before the date of the prospectus or pro forma prospectus, as applicable, a partner, director or executive officer of any issuer that, while that person was acting in that capacity, or within one year of that person ceasing to act in that capacity, became bankrupt, made a proposal under any legislation relating to bankruptcy or insolvency or was subject to or instituted any proceedings, arrangement or compromise with creditors or had a receiver, receiver manager or trustee appointed to hold its assets, or

(b) within the 10 years before the date of the prospectus or pro forma prospectus, as applicable, became bankrupt, made a proposal under any legislation relating to bankruptcy or insolvency, or become subject to or instituted any proceedings, arrangement or compromise with creditors, or had a receiver, receiver manager or trustee appointed to hold the assets of the partner, director or executive officer.

INSTRUCTIONS

(1) If any of the duties or functions of the investment fund manager are performed by another entity, the disclosure required under subsections (2), (3), (4) and (5) must also be provided for that entity.

(2) The disclosure required by subsections (6) and (8) also applies to any personal holding companies of any of the persons referred to in subsections (6) and (8).

(3) A management cease trade order that applies to directors and executive officers of the scholarship plan is an "order" for the purposes of paragraph (10)(a) and must be disclosed, whether or not the director, chief executive officer or chief financial officer was specifically named in the order.

2.3 — Trustee

Under the sub-heading "Trustee", provide details of the trustee of the scholarship plan, including the municipality and the province or country where the trustee principally provides its services to the scholarship plan.

2.4 — The Foundation

(1) Under the sub-heading "The Foundation", state the name and municipal address of the Foundation.

(2) Describe the role of the Foundation, including its mandate and responsibilities.

(3) List the names and municipality of residence of the directors and executive officers of the Foundation, the respective positions and offices held with the Foundation, and their respective principal occupations at, or within the five years preceding, the date of the prospectus.

(4) If a director or executive officer of the Foundation has held more than one office with the Foundation within the last five years, state only the current office held.

(5) If the Foundation provides reports of its activities to subscribers, provide information about how frequently reports are prepared, how a subscriber may obtain a copy of the report, and whether there is any cost to obtaining a report.

2.5 — Independent Review Committee

(1) Under the sub-heading "Independent review committee", briefly describe the independent review committee of the scholarship plan, including

(a) the mandate and responsibilities of the independent review committee, and

(b) the composition of the independent review committee, including the names of its members, and the reasons for any change in its composition since the date of the most recently filed prospectus of the scholarship plan, as applicable.

(2) State the following using the same or substantially similar wording:

At least annually, the independent review committee prepares a report of its activities for subscribers that is available on the [scholarship plan's/investment fund family's] Internet site at [*insert scholarship plan's Internet site address*], or at the subscriber's request at no cost, by contacting the [scholarship plan/ investment fund family] at [scholarship plan's/investment fund family's email address].

2.6 — Other Groups

Under separate sub-headings with the name of each applicable body or group, provide detailed information describing any other body or group that has responsibility for plan governance or performs any kind of oversight function over the scholarship plan and its activities, and the extent to which its members are independent of the investment fund manager of the scholarship plan.

INSTRUCTION

For greater certainty, an applicable body or group includes any committees or sub-committees of the investment fund manager or the Foundation that are established for a specific purpose in respect of the scholarship plan, as well as any third-party dispute resolution service to which the scholarship plans belong or subscribe to.

2.7 — Remuneration of Directors, Officers, Trustees and Independent Review Committee Members

(1) Under the sub-heading "Compensation of directors, officers, trustees, and independent review committee members", if the management functions of the scholarship plan are carried out by employees of the scholarship plan, provide for each employee the disclosure concerning executive compensation that is required to be provided for executive officers of an issuer under securities legislation.

(2) Describe any arrangements under which compensation was paid or payable directly or indirectly by the scholarship plan during the most recently completed financial year of the scholarship plan, for the services of the directors of the scholarship plan, the directors of the Foundation or other independent board of governors or advisory board that may perform a similar function, and the members of the independent review committee of the scholarship plan and include the amounts paid, the name of the individual and any expenses reimbursed by the scholarship plan to the individual:

(a) in any of those capacities, including any additional amounts payable for committee participation or special assignments;

(b) in the capacity as a consultant or expert.

(3) For a scholarship plan that is a trust, describe the arrangements, including the amounts paid and expenses reimbursed, under which compensation was paid or payable by the scholarship plan during the most recently completed financial year of the scholarship plan for the services of the trustee or trustees of the scholarship plan.

INSTRUCTION

The disclosure required under subsection 2.5(1) regarding executive compensation for management functions carried out by employees of a scholarship plan must be made in accordance with the disclosure requirements of Form 51-102F6 Statement of Executive Compensation.

2.8 — Portfolio Adviser

(1) Under the sub-heading "Portfolio adviser" if the investment fund manager provides portfolio management services in connection with the scholarship plan, state that fact.

(2) If the investment fund manager does not provide portfolio management services to the scholarship plan, state the name(s) and municipality and the province or country of the principal or head office for each portfolio adviser of the scholarship plan.

(3) State

(a) the extent to which investment decisions are made by certain individuals employed by the investment fund manager or a portfolio adviser and whether those decisions are subject to the oversight, approval or ratification of a committee, and

(b) the name, title and length of time of service of the persons employed by or associated with the investment fund manager or a portfolio adviser of the scholarship plan who are principally responsible for the day-to-day management of a material portion of the portfolio of the scholarship plan, implementing a particular material strategy or managing a particular segment of the portfolio of the scholarship plan, and each person's business experience in the last five years.

(4) Under the sub-sub-heading "Details of the portfolio advisory agreement", provide a brief description of the essential details of any portfolio advisory agreement that a portfolio adviser has entered into or will be entering into with the scholarship plan or the investment fund manager of the scholarship plan, including any termination rights.

2.9 — Principal Distributor

(1) Under the sub-heading "Principal distributor", state the name and address of the principal distributor of the scholarship plan.

(2) Describe the circumstances under which any agreement with the principal distributor of the scholarship plan may be terminated, and include a brief description of the essential terms of this agreement.

2.10 — Dealer Compensation

(1) Under the sub-heading "Dealer compensation", describe

(a) all compensation payable by members of the organization of the scholarship plan to all principal distributors and any participating dealers of the scholarship plan, and

(b) the sales practices followed by the members of the organization of the scholarship plan for distribution of securities of the scholarship plan.

(2) Disclose, under the sub-sub-heading "Dealer compensation from management fees", the approximate percentage obtained from a fraction

(a) the numerator of which is the aggregate amount of cash paid to registered dealers in the last completed financial year of the investment fund manager of the scholarship plan, for payments made

(i) by

(A) the investment fund manager of the scholarship plan, or

(B) an associate or an affiliate of the investment fund manager,

    (ii) in order to

        (A) pay compensation to registered dealers in connection with the distribution of securities of the scholarship plan or scholarship plans that are members of the same investment fund family as the scholarship plan, or

        (B) pay for any marketing, fund promotion or educational activity in connection with the scholarship plan or scholarship plans that are members of the same investment fund family as the scholarship plan, and

(b) the denominator of which is the aggregate amount of management or administrative fees received by the investment fund manager of the scholarship plan and all other scholarship plans in the same investment fund family as the scholarship plan in the last completed financial year of the investment fund manager.

INSTRUCTIONS

(1) Briefly state the compensation paid and the sales practices followed by the members of the organization of the scholarship plan in a concise and explicit manner. The term "member of the organization" has the same meaning as in NI 81-105, except that "scholarship plan" is substituted for "mutual fund" in this Form.

(2) The disclosure presented under this Item must be described as information about the approximate percentage of management fees paid by scholarship plans in the same investment fund family as the scholarship plan that were used to fund commissions or other promotional activities of the investment fund family in the most recently completed financial year of the investment fund manager of the scholarship plan.

(3) The calculations made under this Item must take into account the payment of sales commissions, other commissions and the costs of participation in co-operative marketing, fund promotion and educational conferences.

(4) If the investment fund manager of the scholarship plan charges an "all-inclusive fee", which includes the management or administrative fee, and other types of fees normally paid by the scholarship plan, such as custodian, trustee or portfolio management fees, only the portion of that all-inclusive fee that is attributable to the management or administrative fees payable to the investment fund manager must be used in calculating the denominator referred to in paragraph 2.10(2)(b).

2.11 — Custodian

(1) Under the sub-heading "Custodian", state the name, municipality of the principal or head office, and nature of business of the custodian and any principal sub-custodian of the scholarship plan.

(2) Describe generally the sub-custodial arrangements of the scholarship plan.

INSTRUCTION

A "principal sub-custodian" is a sub-custodian to whom custodial authority has been delegated in respect of a material portion or segment of the portfolio assets of the scholarship plan.

2.12 — Auditor

Under the sub-heading "Auditor", state the name and address of the auditor of the scholarship plan.

2.13 — Transfer Agent and Registrar

Under the sub-heading "Transfer agent and registrar", for each class or series of securities offered by the scholarship plan under the prospectus, state the name of the scholarship plan's transfer agent(s), registrar(s), trustee, or other agent appointed by the scholarship plan to maintain the securities register and the register of transfers for such securities and indicate the location (by municipalities) of each of the offices of the scholarship plan or transfer agent, registrar, trustee or other agent where the securities register and register of transfers are maintained or transfers of securities are recorded.

2.14 — Promoter

(1) Under the sub-heading "Promoter", for a person or company that is, or has been within the two years immediately preceding the date of the prospectus or pro forma prospectus, a promoter of the scholarship plan, and if that person or company is not otherwise identified as the investment fund manager or dealer of the scholarship plan, state

    (a) the person or company's name and municipality and the province or country of residence,

    (b) the number and percentage of each class or series of voting securities and equity securities of the scholarship plan or any of its subsidiaries owned, or controlled or directed, directly or indirectly, by the person or company,

    (c) the nature and amount of anything of value, including money, property, contracts, options or rights of any kind, received or to be received by the promoter, directly or indirectly from the scholarship plan or from an associate or an affiliate of the scholarship plan, and the nature and amount of any assets, services or other consideration received or to be received by the scholarship plan, or an associate or an affiliate of the scholarship plan, in return, and

    (d) for an asset acquired within the two years before the date of the preliminary prospectus or pro forma prospectus, or to be acquired, by the scholarship plan or by an associate or an affiliate of the scholarship plan from a promoter,

        (i) the consideration paid or to be paid for the asset and the method by which the consideration has been or will be determined,

        (ii) the person or company making the determination referred to in subparagraph (i) and the person's or company's relationship with the scholarship plan, the promoter or an associate or an affiliate of the scholarship plan or of the promoter, and

        (iii) the date that the asset was acquired by the promoter and the cost of the asset to the promoter.

(2) If a promoter referred to in subsection (1) is, as at the date of the prospectus or pro forma prospectus, as applicable, or was within 10 years before the date of the prospectus or pro forma prospectus, as applicable, a director, chief executive officer or chief financial officer of any person or company that was subject to an order that was issued while the promoter was acting in the capacity of director, chief executive officer or chief financial officer, state the fact and describe the basis on which the order was made and whether the order is still in effect.

(3) If a promoter referred to in subsection (1) is, as at the date of the prospectus or pro forma prospectus, as applicable, or was within 10 years before the date of the prospectus or pro forma prospectus, as applicable, a director, chief executive officer or chief financial officer of any person or company that was subject to an order that was issued after the promoter ceased to be a director, chief executive officer or chief financial officer and which resulted from an event that occurred while the promoter was acting in the capacity as director, chief executive officer or chief financial officer, state that fact and describe the basis on which the order was made and whether the order is still in effect.

(4) For the purposes of subsections (2) and (3), "order" means any of the following, if in effect for a period of more than 30 consecutive days:

(a) a cease trade order;

(b) an order similar to a cease trade order;

(c) an order that denied the relevant person or company access to any exemption under securities legislation.

(5) State if a promoter referred to in subsection (1):

(a) is, as at the date of the prospectus or pro forma prospectus, as applicable, or has been within the 10 years before the date of the prospectus or pro forma prospectus, as applicable, a partner, director or executive officer of any person or company that, while the promoter was acting in that capacity, or within a year of that person ceasing to act in that capacity, became bankrupt, made a proposal under any legislation relating to bankruptcy or insolvency or was subject to or instituted any proceedings, arrangement or compromise with creditors or had a receiver, receiver manager or trustee appointed to hold its assets;

(b) within the 10 years before the date of the prospectus or pro forma prospectus, as applicable, became bankrupt, made a proposal under any legislation relating to bankruptcy or insolvency, or was subject to or instituted any proceeding, arrangement or compromise with creditors, or had a receiver, receiver manager or trustee appointed to hold the assets of the promoter.

INSTRUCTIONS

(1) The disclosure required by subsections (2), (3) and (5) also applies to any personal holding companies of any of the persons referred to in subsections (2), (3), and (5).

(2) A management cease trade order that applies to a promoter referred to in subsection (1) is an "order" for the purposes of subsections (2) and (3) and must be disclosed, whether or not the director, chief executive officer or chief financial officer was named in the order.

(3) The disclosure requirement in subsection (2) applies only if the promoter was a director, chief executive officer or chief financial officer when the order was issued against the person or company. The scholarship plan does not have to provide disclosure if the promoter became a director, chief executive officer or chief financial officer after the order was issued.

2.15 — Other Service Providers

Under the sub-heading "Other service providers", state the name, municipality of the principal or head office, and the nature of business of each other person or company that provides services relating to portfolio valuation, securityholder records, fund accounting or other material services, in respect of the scholarship plan, and describe the material features of the contractual arrangements by which the person or company has been retained.

2.16 — Ownership of the Investment Fund Manager and Other Service Providers

(1) The information required in response to this Item must be given as of a specified date within 30 days before the date of the prospectus.

(2) Under the sub-heading "Ownership of the manager and other service providers", disclose the percentage of securities of each class or series of voting securities of the investment fund manager of the scholarship plan owned of record or beneficially by each person or company that owns of record, or is known by the investment fund manager to beneficially own more than 10% of any class or series of voting securities of the investment fund manager, and disclose whether the securities are owned both of record and beneficially, of record only, or beneficially only.

(3) For any person or company that is named in response to subsection (2), disclose the name of any person or company of which the first-mentioned person or company is a "controlled entity".

(4) If any person or company named in subsection (2) owns of record or beneficially, more than 10% of any class or series of voting securities of the principal distributor of the scholarship plan, disclose the number and percentage of securities of the class or series so owned.

(5) Disclose the percentage of securities of each class or series of voting or equity securities beneficially owned in aggregate,

(a) by all the directors and executive officers of the scholarship plan in each of

(i) the investment fund manager, and

(ii) any person or company that provides services to the scholarship plan or the investment fund manager; and

(b) by all the directors and executive officers of the investment fund manager of the scholarship plan in each of

(i) the investment fund manager, and

(ii) any person or company that provides services to the scholarship plan or the investment fund manager;

(c) by all the members of the independent review committee of the scholarship plan in each of

(i) the investment fund manager, and

(ii) any person or company that provides services to the scholarship plan or the investment fund manager; and

(d) by all the directors and executive officers of the foundation in each of

(i) the investment fund manager, and

(ii) any person or company that provides services to the scholarship plan or the investment fund manager.

INSTRUCTION

A person or company is a "controlled entity" of another person or company if any of the following apply:

(a) in the case of the person or company

(i) voting securities of the first-mentioned person or company carrying more than 50% of the votes for the election of directors are held, otherwise than by way of security only, by or for the benefit of the second-mentioned person or company, and

(ii) the votes carried by the securities are entitled, if exercised, to elect a majority of the directors of the first-mentioned person or company;

(b) in the case of a partnership that does not have directors, other than a limited partnership, the second-mentioned person or company holds more than 50% of the interests in the partnership;

(c) in the case of a limited partnership, the general partner is the second-mentioned entity or company.

2.17 — Affiliates of the Investment Fund Manager

(1) If any person or company that provides services to the scholarship plan or the investment fund manager in relation to the scholarship plan is an affiliate of the investment fund manager, illustrate the relationships of those affiliates in the form of an appropriately labelled diagram, under the sub-heading "Affiliates of the manager".

(2) Identify any individual who is a director or executive officer of the scholarship plan or the investment fund manager and also of any affiliate of the investment fund manager described in response to subsection (1), and give particulars of the relationship.

Item 3 — Experts

3.1 — Names of Experts

Under the heading "Experts who contributed to this prospectus", name each person or company

(a) who is named as having prepared or certified a report, valuation, statement or opinion in the prospectus or any amendment to the prospectus, and

(b) whose profession or business gives authority to the report, valuation, statement or opinion made by the person or company.

3.2 — Interests of Experts

(1) Disclose all registered or beneficial ownership in any securities, assets or other property of the scholarship plan or of an associate or an affiliate of the scholarship plan received or to be received by a person or company whose profession or business gives authority to a statement made by the person or company and who is named as having prepared or certified a part of the scholarship plan prospectus or prepared or certified a report, valuation, statement or opinion described or included in the prospectus.

(2) For the purpose of subsection (1), if the ownership is less than 1%, a general statement to that effect is sufficient.

(3) If an individual, or a director, officer or employee of a person or company, referred to in subsection (1), is or is expected to be elected, appointed or employed as a director, officer or employee of the scholarship plan or of any associate or affiliate of the scholarship plan, disclose that fact.

(4) Despite subsection (1), an auditor who is independent in accordance with the auditor's rules of professional conduct in a jurisdiction of Canada or has performed an audit in accordance with the U.S. GAAS is not required to provide the disclosure required by subsection (1) if there is disclosure that the auditor is independent in accordance with the auditor's rules of professional conduct in a jurisdiction of Canada or that the auditor has complied with the SEC's rules on auditor independence.

INSTRUCTION

In addition to the scholarship plan's current auditor, the disclosure referred to in section 3.2 must be provided for the scholarship plan's predecessor auditor for those periods for which it was the scholarship plan's auditor.

Item 4 — Subscriber Matters

4.1 — Subscriber Matters

Under the heading, "Subscriber matters" and the sub-heading "Meetings of subscribers", describe the circumstances, processes and procedures for holding a subscriber meeting and for any extraordinary resolutions.

4.2 — Matters Requiring Subscriber Approval

Under the sub-heading "Matters requiring subscriber approval", describe the matters that require subscriber approval.

4.3 — Amendments to Declaration of Trust

For a scholarship plan established pursuant to a declaration of trust, under the sub-heading "Amendments to the declaration of trust", describe the circumstances, processes and procedures required to amend the declaration of trust.

4.4 — Reporting to Subscribers and Beneficiaries

Under the sub-heading "Reporting to subscribers and beneficiaries", describe the information or reports that will be delivered or made available to subscribers and beneficiaries and the frequency with which such information or reports will be delivered or made available to subscribers, including any requirements under securities legislation.

Item 5 — Business Practices

5.1 — Policies

Describe, under the heading "Business Practices" with the sub-heading "Our policies", the policies, practices and guidelines of the scholarship plan or the investment fund manager relating to business practices, sales practices, risk management controls and internal conflicts of interest and, if the scholarship plan or the investment fund manager of the scholarship plan has no such policies, practices or guidelines, state that fact.

5.2 — Brokerage Arrangements

(1) If any brokerage transactions involving the client brokerage commissions of the scholarship plan have been or might be directed to a dealer in return for the provision of any good or service, by the dealer or a third party, other than order execution, state, under the sub-heading "Brokerage arrangements"

   (a) the process for, and factors considered in, selecting a dealer to effect securities transactions for the scholarship plan, including whether receiving goods or services in addition to order execution is a factor, and whether and how the process may differ for a dealer that is an affiliated entity,

   (b) the nature of the arrangements under which order execution goods and services or research goods and services might be provided,

   (c) each type of good or service, other than order execution, that might be provided, and

   (d) the method by which the portfolio adviser makes a good faith determination that the scholarship plan, on whose behalf the portfolio adviser directs any brokerage transactions involving client brokerage commissions to a dealer in return for the provision of any order execution goods and services or research goods and services, by the dealer or a third party, receives reasonable benefit considering both the use of the goods or services and the amount of client brokerage commissions paid.

(2) Since the date of the last prospectus, if any brokerage transactions involving the client brokerage commissions of the scholarship plan have been or might be directed to a dealer in return for the provision of any good or service by the dealer or a third party, other than order execution, state

   (a) each type of good or service, other than order execution, that has been provided to the manager or portfolio adviser of the scholarship plan, and

   (b) the name of any affiliated entity that provided any good or service referred to in paragraph (a), separately identifying each affiliated entity and each type of good or service provided by each affiliated entity.

(3) If any brokerage transactions involving the client brokerage commissions of the scholarship plan have been or might be directed to a dealer in return for the provision of any good or service, by the dealer or a third party, other than order execution, state that the name of any other dealer or third party that provided a good or service referred to in paragraph (2)(a), that was not disclosed under paragraph (2)(b), will be provided upon request by contacting the scholarship plan, and provide a telephone number and email address for the scholarship plan.

INSTRUCTION

Terms defined in National Instrument 23-102 Use of Client Brokerage Commissions *have the same meaning where used in this Item.*

5.3 — Valuation of Portfolio Investments

(1) Under the sub-heading "Valuation of portfolio investments", describe the methods used to value the various types or classes of portfolio assets of the scholarship plan and its liabilities.

(2) If the valuation principles and practices established by the investment fund manager differ from Canadian GAAP, describe the differences.

(3) If the investment fund manager has discretion to deviate from the scholarship plan's valuation practices described in subsection (1), disclose when and to what extent that discretion may be exercised and, if it has been exercised in the past three years, provide an example of how it has been exercised or, if it has not been exercised in the past three years, state that fact.

5.4 — Proxy Voting Disclosure for Portfolio Securities Held

(1) Unless the scholarship plan invests exclusively in non-voting securities, under the sub-heading "Proxy voting", describe the policies and procedures that the scholarship plan follows when voting proxies relating to portfolio securities, including

   (a) the procedures followed when a vote presents a conflict between the interests of securityholders and those of the scholarship plan's investment fund manager, portfolio adviser, or any associate or affiliate of the scholarship plan, its investment fund manager or its portfolio adviser, and

   (b) any policies and procedures of the scholarship plan's portfolio adviser, or any other third party that the scholarship plan follows, or that are followed on the scholarship plan's behalf, to determine how to vote proxies relating to portfolio securities.

(2) State the following:

> The policies and procedures that the scholarship plan follows when voting proxies relating to portfolio securities are available on request, at no cost, by calling *[insert toll-free/collect call telephone number]* or by writing to *[insert mailing address]*.

(3) State that the scholarship plan's proxy voting record for the most recent period ended June 30 of each year is available free of charge to any securityholder of the scholarship plan upon request at any time after August 31 of that year. Provide the scholarship plan's website address where the proxy voting record is available for review.

Item 6 — Conflicts of Interest

6.1 — Conflicts of Interest

Under the heading "Conflicts of interest", disclose particulars of existing or potential material conflicts of interest between

(a) the scholarship plan and the foundation or any partner, director or executive officer of the foundation,

(b) the scholarship plan and the investment fund manager or promoter or any partner, director or executive officer of the investment fund manager or promoter, and

(c) the scholarship plan and the portfolio adviser or any partner, director or executive officer of the portfolio adviser of the scholarship plan.

6.2 — Interests of Management and Others in Material Transactions

(1) Under the sub-heading "Interests of management and others in material transactions", describe, and state the approximate amount of, any material interest, direct or indirect, of any of the following persons or companies in any transaction within the three years before the date of the prospectus or pro forma prospectus that has materially affected or is reasonably expected to materially affect the scholarship plan:

(a) a partner, director or executive officer of the investment fund manager;

(b) a person or company that owns, or controls or directs, directly or indirectly, more than 10% of any class or series of the outstanding voting securities of the scholarship plan or the investment fund manager;

(c) an associate or an affiliate of any of the persons or companies referred to in paragraph (a) or (b).

Item 7 — Material Contracts

7.1 — Material Contracts

(1) Under the heading "Key business documents", list and provide particulars of

(a) the subscribers' sales agreement or contract,

(b) the articles of incorporation, the declaration of trust or trust agreement of the scholarship plan or any other constating document,

(c) any agreement of the scholarship plan or trustee with the investment fund manager of the scholarship plan,

(d) any agreement of the scholarship plan, the investment fund manager or trustee with the portfolio adviser of the scholarship plan,

(e) any agreement of the scholarship plan, the investment fund manager or trustee with the custodian of the scholarship plan,

(f) any agreement of the scholarship plan, the investment fund manager or trustee with the principal distributor of the scholarship plan,

(g) any other contract or agreement that can reasonably be regarded as material to an investor in the securities of the scholarship plan, and

(h) any contract or agreement with governmental bodies to assist beneficiaries in obtaining government grants and incentives.

(2) State a reasonable time and place where the contracts or agreements listed in response to subsection (1) may be inspected by prospective or existing subscribers.

(3) Include, in describing the particulars of a contract, the date of, parties to, consideration paid by the scholarship plan under, key terms including termination provisions of, and the general nature of the contract.

INSTRUCTION

Provide a list of all the contracts for which particulars must be given under this Item and indicating which of those contracts are described elsewhere in the prospectus, if applicable. Provide particulars only for those contracts that are not described elsewhere in the prospectus.

Item 8 — Legal Matters

8.1 — Exemptions and Approvals

Under the heading "Legal matters" with the sub-heading "Exemptions and approvals under securities laws", describe all exemptions from or approvals under securities legislation that are not otherwise disclosed under Item 9 of Part B or Item 9 of Part C of this Form, as applicable, obtained by the scholarship plan or the investment fund manager that continue to be relied upon by the scholarship plan or the investment fund manager, including all exemptions to be evidenced by the issuance of a receipt for the prospectus pursuant to section 19.3 of the Instrument.

8.2 — Legal and Administrative Proceedings

(1) Under the sub-heading "Legal and administrative proceedings", describe briefly any ongoing legal and administrative proceedings material to the scholarship plan, to which the scholarship plan, the investment fund manager, the promoter, the foundation, or the principal dealer is a party.

(2) For all matters disclosed under subsection (1), state

    (a) the name of the court or agency having jurisdiction,

    (b) the date on which the proceeding commenced,

    (c) the principal parties to the proceeding,

    (d) the nature of the proceeding and, if applicable, the amount claimed, and

    (e) whether the proceedings are being contested and the present status of the proceedings.

(3) Provide similar disclosure about any proceedings known to be contemplated.

(4) If the investment fund manager, the foundation, or promoter of the scholarship plan, or a director or officer of the scholarship plan or the partner, director or officer of the investment fund manager or the foundation has, within the 10 years before the date of the prospectus, been subject to any penalties or sanctions imposed by a court or securities regulator relating to trading in securities, promotion or management of an investment fund, or theft or fraud, or has entered into a settlement agreement with a regulatory authority in relation to any of these matters, describe the penalties or sanctions imposed and the ground on which they were imposed or the terms of the settlement agreement.

Item 9 — Certificates

9.1 — Certificate of the Scholarship Plan

Include a certificate of the scholarship plan in the following form:

> This prospectus, together with the documents incorporated herein by reference, constitutes full, true and plain disclosure of all material facts relating to the securities offered by the prospectus, as required by the securities legislation of [*insert the jurisdictions in which qualified*].

9.2 — Certificate of the Investment Fund Manager

Include a certificate of the investment fund manager of the scholarship plan in the same form as the certificate of the scholarship plan.

9.3 — Certificate of the Principal Distributor

If there is a principal distributor of the scholarship plan, include a certificate of the principal distributor of the scholarship plan in the same form as the certificate of the scholarship plan.

9.4 — Certificate of the Promoter

If there is a promoter of the scholarship plan, include a certificate of each promoter of the scholarship plan in the same form as the certificate of the scholarship plan.

9.5 — Amendments

(1) For an amendment to a scholarship plan prospectus that does not restate the prospectus, change "prospectus" to "prospectus dated [insert date] as amended by this amendment" wherever it appears in the statements in sections 9.1 to 9.4.

(2) For an amended and restated scholarship plan prospectus, change "prospectus" to "amended and restated prospectus" wherever it appears in the statements in sections 9.1 to 9.4.

Companion Policy 41-101CP — Companion Policy to National Instrument 41-101 General Prospectus Requirements

Table of Contents

Part 4:
DISTRIBUTIONS

PART 1 — INTRODUCTION, INTERRELATIONSHIP WITH SECURITIES LEGISLATION, AND DEFINITIONS

1.1 Introduction and purpose — This Policy describes how the provincial and territorial securities regulatory authorities (or "we") intend to interpret or apply the provisions of the Instrument. Some terms used in this Policy are defined or interpreted in the Instrument, NI 14-101, or a definition instrument in force in the jurisdiction.

1.2 Interrelationship with other securities legislation — (1) This Policy — The Instrument applies to any prospectus filed under securities legislation and any distribution of securities subject to the prospectus requirement, other than a prospectus filed under NI 81-101 or a distribution of securities under such a prospectus, or unless otherwise stated. Parts of this Policy may not apply to all issuers.

(2) Local securities legislation — The Instrument, while being the primary instrument regulating prospectus distributions, is not exhaustive. Issuers should refer to the implementing law of the jurisdictions and other securities legislation of the local jurisdiction for additional requirements that may apply to the issuer's prospectus distribution.

(3) Continuous disclosure (NI 51-102 and NI 81-106) — NI 51-102, NI 81-106 and other securities legislation imposes ongoing disclosure and filing obligations on reporting issuers. The regulator may consider issues raised in the context of a continuous disclosure review when determining whether it is in the public interest to refuse to issue a receipt for a prospectus. Consequently, unresolved issues may delay or prevent the issuance of a receipt.

Reporting issuers are generally required to file periodic and timely disclosure documents under applicable securities legislation. Reporting issuers may also be required to file periodic and timely disclosure documents pursuant to an order issued by the securities regulatory authority or an undertaking to the securities regulatory authority. Failure to comply with any requirement to file periodic and timely disclosure documents could cause the regulator to refuse a receipt for the prospectus.

(4) Short form prospectus distributions (NI 44-101) — As set out in section 2.1 of NI 44-101, an issuer must not file a prospectus in the form of Form 44-101F1 unless the issuer is qualified under any of sections 2.2 through 2.6 of NI 44-101 to file a short form prospectus. An issuer that is qualified to file a short form prospectus must satisfy the requirements of NI 44-101, including the filing requirements of Part 4 of NI 44-101, as well as any applicable requirements of the Instrument. Therefore, issuers qualified to file a short form prospectus and selling securityholders of those issuers that wish to distribute securities under the short form system should refer to the Instrument, this Policy, and NI 44-101 and its companion policy.

(5) Shelf distributions (NI 44-102) — Issuers qualified under NI 44-101 to file a prospectus in the form of a short form prospectus and their securityholders can distribute securities under a short form prospectus using the shelf distribution procedures under NI 44-102. The companion policy to NI 44-102 explains that the distribution of securities under the shelf system is governed by the requirements and procedures of NI 44-101 and securities legislation, except as supplemented or varied by NI 44-102. Therefore, issuers qualified to file a short form prospectus and selling securityholders of those issuers that wish to distribute securities under the shelf system should refer to the Instrument, this Policy, NI 44-101 and its companion policy, and NI 44-102 and its companion policy.

(6) PREP procedures (NI 44-103) — NI 44-103 contains the post-receipt pricing (PREP) procedures. All issuers and selling securityholders can use the PREP procedures of NI 44-103 to distribute securities, other than rights under a rights offering. Issuers and selling securityholders that wish to

distribute securities using the PREP procedures as provided for in NI 44-103 should refer to the Instrument, this Policy, and NI 44-103 and its companion policy. Issuers and selling securityholders that wish to distribute securities under a short form prospectus using the PREP procedures should also refer to NI 44-101 and its companion policy for any additional requirements.

(7) **Process for prospectus reviews in multiple jurisdictions (NP 11-202)** — National Policy 11-202 *Process for Prospectus Reviews in Multiple Jurisdictions* ("NP 11-202") describes the process for filing and review of prospectuses, including investment fund and shelf prospectuses, amendments to prospectuses and related materials in multiple jurisdictions. NP 11-202 represents the means by which an issuer can enjoy the benefits of coordinated review by the securities regulatory authorities in the various jurisdictions in which the issuer has filed a prospectus. Under NP 11-202, one securities regulatory authority acts as the principal regulator for all materials relating to a filer.

1.3 Definitions — (1) **Asset-backed security** — The definition of "asset-backed security" is the same definition used in NI 51-102.

The definition is designed to be flexible to accommodate future developments in asset-backed securities. For example, it does not include a list of "eligible" assets that can be securitized. Instead, the definition is broad, referring to "receivables or other financial assets" that by their terms convert into cash within a finite time period. These would include, among other things, notes, leases, instalment contracts and interest rate swaps, as well as other financial assets, such as loans, credit card receivables, accounts receivable and franchise or servicing arrangements. The reference to "and any rights or other assets..." in the definition is sufficiently broad to include "ancillary" or "incidental" assets, such as guarantees, letters of credit, financial insurance or other instruments provided as a credit enhancement for the securities of the issuer or which support the underlying assets in the pool, as well as cash arising upon collection of the underlying assets that may be reinvested in short-term debt obligations.

The term, a "discrete pool" of assets, can refer to a single group of assets as a "pool" or to multiple groups of assets as a "pool". For example, a group or pool of credit card receivables and a pool of mortgage receivables can, together, constitute a "discrete pool" of assets. The reference to a "discrete pool" of assets is qualified by the phrase "fixed or revolving" to clarify that the definition covers "revolving" credit arrangements, such as credit card and short-term trade receivables, where balances owing revolve due to periodic payments and write-offs.

While typically a pool of securitized assets will consist of financial assets owed by more than one obligor, the definition does not currently include a limit on the percentage of the pool of securitized assets that can be represented by one or more financial assets owing by the same or related obligors (sometimes referred to as an "asset concentration test").

(2) **Business day** — Section 1.1 of the Instrument defines business day as any day other than a Saturday, Sunday or a statutory holiday. In some cases, a statutory holiday may only be a statutory holiday in one jurisdiction. The definition of business day should be applied in each local jurisdiction in which a prospectus is being filed. For example, subsection 2.3(2) of the Instrument states that an issuer must not file a prospectus more than three business days after the date of the prospectus. A prospectus is dated Day 1. Day 2 is a statutory holiday in Québec but not in Alberta. If the prospectus is filed in both Alberta and Québec, it must be filed no later than Day 4, despite the fact that Day 2 was not a business day in Québec. If the prospectus is filed only in Québec, it could be filed on Day 5.

(3) **Accounting terms** — The Instrument uses accounting terms that are defined or used in Canadian GAAP applicable to publicly accountable enterprises. In certain cases, some of those terms are defined differently in securities legislation. In deciding which meaning applies, you should consider that NI 14-101 provides that a term used in the Instrument and defined in the securities statute of a local jurisdiction has the meaning given to it in the statute unless: (a) the definition in that statute is restricted to a specific portion of the statute that does not govern prospectuses; or (b) the context otherwise requires.

(4) **Acceptable accounting principles other than Canadian GAAP applicable to publicly accountable enterprises** — If an issuer is permitted under NI 52-107 to file financial statements in accordance with acceptable accounting principles other than Canadian GAAP applicable to publicly accountable enterprises, then the issuer may interpret any reference in the Instrument to a term or provision defined or used in Canadian GAAP applicable to publicly accountable enterprises as a reference to the corresponding term or provision in the other acceptable accounting principles.

(5) **Financial statements prepared in accordance with different accounting principles** — Issuers intending to include financial statements that are prepared in accordance with different accounting principles should consider the guidance in section 2.8 of Companion Policy 52-107CP *Acceptable Accounting Principles and Auditing Standards*.

(6) **Rate-regulated activities** — If a qualifying entity is relying on the exemption in paragraph 5.4(1)(a) of NI 52-107, then the qualifying entity may interpret any reference in the Instrument to a term or provision defined or used in Canadian GAAP applicable to publicly accountable enterprises as a reference to the corresponding term or provision in Part V of the Handbook.

PART 2 — GENERAL REQUIREMENTS

2.1 Experience of officers and directors — Securities legislation requires that a securities regulatory authority or regulator refuse to issue a receipt for a prospectus if it appears that the proceeds received from the sale of securities to be paid to the treasury of the issuer, together with other resources of the issuer, will be insufficient to accomplish the purposes stated in the prospectus. In addition to financial resources, resources include people. If a sufficient number of the directors and officers of the issuer do not have relevant knowledge and experience, the securities regulatory authority or regulator may conclude that the human and other resources are insufficient to accomplish these purposes. If the requisite knowledge and experience are not possessed by the directors and officers, a securities regulatory authority or regulator may be satisfied that the human and other resources are sufficient if it is shown that the issuer has contracted to obtain the knowledge and experience from others.

2.2 Role of underwriter — The due diligence investigation undertaken by an underwriter in relation to the business of the issuer often results in enhanced quality of disclosure in the prospectus. In addition, an underwriter typically provides valuable advice regarding the pricing and marketing of securities. For these reasons, we strongly encourage underwriter participation in prospectus offerings, particularly where the offering is an initial public offering.

2.2.1 Minimum offering amount — If the distribution of securities is being done on a best efforts basis, an issuer will need to determine if a minimum offering is required for the issuer to achieve one or more of the stated purposes of the offering, as expressed in the *"Use of Proceeds"* section of the prospectus. If this is the case, the issuer will need to provide a minimum and maximum offering amount. Otherwise, the issuer is required to provide the cautionary statement prescribed in paragraph 1.4(3)(b) of Form 41-101F1.

Although an issuer may determine that a minimum offering amount is not necessary for the prospectus offering, a regulator may reasonably infer that a minimum offering amount is appropriate in certain circumstances. This could occur, for example, if we have concerns that a minimum amount of proceeds must be raised in order for the issuer to achieve its stated objectives. Also, if we have concerns about an issuer continuing as a going concern, we may take the view that the issuer cannot achieve its stated objectives unless a minimum offering amount is raised. The imposition of a minimum offering amount by a regulator derives from the general responsibility of a regulator under securities laws to refuse a receipt for a prospectus if it appears that the aggregate of the proceeds from the sale of the securities under the prospectus and other resources of the issuer are insufficient to accomplish the purposes stated in the prospectus, or if it would not be in the public interest to issue a receipt. A benefit of the imposition of a minimum offering amount is that if the issuer fails to raise the minimum amount, investors benefit from an investor protection mechanism that facilitates the return of their subscription funds to them, if previously deposited.

2.3 Indirect distributions — Securities legislation prohibits a person from distributing a security unless a prospectus is filed and receipted or the distribution is exempt from the prospectus requirement. Securities legislation also prohibits a person from trading in a security where the trade would be a distribution of such security, unless a prospectus is filed and receipted or the distribution is exempt from the prospectus requirement. Securities legislation defines distribution as including a trade in a security that has not been previously issued, a trade out of a control block and any transaction or series of transactions involving a purchase and sale of or a repurchase and resale in the course of or incidental to a distribution. In Québec, the definition of "distribution" is broad enough to include these transactions.

Occasionally, a prospectus is filed to qualify securities for sale to one purchaser or to a small group of related purchasers where it appears that the purchaser does not have a *bona fide* intention to invest in the securities but rather is acquiring the securities with a view to immediately reselling them in the secondary market. This can be the case where the purchaser is a lender to the issuer or where the securities are issued as consideration for the acquisition of assets.

Where the offering and subsequent resale are in substance a single distribution, in order to comply with securities legislation, the distribution to the public purchasers should be made by way of prospectus in order that the subsequent purchasers have the benefit of prospectus disclosure and all the rights and remedies provided to prospectus purchasers under securities legislation.

Considerations relevant to determining whether a distribution under a prospectus is only one transaction in a series of transactions in the course of or incidental to the ultimate distribution include:

- the number of persons or companies who are likely to purchase securities in each transaction;
- whether the purchasers' traditional business is that of financing as opposed to investing;
- whether a purchaser is likely to acquire more of a specified class of securities of the issuer than it is legally entitled to, or practically wishes to, hold (e.g., more than 10% of a class of equity securities where the purchaser wishes to avoid becoming an insider or 20% of a class of equity securities where the purchaser wishes to avoid becoming a control person);
- the type of security distributed (e.g., loan repayment rights) and whether or not the security is convertible into publicly traded securities of the issuer;
- whether the purchase price of the securities is set at a substantial discount to their market price; and
- whether the purchaser is committed to hold the securities it acquires for any specified time period.

2.4 Over-allocation — Underwriters of a distribution may over-allocate a distribution in order to hold a short position in the securities following closing. This over-allocation position allows the underwriters to engage in limited market stabilization to compensate for the increased liquidity in the market following the distribution. If the market price of the securities decreases following the closing of the distribution, the short position created by the over-allocation position may be filled through purchases in the market. This creates upward pressure on the price of the securities. If the market price of the securities increases following the closing of the distribution, the over-allocation position may be filled through the exercise of an over-allotment option (at the issue offering price). Underwriters would not generally engage in market stabilization activities without the protection provided by an over-allotment option.

Over-allotment options are permitted solely to facilitate the over-allocation of the distribution and consequent market stabilization. Accordingly, an over-allotment option may only be exercised for the purpose of filling the underwriters' over-allocation position. The exercise of an over-allotment option for any other purpose would raise public policy concerns.

To form part of the over-allocation position, securities must be sold to *bona fide* purchasers as of the closing of the offering. Securities held by an underwriter or in proprietary accounts of an underwriter for sale at a future date do not form part of the over-allocation position. Further, as discussed below, section 11.2 of the Instrument restricts the distribution of securities under a prospectus to an underwriter. Since section 11.1 of the Instrument requires that all securities that are sold to create the over-allocation position be distributed under the prospectus, securities cannot be sold to an underwriter to increase the size of the over-allocation position.

2.5 Distribution of securities under a prospectus to an underwriter — Section 11.2 of the Instrument restricts the distribution of securities under a prospectus to a person acting as an underwriter. Issuers should determine the 10% limit in that section as if all convertible or exchangeable securities offered under the prospectus were exercised for the underlying securities.

2.6 Certificates — (1) Public interest — Securities legislation provides the regulator with discretion to refuse a receipt for a prospectus where it is not in the public interest to issue the receipt. Securities legislation imposes statutory liability in connection with prospectus disclosure to provide investors with a remedy if a prospectus does not contain full, true and plain disclosure of all material facts relating to the securities being distributed and to protect the integrity of the Canadian public markets. Where an offering is structured in a manner that circumvents the objects and purposes of securities legislation and results in a person or company accessing the Canadian public markets, who is not clearly accountable for the information in the prospectus, the regulator may have significant public interest concerns. Such public interest concerns will be addressed on a case by case basis as part of the analysis of whether a receipt should be issued for a final prospectus. There may be circumstances in which it will be appropriate for the regulator to request a person or company, that is not otherwise required to do so, to certify a prospectus as a means of resolving such public interest concerns. For example, where it appears that a person or company is organizing its business and affairs to avoid a requirement to sign a prospectus certificate or to avoid prospectus liability, a regulator may conclude that there is sufficient public interest concerns that the regulator should require that person or company to certify a prospectus.

(2) Discretion of the regulator to request certificates — Subsection 5.15(1) of the Instrument provides the regulator in each jurisdiction except Ontario with the discretion to require additional certificates. The exercise of this discretion will generally be informed by public interest concerns, including those discussed in subsection (1) above.

(3) Signatories — Part 5 of the Instrument contains requirements regarding who must sign prospectus certificates. Certificates signed on behalf of the identified signatories by an agent or attorney will generally not be acceptable. For example, an income trust issuer with an active board of trustees would be required to arrange for the signature of two trustees on behalf of the board, rather than the signature of an attorney or agent.

(4) Trustee certificates — Subsection 5.5(4) of the Instrument provides an exception to the trust certificate requirement where the trustees of the issuer do not perform functions similar to those of corporate directors. In this type of situation, a prospectus certificate is instead required from two

individuals who do perform those functions for the issuer on behalf of all such individuals. In a situation where a regulated trust company is a trustee but does not perform functions similar to those of corporate directors, the regulated trust company and its officers and directors will not be required to sign a prospectus certificate if two other individuals who perform those functions do provide a certificate.

(5) Chief executive officer and chief financial officer — The Instrument and other securities legislation require that prospectus certificates of certain persons or companies are to be signed by the chief executive officer and chief financial officer of such persons or companies. The terms chief executive officer and chief financial officer should be read to include the individuals who have the responsibilities normally associated with these positions or act in a similar capacity. This determination should be made irrespective of an individual's corporate title or whether that individual is employed directly or acts pursuant to an agreement or understanding.

(6) Selling securityholder certificates — Subsection 5.13(1) of the Instrument provides the regulator in each jurisdiction except Ontario with the discretion to require selling securityholders to sign a prospectus certificate. Under securities legislation, selling securityholders are liable for misrepresentations in a prospectus whether or not they sign a prospectus certificate. There are circumstances, however, where the regulator may determine that it is in the public interest to require the selling securityholder to affirmatively certify the prospectus. Generally, the regulator would only exercise this discretion where the securities being distributed by the selling securityholder represent a substantial portion of the securities being distributed under the prospectus.

2.7 Promoters of issuers of asset-backed securities — Securities legislation in some jurisdictions in Canada define "promoter" and require, in certain circumstances, a promoter of an issuer to assume statutory liability for prospectus disclosure. Asset-backed securities are commonly issued by a "special purpose" entity, established for the sole purpose of facilitating one or more asset-backed offerings. The securities regulatory authorities are of the opinion that special purpose issuers of asset-backed securities will have a promoter because someone will typically have taken the initiative in founding, organizing or substantially reorganizing the business of the issuer. We interpret the business of such issuers to include the business of issuing asset-backed securities and entering into the supporting contractual arrangements.

For example, in the context of a securitization program under which assets of one or more related entities are financed by issuing asset-backed securities (sometimes called a "single seller program"), we will usually consider an entity transferring or originating a significant portion of such assets, an entity initially agreeing to provide on-going collection, administrative or similar services to the issuer, and the entity for whose primary economic benefit the asset-backed program is established, to be a promoter of the issuer if it took the initiative in founding, organizing or substantially reorganizing the business of the issuer. Persons or companies contracting with the issuer to provide credit enhancements, liquidity facilities or hedging arrangements or to be a replacement servicer of assets, and investors who acquire subordinated investments issued by the issuer, will not typically be promoters of the issuer solely by virtue of such involvement.

In the context of a securitization program established to finance assets acquired from numerous unrelated entities (sometimes called a "multi-seller program"), we will usually consider the person or company (frequently a bank or an investment bank) establishing and administering the program in consideration for the payment of an on-going fee, for example, to be a promoter of the issuer if it took the initiative in founding, organizing or substantially reorganizing the business of the issuer. Individual sellers of the assets into a multi-seller program are not ordinarily considered to be promoters of the issuer, despite the economic benefits accruing to such persons or companies from utilizing the program. As with single-seller programs, other persons or companies contracting with the issuer to provide services or other benefits to the issuer of the asset-backed securities will not typically be promoters of the issuer solely by virtue of such involvement.

Where an entity is determined to be a promoter of an issuer at the time of the issuer's initial public offering, the entity continues to be a promoter of the issuer, in the case of subsequent offerings by the issuer, if the entity's relationship to the issuer and involvement in the offerings remains substantially the same. Accordingly, where an entity establishes a special purpose issuer to act as a dedicated securitization vehicle, and the prospectus filed in connection with a subsequent offering continues to include disclosure relating to the entity's securitization program, we will expect the entity to certify the prospectus as a promoter.

While we have included this discussion of promoters as guidance to issuers of asset-backed securities, the question of whether a particular person or company is a "promoter" of an issuer is ultimately a question of fact to be determined in light of the particular circumstances.

2.8 Special warrants — (1) Distributions to resale market — In certain special warrant transactions, the dealer involved in the private placement may itself have purchased special warrants from the issuer on an exempt basis, despite not disclosing any commitment to do so.

Securities legislation generally requires that a dealer not acting as agent of the purchaser who receives an order or subscription for a security offered in a distribution to which a prospectus requirement applies to deliver to the purchaser the latest prospectus. Where a dealer acquires special warrants, with a view to exercising them and reselling the underlying securities, such a resale would be a distribution that must be made by way of a prospectus or pursuant to an exemption from the prospectus requirements.

It is a requirement, therefore, that any dealer who has acquired special warrants with a view to their distribution or the distribution of the underlying securities deliver a prospectus during the period of distribution to its purchasers (where the sale to such purchasers is made otherwise than pursuant to a prospectus exemption) in order that such purchasers have the benefit of all rights and remedies provided to prospectus purchasers under securities legislation. In Québec, prospectus purchasers are notably conferred with a contractual right of rescission under s. 1443 of the Québec Civil Code.

In connection with its prospectus review procedure, the regulator may request information from the issuer of all beneficial purchasers of special warrants. The regulator will generally keep this information confidential.

(2) Underwriters' certificate and due diligence — While the special warrant transaction is, in form, two separate distributions, the first an exempt private placement distribution and the second a conversion of the warrants under a prospectus, such a transaction is, in substance, a single distribution under a prospectus of the underlying securities to the warrant investors.

The registrants involved in placing the special warrants are, therefore, also involved in the prospectus distribution and such registrants in a contractual relationship with the issuer must include their certificate in the prospectus under subsection 5.9(1) of the Instrument or other securities legislation. We note that the resulting incentive to such registrants to participate in the due diligence investigation of the issuer is also beneficial to the secondary market.

The obligation to deliver an underwriter's certificate as described in this Policy does not extend the scope of distributions any registrant is authorized to make under applicable securities legislation.

(3) Contractual right of rescission — Under section 2.4 of the Instrument, an issuer must not file a prospectus or an amendment to a prospectus to qualify the distribution of securities issued on the exercise of special warrants or other securities acquired on a prospectus-exempt basis, unless the issuer has provided holders of the special warrants or other securities with a contractual right of rescission. We would not generally consider the

disclosure of the contractual right of rescission in the prospectus as satisfying this condition unless there is a prior contract between the issuer and the holder of the special warrant or other security under which the issuer granted this right to the holder.

2.9 Offerings of convertible, exchangeable or exercisable securities — Investor protection concerns may arise where the distribution of a convertible, exchangeable or exercisable security is qualified under a prospectus and the subsequent conversion, exchange or exercise of this security is made on a prospectus-exempt basis. Specifically, this concern arises when the subsequent conversion, exchange or exercise occurs within a short period of time — generally 180 days or less — following the purchase of the original security.

The concerns arise because the conversion, exchange or exercise feature of the security may operate to limit or "strip away" the remedies available to an investor for a misrepresentation in a prospectus.

In particular, we are concerned about offerings of subscription receipts, or other types of securities which may be convertible, exchangeable or exercisable within a short period of time following the purchase of the original security (generally 180 days or less), where the investor, when purchasing the subscription receipt, or other similar type of security, is in effect also making an investment decision in respect of the underlying security.

Public interest concerns arise if the subsequent distribution of the underlying security is not part of the initial distribution and is not qualified by the prospectus. These concerns arise because when the security is converted, exchanged or exercised prior to the end of the statutory period for a right of action for rescission under securities legislation (which in many jurisdictions is 180 days from the date of purchase of the original security), the purchaser of a convertible, exchangeable or exercisable security does not retain the same rights to rescission because the convertible, exchangeable or exercisable security that was issued under the prospectus has been replaced by the underlying security. In these circumstances, the original purchaser should retain the benefit of any remaining statutory right of rescission that would otherwise apply in respect of the convertible, exchangeable or exercisable security. As such, the issuer should provide the original purchaser of the convertible, exchangeable or exercisable security with a contractual right of rescission in respect of the conversion, exchange or exercise transaction.

In some cases, the subsequent distribution of the underlying security may be part of the initial distribution as it is part of a series of transactions involving further purchases and sales in the course of or incidental to a distribution. If this is the case the issuer should consider whether its prospectus should qualify the distribution of both the subscription receipt, or other similar type of security, as well as the underlying security.

The guidance above would not apply to an offering of warrants where the warrants may reasonably be regarded as incidental to the offering as a whole. For example, in the case of a typical special warrant offering, the special warrant converts into i) a common share, and ii) a common share purchase warrant (or a fraction thereof). In such cases, we have generally accepted that the common share purchase warrant component merely represents a "sweetener", and that the primary investment decision relates to the common share underlying the special warrant. This would also generally be the case with a unit offering where the unit consists of a common share, and a common share purchase warrant. Therefore, the regulator would not generally request that the issuer provide the original purchaser with a contractual right of rescission in respect of the sweetener warrants.

2.10 Lapse date — An amendment to a prospectus, even if it amends and restates the prospectus, does not change the lapse date under section 17.2 of the Instrument or other securities legislation.

2.11 Rights offerings — (1) The regulator or, in Québec, the securities regulatory authority may refuse to issue a receipt for a prospectus filed for a rights offering under which rights are issued if the rights are exercisable into convertible securities that require an additional payment by the holder on conversion and the securities underlying the convertible securities are not qualified under the prospectus. This will ensure that the remedies for misrepresentation in the prospectus are available to the person or company who pays value.

(2) Subparagraph 8A.2(1)(d)(ii) of the Instrument provides that if there is no published market for the securities, the subscription price must be lower than fair value unless the issuer restricts all insiders from increasing their proportionate interest in the issuer through the rights offering or a stand-by commitment. Under subsection 8A.2(2), the issuer must deliver to the regulator or, in Québec, the securities regulatory authority evidence of fair value. For this purpose, the regulator will consider such things as fairness opinions, valuations and letters from registered dealers as evidence of the fair value.

(3) Under paragraph 8A.4(b) of the Instrument, if there is a stand-by commitment for a rights offering, the issuer must deliver to the regulator or, in Québec, the securities regulatory authority evidence that the person or company providing the stand-by commitment has the financial ability to carry out the stand-by commitment. For this purpose, the regulator or, in Québec, the securities regulatory authority may consider any of the following:

- a statement of net worth attested to by the person or company making the commitment,
- a bank letter of credit,
- the most recent audited financial statements of the person or company making the commitment,
- other evidence that provides comfort to the regulator or, in Québec, the securities regulatory authority.

PART 3 — FILING AND RECEIPTING REQUIREMENTS

3.1 Extension of 90-day period for issuance of final receipt — The effect of subsection 2.3(1) of the Instrument is to ensure that issues are not being marketed by means of preliminary prospectuses containing outdated information.

3.2 Confidential material change reports — An issuer cannot meet the standard of "full, true and plain" disclosure, while a material change report has been filed but remains undisclosed publicly. Accordingly, an issuer who has filed a confidential material change report may not file a prospectus until the material change that is the subject of the report is generally disclosed or the decision to implement the change has been rejected and the issuer so notified the regulator of each jurisdiction where the confidential material change report was filed, and an issuer may not file a confidential material change report during a distribution and continue with the distribution. If circumstances arise that cause an issuer to file a confidential material change report during the distribution period of securities under a prospectus, the issuer should cease all activities related to the distribution until

(a) the material change is generally disclosed and an amendment to the prospectus is filed, if required, or

(b) the decision to implement the material change has been rejected and the issuer has so notified the regulator of each jurisdiction where the confidential material change report was filed.

3.3 Supporting documents — Material that is filed in a jurisdiction will be made available for public inspection in that jurisdiction, subject to the provisions of securities legislation in the local jurisdiction regarding confidentiality of filed material. Material that is delivered to a regulator, but not filed, is not generally required under securities legislation to be made available for public inspection.

Part 4: DISTRIBUTIONS

3.4 Consents of lawyers — The names of lawyers or law firms frequently appear in prospectuses in two ways. First, the underwriters, the issuer and selling securityholders may name the lawyers upon whose advice they are relying. Second, the opinions of counsel that the securities may be eligible for investment under certain statutes may be expressed or opinions on the tax consequences of the investment may be given.

In the first case, we are of the view that the lawyer is not, in the words of subsection 10.1(1.1) of the Instrument, named as having prepared or certified a part of the prospectus and is not named as having prepared or certified a report, valuation, statement or opinion referred to in the prospectus. Accordingly, this subsection does not require the written consent of the lawyer. In the second case, because the opinions or similar reports are prepared for the purpose of inclusion in the prospectus, we are of the view that this subsection applies and requires the consent.

3.5 Documents affecting the rights of securityholders — (1) Subclause 9.1(a)(ii)(A) of the Instrument requires issuers to file copies of their articles of incorporation, amalgamation, continuation or any other constating or establishing documents, unless the document is a statutory or regulatory instrument. This carve out for a statutory or regulatory instrument is very narrow. For example, the carve out would apply to Schedule I or Schedule II banks under the *Bank Act*, whose charter is the *Bank Act*. It would not apply when only the form of the constating document is prescribed under statute or regulation, such as articles under the *Canada Business Corporations Act*.

(2) Subclause 9.1(a)(ii)(E) of the Instrument requires issuers to file copies of contracts that can reasonably be regarded as materially affecting the rights of their securityholders generally. A warrant indenture is one example of this type of contract. We would expect that contracts entered into in the ordinary course of business would not usually affect the rights of securityholders generally, and so would not be required to be filed under this subclause.

3.5.1 Personal information forms — (1) If issuers are relying upon a previously delivered personal information form or predecessor personal information form pursuant to subsections 9.1(2) or 9.1(3) of the Instrument, issuers are reminded of paragraphs 9.1(2)(b) and 9.1(3)(b), which require that the responses to certain questions in the form must still be correct. Accordingly, in order to meet these requirements issuers should obtain appropriate confirmations from the individual concerned.

(2) Paragraph 9.1(2)(c) of the Instrument requires that in certain circumstances an issuer deliver a copy of a previously delivered personal information form, or "alternative information that is satisfactory to the regulator". Our interpretation of what would potentially be alternative information satisfactory to the regulator is, with respect to the previous delivery of an individual's personal information form, the System for Electronic Document Analysis and Retrieval (SEDAR) project number and name of issuer. In most cases this information will be sufficient. Staff will contact issuers in cases where it is not. Issuers wishing to proceed in this manner should provide the information in the cover letter for the preliminary or pro forma long form prospectus.

(3) If an issuer is delivering a copy of a previously delivered personal information form pursuant to paragraph 9.1(2)(c) of the Instrument, the issuer should deliver it as a personal information form on SEDAR, in the same way that a new personal information form would be delivered.

3.6 Material contracts — (1) **Definition** — Under section 1.1 of the Instrument, a material contract is defined as a contract that an issuer or any of its subsidiaries is a party to, that is material to the issuer. A material contract generally includes a schedule, side letter or exhibit referred to in the material contract and any amendment to the material contract. The redaction and omission provisions in subsections 9.3(3) and (4) of the Instrument apply to these schedules, side letters, exhibits or amendments.

(2) **Filing requirements** — Subject to the exceptions in paragraphs 9.3(2)(a) through (f) of the Instrument, subsection 9.3(2) of the Instrument provides an exemption from the filing requirement for a material contract entered into in the ordinary course of business. Whether an issuer entered into a material contract in the ordinary course of business is a question of fact that the issuer should consider in the context of its business and industry.

Paragraphs 9.3(2)(a) through (f) of the Instrument describe specific types of material contracts that are not eligible for the ordinary course of business exemption. Accordingly, if subsection 9.3(1) of the Instrument requires an issuer to file a material contract of a type described in these paragraphs, the issuer must file that material contract even if the issuer entered into it in the ordinary course of business.

(3) **Contract of employment** — Paragraph 9.3(2)(a) of the Instrument provides that a material contract with certain individuals is not eligible for the ordinary course of business exemption, unless it is a "contract of employment". One way for issuers to determine whether a contract is a contract of employment is to consider whether the contract contains payment or other provisions that are required disclosure under Form 51-102F6 as if the individual were a named executive officer or director of the issuer.

(4) **External management and external administration agreements** — Under paragraph 9.3(2)(e) of the Instrument, external management and external administration agreements are not eligible for the ordinary course of business exemption. External management and external administration agreements include agreements between the issuer and a third party, the issuer's parent entity, or an affiliate of the issuer, under which the latter provides management or other administrative services to the issuer.

(5) **Material contracts on which the issuer's business is substantially dependent** — Paragraph 9.3(2)(f) of the Instrument provides that a material contract on which the "issuer's business is substantially dependent" is not eligible for the ordinary course of business exemption. Generally, a contract on which the issuer's business is substantially dependent is a contract so significant that the issuer's business depends on the continuance of the contract. Some examples of this type of contract include

> (a) a financing or credit agreement providing a majority of the issuer's capital requirements for which alternative financing is not readily available at comparable terms,
>
> (b) a contract calling for the acquisition or sale of substantially all of the issuer's property, plant and equipment, long-lived assets, or total assets, and
>
> (c) an option, joint venture, purchase or other agreement relating to a mining or oil and gas property that represents a majority of the issuer's business.

(6) **Confidentiality provisions** — Under subsection 9.3(3) of the Instrument, an issuer may omit or redact a provision of a material contract that is required to be filed if an executive officer of the issuer reasonably believes that disclosure of the omitted or redacted provision would violate a confidentiality provision. A provision of the type described in paragraphs 9.3(4)(a), (b) or (c) of the Instrument may not be omitted or redacted even if disclosure would violate a confidentiality provision, including a blanket confidentiality provision covering the entire material contract.

When negotiating material contracts with third parties, reporting issuers should consider their disclosure obligations under securities legislation. A regulator or securities regulatory authority may consider granting an exemption to permit a provision of the type listed in subsection 9.3(4) of the Instrument to be redacted if

> (a) the disclosure of that provision would violate a confidentiality provision, and
>
> (b) the material contract was negotiated before the effective date of the Instrument.

The regulator may consider the following factors, among others, in deciding whether to grant an exemption:

(c) whether an executive officer of the issuer reasonably believes that the disclosure of the provision would be prejudicial to the interests of the issuer;

(d) whether the issuer is unable to obtain a waiver of the confidentiality provision from the other party.

(7) Disclosure seriously prejudicial to interests of issuer — Under subsection 9.3(3) of the Instrument, an issuer may omit or redact certain provisions of a material contract that is required to be filed if an executive officer of the issuer reasonably believes that disclosure of the omitted or redacted provision would be seriously prejudicial to the interests of the issuer. One example of disclosure that may be seriously prejudicial to the interests of the issuer is disclosure of information in violation of applicable Canadian privacy legislation. However, in situations where securities legislation requires disclosure of the particular type of information, applicable privacy legislation generally provides an exemption for the disclosure. Generally, disclosure of information that an issuer or other party has already publicly disclosed is not seriously prejudicial to the interests of the issuer.

(8) Terms necessary for understanding impact on business of issuer — An issuer may not omit or redact a provision of a type described in paragraph 9.3(4)(a), (b), or (c) of the Instrument. Paragraph 9.3(4)(c) of the Instrument provides that an issuer may not omit or redact "terms necessary for understanding the impact of the material contract on the business of the issuer". Terms that may be necessary for understanding the impact of the material contract on the business of the issuer include the following:

(a) the duration and nature of a patent, trademark, license, franchise, concession, or similar agreement;

(b) disclosure about related party transactions;

(c) contingency, indemnification, anti-assignability, take-or-pay clauses, or change-of-control clauses.

(9) Summary of omitted or redacted provisions — Under subsection 9.3(5) of the Instrument, an issuer must include a description of the type of information that has been omitted or redacted in the copy of the material contract filed by the issuer. A brief one-sentence description immediately following the omitted or redacted information is generally sufficient.

3.7 Response letters and marked up copies — In response to a comment letter for a preliminary prospectus, an issuer should include draft wording for the changes it proposes to make to a prospectus to address staff's comments. When the comments of the various securities regulators have been resolved, an issuer should clearly mark a draft of the prospectus with all proposed changes from the preliminary prospectus and submit it as far as possible in advance of the filing of final material. These procedures may prevent delay in the issuing of a receipt for the prospectus, particularly if the number or extent of changes are substantial.

3.8 Undertaking in respect of credit supporter disclosure, including financial statements — Under subparagraph 9.2(a)(x) of the Instrument, an issuer must file an undertaking to file the periodic and timely disclosure of a credit supporter. For credit supporters that are reporting issuers with a current AIF (as defined in NI 44-101), the undertaking will likely be to continue to file the documents it is required to file under NI 51-102. For credit supporters registered under the 1934 Act, the undertaking will likely be to file the types of documents that would be required to be incorporated by reference into a Form S-3 or Form F-3 registration statement. For other credit supporters, the types of documents to be filed pursuant to the undertaking will be determined through discussions with the regulators on a case-by-case basis.

If an issuer, a parent credit supporter, and a subsidiary credit supporter satisfy the conditions of the exemption in section 34.3 of Form 41-101F1, an undertaking may provide that the subsidiary credit supporter will file periodic and timely disclosure if the issuer and the credit supporters no longer satisfy the conditions of the exemption in that section.

If an issuer and a credit supporter satisfy the conditions the exemption in section 34.4 of Form 41-101F1, an undertaking may provide that the credit supporter will file periodic and timely disclosure if the issuer and the credit supporter no longer satisfy the conditions of the exemption in that section.

For the purposes of such an undertaking, references to disclosure included in the prospectus should be replaced with references to the issuer or parent credit supporter's continuous disclosure filings. For example, if an issuer and subsidiary credit supporter(s) plan to continue to satisfy the conditions of the exemption in section 34.4 of Form 41-101F1 for continuous disclosure filings, the undertaking should provide that the issuer will file with its consolidated financial statements,

(a) a statement that the financial results of the credit supporter(s) are included in the consolidated financial results of the issuer if

(i) the issuer continues to have limited independent operations, and

(ii) the impact of any subsidiaries of the issuer on a combined basis, excluding the credit supporter(s) but including any subsidiaries of the credit supporter(s) that are not themselves credit supporters, on the consolidated financial statements of the issuer continues to be minor, or

(b) for any periods covered by issuer's consolidated financial statements, consolidating summary financial information for the issuer presented in the format set out in subparagraph 34.4(e)(ii) of Form 41-101F1.

3.9 Disclosure of investigations or proceedings — Securities legislation provides that, subject to certain conditions, the securities regulatory authorities or the regulator must issue a receipt for a prospectus unless it appears that it would not be in the public interest to do so. The securities regulatory authority or the regulator will consider whether there are ongoing or recently concluded investigations or proceedings relating to

- an issuer,
- a promoter,
- a principal securityholder, director or officer of the issuer, or
- an underwriter or other person or company involved in a proposed distribution

when it determines if it should refuse to issue a receipt for the prospectus. That decision will be made on a case-by-case basis and will depend upon the facts known at the time.

If the facts and circumstances do not warrant the denial of a receipt for a prospectus, securities legislation nonetheless imposes an obligation to provide full, true and plain disclosure of all material facts relating to the securities offered by the prospectus. Disclosure of an ongoing or recently concluded investigation or proceeding relating to a person or company involved in a proposed distribution may be necessary to meet this standard. The circumstances in which disclosure will be required and the nature and extent of the disclosure will also be determined on a case-by-case basis. In making this determination, all relevant facts, including the allegations that gave rise to the investigation or proceeding, the status of the investigation or proceeding, the seriousness of the alleged breaches that are the subject of the investigation or proceeding and the degree of involvement in the proposed distribution by the person or company under investigation will be considered.

3.10 Amendments — (1) Subsection 6.5(1) of the Instrument and other securities legislation provides that if a material adverse change occurs after a receipt for a preliminary prospectus is obtained, an amendment to the preliminary prospectus must be filed as soon as practicable, but in any event within 10 days after the change occurs. If a preliminary prospectus indicates the number or value of the securities to be distributed under the prospectus, an increase in the number or value is, absent unusual circumstances, unlikely to constitute a material adverse change requiring an amendment to the preliminary prospectus.

(2) If, after filing a preliminary prospectus, an issuer decides to attach or add to the securities offered under a prospectus a right to convert into, or a warrant to acquire, the security of the issuer being offered under the preliminary prospectus, the attachment or addition of the conversion feature or warrant is, absent unusual circumstances, unlikely to constitute a material adverse change requiring an amendment to the preliminary prospectus.

(3) Securities legislation provides that no person or company shall distribute securities, unless a preliminary prospectus and a prospectus have been filed and receipts have been issued by the securities regulatory authority or regulator. If an issuer intends to add a new class of securities to the distribution under the prospectus after the preliminary prospectus has been filed and receipted, we interpret this requirement to mean an issuer must file an amended and restated preliminary prospectus.

Similarly, if an issuer wishes to add a new class of securities to a prospectus before the distribution under that prospectus is completed the issuer must file a preliminary prospectus for that class of securities and an amended and restated prospectus and obtain receipts for both the preliminary prospectus and the amended prospectus. Alternatively the issuer may file a separate preliminary prospectus and prospectus for the new class of securities. We interpret this requirement to also apply to mutual funds. If a mutual fund adds a new class or series of securities to a prospectus that is referable to a new separate portfolio of assets, a preliminary prospectus must be filed. However, if the new class or series of securities is referable to an existing portfolio of assets, the new class or series may be added by way of amendment.

(4) Any changes to the terms or conditions of the security being distributed, such as the deletion of a conversion feature, may constitute a material adverse change requiring an amendment to the preliminary prospectus.

(5) Under securities legislation, a regulator must not issue a receipt for a prospectus in certain circumstances, including if the regulator considers it prejudicial to the public interest to do so. The purpose of subsection 6.6(3) of the Instrument is to clarify that these receipt refusal grounds apply to an amendment to a final prospectus or a final short form prospectus in certain jurisdictions.

(6) Marketing materials prepared under section 13.7 or 13.8 of the Instrument cannot amend a preliminary prospectus, a final prospectus or any amendment.

3.11 Reduced price distributions — Subsection 7.2(3) of the Instrument permits an issuer to reduce the offering price of the securities being distributed without filing an amendment to the prospectus if certain conditions are satisfied. Satisfying the conditions in this subsection means the underwriter's compensation should decrease by the amount that the aggregate price paid by purchasers for the securities is less than the gross proceeds paid by the underwriter to the issuer or selling securityholder. Section 20.8 of Form 41-101F1 requires disclosure of this fact.

3.12 Licences, registrations and approvals — For the purposes of section 10.2 of the Instrument, we would generally conclude that an issuer has all material licences, registrations and approvals necessary for the stated principal use of proceeds if the issuer could use a material portion of the proceeds of the distribution in the manner described in the prospectus without obtaining the licence, registration or approval.

3.13 Registration requirements — Issuers filing a prospectus and other market participants are reminded to ensure that members of underwriting syndicates are in compliance with registration requirements under securities legislation in each jurisdiction in which syndicate members are participating in the distribution of securities under the prospectus. Failure to comply with the registration requirements could cause the regulator to refuse to issue a receipt for the prospectus.

PART 4 — GENERAL CONTENT OF LONG FORM PROSPECTUS

4.1 Style of long form prospectus — Securities legislation requires that a long form prospectus contain "full, true and plain" disclosure. Issuers should apply plain language principles when they prepare a long form prospectus including:

- using short sentences;
- using definite everyday language;
- using the active voice;
- avoiding superfluous words;
- organizing the document into clear, concise sections, paragraphs and sentences;
- avoiding jargon;
- using personal pronouns to speak directly to the reader;
- avoiding reliance on glossaries and defined terms unless it facilitates understanding of the disclosure;
- avoiding vague boilerplate wording;
- avoiding abstract terms by using more concrete terms or examples;
- avoiding multiple negatives;
- using technical terms only when necessary and explaining those terms;
- using charts, tables and examples where it makes disclosure easier to understand.

Question and answer and bullet point formats are consistent with the disclosure requirements of the Instrument.

4.1.1 Plan summary for a scholarship plan — To help write the plan summary for a scholarship plan in plain language, scholarship plan providers may use the Flesch-Kincaid methodology to assess the readability of a plan summary. The Flesch-Kincaid grade level scale is a methodology that rates the readability of a text to a corresponding grade level and can be determined by the use of Flesch-Kincaid tests built into commonly used word processing programs. For French-language documents, scholarship plan providers may wish to consider using other appropriate readability tools.

4.2 Pricing disclosure — (1) If the offering price or the number of securities being distributed, or an estimate of the range of the offering price or the number of securities being distributed, has been publicly disclosed in a jurisdiction or a foreign jurisdiction as of the date of the preliminary long form prospectus, section 1.7 of Form 41-101F1 requires the issuer to disclose that information in the preliminary long form prospectus. For example, if an issuer has previously disclosed this information in a public filing or a press release, in a foreign jurisdiction, the information must also be disclosed in the preliminary long form prospectus. If the issuer discloses this information in the preliminary long form prospectus, we will not consider a difference between this information and the actual offering price or number of securities being distributed to be, in itself, a material adverse change for which the issuer must file an amended preliminary long form prospectus.

(2) No disclosure is required under section 1.7 of Form 41-101F1 if the offering price or size of the offering has not been disclosed as of the date of the preliminary long form prospectus. However, given the materiality of pricing or offering size information, subsequent disclosure of this information on a selective basis could constitute conduct that is prejudicial to the public interest.

(3) If a minimum offering amount is not provided and the issuer faces significant short-term expenditures or commitments, the issuer must provide additional disclosure as required under subsections 6.3(3) and (4) of Form 41-101F1 or subsections 4.2(3) and (4) of Form 44-101F1. The issuer must provide disclosure of how it will use the proceeds at different thresholds, describing what business objectives will be accomplished at each threshold as well as the priority of how the proceeds will be used. In describing the use of proceeds under each threshold, the disclosure must also include an assessment of the impact of raising this amount on the issuer's liquidity, operations, capital resources and solvency.

Disclosures that may be necessary to understand this impact may include the following examples:

(a) for issuers without significant revenue and available working capital, disclose the anticipated length of time that the proceeds at each threshold will suffice to meet expected cash requirements;

(b) for issuers that have or anticipate having within the next 12 months any cash flow or liquidity problems, disclose how the proceeds at each threshold may impact the issuer's ability to continue in operation for the foreseeable future and realize assets and discharge liabilities in the normal course of operations;

(c) for issuers that have significant projects that have not yet commenced operations and the projects have therefore not yet generated revenue, describe how the proceeds at each threshold may impact the anticipated timing and costs of the project and other critical milestones;

(d) for issuers that have exploration and development expenditures or research and development expenditures required to maintain properties or agreements in good standing, describe how the proceeds at each threshold may impact these properties or agreements.

If the issuer anticipates additional funds from other sources are to be used in conjunction with the proceeds and the available working capital, the issuer will need to sufficiently describe the amounts of those funds, the source of those funds and whether those funds are firm or contingent. If the funds are contingent, the issuer should describe the nature of the contingency.

Depending on the particular circumstances of the issuer, one or more of the above examples may require the provision of a minimum offering amount in the prospectus. Refer to section 2.2.1 of this Policy for additional guidance.

4.3 Principal purposes — generally — (1) Subsection 6.3(1) of Form 41-101F1 requires disclosure of each of the principal purposes for which the issuer will use the net proceeds. If an issuer has negative cash flow from operating activities in its most recently completed financial year for which financial statements have been included in the long form prospectus, the issuer should prominently disclose that fact in the use of proceeds section of the long form prospectus. The issuer should also disclose whether, and if so, to what extent, the issuer will use the proceeds of the distribution to fund any anticipated negative cash flow from operating activities in future periods. An issuer should disclose negative cash flow from operating activities as a risk factor under subsection 21.1(1) of Form 41-101F1. For the purposes of this section, in determining cash flow from operating activities, the issuer must include cash payments related to dividends and borrowing costs.

(2) For the purposes of the disclosure required under section 6.3 of Form 41-101F1, the phrase "for general corporate purposes" is not generally sufficient.

4.4 MD&A — (1) Additional information for venture issuers without significant revenue — Section 8.6 of Form 41-101F1 requires certain venture issuers and IPO venture issuers to disclose a breakdown of material costs whether expensed or recognized as assets. A component of cost is generally considered to be a material component if it exceeds the greater of

(a) 20% of the total amount of the class, and

(b) $25,000.

(2) Disclosure of outstanding security data — Section 8.4 of Form 41-101F1 requires disclosure of information relating to the outstanding securities of the issuer as of the latest practicable date. The "latest practicable date" should be as close as possible to the date of the long form prospectus. Disclosing the number of securities outstanding at the most recently completed financial period is generally not sufficient to meet this requirement.

(3) Additional disclosure for issuers with significant equity investees — Section 8.8 of Form 41-101F1 requires issuers with significant equity investees to provide in their long form prospectuses summarized information about the equity investee. Generally, we will consider that an equity investee is significant if, using the financial statements of the equity investee and the issuer as at the issuer's financial year-end,

either of the following apply:

(a) for an issuer that is not a venture issuer or an IPO venture issuer, the equity investee would meet the thresholds for the significance tests in Item 35 of Form 41-101F1;

(b) for a venture issuer or an IPO venture issuer, the equity investee would meet the thresholds for the significance tests in Item 35 of Form 41-101F1 if "100 percent" is read as "40 percent".

4.5 Distribution of asset-backed securities — Section 10.3 of Form 41-101F1 specifies additional disclosure that applies to distributions of asset-backed securities. Disclosure for a special purpose issuer of asset-backed securities will generally explain

• the nature, performance and servicing of the underlying pool of financial assets,

• the structure of the securities and dedicated cash flows, and

• any third party or internal support arrangements established to protect holders of the asset-backed securities from losses associated with non-performance of the financial assets or disruptions in payment.

The nature and extent of required disclosure may vary depending on the type and attributes of the underlying pool and the contractual arrangements through which holders of the asset-backed securities take their interest in such assets.

An issuer of asset-backed securities should consider the following factors when preparing its long form prospectus:

(a) The extent of disclosure respecting an issuer will depend on the extent of the issuer's on-going involvement in the conversion of the assets comprising the pool to cash and the distribution of cash to securityholders; this involvement may, in turn, vary dramatically depending on the type, quality and attributes of the assets comprising the pool and on the overall structure of the transaction.

1253

Part 4:
DISTRIBUTIONS

(b) Disclosure about the business and affairs of the issuer should relate to the financial assets underlying the asset-backed securities.

(c) Disclosure about the originator or the seller of the underlying financial assets will often be relevant to investors in the asset-backed securities particularly where the originator or seller has an on-going involvement with the financial assets comprising the pool. For example, if asset-backed securities are serviced with the cash flows from a revolving pool of receivables, an evaluation of the nature and reliability of the future origination or the future sales of underlying assets by the seller to or through the issuer may be a critical aspect of an investor's investment decision.

To address this, the focus of disclosure respecting an originator or seller of the underlying financial assets should deal with whether there are current circumstances that indicate that the originator or seller will not generate adequate assets in the future to avoid an early liquidation of the pool and, correspondingly, an early payment of the asset-backed securities. Summary historical financial information respecting the originator or seller will ordinarily be adequate to satisfy the disclosure requirements applicable to the originator or seller in circumstances where the originator or seller has an ongoing relationship with the assets comprising the pool.

Subsection 10.3(10) of Form 41-101F1 requires issuers of asset-backed securities to describe any person or company who originated, sold or deposited a material portion of the financial assets comprising the pool, irrespective of whether the person or company has an on-going relationship with the assets comprising the pool. The securities regulatory authorities consider 33⅓;% of the dollar value of the financial assets comprising the pool to be a material portion in this context.

4.6 Distribution of derivatives and underlying securities — (1) Section 10.4 of Form 41-101F1 specifies additional disclosure applicable to distributions of derivatives. This prescribed disclosure is formulated in general terms for issuers to customize appropriately in particular circumstances.

(2) If the securities being distributed are convertible into or exchangeable for other securities, or are a derivative of, or otherwise linked to, other securities, a description of the material attributes of the underlying securities will generally be necessary to meet the requirements of securities legislation that a long form prospectus contain full, true and plain disclosure of all material facts concerning the securities being distributed.

4.7 Restricted securities — Section 10.6 of Form 41-101F1 specifies additional disclosure for restricted securities, including a detailed description of any significant provisions under applicable corporate and securities law that do not apply to the holders of the restricted securities but do apply to the holders of another class of equity securities. An example of such provisions would be rights under takeover bids.

4.8 Credit supporter disclosure — A long form prospectus must include, under Item 33 of Form 41-101F1, disclosure about any credit supporters that have provided a guarantee or alternative credit support for all or substantially all of the payments to be made under the securities being distributed. Disclosure about a credit supporter may be required even if the credit supporter has not provided full and unconditional credit support.

4.9 Exemptions for certain issues of guaranteed securities — Requiring disclosure about the issuer and any applicable credit supporters in a long form prospectus may result in unnecessary disclosure in some instances. Item 34 of Form 41-101F1 provides exemptions from the requirement to include both issuer and credit supporter disclosure where such disclosure is not necessary to ensure that the long form prospectus includes full, true and plain disclosure of all material facts concerning the securities to be distributed.

These exemptions are based on the principle that, in these instances, investors will generally require issuer disclosure or credit supporter disclosure to make an informed investment decision. These exemptions are not intended to be comprehensive and issuers may apply for exemptive relief from the requirement to provide both issuer and credit supporter disclosure, as appropriate.

4.10 Previously disclosed material forward-looking information — If an issuer, at the time it files a long form prospectus,

(a) has previously disclosed to the public material forward-looking information for a period that is not yet complete, and

(b) is aware of events and circumstances that are reasonably likely to cause actual results to differ materially from the material forward-looking information,

the issuer should discuss those events and circumstances, and the expected differences from the material forward-looking information, in the long form prospectus.

PART 5 — CONTENT OF LONG FORM PROSPECTUS (FINANCIAL STATEMENTS)

5.1 Exemptions from financial disclosure requirements — Request for exemptions from financial disclosure should be made in accordance with Part 19 of the Instrument, which requires the issuer to make submissions in writing along with the reasons for the request. Written submissions should be filed at the time the preliminary long form prospectus is filed, and include any proposed alternative disclosure. If the application involves a novel and substantive issue or raises a novel public policy concern, issuers should use the pre-filing procedures under NP 11-202. Issuers that are not filing their prospectuses under NP 11-202 should also follow the principles outlined and procedures set out in NP 11-202.

5.1.1 Presentation of Financial Results — Canadian GAAP applicable to publicly accountable enterprises provides an issuer two alternatives in presenting its income: (a) in one single statement of comprehensive income, or (b) in a statement of comprehensive income with a separate income statement. If an issuer presents its income using the second alternative, both statements must be filed to satisfy the requirements of this Instrument. (See subsections 32.2(1.1) and 32.3(3) of Form 41-101F1).

5.2 General financial statement requirements — If an issuer has filed annual financial statements or interim financial report for periods that are more recent than those that the issuer must otherwise include in a long form prospectus before it files the prospectus, sections 32.6 and 35.8 of Form 41-101F1 require the issuer to include those financial statements in the long form prospectus. Issuers should update the disclosure in the prospectus accordingly in order to satisfy the requirement that the long form prospectus contain full, true and plain disclosure of all material facts relating to the securities being distributed. However, if historical financial information derived from more recent annual financial statements or interim financial report is released to the public by the issuer before the financial statements are filed, the prospectus should include the information included in the news release or public communication. There is no specific requirement in the Instrument to otherwise update the prospectus, or pro forma financial statements to reflect the more recent information.

We think the directors of an issuer should endeavor to consider and approve financial statements in a timely manner and should not delay the approval and filing of the financial statements for the purpose of avoiding their inclusion in a long form prospectus. Once the directors have approved an issuer's financial statements, the issuer should file them as soon as possible.

5.3 Interpretation of issuer — primary business — (1) An issuer is required to provide historical financial statements under Item 32 of Form 41-101F1 for a business or related businesses that a reasonable investor would regard as the primary business of the issuer. However, if the issuer is a reporting issuer whose principal assets are not cash, cash equivalents or an exchange listing, and the acquisition of the primary business represents a significant acquisition for the issuer, the reporting issuer is subject to the requirements of Item 35 in respect of the financial statement and other disclosure for the acquisition.

An acquisition does not include a reverse takeover, as defined in NI 41-101 which cross-references the meaning of acquisition as used in Part 8 of NI 51-102. Therefore a reporting issuer cannot rely on the exemption in subsection 32.1(2) if the applicable transaction is a reverse takeover.

Examples of when a reasonable investor would regard the primary business of the issuer to be the acquired business or related businesses, thereby triggering the application of Item 32, are when the acquisition(s) was

    (a) a reverse takeover,

    (b) a qualifying transaction for a Capital Pool Company, or

    (c) an acquisition that is a significant acquisition at over the 100% level under subsection 35.1(4) of Form 41-101F1.

The issuer should consider the facts of each situation to determine whether a reasonable investor would regard the primary business of the issuer to be the acquired business or related businesses.

(2) The periods for which the issuer must provide financial statements under Item 32 of Form 41-101F1 for an acquired business or businesses that are regarded as the primary business of the issuer should be determined in reference to sections 32.2 and 32.3 of Form 41-101F1, and with the same exceptions, where applicable, set out in paragraphs 32.4(a) through (e) of Form 41-101F1. For example, for an issuer that is a reporting issuer in at least one jurisdiction immediately before filing a long form prospectus, the reference to three years in subparagraph 32.2(6)(a) of Form 41-101F1 should be read as two years under paragraphs 32.4(a), (b), (d) and (e) of Form 41-101F1.

The issuer must also consider the necessity of including pro forma financial statements pursuant to section 32.7 of Form 41-101F1 to illustrate the impact of the acquisition of the primary business on the issuer's financial position and results of operations. For additional guidance, an issuer should refer to section 5.10 of this Policy.

5.4 Interpretation of issuer — predecessor entity — (1) An issuer is required to provide historical financial statements under Item 32 of the Form 41-101F1 for any predecessor entity. This includes financial statements of acquired businesses that are unrelated and not otherwise individually significant, but together form the basis of the business of the issuer. However, if the issuer is a reporting issuer whose principal assets are not cash, cash equivalents or an exchange listing, and the acquisition of the predecessor entity represents a significant acquisition for the issuer, the reporting issuer is subject to the requirements of Item 35 in respect of the financial statement and other disclosure for the acquisition.

The issuer must also consider the necessity of including pro forma financial statements pursuant to section 32.7 of Form 41-101F1 to illustrate the impact of the acquisition of the predecessor entity on the issuer's financial position and results of operations. For additional guidance, an issuer should refer to section 5.10 of this Policy.

(2) If an issuer determines the financial statements of certain acquired businesses referred to in subsection (1) are not relevant, the issuer should utilize the pre-filing procedures in NP 11-202 to determine whether it would require an exemption from the requirement to include these financial statements.

5.5 Sufficiency of financial history included in a long form prospectus — (1) Item 32 of Form 41-101F1 prescribes the issuer financial statements that must be included in a long form prospectus. We recognize that an issuer, at the time of filing a long form prospectus, may have been in existence for less than one year. We expect that in many situations the limited historical financial statement information that is available for such an issuer may be adequately supplemented by other relevant information disclosed in the long form prospectus. However, if the issuer cannot provide financial statements for a period of at least 12 months and the long form prospectus does not otherwise contain information concerning the business conducted or to be conducted by the issuer that is sufficient to enable an investor to make an informed investment decision, a securities regulatory authority or regulator may consider this a key factor when deciding whether it should refuse to issue a receipt for the long form prospectus.

(2) A reference to a prospectus includes a preliminary prospectus. Consequently, the time references in sections 32.2, 32.3, 35.5 and 35.6 of Form 41-101F1 should be considered as at the date of the preliminary long form prospectus and again at the date of the final long form prospectus for both the issuer and any business acquired or to be acquired. Depending on the period of time between the dates of the preliminary and final long form prospectuses, an issuer may have to include more recent financial statements.

(3) An issuer is subject to certain additional disclosure requirements when it discloses an interim financial report for a period in the year of adopting IFRS, as set out in subparagraph 32.3(2)(e) and subsection 32.3(4) of Form 41-101F1. These requirements only apply to interim financial reports relating to periods in the year of adopting IFRS and therefore do not apply if the prospectus includes annual financial statements prepared in accordance with IFRS.

An issuer is required to provide an opening IFRS statement of financial position at the date of transition to IFRS. An issuer with, for example, a year-end of December 31, 2010 that files a prospectus for which it must include its first interim financial report in the year of adopting IFRS for the period ended March 31, 2011, must generally provide an opening IFRS statement of financial position at January 1, 2010.

An issuer must also include various reconciliations required by IFRS 1 to explain how the transition from previous GAAP to IFRS has affected its reported financial position, financial performance and cash flows. In the first interim period IFRS 1 requires certain additional reconciliations which relate to annual periods and the date of transition to IFRS. Where an issuer that was not a reporting issuer in at least one jurisdiction immediately before filing the prospectus includes an interim financial report in respect of the second or third interim period in the year of adopting IFRS, subsection 32.3(4) of Form 41-101F1 requires these additional reconciliations to be included in the prospectus. Alternatively, pursuant to subsection 32.3(4) of Form 41-101F1, the issuer may include the first interim financial report in the year of adopting IFRS as this report includes the required reconciliations.

These additional reconciliations may be summarized as follows:

- reconciliations of the issuer's equity presented in accordance with previous GAAP to its equity in accordance with IFRS for the date of transition to IFRS (January 1, 2010 in the above-noted example);
- reconciliations of the issuer's equity presented in accordance with previous GAAP to its equity in accordance with IFRS for the end of the latest period presented in the issuer's most recent annual financial statements in accordance with previous GAAP (December 31, 2010 in the above-noted example); and
- a reconciliation of the issuer's total comprehensive income (or total profit or loss) presented in accordance with previous GAAP to its total comprehensive income in accordance with IFRS for the latest period in the issuer's most recent annual financial statements presented in the prospectus in accordance with previous GAAP (year ended December 31, 2010 in the above-noted example).

The reconciliations summarized above must give sufficient detail to enable investors to understand the material adjustments to the statement of financial position, statement of comprehensive income and statement of cash flows.

5.6 Applications for exemption from requirement to include financial statements of the issuer — (1) We believe investors should receive in a long form prospectus for an IPO no less than three years of audited historical financial statements and that relief from the financial statements requirements should be granted only in unusual circumstances and generally not related solely to the cost or the time involved in preparing and auditing the financial statements.

(2) In view of our reluctance to grant exemptions from the requirement to include audited historical financial statements, issuers seeking relief should consult with staff on a pre-filing basis.

(3) Considerations relevant to granting an exemption from the requirement to include financial statements, generally for the years immediately preceding the issuer's most recently completed financial year, may include the following:

The issuer's historical accounting records have been destroyed and cannot be reconstructed.

(a) In this case, as a condition of granting the exemption, the issuer may be requested by a securities regulatory authority or regulator to

(i) represent in writing to the securities regulatory authority or regulator, no later than the time the preliminary long form prospectus is filed, that the issuer made every reasonable effort to obtain copies of, or reconstruct, the historical accounting records necessary to prepare and audit the financial statements, but such efforts were unsuccessful, and

(ii) disclose in the long form prospectus the fact that the historical accounting records have been destroyed and cannot be reconstructed.

The issuer has emerged from bankruptcy and current management is denied access to the historical accounting records necessary to audit the financial statements.

(b) In this case, as a condition of granting the exemption, the issuer may be requested by a securities regulatory authority or regulator to

(i) represent in writing to the securities regulatory authority or regulator, no later than the time the preliminary long form prospectus is filed, that the issuer has made every reasonable effort to obtain access to, or copies of, the historical accounting records necessary to audit the financial statements but that such efforts were unsuccessful, and

(ii) disclose in the long form prospectus the fact that the issuer has emerged from bankruptcy and current management is denied access to the historical accounting records.

The issuer has undergone a fundamental change in the nature of its business or operations affecting a majority of its operations and all, or substantially all, of the executive officers and directors of the company have changed.

(c) The evolution of a business or progression along a development cycle will not be considered to be a fundamental change in an issuer's business or operations. Relief from the requirement to include financial statements of the issuer required by the Instrument for the year in which the change occurred, or for the most recently completed financial year if the change in operations occurred during the issuer's current financial year, generally will not be granted.

(4) If, in unusual circumstances, relief from Part 4 of the Instrument is granted, additional financial information will likely be requested to allow a reader to gain a similar understanding of the entity's financial position and prospects as one would gain from the information required in Part 4 of the Instrument.

Examples of acceptable additional information include an audited interim financial report, audited divisional statements of comprehensive income or cash flows, financial statements accompanied by an auditor's report that expresses a modified opinion, or audited statements of net operating income.

5.7 Additional information — An issuer may find it necessary, in order to meet the requirement for full, true and plain disclosure contained in securities legislation, to include certain additional information in its long form prospectus, such as separate financial statements of a subsidiary of the issuer in a long form prospectus, even if the financial statements of the subsidiary are included in the consolidated financial statements of the issuer. For example, separate financial statements of a subsidiary may be necessary to help explain the risk profile and nature of the operations of the subsidiary.

5.8 Audit and review of financial statements included or incorporated by reference into a long form prospectus — (1) Part 4 of the Instrument requires that all financial statements included in a long form prospectus be audited, except financial statements specifically exempted in the Instrument. This requirement extends to financial statements of subsidiaries and other entities even if the financial statements are not required to be included in the long form prospectus but have been included at the discretion of the issuer.

(2) NI 52-107 requires that financial statements, other than acquisition statements, that are required to be audited by securities legislation, such as this Instrument, be accompanied by an auditor's report that expresses an unmodified opinion if they were audited in accordance with Canadian GAAS or International Standards on Auditing, or contain an unqualified opinion if they were audited in accordance with U.S. PCAOB GAAS. This requirement applies to all financial statements included in the long form prospectus under Item 32 of Form 41-101F1, including financial statements from entities acquired or to be acquired that are the primary business or the predecessor of the issuer. For greater clarity, subsections 3.12(3) and 4.12(6) of NI 52-107 only apply to financial statements included in the long form prospectus pursuant to Item 35 of Form 41-101F1. Relief may be granted to non-reporting issuers in appropriate circumstances to permit the auditor's report on financial statements to contain a qualified opinion relating to opening inventory if there is a subsequent audited period of at least six months on which the auditor's report expresses an unmodified opinion and the business is not seasonal. Issuers requesting this relief should be aware that NI 51-102 requires an issuer's comparative financial statements be accompanied by an auditors' report that expresses an unmodified opinion.

5.9 Financial statement disclosure for significant acquisitions — (1) Applicable principles in NI 51-102 — Generally, it is intended that the disclosure requirements set out in Item 35 of Form 41-101F1 for significant acquisitions follow the requirements in Part 8 of NI 51-102. The guidance in Part 8 of the companion policy to NI 51-102 ("51-102CP") apply to any disclosure of a significant business acquisition in a long form prospectus required by Item 35 of Form 41-101F1, except

(a) any headings in Part 8 of 51-102CP should be disregarded,

(b) subsections 8.1(1), 8.1(5), 8.7(8), and 8.10(2) of 51-102CP do not apply,

(c) other than in subsections 8.3(4) and 8.7(7) of 51-102CP, any references to a "reporting issuer" should be read as an "issuer",

(d) any references to the "Instrument" should be read as "NI 51-102",

(e) any references to a provision in NI 51-102 in 51-102CP should be read to include the following "as it applies to a long form prospectus pursuant to Item 35 of Form 41-101F1",

(f) any references to "business acquisition report" should be read as "long form prospectus",

(g) in subsection 8.1(2) of 51-102CP, the term "file a copy of the documents as its business acquisition report" should be read as "include that disclosure in its long form prospectus in lieu of the significant acquisition disclosure required under Item 35 of Form 41-101F1",

(h) in subsection 8.2(1) of 51-102CP,

    (i) the term "The test" should be read as "For any completed acquisition, the test",

    (ii) the sentence "For any proposed acquisition of a business or related businesses by an issuer that has progressed to a state where a reasonable person would believe that the likelihood of the issuer completing the acquisition is high, the test must be applied using the financial statements included in the long form prospectus." should be added after "the business.", and

    (iii) the term "business acquisition report will be required to be filed" should be read as "disclosure regarding the significant acquisition is required to be included in the issuer's long form prospectus",

(i) in subsection 8.3(1) of 51-102CP, the term "filing a business acquisition report" should be read as "the financial statements used for the optional tests",

(j) in section 8.5, and subsection 8.7(4), of 51-102CP, the term "filed" wherever it occurs, should be read as "included in the long form prospectus",

(k) in subsection 8.7(1) of 51-102CP, the term "as already filed" should be read as "included in the long form prospectus",

(l) in subsection 8.7(2) of 51-102CP, the term "filed under the Instrument" should be read as "included in the long form prospectus",

(m) in subsection 8.7(4) of 51-102CP, the term "presented" should be read as "for which financial statements are included in the prospectus",

(n) in subsection 8.7(6) of 51-102CP, the term "for which financial statements are included in the long form prospectus" should be added after "financial year",

(o) in paragraph 8.8(a) of 51-102CP, the term "prior to the deadline for filing the business acquisition report" should be read as "using the pre-filing procedures referred to in section 5.1 of this Policy",

(p) in subsection 8.9(1) of 51-102CP, the term "before the filing deadline for the business acquisition report and before the closing date of the transaction, if applicable. Reporting issuers are reminded that many securities regulatory authorities and regulators do not have the power to grant retroactive relief" should be read as "using the pre-filing procedures referred to in section 5.1 of this Policy", and

(q) in subparagraphs 8.9(4)(a)(i) and 8.9(4)(b)(i) of 51-102CP, the term "no later than the time the business acquisition report is required to be filed" wherever it occurs should be read as "using the pre-filing procedures referred to in section 5.1 of this Policy".

(r) in subparagraph 8.10(1) of 51-102CP, the term "but must be reviewed" should be added after "may be unaudited".

(2) Completed significant acquisitions and the obligation to provide business acquisition report level disclosure for a non-reporting issuer — For an issuer that is not a reporting issuer in any jurisdiction immediately before filing the long form prospectus (a "non-reporting issuer"), the long form prospectus disclosure requirements for a significant acquisition are generally intended to mirror those for reporting issuers subject to Part 8 of NI 51-102. To determine whether an acquisition is significant, non-reporting issuers would first look to the guidance under section 8.3 of NI 51-102. The initial test for significance would be calculated based on the financial statements of the issuer and acquired business or related businesses for the most recently completed financial year of each that ended before the acquisition date.

To recognize the possible growth of a non-reporting issuer between the date of its most recently completed year end and the acquisition date and the corresponding potential decline in significance of the acquisition to the issuer, issuers should refer to the guidance in paragraph 35.1(4)(b) of Form 41-101F1 to perform the optional test. The applicable time period for this optional test for the issuer is the most recently completed interim period or financial year for which financial statements of the issuer are included in the prospectus and for the acquired business or related businesses is the most recently completed interim period or financial year ended before the date of the long form prospectus

The significance thresholds for IPO venture issuers are identical to the significance thresholds for venture issuers.

The timing of the disclosure requirements set out in subsection 35.3(1) of Form 41-101F1 are based on the principles under section 8.2 of NI 51-102. For reporting issuers, subsection 8.2(2) of NI 51-102 sets out the timing of disclosures for significant acquisitions where the acquisition occurs within 45 days after the year end of the acquired business. However, for IPO venture issuers, paragraph 35.3(1)(d) imposes a disclosure requirement for all significant acquisitions completed more than 90 days before the date of the long form prospectus, where the acquisition occurs within 45 days after the year end of the acquired business. This differs from the business acquisition report filing deadline for venture issuers under paragraph 8.2(2)(b) of NI 51-102 where the business acquisition report deadline for any significant acquisition where the acquisition occurs within 45 days after the year end of the acquired business is within 120 days after the acquisition date.

(3) Probable acquisitions — When interpreting the phrase "where a reasonable person would believe that the likelihood of the acquisition being completed is high", it is our view that the following factors may be relevant in determining whether the likelihood of an acquisition being completed is high:

    (a) whether the acquisition has been publicly announced;

    (b) whether the acquisition is the subject of an executed agreement;

    (c) the nature of conditions to the completion of the acquisition including any material third party consents required.

The test of whether a proposed acquisition "has progressed to a state where a reasonable person would believe that the likelihood of the acquisition being completed is high" is an objective, rather than subjective, test in that the question turns on what a "reasonable person" would believe. It is not sufficient for an officer of an issuer to determine that he or she personally believes that the likelihood of the acquisition being completed is or is not high. The officer must form an opinion as to what a reasonable person would believe in the circumstances. In the event of a dispute, an objective test requires an adjudicator to decide whether a reasonable person would believe in the circumstances that the likelihood of an acquisition being completed was high. By contrast, if the disclosure requirement involved a subjective test, the adjudicator would assess an individual's credibility and decide whether the personal opinion of the individual as to whether the likelihood of the acquisition being completed was high was an honestly held opinion. Formulating the disclosure requirement using an objective test rather than a subjective test strengthens the basis upon which the regulator may object to an issuer's application of the test in particular circumstances.

We generally presume that the inclusion of financial statements or other information is required for all acquisitions that are, or would be, significant under Part 8 of NI 51-102. Reporting issuers can rebut this presumption if they can provide evidence that the financial statements or other information are not required for full, true and plain disclosure.

(4) Satisfactory alternative financial statements or other information — Issuers must satisfy the disclosure requirements in section 35.5 or section 35.6 of Form 41-101F1 by including either:

(i) the financial statements or other information that would be required by Part 8 of NI 51-102; or

(ii) satisfactory alternative financial statements or other information.

Satisfactory alternative financial statements or other information may be provided to satisfy the requirements of subsection 35.5(3) or subsection 35.6(3) of Form 41-101F1 when the financial statements or other information that would be required by Part 8 of NI 51-102 relate to a financial year ended within 90 days before the date of the long form prospectus or an interim period ended within 60 days before the date of the long form prospectus for issuers that are venture issuers, and 45 days for issuers that are not venture issuers. In these circumstances, we believe that satisfactory alternative financial statements or other information would not have to include any financial statements or other information for the acquisition or probable acquisition related to:

(a) a financial year ended within 90 days before the date of the long form prospectus; or

(b) an interim period ended within 60 days before the date of the long form prospectus for issuers that are venture issuers, and 45 days for issuers that are not venture issuers.

An example of satisfactory alternative financial statements or other information that we will generally find acceptable would be:

(c) comparative annual financial statements or other information for the acquisition or probable acquisition for at least the number of financial years as would be required under Part 8 of NI 51-102 that ended more than 90 days before the date of the long form prospectus, audited for the most recently completed financial period in accordance with section 4.2 of the Instrument, and reviewed for the comparative period in accordance with section 4.3 of the Instrument;

(d) a comparative interim financial report or other information for the acquisition or probable acquisition for any interim period ended subsequent to the latest annual financial statements included in the long form prospectus and more than 60 days before the date of the long form prospectus for issuers that are venture issuers, and 45 days for issuers that are not venture issuers reviewed in accordance with section 4.3 of the Instrument; and

(e) pro forma financial statements or other information required under Part 8 of NI 51-102.

If the issuer intends to include financial statements as set out in the example above as satisfactory alternative financial statements, we ask that this be highlighted in the cover letter to the long form prospectus. If the issuer does not intend to include financial statements or other information, or intends to file financial statements or other information that are different from those set out above, the issuer should use the pre-filing procedures in NP 11-202.

(5) Acquired business has recently completed an acquisition — When an issuer acquires a business or related businesses that has itself recently acquired another business or related businesses (an "indirect acquisition"), the issuer should consider whether long form prospectus disclosure about the indirect acquisition, including historical financial statements, is necessary to satisfy the requirement that the long form prospectus contain full, true and plain disclosure of all material facts relating to the securities being distributed. In making this determination, the issuer should consider the following factors:

- if the indirect acquisition would meet any of the significance tests in section 35.1(4) of Form 41-101F1 when the issuer applies each of those tests to its proportionate interest in the indirect acquisition of the business;

- if the amount of time between the separate acquisitions is such that the effect of the first acquisition is not adequately reflected in the results of the business or related businesses the issuer is acquiring.

(6) Financial statements or other information — Paragraphs 35.5(2)(b) and 35.6(2)(b) discuss financial statements or other information for the acquired business or related businesses. This "other information" is intended to capture the financial information disclosures required under Part 8 of NI 51-102 other than financial statements. An example of "other information" would include the operating statements, property descriptions, production volumes and reserves disclosures described under section 8.10 of NI 51-102.

(7) Section 3.11 of NI 52-107 permits acquisition statements included in a business acquisition report or prospectus to be prepared in accordance with Canadian GAAP applicable to private enterprises in certain circumstances. The ability to present acquisition statements using Canadian GAAP applicable to private enterprises would not extend to a situation where an entity acquired or to be acquired is considered the primary business or the predecessor of the issuer and the issuer must provide financial statements for this acquisition under Item 32.

5.10 Financial statements for acquisitions of a predecessor entity, a business or businesses acquired by reporting and non-reporting issuers — (1) The financial statements for acquisitions of a predecessor entity, a business or businesses acquired by the issuer, or other entity must be included in the prospectus under Item 32 of Form 41-101F1, if the entities or businesses satisfy the conditions of paragraph 32.1(1)(a), (b), or (c) unless, as contemplated in subsection 32.1(2) with respect to paragraph 32.1(1)(a) or (b)

(a) the issuer was a reporting issuer in any jurisdiction of Canada on the acquisition date in the case of a completed acquisition or immediately prior to the prospectus filing in the case of a proposed acquisition,

(b) the issuer did not have only cash, cash equivalents or an exchange listing as its principal asset, and

(c) the issuer provides disclosure under Item 35 of Form 41-101F1.

The disclosure requirements applicable to a reporting issuer in Item 35 are intended to reflect the requirements that would be prescribed for such acquisitions in the reporting issuer's business acquisition report.

(2) An issuer that is subject to Item 32 must also consider the necessity of including pro forma financial statements pursuant to section 32.7 of Form 41-101F1 to illustrate the impact of the acquisition on the issuer's financial position and results of operations. However, these pro forma financial statements are only required if their inclusion is necessary for the prospectus to contain full, true and plain disclosure of all material facts relating to the securities being distributed. Examples of when pro forma financial statements would likely be necessary are in cases where:

(a) the issuer has acquired multiple businesses over the relevant period; or

(b) the issuer has an active business and has acquired another business that will constitute its primary business going forward.

In certain circumstances, an issuer may need to disclose multiple acquisitions in its prospectus where the acquisitions include an acquisition of a primary business or predecessor entity to which section 32.1 of Form 41-101F1 applies and a significant acquisition to which only item 35 of Form 41-101F1 applies. In this case, the issuer may wish to present one set of pro forma financial statements reflecting the results of all of the acquisitions, as contemplated separately in each of sections 32.8 and 35.7 of Form 41-101F1. The securities regulatory authority or regulator would not generally object to providing this relief. However the issuer must request the relief when filing its preliminary prospectus.

PART 6 — ADVERTISING OR MARKETING ACTIVITIES IN CONNECTION WITH PROSPECTUS OFFERINGS OF ISSUERS OTHER THAN INVESTMENT FUNDS

6.0 This Part applies to issuers other than investment funds filing a prospectus in the form of Form 41-101F2 or Form 41-101F3.

6.1 **Scope** — (1) The discussion below is focused on the impact of the prospectus requirement on advertising or marketing activities in connection with a prospectus offering.

(2) Issuers and other persons or companies that engage in advertising or marketing activities should also consider the impact of the requirement to register as a dealer in each jurisdiction where such advertising or marketing activities are undertaken. In particular, the persons or companies would have to consider whether their activities result in the party being in the business of trading in securities. For further information, refer to section 1.3 of Companion Policy 31-103CP *Registration Requirements, Exemptions and Ongoing Registrant Obligations*.

(3) Advertising or marketing activities are also subject to regulation under securities legislation and other rules, including those relating to disclosure, and insider trading and registration, which are not discussed below.

6.2 **The prospectus requirement** — (1) Securities legislation generally provides that no one may trade in a security where that trade would be a distribution unless the prospectus requirement has been satisfied, or an exemption is available.

(2) The analysis of whether any particular advertising or marketing activities is prohibited by virtue of the prospectus requirement turns largely on whether the activities constitute a trade and, if so, whether such a trade would constitute a distribution.

(3) In Québec, since securities legislation has been designed without the notion of a "trade", the analysis is dependent solely on whether the advertising or marketing activities constitute a distribution.

(4) **Definition of "trade"** — Securities legislation (other than the securities legislation of Québec) defines a "trade" in a non-exhaustive manner to include, among other things

- any sale or disposition of a security for valuable consideration,
- any receipt by a registrant of an order to buy or sell a security, and
- any act, advertisement, solicitation, conduct or negotiation directly or indirectly in furtherance of any of the foregoing.

(5) Any advertising or marketing activities that can be reasonably regarded as intended to promote a distribution of securities would be "conduct directly or indirectly in furtherance" of the distribution of a security and, therefore, would fall within the definition of a trade.

(6) **Definition of distribution** — Even though advertising or marketing activities constitute a "trade" for the purposes of securities legislation (other than the securities legislation of Québec), they would be prohibited by virtue of the prospectus requirement only if they also constitute a distribution under securities legislation. Securities legislation (other than the securities legislation of Québec) defines a distribution to include a "trade" in, among other things, previously unissued securities and securities that form part of a control block.

(7) The definition of distribution under the securities legislation of Québec includes the endeavour to obtain or the obtaining of subscribers or purchasers of previously unissued securities.

(8) **Prospectus exemptions** — It has been suggested by some that advertising or marketing activities, even if clearly made in furtherance of a distribution, could be undertaken in certain circumstances on a prospectus exempt basis. Specifically, it has been suggested that if an exemption from the prospectus requirement is available in respect of a specific distribution (even though the securities will be distributed under a prospectus), advertising or marketing related to such distribution would be exempt from the prospectus requirement. This analysis is premised on an argument that the advertising or marketing activities constitute one distribution that is exempt from the prospectus requirement while the actual sale of the security to the purchaser constitutes a second discrete distribution effected pursuant to the prospectus.

(9) We are of the view that this analysis is contrary to securities legislation. In these circumstances, the distribution in respect of which the advertising or marketing activities are undertaken is the distribution pursuant to the anticipated prospectus. Advertising or marketing must be viewed in the context of the prospectus offering and as an activity in furtherance of that distribution. If it were otherwise, the overriding concerns implicit and explicit in securities legislation regarding equal access to information, conditioning of the market, tipping and insider trading, and the provisions of the legislation designed to ensure such access to information and curb such abuses, could be easily circumvented.

Although the "testing of the waters" exemption in subsection 13.4(2) of the Instrument allows an investment dealer to solicit expressions of interest from accredited investors before the filing of a preliminary prospectus for an initial public offering, we note that the exemption is

- a limited accommodation to issuers and investment dealers that want a greater opportunity to confidentially test the waters before filing a preliminary prospectus for an initial public offering, and
- subject to a number of conditions to address our regulatory concerns, including conditions to deter conditioning of the market.

(10) We recognize that an issuer and a dealer may have a demonstrable *bona fide* intention to effect an exempt distribution and this distribution may be abandoned in favour of a prospectus offering. In these very limited circumstances, there may be two separate distributions. From the time when it is reasonable for a dealer to expect that a *bona fide* exempt distribution will be abandoned in favour of a prospectus offering, the general rules relating to advertising or marketing activities that constitute an act in furtherance of a distribution will apply.

6.3 **Advertising or marketing activities** — (1) The prospectus requirement applies to any act, advertisement, solicitation, conduct or negotiation directly or indirectly in furtherance of a distribution unless a prospectus exemption is available. Accordingly, advertising or marketing activities intended to promote the distribution of securities, in any form, would be prohibited by virtue of the prospectus requirement. Advertising or marketing activities subject to the prospectus requirement may be oral, written or electronic and include the following:

- television or radio advertisements or commentaries;
- published materials;

- correspondence;
- records;
- videotapes or other similar material;
- market letters;
- research reports;
- circulars;
- promotional seminar text;
- telemarketing scripts;
- reprints or excerpts of any other sales literature.

(2) Advertising or marketing activities that are not in furtherance of a distribution of securities would not generally fall within the definition of a distribution and, therefore, would not be prohibited by virtue of the prospectus requirement. The following activities would not generally be subject to the prospectus requirement:

- advertising and publicity campaigns that are aimed at either selling products or services of the issuer or raising public awareness of the issuer;
- communication of factual information concerning the business of the issuer that is released in a manner, timing and form that is consistent with the regular past communications practices of the issuer if that communication does not refer to or suggest the distribution of securities;
- the release or filing of information that is required to be released or filed pursuant to securities legislation.

(3) Any activities that form part of a plan or series of activities undertaken in anticipation or in furtherance of a distribution would usually trigger the prospectus requirement, even if they would be permissible if viewed in isolation. Similarly, we may still consider advertising or marketing activities that do not indicate that a distribution of securities is contemplated to be in furtherance of a distribution by virtue of their timing and content. In particular, where a private placement or other exempt distribution occurs prior to or contemporaneously with a prospectus offering, we may consider activities undertaken in connection with the exempt distribution as being in furtherance of the prospectus offering.

6.3A Research reports — (1) In order to address regulatory concerns such as conditioning of the market, an investment dealer involved with a potential prospectus offering for an issuer should not issue a research report on the issuer or provide media commentary on the issuer prior to the filing of a preliminary prospectus, the announcement of a bought deal under section 7.2 of NI 44-101 or the filing of a shelf prospectus supplement under NI 44-102, unless the investment dealer has appropriate "ethical wall" policies and procedures in place between:

- the business unit that proposes to issue the research report or provide media commentary, and
- the business unit that proposes to act as underwriter for the distribution.

We understand that many investment dealers have adopted written ethical wall policies and procedures designed to contain non-public information about an issuer and assist the investment dealer and its officers and employees in complying with applicable securities laws relating to insider trading and trading by "tippees" (these laws are summarized in sections 3.1 and 3.2 of National Policy 51-201 *Disclosure Standards*).

(2) Any research reports would have to comply with section 7.7 of the Universal Market Integrity Rules of the Investment Industry Regulatory Organization of Canada and any applicable local rule.

6.4 Pre-marketing and solicitation of expressions of interest in the context of a bought deal — (1) In general, any advertising or marketing activities undertaken in connection with a prospectus prior to the issuance of a receipt for the preliminary prospectus are prohibited under securities legislation by virtue of the prospectus requirement.

(2) In the context of a bought deal, a limited exemption to the prospectus requirement has been provided in Part 7 of NI 44-101. The exemption to is limited to communications by a dealer, directly or through any of its directors, officers, employees or agents, with any person or company (other than another dealer) for the purpose of obtaining from that person or company information as to the interest that it, or any person or company that it represents, may have in purchasing securities of the type that are proposed to be distributed, prior to a preliminary prospectus relating to those securities being filed with the relevant securities regulatory authorities.

(3) The conditions set out in Part 7 of NI 44-101, including the entering into of a bought deal agreement between the issuer and an underwriter or underwriters who have agreed to purchase the securities and the issuance and filing of a news release announcing the agreement, must be satisfied prior to any solicitation of expressions of interest.

(4) We consider that a distribution of securities commences at the time when

- a dealer has had discussions with an issuer or a selling securityholder, or with another dealer that has had discussions with an issuer or a selling securityholder about the distribution, and
- those distribution discussions are of sufficient specificity that it is reasonable to expect that the dealer (alone or together with other dealers) will propose to the issuer or the selling securityholder an underwriting of the securities.

CSA staff do not agree with interpretations that a distribution of securities does not commence until a later time (e.g., when a proposed engagement letter or a proposal for an underwriting of securities with indicative terms is provided by a dealer to an issuer or a selling securityholder).

Similarly, we do not agree with interpretations that if an issuer rejects a proposed engagement letter or a proposal for an underwriting from a dealer, the "distribution" has ended and the dealer could immediately resume communications with potential investors concerning their interest in purchasing securities from the issuer. In these situations, we expect the dealer not to resume communications with potential investors until after a "cooling off" period. We have concerns that such interpretations would allow dealers to circumvent the pre-marketing restrictions by continuing to test the waters between a series of rejected proposals in close succession until the issuer finally accepts a proposal.

By way of example, the following are situations which would indicate that "sufficient specificity" has occurred and a distribution of securities has commenced:

- Following discussions with an issuer, a dealer provides the issuer with a document outlining possible prospectus financing scenarios at one or more specified share price ranges. Subsequently, management of the issuer recommends to its board of directors that the issuer pursue a prospectus financing at a share price range contemplated by the dealer, the directors of the issuer give management broad authority to execute on a prospectus financing opportunity within that share price range if one arose and the dealer is advised of this approval.

- Following discussions with an issuer, a dealer advises the issuer that the market was looking good for a possible prospectus offering and that the dealer would likely provide indicative terms for an offering later that day.

CSA staff are aware that a practice has developed for "non-deal road shows" where issuers and dealers will meet with institutional investors to discuss the business and affairs of the issuer. If such a non-deal road show was undertaken in anticipation of a prospectus offering, it would generally be prohibited under securities legislation by virtue of the prospectus requirement.

CSA staff would also have selective disclosure concerns if the issuer provided the institutional investors with material information that has not been publicly disclosed. In this regard, see the guidance in Part V of National Policy 51-201 *Disclosure Standards*.

(5) We understand that many dealers communicate on a regular basis with clients and prospective clients concerning their interest in purchasing various securities of various issuers. We will not generally consider such ordinary course communications as being made in furtherance of a distribution. However, from the commencement of a distribution, communications by the dealer, with a person or company designed to have the effect of determining the interest that it, or any person or company that it represents, may have in purchasing securities of the type that are the subject of distribution discussions, that are undertaken by any director, officer, employee or agent of the dealer

  (a) who participated in or had actual knowledge of the distribution discussions, or

  (b) whose communications were directed, suggested or induced by a person referred to in (a), or another person acting directly or indirectly at or upon the direction, suggestion or inducement of a person referred to in (a),

are considered to be in furtherance of the distribution and contrary to securities legislation.

(6) From the commencement of the distribution no communications, market making, or other principal trading activities in securities of the type that are the subject of distribution discussions may be undertaken by a person referred to in paragraph 5(a), above, or at or upon the direction, suggestion or inducement of a person or persons referred to in paragraph 5(a) or (b) above until the earliest of

- the issuance of a receipt for a preliminary prospectus in respect of the distribution,

- the time at which a news release that announces the entering into of a bought deal agreement in respect of a bought deal is issued and filed in accordance with Part 7 of NI 44-101, and

- the time at which the dealer determines not to pursue the distribution.

(7) We note that the Investment Industry Regulatory Organization of Canada has adopted IIROC Rule 29.13 which is consistent with the above discussion relating to pre-marketing of bought deals of equity securities. However, the principles articulated above apply to all offerings, whether of debt or equity securities, or a combination.

(8) The bought deal exemption in Part 7 of NI 44-101 is a limited accommodation to facilitate issuers seeking certainty of financing. This policy rationale is reflected in the terms and conditions of the exemption. In particular, in order for the exemption to be available for use, the issuer must have entered into a bought deal agreement with an underwriter who has, or underwriters who have, agreed to purchase the securities on a firm commitment basis. The definition of bought deal agreement in subsection 7.1(1) in NI 44-101 provides that a bought deal agreement must not have:

- a "market-out clause" (as defined in subsection 7.1(1) of NI 44-101),

- an upsizing option (other than an over-allotment option as defined in section 1.1 of the Instrument), or

- a confirmation clause (other than a confirmation clause that complies with section 7.4 of NI 44-101).

(9) Section 7.3 of NI 44-101 allows a bought deal agreement to be modified in certain circumstances. Subsection 7.3(2) sets out conditions for any amendment to increase the number of securities to be purchased by the underwriters. Subsection 7.3(4) sets out conditions for any amendment to provide for a different type of securities to be purchased by the underwriters, and a different price for the securities. Subsection 7.3(5) sets out conditions for any amendment to add additional underwriters or remove an underwriter. Subsection 7.3(6) provides that a bought deal agreement may be replaced with a more extended form of underwriting agreement if the more extended form of underwriting agreement complies with the terms and conditions that apply to a bought deal agreement under Part 7 of NI 44-101. Subsection 7.3(7) provides that the parties may agree to terminate a bought deal agreement if the parties decide not to proceed with the distribution. However, section 7.3 is not intended to prevent a party from exercising a termination right under a provision in a bought deal agreement, or a more extended form of underwriting agreement, that permits a party to terminate the agreement if:

- another party or person performs, or fails to perform, certain actions, or

- certain events occur or fail to occur.

(10) Subsection 7.3(3) of NI 44-101 provides that a bought deal agreement may be amended to reduce the number of securities to be purchased, or the price of the securities, provided the amendment is made on or after the date which is four business days after the date the original agreement was entered into. As noted above, the policy rationale of the bought deal exemption is to facilitate issuers seeking certainty of financing. This policy rationale has not been met when a bought deal agreement is amended to provide for a smaller offering or a lower share price, particularly within a short period of time after the original agreement has been signed. If an underwriter does not wish to assume the risk of a bought deal, the underwriter may want to consider proposing a fully marketed offering to the issuer, rather than a bought deal.

(11) Section 7.4 of NI 44-101 provides that a bought deal agreement may not contain a confirmation clause (as defined in section 7.1 of NI 44-101) unless certain conditions apply. In particular, confirmation clauses are not permitted unless the confirmation period is only between the day on which the bought deal agreement is signed, and the next business day.

Since "sufficient specificity", as discussed in subsection (4), will have occurred before the time the signed bought deal agreement is presented to the issuer pursuant to paragraph 7.4(1)(a) of NI 44-101, underwriters cannot communicate with investors about the issuer or the distribution until the bought deal agreement is signed by the issuer, confirmed by the lead underwriter in accordance with section 7.4 of NI 44-101, and announced in a news release. Furthermore, the issuer and underwriters would be bound by insider trading and tippee prohibitions in securities legislation until the news release announcing the bought deal has been broadly disseminated.

(12) We note that the use of confirmation clauses in bought deal agreements under Part 7 of NI 44-101 is different from the practice of "overnight marketed deals". In an overnight marketed offering, the issuer is not relying on the bought deal exemption in Part 7 of NI 44-101. Instead, in a typical overnight marketing offering,

- On the first day (day 1), the issuer will file a preliminary prospectus with "bullets" for size of the offering and the price per security.

- After a receipt for the preliminary prospectus is issued on day 1, the underwriters will, after the close of trading, market the deal "overnight" to institutional and other investors.

- On the morning of the second day (day 2), the underwriters will provide the issuer with details of the proposed size of the offering and the price per security. If the issuer accepts the proposed terms, the issuer and the underwriters will sign an agreement in which the underwriters agree to purchase the base amount of the offering on a firm commitment basis. The issuer will then issue and file a news release announcing the agreement.

- Later on day 2, the issuer will file an amended and restated preliminary prospectus that discloses the agreement, the size of the offering and the price per security.

- Alternatively, if the issuer does not accept the terms proposed by the underwriters after the overnight marketing, the issuer will withdraw the preliminary prospectus.

(13) We note that underwriters often specify in a bought deal agreement, or a more extended form of underwriting agreement, that the issuer must file and obtain a receipt for the final prospectus within a short period of time after the first comment letter in respect of the preliminary prospectus is issued by staff of the principal regulator under National Policy 11-202 *Process for Prospectus Reviews in Multiple Jurisdictions*. However, issues may arise in the first comment letter that cannot be resolved within the time frame contemplated in the bought deal agreement or the underwriting agreement. Accordingly, issuers and underwriters should not expect that all comments can be resolved within a particular period of time.

As noted above, the policy rationale of the bought deal exemption is to facilitate issuers seeking certainty of financing. This policy rationale may not have been met if a bought deal agreement is terminated because regulatory comments are not settled within a short period of time after the first comment letter. If an underwriter does not want to assume the risk of a bought deal and allow for a reasonable period of time for the issuer to settle any comments from staff of the principal regulator, the underwriter may want to consider proposing a fully marketed offering to the issuer, rather than a bought deal.

(14) If an underwriter enters into an engagement letter, or similar agreement, with an issuer solely for the purpose of conducting due diligence before a potential bought deal under Part 7 of NI 44-101, that event will not, in and of itself, indicate that "sufficient specificity" has been achieved as discussed in subsection (4), provided that the engagement letter does not contain any other information which indicates that "it is reasonable to expect that the dealer will propose to the issuer an underwriting of securities".

If permitted by the issuer, an underwriter may want to conduct sufficient due diligence before proposing a bought deal under Part 7 of NI 44-101. Where an issuer is required to file technical reports under National Instrument 43-101 *Standards of Disclosure for Mineral Projects*, the underwriter may want to confirm, as part of its due diligence before proposing a bought deal, that the issuer's technical reports are compliant with the requirements of that instrument.

As noted above, the policy rationale of the bought deal exemption is to facilitate issuers seeking certainty of financing. While we recognize that a bought deal agreement or a more extended form of underwriting agreement often contain provisions giving the underwriters a right to terminate the agreement under a "due diligence out", these provisions should not be used in a way that would defeat the policy rationale of the bought deal exemption.

Where underwriters are not willing or able to conduct sufficient due diligence in advance of proposing a bought deal to an issuer, the underwriters may want to consider proposing a fully marketed offering to the issuer, rather than a bought deal.

6.4A Testing of the waters exemption — IPO issuers — (1) The testing of the waters exemption for issuers planning to conduct an initial public offering (IPO issuers) in subsection 13.4(2) of the Instrument is intended for issuers that have a reasonable expectation of filing a long form prospectus in respect of an initial public offering (IPO) in at least one jurisdiction of Canada. The exemption permits an IPO issuer, through an investment dealer, to determine interest in a potential IPO through limited confidential communication with accredited investors. The purpose of the exemption is to provide a way for an IPO issuer to ascertain if there is adequate investor interest before starting the IPO process and incurring costs (e.g., retaining advisors to engage in formal due diligence activities and draft a preliminary prospectus).

The exemption is not intended to allow an investment dealer to "pre-sell" the IPO and "fill their book" before the filing of a preliminary prospectus. Consequently, subsection 13.4(4) of the Instrument provides that if any investment dealer solicits an expression of interest under the exemption, the issuer must not file a preliminary prospectus in respect of an IPO until the date which is at least 15 days after the date on which an investment dealer last solicited an expression of interest from an accredited investor under the exemption.

(2) The testing of the waters exemption for IPO issuers permits an investment dealer to solicit expressions of interest from accredited investors if the conditions of the exemption are met. Any investment dealer relying on this exemption would be required to be registered as an investment dealer (unless an exemption from registration is available in the circumstances) in any jurisdiction where it engages in the business of trading, including engaging in acts in furtherance of a trade (which would include soliciting expressions of interest).

(3) In order for the exemption to be used, paragraph 13.4(2)(b) of the Instrument provides that the IPO issuer must not be a "public issuer", as defined in subsection 13.4(1). This means that the IPO issuer must not be a public company in any country, and must not have its securities traded in any country on a stock exchange, marketplace or any other facility for bringing together buyers and sellers of securities and with respect to which trade data is publicly reported. Similarly, subsection 13.4(7) of the Instrument provides that the exemption is not available for use if:

- any of the IPO issuer's securities are held by a control person that is a public issuer, and

- the IPO of the IPO issuer would be a material fact or material change with respect to the control person.

(4) Subsection 13.4(5) of the Instrument requires an issuer to keep a written record of any investment dealer that it authorized to act on its behalf in making solicitations in reliance on the testing of the waters exemption for IPO issuers in subsection 13.4(2) of the Instrument. The issuer must also keep copies of the written authorizations referred to in paragraph 13.4(2)(d) of the Instrument. To meet this requirement, we would expect the issuer to record the name of a contact person for each investment dealer that it authorized and contact information for that person. During compliance reviews, securities regulators may ask the issuer to provide them with copies of these documents.

(5) The testing of the waters exemption for IPO issuers may be used at the same time by more than one investment dealer in respect of the same issuer, provided that the issuer has authorized each investment dealer in accordance with paragraph 13.4(2)(d) of the Instrument.

(6) Paragraph 13.4(6)(a) of the Instrument requires an investment dealer to keep a written record of the accredited investors that it solicits pursuant to the exemption, a copy of any written material and written approval referred to in subparagraph 13.4(3)(a)(i) and a copy of the written confirmations referred to in paragraph 13.4(3)(b). To meet this requirement, we would expect the investment dealer to record the name of the contact person for each

accredited investor that it solicited and contact information for that person. During compliance reviews, securities regulators may ask the investment dealer to provide them with copies of these documents.

(7) An investment dealer soliciting expressions of interest in accordance with the testing of the waters exemption for IPO issuers in subsection 13.4(2) of the Instrument may only solicit expressions of interest from an accredited investor if certain conditions are met. One condition in paragraph 13.4(3)(b) of the Instrument is that before providing the investor with information about the proposed offering, the investment dealer must obtain confirmation in writing from the investor that the investor will keep information about the proposed offering confidential, and will not use the information for any purpose other than assessing the investor's interest in the offering, until the earlier of the information being generally disclosed in a preliminary long form prospectus, or the issuer confirming in writing that it will not be pursuing the potential offering. An investment dealer may obtain this written confirmation from an accredited investor by return email. Here is a sample email that an investment dealer could use:

> *We want to provide you with information about a proposed initial public offering of securities. Before we can provide you with this information, you must confirm by return email that*:
>
> - *You agree to receive certain confidential information about a proposed initial public offering by an issuer.*
>
> - *You agree to keep the information about the proposed offering confidential and not to use the information for any purpose other than assessing your interest in the offering, until the earlier of (i) the information being generally disclosed in a preliminary prospectus or otherwise, or (ii) the issuer confirming in writing that it will not be pursuing the potential offering.*

An accredited investor may respond to this email by simply stating "I so confirm".

We remind investment dealers and accredited investors that they should not be using the information received under the testing of the waters exemption for IPO issuers in a way that may be considered abusive. For example, we would consider it inappropriate for an accredited investor to use information about the IPO issuer to make decisions about trading in securities of competitors of the IPO issuer. We note that CSA staff may investigate subsequent trading in securities of competitors of IPO issuers that have used the testing of the waters exemption.

(8) Subparagraph 13.4(3)(a)(i) of the Instrument requires that any written materials used by an investment dealer to solicit expressions of interest under the testing of the waters exemption be approved by the issuer. We remind issuers and investment dealers that:

- Any preliminary prospectus filed by the issuer subsequent to the solicitation must contain full, true and plain disclosure of all material facts.

- Selective disclosure concerns would arise if accredited investors were provided with material facts that are not disclosed in any subsequent preliminary prospectus.

(9) We would expect an investment dealer seeking to solicit accredited investors in reliance on the testing of the waters exemption for IPO issuers to:

- conduct reasonable diligence to determine that an investor is an accredited investor before soliciting the investor, and

- retain all documentation that they receive in this regard.

(10) Since soliciting accredited investors under the testing of the waters exemption for IPO issuers would be an act in furtherance of a trade, an issuer and an investment dealer acting on behalf of the issuer would not be able to rely on the exemption if the issuer was subject to a cease trade order.

(11) We refer issuers and investment dealers to the guidance in section 6.10 of this Policy. We note that issuers and investment dealers should have procedures in place to prevent "leaks" of information before the filing of a preliminary prospectus for an initial public offering.

6.5 Advertising or marketing activities during the waiting period — (1) Securities legislation provides for certain exceptions to the prospectus requirement for limited advertising or marketing activities during the waiting period between the issuance of the receipt for the preliminary prospectus and the receipt for the final prospectus. Despite the prospectus requirement, it is permissible during the waiting period to

(a) distribute a preliminary prospectus notice (as defined in the Instrument) that

- "identifies" the securities proposed to be issued,

- states the price of such securities, if then determined, and

- states the name and address of a person or company from whom purchases of securities may be made,

provided that any such notice states the name and address of a person or company from whom a preliminary prospectus may be obtained and contains the legend required by subsection 13.1(1) of the Instrument;

(b) distribute the preliminary prospectus;

(c) provide standard term sheets, if the conditions in section 13.5 of the Instrument are complied with;

(d) provide marketing materials, if the conditions in section 13.7 of the Instrument are complied with; and

(e) solicit expressions of interest from a prospective purchaser, if prior to such solicitation or forthwith after the prospective purchaser indicates an interest in purchasing the securities, a copy of the preliminary prospectus is forwarded to the prospective purchaser.

(2) The use of any other marketing information or materials during the waiting period would result in the violation of the prospectus requirement.

(3) The "identification" of the security contemplated by paragraph 6.5(1)(a) above does not permit an issuer or dealer to include a summary of the commercial features of the issue. These details are set out in the preliminary prospectus which is intended as the main disclosure vehicle pending the issuance of the final receipt. The purpose of the permitted advertising or marketing activities during the waiting period is essentially to alert the public to the availability of the preliminary prospectus.

(4) For the purpose of identifying a security contemplated by paragraph 6.5(1)(a) above, the advertising or marketing material may only

- indicate whether a security represents debt or a share in a company or an interest in a non-corporate entity (e.g. a unit of undivided ownership in a film property) or a partnership interest,

- name the issuer if the issuer is a reporting issuer, or name and describe briefly the business of the issuer if the issuer is not already a reporting issuer (the description of the business should be cast in general terms and should not attempt to summarize the proposed use of proceeds),

- indicate, without giving details, whether the security qualifies the holder for special tax treatment, and

- indicate how many securities will be made available.

Part 4:
DISTRIBUTIONS

6.5A Standard term sheets — (1) The standard term sheet provisions in sections 13.5 and 13.6 of the Instrument, section 7.5 of NI 44-101, section 9A.2 of NI 44-102 and section 4A.2 of NI 44-103 permit an investment dealer to provide a standard term sheet to a potential investor if the conditions of the applicable provision are met.

Any investment dealer relying on these provisions would be required to be registered as an investment dealer (unless an exemption from registration is available in the circumstance) in any jurisdiction where it engages in the business of trading, including engaging in acts in furtherance of a trade (which would include providing a standard term sheet to an investor).

(2) The Instrument defines "standard term sheet" to mean a written communication regarding a distribution of securities under a prospectus that contains no information other than that referred to in subsections 13.5(2) and (3) or subsections 13.6(2) and (3) of the Instrument, subsections 7.5(2) and (3) of NI 44-101, subsections 9A.2(2) and (3) of NI 44-102 or subsections 4A.2(2) and (3) of NI 44-103 relating to an issuer, securities or an offering. A standard term sheet does not include a preliminary prospectus notice or a final prospectus notice, each as defined in the Instrument.

(3) Standard term sheets are subject to the provisions in applicable securities legislation which prohibit misleading or untrue statements. Furthermore, standard term sheets must contain the legends required by subsections 13.5(2) and 13.6(2) of the Instrument, subsection 7.5(2) of NI 44-101, subsection 9A.2(2) of NI 44-102 and subsection 4A.2(2) of NI 44-103, as applicable.

(4) In the case of a standard term sheet provided during the waiting period or after a receipt for the final prospectus, paragraphs 13.5(1)(b) and 13.6(1)(b) of the Instrument require that, other than contact information for the investment dealer or underwriters, all information in the standard term sheet concerning the issuer, the securities or the offering must be disclosed in, or derived from, the preliminary prospectus or the final prospectus, respectively.

Similarly, in the case of a standard term sheet for a bought deal under Part 7 of NI 44-101 that is provided before the filing of the preliminary prospectus, paragraph 7.5(1)(c) of NI 44-101 requires that all information in the standard term sheet must either:

- currently be disclosed in, or derived from, a document referred to in subparagraph 7.5(1)(c)(i) of NI 44-101, or

- later be disclosed in, or derived from, the preliminary prospectus that is subsequently filed.

In the case of a standard term sheet for a tranche of securities to be offered under the shelf procedures (a draw-down) pursuant to a final base shelf prospectus, paragraph 9A.2(1)(b) of NI 44-102 provides that all information in the standard term sheet must either:

- currently be disclosed in, or derived from, a document referred to in subparagraph 9A.2(1)(b)(i) of NI 44-102, or

- later be disclosed in, or derived from, an applicable shelf prospectus supplement that is subsequently filed.

In the case of a standard term sheet after a receipt for a final base PREP prospectus, paragraph 4A.2(1)(b) of NI 44-103 provides that all information in the standard term sheet must either:

- currently be disclosed in, or derived from, a document referred to in subparagraph 4A.2(1)(b)(i) of NI 44-103, or

- later be disclosed in, or derived from, the supplemented PREP prospectus that is subsequently filed.

In this regard, if an investment dealer includes information in a standard term sheet for a bought deal, a draw-down under a shelf prospectus or an offering under the PREP procedures that is not currently on the public record, the investment dealer and the issuer should be mindful of selective disclosure concerns and take measures to ensure compliance with applicable securities laws relating to selective disclosure, insider trading and trading by "tippees" (these laws are summarized in sections 3.1 and 3.2 of National Policy 51-201 *Disclosure Standards*). For example, if the information could affect the market price of the issuer's securities, it should be broadly disseminated in a news release before being included in a standard term sheet. If the information was a material change, it would be subject to the material change news release and reporting requirements set out in Part 7 of National Instrument 51-102 *Continuous Disclosure Obligations*.

(5) A standard term sheet must not be provided unless a receipt for the relevant prospectus has been issued in the local jurisdiction. Similarly, in the case of a standard term sheet for a bought deal under Part 7 of NI 44-101 that is provided before the filing of the preliminary prospectus, the standard term sheet must not be provided unless the preliminary prospectus will be filed in the local jurisdiction.

6.5B Marketing materials — (1) The marketing materials provisions in sections 13.7 and 13.8 of the Instrument, section 7.6 of NI 44-101, section 9A.3 of NI 44-102 and section 4A.3 of NI 44-103 permit an investment dealer to provide marketing materials to a potential investor if the conditions of the applicable provision are met.

Any investment dealer relying on these provisions would be required to be registered as an investment dealer (unless an exemption from registration is available in the circumstance) in any jurisdiction where it engages in the business of trading, including engaging in acts in furtherance of a trade (which would include providing marketing materials to an investor).

(2) The Instrument defines "marketing materials" to mean written communications intended for potential investors regarding a distribution of securities under a prospectus that contain material facts relating to an issuer, securities or an offering. The definition does not include a standard term sheet, a preliminary prospectus notice or a final prospectus notice. The definition is not intended to include other communications from an investment dealer to an investor, such as a cover letter or email that encloses a copy of a prospectus, a standard term sheet or marketing materials, but does not include any material facts about issuer, securities or an offering.

(3) The applicable interpretation provisions in the prospectus rules clarify that a reference to "provide" in sections 13.7 and 13.8 of the Instrument, section 7.6 of NI 44-101, section 9A.3 of NI 44-102 and section 4A.3 of NI 44-103 includes showing marketing materials to an investor without allowing the investor to retain or make a copy of the materials. This means that the rules apply not only to situations where marketing materials are physically provided to a potential investor, but also to situations where a potential investor is shown marketing materials but is not permitted to retain a copy. For example, the rules would apply where a potential investor is shown a paper copy of marketing materials during a meeting or other interaction with a broker, but is not permitted to retain the paper copy. Similarly, the rules would apply where a potential investor is shown a version of marketing materials on a projector screen or laptop computer.

(4) Marketing materials are subject to provisions in applicable securities legislation which prohibit misleading or untrue statements. Accordingly, the issuer and investment dealers involved should have a reasonable, factual basis for any statement in marketing materials. We remind issuers to be cautious when including disclosure in marketing materials about mineral projects. Where this is the case, the disclosure would be considered "written disclosure" within the meaning of National Instrument 43-101 *Standards of Disclosure for Mineral Projects* and would have to comply with the requirements of that instrument.

Marketing materials must contain the legends, or words to the same effect, referred to in subsections 13.7(5) and 13.8(5) of the Instrument, subsection 7.6(5) of NI 44-101, subsection 9A.3(5) of NI 44-102 and subsection 4A.3(6) of NI 44-103, as applicable.

Furthermore, paragraphs 13.7(1)(c) and 13.8(1)(c) of the Instrument, paragraph 9A.3(1)(c) of NI 44-102 and paragraph 4A.3(1)(c) of NI 44-103 provide that if the cover page or the summary of the prospectus contains cautionary language, other than prescribed language, in bold type (e.g., the suitability of the investment, a material condition to the closing of the offering or a key risk factor), the marketing materials must contain the same cautionary language. For example, if the cover page of the prospectus contained cautionary language in bold type that the offering is suitable only to those investors who are prepared to risk the loss of their entire investment, the marketing materials must contain the same warning. In contrast, the requirement would not apply to prescribed language that is required to be presented in bold type on the cover page of a prospectus (e.g., section 1.8 and subsections 1.9(3) and 1.11(5) of Form 41-101F1).

(5) In the case of marketing materials provided during the waiting period or after a receipt for the final prospectus, paragraphs 13.7(1)(b) and 13.8(1)(b) of the Instrument require that, other than contact information for the investment dealer or underwriters and any comparables, all information in the marketing materials concerning the issuer, the securities or the offering must be disclosed in, or derived from, the preliminary prospectus or the final prospectus, respectively. For example, marketing materials provided during the waiting period could only include an estimate of the range of the offering price or the number of securities if that estimate was in the preliminary prospectus or any amendment.

Similarly, in the case of marketing materials for a bought deal under Part 7 of NI 44-101 that are provided before the filing of the preliminary prospectus, paragraph 7.6(1)(c) of NI 44-101 requires that all information in the marketing materials must either:

- currently be disclosed in, or derived from, a document referred to in subparagraph 7.6(1)(c)(i) of NI 44-101, or

- later be disclosed in, or derived from, the preliminary prospectus that is subsequently filed.

In the case of marketing materials for a draw-down under a final base shelf prospectus, paragraph 9A.3(1)(b) of NI 44-102 provides that all information in the marketing materials must either:

- currently be disclosed in, or derived from, a document referred to in subparagraph 9A.3(1)(b)(i) of NI 44-102, or

- later be disclosed in, or derived from, an applicable shelf prospectus supplement that is subsequently filed.

In the case of marketing materials after a receipt for a final base PREP prospectus, paragraph 4A.3(1)(b) of NI 44-103 provides that all information in the marketing materials must either:

- currently be disclosed in, or derived from, a document referred to in subparagraph 4A.3(1)(b)(i) of NI 44-103, or

- later be disclosed in, or derived from, the supplemented PREP prospectus that is subsequently filed.

In this regard, if an issuer and an investment dealer include information in marketing materials for a bought deal, a draw-down under a shelf prospectus or an offering under the PREP procedures that is not currently on the public record, the issuer and the investment dealer should be mindful of selective disclosure concerns and take measures to ensure compliance with applicable securities laws relating to selective disclosure, insider trading and trading by "tippees" (these laws are summarized in sections 3.1 and 3.2 of National Policy 51-201 *Disclosure Standards*). For example, if the information could affect the market price of the issuer's securities, it should be broadly disseminated in a news release before being included in marketing materials. If the information was a material change, it would be subject to the material change news release and reporting requirements set out in Part 7 of National Instrument 51-102 *Continuous Disclosure Obligations*.

Under the above provisions, it is permissible for marketing materials to include information derived from the prospectus and information that is presented in a manner that differs from the manner of presentation in the prospectus. For example, it is permissible for marketing materials to summarize information from the relevant prospectus or to include graphs or charts based on numbers in the relevant prospectus.

(6) The term "comparables" is defined in each of the prospectus rules to mean information that compares an issuer to other issuers. Comparables may be based on various factors including, but not limited to, market capitalization, the trading price of the securities on a marketplace or other attributes. If an issuer and an investment dealer want to avoid statutory civil liability for comparables in marketing materials, they must comply with subsections 13.7(4) and 13.8(4) of the Instrument, subsection 7.6(4) of NI 44-101, subsection 9A.3(4) of NI 44-102 and subsection 4A.3(5) of NI 44-103, as applicable. Under these provisions, the issuer may remove any comparables and any disclosure relating to those comparables from the template version of the marketing materials before filing it if:

- The comparables, and any disclosure relating to the comparables, are in a separate section of the template version of the marketing materials.

- The template version of the marketing materials that is filed contains a note advising that the comparables, and any disclosure relating to the comparables, were removed. The note must appear immediately after where the removed comparables and related disclosure would have been.

- If the prospectus is filed in the local jurisdiction, a complete template version of the marketing materials containing the comparables, and any disclosure relating to the comparables, is delivered to the securities regulatory authority. Subject to access to information legislation in each jurisdiction, if a complete template version of the marketing materials is delivered under the applicable prospectus rule, the securities regulatory authority or regulator in each jurisdiction will not make these documents available to the public.

- The complete template version of the marketing materials contains the disclosure referred to in paragraph 13.7(4)(d) of the Instrument.

However, any comparables included in marketing materials provided to an investor would be subject to the provisions in applicable securities legislation which prohibit misleading or untrue statements.

(7) Paragraphs 13.7(1)(d) and 13.8(1)(d) of the Instrument, paragraph 7.6(1)(d) of NI 44-101, paragraph 9A.3(1)(d) of NI 44-102 and paragraph 4A.3(1)(d) of NI 44-103 provide that a template version of the marketing materials must be approved in writing by the issuer and the lead underwriter before the marketing materials are provided to an investor. This written approval may be given by email.

"Template version" is defined in section 1.1 of the Instrument to mean a version of a document with spaces for information to be added in accordance with subsection 13.7(2) or 13.8(2) of the Instrument, subsection 7.6(2) of NI 44-101, subsection 9A.3(2) of NI 44-102 or subsection 4A.3(3) of NI 44-103. "Limited-use version" is defined to mean a template version in which the spaces for information have been completed in accordance with those provisions. A template version can have no other spaces for information to be added in a limited-use version.

The above provisions specify that if a template version of the marketing materials is approved in writing by the issuer and the lead underwriter and filed, an investment dealer may provide a limited-use version of the marketing materials that:

- has a date that is different than the template version,

- contains a cover page referring to the investment dealer or underwriters or a particular investor or group of investors,

- contains contact information for the investment dealer or underwriters,

- has text in a format, including the type's font, colour or size, that is different than the template version, or

- in the case of a limited-use version of the marketing materials provided after a receipt for a final base PREP prospectus, contains the information referred to in paragraph 4A.3(3)(e) of NI 44-103 (the PREP information).

Consequently, other than spaces for a date, a cover page, the contact information or the PREP information described above, a template version of the marketing materials must contain all the information that the issuer and the underwriters would like an investment dealer to be able to provide in a limited-use version.

However, the prospectus rules provide that if the template version of the marketing materials is divided into separate sections for separate subjects, an investment dealer may provide a limited-use version of the marketing materials that includes only one or more of those separate sections.

(8) In the case of marketing materials provided during the waiting period or after a receipt for the final prospectus, paragraphs 13.7(1)(g) and 13.8(1)(g) of the Instrument require that the marketing materials be provided with a copy of the preliminary prospectus or the final prospectus, respectively, and any amendment. The marketing materials can only be provided if a receipt for the relevant prospectus has been issued in the local jurisdiction.

Similarly, in the case of marketing materials for a bought deal under Part 7 of NI 44-101 that are provided before the filing of the preliminary prospectus, the marketing materials can only be provided if the prospectus will be filed in the local jurisdiction. Paragraph 7.6(1)(g) of NI 44-101 requires that upon issuance of a receipt for the preliminary prospectus for the bought deal, a copy of that prospectus must be sent to each potential investor that received the marketing materials and expressed an interest in acquiring the securities.

In the case of marketing materials for a draw-down under a final base shelf prospectus, the marketing materials can only be provided if a receipt for the final base shelf prospectus has been issued in the local jurisdiction. Paragraph 9A.3(1)(g) of NI 44-102 requires that the marketing materials be provided with a copy of the final base shelf prospectus, any amendment to the final base shelf prospectus and any applicable shelf prospectus supplement that has been filed.

In the case of marketing materials provided after a receipt for a final base PREP prospectus, the marketing materials can only be provided if a receipt for the final base PREP prospectus has been issued in the local jurisdiction. Paragraph 4A.3(1)(g) of NI 44-103 requires that the marketing materials be provided with a copy of:

- the final base PREP prospectus and any amendment, or

- if it has been filed, the supplemented PREP prospectus and any amendment.

National Policy 11-201 *Electronic Delivery of Documents* sets out the circumstances in which a prospectus can be delivered by electronic means. If the investment dealer previously delivered a paper or electronic copy of the prospectus and any amendment to an investor in accordance with applicable securities legislation, it can include a hyperlink to an electronic copy of the prospectus and any amendment with any subsequent marketing materials sent to the investor if no additional amendment to the prospectus has been filed and receipted. The investment dealer should ensure that it is clear to the recipient which of the documents being delivered in the hyperlink constitute the prospectus.

(9) Paragraphs 13.7(1)(e) and 13.8(1)(e) of the Instrument, paragraph 7.6(1)(e) of NI 44-101, paragraph 9A.3(1)(e) of NI 44-102 and paragraph 4A.3(1)(e) of NI 44-103 require that a template version of the marketing materials must be filed on SEDAR on or before the day that the marketing materials are first provided to an investor. In this regard,

- If an investment dealer wants to rely on section 13.7 of the Instrument and provide marketing materials to an investor on the same day that the preliminary prospectus is filed and receipted, the template version of the marketing materials should be filed with the preliminary prospectus pursuant to subparagraph 9.1(1)(a)(vii) of the Instrument or subparagraph 4.1(1)(a)(vii) of NI 44-101, as applicable.

- If an investment dealer wants to rely on section 13.8 of the Instrument and provide marketing materials to an investor on the same day that the final prospectus is filed and receipted, the template version of the marketing materials should be filed with the final prospectus pursuant to subparagraph 9.2(a)(xiv) of the Instrument or subparagraph 4.2(a)(xii) of NI 44-101, as applicable.

- When a template version of the marketing materials is filed on SEDAR as part of a prospectus filing, they will generally be made public within one business day. However, in the case of a template version of marketing materials for a bought deal under section 7.6 of NI 44-101, the template version of the marketing materials will not be made public on SEDAR until after the preliminary prospectus is filed and receipted.

- Staff of securities regulatory authorities will not be "pre-clearing" a template version of the marketing materials.

- If an issuer files a template version of marketing materials after staff of a securities regulatory authority have completed their review of a preliminary prospectus filing and indicated that they are "clear for final" on SEDAR, the filing of the template version of the marketing materials may result in staff revising the filing's SEDAR status to indicate that staff are "not clear for final" so that staff may have an opportunity to review the template version of the marketing materials.

(10) As noted in Item 36A.1 of Form 41-101F1 and Item 11.6 of Form 44-101F1, marketing materials do not, as a matter of law, amend a preliminary prospectus, a final prospectus or any amendment.

(11) The template version of the marketing materials filed on SEDAR is required to be included in the final prospectus or incorporated by reference into the final prospectus. An investor who purchases a security distributed under the final prospectus may therefore have remedies under the civil liability provisions of applicable securities legislation if the template version of the marketing materials contains a misrepresentation. Furthermore, an investor who purchases a security of the issuer on the secondary market may have remedies under the civil liability for secondary market disclosure provisions of applicable securities legislation if the template version of the marketing materials contains a misrepresentation since:

> the template version of the marketing materials is required to be included in the final prospectus or incorporated by reference into the final prospectus (a final prospectus is a "core document" under the secondary market liability provisions), and

> - the template version of the marketing materials is required to be filed and is therefore a "document" under the secondary market liability provisions.

(12) If a final prospectus or any amendment modifies a statement of material fact that appeared in marketing materials provided during the waiting period, the issuer is required to:

- prepare and file, at the time the issuer files the final prospectus or any amendment, a revised template version of the marketing materials that is blacklined to show the modified statement, and

- include in the final prospectus, or any amendment, the disclosure referred to in subsection 36A.1(3) of Form 41-101F1 or subsection 11.6(3) of Form 44-101F1, as applicable.

Similar provisions apply for a draw-down under a base shelf prospectus or an offering under the PREP procedures.

If the blacklining software of the issuer or the issuer's service provider has formatting problems or does not function well with certain kinds of documents or formats, the issuer should try to correct the formatting problems or use another method to reflect changes to the marketing materials, such as using the bold type and underlining features of a software package in order to provide easy-to-read blacklines for filing on SEDAR.

(13) For guidance on marketing materials for income trusts and other indirect offerings, see Part 5 of National Policy 41-201 *Income Trusts and Other Indirect Offerings*.

6.5C Standard term sheets and marketing materials — general — In addition to the requirements on standard term sheets and marketing materials in the applicable prospectus rule, issuers and investment dealers should review other securities legislation for limitations and prohibitions on advertising intended to promote interest in an issuer or its securities. For example,

- A standard term sheet and any marketing materials must not contain any representations prohibited by securities legislation, such as:

  - prohibited representations on resales, repurchases or refunds, and

  - prohibited representations on future value.

- A standard term sheet and any marketing materials must comply with the requirements of securities legislation on listing representations.

6.6 Green sheets — (1) Some dealers prepare summaries of the principal terms of an offering, sometimes referred to as green sheets, for the information of their registered representatives during the waiting period. However, distributing the green sheet to the public would generally contravene the prospectus requirement unless the green sheet complies with the provisions in the applicable prospectus rule relating to standard term sheets or marketing materials, or other securities legislation relating to information that can be distributed during a prospectus offering.

(2) Including material information in a green sheet or other marketing communication that is not contained in the preliminary prospectus could indicate a failure to provide in the preliminary prospectus full, true and plain disclosure of all material facts relating to the securities offered by the prospectus and result in the prospectus certificate constituting a misrepresentation. For additional guidance on pricing information in a green sheet, see subsection 4.2(2) of this Policy and subsection 4.3(2) of 44-101CP.

(3) We may request copies of green sheets as part of our prospectus review procedures. Any discrepancies between the content of a green sheet and the preliminary prospectus could result in the delay or refusal of a receipt for a final prospectus and, in appropriate circumstances, could result in enforcement action.

(4) For guidance on green sheets for income trusts or other indirect offerings, see Part 5 *Sales and Marketing Materials* of National Policy 41-201 *Income Trusts and Other Indirect Offerings*.

6.7 Advertising or marketing activities that are permitted during the waiting period may also be undertaken on a similar basis after a receipt has been issued for the final prospectus. In addition, the prospectus and any document filed with or referred to in the prospectus may be distributed.

6.8 Sanctions and enforcement — Any contravention of the prospectus requirement through advertising or marketing activities is a serious matter that could result in a cease trade order in respect of the preliminary prospectus to which such advertising or marketing activities relate. In addition, a receipt for a final prospectus relating to any such offering may be refused. In appropriate circumstances, enforcement proceedings may be initiated.

6.9 Media reports and coverage — (1) We recognize that an issuer does not have control over media coverage; however, an issuer should take appropriate precautions to ensure that media coverage which can reasonably be considered to be in furtherance of a distribution of securities does not occur after a decision has been made to file a preliminary prospectus or during the waiting period.

(2) We may investigate the circumstances surrounding media coverage of an issuer which appears immediately prior to or during the waiting period and which can reasonably be considered as being in furtherance of a distribution of securities. Action will be taken in appropriate circumstances.

(3) Nevertheless, we realize that reporting issuers need to consider whether the decision to pursue a potential offering is a material change under applicable securities legislation. If the decision is a material change, the news release and material change report requirements in Part 7 of NI 51-102 and other securities legislation apply. However, in order to avoid contravening the pre-marketing restrictions under applicable securities legislation, any news release and material change report filed before the filing of a preliminary prospectus or the announcement of a bought deal under section 7.2 of NI 44-101 should be carefully drafted so that it could not be reasonably regarded as intended to promote a distribution of securities or condition the market. The information in the news release and material change report should be limited to identifying the securities proposed to be issued without a summary of the commercial features of the issue (those details should instead be dealt with in the preliminary prospectus which is intended to be the main disclosure vehicle).

Furthermore, after the filing of the news release,

- the issuer should not grant media interviews on the proposed offering, and

- an investment dealer would not be able to solicit expressions of interest until a receipt has been issued for a preliminary prospectus or a bought deal was announced in compliance with section 7.2 of NI 44-101.

6.10 Disclosure practices — At a minimum, participants in all prospectus distributions should consider the following to avoid contravening securities legislation:

- We do not consider it appropriate for a director or an officer of an issuer to give interviews to the media immediately prior to or during the waiting period. It may be appropriate, however, for a director or officer to respond to unsolicited inquiries of a factual nature made by shareholders, securities analysts, financial analysts, the media and others who have an interest in such information.

- Because of the prospectus requirement, an issuer should avoid providing information during a prospectus distribution that goes beyond what is disclosed in the prospectus. Therefore, during the prospectus distribution (which commences as described in subsection 6.4(4) of this Policy and ends following closing), a director or officer of an issuer should only make a statement constituting a forecast, projection or prediction with respect to future financial performance if the statement is also contained in the prospectus. Forward-looking information included in a prospectus must comply with sections 4A.2 and 4A.3 and Part 4B, as applicable, of NI 51-102.

Part 4:
DISTRIBUTIONS

- We understand that underwriters and legal counsel sometimes only advise the working group members of the pre-marketing and marketing restrictions under securities legislation. However, there are often situations where officers and directors of the issuer outside of the working group also come into contact with the media before or after the filing of a preliminary prospectus. Any discussions between these individuals and the media will also be subject to these same restrictions. Working group members, including underwriters and legal counsel, will usually want to ensure that any other officers and directors of the issuer (as well as the officers and directors of a promoter or a selling securityholder) who may come into contact with the media are also fully aware of the marketing and disclosure restrictions.

- One way for issuers, dealers and other market participants to ensure that advertising or marketing activities contrary to securities legislation are not undertaken (intentionally or through inadvertence) is to develop, implement, maintain and enforce disclosure procedures.

If a director or officer of an issuer (or a promoter, selling securityholder, underwriter or any other party involved with a pending offering) makes a statement to the media after a decision has been made to file a preliminary prospectus or during the waiting period, our regulatory concerns include circumvention of the pre-marketing and marketing restrictions, selective disclosure and unequal access to information, conditioning of the market and the lack of prospectus liability. In addition to the sanctions and enforcement proceedings discussed in section 6.8 of this Policy, staff of a securities regulatory authority may require the issuer to take other remedial action, such as:

- explaining why the issuer's disclosure procedures failed to prevent the party from making the statement to the media and how those procedures will be improved,

- instituting a "cooling-off period" before the filing of the final prospectus,

- including the statement in the prospectus so that it will be subject to statutory civil liability, or

- issuing a news release refuting the statement if it cannot be included in the prospectus (e.g., because the statement is incorrect or unduly promotional) and disclosing the reasons for the news release in the prospectus.

6.11 Misleading or untrue statements — In addition to the prohibitions on advertising or marketing activities that result from the prospectus requirement, securities legislation in certain jurisdictions prohibits any person or company from making any misleading or untrue statements that would reasonably be expected to have a significant effect on the market value of securities. Therefore, in addition to ensuring that advertising or marketing activities are carried out in compliance with the prospectus requirement, issuers, dealers and their advisors must ensure that any statements made in the course of advertising or marketing activities are not untrue or misleading and otherwise comply with securities legislation.

6.12 Road shows — (1) Sections 13.9 and 13.10 of the Instrument, section 7.7 of NI 44-101, section 9A.4 of NI 44-102 and section 4A.4 of NI 44-103 provide for road shows for investors. These provisions and the definition of "road show" in section 1.1 of NI 41-101 apply to road shows conducted in person, by telephone conference call, on the internet or by other electronic means. The provisions also apply if an investment dealer records a live road show and later makes an audio or audio-visual version of the recorded road show available to investors.

(2) Although members of the media may attend a road show, they should not be specifically invited to the road show by the issuer or by an investment dealer. We note that road shows are intended to be presentations for potential investors and not press conferences for members of the media. Furthermore, issuers and investment dealers should not market a prospectus offering in the media. In this regard, see the guidance in sections 6.9 and 6.10 of this Policy.

(3) Subsections 13.9(3) and 13.10(3) of the Instrument, subsection 7.7(3) of NI 44-101, subsection 9A.4(3) of NI 44-102 and subsection 4A.4(3) of NI 44-103 provide that if an investment dealer conducts a road show, the investment dealer must establish and follow reasonable procedures to:

- ask any investor attending the road show in person, by telephone conference call, on the internet or by other electronic means to provide their name and contact information;

- keep a record of any information provided by the investor; and

- provide the investor with a copy of the relevant prospectus and any amendment.

However, section 13.11 of the Instrument and section 4A.5 of NI 44-103 provide an exception so that, in the case of a road show for certain U.S. cross-border initial public offerings, an investor attending the road show can provide their name and contact information on a voluntary basis.

For a road show held on the internet or by other electronic means, please see the recommended procedures in section 2.7 of National Policy 47-201 *Trading Securities Using the Internet and Other Electronic Means* and, in Québec, *Notice 47-201 relating to Trading Securities Using the Internet and Other Electronic Means.*

(4) An investment dealer must not provide marketing materials to investors attending a road show unless the materials comply with the relevant marketing materials provisions in sections 13.7 and 13.8 of the Instrument, section 7.6 of NI 44-101, section 9A.3 of NI 44-102 and section 4A.3 of NI 44-103, as applicable. In this context, see the discussion on the meaning of "provide" in subsection 6.5B(3) of this Policy. For example, the provisions would apply where a potential investor is shown a version of marketing materials on a projector screen during a road show conducted in person. Similarly, the provisions would apply where a potential investor is able to view a slide show version of marketing materials during a road show presented online, whether live or recorded.

The above provisions require that a template version of the marketing materials be filed on SEDAR on or before the day they are first provided and included in, or incorporated by reference into, the relevant prospectus.

However, section 13.12 of the Instrument, section 7.8 of NI 44-101, section 9A.5 of NI 44-102 and section 4A.6 of NI 44-103 provide an exception from these filing and incorporation requirements for marketing materials in connection with road shows for certain U.S. cross-border offerings. The exception does not apply to marketing materials other than the marketing materials provided in connection with the road show. Among other things, an issuer relying on the exception must deliver a template version of the marketing materials to the securities regulatory authority in each jurisdiction of Canada where the prospectus was filed. Subject to access to information legislation in each jurisdiction, it is the policy of the securities regulatory authority or regulator in each jurisdiction that the template version of the marketing materials delivered under the applicable prospectus rule will not be made available to the public.

(5) In the past, issuers conducting internet road shows for cross-border IPOs applied for relief from the waiting period restrictions in Canadian securities legislation. However, given the above-noted road show provisions and the exceptions for certain U.S. cross-border offerings, we do not anticipate a need for similar relief in the future and will instead expect these issuers to comply with the applicable road show provision.

In the past, issuers conducting internet road shows for cross-border IPOs also applied for relief from the dealer registration requirements of Canadian securities legislation. However, if a road show is conducted on behalf of an issuer under the above-noted road show provisions, the issuer will not require relief from the dealer registration requirement since the road show will be conducted by an investment dealer that is registered in the appropriate jurisdictions (see subsection 6.12(6) of this Policy). Consequently, we do not expect to grant the relief from the dealer registration requirements that has been granted in the past to cross-border IPO issuers.

(6) The road show provisions permit an investment dealer to conduct a road show for potential investors if the conditions of the applicable provision are met. As noted above, a road show may be conducted in person, by telephone conference call, on the internet or by other electronic means. Unless an exemption from the requirement to register as a dealer is available in the circumstances, any investment dealer relying on one of these provisions would have to be registered as an investment dealer in any jurisdiction where it engages in the business of trading, including engaging in acts in furtherance of a trade (which would include conducting a road show for potential investors). For example, if one or more investment dealers acting as underwriters for a prospectus offering allow potential investors in each jurisdiction of Canada to participate in a road show that the dealers conduct by telephone conference call, then at least one of those dealers must be registered as an investment dealer in every jurisdiction of Canada.

(7) Issuers should note the following with respect to oral statements made at a road show:

- In giving oral presentations at a road show, issuers should generally only discuss information that is contained in, or derived from, the relevant prospectus that has been filed on SEDAR.

- We recognize that issuers need to respond to questions from investors at a road show. In responding to these questions, issuers should avoid making selective disclosure.

- In particular, issuers should take measures to ensure compliance with applicable securities laws relating to selective disclosure, insider trading and trading by "tippees" when:

  - participating in a road show, and

  - including information in marketing materials for a bought deal road show before the filing of a preliminary prospectus that is not in the bought deal news release or the other continuous disclosure documents filed by the issuer.

These laws are summarized in sections 3.1 and 3.2 of National Policy 51-201 *Disclosure Standards*.

- If an issuer discloses material facts at a road show that are not in a preliminary prospectus that has been filed on SEDAR, the final prospectus should contain that information in order to comply with the statutory requirement that the final prospectus contain full, true and plain disclosure of all material facts.

- Depending on the context, oral statements of a "responsible issuer", as defined in securities legislation, at a road show may be "public oral statements", as defined in securities legislation, and subject to statutory provisions for secondary market civil liability.

- Depending on the nature of the statement, oral statements of an issuer at a road show in relation to mineral projects may fall within the purview of National Instrument 43-101 *Standards of Disclosure for Mineral Projects*.

- Oral statements made during a road show are subject to the provisions of securities legislation against making misleading or untrue statements.

PART 6A — ADVERTISING AND MARKETING IN CONNECTION WITH PROSPECTUS OFFERINGS OF INVESTMENT FUNDS

6A.1 Application — This Part applies to investment funds filing a prospectus in the form of Form 41-101F2 or Form 41-101F3.

6A.2 Scope — (1) The discussion below is focused on the impact of the prospectus requirement on advertising or marketing activities in connection with a prospectus offering.

(2) Issuers and other persons or companies that engage in advertising or marketing activities should also consider the impact of the requirement to register as a dealer in each jurisdiction where such advertising or marketing activities are undertaken. In particular, the persons or companies would have to consider whether their activities result in the party being in the business of trading in securities. For further information, refer to section 1.3 of Companion Policy 31-103CP *Registration Requirements, Exemptions and Ongoing Registrant Obligations*.

(3) Advertising or marketing activities are also subject to regulation under securities legislation and other rules, including those relating to disclosure, and insider trading and registration, which are not discussed below.

6A.3 The prospectus requirement — (1) Securities legislation generally provides that no one may trade in a security where that trade would be a distribution unless the prospectus requirement has been satisfied, or an exemption is available.

(2) The analysis of whether any particular advertising or marketing activity is prohibited by virtue of the prospectus requirement turns largely on whether the activity constitutes a trade and, if so, whether such a trade would constitute a distribution.

(3) In Québec, since securities legislation has been designed without the notion of a "trade", the analysis is dependent solely on whether the advertising or marketing activities constitute a distribution.

(4) Definition of "trade" — Securities legislation (other than the securities legislation of Québec) defines a "trade" in a non-exhaustive manner to include, among other things:

- any sale or disposition of a security for valuable consideration,

- any receipt by a registrant of an order to buy or sell a security, or

- any act, advertisement, solicitation, conduct or negotiation directly or indirectly in furtherance of any of the foregoing.

(5) Any advertising or marketing activities that can be reasonably regarded as intended to promote a distribution of securities would be "conduct in furtherance" of the distribution of a security and, therefore, would fall within the definition of a trade.

(6) Definition of distribution — Even though advertising or marketing activities constitute a "trade" for the purposes of securities legislation (other than the securities legislation of Québec), they would be prohibited by virtue of the prospectus requirement only if they also constitute a distribution under securities legislation. Securities legislation (other than the securities legislation of Québec) defines a distribution to include a "trade" in, among other things, previously unissued securities and securities that form part of a control block.

(7) The definition of distribution under the securities legislation of Québec includes the endeavour to obtain or the obtaining of subscribers or purchasers of previously unissued securities.

(8) Prospectus exemptions — It has been suggested by some that advertising or marketing activities, even if clearly made in furtherance of a distribution, could be undertaken in certain circumstances on a prospectus exempt basis. Specifically, it has been suggested that if an exemption from the prospectus requirement is available in respect of a specific distribution (even though the securities will be distributed under a prospectus), advertising or marketing related to such distribution would be exempt from the prospectus requirement. This analysis is premised on an argument that the advertising or marketing activities constitute one distribution that is exempt from the prospectus requirement while the actual sale of the security to the purchaser constitutes a second discrete distribution effected pursuant to the prospectus.

(9) We are of the view that this analysis is contrary to securities legislation. In these circumstances, the distribution in respect of which the advertising or marketing activities are undertaken is the distribution pursuant to the anticipated prospectus. Advertising or marketing must be viewed in the context of the prospectus offering and as an activity in furtherance of that distribution. If it were otherwise, the overriding concerns implicit and explicit in securities legislation regarding equal access to information, conditioning of the market, tipping and insider trading, and the provisions of the legislation designed to ensure such access to information and curb such abuses, could be easily circumvented.

(10) We recognize that an issuer and a dealer may have a demonstrable *bona fide* intention to effect an exempt distribution and this distribution may be abandoned in favour of a prospectus offering. In these very limited circumstances, there may be two separate distributions. From the time when it is reasonable for a dealer to expect that a *bona fide* exempt distribution will be abandoned in favour of a prospectus offering, the general rules relating to advertising or marketing activities that constitute an act in furtherance of a distribution will apply.

6A.4 Advertising or marketing activities — (1) The prospectus requirement applies to any act, advertisement, solicitation, conduct or negotiation directly or indirectly in furtherance of a distribution unless a prospectus exemption is available. Accordingly, advertising or marketing activities intended to promote the distribution of securities, in any form, would be prohibited by virtue of the prospectus requirement. Advertising or marketing activities subject to the prospectus requirement may be oral, written or electronic and include the following:

- television or radio advertisements or commentaries;

- published materials;

- correspondence;

- records;

- videotapes or similar material;

- market letters;

- research reports;

- circulars;

- promotional seminar text;

- telemarketing scripts;

- reprints or excerpts of any other sales literature.

(2) Advertising or marketing activities that are not in furtherance of a distribution of securities would not generally fall within the definition of a distribution and, therefore, would not be prohibited by virtue of the prospectus requirement. The following activities would not generally be subject to the prospectus requirement:

- advertising and publicity campaigns that are aimed at either selling products or services of the issuer or raising public awareness of the issuer;

- communication of factual information concerning the business of the issuer that is released in a manner, timing and form that is consistent with the regular past communications practices of the issuer if that communication does not refer to or suggest the distribution of securities;

- the release or filing of information that is required to be released or filed pursuant to securities legislation.

(3) Any activities that form part of a plan or series of activities undertaken in anticipation or in furtherance of a distribution would usually trigger the prospectus requirement, even if they would be permissible if viewed in isolation. Similarly, we may still consider advertising or marketing activities that do not indicate that a distribution of securities is contemplated to be in furtherance of a distribution by virtue of their timing and content. In particular, where a private placement or other exempt distribution occurs prior to or contemporaneously with a prospectus offering, we may consider activities undertaken in connection with the exempt distribution as being in furtherance of the prospectus offering.

6A.5 Pre-marketing and solicitation of expressions of interest — (1) In general, any advertising or marketing activities undertaken in connection with a prospectus prior to the issuance of a receipt for the preliminary prospectus are prohibited under securities legislation by virtue of the prospectus requirement.

(2) A distribution of securities commences at the time when:

- a dealer has had discussions with an issuer or a selling securityholder, or with another dealer that has had discussions with an issuer or a selling securityholder about the distribution, and

- those distribution discussions are of sufficient specificity that it is reasonable to expect that the dealer (alone or together with other dealers) will propose to the issuer or the selling securityholder an underwriting of the securities.

(3) We understand that many dealers communicate on a regular basis with clients and prospective clients concerning their interest in purchasing various securities of various issuers. We will not generally consider such ordinary course communications as being made in furtherance of a distribution. However, from the commencement of a distribution, communications by the dealer, with a person or company designed to have the effect of determining the interest that it, or any person or company that it represents, may have in purchasing securities of the type that are the subject of distribution discussions, that are undertaken by any director, officer, employee or agent of the dealer

(a) who participated in or had actual knowledge of the distribution discussions, or

(b) whose communications were directed, suggested or induced by a person referred to in (a), or another person acting directly or indirectly at or upon the direction, suggestion or inducement of a person referred to in (a),

are considered to be in furtherance of the distribution and contrary to securities legislation.

(4) From the commencement of the distribution no communications, market making, or other principal trading activities in securities of the type that are the subject of distribution discussions may be undertaken by a person referred to in paragraph 3(a) above, or at or upon the direction, suggestion or inducement of a person or persons referred to in paragraph 3(a) or (b) until the earliest of

- the issuance of a receipt for a preliminary prospectus in respect of the distribution, and

- the time at which the dealer determines not to pursue the distribution.

6A.6 Advertising or marketing activities during the waiting period — (1) Securities legislation provides an exception to the prospectus requirement for limited advertising or marketing activities during the waiting period between the issuance of the receipt for the preliminary prospectus and the receipt for the final prospectus. Despite the prospectus requirement, it is permissible during the waiting period to:

(a) distribute a preliminary prospectus notice (as defined in the Instrument) that:

- "identifies" the securities proposed to be issued,

- states the price of such securities, if then determined, and

- states the name and address of a person or company from whom purchases of securities may be made,

provided that any such notice states the name and address of a person or company from whom a preliminary prospectus may be obtained,

(b) distribute the preliminary prospectus, and

(c) solicit expressions of interest from a prospective purchaser, if prior to such solicitation or forthwith after the prospectus purchaser indicates an interest in purchasing the securities, a copy of the preliminary prospectus is forwarded to the prospectus purchaser.

(2) The use of any other marketing information or materials during the waiting period would result in the violation of the prospectus requirement.

(3) The "identification" of the security contemplated by paragraph 6A.6(1)(a) above does not permit an issuer or dealer to include a summary of the commercial features of the issue. These details are set out in the preliminary prospectus which is intended as the main disclosure vehicle pending the issuance of the final receipt. The purpose of the permitted advertising or marketing activities during the waiting period is essentially to alert the public to the availability of the preliminary prospectus.

(4) For the purpose of identifying a security as contemplated by paragraph 6A.6(1)(a) above, the advertising or marketing material may only:

- indicate whether a security represents debt or a share in an incorporated entity or an interest in a non-corporate entity,

- name the issuer if the issuer is a reporting issuer, or name and describe briefly the business of the issuer if the issuer is not already a reporting issuer (the description of the business should be cast in general terms and should not attempt to summarize the proposed use of proceeds),

- indicate, without giving details, whether the security qualifies the holder for special tax treatment, and

- indicate how many securities will be available.

6A.7 Green Sheets — (1) Some dealers prepare summaries of the principal terms of an offering, sometimes referred to as green sheets. Typically green sheets include information beyond the limited information for which an exemption to the prospectus requirement is available during the waiting period. If so, we would consider the distribution of a green sheet to a potential investor to contravene the prospectus requirement.

(2) Including material information in a green sheet or other marketing communication that is not contained in the preliminary prospectus could indicate a failure to provide in the preliminary prospectus full, true and plain disclosure of all material facts relating to the securities offered by the prospectus and result in the prospectus certificate containing a misrepresentation.

(3) We may request copies of green sheets and other advertising or marketing materials as part of our prospectus review procedures. Any discrepancies between the content of a green sheet and the preliminary prospectus could result in the delay or refusal of a receipt for a final prospectus and, in appropriate circumstances, could result in enforcement action.

6A.8 Advertising or marketing activities following the issuance of a receipt for a final prospectus — Advertising or marketing activities that are not prohibited by the prospectus requirement during the waiting period may also be undertaken on the same basis after a receipt has been issued for the final prospectus relating to the distribution. In addition, the prospectus and any document filed with or referred to in the prospectus may be distributed.

6A.9 Sanctions and enforcement — Any contravention of the prospectus requirement through advertising or marketing activities is a serious matter that could result in a cease trade order in respect of the preliminary prospectus to which such advertising or marketing activities relate. In addition, a receipt for a final prospectus relating to any such offering may be refused. In appropriate circumstances, enforcement proceedings may be initiated.

6A.10 Media reports and coverage — (1) We recognize that an issuer does not have control over media coverage; however, an issuer should take appropriate precautions to ensure that media coverage which can reasonably be considered to be in furtherance of a distribution of securities does not occur after a decision has been made to file a preliminary prospectus or during the waiting period.

(2) We may investigate the circumstances surrounding media coverage of an issuer which appears immediately prior to or during the waiting period and which can reasonably be considered as being in furtherance of a distribution of securities. Action will be taken in appropriate circumstances.

6A.11 Disclosure practices — At a minimum, participants in all prospectus distributions should consider the following practices to avoid contravening securities legislation:

- We do not consider it appropriate for a director or an officer of an issuer to give interviews to the media immediately prior to or during the waiting period. It may be appropriate, however, for a director or officer to respond to unsolicited inquiries of a factual nature made by shareholders, securities analysts, financial analysts, the media and others who have a legitimate interest in such information.

- Because of the prospectus requirement, an issuer is not permitted to provide information during a prospectus distribution that goes beyond what is disclosed in the prospectus. Therefore, during the prospectus distribution (which commences as described in subsection 6A.5(2) of this Policy and ends following closing), a director or officer of an issuer can only make a statement constituting a forecast, projection or prediction with respect to future financial performance if the statement is also contained in the prospectus.

- We understand that underwriters and legal counsel sometimes only advise the working group members of the pre-marketing and marketing restrictions under securities legislation. However, there are often situations where officers and directors of the issuer outside of the working group also come into contact with the media before or after the filing of a preliminary prospectus. Any discussions between these individuals and

Part 4:
DISTRIBUTIONS

the media will also be subject to these same restrictions. Working group members, including underwriters and legal counsel, will usually want to ensure that any other officers and directors of the issuer (as well as the officers and directors of a promoter or a selling securityholder) who may come into contact with the media are also fully aware of the marketing and disclosure restrictions.

- One way for issuers, dealers and other market participants to ensure that advertising or marketing activities contrary to securities legislation are not undertaken (intentionally or through inadvertence) is to develop, implement, maintain and enforce disclosure procedures.

6A.12 Misleading or untrue statements — In addition to the prohibitions on advertising and marketing activities that result from the prospectus requirement, securities legislation in certain jurisdictions prohibits any person or company from making any misleading or untrue statement that would reasonably be expected to have a significant effect on the market value of securities. Therefore, in addition to ensuring that advertising or marketing activities are carried out in compliance with the prospectus requirement, issuers, dealers and their advisers must ensure that any statements made in the course of advertising or marketing activities are not untrue or misleading and otherwise comply with securities legislation.

PART 7 — TRANSITION

7.1 Transition — Application of Amendments — The amendments to the Instrument and this Policy which came into effect on January 1, 2011 only apply to a preliminary prospectus, an amendment to a preliminary prospectus, a final prospectus or an amendment to a final prospectus of an issuer which includes financial statements of the issuer in respect of periods relating to financial years beginning on or after January 1, 2011.

Appendix A — Financial Statement Disclosure Requirements for Significant Acquisitions

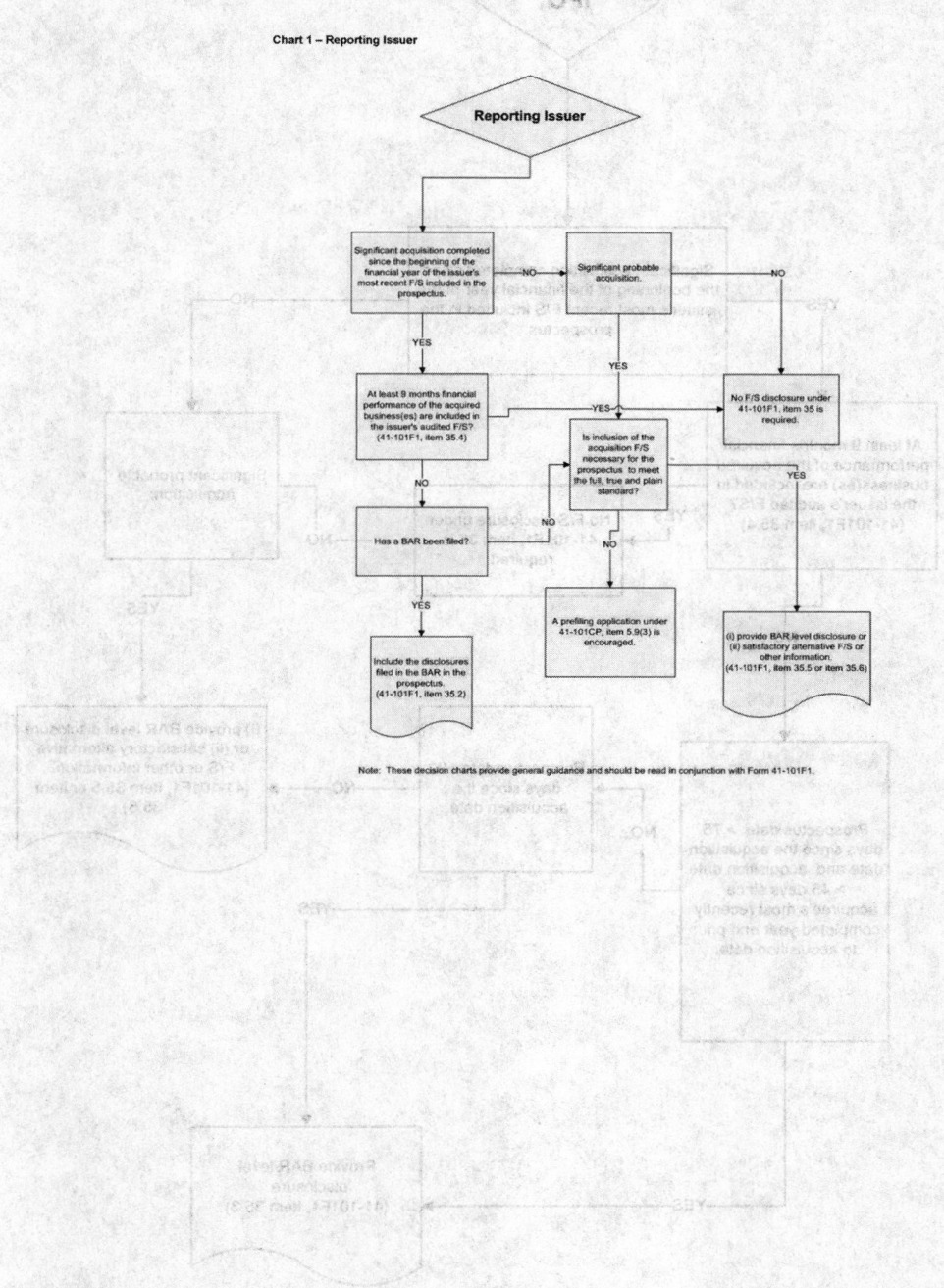

Chart 1 – Reporting Issuer

Note: These decision charts provide general guidance and should be read in conjunction with Form 41-101F1.

Chart 2 – Non-Reporting Issuer

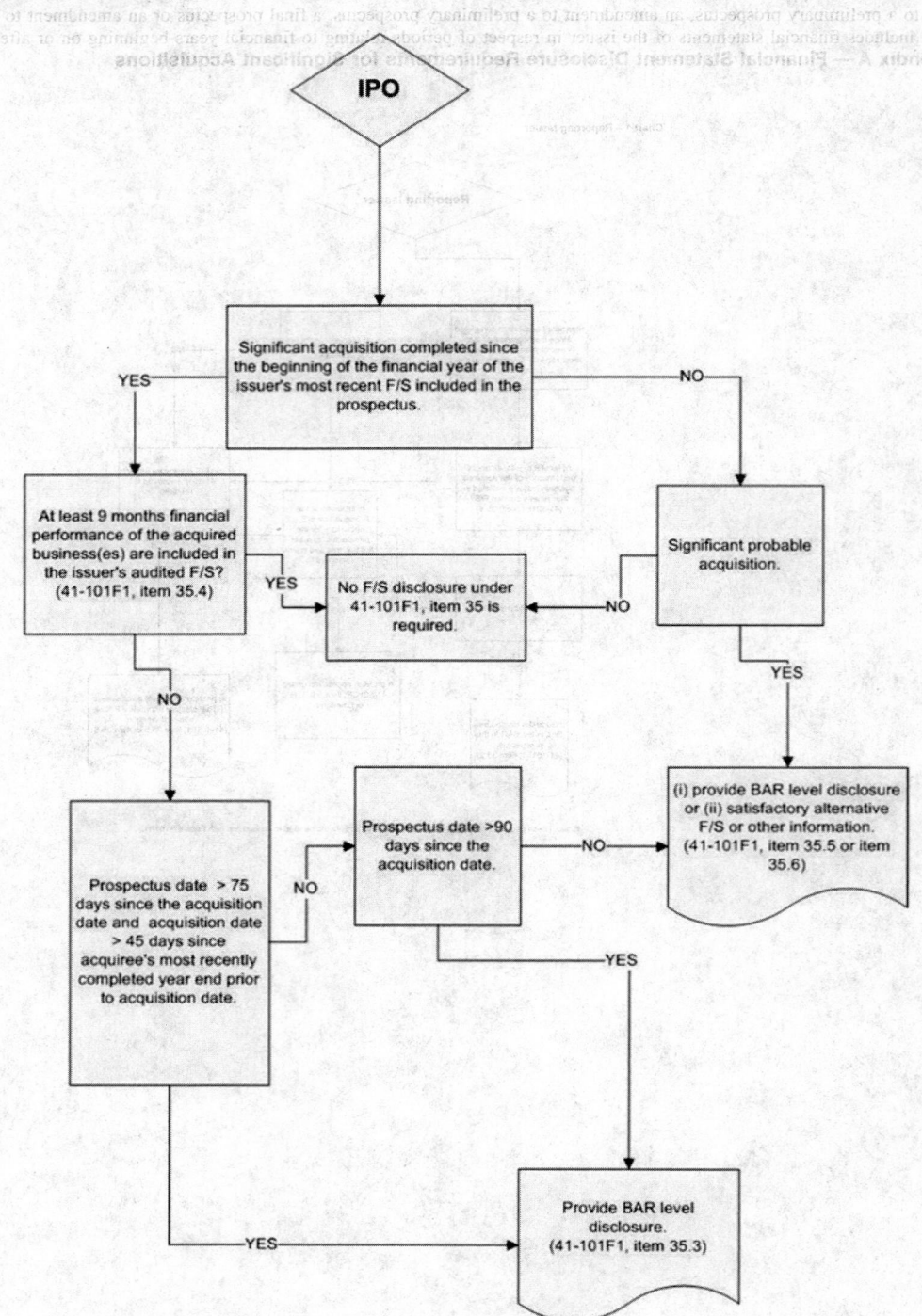

Note: These decision charts provide general guidance and should be read in conjunction with Form 41-101F1.

Adoption of Policy: (2008) 31 O.S.C.B. (Supp. 2) 139 and (2007) 30 O.S.C.B. (Supp. 7) 1 (Dec. 21, 2007); Request for Comments: (2006) 29 O.S.C.B. (Supp. 3) 1 (Dec. 22, 2006).

Adoption of Amendment to Policy: (2010) 33 O.S.C.B. (Supp. 5) 93 and (Supp. 3) 161; Request for Comments: (2009) 32 O.S.C.B. (Supp. 6) 201.

Adoption of Amendment to Policy: (2013) 36 O.S.C.B. 4913 and (Supp. 2) 1; Request for Comments: (2011) 34 O.S.C.B. (Supp. 4) 1.

Adoption of Amendment to Policy: (2013) 36 O.S.C.B. 7994 and (Supp. 4) 1; Request for Comments: (2011) 34 O.S.C.B. 11829

Policies and Orders: CSAN 51-336.

National Policy 41-201 — Income Trusts and Other Indirect Offerings

Date: December 3, 2004; replaced effective July 6, 2007 and amended effective December 31, 2007, December 15, 2008, January 1, 2011 and August 13, 2013

27 O.S.C.B. 9685, 30 O.S.C.B. 6080, 30 O.S.C.B. 10523, 31 O.S.C.B. 11350, 33 O.S.C.B. 10467 and 36 O.S.C.B. 8016

Table of Contents

4.5.3 What disclosure do we expect about the accountibility of the vendors?

4.5.4 What are our concerns about the nature and extent of the representations and indemnities provided by vendors in the acquisition agreement?

PART 5 SALES AND MARKETING MATERIALS

5.1 What are our concerns about sales and marketing materials?

5.2 What information do we expect green sheets and marketing materials to contain?

5.3 Do we expect income trusts to provide us with copies of their green sheets and marketing materials?

PART 6 CONTINUOUS DISCLOSURE-SPECIFIC ISSUES

6.1 What continuous disclosure do we expect about the operating entity?

6.2 Comparative financial information

6.3 Recognition of intangible assets

6.4 Are "insiders" of the operating entity also insiders of the income trust for purposes of insider reporting obligations?

6.5 MD&A

6.5.1 Risks and uncertainties

6.5.2 Discussion of distributed cash

PART 7 CORPORATE GOVERNANCE

7.1 CEO/CFO certification, audit committees, and effective corporate governance

7.2 Broader corporate law concerns

PART 8 OTHER ISSUES

8.1 Income trust names

PART 1 — INTRODUCTION

1.1 What is the purpose of the policy? — It is a fundamental principle that everyone investing in securities should have access to sufficient information to make an informed investment decision. The Canadian Securities Administrators (the CSA or we) believe that there are distinct attributes of an investment in income trust units that should be clearly disclosed.

Within our securities regulatory framework, raising capital in the public markets results in certain rights and obligations attaching to issuers and investors. We believe that it would be beneficial to express our view in a policy about how the existing regulatory framework applies to non-corporate issuers (such as income trusts) and to indirect offering structures in order to minimize inconsistent interpretations and to better ensure that the principles underlying the requirements are preserved. Our concerns relate to the quality and nature of prospectus and continuous disclosure, accountability for prospectus disclosure and liability for insider trading. We have drafted a policy rather than a rule because we believe that the existing regulatory requirements capture the necessary regulatory outcomes relating to income trusts and other indirect offering structures. Our goal is to provide guidance and recommendations about how income trusts and other indirect offering structures fit within the existing regulatory requirements rather than create new regulatory requirements for income trusts and other indirect offering structures. We also identify factors that relate to the exercise of the regulator's discretion in a prospectus offering.

This policy provides guidance and clarification by all jurisdictions represented by the CSA. The guidance generally relates to the requirements of National Instrument 51-102 *Continuous Disclosure Obligations* and the prospectus requirements in each jurisdiction. Although the primary focus of this policy is on income trusts, we believe that much of the guidance and clarification that we provide is useful for other indirect offering structures. As well, the guidance may apply more generally to issuers that offer securities which entitle holders of those securities to net cash flow generated by the issuer's business or its properties. We provide guidance about prospectus disclosure and prospectus liability to minimize situations where staff might recommend against issuance of a receipt for a prospectus where it would appear that the offering may be contrary to the public interest due to insufficient disclosure, the structure of the offering, or other factors.

Although the focus of this policy is on the income trust structure in the context of offerings by way of prospectus, these principles also apply to income trust structures in other contexts, such as the reorganization of a corporate entity into a trust. Although an offering document is not prepared in a reorganization, we expect that the information circular provided to relevant security holders, and that contains prospectus-level disclosure, will follow the principles set out in this policy. In addition when we are determining whether to grant exemptive relief to an income trust issuer in connection with a reorganization or other similar transaction, we will consider the principles described in Part 3 of this policy.

This policy may also apply to income trusts in the fulfillment of their continuous disclosure obligations.

1.2 What do we mean when we refer to an income trust in this policy? — When we refer to an income trust or issuer in this policy, we are referring to a trust or other entity (including corporate and non-corporate entities) that issues securities which provide for participation by the holder in net cash flows generated by: (i) an underlying business owned by the trust or other entity, or (ii) the income-producing properties owned by the trust or other entity. This includes business income trusts, real estate investment trusts and royalty trusts. In our view, this does not include an entity that falls within the definition of "investment fund" contained in National Instrument 81-106 *Investment Fund Continuous Disclosure*, or an entity that issues asset-backed securities or capital trust securities.

1.3 What is an operating entity? — In the most basic income trust structure, the operating entity is: (i) a subsidiary of the income trust with an underlying business, or (ii) income-producing properties owned directly by the income trust. In more complex structures, there may be a number of intervening entities above the operating entity. Generally, the operating entity is the first entity in the structure that has an underlying business that generates cash flows. There may be more than one operating entity in the income trust structure.

In addition to identifying the operating entity, it is also important to understand the operating entity's business. In some cases, its business is to own, operate and produce revenues from its assets. In other cases, its business is to own an interest in a joint venture or to derive a revenue stream from holding a portfolio of investments or financial instruments.

1.4 How is an income trust structured? — Typically, an income trust holds a combination of debt and equity or royalty interests in an entity owning or operating a business. Net cash flows generated by the operating entity's business are distributed to the income trust. The income trust then distributes some or all of that cash flow to its investors (referred to as unitholders or investors).

1.5 What is an income trust offering? — In a typical income trust offering, an income trust is created to distribute units to the public. The income trust then uses the proceeds from the offering to acquire debt and equity or royalty interests in the operating entity, or interests in income producing properties. We view the income trust offering as a form of indirect offering. Instead of offering their securities directly to the public, the vendors sell their interests in the operating entity to the income trust. The income trust purchases those interests with proceeds that it raises through its offering of units to the public. The interests in the operating entity that the income trust acquires are thus indirectly offered to the public. Through their direct investment in units of the income trust, unitholders hold an indirect interest in the operating entity.

By issuing units under a prospectus, the income trust becomes a reporting issuer (or equivalent) under applicable securities laws. The operating entity typically remains a non-reporting issuer.

1.6 How does an indirect offering differ from a direct offering? — In a conventional direct offering, interests in the operating entity are offered to the public through a public distribution of the operating entity's securities. By contrast, in an indirect offering, interests in the operating entity are not offered directly to the public but are instead acquired by a separate entity (for example, an income trust or its subsidiary). The securities of this separate entity, such as units of a trust, are offered to the public under a prospectus. The issuer applies the proceeds of the offering to satisfy the purchase price of the interests in the operating entity.

In a direct initial public offering, an issuer may choose to finance the acquisition of another business with proceeds raised under the offering. In that scenario, the issuer and the vendors of the business are generally arm's length parties. This differs from the structure of an indirect offering, such as the initial public offering by most income trusts, where the income trust and the vendors of the business are not arm's length parties.

In an indirect offering, the vendors negotiate the terms of the purchase of the business by the income trust, and are also involved in the negotiation of the terms of the public offering with the underwriter(s).

If vendors initiate or are involved in the initial public offering process, we believe that they are effectively accessing the capital markets themselves. We consider them to be non-arm's length vendors. This fact gives rise to the concerns that we describe in Part 4. Non-arm's length vendors that are involved in a follow-on offering are also effectively accessing the capital markets through an indirect offering, and the concerns that we describe in Part 4 are equally applicable.

PART 2 — DISTRIBUTABLE CASH

2.1 What is distributable cash? — Distributable cash is a term used to refer to the net cash generated by the income trust's businesses or assets that is available for distribution, at the discretion of the income trust, to the income trust's unitholders. Some issuers have referred to net cash available for distribution by a term other than distributable cash. In this policy "distributable cash" includes all such other terms used to describe the amount available for distribution to an income trust's or other indirect offering structure's securityholders (e.g. distributable income).

The cash that is available to an income trust for distribution per unit varies with the operating performance of the income trust's business or assets, its capital requirements, debt obligations and the number of units outstanding.

Income trust distributions are, for Canadian tax purposes, composed of different types of payments that are referred to as "returns on capital" or "returns of capital." These terms are also used more generally, to make an economic rather than a tax-driven distinction. The underlying concern is that the amount of cash distributed by an income trust may sometimes be greater than what it can safely distribute without eroding its productive capacity and threatening the sustainability of its distributions. In this situation, the "excess" amount of the distribution may be regarded as an economic "return of capital." We are concerned that disclosure by income trusts has not always been sufficiently plain to allow an investor to assess whether a possible concern exists in this respect.

Please refer to subsection 6.5.2 for guidance on how issuers can address these concerns.

2.2 Do income trusts provide investors with a consistent rate of return? — No. In many ways, investing in an income trust is more like an investment in an equity security rather than in a debt security. A fundamental characteristic that distinguishes income trust units from traditional fixed-income securities is that the income trust does not have a fixed obligation to make payments to investors. In other words, it has the ability to reduce or suspend distributions if circumstances warrant (see section 2.3 below for further details). In contrast to a traditional fixed-income security, the trust's ability to consistently make distributions to unitholders is closely tied to the operations of the operating entity or the performance of the income trust's assets. The performance of the operating entity may fluctuate from period to period, which might impact both the distributions paid and value of the issuer's units.

Unlike an issuer of a fixed-income security, an income trust does not promise to return the initial purchase price of the unit bought by the investor on a certain date in the future. Investors who choose to liquidate their holdings would generally do so by selling their unit(s) in the market at the prevailing market price.

In addition, unlike interest payments on an interest-bearing debt security, income trust cash distributions are, for Canadian tax purposes, composed of different types of payments (portions of which may be fully or partially taxable or may constitute tax-deferred returns of capital). The composition for tax purposes of those distributions may change over time, thus affecting the after-tax return to investors. Therefore, a unitholder's rate of return over a defined period may not be comparable to the rate of return on a fixed-income security that provides a "return on capital" over the same period. This is because a unitholder in an income trust may receive distributions that constitute a "return of capital" to some extent during the period. Returns on capital are generally taxed as ordinary income or as dividends in the hands of a unitholder. Returns of capital are generally tax-deferred (and reduce the unitholder's cost base in the unit for tax purposes).

2.3 How do the distribution policies of the income trust and the operating entity affect an investor's rate of return? — The distribution policy of the income trust generally stipulates that payments that the income trust receives from the operating entity (such as interest payments on the debt and dividends paid to common shareholders) will be distributed to unitholders. The distribution policy of the operating entity will generally stipulate that distributions to the income trust will be restricted if the operating entity breaches its covenants with third-party lenders (such as covenants requiring the operating entity to maintain specified financial ratios or to satisfy its interest and other expense obligations). Other operating entity obligations such as funding employee incentive plans or funding capital expenditures will frequently rank in priority to the operating entity's obligations to the income trust. In addition, the operating entity, or the income trust, might retain a portion of available distributable cash as a reserve. Funds in this reserve may be drawn upon to fund future distributions if distributable cash generated is below targeted amounts in any period.

2.4 What prospectus cover page disclosure do we expect about distributable cash? — To ensure that the information described in sections 2.1, 2.2 and 2.3 is adequately communicated to investors, we recommend that issuers consider including language substantively similar to the following on the prospectus cover page:

A return on your investment in • is not comparable to the return on an investment in a fixed-income security. The recovery of your initial investment is at risk, and the anticipated return on your investment is based on many performance assumptions. Although the income trust intends to make distributions of its available cash to you, these cash distributions may be reduced or suspended. The actual amount distributed will depend on numerous factors including: [insert a discussion of the principal factors particular to this specific offering that could affect the predictability of cash flow to unitholders]. In addition, the market value of the units may decline if the income trust is unable to meet its cash distribution targets in the future, and that decline may be significant.

It is important for you to consider the particular risk factors that may affect the industry in which you are investing, and therefore the stability of the distributions that you receive. See, for example, ***, under the section "Risk Factors" [insert specific cross-reference to principal factors that could affect the predictability of cash flow to unitholders]. That section also describes the issuer's assessment of those risk factors, as well as the potential consequences to you if a risk should occur.

The after-tax return from an investment in units to unitholders subject to Canadian income tax can be made up of both a return on and a return of capital. That composition may change over time, thus affecting your after-tax return. [If a forecast has been prepared, include specific disclosure about the estimated portion of the investment that will be taxed as a return on capital and the estimated portion that will be taxed as return of capital. If the issuer cannot estimate the portion that will be a return of capital, state that it is unable to reasonably estimate the return of capital on anticipated distributions, and that this amount might vary materially from period to period.] Returns on capital are generally taxed as ordinary income or as dividends in the hands of a unitholder. Returns of capital are generally tax-deferred (and reduce the unitholder's cost base in the unit for tax purposes).

2.5 What disclosure should be provided for distributable cash? — As required by the accounting principles an issuer uses to prepare its financial statements (the issuer's GAAP), an income trust must disclose the cash distributed to unitholders in its financial statements. Income trusts may also disclose distributable cash. Income trusts generally include disclosure about historical distributable cash in continuous disclosure documents and estimated distributable cash in their prospectuses. We have concluded that distributable cash is a cash flow measure, not an income measure. To ensure readers understand the composition and relevance of distributable cash, income trusts should reconcile distributable cash to cash flows from operating activities. In determining cash flows from operating activities, income trusts should include borrowing costs and changes during the period in non-cash working capital balances.

Specifically, income trusts should:

(i) state explicitly that distributable cash does not have any standardized meaning prescribed by the issuer's GAAP and is therefore unlikely to be comparable to similar measures presented by other issuers;

(ii) present cash flows from operating activities with equal or greater prominence than distributable cash;

(iii) explain why distributable cash provides useful information to investors and how management uses distributable cash as a financial measure;

(iv) provide a clear quantitative reconciliation from distributable cash to cash flows from operating activities, and refer to the reconciliation where distributable cash first appears in the disclosure document, or in the case of content on a website, in a manner that meets this objective (for example, by providing a link to the reconciliation); and

(v) explain any changes in the composition of distributable cash when compared to previously disclosed measures.

2.6 What format of distributable cash reconciliation should be used? — When presenting a reconciliation of distributable cash to cash flows from operating activities, income trusts should discuss any adjustments included in the reconciliation and these adjustments should be grouped separately based on the nature of the adjustment. In addition, income trusts should avoid reconciling cash flows from operating activities to a subtotal that is not a minimum line item in the financial statements required by the issuer's GAAP (for example, profit or loss is a minimum line item).

An issuer might group adjustments to cash flows from operating activities included in a reconciliation of distributable cash as follows:

a. Capital adjustments — Adjustments for capital expenditures, whether to maintain productive capacity of the issuer or otherwise, should be included here and may be based on actual capital expenditures. An issuer that does not intend to maintain productive capacity (for example, in the case of depleting assets) should clearly state this in its distributable cash reconciliation.

Other examples of adjustments that might be included in this section include provisions for maintaining or replacing mineral reserves.

An issuer may include within this grouping a sub-total of cash flows from operating activities after deducting capital expenditures incurred during the period.

b. Non-recurring adjustments — Generally, an item is considered non-recurring if a similar loss or gain is not reasonably likely to occur within the next two years or if it has not occurred during the prior two years. An example of a non-recurring item is a payment in connection with litigation or a penalty that was levied in the current year and is not expected to be incurred going forward.

c. Other adjustments including discretionary items — We recognize that, in limited circumstances, certain adjustments may not properly be classified as non-recurring or capital adjustments. Some examples of such adjustments include amounts for decommissioning, restoration and similar liabilities or external restrictions imposed on the issuer that limit their ability to pay distributions. Where an adjustment is discretionary in nature, we expect income trusts to clearly explain the basis for inclusion of the adjustment and any underlying assumptions which are being relied upon.

2.7 What disclosure do we expect about the adjustments and assumptions underlying distributable cash? — Income trusts should consider how best to provide transparency about the presentation of each adjusting item included in a reconciliation of distributable cash, including a discussion of the work that was done by the issuer to ensure the completeness and reasonableness of the information.

Generally, to achieve acceptable transparency, the reconciliation of distributable cash to cash flows from operating activities should be accompanied by detailed disclosure that:

(i) explains the purpose and relevance of the distributable cash information;

(ii) describes the extent to which actual financial results are incorporated into the reconciliation;

(iii) explicitly states that the reconciliation has been prepared using reasonable and supportable assumptions, all of which reflect the income trust's planned courses of action given management's judgment about the most probable set of economic conditions; and

(iv) cautions investors that actual results may vary, perhaps materially, from the forward-looking adjustments.

Further adjustments made in the reconciliation of distributable cash to cash flows from operating activities should be supported by:

(i) a detailed discussion of the nature of the adjustments;

(ii) a description of the underlying assumptions used in preparing each element of the forward-looking information and the forward-looking information as a whole, including how those assumptions are supported; and

(iii) a discussion of the specific risks and uncertainties that may affect each individual assumption and that may cause actual results to differ materially from the distributable cash figure.

For assumptions to be supportable, they should take into account the past performance of the underlying operating entity, the performance of other entities engaged in similar activities, and any other sources that provide objective corroboration of the assumptions used. Further, for assumptions to be considered reasonable, we believe that they should be consistent with the anticipated plans of the income trust.

In some circumstances, assumptions may be consistent with the issuer's anticipated plans but may not provide an adequate level of transparency about the sustainability of distributable cash. It is important for income trusts to disclose all factors, events or conditions that are likely to occur in the future that may impact the sustainability of future distributions.

For example, capital expenditures to replace productive capacity may be relatively low in initial years but may rise significantly in later years. In these instances, adequate disclosure of the adjustment for estimated future capital maintenance expenditures might include a discussion of the time period over which the income trust anticipates incurring capital maintenance expenditures at the level disclosed and any expected long-term plans to replace productive capacity. A clear and complete explanation should be provided of the reasons why these provisions will be adequate to cover future capital requirements and why these amounts vary from historical amounts, if applicable.

Another example of providing adequate transparency about the sustainability of distributable cash relates to instances where an issuer makes prior arrangements with investors. For example, for some income trusts, the original vendors' entitlement to cash distributions based on their continuing interest is subordinated to that of other investors. The original vendors will not receive cash distributions for a defined period of time if the estimated level of distributable cash disclosed in the prospectus is not achieved. Distributable cash available for distribution to other investors may be higher in the short term while cash distributions are not paid to the original vendors, but may decrease once the subordination conditions are satisfied. In these instances, the key terms and impact of these arrangements should be summarized in proximity to the distributable cash information.

2.8 When should the estimate of distributable cash be derived from a forecast? — When estimated distributable cash information contained in a prospectus includes forward-looking adjustments that are based on significant assumptions and those adjustments materially affect estimated distributable cash, the quantitative reconciliation discussed in section 2.5 should begin with cash flows from operating activities derived from future-oriented financial information (FOFI) that complies with sections 4A and 4B of National Instrument 51-102 *Continuous Disclosure Obligations*. The FOFI should reflect these forward-looking adjustments and the FOFI should be included in the prospectus.

FOFI may not be necessary if the adjusting items are derived from historical amounts and the adjusting items can be adequately explained by alternative disclosures. Alternative disclosures may include:

(i) historical financial statements that support the adjustments. In some cases, a recent acquisition may not be considered significant under the significant acquisition tests set out in OSC Rule 41-501 *General Prospectus Requirements* (Rule 41-501) (or its successor) or the equivalent rule in the applicable jurisdiction for purposes of providing financial statements of the acquired entity. However, the acquisition's anticipated impact on distributable cash may be material. In these cases, income trusts may choose to provide financial statements of the acquired entity in the prospectus in addition to those required by Rule 41-501, and, when appropriate, include financial information from the acquired entity's financial statements in the issuer's pro forma financial statements; or

(ii) other historical financial information that supports the calculation of the adjustments.

In some cases, distributable cash disclosure may contain adjusting items that are based on recent contracts or agreements for which historical financial statements or other historical financial information is not available. In these cases, issuers may instead disclose a detailed description of the contract or agreement including relevant terms and conditions of the contractual commitment and any other financial information that supports the amount of the adjusting item.

PART 3 — OTHER DISCLOSURE ISSUES

A. — Material debt

3.1 Why are we concerned about material debt? — We are concerned about debt obligations that are incurred by the operating entity or other entity that rank before unitholders' entitlement to receive cash distributions. Although many non-income trust issuers have similar, or less conservative, capital structures, we are particularly concerned about the sensitivity of income trusts to cash flows. Specifically, we are concerned about reductions in distributions that might arise from increases in interest expense on floating-rate debt, a breach of financial covenants, a refinancing on less advantageous terms, or a failure to refinance.

3.2 What disclosure do we expect about material debt? — The principal terms of the material debt should be included in an income trust prospectus and in the income trust's Annual Information Form (AIF) filed under National Instrument 51-102 *Continuous Disclosure Obligations*, or its successor (NI 51-102). This would include the following information about the debt:

(i) the principal amount and the anticipated amount to be outstanding when the offering is closed,

(ii) the term and interest rate (including whether the rate is fixed or floating),

(iii) the terms on which the debt is renewable, and the extent to which those terms could have an impact on the ability to distribute cash,

(iv) the priority of the debt relative to the securities of the operating entity held by the income trust,

(v) any security granted by the income trust to the lender over the operating entity's assets, and

(vi) any other covenant(s) that could restrict the ability to distribute cash.

3.3 Are agreements relating to the material debt considered to be material contracts of the income trust? — We consider that in most cases, agreements relating to material debt that have been negotiated with a lender other than the income trust, will be material contracts pursuant to Rule 41-501 and NI 51-102 (or their respective successors) if those agreements have a direct correlation with the anticipated cash distributions. For example, distributions from the operating entity to the income trust may be restricted if the operating entity fails to maintain certain covenants under a credit agreement. If the agreement contains terms that have a direct correlation with the anticipated cash distributions, and will be entered into on or about closing, it should be listed as a material contract in the prospectus and AIF. We also expect a copy of the material agreement and any amendments to be filed on SEDAR.

3.4 Do we expect the income trust to include a separate risk factor about the material debt? — Yes. We expect the income trust to include a separate risk factor about the material debt in the income trust's prospectus and AIF. A full and complete discussion of this risk factor would usually include the following:

    (i) the need for the borrower to refinance the debt when the term of that debt expires,

    (ii) the potential negative impact on the ability of the issuer and/or its subsidiaries to make distributions if the debt is replaced by new debt that has less favourable terms,

    (iii) the impact on distributable cash if the borrower cannot refinance the debt, and

    (iv) the fact that the ability of the operating entity to make distributions, directly or indirectly, to the income trust may be restricted if the borrower fails to maintain certain covenants under the credit agreement (such as a failure to maintain certain customary financial ratios).

B. — Stability ratings

3.5 What is a stability rating? — A stability rating is an opinion of an independent rating agency about the relative stability and sustainability of an income trust's cash distribution stream. Standard & Poor's (S&P's) and Dominion Bond Rating Services (DBRS) currently provide stability ratings on Canadian income trusts. A stability rating reflects the rating agency's assessment of an income trust's underlying business model, and the sustainability and variability in cash flow generation in the medium to long-term. The objective of these stability ratings is to compare the stability of rated Canadian income trusts with one another within a particular sector or industry.

3.6 Does an income trust need to obtain a stability rating? — No. However, the CSA believes that stability ratings by rating agencies, such as S&P's and DBRS, can provide useful information to investors.

Some investors who choose to invest in income trust units may base that decision primarily on the cash flow generated by the operating entity. Distributable cash is often presented as a measure of the issuer's potential to generate cash for distribution. Stability ratings can supplement the presentation of distributable cash to provide an independent opinion on the ability of an income trust to meet its distributable cash targets consistently over a period of time relative to other rated Canadian income trusts within a particular sector or industry.

3.7 What disclosure do we expect about an income trust's stability rating? — If an income trust has asked for and received a stability rating, the rating should be described on the cover page of the prospectus and in the income trust's AIF. The income trust should include disclosure about the rating in accordance with section 10.8 of Ontario Securities Commission Form 41-501F1 Information Required in a Prospectus (or its successor), section 10.8 of Schedule 1 Information Required in a Prospectus to Quebec's Regulation Q-28 respecting General Prospectus Requirements (or its successor), section 7.9 of Form 44-101F1 Short Form Prospectus (or its successor) or item 7.3 of Form 51-102F2 (or its successor). This disclosure should explain that a rating measures an income trust's stability relative to other rated Canadian income trusts within a particular sector or industry. Issuers are required to make timely disclosure of any material change in their affairs, which we believe would include any change in a stability rating that constitutes a material change.

We understand that some stability ratings are provided to income trusts on an unsolicited basis. These ratings are not based on discussions with the income trust but, rather, on publicly available information. Our disclosure expectations do not extend to unsolicited stability ratings.

C. — Executive compensation

3.8 What disclosure do we expect the income trust to provide about executive compensation for the operating entity? — We believe that the executive compensation of the operating entity's executives is important information for investors. The income trust should provide that information in its prospectus and information circular as if the operating entity were a subsidiary of the income trust.

3.9 What disclosure do we expect about the income trust's management contracts and management incentive plans? — We believe that the material terms of management contracts and management incentive plans are relevant information for investors if the terms of those contracts or plans have an impact on distributable cash. For example, if the term "distributable cash" is defined in a unique way in a management contract, we expect that term of the contract to be described. A further example would be information about why an issuer has decided to use an external management company rather than retain an internal management structure or, conversely, why an issuer has internalized management. Adequate information about those contracts and plans should be included in applicable disclosure documents. Even if those contracts and plans have not been finalized prior to the filing of an initial public offering (final) prospectus, the anticipated material terms should still be described in the prospectus.

3.10 Do we expect management contracts and management incentive plans to be filed on SEDAR? — We expect the material contracts and plans referred to in section 3.9 to be filed on SEDAR. If those material contracts and plans have not been finalized before filing a prospectus, we expect the income trust to provide an undertaking from the income trust and the operating entity to securities regulatory authorities that those contracts and plans will be filed as soon as practicable after execution.

D. — Risk factors

3.11 General — Income trusts are required to disclose all material risk factors relating to the offering pursuant to a prospectus. A complete discussion of risk factors for an income trust should include the principal factors related to the specific offering that could affect the predictability of cash flow distributions to unitholders. It would also include an assessment of the likelihood of a risk occurring as well as the potential consequences to a unitholder if a risk should occur. Relevant risk factors may include risks relating to the operating entity business, the potential inapplicability to unitholders of certain corporate law rights and remedies, the potential inapplicability of insolvency and restructuring legislation in the trust context, and other factors relevant to income trusts and other indirect offerings that we have described in this policy. For income trusts, risk factor disclosure is also required on an ongoing basis in the issuer's AIF in accordance with Item 5.2 of Form 51-102F2 (or its successor).

PART 4 — OFFERING-SPECIFIC ISSUES

A. — Determination of offering price

4.1 What disclosure do we expect about the determination of the price of an income trust's units? — We do not require that income trusts obtain a third-party valuation of the operating entity interests to be acquired (unless that valuation is otherwise required under securities legislation). However, if a third-party valuation is obtained in connection with an initial public offering, the income trust should describe the valuation in the prospectus. The description should identify the parties involved, the principal variables and assumptions used in the valuation (particularly those which could, if adversely altered, cause a deterioration in the value of the issuer's investment). If no third-party valuation is obtained, the prospectus should disclose that fact and state that the price of the issuer's units was determined solely through negotiation between the operating entity security holders and the underwriter(s).

B. — Prospectus liability

4.2 What is the regulatory framework? — The central element of the prospectus system is the requirement that disclosure of all material facts relating to the offered securities and the issuer be provided so that investors can make informed investment decisions.

Although the prospectus serves a role in marketing securities, from a regulatory perspective it is also a disclosure document that can give rise to regulatory and civil liability. To provide discipline on prospectus disclosure, and to protect the integrity of the Canadian public markets, securities legislation prohibits certain persons involved in a public offering from making a misrepresentation (as defined in applicable securities legislation) in a prospectus. Where a prospectus contains a misrepresentation, investors may have the right to either rescind their purchases or to claim damages from the issuer or selling security holder, every director of the issuer, any promoters of the issuer, the underwriter(s) and certain other parties. Each of those parties (including each selling security holder) is jointly and severally liable for the damages suffered by investors as a result of the misrepresentation(s). Although "selling security holder" is not defined under applicable securities laws, the term is generally considered to mean persons who are selling securities of the class being distributed under the prospectus.

4.3 How does the regulatory framework related to prospectus liability apply to indirect offerings? — In an indirect offering, the issuer uses the proceeds to acquire a business (and perhaps to repay indebtedness), and the disclosure (including financial disclosure) in the prospectus describes both the acquired business and the issuer. The proceeds are not retained by the issuer, and any prospectus misrepresentation that adversely affects the value of the acquired business may diminish the issuer's ability to satisfy a damages claim.

An underwriter's statutory liability in an indirect offering is the same as it is in a conventional direct offering. Underwriters sign a certificate about the disclosure contained in the issuer's prospectus and are potentially liable for a misrepresentation in the prospectus.

In an indirect offering, the former owners of the operating entity (referred to as vendors) who sell their ownership interests in the operating entity to the issuer and who are effectively accessing the public markets to liquidate their holdings, are not generally considered to be "selling security holders" within the meaning of securities legislation, as they are not selling the securities being offered under the prospectus. As a result, vendors who indirectly receive part of the proceeds of the offering in exchange for their operating entity interests do not (unless they qualify as promoters, see below) have statutory liability for a misrepresentation in a prospectus as they would if their interest in the operating entity had been distributed directly to the public. Vendors of businesses to conventional issuers undertaking a direct offering would also not be considered "selling security holders" although they indirectly receive offering proceeds. However, as noted above, we believe those circumstances differ from an indirect offering because access to the public markets is being initiated primarily not by those vendors but by the conventional issuer.

4.4 Promoter liability — 4.4.1 What is the meaning of promoter? — Persons that are promoters of an issuer within the meaning of securities legislation are required to sign the issuer's prospectus in that capacity. As a consequence, those persons assume joint and several liability for prospectus misrepresentations up to a maximum amount equal to the gross proceeds of the offering. The term "promoter" is defined differently in provincial securities legislation across the CSA jurisdictions. It is not defined in the Securities Act (Québec), and a broad approach is taken in Québec with respect to examining those persons who would be considered promoters. We believe that a vendor that receives, directly or indirectly, a significant portion of the offering proceeds as consideration for services or property in connection with the founding or organizing of the business of an income trust issuer, is a promoter and should sign the prospectus in that capacity.

4.4.2 What constitutes the "business" of the income trust? — In the context of indirect offerings, there appears to be uncertainty about whether the "business of an issuer", as that phrase is used in the definition of "promoter" in some of the CSA jurisdictions, refers to the business of the issuer (the income trust) or to the business of the operating entity. More specifically, the question is whether the test depends on a person's involvement in the founding, organization or substantial reorganization of the operating entity's business, or whether involvement in the founding, organization, or substantial reorganization of the income trust itself will make a person a promoter.

We believe that in most cases, the business of the income trust issuer is primarily to complete the public offering and to acquire the interest in the operating entity. Therefore, we generally focus on a person's involvement in the founding, organization, or substantial reorganization of the income trust itself.

We also believe that any person who initiated or took part in the formation, organization or substantial reorganization (as those terms are often used in the definition of "promoter") of the operating entity would not cease to be a promoter under the offering solely due to use of an indirect offering structure. The relationship between the income trust and the operating entity is not sufficiently at arm's length to support this result. The question of whether a person takes part in the founding, organizing or substantial reorganizing of the income trust's business and of the operating entity's business is one of fact. Therefore, this determination should be made by the income trust and the underwriter(s) after reviewing the relevant facts.

4.4.3 What disclosure do we expect about the implications of the operating entity being identified as a promoter? — Where the operating entity signs the prospectus as promoter but the vendors are retaining no interest, or only a nominal interest, in the operating entity upon closing of the offering, the right to claim damages from the operating entity for misrepresentations offers limited or no additional benefit to investors. This is because all or a substantial majority of the interests in the operating entity are acquired by the income trust. Therefore, the prospectus should explain that, despite the operating entity's statutory liability for a misrepresentation in the prospectus, there will be little or no practical benefit to investors who choose to exercise those rights against the operating entity. This is because a successful judgment would result in a deterioration of the operating entity's value (frequently the sole asset of the income trust) and a resulting decline in the value of the investor's securities of the income trust. It is also likely that the operating entity would have a limited ability to satisfy such a claim.

We believe this type of disclosure would be helpful to investors who may not understand the implications of the operating entity being identified as a promoter of the income trust, as is often the case.

Conversely, where the vendors retain a meaningful interest in the operating entity, the characterization of the operating entity as a promoter will offer an additional benefit because the value in the operating entity held by vendors as their retained interest would be potentially available to contribute to satisfying a damages claim without investors suffering a corresponding decline in the value of their securities of the income trust.

4.5 Contractual accountability — 4.5.1 What accountability for prospectus disclosure is typically assumed by vendors through contractual arrangements? — Our review of indirect offering prospectuses indicates that in situations where vendors have not signed the prospectus, they typically assume, by contract, responsibility for matters relating to the operating entity's business. Vendors typically provide representations and warranties about the operating entity and its business to the issuer under the acquisition agreement pursuant to which the vendors sell, and the issuer acquires, the operating entity interests. As well, in several indirect offerings, the vendors have provided a representation in the acquisition agreement about the absence of any misrepresentation in the prospectus (a prospectus representation).

4.5.2 What are our concerns about the application of the regulatory requirements to indirect offerings? — We are concerned that:

(i) investors in indirect offering structures may not appreciate that there is not always a statutory right of action against the vendors as there would be in a direct offering if the vendors were considered "selling security holders",

(ii) prospectus representations may not be given by vendors in circumstances where we would consider those representations to be appropriate,

(iii) prospectus disclosure of the vendors' representations and warranties, and limitations, in the acquisition agreement may not be sufficiently detailed or clearly set out to permit investors to understand the vendors' contractual accountability, and

(iv) the vendors' representations and warranties may not adequately address the potential loss of rights and remedies that securities legislation would provide to investors in a direct offering.

4.5.3 What disclosure do we expect about the accountability of the vendors? — To address the concerns described in subsection 4.5.2, prospectuses relating to indirect offerings, where part of the proceeds are being paid to vendors, should:

(i) include a clear statement that investors may not have a direct statutory right of action against each vendor for a misrepresentation in the prospectus unless that vendor is a promoter or director of the issuer, or is otherwise required to sign the prospectus,

(ii) include a detailed description of the vendors' representations, warranties and indemnities contained in the acquisition agreement (and any significant related limitations) and details about the negotiations (including the parties involved), together with a summary of these items in the summary section of the prospectus,

(iii) identify the acquisition agreement as a material contract and provide disclosure advising investors to review the terms of the acquisition agreement for a complete description of the vendors' representations, warranties and indemnities, and related limitations, and

(iv) identify what measures have been implemented to provide investors with rights and remedies against the vendors in lieu of those afforded by securities legislation in a direct offering.

The summary of the relevant acquisition agreement provisions should include clear disclosure about the following:

(i) the aggregate cash proceeds being paid to the vendors for the sale of their operating entity interests,

(ii) the nature of the representations and warranties provided by the vendors, including any significant qualifications, and specifically whether a prospectus representation is provided,

(iii) the period of time that the representations and warranties will survive after closing,

(iv) any monetary limits on the vendors' indemnity obligations, and

(v) any other limitations on, or qualifications to, the vendors' indemnity obligations.

The summary of the acquisition agreement provisions should provide investors with a clear description of the extent to which the vendors are supporting, with meaningful indemnities, the representations and warranties in favour of the issuer.

CSA staff may consider recommending against the issuance of a receipt for a prospectus if vendors receive cash proceeds from an indirect offering by selling their operating entity interests and do not take appropriate responsibility (directly or indirectly) for the information provided in the prospectus through the acquisition agreement, or as a result of signing the prospectus, or otherwise.

4.5.4 What are our concerns about the nature and extent of the representations, warranties and indemnities provided by vendors in the acquisition agreement? — Circumstances, including the nature of the operating entity and its business and the nature and extent of the vendors' interests (individually and in the aggregate) and their involvement in the operating entity, will affect the types of representations, warranties and indemnities that can reasonably be expected to be provided to the issuer by vendors in the context of an indirect offering.

Examples of circumstances where we have had concerns about vendors not taking appropriate responsibility in the context of indirect offerings have included situations where:

(i) certain vendors, who we refer to as active vendors, such as:

• vendors that affect materially the control of the operating entity prior to the offering, and who are involved in the offering process and/or the management or supervision of management of the operating entity prior to the offering,

• vendors that influence (whether alone or in conjunction with others) the offering process, and

• members of senior management of the operating entity,

sell a substantial portion of their interest in the operating entity to the issuer on closing but do not

a. sign the prospectus as promoter, or

b. provide a prospectus representation in the acquisition agreement;

(ii) a vendor's obligation to indemnify the issuer if the prospectus contains a misrepresentation is limited to an amount less than the proceeds received by the vendor from the sale of the vendor's interest in the operating entity or is subject to a deductible or other threshold that precludes claims against the vendor that are not, individually or in the aggregate, above a certain value; and

(iii) the vendor's responsibility for the information on which the offering is based is reduced unduly, having regard to the nature of the vendor's investment, as a result of the period during which claims may be asserted against the vendor for a prospectus misrepresentation being significantly shorter than the period in which claims may be asserted against the issuer for a prospectus misrepresentation.

If an active vendor's liability for a misrepresentation in the acquisition agreement is conditional on the active vendor having knowledge of the misrepresentation, we expect that the active vendor would generally have a corresponding obligation to take reasonable steps to confirm the accuracy of the representation. For example, a non-management active vendor should make appropriate inquiries of management of the operating entity.

The CSA acknowledges that there may be constraints on the indemnities that certain vendors can provide and the survival period of those indemnities. In assessing whether the vendors have taken appropriate responsibility (directly or indirectly) for the information provided as a basis for the offering, we will generally assess the entire framework of representations, warranties and indemnities provided by the vendors as a group, as opposed to assessing each component or vendor individually. We believe this approach is consistent with the commercial realities within which the parties to these transactions allocate the risks and rewards of the transactions.

PART 5 — SALES AND MARKETING MATERIALS

5.1 What are our concerns about sales and marketing materials? — Registrants often solicit interest from potential investors during the "waiting period" between the issuance of a receipt for a preliminary prospectus and the issuance of a receipt for the prospectus, and in the period following the receipt for the prospectus until the primary distribution is completed. Along with the distribution of the preliminary prospectus (or prospectus, if then available) to potential investors, that process often involves the preparation and distribution of materials such as:

- green sheets, for the benefit of registered salespersons and banking group members; or

- standard term sheets or marketing materials prepared in accordance with National Instrument 41-101 *General Prospectus Requirements* and other prospectus rules.

The information included in green sheets is typically a simplified summary version of the disclosure in the prospectus, and should be limited to information included in, or directly derivable from, the prospectus (the exceptions are information about the basic terms of comparable offerings and general market information not specific to the issuer).

The information included in standard term sheets and marketing materials must comply with the conditions in National Instrument 41-101 *General Prospectus Requirements* and other prospectus rules.

Green sheets and marketing materials used in the context of income trust offerings often include prominent reference to "yield". We are concerned that expressions of "yield" in these marketing materials may not be clearly understood, both because the term itself may have connotations or common usages that are not consistent with the attributes of income trust units and because the relationship between the "yield" described in the marketing materials and the information in the prospectus may not be clear.

"Yield" is generally used in the context of income trust offerings to refer to the return that would be generated over a one-year period, as a percentage of the offering price of the units, if the amounts intended to be distributed by the income trust according to its distribution policy are so distributed. In connection with their ongoing approach to disclosure, issuers should carefully consider yield expectations previously communicated to investors through marketing materials or otherwise. Whether and to what extent those yield expectations are met are important aspects of overall disclosure of performance. Issuers should include in their interim and annual MD&A, where applicable, a comparison between the expected yield figure previously communicated and the actual yield.

5.2 What information do we expect green sheets and marketing materials to contain? — We are concerned that use of the term "yield" in green sheets and marketing materials may imply that the entitlement of unitholders to distributions is fixed. We expect expressions of yield to be accompanied by disclosure that, unlike fixed-income securities, there is no obligation of the income trust to distribute to unitholders any fixed amount, and reductions in, or suspensions of, cash distributions may occur that would reduce yield based on the offering price.

A related concern is that disclosure of a yield in green sheets may cause confusion because yield is not typically disclosed in the prospectus. If a green sheet contains an expression of yield, we expect the statement to be tied to the disclosure in the prospectus on which the marketing is based (including, in particular, the pro forma presentation of distributable cash in the prospectus). Specifically, expressions of yield in green sheets for income trust offerings should be accompanied by disclosure indicating the proportion of the pro forma distributable cash (as set out in the prospectus) that the stated yield would represent. Guidance for disclosure about distributable cash in green sheets is set out in section 6.5.2 of this policy.

Under National Instrument 41-101 *General Prospectus Requirements* and other prospectus rules, all information in marketing materials must generally be disclosed in, or derived from, the prospectus on which the marketing is based.

In addition, if reference is made to tax efficiencies that may be realized on distributions (such as returns of capital to investors), we expect that disclosure to be clear and, to the extent practical, quantified. For example, the estimated tax-deferred portion of distributions for the foreseeable period, and the tax implications, should be clearly stated or cross-referenced.

5.3 Do we expect income trusts to provide us with copies of their green sheets and marketing materials? — Income trust issuers should provide copies of all green sheets to the securities regulatory authorities when filing the preliminary prospectus, together with separate documentation providing a clear and concise explanation of how the yield figure (if contained in the green sheet) is derived from the prospectus disclosure. In addition, we may request that additional sales and marketing materials used in connection with an income trust offering be provided.

Under National Instrument 41-101 *General Prospectus Requirements* and other prospectus rules, a template version of marketing materials must be filed on or before the day that the marketing materials are first provided.

PART 6 — CONTINUOUS DISCLOSURE-SPECIFIC ISSUES

6.1 What continuous disclosure do we expect about the operating entity? — An income trust's performance and prospects depend primarily on the performance and operations of the operating entity. To make an informed decision about investing in an income trust's units, an investor generally needs comprehensive information about the operating entity, including: (i) the operating entity's interim financial reports and annual financial statements together with corresponding MD&A for the relevant periods, (ii) complete business disclosure about the operating entity of the scope expected in an annual information form, and (iii) press releases and material change reports about any material changes in the business, operations or capital of the operating entity.

If a business acquisition report (a BAR) is filed for the acquisition by the income trust of the operating entity, in accordance with Part 8 of NI 51-102 (or its successor), the income trust must include within the BAR updated financial information about the operating entity.

To the extent the securities laws in some CSA jurisdictions are ambiguous about whether the disclosure described above about the operating entity is required by a reporting issuer that is an income trust or other non-corporate entity, the income trust issuer should file one or more undertakings with the

Part 4:
DISTRIBUTIONS

regulatory authorities prior to receiving a receipt for a prospectus, completing a plan of arrangement involving an operating entity or otherwise acquiring a direct or indirect interest in an operating entity. The following is an example of an undertaking that we would expect:

(A) in complying with its reporting issuer obligations, the income trust will treat the operating entity as a subsidiary of the income trust; however, if generally accepted accounting principles (GAAP) used by the income trust prohibit the consolidation of financial information of the operating entity and the income trust, then for as long as the operating entity (including any of its significant business interests) represents a significant asset of the income trust, the income trust will provide unitholders with separate audited annual financial statements and interim financial reports, prepared in accordance with the same GAAP as the income trust's financial statements, and related management's discussion and analysis, prepared in accordance with National Instrument 51-102 — *Continuous Disclosure Obligations* or its successor, for the operating entity (including information about any of its significant business interests), and

(B) the income trust will annually certify that it has complied with this undertaking, and file the certificate on SEDAR concurrently with the filing of its annual financial statements.

We recognize that there may be circumstances where the income trust does not have direct access to the operating entity's financial information. For example, in situations where the income trust holds less than a 50% interest in an operating entity, it may be difficult for the income trust to have direct access to that operating entity's financial information. If so, the income trust should ensure that it can follow the guidance described in this section 6.1 either through the terms of the acquisition agreement or otherwise.

6.2 Comparative financial information — Most income trusts are the continuation of an existing business that was previously operated under a different legal form (for example, a corporation). We believe that the change in legal form does not alter the substance of the business operations and therefore does not prevent an income trust from presenting comparative financial information for the underlying business during its initial interim and annual periods including the interim period during which the trust came into existence.

For those acquisitions accounted for by the acquisition method, income trusts should provide comparative financial information for the predecessor business in their interim and annual MD&A. For trusts that are created on a date within a given interim period, the trust's first interim MD&A should include both financial information about the predecessor business (from the beginning of the applicable interim period to the date of the creation of the trust) and financial information about the trust (beginning as of the date of its creation). Examples of relevant comparative information would include, but would not be limited to, the following:

- revenue,
- cost of sales,
- gross margin,
- general and administrative expenses, and
- profit or loss.

In situations where the transfer of the operating business into an income trust is accounted for at carrying amounts, we expect the income trust to provide comparative information for the operations of the business under the previous legal entity.

Where an issuer believes that providing comparative information would not be appropriate, such as where the income trust is formed as a result of multiple acquisitions, we encourage the issuer to discuss the circumstances with the relevant securities regulatory authority(ies) prior to filing the applicable continuous disclosure document(s).

6.3 Recognition of intangible assets — An issuer's GAAP requires the appropriate recognition of intangible assets acquired in business combinations. In addition, an issuer's GAAP generally requires that intangible assets acquired be measured at their acquisition date fair value. To assist investors in understanding the valuation process of the intangible assets, income trusts should provide in the offering document a description of the method(s) used to value the intangible assets.

6.4 Are "insiders" of the operating entity also insiders of the income trust for purposes of insider reporting obligations? — Consistent with our view that the performance and prospects of an income trust depend on the performance and prospects of the operating entity, we believe each person who would be an "insider" (as that term is defined in applicable securities legislation) of the operating entity if the operating entity were a reporting issuer should comply with insider reporting requirements as if that person were also an insider of the income trust.

To the extent securities laws in certain CSA jurisdictions are ambiguous about whether insiders of the operating entity are also insiders of the income trust or other non-corporate entity, that issuer is expected to file an undertaking with the regulatory authorities prior to receiving a receipt for a prospectus, completing a plan of arrangement involving an operating entity or otherwise acquiring a direct or indirect interest in an operating entity. We expect the undertaking to provide that for so long as the income trust is a reporting issuer, the income trust will take the appropriate measures to require each person who would be an insider of the operating entity or a person or company in a special relationship with the operating entity if the operating entity were a reporting issuer to: (i) file insider reports about trades in units of the income trust (including securities which are exchangeable into units of the income trust), and (ii) comply with statutory prohibitions against insider trading. We expect the income trust to annually certify in the certificate described in section 6.1(B) above that it has complied with this undertaking.

We are concerned that additional persons that may possess material undisclosed information about the income trust may: (i) not fall within the definition of "insider" (as that term is defined in applicable securities legislation) or (ii) not be caught by the undertaking. As a result, there may be situations where we will require that additional undertakings be provided. The income trust will need to obtain the relevant contractual commitments from these persons and entities in order to comply with the undertakings referred to above.

Recent amendments to securities legislation in Alberta deem insiders of operating entities and management companies to be insiders of the income trust. The CSA is in the process of developing a proposed national rule that would harmonize and streamline the requirements for insiders of reporting issuers to file insider reports. We expect that the proposed national rule will include harmonized requirements for insiders of operating companies and management companies to file insider reports about their transactions involving securities of the income trust. Pending the implementation of the proposed national insider reporting rule, we will continue to require income trusts to provide the undertaking described above.

6.5 MD&A — 6.5.1 Risks and uncertainties — Under Form 51-102F1, an income trust must discuss important trends and risks that have affected the operating entity's financial statements, and trends and risks that are reasonably likely to affect them in the future. Although the instructions in Form 51-102F1 do not specifically state it, to meet the requirement to disclose risks, income trusts should provide a detailed risk factor discussion about the potential commitment to replace and maintain capital assets, including a quantitative discussion about expected annual capital maintenance expenditure levels relative to current levels, and the expected effect on distributions.

6.5.2 Discussion of distributed cash — Although most income trusts intend to make distributions of their available cash to unitholders, these cash distributions are not assured. The actual amount distributed depends on numerous factors, including the operating entity's financial performance, debt covenants and obligations, working capital requirements and future capital requirements. It is important for unitholders to have information about the source(s) of the distributed cash that they receive, including whether the issuer borrowed amounts to finance distributions, and whether distributions include amounts that are not properly classified as a return on capital. Although the instructions in Form 51-102F1 do not specifically state it, to meet the disclosure requirements for liquidity in Form 51-102F1, income trusts should provide sufficient disclosure about their sources of funding relating to current and future cash distributions so that unitholders can understand what portion, if any, of the distributions they receive were funded by sources other than cash flows from operating activities. Also, income trusts should quantify these amounts and discuss the impact on the trust's long-term ability to sustain distributions if sources other than cash flows from operating activities are being used to fund distributions. In determining cash flows from operating activities, the issuer should include borrowing costs.

An income trust can overcome the concerns noted in section 2.1 and in this subsection by providing information in its interim and annual MD&A that summarizes the main elements of its performance that are necessary to assess the sustainability of its cash distributions. One way to summarize this information is by using a table similar to the following:

		For the most recently completed quarter	Accumulated for the current fiscal years (Year 1)	Previously completed fiscal year	
				(Year 2)	(Year 3)
A.	Cash flows from operating activities*	$ XX	$ XX	$ XX	$ XX
B.	Profit or loss	$ XX	$ XX	$ XX	$ XX
C.	Actual cash distributions paid or payable relating to the period**	$ XX	$ XX	$ XX	$ XX
D.	Excess (shortfall) of cash flows from operating activities over cash distributions paid (A)-(C)***	$ XX	$ XX	$ XX	$ XX
E.	Excess (shortfall) of profit or loss over cash distributions paid (B)-(C)***	$ XX	$ XX	$ XX	$ XX

Notes:

*   Takes into account changes in non-cash working capital balances and includes borrowing cost

**   Includes distributions paid or payable on all classes of units and any special distributions paid or payable during the period

***   Income trusts might choose to present the excess (shortfall) in lines D and/or E in the form of a ratio or percentage. In these instances, we expect this ratio or percentage to be determined based solely on amounts included in lines A, B, and C, as applicable, from the above table.

The above table provides clear disclosure about the relationship between cash flows from operating activities and profit or loss, and historical distributed cash amounts.

When cash distributions are greater than either profit or loss or cash flow from operating activities, creating a shortfall in any of the columns in the above table, disclosure of the following, as applicable, will help to provide a balanced discussion of the issuer's financial performance and financial condition:

(i) why the trust has chosen to make distributions partly representing an economic return of capital, or, alternatively, why it does not believe that any portion of those distributions should be regarded as an economic return of capital,

(ii) a quantification and description of the sources of cash used to fund the shortfall,

(iii) the obligations of the issuer or its subsidiaries in connection with the sources of cash used to fund the shortfall, including repayment terms and interest payable,

(iv) whether any material contract was amended in connection with the funding of the shortfall and whether any waivers or consents were obtained,

(v) whether the issuer expects that cash distributions will continue, for the foreseeable future, to exceed profit or loss and/or cash flow from operating activities. If so, the trust should specifically address what implications this has for the sustainability of distributions. If not, the issuer should explain the reasons why it does not expect the situation to continue, and

(vi) whether the issuer anticipates that cash distributions may be suspended in the foreseeable future.

In determining cash flows from operating activities, the issuer should include borrowing costs.

If cash distributions paid do not equal distributable cash, the issuer should also discuss the reasons for the difference between the two amounts. If cash distributions paid materially exceed distributable cash, the disclosure of distributable cash should include a detailed explanation of how the additional distributions were financed as this impacts the issuer's liquidity. Generic boiler-plate language about the issuer's sources of available capital or financing or simply pointing the reader to the statement of cash flows for further information is not sufficient. When distributions paid are materially less than distributable cash, the disclosure of the amounts distributed should include an explanation of why distributable cash was not fully distributed.

In order to meet the requirements for MD&A, disclosure of an issuer's distributable cash for a period should be accompanied by the information referred to in sections 2.5, 2.6, 2.7 and 2.8, as applicable, as well as the above table and accompanying narrative. Issuers should also refer to the guidance in sections 2.5, 2.6, 2.7, 2.8 and 6.5.2 of this policy when considering how to present disclosure of an issuer's distributable cash, including disclosure contained in:

- annual and interim MD&A,
- news releases, and
- sales and other materials such as:
- green sheets, and
- marketing materials prepared in accordance with National Instrument 41-101 *General Prospectus Requirements* and other prospectus rules.

See also Part 5 of this policy.

PART 7 — CORPORATE GOVERNANCE

7.1 CEO/CFO certification, audit committees, and effective corporate governance — How each of the issuer and the operating entity will discharge their governance responsibilities is important information for investors. Issuers should provide prospectus disclosure about how each of the issuer and the operating entity will satisfy governance responsibilities including how they will comply with the following instruments or their successors as applicable in each jurisdiction:

(a) National Instrument 52-109 *Certification of Disclosure in Issuers' Annual and Interim Filings* (NI 52-109),

(b) Multilateral Instrument 52-110 *Audit Committees* or BCI 52-509 *Audit Committees*, as applicable [now NI 52-110], and

(c) National Instrument 58-101 *Disclosure of Corporate Governance Practices*.

For example, the issuer should consider disclosing which persons will be signing as chief executive officer and/or chief financial officer to meet the requirements of NI 52-109.

In particular, income trusts should refer to the following sections of the above-noted instruments or the related companion policies for specific guidance about income trusts and other similar structures:

(a) section 3.2 of Companion Policy 52-109CP to National Instrument 52-109 *Certification of Disclosure in Issuers' Annual and Interim Filings*,

(b) section 1.2 of Companion Policy 52-110CP to Multilateral Instrument 52-110 *Audit Committees* [now NI 52-110], and

(c) section 1.2 of National Policy 58-201 *Corporate Governance Guidelines*.

7.2 Broader corporate law concerns — Corporations are governed by corporate statutes regulating their key obligations and the rights afforded to their shareholders. There is no equivalent statutory regime governing non-corporate entities like income trusts. Investors must look to the declaration of trust of each trust to determine the key obligations of the trust and unitholder rights and protections. It is important that unitholders understand that the provisions of the declarations of trust may differ from the minimum standards required under applicable corporate statutes and among various income trusts.

To facilitate unitholders' understanding of these differences, issuers should compare the rights and obligations generally available to corporate shareholders under applicable corporate statutes with those provided in the declaration of trust, highlighting any material differences. For example, under corporate law a corporation is required to hold an annual meeting enabling shareholders to exercise the right to elect directors to the board. If the declaration of trust does not enable unitholders to elect the directors to the board of the income trust, this fact should be clearly identified.

Because we are concerned that a unitholder may not be afforded the same protections, rights and remedies as a shareholder in a corporation, issuers should also provide the following disclosure in the issuer's AIF (if an AIF is filed) and any prospectus filed by the issuer:

A unitholder in the income trust has all of the material protections, rights and remedies a shareholder would have under the *Canada Business Corporations Act*. These protections, rights and remedies are contained in the [trust indenture, dated ***].

OR

A unitholder in the income trust has all of the material protections, rights and remedies a shareholder would have under the CBCA, except for the following: [list protections, rights and remedies that are not available to a unitholder.] The protections, rights and remedies available to a unitholder are contained in the [trust indenture, dated ***].

Some corporate legislation such as section 21 of the Canada Business Corporations Act provides a mechanism for persons to request a shareholder list for the purpose of making an offer to acquire securities of a corporation. An income trust that refuses to provide a unitholders' list should refer to National Policy 62-202 — *Take-Over Bids — Defensive Tactics* or in Québec Notice 62-202 *Relating to Take-Over Bids — Defensive Tactics* in the case of a potential offeror requesting a unitholders' list. If refusal to provide such a list is likely to deny or severely limit the ability of unitholders to receive or respond to a take-over bid or a competing bid, Canadian securities regulatory authorities may take action.

PART 8 — PART 8 — OTHER ISSUES

8.1 Income trust names — As discussed above in section 1.2, this policy is intended to address income trusts, not "investment funds" as defined in National Instrument 81-106 *Investment Fund Continuous Disclosure*, or an entity that issues asset-backed securities or capital trust securities. On its initial formation an income trust should exercise caution to ensure that its disclosure makes it clear to investors that it is not an investment fund or mutual fund. Income trusts should avoid adopting a name that may mislead investors as to the nature of the issuer's structure or business purpose. By using terms such as 'equity fund' or 'income growth' in the name, an issuer may be inadvertently suggesting that it is an investment fund or mutual fund. Investors should be provided with a clear understanding of the structure of the issuer and the nature of the securities that they are investing in.

Adoption of Policy: (2004) 27 O.S.C.B. 9651; Requests for Comments: (2003) 26 O.S.C.B. 6971.

Adoption of Amended Policy: (2007) 30 O.S.C.B. 6067; Request for Comments: 30 O.S.C.B. 49.

Adoption of Amendment to Policy: (2007) 30 O.S.C.B. 8539 and 10523.

Adoption of Amendment to Policy: (2008) 32 O.S.C.B. 11350.

Adoption of Amendment to Policy: (2010) 33 O.S.C.B. 10467.

Adoption of Amendment to Policy: (2013) 36 O.S.C.B. 8016 and 36 O.S.C.B. (Supp. 4) 1; Request for Comments (2011) 34 O.S.C.B. 11829.

Policies and Orders: CSAN 51-310, 51-319, 52-306.

CSA Staff Notice 41-305 — Share Structure Issues — Initial Public Offerings

Date: September 24, 2010

33 O.S.C.B. 8469

Purpose

Before issuing a receipt for a prospectus, staff of the Canadian Securities Administrators generally consider factors to assess whether a prospectus offering is contrary to the public interest.

We have encountered a number of initial public offerings (IPOs) by issuers with share structures that lead us to question whether those share structures are contrary to the public interest. In those cases, we generally recommend that the decision-maker refuse to issue a receipt for the prospectus.

This notice explains the factors we consider when assessing a proposed share structure in an IPO.

Background information

An IPO by a company that has already issued an unusually large number of shares for nominal cash consideration (or for assets or business development where the value is not readily supportable) may raise public interest concerns related to the company's capital structure. These concerns are heightened when:

- the business has a limited history of operations or development for which there are no other clear proxies for valuation,
- the IPO financing is relatively small.

We are concerned with these structures because:

- the large number of nominally priced shares can create a platform for future market manipulation, and
- the dilution of invested capital caused by existing shares issued for nominal amounts means that IPO investors receive an unconscionably low percentage of ownership compared to the amount of capital they are investing.

The TSX Venture Exchange and the CNSX have both published notices setting out guidelines that aimed to address these issues. We think the notices have addressed some of the issues. However, because we still encounter these issues, it is still appropriate for us to tell the market that we may also object to an issuer's share structure.

When we first issued National Policy 46-201 *Escrow for Initial Public Offerings* (NP 46-201) in 2002, we mentioned in our publication notices that issues associated with nominally-priced stock were better addressed by underwriters appropriately exercising their responsibilities related to IPO pricing and timing.

In addition, section 2.4 of NP 46-201 indicates that securities regulators will generally consider imposing additional escrow if:

- an underwriter has not signed the IPO prospectus;
- the issuer has not applied to have its securities listed on a Canadian exchange, or a Canadian exchange has not agreed to list the securities distributed under the IPO prospectus; or
- there are other exceptional circumstances.

The Notice we issued with NP 46-201 indicated that securities regulators would rely on management of the issuer, underwriters and stock exchanges to assess the appropriateness of share capital structures. That is still the case with the majority of issuers. However, our recent experience is that issuers still file prospectuses with capital structures that raise public interest concerns.

General

As structuring issues are complex, we consider many qualitative and quantitative factors when evaluating the acceptability of IPO share structures.

We consider how the IPO price compares to the average share price paid by the Founders[1]. We may object when the IPO price significantly exceeds the average price paid by the Founders. We are concerned with structures in which the Founders have paid a nominal amount for a large block of shares compared to the IPO price.

We assess the proportion of capital proposed to be contributed by the IPO purchasers in comparison to the percentage of ownership the IPO purchasers will receive in return. We may object when the IPO purchasers are being invited to contribute an amount of capital that will be significantly disproportionate to their equity interest on completion of the offering.

We consider the average capital contributed per share for all issued and outstanding shares on completion of the offering and compare it to the purchase price per share of the IPO. We may be concerned if a large block of Founders' shares issued for nominal amounts reduces the average capital contributed per share significantly in comparison to the IPO price.

---

[1]Generally, the term "Founders": means anyone who is a director, officer, promoter or insider of the issuer. In some instances, Founders may be a subset of this group.

Other factors considered in evaluating acceptable share structures include:

- *Prior development of business or concept:* If the Founders have spent time, effort or resources developing a business, then a structure containing significant Founders' shares may be appropriate. We would not normally object to these structures when they represent a realization of business development efforts or otherwise demonstrate value. We may request that the issuer explain and justify the size of the Founder's position and the discount it represents relative to the IPO price. We will consider relevant facts and circumstances, traditional valuation techniques that support the position, and other forms of third party corroboration of the value of the position such as significant pre-IPO arm's length financing activities.

- *Distribution of Founders' shares:* In some cases, some of the Founders may have received their shares at a significantly lower average price than other Founders. In these cases, we may be concerned with some of the Founders' shares but not others.

- *Cash invested by Founders and length of time invested:* Generally the greater the amount of cash the Founders have invested and the longer it has been actively used as part of the issuer's capital structure and development of its business, the more likely a given structure will be acceptable.

- *Warrants and options:* If there are significant convertible securities outstanding at exercise prices lower than the IPO price, we may include these securities in our analysis. If the number is large enough or the exercise price is low enough, the presence of these convertible securities may lead us to object to an otherwise acceptable share structure.

This CSA Staff Notice is not meant to provide certainty for every possible scenario and allow the reader to definitively determine if a given structure is acceptable or not. Rather it is intended to provide some insight regarding factors we consider when evaluating proposed share structures.

We will continue to monitor this issue and consider what further guidance or policy changes may be appropriate.

CSA Staff Notice 41-307 — Corporate Finance Prospectus Guidance — Concerns Regarding an Issuer's Financial Condition and the Sufficiency of Proceeds from a Prospectus Offering

Date: **March 2, 2012**
35 O.S.C.B. 2036

The purpose of this staff notice is to alert issuers (other than investment fund issuers) and their advisors about our approach where there are concerns regarding the financial condition of an issuer and/or the sufficiency of proceeds in the context of a prospectus offering.[1] In limited circumstances, these concerns may affect our ability to recommend that a receipt be issued for a prospectus. This staff notice applies to all prospectus reviews, regardless of whether the offering is an IPO, new issue or secondary offering.

In this notice, we describe issues that have arisen in past prospectus reviews and explain the types of comments we have raised about an issuer's financial condition and/or the sufficiency of proceeds.

This guidance applies to issuers that have short-term liquidity concerns and/or offerings that do not appear to be raising sufficient proceeds. We recognize the importance of capital formation in Canada, and this guidance is not intended to inhibit capital raising through a prospectus offering other than where there are significant investor protection concerns.

Significant concerns may result in receipt refusal

Securities legislation provides that the authorized decision maker must issue a receipt for a prospectus unless it appears to the decision maker that it is not in the public interest to do so or for motives enumerated in securities legislation.[2]

Securities legislation also provides that the decision maker shall not issue a receipt for a prospectus or an amendment to a prospectus in specified circumstances. For example, a decision maker is prohibited from issuing a receipt for a prospectus if it appears that the proceeds from the prospectus offering, along with the issuer's other resources, will be insufficient to accomplish the purpose of the issue stated in the prospectus (the sufficiency of proceeds receipt refusal provision).[3]

As a result of these statutory provisions, consideration of an issuer's financial condition is a critical part of every prospectus review. A prospectus must contain clear disclosure on how the issuer intends to use the proceeds raised in the offering as well as disclosure of the issuer's financial condition, including any liquidity concerns. This disclosure is important to investors because it provides warnings about significant risks that the issuer is facing or may face in the short term and may help investors avoid or minimize negative consequences when making investment decisions. Relevant information in this context may include disclosure on negative cash flow from operating activities, working capital deficiencies, net losses and significant going concern risks.

However, disclosure on its own may not be sufficient to satisfy receipt refusal concerns in certain circumstances. For example, a recommendation of receipt refusal may be appropriate where an issuer lacks sufficient funds to continue operations, or if the proceeds from the prospectus offering will be insufficient to accomplish the purpose of the offering. When conducting prospectus reviews, we may consider the anticipated proceeds from a prospectus offering to be insufficient if they are raised:

- for a specific purpose but do not address the issuer's short-term liquidity requirements

---

[1] For additional guidance see OSC Staff Notice 52-719 Going Concern Disclosure Review (OSC Staff Notice 52-719).

[2] Relevant statutory provisions include: s. 120(1) of the *Securities Act* (Alberta), s. 65(2) of the *Securities Act* (British Columbia), s. 61(1) of the *Securities Act* (Ontario) and ss. 14 and 15 of the *Securities Act* (Quebec).

[3] See s. 120(2)(c) of the *Securities Act* (Alberta), s. 120(2)(c) of the *Securities Act* (British Columbia), s. 61(2)(c) of the *Securities Act* (Ontario) and s. 15(3) of the *Securities Act* (Quebec).

- through a best efforts offering without a minimum subscription, or a minimum subscription that does not appear to be sufficient to satisfy the issuer's short-term liquidity requirements, or

- through a shelf prospectus offering that can be drawn down in small increments that, when considered separately, may not be sufficient to satisfy the issuer's short-term liquidity requirements.

A principal purpose of the sufficiency of proceeds receipt refusal provision is to protect the integrity of the capital markets, which would be harmed if an issuer ceased operations on account of insufficient funds shortly after completing a public securities offering.

We have concerns with the potential implications to investors who invest in issuers that may not be able to continue operations for a reasonable period of time. We consider that an issuer should have sufficient resources to meet its short-term liquidity requirements. This will vary depending on the circumstances of each issuer. The table below sets out some guidelines.

Type of Issuer	Resources to meet short-term liquidity requirements
Exploration stage issuer	Sufficient to reach completion of the next phase of a project
Development stage issuer	Sufficient to achieve the issuer's next significant milestone
Research & development issuer	Sufficient to achieve progress on the development of a key product
Issuer with active operations	Ability to continue operations for the short term

Potential receipt refusal

The decision maker will not issue a receipt for a prospectus where:
- it appears that the prospectus inadequately discloses an issuer's financial condition and going concern risk, or
- there is adequate disclosure about the issuer's financial condition, but it appears that either the sufficiency of proceeds receipt refusal provision is applicable or that it is not in the public interest to issue the receipt.

Areas of focus

We may raise comments during the prospectus review process where we have identified concerns about an issuer's financial condition and/or sufficiency of proceeds. This staff notice discusses the following five issues in respect of which we may raise comments:

1. Missing information regarding offering amount and pricing
2. Offering structure
3. Use of proceeds disclosure
4. Risk factor disclosure
5. Representations to support ability to continue operations

This list of issues is not exhaustive. The types of comments we raise in these circumstances may change and we will continue to assess and review each prospectus on its own merits.

1. — Missing information regarding offering amount and pricing

We require information regarding the size of the offering to assess whether the sufficiency of proceeds receipt refusal provision is applicable and whether it is in the public interest for the decision maker to issue a receipt. If a preliminary prospectus is filed with the offering amount and pricing information bulleted, we will issue a comment that we require a reasonable opportunity to review a blackline of the draft form of final prospectus (using strike through format for deletions of text) before being in a position to clear the final prospectus. The blackline should include the information currently bulleted in the preliminary prospectus, such as the offering amount, pricing and use of proceeds. If providing this information is not practicable, we may accept an estimate or range of these figures, as applicable. Issuers should note that we may have additional comments based on any new information disclosed in the blackline.

Practice point

In order to avoid unanticipated delays, issuers should ensure that the blackline of the draft form of final prospectus is filed not less than two business days prior to filing final materials.

We may also request a copy of any green sheets (and/or similar marketing materials) used in connection with an offering. A review of the green sheet allows us to assess at an early stage the financial condition of the issuer in the context of the then anticipated offering amount. It will also show whether the final offering amount is substantially less than originally anticipated.

2. — Offering structure

We will review the overall structure of the proposed offering in the context of the issuer's financial condition.

While there is no requirement to have a minimum subscription for an offering in National Instrument 41-101 *General Prospectus Requirements* or National Instrument 44-101 *Short Form Prospectus Distributions),* the absence of a minimum subscription could be a significant concern where there are questions about the issuer's financial condition or where a minimum amount of proceeds appears necessary to meet the stated purpose of the offering. Accordingly, we may raise the following types of comments depending on the structure of an offering, tailored to the particular circumstances of the issuer. Ultimately, an issuer may need to change the structure of an offering to address concerns regarding the issuer's financial condition.

Best efforts agency offering

1. Is there a minimum subscription?

2. If not, explain how the stated purpose of the offering and the use of proceeds will be achieved absent a minimum subscription.

3. Disclose and discuss, both qualitatively and quantitatively:

- how the proceeds will be used by the issuer, with reference to various potential thresholds of proceeds raised, in the event the issuer raises less than the maximum subscription, and
- the impact (if any) on its liquidity, operations, capital resources and solvency.

Base shelf prospectus offering

We may take the view that a base shelf prospectus is not appropriate given the issuer's financial condition and uncertainty of financing. Under a base shelf prospectus, an issuer may raise small amounts of capital in increments over the period of 25 months. We may request submissions on the following:

- the issuer's rationale for filing a base shelf prospectus
- whether the issuer intends to file a prospectus supplement in the near future, and if so, the type of securities to be offered, the proceeds that are contemplated to be raised and the manner in which the proceeds will be used
- the availability of other sources of financing to provide working capital and fund the issuer's business if sufficient financing cannot be raised
- the proposed nature and timing of the offerings under the base shelf prospectus, including:
  - involvement of an agent or underwriter, if any
  - use of a minimum subscription amount below which an offering will not proceed
  - specific use of proceeds for offerings contemplated in the next 12 months
- details regarding concrete development milestones that would advance the issuer's business objectives and are expected to be completed in the next 12 months, including:
  - a description of the milestone
  - expected timing of completion, and
  - financing requirements.

In order to address the concern that incremental drawdowns may be insufficient to satisfy an issuer's short-term liquidity requirements, we may request that the issuer:

- file a short form prospectus with a minimum subscription
- file a short form prospectus with a fully underwritten commitment, and/or
- arrange for additional sources of financing.

Rights offering

We may raise a comment regarding alternatives to a minimum subscription, such as a stand-by commitment, where there is a concern about the sufficiency of proceeds to meet the stated objectives of the offering or there is a concern about the issuer's financial condition.

3. — *Use of proceeds disclosure*

The use of proceeds disclosure in a prospectus informs our consideration of whether the proceeds of the offering will be sufficient to accomplish the stated purpose of the offering. We will assess whether the use of proceeds disclosure complies with all of the applicable requirements in Item 6 of Form 41-101F1 *Information Required in a Prospectus* (Form 41-101F1) or Item 4 of Form 44-101F1 *Short Form Prospectus* (Form 44-101F1).

We have noted inadequate use of proceeds disclosure in the following areas:

- principal purposes of the proceeds
- business objectives and milestones, and
- negative cash flow from operating activities.

An example of the type of disclosure that does not provide sufficient detail on the allocation of proceeds is set out below.

Example of insufficient use of proceeds disclosure

The net proceeds to the Corporation will be combined with the Corporation's working capital for total available funds of approximately $3,000,000. The estimated net proceeds to the Corporation from this Offering are estimated as indicated below:

Principal Purpose	Amount
Exploration Activities	$2,000,000
General Corporate Purposes	$1,000,000
Total Available Funds	**$3,000,000**

The net cash proceeds from the Offering will be used by the Corporation for exploration activities and general corporate purposes. The Corporation expects to accomplish the business objectives described in this Prospectus using the Total Available Funds. The Corporation intends to spend the funds available to it as stated in this Prospectus. There may be circumstances where, for sound business reasons, a reallocation of funds may be necessary.

The guidance below sets out the type of information we would expect to be included in the use of proceeds disclosure.

Principal purposes of the proceeds

Where the disclosure is overly general, we may request that the issuer provide additional information, such as:

- a breakdown of the proceeds towards a certain phase of a project, in the case of an exploration or development stage issuer

- a breakdown of the proceeds towards capital expenditures

- a breakdown of proceeds allocated to general and administrative expenditures, and

- clarification of how proceeds raised under recent financings have been or are being allocated.

If the offering is subject to a minimum subscription, the use of proceeds for both the minimum and maximum subscription must be disclosed. The disclosure should provide adjustments in spending if the proceeds raised are less than the maximum amount. This disclosure should be provided where:

- closing of the distribution is not subject to a minimum offering amount

- the distribution is on a best efforts basis, and

- the issuer has significant short-term non-discretionary expenditures.

Short-term non-discretionary expenditures include those for general corporate purposes, or significant short-term capital or contractual commitments, and an issuer may not have other readily accessible resources to satisfy those expenditures or commitments. We may request that the issuer discuss, both quantitatively and qualitatively, how the proceeds will be used with reference to various potential thresholds of proceeds raised, in the event the issuer raises less than the maximum subscription, and the resulting impact on the issuer's liquidity, operations, capital resources and solvency.

Finally, we remind issuers that statements such as "for general corporate purposes", are not considered to be sufficient disclosure[4].

Business objectives and milestones

Where an issuer has not sufficiently described each significant event that must occur for the business objectives to be accomplished, we will request additional disclosure of each event as well as the specific time period in which each event is expected to occur and the costs related to it. Generally, we expect that the proceeds from the offering will be sufficient to meet the issuer's working capital and operational needs until its next significant milestone.

In the case of a mining issuer, the use of proceeds disclosure should be consistent with the recommendation and budget in the issuer's technical report(s). We take the view that general statements referring to completion of a "phase" of an exploration program may not be sufficient. We may request a further breakdown of the exploration activities contemplated in each phase, as the case may be, and the relevant time period to complete such activities.

Negative cash flow from operating activities

An issuer with negative cash flow from operating activities in its most recently completed financial year for which financial statements have been included in the prospectus should:

- prominently disclose that fact in the use of proceeds section of the prospectus

- disclose whether, and if so, to what extent, it will use the proceeds of the distribution to fund any anticipated negative cash flow from operating activities in future periods, and

- disclose negative cash flow from operating activities as a risk factor[5].

We may also request additional information be disclosed in the prospectus relating to:

- the issuer's most current working capital amount

- the issuer's cash burn rate on a monthly or quarterly basis

- the period of time that the proceeds of the offering are expected to fund operations, and

- any significant debt obligations maturing in the short term.

[4]As stated in subsection 4.3(2) of Companion Policy to National Instrument 41-101 General Prospectus Requirements (Companion Policy 41-101CP) and subsection 4.4(2) of Companion Policy to National Instrument 44-101 Short Form Prospectus Distributions (Companion Policy 44-101CP),

[5]See the guidance set out in subsection 4.3(1) of Companion Policy 41-101CP and subsection 4.4(1) of Companion Policy 44-101CP.

Item 6.2 of Form 41-101F1 requires additional disclosure of certain information relating to junior issuers, such as disclosure of the total funds available, and the following breakdown of those funds:

- the estimated net proceeds from the sale of the securities offered under the prospectus

- the estimated consolidated working capital (deficiency) as at the most recent month end before filing the prospectus, and

- the total other funds available to be used to achieve the principal purposes identified by the junior issuer pursuant to this item.

Practice point

Depending on the circumstances, we may take the view that this disclosure is a material fact for issuers that are not technically junior issuers and that this disclosure should be included in a prospectus in order to meet the requirement to provide "full, true and plain disclosure of all material facts".

---

4. — Risk factor disclosure

Item 21.1 of Form 41-101F1 and item 17.1 of Form 44-101F1 require disclosure of risk factors relating to an issuer and its business, such as cash flow and liquidity problems. The accompanying instructions provide guidance that the risks should be disclosed in order of seriousness, from the most serious to the least serious. We have noted insufficient or boilerplate disclosure in the prospectus for many key risk factors related to an issuer's financial condition.

Example of insufficient boilerplate risk factor disclosure

The Corporation's ability to continue as a going concern is dependent upon its ability to obtain adequate financing and to reach profitable levels of operation. The Corporation has no proven history of performance, earnings or success.

Issuer's financial condition

A prospectus should clearly disclose an issuer's going concern risk to allow readers to make an informed investment decision. This disclosure should explain the uncertainties that may create going concern risk and how the issuer is addressing that risk. As previously noted, even if the risk is adequately disclosed, we will exercise judgement to assess whether the sufficiency of proceeds receipt refusal provision is applicable or if there is a public interest concern in issuing a receipt.

When preparing risk factor disclosure about financial condition, issuers should consider disclosing the following:

- quantification of losses, working capital deficit, negative cash flow from operating activities, debt levels

- how the issuer expects to remedy the liquidity or solvency issues

- other sources of financing available to the issuer

- the implications to the issuer's liquidity, capital resources, operations (i.e. scaling back exploration activities, capital expenditures, research and development expenditures, general and administrative expenditures etc.) and its ability to remain a going concern, and

- the period of time the proceeds raised under the prospectus are expected to fund operations.

In many circumstances, an issuer with going concern risk should include the disclosure required by item 8.7 of Form 41-101F1 for junior issuers. This item requires disclosure of:

- the period of time the proceeds raised under the prospectus are expected to fund operations

- the estimated total operating costs necessary for the issuer to achieve its stated business objectives during that period of time, and

- the estimated amount of other material capital expenditures during that period of time.

Practice Point

While item 8.7 of Form 41-101F1 applies specifically to junior issuers, this information may constitute a material fact for other issuers depending on their particular circumstances, and in that case, we may request this disclosure.

Risk associated with negative cash flow from operating activities

Issuers are reminded that section 4.3 of Companion Policy 41-101CP and section 4.4 of Companion Policy 44-101CP provide that issuers should disclose negative cash flow from operating activities as a risk factor.

Risk associated with offering structure — no minimum subscription

Where the offering is being conducted on a best efforts agency basis and we have accepted that a minimum subscription is not required, we generally expect the issuer to include on the face page of the prospectus disclosure that there is no minimum amount of funds that must be raised under the offering. This disclosure should clearly state that an investor will not generally be entitled to a return of its investment if only a small proportion of the disclosed offering amount is in fact raised.

5. — Representations to support ability to continue operations

We take the view that an issuer contemplating an offering should be able to continue its operations for a reasonable period of time and meet its short-term liquidity requirements as described on page two of this staff notice. The length of time the issuer will be able to continue operations will vary among industries and among issuers within an industry group. Accordingly, issuers should anticipate comments regarding their ability to continue operations as a going concern.

Representation regarding ability to continue operations

In order to assess whether we have a receipt refusal concern, we may ask the issuer to provide us with a written representation of the number of months that it will be able to continue its operations given its financial condition. The proceeds from the offering should only be considered when making this determination where the offering is a bought deal, or where there is a minimum subscription or stand-by commitment. We will generally also request that this representation be disclosed in the prospectus. The rationale for requiring this disclosure is that, in our view, this information is a material fact in the particular circumstances of the issuer due to concerns over its financial condition. We may take the view that the absence of this information may either be an omission of a material fact or raise a public interest concern.

Support for representations regarding ability to continue operations

It is the issuer's responsibility to determine the number of months during which it expects to be able to continue its operations given its financial condition. In some instances, the issuer's representations about its ability to continue as a going concern and the period during which it expects to be able to continue operations may:

- be inconsistent with the issuer's historical statement of cash flows (in particular, its cash flows from operating activities)

- be inconsistent with the disclosure in the preliminary prospectus, including disclosure regarding current and expected profitability, debt repayment schedules and potential sources of additional financing, or

- otherwise appear to be unreasonable.

In these cases, we may request that the issuer provide us with a cash flow forecast to support its assumed period of liquidity (i.e. ability to continue operations). As noted above, the proceeds of the offering should only be considered in an issuer's cash flow forecast where the offering is a bought deal or where there is a minimum subscription or stand-by commitment. If a forecast is provided, we will assess whether the assumptions are consistent with the disclosure made in the prospectus as well as the issuer's historical financial performance.

The cash flow forecast should project the issuer's cash flow from operating activities for the period of time the issuer has represented that it can continue operations. The forecast should take the form of a statement of cash flows as presented in the issuer's financial statements in accordance with International Financial Reporting Standards (IFRS). The forecast must be accompanied by a set of robust assumptions to support management's estimates. We may need supporting schedules and further details in order to assess the reasonableness of the assumptions made by the issuer. See the discussion below about whether this disclosure constitutes forward-looking information (FLI) and forward looking financial information (FOFI).

Practice Point

In the limited circumstances where we request a cash flow forecast, we may request additional disclosure in the prospectus. Specifically, we may ask that the following be included in the prospectus:

- the forecast in its entirety along with all significant assumptions and the material risk factors that could cause actual results to differ materially from the forecast, or

- significant portions of the forecast or material factors and assumptions used to develop the forecast.

This information supports the representation regarding the issuer's ability to continue operations and may inform investors' investment decisions. We may conclude that, in certain cases, the forecast represents a material fact in the particular circumstances of the issuer due to concerns over its financial condition. Any disclosure included in the prospectus is subject to liability provisions.

Forward-looking information and future oriented financial information

A representation regarding an issuer's ability to continue operations constitutes FLI as defined in securities legislation. Generally, FLI means disclosure regarding possible events, conditions or results of operations that is based on assumptions about future economic conditions and courses of action[6]. Depending on its content, this representation may or may not also be FOFI. When this disclosure is included in the prospectus, the disclosure must comply with the FLI and FOFI requirements in Parts 4A and 4B of National Instrument 51-102 *Continuous Disclosure Obligations* (NI 51-102).

Any cash flow forecast and related factors and assumptions provided to support this representation may also be subject to FLI and FOFI requirements.

Issuers will be required to update previously disclosed material FLI in Management's Discussion & Analysis in accordance with section 5.8 of NI 51-102.

---

[6]For the definition of FLI see s. 1(1) of the *Securities Act* (Alberta), s. 1(1) of the *Securities Act* (British Columbia), s. 1(1) of the *Securities Act* (Ontario) and s. 5 of the *Securities Act* (Quebec).

Conclusion

We will continue to raise comments in respect of the financial condition of an issuer and the sufficiency of proceeds from a prospectus offering where the concerns discussed above are identified. Additional disclosure may be required in a prospectus, depending on the particular circumstance of the issuer. In some cases where there are significant investor protection concerns, we may recommend that a receipt for a prospectus not be issued.

OSC Rule 41-501 — General Prospectus Requirements

Date: December 15, 2000, as amended effective September 30, 2003, March 30, 2004 (by Rule 51-801), November 1, 2006 and December 31, 2007

23 O.S.C.B. (Supp) 767; 26 O.S.C.B. 5555, 29 O.S.C.B. 8852, 30 O.S.C.B. 10511 and 10526

[Repealed by Rule 41-801]

Final Rule: 23 O.S.C.B. (Supp) 835 (December 15, 2000); Approval by OSC: 23 O.S.C.B. 631 (October 13, 2000); Request for Comments: 22 O.S.C.B. (LF Supp 2) 1 (December 17, 1999), 22 O.S.C.B. (LF Supp) 1 (July 23, 1999) and 20 O.S.C.B. (Supp) 1 (May 2, 1997).

Amendment to Rule: Approval by OSC: (2003) 26 O.S.C.B. 5517; Request for Comments: (2003) 26 O.S.C.B. 587 and (2003) 26 O.S.C.B. 505.

Amendment to Rule: (2006) 29 O.S.C.B. 8852; Approval by OSC: (2006) 29 O.S.C.B. (Supp-1) 1; Request for Comments: (2005) 28 O.S.C.B. (Supp-2) 1 and (2004) 27 O.S.C.B. 465.

Amendment to Rule: (2007) 30 O.S.C.B. 10526; Approval by OSC: (2007) 30 O.S.C.B. 8539.

Amendment to Rule: (2007) 30 O.S.C.B. 10511; Approval by OSC: (2007) 30 O.S.C.B. 8570.

Companion Policy 41-501CP — To Rule 41-501 General Prospectus Requirements

Date: December 15, 2000, as amended effective December 31, 2007

23 O.S.C.B. (Supp) 839, as amended 30 O.S.C.B. 10525

[Rescinded]

Adoption by OSC: 23 O.S.C.B. (Supp) 835 (December 15, 2000) and 23 O.S.C.B. 631 (October 13, 2000); Request for Comments: 22 O.S.C.B. (LF Supp 2) 1 (December 17, 1999), 22 O.S.C.B. (LF Supp) 1 (July 23, 1999) and 20 O.S.C.B. (Supp) 1 (May 2, 1997).

Adoption of Amendment to Policy: (2007) 30 O.S.C.B. 8539 and 10525.

OSC Rule 41-502 — Prospectus Requirements for Mutual Funds

Date: April 20, 2001, as amended effective June 1, 2005

24 O.S.C.B. 2474 and 28 O.S.C.B. 4978

[Revoked by Rule 41-801]

Final Rule: 24 O.S.C.B. 2474 (April 20, 2001); Approval by OSC: 24 O.S.C.B. 455 (January 19, 2001); Request for Comments: 20 O.S.C.B. (Supp 2) 135 (June 27, 1997).

Amendment to Rule: (2005) 28 O.S.C.B. 4978; Approval by OSC: (2005) 28 O.S.C.B. (Supp-1) 55; Request for Comments: (2004) 27 O.S.C.B. 5157 and (2002) 25 O.S.C.B. 6273.

Companion Policy 41-502CP — To Ontario Securities Commission Rule 41-502 Prospectus Requirements for Mutual Funds

[Rescinded]

Adoption by OSC: 24 O.S.C.B. 2474 (April 20, 2001) and 24 O.S.C.B. 455 (January 19, 2001); Request for Comments: 20 O.S.C.B. (Supp 2) 135 (June 27, 1997).

OSC Policy 41-601 — Capital Pool Companies

Date: April 12, 2002

25 O.S.C.B. 2073

Introduction

The Canadian Venture Exchange Inc. ("CDNX") currently operates a capital pool company program (the "Program") in each of Alberta, Saskatchewan, Manitoba and British Columbia. The Program was designed as a corporate finance vehicle to provide businesses with an opportunity to obtain financing earlier in their development than might otherwise be possible through a normal initial public offering (an "IPO"). The Program permits an IPO to be conducted and a CDNX listing to be achieved by a newly created capital pool company (a "CPC") which has no assets, other than cash, and which has not commenced commercial operations. The CPC then uses this pool of funds to identify and evaluate assets or businesses which, when acquired (a "Qualifying Transaction"), qualify the resulting issuer (the "Resulting Issuer") for listing as a regular Tier 1 or Tier 2 issuer on CDNX.

This Policy sets out the views of the Commission as to whether issuers participating in the Program should be permitted to conduct public offerings in Ontario.

Background

In 1986 the Junior Capital Pool ("JCP") program, a predecessor to the Program, was initiated in Alberta through the co-operation of the Alberta Securities Commission and The Alberta Stock Exchange. In 1997, the British Columbia Securities Commission and the Vancouver Stock Exchange adopted a similar program, the Venture Capital Pool ("VCP") program, for use in British Columbia. The current Program, created following the merger of the Vancouver Stock Exchange and The Alberta Stock Exchange in November 1999, replaced the existing VCP and JCP programs. Prior to the merger of the Winnipeg Stock Exchange with CDNX in November 2000 and the subsequent approval of the Program by the Manitoba Securities Commission, a similar junior capital program, known as the Keystone Company program, was previously available in Manitoba.

Staff of the Commission, the Alberta Securities Commission, the British Columbia Securities Commission, the Manitoba Securities Commission and the Saskatchewan Securities Commission have worked together with CDNX to develop a revised version of the Program to operate in each of their respective jurisdictions (collectively, the "CPC Jurisdictions"). Such an initiative will, among other things, assist in harmonizing the ability of entrepreneurs to raise venture capital in the CPC Jurisdictions.

Operation of the Program

The Program is currently governed by CDNX Policy 2.4 Capital Pool Companies ("CDNX Policy 2.4"). CDNX Policy 2.4 provides that an issuer wishing to participate in the Program must file a preliminary prospectus and related supporting documents with CDNX as well as with each of the securities regulatory authorities in whose jurisdictions the proposed distribution will be made. A CPC prospectus that is filed in Ontario will be reviewed by the staff of both CDNX and the Commission. Upon the issuance of a receipt for a final prospectus and the completion of its IPO, securities of a CPC will trade on Tier 2 of CDNX. A CPC will have 18 months following its IPO in which to identify and complete a Qualifying Transaction. However, as soon as a CPC reaches an "agreement in principle" (as defined below) with respect to a proposed Qualifying Transaction, it must issue a comprehensive news release. The Program requires each CPC to seek the approval of both CDNX and a majority of its minority shareholders prior to completing the Qualifying Transaction. In connection with obtaining such shareholder approval, the CPC must prepare a comprehensive information circular containing full, true and plain disclosure concerning the CPC and the Target Company. The information circular will be reviewed by CDNX before it is mailed to shareholders of the CPC.

As CDNX has incorporated the disclosure requirements of Commission Rule 41-501 General Prospectus Requirements ("Rule 41-501") into CDNX Policy 2.4 and the related information circular form, the information circular must contain the same information as a company would be required to disclose if it filed a prospectus.

The Program will not be available to issuers if, prior to the completion of its IPO, an agreement in principle has been reached with respect to a proposed Qualifying Transaction. An "agreement in principle" includes any enforceable agreement or any other agreement or similar commitment which identifies the fundamental terms upon which the parties agree or intend to agree which:

- identifies assets or a business to be acquired which would reasonably appear to constitute "significant assets", the acquisition of which would reasonably appear to constitute a Qualifying Transaction;

- identifies the parties to the Qualifying Transaction;

- identifies the consideration to be paid for the "significant assets" or otherwise identifies the means by which the consideration will be determined; and

- identifies the conditions to any further formal agreements to complete the transaction, and

in respect of which there are no material conditions to closing (other than receipt of shareholder approval and CDNX acceptance), the satisfaction of which is dependent upon third parties and beyond the reasonable control of the non-arm's length parties to the CPC or the non-arm's length parties to the Qualifying Transaction. Both CDNX and the securities regulatory authorities in the CPC Jurisdictions are of the view that if the issuer has reached an agreement in principle, it is able to, and should, prepare a regular prospectus.

Further information regarding the operation of the Program can be found by consulting the CDNX Corporate Finance Manual and CDNX Policy 2.4.

Historical Concerns versus Anticipated Benefits of the Program

Historically, the Director has been reluctant to issue a receipt for a prospectus where the prospectus revealed the issuer to have neither a business nor operations and no assets, other than cash. In *Re Loki Resources Inc.* (1984), 7 O.S.C.B. 583 the Director noted that where an issuer has neither assets to appraise nor business activities to evaluate, nor any present expectation of either assets or activities, meaningful information regarding an issuer cannot be provided to market participants. Accordingly, in such an instance, the benefits of 'reporting issuer status', including the ability of its securities to freely trade in the market following the expiry of any applicable hold period, should not be conferred upon the issuer. This approach was supported by the subsequent Commission decision In *Re Inland National Capital Inc.* (1996), 19 O.S.C.B. 2053.

While the concerns expressed in *Loki* and *Inland National Capital* remain relevant today, the Commission is aware that the implementation of the Program in Ontario may also confer benefits upon Ontario's capital markets by providing entrepreneurs and emerging businesses access to the financial and other resources necessary for such enterprises to fully develop. Moreover, the Commission has also noted that the Program provides certain investor protection provisions that were unavailable in the *Loki* and *Inland National Capital* cases, which, in the view of the Commission, help mitigate the potential for harm to investors identified in those decisions. These provisions include the following:

- management of a CPC is scrutinized by CDNX to ensure that management has experience appropriate to the running of a public company and the completion of a Qualifying Transaction; management's track record must also be disclosed in the CPC prospectus to allow potential investors a basis upon which to make an investment decision;

- the risk of the investment is clearly and prominently disclosed throughout the CPC prospectus;

- directors and officers of a CPC must contribute a minimum amount of cash prior to an IPO, and a CPC may raise only a limited amount of cash under the CPC prospectus; furthermore, a CPC is subject to strict regulation of private placements prior to the completion of its Qualifying Transaction;

- the amount that may be invested by any one individual during an IPO is limited to 2% of the shares issued under the CPC prospectus, and no more than 4% of the shares issued under the CPC prospectus may be purchased by an investor and his or her associates and affiliates during the IPO;

- most shares held by non-arm's length parties of a CPC are escrowed until the completion of the Qualifying Transaction and then are released in stages;

- when a CPC reaches an "agreement in principle" to acquire the business or assets that will be the subject of the Qualifying Transaction, trading in its shares is halted until a detailed press release describing the transaction is issued, a sponsor is retained (unless waived) and CDNX staff is satisfied that there are not obvious reasons why the Qualifying Transaction cannot be completed;

- each CPC must file and distribute to its shareholders an information circular which is subject to review and which must provide prospectus level disclosure of the Qualifying Transaction and the Resulting Issuer in accordance with CDNX requirements (which incorporate the Commission's prospectus requirements as set out in Rule 41-501);

- CDNX staff will closely monitor secondary trading in securities of CPCs to help guard against insider trading; and

- a CPC which fails to complete its Qualifying Transaction within 18 months may be suspended or de-listed and potentially subject to a cease trade order, thereby ensuring that secondary trading in shares of the CPC does not continue indefinitely.

In discharging its statutory duty, the Commission must have consideration for the purposes of the *Securities Act* (the "Act"). Section 1.1 of the Act states that the purposes of the Act are (a) to provide protection to investors from unfair, improper or fraudulent practice, and (b) to foster fair and efficient capital markets and confidence in capital markets. Section 2.1 of the Act provides that, in pursuing the purposes of the Act, the Commission shall have regard to certain fundamental principles, including the following:

- Balancing the importance to be given to each of the purposes of this Act may be required in specific cases.

- The Commission should, subject to an appropriate system of supervision, use the enforcement capability and regulatory expertise of recognized self-regulatory organizations.

- The integration of capital markets is supported and promoted by the sound and responsible harmonization and co-ordination of securities regulation regimes.

- Business and regulatory costs and other restrictions on the business and investment activities of market participants should be proportionate to the significance of the regulatory objectives sought to be realized.

Upon considering the Program and balancing the purposes and principles underlying the Act, the Commission has decided that it would not be prejudicial to the public interest to permit the operation of the Program in Ontario.

Availability of CDNX Program in Ontario

As the Commission has determined that it would not be prejudicial to the public interest to permit CPCs to conduct initial public offerings in Ontario, the Director is generally willing to issue a final receipt for a CPC's prospectus on the basis of the issuer's participation in the Program.

On the basis of the *Loki* and *Inland National Capital* cases, however, it is unlikely that, in the absence of an issuer's participation in the Program, the Director will consider it to be in the public interest to issue such a receipt to a 'shell issuer'. Issuers contemplating participation in the Program should therefore be cautioned that the Director will consider issuing a cease trade order in respect of the securities of a CPC if such CPC is de-listed on account of its failure to complete its Qualifying Transaction or otherwise comply with the Program.

Future Review of the Program

Five years after the adoption of the Program in Ontario, the Commission intends to review the functioning of the Program to assess the benefits it confers upon Ontario's capital markets. In unusual circumstances, the Commission may decide to review the operation of the Program at an earlier date.

Continuing Compliance with Ontario Securities Legislation

Program participants are reminded of their obligations to comply with Ontario securities legislation, including, without limitation, Commission Rule 41-501. In certain circumstances, the CPC's negotiations regarding its Qualifying Transaction may have progressed to the stage where the CPC has a "significant probable acquisition" (as defined in Rule 41-501) but not an "agreement in principle". In this situation, where compliance with Parts 6 and 7 of Rule 41-501 will require a CPC to include in a CPC prospectus financial statements relating to one or more proposed acquisitions, the Director will be prepared to consider, upon application, exempting the CPC from such requirement as the requirement may be inappropriate in the context of the Program.

Adoption by OSC: (2002) 25 O.S.C.B. 2073: Request for Comments: (2001) 24 O.S.C.B. 5317.

OSC Staff Notice 41-701 — Issuance of Receipts for Preliminary Prospectus and Prospectuses (previous version published May 2, 1997)

Date: **July 29, 2005**
28 O.S.C.B. 6376

This notice is being issued to remind issuers and their advisors wishing to receive a receipt for either a preliminary prospectus or a prospectus on a specific day that the preliminary prospectus or prospectus and all accompanying material should be received by us in acceptable form on or before 12:00 noon on the day that the receipt is required. If you are filing a prospectus for an investment fund during peak filing periods, please note that it may take longer to issue final receipts. In those cases, we will use our best efforts to issue a final receipt within 24 hours.

If materials are filed after 12:00 noon, the receipt will normally be issued before noon on the next business day and dated as of that day. If you anticipate filing a prospectus within a reasonable period of time after 12:00 noon and you need a receipt issued that day, please make special arrangements in advance with the Corporate Finance or Investment Funds staff member assigned to review the prospectus. We will attempt to accommodate these requests, but there is no assurance that a receipt will be issued on the date requested if the filing is made after noon.

Special accommodation will be made for the issuance of receipts for certain preliminary short form prospectuses. Issuers that have entered into bought deals in which marketing efforts have been made in reliance on section 14.1 of National Instrument 44-101 *Short Form Prospectus Distributions* must file a preliminary short form prospectus and obtain a receipt dated within two business days of the date the underwriting agreement is entered into. In this situation, provided that the covering letter that accompanies the short form preliminary prospectus refers to the National Instrument and that acceptable material is filed before 3:00 p.m. on a business day, every effort will be made to ensure that a receipt for the preliminary short form prospectus is dated and issued on the day of filing.

OSC Staff Notice 41-702 — Prospectus Practice Directive #1 — Personal Information Forms and Other Procedural Matters Regarding Preliminary Prospectus Filings

Date: **April 1, 2011**
34 O.S.C.B. 3725

The purpose of this practice directive is to alert issuers (including investment fund issuers) and their advisors of:

- procedural changes to facilitate our review of personal information forms filed by directors, executive officers and other individuals, and

- common deficiencies in preliminary prospectus filings.

It also reminds issuers and their advisors of the timing for filing preliminary prospectus materials and the issuance of receipts.

This practice directive is intended to assist issuers and their advisors. It has been prepared by staff of the Corporate Finance Branch and Investment Funds Branch. The views it expresses do not necessarily reflect the views of the Commission or the Canadian Securities Administrators.

Procedures for personal information forms

Under the general prospectus rules, an issuer is required to:

- deliver a personal information form (including a certificate and consent) and an issuer authorization form (collectively, a PIF), or

- have previously filed or delivered a PIF or other acceptable authorization document, for each director, executive officer and promoter of the issuer (and, if the promoter in not an individual, each director and executive officer of the promoter) concurrent with the filing of a preliminary prospectus.[1]

Under the prospectus rules applicable to investment funds, PIFs are also required to be delivered, or to have previously been filed or delivered, for each director and executive officer of the manager of the investment fund issuer, as applicable.[2]

A summary of updated procedures to accommodate our expeditious review of PIFs, and a discussion of common deficiencies with PIF filings, is set out below.

---

[1]The specific PIF delivery requirements for issuers are described, as applicable, in paragraph 9.1(b)(ii) of NI 41-101 and in paragraph 4.1(b)(i) of NI 44-101.

[2]The specific PIF delivery requirements for investment fund issuers are described, as applicable, in paragraph 9.1(b)(ii) of NI 41-101, paragraph 4.1(b)(i) of NI 44-101 and paragraph 2.3(b)(ii) of NI 81-101.

Procedural matters

To facilitate our review of PIFs, issuers are advised to provide the following information in the cover letter accompanying the materials filed with a preliminary prospectus:

- the name of: (i) each current director, executive officer and promoter of the issuer (and, if the promoter is not an individual, each director and executive officer of the promoter) and, (ii) if the issuer is an investment fund, each director and executive officer of the manager of the investment fund issuer, as applicable (collectively, the individuals).

- for each of the individuals, an indication as to whether a PIF has been delivered with the preliminary prospectus or a PIF or other acceptable authorization document for the individual was previously filed or delivered, and

- for each of the individuals for whom the issuer has not delivered a PIF because a PIF or other acceptable authorization document was previously filed, the SEDAR project number and submission number under which the PIF or other acceptable authorization document was previously filed.

Where an issuer is submitting its first preliminary prospectus for which the OSC will act as its principal regulator, the issuer should either file a new PIF or refile a PIF or other acceptable authorization document that was previously filed with its previous principal regulator for each applicable individual.

Where an issuer has reason to believe that information contained in a PIF previously filed or delivered by an individual has materially changed, the issuer should deliver a new PIF for that individual concurrent with filing its preliminary prospectus.

Common deficiencies with PIF filings

Issuers and their advisors should pay careful attention to ensure that each PIF is fully completed by each applicable individual. In particular, we note the following deficiencies in PIF submissions that may cause delays in our review process:

- incorrect issuer name provided in the PIF

- missing or incomplete name of individual and date of birth information (i.e. middle initial provided, rather than full middle name)

- missing yes/no response to a question in any of Parts 6–9 of the PIF concerning offences, bankruptcy, regulatory proceedings and civil proceedings

- failure to provide details concerning a positive response to a question in any of Parts 6–9 of the PIF in an attachment to the PIF

- individual's certificate and consent not provided with the PIF

- individual's certificate and consent missing the name or signature of the individual, or the date of execution, and

- written responses to questions in the PIF are illegible.

Other procedural matters when filing a preliminary prospectus

We continue to see certain deficiencies that can cause unnecessary delays in issuing a receipt for a preliminary prospectus and often result in additional communication among us, issuers and/or their advisors.

Accordingly, we remind issuers and their advisors to ensure the following:

Prior discussions with staff	•	Details of prior discussions with staff regarding prospectus filing issues should be set out in the cover letter accompanying a preliminary prospectus filing.
Preliminary prospectus face page disclosure	•	The "red herring" statement provides the specified disclosure regarding the jurisdictions in Canada in which the issuer intends to offer securities under the prospectus (per Item 1.2 of Form 41-101F1, Item 1.1 of Form 41-101F2, Item 1.2 of Form 44-101F1 and Item 1 of Form 81-101F1, and the related Instruction in the prospectus forms, as applicable). A generic statement that securities will be offered in "certain" jurisdictions is not acceptable.
Preliminary prospectus amendment face page disclosure	•	An amendment to a preliminary prospectus identifies the name and date of the original prospectus that is being amended or amended and restated (as set out in subsection 6.1(2) of NI 41-101 and subsection 2.2(3) of NI 81-101).
Documents incorporated by reference	•	All documents incorporated by reference into a preliminary short form prospectus have, as of the date of filing the preliminary prospectus, been filed with each jurisdiction in which the preliminary short form prospectus is filed (as noted in subsection 2.1(3) of 44-101CP).
Prospectus certificates	•	Prospectus certificates in the preliminary prospectus comply with applicable requirements.
Short form prospectus qualification certificate	•	The issuer qualification certificate filed pursuant to section 4.1 of NI 44-101 is dated as of the date of the preliminary short form prospectus and refers to the correct issuer name and date of the preliminary short form prospectus.
Expert consent letters	•	All expert consent letters refer to the correct issuer and accurately identify the type and date of the preliminary prospectus.

Issuer confirmation letter pursuant to section 7.2 of NP 11-202	• The issuer confirmation letter filed pursuant to subsection 7.2(2) of NP 11-202 specifies in respect of paragraph (d) that *either*: (i) at least one underwriter that signed the prospectus certificate is registered in each jurisdiction in which the issuer will offer the securities, *or* (ii) at least one underwriter that has signed a prospectus certificate has filed an application for registration or for an exemption from registration in each jurisdiction in which the issuer will offer the securities.
SEDAR — NI 13-101	• Documents filed with a preliminary prospectus are filed under the correct "Filing Type" and "Filing Subtype" as prescribed in the SEDAR Filer Manual. • Only documents from one "Filing Subtype" are filed under a single submission as prescribed in paragraph 8.3(e) of the SEDAR Filer Manual.
Fees	• Activity fees and participation fees are paid as required under OSC Rule 13-502 *Fees*. • The correct fee description and fee code for each type and form of preliminary prospectus or pro forma prospectus is used when attaching an activity fee in SEDAR.

Timing for filing preliminary prospectus materials and the issuance of receipts

General timing guidelines

We remind issuers and their advisors of OSC Staff Notice 41-701 *Issuance of Receipts for Preliminary Prospectuses and Prospectuses* (dated July 29, 2005). It sets out the following deadlines for filing preliminary prospectus materials where the issuer wishes to receive a receipt for the preliminary prospectus on the same day as the filing.

Nature of prospectus offering	Timing for filing preliminary prospectus and all accompanying materials in acceptable form
Preliminary prospectuses generally	12 p.m. (EST) on the day that the receipt is required If preliminary prospectus materials are filed after 12 p.m. (EST), the receipt will normally be issued before 12 p.m. (EST) on the next business day and dated as of that day. If you anticipate filing a prospectus within a reasonable period of time after 12:00 p.m. (EST) and you need a receipt issued that day, please make special arrangements in advance with our Review Officer. We will attempt to accommodate these requests, but there is no assurance that a receipt will be issued on the date requested if the filing is made after 12 p.m. (EST)
Preliminary short form prospectuses where the issuer has entered into a bought deal in which marketing efforts have been made in reliance on section 7.1 of NI 44-101	3 p.m. (EST) on the day that the receipt is required provided that: • the issuer has advised our Review Officer before 12 p.m. (EST) that the preliminary prospectus will be filed by 3 p.m. (EST) on that day, and • the cover letter that accompanies the preliminary short form prospectus indicates the issuer's reliance on section 7.1 of NI 44-101

If a preliminary prospectus and all accompanying materials are filed *in acceptable form* by the applicable deadline above, we will make every reasonable effort to issue a receipt for the preliminary prospectus on the day of filing.

Timing guidelines for overnight marketed deals

- The issuer should advise the Review Officer by email at ProspectusReviewOfficer@osc.gov.on.ca as soon as possible on the morning of the day a receipt is required that it intends to conduct an overnight marketed deal and that it will therefore request that the receipt for the preliminary prospectus be issued after markets close that day (i.e. 4:00 p.m. (EST)).

- The issuer should explain in the email to the Review Officer the reasons for the proposed specified receipt issuance time.

- If the Review Officer is advised of an overnight marketed deal on the morning of the day a receipt is required, and the preliminary prospectus and all accompanying materials are filed in acceptable form before 12 p.m. (EST) on that day, we will make every reasonable effort to issue the receipt for the preliminary prospectus on or after the time requested on the day of filing.

OSC Staff Notice 41-703 — Corporate Finance Prospectus Practice Directive #2 — Exemption from Certain Prospectus Requirements to be Evidenced by a Receipt

Date: April 1, 2011

34 O.S.C.B. 3727

The purpose of this practice directive is to alert issuers (other than investment funds) and their advisors of the procedural steps an issuer should follow when making an application for an exemption from certain requirements, as described below, where the exemption will be evidenced by the issuance of a receipt for a final prospectus (or an amendment to a final prospectus).

This practice directive is intended to assist issuers and their advisors. It has been prepared by staff of the Corporate Finance Branch and the views it expresses do not necessarily reflect the views of the Commission or the Canadian Securities Administrators.

Exemption sought

The issuance of a receipt for a final prospectus in connection with a proposed offering can evidence the granting of an exemption from the requirements of the following rules (referred to as the applicable prospectus requirements):

- National Instrument 41-101 *General Prospectus Requirements* (NI 41-101). Note that an exemption from subsection 2.2(2) of NI 41-101 cannot be evidenced by a final receipt. See Part 19 of NI 41-101.

- National Instrument 44-101 *Short Form Prospectus Distributions* (NI 44-101). Note that an exemption from Part 2 of NI 44-101 cannot be evidenced by a final receipt. See Part 8 of NI 44-101.

- National Instrument 44-102 *Shelf Distributions* (NI 44-102). Note that an exemption from Part 2 of NI 44-102 cannot be evidenced by a final receipt. See Part 11 of NI 44-102.

- National Instrument 44-103 *Post-Receipt Pricing* (NI 44-103). See Part 6 of NI 44-103.

- National Instrument 71-101 *The Multijurisdictional Disclosure System* (NI 71-101). See Part 21 of NI 71-101.

- National Instrument 52-107 *Acceptable Accounting Principles and Auditing Standards* (NI 52-107). See Part 5 of NI 52-107.

Procedural matters when making an application for an exemption to be evidenced by a receipt

We continue to see certain deficiencies that can cause unnecessary delays when reviewing an application for an exemption from the applicable prospectus requirements where the exemption will be evidenced by a receipt for the final prospectus. These deficiencies often result in additional communication among us, issuers and/or their advisors.

Accordingly, issuers and their advisors should note the following when submitting an application for an exemption from the applicable prospectus requirements to be evidenced by the prospectus receipt:

Content of application	An application must be made to the regulator for the exemption. The application should be set out in a separate cover letter and contain: • the exemption sought, • an explanation for why the exemption is needed (e.g., if there is a provision the issuer would like to rely on but cannot, explain why the issuer cannot rely on it), • the issuer's submissions on why the exemption should be granted, and in particular, why, in the issuer's view, granting the exemption would not be prejudicial to the public interest, • how the key facts support granting the exemption, and • any past exemptions that are relevant to the application.
Application to be filed on SEDAR	The application should be filed through SEDAR under the same project number as the prospectus to which the application relates (so that the application is transparent to other regulators). If known at the time, the issuer should reference the application in the cover letter to the preliminary prospectus and file a copy of the application through SEDAR at the time of filing the materials for the preliminary prospectus to which the application relates.
Application to be made public	Please note that staff will generally place on the public file a copy of the application and the written acknowledgement from the regulator that the issuance of a receipt for the final prospectus will evidence the granting of the exemption (unless confidentiality has been requested in which case, they will be made public once confidentiality has been lifted). As a result, these documents will be made available to members of the public on request. They will not be made public under the issuer's profile on the SEDAR website (www.sedar.com).
Prospectus disclosure	Where the exemption is granted, the issuer must describe the application and the resolution in the final prospectus to ensure transparency to investors and to the marketplace.

Please note that an issuer seeking a pre-filing interpretation or a waiver application exemption before the issuance of a receipt may submit the pre-filing or waiver application sufficiently in advance of the filing of the related materials to avoid delays in issuance of the receipt. Please refer to Part 8 of National Policy 11-202 *Process for Prospectus Reviews in Multiple Jurisdictions*.

OSC Rule 41-801 — Implementing National Instrument 41-101 General Prospectus Requirements and Consequential Amendments

Date: March 17, 2008

31 O.S.C.B. (Supp. 2) 259

PART 1 — DEFINITIONS

1.1 Definitions — (1) In this Rule, "NI 41-101" means National Instrument 41-101 *General Prospectus Requirements*.

(2) Each term used in this Rule that is defined or interpreted in NI 41-101 has the meaning ascribed to it in NI 41-101.

PART 2 — INTERRELATIONSHIP WITH LEGISLATION

2.1 Short Form of Prospectus for Purposes of Section 63 of the Act — A preliminary short form prospectus and a short form prospectus prepared and certified in accordance with NI 41-101 and NI 44-101 is a short form of preliminary prospectus and a short form of prospectus in the prescribed form, respectively, for the purposes of section 63 of the *Securities Act* (Ontario).

2.2 Amendments — Exemption — Section 57(2.2) of the *Securities Act* (Ontario) does not apply to an investment fund in continuous distribution.

PART 3 — REPEAL

3.1 Repeal — Ontario Securities Commission Rule 41-501 *General Prospectus Requirements* is repealed.

3.2 Ontario Securities Commission Rule 41-502 *Prospectus Requirements for Mutual Funds* is repealed.

PART 4 — EFFECTIVE DATE

4.1 Effective Date — This Rule comes into force on March 17, 2008.

Final Rule: (2008) 31 O.S.C.B. (Supp. 2) 259 (March 7, 2008); Approved by OSC: (2007) 30 O.S.C.B. (Supp. 7) 1 (Dec. 21, 2007); Request for Comments: (2006) 29 O.S.C.B. (Supp. 3) 1 (Dec. 22, 2006).

4.2 — Prospectus Contents — Financial Matters

4.3 — Prospectus Filing Matters

See also NPS 11-202.

National Instrument 43-101 — Standards of Disclosure for Mineral Projects

Date: January 12, 2001; replaced December 30, 2005; replaced June 30, 2011; amended May 9, 2016
24 O.S.C.B. 303, 28 O.S.C.B. 10355, 34 O.S.C.B. 7043 and 39 O.S.C.B. (Supp. 1) 53

Table of Contents

PART 1 — DEFINITIONS AND INTERPRETATION

1.1 Definitions — In this Instrument

"acceptable foreign code" means the JORC Code, the PERC Code, the SAMREC Code, SEC Industry Guide 7, the Certification Code, or any other code, generally accepted in a foreign jurisdiction, that defines mineral resources and mineral reserves in a manner that is consistent with mineral resource and mineral reserve definitions and categories set out in sections 1.2 and 1.3;

"adjacent property" means a property

(a) in which the issuer does not have an interest;

(b) that has a boundary reasonably proximate to the property being reported on; and

(c) that has geological characteristics similar to those of the property being reported on;

"advanced property" means a property that has

(a) mineral reserves, or

(b) mineral resources the potential economic viability of which is supported by a preliminary economic assessment, a pre-feasibility study or a feasibility study;

"Certification Code" means the Certification Code for Exploration Prospects, Mineral Resources and Ore Reserves prepared by the Mineral Resources Committee of the Institution of Mining Engineers of Chile, as amended;

"data verification" means the process of confirming that data has been generated with proper procedures, has been accurately transcribed from the original source and is suitable to be used;

"disclosure" means any oral statement or written disclosure made by or on behalf of an issuer and intended to be, or reasonably likely to be, made available to the public in a jurisdiction of Canada, whether or not filed under securities legislation, but does not include written disclosure that is made available to the public only by reason of having been filed with a government or agency of government pursuant to a requirement of law other than securities legislation;

"early stage exploration property" means a property for which the technical report being filed has

(a) no current mineral resources or mineral reserves defined; and

(b) no drilling or trenching proposed;

"effective date" means, with reference to a technical report, the date of the most recent scientific or technical information included in the technical report;

"exploration information" means geological, geophysical, geochemical, sampling, drilling, trenching, analytical testing, assaying, mineralogical, metallurgical, and other similar information concerning a particular property that is derived from activities undertaken to locate, investigate, define, or delineate a mineral prospect or mineral deposit;

"historical estimate" means an estimate of the quantity, grade, or metal or mineral content of a deposit that an issuer has not verified as a current mineral resource or mineral reserve, and which was prepared before the issuer acquiring, or entering into an agreement to acquire, an interest in the property that contains the deposit;

"initial deposit period" has the meaning ascribed to that term in section 1.1 of National Instrument 62-104 *Take-Over Bids and Issuer Bids*.

"JORC Code" means the Australasian Code for Reporting of Exploration Results, Mineral Resources and Ore Reserves prepared by the Joint Ore Reserves Committee of the Australasian Institute of Mining and Metallurgy, Australian Institute of Geoscientists and Minerals Council of Australia, as amended;

"mineral project" means any exploration, development or production activity, including a royalty or similar interest in these activities, in respect of diamonds, natural solid inorganic material, or natural solid fossilized organic material including base and precious metals, coal, and industrial minerals;

"PERC Code" means the Pan-European Code for Reporting of Exploration Results, Mineral Resources and Reserves prepared by the Pan-European Reserves and Resources Reporting Committee, as amended;

"preliminary economic assessment" means a study, other than a pre-feasibility or feasibility study, that includes an economic analysis of the potential viability of mineral resources;

"producing issuer" means an issuer with annual audited financial statements that disclose

(a) gross revenue, derived from mining operations, of at least $30 million Canadian for the issuer's most recently completed financial year; and

(b) gross revenue, derived from mining operations, of at least $90 million Canadian in the aggregate for the issuer's three most recently completed financial years;

"professional association" means a self-regulatory organization of engineers, geoscientists or both engineers and geoscientists that

(a) is

(i) given authority or recognition by statute in a jurisdiction of Canada, or

(ii) a foreign association that is generally accepted within the international mining community as a reputable professional association;

(b) admits individuals on the basis of their academic qualifications, experience, and ethical fitness;

(c) requires compliance with the professional standards of competence and ethics established by the organization;

(d) requires or encourages continuing professional development; and

(e) has and applies disciplinary powers, including the power to suspend or expel a member regardless of where the member practises or resides;

"qualified person" means an individual who

(a) is an engineer or geoscientist with a university degree, or equivalent accreditation, in an area of geoscience, or engineering, relating to mineral exploration or mining;

(b) has at least five years of experience in mineral exploration, mine development or operation, or mineral project assessment, or any combination of these, that is relevant to his or her professional degree or area of practice;

(c) has experience relevant to the subject matter of the mineral project and the technical report;

(d) is in good standing with a professional association; and

(e) in the case of a professional association in a foreign jurisdiction, has a membership designation that

(i) requires attainment of a position of responsibility in their profession that requires the exercise of independent judgment; and

(ii) requires

A. a favourable confidential peer evaluation of the individual's character, professional judgement, experience, and ethical fitness; or

B. a recommendation for membership by at least two peers, and demonstrated prominence or expertise in the field of mineral exploration or mining;

"quantity" means either tonnage or volume, depending on which term is the standard in the mining industry for the type of mineral;

"SAMREC Code" means the South African Code for the Reporting of Exploration Results, Mineral Resources and Mineral Reserves prepared by the South African Mineral Resource Committee (SAMREC) under the Joint Auspices of the Southern African Institute of Mining and Metallurgy and the Geological Society of South Africa, as amended;

"SEC Industry Guide 7" means the mining industry guide entitled "Description of Property by Issuers Engaged or to be Engaged in Significant Mining Operations" contained in the *Securities Act* Industry Guides published by the United States Securities and Exchange Commission, as amended;

"specified exchange" means the Australian Stock Exchange, the Johannesburg Stock Exchange, the London Stock Exchange Main Market, the Nasdaq Stock Market, the New York Stock Exchange, or the Hong Kong Stock Exchange;

"technical report" means a report prepared and filed in accordance with this Instrument and Form 43-101F1 Technical Report that includes, in summary form, all material scientific and technical information in respect of the subject property as of the effective date of the technical report; and

"written disclosure" includes any writing, picture, map, or other printed representation whether produced, stored or disseminated on paper or electronically, including websites.

1.2 Mineral Resource — In this Instrument, the terms "mineral resource", "inferred mineral resource", "indicated mineral resource" and "measured mineral resource" have the meanings ascribed to those terms by the Canadian Institute of Mining, Metallurgy and Petroleum, as the CIM Definition Standards on Mineral Resources and Mineral Reserves adopted by CIM Council, as amended.

1.3 Mineral Reserve — In this Instrument, the terms "mineral reserve", "probable mineral reserve" and "proven mineral reserve" have the meanings ascribed to those terms by the Canadian Institute of Mining, Metallurgy and Petroleum, as the CIM Definition Standards on Mineral Resources and Mineral Reserves adopted by CIM Council, as amended.

1.4 Mining Studies — In this Instrument, the terms "preliminary feasibility study", "pre-feasibility study" and "feasibility study" have the meanings ascribed to those terms by the Canadian Institute of Mining, Metallurgy and Petroleum, as the CIM Definition Standards on Mineral Resources and Mineral Reserves adopted by CIM Council, as amended.

1.5 Independence — In this Instrument, a qualified person is independent of an issuer if there is no circumstance that, in the opinion of a reasonable person aware of all relevant facts, could interfere with the qualified person's judgment regarding the preparation of the technical report.

PART 2 — REQUIREMENTS APPLICABLE TO ALL DISCLOSURE

2.1 Requirements Applicable to All Disclosure — All disclosure of scientific or technical information made by an issuer, including disclosure of a mineral resource or mineral reserve, concerning a mineral project on a property material to the issuer must be

(a) based upon information prepared by or under the supervision of a qualified person; or

(b) approved by a qualified person.

2.2 All Disclosure of Mineral Resources or Mineral Reserves — An issuer must not disclose any information about a mineral resource or mineral reserve unless the disclosure

(a) uses only the applicable mineral resource and mineral reserve categories set out in sections 1.2 and 1.3;

(b) reports each category of mineral resources and mineral reserves separately, and states the extent, if any, to which mineral reserves are included in total mineral resources;

(c) does not add inferred mineral resources to the other categories of mineral resources; and

(d) states the grade or quality and the quantity for each category of the mineral resources and mineral reserves if the quantity of contained metal or mineral is included in the disclosure.

2.3 Restricted Disclosure — (1) An issuer must not disclose

(a) the quantity, grade, or metal or mineral content of a deposit that has not been categorized as an inferred mineral resource, an indicated mineral resource, a measured mineral resource, a probable mineral reserve, or a proven mineral reserve;

(b) the results of an economic analysis that includes or is based on inferred mineral resources or an estimate permitted under subsection 2.3(2) or section 2.4;

(c) the gross value of metal or mineral in a deposit or a sampled interval or drill intersection; or

(d) a metal or mineral equivalent grade for a multiple commodity deposit, sampled interval, or drill intersection, unless it also discloses the grade of each metal or mineral used to establish the metal or mineral equivalent grade.

(2) Despite paragraph (1)(a), an issuer may disclose in writing the potential quantity and grade, expressed as ranges, of a target for further exploration if the disclosure

(a) states with equal prominence that the potential quantity and grade is conceptual in nature, that there has been insufficient exploration to define a mineral resource and that it is uncertain if further exploration will result in the target being delineated as a mineral resource; and

(b) states the basis on which the disclosed potential quantity and grade has been determined.

(3) Despite paragraph (1)(b), an issuer may disclose the results of a preliminary economic assessment that includes or is based on inferred mineral resources if the disclosure

(a) states with equal prominence that the preliminary economic assessment is preliminary in nature, that it includes inferred mineral resources that are considered too speculative geologically to have the economic considerations applied to them that would enable them to be categorized as mineral reserves, and there is no certainty that the preliminary economic assessment will be realized;

(b) states the basis for the preliminary economic assessment and any qualifications and assumptions made by the qualified person; and

(c) describes the impact of the preliminary economic assessment on the results of any pre-feasibility or feasibility study in respect of the subject property.

(4) An issuer must not use the term preliminary feasibility study, pre-feasibility study or feasibility study when referring to a study unless the study satisfies the criteria set out in the definition of the applicable term in section 1.4.

2.4 Disclosure of Historical Estimates — Despite section 2.2, an issuer may disclose an historical estimate, using the original terminology, if the disclosure

(a) identifies the source and date of the historical estimate, including any existing technical report;

(b) comments on the relevance and reliability of the historical estimate;

(c) to the extent known, provides the key assumptions, parameters, and methods used to prepare the historical estimate;

(d) states whether the historical estimate uses categories other than the ones set out in sections 1.2 and 1.3 and, if so, includes an explanation of the differences;

(e) includes any more recent estimates or data available to the issuer;

(f) comments on what work needs to be done to upgrade or verify the historical estimate as current mineral resources or mineral reserves; and

(g) states with equal prominence that

(i) a qualified person has not done sufficient work to classify the historical estimate as current mineral resources or mineral reserves; and

(ii) the issuer is not treating the historical estimate as current mineral resources or mineral reserves.

PART 3 — ADDITIONAL REQUIREMENTS FOR WRITTEN DISCLOSURE

3.1 Written Disclosure to Include Name of Qualified Person — If an issuer discloses in writing scientific or technical information about a mineral project on a property material to the issuer, the issuer must include in the written disclosure the name and the relationship to the issuer of the qualified person who

(a) prepared or supervised the preparation of the information that forms the basis for the written disclosure; or

(b) approved the written disclosure.

3.2 Written Disclosure to Include Data Verification — If an issuer discloses in writing scientific or technical information about a mineral project on a property material to the issuer, the issuer must include in the written disclosure

(a) a statement whether a qualified person has verified the data disclosed, including sampling, analytical, and test data underlying the information or opinions contained in the written disclosure;

(b) a description of how the data was verified and any limitations on the verification process; and

(c) an explanation of any failure to verify the data.

3.3 Requirements Applicable to Written Disclosure of Exploration Information — (1) If an issuer discloses in writing exploration information about a mineral project on a property material to the issuer, the issuer must include in the written disclosure a summary of

(a) the material results of surveys and investigations regarding the property;

(b) the interpretation of the exploration information; and

(c) the quality assurance program and quality control measures applied during the execution of the work being reported on.

(2) If an issuer discloses in writing sample, analytical or testing results on a property material to the issuer, the issuer must include in the written disclosure, with respect to the results being disclosed,

(a) the location and type of the samples;

(b) the location, azimuth, and dip of the drill holes and the depth of the sample intervals;

(c) a summary of the relevant analytical values, widths, and to the extent known, the true widths of the mineralized zone;

(d) the results of any significantly higher grade intervals within a lower grade intersection;

(e) any drilling, sampling, recovery, or other factors that could materially affect the accuracy or reliability of the data referred to in this subsection; and

(f) a summary description of the type of analytical or testing procedures utilized, sample size, the name and location of each analytical or testing laboratory used, and any relationship of the laboratory to the issuer.

3.4 Requirements Applicable to Written Disclosure of Mineral Resources and Mineral Reserves — If an issuer discloses in writing mineral resources or mineral reserves on a property material to the issuer, the issuer must include in the written disclosure

(a) the effective date of each estimate of mineral resources and mineral reserves;

(b) the quantity and grade or quality of each category of mineral resources and mineral reserves;

(c) the key assumptions, parameters, and methods used to estimate the mineral resources and mineral reserves;

(d) the identification of any known legal, political, environmental, or other risks that could materially affect the potential development of the mineral resources or mineral reserves; and

(e) if the disclosure includes the results of an economic analysis of mineral resources, an equally prominent statement that mineral resources that are not mineral reserves do not have demonstrated economic viability.

3.5 Exception for Written Disclosure Already Filed — Sections 3.2 and 3.3 and paragraphs (a), (c) and (d) of section 3.4 do not apply if the issuer includes in the written disclosure a reference to the title and date of a document previously filed by the issuer that complies with those requirements.

PART 4 — OBLIGATION TO FILE A TECHNICAL REPORT

4.1 Obligation to File a Technical Report Upon Becoming a Reporting Issuer — (1) Upon becoming a reporting issuer in a jurisdiction of Canada an issuer must file in that jurisdiction a technical report for each mineral property material to the issuer.

(2) Subsection (1) does not apply if the issuer is a reporting issuer in a jurisdiction of Canada and subsequently becomes a reporting issuer in another jurisdiction of Canada.

(3) Subsection (1) does not apply if

(a) the issuer previously filed a technical report for the property;

(b) at the date the issuer becomes a reporting issuer, there is no new material scientific or technical information concerning the subject property not included in the previously filed technical report; and

(c) the previously filed technical report meets any independence requirements under section 5.3.

4.2 Obligation to File a Technical Report in Connection with Certain Written Disclosure about Mineral Projects on Material Properties — (1) An issuer must file a technical report to support scientific or technical information that relates to a mineral project on a property material to the issuer, or in the case of paragraph (c), the resulting issuer, if the information is contained in any of the following documents filed or made available to the public in a jurisdiction of Canada:

(a) a preliminary prospectus, other than a preliminary short form prospectus filed in accordance with National Instrument 44-101 *Short Form Prospectus Distributions*;

(b) a preliminary short form prospectus filed in accordance with National Instrument 44-101 *Short Form Prospectus Distributions* that discloses for the first time

(i) mineral resources, mineral reserves or the results of a preliminary economic assessment on the property that constitute a material change in relation to the issuer; or

(ii) a change in mineral resources, mineral reserves or the results of a preliminary economic assessment from the most recently filed technical report if the change constitutes a material change in relation to the issuer;

(c) an information or proxy circular concerning a direct or indirect acquisition of a mineral property where the issuer or resulting issuer issues securities as consideration;

(d) an offering memorandum, other than an offering memorandum delivered solely to accredited investors as defined under securities legislation;

(e) for a reporting issuer, a rights offering circular;

(f) an annual information form;

(g) a valuation required to be prepared and filed under securities legislation;

(h) an offering document that complies with and is filed in accordance with Policy 4.6 — *Public Offering by Short Form Offering Document* and Exchange Form 4H — *Short Form Offering Document,* of the TSX Venture Exchange, as amended;

(i) a take-over bid circular that discloses mineral resources, mineral reserves or the results of a preliminary economic assessment on the property if securities of the offeror are being offered in exchange on the take-over bid; and

(j) any written disclosure made by or on behalf of an issuer, other than in a document described in paragraphs (a) to (i), that discloses for the first time

(i) mineral resources, mineral reserves or the results of a preliminary economic assessment on the property that constitute a material change in relation to the issuer; or

(ii) a change in mineral resources, mineral reserves or the results of a preliminary economic assessment from the most recently filed technical report if the change constitutes a material change in relation to the issuer.

(2) Subsection (1) does not apply for disclosure of an historical estimate in a document referred to in paragraph (1)(j) if the disclosure is made in accordance with subsection 2.4.

(3) If a technical report is filed under paragraph (1)(a) or (b), and new material scientific or technical information concerning the subject property becomes available before the filing of the final version of the prospectus or short form prospectus, the issuer must file an updated technical report or an addendum to the technical report with the final version of the prospectus or short form prospectus.

(4) The issuer must file the technical report referred to in subsection (1) not later than the time it files or makes available to the public the document listed in subsection (1) that the technical report supports.

(5) Despite subsection (4), an issuer must

    (a) file a technical report supporting disclosure under paragraph (1)(j) not later than

        (i) if the disclosure is also contained in a preliminary short form prospectus, the earlier of 45 days after the date of the disclosure and the date of filing the preliminary short form prospectus;

        (ii) if the disclosure is also contained in a directors' circular, the earlier of 45 days after the date of the disclosure and 3 business days before the expiry of the initial deposit period; and

        (iii) in all other cases, 45 days after the date of the disclosure;

    (b) issue a news release at the time it files the technical report disclosing the filing of the technical report and reconciling any material differences in the mineral resources, mineral reserves or results of a preliminary economic assessment, between the technical report and the issuer's earlier disclosure under paragraph (1)(j).

(6) Despite subsection (4), if a property referred to in an annual information form first becomes material to the issuer less than 30 days before the filing deadline for the annual information form, the issuer must file the technical report within 45 days of the date that the property first became material to the issuer.

(7) Despite subsection (4) and paragraph (5)(a), an issuer is not required to file a technical report within 45 days to support disclosure under subparagraph (1)(j)(i), if

    (a) the mineral resources, mineral reserves or results of a preliminary economic assessment

        (i) were prepared by or on behalf of another issuer who holds or previously held an interest in the property;

        (ii) were disclosed by the other issuer in a document listed in subsection (1); and

        (iii) are supported by a technical report filed by the other issuer;

    (b) the issuer, in its disclosure under subparagraph (1)(j)(i),

        (i) identifies the title and effective date of the previous technical report and the name of the other issuer that filed it;

        (ii) names the qualified person who reviewed the technical report on behalf of the issuer; and

        (iii) states with equal prominence that, to the best of the issuer's knowledge, information, and belief, there is no new material scientific or technical information that would make the disclosure of the mineral resources, mineral reserves or results of a preliminary economic assessment inaccurate or misleading; and

    (c) the issuer files a technical report supporting its disclosure of the mineral resources, mineral reserves or results of a preliminary economic assessment;

        (i) if the disclosure is also contained in a preliminary short form prospectus, by the earlier of 180 days after the date of the disclosure and the date of filing the short form prospectus; and

        (ii) in all other cases, within 180 days after the date of the disclosure.

(8) Subsection (1) does not apply if

    (a) the issuer previously filed a technical report that supports the scientific or technical information in the document;

    (b) at the date of filing the document, there is no new material scientific or technical information concerning the subject property not included in the previously filed technical report; and

    (c) the previously filed technical report meets any independence requirements under section 5.3.

4.3 Required Form of Technical Report — A technical report that is required to be filed under this Part must be prepared

    (a) in English or French; and

    (b) in accordance with Form 43-101F1.

PART 5 — AUTHOR OF TECHNICAL REPORT

5.1 Prepared by a Qualified Person — A technical report must be prepared by or under the supervision of one or more qualified persons.

5.2 Execution of Technical Report — A technical report must be dated, signed and, if the qualified person has a seal, sealed by

    (a) each qualified person who is responsible for preparing or supervising the preparation of all or part of the report; or

    (b) a person or company whose principal business is providing engineering or geoscientific services if each qualified person responsible for preparing or supervising the preparation of all or part of the report is an employee, officer, or director of that person or company.

5.3 Independent Technical Report — (1) A technical report required under any of the following provisions of this Instrument must be prepared by or under the supervision of one or more qualified persons that are, at the effective and filing dates of the technical report, all independent of the issuer:

    (a) section 4.1;

    (b) paragraphs (a) and (g) of subsection 4.2(1); or

    (c) paragraphs (b), (c), (d), (e), (f), (h), (i) and (j) of subsection 4.2(1), if the document discloses

        (i) for the first time mineral resources, mineral reserves or the results of a preliminary economic assessment on a property material to the issuer, or

        (ii) a 100 percent or greater change in the total mineral resources or total mineral reserves on a property material to the issuer, since the issuer's most recently filed independent technical report in respect of the property.

(2) Despite subsection (1), a technical report required to be filed by a producing issuer under paragraph (1)(a) is not required to be prepared by or under the supervision of an independent qualified person if the securities of the issuer trade on a specified exchange.

(3) Despite subsection (1), a technical report required to be filed by a producing issuer under paragraph (1)(b) or (c) is not required to be prepared by or under the supervision of an independent qualified person.

(4) Despite subsection (1), a technical report required to be filed by an issuer concerning a property which is or will be the subject of a joint venture with a producing issuer is not required to be prepared by or under the supervision of an independent qualified person, if the qualified person preparing or supervising the preparation of the report relies on scientific and technical information prepared by or under the supervision of a qualified person that is an employee or consultant of the producing issuer.

PART 6 — PREPARATION OF TECHNICAL REPORT

6.1 The Technical Report — A technical report must be based on all available data relevant to the disclosure that it supports.

6.2 Current Personal Inspection — (1) Before an issuer files a technical report, the issuer must have at least one qualified person who is responsible for preparing or supervising the preparation of all or part of the technical report complete a current inspection on the property that is the subject of the technical report.

(2) Subsection (1) does not apply to an issuer provided that

(a) the property that is the subject of the technical report is an early stage exploration property;

(b) seasonal weather conditions prevent a qualified person from accessing any part of the property or obtaining beneficial information from it; and

(c) the issuer discloses in the technical report, and in the disclosure that the technical report supports, that a personal inspection by a qualified person was not conducted, the reasons why, and the intended time frame to complete the personal inspection.

(3) If an issuer relies on subsection (2), the issuer must

(a) as soon as practical, have at least one qualified person who is responsible for preparing or supervising the preparation of all or part of the technical report complete a current inspection on the property that is the subject of the technical report; and

(b) promptly file a technical report and the certificates and consents required under Part 8 of this Instrument.

6.3 Maintenance of Records — An issuer must keep for 7 years copies of assay and other analytical certificates, drill logs, and other information referenced in the technical report or used as a basis for the technical report.

6.4 Limitation on Disclaimers — (1) An issuer must not file a technical report that contains a disclaimer by any qualified person responsible for preparing or supervising the preparation of all or part of the report that

(a) disclaims responsibility for, or limits reliance by another party on, any information in the part of the report the qualified person prepared or supervised the preparation of; or

(b) limits the use or publication of the report in a manner that interferes with the issuer's obligation to reproduce the report by filing it on SEDAR.

(2) Despite subsection (1), an issuer may file a technical report that includes a disclaimer in accordance with Item 3 of Form 43-101F1.

PART 7 — USE OF FOREIGN CODE

7.1 Use of Foreign Code — (1) Despite section 2.2, an issuer may make disclosure and file a technical report that uses the mineral resource and mineral reserve categories of an acceptable foreign code, if the issuer

(a) is incorporated or organized in a foreign jurisdiction; or

(b) is incorporated or organized under the laws of Canada or a jurisdiction of Canada, for its properties located in a foreign jurisdiction.

(2) If an issuer relies on subsection (1), the issuer must include in the technical report a reconciliation of any material differences between the mineral resource and mineral reserve categories used and the categories set out in sections 1.2 and 1.3.

PART 8 — CERTIFICATES AND CONSENTS OF QUALIFIED PERSONS FOR TECHNICAL REPORTS

8.1 Certificates of Qualified Persons — (1) An issuer must, when filing a technical report, file a certificate that is dated, signed, and if the signatory has a seal, sealed, of each qualified person responsible for preparing or supervising the preparation of all or part of the technical report.

(2) A certificate under subsection (1) must state

(a) the name, address, and occupation of the qualified person;

(b) the title and effective date of the technical report to which the certificate applies;

(c) the qualified person's qualifications, including a brief summary of relevant experience, the name of all professional associations to which the qualified person belongs, and that the qualified person is a "qualified person" for purposes of this Instrument;

(d) the date and duration of the qualified person's most recent personal inspection of each property, if applicable;

(e) the item or items of the technical report for which the qualified person is responsible;

(f) whether the qualified person is independent of the issuer as described in section 1.5;

(g) what prior involvement, if any, the qualified person has had with the property that is the subject of the technical report;

(h) that the qualified person has read this Instrument and the technical report, or part that the qualified person is responsible for, has been prepared in compliance with this Instrument; and

(i) that, at the effective date of the technical report, to the best of the qualified person's knowledge, information, and belief, the technical report, or part that the qualified person is responsible for, contains all scientific and technical information that is required to be disclosed to make the technical report not misleading.

8.2 Addressed to Issuer — All technical reports must be addressed to the issuer.

8.3 Consents of Qualified Persons — (1) An issuer must, when filing a technical report, file a statement of each qualified person responsible for preparing or supervising the preparation of all or part of the technical report, dated, and signed by the qualified person

    (a) consenting to the public filing of the technical report;

    (b) identifying the document that the technical report supports;

    (c) consenting to the use of extracts from, or a summary of, the technical report in the document; and

    (d) confirming that the qualified person has read the document and that it fairly and accurately represents the information in the technical report or part that the qualified person is responsible for.

(2) Paragraphs (1)(b), (c) and (d) do not apply to a consent filed with a technical report filed under section 4.1.

(3) If an issuer relies on subsection (2), the issuer must file an updated consent that includes paragraphs (1)(b), (c) and (d) for the first subsequent use of the technical report to support disclosure in a document filed under subsection 4.2(1).

PART 9 — EXEMPTIONS

9.1 Authority to Grant Exemptions — (1) The regulator or the securities regulatory authority may, on application, grant an exemption from this Instrument, in whole or in part, subject to such conditions or restrictions as may be imposed in the exemption in response to an application.

(2) Despite subsection (1), in Ontario, only the regulator may grant such an exemption.

(3) Except in Ontario, an exemption referred to in subsection (1) is granted under the statute referred to in Appendix B to National Instrument 14-101 *Definitions* opposite the name of the local jurisdiction.

9.2 Exemptions for Royalty or Similar Interests — (1) An issuer whose interest in a mineral project is only a royalty or similar interest is not required to file a technical report to support disclosure in a document under subsection 4.2(1) if

    (a) the operator or owner of the mineral project is

        (i) a reporting issuer in a jurisdiction of Canada, or

        (ii) a producing issuer whose securities trade on a specified exchange and that discloses mineral resources and mineral reserves under an acceptable foreign code;

    (b) the issuer identifies in its document under subsection 4.2(1) the source of the scientific and technical information; and

    (c) the operator or owner of the mineral project has disclosed the scientific and technical information that is material to the issuer.

(2) An issuer whose interest in a mineral project is only a royalty or similar interest and that does not qualify to use the exemption in subsection (1) is not required to

    (a) comply with section 6.2; and

    (b) complete those items under Form 43-101F1 that require data verification, inspection of documents, or personal inspection of the property to complete those items.

(3) Paragraphs (2)(a) and (b) only apply if the issuer

    (a) has requested but has not received access to the necessary data from the operator or owner and is not able to obtain the necessary information from the public domain;

    (b) under Item 3 of Form 43-101F1, states the issuer has requested but has not received access to the necessary data from the operator or owner and is not able to obtain the necessary information from the public domain and describes the content referred to under each item of Form 43-101F1 that the issuer did not complete; and

    (c) includes in all scientific and technical disclosure a statement that the issuer has an exemption from completing certain items under Form 43-101F1 in the technical report required to be filed and includes a reference to the title and effective date of that technical report.

9.3 Exemption for Certain Types of Filings — This Instrument does not apply if the only reason an issuer files written disclosure of scientific or technical information is to comply with the requirement under securities legislation to file a copy of a record or disclosure material that was filed with a securities commission, exchange, or regulatory authority in another jurisdiction.

PART 10 — EFFECTIVE DATE AND REPEAL

10.1 Effective Date — This Instrument comes into force on June 30, 2011.

10.2 Repeal — National Instrument 43-101 *Standards of Disclosure for Mineral Projects,* which came into force on December 30, 2005, is repealed.

Final Rule: (2001) 24 O.S.C.B. 303; Approval by OSC: (2000) 23 O.S.C.B. 7815; Request for Comments: (2000) 23 O.S.C.B. 2159 and (1998) 21 O.S.C.B. 4213. Replaced NPS 2-A.

Revised Rule: (2005) 28 O.S.C.B. 10355; Approval by OSC: 28 O.S.C.B. 8117; Request for Comments: 27 O.S.C.B. 7699.

Revised Rule: (2011) 34 O.S.C.B. 7043; Approval by OSC: (2011) 34 O.S.C.B. (Supp. 2) 1; Request for Comments: (2010) 33 O.S.C.B. 3703.

Amendment to Rule: (2016) 39 O.S.C.B. (Supp. 1) 55

Policies and Orders: NPS 43-101CP, 22; CSAN 43-306, 43-307, 43-308, 51-336; OSCN 43-704, 43-705.

Form 43-101F1 — Technical Report

Contents of the Technical Report

Title Page

Date and Signature Page

Table of Contents

Illustrations

Item 1: Summary

Item 2: Introduction

Item 3: Reliance on Other Experts

Item 4: Property Description and Location

Item 5: Accessibility, Climate, Local Resources, Infrastructure and Physiography

Item 6: History

Item 7: Geological Setting and Mineralization

Item 8: Deposit Types

Item 9: Exploration

Item 10: Drilling

Item 11: Sample Preparation, Analyses and Security

Item 12: Data Verification

Item 13: Mineral Processing and Metallurgical Testing

Item 14: Mineral Resource Estimates

Item 15: Mineral Reserve Estimates

Item 16: Mining Methods

Item 17: Recovery Methods

Item 18: Project Infrastructure

Item 19: Market Studies and Contracts

Item 20: Environmental Studies, Permitting and Social or Community Impact

Item 21: Capital and Operating Costs

Item 22: Economic Analysis

Item 23: Adjacent Properties

Item 24: Other Relevant Data and Information

Item 25: Interpretation and Conclusions

Item 26: Recommendations

Item 27: References

INSTRUCTIONS

(1) The objective of the technical report is to provide a summary of material scientific and technical information concerning mineral exploration, development, and production activities on a mineral property that is material to an issuer. This Form sets out the requirements for the preparation and content of a technical report.

(2) Terms used in this Form that are defined or interpreted in National Instrument 43-101 Standards of Disclosure for Mineral Projects (the "Instrument") will have that definition or interpretation. In addition, a general definition instrument has been adopted as National Instrument 14-101 Definitions that contains definitions of certain terms used in more than one national instrument. Readers of this Form should review both these national instruments for defined terms.

(3) The qualified person preparing the technical report should keep in mind that the intended audience is the investing public and their advisors who, in most cases, will not be mining experts. Therefore, to the extent possible, technical reports should be simplified and understandable to a reasonable investor. However, the technical report should include sufficient context and cautionary language to allow a reasonable investor to understand the nature, importance, and limitations of the data, interpretations, and conclusions summarized in the technical report.

(4) The qualified person preparing the technical report must use all of the headings of Items 1 to 14 and 23 to 27 in this Form and provide the information specified under each heading. For advanced properties, the qualified person must also use the headings of Items 15 to 22 and include the information required under each of these headings. The qualified person may create sub-headings. Disclosure included under one heading is not required to be repeated under another heading.

(5) The qualified person preparing the technical report may refer to information in a technical report previously filed by the issuer for the subject property if the information is still current and the technical report identifies the title, date and author of the previously filed technical report. However, the qualified person must still summarize or quote the referenced information in the current technical report and may not disclaim responsibility for the referenced information. Except as permitted by subsection 4.2(3) of the Instrument, an issuer may not update or revise a previously filed technical report by filing an addendum.

(6) While the Form mandates the headings and general format of the technical report, the qualified person preparing the technical report is responsible for determining the level of detail required under each Item based on the qualified person's assessment of the relevance and significance of the information.

(7) The technical report may only contain disclaimers that are in accordance with section 6.4 of the Instrument and Item 3 of this Form.

(8) Since a technical report is a summary document the inclusion and filing of comprehensive appendices is not generally necessary to comply with the requirements of the Form.

(9) The Instrument requires certificates and consents of qualified persons, prepared in accordance with sections 8.1 and 8.3 respectively, to be filed at the same time as the technical report. The Instrument does not specifically require the issuer to file the certificate of qualified person as a separate

document. It is generally acceptable for the qualified person to include the certificate in the technical report and to use the certificate as the date and signature page.

Contents of the Technical Report

Title Page — Include a title page setting out the title of the technical report, the general location of the mineral project, the name and professional designation of each qualified person, and the effective date of the technical report.

Date and Signature Page — The technical report must have a signature page, at either the beginning or end of the technical report, signed in accordance with section 5.2 of the Instrument. The effective date of the technical report and date of signing must be on the signature page.

Table of Contents — Provide a table of contents listing the contents of the technical report, including figures and tables.

Illustrations — Technical reports must be illustrated by legible maps, plans and sections, all prepared at an appropriate scale to distinguish important features. Maps must be dated and include a legend, author or information source, a scale in bar or grid form, and an arrow indicating north. All technical reports must be accompanied by a location or index map and a compilation map outlining the general geology of the property. In addition, all technical reports must include more detailed maps showing all important features described in the text, relative to the property boundaries, including but not limited to

(a) for exploration projects, areas of previous or historical exploration, and the location of known mineralization, geochemical or geophysical anomalies, drilling, and mineral deposits;

(b) for advanced properties other than properties under development or in production, the location and surficial outline of mineral resources, mineral reserves, and, to the extent known, areas for potential access and infrastructure; and

(c) for properties under development or in production, the location of pit limits or underground development, plant sites, tailings storage areas, waste disposal areas, and all other significant infrastructure features.

If information is used from other sources in preparing maps, drawings, or diagrams, disclose the source of the information. If adjacent or nearby properties have an important bearing on the potential of the subject property, the location of the properties and any relevant mineralized structures discussed in the report must be shown in relationship to the subject property.

INSTRUCTION: Summarize and simplify the illustrations so that they are legible and suitable for electronic filing. For ease of reference, consider inserting the illustration in the text of the report in relative proximity to the text they illustrate.

Requirements for All Technical Reports

Item 1: Summary — Briefly summarize important information in the technical report, including property description and ownership, geology and mineralization, the status of exploration, development and operations, mineral resource and mineral reserve estimates, and the qualified person's conclusions and recommendations.

Item 2: Introduction — Include a description of

(a) the issuer for whom the technical report is prepared;

(b) the terms of reference and purpose for which the technical report was prepared;

(c) the sources of information and data contained in the technical report or used in its preparation, with citations if applicable; and

(d) the details of the personal inspection on the property by each qualified person or, if applicable, the reason why a personal inspection has not been completed.

Item 3: Reliance on Other Experts — A qualified person who prepares or supervises the preparation of all or part of a technical report may include a limited disclaimer of responsibility if:

(a) The qualified person is relying on a report, opinion, or statement of another expert who is not a qualified person, or on information provided by the issuer, concerning legal, political, environmental, or tax matters relevant to the technical report, and the qualified person identifies

(i) the source of the information relied upon, including the date, title, and author of any report, opinion, or statement;

(ii) the extent of reliance; and

(iii) the portions of the technical report to which the disclaimer applies.

(b) The qualified person is relying on a report, opinion, or statement of another expert who is not a qualified person, concerning diamond or other gemstone valuations, or the pricing of commodities for which pricing is not publicly available, and the qualified person discloses

(i) the date, title, and author of the report, opinion, or statement;

(ii) the qualifications of the other expert and why it is reasonable for the qualified person to rely on the other expert;

(iii) any significant risks associated with the valuation or pricing; and

(iv) any steps the qualified person took to verify the information provided.

Item 4: Property Description and Location — To the extent applicable, describe

(a) the area of the property in hectares or other appropriate units;

(b) the location, reported by an easily recognizable geographic and grid location system;

(c) the type of mineral tenure (claim, license, lease, etc.) and the identifying name or number of each;

(d) the nature and extent of the issuer's title to, or interest in, the property including surface rights, legal access, the obligations that must be met to retain the property, and the expiration date of claims, licences, or other property tenure rights;

(e) to the extent known, the terms of any royalties, back-in rights, payments, or other agreements and encumbrances to which the property is subject;

(f) To the extent known, all environmental liabilities to which the property is subject;

(g) to the extent known, the permits that must be acquired to conduct the work proposed for the property, and if the permits have been obtained; and

(h) to the extent known, any other significant factors and risks that may affect access, title, or the right or ability to perform work on the property.

Item 5: Accessibility, Climate, Local Resources, Infrastructure and Physiography — Describe

(a) topography, elevation, and vegetation;

(b) the means of access to the property;

(c) the proximity of the property to a population centre, and the nature of transport;

(d) to the extent relevant to the mineral project, the climate and the length of the operating season; and

(e) to the extent relevant to the mineral project, the sufficiency of surface rights for mining operations, the availability and sources of power, water, mining personnel, potential tailings storage areas, potential waste disposal areas, heap leach pad areas, and potential processing plant sites.

Item 6: History — To the extent known, describe

(a) the prior ownership of the property and ownership changes;

(b) the type, amount, quantity, and general results of exploration and development work undertaken by any previous owners or operators;

(c) any significant historical mineral resource and mineral reserve estimates in accordance with section 2.4 of the Instrument; and

(d) any production from the property.

INSTRUCTION: If the technical report includes work that was conducted outside the current property boundaries, clearly distinguish this work from the work conducted on the property that is the subject of the technical report.

Item 7: Geological Setting and Mineralization — Describe

(a) the regional, local, and property geology; and

(b) the significant mineralized zones encountered on the property, including a summary of the surrounding rock types, relevant geological controls, and the length, width, depth, and continuity of the mineralization, together with a description of the type, character, and distribution of the mineralization.

Item 8: Deposit Types — Describe the mineral deposit type(s) being investigated or being explored for and the geological model or concepts being applied in the investigation and on the basis of which the exploration program is planned.

Item 9: Exploration — Briefly describe the nature and extent of all relevant exploration work other than drilling, conducted by or on behalf of, the issuer, including

(a) the procedures and parameters relating to the surveys and investigations;

(b) the sampling methods and sample quality, including whether the samples are representative, and any factors that may have resulted in sample biases;

(c) relevant information of location, number, type, nature, and spacing or density of samples collected, and the size of the area covered; and

(d) the significant results and interpretation of the exploration information.

INSTRUCTION: If exploration results from previous operators are included, clearly identify the work conducted by or on behalf of the issuer.

Item 10: Drilling — Describe

(a) the type and extent of drilling including the procedures followed and a summary and interpretation of all relevant results;

(b) any drilling, sampling, or recovery factors that could materially impact the accuracy and reliability of the results;

(c) for a property other than an advanced property

(i) the location, azimuth, and dip of any drill hole, and the depth of the relevant sample intervals;

(ii) the relationship between the sample length and the true thickness of the mineralization, if known, and if the orientation of the mineralization is unknown, state this; and

(iii) the results of any significantly higher grade intervals within a lower grade intersection.

INSTRUCTIONS:

(1) For properties with mineral resource estimates, the qualified person may meet the requirements under Item 10(c) by providing a drill plan and representative examples of drill sections through the mineral deposit.

(2) If drill results from previous operators are included, clearly identify the results of drilling conducted by or on behalf of the issuer.

Item 11: Sample Preparation, Analyses, and Security — Describe

(a) sample preparation methods and quality control measures employed before dispatch of samples to an analytical or testing laboratory, the method or process of sample splitting and reduction, and the security measures taken to ensure the validity and integrity of samples taken;

(b) relevant information regarding sample preparation, assaying and analytical procedures used, the name and location of the analytical or testing laboratories, the relationship of the laboratory to the issuer, and whether the laboratories are certified by any standards association and the particulars of any certification;

(c) a summary of the nature, extent, and results of quality control procedures employed and quality assurance actions taken or recommended to provide adequate confidence in the data collection and processing; and

(d) the author's opinion on the adequacy of sample preparation, security, and analytical procedures.

Item 12: Data Verification — Describe the steps taken by the qualified person to verify the data in the technical report, including

(a) the data verification procedures applied by the qualified person;

(b) any limitations on or failure to conduct such verification, and the reasons for any such limitations or failure; and

(c) the qualified person's opinion on the adequacy of the data for the purposes used in the technical report.

Item 13: Mineral Processing and Metallurgical Testing — If mineral processing or metallurgical testing analyses have been carried out, discuss

(a) the nature and extent of the testing and analytical procedures, and provide a summary of the relevant results;

(b) the basis for any assumptions or predictions regarding recovery estimates;

(c) to the extent known, the degree to which the test samples are representative of the various types and styles of mineralization and the mineral deposit as a whole; and

(d) to the extent known, any processing factors or deleterious elements that could have a significant effect on potential economic extraction.

Item 14: Mineral Resource Estimates — A technical report disclosing mineral resources must

(a) provide sufficient discussion of the key assumptions, parameters, and methods used to estimate the mineral resources, for a reasonably informed reader to understand the basis for the estimate and how it was generated;

(b) comply with all disclosure requirements for mineral resources set out in the Instrument, including sections 2.2, 2.3, and 3.4;

(c) when the grade for a multiple commodity mineral resource is reported as metal or mineral equivalent, report the individual grade of each metal or mineral and the metal prices, recoveries, and any other relevant conversion factors used to estimate the metal or mineral equivalent grade; and

(d) include a general discussion on the extent to which the mineral resource estimates could be materially affected by any known environmental, permitting, legal, title, taxation, socio-economic, marketing, political, or other relevant factors.

INSTRUCTIONS:

(1) A statement of quantity and grade or quality is an estimate and should be rounded to reflect the fact that it is an approximation.

(2) Where multiple cut-off grade scenarios are presented, the qualified person must identify and highlight the base case, or preferred scenario. All estimates resulting from each of the cut-off grade scenarios must meet the test of reasonable prospect of economic extraction.

Additional Requirements for Advanced Property Technical Reports

Item 15: Mineral Reserve Estimates — A technical report disclosing mineral reserves must

(a) provide sufficient discussion and detail of the key assumptions, parameters, and methods used for a reasonably informed reader to understand how the qualified person converted the mineral resources to mineral reserves;

(b) comply with all disclosure requirements for mineral reserves set out in the Instrument, including sections 2.2, 2.3, and 3.4;

(c) when the grade for a multiple commodity mineral reserve is reported as metal or mineral equivalent, report the individual grade of each metal or mineral and the metal prices, recoveries, and any other relevant conversion factors used to estimate the metal or mineral equivalent grade; and

(d) discuss the extent to which the mineral reserve estimates could be materially affected by mining, metallurgical, infrastructure, permitting, and other relevant factors.

Item 16: Mining Methods — Discuss the current or proposed mining methods and provide a summary of the relevant information used to establish the amenability or potential amenability of the mineral resources or mineral reserves to the proposed mining methods. Consider and, where relevant, include

(a) geotechnical, hydrological, and other parameters relevant to mine or pit designs and plans;

(b) production rates, expected mine life, mining unit dimensions, and mining dilution factors used;

(c) requirements for stripping, underground development, and backfilling; and

(d) required mining fleet and machinery.

INSTRUCTION: Preliminary economic assessments, pre-feasibility studies, and feasibility studies generally analyse and assess the same geological, engineering, and economic factors with increasing detail and precision. Therefore, the criteria for Items 16 to 22 can be used as a framework for reporting the results of all three studies.

Item 17: Recovery Methods — Discuss reasonably available information on test or operating results relating to the recoverability of the valuable component or commodity and amenability of the mineralization to the proposed processing methods. Consider and, where relevant, include

(a) a description or flow sheet of any current or proposed process plant;

(b) plant design, equipment characteristics and specifications, as applicable; and

(c) current or projected requirements for energy, water, and process materials.

Item 18: Project Infrastructure — Provide a summary of infrastructure and logistic requirements for the project, which could include roads, rail, port facilities, dams, dumps, stockpiles, leach pads, tailings disposal, power, and pipelines, as applicable.

Item 19: Market Studies and Contracts

(a) Provide a summary of reasonably available information concerning markets for the issuer's production, including the nature and material terms of any agency relationships. Discuss the nature of any studies or analyses completed by the issuer, including any relevant market studies, commodity price projections, product valuations, market entry strategies, or product specification requirements. Confirm that the qualified person has reviewed these studies and analyses and that the results support the assumptions in the technical report.

(b) Identify any contracts material to the issuer that are required for property development, including mining, concentrating, smelting, refining, transportation, handling, sales and hedging, and forward sales contracts or arrangements. State which contracts are in place and which are still under negotiation. For contracts that are in place, discuss whether the terms, rates or charges are within industry norms.

Item 20: Environmental Studies, Permitting, and Social or Community Impact — Discuss reasonably available information on environmental, permitting, and social or community factors related to the project. Consider and, where relevant, include

(a) a summary of the results of any environmental studies and a discussion of any known environmental issues that could materially impact the issuer's ability to extract the mineral resources or mineral reserves;

(b) requirements and plans for waste and tailings disposal, site monitoring, and water management both during operations and post mine closure;

(c) project permitting requirements, the status of any permit applications, and any known requirements to post performance or reclamation bonds;

(d) a discussion of any potential social or community related requirements and plans for the project and the status of any negotiations or agreements with local communities; and

(e) a discussion of mine closure (remediation and reclamation) requirements and costs.

Item 21: Capital and Operating Costs — Provide a summary of capital and operating cost estimates, with the major components set out in tabular form. Explain and justify the basis for the cost estimates.

Item 22: Economic Analysis — Provide an economic analysis for the project that includes

(a) a clear statement of and justification for the principal assumptions;

(b) cash flow forecasts on an annual basis using mineral reserves or mineral resources and an annual production schedule for the life of project;

(c) a discussion of net present value (NPV), internal rate of return (IRR), and payback period of capital with imputed or actual interest;

(d) a summary of the taxes, royalties, and other government levies or interests applicable to the mineral project or to production, and to revenue or income from the mineral project; and

(e) sensitivity or other analysis using variants in commodity price, grade, capital and operating costs, or other significant parameters, as appropriate, and discuss the impact of the results.

INSTRUCTIONS:

(1) Producing issuers may exclude the information required under Item 22 for technical reports on properties currently in production unless the technical report includes a material expansion of current production.

(2) The economic analysis in technical reports must comply with paragraphs 2.3(1)(b) and (c), subsections 2.3(3) and (4), and paragraph 3.4(e), of the Instrument, including any required cautionary language.

Requirements for All Technical Reports

Item 23: Adjacent Properties — A technical report may include relevant information concerning an adjacent property if

(a) such information was publicly disclosed by the owner or operator of the adjacent property;

(b) the source of the information is identified;

(c) the technical report states that its qualified person has been unable to verify the information and that the information is not necessarily indicative of the mineralization on the property that is the subject of the technical report;

(d) the technical report clearly distinguishes between the information from the adjacent property and the information from the property that is the subject of the technical report; and

(e) any historical estimates of mineral resources or mineral reserves are disclosed in accordance with paragraph 2.4(a) of the Instrument.

Item 24: Other Relevant Data and Information — Include any additional information or explanation necessary to make the technical report understandable and not misleading.

Item 25: Interpretation and Conclusions — Summarize the relevant results and interpretations of the information and analysis being reported on. Discuss any significant risks and uncertainties that could reasonably be expected to affect the reliability or confidence in the exploration information, mineral resource or mineral reserve estimates, or projected economic outcomes. Discuss any reasonably foreseeable impacts of these risks and uncertainties to the project's potential economic viability or continued viability. A technical report concerning exploration information must include the conclusions of the qualified person.

Item 26: Recommendations — Provide particulars of recommended work programs and a breakdown of costs for each phase. If successive phases of work are recommended, each phase must culminate in a decision point. The recommendations must not apply to more than two phases of work. The recommendations must state whether advancing to a subsequent phase is contingent on positive results in the previous phase.

INSTRUCTION:In some specific cases, the qualified person may not be in a position to make meaningful recommendations for further work. Generally, these situations will be limited to properties under development or in production where material exploration activities and engineering studies have largely concluded. In such cases, the qualified person should explain why they are not making further recommendations.

Item 27: References — Include a detailed list of all references cited in the technical report.

Companion Policy 43-101CP — To National Instrument 43-101 Standards of Disclosure for Mineral Projects

Table of Contents

This companion policy (the "Policy") sets out the views of the Canadian securities regulatory authorities (the "securities regulatory authorities" or "we") as to how we interpret and apply certain provisions of National Instrument 43-101 and Form 43-101F1 (the "Instrument").

General Guidance

(1) **Application of the Instrument** — The definition of "disclosure" in the Instrument includes oral and written disclosure. The Instrument establishes standards for disclosure of scientific and technical information regarding mineral projects and requires that the disclosure be based on a technical report or other information prepared by or under the supervision of a qualified person. The Instrument does not apply to disclosure concerning petroleum, natural gas, bituminous sands or shales, groundwater, coal bed methane, or other substances that do not fall within the meaning of the term "mineral project" in section 1.1 of the Instrument.

(2) **Supplements Other Requirements** — The Instrument supplements other continuous disclosure requirements of securities legislation that apply to reporting issuers in all business sectors.

(3) **Forward-Looking Information** — Part 4 of National Instrument 51-102 *Continuous Disclosure Obligations* (NI 51-102) sets out the requirements for disclosing forward-looking information. Frequently, scientific and technical information about a mineral project includes or is based on forward-looking information. A mining issuer must comply with the requirements of Part 4A of NI 51-102, including identifying forward-looking information, stating material factors and assumptions used, and providing the required cautions. Examples of forward-looking information include metal price assumptions, cash flow forecasts, projected capital and operating costs, metal or mineral recoveries, mine life and production rates, and other assumptions used in preliminary economic assessments, pre-feasibility studies, and feasibility studies.

(4) **Materiality** — An issuer should determine materiality in the context of the issuer's overall business and financial condition taking into account qualitative and quantitative factors, assessed in respect of the issuer as a whole.

In making materiality judgements, an issuer should consider a number of factors that cannot be captured in a simple bright-line standard or test, including the potential effect on both the market price and value of the issuer's securities in light of the current market activity. An assessment of materiality depends on the context. Information that is immaterial today could be material tomorrow; an item of information that is immaterial alone could be material if it is aggregated with other items.

(5) **Property Material to the Issuer** — An actively trading mining issuer, in most circumstances, will have at least one material property. We will generally assess an issuer's view of the materiality of a property based on the issuer's disclosure record, its deployment of resources, and other indicators. For example, we will likely conclude that a property is material if

    (a) the issuer's disclosure record is focused on the property;

    (b) the issuer's disclosure indicates or suggests the results are significant or important;

    (c) the cumulative and projected acquisition costs or proposed exploration expenditures are significant compared to the issuer's other material properties; or

    (d) the issuer is raising significant money or devoting significant resources to the exploration and development of the property.

In determining if a property is material, the issuer should consider how important or significant the property is to the issuer's overall business and in comparison to its other properties. For example

    (e) more advanced stage properties will, in most cases, be more material than earlier stage properties;

    (f) historical expenditures or book value might not be a good indicator of materiality for an inactive property if the issuer is focussing its resources on new properties;

    (g) a small interest in a sizeable property might, in the circumstances, not be material to the issuer;

    (h) a royalty or similar interest in an advanced property could be material to the issuer in comparison to its active projects; or

    (i) several non-material properties in an area or region, when taken as a whole, could be material to the issuer.

(6) **Industry Best Practices Guidelines** — While the Instrument sets standards for disclosure of scientific and technical information about a mineral project, the standards and methodologies for collecting, analysing, and verifying this information are the responsibility of the qualified person. The Canadian Institute of Mining, Metallurgy and Petroleum ("CIM") has published and adopted several industry best practice guidelines to assist qualified persons and other industry practitioners. These guidelines, as amended and supplemented, are posted on www.cim.org, and include

 (a) Exploration Best Practice Guidelines — adopted August 20, 2000;

 (b) Guidelines for Reporting of Diamond Exploration Results — adopted March 9, 2003; and

 (c) Estimation of Mineral Resources and Mineral Reserves Best Practice Guidelines — adopted November 23, 2003, and related commodity-specific appendices.

The Instrument does not specifically require the qualified person to follow the CIM best practices guidelines. However, we think that a qualified person, acting in compliance with the professional standards of competence and ethics established by their professional association, will generally use procedures and methodologies that are consistent with industry standard practices, as established by CIM or similar organizations in other jurisdictions. Issuers that disclose scientific and technical information that does not conform to industry standard practices could be making misleading disclosure, which is an offence under securities legislation.

(7) **Objective Standard of Reasonableness** — Where a determination about the definitions or application of a requirement in the Instrument turns on reasonableness, the test is objective, not subjective. It is not sufficient for an officer of an issuer or a qualified person to determine that they personally believe the matter under consideration. The individual must form an opinion as to what a reasonable person would believe in the circumstances.

(8) **Improper Use of Terms in the French Language** — For an issuer preparing its disclosure using the French language, the words "gisement" and "gîte" have different meanings and using them interchangeably or in the wrong context may be misleading. The word "gisement" means a mineral deposit that is a continuous, well-defined mass of material containing a sufficient volume of mineralized material that can be or has been mined legally and economically. The word "gîte" means a mineral deposit that is a continuous, defined mass of material, containing a volume of mineralized material that has had no demonstration of economic viability.

PART 1 — DEFINITIONS AND INTERPRETATION

1.1 Definitions — (1) "acceptable foreign code" — The definition of "acceptable foreign code" in the Instrument lists five internationally recognized foreign codes that govern the estimation and disclosure of mineral resources and mineral reserves. The JORC Code, PERC Code, SAMREC Code, and Certification Code use mineral resource and mineral reserve definitions and categories that are substantially the same as the CIM definitions mandated in the Instrument. These codes also use mineral resource and mineral reserve categories that are based on or consistent with the International Reporting Template, published by the Committee for Mineral Reserves International Reporting Standards ("the CRIRSCO Template"), as amended.

We think other foreign codes will generally meet the test in the definition if they

 (a) have been adopted or recognized by appropriate government authorities or professional organizations in the foreign jurisdiction; and

 (b) use mineral resource and mineral reserve categories that are based on the CRIRSCO Template, and are substantially the same as the CIM definitions mandated in the Instrument, the JORC Code, the PERC Code, the SAMREC Code, and the Certification Code, as amended and supplemented.

Appendix A.1 to the Policy provides a list of additional codes that we think satisfy the definition of "acceptable foreign code". We will publish updates to the list periodically. We will also consider submissions from market participants regarding the proposed addition of foreign codes to the list. Submissions should explain the basis for concluding that the proposed foreign code meets the test in the definition and include appropriate supporting documentation.

(2) "effective date" — This is the cut-off date for the scientific and technical information included in the technical report. Under section 8.1 of the Instrument, the qualified person must provide their certificate as at the effective date of the technical report and specify this date in their certificate. The effective date can precede the date of signing the technical report but if there is too long a period between these dates, the issuer is exposed to the risk that new material information could become available and the technical report would then not be current.

(3) "mineral project" — The definition of "mineral project" in the Instrument includes a royalty or similar interest. Scientific and technical disclosure regarding all types of royalty interests in a mineral project is subject to the Instrument.

(4) "preliminary economic assessment" — The term "preliminary economic assessment", which can include a study commonly referred to as a scoping study, is defined in the Instrument. A preliminary economic assessment might be based on measured, indicated, or inferred mineral resources, or a combination of any of these. We consider these types of economic analyses to include disclosure of forecast mine production rates that might contain capital costs to develop and sustain the mining operation, operating costs, and projected cash flows.

(5) "professional association" — Paragraph (a)(ii) of the definition of "professional association" in the Instrument includes a test for determining what constitutes an acceptable foreign association. In assessing whether we think a foreign professional association meets this test, we will consider the reputation of the association and whether it is substantially similar to a professional association in a jurisdiction of Canada.

Appendix A to the Policy provides a list of the foreign associations that we think meet all the tests in the definition as of the effective date of the Instrument. We will publish updates to the list periodically. An issuer that wishes to rely on a qualified person that is a member of a professional association not included in Appendix A but which the issuer believes meets the tests in the Instrument, may make submissions to have the association added to Appendix A. Submissions should include appropriate supporting documentation. The issuer should allow sufficient time for its submissions to be considered before naming the qualified person in connection with its disclosure or filing any technical report signed by the qualified person.

The listing of a professional association on Appendix A is only for purposes of the Instrument and does not supersede or alter local requirements where geoscience or engineering is a regulated profession.

(6) definitions that include "property" — The Instrument defines two different types of properties (early stage exploration, advanced) and requires a technical report to summarize material information about the subject property. We consider a property, in the context of the Instrument, to include multiple mineral claims or other documents of title that are contiguous or in such close proximity that any underlying mineral deposits would likely be developed using common infrastructure.

(7) "qualified person" — The definition of "qualified person" in the Instrument does not include engineering and geoscience technicians, engineers and geoscientists in training, and equivalent designations that restrict the individual's scope of practice or require the individual to practise under the supervision of another professional engineer, professional geoscientist, or equivalent.

Paragraph (d) of the definition requires a qualified person to be "in good standing with a professional association". We interpret this to include satisfying any related registration, licensing, or similar requirements. Canadian provincial and territorial legislation requires a qualified person to be registered if practising in a jurisdiction of Canada. It is the responsibility of the qualified person, in compliance with their professional association's code of ethics, to comply with laws requiring licensure of geoscientists and engineers.

Paragraph (e) of the definition includes a test for what constitutes an acceptable membership designation in a foreign professional association. Appendix A to the Policy provides a list of the membership designations that we think meet this test as of the effective date of the Instrument. We will update the list periodically. In assessing whether we think a membership designation meets the test, we will consider whether it is substantially similar to a membership designation in a professional association in a jurisdiction of Canada.

Subparagraph (e)(ii)(B) includes the concept of "demonstrated expertise in the field of mineral exploration or mining". We generally interpret this to mean having at least five years of professional experience and satisfying an additional entrance requirement relating to level of responsibility. Some examples of such a requirement are:

(a) at least three years in a position of responsibility where the person was depended on for significant participation and decision-making;

(b) experience of a responsible nature and involving the exercise of independent judgment in at least three of those years;

(c) at least five years in a position of major responsibility, or a senior technical position of responsibility.

(8) "technical report" — A report may constitute a "technical report" as defined in the Instrument, even if prepared considerably before the date the technical report is required to be filed, provided the information in the technical report remains accurate and complete as at the required filing date. However, a report that an issuer files that is not required under the Instrument will not be considered a technical report until the Instrument requires the issuer to file it *and* the issuer has filed the required certificates and consents of qualified persons.

The definition requires the technical report to include a summary of all material information about the subject property. The qualified person is responsible for preparing the technical report. Therefore, it is the qualified person, not the issuer, who has the responsibility of determining the materiality of the scientific or technical information to be included in the technical report.

1.5 Independence — (1) Guidance on Independence — Section 1.5 of the Instrument provides the test an issuer and a qualified person must apply to determine whether a qualified person is independent of the issuer. When an independent qualified person is required, an issuer must always apply the test in section 1.5 to confirm that the requirement is met.

Applying this test, the following are examples of when we would consider that a qualified person is not independent. These examples are not a complete list of non-independence situations.

We consider a qualified person is not independent when the qualified person

(a) is an employee, insider, or director of the issuer;

(b) is an employee, insider, or director of a related party of the issuer;

(c) is a partner of any person or company in paragraph (a) or (b);

(d) holds or expects to hold securities, either directly or indirectly, of the issuer or a related party of the issuer;

(e) holds or expects to hold securities, either directly or indirectly, in another issuer that has a direct or indirect interest in the property that is the subject of the technical report or in an adjacent property;

(f) is an employee, insider, or director of another issuer that has a direct or indirect interest in the property that is the subject of the technical report or in an adjacent property;

(g) has or expects to have, directly or indirectly, an ownership, royalty, or other interest in the property that is the subject of the technical report or an adjacent property; or

(h) has received the majority of their income, either directly or indirectly, in the three years preceding the date of the technical report from the issuer or a related party of the issuer.

For the purposes of (d) above, a related party of the issuer means an affiliate, associate, subsidiary, or control person of the issuer as those terms are defined in securities legislation.

(2) Independence Not Compromised — In some cases, it might be reasonable to consider the qualified person's independence is not compromised even though the qualified person holds an interest in the issuer's securities, the securities of another issuer with an interest in the subject property, or in an adjacent property. The issuer needs to determine whether a reasonable person would consider such interest would interfere with the qualified person's judgement regarding the preparation of the technical report.

PART 2 — REQUIREMENTS APPLICABLE TO ALL DISCLOSURE

2.1 Requirements Applicable to All Disclosure — (1) Disclosure is the Responsibility of the Issuer — Primary responsibility for public disclosure remains with the issuer and its directors and officers. The qualified person is responsible for preparing or supervising the preparation of the technical report and providing scientific and technical advice in accordance with applicable professional standards. The proper use, by or on behalf of the issuer, of the technical report and other scientific and technical information provided by the qualified person is the responsibility of the issuer and its directors and officers.

The onus is on the issuer and its directors and officers and, in the case of a document filed with a securities regulatory authority, each signatory to the document, to ensure that disclosure in the document is consistent with the related technical report or advice. An issuer should consider having the qualified person review disclosure that summarizes or restates the technical report or the technical advice or opinion to ensure that the disclosure is accurate.

(2) Material Information not yet Confirmed by a Qualified Person — Securities legislation requires an issuer to disclose material facts and to make timely disclosure of material changes. We recognize that there can be circumstances in which an issuer expects that certain information concerning a mineral project may be material notwithstanding the fact that a qualified person has not prepared or supervised the preparation of the information. In this situation, the issuer may file a confidential material change report concerning this information while a qualified person reviews the information. Once a qualified person has confirmed the information, the issuer can issue a news release and the basis of confidentiality will end.

During the period of confidentiality, persons in a special relationship to the issuer are prohibited from tipping or trading until the information is disclosed to the public. National Policy 51-201 *Disclosure Standards* provides further guidance about materiality and timely disclosure obligations.

(3) Use of Plain Language — An issuer should apply plain language principles when preparing disclosure regarding mineral projects on its material properties, keeping in mind that the investing public are often not mining experts. An issuer should present written disclosure in an easy to read format using clear and unambiguous language and, wherever possible, should present data in table format. This includes information in the technical report, to the extent possible. We recognize that the technical report does not always lend itself well to plain language and therefore the issuer might want to consult the responsible qualified person when restating the data and conclusions from a technical report in its public disclosure.

2.2 All Disclosure of Mineral Resources or Mineral Reserves — Use of GSC Paper 88-21 A qualified person estimating mineral resources or mineral reserves for coal may follow the guidelines of Paper 88-21 of the Geological Survey of Canada: A Standardized Coal Resource/Reserve Reporting System for Canada, as amended ("Paper 88-21"). However, for all disclosure of mineral resources or mineral reserves for coal, section 2.2 of the Instrument requires an issuer to use the equivalent mineral resource or mineral reserve categories set out in the CIM Definition Standards and not the categories set out in Paper 88-21.

2.3 Restricted Disclosure — (1) Economic Analysis — Subject to subsection 2.3(3) of the Instrument, paragraph 2.3(1)(b) of the Instrument prohibits the disclosure of the results of an economic analysis that includes or is based on inferred mineral resources, an historical estimate, or an exploration target.

CIM considers the confidence in inferred mineral resources is insufficient to allow the meaningful application of technical and economic parameters or to enable an evaluation of economic viability worthy of public disclosure. The Instrument extends this prohibition to exploration targets because such targets are conceptual and have even less confidence than inferred mineral resources. The Instrument also extends the prohibition to historical estimates because they have not been demonstrated or verified to the standards required for mineral resources or mineral reserves and, therefore, cannot be used in an economic analysis suitable for public disclosure.

(2) Use of Term "Ore" — We consider the use of the word "ore" in the context of mineral resource estimates to be potentially misleading because "ore" implies technical feasibility and economic viability that should only be attributed to mineral reserves.

(3) Exceptions — The Instrument permits an issuer to disclose the results of an economic analysis that uses inferred mineral resources, provided the issuer complies with the requirements of subsection 2.3(3). The issuer must also include the cautionary statement under paragraph 3.4(e) of the Instrument, which applies to disclosure of all economic analyses of mineral resources, to further alert investors to the limitations of the information. The exception under subsection 2.3(3) does not allow an issuer to disclose the results of an economic analysis using an exploration target or an historical estimate.

(4) Impact of Preliminary Economic Assessment on Previous Feasibility or Pre- Feasibility Studies — An issuer may disclose the results of a preliminary economic assessment that includes inferred mineral resources, after it has completed a feasibility study or pre-feasibility study that establishes mineral reserves, if the disclosure complies with subsection 2.3(3) of the Instrument. Under paragraph 2.3(3)(c), the issuer must discuss the impact of the preliminary economic assessment on the mineral reserves and feasibility study or pre-feasibility study. This means considering and disclosing whether the existing mineral reserves and feasibility study or pre-feasibility study are still current and valid in light of the key assumptions and parameters used in the preliminary economic assessment.

For example, if the preliminary economic assessment considers the potential economic viability of developing a satellite deposit in conjunction with the main development project, then the existing mineral reserves, feasibility study, and production scenario could still be current. However, if the preliminary economic assessment significantly modifies the key variables in the feasibility study, including metal prices, mine plan, and costs, the feasibility study and mineral reserves might no longer be current.

(5) Gross Value of Metal or Mineral — We interpret gross metal value or gross mineral value to include any representation of the potential monetary value of the metal or mineral in the ground that does not take into consideration the costs, recoveries, and other relevant factors associated with the extraction and recovery of the metal or mineral. We think this type of disclosure is misleading because it overstates the potential value of the mineral deposit.

(6) Cautionary Language and Explanations — The requirements of subsections 2.3(2), 2.3(3), and 3.4(e) of the Instrument mean the issuer must include the required cautionary statements and explanations *each time* it makes the disclosure permitted by these exceptions. These subsections also require the cautionary statements to have equal prominence with the rest of the disclosure. We interpret this to mean equal size type and proximate location. The issuer should consider including the cautionary language and explanations in the same paragraph as, or immediately following, the disclosure permitted by these exceptions.

2.4 Disclosure of Historical Estimates — (1) Required Disclosure — An issuer may disclose an estimate of resources or reserves made before it entered into an agreement to acquire an interest in the property, provided the issuer complies with the conditions set out in section 2.4 of the Instrument. Under this requirement, the issuer must provide the required disclosure *each time* it discloses the historical estimate, until the issuer has verified the historical estimate as a current mineral resource or mineral reserve. The required cautionary statements must also have equal prominence (see the discussion in subsection 2.3(6) of the Policy).

(2) Source and Date — Under paragraph 2.4(a) of the Instrument, the issuer must disclose the source and date of the historical estimate. This means the original source and date of the estimate, not third party documents, databases or other sources, including government databases, which may also report the historical estimate.

(3) Suitability for Public Disclosure — Under paragraph 2.4(b) of the Instrument, an issuer that discloses an historical estimate must comment on its relevance and reliability. In determining whether to disclose an historical estimate, an issuer should consider whether the historical estimate is suitable for public disclosure.

(4) Historical Estimate Categories — Under paragraph 2.4(d) of the Instrument, an issuer must explain any differences between the categories used in the historical estimate and those set out in sections 1.2 and 1.3 of the Instrument. If the historical estimate was prepared using an acceptable foreign code, the issuer may satisfy this requirement by identifying the acceptable foreign code.

(5) Technical Report Trigger — The disclosure of an historical estimate will not trigger the requirement to file a technical report under paragraph 4.2(1)(j) of the Instrument if the issuer discloses the historical estimate in accordance with section 2.4 of the Instrument, including the cautionary statements required under paragraph 2.4(g).

An issuer could trigger the filing of a technical report under paragraph 4.2(1)(j) if it discloses the historical estimate in a manner that suggests or treats the historical estimate as a current mineral resource or mineral reserve. We will consider an issuer is treating the historical estimate as a current mineral resource or mineral reserve in its disclosure if, for example, it

(a) uses the historical estimate in an economic analysis or as the basis for a production decision;

(b) states it will be adding on or building on the historical estimate; or

(c) adds the historical estimate to current mineral resource or mineral reserve estimates.

PART 3 — ADDITIONAL REQUIREMENTS FOR WRITTEN DISCLOSURE

3.3 Requirements Applicable to Written Disclosure of Exploration Information — Adjacent Property Information — It is an offence under securities legislation to make misleading disclosure. An issuer may disclose in writing scientific and technical information about an adjacent property. However, in order for the disclosure not to be misleading, the issuer should clearly distinguish between the information from the adjacent property and its own property and not state or imply the issuer will obtain similar information from its own property.

3.5 Exception for Written Disclosure Already Filed — Section 3.5 of the Instrument provides that the disclosure requirements of sections 3.2 and 3.3 and paragraphs 3.4(a), (c) and (d) of the Instrument may be satisfied by referring to a previously filed document that includes the required disclosure. However, the disclosure as a whole must be factual, complete, and balanced and not present or omit information in a manner that is misleading.

PART 4 — OBLIGATION TO FILE A TECHNICAL REPORT

4.2 Obligation to File a Technical Report in Connection with Certain Written Disclosure about Mineral Projects on Material Properties — (1) **Information Circular Trigger (4.2(1)(c))** —

(a) The requirement for "prospectus-level disclosure" in an information circular does not make this document a "prospectus" such that the prospectus trigger applies. The information circular is a separate trigger that applies only in certain situations specified in the Instrument.

(b) Paragraph 4.2(1)(c) of the Instrument requires the issuer to file technical reports for properties that will be material to the resulting issuer. Often the resulting issuer is not the issuer filing the information circular. In determining if it must file a technical report on a particular property, the issuer should consider if the property will be material to the resulting issuer after the completion of the proposed transaction.

(c) Our view is that the issuer filing the information circular does not need to file a technical report on its SEDAR profile if

(i) the other party to the transaction has filed the technical report;

(ii) the information circular refers to the other party's SEDAR profile; and

(iii) on completion of the transaction, technical reports for all material properties are filed on the resulting issuer's SEDAR profile or the SEDAR profile of a wholly-owned subsidiary.

(2) **Take-Over Bid Circular Trigger (4.2(1)(i))** — For purposes of the take-over bid circular, the issuer referred to in the introductory language of subsection 4.2(1) of the Instrument and the offeror referred to in paragraph (i) of this subsection are the same entity. Since the offeror is the issuer that files the circular, the technical report trigger applies to properties that are material to the offeror.

(3) **First Time Disclosure Trigger (4.2(1)(j)(i))** — In most cases, we think that first time disclosure of mineral resources, mineral reserves, or the results of a preliminary economic assessment, on a property material to the issuer will constitute a material change in the affairs of the issuer.

(4) **Property Acquisitions — 45-Day Filing Requirement** — Subsection 4.2(5) of the Instrument requires an issuer in certain cases to file a technical report within 45 days to support first time disclosure of mineral resources, mineral reserves, or the results of a preliminary economic assessment, on a property material to the issuer. Property materiality is not contingent on the issuer having acquired an actual interest in the property or having formal agreements in place. In many cases, the property will become material at the letter of intent stage, even if subject to conditions such as the approval of a third party or completion of a due diligence review. In such cases, the 45-day period will begin to run from the time the issuer first discloses the mineral resources, mineral reserves, or results of a preliminary economic assessment.

(5) **Property Acquisitions — Other Alternatives for Disclosure of Previous Estimates** — If an issuer options or agrees to buy a property material to the issuer, any previous estimates of mineral resources or mineral reserves on the property will be in many cases material information that the issuer must disclose.

The issuer has a number of options available for disclosing the previous estimate without triggering a technical report within 45 days. If the previous estimate is not well-documented, the issuer may choose to disclose this information as an exploration target, in compliance with subsection 2.3(2) of the Instrument. Alternatively, the issuer may be able to disclose the previous estimate as an historical estimate, in compliance with section 2.4 of the Instrument. Both these options require the issuer to include certain cautionary language and prohibit the issuer from using the previous estimates in an economic analysis.

In circumstances where the previous estimate is supported by a technical report prepared for another issuer, the issuer may be able to disclose the previous estimate as a mineral resource or mineral reserve, in compliance with subsection 4.2(7) of the Instrument. In this case, the issuer will still be required to file a technical report. However, it will have up to 180 days to do so.

(6) **Production Decision** — The Instrument does not require an issuer to file a technical report to support a production decision because the decision to put a mineral project into production is the responsibility of the issuer, based on information provided by qualified persons. The development of a mining operation typically involves large capital expenditures and a high degree of risk and uncertainty. To reduce this risk and uncertainty, the issuer typically makes its production decision based on a comprehensive feasibility study of established mineral reserves.

We recognize that there might be situations where the issuer decides to put a mineral project into production without first establishing mineral reserves supported by a technical report and completing a feasibility study. Historically, such projects have a much higher risk of economic or technical failure. To avoid making misleading disclosure, the issuer should disclose that it is not basing its production decision on a feasibility study of mineral reserves demonstrating economic and technical viability and should provide adequate disclosure of the increased uncertainty and the specific economic and technical risks of failure associated with its production decision.

Under paragraph 1.4(e) of Form 51-102F1, an issuer must also disclose in its MD&A whether a production decision or other significant development is based on a technical report.

(7) **Shelf Life of Technical Reports** — Economic analyses in technical reports are based on commodity prices, costs, sales, revenue, and other assumptions and projections that can change significantly over short periods of time. As a result, economic information in a technical report can quickly become outdated. Continued reference to outdated technical reports or economic projections without appropriate context and cautionary language could result in misleading disclosure. Where an issuer has triggered the requirement to file a technical report under subsection 4.2(1), it should

consider the current validity of economic assumptions in its existing technical report to determine if the technical report is still current. An issuer might be able to extend the life of a technical report by having a qualified person include appropriate sensitivity analyses of the key economic variables.

(8) **Technical Reports Must be Current and Complete** — A "technical report" as defined in the Instrument must include in summary form *all* material scientific and technical information about the property. Any time an issuer is required to file a technical report, that report must be complete and current. There should only be one current technical report on a property at any point in time. When an issuer files a new technical report, it will replace any previously filed technical report as the current technical report on that property. This means the new technical report must include any material information documented in a previously filed technical report, to the extent that this information is still current and relevant.

If an issuer gets a new qualified person to update a previously filed technical report prepared by a different qualified person, the new qualified person must take responsibility for the entire technical report, including any information referenced or summarized from a previous technical report.

(9) **Limited Provision for Addendums** — The only exception to the requirement to file a complete technical report is under subsection 4.2(3) of the Instrument. An issuer may file an addendum if it is for a technical report that it originally filed with a preliminary short form prospectus or preliminary long form prospectus and new material scientific or technical information becomes available before the issuance of the final receipt.

(10) **Exception from Requirement to File Technical Report if Information Included in a Previously Filed Technical Report** — Subsection 4.2(8) of the Instrument provides an exemption from the technical report filing requirement if the disclosure document does not contain any new material scientific or technical information about a property that is the subject of a previously filed technical report.

In our view, a change to mineral resources or reserves due to mining depletion from a producing property generally will not constitute new material scientific or technical information as the change should be reasonably predictable based on an issuer's continuous disclosure record.

(11) **Filing on SEDAR** — If an issuer is required under National Instrument 13-101 *System for Electronic Document Analysis and Retrieval (SEDAR)* to be an electronic filer, then all technical reports must be prepared so that the issuer can file them on SEDAR. Figures required in the technical report must be included in the technical report filed on SEDAR and therefore should be prepared in electronic format.

(12) **Reports Not Required by the Instrument** — The securities regulatory authorities in most Canadian jurisdictions require an issuer to file, if not already filed with them, any record or disclosure material that the issuer files with any other securities regulator, including geological reports filed with stock exchanges. In other cases, an issuer might wish to file voluntarily a report in the form of a technical report. The Instrument does not prohibit an issuer from filing such reports in these situations. However, any document purporting to be a technical report must comply with the Instrument.

When an issuer files a report in the form of a technical report that is not required to be filed by the Instrument, the issuer is not required to file a consent of qualified person that complies with subsection 8.3(1) of the Instrument. The issuer should consider filing a cover letter with the report explaining why the issuer is filing the report and indicating that it is not filing the report as a requirement of the Instrument. Alternatively, the issuer should consider filing a modified consent with the report that provides the same information.

(13) **Preliminary Short Form Prospectus** — Under paragraph 4.2(1)(b) of the Instrument, an issuer must file a technical report with a preliminary short form prospectus if the prospectus discloses for the first time mineral resources, mineral reserves, or the results of a preliminary economic assessment that constitute a material change in relation to the issuer, or a change in this information, if the change constitutes a material change in relation to the issuer.

If this information is not disclosed for the first time in the preliminary short form prospectus itself, but is repeated or incorporated by reference into the preliminary short form prospectus, the technical report must still be filed at the same time as the preliminary short form prospectus. Subsections 4.2(5) and (7) of the Instrument, in certain limited circumstances, permit the delayed filing of a technical report. For example, an issuer normally has 45 days, or in some cases 180 days, to file a technical report supporting the first time disclosure of a mineral resource. However, if a preliminary short form prospectus that includes the prescribed disclosure is filed during the period of the delay, subparagraphs 4.2(5)(a)(i) and 4.2(7)(c)(i) require the technical report to be filed on the date of filing the preliminary short form prospectus.

(14) **Triggers with Thresholds** — The technical report triggers in paragraphs 4.2(1)(b), (i) and (j) only apply if the relevant disclosure meets certain thresholds. In these cases, the technical report filing requirement is triggered only for the material property or properties that meet the thresholds.

(15) **Triggers with Permitted Filing Delays** — Subsections 4.2(5), (6) and (7) allow technical reports in certain circumstances to be filed later than the disclosure documents they support. In these cases, once the requirement to file the technical report has been triggered, the issuer remains subject to the requirement irrespective of subsequent developments relating to the property, including, for example, the sale or abandonment of the property.

4.3 Required Form of Technical Report — (1) **Review** — Disclosure and technical reports filed under the Instrument may be subject to review by the securities regulatory authorities. If an issuer that is required to file a technical report under the Instrument files a technical report that does not meet the requirements of the Instrument, the issuer has not complied with securities legislation. This includes filing certificates and consents that do not comply with subsections 8.1(2) and 8.3(1) of the Instrument.

(2) **Filing Other Scientific and Technical Reports** — An issuer might have other reports or documents containing scientific or technical information, prepared by or under the supervision of a qualified person, which are not in the form of a technical report. We consider that filing such information on SEDAR as a technical report could be misleading. An issuer wishing to provide public access to these documents should consider posting them on its website.

(3) **Preparation in English or French** — Section 4.3 of the Instrument requires a technical report to be prepared in English or French. Reports prepared in a different language and translated into English or French are not acceptable due to the highly technical nature of the disclosure and the difficulties of ensuring accurate and reliable translations.

PART 5 — AUTHOR OF THE TECHNICAL REPORT

5.1 Prepared by a Qualified Person — (1) **Selection of Qualified Person** — It is the responsibility of the issuer and its directors and officers to retain a qualified person who meets the criteria listed under the definition of qualified person in the Instrument, including having the relevant experience and competence for the subject matter of the technical report.

(2) **Assistance of Non-Qualified Persons** — A person who is not a qualified person may work on a project. If a qualified person relies on the work of a non-qualified person to prepare a technical report or to provide information or advice to the issuer, the qualified person must take responsibility for that work, information, or advice. The qualified person must take whatever steps are appropriate, in their professional judgement, to ensure that the work, information, or advice that they rely on is sound.

(3) **Exemption from Qualified Person Requirement** — The securities regulatory authorities will rarely grant requests for exemption from the requirement that the qualified person belong to a professional association.

(4) More than One Qualified Person — Section 5.1 of the Instrument provides that one or more qualified persons must prepare or supervise the preparation of a technical report. Some technical reports, particularly for advanced properties, could require the involvement of several qualified persons with different areas of expertise. In that case, each qualified person taking responsibility for a part of the technical report must sign the technical report and provide a certificate and consent under Part 8 of the Instrument.

However, section 5.2 and Part 8 of the Instrument allow qualified persons who supervised the preparation of all or part of the technical report to take overall responsibility for the work conducted under their supervision by other qualified persons. While supervising qualified persons do not need to be experts in all aspects of the work they supervise, they should be sufficiently knowledgeable about the subject matter to understand the information and opinions for which they are accepting responsibility. Where there are supervising qualified persons, only the supervising qualified persons must sign the technical report and provide their certificates and consents.

(5) A Qualified Person Must Be Responsible for All Items of Technical Report — Section 5.1 of the Instrument requires a technical report to be prepared by or under the supervision of one or more qualified persons. By implication, this means that at least one qualified person must take responsibility for each section or item of the technical report, including any information incorporated from previously filed technical reports. If the qualified person, in response to a particular item, refers to the equivalent item in a previously filed technical report, the qualified person is implicitly saying that the information is still reliable and current and there have been no material changes. This would normally involve the qualified person doing a certain amount of background work and validation.

(6) Previous Mineral Resources or Mineral Reserves — When a technical report includes a mineral resource or mineral reserve estimate prepared by another qualified person for a previously filed technical report, under section 5.2 and Part 8 of the Instrument, one of the qualified persons preparing the new technical report must take responsibility for those estimates. In doing this, that qualified person should make whatever investigations are necessary to reasonably rely on the estimates.

5.2 Execution of Technical Report — Section 5.2 and subsection 8.1(1) of the Instrument require the qualified person to date, sign, and if the qualified person has a seal, seal the technical report and certificate. Section 8.3 of the Instrument requires the qualified person to date and sign the consent. If a person's name appears in an electronic document with (signed by) or (sealed) next to the person's name or there is a similar indication in the document, the securities regulatory authorities will consider that the person has signed and sealed the document. Although not required, the qualified person may sign or seal maps and drawings in the same manner.

5.3 Independent Technical Report — (1) Independent Qualified Persons — Subsection 5.3(1) of the Instrument requires that one or more independent qualified persons prepare or supervise the preparation of the independent technical report. This subsection does not preclude non-independent qualified persons from co-authoring or assisting in the preparation of the technical report. However, to meet the independence requirement, the independent qualified persons must assume overall responsibility for all items of the technical report.

(2) Hundred Percent or Greater Change — Subparagraph 5.3(1)(c)(ii) of the Instrument requires the issuer to file an independent technical report to support its disclosure of a 100 percent or greater change in total mineral resources or total mineral reserves. We interpret this to mean a 100 percent or greater change in either the total tonnage or volume, or total contained metal or mineral content, of the mineral resource or mineral reserve. We also interpret the 100 percent or greater change to apply to mineral resources and mineral reserves separately. Therefore, a 100 percent or greater change in mineral resources on a material property will require the issuer to file an independent technical report regardless of any changes to mineral reserves, and vice versa.

(3) Objectivity of Author — We could question the objectivity of the author based on our review of a technical report. In order to preserve the requirement for independence of the qualified person, we could ask the issuer to provide further information, additional disclosure, or the opinion or involvement of another qualified person to address concerns about possible bias or partiality on the part of the author of a technical report.

PART 6 — PREPARATION OF TECHNICAL REPORT

6.1 The Technical Report — Summary of Material Information — Section 1.1 of the Instrument defines a technical report as a report that provides a *summary* of all material scientific and technical information about a property. Instruction (1) to Form 43-101F1 includes similar language. The target audience for technical reports are members of the investing public, many of whom have limited geological and mining expertise. To avoid misleading disclosure, technical reports must provide sufficient detail for a reasonably knowledgeable person to understand the nature and significance of the results, interpretation, conclusions, and recommendations presented in the technical report. However, we do not think that technical reports need to be a repository of all technical data and information about a property or include extensive geostatistical analysis, charts, data tables, assay certificate, drill logs, appendices, and other supporting technical information.

In addition, SEDAR might not be able to accommodate large technical report files. An issuer could have difficulty filing, and more importantly, the public could have difficulty accessing and downloading, large technical reports. An issuer should consider limiting the size of its technical reports to facilitate filing and public access to the reports.

6.2 Current Personal Inspection — (1) Meaning — The current personal inspection referred to in subsection 6.2(1) of the Instrument is the most recent personal inspection of the property, provided there is no new material scientific or technical information about the property since that personal inspection. A personal inspection may constitute a current personal inspection even if the qualified person conducted the personal inspection considerably before the filing date of the technical report, if there is no new material scientific or technical information about the property at the filing date. However, since the qualified person is certifying that the technical report contains all material information about the property, the qualified person should consider taking the necessary steps to verify independently that there has been no material work done on the property since their last site visit.

(2) Importance of Personal Inspection — We consider current personal inspections under section 6.2 of the Instrument to be particularly important because they enable qualified persons to become familiar with conditions on the property. Qualified persons can observe the geology and mineralization, verify the work done and, on that basis, design or review and recommend to the issuer an appropriate exploration or development program. A current personal inspection is required even for properties with poor exposure. In such cases, it could be relevant for a qualified person to observe the depth and type of the overburden and cultural effects that could interfere with the results of the geophysics.

It is the responsibility of the issuer to arrange its affairs so that a qualified person can carry out a current personal inspection. A qualified person, or where required, an independent qualified person, must visit the site and cannot delegate the personal inspection requirement.

(3) More than One Qualified Person — Subsection 6.2(1) of the Instrument requires at least one qualified person who is responsible for preparing or supervising the preparation of the technical report to inspect the property. This is the minimum standard for a current personal inspection. There could be cases in advanced mineral projects where the qualified persons consider it necessary for more than one qualified person to conduct current personal inspections of the property, taking into account the nature of the work on the property and the different expertise required to prepare the technical report.

6.3 Maintenance of Records — Section 6.3 of the Instrument requires an issuer to keep copies of underlying or supporting exploration information for at least 7 years. In our view, the issuer could satisfy this requirement by keeping records in any accessible format, not necessarily in hard copies.

6.4 Limitation on Disclaimers — Paragraph 6.4(1)(a) of the Instrument prohibits certain disclaimers in technical reports.

These disclaimers are also potentially misleading disclosure because, in certain circumstances, securities legislation provides investors with a statutory right of action against a qualified person for a misrepresentation in disclosure that is based upon the qualified person's technical report. That right of action exists despite any disclaimer to the contrary that appears in the technical report. The securities regulatory authorities will generally require the issuer to have its qualified person remove any blanket disclaimers in a technical report that the issuer uses to support its public offering document.

Item 3 of Form 43-101F1 permits a qualified person to insert a limited disclaimer of responsibility in certain specified circumstances.

PART 7 — USE OF FOREIGN CODE

7.1 Use of Foreign Code — Use of Foreign Codes other than Acceptable Foreign Codes — Section 2.2 and Part 7 of the Instrument require an issuer to disclose mineral resources or mineral reserves using either the CIM Definition Standards or an "acceptable foreign code" as defined in the Instrument. If an issuer wishes to announce an acquisition or proposed acquisition of a property that contains estimates of quantity and grade that are not in accordance with the CIM Definition Standards or an acceptable foreign code, the issuer might be able to disclose the estimate as an historical estimate, in compliance with section 2.4 of the Instrument. However, it might be more appropriate for the issuer to disclose the estimate as an exploration target, in compliance with subsection 2.3(2) of the Instrument, if the supporting information for the estimate is not well-documented or if the estimate is not comparable to a category in the CIM Definition Standards or an acceptable foreign code.

PART 8 — CERTIFICATES AND CONSENTS OF QUALIFIED PERSONS FOR TECHNICAL REPORTS

8.1 Certificates of Qualified Persons — (1) Certificates Apply to the Entire Technical Report — Section 8.1 of the Instrument requires certificates that apply to the entire technical report, including any sections that refer to information in a previously filed technical report. At least one qualified person must take responsibility for each Item required by Form 43-101F1.

(2) Deficient Certificates — Certificates must include all the statements required by subsection 8.1(2) of the Instrument. An issuer that files certificates with required statements that are missing or altered to change the intended meaning has not complied with the Instrument.

8.2 Addressed to Issuer — We consider that the technical report is addressed to the issuer if the issuer's name appears on the title page as the party for which the qualified person prepared the technical report. We also consider that the technical report is addressed to the issuer filing the technical report if it is addressed to an issuer that is or will become a wholly-owned subsidiary of the issuer filing the technical report.

8.3 Consents of Qualified Persons — (1) Consent of Experts — If the technical report supports disclosure in a prospectus, the qualified person will likely have to provide an expert consent under the prospectus rules (section 8.1 of National Instrument 41-101 *General Prospectus Requirements* and section 4.1 of National Instrument 44-101 *Short Form Prospectus Distributions*), in addition to any consent of qualified person required under the Instrument.

(2) Deficient Consents — Consents must include all the statements required by subsection 8.3(1) of the Instrument. An issuer that files consents with required statements that are missing or altered to change the intended meaning has not complied with the Instrument. Appendix B to the Policy provides an example of an acceptable consent of a qualified person.

(3) Modified Consents under Subsection 8.3(2) — Subsection 8.3(1) of the Instrument requires the qualified person to identify and read the disclosure that the technical report supports and certify that the disclosure accurately represents the information in the technical report. We recognize that an issuer can become a reporting issuer in a jurisdiction of Canada without the requirement to file a disclosure document listed in subsection 4.2(1) of the Instrument. In these cases, the issuer has the option of filing a modified consent under subsection 8.3(2) of the Instrument that excludes the statements in paragraphs 8.3(1)(b), (c) and (d).

(4) Filing of Full Consent Required — If an issuer files a modified consent under subsection 8.3(2) of the Instrument, it must still file a full consent the next time it files a disclosure document that would normally trigger the filing of a technical report under subsection 4.2(1) of the Instrument. This requirement is set out in subsection 8.3(3) of the Instrument.

(5) Filing of Consent for Technical Reports Not Required by the Instrument — Where an issuer files a technical report voluntarily or as a requirement of a Canadian stock exchange, and the filing is not also required under the Instrument, the report is not a "technical report" subject to the consent requirements under subsection 8.3(1) of the Instrument. Therefore, when the issuer subsequently files a disclosure document that would normally trigger the filing of a technical report under subsection 4.2(1) of the Instrument, the issuer must file the consents of qualified persons in accordance with subsection 8.3(1).

If an issuer files a Filing Statement or other prospectus-level disclosure document with a Canadian stock exchange, and the filing is not also required under the Instrument, the issuer may choose or be required by the stock exchange to file a full consent that includes paragraphs 8.3(1)(b), (c) and (d) of the Instrument as they relate to the Filing Statement or other disclosure document.

PART 9 — EXEMPTIONS

9.2 Exemptions for Royalty or Similar Interests — (1) Royalty or Similar Interest — We consider a "royalty or similar interest" to include a gross overriding royalty, net smelter return, net profit interest, free carried interest, and a product tonnage royalty. We also consider a "royalty or similar interest" to include an interest in a revenue or commodity stream from a proposed or current mining operation, such as the right to purchase certain commodities produced from the operation.

(2) Limitation on Exemptions — The term "royalty or similar interest" does not include a participating or carried interest. Therefore, these exemptions do not apply where the issuer also has a participating or carried interest in the property or the mining operation, either direct or indirect.

(3) Non-Reporting Subsidiaries Included — Properties indirectly owned by an owner or operator that is a reporting issuer in a jurisdiction of Canada, through a subsidiary that is not a reporting issuer, would satisfy the condition of subparagraph 9.2(1)(a)(i) of the Instrument.

(4) **Consideration of Liability** — Holders of royalty or similar interests relying on the exemption in subsection 9.2(1) of the Instrument should consider, in the absence of a technical report of the royalty holder, who will be liable under applicable securities legislation for any misrepresentations in the royalty holder's scientific or technical information.

APPENDIX A — ACCEPTED FOREIGN ASSOCIATIONS AND MEMBERSHIP DESIGNATIONS

Foreign Association	Membership Designation
American Institute of Professional Geologists (AIPG)	Certified Professional Geologist (CPG)
The Society for Mining, Metallurgy and Exploration, Inc. (SME)	Registered Member
Mining and Metallurgical Society of America (MMSA)	Qualified Professional (QP)
Any state in the United States of America	Licensed or certified as a professional engineer
European Federation of Geologists (EFG)	European Geologist (EurGeol)
Institute of Geologists of Ireland (IGI)	Professional Member (PGeo)
Institute of Materials, Minerals and Mining (IMMM)	Professional Member (MIMMM), Fellow (FIMMM), Chartered Scientist (CSi MIMMM), or Chartered Engineer (CEng MIMMM)
Geological Society of London (GSL)	Chartered Geologist (CGeol)
Australasian Institute of Mining and Metallurgy (AusIMM)	Fellow (FAusIMM) or Chartered Professional Member or Fellow [MAusIMM (CP), FAusIMM (CP)]
Australian Institute of Geoscientists (AIG)	Member (MAIG), Fellow (FAIG) or Registered Professional Geoscientist Member or Fellow (MAIG RPGeo, FAIG RPGeo)
The Institution of Engineers Australia[1] (Engineers Australia)	Chartered Professional Engineer (CPEng)
The Institution of Professional Engineers New Zealand[2] (Engineers New Zealand, IPENZ)	Chartered Professional Engineer (CPEng)
Southern African Institute of Mining and Metallurgy (SAIMM)	Fellow (FSAIMM)
South African Council for Natural Scientific Professions (SACNASP)	Professional Natural Scientist (Pr.Sci.Nat.)
Engineering Council of South Africa (ECSA)	Professional Engineer (Pr.Eng.) or Professional Certificated Engineer (Pr.Cert.Eng.)
Comisión Calificadora de Competencias en Recursos y Reservas Mineras (Chilean Mining Commission)	Registered Member
Russian Society of Subsoil Use Experts[3] (OERN)	Expert

Notes:

1   As of August 16, 2012.

2   As of February 21, 2013.

3   As of February 25, 2016.

[Editor's note: see 43-308.]

APPENDIX A.1 — ADDITIONAL ACCEPTABLE FOREIGN CODES

Russian Code for the Public Reporting of Exploration Results, Mineral Resources and Mineral Reserves[1] (NAEN Code)

APPENDIX B — EXAMPLE OF CONSENT OF QUALIFIED PERSON

[QP's Letterhead] or
[Insert name of QP]
[Insert name of QP's company]
[Insert address of QP or QP's company]

Consent of Qualified Person

I, [name of QP], consent to the public filing of the technical report titled [insert title of report] and dated [insert date of report] (the "Technical Report") by [insert name of issuer filing the report].

I also consent to any extracts from or a summary of the Technical Report in the [insert date and type of disclosure document (i.e. news release, prospectus, AIF, etc.)] of [insert name of issuer making disclosure].

I certify that I have read [date and type of document (i.e. news release, prospectus, AIF, etc.) that the report supports] being filed by [insert name of issuer] and that it fairly and accurately represents the information in the sections of the technical report for which I am responsible.

Dated this [insert date].

.... Signature of Qualified Person [Seal or Stamp]

.... Print name of Qualified Person

Adoption by OSC: (2001) 24 O.S.C.B. 303 and (2000) 23 O.S.C.B. 7815; Request for Comments: (2000) 23 O.S.C.B. 2159 and (1998) 21 O.S.C.B. 4213.

---

[1]As of February 25, 2016.

Adoption of Revised Policy: (2005) 28 O.S.C.B. 10375 and 8117; Request for Comments: 27 O.S.C.B. 7699.

Adoption of Revised Policy: (2011) 34 O.S.C.B. 7067 and (Supp. 2) 1; Request for Comments: (2010) 33 O.S.C.B. 3703.

Amendments to Revised Policy: (2016), 39 O.S.C.B. 1793

Rules: NI 45-101, s. 3.1.

Policies and Orders: CSAN 43-308.

National Policy 43-201 — Mutual Reliance Review System for Prospectuses

Date: November 19, 1999, as amended January 25, 2002 and September 19, 2005

22 O.S.C.B. 7320, 25 O.S.C.B. 485 and 28 O.S.C.B. 7139

[Rescinded (2008) 31 O.S.C.B. 1009; replaced by NPS 11-202]

Adoption by OSC: (1999) 22 O.S.C.B. 7308; Request for Comments: (1998) 21 O.S.C.B. 3889; Replaced NPS 1. Amendment to Policy: 25 O.S.C.B. 485 (January 25, 2002).

Amendment to Policy: (2005) 28 O.S.C.B. 7139.

CSA Staff Notice 43-306 — Technical Reports Filed for Prospectus Offerings

Date: June 2, 2006

29 O.S.C.B. 4508

Purpose

Staff of the Canadian Securities Administrators (the CSA or we) are giving notice of a planned change in the administrative practices related to:

- public access to technical reports and related materials filed with preliminary prospectuses,

- and the technical materials an issuer must file before a member of the CSA will issue a receipt for a preliminary prospectus.

Background

National Instrument 43-1 01 *Standards of Disclosure for Mineral Projects* (NI 43-101) requires mining issuers to file in specified circumstances technical reports prepared and certified by qualified persons (QPs).

Public access to technical reports

Canadian securities legislation requires CSA members to make filed documents publicly available. For documents filed on SEDAR, we generally provide public access on sedar.com. However, as a matter of practice, we have not made the technical reports filed with a preliminary prospectus publicly available on SEDAR until after we issue a receipt for the final prospectus. For all preliminary prospectus filings on and after *July 1, 2006*, we will make these technical reports (and the QPs' certificates and consents) publicly available on SEDAR at the same time we make the preliminary prospectus public. Generally, that will be immediately after filing. Issuers may apply to have these documents kept confidential but we would only grant this request in exceptional circumstances.

Filing of technical reports, QP certificates and consents

If an issuer's filing of a preliminary prospectus triggers a requirement for the issuer to file a technical report, subsection 4.2(4) of NI 43-101 requires the issuer to file the technical report at the same time it files the preliminary prospectus. Part 8 of NI 43-101 requires the issuer to also file a certificate and consent of each QP responsible for preparing or supervising the preparation of each portion of the technical report. As a matter of practice, we have not always required the issuer to file all technical documents (particularly the certificates and consents) before we would issue a receipt for the preliminary prospectus. However, effective immediately, we will generally not issue a receipt for the preliminary prospectus until the issuer files these required documents.

If an issuer files an amended technical report between the filing of the preliminary and final prospectus, NI 43-101 requires the issuer to file new QP certificates and consents with the amended technical report.

Consents of experts in connection with final prospectuses

Prospectus rules require an issuer to file with its final prospectus consents of experts. The rules apply in specific circumstances and require the consents to contain specific language. These requirements are separate from the consent requirements for QPs, contained in NI 43-101. The consents of a QP filed with a final prospectus must meet the requirements of the prospectus rules and NI 43-101.

CSA Staff Notice 43-307 — Mining Technical Reports — Preliminary Economic Assessments

Date: August 16, 2012

35 O.S.C.B. 7597

Introduction

This notice sets out staff's position on several issues regarding the use and disclosure of a "preliminary economic assessment" (**PEA**), as defined in revised National Instrument 43-101 *Standards of Disclosure for Mineral Projects* (**NI 43-101**), which came into force on June 30, 2011.

The economic analysis by way of a PEA is generally the first signal to the public that a mineral project has potential viability. Given the significance of this milestone in the evolution of any mineral project, the market views PEA results as important information.

NI 43-101 defines a PEA as a study, other than a pre-feasibility study (**PFS**) or feasibility study (**FS**), which includes an economic analysis of the potential viability of mineral resources. The terms PFS and FS have the meanings ascribed by the CIM Definition Standards for Mineral Resources and Mineral Reserves, as amended.

When preparing technical reports under revised Form 43-101F1 *Technical Report*, Items 16 to 22 provide a framework for reporting on a PEA, PFS, or FS. Although these studies generally analyse and assess the same geological, engineering, and economic factors, the level of detail, precision, and confidence in the outcomes is significantly different.

PEA as a Proxy for a PFS

We are seeing situations where issuers represent that their PEA, or components of it, have been or will be done at or close to the level of a PFS. In extreme cases, the issuers are representing that the study is a PFS but for the inclusion of inferred mineral resources. In other cases, issuers appear to be treating the PEA as a substitute or proxy for a PFS.

Staff's position

The definition of PEA has two key elements that distinguish it from other studies. First, by definition, it *cannot* be a PFS or FS. Second, a PEA can only demonstrate the *potential* viability of mineral resources. PFS and FS are more comprehensive studies and, therefore, are sufficient to demonstrate the technical and economic viability of a mineral project.

Section 2.3(1)(b) of NI 43-101 does not allow issuers to include inferred mineral resources in a PFS-level economic analysis, whereas section 2.3(3) of NI 43-101 allows issuers to include inferred mineral resources in a PEA. Issuers that blur the boundary between a PEA and a PFS by stating that some or all of the components of the PEA are done at the level of a PFS, run the risk that we may challenge whether the study meets the definition of a PEA. We recommend that issuers do not:

- describe a study as a PEA unless it clearly falls into the definition of a PEA, or

- compare their PEA or any components of it to the standards of a PFS if the study includes inferred mineral resources

Under the second element of the definition, a PEA is a conceptual study of the potential viability of mineral resources. In this context, section 3.4(e) of NI 43-101 requires specific cautionary language indicating that the economic viability of the mineral resources has not been demonstrated. This cautionary language is in addition to the cautionary statement for inferred mineral resources required by section 2.3(3)(a). Any disclosure that implies the PEA has demonstrated economic or technical viability would be contrary to NI 43-101 and the definition of PEA.

We may take the position that an issuer is treating the PEA as a PFS if the issuer:

- does not include the section 3.4(e) cautionary statement with equal prominence each time it discloses the economic analysis of the mineral resources

- uses the PEA as a basis to justify going directly to a FS or a production decision

- discloses mining or mineable mineral resources or uses the term "ore", which is essentially treating mineral resources as mineral reserves, or

- otherwise states or implies that economic viability of the mineral resources has been demonstrated

We caution issuers to ensure that their disclosure of the results of a PEA is not misleading by providing appropriate context, cautionary statements, and discussion of risk sufficient for the public to understand the importance and limitations of the results of the PEA.

PEA Done in Conjunction with a PFS or FS

We are seeing situations where issuers prepare a PEA using inferred mineral resources, concurrently with or as an add-on or update to their PFS or FS. In some cases, the issuer's explanation for doing this is that the issuer has only completed the technical and economic analysis of the inferred mineral resources to the level of a PEA. We are concerned that this interpretation could lead to issuers indirectly including inferred mineral resources in their PFS or FS, in contravention of the section 2.3(1)(b) restriction on including inferred mineral resources in an economic analysis.

Staff's position

CSA broadened the definition of PEA in response to industry concerns that issuers needed to be able to take a step back and re-scope advanced stage projects based on new information or alternative production scenarios. In this context, the revised definition is based on the premise that the issuer is contemplating a significant change in the existing or proposed operation that is materially different from the previous mining study. In most cases, this will also involve considerably different economic parameters and capital investments. Examples of a significant change are a different scale of proposed operation (higher or lower throughput), a different scope of operation (higher or lower grade), the inclusion of other types of mineralization (oxide vs. sulphide), the use of alternative mining methods (open pit vs. underground), or the use of alternative processing technology.

By definition, a PEA is a study other than a PFS or FS. We generally consider that two parallel studies done concurrently or in close time proximity to each other are not in substance separate studies, but components of the same study. Therefore, a study that includes an economic analysis of the potential viability of mineral resources that is done concurrently with or as part of a PFS or FS is not, in our view, a PEA if it:

- has the net effect of incorporating inferred mineral resources into the PFS or FS, even as a sensitivity analysis

- updates, adds to or modifies a PFS or FS to include more optimistic assumptions and parameters not supported by the original study, or

- is a PFS or FS in all respects except name

PEA Disclosure and Technical Report Triggers

In some cases, issuers are disclosing results of potential economic outcomes for their material mineral properties that are not supported by a technical report.

Staff's position

Investors may place significant reliance and make investment decisions based on potential economic outcomes disclosed by the issuer about its material mineral properties. Because this information is significant, it could trigger the filing of a supporting technical report depending upon the materiality of the information to the issuer.

An issuer could trigger the requirement to file a technical report, under section 4.2(1)(j) of NI 43-101, to support disclosure of the results of a PEA if the disclosure is:

- contained in the issuer's corporate presentations, fact sheets, investor relations materials or any statement on the issuer's website, or

- posted or linked from third party documents, reports or articles or otherwise adopted and disseminated by the issuer

Potentially Misleading PEA Results

We are seeing situations where issuers and qualified persons appear to use overly optimistic or highly aggressive assumptions in the PEA, or methodologies that diverge significantly from industry best practice guidelines and standards for exploration and mineral resources. We are concerned that these practices could result in disclosure that is misleading if it is inconsistent with the comparable work of other qualified persons.

Staff's position

Part 4 of National Instrument 51-102 *Continuous Disclosure Obligations* (**NI 51-102**), sets out the requirements for disclosing forward-looking information. The results of a PEA include, or are based on, forward-looking information that is subject to the requirements of Part 4A of NI 51-102. Under Part 4A, an issuer must not disclose forward-looking information unless the issuer has a reasonable basis for the forward-looking information. Hence, any assumption under the PEA must have a reasonable basis in the context of the mineral project. Where we have concerns that some assumptions are overly optimistic or aggressive, we may challenge the qualified person to explain or justify the assumptions, or failing that, ask them to revise the PEA to take a more conservative or reasonable approach.

As discussed in Companion Policy 43-101CP, we think qualified persons acting in compliance with the professional standards of competence and ethics of their professional association will generally use procedures and methods that are consistent with industry best practices and standards. In circumstances where significant divergence might be justified, issuers should consider disclosing the nature of and basis for the divergence to ensure that their disclosure is not misleading.

PEA Disclosure that Includes By-products

In some cases, issuers are disclosing the results of a PEA that includes projected cash flows for by-product commodities that are not included in the mineral resource estimate. This situation can arise where there is insufficient data for the grades of the by-products to be reasonably estimated or estimated to the level of confidence of the mineral resource.

Staff's Position

We consider the inclusion of such by-product commodities in the PEA to be misleading and contrary to the definition of PEA because these commodities are not part of the mineral resource. We caution issuers not to include cash flow projections for any commodity or part of a commodity that has not been properly categorised as a measured, indicated or inferred mineral resource.

Qualified Person — Relevant Experience

We are seeing situations where individuals are taking responsibility for technical reports or parts of reports that support the results of a PEA, while not fully complying with the requirement to have experience relevant to the subject matter of the mineral project and the technical report.

Staff's Position

In addition to the relevant experience requirement in paragraph (c) of the qualified person definition under NI 43-101, CIM definitions provide guidance relating to the qualified person's competence and relevant experience in the commodity, type of deposit, and situation under consideration. In addition, professional associations recognized under NI 43-101 have codes of ethics that may restrict the practice of members based on their area of expertise and competence.

Where we have concerns that a qualified person does not have relevant experience, we will challenge the qualified person to explain or justify their relevant experience, or failing that, ask for a revised technical report from additional qualified persons.

Consequences of Material Deficiencies or Errors

When we identify material NI 43-101 disclosure deficiencies in required documents, we will generally request that the issuer correct the deficiency by restating and re-filing the documents. Where the issuer fails to comply with the request, we may place the issuer on our reporting issuer default lists, seek a commission order requiring the issuer to re-file the documents, or issue a cease trade order until the issuer corrects the deficiency. Even if the issuer corrects the deficiency, we may still pursue enforcement or other regulatory action for the original breach, depending on the circumstances.

If an issuer is considering a prospectus offering, the review of the prospectus filing could take more time if issues such as those noted above are present. Where there are material deficiencies, we may recommend against issuing a receipt for the prospectus.

Issuers should bear in mind that, in any circumstances, correcting material deficiencies or hiring additional qualified persons to certify deficient parts of a technical report can be complex, costly and time-consuming for the issuer.

For further guidance on this issue, please see CSA Staff Notice 51-312 *Harmonized Continuous Disclosure Review Program* and CSA Notice 51-322 *Reporting Issuer Defaults*.

CSA Staff Notice 43-308 — Professional Associations under NI 43-101 Standards of Disclosure for Mineral Projects

Date: **August 16, 2012, revised February 21, 2013**

35 O.S.C.B. 7601 and 36 O.S.C.B. 1849

Introduction

This Notice confirms staff's view that certain professional organizations meet the tests set out in National Instrument 43-101 *Standards of Disclosure for Mineral Projects* (**NI 43-101**) for professional associations and membership designations.

As noted in subsections 1.1(5) and 1.1(7) of Companion Policy 43-101CP (the **Companion Policy**), Canadian securities regulatory authorities will periodically update the list of foreign professional associations and membership designations in Appendix A of the Companion Policy. Staff may communicate its interpretation of the tests in NI 43-101 as they apply to other foreign professional associations by revisions to this Notice between periodic updates of the Companion Policy.

Addition to the List of Foreign Associations and Membership Designations

After considering submissions received, in staff's view the organizations identified below meet the definition of a "professional association" in NI 43-101, and the membership designations below meet the criteria in paragraph (e) of the definition of "qualified person" in NI 43-101.

Foreign Association	Membership Designation	Date of Determination
The Institution of Engineers Australia (Engineers Australia)	Chartered Professional Engineer (CPEng)	May 29, 2012
The Institution of Professional Engineers New Zealand (Engineers New Zealand, IPENZ)	Chartered Professional Engineer (CPEng)	November 5, 2012

These associations and membership designations should be considered additions to the list of accepted foreign associations and membership designations in Appendix A of the Companion Policy.

Issuers filing technical reports where an author holds a designation listed in this Notice should note that the author must still meet all other elements of the definition of "qualified person" in section 1.1 of NI 43-101, including the requirements for relevant education and professional experience.

CSA Staff Notice 43-309 — Review of Website Investor Presentations by Mining Issuers

Date: **April 9, 2015**

38 O.S.C.B. 3305

1. — Introduction

This notice summarizes the findings of a review (the *Review*) of investor presentations on mining issuers' websites, conducted by staff of the British Columbia Securities Commission (*BCSC*), the Ontario Securities Commission (*OSC*), and the Autorité des marchés financiers (*AMF*) (collectively, the *Principal Mining Jurisdictions* or *we*). We also provide practical information to assist mining issuers in designing investor presentations and websites that meet their disclosure obligations.

The Review assessed investor presentations' compliance with the requirements of National Instrument 43-101 *Standards of Disclosure for Mineral Projects* (*NI 43-101*). In addition, we reviewed the forward looking information (*FLI*) against the requirements of Part 4A of National Instrument 51-102 *Continuous Disclosure Obligations* (*NI 51-102*).

We expect mining issuers to use this notice as a self-assessment tool to strengthen their compliance with securities laws, in particular NI 43-101 and FLI disclosure requirements.

2. — Summary of Results

2.1 — Key Findings

The results of our review highlight the need for mining issuers to improve their disclosure in order to comply with the following requirements of NI 43-101:

- *Naming the qualified person (QP)*: review of technical information by a QP directly improves compliance with requirements

- *Preliminary economic assessments (PEA):* providing required cautionary statements ensures proper understanding of the PEA results' limitations

- *Mineral resources and mineral reserves*: a clear statement whether mineral resources include or exclude mineral reserves is essential to avoid misleading disclosure

- *Exploration targets*: potential quantity and grade must be expressed as a range and be accompanied by the required statements outlining the target limitations

- *Historical estimates*: disclosure must include source, date, reliability, key assumptions and be accompanied by the required cautionary statements.

2.2 — Overall Assessment

In general we found there is room for improvement for mining issuers to comply with disclosure requirements.

Some issuers use terms and statements that could be interpreted as overly promotional or misleading, potentially resulting in a misrepresentation. Terms such as "world-class", "spectacular", "production ready", or "ore" may be used inappropriately in certain circumstances. Misuse of such terms was more commonly seen with exploration or mineral resource stage issuers.

Issuers at the mineral resource stage or earlier sometimes disclose anticipated economic outcomes for their mineral project such as production rate, capital and operating costs, or mine life suggesting that their project is at a more advanced stage of development than is supported by the existing technical report. Such disclosure may trigger the filing of a technical report to support the economic projections.

Based on an overall assessment of 130 investor presentations for compliance with NI 43-101 and FLI requirements, as well as whether the information was balanced and not overly promotional, we assigned a rating to each of the investor presentations as "substantial compliance", "minor non-compliance", or "major non-compliance".

Of the 130 investor presentations, 54 presentations provided the name of the QP that approved the disclosure, and stated that QP's relationship to the issuer, as required by section 3.1 of NI 43-101. Those 54 presentations were rated as having substantial compliance or minor non-compliance 85% of the time, a significant improvement over the full population of presentations.

As demonstrated in the following pie charts, the rating and overall compliance with NI 43-101 disclosure requirements increased significantly among investor presentations reviewed by a QP. We saw improvement in disclosure of exploration targets, mineral resources and mineral reserves, historical estimates and exploration information. No improvement was noted with disclosure of economic studies. Issuers are reminded of the requirement to name the QP responsible for approving the disclosure to ensure that the information complies with NI 43-101.

Overall Assessment

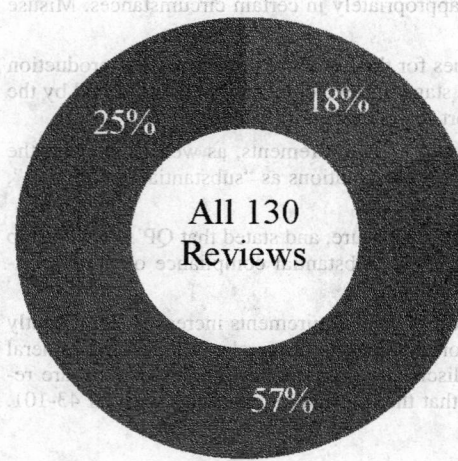

All 130 Reviews

- ■ Substantial Compliance
- ■ Minor Non-Compliance
- ■ Major Non-Compliance

25%   18%   57%

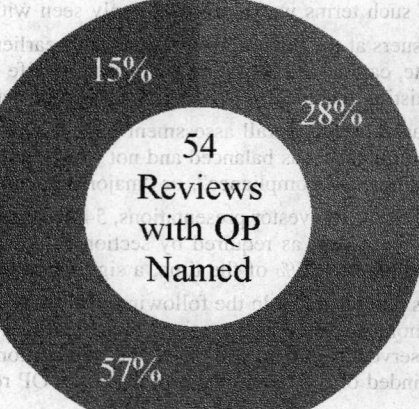

54 Reviews with QP Named

15%   28%   57%

2.3 — Actions Taken

Of the 130 investor presentations reviewed, we sent letters to 49 mining issuers requiring them to amend their investor presentations and correct the non-compliant disclosure. As shown in the bar graph below, this resulted in a range of outcomes from mining issuers confirming future compliance with the requirements, to issuing a corrective news release, to filing or refiling a technical report.

The majority of the corrective news releases and technical report filings or refilings resulted from non-compliant disclosure of economic studies, PEAs, mineral resources, mineral reserves, exploration targets, historical estimates, or overly promotional language.

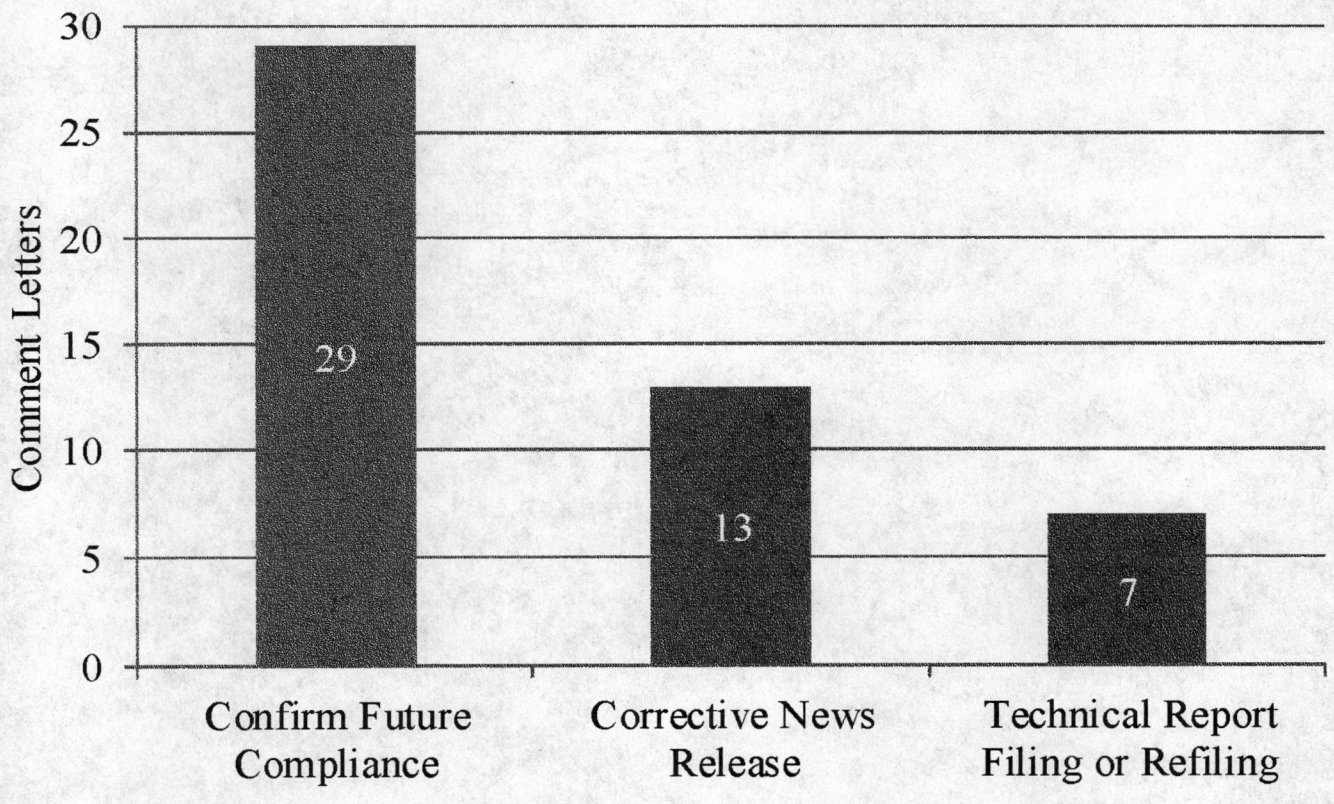

Outcomes

3. — Purpose and Objective

Mining issuers make up approximately 43% (1,600) of the total number of reporting issuers overseen by CSA jurisdictions[1] . Approximately 94% of all mining issuers listed on the Toronto Stock Exchange (*TSX*), TSX Venture Exchange (*TSXV*), and the Canadian Stock Exchange (*CSE*) are regulated by the BCSC, OSC or AMF which maintain a staff of specialized mining professionals to review disclosure by mining issuers based in their respective jurisdictions.

Investor presentations and other forms of investor relations materials contained on mining issuers' websites provide a powerful tool for communication. Information found on issuer websites is captured by the definition of "written disclosure" in NI 43-101 and disclosure requirements apply.

We often observe non-compliance with disclosure on mining issuers' websites such as investor presentations, fact sheets, media articles, and links to third party content. Our Review was intended to provide data and analysis to better understand the nature, extent and compliance of the disclosure in investor presentations in order to better assist mining issuers and their investor relations personnel to improve their disclosure to investors.

4. — Profile of Issuers Reviewed

Approximately 88% of all mining issuers listed on the TSX, TSXV, and the CSE are at the pre-production stage. Our review focused on a sample of 130 mining issuers at the pre-production stage from the Principal Mining Jurisdictions with investor presentations dated between December 2013 and October 2014. The following pie charts provide details of the profile of the mining issuers reviewed in our sample including stock exchange listing, development stage, project location, and main commodity.

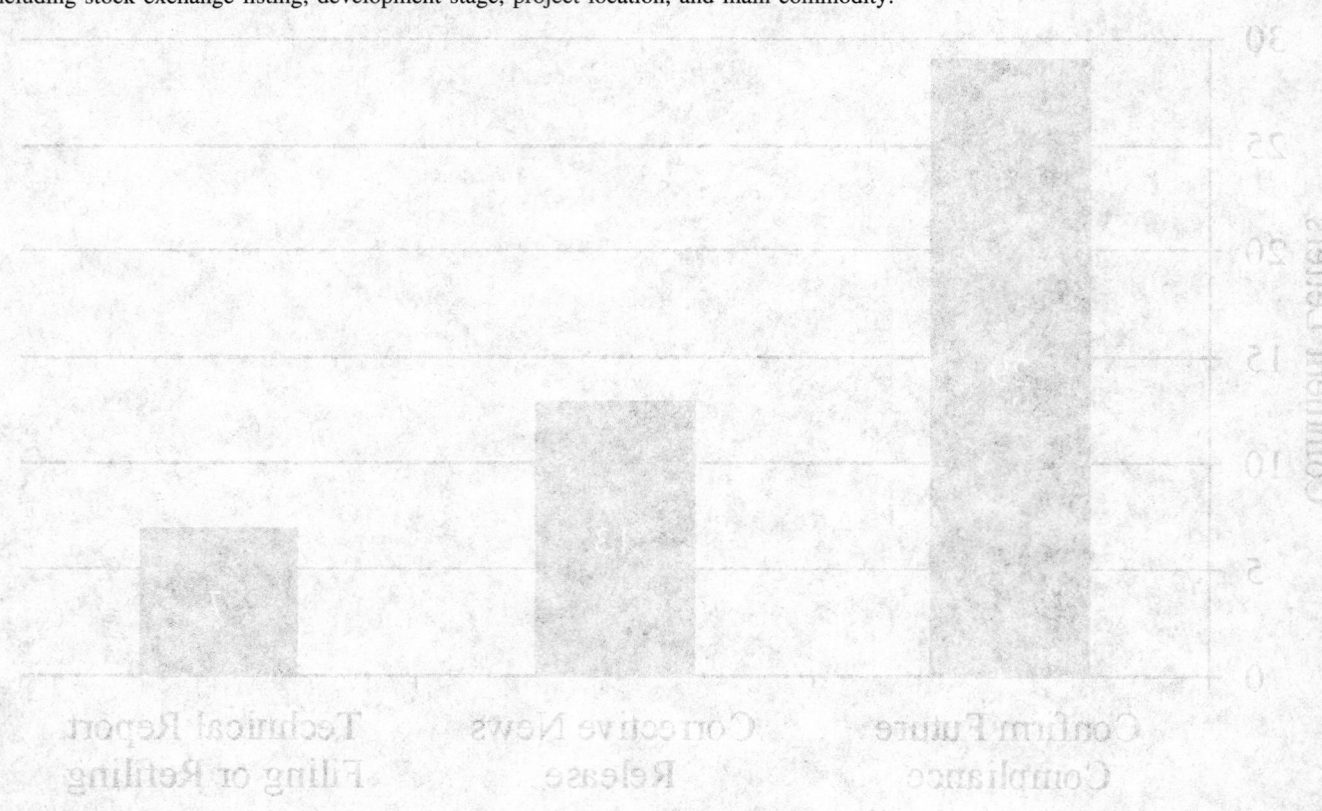

---

[1]As at December 2014.

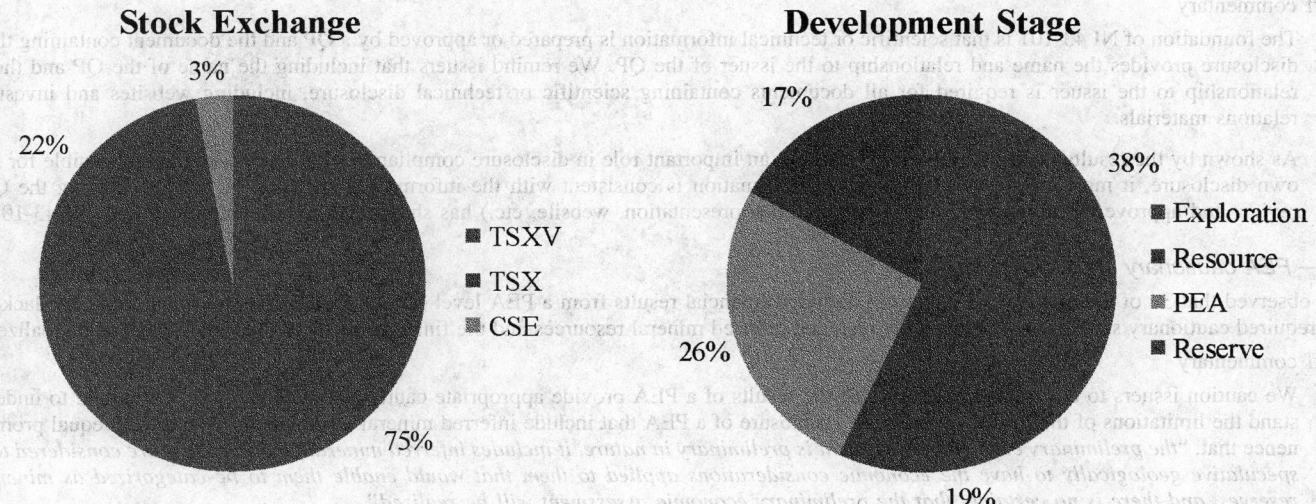

Stock Exchange

- TSXV
- TSX
- CSE

3%
22%
75%

Development Stage

17%
38%
26%
19%

- Exploration
- Resource
- PEA
- Reserve

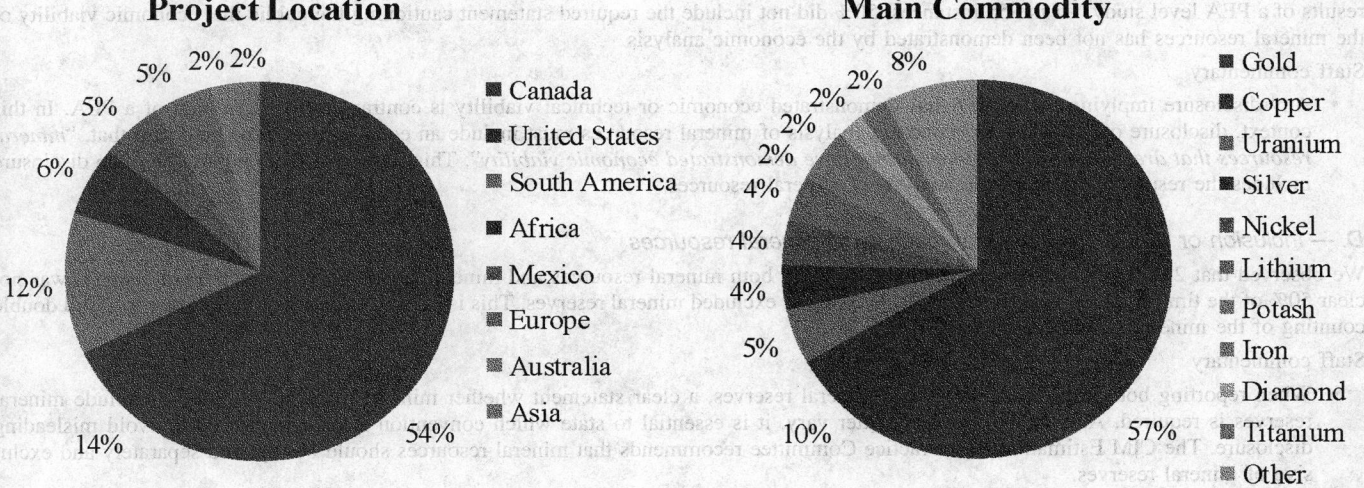

Project Location

5% 2% 2%
5%
6%
12%
14%
54%

- Canada
- United States
- South America
- Africa
- Mexico
- Europe
- Australia
- Asia

Main Commodity

8% 2% 2%
2%
2%
2%
4%
4%
4%
5%
10%
57%

- Gold
- Copper
- Uranium
- Silver
- Nickel
- Lithium
- Potash
- Iron
- Diamond
- Titanium
- Other

5. — NI 43-101 Compliance

The results of our Review are presented according to the following thresholds of non-compliance: High Level of Non-Compliance (greater than 50% of investor presentations reviewed) and Areas for Additional Improvement (between 30% and 50% of investor presentations reviewed). When discussing the Review findings the number of investor presentations that included the particular disclosure is provided followed by the percentage of presentations that did not comply with NI 43-101 requirements. After each Review finding, staff commentary is provided on specific disclosure requirements and reminders for mining issuers. See Appendix A for an overall summary of the 130 investor presentation Review and Appendix B for details of the Review measures and references to the applicable NI 43-101 requirements.

5.1 — High Level of Non-Compliance

A. — Naming the QP

Of the 130 investor presentations reviewed we found that only 54 provided the QP's name and their relationship to the issuer resulting in 58% non-compliance.

Staff commentary

- The foundation of NI 43-101 is that scientific or technical information is prepared or approved by a QP and the document containing this disclosure provides the name and relationship to the issuer of the QP. We remind issuers that including the name of the QP and their relationship to the issuer is required for all documents containing scientific or technical disclosure, including websites and investor relations materials.

- As shown by the results of this Review, the QP plays an important role in disclosure compliance. While the issuer is responsible for its own disclosure, it must ensure that the technical information is consistent with the information provided by the QP. Having the QP review and approve the disclosure (such as the investor presentation, website, etc.) has shown improved compliance with NI 43-101.

B. — PEA cautionary statements

We observed that 34 of the investor presentations included financial results from a PEA level economic analysis and found that 56% lacked the required cautionary statements that the study included inferred mineral resources and the financial results of the PEA may not be realized.

Staff commentary

- We caution issuers to ensure that disclosure of the results of a PEA provide appropriate cautionary statements for the public to understand the limitations of the results of the PEA. Disclosure of a PEA that include inferred mineral resources must state with equal prominence that, "*the preliminary economic assessment is preliminary in nature, it includes inferred mineral resources that are considered too speculative geologically to have the economic considerations applied to them that would enable them to be categorized as mineral reserves, and there is no certainty that the preliminary economic assessment will be realized*".

C. — Caution that mineral resources are not mineral reserves

We noted that 56 of the investor presentations included financial results of an economic analysis of mineral resources, 34 of which were results of a PEA level study. Of the 56 instances, 50% did not include the required statement cautioning the public that economic viability of the mineral resources has not been demonstrated by the economic analysis.

Staff commentary

- Any disclosure implying that a PEA has demonstrated economic or technical viability is contrary to the definition of a PEA. In this context, disclosure of results of an economic analysis of mineral resources must include an equally prominent statement that, "*mineral resources that are not mineral reserves do not have demonstrated economic viability*". This caution is required any time the disclosure includes the results of an economic analysis of mineral resources.

D. — Inclusion or exclusion of mineral reserves in mineral resources

We observed that 22 of the investor presentations disclosed both mineral resources and mineral reserves. For these presentations, it was not clear 50% of the time whether mineral resources included or excluded mineral reserves. This is important information in order to avoid double counting of the mineral resource estimate.

Staff commentary

- When reporting both mineral resources and mineral reserves, a clear statement whether mineral resources include or exclude mineral reserves is required. As practices on this matter vary, it is essential to state which convention is being followed to avoid misleading disclosure. The CIM Estimation Best Practice Committee recommends that mineral resources should be reported separately and exclusive of mineral reserves.

E. — Exploration targets

We observed that only 14 of the investor presentations included disclosure of an exploration target, but this disclosure was non-compliant 79% of the time. This significant level of non-compliance is related to either failing to express the target as ranges or not including the required cautions, or both.

Staff commentary

- Staff has significant concerns about the disclosure of exploration targets, which are not mineral resource estimates and cannot be used the way a mineral resource estimate would be. If a mining issuer chooses to disclose an exploration target, it must provide a reasonable basis for the target and also make the public aware of the target's limitations. Both the potential quantity and grade of the exploration target must be expressed as ranges and be accompanied by an equally prominent statement that, "*the potential quantity and grade is conceptual in nature, there has been insufficient exploration to define a mineral resource*" and that "*it is uncertain if further exploration will result in the target being delineated as a mineral resource*".

F. — Historical estimates

Our Review observed that 30 of the investor presentations included disclosure of an historical estimate, but this disclosure was non-compliant 60% of the time.

Staff commentary

- Disclosure of historical estimates continues to need improvement in order to comply with the requirements. Simply saying "not NI 43-101 compliant" does not meet that requirement. Issuers are reminded that the required information about the source, date, reliability, key assumptions and other factors must be provided each time the historical estimate is disclosed. In addition, an equally prominent statement is required alerting the public that, "*a qualified person has not done sufficient work to classify the historical estimate as current mineral resources or mineral reserves*" and "*the issuer is not treating the historical estimate as current mineral resources or mineral reserves*".

G. — Exploration information about quality assurance/quality control and naming the laboratory

We found that 86 of the investor presentations disclosed analytical or testing results, with 67% failing to disclose a summary of the quality assurance program and quality control measures applied and 71% failing to provide the name and location of the testing laboratory used.

Staff commentary

- Issuers may be able to comply with the disclosure requirements concerning exploration information by including in the written disclosure a reference to the title and date of a document previously filed on SEDAR that contains the exploration information. This may include previously filed documents such as news releases and technical reports. As discussed below, relying on previously filed documents is acceptable to satisfy some of the disclosure requirements in Part 3 of NI 43-101.

H. — Data verification

Of the 130 investor presentations reviewed only 47 included any reference to a statement that the QP had verified the data resulting in 64% non-compliance.

Staff commentary

- Data verification is the process of confirming that the data underlying the written disclosure has been properly generated, was accurately transcribed, and is suitable for the purpose that the data is used. NI 43-101 requires the issuer to include a statement regarding verification of the data by the QP in the document containing the written disclosure.

- As noted above with exploration information, disclosure regarding data verification may be made compliant by referencing the title and date of a document previously filed by the issuer that contains the required data verification statement information by the QP.

5.2 — Areas for Additional Improvement

A. — Taxes in economic studies

We found that 56 of the investor presentations included financial results from economic studies (34 PEA level and 22 pre-feasibility or feasibility level). Of these 56 instances, 37% reported only pre-tax financial results or provided no information about the tax rate for the mineral project. Surprisingly, the level of pre-tax only financial results was higher for projects at a pre-feasibility or feasibility level than at a PEA level.

Staff commentary

- Reporting only pre-tax financial results for an "advanced property", which includes results of a PEA, pre-feasibility or feasibility study does not provide complete and balanced information for investors to appropriately assess the financial results. In order to properly evaluate the potential viability of mineral resources in a PEA, or to demonstrate viability in a pre-feasibility or feasibility study, the cash flow model needs to include assumptions that have an economic impact such as taxes, royalties, and other government levies.

B. — Metal price assumptions used in mineral resources and mineral reserves

Eighty-one of the investor presentations disclosed mineral resources and 22 of these also disclosed mineral reserves. We found that 30% of the time no information was provided about the assumed metal price used for determining the mineral estimates.

Staff commentary

- Metal or commodity price assumptions are key factors in establishing the cut-off grade for both mineral resources and mineral reserves and these assumptions can have a significant impact on the size of the mineral estimate. For this reason, it is important that the assumed metal or commodity price, and the cut-off grade, be clearly stated. Issuers are also reminded to provide the effective date of the reported estimate.

- Providing a complete table of current mineral resources and mineral reserves with all material assumptions in an appendix to the investor presentation may assist in providing the required information. Issuers may also be able to satisfy the requirement to disclose key assumptions by referencing the title and date of a document previously filed by the issuer that contains the required information. Nevertheless, if the assumed metal or commodity price is significantly below or above current prices, issuers should make sure the disclosure is not misleading by clearly stating the key assumptions.

C. — Drilling information regarding true widths and significantly higher grade intervals

We observed that 70 of the investor presentations included drilling results. Of these, 38% did not include information on true widths of mineralized zones and 42% did not provide results of significantly higher grade intervals enclosed in a lower grade intersection. This type of information is particularly important for early stage projects.

Staff commentary

- When drilling results are reported, it is important that investors be provided with information about the nature and context of the results such as true width and higher grade intersections. Without this information the drilling results, especially at the exploration stage, may be potentially misleading.

- In some cases, including representative drill sections or other figures showing mineralized intervals may assist in providing the necessary information in investor presentations. Mining issuers may also be able to rely on a previously filed document that contains the required information.

5.3 — Technical Report Triggers

Technical reports are a key disclosure document under NI 43-101, supporting a mining issuer's disclosure about its material mineral properties. Our Review identified 81 investor presentations that disclosed mineral resources, mineral reserves, or results of a PEA. First time written disclosure of mineral resources, mineral reserves, or results of a PEA, or a change to any of these that constitutes a material change for the issuer triggers the filing of a technical report.

We noted that five of the 81 investor presentations (6%) disclosed financial results of an economic analysis (*e.g.* PEA or scoping study) that were not supported by a technical report.

Staff commentary

- Notwithstanding the fact that our review showed a high level of compliance, we have determined that a highlight of this requirement is warranted based on the relative gravity of not complying with the technical report trigger.

- We have significant concerns when information provided on a mining issuer's website includes PEA disclosure that is not supported by the existing technical report. Disclosing economic projections in investor presentations, fact sheets, posted or linked third party reports, or any statements on the issuer's website may trigger the filing of a technical report to support the disclosure.

- Mining issuers are reminded that we consider that the issuer has disclosed the results of a PEA, or similar type of economic analysis, when the disclosure includes information such as forecast mine production rates that might contain capital costs to develop and sustain the mining operation, operating costs, and projected cash flows.

6. — FLI Compliance

The majority of investor presentations included FLI disclosure, often on slide two. We observed that 54% did not provide information required by paragraph 4A.3(c) of NI 51-102 concerning the material factors and assumptions used to develop the FLI. We expect that mining issuers will follow General Guidance (3) of Companion Policy 43-101CP indicating that FLI includes metal price assumptions used in mineral resource and mineral reserve estimates as well as other assumptions used in economic analysis and financial projections based on engineering studies.

7. — Overly Promotional Terms and Potentially Misleading Information

During the course of the Review, we also assessed the investor presentations for terms and statements that may be overly promotional or misleading, potentially resulting in a misrepresentation[2] under securities legislation in a jurisdiction of Canada.

Terms which may be used inappropriately in certain circumstances include, "world-class", "spectacular and exceptional results", "production ready", "ore" in relation to mineral resources, and "management estimates". We noted that 38% of the investor presentations included statements that could be considered overly promotional or misleading, especially exploration stage and mineral resource stage issuers, by portraying their project to be at a more advanced stage of development.

8. — Conclusions

We expect mining issuers to use this notice to strengthen their compliance with securities legislation and improve their disclosure to investors. Having the QP review technical disclosure in investor presentations and other website disclosure is an important step in improving compliance with NI 43-101.

We will continue the review of mining issuers' website disclosure as part of our overall continuous disclosure review program. When we identify material disclosure deficiencies, we will request that the issuer correct the deficiency by amending or removing the website disclosure and filing a clarifying or retracting news release. We may place the issuer on the reporting issuer default list and where the issuer fails to comply with the requests we may consider issuing a cease trade order until the issuer corrects the deficiency.

If an issuer is considering a prospectus offering, the review of the prospectus filing will likely be deferred if issues such as those noted above are present.

---

[2]Misrepresentation as defined under securities legislation in each of the Canadian jurisdictions. Though the wording of the definition of "misrepresentation" differs slightly, in substance this definition is harmonized in all jurisdictions.

For further guidance on this issue, please see CSA Staff Notice 51-312 *Harmonized Continuous Disclosure Review Program* and CSA Notice 51-322 *Reporting Issuer Defaults*.

Questions

Please refer your questions to any of the following people:

Chris Collins
Chief Mining Advisor, Corporate Finance
British Columbia Securities Commission
604-899-6616
Toll-free 800-373-6393
ccollins@bcsc.bc.ca

Ian McCartney
Senior Geologist, Corporate Finance
British Columbia Securities Commission
604-899-6519
Toll-free 800-373-6393
imccartney@bcsc.bc.ca

Darin Wasylik
Senior Geologist, Corporate Finance
British Columbia Securities Commission
604 899-6517
Toll-free 800-373-6393
dwasylik@bcsc.bc.ca

Craig Waldie
Senior Geologist, Corporate Finance
Ontario Securities Commission
416-593-8308
Toll-free 877-785-1555
cwaldie@osc.gov.on.ca

James Whyte
Senior Geologist, Corporate Finance
Ontario Securities Commission
416-593-2168
Toll-free 877-785-1555
jwhyte@osc.gov.on.ca

Luc Arsenault
Géologue
Autorité des marchés financiers
514-395-0337, ext. 4373
Toll-free 877-525-0337, ext. 4373
luc.arsenault@lautorite.qc.ca

André Laferrière
Géologue
Autorité des marchés financiers
514-395-0337 ext. 4374
Toll-free 877-525-0337 ext. 4374
andre.laferriere@lautorite.qc.ca

Appendix A — Results of 130 Investor Presentation Reviews

The following chart provides a summary of the 130 investor presentations reviewed and the percentage of non-compliance compared to particular disclosure requirements in NI 43-101. The non-compliance percentage is relative to the number of occurrences of the particular disclosure (population size). Disclosure requirements are grouped and colour-coded by type of disclosure, such as Economic studies.

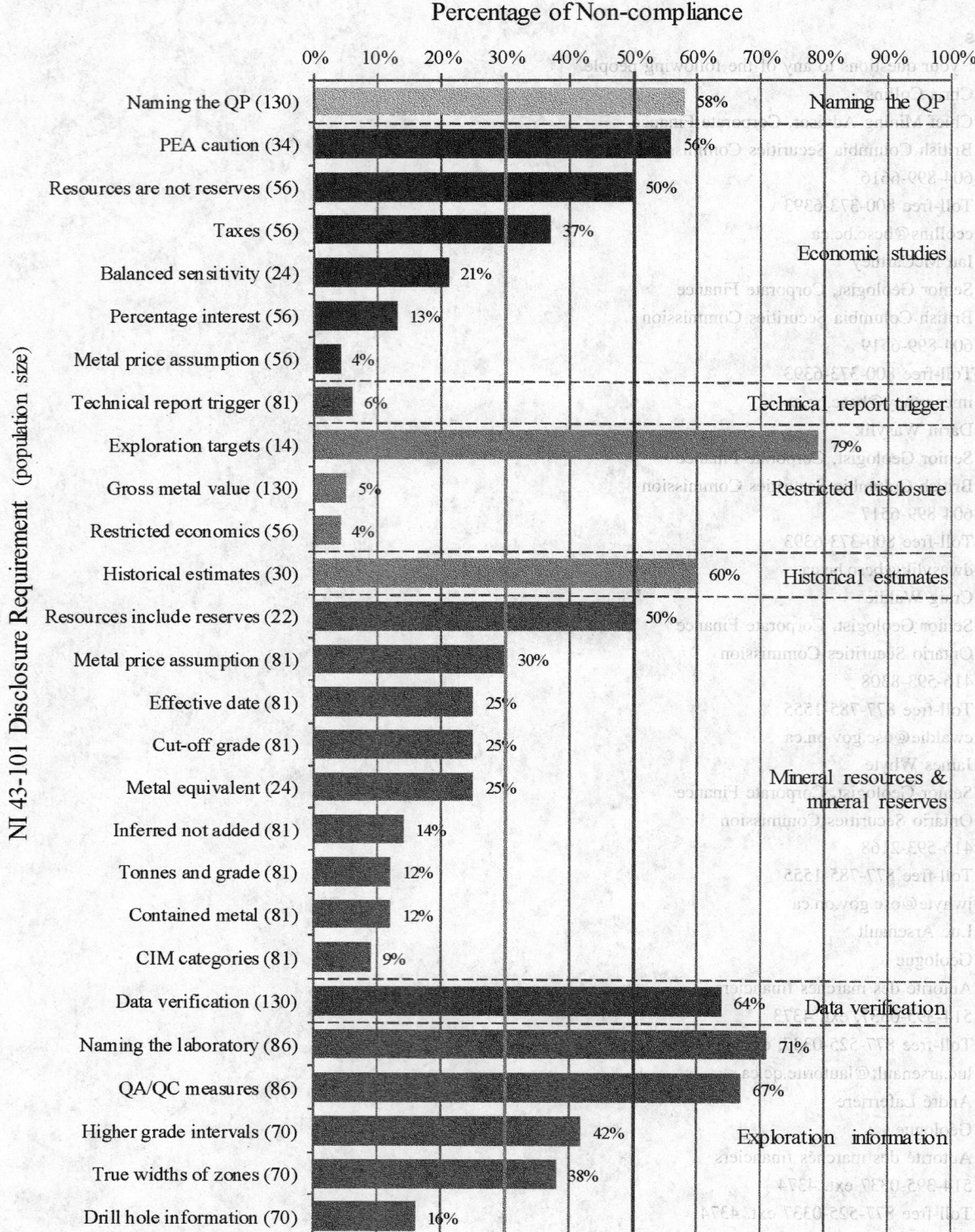

Percentage of Non-compliance

Appendix B — Review Measures in Appendix A with Reference to Provisions of NI 43-101

Note: Review measures below are grouped and listed in the same order as the results in Appendix A.

Naming the QP	s. 3.1 requires issuers to name the QP responsible for the technical disclosure and their relationship to the issuer
Economic studies	
PEA caution	ss. 2.3(3) requires disclosure of a PEA that includes inferred mineral resources provide the mandatory cautionary statements
Resources are not reserves	para. 3.4(e) requires a statement that mineral resources that are not mineral reserves do not have demonstrated economic viability if results of an economic analysis of mineral resources is provided
Taxes	Item 22(d) of Form 43-101F1 requires a summary of taxes applicable to the mineral project
Balanced sensitivity	s. 3.5 of 43-101CP states that disclosure must be factual, complete, and balanced and not present or omit information in a manner that is misleading — such as an unbalanced sensitivity analysis
Percentage interest	s. 3.5 of 43-101CP states that disclosure must be factual, complete, and balanced and not present or omit information in a manner that is misleading — such as not stating that the issuer only holds a minor percentage interest in a mineral project
Metal price assumption	Item 22(a) of Form 43-101F1 requires a clear statement of the principal assumptions used in an economic analysis — such as assumed metal price
Technical report trigger	para. 4.2(1)(j) requires that first time written disclosure of mineral resources, mineral reserves or the results of a PEA, or a change to any of these that is a material change to the issuer, must be supported by a technical report
Restricted disclosure	
Exploration targets	ss. 2.3(2) permits disclosure of exploration targets expressed as ranges of potential quantity and grade and subject to the inclusion of mandatory cautionary statements and other information
Gross metal value	para. 2.3(1)(c) prohibits issuers from disclosing gross value of metal or mineral in a deposit or sampled interval
Restricted economics	para. 2.3(1)(b) prohibits the disclosure of economic analysis using inferred mineral resources (except as allowed in a PEA), historical estimates, or exploration targets
Historical estimates	s. 2.4 requires specific information and mandatory cautionary statements when disclosing historical estimates
Mineral resources & mineral reserves	
Resources include reserves	para. 2.2(b) requires a statement whether mineral reserves are included in mineral resources
Metal price assumption	para. 3.4(c) requires disclosure of key assumptions (such as assumed metal price) used to determine the mineral resources and mineral reserves
Metal equivalent	para. 2.3(1)(d) requires that disclosure of a metal equivalent grade also state the grade of each metal used to establish the metal equivalent grade
Effective date	para. 3.4(a) requires that the effective date of a mineral resource and mineral reserve be disclosed if the mineral estimate is reported
Cut-off grade	para. 3.4(c) requires disclosure of key assumptions (such as cut-off grade) used to determine the mineral resources and mineral reserves

Inferred not added	para. 2.2(c) prohibits the addition of inferred resources to other categories of mineral resources
Tonnes and grade	para. 3.4(b) requires the quantity and grade of each category of mineral resources and mineral reserves be disclosed
Contained metal	para. 2.2 (d) requires that disclosure of contained metal also state the grade and quantity for each category of mineral resources and mineral reserves
CIM categories	para. 2.2(a) requires the use of only accepted mineral resource and mineral reserve categories as prescribed by the Canadian Institute of Mining, Metallurgy and Petroleum (CIM)
Data verification	s. 3.2 requires issuers to include a statement whether a QP has verified the data disclosed, how it was verified and reasons for any failure to verify

Exploration information

Name of laboratory	para. 3.3(2)(f) requires disclosure of the name and location of the testing laboratory used and any relationship to the issuer
QA/QC measures	para. 3.3(1)(c) requires disclosure of a summary of the quality assurance program and quality control measures applied
Higher grade intervals	para. 3.3(2)(d) requires disclosure of any significantly higher grade intervals forming part of a lower grade intersection
True widths of zones	para. 3.3(2)(c) requires disclosure of true widths of mineralized zones, to the extent known
Drill hole information	para. 3.3(2)(b) requires disclosure of drilling information to include the location, azimuth and dip of the drill holes and the sample interval depth

OSC Staff Notice 43-704 — Mineral Brine Projects and National Instrument 43-101 Standards of Disclosure for Mineral Projects

Date: July 22, 2011

34 O.S.C.B. 7977

Purpose

This staff notice provides guidance on the application of National Instrument 43-101 *Standards of Disclosure for Mineral Projects* (**NI 43-101**) in Ontario to issuers with mineral brine projects such as lithium. It has been prepared by staff of the Corporate Finance Branch of the Ontario Securities Commission (**OSC**) and the views it expresses do not necessarily reflect the views of the OSC, other jurisdictions, or the Canadian Securities Administrators.

Recent industry developments have led to an expansion in the exploration for lithium. Currently, this exploration appears to be focused on projects where the lithium is hosted in liquid brine rather than in hard rock sources. Since the summer of 2009, staff of the OSC have seen an increase in reporting issuers working on such mineral brine projects.

Summary

We are providing guidance in three areas:

1. Application of NI 43-101	Do mineral brine projects fall within the definition of "mineral project" in section 1.1 of NI 43-101 and are they, as a result, subject to the requirements of NI 43-101 in Ontario?
2. CIM definitions	Given that NI 43-101 relies on the Canadian Institute of Mining Metallurgy and Petroleum (**CIM**) definitions of "mineral resource" and "mineral reserve" and CIM has not provided an official interpretation of whether a resource or reserve on a mineral brine project falls within these definitions, what is the impact on an issuer's disclosure of resources or reserves?
3. Scientific and technical disclosure	What issues should be considered when preparing disclosure of scientific or technical information, including a technical report?

Guidance

1. — Application of NI 43-101

In our view mineral brine projects are mineral projects as defined in NI 43-101. Under section 1.1 of NI 43-101, "mineral project" means any exploration, development or production activity . . . in respect of . . . natural solid inorganic material . . . including industrial minerals. The mining activity in a mineral brine project is in respect of lithium salts and other salts that are natural solid inorganic material.

We also think that it is in the public interest for mineral brine projects to be subject to the requirements of NI 43-101. NI 43-101 provides a proper and rigorous disclosure framework for mineral projects hosted in a brine.

General Guidance (1) of Companion Policy 43-101CP *To National Instrument 43-101 Standards of Disclosure for Mineral Projects* provides guidance that NI 43-101 does not apply to disclosure concerning "groundwater". We do not think that this guidance regarding groundwater applies to natural solid inorganic materials dissolved in a liquid host medium. Rather, we think that this guidance refers either to: (i) groundwater as a waste product in the process of petroleum extraction, or (ii) potable water. We note that the other materials explicitly named in that section of the Companion Policy are materials generally associated with the oil and gas industry, which are generally subject to the requirements of National Instrument 51-101 *Standards of Disclosure for Oil and Gas Activities*.

2. — CIM definitions

Sections 1.2 and 1.3 of NI 43-101 provide that the terms "mineral resource" and "mineral reserve" have the meanings ascribed to those terms by CIM. We think that a mineral brine project is a "mineral project" under NI 43-101 regardless of whether a resource or reserve on the project falls within the CIM definitions of "mineral resources" or "mineral reserves". However, in the absence of an official interpretation from CIM, whether a resource or reserve on a mineral brine project falls within these CIM definitions may be unclear.

Regardless of whether an issuer or a qualified person takes the view that a resource or reserve on a mineral brine project falls within or outside these CIM definitions, any scientific or technical information on the mineral project should disclose the issuer's or the qualified person's view on this issue. In addition, if an issuer or a qualified person takes the view that a resource or reserve on a mineral brine project falls outside the CIM definitions, the issuer should also disclose how it intends to comply with any requirements of NI 43-101 that rely on these CIM definitions. For example, the issuer should disclose how it will comply with the technical report triggers in section 4.2 of NI 43-101 given its view that a resource or reserve on a mineral brine project falls outside the CIM definitions.

3. — Scientific or technical disclosure

Scientific and technical information about a mineral brine project must satisfy the requirements of NI 43-101. A technical report supporting scientific or technical information about a mineral brine project must satisfy the requirements of Form 43-101F1 *Technical Report* (**Form 43-101F1**) and provide a summary of scientific and technical information concerning mineral exploration, development and production activities on a mineral project that is material to the issuer.

A technical report prepared in respect of a mineral brine project should reflect some issues that are specific to brine-hosted deposits. The following table identifies some considerations for mineral brine projects. This list is not exhaustive, and the qualified person would be expected to take the particular circumstances into account when preparing this disclosure.

Issue	Form 43-101F1 Item	Considerations for Mineral Brine Projects
Mineral Rights	Item 4: Property Description and Location	Nature of the mineral tenure and any potential risks and uncertainties regarding "ownership" of the brine.
Climate	Item 5: Accessibility, Climate, Local Resources, Infrastructure and Physiography	Relevant meteorological data such as solar radiation, precipitation, wind, etc.
Geology and Mineralization	Item 7: Geological Setting and Mineralization	Hydrological aspects of the property such as surface and groundwater, water balance, and geology of the aquifer; characteristics of the brine body such as its geometry, chemical composition, variability, grade, etc.
Deposit Types	Item 8: Deposit Types	Characteristics of the host salar (salt flat), associated hydrogeology, aquifer boundaries, physical properties, etc.
Sampling	Item 11: Sample Preparation, Analyses and Security	Controls and protocols for brine sampling and preservation and determination of key variables such as porosity, specific yield, permeability, etc.
Mineral Resource Estimates	Item 14: Mineral Resource Estimates	Key variables such as brine volume and grade, aquifer geometry, effective porosity, specific yield, flow rate, recoverability, etc. in order to meet the definition of reasonable prospects of economic extraction.
Mineral Reserve Estimates	Item 15: Mineral Reserve Estimates	Key variables such as hydraulic conductivity, recovery, brine behaviour and grade variation over time, etc. and fluid flow simulation models in order to demonstrate that economic extraction can be justified.
Mining Method	Item 16: Mining Methods	Relevant information related to the design of the well field, infrastructure, pumping rate, brine body response to extraction, etc.

Sections 3.3 and 3.4 of NI 43-101 set out requirements for written disclosure about mineral projects, and are intended to ensure that disclosure of exploration information and mineral resource and reserve estimates are presented in context. Because a mineral brine project is a "mineral project" within the meaning of NI 43-101, disclosure about mineral brine projects must meet the requirements of Part 3.

Issuers and qualified persons should interpret the requirements of Part 3 as mandating disclosure of background information that is relevant to the exploration results or resource or reserve estimates being disclosed, even though the information may be specifically relevant only in the case of a mineral brine project.

We also think that issuers should include cautionary language with any scientific or technical information regarding a mineral brine project to emphasize the differences between such projects and traditional hard rock projects.

OSC Staff Notice 43-705 — Report on Staff's Review of Technical Reports by Ontario Mining Issuers

Date: **June 27, 2013**

36 O.S.C.B. 6427

1. — Introduction

Staff of the Ontario Securities Commission (**OSC**) conducted a review (the **Review**) of a subset of Form 43-101F1 *Technical Reports* (**Form 43-101F1**) filed by Ontario mining issuers. The purposes of the Review was to assess whether the technical reports filed by Ontario mining issuers (the **Technical Reports**) complied with the recent revisions to National Instrument 43-101 *Standards of Disclosure for Mineral Projects* (**NI 43-101**) and Form 43-101F1 adopted by the Canadian Securities Administrators (**CSA**).

The purpose of this notice is to:

- summarize the results of the Review and

- provide guidance for mining issuers and qualified persons on compliance with Form 43-101F1 in the areas of concern identified during the Review.

Summary of results and future action

We found an unacceptable level of compliance with Form 43-101F1. Forty (80%) of the total number of Technical Reports reviewed had some form of non-compliance with the requirements of Form 43-101F1. Approximately 40% of the Technical Reports reviewed had at least one major non-compliance concern. We view this level of major non-compliance with the disclosure requirements of Form 43-101F1 to be unacceptable. Although significant efforts have been made to comply with the disclosure requirements in NI 43-101, issuers and qualified persons need to further improve their disclosure. We will continue to actively review Technical Reports by Ontario mining issuers as part of our overall continuous disclosure (**CD**) review program.

Issuers should anticipate staff requests for refilings, additional disclosure, or other staff action, where appropriate, if an issuer and qualified person have not fully met the requirements of Form 43-101F1 and NI 43-101. Please note that the issues raised in a review will be taken into consideration when determining whether a prospectus receipt should be issued. Unresolved issues may delay the prospectus receipt, particularly for short form prospectus filings.

1.1 — Background

As outlined in CSA Notice *Repeal and Replacement of National Instrument 43-101 Standards of Disclosure for Mineral Projects, Form 43-101F1 Technical Reports, and Companion Policy 43-101CP* dated April 8, 2011, the revised NI 43-101 came into force in all CSA jurisdictions on June 30, 2011.

NI 43-101 became effective on February 1, 2001 with minor revisions made in December 2005. The goal of the June 30, 2011 revisions was to maintain the benefits of NI 43-101, including investor protection, transparent disclosure and promoting market integrity, while making compliance simpler in some areas and less costly for mining issuers. NI 43-101 applies to all disclosure of scientific or technical information made by an issuer, including disclosure of mineral resources and mineral reserves, and requires a technical report be filed on a material mineral property when triggered by NI 43-101. In all cases, public disclosure of scientific or technical information must be prepared by or under the supervision of a qualified person or approved by a qualified person.

While the qualified person is responsible for preparing the Technical Report, the issuer is responsible for retaining a qualified person with the appropriate relevant experience and filing the Technical Report prepared in compliance with Form 43-101F1 and NI 43-101.

As at December 31, 2012, there were 457 Ontario mining issuers with a combined market capitalization of more than $181 billion, representing 21% of Ontario's overall market capitalization. Approximately 41% of Ontario mining issuers are listed on the Toronto Stock Exchange (**TSX**) and represent 98% of the market capitalization of the mining issuers in Ontario.

2. — Review Results

2.1 — Scope of Review

There were 460 Technical Reports by 238 Ontario mining issuers filed on SEDAR between June 30, 2011 and June 29, 2012. The scope of the Review was limited to a sample of 50 Technical Reports chosen based on certain identifiable characteristics including the main exchange listing of the issuer, the location of the mineral property, the type of mineral deposit and the stage of development of the mineral property. The selection process was aimed at finding a representative sample of issuers in the Ontario public markets for the Review.

The Review focused on compliance with various aspects of NI 43-101, including:

- the revised Form 43-101F1
- the revised definitions of "qualified person" and "professional association"
- changes in the requirement to file a Technical Report and
- the certificate of the qualified person.

2.2 — Technical Reports reviewed

We reviewed approximately 10% of the Technical Reports (50 out of 460) filed on SEDAR by Ontario mining issuers. Our sample included 27 Technical Reports by issuers listed on the TSX and 16 listed on the TSX Venture Exchange (**TSXV**). The remaining seven Technical Reports were by issuers either listed on the Canadian National Stock Exchange or unlisted.

Fifty percent of the issuers had a market capitalization of over $25 million with 25% of these having a market capitalization of greater than $100 million. In terms of stage of development, the majority (59%) of issuers were at the mineral resource stage, 26% at the development or production stage and 15% at the exploration stage.

Most of the mineral properties described in the Technical Reports were located in North America (44%) while others were located in either South America (22%), Africa (20%), Russia or China (8%) or Australia (6%). The three primary mineral commodities discussed in the Technical Reports were gold (46%), copper (12%) or iron (10%).

The majority of the Technical Reports were authored by qualified persons from independent consulting firms with 54% from regional firms and 20% from global firms. Independent sole proprietor qualified persons authored 14% of the Technical Reports while 12% were prepared by in-house qualified persons.

A summary of the characteristics of the Ontario mining issuers, their stage of development and the location and main type of commodity based on the 50 Technical Reports reviewed is set out below:

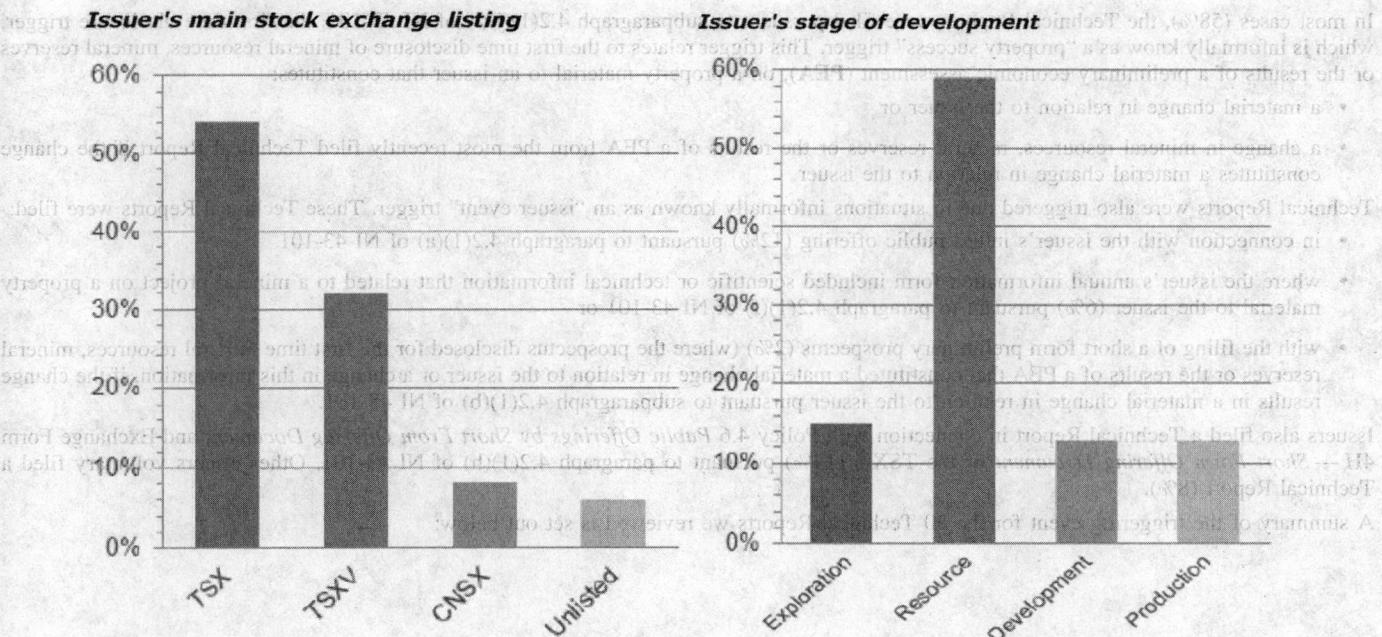

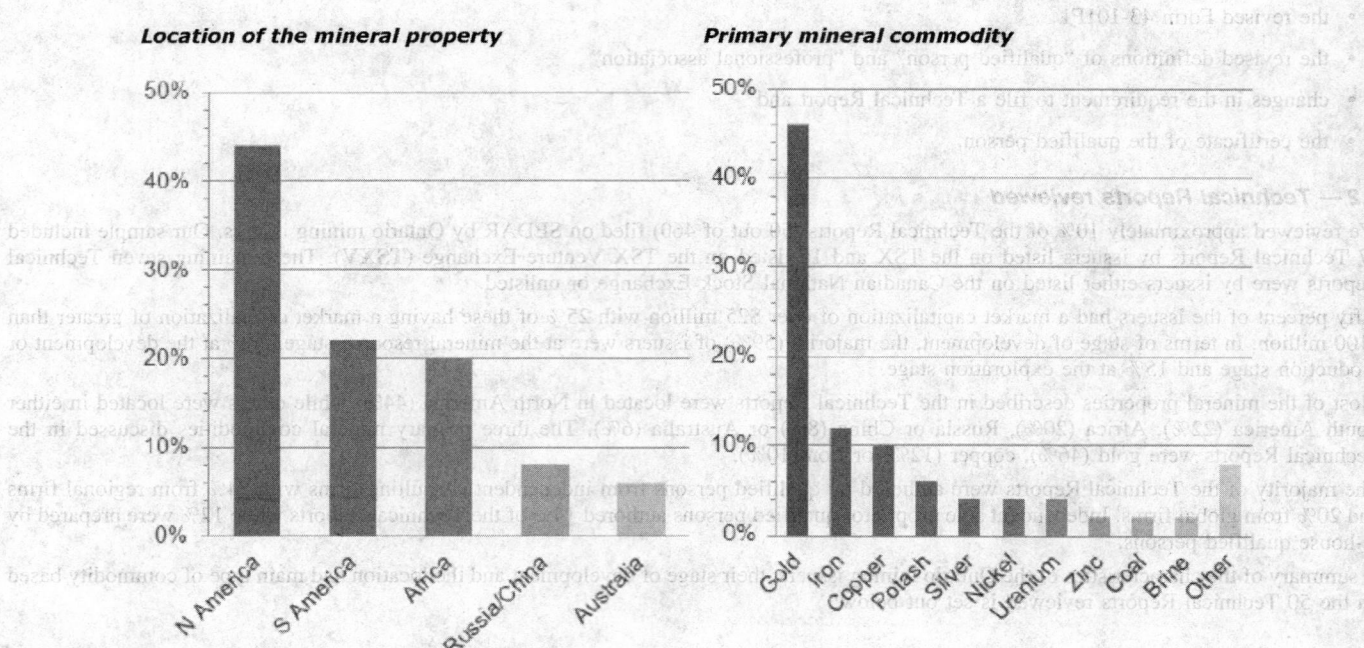

In most cases (58%), the Technical Reports were filed pursuant to subparagraph 4.2(1)(j)(i) of NI 43-101, the first time disclosure trigger, which is informally know as a "property success" trigger. This trigger relates to the first time disclosure of mineral resources, mineral reserves or the results of a preliminary economic assessment (**PEA**), on a property material to an issuer that constitutes:

- a material change in relation to the issuer or

- a change in mineral resources, mineral reserves or the results of a PEA from the most recently filed Technical Report if the change constitutes a material change in relation to the issuer.

Technical Reports were also triggered due to situations informally known as an "issuer event" trigger. These Technical Reports were filed:

- in connection with the issuer's initial public offering (12%) pursuant to paragraph 4.2(1)(a) of NI 43-101

- where the issuer's annual information form included scientific or technical information that related to a mineral project on a property material to the issuer (6%) pursuant to paragraph 4.2(1)(f) of NI 43-101 or

- with the filing of a short form preliminary prospectus (2%) (where the prospectus disclosed for the first time mineral resources, mineral reserves or the results of a PEA that constituted a material change in relation to the issuer or a change in this information, if the change results in a material change in relation to the issuer pursuant to subparagraph 4.2(1)(b) of NI 43-101.

Issuers also filed a Technical Report in connection with Policy 4.6 *Public Offerings by Short From Offering Document* and Exchange Form 4H — *Short Form Offering Document* of the TSXV (14%) pursuant to paragraph 4.2(1)(h) of NI 43-101. Other issuers voluntary filed a Technical Report (8%).

A summary of the triggering event for the 50 Technical Reports we reviewed is set out below:

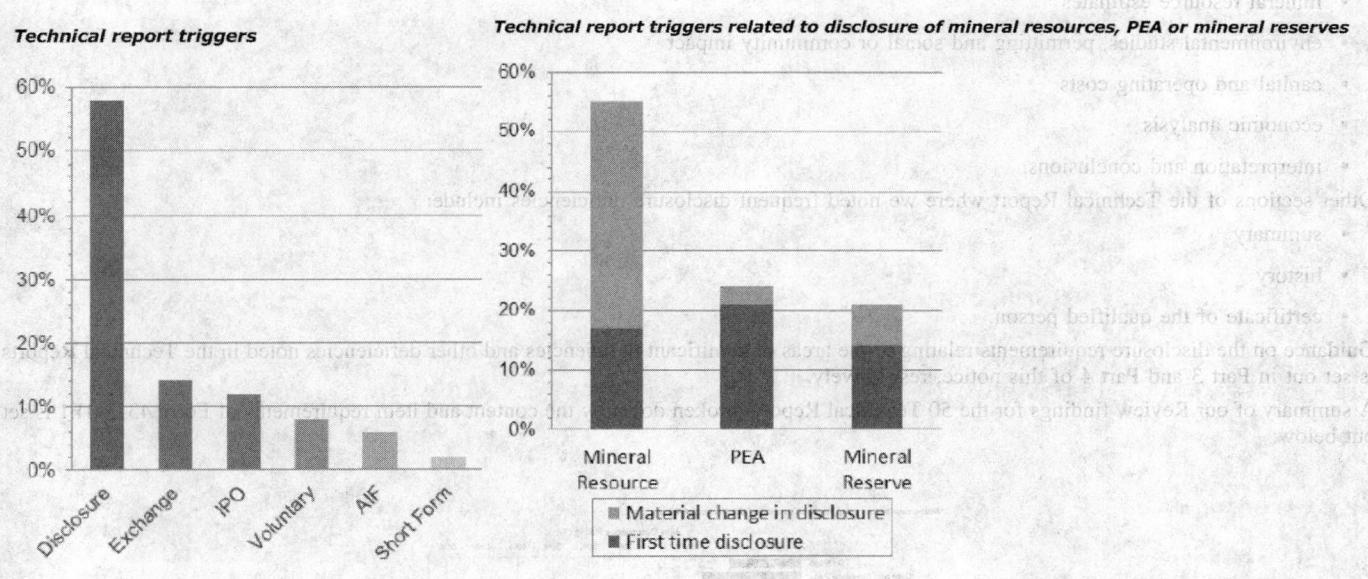

Technical report triggers

Technical report triggers related to disclosure of mineral resources, PEA or mineral reserves

■ Material change in disclosure
■ First time disclosure

We reviewed each of the 50 Technical Reports to determine whether each Technical Report complied with the requirements in Form 43-101F1 and NI 43-101. We remind issuers and qualified persons that staff does not review all Technical Reports filed on SEDAR and cannot approve or certify compliance of any Technical Report.

2.3 — Summary of Review and comments

Approximately 40% of the Technical Reports reviewed had at least one major non-compliance concern. We view this level of non-compliance with the disclosure requirements of Form 43-101F1 to be unacceptable. Although significant efforts have been made to comply with the requirements of Form 43-101F1, issuers and qualified persons need to further improve their disclosure.

2.4 — Guidance

This notice sets out guidance to mining issuers and qualified persons on the existing requirements in NI 43-101 and Form 43-101F1. It is intended to clarify existing disclosure requirements relating to Technical Reports and does not create any new legal requirements or modify existing ones. It is also intended to alert mining issuers and qualified persons by identifying common deficiencies to assist in determining what information in Technical Reports needs to be disclosed, enhanced or supplemented to comply with Form 43-101F1. Issuers and qualified persons should consider this guidance when preparing their Technical Reports.

2.5 — Summary of results

We found an unacceptable level of compliance with Form 43-101F1. Forty (80%) of the total number of Technical Reports reviewed had some form of non-compliance with the requirements of Form 43-101F1. Twenty (40%) of the Technical Reports reviewed had major non-compliance concerns.

We are particularly concerned with the major non-compliance issues noted in the Technical Reports reviewed as these deficiencies may have a significant impact on investors. Technical Reports are a key disclosure document for mining issuers and investors and their advisors may place significant reliance and make investment decisions based on the disclosure in Technical Reports.

A summary of our overall Review findings for the 50 Technical Reports is set out below:

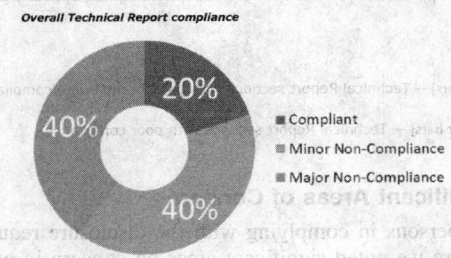

Overall Technical Report compliance

■ Compliant
■ Minor Non-Compliance
■ Major Non-Compliance

The results of the Review identified frequent disclosure deficiencies, some of which may significantly impact investors.

The significant deficiencies include the following sections of the Technical Report:

- mineral resource estimates
- environmental studies, permitting and social or community impact
- capital and operating costs
- economic analysis
- interpretation and conclusions.

Other sections of the Technical Report where we noted frequent disclosure deficiencies include:

- summary
- history
- certificate of the qualified person.

Guidance on the disclosure requirements relating to the areas of significant deficiencies and other deficiencies noted in the Technical Reports is set out in Part 3 and Part 4 of this notice, respectively.

A summary of our Review findings for the 50 Technical Reports broken down by the content and item requirements of Form 43-101F1 is set out below:

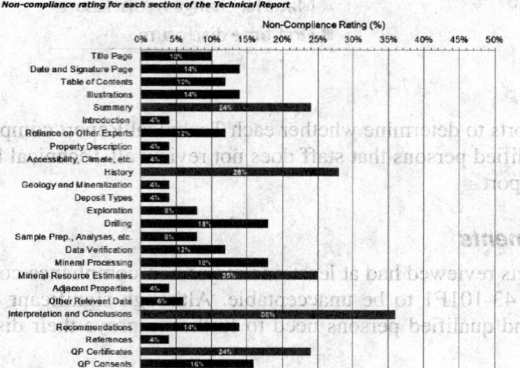

Out of the 50 Technical Reports reviewed, 19 were in relation to advanced properties. A summary of our Review findings for the additional requirements of Form 43-101F1 for an advanced property is set out below:

Legend:

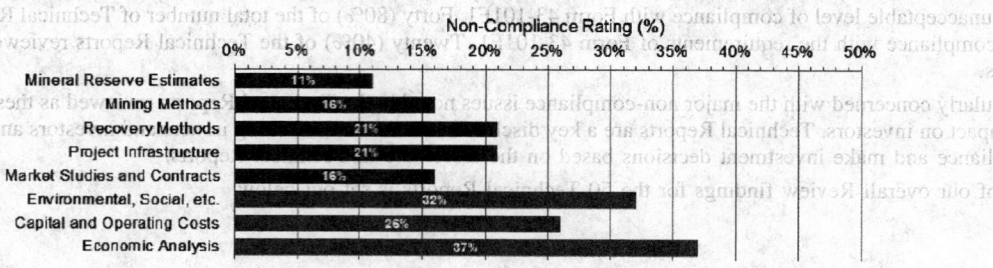

Legend:

Blue bars [Editor's note: darker bars] -- Technical Report sections with good to moderate compliance

Orange bars [Editor's note: lighter bars] -- Technical Report sections with poor compliance

3. — Guidance for Mining Issuers in Significant Areas of Concern

To further assist mining issuers and qualified persons in complying with the disclosure requirements in Form 43-101F1, we have set out guidance for the Technical Report sections where we noted significant areas on concern in our Review.

A. — Mineral resource estimate

Disclosure requirement

Assumptions regarding "reasonable prospects for economic extraction" must be disclosed under subsection 3.4(c) of the NI 43-101.

Item 14 of Form 43-101F1 requires a Technical Report disclosing mineral resources to provide, among other things, sufficient discussion of the key assumptions, parameters and methods used to estimate the mineral resources for a reasonably informed reader to understand the basis for the estimate and how it was generated.

Findings of Review

Our Review found that 25% of the Technical Reports disclosing mineral resource estimates did not provide the required information. In some cases the Technical Reports did not include disclosure as to how "reasonable prospects for economic extraction" were established or what cut-off grade was used to estimate the mineral resource. We also found that many Technical Reports did not clearly disclose the assumed metal price or factors related to the mining scenario or mineral processing recovery. We have also noted that, where a mineral reserve is disclosed, the required statement whether the reserve is included in or excluded from the mineral resource may be absent or not prominent.

Commentary

Qualified persons are reminded that mineral resources, by definition, must have reasonable prospects for economic extraction based on justifiable technical and economic factors. These factors are typically reflected in the cut-off grade and metal price assumptions and other constraints such as the geological model, conceptual pit shell or mine model. The Canadian Institute of Mining, Metallurgy and Petroleum's Best Practice Guidelines for Estimation of Mineral Resources and Mineral Reserves provide guidance on the constraints that should be considered in resource estimation and disclosed as part of a statement of mineral resources. We expect qualified persons to use procedures and methodologies that are consistent with industry best practices.

If an issuer discloses in writing mineral resources on a property material to the issuer, the issuer must include in the written disclosure, amongst other things, the key assumptions, parameters and methods used by the qualified person to estimate the mineral resources.

Qualified persons and issuers are reminded to provide the key assumptions, parameters and methods to support the basis for estimating the mineral resource as required under subsection 3.4(c) of NI 43-101.

B. — Environmental studies, permitting and social or community impact

Disclosure requirement

Item 20 of Form 43-101F1 requires that a Technical Report for an "advanced property" discuss reasonably available information on environmental permits and social or community factors related to the mineral project. Specifically, with regards to social or community impact, Item 20 requires a discussion of any potential social or community related requirements and plans for the project and the status of any negotiations or agreements with local communities. It also requires the qualified person to include a discussion of mine closure (remediation and reclamation) requirements and costs.

Findings of Review

Our Review found that 32% of the Technical Reports on advanced properties did not adequately disclose information related to environmental permits or the social or community impacts of developing the mineral project. We also found that some Technical Reports did not disclose how surface rights issues would be addressed or whether there was an exploration agreement in place or under negotiation with local First Nation communities.

Commentary

In some recent cases, the inability to advance projects has been related to surface and community issues rather than geological or technical issues.

Issuers are reminded that National Instrument 41-101 *General Prospectus Requirements* requires issuers to file material contracts that are entered in the ordinary course of business. A material contract is a contract to which a reporting issuer or any of its subsidiaries is a party that is material to the reporting issuer and generally includes a schedule, side letter or exhibit referred to in the material contract as well as any amendment to the material contract. When negotiating material contracts and agreements with local First Nation communities, issuers should consider this filing requirement, including with respect to any confidentiality obligations in such contracts.

Qualified persons are reminded to include a discussion of any potential social or community related requirements and plans for the project and the status of any negotiations or agreements with local communities and a discussion of mine closure (remediation and reclamation) requirements and costs in Technical Reports on an "advanced property".

C. — Capital and operating costs

Disclosure requirement

Item 21 of Form 43-101F1 requires the Technical Report for an "advanced property" to include a summary of capital and operating cost estimates, with the major components set out in tabular form. The summary must explain and justify the basis for the cost estimates.

Findings of Review

We found that 26% of the Technical Reports on advanced properties did not adequately disclose information required by Item 21 of Form 43-101F1. In some cases, the main components of the capital cost estimate were not provided. In other cases, the Technical Report did not provide justification for how the operating cost estimate was determined or why certain costs were assumed.

Commentary

It is important for qualified persons to include disclosure of the main components of the estimated capital and operating costs and the basis for these costs.

Cost estimates should not be a single bottom-line number. Qualified persons are reminded to provide more context and justification for capital and operating cost estimates included in Technical Reports for an "advanced property".

D. — Economic analysis

Disclosure requirement

Item 22 of Form 43-101F1 requires that the Technical Report for an "advanced property" provide an economic analysis for the mineral project. The economic analysis must include a clear statement of and justification for the principal assumptions and cash flow forecasts on an annual basis using mineral reserves or mineral resources and an annual production schedule for the life of the project. It must also include a discussion of net present value, internal rate of return and payback period of capital with imputed or actual interest. Specifically, Item 22(d) of Form 43-101F1 requires that the economic analysis include a summary of the taxes, royalties and other governmental levies or interests applicable to the mineral project or to production and to revenue or income from the mineral project. Finally, Item 22(e) of Form 43-101F1 requires that the economic analysis include sensitivity or other analysis using variants in commodity price, grade, capital and operating costs or other significant parameters as appropriate, and a discussion of the impact of the results.

Findings of Review

We found that 37% of the Technical Reports on advanced properties did not sufficiently disclose the economic analysis information required by Item 22 of Form 43-101F1. We found that some Technical Reports did not provide cash flows on an annual basis or provide an appropriate sensitivity analysis with related impacts on the economic analysis. We also found that 40% of the Technical Reports on mineral projects at a PEA-stage did not adequately address the issue of taxes applicable to the mineral project.

Commentary

Reporting of only pre-tax cash flows in a Technical Report for an advanced property which includes results of a PEA, pre-feasibility or feasibility study does not meet the disclosure requirement Item 22(d) of Form 43-101F1 or provide sufficient information for investors to properly assess the mineral project. Additionally, our Review noted some instances of very limited ranges of sensitivities or only up-side sensitivities which may not reflect the true nature of the project risk as required by Item 22(e) of Form 43-101F1.

It is potentially misleading for a Technical Report on an "advanced property" to disclose only pre-tax cash flows and economic outcomes or to disclose only positive metal price changes or only up-side sensitivity analysis.

E. — Interpretation and conclusions

Disclosure requirement

Item 25 of Form 43-101F1 requires the Technical Report to summarize the relevant results and interpretations of the information and analysis being reported on. Specifically, it includes a new requirement to discuss any significant risks and uncertainties and any related reasonably foreseeable impacts of these risks and uncertainties. The interpretation and conclusions section is required to include a discussion on any significant risks and uncertainties that could reasonably be expected to affect the reliability or confidence in the exploration information, mineral resource or mineral reserve estimates or projected economic outcomes. The Technical Report should also include a discussion of any reasonably foreseeable impacts of these risks and uncertainties to the project's potential economic viability or continued viability. A Technical Report concerning exploration information must include the conclusions of the qualified person.

Findings of Review

Our Review revealed that 36% of Technical Reports reviewed did not disclose project specific risks and uncertainties such as the availability of water rights, use of a novel mineral processing technology or the potential impact of a civil war in the region.

Commentary

Item 25 of Form 43-101 requires the qualified person to include in the Technical Report a clear overview of the main risks, uncertainties and potential impacts of these risks and uncertainties on the mineral project and its potential future development. Some Technical Reports reviewed contained a concise summary table which clearly provided this information.

Qualified persons should consider including in the Technical Report a table showing the significant project specific risks, potential outcomes and mitigating factors along with supplementary discussions. Possible opportunities may also be included, if reasonable.

4. — Guidance for Mining Issuers in Other Areas of Concern

To further assist mining issuers and qualified persons in complying with the disclosure requirements in Form 43-101F1, we have set out guidance for the Technical Report sections where we noted other areas of concern in our Review.

A. — Summary

Disclosure requirement

Item 1 of Form 43-101F1 requires a brief summary of important information in the Technical Report, including property description, ownership, geology and mineralization, the status of exploration, development and operations, mineral resource and mineral reserve estimates and the qualified person's conclusions and recommendations.

Findings of Review

Our Review found that 24% of the Technical Reports did not provide a summary that met the requirements in Form 43-101F1 and did not provide a useful overview of the important information and key findings about the mineral project in particular. Some Technical Reports with mineral resource estimates or PEA outcomes did not include this information in the summary. Where other report items were deficient, the deficiencies often also appeared in the summary.

Commentary

The summary is a key part of the Technical Report and needs to include important information relative to the stage of development of the mineral property. If a mineral resource has been estimated or a PEA has been disclosed the actual numbers and key findings need to be included in the summary. A qualified person may refer to section 5.4 of Form 51-102F2 *Annual Information Form* as a possible template for what to include in the summary of a Technical Report.

A qualified person is reminded to briefly summarize important information and "key findings" about the property including:

- property description and ownership

- data verification and site visits

- mineral resource and mineral reserve estimates (if applicable)

- mining studies and economic analysis (if applicable)

- qualified person's conclusions and recommendations.

B. — History

Disclosure requirement

Item 6 of Form 43-101F1 requires a description of:
- the prior ownership of the property and ownership changes

- the type, amount, quantity and general results of exploration and development work undertaken by any previous owners or operators

- any significant historical estimates in accordance with the requirements and cautionary language in section 2.4 of NI 43-101 and

- any production from the property.

If the Technical Report includes work that was conducted outside the issuer's current property boundaries, the disclosure should distinguish this work from the work conducted on the property that is the subject of the Technical Report.

Findings of Review

We observed that 28% of the Technical Reports reviewed did not include the cautionary statements required by section 2.4 of NI 43-101 when a historical estimate was disclosed.

Commentary

Simply stating that the historical estimate is not compliant with NI 43-101 does not satisfy the requirements of NI 43-101. Subsection 2.4(g) of the NI 43-101 requires that each time a historical estimate is disclosed, either in the Technical Report or in the issuer's other disclosure, the cautionary language must be stated with equal prominence that:

- a qualified person has not done sufficient work to classify the historical estimate as a current resource estimate and

- the issuer is not treating the historical estimate as a current resource estimate.

Qualified persons and issuers are reminded to include the required cautionary language as set out in section 2.4 of NI 43-101 every time a historical estimate is disclosed.

C. — Qualified person certificate

Disclosure requirements

Subsection 8.1(1) of NI 43-101 requires an issuer, when filing a Technical Report, to file a certificate that is dated, signed, and if the signatory has a seal, sealed, for each qualified person responsible for preparing or supervising the preparation of all or part of the Technical Report.

Additionally, paragraph 8.1(2) of NI 43-101 provides a list of the specific information and statements required to be included in the qualified person(s) certificate including, but not limited to, the qualified person's qualifications, brief summary of their relevant experience and the item(s) of the Technical Report for which the qualified person is responsible.

Findings of Review

We found that 24% of the qualified person(s) certificates were deficient. In some instances, the certificate was not dated or signed. In other cases, the qualified person(s) did not include which items of the Technical Report they were responsible for or a summary of their relevant experience related to the commodity, type of mineral deposit and situation under consideration that they were responsible for in the Technical Report.

Commentary

It is important to ensure that each section of the Technical Report has a qualified person with the appropriate relevant experience taking responsibility for the information provided.

Qualified persons are reminded to include all the required statements as per subsection 8.1(2) of NI 43-101. The qualified person's certificate is one of the first things checked by the regulators when reviewing a Technical Report.

5. — Governance Structures Around Form 43-101F1 and NI 43-101

The qualified person is responsible for preparing or supervising the preparation of the Technical Report and providing scientific and technical advice in accordance with applicable professional standards pursuant to section 2.1 of NI 43-101. Section 2.1 of the Companion Policy to NI 43-101 provides that primary responsibility for the disclosure in an issuer's Technical Report, and the proper use of the scientific and technical information provided by the qualified person, is the responsibility of the issuer and its directors and officers.

The onus is on the issuer and its directors and officers and, in the case of a document filed with a securities regulatory authority, each signatory to the document, to ensure that disclosure in the document is consistent with the related Technical Report or advice. An issuer should consider having the qualified person review disclosure that summarizes or restates the Technical Report or the technical advice or opinion to ensure that the disclosure is accurate.

In our view, while there is no statutory requirement that directors review the issuer's Technical Reports in full, each issuer should determine how it can meet our expectations with regards to the disclosure responsibility set out in section 2.1 of the Companion Policy to NI 43-101. In fulfilling their oversight function relating to the Technical Report, a board of directors should consider the composition and technical skill set of the board of directors, its various committees and the management team in order to ensure that it can meet the issuer's responsibilities for mining-related disclosure.

6. — Conclusions and Questions

Mining issuers and qualified persons should consider NI 43-101, Form 43-101F1 and the guidance in this notice when preparing their Technical Reports to ensure that each Technical Report complies with securities legislation and provides investors with meaningful information for making investment decisions. It is important for investors to have accurate and meaningful information about a mineral property material to the issuer.

We will continue the review of Technical Reports of Ontario mining issuers as part of our overall CD program. Issuers should anticipate staff requests for re-filings or other staff action, where appropriate, if an issuer has not fully met the requirements of Form 43-101F1 and NI 43-101. Please note that the issues raised in a review will be taken into consideration when determining whether a prospectus receipt should be issued. Unresolved issues may delay the prospectus receipt, particularly for short form prospectus filings.

4.4 — Alternative Forms of Prospectus

National Instrument 44-101 — Short Form Prospectus Distributions

Date: December 22, 2000, as amended effective September 30, 2003, March 30, 2004 and January 4, 2005; replaced effective December 30, 2005, as amended effective September 6, 2006, December 29, 2006, December 31, 2007, March 17, 2008, January 1, 2011, June 30, 2011, April 20, 2012, May 14, 2013, May 31, 2013, August 13, 2015, November 17, 2015 and December 8, 2015.

23 O.S.C.B. (Supp) 867, 26 O.S.C.B. 5547, 26 O.S.C.B. (Supp-3) 55, 28 O.S.C.B. 83, 28 O.S.C.B. 10385, 29 O.S.C.B. 7085, 29 O.S.C.B. (Supp. 2) 26, 30 O.S.C.B. 10520, 31 O.S.C.B. (Supp. 2) 171, 33 O.S.C.B. (Supp. 5) 97, 34 O.S.C.B. 7083, 35 O.S.C.B. 2383, 36 O.S.C.B. 4917, 36 O.S.C.B. 2619, 36 O.S.C.B. 8018, 38 O.S.C.B. 7551, 38 O.S.C.B. 8319 and 38 O.S.C.B. 9328.

Table of Contents

PART 1 — DEFINITIONS AND INTERPRETATIONS

1.1 Definitions — In this Instrument

"AIF" has the same meaning as in NI 51-102 for a reporting issuer other than an investment fund, and for an investment fund means an annual information form as such term is used in NI 81-106;

"applicable CD rule" means, for a reporting issuer other than an investment fund, NI 51-102 and, for an investment fund, NI 81-106;

"cash equivalent" means an evidence of indebtedness that has a remaining term to maturity of 365 days or less and that is issued, or fully and unconditionally guaranteed as to principal and interest, by

(a) the government of Canada or the government of a jurisdiction of Canada,

(b) the government of the United States of America, the government of one of the states of the United States of America, the government of another sovereign state or a permitted supranational agency, if, in each case, the evidence of indebtedness has a designated rating, or

(c) a Canadian financial institution, or other entity that is regulated as a banking institution, loan corporation, trust company, or insurance company or credit union by the government, or an agency of the government, of the country under whose laws the entity is incorporated or organized or a political subdivision of that country, if, in either case, the Canadian financial institution or other entity has outstanding short term debt securities that have received a designated rating from any designated rating organization or its DRO affiliate;

"cash settled derivative" means a derivative, the terms of which provide for settlement only by means of cash or cash equivalent the amount of which is determinable by reference to the underlying interest of the derivative;

"current AIF" means,

(a) if the issuer has filed an AIF for its most recently completed financial year, that AIF, or

(b) the issuer's AIF filed for the financial year immediately preceding its most recently completed financial year if

(i) the issuer has not filed an AIF for its most recently completed financial year, and

(ii) the issuer is not yet required under the applicable CD rule to have filed its annual financial statements for its most recently completed financial year, "current annual financial statements" means,

(a) if the issuer has filed its comparative annual financial statements in accordance with the applicable CD rule for its most recently completed financial year, those financial statements together with the auditor's report accompanying the financial statements and, if there has been a change of auditors since the comparative period, an auditor's report on the financial statements for the comparative period, or

(b) the issuer's comparative annual financial statements filed for the financial year immediately preceding its most recently completed financial year, together with the auditor's report accompanying the financial statements and, if there has been a change of auditors since the comparative period, an auditor's report on the financial statements for the comparative period if

(i) the issuer has not filed its comparative annual financial statements for its most recently completed financial year, and

(ii) the issuer is not yet required under the applicable CD rule to have filed its annual financial statements for its most recently completed financial year;

"designated rating" means, for a security, a rating issued by a designated rating organization, or its DRO affiliate, that is at or above one of the following rating categories or that is at or above a category that replaces one of the following rating categories:

Designated Rating Organization	Long Term Debt	Short Term Debt	Preferred Shares
DBRS Limited	BBB	R-2	Pfd-3
Fitch, Inc.	BBB	F3	BBB
Moody's Canada Inc.	Baa	Prime-3	"baaa"
Standard & Poor's Ratings Services (Canada)	BBB	A-3	P-3

"designated rating organization" means

(a) each of DBRS Limited, Fitch, Inc., Moody's Canada Inc., Standard & Poor's Ratings Services (Canada), including their DRO affiliates; or

(b) any other credit rating organization that has been designated under securities legislation;

"DRO affiliate" has the same meaning as in section 1 of National Instrument 25-101 *Designated Rating Organizations*;

"material change report" means, for a reporting issuer other than an investment fund, a completed Form 51-102F3, and for an investment fund, a completed Form 51-102F3 *Material Change Report* of NI 51-102 adjusted as directed by NI 81-106;

"MD&A" has the same meaning as in NI 51-102 in relation to a reporting issuer other than an investment fund, and in relation to an investment fund means an annual or interim management report of fund performance as defined in NI 81-106;

"NI 13-101" means National Instrument 13-101 *System for Electronic Document Analysis and Retrieval (SEDAR)*;

"NI 41-101" means National Instrument 41-101 *General Prospectus Requirements*;

"permitted supranational agency" means the International Bank for Reconstruction and Development, the International Finance Corporation, the Inter-American Development Bank, the Asian Development Bank, the Caribbean Development Bank, the European Bank for Reconstruction and Development, the African Development Bank and any person or company prescribed under paragraph (g) of the definition of "foreign property" in subsection 206(1) of the ITA;

"reverse takeover acquiree" has the same meaning as in section 1.1 of NI 51-102;

"short form eligible exchange" means each of the Toronto Stock Exchange, Tier 1 and Tier 2 of the TSX Venture Exchange, Aequitas NEO Exchange Inc., and the Canadian Securities Exchange;

"successor issuer" means

(a) except for an issuer which, in the case where the restructuring transaction involved a divestiture of a portion of a reporting issuer's business, succeeded to or otherwise acquired less than substantially all of the business divested, an issuer that meets any of the following requirements:

(i) it was a reverse takeover acquiree in a completed reverse takeover;

(ii) it was formed as a result of a completed restructuring transaction;

(iii) it participated in a restructuring transaction and its existence continued following the completion of the restructuring transaction; or

(b) an issuer that issued securities to the securityholders of a second issuer that was a reporting issuer, in a reorganization that did not alter those securityholders' proportionate interest in the second issuer or the second issuer's proportionate interest in its assets;

"underlying interest" means, for a derivative, the security, commodity, financial instrument, currency, interest rate, foreign exchange rate, economic indicator, index, basket, agreement, benchmark or any other reference, interest or variable, and, if applicable, the relationship between any of the foregoing, from, to or on which the market price, value or any payment obligation of the derivative is derived, referenced or based; and

"U.S. credit supporter" means a credit supporter that

(a) is incorporated or organized under the laws of the United States of America or any state or territory of the United States of America or the District of Columbia,

(b) either

(i) has a class of securities registered under section 12(b) or section 12(g) of the 1934 Act, or

(ii) is required to file reports under section 15(d) of the 1934 Act,

(c) has filed with the SEC all 1934 Act filings for a period of 12 calendar months immediately before the filing of the preliminary short form prospectus,

(d) is not registered or required to be registered as an investment company under the *Investment Company Act of 1940* of the United States of America, and

(e) is not a commodity pool issuer as defined in National Instrument 71-101 *The Multijurisdictional Disclosure System*;

1.1.1 Definitions in NI 41-101 — Every term that is defined or interpreted in NI 41-101, the definition or interpretation of which is not restricted to a specific portion of NI 41-101, has, if used in this Instrument, the meaning ascribed to it in NI 41-101, unless otherwise defined or interpreted in this Instrument.

1.2 References to Information Included in a Document — References in this Instrument to information included in a document refer to both information contained directly in the document and information incorporated by reference in the document.

1.3 References to Information to be Included in a Document — Provisions of this Instrument that require an issuer to include information in a document require an issuer either to insert the information directly in the document or to incorporate the information in the document by reference.

1.4 Interpretation of "short form prospectus" — In this Instrument, other than in Parts 4 through 8 or unless otherwise stated, a reference to a short form prospectus includes a preliminary short form prospectus.

PART 2 — QUALIFICATION TO FILE A PROSPECTUS IN THE FORM OF A SHORT FORM PROSPECTUS

2.1 Short Form Prospectus — (1) An issuer shall not file a prospectus in the form of Form 44-101F1 of this Instrument unless the issuer is qualified under any of sections 2.2 through 2.6 to file a prospectus in the form of a short form prospectus.

(2) An issuer that is qualified under any of sections 2.2 through 2.6 to file a prospectus in the form of a short form prospectus for a distribution may file, for that distribution,

(a) a preliminary prospectus, prepared and certified in the form of Form 44-101F1; and

(b) a prospectus, prepared and certified in the form of Form 44-101F1.

2.2 Basic Qualification Criteria — An issuer is qualified to file a prospectus in the form of a short form prospectus for a distribution of any of its securities in the local jurisdiction, if the following criteria are satisfied:

(a) the issuer is an electronic filer under NI 13-101;

(b) the issuer is a reporting issuer in at least one jurisdiction of Canada;

(c) the issuer has filed with the securities regulatory authority in each jurisdiction in which it is a reporting issuer all periodic and timely disclosure documents that it is required to have filed in that jurisdiction

(i) under applicable securities legislation,

(ii) pursuant to an order issued by the securities regulatory authority, or

(iii) pursuant to an undertaking to the securities regulatory authority;

(d) the issuer has, in at least one jurisdiction in which it is a reporting issuer,

(i) current annual financial statements, and

(ii) a current AIF;

(e) the issuer's equity securities are listed and posted for trading on a short form eligible exchange and the issuer is not an issuer

(i) whose operations have ceased, or

(ii) whose principal asset is cash, cash equivalents, or its exchange listing.

2.3 Alternative Qualification Criteria for Issuers of Designated Rating Non-Convertible Securities — (1) An issuer is qualified to file a prospectus in the form of a short form prospectus for a distribution of non-convertible securities in the local jurisdiction, if the following criteria are satisfied:

(a) the issuer is an electronic filer under NI 13-101;

(b) the issuer is a reporting issuer in at least one jurisdiction of Canada;

(c) the issuer has filed with the securities regulatory authority in each jurisdiction in which it is a reporting issuer all periodic and timely disclosure documents that it is required to have filed in that jurisdiction

(i) under applicable securities legislation,

(ii) pursuant to an order issued by the securities regulatory authority, or

(iii) pursuant to an undertaking to the securities regulatory authority;

(d) the issuer has, in at least one jurisdiction in which it is a reporting issuer,

(i) current annual financial statements, and

(ii) a current AIF;

(e) the securities to be distributed

(i) have received a designated rating on a provisional basis,

(ii) are not the subject of an announcement by a designated rating organization or its DRO affiliate, of which the issuer is or ought reasonably to be aware, that the designated rating given by the organization may be down-graded to a rating category that would not be a designated rating, and

(iii) have not received a provisional or final rating lower than a designated rating from any designated rating organization or its DRO affiliate.

(2) Paragraph (1)(e) does not apply to an issuer filing a short form prospectus that is a base shelf prospectus under NI 44-102.

2.4 Alternative Qualification Criteria for Issuers of Guaranteed Non-Convertible Debt Securities, Preferred Shares and Cash Settled Derivatives — (1) An issuer is qualified to file a prospectus in the form of a short form prospectus for a distribution of non-convertible debt securities, non-convertible preferred shares or non-convertible cash settled derivatives in the local jurisdiction, if the following criteria are satisfied:

(a) a credit supporter has provided full and unconditional credit support for the securities being distributed,

(b) at least one of the following is true:

(i) the credit supporter satisfies the criteria in paragraphs 2.2(a), (b), (c) and (d) if the word "issuer" is replaced with "credit supporter" wherever it occurs;

Part 4:
DISTRIBUTIONS

(ii) the credit supporter is a U.S. credit supporter and the issuer is incorporated or organized under the laws of Canada or a jurisdiction of Canada;

(c) unless the credit supporter satisfies the criteria in paragraph 2.2(e) if the word "issuer" is replaced with "credit supporter" wherever it occurs, at the time the preliminary short form prospectus is filed

(i) the credit supporter has outstanding non-convertible securities that

(A) have received a designated rating,

(B) have not been the subject of an announcement by a designated rating organization or its DRO affiliate, of which the issuer is or ought reasonably to be aware, that the designated rating given by the organization may be down-graded to a rating category that would not be a designated rating, and

(C) have not received a rating lower than a designated rating from any designated rating organization or its DRO affiliate, and

(ii) the securities to be issued by the issuer

(A) have received a designated rating on a provisional basis,

(B) have not been the subject of an announcement by a designated rating organization or its DRO affiliate, of which the issuer is or ought reasonably to be aware, that the designated rating given by the organization may be down-graded to a rating category that would not be a designated rating, and

(C) have not received a provisional or final rating lower than a designated rating from any designated rating organization or its DRO affiliate.

(2) Subparagraph (1)(c)(ii) does not apply to an issuer filing a short form prospectus that is a base shelf prospectus under NI 44-102.

2.5 Alternative Qualification Criteria for Issuers of Guaranteed Convertible Debt Securities or Preferred Shares — An issuer is qualified to file a prospectus in the form of a short form prospectus for a distribution of convertible debt securities or convertible preferred shares in the local jurisdiction, if the following criteria are satisfied:

(a) the debt securities or the preferred shares are convertible into securities of a credit supporter that has provided full and unconditional credit support for the securities being distributed;

(b) the credit supporter satisfies the criteria in section 2.2 if the word "issuer" is replaced with "credit supporter" wherever it occurs.

2.6 Alternative Qualification Criteria for Issuers of Asset-Backed Securities — (1) An issuer established in connection with a distribution of asset-backed securities is qualified to file a prospectus in the form of a short form prospectus for a distribution of asset-backed securities in the local jurisdiction, if the following criteria are satisfied:

(a) the issuer is an electronic filer under NI 13-101;

(b) the issuer has, in at least one jurisdiction of Canada,

(i) current annual financial statements, and

(ii) a current AIF;

(c) the asset-backed securities to be distributed

(i) have received a designated rating on a provisional basis,

(ii) have not been the subject of an announcement by a designated rating organization or its DRO affiliate, of which the issuer is or ought reasonably to be aware, that the designated rating given by the organization may be down-graded to a rating category that would not be a designated rating, and

(iii) have not received a provisional or final rating lower than a designated rating from any designated rating organization or its DRO affiliate.

(2) Paragraph (1)(c) does not apply to an issuer filing a short form prospectus that is a base shelf prospectus under NI 44-102.

2.7 Exemptions for Reporting Issuers that Previously Filed a Prospectus and Successor Issuers — (1) Paragraphs 2.2(d), 2.3(1)(d) and 2.6(1)(b) do not apply to an issuer if

(a) the issuer is not exempt from the requirement in the applicable CD rule to file any annual financial statements within a prescribed period after its financial year end, but the issuer has not yet been required under the applicable CD rule to file annual financial statements, and

(b) unless the issuer is seeking qualification under section 2.6, the issuer has filed and obtained a receipt for a final prospectus that included the issuer's or each predecessor entity's comparative annual financial statements for its most recently completed financial year or the financial year immediately preceding its most recently completed financial year, together with the auditor's report accompanying those financial statements and, if there has been a change of auditors since the comparative period, an auditor's report on the financial statements for the comparative period.

(1.1) Subparagraphs 2.2(d)(ii), 2.3(1)(d)(ii) and 2.6(1)(b)(ii) do not apply to an issuer if

(a) the issuer has filed annual financial statements as required under the applicable CD rule, and

(b) unless the issuer is seeking qualification under section 2.6, the issuer has filed and obtained a receipt for a final prospectus that included the issuer's or each predecessor entity's comparative annual financial statements for its most recently completed financial year or the financial year immediately preceding its most recently completed financial year, together with the auditor's report accompanying those financial statements and, if there has been a change of auditors since the comparative period, an auditor's report on the financial statements for the comparative period.

(2) Paragraphs 2.2(d), 2.3(1)(d) and 2.6(1)(b) do not apply to a successor issuer if

(a) the successor issuer is not exempt from the requirement in the applicable CD rule to file annual financial statements within a prescribed period after its financial year end, but the successor issuer has not yet, since the completion of the restructuring transaction or the reorganization described in paragraph (b) of the definition of "successor issuer", which resulted in the successor issuer, been required under the applicable CD rule to file annual financial statements, and

(b) an information circular relating to the restructuring transaction or the reorganization described in paragraph (b) of the definition of "successor issuer", in which the successor issuer participated or which resulted in the successor issuer was filed by the successor issuer or an issuer that was a party to the restructuring transaction or reorganization, and such information circular

(i) complied with applicable securities legislation, and

(ii) in the case of a restructuring transaction included disclosure in accordance with Item 14.2 or 14.5 of Form 51-102F5 for the successor issuer.

(3) Paragraphs 2.2(d), 2.3(1)(d) and 2.6(1)(b) do not apply to an issuer if

(a) the issuer is not exempt from the requirement in the applicable CD rule to file annual financial statements within a prescribed period after its financial year end, but the issuer has not yet, since the completion of a qualifying transaction or reverse takeover (as both terms are defined in the TSX Venture Exchange Corporate Finance Manual, as amended from time to time) been required under the applicable CD rule to file annual financial statements, and

(b) a CPC filing statement as defined in the TSX Venture Exchange Corporate Finance Manual as amended from time to time, or other filing statement of the TSX Venture Exchange was filed by the issuer and,

(i) in the case of a CPC filing statement, the statement

(A) was filed in connection with a qualifying transaction, and

(B) complied with the TSX Venture Exchange Corporate Finance Manual, as amended from time to time, in respect of the qualifying transaction; or

(ii) in the case of a TSX Venture Exchange filing statement, other than a CPC filing statement, the statement

(A) was filed in connection with a reverse takeover, and

(B) complied with TSX Venture Exchange Corporate Finance Manual, as amended from time to time, in respect of the reverse takeover.

2.8 Notice of Intention and Transition — (1) An issuer is not qualified to file a short form prospectus under this Part unless it has filed a notice declaring its intention to be qualified to file a short form prospectus at least 10 business days prior to the issuer filing its first preliminary short form prospectus after the notice

(a) with its notice regulator, and

(b) in substantially the form of Appendix A.

(2) The notice under subsection (1) is effective until withdrawn.

(3) For the purposes of subsection (1), "notice regulator" means, as determined on the date the notice is filed, the securities regulatory authority or regulator of the jurisdiction of Canada

(a) in which the issuer's head office is located, if the issuer is not an investment fund and the issuer is a reporting issuer in that jurisdiction,

(b) in which the investment fund manager's head office is located, if the issuer is an investment fund and the issuer is a reporting issuer in that jurisdiction, or

(c) with which the issuer has determined that it has the most significant connection, if paragraphs (a) and (b) do not apply to the issuer.

(4) For the purposes of this section, if, on December 29, 2005, an issuer had a current AIF under National Instrument 44-101 *Short Form Prospectus Distributions* that was in force on December 29, 2005, the issuer is deemed to have filed a notice on December 14, 2005 declaring its intention to be qualified to file a short form prospectus.

(5) [repealed]

(6) The 10 business day period referred to in subsection (1) does not apply if

(a) an issuer is relying on section 2.4 or 2.5 and the following requirements are met:

(i) the issuer satisfies section 2.4 or 2.5, as applicable, at the time of filing its short form prospectus;

(ii) the issuer files its notice of intention before or concurrently with the filing of its preliminary short form prospectus; and

(iii) the issuer's credit supporter

(A) previously filed a notice of intention under subsection (1) which has not been withdrawn; or

(B) is deemed to have filed a notice of intention under subsection (4); or

(b) an issuer is a successor issuer and the following requirements are met:

(i) the issuer satisfies

(A) section 2.2, 2.3 or 2.6, and

(B) subsection 2.7(2);

(ii) the issuer files its notice of intention before or concurrently with the filing of its preliminary short form prospectus; and

(iii) the issuer has acquired substantially all of its business from a person or company that

(A) previously filed a notice of intention under subsection (1) which has not been withdrawn; or

(B) is deemed to have filed a notice of intention under subsection (4).

PART 3 — DEEMED INCORPORATION BY REFERENCE

3.1 Deemed Incorporation by Reference of Filed Documents — If an issuer does not incorporate by reference in its short form prospectus a document required to be incorporated by reference under section 11.1 or 12.1 of Form 44-101F1, the document is deemed for purposes of securities legislation to be incorporated by reference in the issuer's short form prospectus as of the date of the short form prospectus to the extent not otherwise modified or superseded by a statement contained in the short form prospectus or in any other subsequently filed document that also is, or is deemed to be, incorporated by reference in the short form prospectus.

3.2 Deemed Incorporation by Reference of Subsequently Filed Documents — If an issuer does not incorporate by reference in its short form prospectus a subsequently filed document required to be incorporated by reference under section 11.2 or 12.1 of Form 44-101F1, the document is deemed for purposes of securities legislation to be incorporated by reference in the issuer's short form prospectus as of the date the issuer filed the document to the extent not otherwise modified or superseded by a statement contained in the short form prospectus or in any other subsequently filed document that also is, or is deemed to be, incorporated by reference in the short form prospectus.

3.3 Incorporation by Reference — A document deemed by this Instrument to be incorporated by reference in another document is deemed for purposes of securities legislation to be incorporated by reference in the other document.

PART 4 — FILING REQUIREMENTS FOR A SHORT FORM PROSPECTUS

4.1 Required Documents for Filing a Preliminary Short Form Prospectus — (1) An issuer that files a preliminary short form prospectus shall

(a) file the following with the preliminary short form prospectus:

(i) **Signed Copy** — a signed copy of the preliminary short form prospectus;

(ii) **Qualification Certificate** — a certificate, dated as of the date of the preliminary short form prospectus, executed on behalf of the issuer by one of its executive officers

(A) specifying which of the qualification criteria set out in Part 2 the issuer is relying on in order to be qualified to file a prospectus in the form of a short form prospectus, and

(B) certifying that

(I) all of those qualification criteria have been satisfied, and

(II) all of the material incorporated by reference in the preliminary short form prospectus and not previously filed is being filed with the preliminary short form prospectus;

(iii) **Material Incorporated by Reference** — copies of all material incorporated by reference in the preliminary short form prospectus and not previously filed;

(iv) **Documents Affecting the Rights of Securityholders** — a copy of any document required to be filed under subsection 12.1(1) of NI 51-102 or section 16.4 of NI 81-106, as applicable, that relates to the securities being distributed, and that has not previously been filed;

(iv.1) **Material Contracts** — a copy of any material contract required to be filed under section 12.2 of NI 51-102 or section 16.4 of NI 81-106 that has not previously been filed;

(v) **Mining Reports** — if the issuer has a mineral project, the technical reports required to be filed with a preliminary short form prospectus under NI 43-101;

(vi) **Reports and Valuations** — a copy of each report or valuation referred to in the preliminary short form prospectus for which a consent is required to be filed under section 10.1 of NI 41-101 and that has not previously been filed, other than a technical report that

(A) deals with a mineral project or oil and gas activities, and

(B) is not otherwise required to be filed under paragraph (v); and

(vii) **Marketing Materials** — a copy of any template version of the marketing materials required to be filed under paragraph 7.6(1)(e) of this Instrument or paragraph 13.7(1)(e) of NI 41-101 that has not previously been filed; and

(b) deliver to the regulator, concurrently with the filing of the preliminary short form prospectus, the following:

(i) **Personal Information Form and Authorization to Collect, Use and Disclose Personal Information** — a completed personal information form for,

(A) each director and executive officer of an issuer;

(B) if the issuer is an investment fund, each director and executive officer of the manager of the issuer;

(C) each promoter of the issuer;

(D) if the promoter is not an individual, each director and executive officer of the promoter; and

(ii) **Auditor's Comfort Letter Regarding Audited Financial Statements** — if a financial statement of an issuer or a business included in, or incorporated by reference into, a preliminary short form prospectus is accompanied by an unsigned auditor's report, a signed letter addressed to the regulator from the auditor of the issuer or of the business, as applicable, prepared in accordance with the form suggested for this circumstance in the Handbook; and

(iii) **Marketing Materials** — a copy of any template version of the marketing materials required to be delivered under paragraph 7.6(4)(c) or 7.8(2)(c) of this Instrument or paragraph 13.7(4)(c) or 13.12(2)(c) of NI 41-101 that has not previously been delivered.

(2) Despite subparagraph (1)(b)(i), an issuer is not required to deliver to the regulator a personal information form for an individual if the issuer, another issuer or, if the issuer is an investment fund, the manager of the investment fund issuer or another investment fund issuer, previously delivered a personal information form for the individual and all of the following are satisfied:

(a) the certificate and consent included in or attached to the personal information form was executed by the individual within three years preceding the date of filing of the preliminary short form prospectus;

(b) the responses given by the individual to questions 6 through 10 of the individual's personal information form are correct as at a date that is within 30 days of the filing of the preliminary short form prospectus;

(c) if the personal information form was previously delivered to the regulator by another issuer, the issuer delivers to the regulator, concurrently with the filing of the preliminary short form prospectus, a copy of the previously delivered personal information form, or alternative information that is satisfactory to the regulator.

(3) Until May 14, 2016, subparagraph (1)(b)(i) does not apply to an issuer in respect of the delivery of a personal information form for an individual if the issuer or, if the issuer is an investment fund, the manager of the investment fund issuer, previously delivered to the regulator a predecessor personal information form for the individual and all of the following are satisfied:

(a) the certificate and consent included in or attached to the predecessor personal information form was executed by the individual within three years preceding the date of filing of the preliminary short form prospectus;

(b) the responses given by the individual to questions 4(B) and (C) and questions 6 through 9 or, in the case of a TSX/TSXV personal information form in effect after September 8, 2011, questions 6 through 10, of the individual's predecessor personal information form are correct as at a date that is within 30 days of the filing of the preliminary short form prospectus.

4.2 Required Documents for Filing a Short Form Prospectus — An issuer that files a short form prospectus shall

(a) file the following with the short form prospectus:

(i) **Signed Copy** — a signed copy of the short form prospectus;

(ii) **Material Incorporated by Reference** — copies of all material incorporated by reference in the short form prospectus and not previously filed;

(iii) **Documents Affecting the Rights of Securityholders** — a copy of any document described under subparagraph 4.1(a)(iv) that has not previously been filed;

(iii.1) **Material Contracts** — a copy of any material contract described under subparagraph 4.1(a)(iv.1) that has not previously been filed;

(iv) **Other Reports and Valuations** — a copy of any report or valuation referred to in the short form prospectus, for which a consent is required to be filed under section 10.1 of NI 41-101 and that has not previously been filed, other than a technical report that

(A) deals with a mineral project or oil and gas activities of the issuer, and

(B) is not otherwise required to be filed under subparagraph 4.1(a)(v) or (vi);

(v) **Issuer's Submission to Jurisdiction** — a submission to jurisdiction and appointment of agent for service of process of the issuer in the form set out in Appendix B of NI 41-101, if an issuer is incorporated or organized in a foreign jurisdiction and does not have an office in Canada;

(vi) **Non-Issuer's Submission to Jurisdiction** — a submission to jurisdiction and appointment of agent for service of process of

(A) each selling securityholder,

(A.1) each director of the issuer, and

(B) any other person or company that provides or signs a certificate under Part 5 of NI 41-101 or other securities legislation, other than an issuer,

in the form set out in Appendix C of NI 41-101, if the person or company is incorporated or organized under a foreign jurisdiction and does not have an office in Canada or is an individual who resides outside of Canada;

(vii) **Expert's Consents** — the consents required to be filed under section 10.1 of NI 41-101;

(viii) **Credit Supporter's Consent** — the written consent of the credit supporter to the inclusion of its financial statements in the short form prospectus, if financial statements of a credit supporter are required under section 12.1 of Form 44-101F1 to be included in a short form prospectus and a certificate of the credit supporter is not required under section 5.12 of NI 41-101 to be included in the short form prospectus;

(ix) **Undertaking in Respect of Credit Supporter Disclosure** — an undertaking of the issuer to file the periodic and timely disclosure of a credit supporter similar to the disclosure provided under section 12.1 of Form 44-101F1, for so long as the securities being distributed are issued and outstanding;

(x) **Undertaking to File Agreements, Contracts and Material Contracts** — if an agreement or contract referred to in subparagraph (iii) or a material contract under subparagraph (iii.1) has not been executed before the filing of the final short form prospectus but will be executed on or before the completion of the distribution, the issuer must file with the securities regulatory authority, no later than the time of filing of the final short form prospectus, an undertaking of the issuer to the securities regulatory authority to file the agreement, contract or material contract promptly and in any event no later than seven days after the execution of the agreement, contract or material contract;

(x.1) **Undertaking to File Unexecuted Documents** — if a document referred to in subparagraph (iii) does not need to be executed in order to become effective and has not become effective before the filing of the final short form prospectus, but will become effective on or before the completion of the distribution, the issuer must file with the securities regulatory authority, no later than the time of filing of the final short form prospectus, an undertaking of the issuer to the securities regulatory authority to file the document promptly and in any event no later than seven days after the document becomes effective;

(xi) **Undertaking in Respect of Restricted Securities** — for distributions of non-voting securities an undertaking of the issuer to give notice to holders of non-voting securities of a meeting of securityholders if a notice of such meeting is given to its registered holders of voting securities; and

(xii) **Marketing Materials** — a copy of any template version of the marketing materials required to be filed under paragraph 7.6(1)(e) or 7.6(7)(a) of this Instrument or paragraph 13.7(1)(e), 13.7(7)(a) or 13.8(1)(e) of NI 41-101 that has not previously been filed; and,

(b) deliver to the regulator, no later than the filing of the short form prospectus,

(i) a copy of the short form prospectus, blacklined to show changes from the preliminary short form prospectus,

(ii) if the issuer has made an application to list the securities being distributed on an exchange in Canada, a copy of a communication in writing from the exchange stating that the application for listing has been made and has been accepted subject to the issuer meeting the requirements for listing of the exchange;

(iii) a copy of any template version of the marketing materials required to be delivered under paragraph 7.6(4)(c) or 7.8(2)(c) of this Instrument or paragraph 13.7(4)(c) or 13.12(2)(c) of NI 41-101 that has not previously been delivered,

(iv) the evidence of financial ability required to be delivered under section 8A.4 of NI 41-101 if it has not previously been delivered, and

(v) the evidence of fair value required to be delivered under subsection 8A.2(2) of NI 41-101 if it has not previously been delivered.

4.2.1 Alternative Consent — (1) Despite subparagraph 4.2(a)(vii), if the expert whose consent is required is a "qualified person" as defined in NI 43-101, the issuer is not required to file the consent of the qualified person if

(a) the qualified person's consent is required in connection with a technical report that was not required to be filed with the preliminary short form prospectus,

(b) the qualified person was employed by a person or company at the date of signing the technical report,

(c) the principal business of the person or company is providing engineering or geoscientific services, and

(d) the issuer files the consent of the person or company.

(2) A consent filed under subsection (1) must be signed by an individual who is an authorized signatory of the person or company and who falls within paragraphs (a), (b), (d) and (e) of the definition of "qualified person" in NI 43-101.

4.3 Review of Unaudited Financial Statements — (1) Subject to subsection (2), any unaudited financial statements, other than *pro forma* financial statements, included in, or incorporated by reference into, a short form prospectus must have been reviewed in accordance with the relevant standards set out in the Handbook for a review of financial statements by the person or company's auditor or a public accountant's review of financial statements.

(2) If NI 52-107 permits the financial statements of the person or company in subsection (1) to be audited in accordance with

(a) U.S. AICPA GAAS, the unaudited financial statements may be reviewed in accordance with the review standards issued by the American Institute of Certified Public Accountants,

(a.1) U.S. PCAOB GAAS, the unaudited financial statements may be reviewed in accordance with the review standards issued by the Public Company Accounting Oversight Board (United States of America),

(b) International Standards on Auditing, the unaudited financial statements may be reviewed in accordance with International Standards on Review Engagement issued by the International Auditing and Assurance Standards Board, or

(c) auditing standards that meet the foreign disclosure requirements of the designated foreign jurisdiction to which the issuer is subject, the unaudited financial statements

    (i) may be reviewed in accordance with review standards that meet the foreign disclosure requirements of the designated foreign jurisdiction, or

    (ii) do not have to be reviewed if

        (A) the designated foreign jurisdiction does not have review standards for unaudited financial statements, and

        (B) the short form prospectus includes disclosure that the unaudited financial statements have not been reviewed.

PART 5 — [REPEALED]

PART 6 — [REPEALED]

PART 7 — SOLICITATIONS OF EXPRESSIONS OF INTEREST

7.1 Definitions and Interpretations — (1) In this Part:

"bought deal agreement" means a written agreement

(a) under which one or more underwriters has agreed to purchase all securities of an issuer that are to be offered in a distribution under a short form prospectus on a firm commitment basis, other than securities issuable on the exercise of an over-allotment option,

(b) that does not have a market-out clause,

(c) that, other than an over-allotment option, does not provide an option for any party to increase the number of securities to be purchased, and

(d) that, other than what is agreed to under a confirmation clause that complies with section 7.4, is not conditional on one or more additional underwriters agreeing to purchase any of the securities offered;

"comparables" means information that compares an issuer to other issuers;

"confirmation clause" means a provision in a bought deal agreement that provides that the agreement is conditional on the lead underwriter confirming that one or more additional underwriters has agreed to purchase certain of the securities offered;

"market-out clause" means a provision in an agreement which permits an underwriter to terminate its commitment, or underwriters to terminate their commitment, to purchase securities in the event that the securities cannot be marketed profitably due to market conditions;

"U.S. cross-border offering" means an offering of securities of an issuer being made contemporaneously in the United States of America and Canada by way of a prospectus filed with a securities regulatory authority in a jurisdiction of Canada and a U.S. prospectus filed with the SEC;

"U.S. prospectus" means a prospectus that has been prepared in accordance with the disclosure and other requirements of U.S. federal securities law for an offering of securities registered under the 1933 Act.

(2) In this Part, for greater certainty, a reference to "provides" includes showing a document to a person without allowing the person to retain or make a copy of the document.

7.2 Solicitations of Expressions of Interest — Subject to subsection 7.4(2), the prospectus requirement does not apply to a solicitation of an expression of interest made before the issuance of a receipt for a preliminary short form prospectus for securities to be qualified for distribution under a short form prospectus pursuant to this Instrument or for securities to be issued or transferred pursuant to an over-allotment option that are qualified for distribution under a short form prospectus pursuant to this Instrument, if

(a) before the solicitation,

    (i) the issuer has entered into a bought deal agreement;

    (ii) the bought deal agreement has fixed the terms of the distribution, including, for greater certainty, the number and type of securities and the price per security, and requires that the issuer file a preliminary short form prospectus for the securities not more than four business days after the date that the bought deal agreement was entered into; and

    (iii) immediately upon entering into the bought deal agreement, the issuer issued and filed a news release announcing the agreement,

(b) the issuer files a preliminary short form prospectus for the securities pursuant to this Instrument within four business days after the date that the bought deal agreement was entered into,

(c) upon issuance of a receipt for the preliminary short form prospectus, a copy of the preliminary short form prospectus is sent to each person or company that, in response to the solicitation, expressed an interest in acquiring the securities, and

(d) except for a bought deal agreement under paragraph (a) or a more extended form of underwriting agreement referred to in subsection 7.3(6), no agreement of purchase and sale for the securities is entered into until the short form prospectus has been filed and a receipt has been issued.

7.3 Amendment or Termination of Bought Deal Agreement — (1) Except as provided in subsections (2) to (7), a party to a bought deal agreement referred to in paragraph 7.2(a) must not agree to modify the terms of a distribution provided for under a bought deal agreement.

(2) The parties to a bought deal agreement referred to in paragraph 7.2(a) may increase the number of securities to be purchased by an underwriter or underwriters, if

(a) the number of additional securities to be purchased does not exceed 100% of the total of the base offering contemplated by the original agreement plus any securities that would be acquired upon the exercise of an over-allotment option;

(b) the type of securities to be purchased, and the price per security, is the same as under the original agreement;

(c) the issuer files a preliminary short form prospectus for the increased number of securities in accordance with this Instrument within four business days after the date that the original agreement was entered into;

(d) immediately upon agreeing to change the number of securities to be purchased, the issuer issued and filed a news release announcing the amendment;

(e) no previous amendment has been made to the original agreement to increase the number of securities to be purchased; and

(f) the amended agreement is a bought deal agreement and the conditions in section 7.2 are complied with.

(3) The parties to a bought deal agreement referred to in paragraph 7.2(a) may reduce the number of securities to be purchased, or the price of the securities, if the amendment is made on or after the date which is four business days after the date the original agreement was entered into.

(4) The parties to a bought deal agreement referred to in paragraph 7.2(a) may provide for a different type of securities to be purchased by the underwriter or underwriters, and a different price for the securities, if

(a) in the case where a different type of securities is to be substituted in whole or in part for the securities that were the subject of the original agreement, or offered in addition to the securities that were the subject of the original agreement, the aggregate dollar amount of the securities to be purchased by the underwriter or underwriters on a firm commitment basis under the amended agreement is the same as the aggregate dollar amount of the securities that were to be purchased by the underwriter or underwriters on a firm commitment basis under the original agreement or under an agreement amended in accordance with subsection (2);

(b) before a solicitation of an expression of interest in the different type of securities and immediately upon entering into the amendment to the original agreement, the issuer issued and filed a news release announcing the amendment;

(c) the issuer files a preliminary short form prospectus for the different type of securities pursuant to this Instrument within four business days after the date that the original agreement was entered into;

(d) no previous amendment has been made to the original agreement to provide for a different type of securities to be purchased; and

(e) the amended agreement is a bought deal agreement and the conditions in section 7.2 are complied with.

(5) The parties to a bought deal agreement referred to in paragraph 7.2(a) may add or remove an underwriter or adjust the number of securities to be purchased by each underwriter on a proportionate basis, if

(a) the aggregate dollar amount of the securities to be purchased by the underwriter or underwriters on a firm commitment basis under the amended agreement is the same as the aggregate dollar amount of the securities that were to be purchased by the underwriter or underwriters on a firm commitment basis under the original agreement or under an agreement amended in accordance with subsection (2); and

(b) the amended agreement is a bought deal agreement and the conditions in section 7.2 are complied with.

(6) The parties to a bought deal agreement referred to in paragraph 7.2(a) may replace the bought deal agreement with a more extended form of underwriting agreement that includes, without limitation, termination rights, if the more extended form of underwriting agreement complies with the terms and conditions that apply to a bought deal agreement under this Part.

(7) The parties to a bought deal agreement referred to in paragraph 7.2(a) may agree to terminate the agreement if the parties decide not to proceed with the distribution.

7.4 Confirmation Clause — (1) A bought deal agreement referred to in paragraph 7.2(a) must not contain a confirmation clause unless

(a) under the bought deal agreement, the lead underwriter must provide the issuer with a copy of the agreement that has been signed by the lead underwriter;

(b) the issuer signs the bought deal agreement on the same day that the lead underwriter provides the agreement in accordance with paragraph (a);

(c) the lead underwriter has discussions with other investment dealers regarding their participation in the distribution as additional underwriters; and

(d) on the business day after the day that the lead underwriter provides the agreement in accordance with paragraph (a), the lead underwriter provides notice in writing to the issuer that

(i) the lead underwriter has confirmed the terms of the boughtdeal agreement, or

(ii) the lead underwriter will not be confirming the terms of the bought deal agreement and the agreement has been terminated.

(2) Where an issuer has entered into a bought deal agreement that has been confirmed in accordance with subsection (1), the prospectus requirement does not apply to a solicitation of an expression of interest made before the issuance of a receipt for a preliminary short form prospectus for securities

to be qualified for distribution under a short form prospectus pursuant to this Instrument, or for securities to be issued or transferred pursuant to an over-allotment option that are qualified for distribution under a short form prospectus pursuant to this Instrument, if

    (a) before the solicitation,

        (i) the bought deal agreement has fixed the terms of the distribution, including, for greater certainty, the number and type of securities and the price per security, and requires that the issuer file a preliminary short form prospectus for the securities not more than four business days after the date that the lead underwriter provides the notice in accordance with subparagraph (1)(d)(i); and

        (ii) immediately after the lead underwriter provides the notice in accordance with subparagraph (1)(d)(i), the issuer issues the news release referred to in subparagraph 7.2(a)(iii),

    (b) the issuer files a preliminary short form prospectus for the securities pursuant to this Instrument within four business days after the date that the lead underwriter provides the notice in accordance with subparagraph (1)(d)(i),

    (c) upon issuance of a receipt for the preliminary short form prospectus, a copy of the preliminary short form prospectus is sent to each person or company that, in response to the solicitation, expressed an interest in acquiring the securities, and

    (d) except for a bought deal agreement under paragraph 7.2(a), no agreement of purchase and sale for the securities is entered into until the short form prospectus has been filed and a receipt has been issued.

7.5 Standard Term Sheets after Announcement of Bought Deal but before a Receipt for a Preliminary Short Form Prospectus — (1) An investment dealer that provides a standard term sheet to a potential investor before the issuance of a receipt for a preliminary short form prospectus is exempt from the prospectus requirement with respect to providing the standard term sheet if

    (a) the standard term sheet complies with subsections (2) and (3);

    (b) the issuer is relying on the exemption in section 7.2 and has complied with paragraph 7.2(a);

    (c) other than contact information for the investment dealer or underwriters, all information in the standard term sheet concerning the issuer, the securities or the offering

        (i) is disclosed in, or derived from,

            (A) the news release described in subparagraph 7.2(a)(iii), or

            (B) a document referred to in subsection 11.1(1) of Form 44-101F1 that the issuer has filed, or

        (ii) will be disclosed in, or derived from, the preliminary short form prospectus that is subsequently filed; and

    (d) the preliminary short form prospectus will be filed in the local jurisdiction.

(2) A standard term sheet provided under subsection (1) must be dated and include the following legend, or words to the same effect, on the first page:

A preliminary short form prospectus containing important information relating to the securities described in this document has not yet been filed with the securities regulatory authorit[y/ies] in [each of/certain of the provinces/provinces and territories of Canada].

Copies of the preliminary short form prospectus may be obtained from *[insert contact information for the investment dealer or underwriters]*. There will not be any sale or any acceptance of an offer to buy the securities until a receipt for the final short form prospectus has been issued.

This document does not provide full disclosure of all material facts relating to the securities offered. Investors should read the preliminary short form prospectus, final short form prospectus and any amendment, for disclosure of those facts, especially risk factors relating to the securities offered, before making an investment decision.

(3) A standard term sheet provided under subsection (1) may contain only the information referred to in subsection (2) and the information referred to in subsection 13.5(3) of NI 41-101.

7.6 Marketing Materials after Announcement of Bought Deal but before a Receipt for a Preliminary Short Form Prospectus — (1) An investment dealer that provides marketing materials to a potential investor before the issuance of a receipt for a preliminary short form prospectus is exempt from the prospectus requirement with respect to providing the marketing materials if

    (a) the marketing materials comply with subsections (2) to (8);

    (b) the issuer is relying on the exemption in section 7.2 and has complied with paragraph 7.2(a);

    (c) other than contact information for the investment dealer or underwriters and any comparables, all information in the marketing materials concerning the issuer, the securities or the offering

        (i) is disclosed in, or derived from,

            (A) the news release described in subparagraph 7.2(a)(iii), or

            (B) a document referred to in subsection 11.1(1) of Form 44-101F1 that the issuer has filed, or

        (ii) will be disclosed in, or derived from, the preliminary short form prospectus that is subsequently filed;

    (d) a template version of the marketing materials is approved in writing by the issuer and the lead underwriter before the marketing materials are provided;

    (e) a template version of the marketing materials is filed on or before the day that the marketing materials are first provided;

    (f) the preliminary short form prospectus will be filed in the local jurisdiction; and

    (g) upon issuance of a receipt for the preliminary short form prospectus, a copy of the preliminary short form prospectus is sent to each person or company that received the marketing materials and expressed an interest in acquiring the securities.

(2) If a template version of the marketing materials is approved in writing by the issuer and lead underwriter under paragraph (1)(d) and filed under paragraph (1)(e), an investment dealer may provide a limited-use version of the marketing materials that

    (a) has a date that is different than the template version;

    (b) contains a cover page referring to the investment dealer or underwriters or a particular investor or group of investors;

    (c) contains contact information for the investment dealer or underwriters; or

    (d) has text in a format, including the type's font, colour or size, that is different than the template version.

(3) If a template version of the marketing materials is divided into separate sections for separate subjects and is approved in writing by the issuer and lead underwriter under paragraph (1)(d), and that template version is filed under paragraph (1)(e), an investment dealer may provide a limited-use version of the marketing materials that includes only one or more of those separate sections.

(4) The issuer may remove any comparables, and any disclosure relating to those comparables, from the template version of the marketing materials before filing it under paragraph (1)(e) or (7)(a) if

(a) the comparables, and any disclosure relating to the comparables, are in a separate section of the template version of the marketing materials;

(b) the template version of the marketing materials that is filed contains a note advising that the comparables, and any disclosure relating to the comparables, were removed in accordance with this subsection, provided that the note appears immediately after where the removed comparables and related disclosure would have been;

(c) if the preliminary short form prospectus is subsequently filed in the local jurisdiction, a complete template version of the marketing materials is delivered to the securities regulatory authority; and

(d) the complete template version of the marketing materials contains the disclosure referred to in paragraph 13.7(4)(d) of NI 41-101.

(5) Marketing materials provided under subsection (1) must be dated and include the following legend, or words to the same effect, on the first page:

A preliminary short form prospectus containing important information relating to the securities described in this document has not yet been filed with the securities regulatory authorit[y/ies] in [each of/certain of the provinces/provinces and territories of Canada]. A copy of the preliminary short form prospectus is required to be delivered to any investor that received this document and expressed an interest in acquiring the securities.

There will not be any sale or any acceptance of an offer to buy the securities until a receipt for the final short form prospectus has been issued.

This document does not provide full disclosure of all material facts relating to the securities offered. Investors should read the preliminary short form prospectus, final short form prospectus and any amendment, for disclosure of those facts, especially risk factors relating to the securities offered, before making an investment decision.

(6) If marketing materials are provided before the issuance of a receipt for a preliminary short form prospectus under subsection (1), the issuer must include the template version of the marketing materials filed under paragraph (1)(e) in its final short form prospectus or incorporate by reference the template version of the marketing materials filed under paragraph (1)(e) into its final short form prospectus in the manner described in subsection 11.6(1) of Form 44-101F1.

(7) If the final short form prospectus or any amendment modifies a statement of a material fact that appeared in marketing materials provided before the issuance of a receipt for the preliminary short form prospectus under subsection (1), the issuer must

(a) prepare and file, at the time the issuer files the final short form prospectus or any amendment, a revised template version of the marketing materials that is blacklined to show the modified statement, and

(b) include in the final short form prospectus, or any amendment, the disclosure required by subsection 11.6(3) of Form 44-101F1.

(8) A revised template version of the marketing materials filed under subsection (7) must comply with section 13.8 of NI 41-101.

(9) If marketing materials are provided before the issuance of a receipt for a preliminary short form prospectus under subsection (1) but the issuer does not comply with subsection (6), the marketing materials are deemed for purposes of securities legislation to be incorporated into the issuer's final short form prospectus as of the date of the final short form prospectus to the extent not otherwise expressly modified or superseded by a statement contained in the final short form prospectus.

7.7 Road Shows after Announcement of Bought Deal but before a Receipt for a Preliminary Short Form Prospectus — (1) An investment dealer that conducts a road show for potential investors before the issuance of a receipt for a preliminary short form prospectus is exempt from the prospectus requirement with respect to the road show if

(a) the road show complies with subsections (2) to (4);

(b) the issuer is relying on the exemption in section 7.2 and has complied with paragraph 7.2(a); and

(c) the preliminary short form prospectus will be filed in the local jurisdiction.

(2) Subject to section 7.8, an investment dealer must not provide marketing materials to an investor attending a road show conducted under subsection (1) unless the marketing materials are provided in accordance with section 7.6.

(3) If an investment dealer conducts a road show, the investment dealer must establish and follow reasonable procedures to

(a) ask any investor attending the road show in person, by telephone conference call, on the internet or by other electronic means to provide their name and contact information;

(b) keep a record of any information provided by the investor; and

(c) upon issuance of a receipt for the preliminary prospectus, provide the investor with a copy of the preliminary prospectus and any amendment.

(4) If an investment dealer permits an investor, other than an accredited investor, to attend a road show, the investment dealer must commence the road show with the oral reading of the following statement or a statement to the same effect:

This presentation does not provide full disclosure of all material facts relating to the securities offered. Investors should read the preliminary prospectus, the final prospectus and any amendment for disclosure of those facts, especially risk factors relating to the securities offered, before making an investment decision.

7.8 Exception from Filing and Incorporation Requirements for Road Shows for Certain U.S. Cross-border Offerings — (1) Subject to subsections (2) to (4), if an investment dealer provides marketing materials to a potential investor in connection with a road show for a U.S. cross-border offering, the following provisions do not apply to the template version of the marketing materials relating to the road show:

(a) paragraph 7.6(1)(e);

(b) subsections 7.6(6) to (9);

(c) paragraphs 11.6(1)(b) and (c), paragraph 11.6(3)(b) and subsection 11.6(4) of Form 44-101F1.

(2) Subsection (1) does not apply unless

    (a) the underwriters have a reasonable expectation that the securities offered under the U.S. cross-border offering will be sold primarily in the United States of America;

    (b) the issuer and the underwriters who sign the final short form prospectus filed in the local jurisdiction provide a contractual right containing the language set out in subsection 36A.1(5) of Form 41-101F1, or words to the same effect, except that the language may specify that the contractual right does not apply to any comparables provided in accordance with subsection (3); and

    (c) if the prospectus is filed in the local jurisdiction, the template version of the marketing materials relating to the road show is delivered to the securities regulatory authority.

(3) If the template version of the marketing materials relating to the road show contains comparables, the template version of the marketing materials must contain the disclosure referred to in paragraph 13.7(4)(d) of NI 41-101.

(4) For greater certainty, subsection (1) does not apply to marketing materials other than the marketing materials provided in connection with the road show.

PART 8 — EXEMPTION

8.1 Exemption — (1) The regulator or the securities regulatory authority may grant an exemption from the provisions of this Instrument, in whole or in part, subject to such conditions or restrictions as may be imposed in the exemption.

(2) Despite subsection (1), in Ontario only the regulator may grant such an exemption.

(3) An application made to the securities regulatory authority or regulator for an exemption from the provisions of this Instrument shall include a letter or memorandum describing the matters relating to the exemption, and indicating why consideration should be given to the granting of the exemption.

(4) Except in Ontario, an exemption referred to in subsection (1) is granted under the statute referred to in Appendix B of National Instrument 14-101 *Definitions* opposite the name of the local jurisdiction.

8.2 Evidence of Exemption — (1) Subject to subsection (2) and without limiting the manner in which an exemption under this Part may be evidenced, the granting under this Part of an exemption, other than an exemption, in whole or in part, from Part 2, may be evidenced by the issuance of a receipt for a short form prospectus or an amendment to a short form prospectus.

(2) The issuance of a receipt for a final short form prospectus or an amendment to a final short form prospectus is not evidence that the exemption has been granted unless

    (a) the person or company that sought the exemption sent to the regulator

        (i) the letter or memorandum referred to in subsection 8.1(3), on or before the date of the filing of the preliminary short form prospectus, or

        (ii) the letter or memorandum referred to in subsection 8.1(3) after the date of the filing of the preliminary short form prospectus and received a written acknowledgement from the regulator that the exemption may be evidenced in the manner set out in subsection (1), and

    (b) the regulator has not before, or concurrently with, the issuance of the receipt sent notice to the person or company that sought the exemption, that the exemption sought may not be evidenced in the manner set out in subsection (1).

PART 9 — TRANSITION, REPEAL AND EFFECTIVE DATE

9.1 Applicable Rules — A short form prospectus may, at the issuer's option be prepared in accordance with securities legislation in effect at either the date of issuance of a receipt for the preliminary short form prospectus or the date of issuance of a receipt for the short form prospectus.

9.2 Repeal — National Instrument 44-101 *Short Form Prospectus Distributions* and Form 44-101F3 *Short Form Prospectus*, both of which came into force on December 31, 2000, are repealed on December 30, 2005.

9.3 Effective Date — This Instrument comes into force on December 30, 2005.

Appendix A — Notice Declaring Intention to be Qualified under National Instrument 44-101 Short Form Prospectus Distributions ("NI 44-101")

[date]

To: [the issuer's notice regulator (as defined in subsection 2.8(2) of NI 44-101), and any other securities regulatory authority or regulator of a jurisdiction of Canada with whom the issuer may voluntarily file this notice]

[name of issuer] (the "Issuer") intends to be qualified to file a short form prospectus under NI 44-101. The Issuer acknowledges that it must satisfy all applicable qualification criteria prior to filing a preliminary short form prospectus. This notice does not evidence the Issuer's intent to file a short form prospectus, to enter into any particular financing or transaction or to become a reporting issuer in any jurisdiction. This notice will remain in effect until withdrawn by the Issuer.

[signature of Issuer]

[name and title of duly authorized signing officer of Issuer]

Final Rule: (2000) 23 O.S.C.B. (Supp) 867 (December 22, 2000); Approval by OSC: (2000) 23 O.S.C.B. (Supp) 419 (October 13, 2000); Request for Comments: (1999) 22 O.S.C.B. (POP Supp 2) 1 (December 17, 1999), (1999) 22 O.S.C.B. (POP Supp) 1 (July 23, 1999) and (1998) 21 O.S.C.B. 1138 (February 20, 1998). Replaced NPS 47.

Amendment to Rule: Approval by OSC: (2003) 26 O.S.C.B. 5517; Request for Comments: (2003) 26 O.S.C.B. 587 and (2002) 25 O.S.C.B. 505.

Amendment to Rule: Approval by OSC: (2003) 26 O.S.C.B. (Supp-3) 55 (December 19, 2003); Request for Comments: (2003) 26 O.S.C.B. 4577 and (2002) 25 O.S.C.B. 3701.

Amendment to Rule: (2005) 28 O.S.C.B. 83; Approval by OSC: (2004) 27 O.S.C.B. 8710 (revised 27 O.S.C.B. 9181); Request for Comments: (2004) O.S.C.B. 1383.

Revised Rule: (2005) 28 O.S.C.B. 10385; Approval by OSC: (2005) 28 O.S.C.B. 8569; Request for Comments: (2005) 28 O.S.C.B. 228.

Amendment to Rule: (2006) 29 O.S.C.B. 7085; Approval by OSC: 29 O.S.C.B. 5731.

Amendment to Rule: Approval by OSC: (2006) 29 O.S.C.B. (Supp-2) 1; Request for Comments: (2005) 28 O.S.C.B. 9845.

Amendment to Rule: (2007) O.S.C.B. 10520; Approval by OSC: (2007) 30 O.S.C.B. 8539.

Amendment to Rule: (2008) 31 O.S.C.B. (Supp. 2) 117 (March 7, 2008); Approval by OSC: (2007) 30 O.S.C.B. (Supp. 7) 1 (Dec. 21, 2007); Request for Comments: (2006) 29 O.S.C.B. (Supp. 3) 1 (Dec. 22, 2006).

Amendment to Rule: (2010) 33 O.S.C.B. (Supp. 5) 97; Approval by OSC: (2010) 33 O.S.C.B. (Supp. 3) 161; Request for Comments: (2009) 32 O.S.C.B. (Supp. 6) 201.

Amendment to Rule: (2011) 34 O.S.C.B. 7083; Approval by OSC: (2011) 34 O.S.C.B. (Supp. 2) 1; Request for Comments: (2010) 33 O.S.C.B. 3703.

Amendment to Rule: (2012) 35 O.S.C.B. 3294; Approval by OSC: (2012) 35 O.S.C.B. 2383 and 913; Request for Comments: (2011) 34 O.S.C.B. 3249 and (2010) 33 O.S.C.B. 6353.

Amendment to Rule: (2013) 36 O.S.C.B. 4925; Approval by OSC: (2013) 36 O.S.C.B. (Supp. 2) 1; Request for Comments: (2011) 34 O.S.C.B. (Supp. 4) 1.

Amendment to Rule: Approval by OSC: (2013) 36 O.S.C.B. 2619; Request for Comments: (2012) 35 O.S.C.B. 6887.

Amendment to Rule: (2013) 36 O.S.C.B. 8018; Approval by OSC: (2013) 36 O.S.C.B. (Supp. 4) 1; Request for Comments: (2011) 34 O.S.C.B. 11829.

Amendment to Rule: (2015) 38 O.S.C.B. 9255; Approval by OSC: (2015) 38 O.S.C.B. 7551.

Related Provisions: OSA Parts XV and XVI.

Rules: NI 41-101, 43-101, 44-102, 44-103, 33-105, 51-101, 51-102, 52-107; Rule 44-801, 51-501, 13-502, App. C, Item A.

Policies and Orders: NPS 41-101CP, 44-101CP, 43-201, 11-202, CSAN 41-307, 42-303, 44-301, 47-302, 51-338; OSCN 41-702, 41-703.

Form 44-101F1 — Short Form Prospectus

Table of Contents

Item 14 Relationship between Issuer or Selling Securityholder and Underwriter

    14.1 Relationship between Issuer or Selling Securityholder and Underwriter

Item 15 Interest of Experts

    15.1 Names of Experts

    15.2 Interest of Experts

    15.3 Exemption

Item 16 Promoters

    16.1 Promoters

Item 17 Risk Factors

    17.1 Risk Factors

Item 18 Other Material Facts

    18.1 Other Material Facts

Item 19 Exemptions from the Instrument

    19.1 Exemptions from the Instrument

Item 20 Statutory Rights of Withdrawal and Rescission

    20.1 General

    20.2 Non-fixed Price Offerings

    20.3 Convertible, Exchangeable or Exercisable Securities

Item 21 Certificates

    21.1 Certificates

    21.2 Issuer Certificate Form

    21.3 Underwriter Certificate Form

    21.4 Amendments

INSTRUCTIONS

(1) The objective of the short form prospectus is to provide information concerning the issuer that an investor needs in order to make an informed investment decision. This Form sets out specific disclosure requirements that are in addition to the general requirement under securities legislation to provide full, true and plain disclosure of all material facts relating to the securities to be distributed. Certain rules of specific application impose prospectus disclosure obligations in addition to those described in this Form.

(2) Terms used and not defined in this Form that are defined or interpreted in the Instrument or NI 41-101 bear that definition or interpretation. Other definitions are set out in NI 14-101.

(3) In determining the degree of detail required, a standard of materiality must be applied. Materiality is a matter of judgement in the particular circumstance, and is determined in relation to an item's significance to investors, analysts and other users of information. An item of information, or an aggregate of items, is considered material if it is probable that its omission or misstatement would influence or change an investment decision with respect to the issuer's securities. In determining whether information is material, take into account both quantitative and qualitative factors. The potential significance of items must be considered individually rather than on a net basis, if the items have an offsetting effect.

(4) Unless an item specifically requires disclosure only in the preliminary short form prospectus, the disclosure requirements set out in this Form apply to both the preliminary short form prospectus and the short form prospectus. Details concerning the price and other matters dependent upon or relating to price, such as the number of securities being distributed, may be left out of the preliminary short form prospectus, along with specifics concerning the plan of distribution, to the extent that these matters have not been decided.

(5) Any information required in a short form prospectus may be incorporated by reference in the short form prospectus, other than confidential material change reports. Clearly identify in a short form prospectus any document incorporated by reference. If an excerpt of a document is incorporated by reference, clearly identify the excerpt in the short form prospectus by caption and paragraph of the document. Any material incorporated by reference in a short form prospectus is required under sections 4.1 and 4.2 of the Instrument to be filed with the short form prospectus unless it has been previously filed.

(6) The disclosure must be understandable to readers and presented in an easy-to-read format. The presentation of information should comply with the plain language principles listed in section 4.2 of Companion Policy 44-101CP Short Form Prospectus Distributions. If technical terms are required, clear and concise explanations should be included.

(7) No reference need be made to inapplicable items and, unless otherwise required in this Form, negative answers to items may be omitted.

(8) Where the term "issuer" is used, it may be necessary, in order to meet the requirement for full, true and plain disclosure of all material facts, to also include disclosure with respect to persons or companies that the issuer is required, under the issuer's GAAP, to consolidate, proportionately consolidate or account for using the equity method (for example, including "subsidiaries" as that term is used in Canadian GAAP applicable to publicly accountable enterprises). If it is more likely than not that a person or company will become an entity that the issuer will be required, under the issuer's GAAP, to consolidate, proportionately consolidate or account for using the equity method, it may be necessary to also include disclosure with respect to the person or company.

(9) An issuer that is a special purpose entity may have to modify the disclosure items to reflect the special purpose nature of its business.

(10) If disclosure is required as of a specific date and there has been a material change or change that is otherwise significant in the required information subsequent to that date, present the information as of the date of the change or a date subsequent to the change instead.

(11) If the term "class" is used in any item to describe securities, the term includes a series of a class.

(12) Disclosure in a preliminary short form prospectus or short form prospectus must be consistent with NI 51-101 if the issuer is engaged in oil and gas activities (as defined in NI 51-101).

(13) Forward-looking information included in a short form prospectus must comply with section 4A.2 of NI 51-102 and must include the disclosure described in section 4A.3 of NI 51-102. In addition to the foregoing, FOFI or a financial outlook, each as defined in NI 51-102, included in a short form prospectus must comply with Part 4B of NI 51-102. If the forward-looking information relates to an issuer or other entity that is not a reporting issuer, section 4A.2, section 4A.3 and Part 4B of NI 51-102 apply as if the issuer or other entity were a reporting issuer.

(14) If an issuer discloses financial information in a short form prospectus in a currency other than the Canadian dollar, prominently display the presentation currency.

(15) Except as otherwise required or permitted, include information in a narrative form. The issuer may include graphs, photographs, maps, artwork or other forms of illustration, if relevant to the business of the issuer or the distribution and not misleading. Include descriptive headings. Except for information that appears in a summary, information required under more than one Item need not be repeated.

(16) Certain requirements in this Form make reference to requirements in another instrument or form. Unless this Form states otherwise, issuers must also follow the instructions or requirements in the other instrument or form.

(17) Wherever this Form uses the word "subsidiary", the term includes companies and other types of business organizations such as partnerships, trusts, and other unincorporated business entities.

(18) Issuers must supplement any disclosure incorporated by reference into a short form prospectus if that supplemented disclosure is necessary to ensure that the short form prospectus provides full, true and plain disclosure of all material facts related to the securities to be distributed as required under Item 18 of this Form.

Item 1 — Cover Page Disclosure

1.1 Required Language — State in italics at the top of the cover page the following:

> No securities regulatory authority has expressed an opinion about these securities and it is an offence to claim otherwise.

1.2 Preliminary Short Form Prospectus Disclosure — Every preliminary short form prospectus shall have printed in red ink and italics on the top of the cover page the following, with the bracketed information completed:

> A copy of this preliminary short form prospectus has been filed with the securities regulatory authority[ies] in [each of/certain of the provinces/provinces and territories of Canada] but has not yet become final for the purpose of the sale of securities. Information contained in this preliminary short form prospectus may not be complete and may have to be amended. The securities may not be sold until a receipt for the short form prospectus is obtained from the securities regulatory authority[ies].

INSTRUCTION

Issuers shall complete the bracketed information by

> *(a) inserting the names of each jurisdiction in which the issuer intends to offer securities under the short form prospectus;*

> *(b) stating that the filing has been made in each of the provinces of Canada or each of the provinces and territories of Canada; or*

> *(c) identifying the filing jurisdictions by exception (i.e., every province of Canada or every province and territory of Canada, except [excluded jurisdiction]).*

1.3 Disclosure Concerning Documents Incorporated by Reference — State the following in italics on the cover page, with the first sentence in boldface type and the bracketed information completed:

> Information has been incorporated by reference in this prospectus from documents filed with securities commissions or similar authorities in Canada. Copies of the documents incorporated herein by reference may be obtained on request without charge from the secretary of the issuer at [insert complete address and telephone number], and are also available electronically at www.sedar.com.

1.4 Basic Disclosure about the Distribution — State the following, immediately below the disclosure required under sections 1.1, 1.2 and 1.3, with the bracketed information completed:

[PRELIMINARY] SHORT FORM PROSPECTUS

[INITIAL PUBLIC OFFERING OR NEW ISSUE AND/OR SECONDARY OFFERING]

(Date)

[Name of Issuer]

[number and type of securities qualified for distribution under the short form prospectus, including any options or warrants, and the price per security]

1.5 Name and Address of Issuer — State the full corporate name of the issuer or, if the issuer is an unincorporated entity, the full name under which the entity exists and carries on business and the address(es) of the issuer's head and registered office.

1.6 Distribution

(1) If the securities are being distributed for cash, provide the information called for below, in substantially the following tabular form or in a note to the table:

	Price to public (a)	Underwriting discounts or commissions (b)	Proceeds to issuer or selling securityholders (c)
Per security			
Total			

(2) Describe the terms of any over-allotment option or any option to increase the size of the distribution before closing.

(2.1) If there may be an over-allocation position provide the following disclosure:

> A purchaser who acquires [*insert type of securities qualified for distribution under the prospectus*] forming part of the underwriters' over-allocation position acquires those securities under this short form prospectus, regardless of whether the over-allocation position is ultimately filled through the exercise of the over-allotment option or secondary market purchases.

(3) If the distribution of the securities is to be on a best efforts basis, and a minimum offering amount

(a) is required for the issuer to achieve one or more of the purposes of the offering, provide totals for both the minimum and maximum offering amount, or

(b) is not required for the issuer to achieve any of the purposes of the offering, state the following in boldface type:

There is no minimum amount of funds that must be raised under this offering. This means that the issuer could complete this offering after raising only a small proportion of the offering amount set out above.

(3.1) If a minimum subscription amount is required from each subscriber, provide details of the minimum subscription requirements in the table required under subsection (1).

(4) If debt securities are distributed at a premium or a discount, state in boldface type the effective yield if held to maturity.

(5) Disclose separately those securities that are underwritten, those under option and those to be sold on a best efforts basis and, in the case of a best efforts distribution, the latest date that the distribution is to remain open.

(6) In column (b) of the table, disclose only commissions paid or payable in cash by the issuer or selling securityholder and discounts granted. Set out in a note to the table

(a) commissions or other consideration paid or payable by persons or companies other than the issuer or selling securityholder;

(b) consideration other than discounts granted and cash paid or payable by the issuer or selling securityholder, other than securities described in section 1.10 below; and

(c) any finder's fees or similar required payment.

(7) If a security is being distributed for the account of a selling securityholder, state the name of the selling securityholder and a cross-reference to the applicable section in the short form prospectus where further information about the selling securityholder is provided. State the portion of expenses of the distribution to be borne by the selling securityholder and, if none of the expenses of the distribution are being borne by the selling securityholder, include a statement to that effect and discuss the reasons why this is the case.

INSTRUCTIONS

(1) Estimate amounts, if necessary. For non-fixed price distributions that are being made on a best efforts basis, disclosure of the information called for by the table may be set forth as a percentage or a range of percentages and need not be set forth in tabular form.

(2) If debt securities are being distributed, also express the information in the table as a percentage.

1.6.1 Offering price in currency other than Canadian dollar — If the offering price of the securities being distributed is disclosed in a currency other than the Canadian dollar, disclose in boldface type the currency.

1.7 Non-Fixed Price Distributions — If the securities are being distributed at non-fixed prices, disclose

(a) the discount allowed or commission payable to the underwriter;

(b) any other compensation payable to the underwriter and, if applicable, that the underwriter's compensation will be increased or decreased by the amount by which the aggregate price paid for the securities by the purchasers exceeds or is less than the gross proceeds paid by the underwriter to the issuer or selling securityholder;

(c) that the securities to be distributed under the short form prospectus will be distributed, as applicable, at

(i) prices determined by reference to the prevailing price of a specified security in a specified market,

(ii) market prices prevailing at the time of sale, or

(iii) prices to be negotiated with purchasers;

(d) that prices may vary from purchaser to purchaser and during the period of distribution;

(e) if the price of the securities is to be determined by reference to the prevailing price of a specified security in a specified market, the price of the specified security in the specified market at the latest practicable date;

(f) if the price of the securities will be the market price prevailing at the time of sale, the market price at the latest practicable date; and

(g) the net proceeds or, if the distribution is to be made on a best efforts basis, the minimum amount of net proceeds, if any, to be received by the issuer or selling securityholder.

1.7.1 Pricing Disclosure — If the offering price or the number of securities being distributed, or an estimate of the range of the offering price or of the number of securities being distributed, has been publicly disclosed in a jurisdiction or a foreign jurisdiction as of the date of the preliminary short form prospectus, include this information in the preliminary short form prospectus.

1.8 Reduced Price Distributions — If an underwriter wishes to be able to decrease the price at which securities are distributed for cash from the initial offering price disclosed in the short form prospectus, include in boldface type a cross-reference to the section in the short form prospectus where disclosure concerning the possible price decrease is provided.

1.9 Market for Securities

(1) Identify the exchange(s) and quotation system(s), if any, on which securities of the issuer of the same class or series as the securities being distributed are traded or quoted and the market price of those securities as of the latest practicable date.

(2) Disclose any intention to stabilize the market and provide a cross-reference to the section in the short form prospectus where further information about market stabilization is provided.

(3) If no market for the securities being distributed under the short form prospectus exists or is expected to exist upon completion of the distribution, state the following in boldface type:

There is no market through which these securities may be sold and purchasers may not be able to resell securities purchased under the short form prospectus. This may affect the pricing of the securities in the secondary market, the transparency and availability of trading prices, the liquidity of the securities, and the extent of issuer regulation. See Risk Factors.

1.10 Underwriter(s)

(1) State the name of each underwriter.

(2) If applicable, comply with the requirements of NI 33-105 for front page prospectus disclosure.

(3) If an underwriter has agreed to purchase all of the securities being distributed at a specified price and the underwriter's obligations are subject to conditions, state the following, with the bracketed information completed:

> We, as principals, conditionally offer these securities, subject to prior sale, if, as and when issued by [name of issuer] and accepted by us in accordance with the conditions contained in the underwriting agreement referred to under Plan of Distribution.

(4) If an underwriter has agreed to purchase a specified number or principal amount of the securities at a specified price, state that the securities are to be taken up by the underwriter, if at all, on or before a date not later than 42 days after the date of the receipt for the short form prospectus.

(5) If there is no underwriter involved in the distribution, provide a statement in boldface type to the effect that no underwriter has been involved in the preparation of the short form prospectus or performed any review of the contents of the short form prospectus.

(6) Provide the following tabular information:

Underwriter's Position	Maximum size or number of securities available	Exercise period or Acquisition date	Exercise price or average acquisition price
Over-allotment option			
Compensation option			
Any other option granted by issuer or insider of issuer to underwriter			
Total securities under option issuable to underwriter			
Other compensation securities issuable to underwriter			

INSTRUCTIONS

If the underwriter has been granted compensation securities, state, in a footnote, whether the prospectus qualifies the grant of all or part of the compensation securities and provide a cross-reference to the applicable section in the prospectus where further information about the compensation securities is provided.

1.11 Enforcement of Judgments Against Foreign Persons or Companies — If the issuer, a director of the issuer, a selling securityholder, or any other person or company that is signing or providing a certificate under Part 5 of NI 41-101 or other securities legislation, or any person or company for whom the issuer is required to file a consent under Part 10 of NI 41-101, is incorporated, continued, or otherwise organized under the laws of a foreign jurisdiction or resides outside of Canada, state the following on the cover page or under a separate heading elsewhere in the prospectus, with the bracketed information completed:

> The [issuer, director of the issuer, selling securityholder, or other person or company] is incorporated, continued or otherwise organized under the laws of a foreign jurisdiction or resides outside of Canada.
>
> [the person or company named below] has appointed the following agent(s) for service of process:

Name of Person or Company	Name and Address of Agent

> Purchasers are advised that it may not be possible for investors to enforce judgments obtained in Canada against any person or company that is incorporated, continued or otherwise organized under the laws of a foreign jurisdiction or resides outside of Canada, even if the party has appointed an agent for service of process

1.12 Restricted Securities

(1) Describe the number and class or classes of restricted securities being distributed using the appropriate restricted security terms in the same type face and type size as the rest of the description.

(2) If the securities being distributed are restricted securities and the holders of the securities do not have the right to participate in a takeover bid made for other equity securities of the issuer, disclose that fact.

1.13 Earnings Coverage Ratios — If any of the earnings coverage ratios required to be disclosed under section 6.1 is less than one-to-one, disclose this fact in boldface type.

Item 2 — Summary Description of Business

2.1 Summary of Description of Business — Provide a brief summary on a consolidated basis of the business carried on and intended to be carried on by the issuer.

Item 3 — Consolidated Capitalization

3.1 Consolidated Capitalization — Describe any material change in, and the effect of the material change on, the share and loan capital of the issuer, on a consolidated basis, since the date of the issuer's financial statements most recently filed in accordance with the applicable CD rule, including any material change that will result from the issuance of the securities being distributed under the short form prospectus.

Item 4 — Use of Proceeds

4.1 Proceeds

(1) State the estimated net proceeds to be received by the issuer or selling securityholder or, in the case of a non-fixed price distribution or a distribution to be made on a best efforts basis, the minimum amount, if any, of net proceeds to be received by the issuer or selling securityholder from the sale of the securities distributed.

(2) State the particulars of any provisions or arrangements made for holding any part of the net proceeds of the distribution in trust or escrow subject to the fulfillment of conditions.

(3) If the short form prospectus is used for a special warrant or similar transaction, state the amount that has been received by the issuer of the special warrants or similar securities on the sale of the special warrants or similar securities.

4.2 Principal Purposes — Generally

(1) Describe in reasonable detail and, if appropriate, using tabular form, each of the principal purposes, with approximate amounts, for which the net proceeds will be used by the issuer.

(2) If the closing of the distribution is subject to a minimum offering amount, provide disclosure of the use of proceeds for the minimum and maximum offering amounts.

(3) If the following apply, disclose how the proceeds will be used by the issuer, with reference to various potential thresholds of proceeds raised, in the event that the issuer raises less than the maximum offering amount:

(a) the closing of the distribution is not subject to a minimum offering amount;

(b) the distribution is to be on a best efforts basis; and

(c) the issuer has significant short-term non-discretionary expenditures including those for general corporate purposes, or significant short-term capital or contractual commitments, and may not have other readily accessible resources to satisfy those expenditures or commitments.

(4) If the issuer is required to provide disclosure under subsection (3), the issuer must discuss, in respect of each threshold, the impact, if any, of raising each threshold amount on its liquidity, operations, capital resources and solvency.

INSTRUCTIONS

If the issuer is required to disclose the use of proceeds at various thresholds under subsections 4.2(3) and (4), include as an example a threshold that reflects the receipt of 15% of the offering or less.

4.3 Principal Purposes — Indebtedness

(1) If more than 10% of the net proceeds will be used to reduce or retire indebtedness and the indebtedness was incurred within the two preceding years, describe the principal purposes for which the proceeds of the indebtedness were used.

(2) If the creditor is an insider, associate or affiliate of the issuer, identify the creditor and the nature of the relationship to the issuer and disclose the outstanding amount owed.

4.4 Principal Purposes — Asset Acquisition

(1) If more than 10% of the net proceeds are to be used to acquire assets, describe the assets.

(2) If known, disclose the particulars of the purchase price being paid for or being allocated to the assets or categories of assets, including intangible assets.

(3) If the vendor of the assets is an insider, associate or affiliate of the issuer, identify the vendor and the nature of the relationship to the issuer, and disclose the method used in determining the purchase price.

(4) Describe the nature of the title to or interest in the assets to be acquired by the issuer.

(5) If part of the consideration for the acquisition of the assets consists of securities of the issuer, give brief particulars of the class, number or amount, voting rights, if any, and other appropriate information relating to the securities, including particulars of the issuance of securities of the same class within the two preceding years.

4.5 Principal Purposes — Insiders, etc. — If an insider, associate or affiliate of the issuer will receive more than 10% of the net proceeds, identify the insider, associate or affiliate and the nature of the relationship to the issuer, and disclose the amount of net proceeds to be received.

4.6 Principal Purposes — Research and Development — If more than 10% of the net proceeds from the distribution will be used for research and development of products or services, describe

(a) the timing and stage of research and development programs that management anticipates will be reached using such proceeds,

(b) the major components of the proposed programs that will be funded using the proceeds from the distribution, including an estimate of anticipated costs,

(c) if the issuer is conducting its own research and development, is subcontracting out the research and development or is using a combination of those methods, and

(d) the additional steps required to reach commercial production and an estimate of costs and timing.

4.7 Business Objectives and Milestones

(1) State the business objectives that the issuer expects to accomplish using the net proceeds of the distribution under section 4.1.

(2) Describe each significant event that must occur for the business objectives described under subsection (1) to be accomplished and state the specific time period in which each event is expected to occur and the costs related to each event.

4.8 Unallocated Funds in Trust or Escrow

(1) Disclose that unallocated funds will be placed in a trust or escrow account, invested or added to the working capital of the issuer.

(2) Give details of the arrangements made for, and the persons or companies responsible for,

(a) the supervision of the trust or escrow account or the investment of unallocated funds, and

(b) the investment policy to be followed.

4.9 Other Sources of Funding — If any material amounts of other funds are to be used in conjunction with the proceeds, state the amounts and sources of the other funds.

4.10 Financing by Special Warrants, etc.

(1) If the short form prospectus is used to qualify the distribution of securities issued upon the exercise of special warrants or the exercise of other securities acquired on a prospectus-exempt basis, describe the principal purposes for which the proceeds of the prospectus-exempt financing were used or are to be used.

(2) If all or a portion of the funds have been spent, explain how the funds were spent.

Item 5 — Plan of Distribution

5.1 Disclosure of Conditions to Underwriters' Obligations — If securities are distributed by an underwriter that has agreed to purchase all of the securities at a specified price and the underwriter's obligations are subject to conditions,

    (a) include a statement in substantially the following form, with the bracketed information completed and with modifications necessary to reflect the terms of the distribution:

> "Under an agreement dated [insert date of agreement] between [insert name of issuer or selling securityholder] and [insert name(s) of underwriter(s)], as underwriter[s], [insert name of issuer or selling securityholder] has agreed to sell and the underwriter[s] [has/have] agreed to purchase on [insert closing date] the securities at a price of [insert offering price], payable in cash to [insert name of issuer or selling securityholder] against delivery. The obligations of the underwriter[s] under the agreement may be terminated at [its/their] discretion on the basis of [describe any "market out", "disaster out", "material change out" or similar provision] and may also be terminated upon the occurrence of certain stated events. The underwriter[s] [is/are], however, obligated to take up and pay for all of the securities if any of the securities are purchased under the agreement."

    , and

    (b) describe any other conditions and indicate any information known that is relevant to whether such conditions will be satisfied.

5.2 Best Efforts Offering — Outline briefly the plan of distribution of any securities being distributed other than on the basis described in section 5.1.

5.3 Determination of Price — Disclose the method by which the distribution price has been or will be determined and, if estimates have been provided, explain the process for determining the estimates.

5.4 Stabilization — If the issuer, a selling securityholder or an underwriter knows or has reason to believe that there is an intention to over-allot or that the price of any security may be stabilized to facilitate the distribution of the securities, describe the nature of these transactions, including the anticipated size of any over-allocation position, and explain how the transactions are expected to affect the price of the securities.

5.4.1 Underwriting Discounts — Interests of Management and Others in Material Transactions — Disclose any material underwriting discounts or commissions on the sale of securities by the issuer if any of the persons or companies listed under section 13.1 of Form 51-102F2 were or are to be an underwriter or are associates, affiliates or partners of a person or company that was or is to be an underwriter.

5.5 Minimum Distribution — If securities are being distributed on a best efforts basis and minimum funds are to be raised, state

    (a) the minimum funds to be raised,

    (b) that the issuer must appoint a registered dealer authorized to make the distribution, a Canadian financial institution, or a lawyer who is a practicing member in good standing with a law society of a jurisdiction in which the securities are being distributed, or a notary in Québec, to hold in trust all funds received from subscriptions until the minimum amount of funds stipulated in paragraph (a) has been raised, and

    (c) that if the minimum amount of funds is not raised within the distribution period, the trustee must return the funds to the subscribers without any deductions.

5.5.1 Approvals — If the proceeds of the distribution will be used to substantially fund a material undertaking that would constitute a material departure from the business or operations of the issuer and the issuer has not obtained all material licences, registrations and approvals necessary for the stated principal use of proceeds, include a statement that

    (a) the issuer must appoint a registered dealer authorized to make the distribution, a Canadian financial institution, or a lawyer who is a practicing member in good standing with a law society of a jurisdiction in which the securities are being distributed, or a notary in Québec, to hold in trust all funds received from subscriptions until all material licenses, registrations and approvals necessary for the stated principal use of proceeds have been obtained, and

    (b) if all material licenses, registrations and approvals necessary for the operation of the material undertaking have not been obtained within 90 days from the date of receipt of the final short form prospectus, the trustee must return the funds to subscribers.

5.6 Reduced Price Distributions — If the underwriter may decrease the offering price after the underwriter has made a reasonable effort to sell all of the securities at the initial offering price disclosed in the short form prospectus in accordance with the procedures permitted by the Instrument, disclose this fact and that the compensation realised by the underwriter will be decreased by the amount that the aggregate price paid by purchasers for the securities is less than the gross proceeds paid by the underwriter to the issuer or selling securityholder.

5.7 Listing Application — If application has been made to list or quote the securities being distributed, include a statement in substantially the following form with the bracketed information completed:

> The issuer has applied to [list/quote] the securities distributed under this short form prospectus on [name of exchange or other market]. [Listing/Quotation] will be subject to the issuer fulfilling all the listing requirements of [name of exchange or other market].

5.8 Conditional Listing Approval — If application has been made to list or quote the securities being distributed and conditional listing approval has been received, include a statement in substantially the following form, with the bracketed information completed:

> [name of exchange or other market] has conditionally approved the [listing/quotation] of these securities. [Listing/Quotation] is subject to the [name of the issuer] fulfilling all of the requirements of the [name of exchange or market] on or before [date], [including distribution of these securities to a minimum number of public securityholders.]

5.9 Constraints — If there are constraints imposed on the ownership of securities of the issuer to ensure that the issuer has a required level of Canadian ownership, describe the mechanism, if any, by which the level of Canadian ownership of the securities of the issuer will be monitored and maintained.

5.10 Special Warrants Acquired by Underwriters or Agents — Disclose the number and dollar value of any special warrants acquired by any underwriter or agent and the percentage of the distribution represented by those special warrants.

Item 6 — Earnings Coverage Ratios

6.1 Earnings Coverage Ratios

(1) If the securities being distributed are debt securities having a term to maturity in excess of one year or are preferred shares, disclose the following earnings coverage ratios adjusted in accordance with subsection (2):

    (a) the earnings coverage ratio based on the most recent 12-month period included in the issuer's current annual financial statements included in the short form prospectus,

(b) if there has been a change in year end and the issuer's most recent financial year is less than nine months in length, the earnings coverage calculation for its old financial year, and

(c) the earnings coverage ratio based on the 12-month period ended on the last day of the most recently completed period for which an interim financial report of the issuer has been included in the short form prospectus.

(2) Adjust the ratios referred to in subsection (1) to reflect

(a) the issuance of the securities being distributed under the short form prospectus, based on the price at which these securities are expected to be distributed;

(b) in the case of a distribution of preferred shares,

(i) the issuance of all preferred shares since the date of the annual financial statements or interim financial report, and

(ii) the repurchase, redemption or other retirement of all preferred shares repurchased, redeemed, or otherwise retired since the date of the annual financial statements or interim financial report and of all preferred shares to be repurchased, redeemed, or otherwise retired from the proceeds to be realized from the sale of securities under the short form prospectus;

(c) the issuance of all financial liabilities, as defined in accordance with the issuer's GAAP since the date of the annual financial statements or interim financial report; and

(d) the repayment, redemption or other retirement of all financial liabilities, as defined in accordance with the issuer's GAAP, since the date of the annual financial statements or interim financial report and all financial liabilities to be repaid or redeemed from the proceeds to be realized from the sale of securities distributed under the short form prospectus.

(3) [repealed]

(4) If the earnings coverage ratio is less than one-to-one, disclose in the short form prospectus the dollar amount of the numerator required to achieve a ratio of one-to-one.

(5) If the short form prospectus includes a *pro forma* income statement, calculate the *pro forma* earnings coverage ratios for the periods of the *pro forma* income statement, and disclose them in the short form prospectus.

INSTRUCTIONS

(1) Cash flow coverage may be disclosed but only as a supplement to earnings coverage and only if the method of calculation is fully disclosed.

(2) Earnings coverage is calculated by dividing an entity's profit or loss attributable to owners of the parent (the numerator) by its borrowing costs and dividend obligations (the denominator).

(3) For the earnings coverage calculation

(a) the numerator should be calculated using consolidated profit or loss attributable to owners of the parent before borrowing costs and income taxes;

(b) imputed interest income from the proceeds of a distribution should not be added to the numerator;

(c) [repealed];

(d) for distributions of debt securities, the appropriate denominator is borrowing costs, after giving effect to the new debt securities issue and any retirement of obligations, plus the borrowing costs that have been capitalized during the period;

(e) for distributions of preferred shares

(i) the appropriate denominator is dividends declared during the period, together with undeclared dividends on cumulative preferred shares, after giving effect to the new preferred share issue, plus the issuer's annual borrowing cost requirements, including the borrowing costs that have been capitalized during the period, less any retirement of obligations, and

(ii) dividends should be grossed-up to a before-tax equivalent using the issuer's effective income tax rate; and

(f) for distributions of both debt securities and preferred shares, the appropriate denominator is the same as for a preferred share issue, except that the denominator should also reflect the effect of the debt securities being offered pursuant to the short form prospectus.

(4) The denominator represents a pro forma calculation of the aggregate of an issuer's borrowing cost obligations on all financial liabilities and dividend obligations (including both dividends declared and undeclared dividends on cumulative preferred shares) with respect to all outstanding preferred shares, as adjusted to reflect

(a) the issuance of all financial liabilities and, in addition in the case of an issuance of preferred shares, all preferred shares issued, since the date of the annual financial statements or interim financial report;

(b) the issuance of the securities that are to be distributed under the short form prospectus, based on a reasonable estimate of the price at which these securities will be distributed; and

(c) the repayment or redemption of all financial liabilities since the date of the annual financial statements or interim financial report, all financial liabilities to be repaid or redeemed from the proceeds to be realized from the sale of securities under the short form prospectus and, in addition, in the case of an issuance of preferred shares, all preferred shares repaid or redeemed since the date of the annual financial statements or interim financial report and all preferred shares to be repaid or redeemed from the proceeds to be realized from the sale of securities under the short form prospectus.

(5) [repealed]

(6) For debt securities, disclosure of earnings coverage shall include language similar to the following, with the bracketed and bulleted information completed:

[Name of the issuer]'s borrowing cost requirements, after giving effect to the issue of [the debt securities to be distributed under the short form prospectus], amounted to $• for the 12 months ended •. [Name of the issuer]'s profit or loss attributable to owners of the parent before borrowing costs and income tax for the 12 months then ended was $•, which is • times [name of the issuer]'s borrowing cost requirements for this period.

(7) For preferred share issues, disclosure of earnings coverage shall include language similar to the following, with the bracketed and bulleted information completed:

> *[Name of the issuer]'s dividend requirements on all of its preferred shares, after giving effect to the issue of [the preferred shares to be distributed under the short form prospectus], and adjusted to a before-tax equivalent using an effective income tax rate of •%, amounted to $• for the 12 months ended •. [Name of the issuer]'s borrowing cost requirements for the 12 months then ended amounted to $•. [Name of the issuer]'s profit or loss attributable to owners of the parent before borrowing costs and income tax for the 12 months ended • was $•, which is • times [name of the issuer]'s aggregate dividend and borrowing cost requirements for this period.*

(8) [repealed]

(9) Other earnings coverage calculations may be included as supplementary disclosure to the required earnings coverage calculations outlined above as long as their derivation is disclosed and they are not given greater prominence than the required earnings coverage calculations.

Item 7 — Description of Securities Being Distributed

7.1 Equity Securities — If equity securities are being distributed, state the description or the designation of the class of the equity securities and describe all material attributes and characteristics that are not described elsewhere in a document incorporated by reference in the short form prospectus including, as applicable,

> (a) dividend rights;
>
> (b) voting rights;
>
> (c) rights upon dissolution or winding up;
>
> (d) pre-emptive rights;
>
> (e) conversion or exchange rights;
>
> (f) redemption, retraction, purchase for cancellation or surrender provisions;
>
> (g) sinking or purchase fund provisions;
>
> (h) provisions permitting or restricting the issuance of additional securities and any other material restrictions; and
>
> (i) provisions requiring a securityholder to contribute additional capital.

7.2 Debt Securities — If debt securities are being distributed, describe all material attributes and characteristics of the indebtedness and the security, if any, for the debt that are not described elsewhere in a document incorporated by reference in the short form prospectus, including

> (a) provisions for interest rate, maturity and premium, if any;
>
> (b) conversion or exchange rights;
>
> (c) redemption, retraction, purchase for cancellation or surrender provisions;
>
> (d) sinking or purchase fund provisions;
>
> (e) the nature and priority of any security for the debt securities, briefly identifying the principal properties subject to lien or charge;
>
> (f) provisions permitting or restricting the issuance of additional securities, the incurring of additional indebtedness and other material negative covenants including restrictions against payment of dividends and restrictions against giving security on the assets of the issuer or its subsidiaries and provisions as to the release or substitution of assets securing the debt securities;
>
> (g) the name of the trustee under any indenture relating to the debt securities and the nature of any material relationship between the trustee or any of its affiliates and the issuer or any of its affiliates; and
>
> (h) any financial arrangements between the issuer and any of its affiliates or among its affiliates that could affect the security for the indebtedness.

7.3 Asset-backed Securities — (1) This section applies only if any asset-backed securities are being distributed.

(2) Describe the material attributes and characteristics of the asset-backed securities, including

> (a) the rate of interest or stipulated yield and any premium,
>
> (b) the date for repayment of principal or return of capital and any circumstances in which payments of principal or capital may be made before such date, including any redemption or pre-payment obligations or privileges of the issuer and any events that may trigger early liquidation or amortization of the underlying pool of financial assets,
>
> (c) provisions for the accumulation of cash flows to provide for the repayment of principal or return of capital,
>
> (d) provisions permitting or restricting the issuance of additional securities and any other material negative covenants applicable to the issuer,
>
> (e) the nature, order and priority of the entitlements of holders of asset-backed securities and any other entitled persons or companies to receive cash flows generated from the underlying pool of financial assets, and
>
> (f) any events, covenants, standards or preconditions that may reasonably be expected to affect the timing or amount of payments or distributions to be made under the asset-backed securities, including those that are dependent or based on the economic performance of the underlying pool of financial assets.

(3) Provide financial disclosure that describes the underlying pool of financial assets, for the period from the date as at which the following information was presented in the issuer's current AIF to a date not more than 90 days before the date of the issuance of a receipt for the preliminary short form prospectus, of

> (a) the composition of the pool as at the end of the period,
>
> (b) profit and losses from the pool for the period presented on at least an annual basis or such shorter period as is reasonable given the nature of the underlying pool of assets,
>
> (c) the payment, prepayment and collection experience of the pool for the period on at least an annual basis or such shorter period as is reasonable given the nature of the underlying pool of assets;
>
> (d) servicing and other administrative fees, and

(e) any significant variances experienced in the matters referred to in paragraphs (a) through (d).

(4) Describe the type of financial assets, the manner in which the financial assets originated or will originate and, if applicable, the mechanism and terms of the agreement governing the transfer of the financial assets comprising the underlying pool to or through the issuer, including the consideration paid for the financial assets.

(5) Describe any person or company who

(a) originated, sold or deposited a material portion of the financial assets comprising the pool, or has agreed to do so,

(b) acts, or has agreed to act, as a trustee, custodian, bailee or agent of the issuer or any holder of the asset-backed securities, or in a similar capacity,

(c) administers or services a material portion of the financial assets comprising the pool or provides administrative or managerial services to the issuer, or has agreed to do so, on a conditional basis or otherwise, if

(i) finding a replacement provider of the services at a cost comparable to the cost of the current provider is not reasonably likely,

(ii) a replacement provider of the services is likely to achieve materially worse results than the current provider,

(iii) the current provider of the services is likely to default in its service obligations because of its current financial condition, or

(iv) the disclosure is otherwise material,

(d) provides a guarantee, alternative credit support or other credit enhancement to support the obligations of the issuer under the asset-backed securities or the performance of some or all of the financial assets in the pool, or has agreed to do so, or

(e) lends to the issuer in order to facilitate the timely payment or repayment of amounts payable under the asset-backed securities, or has agreed to do so.

(6) Describe the general business activities and material responsibilities under the asset-backed securities of a person or company referred to in subsection (5).

(7) Describe the terms of any material relationships between

(a) any of the persons or companies referred to in subsection (5) or any of their respective affiliates, and

(b) the issuer.

(8) Describe any provisions relating to termination of services or responsibilities of any of the persons or companies referred to in subsection (5) and the terms on which a replacement may be appointed.

(9) Describe any risk factors associated with the asset-backed securities, including disclosure of material risks associated with changes in interest rates or prepayment levels, and any circumstances where payments on the asset-backed securities could be impaired or disrupted as a result of any reasonably foreseeable event that may delay, divert or disrupt the cash flows dedicated to service the asset-backed securities.

INSTRUCTIONS

(1) Present the information required under subsection (3) in a manner that will enable a reader to easily determine whether, and the extent to which, the events, covenants, standards and preconditions referred to in paragraph (2)(f) have occurred, are being satisfied or may be satisfied.

(2) If the information required under subsection (3) is not compiled specifically from the underlying pool of financial assets, but is compiled from a larger pool of the same assets from which the securitized assets are randomly selected so that the performance of the larger pool is representative of the performance of the pool of securitized assets, then an issuer may comply with subsection (3) by providing the financial disclosure required based on the larger pool and disclosing that it has done so.

(3) Issuers are required to summarize contractual arrangements in plain language and may not merely restate the text of the contracts referred to. The use of diagrams to illustrate the roles of, and the relationship among, the persons and companies referred to in subsection (5) and the contractual arrangements underlying the asset-backed securities is encouraged.

7.4 Derivatives — If derivatives are being distributed, describe fully the material attributes and characteristics of the derivatives, including

(a) the calculation of the value or payment obligations under the derivatives;

(b) the exercise of the derivatives;

(c) settlements that are the result of the exercise of the derivatives;

(d) the underlying interest of the derivatives;

(e) the role of a calculation expert in connection with the derivatives;

(f) the role of any credit supporter of the derivatives; and

(g) the risk factors associated with the derivatives.

7.5 Other Securities — If securities other than equity securities, debt securities, asset-backed securities or derivatives are being distributed, describe fully the material attributes and characteristics of those securities.

7.6 Special Warrants, etc. — If the short form prospectus is used to qualify the distribution of securities issued upon the exercise of special warrants or other securities acquired on a prospectus-exempt basis, state the following:

"The issuer has granted to each holder of a special warrant a contractual right of rescission of the prospectus-exempt transaction under which the special warrant was initially acquired. The contractual right of rescission provides that if a holder of a special warrant who acquires another security of the issuer on exercise of the special warrant as provided for in the prospectus is, or becomes, entitled under the securities legislation of a jurisdiction to the remedy of rescission because of the short form prospectus or an amendment to the short form prospectus containing a misrepresentation,

(a) the holder is entitled to rescission of both the holder's exercise of its special warrant and the private placement transaction under which the special warrant was initially acquired,

(b) the holder is entitled in connection with the rescission to a full refund of all consideration paid to the underwriter or issuer, as the case may be, on the acquisition of the special warrant, and

(c) if the holder is a permitted assignee of the interest of the original special warrant subscriber, the holder is entitled to exercise the rights of rescission and refund as if the holder was the original subscriber."

7.7 Restricted Securities

(1) If the issuer has outstanding, or proposes to distribute under a short form prospectus restricted securities, subject securities or securities that are, directly or indirectly, convertible into or exercisable or exchangeable for restricted securities or subject securities, provide a detailed description of

(a) the voting rights attached to the restricted securities that are the subject of the distribution or that will result from the distribution, either directly or following a conversion, exchange or exercise, and the voting rights, if any, attached to the securities of any other class of securities of the issuer that are the same as or greater than, on a per security basis, those attached to the restricted securities,

(b) any significant provisions under applicable corporate and securities law that do not apply to the holders of the restricted securities that are the subject of the distribution or that will result from the distribution, either directly or following a conversion, exchange or exercise, but do apply to the holders of another class of equity securities, and the extent of any rights provided in the constating documents or otherwise for the protection of holders of the restricted securities,

(c) any rights under applicable corporate law, in the constating documents or otherwise, of holders of restricted securities that are the subject of the distribution or that will result from the distribution, either directly or following a conversion, exchange or exercise, to attend, in person or by proxy, meetings of holders of equity securities of the issuer and to speak at the meetings to the same extent that holders of equity securities are entitled, and

(d) how the issuer complied with, or basis upon which it was exempt from, the requirements of Part 12 of NI 41-101.

(2) If holders of restricted securities do not have all of the rights referred to in subsection (1) the detailed description referred to in that subsection must include, in boldface, a statement of the rights the holders do not have.

(3) If the issuer is required to include the disclosure referred to in subsection (1), state the percentage of the aggregate voting rights attached to the issuer's securities that will be represented by restricted securities after effect has been given to the issuance of the securities being offered.

7.8 Modification of Terms — Describe provisions about the modification, amendment or variation of any rights or other terms attached to the securities being distributed. If the rights of holders of securities may be modified otherwise than in accordance with the provisions attached to the securities or the provisions of the governing statute relating to the securities, explain briefly.

7.9 Ratings (1) If the issuer has asked for and received a credit rating, or if the issuer is aware that it has received any other kind of rating, including a stability rating or a provisional rating, from one or more credit rating organizations for the securities being distributed, and the rating or ratings continue in effect, disclose

(a) each rating received from a credit rating organization;

(b) for each rating disclosed under paragraph (a), the name of the credit rating organization that has assigned the rating;

(c) a definition or description of the category in which each credit rating organization rated the securities and the relative rank of each rating within the organization's overall classification system;

(d) an explanation of what the rating addresses and what attributes, if any, of the securities are not addressed by the rating;

(e) any factors or considerations identified by the credit rating organization as giving rise to unusual risks associated with the securities;

(f) a statement that a credit rating or a stability rating is not a recommendation to buy, sell or hold securities and may be subject to revision or withdrawal at any time by the credit rating organization; and

(g) any announcement made by, or any proposed announcement known to the issuer that is to be made by, a credit rating organization to the effect that the organization is reviewing or intends to revise or withdraw a rating previously assigned and required to be disclosed under this section.

(2) If payments were, or reasonably will be, made to a credit rating organization that provided a rating described in subsection (1), state that fact and state whether any payments were made to the credit rating organization in respect of any other service provided to the issuer by the credit rating organization during the last two years.

INSTRUCTIONS

There may be factors relating to a security that are not addressed by a credit rating organization when they give a rating. For example, in the case of cash settled derivative instruments, factors in addition to the creditworthiness of the issuer, such as the continued subsistence of the underlying interest or the volatility of the price, value or level of the underlying interest may be reflected in the rating analysis. Rather than being addressed in the rating itself, these factors may be described by a credit rating organization by way of a superscript or other notation to a rating. Any such attributes must be discussed in the disclosure under this section.

A provisional rating received before the issuer's most recently completed financial year is not required to be disclosed under this section.

7.10 Other Attributes

(1) If the rights attaching to the securities being distributed are materially limited or qualified by the rights of any other class of securities, or if any other class of securities ranks ahead of or equally with the securities being distributed, include information about the other securities that will enable investors to understand the rights attaching to the securities being distributed.

(2) If securities of the class being distributed may be partially redeemed or repurchased, state the manner of selecting the securities to be redeemed or repurchased.

INSTRUCTION

This Item requires only a brief summary of the provisions that are material from an investment standpoint. The provisions attaching to the securities being distributed or any other class of securities do not need to be set out in full. They may, in the issuer's discretion, be attached as a schedule to the short form prospectus.

Item 7A — Prior Sales

7A.1 Prior Sales — For each class or series of securities of the issuer distributed under the short form prospectus and for securities that are convertible or exchangeable into those classes or series of securities, state, for the 12-month period before the date of the short form prospectus,

(a) the price at which the securities have been issued or are to be issued by the issuer or sold by the selling securityholder,

(b) the number of securities issued or sold at that price, and

(c) the date on which the securities were issued or sold.

7A.2 Trading Price and Volume

(1) For the following securities of the issuer that are traded or quoted on a Canadian marketplace, identify the marketplace and the price ranges and volume traded or quoted on the Canadian marketplace on which the greatest volume of trading or quotation for the securities generally occurs:

    (a) each class or series of securities of the issuer distributed under the short form prospectus;

    (b) securities of the issuer into which those classes or series of securities are convertible or exchangeable.

(2) For the following securities of the issuer that are not traded or quoted on a Canadian marketplace, but are traded or quoted on a foreign marketplace, identify the foreign marketplace and the price ranges and volume traded or quoted on the foreign marketplace on which the greatest volume or quotation for the securities generally occurs:

    (a) each class or series of securities of the issuer distributed under the short form prospectus;

    (b) securities of the issuer into which those classes or series of securities are convertible or exchangeable.

(3) Provide the information required under subsections (1) and (2) on a monthly basis for each month or, if applicable, partial months of the 12-month period before the date of the short form prospectus.

Item 8 — Selling Securityholder

8.1 Selling Securityholder

(1) If any securities are being distributed for the account of a securityholder, provide the following information for each securityholder:

    1. The name.

    2. The number or amount of securities owned, controlled or directed of the class being distributed.

    3. The number or amount of securities of the class being distributed for the account of the securityholder.

    4. The number or amount of securities of the issuer of any class to be owned, controlled or directed after the distribution, and the percentage that number or amount represents of the total outstanding.

    5. Whether the securities referred to in paragraph 2, 3 or 4 are owned both of record and beneficially, of record only, or beneficially only.

(2) If securities are being distributed in connection with a restructuring transaction, indicate, to the extent known, the holdings of each person or company described in paragraph 1. of subsection (1) that will exist after effect has been given to the transaction.

(3) If any of the securities being distributed are being distributed for the account of a securityholder and those securities were purchased by the selling securityholder within the two years preceding the date of the short form prospectus, state the date the selling securityholder acquired the securities and, if the securities were acquired in the 12 months preceding the date of the short form prospectus, the cost to the securityholder in the aggregate and on an average cost-per-security basis.

(4) If, to the knowledge of the issuer or the underwriter of the securities being distributed, any selling securityholder is an associate or affiliate of another person or company named as a principal holder of voting securities in the issuer's information circular required to be incorporated by reference under paragraph 7. of subsection 11.1(1), disclose, to the extent known, the material facts of the relationship, including any basis for influence over the issuer held by the person or company other than the holding of voting securities of the issuer.

(5) In addition to the above, include in a footnote to the table the required calculation(s) on a fully-diluted basis.

(6) Describe any material change to the information required to be included in the short form prospectus under subsection (1) to the date of the short form prospectus.

INSTRUCTION

If a company, partnership, trust or other unincorporated entity is a selling securityholder, disclose, to the extent known, the name of each individual who, through ownership of or control or direction over the securities of that company, trust or other unincorporated entity, or membership in the partnership, as the case may be, is a principal securityholder of that entity.

Item 9 — Mineral Property

9.1 Mineral Property — If a material part of the proceeds of the distribution is to be expended on a particular mineral property and if the current AIF does not contain the disclosure required under section 5.4 of Form 51-102F2 for the property or that disclosure is inadequate or incorrect due to changes, disclose the information required under section 5.4 of Form 51-102F2.

Item 10 — Recently Completed and Probable Acquisitions

10.1 Application and Definitions — This Item does not apply to a completed or proposed transaction by the issuer that was or will be accounted for as a reverse takeover or a transaction that is a proposed reverse takeover that has progressed to a state where a reasonable person would believe that the likelihood of the reverse takeover being completed is high.

10.2 Significant Acquisitions

(1) Describe any acquisition

    (a) that the issuer has completed within 75 days prior to the date of the short form prospectus;

    (b) that is a significant acquisition for the purposes of Part 8 of NI 51-102; and

    (c) for which the issuer has not yet filed a business acquisition report under NI 51-102.

(2) Describe any proposed acquisition by an issuer that

    (a) has progressed to a state where a reasonable person would believe that the likelihood of the issuer completing the acquisition is high; and

    (b) would be a significant acquisition for the purposes of Part 8 of NI 51-102 if completed as of the date of the short form prospectus.

(3) If disclosure about an acquisition or proposed acquisition is required under subsection (1) or (2), include financial statements of or other information about the acquisition or proposed acquisition if the inclusion of the financial statements is necessary for the short form prospectus to contain full, true and plain disclosure of all the material facts relating to the securities being distributed.

(4) The requirement to include financial statements or other information under subsection (3) must be satisfied by including

(a) the financial statements or other information that will be required to be included in, or incorporated by reference into, a business acquisition report filed under Part 8 of NI 51-102, or

(b) satisfactory alternative financial statements or other information.

INSTRUCTION

For the description of the acquisition or proposed acquisition, include the information required by sections 2.1 through 2.6 of Form 51-102F4. For a proposed acquisition, modify this information as necessary to convey that the acquisition is not yet completed.

Item 10A — Reverse Takeover and Probable Reverse Takeover

10A.1 Completed Reverse Takeover Disclosure — If the issuer has completed a reverse takeover since the end of the financial year in respect of which the issuer's current AIF is incorporated by reference into the short form prospectus under paragraph 1. of subsection 11.1(1), provide disclosure about the reverse takeover acquirer by complying with the following:

1. If the reverse takeover acquirer satisfies the criteria set out in paragraphs 2.2(a), (b), (c), and (d) of the Instrument, incorporate by reference into the short form prospectus all documents that would be required to be incorporated by reference under Item 11 if the reverse takeover acquirer were the issuer of the securities.

2. If paragraph 1 does not apply to the reverse takeover acquirer, include in the short form prospectus the same disclosure about the reverse takeover acquirer that would be required to be contained in Form 41-101F1 if the reverse takeover acquirer were the issuer of the securities being distributed and the reverse takeover acquirer were distributing those securities by way of the short form prospectus.

10A.2 Probable Reverse Takeover Disclosure — If the issuer is involved in a proposed reverse takeover that has progressed to a state where a reasonable person would believe that the likelihood of the reverse takeover being completed is high, provide disclosure about the reverse takeover acquirer by complying with the following:

1. If the reverse takeover acquirer satisfies the criteria set out in paragraphs 2.2(a), (b), (c), and (d) of the Instrument, incorporate by reference into the short form prospectus all documents that would be required to be incorporated by reference under Item 11 if the reverse takeover acquirer were the issuer of the securities.

2. If paragraph 1 does not apply to the reverse takeover acquirer, include in the short form prospectus the same disclosure about the reverse takeover acquirer that would be required to be contained in Form 41-101F1, if the reverse takeover acquirer were the issuer of the securities being distributed and the reverse takeover acquirer were distributing those securities by way of the short form prospectus.

Item 11 — Documents Incorporated by Reference

11.1 Mandatory Incorporation by Reference

(1) In addition to any other document that an issuer may choose to incorporate by reference, specifically incorporate by reference in the short form prospectus, by means of a statement in the short form prospectus to that effect, the documents set forth below:

1. The issuer's current AIF, if it has one.

2. The issuer's current annual financial statements, if any, and related MD&A.

3. The issuer's interim financial report most recently filed or required to have been filed under the applicable CD rule in respect of an interim period, if any, subsequent to the financial year in respect of which the issuer has filed its current annual financial statements or has included annual financial statements in the short form prospectus, and the related interim MD&A.

4. If, before the short form prospectus is filed, historical financial information about the issuer for a financial period more recent than the period for which financial statements are required under paragraphs 2 and 3 is publicly disseminated by, or on behalf of, the issuer through news release or otherwise, the content of the news release or public communication.

5. Any material change report, except a confidential material change report, filed under Part 7 of NI 51-102 or Part 11 of NI 81-106 since the end of the financial year in respect of which the issuer's current AIF is filed.

6. Any business acquisition report filed by the issuer under Part 8 of NI 51-102 for acquisitions completed since the beginning of the financial year in respect of which the issuer's current AIF is filed, unless the issuer

(a) incorporated the BAR by reference into its current AIF, or

(b) incorporated at least 9 months of the acquired business or related businesses operations into the issuer's current annual financial statements.

7. Any information circular filed by the issuer under Part 9 of NI 51-102 or Part 12 of NI 81-106 since the beginning of the financial year in respect of which the issuer's current AIF is filed, other than an information circular prepared in connection with an annual general meeting if the issuer has filed and incorporated by reference an information circular for a subsequent annual general meeting.

8. The most recent Form 51-101F1, Form 51-101F2 and Form 51-101F3, filed by an SEC issuer, unless

(a) the issuer's current AIF is in the form of Form 51-102F2; or

(b) the issuer is otherwise exempted from the requirements of NI 51-101.

9. Any other disclosure document which the issuer has filed pursuant to an undertaking to a provincial and territorial securities regulatory authority since the beginning of the financial year in respect of which the issuer's current AIF is filed.

10. Any other disclosure document of the type listed in paragraphs 1 through 8 that the issuer has filed pursuant to an exemption from any requirement under securities legislation since the beginning of the financial year in respect of which the issuer's current AIF is filed.

(2) In the statement incorporating the documents listed in subsection (1) by reference in a short form prospectus, clarify that applicable portions of the documents are not incorporated by reference to the extent their contents are modified or superseded by a statement contained in the short form prospectus or in any other subsequently filed document that is also incorporated by reference in the short form prospectus.

(3) Despite paragraph 7 of subsection (1), an issuer may exclude from its short form prospectus a report, valuation, statement or opinion of a person or company contained in an information circular prepared in connection with a special meeting of securityholders of the issuer, and any references therein, if

(a) the report is not an auditor's report in respect of financial statements of a person or company; and

(b) the report, valuation, statement or opinion was prepared in respect of a specific transaction contemplated in the information circular, unrelated to the distribution of securities under the short form prospectus, and that transaction has been abandoned or completed.

INSTRUCTIONS

(1) Paragraph 4 of subsection (1) requires issuers to incorporate only the news release or other public communication through which more recent financial information is released to the public. However, if the financial statements from which the information in the news release has been derived have been filed, then the financial statements must be incorporated by reference.

(2) Issuers must provide a list of the material change reports and business acquisition reports required under paragraphs 5 and 6 of subsection (1), giving the date of filing and briefly describing the material change or acquisition, as the case may be, in respect of which the report was filed.

(3) Any material incorporated by reference in a short form prospectus is required under sections 4.1 and 4.2 of the Instrument to be filed with the short form prospectus unless it has been previously filed.

11.2 Mandatory Incorporation by Reference of Future Documents — State that any documents, of the type described in section 11.1, if filed by the issuer after the date of the short form prospectus and before the termination of the distribution, are deemed to be incorporated by reference in the short form prospectus.

11.3 Issuers without a Current AIF or Current Annual Financial Statements

(1) If the issuer does not have a current AIF or current annual financial statements and is relying on the exemption in subsection 2.7(1) of the Instrument, include the disclosure, including financial statements and related MD&A, that would otherwise have been required to have been included in a current AIF and current annual financial statements and related MD&A under section 11.1.

(2) If the issuer does not have a current AIF or current annual financial statements and is relying on the exemption in subsection 2.7(2) or 2.7(3) of the Instrument, include the disclosure, including financial statements, provided in accordance with

(a) Section 14.2 or 14.5 of Form 51-102F5 in the information circular referred to in paragraph 2.7(2)(b) of the Instrument; or

(b) the policies and requirements of the TSX Venture Exchange for disclosure of a qualifying transaction in a CPC filing statement or a reverse takeover in a filing statement referred to in paragraph 2.7(3)(b) of the Instrument.

INSTRUCTION

(1) If an issuer is required to include disclosure under subsection 11.3(2), it must include the historical financial statements of any entity that was a party to the restructuring transaction and any other information contained in the information circular, CPC filing statement or other filing statement of the TSX Venture Exchange that was used to construct financial statements for the issuer.

(2) The disclosure referenced in instruction (1) must be presented in a way that supplements, but does not replace, the disclosure required to be made for a transaction that constitutes a significant acquisition for the issuer or a reverse takeover in which the issuer was involved.

11.4 Significant Acquisition for Which No Business Acquisition Report is Filed

(1) If the issuer has,

(a) since the beginning of the most recently completed financial year in respect of which annual financial statements are included in the short form prospectus; and

(b) more than 75 days prior to the date of filing the preliminary short form prospectus; completed a transaction that would have been a significant acquisition for the purposes of Part 8 of NI 51-102 if the issuer had been a reporting issuer at the time of the transaction, and the issuer has not filed a business acquisition report in respect of the transaction, include the financial statements and other information in respect of the transaction that is prescribed by Form 51-102F4.

INSTRUCTION

Disclosure required by section 11.3 or 11.4 to be included in the short form prospectus may be incorporated by reference from another document or included directly in the short form prospectus.

11.5 Additional Disclosure for Issuers of Asset-Backed Securities — If the issuer has not filed or has not been required to file interim financial statements and related MD&A in respect of an interim period subsequent to the financial year in respect of which it has included annual financial statements in the short form prospectus because it is not a reporting issuer and is qualifying to file the short form prospectus under section 2.6 of the Instrument, include the interim financial statements and related MD&A that the issuer would have been required to incorporate by reference under paragraph 3 of subsection 11.1(1) if the issuer were a reporting issuer at the relevant time.

11.6 Marketing Materials

(1) If marketing materials were provided under subsection 7.6(1) of the Instrument or subsection 13.7(1) or 13.8(1) of NI 41-101, the issuer must

(a) include a section under the heading "Marketing Materials" proximate to the beginning of the short form prospectus that contains the disclosure required by this Item,

(b) subject to subsection (2), include the template version of the marketing materials filed under the Instrument or NI 41-101 in the final short form prospectus, or incorporate by reference the template version of the marketing materials filed under the Instrument or NI 41-101 into the final short form prospectus, and

(c) indicate that the template version of the marketing materials is not part of the final short form prospectus to the extent that the contents of the template version of the marketing materials have been modified or superseded by a statement contained in the final short form prospectus.

(2) An issuer may comply with paragraph (1)(b) by including the template version of the marketing materials filed under the Instrument or NI 41-101 in the section of the short form prospectus under the heading "Marketing Materials" or in an appendix to the short form prospectus that is referred to in that section.

(3) If the final short form prospectus or any amendment modifies a statement of material fact that appeared in marketing materials provided earlier,

(a) provide details of how the statement in the marketing materials has been modified, and

(b) disclose that, pursuant to subsection 7.6(7) of the Instrument or subsection 13.7(8) or 13.8(8) of NI 41-101,

(i) the issuer has prepared a revised template version of the marketing materials which has been blacklined to show the modified statement, and

(ii) the revised template version of the marketing materials can be viewed under the issuer's profile on www.sedar.com.

(4) State that any template version of the marketing materials filed under NI 41-101 after the date of the final short form prospectus and before the termination of the distribution is deemed to be incorporated into the final short form prospectus.

(5) If the issuer relies on the exception in subsection 7.8(1) of the Instrument or subsection 13.12(1) of NI 41-101, include the statement set out in subsection 36.A.1(5) of Form 41-101F1, or words to the same effect.

GUIDANCE

Marketing materials do not, as a matter of law, amend a preliminary short form prospectus, a final short form prospectus or any amendment.

Item 12 — Additional Disclosure for Issues of Guaranteed Securities

12.1 Credit Supporter Disclosure — Provide disclosure about each credit supporter, if any, that has provided a guarantee or alternative credit support for all or substantially all of the payments to be made under the securities to be distributed, by complying with the following:

1. If the credit supporter is a reporting issuer in at least one jurisdiction and has a current AIF, incorporating by reference into the short form prospectus all documents that would be required to be incorporated by reference under Item 11 if the credit supporter were the issuer of the securities.

2. If the credit supporter is not a reporting issuer in any jurisdiction and has a class of securities registered under section 12(b) or 12(g) of the 1934 Act, or is required to file reports under section 15(d) of the 1934 Act, incorporating by reference into the short form prospectus all 1934 Act filings that would be required to be incorporated by reference in a Form S-3 or Form F-3 registration statement filed under the 1933 Act if the securities distributed under the short form prospectus were being registered on Form S-3 or Form F-3.

3. If neither paragraph 1 nor paragraph 2 applies to the credit supporter, providing directly in the short form prospectus the same disclosure that would be contained in the short form prospectus through the incorporation by reference of the documents referred to in Item 11 if the credit supporter were the issuer of the securities and those documents had been prepared by the credit supporter.

4. Providing such other information about the credit supporter as is necessary to provide full, true and plain disclosure of all material facts concerning the securities to be distributed, including the credit supporter's earnings coverage ratios under Item 6 as if the credit supporter were the issuer of the securities.

Item 13 — Exemptions for Certain Issues of Guaranteed Securities

13.1 Definitions and Interpretation

(1) In this Item

(a) the impact of subsidiaries, on a combined basis, on the financial results of the parent entity is "minor" if each item of the summary financial information of the subsidiaries, on a combined basis, represents less than 3% of the total consolidated amounts,

(b) a parent entity has "limited independent operations" if each item of its summary financial information represents less than 3% of the total consolidated amounts,

(c) a subsidiary is a "finance subsidiary" if it has minimal assets, operations, revenue or cash flows other than those related to the issuance, administration and repayment of the security being distributed and any other securities guaranteed by its parent entity,

(d) "parent credit supporter" means a credit supporter of which the issuer is a subsidiary,

(e) "parent entity" means a parent credit supporter for the purposes of sections 13.2 and 13.3 and an issuer for the purpose of section 13.4,

(f) "subsidiary credit supporter" means a credit supporter that is a subsidiary of the parent credit supporter, and

(g) "summary financial information" includes the following line items:

(i) revenue;

(ii) profit or loss from continuing operations attributable to owners of the parent;

(iii) profit or loss attributable to owners of the parent; and

(iv) unless the issuer's GAAP permits the preparation of the credit support issuer's statement of financial position without classifying assets and liabilities between current and non-current and the credit support issuer provides alternative meaningful financial information which is more appropriate to the industry,

(A) current assets;

(B) non-current assets;

(C) current liabilities; and

(D) non-current liabilities.

INSTRUCTION

See section 1.1 of NI 41-101 for the definitions of "profit or loss attributable to owners of the parent" and "profit or loss from continuing operations attributable to owners of the parent".

(2) For the purposes of this Item, consolidating summary financial information must be prepared on the following basis

(a) an entity's annual or interim summary financial information must be derived from the entity's financial information underlying the corresponding consolidated financial statements of the parent entity included in the short form prospectus,

(b) the parent entity column must account for investments in all subsidiaries under the equity method, and

(c) all subsidiary entity columns must account for investments in non-credit supporter subsidiaries under the equity method.

13.2 Issuer is Wholly-owned Subsidiary of Parent Credit Supporter — Despite Items 6 and 11, an issuer is not required to incorporate by reference into the short form prospectus any of its documents under paragraphs 1 to 4 and 6 to 8 of subsection 11.1(1) or include in the short form prospectus its earning coverage ratios under section 6.1, if

(a) a parent credit supporter has provided full and unconditional credit support for the securities being distributed;

(b) the parent credit supporter satisfies the criterion in paragraph 2.4(1)(b) of the Instrument;

(c) the securities being distributed are non-convertible debt securities, non-convertible preferred shares, or convertible debt securities or convertible preferred shares that are convertible, in each case, into non-convertible securities of the parent credit supporter;

(d) the parent credit supporter is the beneficial owner of all the issued and outstanding equity securities of the issuer;

(e) no other subsidiary of the parent credit supporter has provided a guarantee or alternative credit support for all or substantially all of the payments to be made under the securities being distributed;

(f) the issuer includes in the short form prospectus either

(i) a statement that the financial results of the issuer are included in the consolidated financial results of the parent credit supporter, if

(A) the issuer is a finance subsidiary, and

(B) the impact of any subsidiaries of the parent credit supporter on a combined basis, excluding the issuer, on the consolidated financial results of the parent credit supporter is minor, or

(ii) for the periods covered by the parent credit supporter's consolidated interim financial report and consolidated annual financial statements included in the short form prospectus under section 12.1, consolidating summary financial information for the parent credit supporter presented with a separate column for each of the following:

(A) the parent credit supporter;

(B) the issuer;

(C) any other subsidiaries of the parent credit supporter on a combined basis;

(D) consolidating adjustments;

(E) the total consolidated amounts.

13.3 Issuer is Wholly-owned Subsidiary of, and One or More Subsidiary Credit Supporters Controlled by, Parent Credit Supporter

(1) Despite Items 6, 11 and 12, an issuer is not required to incorporate by reference into the short form prospectus any of its documents under paragraphs 1 to 4 and 6 to 8 of subsection 11.1(1), or include in the short form prospectus its earning coverage ratios under section 6.1, or include in the short form prospectus the disclosure of one or more subsidiary credit supporters required by section 12.1, if

(a) a parent credit supporter and one or more subsidiary credit supporters have each provided full and unconditional credit support for the securities being distributed;

(b) the parent credit supporter satisfies the criterion in paragraph 2.4(1)(b) of the Instrument;

(c) the guarantees or alternative credit supports are joint and several;

(d) the securities being distributed are non-convertible debt securities, non-convertible preferred shares, or convertible debt securities or convertible preferred shares that are convertible, in each case, into non-convertible securities of the parent credit supporter;

(e) the parent credit supporter is the beneficial owner of all the issued and outstanding equity securities of the issuer;

(f) the parent credit supporter controls each subsidiary credit supporter and the parent credit supporter has consolidated the financial statements of each subsidiary credit supporter into the parent credit supporter's financial statements that are included in the short form prospectus; and

(g) the issuer includes in the short form prospectus for the periods covered by the parent credit supporter's financial statements included in the short form prospectus under section 12.1, consolidating summary financial information for the parent credit supporter presented with a separate column for each of the following:

(i) the parent credit supporter;

(ii) the issuer;

(iii) each subsidiary credit supporter on a combined basis;

(iv) any other subsidiaries of the parent credit supporter on a combined basis;

(v) consolidating adjustments;

(vi) the total consolidated amounts.

(2) Despite paragraph (1)(g)

(a) if the impact of any subsidiaries of the parent credit supporter on a combined basis, excluding the issuer and all subsidiary credit supporters, on the consolidated financial results of the parent credit supporter is minor, column (iv) may be combined with another column, and

(b) if the issuer is a finance subsidiary, column (ii) may be combined with another column.

13.4 One or More Credit Supporters Controlled by Issuer — Despite Item 12, an issuer is not required to include in the short form prospectus the credit supporter disclosure for one or more credit supporters required by section 12.1, if

(a) one or more credit supporters have each provided full and unconditional credit support for the securities being distributed,

(b) if there is more than one credit supporter, the guarantee or alternative credit supports are joint and several,

(c) the securities being distributed are non-convertible debt securities or non-convertible preferred shares, or convertible debt securities or convertible preferred shares that are convertible, in each case, into non-convertible securities of the issuer,

(d) the issuer controls each credit supporter and the issuer has consolidated the financial statements of each credit supporter into the issuer's financial statements that are included in the short form prospectus, and

Part 4:
DISTRIBUTIONS

(e) the issuer includes in the short form prospectus either

    (i) a statement that the financial results of the credit supporter(s) are included in the consolidated financial results of the issuer, if

        (A) the issuer has limited independent operations, and

        (B) the impact of any subsidiaries of the issuer on a combined basis, excluding the credit supporter(s) but including any subsidiaries of the credit supporter(s) that are not themselves credit supporters, on the consolidated financial results of the issuer is minor, or

    (ii) for the periods covered by the issuer's financial statements included in the short form prospectus under Item 11, consolidating summary financial information for the issuer, presented with a separate column for each of the following:

        (A) the issuer;

        (B) the credit supporters on a combined basis;

        (C) any other subsidiaries of the issuer on a combined basis;

        (D) consolidating adjustments;

        (E) the total consolidated amounts.

Item 14 — Relationship between Issuer or Selling Securityholder and Underwriter

14.1 Relationship between Issuer or Selling Securityholder and Underwriter

(1) If the issuer or selling securityholder is a connected issuer or related issuer of an underwriter of the distribution, or if the issuer or selling securityholder is also an underwriter of the distribution, comply with the requirements of NI 33-105.

(2) For the purposes of subsection (1), "connected issuer" and "related issuer" have the same meaning as in NI 33-105.

Item 15 — Interest of Experts

15.1 Names of Experts — Name each person or company

    (a) who is named as having prepared or certified a report, valuation, statement or opinion in the short form prospectus or an amendment to the short form prospectus, either directly or in a document incorporated by reference; and

    (b) whose profession or business gives authority to the report, valuation, statement or opinion made by the person or company.

15.2 Interest of Experts — For each person or company referred to in section 15.1, provide the disclosure that would be required under section 16.2 of Form 51-102F2, as of the date of the short form prospectus, as if that person or company were a person or company referred to in section 16.1 of Form 51-102F2.

15.3 Exemption — Sections 15.1 and 15.2 do not apply to a person or company if the disclosure regarding the person or company required under section 15.2 is already disclosed in the issuer's current AIF and the disclosure is correct as at the date of the prospectus.

Item 16 — Promoters

16.1 Promoters

(1) For a person or company that is, or has been within the two years immediately preceding the date of the short form prospectus, a promoter of the issuer or subsidiary of the issuer state, to the extent not disclosed elsewhere in a document incorporated by reference in the short form prospectus,

    (a) the person or company's name;

    (b) the number and percentage of each class of voting securities and equity securities of the issuer or any of its subsidiaries beneficially owned, or controlled or directed, directly or indirectly, by the person or company;

    (c) the nature and amount of anything of value, including money, property, contracts, options or rights of any kind received or to be received by the promoter, directly or indirectly, from the issuer or from a subsidiary of the issuer, and the nature and amount of any assets, services or other consideration received or to be received by the issuer or a subsidiary of the issuer in return; and

    (d) for an asset acquired within the two years before the date of the preliminary short form prospectus, or to be acquired, by the issuer or by a subsidiary of the issuer from a promoter,

        (i) the consideration paid or to be paid for the asset and the method by which the consideration has been or will be determined,

        (ii) the person or company making the determination referred to in subparagraph (i) and the person or company's relationship with the issuer or the promoter or an affiliate of the issuer or of the promoter, and

        (iii) the date that the asset was acquired by the promoter and the cost of the asset to the promoter.

(2) If a promoter referred to in subsection (1) is, as at the date of the preliminary short form prospectus, or was within 10 years before the date of the preliminary short form prospectus, a director, chief executive officer or chief financial officer of any person or company that

    (a) was subject to an order that was issued while the promoter was acting in the capacity as director, chief executive officer or chief financial officer, or

    (b) was subject to an order that was issued after the promoter ceased to be a director, chief executive officer or chief financial officer and which resulted from an event that occurred while the promoter was acting in the capacity as director, chief executive officer or chief financial officer,

state the fact and describe the basis on which the order was made and whether the order is still in effect.

(3) For the purposes of subsection (2), "order" means:

    (a) a cease trade order,

    (b) an order similar to a cease trade order, or

    (c) an order that denied the relevant person or company access to any exemption under securities legislation,

that was in effect for a period of more than 30 consecutive days.

(4) If a promoter referred to in subsection (1)

(a) is, at the date of the preliminary short form prospectus, or has been within the 10 years before the date of the preliminary short form prospectus, a director or executive officer of any person or company that, while the promoter was acting in that capacity, or within a year of that person ceasing to act in that capacity, became bankrupt, made a proposal under any legislation relating to bankruptcy or insolvency or was subject to or instituted any proceedings, arrangement or compromise with creditors or had a receiver, receiver manager or trustee appointed to hold its assets, state the fact, or

(b) has, within the 10 years before the date of the preliminary short form prospectus, become bankrupt, made a proposal under any legislation relating to bankruptcy or insolvency, or became subject to or instituted any proceedings, arrangement or compromise with creditors, or had a receiver, receiver manager or trustee appointed to hold the assets of the promoter, state the fact.

(5) Describe the penalties or sanctions imposed and the grounds on which they were imposed or the terms of the settlement agreement and the circumstances that gave rise to the settlement agreement, if a promoter referred to in subsection (1) has been subject to

(a) any penalties or sanctions imposed by a court relating to provincial and territorial securities legislation or by a provincial and territorial securities regulatory authority or has entered into a settlement agreement with a provincial and territorial securities regulatory authority; or

(b) any other penalties or sanctions imposed by a court or regulatory body that would be likely to be considered important to a reasonable investor in making an investment decision.

(6) Despite subsection (5), no disclosure is required of a settlement agreement entered into before December 31, 2000 unless the disclosure would likely be considered important to a reasonable investor in making an investment decision.

INSTRUCTIONS

(1) The disclosure required by subsections (2), (4) and (5) also applies to any personal holding companies of any of the persons referred to in subsections (2), (4), and (5).

(2) A management cease trade order which applies to a promoter referred to in subsection (1) is an "order" for the purposes of paragraph (2)(a) and must be disclosed, whether or not the director, chief executive officer or chief financial officer was named in the order.

(3) For the purposes of this section, a late filing fee, such as a filing fee that applies to the late filing of an insider report, is not a "penalty or sanction".

(4) The disclosure in paragraph (2)(a) only applies if the promoter was a director, chief executive officer or chief financial officer when the order was issued against the person or company. The issuer does not have to provide disclosure if the promoter became a director, chief executive officer or chief financial officer after the order was issued.

Item 17 — Risk Factors

17.1 Risk Factors — Describe the factors material to the issuer that a reasonable investor would consider relevant to an investment in the securities being distributed.

INSTRUCTIONS

(1) Issuers may cross-reference to specific risk factors relevant to the securities being distributed that are discussed in their current AIF.

(2) Disclose risks in the order of seriousness from the most serious to the least serious.

(3) A risk factor should not be de-emphasized by including excessive caveats or conditions.

Item 18 — Other Material Facts

18.1 Other Material Facts — Give particulars of any material facts about the securities being distributed that are not disclosed under any other items or in the documents incorporated by reference into the short form prospectus and are necessary in order for the short form prospectus to contain full, true and plain disclosure of all material facts relating to the securities to be distributed.

Item 19 — Exemptions from the Instrument

19.1 Exemptions from the Instrument — List all exemptions from the provisions of the Instrument, including this Form, granted to the issuer applicable to the distribution or the short form prospectus, including all exemptions to be evidenced by the issuance of a receipt for the short form prospectus pursuant to section 8.2 of the Instrument.

Item 20 — Statutory Rights of Withdrawal and Rescission

20.1 General — Include a statement in substantially the following form, with the bracketed information completed:

Securities legislation in [certain of the provinces [and territories] of Canada/the Province of [insert name of local jurisdiction, if applicable]] provides purchasers with the right to withdraw from an agreement to purchase securities. This right may be exercised within two business days after receipt or deemed receipt of a prospectus and any amendment. [In several of the provinces/provinces and territories,] [T/t]he securities legislation further provides a purchaser with remedies for rescission [or [, in some jurisdictions,] revisions of the price or damages] if the prospectus and any amendment contains a misrepresentation or is not delivered to the purchaser, provided that the remedies for rescission [, revisions of the price or damages] are exercised by the purchaser within the time limit prescribed by the securities legislation of the purchaser's province [or territory]. The purchaser should refer to any applicable provisions of the securities legislation of the purchaser's province [or territory] for the particulars of these rights or consult with a legal adviser.

20.2 Non-fixed Price Offerings — In the case of a non-fixed price offering, replace, if applicable in the jurisdiction in which the short form prospectus is filed, the second sentence in the legend in section 20.1 with a statement in substantially the following form:

This right may only be exercised within two business days after receipt or deemed receipt of a prospectus and any amendment, irrespective of the determination at a later date of the purchase price of the securities distributed.

20.3 Convertible, Exchangeable or Exercisable Securities — In the case of an offering of convertible, exchangeable or exercisable securities in which additional amounts are payable or may become payable upon conversion, exchange or exercise, provide a statement in the following form:

In an offering of [state name of convertible, exchangeable or exercisable securities], investors are cautioned that the statutory right of action for damages for a misrepresentation contained in the prospectus is limited, in certain provincial [and territorial] securities legislation, to the price at which the [state name of convertible, exchangeable or exercisable securities] is offered to the public under the prospectus offering. This means that, under the securities legislation of certain provinces [and territories], if the purchaser pays additional amounts upon [conversion, exchange or exercise] of the security, those amounts may not be recoverable under the statutory right of action for damages that applies in those provinces [and territories]. The purchaser should refer to any applicable provisions of the securities legislation of the purchaser's province [or territory] for the particulars of this right of action for damages or consult with a legal adviser.

INSTRUCTION

For greater certainty, in the case of a short form prospectus that is a base shelf prospectus under NI 44-102, issuers must include the above statement, unless it is stated in the base shelf prospectus that no convertible, exchangeable or exercisable securities will be offered, or that such securities may be offered but no amounts will be payable to convert, exchange or exercise those securities.

Item 21 — Certificates

21.1 Certificates — Include the certificates required by Part 5 of NI 41-101 or by other securities legislation.

21.2 Issuer Certificate Form — An issuer certificate form must state

This short form prospectus, together with the documents incorporated by reference, constitutes full, true and plain disclosure of all material facts relating to the securities offered by this short form prospectus as required by the securities legislation of [insert the jurisdictions in which qualified].

21.3 Underwriter Certificate Form — An underwriter certificate form must state

To the best of our knowledge, information and belief, this short form prospectus, together with the documents incorporated by reference, constitutes full, true and plain disclosure of all material facts relating to the securities offered by this short form prospectus as required by the securities legislation of [insert the jurisdictions in which qualified].

21.4 Amendments

(1) For an amendment to a short form prospectus that does not restate the short form prospectus, change "short form prospectus" to "short form prospectus dated [insert date] as amended by this amendment" wherever it appears in the statements in sections 21.2 and 21.3.

(2) For an amended and restated short form prospectus, change "short form prospectus" to "amended and restated short form prospectus" wherever it appears in the statements in sections 21.2 and 21.3.

Companion Policy 44-101CP — To National Instrument 44-101 Short Form Prospectus Distributions

Table of Contents

PART 1 — INTRODUCTION AND DEFINITIONS

1.1 Introduction and Purpose — National Instrument 44-101 *Short Form Prospectus Distributions* ("NI 44-101") sets out the substantive tests for an issuer to qualify to file a prospectus in the form of a short form prospectus. The purpose of NI 44-101 is to shorten the time period in which, and streamline the procedures by which, qualified issuers and their selling securityholders can obtain access to the Canadian capital markets through a prospectus offering.

British Columbia, Alberta, Ontario, Manitoba, Nova Scotia and New Brunswick have adopted NI 44-101 by way of rule. Saskatchewan and Québec have adopted it by way of regulation. All other jurisdictions have adopted NI 44-101 by way of related blanket ruling or order. Each jurisdiction implements NI 44-101 by one or more instruments forming part of the law of that jurisdiction (referred to as the "implementing law of the jurisdiction"). Depending on the jurisdiction, the implementing law of the jurisdiction can take the form of regulation, rule, ruling or order.

This Companion Policy to NI 44-101 (also referred to as "this Companion Policy" or this "Policy") provides information relating to the manner in which the provisions of NI 44-101 are intended to be interpreted or applied by the provincial and territorial securities regulatory authorities, as well as the exercise of discretion under NI 44-101. The Companion Policy to NI 41-101 provides guidance for prospectuses filed under securities legislation including short form prospectuses. Issuers should refer to the Companion Policy to NI 41-101 as well as this Policy.

Terms used and not defined in this Companion Policy that are defined or interpreted in NI 44-101, NI 41-101 or a definition instrument in force in the jurisdiction should be read in accordance with NI 44-101, NI 41-101 or the definition instrument, unless the context otherwise requires.

To the extent that any provision of this Policy is inconsistent or conflicts with the applicable provisions of NI 44-101 and NI 41-101 in those jurisdictions that have adopted NI 44-101 by way of related blanket ruling or order, the provisions of NI 44-101 and NI 41-101 prevail over the provisions of this Policy.

1.2 Interrelationship with Local Securities Legislation — NI 44-101 and NI 41-101, while being the primary instruments regulating short form prospectus distributions, are not exhaustive. Issuers are reminded to refer to the implementing law of the jurisdiction and other securities legislation of the local jurisdiction for additional requirements that may be applicable to the issuer's short form prospectus distribution.

1.3 Interrelationship with Continuous Disclosure (NI 51-102 and NI 81-106) — The short form prospectus distribution system established under NI 44-101 is based on the continuous disclosure filings of reporting issuers pursuant to NI 51-102 or, in the case of an investment fund, NI 81-106. Issuers who wish to use the system should be mindful of their ongoing disclosure and filing obligations under the applicable CD rule. Issues raised in the context of a continuous disclosure review may be taken into consideration by the regulator when determining whether it is in the public interest to refuse to issue a receipt for a short form prospectus. Consequently, unresolved issues may delay or prevent the issuance of a receipt.

1.4 Process for Prospectus Reviews in Multiple Jurisdictions (NP 11-202) — National Policy 11-202 *Process for Prospectus Reviews in Multiple Jurisdictions* ("NP 11-202") describes the process for filing and review of prospectuses, including investment fund and shelf prospectuses, amendments to prospectuses and related materials in multiple jurisdictions. NP 11-202 represents the means by which an issuer can enjoy the benefits of co-ordinated review by the securities regulatory authorities in the various jurisdictions in which the issuer has filed a prospectus. Under NP 11-202, one securities regulatory authority acts as the principal regulator for all materials relating to a filer.

1.5 Interrelationship with Shelf Distributions (NI 44-102) — Issuers qualified under NI 44-101 to file a prospectus in the form of a short form prospectus and their securityholders can distribute securities under a short form prospectus using the shelf distribution procedures under NI 44-102. The Companion Policy to NI 44-102 explains that the distribution of securities under the shelf system is governed by the requirements and procedures of NI 44-101 and securities legislation, except as supplemented or varied by NI 44-102. Therefore, issuers qualified to file a prospectus in the form of a short form prospectus and selling securityholders of those issuers that wish to distribute securities under the shelf system should have regard to NI 44-101 and this Policy first, and then refer to NI 44-102 and the accompanying policy for any additional requirements.

1.6 Interrelationship with PREP Procedures (NI 44-103) — NI 44-103 contains the post-receipt pricing procedures (the "PREP procedures"). All issuers and selling securityholders can use the PREP procedures of NI 44-103 to distribute securities, other than rights under a rights offering. Issuers and selling securityholders that wish to distribute securities under a prospectus in the form of a short form prospectus using the PREP procedures should have regard to NI 44-101 and this Policy first, and then refer to NI 44-103 and the accompanying policy for any additional requirements.

1.7 Definitions — (1) **Designated rating** — Cash settled derivatives are covenant-based instruments that may be rated on a similar basis to debt securities. In addition to the creditworthiness of the issuer, other factors such as the continued subsistence of the underlying interest or the volatility of the price, value or level of the underlying interest may be reflected in the rating analysis for cash settled derivatives. These additional factors may be described by a designated rating organization or its DRO affiliate by way of a superscript or other notation to a rating. The inclusion of such notations for covenant-based instruments that otherwise fall within one of the categories of a designated rating does not detract from the rating being considered to be a designated rating for the purposes of NI 44-101.

A designated rating organization or its DRO affiliate may also restrict its rating to securities of an issuer that are denominated in local currency. This restriction may be denoted, for example, by the designation "LC". The inclusion of such a designation in a rating that would otherwise fall within one of the categories of a designated rating does not detract from the rating being considered to be a designated rating for the purposes of NI 44-101.

(1.1) **Predecessor terms** — We recognize there are existing contracts that use the predecessor terms "approved credit rating", "approved rating" and "approved credit rating organization". The content of the new definitions "designated rating" and "designated rating organization" is substantially the same as the content of their respective predecessor terms, only the terminology has changed. Therefore, it is reasonable to interpret the predecessor terms as having the same meaning as the definition of "designated rating" and "designated rating organization" in NI 44-101, as applicable

(2) **Asset-backed security** — Issuers should refer to section 1.3(1) of the Companion Policy to NI 41-101.

(3) **Current AIF** — An issuer's AIF filed under the applicable CD rule is a "current AIF" until the issuer files an AIF for the next financial year, or is required by the applicable CD rule to have filed its annual financial statements for the next financial year. If an issuer fails to file a new AIF by the filing deadline under the applicable CD rule for its annual financial statements, it will not have a current AIF and will not qualify under NI 44-101 to file a prospectus in the form of a short form prospectus. If an issuer files a revised or amended AIF for the same financial year as an AIF that has previously been filed, the most recently filed AIF will be the issuer's current AIF.

An issuer that is a *venture issuer* for the purpose of NI 51-102, and certain investment funds, may have no obligation under the applicable CD rule to file an AIF. However, to qualify under NI 44-101 to file a prospectus in the form of a short form prospectus, that issuer will be required to file an AIF in accordance with the applicable CD rule so as to have a "current AIF". A current AIF filed by an issuer that is a venture issuer for the purposes of NI 51-102 can be expected to expire later than a non-venture issuer's AIF, due to the fact that the deadlines for filing annual financial statements under NI 51-102 are later for venture issuers than for other issuers.

(4) **Current annual financial statements** — An issuer's comparative annual financial statements filed under the applicable CD rule, together with the accompanying auditor's report, are "current annual financial statements" until the issuer files, or is required under the applicable CD rule to have filed, its comparative annual financial statements for the next financial year. If an issuer fails to file its comparative annual financial statements by the filing deadline under the applicable CD rule, it will not have current annual financial statements and will not be qualified under NI 44-101 to file a prospectus in the form of a short form prospectus.

Where there has been a change of auditor and the new auditor has not audited the comparative period, the report of the predecessor auditor on the comparative period must be included in the prospectus. The issuer may file the report of the predecessor auditor on the comparative period with the annual financial statements that are being incorporated by reference into the short form prospectus, and clearly incorporate by reference the predecessor auditor's report in addition to the new auditor's report. Alternatively, the issuer can incorporate by reference into the short form prospectus its comparative financial statements filed for the previous year, including the audit reports thereon.

(5) **Successor Issuer** — A successor issuer is defined to include a reverse takeover acquiree in a completed reverse takeover. Alternatively, the definition of "successor issuer" requires that the issuer was formed "as a result of a restructuring transaction" or that the issuer participate in the restructuring transaction and continue to exist following completion of the restructuring transaction. In both instances, prospectus level disclosure or comparable disclosure prescribed by the TSX Venture Exchange for such issuer must be provided in an information circular or similar disclosure document pursuant to subsections 2.7(2) and (3) of NI 44-101. In the case of an amalgamation, the amalgamated corporation is regarded by the securities regulatory authorities as having been formed "as a result of a restructuring transaction". The definition of "successor issuer" also contains an exclusion applicable to divestitures. For example, an issuer may carry out a restructuring transaction that results in the distribution to securityholders of a portion of its business or the transfer of a portion of its business to another issuer. In that case, the entity that carries on the portion of the business that was "spun-off" is not a successor issuer within the meaning of the definition.

However, if the divestiture represents a divestiture of substantially all of the business of the predecessor entity to the issuer, the issuer would be considered a successor issuer. In such circumstances, the financial information concerning the predecessor entity should be representative of the financial information of the successor issuer. Therefore, if an issuer is relying on this basis for short form prospectus qualification, it must ensure that the financial statements of the predecessor entity are a relevant, accurate proxy for its financial statements as a successor issuer.

An issuer may also be considered a successor issuer to a second issuer where there has been an internal reorganization of the second issuer, provided that the conditions in paragraph (b) of the definition of "successor issuer" are met. In particular, the internal reorganization must not result in an alteration of the securityholders' proportionate interest in the second issuer nor the second issuer's proportionate interest in its assets. For example, this may arise in an internal reorganization in which all of the securityholders of the second issuer exchange their securities in the second issuer for securities of the successor issuer. The second issuer would become a subsidiary of the successor issuer and its ownership in its assets would remain the same. The successor issuer definition was expanded to include this type of internal reorganization as it may not be considered a "restructuring transaction" as defined in NI 51-102 by virtue of the exclusion found at the end of the definition of "restructuring transaction".

1.8 Bought Deal Provisions — Issuers and investment dealers relying on the bought deal provisions in Part 7 of NI 44-101 should refer to the guidance in Part 6 of the Companion Policy to NI 41-101.

1.9 Marketing Activities — Issuers and investment dealers should also refer to the guidance on marketing activities in Part 6 of the Companion Policy to NI 41-101. While NI 44-101 has provisions on marketing after the announcement of a bought deal and before a receipt for a preliminary short form prospectus, NI 41-101 has general provisions that apply to marketing during the waiting period and after a receipt for a final prospectus.

PART 2 — QUALIFICATION TO FILE A PROSPECTUS IN THE FORM OF A SHORT FORM PROSPECTUS

2.1 Basic Qualification Criteria — Reporting Issuers with Equity Securities Listed on a Short Form Eligible Exchange (Section 2.2 of NI 44-101) — (1) Section 2.2 of NI 44-101 provides that an issuer with equity securities listed and posted for trading on a short form eligible exchange and that is up-to-date in its periodic and timely disclosure filings in all jurisdictions in which it is a reporting issuer satisfies the criteria for being qualified to file a prospectus in the form of a short form prospectus if it meets the other general qualification criteria. In addition to the listing requirement, the issuer may not be an issuer whose operations have ceased or whose principal asset is its exchange listing. The purpose of this requirement is to ensure that eligible issuers have an operating business in respect of which the issuer must provide current disclosure through application of the applicable CD rule.

The basic qualification criteria are structured to allow most Canadian listed issuers to participate in the expedited offering system created by NI 44-101, provided their public disclosure record provides investors with satisfactory and sufficient information about the issuer and its business, operations or capital. The securities regulatory authorities believe that it is in the public interest to allow an issuer's public disclosure to be incorporated into a short form prospectus, provided that the resulting prospectus provides prospective investors with full, true and plain disclosure about the issuer and the securities being distributed. The securities regulatory authority may not be prepared to issue a receipt for a short form prospectus if the prospectus, together with the documents incorporated by reference, fails to provide such full, true and plain disclosure. In such circumstances, the securities regulatory authority may require, in the public interest, that the issuer utilize the long form prospectus regime. In addition, the securities regulatory authority may also require that the issuer utilize the long form prospectus regime if the offering is, in essence, an initial public offering by a business or if:

(a) the offering is for the purpose of financing a dormant or inactive issuer whether or not the issuer intends to use the proceeds to reactivate the issuer or to acquire an active business; or

(b) the offering is for the purpose of financing a material undertaking that would constitute a material departure from the business or operations of the issuer as at the date of its current annual financial statements and current AIF.

(2) A new reporting issuer or a successor issuer may satisfy the criteria to have current annual financial statements or a current AIF by filing its comparative annual financial statements or an AIF, respectively, in accordance with NI 51-102 or NI 81-106, as applicable, for its most recently completed financial year. It is not necessary that the issuer be required by the applicable CD rule to have filed such documents. An issuer may voluntarily choose to file either of these documents in accordance with the applicable CD rule for the purposes of satisfying the eligibility criteria under NI 44-101.

Alternatively, an issuer may rely on the exemption from the requirement to file such documents in section 2.7 of NI 44-101. That section provides an exemption from the current AIF and current annual financial statement requirements for new reporting issuers and successor issuers who have not yet been required to file such documents and who have filed a prospectus or information circular containing disclosure which would have been included in such documents had they been filed under the applicable CD rule.

(3) An issuer need not have filed all of its continuous disclosure filings in the local jurisdiction in order to be qualified to file a short form prospectus, but under sections 4.1 and 4.2 of NI 44-101 it will be required to file in the local jurisdiction all documents incorporated by reference into the short form prospectus no later than the date of filing the preliminary short form prospectus. However, if the divestiture represents a divestiture of substantially all of the business of the predecessor entity to the issuer, the issuer would be considered a successor issuer. In such circumstances, the financial information concerning the predecessor entity should be representative of the financial information of the successor issuer. Therefore, if an issuer is relying on this basis for short form prospectus qualification, it must ensure that the financial statements of the predecessor entity are a relevant, accurate proxy for its financial statements as a successor issuer.

An issuer may also be considered a successor issuer to a second issuer where there has been an internal reorganization of the second issuer, provided that the conditions in paragraph (b) of the definition of "successor issuer" are met. In particular, the internal reorganization must not result in an alteration of the securityholders' proportionate interest in the second issuer nor the second issuer's proportionate interest in its assets. For example, this may arise in an internal reorganization in which all of the securityholders of the second issuer exchange their securities in the second issuer for securities of the successor issuer. The second issuer would become a subsidiary of the successor issuer and its ownership in its assets would remain the same. The successor issuer definition was expanded to include this type of internal reorganization as it may not be considered a "restructuring transaction" as defined in NI 51-102 by virtue of the exclusion found at the end of the definition of "restructuring transaction".

2.2 Alternative Qualification Criteria — Issuers that are Not Listed (Sections 2.3, 2.4, 2.5 and 2.6 of NI 44-101) — Issuers that do not have equity securities listed and posted for trading on a short form eligible exchange in Canada may nonetheless be qualified to file a prospectus in the form of a short form prospectus under the following alternative qualification criteria of NI 44-101:

1. Section 2.3, which applies to issuers which are reporting issuers in at least one jurisdiction, and who are intending to issue non-convertible securities with a provisional designated rating.

2. Section 2.4, which applies to issuers of non-convertible debt securities, non-convertible preferred shares or non-convertible cash settled derivatives, if another person or company that satisfies prescribed criteria provides full and unconditional credit support for the payments to be made by the issuer of the securities.

3. Section 2.5, which applies to issuers of convertible debt securities or convertible preferred shares, if the securities are convertible into securities of a credit supporter that satisfies prescribed criteria and provides full and unconditional credit support for the payments to be made by the issuer of the securities.

4. Section 2.6, which applies to issuers of asset-backed securities.

Under sections 2.4, 2.5 and 2.6 of NI 44-101, an issuer is not required to be a reporting issuer in any jurisdiction in order to qualify to file a prospectus in the form of a short form prospectus. Section 2.3 requires the issuer to be a reporting issuer in at least one jurisdiction of Canada.

2.3 Alternative Qualification Criteria — Issuers of Guaranteed Debt Securities, Preferred Shares and Cash Settled Derivatives (Sections 2.4 and 2.5 of NI 44-101) — Sections 2.4 and 2.5 of NI 44-101 allow an issuer to qualify to file a prospectus in the form of a short form prospectus based on full and unconditional credit support, which may take the form of a guarantee or alternative credit support. The securities regulatory authorities are of the view that a person or company that provides the full and unconditional guarantee or alternative credit support is not, simply by providing that guarantee or alternative credit support, issuing a security.

2.4 Alternative Qualification Criteria — Issuers of Asset-Backed Securities (Section 2.6 of NI 44-101) — (1) In order to be qualified to file a prospectus in the form of a short form prospectus under section 2.6 of NI 44-101, an issuer must have been established in connection with a distribution of asset-backed securities. Ordinarily, asset-backed securities are issued by special purpose issuers established for the sole purpose of purchasing financial assets with the proceeds of one or more distributions of these securities. This ensures that the credit and performance attributes of the asset-backed securities are dependent on the underlying financial assets, rather than upon concerns relating to ancillary business activities and their attendant risks. Qualification to file a prospectus in the form of a short form prospectus under section 2.6 of NI 44-101 has been limited to special purpose issuers to avoid the possibility that an otherwise ineligible issuer would structure securities falling within the definition of "asset-backed security".

(2) The qualification criteria for a distribution of asset-backed securities under a prospectus in the form of a short form prospectus are intended to provide sufficient flexibility to accommodate future developments. To qualify under section 2.6 of NI 44-101, the securities to be distributed must satisfy the following two criteria:

1. First, the payment obligations on the securities must be serviced primarily by the cash flows of a pool of discrete liquidating assets such as accounts receivable, instalment sales contracts, leases or other assets that by their terms convert into cash within a specified or determinable period of time.

2. Second, the securities must (i) receive a designated rating on a provisional basis, (ii) not have been the subject of an announcement regarding a downgrade to a rating that is not a designated rating, and (iii) not have received a provisional or final rating lower than a designated rating from any designated rating organization or its DRO affiliate.

The qualification criteria do not distinguish between pass-through (i.e., equity) and pay-through (i.e., debt) asset-backed securities. Consequently, both pay-through and pass-through securities, as well as residual or subordinate interests, may be distributed under a prospectus in the form of a short form prospectus if all other applicable requirements are met.

2.5 Timely and Periodic Disclosure Documents — To be qualified to file a short form prospectus under sections 2.2 and 2.3 of NI 44-101, an issuer must file with the securities regulatory authority in each jurisdiction in which it is a reporting issuer all periodic and timely disclosure documents that it is required to have filed in that jurisdiction under applicable securities legislation, pursuant to an order issued by the securities regulatory authority, or pursuant to an undertaking to the securities regulatory authority. Similarly, a credit supporter must satisfy this qualification criterion for an issuer to be qualified to file a short form prospectus under sections 2.4 and 2.5 of NI 44-101.

This qualification criterion applies to all disclosure documents including, if applicable, a disclosure document the issuer or credit supporter (i) has undertaken to file with a provincial or territorial securities regulatory authority, (ii) must file pursuant to a condition in a written order or decision granting exemptive relief to the issuer or credit supporter from a requirement to file periodic and timely disclosure documents, (iii) must file pursuant to a condition in securities legislation exempting the issuer or credit supporter from a requirement to file periodic and timely disclosure documents, and (iv) has represented that it will file pursuant to a representation in a written order or decision granting exemptive relief to the issuer or credit supporter from a requirement to file periodic and timely disclosure documents. These disclosure documents must be incorporated by reference into a short form prospectus pursuant to paragraph 9 or 10 of subsection 11.1(1) of Form 44-101F1.

2.6 Notice Declaring Intention — Subsection 2.8(1) of NI 44-101 provides that an issuer is not qualified to file a short form prospectus under Part 2 of NI 44-101 unless it has filed, with its notice regulator, a notice declaring its intention to be qualified to file a short form prospectus under NI 44-101. This notice must be filed in substantially the form of Appendix A of NI 44-101 at least 10 business days prior to the issuer filing its first preliminary short form prospectus. This is a new requirement that came into effect on December 30, 2005. The securities regulatory authorities expect that this notice will be a one-time filing for issuers that intend to be participants in the short form prospectus distribution system established under NI 44-101. Subsection 2.8(2) provides that this notice is operative until withdrawn. Though the notice must be filed with the notice regulator, an issuer may voluntarily file the notice with any other securities regulatory authority or regulator of a jurisdiction of Canada.

Subsection 2.8(4) of NI 44-101 is a transitional provision that has the effect of deeming issuers that, as of December 29, 2005, have a current AIF under the pre-December 30, 2005 short form prospectus distribution system to have filed this notice and no additional filing is required to satisfy the notice requirements set out in subsection 2.8(1) of NI 44-101.

PART 3 — FILING AND RECEIPTING OF SHORT FORM PROSPECTUS

3.1 Previously filed documents — Sections 4.1 and 4.2 of NI 44-101 require the filing of specified documents that have not been previously filed. Issuers that are relying on previous filing of these specified documents are reminded that the documents should have been filed on the issuer's filer profile for SEDAR.

3.2 Confidential Material Change Reports — Confidential material change reports cannot be incorporated by reference into a short form prospectus. Issuers should refer to section 3.2 of the Companion Policy to NI 41-101 for further guidance.

3.2.1 Personal information forms — (1) If issuers are relying upon a previously delivered personal information form or predecessor personal information form pursuant to subsections 4.1(2) or 4.1(3) of NI 44-101, issuers are reminded of paragraphs 4.1(2)(b) and 4.1(3)(b), which require that the responses to certain questions in the form must still be correct. Accordingly, in order to meet these requirements issuers should obtain appropriate confirmations from the individual concerned.

(2) Paragraph 4.1(2)(c) of NI 44-101 requires that in certain circumstances an issuer deliver a copy of a previously delivered personal information form, or "alternative information that is satisfactory to the regulator". Our interpretation of what would potentially be alternative information that is satisfactory to the regulator is, with respect to the previous delivery of an individual's personal information form, the System for Electronic Document Analysis and Retrieval (SEDAR) project number and name of issuer. In most cases this information will be sufficient. Staff will contact issuers in cases where it is not. Issuers wishing to proceed in this manner should provide the information in the cover letter for the preliminary short form prospectus.

(3) If an issuer is delivering a copy of a previously delivered personal information form pursuant to paragraph 4.1(2)(c) of NI 44-101, the issuer should deliver it as a personal information form on SEDAR, in the same way that a new personal information form would be delivered.

3.3 Supporting Documents — Issuers should refer to section 3.3 of the Companion Policy to NI 41-101.

3.4 Experts' Consent — Issuers are reminded that under section 10.1 of NI 41-101 an auditor's consent is required to be filed for audited financial statements that are included as part of other continuous disclosure filings that are incorporated by reference into a short form prospectus. For example, a separate auditor's consent is required for each set of audited financial statements that are included as part of a business acquisition report or an information circular incorporated by reference into a short form prospectus. Issuers should also refer to section 3.4 of the Companion Policy to NI 41-101 for further guidance.

3.4.1 Special meeting information circular — Subsection 11.1(3) of Form 44-101F1 sets out certain circumstances where an issuer is not required to incorporate by reference into its prospectus a report, valuation, statement or opinion of an expert that is indirectly incorporated by reference into its prospectus through the incorporation by reference of an information circular prepared for a special meeting of the issuer. A special meeting information circular often relates to a restructuring transaction of an issuer or other special business of the issuer. In these circumstances, the issuer or its board of directors may engage an expert to provide an opinion that is specific to the business that will be considered at the special meeting of securityholders. For example, the board may retain a person or company to provide a fairness opinion which would assist the board in determining whether to recommend the approval of the proposed transaction to its securityholders. Similarly, the issuer may include a tax opinion in the information circular to illustrate the tax consequences of the proposed transaction to its securityholders. Pursuant to subsection 11.1(3), we would not require the incorporation by reference of these particular opinions, provided that these opinions were prepared in respect of the specific transaction contemplated in the information circular and this transaction has been completed or abandoned prior to the filing of the prospectus.

3.5 Undertaking in Respect of Credit Supporter Disclosure — Under subparagraph 4.2(a)(ix) of NI 44-101, an issuer must file an undertaking to file the periodic and timely disclosure of a credit supporter. For credit supporters that are reporting issuers with a current AIF, the undertaking will likely be to continue to file the documents it is required to file under NI 51-102. For credit supporters registered under the 1934 Act, the undertaking will likely be to file the types of documents that would be required to be incorporated by reference into a Form S-3 or Form F-3 registration statement. For other credit supporters, the types of documents to be filed pursuant to the undertaking will be determined through discussions with the regulators on a case-by-case basis.

If an issuer, a parent credit supporter, and a subsidiary credit supporter satisfy the conditions of the exemption in section 13.3 of Form 44-101F1, an undertaking may provide that the subsidiary credit supporter will file periodic and timely disclosure if the issuer and the credit supporters no longer satisfy the conditions of the exemption in that section.

If an issuer and a credit supporter satisfy the conditions of the exemption in section 13.4 of Form 44-101F1, an undertaking may provide that the credit supporter will file periodic and timely disclosure if the issuer and the credit supporter no longer satisfy the conditions of the exemption in that section.

For the purposes of such an undertaking, references to disclosure included in the short form prospectus should be replaced with references to the issuer or parent credit supporter's continuous disclosure filings. For example, if an issuer and subsidiary credit supporter(s) plan to continue to satisfy the conditions of the exemption in section 13.4 of Form 44-101F1 for continuous disclosure filings, the undertaking should provide that the issuer will file with its consolidated financial statements,

    (a) a statement that the financial results of the credit supporter(s) are included in the consolidated financial results of the issuer if

        (i) the issuer continues to have limited independent operations, and

        (ii) the impact of any subsidiaries of the issuer on a combined basis, excluding the credit supporter(s) but including any subsidiaries of the credit supporter(s) that are not themselves credit supporters, on the consolidated financial statements of the issuer continues to be minor, or

    (b) for any periods covered by issuer's consolidated financial statements, consolidating summary financial information for the issuer presented in the format set out in subparagraph 13.4(e)(ii) of Form 44-101F1.

3.6 Amendments and Incorporation by Reference of Subsequently Filed Material Change Reports or Marketing Materials — The requirement in NI 41-101 and securities legislation for the filing of an amendment to a preliminary prospectus and prospectus is not satisfied by the incorporation by reference in a preliminary short form prospectus or a short form prospectus of a subsequently filed material change report or a subsequently filed template version of marketing materials. Issuers should refer to the Companion Policy to NI 41-101 for further guidance regarding amendments.

3.7 Short Form Prospectus Review — No target time frame applies to the review of a short form prospectus of an issuer if the issuer has not elected to use the process set out in NP 11-202.

3.8 Review time frames for "equity line" short form prospectuses — An issuer that is eligible to use the short form prospectus system may file a preliminary short form prospectus relating to the distribution of securities in connection with an "equity line" financing. Under an equity line arrangement, the issuer typically enters into an agreement with one or more purchasers which provides that, over a certain term, the issuer may from time to time require the purchasers to subscribe for a certain number of securities of the issuer usually at a discount from the market price. Equity line financing raises a number of important policy issues relating to the appropriate treatment of such offerings under existing securities law. Accordingly, these prospectuses will generally be reviewed within the time periods applicable to a long form prospectus.

3.9 Registration Requirements — Issuers should refer to section 3.13 of the Companion Policy to NI 41-101 for further guidance.

3.10 No Minimum Offering Amount — Issuers distributing securities on a best efforts basis that have not specified a minimum offering amount in their prospectus, should refer to section 2.2.1 and subsection 4.3(3) of the Companion Policy to NI 41-101 for further guidance.

PART 4 — CONTENT OF SHORT FORM PROSPECTUS

4.1 Prospectus Liability — Nothing in the short form prospectus regime established by NI 44-101 is intended to provide relief from liability arising under the provisions of securities legislation of any jurisdiction in which a short form prospectus is filed if the short form prospectus contains an untrue statement of a material fact or omits to state a material fact that is required to be stated therein or that is necessary to make a statement not misleading in light of the circumstances in which it was made.

4.2 Style of Short Form Prospectus — Securities legislation requires that a short form prospectus contain "full, true and plain" disclosure of the securities to be distributed. Issuers should apply plain language principles when they prepare a short form prospectus, including:

- using short sentences;
- using definite everyday language;
- using the active voice;
- avoiding superfluous words;
- organizing the document into clear, concise sections, paragraphs and sentences;
- avoiding jargon;
- using personal pronouns to speak directly to the reader;
- avoiding reliance on glossaries and defined terms unless it facilitates understanding of the disclosure;

- avoiding vague boilerplate wording;
- avoiding abstract terms by using more concrete terms or examples;
- avoiding multiple negatives;
- using technical terms only when necessary and explaining those terms;
- using charts, tables and examples where it makes disclosure easier to understand.

Question and answer and bullet point formats are consistent with the disclosure requirements of NI 44-101.

4.3 Pricing Disclosure — (1) If the offering price or the number of securities being distributed, or an estimate of the range of the offering price or the number of securities being distributed, has been publicly disclosed in a jurisdiction or a foreign jurisdiction as of the date of the preliminary short form prospectus, section 1.7.1 of Form 44-101F1 requires the issuer to disclose that information in the preliminary short form prospectus. For example, if an issuer has previously disclosed this information in a public filing or a press release, in a foreign jurisdiction, the information must also be disclosed in the preliminary short form prospectus. If the issuer discloses this information in the preliminary short form prospectus, we will not consider a difference between this information and the actual offering price or number of securities being distributed to be, in itself, a material adverse change for which the issuer must file an amended preliminary short form prospectus.

(2) No disclosure is required under section 1.7.1 of Form 44-101F1 if the offering price or size of the offering has not been disclosed as of the date of the preliminary short form prospectus. However, given the materiality of pricing or offering size information, subsequent disclosure of this information on a selective basis could constitute conduct that is prejudicial to the public interest.

4.4 Principal Purposes — Generally — (1) Section 4.2 of Form 44-101F1 requires disclosure of each of the principal purposes for which the net proceeds will be used by an issuer. If an issuer has negative operating cash flow in its most recently completed financial year for which financial statements have been included in the short form prospectus, the issuer should disclose prominently that fact in the use of proceeds section of the short form prospectus. The issuer should also disclose whether, and if so, to what extent, the proceeds of the distribution will be used to fund any anticipated negative cash flow from operating activities in future periods. An issuer should disclose negative cash flow from operating activities as a risk factor under subsection 17.1(1) of Form 44-101F1 or section 5.2 in NI 51-102F2. For the purposes of this section, in determining cash flow from operating activities, the issuer must include cash payments related to dividends and borrowing costs.

(2) For the purposes of the disclosure required under section 4.2 of Form 44-101F1, the phrase "for general corporate purposes" is not generally sufficient.

4.5 Distribution of Asset-backed Securities — Section 7.3 of Form 44-101F1 specifies additional disclosure that applies to distributions of asset-backed securities. Disclosure for a special purpose issuer of asset-backed securities will generally explain

- the nature, performance and servicing of the underlying pool of financial assets,
- the structure of the securities and dedicated cash flows, and
- any third party or internal support arrangements established to protect holders of the asset-backed securities from losses associated with non-performance of the financial assets or disruptions in payment.

The nature and extent of required disclosure may vary depending on the type and attributes of the underlying pool and the contractual arrangements through which holders of the asset-backed securities take their interest in such assets.

An issuer of asset-backed securities should consider these factors when preparing its short form prospectus:

(a) The extent of disclosure respecting an issuer will depend on the extent of the issuer's on-going involvement in the conversion of the assets comprising the pool to cash and the distribution of cash to securityholders; this involvement may, in turn, vary dramatically depending on the type, quality and attributes of the assets comprising the pool and on the overall structure of the transaction.

(b) Requested disclosure respecting the business and affairs of the issuer should be interpreted to apply to the financial assets underlying the asset-backed securities.

(c) Disclosure respecting the originator or the seller of the underlying financial assets will be relevant to investors in the asset-backed securities particularly in circumstances where the originator or seller has an on-going relationship with the financial assets comprising the pool. For example, if asset-backed securities are serviced with the cash flows from a revolving pool of receivables, an evaluation of the nature and reliability of the future origination or the future sales of underlying assets by the seller to or through the issuer may be a critical aspect of an investor's investment decision.

To address this, the focus of disclosure respecting an originator or seller of the underlying financial assets should deal with whether there are current circumstances that indicate that the originator or seller will not generate adequate assets in the future to avoid an early liquidation of the pool and, correspondingly, an early payment of the asset-backed securities. Summary historical financial information respecting the originator or seller will ordinarily be adequate to satisfy the disclosure requirements applicable to the originator or seller in circumstances where the originator or seller has an ongoing relationship with the assets comprising the pool.

Subsection 7.3(5) of Form 44-101F1 requires issuers of asset-backed securities to describe any person or company who originated, sold or deposited a material portion of the financial assets comprising the pool, irrespective of whether the person or company has an on-going relationship with the assets comprising the pool. The securities regulatory authorities consider 331/3% of the dollar value of the financial assets comprising the pool to be a material portion in this context.

4.6 Distribution of Derivatives — Section 7.4 of Form 44-101F1 specifies additional disclosure applicable to distributions of derivatives. This prescribed disclosure is formulated in general terms for issuers to customize appropriately in particular circumstances.

4.7 Underlying Securities — If securities being distributed are convertible into or exchangeable for other securities, or are a derivative of, or otherwise linked to, other securities, a description of the material attributes of the underlying securities would generally be necessary to meet the requirement of securities legislation that a prospectus contain full, true and plain disclosure of all material facts relating to the securities being distributed.

4.8 Restricted Securities — Section 7.7 of Form 44-101F1 specifies additional disclosure applicable to restricted securities, including a detailed description of any significant provisions under applicable corporate and securities law that do not apply to the holders of the restricted securities but do apply to the holders of another class of equity securities. An example of such provisions would be rights under takeover bids.

4.9 Recent and Proposed Acquisitions — (1) Subsection 10.2(2) of Form 44-101F1 requires prescribed disclosure of a proposed acquisition that has progressed to a state "where a reasonable person would believe that the likelihood of the acquisition being completed is high" and that would, if completed on the date of the short form prospectus, be a significant acquisition for the purposes of Part 8 of NI 51-102. When interpreting the phrase "where a reasonable person would believe that the likelihood of the acquisition being completed is high", it is our view that the following factors may be relevant in determining whether the likelihood of an acquisition being completed is high:

(a) whether the acquisition has been publicly announced;

(b) whether the acquisition is the subject of an executed agreement; and

(c) the nature of conditions to the completion of the acquisition including any material third party consents required.

The test of whether a proposed acquisition "has progressed to a state where a reasonable person would believe that the likelihood of the acquisition being completed is high" is an objective, rather than subjective, test in that the question turns on what a "reasonable person" would believe. It is not sufficient for an officer of an issuer to determine that he or she personally believes that the likelihood of the acquisition being completed is or is not high. The officer must form an opinion as to what a reasonable person would believe in the circumstances. In the event of a dispute, an objective test requires an adjudicator to decide whether a reasonable person would believe in the circumstances that the likelihood of an acquisition being completed was high. By contrast, if the disclosure requirement involved a subjective test, the adjudicator would assess an individual's credibility and decide whether the personal opinion of the individual as to whether the likelihood of the acquisition being completed was high was an honestly held opinion. Formulating the disclosure requirement using an objective test rather than a subjective test strengthens the basis upon which the regulator may object to an issuer's application of the test in particular circumstances.

(2) Subsection 10.2(3) of Form 44-101F1 requires inclusion of the financial statements or other information relating to certain acquisitions or proposed acquisitions if the inclusion of the financial statements or other information is necessary in order for the short form prospectus to contain full, true and plain disclosure of all material facts relating to the securities being distributed. We generally presume that the inclusion of financial statements or other information is required for all acquisitions that are, or would be, significant under Part 8 of NI 51-102. Issuers can rebut this presumption if they can provide evidence that the financial statements or other information are not required for full, true and plain disclosure.

Subsection 10.2(4) of Form 44-101F1 provides that issuers must satisfy the requirements of subsection 10.2 (3) of Form 44-101F1 by including either:

(i) the financial statements or other information that would be required by Part 8 of NI 51-102; or

(ii) satisfactory alternative financial statements or other information.

Satisfactory alternative financial statements or other information may be provided to satisfy the requirements of subsection 10.2(3) when the financial statements or other information that would be required by Part 8 of NI 51-102 relate to a financial year ended within 90 days before the date of the prospectus or an interim period ended within 60 days before the date of the prospectus for issuers that are venture issuers, and 45 days for issuers that are not venture issuers. In these circumstances, we believe that satisfactory alternative financial statements or other information would not have to include any financial statements or other information for the acquisition or probable acquisition related to:

(a) a financial year ended within 90 days before the date of the short form prospectus; or

(b) an interim period ended within 60 days before the date of the short form prospectus for issuers that are venture issuers, and 45 days for issuers that are not venture issuers.

An example of satisfactory alternative financial statements or other information that we will generally find acceptable would be:

(c) comparative annual financial statements or other information for the acquisition or probable acquisition for at least the number of financial years as would be required under Part 8 of NI 51-102 that ended more than 90 days before the date of the short form prospectus, audited for the most recently completed financial period in accordance with NI 52-107, and reviewed for the comparative period in accordance with section 4.3 of NI 44-101;

(d) a comparative interim financial report or other information for the acquisition or probable acquisition for any interim period ended subsequent to the latest annual financial statements included in the short form prospectus and more than 60 days before the date of the short form prospectus for issuers that are venture issuers, and 45 days for issuers that are not venture issuers reviewed in accordance with section 4.3 of NI 44-101; and

(e) pro forma financial statements or other information required under Part 8 of NI 51-102.

If the issuer intends to include financial statements as set out in the example above as satisfactory alternative financial statements or other information, we ask that this be highlighted in the cover letter to the prospectus. If the issuer does not intend to include financial statements or other information, or intends to file financial statements or other information that are different from those set out above, we encourage the utilization of pre-filing procedures.

(3) When an issuer acquires a business or related businesses that has itself recently acquired another business or related businesses (an "indirect acquisition"), the issuer should consider whether prospectus disclosure about the indirect acquisition, including historical financial statements, is necessary to satisfy the requirement that the prospectus contain full, true and plain disclosure of all material facts relating to the securities being distributed. In making this determination, the issuer should consider the following factors:

• if the indirect acquisition would meet any of the significance tests in Part 8 of NI 51-102 when the issuer applies each of those tests to its proportionate interest in the indirect acquisition of the business; and

• if the amount of time between the separate acquisitions is such that the effect of the first acquisition is not adequately reflected in the results of the business or related businesses the issuer is acquiring.

(4) Subsection 10.2(3) discusses financial statements or other information for the completed or proposed acquisition of the business or related businesses. This "other information" is intended to capture the financial information disclosures required under Part 8 of NI 51-102 other than financial statements. An example of "other information" would include the operating statements, property descriptions, production volumes and reserves disclosures described under section 8.10 of NI 51-102.

4.10 Updated pro forma financial statements to date of prospectus — In addition to the pro forma financial statements for completed acquisitions that are required to be included in a business acquisition report incorporated by reference into a prospectus under Item 11 of Form 44-101F1, an issuer may include a set of pro forma financial statement prepared as at the date of the prospectus.

4.11 General Financial Statement Requirements — A reporting issuer is required under the applicable CD rule to file its annual financial statements and related MD&A 90 days after year end (or 120 days if the issuer is a *venture issuer* as defined in NI 51-102). Certain transition rules in the applicable CD rule apply to the first interim financial report required to be filed in the year of adopting IFRS in respect of an interim period beginning on or after January 1, 2011. Otherwise, an interim financial report and related MD&A must be filed 45 days after the last day of an interim period (or 60 days for a venture issuer). The financial statement requirements in NI 44-101 are based on these continuous disclosure reporting time frames and do not impose accelerated filing deadlines for a reporting issuer's financial statements. However, to the extent an issuer has filed financial statements in advance of the deadline for doing so, those financial statements must be incorporated by reference in the short form prospectus. We are of the view that directors of an issuer should endeavor to consider and approve financial statements in a timely manner and should not delay the approval and filing of the financial statements for the purpose of avoiding their inclusion in a short form prospectus. Once the financial statements have been approved, they should be filed as soon as possible.

4.12 Credit Supporter Disclosure — In addition to the issuer's documents required to be incorporated by reference under sections 11.1 and 11.2 of Form 44-101F1 and the issuer's earnings coverage ratios required to be included under Item 6 of Form 44-101F1, a short form prospectus must include, under section 12.1 of Form 44-101F1, disclosure about any credit supporters that have provided a guarantee or alternative credit support for all or substantially all of the payments to be made under the securities being distributed. Accordingly, disclosure about a credit supporter may be required even if the credit supporter has not provided full and unconditional credit support.

4.13 Exemptions for Certain Issues of Guaranteed Securities — Requiring disclosure about the issuer and any applicable credit supporters in a short form prospectus may result in unnecessary disclosure in some instances. Item 13 of Form 44-101F1 provides exemptions from the requirement to include both issuer and credit supporter disclosure where such disclosure is not necessary to ensure that the short form prospectus includes full, true and plain disclosure of all material facts concerning the securities to be distributed.

The exemptions in Item 13 of Form 44-101F1 are based on the principle that, in these instances, investors will generally require either issuer disclosure or credit supporter disclosure to make an informed investment decision. The exemptions set out in Item 13 of Form 44-101F1 are not intended to be comprehensive and issuers may apply for exemptive relief from the requirement to provide both issuer and credit supporter disclosure, as appropriate.

4.14 Previously Disclosed Material Forward-Looking Information — If an issuer, at the time it files a short form prospectus,

1. has previously disclosed to the public material forward-looking information for a period that is not yet complete;

2. is aware of events and circumstances that are reasonably likely to cause actual results to differ materially from the material forward-looking information; and

3. has not filed an MD&A with the securities regulatory authorities that discusses those events and circumstances and expected differences from the material forward-looking information, as required by section 5.8 of NI 51-102,

the issuer should discuss those events and circumstances, and the expected differences from the material forward-looking information, in the short form prospectus.

PART 5 — CERTIFICATES

5.1 General — Issuers should refer to section 2.6 of the Companion Policy to NI 41-101.

PART 6 — TRANSITION

6.1 Transition — The amendments to NI 44-101 and this Policy which came into effect on January 1, 2011 only apply to a preliminary short form prospectus, an amendment to a preliminary short form prospectus, a final short form prospectus or an amendment to a final short form prospectus of an issuer which includes or incorporates by reference financial statements of the issuer in respect of periods relating to financial years beginning on or after January 1, 2011.

Adoption by OSC: (2000) 23 O.S.C.B. (Supp) 867 (December 22, 2000) and (2000) 23 O.S.C.B. (Supp) 419 (October 13, 2000); Request for Comments: (1999) 22 O.S.C.B. (POP Supp 2) (December 17, 1999), (1999) 22 O.S.C.B. (POP Supp) 1 (July 23, 1999) and (1998) 21 O.S.C.B. 1138 (February 20, 1998).

Adoption of Amendment by OSC: (2003) 26 O.S.C.B. (Supp-3) 55 (December 19, 2003); Request for Comments: (2003) 26 O.S.C.B. 4577 and (2002) 25 O.S.C.B. 3301.

Adoption of Amendments by OSC: (2005) 28 O.S.C.B. 83 and (2004) 27 O.S.C.B. 8710.

Adoption of Revised Policy by OSC: (2005) 28 O.S.C.B. 10435 and 8569; Request for Comments: (2005) 28 O.S.C.B. 228.

Adoption of Amendment to Policy by OSC: (2007) 30 O.S.C.B. 10520 and 8539.

Adoption of Revised Policy by OSC: (2008) 31 O.S.C.B. (Supp. 2) 199 (March 7, 2008) and (2007) 30 O.S.C.B. (Supp. 7) 1 (Dec. 21, 2007); Request for Comments: (2006) 29 O.S.C.B. (Supp. 3) 1 (Dec. 22, 2006).

Adoption of Amendment to Policy by OSC: (2010) 33 O.S.C.B. (Supp. 5) 100 and (Supp. 3) 161; Request for Comments: (2009) 32 O.S.C.B. (Supp. 6) 201.

Adoption of Amendment to Policy by OSC: (2013) 36 O.S.C.B. 4917 and (Supp. 2) 1; Request for Comments: (2011) 34 O.S.C.B. (Supp. 4) 1.

Adoption of Amendment to Policy by OSC: (2013) 36 O.S.C.B. 2619; Request for Comments: (2012) 35 O.S.C.B. 6887.

Adoption of Amendment to Policy by OSC: (2013) 36 O.S.C.B. 8027 and (Supp. 4) 1; Request for Comments: (2011) 34 O.S.C.B. 11829

National Instrument 44-102 — Shelf Distributions

Date: December 22, 2000, as amended effective December 30, 2005, March 17, 2008, January 1, 2011, May 14, 2013, May 31, 2013, August 13, 2013 and September 22, 2014

23 O.S.C.B. (Supp) 985 and 28 O.S.C.B. 10449, 31 O.S.C.B. (Supp. 2) 211, 33 O.S.C.B. (Supp. 5) 101, 36 O.S.C.B. 4927, 36 O.S.C.B. 2619, 36 O.S.C.B. 8028 and [37 O.S.C.B. (supp 4)]

Table of Contents

Part 4:
DISTRIBUTIONS

9A.4 Road Shows after a Receipt for a Final Base Shelf Prospectus

9A.5 Exception from Filing and Incorporation Requirements for Road Shows for Certain U.S. Cross-Border Offerings

PART 10 [REPEALED]

PART 11 EXEMPTIONS

11.1 Exemption

11.2 Evidence of Exemption

APPENDIX A METHOD 1 FOR FORM OF SHELF PROSPECTUS CERTIFICATES

APPENDIX B METHOD 2 FOR FORM OF SHELF PROSPECTUS CERTIFICATES

PART 1 — DEFINITIONS AND INTERPRETATION

1.1 Definitions — (1) In this Instrument

"acting jointly or in concert" has the meaning ascribed to that phrase in securities legislation;

"at-the-market distribution" means a non-fixed price distribution of equity securities under the shelf procedures into a pre-existing trading market in which securities of the same class are traded;

"base shelf prospectus" means a short form prospectus that is prepared in the form required under NI 44-101 as varied in accordance with this Instrument;

"clearing corporation" has the meaning ascribed to that term in National Instrument 81-102 *Investment Funds*;

"conventional convertible security" means a security of an issuer that is, according to its terms, convertible into, or exchangeable for, other securities of the issuer, or of an affiliate of the issuer;

"conventional warrant or right" means a security of an issuer, other than a clearing corporation, that gives the holder the right to purchase securities of the issuer or of an affiliate of the issuer;

"index participation unit" means a security traded on a stock exchange in Canada or the United States and issued by an issuer the only purpose of which is to

(a) hold the securities that are included in a specified widely quoted market index in substantially the same proportion as those securities are reflected in the index;or

(b) invest in a manner that causes the issuer to replicate the performance of that index;

"method 1" means the method described in Appendix A of providing forward looking forms of prospectus certificates in a base shelf prospectus or in a shelf prospectus supplement that establishes an MTN program or continuous distribution;

"method 2" means the method described in Appendix B of providing non-forward looking forms of prospectus certificates in a base shelf prospectus and a shelf prospectus supplement;

"MTN program" means a continuous distribution of debt securities in which the specific variable terms of the individual debt securities and the method of distribution of those securities are determined at the time of the distribution;

"novel" means,

(a) for a specified derivative proposed to be distributed using the shelf procedures and that has an underlying interest that is not a security of the issuer,

(i) a derivative of a type that has not been distributed by the issuer by way of prospectus in a jurisdiction of Canada before the proposed distribution, or

(ii) a derivative of a type that has been distributed by the issuer by way of prospectus in a jurisdiction of Canada before the proposed distribution, if

(A) the attributes of the derivative differ materially from the attributes of derivatives of the same type previously distributed by the issuer by way of prospectus,

(B) the structure and contractual arrangements underlying the derivative differ materially from the structure and contractual arrangements underlying derivatives of the same type previously distributed by the issuer by way of prospectus, or

(C) the type of the underlying interest for the derivative differs materially from the type of underlying interest for derivatives of the same type previously distributed by the issuer by way of prospectus, and

(b) for an asset-backed security proposed to be distributed using the shelf procedures

(i) a security of a type that has not been distributed by way of prospectus in a jurisdiction of Canada before the proposed distribution, or

(ii) a security of a type that has been distributed by way of prospectus in a jurisdiction of Canada before the proposed distribution, if

(A) the attributes of the security differ materially from the attributes of securities of the same type previously distributed by way of prospectus,

(B) the structure and contractual arrangements underlying the security differ materially from the structure and contractual arrangements underlying securities of the same type previously distributed by way of prospectus, or

(C) the type of financial assets servicing the security differ materially from the type of financial assets servicing securities of the same type previously distributed by way of prospectus;

"pricing supplement" means a shelf prospectus supplement that contains the price of securities distributed under an MTN program or other continuous distribution using the shelf procedures;

"shelf information" means the information permitted by this Instrument to be omitted from a base shelf prospectus;

"shelf procedures" means the requirements in this Instrument for the distribution of securities under a base shelf prospectus and a shelf prospectus supplement;

"shelf prospectus supplement" means a supplement to a base shelf prospectus, containing some or all of the information omitted from the base shelf prospectus as permitted by this Instrument;

"specified derivative" means an instrument, agreement or security, the market price, value or payment obligations of which are derived from, referenced to, or based on an underlying interest, other than one that is also

(a) a conventional convertible security,

(b) a specified asset-backed security,

(c) an index participation unit,

(d) a government or corporate strip bond,

(e) a capital, equity dividend or income share of a subdivided equity or fixed income security,

(f) a conventional warrant or right, or

(g) a special warrant; and

"stabilization provisions" means those provisions of securities legislation that prohibit an issuer, selling securityholder, underwriter or dealer, or an affiliate of any of the foregoing persons or companies, or any person or company acting jointly or in concert with any of them from trading in securities being distributed by way of prospectus during the period of distribution.

(2) Every term that is defined or interpreted in NI 41-101 or NI 44-101, the definition or interpretation of which is not restricted to a specific portion of NI 41-101 or NI 44-101, has, if used in this Instrument, the meaning ascribed to it in NI 41-101 or NI 44-101, unless otherwise defined or interpreted in this Instrument.

1.2 Amendments — References in this Instrument, other than in Appendix A and Appendix B, to an amendment to a prospectus include both an amendment that does not fully restate the text of a prospectus and an amended and restated prospectus.

PART 2 — SHELF QUALIFICATION AND PERIOD OF RECEIPT EFFECTIVENESS

2.1 General — An issuer shall not file a short form prospectus that is a base shelf prospectus, unless the issuer is qualified to do so under this Instrument.

2.2 Shelf Qualification for Distributions Qualified under Section 2.2 of NI 44-101 (Basic Qualification) — (1) An issuer is qualified to file a preliminary short form prospectus that is a preliminary base shelf prospectus if, at the time of filing, the issuer is qualified under section 2.2 of NI 44-101 to file a prospectus in the form of a short form prospectus.

(2) An issuer that has filed a preliminary base shelf prospectus in reliance on the qualification criteria in subsection (1) is qualified to file a short form prospectus that is the corresponding base shelf prospectus.

(3) A receipt issued for a base shelf prospectus of an issuer qualified under subsection (2) is effective until the earliest of

(a) the date 25 months from the date of its issue;

(b) the time immediately before the entering into of an agreement of purchase and sale for a security to be sold under the base shelf prospectus, if at that time

(i) the issuer does not have current annual financial statements and does not satisfy the requirements of the exemption in either of subsection 2.7(1) or (2) of NI 44-101,

(ii) the issuer does not have a current AIF and does not satisfy the requirements of the exemption in either of subsection 2.7(1) or (2) of NI 44-101,

(iii) the issuer's equity securities are not listed or posted for trading on a short form eligible exchange,

(iv) the issuer is an issuer

(A) whose operations have ceased, or

(B) whose principal asset is cash, cash equivalents, or its exchange listing, or

(v) the issuer has withdrawn its notice declaring the issuer's intention to be qualified to file a short form prospectus under NI 44-101; and

(c) in Ontario, the lapse date prescribed by securities legislation.

2.3 Shelf Qualification for Distributions Qualified under Section 2.3 of NI 44-101 (Designated Rating Non-Convertible Securities) — (1) An issuer is qualified to file a preliminary short form prospectus that is a preliminary base shelf prospectus for designated rating non-convertible securities if, at the time of filing, the issuer

(a) is qualified under section 2.3 of NI 44-101 to file a prospectus in the form of a short form prospectus; and

(b) has reasonable grounds for believing that, if it were to distribute securities under the base shelf prospectus, the securities distributed would receive a designated rating and would not receive a rating lower than a designated rating from any designated rating organization or its DRO affiliate.

(2) An issuer that has filed a preliminary base shelf prospectus in reliance on the qualification criteria in subsection (1) is qualified to file a short form prospectus that is the corresponding base shelf prospectus if, at the time of the filing of the base shelf prospectus, the issuer has reasonable grounds for believing that, if it were to distribute non-convertible securities under the base shelf prospectus, the securities distributed would receive a designated rating and would not receive a rating lower than a designated rating from any designated rating organization or its DRO affiliate.

(3) A receipt issued for a base shelf prospectus of an issuer filed under subsection (2) is effective until the earliest of

(a) the date 25 months from the date of its issue;

(b) the time immediately before the entering into of an agreement of purchase and sale for a security to be sold under the base shelf prospectus, if at that time

(i) the issuer does not have current annual financial statements and does not satisfy the requirements of the exemption in either of subsection 2.7(1) or (2) of NI 44-101,

(ii) the issuer does not have a current AIF and does not satisfy the requirements of the exemption in either of subsection 2.7(1) or (2) of NI 44-101,

(iii) the issuer has withdrawn its notice declaring the issuer's intention to be qualified to file a short form prospectus under NI 44-101, or

(iv) the securities to which the agreement relates

(A) have not received a final designated rating,

(B) are the subject of an announcement by a designated rating organization or its DRO affiliate, of which the issuer is or ought reasonably to be aware, that the designated rating given by the organization may be down-graded to a rating category that would not be a designated rating, or

(C) have received a provisional or final rating lower than an designated rating from any designated rating organization or its DRO affiliate; and

(c) in Ontario, the lapse date prescribed by securities legislation.

2.4 Shelf Qualification for Distributions under Section 2.4 of NI 44-101 (Guaranteed Non-Convertible Debt Securities, Preferred Shares and Cash Settled Derivatives) — (1) An issuer is qualified to file a short form prospectus that is a preliminary base shelf prospectus for non-convertible debt securities, non-convertible preferred shares or non-convertible cash settled derivatives if, at the time of filing, the issuer is qualified under section 2.4 of NI 44-101 to file a prospectus in the form of a short form prospectus.

(2) An issuer that has filed a preliminary base shelf prospectus in reliance on subsection (1) is qualified to file a short form prospectus that is the corresponding base shelf prospectus.

(3) A receipt issued for a base shelf prospectus of an issuer qualified under subsection (2) is effective until the earliest of

(a) the date 25 months from the date of its issue;

(b) the time immediately before the entering into of an agreement of purchase and sale for a security to be sold under the base shelf prospectus, if at that time

(i) a credit supporter has not provided full and unconditional credit support for the securities to which the shelf prospectus supplement relates,

(ii) unless the requirements of subparagraph 2.4(1)(b)(ii) of NI 44-101, but not the requirements of subparagraph 2.4(1)(b)(i) of NI 44-101, were satisfied at the time the issuer filed its base shelf prospectus, the credit supporter does not have current annual financial statements and does not satisfy the requirements of the exemption in either of subsection 2.7(1) or (2) of NI 44-101,

(iii) unless the requirements of subparagraph 2.4(1)(b)(ii) of NI 44-101, but not the requirements of subparagraph 2.4(1)(b)(i) of NI 44-101, were satisfied at the time the issuer filed its base shelf prospectus, the credit supporter does not have a current AIF and does not satisfy the requirements of the exemption in either of subsection 2.7(1) or (2) of NI 44-101,

(iv) the issuer has withdrawn its notice declaring the issuer's intention to be qualified to file a short form prospectus under NI 44-101, or

(v) either of the following is true

(A) the credit supporter's equity securities are not listed or posted for trading on a short form eligible exchange, or

(B) the credit supporter is a credit supporter

(I) whose operations have ceased, or

(II) whose principal asset is cash, cash equivalents, or its exchange listing, and

either of the following is true:

(C) the credit supporter does not have issued and outstanding non-convertible securities that

(I) have received a designated rating,

(II) have not been the subject of an announcement by a designated rating organization or its DRO affiliate, of which the issuer is or ought reasonably to be aware, that the designated rating given by the organization may be down-graded to a rating category that would not be a designated rating, and

(III) have not received a rating lower than a designated rating from any designated rating organization or its DRO affiliate, or

(D) the securities to which the agreement relates

(I) have not received a final designated rating,

(II) have been the subject of an announcement by a designated rating organization or its DRO affiliate, of which the issuer is or ought reasonably to be aware, that the designated rating given by the organization may be down-graded to a rating category that would not be a designated rating, and

(III) have received a provisional or final rating lower than a designated rating from any designated rating organization or its DRO affiliate; and

(c) in Ontario, the lapse date prescribed by securities legislation.

2.5 Shelf Qualification for Distributions under Section 2.5 of NI 44-101 (Guaranteed Convertible Debt Securities or Preferred Shares) — (1) An issuer is qualified to file a short form prospectus that is a preliminary base shelf prospectus for convertible debt securities and convertible preferred shares if, at the time of filing, the issuer is qualified under section 2.5 of NI 44-101 to file a prospectus in the form of a short form prospectus.

(2) An issuer that has filed a preliminary base shelf prospectus in reliance on subsection (1) is qualified to file a short form prospectus that is the corresponding base shelf prospectus.

(3) A receipt issued for a base shelf prospectus qualified under subsection (2) is effective until the earliest of

(a) the date 25 months from the date of its issue;

(b) the time immediately before the entering into of an agreement of purchase and sale for a security to be sold under the base shelf prospectus, if at that time

(i) the securities to which the agreement relates are not convertible into securities of a credit supporter that has provided full and unconditional credit support for the securities being distributed,

(ii) the credit supporter does not have current annual financial statements and does not satisfy the requirements of the exemption in either of subsection 2.7(1) or (2) of NI 44-101,

(iii) the credit supporter does not have a current AIF and does not satisfy the requirements of the exemption in either of subsection 2.7(1) or (2) of NI 44-101,

(iv) the credit supporter's equity securities are not listed or posted for trading on a short form eligible exchange,

(v) the credit supporter is a credit supporter

(A) whose operations have ceased, or

(B) whose principal asset is cash, cash equivalents, or its exchange listing, or

(vi) the issuer has withdrawn its notice declaring the issuer's intention to be qualified to file a short form prospectus under NI 44-101; and

(c) in Ontario, the lapse date prescribed by securities legislation.

2.6 Shelf Qualification for Distributions under Section 2.6 of NI 44-101 (Asset-Backed Securities) — (1) An issuer that is qualified under section 2.6 of NI 44-101 to file a prospectus in the form of a short form prospectus may file a preliminary base shelf prospectus for asset-backed securities if, at the time of filing, the issuer has reasonable grounds for believing that

(a) all asset-backed securities that it may distribute under the base shelf prospectus will receive a designated rating; and

(b) no asset-backed securities that it may distribute under the base shelf prospectus will receive a rating lower than a designated rating from any designated rating organization or its DRO affiliate.

(2) An issuer that has filed a preliminary base shelf prospectus in reliance on the qualification criteria in section 2.6 of NI 44-101 may file the corresponding base shelf prospectus if, at the time of the filing of the base shelf prospectus, the issuer has reasonable grounds for believing that

(a) all asset-backed securities that it may distribute under the base shelf prospectus will receive a designated rating; and

(b) no asset-backed securities that it may distribute under the base shelf prospectus will receive a rating lower than a designated rating from any designated rating organization or its DRO affiliate.

(3) A receipt issued for a base shelf prospectus qualified under subsection (2) is effective for a distribution of asset-backed securities until the earliest of

(a) the date 25 months from the date of its issue;

(b) the time immediately before the entering into of an agreement of purchase and sale for an asset-backed security to be sold under the base shelf prospectus, if at that time

(i) the issuer does not have current annual financial statements and does not satisfy the requirements of the exemption in either of subsection 2.7(1) or (2) of NI 44-101,

(ii) the issuer does not have a current AIF and does not satisfy the requirements of the exemption in either of subsection 2.7(1) or (2) of NI 44-101, or

(iii) the asset-backed securities to which the agreement relates

(A) have not received a final designated rating,

(B) have been the subject of an announcement by an designated rating organization or its DRO affiliate, of which the issuer is or ought reasonably to be aware, that the designated rating given by the organization may be down-graded to a rating category that would not be a designated rating, or

(C) have received a provisional or final rating lower than a designated rating from any designated rating organization or its DRO affiliate; and

(c) in Ontario, the lapse date prescribed by securities legislation.

2.7 Lapse Date — Ontario — In Ontario, the lapse date prescribed by securities legislation for a receipt issued for a base shelf prospectus is extended to the date 25 months from the date of issuance of the receipt.

2.8 [Repealed]

2.9 Limitation on Offerings — Despite any provision in this Instrument, the shelf procedures shall not be used for a distribution of rights under a rights offering.

PART 3 — UNALLOCATED SHELF

3.1 Unallocated Shelf Permitted — A base shelf prospectus may pertain to more than one type of security for which the issuer is qualified to file a prospectus in the form of a short form prospectus.

3.2 Distributions of Equity Securities Under Unallocated Shelf — An issuer or selling securityholder that forms a reasonable expectation that a distribution of a tranche of equity securities will proceed under a base shelf prospectus that is not specifically restricted to equity securities shall immediately issue a news release that announces the intention to proceed with the distribution.

PART 4 — DISTRIBUTIONS OF NOVEL DERIVATIVES OR ASSET-BACKED SECURITIES UNDER SHELF

4.1 Distributions of Novel Derivatives or Asset-Backed Securities Under Shelf — (1) If a base shelf prospectus pertains to specified derivatives or asset-backed securities, the issuer or the selling securityholder, as the case may be, shall file before or concurrently with the base shelf prospectus an undertaking that it will not distribute in the local jurisdiction under the base shelf prospectus specified derivatives or asset-backed securities, as the case may be, that, at the time of distribution, are novel without pre-clearing with the regulator in accordance with subsection (2) the disclosure to be contained in a shelf prospectus supplement pertaining to the distribution of the novel specified derivatives or asset-backed securities.

(2) The undertaking referred to in subsection (1) shall state that the issuer or the selling securityholder, as the case may be, shall not distribute in the local jurisdiction specified derivatives or asset-backed securities that, at the time of distribution, are novel, unless

(a) the draft shelf prospectus supplement or, if more than one shelf prospectus supplement is to be used, the draft shelf prospectus supplements, pertaining to the distribution of the novel specified derivatives or asset-backed securities have been delivered to the regulator in substantially final form; and

(b) either

(i) the regulator has confirmed his or her acceptance of each draft shelf prospectus supplement in substantially final form or each shelf prospectus supplement in final form, or

(ii) 10 business days have elapsed since the date of delivery to the regulator of each draft shelf prospectus supplement in substantially final form and the regulator has not provided written comments on the draft shelf prospectus supplement.

PART 5 — BASE SHELF PROSPECTUSES

5.1 Opting out of the Shelf Procedures After a Preliminary Prospectus has been Receipted — An issuer that has filed a preliminary base shelf prospectus shall not file a short form prospectus for the distribution that is not a base shelf prospectus unless the issuer files

(a) either

(i) an amended preliminary short form prospectus in accordance with NI 44-101 that is not a preliminary base shelf prospectus, or

(ii) a new preliminary short form prospectus that is not a preliminary base shelf prospectus; and

(b) a covering letter stating that the issuer or the selling securityholder, as the case may be, has decided not to use the shelf procedures for the distribution.

5.2 Opting into the Shelf Procedures After a Preliminary Prospectus has been Receipted — An issuer that has filed a preliminary short form prospectus that is not a preliminary base shelf prospectus shall not file a base shelf prospectus for the distribution unless the issuer files

(a) either

(i) an amended preliminary base shelf prospectus in accordance with this Instrument, or

(ii) a new preliminary short form prospectus that is a preliminary base shelf prospectus in accordance with this Instrument; and

(b) a covering letter stating that the issuer or the selling securityholder, as the case may be, has decided to use the shelf procedures for the distribution.

5.3 Form of Base Shelf Prospectus — Despite NI 44-101, a short form prospectus that is a base shelf prospectus may vary from Form 44-101F1 to the extent required or permitted by this Instrument.

5.4 Dollar Value of Securities — A base shelf prospectus shall pertain to no more than the dollar value of securities that the issuer or selling securityholder proposing to distribute securities under the base shelf prospectus reasonably expects, at the time the base shelf prospectus is filed, to distribute within 25 months after the date of the receipt for the base shelf prospectus.

5.5 Required Disclosure — A base shelf prospectus shall contain the following:

1. A statement at the top of the cover page identifying the short form prospectus as a base shelf prospectus.

2. The following statement in red ink in *italics* on the cover page:

> *"This short form prospectus has been filed under legislation in [insert name[s] of the jurisdiction[s] where qualified] that permits certain information about these securities to be determined after this prospectus has become final and that permits the omission from this prospectus of that information. The legislation requires the delivery to purchasers of a prospectus supplement containing the omitted information within a specified period of time after agreeing to purchase any of these securities."*

3. A statement that all shelf information omitted from the base shelf prospectus will be contained in one or more shelf prospectus supplements that will be delivered to purchasers together with the base shelf prospectus.

4. A statement that each shelf prospectus supplement will be incorporated by reference into the base shelf prospectus for the purposes of securities legislation as of the date of the shelf prospectus supplement and only for the purposes of the distribution of the securities to which the shelf prospectus supplement pertains.

5. A statement of the aggregate dollar amount of securities that may be raised under the base shelf prospectus.

6. Disclosure of the types of securities that may be distributed under the base shelf prospectus.

7. If an undertaking is required to be filed under subsection 4.1(1), a statement that the issuer or the selling securityholder, as the case may be, has filed an undertaking that it will not distribute specified derivatives or asset-backed securities, as the case may be, that, at the time of distribution, are novel without pre-clearing with the regulator the disclosure to be contained in the shelf prospectus supplement pertaining to the distribution of the novel specified derivatives or asset-backed securities.

8. The prospectus certificates required by Part 5 of NI 41-101 or other securities legislation, in the issuer certificate form or underwriter certificate form prescribed by

(a) method 1, if

(i) the base shelf prospectus is being used to establish an MTN program or other continuous distribution, or

(ii) method 2 has not been elected; or

(b) method 2, if method 2 has been elected.

9. List all exemptions from the provisions of this Instrument granted to the issuer applicable to the base shelf prospectus, including all exemptions to be evidenced by the issuance of a receipt for the base shelf prospectus pursuant to section 11.2.

5.6 Disclosure that may be Omitted — If the specified circumstances exist, a base shelf prospectus may omit the following information:

1. The variable terms of the securities that may be distributed under the base shelf prospectus, if not known on the date the base shelf prospectus is filed.

2. The dollar amount, size and other specific terms of each tranche of securities that may be distributed under the base shelf prospectus, if not known on the date the base shelf prospectus is filed.

3. The variable terms of the plans of distribution for the securities that may be distributed under the base shelf prospectus, if not known on the date the base shelf prospectus is filed.

4. The name and prospectus certificate of an underwriter if, at the time of the filing of the base shelf prospectus, no underwriter is, and it is not known to the issuer that a particular underwriter will be, in a contractual relationship with the issuer or selling securityholder requiring the underwriter to distribute under the base shelf prospectus.

5. If one or more underwriters have agreed to purchase the securities to be distributed under the base shelf prospectus at a specified price, the statement required under Form 44-101F1 that the securities are to be taken up by the underwriters, if at all, on or before a specified date.

6. If the securities to be distributed under the base shelf prospectus are underwritten on a best efforts basis for which a minimum amount of funds are required by an issuer, the disclosure required under Form 44-101F1 concerning the maximum length of time for which the distribution may continue and concerning the disposition of subscription funds.

6.1 The information required under item 7A of Form 44-101F1 for securities that may be distributed under the base shelf prospectus, if the specific series or class of securities that will be distributed under the base shelf prospectus is not known on the date the base shelf prospectus is filed.

7. Any other information that pertains only to a specific distribution of securities under the base shelf prospectus, if not known on the date the base shelf prospectus is filed.

8. Any other information required under NI 44-101 or other securities legislation that is not known and cannot be ascertained at the time of filing of the base shelf prospectus.

5.7 Issue of Receipt — Despite the omission of shelf information, the regulator may issue a receipt for a base shelf prospectus.

5.8 Amendments — If a material change occurs at a time when no securities are being distributed under a base shelf prospectus, the provisions in Part 6 of NI 41-101 or other securities legislation that require the filing of an amendment to a prospectus if a material change occurs are satisfied by

(a) the filing of a material change report, and

(b) the incorporation by reference in the base shelf prospectus of the material change report.

PART 6 — SHELF PROSPECTUS SUPPLEMENTS

6.1 Requirement to Use Shelf Prospectus Supplements — An issuer or selling securityholder that distributes securities under a base shelf prospectus shall supplement the disclosure in the base shelf prospectus with a shelf prospectus supplement, or more than one shelf prospectus supplement, in order for the prospectus to contain full, true and plain disclosure of all material facts relating to the securities distributed under the prospectus.

6.2 Incorporation by Reference — (1) An issuer shall incorporate by reference in the corresponding base shelf prospectus, by means of a statement in the base shelf prospectus, each shelf prospectus supplement referred to in section 6.1 as of the date of the shelf prospectus supplement and only for purposes of the distribution to which the shelf prospectus supplement pertains.

(2) If an issuer does not incorporate by reference in a base shelf prospectus a shelf prospectus supplement required to be incorporated by reference under subsection (1), the shelf prospectus supplement is conclusively deemed for purposes of securities legislation to be incorporated by reference in the issuer's base shelf prospectus as of the date of the shelf prospectus supplement and only for purposes of the distribution to which the shelf prospectus supplement pertains.

(3) Subject to subsection (4) any unaudited financial statements, other than *pro forma* financial statements, incorporated by reference into the base shelf prospectus but filed after the date of filing the base shelf prospectus must have been reviewed in accordance with the relevant standards set out in the Handbook for a review of financial statements by a person or company's auditor or a public accountant's review of financial statements.

(4) If NI 52-107 permits the financial statements of the person or company in subsection (3) to be audited in accordance with

(a) U.S. AICPA GAAS, the unaudited financial statements may be reviewed in accordance with the review standards issued by the American Institute of Certified Public Accountants,

(a.1) U.S. PCAOB GAAS, the unaudited financial statements may be reviewed in accordance with the review standards issued by the Public Company Accounting Oversight Board (United States of America),

(b) International Standards on Auditing, the unaudited financial statements may be reviewed in accordance with International Standards on Review Engagement issued by the International Auditing and Assurance Standards Board, or

(c) auditing standards that meet the foreign disclosure requirements of the designated foreign jurisdiction to which the issuer is subject, the unaudited financial statements

(i) may be reviewed in accordance with review standards that meet the foreign disclosure requirements of the designated foreign jurisdiction, or

(ii) do not have to be reviewed if

(A) the designated foreign jurisdiction does not have review standards for unaudited financial statements, and

(B) the base shelf prospectus includes disclosure that the unaudited financial statements have not been reviewed.

(5) The review specified in subsection (3), if applicable, must have been completed

(a) if the base shelf prospectus established an MTN program or other continuous offering, no later than filing of the unaudited financial statements; or

(b) in all other circumstances, no later than the next filing of a shelf supplement.

6.3 Shelf Prospectus Supplement Disclosure — (1) A shelf prospectus supplement shall contain the following:

1. The name of the issuer on the cover page.

2. The dates of the corresponding base shelf prospectus and of each previously filed shelf prospectus supplement corresponding to the same base shelf prospectus and pertaining to the same distribution, on the cover page.

3. The prospectus certificates required by Part 5 of NI 41-101 and other securities legislation, in the issuer certificate form or underwriter certificate form prescribed by

(a) method 1, if the shelf prospectus supplement establishes an MTN program or other continuous distribution; or

(b) method 2, if the prospectus certificate forms prescribed by method 1 have not been included in the corresponding base shelf prospectus and if method 1 is not mandatory under paragraph (a).

4. A list of each document that is incorporated by reference into the corresponding base shelf prospectus as of the date of the shelf prospectus supplement and provides disclosure pertaining to the securities being distributed under the shelf prospectus supplement.

(2) If only one shelf prospectus supplement is used to supplement the disclosure in the corresponding base shelf prospectus pertaining to a distribution of securities, that shelf prospectus supplement shall contain the following, and if more than one shelf prospectus supplement is used to supplement the disclosure in the corresponding base shelf prospectus pertaining to a distribution of securities, the shelf prospectus supplements used shall, together, contain the following:

1. All of the shelf information pertaining to the distribution of securities that was not disclosed in the corresponding base shelf prospectus.

2. All material facts relating to the securities to be distributed and all other information required under securities legislation to be disclosed in a short form prospectus that is not disclosed, either directly or through incorporation by reference, in the corresponding base shelf prospectus.

6.4 Filing Requirement For Shelf Prospectus Supplements — (1) A shelf prospectus supplement shall be filed in the local jurisdiction if a base shelf prospectus to which the shelf prospectus supplement pertains was filed in the local jurisdiction.

(2) A shelf prospectus supplement that is required to be filed under subsection (1) shall be filed,

(a) if the shelf prospectus supplement pertains to a distribution of securities, other than an MTN program or other continuous distribution, on or before the earlier of

(i) the date the shelf prospectus supplement was first sent or delivered to a purchaser or a prospective purchaser, and

(ii) the date two business days after the offering price of the securities to which it pertains is determined; or

(b) in all other circumstances, on or before the date two business days after the date the shelf prospectus supplement was first sent or delivered to a purchaser or a prospective purchaser.

6.5 Underwriters' Conflicts of Interest — For a distribution of securities under a base shelf prospectus, the provisions of National Instrument 33-105 *Underwriting Conflicts*

(a) concerning the participation of independent underwriters shall be satisfied

(i) on a tranche-by-tranche basis for a distribution other than an MTN program or other continuous distribution, or

(ii) on the basis of the total dollar amount of securities that, at any given time, have been or are being distributed under the program or distribution for a distribution of securities under an MTN program or other continuous distribution; and

(b) concerning disclosure, to the extent not previously satisfied in the base shelf prospectus, shall be satisfied by including the prescribed disclosure in a shelf prospectus supplement pertaining to the distribution.

6.6 Market Stabilization — The stabilization provisions shall be satisfied on a tranche-by-tranche basis for a non-continuous distribution of securities under a base shelf prospectus.

6.7 Delivery Requirement — The shelf prospectus supplement or supplements that, together with the corresponding base shelf prospectus, contain full, true and plain disclosure of all material facts relating to the securities being distributed shall be sent by prepaid mail or delivered to a purchaser of the securities with the base shelf prospectus.

6.8 Disclosure that may be Omitted — A shelf prospectus supplement may omit any prospectus certificates required by Part 5 of NI 41-101 or other securities legislation, if the person or company required to sign the certificate signed a prospectus certificate in the issuer certificate form or underwriter certificate form prescribed by method 1 included in a base shelf prospectus or a shelf prospectus supplement qualifying the securities being distributed.

PART 7 — SHELF SUPPORTING DOCUMENTS

7.1 General — The provisions of NI 44-101 requiring the filing of supporting documents with a preliminary short form prospectus, a short form prospectus or a prospectus amendment apply to a filing of a preliminary base shelf prospectus, a base shelf prospectus or an amendment to a preliminary base shelf prospectus or to a base shelf prospectus, except to the extent varied in this Part.

7.2 Consents — (1) If any notary in Québec, solicitor, auditor, accountant, engineer or appraiser, or any other person or company whose profession or business gives authority to a statement made by that person or company, is

(a) named in a document that is

(i) incorporated by reference into a base shelf prospectus, and

(ii) filed after the date of filing of the base shelf prospectus; and

(b) named in the document

(i) as having prepared or certified any part of the base shelf prospectus, amendment or shelf prospectus supplement,

(ii) as having opined on financial statements from which selected information included in the base shelf prospectus, amendment or shelf prospectus supplement has been derived and which audit opinion is referred to in the base shelf prospectus, amendment or shelf prospectus supplement directly or in a document incorporated by reference, or

(iii) as having prepared or certified a report, valuation, statement or opinion referred to in the base shelf prospectus, amendment or shelf prospectus supplement, directly or in a document incorporated by reference,

the issuer shall file the written consent of the person or company to being named and to the use of that report, valuation, statement or opinion in accordance with subsection (2).

(1.1) Despite subsection (1), if the expert whose consent is required is a "qualified person" as defined in NI 43-101, the issuer is not required to file the consent of the qualified person if

(a) the qualified person's consent is required in connection with a technical report that was not required to be filed with the preliminary base shelf prospectus,

(b) the qualified person was employed by a person or company at the date of signing the technical report,

(c) the principal business of the person or company is providing engineering or geoscientific services, and

(d) the issuer files the consent of the person or company.

(1.2) A consent filed under subsection (1.1) must be signed by an individual who is an authorized signatory of the person or company and who falls within paragraphs (a), (b), (d) and (e) of the definition of "qualified person" in NI 43-101.

(2) A consent of an expert required under subsection (1) or subsections (1.1) and (1.2) shall be filed in accordance with the following:

1. If the document in which the expert is named is incorporated by reference into the base shelf prospectus by means of a statement to that effect in the base shelf prospectus, the consent shall be filed

(a) no later than the time the document is filed, if the base shelf prospectus establishes an MTN program or other continuous distribution; and

(b) in all other circumstances, no later than the time of the next filing of a shelf prospectus supplement corresponding to the base shelf prospectus.

2. If the document in which the expert is named is incorporated by reference into a shelf prospectus supplement by means of a statement to that effect in the shelf prospectus supplement and filed before or concurrently with the shelf prospectus supplement, the consent shall be filed no later than the time the shelf prospectus supplement is filed.

3. If the document in which the expert is named is incorporated by reference into a shelf prospectus supplement by means of a statement to that effect in the shelf prospectus supplement and filed after the shelf prospectus supplement is filed, the consent shall be filed no later than the time the document is filed.

7.3 [Repealed]

7.4 Underwriting Agreements — (1) If, at the time an issuer files a base shelf prospectus, no underwriter is in a contractual relationship with the issuer or selling securityholder requiring the underwriter to distribute securities under the base shelf prospectus, the issuer is not required to file a copy of an underwriting agreement with the base shelf prospectus.

(2) If an underwriter enters into a contractual relationship with an issuer or selling securityholder requiring the underwriter to distribute securities under a base shelf prospectus after the base shelf prospectus is filed, the issuer shall file a copy of the underwriting agreement pertaining to the distribution concurrently with the next shelf prospectus supplement filed pertaining to that distribution.

PART 8 — MEDIUM TERM NOTE PROGRAMS AND OTHER CONTINUOUS DISTRIBUTIONS UNDER SHELF

8.1 General — An issuer that is qualified under Part 2 to file a base shelf prospectus for securities may distribute those securities by way of an MTN program or other continuous distribution, if it files

(a) a base shelf prospectus or a shelf prospectus supplement that establishes the program or distribution; and

(b) a pricing supplement.

8.2 Additional Disclosure Requirements — (1) Despite section 5.6, a base shelf prospectus or shelf prospectus supplement that establishes an MTN program or other continuous distribution shall contain the following:

1. A description of the method of distribution, including the name of any underwriter involved in the distribution and the amount of any underwriting fee, discount or commission.

2. A description of the intended parameters of the terms of the MTN program or other continuous distribution.

3. At the option of the issuer or selling securityholder proposing to distribute securities under the MTN program or other continuous distribution, a statement that the issuer or selling securityholder, as the case may be, reserves the right to issue securities under the MTN program or other continuous distribution on terms outside the intended parameters disclosed under paragraph 2.

(2) A pricing supplement for an MTN program or other continuous distribution under the shelf procedures shall contain the following:

1. The terms of the securities distributed that are not disclosed in the base shelf prospectus or shelf prospectus supplement establishing the MTN program or other continuous distribution.

2. A list of each document that is incorporated by reference into the corresponding base shelf prospectus as of the date of the pricing supplement and that provides disclosure pertaining to the securities being distributed under the MTN program or other continuous distribution.

8.3 Filing Requirement — If an issuer sends or delivers to a purchaser or a prospective purchaser in the local jurisdiction a pricing supplement in a particular month, the issuer shall, despite section 6.4, file within seven days after the end of the month

(a) a copy of each pricing supplement sent or delivered to a purchaser or prospective purchaser during the month, if the pricing supplement had not previously been sent or delivered to any purchaser or prospective purchaser; or

(b) a summary of the information contained in each pricing supplement sent or delivered to a purchaser or prospective purchaser during the month, including

(i) a list of the pricing supplements referred to in paragraph (a),

(ii) the terms of the securities distributed under each pricing supplement sent or delivered to a purchaser or a prospective purchaser during the month, and

(iii) the aggregate amount of securities distributed under each pricing supplement sent or delivered to a purchaser or a prospective purchaser during the month.

8.4 Requirement to Update Earnings Coverage Ratios — An issuer distributing securities by way of an MTN program or other continuous distribution using the shelf procedures shall

(a) calculate updated earnings coverage ratios for the ratios contained in its base shelf prospectus each time the issuer prepares an interim financial report or audited annual financial statements, using the 12 month period that ended on the last day of the most recently completed financial period; and

(b) file the updated earnings coverage ratios, concurrently with the filing of its financial statements, either

(i) as an exhibit to the financial statements, or

(ii) as a shelf prospectus supplement corresponding to the base shelf prospectus.

PART 9 — AT-THE-MARKET DISTRIBUTIONS OF EQUITY SECURITIES UNDER SHELF

9.1 At-the-Market Distributions of Equity Securities Under Shelf — (1) Despite section 7.2 of NI 41-101, equity securities may be distributed by way of an at-the-market distribution using the shelf procedures if the market value of equity securities distributed does not exceed 10% of the aggregate market value of the issuer's outstanding equity securities of the same class as the class of securities distributed, calculated in accordance with section 9.2, as at the last trading day of the month before the month in which the first trade under the at-the-market distribution is made.

(2) No underwriter or dealer distributing equity securities by way of an at-the-market distribution, or any affiliate of such an underwriter or dealer, or any person or company acting jointly or in concert with such an underwriter or dealer, shall, in connection with the distribution, over-allot the securities or effect a transaction that is intended to stabilize or maintain the market price of the securities.

(3) An issuer shall include in a base shelf prospectus or shelf prospectus supplement pertaining to an at-the-market distribution a statement that no underwriter or dealer involved in the distribution, no affiliate of such an underwriter or dealer and no person or company acting jointly or in concert with such an underwriter or dealer has over-allotted, or will over-allot, securities in connection with the distribution or effect any other transactions that are intended to stabilize or maintain the market price of the securities.

9.2 Market Value Calculation — (1) For the purposes of this Part,

(a) the aggregate market value of the equity securities of an issuer on a date is the aggregate of the market value of each class of its equity securities on the date, calculated by multiplying

(i) the total number of equity securities of the class outstanding on the date, by

(ii) the closing price on the date of the equity securities of the class on the exchange in Canada on which that class of equity securities is principally traded; and

(b) instalment receipts may, at the option of the issuer, be deemed to be equity securities if

(i) the instalment receipts are listed and posted for trading on an exchange in Canada, and

(ii) the outstanding equity securities, the beneficial ownership of which is evidenced by the instalment receipts, are not listed and posted for trading on an exchange in Canada.

(2) For the purposes of subsection (1), in calculating the total number of equity securities of a class outstanding, an issuer shall exclude those equity securities of the class that are beneficially owned, or controlled or directed, directly or indirectly, by persons or companies that, alone or together with their respective affiliates and associated parties, beneficially own, or control or direct, directly or indirectly, more than 10% of the outstanding equity securities of the issuer.

(3) Despite subsection (2), if a portfolio manager of a pension fund or investment fund, alone or together with its affiliates and associated parties, exercises control or direction, directly or indirectly, in the aggregate over more than 10% of the outstanding equity securities of an issuer, and the fund beneficially owns, or controls or directs, directly or indirectly, 10% or less of the issued and outstanding equity securities of the issuer, the securities that the fund beneficially owns, or controls or directs, directly or indirectly, are not excluded unless the portfolio manager is an affiliate of the issuer.

PART 9A — MARKETING IN CONNECTION WITH SHELF DISTRIBUTIONS

9A.1 Definitions — (1) In this Part,

"comparables" means information that compares an issuer to other issuers;

"U.S. cross-border offering" means an offering of securities of an issuer being made contemporaneously in the United States of America and Canada by way of a prospectus filed with a securities regulatory authority in a jurisdiction of Canada and a U.S. prospectus filed with the SEC;

"U.S. prospectus" means a prospectus that has been prepared in accordance with the disclosure and other requirements of U.S. federal securities law for an offering of securities registered under the 1933 Act.

(2) In this Part, for greater certainty, a reference to "provides" includes showing a document to a person without allowing the person to retain or make a copy of the document.

9A.2 Standard Term Sheets after a Receipt for a Final Base Shelf Prospectus — (1) An investment dealer must not provide a standard term sheet to a potential investor after a receipt for a final base shelf prospectus or any amendment is issued unless

(a) the standard term sheet complies with subsections (2) and (3);

(b) other than contact information for the investment dealer or underwriters, all information in the standard term sheet concerning the issuer, the securities or the offering

(i) is disclosed in, or derived from, the final base shelf prospectus, any amendment or an applicable shelf prospectus supplement that has been filed, or

(ii) will be disclosed in, or derived from, an applicable shelf prospectus supplement that is subsequently filed; and

(c) a receipt for the final base shelf prospectus has been issued in the local jurisdiction.

(2) A standard term sheet provided under subsection (1) must be dated and include the following legend, or words to the same effect, on the first page:

A final base shelf prospectus containing important information relating to the securities described in this document has been filed with the securities regulatory authorit[y/ies] in [each of/certain of the provinces/provinces and territories of Canada].

Copies of the final base shelf prospectus, and any applicable shelf prospectus supplement, may be obtained from *[insert contact information for the investment dealer or underwriters]*.

This document does not provide full disclosure of all material facts relating to the securities offered. Investors should read the final base shelf prospectus, any amendment and any applicable shelf prospectus supplement for disclosure of those facts, especially risk factors relating to the securities offered, before making an investment decision.

(3) A standard term sheet provided under subsection (1) may contain only the information referred to in subsection (2) and the information referred to in subsection 13.5(3) of NI 41-101.

9A.3 Marketing Materials after a Receipt for a Final Base Shelf Prospectus — (1) An investment dealer must not provide marketing materials to a potential investor after a receipt for a final base shelf prospectus or any amendment is issued unless

(a) the marketing materials comply with subsections (2) to (8);

(b) other than contact information for the investment dealer or underwriters and any comparables, all information in the marketing materials concerning the issuer, the securities or the offering

(i) is disclosed in, or derived from, the final base shelf prospectus, any amendment or an applicable shelf prospectus supplement that has been filed, or

(ii) will be disclosed in, or derived from, an applicable shelf prospectus supplement that is subsequently filed;

(c) other than prescribed language, the marketing materials contain the same cautionary language in bold type as contained on the cover page, and in the summary, of the final base shelf prospectus;

(d) a template version of the marketing materials is approved in writing by the issuer and the lead underwriter before the marketing materials are provided;

(e) a template version of the marketing materials is filed on or before the day that the marketing materials are first provided;

(f) a receipt for the final base shelf prospectus has been issued in the local jurisdiction; and

(g) the investment dealer provides a copy of the final base shelf prospectus, any amendment and any applicable shelf prospectus supplement that has been filed, with the marketing materials.

(2) If a template version of the marketing materials is approved in writing by the issuer and lead underwriter under paragraph (1)(d) and filed under paragraph (1)(e), an investment dealer may provide a limited-use version of the marketing materials that

(a) has a date that is different than the template version;

(b) contains a cover page referring to the investment dealer or underwriters or a particular investor or group of investors;

(c) contains contact information for the investment dealer or underwriters; or

(d) has text in a format, including the type's font, colour or size, that is different than the template version.

(3) If a template version of the marketing materials is divided into separate sections for separate subjects and is approved in writing by the issuer and lead underwriter under paragraph (1)(d), and that template version is filed under paragraph (1)(e), an investment dealer may provide a limited-use version of the marketing materials that includes only one or more of those separate sections.

(4) The issuer may remove any comparables, and any disclosure relating to those comparables, from the template version of the marketing materials before filing it under paragraph (1)(e) or subparagraph (7)(b)(ii) if

(a) the comparables, and any disclosure relating to the comparables, are in a separate section of the template version of the marketing materials;

(b) the template version of the marketing materials that is filed contains a note advising that the comparables, and any disclosure relating to the comparables, were removed in accordance with this subsection, provided that the note appears immediately after where the removed comparables and related disclosure would have been;

(c) if the prospectus is filed in the local jurisdiction, a complete template version of the marketing materials containing the comparables, and any disclosure relating to the comparables, is delivered to the securities regulatory authority; and

(d) the complete template version of the marketing materials contains the disclosure referred to in paragraph 13.7(4)(d) of NI 41-101.

(5) Marketing materials provided under subsection (1) must be dated and include the following legend, or words to the same effect, on the first page:

A final base shelf prospectus containing important information relating to the securities described in this document has been filed with the securities regulatory authorit[y/ies] in [each of/certain of the provinces/provinces and territories of Canada]. A copy of the final base shelf prospectus, any amendment to the final base shelf prospectus and any applicable shelf prospectus supplement that has been filed, is required to be delivered with this document.

This document does not provide full disclosure of all material facts relating to the securities offered. Investors should read the final base shelf prospectus, any amendment and any applicable shelf prospectus supplement for disclosure of those facts, especially risk factors relating to the securities offered, before making an investment decision.

(6) An investment dealer must not provide marketing materials under subsection (1) after a receipt for the final base shelf prospectus is issued and after the applicable shelf prospectus supplement is filed unless the issuer

(a) has included the template version of the marketing materials filed under paragraph (1)(e) in the applicable shelf prospectus supplement, or incorporated by reference the template version of the marketing materials filed under paragraph (1)(e) into the applicable shelf prospectus supplement in the manner described in paragraph 4 of subsection 6.3(1), or

(b) has included in the applicable base shelf prospectus a statement that any template version of the marketing materials filed after the date of the shelf prospectus supplement and before the termination of the distribution is deemed to be incorporated into the shelf prospectus supplement.

(7) If marketing materials are provided under subsection (1) after a receipt for the final base shelf prospectus is issued but before the applicable shelf prospectus supplement is filed, the issuer must

(a) include the template version of the marketing materials filed under paragraph (1)(e) in the applicable shelf prospectus supplement, or incorporate by reference the template version of the marketing materials filed under paragraph (1)(e) into the applicable shelf prospectus supplement in the manner described in paragraph 4 of subsection 6.3(1); and

(b) if the applicable shelf prospectus supplement modifies a statement of material fact that appeared in marketing materials provided earlier under subsection (1),

(i) indicate in the shelf prospectus supplement that the template version of the marketing materials is not part of the shelf prospectus supplement to the extent that the contents of the template version of the marketing materials have been modified or superseded by a statement contained in the shelf prospectus supplement,

(ii) prepare and file, at the time the issuer files the shelf prospectus supplement, a revised template version of the marketing materials that is blacklined to show the modified statement,

(iii) provide details in the shelf prospectus supplement of how the statement in the marketing materials has been modified, and

(iv) disclose in the shelf prospectus supplement that pursuant to subsection (7),

(A) the issuer has prepared a revised template version of the marketing materials which has been blacklined to show the modified statement, and

(B) the revised template version of the marketing materials can be viewed under the issuer's profile on www.sedar.com.

(8) Any revised template version of the marketing materials filed under subsection (7) must comply with this section.

(9) If marketing materials are provided under subsection (1) but the issuer did not comply with subsection (6) or paragraph (7)(a), as applicable, the marketing materials are deemed for purposes of securities legislation to be incorporated into the applicable shelf prospectus supplement as of the date of the shelf prospectus supplement to the extent not otherwise expressly modified or superseded by a statement contained in the shelf prospectus supplement.

9A.4 Road Shows after a Receipt for a Final Base Shelf Prospectus — (1) An investment dealer must not conduct a road show for potential investors after a receipt for a final base shelf prospectus or any amendment is issued unless

(a) the road show complies with subsections (2) to (4); and

(b) a receipt for the final base shelf prospectus has been issued in the local jurisdiction.

(2) Subject to section 9A.5, an investment dealer must not provide marketing materials to investors attending a road show conducted under subsection (1) unless the marketing materials are provided in accordance with section 9A.3.

(3) If any investment dealer conducts a road show, the investment dealer must establish and follow reasonable procedures to

(a) ask any investor attending the road show in person, by telephone conference call, on the internet or by other electronic means to provide their name and contact information;

(b) keep a record of any information provided by the investor; and

(c) provide the investor with a copy of the final base shelf prospectus, any amendment to the final base shelf prospectus and any applicable shelf prospectus supplement that has been filed.

(4) If an investment dealer permits an investor, other than an accredited investor, to attend a road show, the investment dealer must commence the road show with the oral reading of the following statement or a statement to the same effect:

This presentation does not provide full disclosure of all material facts relating to the securities offered. Investors should read the final base shelf prospectus, any amendment and any applicable shelf prospectus supplement for disclosure of those facts, especially risk factors relating to the securities offered, before making an investment decision.

9A.5 Exception from Filing and Incorporation Requirements for Road Shows for Certain U.S. Cross-border Offerings — (1) Subject to subsections (2) to (4), if an investment dealer provides marketing materials to a potential investor in connection with a road show for a U.S. cross-border offering, the following provisions do not apply to the template version of the marketing materials relating to the road show:

(a) paragraph 9A.3(1)(e);

(b) subsections 9A.3(6) to (9).

(2) Subsection (1) does not apply unless

(a) the underwriters have a reasonable expectation that the securities offered under the U.S. cross-border offering will be sold primarily in the United States of America;

(b) the issuer and the underwriters who sign the base shelf prospectus or the applicable shelf prospectus supplement filed in the local jurisdiction provide a contractual right containing the language set out in subsection 36A.1(5) of Form 41-101F1, or words to the same effect, except that the language may specify that the contractual right does not apply to any comparables provided in accordance with subsection (3); and
materials relating to the road show is delivered to the securities regulatory authority.

(3) If the template version of the marketing materials relating to the road show contains comparables, the template version of the marketing materials must contain the disclosure referred to in paragraph 13.7(4)(d) of NI 41-101.

(4) For greater certainty, subsection (1) does not apply to marketing materials other than the marketing materials provided in connection with the road show.

PART 10 — [REPEALED]

PART 11 — EXEMPTIONS

11.1 **Exemption** — (1) The regulator or the securities regulatory authority may grant an exemption from this Instrument, in whole or in part, subject to such conditions or restrictions as may be imposed in the exemption.

(2) Despite subsection (1), in Ontario only the regulator may grant such an exemption.

(2.1) Except in Ontario, an exemption referred to in subsection (1) is granted under the statute referred to in Appendix B of National Instrument 14-101 *Definitions* opposite the name of the local jurisdiction.

(3) An application made to the securities regulatory authority or regulator for an exemption from this Instrument shall include a letter or memorandum describing the matters relating to the exemption, and indicating why consideration should be given to the granting of the exemption.

11.2 **Evidence of Exemption** — (1) Subject to subsection (2) and without limiting the manner in which an exemption under this Part may be evidenced, the granting under this Part of an exemption, other than an exemption, in whole or in part from Part 2, may be evidenced by the issuance of a receipt for a base shelf prospectus or an amendment to a base shelf prospectus.

(2) The issuance of a receipt for a base shelf prospectus or an amendment to a base shelf prospectus is not evidence that the exemption is being granted unless

(a) the person or company that sought the exemption sent to the regulator

  (i) the letter or memorandum referred to in subsection 11.1(3), on or before the date of the filing of the base shelf prospectus or an amendment to a base shelf prospectus, or

  (ii) the letter or memorandum referred to in subsection 11.1(3) after the date of the filing of the base shelf prospectus or an amendment to a base shelf prospectus and received a written acknowledgement from the regulator that the exemption may be evidenced in the manner set out in subsection (1), and

(b) the regulator has not before, or concurrently with, the issuance of the receipt sent notice to the person or company that sought the exemption, that the exemption sought may not be evidenced in the manner set out in subsection (1).

PART 12 — EFFECTIVE DATE

12.1 **Effective Date** — This Instrument shall come into force on December 31, 2000.

APPENDIX A — METHOD 1 FOR FORM OF SHELF PROSPECTUS CERTIFICATES

METHOD 1: FORWARD LOOKING FORM OF CERTIFICATES TO BE INCLUDED IN BASE SHELF PROSPECTUSES OR SUPPLEMENTS ESTABLISHING AN MTN PROGRAM OR OTHER CONTINUOUS DISTRIBUTION

Part 1 — Base Shelf Prospectuses

1.1 — Issuer Certificate Form

If a base shelf prospectus establishes an MTN program or other continuous distribution, or if method 2 has not been elected by an issuer, an issuer certificate form in the preliminary base shelf prospectus and the base shelf prospectus must state:

> This short form prospectus, together with the documents incorporated in this prospectus by reference, will, as of the date of the last supplement to this prospectus relating to the securities offered by this prospectus and the supplement(s), constitute full, true and plain disclosure of all material facts relating to the securities offered by this prospectus and the supplement(s) as required by the securities legislation of [insert name of each jurisdiction in which qualified].

1.2 — Underwriter Certificate Form

If the base shelf prospectus establishes an MTN program or other continuous distribution or if method 2 has not been elected by the underwriter, an underwriter certificate form in the preliminary base shelf prospectus and the base shelf prospectus must state:

> To the best of our knowledge, information and belief, this short form prospectus, together with the documents incorporated in this prospectus by reference will, as of the date of the last supplement to this prospectus relating to the securities offered by this prospectus and the supplement(s), constitute full, true and plain disclosure of all material facts relating to the securities offered by this prospectus and the supplement(s) as required by the securities legislation of [insert name of each jurisdiction in which qualified].

1.3 — [Repealed]

1.4 — Amendments

(1) For an amendment to a base shelf prospectus in respect of a base shelf prospectus that included the issuer certificate form and underwriter certificate form in sections 1.1 and 1.2, and if the amendment does not restate the prospectus, change "this short form prospectus" to "the short form prospectus dated [insert date] as amended by this amendment" wherever it appears in the statements in sections 1.1 and 1.2.

(2) For an amended and restated base shelf prospectus in respect of a base shelf prospectus that included the issuer certificate form and underwriter certificate form in sections 1.1 and 1.2, change "this short form prospectus" and replace it with "this amended and restated short form prospectus" wherever it appears in the statements in sections 1.1 and 1.2.

Part 2 — Shelf Prospectus Supplements establishing an MTN Program

2.1 — Issuer Certificate Form

If an issuer certificate form described in section 1.1 was not included in the corresponding base shelf prospectus, an issuer certificate form in a shelf prospectus supplement that establishes an MTN program or other continuous distribution must state:

> The short form prospectus, together with the documents incorporated in the prospectus by reference, as supplemented by the foregoing, will, as of the date of the last supplement to the prospectus relating to the securities offered by the prospectus and the supplement(s), constitute full, true and plain disclosure of all material facts relating to the securities offered by the prospectus and the supplement(s) as required by the securities legislation of [insert name of each jurisdiction in which qualified].

2.2 — Underwriter Certificate Form

If an underwriter's certificate form described in section 1.2 was not included in the corresponding base shelf prospectus, an underwriter certificate form in a shelf prospectus supplement that establishes an MTN program or other continuous distribution must state:

> To the best of our knowledge, information and belief, the short form prospectus, together with the documents incorporated in the prospectus by reference, as supplemented by the foregoing, will, as of the date of the last supplement to the prospectus relating to the securities offered by the prospectus and the supplement(s), constitute full, true and plain disclosure of all material facts relating to the securities offered by the prospectus and the supplement as required by the securities legislation of [insert name of jurisdiction in which qualified].

2.3 — [Repealed]

2.4 — Amendments

(1) For an amendment to a shelf prospectus supplement in respect of a shelf prospectus supplement that included the issuer certificate form and underwriter certificate form in sections 2.1 and 2.2, and if the amendment does not restate the prospectus, add ", as it amends the shelf prospectus supplement dated [insert date]" after "the foregoing," wherever it appears in the statements in sections 2.1 and 2.2.

(2) For an amended and restated shelf prospectus supplement in respect of a shelf prospectus supplement that included the issuer certificate form and underwriter certificate form in sections 2.1 and 2.2, include the issuer certificate form and the underwriter certificate form in sections 2.1 and 2.2.

APPENDIX B — METHOD 2 FOR FORM OF SHELF PROSPECTUS CERTIFICATES

METHOD 2: NON-FORWARD LOOKING FORM OF PROSPECTUS CERTIFICATES TO BE INCLUDED IN BOTH BASE SHELF PROSPECTUSES AND SUPPLEMENTS

Part 1 — Base Shelf Prospectus

1.1 — Issuer Certificate Form

If method 2 is elected by an issuer, an issuer certificate form in the preliminary base shelf prospectus and the base shelf prospectus must state:

> This short form prospectus, together with the documents incorporated in this prospectus by reference, constitutes full, true and plain disclosure of all material facts relating to the securities offered by this prospectus as required by the securities legislation of [insert name of each jurisdiction in which qualified].

1.2 — Underwriter Certificate Form

If method 2 is elected by an underwriter, an underwriter certificate form in the preliminary base shelf prospectus and the base shelf prospectus must state:

> To the best of our knowledge, information and belief, this short form prospectus, together with the documents incorporated in this prospectus by reference, constitutes full, true and plain disclosure of all material facts relating to the securities offered by this prospectus as required by the securities legislation of [insert name of each jurisdiction in which qualified].

1.3 — [Repealed]

1.4 — Amendments

(1) For an amendment to a base shelf prospectus in respect of a base shelf prospectus that included the issuer certificate form and underwriter certificate form in sections 1.1 and 1.2, and if the amendment does not restate the prospectus, change "this short form prospectus" to "the short form prospectus dated [insert date] as amended by this amendment" wherever it appears in the statements in sections 1.1 and 1.2.

(2) For an amended and restated base shelf prospectus in respect of a base shelf prospectus that included the issuer certificate form and underwriter certificate form in sections 1.1 and 1.2, change "this short form prospectus" to "this amended and restated short form prospectus" wherever it appears in the statements in sections 1.1 and 1.2.

Part 2 — Shelf Prospectus Supplement

2.1 — Issuer Certificate Form

If method 2 is elected by an issuer, an issuer certificate form in a shelf prospectus supplement must state:

> The short form prospectus, together with the documents incorporated in the prospectus by reference, as supplemented by the foregoing, constitutes full, true and plain disclosure of all material facts relating to the securities offered by the prospectus and this supplement as required by the securities legislation of [insert name of each jurisdiction in which qualified].

2.2 — Underwriter Certificate Form

If method 2 is elected by an underwriter, an underwriter certificate form in a shelf prospectus supplement must state:

> To the best of our knowledge, information and belief, the short form prospectus, together with the documents incorporated in the prospectus by reference, as supplemented by the foregoing, constitutes full, true and plain disclosure of all material facts relating to the securities offered by the prospectus and this supplement as required by the securities legislation of [insert name of jurisdiction in which qualified].

2.3 — [Repealed]

2.4 — Amendments

(1) For an amendment to a shelf prospectus supplement in respect of a shelf prospectus supplement that included the issuer certificate form and underwriter certificate form in sections 2.1 and 2.2, and if the amendment does not restate the prospectus, add ", as it amends the shelf prospectus supplement dated [insert date]" after "the foregoing," wherever it appears in the statements in sections 2.1 and 2.2.

(2) For an amended and restated shelf prospectus supplement in respect of a shelf prospectus supplement that included the issuer certificate form and underwriter certificate form in sections 2.1 and 2.2, include the issuer certificate form and the underwriter certificate form in sections 2.1 and 2.2.

Final Rule: 23 O.S.C.B. (Supp) 985 (December 22, 2000); Approval by OSC: 23 O.S.C.B. (Supp) 565 (October 13, 2000); Request for Comments: (1998) 21 O.S.C.B. 6191. Replaced, in part, NPS 44.

Amendments: 28 O.S.C.B. 10449; Approval by OSC: 28 O.S.C.B. 8569; Request for Comments: 28 O.S.C.B. 228.

Amendments to Rule: (2008) 31 O.S.C.B. (Supp. 2) 211 (March 7, 2008); Approval by OSC: (2007) 30 O.S.C.B. (Supp. 7) 1 (Dec. 21, 2007); Request for Comments: (2006) 29 O.S.C.B. (Supp. 3) 1 (Dec. 22, 2006).

Amendments to Rule: (2010) 33 O.S.C.B. (Supp. 5) 101; Approval by OSC: (2010) 33 O.S.C.B. (Supp. 3) 161; Request for Comments: (2009) 32 O.S.C.B. (Supp. 6) 201.

Amendments to Rule: (2013) 36 O.S.C.B. 4927; Approval by OSC: (2013) 36 O.S.C.B. (Supp. 2) 1; Request for Comments: (2011) 34 O.S.C.B. (Supp. 4) 1.

Amendments to Rule: Approval by OSC: (2013) 36 O.S.C.B. 2619; Request for Comments: (2012) 35 O.S.C.B. 6887.

Amendments to Rule: (2013) 36 O.S.C.B. 8028; Approved by OSC: (2013) 36 O.S.C.B. (Supp. 4) 1; Request for Comments: (2011) 34 O.S.C.B. 11829

Amendments to Rule: Approval by OSC: (2014) 37 O.S.C.B. (Supp 4) 128; Request for Comments: (2013) 36 O.S.C.B. (Supp 3)

Rules: NI 44-101, 44-103; Rule 13-502, App. C, Item A.

Policies and Orders: NPS 44-102CP, 11-202; CSAN 44-304; OSCN 41-703.

Companion Policy 44-102CP — To National Instrument 44-102 Shelf Distributions

Table of Contents

PART 1 — GENERAL

1.1 Relationship of the National Instrument to Securities Legislation — (1) Issuers are reminded that the rules and procedures contained in National Instrument 44-102 for distributions made under the shelf procedures should be read in conjunction with other provisions of securities legislation in each jurisdiction in which a distribution is being made.

(2) A distribution under a short form prospectus using the shelf procedures is subject to all the requirements of National Instrument 44-101 *Short Form Prospectus Distributions*, some of the requirements of National Instrument 41-101 *General Prospectus Requirements*, and other provisions of securities legislation, as supplemented or varied by NI 44-102 and the implementing law of the jurisdiction. Reference is made to section 1.5 of the Companion Policy to NI 44-101 for a discussion of the relationship between NI 44-101 and NI 44-102, and to subsection 1.2(5) of the Companion Policy to NI 41-101 for a discussion of the relationship among NI 41-101, NI 44-101 and NI 44-102.

1.2 Liability — (1) The securities regulatory authorities are of the view that an issuer's prospectus certificate contained in an amendment to a base shelf prospectus filed under the shelf procedures supersedes and replaces the issuer's certificate contained in the base shelf prospectus. Accordingly, an officer who signed the later dated certificate and the directors at the time the amendment was filed would be subject to statutory civil liability to purchasers of securities under the amended base shelf prospectus.

(2) The securities regulatory authorities are of the view that an issuer's prospectus certificate contained in a shelf prospectus supplement filed under the shelf procedures supersedes and replaces the issuer's certificate contained in the base shelf prospectus for purposes of the distribution of securities under the shelf prospectus supplement. Accordingly, an officer who signed the later dated certificate and the directors at the time the supplement was filed would be subject to statutory civil liability to purchasers of securities under the shelf prospectus supplement.

1.3 Marketing before the Filing of a Shelf Prospectus Supplement — After a receipt has been issued for a base shelf prospectus, we do not have the same regulatory concerns about "marketing" before the filing of a shelf prospectus supplement as we do about "pre-marketing" before the filing of a short form prospectus or a long form prospectus (see section 6.4 of Companion Policy 41-101CP).

A preliminary form of shelf prospectus supplement describing a tranche of securities to be offered under the shelf procedures (a draw-down) may be used in marketing the securities before the public offering price is determined. Issuers are reminded that the ability to use a preliminary form of shelf prospectus supplement in this manner for a distribution of equity securities under an unallocated base shelf prospectus is subject to the requirement in section 3.2 of National Instrument 44-102 to issue a news release once the issuer or selling securityholder has formed a reasonable expectation that the distribution will proceed.

Issuers should also consider whether the decision to pursue a draw-down under an allocated base shelf prospectus is a material change under applicable securities legislation. If the decision is a material change, the news release and material change report requirements in Part 7 of NI 51-102 and other securities legislation apply.

In order to address selective disclosure concerns, an issuer will generally file any preliminary form of shelf prospectus supplement on SEDAR and ask their principal regulator to make it public. However, staff of securities regulatory authorities will not be "pre-clearing" any preliminary form of shelf prospectus supplement (unless the issuer is filing a draft supplement pursuant to an undertaking previously given to securities regulatory authorities).

If an issuer does not issue a news release about a potential draw-down under a base shelf prospectus, then the relevant investment dealers should consider measures to ensure compliance with applicable securities laws relating to selective disclosure, insider trading and trading by "tippees" (these laws are summarized in sections 3.1 and 3.2 of National Policy 51-201 *Disclosure Standards*) before circulating a preliminary form of shelf prospectus supplement to investors.

Issuers and investment dealers should also refer to the guidance on marketing activities in Part 6 of the Companion Policy to NI 41-101. While NI 44-102 has provisions on marketing after a receipt for a final base shelf prospectus, NI 41-101 has general provisions that apply to marketing during the waiting period.

PART 2 — SHELF PROCEDURES

2.1 Shelf Qualification — (1) The principle guiding the qualification provisions of NI 44-102 is that any distribution under a short form prospectus, other than rights offerings, may be effected using the shelf procedures.

(2) A distribution using the shelf procedures is necessarily a distribution under a short form prospectus. Therefore, issuers must be qualified to file a prospectus in the form of a short form prospectus under NI 44-101 and must satisfy the additional qualification criteria under Part 2 of NI 44-102.

2.2 Period of Receipt Effectiveness — (1) NI 44-102 provides that a receipt for a base shelf prospectus is effective until the earliest of the following three events: (i) the date 25 months from the date of the issuance of a receipt for the base shelf prospectus, (ii) the time immediately before selling the securities, if certain prescribed conditions relating to the issuer's qualification to file a prospectus in the form of a short form prospectus are not satisfied, and (iii) in Ontario, the lapse date of the receipt prescribed by securities legislation, if no relief has been granted to the issuer through a blanket ruling or upon application by the issuer. This receipt expiry mechanism is designed to impose a limit of, essentially, two years on shelf distributions under the same base shelf prospectus and to prevent distributions of securities under a base shelf prospectus if the issuer would no longer be qualified under NI 44-101.

(2) The securities legislation in some jurisdictions provides that a prospectus receipt does not continue to be effective for more than one year absent relief granted by the securities regulatory authority in that jurisdiction. Some of these jurisdictions have provided blanket relief for receipts issued for base shelf prospectuses.

2.3 Unallocated Shelf — (1) Section 3.1 of NI 44-102 provides that a base shelf prospectus may pertain to different types of securities. This allows a base shelf prospectus to be used to distribute any combination of debt securities, preferred shares, derivatives, asset-backed securities and equity securities, for which the issuer is eligible to participate in the short form prospectus distributions system.

(2) In the case of an unallocated base shelf prospectus, section 3.2 of NI 44-102 requires an issuer or a selling securityholder to issue a news release immediately upon having formed a reasonable expectation that a distribution of equity securities under the unallocated shelf prospectus will proceed. An issuer or selling securityholder will generally only have formed such a reasonable expectation upon having discussions with an underwriter concerning the distribution of some specificity and certainty.

2.4 Distributions of Novel Derivatives and Asset-Backed Securities using the Shelf Procedures — (1) The securities regulatory authorities recognize the utility of the shelf procedures for distributions of derivatives and asset-backed securities in order to permit tranches of these products to be priced and distributed expeditiously to take advantage of market opportunities, without the need for regulatory approval.

(2) However, the securities regulatory authorities are also aware of the complexities that may be associated with distributions of specified derivatives and asset-backed securities. All material attributes of the products, and the risks associated with them, should be disclosed in either the base shelf prospectus or the shelf prospectus supplement. The securities regulatory authorities also want to ensure that prospectus investors of such products are entitled to the appropriate rights at the time of their investment as contemplated by applicable securities laws. Reference is made to section 4.8 of Companion Policy NI 44-101CP for a discussion of these issues. The securities regulatory authorities have attempted to balance these objectives in formulating NI 44-102.

(3) The requirements relating to the clearance of distributions of derivatives or asset-backed securities make a distinction between "novel" and "non-novel" products. If a base shelf prospectus pertains to specified derivatives or asset-backed securities, the issuer or selling securityholder, as the case may be, must file an undertaking under section 4.1 of NI 44-102 with its base shelf prospectus. This includes any circumstances where a base shelf prospectus, including, if applicable, an unallocated shelf prospectus, may be used together with a prospectus supplement to qualify novel products. The undertaking must state that the issuer or the selling securityholder, as the case may be, will not distribute under the base shelf prospectus specified

derivatives or asset-backed securities that at the time of distribution are novel without pre-clearing the disclosure in shelf prospectus supplements with the regulator.

(4) The term "novel" has a different meaning depending on whether it pertains to specified derivatives or asset-backed securities. In the case of asset-backed securities, the term is intended to apply to a distribution of asset-backed securities that is structured in a manner that differs materially from the manner in which any public distribution that has previously taken place in a jurisdiction was structured. In the case of specified derivatives, an issuer or selling securityholder must pre-clear any distribution of derivative securities that are of a type that have not previously been distributed to the public by the issuer.

(5) The securities regulatory authorities are of the view that the definition of the term "novel" should be read relatively restrictively. A security would not be novel merely because a new underlying interest was used. For example, where the underlying interest is a market index, the use of a different market index would not be considered "novel", provided that information about the index methodology, the constituents that make up the index, as well as the daily index level, are available to the public. However, in circumstances where an issuer or its advisor is uncertain if a product is novel, the securities regulatory authorities encourage the issuer to either treat products as novel or to seek input from staff prior to filing a base shelf prospectus or prospectus supplement, as the case may be.

(6) If the product is not novel, then the shelf prospectus supplements concerning the product need not be reviewed by the securities regulatory authorities. The securities regulatory authorities are of the view that the disclosure in shelf prospectus supplements in such circumstances should be no less comprehensive than the disclosure that has previously been reviewed by a securities regulatory authority in a jurisdiction. The securities regulatory authorities also believe that the rights provided to investors in such products should be no less comprehensive than the rights provided in offerings previously reviewed by a securities regulatory authority in a jurisdiction.

(7) The securities regulatory authorities have a particular interest in reviewing novel specified derivatives that are functionally similar to investment fund products. These products have generally taken the form of linked notes issued under a medium term note program. These derivatives provide returns that are similar to investment fund products but are not necessarily subject to the investment funds regulatory regime. As a result, the securities regulatory authorities will review such offerings while keeping investment fund conflicts and disclosure concerns in mind.

(8) In circumstances where it is apparent to the issuer or selling securityholder that a specified derivative that is subject to the pre-clearance process is similar to a specified derivative that has already been subject to the pre-clearance process, the issuer or selling securityholder is encouraged, for the purpose of expediting the pre-clearance process, to file along with the shelf prospectus supplement a blackline to the relevant precedent shelf prospectus supplement. The issuer or selling securityholder is also encouraged to provide a cover letter setting out the material attributes of the specified derivative that differ from the securities offered under the precedent shelf prospectus.

2.5 Information that may be Omitted from a Base Shelf Prospectus — (1) Paragraph 1 of section 5.6 of NI 44-102 provides that a base shelf prospectus may omit the variable terms, if not known, of the securities that may be distributed under it. The types of variable information that may be omitted from the base shelf prospectus include

(a) the designation of the tranche;

(b) maturities;

(c) denominations;

(d) interest or dividend provisions;

(e) purchase, redemption and retraction provisions;

(f) conversion or exchange provisions;

(g) the terms for extension or early repayment;

(h) the currencies in which the securities are issued or payable;

(i) sinking fund provisions; and

(j) any special covenants or other terms applicable to the securities of the tranche.

(2) Paragraph 3 of section 5.6 of NI 44-102 provides that a base shelf prospectus may omit information, if not known, relating to the variable terms of the plans of distribution for the securities that may be distributed under the base shelf prospectus. These variable terms may include

(a) if the shelf prospectus sets forth alternative methods of distribution, the method that will be applicable to each tranche of securities distributed under the shelf prospectus; and

(b) for each tranche of securities distributed under the shelf prospectus, the specific terms not included in the description of the applicable method of distribution in the shelf prospectus, including, if applicable

(i) the names of any underwriters, and

(ii) the distribution spread and underwriting fees, discounts and commissions.

(3) Paragraph 7 of section 5.6 of NI 44-102 provides that a base shelf prospectus may omit other information, if not known, that pertains only to a specific distribution of securities under the base shelf prospectus. This information may include

(a) the public offering price;

(b) delivery dates;

(c) legal opinions regarding the eligibility for investment of the securities and tax matters;

(d) statements regarding listing of the securities;

(e) actual amount of proceeds on the distribution; and

(f) information about the use of proceeds.

2.6 Shelf Prospectus Supplements — (1) The ability to file a shelf prospectus supplement does not prevent the filing of a shelf prospectus amendment to supply some or all of the information that is permitted to be included in a prospectus supplement.

(2) Under subsection 6.3(2) of NI 44-102, the shelf prospectus supplements used in a distribution must contain all omitted shelf information as well as all information necessary for the base shelf prospectus to comply with the disclosure requirements for a short form prospectus. For example, if the securities being distributed using the shelf procedures are rated, that rating must be disclosed in a shelf prospectus supplement because NI 44-101

requires all ratings, including provisional ratings, received from one or more designated rating organizations or their DRO affiliates for the securities to be distributed and continuing in effect, to be disclosed in a short form prospectus.

(3) Section 6.7 of NI 44-102 provides that all shelf prospectus supplements pertaining to the securities being distributed under a base shelf prospectus shall be sent by prepaid mail or delivered to purchasers of the securities concurrently with the base shelf prospectus. A shelf prospectus supplement may take the form of a "sticker", a "wrap-around" or a one or more page supplement to a base shelf prospectus.

2.6.1 Expert's Consent — Section 7.2 of NI 44-102 provides that if a document (the "Document") containing an expert's report, valuation, statement of opinion is incorporated by reference into a base shelf prospectus and filed after the filing of the base shelf prospectus, the issuer must file the written consent of the expert in accordance with deadlines that vary with the circumstances. For example, issuers are reminded that separate auditor's consents are required at the filing of the base shelf prospectus and in each subsequent shelf prospectus supplement for each set of audited financial statements incorporated by reference for which a consent was not previously filed. The following is intended to illustrate the required timing for the filing of the expert's consents:

Type of Prospectus Filed	Timing of inclusion of expert's report	Timing of filing of expert's consent
MTN or non-MTN base shelf prospectus	Expert's report included in the base shelf prospectus at the date the base shelf prospectus is filed.	Expert's consent is filed at the date the prospectus is filed.
MTN base shelf prospectus	Expert's report included in a Document, filed after the base shelf prospectus is filed, that is incorporated by reference into the prospectus.	Expert's consent is filed at the date the Document is filed.
Non-MTN base shelf prospectus	Expert's report included in a Document, filed after the base shelf prospectus is filed, that is incorporated by reference into the prospectus.	Expert's consent is filed no later than the date of filing of the next prospectus supplement corresponding to the base shelf prospectus or the date the Document is filed.

2.7 Firm Commitment Distributions — Paragraph 5 of section 5.6 of NI 44-102 provides that a base shelf prospectus for securities to be distributed by one or more underwriters that have agreed to purchase the securities at a specified price may omit the statement that the securities are to be taken up by the underwriters, if at all, on or before a specified date. This paragraph provides an exemption from the requirement of securities legislation that this disclosure be contained in a prospectus. Issuers are reminded that paragraph 1 of subsection 6.3(2) of NI 44-102 requires all information that was omitted from the base shelf prospectus to be included in a shelf prospectus supplement. Therefore, it is necessary to include in a shelf prospectus supplement the disclosure required under securities legislation relating to specific distributions that are being effected on a firm commitment basis.

2.8 Best Efforts Distributions — Paragraph 6 of section 5.6 of NI 44-102 similarly provides that a base shelf prospectus for a distribution of securities underwritten on a best efforts basis for which a minimum amount of funds are required by an issuer may omit disclosure required under securities legislation concerning the maximum length of time for which the distribution can continue and concerning the disposition of subscription funds. Issuers are reminded that paragraph 1 of subsection 6.3(2) of NI 44-102 requires all information that was omitted from the base shelf prospectus to be included in a shelf prospectus supplement. Therefore, it is necessary to include in a shelf prospectus supplement the disclosure required under securities legislation relating to specific distributions that are being effected on a best efforts basis.

2.9 Delivery Obligations — The securities regulatory authorities are of the view that statutory rights of rescission or withdrawal commence from the time of the purchaser's receipt of all relevant shelf prospectus supplements. It is only at this time that the entire prospectus has been delivered.

PART 3 — SHELF PROSPECTUS AMENDMENTS

3.1 Shelf Prospectus Amendments — (1) Part 6 of NI 41-101 or other securities legislation in a number of jurisdictions requires that an amendment to a prospectus be filed if a material change occurs after the receipt for the prospectus is obtained but before the completion of the distribution under that prospectus. These requirements apply to base shelf prospectuses.

(2) Section 5.8 of NI 44-102 permits, in limited circumstances, the requirement in Part 6 of NI 41-101 or other securities legislation to file an amendment to be satisfied by the incorporation by reference of material change reports filed after the base shelf prospectus has been receipted. This is an exception to the general principle set out in section 3.6 of the Companion Policy to NI 44-101. That section provides that the requirement in NI 41-101 or other securities legislation to file an amendment is not satisfied by the incorporation by reference of material change reports filed after the short form prospectus has been receipted. The exception in section 5.8 of NI 44-102 is limited to periods in which no securities are being distributed under the base shelf prospectus.

(3) If securities are being distributed under a base shelf prospectus, the general principle referred in subsection (2) applies. The requirement of NI 41-101 or other securities legislation to file an amendment to a prospectus if a material change occurs may be satisfied by filing an amendment which is also a material change report. In these circumstances, the material change report would:

    (a) state that the base shelf prospectus is amended and supplemented by the contents of the material change report; and

    (b) contain the certificates required to be contained in an amendment.

(4) If an issuer wishes to add securities to its base shelf prospectus it may do so prior to issuing all of the securities qualified by the base shelf prospectus by filing an amendment to the base shelf prospectus. This will not extend the life of the base shelf prospectus.

PART 4 — PROSPECTUS CERTIFICATES

4.1 Prospectus Certificates — (1) Appendix A and Appendix B of NI 44-102 provide for two alternate methods of preparing forms of prospectus certificates. Unless a particular method is prescribed, the choice of method may be changed between the date of filing of the preliminary base shelf prospectus and the date of filing of the base shelf prospectus. Furthermore, the method elected need not be the same.

(2) Method 1 requires that forward-looking forms of prospectus certificates be included in a base shelf prospectus. Doing so allows the use of shelf prospectus supplements that do not contain prospectus certificates as set out in section 6.8 of NI 44-102. Method 2 requires forms of prospectus certificates that speak only to the present to be included in both the base shelf prospectus and each shelf prospectus supplement.

(3) Method 1 is mandatory for a base shelf prospectus that establishes an MTN program. If an MTN program is established in a shelf prospectus supplement, method 1 is mandatory and prescribes that forward-looking forms of certificates be included, unless they were already included in the base shelf prospectus.

Adoption by OSC: 23 O.S.C.B. (Supp) 985 (December 22, 2000) and 23 O.S.C.B. (Supp) 565 (October 13, 2000); Request for Comments: (1998) 21 O.S.C.B. 6191.

Rules: Rule 41-501; NI 41-101, 41-102.

Adoption of Amendments: 28 O.S.C.B. 10456 and 8569; Request for Comments: 28 O.S.C.B. 228.

Adoption of Amendments: 31 O.S.C.B. (Supp. 2) 218 (March 7, 2008) and 30 O.S.C.B. (Supp. 7) 1 (Dec. 21, 2007); Request for Comments: 29 O.S.C.B. (Supp. 3) 1 (Dec. 22, 2006).

Adoption of Amendment: (2013) 36 O.S.C.B. 4928 and (Supp. 2) 1; Request for Comments: (2011) 34 O.S.C.B. (Supp. 4) 1.

Adoption of Amendment: (2013) 36 O.S.C.B. 2619; Request for Comments: (2012) 35 O.S.C.B. 6887.

Adoption of Amendment: (2003) 36 O.S.C.B. 8033 and (Supp. 4) 1; Request for Comments: (2011) 34 O.S.C.B. 11829

Policies and Orders: NPS 41-101CP.

National Instrument 44-103 — Post-Receipt Pricing

Date: **December 22, 2000, as amended effective December 30, 2005, March 17, 2008 and August 13, 2013**

23 O.S.C.B. (Supp) 1013, 28 O.S.C.B. 10458, 31 O.S.C.B. (Supp. 2) 221 and 36 O.S.C.B. 8034

Table of Contents

PART 1 — DEFINITIONS AND INTERPRETATION

1.1 Definitions — (1) In this Instrument

"base PREP prospectus" means a prospectus that at the time of issuance of a receipt for the prospectus omits some or all of the PREP information as permitted by this Instrument;

"PREP information" means the information permitted by this Instrument to be omitted from a base PREP prospectus;

"PREP procedures" means the requirements in this Instrument for the distribution under a base PREP prospectus and a supplemented PREP prospectus of securities, the price of which is determined after a receipt has been obtained for the base PREP prospectus; and

"supplemented PREP prospectus" means a prospectus filed under the PREP procedures containing PREP information.

(2) Every term that is defined or interpreted in NI 41-101 or NI 44-101, the definition or interpretation of which is not restricted to a specific portion of NI 41-101 or NI 44-101, has, if used in this Instrument, the meaning ascribed to it in NI 41-101 or NI 44-101, unless otherwise defined or interpreted in this Instrument.

1.2 Amendments — References in this Instrument to an amendment to a prospectus include both an amendment that does not fully restate the text of a prospectus and an amended and restated prospectus.

PART 2 — USE OF THE PREP PROCEDURES

2.1 Prohibited Offerings — Despite the other provisions of this Instrument, the PREP procedures shall not be used for a distribution of rights under a rights offering.

2.2 Opting out of the PREP Procedures After a Preliminary Prospectus has been Receipted and before a Prospectus has been Receipted — An issuer that has obtained a receipt for a preliminary base PREP prospectus for a distribution of securities shall not file a prospectus for the distribution that is not a base PREP prospectus, unless the issuer files a covering letter, before or concurrently with the filing of the prospectus, stating that the issuer or the selling securityholder, as the case may be, has decided not to use the PREP procedures for the distribution.

2.3 Opting into the PREP Procedures After a Preliminary Prospectus has been Receipted and before the Prospectus has been Receipted — An issuer that has obtained a receipt for a preliminary prospectus that is not a preliminary base PREP prospectus for a distribution of securities shall not file a base PREP prospectus for the distribution, unless the issuer files a covering letter, before or concurrently with the base PREP prospectus, stating that the issuer or the selling securityholder, as the case may be, has decided to use the PREP procedures for the distribution.

2.4 Opting out of the PREP Procedures After a Prospectus has been Receipted — If a receipt has been issued for a base PREP prospectus for a distribution of securities and the issuer or the selling securityholder decides, before a supplemented PREP prospectus is filed, no longer to use the PREP procedures for the distribution, the issuer shall file

(a) either

(i) an amended prospectus that is not a base PREP prospectus or a supplemented PREP prospectus, or

(ii) a new preliminary prospectus that is not a preliminary base PREP prospectus; and

(b) a covering letter stating that the issuer or the selling securityholder, as the case may be, has decided not to use the PREP procedures for the distribution.

PART 3 — BASE PREP PROSPECTUSES

3.1 Form of Base PREP Prospectus — The required form of prospectus under securities legislation may be varied for a PREP prospectus to the extent provided for in this Instrument.

3.2 Required Disclosure — (1) A base PREP prospectus of an issuer shall contain the following:

1. A statement at the top of the cover page identifying the prospectus as a base PREP prospectus.

2. The following statement in red ink and in *italics* on the cover page:

   "This [insert throughout, if applicable, "short form"] prospectus has been filed under procedures in [insert names of each jurisdiction where qualified] that permit certain information about these securities to be determined after the prospectus has become final and that permit the omission of that information from this prospectus. The procedures require the delivery to purchasers of a supplemented PREP prospectus containing the omitted information within a specified period of time after agreeing to purchase any of these securities."

3. A statement that all disclosure contained in a supplemented PREP prospectus that is not contained in the base PREP prospectus will be incorporated by reference into the base PREP prospectus as of the date of the supplemented PREP prospectus.

4. If securities other than shares are being distributed, a statement of the aggregate dollar amount of securities to which the base PREP prospectus pertains.

5. If shares are being distributed,

   (a) the aggregate dollar amount of the shares to which the base PREP prospectus pertains, if

   (i) the proceeds of the offering are to be applied to a specific purpose identified in the prospectus and a minimum amount must be raised through the offering in order to accomplish the purpose, and

   (ii) there is no pre-existing trading market in which securities of the same class as the securities to be distributed under the prospectus are traded; or

   (b) either the aggregate number, or the aggregate dollar amount, of the shares to which the base PREP prospectus pertains.

6. Any earnings coverage ratios required under securities legislation, which may be expressed as ranges based on a reasonable estimate of the PREP information.

7. The prospectus certificates required by Part 5 of NI 41-101 and other securities legislation,

(a) in the following issuer certificate form:

"The [insert, if applicable, "short form"] prospectus, together with the documents and information incorporated by reference, will, as of the date of the supplemented prospectus providing the information permitted to be omitted from this prospectus, constitute, full, true and plain disclosure of all material facts relating to the securities offered by this prospectus as required under the securities legislation of [insert name of each jurisdiction in which qualified]."; and

(b) in the following underwriter certificate form:

"To the best of our knowledge, information and belief, this [insert, if applicable "short form"] prospectus, together with the documents and information incorporated by reference, will, as of the date of the supplemented prospectus providing the information permitted to be omitted from this prospectus, constitute full, true and plain disclosure of all material facts relating to the securities offered by this prospectus as required under the securities legislation of [insert name of each jurisdiction in which qualified]."

8. [Repealed]

9. [Repealed]

10. List all exemptions from the provisions of this Instrument granted to the issuer applicable to the base PREP prospectus, including all exemptions to be evidenced by the issuance of a receipt for the base PREP prospectus pursuant to section 6.2.

(2) Despite subsection (1), a preliminary base PREP prospectus is not required to contain the information required in paragraphs 4, 5 and 6 of subsection (1), if the information is not known at the time of filing the preliminary base PREP prospectus.

3.3 Disclosure that may be Omitted — A base PREP prospectus may omit the following:

1. The public offering price of the securities to be distributed.

2. The amount of cash underwriting fees, discounts and commissions for the distribution of the securities.

3. The net proceeds of the distribution.

4. If shares are being distributed and only the aggregate number of securities to be distributed is disclosed and the aggregate dollar amount of shares is not required to be disclosed under paragraph 5 of subsection 3.2(1), the gross proceeds of the distribution.

5. Any dividend or interest rate of the securities to be distributed.

6. Any dividend or interest payment dates, record dates and any dates from which dividends or interest accrue for the securities to be distributed.

7. Any redemption, purchase for cancellation, conversion and exchange prices of the securities.

8. The identity of the members of the underwriting syndicate, other than the lead underwriter and any co-lead underwriter, and the disclosure required under Item 14 of Form 44-101F1 or Item 25 of Form 41-101F1.

9. The delivery dates of securities to be purchased under the distribution.

10. If one or more underwriters have agreed to purchase the securities to be distributed at a specified price, the statement required under securities legislation that the securities are to be taken up by the underwriters, if at all, on or before a specified date.

11. If the securities to be distributed are underwritten on a best efforts basis for which a minimum amount of funds are required by an issuer, disclosure required under securities legislation concerning the maximum length of time for which the distribution may continue and concerning the disposition of subscription funds.

12. Other terms of the securities to be distributed that are mathematically derivable from any of the information referred to in paragraphs 1 through 11.

3.4 Issuance of Receipt — Despite the omission of PREP information, the regulator may issue a receipt for a base PREP prospectus.

3.5 Expiry of Receipt — (1) Subject to subsection (2), a receipt issued for a base PREP prospectus expires 90 days after issuance unless a supplemented PREP prospectus is filed within the 90 day period.

(2) If a supplemented PREP prospectus is not filed within 20 days of the filing of a base PREP prospectus, the receipt issued for the base PREP prospectus expires at the time immediately before the entering into of the first agreement of purchase and sale for a security to which the base PREP prospectus pertains, unless a receipt has been issued within the preceding 20 days for an amended base PREP prospectus that updates to the date of the filing of the amended base PREP prospectus all of the disclosure contained in the base PREP prospectus.

3.6 Amendment to a Base PREP Prospectus — (1) For an amendment to a base PREP prospectus, other than an amendment filed under section 2.4 to opt out of the PREP procedures, in respect of a base PREP prospectus that included the issuer certificate form or the underwriter certificate form in subsection 3.2(1), and if the amendment is not a restatement of the base PREP prospectus, insert the phrase "as amended by this amendment" after the reference in each certificate form to the prospectus.

(2) For an amended and restated base PREP prospectus, other than an amended and restated base PREP prospectus filed under section 2.4 to opt out of the PREP procedures, in respect of a base PREP prospectus that included the issuer certificate form or the underwriter certificate form in subsection 3.2(1), preface the reference to the prospectus in each certificate form with the phrase "this amended and restated".

PART 4 — SUPPLEMENTED PREP PROSPECTUSES

4.1 Requirement to Use a Supplemented PREP Prospectus — An issuer or selling securityholder that distributes securities under a base PREP prospectus shall supplement the disclosure in the base PREP prospectus with a supplemented PREP prospectus in order for the prospectus to contain full, true and plain disclosure of all material facts relating to the securities distributed under the prospectus.

4.2 Incorporation by Reference — The content of a supplemented PREP prospectus that is not also contained in the corresponding base PREP prospectus is incorporated by reference in the base PREP prospectus as of the date of the supplemented PREP prospectus.

4.3 Restriction on Changes — A supplemented PREP prospectus shall be identical to the corresponding base PREP prospectus, except for the changes permitted or required under this Part.

4.4 Changes in the Size of Distribution — (1) The size of the distribution as disclosed in the base PREP prospectus under paragraph 4 or 5 of subsection 3.2(1) may be increased or decreased by up to 20% in a supplemented PREP prospectus.

(2) If the size of the distribution as disclosed in the base PREP prospectus under paragraph 4 or 5 of subsection 3.2(1) is increased or decreased by up to 20% in a supplemented PREP prospectus and that increase or decrease is a material change, the provisions of Part 6 of NI 41-101 or other securities legislation that require the filing of an amendment to a prospectus if a material change occurs are satisfied by the filing of the supplemented PREP prospectus.

(3) Despite the provisions of securities legislation regarding the prescribed form of issuer certificate form and underwriter certificate form for prospectus amendments, a supplemented PREP prospectus filed in order to satisfy provisions of Part 6 of NI 41-101 or other securities legislation that require the filing of an amendment to a prospectus if a material change occurs shall contain the issuer certificate form and underwriter certificate form required in subsection 4.5(2).

4.5 Required Disclosure — (1) A supplemented PREP prospectus shall be dated the date that the public offering price of the securities is determined.

(2) A supplemented PREP prospectus shall contain the following:

1. All of the PREP information omitted from the base PREP prospectus.

2. Instead of the earnings coverage ratios expressed as ranges based on a reasonable estimate of the PREP information as permitted under paragraph 6 of subsection 3.2(1), the earnings coverage ratios required under securities legislation.

3. The prospectus certificates required by Part 5 of NI 41-101 or other securities legislation,

    (a) in the following issuer certificate form:

        "This [insert, if applicable, "short form"] prospectus [insert in the case of a short form prospectus distribution — ", together with the documents incorporated by reference"] constitutes full, true and plain disclosure of all material facts relating to the securities offered by this prospectus as required under securities legislation of [insert name of each jurisdiction in which qualified]."; and

    (b) in the following underwriter certificate form:

        "To the best of our knowledge, information and belief, this [insert, if applicable, "short form"] prospectus [insert in the case of a short form prospectus distribution — ", together with the documents incorporated by reference,"] constitutes full, true and plain disclosure of all material facts relating to securities offered by this prospectus as required under the securities legislation of [insert name of each jurisdiction in which qualified]."

    4. [Repealed]

    5. [Repealed]

    6. A list and brief description of each document that has been incorporated by reference in the base PREP prospectus since the issuance of a receipt for the base PREP prospectus.

4.6 Legend to be Omitted — A supplemented PREP prospectus shall omit the legend required under paragraph 2 of subsection 3.2(1).

4.7 Amendment to a Supplemented PREP Prospectus — An amendment to a supplemented PREP prospectus shall contain the form of certificates set out in subsection 4.5(2) for a supplemented PREP prospectus with the following changes:

1. If the amendment is not a restatement of the supplemented PREP prospectus, the phrase "as amended by this amendment" inserted after the reference in each certificate form to the prospectus.

2. If the amendment is an amended and restated supplemented PREP prospectus, the reference in each certificate form to the prospectus prefaced by the phrase "this amended and restated".

4.8 Timing of Filing of Supplemented PREP Prospectus — If securities are distributed using the PREP procedures in the local jurisdiction, a supplemented PREP prospectus prepared in accordance with this Instrument shall be filed in the local jurisdiction by the second business day following the date of the determination of the information omitted from the base PREP prospectus.

4.9 Delivery Requirement — If securities are being distributed using the PREP procedures, the requirement under securities legislation to deliver a prospectus to a purchaser of securities shall be satisfied by the delivery of a supplemented PREP prospectus.

4.10 Underwriting Agreements — Despite the provisions of Part 9 of NI 41-101, an underwriting agreement or other material contract that relates to a distribution of securities that cannot be completed until the distribution is priced and that is required under Part 9 of NI 41-101 to be filed with a prospectus

    (a) shall be filed with the base PREP prospectus in draft form and may omit PREP information; and

    (b) shall be refiled in final form, together with the supplemented PREP prospectus or base PREP prospectus amendment containing the PREP information and a copy of the agreement, blacklined against the draft form filed under paragraph (a).

PART 4A — MARKETING IN CONNECTION WITH THE PREP PROCEDURES

4A.1 Definitions — (1) In this Part,

"comparables" means information that compares an issuer to other issuers;

"U.S. cross-border initial public offering" means an initial public offering of securities of an issuer being made contemporaneously in the United States of America and Canada by way of a prospectus filed with a securities regulatory authority in a jurisdiction of Canada and a U.S. prospectus filed with the SEC;

"U.S. cross-border offering" means an offering of securities of an issuer being made contemporaneously in the United States of America and Canada by way of a prospectus filed with a securities regulatory authority in a jurisdiction of Canada and a U.S. prospectus filed with the SEC, and includes a U.S. cross-border initial public offering;

"U.S. prospectus" means a prospectus that has been prepared in accordance with the disclosure and other requirements of U.S. federal securities law for an offering of securities registered under the 1933 Act.

(2) In this Part, for greater certainty, a reference to "provides" includes showing a document to a person without allowing the person to retain or make a copy of the document.

4A.2 Standard Term Sheets after a Receipt for a Final Base PREP Prospectus — (1) An investment dealer must not provide a standard term sheet to a potential investor after a receipt for a final base PREP prospectus or any amendment is issued unless

    (a) the standard term sheet complies with subsections (2) and (3);

    (b) other than contact information for the investment dealer or underwriters, all information in the standard term sheet concerning the issuer, the securities or the offering

        (i) is disclosed in, or derived from, the final base PREP prospectus, the supplemented PREP prospectus or any amendment that has been filed, or

        (ii) will be disclosed in, or derived from, the supplemented PREP prospectus that is subsequently filed; and

    (c) a receipt for the final base PREP prospectus has been issued in the local jurisdiction.

(2) A standard term sheet provided under subsection (1) must be dated and include the following legend, or words to the same effect, on the first page:

A [final base PREP prospectus/supplemented PREP prospectus] containing important information relating to the securities described in this document has been filed with the securities regulatory authorit[y/ies] in [each of/certain of the provinces/provinces and territories of Canada].

Copies of the [final base PREP prospectus/supplemented PREP prospectus] may be obtained from *[insert contact information for the investment dealer or underwriters].*

This document does not provide full disclosure of all material facts relating to the securities offered. Investors should read the supplemented PREP prospectus and any amendment for disclosure of those facts, especially risk factors relating to the securities offered, before making an investment decision.

(3) A standard term sheet provided under subsection (1) may contain only the information referred to in subsection (2) and the information referred to in subsection 13.5(3) of NI 41-101.

4A.3 Marketing Materials after a Receipt for a Final Base PREP Prospectus — (1) An investment dealer must not provide marketing materials to a potential investor after a receipt for a final base PREP prospectus or any amendment is issued unless

    (a) the marketing materials comply with subsections (2) to (9);

    (b) other than contact information for the investment dealer or underwriters and any comparables, all information in the marketing materials concerning the issuer, the securities or the offering

        (i) is disclosed in, or derived from, the final base PREP prospectus, the supplemented PREP prospectus or any amendment that has been filed, or

        (ii) will be disclosed in, or derived from, the supplemented PREP prospectus that is subsequently filed;

    (c) other than prescribed language, the marketing materials contain the same cautionary language in bold type as contained on the cover page, and in the summary, of the final base PREP prospectus;

    (d) a template version of the marketing materials is approved in writing by the issuer and the lead underwriter before the marketing materials are provided;

    (e) a template version of the marketing materials is filed on or before the day that the marketing materials are first provided;

    (f) a receipt for the final base PREP prospectus has been issued in the local jurisdiction; and

    (g) the investment dealer provides the marketing materials with a copy of

        (i) the final base PREP prospectus and any amendment, or

        (ii) if it has been filed, the supplemented PREP prospectus and any amendment.

(2) A template version of the marketing materials filed under paragraph 1(e) may contain blank spaces for the PREP information set out in section 3.3, provided that the omitted information is contained in the supplemented PREP prospectus that is subsequently filed.

(3) If a template version of the marketing materials is approved in writing by the issuer and lead underwriter under paragraph 1(d) and filed under paragraph 1(e), an investment dealer may provide a limited-use version of the marketing materials that

    (a) has a date that is different than the template version;

    (b) contains a cover page referring to the investment dealer or underwriters or a particular investor or group of investors;

    (c) contains contact information for the investment dealer or underwriters;

    (d) has text in a format, including the type's font, colour or size, that is different than the template version; or

    (e) contains the omitted information referred to in subsection (2), provided that the omitted information is contained in the supplemented PREP prospectus that is subsequently filed.

(4) If a template version of the marketing materials is divided into separate sections for separate subjects and is approved in writing by the issuer and lead underwriter under paragraph (1)(d), and that template version is filed under paragraph (1)(e), an investment dealer may provide a limited-use version of the marketing materials that includes only one or more of those separate sections.

(5) The issuer may remove any comparables, and any disclosure relating to those comparables, from the template version of the marketing materials before filing it under paragraph (1)(e) or (8)(b) if

    (a) the comparables, and any disclosure relating to the comparables, are in a separate section of the template version of the marketing materials;

    (b) the template version of the marketing materials that is filed contains a note advising that the comparables, and any disclosure relating to the comparables, were removed in accordance with this subsection, provided that the note appears immediately after where the removed comparables and related disclosure would have been;

(c) if the prospectus is filed in the local jurisdiction, a complete template version of the marketing materials containing the comparables, and any disclosure relating to the comparables, is delivered to the securities regulatory authority; and

(d) the complete template version of the marketing materials contains the disclosure referred to in paragraph 13.7(4)(d) of NI 41-101.

(6) Marketing materials provided under subsection (1) must be dated and include the following legend, or words to the same effect, on the first page:

A [final base PREP prospectus/supplemented PREP prospectus] containing important information relating to the securities described in this document has been filed with the securities regulatory authorit[y/ies] in [each of/certain of the provinces/provinces and territories of Canada]. A copy of the [final base PREP prospectus/supplemented PREP prospectus], and any amendment, is required to be delivered with this document.

This document does not provide full disclosure of all material facts relating to the securities offered. Investors should read the supplemented PREP prospectus and any amendment for disclosure of those facts, especially risk factors relating to the securities offered, before making an investment decision.

(7) An investment dealer must not provide marketing materials under subsection (1) after a receipt for the final base PREP prospectus is issued unless the issuer

(a) has included the template version of the marketing materials filed under paragraph (1)(e) in the final base PREP prospectus, and any amendment, or incorporated by reference the template version of the marketing materials filed under paragraph (1)(e) into the final base PREP prospectus, and any amendment, in the manner described in subsection 36A.1(1) of Form 41-101F1 or subsection 11.6(1) of Form 44-101F1, as applicable, or

(b) has included in the final base PREP prospectus a statement that any template version of the marketing materials filed after the date of the final base PREP prospectus and before the termination of the distribution is deemed to be incorporated into the final base PREP prospectus.

(8) If an amendment to a final base PREP prospectus or a supplemented PREP prospectus modifies a statement of material fact that appeared in marketing materials provided under subsection (1), the issuer must

(a) indicate in the amendment that the template version of the marketing materials is not part of the final base PREP prospectus or supplemented PREP prospectus, as amended, to the extent that the contents of the template version of the marketing materials have been modified or superseded by a statement contained in the amendment;

(b) prepare and file, at the time the issuer files the amendment to the final base PREP prospectus or supplemented PREP prospectus, as applicable, a revised template version of the marketing materials that is blacklined to show the modified statement; and

(c) include in the amendment to the final base PREP prospectus or supplemented PREP prospectus, as applicable, the disclosure required by subsection 36A.1(3) of Form 41-101F1 or subsection 11.6(3) of Form 44-101F1, as applicable.

(9) Any revised template version of the marketing materials filed under subsection (8) must comply with this section.

(10) If marketing materials are provided under subsection (1) but the issuer did not comply with subsection (7), the marketing materials are deemed for purposes of securities legislation to be incorporated into the final base PREP prospectus as of the date of the final base PREP prospectus to the extent not otherwise expressly modified or superseded by a statement contained in the final base PREP prospectus.

4A.4 Road Shows after a Receipt for a Final Base PREP Prospectus — (1) An investment dealer must not conduct a road show for potential investors after a receipt for a final base PREP prospectus or any amendment is issued unless

(a) the road show complies with subsections (2) to (4); and

(b) a receipt for the final base PREP prospectus has been issued in the local jurisdiction.

(2) Subject to section 4A.6, an investment dealer must not provide marketing materials to investors attending a road show conducted under subsection (1) unless the marketing materials are provided in accordance with section 4A.3.

(3) If an investment dealer conducts a road show, the investment dealer must establish and follow reasonable procedures to

(a) ask any investor attending the road show in person, by telephone conference call, on the internet or by other electronic means to provide their name and contact information;

(b) keep a record of any information provided by the investor; and

(c) provide the investor with a copy of

(i) the final base PREP prospectus and any amendment, or

(ii) if it has been filed, the supplemented PREP prospectus and any amendment.

(4) If an investment dealer permits an investor, other than an accredited investor, to attend a road show, the investment dealer must commence the road show with the oral reading of the following statement or a statement to the same effect:

This presentation does not provide full disclosure of all material facts relating to the securities offered. Investors should read the supplemented PREP prospectus and any amendment for disclosure of those facts, especially risk factors relating to the securities offered, before making an investment decision.

4A.5 Exception from Procedures for Road Shows for Certain U.S. Cross-border Initial Public Offerings — (1) Subject to subsection (2), paragraphs 4A.4(3)(a) and (b) do not apply to an investment dealer that conducts a road show in connection with a U.S. cross-border initial public offering.

(2) Subsection (1) does not apply unless

(a) the issuer is relying on the exemption from U.S. filing requirements in Rule 433(d)(8)(ii) under the 1933 Act in respect of the road show; and

(b) the investment dealer establishes and follows reasonable procedures to

(i) ask any investor attending the road show in person, by telephone conference call, on the internet or by other electronic means to voluntarily provide their name and contact information; and

(ii) keep a record of any information voluntarily provided by the investor.

4A.6 Exception from Filing and Incorporation Requirements for Road Shows for Certain U.S. Cross-border Offerings — (1) Subject to sub-sections (2) to (4), if an investment dealer provides marketing materials to a potential investor in connection with a road show for a U.S. cross-border offering, the following provisions do not apply to the template version of the marketing materials relating to the road show:

(a) paragraph 4A.3(1)(e);

(b) subsections 4A.3(7) to (10).

(2) Subsection (1) does not apply unless

(a) the underwriters have a reasonable expectation that the securities offered under the U.S. cross-border offering will be sold primarily in the United States of America;

(b) the issuer and the underwriters who sign the base PREP prospectus or the supplemented PREP prospectus filed in the local jurisdiction provide a contractual right containing the language set out in subsection 36A.1(5) of Form 41-101F1, or words to the same effect, except that the language may specify that the contractual right does not apply to any comparables provided in accordance with subsection (3); and

(c) if the base PREP prospectus has been filed in the local jurisdiction, the template version of the marketing materials relating to the road show is delivered to the securities regulatory authority.

(3) If the template version of the marketing materials relating to the road show contains comparables, the template version of the marketing materials must contain the disclosure referred to in paragraph 13.7(4)(d) of NI 41-101.

(4) For greater certainty, subsection (1) does not apply to marketing materials other than the marketing materials provided in connection with the road show.

PART 5 — [REPEALED]

PART 6 — EXEMPTIONS

6.1 Exemption — (1) The regulator or the securities regulatory authority may grant an exemption from this Instrument, in whole or in part, subject to such conditions or restrictions as may be imposed in the exemption.

(2) Despite subsection (1), in Ontario, only the regulator may grant such an exemption.

(2.1) Except in Ontario, an exemption referred to in subsection (1) is granted under the statute referred to in Appendix B of National Instrument 14-101 *Definitions* opposite the name of the local jurisdiction.

(3) An application made to the securities regulatory authority or regulator for an exemption from this Instrument shall include a letter or memorandum describing the matters relating to the exemption, and indicating why consideration should be given to the granting of the exemption.

6.2 Evidence of Exemption — (1) Subject to subsection (2) and without limiting the manner in which an exemption under this Part may be evidenced, the granting of an exemption under this Part may be evidenced by the issuance of a receipt for a base PREP prospectus or an amendment to a base PREP prospectus.

(2) The issuance of a receipt for a base PREP prospectus or an amendment to a base PREP prospectus is not evidence that the exemption is being granted unless

(a) the person or company that sought the exemption sent to the regulator

(i) the letter or memorandum referred to in subsection 6.1(3), on or before the date of the filing of the preliminary base PREP prospectus, or

(ii) the letter or memorandum referred to in subsection 6.1(3) after the date of the filing of the preliminary base PREP prospectus and received a written acknowledgement from the regulator that the exemption may be evidenced in the manner set out in subsection (1), and

(b) the regulator has not before, or concurrently with, the issuance of the receipt sent notice to the person or company that sought the exemption, that the exemption sought may not be evidenced in the manner set out in subsection (1).

PART 7 — EFFECTIVE DATE

7.1 Effective Date — This Instrument shall come into force on December 31, 2000.

Final Rule: 23 O.S.C.B. (Supp) 1013 (December 22, 2000); Approval by OSC: 23 O.S.C.B. (Supp) 599 (October 13, 2000); Request for Comments: (1998) 21 O.S.C.B. 6233; Replaced, in part, NPS 44.

Amendments to Rule: 28 O.S.C.B. 10458; Approval by OSC: 28 O.S.C.B. 8569; Request for Comments: 28 O.S.C.B. 228.

Amendments to Rule: 31 O.S.C.B. (Supp. 2) 221 (March 7, 2008); Approval by OSC: 30 O.S.C.B. (Supp. 7) 1 (Dec. 21, 2007); Request for Comments: 29 O.S.C.B. (Supp. 3) 1 (Dec. 22, 2006).

Amendments to Rule: (2013) 36 O.S.C.B. 8034; Approval by OSC: (2013) 36 O.S.C.B. (Supp. 4) 1; Request for Comments: (2011) 34 O.S.C.B. 11829.

Rules: NI 41-101, 44-101.

Policies and Orders: NPS 44-103CP, 11-202; OSCN 41-703.

Companion Policy 44-103CP — To National Instrument 44-103 Post-Receipt Pricing

PART 1 — INTRODUCTION

1.1 Implementation of the Instrument — Certain jurisdictions have implemented National Instrument 44-103 Post-Receipt Pricing (the "Instrument") by one or more instruments forming part of securities legislation or securities directions in the jurisdiction. As a result, the provisions of the Instrument apply in those jurisdictions to the extent provided by, and except as modified by, the implementing law of the jurisdiction.

1.2 Availability of PREP Procedures — Access to the PREP procedures is not restricted to issuers qualified to file a prospectus in the form of a short form prospectus. Any issuer that wishes to use the PREP procedures, or enable a selling securityholder to use the PREP procedures, to distribute securities may file a prospectus that is a base PREP prospectus.

1.3 Relationship of the Instrument to Securities Legislation — (1) Issuers are reminded that the rules and procedures contained in the Instrument for distributions made using the PREP procedures should be read in conjunction with other provisions of securities legislation in each jurisdiction in which a distribution is being made.

(2) A distribution under a short form prospectus using the PREP procedures is subject to all the requirements of National Instrument 44-101 *Short Form Prospectus Distributions*, some of the requirements of National Instrument 41-101 *General Prospectus Requirements* and other provisions of securities legislation, as supplemented or varied by the Instrument and the implementing law of the jurisdiction. Reference is made to Part 1 of the Companion Policy to NI 44-101 for a discussion of the relationship between NI 44-101 and various other pieces of securities legislation and section 1.2 of the Companion Policy to NI 41-101 for a discussion of the relationship between NI 41-101 and various other pieces of securities legislation.

(3) Similarly, a distribution using the PREP procedures not made under a short form prospectus is subject to securities legislation, as supplemented or varied by the Instrument and the implementing law of the jurisdiction, including NI 41-101.

PART 2 — PROSPECTUS AMENDMENTS

2.1 Prospectus Amendments — (1) Section 4.4 of the Instrument provides that the size of an offering may be increased or decreased by up to 20% between the filing of the prospectus and the filing of the supplemented PREP prospectus. The section further provides that, in cases where such a change in the size of the offering constitutes a material change, the requirement in Part 6 of NI 41-101 or other securities legislation to file an amendment if a material change occurs may be satisfied by filing the supplemented PREP prospectus. The form of certificates required in the supplemented PREP prospectus are those set out in subsection 4.5(2) of the Instrument. For changes in the size of the offering by more than 20% that constitute a material change, this flexibility in filing of the amendment is not available.

(2) The securities regulatory authorities are of the view that an issuer's ability to use the PREP procedures does not prevent the filing of a prospectus amendment to make some or all of the changes to the prospectus that are permitted to be made by a supplemented PREP prospectus.

PART 3 — PREP PROCEDURES

3.1 Firm Commitment Distributions — Paragraph 10 of section 3.3 of the Instrument provides that a base PREP prospectus for securities to be distributed by one or more underwriters that have agreed to purchase the securities at a specified price is not required to indicate that the securities are to be taken up by the underwriters, if at all, on or before a specified date. This subsection provides an exemption from the requirement of securities legislation that this disclosure must be contained in a prospectus. Issuers are reminded that paragraph 1 of subsection 4.5(2) requires all information omitted from a base PREP prospectus to be included in a supplemented PREP prospectus. Therefore, it is necessary to comply with the relevant requirement of securities legislation in a supplemented PREP prospectus relating to specific distributions that are being effected on a firm commitment basis.

3.2 Best Efforts Distributions — Similarly, paragraph 11 of section 3.3 of the Instrument provides that a base PREP prospectus for a distribution of securities underwritten on a best efforts basis for which a minimum amount of funds are required by an issuer is not required to include disclosure required under securities legislation concerning the maximum length of time for which the distribution may continue and concerning the disposition of subscription funds. Issuers are reminded, as in the previous subsection, that paragraph 1 of subsection 4.5(2) requires all information omitted from a base PREP prospectus to be included in a supplemented PREP prospectus. Therefore, it is necessary to comply with the relevant requirement of securities legislation in a supplemented PREP prospectus relating to specific distributions that are being effected on a best efforts basis. Issuers are also reminded that where PREP procedures are used in connection with securities offered on a best efforts basis for which a minimum amount of funds are required, the issuer may not reduce the size of the distribution pursuant to section 4.4 of the Instrument in a supplemented PREP prospectus to a size that would yield less than the minimum amount of funds.

3.3 Rights of Rescission or Withdrawal — The securities regulatory authorities are of the view that statutory rights of rescission or withdrawal commence from the time of the purchaser's receipt of a supplemented PREP prospectus. It is only at this time that the entire prospectus has been delivered.

3.4 Supplemented Prospectus not an Amendment — The securities regulatory authorities do not consider a supplemented PREP prospectus to constitute an amendment to a prospectus within the meaning of Part 6 of NI 41-101 or other securities legislation.

3.5 Marketing Activities — Issuers and investment dealers should also refer to the guidance on marketing activities in Part 6 of the Companion Policy to NI 41-101. While the Instrument has provisions on marketing after a receipt for a final base PREP prospectus, NI 41-101 has general provisions that apply to marketing during the waiting period.

Adoption by OSC: 23 O.S.C.B. (Supp) 1013 (December 22, 2000) and 23 O.S.C.B. (Supp) 599 (October 13, 2000); Request for Comments: (1998) 21 O.S.C.B. 6233.

Adoption of Amendments: 28 O.S.C.B. 10460 and 8569; Request for Comments: 28 O.S.C.B. 228.

Adoption of Amendments: 31 O.S.C.B. (Supp. 2) 224 (March 7, 2008) and 30 O.S.C.B. (Supp. 7) 1 (Dec. 21, 2007); Request for Comments: 29 O.S.C.B. (Supp. 3) 1 (Dec. 22, 2006).

Adoption of Amendments: (2013) 36 O.S.C.B. 8039 and (Supp. 4) 1; Request for Comments: (2011) 34 O.S.C.B. 11829.

Rules: NI 44-101, 44-103.

Policies and Orders: NPS 41-101CP, 44-101CP.

CSA Staff Notice 44-304 — Linked Notes Distributed under Shelf Prospectus System

Date: **July 20, 2007**

30 O.S.C.B. 6425

Introduction

CSA staff (we) have noticed an increase in the use of the shelf prospectus system for the distribution of linked notes. For purposes of this notice, a linked note is a specified derivative (as defined in National Instrument 44-102 *Shelf Distributions* (NI 44-102)) for which the amount payable is determined by reference to the price, value or level of an underlying interest that is unrelated to the operations or securities of the linked note issuer.

These linked notes are generally securities issued as part of a medium term note program established by a bank or another financial institution. The underlying interest is frequently one or more stock indices, equities, commodities, investment funds or notional reference portfolios. Linked notes are frequently targeted at the retail market.

This Notice provides guidance to issuers that intend to qualify linked notes for distribution by way of a shelf prospectus. It includes:

- a description of the concerns we have identified in prospectus disclosure for linked notes offered under the shelf prospectus system;

- a description of some things we think an issuer of linked notes should consider in deciding how to comply with the requirement for a prospectus to provide full, true and plain disclosure of all material facts relating to the securities being offered (the full, true and plain disclosure requirement);

- notice to issuers of linked notes that, before exercising our discretion to receipt a base shelf prospectus that qualifies linked notes, we will ask the issuer to file an undertaking to pre-clear prospectus supplements or templates of prospectus supplements pertaining to linked notes that the issuer has not previously distributed in a jurisdiction in Canada; and

- a description of the pre-clearance process we will follow.

Disclosure concerns

The substantive details of linked note offerings are not typically contained in the base shelf prospectus — a document that is subject to regulatory review in advance of distribution. Often those details are set out in a lengthy prospectus supplement. Unless the issuer considers the prospectus supplement to be for a "novel" derivative that is subject to regulatory pre-clearance under NI 44-102, it is generally filed with the regulators after the distribution has already taken place. As a result, any review of the prospectus supplement is on a post-distribution basis.

Since summer 2006, we have asked issuers filing base shelf prospectuses to file interim undertakings to pre-clear certain prospectus supplements pertaining to linked notes before exercising our discretion to receipt the base shelf prospectus. As a result, we have reviewed and pre-cleared most of the prospectus supplements qualifying linked note distributions since that time. In many of these cases, our review resulted in the inclusion of additional disclosure that we think was necessary for the shelf prospectus, the prospectus supplement and documents incorporated by reference to comply with the full, true and plain disclosure requirement. The general disclosure matters discussed below highlight the focus of our pre-clearance reviews.

Disclosure in prospectus supplements about linked notes

Under the securities legislation of each jurisdiction, an issuer's prospectus must provide full, true and plain disclosure of all material facts relating to the securities offered by the prospectus. When an issuer is using the shelf prospectus system under NI 44-102, the full, true and plain disclosure requirement can be met by the combination of disclosure in the base shelf prospectus, the prospectus supplement and other documents the instrument permits the issuer to incorporate by reference.

This Notice describes some areas we think an issuer should consider in meeting the full, true and plain disclosure requirement for linked note offerings. CSA staff are currently applying the disclosure standards discussed below in reviewing prospectus supplements that are submitted for pre-clearance.

General disclosure matters

(a) — Clear description of linked note

When the prospectus supplement or the base prospectus is offering linked notes, issuers should consider what information investors and their advisers would need to assess the nature of that security. Issuers may find that describing the linked notes in plain language, without being overly technical or relying on the use of complex jargon, will help a person trying to understand the nature of the security.

(b) — Cover page disclosure

Given the unique characteristics of linked notes, issuers should consider whether investors and advisers would benefit from additional disclosure about the linked notes on the cover page of the prospectus supplement. Some examples of disclosure an issuer could consider are:

- explaining the linked note is a derivative product;

- informing readers that the linked note does not represent a direct investment in the underlying interest;

- describing whether an investor has any direct rights with respect to the underlying interest; and

- a summary of the key features of the investment including the underlying interest, the payout formula and the extent to which the investor's principal investment is at risk.

(c) — Limits on investment returns

If a feature of a particular linked note is a limit on the return the issuer will pay to investors, we will generally conclude that the prospectus does not meet the full, true and plain disclosure requirement unless the shelf prospectus or prospectus supplement clearly explains that investors' returns will be capped at a certain amount and that they will not be able to participate in any returns on the underlying interest that exceed that maximum.

(d) — Principal protection

In most linked note offerings some or all of the principal amount invested is at risk. In those cases where the issuer or another entity guarantees that an investor will receive some or all of the principal amount invested, we will generally conclude that the shelf prospectus and the prospectus supplement does not meet the full, true and plain disclosure requirement unless the issuer discloses that the principal protection depends on the creditworthiness of the issuer or guarantor. If principal protection only applies where the linked notes are held to maturity, this fact should also be disclosed in the prospectus supplement. The issuer should also disclose whether or not the linked notes qualify as a product covered by the Canada Deposit Insurance Corporation or any other similar product insurer.

(e) — Past performance

Where the prospectus supplement contains past performance information for the underlying interest, the prospectus supplement should clearly state that past performance is not an indicator of future performance. Information provided should not include only the best periods for past performance while ignoring negative periods. This disclosure would be necessary to meet the full, true and plain disclosure requirement.

Issuers can refer to Item 4 of Part B of Form 81-106F1 *Contents of Annual and Interim Management Report of Fund Performance* for further guidance on presentation of past performance information.

(f) — Use of hypothetical calculation examples

Where an issuer uses hypothetical examples to illustrate how payouts for a linked note are calculated, the issuer should use reasonable and balanced assumptions and should disclose those assumptions. In particular, it may be misleading to emphasize potential gains while minimizing the risk of loss. It should also be clear that the hypothetical examples are not indicators of future results. This disclosure would generally be necessary to meet the full, true and plain disclosure requirement.

(g) — Use of total return figures

If total return figures are used in the presentation of past performance data or assumptions for hypothetical calculation examples, the issuer should also refer to the equivalent compound annual returns in an equally prominent way in the prospectus supplement to meet the full, true and plain disclosure requirement.

(h) — Benefit to issuer or affiliates of the issuer

For the purposes of the full, true and plain disclosure requirement, the issuer should clearly identify any benefits that will accrue to it or to any other parties that are involved in structuring or administering the linked note offering.

(i) — Full explanation and transparency of fees and expenses

The full, true and plain disclosure requirement requires a clear and full explanation of fees that an investor will be paying. An issuer should clearly disclose any direct or indirect fees, expenses, costs or other charges that may be imposed on investors in linked notes. This would include any charges embedded in the formula used to determine payment at maturity, or in the offering price of the linked notes. For example, disclosure should be made of any fees or costs associated with enhanced participation rates, principal protection and any hedging activities undertaken by the issuer or any other party involved in product structuring on behalf of the issuer.

Issuers should consider what format the disclosure could take that would make the information easy to understand. For example, including all applicable fees, charges and expenses an investor would pay in a single table might be a useful format for this disclosure. This would allow investors to more easily determine the total cost of investing in a linked note without having to refer to various sections of the prospectus supplement.

(j) — Conflicts of interest

We think that it is important for investors to understand where issuer and investor interests in a linked note might conflict. To meet the full, true and plain disclosure requirement, the prospectus supplement should disclose any actual or potential conflicts of interest that might arise from the different roles an issuer and its affiliates could have in connection with a linked note offering. Risk factor disclosure should also address these conflicts. Without this disclosure, investors may find it difficult to make an informed investment decision.

Investors may also find it helpful to understand how issuers will address situations where the issuer finds that its interests conflict with those of an investor. One way an issuer could do this is to disclose any policies or processes it has in place to deal with conflicts of interest or perceived conflicts identified by the issuer.

Some examples of conflicts we have seen, and how some issuers have resolved them, are:

1. Where an issuer or an affiliate of the issuer is also the calculation agent for the linked notes, the issuer provided disclosure to enable an investor to understand any risk that the calculation agent might not make decisions in the investor's favour.

2. A calculation, valuation or determination that the calculation agent must make for a linked note may require the calculation agent to apply material discretion or may not be based on information or calculation methodologies utilized by or derived from independent third party sources. In these situations, we have seen prospectus disclosure indicating that the calculation agent/issuer has a policy that would appoint an independent calculation expert to confirm its calculation, valuation or determination.

3. A conflict or perceived conflict may arise because an investor cannot easily verify payouts for certain linked notes. This might arise where the calculation formula the agent uses to determine payout amounts is complex, such as where the calculation depends not only on the final value of the underlying interest but also on the performance pattern of the underlying interest during the term of the note. Such complexities are compounded when the issuer or agent of the issuer has discretion to change the composition of the underlying interest. In situations like these, we have seen some issuers develop and disclose that they have an independent and objective review of the calculation process to deal with the potential conflict.

4. Some linked notes are linked to a portfolio or basket of underlying interests that may change from time to time in the discretion of the issuer or an investment manager retained by the issuer. This structure may generate additional conflicts. For these products, some issuers have appointed an independent committee made up of three independent members to oversee how the issuer handles the conflicts of interest. The issuers' prospectus disclosure has addressed how this type of body could assist the issuer to revolve the conflicts of interest it identified.

(k) — Continuous disclosure

Because linked notes often constitute unsecured debt obligations of the issuer, an investor purchasing these notes would usually want to understand the credit quality of the issuer. As part of their investment decision, investors would also want to understand how they will be able to monitor changes in the underlying interest from which the linked note derives its value. When considering the full, true and plain disclosure requirement, issuers should think about informing investors on how they can obtain on-going information about the issuer, the underlying interest and the performance of the linked notes.

(l) — Risk disclosure

An issuer will generally find it difficult to meet the full, true and plain disclosure requirement without adequately disclosing the risks relating to the issuer and the particular linked note it is offering. The issuer should highlight any features of linked notes that differ from conventional debt securities, as well as the additional risks that may result from those differences. Risks for the investor will also usually be different than if the investor held the underlying interest directly. As a result, where an investor in a linked note does not have the same rights as it would if it held the underlying interest directly, we will generally consider that disclosing this information is necessary to meet the full, true and plain disclosure requirement.

(m) — Suitability statement

Given the complexity of linked notes, it is important that issuers consider including a brief description of the suitability of a linked note for particular investors. This description may include the characteristics of investors for whom the linked note may or may not be a suitable investment.

(n) — Secondary market and early redemption

If the linked note is redeemable, the full, true and plain disclosure requirement requires a description of how the redemption price is determined. In addition, where the issuer or a related entity intends to maintain a secondary market for its linked notes, the full, true and plain disclosure requirement would be satisfied by describing how bid-ask pricing is determined, as well as the limitations or conditions affecting the issuer's commitment to maintain a secondary market. Where principal protection is a feature of the linked note, it should be made clear, if it is the case, that investors will not benefit from this feature if they liquidate their investment prior to maturity.

(o) — Underlying interest

In order to satisfy the full, true and plain disclosure requirement issuers must provide sufficient information regarding the underlying interest in order to allow investors to make an informed investment decision. As a result, issuers should consider whether the disclosure in the base prospectus or prospectus supplement would provide investors with sufficient information about the underlying interest so that an investor can fully understand the nature of its exposure under the linked note.

We have seen many linked note offerings use a market index or a basket of market indices as the underlying interest. Where this is the case, issuers may want to consider whether the indices on which they are basing the offering are "publicly available". We would generally consider a market index to be publicly available if there is market transparency of the index methodology, the constituents that make up the index, and the calculation of the index through information that is published and circulated to the public on a regular basis.

In some cases we believe that it would be difficult for an investor to readily access information about an underlying interest. In order to meet the full, true and plain disclosure requirement, issuers of linked notes tied to these underlying interests should pay special attention to whether adequate information about the underlying interest will be made available to investors. Areas where we think this could be particularly difficult are:

- proprietary indices established by the issuer or an affiliate of the issuer;

- hedge funds and hedge fund replication strategies; and

- any reference asset or interest for which there is no information in the public domain.

Specific disclosure for equity linked notes

Some linked notes (often called equity linked notes) provide a return based on the performance of an underlying security of a single underlying issuer or a static basket of underlying securities of one or more underlying issuer(s), where the issuer of the note and the underlying issuers (i.e. the issuers the note is linked to) are not the same. For the purposes of this Notice, equity linked notes do not include notes where the underlying issuer is an investment fund or the basket of underlying securities is a managed portfolio.

Investors in equity linked notes generally need specific information about the underlying issuer(s) to make informed investment decisions. This part of the Notice provides an issuer of equity linked notes with guidance on the disclosure it should consider including in its prospectus supplement to satisfy the full, true and plain disclosure requirement.

(a) — Underlying issuer

An issuer of equity linked notes can meet the full, true and plain disclosure requirement in a number of different ways:

1. The issuer could include, or incorporate by reference, prospectus-level disclosure about an underlying issuer directly in its prospectus supplement. directly in its prospectus supplement.

2. The issuer could include "abbreviated disclosure" about an underlying issuer in its prospectus supplement if there is sufficient market interest and publicly available information about the underlying issuer. An issuer that chooses to include only abbreviated disclosure should consider whether that abbreviated disclosure satisfies the full, true and plain disclosure requirement. We will generally consider that the full, true and plain disclosure requirement is not met unless the disclosure includes, at a minimum:

- a brief description of the name and business of each underlying issuer;

- disclosure about the availability of information about each underlying issuer (on, for example, SEDAR); and

- information concerning the market price of each underlying security (as, for example, quoted on the exchange on which the underlying security is listed).

We will generally consider that there is sufficient market interest and publicly available information about an underlying issuer if the underlying issuer:

- is a reporting issuer in at least one jurisdiction of Canada and has been a reporting issuer in a jurisdiction of Canada for at least 12 months;

- is *not* on a list that identifies those reporting issuers that have been noted in default in a relevant jurisdiction in Canada, as described in CSA Notice 51-322 *Reporting Issuer Defaults*;

- has filed a current AIF in at least one jurisdiction in which it is a reporting issuer;

- has listed the underlying security on a short form eligible exchange (as defined in National Instrument 44-101 *Short Form Prospectus Distributions*);

- is not an issuer whose operations have ceased or whose principal asset is cash, cash equivalents or its exchange listing;

- is an electronic filer under National Instrument 13-101 *System for Electronic Document Analysis and Retrieval (SEDAR)*; and

- has a market capitalization of at least Cdn$75 million.

3. The issuer could include other alternative disclosure provided the full, true and plain disclosure requirement is met.

(b) — Direct or indirect financing benefit

To meet the full, true and plain disclosure requirement, the prospectus supplement should disclose whether each underlying issuer will receive a direct or indirect financing benefit from the distribution of the equity linked notes.

Whether an underlying issuer receives a direct or indirect financing benefit will depend on the facts and circumstances of a particular distribution. We may consider that an underlying issuer receives a financing benefit if the issuer of the equity linked notes has purchased securities of the same type as the underlying security directly from the underlying issuer within a proximate period of time to the distribution of the equity linked notes.

If an underlying issuer will receive a direct or indirect financing benefit, both the issuer of the equity linked note and the underlying issuer should refer to National Policy 41-201 *Income Trusts and Other Indirect Offerings* for further guidance.

(c) — Physical delivery of underlying security

Certain equity linked notes may provide for the physical delivery of underlying securities at maturity. In this case, the prospectus supplement should disclose whether the underlying securities to be delivered will be subject to any resale restrictions under National Instrument 45-102 *Resale of Securities*. We understand that in most circumstances the underlying securities to be delivered will be freely tradeable.

Undertaking to pre-clear prospectus supplements

Due to our public interest concerns, before the securities regulators issue a final receipt for a base shelf prospectus that qualifies linked notes, issuers will be asked to file an undertaking to pre-clear prospectus supplements or templates for prospectus supplements pertaining to linked notes that the issuer has not previously distributed in a jurisdiction in Canada. These undertakings are in addition to the undertakings that are required under Part 4 of NI 44-102 for novel specified derivatives and asset backed securities.

The undertaking is not intended to capture "plain vanilla" debt securities where payment of the principal is guaranteed and the return is not linked to a derivative instrument. It is also not intended to capture derivatives of an issuer that are linked to the issuer's own securities, such as "plain vanilla" options and warrants.

A proposal to amend NI 44-102, which mirrors the broadened pre-clearance approach set out in this Notice, was published for comment on December 21, 2006. The comment period closed on March 31, 2007.

Issuer speed to market concerns

We recognize that issuers are concerned that the pre-clearance process could potentially affect their ability to take immediate advantage of perceived market opportunities. We have attempted to address this concern in the following three ways:

(a) — Pre-clearance of templates of prospectus supplements

An issuer may submit for review a template of a prospectus supplement that it will use for future linked note offerings. To assist CSA staff in a review, the template should usually include most of the disclosure that the issuer would include in the prospectus supplement; however, the issuer may omit certain disclosure relating to information that the issuer would only know when the particular linked note distribution is identified. CSA staff would treat a pre-cleared template as supporting all subsequent offerings of linked notes by the issuer that are identical or substantially similar to the linked note described in the template.

(b) — No pre-clearance of new tranches or series of previously issued linked notes

We will generally not ask an issuer to pre-clear a prospectus supplement that pertains to a new tranche or series of previously issued linked notes for which the issuer pre-cleared a prospectus supplement.

We will also generally not ask an issuer to pre-clear a prospectus supplement that pertains to a linked note that is not materially different from a previously issued linked note for which the issuer pre-cleared a prospectus supplement. We would not usually consider a change in the underlying interest to be a material difference unless it was a different type of underlying interest. For example, if the underlying interest is a publicly available market index, we do not think it is a material difference to use a different publicly available market index. Changing the underlying interest to a mutual fund or a notional reference portfolio, however, would likely result in the need for pre-clearance. We would also not consider a change to features such as the term to maturity or the level of principal protection to be material. We would usually consider introducing a new fee or a change to the payout mechanism to be a material difference.

(c) — Shortened review time

The time period to provide initial comments on a prospectus supplement or a template of a prospectus supplement submitted for pre-clearance will be shortened from the 21 days set out in Part 4 of NI 44-102 to 10 working days. This shorter timeframe is consistent with the review period outlined in subsection 5.3(2) of National Policy 43-201 *Mutual Reliance Review System for Prospectuses* for complex offerings distributed under a short-form prospectus.

Pre-clearance process

The following is a summary of the process CSA staff will follow to pre-clear a prospectus supplement or template of a prospectus supplement:

- an issuer will file the prospectus supplement or template of a prospectus supplement and any other relevant material through SEDAR;

- the filing should be under the same SEDAR project number as the final base shelf prospectus;

- the filing subtype should be "prospectus supplement" and the document type should be "draft shelf prospectus supplement";

- the filing should remain private;

- the filing should include a cover letter requesting pre-clearance of the prospectus supplement or template of a prospectus supplement;

- an issuer should identify, where possible, in the cover letter any previously issued linked notes of the issuer or other issuers that are similar to the linked notes being pre-cleared;

- the principal regulator will coordinate the receipt of comments from all jurisdictions where pre-clearance is sought;

- an initial comment letter will be issued through SEDAR within 10 working days of receiving the request for pre-clearance;

- the issuer should file its response to the initial comment letter through SEDAR;

- once all comments have been resolved, a letter confirming acceptance of the prospectus supplement will be issued through SEDAR; and

- a copy of the final version of the prospectus supplement or template of a prospectus supplement, which incorporates all changes required to address comments raised during the review, will be attached to the acceptance letter.

Once the issuer gets the acceptance letter, it may offer identical or substantially similar products based on that prospectus supplement or template of a prospectus supplement without the need for further pre-clearance. When filing the prospectus supplement for subsequent offerings based on the pre-cleared prospectus supplement or template of a prospectus supplement the issuer should:

- include a cover letter referring to the acceptance letter for the pre-cleared prospectus supplement or template of a prospectus supplement and setting out the basis for determining that pre-clearance of the current prospectus supplement is not required; and

- file a blacklined document showing a comparison of the current prospectus supplement against the pre-cleared prospectus supplement or template of a prospectus supplement.

Where an issuer is uncertain whether a prospectus supplement for a new offering would need to be pre-cleared, we would encourage the issuer to either treat the product as novel or to seek input from CSA staff prior to proceeding with the offering.

Future Action

We will continue to monitor linked note offerings as both the nature of linked notes and the regulatory landscape evolve. We may provide additional guidance by updating this Notice or propose additional amendments to NI 44-102 or other instruments.

CSA Staff Notice 44-305 — 2015 Update — Structured Notes Distributed under the Shelf Prospectus System

Date: **January 22, 2015**

38 O.S.C.B. 555

Purpose

This notice sets out the views of CSA staff (we) regarding issues in connection with offerings of structured notes under the shelf prospectus system. This notice supplements and should be read together with CSA Staff Notice 44-304 *Linked Notes Distributed Under Shelf Prospectus System* (SN 44-304). We have used the term "structured notes" instead of "linked notes" in this notice as that seems to be the term most used by the industry.

A structured note, or linked note, is a specified derivative, as defined in NI 44-102 *Shelf Distributions* (NI 44-102), for which the amount payable is determined by reference to the price, value or level of an underlying interest that is unrelated to the operations or securities of the structured note issuer. Structured notes issued under the shelf prospectus system are generally non-principal protected securities issued by a bank or another financial institution. The underlying interests frequently include one or more stock indices, exchange-traded funds (ETFs), equities or notional reference portfolios.

Background

We discussed structured notes previously in SN 44-304. Since that time, the industry has continued to grow and the shelf prospectus system has evolved as an alternative distribution channel for retail investment products. Also, the Task Force on Unregulated Financial Markets and Products (TFUMP), a multilateral group of staff experts from various members of the International Organization of Securities Commissions (IOSCO), released its final report in December 2013. The TFUMP analyzed trends and developments in the retail structured product market and related regulatory issues encountered by IOSCO members.

We regulate structured notes primarily through our reviews of prospectus supplements filed for pre-clearance pursuant to undertakings that issuers provide under Part 4 of NI 44-102. As the industry continues to evolve, so does our regulatory approach. One of the challenges is to ensure consistency, where appropriate, in how we regulate structured notes and other types of products sold to retail investors, such as investment funds. CSA staff look to investment fund regulatory requirements and developments, where practicable, as a guide in conducting our reviews. Our regulatory approach also considers the guidance provided in the TFUMP report.

This notice updates and supplements SN 44-304 regarding:

- disclosure issuers should consider when preparing prospectus supplements for their structured notes;

- disclosure issuers should consider providing regarding their structured notes on an on-going basis; and

- the filing process to pre-clear novel supplements and for subsequent offerings of pre-cleared products.

1. — Disclosure — Prospectus Supplements

The substantive details of structured note offerings are not generally contained in the base shelf prospectus, but rather in the prospectus supplement filed subsequently. Under the securities legislation of each jurisdiction, an issuer's prospectus must provide full, true and plain disclosure of all material facts relating to the securities offered by the prospectus.

1.1 — Fees, expenses, product pricing and estimates of fair value

SN 44-304 discusses CSA staff's view that the full, true and plain disclosure requirement requires a clear and full explanation of fees that an investor will be paying. With respect to investment funds, the CSA has focused on initiatives aimed at improving the transparency of mutual fund fees and embedded commissions as a way to enable retail investors to better understand the costs of investing and to make more informed investment decisions.

Structured note issuers should similarly ensure that their disclosure provides sufficient transparency regarding fees including any financial benefits the issuer may embed into the structuring and pricing of the notes. The disclosure should enable an investor to readily assess the costs of investing in the note and the potential financial benefit the issuer and dealer will receive from the sale of the note. The disclosure required will vary depending upon the fee structure and whether the issuer has embedded a profit component into the offering price of the note.

Some structured note issuers charge fees on a basis similar to investment fund managers. These fees may include on-going management or administrative fees, sales commissions and on-going service fees or embedded trailing commissions paid to advisors. For structured notes that charge fees on a similar basis as investment funds, we would expect that the prospectus supplement include a table similar to those typically provided in investment fund prospectuses that clearly summarize all relevant fees in one easy to read section.[1] Issuers should also consider disclosing the dollar value of fees per note an investor can expect to pay on an annual basis and the total dollar value of fees if they hold the note to maturity.

In addition to the above-noted fees, the offering price of a structured note often embeds an estimated profit for the issuer as the offering price will be greater than the issuer's estimated costs to structure, distribute and hedge the note. This applies, in particular, in connection with structured notes that make use of embedded derivatives to provide different returns. It is our understanding that the issuer's estimate of the note's fair value and its potential profit is based on its valuation of the economic components embedded in the note at the time of issuance. Unlike other jurisdictions, such as the U.S. for instance, we have not consistently requested that issuers disclose their estimate of the note's fair value and potential profit.

In our view, this disclosure would provide improved transparency regarding the pricing and structuring of notes that make use of embedded derivatives and help ensure that investors better understand that the offering price of the note embeds an estimated profit margin. Consequently, CSA staff will, going forward, generally ask issuers to include the following in their structured note supplements:

- cover page disclosure of the issuer's estimate of the note's fair value based on its valuation of the economic components that could be combined to provide the same exposure as the structured note;

  - a brief explanation that the fair value of the note is based on the issuer's estimate of the value of the note's economic components and a brief description of what those components are;

  - explanation regarding why the issuer's estimate of the note's fair value may be different from the offering price including whether the offering price includes an estimated profit for the issuer and what fees, costs or other amounts that the issuer adds to its estimate of the note's fair value; and

  - explanation that the issuer's estimate of the note's fair value may differ from the price at which an investor can sell the note in the secondary market and why.

We suggest that, other than the cover page disclosure, the foregoing disclosure regarding the issuer's estimate of the note's fair value appear under its own separate heading and, as appropriate, be included in the risk factor disclosure.

Further, CSA staff will generally ask issuers to include a statement in their base shelf prospectus or in structured note supplements that they have adopted written policies and procedures for determining the fair value of the note which include: (i) the methodologies used for valuing each type of component embedded in the note, (ii) the methods by which the issuer will review and test valuations to assess the quality of the prices obtained as well as the general functioning of the valuation process, and (iii) conflicts of interest. CSA staff may also request, on a confidential basis as part of a pre-clearance review, that issuers provide a description of the valuation models and assumptions used to estimate the fair value of a particular note.

1.2 — What type of investor is the note designed for

In SN 44-304, we asked issuers to provide a brief description of the suitability of a structured note, including the characteristics of investors for whom the note may or may not be a suitable investment. This disclosure should provide investors with a quick overview of the note's key features, economic exposure, return profile, risks and what the issuer views to be the unique value-add of the product.

More recently, we have also been requesting that, in certain instances, issuers disclose relevant factors against which an investor can compare an investment in the note versus holding its underlying interest(s) directly, particularly when the underlying interest(s) is already easily available. Examples of factors that issuers should consider discussing include differences in the return profiles between the note and holding the underlying interest(s), terms to maturity, tax implications, any incremental costs associated with different fee structures between the note and the underlying interest(s), the primary means through which liquidity is provided including any differences in the investor's ability to re-sell the product over a secondary market or investor redemption rights and the relative treatment of any distributions paid out.

1.3 — Underlying Interests — Transparency, Quantitative Models, Investment Funds and Fixed Income Securities

Transparency

A structured note's underlying interest or reference asset must be sufficiently publicly transparent to enable the issuer to satisfy the full, true and plain disclosure requirement. Prospectus supplements must provide sufficient information regarding a note's underlying interest or reference asset in order to allow investors to make an informed decision. This is relatively straightforward when the underlying interest or reference asset is a public entity that is subject to some form of continuous disclosure regime.

---

[1]See, for instance, Item 3.6 of Form 41-101F2 *Information Required in an Investment Funds Prospectus* and Item 8 Part A of Form 81-101F1 *Contents of Simplified Prospectus.*

Underlying interests for which providing full, true and plain disclosure may be particularly difficult include:

- some proprietary indices established by the issuer or an affiliate of the issuer;

- hedge funds and hedge fund replication strategies; and

- reference assets or interests for which there is no information in the public domain such as, for instance, a private discretionary managed account or portfolio of investments.

We will generally not recommend that an acceptance letter be provided in connection with prospectus supplements for notes linked to the foregoing underlying interests.

Quantitative Models

We have pre-cleared notes linked to the performance of quantitative models where the composition of the portfolio is dictated exclusively by the non-discretionary financial criteria of the model, but for the very limited discretion to substitute components of the underlying portfolio in exceptional circumstances. In such instances, we have asked issuers to provide disclosure regarding:

- the quantitative model including its methodology and financial criteria;

- the initial portfolio holdings under the model and the initial portfolio value;

- how transactions in the portfolio will be valued even when the portfolio only exists on a notional basis; and

- how investors may access on-going information regarding the portfolio free of charge.

Investment Funds

Notes linked to publicly offered investment funds that are actively managed and are not index participation units, as defined under National Instrument 81-102 *Investment Funds*, generally raise significant policy concerns. CSA staff generally consider all such notes to be novel for the purposes of the undertakings provided under NI 44-102. Consequently, an issuer should file all such notes for pre-clearance. Issuers should also be aware that the review period may be longer than normal given the policy issues such notes raise.

Our concerns include:

- whether the note is converging into an investment fund;

- whether the note constitutes an indirect offering of the underlying investment fund;

- the relative benefits of the note, particularly since the underlying investment fund is generally already available to retail investors; and

- potential investor confusion regarding the two different products and in making a decision to invest in the structured note or the investment fund directly.

We suggest that the disclosure provided in prospectus supplements for notes linked to actively managed investment funds that are not index participation units include:

- clear bolded textbox disclosure on the cover page indicating that investors are buying notes, not the underlying investment funds, which carry different risks, have a different fee structure, and are subject to a different regulatory regime than the underlying investment funds. Investors will not receive any ongoing disclosure regarding the underlying investment funds that would be received by investors of the underlying investment funds; and

- a clear explanation of the differences between an investment in the note and a direct investment in the underlying fund. See section 1.2 above for examples of the factors that should be explained to investors.

CSA staff continue to consider whether to recommend that an acceptance letter be provided in these instances. Accordingly, issuers should file for pre-clearance every prospectus supplement for notes linked to investment funds that are not index participation units. We will continue to actively monitor these types of notes.

Fixed income securities

We have pre-cleared notes linked to the performance of fixed income securities, such as government bonds and investment grade corporate bonds, where there is sufficient market interest and publicly available information about the underlying issuer. In these instances, CSA staff will usually request that issuers ensure that adequate information about the underlying security is available to investors throughout the term of the notes including providing investors with access to the market value of the underlying bonds on a daily basis free of charge[2] . One way to accomplish this objective is for the issuer to post daily the bid and offering price for each underlying bond on its website.

If the composition of the portfolio of underlying bonds may change during the term of the note, we also request that issuers ensure that prices used for the purpose of notional sales and purchases are obtained through a process involving independent third parties. One way to accomplish this objective is by requiring the issuer's calculation agent to obtain different quotations from at least three reputable investment dealers independent from the issuer and use, for notional sales, the highest bid price available and, for notional purchases, the lowest ask price available.

---

[2]If the market prices for the underlying bonds are available only on paying platforms (e.g. Bloomberg), that information is not considered as available to investors free of charge.

In the case of notes linked to investment grade corporate bonds, CSA staff will also consider the liquidity of the market for the underlying bonds. We expect the market for underlying corporate bonds to have a highly liquid secondary market. Underlying bonds that are not used as a component of any benchmark index that provides a broad measure of the bond market will generally not meet staff expectations.

1.4 — Subscriptions In-kind or Exchange Offers

In some instances, we have observed issuers providing investors with the option of paying their subscription price for a note in-kind by exchanging any existing holdings they may have in the note's underlying interest. For example, an investor could pay the subscription price for a note linked to an ETF by tendering any units it already holds in the ETF. In such instances, the disclosure described in section 1.2 should explain the factors an investor should consider in making a decision to continue to hold the underlying interest directly or to invest in the note. In the context of equity linked notes, such exchanges may also raise the financing benefit concerns discussed in section 1.10 below.

1.5 — Hypothetical or back-tested performance data

We have reviewed some prospectus supplements, for quantitative models in particular, that sought to include hypothetical or back-tested performance data regarding how the model or strategy would have performed had it been in existence over a specified historical performance period. We are concerned that the disclosure of such information in the prospectus supplement has the potential to be overly promotional and misleading. Consequently, we have requested its removal in our pre-clearance reviews.

We continue to review this issue and monitor regulatory developments in other IOSCO jurisdictions. We may also, in some instances, request that issuers provide, for our information only, hypothetical or back-tested performance data along with the mathematical formulas used.

1.6 — Index linked notes — pricing versus total return index

In order to satisfy the full, true and plain disclosure requirement, CSA staff generally expect that issuers of notes linked to underlying indices will clearly disclose in the prospectus supplement whether the note is linked to the pricing index or total return index. We ask that this information be prominently disclosed on the cover page of the supplement in bold print. Further, the supplement should explain the expected difference in performance between the price index and the total return index so that an investor will have a better understanding regarding the potential distributions they will be foregoing.

1.7 — Disclaimers of liability for third party information

CSA staff have seen disclaimers in prospectus supplements that relate to the accuracy of third party information disclosed in the prospectus that is publicly available. The disclaimers indicate that the issuer is not responsible for, or that the investors have no recourse against the issuer in connection with, information provided by third parties, including information relating to the underlying interests and the underlying interests' issuer. The disclaimers are also sometimes accompanied by cautionary language that investors should not place undue reliance on such information.

We believe that such disclaimers and cautionary language do not reflect the liability for prospectus misrepresentations under securities law. Securities legislation makes an issuer liable for any misrepresentation in a prospectus, even if the misrepresentation in the prospectus is based upon information included from a reliable third party source. The only defence to a misrepresentation claim available to an issuer is that the investor making the claim was aware of the misrepresentation at the time of purchase. As issuers are unable to completely disclaim liability for third party information in a prospectus supplement, we will generally request that such disclaimers and cautionary language regarding undue reliance be removed.

Issuers, however, may include disclosure in prospectus supplements with respect to third party information that clearly identifies the information as third party information and states that the issuer has not verified and makes no representation regarding the accuracy or completeness of such information.

1.8 — Clarity that structured notes are not fixed income securities

In order to help ensure that investors understand that structured notes are not fixed income securities, CSA staff ask issuers to include textbox disclosure on the cover page of their prospectus supplements which highlights, as appropriate, that:

- structured notes are not fixed income securities and are not designed to be alternatives to fixed income or money market instruments; and

- the notes are structured products that possess downside risk.

We also may request further disclosure, particularly in connection with notes that offer the potential for fixed return payments contingent on the performance of the note's underlying interest, such as auto-callables and reverse convertibles.

1.9 — Use of hypothetical calculation examples

Issuers often provide hypothetical return calculation examples in prospectus supplements to illustrate how payouts for a structured note are calculated under various scenarios. As discussed in SN 44-304, calculation examples should use reasonable and balanced assumptions. We will generally request that issuers provide examples assuming at least three scenarios (negative, neutral and positive) and that issuers disclose the most negative scenario first.

1.10 — Disclosure specific to equity linked notes — direct or indirect financing benefit

SN 44-304 discusses our views regarding direct or indirect financing benefits in connection with equity linked notes. Equity linked notes provide a return based on the performance of an underlying security of a single underlying issuer or a static basket of underlying securities of one or more underlying issuer(s).

SN 44-304 provides that to meet the full, true and plain disclosure requirement, the prospectus should disclose whether each underlying issuer will receive a direct or indirect financing benefit from the distribution of the equity linked notes. Whether an underlying issuer receives a direct or indirect financing benefit will depend on the facts and circumstances of a particular distribution. We may consider that an issuer receives a financing benefit if, in addition to any limited purchases made pursuant to its hedging activities in connection with the note, the issuer of the equity linked note has purchased securities of the same type as the underlying security directly from the underlying issuer within a proximate period of time to the distribution of the equity linked notes.

We understand that employees responsible for the issuance of equity linked notes may not be privy to any information regarding the primary market purchases of a security of an underlying issuer made by other employees of the notes issuer. We understand that as a result of "ethical walls" between different groups of employees within the organizational structure of the notes issuer, consideration of whether the notes issuer has purchased securities of the underlying issuer within a proximate period of time to the distribution of the equity linked notes may be impractical. Our concerns regarding a direct or indirect financing benefit to the underlying issuer may be addressed through disclosure if the notes issuer relies on the existence of "ethical walls" within their organizational structure.

2. — On-going Disclosure

The continuous disclosure requirements under securities legislation that apply to structured note issuers do not contemplate the distribution of retail investment products by those issuers. Consequently, potential gaps exist between the information structured note issuers are required to file and the additional information that may be relevant on an on-going basis to structured note investors.

Structured note issuers are subject to the on-going reporting requirements designed for operating businesses under National Instrument 51-102 *Continuous Disclosure Obligations*. These requirements focus on disclosure regarding the overall financial condition and operating results of the issuer. This can provide useful information regarding the issuer's overall credit quality and its ability to meet its obligations under the note, but somewhat limited information regarding the note itself.

Investment funds are subject to National Instrument 81-106 *Investment Fund Continuous Disclosure* which requires them to file on-going disclosure tailored specifically to the investment products being sold. Amongst other requirements, investment funds must publish daily net asset values and quarterly portfolio holdings, as well as file regular financial statements and management reports of fund performance for the funds.

SN 44-304 suggests that issuers inform investors how they can obtain additional on-going information regarding structured notes. More recently, issuers have been disclosing in their prospectus supplements a website on which they will publish additional on-going information about the note being offered. The information that is relevant to investors and the frequency with which it should be provided will vary depending on the type of note being offered.

Information that CSA staff expect issuers to consider disclosing on their websites going forward for each structured note during the term of the note and for a reasonable period afterwards, as appropriate, includes:

- composition of the underlying portfolio to which the note is linked;

- initial price or level of the underlying interest;

- the current and historical daily bid prices for the note where the issuer or a related entity of the issuer intends to maintain a secondary market;

- the daily indicative value of the note applying the payment formula under the note to the current value of the underlying interest;

- the daily current value of the underlying interest, obtained from a reliable and independent source;

- the amount of any early trading charge;

- any relevant trigger, barrier level or cap which can impact the return on the note;

- details about any call feature including call price and observation date;

- quarterly portfolio holdings;

- changes to the underlying portfolio or exposure and the prices/levels at which the changes or notional trades were made;

- distributions/coupons/return of capital payments including how they have been calculated;

- product fees that have accrued or been paid, broken down by each component;

- annual compounded rates of return for notes that have reached maturity;

- the existence of any special circumstances, market disruption or extraordinary events;

- where an investor can find more information regarding the underlying interest; and

- links to all of the disclosure documents related to the structured note offering.

The foregoing list is not exhaustive. CSA staff may request that issuers provide additional or different information as part of the pre-clearance process or on-going review of prospectus supplements.

3. — Process

3.1 — Pre-clearance — filing supplement templates on SEDAR

SN 44-304 describes the pre-clearance process for novel structured notes. Under this process, issuers file pricing supplement templates for review under the same SEDAR project number as the base shelf prospectus. Given the high volume of filings this can create under a single project number, we encourage issuers to notify staff in the principal regulator's jurisdiction via email to alert them that a supplement has been filed for pre-clearance. CSA staff will use its best efforts to review the materials filed for pre-clearance and provide a first comment letter within 10 business days.

In order to facilitate our tracking of multiple pre-clearance requests, we request that issuers not bundle multiple supplements together into the same submission. In instances where an issuer wishes to pre-clear multiple supplements at the same time, please file each supplement as a separate pre-clearance request and submission under the relevant SEDAR project number.

3.2 — Pre-clearance — cover letters

In addition to the guidance provided in SN 44-304, CSA staff also request that issuers provide the following information in the cover letter requesting pre-clearance:

- a brief description of what the issuer considers to be novel about the product for the purposes of the undertakings provided under NI 44-102;

- a brief description of the process followed by the issuer to design the product, including the assessment performed to identify investors' needs; and

- additional measures, if any, beyond the issuer's normal policies and procedures that will be taken to ensure that the product is promoted appropriately, including how the dealer's sales representatives will be educated regarding the novel features of this product.

3.3 — Subsequent offerings of pre-cleared products

In order to better facilitate the administration and tracking of prospectus supplements filed in connection with subsequent offerings that are based on a pre-cleared prospectus supplement or template of a prospectus supplement, we request that the issuer:

- include a cover letter that refers to the acceptance letter the issuer is relying upon including the SEDAR project number and submission number and that explains why, in its view, pre-clearance of the current prospectus supplement is not required;

- file a copy of the acceptance letter the issuer is relying upon;

- file a black-lined document showing a comparison of the current prospectus supplement against the pre-cleared prospectus supplement or template; and

- please not bundle multiple offerings together into the same submission on SEDAR, but rather file each supplement as a separate submission under the relevant SEDAR project number.

We also remind issuers to pay the requisite filing fees in connection with each subsequent offering[3].

3.4 — Undertaking for notes linked to equity securities that are not listed on a Canadian stock exchange

CSA staff have been requesting that issuers file an undertaking (the Unlisted Issuer Undertaking) in connection with notes qualified under a base prospectus that may be linked to equity securities and that are not listed on a Canadian stock exchange. This undertaking is requested in addition to the undertaking required to be filed under Part 4 of NI 44-102 in connection with distributions of novel specified derivatives. Pursuant to the Unlisted Issuer Undertaking, issuers commit to not proceed with a distribution of notes linked to equity securities that are not listed on a Canadian stock exchange without first filing a draft prospectus supplement for pre-clearance. The undertakings generally contain carve-outs, subject to certain conditions, for SEC well-known seasoned issuers, other U.S. issuers listed on a national securities exchange registered with the SEC and U.S. 40 Act Companies that issue index participation units.

Next Steps

CSA staff will continue to review structured notes filed for pre-clearance and monitor the development of the structured note industry generally. We will continue to consider what gaps may exist under our regulatory approach to structured notes and whether more formal regulatory requirements may become necessary to ensure we are regulating like products in a consistent way to achieve investor protection and fair and efficient capital markets. In the interim, we will continue to provide updates regarding our views, concerns or initiatives in connection with structured notes as necessary.

Questions

Please refer your questions to any of the following people:

Ontario

Darren McKall — Manager
Investment Funds and Structured Products

---

[3]In Ontario, each supplement must be accompanied by a $500 activity fee under OSC Rule 13-502 — *Fees*.

Ontario Securities Commission

(416) 593-8118

dmckall@osc.gov.on.ca

Doug Welsh — Senior Legal Counsel

Investment Funds and Structured Products

Ontario Securities Commission

(416) 593-8068

dwelsh@osc.gov.on.ca

Quebec

Marc-Olivier St-Jacques

Securities Analyst, Corporate Finance

(514) 395-0337, ext: 4424

marco.st-jacques@lautorite.qc.ca

Sophie Fournier, CFA

Analyst, Investment Funds

(514) 395-0337, ext: 4426

sophie.fournier@lautorite.qc.ca

OSC Rule 44-801 — Implementing National Instrument 44-101 — Short Form Prospectus Distributions

Date: **April 13, 2001**

24 O.S.C.B. 2334

[Repealed 31 O.S.C.B. (Supp. 2) 263 (March 7, 2008)]

Final Rule: 24 O.S.C.B. 2334 (April 13, 2001); Approval by OSC: 24 O.S.C.B. 937 (February 9, 2001); Request for Comments: 22 O.S.C.B. (POP Supp 2) 129 (December 17, 1999), 22 O.S.C.B. (POP Supp) 3 (July 23, 1999) and 21 O.S.C.B. 1138 (February 20, 1998).

4.5 — Prospectus Exempt Distributions

National Instrument 45-101 — Rights Offerings

Date: **July 20, 2001, as amended effective September 30, 2003, September 14, 2005, December 31, 2007, March 17, 2008 and June 30, 2011**

Date: **Repealed effective December 8, 2015**

24 O.S.C.B. 4397, 26 O.S.C.B. 5552, 28 O.S.C.B. (Supp-4) 119, 30 O.S.C.B. 10521, 31 O.S.C.B. (Supp. 2) 225, 34 O.S.C.B. 7086 and 38 O.S.C.B. 8321.

[Editor's note: This verson reflects changes that are scheduled to come into force on Decmber 8, 2015. For the complete text of 45-101, please see the 58th edition of this work.]

Adoption by OSC: 24 O.S.C.B. 4397 (July 20, 2001) and 24 O.S.C.B. 2667 (April 27, 2001); Request for Comments: (2000) 23 O.S.C.B. 5547 and (1997) 20 O.S.C.B. 6097.

Amendment to Policy: (2003) 26 O.S.C.B. 5517; Request for Comments: (2003) 26 O.S.C.B. 587.

Repeal by OSC: 38 O.S.C.B. 8321.

National Instrument 45-102 — Resale of Securities

Date: **November 23, 2001, as amended September 30, 2003; replaced effective March 30, 2004, as amended effective September 14, 2005, September 28, 2009, May 6, 2011, May 5, 2015 and January 25, 2016**

24 O.S.C.B. 7029, 26 O.S.C.B. 5554, 27 O.S.C.B. 3580, 28 O.S.C.B. (Supp-4) 121, 32 O.S.C.B. (Supp. 5) 115, 34 O.S.C.B. 5171, 38 O.S.C.B. 4166, 38 O.S.C.B. 8320 and 38 O.S.C.B. (Supp. 4) 74.

[Editor's note: This version of the Instrument reflects changes scheduled to come into force in Ontario on January 13, 2016, and in Alberta, New Brunswick, Nova Scotia, Québec and Saskatchewan on April 30, 2016. It also reflects amendments scheduled to come into force on January 25, 2016.]

Table of Contents

PART 1 — DEFINITIONS

1.1 Definitions — In this Instrument

"control distribution" means a trade described in the provisions of securities legislation listed in Appendix A;

"convertible security" means a security of an issuer that is convertible into, or carries the right of the holder to purchase or otherwise acquire, or of the issuer to cause the purchase or acquisition of, a security of the same issuer;

"distribution date" means

(a) in respect of a trade that is not a control distribution, the date the security that is the subject of the trade was distributed in reliance on an exemption from the prospectus requirement by the issuer or, in the case of a control distribution, by the selling security holder,

(b) in respect of a trade that is a control distribution, the date the security that is the subject of the trade was acquired by the selling security holder,

(c) in respect of a trade of an underlying security that is not a control distribution, the date the convertible security, exchangeable security or multiple convertible security that, directly or indirectly, entitled or required the holder to acquire the underlying security was distributed in reliance on an exemption from the prospectus requirement by the issuer or, in the case of a control distribution, by the selling security holder, or

(d) in respect of a trade of an underlying security that is a control distribution, the date the convertible security, exchangeable security or multiple convertible security that, directly or indirectly, entitled or required the holder to acquire the underlying security was acquired by the selling security holder;

"exchangeable security" means a security of an issuer that is exchangeable for, or carries the right of the holder to purchase or otherwise acquire, or of the issuer to cause the purchase or acquisition of, a security of another issuer;

"MI 45-102" means this Instrument prior to its amendment on September 14, 2005;

"MI 45-103" means Multilateral Instrument 45-103 *Capital Raising Exemptions* prior to its repeal on September 14, 2005;

"MI 45-105" means Multilateral Instrument 45-105 *Trades to Employees, Senior Officers, Directors, and Consultants* prior to its repeal on September 14, 2005;

"multiple convertible security" means a security of an issuer that is convertible into, or exchangeable for, or carries the right of the holder to purchase or otherwise acquire, or of the issuer to cause the purchase or acquisition of, a convertible security, an exchangeable security or another multiple convertible security;

"NI 45-106" means National Instrument 45-106 *Prospectus Exemptions*;

"private company" has the same meaning as in securities legislation;

"private issuer" means, as the context requires,

(a) a private issuer as defined in securities legislation,

(b) a private issuer as defined in NI 45-106, or

(c) in Ontario, for purposes of the definition of a private issuer as it existed in 1998 OSC Rule 45-501 (as defined in the Ontario transitional provisions in Appendix D) prior to its repeal on November 30, 2001, a person that

(i) is not a reporting issuer or a mutual fund,

(ii) is an issuer all of whose issued and outstanding shares

(A) are subject to restrictions on transfer contained in the constating documents of the issuer or one or more agreements among the issuer and the holders of its securities; and

(B) are beneficially owned, directly or indirectly, by not more than 50 persons or companies, counting any two or more joint registered holders as one beneficial owner, exclusive of persons

(I) that are employed by the issuer or an affiliated entity of the issuer, or

(II) that beneficially owned, directly or indirectly, shares of the issuer while employed by it or an affiliated entity of it and at all times since ceasing to be so employed have continued to beneficially own, directly or indirectly, at least one share of the issuer, and

(iii) has not distributed any securities to the public;

"SEDAR" has the same meaning as in National Instrument 13-101 *System for Electronic Document Analysis and Retrieval (SEDAR)*; and

"trade" in Québec, has the same meaning as in NI 45-106;

"underlying security" means a security issued or transferred, or to be issued or transferred, in accordance with the terms of a convertible security, an exchangeable security or a multiple convertible security.

PART 2 — FIRST TRADES

2.1 Application — In Manitoba, sections 2.2 to 2.7 and 2.10 to 2.14 do not apply.

2.2 Removal of Resale Provisions — In Newfoundland and Labrador, and Ontario, the provisions in securities legislation listed in Appendix C, respectively, do not apply.

2.3 Section 2.5 Applies — If a security was distributed under any of the provisions listed in Appendix D, the first trade of that security is subject to section 2.5.

2.4 Section 2.6 Applies — If a security was distributed under any of the provisions listed in Appendix E, the first trade of that security is subject to section 2.6.

2.5 Restricted Period — (1) Unless the conditions in subsection (2) are satisfied, a trade that is specified by section 2.3 or other securities legislation to be subject to this section is a distribution.

(2) Subject to subsection (3), for the purposes of subsection (1) the conditions are:

1. The issuer is and has been a reporting issuer in a jurisdiction of Canada for the four months immediately preceding the trade.

2. At least four months have elapsed from the distribution date.

3. If the distribution date is on or after March 30, 2004, or, in Québec, on or after September 14, 2005, and either of the following apply:

(i) if the issuer was a reporting issuer on the distribution date, the certificate representing the security, if any, carries a legend stating:

Unless permitted under securities legislation, the holder of this security must not trade the security before *[insert the date that is 4 months and a day after the distribution date]*";

or

(ii) if the issuer was not a reporting issuer on the distribution date, the certificate representing the security, if any, carries a legend stating:

Unless permitted under securities legislation, the holder of this security must not trade the security before the date that is 4 months and a day after the later of (i) *[insert the distribution date]*, and (ii) the date the issuer became a reporting issuer in any province or territory.

3.1 If the security is entered into a direct registration or other electronic book-entry system, or if the purchaser did not directly receive a certificate representing the security, the purchaser received written notice containing the legend restriction notation set out in subparagraphs (i) or (ii) of item 3.

4. The trade is not a control distribution.

5. No unusual effort is made to prepare the market or to create a demand for the security that is the subject of the trade.

6. No extraordinary commission or consideration is paid to a person or company in respect of the trade.

7. If the selling security holder is an insider or officer of the issuer, the selling security holder has no reasonable grounds to believe that the issuer is in default of securities legislation.

(3) Items 3 and 3.1 of subsection (2) do not apply to a trade of an underlying security if the underlying security is issued at least four months after the later of

(a) the distribution date, and

(b) the date the issuer became a reporting issuer in any jurisdiction of Canada.

2.6 Seasoning Period — (1) Unless the conditions in subsection (3) are satisfied, a trade that is specified by section 2.4 or other securities legislation to be subject to this section is a distribution.

(2) The first trade of securities issued by a private company or private issuer made after the issuer has ceased to be a private company or private issuer is a distribution unless the conditions in subsection (3) are satisfied.

(3) For the purposes of subsections (1) and (2), the conditions are:

1. The issuer is and has been a reporting issuer in a jurisdiction of Canada for the four months immediately preceding the trade.

2. The trade is not a control distribution.

3. No unusual effort is made to prepare the market or to create a demand for the security that is the subject of the trade.

4. No extraordinary commission or consideration is paid to a person or company in respect of the trade.

5. If the selling security holder is an insider or officer of the issuer, the selling security holder has no reasonable grounds to believe that the issuer is in default of securities legislation.

2.7 Exemption for a Trade if the Issuer Becomes a Reporting Issuer After the Distribution Date — Item 1 of subsection 2.5(2), 2.6(3) or 2.8(2) does not apply if the issuer became a reporting issuer after the distribution date by filing a prospectus in a jurisdiction listed in Appendix B and is a reporting issuer in a jurisdiction of Canada at the time of the trade.

2.8 Exemption for a Trade by a Control Person — (1) The prospectus requirement does not apply to a control distribution, or a distribution by a lender, pledgee, mortgagee or other encumbrancer for the purpose of liquidating a debt made in good faith by selling or offering for sale a security pledged, mortgaged or otherwise encumbered in good faith as collateral for the debt if the security was acquired by the lender, pledgee, mortgagee or other encumbrancer in a control distribution, if the conditions in subsection (2) are satisfied.

(2) For the purposes of subsection (1), the conditions are:

1. The issuer is and has been a reporting issuer in a jurisdiction of Canada for the four months immediately preceding the trade.

2. The selling security holder, or the lender, pledgee, mortgagee or other encumbrancer if the distribution is for the purpose of liquidating a debt, has held the securities for at least four months.

3. No unusual effort is made to prepare the market or to create a demand for the security that is the subject of the trade.

4. No extraordinary commission or consideration is paid to a person or company in respect of the trade.

5. The selling security holder has no reasonable grounds to believe that the issuer is in default of securities legislation.

(3) The selling security holder, or the lender, pledgee, mortgagee or other encumbrancer if the distribution is for the purpose of liquidating a debt, under subsection (2) must

(a) complete and sign a Form 45-102F1 no earlier than one business day before the Form 45-102F1 is filed;

(b) file the completed and signed Form 45-102F1 on SEDAR at least seven days before the first trade of the securities that is part of the distribution; and

(c) file, within three days after the completion of any trade, an insider report prepared in accordance with either Form 55-102F2 or Form 55-102F6 under National Instrument 55-102 *System for Electronic Disclosure by Insiders (SEDI)*.

(4) A Form 45-102F1 filed under subsection (3) expires on the earlier of

(a) thirty days after the date the Form 45-102F1 was filed, and

(b) the date the selling security holder, or the lender, pledgee, mortgagee or other encumbrancer, files the last of the insider reports reflecting the sale of all securities referred to in the Form 45-102F1.

(5) A selling security holder, or the lender, pledgee, mortgagee or other encumbrancer must not file a new Form 45-102F1 in respect of a class of securities of a reporting issuer until the Form 45-102F1 in respect of that class of securities previously filed by that person or company has expired.

2.9 Determining Time Periods — (1) In determining the period of time that an issuer was a reporting issuer in a jurisdiction of Canada for the purposes of section 2.5, 2.6 or 2.8, if the issuer was a party to an amalgamation, merger, reorganization or arrangement, the selling security holder may include the period of time that one of the parties to the amalgamation, merger, reorganization or arrangement was a reporting issuer in a jurisdiction of Canada immediately before the amalgamation, merger, reorganization or arrangement.

(2) In determining the period of time that a selling security holder has held a security for the purposes of section 2.5 or 2.8, if the selling security holder acquired the security from an affiliate of the selling security holder, the selling security holder may include the period of time that the affiliate held the security.

(3) In determining the period of time that a selling security holder has held an underlying security for the purposes of section 2.8, the selling security holder may include the period of time the selling security holder held the convertible security, exchangeable security or multiple convertible security.

(4) In determining the period of time that a lender, pledgee, mortgagee or other encumbrancer has held a security under item 2 of subsection 2.8(2), the selling security holder may include the period of time the debtor held the security.

(5) In determining the period of time that a lender, pledgee, mortgagee or other encumbrancer has held an underlying security under item 2 of subsection 2.8(2), the selling security holder may include the period of time the debtor held the convertible security, exchangeable security or multiple convertible security.

2.10 Exemption for a Trade in an Underlying Security if the Convertible Security, Exchangeable Security or Multiple Convertible Security is Qualified by a Prospectus — Section 2.6 does not apply to a trade in an underlying security issued or transferred under the terms of a convertible security, exchangeable security or multiple convertible security if

(a) a receipt was obtained for a prospectus qualifying the distribution of the convertible security, exchangeable security or multiple convertible security;

(b) the trade is not a control distribution; and

(c) the issuer of the underlying security is a reporting issuer at the time of the trade.

2.11 Exemption for a Trade in a Security Acquired in a Take-over Bid or Issuer Bid — Section 2.6 does not apply to a trade of a security of an offeror if

(a) a securities exchange take-over bid circular or securities exchange issuer bid circular relating to the distribution of the security was filed by the offeror on SEDAR;

(b) the trade is not a control distribution; and

(c) the offeror was a reporting issuer on the date the securities of the offeree issuer were first taken up under the take-over bid or issuer bid.

2.12 Exemption for a Trade in an Underlying Security if the Convertible Security, Exchangeable Security or Multiple Convertible Security is Qualified by a Securities Exchange Take-over Bid Circular or Issuer Bid Circular — Section 2.6 does not apply to a trade in an underlying security issued or transferred under the terms of a convertible security, exchangeable security or multiple convertible security if

> (a) a securities exchange take-over bid circular or a securities exchange issuer bid circular relating to the distribution of the convertible security, exchangeable security or multiple convertible security was filed by the offeror on SEDAR;

> (b) the trade is not a control distribution;

> (c) the offeror was a reporting issuer on the date the securities of the offeree issuer were first taken up under the take-over bid or issuer bid; and

> (d) the issuer of the underlying security is a reporting issuer at the time of the trade.

2.13 Trades by Underwriters — A trade by an underwriter of securities distributed under any of the provisions listed in Appendix F is a distribution.

2.14 First Trades in Securities of a Non-Reporting Issuer Distributed under a Prospectus Exemption — (1) The prospectus requirement does not apply to the first trade of a security distributed under an exemption from the prospectus requirement if

> (a) the issuer of the security

>> (i) was not a reporting issuer in any jurisdiction of Canada at the distribution date, or

>> (ii) is not a reporting issuer in any jurisdiction of Canada at the date of the trade;

> (b) at the distribution date, after giving effect to the issue of the security and any other securities of the same class or series that were issued at the same time as or as part of the same distribution as the security, residents of Canada

>> (i) did not own directly or indirectly more than 10 percent of the outstanding securities of the class or series, and

>> (ii) did not represent in number more than 10 percent of the total number of owners directly or indirectly of securities of the class or series; and

> (c) the trade is made

>> (i) through an exchange, or a market, outside of Canada, or

>> (iii) to a person or company outside of Canada.

(2) The prospectus requirement does not apply to the first trade of an underlying security if

> (a) the convertible security, exchangeable security or multiple convertible security that, directly or indirectly, entitled or required the holder to acquire the underlying security was distributed under an exemption from the prospectus requirement;

> (b) the issuer of the underlying security

>> (i) was not a reporting issuer in any jurisdiction of Canada at the distribution date of the convertible security, exchangeable security or multiple convertible security, or

>> (ii) is not a reporting issuer in any jurisdiction of Canada at the date of the trade;

> (c) the conditions in paragraph (1)(b) would have been satisfied for the underlying security at the time of the initial distribution of the convertible security, exchangeable security or multiple convertible security; and

> (d) the condition in paragraph (1)(c) is satisfied.

PART 3 — EXEMPTION

3.1 Exemption — (1) The regulator or the securities regulatory authority may grant an exemption from this Instrument, in whole or in part, subject to such conditions or restrictions as may be imposed in the exemption.

(2) Despite subsection (1), in Ontario, only the regulator may grant such an exemption.

PART 4 — EFFECTIVE DATE

4.1 Effective Date — This Instrument comes into force on March 30, 2004.

APPENDIX A — TO NATIONAL INSTRUMENT 45-102 RESALE OF SECURITIES — CONTROL DISTRIBUTIONS

JURISDICTION	SECURITIES LEGISLATION REFERENCE
Alberta	Definition of "control person" in section 1(l) and subclause (iii) of the definition of "distribution" contained in section 1(p) of the *Securities Act* (Alberta)
British Columbia	Paragraph (c) of the definition of "distribution" contained in section 1(1) of the *Securities Act* (British Columbia)
Manitoba	Paragraph (b) of the definition of "primary distribution to the public" contained in subsection 1(1) of the *Securities Act* (Manitoba)
Newfoundland and Labrador	Clause 2(1)(l)(iii) of the *Securities Act* (Newfoundland and Labrador)
New Brunswick	Definition of "control person" and clause (c) of the definition of "distribution" contained in subsection 1(1) of the *Securities Act* (New Brunswick)

JURISDICTION	SECURITIES LEGISLATION REFERENCE
Northwest Territories	Definition of "control person" in subsection 1(1) and paragraph (c) of the definition of "distribution" contained in subsection 1(1) of the *Securities Act* (Northwest Territories)
Nova Scotia	Clause 2(1)(l)(iii) of the *Securities Act* (Nova Scotia)
Nunavut	Definition of "control person" in subsection 1(1) and paragraph (c) of the definition of "distribution" contained in subsection 1(1) of the *Securities Act* (Nunavut)
Ontario	Paragraph (c) of the definition of "distribution" contained in subsection 1(1) of the *Securities Act* (Ontario)
Prince Edward Island	Clause 1(e) and subclause 1(k)(iii) of the *Securities Act* (Prince Edward Island)
Québec	Paragraph 9 of the definition of "distribution" contained in section 5 of the *Securities Act* (Québec)
Saskatchewan	Subclauses 2(1)(r)(iii), (iv) and (v) of *The Securities Act*, 1988 (Saskatchewan)
Yukon	Definition of "control person" in subsection 1(1) and paragraph (c) of the definition of "distribution" contained in subsection 1(1) of the *Securities Act* (Yukon)

APPENDIX B — TO NATIONAL INSTRUMENT 45-102 RESALE OF SECURITIES — REPORTING ISSUER JURISDICTIONS

Alberta

British Columbia

Manitoba

New Brunswick

Nova Scotia

Ontario

Québec

Saskatchewan

APPENDIX C — TO NATIONAL INSTRUMENT 45-102 RESALE OF SECURITIES — NON-APPLICABLE RESALE PROVISIONS

(Section 2.2)

JURISDICTION	SECURITIES LEGISLATION REFERENCE
Newfoundland and Labrador	Clause 54(5)(a), subsections 54(7), 54(9), 54(10), 73(4), 73(5), 73(6) as it relates to clause 72(1)(r), 73(7) but not as it relates to subsection 54(6) and 54(7), 73(12), 73(18), 73(19) and 73(24) of the Securities Act (Newfoundland and Labrador)
Ontario	Subsections 72(4), 72(5), 72(6) as it relates to clause 72(1)(r), and 72(7) of the *Securities Act* (Ontario), in each case prior to section 11 of Schedule 26 of the *Budget Measures Act, 2009* being proclaimed in force.

APPENDIX D — TO NATIONAL INSTRUMENT 45-102 RESALE OF SECURITIES — RESTRICTED PERIOD TRADES

(Section 2.3)

1. Except in Manitoba, the following exemptions from the prospectus requirement in NI 45-106:

- section 2.3 [*Accredited investor (except in Ontario)*];

- section 2.5 [*Family, friends and business associates*];

- section 2.8 [*Affiliates*];

- section 2.9 [*Offering memorandum*];

- section 2.10 [*Minimum amount investment*];

- section 2.12 [*Asset acquisition*];

- section 2.13 [*Petroleum, natural gas and mining properties*];

- section 2.14 [*Securities for debt*];

- section 2.19 [*Additional investment in investment funds*];

- section 2.30 [*Isolated distribution by issuer*];

- section 2.31 [*Dividends and distributions*], if the security was acquired in the circumstances referred to in subsection 2.31(2) and that security was initially acquired by the issuer under

  (a) one of the exemptions listed in this Appendix,

  (b) an exemption from the prospectus requirement that specifies that the first trade is subject to section 2.5 of this Instrument, or

  (c) an exemption from the prospectus requirement that specified prior to September 14, 2005 that the first trade was subject to section 2.5 of MI 45-102;

- section 2.40 [*RRSP/RRIF/TFSA*], if the security acquired under section 2.40 was initially acquired by an individual or an associate of the individual or a RRSP, RRIF, or TFSA established for or by that individual or under which that individual is a beneficiary under

  (a) one of the exemptions listed in this Appendix,

  (b) an exemption from the prospectus requirement that specifies that the first trade is subject to section 2.5 of this Instrument, or

  (c) an exemption from the prospectus requirement that specified prior to September 14, 2005 that the first trade was subject to section 2.5 of MI 45-102;

- section 2.42 [*Conversion, exchange or exercise*], if the security acquired in the circumstances referred to in paragraph 2.42(1)(a) was acquired in accordance with the terms and conditions of a previously issued security and that previously issued security was distributed under

  (a) one of the exemptions listed in this Appendix,

  (b) an exemption from the prospectus requirement that specifies that the first trade is subject to section 2.5 of this Instrument, or

  (c) an exemption from the prospectus requirement that specified prior to September 14, 2005 that the first trade was subject to section 2.5 of MI 45-102;

- section 5.2 [*TSX Venture exchange offering*], if the security acquired under section 5.2 was acquired by

  (a) a purchaser that, at the time the security was acquired, was an insider or promoter of the issuer of the security, the issuer's underwriter, or a member of the underwriter's "professional group" (as defined in National Instrument 33-105 *Underwriting Conflicts*), or

  (b) any other purchaser in excess of $40,000 for the portion of the securities in excess of 40,000;

  as well as the following local exemptions from the prospectus requirement:

- section 3.1 of Alberta Securities Commission Rule 72-501 *Distributions to Purchasers Outside Alberta*;

- clauses 77(1)(u) and (w) and subclauses 77(1)(ab)(ii) and (iii) of the *Securities Act* (Nova Scotia); section 73.3 of the *Securities Act* (Ontario) [*Accredited Investor*];

- an exemption from the prospectus requirement in a jurisdiction of Canada that specifies that the first trade is subject to section 2.5 of NI 45-102.

2. In Ontario, Québec, New Brunswick and Nova Scotia, the exemption from the prospectus requirement in section 5 [*Crowdfunding prospectus exemption*] of Multilateral Instrument 45-108 *Crowdfunding*.

Transitional and Other Provisions

1. General — An exemption from the prospectus requirement listed in Appendix D of MI 45-102 in effect on March 30, 2004 or an exemption from the prospectus requirement that specified prior to September 14, 2005 that the first trade was subject to section 2.5 of MI 45-102. The exemptions listed in Appendix D on March 30, 2004 were:

- Sections 131(1)(b), (c), (l), and (m) of the *Securities Act* (Alberta);

- Section 122(d) and 122.2 of the Alberta Securities Commission Rules, section 3.1 of Alberta Securities Commission Rule 72-501 *Distributions to Purchasers Outside Alberta*, subsections 3.1(2), 4.1(2), 4.1(4), and 5.1(2) of MI 45-103 or an exemption from the prospectus requirement that specifies that the first trade is subject to section 2.5 of MI 45-102;

- Section 131(1)(f)(iii) of the *Securities Act* (Alberta), if the right to purchase, convert or exchange was previously acquired under one of the above-listed exemptions under the *Securities Act* (Alberta), the Alberta Securities Commission Rules or MI 45-103, or under an exemption from the prospectus requirement that specifies that the first trade is subject to section 2.5 of MI 45-102;

- Sections 74(2)(1) to (6), (16), (18), (19), (23) and (25) of the *Securities Act* (British Columbia);

- Sections 128(a), (b), (c), (e), (f) and (h) of the *Securities Rules* (British Columbia) and subsections 3.1(2), 4.1(2), 4.1(4), and 5.1(2) of MI 45-103 or an exemption from the prospectus requirement that specifies that the first trade is subject to section 2.5 of MI 45-102;

- Sections 74(2)(11)(ii), 74(2)(11)(iii) and 74(2)(13) of the *Securities Act* (British Columbia) if the security acquired by the selling security holder or the right to purchase, convert or exchange or otherwise acquire, was initially acquired by a person or company under any of the sections of the *Securities Act* (British Columbia), the *Securities Rules* (British Columbia) or MI 45-103 referred to in this Appendix, or under an exemption from the prospectus requirement that specifies that the first trade is subject to section 2.5 of MI 45-102;

- Section 74(2)(12) of the *Securities Act* (British Columbia) if the security acquired by the selling security holder under the realization on collateral was initially acquired by a person or company under any of the sections of the *Securities Act* (British Columbia), the *Securities Rules* (British Columbia) or MI 45-103 referred to in this Appendix, or under an exemption from the prospectus requirement that specifies that the first trade is subject to section 2.5 of MI 45-102;

- Clauses 54(3)(f) and (g) and 73(1)(a), (b), (c), (d), (h), (l), (m), (p) and (q) of the *Securities Act* (Newfoundland and Labrador), subsections 3.1(2), 4.1(2), 4.1(4), and 5.1(2) of MI 45-103, or an exemption from the prospectus requirement that specifies that the first trade is subject to section 2.5 of MI 45-102;

- Subclause 73(1)(f)(iii) of the *Securities Act* (Newfoundland and Labrador) if the right to purchase, convert or exchange was previously acquired under one of the above listed exemptions under the *Securities Act* (Newfoundland and Labrador) or MI 45-103, or under an exemption from the prospectus requirement that specifies that the first trade is subject to section 2.5 of MI 45-102;

- Paragraphs 3(a), (b), (c), (k), (l), (m), (r), (s), (t), (u), (w) and (z) of Blanket Order No. 1 of the Registrar of Securities (Northwest Territories), subsections 3.1(2), 4.1(2), 4.1(4), 5.1(2) of MI 45-103 or an exemption from the prospectus requirement that specifies that the first trade is subject to section 2.5 of MI 45-102;

- Subparagraph 3(e)(iii) of Blanket Order No. 1 of the Registrar of Securities (Northwest Territories) if the right to purchase, convert or exchange was previously acquired under one of the above-listed exemptions under Blanket Order No. 1 of the Registrar of Securities (Northwest Territories) or MI 45-103, or under an exemption from the prospectus requirement that specifies that the first trade is subject to section 2.5 of MI 45-102;

- Clauses 77(1)(a), (b), (c), (d), (l), (m), (p), (q), (u), (w), (y), (ab) and (ad) of the *Securities Act* (Nova Scotia), subsections 3.1(2), 4.1(2), 4.1(4), and 5.1(2) of MI 45-103 or an exemption from the prospectus requirement that specifies that the first trade is subject to section 2.5 of MI 45-102;

- Subclause 77(1)(f)(iii) of the *Securities Act* (Nova Scotia) if the right to purchase, convert or exchange was previously acquired under one of the above listed exemptions under the *Securities Act* (Nova Scotia) or MI 45-103, or under an exemption from the prospectus requirement that specifies that the first trade is subject to section 2.5 of MI 45-102;

- Paragraphs 3(a), (b), (c), (k), (l), (m), (r), (s), (t), (u), (w) and (z) of Blanket Order No.1 of the Registrar of Securities (Nunavut), subsections 3.1(2), 4.1(2), 4.1(4), and 5.1(2) of MI 45-103 or an exemption from the prospectus requirement that specifies that the first trade is subject to section 2.5 of MI 45-102;

- Subparagraph 3(e)(iii) of Blanket Order No.1 of the Registrar of Securities (Nunavut) if the right to purchase, convert or exchange was previously acquired under one of the above-listed exemptions under Blanket Order No. 1 of the Registrar of Securities (Nunavut) or MI 45-103, or under an exemption from the prospectus requirement that specifies that the first trade is subject to section 2.5 of MI 45-102;

- Clauses 13(1)(a), (b), (c), (g) and (i) of the *Securities Act* (Prince Edward Island), subsections 3.1(2), 4.1(2), 4.1(4), and 5.1(2) of MI 45-103 or under an exemption from the prospectus requirement that specifies that the first trade is subject to section 2.5 of MI 45-102;

- Subclause 13(1)(e)(iii) of the *Securities Act* (Prince Edward Island) if the right to purchase, convert or exchange was previously acquired under one the above-listed exemptions under the *Securities Act* (Prince Edward Island) or under an exemption from the prospectus requirement that specifies that the first trade is subject to section 2.5 of MI 45-102;

- Subclauses 81(1)(f)(iii) and (iv) of *The Securities Act, 1988* (Saskatchewan) if the convertible security, exchangeable security or multiple convertible security was acquired under one of the exemptions of *The Securities Act, 1988* (Saskatchewan) or MI 45-103 referred to in this Appendix or under an exemption from the prospectus requirement that specifies that the first trade is subject to section 2.5 of MI 45-102;

- Clause 81(1)(e) of *The Securities Act, 1988* (Saskatchewan) if the person or company from whom the securities were acquired obtained the securities under one of the exemptions of *The Securities Act, 1988* (Saskatchewan) referred to in this Appendix;

2. Québec Provisions

- Sections 43, 47, 48 and 51 of the *Securities Act* (Québec) as they read prior to their amendment or repeal by sections 7 and 8 of *An Act to amend the Securities Act and other legislative provisions*;

- Prospectus and registration exemptions granted pursuant to section 263 of the *Securities Act* (Québec) before March 30, 2004 if the exemption included as a condition a restricted period of 12 months.

3. Ontario Provisions

Definitions

In this Appendix

"1998 OSC Rule 45-501" means the Ontario Securities Commission Rule 45-501 *Exempt Distributions* that came into force on December 22, 1998;

"2001 OSC Rule 45-501" means the Ontario Securities Commission Rule 45-501 *Exempt Distributions* that came into force on November 30, 2001;

"2004 OSC Rule 45-501" means the Ontario Securities Commission Rule 45-501 *Exempt Distributions* that came into force on January 12, 2004;

"2005 OSC Rule 45-501" means the Ontario Securities Commission Rule 45-501 *Ontario Prospectus and Registration Exemptions* that came into force on September 14, 2005;

"2005 NI 45-106" means the National Instrument 45-106 *Prospectus and Registration Exemptions* that came into effect on September 14, 2005;

"2009 NI 45-106" means the National Instrument 45-106 *Prospectus and Registration Exemptions* that came into effect on September 28, 2009;

"2009 OSC Rule 45-501" means the Ontario Securities Commission Rule 45-501 *Ontario Prospectus and Registration Exemption* that came into force on the later of (a) September 28, 2009 and (b) the day on which sections 5 and 11, subsection 12(1) and section 13 of Schedule 26 of the *Budget Measures Act, 2009* were proclaimed into force;

"convertible security" means, in Ontario, a security of an issuer that is convertible into, or carries the right of the holder to purchase, or of the issuer to cause the purchase of, a security of the same issuer;

"exchangeable security" means, in Ontario, a security of an issuer that is exchangeable for, or carries the right of the holder to purchase, or the right of the issuer to cause the purchase of, a security of another issuer;

"exchange issuer" means, in Ontario, an issuer that distributes securities of a reporting issuer held by it in accordance with the terms of an exchangeable security of its own issue;

"**multiple convertible security**" means, in Ontario, a security of an issuer that is convertible into or exchangeable for, or carries the right of the holder to purchase, or of the issuer or exchange issuer to cause the purchase of, a convertible security, an exchangeable security or another multiple convertible security;

"**OSC Rule 45-502**" means Ontario Securities Commission Rule 45-502 *Dividend or Interest Reinvestment and Stock Dividend Plans*;

"**Type 1 trade**" means, in Ontario, a distribution in a security under an exemption from the prospectus requirement in any of the following:

(a) clause 72(1)(a), (b), (c), (d), (l), (m), (p) or (q) of the *Securities Act* (Ontario), in each case prior to section 11 of Schedule 26 of the *Budget Measures Act, 2009* being proclaimed in force;

(b) section 2.4, 2.5 or 2.11 of the 1998 OSC Rule 45-501;

(c) section 2.3, 2.12, 2.13 or 2.14 of the 2001 OSC Rule 45-501;

(d) section 2.3, 2.12, 2.13, 2.14 or 2.16 of the 2004 OSC Rule 45-501;

(e) section 2.1 and section 2.2 of the 2009 OSC Rule 45-501, and

"**underlying security**" means, in Ontario, a security issued or transferred, or to be issued or transferred, in accordance with the terms of a convertible security, an exchangeable security or a multiple convertible security.

(a) — Securities Act (Ontario)

Clauses 72(1)(a), (b), (c), (d), (l), (m), (p) and (q) of the *Securities Act* (Ontario) and subclause 72(1)(f)(iii) of the *Securities Act* (Ontario) if the right to purchase, convert or exchange was previously acquired under one of the above-listed exemptions under the *Securities Act* (Ontario), in each case prior to section 11 of Schedule 26 of the *Budget Measures Act, 2009* being proclaimed in force, or an exemption from the prospectus requirement that specifies that the first trade is subject to section 2.5 of MI 45-102

- Section 73.5 of the *Securities Act* (Ontario) [*Government incentive security*],

(a.1) — National Instrument 45-106

- Section 2.3 of National Instrument 45-106 *Prospectus and Registration Exemptions* prior to subsection 12(2) of Schedule 26 of the *Budget Measures Act, 2009* being proclaimed in force.

(a.2) — 2005 NI 45-106 and 2009 NI 45-106

Section 2.7 of the 2005 NI 45-106 and the 2009 NI 45-106.

(b) — 2005 OSC Rule 45-501 and 2009 OSC Rule 45-501

- Section 2.1 of the 2005 OSC Rule 45-501 and sections 2.1 and 2.2 of the 2009 OSC Rule 45-501.

(c) — 2001 OSC Rule 45-501 and 2004 OSC Rule 45-501

Section 2.3 of the 2001 OSC Rule 45-501 and the 2004 OSC Rule 45-501;

Section 2.11 of the 2001 OSC Rule 45-501 and the 2004 OSC Rule 45-501 if section 2.5 of MI 45-102 would have been applicable to a first trade in that security by the person making the exempt distribution under section 2.11 of the 2001 OSC Rule 45-501 or the 2004 OSC Rule 45-501;

Section 2.12 of the 2001 OSC Rule 45-501 and the 2004 OSC Rule 45-501;

Section 2.13 of the 2001 OSC Rule 45-501 and the 2004 OSC Rule 45-501;

Section 2.14 of the 2001 OSC Rule 45-501 and the 2004 OSC Rule 45-501;

Section 2.16 of the 2004 OSC Rule 45-501.

(d) — 1998 OSC Rule 45-501

Section 2.4 of the 1998 OSC Rule 45-501

Section 2.5 of the 1998 OSC Rule 45-501

Section 2.11 of the 1998 OSC Rule 45-501

(e) — Other

Any provision under which an underlying security was distributed on conversion or exchange of a multiple convertible security, convertible security or exchangeable security acquired in a Type 1 trade or in a trade under section 2.4, 2.5 or 2.11 of the 1998 OSC Rule 45-501.

4. New Brunswick Provisions

In this Appendix

"**2004 NB LR 45-501**" means the New Brunswick Securities Commission Local Rule 45-501 that came into force on September 29, 2004;

A. Subsections 2.3(3), 2.5(2), 2.6(7), 2.7(2), 2.8(2), 2.10(2), 2.11(2), 2.12(2) and 2.17(2) of 2004 NB LR 45-501

B. Subsection 2.41(2) of 2004 NB LR 45-501 (if the security acquired under section 2.4 was initially acquired by an individual or an associate of the individual or an RRSP or RRIF established for or by that individual or under which that individual is a beneficiary under

(a) one of the exemptions in NB LR 45-501 listed in paragraph A, or

(b) an exemption from the prospectus requirement that specifies that the first trade is subject to section 2.5 of Multilateral Instrument 45-102 *Resale of Securities*)

C. Subsection 2.43(3) (if the security acquired under paragraph 2.43(1)(a) was acquired in accordance with the terms and conditions of a previously issued security under

(a) one of the exemptions in 2005 NB LR 45-501 listed in paragraph A, or

(b) an exemption from the prospectus requirement that specifies that the first trade is subject to section 2.5 of Multilateral Instrument, 45-102 *Resale of Securities*)

D. Section 5.2 of 2004 NB LR 45-501

APPENDIX E — TO NATIONAL INSTRUMENT 45-102 RESALE OF SECURITIES — SEASONING PERIOD TRADES

(Section 2.4)

1. Except in Manitoba, the following exemptions from the prospectus requirement in NI 45-106:

- section 2.1 [*Rights offering — reporting issuer*];
- section 2.1.1 [*Rights offering — stand-by commitment*];
- section 2.1.2 [*Rights offering — issuer with a minimal connection to Canada*]
- section 2.2 [*Reinvestment plan*];
- section 2.4 [*Private issuer*], except in Ontario;
- section 2.11 [*Business combination and reorganization*];
- section 2.16 [*Take-over bid and issuer bid*];
- section 2.17 [*Offer to acquire to security holder outside local jurisdiction*];
- section 2.18 [*Investment fund reinvestment*];
- section 2.20 [*Private investment club*];
- section 2.21 [*Private investment fund — loan and trust pools*];
- section 2.24 [*Employee, executive officer, director and consultant*];
- section 2.26 [*Distributions among current or former employees, executive officers, directors or consultants of non-reporting issuer*];
- section 2.27 [*Permitted transferees*];
- section 2.31 [*Dividends and distributions*], if the security was acquired in the circumstances referred to in subsection 2.31(2), that security was initially acquired by the issuer under

  (a) one of the exemptions listed in this Appendix,

  (b) an exemption from the prospectus requirement that specifies that the first trade is subject to section 2.6 of this Instrument, or

  (c) an exemption from the prospectus requirement that specified prior to September 14, 2005 that the first trade was subject to section 2.6 of MI 45-102;

- section 2.40 [*RRSP/RRIF/TFSA*], if the security acquired under section 2.40 was initially acquired by an individual or an associate of the individual or a RRSP, RRIF, or TFSA established for or by that individual or under which that individual is a beneficiary under

  (a) one of the exemptions listed in this Appendix,

  (b) an exemption from the prospectus requirement that specifies that the first trade is subject to section 2.6 of this Instrument, or

  (c) an exemption from the prospectus requirement that specified prior to September 14, 2005 that the first trade was subject to section 2.6 of MI 45-102;

- section 2.42 [*Conversion, exchange or exercise — security of own issue*], if the security acquired in the circumstances referred to in paragraph 2.42(1)(a) was acquired in accordance with the terms and conditions of a previously issued security and that previously issued security was distributed under

  (a) one of the exemptions listed in this Appendix,

  (b) an exemption from the prospectus requirement that specifies that the first trade is subject to section 2.6 of this Instrument, or

  (c) an exemption from the prospectus requirement that specified prior to September 14, 2005 that the first trade was subject to section 2.6 of MI 45-102;

- section 2.42 [*Conversion, exchange or exercise — security of a reporting issuer*] for a security being traded in the circumstances referred to in clause (b) of subsection 2.42(1);

as well as the following local exemptions from the prospectus requirement:

- Alberta Securities Commission Rule 45-502 *Trade with RESP*, if not included in Appendix D;
- Nova Scotia Securities Commission Blanket Order No. 46;
- Section 73.4 of the *Securities Act* (Ontario) [*Private issuer*];
- Prince Edward Island Local Rule 45-510 — *Exempt Distributions — Exemptions for Trades Pursuant to Take-over Bids and Issuer Bids*;
- an exemption from the prospectus requirement in a jurisdiction of Canada that specifies that the first trade is subject to section 2.6 of NI 45-102.

Transitional and Other Provisions

1. — General

An exemption from the prospectus requirement listed in Appendix E of MI 45-102 in effect on March 30, 2004 or an exemption from the prospectus requirement that specified prior to September 14, 2005 that the first trade was subject to section 2.6 of MI 45-102. The exemptions listed in Appendix E of MI 45-102 on March 30, 2004 were:

- Section 131(1)(f) if not included in Appendix D of this Instrument, sections 131(h), (i), (j), (k), and (y) of the *Securities Act* (Alberta) and sections 107(1)(j.1) and (k.1) prior to their repeal by section 5 of the *Securities Amendment Act, 1989* (Alberta), subsection 2.1(2) of MI 45-103 and sections 2.1, 2.2, 2.3 and 2.4 of MI 45-105 or under an exemption from the prospectus requirement that specifies that the first trade is subject to section 2.6 of MI 45-102;

- Section 74(2)(11)(iii) if not included in Appendix D or F and sections 74(2)(7), (8) if not included in Appendix F, (9) to (11), (13), (22) and (24) of the *Securities Act* (British Columbia);

- Section 128(g) of the *Securities Rules* (British Columbia), section 2.1(2) of MI 45-103 and sections 2.1, 2.2, 2.3 and 2.4 of MI 45-105 or under an exemption from the prospectus requirement that specifies that the first trade is subject to section 2.6 of MI 45-102;

- Section 74(2)(12) of the *Securities Act* (British Columbia), if the security acquired by the selling security holder under the realization on collateral was initially acquired by a person or company under any of the sections of the *Securities Act* (British Columbia), the *Securities Rules* (British Columbia) or a multilateral instrument referred to in this Appendix or under an exemption from the prospectus requirement that specifies that the first trade is subject to section 2.6 of MI 45-102;

- Clauses 54(3) and 73(1)(f) if not included in Appendix D or F of this Instrument, (i) if not included in Appendix F, (j), (k) and (n) of the *Securities Act* (Newfoundland and Labrador), subsection 2.1(2) of MI 45-103 and sections 2.1, 2.2, 2.3 and 2.4 of MI 45-105 or under an exemption from the prospectus requirement that specifies that the first trade is subject to section 2.6 of MI 45-102;

- Paragraphs 3(e), (f), (g), (h), (i), (n), (x), (y) and (mm) of Blanket Order No. 1 of the Registrar of Securities (Northwest Territories), except for a trade made under subparagraph 3(e)(iii) of Blanket Order No. 1 of the Registrar of Securities (Northwest Territories) that is included in Appendix D or F of this Instrument or a trade made under paragraph 3(g) that is included in Appendix F of this Instrument, subsection 2.1(2) of MI 45-103 and sections 2.1, 2.2, 2.3 and 2.4 of MI 45-105 or under an exemption from the prospectus requirement that specifies that the first trade is subject to section 2.6 of MI 45-102;

- Clause 77(1)(f) of the *Securities Act* (Nova Scotia) if not included in Appendix D or F of this Instrument, and clauses 77(1)(h), (i) if not included in Appendix F, (j), (k), (n), (v), (va), (ac), (ae) and (af) of the *Securities Act* (Nova Scotia), and clause 78(1)(a) of the *Securities Act* (Nova Scotia) as it relates to clause 41(2)(j) of the *Securities Act* (Nova Scotia) and Blanket Order No. 37, 38 if not included in Appendix F, 46 and 45-503 if not included in Appendix F, subsection 2.1(2) of MI 45-103 and sections 2.1, 2.2, 2.3 and 2.4 of MI 45-105 or under an exemption from the prospectus requirement that specifies that the first trade is subject to section 2.6 of MI 45-102;

- Paragraphs 3(e), (f), (g), (h), (i), (n), (x), (y) and (mm) of Blanket Order No. 1 of the Registrar of Securities (Nunavut), except for a trade made under subparagraph 3(e)(iii) of Blanket Order No. 1 of the Registrar of Securities (Nunavut) that is included in Appendix D or F of this Instrument or a trade made under paragraph 3(g) that is included in Appendix F of this Instrument, subsection 2.1(2) of MI 45-103 and sections 2.1, 2.2, 2.3 and 2.4 of MI 45-105 or under an exemption from the prospectus requirement that specifies that the first trade is subject to section 2.6 of MI 45-102;

- Clauses 13(1)(e) if not included in Appendix D or F of this Instrument, (f) if not included in Appendix F, (h) and (k) of the *Securities Act* (Prince Edward Island) or section 3.1 or 3.2 of Rule 45-501, section 1.1 of Prince Edward Island Rule 45-502, section 2.1 or 2.2 of Prince Edward Island Rule 45-506 or section 2.1 or 2.2 of Prince Edward Island Rule 45-510, subsection 2.1(2) of MI 45-103 and sections 2.1, 2.2, 2.3 and 2.4 of MI 45-105 or under an exemption from the prospectus requirement that specifies that the first trade is subject to section 2.6 of MI 45-102;

- Clauses 81(1)(a.1), (e) if not included in Appendix D or F of this Instrument, (f) if not included in Appendix D or F of this Instrument, (f.1), (g), (h), (i) if not included in Appendix F, (i.1), (j), (k), (o), (cc) and (dd) of *The Securities Act, 1988* (Saskatchewan), subsection 2.1(2) of MI 45-103 and sections 2.1, 2.2, 2.3 and 2.4 of MI 45-105 or under an exemption from the prospectus requirement that specifies that the first trade is subject to section 2.6 of MI 45-102.

2. — Québec Provisions

- Sections 50 and 52 of the *Securities Act* (Québec) as they read prior to their repeal by section 8 of *An Act to amend the Securities Act and other legislative provisions*;

- Prospectus and registration exemptions granted pursuant to section 263 of the *Securities Act* (Québec) before March 30, 2004 if the exemption included as a condition a seasoning period of 12 months.

3. — Ontario provisions
Definitions

In this Appendix

"1998 OSC Rule 45-501" means the Ontario Securities Commission Rule 45-501 *Exempt Distributions* that came into force on December 22, 1998;

"2001 OSC Rule 45-501" means the Ontario Securities Commission Rule 45-501 *Exempt Distributions* that came into force on November 30, 2001;

"2004 OSC Rule 45-501" means the Ontario Securities Commission Rule 45-501 *Exempt Distributions* that came into force on January 12, 2004;

"convertible security" means, in Ontario, a security of an issuer that is convertible into, or carries the right of the holder to purchase, or of the issuer to cause the purchase of, a security of the same issuer;

"exchangeable security" means, in Ontario, a security of an issuer that is exchangeable for, or carries the right of the holder to purchase, or the right of the issuer to cause the purchase of, a security of another issuer;

"exchange issuer" means, in Ontario, an issuer that distributes securities of a reporting issuer held by it in accordance with the terms of an exchangeable security of its own issue;

"multiple convertible security" means, in Ontario, a security of an issuer that is convertible into or exchangeable for, or carries the right of the holder to purchase, or of the issuer or exchange issuer to cause the purchase of, a convertible security, an exchangeable security or another multiple convertible security;

"OSC Rule 45-502" means Ontario Securities Commission Rule 45-502 *Dividend or Interest Reinvestment and Stock Dividend Plans*;

"OSC Rule 45-503" means Ontario Securities Commission Rule 45-503 *Trades to Employees, Executives and Consultants*;

"Type 1 trade" means, in Ontario, a distribution in a security under an exemption from the prospectus requirement in:

(a) clause 72(1)(a), (b), (c), (d), (l), (m), (p) or (q) of the *Securities Act* (Ontario), in each case prior to section 11 of Schedule 26 of the *Budget Measures Act, 2009* being proclaimed in force;

(b) section 2.4, 2.5 or 2.11 of the 1998 OSC Rule 45-501;

(c) section 2.3, 2.12, 2.13 or 2.14 of the 2001 OSC Rule 45-501; or

(d) section 2.3, 2.12, 2.13, 2.14 or 2.16 of the 2004 OSC Rule 45-501; and

"Type 2 trade" means, in Ontario, a distribution in a security under an exemption from the prospectus requirement in:

(a) clause 72(1)(f) of the *Securities Act* (Ontario), prior to section 11 of Schedule 26 of the *Budget Measures Act, 2009* being proclaimed in force, other than a distribution to an associated consultant or investor consultant as defined in OSC Rule 45-503 or a distribution to an associated consultant or investor relations person as defined in MI 45-105;

(b) clause 72(1)(h), (i), (j), (k) or (n) of the *Securities Act* (Ontario), in each case prior to section 11 of Schedule 26 of the *Budget Measures Act, 2009* being proclaimed in force; or

(c) section 2.5, 2.8 or 2.15 of the 2001 OSC Rule 45-501; or

(d) section 2.5, 2.8 or 2.15 of the 2004 OSC Rule 45-501; and

"underlying security" means, in Ontario, a security issued or transferred, or to be issued or transferred, in accordance with the terms of a convertible security, an exchangeable security or a multiple convertible security.

(a) — Securities Act (Ontario)

Clauses 72(1)(f), (i) if not included in Appendix F, (j), (k) and (n) of the *Securities Act* (Ontario), in each case prior to section 11 of Schedule 26 of the *Budget Measures Act, 2009* being proclaimed in force, except for a trade made under 72(1)(f)(iii) of the Securities Act (Ontario), prior to section 11 of Schedule 26 of the *Budget Measures Act, 2009* being proclaimed in force, that is:

(i) included in Appendix D or F of this Instrument, or

(ii) contemplated by section 6.5 of 2004 OSC Rule 45-501; and

an exemption from the prospectus requirement that specifies that the first trade is subject to section 2.6 of MI 45-102

Clause 72(1)(h) of the *Securities Act* (Ontario) except for a distribution under clause 72(1)(h) of the *Securities Act* (Ontario) of an underlying security that was distributed on conversion or exchange of a multiple convertible security, convertible security or exchangeable security acquired in a Type 1 trade, in each case prior to section 11 of Schedule 26 of the *Budget Measures Act, 2009* being proclaimed in force.

(a.1) — National Instrument 45-106

Section 2.4 of National Instrument 45-106 *Prospectus and Registration Exemptions* prior to subsection 12(2) of Schedule 26 of the *Budget Measures Act, 2009* being proclaimed in force.

(b) — 2001 OSC Rule 45-501 and 2004 OSC Rule 45-501

Section 2.1 of the 2001 OSC Rule 45-501 and the 2004 OSC Rule 45-501;

Section 2.5 of the 2001 OSC Rule 45-501 and the 2004 OSC Rule 45-501;

Section 2.6 of the 2001 OSC Rule 45-501 and the 2004 OSC Rule 45-501 if an underlying security was distributed under section 2.6 of the 2001 OSC Rule 45-501 or the 2004 OSC Rule 45-501 on a forced conversion or exchange of a multiple convertible security, convertible security or exchangeable security acquired:

(a) in a Type 2 trade;

(b) under section 2.2, 3.1, 3.2, 3.3, 5.1 or 8.1 of OSC Rule 45-503, other than a trade by an associated consultant or investor consultant as defined in OSC Rule 45-503; or

(c) under a provision in Part 2 of MI 45-105;

Section 2.7 of the 2001 OSC Rule 45-501 and the 2004 OSC Rule 45-501 if an underlying security was distributed under section 2.7 of the 2001 OSC Rule 45-501 or the 2004 OSC Rule 45-501 on a forced conversion or exchange of a multiple convertible security, convertible security or exchangeable security acquired:

(a) in a Type 2 trade;

(b) under section 2.2, 3.1, 3.2, 3.3, 5.1 or 8.1 of OSC Rule 45-503, other than a trade by an associated consultant or investor consultant as defined in OSC Rule 45-503; or

(c) under a provision in Part 2 of MI 45-105;

Section 2.8 of the 2001 OSC Rule 45-501 and the 2004 OSC Rule 45-501;

Section 2.11 of the 2001 OSC Rule 45-501 and the 2004 OSC Rule 45-501 if section 2.6 of MI 45-102 would have been applicable to a first trade in that security by the person making the exempt distribution under section 2.11 of the 2001 OSC Rule 45-501 or the 2004 OSC Rule 45-501;

Section 2.15 of the 2004 OSC Rule 45-501.

(c) — 1998 OSC Rule 45-501

Section 2.7 of the 1998 OSC Rule 45-501;

Section 2.8 of the 1998 OSC Rule 45-501;

Section 2.9 of the 1998 OSC Rule 45-501 if an underlying security was distributed under section 2.9 of the 1998 OSC Rule 45-501 on a forced conversion or exchange of a multiple convertible security, convertible security or exchangeable security acquired by the holder in a Type 2 trade;

Section 2.10 of the 1998 OSC Rule 45-501 if an underlying security was distributed under section 2.10 of the 1998 OSC Rule 45-501 on a forced conversion or exchange of a multiple convertible security, convertible security or exchangeable security acquired by the holder in a Type 2 trade;

Section 2.17 of the 1998 OSC Rule 45-501;

Subsection 2.18(1) of the 1998 OSC Rule 45-501 after the issuer had ceased to be a private issuer for the purposes of the *Securities Act* (British Columbia).

(d) — Other

Sections 2.1 and 3.1 of Ontario Securities Commission Rule 45-502.

4. — New Brunswick Provisions

In this Appendix

"**2004 NB LR 45-501**" means the New Brunswick Securities Commission Local Rule 45-501 that came into force on September 29, 2004;

   A. Subsections 2.1(2), 2.2(3), 2.4(2), 2.9(2), 2.14(2), 2.16(3), 2.18(2), 2.19(2), 2.22(4), 2.25(3), 2.26(4), 2.29(3), 2.30(2) and 2.31(3) of 2004 NB LR 45-501

   B. Subsection 2.41(2) of 2004 NB LR 45-501 (if the security acquired under section 2.4 was initially acquired by an individual or an associate of the individual or an RRSP or RRIF established for or by that individual or under which that individual is a beneficiary under

   (a) one of the exemptions in NB LR 45-501 listed in paragraph A, or

   (b) an exemption from the prospectus requirement that specifies that the first trade is subject to section 2.5 of Multilateral Instrument 45-102 *Resale of Securities*)

   C. Subsection 2.43(3) (if the security acquired under paragraph 2.43(1)(a) was acquired in accordance with the terms and conditions of a previously issued security under

   (a) one of the exemptions in 2005 NB LR 45-501 listed in paragraph A, or

   (b) an exemption from the prospectus requirement that specifies that the first trade is subject to section 2.5 of Multilateral Instrument, 45-102 *Resale of Securities*)

APPENDIX F — TO NATIONAL INSTRUMENT 45-102 RESALE OF SECURITIES — UNDERWRITERS

(Section 2.13)

Section 2.33 [*Acting as underwriter*] of NI 45-106 and section 2.11 [*Business combination and reorganization*] or subsection 2.42(1) [*Conversion, exchange or exercise*] of NI 45-106, if the original security was acquired under section 2.33 of NI 45-106 or one of the underwriter exemptions in the transitional provisions listed below.

Transitional Provisions:

Except in New Brunswick, an exemption from the prospectus requirement listed in Appendix F of MI 45-102 in effect on March 30, 2004. Except in New Brunswick, exemptions listed in Appendix F of MI 45-102 on March 30, 2004 were:

- Section 74(2)(15) of the *Securities Act* (British Columbia) and section 74(2)(8) or 74(2)(11)(iii) of the *Securities Act* (British Columbia) if the original security was acquired under section 74(2)(15) of the *Securities Act* (British Columbia);

- Clause 73(1)(r) of the *Securities Act* (Newfoundland and Labrador) and section 73(1)(i) or 73(1)(f)(iii) of the *Securities Act* (Newfoundland and Labrador) if the original security was acquired under section 73(1)(r) of the *Securities Act* (Newfoundland and Labrador);

- Paragraph 3(v) of Blanket Order No. 1 of the Registrar of Securities (Northwest Territories) and paragraph 3(g) or subparagraph 3(e)(iii) of Blanket Order No. 1 of the Registrar of Securities (Northwest Territories) if the original security was acquired under paragraph 3(v) of Blanket Order No. 1 of the Registrar of Securities (Northwest Territories);

- Clause 77(1)(r) of the *Securities Act* (Nova Scotia) and clause 77(1)(i) or 77(1)(f)(iii) of the *Securities Act* (Nova Scotia) or Blanket Order No. 38 or 45-503 if the original security was acquired under clause 77(1)(r) of the *Securities Act* (Nova Scotia);

- Paragraph 3(v) of Blanket Order No. 1 of the Registrar of Securities (Nunavut) and paragraph 3(g) or subparagraph 3(e)(iii) of Blanket Order No. 1 of the Registrar of Securities (Nunavut) if the original security was acquired under paragraph 3(v) of Blanket Order No. 1 of the Registrar of Securities (Nunavut);

- Clause 72(1)(f)(iii) of the *Securities Act* (Ontario) if the original security was acquired under clause 72(1)(r) of the *Securities Act* (Ontario), in each case prior to section 11 of Schedule 26 the *Budget Measures Act, 2009* being proclaimed in force;

- Clause 72(1)(i) of the *Securities Act* (Ontario) if the original security was acquired under clause 72(1)(r) of the *Securities Act* (Ontario), in each case prior to section 11 of Schedule 26 of the *Budget Measures Act, 2009* being proclaimed in force;

- Clause 72(1)(r) of the *Securities Act* (Ontario), in each case prior to section 11 of Schedule 26 of the *Budget Measures Act, 2009* being proclaimed in force;

- Section 2.1 of Prince Edward Island Rule 45-509 and subclause 13(1)(e)(iii) or clause 13(1)(f) of the *Securities Act* (Prince Edward Island) or section 1.1 of Prince Edward Island Rule 45-502 if the original security was acquired under section 2.1 of Prince Edward Island Rule 45-509;

- Section 55 of the *Securities Act* (Québec) as it read prior to its repeal by section 8 of *An Act to amend the Securities Act and other legislative provisions*; and

- Clause 81(1)(u) of *The Securities Act, 1988* (Saskatchewan) and clause 81(1)(i) or subclause 81(1)(f)(iii) of *The Securities Act, 1988* (Saskatchewan) if the original security was acquired under clause 81(1)(u) of *The Securities Act, 1988* (Saskatchewan).

New Brunswick Provisions:

In New Brunswick, an exemption from the prospectus requirement listed in New Brunswick Securities Commission Local Rule 45-501 in effect on September 29, 2004 (2004 NB LR 45-501).

In New Brunswick, the exemptions listed in 2004 NB LR 45-501 were:

- Subsection 2.33(2); and

- Subsection 2.43(3) if the original security was acquired under section 2.09.

Final Rule: (2001) 24 O.S.C.B. 7029; Approval by OSC: (2001) 24 O.S.C.B. 5511; A version of this MI was approved by the OSC, (2001) 24 O.S.C.B. 2437 but withdrawn by the OSC, (2001) 24 O.S.C.B. 3133. Request for Comments: (2000) 23 O.S.C.B. 6238.

Approval of Amendment by OSC: (2003) 26 O.S.C.B. 5517; Request for Comments: (2003) 26 O.S.C.B. 587 and (2002) 26 O.S.C.B. 505.

Amendment to Rule: (2004) 27 O.S.C.B. 3580; Approval by OSC: (2003) 26 O.S.C.B. 8217; Request for Comments: (2003) 26 O.S.C.B. 991.

Amendment to Rule: (2005) 28 O.S.C.B. (Supp-4) 121; Approval by OSC: (2005) 28 O.S.C.B. (Supp-3) 88; Request for Comments: (2004) 27 O.S.C.B. (Supp-3) 1.

Amendment to Rule: (2009) 32 O.S.C.B. (Supp. 5) 115; Approval by OSC: (2009) 32 O.S.C.B. (Supp. 3) 1; Request for Comments: (2009) 32 O.S.C.B. 4233 and (2008) 31 O.S.C.B. (Supp. 1) 1.

Amendment to Rule: CSAN 11-314.

Amendment to Rule: (2015) 38 O.S.C.B. 4166.

Form 45-102F1 — Notice of Intention to Distribute Securities under Section 2.8 of NI 45-102 Resale of Securities

Reporting issuer

1. Name of reporting issuer:

Selling security holder

2. Your name:

3. The offices or positions you hold in the reporting issuer:

4. Are you selling securities as a lender, pledgee, mortgagee or other encumbrancer?

5. Number and class of securities of the reporting issuer you beneficially own:

Distribution

6. Number and class of securities you propose to sell:

7. Will you sell the securities privately or on an exchange or market? If on an exchange or market, provide the name.

Warning

It is an offence to submit information that, in a material respect and in light of the circumstances in which it is submitted, is misleading or untrue.

Certificate

I certify that

    (1) I have no knowledge of a material fact or material change with respect to the issuer of the securities that has not been generally disclosed; and

    (2) the information given in this form is true and complete.

Date ....

.... Your name (Selling security holder)

.... Your signature (or if a company, the signature of your authorized signatory)

.... Name of your authorized signatory

INSTRUCTION:

File this form electronically through SEDAR with the securities regulatory authority or regulator in each jurisdiction where you sell securities and with the Canadian exchange on which the securities are listed. If the securities are being sold on an exchange, the form should be filed in every jurisdiction across Canada.

Notice to selling security holders — collection and use of personal information

The personal information required in this form is collected for and used by the listed securities regulatory authorities or regulators to administer and enforce securities legislation in their jurisdictions. This form is publicly available by authority of National Instrument 45-102 and the securities legislation in each of the jurisdictions. The personal information collected will not be used or disclosed other than for the stated purposes without first obtaining your consent. Corporate filers should seek the consent of any individuals whose personal information appears in this form before filing this form.

If you have questions about the collection and use of your personal information, or the personal information of your authorized signatory, contact any of the securities regulatory authorities or regulators listed below.

British Columbia Securities Commission

P.O. Box 10142, Pacific Centre

701 West Georgia Street

Vancouver, BC V7Y 1L2

Attention: Assistant Manager, Financial Reporting

Telephone: (604) 899-6805 or (800) 373-6393 (in B.C.)

Facsimile: (604) 899-6506

Alberta Securities Commission

Suite 600, 250 — 5th Street SW

Calgary, AB T2P 0R4

Attention: Information Officer

Telephone: (403) 297-6454

Facsimile: (403) 297-6156

Saskatchewan Financial Services Commission

Securities Division

601 - 1919 Saskatchewan Drive

Regina, SK S4P 4H2

Attention: Deputy Director, Legal/Registration

Telephone: (306) 787-5879

Facsimile: (306) 787-5899

Ontario Securities Commission

20 Queen Street West

22nd Floor

Toronto, ON M5H 3S8

Telephone: (416) 593-8314

Toll free in Canada: 1-877-785-1555

Facsimile: (416) 593-8122

Public official contact regarding collection of personal information:

Inquiries Officer

Autorité des marchés financiers

Tour de la Bourse

800 square Victoria

C.P. 246, 22e étage

Montréal, Québec H4Z 1G3

Attention: Responsable de l'accès à l'information

Telephone: (514) 395-0337

Toll free: 1-877-525-0337

Facsimile: (514) 873-6155 (For filing purposes only)

Facsimile: (514) 864-6381 (For privacy requests only)

www.lautorite.qc.ca

New Brunswick Securities Commission

85 Charlotte Street, Suite 300

Saint John, New Brunswick E2L 2J2

Telephone: (506) 658-3060

Toll Free in New Brunswick 1-866-933-2222

Facsimile: (506) 658-3059

Nova Scotia Securities Commission

Suite 400, 5251 Duke Street

Halifax, NS B3J 1P3

Attention: Corporate Finance

Telephone: (902) 424-7768

Facsimile: (902) 424-4625

Prince Edward Island Securities Office

95 Rochford Street, 4th Floor Shaw Building

P.O. Box 2000

Charlottetown, Prince Edward Island C1A 7N8

Telephone: (902) 368-4569

Facsimile: (902) 368-5283

Government of Newfoundland and Labrador

Financial Services Regulation Division

P.O. Box 8700

Confederation Building

2nd Floor, West Block

Prince Philip Drive

St. John's, NFLD A1B 4J6

Attention: Director of Securities

Telephone: (709) 729-4189

Facsimile: (709) 729-6187

Government of Yukon

Office of the Yukon Superintendent of Securities

Government of Yukon

Department of Community Services

307 Black Street, 1st Floor

PO Box 2703 (C-6)

Whitehorse, Yukon Y1A 2C6

Telephone: 867-667-5466

Facsimile: 867-393-6251

http://www.community.gov.yk.ca/corp/securities_about.html

Government of Northwest Territories

Office of the Superintendent of Securities

Deputy Superintendent, Legal & Enforcement

P.O. Box 1320

Yellowknife, NT X1A 2L9

Attention: Deputy Superintendent of Securities

Telephone: (867) 920-8984

Facsimile: (867) 873-0243

Department of Justice, Nunavut Legal Registries Division

P.O. Box 1000, Station 570

1st Floor, Brown Building

Iqaluit, NT X0A 0H0

Attention: Director, Legal Registries Division

Telephone: (867) 975-6590

Facsimile: (867) 975-6594

Companion Policy 45-102CP — To National Instrument 45-102 Resale of Securities

Date: November 23, 2001; replaced effective March 30, 2004, as amended effective September 14, 2005; amended and restated September 28, 2009

24 O.S.C.B. 5540; 27 O.S.C.B. 3598; 28 O.S.C.B. (Supp-4) 136; 32 O.S.C.B. (Supp. 5) 141

1.1 Application — (1) National Instrument 45-102 (NI 45-102) has been implemented in all jurisdictions.

(2) Except for sections 2.1, 2.8 and 2.9, Part 2 of NI 45-102 does not apply in Manitoba.

1.2 Purpose — (1) NI 45-102 provides that first trades of securities distributed under certain exemptions from the prospectus requirement are distributions unless certain conditions are met. The conditions impose restrictions on the resale of the securities. If the securities were distributed under any of the provisions listed in Appendix D to NI 45-102 or under other securities legislation which specifies that the first trade is subject to section 2.5 of NI

45-102, the conditions include that the issuer is and has been a reporting issuer for a four month seasoning period and that a four month restricted period has elapsed from the date of the initial distribution. If the securities were distributed under any of the provisions listed in Appendix E to NI 45-102 or under other securities legislation which specifies that the first trade is subject to section 2.6 of NI 45-102, the conditions include that the issuer is and has been a reporting issuer for a four month seasoning period. NI 45-102 also provides an exemption for a control distribution and a sale by a pledgee of pledged securities if the sale would be a distribution for the purposes of securities legislation.

(2) Appendices D and E to NI 45-102 list the harmonized exemptions in National Instrument 45-106 *Prospectus Exemptions* (NI 45-106) and local exemptions that are subject to the resale restrictions under section 2.5 or 2.6 of NI 45-102, while Appendix F lists the harmonized exemptions in NI 45-106 applicable to underwriters. Each of these appendices also contains transitional provisions applicable to securities acquired under exemptions listed in the Appendices to MI 45-102 as Appendices D, E and F read on March 30, 2004. For all local exemptions that remain in force, you should look to the local instrument itself to see if it specifies that the securities acquired are subject to section 2.5 or 2.6 of NI 45-102 as well as to Appendix D and E to NI 45-102. You may also wish to consult the CSA Staff Notice 45-304 listing local registration and prospectus exemptions in place in each jurisdiction of Canada, which the CSA will update periodically.

(3) Nothing in NI 45-102 is intended to restrict the ability of a purchaser to resell securities during the restricted period or seasoning period under a prospectus or an exemption from the prospectus requirement. This includes the further exemption found in section 2.14. For example, if a person or company obtains a discretionary exemption order or ruling that imposes any of the resale restrictions contained in section 2.5, 2.6 or 2.8 on a security that is the subject of the order or ruling, the person or company may rely on section 2.14 to resell the security.

1.3 Open System Jurisdiction — Sections 2.5 and 2.6 of NI 45-102 do not apply in Manitoba because Manitoba does not impose restrictions on first trades in securities distributed under an exemption from the prospectus requirement in those jurisdictions unless the trade is a control distribution.

1.4 Example of Application of Section 2.5 — If an issuer distributes securities to a purchaser in British Columbia, the issuer must file a prospectus or rely upon a prospectus exemption under the securities legislation of British Columbia. If the issuer relies upon a British Columbia prospectus exemption listed in Appendix D to NI 45-102, section 2.3 of NI 45-102 applies and the first trade of the securities is subject to section 2.5 of NI 45-102. Section 2.5 provides that the first trade is a distribution unless, among other conditions, a four month restricted period has elapsed. If the British Columbia purchaser seeks to resell the securities into Ontario, a prospectus must be filed in Ontario or a prospectus exemption relied upon unless the conditions in subsection 2.5(2) of NI 45-102 are satisfied.

1.5 Reporting Issuer Status — Reporting issuer status in any jurisdiction will satisfy the reporting issuer requirements in subsections 2.5(2), 2.6(3) and 2.8(2) of NI 45-102. See section 1.11 for guidance if an issuer becomes a reporting issuer by filing a prospectus after the distribution date.

1.6 Legending of Securities — (1) Items 3 and 3.1 of subsection 2.5(2) of NI 45-102 impose legend or legend notation requirements for securities distributed under any of the provisions listed in Appendix D to NI 45-102 or another prospectus exemption of any jurisdiction subject to the resale restrictions in subsection 2.5(2) of NI 45-102. This requirement applies to securities transferred during the restricted period, whether to initial or subsequent transferees. However, because of the definition of "distribution date", in the case of most resales, the subsequent purchaser's restricted period will expire four months and a day after the original distribution date.

(2) If the security is entered into a direct registration or other electronic book-entry system, or where a certificate representing the security is not issued directly to a purchaser, the issuer must provide written notice of the legend restriction notation to the purchaser. We would consider providing written notice of the legend restriction notation to the purchaser in a subscription agreement or including the legend restriction notation in an ownership statement issued under a direct registration system or other electronic book-entry system delivered directly to the purchaser to be ways of meeting the written notice requirement.

(3) In addition to the written notice condition contemplated in item 3.1 of subsection 2.5(2), issuers may want to assist purchasers of restricted securities with compliance with the resale restrictions in item 2 of subsection 2.5(2) through other means. For example, issuers can request that the direct registration or electronic book-entry system in which the security is entered apply any available procedures to identify the restricted nature of the security, such as the assignment of a separate CUSIP or ISIN number to the security for the duration of the restricted period. There may be alternative procedures available depending on the capabilities of the particular direct registration system or other electronic book-entry system.

(4) Issuers may add additional wording to that found in item 3 of subsection 2.5(2) of NI 45-102. If you supplement the specified text of the legend on the certificate or the legend notation on the written notice, that additional wording cannot alter the meaning of the specified wording. You should also look to section 1.10 for further guidance on the legending of convertible and underlying securities.

(5) A reference to a purchaser of a security in items 3 and 3.1 of subsection 2.5(2) of NI 45-102 means a person who makes the investment decision about the acquisition of a security. In most cases, the person making the investment decision will be the beneficial owner of the security. In some cases, however, the person making the investment decision will not be the beneficial owner. In the case of a fully managed account, the manager may be making the investment decision. In the case of a trust, the trustee may be making the investment decision. There may be other examples where the person making the investment decision is not the beneficial owner of the security.

1.7 Removal of Legend — NI 45-102 does not preclude an issuer or its transfer agent from removing a legend once the requirements in subsection 2.5(2)3 have been satisfied. The parties involved in a transfer of securities would not be prevented from transferring those securities even if the legend on the certificate was stale-dated. The transferor should, however, verify exchange rules to determine if removal of the legend is necessary to effect "good delivery".

1.8 Calculation of Restricted and Seasoning Periods — The restricted period in item 2 of subsection 2.5(2) of NI 45-102 is calculated from the distribution date, that is, the date the securities were distributed in reliance on an exemption from the prospectus requirement by the issuer or a control person. For example, if an issuer or control person distributes securities under a private placement exemption to a purchaser in Saskatchewan and the private placee resells the securities during the restricted period to a purchaser in Alberta under a further private placement exemption, upon resale by the Alberta purchaser, that purchaser will determine whether the restricted period has expired by calculating the time period from the date the issuer or control person distributed the securities to the Saskatchewan purchaser.

1.9 No Unusual Effort — Persons interested in the meaning of the concept of "no unusual effort is made to prepare the market or to create a demand for the security that is the subject of the trade" found in subsections 2.5(2), 2.6(3) and 2.8(2) of NI 45-102 should look to the case law, in particular the order of the Ontario Securities Commission dated April 24, 1985 in the matter of Daon Development Corporation and Daon Corporation as well as to the definition of unusual effort in section 4 of the Alberta Securities Commission Rules.

1.10 Underlying Securities — The restricted period or seasoning period applicable to trades in underlying securities is calculated from the distribution date of the convertible security, exchangeable security or multiple convertible security. If the applicable restricted period or seasoning period expired prior to the conversion or exchange, subsection 2.5(3) provides that an issuer is not required to place a legend on the certificate representing the underlying securities or a legend restriction notation in the written notice.

1.11 Becoming a Reporting Issuer By Filing a Prospectus After the Distribution Date — If an issuer is not a reporting issuer at the distribution date but subsequently becomes a reporting issuer after the distribution date by filing and obtaining a receipt for a prospectus in one of the jurisdictions listed in Appendix B, section 2.7 of NI 45-102 provides that the four month seasoning requirement in sections 2.5, 2.6 and 2.8 of NI 45-102 does not apply. This means that the securities issued prior to the prospectus being filed may then be resold, provided however that the restricted period under section 2.5 or 2.8 of NI 45-102 has expired.

For example, if, on September 28, 2009, an issuer that is not a reporting issuer in any jurisdiction issues securities which are subject to section 2.5 to purchasers under a private placement and the issuer subsequently receives a receipt for its initial public offering prospectus on October 28, 2009, then those purchasers can resell the securities acquired under the private placement on January 29, 2010, being the date that is four months and a day from the original distribution date, provided that the conditions in subsection 2.5(2) are satisfied.

1.12 Realization of Pledged Securities — The prospectus exemption in section 2.8 of NI 45-102 is available for realizations of pledged securities under either a power of sale or by way of foreclosure. This means that a pledgee, mortgagee or other encumbrancer can rely on the exemption in section 2.8 of NI 45-102 to immediately effect a resale of pledged securities under a power of sale or to foreclose and take the securities on its own books for subsequent resale.

1.13 Securities Exchange Take-over Bid or Issuer Bid — Section 2.11 of NI 45-102 provides relief from the seasoning requirement for a trade of securities issued in connection with a securities exchange take-over bid or securities exchange issuer bid if a securities exchange take-over bid circular or securities exchange issuer bid circular is filed by the offeror under securities legislation of the local jurisdiction. A bid circular may be filed for either a formal bid or an exempt bid. The basis for this exemption is that a securities exchange take-over bid circular or securities exchange issuer bid circular for a formal bid is required to contain prospectus-level disclosure for the offeror or other issuer whose securities are being offered in exchange for the securities of the offeree issuer. If a take-over bid circular or issuer bid circular is prepared in connection with an exempt bid, the circular must meet the disclosure standards in securities legislation relating to the form and content of a take-over bid circular or issuer bid circular, as the case may be, for a formal bid for the exemption in section 2.11 to be available.

1.14 Exemptions for Certain Trades in the Local Jurisdiction — The exemption in section 2.10 of NI 45-102 is subject to a condition that the issuer of the underlying security was a reporting issuer in the local jurisdiction at the time of the trade. The exemptions in sections 2.11 and 2.12 of NI 45-102 are subject to a condition that the offeror was a reporting issuer in the local jurisdiction on the date securities of the offeree issuer are first taken up under the take-over bid or issuer bid and, in the case of the exemption in section 2.12, an additional condition that issuer of the underlying security was a reporting issuer in the local jurisdiction at the time of the trade. Issuers cannot rely on a prospectus filed in another jurisdiction nor can an offeror rely on a take-over bid circular or issuer bid circular filed in another jurisdiction to satisfy these conditions.

1.15 Resales of Securities of a Non-Reporting Issuer — (1) For the purposes of section 2.14 of NI 45-102, in determining the percentage of the outstanding securities of the class or series that are directly or indirectly owned by residents of Canada and the number of owners directly or indirectly that are residents of Canada, an issuer should use reasonable efforts to

   (a) determine securities held of record by a broker, dealer, bank, trust company or nominee for any of them for the accounts of customers resident in Canada;

   (b) count securities beneficially owned by residents of Canada as reported on reports of beneficial ownership; and

   (c) assume that a customer is a resident of the jurisdiction or foreign jurisdiction in which the nominee has its principal place of business if, after reasonable inquiry, information regarding the jurisdiction or foreign jurisdiction of residence of the customer is unavailable.

(2) Lists of beneficial owners of securities maintained by intermediaries under SEC Rule 14a-13 under the 1934 Act or other securities law analogous to National Instrument 54-101 Communication *with Beneficial Owners of Securities of a Reporting Issuer* may be useful in determining the percentages referred to in subsection (1).

(3) There is no requirement to place a legend on the securities in order to rely on the exemption in section 2.14 of NI 45-102.

1.16 Filing of Form 45-102F1 — Section 2.8 of NI 45-102 provides that the prospectus requirement does not apply to a control distribution if the conditions in section 2.8 are met. Selling security holders are required to give advance notice of intention to resell their securities under subsection 2.8(3) of NI 45-102 by filing a completed and signed Form 45-102F1. Under subsection 2.8(4), the advance notice expires on the earlier of the date the selling security holder files the last of the insider reports reflecting the sale of all securities referred to in the Form and 30 days after the Form 45-102F1 is filed. A new Form 45-102F1 must be filed in accordance with subsection 2.8(3) if the selling security holder wishes to continue to resell securities from a control block. Form 45-102F1 should be filed through SEDAR under the issuer's profile under "*Continuous Disclosure — Resale of Securities (NI 45-102) — Form 45-102F1*" in the jurisdiction of the issuer's principal regulator under National Policy 11-202 *Process for Prospectus Reviews in Multiple Jurisdictions*. Consult National Instrument 13-101 *System for Electronic Document Analysis and Retrieval (SEDAR)* and the current CSA SEDAR Filer Manual (including code updates) for further information about filing documents electronically.

1.17 Application of section 2.10 — Section 2.10 of NI 45-102 applies when securities qualified by a prospectus are convertible into or exchangeable for securities of a reporting issuer other than the issuer of the convertible or exchangeable securities. Those securities would be converted or exchanged in reliance on the prospectus exemption in paragraph 2.42(1)(b) of NI 45-106. As a result, those securities would be subject to a seasoning period requirement because distributions under subsection 2.42(1) of NI 45-106 for a security being distributed in the circumstances referred to in clause (b) of subsection 2.42(1) are listed in Appendix E of NI 45-102. Section 2.10 removes the seasoning period requirement for the underlying securities provided the requirements of that section are met.

Adoption by OSC: (2001) 24 O.S.C.B. 7029 and 5511; Request for Comments: (2000) 23 O.S.C.B. 6238.

Adoption of amended version: (2004) 27 O.S.C.B. 3598 and (2003) 26 O.S.C.B. 8248; Request for Comments: (2003) 26 O.S.C.B. 991.

Adoption of amendments: (2005) 28 O.S.C.B. (Supp-4) 136 and (2005) 28 O.S.C.B. (Supp-3) 103; Request for Comments: (2004) 27 O.S.C.B. (Supp-3) 1.

Adoption of amended version: (2009) 32 O.S.C.B. (Supp. 5) 141 and 32 O.S.C.B. (Supp. 3) 1; Request for Comments: (2009) 32 O.S.C.B. 4233 and (2008) 31 O.S.C.B. (Supp. 1) 1.

Part 4: DISTRIBUTIONS

Multilateral Instrument 45-105 — Trades to Employees, Senior Officers, Directors, and Consultants

[Repealed upon the coming into force of NI 45-106]

Final Rule: (2003) 26 O.S.C.B. 5993; Approval by OSC: (2003) 26 O.S.C.B 4167; Request for Comments: (2003) 26 O.S.C.B. 7205.

Amendment to Rule: (2003) 26 O.S.C.B. 7353; Approval by OSC: (2003) 26 O.S.C.B. 6315.

Repeal: (2005) 28 O.S.C.B. (Supp-4) 117; Adoption by OSC: (2005) 28 O.S.C.B. (Supp-3) 83; Request for Comments: (2004) 27 O.S.C.B. (Supp-3) 1.

45-106 — Summary of Key Capital Raising Prospectus Exemptions in Ontario

January 28, 2016

TABLE OF CONTENTS

The information provided in this summary describes each prospectus exemption as it applies in Ontario only. It is provided for general informational purposes only and does not constitute legal or accounting advice. Information has been summarized and paraphrased for publication purposes. Responsibility for making required disclosure and complying with applicable securities legislation remains with the company. Information in this summary reflects securities legislation and other relevant standards that are in effect as of the date of the publication of this summary.

Background

This summary provides an overview of key capital raising prospectus exemptions in Ontario that were amended or introduced as a result of the Ontario Securities Commission's (OSC) broad review of the exempt market regulatory regime (the Exempt Market Review) beginning in 2011.

Original scope of the review

The original scope of the Exempt Market Review was on the existing accredited investor and minimum amount investment prospectus exemptions. The original purpose of the review was to assess whether the two exemptions remained appropriate given the investor protection concerns associated with these exemptions that were highlighted during the financial crisis in 2007-2008. The OSC worked with the Canadian Securities Administrators (CSA) to publish final amendments to these two exemptions, which came into force in Ontario on May 5, 2015.

Expanded OSC review

As a result of feedback received during the original Exempt Market Review, in 2012 the OSC decided to expand the focus of the review to consider whether there was potential to facilitate greater access to capital through the exempt market, particularly for start-ups and small and medium-sized enterprises (SMEs), while maintaining an appropriate level of investor protection. On March 20, 2014, the OSC published a proposal to introduce four new capital raising prospectus exemptions in Ontario.

Since that time,

- the existing security holder prospectus exemption came into force in Ontario on February 11, 2015,

- the family, friends and business associates (FFBA) prospectus exemption came into force in Ontario on May 5, 2015,

- the offering memorandum (OM) prospectus exemption came into force in Ontario on January 13, 2016, and
- the crowdfunding prospectus exemption came into force in Ontario on January 25, 2016.

The OSC also worked with other CSA members to see if the existing rights offering prospectus exemption available across Canada could be streamlined to improve its efficiency and effectiveness. Final amendments to the existing rights offering prospectus exemption were published by the CSA on September 24, 2015 and came into force in Ontario on December 8, 2015.

Links to more information

- For further information on the **accredited investor and minimum amount investment prospectus exemptions**, please see the Notice of Amendments published on February 19, 2015: https://www.osc.gov.on.ca/en/SecuritiesLaw_ni_20150219_45-106_amendments.htm

- For further information on the **existing security holder prospectus exemption**, please see the Notice of Amendments published on November 27, 2014: https://www.osc.gov.on.ca/en/SecuritiesLaw_rule_20141127_45-501-amd-prospectus-registration.htm

- For further information on the **FFBA prospectus exemption**, please see the Notice of Amendments published on February 19, 2015: https://www.osc.gov.on.ca/en/SecuritiesLaw_ni_20150219_45-106_amendments.htm

- For further information on the **OM prospectus exemption**, please see the Notice of Amendments published on October 29, 2015: https://www.osc.gov.on.ca/en/SecuritiesLaw_ni_20151029_45-106_amendments.htm

- For further information on the **crowdfunding prospectus exemption**, please see the Notice of Publication published on November 5, 2015: http://www.osc.gov.on.ca/en/SecuritiesLaw_csa_20151105_45-108_multilateral-crowdfunding.htm

- For further information on the **rights offering prospectus exemption**, please see the Notice of Amendments published on September 24, 2015: https://www.osc.gov.on.ca/en/SecuritiesLaw_ni_20150924_45-106_amd-rights-offerings.htm

Purpose of Summary

The purpose of this summary is to highlight features of the key capital raising prospectus exemptions available in Ontario following the Exempt Market Review. Table 1 provides a high-level comparison of these prospectus exemptions. Tables 2 to 8 provide an overview of each of the prospectus exemptions.

Please note that the availability of a prospectus exemption to distribute securities does not mean there is a corresponding registration exemption. An issuer distributing securities under one or more of these prospectus exemptions must consider whether its activities result in it being "in the business" of trading in securities. An issuer that is "in the business" of trading in securities, would generally be subject to the dealer registration requirement. The Companion Policy to National Instrument 31-103 *Registration, Exemptions and Ongoing Registrant Obligations* (NI 31-103) provides a list of factors we consider in determining whether the activity is for a business purpose and, therefore, subject to the dealer registration requirement.

Table 1: Comparison Table of Key Capital Raising Prospectus Exemptions in Ontario

	Accredited Investor	Crowdfunding	Existing Security Holder	FFBA	Minimum Amount Investment	OM	Rights Offering
Who can use the exemption?	All companies[1] and investment funds	Canadian companies except blind pools	Public companies listed on specified exchanges	All companies	All companies and investment funds	All companies	Public companies[2]
Who can buy securities under the exemption?	Accredited investors	Any investor	Existing security holders holding the type of security being offered	Specified principals of the company, specified family members, close personal friends, close business associates	Non-individual investors	Any investor	Rights to purchase a security issued by the company are distributed to each security holder. Rights holders may exercise their right to acquire the security.

Table 1: Comparison Table of Key Capital Raising Prospectus Exemptions in Ontario

	Accredited Investor	Crowdfunding	Existing Security Holder	FFBA	Minimum Amount Investment	OM	Rights Offering
Are there limits on how much investors can invest under the exemption?	No	Yes, for retail investors and accredited investors	Yes, unless suitability advice is obtained from an investment dealer	No	No, but the purchase price of the securities must be at least $150,000	Yes, for individual investors except accredited investors or investors who qualify under the FFBA exemption	No
Is disclosure required to be provided to investors at the point of sale?	No	Yes	No	No	No	Yes	Yes
Do investors have the right to withdraw from the investment after buying the securities?	No	Yes	No	No	No	Yes	No
Are the securities subject to restrictions the first time they are resold?	Yes	Yes	Yes	Yes	Yes	Yes	Generally freely tradeable
Does a report of exempt distribution have to be filed with the OSC?	Yes	Yes	Yes	Yes	Yes	Yes	No

Notes:

1   References to companies in this document include corporate and non-corporate entities, but do not include investment funds.

2   In general, a public company is a company whose shares are bought and sold by the general public on a stock market or exchange.

Table 2: Overview of the Accredited Investor Prospectus Exemption in Ontario

What is the purpose of the exemption?	Allows companies to cost-effectively raise funds from investors who have certain characteristics, such as the ability to withstand financial loss and the financial resources to obtain expert advice.
Who can use the exemption?	All companies and investment funds.
Who can buy securities under the exemption?	An accredited investor, which includes an individual with income, net assets or financial assets that exceed the amounts set out in the exemption.[3] Accredited investors also include non-individuals, such as Canadian and foreign governments, Canadian financial institutions, pension funds, charities and other entities set out in the exemption.
Are there limits on how much investors can invest under the exemption?	NO
Is a risk acknowledgement form required?	YES. A risk acknowledgement form is required to be completed and signed by individual accredited investors, except those who qualify as permitted clients.[4] Investors must indicate in the form how they meet the criteria for an accredited investor. The form also requires identification of any salesperson who meets with or provides information to the investor with respect to the investment.

Table 2: Overview of the Accredited Investor Prospectus Exemption in Ontario

Is disclosure required to be provided to investors at the point of sale?	NO
Do investors have the right to withdraw from the investment after buying the securities?	NO
Are the securities subject to restrictions the first time they are resold?	YES. Securities of a public company are subject to a 4-month hold period (subject to certain other conditions being met). Securities of a non-public company are subject to an indefinite hold period and can only be resold under another prospectus exemption or under a prospectus.
Does a report of exempt distribution have to be filed with the OSC?	YES. A report of exempt distribution must be filed by a company within 10 days of the distribution and by an investment fund no later than 30 days after the financial year-end of the investment fund.

Notes:

3   Under National Instrument 45-106 *Prospectus Exemptions*, an accredited investor means an individual with:

- Net income before taxes was more than $200,000 in each of the two most recent calendar years and is expected to be more than $200,000 in the current calendar year

- Net income before taxes combined with a spouse was more than $300,000 in each of the two most recent calendar years and their combined net income is expected to be more than $300,000 in the current calendar year

- Financial assets, alone or with a spouse, of more than $1 million before taxes but net of related liabilities

- Net assets, alone or with a spouse, worth more than $5 million

4   A permitted client is defined under NI 31-103.

Table 3: Overview of the Crowdfunding Prospectus Exemption in Ontario

What is the purpose of the exemption?	Allows Canadian companies, particularly start-ups and SMEs, in their early stages of development, to raise funds online from the public through a single funding portal registered with securities regulators.
Who can use the exemption?	All companies incorporated or organized in Canada, with their head office in Canada, a majority of their directors resident in Canada, and their principal operating subsidiary (if any) incorporated or organized in Canada or the USA. Blind pools and investment funds cannot use the exemption.
Who can buy securities under the exemption?	Any investor.
Are there limits on how much investors can invest under the exemption?	YES • A retail investor cannot invest more than $2,500 per investment, and cannot invest more than $10,000 in total in the same calendar year. • An accredited investor (other than a permitted client) cannot invest more than $25,000 per investment, and cannot invest more than $50,000 in total in the same calendar year. There are no investment limits for permitted clients.
Is a risk acknowledgement form required?	YES. Investors must complete and sign a risk acknowledgment form requiring them to positively confirm having read and understood the risk warnings and information in the crowdfunding offering document. An investor must also complete a form confirming that the investor is within the investment limits, where applicable.

Table 3: Overview of the Crowdfunding Prospectus Exemption in Ontario	
Is disclosure required to be provided to investors at the point of sale?	YES. A crowdfunding offering document must be provided to investors. An issuer may also provide purchasers with a term sheet, a video or other materials summarizing the information in the crowdfunding offering document.
Do investors have the right to withdraw from the investment after buying the securities?	YES. Investors have the right to withdraw from an agreement to buy the securities within 48 hours.
Are the securities subject to restrictions the first time they are resold?	YES. Securities of a public company are subject to a 4-month hold period (subject to certain other conditions being met). Securities of a non-public company are subject to an indefinite hold period and can only be resold under another prospectus exemption or under a prospectus.
Does a report of exempt distribution have to be filed with the OSC?	YES. A report of exempt distribution must be filed within 10 days of the distribution.

Table 4: Overview of the Existing Security Holder Prospectus Exemption in Ontario	
What is the purpose of the exemption?	Allows public companies listed on specified exchanges (listed below) to cost-effectively raise funds from existing security holders holding securities.
Who can use the exemption?	Public companies listed on the Toronto Stock Exchange, TSX Venture Exchange, Canadian Securities Exchange or Aequitas NEO Exchange. Investment funds cannot use the exemption.
Who can buy securities under the exemption?	Existing security holders that hold the type of listed security of the company being offered. The offer must be made to all security holders.
Are there limits on how much investors can invest under the exemption?	YES. There is an investment limit of $15,000 per investor in any 12 month period, which can be exceeded if the investor has obtained advice regarding the suitability of the investment from an investment dealer.
Is a risk acknowledgement form required?	NO
Is disclosure required to be provided to investors at the point of sale?	NO. However, the company is required to issue a news release about the proposed sale of the securities and file any offering materials (other than the subscription agreement) with securities regulators on the same day it provides materials to investors.
Do investors have the right to withdraw from the investment after buying the securities?	NO
Are the securities subject to restrictions the first time they are resold?	YES. Securities of a public company are subject to a 4-month hold period (subject to certain other conditions being met).
Does a report of exempt distribution have to be filed with the OSC?	YES. A report of exempt distribution must be filed within 10 days of the distribution.

Table 5: Overview of the FFBA Prospectus Exemption in Ontario	
What is the purpose of the exemption?	Allows early stage companies to raise capital from investors who are principals of the business or within the personal networks of the principals of the business.

Table 5: Overview of the FFBA Prospectus Exemption in Ontario

Who can use the exemption?	All companies. Investment funds cannot use the exemption.
Who can buy securities under the exemption?	• Director, executive officer, control person or founder of the company, or
	• Specified family member, close personal friend or close business associate of a director, executive officer, control person or founder of the company.
Are there limits on how much investors can invest under the exemption?	NO
Is a risk acknowledgement form required?	YES A risk acknowledgment form must be completed and signed by: • the investor, • the director, executive officer, control person or founder of the issuer with whom the investor has asserted the relationship, if applicable, and • the issuer. The investor must disclose, if applicable: • the identity of the director, executive officer, control person or found of the issuer with whom they assert a relationship, • that person's position at or relationship with the issuer, • the category of the relationship asserted by the investor, and • how long the investor has known that person.
Is disclosure required to be provided to investors at the point of sale?	NO
Do investors have the right to withdraw from the investment after buying the securities?	NO
Are the securities subject to restrictions the first time they are resold?	YES. Securities of a public company are subject to a 4-month hold period (subject to certain other conditions being met). Securities of a non-public company are subject to an indefinite hold period and can only be resold under another prospectus exemption or under a prospectus.
Does a report of exempt distribution have to be filed with the OSC?	YES. A report of exempt distribution must be filed within 10 days of the distribution.

Table 6: Overview of the Minimum Amount Investment Prospectus Exemption in Ontario

What is the purpose of the exemption?	Allows companies to cost-effectively raise funds from investors (who are not individuals) that have the ability to withstand financial loss and the financial resources to obtain expert advice.
Who can use the exemption?	All companies and investment funds.
Who can buy securities under the exemption?	Any investor that is not an individual.
Are there limits on how much investors can invest under the exemption?	NO. However, the purchase price of the securities purchased by the investor must be at least $150,000, which must be paid in cash at the time of distribution.

Table 6: Overview of the Minimum Amount Investment Prospectus Exemption in Ontario

Is a risk acknowledgement form required?	NO
Is disclosure required to be provided to investors at the point of sale?	NO
Do investors have the right to withdraw from the investment after buying the securities?	NO
Are the securities subject to restrictions the first time they are resold?	YES. Securities of a public company are subject to a 4-month hold period (subject to certain other conditions being met). Securities of a non-public company are subject to an indefinite hold period and can only be resold under another prospectus exemption or under a prospectus.
Does a report of exempt distribution have to be filed with the OSC?	YES. A report of exempt distribution must be filed by a company within 10 days of the distribution and by an investment fund no later than 30 days after the financial year-end of the investment fund.

Table 7: Overview of the OM Prospectus Exemption in Ontario

What is the purpose of the exemption?	Allows companies at different stages of development, including SMEs, to raise funds from a wide range of investors based on an OM being made available to investors.
Who can use the exemption?	All companies. Investment funds cannot use the exemption.
Who can buy securities under the exemption?	Any investor.
Are there limits on how much investors can invest under the exemption?	YES. Investment limits apply depending on whether the investor is an individual or not, and whether the investor is an eligible investor or non-eligible investor: • An eligible investor is a person with net income or net assets that exceed the amounts set out in the exemption.[5] An eligible investor also includes an accredited investor, an investor that qualifies under the FFBA exemption and a number of other listed entities set out in the OM exemption. • A non-eligible investor can also buy securities under the exemption. However, non-eligible investors are subject to more restrictive investment limits than eligible investors. The following investment limits apply: • For a non-eligible investor that is an individual, the purchase price for all securities purchased under the exemption in the preceding 12 months cannot be more than $10,000. • For an eligible investor that is an individual, the purchase price for all securities purchased under the exemption in the preceding 12 months cannot be more than $30,000. • For an eligible investor that is an individual that receives advice from a portfolio manager, investment dealer or exempt market dealer that an investment above $30,000 is suitable, the price for all the securities purchased by the investor under the exemption in the preceding 12 months cannot be more than $100,000.

Table 7: Overview of the OM Prospectus Exemption in Ontario	
	There are no investment limits for individual investors that are accredited investors or qualify under the FFBA exemption. There are also no investment limits for investors that are not individuals, such as companies.
Is a risk acknowledgement form required?	YES. All investors must complete and sign a risk acknowledgment form. In addition, individual investors must complete two schedules in conjunction with the form: • One schedule asks investors to confirm their status, as an eligible investor, non-eligible investor, accredited investor or an investor who would qualify under the FFBA exemption. • The other schedule requires confirmation that that the investor is within the investment limits, where applicable.
Is disclosure required to be provided to investors at the point of sale?	YES. An OM in the required form must be provided to investors. Any marketing materials used by the company must also be incorporated by reference in the OM.
Do investors have the right to withdraw from the investment after buying the securities?	YES. Investors have the right to withdraw from an agreement to buy the securities within two business days.
Are the securities subject to restrictions the first time they are resold?	YES. Securities of a public company are subject to a 4-month hold period (subject to certain other conditions being met). Securities of a non-public company are subject to an indefinite hold period and can only be resold under another prospectus exemption or under a prospectus.
Does a report of exempt distribution have to be filed with the OSC?	YES. A report of exempt distribution must be filed within 10 days of the distribution.

Notes:

5   Under the OM exemption, an investor can qualify as an eligible investor under certain income and asset tests. For example, an eligible investor includes a person whose:

   • Net assets, alone or with a spouse, in the case of an individual, exceeds $400,000

   • Net income before taxes exceeded $75,000 in each of the two most recent calendar years and who reasonably expects to exceed that level in the current calendar year

   • Net income before taxes, alone or with a spouse, in the case of an individual, exceeded $125,000 in each of the two most recent calendar years and who reasonably expects to exceed that income level in the current calendar year.

Table 8: Overview of the Rights Offering Prospectus Exemption in Ontario	
What is the purpose of the exemption?	Allows public companies to quickly and cost-effectively raise funds from existing security holders holding securities of the company.
Who can use the exemption?	Public companies. Investment funds subject to National Instrument 81-102 *Investment Funds* cannot use the exemption.
Who can buy securities under the exemption?	Rights to purchase a security issued by the company are distributed to each security holder on a pro rata basis.[6] Rights holders may exercise their right to acquire the security.
Are there limits on how much investors can invest under the exemption?	NO

Table 8: Overview of the Rights Offering Prospectus Exemption in Ontario

Is a risk acknowledgment form required?	NO
Is disclosure required to be provided to investors at the point of sale?	YES. A rights offering circular in a question and answer format must be filed on SEDAR and a rights offering notice must be sent to investors and filed on SEDAR informing them about how to access the rights offering circular electronically.
Do investors have the right to withdraw from the investment after buying the securities?	NO
Are the securities subject to restrictions the first time they are resold?	Securities are only subject to a seasoning period on resale and are therefore generally freely tradeable.
Does a report of exempt distribution have to be filed with the OSC?	NO

Notes:

6   This means that the company must offer the rights to all security holders holding securities of that class.

National Instrument 45-106 — Prospectus Exemptions

Date: September 14, 2005, as amended effective January 6, 2006, December 31, 2007; replaced effective September 28, 2009, as amended effective January 1, 2011, May 6, 2011, June 30, 2011, October 3, 2011 (B.C. only), May 31, 2013, September 22, 2014, May 5, 2015, June 25, 2015, November 17, 2015, December 3, 2015, January 13, 2016; and June 30, 2016.

28 O.S.C.B. (Supp-4) 3, 29 O.S.C.B. 75, 30 O.S.C.B. 10522, 32 O.S.C.B. (Supp. 5) 1, 33 O.S.C.B. (Supp. 5) 111, 34 O.S.C.B. 5171, 34 O.S.C.B. 7085, 35 O.S.C.B. 3589, 36 O.S.C.B. 2619, 37 O.S.C.B. (Supp 4), 38 O.S.C.B. (Supp 1), 38 O.S.C.B. 5801, 38 O.S.C.B. 7551, 38 O.S.C.B. (Supp. 3) 12 and 39 O.S.C.B. 3286.

[This version of the Instrument reflects changes scheduled to come into force on June 30, 2016. For a version of this Instrument without those changes, please see the 59th ed.]

Text boxes in this Instrument located above sections 2.1 to 2.5, 2.7 to 2.21, 2.24, 2.26, 2.27, and 2.30 to 2.43 refer to National Instrument 45-102 Resale of Securities. These text boxes do not form part of this Instrument.

Text boxes in this Instrument located below the definition of "accredited investor" in section 1.1 and below sections 2.3, 2.4, 2.34, 2.36, 2.37 and 2.41 refer to the Securities Act (Ontario). These text boxes do not form part of this Instrument. [Editor's note: The text boxes are shown in bold italics.]

PART 1 — DEFINITIONS AND INTERPRETATION

1.1 Definitions — In this Instrument

"accredited investor" means

(a) except in Ontario, a Canadian financial institution, or a Schedule III bank,

(b) except in Ontario, the Business Development Bank of Canada incorporated under the *Business Development Bank of Canada Act* (Canada),

(c) except in Ontario, a subsidiary of any person referred to in paragraphs (a) or (b), if the person owns all of the voting securities of the subsidiary, except the voting securities required by law to be owned by directors of that subsidiary,

(d) except in Ontario, a person registered under the securities legislation of a jurisdiction of Canada as an adviser or dealer,

(e) an individual registered under the securities legislation of a jurisdiction of Canada as a representative of a person referred to in paragraph (d),

(e.1) an individual formerly registered under the securities legislation of a jurisdiction of Canada, other than an individual formerly registered solely as a representative of a limited market dealer under one or both of the *Securities Act* (Ontario) or the *Securities Act* (Newfoundland and Labrador),

(f) except in Ontario, the Government of Canada or a jurisdiction of Canada, or any crown corporation, agency or wholly owned entity of the Government of Canada or a jurisdiction of Canada,

(g) except in Ontario, a municipality, public board or commission in Canada and a metropolitan community, school board, the Comité de gestion de la taxe scolaire de l'île de Montréal or an intermunicipal management board in Québec,

(h) except in Ontario, any national, federal, state, provincial, territorial or municipal government of or in any foreign jurisdiction, or any agency of that government,

(i) except in Ontario, a pension fund that is regulated by the Office of the Superintendent of Financial Institutions (Canada), a pension commission or similar regulatory authority of a jurisdiction of Canada,

(j) an individual who, either alone or with a spouse, beneficially owns financial assets having an aggregate realizable value that, before taxes but net of any related liabilities, exceeds $1 000 000,

(j.1) an individual who beneficially owns financial assets having an aggregate realizable value that, before taxes but net of any related liabilities, exceeds $5 000 000,

(k) an individual whose net income before taxes exceeded $200 000 in each of the 2 most recent calendar years or whose net income before taxes combined with that of a spouse exceeded $300 000 in each of the 2 most recent calendar years and who, in either case, reasonably expects to exceed that net income level in the current calendar year,

(l) an individual who, either alone or with a spouse, has net assets of at least $5 000 000,

(m) a person, other than an individual or investment fund, that has net assets of at least $5 000 000 as shown on its most recently prepared financial statements,

(n) an investment fund that distributes or has distributed its securities only to

(i) a person that is or was an accredited investor at the time of the distribution,

(ii) a person that acquires or acquired securities in the circumstances referred to in sections 2.10 [*Minimum amount investment*], or 2.19 [*Additional investment in investment funds*], or

(iii) a person described in paragraph (i) or (ii) that acquires or acquired securities under section 2.18 [*Investment fund reinvestment*],

(o) an investment fund that distributes or has distributed securities under a prospectus in a jurisdiction of Canada for which the regulator or, in Québec, the securities regulatory authority, has issued a receipt,

(p) a trust company or trust corporation registered or authorized to carry on business under the *Trust and Loan Companies Act* (Canada) or under comparable legislation in a jurisdiction of Canada or a foreign jurisdiction, acting on behalf of a fully managed account managed by the trust company or trust corporation, as the case may be,

(q) a person acting on behalf of a fully managed account managed by that person, if that person is registered or authorized to carry on business as an adviser or the equivalent under the securities legislation of a jurisdiction of Canada or a foreign jurisdiction,

(r) a registered charity under the *Income Tax Act* (Canada) that, in regard to the trade, has obtained advice from an eligibility adviser or an adviser registered under the securities legislation of the jurisdiction of the registered charity to give advice on the securities being traded,

(s) an entity organized in a foreign jurisdiction that is analogous to any of the entities referred to in paragraphs (a) to (d) or paragraph (i) in form and function,

(t) a person in respect of which all of the owners of interests, direct, indirect or beneficial, except the voting securities required by law to be owned by directors, are persons that are accredited investors,

(u) an investment fund that is advised by a person registered as an adviser or a person that is exempt from registration as an adviser,

(v) a person that is recognized or designated by the securities regulatory authority or, except in Ontario and Québec, the regulator as an accredited investor, or

(w) a trust established by an accredited investor for the benefit of the accredited investor's family members of which a majority of the trustees are accredited investors and all of the beneficiaries are the accredited investor's spouse, a former spouse of the accredited investor or a parent, grandparent, brother, sister, child or grandchild of that accredited investor, of that accredited investor's spouse or of that accredited investor's former spouse;

In Ontario, paragraphs (a) to (h) of subsection 73.3(1) of the Securities Act (Ontario) correspond to paragraphs (a) to (d) and paragraphs (f) to (i) of the definition of "accredited investor" in section 1.1 of this Instrument.

"acquisition date" has the same meaning as in the issuer's GAAP;

"AIF" means

(a) an AIF as defined in National Instrument 51-102 *Continuous Disclosure Obligations*,

(b) a prospectus filed in a jurisdiction, other than a prospectus filed under a CPC instrument, if the issuer has not filed or been required to file an AIF or annual financial statements under National Instrument 51-102 *Continuous Disclosure Obligations*, or

(c) a QT circular if the issuer has not filed or been required to file annual financial statements under National Instrument 51-102 *Continuous Disclosure Obligations* subsequent to filing a QT circular;

"asset pool" means a pool of cash-flow generating assets in which an issuer of a securitized product has a direct or indirect ownership or security interest;

"asset transaction" means a transaction or series of transactions in which a conduit acquires a direct or indirect ownership or security interest in an asset pool in connection with issuing a short-term securitized product;

"bank" means a bank named in Schedule I or II of the *Bank Act* (Canada);

"Canadian financial institution" means

(a) an association governed by the *Cooperative Credit Associations Act* (Canada) or a central cooperative credit society for which an order has been made under section 473(1) of that Act, or

(b) a bank, loan corporation, trust company, trust corporation, insurance company, treasury branch, credit union, caisse populaire, financial services cooperative, or league that, in each case, is authorized by an enactment of Canada or a jurisdiction of Canada to carry on business in Canada or a jurisdiction of Canada;

"conduit" means an issuer of a short-term securitized product

(a) created to conduct one or more asset transactions, and

(b) in respect of which it is reasonable for the issuer to expect that, in the event of a bankruptcy or insolvency proceeding under the *Bankruptcy and Insolvency Act* (Canada), the *Companies Creditors' Arrangement Act* (Canada) or a proceeding under similar legislation in Canada, a jurisdiction of Canada or a foreign jurisdiction,

(i) none of the assets in an asset pool of the issuer in which the issuer has an ownership interest will be consolidated with the assets of a third party that transferred or participated in the transfer of assets to the issuer prior to satisfaction in full of all securitized products that are backed in whole or in part by the assets transferred by the third party, or

(ii) for the assets in an asset pool of the issuer in which the issuer has a security interest, the issuer will realize against the assets in that asset pool in priority to the claims of other persons;

"CPC instrument" means a rule, regulation or policy of the TSX Venture Exchange Inc. that applies only to capital pool companies, and, in Québec, includes Policy Statement 41-601Q, Capital Pool Companies;

"credit enhancement" means a method used to reduce the credit risk of a series or class of securitized product;

"debt security" means any bond, debenture, note or similar instrument representing indebtedness, whether secured or unsecured;

"designated rating" has the same meaning as in National Instrument 81-102 *Investment Funds*;

"designated rating organization" has the same meaning as in National Instrument 81-102 *Investment Funds*;

"director" means

(a) a member of the board of directors of a company or an individual who performs similar functions for a company, and

(b) with respect to a person that is not a company, an individual who performs functions similar to those of a director of a company;

"DRO affiliate" has the same meaning as in section 1 of National Instrument 25-101 *Designated Rating Organizations*;

"eligibility adviser" means

    (a) a person that is registered as an investment dealer and authorized to give advice with respect to the type of security being distributed, and

    (b) in Manitoba, also means a lawyer who is a practicing member in good standing with a law society of a jurisdiction of Canada or a public accountant who is a member in good standing of an institute or association of chartered accountants, certified general accountants or certified management accountants in a jurisdiction of Canada provided that the lawyer or public accountant must not

        (i) have a professional, business or personal relationship with the issuer, or any of its directors, executive officers, founders, or control persons, and

        (ii) have acted for or been retained personally or otherwise as an employee, executive officer, director, associate or partner of a person that has acted for or been retained by the issuer or any of its directors, executive officers, founders or control persons within the previous 12 months;

"eligible investor" means

    (a) a person whose

        (i) net assets, alone or with a spouse, in the case of an individual, exceed $400 000,

        (ii) net income before taxes exceeded $75 000 in each of the 2 most recent calendar years and who reasonably expects to exceed that income level in the current calendar year, or

        (iii) net income before taxes, alone or with a spouse, in the case of an individual, exceeded $125 000 in each of the 2 most recent calendar years and who reasonably expects to exceed that income level in the current calendar year,

    (b) a person of which a majority of the voting securities are beneficially owned by eligible investors or a majority of the directors are eligible investors,

    (c) a general partnership of which all of the partners are eligible investors,

    (d) a limited partnership of which the majority of the general partners are eligible investors,

    (e) a trust or estate in which all of the beneficiaries or a majority of the trustees or executors are eligible investors,

    (f) an accredited investor,

    (g) a person described in section 2.5 [*Family, friends and business associates*], or

    (h) in Manitoba, Northwest Territories, Nunavut, Prince Edward Island and Yukon, a person that has obtained advice regarding the suitability of the investment and, if the person is resident in a jurisdiction of Canada, that advice has been obtained from an eligibility adviser;

"executive officer" means, for an issuer, an individual who is

    (a) a chair, vice-chair or president,

    (b) a vice-president in charge of a principal business unit, division or function including sales, finance or production, or

    (c) performing a policy-making function in respect of the issuer;

"financial assets" means

    (a) cash,

    (b) securities, or

    (c) a contract of insurance, a deposit or an evidence of a deposit that is not a security for the purposes of securities legislation;

"financial statements" includes interim financial reports;

"founder" means, in respect of an issuer, a person who,

    (a) acting alone, in conjunction, or in concert with one or more persons, directly or indirectly, takes the initiative in founding, organizing or substantially reorganizing the business of the issuer, and

    (b) at the time of the distribution or trade is actively involved in the business of the issuer;

"fully managed account" means an account of a client for which a person makes the investment decisions if that person has full discretion to trade in securities for the account without requiring the client's express consent to a transaction;

"investment fund" has the same meaning as in National Instrument 81-106 *Investment Fund Continuous Disclosure*;

"issuer's GAAP" has the same meaning as in National Instrument 52-107 *Acceptable Accounting Principles and Auditing Standards*;

"liquidity provider" means a person that is obligated to provide funds to a conduit to enable the conduit to pay principal or interest in respect of a maturing securitized product;

"marketplace" has the same meaning as in National Instrument 21-101 *Marketplace Operation*;

"MD&A" has the same meaning as in National Instrument 51-102 *Continuous Disclosure Obligations*;

"non-redeemable investment fund" has the same meaning as in National Instrument 81-106 *Investment Fund Continuous Disclosure*;

"person" includes

    (a) an individual,

    (b) a corporation,

    (c) a partnership, trust, fund and an association, syndicate, organization or other organized group of persons, whether incorporated or not, and

    (d) an individual or other person in that person's capacity as a trustee, executor, administrator or personal or other legal representative;

"private enterprise" has the same meaning as in Part 3 of National Instrument 52-107 *Acceptable Accounting Principles and Auditing Standards*;

"publicly accountable enterprise" has the same meaning as in Part 3 of National Instrument 52-107 *Acceptable Accounting Principles and Auditing Standards*;

"QT circular" means an information circular or filing statement in respect of a qualifying transaction for a capital pool company filed under a CPC instrument;

"qualifying issuer" means a reporting issuer in a jurisdiction of Canada that

    (a) is a SEDAR filer,

    (b) has filed all documents required to be filed under the securities legislation of that jurisdiction, and

    (c) if not required to file an AIF, has filed in the jurisdiction,

        (i) an AIF for its most recently completed financial year for which annual statements are required to be filed, and

        (ii) copies of all material incorporated by reference in the AIF not previously filed;

"related liabilities" means

    (a) liabilities incurred or assumed for the purpose of financing the acquisition or ownership of financial assets, or

    (b) liabilities that are secured by financial assets;

"retrospective" has the same meaning as in Canadian GAAP applicable to publicly accountable enterprises;

"retrospectively" has the same meaning as in Canadian GAAP applicable to publicly accountable enterprises;

"RRIF" means a registered retirement income fund as defined in the *Income Tax Act* (Canada);

"RRSP" means a registered retirement savings plan as defined in the *Income Tax Act* (Canada);

"Schedule III bank" means an authorized foreign bank named in Schedule III of the *Bank Act* (Canada);

"securitized product" means a security that

    (a) is governed by a trust indenture or similar agreement setting out the rights and protections applicable to a holder of the security,

    (b) provides a holder with a direct or indirect ownership or security interest in one or more asset pools, and

    (c) entitles a holder to one or more payments of principal or interest primarily obtained from one or more of the following:

        (i) the proceeds from the distribution of securitized products;

        (ii) the cash flows generated by one or more asset pools

        (iii) the proceeds obtained on the liquidation of one or more assets in one or more asset pools;

"SEDAR filer" means an issuer that is an electronic filer under National Instrument 13-101 *System for Electronic Document Analysis and Retrieval (SEDAR)*;

"self-directed RESP" means an educational savings plan registered under the *Income Tax Act* (Canada)

    (a) that is structured so that a contribution by a subscriber to the plan is deposited directly into an account in the name of the subscriber, and

    (b) under which the subscriber maintains control and direction over the plan to direct how the assets of the plan are to be held, invested or reinvested subject to compliance with the *Income Tax Act* (Canada).

"short-term securitized product" means a securitized product that is a negotiable promissory note or commercial paper that matures not more than one year from the date of issue;

"spouse" means, an individual who,

    (a) is married to another individual and is not living separate and apart within the meaning of the *Divorce Act* (Canada), from the other individual,

    (b) is living with another individual in a marriage-like relationship, including a marriage-like relationship between individuals of the same gender, or

    (c) in Alberta, is an individual referred to in paragraph (a) or (b), or is an adult interdependent partner within the meaning of the *Adult Interdependent Relationships Act* (Alberta);

"subsidiary" means an issuer that is controlled directly or indirectly by another issuer and includes a subsidiary of that subsidiary;

"TFSA" means a tax-free savings account as described in the *Income Tax Act* (Canada).

1.1.1 In this Instrument, in Alberta, New Brunswick, Nova Scotia, Ontario, Québec and Saskatchewan

"date of transition to IFRS" has the same meaning as in National Instrument 51-102 *Continuous Disclosure Obligations*;

"exempt market dealer" has the same meaning as in National Instrument 31-103 *Registration Requirements, Exemptions and Ongoing Registrant Obligations*;

"first IFRS financial statements" has the same meaning as in National Instrument 51-102 *Continuous Disclosure Obligations*;

"investment dealer" has the same meaning as in National Instrument 31-103 *Registration Requirements, Exemptions and Ongoing Registrant Obligations*;

"new financial year" means the financial year of an issuer that immediately follows a transition year;

"old financial year" means the financial year of an issuer that immediately precedes a transition year;

"OM marketing materials" means a written communication, other than an OM standard term sheet, intended for prospective purchasers regarding a distribution of securities under an offering memorandum delivered under section 2.9 [*Offering memorandum*] that contains material facts relating to an issuer, securities or an offering;

"OM standard term sheet" means a written communication intended for prospective purchasers regarding a distribution of securities under an offering memorandum delivered under section 2.9 [*Offering memorandum*] that

    (a) is dated,

    (b) includes the following legend, or words to the same effect, on the first page:

        "This document does not provide disclosure of all information required for an investor to make an informed investment decision. Investors should read the offering memorandum, especially the risk factors relating to the securities offered, before making an investment decision.",

Part 4:
DISTRIBUTIONS

(c) contains only the following information in respect of the issuer, the securities or the offering:

    (i) the name of the issuer;

    (ii) the jurisdiction or foreign jurisdiction in which the issuer's head office is located;

    (iii) the statute under which the issuer is incorporated, continued or organized or, if the issuer is an unincorporated entity, the laws of the jurisdiction or foreign jurisdiction under which it is established and exists;

    (iv) a brief description of the business of the issuer;

    (v) a brief description of the securities;

    (vi) the price or price range of the securities;

    (vii) the total number or dollar amount of the securities, or range of the total number or dollar amount of the securities;

    (viii) the names of any agent, finder or other intermediary, whether registered or not, involved with the offering and the amount of any commission, fee or discount payable to them;

    (ix) the proposed or expected closing date of the offering;

    (x) a brief description of the use of proceeds;

    (xi) the exchange on which the securities are proposed to be listed, if any, provided that the OM standard term sheet complies with the requirements of securities legislation for listing representations;

    (xii) in the case of debt securities, the maturity date of the debt securities and a brief description of any interest payable on the debt securities;

    (xiii) in the case of preferred shares, a brief description of any dividends payable on the securities;

    (xiv) in the case of convertible securities, a brief description of the underlying securities into which the convertible securities are convertible;

    (xv) in the case of exchangeable securities, a brief description of the underlying securities into which the exchangeable securities are exchangeable;

    (xvi) in the case of restricted securities, a brief description of the restriction;

    (xvii) in the case of securities for which a credit supporter has provided a guarantee or alternative credit support, a brief description of the credit supporter and the guarantee or alternative credit support provided;

    (xviii) whether the securities are redeemable or retractable;

    (xvix) a statement that the securities are eligible, or are expected to be eligible, for investment in registered retirement savings plans, tax-free savings accounts or other registered plans, if the issuer has received, or reasonably expects to receive, a legal opinion that the securities are so eligible;

    (xx) contact information for the issuer or any registrant involved, and

(d) for the purposes of paragraph (c), "brief description" means a description consisting of no more than three lines of text in type that is at least as large as that used generally in the body of the OM standard term sheet;

"portfolio manager" has the same meaning as in National Instrument 31-103 *Registration Requirements, Exemptions and Ongoing Registrant Obligations*;

"SEC issuer" has the same meaning as in National Instrument 51-102 *Continuous Disclosure Obligations*;

"specified derivative" has the same meaning as in National Instrument 44-102 *Shelf Distributions*;

"structured finance product" has the same meaning as in National Instrument 25-101 *Designated Rating Organizations*;

"transition year" means the financial year of an issuer in which the issuer has changed its financial year end;

"U.S. laws" has the same meaning as in National Instrument 51-102 *Continuous Disclosure Obligations*.

1.2 Interpretation of indirect interest — For the purposes of paragraph (t) of the definition of "accredited investor" in section 1.1, in British Columbia, an indirect interest means an economic interest in the person referred to in that paragraph.

1.3 Affiliate — For the purpose of this Instrument, an issuer is an affiliate of another issuer if

    (a) one of them is the subsidiary of the other, or

    (b) each of them is controlled by the same person.

1.4 Control — Except in Part 2, Division 4, for the purpose of this Instrument, a person (first person) is considered to control another person (second person) if

    (a) the first person beneficially owns or directly or indirectly exercises control or direction over securities of the second person carrying votes which, if exercised, would entitle the first person to elect a majority of the directors of the second person, unless that first person holds the voting securities only to secure an obligation,

    (b) the second person is a partnership, other than a limited partnership, and the first person holds more than 50% of the interests of the partnership, or

    (c) the second person is a limited partnership and the general partner of the limited partnership is the first person.

1.5 Registration requirement — (1) An exemption in this Instrument that refers to a registered dealer is only available for a trade in a security if the dealer is registered in a category that permits the trade described in the exemption.

1.6 Definition of distribution — Manitoba — For the purpose of this Instrument, in Manitoba, "distribution" means a primary distribution to the public.

1.7 Definition of trade — Québec — For the purpose of this Instrument, in Québec, "trade" refers to any of the following activities:

(a) the activities described in the definition of "dealer" in section 5 of the *Securities Act* (R.S.Q., c. V-1.1), including the following activities:

(i) the sale or disposition of a security by onerous title, whether the terms of payment be on margin, installment or otherwise, but does not include a transfer or the giving in guarantee of securities in connection with a debt or the purchase of a security, except as provided in paragraph (b);

(ii) participation as a trader in any transaction in a security through the facilities of an exchange or a quotation and trade reporting system;

(iii) the receipt by a registrant of an order to buy or sell a security;

(b) a transfer or the giving in guarantee of securities of an issuer from the holdings of a control person in connection with a debt.

1.8 Designation of insider — For the purpose of this Instrument, in Ontario, the following classes of persons are designated as insiders:

(a) a director or an officer of an issuer;

(b) a director or an officer of a person that is an insider or a subsidiary of an issuer;

(c) a person that has

(i) beneficial ownership of, or control or direction over, directly or indirectly, securities of an issuer carrying more than 10% of the voting rights attached to all the issuer's outstanding voting securities, excluding, for the purpose of the calculation of the percentage held, any securities held by the person as underwriter in the course of a distribution, or

(ii) a combination of beneficial ownership of, and control or direction over, directly or indirectly, securities of an issuer carrying more than 10% of the voting rights attached to all the issuer's outstanding voting securities, excluding, for the purpose of the calculation of the percentage held, any securities held by the person as underwriter in the course of a distribution;

(d) an issuer that has purchased, redeemed or otherwise acquired a security of its own issue, for so long as it continues to hold that security.

In Ontario, subsection 73.3(2) of the **Securities Act** *(Ontario) provides a similar exemption to the exemption in subsection 2.3(1) of this Instrument.*

PART 2 — PROSPECTUS EXEMPTIONS

DIVISION 1 — CAPITAL RAISING EXEMPTIONS

Rights offering — reporting issuer

Refer to Appendix E of National Instrument 45-102 **Resale of Securities**. *First trades are subject to a seasoning period on resale.*

2.1 (1) In this section and sections 2.1.1, 2.1.2, 2.1.3 and 2.1.4,

"additional subscription privilege" means a privilege, granted to a holder of a right, to subscribe for a security not subscribed for by any holder under a basic subscription privilege;

"basic subscription privilege" means a privilege to subscribe for the number or amount of securities set out in a rights certificate held by the holder of the rights certificate;

"closing date" means the date of completion of the distribution of the securities issued upon exercise of the rights issued under this section;

"listing representation" means a representation that a security will be listed or quoted, or that an application has been or will be made to list or quote the security, either on an exchange or on a quotation and trade reporting system, in a foreign jurisdiction;

"listing representation prohibition" means the provisions of securities legislation set out in Appendix C;

"managing dealer" means a person that has entered into an agreement with an issuer under which the person has agreed to organize and participate in the solicitation of the exercise of the rights issued by the issuer;

"market price" means, for securities of a class for which there is a published market,

(a) except as provided in paragraph (b),

(i) if the published market provides a closing price, the simple average of the closing price of securities of that class on the published market for each of the trading days on which there was a closing price falling not more than 20 trading days immediately before the day as of which the market price is being determined, or

(ii) if the published market does not provide a closing price, but provides only the highest and lowest prices of securities of the class traded, the average of the simple averages of the highest and lowest prices of securities of the class on the published market for each of the trading days on which there were highest and lowest prices falling not more than 20 trading days immediately before the day as of which the market price is being determined, or

(b) if trading of securities of the class on the published market has occurred on fewer than 10 of the immediately preceding 20 trading days, the average of the following amounts established for each of the 20 trading days immediately before the day as of which the market price is being determined:

(i) the average of the closing bid and closing ask prices for each day on which there was no trading;

(ii) if the published market

(A) provides a closing price of securities of the class for each day that there was trading, the closing price, or

(B) provides only the highest and lowest prices, the average of the highest and lowest prices of securities of that class for each day that there was trading;

(c) the issuer has complied with the applicable requirements of National Instrument 45-101 *Rights Offerings*.

"published market" means, for a class of securities, a marketplace on which the securities are traded, if the prices at which they have been traded on that marketplace are regularly

(a) disseminated electronically, or

(b) published in a newspaper or business or financial publication of general and regular paid circulation;

"rights offering circular" means a completed Form 45-106F15 *Rights Offering Circular for Reporting Issuers*;

"rights offering notice" means a completed Form 45-106F14 *Rights Offering Notice for Reporting Issuers*;

"secondary market liability provisions" means the provisions of securities legislation set out in Appendix D opposite the name of the local jurisdiction;

"soliciting dealer" means a person whose interest in a distribution of rights is limited to soliciting the exercise of the rights by holders of those rights;

"stand-by commitment" means an agreement by a person to acquire the securities of an issuer not subscribed for under the basic subscription privilege or the additional subscription privilege;

"stand-by guarantor" means a person who agrees to provide the stand-by commitment.

(2) For the purpose of the definition of "market price", if there is more than one published market for a security and

    (a) only one of the published markets is in Canada, the market price is determined solely by reference to that market,

    (b) more than one of the published markets is in Canada, the market price is determined solely by reference to the published market in Canada on which the greatest volume of trading in the particular class of securities occurred during the 20 trading days immediately before the date as of which the market price is being determined, and

    (c) none of the published markets are in Canada, the market price is determined solely by reference to the published market on which the greatest volume of trading in the particular class of securities occurred during the 20 trading days immediately before the date as of which the market price is being determined.

(3) The prospectus requirement does not apply to a distribution by an issuer, of a right to purchase a security of the issuer's own issue, to a security holder of the issuer if all of the following apply:

    (a) the issuer is a reporting issuer in at least one jurisdiction of Canada;

    (b) if the issuer is a reporting issuer in the local jurisdiction, the issuer has filed all periodic and timely disclosure documents that it is required to have filed in that jurisdiction as required by each of the following:

        (i) applicable securities legislation;

        (ii) an order issued by the regulator or, in Québec, the securities regulatory authority;

        (iii) an undertaking to the regulator or, in Québec, the securities regulatory authority;

    (c) before the commencement of the exercise period for the rights, the issuer files and sends the rights offering notice to all security holders, resident in Canada, of the class of securities to be issued upon exercise of the rights;

    (d) concurrently with filing the rights offering notice, the issuer files a rights offering circular;

    (e) the basic subscription privilege is available on a pro rata basis to the security holders, resident in Canada, of the class of securities to be distributed upon the exercise of the rights;

    (f) in Québec, the documents filed under paragraphs (c) and (d) are prepared in French or in French and English;

    (g) the subscription price for a security to be issued upon the exercise of a right is:

        (i) if there is a published market for the security, lower than the market price of the security on the day the rights offering notice is filed, or

        (ii) if there is no published market for the security, lower than the fair value of the security on the day the rights offering notice is filed unless the issuer restricts all of its insiders from increasing their proportionate interest in the issuer through the exercise of the rights distributed or through a stand-by commitment;

    (h) if the distribution includes an additional subscription privilege, all of the following apply:

        (i) the issuer grants the additional subscription privilege to all holders of the rights;

        (ii) each holder of a right is entitled to receive, upon the exercise of the additional subscription privilege, the number or amount of securities equal to the lesser of

            (A) the number or amount of securities subscribed for by the holder under the additional subscription privilege, and

            (B) the number or amount calculated in accordance with the following formula:

        $x(y/z)$ where

        x = the aggregate number or amount of securities available through unexercised rights after giving effect to the basic subscription privilege;

        y = the number of rights exercised by the holder under the basic subscription privilege;

        z = the aggregate number of rights exercised under the basic subscription privilege by holders of the rights that have subscribed for securities under the additional subscription privilege;

        (iii) all unexercised rights have been allocated on a pro rata basis to holders who subscribed for additional securities under the additional subscription privilege;

        (iv) the subscription price for the additional subscription privilege is the same as the subscription price for the basic subscription privilege;

    (i) if the issuer enters into a stand-by commitment, all of the following apply:

        (i) the issuer has granted an additional subscription privilege to all holders of the rights;

        (ii) the issuer has included a statement in the rights offering circular that the issuer has confirmed that the stand-by guarantor has the financial ability to carry out its stand-by commitment;

        (iii) the subscription price under the stand-by commitment is the same as the subscription price under the basic subscription privilege;

(j) if the issuer has stated in its rights offering circular that no security will be issued upon the exercise of a right unless a stand-by commitment is provided, or unless proceeds of no less than the stated minimum amount are received by the issuer, all of the following apply:

    (i) the issuer has appointed a depository to hold all money received upon the exercise of the rights until either the stand-by commitment is provided or the stated minimum amount is received and the depository is one of the following:

        (A) a Canadian financial institution;

        (B) a registrant in the jurisdiction in which the funds are proposed to be held that is acting as managing dealer for the distribution of the rights or, if there is no managing dealer for the distribution of the rights, that is acting as a soliciting dealer;

    (ii) the issuer and the depository have entered into an agreement, the terms of which require the depository to return the money referred to in subparagraph (i) in full to the holders of rights that have subscribed for securities under the distribution of the rights if the stand-by commitment is not provided or if the stated minimum amount is not received by the depository during the exercise period for the rights;

(k) the rights offering circular contains the following statement:

"There is no material fact or material change about [name of issuer] that has not been generally disclosed".

(4) An issuer must not file an amendment to a rights offering circular filed under paragraph (3)(d) unless

    (a) the amendment amends and restates the rights offering circular,

    (b) the issuer files the amended rights offering circular before the earlier of

        (i) the listing date of the rights, if the issuer lists the rights for trading, and

        (ii) the date the exercise period for the rights commences, and

    (c) the issuer issues and files a news release explaining the reason for the amendment concurrently with the filing of the amended rights offering circular.

(5) On the closing date or as soon as practicable following the closing date, the issuer must issue and file a news release containing all of the following information:

    (a) the aggregate gross proceeds of the distribution;

    (b) the number or amount of securities distributed under the basic subscription privilege to

        (i) all persons who were insiders before the distribution or became insiders as a result of the distribution, as a group, to the knowledge of the issuer after reasonable inquiry, and

        (ii) all other persons, as a group;

    (c) the number or amount of securities distributed under the additional subscription privilege to

        (i) all persons who were insiders before the distribution or became insiders as a result of the distribution, as a group, to the knowledge of the issuer after reasonable inquiry, and

        (ii) all other persons, as a group;

    (d) the number or amount of securities distributed under any stand-by commitment;

    (e) the number or amount of securities of the class issued and outstanding as of the closing date;

    (f) the amount of any fees or commissions paid in connection with the distribution.

(6) Subsection (3) does not apply to a distribution of rights if any of the following apply:

    (a) there would be an increase of more than 100% in the number, or, in the case of debt, the principal amount, of the outstanding securities of the class to be issued upon the exercise of the rights, assuming the exercise of all rights issued under a distribution of rights by the issuer during the 12 months immediately before the date of the rights offering circular;

    (b) the exercise period for the rights is less than 21 days, or more than 90 days, and commences after the day the rights offering notice is sent to security holders;

    (c) the issuer has entered into an agreement that provides for the payment of a fee to a person for soliciting the exercise of rights by holders of rights that were not security holders of the issuer immediately before the distribution under subsection (3) and that fee is higher than the fee payable for soliciting the exercise of rights by holders of rights that were security holders at that time.

Rights offering — stand-by commitment

Refer to Appendix E of National Instrument 45-102 Resale of Securities. *First trades are subject to a seasoning period on resale.*

2.1.1 The prospectus requirement does not apply to the distribution of a security by an issuer to a stand-by guarantor as part of a distribution under section 2.1 if the stand-by guarantor acquires the security as principal.

Rights offering — issuer with a minimal connection to Canada

Refer to Appendix E of National Instrument 45-102 Resale of Securities. *First trades are subject to a seasoning period on resale.*

2.1.2 (1) The prospectus requirement does not apply to a distribution by an issuer, of a right to purchase a security of the issuer's own issue, to a security holder of the issuer if all of the following apply:

    (a) to the knowledge of the issuer after reasonable inquiry,

        (i) the number of beneficial holders of the class for which the rights are issued that are resident in Canada does not constitute 10% or more of all holders of that class, and

        (ii) the number or amount of securities of the issuer of the class for which the rights are issued that are beneficially held by security holders that are resident in Canada does not constitute, in the aggregate, 10% or more of the outstanding securities of that class;

Part 4:
DISTRIBUTIONS

(b) all materials sent to any other security holders for the distribution of the rights are concurrently filed and sent to each security holder of the issuer that is resident in Canada;

(c) the issuer files a written notice that it is relying on this exemption and a certificate that states that, to the knowledge of the person signing the certificate after reasonable inquiry,

(i) the number of beneficial holders of the class for which the rights are issued that are resident in Canada does not constitute 10% or more of all holders of that class, and

(ii) the number or amount of securities of the issuer of the class for which the rights are issued that are beneficially held by security holders that are resident in Canada does not constitute, in the aggregate, 10% or more of the outstanding securities of that class.

(2) For the purposes of paragraph (1)(c), a certificate of an issuer must be signed,

(a) if the issuer is a limited partnership, by an officer or director of the general partner of the issuer,

(b) if the issuer is a trust, by a trustee or officer or director of a trustee of the issuer, or

(c) in any other case, by an officer or director of the issuer.

2.1.3 Rights offering — listing representation exemption — The listing representation prohibition does not apply to a listing representation made in a rights offering circular for a distribution of rights conducted under section 2.1.2 if the listing representation is not a misrepresentation.

2.1.4 Rights offering — civil liability for secondary market disclosure — (1) The secondary market liability provisions apply to

(a) the acquisition of an issuer's security pursuant to the exemption from the prospectus requirement set out in section 2.1, and

(b) the acquisition of an issuer's security pursuant to the exemption from the prospectus requirement set out in section 2.42 if the security previously issued by the issuer was acquired pursuant to the exemption set out in section 2.1.

(2) For greater certainty, in British Columbia, the classes of acquisitions referred to in subsection (1) are prescribed classes of acquisitions under paragraph 140.2(b) of the *Securities Act* (British Columbia).

Reinvestment plan

Refer to Appendix E of National Instrument 45-102** Resale of Securities. **First trades are subject to a seasoning period on resale.

2.2 (1) Subject to subsections (3), (4) and (5), the prospectus requirement does not apply to the following distributions by an issuer, or by a trustee, custodian or administrator acting for or on behalf of the issuer, to a security holder of the issuer if the distributions are permitted by a plan of the issuer:

(a) a distribution of a security of the issuer's own issue if a dividend or distribution out of earnings, surplus, capital or other sources payable in respect of the issuer's securities is applied to the purchase of the security, and

(b) subject to subsection (2), a distribution of a security of the issuer's own issue if the security holder makes an optional cash payment to purchase the security of the issuer that trades on a marketplace.

(2) Subsection (1) does not apply unless the aggregate number of securities issued under the optional cash payment referred to in subsection (1)(b) does not exceed, in the financial year of the issuer during which the distribution takes place, 2% of the issued and outstanding securities of the class to which the plan relates as at the beginning of the financial year.

(3) A plan that permits a distribution described in subsection (1)(a) or (b) must be available to every security holder in Canada to which the dividend or distribution out of earnings, surplus, capital or other sources is available.

(4) Subsection (1) does not apply to a distribution of a security of an investment fund.

(5) If the security distributed under a plan described in subsection (1) is of a different class or series than the class or series of the security to which the dividend or distribution is attributable, the issuer or the trustee, custodian or administrator must have provided to each participant that is eligible to receive a security under the plan either a description of the material attributes and characteristics of the security distributed under the plan or notice of a source from which the participant can obtain the information without charge.

Accredited investor

Refer to Appendix D of National Instrument 45-102** Resale of Securities. **First trades are subject to a restricted period on resale.

2.3 (0.1) In this section, "accredited investor exemption" means

(a) in a jurisdiction other than Ontario, the prospectus exemption under subsection (1), and

(b) in Ontario, the prospectus exemption under subsection 73.3(2) of the *Securities Act* (Ontario).

(1) The prospectus requirement does not apply to a distribution of a security if the purchaser purchases the security as principal and is an accredited investor.

(2) Subject to subsection (3), for the purpose of the accredited investor exemption, a trust company or trust corporation described in paragraph (p) of the definition of "accredited investor" in section 1.1 [*Definitions*] is deemed to be purchasing as principal.

(3) Subsection (2) does not apply to a trust company or trust corporation registered under the laws of Prince Edward Island that is not registered or authorized under the *Trust and Loan Companies Act* (Canada) or under comparable legislation in another jurisdiction of Canada.

(4) For the purpose of the accredited investor exemption, a person described in paragraph (q) of the definition of "accredited investor" in section 1.1 [*Definitions*] is deemed to be purchasing as principal.

(5) The accredited investor exemption does not apply to a distribution of a security to a person if the person was created, or is used, solely to purchase or hold securities as an accredited investor described in paragraph (m) of the definition of "accredited investor" in section 1.1 [*Definitions*].

(6) The accredited investor exemption does not apply to a distribution of a security to an individual described in paragraphs (j), (k) or (l) of the definition of "accredited investor" in section 1.1 [*Definitions*] unless the person distributing the security obtains from the individual a signed risk acknowledgement in the required form at the same time or before that individual signs the agreement to purchase the security.

(7) A person relying on the accredited investor exemption to distribute a security to an individual described in paragraphs (j), (k) or (l) of the definition of "accredited investor" in section 1.1 [*Definitions*] must retain the signed risk acknowledgement required in subsection (6) of this section for 8 years after the distribution.

(8) Subsection (1) does not apply in Ontario.

In Ontario, subsection 73.3(2) of the **Securities Act (Ontario)** *provides a similar exemption to the exemption in subsection 2.3(1) of this Instrument.*

Private issuer

Refer to Appendix E of National Instrument 45-102 **Resale of Securities.** *First trades are subject to a seasoning period on resale.*

2.4 (1) In this section,

"private issuer" means an issuer

(a) that is not a reporting issuer or an investment fund,

(b) the securities of which, other than non-convertible debt securities,

(i) are subject to restrictions on transfer that are contained in the issuer's constating documents or security holders' agreements, and

(ii) are beneficially owned by not more than 50 persons, not including employees and former employees of the issuer or its affiliates, provided that each person is counted as one beneficial owner unless the person is created or used solely to purchase or hold securities of the issuer in which case each beneficial owner or each beneficiary of the person, as the case may be, must be counted as a separate beneficial owner, and

(c) that

(i) has distributed its securities only to persons described in subsection (2), or

(ii) has completed a transaction and immediately following the completion of the transaction, its securities were beneficially owned only by persons described in subsection (2) and since the completion of the transaction has distributed its securities only to persons described in subsection (2).

(2) The prospectus requirement does not apply to a distribution of a security of a private issuer to a person who purchases the security as principal and is

(a) a director, officer, employee, founder or control person of the issuer,

(b) a director, officer or employee of an affiliate of the issuer,

(c) a spouse, parent, grandparent, brother, sister, child or grandchild of a director, executive officer, founder or control person of the issuer,

(d) a parent, grandparent, brother, sister, child or grandchild of the spouse of a director, executive officer, founder or control person of the issuer,

(e) a close personal friend of a director, executive officer, founder or control person of the issuer,

(f) a close business associate of a director, executive officer, founder or control person of the issuer,

(g) a spouse, parent, grandparent, brother, sister, child or grandchild of the selling security holder or of the selling security holder's spouse,

(h) a security holder of the issuer,

(i) an accredited investor,

(j) a person of which a majority of the voting securities are beneficially owned by, or a majority of the directors are, persons described in paragraphs (a) to (i),

(k) a trust or estate of which all of the beneficiaries or a majority of the trustees or executors are persons described in paragraphs (a) to (i), or

(l) a person that is not the public.

(2.1) The following persons are prescribed for purposes of subsection 73.4(2) of the *Securities Act* (Ontario):

(a) a director, officer, employee, founder or control person of the issuer,

(b) a director, officer or employee of an affiliate of the issuer,

(c) a spouse, parent, grandparent, brother, sister, child or grandchild of a director, executive officer, founder or control person of the issuer,

(d) a parent, grandparent, brother, sister, child or grandchild of the spouse of a director, executive officer, founder or control person of the issuer,

(e) a close personal friend of a director, executive officer, founder or control person of the issuer,

(f) a close business associate of a director, executive officer, founder or control person of the issuer,

(g) a spouse, parent, grandparent, brother, sister, child or grandchild of the selling security holder or of the selling security holder's spouse,

(h) a security holder of the issuer,

(i) an accredited investor,

(j) a person of which a majority of the voting securities are beneficially owned by, or a majority of the directors are, persons described in paragraphs (a) to (i),

(k) a trust or estate of which all of the beneficiaries or a majority of the trustees or executors are persons described in paragraphs (a) to (i), or

(l) a person that is not the public.

(3) Except for a distribution to an accredited investor, no commission or finder's fee may be paid to any director, officer, founder or control person of an issuer in connection with a distribution under subsection (2) or, in Ontario, a distribution under subsection 73.4(2) of the *Securities Act* (Ontario).

(4) Subsection (2) does not apply to a distribution of a short-term securitized product.

(5) Subsection (2) does not apply in Ontario.

In Ontario, subsection 73.4(2) of the **Securities Act** *(Ontario) provides a similar exemption to the exemption in subsection 2.4(2) of this Instrument.*

Family, friends and business associates

Refer to Appendix D of National Instrument 45-102 **Resale of Securities**. *First trades are subject to a restricted period on resale.*

2.5 (1) Subject to section 2.6 [*Family, friends and business associates — Saskatchewan*] and section 2.6.1 [*Family, friends and business associates — Ontario*], the prospectus requirement does not apply to a distribution of a security to a person who purchases the security as principal and is

    (a) a director, executive officer or control person of the issuer, or of an affiliate of the issuer,

    (b) a spouse, parent, grandparent, brother, sister, child or grandchild of a director, executive officer or control person of the issuer, or of an affiliate of the issuer,

    (c) a parent, grandparent, brother, sister, child or grandchild of the spouse of a director, executive officer or control person of the issuer or of an affiliate of the issuer,

    (d) a close personal friend of a director, executive officer or control person of the issuer, or of an affiliate of the issuer,

    (e) a close business associate of a director, executive officer or control person of the issuer, or of an affiliate of the issuer,

    (f) a founder of the issuer or a spouse, parent, grandparent, brother, sister, child, grandchild, close personal friend or close business associate of a founder of the issuer,

    (g) a parent, grandparent, brother, sister, child or grandchild of a spouse of a founder of the issuer,

    (h) a person of which a majority of the voting securities are beneficially owned by, or a majority of the directors are, persons described in paragraphs (a) to (g), or

    (i) a trust or estate of which all of the beneficiaries or a majority of the trustees or executors are persons described in paragraphs (a) to (g).

(2) No commission or finder's fee may be paid to any director, officer, founder, or control person of an issuer or an affiliate of the issuer in connection with a distribution under subsection (1).

(3) Subsection (1) does not apply to a distribution of a short-term securitized product or, in Ontario, a distribution under subsection 73.4(2) of the *Securities Act* (Ontario).

Family, friends and business associates — Saskatchewan

2.6 (1) In Saskatchewan, section 2.5 [*Family, friends and business associates*] does not apply unless the person making the distribution obtains a signed risk acknowledgement from the purchaser in the required form for a distribution to

    (a) a person described in section 2.5(1) (d) or (e) [*Family, friends and business associates*],

    (b) a close personal friend or close business associate of a founder of the issuer, or

    (c) a person described in section 2.5(1)(h) or (i) [*Family, friends and business associates*] if the distribution is based in whole or in part on a close personal friendship or close business association.

(2) The person making the distribution must retain the required form referred to in subsection (1) for 8 years after the distribution.

(3) Subsection (1) does not apply to a distribution of a short-term securitized product.

Family, friends and business associates — Ontario

2.6.1 (1) In Ontario, section 2.5 [*Family, friends and business associates*] does not apply to a distribution of a security of an issuer unless all of the following are satisfied:

    (a) the issuer is not an investment fund;

    (b) the person making the distribution obtains a risk acknowledgement signed by all of the following:

        (i) the purchaser;

        (ii) an executive officer of the issuer other than the purchaser;

        (iii) if the purchaser is a person referred to under paragraph 2.5(1)(b), the director, executive officer or control person of the issuer or an affiliate of the issuer who has the specified relationship with the purchaser;

        (iv) if the purchaser is a person referred to under paragraph 2.5(1)(c), the director, executive officer or control person of the issuer or an affiliate of the issuer whose spouse has the specified relationship with the purchaser;

        (v) if the purchaser is a person referred to under paragraph 2.5(1)(d) or (e), the director, executive officer or control person of the issuer or an affiliate of the issuer who is a close personal friend or a close business associate of the purchaser; and

        (vi) the founder of the issuer, if the purchaser is a person referred to in paragraph 2.5(1)(f) or (g) other than the founder of the issuer.

(2) The person making the distribution must retain the required form referred to in subsection (1) for 8 years after the distribution.

Founder, control person and family — Ontario

2.7 [Repealed.]

Affiliates

Refer to Appendix D of National Instrument 45-102 Resale of Securities. *First trades are subject to a restricted period on resale.*

2.8 The prospectus requirement does not apply to a distribution by an issuer of a security of its own issue to an affiliate of the issuer that is purchasing as principal.

Offering memorandum

Refer to Appendix D of National Instrument 45-102 Resale of Securities. *First trades are subject to a restricted period on resale.*

2.9 (1) In British Columbia and Newfoundland and Labrador, the prospectus requirement does not apply to a distribution by an issuer of a security of its own issue to a purchaser if

(a) the purchaser purchases the security as principal, and

(b) at the same time or before the purchaser signs the agreement to purchase the security, the issuer

(i) delivers an offering memorandum to the purchaser in compliance with subsections (5) to (13), and

(ii) obtains a signed risk acknowledgement from the purchaser in compliance with subsection (15).

(2) In Manitoba, Northwest Territories, Nunavut, Prince Edward Island and Yukon, the prospectus requirement does not apply to a distribution by an issuer of a security of its own issue to a purchaser if

(a) the purchaser purchases the security as principal,

(b) the purchaser is an eligible investor or the acquisition cost to the purchaser does not exceed $10 000,

(c) at the same time or before the purchaser signs the agreement to purchase the security, the issuer

(i) delivers an offering memorandum to the purchaser in compliance with subsections (5) to (13), and

(ii) obtains a signed risk acknowledgement from the purchaser in compliance with subsection (15), and

(d) if the issuer is an investment fund, the investment fund is

(i) a non-redeemable investment fund, or

(ii) a mutual fund that is a reporting issuer.

(2.1) In Alberta, New Brunswick, Nova Scotia, Ontario, Québec and Saskatchewan, the prospectus requirement does not apply to a distribution by an issuer of a security of its own issue to a purchaser if

(a) the purchaser purchases the security as principal,

(b) the acquisition cost of all securities acquired by a purchaser who is an individual under this section in the preceding 12 months does not exceed the following amounts:

(i) in the case of a purchaser that is not an eligible investor, $10 000;

(ii) in the case of a purchaser that is an eligible investor, $30 000;

(iii) in the case of a purchaser that is an eligible investor and that received advice from a portfolio manager, investment dealer or exempt market dealer that the investment is suitable, $100 000,

(c) at the same time or before the purchaser signs the agreement to purchase the security, the issuer

(i) delivers an offering memorandum to the purchaser in compliance with subsections (5) to (13), and

(ii) obtains a signed risk acknowledgement from the purchaser in compliance with subsection (15), and

(d) the security distributed by the issuer is not either of the following:

(i) a specified derivative;

(ii) a structured finance product.

(2.2) The prospectus exemption described in subsection (2.1) is not available

(a) in Alberta, Nova Scotia and Saskatchewan, to an issuer that is an investment fund, unless the issuer is a non-redeemable investment fund or a mutual fund that is a reporting issuer, or

(b) in New Brunswick, Ontario and Québec, to an issuer that is an investment fund.

(2.3) The investment limits described in subparagraphs (2.1)(b)(ii) and (iii) do not apply if the purchaser is

(a) an accredited investor,

(b) a person described in subsection 2.5(1) [*Family, friends and business associates*].

(3) In Manitoba, Northwest Territories, Nunavut, Prince Edward Island and Yukon, this section does not apply to a distribution of a security to a person described in paragraph (a) of the definition of "eligible investor" in section 1.1 [*Definitions*] if that person was created, or is used, solely to purchase or hold securities in reliance on the exemption from the prospectus requirement set out in subsection (2).

(3.0.1) In Alberta, New Brunswick, Nova Scotia, Ontario, Québec and Saskatchewan, this section does not apply to a distribution of a security to a person that was created, or is used, solely to purchase or hold securities in reliance on the exemption from the prospectus requirement set out in subsection (2.1).

(3.1) Subsections (1), (2) and (2.1) do not apply to a distribution of a short-term securitized product.

(4) No commission or finder's fee may be paid to any person, other than a registered dealer, in connection with a distribution to a purchaser in the Northwest Territories, Nunavut and Yukon under subsection (2).

(5) An offering memorandum delivered under this section must be in the required form.

(5.1) In Alberta, New Brunswick, Nova Scotia, Ontario, Québec and Saskatchewan, an offering memorandum delivered under subsection (2.1)

    (a) must incorporate by reference, by way of a statement in the offering memorandum, OM marketing materials related to each distribution under the offering memorandum and delivered or made reasonably available to a prospective purchaser before the termination of the distribution, and

    (b) is deemed to incorporate by reference OM marketing materials related to each distribution under the offering memorandum and delivered or made reasonably available to a prospective purchaser before the termination of the distribution.

(5.2) A portfolio manager, investment dealer or exempt market dealer must not distribute OM marketing materials unless the OM marketing materials have been approved in writing by the issuer.

(6) If the securities legislation where the purchaser is resident does not provide a comparable right, an offering memorandum delivered under this section must provide the purchaser with a contractual right to cancel the agreement to purchase the security by delivering a notice to the issuer not later than midnight on the 2nd business day after the purchaser signs the agreement to purchase the security.

(7) If the securities legislation where the purchaser is resident does not provide statutory rights of action in the event of a misrepresentation in an offering memorandum delivered under this section, the offering memorandum must contain a contractual right of action against the issuer for rescission or damages that

    (a) is available to the purchaser if the offering memorandum, or any information or documents incorporated or deemed to be incorporated by reference into the offering memorandum, contains a misrepresentation, without regard to whether the purchaser relied on the misrepresentation,

    (b) is enforceable by the purchaser delivering a notice to the issuer

        (i) in the case of an action for rescission, within 180 days after the purchaser signs the agreement to purchase the security, or

        (ii) in the case of an action for damages, before the earlier of

            A) 180 days after the purchaser first has knowledge of the facts giving rise to the cause of action, or

            B) 3 years after the date the purchaser signs the agreement to purchase the security,

    (c) is subject to the defence that the purchaser had knowledge of the misrepresentation,

    (d) in the case of an action for damages, provides that the amount recoverable

        (i) must not exceed the price at which the security was offered, and

        (ii) does not include all or any part of the damages that the issuer proves does not represent the depreciation in value of the security resulting from the misrepresentation, and

    (e) is in addition to, and does not detract from, any other right of the purchaser.

(8) An offering memorandum delivered under this section must contain a certificate that states the following:

"This offering memorandum does not contain a misrepresentation."

(9) If the issuer is a company, a certificate under subsection (8) must be signed

    (a) by the issuer's chief executive officer and chief financial officer or, if the issuer does not have a chief executive officer or chief financial officer, an individual acting in that capacity,

    (b) on behalf of the directors of the issuer, by

        (i) any 2 directors who are authorized to sign, other than the persons referred to in paragraph (a), or

        (ii) all the directors of the issuer, and

    (c) by each promoter of the issuer.

(10) If the issuer is a trust, a certificate under subsection (8) must be signed by

    (a) the individuals who perform functions for the issuer similar to those performed by the chief executive officer and the chief financial officer of a company, and

    (b) each trustee and the manager of the issuer.

(10.1) If a trustee or the manager that is signing the certificate of the issuer is

    (a) an individual, the individual must sign the certificate,

    (b) a company, the certificate must be signed

        (i) by the chief executive officer and the chief financial officer of the trustee or the manager, and

        (ii) on behalf of the board of directors of the trustee or the manager, by

            (A) any two directors of the trustee or the manager, other than the persons referred to in subparagraph (i), or

            (B) all of the directors of the trustee or the manager,

    (c) a limited partnership, the certificate must be signed by each general partner of the limited partnership as described in subsection (11.1) in relation to an issuer that is a limited partnership, or

    (d) not referred to in paragraphs (a), (b) or (c), the certificate may be signed by any person or company with authority to act on behalf of the trustee or the manager.

(10.2) Despite subsections (10) and (10.1), if the issuer is an investment fund and the declaration of trust, trust indenture or trust agreement establishing the investment fund delegates the authority to do so, or otherwise authorizes an individual or company to do so, the certificate may be signed by the individual or company to whom the authority is delegated or that is authorized to sign the certificate.

(10.3) Despite subsections (10) and (10.1), if the trustees of an issuer, other than an investment fund, do not perform functions for the issuer similar to those performed by the directors of a company, the trustees are not required to sign the certificate of the issuer if at least two individuals who perform functions for the issuer similar to those performed by the directors of a company sign the certificate.

(11) If the issuer is a limited partnership, a certificate under subsection (8) must be signed by

(a) each individual who performs a function for the issuer similar to any of those performed by the chief executive officer or the chief financial officer of a company, and

(b) each general partner of the issuer.

(11.1) If a general partner of the issuer is

(a) an individual, the individual must sign the certificate,

(b) a company, the certificate must be signed

(i) by the chief executive officer and the chief financial officer of the general partner, and

(ii) on behalf of the board of directors of the general partner, by

(A) any two directors of the general partner, other than the persons referred to in subparagraph (i), or

(B) all of the directors of the general partner,

(c) a limited partnership, the certificate must be signed by each general partner of the limited partnership and, for greater certainty, this subsection applies to each general partner required to sign,

(d) a trust, the certificate must be signed by the trustees of the general partner as described in subsection 10 in relation to an issuer that is a trust, or

(e) not referred to in paragraphs (a) to (d), the certificate may be signed by any person or company with authority to act on behalf of the general partner.

(12) If an issuer is not a company, trust or limited partnership, a certificate under subsection (8) must be signed by the persons that, in relation to the issuer, are in a similar position or perform a similar function to any of the persons referred to in subsections (9), (10), (10.1), (10.2), (10.3), (11) and (11.1).

(13) A certificate under subsection (8) must be true

(a) at the date the certificate is signed, and

(b) at the date the offering memorandum is delivered to the purchaser.

(14) If a certificate under subsection (8) ceases to be true after it is delivered to the purchaser, the issuer cannot accept an agreement to purchase the security from the purchaser unless

(a) the purchaser receives an update of the offering memorandum,

(b) the update of the offering memorandum contains a newly dated certificate signed in compliance with subsection (9), (10), (10.1), (10.2), (10.3), (11) or (11.1) and

(c) the purchaser re-signs the agreement to purchase the security.

(15) A risk acknowledgement under subsection (1), (2) or (2.1) must be in the required form and an issuer relying on subsection (1), (2) or (2.1) must retain the signed risk acknowledgment for 8 years after the distribution.

(16) The issuer must

(a) hold in trust all consideration received from the purchaser in connection with a distribution of a security under subsection (1), (2) or (2.1) until midnight on the 2nd business day after the purchaser signs the agreement to purchase the security, and

(b) return all consideration to the purchaser promptly if the purchaser exercises the right to cancel the agreement to purchase the security described under subsection (6).

(17) The issuer must file a copy of an offering memorandum delivered under this section and any update of a previously filed offering memorandum with the securities regulatory authority on or before the 10th day after the distribution under the offering memorandum or update of the offering memorandum.

(17.1) In Alberta, New Brunswick, Nova Scotia, Ontario, Québec and Saskatchewan, the issuer must file with the securities regulatory authority a copy of all OM marketing materials required or deemed to be incorporated by reference into an offering memorandum delivered under this section,

(a) if the OM marketing materials are prepared on or before the filing of the offering memorandum, concurrently with the filing of the offering memorandum, or

(b) if the OM marketing materials are prepared after the filing of the offering memorandum, within 10 days of the OM marketing materials being delivered or made reasonably available to a prospective purchaser.

(17.2) OM marketing materials filed under subsection (17.1) must include a cover page clearly identifying the offering memorandum to which they relate.

(17.3) Subsections (17.4) to (17.21) apply to issuers that rely on subsection (2.1) and that are not reporting issuers in any jurisdiction of Canada.

(17.4) In Alberta, an issuer must, within 120 days after the end of each of its financial years, file with the securities regulatory authority annual financial statements and make them reasonably available to each holder of a security acquired under subsection (2.1).

(17.5) In New Brunswick, Ontario, Québec and Saskatchewan, an issuer must, within 120 days after the end of each of its financial years, deliver annual financial statements to the securities regulatory authority and make them reasonably available to each holder of a security acquired under subsection (2.1).

(17.6) In Nova Scotia, an issuer must, within 120 days after the end of each of its financial years, make reasonably available annual financial statements to each holder of a security acquired under subsection (2.1).

(17.7) Despite subsections (17.4), (17.5) and (17.6), as applicable, if an issuer is required to file, deliver or make reasonably available annual financial statements for a financial year that ended before the issuer distributed securities under subsection (2.1) for the first time, those annual financial statements must be filed in Alberta, delivered in New Brunswick, Ontario, Québec and Saskatchewan or made reasonably available in Nova Scotia, as applicable, on or before the later of

(a) the 60th day after the issuer first distributes securities under subsection (2.1), and

(b) the deadline in subsection (17.4), (17.5) or (17.6), as applicable, to file, deliver or make reasonably available the annual financial statements.

(17.8) The annual financial statements of an issuer referred to in subsections (17.4), (17.5) and (17.6) must include

(a) a statement of comprehensive income, a statement of changes in equity, and a statement of cash flows for

(i) the most recently completed financial year, and

(ii) the financial year immediately preceding the most recently completed financial year, if any,

(b) a statement of financial position as at the end of each of the periods referred to in paragraph (a),

(c) in the following circumstances, a statement of financial position as at the beginning of the financial year immediately preceding the most recently completed financial year:

(i) the issuer discloses in its annual financial statements an unreserved statement of compliance with IFRS, and

(ii) the issuer

(A) applies an accounting policy retrospectively in its annual financial statements,

(B) makes a retrospective restatement of items in its annual financial statements, or

(C) reclassifies items in its annual financial statements,

(d) in the case of the issuer's first IFRS financial statements, the opening IFRS statement of financial position at the date of transition to IFRS, and

(e) notes to the annual financial statements.

(17.9) If the annual financial statements referred to in subsection (17.8) present the components of profit or loss in a separate income statement, the separate income statement must be displayed immediately before the statement of comprehensive income referred to in subsection (17.8).

(17.10) The annual financial statements referred to in subsection (17.8) must be audited.

(17.11) Despite subsection (17.10), for the first annual financial statements of an issuer referred to in subsections (17.4), (17.5) and (17.6), comparative information relating to the preceding financial year is not required to be audited if it has not been previously audited.

(17.12) Any period referred to in subsection (17.8) that has not been audited must be clearly labelled as unaudited.

(17.13) In Alberta, New Brunswick, Ontario, Québec and Saskatchewan, if an issuer decides to change its financial year end by more than 14 days, it must deliver to the securities regulatory authority and make reasonably available to each holder of a security acquired under subsection (2.1) a notice containing the information set out in subsection (17.15) as soon as practicable and, in any event, no later than the earlier of

(a) the deadline, based on the issuer's old financial year end, for the next annual financial statements referred to in subsections (17.4) and (17.5), and

(b) the deadline, based on the issuer's new financial year end, for the next annual financial statements referred to in subsections (17.4) and (17.5).

(17.14) In Nova Scotia, if an issuer decides to change its financial year end by more than 14 days, it must make reasonably available to each holder of a security acquired under subsection (2.1) a notice containing the information set out in subsection (17.15) as soon as practicable and, in any event, no later than the earlier of

(a) the deadline, based on the issuer's old financial year end, for the next annual financial statements referred to in subsection (17.6), and

(b) the deadline, based on the issuer's new financial year end, for the next annual financial statements referred to in subsection (17.6).

(17.15) The notice referred to in subsections (17.13) and (17.14) must state

(a) that the issuer has decided to change its financial year end,

(b) the reason for the change,

(c) the issuer's old financial year end,

(d) the issuer's new financial year end,

(e) the length and ending date of the periods, including the comparative periods, of the annual financial statements referred to in subsections (17.4), (17.5) and (17.6) for the issuer's transition year and its new financial year, and

(f) the filing deadline for the annual financial statements for the issuer's transition year.

(17.16) If a transition year is less than 9 months in length, the issuer must include as comparative financial information to its annual financial statements for its new financial year

(a) a statement of financial position, a statement of comprehensive income, a statement of changes in equity, a statement of cash flows, and notes to the financial statements for its transition year,

(b) a statement of financial position, a statement of comprehensive income, a statement of changes in equity, a statement of cash flows, and notes to the financial statements for its old financial year,

(c) in the following circumstances, a statement of financial position as at the beginning of the old financial year:

(i) the issuer discloses in its annual financial statements an unreserved statement of compliance with IFRS, and

(ii) the issuer

(A) applies an accounting policy retrospectively in its annual financial statements,

(B) makes a retrospective restatement of items in its annual financial statements, or

(C) reclassifies items in its annual financial statements, and

(d) in the case of the issuer's first IFRS financial statements, the opening IFRS statement of financial position at the date of transition to IFRS.

(17.17) A transition year must not exceed 15 months.

(17.18) An SEC issuer satisfies subsections (17.13), (17.14) and (17.16) if

(a) it complies with the requirements of U.S. laws relating to a change of fiscal year, and

(b) it delivers a copy of all materials required by U.S. laws relating to a change in fiscal year to the securities regulatory authority at the same time as, or as soon as practicable after, they are filed with or furnished to the SEC and, in any event, no later than 120 days after the end of its most recently completed financial year.

(17.19) The financial statements of an issuer referred to in subsections (17.4), (17.5) and (17.6) must be accompanied by a notice of the issuer disclosing in reasonable detail the use of the aggregate gross proceeds raised by the issuer under section 2.9 in accordance with Form 45-106F16, unless the issuer has previously disclosed the use of the aggregate gross proceeds in accordance with Form 45-106F16.

(17.20) In New Brunswick, Nova Scotia and Ontario, an issuer must make reasonably available to each holder of a security acquired under subsection (2.1) a notice of each of the following events in accordance with Form 45-106F17, within 10 days of the occurrence of the event:

(a) a discontinuation of the issuer's business;

(b) a change in the issuer's industry;

(c) a change of control of the issuer.

(17.21) An issuer is required to make the disclosure required respectively by subsections (17.4), (17.5), (17.6), (17.19) and (17.20) until the earliest of

(a) the date the issuer becomes a reporting issuer in any jurisdiction of Canada, and

(b) the date the issuer ceases to carry on business.

(17.22) In Ontario, an issuer that is not a reporting issuer in Ontario that distributes securities in reliance on the exemption in subsection (2.1) is designated a market participant under the *Securities Act* (Ontario).

(17.23) In New Brunswick, an issuer that is not a reporting issuer in New Brunswick that distributes securities in reliance on the exemption in subsection (2.1) is designated a market participant under the *Securities Act* (New Brunswick).

(18) Repealed. [B.C. Reg. 86/2011, s. (e).]

Minimum amount investment

Refer to Appendix D of National Instrument 45-102 **Resale of Securities.** *First trades are subject to a restricted period on resale.*

2.10 (1) The prospectus requirement does not apply to a distribution of a security to a person if all of the following apply:

(a) that person is not an individual;

(b) that person purchases as principal;

(c) the security has an acquisition cost to that person of not less than $150 000 paid in cash at the time of the distribution;

(d) the distribution is of a security of a single issuer.

(2) Subsection (1) does not apply to a distribution of a security to a person if the person was created, or is used, solely to purchase or hold securities in reliance on this exemption from the prospectus requirement set out in subsection (1).

DIVISION 2 — TRANSACTION EXEMPTIONS

Business combination and reorganization

Refer to Appendix E of National Instrument 45-102 **Resale of Securities.** *First trades are subject to a seasoning period on resale.*

2.11 The prospectus requirement does not apply to a distribution of a security in connection with

(a) an amalgamation, merger, reorganization or arrangement that is under a statutory procedure,

(b) an amalgamation, merger, reorganization or arrangement that

(i) is described in an information circular made pursuant to National Instrument 51-102 *Continuous Disclosure Obligations* or in a similar disclosure record and the information circular or similar disclosure record is delivered to each security holder whose approval of the amalgamation, merger, reorganization or arrangement is required before it can proceed, and

(ii) is approved by the security holders referred to in subparagraph (i), or

(c) a dissolution or winding-up of the issuer.

Asset acquisition

Refer to Appendix D of National Instrument 45-102 **Resale of Securities.** *First trades are subject to a restricted period on resale.*

2.12 The prospectus requirement does not apply to a distribution by an issuer of a security of its own issue to a person as consideration for the acquisition, directly or indirectly, of the assets of the person, if those assets have a fair value of not less than $150 000.

Petroleum, natural gas and mining properties

Refer to Appendix D of National Instrument 45-102 **Resale of Securities.** *First trades are subject to a restricted period on resale.*

2.13 The prospectus requirement does not apply to a distribution by an issuer of a security of its own issue as consideration for the acquisition, directly or indirectly, of petroleum, natural gas or mining properties or any interest in them.

Securities for debt

Refer to Appendix D of National Instrument 45-102 **Resale of Securities.** *First trades are subject to a restricted period on resale.*

2.14 The prospectus requirement does not apply to a distribution by a reporting issuer of a security of its own issue to a creditor to settle a bona fide debt of that reporting issuer.

Issuer acquisition or redemption

This provision is not cited in any Appendix of National Instrument 45-102 **Resale of Securities.**

2.15 The prospectus requirement does not apply to a distribution of a security to the issuer of the security.

Take-over bid and issuer bid

Refer to section 2.11 or Appendix E of National Instrument 45-102 **Resale of Securities.** *First trades are subject to a seasoning period on resale unless the requirements of section 2.11 of National Instrument 45-102 are met.*

2.16 The prospectus requirement does not apply to a distribution of a security in connection with a take-over bid in a jurisdiction of Canada or an issuer bid in a jurisdiction of Canada.

Offer to acquire to security holder outside local jurisdiction

Refer to Appendix E of National Instrument 45-102 **Resale of Securities.** *First trades are subject to a seasoning period on resale.*

2.17 The prospectus requirement does not apply to a distribution by a security holder outside the local jurisdiction to a person in the local jurisdiction if the distribution would have been in connection with a take-over bid or issuer bid made by that person were it not for the fact that the security holder is outside of the local jurisdiction.

DIVISION 3 — INVESTMENT FUND EXEMPTIONS

Investment fund reinvestment

Refer to Appendix E of National Instrument 45-102 **Resale of Securities.** *First trades are subject to a seasoning period on resale.*

2.18 (1) Subject to subsections (3), (4), (5) and (6), the prospectus requirement does not apply to the following distributions by an investment fund, and the investment fund manager of the fund, to a security holder of the investment fund if the distributions are permitted by a plan of the investment fund:

(a) a distribution of a security of the investment fund's own issue if a dividend or distribution out of earnings, surplus, capital or other sources payable in respect of the investment fund's securities is applied to the purchase of the security that is of the same class or series as the securities to which the dividend or distribution out of earnings, surplus, capital or other sources is attributable, and

(b) subject to subsection (2), a distribution of a security of the investment fund's own issue if the security holder makes an optional cash payment to purchase the security of the investment fund that is of the same class or series of securities described in paragraph (a) that trade on a marketplace.

(2) The aggregate number of securities issued under the optional cash payment referred to in subsection (1) (b) must not exceed, in any financial year of the investment fund during which the distribution takes place, 2% of the issued and outstanding securities of the class to which the plan relates as at the beginning of the financial year.

(3) A plan that permits the distributions described in subsection (1) must be available to every security holder in Canada to which the dividend or distribution out of earnings, surplus, capital or other sources is available.

(4) A person must not charge a fee for a distribution described in subsection (1).

(5) An investment fund that is a reporting issuer and in continuous distribution must set out in its current prospectus:

(a) details of any deferred or contingent sales charge or redemption fee that is payable at the time of the redemption of the security,

(b) any right that the security holder has to make an election to receive cash instead of securities on the payment of a dividend or making of a distribution by the investment fund, and

(c) instructions on how the right referred to in paragraph (b) can be exercised.

(6) An investment fund that is a reporting issuer and is not in continuous distribution must provide the information required by subsection (5) in its prospectus, annual information form or a material change report.

Additional investment in investment funds

Refer to Appendix D of National Instrument 45-102 **Resale of Securities.** *First trades are subject to a restricted period on resale.*

2.19 The prospectus requirement does not apply to a distribution by an investment fund, or the investment fund manager of the fund, of a security of the investment fund's own issue to a security holder of the investment fund if

(a) the security holder initially acquired securities of the investment fund as principal for an acquisition cost of not less than $150 000 paid in cash at the time of the distribution,

(b) the distribution is of a security of the same class or series as the securities initially acquired, as described in paragraph (a), and

(c) the security holder, as at the date of the distribution, holds securities of the investment fund that have

(i) an acquisition cost of not less than $150 000, or

(ii) a net asset value of not less than $150 000.

Private investment club

Refer to Appendix E of National Instrument 45-102 **Resale of Securities.** *First trades are subject to a seasoning period on resale.*

2.20 The prospectus requirement does not apply to a distribution of a security of an investment fund if the investment fund

(a) has no more than 50 beneficial security holders,

(b) does not seek and has never sought to borrow money from the public,

(c) does not distribute and has never distributed its securities to the public,

(d) does not pay or give any remuneration for investment management or administration advice in respect of trades in securities, except normal brokerage fees, and

(e) for the purpose of financing the operations of the investment fund, requires security holders to make contributions in proportion to the value of the securities held by them.

Private investment fund — loan and trust pools

Refer to Appendix E of National Instrument 45-102 **Resale of Securities.** *First trades are subject to a seasoning period on resale.*

2.21 (1) Subject to subsection (2), the prospectus requirement does not apply to a distribution of a security of an investment fund if the investment fund

(a) is administered by a trust company or trust corporation that is registered or authorized by an enactment of Canada or a jurisdiction of Canada to carry on business in Canada or a jurisdiction of Canada,

(b) has no promoter or investment fund manager other than the trust company or trust corporation referred to in paragraph (a), and

(c) co-mingles the money of different estates and trusts for the purpose of facilitating investment.

(2) A trust company or trust corporation registered under the laws of Prince Edward Island that is not registered under the *Trust and Loan Companies Act* (Canada) or under comparable legislation in another jurisdiction of Canada is not a trust company or trust corporation for the purpose of subparagraph (1)(a).

DIVISION 4 — EMPLOYEE, EXECUTIVE OFFICER, DIRECTOR AND CONSULTANT EXEMPTIONS

Definitions

2.22 In this Division

"associate", when used to indicate a relationship with a person, means

(a) an issuer of which the person beneficially owns or controls, directly or indirectly, voting securities entitling the person to more than 10% of the voting rights attached to outstanding voting securities of the issuer,

(b) any partner of the person,

(c) any trust or estate in which the person has a substantial beneficial interest or in respect of which the person serves as trustee or executor or in a similar capacity, or

(d) in the case of an individual, a relative of that individual, including

(i) a spouse of that individual, or

(ii) a relative of that individual's spouse

if the relative has the same home as that individual;

"associated consultant" means, for an issuer, a consultant of the issuer or of a related entity of the issuer if

(a) the consultant is an associate of the issuer or of a related entity of the issuer, or

(b) the issuer or a related entity of the issuer is an associate of the consultant;

"compensation" means an issuance of securities in exchange for services provided or to be provided and includes an issuance of securities for the purpose of providing an incentive;

"consultant" means, for an issuer, a person, other than an employee, executive officer, or director of the issuer or of a related entity of the issuer, that

(a) is engaged to provide services to the issuer or a related entity of the issuer, other than services provided in relation to a distribution,

(b) provides the services under a written contract with the issuer or a related entity of the issuer, and

(c) spends or will spend a significant amount of time and attention on the affairs and business of the issuer or a related entity of the issuer

and includes

(d) for an individual consultant, a corporation of which the individual consultant is an employee or shareholder, and a partnership of which the individual consultant is an employee or partner, and

(e) for a consultant that is not an individual, an employee, executive officer, or director of the consultant, provided that the individual employee, executive officer, or director spends or will spend a significant amount of time and attention on the affairs and business of the issuer or a related entity of the issuer.

"holding entity" means a person that is controlled by an individual;

"investor relations activities" means activities or communications, by or on behalf of an issuer or a security holder of the issuer, that promote or could reasonably be expected to promote the purchase or sale of securities of the issuer, but does not include

(a) the dissemination of information or preparation of records in the ordinary course of the business of the issuer

(i) to promote the sale of products or services of the issuer, or

(ii) to raise public awareness of the issuer

that cannot reasonably be considered to promote the purchase or sale of securities of the issuer,

(b) activities or communications necessary to comply with the requirements of

(i) securities legislation of any jurisdiction of Canada,

(ii) the securities laws of any foreign jurisdiction governing the issuer, or

(iii) any exchange or market on which the issuer's securities trade, or

(c) activities or communications necessary to follow securities directions of any jurisdiction of Canada;

"investor relations person" means a person that is a registrant or that provides services that include investor relations activities;

"issuer bid requirements" means the requirements under securities legislation that apply to an issuer bid;

"listed issuer" means an issuer, any of the securities of which

(a) are listed and not suspended, or the equivalent, from trading on

(i) TSX Inc.,

(ii) TSX Venture Exchange Inc.,

(ii.1) Aequitas NEO Exchange Inc.,

(iii) NYSE Amex Equities,

(iv) The New York Stock Exchange,

(v) the London Stock Exchange, or

(b) are quoted on the Nasdaq Stock Market;

"permitted assign" means, for a person that is an employee, executive officer, director or consultant of an issuer or of a related entity of the issuer,

(a) a trustee, custodian, or administrator acting on behalf of, or for the benefit of the person,

(b) a holding entity of the person,

(c) a RRSP, RRIF, or TFSA of the person,

(d) a spouse of the person,

(e) a trustee, custodian, or administrator acting on behalf of, or for the benefit of the spouse of the person,

(f) a holding entity of the spouse of the person, or

(g) a RRSP, RRIF, or TFSA of the spouse of the person;

"plan" means a plan or program established or maintained by an issuer providing for the acquisition of securities of the issuer by persons described in section 2.24(1) [*Employee, executive officer, director and consultant*] as compensation;

"related entity" means, for an issuer, a person that controls or is controlled by the issuer or that is controlled by the same person that controls the issuer;

"related person" means, for an issuer,

(a) a director or executive officer of the issuer or of a related entity of the issuer,

(b) an associate of a director or executive officer of the issuer or of a related entity of the issuer, or

(c) a permitted assign of a director or executive officer of the issuer or of a related entity of the issuer;

"security holder approval" means an approval for the issuance of securities of an issuer as compensation or under a plan

(a) given by a majority of the votes cast at a meeting of security holders of the issuer other than votes attaching to securities beneficially owned by related persons to whom securities may be issued as compensation or under that plan, or

(b) evidenced by a resolution signed by all the security holders entitled to vote at a meeting, if the issuer is not required to hold a meeting; and

"support agreement" includes an agreement to provide assistance in the maintenance or servicing of indebtedness of the borrower and an agreement to provide consideration for the purpose of maintaining or servicing indebtedness of the borrower.

Interpretation

2.23 (1) In this Division, a person (first person) is considered to control another person (second person) if the first person, directly or indirectly, has the power to direct the management and policies of the second person by virtue of

(a) ownership of or direction over voting securities in the second person,

(b) a written agreement or indenture,

(c) being the general partner or controlling the general partner of the second person, or

(d) being a trustee of the second person.

(2) In this Division, participation in a distribution is considered voluntary if

(a) in the case of an employee or the employee's permitted assign, the employee or the employee's permitted assign is not induced to participate in the distribution by expectation of employment or continued employment of the employee with the issuer or a related entity of the issuer,

(b) in the case of an executive officer or the executive officer's permitted assign, the executive officer or the executive officer's permitted assign is not induced to participate in the distribution by expectation of appointment, employment, continued appointment or continued employment of the executive officer with the issuer or a related entity of the issuer,

(c) in the case of a consultant or the consultant's permitted assign, the consultant or the consultant's permitted assign is not induced to participate in the distribution by expectation of engagement of the consultant to provide services or continued engagement of the consultant to provide services to the issuer or a related entity of the issuer, and

(d) in the case of an employee of a consultant, the individual is not induced by the issuer, a related entity of the issuer, or the consultant to participate in the distribution by expectation of employment or continued employment with the consultant.

Employee, executive officer, director and consultant

Refer to Appendix E of National Instrument 45-102 **Resale of Securities.** *First trades are subject to a seasoning period on resale.*

2.24 (1) Subject to section 2.25 [*Unlisted reporting issuer exception*], the prospectus requirement does not apply to a distribution

(a) by an issuer in a security of its own issue, or

(b) by a control person of an issuer of a security of the issuer or of an option to acquire a security of the issuer,

with

(c) an employee, executive officer, director or consultant of the issuer,

(d) an employee, executive officer, director or consultant of a related entity of the issuer, or

(e) a permitted assign of a person referred to in paragraphs (c) or (d)

if participation in the distribution is voluntary.

(2) For the purposes of subsection (1), a person referred to in paragraph (c), (d) or (e) includes a trustee, custodian or administrator acting as agent for that person for the purpose of facilitating a trade.

Unlisted reporting issuer exception

2.25 (1) For the purpose of this section, "unlisted reporting issuer" means a reporting issuer in a jurisdiction of Canada that is not a listed issuer.

(2) Subject to subsection (3), section 2.24 [*Employee, executive officer, director and consultant*] does not apply to a distribution to an employee or consultant of the unlisted reporting issuer who is an investor relations person of the issuer, an associated consultant of the issuer, an executive officer of the issuer, a director of the issuer, or a permitted assign of those persons if, after the distribution,

(a) the number of securities, calculated on a fully diluted basis, reserved for issuance under options granted to

(i) related persons, exceeds 10% of the outstanding securities of the issuer, or

(ii) a related person, exceeds 5% of the outstanding securities of the issuer, or

(b) the number of securities, calculated on a fully diluted basis, issued within 12 months to

(i) related persons, exceeds 10% of the outstanding securities of the issuer, or

(ii) a related person and the associates of the related person, exceeds 5% of the outstanding securities of the issuer.

(3) Subsection (2) does not apply to a distribution if the unlisted reporting issuer

(a) obtains security holder approval, and

(b) before obtaining security holder approval, provides security holders with the following information in sufficient detail to permit security holders to form a reasoned judgment concerning the matter:

(i) the eligibility of employees, executive officers, directors, and consultants to be issued or granted securities as compensation or under a plan;

(ii) the maximum number of securities that may be issued, or in the case of options, the number of securities that may be issued on exercise of the options, as compensation or under a plan;

(iii) particulars relating to any financial assistance or support agreement to be provided to participants by the issuer or any related entity of the issuer to facilitate the purchase of securities as compensation or under a plan, including whether the assistance or support is to be provided on a full-, part-, or non-recourse basis;

(iv) in the case of options, the maximum term and the basis for the determination of the exercise price;

(v) particulars relating to the options or other entitlements to be granted as compensation or under a plan, including transferability; and

(vi) the number of votes attaching to securities that, to the issuer's knowledge at the time the information is provided, will not be included for the purpose of determining whether security holder approval has been obtained.

Distributions among current or former employees, executive officers, directors, or consultants of non-reporting issuer

Refer to Appendix E of National Instrument 45-102 **Resale of Securities.** *First trades are subject to a seasoning period on resale.*

2.26 (1) Subject to subsection (2), the prospectus requirement does not apply to a distribution of a security of an issuer by

(a) a current or former employee, executive officer, director, or consultant of the issuer or related entity of the issuer, or

(b) a permitted assign of a person referred to in paragraph (a),

to

(c) an employee, executive officer, director, or consultant of the issuer or a related entity of the issuer, or

(d) a permitted assign of the employee, executive officer, director, or consultant.

(2) The exemption in subsection (1) is only available if

(a) participation in the distribution is voluntary,

(b) the issuer of the security is not a reporting issuer in any jurisdiction of Canada, and

(c) the price of the security being distributed is established by a generally applicable formula contained in a written agreement among some or all of the security holders of the issuer to which the transferee is or will become a party.

Permitted transferees

Refer to Appendix E of National Instrument 45-102 **Resale of Securities**. *First trades are subject to a seasoning period on resale.*

2.27 (1) Subject to section 2.28, the prospectus requirement does not apply to a distribution of a security of an issuer acquired by a person described in section 2.24(1)[*Employee, executive officer, director and consultant*] under a plan of the issuer if the distribution

(a) is between

(i) a person who is an employee, executive officer, director or consultant of the issuer or a related entity of the issuer, and

(ii) the permitted assign of that person,

or

(b) is between permitted assigns of that person.

(2) Subject to section 2.28, the prospectus requirement does not apply to a distribution of a security of an issuer by a trustee, custodian or administrator acting on behalf, or for the benefit, of employees, executive officers, directors or consultants of the issuer or a related entity of the issuer, to

(a) an employee, executive officer, director or consultant of the issuer or a related entity of the issuer, or

(b) a permitted assign of a person referred to in paragraph (a),

if the security was acquired from

(c) an employee, executive officer, director or consultant of the issuer or a related entity of the issuer, or

(d) the permitted assign of a person referred to in paragraph (c).

(3) For the purposes of the exemptions in subsection (1) and paragraphs (2) (c) and (d), all references to employee, executive officer, director, or consultant include a former employee, executive officer, director, or consultant.

Limitation re: permitted transferees

2.28 The exemption from the prospectus requirement under subsection 2.27(1) or (2) is only available if the security was acquired

(a) by a person described in section 2.24(1) [*Employee, executive officer, director, and consultant*] under any exemption that makes the resale of the security subject to section 2.6 of National Instrument 45-102 *Resale of Securities*, or

(b) in Manitoba, by a person described in section 2.24(1) [*Employee, executive officer, director, and consultant*].

Issuer bid

2.29 The issuer bid requirements do not apply to the acquisition by an issuer of a security of its own issue that was acquired by a person described in section 2.24(1) [*Employee, executive officer, director, and consultant*] if

(a) the purpose of the acquisition by the issuer is to

(i) fulfill withholding tax obligations, or

(ii) provide payment of the exercise price of a stock option,

(b) the acquisition by the issuer is made in accordance with the terms of a plan that specifies how the value of the securities acquired by the issuer is determined,

(c) in the case of securities acquired as payment of the exercise price of a stock option, the date of exercise of the option is chosen by the option holder, and

(d) the aggregate number of securities acquired by the issuer within a 12 month period under this section does not exceed 5% of the outstanding securities of the class or series at the beginning of the period.

DIVISION 5 — MISCELLANEOUS EXEMPTIONS

Isolated distribution by issuer

Refer to Appendix D of National Instrument 45-102 **Resale of Securities**. *First trades are subject to a restricted period.*

2.30 The prospectus requirement does not apply to a distribution by an issuer of a security of its own issue if the distribution is an isolated distribution and is not made

(a) in the course of continued and successive transactions of a like nature, and

(b) by a person whose usual business is trading in securities.

Dividends and distributions

Subsection (1) is cited in Appendix E of National Instrument 45-102 **Resale of Securities**. *First trades are subject to a seasoning period on resale.*

Subsection (2) is cited in Appendix D and Appendix E of National Instrument 45-102. Resale restriction is determined by the exemption under which the previously issued security was first acquired.

2.31 (1) The prospectus requirement does not apply to a distribution by an issuer of a security of its own issue to a security holder of the issuer as a dividend or distribution out of earnings, surplus, capital or other sources.

(2) The prospectus requirement does not apply to a distribution by an issuer to a security holder of the issuer of a security of a reporting issuer as an in specie dividend or distribution out of earnings or surplus.

Distribution to lender by control person for collateral

This provision is not cited in any Appendix of National Instrument 45-02 **Resale of Securities.** *Trades by a lender, pledgee, mortgagee or other encumbrancer to realize on a debt are regulated by section 2.8 of National Instrument 45-102.*

2.32 The prospectus requirement does not apply to a distribution of a security of an issuer to a lender, pledgee, mortgagee or other encumbrancer from the holdings of a control person of the issuer for the purpose of giving collateral for a bona fide debt of the control person.

Acting as underwriter

Refer to Appendix F of National Instrument 45-102 **Resale of Securities.** *First trades are a distribution.*

2.33 The prospectus requirement does not apply to a distribution of a security between a person and a purchaser acting as an underwriter or between or among persons acting as underwriters.

Specified debt

This provision is not cited in any Appendix of National Instrument 45-102 **Resale of Securities.** *These securities are free trading.*

2.34 (1) In this section, "permitted supranational agency" means

(a) the African Development Bank, established by the Agreement Establishing the African Development Bank which came into force on September 10, 1964, that Canada became a member of on December 30, 1982;

(b) the Asian Development Bank, established under a resolution adopted by the United Nations Economic and Social Commission for Asia and the Pacific in 1965;

(c) the Caribbean Development Bank, established by the Agreement Establishing the Caribbean Development Bank which came into force on January 26, 1970, as amended, that Canada is a founding member of;

(d) the European Bank for Reconstruction and Development, established by the Agreement Establishing the European Bank for Reconstruction and Development and approved by the *European Bank for Reconstruction and Development Agreement Act* (Canada), that Canada is a founding member of;

(e) the Inter-American Development Bank, established by the Agreement establishing the Inter-American Development Bank which became effective December 30, 1959, as amended from time to time, that Canada is a member of;

(f) the International Bank for Reconstruction and Development, established by the Agreement for an International Bank for Reconstruction and Development approved by the *Bretton Woods and Related Agreements Act* (Canada); and

(g) the International Finance Corporation, established by Articles of Agreement approved by the *Bretton Woods and Related Agreements Act* (Canada).

(2) The prospectus requirement does not apply to a distribution of

(a) a debt security issued by or guaranteed by the Government of Canada or the government of a jurisdiction of Canada,

(b) a debt security issued by or guaranteed by a government of a foreign jurisdiction if the debt security has a designated rating from a designated rating organization or its DRO affiliate,

(c) a debt security issued by or guaranteed by a municipal corporation in Canada, or secured by or payable out of rates or taxes levied under the law of a jurisdiction of Canada on property in the jurisdiction and collectable by or through the municipality in which the property is situated,

(d) a debt security issued by or guaranteed by a Canadian financial institution or a Schedule III bank, other than debt securities that are subordinate in right of payment to deposits held by the issuer or guarantor of those debt securities,

(d.1) in Ontario, a debt security issued by or guaranteed by a loan corporation, trust company, trust corporation, insurance company, treasury branch, credit union, caisse populaire, financial services cooperative, or league that, in each case, is authorized by an enactment of a jurisdiction of Canada other than Ontario to carry on business in a jurisdiction of Canada, other than debt securities that are subordinate in right of payment to deposits held by the issuer or guarantor of those debt securities,

(e) a debt security issued by the Comité de gestion de la taxe scolaire de l'île de Montréal, or

(f) a debt security issued by or guaranteed by a permitted supranational agency if the debt securities are payable in the currency of Canada or the United States of America.

(3) Paragraphs (2)(a), (c) and (d) do not apply in Ontario.

In Ontario, subsections 73(1)(a) and (2) of the **Securities Act** *(Ontario) provide similar exemptions to the exemptions in paragraphs (2)(a), and (c) of this Instrument.*

In Ontario, subsections 73.1(1) and (2) of the **Securities Act** *(Ontario), read together, provide a similar exemption to the exemption in paragraph 2(d) of this Instrument.*

Short-term debt

This provision is not cited in any Appendix of National Instrument 45-102 **Resale of Securities.** *These securities are free trading.*

2.35 (1) The prospectus requirement does not apply to a distribution of a negotiable promissory note or commercial paper if all of the following apply:

(a) the note or commercial paper matures not more than one year from the date of issue;

(b) the note or commercial paper has a credit rating from a designated rating organization, or its DRO affiliate, that is at or above one of the following rating categories or that is at or above a rating category that replaces one of the following rating categories:

(i) R-1(low) if issued by DBRS Limited;

(ii) F1 if issued by Fitch, Inc.;

(iii) P-1 if issued by Moody's Canada Inc.;

(iv) A-1(Low) (Canada national scale) if issued by Standard & Ratings Services (Canada);

(c) the note or commercial paper has no credit rating from a designated rating organization, or its DRO affiliate, that is below one of the following rating categories or that is below a rating category that replaces one of the following rating categories:

(i) R-1(low) if issued by DBRS Limited;

(ii) F2 if issued by Fitch, Inc.;

(iii) P-2 if issued by Moody's Canada Inc.;

(iv) A-1(Low) (Canada national scale) or A-2 (global scale) if issued by Standard & Poor's Ratings Services (Canada).

(2) Subsection (1) does not apply to a distribution of a negotiable promissory note or commercial paper if either of the following applies:

(a) the note or commercial paper is a securitized product;

(b) the note or commercial paper is convertible or exchangeable into or accompanied by a right to purchase another security other than a security described in subsection (1).

Short-term securitized products

2.35.1 The prospectus requirement does not apply to a distribution of a short-term securitized product if all of the following apply:

(a) the short-term securitized product is a security described in section 2.35.2;

(b) the conduit issuing the short-term securitized product complies with section 2.35.4;

(c) the short-term securitized product is not convertible or exchangeable into or accompanied by a right to purchase another security other than a security described in paragraph (a) and for which disclosure is provided pursuant to paragraph (b).

Limitations on short-term securitized product exemption

2.35.2 All of the following must apply to a short-term securitized product distributed under section 2.35.1:

(a) the short-term securitized product is of a series or class of securitized product to which all of the following apply:

(i) it has a credit rating from not less than two designated rating organizations, or their respective DRO affiliate, and at least one of the credit ratings is at or above one of the following rating categories or is at or above a rating category that replaces one of the following rating categories:

(A) R-1(high)(sf) if issued by DBRS Limited;

(B) F1+sf if issued by Fitch, Inc.;

(C) P-1(sf) if issued by Moody's Canada Inc.;

(D) A-1(High)(sf) (Canada national scale) or A-1+(sf) (global scale) if issued by Standard & Poor's Ratings Services (Canada);

(ii) it has no credit rating from a designated rating organization, or its DRO affiliate, that is below one of the following rating categories or that is below a rating category that replaces one of the following rating categories:

(A) R-1(low)(sf) if issued by DBRS Limited;

(B) F2sf if issued by Fitch, Inc.;

(C) P-2(sf) if issued by Moody's Canada Inc.;

(D) A-1(Low)(sf) (Canada national scale) or A-2(sf) (global scale) if issued by Standard & Poor's Ratings Services (Canada);

(iii) the conduit has entered into one or more agreements that, subject to section 2.35.3, obligate one or more liquidity providers to provide funds to the conduit to enable the conduit to satisfy all of its obligations to pay principal or interest as that series or class of short-term securitized product matures;

(iv) all of the following apply to each liquidity provider:

(A) the liquidity provider is a deposit-taking institution;

(B) the liquidity provider is regulated or approved to carry on business in Canada by one or both of the following:

1. the Office of the Superintendent of Financial Institutions (Canada);

2. a government department or regulatory authority of Canada, or of a jurisdiction of Canada responsible for regulating deposit-taking institutions;

(C) the liquidity provider has a rating from each of the designated rating organizations providing a rating on the short-term securitized product under subparagraph 2.35.2(a)(i), or their respective DRO affiliate, for its senior, unsecured short-term debt, none of which is dependent upon a guarantee by a third party, and each rating from such designated rating organizations, or their respective DRO affiliate, is at or above the following rating categories or is at or above a rating category that replaces one of the following rating categories:

1. R-1(low) if issued by DBRS Limited;

2. F2 if issued by Fitch, Inc.;

3. P-2 if issued by Moody's Canada Inc.;

4. A-1(Low) (Canada national scale) or A-2 (global scale) if issued by Standard & Poor's Ratings Services (Canada);

(b) if the conduit has issued more than one series or class of short-term securitized product, the short-term securitized product to be distributed under section 2.35.1, when issued, will not in the event of bankruptcy, insolvency or winding-up of the conduit be subordinate in priority of claim to any other outstanding series or class of short-term securitized product issued by the conduit in respect of any asset pool backing the short-term securitized product to be distributed under section 2.35.1;

(c) the conduit has provided an undertaking to or has agreed in writing with the purchaser of the short-term securitized product or an agent, custodian or trustee appointed to act on behalf of purchasers of that series or class of short-term securitized product, that any asset pool of the conduit will consist only of one or more of the following:

    (i) a bond;

    (ii) a mortgage;

    (iii) a lease;

    (iv) a loan;

    (v) a receivable;

    (vi) a royalty;

    (vii) any real or personal property securing or forming part of that asset pool.

Exceptions relating to liquidity agreements

2.35.3 (1) Despite subparagraph 2.35.2(a)(iii), an agreement with a liquidity provider may provide that a liquidity provider is not obligated to advance funds in respect of a series or class of short-term securitized product distributed under section 2.35.1 if the conduit is subject to any of the following:

    (a) bankruptcy, or insolvency proceedings under the *Bankruptcy and Insolvency Act* (Canada);

    (b) an arrangement under the *Companies Creditors' Arrangement Act* (Canada);

    (c) proceedings similar to those referred to in paragraph (a) or (b) under the laws of Canada or a jurisdiction of Canada or a foreign jurisdiction.

(2) Despite subparagraph 2.35.2(a)(iii), an agreement with a liquidity provider may provide that a liquidity provider is not obligated to advance funds in respect of a series or class of short-term securitized product distributed under section 2.35.1 that exceed the sum of the following:

    (a) the aggregate value of the non-defaulted assets in the asset pool to which the agreement relates;

    (b) the amount of credit enhancement applicable to the asset pool to which the agreement relates.

Disclosure requirements

2.35.4 (1) A conduit that distributes a short-term securitized product under section 2.35.1 must, on or before the date a purchaser purchases the short-term securitized product, do all of the following:

    (a) provide to or make reasonably available to the purchaser an information memorandum prepared in accordance with Form 45-106F7 *Information Memorandum for Short-term Securitized Products Distributed under Section 2.35.1*;

    (b) provide an undertaking to or agree in writing with the purchaser, or with an agent, custodian or trustee appointed to act on behalf of purchasers of that series or class of securitized product, to

        (i) for so long as a short-term securitized product of that class remains outstanding, prepare the documents specified in subsections (5) and (6) within the time periods specified in those subsections, and

        (ii) provide to or make reasonably available to each holder of a short-term securitized product of that series or class, the documents specified in subsections (5) and (6).

(2) Subsection (1) does not apply to a conduit distributing a short-term securitized product under section 2.35.1 if

    (a) the conduit has previously distributed a short-term securitized product of the same series or class as the short-term securitized product to be distributed,

    (b) in connection with that previous distribution the conduit prepared an information memorandum that complied with paragraph (1)(a), and

    (c) the conduit, on or before the time each purchaser in the current distribution purchases a short-term securitized product, does each of the following:

        (i) provides to or makes reasonably available to the purchaser the information memorandum prepared in connection with the previous distribution;

        (ii) provides to or makes reasonably available to the purchaser all documents specified in subsections (5) and (6) that have been prepared in respect of that series or class of short-term securitized product.

(3) A conduit must, on or before the 10th day following a distribution of a short-term securitized product under section 2.35.1, do each of the following:

    (a) provide to or make reasonably available to the securities regulator either of the following:

        (i) the information memorandum required under paragraph (1)(a);

        (ii) if the conduit is relying on subsection (2), the documents referred to in paragraph (c) of subsection (2);

    (b) subject to subsection (4), deliver to the securities regulator an undertaking that it will, in respect of that series or class of short-term securitized product,

        (i) provide to or make reasonably available to the securities regulator the documents specified in subsections (5) and (6), and

        (ii) promptly deliver to the securities regulator each document specified in subsections (5) and (6) that is requested by the securities regulator.

(4) Paragraph (3)(b) does not apply if

    (a) the conduit has delivered an undertaking to the securities regulator under paragraph (3)(b) in respect of a previous distribution of a securitized product that is of the same series or class as the short-term securitized product currently being distributed, and

    (b) the undertaking referred to in paragraph (a) applies in respect of the current distribution.

(5) For the purpose of subsection 2.35.4(1), the undertaking or agreement must require the conduit to prepare a monthly disclosure report relating to the series or class of short-term securitized product that is

    (a) prepared in accordance with Form 45-106F8 *Monthly Disclosure Report for Short-term Securitized Products Distributed under Section 2.35.1,*

    (b) current as at the last business day of each month, and

    (c) no later than 50 days from the end of the most recent month to which it relates, made reasonably available to each holder of that series or class of the conduit's short-term securitized product.

(6) For the purpose of subsection 2.35.4(1), the undertaking or agreement must require the conduit to prepare a timely disclosure report, providing the information specified in subsection (7), in each of the following circumstances:

    (a) a downgrade in one or more of the conduit's credit ratings;

    (b) failure by the conduit to make any required payment of principal or interest on the series or class of short-term securitized product;

    (c) the occurrence of a change or event that the conduit would reasonably expect to have a significant adverse effect on the payment of principal or interest on the series or class of short-term securitized product.

(7) The timely disclosure report referred to in subsection (6) must

    (a) describe the nature and substance of the change or event and the actual or potential effect on any payment of principal or interest to a holder of that series or class of short-term securitized product, and

    (b) be provided to or made reasonably available to holders of that series or class of short-term securitized product no later than the second business day after the conduit becomes aware of the change or event.

Mortgages

This provision is not cited in any Appendix of National Instrument 45-102 **Resale of Securities.** *These securities are free trading.*

2.36 (1) In this section, "syndicated mortgage" means a mortgage in which 2 or more persons participate, directly or indirectly, as a lender in a debt obligation that is secured by the mortgage.

(2) Except in Ontario, and subject to subsection (3), the prospectus requirement does not apply to a distribution of a mortgage on real property in a jurisdiction of Canada by a person who is registered or licensed, or exempted from registration or licensing, under mortgage brokerage or mortgage dealer legislation of that jurisdiction.

(3) In Alberta, British Columbia, Manitoba, Québec and Saskatchewan, subsection (2) does not apply to a distribution of a syndicated mortgage.

In Ontario, subsection 73.2(3) of the **Securities Act** *(Ontario) provides a similar exemption to the exemption in subsection (2).*

Personal property security legislation

This provision is not cited in any Appendix of National Instrument 45-102 **Resale of Securities.** *These securities are free trading.*

2.37 Except in Ontario, the prospectus requirement does not apply to a distribution to a person, other than an individual, in a security evidencing indebtedness secured by or under a security agreement, secured in accordance with personal property security legislation of a jurisdiction of Canada that provides for the granting of security in personal property.

In Ontario, subsection 73.2(1) of the **Securities Act** *(Ontario) provides a similar exemption to the exemption in section 2.37.*

Not for profit issuer

This provision is not cited in any Appendix of National Instrument 45-102 **Resale of Securities.** *These securities are free trading.*

2.38 The prospectus requirement does not apply to a distribution by an issuer that is organized exclusively for educational, benevolent, fraternal, charitable, religious or recreational purposes and not for profit in a security of its own issue if

    (a) no part of the net earnings benefit any security holder of the issuer, and

    (b) no commission or other remuneration is paid in connection with the sale of the security.

Variable insurance contract

This provision is not cited in any Appendix of National Instrument 45-102 **Resale of Securities.** *These securities are free trading.*

2.39 (1) In this section,

    (a) "contract", "group insurance", "insurance company", "life insurance" and "policy" have the respective meanings assigned to them in the legislation for a jurisdiction referenced in Appendix A.

    (b) "variable insurance contract" means a contract of life insurance under which the interest of the purchaser is valued for purposes of conversion or surrender by reference to the value of a proportionate interest in a specified portfolio of assets.

(2) The prospectus requirement does not apply to a distribution of a variable insurance contract by an insurance company if the variable insurance contract is

    (a) a contract of group insurance,

    (b) a whole life insurance contract providing for the payment at maturity of an amount not less than 75% of the premium paid up to age 75 years for a benefit payable at maturity,

    (c) an arrangement for the investment of policy dividends and policy proceeds in a separate and distinct fund to which contributions are made only from policy dividends and policy proceeds, or

    (d) a variable life annuity.

RRSP/RRIF/TFSA

Refer to Appendix D and Appendix E of National Instrument 45-102 **Resale of Securities.** *The resale restriction is determined by the exemption under which the security was first acquired.*

2.40 The prospectus requirement does not apply to a distribution of a security between

(a) an individual or an associate of the individual, and

(b) a RRSP, RRIF, or TFSA

(i) established for or by the individual, or

(ii) under which the individual is a beneficiary.

Schedule III banks and cooperative associations — evidence of deposit

This provision is not cited in any Appendix of National Instrument 45-102 **Resale of Securities.** *These securities are free trading.*

2.41 Except in Ontario, the prospectus requirement does not apply to a distribution of an evidence of deposit issued by a Schedule III bank or an association governed by the *Cooperative Credit Associations Act* (Canada).

In Ontario, clause (e) of the definition of "security" in subsection 1(1) of the **Securities Act** *(Ontario) excludes these evidences of deposit from the definition of "security".*

Conversion, exchange, or exercise

Subsection (1)(a) is cited in Appendix D and Appendix E of National Instrument 45-102 **Resale of Securities.** *Resale restriction is determined by the exemption under which the previously issued security was first acquired.*

Subsection (1)(b) is cited in Appendix E of National Instrument 45-102 **Resale of Securities.** *First trades are subject to a seasoning period on resale, unless the requirements of section 2.10 of NI 45-102 are met.*

2.42 (1) The prospectus requirement does not apply to a distribution by an issuer if

(a) the issuer distributes a security of its own issue to a security holder of the issuer in accordance with the terms and conditions of a security previously issued by that issuer, or

(b) subject to subsection (2), the issuer distributes a security of a reporting issuer held by it to a security holder of the issuer in accordance with the terms and conditions of a security previously issued by that issuer.

(2) Subsection (1)(b) does not apply unless

(a) the issuer has given the regulator or, in Québec, the securities regulatory authority, prior written notice stating the date, amount, nature and conditions of the distribution, and

(b) the regulator or, in Québec, the securities regulatory authority, has not objected in writing to the distribution within 10 days of receipt of the notice referred to in paragraph (a) or, if the regulator or securities regulatory authority objects to the distribution, the issuer must deliver to the regulator or securities regulatory authority information relating to the securities that is satisfactory to and accepted by the regulator or securities regulatory authority.

Self-directed registered educational savings plans

This provision is not cited in any Appendix of National Instrument 45-102 **Resale of Securities.** *These securities are free trading.*

2.43 The prospectus requirement does not apply to a distribution of a self-directed RESP to a subscriber if

(a) the distribution is conducted by

(i) a dealing representative of a mutual fund dealer who is acting on behalf of the mutual fund dealer,

(ii) a Canadian financial institution, or,

(iii) in Ontario, a financial intermediary, and

(b) the self-directed RESP restricts its investments in securities to securities in which the person who distributes the self-directed RESP is permitted to distribute.

PART 3

[Repealed.]

Under section 8.5 of this Instrument, Part 3 was no longer available in any jurisdiction. In British Columbia, Part 3 was repealed by B.C. Reg. 227/2009. All other jurisdictions will repeal Part 3 in these amendments.

PART 4 — CONTROL BLOCK DISTRIBUTIONS

Control block distributions

4.1 (1) In this Part,

"control block distribution" means a trade to which the provisions of securities legislation listed in Appendix B apply.

(2) Terms defined or interpreted in National Instrument 62-103 *The Early Warning System and Related Take-over Bid and Insider Reporting Issues* and used in this Part have the same meaning as is assigned to them in that Instrument.

(3) The prospectus requirement does not apply to a control block distribution by an eligible institutional investor of a reporting issuer's securities if

(a) the eligible institutional investor

(i) has filed the reports required under the early warning requirements or files the reports required under Part 4 of National Instrument 62-103 *The Early Warning System and Related Take-over Bid and Insider Reporting Issues*,

(ii) does not have knowledge of any material fact or material change with respect to the reporting issuer that has not been generally disclosed,

(iii) does not receive in the ordinary course of its business and investment activities knowledge of any material fact or material change with respect to the reporting issuer that has not been generally disclosed, and

(iv) either alone or together with any joint actors, does not possess effective control of the reporting issuer,

(b) there are no directors or officers of the reporting issuer who were, or could reasonably be seen to have been, selected, nominated or designated by the eligible institutional investor or any joint actor,

(c) the control block distribution is made in the ordinary course of business or investment activity of the eligible institutional investor,

(d) securities legislation would not require the securities to be held for a specified period of time if the trade were not a control block distribution,

(e) no unusual effort is made to prepare the market or to create a demand for the securities, and

(f) no extraordinary commission or consideration is paid in respect of the control block distribution.

(4) An eligible institutional investor that makes a distribution in reliance on subsection (3) must file a letter within 10 days after the distribution that describes the date and size of the distribution, the market on which it was made and the price at which the securities being distributed were sold.

Distributions by a control person after a take-over bid

4.2 (1) Subject to subsection (2), the prospectus requirement does not apply to a distribution in a security from the holdings of a control person acquired under a take-over bid for which a take-over bid circular was issued and filed if

(a) the issuer whose securities are being acquired under the take-over bid has been a reporting issuer for at least 4 months at the date of the take-over bid,

(b) the intention to make the distribution is disclosed in the take-over bid circular issued in respect of the take-over bid,

(c) the distribution is made within the period beginning on the date of the expiry of the bid and ending 20 days after that date,

(d) a notice of intention to distribute securities in Form 45-102F1 *Notice of Intention to Distribute Securities* under Section 2.8 of NI 45-102 *Resale of Securities* under National Instrument 45-102 *Resale of Securities* is filed before the distribution,

(e) an insider report of the distribution in Form 55-102F2 *Insider Report* or Form 55-102F6 *Insider Report*, as applicable, under National Instrument 55-102 *System for Electronic Disclosure by Insiders (SEDI)* is filed within 3 days after the completion of the distribution,

(f) no unusual effort is made to prepare the market or to create a demand for the security, and

(g) no extraordinary commission or consideration is paid in respect of the distribution.

(2) A control person referred to in subsection (1) is not required to comply with subsection (1)(b) if

(a) another person makes a competing take-over bid for securities of the issuer for which the take-over bid circular is issued, and

(b) the control person sells those securities to that other person for a consideration that is not greater than the consideration offered by that other person under its take-over bid.

PART 5 — OFFERINGS BY TSX VENTURE EXCHANGE OFFERING DOCUMENT

Application and interpretation

5.1 (1) This Part does not apply in Ontario.

(2) In this Part

"exchange policy" means Exchange Policy 4.6 — *Public Offering by Short Form Offering Document* and Exchange Form 4H — *Short Form Offering Document*, of the TSX Venture Exchange as amended from time to time;

"gross proceeds" means the gross proceeds that are required to be paid to the issuer for listed securities distributed under a TSX Venture exchange offering document;

"listed security" means a security of a class listed on the TSX Venture Exchange;

"prior exchange offering" means a distribution of securities by an issuer under a TSX Venture exchange offering document that was completed during the 12-month period immediately preceding the date of the TSX Venture exchange offering document;

"subsequently triggered report" means a material change report that must be filed no later than 10 days after a material change under securities legislation as a result of a material change that occurs after the date the TSX Venture exchange offering document is certified but before a purchaser enters into an agreement of purchase and sale;

"TSX Venture Exchange" means the TSX Venture Exchange Inc.;

"TSX Venture exchange offering document" means an offering document that complies with the exchange policy;

"warrant" means a warrant of an issuer distributed under a TSX Venture exchange offering document that entitles the holder to acquire a listed security or a portion of a listed security of the same issuer.

TSX Venture Exchange offering

Refer to Appendix D of National Instrument 45-102 Resale of Securities. *These securities are free trading unless the security is acquired by*

(i) *a purchaser that, at the time the security was acquired, was an insider or promoter of the issuer of the security, an underwriter of the issuer, or a member of the underwriter's professional group, or*

(ii) *any other purchaser in excess of $40 000 for the portion of the securities in excess of $40 000.*

The first trade by purchasers under (i) and (ii) are subject to a restricted period.

5.2 The prospectus requirement does not apply to a distribution by an issuer in a security of its own issue if

(a) the issuer has filed an AIF in a jurisdiction of Canada,

(b) the issuer is a SEDAR filer,

(c) the issuer is a reporting issuer in a jurisdiction of Canada and has filed in a jurisdiction of Canada

(i) a TSX Venture exchange offering document,

(ii) all documents required to be filed under the securities legislation of that jurisdiction, and

(iii) any subsequently triggered report,

(d) the distribution is of listed securities or units consisting of listed securities and warrants,

(e) the issuer has filed with the TSX Venture Exchange a TSX Venture exchange offering document in respect of the distribution, that

(i) incorporates by reference the following documents of the issuer filed with the securities regulatory authority in any jurisdiction of Canada:

A) the AIF;

B) the most recent annual financial statements and the MD&A relating to those financial statements;

C) all unaudited interim financial reports and the MD&A relating to those financial reports, filed after the date of the AIF but before or on the date of the TSX Venture exchange offering document;

D) all material change reports filed after the date of the AIF but before or on the date of the TSX Venture exchange offering document, and

E) all documents required under National Instrument 43-101 *Standards of Disclosure for Mineral Projects* and National Instrument 51-101 *Standards of Disclosure for Oil and Gas Activities* filed on or after the date of the AIF but before or on the date of the TSX Venture exchange offering document,

(ii) deems any subsequently triggered report required to be delivered to a purchaser under this Part to be incorporated by reference,

(iii) grants to purchasers contractual rights of action in the event of a misrepresentation, as required by the exchange policy,

(iv) grants to purchasers contractual rights of withdrawal, as required by the exchange policy, and

(v) contains all the certificates required by the exchange policy,

(f) the distribution is conducted in accordance with the exchange policy,

(g) the issuer or the underwriter delivers the TSX Venture exchange offering document and any subsequently triggered report to each purchaser

(i) before the issuer or the underwriter enters into the written confirmation of purchase and sale resulting from an order or subscription for securities being distributed under the TSX Venture exchange offering document, or

(ii) not later than midnight on the 2nd business day after the agreement of purchase and sale is entered into,

(h) the listed securities issued under the TSX Venture exchange offering document, when added to the listed securities of the same class issued under prior exchange offerings, do not exceed

(i) the number of securities of the same class outstanding immediately before the issuer distributes securities of the same class under the TSX Venture exchange offering document, or

(ii) the number of securities of the same class outstanding immediately before a prior exchange offering,

(i) the gross proceeds under the TSX Venture exchange offering document, when added to the gross proceeds from prior exchange offerings do not exceed $2 million,

(j) no purchaser acquires more than 20% of the securities distributed under the TSX Venture exchange offering document, and

(k) no more than 50% of the securities distributed under the TSX Venture exchange offering document are subject to section 2.5 of National Instrument 45-102 *Resale of Securities.*

Underwriter obligations

5.3 An underwriter that qualifies as a "sponsor" under TSX Venture Exchange Policy 2.2 — *Sponsorship and Sponsorship Requirements* as amended from time to time must sign the TSX Venture exchange offering document and comply with TSX Venture Exchange Appendix 4A — *Due Diligence Report* in connection with the distribution.

PART 6 — REPORTING REQUIREMENTS

6.1 Report of exempt distribution — (1) Subject to subsection (2) and section 6.2 [*When report not required*], issuers that distribute their own securities and underwriters that distribute securities they acquired under section 2.33 must file a completed report if they make the distribution under one or more of the following exemptions:

(a) section 2.3 [*Accredited investor*] or, in Ontario, section 73.3 of the *Securities Act* (Ontario) [*Accredited investor*];

    (b) section 2.5 [*Family, friends and business associates*];

    (c) subsection 2.9(1), (2) or (2.1) [*Offering memorandum*]

    (d) section 2.10 [*Minimum amount investment*];

    (e) section 2.12 [*Asset acquisition*];

    (f) section 2.13 [*Petroleum, natural gas and mining properties*];

    (g) section 2.14 [*Securities for debt*];

    (h) section 2.19 [*Additional investment in investment funds*];

    (i) section 2.30 [*Isolated distribution by issuer*];

    (j) section 5.2 [*TSX Venture Exchange offering*].

(2) The issuer or underwriter must file the report in the jurisdiction where the distribution takes place no later than 10 days after the distribution.

6.2 When report not required — (1) An issuer is not required to file a report under section 6.1(1)(a) [*Report of exempt distribution*] for a distribution of a debt security of its own issue or, concurrently with the distribution of the debt security, an equity security of its own issue, to a Canadian financial institution or a Schedule III bank.

(2) An investment fund is not required to file a report under section 6.1 [*Report of exempt distribution*] for a distribution under section 2.3 [*Accredited investor*], section 2.10 [*Minimum amount investment*] or section 2.19 [*Additional investment in investment funds*], or section 73.3 of the *Securities Act* (Ontario) [*Accredited investor*], if the investment fund files the report not later than 30 days after the end of the calendar year.

6.3 Required form of report of exempt distribution — (1) The required form of report under section 6.1 [*Report of exempt distribution*] is Form 45-106F1.

(2) Except in Manitoba, an issuer that makes a distribution under an exemption from a prospectus requirement not provided for in this Instrument is exempt from the requirements in securities legislation to file a report of exempt trade or exempt distribution in the required form if the issuer files a report of exempt distribution in accordance with Form 45-106F1.

6.4 Required form of offering memorandum — (1) The required form of offering memorandum under section 2.9 [*Offering memorandum*] is Form 45-106F2.

(2) Despite subsection (1), a qualifying issuer may prepare an offering memorandum in accordance with Form 45-106F3.

6.5 Required form of risk acknowledgement — (0.1) The required form of risk acknowledgement under subsection 2.3(6) [*Accredited investor*] is Form 45-106F9.

(1) The required form of risk acknowledgement under subsection 2.9(15) [*Offering memorandum*] is Form 45-106F4.

(1.1) In Alberta, New Brunswick, Nova Scotia, Ontario, Québec and Saskatchewan, the required form of risk acknowledgement for individual investors includes Schedule 1 *Classification of Investors Under the Offering Memorandum Exemption* and Schedule 2 *Investment Limits for Investors Under the Offering Memorandum Exemption* to Form 45-106F4.

(2) In Saskatchewan, the required form of risk acknowledgement under section 2.6 [*Family, friends and business associates — Saskatchewan*] is Form 45-106F5.

(3) In Ontario, the required form of risk acknowledgement under section 2.6.1 [*Family, friends and business associates — Ontario*] is Form 45-106F12.

6.6 [Repealed]

PART 7 — EXEMPTION

7.1 Exemption — (1) Subject to subsection (2), the regulator or the securities regulatory authority may grant an exemption to this Instrument, in whole or in part, subject to such conditions or restrictions as may be imposed in the exemption.

(2) In Ontario, only the regulator may grant an exemption and only from Part 6, in whole or in part, subject to such conditions or restrictions as may be imposed in the exemption.

(3) Except in Ontario, an exemption referred to in subsection (1) is granted under the statute referred to in Appendix B of National Instrument 14-101 *Definitions* opposite the name of the local jurisdiction.

PART 8 — TRANSITIONAL, COMING INTO FORCE

8.1 Additional investment — investment funds — exemption from prospectus requirement — The prospectus requirement does not apply to a distribution by an investment fund in a security of its own issue to a purchaser that initially acquired the security as principal before this Instrument came into force if

    (a) the security was initially acquired under any of the following provisions:

        (i) in Alberta, sections 86(e) and 131(1)(d) of the *Securities Act* (Alberta) as they existed prior to their repeal by sections 9(a) and 13 of the *Securities Amendment Act* (Alberta), 2003 SA c.32 and sections 66.2 and 122.2 of the *Alberta Securities Commission Rules* (*General*);

        (ii) in British Columbia, sections 45(2) (5) and (22), and 74(2) (4) and (19) of the *Securities Act* (British Columbia),

        (iii) in Manitoba, sections 19(3) and 58(1)(a) of the *Securities Act* (Manitoba) and section 90 of the *Securities Regulation* MR 491/88R;

        (iv) in New Brunswick, section 2.8 of Local Rule 45-501 *Prospectus and Registration Exemptions*;

        (v) in Newfoundland and Labrador, sections 36(1)(e) and 73(1)(d) of the *Securities Act* (Newfoundland and Labrador);

        (vi) in Nova Scotia, sections 41(1)(e) and 77(1)(d) of the *Securities Act* (Nova Scotia);

        (vii) in Northwest Territories, section 3(c) and (z) of Blanket Order No. 1;

        (viii) in Nunavut, section 3(c) and (z) of Blanket Order No. 1;

(ix) in Ontario, sections 35(1)5 and 72(1)(d) of the *Securities Act* (Ontario) and section 2.12 of Ontario Securities Commission Rule 45-501 *Exempt Distributions* that came into force on January 12, 2004;

(x) in Prince Edward Island, section 2(3)(d) of the *Securities Act* (Prince Edward Island) and Prince Edward Island Local Rule 45-512 — Exempt Distributions — Exemption for Purchase of Mutual Fund Securities;

(xi) in Québec, section 51 and 155.1(2) of the *Securities Act* (Québec);

(xii) in Saskatchewan, sections 39(1)(e) and 81(1)(d) of the *The Securities Act, 1988* (Saskatchewan).

(b) the distribution is of a security of the same class or series as the initial distribution, and

(c) the security holder, as at the date of the distribution, holds securities of the investment fund that have

(i) an acquisition cost of not less than the minimum amount prescribed by securities legislation referred to in paragraph (a) under which the initial distribution was conducted, or

(ii) a net asset value of not less than the minimum amount prescribed by securities legislation referred to in paragraph (a) under which the initial distribution was conducted.

8.1.1 [Repealed.]

In British Columbia section 8.1.1 was repealed by B.C. Reg. 227/2009. All other jurisdictions will repeal section 8.1.1 in these amendments.

8.2 Definition of "accredited investor" — investment fund — An investment fund that distributed its securities to persons pursuant to any of the following provisions is an investment fund under paragraph (n)(ii) of the definition of "accredited investor":

(a) in Alberta, sections 86(e) and 131(1)(d) of the *Securities Act* (Alberta) as they existed prior to their repeal by sections 9(a) and 13 of the *Securities Amendment Act* (Alberta), 2003 SA c.32 and sections 66.2 and 122.2 of the *Alberta Securities Commission Rules (General)*;

(b) in British Columbia, sections 45(2) (5) and (22), and 74(2) (4) and (19) of the *Securities Act* (British Columbia),

(c) in Manitoba, sections 19(3) and 58(1)(a) of the *Securities Act* (Manitoba) and section 90 of the *Securities Regulation* MR 491/88R;

(d) in New Brunswick, section 2.8 of Local Rule 45-501 *Prospectus and Registration Exemptions*;

(e) in Newfoundland and Labrador, sections 36(1)(e) and 73(1)(d) of the *Securities Act* (Newfoundland and Labrador);

(f) in Nova Scotia, sections 41(1)(e) and 77(1)(d) of the *Securities Act* (Nova Scotia);

(g) in Northwest Territories, section 3(c) and (z) of Blanket Order No. 2;

(h) in Nunavut, section 3(c) and (z) of Blanket Order No. 3;

(i) in Ontario, sections 35(1)5 and 72(1)(d) of the *Securities Act* (Ontario) and section 2.12 of Ontario Securities Commission Rule 45-501 *Exempt Distributions* that came into force on January 12, 2004;

(j) in Prince Edward Island, section 2(3)(d) of the *Securities Act* (Prince Edward Island) and Prince Edward Island Local Rule 45-512 -*Exempt Distributions — Exemption for Purchase of Mutual Fund Securities*;

(k) in Québec, section 51 and 155.1(2) of the *Securities Act* (Québec);

(l) in Saskatchewan, sections 39(1)(e) and 81(1)(d) of the *The Securities Act, 1988* (Saskatchewan).

8.3 Transition — Closely-held issuer — exemption from prospectus requirement — (1) In this section,

"2001 OSC Rule 45-501" means the Ontario Securities Commission Rule 45-501 *Exempt Distributions* that came into force on November 30, 2001;

"2004 OSC Rule 45-501" means the Ontario Securities Commission Rule 45-501 *Exempt Distributions* that came into force on January 12, 2004;

"closely-held issuer" has the same meaning as in 2004 OSC Rule 45-501;

(2) The prospectus requirement does not apply to a distribution of a security that was previously distributed by a closely-held issuer under section 2.1 of 2001 OSC Rule 45-501, or under section 2.1 of 2004 OSC Rule 45-501, to a person who purchases the security as principal and is

(a) a director, officer, employee, founder or control person of the issuer,

(b) a spouse, parent, grandparent, brother, sister or child of a director, executive officer, founder or control person of the issuer,

(c) a parent, grandparent, brother, sister or child of the spouse of a director, executive officer, founder or control person of the issuer,

(d) a close personal friend of a director, executive officer, founder or control person of the issuer,

(e) a close business associate of a director, executive officer, founder or control person of the issuer,

(f) a spouse, parent, grandparent, brother, sister or child of the selling security holder or of the selling security holder's spouse,

(g) a security holder of the issuer,

(h) an accredited investor,

(i) a person of which a majority of the voting securities are beneficially owned by, or a majority of the directors are, persons described in paragraphs (a) to (h),

(j) a trust or estate of which all of the beneficiaries or a majority of the trustees or executors are persons described in paragraphs (a) to (h), or

(k) a person that is not the public.

8.3.1 [Repealed.]

In British Columbia section 8.3.1 was repealed by B.C. Reg. 227/2009. All other jurisdictions will repeal section 8.3.1 in these amendments.

8.4 Transition — reinvestment plan — Despite subsection 2.2(5), if an issuer's reinvestment plan was established before September 28, 2009, and provides for the distribution of a security that is of a different class or series than the class or series of the security to which the dividend or distribution is attributable, the issuer or the trustee, custodian or administrator of the plan must provide to each person who is already a participant the description of the material attributes and characteristics of the securities traded under the plan or notice of a source from which the participant can obtain the information not later than 140 days after the next financial year end of the issuer ending on or after September 28, 2009.

8.4.1 Transition — offering memorandum exemption — update of offering memorandum — Despite subsection 2.9(5.1), in Alberta, New Brunswick, Nova Scotia, Québec and Saskatchewan, an issuer is not required to update an offering memorandum that was filed in the local jurisdiction before April 30, 2016, solely to incorporate the statement required under paragraph 2.9(5.1)(a), unless the offering memorandum would otherwise be required to be updated pursuant to subsection 2.9(14) or Instruction B.12 of Form 45-106F2 *Offering Memorandum for Non-Qualifying Issuers*.

8.4.2 Transition — offering — memorandum exemption — marketing materials — Despite paragraph 2.9(17.1)(a), in Alberta, New Brunswick, Nova Scotia, Québec and Saskatchewan, OM marketing materials that relate to an offering memorandum that was filed in the local jurisdiction before April 30, 2016 and that are delivered or made reasonably available after April 30, 2016 must be filed within 10 days from the earlier of delivery to, or being made reasonably available to, a prospective purchaser.

8.4.3 Transition — investment funds — required form of report — Despite section 6.3, an investment fund that files a report on or before the date required by subsection 6.2(2) for a distribution that occurred before January 1, 2017 may file a report prepared in accordance with the version of Form 45-106F1 in force on June 29, 2016.

8.5 [Repealed.]

In British Columbia section 8.5 was repealed by B.C. Reg. 227/2009. All other jurisdictions will repeal section 8.5 in these amendments.

8.6 Repeal of former instrument — National Instrument 45-106 *Prospectus and Registration Exemptions* which came into force on September 14, 2005 is repealed on September 28, 2009.

8.7 Effective date — (1) Except in Ontario, this Instrument comes into force on September 28, 2009.

(2) In Ontario, this Instrument comes into force on the later of the following:

     a) September 28, 2009;

     (b) the day on which sections 5 and 11, subsection 12(1) and section 13 of Schedule 26 of the *Budget Measures Act, 2009* are proclaimed in force.

APPENDIX A — TO NATIONAL INSTRUMENT 45-106 PROSPECTUS EXEMPTIONS

Variable insurance contract exemption (section 2.39)

JURISDICTION	LEGISLATION REFERENCE
ALBERTA	"contract of insurance", "group insurance", "life insurance", and "policy" have the respective meanings assigned to them under the *Insurance Act* (Alberta) and the regulations under that Act.
	"insurance company" means an insurer as defined in the *Insurance Act* (Alberta) that is licensed under that Act.
BRITISH COLUMBIA	"contract", "group insurance", and "policy" have the respective meanings assigned to them under the *Insurance Act* (British Columbia) and the regulations under that Act.
	"life insurance" has the respective meaning assigned to it under the *Financial Institutions Act* (British Columbia) and the regulations under that Act.
	"insurance company" means an insurance company, or an extraprovincial insurance corporation, authorized to carry on insurance business under the *Financial Institutions Act* (British Columbia).
MANITOBA	"contract of insurance", "group insurance", "life insurance", and "policy" have the respective meanings assigned to them under the *Insurance Act* (Manitoba) and the regulations under that Act.
	"insurance company" means an insurer as defined in the *Insurance Act* (Manitoba) that is licensed under that Act.
NEW BRUNSWICK	"contract of insurance", "group insurance", "life insurance", and "policy" have the respective meanings assigned to them under the *Insurance Act* (New Brunswick) and the regulations under that Act.
	"insurance company" means an insurer as defined in the *Insurance Act* (New Brunswick) that is licensed under that Act.
NORTHWEST TERRITORIES	"contract", "group insurance", "life insurance", and "policy" have the respective meanings assigned to them under the *Insurance Act* (Northwest Territories).
	"insurance company" means an insurer as defined in the *Insurance Act* (Northwest Territories) that is licensed under that Act.

JURISDICTION	LEGISLATION REFERENCE
NOVA SCOTIA	"contract", "group insurance", "life insurance", and "policy" have the respective meanings assigned to them under the *Insurance Act* (Nova Scotia) and the regulations under that Act.
	"insurance company" has the same meaning as in section 3(1)(a) of the *General Securities Rules* (Nova Scotia).
ONTARIO	"contract", "group insurance", and "policy" have the respective meanings assigned to them in section 1 and 171 of the *Insurance Act* (Ontario).
	"life insurance" has the respective meaning assigned to it in Schedule 1 by Order of the Superintendent of Financial Services.
	"insurance company" has the same meaning as in section 1(2) of the *General Regulation* (Ont. Reg. 1015).
QUÉBEC	"contract of insurance", "group insurance", "life insurance", and "policy" have the respective meanings assigned to them under the Civil Code of Québec.
	"insurance company" means an insurer holding a license under the Act respecting insurance (R.S.Q., c. A-32).
PRINCE EDWARD ISLAND	"contract", "group insurance", "insurer", "life insurance and "policy" have the respective meanings assigned to them in sections 1 and 174 of the *Insurance Act* (Prince Edward Island).
	"insurance company" means an insurance company licensed under the *Insurance Act* (R.S.P.E.I. 1988, Cap. I-4),
SASKATCHEWAN	"contract", "life insurance" and "policy" have the respective meanings assigned to them in section 2 of *The Saskatchewan Insurance Act* (Saskatchewan).
	"group insurance" has the respective meaning assigned to it in section 133 of *The Saskatchewan Insurance Act* (Saskatchewan).
	"insurance company" means an issuer licensed under *The Saskatchewan Insurance Act* (Saskatchewan).
YUKON	"contract", "group", "life insurance" and "policy" have the respective meanings assigned to them under the *Insurance Act* (Yukon) and the regulations made under that Act.
	"insurance company" means an insurer as defined in the *Insurance Act* (Yukon) that is licensed under that Act.

APPENDIX B — TO NATIONAL INSTRUMENT 45-106 PROSPECTUS EXEMPTIONS

Control Block Distributions (PART 4)

JURISDICTION	LEGISLATION REFERENCE
ALBERTA	Section 1(p)(iii) of the *Securities Act* (Alberta)
BRITISH COLUMBIA	Paragraph (c) of the definition of "distribution" contained in section 1 of the *Securities Act* (British Columbia)
MANITOBA	Section 1(b) of the definition of "primary distribution to the public" contained in subsection 1(1) of the *Securities Act* (Manitoba)
NEW BRUNSWICK	Paragraph (c) of the definition of "distribution" contained in section 1(1) of the *Securities Act* (New Brunswick)
NEWFOUNDLAND AND LABRADOR	Section 2(1)(1)(iii) of the *Securities Act* (Newfoundland and Labrador)
NORTHWEST TERRITORIES	Paragraph (c) of the definition of "distribution" in subsection 1(1) of the *Securities Act* (Northwest Territories)
NOVA SCOTIA	Section 2(1)(1)(iii) of the *Securities Act* (Nova Scotia)
ONTARIO	Paragraph (c) of the definition of "distribution" contained in subsection 1(1) of the *Securities Act* (Ontario)
PRINCE EDWARD ISLAND	Section 1(f)(iii) of the *Securities Act* (Prince Edward Island)

JURISDICTION	LEGISLATION REFERENCE
QUÉBEC	Paragraph 9 of the definition of "distribution" contained section 5 of the *Securities Act* (Québec)
SASKATCHEWAN	Section 2(1)(r)(iii) of *The Securities Act, 1988* (Saskatchewan)
YUKON	Paragraph (c) of the definition of "distribution" in subsection 1(1) of the *Securities Act* (Yukon)

APPENDIX C — TO NATIONAL INSTRUMENT 45-106 PROSPECTUS EXEMPTIONS

Listing Representation Prohibitions

JURISDICTION	SECURITIES LEGISLATION REFERENCE
ALBERTA	Subsection 92(3) of the *Securities Act* (Alberta)
MANITOBA	Subsection 69(3) of *The Securities Act* (Manitoba)
NEW BRUNSWICK	Subsection 58(3) of the *Securities Act* (New Brunswick)
NEWFOUNDLAND AND LABRADOR	Subsection 39(3) of the *Securities Act* (Newfoundland and Labrador)
NORTHWEST TERRITORIES	Subsection 147(1) of the *Securities Act* (Northwest Territories)
NOVA SCOTIA	Subsection 44(3) of the *Securities Act* (Nova Scotia)
NUNAVUT	Subsection 147(1) of the *Securities Act* (Nunavut)
ONTARIO	Subsection 38(3) of the *Securities Act* (Ontario)
PRINCE EDWARD ISLAND	Subsection 147(1) of the *Securities Act* (Prince Edward Island)
QUÉBEC	Subsection 199(4) of the *Securities Act* (Québec)
SASKATCHEWAN	Subsection 44(3) of *The Securities Act, 1988* (Saskatchewan)
YUKON	Subsection 147(1) of the *Securities Act* (Yukon)

APPENDIX D — TO NATIONAL INSTRUMENT 45-106 PROSPECTUS EXEMPTIONS

Secondary Market Liability Provisions

JURISDICTION	SECURITIES LEGISLATION REFERENCE
ALBERTA	Part 17.01 of the *Securities Act* (Alberta)
BRITISH COLUMBIA	Part 16.1 of the *Securities Act* (British Columbia)
MANITOBA	Part XVIII of *The Securities Act* (Manitoba)
NEW BRUNSWICK	Part 11.1 of the *Securities Act* (New Brunswick)
NEWFOUNDLAND AND LABRADOR	Part XXII.1 of the *Securities Act* (Newfoundland and Labrador)
NORTHWEST TERRITORIES	Part 14 of the *Securities Act* (Northwest Territories)
NOVA SCOTIA	Sections 146A to 146N of the *Securities Act* (Nova Scotia)
NUNAVUT	Part 14 of the *Securities Act* (Nunavut)

JURISDICTION	SECURITIES LEGISLATION REFERENCE
ONTARIO	Part XXIII.1 of the *Securities Act* (Ontario)
PRINCE EDWARD ISLAND	Part 14 of the *Securities Act* (Prince Edward Island)
QUÉBEC	Division II of Chapter II of Title VIII of the *Securities Act* (Québec)
SASKATCHEWAN	Part XVIII.1 of *The Securities Act, 1988* (Saskatchewan)
YUKON	Part 14 of the *Securities Act* (Yukon)

Final Rule: (2005) 28 O.S.C.B. (Supp-4) 3; Approval by OSC: (2005) 28 O.S.C.B. (Supp-3) 1; Request for Comments: (2004) 27 O.S.C.B. (Supp-3) 1.

Amendment: (2006) 29 O.S.C.B. 75; Approval by OSC: (2005) 28 O.S.C.B. 9841.

Amendment: (2007) 30 O.S.C.B. 10522; Approval by OSC: (2007) 30 O.S.C.B. 8539.

Revised Rule: (2009) 32 O.S.C.B. (Supp. 5) 1; Approval by OSC: (2009) 32 O.S.C.B. (Supp. 3) 1; Request for Comments: (2009) 32 O.S.C.B. 4233 and (2008) 31 O.S.C.B. (Supp. 1) 1.

Amendment to Rule: (2010) 33 O.S.C.B. (Supp. 5) 111; Approval by OSC: (2010) 33 O.S.C.B. (Supp. 3) 213; Request for Comments: (2009) 32 O.S.C.B. 8464.

Amendment to Rule: CSAN 11-314.

Amendment to Rule: (2011) 34 O.S.C.B. 7085; Approval by OSC: (2011) 34 O.S.C.B. (Supp. 2) 1; Request for Comments: (2010) 33 O.S.C.B. 3703.

Amendment to Rule (B.C. only): CSAN 11-716.

Amendment to Rule: Approval by OSC: (2013) 36 O.S.C.B. 2619; Request for Comments: (2012) 35 O.S.C.B. 6887.

Amendment to Rule: Approval by OSC: (2014) 37 O.S.C.B. (Supp 4) 128; Request for Commments: (2013) 36 O.S.C.B. (Supp 3).

Amendment to Rule: Approval by OSC: (2015) 38 O.S.C.B. (Supp. 1) 7, 67 and 177; Request for Comment: (2014) 37 O.S.C.B. 1043 and (2014) 37 O.S.C.B. (Supp. 3).

Amendment to Rule: (2015) 38 OSCB 9255; Approval by OSC: (2015) 38 O.S.C.B. 7551.

Amendment to Rule: Approval by OSC: (2015), 38 O.S.C.B. 4162.

Amendment to Rule: Approval by OSC: (2015) 38 O.S.C.B. 5801.

Rules: NI 45-102; Rule 45-501.

Policies and Orders: CSAN 33-327, 45-304, 45-308; OSCN 33-735, 45-708, 45-709.

Form 45-106F1 — Report of Exempt Distribution

A. — General Instructions

1. — Filing instructions

An issuer or underwriter that is required to file a report of exempt distribution and pay the applicable fee must file the report and pay the fee as follows:

- **In British Columbia** — through BCSC eServices at http://www.bcsc.bc.ca.

- **In Ontario** — through the online e-form available at http://www.osc.gov.on.ca.

- **In all other jurisdictions** — through the System for Electronic Document Analysis and Retrieval (SEDAR) in accordance with National Instrument 13-101 *System for Electronic Document Analysis and Retrieval (SEDAR)* if required, or otherwise with the securities regulatory authority or regulator, as applicable, in the applicable jurisdictions at the addresses listed at the end of this form.

The issuer or underwriter must file the report in a jurisdiction of Canada if the distribution occurs in the jurisdiction. If a distribution is made in more than one jurisdiction of Canada, the issuer or underwriter may satisfy its obligation to file the report by completing a single report identifying all purchasers, and file the report in each jurisdiction of Canada in which the distribution occurs. Filing fees payable in a particular jurisdiction are not affected by identifying all purchasers in a single report.

In order to determine the applicable fee in a particular jurisdiction of Canada, consult the securities legislation of that jurisdiction.

2. — Issuers located outside of Canada

If an issuer located outside of Canada determines that a distribution has taken place in a jurisdiction of Canada, include information about purchasers resident in that jurisdiction only.

3. — Multiple distributions

An issuer may use one report for multiple distributions occurring within 10 days of each other, provided the report is filed on or before the 10th day following the first distribution date. However, an investment fund issuer that is relying on the exemptions set out in subsection 6.2(2) of NI 45-106 may file the report annually in accordance with that subsection.

4. — References to purchaser

References to a purchaser in this form are to the beneficial owner of the securities.

However, if a trust company, trust corporation, or registered adviser described in paragraph (p) or (q) of the definition of "accredited investor" in section 1.1 of NI 45-106 has purchased the securities on behalf of a fully managed account, provide information about the trust company, trust corporation or registered adviser only; do not include information about the beneficial owner of the fully managed account.

5. — References to issuer

References to "issuer" in this form include an investment fund issuer and a non-investment fund issuer, unless otherwise specified.

6. — Investment fund issuers

If the issuer is an investment fund, complete Items 1–3, 6–8, 10, 11 and Schedule 1 of this form.

7. — Mortgage investment entities

If the issuer is a mortgage investment entity, complete all applicable items of this form other than Item 6.

8. — Language

The report must be filed in English or in French. In Québec, the issuer or underwriter must comply with linguistic rights and obligations prescribed by Québec law.

9. — Currency

All dollar amounts in the report must be in Canadian dollars. If the distribution was made or any compensation was paid in connection with the distribution in a foreign currency, convert the currency to Canadian dollars using the daily noon exchange rate of the Bank of Canada on the distribution date. If the distribution date occurs on a date when the daily noon exchange rate of the Bank of Canada is not available, convert the currency to Canadian dollars using the most recent closing exchange rate of the Bank of Canada available before the distribution date. For investment funds in continuous distribution, convert the currency to Canadian dollars using the average daily noon exchange rate of the Bank of Canada for the distribution period covered by the report.

If the Bank of Canada no longer publishes a daily noon exchange rate and closing exchange rate, convert foreign currency using the daily single indicative exchange rate of the Bank of Canada in the same manner described in each of the three scenarios above.

If the distribution was not made in Canadian dollars, provide the foreign currency in Item 7(a) of the report.

10. — Date of information in report

Unless otherwise indicated in this form, provide the information as of the distribution end date.

11. — Date of formation

For the date of formation, provide the date on which the issuer was incorporated, continued or organized (formed). If the issuer resulted from an amalgamation, arrangement, merger or reorganization, provide the date of the most recent amalgamation, arrangement, merger or reorganization.

12. — Security codes

Wherever this form requires disclosure of the type of security, use the following security codes:

Security code	Security type
BND	Bonds
CER	Certificates (*including pass-through certificates, trust certificates*)
CMS	Common shares
CVD	Convertible debentures
CVN	Convertible notes
CVP	Convertible preferred shares
DEB	Debentures
FTS	Flow-through shares
FTU	Flow-through units
LPU	Limited partnership units

Security code	Security type
NOT	Notes *(include all types of notes except convertible notes)*
OPT	Options
PRS	Preferred shares
RTS	Rights
UBS	Units of bundled securities *(such as a unit consisting of a common share and a warrant)*
UNT	Units *(exclude units of bundled securities, include trust units and mutual fund units)*
WNT	Warrants
OTH	Other securities not included above *(if selected, provide details of security type in Item 7d)*

B. — Terms used in the form

1. For the purposes of this form:

"designated foreign jurisdiction" means Australia, France, Germany, Hong Kong, Italy, Japan, Mexico, the Netherlands, New Zealand, Singapore, South Africa, Spain, Sweden, Switzerland or the United Kingdom of Great Britain and Northern Ireland;

"eligible foreign security" means a security offered primarily in a foreign jurisdiction as part of a distribution of securities in either of the following circumstances:

    (a) the security is issued by an issuer

        (i) that is incorporated, formed or created under the laws of a foreign jurisdiction,

        (ii) that is not a reporting issuer in a jurisdiction of Canada,

        (iii) that has its head office outside of Canada, and

        (iv) that has a majority of the executive officers and a majority of the directors ordinarily resident outside of Canada;

    (b) the security is issued or guaranteed by the government of a foreign jurisdiction;

"foreign public issuer" means an issuer where any of the following apply:

    (a) the issuer has a class of securities registered under section 12 of the 1934 Act;

    (b) the issuer is required to file reports under section 15(d) of the 1934 Act;

    (c) the issuer is required to provide disclosure relating to the issuer and the trading in its securities to the public, to security holders of the issuer or to a regulatory authority and that disclosure is publicly available in a designated foreign jurisdiction;

"legal entity identifier" means a unique identification code assigned to the person

    (a) in accordance with the standards set by the Global Legal Entity Identifier System, or

    (b) that complies with the standards established by the Legal Entity Identifier Regulatory Oversight Committee for pre-legal entity identifiers;

"permitted client" has the same meaning as in National Instrument 31-103 *Registration Requirements, Exemptions and Ongoing Registrant Obligations*;

"SEDAR profile" means a filer profile required under section 5.1 of National Instrument 13-101 *System for Electronic Document Analysis and Retrieval (SEDAR)*.

2. For the purposes of this form, a person is connected with an issuer or an investment fund manager if either of the following applies:

    (a) one of them is controlled by the other;

    (b) each of them is controlled by the same person.

Form 45-106F1 — Report of Exempt Distribution
IT IS AN OFFENCE TO MAKE A MISREPRESENTATION IN THIS REPORT

ITEM 1 – REPORT TYPE

☐ New report

☐ Amended report   If amended, provide filing date of report that is being amended. ☐☐☐ (YYYY-MM-DD)

ITEM 2 – PARTY CERTIFYING THE REPORT

Indicate the party certifying the report (select only one). For guidance regarding whether an issuer is an investment fund, refer to section 1.1 of National Instrument 81-106 Investment Fund Continuous Disclosure *and the companion policy to NI 81-106.*

☐ Investment fund issuer

☐ Issuer (other than an investment fund)

☐ Underwriter

ITEM 3 – ISSUER NAME AND OTHER IDENTIFIERS

Provide the following information about the issuer, or if the issuer is an investment fund, about the fund.

Full legal name

Previous full legal name
If the issuer's name changed in the last 12 months, provide most recent previous legal name.

Website   (if applicable)

If the issuer has a legal entity identifier, provide below. Refer to Part B of the Instructions for the definition of "legal entity identifier".

Legal entity identifier

ITEM 4 – UNDERWRITER INFORMATION

If an underwriter is completing the report, provide the underwriter's full legal name and firm National Registration Database (NRD) number.

Full legal name

Firm NRD number ☐☐☐☐☐☐☐ (if applicable)

If the underwriter does not have a firm NRD number, provide the head office contact information of the underwriter.

Street address

Municipality   Province/State

Country   Postal code/Zip code

Telephone number   Website   (if applicable)

ITEM 5 – ISSUER INFORMATION

If the issuer is an investment fund, do not complete Item 5. Proceed to Item 6.

a) Primary industry

Provide the issuer's North American Industry Classification Standard (NAICS) code (6 digits only) that corresponds to the issuer's primary business activity. For more information on finding the NAICS industry code go to **Statistics Canada's NAICS industry search tool**.

NAICS industry code [ ][ ][ ][ ][ ][ ]

If the issuer is in the **mining industry,** indicate the stage of operations. This does not apply to issuers that provide services to issuers operating in the mining industry. Select the category that best describes the issuer's stage of operations.

[ ] Exploration   [ ] Development   [ ] Production

Is the issuer's primary business to invest all or substantially all of its assets in any of the following? If yes, select all that apply.

[ ] Mortgages   [ ] Real estate   [ ] Commercial/business debt   [ ] Consumer debt   [ ] Private companies

b) Number of employees

Number of employees: [ ] 0 – 49   [ ] 50 – 99   [ ] 100 – 499   [ ] 500 or more

c) SEDAR profile number

Does the issuer have a SEDAR profile?

[ ] No   [ ] Yes   If yes, provide SEDAR profile number [ ][ ][ ][ ][ ][ ][ ][ ]

If the issuer does not have a SEDAR profile complete Item 5(d) – (h).

d) Head office address

Street address		Province/State	
Municipality		Postal code/Zip code	
Country		Telephone number	

e) Date of formation and financial year-end

Date of formation [ ][ ][ ]   Financial year-end [ ][ ]
YYYY   MM   DD   MM   DD

f) Reporting issuer status

Is the issuer a reporting issuer in any jurisdiction of Canada?   [ ] No   [ ] Yes

If yes, select the jurisdictions of Canada in which the issuer is a reporting issuer.

[ ] All   [ ] AB   [ ] BC   [ ] MB   [ ] NB   [ ] NL   [ ] NT
[ ] NS   [ ] NU   [ ] ON   [ ] PE   [ ] QC   [ ] SK   [ ] YT

g) Public listing status

If the issuer has a CUSIP number, provide below (first 6 digits only)

CUSIP number [ ][ ][ ][ ][ ][ ]

If the issuer is publicly listed, provide the names of all exchanges on which its securities are listed. Include only the names of exchanges for which the issuer has applied for and received a listing, which excludes, for example, automated trading systems.

Exchange names [ ] [ ] [ ]

h) Size of issuer's assets

Select the size of the issuer's assets for its most recent financial year-end (Canadian $). If the issuer has not existed for a full financial year, provide the size of the issuer's assets at the distribution end date.

[ ] $0 to under $5M   [ ] $5M to under $25M   [ ] $25M to under $100M
[ ] $100M to under $500M   [ ] $500M to under $1B   [ ] $1B or over

ITEM 6 – INVESTMENT FUND ISSUER INFORMATION

If the issuer is an investment fund, provide the following information.

a) Investment fund manager information

Full legal name

Firm NRD Number [ ][ ][ ][ ][ ][ ][ ] **(if applicable)**

If the investment fund manager does not have a firm NRD number, provide the head office contact information of the investment fund manager.

Street Address

Municipality   Province/State

Country   Postal code/Zip code

Telephone number   Website (if applicable)

b) Type of investment fund

Type of investment fund that most accurately identifies the issuer (select only one).

[ ] Money market   [ ] Equity   [ ] Fixed income

[ ] Balanced   [ ] Alternative strategies   [ ] Other (describe)

Indicate whether one or both of the following apply to the investment fund.

[ ] Invests primarily in other investment fund issuers

[ ] Is a UCITs Fund[1]

[1]*Undertaking for the Collective Investment of Transferable Securities funds (UCITs Funds) are investment funds regulated by the European Union (EU) directives that allow collective investment schemes to operate throughout the EU on a passport basis on authorization from one member state.*

c) Date of formation and financial year-end of the investment fund

Date of formation [| |]   Financial year-end [|]
                  YYYY   MM   DD   MM   DD

d) Reporting issuer status of the investment fund

Is the investment fund a reporting issuer in any jurisdiction of Canada?   [ ] No   [ ] Yes

If yes, select the jurisdictions of Canada in which the investment fund is a reporting issuer.

[ ] All   [ ] AB   [ ] BC   [ ] MB   [ ] NB   [ ] NL   [ ] NT

[ ] NS   [ ] NU   [ ] ON   [ ] PE   [ ] QC   [ ] SK   [ ] YT

e) Public listing status of the investment fund

If the investment fund has a CUSIP number, provide below (first 6 digits only).

CUSIP number [ ][ ][ ][ ][ ][ ]

If the investment fund is publicly listed, provide the names of all exchanges on which its securities are listed. Include only the names of exchanges for which the investment fund has applied for and received a listing, which excludes, for example, automated trading systems.

Exchange names

f) Net asset value (NAV) of the investment fund

Select the NAV range of the investment fund as of the date of the most recent NAV calculation (Canadian $).

[ ] $0 to under $5M   [ ] $5M to under $25M   [ ] $25M to under $100M

[ ] $100M to under $500M   [ ] $500M to under $1B   [ ] $1B or over   Date of NAV calculation: [| |]
                                                                                                          YYYY   MM   DD

ITEM 7 – INFORMATION ABOUT THE DISTRIBUTION

If an issuer located outside of Canada completes a distribution in a jurisdiction of Canada, include in Item 7 and Schedule 1 information about purchasers resident in that jurisdiction of Canada only. Do not include in Item 7 securities issued as payment of commissions or finder's fees, which should be disclosed in Item 8. The information provided in Item 7 must reconcile with the information provided in Schedule 1 of the report.

a) Currency

Select the currency or currencies in which the distribution was made. All dollar amounts provided in the report must be in Canadian dollars.

☐ Canadian dollar   ☐ US dollar   ☐ Euro   Other (describe) _____

b) Distribution date(s)

State the distribution start and end dates. If the report is being filed for securities distributed on only one distribution date, provide the distribution date as both the start and end dates. If the report is being filed for securities distributed on a continuous basis, include the start and end dates for the distribution period covered by the report.

Start date [| |]   YYYY MM DD   End date [| |]   YYYY MM DD

c) Detailed purchaser information

Complete Schedule 1 of this form for each purchaser and attach the schedule to the completed report.

d) Types of securities distributed

Provide the following information for all distributions that take place in a jurisdiction of Canada on a per security basis. Refer to Part A of the Instructions for how to indicate the security code. If providing the CUSIP number, indicate the full 9-digit CUSIP number assigned to the security being distributed.

Security code	CUSIP number (if applicable)	Description of security	Number of securities	Canadian $		
				Single or lowest price	Highest price	Total amount

e) Details of rights and convertible/exchangeable securities

If any rights (e.g. warrants, options) were distributed, provide the exercise price and expiry date for each right. If any convertible/exchangeable securities were distributed, provide the conversion ratio and describe any other terms for each convertible/exchangeable security.

Security code	Underlying security code	Exercise price (Canadian $)		Expiry date (YYYY-MM-DD)	Conversion ratio	Describe other terms (if applicable)
		Lowest	Highest			

f) Summary of the distribution by jurisdiction and exemption

State the total dollar amount of securities distributed and the number of purchasers for each jurisdiction of Canada and foreign jurisdiction where a purchaser resides and for each exemption relied on in Canada for that distribution. However, if an issuer located outside of Canada completes a distribution in a jurisdiction of Canada, include distributions to purchasers resident in that jurisdiction of Canada only.

This table requires a separate line item for: (i) each jurisdiction where a purchaser resides, (ii) each exemption relied on in the jurisdiction where a purchaser resides, if a purchaser resides in a jurisdiction of Canada, and (iii) each exemption relied on in Canada, if a purchaser resides in a foreign jurisdiction.

For jurisdictions within Canada, state the province or territory, otherwise state the country.

Province or country	Exemption relied on	Number of purchasers	Total amount (Canadian $)
Total dollar amount of securities distributed			
Total number of unique purchasers[2]			

[2]*In calculating the total number of unique purchasers to which the issuer distributed securities, count each purchaser only once, regardless of whether the issuer distributed multiple types of securities to, and relied on multiple exemptions for, that purchaser.*

g)   Net proceeds to the investment fund by jurisdiction

If the issuer is an investment fund, provide the net proceeds to the investment fund for each jurisdiction of Canada and foreign jurisdiction where a purchaser resides.[3] If an issuer located outside of Canada completes a distribution in a jurisdiction of Canada, include net proceeds for that jurisdiction of Canada only. For jurisdictions within Canada, state the province or territory, otherwise state the country.

Province or country	Net proceeds (Canadian $)
Total net proceeds to the investment fund	

[3]*"Net proceeds" means the gross proceeds realized in the jurisdiction from the distributions for which the report is being filed, less the gross redemptions that occurred during the distribution period covered by the report.*

h)   Offering materials - This section applies only in Saskatchewan, Ontario, Québec, New Brunswick and Nova Scotia.

If a distribution has occurred in Saskatchewan, Ontario, Québec, New Brunswick or Nova Scotia, complete the table below by listing the offering materials that are required under the prospectus exemption relied on to be filed with or delivered to the securities regulatory authority or regulator in those jurisdictions.

In Ontario, if the offering materials listed in the table are required to be filed with or delivered to the Ontario Securities Commission (OSC), attach an electronic version of the offering materials that have not been previously filed with or delivered to the OSC.

	Description	Date of document or other material (YYYY-MM-DD)	Previously filed with or delivered to regulator? (Y/N)	Date previously filed or delivered (YYYY-MM-DD)
1.				
2.				
3.				

ITEM 8 – COMPENSATION INFORMATION

Provide information for each person (as defined in NI 45-106) to whom the issuer directly provides, or will provide, any compensation in connection with the distribution. **Complete additional copies of this page if more than one person was, or will be, compensated.**

Indicate whether any compensation was paid, or will be paid, in connection with the distribution.

[ ] No   [ ] Yes   If yes, indicate number of persons compensated. [ ]

a)   Name of person compensated and registration status

Indicate whether the person compensated is a registrant.

[ ] No   [ ] Yes

If the person compensated is an individual, provide the name of the individual.

Full legal name of individual [Family name | First given name | Secondary given names]

If the person compensated is not an individual, provide the following information.

Full legal name of non-individual [   ]

Firm NRD number [ ][ ][ ][ ][ ][ ][ ]   (if applicable)

Indicate whether the person compensated facilitated the distribution through a funding portal or an internet-based portal.

[ ] No   [ ] Yes

b)   Business contact information

If a firm NRD number is not provided in Item 8(a), provide the business contact information of the person being compensated.

Street address	[ ]		
Municipality	[ ]	Province/State	[ ]
Country	[ ]	Postal code/Zip code	[ ]
Email address	[ ]	Telephone number	[ ]

c)   Relationship to issuer or investment fund manager

Indicate the person's relationship with the issuer or investment fund manager (select all that apply). Refer to the meaning of "connected" in Part B(2) of the Instructions and the meaning of "control" in section 1.4 of NI 45-106 for the purposes of completing this section.

[ ] Connected with the issuer or investment fund manager

[ ] Insider of the issuer (other than an investment fund)

[ ] Director or officer of the investment fund or investment fund manager

[ ] Employee of the issuer or investment fund manager

[ ] None of the above

d)   Compensation details

Provide details of all compensation paid, or to be paid, to the person identified in Item 8(a) in connection with the distribution. Provide all amounts in Canadian dollars. Include cash commissions, securities-based compensation, gifts, discounts or other compensation. Do not report payments for services incidental to the distribution, such as clerical, printing, legal or accounting services. An issuer is not required to ask for details about, or report on, internal allocation arrangements with the directors, officers or employees of a non-individual compensated by the issuer.

Cash commissions paid [   ]

Value of all securities distributed as compensation[4] [   ]

	Security code 1	Security code 2	Security code 3
Security codes	[ ][ ][ ]	[ ][ ][ ]	[ ][ ][ ]

Describe terms of warrants, options or other rights [   ]

Other compensation[5] [   ]   Describe [   ]

Total compensation paid [   ]

[ ] Check box if the person will or may receive any deferred compensation (describe the terms below)

[   ]

[4]*Provide the aggregate value of all securities distributed as compensation, excluding options, warrants or other rights exercisable to acquire additional securities of the issuer. Indicate the security codes for all securities distributed as compensation, including options, warrants or other rights exercisable to acquire additional securities of the issuer.*

[5]*Do not include deferred compensation.*

ITEM 9 – DIRECTORS, EXECUTIVE OFFICERS AND PROMOTERS OF THE ISSUER

If the issuer is an investment fund, do not complete Item 9. Proceed to Item 10.

Indicate whether the issuer is any of the following (select all that apply).

☐ Reporting issuer in any jurisdiction of Canada

☐ Foreign public issuer

☐ Wholly owned subsidiary of a reporting issuer in any jurisdiction of Canada[6]

    Provide name of reporting issuer [_____]

☐ Wholly owned subsidiary of a foreign public issuer[6]

    Provide name of foreign public issuer [_____]

☐ Issuer distributing eligible foreign securities only to permitted clients[7]

If the issuer is at least one of the above, do not complete Item 9(a) – (c). Proceed to Item 10.

[6]An issuer is a wholly owned subsidiary of a reporting issuer or a foreign public issuer if all of the issuer's outstanding voting securities, other than securities that are required by law to be owned by its directors, are beneficially owned by the reporting issuer or the foreign public issuer, respectively.

[7]Check this box if it applies to the current distribution even if the issuer made previous distributions of other types of securities to non-permitted clients. Refer to the definitions of "eligible foreign security" and "permitted client" in Part B(1) of the Instructions.

☐ **If the issuer is none of the above, check this box and complete Item 9(a) – (c).**

a)   Directors, executive officers and promoters of the issuer

Provide the following information for each director, executive officer and promoter of the issuer. For locations within Canada, state the province or territory, otherwise state the country. For "Relationship to issuer", "D" – Director, "O" – Executive Officer, "P" – Promoter.

Organization or company name	Family name	First given name	Secondary given names	Business location of non-individual or residential jurisdiction of individual	Relationship to issuer (select all that apply)		
				Province or country	D	O	P

b)   Promoter information

If the promoter listed above is not an individual, provide the following information for each director and executive officer of the promoter. For locations within Canada, state the province or territory, otherwise state the country. For "Relationship to promoter", "D" – Director, "O" – Executive Officer.

Organization or company name	Family name	First given name	Secondary given names	Residential jurisdiction of individual	Relationship to promoter (select one or both if applicable)	
				Province or country	D	O

c)   Residential address of each individual

Complete Schedule 2 of this form providing the full residential address for each individual listed in Item 9(a) and (b) and attach to the completed report. Schedule 2 also requires information to be provided about control persons.

ITEM 10 – CERTIFICATION

Provide the following certification and business contact information of an officer or director of the issuer or underwriter. If the issuer or underwriter is not a company, an individual who performs functions similar to that of a director or officer may certify the report. For example, if the issuer is a trust, the report may be certified by the issuer's trustee. If the issuer is an investment fund, a director or officer of the investment fund manager (or, if the investment fund manager is not a company, an individual who performs similar functions) may certify the report if the director or officer has been authorized to do so by the investment fund.

The certification may not be delegated to an agent or other individual preparing the report on behalf of the issuer or underwriter. If the individual completing and filing the report is different from the individual certifying the report, provide their name and contact details in Item 11.

The signature on the report must be in typed form rather than handwritten form. The report may include an electronic signature provided the name of the signatory is also in typed form.

IT IS AN OFFENCE TO MAKE A MISREPRESENTATION IN THIS REPORT

By completing the information below, I certify to the securities regulatory authority or regulator that:

- I have read and understand this report; and
- all of the information provided in this report is true.

Full legal name			
	Family name	First given name	Secondary given names

Title

Name of issuer/underwriter/ investment fund manager

Telephone number   Email address

Signature   Date

YYYY   MM   DD

ITEM 11 – CONTACT PERSON

Provide the following business contact information for the individual that the securities regulatory authority or regulator may contact with any questions regarding the contents of this report, if different than the individual certifying the report in Item 10.

☐ Same as individual certifying the report

Full legal name				Title	
	Family name	First given name	Secondary given names		

Name of company

Telephone number   Email address

Notice – Collection and use of personal information

The personal information required under this form is collected on behalf of and used by the securities regulatory authority or regulator under the authority granted in securities legislation for the purposes of the administration and enforcement of the securities legislation.

If you have any questions about the collection and use of this information, contact the securities regulatory authority or regulator in the local jurisdiction(s) where the report is filed, at the address(es) listed at the end of this form.

The attached Schedules 1 and 2 may contain personal information of individuals and details of the distribution(s). The information in Schedules 1 and 2 will not be placed on the public file of any securities regulatory authority or regulator. However, freedom of information legislation may require the securities regulatory authority or regulator to make this information available if requested.

By signing this report, the issuer/underwriter confirms that each individual listed in Schedule 1 or 2 of the report who is resident in a jurisdiction of Canada:

a) has been notified by the issuer/underwriter of the delivery to the securities regulatory authority or regulator of the information pertaining to the individual as set out in Schedule 1 or 2, that this information is being collected by the securities regulatory authority or regulator under the authority granted in securities legislation, that this information is being collected for the purposes of the administration and enforcement of the securities legislation of the local jurisdiction, and of the title, business address and business telephone number of the public official in the local jurisdiction, as set out in this form, who can answer questions about the security regulatory authority's or regulator's indirect collection of the information, and

b) has authorized the indirect collection of the information by the securities regulatory authority or regulator.

Schedule 1 — To Form 45-106F1 (Confidential Purchaser Information)

Schedule 1 must be filed in the format of an Excel spreadsheet in a form acceptable to the securities regulatory authority or regulator.

The information in this schedule will not be placed on the public file of any securities regulatory authority or regulator. However, freedom of information legislation may require the securities regulatory authority or regulator to make this information available if requested.

a) General information *(provide only once)*

1. Name of issuer
2. Certification date (YYYY-MM-DD)

Provide the following information for each purchaser that participated in the distribution. For each purchaser, create separate entries for each distribution date, security type and exemption relied on for the distribution.

b) Legal name of purchaser

1. Family name
2. First given name
3. Secondary given names
4. Full legal name of non-individual *(if applicable)*

c) Contact information of purchaser

1. Residential street address
2. Municipality
3. Province/State
4. Postal code/Zip code
5. Country
6. Telephone number
7. Email address *(if available)*

d) Details of securities purchased

1. Date of distribution (YYYY-MM-DD)
2. Number of securities
3. Security code
4. Amount paid (Canadian $)

e) Details of exemption relied on

1. Rule, section and subsection number

2. If relying on section 2.3 [*Accredited investor*] of NI 45-106, provide the paragraph number in the definition of "accredited investor" in section 1.1 of NI 45-106 that applies to the purchaser. *(select only one)*

3. If relying on section 2.5 [*Family, friends and business associates*] of NI 45-106, provide:

   a. the paragraph number in subsection 2.5(1) that applies to the purchaser *(select only one)*; and

   b. if relying on paragraphs 2.5(1)(b) to (i), provide:

      i. the name of the director, executive officer, control person, or founder of the issuer or affiliate of the issuer claiming a relationship to the purchaser. *(Note: if Item 9(a) has been completed, the name of the director, executive officer or control person must be consistent with the name provided in Item 9 and Schedule 2.)*

      ii. the position of the director, executive officer, control person, or founder of the issuer or affiliate of the issuer claiming a relationship to the purchaser.

4. If relying on subsection 2.9(2) or, in Alberta, New Brunswick, Nova Scotia, Ontario, Québec, or Saskatchewan, subsection 2.9(2.1) [*Offering memorandum*] of NI 45-106 and the purchaser is an eligible investor, provide the paragraph number in the definition of "eligible investor" in section 1.1 of NI 45-106 that applies to the purchaser. *(select only one)*

f) Other information

1. Is the purchaser a registrant? (Y/N)

2. Is the purchaser an insider of the issuer? (Y/N) *(not applicable if the issuer is an investment fund)*

3. Full legal name of person compensated for distribution to purchaser. *If the person compensated is a registered firm, provide the firm NRD number only. (Note: the name must be consistent with name of the person compensated as provided in Item 8.)*

Instructions for Schedule 1

Any securities issued as payment for commissions or finder's fees must be disclosed in Item 8 of the report, not in Schedule 1.

Details of exemption relied on — When identifying the exemption the issuer relied on for the distribution to each purchaser, refer to the rule, statute or instrument in which the exemption is provided and identify the specific section and, if applicable, subsection or paragraph. For example, if the issuer is relying on an exemption in a National Instrument, refer to the number of the National Instrument, and the subsection or paragraph number of the specific provision. If the issuer is relying on an exemption in a local blanket order, refer to the blanket order by number.

For exemptions that require the purchaser to meet certain characteristics, such as the exemption in section 2.3 [*Accredited investor*], section 2.5 [*Family, friends and business associates*] or subsection 2.9(2) or, in Alberta, New Brunswick, Nova Scotia, Ontario, Québec, or Saskatchewan, subsection 2.9(2.1) [*Offering memorandum*] of NI 45-106, provide the specific paragraph in the definition of those terms that applies to each purchaser.

Reports filed under paragraph 6.1(1)(j) [*TSX Venture Exchange offering*] **of NI 45-106** — For reports filed under paragraph 6.1(1)(j) [*TSX Venture Exchange offering*] of NI 45-106, Schedule 1 needs to list the total number of purchasers by jurisdiction only, and is not required to include the name, residential address, telephone number or email address of the purchasers.

Schedule 2 — To Form 45-106F1 (Confidential Director, Executive Officer, Promoter and Control Person Information)

Schedule 2 must be filed in the format of an Excel spreadsheet in a form acceptable to the securities regulatory authority or regulator.

Complete the following only if Item 9(a) is required to be completed. **This schedule also requires information to be provided about control persons of the issuer at the time of the distribution.**

The information in this schedule will not be placed on the public file of any securities regulatory authority or regulator. However, freedom of information legislation may require the securities regulatory authority or regulator to make this information available if requested.

a) General information (*provide only once*)

1. Name of issuer
2. Certification date (YYYY-MM-DD)

b) Business contact information of Chief Executive Officer (*if not provided in Item 10 or 11 of report*)

1. Email address
2. Telephone number

c) Residential address of directors, executive officers, promoters and control persons of the issuer

Provide the following information for each individual who is a director, executive officer, promoter or control person of the issuer at the time of the distribution. If the promoter or control person is not an individual, provide the following information for each director and executive officer of the promoter and control person. (Note: names of directors, executive officers and promoters must be consistent with the information in Item 9 of the report, if required to be provided.)

1. Family name
2. First given name
3. Secondary given names
4. Residential street address
5. Municipality
6. Province/State
7. Postal code/Zip code
8. Country
9. Indicate whether the individual is a control person, or a director and/or executive officer of a control person (*if applicable*)

d) Non-individual control persons (*if applicable*)

If the control person is not an individual, provide the following information. For locations within Canada, state the province or territory, otherwise state the country.

1. Organization or company name
2. Province or country of business location

Questions:

Refer any questions to:

Alberta Securities Commission

Suite 600, 250 - 5th Street SW

Calgary, Alberta T2P 0R4

Telephone: (403) 297-6454

Toll free in Canada: 1-877-355-0585

Facsimile: (403) 297-2082

British Columbia Securities Commission

P.O. Box 10142, Pacific Centre

701 West Georgia Street

Vancouver, British Columbia V7Y 1L2

Inquiries: (604) 899-6854

Toll free in Canada: 1-800-373-6393

Facsimile: (604) 899-6581

Email: inquiries@bcsc.bc.ca

The Manitoba Securities Commission

500 - 400 St. Mary Avenue

Winnipeg, Manitoba R3C 4K5

Telephone: (204) 945-2548

Toll free in Manitoba 1-800-655-5244

Facsimile: (204) 945-0330

Financial and Consumer Services Commission (New Brunswick)

85 Charlotte Street, Suite 300

Saint John, New Brunswick E2L 2J2

Telephone: (506) 658-3060

Toll free in Canada: 1-866-933-2222

Facsimile: (506) 658-3059

Email: info@fcnb.ca

Government of Newfoundland and Labrador

Financial Services Regulation Division

P.O. Box 8700

Confederation Building

2nd Floor, West Block

Prince Philip Drive

St. John's, Newfoundland and Labrador A1B 4J6

Attention: Director of Securities

Telephone: (709) 729-4189

Facsimile: (709) 729-6187

Government of the Northwest Territories

Office of the Superintendent of Securities

P.O. Box 1320

Yellowknife, Northwest Territories X1A 2L9

Attention: Deputy Superintendent, Legal & Enforcement

Telephone: (867) 920-8984

Facsimile: (867) 873-0243

Nova Scotia Securities Commission

Suite 400, 5251 Duke Street

Duke Tower

P.O. Box 458

Halifax, Nova Scotia B3J 2P8

Telephone: (902) 424-7768

Facsimile: (902) 424-4625

Government of Nunavut

Department of Justice

Legal Registries Division

P.O. Box 1000, Station 570

1st Floor, Brown Building

Iqaluit, Nunavut X0A 0H0

Telephone: (867) 975-6590

Facsimile: (867) 975-6594

Ontario Securities Commission

20 Queen Street West, 22nd Floor

Toronto, Ontario M5H 3S8

Telephone: (416) 593- 8314

Toll free in Canada: 1-877-785-1555

Facsimile: (416) 593-8122

Email: exemptmarketfilings@osc.gov.on.ca

Public official contact regarding indirect collection of information:

Inquiries Officer

Prince Edward Island Securities Office

95 Rochford Street, 4th Floor Shaw Building

P.O. Box 2000

Charlottetown, Prince Edward Island C1A 7N8

Telephone: (902) 368-4569

Facsimile: (902) 368-5283

Autorité des marchés financiers

800, Square Victoria, 22e étage

C.P. 246, Tour de la Bourse

Montréal, Québec H4Z 1G3

Telephone: (514) 395-0337 or 1-877-525-0337

Facsimile: (514) 873-6155 (For filing purposes only)

Facsimile: (514) 864-6381 (For privacy requests only)

Email: financementdessocietes@lautorite.qc.ca (For corporate finance issuers); fonds_dinvestissement@lautorite.qc.ca (For investment fund issuers)

Financial and Consumer Affairs Authority of Saskatchewan

Suite 601 - 1919 Saskatchewan Drive

Regina, Saskatchewan S4P 4H2

Telephone: (306) 787-5879

Facsimile: (306) 787-5899

Government of Yukon

Department of Community Services

Law Centre, 3rd Floor

2130 Second Avenue

Whitehorse, Yukon Y1A 5H6

Telephone: (867) 667-5314

Facsimile: (867) 393-6251

Form 45-106F2 — Offering Memorandum for Non-Qualifying Issuers

Date: [Insert the date from the certificate page.]

The Issuer

Name:

Head office:

    Address:

    Phone #:

    E-mail address:

    Fax #:

Currently listed or quoted? [If no, state in bold type: **"These securities do not trade on any exchange or market"**. If yes, state where, e.g., TSX/TSX Venture Exchange.]

Reporting issuer? [Yes/No. If yes, state where.]

SEDAR filer? [Yes/No]

The Offering

Securities offered:

Price per security:

Minimum/Maximum offering: [If there is no minimum, state in bold type: "**There is no minimum.**" and also state in bold type: "**You may be the only purchaser.**"]

State in bold type: **Funds available under the offering may not be sufficient to accomplish our proposed objectives.**

Minimum subscription amount: [State the minimum amount each investor must invest, or state "There is no minimum subscription amount an investor must invest."]

Payment terms:

Proposed closing date(s):

Income tax consequences: There are important tax consequences to these securities. See item 6. [If income tax consequences are not material, delete this item.]

Selling agent? [Yes/No. If yes, state "See item 7". The name of the selling agent may also be stated.]

Resale restrictions

State: "You will be restricted from selling your securities for [4 months and a day/an indefinite period]. See item 10."

Purchaser's rights

State: "You have 2 business days to cancel your agreement to purchase these securities. If there is a misrepresentation in this offering memorandum, you have the right to sue either for damages or to cancel the agreement. See item 11."

State in bold type:

"No securities regulatory authority or regulator has assessed the merits of these securities or reviewed this offering memorandum. Any representation to the contrary is an offence. This is a risky investment. See item 8."

[All of the above information must appear on a single cover page.]

Item 1 — Use of Available Funds

1.1 *Funds* — Using the following table, disclose the funds available as a result of the offering. If the issuer plans to combine additional sources of funding with the available funds from the offering to achieve its principal capital-raising purpose, please provide details about each additional source of funding. If there is no minimum offering, state "$0" as the minimum.

Disclose also the amount of any working capital deficiency, if any, of the issuer as at a date not more than 30 days prior to the date of the offering memorandum. If the working capital deficiency will not be eliminated by the use of available funds, state how the issuer intends to eliminate or manage the deficiency.

		Assuming min. offering	Assuming max. offering
A.	Amount to be raised by this offering	$	$
B.	Selling commissions and fees	$	$
C.	Estimated offering costs (e.g., legal, accounting, audit.)	$	$
D.	Available funds: D = A - (B+C)	$	$
E.	Additional sources of funding required	$	$
F.	Working capital deficiency	$	$
G.	Total: G = (D+E) - F	$	$

1.2 *Use of Available Funds* — Using the following table, provide a detailed breakdown of how the issuer will use the available funds. If any of the available funds will be paid to a related party, disclose in a note to the table the name of the related party, the relationship to the issuer, and the amount. If the issuer has a working capital deficiency, disclose the portion, if any, of the available funds to be applied against the working capital deficiency. If more than 10% of the available funds will be used by the issuer to pay debt and the issuer incurred the debt within the two preceding financial years, describe why the debt was incurred.

Description of intended use of available funds listed in order of priority	Assuming min. offering	Assuming max. offering
	$	$
	$	$
Total: Equal to G in the Funds table above	$	$

1.3 *Reallocation* — The available funds must be used for the purposes disclosed in the offering memorandum. The board of directors can reallocate the proceeds to other uses only for sound business reasons. If the available funds may be reallocated, include the following statement:

We intend to spend the available funds as stated. We will reallocate funds only for sound business reasons.

Item 2 — Business of [name of issuer or other term used to refer to issuer]

2.1 *Structure* — State the business structure (e.g., partnership, corporation or trust), the statute and the province, state or other jurisdiction under which the issuer is incorporated, continued or organized, and the date of incorporation, continuance or organization.

2.2 *Our Business* — Describe the issuer's business. The disclosure must provide sufficient information to enable a prospective purchaser to make an informed investment decision. For a non-resource issuer this disclosure may include principal products or services, operations, market, marketing plans and strategies and a discussion of the issuer's current and prospective competitors. For a resource issuer this will require a description of principal properties (including interest held) and a summary of material information including, if applicable: the stage of development, reserves, geology, operations, production and mineral reserves or mineral resources being explored or developed. A resource issuer disclosing scientific or technical information for a mineral project must follow General Instruction A.8 of this Form. A resource issuer disclosing information about its oil and gas activities must follow General Instruction A.9 of this Form.

2.3 *Development of Business* — Describe (generally, in one or two paragraphs) the general development of the issuer's business over at least its two most recently completed financial years and any subsequent period. Include the major events that have occurred or conditions that have influenced (favourably or unfavourably) the development of the issuer.

2.4 *Long Term Objectives* — Describe each significant event that must occur to accomplish the issuer's long term objectives, state the specific time period in which each event is expected to occur, and the costs related to each event.

2.5 *Short Term Objectives and How We Intend to Achieve Them*

(a) Disclose the issuer's objectives for the next 12 months.

(b) Using the following table, disclose how the issuer intends to meet those objectives for the next 12 months.

What we must do and how we will do it	Target completion date or, if not known, number of months to complete	Our cost to complete
		$
		$

2.6 *Insufficient Funds*

If applicable, disclose that the funds available as a result of the offering either may not or will not be sufficient to accomplish all of the issuer's proposed objectives and there is no assurance that alternative financing will be available. If alternative financing has been arranged, disclose the amount, source and all outstanding conditions that must be satisfied.

2.7 *Material Agreements* — Disclose the key terms of all material agreements

(a) to which the issuer is currently a party, or

(b) with a related party including the following information:

(i) if the agreement is with a related party, the name of the related party and the relationship,

(ii) a description of any asset, property or interest acquired, disposed of, leased, under option, etc.,

(iii) a description of any service provided,

(iv) purchase price and payment terms (e.g., paid in instalments, cash, securities or work commitments),

(v) the principal amount of any debenture or loan, the repayment terms, security, due date and interest rate,

(vi) the date of the agreement,

(vii) the amount of any finder's fee or commission paid or payable to a related party in connection with the agreement,

(viii) any material outstanding obligations under the agreement, and

(ix) for any transaction involving the purchase of assets by or sale of assets to the issuer from a related party, state the cost of the assets to the related party, and the cost of the assets to the issuer.

Item 3 — Interests of Directors, Management, Promoters and Principal Holders

3.1 *Compensation and Securities Held* — Using the following table, provide the specified information about each director, officer and promoter of the issuer and each person who, directly or indirectly, beneficially owns or controls 10% or more of any class of voting securities of the issuer (a "principal holder"). If the principal holder is not an individual, state in a note to the table the name of any person that, directly or indirectly, beneficially owns or controls more than 50% of the voting rights of the principal holder. If the issuer has not completed its first financial year, then include compensation paid since inception. Compensation includes any form of remuneration including cash, shares and options.

Name and municipality of principal residence	Positions held (e.g., director, officer, promoter and/or principal holder) and the date of obtaining that position	Compensation paid by issuer or related party in the most recently completed financial year and the compensation anticipated to be paid in the current financial year	Number, type and percentage of securities of the issuer held after completion of min. offering	Number, type and percentage of securities of the issuer held after completion of max. offering

3.2 *Management Experience* — Using the following table, disclose the principal occupations of the directors and executive officers over the past five years. In addition, for each individual, describe any relevant experience in a business similar to the issuer's.

Name	Principal occupation and related experience

3.3 *Penalties, Sanctions and Bankruptcy*

(a) Disclose any penalty or sanction (including the reason for it and whether it is currently in effect) that has been in effect during the last 10 years, or any cease trade order that has been in effect for a period of more than 30 consecutive days during the past 10 years against

    (i) a director, executive officer or control person of the issuer, or

    (ii) an issuer of which a person referred to in (i) above was a director, executive officer or control person at the time.

(b) Disclose any declaration of bankruptcy, voluntary assignment in bankruptcy, proposal under any bankruptcy or insolvency legislation, proceedings, arrangement or compromise with creditors or appointment of a receiver, receiver manager or trustee to hold assets, that has been in effect during the last 10 years with regard to any

    (i) director, executive officer or control person of the issuer, or

    (ii) issuer of which a person referred to in (i) above was a director, executive officer or control person at that time.

3.4 *Loans* — Disclose the principal amount of any debenture or loan, the repayment terms, security, due date and interest rate due to or from the directors, management, promoters and principal holders as at a date not more than 30 days prior to the date of the offering memorandum.

Item 4 — Capital Structure

4.1 *Share Capital* — Using the following table, provide the required information about outstanding securities of the issuer (including options, warrants and other securities convertible into shares). If necessary, notes to the table may be added to describe the material terms of the securities.

Description of security

Number authorized to be issued

Description of security	Number authorized to be issued	Price per security	Number outstanding as at [a date not more than 30 days prior to the offering memorandum date]	Number outstanding after min. offering	Number outstanding after max. offering

4.2 *Long Term Debt Securities* — Using the following table, provide the required information about outstanding long term debt of the issuer. Disclose the portion of the debt due within 12 months of the date of the offering memorandum. If the securities being offered are debt securities, add a column to the table disclosing the amount of debt that will be outstanding after both the minimum and maximum offering. If the debt is owed to a related party, indicate that in a note to the table and identify the related party.

Description of long term debt (including whether secured)	Interest rate	Repayment terms	Amount outstanding at [a date not more than 30 days prior to the offering memorandum date]
			$
			$

4.3 *Prior Sales* — If the issuer has issued any securities of the class being offered under the offering memorandum (or convertible or exchangeable into the class being offered under the offering memorandum) within the last 12 months, use the following table to provide the information specified. If securities were issued in exchange for assets or services, describe in a note to the table the assets or services that were provided.

Date of issuance	Type of security issued	Number of securities issued	Price per security	Total funds received

Item 5 — Securities Offered

5.1 *Terms of Securities* — Describe the material terms of the securities being offered, including:

    (a) voting rights or restrictions on voting,

    (b) conversion or exercise price and date of expiry,

    (c) rights of redemption or retraction, and

    (d) interest rates or dividend rates.

5.2 *Subscription Procedure*

(a) Describe how a purchaser can subscribe for the securities and the method of payment.

(b) State that the consideration will be held in trust and the period that it will be held (refer at least to the mandatory two day period).

(c) Disclose any conditions to closing, e.g., receipt of additional funds from other sources. If there is a minimum offering, disclose when consideration will be returned to purchasers if the minimum is not met, and whether the issuer will pay the purchasers interest on consideration.

Item 6 — Income Tax Consequences and RRSP Eligibility

6.1 State: "You should consult your own professional advisers to obtain advice on the income tax consequences that apply to you."

6.2 If income tax consequences are a material aspect of the securities being offered (e.g., flow-through shares), provide

(a) a summary of the significant income tax consequences to Canadian residents, and

(b) the name of the person providing the income tax disclosure in (a).

6.3 Provide advice regarding the RRSP eligibility of the securities and the name of the person providing the advice or state "Not all securities are eligible for investment in a registered retirement savings plan (RRSP). You should consult your own professional advisers to obtain advice on the RRSP eligibility of these securities."

Item 7 — Compensation Paid to Sellers and Finders

If any person has or will receive any compensation (e.g., commission, corporate finance fee or finder's fee) in connection with the offering, provide the following information to the extent applicable:

(a) a description of each type of compensation and the estimated amount to be paid for each type,

(b) if a commission is being paid, the percentage that the commission will represent of the gross proceeds of the offering (assuming both the minimum and maximum offering),

(c) details of any broker's warrants or agent's option (including number of securities under option, exercise price and expiry date), and

(d) if any portion of the compensation will be paid in securities, details of the securities (including number, type and, if options or warrants, the exercise price and expiry date).

Item 8 — Risk Factors

Describe in order of importance, starting with the most important, the risk factors material to the issuer that a reasonable investor would consider important in deciding whether to buy the issuer's securities. Risk factors will generally fall into the following three categories:

(a) Investment Risk — risks that are specific to the securities being offered. Some examples include

- arbitrary determination of price,
- no market or an illiquid market for the securities,
- resale restrictions, and
- subordination of debt securities.

(b) Issuer Risk — risks that are specific to the issuer. Some examples include

- insufficient funds to accomplish the issuer's business objectives,
- no history or a limited history of revenue or profits,
- lack of specific management or technical expertise,
- management's regulatory and business track record,
- dependence on key employees, suppliers or agreements,
- dependence on financial viability of guarantor,
- pending and outstanding litigation, and
- political risk factors.

(c) Industry Risk — risks faced by the issuer because of the industry in which it operates. Some examples include

- environmental and industry regulation,
- product obsolescence, and
- competition.

Item 9 — Reporting Obligations

9.1 Disclose the documents, including any financial information required by the issuer's corporate legislation, constating documents, or other documents under which the issuer is organized, that will be sent to purchasers on an annual or on-going basis. If the issuer is not required to send any documents to the purchasers on an annual or on-going basis, state in bold type: **"We are not required to send you any documents on an annual or ongoing basis."**

9.2 If corporate or securities information about the issuer is available from a government, securities regulatory authority or regulator, SRO or quotation and trade reporting system, disclose where that information can be located (including website address).

Item 10 — Resale Restrictions

10.1 General Statement — For trades in Alberta, British Columbia, New Brunswick, Newfoundland and Labrador, Northwest Territories, Nova Scotia, Nunavut, Ontario, Prince Edward Island, Québec, Saskatchewan and Yukon, state:

> "These securities will be subject to a number of resale restrictions, including a restriction on trading. Until the restriction on trading expires, you will not be able to trade the securities unless you comply with an exemption from the prospectus and registration requirements under securities legislation."

10.2 Restricted Period — For trades in Alberta, British Columbia, New Brunswick, Newfoundland and Labrador, Northwest Territories, Nova Scotia, Nunavut, Ontario, Prince Edward Island, Québec, Saskatchewan and Yukon state one of the following, as applicable:

> (a) If the issuer is not a reporting issuer in a jurisdiction at the distribution date state:
>
> > "Unless permitted under securities legislation, you cannot trade the securities before the date that is 4 months and a day after the date [insert name of issuer or other term used to refer to the issuer] becomes a reporting issuer in any province or territory of Canada."
>
> (b) If the issuer is a reporting issuer in a jurisdiction at the distribution date state:
>
> > "Unless permitted under securities legislation, you cannot trade the securities before the date that is 4 months and a day after the distribution date."

10.3 Manitoba Resale Restrictions — For trades in Manitoba, if the issuer will not be a reporting issuer in a jurisdiction at the time the security is acquired by the purchaser state:

> "Unless permitted under securities legislation, you must not trade the securities without the prior written consent of the regulator in Manitoba unless
>
> > (a) [name of issuer or other term used to refer to issuer] has filed a prospectus with the regulator in Manitoba with respect to the securities you have purchased and the regulator in Manitoba has issued a receipt for that prospectus, or
> >
> > (b) you have held the securities for at least 12 months.
>
> The regulator in Manitoba will consent to your trade if the regulator is of the opinion that to do so is not prejudicial to the public interest."

Item 11 — Purchasers' Rights

State the following:

> "If you purchase these securities you will have certain rights, some of which are described below. For information about your rights you should consult a lawyer.
>
> **(1)** Two Day Cancellation Right — You can cancel your agreement to purchase these securities. To do so, you must send a notice to us by midnight on the 2nd business day after you sign the agreement to buy the securities.
>
> **(2)** Statutory Rights of Action in the Event of a Misrepresentation — [Insert this section only if the securities legislation of the jurisdiction in which the trade occurs provides purchasers with statutory rights in the event of a misrepresentation in an offering memorandum. Modify the language, if necessary, to conform to the statutory rights.] If there is a misrepresentation in this offering memorandum, you have a statutory right to sue:
>
> > (a) [name of issuer or other term used to refer to issuer] to cancel your agreement to buy these securities, or
> >
> > (b) for damages against [state the name of issuer or other term used to refer to issuer and the title of any other person against whom the rights are available].
>
> This statutory right to sue is available to you whether or not you relied on the misrepresentation. However, there are various defences available to the persons or companies that you have a right to sue. In particular, they have a defence if you knew of the misrepresentation when you purchased the securities.
>
> If you intend to rely on the rights described in (a) or (b) above, you must do so within strict time limitations. You must commence your action to cancel the agreement within [state time period provided by the securities legislation]. You must commence your action for damages within [state time period provided by the securities legislation.]
>
> **(3)** Contractual Rights of Action in the Event of a Misrepresentation — [Insert this section only if the securities legislation of the jurisdiction in which the purchaser is resident does not provide purchasers with statutory rights in the event of a misrepresentation in an offering memorandum.] If there is a misrepresentation in this offering memorandum, you have a contractual right to sue [name of issuer or other term used to refer to issuer]:
>
> > (a) to cancel your agreement to buy these securities, or
> >
> > (b) for damages.
>
> This contractual right to sue is available to you whether or not you relied on the misrepresentation. However, in an action for damages, the amount you may recover will not exceed the price that you paid for your securities and will not include any part of the damages that [name of issuer or other term used to refer to issuer] proves does not represent the depreciation in value of the securities resulting from the misrepresentation. [Name of issuer or other term used to refer to issuer] has a defence if it proves that you knew of the misrepresentation when you purchased the securities.
>
> If you intend to rely on the rights described in (a) or (b) above, you must do so within strict time limitations. You must commence your action to cancel the agreement within 180 days after you signed the agreement to purchase the securities. You must commence your action for damages within the earlier of 180 days after learning of the misrepresentation and 3 years after you signed the agreement to purchase the securities."

Item 12 — Financial Statements

Include in the offering memorandum immediately before the certificate page of the offering memorandum all required financial statements as set out in the Instructions.

Item 13 — Date and Certificate

State the following on the certificate page of the offering memorandum:

"Dated [insert the date the certificate page of the offering memorandum is signed].

This offering memorandum does not contain a misrepresentation."

Instructions for Completing — 45-106F2 Offering Memorandum for Non-Qualifying Issuers

A. — General Instructions

1. Draft the offering memorandum so that it is easy to read and understand. Be concise and use clear, plain language. Avoid technical terms. If technical terms are necessary, provide definitions.

2. Address the items required by the form in the order set out in the form. However, it is not necessary to provide disclosure about an item that does not apply.

3. The issuer may include additional information in the offering memorandum other than that specifically required by the form. An offering memorandum is generally not required to contain the level of detail and extent of disclosure required by a prospectus. Generally, this description should not exceed 2 pages. However, an offering memorandum must provide a prospective purchaser with sufficient information to make an informed investment decision.

4. The issuer may wrap the offering memorandum around a prospectus or similar document. However, all matters required to be disclosed by the offering memorandum must be addressed and the offering memorandum must provide a cross-reference to the page number or heading in the wrapped document where the relevant information is contained. The certificate to the offering memorandum must be modified to indicate that the offering memorandum, including the document around which it is wrapped, does not contain a misrepresentation.

5. It is an offence to make a misrepresentation in the offering memorandum. This applies both to information that is required by the form and to additional information that is provided. Include particulars of any material facts, which have not been disclosed under any of the Item numbers and for which failure to disclose would constitute a misrepresentation in the offering memorandum. Refer also to section 3.8(3) of Companion Policy 45-106CP for additional information.

6. When the term "related party" is used in this form, it refers to:

(a) a director, officer, promoter or control person of the issuer,

(b) in regard to a person referred to in (a), a child, parent, grandparent or sibling, or other relative living in the same residence,

(c) in regard to a person referred to in (a) or (b), his or her spouse or a person with whom he or she is living in a marriage-like relationship,

(d) an insider of the issuer,

(e) a company controlled by one or more individuals referred to in (a) to (d), and

(f) in the case of an insider, promoter or control person that is not an individual, any person that controls that insider, promoter or control person.

(If the issuer is not a reporting issuer, the reference to "insider" includes persons or companies who would be insiders of the issuer if that issuer were a reporting issuer.)

7. Disclosure is required in item 3.1 of compensation paid directly or indirectly by the issuer or a related party to a director, officer, promoter and/or principal holder if the issuer receives a direct benefit from such compensation paid.

8. Refer to National Instrument 43-101 *Standards of Disclosure for Mineral Projects* (NI 43-101) when disclosing scientific or technical information for a mineral project of the issuer.

9. If an oil and gas issuer is disclosing information about its oil and gas activities, it must ensure that the information is disclosed in accordance with Part 4 and Part 5 of National Instrument 51-101 Standards of Disclosure for Oil and Gas Activities (NI 51-101). Under section 5.3 of NI 51-101, disclosure of reserves or resources must be consistent with the reserves and resources terminology and categories set out in the Canadian Oil and Gas Evaluation Handbook. For the purposes of this instruction, references to reporting issuer in Part 4 and Part 5 of NI 51-101 will be deemed to include all issuers.

10. Securities legislation restricts what can be told to investors about the issuer's intent to list or quote securities on an exchange or market. Refer to applicable securities legislation before making any such statements.

11. If an issuer uses this form in connection with a distribution under an exemption other than section 2.9 (*offering memorandum*) of National Instrument 45-106 *Prospectus Exemptions*, the issuer must modify the disclosure in item 11 to correctly describe the purchaser's rights. If a purchaser does not have statutory or contractual rights of action in the event of a misrepresentation in the offering memorandum, that fact must be stated in bold on the face page.

12. During the course of a distribution of securities, any material forward-looking information disseminated must only be that which is set out in the offering memorandum. If an extract of FOFI, as defined in National Instrument 51-102 *Continuous Disclosure Obligations* (NI 51-102), is disseminated, the extract or summary must be reasonably balanced and have a cautionary note in boldface stating that the information presented is not complete and that complete FOFI is included in the offering memorandum.

B. — Financial Statements — General

1. All financial statements, operating statements for an oil and gas property that is an acquired business or a business to be acquired, and summarized financial information as to the aggregated amounts of assets, liabilities, revenue and profit or loss of an acquired business or business to be acquired that is, or will be, an investment accounted for by the issuer using the equity method included in the offering memoran-

dum must comply with National Instrument 52-107 *Acceptable Accounting Principles and Auditing Standards*, regardless of whether the issuer is a reporting issuer or not.

Under National Instrument 52-107 *Acceptable Accounting Principles and Auditing Standards*, financial statements are generally required to be prepared in accordance with Canadian GAAP applicable to publicly accountable enterprises. An issuer using this form cannot use Canadian GAAP applicable to private enterprises, except, subject to the requirements of NI 52-107, certain issuers may use Canadian GAAP applicable to private enterprises for financial statements for a business referred to in C.1. An issuer that is not a reporting issuer may prepare acquisition statements in accordance with the requirements of NI 52-107 as if the issuer were a venture issuer as defined in NI 51-102. For the purposes of Form 45-106F2, the "applicable time" in the definition of a venture issuer is the acquisition date.

2. Include all financial statements required by these instructions in the offering memorandum immediately before the certificate page of the offering memorandum.

3. If the issuer has not completed one financial year or its first financial year end is less than 120 days from the date of the offering memorandum, include in the offering memorandum financial statements of the issuer consisting of:

(a) a statement of comprehensive income, a statement of changes in equity and a statement of cash flows for the period from inception to a date not more than 90 days before the date of the offering memorandum,

(b) a statement of financial position as at the end of the period referred to in paragraph (a), and

(c) notes to the financial statements.

4. If the issuer has completed one or more financial years, include in the offering memorandum annual financial statements of the issuer consisting of:

(a) a statement of comprehensive income, a statement of changes in equity and a statement of cash flows for

(i) the most recently completed financial year that ended more than 120 days before the date of the offering memorandum, and

(ii) the financial year immediately preceding the financial year in clause (i), if any,

(b) a statement of financial position as at the end of each of the periods referred to in paragraph (a), and

(c) a statement of financial position as at the beginning of the earliest comparative period for which financial statements that are included in the offering memorandum comply with IFRS in the case of an issuer that

(i) discloses in its annual financial statements an unreserved statement of compliance with IFRS, and

(ii) does any of the following:

(A) applies an accounting policy retrospectively in its annual financial statements;

(B) makes a retrospective restatement of items in its annual financial statements;

(C) reclassifies items in its annual financial statements,

(d) in the case of an issuer's first IFRS financial statements as defined in NI 51-102, the opening IFRS statement of financial position at the date of transition to IFRS as defined in NI 51-102, and

(e) notes to the financial statements.

4.1 If an issuer presents the components of profit or loss in a separate income statement, the separate income statement must be displayed immediately before the statement of comprehensive income filed under Item 4 above.

5. If the issuer has completed one or more financial years, include in the offering memorandum an interim financial report of the issuer comprised of:

(a) a statement of comprehensive income, a statement of changes in equity and a statement of cash flows for the most recently completed interim period that ended

(i) more than 60 days before the date of the offering memorandum, and

(ii) after the year-end date of the financial statements required under B.4(a)(i),

(b) a statement of comprehensive income, a statement of changes in equity and a statement of cash flows for the corresponding period in the immediately preceding financial year, if any,

(c) a statement of financial position as at the end of the period required by paragraph (a) and the end of the immediately preceding financial year

(d) a statement of financial position as at the beginning of the earliest comparative period for which financial statements that are included in the offering memorandum comply with IFRS in the case of an issuer that

(i) discloses in its interim financial report an unreserved statement of compliance with International Accounting Standard 34 *Interim Financial Reporting*, and

(ii) does any of the following:

(A) applies an accounting policy retrospectively in its interim financial report;

(B) makes a retrospective restatement of items in its interim financial report;

(C) reclassifies items in its interim financial report,

(e) in the case of the first interim financial report in the year of adopting IFRS, the opening IFRS statement of financial position at the date of transition to IFRS,

(f) for an issuer that is not a reporting issuer in at least one jurisdiction of Canada immediately before filing the offering memorandum, if the issuer is including an interim financial report of the issuer for the second or third interim period in the year of adopting IFRS include

    (i) the issuer's first interim financial report in the year of adopting IFRS, or

    (ii) both

        (A) the opening IFRS statement of financial position at the date of transition to IFRS, and

        (B) the annual and date of transition to IFRS reconciliations required by IFRS 1 *First-time Adoption of International Financial Reporting Standards* to explain how the transition from previous GAAP to IFRS affected the issuer's reported financial position, financial performance and cash flows, and

  (g) notes to the financial statements.

5.1 If an issuer presents the components of profit or loss in a separate income statement, the separate income statement must be displayed immediately before the statement of comprehensive income filed under item 5 above.

6. An issuer is not required to include the comparative financial information for the period in B.4.(a)(ii) in an offering memorandum if the issuer includes financial statements for a financial year ended less than 120 days before the date of the offering memorandum.

7. For an issuer that is not an investment fund, the term "interim period" has the meaning set out in NI 51-102. In most cases, an interim period is a period ending nine, six, or three months before the end of a financial year. For an issuer that is an investment fund, the term "interim period" has the meaning set out in National Instrument 81-106 — *Investment Fund Continuous Disclosure* (NI 81-106).

8. The comparative financial information required under B.5(b) and (c) may be omitted if the issuer has not previously prepared financial statements in accordance with its current or, if applicable, its previous GAAP.

9. The financial statements required by B.3 and the financial statements of the most recently completed financial period referred to in B.4 must be audited. The financial statements required under B.5, B.6 and the comparative financial information required by B.4 may be unaudited; however, if any of those financial statements have been audited, the auditor's report must be included in the offering memorandum.

10. Refer to National Instrument 52-108 *Auditor Oversight* for requirements relating to reporting issuers and public accounting firms.

11. All unaudited financial statements and unaudited comparatives must be clearly labelled as unaudited.

12. If the offering memorandum does not contain audited financial statements for the issuer's most recently completed financial year, and if the distribution is ongoing, update the offering memorandum to include the annual audited financial statements and the accompanying auditor's report as soon as the issuer has approved the audited financial statements, but in any event no later than the 120th day following the financial year end.

13. The offering memorandum does not have to be updated to include interim financial reports for periods completed after the date that is 60 days before the date of the offering memorandum unless it is necessary to prevent the offering memorandum from containing a misrepresentation.

14. Forward looking information, as defined in NI 51-102, included in an offering memorandum must comply with section 4A.2 of NI 51-102 and must include the disclosure described in section 4A.3 of NI 51-102. In addition to the foregoing, FOFI or a financial outlook, each as defined in NI 51-102, included in an offering memorandum must comply with Part 4B of NI 51-102. For an issuer that is not a reporting issuer, references to "reporting issuer" in section 4A.2, section 4A.3 and Part 4B of NI 51-102 should be read as references to an "issuer". Additional guidance may be found in the companion policy to NI 51-102.

15. If the issuer is a limited partnership, in addition to the financial statements required for the issuer, include in the offering memorandum the financial statements in accordance with Part B for the general partner and, if the limited partnership has active operations, for the limited partnership.

16. Despite section B.5, an issuer may include a comparative interim financial report of the issuer for the most recent interim period, if any, ended

  (a) subsequent to the most recent financial year in respect of which annual financial statements of the issuer are included in the offering memorandum, and

  (b) more than 90 days before the date of the offering memorandum.

This section does not apply unless

  (a) the comparative interim financial report is the first interim financial report required to be filed in the year of adopting IFRS, and the issuer is disclosing, for the first time, a statement of compliance with International Accounting Standard 34 *Interim Financial Reporting*,

  (b) the issuer is a reporting issuer in the local jurisdiction immediately before the date of the offering memorandum, and

  (c) the offering memorandum is dated before June 29, 2012.

C. — Financial Statements — Business Acquisitions

1. If the issuer

  (a) has acquired a business during the past two years and the audited financial statements of the issuer included in the offering memorandum do not include the results of the acquired business for 9 consecutive months, or

  (b) is proposing to acquire a business and the acquisition has progressed to a state where a reasonable person would believe that the likelihood of the acquisition being completed is high,

  include the financial statements specified in C.4 for the business if either of the tests in C.2 is met, irrespective of how the issuer accounts, or will account, for the acquisition.

2. Include the financial statements specified in C.4 for a business referred to in C.1 if either:

(a) the issuer's proportionate share of the consolidated assets of the business exceeds 40% of the consolidated assets of the issuer calculated using the annual financial statements of each of the issuer and the business for the most recently completed financial year of each that ended before the acquisition date or, for a proposed acquisition, the date of the offering memorandum or

(b) the issuer's consolidated investments in and advances to the business as at the acquisition date or the proposed acquisition date exceeds 40% of the consolidated assets of the issuer, excluding any investments in or advances to the business, as at the last day of the issuer's most recently completed financial year that ended before the acquisition date or the date of the offering memorandum for a proposed acquisition. For information about how to perform the investment test in this paragraph, please refer to subsections 8.3(4.1) and (4.2) of NI 51-102. Additional guidance may be found in the companion policy to NI 51-102.

2.1 [repealed]

3. If an issuer or a business has not yet completed a financial year, or its first financial year ended within 120 days of the offering memorandum date, use the financial statements referred to in B.3 to make the calculations in C.2.

4. If under C.2 you must include in an offering memorandum financial statements for a business, the financial statements must include:

(a) If the business has not completed one financial year or its first financial year end is less than 120 days from the date of the offering memorandum

     (i) a statement of comprehensive income, a statement of changes in equity and a statement of cash flows.

         A) for the period from inception to a date not more than 90 days before the date of the offering memorandum, or

         B) if the acquisition date precedes the ending date of the period referred to in (A), for the period from inception to the acquisition date or a date not more than 45 days before the acquisition date,

     (ii) a statement of financial position dated as at the end of the period referred to in clause (i), and

     (iii) notes to the financial statements.

(b) If the business has completed one or more financial years include

     (i) annual financial statements comprised of:

         A) a statement of comprehensive income, a statement of changes in equity and a statement of cash flows for the following annual periods:

             i. the most recently completed financial year that ended before the acquisition date and more than 120 days before the date of the offering memorandum, and

             ii. the financial year immediately preceding the most recently completed financial year specified in clause i, if any,

         B) a statement of financial position as at the end of each of the periods specified in (A),

         C) notes to the financial statements, and

     (ii) an interim financial report comprised of

         A) either

             i. a statement of comprehensive income, a statement of changes in equity and a statement of cash flows for the most recently completed year-to-date interim period ending on the last date of the interim period that ended before the acquisition date and more than 60 days before the date of the offering memorandum and ended after the date of the financial statements required under subclause (b)(i)(A)(i), and a statement of comprehensive income and a statement of changes in equity for the three month period ending on the last date of the interim period that ended before the acquisition date and more than 60 days before the date of the offering memorandum and ended after the date of the financial statements required under subclause (b)(i)(A)(i), or

             ii. a statement of comprehensive income, a statement of changes in equity and a statement of cash flows for the period from the first day after the financial year referred to in subparagraph (b)(i) to a date before the acquisition date and after the period end in subclause (b)(ii)(A)(i),

         B) a statement of comprehensive income, a statement of changes in equity and a statement of cash flows for the corresponding period in the immediately preceding financial year, if any,

         C) a statement of financial position as at the end of the period required by clause (A) and the end of the immediately preceding financial year, and

         D) notes to the financial statements.

Refer to Instruction B.7 for the meaning of "interim period".

5. The information for the most recently completed financial period referred to in C.4(b)(i) must be audited and accompanied by an auditor's report. The financial statements required under C.4(a), C.4(b)(ii) and the comparative financial information required by C.4(b)(i) may be unaudited; however, if those financial statements or comparative financial information have been audited, the auditor's report must be included in the offering memorandum.

6. If the offering memorandum does not contain audited financial statements for a business referred to in C.1 for the business's most recently completed financial year that ended before the acquisition date and the distribution is ongoing, update the offering memorandum to include those financial statements accompanied by an auditor's report when they are available, but in any event no later than the date 120 days following the year-end.

7. The term "business" should be evaluated in light of the facts and circumstances involved. Generally, a separate entity or a subsidiary or division of an entity is a business and, in certain circumstances, a lesser component of an entity may also constitute a business, whether or not the subject of the acquisition previously prepared financial statements. The subject of an acquisition should be considered a business where there is, or the issuer expects there will be, continuity of operations. The issuer should consider:

(a) whether the nature of the revenue producing activity or potential revenue producing activity will remain generally the same after the acquisition, and

(b) whether any of the physical facilities, employees, marketing systems, sales forces, customers, operating rights, production techniques or trade names are acquired by the issuer instead of remaining with the vendor after the acquisition.

8. If a transaction or a proposed transaction for which the likelihood of the transaction being completed is high has been or will be a reverse take-over as defined in NI 51-102, include financial statements for the legal subsidiary in the offering memorandum in accordance with Part A. The legal parent is considered to be the business acquired. C.1 may also require financial statements of the legal parent.

9. An issuer satisfies the requirements in C.4 if the issuer includes in the offering memorandum the financial statements required in a business acquisition report under NI 51-102.

D. — Financial Statement — Exemptions

1. An issuer will satisfy the financial statement requirements of this form if it includes the financial statements required by securities legislation for a prospectus.

2. Notwithstanding the requirements in section 3.3(1)(a)(i) of National Instrument 52-107 *Acceptable Accounting Principles and Auditing Standards*, an auditor's report that accompanies financial statements of an issuer or a business contained in an offering memorandum of a non-reporting issuer may express a qualification of opinion relating to inventory if

(a) the issuer includes in the offering memorandum a statement of financial position that is for a date that is subsequent to the date to which the qualification relates, and

(b) the statement of financial position referred to in paragraph (a) is accompanied by an auditor's report that does not express a qualification of opinion relating to closing inventory, and

(c) the issuer has not previously filed financial statements for the same entity accompanied by an auditor's report for a prior year that expressed a qualification of opinion relating to inventory.

3. If an issuer has, or will account for a business referred to in C.1 using the equity method, then financial statements for a business required by Part C are not required to be included if:

(a) the offering memorandum includes disclosure for the periods for which financial statements are otherwise required under Part C that:

(i) summarizes information as to the aggregated amounts of assets, liabilities, revenue and profit or loss of the business, and

(ii) describes the issuer's proportionate interest in the business and any contingent issuance of securities by the business that might significantly affect the issuer's share of profit or loss;

(b) the financial information provided under D.3(a) for the most recently completed financial year has been audited, or has been derived from audited financial statements of the business; and

(c) the offering memorandum discloses that:

(i) the financial information provided under D.3(a) for any completed financial year has been audited, or identifies the audited financial statements from which the financial information provided under D.3(a) has been derived; and

(ii) the audit opinion with respect to the financial information or financial statements referred to in D.3(c)(i) was an unmodified opinion.

4. Financial statements relating to the acquisition or proposed acquisition of a business that is an interest in an oil and gas property are not required to be included in an offering memorandum if the acquisition is significant based only on the asset test or:

(a) the issuer is unable to provide the financial statements in respect of the significant acquisition otherwise required because those financial statements do not exist or the issuer does not have access to those financial statements,

(b) the acquisition was not or will not be a reverse take-over as defined in NI 51-102, and

(c) [repealed]

(d) the offering memorandum contains alternative disclosure for the business which includes:

(i) an operating statement for the business or related businesses for each of the financial periods for which financial statements would, but for this section, be required under C.4 prepared in accordance with subsection 3.11(5) of National Instrument 52-107 *Acceptable Accounting Principles and Auditing Standards*. The operating statement for the most recently completed financial period referred to in C.4(b)(i) must be audited.

(ii) a description of the property or properties and the interest acquired by the issuer,

(iii) information with respect to the estimated reserves and related future net revenue attributable to the business, the material assumptions used in preparing the estimates and the identity and relationship to the issuer or to the seller of the person who prepared the estimates,

(iv) actual production volumes of the property for the most recently completed year, and

(v) estimated production volumes of the property for the first year reflected in the estimate disclosed under D.4(d)(iv).

5. Financial statements for a business that is an interest in an oil and gas property, or for the acquisition or proposed acquisition by an issuer of a property, are not required to be audited if during the 12 months preceding the acquisition date or the proposed acquisition date, the daily average production of the property on a barrel of oil equivalent basis (with gas converted to oil in the ratio of six thousand cubic feet of gas being the equivalent of one barrel of oil) is less than 20 per cent of the total daily average production of the seller for the same or similar periods and:

(i) despite reasonable efforts during the purchase negotiations, the issuer was prohibited from including in the purchase agreement the rights to obtain an audited operating statement of the property,

(ii) the purchase agreement includes representations and warranties by the seller that the amounts presented in the operating statement agree to the seller's books and records, and

(iii) the offering memorandum discloses

     1. that the issuer was unable to obtain an audited operating statement,

     2. the reasons for that inability,

     3. the fact that the purchase agreement includes the representations and warranties referred to in D.5(ii), and

     4. that the results presented in the operating statements may have been materially different if the statements had been audited.

Form 45-106F3 — Offering Memorandum for Qualifying Issuers

Date: [Insert the date from the certificate page.]

The Issuer

Name:

Head office:

     Address:

     Phone #:

     E-mail address:

     Fax #:

Where currently listed or quoted? [e.g., TSX/TSX Venture Exchange]

Jurisdictions in which the issuer is a reporting issuer:

The Offering

Securities offered:

Price per security:

Minimum/Maximum offering: [If there is no minimum state in bold: **"There is no minimum."** and also state in bold type: **"You may be the only purchaser."**]

State in bold type: **Funds available under the offering may not be sufficient to accomplish our proposed objectives.**

Minimum subscription amount: [State the minimum amount each investor must invest, or state "There is no minimum subscription amount an investor must invest."]

Payment terms:

Proposed closing date(s):

Income Tax consequences: "There are important tax consequences to these securities. See item 6." [If income tax consequences are not material, delete this item.]

Selling agent? [Yes/No. If yes, state "See item 7". The name of the selling agent may also be stated.]

Resale restrictions

State: "You will be restricted from selling your securities for 4 months and a day. See item 10".

Purchaser's rights

State: "You have 2 business days to cancel your agreement to purchase these securities. If there is a misrepresentation in this offering memorandum, you have the right to sue either for damages or to cancel the agreement. See item 11."

State in bold type:

     "No securities regulatory authority or regulator has assessed the merits of these securities or reviewed this offering memorandum. Any representation to the contrary is an offence. This is a risky investment. See item 8."

[All of the above information must appear on a single cover page.]

Item 1 — Use of Available Funds

1.1 *Available Funds* — Using the following table, disclose the funds available as a result of the offering. If the issuer plans to combine additional sources of funding with the available funds from the offering to achieve its principal capital-raising purpose, please provide details about each additional source of funding. If there is no minimum offering, state "$0" as the minimum.

Disclose also the amount of any working capital deficiency, if any, of the issuer as at a date not more than 30 days prior to the date of the offering memorandum. If the working capital deficiency will not be eliminated by the use of available funds, state how the issuer intends to eliminate or manage the deficiency.

		Assuming min. offering	Assuming max. offering
A	Amount to be raised by this offering	$	$
B	Selling commissions and fees	$	$
C	Estimated offering costs (e.g., legal, accounting, audit)	$	$
D	Available funds: D = A - (B+C)	$	$
E.	Additional sources of funding required	$	$
F.	Working capital deficiency	$	$
G.	Total: G = (D+E) - F	$	$

1.2 *Use of Available Funds* — Using the following table, provide a detailed breakdown of how the issuer will use the available funds. If any of the available funds will be paid to an insider, associate or affiliate of the issuer, disclose in a note to the table the name of the insider, associate or affiliate, the relationship to the issuer, and the amount. If the issuer has a working capital deficiency, disclose the portion, if any, of the available funds to be applied against the working capital deficiency. If more than 10% of the available funds will be used by the issuer to pay debt and the issuer incurred the debt within the two preceding financial years, describe why the debt was incurred.

Description of intended use of available funds listed in order of priority.	Assuming min. offering	Assuming max. offering
	$	$
	$	$
Total: Equal to G in the Funds table above	$	$

1.3 *Reallocation* — The available funds must be used for the purposes disclosed in the offering memorandum. The board of directors can reallocate the proceeds to other uses only for sound business reasons. If the available funds may be reallocated, include the following statement:

"We intend to spend the available funds as stated. We will reallocate funds only for sound business reasons."

1.4 *Insufficient Funds* — If applicable, disclose that the funds available as a result of the offering either may not or will not be sufficient to accomplish all of the issuer's proposed objectives and that there is no assurance that alternative financing will be available. If alternative financing has been arranged, disclose the amount, source and any outstanding conditions that must be satisfied.

Item 2 — Information About [name of issuer or other term used to refer to issuer]

2.1 *Business Summary* — Briefly (in one or two paragraphs) describe the business intended to be carried on by the issuer over the next 12 months. State whether this represents a change of business. The disclosure must provide sufficient information to enable a prospective purchaser to make an informed investment decision. If the issuer is a non-resource issuer, describe the products that the issuer is or will be developing or producing and the stage of development of each of the products. If the issuer is a resource issuer, state: whether the issuer's principal properties are primarily in the exploration or in the development or production stage; what resources the issuer is engaged in exploring, developing or producing; and the locations of the issuer's principal properties. A resource issuer who discloses information about its oil and gas activities must follow General Instruction A-9 of this Form.

2.2 *Existing Documents Incorporated by Reference* — State:

"Information has been incorporated by reference into this offering memorandum from documents listed in the table below, which have been filed with securities regulatory authorities or regulators in Canada. The documents incorporated by reference are available for viewing on the SEDAR website at *www.sedar.com*. In addition, copies of the documents may be obtained on request without charge from [insert complete address and telephone and the name of a contact person].

Documents listed in the table and information provided in those documents are not incorporated by reference to the extent that their contents are modified or superseded by a statement in this offering memorandum or in any other subsequently filed document that is also incorporated by reference in this offering memorandum."

Using the following table, list all of the documents incorporated by reference (as required by Instruction D.1):

Description of document (In the case of material change reports, provide a brief description of the nature of the material change)	Date of document

2.3 *Existing Documents Not Incorporated by Reference* — State:

"Other documents available on the SEDAR website (for example, most press releases, take-over bid circulars, prospectuses and rights offering circulars) are not incorporated by reference into this offering memorandum unless they are specifically referenced in the table above. Your rights as described in item 11 of this offering memorandum apply only in respect of information contained in this offering memorandum and documents or information incorporated by reference."

2.4 *Existing Information Not Incorporated by Reference* — Certain specified information (as outlined in Instruction D.2) contained in the documents incorporated by reference may be, but is not required to be, incorporated by reference into the offering memorandum. If the issuer does not wish to incorporate that information into the offering memorandum, the issuer must state that and include a statement in the offering memorandum identifying:

(a) the information that is not being incorporated by reference, and

(b) the document in which the information is contained.

2.5 *Future Documents Not Incorporated by Reference* — State:

"Documents filed after the date of this offering memorandum are not deemed to be incorporated into this offering memorandum. However, if you subscribe for securities and an event occurs, or there is a change in our business or affairs, that makes the certificate to this offering memorandum no longer true, we will provide you with an update of this offering memorandum, including a newly dated and signed certificate, and will not accept your subscription until you have re-signed the agreement to purchase the securities."

Item 3 — Interests of Directors, Executive Officers, Promoters and Principal Holders

3.1 Using the following table, provide information about each director, executive officer, promoter and each person who, directly or indirectly, beneficially owns or controls 10% or more of any class of voting securities of the issuer (a "principal holder"). If the principal holder is not an individual, state in a note to the table the name of any person or company that, directly or indirectly, beneficially owns or controls more than 50% of the voting rights of the principal holder.

Name and municipality of principal residence	Position(s) with the issuer

3.2 State: "You can obtain further information about directors and executive officers from [insert the name and date of the document(s) with the most current information, e.g., management information circular, annual information form or material change report]."

3.3 State: "Current information regarding the securities held by directors, executive officers and principal holders can be obtained from [refer to the SEDI website at www.sedi.ca or, if information cannot be obtained from the SEDI website, refer to the securities regulatory authority(ies) or regulator(s) from which the information can be obtained, including any website(s)]. [Name of issuer or other term used to refer to issuer] can not guarantee the accuracy of this information."

3.4 *Loans* — Disclose the principal amount of any debenture or loan, the repayment terms, security, due date and interest rate due to or from the directors, management, promoters and principal holders as at a date not more than 30 days prior to the date of the offering memorandum.

Item 4 — Capital Structure

Using the following table, provide the required information about outstanding securities of the issuer (including options, warrants and other securities convertible into shares). If necessary, notes to the table may be added to describe the material terms of the securities.

Description of security	Number authorized to be issued	Price per security	Number outstanding as at [a date not more than 30 days prior to the offering memorandum date]	Number outstanding after min. offering	Number outstanding after max. offering

Item 5 — Securities Offered

5.1 *Terms of Securities* — Describe the material terms of the securities being offered, including:

(a) voting rights or restrictions on voting,

(b) conversion or exercise price and date of expiry,

(c) rights of redemption or retraction, and

(d) interest rates or dividend rates.

5.2 *Subscription Procedure*

(a) Describe how a purchaser can subscribe for the securities and the method of payment.

(b) State that the consideration will be held in trust and the period that it will be held (refer at least to the mandatory two day period).

(c) Disclose any conditions to closing e.g., receipt of additional funds from other sources. If there is a minimum offering, disclose when consideration will be returned to purchasers if the minimum is not met.

Item 6 — Income Tax Consequences and RRSP Eligibility

6.1 State: "You should consult your own professional advisers to obtain advice on the income tax consequences that apply to you".

6.2 If income tax consequences are a material aspect of the securities being offered (e.g., flow-through shares), provide

(a) a summary of the significant income tax consequences to Canadian residents, and

(b) the name of the person or company providing the income tax disclosure in (a).

6.3 Provide advice regarding the RRSP eligibility of the securities and the name of the person or company providing the advice or state "Not all securities are eligible for investment in a registered retirement savings plan (RRSP). You should consult your own professional advisers to obtain advice on the RRSP eligibility of these securities."

Item 7 — Compensation Paid to Sellers and Finders

If any person or company has or will receive any compensation (e.g., commission, corporate finance fee or finder's fee) in connection with the offering, provide the following information to the extent applicable:

(a) a description of each type of compensation and the estimated amount to be paid for each type,

(b) if a commission is being paid, the percentage that the commission will represent of the gross proceeds of the offering (assuming both the minimum and maximum offering),

(c) details of any broker's warrants or agent's option (including number of securities under option, exercise price and expiry date), and

(d) if any portion of the compensation will be paid in securities, details of the securities (including number, type and, if options or warrants, the exercise price and expiry date).

Item 8 — Risk Factors

Describe in order of importance, starting with the most important, the risk factors material to the issuer that a reasonable investor would consider important in deciding whether to buy the issuer's securities.

Risk factors will generally fall into the following three categories:

(a) Investment Risk — risks that are specific to the securities being offered. Some examples include

- arbitrary determination of price,
- no market or an illiquid market for the securities,
- resale restrictions, and
- subordination of debt securities.

(b) Issuer Risk — risks that are specific to the issuer. Some examples include

- insufficient funds to accomplish the issuer's business objectives,
- no history or a limited history of revenue or profits,
- lack of specific management or technical expertise,
- management's regulatory and business track record,
- dependence on key employees, suppliers or agreements,
- dependence on financial viability of guarantor,
- pending and outstanding litigation, and
- political risk factors.

(c) Industry Risk — risks faced by the issuer because of the industry in which it operates. Some examples include

- environmental and industry regulation,
- product obsolescence, and
- competition.

Item 9 — Reporting Obligations

9.1 Disclose the documents that will be sent to purchasers on an annual or on-going basis.

9.2 If corporate or securities information about the issuer is available from a government, securities regulatory authority or regulator, SRO or quotation and trade reporting system, disclose where that information can be located (including website address).

Item 10 — Resale Restrictions

For trades in Alberta, British Columbia, New Brunswick, Newfoundland and Labrador, Northwest Territories, Nova Scotia, Nunavut, Ontario, Prince Edward Island, Québec, Saskatchewan and Yukon, state:

"These securities will be subject to a number of resale restrictions, including a restriction on trading. Until the restriction on trading expires, you will not be able to trade the securities unless you comply with an exemption from the prospectus and registration requirements under securities legislation.

Unless permitted under securities legislation, you cannot trade the securities before the date that is 4 months and a day after the distribution date."

Item 11 — Purchasers' Rights

State the following:

"If you purchase these securities you will have certain rights, some of which are described below. For information about your rights you should consult a lawyer.

(1) Two -Day Cancellation Right — You can cancel your agreement to purchase these securities. To do so, you must send a notice to us by midnight on the 2nd business day after you sign the agreement to buy the securities.

(2) Statutory Rights of Action in the Event of a Misrepresentation — [Insert this section only if the securities legislation of the jurisdiction in which the trade occurs provides purchasers with statutory rights in the event of a misrepresentation in an offering memorandum. Modify the language, if necessary, to conform to the statutory rights.] If there is a misrepresentation in this offering memorandum, you have a statutory right to sue:

(a) [name of issuer or other term used to refer to issuer] to cancel your agreement to buy these securities, or

(b) for damages against [state the name of issuer or other term used to refer to issuer and the title of any other person or company against whom the rights are available].

This statutory right to sue is available to you whether or not you relied on the misrepresentation. However, there are various defences available to the persons or companies that you have a right to sue. In particular, they have a defence if you knew of the misrepresentation when you purchased the securities.

If you intend to rely on the rights described in (a) or (b) above, you must do so within strict time limitations. You must commence your action to cancel the agreement within [state time period provided by the securities legislation]. You must commence your action for damages within [state time period provided by the securities legislation].

(3) Contractual Rights of Action in the Event of a Misrepresentation — [Insert this section only if the securities legislation of the jurisdiction in which the purchaser is resident does not provide purchasers with statutory rights in the event of a misrepresentation in an offering memorandum.] If there is a misrepresentation in this offering memorandum, you have a contractual right to sue [name of issuer or other term used to refer to issuer]:

(a) to cancel your agreement to buy these securities, or

(b) for damages.

This contractual right to sue is available to you whether or not you relied on the misrepresentation. However, in an action for damages, the amount you may recover will not exceed the price that you paid for your securities and will not include any part of the damages that [name of issuer or other term used to refer to issuer] proves does not represent the depreciation in value of the securities resulting from the misrepresentation. [Name of issuer or other term used to refer to issuer] has a defence if it proves that you knew of the misrepresentation when you purchased the securities.

If you intend to rely on the rights described in (a) or (b) above, you must do so within strict time limitations. You must commence your action to cancel the agreement within 180 days after you signed the agreement to purchase the securities. You must commence your action for damages within the earlier of 180 days after learning of the misrepresentation and 3 years after you signed the agreement to purchase the securities."

Item 12 — Date and Certificate

State the following on the certificate page of the offering memorandum:

"Dated [insert the date the certificate page of the offering memorandum is signed].

This offering memorandum does not contain a misrepresentation."

Instructions for Completing — Form 45-106F3 Offering Memorandum for Qualifying Issuers

A. — General Instructions

1. Only a "qualifying issuer" may use this form.

2. An issuer using this form to draft an offering memorandum must incorporate by reference certain parts of its existing continuous disclosure base. An issuer that does not want to do this must use Form 45-106F2 *Offering Memorandum for Non-Qualifying Issuers*.

3. Draft the offering memorandum so that it is easy to read and understand. Be concise and use clear, plain language. Avoid technical terms. If technical terms are necessary, provide definitions.

4. Address the items required by the form in the order set out in the form. However, it is not necessary to provide disclosure about an item that does not apply.

5. The issuer may include additional information in the offering memorandum other than that specifically required by the form. The offering memorandum is generally not required to contain the level of detail and extent of disclosure required by a prospectus. However, an offering memorandum must provide a prospective purchaser with sufficient information to make an informed investment decision.

6. The issuer may wrap the offering memorandum around a prospectus or similar document. However, all matters required to be disclosed by the offering memorandum must be addressed and the offering memorandum must provide a cross-reference to the page number or heading in the wrapped document where the relevant information is contained. The certificate to the offering memorandum must be modified to indicate that the offering memorandum, including the document around which it is wrapped, does not contain a misrepresentation.

7. It is an offence to make a misrepresentation in the offering memorandum. This applies both to information that is required by the form and to additional information that is provided. Include particulars of any material facts, which have not been disclosed under any of the Item numbers and for which failure to disclose would constitute a misrepresentation in the offering memorandum. Refer also to section 3.8(3) of Companion Policy 45-106CP for additional information.

8. Refer to National Instrument 43-101 *Standards of Disclosure for Mineral Projects* (NI 43-101) when disclosing scientific or technical information for a mineral project of the issuer.

9. If an oil and gas issuer is disclosing information about its oil and gas activities, it must ensure that the information is disclosed in accordance with Part 4 and Part 5 of National Instrument 51-101 Standards of Disclosure for Oil and Gas Activities (NI 51-101). Under section 5.3 of NI

51-101, disclosure of reserves or resources must be consistent with the reserves and resources terminology and categories set out in the Canadian Oil and Gas Evaluation Handbook. For the purposes of this instruction, references to reporting issuer in Part 4 and Part 5 of NI 51-101 will be deemed to include all issuers.

10. Securities legislation restricts what can be told to investors about the issuer's intent to list or quote securities on an exchange or market. Refer to applicable securities legislation before making any such statements.

11. If an issuer uses this form in connection with a distribution under an exemption other than section 2.9 (*offering memorandum*) of National Instrument 45-106 *Prospectus Exemptions*, the issuer must modify the disclosure in item 12 to correctly describe the purchaser's rights. If a purchaser does not have statutory or contractual rights of action in the event of a misrepresentation in the offering memorandum, that fact must be stated in bold on the face page.

12. During the course of a distribution of securities, any material forward-looking information disseminated must only be that which is set out in the offering memorandum. If an extract of FOFI, as defined in NI 51-102 *Continuous Disclosure Obligations* (NI 51-102), is disseminated, the extract or summary must be reasonably balanced and have a cautionary note in boldface stating that the information presented is not complete and that complete FOFI is included in the offering memorandum.

B. — Financial Statements

1. All financial statements incorporated by reference into the offering memorandum must comply with NI 51-102 and National Instrument 52-107 *Acceptable Accounting Principles and Auditing Standards*.

2. Forward-looking information included in an offering memorandum must comply with section 4A.2 of NI 51-102 and must include the disclosure described in section 4A.3 of NI 51-102. In addition to the foregoing, FOFI or a financial outlook, each as defined in NI 51-102, included in an offering memorandum must comply with Part 4B of NI 51-102. Additional guidance may be found in the companion policy to NI 51-102.

C. — Required Updates to the Offering Memorandum

1. If the offering memorandum does not incorporate by reference the issuer's AIF, and audited financial statements for its most recently completed financial year, update the offering memorandum for any financial statements that are required to be filed prior to the distribution to incorporate by reference the documents as soon as the documents are filed on SEDAR.

2. Except for documents referred to in C.1, the offering memorandum does not have to be updated to incorporate by reference interim financial reports or other documents referred to in D.1 unless it is necessary to do so to prevent the offering memorandum from containing a misrepresentation.

D. — Information about the Issuer

1. *Existing Documents Incorporated by Reference* — In addition to any other document that an issuer may choose to incorporate by reference, the issuer must incorporate the following documents:

(a) the issuer's AIF for the issuer's most recently completed financial year for which annual financial statements are either required to be filed or have been filed,

(b) material change reports, except confidential material change reports, filed since the end of the financial year in respect of which the issuer's AIF is filed,

(c) the interim financial report for the issuer's most recently completed interim period for which the issuer prepares an interim financial report that is required to be filed or have been filed and which ends after the most recently completed financial year referred to in (d),

(d) the comparative financial statements, together with the accompanying auditor's report, for the issuer's most recently completed financial year for which annual financial statements are required to be filed or have been filed,

(e) if, before the offering memorandum is filed, financial information about the issuer for a financial period more recent than the period for which financial statements are required under D.1(c) and (d) is publicly disseminated by, or on behalf of, the issuer through news release or otherwise, the content of the news release or public communication,

(f) management's discussion and analysis (MD&A) as required under NI 51-102 for the period specified in D.1(c) and D.1(d),

(g) each business acquisition report required to be filed under NI 51-102 for acquisitions completed since the beginning of the financial year in respect of which the issuer's AIF is filed, unless the issuer incorporated the business acquisition report by reference into its AIF for its most recently completed financial year for which annual financial statements are either required to be filed or have been filed, or incorporated at least 9 months of the acquired business or related businesses operations into the issuer's most recent audited financial statements,

(h) any information circular filed by the issuer since the beginning of the financial year in respect of which the issuer's most recent AIF is filed, other than an information circular prepared in connection with an annual general meeting if the issuer has filed and incorporated by reference an information circular for a subsequent annual general meeting,

(i) if the issuer has oil and gas activities, as defined in National Instrument 51-101 *Standards of Disclosure for Oil and Gas Activities*, the most recent Form 51-101F1, Form 51-101F2 and Form 51-101F3, filed by an SEC issuer, unless

(i) the issuer's current AIF is in the form of Form 51-102F2; or

(ii) the issuer is otherwise exempted from the requirements of NI 51-101,

(j) any other disclosure document which the issuer has filed pursuant to an undertaking to a provincial and territorial securities regulatory authority or regulator since the beginning of the financial year in respect of which the issuer's most recent AIF is filed, and

(k) any other disclosure document of the type listed above that the issuer has filed pursuant to an exemption from any requirement under securities legislation since the beginning of the financial year in respect of which the issuer's most recent AIF is filed.

2. *Mineral Property* — If a material part of the funds available as a result of the distribution is to be expended on a particular mineral property and if the issuer's most recent AIF does not contain the disclosure required under section 5.4 of Form 51-102F2 for the property or that disclosure is inadequate or incorrect due to changes, disclose the information required under section 5.4 of Form 51-102F2.

An issuer may incorporate any additional document provided that the document is available for viewing on the SEDAR website and that, on request by a purchaser, the issuer provides a copy of the document to the purchaser, without charge.

Form 45-106F4 — Risk Acknowledgement

Risk Acknowledgement

- I acknowledge that this is a risky investment.

- I am investing entirely at my own risk.

- No securities regulatory authority or regulator has evaluated or endorsed the merits of these securities or the disclosure in the offering memorandum.

- The person selling me these securities is not registered with a securities regulatory authority or regulator and has no duty to tell me whether this investment is suitable for me. *[Instruction: Delete if sold by registrant]*

- I will not be able to sell these securities except in very limited circumstances. I may never be able to sell these securities. *[Instruction: Delete if issuer is reporting]*

- The securities are redeemable, but I may only be able to redeem them in limited circumstances. *[Instruction: Delete if securities are not redeemable]*

- I will not be able to sell these securities for 4 months. *[Instruction: Delete if issuer is not reporting or if the purchaser is a Manitoba resident]*

- I could lose all the money I invest.

I am investing $_____ [total consideration] in total; this includes any amount I am obliged to pay in future. _____ [name of issuer] will pay $_____ [amount of fee or commission] of this to _____ [name of person selling the securities] as a fee or commission.

I acknowledge that this is a risky investment and that I could lose all the money I invest.

_____   _____
Date   Signature of Purchaser

                                            Print name of Purchaser

Sign 2 copies of this document. Keep one copy for your records.

WARNING

You have 2 business days to cancel your purchase *[Instruction: The issuer must complete this section before giving the form to the purchaser.]*

To do so, send a notice to [name of issuer] stating that you want to cancel your purchase. You must send the notice before midnight on the 2nd business day after you sign the agreement to purchase the securities. You can send the notice by fax or email or deliver it in person to [name of issuer] at its business address. Keep a copy of the notice for your records.

Issuer Name and Address:

Fax:

E-mail:

You are buying Exempt Market Securities

They are called *exempt market securities* because two parts of securities law do not apply to them. If an issuer wants to sell *exempt market securities* to you:

- the issuer does not have to give you a prospectus (a document that describes the investment in detail and gives you some legal protections), and

- the securities do not have to be sold by an investment dealer registered with a securities regulatory authority or regulator.

There are restrictions on your ability to resell *exempt market securities*. Exempt market securities are more risky than other securities.

You will receive an offering memorandum Read the offering memorandum carefully because it has important information about the issuer and its securities. Keep the offering memorandum because you have rights based on it. Talk to a lawyer for details about these rights.

You will not receive advice *[Instruction: Delete if sold by registrant]*

You will not get professional advice about whether the investment is suitable for you. But you can still seek that advice from a registered adviser or registered dealer. In Manitoba, Northwest Territories, Nunavut, Prince Edward Island and Yukon to qualify as an eligible investor, you may be required to obtain that advice.

The securities you are buying are not listed*[Instruction: Delete if securities are listed or quoted]*

The securities you are buying are not listed on any stock exchange, and they may never be listed. You may never be able to sell these securities.

The issuer of your securities is a non-reporting issuer*[Instruction: Delete if issuer is reporting]*

A *non-reporting issuer* does not have to publish financial information or notify the public of changes in its business. You may not receive ongoing information about this issuer.

For more information on the exempt market, call your local securities regulatory authority or regulator. *[Instruction: Insert the name, telephone number and website address of the securities regulatory authority or regulator in the jurisdiction in which you are selling these securities.]*

[Instruction: The purchaser must sign 2 copies of this form. The purchaser and the issuer must each receive a signed copy.]

Schedule 1 — *Classification of Investors Under the Offering Memorandum Exemption*

Instructions: This schedule must be completed together with the Risk Acknowledgement Form and Schedule 2 by individuals purchasing securities under the exemption (the offering memorandum exemption) in subsection 2.9(2.1) of National Instrument 45-106 *Prospectus Exemptions* (NI 45-106) in Alberta, New Brunswick, Nova Scotia, Ontario, Québec and Saskatchewan.

How you qualify to buy securities under the offering memorandum exemption		Initial the statement under A, B, C or D containing the criteria that applies to you. (You may initial more than one statement.) If you initial a statement under B or C, you are not required to complete A.
A. You are an eligible investor because:		*Your initials*
ELIGIBLE INVESTOR	Your net income before taxes was more than $75,000 in each of the 2 most recent calendar years, and you expect it to be more than $75,000 in this calendar year. (You can find your net income before taxes on your personal income tax return.)	
	Your net income before taxes combined with your spouse's was more than $125,000 in each of the 2 most recent calendar years, and you expect your combined net income to be more than $125,000 in this calendar year. (You can find your net income before taxes on your personal income tax return.)	
	Either alone or with your spouse, you have net assets worth more than $400,000. (Your net assets are your total assets, including real estate, minus your total debt including any mortgage on your property.)	
B. You are an eligible investor, as a person described in section 2.3 [Accredited investor] of NI 45-106 or, as applicable in Ontario, subsection 7.3(3) of the Securities Act (Ontario), because:		*Your initials*
ACCREDITED INVESTOR	Your net income before taxes was more than $200,000 in each of the 2 most recent calendar years, and you expect it to be more than $200,000 in this calendar year. (You can find your net income before taxes on your personal income tax return.)	
	Your net income before taxes combined with your spouse's was more than $300,000 in each of the 2 most recent calendar years, and you expect your combined net income before taxes to be more than $300,000 in the current calendar year.	
	Either alone or with your spouse, you own more than $1 million in cash and securities, after subtracting any debt related to the cash and securities.	
	Either alone or with your spouse, you have net assets worth more than $5 million. (Your net assets are your total assets (including real estate) minus your total debt.)	

C. You are an eligible investor, as a person described in section 2.5 [Family, friends and business associates] of NI 45-106, because:		Your initials
	You are:	
	1) [check all applicable boxes]	
	❑ a director of the issuer or an affiliate of the issuer	
	❑ an executive officer of the issuer or an affiliate of the issuer	
	❑ a control person of the issuer or an affiliate of the issuer	
	❑ a founder of the issuer	
	OR	
	2) [check all applicable boxes]	
	❑ a person of which a majority of the voting securities are beneficially owned by, or a majority of the directors are, (i) individuals listed in (1) above and/or (ii) family members, close personal friends or close business associates of individuals listed in (1) above	
	❑ a trust or estate of which all of the beneficiaries or a majority of the trustees or executors are (i) individuals listed in (1) above and/or (ii) family members, close personal friends or close business associates of individuals listed in (1) above	
FAMILY, FRIENDS AND BUSINESS ASSOCIATES	You are a family member of .... [Instruction: Insert the name of the person who is your relative either directly or through his or her spouse], who holds the following position at the issuer or an affiliate of the issuer:	
	You are the .... of that person or that person's spouse. [Instruction: To qualify for this investment, you must be (a) the spouse of the person listed above or (b) the parent, grandparent, brother, sister, child or grandchild of that person or that person's spouse.]	
	You are a close personal friend of .... [Instruction: Insert the name of your close personal friend], who holds the following position at the issuer or an affiliate of the issuer: .... You have known that person for .... years.	
	You are a close business associate of .... [Instruction: Insert the name of your close business associate], who holds the following position at the issuer or an affiliate of the issuer: .... You have known that person for .... years.	

D. You are not an eligible investor.		Your initials
NOT AN ELIGIBLE INVESTOR	You acknowledge that you are not an eligible investor.	

Schedule 2 — *Investment Limits for Investors Under the Offering Memorandum Exemption*

Instructions: This schedule must be completed together with the Risk Acknowledgement Form and Schedule 1 by individuals purchasing securities under the exemption (the offering memorandum exemption) in subsection 2.9(2.1) of National Instrument 45-106 *Prospectus Exemptions* (NI 45-106) in Alberta, New Brunswick, Nova Scotia, Ontario, Québec and Saskatchewan.

SECTION 1 TO BE COMPLETED BY THE PURCHASER	1. Investment limits you are subject to when purchasing securities under the offering memorandum exemption	You may be subject to annual investment limits that apply to all securities acquired under the offering memorandum exemption in a 12 month period, depending on the criteria under which you qualify as identified in Schedule 1. Initial the statement that applies to you.

A. You are an eligible investor.		Your initials
ELIGIBLE INVES-TOR	As an eligible investor that is an individual, you cannot invest more than *$30,000* in all offering memorandum exemption investments made in the previous 12 months, unless you have received advice from a portfolio manager, investment dealer or exempt market dealer, as identified in section 2 of this schedule, that your investment is suitable. Initial one of the following statements:	
	You confirm that, after taking into account your investment of $ .... today in this issuer, you have not exceeded your investment limit of $30,000 in all offering memorandum exemption investments made in the previous 12 months.	
	You confirm that you received advice from a portfolio manager, investment dealer or exempt market dealer, as identified in section 2 of this schedule that the following investment is suitable.	
	You confirm that, after taking into account your investment of $ .... today in this issuer, you have not exceeded your investment limit in all offering memorandum exemption investments made in the previous 12 months of $100,000.	

B. You are an eligible investor, as a person described in section 2.3 *[Accredited investor]* of NI 45- 106 or, as applicable in Ontario, subsection 7.3(3) of the Securities Act (Ontario).		Your initials
ACCREDITED IN-VESTOR	You acknowledge that, by qualifying as an eligible investor as a person described in section 2.3 *[Accredited investor]*, you are not subject to investment limits.	

C. You are an eligible investor, as a person described in section 2.5 *[Family, friends and business associates]* of NI 45-106.		Your initials
FAMILY, FRIENDS AND BUSINESS ASSOCIATES	You acknowledge that, by qualifying as an eligible investor as a person described in section 2.5 *[Family, friends and business associates]*, you are not subject to investment limits.	

D. You are not an eligible investor.		Your initials
NOT AN ELIGI-BLE INVESTOR	You acknowledge that you cannot invest more than *$10,000* in all offering memorandum exemption investments made in the previous 12 months.	
	You confirm that, after taking into account your investment of $ .... today in this issuer, you have not exceeded your investment limit of $10,000 in all offering memorandum exemption investments made in the previous 12 months.	

SECTION 2 TO BE COMPLETED BY THE REGISTRANT

2. *Registrant information*

[Instruction: this section must only be completed if an investor has received advice from a portfolio manager, investment dealer or exempt market dealer concerning his or her investment.]

First and last name of registrant (please print):

Registered as:

[Instruction: indicate whether registered as a dealing representative or advising representative]

Telephone:	Email:

Name of firm:

[Instruction: indicate whether registered as an exempt market dealer, investment dealer or portfolio manager.]

Date:

Form 45-106F5 — Risk Acknowledgement

Risk Acknowledgement
Saskatchewan Close Personal Friends and Close Business Associates

I acknowledge that this is a risky investment:

- I am investing entirely at my own risk.

- No securities regulatory authority or regulator has evaluated or endorsed the merits of these securities.

- The person selling me these securities is not registered with a securities regulatory authority or regulator and has no duty to tell me whether this investment is suitable for me. *[Instruction: Delete if sold by registrant]*

- I will not be able to sell these securities except in very limited circumstances. I may never be able to sell these securities. *[Instruction: Delete if issuer is reporting]*

- The securities are redeemable, but I may only be able to redeem them in limited circumstances. *[Instruction: Delete if securities are not redeemable]*

- I will not be able to sell these securities for 4 months. *[Instruction: Delete if issuer is not reporting]*

- I could lose all the money I invest.

- I do not have a 2-day right to cancel my purchase of these securities or the statutory rights of action for misrepresentation I would have if I were purchasing the securities under a prospectus. I do have a 2-day right to cancel my purchase of these securities if I receive an amended offering document.

I am investing $_____ [total consideration] in total; this includes any amount I am obliged to pay in future.

I am a **close** personal friend or **close** business associate of _____ [state name], who is a _____ [state title - founder, director, executive officer or control person] of _____ [state name of issuer or its affiliate – if an affiliate state "an affiliate of the issuer" and give the issuer's name].

I acknowledge that I am purchasing based on my close relationship with _____ [state name of founder, director, executive officer or control person] whom I know well enough and for a sufficient period of time to be able to assess her/his capabilities and trustworthiness.

I acknowledge that this is a risky investment and that I could lose all the money I invest.

_____   _____
Date   Signature of Purchaser

                                                             _____
                                                             Print name of Purchaser

Sign 2 copies of this document. Keep one copy for your records.

WARNING

You are buying Exempt Market Securities

They are called *exempt market securities* because two parts of securities law do not apply to them. If an issuer wants to sell *exempt market securities* to you:

- the issuer does not have to give you a prospectus (a document that describes the investment in detail and gives you some legal protections), and

- the securities do not have to be sold by an investment dealer registered with a securities regulatory authority or regulator.

There are restrictions on your ability to resell *exempt market securities*. Exempt market securities are more risky than other securities.

You may not receive any written information about the issuer or its business

If you have any questions about the issuer or its business, ask for written clarification before you purchase the securities. You should consult your own professional advisers before investing in the securities.

You will not receive advice *[Instruction: Delete if sold by registrant]*

Unless you consult your own professional advisers, you will not get professional advice about whether the investment is suitable for you.

The issuer of your securities is a non-reporting issuer*[Instruction: Delete if issuer is reporting]*

A *non-reporting issuer* does not have to publish financial information or notify the public of changes in its business. You may not receive ongoing information about this issuer. You can only sell the securities of a non-reporting issuer in very limited circumstances. You may never be able to sell these securities.

The securities you are buying are not listed*[Instruction: Delete if securities are listed or quoted]*

The securities you are buying are not listed on any stock exchange, and they may never be listed. There may be no market for these securities. You may never be able to sell these securities.

For more information on the exempt market, refer to the Saskatchewan Financial Services Commission's website at *http://www.sfsc.gov.sk.ca*.

[Instruction: The purchaser must sign 2 copies of this form. The purchaser and the issuer must each receive a signed copy.]

Form 45-106F6

[Repealed]

Form 45-106F7 — Information Memorandum for Short-term Securitized Products Distributed under Section 2.35.1

Instructions:

(1) Using language that is plain and easy to understand by the type of purchaser to whom the issuer's short-term securitized products are offered, provide the information required by this form. No reference need be made to inapplicable items and, unless otherwise required by this form, negative answers may be omitted.

(2) An information memorandum may be used to disclose information about more than one series or class of short-term securitized product. If so, the disclosure required by this form must be provided for each series or class of short-term securitized product distributed under the information memorandum.

(3) This form requires disclosure of certain items, matters or other information referred to as "material". Information is "material if knowledge of it could reasonably be expected to affect a reasonable investor's decision whether to buy, sell or hold a short-term securitized product.

(4) Include a glossary that defines all technical terms, and includes the following definition:

"*sponsor*" means a person or group of affiliated persons that organizes or initiates the formation of a conduit.

Item 1: — Significant Parties

1.1 Provide the conduit's legal name.

1.2 Disclose the conduit's jurisdiction and form of organization.

1.3 Identify each sponsor of the conduit and disclose

(a) whether or not it is a Canadian bank, Schedule II foreign bank subsidiary or Schedule III bank, and

(b) if it is not a financial institution referred to in paragraph (a), whether there is a government department or regulatory authority responsible for overseeing it and, if applicable, the name of the government department or regulatory authority.

1.4 Briefly describe the conduit's structure, business and operations and the key documents that establish the conduit and govern its business and operations.

1.5 Identify each other party, excluding any liquidity provider or any credit enhancement provider for whom disclosure is not required under item 4, that is primarily responsible under the terms of the key documents referred to in section 1.4 for a significant role in the conduit's structure or operations and briefly describe that party's role.

Item 2: — Structure

Include one or more diagrams or descriptions that provide the following information in summary form:

(a) how the conduit acquires assets and issues securitized product;

(b) liquidity facilities available to the conduit as disclosed in item 4;

(c) credit enhancements available to the conduit as disclosed in item 4;

(d) material agreements as disclosed in item 9;

(e) the structure of one or more common types of asset transactions into which the conduit may enter.

Item 3: — Eligible assets and asset transactions

3.1 Briefly describe the types of asset transactions into which the conduit expects to enter. If applicable, state that the conduit expects to finance the acquisition, origination or refinancing of asset pools from the proceeds of issuing short-term securitized products. Describe any other methods the conduit expects to employ to finance the acquisition, origination or refinancing of asset pools.

3.2 Briefly describe the types of asset eligibility criteria the conduit applies or anticipates applying when entering into asset transactions.

3.3 Briefly describe the types of due diligence or verification procedures that the conduit applies or anticipates applying to asset transactions and asset pools.

3.4 Briefly describe the conduit's approach to concentration limits, liquidity support and credit enhancement in respect of its asset transactions and asset pools.

3.5 Disclose the types of assets that the conduit is permitted to hold in its asset pools.

3.6 Briefly describe how the conduit uses or anticipates using derivatives for the purpose of hedging.

Item 4: — Interest alignment, program-wide liquidity support and program-wide credit enhancement

4.1 Briefly describe how the interests of investors are aligned with the interests of the conduit, the sponsor and the parties to asset transactions entered into by the conduit, including any requirement of law that the conduit or the sponsor retain an interest in one or more of the conduit's asset pools or be exposed to the credit risk of assets in one or more of the conduit's asset pools.

4.2 Briefly describe any standard liquidity support arrangements the conduit has entered into or anticipates entering into, excluding liquidity support arrangements that are particular to an asset transaction or asset pool. Include the following information in the description:

    (a) the name of each existing liquidity provider;

    (b) any minimum credit rating a liquidity provider must have under the terms of the key documents referred to in section 1.4;

    (c) the nature of the liquidity support;

    (d) a summary of the material terms of each liquidity agreement, including all material conditions to or limitations on the obligation of a liquidity provider to provide liquidity support;

    (e) any limitations on the obligation of a liquidity provider to provide same-day funding.

4.3 Briefly describe any standard credit enhancement arrangements that the conduit has entered into or anticipates entering into, excluding credit enhancement arrangements that are particular to an asset transaction or asset pool. Include the following information in the description:

    (a) the name of each existing credit enhancement provider;

    (b) any minimum credit rating a credit enhancement provider must have under the terms of the key documents referred to in section 1.4;

    (c) the form of the credit enhancement;

    (d) a summary of the material terms of each credit enhancement agreement, including all material conditions to or limitations on the obligation of a credit enhancement provider to provide credit support.

Item 5: — Ownership or security interests in asset pool and priority of payments

5.1 Disclose the ownership or security interest a holder of a short-term securitized product will have in the conduit's asset pools.

5.2 If any other party other than the conduit has or is anticipated to have an ownership or security interest in one or more of the conduit's asset pools, briefly describe the following:

    (a) the party's role in the conduit's structure or operations;

    (b) the nature of its interest in the asset pool;

    (c) the priority of its claims in the event of the conduit's insolvency.

Item 6: — Compliance or termination events

6.1 Briefly describe any events or circumstances that would, pursuant to the terms of the conduit's governing documents or material agreements in item 9, constitute an event of default or require the conduit to cease issuing short-term securitized products.

6.2 Briefly describe the types of methods the conduit will use to monitor the performance of or identify adverse changes to an asset pool, such as portfolio performance tests.

6.3 Briefly describe any other structural features that are intended to reduce the risk of loss for a holder of the series or class of short-term securitized products or to protect the holder from material deterioration in respect of either or both of the following:

    (a) the credit quality or performance of assets in an asset pool;

    (b) the ability of a party in Item 4 to perform its obligations to the conduit.

Item 7: — Description of short-term securitized product and offering

Describe the short-term securitized products to be distributed and the distribution procedure and include the following information:

    (a) whether short-term securitized products will be issued in certificated (registered or bearer) form or book-entry form and the delivery procedures;

    (b) whether short-term securitized products will be sold on a discount basis or on an interest-bearing basis;

    (c) the denominations in which short-term securitized products may be issued;

    (d) the permitted maturity period for the short-term securitized products, and the ability of the conduit to extend maturity;

    (e) the ability of either an investor to redeem prior to maturity or of the conduit to repay prior to maturity;

    (f) the maximum aggregate principal amount of short-term securitized products permitted to be outstanding at any one time, or a statement that there is no limit on the maximum aggregate principal amount of short-term securitized products outstanding at any one time;

    (g) the key risks related to the conduit that could cause a delay in or non-payment of principal or interest on the short-term securitized product.

Item 8: — Additional information about the conduit

8.1 Disclose if the conduit has issued and outstanding, or anticipates issuing, any securities other than the series or class of short-term securitized product to which the information memorandum relates. If the conduit has issued and outstanding, or anticipates issuing, any security other than the series or class of short-term securitized product to which the information memorandum relates, describe that other security, its credit rating, if applicable, and how it will rank, in the event of insolvency of the conduit, relative to the series or class of the conduit's short-term securitized product to which the information memorandum relates.

8.2 Disclose how a potential purchaser can obtain access to disclosure that the conduit is required to provide or make reasonably available in connection with a purchase of a short-term securitized product of the conduit.

8.3 Disclose how a holder of a short-term securitized product of the conduit can obtain access to the disclosure the conduit is required to provide or make reasonably available to a holder of a short-term securitized product of the conduit.

Item 9: — Material agreements

9.1 If not disclosed elsewhere in the information memorandum, identify and summarize each agreement to which the conduit is a party and that is material to the conduit's business and operations, excluding agreements that are particular to an asset transaction or asset pool.

9.2 If material and not disclosed elsewhere in the information memorandum, describe the ability of a person to waive or modify the requirements, activities or standards that would apply under an agreement referred to in section 9.1.

Item 10: — Date of information memorandum

State the date of the information memorandum.

Item 11: — Representation that no misrepresentation

State the following in the information memorandum:

"**This information memorandum does not contain a misrepresentation regarding the conduit, its structure, or operations.**"

Form 45-106F8 — Monthly Disclosure Report for Short-term Securitized Products Distributed under Section 2.35.1

Instructions:

(1) Using language that is plain and easy to understand by the type of purchaser to whom the issuer's short-term securitized products are offered, provide the information required by this form. No reference need be made to inapplicable items and, unless otherwise required by this form, negative answers may be omitted.

(2) A monthly disclosure report may be used to disclose information about more than one series or class of short-term securitized product. If so, the disclosure required by this form must be provided for each series or class of short-term securitized product to which the monthly disclosure report relates.

(3) This form requires disclosure of certain items, matters or other information referred to as "material". Information is "material" if knowledge of it could reasonably be expected to affect a reasonable investor's decision whether to buy, sell or hold a short-term securitized product.

(4) Include or incorporate by reference a glossary that defines all technical terms, and includes each of the following definitions:

"*seller*" means, in connection with an asset transaction, a person or group of affiliated persons that originates or acquires cash-flow generating assets and sells or otherwise transfers, either directly or indirectly, an ownership or security interest in such assets to a conduit, which assets form one or more asset pools of the conduit.

"*sponsor*" means a person or group of affiliated persons that organizes or initiates the formation of a conduit;

Item 1: — Summary of conduit operations and asset pools

Provide a summary of the conduit's operations and asset pools as at the last day of the month for which the monthly disclosure report applies that includes the following:

(a) the total face value of securitized product outstanding;

(b) the aggregate outstanding asset balance of the asset pools;

(c) the number of asset pools in which the conduit has an ownership or security interest;

(d) the number and dollar amount of new asset pools added during the month or other information that in conjunction with information in the report for the prior monthly period will permit an investor to easily calculate such amounts;

(e) the number and dollar amount of asset pools repaid during the month or other information that in conjunction with information in the report for the prior monthly period will permit an investor to easily calculate such amounts;

(f) each type of asset in the conduit's asset pools, expressed as a percentage of the total assets of the conduit's asset pools.

Item 2: — Asset transaction information

Provide the following information regarding each of the conduit's asset pools in one or more tables or diagrams as at the last day of the month to which the monthly disclosure report applies:

(a) the type of assets in the asset pool, including whether the assets are revolving or amortizing;

(b) an identifier such as an asset pool, asset transaction or seller number;

(c) the industry of the person or group of affiliated persons that originated the assets;

(d) whether each seller or applicable performance guarantor has an investment grade rating;

(e) the amount of any conduit commitment to acquire assets from a seller for the asset pool;

(f) the balance outstanding on the asset pool;

(g) if available, the number of assets or obligors in the asset pool.

Item 3: — Asset transaction credit enhancement

Provide the following information regarding each of the conduit's asset transactions in one or more tables as at the last day of the month to which the monthly disclosure report applies:

(a) the form of each credit enhancement;

(b) the amount of credit enhancement expressed in either of the following forms:

(i) a dollar amount;

(ii) a percentage, including the basis of presentation.

Item 4: — Asset transaction performance

Provide the following information regarding each of the conduit's asset transactions in one or more tables as at the last day of the month to which the monthly disclosure report applies:

(a) the default or loss ratio for the month, including the basis of presentation;

(b) information with respect to default experience both for the most recent period and over an extended period of time in the form of ratios or otherwise, provided on a consistent basis for that asset transaction in each monthly disclosure report;

(c) defaults for the month relative to available credit enhancement.

Item 5: — Compliance and termination events

Disclose the occurrence of any events or circumstances that the conduit would reasonably expect to have a significant adverse effect on the payment of principal or interest on the series or class of short-term securitized product or require the conduit to cease issuing short-term securitized products.

Item 6: — Report Information

State each of the following:

(a) date of the report;

(b) period covered by the report;

(c) contact information, including name, phone number and email address of a contact person for the conduit.

Transitional provisions

14.(1) An information memorandum that is provided to or made reasonably available to a purchaser pursuant to paragraph 2.35.4(1)(a), as enacted by section 9 of this Instrument, need only be prepared in accordance with Form 45-106F7 *Information Memorandum for Short-term Securitized Products Distributed under Section 2.35.1* for a distribution of a short term securitized product that takes place on or after November 5, 2015.

(2) A monthly disclosure report that is provided to or made reasonably available to a holder of a short-term securitized product pursuant to an undertaking or agreement in writing required by paragraph 2.35.4(1)(b), as enacted by section 9 of this Instrument, need not be prepared in accordance with Form 45-106F8 *Monthly Disclosure Report for Short-term Securitized Products Distributed under Section 2.35.1* for an asset transaction that a conduit entered into on or before November 5, 2015.

Form 45-106F9 — Form for Individual Accredited Investors

WARNING!
This investment is risky. Don't invest unless you can afford to lose all the money you pay for this investment.

SECTION 1 TO BE COMPLETED BY THE ISSUER OR SELLING SECURITY HOLDER

1. About your investment

Type of securities: *[Instruction: Include a short description, e.g., common shares.]*	Issuer:

Purchased from: *[Instruction: Indicate whether securities are purchased from the issuer or a selling security holder.]*

SECTIONS 2 TO 4 TO BE COMPLETED BY THE PURCHASER
2. Risk acknowledgement

This investment is risky. Initial that you understand that:	**Your initials**
Risk of loss — You could lose your entire investment of $........... *[Instruction: Insert the total dollar amount of the investment.]*	
Liquidity risk — You may not be able to sell your investment quickly — or at all.	
Lack of information — You may receive little or no information about your investment.	
Lack of advice — You will not receive advice from the salesperson about whether this investment is suitable for you unless the salesperson is registered. The salesperson is the person who meets with, or provides information to, you about making this investment. To check whether the salesperson is registered, go to www.aretheyregistered.ca.	
3. Accredited investor status	

You must meet at least **one** of the following criteria to be able to make this investment. Initial the statement that applies to you. (You may initial more than one statement.) The person identified in section 6 is responsible for ensuring that you meet the definition of accredited investor. That person, or the salesperson identified in section 5, can help you if you have questions about whether you meet these criteria.

	Your initials
• Your net income before taxes was more than $200,000 in each of the 2 most recent calendar years, and you expect it to be more than $200,000 in the current calendar year. (You can find your net income before taxes on your personal income tax return.)	
• Your net income before taxes combined with your spouse's was more than $300,000 in each of the 2 most recent calendar years, and you expect your combined net income before taxes to be more than $300,000 in the current calendar year.	
• Either alone or with your spouse, you own more than $1 million in cash and securities, after subtracting any debt related to the cash and securities.	
• Either alone or with your spouse, you have net assets worth more than $5 million.(Your net assets are your total assets (including real estate) minus your total debt.)	

4. Your name and signature

By signing this form, you confirm that you have read this form and you understand the risks of making this investment as identified in this form.

First and last name(please print):

Signature:	Date:

SECTION 5 TO BE COMPLETED BY THE SALESPERSON

5. Salesperson information

[Instruction: The salesperson is the person who meets with, or provides information to, the purchaser with respect to making this investment. That could include a representative of the issuer or selling security holder, a registrant or a person who is exempt from the registration requirement.]

First and last name of salesperson (please print):

Telephone:	Email:

Name of firm (if registered):

SECTION 6 TO BE COMPLETED BY THE ISSUER OR SELLING SECURITY HOLDER

6. For more information about this investment

For investment in a non-investment fund

[Insert name of issuer/selling security holder]
[Insert address of issuer/selling security holder]
[Insert contact person name, if applicable]
[Insert telephone number]
[Insert email address]
[Insert website address, if applicable]

For investment in an investment fund

[Insert name of investment fund]
[Insert name of investment fund manager]
[Insert address of investment fund manager]
[Insert telephone number of investment fund manager]
[Insert email address of investment fund manager]
[If investment is purchased from a selling security holder, also insert name, address, telephone number and email address of selling security holder here]

For more information about prospectus exemptions, contact your local securities regulator. You can find contact information at www.securities-administrators.ca.

Form instructions:

1. This form does not mandate the use of a specific font size or style but the font must be legible.

2. The information in sections 1, 5 and 6 must be completed before the purchaser completes and signs the form.

3. The purchaser must sign this form. Each of the purchaser and the issuer or selling security holder must receive a copy of this form signed by the purchaser. The issuer or selling security holder is required to keep a copy of this form for 8 years after the distribution.

45-106F10 [reserved]

45-106F11 [reserved]

Form 45-106F12 — Risk Acknowledgement Form for Family, Friend and Business Associate Investors

WARNING!
This investment is risky. Don't invest unless you can afford to lose all the money you pay for this investment.

SECTION 1 TO BE COMPLETED BY THE ISSUER

1. About your investment

Type of securities: *[Instruction: Include a short description, e.g., common shares.]*	Issuer:

SECTIONS 2 TO 4 TO BE COMPLETED BY THE PURCHASER

2. Risk acknowledgement

This investment is risky. Initial that you understand that:	**Your initials**
Risk of loss — You could lose your entire investment of $........... *[Instruction: Insert the total dollar amount of the investment.]*	
Liquidity risk — You may not be able to sell your investment quickly — or at all.	
Lack of information — You may receive little or no information about your investment. The information you receive may be limited to the information provided to you by the family member, friend or close business associate specified in section 3 of this form.	

3. Family, friend or business associate status

You must meet one of the following criteria to be able to make this investment. Initial the statement that applies to you:	**Your initials**

A) You are:

     1) *[check all applicable boxes]*

         ❏ a director of the issuer or an affiliate of the issuer

         ❏ an executive officer of the issuer or an affiliate of the issuer

         ❏ a control person of the issuer or an affiliate of the issuer

         ❏ a founder of the issuer

    OR

     2 *[check all applicable boxes]*

         ❏ a person of which a majority of the voting securities are beneficially owned by, or a majority of the directors are, (i) individuals listed in (1) above and/or (ii) family members, close personal friends or close business associates of individuals listed in (1) above

         ❏ a trust or estate of which all of the beneficiaries or a majority of the trustees or executors are (i) individuals listed in (1) above and/or (ii) family members, close personal friends or close business associates of individuals listed in (1) above

B) You are a family member of _____ *[Instruction: Insert the name of the person who is your relative either directly or through his or her spouse]*, who holds the following position at the issuer or an affiliate of the issuer: _____ .

You are the _____ of that person or that person's spouse.

[Instruction: To qualify for this investment, you must be (a) the spouse of the person listed above or (b) the parent, grandparent, brother, sister, child or grandchild of that person or that person's spouse.]

C) You are a close personal friend of _____ *[Instruction: Insert the name of your close personal friend]*, who holds the following position at the issuer or an affiliate of the issuer: _____

You have known that person for _____ years.

D) You are a close business associate of _____ *[Instruction: Insert the name of your close business associae]*, who holds the following position at the issuer or an affiliate of the issuer:

You have known that person for _____ years.

4. Your name and signature

By signing this form, you confirm that you have read this form and you understand the risks of making this investment as identified in this form. You also confirm that you are eligible to make this investment because you are a family member, close personal friend or close business associate of the person identified in section 5 of this form.

First and last name (please print):

Signature: Date:

SECTION 5 TO BE COMPLETED BY PERSON WHO CLAIMS THE CLOSE PERSONAL RELATIONSHIP, IF APPLICABLE

5. Contact person at the issuer or an affiliate of the issuer

[Instruction: To be completed by the director, executive officer, control person or founder with whom the purchaser has a close personal relationship indicated under sections 3B, C or D of this form.]

By signing this form, you confirm that you have, or your spouse has, the following relationship with the purchaser: [*check the box that applies*]

- ❏ family relationship as set out in section 3B of this form
- ❏ close personal friendship as set out in section 3C of this form
- ❏ close business associate relationship as set out in section 3D of this form

First and last name of contact person *[please print]*:

Position with the issuer or affiliate of the issuer (director, executive officer, control person or founder):

Telephone: Email:

Signature: Date:

SECTION 6 TO BE COMPLETED BY THE ISSUER

6. For more information about this investment

[Insert name of issuer]
[Insert address of issuer]
[Insert contact person name]
[Insert telephone number]
[Insert email address]
[Insert website address, if applicable]

For more information about prospectus exemptions, contact your local securities regulator. You can find contact information at www.securities-administrators.ca.

Signature of executive officer of the issuer (other than the purchaser):   Date:

Form instructions

1. This form does not mandate the use of a specific font size or style but the font must be legible.

2. The information in sections 1, 5 and 6 must be completed before the purchaser completes and signs the form.

3. The purchaser, an executive officer who is not the purchaser and, if applicable, the person who claims the close personal relationship to the purchaser must sign this form. Each of the purchaser, contact person at the issuer and the issuer must receive a copy of this form signed by the purchaser. The issuer is required to keep a copy of this form for 8 years after the distribution.

4. The detailed relationships required to purchase securities under this exemption are set out in section 2.5 of National Instrument 45-106 Prospectus and Registration Exemptions. For guidance on the meaning of "close personal friend" and "close business associate", please refer to sections 2.7 and 2.8, respectively, of Companion Policy 45-106CP Prospectus and Registration Exemptions.

This is the form of notice you must use for a distribution of rights under section 2.1 of National Instrument 45-106 *Prospectus Exemptions*. In this form, a distribution of rights is sometimes referred to as a "rights offering".

Form 45-106F14 — Rights Offering Notice for Reporting Issuers

This is the form of notice you must use for a distribution of rights under section 2.1 of National Instrument 45-106 *Prospectus Exemptions*. In this form, a distribution of rights is sometimes referred to as a "rights offering".

Part 1 General Instructions

Deliver this rights offering notice to each security holder eligible to receive rights under the rights offering. Using plain language, prepare the rights offering notice using a question-and-answer format.

Guidance

We do not expect the rights offering notice to be longer than two pages in length.

Part 2 The Rights Offering Notice

1. Basic information

State the following with the bracketed information completed:

"[Name   of   issuer]

Notice to security holders — [Date]"

If you have less than 12 months of working capital and are aware of material uncertainties that may cast significant doubt upon your ability to continue as a going concern, include the following language in bold immediately below the date of the rights offering notice:

"We currently have sufficient working capital to last [insert the number of months of working capital as at the date of the rights offering circular] months. We require [insert the percentage of the rights offering required to be taken up]% of the offering to last 12 months."

2. Who can participate in the rights offering?

State the record date and identify which class of securities is subject to the offering.

3. Who is eligible to receive rights?

List the jurisdictions in which the issuer is offering rights.

Explain how a security holder in a foreign jurisdiction can acquire the rights and the securities issuable upon the exercise of the rights.

4. How many rights are we offering?

State the total number of rights offered.

5. How many rights will you receive?

State the number of rights a security holder on the record date will receive for every security held as of the record date.

6. What does one right entitle you to receive?

State the number of rights required to acquire a security upon the exercise of the rights. Also state the subscription price.

7. How will you receive your rights

Include a rights certificate with the rights offering notice if the rights offering notice is being delivered to a registered security holder and direct the security holder's attention to this certificate

If you are delivering the rights offering notice to a security holder in a foreign jurisdiction, provide instructions on how that security holder can receive its rights certificate.

8. When and how can you exercise your rights?

State when the exercise period ends for security holders who have their rights certificate.

Also, provide instructions on how to exercise the rights to security holders whose securities are held in a brokerage account.

9. What are the next steps?

Include the following statement, using wording substantially similar to the following:

"This document contains key information you should know about [insert name of issuer]. You can find more details in the issuer's rights offering circular. To obtain a copy, visit [insert name of issuer]'s profile on the SEDAR website, visit [insert the website of the issuer], ask your dealer representative for a copy or contact [insert name of contact person of the issuer] at [insert the phone number or email of the contact person of the issuer]. You should read the rights offering circular, along with [insert name of issuer]'s continuous disclosure record, to make an informed decision."

10. Signature

Sign the rights offering notice. State the name and title of the person signing the rights offering notice.

Form 45-106F15 — Rights Offering Circular for Reporting Issuers

PART 1 INSTRUCTIONS

    1. Overview of the rights offering circular

    2. Incorporating information by reference

    3. Plain language

    4. Format

    5. Omitting information

    6. Date of information

PART 1 INSTRUCTIONS

1. Overview of the rights offering circular

This is the form of circular you must use for a distribution of rights under section 2.1 of National Instrument 45-106 *Prospectus Exemptions*. In this form, a distribution of rights is sometimes referred to as a "rights offering".

The objective of the rights offering circular is to provide information about the rights offering and details on how an existing security holder can exercise the rights.

Prepare the rights offering circular using a question-and-answer format.

Guidance

We do not expect the rights offering circular to be longer than 10 pages.

2. Incorporating information by reference

You must not incorporate information into the rights offering circular by reference.

3. Plain language

Use plain, easy to understand language in preparing the rights offering circular. Avoid technical terms but if they are necessary, explain them in a clear and concise manner.

4. Format

Except as otherwise stated, use the questions presented in this form as headings in the rights offering circular. To make the rights offering circular easier to understand, present information in tables.

5. Omitting information

Unless this form indicates otherwise, you are not required to complete an item in this form if it does not apply.

6. Date of information

Unless this form indicates otherwise, present the information in this form as of the date of the rights offering circular.

7. Forward-looking information

If you disclose forward-looking information in the rights offering circular, you must comply with Part 4A.3 of National Instrument 51-102 *Continuous Disclosure Obligations*.

PART 2 SUMMARY OF OFFERING

8. Required statement

State in italics, at the top of the cover page, the following:

> *"This rights offering circular is prepared by management. No securities regulatory authority or regulator has assessed the merits of these securities or reviewed this circular. Any representation to the contrary is an offence.*
>
> *This is the circular we referred to in the* [insert date of the rights offering notice] *rights offering notice, which you should have already received. Your rights certificate and relevant forms were enclosed with the rights offering notice. This circular should be read in conjunction with the rights offering notice and our continuous disclosure prior to making an investment decision."*

Guidance

We remind issuers and their executives that they are liable under secondary market liability provisions for the disclosure in this rights offering circular.

9. Basic disclosure about the distribution

Immediately below the statement referred to in item 8, state the following with the bracketed information completed:

> "Rights offering circular   [Date]
>
>   [Name of Issuer]"

If you have less than 12 months of working capital and are aware of material uncertainties that may cast significant doubt upon your ability to continue as a going concern, state the following in bold immediately below the name of the issuer:

> **"We currently have sufficient working capital to last [insert the number of months of working capital as at the date of the rights offering circular] months. We require [insert the percentage of the rights offering required to be taken up]% of the offering to last 12 months."**

10. Purpose of the rights offering circular

State the following in bold:

> **"Why are you reading this circular?"**

Explain the purpose of the rights offering circular. State that the rights offering circular provides details about the rights offering and refer to the rights offering notice that you sent to security holders.

11. Securities offered

State the following in bold:

> **"What is being offered?"**

Provide the number of rights you are offering to each security holder under the rights offering. If your outstanding share capital includes more than one class or type of security, identify which security holders are eligible to receive rights. Include the record date the issuer will use to determine which security holders are eligible to receive rights.

12. Right entitlement

State the following in bold:

> **"What do[es] [insert number of rights] right[s] entitle you to receive?"**

Explain what the security holder will receive upon the exercise of the rights. Also include the number of rights needed to acquire the underlying security.

13. Subscription price

State the following in bold:

> **"What is the subscription price?"**

Provide the price a security holder must pay to exercise the rights. If there is no published market for the securities, either explain how you determined the fair value of the securities or explain that no insider will be able to increase their proportionate interest through the rights offering.

Guidance

Refer to paragraph 2.1(3)(g) of NI 45-106 which provides that the subscription price must be lower than the market price if there is a published market for the securities. If there is no published market, either the subscription price must be lower than the fair value of the securities or insiders are not permitted to increase their proportionate interest in the issuer through the rights offering.

14. Expiry of offer

State the following in bold:

> **"When does the offer expire?"**

Provide the date and time that the offer expires.

Guidance

Refer to paragraph 2.1(6)(b) of NI 45-106 which provides that the prospectus exemption is not available where the exercise period for the rights is less than 21 days or more than 90 days after the day the rights offering notice is sent to security holders.

15. Description of the securities

State the following in bold:

> **"What are the significant attributes of the rights issued under the rights offering and the securities to be issued upon the exercise of the rights?"**

Describe the significant attributes of the rights and securities to be issued upon exercise of the rights. Include in the description the number of outstanding securities of the class of securities issuable upon exercise of the rights, as of the date of the rights offering circular.

17. Listing of securities

State the following in bold:

> **"Where will the rights and the securities issuable upon the exercise of the rights be listed for trading?"**

Identify the exchange(s) and quotation system(s), if any, on which the rights and underlying securities are listed, traded or quoted. If no market exists, or is expected to exist, state the following in bold:

> **"There is no market through which these [rights and/or underlying securities] may be sold."**

PART 3 USE OF AVAILABLE FUNDS

18. Available funds

State the following in bold:

> **"What will our available funds be upon the closing of the rights offering?"**

Using the following table, disclose the available funds after the rights offering. If you plan to combine additional sources of funding with the offering proceeds to achieve your principal capital-raising purpose, provide details about each additional source of funding.

If there is no minimum offering or stand-by commitment, or if the minimum offering or stand-by commitment represents less than 75% of the rights offering, include threshold disclosure if only 15%, 50% or 75% of the entire offering is taken up.

Disclose the amount of working capital deficiency, if any, of the issuer as of the most recent month end. If the available funds will not eliminate the working capital deficiency, state how you intend to eliminate or manage the deficiency. If there has been a significant change in the working capital since the most recently audited annual financial statements, explain those changes.

Guidance

We would consider a significant change to include a change in the working capital that results in material uncertainty regarding the issuer's going concern assumption, or a change in the working capital balance from positive to deficiency or vice versa.

		Assuming minimum offering or stand-by commitment only	Assuming 15% of offering	Assuming 50% of offering	Assuming 75% of offering	Assuming 100% of offering
A	Amount to be raised by this offering	$	$	$	$	$
B	Selling commissions and fees	$	$	$	$	$
C	Estimated offering costs (e.g., legal, accounting, audit)	$	$	$	$	$
D	Available funds: D = A - (B+C)	$	$	$	$	$
E	Additional sources of funding required	$	$	$	$	$
F	Working capital deficiency	$	$	$	$	$
G	Total: G = (D+E) - F	$	$	$	$	$

19. Use of available funds

State the following in bold:

"How will we use the available funds?"

Using the following table, provide a detailed breakdown of how you will use the available funds. Describe in reasonable detail each of the principal purposes, with approximate amounts.

Description of intended use of available funds listed in order of priority.	Assuming minimum offering or stand-by commitment only	Assuming 15% of offering	Assuming 50% of offering	Assuming 75% of offering	Assuming 100% of offering
	$	$	$	$	$
	$	$	$	$	$
Total: Equal to G in the available funds in item 18	$	$	$	$	$

If there is no minimum offering or stand-by commitment, or if the minimum offering or stand-by commitment represents less than 75% of the rights offering, include threshold disclosure if only 15%, 50% or 75% of the entire offering is taken up.

Instructions:

1. If the issuer has significant short-term liquidity requirements, discuss, for each threshold amount (i.e., 15%, 50% and 75%), the impact, if any, of raising that amount on its liquidity, operations, capital resources and solvency. Short-term liquidity requirements include non-discretionary expenditures for general corporate purposes and overhead expenses, significant short-term capital or contractual commitments, and expenditures required to achieve stated business objectives.

When discussing the impact of raising each threshold amount on your liquidity, operations, capital resources and solvency, include all of the following in the discussion:

- *which expenditures will take priority at each threshold, and what effect this allocation would have on your operations and business objectives and milestones;*
- *the risks of defaulting on payments as they become due, and what effect the defaults would have on your operations;*
- *an analysis of your ability to generate sufficient amounts of cash and cash equivalents from other sources, the circumstances that could affect those sources and management's assumptions in conducting this analysis.*

State the minimum amount required to meet the short-term liquidity requirements. In the event that the available funds could be less than the amount required to meet the short-term liquidity requirements, describe how management plans to discharge its liabilities as they become due. Include the assumptions management used in its plans.

If the available funds could be insufficient to cover the issuer's short-term liquidity requirements and overhead expenses for the next 12 months, include management's assessment of the issuer's ability to continue as a going concern. If there are material uncertainties that cast significant doubt upon the issuer's ability to continue as a going concern, state this fact in bold.

2. If you will use more than 10% of available funds to reduce or retire indebtedness and the indebtedness was incurred within the two preceding years, describe the principal purposes for which the indebtedness was used. If the creditor is an insider, associate or affiliate of the issuer, identify the creditor and the nature of the relationship to the issuer and disclose the outstanding amount owed.

3. If you will use more than 10% of available funds to acquire assets, describe the assets. If known, disclose the particulars of the purchase price being paid for or being allocated to the assets or categories of assets, including intangible assets. If the vendor of the asset is an insider, associate or affiliate of the issuer, identify the vendor and nature of the relationship to the issuer, and disclose the method used to determine the purchase price.

4. If any of the available funds will be paid to an insider, associate or affiliate of the issuer, disclose in a note to the use of available funds table in item 19 the name of the insider, associate or affiliate, the relationship to the issuer, and the amount to be paid.

5. If you will use more than 10% of available funds for research and development of products or services,

    a. describe the timing and stage of research and development that management anticipates will be reached using the funds,

    b. describe the major components of the proposed programs you will use the available funds for, including an estimate of anticipated costs,

    c. state if you are conducting your own research and development, are subcontracting out the research and development or are using a combination of those methods, and

    d. describe the additional steps required to reach commercial production and an estimate of costs and timing.

6. If you may reallocate available funds, include the following statement:

    "We intend to spend the available funds as stated. We will reallocate funds only for sound business reasons."

20. How long will the available funds last?

State the following in bold:

    "How long will the available funds last?"

Explain how long management anticipates the available funds will last. If you do not have adequate funds to cover anticipated expenses for the next 12 months, state the sources of financing that the issuer has arranged but not yet used. Also, provide an analysis of the issuer's ability to generate sufficient amounts of cash and cash equivalents in the short term and the long term to maintain capacity, and to meet planned growth or to fund development activities. You should describe sources of funding and circumstances that could affect those sources that are reasonably likely to occur. If this results in material uncertainties that cast significant doubt upon the issuer's ability to continue as a going concern, disclose this fact.

If you expect the available funds to last for more than 12 months, state this expectation.

PART 4 INSIDER PARTICIPATION

21. Intention of insiders

State the following in bold:

    "Will insiders be participating?"

Provide the answer. If "yes", provide details of insiders' intentions to exercise their rights, to the extent known to the issuer after reasonable inquiry.

22. Holders of at least 10% before and after the rights offering

State the following in bold:

    "Who are the holders of 10% or more of our securities before and after the rights offering?"

Provide this information in the following tabular form, to the extent known to the issuer after reasonable inquiry:

Name	Holdings before the offering	Holdings after the offering
[Name of security holder]	[State the number or amount of securities held and the percentage of security holdings this represents]	[State the number or amount of securities held and the percentage of security holdings this represents]

PART 5 DILUTION

23. Dilution

State the following in bold:

    "If you do not exercise your rights, by how much will your security holdings be diluted?"

Provide a percentage in the rights offering circular and state the assumptions used, as appropriate.

PART 6 STAND-BY COMMITMENT

24. Stand-by guarantor

State the following in bold:

    "Who is the stand-by guarantor and what are the fees?"

Explain the nature of the issuer's relationship with the stand-by guarantor including whether, and the basis on which, if applicable, the stand-by guarantor is a related party of the issuer. Describe the stand-by commitment and the material terms of the basis on which the stand-by guarantor may terminate the obligation under the stand-by commitment.

Instructions:

> In determining if a stand-by guarantor is a related party, you should refer to the issuer's GAAP which has the same meaning as in *National Instrument 52-107 Acceptable Accounting Principles and Auditing Standards.*

25. Financial ability of the stand-by guarantor

State the following in bold:

> **"Have we confirmed that the stand-by guarantor has the financial ability to carry out its stand-by commitment?"**

If the offering has a stand-by commitment, state that you have confirmed that the stand-by guarantor has the financial ability to carry out its stand-by commitment.

26. Security holdings of the stand-by guarantor

State the following in bold:

> **"What are the security holdings of the stand-by guarantor before and after the rights offering?"**

Provide a percentage in the rights offering circular and state the assumptions used, as appropriate.

Name	Holdings before the offering	Holdings after the offering
[Name of stand-by guarantor]	[State the number or amount of securities held and the percentage of security holdings this represents]	[State the number or amount of securities held and the percentage of security holdings this represents]

PART 7 MANAGING DEALER, SOLICITING DEALER AND UNDERWRITING CONFLICTS

27. The managing dealer, the soliciting dealer and their fees

State the following in bold:

> **"Who is the [managing dealer/soliciting dealer] and what are its fees?"**

Identify the managing dealer, if any, and the soliciting dealer, if any, and describe the commissions or fees payable to them.

28. Managing dealer/soliciting dealer conflicts

State the following in bold:

> **"Does the [managing dealer/soliciting dealer] have a conflict of interest?"**

If disclosure is required by National Instrument 33-105 *Underwriting Conflicts*, include that disclosure.

PART 8 HOW TO EXERCISE THE RIGHTS

29. Security holders who are registered holders

State the following in bold:

> **"How does a security holder that is a registered holder participate in the rights offering?"**

Explain how a registered holder can participate in the rights offering.

30. Security holders who are not registered holders

State the following in bold:

> **"How does a security holder that is not a registered holder participate in the rights offering?"**

Explain how a security holder who is not a registered holder can participate in the rights offering.

31. Eligibility to participate

State the following in bold:

> **"Who is eligible to receive rights?"**

List the jurisdictions in which you are making the rights offering.

Explain how a security holder in a foreign jurisdiction can acquire the rights and securities issuable upon the exercise of the rights.

32. Additional subscription privilege

State the following in bold:

> **"What is the additional subscription privilege and how can you exercise this privilege?"**

Describe the additional subscription privilege and explain how a holder of rights who has exercised the basic subscription privilege can exercise the additional subscription privilege.

33. Transfer of rights

State the following in bold:

> **"How does a rights holder sell or transfer rights?"**

Explain how a holder of rights can sell or transfer rights. If the rights will be listed on an exchange, provide further details related to the trading of the rights on the exchange.

34. Trading of underlying securities

State the following in bold:

> **"When can you trade securities issuable upon the exercise of your rights?"**

State when a security holder can trade the securities issuable upon the exercise of the rights.

35. Resale restrictions

State the following in bold:

> **"Are there restrictions on the resale of securities?"**

If the issuer is offering rights in one or more jurisdictions where there are restrictions on the resale of securities, include a statement disclosing when those rights and underlying securities will become freely tradable and that until then such securities may not be resold except pursuant to a prospectus or prospectus exemption, which may be available only in limited circumstances.

36. Fractional securities upon exercise of the rights

State the following in bold:

> **"Will we issue fractional underlying securities upon exercise of the rights?"**

Respond "yes" or "no" and explain (if necessary).

PART 9 APPOINTMENT OF DEPOSITORY

37. Depository

State the following in bold:

> **"Who is the depository?"**

If the rights offering is subject to a minimum offering amount, or if there is a stand-by commitment, state the name of the depository you appointed to hold all money received upon exercise of the rights until the minimum offering amount or stand-by commitment is received or until the money is returned.

38. Release of funds from depository

State the following in bold:

> **"What happens if we do not raise the [minimum offering amount] or if we do not receive funds from the stand-by guarantor?"**

If the offering is subject to a minimum offering amount, or if there is a stand-by commitment, state that you have entered into an agreement with the depository under which the depository will return the money held by it to holders of rights that have already subscribed for securities under the offering, if you do not raise the minimum offering amount or receive funds from the stand-by guarantor.

PART 10 FOREIGN ISSUERS

39. Foreign issuers

State the following in bold:

> **"How can you enforce a judgment against us?"**

If the issuer is incorporated, continued, or otherwise organized under the laws of a foreign jurisdiction or resides outside of Canada, state the following:

> "[The issuer] is incorporated, continued or otherwise organized under the laws of a foreign jurisdiction or resides outside of Canada. It may not be possible for investors to enforce judgments obtained in Canada against any person or company that is incorporated, continued or otherwise organized under the laws of a foreign jurisdiction or resides outside of Canada."

PART 11 ADDITIONAL INFORMATION

40. Additional information

State the following in bold:

> **"Where can you find more information about us?"**

Provide the SEDAR website address and state that a security holder can access the issuer's continuous disclosure from that site. If applicable, provide the issuer's website address.

PART 12 MATERIAL FACTS AND MATERIAL CHANGES

41. Material facts and material changes

State the following in bold:

> **"There is no material fact or material change about the issuer that has not been generally disclosed."**

If there is a material fact or material change about the issuer that has not been generally disclosed, add disclosure of that material fact or material change.

Guidance

Issuers should be aware that disclosing a material change in the rights offering circular does not relieve the issuer of the requirement to issue a news release and file a material change report as required by Part 7 of NI 51-102.

Form 45-106F16 — Notice of Use of Proceeds

	[Insert issuer name]	

For the financial year ended *[Insert end date of most recently completed financial year]*

Date: *[Specify the date of the Notice. The date must be no earlier than the date of the auditor's report on the financial statements for the issuer's most recently completed financial year.]*

[Provide the information specified in the following table.]

1	**Opening Proceeds**		
	(A)	*Closing unused proceeds balance from the last Notice in Form 45-106F16 filed, if any*	$
	(B)	*Proceeds raised in the most recently completed financial year*	$
	(C)	*Total opening proceeds [Line (C) = Line (A) + Line (B)]*	$
2	**Proceeds Used During the Most Recently Completed Financial Year**		
		[Provide in reasonable detail a breakdown of all proceeds used in the most recently completed financial year, including proceeds used to pay the following, as applicable: *i. selling commissions and fees* *ii. other offering costs* *iii. amounts paid in respect of each use of available funds identified in the offering memorandum* *iv. each other principal use of proceeds, identified separately]*	$
	(D)	*Total used proceeds [Line (D) is the sum of the uses of proceeds itemized in this section 2 of the table, and must equal the aggregate gross proceeds used during the most recently completed financial year.]*	$
3	**Closing Unused Proceeds**		
	(E)	*Closing unused proceeds [Line (E) = Line (C) - Line (D)]*	$

[If any of the proceeds required to be disclosed in this table were paid directly or indirectly to a related party (as defined in Instruction A.6 of Form 45-106F2 Offering Memorandum Form for Non-Qualifying Issuers) of the issuer, state in each case the name of the related party to whom the payment was made, their relationship to the issuer and the amount paid to the related party.]

Instructions for Completing Form 45-106F16 *Notice of Use of Proceeds*

1. The amount for Line (A) is taken from Line (E) in the prior year's Notice of Use of Proceeds (Notice), if applicable. If a Notice was not required in the prior year, then the amount for Line (A) is $nil.

2. The amount for Line (B) is the aggregate gross proceeds raised in all jurisdictions in Canada under section 2.9 *[Offering memorandum]* of National Instrument 45-106 (the OM exemption) during the most recently completed financial year. If an issuer raised funds in reliance on other prospectus exemptions concurrently with the OM exemption during the year and it is impractical to separately track proceeds raised only under the OM exemption, the issuer can provide the disclosure outlined in the table for the aggregate gross proceeds raised under all prospectus exemptions during the most recently completed financial year.

3. If Line (C) is $nil, then the issuer does not have an obligation to file, deliver or make reasonably available the Notice for that financial year.

4. In Section 2 of the table, the issuer must provide a breakdown in reasonable detail of the uses of the aggregate gross proceeds during the most recently completed financial year. Issuers should ensure that the disclosure is specific enough and provides sufficient detail for an investor to understand how the proceeds have been used.

5. Both direct and indirect payments to related parties must be disclosed. An example of an indirect payment could include repayment of a debt that was incurred for a prior payment to a related party.

6. Proceeds invested on a temporary basis would not generally be considered to have been used.

Form 45-106F17 — Notice of Specified Key Events

This is the form required under subsection 2.9(17.20) of National Instrument 45-106 *Prospectus Exemptions* (NI 45-106) in New Brunswick, Nova Scotia and Ontario to make available notice of specified key events to holders of securities acquired under subsection 2.9(2.1) of NI 45-106.

Full legal name	

Street address		Province/State	
Municipality		Postal code/Zip code	
Website		Country	

2. Specified Key Event

Provide the following information.

The event, as described in section 3, is: *[Select one or more type of event from the list below]*

❑ a discontinuation of the issuer's business

❑ a change in the issuer's industry

❑ a change of control of the issuer

Date on which the event occurred (yyyy/mm/dd): | .... / .... / .... |

3. Event Description

Provide a brief description of the event identified in section 2.

....

4. Contact Person

Provide the following information for a person at the issuer who can be contacted regarding the event described in section 3.

| Name | | Title | |
| Email address | | Telephone number | |

Date of notice (yyyy/mm/dd): | .... / .... / .... |

Companion Policy 45-106CP — Prospectus Exemptions

PART 1 — INTRODUCTION

1.1 Purpose

1.2 All trades and distributions are subject to securities legislation

1.3 Multi-jurisdictional distributions

1.4 Other exemptions

1.5 Discretionary relief

1.6 Registration business trigger for trading and advising

1.7 Underwriters

1.8 Persons created to use exemptions ("syndication")

1.9 Responsibility for compliance and verifying purchaser status

1.10 Prohibited activities

PART 2 — INTERPRETATION

2.1 Definitions

2.2 Executive officer ("policy making function")

2.3 Directors, executive officers and officers of non-corporate issuers

2.4 Founder

2.5 Investment fund

2.6 Affiliate, control and related entity

2.7 Close personal friend

2.8 Close business associate

2.9 Indirect interest

PART 3 — CAPITAL RAISING EXEMPTIONS

3.1 Soliciting purchasers

3.2 Soliciting purchasers — Newfoundland and Labrador and Ontario

3.3 Advertising

3.3.1 Advertising and marketing materials under the offering memorandum exemption

3.4 Restrictions on finders fees or commissions

3.4.01 Payment of Finder's Fees or Commissions to Any Person

3.4.1 Reinvestment plans

3.5 Accredited investor

3.6 Private issuer

3.7 Family, friends and business associates

3.8 Offering memorandum

3.9 Minimum amount investment

3.10 Rights offering — reporting issuer

PART 1 — INTRODUCTION

National Instrument 45-106 *Prospectus Exemptions* (NI 45-106) provides: (i) exemptions from the prospectus requirement and (ii) one exemption from the issuer bid requirements. It does not provide exemptions from the requirement to be registered as a dealer, adviser or investment fund manager. National Instrument 31-103 *Registration Requirements, Exemptions and Ongoing Registrant Obligations* ("NI 31-103") contains some exemptions from the registration requirement.

1.1 **Purpose** — The purpose of this Companion Policy is to help users understand how the provincial and territorial securities regulatory authorities and regulators interpret or apply certain provisions of NI 45-106. This Companion Policy includes explanations, discussion and examples of the application of various parts of NI 45-106.

1.2 **All distributions and other trades are subject to securities legislation** — The securities legislation of a local jurisdiction applies to any trade in, or distribution of, a security in the local jurisdiction, whether or not the issuer of the security is a reporting issuer in that jurisdiction. Likewise, the definition of "trade" in securities legislation includes any act, advertisement, solicitation, conduct or negotiation directly or indirectly in furtherance of a trade. A person who engages in these activities, or other trading activities, must comply with the securities legislation of each jurisdiction in which the trade or distribution occurs.

1.3 **Multi-jurisdictional distributions** — A distribution can occur in more than one jurisdiction. If it does, the person conducting the distribution must comply with the securities legislation of each jurisdiction in which the distribution occurs. For example, a distribution from a person in Alberta to a purchaser in British Columbia may be considered a distribution in both jurisdictions.

1.4 **Other exemptions** — In addition to the exemptions in NI 45-106, exemptions may also be available to persons under securities legislation of each local jurisdiction.

1.5 **Discretionary relief** — In addition to the exemptions contained in NI 45-106 and those available under securities legislation of a local jurisdiction, the securities regulatory authority or regulator in each jurisdiction has the discretion to grant exemptions from the prospectus requirement.

1.6 **Registration business trigger for trading and advising** — Securities legislation requires certain persons to be registered if they are any of the following:

- in the business of trading
- in the business of advising
- holding themselves out as being in the business of trading or advising
- acting as an underwriter
- acting as an investment fund manager

NI 31-103 sets out the requirements for registration as well as certain exemptions from these registration requirements.

Issuers relying on prospectus exemptions to distribute securities, or any selling agents they use, may be required to be registered. Companion Policy 31-103CP gives guidance to issuers on how to apply the registration business trigger.

1.7 **Underwriters** — Underwriters should not sell securities to the public without providing a prospectus. If an underwriter purchases securities with a view to distribution, the underwriter should purchase the securities under the prospectus exemption in section 2.33 of NI 45-106. If the underwriter purchases securities under this exemption, the first trade in the securities will be a distribution. As a result, the underwriter will only be able to resell the securities if it can rely on another exemption from the prospectus requirement, or if a prospectus is delivered to the purchasers of the securities.

There may be legitimate transactions where a dealer purchases securities under a prospectus exemption other than the exemption in section 2.33 of NI 45-106; however, these transactions are only appropriate when the dealer purchases the securities with investment intent and not with a view to distribution.

If a dealer purchases securities through a series of exempt transactions in order to avoid the obligation to deliver a prospectus, the transactions will be viewed as a whole to determine if they constitute a distribution. If a transaction is in effect an indirect distribution, a prospectus will be required to qualify the sale of the securities despite the fact that each interim step in the transaction could otherwise be completed under a prospectus exemption. Such indirect distributions cannot be legitimately structured under NI 45-106.

1.8 Persons created to use exemptions ("syndication") — Sections 2.3(5), 2.4(1), 2.9(3), 2.9(3.0.1) and 2.10(2) of NI 45-106 specifically prohibit syndications. A distribution of securities to a person that had no pre-existing purpose and is created or used solely to purchase or hold securities under exemptions (a "syndicate") may be considered a distribution of securities to the persons beneficially owning or controlling the syndicate.

For example, a newly formed company with 15 shareholders is set up with the intention of purchasing $150 000 worth of securities under the minimum amount investment exemption. Each shareholder of the newly formed company contributes $10 000. In this situation the shareholders of the newly formed company are indirectly investing $10 000 when the exemption requires that they each invest $150 000. Consequently, both the newly formed company and its shareholders may need to comply with the requirements of the minimum amount investment exemption, or find an alternative exemption to rely on.

Syndication related concerns should not ordinarily arise if the purchaser under the exemption is a corporation, syndicate, partnership or other form of entity that is pre-existing and has a bona fide purpose other than investing in the securities being sold. However, it is an inappropriate use of these exemptions to indirectly distribute securities when the exemption is not available to directly distribute securities to each person in the syndicate.

1.9 Responsibility for compliance and verifying purchaser status — (1) **Determining whether an exemption is available.** — The prospectus exemptions in NI 45-106 set out specific terms and conditions that must be satisfied in order for the person relying on the exemption to distribute securities. The person relying on a prospectus exemption is responsible for determining whether the terms and conditions of the prospectus exemption are met. That person should retain all necessary documents to demonstrate that they properly relied on the exemption.

Some of the prospectus exemptions in NI 45-106 are available to both issuers and selling security holders. For purposes of this section, the term "seller" refers to the person relying on a prospectus exemption, whether an issuer or a selling security holder.

(2) **Registration related requirements** — Registered dealers and representatives have specific obligations under NI 31-103, including the "know your client," "know your product" and suitability obligations. These obligations apply to securities traded on a marketplace, distributed under a prospectus or distributed under a prospectus exemption.

Registered dealers or representatives may be involved in distributions under prospectus exemptions in different ways. The registered dealer or representative may be acting on behalf of a seller in connection with a distribution using a prospectus exemption.

In both cases, the registered dealer or representative must not only establish that a prospectus exemption is available, it must also comply with its registration obligations. For example, even if a registered dealer or representative has determined that a purchaser qualifies as an accredited investor or eligible investor, the registered dealer or representative must still assess whether the investment is suitable for the purchaser.

(3) **Exemptions based on purchaser characteristics** — Some of the prospectus exemptions in NI 45-106 require the purchaser of the securities to meet certain characteristics or have certain relationships with a director, executive officer, founder or control person of the issuer. These exemptions include:

- Exemptions based on income or asset tests — The accredited investor exemption and the "eligible investor" test in the offering memorandum exemption in some jurisdictions require a purchaser to meet certain income or asset tests in order for securities to be sold in reliance on the exemption.
- Exemptions based on relationships — The private issuer exemption, the family, friends and business associates exemption and the "eligible investor" test in the offering memorandum exemption in some jurisdictions require a relationship between the purchaser and a director, executive officer, founder or control person of the issuer, such as that of a family member, close personal friend, or close business associate.

When distributing securities under these exemptions, the seller will have to obtain information from the purchaser in order to determine whether the purchaser has the requisite income, assets or relationship to meet the terms of the exemption.

It will not be sufficient for the seller to accept standard representations in a subscription agreement or an initial beside a category on Form 45-106F9 *Form for Individual Accredited Investors* unless the seller has taken reasonable steps to verify the representations made by the purchaser.

(4) **Reasonable steps** — Described below are procedures that a seller could implement in order to reasonably confirm that the purchaser meets the conditions for a particular exemption. Whether the types of steps are reasonable will depend on the particular facts and circumstances of the purchaser, the offering and the exemption being relied on, including:

- how the seller identified or located the potential purchaser
- what category of accredited investor or eligible investor the purchaser claims to meet
- what type of relationship the purchaser claims to have and with which director, executive officer, founder or control person of the issuer
- how much and what type of background information is known about the purchaser
- whether the person who meets with, or provides information to, the purchaser is registered

We expect a seller to be in a position to explain why certain steps were not taken or to be able to explain how alternative steps were reasonable in the circumstances. It is the seller that is relying on the prospectus exemption and it is the seller that is responsible to ensure the terms of the exemption are met. If the seller has any reservations about whether the purchaser qualifies under the exemption, the seller should not sell securities to the purchaser in reliance on that exemption.

(a) **Understand the terms and conditions of the exemption** — The seller should fully understand the terms and conditions of the exemption being relied on. "Understanding" includes being able to:

- Explain the terms and conditions — The seller must be able to explain to a purchaser the meaning of the terms and conditions of the particular exemption, including the difference between alternative qualification criteria for the same exemption.

  For example, the accredited investor definition uses the terms "financial assets" and "net assets". In some jurisdictions, the offering memorandum exemption also uses the term "net assets" as part of the eligible investor definition. A seller should be capable of explaining the meaning and differences between the two terms, including describing the specific assets and liabilities that form part of each calculation.

- Apply the specific facts of the purchaser to the terms and conditions — The terms "close personal friend" and "close business associate" used in some exemptions are difficult to define and can mean different things to different people. Sections 2.7 and 2.8 of this Companion Policy provide guidance on the key elements necessary to establish these types of relationships. We have not provided a "bright line" test for these relationships. A seller should understand the key elements of these relationships and be able to evaluate whether the relationship claimed by the purchaser meets those key elements.

(b) **Establish appropriate policies and procedures** — The seller is also responsible for confirming that all parties acting on behalf of the seller in a distribution understand the conditions that must be satisfied to rely on the exemption. This includes any employee, officer, director, agent, finder or other intermediary (whether registered or not) involved in the transaction.

We expect a seller to have policies and procedures in place to confirm that these other parties understand the exemption being relied on, are able to describe the terms of the exemption to purchasers and know what information and documentation must be obtained from purchasers to confirm the conditions of the exemption have been satisfied.

(c) **Verify the purchaser meets the criteria set out in the exemption** — Before discussing the details of an investment with a prospective purchaser, we expect the seller to obtain information that confirms the purchaser meets the criteria set out in the exemption. It would not be sufficient for a seller to rely solely on a form of subscription agreement or other document that only states: "I am an accredited investor" or "I am a friend of a director".

We would also have concerns if a seller only accepted detailed representations or an initial beside a category on the Form 45-106F9 *Form for Individual Accredited Investors* from the purchaser. In both cases, we expect the seller to take additional steps to confirm that the purchaser understood the meaning of what the purchaser was signing or initialing and that the purchaser was truthful in making the representation or initialing the category.

For example,

- Exemptions based on income or asset tests — To assess whether a purchaser is an accredited investor or eligible investor, we expect the seller to ask questions about the purchaser's net income, financial assets or net assets, or to ask other questions designed to elicit details about the purchaser's financial circumstances.

  If the seller has concerns about the purchaser's responses, the seller should make further inquiries about the purchaser's financial circumstances. If the seller still questions the purchaser's eligibility, the seller could ask to see documentation that independently confirms the purchaser's claims.

- Exemptions based on relationships — If an exemption is based on the existence of a specific relationship between the purchaser and a principal of the issuer (such as that of a family member, "close personal friend" or "close business associate"), we expect the seller to ask questions designed to confirm the nature and length of the relationship. The seller should also confirm the nature and length of the relationship with the director, executive officer, founder or control person identified by the purchaser.

  For example, if the purchaser claims to be a close personal friend of a director of an issuer, the seller could ask the purchaser for the name of the director and a description of the nature and length of the purchaser's relationship with the director. The seller could verify with the director that the information is accurate. Based on that factual information, the seller could determine whether the purchaser is a close personal friend of the director for the purposes of the family, friends and business associates exemption.

(d) **Keep relevant and detailed documentation** — The seller should consider what documentation it needs to retain or collect from a purchaser to evidence the steps the seller followed to establish the purchaser met the conditions of the exemption.

The seller should consider whether it is necessary to have the purchaser sign that documentation before distributing securities to that purchaser. For example, if the purchaser claims to be a close personal friend of a director of the issuer, the seller could ask the purchaser to sign a statement giving the name of the director and describing the nature and length of the purchaser's relationship with the director. The seller could also ask the director to sign the statement confirming the relationship. In other cases, the seller may determine it is not necessary for the purchaser to sign the documentation, for example, if the seller is using meeting notes and email communications to demonstrate its verification efforts.

The seller should retain this documentation to evidence the steps the seller has taken to verify the availability of the exemption. Certain exemptions require the seller to obtain a signed risk acknowledgement form from the purchaser and to retain that risk acknowledgement for 8 years after the distribution. The 8-year period reflects the longest limitation period under securities legislation in Canada. The seller should consider local legislation concerning limitation periods when deciding how long to retain other documentation it considers necessary to demonstrate that it complied with the exemption.

The seller should also consider and comply with the requirements under provincial or federal legislation concerning the protection of personal information when collecting and retaining purchaser information.

1.10 Prohibited activities — Securities legislation in certain jurisdictions prohibits any person from making certain representations to a purchaser of securities, including an undertaking about the future value or price of the securities. In certain jurisdictions, these provisions also prohibit a person from making any statement that the person knows or ought reasonably to know is a misrepresentation. These prohibitions apply whether or not a trade or distribution is made under an exemption.

Misrepresentation is defined in securities legislation. The use of exaggeration, innuendo or ambiguity in an oral or written representation about a material fact, or other deceptive behaviour relating to a material fact, might be a misrepresentation.

PART 2 — INTERPRETATION

2.1 Definitions — Unless defined in NI 45-106, terms used in NI 45-106 have the meaning given to them in local securities legislation or in National Instrument 14-101 *Definitions*.

The term "contract of insurance" in the definition of "financial assets" has the meaning assigned to it in the legislation for the jurisdiction referenced in Appendix A of NI 45-106.

2.2 Executive officer ("policy making function") — The definition of "executive officer" in NI 45-106 is based on the definition of the same term contained in National Instrument 51-102 *Continuous Disclosure Obligations* (NI 51-102).

Paragraph (c) of the definition "executive officer" includes individuals that are not employed by the issuer or any of its subsidiaries, but who perform a policy-making function in respect of the issuer.

The definition includes someone who "performs a policy-making function" in respect of the issuer. The CSA is of the view that an individual who "performs a policy-making function" in respect of an issuer is someone who is responsible, solely or jointly with others, for setting the direction of the issuer and is sufficiently knowledgeable of the business and affairs of the issuer so as to be able to respond meaningfully to inquiries from investors about the issuer.

2.3 Directors, executive officers and officers of non-corporate issuers — The term "director" is defined in NI 45-106 and it includes, for non-corporate issuers, individuals who perform functions similar to those of a director of a company.

When the term "officer" is used in NI 45-106, or any of the NI 45-106 forms, a non-corporate issuer should refer to the definitions in securities legislation. Securities legislation in most jurisdictions defines "officer" to include any individual acting in a capacity similar to that of an officer of a company. Therefore, in most jurisdictions, non-corporate issuers must determine which individuals are acting in capacities similar to that of directors and officers of corporate issuers, for the purposes of complying with NI 45-106 and its forms.

For example, the determination of who is acting in the capacity of a director or executive officer may be important where a person intends to distribute securities of a limited partnership under an exemption that is conditional on a relationship with a director or executive officer. The person must conclude that the purchaser has the necessary relationship with an individual who is acting in a capacity with the limited partnership that is similar to that of a director or executive officer of a company.

2.4 Founder — The definition of "founder" includes a requirement that, at the time of the distribution a security the person be actively involved in the business of the issuer. Accordingly, a person who takes the initiative in founding, organizing or substantially reorganizing the business of the issuer within the meaning of the definition but subsequently ceases to be actively engaged in the day to day operations of the business of the issuer would no longer be a "founder" for the purposes of NI 45-106, regardless of the person's degree of prior involvement with the issuer or the extent of the person's continued ownership interest in the issuer.

2.5 Investment fund — Generally, the definition of "investment fund" would not include a trust or other entity that issues securities that entitle the holder to net cash flows generated by: (i) an underlying business owned by the trust or other entity, or (ii) the income-producing properties owned by the trust or other entity. Examples of trusts or other entities that are not included in the definition are business income trusts, real estate investment trusts and royalty trusts.

2.6 Affiliate, control and related entity — (1) *Affiliate* — Section 1.3 of NI 45-106 contains rules for determining whether persons are affiliates for the purposes of NI 45-106, which may be different than those contained in other securities legislation.

(2) *Control* — The concept of control has two different interpretations in NI 45-106. For the purposes of Division 4 of Part 2 (employee, executive officer, director and consultant exemptions), the interpretation of control is contained in section 2.23(1). For the purposes of the rest of NI 45-106, the interpretation of control is found in section 1.4 of NI 45-106. The reason for having two different interpretations of control is that the exemptions for distributions of securities to employees, executive officers, directors and consultants require a broader concept of control than is considered necessary for the rest of NI 45-106 to accommodate the issuance of compensation securities in a wide variety of business structures.

2.7 Close personal friend — For purposes of both the private issuer exemption in section 2.4 of NI 45-106 and the family, friends and business associates exemption in section 2.5 of NI 45-106, a "close personal friend" of a director, executive officer, founder or control person of an issuer is an individual who knows the director, executive officer, founder or control person well enough and has known them for a sufficient period of time to be in a position to assess their capabilities and trustworthiness and to obtain information from them with respect to the investment. The term "close personal friend" can include a family member who is not already specifically identified in the exemptions if the family member satisfies the criteria described above.

We consider the following factors as relevant to this determination:

(a) the length of time the individual has known the director, executive officer, founder or control person,

(b) the nature of the relationship between the individual and the director, executive officer, founder or control person including such matters as the frequency of contacts between them and the level of trust and reliance in the other circumstances, and

(c) the number of "close personal friends" of the director, executive officer, founder or control person to whom securities have been distributed in reliance on the private issuer exemption or the family, friends and business associates exemption.

An individual is not a close personal friend solely because the individual is:

(a) a relative,

(b) a member of the same club, organization, association or religious group,

(c) a co-worker, colleague or associate at the same workplace,

(d) a client, customer, former client or former customer,

(e) a mere acquaintance, or

(f) connected through some form of social media, such as Facebook, Twitter or LinkedIn.

The relationship between the individual and the director, executive officer, founder or control person must be direct. For example, the exemption is not available to a close personal friend of a close personal friend of a director of the issuer.

We would not consider a relationship that is primarily founded on participation in an Internet forum to be that of a close personal friend.

The person relying on the exemption is responsible for determining that the purchaser meets the characteristics required under the exemption. See section 1.9 of this Companion Policy for guidance on how to verify and document purchaser status.

2.8 Close business associate — For the purposes of both the private issuer exemption in section 2.4 of NI 45-106 and the family, friends and business associates exemption in section 2.5 of NI 45-106, a "close business associate" is an individual who has had sufficient prior business dealings with a director, executive officer, founder or control person of the issuer to be in a position to assess their capabilities and trustworthiness and to obtain information from them with respect to the investment.

We consider the following factors as relevant to this determination:

(a) the length of time the individual has known the director, executive officer, founder or control person,

(b) the nature of any specific business relationships between the individual and the director, executive officer, founder or control person, including, for each relationship, when it began, the frequency of contact between them and when it terminated if it is not ongoing, and the level of trust and reliance in the other circumstances,

(c) the nature and number of any business dealings between the individual and the director, executive officer, founder or control person, the length of the period during which they occurred, and the nature and date of the most recent business dealing, and

(d) the number of "close business associates" of the director, executive officer, founder or control person to whom securities have been distributed in reliance on the private issuer exemption or the family, friends and business associates exemption.

An individual is not a close business associate solely because the individual is:

(a) a member of the same club, organization, association or religious group,

(b) a co-worker, colleague or associate at the same workplace,

(c) a client, customer, former client or former customer,

(d) a mere acquaintance, or

(e) connected through some form of social media, such as Facebook, Twitter or LinkedIn.

The relationship between the individual and the director, executive officer, founder or control person must be direct. For example, the exemptions are not available for a close business associate of a close business associate of a director of the issuer.

We would not consider a relationship that is primarily founded on participation in an internet forum to be that of a close business associate.

The person relying on the exemption is responsible for determining that the purchaser meets the characteristics required under the exemption. See section 1.9 of this Companion Policy for guidance on how to verify and document purchaser status.

2.9 Indirect interest — Under paragraph (t) of the definition of "accredited investor" in section 1.1 of NI 45-106, an "accredited investor" includes a person in respect of which all of the owners of interests in that person, direct, indirect or beneficial, are accredited investors. The interpretive provision in section 1.2 of NI 45-106 is needed to confirm the meaning of indirect interest in British Columbia.

PART 3 — CAPITAL RAISING EXEMPTIONS

3.1 Soliciting purchasers — (1) Soliciting purchasers — Alberta, British Columbia, Manitoba, New Brunswick, Newfoundland and Labrador, Northwest Territories, Nova Scotia, Nunavut, Prince Edward Island, Québec, Saskatchewan and Yukon — Part 2, Division 1 (capital raising exemptions) in NI 45-106 does not prohibit the use of registrants, finders, or advertising in any form (for example, Internet, e-mail, direct mail, newspaper or magazine) to solicit purchasers under any of the exemptions. However, use of any of these means to find purchasers under the private issuer exemption in section 2.4 of NI 45-106 or under the family, friends and business associates exemption in section 2.5 of NI 45-106, may give rise to a presumption that the relationship required for use of these exemptions is not present. If, for example, an issuer advertises or pays a commission or finder's fee to a third party to find purchasers under the family, friends and business associates exemption, it suggests that the precondition of a close relationship between the purchaser and the issuer may not exist and therefore the issuer cannot rely on this exemption.

Use of a finder by a private issuer to find an accredited investor, however, would not preclude the private issuer from relying upon the private issuer exemption, provided that all of the other conditions to that exemption are met.

Any solicitation activities that aim to identify a particular category of investor should clearly state the kind of investor being sought and the criteria that investors will be required to meet. Any print materials used to find accredited investors, for example, should clearly and prominently state that only accredited investors should respond to the solicitation.

(2) Soliciting purchasers — Ontario — Part 2, Division 1 (capital raising exemptions) in NI 45-106 does not prohibit the use of registrants, finders, or advertising in any form (for example, Internet, e-mail, direct mail, newspaper or magazine) to solicit purchasers under any of the exemptions.

Any solicitation activities that aim to identify a particular category of investor should clearly state the kind of investor being sought and the criteria that investors will be required to meet. Any print materials used to find accredited investors, for example, should clearly and prominently state that only accredited investors should respond to the solicitation.

The Ontario Securities Commission considers the use of registrants, finders or advertising to find or attract purchasers to be inconsistent with the use of the family, friends and business associates exemption in section 2.5 of NI 45-106 and the private issuer exemption in section 2.4 of NI 45-106 for distributions to family members, close personal friends or close business associates. Since advertising should not be required to find a family member, close personal friend or close business associate, the Ontario Securities Commission does not expect that advertising would be used to find or attract purchasers for distributions made solely under section 2.5 of NI 45-106 or to identify purchasers for distributions made in reliance on that exemption. The Ontario Securities Commission also does not expect that advertising would be used for distributions made solely to family members, close personal friends or close business associates under section 2.4 of NI 45-106 or to identify those types of purchasers for distributions made in reliance on that exemption.

If a distribution is being made in reliance on one or more other prospectus exemptions, advertising in connection with those other exemptions does not prevent concurrent reliance on the family, friends and business associates exemption in section 2.5 or the private issuer exemption in section 2.4 of NI 45-106. Similarly, use of a finder by a private issuer to find an accredited investor would not preclude the private issuer from relying upon the private issuer exemption under section 2.4 of NI 45-106 provided that all of the other conditions to that exemption are met.

3.2 Soliciting purchasers — Ontario — The Ontario Securities Commission takes the position that if an issuer retains an employee whose primary job function is to actively solicit members of the public for the purposes of selling the issuer's securities, the issuer and its employee are in the business of selling securities. Further, if an issuer and its employees are deemed to be in the business of selling securities the Ontario Securities Commission considers both the issuer and its employees to be market intermediaries. This applies whether the issuer and its employees are located in Ontario and solicit members of the public outside of Ontario or whether the issuer and its employees are located outside of Ontario and solicit members of the public in Ontario. Accordingly, in order to be in compliance with securities legislation, these issuers and their employees should be registered under the appropriate category of registration in Ontario.

3.3 Advertising — NI 45-106 does not restrict the use of advertising to solicit or find purchasers. However, issuers and selling security holders should review other securities legislation and securities directions for guidelines, limitations and prohibitions on advertising intended to promote interest in an issuer or its securities. For example, any advertising or marketing communications must not contain a misrepresentation and should be consistent with the issuer's public disclosure record.

3.3.1 Advertising and marketing materials under the offering memorandum exemption — In Alberta, New Brunswick, Nova Scotia, Ontario, Québec and Saskatchewan, an offering memorandum prepared in accordance with the offering memorandum exemption in section 2.9(2.1) of NI 45-106 must incorporate by reference any marketing materials used in relation to a distribution under the offering memorandum exemption. Subsection 2.9(8) of NI 45-106 requires the issuer to sign a certificate that indicates that the offering memorandum does not contain a misrepresentation. As marketing materials are incorporated by reference into the offering memorandum, the issuer must also ensure that the information contained in marketing materials does not contain a misrepresentation.

In these jurisdictions, an issuer or registrant that uses marketing materials as part of an offering made in reliance on the offering memorandum exemption must review the marketing materials to confirm that they are consistent with the offering document and are fair, balanced and not misleading. In addition, these jurisdictions expect an issuer or registrant to determine whether any claims set out in marketing materials adequately refer to information to support these claims and representations. For example, if benchmarks are used for comparison purposes, the issuer or registrant should assess whether the benchmarks are relevant and comparable to the investment in question and confirm the marketing materials:

(a) adequately explain differences between the benchmark and the investment,

(b) make reference to the source of the benchmark and identify the date to which the information is current, and

(c) where relevant, caution purchasers that historical performance is not necessarily indicative of future results.

Issuers that prepare offering memoranda in accordance with Form 45-106F2 *Offering Memorandum for Non-Qualifying Issuers*, are also required to comply with requirements relating to forward-looking information, which are described in Instructions A.12 and B.14 of Form 45-106F2. Issuers cannot disseminate material forward-looking information unless it is contained within the offering memorandum. Additionally, forward-looking information contained in an offering memorandum must comply with certain requirements in National Instrument 51-102 *Continuous Disclosure Obligations*. These requirements also extend to marketing materials that are used in connection with a distribution under the offering memorandum exemption.

In these jurisdictions, if an issuer or registrant intends to rely on marketing materials prepared by a third party, such as an analyst report that rates a security or compares a security with securities of other issuers, the issuer or registrant is expected to perform its own assessment of the marketing materials to confirm that they are fair, balanced and not misleading. For example, if the report has been paid for by the issuer, or if there are other relationships between the analyst and the issuer, it would be inappropriate to describe the report as being an "independent" report. The report should also prominently disclose the fees paid and relationships between the analyst and the issuer. An issuer or registrant should not rely on marketing materials prepared by a third party without independently reviewing the materials prior to use.

A registrant should be aware of other CSA guidance on the review and use of marketing materials and reliance on marketing materials prepared by third parties.

3.4 Restrictions on finder's fees or commissions — The following restrictions apply with respect to certain exemptions under NI 45-106:

(1) no commissions or finder's fees may be paid to directors, officers, founders and control persons in connection with a distribution made under the private issuer exemption or the family, friends and business associates exemption, except in connection with a distribution of a security to an accredited investor under the private issuer exemption; and

(2) in Northwest Territories and Nunavut, only a registered dealer may be paid a commission or finder's fee in connection with a distribution of a security to a purchaser in one of those jurisdictions under the offering memorandum exemption.

3.4.01 Payment of Finder's Fees or Commissions to Any Person — Subsection 2.5(2) of NI 45-106 prohibits the payment of commissions or finder's fees to any director, officer, founder or control person of an issuer or an affiliate of an issuer in connection with a distribution under the family, friends and business associates exemption.

The Ontario Securities Commission considers the payment of fees or commissions to any person, including registrants or finders, to identify, find or introduce one's family members, close personal friends or close business associates to be inconsistent with the family, friends and business associates exemption. However, the Ontario Securities Commission recognizes that fees may be paid to a person in connection with a distribution under the family, friends and business associates exemption in certain circumstances.

For example:

- Documentation and certain other activities — Fees may be paid for the documentation and other activities relating to the closing of the distribution.

- Concurrent reliance on other prospectus exemptions — If distributing securities on the same terms concurrently under one or more other prospectus exemptions in respect of which fees or commissions are being paid, then such fees and commissions may also be paid in respect of securities distributed under the family, friends and business associates exemption.

3.4.1 Reinvestment plans — (1) **When is a plan administrator acting "for or on behalf of the issuer"?** — Section 2.2 of NI 45-106 contains a prospectus exemption for distributions of securities by a trustee, custodian or administrator acting for or on behalf of the issuer. If the trustee, custodian or administrator is engaged by the issuer, the plan administrator acts "for or on behalf of the issuer" and therefore falls within the language contained in section 2.2(1). The fact that the plan administrator may act on or in accordance with instructions of a plan participant, under the plan, does not preclude the administrator from relying on the exemption contained in section 2.2 of NI 45-106.

(2) **Providing a description of material attributes and characteristics of securities** — The reinvestment plan exemption in section 2.2(5) of NI 45-106 includes a requirement, effective September 28, 2009, that if the securities distributed under a reinvestment plan are of a different class or series than the securities to which the dividend or distribution is attributable, the issuer or plan agent must have provided the plan participants with a description of the material attributes and characteristics of the securities being distributed. An issuer or plan agent with an existing reinvestment plan can satisfy this requirement in a number of ways. If plan participants have previously signed a plan agreement or received a copy of a reinvestment plan that included this information, the issuer or plan agent does not need to take any further action for current plan participants. (Future participants should receive the same type of information before their first trade of a security under the plan.)

If plan participants have not received this information in the past, the issuer or plan agent can provide the required information or a reference to a website where the information is available with other materials sent to holders of that class of securities, for example with proxy materials.

(3) **Interest payments** — The exemption in section 2.2 of NI 45-106 may be available where a person invests interest payable on debentures or other similar securities into other securities of the issuer. The words "distributions out of earnings. . .or other sources" cover interest payable on debentures.

3.5 Accredited investor — (1) Individual qualification — financial tests — An individual is an "accredited investor" for the purposes of NI 45-106 if the individual satisfies one of four tests set out in the "accredited investor" definition in section 1.1 of NI 45-106:

- the $1 000 000 financial asset test in paragraph (j)
- the $5 000 000 financial asset test in paragraph (j.1)
- the net income test in paragraph (k)
- the net asset test in paragraph (l)

Three branches of the definition (in paragraphs (j), (k) and (l)) are designed to treat spouses as a single investing unit, so that either spouse qualifies as an "accredited investor" if the combined financial assets of both spouses exceed $1 000 000, the combined net income of both spouses exceeds $300 000, or the combined net assets of both spouses exceeds $5 000 000.

The fourth branch, the $5 000 000 financial asset test, does not treat spouses as a single investing unit. If an individual meets the $5 000 000 financial asset test, they also meet the test to be a "permitted client" under NI 31-103. Permitted clients are entitled to waive the "know your client" and suitability obligations of registered dealers and advisers under NI 31-103. Under subsection 2.3(7) of NI 45-106, an issuer distributing securities under the accredited investor exemption to an individual who meets the $5 000 000 financial asset test in paragraph (j.1) under the definition of "accredited investor" is not required to obtain a signed risk acknowledgement in Form 45-106F9 *Form for Individual Accredited Investors* from that individual.

For the purposes of the financial asset tests in paragraphs (j) and (j.1), "financial assets" are defined in NI 45-106 to mean cash, securities, or a contract of insurance, a deposit or an evidence of a deposit that is not a security for the purposes of securities legislation. These financial assets are generally liquid or relatively easy to liquidate. The value of a purchaser's personal residence is not included in a calculation of financial assets.

By comparison, the net asset test under paragraph (l) means all of the purchaser's total assets minus all of the purchaser's total liabilities. Accordingly, for the purposes of the net asset test, the calculation of total assets would include the value of a purchaser's personal residence and the calculation of total liabilities would include the amount of any liability (such as a mortgage) in respect of the purchaser's personal residence.

If the combined net income of both spouses does not exceed $300 000, but the net income of one of the spouses exceeds $200 000, only the spouse whose net income exceeds $200 000 qualifies as an accredited investor.

(2) Bright-line standards — individuals — The monetary thresholds in the "accredited investor" definition are intended to create "bright-line" standards. Investors who do not satisfy these monetary thresholds do not qualify as accredited investors under the applicable paragraph.

(3) Beneficial ownership of financial assets — Paragraphs (j) and (j.1) of the "accredited investor" definition refer to the beneficial ownership of financial assets. As a general matter, it should not be difficult to determine whether financial assets are beneficially owned by an individual, an individual's spouse, or both, in any particular instance. However, in the case where financial assets are held in a trust or in another type of investment vehicle for the benefit of an individual there may be questions as to whether the individual beneficially owns the financial assets. The following factors are indicative of beneficial ownership of financial assets:

(a) physical or constructive possession of evidence of ownership of the financial asset;

(b) entitlement to receipt of any income generated by the financial asset;

(c) risk of loss of the value of the financial asset; and

(d) the ability to dispose of the financial asset or otherwise deal with it as the individual sees fit.

For example, securities held in a self-directed RRSP, for the sole benefit of an individual, are beneficially owned by that individual. In general, financial assets in a spousal RRSP would also be included for the purposes of the $1 000 000 financial asset test in paragraph (j) because it takes into account financial assets owned beneficially by a spouse. However, financial assets in a spousal RRSP would not be included for purposes of the $5 000 000 financial asset test in paragraph (j.1). Financial assets held in a group RRSP under which the individual does not have the ability to acquire the financial assets and deal with them directly would not meet the beneficial ownership requirements in either paragraph (j) or paragraph (j.1).

(4) Calculation of an individual purchaser's net assets — To calculate a purchaser's net assets under the net asset test in paragraph (l) of the "accredited investor" definition, subtract the purchaser's total liabilities from the purchaser's total assets. The value attributed to assets should reasonably reflect their estimated fair value. Income tax should be considered a liability if the obligation to pay it is outstanding at the time of the distribution of the security.

(4.1) Risk acknowledgement from individual investors — Persons relying on the accredited investor exemption in section 2.3 of NI 45-106 and section 73.3 of the *Securities Act* (Ontario) to distribute securities to individual accredited investors described in paragraphs (j), (k) and (l) of the "accredited investor" definition must obtain a completed and signed risk acknowledgement from that individual accredited investor.

"Individual" is defined in the securities legislation of certain jurisdictions to mean a natural person. The definition specifically excludes partnerships, unincorporated associations, unincorporated syndicates, unincorporated organizations and trusts. It also specifically excludes a natural person acting in the capacity of trustee, executor, administrator or personal or other legal representative.

(5) Financial statements — The minimum net asset threshold of $5 000 000 specified in paragraph (m) of the "accredited investor" definition must, in the case of a non-individual entity, be shown on the entity's "most recently prepared financial statements". The financial statements must be prepared in accordance with applicable generally accepted accounting principles.

(6) Time for assessing qualification — The financial tests prescribed in the accredited investor definition are to be applied only at the time of the distribution of the security. The person is not required to monitor the purchaser's continuing qualification as an accredited investor after the distribution of the security is completed.

(7) Recognition or designation as an "accredited investor" — Paragraph (v) of the "accredited investor" definition in NI 45-106 contemplates that a person may apply to be recognized or designated as an accredited investor by the securities regulatory authorities or, except in Ontario and Québec, the regulators. The securities regulatory authorities or regulators have not adopted any specific criteria for granting accredited investor recognition or designation to applicants, as the securities regulatory authorities or regulators believe that the "accredited investor" definition generally covers all types of persons that do not require the protection of the prospectus requirement. Accordingly, the securities regulatory authorities or regulators expect that applications for accredited investor recognition or designation will be utilized on a very limited basis. If a securities regulatory authority or regulator considers it appropriate in the circumstances, it may grant accredited investor recognition or designation to a person on terms and conditions, including a requirement that the person apply annually for renewal of accredited investor recognition or designation.

(8) Verifying accredited investor status — Persons relying on the accredited investor exemption are responsible for determining whether a purchaser meets the definition of "accredited investor". See section 1.9 of this Companion Policy for guidance on how to verify and document purchaser status.

3.6 Private issuer — (1) **Meaning of "the public"** — Whether or not a person is a member of the public must be determined on the facts of each particular case. The courts have interpreted "the public" very broadly in the context of securities trading. Whether a person is a part of the public will be determined on the particular facts of each case, based on the tests that have developed under the relevant case law. A person who intends to distribute securities, in reliance upon the private issuer prospectus exemption in section 2.4(2) of NI 45-106 to a person not listed in paragraphs (a) through (j) of that section will have to satisfy itself that the distribution of the security is not to the public.

(2) **Meaning of "close personal friend" and "close business associate"** — See sections 2.7 and 2.8 of this Companion Policy for a discussion of the meaning of "close personal friend" and "close business associate".

(2.1) **Meaning of "non-convertible debt securities"** — Paragraph (b) of the definition of private issuer has a number of restrictions that apply to the securities, other than nonconvertible debt securities, of a private issuer. Non-convertible debt securities are debt securities that do not have a right or obligation to exchange or convert into another security of the issuer.

(3) **Business combination of private issuers** — A distribution of securities in connection with an amalgamation, merger, reorganization, arrangement or other statutory procedure involving two private issuers to holders of securities of those issuers is not a distribution of a security to the public, provided that the resulting issuer is a private issuer.

Similarly, a distribution of securities by a private issuer in connection with a share exchange take-over bid for another private issuer is not a distribution of securities to the public, provided the offeror remains a private issuer after completion of the bid.

(4) **Acquisition of a private issuer** — Persons relying on a private issuer exemption in NI 45-106 must be satisfied that the purchaser is not a member of the public. Generally, however, if the owner of a private issuer sells the business of the private issuer by way of a sale of securities, rather than assets, to another party who acquires all of the securities, the sale will not be considered to have been to the public.

(5) **Ceasing to be a private issuer** — The term "private issuer" is defined in section 2.4(1) of NI 45-106. A private issuer can distribute securities only to the persons listed in section 2.4(2) of NI 45-106. If a private issuer distributes securities to a person not listed in section 2.4(2), even under another exemption, it will no longer be a private issuer and will not be able to continue to use the private issuer prospectus exemption in section 2.4(2). For example, if a private issuer distributes securities under the offering memorandum exemption, it will no longer be a private issuer.

Issuers that cease to be private issuers do not automatically become "reporting issuers". They are simply no longer able to rely on the private issuer exemption in section 2.4(1). Such issuers would still be able to use other exemptions to distribute their securities. For example, such issuers could rely on the family, friends and business associates prospectus exemption or the accredited investor prospectus exemption. However, issuers that rely on these prospectus exemptions must file a report of exempt distribution with the securities regulatory authority or regulator in each jurisdiction in which the distribution took place.

An issuer that completes a going private transaction (for example, by way of an amalgamation, squeeze out or a takeover bid with a subsequent statutory compulsory acquisition) can use the private issuer exemption after a going private transaction.

3.7 Family, friends and business associates — (1) **Number of purchasers** — There is no restriction on the number of persons that the issuer may sell securities to under the family, friends and business associates exemption in section 2.5 of NI 45-106. However, an issuer selling securities to a large number of persons under this exemption may give rise to a presumption that not all of the purchasers are family, close personal friends or close business associates and that the exemption may not be available.

(2) **Meaning of "close personal friend" and "close business associate"** — See sections 2.7 and 2.8 of this Companion Policy for a discussion of the meaning of "close personal friend" and "close business associate".

(3) **Risk acknowledgement — Saskatchewan** — Under section 2.6 of NI 45-106, the family, friends and business associates exemption in section 2.5 of NI 45-106 cannot be relied upon in Saskatchewan for a distribution of securities based on a close personal friendship or close business association unless the person obtains a signed "risk acknowledgement" in the required form from the purchaser and retains the form for eight years after the distribution of securities.

3.8 Offering memorandum — (1) **Eligibility criteria — Manitoba, Northwest Territories, Nunavut and Prince Edward Island** — Manitoba, Northwest Territories, Nunavut, Prince Edward Island and Yukon impose eligibility criteria on persons investing under the offering memorandum exemption. In these jurisdictions, the purchaser must be an eligible investor if the purchaser's acquisition cost is more than $10 000.

In determining the acquisition cost to a purchaser who is not an eligible investor, include any future payments that the purchaser will be required to make. Proceeds that may be obtained on exercise of warrants or other rights, or on conversion of convertible securities, are not considered to be part of the acquisition cost unless the purchaser is legally obligated to exercise or convert the securities. The $10 000 maximum acquisition cost is calculated per distribution of security.

Nevertheless, concurrent and consecutive, closely-timed offerings to the same purchaser will usually constitute one distribution of a security. Consequently, when calculating the acquisition cost, all of these offerings by or on behalf of the issuer to the same purchaser who is not an eligible investor would be included. It would be inappropriate for an issuer to try to circumvent the $10 000 threshold by dividing a subscription in excess of $10 000 by one purchaser into a number of smaller subscriptions of $10 000 or less that are made directly or indirectly by the same purchaser.

A purchaser can qualify as an eligible investor under various categories of the definition, including if the purchaser has and has had in prior years either $75 000 pre-tax net income or profit or has $400 000 worth of net assets. In calculating a purchaser's net assets, subtract the purchaser's total liabilities from the purchaser's total assets. The value attributed to assets should reasonably reflect their estimated fair value. Income tax should be considered a liability if the obligation to pay it is outstanding at the time of the distribution of a security.

Another way a purchaser can qualify as an eligible investor is to obtain advice from an eligibility adviser. An eligibility adviser is a person registered as an investment dealer (or in an equivalent category of unrestricted dealer in the purchaser's jurisdiction) that is authorized to give advice with respect to the type of security being distributed. In Manitoba, certain lawyers and public accountants may also act as eligibility advisers.

A registered investment dealer providing advice to a purchaser in these circumstances is expected to comply with the "know your client" and suitability requirements under applicable securities legislation and SRO rules and policies. Some dealers have obtained exemptions from the "know your client" and suitability requirements because they do not provide advice. An assessment of suitability by these dealers is not sufficient to qualify a purchaser as an eligible investor.

(1.1) **Eligibility criteria and investment limits — Alberta, New Brunswick, Nova Scotia, Ontario, Québec and Saskatchewan —**

(a) Eligibility criteria

Alberta, New Brunswick, Nova Scotia, Ontario, Québec and Saskatchewan impose eligibility criteria on persons investing under the offering memorandum exemption.

The qualification criteria for becoming an eligible investor are substantially the same as in the jurisdictions identified in subsection (1), above. Note, however, that in Alberta, New Brunswick, Nova Scotia, Ontario, Québec and Saskatchewan, it is not possible to qualify as an eligible investor by receiving advice from an "eligibility advisor".

A purchaser can qualify as an eligible investor under various categories of the definition, including if the purchaser has and has had in prior years either $75 000 pre-tax net income or profit or has $400 000 worth of net assets. In calculating a purchaser's net assets, subtract the purchaser's total liabilities from the purchaser's total assets. The value attributed to assets should reasonably reflect their estimated fair value. Income tax should be considered a liability if the obligation to pay it is outstanding at the time of the distribution of a security.

(b) Investment limits for individual eligible and non-eligible investors — Both eligible investors and purchasers that do not qualify as eligible investors (non-eligible investors) who are individuals are subject to investment limits under the offering memorandum exemption. In these jurisdictions, non-eligible investors who are individuals are subject to an investment limit of $10 000 and eligible investors who are individuals are subject to an investment limit of $30 000. In both cases, the investment limits apply to all securities acquired by the purchaser under the offering memorandum exemption in the preceding 12 months.

However, an individual purchaser that qualifies as an eligible investor because the investor is an accredited investor or is a person described in the family, friends and business associates exemption, is not subject to an investment limit under the offering memorandum exemption.

The fact that investment limits have been established for eligible and non-eligible investors who are individuals does not mean that these amounts are suitable investments in all cases. If a registrant is involved in a transaction, the registrant must still conduct a suitability assessment to determine that the amount of the investment and the investment itself is suitable for the purchaser. This may result in a lower investment amount for a purchaser.

The $30 000 investment limit may be exceeded by an eligible investor who receives advice from a portfolio manager, investment dealer or exempt market dealer that exceeding the investment limit of $30 000 and the investment itself is suitable for the eligible investor. In this case, the investment limit for all securities acquired by the purchaser under the offering memorandum exemption in the preceding 12 months is $100 000.

In determining the acquisition cost to a purchaser subject to investment limits, include any future payments that the purchaser will be required to make. Proceeds that may be obtained on exercise of warrants or other rights, or on conversion of convertible securities, are not considered to be part of the acquisition cost unless the purchaser is legally obligated to exercise or convert the securities.

"Individual" is defined in the securities legislation of certain jurisdictions to mean a natural person. The definition specifically excludes partnerships, unincorporated associations, unincorporated syndicates, unincorporated organizations and trusts. It also specifically excludes a natural person acting in the capacity of trustee, executor, administrator or personal or other legal representative.

(c) Circumstances when investment limits can be exceeded — The fact that higher investment limits apply to individual eligible investors than individual non-eligible investors does not mean these higher amounts will be suitable in all cases for eligible investors. It is a condition of the offering memorandum exemption that, in order to exceed the $30 000 investment limit, a registrant must determine that an investment above the $30,000 investment limit is suitable for the purchaser. Unless a registrant determines that exceeding the $30 000 investment limit is suitable for the purchaser, the issuer cannot accept a subscription in excess of $30 000 from the purchaser. In this case, the registrant could also not proceed to take instructions from the purchaser to exceed the $30 000 investment limit.

(d) Investment limits apply over a 12-month period — The investment limits for both individual eligible and non-eligible investors apply to the aggregate of all investments made by a purchaser in distributions by different issuers (or multiple offerings by the same issuer) under the offering memorandum exemption during the preceding 12 months, which may or may not be a calendar year. For example, if a purchaser wishes to acquire securities of an issuer under the offering memorandum exemption on January 15, the issuer must include in the calculation all investments made by the purchaser under the offering memorandum exemption beginning on January 16 of the prior year, up to and including the date of the proposed investment.

On each distribution, the issuer must confirm that the amount invested by a purchaser who is an individual does not exceed the applicable limit and should take reasonable steps to do so. This will require the issuer to first understand whether or not the purchaser is an eligible investor. As described above in section 1.9, the issuer should gather information that confirms the purchaser meets the criteria set out in the exemption. As part of this exercise, the issuer should also discuss with the purchaser the investment limits that apply to the purchaser.

In making a determination as to whether a purchaser is within the applicable investment limit, an issuer should obtain appropriate representations from the purchaser that confirm the purchaser has not exceeded the applicable investment limit over the relevant period. Note that we would have concerns if an issuer simply accepted standard representations from a purchaser without taking steps to verify the representations made by the purchaser. For instance, inquiries could be made with respect to other investments made under the offering memorandum exemption during the 12-month period preceding the current investment.

Notwithstanding the representations made by a purchaser in the schedules to the risk acknowledgement form, we expect an issuer to be able to explain what steps were taken to verify the representations made by the purchaser. We recognize that in many circumstances, a registrant may act as agent on behalf of an issuer for this process. In both cases, the guidance in section 1.9 above may also be instructive for this purpose.

(1.2) Role of registrant in providing suitability advice and conflicts of interest — A registrant involved in a distribution of securities pursuant to a prospectus exemption must not only establish that the prospectus exemption is available, it must also comply with its registrant obligations, including know-your-client, know-your-product and suitability. In assessing the level of investment that may be suitable for a purchaser under the offering memorandum exemption, registrants should take into consideration guidance published by the CSA on best practices for conducting a suitability assessment, which includes considering the level of concentration of investments in the client's portfolio.

NI 31-103 and the related companion policy provide a framework that requires registrants to identify and respond to material conflicts of interest that may affect their ability to meet their regulatory obligations, including suitability.

Where a registrant is providing suitability advice to a purchaser in respect of an offering by a related or connected issuer, we expect the registrant that is related or connected to the issuer to be aware of the material conflicts that arise in these circumstances, and to take appropriate steps to respond to the conflicts to ensure it is fulfilling its regulatory obligations. We expect a registrant to be able to demonstrate that it is addressing the conflicts by avoiding or managing and disclosing the conflicts of interest appropriately to ensure compliance with its obligation to deal fairly, honestly and in good faith with clients.

We expect all registrants to be aware of other CSA guidance on registrant obligations with respect to know-your-client, know-your-product and suitability, and identify and respond to conflicts of interest.

(2) **Form of offering memorandum** — There are two forms of offering memorandum: Form 45-106F3, which may be used by qualifying issuers, and Form 45-106F2, which must be used by all other issuers. Form 45-106F3 requires qualifying issuers to incorporate by reference their annual information form (AIF), management's discussion and analysis (MD&A), annual financial statements and subsequent specified continuous disclosure documents required under NI 51-102.

A qualifying issuer is a reporting issuer that has filed an AIF under NI 51-102 and has met all of its other continuous disclosure obligations, including those in NI 51-102, National Instrument 43-101 *Standards of Disclosure for Mineral Projects*, and National Instrument 51-101 *Standards of Disclosure for Oil and Gas Activities*. Under NI 51-102, venture issuers are not required to file AIFs. However, if a venture issuer wants to use Form 45-106F3, the venture issuer must voluntarily file an AIF under NI 51-102 in order to incorporate that AIF into its offering memorandum.

(3) **Date of certificate and required signatories** — The issuer must ensure that the information provided to the purchaser is current and does not contain a misrepresentation. For example, if a material change occurs in the business of the issuer after delivery of an offering memorandum to a potential purchaser, the issuer must give the potential purchaser an update to the offering memorandum before the issuer accepts the agreement to purchase the securities. The update to the offering memorandum may take the form of an amendment describing the material change, a new offering memorandum containing up-to-date disclosure or a material change report, whichever the issuer decides will most effectively inform purchasers.

Whatever form of update the issuer uses, it must include a newly signed and dated certificate as required in the applicable subsection 2.9(9), (10), (10.1), (10.2), (10.3), (11), (11.1), or (12) of NI 45-106.

"Promoter" is defined differently in provincial and territorial securities legislation across CSA jurisdictions. It is generally defined as meaning a person who has taken the initiative in founding, organizing or substantially reorganizing the business of the issuer or who has received consideration over a prescribed amount for services or property or both in connection with founding, organizing or substantially reorganizing the issuer. "Promoter" has not been defined in the *Securities Act* (Québec) and a broad interpretation is taken in Québec in determining who would be considered a promoter.

Under securities legislation, persons who receive consideration solely as underwriting commissions or in consideration of property and who do not otherwise take part in the founding, organizing or substantially reorganizing the issuer are not promoters. Simply selling securities, or in some way facilitating sales in securities, does not make a person a promoter under the offering memorandum exemption.

(4) **Consideration to be held in trust** — The purchaser has, or must be given, the right to cancel the agreement to purchase the securities until midnight on the 2nd business day after signing the agreement. During this period, the issuer must arrange for the consideration to be held in trust on behalf of the purchaser.

It is up to the issuer to decide what arrangements are necessary to preserve the consideration received from the purchaser. The requirement to hold the consideration in trust may be satisfied if, for example, the issuer keeps the purchaser's cheque, without cashing or depositing it, until the expiration of the two business day cancellation period.

It is also the issuer's responsibility to ensure that whoever is holding the consideration promptly returns it to the purchaser if the purchaser cancels the agreement to purchase the securities.

(5) **Filing of offering memorandum** — The issuer is required to file the offering memorandum with the securities regulatory authority or regulator in each of the jurisdictions in which the issuer distributes securities under an offering memorandum exemption. The issuer must file the offering memorandum on or before the 10th day after the distribution.

If the issuer is conducting multiple closings, the offering memorandum must be filed on or before the 10th day after the first closing. Once the offering memorandum has been filed, there is no need to file it again after subsequent closings, unless it has been updated.

(5.1) **Filing of marketing materials** — In Alberta, New Brunswick, Nova Scotia, Ontario, Québec and Saskatchewan, marketing materials used in the context of an offering made in reliance on the offering memorandum exemption must also be filed with the securities regulatory authority. Once the marketing materials have been filed, there is no need to file them again after subsequent closings, unless there is a change to the marketing materials.

(6) **Purchasers' rights** — Unless securities legislation in a purchaser's jurisdiction provides a purchaser with a comparable right of cancellation or revocation, an issuer must give each purchaser under an offering memorandum a contractual right to cancel the agreement to purchase the securities by delivering a notice to the issuer not later than midnight on the 2nd business day after the purchaser signs the agreement.

Unless securities legislation in a purchaser's jurisdiction provides purchasers with comparable statutory rights, the issuer must also give the purchaser a contractual right of action against the issuer in the event the offering memorandum contains a misrepresentation. This contractual right of action must be available to the purchaser regardless of whether the purchaser relied on the misrepresentation when deciding to purchase the securities. This right is similar to that given to a purchaser under a prospectus. The purchaser may claim damages or ask that the agreement be cancelled. If the purchaser wants to cancel the agreement, the purchaser must commence the action within 180 days after signing the agreement to purchase the securities. If the purchaser is seeking damages, the purchaser must commence the action within the earlier of 180 days after learning of the misrepresentation or 3 years after signing the agreement to purchase the securities.

The issuer is required to describe in the offering memorandum any rights available to the purchaser, whether they are provided by the issuer contractually as a condition to the use of the exemption or provided under securities legislation.

(7) **Types of securities that can be distributed under the exemption — Alberta, New Brunswick, Nova Scotia, Ontario, Québec and Saskatchewan** — In Alberta, New Brunswick, Nova Scotia, Ontario, Québec and Saskatchewan, issuers are prohibited from distributing certain types of securities under the offering memorandum exemption, including specified derivatives and structured finance products. Note that this is in addition to the prohibition in subsection 2.9(3.1) against distributions of short-term securitized products under the offering memorandum exemption.

These types of securities have been excluded because the purpose of the exemption is for raising capital and it is not intended to be used to distribute complex or novel securities to purchasers. We would have concerns if issuers relied on the offering memorandum exemption to distribute novel or complex securities, even if they do not fall within the prohibited categories.

(8) **Ongoing disclosure — Alberta, New Brunswick, Nova Scotia, Ontario, Québec and Saskatchewan** — In Alberta, New Brunswick, Ontario, Québec and Saskatchewan, non-reporting issuers that issue securities under the offering memorandum exemption are required, in respect of each financial year, to file or deliver (as applicable) to the securities regulatory authority and make available to purchasers, audited annual financial statements within 120 days from the issuer's financial year end. In Nova Scotia, issuers are not required to file or deliver these financial statements to the securities regulatory authority, but are only required to make them available to purchasers that acquired securities under the offering memorandum exemption.

The following table illustrates when the first audited annual financial statements of an issuer would be due, as required by subsections (17.4), (17.5) and (17.6), following an initial distribution of securities under the offering memorandum exemption. The examples in the table take into account the extension to the filing deadline provided by subsection (17.7).

The following examples assume the issuer's financial year end is December 31.

Date of formation	Date of first distribution under subsection 2.9(2.1)	Deadline for first annual financial statements under subsections 2.9(17.4), (17.5) and (17.6)	Financial periods included in annual financial statements	Notes
January 1, 20X3	April 15, 20X7	June 14, 20X7	December 31, 20X6 and December 31, 20X5	The issuer completes its first distribution under the offering memorandum exemption in subsection 2.9(2.1) before the filing deadline for annual financial statements, which would be April 30, 20X7. Since the distribution was completed so close to the filing deadline, the issuer can take advantage of the extension in subsection 2.9(17.7) and file the statements on June 14, 20X7.
January 1, 20X7	April 15, 20X7	April 30, 20X8	December 31, 20X7	The issuer completes its first distribution under the offering memorandum exemption in subsection 2.9(2.1) before the filing deadline for annual financial statements, which would be April 30, 20X7. However, since the issuer has not completed a financial year, the issuer would not be required to file annual financial statements until April 30, 20X8 for the financial year ended December 31, 20X7.
January 1, 20X3	June 15, 20X7	April 30, 20X8	December 31, 20X7 and December 31, 20X6	The issuer completes its first distribution under the offering memorandum exemption in subsection 2.9(2.1) after the filing deadline for annual financial statements in 20X7. The offering memorandum would already include audited annual financial statements for the year ended December 31, 20X6. The next audited annual financial statements of the issuer would be required to be filed by April 30, 20X8 for the year ended December 31, 20X7.

The requirement to file or deliver (as applicable) to the securities regulatory authority and make available to purchasers annual financial statements continues to apply each year after the initial distribution under subsection 2.9(2.1) until the earlier of (1) the date the issuer becomes a reporting issuer and (2) the date the issuer ceases to carry on business.

(9) Ongoing disclosure — notice of specified key events — New Brunswick, Nova Scotia and Ontario — In addition to audited annual financial statements and a notice of how the proceeds raised under the offering memorandum exemption have been used, non-reporting issuers that issue securities in reliance on the offering memorandum exemption in New Brunswick, Nova Scotia and Ontario must also make available to investors a notice of certain key events, within 10 days of the occurrence of the event. These events are considered to be significant changes in the business of the issuer of which purchasers should be notified. This requirement is in addition to any similar requirement under corporate law and also applies to non-reporting issuers with non-corporate structures, such as trusts or partnerships.

In making a determination as to whether an issuer's industry has changed, issuers may consider whether they would identify a different industry category on Form 45-106F1 *Report of Exempt Distribution* than the category previously identified.

A non-reporting issuer must continue to provide notice of the specified events, if applicable, until the earlier of (i) the date the issuer becomes a reporting issuer or (ii) the date the issuer ceases to carry on business.

(10) Meaning of "make reasonably available" — In Alberta, New Brunswick, Nova Scotia, Ontario, Québec and Saskatchewan, disclosure documents will be considered to have been made reasonably available to each holder of a security acquired under the offering memorandum exemption if the documents are mailed to security holders, or if security holders receive notice that the disclosure documents can be viewed on a public website of the issuer or a website accessible by all holders of securities acquired under subsection 2.9(2.1) of the issuer (such as a password protected website). Issuers should take reasonable steps to enable purchasers to receive or access these documents promptly.

3.9 Minimum amount investment — (1) Baskets of securities — An issuer may wish to distribute more than one kind of security of its own issue, such as shares and debt, in a single transaction under the minimum investment amount exemption. Provided that the shares and debt are sold in units that have a total acquisition cost of not less than $150 000 paid in cash at the time of the distribution of a security, the exemption can, if otherwise available, be used, notwithstanding that the acquisition cost of the shares and the acquisition cost of the debt, taken separately, are both less than $150 000.

(2) Not available for distributions to individuals or syndicates — The minimum amount investment exemption in section 2.10 of NI 45-106 is not available for distributions to individuals. "Individual" is defined in the securities legislation of certain jurisdictions to mean a natural person. The definition specifically excludes partnerships, unincorporated associations, unincorporated syndicates, unincorporated organizations and trusts. It also specifically excludes a natural person acting in the capacity of trustee, executor, administrator or personal or other legal representative.

Subsection 2.10(2) of NI 45-106 specifically prohibits using the minimum amount investment exemption to distribute to persons created or used solely to rely on this exemption. See section 1.8 of this Companion Policy for a discussion of the "anti-syndication" provisions in NI 45-106.

3.10 Rights offering — reporting issuer — (1) Offer available to all security holders in Canada — One of the conditions of the rights offering exemption for reporting issuers in section 2.1 of NI 45-106 is that the issuer must make the basic subscription privilege available on a pro rata basis to every security holder in Canada of the class of securities to be distributed on exercise of the rights, regardless of how many security holders reside in a local jurisdiction.

(2) Market price and fair value — Paragraph 2.1(3)(g) of NI 45-106 provides that if there is no published market for the securities, the subscription price must be lower than fair value unless the issuer restricts all insiders from increasing their proportionate interest in the issuer through the rights offering or a stand-by commitment. If there is no published market for the securities and the issuer restricts all insiders from increasing their proportionate interest in the issuer, the subscription price may be set at any price. Under section 13 of Form 45-106F15, an issuer must explain in its rights offering circular how it determined the fair value of the securities. For these purposes, an issuer could consider a fairness opinion or a valuation.

For the purposes of paragraph 2.1(3)(g) of NI 45-106, insiders will not be prohibited from participating in the offering if the published market price or fair value of the securities falls below the subscription price following filing of the rights offering notice.

The rights offering exemption is not intended to be used by insiders or related parties for the purpose of increasing their proportionate interest in the issuer, although we recognize that as a potential outcome. One of the reasons for the above pricing restrictions, and the similar restrictions in paragraph 2.1(3)(g) for issuers with a published market, is to prevent insiders and other related parties from using the rights offering exemption as a means of taking control of the issuer.

(3) Stand-by commitments — To provide the confirmation in subparagraph 2.1(3)(i)(ii) of NI 45-106 that the stand-by guarantor has the financial ability to carry out its obligations under the stand-by commitment, the issuer could consider the following:

• a statement of net worth attested to by the stand-by guarantor
• a bank letter of credit
• the most recent annual audited financial statements of the stand-by guarantor.

A registered dealer that acquires a security of an issuer as part of the stand-by commitment may use the exemption in section 2.1.1 of NI 45-106. However, we would have concerns if a dealer or other person uses the exemption in section 2.1.1 in a situation where the dealer or other person

(a) is acting as an underwriter with respect to the distribution, and

(b) acquires the security with a view to distribution.

If (a) and (b) apply, the dealer or other person should acquire the security under the exemption in section 2.33 of NI 45-106. Please refer to section 1.7 of this Companion Policy.

(4) Calculation of number of securities — In calculating the number of outstanding securities for purposes of paragraph 2.1(3)(h) of NI 45-106, CSA staff generally take the view that

(a) if

x = the number or amount of securities of the class of the securities that may be or have been issued upon the exercise of rights under all rights offerings made by the issuer in reliance on the exemption during the previous 12 months,

y = the maximum number or amount of securities that may be issued upon exercise of rights under the proposed rights offering, and

z = the number or amount of securities of the class of securities that is issuable upon the exercise of rights under the proposed rights offering that are outstanding as of the date of the rights offering circular;

then

$$\frac{x+y}{z}$$

must be equal to or less than 1,

(b) if the convertible securities that may be acquired under the proposed rights offering may be converted before 12 months after the date of the proposed rights offering, the potential increase in outstanding securities, and specifically, "y" in paragraph (a), should be calculated as if the conversion of those convertible securities had occurred,

(c) despite paragraph (b), if the convertible security is a warrant that forms part of a unit and the warrant has nominal or no value, the potential increase in outstanding securities, and specifically, "y" in paragraph (a), should not be calculated as if the conversion of the warrant had occurred.

One of the conditions of the exemption is that the issuer must make the basic subscription privilege available on a pro rata basis to each security holder of the class of securities to be distributed on exercise of the rights. For clarity, this means that an issuer cannot use a rights offering to distribute a new class of securities.

(5) Investment funds — As a reminder, pursuant to section 9.1.1 of National Instrument 81-102 *Investment Funds* (NI 81-102), investment funds that are subject to NI 81-102 are restricted from issuing warrants or rights.

3.11 Rights offering - issuer with a minimal connection to Canada — It may be difficult for an issuer to determine beneficial ownership of its securities as a result of the book-based system of holding securities. We are of the view that, for the purpose of determining beneficial ownership to comply with the exemption in section 2.1.2 of NI 45-106, procedures comparable to those found in National Instrument 54-101 *Communication with Beneficial Owners of Securities of a Reporting Issuer*, or any successor instrument, are appropriate.

In section 2.1.2(1)(a), the issuer must determine the number of beneficial security holders in Canada and the number of securities held by those security holders "to the issuer's knowledge after reasonable enquiry". We think an issuer could generally satisfy this requirement by relying on its most recently-conducted beneficial ownership search procedures conducted for the purpose of distributing proxy material for a shareholders meeting that occurred within the last 12 months, unless the issuer has reason to believe that it would no longer meet the test in section 2.1.2 of NI 45-106. For example, if, after the previous search procedures, the issuer conducted a financing in Canada that could affect the results, they may not be able to rely on those procedures.

PART 4 — OTHER EXEMPTIONS

4.1 Employee, executive officer, director and consultant exemptions — Trustees, custodians or administrators who engage in activities, contemplated in the prospectus exemption in section 2.27 of NI 45-106, that bring together purchasers and sellers of securities should have regard to the provisions of National Instrument 21-101 *Marketplace Operation* respecting "marketplaces" and "alternative trading systems".

The employee, executive officer, director and consultant exemptions are based on the alignment of economic interests between an issuer and its employees. They may, where available, be used to provide employees and other similar persons with an opportunity to participate in the growth of the employer's business and to compensate persons for the services they provide to an issuer. The securities regulatory authorities or regulators will generally not grant exemptive relief analogous to these exemptions except in very limited circumstances.

4.2 Business combination and reorganization — **(1) Statutory procedure** — The securities regulatory authorities and regulators interpret the phrase "statutory procedure" broadly and are of the view that the prospectus exemption contained in section 2.11 of NI 45-106 applies to all distributions of securities of an issuer that are both part of the procedure and necessary to complete the transaction, regardless of when the distribution of a security occurs.

The prospectus exemption contained in section 2.11 of NI 45-106 exempts distributions of securities in connection with an amalgamation, merger, reorganization or arrangement if the same is done "under a statutory procedure". The securities regulatory authorities or regulators are of the view that the references to statutory procedure in section 2.11 are to any statute of a jurisdiction or foreign jurisdiction under which the entities involved have been incorporated or created and exist or under which the transaction is taking place. This would include, for example, an arrangement under the *Companies' Creditors Arrangement Act* (Canada).

(2) Three-cornered amalgamations — Certain corporate statutes permit a so-called "three-cornered merger or amalgamation" under which two companies will amalgamate or merge and security holders of the amalgamating or merging entities will receive securities of a third party affiliate of one amalgamating or merging entity. The prospectus exemption contained in section 2.11 of NI 45-106 refers to these distributions of a security when they refer to a distribution of a security made in connection with an amalgamation or merger done under a statutory procedure.

(3) Exchangeable shares — A transaction involving a procedure described in the prospectus exemption contained in section 2.11 of NI 45-106 may include an exchangeable share structure to achieve certain tax-planning objectives. For example, where a non-Canadian company seeks to acquire a Canadian company under a plan of arrangement, an exchangeable share structure may be used to allow the Canadian shareholders of the company to be acquired to receive, in substance, shares of the non-Canadian company while avoiding the adverse tax consequences associated with exchanging shares of a Canadian company for shares of a non-Canadian company. Instead of receiving shares of the non-Canadian company directly, the Canadian shareholders receive shares of a Canadian company which, through various contractual arrangements, have economic terms and voting rights that are essentially identical to the shares of the non-Canadian company and permit the holder to exchange such shares, at a time of the holder's choosing, for shares of the non-Canadian company.

Historically, the use of an exchangeable share structure in connection with a statutory procedure has raised a question as to whether the exemption now contained in section 2.11 of NI 45-106 was available for all distributions necessary to complete the transaction. For example, in the case of the acquisition under a plan of arrangement noted above, the use of an exchangeable share structure may result in a delay of several months or even years between the date of the arrangement and the date the shares of the non-Canadian company are distributed to the former shareholders of the acquired company. As a result of this delay, some filers have questioned whether the distribution of the non-Canadian company's shares upon the exercise of the exchangeable shares may still be viewed as being "in connection with" the statutory transaction, and have made application for exemptive relief to address this uncertainty.

The securities regulatory authorities or regulators take the position that the statutory procedure exemption contained in section 2.11 of NI 45-106 refers to all distributions of securities that are necessary to complete an exchangeable share transaction involving a procedure described in section 2.11, even where such distributions occur several months or years after the transaction. In the case of the acquisition noted above, the investment decision of the shareholders of the acquired company at the time of the arrangement represented a decision to, ultimately, exchange their shares for shares of the non-Canadian company. The distribution of such shares upon the exercise of the exchangeable shares does not represent a new investment decision, but merely represents the completion of that original investment decision. Accordingly, additional exemptive relief is not warranted in circumstances where the original transaction was completed in reliance on this exemption.

4.3 Asset acquisition — character of assets to be acquired — When issuing securities, issuers must comply with the requirements under applicable corporate or other governing legislation that the securities be issued for fair value. Where securities are issued for non-cash consideration such as assets or resource properties, it is the responsibility of the issuer and its board of directors to determine the fair market value of the assets or resource properties and to retain records to demonstrate how that fair market value was determined. In some situations, cash assets that make up working capital could also be considered in the total calculation of the fair market value.

4.4 Securities for debt — bona fide debt — A bona fide debt is one that was incurred for value, on commercially reasonable terms and that on the date the debt was incurred the parties believed would be repaid in cash.

A reporting issuer may distribute securities to settle a debt only after the debt becomes due, as evidenced by the creditor issuing an invoice, demand letter or other written statement to the issuer indicating that the debt is due. The securities for debt exemption may not be relied on for the issuance of securities by an issuer to secure a debt that will remain outstanding after the issuance.

4.5 Take-over bid and issuer bid — (1) **Exempt bids** — The terms "take-over bid" and "issuer bid", for the purposes of section 2.16 of NI 45-106, include an exempt take-over bid and exempt issuer bid.

(2) **Bids involving exchangeable shares** — The take-over bid and issuer bid exemptions refer to all distributions necessary to complete a take-over bid or an issuer bid that involves an exchangeable share structure (as described under section 4.2 of this Companion Policy), even where such distributions may occur several months or even years after the bid is completed.

4.6 Isolated distribution — The exemption contained in section 2.30 of NI 45-106 is limited to distribution of a security made by an issuer in a security of its own issue. It is intended that this exemption will only be used rarely and not to distribute securities to multiple purchasers.

4.6.1 Short-term securitized products — (1) **Types of short-term securitized products** — Section 2.35.1 is a prospectus exemption for the distribution of short-term securitized products. Short-term securitized products distributed in Canada are generally asset-backed commercial paper.

(2) **Definition of "asset pool"** — The term "cash-flow generating assets" in the definition of "asset pool" refers to the bonds, mortgages, leases, loans, receivables, or royalties in which a conduit has a direct or indirect ownership or security interest. It does not refer to a security or other instrument through which a conduit obtains an indirect ownership or security interest in underlying cash-flow generating assets. For example, a conduit may enter into an asset transaction whereby it purchases a note from a trust that owns a pool of mortgages, thereby acquiring an indirect ownership or security interest in that pool of mortgages. In this scenario, the "cash-flow generating assets" are the mortgages, not the note.

(3) **Interaction of conditions with credit ratings** — In order for the short-term securitized products prospectus exemption to be available, the short-term securitized product must satisfy certain conditions relating to credit ratings as set out in subparagraphs 2.35.2(a)(i) and (ii). The short-term securitized product and issuing conduit must also satisfy other conditions regarding liquidity support, series or class seniority and asset pool composition as set out in subparagraphs 2.35.2(a)(iii) and (iv) and paragraphs 2.35.2(b) and (c).

Short-term securitized products that satisfy the conditions in the prospectus exemption relating to liquidity support, series or class seniority and asset pool composition may not necessarily satisfy the credit-rating conditions; particularly the requirement in subparagraph 2.35.2(a)(i) that one of the two credit ratings must be at the highest rating category. Designated rating organizations each have their own rating methodologies and may require features that go beyond those specified in the prospectus exemption in order for a short-term securitized product to obtain a credit rating in the highest category.

(4) **Liquidity provider** — Clause 2.35.2(a)(iv)(B) requires a liquidity provider to be a deposit-taking institution regulated or approved to carry on business in Canada by the Office of the Superintendent of Financial Institutions (OSFI) or a Canadian federal or provincial government department or regulatory authority. This provision allows a foreign bank to be a liquidity provider if it is a Schedule II or Schedule III bank that is regulated by OSFI or approved by OSFI to carry on business in Canada.

(5) **Exceptions relating to liquidity agreements** — The intention of subsection 2.35.3(2) is to permit a liquidity agreement to provide that a liquidity provider need not advance funds in respect of assets that have defaulted and that are not covered by any applicable credit enhancement. For purposes of paragraph 2.35.3(2)(a), we expect that the aggregate value of the non-defaulted assets would be the book value, unless some other method of determining the value is specified by the provisions of the applicable liquidity agreement, e.g. discounted value or market value.

(6) **Disclosure — meaning of "make reasonably available"** — Section 2.35.4 requires that each information memorandum and reports on Form 45-106F7 and Form 45-106F8 be made reasonably available both to securities regulators and purchasers of a short-term securitized product.

This requirement could generally be satisfied by a conduit posting the document on a website maintained by it or on its behalf. If a password is used to limit access to the website, we would expect that the password would be promptly provided upon application. We generally would not object if a prospective purchaser, before being provided access to a website on which the documents are posted, would have to agree to keep the information on the website confidential or that it would not provide others with access to the website or the documents available on it.

4.7 Mortgages — In British Columbia, Alberta, Manitoba, Québec and Saskatchewan, NI 45-106 specifically excludes syndicated mortgages from the mortgage prospectus exemption in section 2.36(1). In determining what constitutes a syndicated mortgage, issuers will need to refer to the corresponding definition provided in section 2.36 of NI 45-106.

The mortgage prospectus exemption does not apply to distributions in securities that secure mortgages by bond, debenture, trust deed or similar obligation. The mortgage prospective exemption does not apply to a distribution of, or a trade in, a security that represents an undivided co-ownership interest in a pool of mortgages, such as a pass-through certificate issued by an issuer of asset-backed securities.

4.8 Not for profit issuer — (1) **Eligibility to use this exemption** — This exemption applies to distributions of securities of an issuer that is organized exclusively for educational, benevolent, fraternal, charitable, religious or recreational purposes and not for profit ("not for profit issuer"). To use this exemption, an issuer must be organized exclusively for one or more of the listed purposes and use the funds raised for those purposes.

If an issuer is organized exclusively for one of the listed purposes, but its mandate changes so that it is no longer primarily engaged in the purpose it was organized for, the issuer may no longer be able to rely on this exemption. For example, if an issuer organized exclusively for educational purposes over time devotes more and more of its efforts to lending money, even if it is only to other educational entities, the lending issuer *may* be unable to rely on these exemptions. The same would also be true if one of an issuer's mandates was to provide an investment vehicle for its members. An issuer that issues securities that pay dividends would also not be able to use these exemptions, because no part of the issuer's net earnings can go to any security holder. However, if the securities are debt securities and the issuer agrees to repay the principal amount with or without interest, the security holders are not considered to be receiving part of the net earnings of the issuer. The debt securities may be secured or unsecured.

If investors could receive any special treatment as a result of purchasing securities, the security holders are *not* typically receiving part of the net earnings of the issuer and the sale may still fit within these exemptions. For example, if the not for profit issuer runs a golf course and offers security holders a waiver of greens fees for three years, it could still rely on this exemption, provided all other conditions are met (and the exemption remains available in the relevant jurisdiction(s)).

If, at the time of the distribution of the security, the purchaser has an entitlement to the assets of the issuer on the basis that they would be getting part of the net earnings of the issuer, then the sale would not fit within this exemption.

In Québec, not for profit issuers may still rely on the broad exemption available for not for profit issuers under section 3 of the *Securities Act* (Québec).

(2) **Meaning of "no commission or other remuneration"** — Section 2.38(b) provides that "no commission or other remuneration is paid in connection with the sale of the security". This is intended to ensure that no one is paid to find purchasers of the securities. However, the issuer may pay its legal and accounting advisers for their legal or accounting services in connection with the sale.

PART 5 — FORMS

5.1 Report of exempt distribution — (1) Requirement to file — An issuer that has distributed a security of its own issue under any of the prospectus exemptions listed in section 6.1 of NI 45-106 is required to file a report of exempt distribution, on or before the 10th day after the distribution. Alternatively, if an underwriter distributes securities acquired under section 2.33 of NI 45-106, either the issuer or the underwriter may complete and file the form. If there is a syndicate of underwriters, the lead underwriter may file the form on behalf of the syndicate or each underwriter may file a form relating to the portion of the distribution it was responsible for.

The required form of report is Form 45-106F1 Report of Exempt Distribution.

In determining if it is required to file a report in a particular jurisdiction, the issuer or underwriter should consider the following questions:

(a) Is there a distribution in the jurisdiction? (Please refer to the securities legislation and securities directions of the jurisdiction for guidance, if any, on when a distribution occurs in the jurisdiction.)

(b) If there is a distribution in the jurisdiction, what exemption from the prospectus requirement is the issuer relying on for the distribution of the security?

(c) Does the exemption referred to in paragraph (b) trigger a reporting requirement? (Reports of exempt distribution are required for distributions made in reliance on the prospectus exemptions listed in section 6.1 of NI 45-106. Multilateral Instrument 45-108 *Crowdfunding* and certain local rules and orders.)

A distribution may occur in more than one jurisdiction. In this case, the issuer may complete a single report identifying all purchasers and file the report in each Canadian jurisdiction where the distribution has occurred.

(2) Access to information — The securities legislation of several provinces requires that information filed with the securities regulatory authority or, where applicable, the regulator under such securities legislation, be made available for public inspection during normal business hours except for information that the securities regulatory authority, or where applicable, the regulator,

(a) believes to be personal or other information of such a nature that the desirability of avoiding disclosure thereof in the interest of any affected individual outweighs the desirability of adhering to the principle that information filed with the securities regulatory authority or the regulator, as applicable, be available to the public for inspection,

(b) in Alberta, considers that it would not be prejudicial to the public interest to hold the information in confidence, and

(c) in Québec, considers that access to the information could result in serious prejudice.

Based on the above mentioned provisions of securities legislation, the securities regulatory authorities or regulators, as applicable, have determined that the information listed in Schedule 1 and Schedule 2 of Form 45-106F1 *Report of Exempt Distribution*, discloses personal or other information of such a nature that the desirability of avoiding disclosure of this personal information outweighs the desirability of making the information available to the public for inspection. In addition, in Alberta, the regulator considers that it would not be prejudicial to the public interest to hold the information listed in these schedules in confidence. In Québec, the securities regulatory authority considers that access to these schedules by the public in general could result in serious prejudice and consequently, the information listed in these schedules will not be made publicly available.

(3) Electronic filing of Form 45-106F1 *Report of Exempt Distribution* — Form 45-106F1 is required to be filed electronically in all CSA jurisdictions as described below.

For filings made in British Columbia, issuers are required to file Form 45-106F1 and pay the fees associated with that filing electronically using BCSC Services. This requirement only applies to filings that are required to be made within 10 days of the distribution. It does not apply to filings made annually by investment funds under subsection 6.2(2) of NI 45-106. Please refer to BC Instrument 13-502 *Electronic Filing of Reports of Exempt Distribution* for further information.

For filings made in Ontario, issuers are required to file Form 45-106F1 electronically through the OSC's Electronic Filing Portal and pay the applicable fees. The electronic filing requirement applies to all issuers that file Form 45-106F1, including investment fund issuers that file annually in accordance with subsection 6.2(2) of NI 45-106. Please see OSC Rule 11-501 *Electronic Delivery of Documents to the Ontario Securities Commission* and OSC Rule 13-502 *fees* for further information.

For filings made in any other Canadian jurisdiction except for British Columbia and Ontario, issuers, other than certain foreign issuers, are required to file Form 45-206F1 and pay the fees associated with that filing electronically through the System for Electronic Document Analysis and Retrieval (SEDAR). The electronic filing requirement also applies to investment fund issuers that file annually in accordance with subsection 6.2(2) of NI 45-106. Please refer to National Instrument 13-101 *System for Electronic Document Analysis and Retrieval (SEDAR)* and Multilateral Instrument 13-102 *System fees for SEDAR and NRD* for further information. Foreign issuers that are not required to file Form 45-106F1 electronically through SEDAR should file the report and pay the applicable fees in each of the jurisdictions in which a distribution is made at the addresses listed at the end of the report.

5.2 Forms required under the offering memorandum exemption — NI 45-106 designates two forms of offering memorandum. The first, Form 45-106F2, is for non-qualifying issuers and the second, Form 45-106F3, can only be used by qualifying issuers (as defined in NI 45-106).

The required form of risk acknowledgment under sections 2.9(1), 2.9(2) and 2.9(2.1) of NI 45-106 is Form 45-106F4.

In Alberta, New Brunswick, Nova Scotia, Ontario, Québec and Saskatchewan, Form 45-106F4, required under subsection 2.9(2.1), includes Schedule 1 *Classification of Investors Under the Offering Memorandum Exemption*, with respect to eligibility of individual investors, and Schedule 2 *Investment Limits for Investors Under the Offering Memorandum Exemption*, with respect to investment limits of individual investors.

5.3 Real estate securities — Certain jurisdictions impose alternative or additional disclosure requirements in relation to the distribution of real estate securities by offering memorandum. Refer to securities legislation in the jurisdictions where securities are being distributed.

5.4 Risk acknowledgement form for distributions to close personal friends and close business associates in Saskatchewan — In Saskatchewan, a risk acknowledgment is also required under section 2.6(1) of NI 45-106 if the person intends to rely upon the "family, friends and business associates exemption" in section 2.5 of NI 45-106, which is based on a relationship of close personal friendship or close business association. The form of risk acknowledgement required in these circumstances is Form 45-106F5.

5.5 Risk acknowledgement form for distributions to individual accredited investors — A person relying on the accredited investor exemption in section 2.3 of NI 45-106 and section 73.3 of the *Securities Act* (Ontario) to distribute securities to an individual must obtain a signed risk acknowledgement from that individual accredited investor. Under subsection 2.3(7) of NI 45-106, this requirement does not apply if the individual accredited investor meets the highest threshold to be an individual accredited investor, that is, the individual owns $5 000 000 of financial assets as set out in paragraph (j.1) of the definition of "accredited investor" in section 1.1 of NI 45-106. The required form of risk acknowledgement for the accredited investor exemption is Form 45-106F9 *Form for Individual Accredited Investors*.

PART 6 — RESALE OF SECURITIES ACQUIRED UNDER AN EXEMPTION

6.1 Resale restrictions — In most jurisdictions, securities distributed under a prospectus exemption may be subject to restrictions on their resale. The particular resale, or "first trade", restrictions depend on the parties to the distribution and the particular exemption that was relied upon to distribute the securities. In certain circumstances, no resale restrictions will apply and the securities acquired under an exempt distribution will be freely tradable.

Resale restrictions are imposed under National Instrument 45-102 *Resale of Securities* (NI 45-102). While NI 45-106 contains text boxes providing commentary on resale, these text boxes are intended as guidance only and are not a substitute for reviewing the applicable provisions in NI 45-102 to determine what resale restrictions, if any, apply to the securities in question.

The resale restrictions operate by the resale transaction triggering the prospectus requirement unless certain conditions are satisfied. Securities that are subject to such restrictions in circumstances where the conditions cannot be satisfied may nevertheless be distributed under an exemption from the prospectus requirement, whether under NI 45-106 or other securities legislation.

PART 7 — TRANSITION

7.1 Transition — Application of IFRS amendments — The amendments to NI 45-106 and this Companion Policy which came into effect on January 1, 2011 only apply in respect of an offering memorandum or an amendment to an offering memorandum of an issuer which includes or incorporates by reference financial statements of the issuer in respect of periods relating to financial years beginning on or after January 1, 2011.

Adoption of Policy: (2005) 28 O.S.C.B. (Supp-4) 81 and 28 O.S.C.B. (Supp-3) 1; Request for Comments: (2004) 27 O.S.C.B. 1.

Adoption of amended and restated Policy: (2009) 32 O.S.C.B. (Supp. 5) 99 and 32 O.S.C.B. (Supp. 3) 1; Request for Comments: (2009) 32 O.S.C.B. 4233 and (2008) 31 O.S.C.B. (Supp. 1) 1.

Adoption of Amendments to Policy: (2010) 33 O.S.C.B. (Supp. 5) 117 and (Supp. 3) 213; Request for Comments: (2009) 32 O.S.C.B. 8464.

Multilateral Instrument 45-108 — Crowdfunding

Date: **January 25, 2016**

38 O.S.C.B. (Supp. 4) 11

24. Advertising and general solicitation

25. Access to funding portal

26. Issuer access agreement

27. Obligation to review materials of eligible crowdfunding issuer

28. Denial of issuer access and termination

29. Return of funds

30. Notifications

31. Removal of distribution materials

32. Monitoring purchaser communications

33. Online platform acknowledgement

34. Purchaser requirements prior to purchase

35. Required online platform disclosure

36. Delivery to the issuer

37. Release of funds

38. Reporting requirements

Division 3: Additional requirements, restricted dealer funding portal

39. Prohibition on providing recommendations or advice

40. Restriction on referral arrangements

41. Permitted dealing activities

42. Chief compliance officer

43. Proficiency

Part 4 Exemption

44. Exemption

Part 5 Coming into force

45. Effective date

Appendix A — Signing Requirements for Certificate of a Crowdfunding Offering Document (Section 7)

Form 45-108F1 *Crowdfunding Offering Document*

Form 45-108F2 *Risk Acknowledgement*

Form 45-108F3 *Confirmation of Investment Limits*

Form 45-108F4 *Notice of Specified Key Events*

Form 45-108F5 *Personal Information Form and Authorization to Collect, Use and Disclose Personal Information*

PART 1 — DEFINITIONS AND INTERPRETATION

1. Definitions — In this Instrument

"accredited investor" means

(a) except in Ontario, an accredited investor as defined in National Instrument 45-106 *Prospectus Exemptions*, and

(b) in Ontario, an accredited investor as defined in subsection 73.3(1) of the the *Securities Act*, R.S.O. 1990 c. S.5 and in National Instrument 45-106 *Prospectus Exemptions*;

"aggregate minimum proceeds" means the amount disclosed in item 5.2 of the crowdfunding offering document that is sufficient to accomplish the business objectives of the issuer;

"Canadian Financial Statement Review Standards" means standards for the review of financial statements by a public accountant determined with reference to the Handbook;

"confirmation of investment limits form" means a completed Form 45-108F3 *Confirmation of Investment Limits*;

"crowdfunding offering document" means a completed Form 45-108F1 *Crowdfunding Offering Document* together with any amendment to that document and any document incorporated by reference therein;

"crowdfunding prospectus exemption" means the exemption from the prospectus requirement in section 5 [*Crowdfunding prospectus exemption*];

"distribution period" means the period referred to in the crowdfunding offering document during which an eligible crowdfunding issuer offers its securities to purchasers in reliance on the crowdfunding prospectus exemption;

"eligible crowdfunding issuer" means an issuer if all of the following apply:

(a) the issuer and, if applicable, its parent are incorporated or organized under the laws of Canada or any jurisdiction of Canada;

(b) the head office of the issuer is located in Canada;

(c) a majority of the directors of the issuer are resident in Canada;

(d) the principal operating subsidiary of the issuer, if any, is incorporated or organized under

(i) the laws of Canada or any jurisdiction of Canada, or

(ii) the laws of the United States of America or any state or territory of the United States of America or the District of Columbia;

(e) the issuer is not an investment fund;

"eligible securities" means securities of an eligible crowdfunding issuer having the same price, terms and conditions that are distributed under the crowdfunding prospectus exemption during the distribution period and are any one or more of the following:

(a) a common share;

(b) a non-convertible preference share;

(c) a security convertible into securities referred to in paragraph (a) or (b);

(d) a non-convertible debt security linked to a fixed or floating interest rate;

(e) a unit of a limited partnership;

(f) a flow-through share under the ITA;

"executive officer" means an individual who is

(a) a chair, vice-chair or president,

(b) a chief executive officer or chief financial officer,

(c) a vice-president in charge of a principal business unit, division or function including sales, finance or production, or

(d) performing a policy-making function in respect of the issuer;

"funding portal" means

(a) a registered dealer funding portal, or

(b) a restricted dealer funding portal;

"issuer access agreement" means a written agreement entered into between an eligible crowdfunding issuer and a funding portal in compliance with section 26 [*Issuer access agreement*];

"issuer group" means

(a) an eligible crowdfunding issuer,

(b) an affiliate of the eligible crowdfunding issuer, and

(c) any other issuer

(i) that is engaged in a common enterprise with the eligible crowdfunding issuer or with an affiliate of the eligible crowdfunding issuer, or

(ii) that is controlled, directly or indirectly, by the same person or company or persons or companies that control, directly or indirectly, the eligible crowdfunding issuer;

"permitted client" means a permitted client as defined in National Instrument 31-103 *Registration Requirements, Exemptions and Ongoing Registrant Obligations*;

"personal information form" means a completed Form 45-108F5 *Personal Information Form and Authorization to Collect, Use and Disclose Personal Information*;

"registered dealer funding portal" means a person or company that

(a) is registered in the category of investment dealer or exempt market dealer under National Instrument 31-103 *Registration Requirements, Exemptions and Ongoing Registrant Obligations*, and

(b) acts or proposes to act as an intermediary in a distribution of eligible securities through an online platform in reliance on the crowdfunding prospectus exemption;

"restricted dealer funding portal" means a person or company that

(a) is registered in the category of restricted dealer under National Instrument 31-103 *Registration Requirements, Exemptions and Ongoing Registrant Obligations*,

(b) is authorized under the terms and conditions of its restricted dealer registration to distribute securities under this Instrument,

(c) acts or proposes to act as an intermediary in a distribution of eligible securities through an online platform in reliance on the crowdfunding prospectus exemption,

(d) is not registered in any other registration category, and

(e) in Ontario, is not an affiliate of another registered dealer, registered adviser, or registered investment fund manager;

"right of withdrawal" means the right referred to in section 8 [*Right of withdrawal*] or a comparable right described in securities legislation of the jurisdiction in which the purchaser resides;

"risk acknowledgement form" means a completed Form 45-108F2 *Risk Acknowledgement*;

"SEC issuer" means an SEC issuer as defined in National Instrument 52-107 *Acceptable Accounting Principles and Auditing Standards*;

"U.S. AICPA Financial Statement Review Standards" means the standards of the American Institute of Certified Public Accountants for a review of financial statements by a public accountant, as amended from time to time.

2. Terms defined or interpreted in other instruments — (1) Unless otherwise defined herein, in Part 2 [*Crowdfunding prospectus exemption*], each term has the meaning ascribed, or interpretation given, to it in National Instrument 45-106 *Prospectus Exemptions*.

(2) Unless otherwise defined herein, in Part 3 [*Requirements for funding portals*], each term has the meaning ascribed, or interpretation given, to it in National Instrument 31-103 *Registration Requirements, Exemptions and Ongoing Registrant Obligations*.

3. Purchaser — References to a "client" in a provision of any instrument with which a funding portal is required to comply under Part 3 [*Requirements for funding portals*], must be read as if the references are to a "purchaser".

4. **Specifications — Québec** — (1) In Québec, "trade" in this Instrument refers to any of the following activities:

    (a) the activities described in the definition of "dealer" in section 5 of the Securities Act (chapter V-1.1), including the following activities:

        (i) the sale or disposition of a security by onerous title, whether the terms of payment be on margin, installment or otherwise, but does not include a transfer or the giving in guarantee of securities in connection with a debt or the purchase of a security, except as provided in paragraph (b);

        (ii) participation as a trader in any transaction in a security through the facilities of an exchange or a quotation and trade reporting system;

        (iii) the receipt by a registrant of an order to buy or sell a security;

    (b) a transfer or the giving in guarantee of securities of an issuer from the holdings of a control person in connection with a debt.

(2) In Québec, the crowdfunding offering document and materials that are made available to purchasers by a reporting issuer in accordance with this Instrument are documents authorized by the Autorité des marchés financiers for use in lieu of a prospectus.

(3) In Québec, the crowdfunding offering document and materials that are made available to purchasers in accordance with this Instrument must be drawn up in French only or in French and English.

PART 2 — CROWDFUNDING PROSPECTUS EXEMPTION

DIVISION 1: — DISTRIBUTION REQUIREMENTS

5. **Crowdfunding prospectus exemption** — (1) The prospectus requirement does not apply to a distribution by an eligible crowdfunding issuer of an eligible security of its own issue to a person or company that purchases the security as principal if all of the following apply:

    (a) the issuer offers the securities during the distribution period and the distribution period ends no later than 90 days after the date the issuer first offers its securities to purchasers;

    (b) the total proceeds raised by the issuer group in reliance on the crowdfunding prospectus exemption does not exceed $1,500,000 within the 12 — month period ending on the last day of the distribution period;

    (c) in Ontario, the acquisition cost of the securities acquired by the purchaser

        (i) in the case of a purchaser that is not an accredited investor, does not exceed

            (A) $2,500 for the distribution, and

            (B) $10,000 for all distributions in reliance on the crowdfunding prospectus exemption in the same calendar year,

        (ii) in the case of a purchaser that is an accredited investor that is not a permitted client, does not exceed

            (A) $25,000 for the distribution, and

            (B) $50,000 for all distributions in reliance on the crowdfunding prospectus exemption in the same calendar year, and

        (iii) in the case of a purchaser that is a permitted client, is not limited;

    (d) except in Ontario, the acquisition cost of the securities acquired by the purchaser

        (i) in the case of a purchaser that is not an accredited investor, does not exceed $2,500 for the distribution, and

        (ii) in the case of a purchaser that is an accredited investor, does not exceed $25,000 for the distribution;

    (e) the issuer distributes the securities through a single funding portal;

    (f) before the purchaser enters into an agreement to purchase the securities, the issuer makes available to the purchaser, through the funding portal, a crowdfunding offering document that is in compliance with

        (i) section 7 [*Certificates*] and section 8 [*Right of withdrawal*], and

        (ii) section 9 [*Liability for misrepresentation — reporting issuers*] or section 10 [*Liability for untrue statement — non-reporting issuers*], as applicable.

(2) The crowdfunding prospectus exemption is not available if any of the following apply:

    (a) the proceeds of the distribution are used by the issuer to invest in, merge with or acquire an unspecified business;

    (b) the issuer is not a reporting issuer, and the issuer previously distributed securities in reliance on the crowdfunding prospectus exemption and is not in compliance with any of the following:

        (i) section 15 [*Filing or delivery of distribution materials*];

        (ii) section 16 [*Annual financial statements*];

        (iii) section 17 [*Annual disclosure of use of proceeds*];

        (iv) section 19 [*Period of time for providing ongoing disclosure*];

        (v) section 20 [*Books and records*];

        (vi) in New Brunswick, Nova Scotia and Ontario, section 18 [*Notice of specified key events*];

    (c) the issuer is a reporting issuer and is not in compliance with its reporting obligations under securities legislation, including under this Instrument;

    (d) the issuer has previously commenced a distribution under this section and that distribution has not closed, been withdrawn or otherwise terminated.

6. **Conditions for closing of the distribution** — A distribution in reliance on the crowdfunding prospectus exemption must not close unless

    (a) the right of withdrawal has expired,

    (b) the aggregate minimum proceeds have been raised through one or both of the following:

        (i) the distribution;

(ii) any concurrent distributions by any member of the issuer group, provided that the proceeds from those distributions are unconditionally available to the eligible crowdfunding issuer at the time of closing of the distribution,

(c) the issuer has provided to the funding portal written confirmation of the proceeds of the concurrent distributions referred to in subparagraph (b)(ii), if any,

(d) the issuer has received

(i) the purchase agreement entered into between the issuer and the purchaser,

(ii) a risk acknowledgement form for the purchaser where the purchaser positively confirms having read and understood the risk warnings and the information in the crowdfunding offering document,

(iii) except in Ontario, confirmation and validation that the purchaser is an accredited investor if the acquisition cost is greater than $2,500, and

(iv) in Ontario, a confirmation of investment limits form for the purchaser, and

(e) the closing occurs within 30 days of the end of the distribution period.

7. Certificates — (1) A crowdfunding offering document made available under paragraph 5(1)(f) [*Crowdfunding prospectus exemption*] must contain a certificate executed by the issuer in accordance with the applicable provisions of Appendix A, which

(a) if the issuer is a reporting issuer, states that "*This crowdfunding offering document does not contain a misrepresentation. Purchasers of securities have a right of action in the case of a misrepresentation.*", or

(b) if the issuer is not a reporting issuer, states that "*This crowdfunding offering document does not contain an untrue statement of a material fact. Purchasers of securities have a right of action in the case of an untrue statement of a material fact.*"

(2) A certificate under subsection (1) must be true as at the date the certificate is signed, the date the crowdfunding offering document is made available to purchasers and the time of the closing of the distribution.

(3) If a certificate under subsection (1) ceases to be true after a crowdfunding offering document is made available to a purchaser, the issuer must

(a) amend the crowdfunding offering document and provide a newly dated certificate executed by the issuer in accordance with the applicable provisions of Appendix A, and

(b) provide the amended crowdfunding offering document to the funding portal for the purpose of making it available to purchasers.

8. Right of withdrawal — If the securities legislation of the jurisdiction in which a purchaser resides does not provide a comparable right, the crowdfunding offering document made available to the purchaser under paragraph 5(1)(f) [*Crowdfunding prospectus exemption*] must provide the purchaser with a contractual right to withdraw from any agreement to purchase the security by delivering a notice to the funding portal within 48 hours after the date of the agreement to purchase and any subsequent amendment to the crowdfunding offering document.

9. Liability for misrepresentation — reporting issuers — If the securities legislation of the jurisdiction in which a purchaser resides does not provide a comparable right, the crowdfunding offering document of a reporting issuer, made available to the purchaser under paragraph 5(1)(f) [*Crowdfunding prospectus exemption*], must provide a contractual right of action against the issuer for rescission and damages that

(a) is available to the purchaser if the crowdfunding offering document or other materials made available to the purchaser contain a misrepresentation, without regard to whether the purchaser relied on the misrepresentation,

(b) is enforceable by the purchaser delivering a notice to the issuer

(i) in the case of an action for rescission, within 180 days after the date of purchase by the purchaser, or

(ii) in the case of an action for damages, before the earlier of

(A) 180 days after the purchaser first has knowledge of the facts giving rise to the cause of action, or

(B) 3 years after the date of purchase,

(c) is subject to the defence that the purchaser had knowledge of the misrepresentation,

(d) in the case of an action for damages, provides that the amount recoverable

(i) does not exceed the price at which the security was distributed, and

(ii) does not include all or any part of the damages that the issuer proves do not represent the depreciation in value of the security resulting from the misrepresentation, and

(e) is in addition to, and does not detract from, any other right of the purchaser.

10. Liability for untrue statement — non-reporting issuers — The crowdfunding offering document of an issuer that is not a reporting issuer, made available to a purchaser under paragraph 5(1)(f) [*Crowdfunding prospectus exemption*], must provide a contractual right of action against the issuer for rescission and damages that

(a) is available to the purchaser if the crowdfunding offering document or other materials made available to the purchaser contain an untrue statement of a material fact, without regard to whether the purchaser relied on the statement,

(b) is enforceable by the purchaser delivering a notice to the issuer

(i) in the case of an action for rescission, within 180 days after the date of purchase by the purchaser, or

(ii) in the case of an action for damages, before the earlier of

(A) 180 days after the purchaser first has knowledge of the facts giving rise to the cause of action, or

(B) 3 years after the date of purchase,

(c) is subject to the defence that the purchaser had knowledge of the untrue statement of a material fact,

(d) in the case of an action for damages, provides that the amount recoverable

(i) does not exceed the price at which the security was distributed, and

(ii) does not include all or any part of the damages that the issuer proves do not represent the depreciation in value of the security resulting from the untrue statement of a material fact, and

(e) is in addition to, and does not detract from, any other right of the purchaser.

11. Advertising and general solicitation — (1) An issuer must not, directly or indirectly, advertise a distribution, or solicit purchasers, under the crowdfunding prospectus exemption.

(2) Despite subsection (1), the issuer may inform purchasers that it proposes to distribute securities under the crowdfunding prospectus exemption and may refer purchasers to the funding portal facilitating the distribution.

12. Additional distribution materials — (1) In addition to the crowdfunding offering document required to be made available to a purchaser under paragraph 5(1)(f) [*Crowdfunding prospectus exemption*], an issuer may make available to a purchaser only through the funding portal the following materials:

    (a) a term sheet;

    (b) a video;

    (c) other materials summarizing the information in the crowdfunding offering document.

(2) The materials referred to in subsection (1) must be consistent with the information in the crowdfunding offering document.

(3) If an amended crowdfunding offering document is made available to purchasers, all materials made available to purchasers under this section must be amended, if necessary, and made available to purchasers through the funding portal.

13. Commissions or fees — No person or company in the issuer group or director or executive officer of an issuer in the issuer group may, directly or indirectly, pay a commission, finder's fee, referral fee or similar payment to any person or company in connection with a distribution in reliance on the crowdfunding prospectus exemption, other than to a funding portal.

14. Restriction on lending — No person or company in the issuer group or director or executive officer of an issuer in the issuer group may, directly or indirectly, lend or finance, or arrange lending or financing, for a purchaser to purchase securities of the issuer under the crowdfunding prospectus exemption.

15. Filing or delivery of distribution materials — (1) An issuer must, no later than 10 days after the closing of the distribution, file with the securities regulatory authority or regulator Form 45-106F1 *Report of Exempt Distribution*.

(2) At the same time that the issuer files the form referred to in subsection (1), the issuer must file a copy of the crowdfunding offering document and the materials referred to in paragraphs 12(1)(a) and (c) [*Additional distribution materials*].

(3) Upon request, the issuer must deliver to the securities regulatory authority or regulator any video referred to in paragraph 12(1)(b) [*Additional distribution materials*].

DIVISION 2: — ONGOING DISCLOSURE REQUIREMENTS FOR NON-REPORTING ISSUERS

16. Annual financial statements — (1) An issuer that is not a reporting issuer that has distributed securities under the crowdfunding prospectus exemption must deliver to the securities regulatory authority or regulator and make reasonably available to each purchaser, within 120 days after the end of its most recently completed financial year, the financial statements listed in paragraphs 4.1(1)(a), (b), (c) and (e) [*Comparative annual financial statements and audit*] of National Instrument 51-102 *Continuous Disclosure Obligations*.

(2) The financial statements referred to in subsection (1) must

    (a) be approved by management of the issuer and be accompanied by

        (i) a review report or auditor's report if the amount raised by the issuer under one or more prospectus exemptions from the date of the formation of the issuer until the end of its most recently completed financial year, is $250,000 or more but is less than $750,000, or

        (ii) an auditor's report if the amount raised by the issuer under one or more prospectus exemptions from the date of the formation of the issuer until the end of its most recently completed financial year, is $750,000 or more,

    (b) comply with paragraph 3.2(1)(a) [*Acceptable accounting principles — general requirements*], subparagraph 3.2(1)(b)(i) [*Acceptable accounting principles — general requirements*], and subsection 3.2(5) [*Acceptable accounting principles — general requirements*] of National Instrument 52-107 *Acceptable Accounting Principles and Auditing Standards*, and

    (c) comply with section 3.5 [*Presentation and functional currencies*] of National Instrument 52-107 *Acceptable Accounting Principles and Auditing Standards*.

(3) If the financial statements referred to in subsection (1) are accompanied by a review report, the financial statements must be reviewed in accordance with Canadian Financial Statement Review Standards and the review report must

    (a) not include a reservation or modification,

    (b) identify the financial periods that were subject to review,

    (c) be in the form specified by Canadian Financial Statement Review Standards, and

    (d) refer to IFRS as the applicable financial reporting framework.

(4) If the financial statements referred to in subsection (1) are accompanied by an auditor's report, the auditor's report must be

    (a) prepared in accordance with section 3.3 [*Acceptable auditing standards — general requirements*] of National Instrument 52-107 *Acceptable Accounting Principles and Auditing Standards*, and

    (b) signed by an auditor that complies with section 3.4 [*Acceptable auditors*] of National Instrument 52-107 *Acceptable Accounting Principles and Auditing Standards*.

(5) If the financial statements referred to in subsection (1) are those of an SEC issuer,

    (a) the financial statements may be prepared in accordance with section 3.7 [*Acceptable accounting principles for SEC issuers*] of National Instrument 52-107 *Acceptable Accounting Principles and Auditing Standards*,

    (b) the financial statements may be reviewed in accordance with U.S. AICPA Financial Statement Review Standards and accompanied by a review report prepared in accordance with U.S. AICPA Financial Statement Review Standards that

        (i) does not include a modification or exception,

(ii) identifies the financial periods that were subject to review,

(iii) identifies the review standards used to conduct the review and the accounting principles used to prepare the financial statements, and

(iv) refers to IFRS as the applicable financial reporting framework if the financial statements comply with paragraph 3.2(1)(a) [*Acceptable accounting principles — general requirements*] of National Instrument 52-107 *Acceptable Accounting Principles and Auditing Standards*, and

(c) the financial statements may be audited in accordance with section 3.8 [*Acceptable auditing standards for SEC issuers*] of National Instrument 52-107 *Acceptable Accounting Principles and Auditing Standards*.

(6) If the financial statements referred to in subsection (5) are accompanied by a review report and the statements have been reviewed in accordance with Canadian Financial Statement Review Standards, the review report must be in compliance with paragraphs (3)(a) to (c) and must

(a) refer to IFRS as the applicable financial reporting framework if the financial statements comply with paragraph 3.2(1)(a) [*Acceptable accounting principles — general requirements*] of National Instrument 52-107 *Acceptable Accounting Principles and Auditing Standards*, or

(b) refer to U.S. GAAP as the applicable financial reporting framework if the financial statements comply with section 3.7 [*Acceptable accounting principles for SEC issuers*] of National Instrument 52-107 *Acceptable Accounting Principles and Auditing Standards*.

(7) For the purpose of subsection (3) and paragraph (5)(b), the review report must be prepared and signed by a person or company authorized to sign a review report under the laws of a jurisdiction of Canada or a foreign jurisdiction, and that meets the professional standards of that jurisdiction.

(8) If any of the financial statements referred to in subsection (1) are not accompanied by an auditor's report or a review report prepared by a public accountant, the statements must include the following statement; "These financial statements were not audited or subject to a review by a public accountant, as permitted by securities legislation where an issuer has not raised more than a pre-defined amount under prospectus exemptions."

17. Annual disclosure of use of proceeds — (1) The financial statements of an issuer referred to in section 16 [*Annual financial statements*] and the financial statements required under section 4.1 [*Comparative annual financial statements and audit*] of National Instrument 51-102 *Continuous Disclosure Obligations* must be accompanied by a notice that details, as at the date of the issuer's most recently completed financial year, the use of the gross proceeds received by the issuer from a distribution made under the crowdfunding prospectus exemption.

(2) An issuer is not required to provide the notice referred to in subsection (1) if

(a) the issuer has disclosed in one or more prior notices the use of the entire gross proceeds from the distribution, or

(b) the issuer is no longer required to deliver, and make available to purchasers, annual financial statements.

18. Notice of specified key events — In New Brunswick, Nova Scotia and Ontario, an issuer that is not a reporting issuer that distributes securities in reliance on the crowdfunding prospectus exemption must make reasonably available to each holder of a security acquired under the crowdfunding prospectus exemption, a notice in Form 45-108F4 *Notice of Specified Key Events* of each of the following events within 10 days of their occurrence:

(a) a discontinuation of the issuer's business;

(b) a change in the issuer's industry;

(c) a change of control of the issuer.

19. Period of time for providing ongoing disclosure — The obligations of an issuer that is not a reporting issuer under section 16 [*Annual financial statements*] and, in New Brunswick, Nova Scotia and Ontario, under section 18 [*Notice of specified key events*] apply until the earliest of the following events:

(a) the issuer becomes a reporting issuer;

(b) the issuer has completed a winding up or dissolution;

(c) the securities of the issuer are beneficially owned, directly or indirectly, by fewer than 51 security holders worldwide.

20. Books and records — An issuer that is not a reporting issuer that distributes securities under the crowdfunding prospectus exemption must maintain the following books and records relating to the distribution for 8 years following the closing of the distribution:

(a) the crowdfunding offering document and the materials referred to in subsection 12(1) [*Additional distribution materials*];

(b) the risk acknowledgement forms;

(c) except in Ontario, confirmation and validation that the purchaser is an accredited investor if the acquisition cost is greater than $2,500;

(d) in Ontario, the confirmation of investment limits forms;

(e) the ongoing disclosure documents described in Division 2 [*Ongoing disclosure requirements for non-reporting issuers*];

(f) the aggregate number of securities issued under the crowdfunding prospectus exemption, and the date of issuance and the price for each security;

(g) the names of all security holders of the issuer and the number and the type of securities held by each security holder;

(h) such other books and records as are necessary to record the business activities of the issuer and to comply with this Instrument.

PART 3 — REQUIREMENTS FOR FUNDING PORTALS
DIVISION 1: — REGISTRATION REQUIREMENTS, GENERAL

21. Restricted dealer funding portal — A restricted dealer funding portal and a registered individual of the restricted dealer funding portal that distributes securities in reliance on the crowdfunding prospectus exemption must comply with all of the following:

(a) the requirements in this section and in Division 2 [*Registration requirements, funding portals*] and Division 3 [*Additional requirements, restricted dealer funding portal*] of this Part;

(b) the terms, conditions, restrictions and requirements applicable to a registered dealer and to a registered individual, respectively, including

(i) National Instrument 31-102 *National Registration Database*,

(ii) National Instrument 31-103 *Registration Requirements, Exemptions and Ongoing Registrant Obligations*, except for the following:

    (A) Division 2 of Part 3 [*Education and experience requirements*], except for subsection 3.4(2) [*Proficiency — initial and ongoing*] and section 3.9 [*Exempt market dealer — dealing representative*];

    (B) section 6.2 [*If IIROC approval is revoked or suspended*];

    (C) section 6.3 [*If MFDA approval is revoked or suspended*];

    (D) Part 8 [*Exemptions from the requirement to register*];

    (E) Part 9 [*Membership in a self-regulatory organization*];

    (F) paragraphs 11.5(2)(i), and (j) [*General requirements for records*];

    (G) paragraphs 13.2(2)(c) and (d) and subsection 13.2(6) [*Know your client*];

    (H) section 13.3 [*Suitability*];

    (I) Division 3 of Part 13 [*Referral arrangements*], if the restricted dealer funding portal does not enter into a referral arrangement permitted under subsection 40(2) [*Restriction on referral arrangements*] of this Instrument;

    (J) section 13.13 [*Disclosure when recommending the use of borrowed money*];

    (K) section 13.16 [*Dispute resolution service*];

    (L) paragraphs 14.2(2)(i), (j), (k), (m), and (n) [*Relationship disclosure information*];

    (M) Division 5 of Part 14 [*Reporting to clients*], except for section 14.12 [*Content and delivery of trade confirmation*],

    (iii) National Instrument 33-105 *Underwriting Conflicts*,

    (iv) National Instrument 33-109 *Registration Information*, and

    (v) the requirement to pay fees under securities legislation;

(c) the requirement to deal fairly, honestly and in good faith with purchasers;

(d) any other terms, conditions, restrictions or requirements imposed by a securities regulatory authority or regulator on the restricted dealer funding portal or on a registered individual of the restricted dealer funding portal.

Note: In Ontario, a number of requirements in National Instrument 31-103 *Registration Requirements, Exemptions and Ongoing Registrant Obligations* do not apply because similar requirements are contained in provisions of the *Securities Act* (Ontario). To the extent that (a) one or more requirements of National Instrument 31-103 *Registration Requirements, Exemptions and Ongoing Registrant Obligations* made applicable under section 21 [*Restricted dealer funding portal*] do not apply in Ontario, and (b) there is a similar requirement in the *Securities Act* (Ontario) that is referenced in a note in National Instrument 31-103 *Registration Requirements, Exemptions and Ongoing Registrant Obligations*, a restricted dealer funding portal or a registered individual of the restricted dealer funding portal operating in Ontario is subject to the similar requirement referenced in the *Securities Act* (Ontario).

22. Registered dealer funding portal — A registered dealer funding portal and a registered individual of the registered dealer funding portal that distributes securities in reliance on the crowdfunding prospectus exemption must comply with all of the following:

(a) the requirements in this section and Division 2 [*Registration requirements, funding portals*] of this Part;

(b) the terms, conditions, restrictions or requirements applicable to its registration category and to a registered individual, respectively, under securities legislation.

Note: In Ontario, a number of requirements in National Instrument 31-103 *Registration Requirements, Exemptions and Ongoing Registrant Obligations* do not apply because similar requirements are contained in provisions of the *Securities Act* (Ontario). To the extent that (a) one or more requirements of National Instrument 31-103 *Registration Requirements, Exemptions and Ongoing Registrant Obligations* made applicable under section 22 [*Registered dealer funding portal*] do not apply in Ontario, and (b) there is a similar requirement in the *Securities Act* (Ontario) that is referenced in a note in National Instrument 31-103 *Registration Requirements, Exemptions and Ongoing Registrant Obligations*, a registered dealer funding portal or a registered individual of the registered dealer funding portal operating in Ontario is subject to the similar requirement referenced in the *Securities Act* (Ontario).

DIVISION 2: — REGISTRATION REQUIREMENTS, FUNDING PORTALS

23. Restricted dealing activities — (1) A funding portal and a registered individual of the funding portal must not act as intermediaries in connection with a distribution of or trade in securities of an eligible crowdfunding issuer that is a related issuer of the funding portal.

(2) For the purposes of subsection (1), an issuer is not a related issuer where a funding portal, an affiliate of the funding portal, or any officer, director, significant shareholder, promoter or control person of the funding portal or of any affiliate of the funding portal, has beneficial ownership of, or control or direction over, issued and outstanding voting securities of the issuer, or securities convertible into voting securities of the issuer that alone or together constitute 10 percent or less of the outstanding voting securities of the issuer.

24. Advertising and general solicitation — (1) A funding portal must not, directly or indirectly, advertise a distribution or solicit purchasers under the crowdfunding prospectus exemption.

(2) A funding portal may only make available to purchasers the crowdfunding offering document and the materials under section 12 [*Additional distribution materials*].

(3) A funding portal must ensure that the information about an eligible crowdfunding issuer and a distribution of eligible securities of the issuer is presented or displayed on its online platform in a fair, balanced and reasonable manner.

25. Access to funding portal — (1) Prior to allowing an eligible crowdfunding issuer to access the funding portal for the purposes of posting a distribution, a funding portal must

(a) enter into an issuer access agreement with the issuer,

(b) obtain a personal information form from each director, executive officer and promoter of the issuer, and

(c) conduct or arrange for the following:

(i) backgrounds checks on the issuer;

(ii) criminal record and background checks on each individual referred to in paragraph (b).

(2) In respect of each individual who becomes a director, executive officer or promoter of the issuer during the distribution period, the funding portal must

(a) obtain a personal information form, and

(b) conduct or arrange for criminal record and background checks to be conducted.

26. **Issuer access agreement** — The issuer access agreement referred to in paragraph 25(1)(a) [*Access to funding portal*] must include all of the following:

(a) confirmation that the issuer will comply with the funding portal's policies and procedures concerning information posted by issuers on the funding portal's online platform;

(b) confirmation that the information that the issuer provides to the funding portal or posts on the funding portal's online platform will only contain permitted materials that are reasonably supported, and will not contain a promotional statement, a misrepresentation or an untrue statement of a material fact or otherwise be misleading;

(c) confirmation from each of the issuer and the funding portal that each is responsible for compliance with applicable securities legislation, including compliance with this Instrument;

(d) a requirement that the funding portal must terminate any distribution and report immediately to the securities regulatory authority or regulator if, at any time during the distribution period, it appears to the funding portal that the business of the issuer is not being, or may not be, conducted with integrity;

(e) in Ontario, confirmation that the funding portal is the agent of the issuer for the purposes of a distribution under the crowdfunding prospectus exemption.

27. **Obligation to review materials of eligible crowdfunding issuer** — (1) A funding portal is required to review the crowdfunding offering document, the materials referred to in subsection 12(1) [*Additional distribution materials*], the personal information forms, the results of the criminal record and background checks, and any other information about an issuer or a distribution made available to the funding portal or of which the funding portal is aware.

(2) If it appears to the funding portal that, based upon its review of the information and materials in subsection (1), the disclosure in the crowdfunding offering document and other materials referred to in subsection 12(1) [*Additional distribution materials*] is incorrect, incomplete or misleading, the funding portal must require that the issuer correct, complete or clarify the incorrect, incomplete or misleading disclosure prior to its posting on the funding portal's online platform.

28. **Denial of issuer access and termination** — (1) The funding portal must not allow an issuer access to its online platform for the purposes of a distribution under the crowdfunding prospectus exemption if

(a) after reviewing the information about the issuer or the distribution made available to the funding portal or of which the funding portal is aware, the funding portal makes a good faith determination that

(i) the business of the issuer may not be conducted with integrity because of the past conduct of

(A) the issuer, or

(B) any of the issuer's directors, executive officers, or promoters,

(ii) the issuer is not complying with one or more of its obligations under this Instrument, or

(iii) the crowdfunding offering document or the materials referred to in subsection 12(1) [*Additional distribution materials*] contain a statement or information that constitutes a misrepresentation or an untrue statement of a material fact and the issuer has not corrected the statement or information as requested by the funding portal under section 27 [*Obligation to review materials of eligible crowdfunding issuer*], or

(b) the issuer or any of its directors, executive officers or promoters has pled guilty to or has been found guilty of an offence related to or has entered into a settlement agreement in a matter that involved fraud, or securities violations.

(2) A funding portal must terminate a distribution if, at any time during the distribution period, it appears to the funding portal that the business of the issuer is not being, or may not be, conducted with integrity.

29. **Return of funds** — A funding portal must promptly return to the purchaser all funds or assets received from a purchaser in connection with a distribution under the crowdfunding prospectus exemption if any of the following apply:

(a) the purchaser exercises its right of withdrawal;

(b) the requirements set out in section 6 [*Conditions for closing of the distribution*] are not met;

(c) the issuer withdraws the distribution;

(d) the distribution is otherwise terminated.

30. **Notifications** — If an amended crowdfunding offering document has been made available to purchasers under paragraph 7(3)(b) [*Certificates*], the funding portal must notify each purchaser that entered into an agreement to purchase securities prior to the amended crowdfunding offering document being made available that an amended crowdfunding offering document and, if applicable, other materials referred to in subsection 12(1) [*Additional distribution materials*] have been made available on the funding portal's online platform.

31. **Removal of distribution materials** — A funding portal must remove a crowdfunding offering document and the materials referred to in subsection 12(1) [*Additional distribution materials*] on the earliest of the following:

(a) the end of the distribution period;

(b) the withdrawal of the distribution;

(c) the date on which the funding portal becomes aware that the crowdfunding offering document or the materials may contain a statement or information that is false, deceptive, misleading or that may constitute a misrepresentation or untrue statement of a material fact.

32. Monitoring purchaser communications — If a funding portal establishes an online communication channel through which purchasers may communicate with one another and with the eligible crowdfunding issuer about a distribution, the funding portal must monitor postings and remove any statement by, or information from, the issuer that is inconsistent with the crowdfunding offering document or is not in compliance with this Instrument.

33. Online platform acknowledgement — Prior to allowing a person or company entry to its online platform, a funding portal must require the person or company to acknowledge all of the following:

    (a) that a distribution posted on the funding portal's online platform

        (i) has not been reviewed or approved in any way by a securities regulatory authority or regulator, and

        (ii) is risky and may result in the loss of all or most of an investment;

    (b) that the person or company may receive limited ongoing information about an issuer or an investment made through the funding portal;

    (c) that the person or company is entering an online platform operated by a funding portal that

        (i) is registered in the category of restricted dealer subject to the terms and conditions of this Instrument, and will not provide advice about the suitability of the purchase of the security, or

        (ii) is registered in the category of investment dealer or exempt market dealer, and is required to provide advice about the suitability of the purchase of the security.

34. Purchaser requirements prior to purchase — Prior to a purchaser entering into an agreement to purchase securities under the crowdfunding prospectus exemption, a funding portal must

    (a) obtain from the purchaser a risk acknowledgement form where the purchaser positively confirms having read and understood the risk warnings and the information in the crowdfunding offering document,

    (b) except in Ontario, confirm and validate that the purchaser is an accredited investor if the acquisition cost is greater than $2,500, and

    (c) in Ontario, obtain from the purchaser, and validate, a confirmation of investment limits form.

35. Required online platform disclosure — A funding portal must include on its online platform prominent disclosure of all compensation, including fees, costs and other expenses that the funding portal may charge to, or impose on, an eligible crowdfunding issuer or a purchaser, and any such other disclosure that may be required under securities legislation.

36. Delivery to the issuer — On or before the closing of a distribution, the funding portal must deliver to the issuer the following:

    (a) the purchase agreement entered into between the issuer and the purchaser;

    (b) a risk acknowledgement form from the purchaser where the purchaser positively confirms having read and understood the risk warnings and the information in the crowdfunding offering document;

    (c) except in Ontario, confirmation and validation that the purchaser is an accredited investor, if the acquisition cost is greater than $2,500;

    (d) in Ontario, a confirmation of investment limits form for the purchaser.

37. Release of funds — A funding portal must not release the funds raised under the distribution to the eligible crowdfunding issuer unless the requirements set out in section 6 [*Conditions for closing of the distribution*] have been met.

38. Reporting requirements — (1) A funding portal must immediately notify the securities regulatory authority or regulator in writing if, at any time during the distribution period, the funding portal terminates a distribution pursuant to subsection 28(2) [*Denial of issuer access and termination*].

(2) A funding portal must deliver to the securities regulatory authority or regulator, in a format acceptable to the securities regulatory authority or regulator, within 30 days of the end of the second and fourth quarters of its financial year, a report containing the following information for the immediately preceding two quarters:

    (a) each distribution through the funding portal, including the name of the issuer, the type of security, the amount of the distribution, the industry of the issuer and the number of purchasers participating in the distribution;

    (b) the name and industry of each issuer denied access to the funding portal and the reason for the denial;

    (c) the name and industry of each issuer

        (i) that was granted access to the funding portal but the distribution did not close and the reason the distribution did not close, or

        (ii) that was granted access to the funding portal but was subsequently removed from the funding portal and the reason for removal;

    (d) such other information as a securities regulatory authority or regulator may reasonably request.

DIVISION 3: — ADDITIONAL REQUIREMENTS, RESTRICTED DEALER FUNDING PORTAL

39. Prohibition on providing recommendations or advice — A restricted dealer funding portal and a registered individual of the restricted dealer funding portal must not, directly or indirectly, provide a recommendation or advice to a purchaser

    (a) to purchase securities under the crowdfunding prospectus exemption or in connection with any other trade in a security, or

    (b) to use borrowed money to finance any part of a purchase of securities under the crowdfunding prospectus exemption or in connection with any other trade in a security.

40. Restriction on referral arrangements — (1) A restricted dealer funding portal must not participate in a referral arrangement.

(2) Despite subsection (1), a funding portal may compensate a third party for referring an issuer to the funding portal.

41. Permitted dealing activities — A restricted dealer funding portal and a registered individual of the restricted dealer funding portal may only act as intermediaries in connection with

    (a) a distribution of securities made in reliance on the crowdfunding prospectus exemption, and

(b) except in Ontario, a distribution of securities made in reliance on a start-up crowdfunding registration and prospectus exemptive relief order granted by a securities regulatory authority or regulator, provided that the restricted dealer funding portal and a registered individual of the restricted dealer funding portal are in compliance with the terms, conditions, restrictions and requirements in this Instrument.

42. Chief compliance officer — A restricted dealer funding portal must not designate an individual as its chief compliance officer under section 11.3 [*Designating a chief compliance officer*] of National Instrument 31-103 *Registration Requirements, Exemptions and Ongoing Registrant Obligations* unless the individual has

(a) passed the Exempt Market Products Exam or the Canadian Securities Course Exam,

(b) passed the PDO Exam or the Chief Compliance Officers Qualifying Exam, and

(c) gained 12 months of experience and training that a reasonable person would consider necessary to perform the functions of a chief compliance officer for a restricted dealer funding portal.

43. Proficiency — (1) A restricted dealer funding portal must not permit an individual to perform an activity in connection with a distribution under the crowdfunding prospectus exemption unless the individual has the education, training and experience, which may include appropriate registration, that a reasonable person would consider necessary to perform the activity competently, including understanding the structure, features and risks of the distribution.

(2) For the purposes of subsection (1), the obligation to understand the structure, features and risks of the distribution does not include any obligation to assess

(a) the merits or expected returns of the investment to purchasers, or

(b) the commercial viability of the proposed business or distribution.

PART 4 — EXEMPTION

44. Exemption — (1) Subject to subsection (2), the securities regulatory authority or regulator may grant an exemption from this Instrument, in whole or in part, subject to such conditions or restrictions as may be imposed in the exemption.

(2) Despite subsection (1), in Ontario, only the regulator may grant an exemption.

(3) Except in Ontario, an exemption referred to in subsection (1) is granted under the statute referred to in Appendix B of National Instrument 14-101 *Definitions* opposite the name of the local jurisdiction.

PART 5 — COMING INTO FORCE

45. Effective date — This Instrument comes into force on January 25, 2016.

Appendix A — Signing Requirements for Certificate of a Crowdfunding Offering Document (Section 7)

1. If the eligible crowdfunding issuer is a company, a certificate under paragraph 7(1)(b) [*Certificates*] of the Instrument complies with this section if it is signed

(a) by the issuer's chief executive officer and chief financial officer or, if the issuer does not have a chief executive officer or chief financial officer, an individual acting in that capacity,

(b) on behalf of the directors of the issuer, by

(i) any 2 directors who are authorized to sign, other than the persons referred to in paragraph (a), or

(ii) all the directors of the issuer, and

(c) by each promoter of the issuer.

2. If the eligible crowdfunding issuer is a trust, a certificate under paragraph 7(1)(b) [*Certificates*] of the Instrument complies with this section if it is signed by

(a) the individuals who perform functions for the issuer similar to those performed by the chief executive officer and the chief financial officer of a company, and

(b) each trustee and the manager of the issuer.

3. A certificate under paragraph 7(1)(b) [*Certificates*] of the Instrument complies with this section

(a) if a trustee or manager signing the certificate is an individual, the individual signs the certificate,

(b) if a trustee or manager signing the certificate is a company, the certificate is signed

(i) by the chief executive officer and the chief financial officer of the trustee or the manager, and

(ii) on behalf of the board of directors of the trustee or the manager, by

(A) any two directors of the trustee or the manager, other than the persons referred to in subparagraph (i), or

(B) all of the directors of the trustee or the manager,

(c) if a trustee or manager signing the certificate is a limited partnership, the certificate is signed by each general partner of the limited partnership as described in section 5 in relation to an eligible crowdfunding issuer that is a limited partnership, or

(d) in any other case, the certificate is signed by any person with authority to act on behalf of the trustee or the manager.

4. Despite sections 2 and 3, if the trustees of an eligible crowdfunding issuer, do not perform functions for the issuer similar to those performed by the directors of a company, the trustees are not required to sign the certificate of the issuer if at least two individuals who perform functions for the issuer similar to those performed by the directors of a company sign the certificate.

5. If the eligible crowdfunding issuer is a limited partnership, a certificate under paragraph 7(1)(b) [*Certificates*] of the Instrument complies with this section if it is signed by

    (a) each individual who performs a function for the issuer similar to any of those performed by the chief executive officer or the chief financial officer of a company, and

    (b) each general partner of the issuer.

6. A certificate under paragraph 7(1)(b) [*Certificates*] of the Instrument complies with this section

    (a) if a general partner of the eligible crowdfunding issuer is an individual, the individual signs the certificate,

    (b) if a general partner of the eligible crowdfunding issuer is a company, the certificate is signed

        (i) by the chief executive officer and the chief financial officer of the general partner, and

        (ii) on behalf of the board of directors of the general partner, by

            (A) any two directors of the general partner, other than the persons referred to in subparagraph (i), or

            (B) all of the directors of the general partner,

    (c) if a general partner of the eligible crowdfunding issuer is a limited partnership, the certificate is signed by each general partner of the limited partnership and, for greater certainty, this section applies to each general partner required to sign,

    (d) if a general partner of the eligible crowdfunding issuer is a trust, the certificate is signed by the trustees of the general partner as described in section 2 in relation to an issuer that is a trust, or

    (e) in any other case where there is a general partner of the eligible crowdfunding issuer, the certificate is signed by any person with authority to act on behalf of the general partner.

7. If an eligible crowdfunding issuer is not a company, trust or limited partnership, a certificate under paragraph 7(1)(b) [*Certificates*] of the Instrument complies with this section if it is signed by the persons that, in relation to the issuer, are in a similar position or perform a similar function to any of the persons referred to in section 1, 2, 3, 4, 5 or 6.

Final Rule: (2015) 38 O.S.C.B. (Supp. 4) 11.

Rules: NI 45-102, NI 45-106.

Form 45-108F1 — Crowdfunding Offering Document

Instructions

This Form contains the disclosure items that an eligible crowdfunding issuer offering securities under the crowdfunding prospectus exemption (the *issuer*) must include in a crowdfunding offering document. If any disclosure item is not applicable, include the relevant heading and state "Not applicable" under it.

Use plain language and focus on relevant information that would assist purchasers in making an investment decision. Use tables, charts and other graphic methods of presenting information if this will make the information easier to understand. The information should be balanced and not promotional in nature. A longer document is not necessarily a better document.

Do not disclose forward-looking information unless there is a reasonable basis for the forward-looking information. If material forward-looking information is disclosed, it must be accompanied by disclosure that identifies the forward-looking information as such, and cautions that actual results may vary from the forward-looking information. An example of forward-looking information would be an estimate of the timeline to complete a project.

If this crowdfunding offering document is amended and restated, the document that is made available to purchasers must be labelled as an amended and restated crowdfunding offering document.

This crowdfunding offering document is divided into the following 11 items:

ITEM 1 — Warning to purchasers

ITEM 2 — Brief overview of the issuer

ITEM 3 — Brief overview of the issuer's business

ITEM 4 — What you need to know about the issuer's management

ITEM 5 — What you need to know about the distribution

ITEM 6 — What you need to know about the issuer

ITEM 7 — What you need to know about the funding portal

ITEM 8 — What you need to know about your rights

ITEM 9 — Other relevant information

ITEM 10 — Documents incorporated by reference in this crowdfunding offering document

ITEM 11 — Certificate

Item 1 — Warning to Purchasers

Include the following statement, in bold type:

> *"No securities regulatory authority or regulator has assessed, reviewed or approved the merits of these securities or reviewed this crowdfunding offering document. Any representation to the contrary is an offence. This is a risky investment."*

Item 2 — Brief Overview of the Issuer

2.1 — Issuer information

Provide the following information in the table below:

Full legal name of issuer	
Legal status (form of entity and date and jurisdiction of organization)	
Articles of incorporation, limited partnership agreement or similar document, and shareholder agreement, available at:	
Head office address of issuer	
Telephone	
Fax	
Website URL	
Link(s) to access video(s) relating to this offering (see instruction 1 below)	
Jurisdictions of Canada where the issuer is a reporting issuer (see instruction 2 below)	

Instructions:

1. A video may only be made available on the funding portal's online platform.

2. Disclose each jurisdiction of Canada where the issuer is a reporting issuer. If the issuer is not a reporting issuer, disclose that fact.

2.2 — Issuer contact person

Provide the following information for a contact person at the issuer who is able to answer questions from a purchaser or a securities regulatory authority or regulator:

Full legal name of the contact person	
Position held at the issuer	
Business address	
Business telephone number	
Business email address	

Item 3 — Brief Overview of the Issuer's Business

Briefly explain, in a few lines, the issuer's business and why the issuer is raising funds.

Include the following statement, in bold type:

> *"A more detailed description of the issuer's business is provided below."*

Item 4 — What You Need to Know About the Issuer's Management

Provide the required information in the following table for each executive officer, director, promoter and control person of the issuer.

Instruction: An executive officer is an individual who is: (a) a chair, vice-chair or president; (b) a chief executive officer or chief financial officer; (c) a vice-president in charge of a principal business unit, division or function including sales, finance or production; or (d) performing a policy-making function in respect of the issuer.

Full legal name City, prov/state and country of residence Position at issuer	Principal occupation for the last five years	Expertise, education, and experience that is relevant to the issuer's business	Percentage of time the person spends/will spend on the issuer's business (if less than full time)	Number and type of securities of the issuer owned, directly or indirectly Date securities were acquired and price paid for securities % of the issuer's issued and outstanding securities as of the date of this crowdfunding offering document

State whether each person listed in item 4 or the issuer, as the case may be

(a) has ever pled guilty to or been found guilty of:

(i) a summary conviction or indictable offence under the *Criminal Code* (R.S.C. 1985, c. C-46) of Canada;

(ii) a quasi-criminal offence in any jurisdiction of Canada or a foreign jurisdiction;

(iii) a misdemeanour or felony under the criminal legislation of the United States of America, or any state or territory therein;

(iv) an offence under the criminal legislation of any other foreign jurisdiction,

(b) is or has been the subject of an order (cease trade or otherwise), judgment, decree, sanction, or administrative penalty imposed by a government agency, administrative agency, self-regulatory organization, civil court, or administrative court of Canada or a foreign jurisdiction in the last ten years related to his or her involvement in any type of business, securities, insurance or banking activity,

(c) is or has been the subject of a bankruptcy or insolvency proceeding in the last ten years, and/or

(d) is an executive officer, director, promoter or control person of an issuer that is or has been subject to a proceeding described in paragraphs (a), (b) or (c) above.

Item 5 — What You Need to Know About the Distribution

5.1 — Distribution information

Provide the following information in the table below:

Type of securities being distributed	
Price per security	$
Description of any additional rewards or benefits that are not securities (see instruction 1 below)	
Start of distribution period	
End of distribution period	
Date and description of amendment(s) made to this crowdfunding offering document, if any	
Jurisdiction(s) where securities are being distributed	
Expected proceeds of this distribution (see instruction 2 below)	$
Minimum subscription per purchaser, if applicable	$

Instructions:

1. Include the following statement, in bold type as a footnote to the table if the issuer is offering any rewards or benefits:

"*The disclosure of additional rewards and benefits that are not securities is for information purposes only. A purchaser is cautioned that any rights applicable to a purchaser as result of an offering of rewards or benefits that are not securities are outside the jurisdiction of securities legislation.*"

2. The amount disclosed must be the same as the amount in Row A in the table under Proceeds to be raised in item 5.2.

5.2 — Aggregate proceeds

Insert the relevant dollar amount and include the following statement, in bold type:

"*The issuer requires aggregate minimum proceeds of $ .... to accomplish the business objectives described below.*"

Provide the following information in the tables below:

Proceeds to be raised

A.	Expected proceeds of this distribution	$
B.	Proceeds expected to be received from concurrent distributions, if any, that will be unconditionally available to the issuer at the time of closing of the distribution (see instruction 1 below)	$
C.	*Aggregate minimum proceeds* C = (A+B) (see instruction 2 below)	$
D.	Maximum amount the issuer wants to raise	$

Instructions:

1. The amount disclosed in Row B should reconcile to the information provided in item 5.3.

2. The amount disclosed in Row C must be the same as the amount disclosed in the statement at the beginning of this item.

Use of proceeds

	Description of expenses	Assuming aggregate minimum proceeds	Assuming maximum amount raised, if applicable
A.	Fees to be paid to funding portal (see instructions 1 and 2 below)	$	$
B.	Other expenses of this distribution (see instruction 3 below)	$	$
C.	Funds to accomplish business objectives (see instruction 4)	$	$
D.	*Total* (see instruction 5)	$	$

Instructions:

1. Describe the fees (e.g., commission, arranging fee or other fee) that the funding portal is charging for its services. Describe each type of fee and the estimated amount to be paid for each type. If a commission is being paid, indicate the percentage that the commission will represent of the gross proceeds of the distribution.

2. Disclose the estimated number and value of the issuer's securities to be issued, if any, in consideration for all or a portion of the portal's fees.

3. State the nature of each expense (e.g. legal, accounting, audit) and the estimated amount of the expense.

4. State the business objectives the issuer expects to accomplish using the proceeds to be raised, assuming: (i) the aggregate minimum proceeds are raised; and (ii) if applicable, the maximum amount is raised. Describe each business objective and state the estimated time period for the objective to be accomplished and the costs related to accomplishing it. Each business objective must be included in a separate row in the table.

5. The total dollar amount of the proceeds to be raised must be accounted for in the table. The amount disclosed in Row D under the column Assuming aggregate minimum proceeds *must be the same as the amount in Row C in the table under* Proceeds to be raised *in this item. The amount disclosed in Row D under the column* Assuming maximum amount raised, if applicable *must be the same as the amount in Row D in the table under* Proceeds to be raised *in this item.*

Business Acquisition

If any of the proceeds will be used by the issuer to acquire, invest in, or merge with a business, disclose, for that business, the information required by items 3 and 6.3, together with other relevant information.

5.3 — Concurrent distributions

If the proceeds of a concurrent distribution will be unconditionally available to the issuer at the time of closing of the distribution, provide the following information for each distribution by any member of the issuer group that is intended to be conducted, at least in part, during the distribution period:

(a) type of securities being distributed in concurrent distribution;

(b) proposed size of concurrent distribution;

(c) proposed closing date of concurrent distribution;

(d) price and terms of securities to be distributed in concurrent distribution.

Instruction: If during the course of this distribution: (i) there is any change in the size, type of security, price per security, or other terms and conditions in a concurrent distribution being made by the issuer; (ii) there is any change in the amount of proceeds proposed to be received by the issuer from a concurrent distribution being made by a member of the issuer group, other than the issuer; or (iii) a new distribution is commenced by any member of the issuer group where the proceeds of the distribution will be unconditionally available to the issuer, this crowdfunding offering document must be amended to reflect this development.

5.4 — Description of securities distributed and relevant rights

This security gives you the following rights (choose all that apply):

❑ Voting rights;

❑ Interest or dividends;

❑ Redemption rights;

❑ Rights on dissolution;

❑ Conversion rights: Each security is convertible into ....;

❑ Other (describe) ....

Provide a description of any right to receive interest or dividends.

Other rights or obligations

State whether purchasers will have protections such as tag-along or pre-emptive rights. If no such rights will be provided or are minimal in nature, explain:

(a) the risks associated with being a minority security holder;

(b) that the absence of such rights affects the value of the securities.

Any other restrictions or conditions

Provide a brief summary of any other restrictions or conditions that attach to the securities being distributed.

Dilution

Include the following statement:

"Your percentage of ownership in this issuer may be reduced significantly due to a number of factors beyond your control, such as the rights and characteristics of other securities already issued by the issuer, future issuances of securities by the issuer, and potential changes to the capital structure and/or control of the issuer."

5.5 — Other crowdfunding distributions

For any crowdfunding distribution in which the issuer or an executive officer, director, promoter or control person of the issuer has been involved in the past five years, provide the information below:

For crowdfunding distributions that were started but the issuer did not receive any funds:

(a) the full legal name of the issuer that made the distribution;

(b) the date the distribution was discontinued.

For closed crowdfunding distributions:

(a) the full legal name of the issuer that made the distribution;

(b) the date that the distribution commenced and the date it closed;

(c) the name and website address of the funding portal through which the distribution was made;

(d) the amount raised;

(e) the intended use of proceeds stated in the relevant crowdfunding offering document and the actual use of proceeds.

This information must be provided for each person that has been involved in a crowdfunding distribution in the past five years, whether with the issuer, or with another issuer.

Item 6 — What You Need to Know About the Issuer

6.1 — Issuer's business

Indicate which statement(s) best describe the issuer's operations (select all that apply):

❏ has never conducted operations;

❏ is in the development stage;

❏ is currently conducting operations;

❏ has shown profit in the last financial year.

Briefly describe:

(a) the nature of the issuer's product(s) or service(s);

(b) the industry in which the issuer operates;

(c) the issuer's long term business objectives;

(d) the issuer's assets and whether those assets are owned or leased.

6.2 — Related party relationships and transactions

For purposes of this item, a control person is a person or company that controls, directly or indirectly, more than 20% of the issuer's voting securities prior to the closing of this distribution.

Family relationships

Are there any family relationships between any executive officers, directors, promoters or control persons?   Y ❏   N ❏

If yes, describe the nature of each relationship.

Proceeds to be raised

Will the issuer use any of the proceeds to be raised to:

- acquire assets or services from an executive officer, director, promoter or control person, or   Y ❏   N ❏
an associate of any of them?

- loan money to any executive officer, director, promoter or control person, or an associate of   Y ❏   N ❏
any of them?

- reimburse any executive officer, director, promoter or control person, or an associate of any   Y ❏   N ❏
of them, for assets previously acquired, services previously rendered, monies previously
loaned or advanced, or for any other reason?

If the answer to any of the above is "yes", disclose the relationship between each person and the issuer and the principal terms of each transaction. If assets were acquired from a person, disclose the cost of the asset to the issuer and the method used to determine this cost. Disclose for each person who has been involved in more than one related party transaction, their relationship with the issuer and which of the transactions they have been involved with.

6.3 — Principal risks facing the business

Disclose the risks facing the issuer's business that could result in a purchaser losing the value of the purchaser's investment. Only those risks that are highly significant to the business should be disclosed. The risks should be disclosed in order of most to least significant.

In addition to disclosing the principal risks in this crowdfunding offering document, reporting issuers may incorporate by reference the risk disclosure in their continuous disclosure documents (for example, their annual information form or management discussion & analysis).

Instruction: Explain the risks of investing in the issuer for the purchaser in a meaningful way, avoiding overly general or "boilerplate" disclosure. Disclose both the risk and the factual basis for it. Risks can relate to the issuer's business, its industry, its clients, etc.

Litigation

Disclose any litigation or administrative action that has had or is likely to have a material effect on the issuer's business. Include information not only about present pending litigation or administrative actions, but also past concluded litigation or administrative actions, and potential future claims of which the issuer is aware. Disclose the name of the court, agency or tribunal where the proceeding is pending, a description of the facts underlying the claim and the relief sought, or any information known to the issuer about pending litigation or administrative actions.

6.4 — Financial information

If the issuer is a non-reporting issuer, include the following statement, in bold type:

"The issuer's financial statements have not been provided to or reviewed by a securities regulatory authority or regulator."

Fiscal year end

Month and Day: ....

See Schedule A *Crowdfunding Offering Document — Financial Statement Requirements* to determine which financial statements must be attached to this crowdfunding offering document.

6.5 — Ongoing disclosure

Briefly describe how the issuer intends to communicate with purchasers.

Reporting issuer

If the issuer is a reporting issuer, state that the issuer is subject to reporting obligations under securities legislation and explain how a purchaser can access the issuer's continuous disclosure documents.

Non-reporting issuer

If the issuer is a non-reporting issuer:

(a) state that the issuer has limited disclosure obligations under securities legislation and that the issuer is required to provide only annual financial statements and annual disclosure regarding use of proceeds;

(b) state the nature and frequency of any other disclosure the issuer intends to provide to purchasers;

(c) explain how purchasers can access the disclosure documents referred to in paragraphs (a) and (b).

In New Brunswick, Nova Scotia and Ontario, a non-reporting issuer must make available to each holder of a security acquired under the crowdfunding prospectus exemption, within 10 days of their occurrence, a notice of each of the following events:

(a) a discontinuation of the issuer's business;

(b) a change in the issuer's industry;

(c) a change of control of the issuer.

6.6 — Capital structure

Disclose the following information:

(a) the issuer's capital structure, including the terms and conditions of any other securities that are issued and outstanding as at the date of this crowdfunding offering document and the amount(s) that were paid for the securities;

(b) using the calculation outlined below, the percentage of the issuer's outstanding securities that the securities being distributed will represent on the closing of the distribution:

$$\frac{A}{A + B} = \%$$

A — Number of securities being distributed under this distribution

B — Number of issued and outstanding securities as of the date of this crowdfunding offering document

Instruction: If the issuer has more than one class of outstanding securities, the calculation should be based only on the class of securities that is being distributed. If the securities being distributed are non-convertible debt securities, the calculation should be based on the face value of the debt securities;

(c) the total number of securities reserved or subject to issuance under outstanding options, warrants or rights, the amount(s) that were paid for the securities, and the terms and conditions of those instruments.

6.7 — Connected issuers

If the issuer is a connected issuer to a funding portal, include the disclosure required by Appendix C to National Instrument 33-105 *Underwriting Conflicts* (NI 33-105).

Instruction: The definition of "connected issuer" is provided in NI 33-105.

6.8 — Management compensation

Reporting issuer

If the issuer is a reporting issuer, incorporate by reference the disclosure provided for purposes of item 3 of Form 51-102F6 *Statement of Executive Compensation (Form 51-102F6)* and other information disclosed in the issuer's Form 51-102F6 as needed.

Non-reporting issuer

If the issuer is a non-reporting issuer, provide the following information in the format set out below for each director and the three most highly compensated executive officers (or all executive officers if there are fewer than three):

Name of person and position at issuer	Total compensation paid to that person during the 12 month period preceding commencement of this distribution		Total compensation expected to be paid to that person during the 12 month period following closing of this distribution	
	Cash ($)	Other Compensation	Cash ($)	Other Compensation

Instruction: Describe any non-cash compensation and how it was valued.

6.9 — Mining issuer disclosure

If the issuer is a mining issuer, state that the issuer is subject to the requirements of National Instrument 43-101 *Standards of Disclosure for Mineral Projects* (NI 43-101).

Instruction: Note that NI 43-101 applies to all issuers, including non-reporting issuers.

Item 7 — What You Need to Know About the Funding Portal

State that the issuer is using the services of a funding portal to offer its securities and provide the contact information of the funding portal below:

Full legal name of the funding portal	
Full website address of the funding portal	
Business email address of the funding portal	
Full legal name of the Chief Compliance Officer	
Full legal name of the contact person	
	Business address
	Business telephone number

Include the following statement:

"A purchaser can check if the funding portal is operated by a registered dealer at the following website: www.aretheyregistered.ca"

Item 8 — What You Need to Know About Your Rights

Reporting issuer

If the issuer is a reporting issuer, state that a purchaser has the following contractual rights in connection with the purchase of securities:

(a) if the securities legislation of the jurisdiction in which the purchaser resides does not provide a comparable right, a right of action for damages or rescission if this crowdfunding offering document, or any document or video made available to a purchaser in addition to this crowdfunding offering document, contains a misrepresentation, and

(b) if the securities legislation of the jurisdiction in which the purchaser resides does not provide a comparable right, a right to withdraw from an agreement to purchase securities distributed under this crowdfunding offering document by delivering a notice to the funding portal within 48 hours after the date of subscription.

Non-reporting issuer

If the issuer is a non-reporting issuer, state that a purchaser has the following contractual rights in connection with the purchase of securities:

(a) a right of action for damages or rescission if this crowdfunding offering document, or any document or video made available to a purchaser in addition to this crowdfunding offering document, contains an untrue statement of a material fact, and

(b) if the securities legislation of the jurisdiction in which the purchaser resides does not provide a comparable right, a right to withdraw from an agreement to purchase securities distributed under this crowdfunding offering document by delivering a notice to the funding portal within 48 hours after the date of subscription.

Disclose how a purchaser can find more information about these rights and how to exercise them. The disclosure should include who a purchaser needs to contact, how a purchaser can contact that person and the deadline for a purchaser to do so in order to exercise their rights. The issuer may choose to include a link to the relevant portion of the funding portal's website.

Item 9 — Other Relevant Information

State any other facts that would likely be important to a purchaser purchasing securities under this crowdfunding offering document.

Item 10 — Documents Incorporated by Reference in This Crowdfunding Offering Document

If the issuer is a reporting issuer, include the following disclosure and provide the required information in the table below:

"Information has been incorporated by reference into this crowdfunding offering document from documents listed in the table below, which have been filed with the securities regulatory authorities or regulators in Canada. The documents incorporated by reference are available for viewing on the SEDAR website at www.sedar.com.

Documents listed in the table and information provided in those documents are not incorporated by reference to the extent that their contents are modified or superseded by a statement in this crowdfunding offering document or in any other subsequently filed document that is also incorporated by reference in this crowdfunding offering document."

Description of document (in the case of material change reports, provide a brief description of the nature of the material change)	Date of document

Item 11 — Certificate

11.1 — Insert the date of this crowdfunding offering document and the date it was made available to purchasers through the funding portal and include the following statement, in bold type:

For reporting issuers:

"This crowdfunding offering document does not contain a misrepresentation. Purchasers of securities have a right of action in the case of a misrepresentation."

For non-reporting issuers:

"This crowdfunding offering document does not contain an untrue statement of a material fact. Purchasers of securities have a right of action in the case of an untrue statement of a material fact."

11.2 — For both reporting and non-reporting issuers, provide the signature, date of the signature, name and position of each individual certifying this crowdfunding offering document.

11.3 — If this crowdfunding offering document is signed electronically, include the following statement for each individual certifying the document, in bold type:

"I acknowledge that I am signing this crowdfunding offering document electronically and agree that this is the legal equivalent of my handwritten signature. I will not at any time in the future claim that my electronic signature is not legally binding."

Instruction: See Appendix A of Multilateral Instrument 45-108 Crowdfunding to determine who is required to certify this crowdfunding offering document.

Securities regulatory authorities and regulators of the participating jurisdictions:

Manitoba

The Manitoba Securities Commission
500 — 400 St Mary Avenue
Winnipeg, Manitoba R3C 4K5
Telephone: 204-945-2548
Toll free in Manitoba: 1-800-655-2548
Fax: 204-945-0330
E-mail: exemptions.msc@gov.mb.ca
www.msc.gov.mb.ca

New Brunswick

Financial and Consumer Services Commission
85 Charlotte Street, Suite 300
Saint John, New Brunswick E2L 2J2
Toll free: 1-866-933-2222

	Fax: 506-658-3059
	E-mail: info@fcnb.ca
	www.fcnb.ca
Nova Scotia	Nova Scotia Securities Commission
	Suite 400, 5251 Duke Street
	Halifax, Nova Scotia B3J 1P3
	Telephone: 902-424-7768
	Toll free in Nova Scotia: 1-855-424-2499
	Fax: 902-424-4625
	E-mail: nssc.crowdfunding@novascotia.ca
	www.nssc.gov.ns.ca
Ontario	Ontario Securities Commission
	20 Queen Street West, 22nd Floor
	Toronto, Ontario M5H 3S8
	Telephone: 416-593-8314
	Toll-free (North America): 1-877-785-1555
	Fax: 416-593-8122
	E-mail: inquiries@osc.gov.on.ca
	www.osc.gov.on.ca
Québec	Autorité des marchés financiers
	Direction du financement des sociétés
	800, rue du Square-Victoria, 22nd floor
	P.O. Box 246, tour de la Bourse
	Montréal, Québec H4Z 1G3
	Telephone: 514-395-0337
	Toll free in Québec: 1-877-525-0337
	Fax: 514-873-3090
	E-mail: financement-participatif@lautorite.qc.ca
	www.lautorite.qc.ca

Schedule A — Crowdfunding Offering Document Financial Statement Requirements

1. — In this schedule

"Canadian Financial Statement Review Standards" means standards for the review of financial statements by a public accountant determined with reference to the Handbook;

"SEC issuer" means an SEC issuer as defined in National Instrument 52-107 *Acceptable Accounting Principles and Auditing Standards*;

"U.S. AICPA Financial Statement Review Standards" means the standards of the American Institute of Certified Public Accountants for a review of financial statements by a public accountant, as amended from time to time.

Reporting issuer

2. If the issuer is a reporting issuer, attach as an appendix to this crowdfunding offering document

    (a) the most recent annual financial statements the issuer has filed with the securities regulatory authority or regulator, and

    (b) the most recent interim financial report the issuer has filed with the securities regulatory authority or regulator for an interim period that is subsequent to the financial year covered by the annual financial statements referred to in paragraph (a).

Non-reporting issuer

3. If the issuer is not a reporting issuer

    (a) Attach as an appendix to this crowdfunding offering document the financial statements listed in paragraphs 4.1(1)(a), (b), (c) and (e) [*Comparative annual financial statements and audit*] of National Instrument 51-102 *Continuous Disclosure Obligations*.

    (b) Despite paragraph (a), if the issuer has not completed a financial year, attach as an appendix to this crowdfunding offering document financial statements that include

        (i) a statement of comprehensive income, a statement of changes in equity, and a statement of cash flows for the period from the date of the formation of the issuer to a date not more than 90 days before the date of this crowdfunding offering document,

        (ii) a statement of financial position as at the end of the period referred to in subparagraph (i), and

(iii) notes to the financial statements.

(c) The financial statements referred to in paragraphs (a) and (b), and any other financial statements that are attached as an appendix to this crowdfunding offering document, must

(i) be approved by management and be accompanied by

(A) a review report or auditor's report if the amount raised by the issuer under one or more prospectus exemptions from the date of the formation of the issuer until 90 days before the date of this crowdfunding offering document, is \$250,000 or more but is less than \$750,000, or

(B) an auditor's report if the amount raised by the issuer under one or more prospectus exemptions from the date of the formation of the issuer until 90 days before the date of this crowdfunding offering document, is \$750,000 or more,

(ii) comply with paragraph 3.2(1)(a) [*Acceptable accounting principles — general requirements*], subparagraph 3.2(1)(b)(i) [*Acceptable accounting principles — general requirements*], and subsection 3.2(5) [*Acceptable accounting principles — general requirements*] of National Instrument 52-107 *Acceptable Accounting Principles and Auditing Standards*, and

(iii) comply with section 3.5 [*Presentation and functional currencies*] of National Instrument 52-107 *Acceptable Accounting Principles and Auditing Standards*.

(d) If the financial statements referred to paragraphs (a) and (b), or any other financial statements that are attached as an appendix to this crowdfunding offering document, are accompanied by a review report, the financial statements must be reviewed in accordance with Canadian Financial Statement Review Standards and the review report must

(i) not include a reservation or modification,

(ii) identify the financial periods that were subject to review,

(iii) be in the form specified by Canadian Financial Statement Review Standards, and

(iv) refer to IFRS as the applicable financial reporting framework.

(e) If the financial statements referred to in paragraphs (a) and (b), or any other financial statements that are attached as an appendix to this crowdfunding offering document, are accompanied by an auditor's report, the auditor's report must be

(i) prepared in accordance with section 3.3 [*Acceptable auditing standards — general requirements*] of National Instrument 52-107 *Acceptable Accounting Principles and Auditing Standards*, and

(ii) signed by an auditor that complies with section 3.4 [*Acceptable auditors*] of National Instrument 52-107 *Acceptable Accounting Principles and Auditing Standards*.

(f) If the financial statements referred to in paragraphs (a) and (b), or any other financial statements that are attached as an appendix to this crowdfunding offering document, are those of an SEC issuer,

(i) the statements may be prepared in accordance with section 3.7 [*Acceptable accounting principles for SEC issuers*] of National Instrument 52-107 *Acceptable Accounting Principles and Auditing Standards*,

(ii) the financial statements may be reviewed in accordance with U.S. AICPA Financial Statement Review Standards and accompanied by a review report prepared in accordance with U.S. AICPA Financial Statement Review Standards that

(A) does not include a modification or exception,

(B) identifies the financial periods that were subject to review,

(C) identifies the review standards used to conduct the review and the accounting principles used to prepare the financial statements, and

(D) refers to IFRS as the applicable financial reporting framework if the financial statements comply with paragraph 3.2(1)(a) [*Acceptable accounting principles — general requirements*] of National Instrument 52-107 *Acceptable Accounting Principles and Auditing Standards*, and

(iii) the financial statements may be audited in accordance with section 3.8 [*Acceptable auditing standards for SEC issuers*] of National Instrument 52-107 *Acceptable Accounting Principles and Auditing Standards*.

(g) If the financial statements referred to in paragraph (f) are accompanied by a review report and the statements have been reviewed in accordance with Canadian Financial Statement Review Standards, the review report must be in compliance with subparagraphs 3(d)(i) to (iii) and must

(i) refer to IFRS as the applicable financial reporting framework if the financial statements comply with paragraph 3.2(1)(a) [*Acceptable accounting principles — general requirements*] of National Instrument 52-107 *Acceptable Accounting Principles and Auditing Standards*, or

(ii) refer to U.S. GAAP as the applicable financial reporting framework if the financial statements comply with section 3.7 [*Acceptable accounting principles for SEC issuers*] of National Instrument 52-107 *Acceptable Accounting Principles and Auditing Standards*.

(h) For the purpose of paragraph (d) and subparagraph (f)(ii), the review report must be prepared and signed by a person or company authorized to sign a review report under the laws of a jurisdiction of Canada or a foreign jurisdiction, and that meets the professional standards of that jurisdiction.

(i) If any of the financial statements referred to in paragraphs (a) and (b), or any other financial statements that are attached as an appendix to this crowdfunding offering document, are not accompanied by an auditor's report or a review report prepared by a public accountant, the statements must include the following statement: "*These financial statements were not audited or subject to a review by a public accountant as permitted by securities legislation where an issuer has not raised more than a pre-defined amount under prospectus exemptions."*

Instructions related to financial statement requirements and the disclosure of other financial information

What constitutes an issuer's first financial year — The first financial year of an issuer commences on the date of its incorporation or organization and ends at the close of that financial year.

What would be presented in an issuer's financial statements if the issuer has not completed a financial year — The financial statements would include the financial statements listed in paragraphs 4.1(1)(a), (b), (c) and (e) [Comparative annual financial statements and audit] of National Instrument 51-102 Continuous Disclosure Obligations for the period from the date of the formation of the issuer to a date not more than 90 days before the date of this crowdfunding offering document. The financial statements would not include a comparative period.

What financial years need to be audited or reviewed — If an issuer is required to have an auditor's report or review report accompany its financial statements in accordance with subparagraph 3(c)(i) of this schedule, the financial statements for the most recent period and the comparative period, if any, are both required to be audited or are both required to be reviewed.

Statement required in annual financial statements that have not been audited or reviewed — Paragraph 3(i) of this schedule requires that if an issuer's annual financial statements are not accompanied by an auditor's report or a review report prepared by a public accountant, the financial statements must include a statement that discloses that fact. Consistent with the requirements set out in subparagraph 3(c)(i) of this schedule, an issuer's annual financial statements are not required to be audited or reviewed by a public accountant if the issuer has raised less than $250,000 under one or more prospectus exemptions from the date of the formation of the issuer until 90 days before the date of this crowdfunding offering document.

What financial reporting framework is identified in the financial statements, and any accompanying auditor's report or review report — If an issuer's financial statements are prepared in accordance with Canadian GAAP for publicly accountable enterprises and include an unreserved statement of compliance with IFRS, the auditor's report or review report must refer to IFRS as the applicable financial reporting framework.

There are two options for referring to the financial reporting framework in the applicable financial statements and accompanying auditor's report or review report:

   (a) refer only to IFRS in the notes to the financial statements and in the auditor's report or review report, or

   (b) refer to both IFRS and Canadian GAAP in the notes to the financial statements and in the auditor's report or review report.

Non-GAAP financial measures — An issuer that intends to disclose non-GAAP financial measures in its crowdfunding offering document should refer to CSA guidance for a discussion of staff expectations concerning the use of these measures.

Form 45-108F2 — Risk Acknowledgement

Instructions: This form must be completed by the purchaser before the purchaser enters into an agreement to purchase securities under the exemption in Multilateral Instrument 45-108 Crowdfunding.

Issuer name: i.e., ABC Company

Type of security offered: i.e., common share

WARNING!

   BUYER BEWARE: This investment is risky.

   Don't invest unless you can afford to lose all the money you pay for this investment.

	Yes	No
1. Risk acknowledgement		
Risk of loss — Do you understand that this is a risky investment and that you may lose all the money you pay for this investment?	☐	☐
Liquidity risk — Do you understand that you may never be able to sell this investment?	☐	☐
Lack of information — Do you understand that you may receive little ongoing information about the issuer and/or this investment?	☐	☐
No income — Do you understand that you may not earn any income, such as dividends or interest, on this investment?	☐	☐
2. No approval and no advice		
No approval — Do you understand that this investment has not been reviewed or approved in any way by a securities regulatory authority?	☐	☐
No advice — Do you understand that you will not receive advice about whether this investment is suitable for you to purchase? *[Instructions: Delete if the funding portal is operated by a registered investment dealer or exempt market dealer.]*	☐	☐
3. Limited legal rights		
Limited legal rights — Do you understand that you will not have the same rights as if you purchased under a prospectus or through a stock exchange?	☐	☐

	Yes	No
If you want to know more, you may need to seek professional legal advice.		

4. Purchaser's understanding of this investment

	Yes	No
Investment risks — Have you read this form and do you understand the risks of making this investment?	❏	❏
Offering document — Before you invest, you should read the offering document carefully. The offering document contains important information about this investment. If you have not read the offering document or if you do not understand the information in it, you should not invest. Have you read and do you understand the information in the offering document?	❏	❏

5. Purchaser's acknowledgement

First and last name:	Date:

Electronic signature: By clicking the 'I confirm' button, I acknowledge that I am signing this form electronically and agree that this is the legal equivalent of my handwritten signature. I will not at any time in the future claim that my electronic signature is not legally binding. The date of my electronic signature is the same as my acknowledgement.

6. Additional information

- *You have 48 hours to cancel your purchase from the date of the agreement to purchase the security and any amendment to the crowdfunding offering document of the issuer, by sending a notice to the funding portal at: [Instructions: Provide an email address or a fax number where purchasers can send their notice. Describe any other way purchasers can cancel their purchase.]*

- *To check if the funding portal is operated by a registered dealer, go to www.aretheyregistered.ca*

- *If you want more information about your local securities regulatory authority, go to www.securities-administrators.ca*

Form 45-108F3 — Confirmation of Investment Limits

Instructions: This form must be completed by the purchaser before the purchaser enters into an agreement to purchase securities under the exemption in Multilateral Instrument 45-108 Crowdfunding (the crowdfunding exemption) in Ontario.

How you qualify to buy securities under the crowdfunding exemption: Checkmark the statement under A, B or C that applies to you. You may checkmark more than one statement. If you qualify under B or C, complete the confirmation of investment limits in the relevant section.

A. Permitted Client

You are a permitted client because:

❏ You are an individual who beneficially owns financial assets, as defined in section 1.1 of National Instrument 45-106 *Prospectus Exemptions*, having an aggregate realizable value that, before taxes but net of any related liabilities, exceeds $5 million.

❏ Other — you are a person or company that otherwise falls within the definition of a permitted client in section 1.1 of Part 1 in National Instrument 31-103 *Registration Requirements, Exemptions and Ongoing Registrant Obligations*. Please specify the relevant category: ....

B. Accredited Investor

You are an accredited investor because (check all that apply):

❏ Your net income before taxes was more than $200,000 in each of the 2 most recent calendar years and you expect it to be more than $200,000 in this calendar year. (You can find your net income before taxes on your personal income tax return.)

❏ Your net income before taxes combined with your spouse's was more than $300,000 in each of the 2 most recent calendar years and you expect your combined net income before taxes to be more than $300,000 in the current calendar year.

❏ Either alone or with your spouse, you own more than $1 million in cash and securities, after subtracting any debt related to the cash and securities.

❏ Either alone or with your spouse, you have net assets worth more than $5 million. (Your net assets are your total assets (including real estate) minus your total debt.)

❏ Other — you are a person or company that otherwise falls within the definition of an accredited investor as defined in section 1.1 of National Instrument 45-106 *Prospectus Exemptions* and in subsection 73.3(1) of the *Securities Act*, R.S.O. 1990 c. S.5. Please specify the relevant category: ....

Confirmation (if you are an accredited investor but not a permitted client)

❏ I confirm that, after taking into account my investment of $ .... today in this issuer:

.... I have not invested more than $25,000 in a single crowdfunding investment, and

.... I have not invested more than $50,000 in all of the crowdfunding investments I have made in this calendar year.

C. Retail Investor

You are a retail investor if none of the statements in the previous two sections apply to you.

Part 4:
DISTRIBUTIONS

Confirmation (if you are a retail investor)

❏ I confirm that, after taking into account my investment of $ .... today in this issuer:

.... I have not invested more than $2,500 in a single crowdfunding investment, and

.... I have not invested more than $10,000 in all of the crowdfunding investments I have made in this calendar year.

Purchaser acknowledgement

First and last name:		Date:

Electronic signature: By clicking the 'I confirm' button, I acknowledge that I am signing this form electronically and agree that this is the legal equivalent of my handwritten signature. I will not at any time in the future claim that my electronic signature is not legally binding. The date of my electronic signature is the same as my acknowledgement.

Funding portal information

This section must only be completed if an investor has received advice about this investment from a funding portal registered in the category of an investment dealer or an exempt market dealer.

First and last name of registered individual:

Telephone:		Email:
Name of firm:		Registration Category:

Form 45-108F4 — Notice of Specified Key Events

Instructions: This is the form of notice required under section 18 of Multilateral Instrument 45-108 Crowdfunding in New Brunswick, Nova Scotia and Ontario to be made available to holders of securities acquired under the crowdfunding prospectus exemption.

1. Issuer Name and Address

Full legal name:

Street address:	Province/State:
Municipality:	Postal code/Zip code:
Website:	Country:

2. Specified Key Event

The event, as described in section 3, is (checkmark all that apply):

❏ a discontinuation of the issuer's business

❏ a change in the issuer's industry

❏ a change of control of the issuer

Date on which the event occurred (yyyy/mm/dd):

3. Event Description

Provide a brief description of the event identified in section 2.

....

4. Contact Person

Provide the following information for a person at the issuer who can be contacted regarding the event described in section 3.

Name:	Title:
Email address:	Telephone number:

Date of notice (yyyy/mm/dd): ....

Form 45-108F5 — Personal Information Form and Authorization to Collect, Use and Disclose Personal Information

Instructions: This Personal Information Form and Authorization to Collect, Use and Disclose Personal Information (the "Form") is to be completed by every director, executive officer, and promoter of an eligible crowdfunding issuer relying on the crowdfunding prospectus exemption as set out in Multilateral Instrument 45-108 Crowdfunding.

All Questions

All questions must have a response. The response of "N/A" or "Not Applicable" will not be accepted for any questions, *except* Questions 1(B), 2(iii) and (v) and 5.

Questions 6 to 10

Please place a checkmark (✓) in the appropriate space provided. If your answer to any of questions 6 to 10 is "YES", you *must*, in an attachment, provide complete details, including the circumstances, relevant dates, names of the parties involved and final disposition, if known. *Any attachment must be initialled by the person completing this Form.* Responses must consider all time periods.

If you have received a pardon under the *Criminal Records Act* (Canada) for an Offence that relates to fraud (including any type of fraudulent activity), misappropriation of money or other property, theft, forgery, falsification of books or documents or similar Offences, you must disclose the pardoned Offence in this Form. In such circumstances:

(a) the appropriate written response would be "Yes, pardon granted on (date)"; and

(b) you must provide complete details in an attachment to this Form.

Definitions

"Offence" An offence *includes*:

(a) a summary conviction or indictable offence under the *Criminal Code* (Canada);

(b) a quasi-criminal offence (for example under the *Income Tax Act* (Canada), the *Immigration and Refugee Protection Act* (Canada) or the tax, immigration, drugs, firearms, money laundering or securities legislation of any Canadian or foreign jurisdiction);

(c) a misdemeanour or felony under the criminal legislation of the United States of America, or any state or territory therein; or

(d) an offence under the criminal legislation of any other foreign jurisdiction;

"Proceedings" means:

(a) a civil or criminal proceeding or inquiry which is currently before a court;

(b) a proceeding before an arbitrator or umpire or a person or group of persons authorized by law to make an inquiry and take evidence under oath in the matter;

(c) a proceeding before a tribunal in the exercise of a statutory power of decision making where the tribunal is required by law to hold or afford the parties to the proceeding an opportunity for a hearing before making a decision; or

(d) a proceeding before a self-regulatory entity authorized by law to regulate the operations and the standards of practice and business conduct of its members (including where applicable, issuers listed on a stock exchange) and individuals associated with those members and issuers, in which the self-regulatory entity is required under its by-laws, rules or policies to hold or afford the parties the opportunity to be heard before making a decision, but does not apply to a proceeding in which one or more persons are required to make an investigation and to make a report, with or without recommendations, if the report is for the information or advice of the person to whom it is made and does not in any way bind or limit that person in any decision the person may have the power to make;

"securities regulatory authority" or *"SRA"* means a body created by statute in any Canadian or foreign jurisdiction to administer securities law, regulation and policy (e.g. securities commission), but does not include an exchange or other self-regulatory entity;

"self-regulatory entity" or *"SRE"* means:

(a) a stock, derivatives, commodities, futures or options exchange;

(b) an association of investment, securities, mutual fund, commodities, or future dealers;

(c) an association of investment counsel or portfolio managers;

(d) an association of other professionals (e.g. legal, accounting, engineering); and

(e) any other group, institution or self-regulatory organization, recognized by a securities regulatory authority, that is responsible for the enforcement of rules, policies, disciplines or codes under any applicable legislation, or considered an SRE in another country.

1. Identification of individual completing form

A.	Last name(s):		First name(s):			Full middle name(s) (No initials. If none, please state):	
	Name(s) most commonly known by:						
	Name of issuer:						
	Present or proposed position(s) with the issuer (check (✓) all positions below that are applicable)	(✓)	If director / executive officer disclose the date elected / appointed			If executive officer — provide title If other — provide details	
			MM	DD	YY		
	Director						
	Executive Officer						
	Promoter						
B.	Other than the name given in Question 1A above, provide any legal names, assumed names or nicknames under which you have carried on business or have otherwise been known, including information regarding any name change(s) resulting from marriage, divorce, court order or any other process. Use an attachment if necessary.		From		To		
			MM	YY	MM	YY	

C.	Gender		Date of birth			Place of birth		
	Male ❏		MM	DD	YYYY	City	Province/State	Country
	Female ❏							

D.	Marital Status:	Full name of spouse (include common law):	Occupation of spouse;

E.	Telephone and Facsimile Numbers and Email Address	
	Residential/Cellular: ( )	Facsimile: ( )
	Business: ( )	E-mail*:

Notes:

* Provide an email address that the funding portal may use to contact you regarding this form. Where the securities regulatory authority or regulator (as defined in section1.1 of National Instrument 14-101 *Definitions*) has requested the funding portal to provide it with this form, the securities regulator authority or regulator may also use the email address to contact you. This email address may be used to exchange personal information relating to you.

F.	Residential history
	Provide all residential addresses for the past 10 YEARS starting with your current principal residential address. If you are unable to recall the complete residential address for a period, which is beyond 5 years from the date of completion of this Form, the municipality and province or state and country must be identified. The funding portal reserves the right to require the full address.

Street address, city, province/state, country & postal/zip code	From		To	
	MM	YY	MM	YY

			Yes	No
2.	*Citizenship*			
	(i) Are you a Canadian citizen?		❏	❏
	(ii) Are you a person lawfully in Canada as an immigrant but are not yet a Canadian citizen?		❏	❏
	(iii) If "Yes" to Question 2(ii), the number of years of continuous residence in Canada:			
	(iv) Do you hold citizenship in any country other than Canada?		❏	❏
	(v) If "Yes" to Question 2(iv), the name of the country(ies):			

3. Employment history

Provide your complete employment history for the *5 YEARS* immediately prior to the date of this Form starting with your current employment. Use an attachment if necessary. If you were unemployed during this period of time, state this and identify the period of unemployment.

Employer name	Employer address	Position held	From		To	
			MM	YY	MM	YY

			Yes	No
4. Involvement with issuers				
A.	Are you or have you during the last 10 years ever been a director, officer, promoter, insider or control person for any issuer?		❏	❏
B.	If "YES" to 4A above, provide the names of each issuer. State the position(s) held and the period(s) during which you held the position(s). Use an attachment if necessary.			

Name of issuer	Position(s) held	Market traded on	From		To	
			MM	YY	MM	YY

		Yes	No
C.	While you were a director, officer or insider of an issuer, did any exchange or other self-regulatory entity ever refuse approval for listing or quotation of the issuer, including (i) a listing resulting from a business combination, reverse takeover or similar transaction involving the issuer that is regulated by an SRE or SRA, (ii) a backdoor listing or qualifying acquisition involving the issuer (as those terms are defined in the TSX Company Manual as amended from time to time) or (iii) a qualifying transaction, reverse takeover or change of business involving the issuer (as those terms are defined in the TSX Venture Corporate Finance Manual as amended from time to time)? If yes, attach full particulars.	❏	❏

5. Educational history

A.	Professional designation(s)

Identify any professional designation held and professional associations to which you belong, for example, Barrister & Solicitor, C.P.A., C.A., C.M.A., C.G.A., P.Eng., P.Geol., CFA, etc. and indicate which organization and the date the designations were granted.

Professional Designation and Membership Number	Grantor of designation and Canadian or Foreign Jurisdiction	Date granted MM	YY

Describe the current status of any designation and/or association (e.g. active, retired, non-practicing, suspended).

B.	Provide your post-secondary educational history starting with the most recent.

School	Location	Degree or diploma	Date obtained MM	DD	YY

6. Offences

		Yes	No

If you answer "YES" to any item in Question 6, you *must* provide complete details in an attachment. *If you have received a pardon under the Criminal Records Act (Canada) for an Offence that relates to fraud (including any type of fraudulent activity), misappropriation of money or other property, theft, forgery, falsification of books or documents or similar Offences, you must disclose the pardoned Offence in this Form.*

A.	Have you ever, in any Canadian or foreign jurisdiction, pled guilty to or been found guilty of an Offence?	❏	❏
B.	Are you the subject of any current charge, indictment or proceeding for an Offence, in any Canadian or foreign jurisdiction?	❏	❏
C.	To the best of your knowledge, are you currently or have you *ever* been a director, officer, promoter, insider, or control person of an issuer, in any Canadian or foreign jurisdiction, at the time of events that resulted in the issuer:		❏
	(i) pleading guilty to or being found guilty of an Offence?	❏	❏
	(ii) now being the subject of any charge, indictment or proceeding for an alleged Offence?	❏	❏

7. Bankruptcy

		Yes	No

If you answer "YES" to any item in Question 7, you *must* provide complete details in an attachment and attach a copy of any discharge, release or other applicable document. You must answer "YES" or "NO" for EACH of (A), (B) and (C) below.

A.	Have you, in any Canadian or foreign jurisdiction, within the past *10 years* had a petition in bankruptcy issued against you, made a voluntary assignment in bankruptcy, made a proposal under any bankruptcy or insolvency legislation, been subject to any proceeding, arrangement or compromise with creditors, or had a receiver, receiver-manager or trustee appointed to manage your assets?	❏	❏
B.	Are you now an undischarged bankrupt?	❏	❏

Part 4: DISTRIBUTIONS

		Yes	No
C.	To the best of your knowledge, are you currently or have you *ever* been a director, officer, promoter, insider, or control person of an issuer, in any Canadian or foreign jurisdiction, at the time of events, or for a period of 12 months preceding the time of events, where the issuer:		
	(i) has made a petition in bankruptcy, a voluntary assignment in bankruptcy, a proposal under any bankruptcy or insolvency legislation, been subject to any proceeding, arrangement or compromise with creditors or had a receiver, receiver-manager or trustee appointed to manage the issuer's assets?	❑	❑
	(ii) is now an undischarged bankrupt?	❑	❑

8. Proceedings

		Yes	No
	If you answer "YES" to any item in Question 8, you must provide complete details in an attachment.		
A.	Current proceedings by securities regulatory authority or self regulatory entity.		
	Are you now, in any Canadian or foreign jurisdiction, the subject of:		
	(i) a notice of hearing or similar notice issued by an SRA or SRE?	❑	❑
	(ii) a proceeding of or, to your knowledge, an investigation by, an SRA or SRE?	❑	❑
	(iii) settlement discussions or negotiations for settlement of any nature or kind whatsoever with an SRA or SRE?	❑	❑
B.	Prior proceedings by securities regulatory authority or self regulatory entity. Have you *ever*:		
	(i) been reprimanded, suspended, fined, been the subject of an administrative penalty, or been the subject of any proceedings of any kind whatsoever, in any Canadian or foreign jurisdiction, by an SRA or SRE?	❑	❑
	(ii) had a registration or licence for the trading of securities, exchange or commodity futures contracts, real estate, insurance or mutual fund products cancelled, refused, restricted or suspended by an SRA or SRE?	❑	❑
	(iii) been prohibited or disqualified by an SRA or SRE under securities, corporate or any other legislation from acting as a director or officer of a reporting issuer or been prohibited or restricted by an SRA or SRE from acting as a director, officer or employee of, or an agent or consultant to, a reporting issuer?	❑	❑
	(iv) had a cease trading or similar order issued against you or an order issued against you by an SRA or SRE that denied you the right to use any statutory prospectus or registration exemption?	❑	❑
	(v) had any other proceeding of any kind taken against you by an SRA or SRE?	❑	❑
C.	Settlement agreement(s)		
	Have you ever entered into a settlement agreement with an SRA, SRE, attorney general or comparable official or body, in any Canadian or foreign jurisdiction, in a matter that involved actual or alleged fraud, theft, deceit, misrepresentation, conspiracy, breach of trust, breach of fiduciary duty, insider trading, unregistered trading in securities or exchange or commodity futures contracts, illegal distributions, failure to disclose material facts or changes or similar conduct, or any other settlement agreement with respect to any other violation of securities legislation in a Canadian or foreign jurisdiction or the rules, by-laws or policies of any SRE?	❑	❑
D.	To the best of your knowledge, are you now or have you ever been a director, officer, promoter, insider, or control person of an issuer at the time of such event, in any Canadian or foreign jurisdiction, for which a securities regulatory authority or self-regulatory entity has:		
	(i) refused, restricted, suspended or cancelled the registration or licensing of an issuer to trade securities, exchange or commodity futures contracts, or to sell or trade real estate, insurance or mutual fund products?	❑	❑
	(ii) issued a cease trade or similar order or imposed an administrative penalty of any nature or kind whatsoever against the issuer, other than an order for failure to file financial statements that was revoked within 30 days of its issuance?	❑	❑
	(iii) refused a receipt for a prospectus or other offering document, denied any application for listing or quotation or any other similar application, or issued an order that denied the issuer the right to use any statutory prospectus or registration exemptions?	❑	❑
	(iv) issued a notice of hearing, notice as to a proceeding or similar notice against the issuer?	❑	❑

		Yes	No

(v) commenced any other proceeding of any kind against the issuer, including a trading halt, suspension or delisting of the issuer, in connection with an alleged or actual contravention of an SRA's or SRE's rules, regulations, policies or other requirements, but excluding halts imposed (i) in the normal course for proper dissemination of information, or (ii) pursuant to a business combination, reverse takeover or similar transaction involving the issuer that is regulated by an SRE or SRA, including a qualifying transaction, reverse takeover or change of business involving the issuer (as those terms are defined in the TSX Venture Corporate Finance Manual as amended from time to time)? ☐ ☐

(vi) entered into a settlement agreement with the issuer in a matter that involved actual or alleged fraud, theft, deceit, misrepresentation, conspiracy, breach of trust, breach of fiduciary duty, insider trading, unregistered trading in securities or exchange or commodity futures contracts, illegal distributions, failure to disclose material facts or changes or similar conduct by the issuer, or any other violation of securities legislation or the rules, by-laws or policies of an SRE? ☐ ☐

		Yes	No

9. Civil proceedings

If you answer "YES" to any item in Question 9, you *must* provide complete details in an attachment.

A. Judgment, garnishment and injunctions

Has a court in any Canadian or foreign jurisdiction:

(i) rendered a judgment, ordered garnishment or issued an injunction or similar ban (whether by consent or otherwise) against *you* in a claim based in whole or in part on fraud, theft, deceit, misrepresentation, conspiracy, breach of trust, breach of fiduciary duty, insider trading, unregistered trading, illegal distributions, failure to disclose material facts or changes, or allegations of similar conduct? ☐ ☐

(ii) rendered a judgment, ordered garnishment or issued an injunction or similar ban (whether by consent or otherwise) against *an issuer,* of which you are currently or have ever been a director, officer, promoter, insider or control person in a claim based in whole or in part on fraud, theft, deceit, misrepresentation, conspiracy, breach of trust, breach of fiduciary duty, insider trading, unregistered trading, illegal distributions, failure to disclose material facts or changes, or allegations of similar conduct? ☐ ☐

B. Current claims

(i) Are *you* now subject, in any Canadian or foreign jurisdiction, to a claim that is based in whole or in part on actual or alleged fraud, theft, deceit, misrepresentation, conspiracy, breach of trust, breach of fiduciary duty, insider trading, unregistered trading, illegal distributions, failure to disclose material facts or changes, or allegations of similar conduct? ☐ ☐

(ii) To the best of your knowledge, are you currently or have you ever been a director, officer, promoter, insider or control person of *an issuer* that is now subject, in any Canadian or foreign jurisdiction, to a claim that is based in whole or in part on actual or alleged fraud, theft, deceit, misrepresentation, conspiracy, breach of trust, breach of fiduciary duty, insider trading, unregistered trading, illegal distributions, failure to disclose material facts or changes, or allegations of similar conduct? ☐ ☐

C. Settlement agreement

(i) Have *you* ever entered into a settlement agreement, in any Canadian or foreign jurisdiction, in a civil action that involved actual or alleged fraud, theft, deceit, misrepresentation, conspiracy, breach of trust, breach of fiduciary duty, insider trading, unregistered trading, illegal distributions, failure to disclose material facts or changes, or allegations of similar conduct? ☐ ☐

(ii) To the best of your knowledge, are you currently or have you ever been a director, officer, promoter, insider or control person of *an issuer* that has entered into a settlement agreement, in any Canadian or foreign jurisdiction, in a civil action that involved actual or alleged fraud, theft, deceit, misrepresentation, conspiracy, breach of trust, breach of fiduciary duty, insider trading, unregistered trading, illegal distributions, failure to disclose material facts or changes, or allegations of similar conduct? ☐ ☐

		Yes	No

10. Involvement with other entities

A. Has your employment in a sales, investment or advisory capacity with any employer engaged in the sale of real estate, insurance or mutual funds ever been suspended or terminated for cause? If yes, attach full particulars. ☐ ☐

		Yes	No
B.	Has your employment with a firm or company registered under the securities laws of any Canadian or foreign jurisdiction as a securities dealer, broker, investment advisor or under-writer, ever been suspended or terminated for cause? If yes, attach full particulars.	❑	❑
C.	Has your employment as an officer of an issuer ever been suspended or terminated for cause? If yes, attach full particulars.	❑	❑

Certificate and Consent

I, ... hereby certify that:

(Please Print — Name of Individual)

(a) I have read and understand the questions, cautions, acknowledgement and consent in the personal information form to which this certificate and consent is attached or of which this certificate and consent forms a part (the "Form"), and the answers I have given to the questions in the Form and in any attachments to it are correct, except where stated to be answered to the best of my knowledge, in which case I believe the answers to be correct;

(b) I have been provided with and have read and understand the Personal Information Collection Policy (the "Personal Information Collection Policy") attached hereto as Schedule 1;

(c) I consent to the collection, use and disclosure by the funding portal of the information in the Form and to the collection, use and disclosure by the funding portal of further personal information in accordance with the Personal Information Collection Policy;

(d) I understand that the funding portal may use a third party to conduct the criminal record and background checks and I consent to the use and disclosure by the funding portal to the third party of the information in the Form and to the collection, use and disclosure by the third party of the information in the Form and of further personal information in order to provide these services to the funding portal;

(e) I am aware that I am providing the Form to a funding portal, who upon request, will provide the Form and all further personal information in accordance with the Personal Information Collection Policy to the securities regulatory authorities or regulators (as defined in section 1.1 of National Instrument 14-101 *Definitions*) and consent to such disclosure to, and the collection, use and disclosure by, the securities regulatory authorities or regulators and I understand that I am under the jurisdiction of the securities regulatory authorities and the regulators to which this Form may be provided, and that it is a breach of securities legislation to provide false or misleading information to the securities regulatory authorities and the regulators.

....

Date

....

Signature of Person Completing this Form

Schedule 1 — Personal Information Collection Policy

The funding portal collects, uses and discloses personal information from every director, executive officer, and promoter of an issuer relying on the crowdfunding prospectus exemption for the purpose of complying with its obligations under Multilateral Instrument 45-108 *Crowdfunding* ("*MI 45-108*"), including conducting criminal record and background checks; verifying the information provided in the Personal Information Form and Authorization to Collect, Use and Disclose Personal Information (the "*Personal Information Form*"); reviewing the crowdfunding offering document and other materials for incorrect, incomplete and misleading information; identifying whether the issuer or any of its directors, executive officers, or promoters has been convicted of an offence related to or has entered into a settlement agreement in a matter that involved fraud or securities law violations; and making a good faith determination as to whether (i) the business of the issuer may not be conducted with integrity; (ii) the issuer is not complying with one or more of its obligations under MI 45-108; and (iii) the crowdfunding offering document and other materials contain a statement or information that constitutes a misrepresentation or an untrue statement of a material fact.

You understand that by signing the certificate and consent in the Personal Information Form, you are consenting to the funding portal collecting and using your personal information in the Personal Information Form, as well as any other information that may be necessary for the purposes described above (the "Information").

You also understand and agree that the Information the funding portal collects about you may also be disclosed, as permitted by law, where its use and disclosure is for the purposes described above. The funding portal may use a third party to conduct the criminal record and background checks and to process the Information, but when this happens, the third party will be carefully selected and obligated to comply with the limited use restrictions described above and with applicable privacy legislation. You understand that by signing the certificate and consent in the Personal Information Form, you are consenting to the funding portal disclosing your Information to, and to the collection, use and disclosure of your Information by, the third party service provider for the purposes of providing these services to the funding portal.

You understand that the funding portal, upon request of the securities regulatory authorities or regulators (as defined in section 1.1 of National Instrument 14-101 *Definitions*), is required to deliver the Information to the securities regulatory authorities or regulators because the issuer has relied upon the crowdfunding prospectus exemption. The securities regulatory authorities and the regulators collect, use and disclose the Information under the authority granted to them under provincial securities legislation for the purpose of enabling the securities regulatory authorities and regulators to administer and enforce provincial securities legislation. You understand that by signing the certificate and consent in the Personal Information Form, you are consenting to disclosure of your Information by the funding portal to the securities regulatory authorities and regulators upon their request.

You also understand that you have a right to be informed of the existence of personal information about you that is kept by funding portals, securities regulatory authorities and regulators, that you have the right to request access to that information, and that you have the right to request that such information be corrected, subject to the provisions of the applicable privacy legislation.

Warning: It is an offence to submit information that, in a material respect and at the time and in the light of the circumstances in which it is submitted, is misleading or untrue.

Questions

If you have any questions about the collection, use, and disclosure of the information you provide, you may contact the funding portal at: *[Instructions: Provide an address and telephone number where an individual who has provided personal information can contact the funding portal.]*

Companion Policy 45-108CP — Crowdfunding

Preamble to Companion Policy

Purpose of this Companion Policy

This Companion Policy sets out how the participating members of the Canadian Securities Administrators (**CSA**) (the "**participating CSA members**" or "**we**") interpret or apply the provisions of Multilateral Instrument 45-108 *Crowdfunding* (the "**Instrument**"), including the required forms, and related securities legislation.

The Instrument provides

    (a) in Part 2, a prospectus exemption for eligible crowdfunding issuers that wish to make a crowdfunding distribution,

    (b) in Part 3, the registration requirements for funding portals, and

    (c) in Part 4, who can grant exemptions from the Instrument.

References to the Instrument

Except for Part 1, all references in this Companion Policy to parts, divisions and sections are to the Instrument, unless otherwise noted. Any general guidance for a part or a division appears immediately after the reference to that part or division name. Any specific guidance on sections in the Instrument follows any general guidance. If there is no guidance for a part, division or section, the numbering in this Companion Policy will skip to the next provision that does have guidance.

Models of crowdfunding

Crowdfunding is a method of funding a project or venture through amounts of money raised from members of the public over the internet via an online portal. There are at least four examples of crowdfunding models:

    (a) the <u>donation model</u>, which is the practice of the crowd donating to a project or venture in exchange for nothing of tangible value;

    (b) the <u>reward model</u>, which is the practice of the crowd donating to a project or venture in exchange for some tangible reward, perk or benefit;

    (c) the <u>pre-purchase model</u>, which is the practice of the crowd donating to a project or venture in exchange for a future tangible reward, such as a consumer product; and

    (d) the securities-based model, which is the practice of the crowd investing in an issuer and its business in exchange for the issuer's securities, which are often equity securities but may include other types of securities, including debt securities.

Applicability of securities legislation

In this Companion Policy, when we refer to a "crowdfunding offering", we are referring to a distribution of securities made in reliance on the crowdfunding prospectus exemption through a funding portal as described in the Instrument.

Crowdfunding activities that are limited to the donation model, reward model and/or pre-purchase model generally will not constitute or involve a distribution of securities. However, crowdfunding offerings using the securities-based model will involve an offering of securities. Issuers that wish to make a crowdfunding offering using the securities-based model will always be subject to securities legislation.

Securities-based and non-securities-based crowdfunding

An issuer may wish to include both securities and non-securities rewards or benefits in a crowdfunding offering. Permitting an issuer to do so may enable an issuer to derive the benefits of both securities-based and non-securities based crowdfunding. An issuer must disclose in item 5.1 of the crowdfunding offering document a description of any additional rewards or benefits being offered that are not securities.

All distributions and other trades are subject to securities legislation

The securities legislation of a local jurisdiction applies to any distribution of a security in that jurisdiction, whether or not the issuer of the security is an issuer in that jurisdiction. A person or company who engages in a distribution must comply with the securities legislation of each jurisdiction in which the distribution occurs. That may include the requirement that such person or company be registered under securities legislation.

A funding portal that carries on business in a jurisdiction (either by facilitating offerings of issuers in that jurisdiction and/or by facilitating offerings to investors in that jurisdiction) must be registered in that jurisdiction.

Multi-jurisdictional distributions

A distribution can occur in more than one jurisdiction. If it does, the person or company conducting the distribution must comply with the securities legislation of each jurisdiction in which the distribution occurs. For example, a distribution from a person or company in Québec to a purchaser in Ontario may be considered a distribution in both jurisdictions.

PART 1 — DEFINITIONS AND INTERPRETATION

Defined terms used in this Companion Policy have the meaning ascribed to them in the Instrument unless otherwise noted.

Terms defined or interpreted in other instruments

    (1) <u>Director</u> — The term "director" referred to in Part 3 is defined in the provincial securities legislation of each of the participating CSA members.

    (2) <u>Officer</u> — The term "officer" referred to in Part 3 is defined in the provincial securities legislation of each of the participating CSA members.

    (3) <u>Principal Regulator</u> — A registered dealer funding portal's principal regulator generally will be determined in accordance with section 4A.1 of Multilateral Instrument 11-102 Passport System. This means that the principal regulator will usually be the securities regulatory authority or regulator in the jurisdiction where the funding portal's head office is located.

    (4) <u>Funding portal</u> — There are two types of funding portals that can facilitate distributions of securities in reliance on the crowdfunding prospectus exemption:

        (a) a funding portal registered in the category of restricted dealer and defined in the Instrument as a restricted dealer funding portal; or

        (b) a funding portal registered in the category of investment dealer or exempt market dealer and defined in the Instrument as a registered dealer funding portal.

    (a) Restricted dealer funding portal

The restricted dealer category is described in paragraph 7.1(2)(e) of National Instrument 31-103 *Registration Requirements, Exemptions and Ongoing Registrant Obligations* (**NI 31-103**) and permits specialized dealers or other intermediaries with an unconventional business model to carry on a limited trading business, subject to terms and conditions restricting their activities. The restricted dealer funding portal is intended to be a specialized type of restricted dealer with limited permitted dealing activities as described in section 41 [*Permitted dealing activities*]. Accordingly, the regulatory framework for a restricted dealer funding portal described in Part 3, including the exemptions from certain usual registrant requirements described in subparagraph 21(b)(ii) [*Restricted dealer funding portal*], is not available to other types of registrants that facilitate the sale of securities through an online portal. A restricted dealer funding portal will not be permitted to obtain dual registration in another registration category.

Except in Ontario, a restricted dealer funding portal may be affiliated with another registered dealer, registered adviser or registered investment fund manager. A restricted dealer funding portal that is affiliated with another registered firm must establish internal controls and appropriate policies and procedures to manage the risks associated with operating an affiliated restricted dealer funding portal. A restricted dealer funding portal should refer to section 13.4 of Companion Policy 31-103 *Registration Requirements, Exemptions and Ongoing Registrant Obligations* (**31-103CP**) to consider ways to identify and respond to conflicts of interest, including avoiding the conflict if it is significant and cannot be managed appropriately. In addition, a restricted dealer funding portal should be aware of other CSA guidance on registrant obligations to identify and respond to conflicts of interest.

(b) Registered dealer funding portal

We recognize that other categories of registered dealers, such as investment dealers and exempt market dealers, may operate online portals that facilitate distributions of securities in reliance on other prospectus exemptions, such as the accredited investor exemption in section 2.3 of National Instrument 45-106 *Prospectus Exemptions* (**NI 45-106**) or the offering memorandum exemption in section 2.9 of NI 45-106. An investment dealer or exempt market dealer may facilitate distributions of securities in reliance on the crowdfunding prospectus exemption; however, they are required to comply with all of their registrant obligations under securities legislation and Divisions 1 and 2 of Part 3.

(5) <u>Registered individual</u> — The term "registered individual" is defined in NI 31-103 and ordinarily refers to an individual who is registered as the ultimate designated person (**UDP**), chief compliance officer (**CCO**) or a dealing or advising representative of a registered firm. A restricted dealer funding portal is not permitted to provide recommendations or advice to purchasers. Therefore, we do not expect a restricted dealer funding portal will require an individual registered as a dealing or advising representative.

PART 2 — CROWDFUNDING PROSPECTUS EXEMPTION

Division 1: — Distribution requirements

Reporting and non-reporting issuers — The definition of "eligible crowdfunding issuer" in section 1 [*Definitions*] outlines certain requirements for the issuer to be eligible to rely on the crowdfunding prospectus exemption. Subject to satisfying these requirements, the crowdfunding prospectus exemption is available to both reporting issuers and non-reporting issuers.

5.1 Crowdfunding prospectus exemption — (1) <u>Distribution period</u> — The Instrument contemplates a distribution period that, in accordance with paragraph 5(1)(a) [*Crowdfunding prospectus exemption*], must end no later than 90 days after the date the issuer first offers its securities to purchasers under the crowdfunding prospectus exemption. If an issuer cannot complete an offering within the distribution period, the distribution period will expire. An issuer may commence a new crowdfunding offering so long as the issuer is in compliance with subsection 5(2) [*Crowdfunding prospectus exemption*].

<u>Issuer group limit</u> — Paragraph 5(1)(b) [*Crowdfunding prospectus exemption*] imposes a $1,500,000 limit on the aggregate proceeds that can be raised by an issuer group under the crowdfunding prospectus exemption within the 12-month period ending on the last day of the distribution period. For example, suppose an issuer group consists of Issuer A, Issuer B and Issuer C. Issuer A proposes to distribute securities under the crowdfunding prospectus exemption and the last day of the distribution period will be March 15, 2015. In this case, the 12-month period to which the $1,500,000 limit applies will commence on March 16, 2014 and end on March 15, 2015. If Issuer B has raised $600,000 under the crowdfunding prospectus exemption during that same 12 month period (i.e., March 16, 2014 to March 15, 2015), the maximum amount Issuer A could raise under the crowdfunding prospectus exemption will be $900,000 ($1,500,000 minus $600,000).

If, in addition, Issuer C proposes to raise a maximum of $300,000 in a concurrent distribution under the crowdfunding prospectus exemption that will end on or prior to March 15, 2015, since this is within the same 12 month period, the maximum amount Issuer A could now raise under the crowdfunding prospectus exemption will be $600,000 ($1,500,000 minus ($600,000 + $300,000)) in order to ensure compliance with the $1,500,000 offering limit for the issuer group.

<u>Investment Limits</u> — Paragraphs 5(1)(c) and (d) [*Crowdfunding prospectus exemption*] impose investment limits on purchasers of securities distributed under the crowdfunding prospectus exemption. In all the jurisdictions, a purchaser that is not an accredited investor is subject to an investment limit of $2,500 per distribution and in Ontario, such purchaser is also subject to an annual investment limit of $10,000 for all distributions made in reliance on the crowdfunding prospectus exemption in the same calendar year. In all jurisdictions, an accredited investor is subject to an investment limit of $25,000 per distribution and in Ontario, an accredited investor is also subject to an annual investment limit of $50,000 for all distributions made in reliance on the crowdfunding prospectus exemption in the same calendar year. In Ontario, an investor that is a permitted client is not subject to an investment limit.

(2) The crowdfunding prospectus exemption is not available to an issuer if any of the conditions in subsection 5(2) [*Crowdfunding prospectus exemption*] apply. For example, an issuer that uses the proceeds to invest in, merge with or acquire an unspecified business, commonly referred to as a blind pool, is excluded from using the crowdfunding prospectus exemption.

6. Conditions for closing of the distribution — <u>Concurrent distributions</u> — Eligible securities are defined in section 1 [*Definitions*]. An eligible crowdfunding issuer can distribute securities under other prospectus exemptions, such as the accredited investor exemption in section 2.3 of NI 45-106 or the offering memorandum exemption in section 2.9 of NI 45-106, during the distribution period. Securities distributed under other prospectus exemptions do not need to have the same price, terms and conditions as those distributed under the crowdfunding prospectus exemption. However, the issuer must ensure compliance with the conditions of the prospectus exemption being relied upon for the distribution. Information about any concurrent distribution, including a concurrent distribution by a member of the issuer group, must be disclosed in the crowdfunding offering document.

<u>Risk acknowledgement form</u> — The issuer must ensure upon closing of the distribution that they receive from the funding portal a Form 45-108F2 *Risk Acknowledgement* (**Form 45-108F2**) from each purchaser in which the purchaser has positively responded to each question in Form 45-108F2.

<u>Confirmation of investment limits</u> — In each jurisdiction other than Ontario, the issuer must ensure upon closing of the distribution that they receive from the funding portal confirmation that the purchaser is an accredited investor if the acquisition cost is greater than $2,500. In Ontario, the issuer must receive a Form 45-108F3 *Confirmation of investment limits* (**Form 45-108F3**) for each purchaser regardless of the acquisition cost to the purchaser.

Part 4: DISTRIBUTIONS

<u>Closing of the distribution</u> — If the closing of the distribution does not take place within 30 days of the end of the distribution period, the funding portal is required to promptly return to the purchaser all funds and assets received from a purchaser in connection with the distribution under the crowdfunding prospectus exemption.

9. Liability for misrepresentation — reporting issuers — In Ontario, the crowdfunding offering document required to be filed by an issuer under the Instrument is considered to be an offering memorandum and the rights available under section 130.1 of the *Securities Act* (Ontario) apply. Refer to Ontario Securities Commission (**OSC**) Rule 45-501 *Ontario Prospectus and Registration Exemptions* and the related Companion Policy for more information. Under section 9 [*Liability for misrepresentation — reporting issuers*], an issuer must provide a purchaser with a contractual right equivalent to the right in section 130.1 of the *Securities Act* (Ontario) for any materials made available to a purchaser in addition to the crowdfunding offering document, if the securities legislation of the jurisdiction in which a purchaser resides does not provide a comparable right.

In Québec, the crowdfunding offering document and any other materials that are made available to purchasers by a reporting issuer are documents authorized by the Autorité des marchés financiers for use in lieu of a prospectus in regards to which rights of action established in section 217 to 221 of *Securities Act* (Québec) may be exercised.

In Nova Scotia, the crowdfunding offering document required to be filed by an issuer under the Instrument is considered to be an offering memorandum and the rights available under section 138 of the *Securities Act* (Nova Scotia) apply. Refer to Nova Scotia Securities Commission Rule 45-501 *Statutory Liability for Misrepresentations in an Offering Memorandum Under Certain Exemptions* from the Prospectus Requirement and the related Companion Policy for more information. Under section 9 [*Liability for misrepresentation — reporting issuers*], an issuer must provide a purchaser with a contractual right equivalent to the right in section 138 of the *Securities Act* (Nova Scotia) for any materials made available to a purchaser in addition to the crowdfunding offering document.

10. Liability for untrue statement — non-reporting issuers — The crowdfunding offering document required to be filed by an issuer that is not a reporting issuer must contain a contractual right of action against the issuer for rescission and damages that is available to the purchaser if the crowdfunding offering document or other permitted materials made available to the purchaser contains an untrue statement of a material fact.

11. Advertising and general solicitation — An eligible crowdfunding issuer cannot advertise the distribution or solicit purchasers, except as permitted in subsection 11(2) [*Advertising and general solicitation*]. An issuer may inform purchasers, including the issuer's customers and clients, that the issuer is proposing to offer its securities under the crowdfunding prospectus exemption and refer the customers and clients to the funding portal facilitating the distribution. This direction can be provided through the use of social media or in paper format. However, in all cases, the direction must be limited to directing the purchasers, including the issuer's customers and clients, to the funding portal's online platform to obtain relevant information about the distribution.

We anticipate that issuers will want to use social media to harness the "wisdom of the crowd" in a crowdfunding offering. Although an issuer cannot advertise the distribution or solicit purchasers, an issuer may participate in communication channels or discussion boards to encourage purchasers to discuss the crowdfunding distribution, if the funding portal establishes one. An issuer is reminded that it cannot post any statement or information on the funding portal's online platform that is inconsistent with the crowdfunding offering document or the Instrument.

13. Commissions or fees — Section 13 [*Commissions or fees*] prohibits payment of a commission, finder's fee, referral fee or similar payment by any person or company in the issuer group to any person or company in connection with a crowdfunding distribution, other than to a funding portal. This is meant to mitigate against potential conflicts of interest. However, this restriction is not intended to prohibit payments to persons or companies as compensation for their services to an issuer in preparing materials in connection with a crowdfunding offering, such as accounting or legal fees.

Division 2 — Ongoing disclosure requirements for non-reporting issuers

Division 2 [*Ongoing disclosure requirements for non-reporting issuers*] prescribes ongoing disclosure obligations for non-reporting issuers that distribute securities under the crowdfunding prospectus exemption.

Non-reporting issuers are required to make available to the purchaser certain ongoing disclosure documents. These include annual financial statements, notices disclosing the use of proceeds, and in New Brunswick, Nova Scotia and Ontario, notices of specified key events. We anticipate issuers generally will choose to make these documents available to purchasers electronically. However, an issuer may also make these documents available in paper format. We expect an issuer to take reasonable steps to ensure that all purchasers receive or have access to the documents promptly.

We consider ongoing disclosure documents to have been made reasonably available to each holder of a security acquired under the crowdfunding prospectus exemption if the documents are made available through the funding portal or are mailed to security holders, or if security holders receive an electronic notice that the annual financial statements, the notices disclosing the use of proceeds, and in New Brunswick, Nova Scotia and Ontario, the notices of specified key events can be viewed on a public website of the issuer or a website accessible by all holders of securities of the issuer that were acquired under the crowdfunding prospectus exemption (such as a password protected website).

For reporting issuers that distribute securities under the crowdfunding prospectus exemption, all applicable continuous disclosure obligations under securities legislation continue to apply.

16. Annual financial statements — <u>What constitutes an issuer's first financial year?</u> — The first financial year of an issuer commences on the date of its incorporation or organization and ends at the close of that financial year.

<u>What financial years need to be audited or reviewed?</u> — If an issuer is required to have an auditor's report or review report accompany its financial statements in accordance with paragraph 16(2)(a) [*Annual financial statements*], the financial statements for the most recent period and the comparative period, if any, are both required to be audited or are both required to be reviewed.

<u>Statement required in annual financial statements that have not been audited or reviewed</u> — Subsection 16(8) [*Annual financial statements*] requires that if an issuer's annual financial statements are not accompanied by an auditor's report or a review report prepared by a public accountant, the financial statements must include a statement which discloses that fact. As set out in subsection 16(2) [*Annual financial statements*], an issuer's annual financial statements are not required to be audited or reviewed by a public accountant if the issuer has raised less than $250,000 under one or more prospectus exemptions from the date of its formation until the end of its most recently completed financial year.

<u>What financial reporting framework is identified in the financial statements and in any accompanying auditor's report or review report?</u> — If an issuer's financial statements are prepared in accordance with Canadian GAAP for publicly accountable enterprises and include an unreserved statement of compliance with IFRS, the auditor's report or review report must refer to IFRS as the applicable financial reporting framework.

There are two options for referring to the financial reporting framework in the applicable financial statements and accompanying auditor's report or review report:

    (a) refer only to IFRS in the notes to the financial statements and in the auditor's report or review report; or

    (b) refer to both IFRS and Canadian GAAP in the notes to the financial statements and in the auditor's report or review report.

<u>Non-GAAP financial measures</u> — An issuer that intends to disclose non-GAAP financial measures, including in its crowdfunding offering document, should refer to CSA guidance for a discussion on staff's expectations concerning the use of these measures.

17. Annual disclosure of use of proceeds — (1) Section 17 [*Annual disclosure of use of proceeds*] requires that an issuer's annual financial statements be accompanied by a notice that discloses in detail, how the gross proceeds raised by the issuer in a distribution under the crowdfunding prospectus exemption have been spent. The information in the notice is to be provided as at the date of the issuer's most recently completed financial year.

While specific disclosure is not prescribed for the notice, issuers should carefully consider whether the disclosure being provided contains sufficient detail for a security holder to understand how the proceeds have been used. For example, the level of detail expected in the notice of proceeds could include a breakdown of the amount of proceeds that were allocated to fees (including management or service provider fees), salaries or other compensation paid, asset purchases made or development costs.

If, at the date of the notice, there are funds raised by the issuer in a distribution under the crowdfunding prospectus exemption that have not been used, the notice should disclose that fact as well as the amount of the unused proceeds. The amount of the proceeds used together with the amount of unused proceeds, if any, should equal the gross proceeds raised by the issuer in the distribution under the crowdfunding prospectus exemption.

We expect the actual use of the proceeds as disclosed in the notice to be consistent with the issuer's intended use of proceeds as disclosed in the crowdfunding offering document.

If the proceeds of a crowdfunding distribution have been distributed to an entity that is related to the issuer (for example, an issuer in the same corporate structure), then the issuer should provide disclosure as to how the proceeds were used by that entity.

18. Notice of specified key events — In addition to annual financial statements and the notice of how the proceeds raised under the crowdfunding prospectus exemption have been used, non-reporting issuers that issue securities in reliance on the crowdfunding prospectus exemption in New Brunswick, Nova Scotia and Ontario must also make available a notice of specified key events to each holder of a security acquired under the crowdfunding prospectus exemption, within 10 days of the occurrence of the event. These events are considered to be significant changes in the business of the issuer that purchasers should be notified of. This requirement is in addition to any similar requirement under corporate law and also applies to non-reporting issuers with non-corporate structures, such as trusts and partnerships.

In making a determination as to whether an issuer's industry has changed, issuers may consider whether they would identify a different industry category on Form 45-106F1 *Report of Exempt Distribution* than the category previously identified.

A non-reporting issuer must continue to provide notice of the specified key events, if applicable, until the earliest of the following events: (i) the issuer becomes a reporting issuer; (ii) the issuer has completed a winding up or dissolution; (iii) the securities of the issuer are beneficially owned, directly or indirectly, by fewer than 51 security holders worldwide.

PART 3 — REQUIREMENTS FOR FUNDING PORTALS

Division 1 — Registration requirements, general

Division 1 [*Registration requirements, general*] sets out the registration requirements for both a restricted dealer funding portal and a registered dealer funding portal.

21. Restricted dealer funding portal — A restricted dealer funding portal and a registered individual of a restricted dealer funding portal must comply with the requirements set out in Part 3.

Although a restricted dealer funding portal is not required to comply with section 13.3 of NI 31-103 or collect client specific know your client information as contemplated by paragraph 13.2(2)(c) of NI 31-103, a restricted dealer funding portal is still required to establish the identity of, and to conduct due diligence on its clients under the general know-your-client obligation set out in section 13.2 of NI 31-103.

22. Registered dealer funding portal — A crowdfunding distribution must be made through a single funding portal. A registered dealer who currently distributes securities online under other prospectus exemptions, such as the accredited investor exemption in section 2.3 of NI 45-106 or the offering memorandum exemption in section 2.9 of NI 45-106, will already have in place the infrastructure required to facilitate distributions of securities under the crowdfunding prospectus exemption through an online platform. However, these registered dealers will be required to ensure they have the necessary policies and procedures in place to comply with Part 3, as applicable. For those registered dealers who do not currently distribute securities online and intend to use the crowdfunding prospectus exemption, they must establish an online funding portal to distribute the securities under the crowdfunding prospectus exemption in accordance with the Instrument.

A registered dealer that proposes to distribute securities under the Instrument must file a Form 33-109F5 *Change of Registration Information* that describes the change in its business operations.

Division 2 — Registration requirements, funding portals

General

Although a funding portal enters into a contractual relationship with an eligible crowdfunding issuer, the funding portal also has a relationship with a purchaser investing through the funding portal. These purchasers are clients of the funding portal. A funding portal and its registered individuals must deal fairly, honestly and in good faith with a purchaser. This is consistent with the obligation imposed on all registered dealers and advisers under securities legislation. As a registrant, we expect a funding portal to follow the letter of the law and also the spirit of the law. For example, a funding portal that requires a purchaser to sign an agreement that contains an inappropriate waiver of liability or that attempts to transfer its responsibilities to the purchaser, is engaging in conduct that is not consistent with the principle of dealing fairly, honestly and in good faith with a purchaser.

A funding portal must be aware of and act in compliance with the terms of the exemption being relied upon for the trade or distribution of the security. For example, the funding portal must confirm and validate that the purchaser is investing within the investment limits set out in the Instrument.

23. Restricted dealing activities — (1) Section 23 [*Restricted dealing activities*] provides that a funding portal and a registered individual of a funding portal must not allow an issuer access to the funding portal if the issuer is a "related issuer" of the funding portal. The definition of a "related issuer" is described in National Instrument 33-105 *Underwriting Conflicts* (**NI 33-105**) and generally refers to a situation where there is cross-ownership between an issuer and a registrant. Subsection 1.2(2) of NI 33-105 provides that an entity is a related issuer to another entity if one of them is an "influential security holder" of the other or if each of them is a related issuer of the same third party.

If a funding portal proposes to allow an issuer that is a connected issuer access to the funding portal, the funding portal should ensure that the issuer's offering documents include the disclosure required by Appendix C to NI 33-105. The definition of a "connected issuer" is described in NI 33-105 and generally refers to a situation where an issuer may not be a related issuer of the registrant, but has some other relationship with the registrant that would cause a reasonable investor to question whether the registrant and the issuer are independent of each other for purposes of the distribution. Refer to NI 33-105 and the related guidance in Companion Policy 33-105CP for more information.

23. (2) A funding portal may accept securities of an issuer as payment of portal access fees or other similar fees, provided that the payment by the issuer does not result in the funding portal holding securities of the issuer that exceed the limit set out in subsection 23(2) [*Restricted dealing activities*]. However, an investment by a funding portal in an issuer that intends to distribute securities through the funding portal, including an investment in the form of securities accepted as payment for fees, may give rise to a conflict of interest. Accordingly, we expect the funding portal to comply with the conflicts of interest provisions in Division 2 of Part 13 of NI 31-103 and related provisions in 31-103CP.

24. **Advertising and general solicitation** — A funding portal cannot advertise the distribution or solicit purchasers, except as permitted in subsection 24(2) [*Advertising and general solicitation*]. Any solicitation or marketing activities, either in print or electronic form that targets specific individuals in connection with a distribution under the crowdfunding prospectus exemption would be a contravention of section 24 [*Advertising and general solicitation*].

A funding portal is not permitted to recommend or endorse a particular issuer or distribution, which includes accepting payment or other benefits from an issuer to highlight or showcase the issuer or its distribution. Such conduct would be considered to be inconsistent with the restriction in section 24 [*Advertising and general solicitation*]. However, a funding portal may advertise its business operations. For example, a funding portal may advertise that it is in the business of distributing securities under the crowdfunding prospectus exemption.

25. **Access to funding portal** — Section 25 [*Access to funding portal*] requires a funding portal to obtain a Form 45-108F5 *Personal Information Form and Authorization to Collect, Use and Disclose Personal Information* (**Form 45-108F5**) from each director, executive officer and promoter of an issuer prior to allowing the issuer access to the funding portal for the purposes of posting a distribution.

Funding portals should ensure all questions in Form 45-108F5 have been answered and additional details provided, where necessary.

At a minimum, we expect the following checks to be conducted by a funding portal:

    (a) regarding issuers:

        (i) the existence of the issuer and its business registration, including a review of the issuer's constating documents;

        (ii) securities and disciplinary enforcement history checks;

        (iii) bankruptcy check; and

        (iv) court record check, where available; and

    (b) regarding directors, executive officers and promoters of the issuer:

        (i) criminal record and securities and disciplinary enforcement history checks;

        (ii) bankruptcy check; and

        (iii) court record check, where available.

While we have outlined the minimum steps we expect a funding portal to take in conducting background checks on the issuer and criminal records and background checks on each director, executive officer and promoter of the issuer, a registered dealer funding portal must also take steps to ensure compliance with its regulatory obligations under securities legislation. For example, we would not consider the minimum checks and requirements outlined in this section by a registered dealer funding portal to be adequate compliance with its know-your-product obligation.

A funding portal may retain a third party to perform these checks. However, the funding portal is responsible and accountable for all functions that it outsources to a third party. A funding portal should have a written agreement that sets out the responsibilities of the parties to the arrangement. A funding portal should consider the guidance provided in Part 11 of 31-103CP on outsourcing.

26. **Issuer access agreement** — We expect the funding portal and the issuer to enter into a written agreement that sets out all material terms and conditions of the arrangement under which a funding portal will grant the issuer access to its online platform. Although section 26 [*Issuer access agreement*] prescribes certain minimum requirements that must be included in an issuer access agreement, we encourage the funding portal and the issuer to also set out other key terms and conditions that will govern the arrangement.

27. **Obligation to review materials of eligible crowdfunding issuer** — (2) If, after reviewing the crowdfunding offering document, the materials referred to in subsection 12(1) [*Additional distribution materials*], the personal information forms, the results of the criminal record and background checks, and any other information about the issuer or the distribution made available to the funding portal or of which the funding portal is aware, the funding portal determines the disclosure in the crowdfunding offering document and other materials referred to in subsection 12(1) [*Additional distribution materials*] is incorrect, incomplete or misleading, it must require the issuer to correct, complete or clarify the disclosure in the crowdfunding offering document and other permitted materials prior to posting on the funding portal's online platform. For example:

    (a) if an issuer's constating documents indicate that the "common shares" contain restrictions on voting or contain redemption rights that allow the issuer to redeem the shares in certain circumstances, or that insiders or promoters of the issuer hold another class of securities that have multiple votes, and the crowdfunding offering document does not contain this disclosure, the funding portal must not grant the issuer access to the funding portal for the purposes of distributing its securities until it is satisfied that the crowdfunding offering document accurately describes the securities being distributed, the capital structure of the issuer, including the percentage ownership of the outstanding securities of the issuer held by the insiders and promoters, and any rights not otherwise available to purchasers;

    (b) if an issuer is part of an issuer group, and the issuer's interest in the business or the assets of the business are owned through one or more subsidiaries, the funding portal should understand the features and risks of the capital structure of the issuer group and assess whether the issuer's disclosures adequately discloses these risks.

Nothing in the Instrument prevents a funding portal from establishing additional criteria that an issuer must satisfy or meet in order to distribute its securities through the funding portal. A funding portal should establish additional criteria or due diligence checks to grant or deny access by an issuer to its online platform for any reason, including any concern of the funding portal that:

(a) the issuer may not be financially responsible in the conduct of its business; or

(b) the issuer has not complied with, or is not complying with, securities legislation or the undertakings, terms and conditions agreed to by the issuer in connection with a distribution under the crowdfunding prospectus exemption or otherwise.

28. Denial of issuer access and termination — (1) Funding portals are expected to play a gatekeeper role in attempting to ensure that issuers comply with the requirements of the crowdfunding prospectus exemption and to maintain the integrity of the capital markets. We expect funding portals to have policies and procedures in place to carry out their gatekeeper function, including measures to reduce the risk of fraud in securities-based crowdfunding. These policies and procedures should include the steps a funding portal follows to review and assess the issuer, the distribution, the crowdfunding offering document and the materials described in subsection 12(1) [*Additional distribution materials*]. At a minimum, we expect a funding portal to:

* establish the identity of an issuer, such as obtaining and reviewing the issuer's articles of incorporation or other constating documents;

* determine the nature of the issuer's business; and

* review the responses provided in Form 45-108F5 and the results of the criminal record and background checks.

If, after reviewing the information provided to the funding portal under the Instrument and any other information about the issuer or the distribution made available to the funding portal or of which the funding portal is aware, the funding portal identifies any discrepancies or causes for concern about an issuer, its directors, executive officers or promoters, the distribution, the crowdfunding offering document or the materials described in subsection 12(1) [*Additional distribution materials*], the funding portal must make all reasonable inquiries to resolve the discrepancies or concerns. This may include asking additional questions of the issuer and its management and ensuring the answers provided resolve the concern to the satisfaction of the funding portal or obtaining and reviewing additional documentation. We expect the funding portal to consider the discrepancy or concern in its determination as to whether or not to grant an issuer access to its online platform.

We expect a funding portal to deny access to an issuer if based on the information the funding portal has, it appears to the funding portal that the issuer has not satisfied the conditions in subsection 28(1) [*Denial of issuer access and termination*]. For example, if it appears to the funding portal that upon a good faith determination the business of the issuer may not be conducted with integrity, including where the funding portal believes the issuer or the distribution is part of a scheme to defraud investors, the funding portal must deny the issuer access. If certain executive officers of the issuer reside in a jurisdiction where background checks and securities and disciplinary enforcement history checks are not readily available to the funding portal, it may determine that it is unable to assess whether the business of the issuer will be conducted with integrity, and thus must deny the issuer access to its platform.

32. Monitoring purchaser communications — A funding portal that establishes an online communication channel, such as a blog or chat room, should have detailed written policies and procedures that outline the steps the funding portal will take to ensure compliance with section 32 [*Monitoring purchaser communications*]. For example, a funding portal may require issuers and purchasers to register to use the online communication channel and each will be assigned a user code or client identifier that enables the funding portal to track the communications of each participant.

If, for example, a purchaser makes an incorrect statement on the blog that the price per share is too high at $50, when the crowdfunding offering document states the price per share is $10, the funding portal would not be required to remove the statement. However, the issuer would be permitted to correct the price through a statement on the blog that the price per share is $10. If, in another example, an issuer makes a statement on the blog that describes how its product works and that information was not disclosed in the crowdfunding offering document, then the funding portal must remove the statement as it is inconsistent with the crowdfunding offering document. However, in this example, an issuer could make a clarifying statement as to how its product works, if necessary, to address a misconception or misunderstanding expressed by a purchaser on the blog.

33. Online platform acknowledgement — Prior to a person or company entering a funding portal's online platform, the funding portal must take reasonable steps to confirm that the person or company understands the risks of investing in securities posted on the funding portal and is advised whether they will or will not receive suitability advice depending on the type of dealer operating the funding portal. We expect that these acknowledgements will be completed electronically through the funding portal and that the funding portal's books and records will include evidence that the funding portal has satisfied this obligation.

34. Purchaser requirements prior to purchase — Prior to a purchaser entering into an agreement to purchase securities under the crowdfunding prospectus exemption, a funding portal must obtain from a purchaser:

(a) a risk acknowledgment form in which the purchaser has positively answered all questions;

(b) except in Ontario, confirmation and validation that the purchaser is an accredited investor if the acquisition cost is greater than $2,500; and

(c) in Ontario, a confirmation of investment limits form and validation of the information contained in the form regardless of the acquisition cost to the purchaser.

A funding portal must not permit a purchaser to acquire securities of the issuer if the purchaser has responded negatively to any of the questions in the risk acknowledgement form.

We anticipate that (a) the risk acknowledgement form, (b) the confirmation and validation of the purchaser's investor status, and (c) where applicable, the confirmation of investment limits form will be completed online through the funding portal facilitating the distribution.

A funding portal should take reasonable steps to confirm that each purchaser proposing to participate in a crowdfunding distribution through its online platform understands and complies with the applicable investment limits. A funding portal must have appropriate policies and procedures in place to confirm and verify the purchaser's investor status, the applicable investment limits and whether the purchaser is in compliance with the applicable investment limits. In Ontario, these procedures must include obtaining a Form 45-108F3 from the purchaser prior to accepting any funds from the purchaser. The funding portal should review the risk acknowledgement form and in Ontario, also review the confirmation of investment limits form to ensure they have been properly completed and executed. If a purchaser specifies that it is an accredited investor or a permitted client, the funding portal will have to obtain further information from the purchaser in order to determine whether the purchaser has the requisite income or assets to meet the terms of the accredited investor or permitted client definition.

Division 3 — Additional requirements, restricted dealer funding portal

39. Prohibition on providing recommendations or advice — Section 39 [*Prohibition on providing recommendations or advice*] provides that a restricted dealer funding portal and a registered individual of the restricted dealer funding portal must not provide a recommendation or advice to a purchaser in connection with a distribution under the crowdfunding prospectus exemption or other trades in a security. This means a restricted dealer funding portal cannot tell a purchaser that the securities are a good investment, that the securities meet the purchaser's investment needs or objectives, or that the purchaser should, for whatever reason, buy the securities.

Some activities may be considered bona fide activities of a restricted dealer funding portal provided that a reasonable person would not construe those activities to be the restricted dealer funding portal providing a recommendation or advice to a purchaser. These activities could include:

(a) using objective criteria to limit the crowdfunding distributions on the funding portal if the objective criteria are disclosed on the funding portal and applied consistently to all distributions on the funding portal;

(b) providing general information and educational materials to purchasers about crowdfunding distributions if the information is presented in a fair, balanced and reasonable manner;

(c) providing search functions or other tools for purchasers to search, sort or categorize crowdfunding distributions available on the funding portal if the search functions are based on objective criteria;

(d) distributing information on the funding portal about a particular issuer or offering to a purchaser based on selection criteria identified by a purchaser; and

(e) providing communication channels or discussion boards to enable purchasers in a crowdfunding distribution to communicate with one another and with representatives of the issuer about a crowdfunding distribution displayed on the funding portal if a communication by a person can be traced back to its author and the funding portal complies with its obligations in section 32 [*Monitoring purchaser communication*].

Restriction on Lending — A restricted dealer funding portal must comply with section 13.12 of NI 31-103 which provides that a registrant must not lend money, extend credit or provide margin to a client. Further, paragraph 39(b) [*Prohibition on providing recommendations or advice*] provides that a restricted dealer funding portal must not recommend that a purchaser use borrowed money to finance any part of the purchase of securities of the issuer under the crowdfunding prospectus exemption. This activity creates a conflict of interest which cannot be properly managed.

To the extent that products sold to a purchaser are structured in a way that results in the restricted dealer funding portal becoming a lender to the purchaser, we will consider the restricted dealer funding portal not to be in compliance with the prohibition in section 13.12 of NI 31-103.

41. Permitted dealing activities — Section 41 [*Permitted dealing activities*] provides that a restricted dealer funding portal and a registered individual of the restricted dealer funding portal may only act as an intermediary in connection with a distribution of securities made in reliance on the crowdfunding prospectus exemption and, except in Ontario, a distribution of securities made in reliance on a start-up crowdfunding registration and prospectus exemptive relief order granted by a securities regulatory authority or regulator. This means that a restricted dealer funding portal is not permitted to engage in a broader range of dealing or advising activities, such as

(a) facilitating distributions of securities in reliance on other prospectus exemptions,

(b) facilitating resales of securities acquired by a purchaser to accredited investors or to other purchasers who are eligible to purchase securities on a prospectus-exempt basis, or

(c) providing underwriting or underwriting-related services to issuers except as otherwise permitted by the Instrument.

The limitation on dealing activities applies only to activities in connection with a distribution of securities under the crowdfunding prospectus exemption and, except in Ontario, a distribution of securities under a start-up crowdfunding exemptive relief order granted by a securities regulatory authority or regulator. A funding portal may engage in other types of crowdfunding activities that do not involve a distribution of securities, including facilitating crowdfunding activities based on a donation model, a reward model or a pre-purchase model. To the extent that a funding portal does engage in crowdfunding activities that do not involve a distribution of securities, it should have separate books and records for its non-securities related crowdfunding activities.

42. Chief Compliance Officer — A restricted dealer funding portal is required to have a UDP and a CCO. The UDP and the CCO can be the same person if they meet the requirements for both registration categories. We prefer funding portals to separate these functions, but we recognize that for a restricted dealer funding portal, it might not be practical.

Section 42 [*Chief compliance officer*] sets out the proficiency requirements for a CCO of a restricted dealer funding portal. The regulator is required to determine an individual's fitness for registration and may exercise discretion in so doing.

The regulator may grant an exemption from any of the education requirements in paragraphs 42(a) and (b) [*Chief compliance officer*] for the CCO of a restricted dealer funding portal if it is satisfied that the individual has qualifications or relevant experience that are equivalent to, or more relevant in the circumstances than, the prescribed requirements.

The experience requirement in paragraph 42(c) [*Chief compliance officer*] may include experience acquired:

- during employment as or with a registered dealer, a registered adviser or an investment fund manager;
- in related investment fields, such as investment banking, advisory services, venture capital or private equity;
- in legal, accounting or consulting practices; or
- in other professional fields that relate to capital raising business activities.

43. Proficiency — Section 43 [*Proficiency*] requires an individual of a restricted dealer funding portal to have the education, training and experience, among other things, to understand the structure, features and risks of the distribution. At a minimum, to comply with the proficiency requirements set out in section 43 [*Proficiency*], we expect a restricted dealer funding portal to review and assess the crowdfunding offering document, the materials referred to in subsection 12(1) [*Additional distribution materials*], the issuer's articles of incorporation and other constating documents. The restricted dealer funding portal must be able to evidence their review of the information provided by the issuer. If the information provided by the issuer is not sufficient to enable the restricted dealer funding portal to understand the structure, features and risks of the distribution, the funding portal must make further inquiries with the issuer to satisfy the proficiency requirement.

Examples of the structure, features and risks of the distribution include:

- return on the investment;

- fee structure;
- time horizon;
- liquidity risk;
- conflict of interest risk; and
- issuer's financial position.

MISCELLANEOUS

Resale of securities distributed under the crowdfunding prospectus exemption

Securities acquired under the crowdfunding prospectus exemption are subject to resale restrictions. Securities of a reporting issuer acquired under the crowdfunding prospectus exemption are subject to a four-month hold period. Securities of a non-reporting issuer cannot be resold in a jurisdiction:

(a) until the issuer becomes a reporting issuer and certain other conditions are met; or

(b) unless the sale is made under another available prospectus exemption.

The crowdfunding prospectus exemption is not available for distributions by selling security holders.

Refer to National Instrument 45-102 *Resale of Securities.*

Adoption of Policy: (2015) 38 O.S.C.B. (Supp. 4) 11.

CSA Staff Notice 45-304 — (Revised) Notice of Local Exemptions Related to NI 45-106 Prospectus Exemptions and NI 31-103 Registration Requirements, Exemptions and Ongoing Registrant Obligations

Date: September 9, 2005 as revised November 27, 2009 and May 21, 2015

28 O.S.C.B. 7469, 33 O.S.C.B. 9781 and 38 O.S.C.B. 4663

The Canadian Securities Administrators (CSA or we) have implemented National Instrument 45-106 *Prospectus Exemptions* (NI 45-106) and National Instrument 31-103 *Registration Requirements, Exemptions and Ongoing Registrant Exemptions* (NI 31-103) in order to consolidate and harmonize most of the prospectus and registration exemptions available under Canadian securities laws. However, there remain a limited number of local exemptions in each jurisdiction.

The CSA are replacing a prior notice issued in September 2005 and amended in November 2009 with this notice listing the prospectus and registration exemptions in each jurisdiction that are not included in NI 45-106 or NI 31-103.

These exemptions are listed in the Appendix by jurisdiction and apply only in that jurisdiction. Although we have attempted to consolidate a list of all remaining exemptions by local jurisdiction, we encourage persons relying on a local exemption to consult the securities legislation of the jurisdiction.

The list of exemptions in the Appendix is up-to-date as of May 21, 2015.

Questions

Questions about any of the local exemptions listed in the Appendix may be referred to the contact(s) for that local jurisdiction listed below:

[Omitted]

Appendix Local Exemptions — Alberta

Alberta Securities Commission Rules

ASC Rule 45-502 *Trade with RESP*

ASC Rule 45-509 *Offering Memorandum for Real Estate Securities*

ASC Rule 45-511 *Local Prospectus Exemptions and Related Requirements*

ASC Rule 45-513 *Prospectus Exemptions for Distributions to Existing Security Holders*

ASC Rule 72-501 *Distributions to Purchasers Outside Alberta*

ASC Rule 91-504 *Strip Bonds*

Blanket Orders

ASC Blanket Order 2005/10/849 *Registration and Prospectus Exemption for Certain Capital Accumulation Plans*

ASC Blanket Order 31-505 *Registration Exemption for Trades in Connection with Certain Prospectus-Exempt Distributions*

ASC Blanket Order 31-530 *Trades and Advice for US-Resident Clients: Dealer and Adviser Registration Exemptions*

ASC Blanket Order 45-515 *Exemption from Certain Financial Statement Requirements of Form 45-106F2 Offering Memorandum for Non-Qualifying Issuers*

ASC Blanket Order 91-506 *Over-the-Counter Trades in Derivatives*

Local Exemptions — British Columbia

Commission Rules

BC Instrument 45-501 *Mortgages*

Blanket Orders

BC Instrument 32-503 *Registration Exemption for Approved Persons of the Mutual Funds Dealers Association of Canada*

BC Instrument 32-513 *Registration Exemption for Trades in Connection with Certain Prospectus Exempt Distributions*

BC Instrument 32-517 *Exemption from Dealer Registration Requirement for Trades in Securities of Mortgage Investment Entities*

BC Instrument 33-517 *Registration and Prospectus Exemption for Persons Registered under the Mortgage Brokers Act*

BC Instrument 32-522 *Exemption from the registration requirement for trades in short-term debt instruments*

BC Instrument 32-525 *Exemption from the dealer registration requirement and the dviser registration requirement in respect of trades and advice for U.S. resident clients*

BC Instrument 45-504 *Trades to trust companies, insurers, and portfolio managers outside British Columbia*

BC Instrument 45-512 *Real Estate Securities*

BC Instrument 45-514 *The Employee Investment Act*

BC Instrument 45-524 *Registration and Prospectus Exemption for Certain Capital Accumulation Plans*

BC Instrument 45-528 *Trades under a realization on collateral given for a debt*

BC Instrument 45-529 *Bonus or Finder's Fee*

BC Instrument 45-530 *Exemptions for securities issued by a cooperative association*

BC Instrument 45-531 *Exemptions for shares or deposits of a credit union*

BC Instrument 45-534 *Exemption from prospectus requirement for certain trades to existing security holders*

BC Instrument 45-535 *Start-up Crowdfunding Registration and Prospectus Exemptions*

BC Instrument 72-502 *Trades in Securities of U.S. Registered Issuers*

BC Instrument 72-503 *Distribution of Securities outside British Columbia*

BC Instrument 72-504 *Distribution of Eurobonds*

BC Instrument 91-501 *Over-The-Counter Derivatives*

BC Instrument 91-502 *Short Term Foreign Exchange Transactions*

BC Instrument 91-503 *Contracts Providing for Physical Delivery of Commodities*

BC Instrument 91-504 *Government Strip Bonds*

BC Instrument 91-505 *Prospectus exemption for put and call options*

Local Exemptions — Manitoba

The Securities Act (Manitoba)

Section 19(1)(c) and 58(1)(a) — Exempt Purchasers

Sections 19(2)(g) and 58(3)(a) — Securities to which *The Cooperatives Act* apply

Sections 19(2)(h) and 58(3)(a) — Securities to which *The Credit Unions and Caisses Populaires Act* apply

Securities Regulation (Manitoba)

Sections 91(a) and (b) of *The Securities Regulation* M.R. 491/88R

Blanket Rulings (Manitoba)

Local Policy 3.17 — Strip Bonds

Blanket Order 45-501 *Exemption from prospectus requirement for certain trades to existing security holders*

Blanket Order 45-502 *Start-up Crowdfunding Prospectus and Registration Exemption*

Local Exemptions — New Brunswick

Rules

Local Rule 45-501 *Prospectus and Registration Exemptions*

Local Rule 45-802 *Implementing National Instrument 45-106 Prospectus and Registration Exemptions*

Local Rule 72-501 *Distribution of Securities to Persons Outside New Brunswick*

Local Rule 81-502 *Registration and Prospectus Exemption for Certain Capital Accumulation Plans*

Local Rule 91-501 *Derivatives*

Blanket Orders

Blanket Order 31-520 *Exemption from the Requirement in NI 31-103 to Register for International Dealers*

Blanket Order 31-521 *Exemption from the Requirement in NI 31-103 to Register for International Advisers*

Blanket Order 32-503 *Exemption From The Dealer Registration Requirement And The Adviser Registration Requirement In Respect Of Trades And Advice For U.S. Resident Clients*

Blanket Order 41-502 *in the matter of Capital Pool Companies*

Blanket Order 44-501 *In the matter of the Lapse Date for Shelf Prospectuses Under National Instrument 44-102 Shelf Distributions*

Blanket Order 44-502 *In the matter of an Exemption for Solicitations of Expressions of Interest*

Blanket Order 45-504 *Exemptions From Certain Financial Statement Requirements Of Form 45-106F2 Offering Memorandum For Non-Qualifying Issuers*

Blanket Order 45-505 *Prospectus Exemption for Distribution to Existing Security Holders*

Blanket Order 45-506 *Start-Up Crowdfunding Registration and Prospectus Exemptions*

Blanket Order 45-507 *Exemptions from certain financial statement requirements of the offering memorandum*

Local Exemptions — Newfoundland and Labrador

Securities Act (Newfoundland and Labrador)

Section 35 (Exemption of advisers)

Section 36 (Exemption of trades)

Local Exemptions — Northwest Territories

Securities Act (Northwest Territories)

Section 2 (Various exemptions from registration requirement)

Blanket Orders

Blanket Order No. 1 — Section 2 (Secondary Market Trading)

Blanket Order No. 1 — Subsection 3(a) (*Bona Fide* Debts of Non-control Persons)

Blanket Order No. 1 — Section 3(b) (Securities of a Cooperative)

Blanket Order No. 1 — Section 3(c) (Distributions commenced in reliance on Blanket Order exemptions in effect prior to September 14, 2005)

Blanket Order No. 2 — Subsection 2(a) (*Bona Fide* Debts of Non-control Persons)

Blanket Order No. 2 — Section 2(b) (Securities of a Cooperative)

Blanket Order No. 2 — Section 2(c) (Trades commenced in reliance on Blanket Order exemptions in effect prior to September 14, 2005)

Local Exemptions — Nova Scotia

Securities Act (Nova Scotia)

Section 41(1) (ama) and (amb) (Registration exemption for securities of a cooperative)

Section 41(2)(i) (Registration exemption for shares of a credit union within the meaning of the *Credit Union Act*)

Section 77(1)(ah) (Prospectus exemption for securities of a cooperative)

Section 78(1)(a) as it relates to section 41(2)(i) (Prospectus exemption for shares of a credit union within the meaning of the *Credit Union Act*)

Rules

NSSC Rule 35-101 *Conditional Exemption from Registration for United States Broker-Dealers and Agents*

Regulations

Section 3 of the *Community Economic — Development Corporations Regulations* — N.S. Reg. 79/98 (Registration and prospectus exemptions for shares of a community economic-development corporation)

Blanket Orders

Blanket Order No. 3 Zero Coupon Strip Bonds

Blanket Order No. 15 Trading in Recognized Options Cleared Through Recognized Clearing Organizations

Blanket Order No. 16 Trading in Commodity Futures Contracts and Commodity Futures Options

Blanket Order No. 24 Certain Certificates for Government Securities

Blanket Order No. 31-527 as varied by Blanket Order No. 31-531 Registration Exemption for Trades in Short-Term Debt Instruments

Blanket Order No. 32A Registration and Prospectus Exemptions for Real Return Bond Strip Bonds

Blanket Order 32-502 Exemption from the Dealer Registration and the Advisor Registration Requirement in respect of Trades and Advice for US Resident Clients

Blanket Order No. 47 Distribution of Mutual Funds Established for Employees of a Company and Its Affiliates

Blanket Order No. 45-507 A Registration and Prospectus Exemption for Certain Capital Accumulation Plans

Blanket Order No. 45-509 Trades in Warrants to Acquire Certain Debt Securities

Blanket Order No. 45-524 Start-up Crowdfunding Registration & Prospectus Exemptions

Blanket Order No. 45-525 Prospectus Exemption For Certain Trades To Existing Security Holders

Local Exemptions — Nunavut

Securities Act (Nunavut)

Section 2 (Various exemptions from registration requirement)

Blanket Orders

Blanket Order No. 1 — Section 2 (Secondary Market Trading)

Blanket Order No. 1 — Subsection 3(a) (*Bona Fide* Debts of Non-control Persons)

Blanket Order No. 1 — Section 3(b) (Securities of a Cooperative)

Blanket Order No. 1 — Section 3(c) (Distributions commenced in reliance on Blanket Order exemptions in effect prior to September 14, 2005)

Blanket Order No. 3 — Subsection 2(a) (*Bona Fide* Debts of Non-control Persons)

Blanket Order No. 3 — Section 2(b) (Securities of a Cooperative)

Blanket Order No. 3 — Section 2(c) (Trades commenced in reliance on Blanket Order exemptions in effect prior to September 14, 2005)

Local Exemptions — Ontario

Securities Act (Ontario)

Section 34 (Exemption from registration requirements, advisers)

Section 35 (Exemption from registration requirements, dealers)

Section 35.1 (Exemption from registration requirement, financial institutions)

Section 73 (Exemption)

Section 73.1 (Exemption from prospectus requirement — securities of financial institutions)

Section 73.2 (Exemption from prospectus requirement — where other legislation applies)

Section 73.3 (Exemption from prospectus requirement — accredited investor)

Section 73.4 (Exemption from prospectus requirement — private issuer)

Section 73.5 (Exemption from prospectus requirement — government incentive securities)

Regulations

Ontario Regulation 85/05 generally *Exemptions respecting the Ontario Financing Authority*

Rules

Ontario Securities Commission Rule 32-501 *Direct Purchase Plans*

Ontario Securities Commission Rule 35-101 *Conditional Exemption from Registration for United States Broker-Dealers and Agents*

Ontario Securities Commission Rule 35-502 *Non Resident Advisers*

Ontario Securities Commission Rule 35-503 *Trades by Certain Members of The Toronto Stock Exchange*

Ontario Securities Commission Rule 45-501 *Ontario Prospectus and Registration Exemptions*

Ontario Securities Commission Rule 91-501 *Strip Bonds*

Ontario Securities Commission Rule 91-502 *Trades in Recognized Options — Rule Under the Securities Act*

Ontario Securities Commission Rule 91-503 *Trades in Commodity Futures Contracts and Commodity Futures Options Entered into on Commodity Futures Exchanges Situate Outside of Ontario — Rule Under the Securities Act*

Local Exemptions — Prince Edward Island

Rules

Local Rule 45-501 — *Exempt Distributions — Co-operative Associations*

Local Rule 45-502 — *Exempt Distributions — Credit Unions*

Local Exemptions — Québec

Securities Act (Québec)

Section 3 (exemptions)

Section 41 (prospectus exemptions)

Securities Regulation (Québec)

Section 192 (registration exemptions)

Derivatives Act (Québec)

Section 7 (over-the-counter derivatives activities or transactions involving accredited counterparties only or in any other case specified by regulation).

Derivatives Regulation

Section 11.14 (registration exemption to the extent the person carries on business solely for an accredited counterparty and its activity involves a standardized derivative that is offered primarily outside Québec)

General exemption decisions

Decision 2000-C-0699: Registration exemption for dealers in respect of trading at a distance on NASDAQ

Decision 2009-PDG-0007: Registration exemption for dealer and adviser activities relative to derivatives with accredited investors

Decision 2015-PDG-0066: Exemption from the risk acknowledgement form requirement for activities relating to derivatives described in decision 2009-PDG-0007

Decision 2015-PDG-0077: Start-up Crowdfunding Prospectus and Registration Exemptions

Local Exemptions — Saskatchewan

General Rulings/Orders

General Ruling/Order 21-901 *Market Facilitation Activities by Issuers in Their Own Securities*

General Ruling/Order 31-904 *Exemption from certain sections of National Instrument 31-103 in connection with transition and grandfathering matters*

General Ruling/Order 31-907 *Exemption from section 3.3 of National Instrument 31-103 Registration Requirements and Exemptions for representatives of scholarship plan dealers*

General Ruling/Order 31-915 *Exemption for mortgage investment entities from the requirement to register as investment fund managers and advisers*

General Ruling/Order 31-916 *Exemption from the Registration Requirement in NI 31-103 for International Dealers*

General Ruling/Order 31-917 *Exemption from the Registration Requirement in NI 31-103 for International Advisors*

General Ruling/Order 31-932 *Exemption from the Dealer Registration Requirement and the Adviser Registration Requirement in Respect of Trades and Advice for U.S. Resident Clients*

General Ruling/Order 43-901 *Trade Unions which Sponsor Labour Sponsored Venture Capital Corporations*

General Ruling/Order 45-902 *Labour-Sponsored Venture Capital Corporations*

General Ruling/Order 45-912 *Co-operatives and Credit Unions*

General Ruling/Order 45-913 *Capital Accumulation Plans*

General Ruling/Order 45-916 *Solicitations of Expressions of Interest*

General Ruling/Order 45-918 *Registration Exemption for Trades in Connection with Certain Prospectus Exempt Distributions*

General Ruling/Order 45-919 *Exemption from restriction on paying commissions and finder fees in offering memorandum exemption in National Instrument 45-106 Prospectus and Registration Exemptions*

General Ruling/Order 45-926 *Exemption from prospectus requirement for certain trades to existing security holders*

General Ruling/Order 45-927 *Exemption from Registration Requirement in NI 31-103 for Trades in Short-Term Debt Instruments*

General Ruling/Order 45-929 *Start-up Crowdfunding Registration and Prospectus Exemptions*

General Ruling/Order 72-901 *Trades to Purchasers Outside of Saskatchewan*

General Ruling/Order 91-904 *Government Warrants*

General Ruling/Order 91-905 *Certain Interests in Government Securities*

General Ruling/Order 91-906 *Strip Bonds*

General Ruling/Order 91-907 *Over-the-Counter Derivatives*

Local Exemptions — Yukon

Registrar's Order 1999/38 *Exemptions relating to Yukon Small Business Investment Tax Credit*

Superintendent's Order 2014/05 *Exemption from Prospectus Requirement for Certain Trades to Existing Security Holders*

Superintendent's Order 2015/01 *Exemption from the Registration Requirement in National Instrument 31-103 For Trades in Short Term Debt Instruments*

Superintendent's Order 2015/05 *Exemption from the dealer registration requirement and the adviser registration requirement in respect of trades and advice for U.S. resident clients*

CSA Staff Notice 45-307 — Regulatory Developments Regarding Securitization

Date: June 18, 2010

33 O.S.C.B. 5470

This Notice provides an update from Canadian Securities Administrators' (CSA) staff on the development of regulatory proposals relating to securitized products, including asset-backed commercial paper (ABCP) and asset-backed securities.

In the October 2008 CSA Consultation Paper 11-405 *Securities Regulatory Proposals Stemming from the 2007-08 Credit Market Turmoil and its Effect on the ABCP Market in Canada* (Consultation Paper), the CSA explored, among other things, securities regulatory proposals in connection with the sale of ABCP. Since that time, the CSA's focus has broadened to encompass all securitized products and to consider their distribution both publicly under a prospectus and in the exempt market under exemptions from the prospectus and registration requirements.

In developing our proposals, we are considering international regulatory and industry developments. These include

- the recommendations of the International Organization of Securities Commissions (IOSCO) entitled "Disclosure Principles for Public Offerings and Listings of Asset-Backed Securities",

- IOSCO's Technical Committee's Task Force report entitled "Unregulated Financial Markets and Products — Final Report", and

- the United States Securities and Exchange Commission's (SEC) notice of proposed rule-making relating to asset-backed securities and other structured finance products.

Exempt market

CSA staff have been considering changes to the current approach to the issuance of securitized products in the exempt market. In addition to reconsidering the use of the short-term debt exemption for the distribution of ABCP, we have been considering whether to impose other conditions in connection with the exempt distribution of securitized products, including requiring disclosure.

Prospectus distributions and continuous disclosure for reporting issuers

Disclosure requirements under Canadian securities legislation for securitized products distributed by prospectus are comprehensive. In light of the IOSCO and SEC proposals, CSA staff are considering enhancements to these requirements. We are also considering proposals for more tailored continuous disclosure for reporting issuers that have distributed securitized products.

Proposed consultations

Our proposals will be designed to address investor protection and market stability concerns, taking into consideration international developments, while recognizing the importance of the securitization markets. We appreciate that some of these proposals could be significant policy changes.

To obtain market input on these issues, we plan to publish materials for comment in fall 2010. We also anticipate additional consultations with interested stakeholders on the scope of the proposals, their impact on investor protection and the implications for the securitization market.

In addition to our securitization proposals, the CSA expects to publish proposals relating to regulation of credit rating organizations in summer 2010.

CSA Staff Notice 45-308 — Guidance for Preparing and Filing Reports of Exempt Distribution under National Instrument 45-106 Prospectus and Registration Exemptions

Date: April 26, 2012

35 O.S.C.B. 4074

Introduction and Purpose

Staff of the Canadian Securities Administrators (Staff or we) are publishing this Staff Notice (the Notice) to highlight issues identified in some reports of exempt distribution filed in Form 45-106F1 *Report of Exempt Distribution* (the F1) under National Instrument 45-106 *Prospectus and Registration Exemptions* (NI 45-106). The Notice also provides guidance to issuers, underwriters and their advisors for preparing and filing the F1.

Background

Securities legislation prohibits issuers and underwriters from distributing securities without a prospectus for which a receipt has been issued. NI 45-106 contains a number of exemptions from the prospectus requirement. Part 6 of NI 45-106 requires issuers or underwriters relying on prospectus exemptions specified in that Part to report exempt distributions, and sets out the form required to be filed and the deadlines for filing. Responsibility for compliance with NI 45-106 rests with the issuer or underwriter purporting to rely on the applicable exemption(s).

The use of a prospectus exemption under NI 45-106 is subject to regulatory oversight and monitoring. Staff may review filings required by NI 45-106 and/or an issuer's or underwriter's reliance on a prospectus exemption as a result of planned compliance-monitoring programmes, observed market activity, or following specific complaints or referrals. Identified non-compliance may result in appropriate corrective action.

Guidance and Identified Issues

Outlined below are issues we have observed when reviewing F1s filed with us. We are communicating these issues to assist issuers, underwriters and their advisors in avoiding similar deficiencies when preparing and filing the F1.

1. — Failing to use the correct form

The required form for a report of exempt distribution is the F1, except in British Columbia (BC). Effective October 3, 2011, the British Columbia Securities Commission (the BCSC) introduced a new form of report of exempt distribution, Form 45-106F6 *British Columbia Report of Exempt Distribution* (the F6).[1]

We have seen instances of issuers or underwriters filing the F6 outside BC. The filing of the F6 is only accepted in BC.

If a distribution occurs in BC and elsewhere, the issuer or underwriter is required to file the F6 with the BCSC[2] *and* file the F1 in the other applicable jurisdictions.

2. — Failing to file the F1 on time

Part 6 of NI 45-106 requires issuers or underwriters relying on certain prospectus exemptions to file the F1 in each applicable jurisdiction where the distribution takes place. Some (but not all) of these prospectus exemptions include:

- the accredited investor exemption (section 2.3 of NI 45-106)
- the family, friends and business associates exemption (section 2.5 of NI 45-106)
- the offering memorandum exemption (section 2.9 of NI 45-106, the OM exemption)
- the minimum amount investment exemption (section 2.10 of NI 45-106)
- the additional investment in investment funds exemption (section 2.19 of NI 45-106)

The deadline for filing the F1 is generally 10 days after the distribution.

Investment funds have the option of filing the F1 on an annual basis, within 30 days of their financial year-end, when relying on section 2.3, 2.10 or 2.19 of NI 45-106. **This option is *not* available for investment funds using the OM exemption** (in jurisdictions where such exemption is available).

Staff have observed that many issuers or underwriters have filed the F1 late and, in some cases, not at all.

3. — Failing to pay the required fee

Some issuers or underwriters have filed the F1 with an incorrect fee or with no fee. Issuers or underwriters must pay the applicable fee in each jurisdiction in which a distribution is made, when the report is filed.

4. — Failing to include a complete list of purchasers in the F1

Some F1s filed by issuers or underwriters only identified purchasers from the jurisdiction in which the F1 was filed, even though the distribution included purchasers from other jurisdictions. If distributions are made in more than one jurisdiction, the issuer or underwriter must complete a single F1 identifying all purchasers, including purchasers that reside in the jurisdiction and those that do not, and file that report in each of the jurisdictions in which the distribution is made (see Instruction 2 of the F1).

5. — Failing to reconcile information in the F1

Issuers or underwriters have frequently reported a different total number of securities distributed, total dollar value raised, number of purchasers and/or exemptions used in items 6 and 7 of the F1 when compared to Schedule I of the F1 (Schedule I). Information in items 5, 6, and 7 of the F1 must reconcile with the information in Schedule I (see Instruction 5 of the F1).

6. — Incorrectly identifying the number of purchasers

Item 7 of the F1 requires the total number of purchasers in each jurisdiction to be reported. The number of purchasers refers to the number of investors and not to the number of securities each purchaser purchased.

---

[1] In BC, the F6 generally must be filed electronically using the BCSC's E-services filing system. See BC Instrument 13-502 *Electronic filing of reports of exempt distribution*. Except in limited circumstances, the BCSC will not accept F6s delivered in paper or via other electronic means (such as a PDF attachment to an email).

[2] In limited cases, the BCSC will accept the F1 instead of the F6. Issuers that have distributed securities in BC should review BC Instrument 45-533 *Exemptions from Form 45-106F6 requirements* to determine if they may file the F1 in BC instead of the F6.

7. — Relying on unavailable exemptions

In certain instances, issuers distributing in more than one jurisdiction, have reported in the F1 distributions under an exemption that is not available in one of the jurisdictions. Issuers or underwriters should note that not all exemptions are available in all jurisdictions. For example, section 2.5 of NI 45-106 *Family, friends and business associates* (the 2.5 exemption) is not available in Ontario, although Ontario offers a similar exemption (section 2.7 of NI 45-106 *Founder, control person and family — Ontario*) (the 2.7 exemption).

An issuer or underwriter should indicate in Schedule I the appropriate exemption for each purchaser. This may require the issuer or underwriter to report (in Schedule I) multiple exemptions relied on for the same purchaser in circumstances where the distribution is made in more than one jurisdiction and the same exemption is not available in those jurisdictions. For example, an issuer or underwriter relying on the 2.5 exemption in Alberta and the 2.7 exemption in Ontario, for a distribution to the same purchaser, would identify both section 2.5 and section 2.7 in Schedule I as the applicable exemptions relied on for that purchaser.

8. — Failing to disclose all commissions and finder's fees

We have observed that some issuers or underwriters are not reporting compensation paid in connection with a distribution. In some of these cases, the payment was not disclosed because it was not called a "commission" or a "finder's fee."

Item 8 of the F1 requires an issuer or underwriter to disclose compensation received or to be received by any person in connection with the distribution. Compensation includes commissions, discounts or other fees or payments of a similar nature, which result from a distribution of securities, regardless of what the payment is called. For example, a "brokerage fee" or "finance fee" for a syndicated mortgage is compensation in connection with a distribution. Compensation does not include payments for services incidental to the distribution (such as clerical, printing, legal or accounting services).

9. — Failing to provide complete information regarding convertible or exchangeable securities distributed

Item 6 of the F1 requires information regarding the security distributed. If the security is convertible or exchangeable into an underlying security, the F1 states that the issuer or underwriter must include:

- a description of the underlying security,

- the terms of conversion or exercise, and

- any expiry date.

10. — Improperly reporting distributions under the minimum amount exemption

In order to rely on the prospectus exemption in section 2.10 *Minimum amount investment* of NI 45-106, the purchase price must be at least $150,000 (among other conditions). If an issuer or underwriter relies on this exemption, it should ensure that the purchase price reported is at least that minimum amount. We also remind issuers or underwriters that it is not permitted to distribute securities under this exemption to multiple purchasers acting in concert or as a "syndicate" in order to pool individual purchases and reach the $150,000 minimum.

11. — Failing to certify the F1

We have received some reports with unsigned certificates. An issuer or underwriter must include the date and the signature of the person identified as signing the F1 in the certificate section of the F1.

CSA Staff Notice 45-308 (Revised) — Guidance for Preparing and Filing Reports of Exempt Distribution under National Instrument 45-106 Prospectus Exemptions

Date: **April 7, 2016**

First Published April 26, 2012, revised June 25, 2015 and April 7, 2016

Purpose

Staff of the Canadian Securities Administrators (**CSA** or **we**) have prepared this revised Staff Notice (this **Notice**) to assist issuers, underwriters and their advisors in preparing and filing the new harmonized report of exempt distribution (the **New Report**) introduced by amendments to National Instrument 45-106 *Prospectus Exemptions* (**NI 45-106**) and related changes to Companion Policy 45-106 *Prospectus Exemptions* published on April 7, 2016 (the **amendments**). The amendments, including the New Report, will come into force on June 30, 2016, provided all necessary ministerial approvals are obtained.

This Notice replaces a prior version of this notice issued on June 25, 2015.

This Notice includes the following documents to assist issuers, underwriters and their advisors to prepare for the transition to, and changes introduced by, the New Report:

- Annex 1 — Tips for Completing and Filing the New Report

- Annex 2 — Checklist of New Information Requirements

- Annex 3 — Frequently Asked Questions

- Annex 4 — Transition to the New Report

We may from time to time reissue this Notice to reflect additional questions or concerns raised about the completion and filing of the New Report.

Background

Issuers and underwriters who rely on certain prospectus exemptions to distribute securities are required to file a report of exempt distribution within the prescribed timeframe. Currently, in all CSA jurisdictions except British Columbia, the form of report is Form 45-106F1 *Report of Exempt Distribution* (**F1**). In British Columbia, the form of report is Form 45-106F6 *British Columbia Report of Exempt Distribution* (**F6**, and together with the F1, **Current Reports**).

The amendments will apply in all CSA jurisdictions and will replace the Current Reports with the New Report for both investment fund issuers and non-investment fund issuers that distribute securities under certain prospectus exemptions.

Annexes to Notice

Annex 1 — Tips for Completing and Filing the New Report

Annex 2 — Checklist of New Information Requirements

Annex 3 — Frequently Asked Questions

Annex 4 — Transition to the New Report

Questions

Please refer your questions to any of the following:

[Names not reproduced]

Annex 1 — Tips for Completing and Filing the New Report

The following are tips to assist issuers, underwriters and advisors in completing and filing the New Report.

1. — File the report on time

Issuers must file the report in each jurisdiction of Canada where the distribution occurred. The deadline for filing the report is generally 10 days after the distribution. If an issuer is filing a report for distributions occurring on multiple dates, such distributions must occur within a 10-day period and the issuer must file the report no later than 10 days after the first distribution date.

Investment fund issuers relying on certain prospectus exemptions have the option of filing the report on an annual basis, within 30 days of the end of the calendar year. This option is only available for investment fund issuers distributing securities in reliance on the following prospectus exemptions in NI 45-106:

- section 2.3 [*Accredited investor*][1]
- section 2.10 [*Minimum amount investment*]
- section 2.19 [*Additional investment in investment funds*]

2. — Pay the required fees

Issuers must pay the applicable fee in each jurisdiction of Canada in which the report is filed. In order to determine the applicable fee in a particular jurisdiction of Canada, consult the securities legislation of that jurisdiction.

Filing fees payable in a particular jurisdiction are not affected by identifying all purchasers in a single report.

3. — Include a complete list of purchasers in the report

Issuers must ensure that Item 7(f) and Schedule 1 include all purchasers that participated in the distribution.

If an issuer located outside of Canada completes a distribution in a jurisdiction of Canada, the issuer is required to provide information in the report about purchasers resident in that jurisdiction of Canada only. See Question 12 in Annex 3 for further guidance on issuers located outside of Canada.

If an issuer makes a distribution in more than one jurisdiction of Canada, the issuer may complete a single report identifying all purchasers, and file that report in each jurisdiction of Canada in which the distribution occurs.

---

[1]This option is also available for investment fund issuers distributing securities in reliance on section 73.3 of the *Securities Act* (Ontario) [*Accredited investor*].

4. — Ensure the information provided in the report and schedules is consistent

Issuers should verify that the information included in the report and schedules is accurate and consistent. In particular, issuers should verify the following:

- The information provided in Item 7 about the distribution date, number and type of securities distributed, total dollar amount of securities distributed, number of purchasers in each jurisdiction and prospectus exemptions relied on, must reconcile with the information provided in Schedule 1.

- The identities of persons compensated provided in Item 8 must reconcile with the information provided in Schedule 1 about the persons compensated for each purchaser.

- The information about directors, executive officers and promoters provided in Item 9 must reconcile with the information provided in Schedule 2.

5. — Correctly identify the total number of purchasers

The table in Item 7(f) requires the total number of unique purchasers to which the issuer distributed securities. To determine the total number of unique purchasers, the issuer should count each purchaser only once, regardless of whether the issuer distributed different types of securities to that purchaser, on different dates, and/or relied on multiple prospectus exemptions for such distributions.

6. — Ensure the purchase price of the securities distributed is correct

If an issuer is relying on the prospectus exemption in section 2.10 [*Minimum amount investment*] of NI 45-106 for distributions to a purchaser, the purchase price paid by that purchaser must be at least $150,000 (among other conditions), and the purchase price provided in Item 7 and Schedule 1 must be at least that minimum amount. An issuer is not permitted to distribute securities under this prospectus exemption to a purchaser that is an individual, or to multiple purchasers acting in concert or as a "syndicate" in order to pool separate purchases and reach the $150,000 minimum.

7. — Ensure that a valid prospectus exemption is available

Not all prospectus exemptions are available in all jurisdictions. An issuer should ensure that a valid prospectus exemption is reported in Item 7(f) and Schedule 1 for each purchaser.

This may require the issuer to report in Item 7(f) and Schedule 1 multiple prospectus exemptions relied on for the same distribution in circumstances where the distribution occurred in more than one jurisdiction and the same prospectus exemption is not available in each of those jurisdictions.

8. — Disclose all compensation paid in connection with the distribution

An issuer must complete Item 8 for each person to whom the issuer directly provides, or will provide, any compensation in connection with the distribution. Compensation includes cash commissions, securities-based compensation, gifts, discounts or other compensation of a similar nature, paid in connection with a distribution of securities, regardless of the term used to describe the payment. For example, we consider a brokerage fee or finance fee to be compensation in connection with a distribution.

Compensation does not include payments for services incidental to the distribution, such as clerical, printing, legal or accounting services.

Item 8 does not require details about internal allocation arrangements with the directors, officers or employees of an entity compensated by the issuer.

9. — Date and certify the report

Item 10 of the report must include the date and the signature of the person certifying the report. The party certifying the report must be a director or officer of the issuer or underwriter. If the issuer or underwriter is not a company, an individual who performs functions similar to that of a director or officer (as determined by the issuer or underwriter) may certify the report.

For example, if the issuer is a trust, the report may be certified by the issuer's trustee. If the issuer is an investment fund, a director or officer of the investment fund manager (or, if the investment fund manager is not a company, an individual who performs similar functions) may certify the report if the director or officer has been authorized to do so by the investment fund.

A filing agent completing the report on an issuer's behalf may not certify or sign the report but must provide their contact details in Item 11.

Annex 2 — Checklist of New Information Requirements

The new information requirements introduced by the New Report are listed in the checklist below. The checklist is designed to assist filers in gathering the required information to complete the New Report.

All issuers		
	❏	Most recent previous legal name (if issuer's name has changed in last 12 months)
	❏	Website of issuer (if issuer has one) and underwriter (if underwriter has one and is not a registrant)
	❏	Legal entity identifier (if issuer has one)
	❏	Firm NRD number for underwriter
	❏	CUSIP numbers of securities distributed (if applicable)

❏	Details about the distribution (number of purchasers and total amount raised) by jurisdiction and prospectus exemption relied on
❏	List of (and if required to be filed with or delivered to the Ontario Securities Commission, electronic copies of) all offering materials required to be filed with or delivered to the securities regulatory authority or regulator for distributions in Saskatchewan, Ontario, Québec, New Brunswick or Nova Scotia
❏	NRD number of registrant compensated (if applicable)
❏	Whether person compensated facilitated distribution through funding portal or internet-based portal
❏	Description of terms of any deferred compensation
❏	Relationship of person compensated to issuer or investment fund manager (connected with issuer or investment fund manager/insider/director or officer/employee/none of the above)

Schedule 1 (non-public)

❏	Email address of purchaser (if provided by purchaser)
❏	Specific prospectus exemption relied on to distribute securities to each purchaser
❏	Identification of whether purchaser is a registrant or insider
❏	Name of person compensated for the distribution for each purchaser

Non-investment fund issuers		
	❏	NAICS industry code
	❏	Stage of operations for issuers in mining industry (exploration/development/production)
	❏	Areas of asset holdings for issuers involved in investment activities (mortgages/real estate/commercial/business debt/consumer debt/private companies)
	❏	Number of employees (within a range)
	❏	SEDAR profile number (if issuer has one)
		If issuer does not have a SEDAR profile number:
	❏	Date of formation
	❏	Financial year-end
	❏	Jurisdictions of Canada where reporting
	❏	CUSIP number (if issuer has one)
	❏	Name of exchanges where publicly listed
	❏	Size of assets (within a range)

Investment fund issuers		
	❏	NRD number of investment fund manager
	❏	Website of investment fund manager (if investment fund manager does not have a firm NRD number and has a website)
	❏	Type of investment fund (money market/equity/fixed income/balanced/alternative strategies/other)
	❏	Date of formation
	❏	Financial year-end
	❏	Jurisdictions of Canada where reporting
	❏	CUSIP number (if issuer has one)
	❏	Name of exchanges where publicly listed
	❏	Net asset value (within a range) and date of calculation
	❏	Net proceeds by jurisdiction

Issuers that are not any of the following: • **investment fund issuers**		
	❏	Names, titles and locations of directors, executives officers and promoters
	❏	If a promoter is not an individual, this information is also required for the directors and executive officers of the promoter

- **reporting issuers and their wholly owned subsidiaries**

- **foreign public issuers and their wholly owned subsidiaries**

- **issuers distributing eligible foreign**

- **securities only to permitted clients**

Schedule 2 (non-public)

❏ Business email address and telephone number of issuer's CEO

❏ Residential addresses of directors, executives officers, promoters and control persons that are individuals

❏ If a promoter or control person is not an individual, this information is required for the directors and executive officers of the promoter and control person

❏ If control person is not an individual:

❏ Organization or company name

❏ Province or country of business location

Annex 3 — Frequently Asked Questions

Filing the report

1. An issuer whose head office is in Alberta distributes securities to a purchaser resident in Saskatchewan. Where is the issuer required to file the report?

The issuer must file a report with the Alberta Securities Commission and with the Financial and Consumer Affairs Authority of Saskatchewan.

The issuer must file a report in each jurisdiction where the distribution occurred. To determine if a distribution has occurred in one or more jurisdictions of Canada, consult applicable securities legislation, securities directions and case law.

For example:

- In Alberta, an issuer should consult Alberta Securities Commission Policy 45-601 *Distributions Outside Alberta*.

- In British Columbia, an issuer should consult BC Interpretation Note 72-702 *Distribution of Securities to Persons Outside British Columbia*.

- In New Brunswick, an issuer should consult Companion Policy to Local Rule 72-501 *Distributions of Securities to Persons Outside New Brunswick*.

- In Québec, an issuer should consult *Avis du personnel de l'Autorité des marchés financiers — Règlement 45-106 sur les dispenses de prospectus et d'inscription : Questions fréquemment posées*.

In all cases, a distribution occurs when a distribution is made to a purchaser resident in that jurisdiction. In most cases, a distribution includes a distribution made by an issuer whose head office is in that jurisdiction (or, in the case of an investment fund, an investment fund whose manager's head office is in that jurisdiction), to purchasers resident outside that jurisdiction. A distribution may also occur in a jurisdiction of Canada if the issuer has a significant connection to that jurisdiction.

If an issuer is uncertain as to whether a distribution has occurred in a jurisdiction of Canada, the issuer should file the report in that jurisdiction.

2. How does an issuer file a report for a distribution to purchasers in every CSA jurisdiction?

Issuers are required to file the report electronically in all CSA jurisdictions, except certain foreign issuers when filing on SEDAR. The British Columbia Securities Commission (**BCSC**) is developing a web-based filing system on eServices to accommodate the structured data format of the report. Issuers filing in British Columbia and Ontario will file the report with the BCSC and Ontario Securities Commission (**OSC**) by completing an electronic form on the BCSC's eServices and the OSC's Electronic Filing Portal, respectively.

In all CSA jurisdictions other than British Columbia and Ontario, issuers, except certain foreign issuers, must file the report on SEDAR in accordance with National Instrument 13-101 *System for Electronic Document Analysis and Retrieval (SEDAR)*. Both the BCSC's eServices and the OSC's Electronic Filing Portal will generate an electronic copy of the completed report, which issuers can then file on SEDAR, if required.

Schedule 1 and Schedule 2 of the report must be filed in .xlsx format using the Excel templates developed by the CSA. The Excel templates are available on the website of each CSA member and at the links below.

- *Schedule 1 template*[2]

- *Schedule 2 template*[3]

3. The issuer distributed securities from June 28, 2016 to July 1, 2016. Should the issuer file the Current Report or the New Report?

Issuers must file the New Report for distributions that occur on or after June 30, 2016. However, if an issuer completes distributions on dates that occur within a 10-day period beginning before and ending after June 30, 2016, the issuer may file either the Current Report or the New Report to report such distributions.

---

[2]http://www.securities-administrators.ca/uploadedFiles/Schedule_1_Form_45-106F1_En.xlsx.

[3]http://www.securities-administrators.ca/uploadedFiles/Schedule_2_Form_45-106F1_En.xlsx.

In this example, the issuer may choose to file either the Current Report or the New Report. The issuer must file the report by July 8, 2016 (10 days after the first distribution date for which the report is being filed).

To provide further clarity on the report that should be filed, please see the examples in Table 1 in Annex 4.

4. Is there a transition period available for investment fund issuers that file reports annually?

Yes, there is a transition period which allows an investment fund issuer filing annually to file either the Current Report or the New Report for distributions that occur before January 1, 2017. For distributions that occur on or after January 1, 2017, all investment fund issuers filing annually must file the New Report.

Investment funds that file annually are no longer required to file annual reports within 30 days of their financial yearend. Beginning on June 30, 2016, all investment fund issuers filing annually must file within 30 days after the end of the calendar year. This means that all investment funds filing annually will be required to file by January 30, 2017 for distributions that occur before January 1, 2017 (that have not been previously reported).

To provide further clarity on the transition period, please see the examples in Table 2 in Annex 4.

Names and identifiers

5. What information should be provided for individuals under family name, first given name and secondary given names in the report?[4]

Family name refers to the individual's last name or surname.

First given name refers to the first name of an individual, used to identify the person from other members of a family, all of whom usually share the same family name.

Secondary given names, often referred to as middle names, refer to all given names of an individual, other than their first given name and family name.

The ordering of family and given names can vary among cultures. Indicate the "family name", "first given name" and "secondary given names" in the appropriate field in the report regardless of the order in which they may be given or traditionally used.

Do not include aliases, nicknames, preferred names, initials or short forms of full names in the name fields of the report.

6. What is a legal entity identifier (LEI)? Does an issuer need to obtain an LEI to complete Item 3 of the report?

An LEI is a globally recognized 20-character alphanumeric code used to identify entities that enter into financial transactions. If an issuer already has an LEI, it must provide the LEI in Item 3. If an issuer does not have an LEI, it is not necessary to obtain one to complete the report.

7. How does an issuer determine its North American Industry Classification Standard (NAICS) code?

NAICS was developed to classify the domestic activities of businesses within North America, and also covers a wide range of industries that exist outside of North America.

If the issuer has already identified a NAICS code for its business, it should use that code. For example, Canadian businesses that file tax returns with the Canada Revenue Agency should use the same NAICS code that they report on those forms.

An issuer that has not already identified a NAICS code should use *Statistics Canada's NAICS search tool*[5] to find its NAICS code. An alternative is the *US Census Bureau's NAICS search tool.*[6]

The online search tools listed above allow an issuer to enter keywords that describe its business, and generate a list of primary business activities containing that keyword and the corresponding NAICS codes. Issuers for which more than one NAICS code may apply should choose the one that most closely describes the issuer's primary business activity. Alternatively, an issuer may browse a list of NAICS market sectors to find the more detailed industry level descriptions and the appropriate 6-digit code that closely matches the issuer's primary business activity.

Below are some examples:

Description of Issuer	Keywords searched	Possible NAICS Codes to consider
ABC-ABS Inc. is structured as a special purpose financial vehicle organized for the securitization of pools of receivables and the issuance of marketable fixed-income securities (asset-backed securities)	"special purpose vehicle" or "securitization"	526981 — Securitization vehicles
ABC Minerals operates as a mining and metals company worldwide. It produces copper, nickel, gold, zinc, platinum-group elements and pyrite.	"zinc" or "copper" or "nickel" or "gold"	212233 — Copper-zinc ore mining 212232 — Nickel-copper ore mining 212220 — Gold and silver ore mining
ABC LP is a private equity fund that invests in a portfolio of private companies. The fund will typically acquire a controlling or substantial minority interest in a portfolio of companies.	"investment firm" or "portfolio companies"	526989 — All other miscellaneous funds and financial vehicles 523920 — Portfolio management

---

[4]Names of individuals are required to be provided in Item 8(a), Items 9(a) and (b), Item 10, Item 11, Schedule 1 and Schedule 2.

[5]http://www23.statcan.gc.ca/imdb/p3VD.pl?Function=getVD&TVD=118464.

[6]http://www.census.gov/eos/www/naics/index.html.

Issuer information

8. The issuer filing the report was formed in 2002 by the completion of a plan of arrangement. Does Item 5(e) of the report require the date(s) of incorporation of the companies that completed the plan of arrangement, or the date of the completion of the plan of arrangement?

In this example, the issuer is not required to provide the incorporation dates of any predecessor entities in Item 5(e), only the date that the issuer was formed by the completion of the plan of arrangement in 2002.

9. How does an issuer determine the number of its employees for Item 5(b) of the report?

Employees are individuals that are employed directly by the issuer and on the issuer's payroll, including full and part-time employees.

Investment fund issuer information

10. What do the different investment fund types in Item 6(b) of the report refer to?

In Item 6(b), an investment fund issuer must select the investment fund type that most accurately describes the issuer based on the following:

- Money Market — An investment fund that invests in cash, cash equivalents and/or short term debt securities, such as government bonds and treasury bills.

- Equity — An investment fund that invests primarily in equity securities of other issuers.

- Fixed Income — An investment fund that invests primarily in fixed income (debt) securities.

- Balanced — An investment fund that invests primarily in a balanced combination of fixed income and equity securities.

- Alternative Strategies — An investment fund that primarily adopts alternative investment strategies, such as short selling, leverage or the use of derivatives, or that invests primarily in alternative asset classes, such as real estate or commodities.

- Other — An investment fund that cannot be classified under one of the above investment fund types. Include a short description of the type of investment fund in the box provided.

11. When would an investment fund issuer be considered to be primarily invested in other investment funds under Item 6(b) of the report?

An investment fund is generally considered a "fund of funds" if a majority of its assets are invested in other funds, under normal market conditions. One factor to consider in determining whether an investment fund issuer is a "fund of funds" is whether its investment objectives specifically state this as a strategy.

Distribution details

12. What does "located outside of Canada" mean in Item 7 of the report?

The onus is on an issuer and its counsel to determine where the issuer is located for the purposes of determining where a distribution has occurred, including whether an issuer is located in a jurisdiction of Canada.

The determination is based on the facts and circumstances of each particular distribution. The issuer should consider the following factors:

- where the issuer's mind and management are primarily located, which may be determined by the location of the issuer's head office or the residences of the issuer's key officers and directors,

- where the issuer's operations are conducted,

- where the issuer administers its business,

- whether any acts in furtherance of a distribution have occurred in a jurisdiction, including active advertisements or solicitations, negotiations, underwriting activities or investor relations activities, and

- where the issuer is incorporated or organized.

The above are examples of the types of factors that an issuer should consider in determining whether it is making a distribution from a jurisdiction, but it is not an exhaustive list.

13. What dates should be provided as the distribution date under Item 7(b) of the report?

If the report is being filed for securities distributed only on a single distribution date, provide this distribution date in Item 7(b) as both the start date and end date. For example, if the report is being filed for securities distributed only on July 1, 2016, provide July 1, 2016 as both the start date and end date.

If the report is being filed for securities distributed on more than one distribution date, in Item 7(b) provide the date of the earliest distribution as the start date and provide the date of the last distribution as the end date. A single report can be filed for distributions occurring on multiple dates only if such distributions occur within a 10-day period and the report is filed no later than 10 days after the first distribution date (other than investment funds that file reports on an annual basis).

For example:

- If the report is being filed for securities distributed on July 1, July 4, July 5 and July 7, 2016, in Item 7(b) provide July 1, 2016 as the start date and July 7, 2016 as the end date.

- If the report is being filed for an investment fund issuer that files annually and has distributed securities on a continuous basis from January 1, 2017 to December 31, 2017, in Item 7(b) provide January 1, 2017 as the start date and December 31, 2017 as the end date.

14. The type of security distributed by the issuer is not on the list of security codes in Instruction 12 of the report. What security code should the issuer provide in Item 7(d) of the report?

The list of security codes in Instruction 12 of the report captures most types of securities distributed by issuers filing reports in Canada. If the security being distributed is not listed, enter "OTH" (for other) as the security code in Item 7(d) and include a description of the security in the box provided. Examples are provided below.

Security code			CUSIP number (if applicable)	Description of security
N	O	T	555555555	6.26% medium term notes
C	E	R	555555556	Commercial mortgage pass-through certificates
U	B	S		Units comprised of one common share and one-half of one non-transferrable share purchase warrant
O	T	H		Syndicated mortgage interest
O	T	H		Global depository receipt

15. How does an issuer determine the number of unique purchasers for Item 7(f) of the report?

For the total number of unique purchasers, each purchaser should only be counted once, regardless of whether the issuer distributed different types of securities to that purchaser, distributed securities on different dates to that purchaser and/or relied on multiple prospectus exemptions for such distributions.

As an example, an issuer located in Alberta distributes (at $10/debenture, $10/common share):

- 100 debentures to Purchaser A in Alberta in reliance on the accredited investor prospectus exemption
- 100 common shares to Purchaser A in Alberta in reliance on the offering memorandum prospectus exemption
- 100 common shares to Purchaser B in Alberta in reliance on the accredited investor prospectus exemption
- 100 common shares to Purchaser C in Ontario in reliance on the family, friends and business associates prospectus exemption
- 100 debentures to Purchaser D in France in reliance on the accredited investor prospectus exemption

In this example, there are a total of 4 unique purchasers.

The table in Item 7(f) requires a separate line item for: (i) each jurisdiction where a purchaser resides, (ii) each exemption relied on in the jurisdiction where a purchaser resides, if a purchaser resides in a jurisdiction of Canada, and (iii) each exemption relied on in Canada, if a purchaser resides in a foreign jurisdiction. The table should be completed as follows:

Province or country	Exemption relied on	Number of purchasers	Total amount (Canadian $)
Alberta	Accredited investor (NI 45-106 s.2.3)	2	2,000
Alberta	Offering memorandum (NI 45-106 s.2.9(2.1))	1	1,000
Ontario	Family, friends and business associates (NI 45-106 s.2.5)	1	1,000
France	Accredited investor (NI 45-106 s.2.3)	1	1,000
Total dollar amount of securities distributed			5,000
Total number of unique purchasers[2]		4	

In Schedule 1, create a separate entry for each distribution date, security type and exemption relied on for the distribution to each purchaser. In the example above, this means there must be two separate entries for Purchaser A in Schedule 1: one entry for the distribution of 100 debentures in reliance on the accredited investor prospectus exemption, and a second entry for the distribution of 100 common shares in reliance on the offering memorandum prospectus exemption.

16. Are marketing materials required to be listed under Item 7(h) of the report?

Yes, if the securities legislation of Saskatchewan, Ontario, Québec, New Brunswick and Nova Scotia requires marketing materials to be filed with or delivered to the securities regulatory authority or regulator in connection with the distribution under the exemption relied on.

Item 7(h) requires issuers to list and provide certain details about offering materials that are required under the exemption relied on to be filed with or delivered to the securities regulatory authority or regulator in connection with the distribution in these jurisdictions. This is a reporting requirement only; the report does not impose any new requirement to deliver or file offering materials.

If marketing materials are required to be filed or delivered under the prospectus exemption relied on for the distribution, the issuer must list such materials in Item 7(h). For example, if an issuer makes a distribution to purchasers in Ontario in reliance on the offering memorandum exemption under section 2.9 of NI 45-106, the issuer must list marketing materials that are required to be incorporated or deemed to be incorporated by reference into the offering memorandum.

Part 4:
DISTRIBUTIONS

In Ontario only, if the offering materials listed in Item 7(h) are required to be filed with or delivered to the OSC, electronic versions of those offering materials are to be attached to and submitted electronically with the report on the OSC's Electronic Filing Portal (if not previously filed with or delivered to the OSC).

Compensation information

17. How does an issuer report compensation paid to two dealers in connection with the distribution?

Item 8 of the report must be completed separately for each dealer to whom the issuer provides compensation in connection with the distribution.

In section f(3) of Schedule 1, the issuer must indicate which of the two dealers received compensation in connection with the distribution to each purchaser by indicating the firm NRD number of the dealer, or the dealer's full legal name if not a registered firm. The firm NRD number or name must be consistent with the information provided in Item 8. If neither of the two dealers received compensation in connection with the distribution to a particular purchaser, then section f(3) of Schedule 1 should be left blank for that purchaser.

As noted in the instructions to Item 8(d), the report does not require disclosure of details about internal allocation arrangements with the directors, officers or employees of entities compensated by the issuer.

18. The issuer entered into a referral arrangement pursuant to which it pays an ongoing annual referral fee to a third party for so long as the purchaser holds the securities distributed. Is the issuer required to disclose the ongoing referral fee in the report? Is the issuer required to do so each year for so long as it pays the referral fee?

If the referral fee is paid in connection with a distribution, the issuer must report the referral fee in Item 8(d) of the report, by checking the box that indicates a person is receiving deferred compensation in connection with the distribution and describing the terms of the referral arrangement in the box provided.

The issuer is not required to report the referral fee every year. If no distributions were made in a particular year that give rise to referral fees being paid, then the referral fee is not required to be reported that year.

19. What do the terms "funding portal" and "internet-based portal" refer to in Item 8(a) of the report?

These terms generally refer to an intermediary that provides an online platform for issuers to offer and sell securities to investors. These include funding portals as defined under Multilateral Instrument 45-108 *Crowdfunding*.

Purchaser information

20. The issuer sold shares to a purchaser that instructed that the shares be registered in the name of its investment adviser. What name is the issuer required to disclose in Schedule 1 of the report?

All references to a purchaser in the report are to the beneficial owner of the securities (with the exception of fully managed accounts described below). In this example, the issuer should provide the name of the beneficial owner as the purchaser in Schedule 1. The investment adviser in this example is the registered, not the beneficial, owner.

Similarly, if a trust or personal holding corporation purchases securities from an issuer, the trust or corporation is the beneficial owner. The names of the trust beneficiaries or shareholders of the holding corporation are not required.

Beneficial owner information is not required in Schedule 1 where a trust company, trust corporation, or registered adviser is deemed to be purchasing the securities as principal on behalf of a fully managed account and the issuer is relying on the exemption described in paragraph (p) or (q) of the definition of "accredited investor" in section 1.1 of NI 45-106 to issue the securities. In that case, only the name of the trust company, trust corporation or registered adviser should be provided in Schedule 1.

21. The issuer does not have a purchaser's email address. What is the issuer required to disclose in section c(7) of Schedule 1 of the report?

If the purchaser has not provided an email address to the issuer, or the purchaser does not have an email address, the issuer may leave section c(7) of Schedule 1 blank for that purchaser.

Annex 4 — Transition to the New Report

This Annex provides further guidance on the report that should be filed as of June 30, 2016, when the amendments come into force.

Issuers other than investment funds filing annually

All issuers, other than investment fund issuers filing reports annually, must use the New Report for distributions that occur on or after June 30, 2016, when the amendments come into force. If an issuer completes a distribution before June 30, 2016, and the deadline to file the report occurs after June 30, 2016, the issuer must file the Current Report. If an issuer completes multiple distributions on dates that occur within a 10-day period beginning before and ending after June 30, 2016, the issuer may file either the Current Report or the New Report to report such distributions.

Please see the examples in Table 1 below for further clarity on the report that should be filed.

TABLE 1: FILING THE NEW REPORT			
	Distribution period covered by report	**Filing deadline[7]**	**Report required**
Issuer	1 June 20, 2016 to June 29, 2016	June 30, 2016	Current Report
Issuer 2	June 21, 2016 to June 30, 2016	July 1, 2016	Current Report *or* New Report

TABLE 1: FILING THE NEW REPORT

	Distribution period covered by report	Filing deadline[7]	Report required
Issuer 3	June 27, 2016	July 7, 2016	Current Report
Issuer 4	June 28, 2016 to July 1, 2016	July 8, 2016	Current Report *or* New Report
Issuer 5	June 30, 2016 to July 8, 2016	July 10, 2016[8]	New Report
Issuer 6	July 4, 2016	July 14, 2016	New Report
Issuer 7	July 5, 2016 to July 14, 2016	July 15, 2016	New Report

Notes:

7   The report must be filed no later than 10 days after the first distribution in the report.

8   If the filing deadline falls on a Saturday, Sunday or another day when the CSA member with which the report being filed is closed, the deadline is the next day on which the CSA member is open.

Investment fund issuers that file annually

Investment funds relying on certain prospectus exemptions may file reports of exempt distribution annually, within 30 days after the end of the calendar year. We have provided a transition period to allow investment fund issuers that file annually to file either the Current Report or the New Report for distributions that occur before January 1, 2017. For distributions that occur on or after January 1, 2017, all investment fund issuers filing annually must file the New Report.

Please see the examples in Table 2 for further clarity on the report that should be filed.

TABLE 2: TRANSITION PERIOD FOR INVESTMENT FUND ISSUERS THAT REPORT ANNUALLY

	Financial year-end	2016		2017		2018	
		Filing deadline	Report required	Filing deadline	Report required	Filing deadline	Report required
Investment Fund Issuer 1	Dec 31	Jan 30, 2016	Current Report — For distributions completed between Jan 1, 2015 and Dec 31, 2015	Jan 30, 2017	Current Report *or* New Report — For distributions completed between Jan 1, 2016 and Dec 31, 2016	Jan 30, 2018	New Report — For distributions completed between Jan 1, 2017 and Dec 31, 2017
Investment Fund Issuer 2	Apr 30	May 30, 2016	Current Report — For distributions completed between May 1, 2015 and Apr 30, 2016	Jan 30, 2017	Current Report *or* New Report — For distributions completed between May 1, 2016 and Dec 31, 2016	Jan 30, 2018	New Report — For distributions completed between Jan 1, 2017 and Dec 31, 2017
Investment Fund Issuer 3	May 31	Jun 30, 2016	Current Report — For distributions completed between Jun 1, 2015 and May 31, 2016	Jan 30, 2017	Current Report *or* New Report — For distributions completed between Jun 1, 2016 and Dec 31, 2016	Jan 30, 2018	New Report — For distributions completed between Jan 1, 2017 and Dec 31, 2017
Investment Fund Issuer 4	Jun 30	N/A	N/A	Jan 30, 2017	Current Report *or* New Report — For distributions completed between Jul, 1 2015 and Dec 31, 2016	Jan 30, 2018	New Report — For distributions completed between Jan 1, 2017 and Dec 31, 2017
Investment Fund Issuer 5	Sept 30	N/A	N/A	Jan 30, 2017	Current Report *or* New Report — For distributions completed between Oct 1, 2015 and Dec 31, 2016	Jan 30, 2018	New Report — For distributions completed between Jan 1, 2017 and Dec 31, 2017

TABLE 2: TRANSITION PERIOD FOR INVESTMENT FUND ISSUERS THAT REPORT ANNUALLY								
		2016			**2017**			**2018**
	Financial year-end	**Filing deadline**	**Report required**	**Filing deadline**	**Report required**	**Filing deadline**	**Report required**	

CSA Staff Notice 45-310 — Update on CSA Staff Consultation Note 45-401 — Review of Minimum Amount and Accredited Investor Exemptions

Date: June 7, 2012

35 O.S.C.B. 5319

[Not reproduced]

CSA Staff Notice 45-314 — Updated List of Current CSA Exempt Market Initiatives

Date: January 28, 2016

39 O.S.C.B. 903

First published March 20, 2014 — Revised January 28, 2016

Introduction

Modernization of the exempt market regulatory regime is a major priority for the Canadian Securities Administrators (CSA). In keeping with this, CSA members have published or adopted a series of significant initiatives related to prospectus exemptions. This notice describes all of these initiatives in one place for the benefit of industry and investors.

Further information about each initiative, and the text of the new exemptions and proposed amendments, is or will be available on the websites of the following CSA websites:

> www.lautorite.qc.ca
> www.albertasecurities.com
> www.bcsc.bc.ca
> nssc.novascotia.ca
> www.fcnb.ca
> www.osc.gov.on.ca
> www.fcaa.gov.sk.ca
> www.mbsecurities.ca

Updated List of Initiatives

Initiatives	Jurisdiction(s)	Summary of Latest Developments	Date
Short-Term Debt			
Short-Term Debt (s. 2.35 of NI 45-106 *Prospectus Exemptions*)	All	In effect: • Amendments to modify the minimum credit rating requirement when an issuer obtains more than one credit rating • Makes this exemption unavailable for securitized products	May 5, 2015
Short-Term Securitized Products (s. 2.35.1 of NI 45-106)	All	In effect: • New prospectus exemption for short-term securitized products (ABCP) with additional credit rating, liquidity and disclosure requirements	May 5, 2015
Accredited Investor, Minimum Amount and Family, Friends and Business Associates			
Accredited Investor	All	In effect:	May 5, 2015

Initiatives	Jurisdiction(s)	Summary of Latest Developments	Date
(s. 2.3 of NI 45-106)		• Amendments to require persons relying on the prospectus exemption to obtain a signed risk acknowledgement from certain individual accredited investors • Expanded guidance on steps issuers can take to verify accredited investor status • Introduced family trusts as a category of accredited investor	
	ON	In effect: • Amendments to the definition of accredited investor to allow fully managed accounts to purchase investment fund securities using the managed account category of the prospectus exemption	May 5, 2015
$150,000 Minimum Amount Investment (s. 2.10 of NI 45-106)	All	In effect: • Amendments to restrict the prospectus exemption to distributions to non-individual investors	May 5, 2015
Family, Friends and Business Associates (s. 2.5 and s. 2.6.1 of NI 45-106)	ON	In effect: • New prospectus exemption for non-investment fund issuers similar to the FFBA exemption in other CSA jurisdictions • Repeal of existing founder, control person and family prospectus exemption	May 5, 2015
Existing Security Holder, Rights Offering and Investment Dealer			
Existing Security Holder (General and blanket orders in jurisdictions other than AB and ON) s. 3 of ASC Rule 45-516	BC, AB, SK, MB, QC, NL, NB, NS, PE, YK, NT, NU	In effect: • New prospectus exemption to allow issuers listed on certain Canadian stock exchanges to distribute securities to existing security holders in prescribed circumstances	March 13, 2014
Prospectus Exemptions for Retail Investors and Existing Security Holders in AB s. 2.9 of OSC Rule 45-501 *Ontario Prospectus and Registration Exemptions* in ON)	ON	In effect: • New prospectus exemption to allow non-investment fund issuers listed on certain Canadian stock exchanges to distribute securities to existing security holders in prescribed circumstances	February 11, 2015
Rights Offering (s. 2.1 of NI 45-106)	All	In effect: • Streamlined prospectus exemption to allow reporting issuers to raise capital by issuing rights to existing security holders • Securities are subject to seasoning period	December 8, 2015
Investment Dealer Exemption (General and blanket orders in jurisdictions other than AB	BC, AB, SK, MB, NB	In effect: • New prospectus exemption to allow issuers listed on a Canadian exchange to raise any amount of money from any investor who has received suitability advice from a registered investment dealer	January 14, 2016

Part 4:
DISTRIBUTIONS

Initiatives	Jurisdiction(s)	Summary of Latest Developments	Date
s. 4 of ASC Rule 45-516 *Prospectus Exemptions for Retail Investors and Existing Security Holders* in AB)			
Offering Memorandum, Crowdfunding and Start-up Business			
Start-up Crowdfunding (*Start-up Crowdfunding* general and blanket orders)	BC, SK, MB, QC, NB, NS	In effect: • New prospectus and registration exemptions for start-up and early stage businesses	May 14, 2015
Start-up Business (proposed MI 45-109 *Prospectus Exemption for Start-up Businesses*)	AB, NU	Published for comment: • Proposed prospectus exemption for small and early-stage businesses	October 19, 2015
Offering Memorandum (s. 2.9 of NI 45-106)	ON	In effect: • New prospectus exemption for noninvestment fund issuers similar to the offering memorandum exemption published by AB, SK, QC, NB and NS on October 29, 2015	January 13, 2016
	AB, SK, QC, NB, NS	Advance notice of adoption: • Amendments to introduce new investor protection measures, including rolling investment limits, incorporation by reference of marketing materials and certain limited disclosure requirements for non-reporting issuers following a distribution	October 29, 2015 (intended to be in force April 30, 2016)
Crowdfunding (MI 45-108 *Crowdfunding*)	SK	Advance notice of adoption: • New prospectus exemption for noninvestment fund issuers • Registration framework for online funding portals as a dealer	January 25, 2016 (implementation date subject to Ministerial approval)
	MB, ON, QC, NB, NS	In effect: • New prospectus exemption for noninvestment fund issuers • Registration framework for online funding portals as a dealer	January 25, 2016
Report of Exempt Distribution			
Report of Exempt Distribution (Proposed Form 45-106F1)	All	Published for comment: • Proposal to introduce harmonized report of exempt distribution in Form 45-106F1	August 13, 2015

Questions

Please refer your questions to any of the following:

[Names not reproduced]

OSC Rule 45-501 — Ontario Prospectus and Registration Exemptions

Date: November 23, 2001, as amended effective March 31, 2003, January 12, 2004 and March 30, 2004; replaced effective September 14, 2005, as amended effective December 31, 2007; replaced effective September 28, 2009, amended February 11, 2015, May 5, 2015, September 8, 2015, December 8, 2015, January 13, 2016 and January 25, 2016.

24 O.S.C.B. 7011, 26 O.S.C.B. 4375, 27 O.S.C.B. 433, 27 O.S.C.B. 3603, 28 O.S.C.B. (Supp-4) 95, 31 O.S.C.B. 10527, 32 O.S.C.B. (Supp. 5) 161, 37 O.S.C.B. 10481, 38 O.S.C.B. (Supp. 1) 12, 169, 38 O.S.C.B. 5798, 38 O.S.C.B. 8277 and 38 O.S.C.B. (Supp. 3) 55.

[This version of the Rule reflects changes scheduled to come into force on January 13th and 25th, 2016. For a version of the Rule without these changes please see the 58th ed.]

Text boxes in this Rule refer to National Instrument 45-102 Resale of Securities. These text boxes are located above sections 2.1 to 2.8. These text boxes do not form part of this Rule. [Editor's Note: The text boxes are shown in bold italics.]

PART 1 — DEFINITIONS AND INTERPRETATION

1.1 Definitions — In this Rule

"bank" means a bank named in Schedule I or II of the *Bank Act* (Canada);

"Canadian financial institution" means

(a) an association governed by the *Cooperative Credit Associations Act* (Canada) or a central cooperative credit society for which an order has been made under section 473(1) of that Act, or

(b) a bank, loan corporation, trust company, trust corporation, insurance company, treasury branch, credit union, caisse populaire, financial services cooperative, or league that, in each case, is authorized by an enactment of Canada or a jurisdiction of Canada to carry on business in Canada or a jurisdiction of Canada;

"**debt security**" means any bond, debenture, note or similar instrument representing indebtedness, whether secured or unsecured;

"**director**" means

(a) a member of the board of directors of a company or an individual who performs similar functions for a company, and

(b) with respect to a person that is not a company, an individual who performs functions similar to those of a director of a company;

"**eligible foreign security**" means a security offered primarily in a foreign jurisdiction as part of a distribution of securities in either of the following circumstances:

(a) the security is issued by an issuer

(i) that is incorporated, formed or created under the laws of a foreign jurisdiction,

(ii) that is not a reporting issuer in a jurisdiction of Canada,

(iii) that has its head office outside of Canada, and

(iv) that has a majority of the executive officers and a majority of the directors ordinarily resident outside of Canada;

(b) the security is issued or guaranteed by the government of a foreign jurisdiction;

"**entity**" means a company, syndicate, partnership, trust or unincorporated organization;

"**executive officer**" means, for an issuer, an individual who is

(a) a chair, vice-chair or president,

(a.1) a chief executive officer or chief financial officer,

(b) a vice-president in charge of a principal business unit, division or function including sales, finance or production, or

(c) performing a policy-making function in respect of the issuer;

"**NI 45-106**" means National Instrument 45-106 *Prospectus Exemptions*;

"**permitted client**" has the same meaning as in section 1.1 of National Instrument 31-103 *Registration Requirements, Exemptions and Ongoing Registrant Obligations*;

"**person**" includes

(a) an individual,

(b) a corporation,

(c) a partnership, trust, fund and an association, syndicate, organization or other organized group of persons, whether incorporated or not, and

(d) an individual or other person in that person's capacity as a trustee, executor, administrator or personal or other legal representative;

"**Schedule III bank**" means an authorized foreign bank named in Schedule III of the *Bank Act* (Canada);

"**spouse**" means an individual who

(a) is married to another individual and is not living separate and apart, within the meaning of the *Divorce Act* (Canada), from the other individual, or

(b) is living with another individual in a marriage-like relationship, including a marriage-like relationship between individuals of the same gender;

"**subsidiary**" means an issuer that is controlled directly or indirectly by another issuer and includes a subsidiary of that subsidiary.

1.2 Affiliate — For the purpose of this Rule, an issuer is an affiliate of another issuer if

(a) one of them is the subsidiary of the other, or

(b) each of them is controlled by the same person.

1.3 Control — For the purpose of this Rule, a person (first person) is considered to control another person (second person) if

(a) the first person beneficially owns or, directly or indirectly, exercises control or direction over securities of the second person carrying votes which, if exercised, would entitle the first person to elect a majority of the directors of the second person, unless that first person holds the voting securities only to secure an obligation,

(b) the second person is a partnership, other than a limited partnership, and the first person holds more than 50% of the interests of the partnership, or

(c) the second person is a limited partnership and the general partner of the limited partnership is the first person.

1.4 Registration requirement — (1) An exemption in this Rule from the dealer registration requirement or from the prospectus requirement, that refers to a registered dealer is only available for a trade in a security if the dealer is registered in a category that permits the trade described in the exemption.

(2) In this Rule, an exemption from the dealer registration requirement is deemed to be an exemption from the underwriter registration requirement.

(3) In this Rule, an exemption from the dealer registration requirement or from the prospectus requirement that refers to a registered adviser is only available for a trade in a security if the adviser is registered in a category that permits the adviser to act as an adviser in the circumstances described in the exemption.

PART 2 — PROSPECTUS EXEMPTIONS

2.0 Government incentive security — The following are prescribed as government incentive securities under subsection 73.5(1) of the Act:

1. a security, or unit or interest in a partnership that invests in a security, that is issued by a company and for which the company has agreed to renounce in favour of the holder of the security, unit or interest, amounts that will constitute Canadian exploration expense, as defined in

subsection 66.1(6) of the ITA, Canadian development expense, as defined in subsection 66.2(5) of the ITA, or Canadian oil and gas property expense, as defined in subsection 66.4(5) of the ITA, or

2. a unit or interest in a partnership or joint venture that is issued in order to fund Canadian exploration expense, as defined in subsection 66.1(6) of the ITA, Canadian development expense, as defined in subsection 66.2(5) of the ITA, or Canadian oil and gas property expense, as defined in subsection 66.4(5) of the ITA;

2.1 Government incentive security —

Refer to Appendix D of National Instrument 45-102 **Resale of Securities**. *First trades are subject to a seasoning period on resale.*

(1) For the purpose of section 73.5 of the Act, the prospectus requirement does not apply to a distribution of a government incentive security by an issuer or a promoter of an issuer of a security of the issuer, if all of the following apply:

(a) in the aggregate in all jurisdictions in Canada, not more than 75 prospective purchasers are solicited resulting in sales to not more than 50 purchasers,

(b) before entering into an agreement of purchase and sale, the prospective purchaser has been supplied with an offering memorandum that includes information

(i) identifying every officer and director of the issuer,

(ii) identifying every promoter of the issuer,

(iii) giving the particulars of the professional qualifications and associations during the five years before the date of the offering memorandum of each officer, director and promoter of the issuer that are relevant to the offering,

(iv) indicating each of the directors that will be devoting his or her full time to the affairs of the issuer, and

(v) describing the right of action referred to in section 130.1 of the Act that is applicable in respect of the offering memorandum,

(c) the prospective purchaser has access to substantially the same information concerning the issuer that a prospectus filed under the Act would provide and,

(i) because of net worth and investment experience or because of consultation with or advice from a person that is not a promoter of the issuer and that is a registered dealer or registered adviser under the Act, is able to evaluate the prospective investment on the basis of information about the investment presented to the prospective purchaser by the issuer or selling security holder, or

(ii) is an executive officer or director of the issuer or of an affiliate of the issuer or a spouse or child of a director or executive officer of the issuer or of an affiliate of the issuer,

(d) the offer and sale of the security is not accompanied by an advertisement and no selling or promotional expenses have been paid or incurred for the offer and sale except for professional services or for services performed by a registered dealer under the Act, and

(e) the promoter, if any, has not acted as a promoter of any other issue of securities under this exemption within the calendar year.

(2) For the purpose of determining the number of purchasers or prospective purchasers under paragraph (1)(a), a corporation, partnership, trust or other entity is counted as one purchaser or prospective purchaser unless the entity has been created, or is being used, primarily for the purpose of purchasing a security of the issuer, in which event each beneficial owner of an equity security of the entity or each beneficiary of the entity, as the case may be, is counted as a separate purchaser or prospective purchaser.

2.2 Government incentive security distributed under section 2.1 —

Refer to Appendix D of National Instrument 45-102 **Resale of Securities**. *First trades are subject to a restricted period on resale.*

The prospectus requirement does not apply to a distribution of a security that was previously distributed under the exemption in section 73.5 of the Act, or a predecessor exemption to section 73.5 of the Act, if each of the parties to the trade is one of the not more than 50 purchasers referred to in the exemption or predecessor exemption.

2.3 Commodity futures option or contract —

This provision will not be cited in any Appendix of National Instrument 45-102 *Resale of Securities*. **These securities are free trading.**

(1) The prospectus requirement does not apply to a distribution of a commodity futures option or commodity futures contract by a hedger through a dealer.

(2) For the purposes of subsection (1), the terms "commodity futures option", "dealer", "commodity futures contract", and "hedger" have the same meaning as in the CFA.

2.4 Security of a co-operative — [Repealed.]

2.5 Membership share of a credit union — [Repealed.]

2.6 Security of a credit union — [Repealed.]

2.7 Execution Act —

This provision will not be cited in any Appendix of National Instrument 45-102 *Resale of Securities*. **These securities are free trading.**

(1) The prospectus requirement does not apply to a distribution of a security by a sheriff under the *Execution Act* if

(a) there is no published market in respect of the security,

(b) the aggregate acquisition cost to the purchaser is not more than $25,000, and

(c) each written notice to the public soliciting offers for the security, or giving notice of the intended auction of the security, is accompanied by a statement substantially as follows:

> These securities are speculative. No representations are made concerning the securities, or the issuer of the securities. No prospectus is available and the protections, rights and remedies arising out of the prospectus provisions of the Securities Act (Ontario) including statutory rights of rescission and damages, will not be available to the purchaser of these securities.

(2) For the purposes of subsection (1), "published market" means, for a security, any market on which the security is traded if the prices at which it has been traded on the market are regularly published in a newspaper or a business or financial publication of general and regular circulation.

2.8 Distributions in mutual fund securities to corporate sponsored plans —

This provision will not be cited in any Appendix of National Instruments 45-102 **Resale of Securities**. ***These securities are free trading.***

The prospectus requirement does not apply to a distribution by a person of

(a) a security of a mutual fund, if the security is sold to a pension plan, deferred profit sharing plan, retirement savings plan or other similar capital accumulation plan maintained by the sponsor of the plan for its employees, and

     (i) the employees deal only with the sponsor in respect of their participation in the plan and the purchase of the security by the plan, or

     (ii) the decision to purchase the security is not made by or at the direction of the employee; or

(b) a security of a mutual fund that

     (i) is administered by a trust corporation registered under the *Loan and Trust Corporations Act*,

     (ii) consists of a pool of funds that

         (A) results from, and is limited to, the combination or commingling of funds of pension or other superannuation plans registered under the ITA, and

         (B) is established by or related to persons that are associates or affiliates of or that otherwise do not deal at arm's length with the promoters of the mutual fund except the trust corporation that administers the fund, and

     (iii) is managed, in whole or in part, by a person who is registered or who is exempt from registration under the Act.

2.9 Distributions to existing security holders — (1) In this section,

"announcement date" means the day that an issuer issues an offering news release;

"investment dealer" has the same meaning as in section 1.1 of National Instrument 31-103 *Registration Requirements, Exemptions and Ongoing Registrant Obligations*;

"listed security" means an equity security of an issuer of a class listed on the Toronto Stock Exchange, the TSX Venture Exchange, the Canadian Securities Exchange or the Aequitas NEO Exchange;

"offering material" means a document purporting to describe the business and affairs of an issuer that has been prepared primarily for delivery to and review by a prospective purchaser so as to assist the prospective purchaser to make an investment decision in respect of securities being sold in a distribution under this section;

"offering news release" means a news release of an issuer announcing its intention to conduct a distribution under this section;

"record date" means the date determined by an issuer that intends to conduct a distribution under this section that is at least one day prior to the announcement date;

"warrant" means a warrant of an issuer that entitles the holder to acquire a listed security or a fraction of a listed security of the same issuer;

"unit" means a listed security and a warrant.

(2) The prospectus requirement does not apply to a distribution by an issuer of a listed security or a unit of its own issue to a security holder of the issuer purchasing as principal if all of the following apply:

     (a) the issuer

         (i) is a reporting issuer in at least one jurisdiction of Canada with a class of listed securities, and

         (ii) is not an investment fund;

     (b) the issuer has filed in each jurisdiction of Canada in which it is a reporting issuer all periodic and timely disclosure documents that it is required to have filed in that jurisdiction as and when required

         (i) under applicable securities legislation,

         (ii) pursuant to an order issued by the regulator or securities regulatory authority, or

         (iii) pursuant to an undertaking to the regulator or securities regulatory authority;

     (c) the issuer has issued and filed an offering news release describing in reasonable detail the proposed distribution, including, without limitation,

         (i) the minimum and maximum number of securities proposed to be distributed under this section and the minimum and maximum aggregate gross proceeds of the distribution,

         (ii) the proposed principal uses, including estimated dollar amounts, of the gross proceeds of the distribution, assuming both the minimum and maximum offering, and

         (iii) a description of how the issuer intends to allocate securities;

     (d) subject to applicable securities laws, the issuer permits each person who, as of the record date, held a listed security of the issuer of the same class and series as the listed securities to be distributed under this section to subscribe for securities in the distribution;

     (e) the purchaser has represented in writing to the issuer that the purchaser held at the record date, and continues to hold, a listed security of the issuer of the same class and series as the listed securities to be distributed under this section;

     (f) the issuer or any salesperson acting on behalf of the issuer in connection with a distribution under this section does not reasonably believe that the representation of the purchaser, referred to in paragraph (e), is untrue;

(g) either:

    (i) the purchaser has obtained advice regarding the suitability of the investment and, if the purchaser is a resident of a jurisdiction of Canada, that advice is from a person registered in that jurisdiction as an investment dealer, or

    (ii) the aggregate of the acquisition cost to the purchaser of securities to be purchased from the issuer under the distribution, when added to the acquisition cost to the purchaser of all other securities of the issuer acquired in reliance on this section in the 12-month period immediately preceding the distribution, does not exceed $15,000.

(3) The issuer must represent to the purchaser in the subscription agreement that

    (a) the issuer's "core documents" and "documents", as those terms are defined in section 138.1 of the Act, do not contain a misrepresentation, and

    (b) there is no material fact or material change related to the issuer which has not been generally disclosed.

(4) A distribution of listed securities or units by an issuer under subsection (2) must not result in an increase of more than 100 percent in the number of outstanding listed securities of the same class.

(5) The exemption in subsection (2) is not available for a distribution of a listed security if the class of listed security has been suspended from trading for failure to comply with the ongoing requirements of the applicable exchange.

(6) Part XXIII.1 of the Act applies to a security distributed under this section.

(7) Other than the subscription agreement, any offering material prepared in connection with a distribution under this section must be filed with the securities regulatory authority by the issuer no later than the day that the offering material was first provided to a potential purchaser.

PART 3 — REGISTRATION EXEMPTIONS

3.0 Application — Part 3, except for sections 3.3 and 3.4, does not apply.

[Editor's Note: Sections 3.01, 3.1, 3.2, 3.5 and 3.6 have been omitted.]

3.3 Commodity futures option or contract — (1) The dealer registration requirement does not apply to a trade in a commodity futures option or commodity futures contract by a hedger through a dealer.

(2) For the purposes of subsection (1), the terms "commodity futures option", "dealer", "commodity futures contract", and "hedger" have the same meaning as in the CFA.

3.4 Security of a co-operative — The dealer registration requirement does not apply to a trade in a security issued by a corporation to which the *Co-operative Corporations Act* applies.

PART 4 — REGISTRATION EXEMPTIONS FOR FINANCIAL INTERMEDIARIES AND SCHEDULE III BANKS

[Repealed.]

PART 5 — OFFERING MEMORANDUM

5.1 Application — This Part only applies to a distribution made in reliance on an exemption from the prospectus requirement in

    (a) section 73.3 of the Act or a predecessor exemption to section 73.3 of the Act [*Accredited investor*],

    (b) section 73.4 of the Act or a predecessor exemption to section 73.4 of the Act [*Private issuer*],

    (b.1) section 2.5 of NI 45-106 [*Family, friends and business associates*]

    (c) [Repealed.]

    (d) section 2.8 of NI 45-106 [*Affiliates*],

    (d.1) section 2.9 of NI 45-106 [*Offering Memorandum*],

    (e) section 2.10 of NI 45-106 [*Minimum amount investment*],

    (f) section 2.19 of NI 45-106 [*Additional investment in investment funds*],

    (f.1) section 5 of Multilateral Instrument 45-108 *Crowdfunding* [*Crowdfunding prospectus exemption*], if the eligible crowdfunding issuer is a reporting issuer, and

    (g) section 73.5 of the Act or a predecessor exemption to section 73.5 of the Act [*Government incentive security*].

5.2 Right of action for damages and right of rescission — (1) The rights referred to in section 130.1 of the Act apply in respect of an offering memorandum delivered to a prospective purchaser.

(2) Despite subsection (1), the rights referred to in section 130.1 of the Act do not apply in respect of an offering memorandum delivered to a prospective purchaser in connection with a distribution made in reliance on the exemption from the prospectus requirement in section 73.3 of the Act or a predecessor exemption to section 73.3 of the Act [*Accredited investor*] if the prospective purchaser is

    (a) a Canadian financial institution or a Schedule III bank,

    (b) the Business Development Bank of Canada incorporated under the *Business Development Bank of Canada Act* (Canada), or

    (c) a subsidiary of any person referred to in paragraphs (a) and (b), if the person owns all of the voting securities of the subsidiary, except the voting securities required by law to be owned by directors of that subsidiary.

5.3 Description of rights in offering memorandum — If a seller delivers an offering memorandum to a prospective purchaser in connection with a distribution to which the rights referred to in section 130.1 of the Act apply, the rights must be described in the offering memorandum.

5.3.1 Alternative compliance with description of rights in an offering memorandum — (1) If a seller delivers an offering memorandum to a prospective purchaser that is a permitted client in connection with a distribution of an eligible foreign security, the requirement in section 5.3 to disclose the rights referred to in section 130.1 of the Act will be considered to have been satisfied if a specified disclosure statement is made in one of the following:

(a) the offering memorandum;

(b) a document delivered to the permitted client which accompanies, but is not part of, the offering memorandum;

(c) a written notice that:

(i) has been delivered to the permitted client by a registered dealer or an international dealer that proposes to make future distributions of securities to the permitted client; and

(ii) which contains a statement to the effect that the disclosure will apply to all future distributions.

(2) For the purpose of subsection (1), a specified disclosure statement must be in the following form or a substantively similar form:

(a) if the statement is made in a document referred to in paragraph 1(a),

Securities legislation in certain provinces or territories of Canada may provide a purchaser with remedies for rescission or damages if the offering memorandum (including any amendment thereto) contains a misrepresentation, provided that the remedies for rescission or damages are exercised by the purchaser within the time limit prescribed by the securities legislation of the purchaser's province or territory. The purchaser should refer to any applicable provisions of the securities legislation of the purchaser's province or territory for particulars of these rights or consult with a legal advisor;

(b) if the statement is made in a document referred to in paragraph (1)(b) or (1)(c),

If, in connection with a distribution of an eligible foreign security as defined in Ontario Securities Commission Rule 45-501 Ontario Prospectus and Registration Exemptions, we deliver to you an offering document that constitutes an offering memorandum under applicable securities laws in Canada, you may have, depending on the province or territory of Canada in which the trade was made to you, remedies for rescission or damages if the offering memorandum (including any amendment thereto) contains a misrepresentation, provided that the remedies for rescission or damages are exercised by you within the time limit prescribed by the securities legislation of your province or territory. You should refer to any applicable provisions of the securities legislation of your province or territory for the particulars of these rights or consult with a legal advisor.

5.4 Delivery of offering memorandum — (1) If an offering memorandum is provided to a prospective purchaser, the seller must deliver to the Commission a copy of the offering memorandum or any amendment to a previously delivered offering memorandum within 10 days of the date of the distribution.

(2) The requirement in subsection (1) does not apply to an offering memorandum prepared and filed with the Commission in accordance with section 2.9 of NI 45-106.

5.5 Exemption from Listing Representation Requirements — Subsection 38(3) of the Act does not apply to any representation made in an offering memorandum in connection with a distribution of an eligible foreign security if all of the following apply:

(a) each purchaser of the security is a permitted client;

(b) the representation does not contain a misrepresentation;

(c) the representation is made in compliance with the by-laws and rules of the exchange or quotation and trade reporting system referred to in the representation.

5.6 Application — Sections 5.3.1 and 5.6 do not apply if a prospectus has been filed with a Canadian securities regulatory authority in connection with the distribution.

PART 6 — REPORTING REQUIREMENTS

6.1 Report of exempt distribution — (1) An issuer that distributes its own securities must file a report if it makes the distribution under

(a) section 73.5 of the Act or a predecessor exemption to section 73.5 of the Act [Government incentive security], or

(b) section 2.9 [Distributions to existing security holders].

(2) The issuer must file the report no later than 10 days after the distribution.

6.2 Required form of report of exempt distribution — (1) The required form of report under paragraph 6.1(1)(a) [Report of exempt distribution] is Form 45-501F1.

(2) The required form of report of exempt distribution under paragraph 6.1(1)(b) [Report of exempt distribution] is Form 45-106F1 *Report of Exempt Distribution*.

PART 7 — EXEMPTION

7.1 Exemption — The Director may grant an exemption to Part 6, in whole or in part, subject to such conditions or restrictions as may be imposed in the exemption.

PART 8 — TRANSITION AND EFFECTIVE DATE

8.1 Revocation of former rule — [Repealed.]

8.2 Effective date — This Rule comes into force on the later of the following:

(a) September 28, 2009;

(b) the day on which sections 5 and 11, subsection 12(1) and section 13 of Schedule 26 of the *Budget Measures Act, 2009* are proclaimed in force.

Replacement Rule: (2009) 32 O.S.C.B. (Supp. 5) 161; Approval by OSC: (2009) 32 O.S.C.B. (Supp. 2) 1; Request for Comments: (2009) 32 O.S.C.B. 4233 and (2008) 31 O.S.C.B. (Supp. 1) 1.

Replacement Rule: (2005) 28 O.S.C.B. (Supp-4) 95; Approval by OSC: (2005) 25 O.S.C.B. (Supp-3) 1; Request for Comments: (2004) 27 O.S.C.B. (Supp-3) 1; Replaced and consolidated certain provisions of the Act, the Regulation and Rules 32-502, 32-503 and 46-501.

Amendment to Rule: (2007) 30 O.S.C.B. 10527; Approval by OSC: (2007) 30 O.S.C.B. 8539.

Revised Rule: (2004) 27 O.S.C.B. 433; Approval by OSC: (2003) 26 O.S.C.B. 7297; Request for Comments: (2003) 26 O.S.C.B. 2965.

Amendment to Revised Rule: (2004) 27 O.S.C.B. 3603; Approval by OSC: (2003) 26 O.S.C.B. 8217; Request for Comments: (2003) 26 O.S.C.B. 99.

Revised Rule: (2001) 24 O.S.C.B. 7011; Approval by OSC: (2001) 24 O.S.C.B. 5544; Request for Comments: (2001) 24 O.S.C.B. 4247 and 2183 and (2000) 23 O.S.C.B. 6205.

Amendment to Rule: (2003) 26 O.S.C.B. 4375; Approval by OSC: (2003) 26 O.S.C.B. 888.

Amendment to Rule: (2015) 38 O.S.C.B. 4156.

Amendment to Rule: (2015) 38 O.S.C.B. 5798.

Amendment to Rule: (2015) 38 O.S.C.B. (Supp. 3) 55.

Amendment to Rule: (2015) 38 O.S.C.B. (Supp. 4) 89.

Final Rule: (1999) 22 O.S.C.B. 139; Approval by OSC: (1998) 21 O.S.C.B. 6541; Request for Comments: (1998) 21 O.S.C.B. 3386 and (1997) 20 O.S.C.B. 5287. Replaced and consolidated certain sections of the Regulation and the following rules which were originally blanket rulings which where deemed to be rules under section 143.1(1) of the Act and remade into rules as follows:

Original Blanket Ruling	Title of Remade Rule
(a) (1994) 17 O.S.C.B. 2877	In the Matter of Trades by Issuers Upon Exercise of Certain Conversion Rights and In the Matter of the First Trade in Securities Acquired Upon Exercise of Such Conversion or Exchange Rights
(b) (1987) 10 O.S.C.B. 5936	In the Matter of Certain Proposed Amendments
(c) (1994) 17 O.S.C.B. 197	In the Matter of Trades by Issuers in Connection with Securities Exchange Issuer Bids and by Holders of Securities of a Company to Another Company in Connection with an Amalgamation, an Arrangement or a Specified Statutory Procedure
(d) (1985) 8 O.S.C.B. 127	In the Matter of Trades in Securities of a Private Company Under the Execution Act
(e) (1994) 17 O.S.C.B. 1178	In the Matter of Dividend Reinvestment Plans

(1997) 20 O.S.C.B. 1218 as amended by (1998) 21 O.S.C.B. 2330-2335.

Rules: NI 45-102, 13-502 App. C, Item B2.

Form 45-501F1 — Report of Exempt Distribution

This is the form required under section 6.1 of Ontario Securities Commission Rule 45-501 for a report of exempt distribution.

Issuer information

Item 1: State the full name of the issuer of the security distributed and the address and telephone number of its head office. If the issuer of the security distributed is an investment fund, state the name of the fund as the issuer, and provide the full name of the manager of the investment fund and the address and telephone number of the head office of the manager. Include the former name of the issuer if its name has changed since last report.

Item 2: State whether the issuer is or is not a reporting issuer and, if reporting, each of the jurisdictions in which it is reporting.

Item 3: Indicate the industry of the issuer by checking the appropriate box next to one of the industries listed below.

❏ Bio-tech

Financial Services

    ❏ investment companies and funds

    ❏ mortgage investment companies

❏ Forestry

❏ Hi-tech

❏ Industrial

Mining

    ❏ exploration/development

    ❏ production

❏ Oil and gas

❏ Real estate

❏ Utilities

❏ Other (describe) ....

Details of distribution

Item 4: Complete Schedule I to this report. Schedule I is designed to assist in completing the remainder of this report.

Item 5: State the distribution date. If the report is being filed for securities distributed on more than one distribution date, state all distribution dates.

Item 6: For each security distributed:

    (a) describe the type of security,

(b) state the total number of securities distributed. If the security is convertible or exchangeable, describe the type of underlying security, the terms of exercise or conversion and any expiry date; and

(c) state the exemption(s) relied on.

Item 7: Complete the following table for each Canadian and foreign jurisdiction where purchasers of the securities reside. Do not include in this table, securities issued as payment for commissions or finder's fees disclosed under item 8, below.

Each jurisdiction where purchasers reside	Number of purchasers	Price per security (Canadian $)[1]	Total dollar value raised from purchasers in the jurisdiction (Canadian $)
Total number of Purchasers			
Total dollar value of distribution in all jurisdictions (Canadian $)			

Notes 1: If securities are issued at different prices list the highest and lowest price the securities were sold for.

Commissions and finder's fees

Item 8: Complete the following table by providing information for each person who has received or will receive compensation in connection with the distribution(s). Compensation includes commissions, discounts or other fees or payments of a similar nature. Do not include payments for services incidental to the distribution, such as clerical, printing, legal or accounting services.

If the securities being issued as compensation are or include convertible securities, such as warrants or options, please add a footnote describing the terms of the convertible securities, including the term and exercise price. Do not include the exercise price of any convertible security in the total dollar value of the compensation unless the securities have been converted.

Full name and address of the person being compensated	Cash (Canadian $)	Compensation paid or to be paid (cash and/or securities)			Total dollar value of compensation (Canadian $)
		Securities			
		Number and type of securities issued	Price per security	Exemption relied on and date of distribution	

Item 9: If a distribution is made to one or more individuals in Ontario, include the attached "Authorization of Indirect Collection of Personal Information for Distribution in Ontario".

Certificate

On behalf of the issuer, I certify that the statements made in this report are true.

Date: ....

.... Name of issuer (please print)

.... Print name, title and telephone number of person signing

.... Signature

Item 10: State the name, title and telephone number of the person who may be contacted with respect to any questions regarding the contents of this report, if different than the person signing the certificate.

IT IS AN OFFENCE TO MAKE A MISREPRESENTATION IN THIS REPORT.

Notice — Collection and use of personal information

The personal information required under this form is collected on behalf of and used by the Ontario Securities Commission under the authority granted in securities legislation for the purposes of the administration and enforcement of the securities legislation.

If you have any questions about the collection and use of this information, contact the Ontario Securities Commission at the following address:

Ontario Securities Commission

Suite 1903, Box 55, 20 Queen Street West

Toronto, Ontario M5H 3S8

Public official contact regarding indirect collection of information:

Administrative Support Clerk

Telephone (416) 593-3684

Authorization of Indirect Collection of Personal Information for Distributions in Ontario

The attached Schedule I contains personal information of purchasers and details of the distribution(s). The issuer hereby confirms that each purchaser listed in Schedule I of this report

(a) has been notified by the issuer

(i) of the delivery to the Ontario Securities Commission of the information pertaining to the person as set out in Schedule I,

(ii) that this information is being collected indirectly by the Ontario Securities Commission under the authority granted to it in securities legislation,

(iii) that this information is being collected for the purposes of the administration and enforcement of Ontario securities legislation, and

(iv) of the title, business address and business telephone number of the public official in Ontario, as set out in this report, who can answer questions about the Ontario Securities Commission's indirect collection of the information, and

(b) has authorized the indirect collection of the information by the Ontario Securities Commission.

Schedule I

Complete the following table.

Do not include in this table, securities issued as payment of commissions or finder's fees disclosed under item 8 of this report.

The information in this schedule will not be placed on the public file of the Ontario Securities Commission. However, freedom of information legislation in Ontario may require the Ontario Securities Commission to make this information available if requested.

Full name, residential address and telephone number of purchaser	Number and type of securities purchased	Total purchase price (Canadian $)	Exemption relied on	Date of distribution

Instructions:

1. File this report and the applicable fee at the following address:

Ontario Securities Commission

Suite 1900, Box 55, 20 Queen Street West

Toronto, Ontario M5H 3S8

Telephone: (416) 593-3682

Facsimile: (416) 593-8252

Public official contact regarding indirect collection of information:

Administrative Support Clerk

Telephone (416) 593-3684

2. References to a purchaser in this report are to the beneficial owner of the securities.

3. If the space provided for any answer is insufficient, additional sheets may be used and must be cross-referenced to the relevant part and properly identified and signed by the person whose signature appears on the report.

4. One report may be used for multiple distributions occurring within 10 days of each other provided that the report is filed on or before the 10th day following the first of such distributions.

5. The information in items 5, 6 and 7 must reconcile with the information in Schedule I of Form 45-501F1. All dollar amounts must be in Canadian dollars.

6. In order to determine the applicable fee, consult Ontario securities legislation.

Companion Policy 45-501CP — To Ontario Securities Commission Rule 45-501 Ontario Prospectus and Registration Exemptions

Date: November 23, 2001 and March 30, 2004; replaced effective September 14, 2005; replaced effective September 28, 2009, as amended February 11, 2015, May 5, 2015, September 8, 2015, January 13, 2016 and January 25, 2016.

24 O.S.C.B. 7011; 27 O.S.C.B. 449, 28 O.S.C.B. (Supp-3) 213, 32 O.S.C.B. (Supp. 5) 177, 37 O.S.C.B. (Supp. 5), 38 O.S.C.B. 4191, 38 O.S.C.B. (Supp. 3) 57 and 38 O.S.C.B. (Supp. 4) 90.

PART 1: APPLICATION

1.1 Introduction

1.2 Purpose

PART 2: OTHER EXEMPTIONS AND DISCRETIONARY RELIEF

2.1 Other exemptions

Part 4: DISTRIBUTIONS

PART 1 — APPLICATION

1.1 Introduction — Ontario Securities Commission Rule 45-501 *Ontario Registration and Prospectus Exemptions* (the Rule) concerns exemptions from the registration requirement and from the prospectus requirement.

1.2 Purpose — The purpose of this companion policy (the Policy) is to help users understand how the Commission interprets or applies certain provisions of the Rule. The Policy includes explanations, discussion and examples of various parts of the Rule.

PART 2 — OTHER EXEMPTIONS AND DISCRETIONARY RELIEF

2.1 Other exemptions — In addition to the exemptions in the Rule, exemptions may also be available to persons under National Instrument 45-106 *Prospectus Exemptions* (NI 45-106) and other provisions of Ontario securities legislation, including exemptions from the registration requirement under National Instrument 31-103 *National Instrument 31-103 Registration Requirements, Exemptions and Ongoing Registrant Obligations* (NI 31-103).

2.2 Discretionary relief — In addition to the exemptions contained in the Rule and those available under other provisions of Ontario securities legislation, the Commission has the discretion to grant exemptions from the prospectus requirement and from the registration requirement.

PART 3 — GENERAL

3.0 Availability of Registration Exemptions — With the exception of the dealer registration exemptions set out in sections 3.3 [*Commodity futures option or contract*] and 3.4 [*Security of a co-operative*], section 3.0 of the Rule withdraws the availability of all of the dealer registration exemptions set out in Part 3 of the Rule after the coming into force of NI 31-103 (and the transition period provided for in section 3.0). The withdrawal of the availability of these registration exemptions reflects the anticipated adoption of a "business trigger" for the dealer registration requirement, as a precondition to the coming into force of NI 31-103.

Under the business trigger, persons who are not in the business of trading in securities will not be subject to the dealer registration requirement and will not require an exemption from the dealer registration requirement for their trading activities. Persons who are in the business of trading securities will generally be required to register as a dealer. The exemption from the dealer registration requirement set out in section 3.3 and 3.4 of the Rule relate to circumstances where the trading activity or person involved in the trading activity is subject to another regulatory regime.

3.1 All distributions are subject to securities legislation — (1) Ontario securities legislation applies to any trade in a security in Ontario, whether or not the issuer of the security is a reporting issuer in Ontario.

(2) The definition of "trade" includes any act, advertisement, solicitation, conduct or negotiation directly or indirectly in furtherance of a trade. A person who engages in these activities, or other trading activities, in Ontario must comply with Ontario securities legislation.

3.2 Multi-jurisdictional distributions — A distribution can occur in more than one jurisdiction. If it does, the person conducting the distribution must comply with the securities legislation of each jurisdiction in which the distribution occurs.

3.3 Responsibility for compliance — A person distributing or trading securities is responsible for determining when an exemption is available. In determining whether an exemption is available, a person may rely on factual representations by a purchaser, provided that the person has no reasonable grounds to believe that those representations are false. However, the person distributing or trading securities is responsible for determining whether, given the facts available, the exemption is available. A person distributing or trading securities under an exemption should retain all necessary documents that show that the person properly relied on the exemption. It is not appropriate for a person to assume an exemption is available.

3.4 Advisers — Subsection 1.4(2) of the Rule provides that an exemption from the dealer registration requirement is an exemption from the underwriter registration requirement. However, it is not an exemption from the adviser registration requirement. The adviser registration requirement is distinct from the dealer registration requirement. Under Ontario securities legislation, persons engaged in the business of, or holding themselves out as being in the business of, advising others as to the investing in or buying or selling of securities are required to be registered as an adviser or have an exemption from this registration requirement. Accordingly, only persons that are registered advisers or exempt from the requirement to be registered as advisers may act as advisers in connection with a trade made under the Rule.

3.5 Underwriters — (1) Underwriters should not sell securities to the public without providing a prospectus. If an underwriter purchases securities with a view to distribution, the underwriter should purchase the securities under the exemption from the prospectus requirement in section 2.33 of NI 45-106. If the underwriter purchases securities under this exemption, the first trade in the securities will be a distribution. As a result, the underwriter will only be able to resell the securities if it can rely on another exemption from the prospectus requirement, or if a prospectus is delivered to the purchasers of the securities.

(2) There may be legitimate transactions where a dealer purchases securities under an exemption from the prospectus requirement other than the exemption in section 2.33 of NI 45-106; however, these transactions are only appropriate when the dealer purchases the securities with investment intent and not with a view to distribution.

(3) If a dealer purchases securities through a series of exempt transactions in order to avoid the obligation to deliver a prospectus, the transactions will be viewed as a whole to determine if they constitute a distribution. If a transaction is in effect an indirect distribution, a prospectus will be required to qualify the sale of the securities despite the fact that each interim step in the transaction could otherwise be completed under an exemption from the prospectus requirement. Such indirect distributions cannot be legitimately structured under NI 45-106 or the Rule.

3.6 Soliciting purchasers — (1) Generally, a person is a market intermediary if the person is in the business of trading in securities as principal or agent. The term "market intermediary" is defined in Ontario Securities Commission Rule 14-501 *Definitions*.

(2) The Commission takes the position that if an issuer retains an employee whose primary job function is to actively solicit members of the public for the purposes of selling the issuer's securities, the issuer and its employees are in the business of selling securities. Further, if an issuer and its employees are deemed to be in the business of selling securities, the Commission considers both the issuer and its employees to be market intermediaries. This applies whether the issuer and its employees are located in Ontario and solicit members of the public outside of Ontario or whether the issuer and its employees are located outside of Ontario and solicit members of the public in Ontario. Accordingly, in order to be in compliance with Ontario securities legislation, these issuers and their employees should be registered under the appropriate category of registration in Ontario.

PART 4 — INTERPRETATION

4.1 Definitions — Unless defined in the Rule, terms used in the Rule have the meaning given to them in Ontario securities legislation, including National Instrument 14-101 *Definitions*.

4.2 Executive officer — (1) The definition of "executive officer" in the Rule is based on the definition of the same term in National Instrument 51-102 *Continuous Disclosure Obligations*.

(2) The definition includes someone who "performs a policy-making function" in respect of an issuer. The Commission is of the view that an individual who "performs a policy-making function" in respect of an issuer is someone who is responsible, solely or jointly with others, for setting the direction of the issuer and is sufficiently knowledgeable of the business and affairs of the issuer so as to be able to respond meaningfully to inquiries from investors about the issuer.

(3) Paragraph (c) of the definition of "executive officer" includes individuals that are not employed by the issuer or any of its subsidiaries, but who perform a policy-making function in respect of the issuer.

4.3 Directors, executive officers and officers of non-corporate issuers — (1) Non-corporate issuers must determine which individuals are acting in capacities similar to that of directors and officers of corporate issuers for the purpose of complying with the Rule.

(2) The term "director" is defined in the Rule and it includes, for non-corporate issuers, individuals who perform functions similar to those of a director of a company.

(3) When the term "officer" is used in the Rule, a non-corporate issuer should refer to the definition in the Act, which defines the term to include any individual acting in a capacity similar to that of an officer of a company.

PART 5 — OFFERING MEMORANDUM

5.1 Definition of offering memorandum — (1) "Offering memorandum" is defined in Ontario Securities Commission Rule 14-501 *Definitions*.

(2) The Commission is of the view that the phrase "prepared primarily for delivery to and review by a prospective purchaser" in the definition of offering memorandum means the document is prepared in contemplation of soliciting an investment from the prospective purchaser.

5.2 Mandatory and voluntary use of offering memorandum — (1) An issuer must prepare an offering memorandum for use in connection with a distribution made in reliance on the prospectus exemption in section 73.5 of the Act [*Government incentive security*].

(2) There is no obligation to prepare an offering memorandum for use in connection with a distribution made in reliance on a prospectus exemption in:

    (a) section 73.3 of the Act [*Accredited investor*],

    (b) section 73.4 of the Act [*Private issuer*],

    (b.1) section 2.5 of NI 45-106 [*Family, friends and business associates*],

    (c) [Repealed.]

    (d) section 2.8 of NI 45-106 [*Affiliates*],

    (e) section 2.10 of NI 45-106 [*Minimum amount investment*], or

    (f) section 2.19 of NI 45-106 [*Additional investment in investment funds*].

Business practice may dictate the preparation of offering material that is delivered voluntarily to a prospective purchaser in connection with a distribution made in reliance on a prospectus exemption in section 73.3 of the Act, 73.4 of the Act, 2.5, 2.8, 2.10 or 2.19 of NI 45-106. This offering material may constitute an "offering memorandum" as defined in Ontario Securities Commission Rule 14-501 *Definitions*.

5.3 Right of action for damages and right of rescission — (1) Part 5 of the Rule provides for the application of the rights referred to in section 130.1 of the Act if an offering memorandum is delivered to a prospective purchaser in connection with a distribution made in reliance on a prospectus exemption in:

    (a) section 73.3 of the Act or a predecessor exemption to section 73.3 of the Act (subject to the provisions of subsection 6.2(2) of the Rule) [*Accredited investor*],

    (b) section 73.4 of the Act or a predecessor exemption to section 73.4 of the Act [*Private issuer*],

    (b.1) section 2.5 of NI 45-106 [*Family, friends and business associates*],

    (c) [Repealed.]

    (d) section 2.8 of NI 45-106 [*Affiliates*],

    (d.1) section 2.9 of NI 45-106 [*Offering memorandum*],

    (e) section 2.10 of NI 45-106 [*Minimum amount investment*],

    (f) section 2.19 of NI 45-106 [*Additional investment in investment funds*], or

    (f.1) section 5 of Multilateral Instrument 45-108 *Crowdfunding* [*Crowdfunding prospectus exemption*], or

    (g) section 73.5 of the Act or a predecessor exemption to section 73.5 of the Act [*Government incentive security*].

The rights apply when the offering memorandum is delivered mandatorily in connection with a distribution made in reliance on the exemption in section 73.5 of the Act or a predecessor exemption to section 73.5 of the Act, in accordance with the requirements of section 2.9 of NI 45-106 [*Offering memorandum*], in accordance with the requirements of section 5 of Multilateral Instrument 45-108 *Crowdfunding* [*Crowdfunding prospectus exemption*],* or voluntarily in connection with a distribution made in reliance on a prospectus exemption in section 73.3 of the Act or a predecessor exemption to section 73.3 of the Act, section 73.4 of the Act or a predecessor exemption to section 73.4 of the Act, 2.5, 2.8, 2.10 or 2.19 of NI 45-106.

(2) A document delivered in connection with a distribution in a security made otherwise than in reliance on the prospectus exemptions referred to in subsection (1) does not give rise to the rights referred to in section 130.1 of the Act or subject the selling security holder to the requirements of Part 5 of the Rule.

5.4 Content of offering memorandum — (1) Other than in the case of an offering memorandum delivered in connection with a distribution made in reliance on the exemption in section 73.5 of the Act or a predecessor exemption to section 73.5 of the Act and section 2.9 of NI 45-106 [*Offering memorandum*], section 5 of 45-108 Multilateral Instrument 45-108 *Crowdfunding* [*Crowdfunding prospectus exemption*],* and subject to subsection (2), Ontario securities legislation generally does not prescribe the content of an offering memorandum. The decision relating to the appropriate disclosure in an offering memorandum generally rests with the issuer, the selling security holder and their advisors.

(2) Under section 5.3 of the Rule, the rights referred to in section 130.1 of the Act must be described in an offering memorandum delivered in connection with a distribution to which the rights apply.

5.5 Review of offering memorandum — (1) Staff may review the form and content of an offering memorandum filed in connection with a distribution made in reliance on the exemption in section 2.9 of NI 45-106 [*Offering memorandum*], the exemption in section 5 of Multilateral Instrument 45-108 *Crowdfunding* [*Crowdfunding prospectus exemption*],* or delivered in connection with a distribution made in reliance on another exemption referred to in Part 5 of the Rule, for the purpose of determining whether the issuer has complied with the requirements, conditions and restrictions of the exemption relied on for the distribution.

(2) If Commission staff becomes aware that an offering memorandum contains a misrepresentation, fails to disclose material information relating to a security that is the subject of a distribution, or the distribution otherwise fails to comply with Ontario securities law, staff may recommend remedial action or, in appropriate circumstances, enforcement action.

5.6 Preliminary offering material — (1) The Commission cautions against the practice of providing preliminary offering material to a prospective purchaser before furnishing a "final" offering memorandum unless the offering material contains a description of the rights referred to in section 130.1 of the Act in situations when the rights apply.

(2) The only material delivered to a prospective purchaser in connection with a distribution made in reliance on a prospectus exemption referred to in section 5.1 of the Rule should be:

    (a) a "term sheet" (representing a skeletal outline of the features of a distribution without dealing extensively with the business or affairs of the issuer of the securities being distributed) or in the case of a distribution made in reliance on the exemption in section 2.9 of NI 45-106 [*Offering memorandum*] an "OM standard term sheet", as that term is defined in NI 45-106,

    (b) an offering memorandum describing the rights referred to in section 130.1 of the Act available to purchasers and complying in all other respects with Ontario securities legislation, and

    (c) in the case of an offering memorandum prepared in accordance with section 2.9 of NI 45-106, OM marketing materials, as that term is defined in NI 45-106; a video, in the case of a distribution made in reliance on the exemption in section 5 of Multilateral Instrument 45-108 *Crowdfunding* [*Crowdfunding prospectus exemption*].*

5.7 Availability of offering memorandum — Subject to *Freedom of Information and Protection of Privacy Act* requests, it is the Commission's policy that an offering memorandum delivered to the Commission under section 5.4 of the Rule will not be made available to the public.

---

*At the direction of the OSC, all of these amendments are scheduled to come into force and coincide with, rather than replace, one another.

PART 6 — REPORTING REQUIREMENTS

6.1 Report of exempt distribution — (1) Section 6.1 of the Rule requires an issuer that has distributed a security of its own issue under section 73.5 of the Act or a predecessor exemption to section 73.5 of the Act [*Government incentive security*] or section 2.9 [*Distributions to existing security holders*] of the Rule to file a report of exempt distribution in the required form, on or before the 10th day after the distribution.

PART 7 — RESALE OF SECURITIES ACQUIRED UNDER AN EXEMPTION

7.1 Resale restrictions — (1) A security distributed under a prospectus exemption may be subject to restrictions on its resale. The particular resale — or "first trade" — restrictions depend on the parties to the trade and the particular exemption from the prospectus requirement that was relied on to distribute the security. In certain circumstances, no resale restrictions will apply and the security acquired under an exempt distribution will be freely tradable.

(2) Resale restrictions are imposed under National Instrument 45-102 *Resale of Securities*. While the Rule contains text boxes providing commentary on resale, these text boxes are intended as guidance only and are not a substitute for reviewing the applicable provisions in National Instrument 45-102 *Resale of Securities* to determine what resale restrictions, if any, apply to the security in question.

(3) The resale restrictions operate by triggering the prospectus requirement unless certain conditions are satisfied. A security that is subject to such restrictions in circumstances where the conditions cannot be satisfied may nevertheless be distributed in reliance on an exemption from the prospectus requirement in the Rule, NI 45-106 or another provision in Ontario securities legislation.

Amended and Restated on the later of the following:

(a) September 28, 2009;

(b) the day on which sections 5 and 11, subsection 12(1) and section 13 of Schedule 26 of the *Budget Measures Act, 2009* are proclaimed in force.

PART 8 — EXISTING SECURITY HOLDER PROSPECTUS EXEMPTION

Distributions to existing security holders

8.1 General — All security holders of the same class of securities must be treated fairly and in a manner that is perceived to be fair in connection with a distribution under section 2.9 of the Rule. The Commission recognizes that distributions to existing security holders are capable of being abusive or unfair. Accordingly, issuers and others who benefit from access to the capital markets have an obligation to treat security holders fairly, and the fulfillment of this obligation is essential to the protection of the public interest in maintaining capital markets that operate efficiently, fairly and with integrity.

8.2 Anti-dilution — While an offer must be made available to all persons who, as of the record date, held a listed security of the issuer of the same class and series as the listed security to be distributed under section 2.9 of the Rule, there is no requirement that an issuer make the offer on a pro rata basis to its security holders. For the purposes of a distribution under section 2.9 of the Rule, if security holders have an identical opportunity under the distribution, then they are considered to be treated identically.

While there is no pro rata requirement, the Commission takes the position that in order to support the fair treatment of all security holders, an issuer should establish, maintain and apply policies and procedures that provide reasonable assurance that the issuer, and, if applicable, each registrant, fairly allocate investment opportunities among the issuer's security holders. However, any distribution under section 2.9 of the Rule cannot result in an increase of more than 100% of the outstanding securities of the same class and section 2.9 of the Rule should not be used in a manner that results in security holders suffering significant dilution.

8.3 Minimum Subscription Amount — Under section 2.9 of the Rule, there is no requirement that an issuer accept all subscriptions from each existing security holder. However, if an issuer were to reject a subscription that was in all respects a valid subscription, it could call into question whether the offering was made available to all security holders of the issuer. While an issuer might not want to accept small subscription amounts because of the administrative burden, for transparency purposes, an issuer should consider clearly disclosing the minimum subscription amount in the offering news release.

Amendment to Policy: (2015) 38 O.S.C.B. (Supp. 1) 175.

Amendment to Policy: (2015) 38 O.S.C.B. (Supp. 1) 20.

Amendment to Policy: (2014) 32 O.S.C.B. 103481.

Adoption of Revised Policy: (2009) 32 O.S.C.B. (Supp. 5) 177 and 32 O.S.C.B. (Supp. 3) 1; Request for Comments: (2009) 32 O.S.C.B. 4233 and (2008) 31 O.S.C.B. (Supp. 1) 1.

Adoption of Revised Policy: (2005) 28 O.S.C.B. (Supp-3) 213 and 28 O.S.C.B. (Supp-3) 1; Request for Comments: (2004) 27 O.S.C.B. (Supp-3) 1.

Adoption of Revised Policy: (2004) 27 O.S.C.B. 449 and (2003) 26 O.S.C.B. 8217; Request for Comments: (2003) 26 O.S.C.B. 2965.

Adoption of Revised Policy: (2001) 24 O.S.C.B. 7011 and 5544; Request for Comments: (2001) 24 O.S.C.B. 4247 and 2183 and (2000) 23 O.S.C.B. 6205.

OSC Rule 45-502 — Dividend or Interest Reinvestment and Stock Dividend Plans

[Revoked by Rule 45-802 and replaced by s. 2.2 of NI 45-106]

Rule 45-502 was revoked by Rule 45-802, effective September 14, 2005. [September 9, 2005: 28 O.S.C.B. (Supp-4)]

OSC Notice 45-705 — Interpretation of Section 130.1 of the Securities Act

Issue: September 5, 2003
Citation: 26 O.S.C.B. 6269

Section 130.1 (*Liability for misrepresentation in offering memorandum*) was introduced in the *Securities Act* through the *More Tax Cuts for Jobs, Growth and Prosperity Act, 1999*. The section was intended to replace the contractual rights of action required by the Regulation under the *Securities Act* to be conferred by issuers upon investors who purchase securities pursuant to certain prospectus exemptions for misrepresentations in an offering memorandum. Section 130.1 also created, for the first time, a statutory right of action for damages or rescission against "a selling security holder on whose behalf the distribution is made".

We understand that some securities practitioners are taking the view that the reference in Section 130.1 to "a selling security holder on whose behalf the distribution is made" could be read to include an underwriter where it purchases securities for resale on a private placement basis. Under this interpretation, the underwriter in an underwritten private placement would be liable to purchasers for a misrepresentation in the offering memorandum and, incidentally, would not have a due diligence defence under Section 130.1. The term "selling security holder" is not defined in the Act.

Staff have been asked for their views on this question. Staff discussed the issue with a group of senior securities lawyers and considered that it would be helpful to underwriters, issuers and their advisors to set forth our views on this matter.

- The extension of rights of action to include both issuers and selling security holders as defendants was intended to overcome a long standing problem under the contractual rights of action provision of the Regulations which, in effect, required that purchasers be given a right against an issuer even in circumstances where the private placement was entirely a secondary offering by a selling shareholder.

- Had the legislation intended to include underwriters in the defendant class, it would have done so expressly, as does Section 130(1)(b) of the *Securities Act*.

- There is no apparent policy rationale for drawing a distinction, as the suggested interpretation of Section 130.1 would require, between underwriters who purchase as principal securities for distribution by private placement and underwriters who act merely as agents in a distribution by private placement. It is noteworthy that under Section 130, underwriters' liability does not turn on whether the underwriter purchases as principal, or sells as agent, but rather whether the underwriter signs the certificate in the prospectus.

- As a matter of statutory interpretation, Section 130.1 must be read in the context of the entire *Securities Act*, including Section 130. Section 130 has always included in the defendant class a selling security holder. It has never been suggested, however, that an underwriter (including one that did not sign the prospectus) might be liable under Section 130(1)(a) as a selling security holder rather than under Section 130(1)(b) as an underwriter. The significance of the distinction under Section 130 is that if the underwriter were liable under (a) it would have no due diligence defence but would have such a defence under (b). The common interpretation of a "selling security holder" and "underwriter" under Section 130 is that they are mutually exclusive.

- Had the intention been to create underwriter liability under Section 130.1, the legislation would have included a due diligence defence for underwriters as there would be no policy basis for subjecting underwriters to a higher standard of liability in the private placement context than in the public offering context.

For the foregoing reasons, Staff is of the view that Section 130.1 was not intended to impose liability for misrepresentations in an offering memorandum on an underwriter in an underwritten private placement.

Questions may be referred to:
[Omitted.]

OSC Staff Notice 45-707 — OSC Broadening Scope of Review of Prospectus Exemptions

Effective: June 7, 2012
Citation: 35 O.S.C.B. 5318

Introduction

On November 10, 2011, CSA staff announced that they are reviewing the $150,000 minimum amount and the accredited investor prospectus exemptions contained in National Instrument 45-106 *Prospectus and Registration Exemptions* (NI 45-106). In light of feedback received from stakeholders to date, OSC staff are broadening the scope of our review to consider whether the OSC should introduce new prospectus exemptions that may assist capital raising for business enterprises while protecting the interests of investors. For instance, we heard from some stakeholders that we should consider prospectus exemptions based on a number of factors, such as the financial resources of a purchaser relative to the size of the investment and the availability of disclosure regarding the investment.

Different capital raising exemptions currently exist in the exempt market across CSA jurisdictions, and as a result, different feedback was received across CSA jurisdictions during consultations on the exempt market. In conducting the broader review, we will continue to work with staff in other CSA jurisdictions.

No decisions regarding changes to the exempt market regulatory regime have been made at this point. In deciding whether changes are necessary or appropriate, we will be governed by our regulatory mandate of:

- protecting investors from unfair, improper or fraudulent practices, and

- fostering fair and efficient capital markets, and confidence in those markets.

Significance of exempt market

The exempt market in Canada has become increasingly important for investors and issuers. The total amount of capital raised through exempt distributions reported to the OSC in 2011 was approximately $142.9 billion. Approximately $86.5 billion of that amount was raised in Ontario. In 2011, approximately $72.8 billion was raised under the accredited investor prospectus exemption in Ontario. The minimum amount prospectus exemption was less used, but in 2011, approximately $3.9 billion was raised under this exemption in Ontario.

We want the exempt market to be an effective mechanism for raising capital for business enterprises, particularly small and medium-sized businesses. However, we need to strike a balance between investor protection and efficient capital raising. In doing so, we need to consider in what circumstances investors do not require the protections afforded by a prospectus offering, including prospectus level disclosure, the provision of statutory rights where there is a misrepresentation and the involvement of a registrant.

CSA consultation

On November 10, 2011, CSA staff published CSA Staff Consultation Note 45-401 *Review of Minimum Amount and Accredited Investor Exemptions*. The consultation note provided summary information regarding the two prospectus exemptions being reviewed and set out a number of specific consultation questions. The comment period closed on February 29, 2012 and 108 comment letters were received.

As part of the consultation process, OSC staff met with over 300 individuals. We held four public consultation sessions in February 2012, which were attended in total by approximately 200 individuals. We also consulted with our Investor Advisory Panel, Securities Advisory Committee, Small Business Advisory Committee and Continuous Disclosure Advisory Committee. In addition, we met with several interested stakeholder groups, including investor representatives, industry members, registrants, other regulators and legal and other advisors.

Key themes from feedback received

A wide range of views were expressed in both the written comment letters and in our consultation sessions. Some of the themes raised with OSC staff were:

- *Diversity of the exempt market.* There are different segments of the exempt market: capital raising traditionally associated with business enterprises, as well as a capital management component, including investments in pooled or hedge funds. There is a wide range of products being sold in the exempt market. A "one size fits all" regulatory approach may not be appropriate or sufficient.

- *Access to the exempt market by issuers.* Many stakeholders expressed concern that any changes to the exempt market regime might restrict access to capital by businesses. Some suggested that access to a broader range of investors through the exempt market may provide better support for small and medium-sized businesses.

- *Access to the exempt market by investors.* Some stakeholders supported "democratization" of the exempt market so that more individuals, rather than simply high net worth or high income individuals, would be able to make investments on a prospectus-exempt basis. Other stakeholders expressed investor protection concerns with broader investor participation in the exempt market given that no disclosure is currently mandated and registrant involvement is not always required.

- *Existing criteria for accredited investor status.* Some stakeholders believe the current financial thresholds for individuals to qualify for accredited investor status are appropriate. Other stakeholders do not think net income or financial assets are an adequate proxy for sophistication. Other stakeholders questioned whether the monetary criteria should be adjusted for inflation. Some stakeholders have suggested that individuals who do not meet the current financial thresholds should nonetheless be able to invest in the exempt market if they have certain attributes of sophistication such as investment or work experience or education, or are relying on the advice of a registrant.

- *Existing minimum purchase amount.* Many stakeholders questioned the rationale for the existing minimum amount prospectus exemption. They felt that it had the effect of causing investors to invest $150,000 in one investment when an investment in smaller amounts or a more diversified approach would have been more appropriate. We also heard that the ability to invest a lump sum of $150,000 does not indicate that an investor is sophisticated or able to withstand the loss of that investment. Some stakeholders indicated that a limit on the maximum amount invested, expressed either as a dollar amount or a percentage of the investor's assets or net income, would be more appropriate than the current minimum amount prospectus exemption.

- *Other options.* There were a number of views on whether there should be prospectus exemptions based on the provision of disclosure to investors and, if so, what form that disclosure should take. Some stakeholders suggested that Ontario should adopt an offering memorandum prospectus exemption, which would allow a broader range of investors to participate in the exempt market on the condition that a minimum level of disclosure is provided to investors. That exemption currently exists in some CSA jurisdictions. Some stakeholders supported more rigorous risk disclosure to enhance investor protection. In addition, there were different views on whether the availability of a prospectus exemption should be contingent on the involvement of a registrant who is subject to know-your-client (or KYC), know-your-product (or KYP) and suitability obligations.

- *Harmonization.* Some commenters encouraged CSA members to renew their efforts to harmonize the current prospectus exemptions that exist in National Instrument 45-106 *Prospectus and Registration Exemptions*. We received feedback that exemptions, which are not totally harmonized across Canada, add undue complexity for investors and costs for issuers.

This is not an exhaustive list of all the comments staff received. We are currently considering all of the comments provided to us by stakeholders, which will inform the next phase of this initiative. We will publish a summary of the comment letters we have received in response to our request for comment on the minimum amount and accredited investor prospectus exemptions.

Next steps for OSC staff

In light of feedback received from stakeholders, we are broadening the scope of our review to consider the exempt market regulatory regime more generally. We will continue to assess whether the existing minimum amount and accredited investor prospectus exemptions remain appropriate or whether changes should be made. We will also consider whether the OSC should introduce other prospectus exemptions to facilitate capital raising for business enterprises. Because this latter consideration was not part of the review of the minimum amount and accredited investor prospectus exemptions, we are giving market participants an opportunity to address that issue before our review of the exempt market is completed.

During this fiscal year, OSC staff will:

- *Publish a second consultation note*. We will publish a second consultation note which will seek further feedback on the exempt market regulatory regime. That consultation note will explore whether the OSC should adopt any new prospectus exemptions and, if so, under what circumstances or terms.

- *Hold further public consultation sessions*. We will hold further public consultation sessions following the publication of the second consultation note. In addition, we will actively reach out to investors and meet with other stakeholders to obtain their feedback.

- *Consider the experience of the other CSA jurisdictions with prospectus exemptions not currently available in Ontario*. Other CSA jurisdictions currently have a form of offering memorandum prospectus exemption and a "friends and family" prospectus exemption, neither of which are currently available in Ontario. On April 26, 2012, CSA staff published Multilateral CSA Staff Notice 45-309 *Guidance for Preparing and Filing an Offering Memorandum under National Instrument 45-106 Prospectus and Registration Exemptions*. The staff notice summarizes common deficiencies in offering memoranda prepared in accordance with Form 45-106F2 *Offering Memorandum for Non-Qualifying Issuers* and provides guidance to improve compliance with the disclosure requirements.

- *Consider developments in other jurisdictions relevant to capital raising in the exempt market*. We will consider the securities regulatory regime for capital raising in the exempt market in other jurisdictions. In particular, we will consider developments in the U.S. with respect to capital raising contained in the *Jumpstart Our Business Startups Act* (or the JOBS Act).

- *Establish an ad hoc advisory committee*. We will establish an ad hoc advisory committee to communicate views to us on possible regulatory approaches to the exempt market. The committee will be comprised of investors, issuer representatives, registrants and legal and other advisors. A separate news release will be published inviting interested stakeholders to apply for membership on this committee.

As noted above, we will publish a summary of the comment letters received on CSA Staff Consultation Note 45-401 *Review of Minimum Amount and Accredited Investor Exemptions*.

OSC Staff Notice 45-708 — Introduction of Electronic Report of Exempt Distribution on Form 45-106F1

Effective: June 21, 2012

Citation: 35 O.S.C.B. 5705

Staff of the Ontario Securities Commission (OSC) want to notify issuers, underwriters and their advisers that an electronic version (the E-form) of Form 45-106F1 *Report of Exempt Distribution* is being made available on the OSC website as of today. Issuers and underwriters that are required to prepare and file a report of exempt distribution on Form 45-106F1 (the Report) may now choose to prepare and file the Report using the E-form, instead of in paper format.

At this time, filing the Report electronically is voluntary, although we anticipate moving towards mandatory electronic filings in the future. Filers may continue to prepare and send in the paper version of the Report. However, we encourage filers to use the E-form whenever possible, as we anticipate that it will be faster and more efficient.

Report of exempt distribution (Form 45-106F1)

Section 6.1 of National Instrument 45-106 *Prospectus and Registration Exemptions* (NI 45-106) requires:

- issuers that distribute their own securities, and

- underwriters that distribute securities they acquired under section 2.33 of NI 45-106 (acting as underwriter) to file a Report if a distribution is made in reliance on certain specified prospectus exemptions. The Report must be filed no later than 10 days after the distribution. In certain cases, investment funds are permitted to file the Report no later than 30 days after the financial year-end of the investment fund.

The exemptions that require the filing of a Report include some of the most commonly used prospectus exemptions in Ontario, including the accredited investor exemption (section 2.3) and the minimum amount investment exemption (section 2.10). The Report contains key information, including the name of the issuer or underwriter that distributed the securities, the exemption(s) relied on to effect the distribution, the type of securities that were distributed and detailed purchaser information. Until now, the Report was only available in paper format in Ontario.

Introducing an electronic version of the Report

The exempt market is a significant part of Ontario's capital markets. The total amount of capital raised through exempt distributions reported to the OSC in 2011 was approximately $142.9 billion. Approximately $86.5 billion of that amount was raised in Ontario. Information contained in filed Reports provides the OSC with insight into this exempt market activity, which would otherwise not be readily available. Having reliable information on exempt distributions is an important tool which may be used to inform the OSC's policy making initiatives.

Every year, thousands of Reports are filed with the OSC. Our goal in providing an E-form is to both make it easier for filers to prepare and file the Report, and also to facilitate the OSC's ability to review the data contained in the Report.

Obtaining the data electronically will make it possible for us to search and sort the data more efficiently and improve the quality of the data we receive.

The information required to be included in the Report has not changed and no new reporting requirements are being added at this time.

Training sessions

We plan to hold public training sessions on preparing and filing the E-form. These sessions will be open to anyone and will be most useful to those responsible for preparing the Report. There are two sessions currently scheduled, as follows:

- Friday July 20, 2012 from 1:00 to 2:30 p.m.
- Wednesday July 25, 2012 from 1:00 to 2:30 p.m.

If you are interested in attending one of these sessions, please contact us at E-formtraining@osc.gov.on.ca by Friday, July 6, 2012 to register.

Answers to key questions about the E-form

We have attached to this notice a list of questions and answers on preparing and filing the E-form. Note also that the OSC is concurrently publishing, along with this notice, a staff notice (OSC Staff Notice 45-709) on tips for preparing and filing the Report. For more detailed guidance on how to comply with the requirements of the Report, see this OSC Staff Notice.

Questions about the electronic report of exempt distribution on Form 45-106F1

1. — Where can I find a link to the E-form?

A link to the E-form can be found on the Ontario Securities Commission (OSC) website at www.osc.gov.on.ca, under the "Frequently Used Forms" section of the website.

2. — If I am required to pay an activity fee when I submit the E-form, how would I do this?

Please mail a cheque to the OSC referencing the confirmation number that you receive when you electronically submit the E-form. The cheque should be made payable to the "Ontario Securities Commission" and mailed to:

> Ontario Securities Commission
> Suite 1903, Box 55
> 20 Queen Street West
> Toronto, Ontario M5H 3S8

For the amount of the fee payable, please refer to OSC Rule 13-502 *Fees*.

3. — How do I save a copy of the E-form once I have started entering the required information?

Click on the "Save" button located on the upper right hand corner of the E-form to save a copy at any time. When you first save the E-form you will be prompted to enter an e-mail address where a link to the saved form will be sent. The link to the saved E-form will remain active for 10 days. You can print a copy or e-mail the link to others for review.

4. — What if an error was made in the E-form I submitted?

You must file an amended E-form by selecting Amended Submission on the Start page and reference the confirmation number that you received when you submitted your Initial Submission when prompted.

5. — How do I sign and certify the E-form?

If you are an officer who is authorized on behalf of the issuer or underwriter to certify that the statements made in the E-form are true, fill in the information on the Certificate page at the end of the E-form and provide your name, title and signature in the appropriate fields.

If you are an agent (i.e. law firm) authorized to submit the E-form on behalf of the person signing the E-form, fill in their information on the Certificate page at the end of the E-form, then check the box to indicate you are authorized to complete and file the E-form on behalf of the person signing the E-form and provide your name and title. Please ensure that you have obtained appropriate authority from the issuer or underwriter to complete and submit the Eform.

6. — Can I provide the Schedule 1 in any document format, including Word or Excel?

Schedule 1 includes specific information about each purchaser that acquired securities in the exempt distribution. We have provided an Excel spreadsheet that can be used for this purpose. Providing a separate spreadsheet will enable filers to save the spreadsheet to their computer and work on it separately from the E-form. This will be useful where there is a large number of purchasers to include in the schedule. In order for us to be able to review and sort the data provided in the Schedule 1, it needs to be in a consistent format. Therefore, at this time, we can only accept the Schedule 1 in the Excel template provided.

7. — Why are there two versions of the E-form?

One version is for non-investment fund issuers and the other version is for investment fund issuers reporting exempt distributions as required by section 6.1 of National Instrument 45-106 *Prospectus and Registration Exemptions*. As non-investment fund issuers and investment fund issuers generally have different filing deadlines for the Report (either 10 days after the distribution for non-investment fund issuers, or in the case of investment fund issuers, up to 30 days after the fund's financial year-end) and different distribution models, providing two versions of the E-form will make it easier for issuers, underwriters and their advisers to file the Report and should also allow OSC staff the ability to better collect the data from each respective segment of the market.

8. — Can I file the E-form with other jurisdictions?

Currently the E-form is available in Ontario only. The only other jurisdiction that currently accepts electronic filing of the Report is British Columbia, however the B.C. system works differently. In addition, B.C. has a separate form of report of exempt distribution on Form 45-106F6 *British Columbia Report of Exempt Distribution* which is different from the E-form.

9. — Do I have to use the E-form to file Reports?

Filing the Report using the E-form is voluntary at this time. We strongly encourage issuers and underwriters to use the E-form as it should make the filing process faster and more efficient. It will also assist the OSC in compiling data on the exempt market. We anticipate moving towards mandatory electronic filing in the future.

10. — What is the deadline for filing the E-form?

Reports are due no later than 10 days after the distribution date. In certain cases, Investment Funds may file the Report not later than 30 days after the financial year-end of the fund. See Part 6 of NI 45-106 for information about filing deadlines.

You may submit the E-form electronically at any time of the day. E-forms submitted and received by the OSC by 11:59 p.m. on the day that they are due will be considered to be filed on time. Ensure that you allow sufficient time for the E-form and any related attachments (such as Schedule 1) to be uploaded and received by the OSC's server.

OSC Staff Notice 45-709 — (Revised) — Tips for Filing Reports of Exempt Distribution

Date: May 21, 2015

38 O.S.C.B. 4672

Purpose

OSC Staff have prepared this notice to provide guidance to issuers, underwriters and their advisors in filing Form 45-106F1 *Report of Exempt Distribution* (Form F1) in Ontario.[1] OSC Staff are replacing a prior notice issued in June 2012 with this notice.

Background

Securities legislation in Ontario prohibits the distribution of securities without a prospectus for which a receipt has been issued. The *Securities Act* (Ontario), National Instrument 45-106 *Prospectus Exemptions* (NI 45-106) and OSC Rule 45-501 *Ontario Prospectus and Registration Exemptions* (OSC Rule 45-501) contain a number of exemptions from the prospectus requirement under which exempt distributions may be made. Part 6 of NI 45-106 and Part 6 of OSC Rule 45-501 require issuers or underwriters relying on certain prospectus exemptions to report exempt distributions and set out the form of report required to be filed as well as the deadlines for filing the report.

Issuers and underwriters involved in exempt distributions must determine when a distribution has occurred in Ontario. For additional guidance on when a distribution has occurred in Ontario, issuers and underwriters should refer to:

- relevant case law, including *Crowe et al. v. Ontario Securities Commission*,
- applicable OSC rules and related companion policies (for example Part 6 of NI 45-106 and related guidance in the companion policy), and
- other relevant notices, such as Interpretation Note 1 *Distributions of Securities Outside Ontario* (March 25, 1983) and proposed Multilateral Instrument 72-101 *Distributions Outside of the Local Jurisdiction* (September 8, 2000).

If there is uncertainty as to whether a distribution has occurred in Ontario, we recommend that the report should also be filed in Ontario.

Tips

The following are tips to assist issuers, underwriters and their advisors in filing Form F1 in Ontario. Please note this staff notice is not meant to be a complete checklist for these reports, but rather a quick reference tool to enable an issuer or underwriter to avoid certain deficiencies in completing and filing reports of exempt distribution.

1. File the report in the correct form

In Ontario, the correct form of report of exempt distribution under NI 45-106 and section 2.9 [*Distributions to existing security holders*] of OSC Rule 45-501 is Form F1. See section 6.3 of NI 45-106 and section 6.2 of OSC Rule Rule 45-501.

---

[1]Subject to subsequent amendments to NI 45-106, CSA Staff Notice 45-308 — *Guidance for Preparing and Filing Reports of Exempt Distribution* under National Instrument 45-106 *Prospectus and Registration Exemptions* also provides guidance on compliance with the reporting requirements in NI 45-106.

The British Columbia Securities Commission (BCSC) has introduced an alternate report of exempt distribution, Form 45-106F6 (Form F6). Subject to certain exceptions, exempt distributions in British Columbia (BC) which occurred on or after October 3, 2011 must be reported to the BCSC using Form F6.[2] Exempt distributions in both BC and Ontario must generally be reported to the BCSC using Form F6 and to the OSC using Form F1.

As of February 19, 2014, it is mandatory to file Form F1 electronically.[3] The electronic form can be found at https://www.osc.gov.on.ca/filings.

2. File the report on time

Reports of exempt distribution are due no later than 10 days after the distribution date. See subsection 6.1(2) of NI 45-106 and of OSC Rule 45-501.

Investment funds are not required to file a report within 10 days of the distribution date for a distribution under section 73.3 of the *Securities Act* (Ontario) [*Accredited investor*], section 2.10 [*Minimum amount*], or section 2.19 [*Additional investment in investment funds*] if the fund files the report not later than 30 days after the financial year-end of the fund. See subsection 6.2(2) of NI 45-106.

3 Identify the correct prospectus exemption relied on for the distribution in Ontario

An issuer or underwriter must indicate in Form F1 the prospectus exemption(s) relied on for the distribution.

Issuers and underwriters should note that the following prospectus exemptions are not available in Ontario:[4] section 2.9 [*Offering memorandum*] and section 5.2 [*TSX Venture Exchange offering*] of NI 45-106.

An issuer or underwriter should indicate in Schedule 1 to Form F1 a valid prospectus exemption for the distribution to each purchaser. This may necessitate reporting in Schedule 1 multiple exemptions relied on for the distribution to the same purchaser where the distribution is made in more than one jurisdiction and the same exemption is not available in those jurisdictions.

4. Ensure that the identified purchase price of the securities distributed is correct

In order to rely on the prospectus exemption in section 2.10 [*Minimum amount investment*], the purchase price must be at least $150,000 (among other conditions). If an issuer or underwriter relies on this exemption, it should ensure that the purchase price set out in item 7 of Form F1 and Schedule 1 to Form F1 is at least that minimum amount.

5. If the purchase price for the securities distributed is $0, provide an explanation

The purchase price for the securities distributed is required to be disclosed in item 7 of Form F1 and Schedule 1 to Form F1. The purchase price may be $0 where no funds are raised, and instead property is being acquired. These distributions may be completed under several different prospectus exemptions. If the distribution is being made under a prospectus exemption other than section 2.12 [*Asset acquisition*] or section 2.13 [*Petroleum, natural gas and mining properties*], the issuer or underwriter should include a footnote explaining the reason for the purchase price of $0.

6. Disclose all commissions and finder's fees

Item 8 of Form F1 requires information regarding compensation received or to be received by any person in connection with the distribution. Compensation includes commissions, discounts or other fees or payments of a similar nature. Compensation does not include payments for services incidental to the distribution (such as clerical, printing, legal or accounting services).

7. Provide complete information regarding convertible or exchangeable securities distributed

Item 6 of Form F1 requires information regarding the security distributed. If the security is convertible or exchangeable into an underlying security, the issuer or underwriter must include in the form:

- a description of the underlying security,
- the terms of conversion or exercise, and
- any expiry date.

8. Ensure that the information in both the Form F1 and Schedule 1 to Form F1 is consistent

The number of purchasers, jurisdiction of residence, price per security and total dollar value raised from purchasers in each jurisdiction must be completed in item 7 of Form F1. Schedule 1 to Form F1 requires an issuer or underwriter to report the name of the purchaser, number and type of securities, total purchase price, prospectus exemption relied on and the date of the distribution. Issuers and underwriters should verify that the information included in item 7 of Form F1 and Schedule 1 is correct and consistent.

---

[2] In limited cases, the BCSC will accept Form F1 instead of Form F6. Issuers that have distributed securities in BC should review BC Instrument 45-533 *Exemptions from Form 45-106F6* to determine if they may file Form F1 in BC instead of Form F6.

[3] See OSC Rule 11-501 *Electronic Delivery of Documents to the Ontario Securities Commission*.

[4] Section 2.5 [*Family, friends and business associates*] of NI 45-106 does not apply to a distribution of a security of an issuer that is an investment fund.

9. Ensure that all purchasers are identified in Schedule 1 to Form F1

Schedule 1 to Form F1 should include a complete list of purchasers under the distribution, including purchasers that reside in Ontario, purchasers that reside in other Canadian jurisdictions and purchasers that reside outside of Canada.

If the distribution is made in more than one Canadian jurisdiction, the issuer or underwriter must complete a single Form F1 identifying all purchasers and file that report in each of the Canadian jurisdictions (other than BC) in which the distribution is made. As noted above, the issuer or underwriter must file a Form F6 with the BCSC.

10. Ensure that the correct number of purchasers is set out in Form F1

Item 7 of Form F1 requires the total number of purchasers in each jurisdiction. The number of purchasers refers to the number of investors and not to the number of securities each purchaser purchased.

11. Date and sign the Form F1

An issuer or underwriter must include the date and the signature of the person identified as signing the form in the certificate section of the Form F1.

12. Ensure that the correct fees are paid

A filing fee must accompany a Form F1 for a distribution of securities of an issuer. Refer to OSC Rule 13-502 *Fees*.

Questions

Questions may be referred to:

[Omitted.]

OSC Staff Notice 45-710 — Considerations for New Capital Raising Prospectus Exemptions

Date: **December 14, 2012**

35 O.S.C.B. 11683

[Not reproduced]

OSC Staff Notice 45-711 — Extension of Consulation Period — OSC Staff Consulation Paper 45-710

Date: **January 24, 2013**

36 O.S.C.B. 1027

[Not reproduced]

OSC Staff Notice 45-713 — Reports of Exempt Distribution — Compliance with Filing Requirements

Date: **November 21, 2013**

36 O.S.C.B. 11195

Purpose of notice

We have prepared this notice to provide guidance on filing reports of exempt distribution (Reports) under National Instrument 45-106 — *Prospectus and Registration Exemptions* (NI 45-106)[1] . In particular, we wish to remind issuers, underwriters and their advisors of:

- the importance of filing Reports and applicable filing fees on time, and

- recent changes to the applicable filing fees.

Background of exempt market and importance of Reports

One of the key principles of Ontario securities law is that securities may not be distributed unless a prospectus is filed with and receipted by the OSC. Only in limited circumstances may securities be distributed without a prospectus. This is typically referred to as an "exempt distribution" that occurs in the "exempt market".

NI 45-106 includes a number of exemptions from the prospectus requirement under which exempt distributions may be made. Issuers, including investment funds, and underwriters are required to report exempt distributions made in reliance on certain of those prospectus exemptions, including the accredited investor and minimum amount investment exemptions.

---

[1]The guidance in this staff notice also applies to reports of exempt distribution required to be filed under OSC Rule 45-501 — *Ontario Prospectus and Registration Exemptions*. Part 6 of that Rule requires that issuers file a report of exempt distribution on or before the 10th day after a distribution in the form prescribed in Form 45-501F1.

Exempt market activity is significant. Based on Reports filed with the OSC, approximately $104 billion was raised in the exempt market in Ontario in 2012. Approximately one-third of this amount was raised by issuers other than investment funds[2].

Importance of Reports

Reports are our primary source of information about activity in the exempt market. They include information about the issuer, the underwriter (if any), the distribution, commissions and finders' fees and the investors.

This information provides us with a more comprehensive understanding of activity in the exempt market, helps us to effectively oversee that market, and informs any future changes we may recommend to the exempt market regulatory regime. As a result, it is important that complete and accurate Reports are filed with the OSC in a timely manner.

Snapshot of requirements to file Reports

Topic	Reminder regarding requirement
Requirement to file a Report	A Report must be filed in connection with a distribution made in reliance on certain prospectus exemptions, including the accredited investor and minimum amount investment exemptions (see Part 6 of NI 45-106).
Form of Report	In Ontario, the prescribed form of Report under NI 45-106 is Form 45-106F1 (see section 6.3 of NI 45-106). Reports can be filed either in paper form or online using the e-form available at: https: // eforms2.osc.gov.on.ca /exemptdistribution/ ProcessFormsServlet? action= open & filename= 45-106F1CF.xfdl & mode=html On October 31, 2013, the OSC published OSC Rule 11-501 — *Electronic Delivery of Documents to the Ontario Securities Commission* in final form and, subject to Ministerial approval, it will come into effect on February 19, 2014. The rule contemplates mandatory electronic filing of certain documents, including Reports. Electronic filing is a convenience to filers and allows for the efficient collection and use of information by the OSC. Electronic filing will: • streamline the submission process and regulatory burden for market participants in Ontario, • improve our data analysis, compliance and enforcement capabilities by requiring more reports in a machine-readable format, and • reduce the effort and time required to process and analyze the documents, allowing the Commission to focus resources on more substantive matters.
Deadline for filing Report	A Report must be filed no later than 10 days after a distribution (see subsection 6.1(2) of NI 45-106). An investment fund relying on the accredited investor, minimum amount investment or additional investment in investment funds exemption may instead file a Report no later than 30 days after its financial year end (see subsection 6.2(2) of NI 45-106). A Report in paper form is considered to be filed when it is received in our office. A Report that uses the e-form is considered to be filed when the e-form has been successfully submitted online to the OSC. A payment is considered to have been made when it is received in our office. If the deadline for filing a Report falls on a Saturday, Sunday, or another day when the OSC is not open, the deadline is the next day the OSC is open.
One Report for multiple distributions	One Report may be used for multiple distributions that occur within 10 days of each other provided the Report is filed on or before the 10th day following the first of those distributions. Distributions that occur over periods longer than 10 days must be split into two or more Reports to meet this requirement (see Instruction 4 to Form 45-106F1).
Filing fee	A $500 fee must be filed with each Report by the deadline (see section 4.1 and section B of Appendix C of OSC Rule 13-502 — Fees (OSC Rule 13-502)).
Late filing fee	If a Report is filed after the deadline, a late fee of $100 per business day applies, up to a maximum of $5,000 per fiscal year of an issuer for all of the issuer's Reports together with reports of exempt distribution required under OSC Rule 45-501 — Ontario Prospectus and Registration Exemptions (OSC Rule 45-501) (see section 4.3 and section A.1 of Appendix D of OSC Rule 13-502).

Summary of changes to filing fees and late filing fees applicable to Reports

Recent changes to OSC Rule 13-502 became effective on April 1, 2013. The following table summarizes the recent changes in filing fees and late filing fees applicable to filing Reports.

---

[2]This data reflects purchases but not redemptions of investment fund securities. The data for distributions of investment fund securities reflects distributions to both individual and institutional investors of both public and private investment fund securities.

Previous Requirements	Amended Requirements
An activity fee of $500 for filing a Report was required to be paid by issuers other than those that paid, or in the case of an investment fund, whose investment fund manager paid, participation fees.	Now, an activity fee of $500 is required to be paid with each Report filed, regardless of whether an issuer (reporting or non-reporting), or in the case of an investment fund, the fund's investment fund manager, paid a participation fee. The activity fee is intended to reflect the average cost to the OSC of reviewing Reports (see section 4.1 and section B of Appendix C of OSC Rule 13-502).
Only reporting issuers were subject to a late fee when a Report was filed after the deadline.	Now, all issuers (reporting and non-reporting) are subject to a late fee when a Report is filed after the deadline.
The maximum late fee of $5,000 per fiscal year was an aggregate fee that applied to the late filing of several documents (such as financial statements, annual information forms, participation fee forms, Reports, etc.).	The fee for a late Report is $100 per business day, up to a maximum of $5,000 per fiscal year of an issuer. This maximum fee now only applies to Reports, and reports of exempt distribution under OSC Rule 45-501, and is in addition to any other late fees that may be charged in connection with other documents (see section 4.3 and section A.1 of Appendix D of OSC Rule 13-502).

OSC Staff Notice 45-714 — Summaries of Exempt Distribution Information

Date: **October 15, 2015**

38 O.S.C.B. 8823

Beginning October 2015, the OSC will be posting on a regular basis summaries of reported exempt distributions on the OSC website at: http://www.osc.gov.on.ca/en/exempt-distributions-summary.htm.

The summaries are based on information contained in reports of exempt distribution (Form 45-106F1) filed with the OSC where Ontario purchasers have been identified. This is similar to the information previously reported in Chapter 8 of our Bulletin.

The summaries include the following information regarding the distribution:

- the submission date of the report

- the name of the issuer of the securities

- the distribution date (or first distribution date where there are multiple distribution dates identified in a single report)

- the amount of capital raised in Ontario, and

- the number of purchasers in Ontario.

The summaries will be posted as Excel files to facilitate the use, search and analysis of the data by stakeholders.

Questions

Please refer your questions to any of the following:

Daphne Wong
Legal Counsel, Corporate Finance
Ontario Securities Commission
416-593-8125
dwong@osc.gov.on.ca

Melissa Schofield
Senior Legal Counsel, Investment Funds and Structured Products
Ontario Securities Commission
416-595-8777
mschofield@osc.gov.on.ca

OSC Rule 45-801 — Implementing Multilateral Instrument 45-105 Trades to Employees, Senior Officers, Directors, and Consultants

Date: **August 8, 2003; as amended effective November 18, 2003 and September 28, 2009**

26 O.S.C.B. 6002; 32 O.S.C.B. (Supp-5) 183

    1.1 Revocation of Rule 45-503 — Ontario Securities Commission Rule 45-503 *Trades to Employees, Executives and Consultants* is revoked.

    1.3 revoked

    1.4 Effective Date — This rule comes into force on August 15, 2003.

Final Rule: (2006) 26 O.S.C.B. 6002; Approval by OSC: (2003) 26 O.S.C.B. 4167; Request for Comments: (2002) 25 O.S.C.B. 7205.

Amendment to Rule: (2003) 26 O.S.C.B. 7353; Approval by OSC: (2003) 26 O.S.C.B. 6315; (2009) 32 O.S.C.B. (Supp. 5) 183; Approval by OSC: (2009) 32 O.S.C.B. (Supp. 3) 325.

OSC Rule 45-802 — Implementing National Instrument 45-106 Prospectus and Registration Exemptions and Ontario Securities Commission Rule 45-501 Ontario Prospectus and Registration Exemptions

Date: September 14, 2005

28 O.S.C.B. (Supp. 4) 138

1.1 *OSC Rule 32-502* — Ontario Securities Commission Rule 32-502 — *Registration Exemption for Certain Trades by Financial Intermediaries* is revoked.

1.2 *OSC Rule 32-503* — Ontario Securities Commission Rule 32-503 — *Registration and Prospectus Exemption for Trades by Financial Intermediaries in Mutual Fund Securities to Corporate Sponsored Plans* is revoked.

1.3 *OSC Rule 45-502* — Ontario Securities Commission Rule 45-502 *Dividend or Interest Reinvestment and Stock Dividend Plans* is revoked.

1.4 *OSC Rule 46-501* — Ontario Securities Commission Rule 46-501 — *Self-Directed Registered Education Savings Plans* is revoked.

1.5 *OSC Rule 81-501* — Ontario Securities Commission Rule 81-501 *Mutual Fund Reinvestment Plans* is revoked.

1.6 *Effective Date* — This Rule comes into force on September 14, 2005.

Final Rule: (2005) 28 O.S.C.B. (Supp. 4) 138; Approval by OSC: (2005) 28 O.S.C.B. (Supp. 3) 220; Request for Comments: (2004) 27 O.S.C.B. (Supp. 3) 1.

4.6 — Requirements Affecting Distributions by Certain Issuers

See also NP 15.

National Policy 46-201 — Escrow for Initial Public Offerings

Date: June 28, 2002, amended November 17, 2015

25 O.S.C.B. 4038 and 38 O.S.C.B. 7551.

Table of Contents

Part VIII Amendment of Release Terms in Escrow Agreements Made Prior to this Policy

8.1 Can the release terms of escrow agreements made prior to this Policy be amended?

PART I — PURPOSE AND INTERPRETATION

1.1 What is the purpose of escrow? — (1) A public investor who buys securities in an initial public offering or an offering to fund a significant change of business relies on the issuer's management and principal securityholders to carry out the plans described in the issuer's prospectus. This is particularly true for issuers with a limited history of operations.

(2) An escrow agreement ties the issuer's management and its principal securityholders to the issuer by restricting their ability to sell their securities for a period of time following the issuer's offering. This gives them an incentive to devote their time and attention to the issuer's business while they are securityholders.

1.2 Interpretation — (1) You should use common sense in applying this Policy to your own circumstances, as we will apply the Policy according to its purpose.

(2) When we refer to securities that a person or company "holds", we mean that the person or company has direct or indirect beneficial ownership of, or control or direction over, the securities.

(3) When we refer to "any share certificates or other evidence...", it should not be construed to require a paper share certificate or other paper evidence of ownership for securities registered electronically if the terms of this Policy and the Form 46-201F1 *Escrow Agreement* are otherwise met.

1.3 Will a Canadian exchange impose additional escrow terms? — A Canadian exchange may impose additional escrow conditions or more stringent release terms.

PART II — APPLICATION OF THE POLICY

2.1 When does this Policy apply? — This Policy applies when an issuer and/or one or more of its securityholders distributes shares or convertible securities (both defined in section 3.7) to the public by prospectus in one of the following ways (an *IPO*):

(a) an initial distribution by the issuer

(b) a distribution by one or more of the issuer's securityholders if it is the initial public distribution of the issuer's securities (e.g., a corporate spin-off)

(c) a distribution, other than an initial distribution, by a reporting issuer and/or one or more of its securityholders, if no escrow has been previously imposed by a securities regulator or a Canadian exchange on the issuer's principals in connection with its current business.

2.2 What are the exceptions? — (1) This Policy does not apply to a distribution by:

(a) an exempt issuer (defined in section 3.2);

(b) a capital pool company under the TSX Venture Exchange Inc. (*TSX Venture*) Policy 2.4;

(c) a Tier 3 issuer listed on the TSX Venture; or

(d) an issuer that, following a business combination, is a successor to issuers whose principals have been subject to escrow requirements.

(2) This Policy generally does not apply to a prospectus that does not offer securities to the public, such as a prospectus that an issuer files with a securities regulator only to become a "reporting issuer".

2.3 How does this Policy apply to special warrant prospectuses? — (1) Special warrants are convertible securities that a principal is required to place in escrow. The principal must also place the securities issued on conversion of the special warrants in escrow, even if the securities are qualified under the prospectus.

(2) A prospectus that only qualifies the securities issued on conversion of special warrants is generally not an IPO prospectus because there are no additional proceeds raised. However, if there is a market for the securities, the prospectus may be considered an IPO prospectus for the purpose of this Policy. Otherwise, the IPO prospectus will be the next prospectus of the issuer that makes a public offering.

2.4 Can securities regulators impose additional or different terms? — A securities regulator may impose additional or different escrow terms if:

(a) an underwriter has not signed the IPO prospectus;

(b) the issuer has not applied to have its securities listed on a Canadian exchange, or a Canadian exchange has not agreed to list the securities distributed under the IPO prospectus; or

(c) there are other exceptional circumstances.

PART III — ESCROW CLASSIFICATIONS

3.1 Escrow classifications — Issuers are classified as either exempt issuers, established issuers or emerging issuers. Whether or not an issuer's securities will be subject to escrow, and the schedule for release of escrow securities from escrow will depend on the classification of the issuer.

3.2 Exempt issuers — Securities regulators do not generally consider that escrow is necessary for an exempt issuer. An *exempt issuer* is an issuer that, after its IPO:

(a) has securities listed on The Toronto Stock Exchange Inc. (*TSX*) and is classified by the TSX as an exempt issuer;

(a.1) has securities listed on Aequitas NEO Exchange Inc. and is a Closed End Fund, Exchange Traded Fund or Exchange Traded Product (as defined in the Aequitas NEO Exchange Inc. Listing Manual as amended from time to time); or

(b) has a market capitalization of at least $100 million. (In calculating market capitalization, multiply the total number of the securities of the same class as the securities offered in the IPO, which are outstanding on completion of the IPO, by the IPO price.)

3.3 Established and emerging issuers — (1) Securities regulators generally consider that escrow is necessary for established and emerging issuers.

(2) An *established issuer* is an issuer that, after its IPO:

(a) has securities listed on the TSX and is not classified by the TSX as an exempt issuer;

Part 4:
DISTRIBUTIONS

(b) has securities listed on the TSX Venture and is a TSX Venture Tier 1 issuer; or

(c) has securities listed on Aequitas NEO Exchange Inc. and is not an exempt issuer.

(3) An *emerging issuer* is an issuer that, after its IPO, is not an exempt issuer or an established issuer.

3.4 When is an issuer classified for escrow purposes? — An issuer is classified based on its circumstances immediately after completion of its IPO. If an emerging issuer becomes an established issuer at a later point, it may have the release schedule changed. See section 4.4.

3.5 Whose securities are subject to escrow? — (1) Securities regulators generally require principals of an emerging or established issuer to place their securities in escrow under an escrow agreement.

(2) A *principal* of an issuer is:

(a) a person or company who acted as a promoter of the issuer within two years before the IPO prospectus

(b) a director or senior officer of the issuer or any of its material operating subsidiaries at the time of the IPO prospectus

(c) a *20% holder* — a person or company that holds securities carrying more than 20% of the voting rights attached to the issuer's outstanding securities immediately before and immediately after the issuer's IPO

(d) a *10% holder* — a person or company that

(i) holds securities carrying more than 10% of the voting rights attached to the issuer's outstanding securities immediately before and immediately after the issuer's IPO and

(ii) has elected or appointed, or has the right to elect or appoint, one or more directors or senior officers of the issuer or any of its material operating subsidiaries.

(3) In calculating these percentages, include securities that may be issued to the holder under outstanding convertible securities in both the holder's securities and the total securities outstanding.

(4) A company, trust, partnership or other entity more than 50% held by one or more principals will be treated as a principal. (In calculating this percentage, include securities of the entity that may be issued to the principals under outstanding convertible securities in both the principals' securities of the entity and the total securities of the entity outstanding.) Any securities of the issuer that this entity holds will be subject to escrow requirements.

(5) A principal's spouse and their relatives that live at the same address as the principal will also be treated as principals and any securities of the issuer they hold will be subject to escrow requirements.

3.6 Are any principals exempt from escrow requirements? — A principal that holds securities carrying less than 1% of the voting rights attached to an issuer's outstanding securities immediately after its IPO is not subject to escrow requirements. (In calculating this percentage, include securities that may be issued to that principal under outstanding convertible securities in both the principal's securities and the total securities outstanding.)

3.7 What types of securities are subject to escrow? — 3.7.1 Escrow securities —

(1) The following securities are subject to escrow (*escrow securities*) if a principal holds them immediately before the issuer's IPO:

(a) **shares** — equity securities that carry the right to participate in earnings and assets remaining on winding-up or liquidation, including common shares, restricted voting shares, subordinate voting shares, multiple voting shares and non-voting shares

(b) **convertible securities** — securities that allow the holder to acquire shares or other convertible securities (such as warrants, special warrants qualified under the IPO prospectus, convertible shares, convertible debentures, rights and options), *except for* non-transferable incentive stock options issued to principals of the issuer to purchase securities solely for cash at a price equal to or greater than the IPO price

(2) Securities will be released from escrow if they are sold in a "permitted secondary offering" which is defined in section 3.8.

3.7.2 Additional escrow securities — Shares and convertible securities that a holder of escrow securities acquires in relation to securities that are in escrow at the time:

(a) as a dividend or other distribution;

(b) on the exercise of a right of purchase, conversion or exchange, including securities received on conversion of special warrants;

(c) on a subdivision, or compulsory or automatic conversion or exchange; or

(d) from a successor issuer in a business combination, if this is required under Part V

(*additional escrow securities*) must be placed in escrow by the holder.

3.8 What is a permitted secondary offering? — (1) A principal may sell its securities in the issuer in the issuer's IPO free of escrow in the following circumstances (*a permitted secondary offering*):

(a) the sale is conducted on a firmly underwritten basis; or

(b) the sale is conducted on a best efforts basis after completion of the sale by the issuer of all or the specified minimum number of its securities offered in the IPO (if any), if the principal is not a promoter, director or senior officer of the issuer or any of its material operating subsidiaries.

(2) The permitted secondary offering must be disclosed in the IPO prospectus.

(3) Any of the principal's remaining unsold escrow securities will continue to be subject to the escrow agreement and released in accordance with the applicable release schedules in the tables set out in sections 4.2.3 and 4.3.3.

3.9 Is there a standard form of escrow agreement? — The terms of escrow are set out in a written escrow agreement among an emerging issuer or an established issuer, an escrow agent and the issuer's principals whose securities are subject to escrow. The standard form of escrow agreement is attached as an Appendix to this Policy. An issuer must file a copy of the signed escrow agreement with securities regulators in the jurisdictions where the issuer files its IPO prospectus.

3.10 Who may be an escrow agent? — A person or company approved by a Canadian exchange to act as a transfer agent may be an escrow agent.

PART IV — RELEASE OF ESCROW SECURITIES FROM ESCROW

4.1 When are escrow securities released from escrow? — (1) The release of escrow securities from escrow will vary depending on the escrow classification of the issuer that issued the securities. Principals of established issuers will have their escrow securities released from escrow over an 18-month period. Principals of emerging issuers will have their escrow securities released over a three-year period. The timing of escrow release will also be affected if a securityholder dies, if an emerging issuer becomes an established issuer, or if an issuer is party to a business combination.

(2) The escrow agreement sets out release procedures for escrow securities.

4.2 Release schedule for an established issuer — **4.2.1 Usual case** — A principal's escrow securities in an established issuer are released as follows:

On the date the issuer's securities are listed on a Canadian exchange *(the listing date)*	1/4 of the escrow securities
6 months after the listing date	1/3 of the remaining escrow securities
12 months after the listing date	1/2 of the remaining escrow securities
18 months after the listing date	The remaining escrow securities

Notes:

* In the simplest case, where there are no changes to the escrow securities initially deposited and no additional escrow securities, the release schedule outlined above results in the escrow securities being released in equal tranches of 25%.

4.2.2 Alternate meaning of "listing date" — If an issuer is an established issuer, an alternate meaning for listing date is the date the issuer completes its IPO if the issuer's securities are listed on a Canadian exchange immediately before its IPO.

4.2.3 If there is a permitted secondary offering —

(1) If a principal has sold in a permitted secondary offering 25% or more of that principal's escrow securities, the principal's escrow securities are released as follows:

For delivery to complete the issuer's IPO	**All escrow securities sold in the permitted secondary offering**
6 months after the listing date	1/3 of the remaining escrow securities
12 months after the listing date	1/2 of the remaining escrow securities
18 months after the listing date	The remaining escrow securities

Notes:

* In the simplest case, where there are no changes to the remaining escrow securities upon completion of the permitted secondary offering and no additional escrow securities, the release schedule outlined above results in the remaining escrow securities being released in equal tranches of 33 1/3%.

(2) If a principal has sold in a permitted secondary offering less than 25% of that principal's escrow securities, the principal's escrow securities are released as follows:

For delivery to complete the issuer's IPO	**All escrow securities sold in the permitted secondary offering**
On the listing date	1/4 of the original number of escrow securities less the escrow securities sold in the permitted secondary offering
6 months after the listing date	1/3 of the remaining escrow securities
12 months after the listing date	1/2 of the remaining escrow securities
18 months after the listing date	The remaining escrow securities

Notes:

* In the simplest case, where there are no changes to the remaining escrow securities upon completion of the permitted secondary offering and no additional escrow securities, the release schedule outlined above results in the remaining escrow securities being released in equal tranches of 33 1/3% after completion of the release on the listing date.

4.2.4 Additional escrow securities — If a holder of escrow securities acquires additional escrow securities, those securities will be added to the securities already in escrow to increase the number of remaining escrow securities. After that, all of the escrow securities will be released in accordance with the applicable release schedule in the tables above.

4.3 Release schedule for an emerging issuer — **4.3.1 Usual case** — A principal's escrow securities in an emerging issuer are released as follows:

On the date the issuer's securities are listed on a Canadian exchange *(the listing date)*	1/10 of the escrow securities
6 months after the listing date	1/6 of the remaining escrow securities
12 months after the listing date	1/5 of the remaining escrow securities
18 months after the listing date	1/4 of the remaining escrow securities
24 months after the listing date	1/3 of the remaining escrow securities
30 months after the listing date	1/2 of the remaining escrow securities

36 months after the listing date

Notes:

*   In the simplest case, where there are no changes to the escrow securities initially deposited and no additional escrow securities, the release schedule outlined above results in the escrow securities being released in equal tranches of 15% after completion of the release on the listing date.

4.3.2 Alternate meaning of "listing date" — If an issuer is an emerging issuer, an alternate meaning for listing date is the date the issuer completes its IPO if:

(a) the issuer's securities are not listed on a Canadian exchange immediately after its IPO; or

(b) the issuer's securities are listed on a Canadian exchange immediately before its IPO.

4.3.3 If there is a permitted secondary offering —

(1) If a principal has sold in a permitted secondary offering 10% or more of that principal's escrow securities, the principal's escrow securities are released as follows:

For delivery to complete the issuer's IPO	All escrow securities sold in the permitted secondary offering
6 months after the listing date	1/6 of the remaining escrow securities
12 months after the listing date	1/5 of the remaining escrow securities
18 months after the listing date	1/4 of the remaining escrow securities
24 months after the listing date	1/3 of the remaining escrow securities
30 months after the listing date	1/2 of the remaining escrow securities
36 months after the listing date	The remaining escrow securities

Notes:

*   In the simplest case, where there are no changes to the remaining escrow securities upon completion of the permitted secondary offering and no additional escrow securities, the release schedule outlined above results in the remaining escrow securities being released in equal tranches of 16 2/3%.

(2) If a principal has sold in a permitted secondary offering less than 10% of that principal's escrow securities, the principal's escrow securities are released as follows:

For delivery to complete the issuer's IPO	All escrow securities sold in the permitted secondary offering
On the listing date	1/10 of the original number of escrow securities less the escrow securities sold in the permitted secondary offering
6 months after the listing date	1/6 of the remaining escrow securities
12 months after the listing date	1/5 of the remaining escrow securities
18 months after the listing date	1/4 of the remaining escrow securities
24 months after the listing date	1/3 of the remaining escrow securities
30 months after the listing date	1/2 of the remaining escrow securities
36 months after the listing date	The remaining escrow securities

Notes:

*   In the simplest case, where there are no changes to the remaining escrow securities upon completion of the permitted secondary offering and no additional escrow securities, the release schedule outlined above results in the remaining escrow securities being released in equal tranches of 16 2/3% after completion of the release on the listing date.

4.3.4 Additional escrow securities — If a holder of escrow securities acquires additional escrow securities, those securities will be added to the securities already in escrow to increase the number of remaining escrow securities. After that, all of the escrow securities will be released in accordance with the applicable release schedule in the tables above.

4.4 What happens if an emerging issuer becomes an established issuer after its IPO? — (1) An emerging issuer becomes an established issuer if it:

(a) lists its securities on the TSX or Aequitas NEO Exchange Inc.;

(b) becomes a TSX Venture Tier 1 issuer; or

(c) lists or quotes its securities on an exchange or market outside Canada that its "principal regulator" under National Policy 43-201 *Mutual Reliance Review System for Prospectuses and Annual Information Forms* (in Quebec under Staff Notice, *Mutual Reliance Review System for Prospectuses and Annual Information Forms*) or, if the issuer has only filed its IPO prospectus in one jurisdiction, the securities regulator in that jurisdiction, is satisfied has minimum listing requirements at least equal to those of TSX Venture Tier 1.

(2) If an emerging issuer becomes an established issuer 18 months or more after its listing date, all escrow securities will be released immediately.

(3) If an emerging issuer becomes an established issuer within 18 months after its listing date, all escrow securities that would have been released to that time, if the issuer was an established issuer on its listing date, will be released immediately. Remaining escrow securities will be released in equal instalments on the day that is 6 months, 12 months and 18 months after the listing date.

4.5 Release of escrow securities on death of holder — If a holder of escrow securities dies, the holder's escrow securities will be released from escrow.

4.6 Release of escrow securities — Once escrow securities are released from escrow, they are no longer escrow securities for the purpose of this Policy.

PART V — BUSINESS COMBINATIONS

5.1 When does this Part apply? — This Part applies to business combinations. A *business combination* is:

(a) a formal take-over bid for all outstanding equity securities of the issuer or which, if successful, would result in a change of control of the issuer

(b) a formal issuer bid for all outstanding equity securities of the issuer

(c) a statutory arrangement

(d) an amalgamation

(e) a merger

(f) a reorganization that has an effect similar to an amalgamation or merger

5.2 Can a holder of escrow securities tender them in a business combination? — (1) Yes, a holder of escrow securities can tender them in a business combination. The tendered escrow securities will be released from escrow and delivered under the business combination if:

(a) the terms and conditions of the business combination have been satisfied or waived; and

(b) the escrow securities have either been taken up and paid for or are subject to an unconditional obligation to be taken up and paid for under the business combination.

(2) The escrow agreement contains special procedures for tendering escrow securities.

5.3 If the holder receives securities of another issuer in exchange for the holder's escrow securities, will the new securities be subject to escrow? — If the holder receives securities of another issuer *(successor issuer)* in exchange for the holder's escrow securities, the new securities will be subject to escrow, if immediately upon completion of the business combination:

(a) the successor issuer is not an exempt issuer (defined in section 3.2)

(b) the holder is a principal (defined in section 3.5) of the successor issuer; and

(c) the holder holds more than 1% of the voting rights attached to the successor issuer's outstanding securities. (In calculating this percentage, include securities that may be issued to the principal under outstanding convertible securities to both the principal's securities and the total securities outstanding.)

5.4 If the new securities are subject to escrow, when will they be released? — (1) If the new securities are subject to escrow, the escrow agent will hold the new securities in escrow on the same terms and conditions, including release dates, as applied to the escrow securities that were exchanged.

(2) However, if the issuer is an emerging issuer, the successor issuer is an established issuer, and the business combination occurs 18 months or more after the issuer's listing date, all escrow securities will be released immediately.

(3) If the issuer is an emerging issuer, the successor issuer is an established issuer and the business combination occurs within 18 months after the issuer's listing date, all escrow securities that would have been released to that time, if the issuer was an established issuer on its listing date, will be released immediately. Remaining escrow securities will be released in equal instalments on the day that is 6 months, 12 months and 18 months after the issuer's listing date.

PART VI — DEALING WITH ESCROW SECURITIES

6.1 Can a holder of escrow securities vote and receive distributions on the escrow securities? — A holder may exercise any voting rights attached to their escrow securities and receive distributions on the holder's escrow securities.

6.2 Restrictions on dealing with escrow securities — *Escrow restricts the ability of holders to deal with their escrow securities while they are in escrow. The standard form of escrow agreement sets out these restrictions. Except to the extent that the escrow agreement expressly permits, a principal cannot sell, transfer, assign, mortgage, enter into a derivative transaction concerning, or otherwise deal in any way with the holder's escrow securities or any related share certificates or other evidence of the escrow securities. A private company, controlled by one or more principals of the issuer, that holds escrow securities of the issuer, may not participate in a transaction that results in a change of its control or a change in the economic exposure of the principals to the risks of holding escrow securities.*

6.3 When can a holder of escrow securities transfer them within escrow? — (1) A holder may transfer escrow securities within escrow:

(a) to existing or, upon their appointment, incoming directors or senior officers of the issuer or any of its material operating subsidiaries, if the issuer's board of directors has approved the transfer;

(b) to a person or company that before the proposed transfer holds more than 20% of the voting rights attached to the issuer's outstanding securities;

(c) to a person or company that after the proposed transfer

(i) will hold more than 10% of the voting rights attached to the issuer's outstanding securities, and

(ii) has the right to elect or appoint one or more directors or senior officers of the issuer or any of its material operating subsidiaries;

(d) to a trustee in bankruptcy or another person or company entitled to escrow securities on the bankruptcy of the holder;

(e) to a financial institution on the realization of escrow securities pledged, mortgaged or charged by the holder to the financial institution as collateral for a loan; or

(f) to or between a registered retirement savings plan (RRSP), registered retirement income fund (RRIF) or other similar registered plan or fund with a trustee, where the annuitant of the RRSP or RRIF, or the beneficiaries of the other registered plan or fund are limited to the holder and his or her spouse, children and parents or, in the case of a trustee of such registered plan or fund, to the annuitant of the RRSP or RRIF, or a beneficiary of the other registered plan or fund, as applicable, or his or her spouse, children and parents.

(2) The escrow agreement sets out transfer procedures for escrow securities.

(3) Securities laws and other legislation may impose additional restrictions on transfer. (See section 7.4.)

6.4 Can a holder pledge, mortgage or charge escrow securities as collateral for a loan? — A holder can pledge, mortgage or charge escrow securities to a financial institution as collateral for a loan. The loan agreement must provide that the escrow securities will remain in escrow if the lender realizes on the escrow securities to satisfy the loan.

6.5 Can a holder exchange or convert convertible escrow securities? — A holder of a convertible security that is in escrow may exchange or convert the security within escrow. Securities acquired on conversion or exchange of convertible escrow securities are additional escrow securities and remain in escrow.

PART VII — GENERAL PROVISIONS

7.1 Amendments to escrow agreement require regulatory approval — The securities regulator in each jurisdiction where the issuer files its IPO prospectus has jurisdiction over the escrow agreement and escrow securities of the issuer. No amendment to an escrow agreement is valid unless the securities regulators that have jurisdiction have approved it.

7.2. Will mutual reliance principles apply to escrow filings? — Yes, the securities regulators will apply mutual reliance principles in administering this Policy. This means the decision of a single regulator will evidence the decision of all securities regulators with jurisdiction.

7.3 What happens if an issuer does not complete its IPO? — If an issuer does not complete its IPO and becomes a reporting issuer in one or more jurisdictions because it has obtained a receipt for its IPO prospectus, its escrow agreement will remain in effect until the securities regulators in those jurisdictions order that the issuer has ceased to be a reporting issuer.

7.4 Do local resale restrictions still apply to escrow securities after they are released from escrow? — Although this Policy may permit the release of escrow securities from escrow or permit a holder to transfer or deal in other ways with escrow securities, other restrictions imposed by securities legislation, securities regulators and Canadian exchanges will still apply.

PART VIII — AMENDMENT OF RELEASE TERMS IN ESCROW AGREEMENTS MADE PRIOR TO THIS POLICY

8.1 Can the release terms of escrow agreements made prior to this Policy be amended? — (1) The securities regulators consent to amendments to escrow agreements made prior to the date of this Policy *(existing escrow agreements)* to reflect the release terms of this Policy on the following conditions:

(a) The issuer's board of directors must have approved the amendment.

(b) All parties to the existing escrow agreement, except parties whose securities are no longer in escrow, must have agreed to the amendment.

(c) The issuer must have obtained any approval by a Canadian exchange required by the existing escrow agreement.

(d) The amendment must have been approved by a majority vote of the securityholders of the issuer, or consented to by securityholders holding a majority of the securities of the issuer, excluding in each case escrow securityholders and their affiliates and associates.

(e) The amendment to the release terms must apply to all escrow securities.

(f) Once the escrow agreement has been amended and these conditions have been met, the issuer must issue a news release at least 60 days before the first release of escrow securities under the amended escrow agreement notifying the market of the amendment and the new release terms.

(g) The issuer's classification as an exempt, established or emerging issuer must be determined at the date of the news release.

(h) The news release must set out the date of the first release of escrow securities under the amended escrow agreement. The first release date must be at least 60 days after the news release and that date will take the place of the listing date for purposes of the appropriate release schedule under this Policy.

(i) If the issuer is an exempt issuer, all escrow securities may be released no earlier than 60 days after the news release, subject to the 10% limit in (k) below.

(j) If the issuer is an emerging or an established issuer, the new release schedule must be the schedule included in this Policy for that class of issuer, subject to the 10% limit in (k) below.

(k) The number of escrow securities to be released at any one time may not exceed 10% of the issuer's outstanding securities at the time of release. Securities remaining in escrow after the last scheduled release will continue to be released from escrow at 6-month intervals until all escrow securities have been released.

(l) Escrow securities must be released on a pro rata basis, with each holder of escrow securities receiving the same percentage of the escrow securities that are released as the percentage of total escrow securities held by the holder.

(m) The issuer must file with the securities regulators in the jurisdictions where it filed its IPO prospectus:

    (i) a copy of the amended escrow agreement, and

    (ii) a certificate of a director or senior officer of the issuer confirming that the escrow agreement has been amended in accordance with this Part.

(2) The parties to an existing escrow agreement may amend the agreement by entering into an agreement in the form of Form 46-201F1 *Escrow Agreement*.

(3) Our consent does not limit the right of a Canadian exchange to impose additional conditions or more stringent release terms.

Appedix 1 — Escrow Agreement

THIS AGREEMENT is made as of the .... day of ...., ...

AMONG:

    (the *"Issuer"*)

AND:

    (the *"Escrow Agent"*)

AND:

EACH OF THE UNDERSIGNED SECURITYHOLDERS OF THE ISSUER

(a "*Securityholder*" or "*you*")

(collectively, the *"Parties"*)

This Agreement is being entered into by the Parties under National Policy 46-201 *Escrow for Initial Public Offerings* (the *Policy*) in connection with the proposed distribution (the *IPO*), by the Issuer, an [established/emerging] issuer, of [describe securities] by prospectus and/or by certain Securityholders, namely [names of Securityholders], of [specify number of securities distributed by each Securityholder and what percentage of each Securityholder's securities that number represents] (the *permitted secondary offering*).

For good and valuable consideration, the Parties agree as follows:

Form 46-201F1 — Escrow Agreement

Table of Contents

PART 10 GENERAL

Part 1 — Escrow

1.1 — Appointment of Escrow Agent

The Issuer and the Securityholders appoint the Escrow Agent to act as escrow agent under this Agreement. The Escrow Agent accepts the appointment.

1.2 — Deposit of Escrow Securities in Escrow

(1) You are depositing the securities *(escrow securities)* listed opposite your name in Schedule "A" with the Escrow Agent to be held in escrow under this Agreement. You will immediately deliver or cause to be delivered to the Escrow Agent any share certificates or other evidence of these securities which you have or which you may later receive.

(2) If you receive any other securities *(additional escrow securities)*:

(a) as a dividend or other distribution on escrow securities;

(b) on the exercise of a right of purchase, conversion or exchange attaching to escrow securities, including securities received on conversion of special warrants;

(c) on a subdivision, or compulsory or automatic conversion or exchange of escrow securities; or

(d) from a successor issuer in a business combination, if Part 6 of this Agreement applies,

you will deposit them in escrow with the Escrow Agent. You will deliver or cause to be delivered to the Escrow Agent any share certificates or other evidence of those additional escrow securities. When this Agreement refers to *escrow securities,* it includes additional escrow securities.

(3) You will immediately deliver to the Escrow Agent any replacement share certificates or other evidence of additional escrow securities issued to you.

1.3 — Direction to Escrow Agent

The Issuer and the Securityholders direct the Escrow Agent to hold the escrow securities in escrow until they are released from escrow under this Agreement.

Part 2 — Release of Escrow Securities

2.1 — Release Schedule for an Established Issuer

2.1.1 — Usual case

If the Issuer is an *established issuer* (as defined in section 3.3 of the Policy) and you have not sold any escrow securities in a permitted secondary offering, your escrow securities will be released as follows:

On ...., 2.........., the date the Issuer's securities are listed on a Canadian exchange *(the listing date)*	1/4 of your escrow securities
6 months after the listing date	1/3 of your remaining escrow securities
12 months after the listing date	1/2 of your remaining escrow securities
18 months after the listing date	your remaining escrow securities

Notes:

*   In the simplest case, where there are no changes to the escrow securities initially deposited and no additional escrow securities, then the release schedule outlined above results in the escrow securities being released in equal tranches of 25%.

2.1.2 — Alternate meaning of "listing date"

If the Issuer is an established issuer, an alternate meaning for *listing date* is the date the Issuer completes its IPO if the Issuer's securities are listed on a Canadian exchange immediately before its IPO.

2.1.3 — If there is a permitted secondary offering

(1) If the Issuer is an established issuer and you have sold in a permitted secondary offering 25% or more of your escrow securities, your escrow securities will be released as follows:

For delivery to complete the IPO	All escrow securities sold by you in the permitted secondary offerinG
6 months after the listing date	1/3 of your remaining escrow securities
12 months after the listing date	1/2 of your remaining escrow securities
18 months after the listing date	your remaining escrow securities

Notes:

*   In the simplest case, where there are no changes to the remaining escrow securities upon completion of the permitted secondary offering and no additional escrow securities, the release schedule outlined above results in the remaining escrow securities being released in equal tranches of 33 1/3%.

(2) If the Issuer is an established issuer and you have sold in a permitted secondary offering less than 25% of your escrow securities, your escrow securities will be released as follows:

For delivery to complete the IPO	All escrow securities sold by you in the permitted secondary offering
On the listing date	1/4 of your original number of escrow securities less the escrow securities sold by you in the permitted secondary offering
6 months after the listing date	1/3 of your remaining escrow securities
12 months after the listing date	1/2 of your remaining escrow securities
18 months after the listing date	your remaining escrow securities

Notes:

*   In the simplest case, where there are no changes to the remaining escrow securities upon completion of the permitted secondary offering and no additional escrow securities, the release schedule outlined above results in the remaining escrow securities being released in equal tranches of 33 1/3% after completion of the release on the listing date.

2.1.4 — Additional escrow securities

If you acquire additional escrow securities, those securities will be added to the securities already in escrow, to increase the number of remaining escrow securities. After that, all of the escrow securities will be released in accordance with the applicable release schedule in the tables above.

2.2 — Release Schedule for an Emerging Issuer

2.2.1 — Usual case

If the Issuer is an *emerging issuer* (as defined in section 3.3 of the Policy) and you have not sold any escrow securities in a permitted secondary offering, your escrow securities will be released as follows:

On ...., 2..........., the date the Issuer's securities are listed on a Canadian exchange *(the listing date)*	1/10 of your escrow securities
6 months after the listing date	1/6 of your remaining escrow securities
12 months after the listing date	1/5 of your remaining escrow securities
18 months after the listing date	1/4 of your remaining escrow securities
24 months after the listing date	1/3 of your remaining escrow securities
30 months after the listing date	1/2 of your remaining escrow securities
36 months after the listing date	your remaining escrow securities

Notes:

*   In the simplest case, where there are no changes to the escrow securities initially deposited and no additional escrow securities, the release schedule outlined above results in the escrow securities being released in equal tranches of 15% after completion of the release on the listing date.

2.2.2 — Alternate meaning of "listing date"

If the Issuer is an emerging issuer, an alternate meaning for *listing date* is the date the Issuer completes its IPO if:

(a) the Issuer's securities are not listed on a Canadian exchange immediately after its IPO; or

(b) the Issuer's securities are listed on a Canadian exchange immediately before its IPO.

2.2.3 — If there is a permitted secondary offering

(1) If the Issuer is an emerging issuer and you have sold in a permitted secondary offering 10% or more of your escrow securities, your escrow securities will be released as follows:

For delivery to complete the IPO	**All escrow securities sold by you in the permitted secondary offering**
6 months after the listing date	1/6 of your remaining escrow securities
12 months after the listing date	1/5 of your remaining escrow securities
18 months after the listing date	1/4 of your remaining escrow securities

For delivery to complete the IPO	All escrow securities sold by you in the permitted secondary offering
24 months after the listing date	1/3 of your remaining escrow securities
30 months after the listing date	1/2 of your remaining escrow securities
36 months after the listing date	your remaining escrow securities

Notes:

*   In the simplest case, where there are no changes to the remaining escrow securities upon completion of the permitted secondary offering and no additional escrow securities, the release schedule outlined above results in the remaining escrow securities being released in equal tranches of 16 2/3%.

(2) If the Issuer is an emerging issuer and you have sold in a permitted secondary offering less than 10% of your escrow securities, your escrow securities will be released as follows:

For delivery to complete the IPO	All escrow securities sold by you in the permitted secondary offering
On the listing date	1/10 of your original number of escrow securities less the escrow securities sold by you in the permitted secondary offering
6 months after the listing date	1/6 of your remaining escrow securities
12 months after the listing date	1/5 of your remaining escrow securities
18 months after the listing date	1/4 of your remaining escrow securities
24 months after the listing date	1/3 of your remaining escrow securities
30 months after the listing date	1/2 of your remaining escrow securities
36 months after the listing date	your remaining escrow securities

Notes:

*   In the simplest case, where there are no changes to the remaining escrow securities upon completion of the permitted secondary offering and no additional escrow securities, the release schedule outlined above results in the remaining escrow securities being released in equal tranches of 16 2/3% after completion of the release on the listing date.

2.2.4 — Additional escrow securities

If you acquire additional escrow securities, those securities will be added to the securities already in escrow, to increase the number of remaining escrow securities. After that, all of the escrow securities will be released in accordance with the applicable release schedule in the tables above.

2.3 — Delivery of Share Certificates for Escrow Securities

The Escrow Agent will send to each Securityholder any share certificates or other evidence of that Securityholder's escrow securities in the possession of the Escrow Agent released from escrow as soon as reasonably practicable after the release.

2.4 — Replacement Certificates

If, on the date a Securityholder's escrow securities are to be released, the Escrow Agent holds a share certificate or other evidence representing more escrow securities than are to be released, the Escrow Agent will deliver the share certificate or other evidence to the Issuer or its transfer agent and request replacement share certificates or other evidence. The Issuer will cause replacement share certificates or other evidence to be prepared and delivered to the Escrow Agent. After the Escrow Agent receives the replacement share certificates or other evidence, the Escrow Agent will send to the Securityholder or at the Securityholder's direction, the replacement share certificate or other evidence of the escrow securities released. The Escrow Agent and Issuer will act as soon as reasonably practicable.

2.5 — Release upon Death

(1) If a Securityholder dies, the Securityholder's escrow securities will be released from escrow. The Escrow Agent will deliver any share certificates or other evidence of the escrow securities in the possession of the Escrow Agent to the Securityholder's legal representative.

(2) Prior to delivery the Escrow Agent must receive:

   (a) a certified copy of the death certificate; and

   (b) any evidence of the legal representative's status that the Escrow Agent may reasonably require.

Part 3 — Early Release on Change of Issuer Status

3.1 — Becoming an Established Issuer

If the Issuer is an emerging issuer on the date of this Agreement and, during this Agreement, the Issuer:

   (a) lists its securities on the Toronto Stock Exchange Inc. or Aequitas NEO Exchange Inc.;

   (b) becomes a TSX Venture Exchange Inc. *(TSX Venture)* Tier 1 issuer; or

   (c) lists or quotes its securities on an exchange or market outside Canada that its "principal regulator" under National Policy 43-201 *Mutual Reliance Review System for Prospectuses and Annual Information Forms* (in Quebec under Staff Notice, *Mutual Reliance Review System for Prospectuses and Annual Information Forms*) or, if the Issuer has only filed its IPO prospectus in one jurisdiction, the securities regulator in that jurisdiction, is satisfied has minimum listing requirements at least equal to those of TSX Venture Tier 1,

then the Issuer becomes an *established issuer*.

3.2 — Release of Escrow Securities

(1) When an emerging issuer becomes an established issuer, the release schedule for its escrow securities changes.

(2) If an emerging issuer becomes an established issuer 18 months or more after its listing date, all escrow securities will be released immediately.

(3) If an emerging issuer becomes an established issuer within 18 months after its listing date, all escrow securities that would have been released to that time, if the Issuer was an established issuer on its listing date, will be released immediately. Remaining escrow securities will be released in equal installments on the day that is 6 months, 12 months and 18 months after the listing date.

3.3 — Filing Requirements

Escrow securities will not be released under this Part until the Issuer does the following:

(a) at least 20 days before the date of the first release of escrow securities under the new release schedule, files with the securities regulators in the jurisdictions in which it is a reporting issuer

(i) a certificate signed by a director or officer of the Issuer authorized to sign stating

(A) that the Issuer has become an established issuer by satisfying one of the conditions in section 3.1 and specifying the condition, and

(B) the number of escrow securities to be released on the first release date under the new release schedule, and

(ii) a copy of a letter or other evidence from the exchange or quotation service confirming that the Issuer has satisfied the condition to become an established issuer; and

(b) at least 10 days before the date of the first release of escrow securities under the new release schedule, issues and files with the securities regulators in the jurisdictions in which it is a reporting issuer a news release disclosing details of the first release of the escrow securities and the change in the release schedule, and sends a copy of such filing to the Escrow Agent.

3.4 — Amendment of Release Schedule

The new release schedule will apply 10 days after the Escrow Agent receives a certificate signed by a director or officer of the Issuer authorized to sign

(a) stating that the Issuer has become an established issuer by satisfying one of the conditions in section 3.1 and specifying the condition;

(b) stating that the release schedule for the Issuer's escrow securities has changed;

(c) stating that the Issuer has issued a news release at least 10 days before the first release date under the new release schedule and specifying the date that the news release was issued; and

(d) specifying the new release schedule.

Part 4 — Dealing With Escrow Securities

4.1 — Restriction on Transfer, etc.

Unless it is expressly permitted in this Agreement, you will not sell, transfer, assign, mortgage, enter into a derivative transaction concerning, or otherwise deal in any way with your escrow securities or any related share certificates or other evidence of the escrow securities. If a Securityholder is a private company controlled by one or more principals (as defined in section 3.5 of the Policy) of the Issuer, the Securityholder may not participate in a transaction that results in a change of its control or a change in the economic exposure of the principals to the risks of holding escrow securities.

4.2 — Pledge, Mortgage or Charge as Collateral for a Loan

You may pledge, mortgage or charge your escrow securities to a financial institution as collateral for a loan, provided that no escrow securities or any share certificates or other evidence of escrow securities will be transferred or delivered by the Escrow Agent to the financial institution for this purpose. The loan agreement must provide that the escrow securities will remain in escrow if the lender realizes on the escrow securities to satisfy the loan.

4.3 — Voting of Escrow Securities

You may exercise any voting rights attached to your escrow securities.

4.4 — Dividends on Escrow Securities

You may receive a dividend or other distribution on your escrow securities, and elect the manner of payment from the standard options offered by the Issuer. If the Escrow Agent receives a dividend or other distribution on your escrow securities, other than additional escrow securities, the Escrow Agent will pay the dividend or other distribution to you on receipt.

4.5 — Exercise of Other Rights Attaching to Escrow Securities

You may exercise your rights to exchange or convert your escrow securities in accordance with this Agreement.

Part 5 — Permitted Transfers Within Escrow

5.1 — Transfer to Directors and Senior Officers

(1) You may transfer escrow securities within escrow to existing or, upon their appointment, incoming directors or senior officers of the Issuer or any of its material operating subsidiaries, if the Issuer's board of directors has approved the transfer.

(2) Prior to the transfer the Escrow Agent must receive:

(a) a certified copy of the resolution of the board of directors of the Issuer approving the transfer;

(b) a certificate signed by a director or officer of the Issuer authorized to sign, stating that the transfer is to a director or senior officer of the Issuer or a material operating subsidiary and that any required approval from the Canadian exchange the Issuer is listed on has been received;

(c) an acknowledgment in the form of Schedule "B" signed by the transferee;

(d) copies of the letters sent to the securities regulators described in subsection (3) accompanying the acknowledgement; and

(e) a transfer power of attorney, completed and executed by the transferor in accordance with the requirements of the Issuer's transfer agent.

(3) At least 10 days prior to the transfer, the Issuer will file a copy of the acknowledgement with the securities regulators in the jurisdictions in which it is a reporting issuer.

5.2 — Transfer to Other Principals

(1) You may transfer escrow securities within escrow:

(a) to a person or company that before the proposed transfer holds more than 20% of the voting rights attached to the Issuer's outstanding securities; or

(b) to a person or company that after the proposed transfer

(i) will hold more than 10% of the voting rights attached to the Issuer's outstanding securities, and

(ii) has the right to elect or appoint one or more directors or senior officers of the Issuer or any of its material operating subsidiaries.

(2) Prior to the transfer the Escrow Agent must receive:

(a) a certificate signed by a director or officer of the Issuer authorized to sign stating that

(i) the transfer is to a person or company that the officer believes, after reasonable investigation, holds more than 20% of the voting rights attached to the Issuer's outstanding securities before the proposed transfer, or

(ii) the transfer is to a person or company that

(A) the officer believes, after reasonable investigation, will hold more than 10% of the voting rights attached to the Issuer's outstanding securities, and

(B) has the right to elect or appoint one or more directors or senior officers of the Issuer or any of its material operating subsidiaries

after the proposed transfer, and

(iii) any required approval from the Canadian exchange the Issuer is listed on has been received;

(b) an acknowledgment in the form of Schedule "B" signed by the transferee;

(c) copies of the letters sent to the securities regulators accompanying the acknowledgement; and

(d) a transfer power of attorney, executed by the transferor in accordance with the requirements of the Issuer's transfer agent.

(3) At least 10 days prior to the transfer, the Issuer will file a copy of the acknowledgement with the securities regulators in the jurisdictions in which it is a reporting issuer.

5.3 — Transfer upon Bankruptcy

(1) You may transfer escrow securities within escrow to a trustee in bankruptcy or another person or company entitled to escrow securities on bankruptcy.

(2) Prior to the transfer, the Escrow Agent must receive:

(a) a certified copy of either

(i) the assignment in bankruptcy filed with the Superintendent of Bankruptcy, or

(ii) the receiving order adjudging the Securityholder bankrupt;

(b) a certified copy of a certificate of appointment of the trustee in bankruptcy;

(c) a transfer power of attorney, completed and executed by the transferor in accordance with the requirements of the Issuer's transfer agent; and

(d) an acknowledgment in the form of Schedule "B" signed by:

(i) the trustee in bankruptcy, or

(ii) on direction from the trustee, with evidence of that direction attached to the acknowledgment form, another person or company legally entitled to the escrow securities.

(3) Within 10 days after the transfer, the transferee of the escrow securities will file a copy of the acknowledgment with the securities regulators in the jurisdictions in which the Issuer is a reporting issuer.

5.4 — Transfer Upon Realization of Pledged, Mortgaged or Charged Escrow Securities

(1) You may transfer within escrow to a financial institution the escrow securities you have pledged, mortgaged or charged under section 4.2 to that financial institution as collateral for a loan on realization of the loan.

(2) Prior to the transfer the Escrow Agent must receive:

(a) a statutory declaration of an officer of the financial institution that the financial institution is legally entitled to the escrow securities;

(b) a transfer power of attorney, executed by the transferor in accordance with the requirements of the Issuer's transfer agent; and

(c) an acknowledgement in the form of Schedule "B" signed by the financial institution.

(3) Within 10 days after the transfer, the transferee of the escrow securities will file a copy of the acknowledgment with the securities regulators in the jurisdictions in which the Issuer is a reporting issuer.

5.5 — Transfer to Certain Plans and Funds

(1) You may transfer escrow securities within escrow to or between a registered retirement savings plan (RRSP), registered retirement income fund (RRIF) or other similar registered plan or fund with a trustee, where the annuitant of the RRSP or RRIF, or the beneficiaries of the other registered plan or fund are limited to you and your spouse, children and parents, or, if you are the trustee of such a registered plan or fund, to the annuitant of the RRSP or RRIF, or a beneficiary of the other registered plan or fund, as applicable, or his or her spouse, children and parents.

(2) Prior to the transfer the Escrow Agent must receive:

(a) evidence from the trustee of the transferee plan or fund, or the trustee's agent, stating that, to the best of the trustee's knowledge, the annuitant of the RRSP or RRIF, or the beneficiaries of the other registered plan or fund do not include any person or company other than you and your spouse, children and parents;

(b) a transfer power of attorney, executed by the transferor in accordance with the requirements of the Issuer's transfer agent; and

(c) an acknowledgement in the form of Schedule "B" signed by the trustee of the plan or fund.

(3) Within 10 days after the transfer, the transferee of the escrow securities will file a copy of the acknowledgment with the securities regulators in the jurisdictions in which the Issuer is a reporting issuer.

5.6 — Effect of Transfer Within Escrow

After the transfer of escrow securities within escrow, the escrow securities will remain in escrow and released from escrow under this Agreement as if no transfer has occurred on the same terms that applied before the transfer. The Escrow Agent will not deliver any share certificates or other evidence of the escrow securities to transferees under this Part 5.

Part 6 — Business Combinations

6.1 — Business Combinations

This Part applies to the following (*business combinations*):

(a) a formal take-over bid for all outstanding equity securities of the Issuer or which, if successful, would result in a change of control of the Issuer

(b) a formal issuer bid for all outstanding equity securities of the Issuer

(c) a statutory arrangement

(d) an amalgamation

(e) a merger

(f) a reorganization that has an effect similar to an amalgamation or merger

6.2 — Delivery to Escrow Agent

You may tender your escrow securities to a person or company in a business combination. At least five business days prior to the date the escrow securities must be tendered under the business combination, you must deliver to the Escrow Agent:

(a) a written direction signed by you that directs the Escrow Agent to deliver to the depositary under the business combination any share certificates or other evidence of the escrow securities and a completed and executed cover letter or similar document and, where required, transfer power of attorney completed and executed for transfer in accordance with the requirements of the depositary, and any other documentation specified or provided by you and required to be delivered to the depositary under the business combination; and

(b) any other information concerning the business combination as the Escrow Agent may reasonably request.

6.3 — Delivery to Depositary

As soon as reasonably practicable, and in any event no later than three business days after the Escrow Agent receives the documents and information required under section 6.2, the Escrow Agent will deliver to the depositary, in accordance with the direction, any share certificates or other evidence of the escrow securities, and a letter addressed to the depositary that

(a) identifies the escrow securities that are being tendered;

(b) states that the escrow securities are held in escrow;

(c) states that the escrow securities are delivered only for the purposes of the business combination and that they will be released from escrow only after the Escrow Agent receives the information described in section 6.4;

(d) if any share certificates or other evidence of the escrow securities have been delivered to the depositary, requires the depositary to return to the Escrow Agent, as soon as practicable, any share certificates or other evidence of escrow securities that are not released from escrow into the business combination; and

(e) where applicable, requires the depositary to deliver or cause to be delivered to the Escrow Agent, as soon as practicable, any share certificates or other evidence of additional escrow securities that you acquire under the business combination.

6.4 — Release of Escrow Securities to Depositary

The Escrow Agent will release from escrow the tendered escrow securities when the Escrow Agent receives a declaration signed by the depositary or, if the direction identifies the depositary as acting on behalf of another person or company in respect of the business combination, by that other person or company, that:

(a) the terms and conditions of the business combination have been met or waived; and

(b) the escrow securities have either been taken up and paid for or are subject to an unconditional obligation to be taken up and paid for under the business combination.

6.5 — Escrow of New Securities

If you receive securities (*new securities*) of another issuer (*successor issuer*) in exchange for your escrow securities, the new securities will be subject to escrow in substitution for the tendered escrow securities if, immediately after completion of the business combination:

(a) the successor issuer is not an *exempt issuer* (as defined in section 3.2 of the Policy);

(b) you are a *principal* (as defined in section 3.5 of the Policy) of the successor issuer; and

(c) you hold more than 1% of the voting rights attached to the successor issuer's outstanding securities (In calculating this percentage, include securities that may be issued to you under outstanding convertible securities in both your securities and the total securities outstanding.)

6.6 — Release from Escrow of New Securities

(1) As soon as reasonably practicable after the Escrow Agent receives:

(a) a certificate from the successor issuer signed by a director or officer of the successor issuer authorized to sign

(i) stating that it is a successor issuer to the Issuer as a result of a business combination and whether it is an emerging issuer or an established issuer under the Policy, and

(ii) listing the Securityholders whose new securities are subject to escrow under section 6.5,

the escrow securities of the Securityholders whose new securities are not subject to escrow under section 6.5 will be released, and the Escrow Agent will send any share certificates or other evidence of the escrow securities in the possession of the Escrow Agent in accordance with section 2.3.

(2) If your new securities are subject to escrow, unless subsection (3) applies, the Escrow Agent will hold your new securities in escrow on the same terms and conditions, including release dates, as applied to the escrow securities that you exchanged.

(3) If the Issuer is

(a) an emerging issuer, the successor issuer is an established issuer, and the business combination occurs 18 months or more after the Issuer's listing date, all escrow securities will be released immediately; and

(b) an emerging issuer, the successor issuer is an established issuer, and the business combination occurs within 18 months after the Issuer's listing date, all escrow securities that would have been released to that time, if the Issuer was an established issuer on its listing date, will be released immediately. Remaining escrow securities will be released in equal instalments on the day that is 6 months, 12 months and 18 months after the Issuer's listing date.

Part 7 — Resignation of Escrow Agent

7.1 — Resignation of Escrow Agent

(1) If the Escrow Agent wishes to resign as escrow agent, the Escrow Agent will give written notice to the Issuer.

(2) If the Issuer wishes to terminate the Escrow Agent as escrow agent, the Issuer will give written notice to the Escrow Agent.

(3) If the Escrow Agent resigns or is terminated, the Issuer will be responsible for ensuring that the Escrow Agent is replaced not later than the resignation or termination date by another escrow agent that is acceptable to the securities regulators having jurisdiction in the matter and that has accepted such appointment, which appointment will be binding on the Issuer and the Securityholders.

(4) The resignation or termination of the Escrow Agent will be effective, and the Escrow Agent will cease to be bound by this Agreement, on the date that is 60 days after the date of receipt of the notices referred to above by the Escrow Agent or Issuer, as applicable, or on such other date as the Escrow Agent and the Issuer may agree upon (the "resignation or termination date"), provided that the resignation or termination date will not be less than 10 business days before a release date.

(5) If the Issuer has not appointed a successor escrow agent within 60 days of the resignation or termination date, the Escrow Agent will apply, at the Issuer's expense, to a court of competent jurisdiction for the appointment of a successor escrow agent, and the duties and responsibilities of the Escrow Agent will cease immediately upon such appointment.

(6) On any new appointment under this section, the successor Escrow Agent will be vested with the same powers, rights, duties and obligations as if it had been originally named herein as Escrow Agent, without any further assurance, conveyance, act or deed. The predecessor Escrow Agent, upon receipt of payment for any outstanding account for its services and expenses then unpaid, will transfer, deliver and pay over to the successor Escrow Agent, who will be entitled to receive, all securities, records or other property on deposit with the predecessor Escrow Agent in relation to this Agreement and the predecessor Escrow Agent will thereupon be discharged as Escrow Agent.

(7) If any changes are made to Part 8 of this Agreement as a result of the appointment of the successor Escrow Agent, those changes must not be inconsistent with the Policy and the terms of this Agreement and the Issuer to this Agreement will file a copy of the new Agreement with the securities regulators with jurisdiction over this Agreement and the escrow securities.

Part 8 — Other Contractual Arrangements

[*You may insert any other contractual arrangements the Parties to this Agreement wish to provide to govern the responsibilities, remuneration, liabilities, and indemnities for the duties of the Escrow Agent or any other matter which the Parties wish to include in this Agreement provided that the terms are not inconsistent with the Policy and the terms of this Agreement.*]

Part 9 — Notices

9.1 — Notice to Escrow Agent

Documents will be considered to have been delivered to the Escrow Agent on the next business day following the date of transmission, if delivered by fax, the date of delivery, if delivered by hand during normal business hours or by prepaid courier, or 5 business days after the date of mailing, if delivered by mail, to the following:

[Name, address, contact person, fax number]

9.2 — Notice to Issuer

Documents will be considered to have been delivered to the Issuer on the next business day following the date of transmission, if delivered by fax, the date of delivery, if delivered by hand during normal business hours or by prepaid courier, or 5 business days after the date of mailing, if delivered by mail, to the following:

[Name, address, contact person, fax number]

9.3 — Deliveries to Securityholders

Documents will be considered to have been delivered to a Securityholder on the date of delivery, if delivered by hand or by prepaid courier, or 5 business days after the date of mailing, if delivered by mail, to the address on the Issuer's share register.

Any share certificates or other evidence of a Securityholder's escrow securities will be sent to the Securityholder's address on the Issuer's share register unless the Securityholder has advised the Escrow Agent in writing otherwise at least ten business days before the escrow securities are released from escrow. The Issuer will provide the Escrow Agent with each Securityholder's address as listed on the Issuer's share register.

9.4 — Change of Address

(1) The Escrow Agent may change its address for delivery by delivering notice of the change of address to the Issuer and to each Securityholder.

(2) The Issuer may change its address for delivery by delivering notice of the change of address to the Escrow Agent and to each Securityholder.

(3) A Securityholder may change that Securityholder's address for delivery by delivering notice of the change of address to the Issuer and to the Escrow Agent.

9.5 — Postal Interruption

A Party to this Agreement will not mail a document it is required to mail under this Agreement if the Party is aware of an actual or impending disruption of postal service.

Part 10 — General

10.1 — Interpretation — "holding securities"

When this Agreement refers to securities that a Securityholder "holds", it means that the Securityholder has direct or indirect beneficial ownership of, or control or direction over, the securities.

10.2 — Further Assurances

The Parties will execute and deliver any further documents and perform any further acts reasonably requested by any of the Parties to this Agreement which are necessary to carry out the intent of this Agreement.

10.3 — Time

Time is of the essence of this Agreement.

10.4 — Incomplete IPO

If the Issuer does not complete its IPO and has become a reporting issuer in one or more jurisdictions because it has obtained a receipt for its IPO prospectus, this Agreement will remain in effect until the securities regulators in those jurisdictions order that the Issuer has ceased to be a reporting issuer.

10.5 — Governing Laws

The laws of [insert principal jurisdiction] (the "Principal Regulator") and the applicable laws of Canada will govern this Agreement.

10.6 — Jurisdiction

The securities regulator in each jurisdiction where the Issuer files its IPO prospectus has jurisdiction over this Agreement and the escrow securities.

10.7 — Consent of Securities Regulators to Amendment

Except for amendments made under Part 3, the securities regulators with jurisdiction must approve any amendment to this Agreement and will apply mutual reliance principles in reviewing any amendments that are filed with them. Therefore, the consent of the Principal Regulator will evidence the consent of all securities regulators with jurisdiction.

10.8 — Counterparts

The Parties may execute this Agreement by fax and in counterparts, each of which will be considered an original and all of which will be one agreement.

10.9 — Singular and Plural

Wherever a singular expression is used in this Agreement, that expression is considered as including the plural or the body corporate where required by the context.

10.10 — Language

This Agreement has been drawn up in the [English/French] language at the request of all Parties. Cette convention a été rédigé en [anglais/français] à la demande de toutes les Parties.

10.11 — Benefit and Binding Effect

This Agreement will benefit and bind the Parties and their heirs, executors, administrators, successors and permitted assigns and all persons claiming through them as if they had been a Party to this Agreement.

10.12 — Entire Agreement

This is the entire agreement among the Parties concerning the subject matter set out in this Agreement and supersedes any and all prior understandings and agreements.

10.13 — Successor to Escrow Agent

Any corporation with which the Escrow Agent may be amalgamated, merged or consolidated, or any corporation succeeding to the business of the Escrow Agent will be the successor of the Escrow Agent under this Agreement without any further act on its part or on the part or any of the Parties, provided that the successor is recognized as a transfer agent by the Canadian exchange the Issuer is listed on (or if the Issuer is not listed on a Canadian exchange, by any Canadian exchange) and notice is given to the securities regulators with jurisdiction.

The Parties have executed and delivered this Agreement as of the date set out above.

Part 4:
DISTRIBUTIONS

[Escrow Agent]

.... Authorized signatory

.... Authorized signatory

[Issuer]

.... Authorized signatory

.... Authorized signatory

If the Securityholder is an individual:

Signed, sealed and delivered by   )

[Securityholder] in the presence of:)

)

)

Signature of Witness   )   ....

)   *[Securityholder]*

)

....   )

Name of Witness   )

)

If the Securityholder is not an individual:

   [Securityholder]

   .... Authorized signatory

   .... Authorized signatory

Schedule "A" "A" — To Escrow Agreement

Securityholder

Name: ....

Securities: ....

Class or description ....

Number ....

Certificate(s) (if applicable) ....

Schedule "B" — To Escrow Agreement

Acknowledgment and Agreement to be Bound

I acknowledge that the securities listed in the attached Schedule "A" (the "escrow securities") have been or will be transferred to me and that the escrow securities are subject to an Escrow Agreement dated .... (the "Escrow Agreement").

For other good and valuable consideration, I agree to be bound by the Escrow Agreement in respect of the escrow securities, as if I were an original signatory to the Escrow Agreement.

Dated at .... on ....

Where the transferee is an individual:

Signed, sealed and delivered by   )

[Transferee] in the presence of:)

)

....   )

Signature of Witness   )

)   ....

)   *[Transferee]*

....   )

Name of Witness   )

Where the transferee is not an individual:

   [Transferee]

   .... Authorized signatory

   .... Authorized signatory

Adopted: (2002) 25 O.S.C.B. 4038; Request for Comments: (2001) 24 O.S.C.B. 5677 and (1998) 21 O.S.C.B. 2927. Replaced OPS 5.9.

Amendment to Rule: (2015) 38 O.S.C.B. 7551.

Policies and Orders: CSAN 41-305.

CSA Notice 46-303 — Prinicipal Protected Notes

Date: July 7, 2006
29 O.S.C.B. 5538

What is the purpose of this notice?

This notice details the concerns of the Canadian Securities Administrators (CSA) about the distribution and sale of Principal Protected Notes (PPNs) and the CSA's proposed course of action.

What is a PPN?

A PPN is an investment product that offers an investor potential returns based on the performance of an underlying investment and a guarantee that the investor will receive, on maturity of the PPN, not less than the principal amount invested. For the purpose of this notice, PPNs include the instruments commonly described as market-linked GICs (Market-Linked GICs) and linked notes (Linked Notes). Market-Linked GICs are described as term deposits that guarantee principal through a CDIC-insured (or equivalent) deposit-taking institution or insurance company, with a return linked to a number of underlying investments, including stock market indices, mutual funds or hedge funds. Linked Notes are described as debt instruments that provide a principal guarantee through the credit-worthiness of the issuer, with returns linked to a variety of underlying investments, including stock market indices, mutual funds, and hedge funds.

What concerns us about PPNs?

Background

The CSA is focussing on the structure and distribution of PPNs because of the recent significant growth in the sale of PPNs to retail investors and the development of increasingly complex structures that pose investment risks that investors may not be fully informed about.

According to the Spring 2005 Investor Economics Report on Market-Linked Instruments, as of December 2004, $21 billion in assets was invested in these investment products, comprised of:

- $15.7 billion in Market-Linked GICs; and

- $5.3 billion in Linked Notes.

By way of comparison, in December 1999, only $9.4 billion was invested in market-linked instruments. From December 1999 to December 2004, the number of market-linked instruments also increased from 67 to 282, and the number of product sponsors (the primary developer and marketer of the product) increased from 20 to 44.

Moreover, the market for PPNs linked to hedge funds has grown steadily from 1999 to 2005. In 1999, 7.5% of the PPN market was invested in hedge-fund linked products. By March, 2005, 24% of the market was invested in these products.[1]

In addition, recent types of PPN products are more complex and pose investment risks that investors may not be fully informed about. The component of each product not covered by the principal protection guarantee has a different degree of risk, which depends on the underlying investment linked to the notes. In some cases, the underlying investment is a hedge fund, fund of funds, or managed futures. Therefore, through the sale of PPNs, intermediaries are selling retail investors products with investment risks that are more like those risks associated with alternative asset classes otherwise not accessible to retail investors without a prospectus.

Our Key Concerns

We understand that many types of PPNs are sold without a prospectus under the prospectus exemption for guaranteed debt[2] or on the basis that they fall outside the scope of provincial securities legislation[3]. Many types of PPNs are more complex and pose more investment risks than the type of product that was contemplated when securities legislation was enacted excluding financial institution deposits from securities regulation and exempting guaranteed debt instruments. Our key concerns about PPN disclosure materials and how PPNs are being sold are:

1. Disclosure — We are concerned that investors are not getting sufficient disclosure to allow them to make an informed investment decision. They are not getting sufficient disclosure about how PPNs are structured, how they work, and the fees and investment risks associated with them. Some of our more specific disclosure-related concerns are:

Disclosure documents and marketing materials — We are concerned that investors may not be getting sufficient disclosure about PPNs, whether in an information statement, offering memorandum, prospectus, or in sales and marketing materials. Some examples are:

- Sales and marketing materials contained poor or overly-promotional presentation of performance returns. For instance, they provided

  - disclosure about the potential upside return of the investment without providing sufficient information to allow an investor to understand how much the underlying investments would need to return, after fees, to deliver the upside that is being promoted,

---

[1]Spring 2005 Investor Economics Report on Market-Linked Instruments, Volume 2, section 2, page 22.

[2]See section 2.34 of National Instrument 45-106 *Prospectus and Registration Exemptions*.

[3]Or, in Québec, also under an applicable exemption (see section 3(9) of the *Securities Act* (Québec)).

- "back-tested" performance returns to show what the performance would have been if the product had existed for a certain period of time without an explanation of why that particular period is being used and that the disclosure is essentially based on hypothetical performance, and

- performance information presented in an unbalanced way.

• Disclosure in information statements provided for many PPNs was lengthy, complex and difficult to understand, particularly in the sections describing the methods used to deliver principal protection and the upside benefit of the return on the linked investment.

• Disclosure materials in some cases lacked a sufficiently understandable description of the structure (both for the guarantee and the underlying investment) and the various participants that stand behind the investment.

Fees — We are concerned that investors might not be aware of the full cost they are paying, or that there is a cost at all, for the guarantee provided with PPNs. In some cases, that cost is the additional fees to cover the insurance policy to back the guarantee. In other cases, there are multiple layers of fees including management fees, performance fees, up-front sales fees, and trailer fees. These fees can significantly reduce the returns that would otherwise be derived from the underlying investments.

Lack of liquidity — We are concerned investors might not be aware that the terms of the PPN frequently do not permit an investor to sell it before maturity, without significant penalty. It also means that investors who wish to sell a PPN before maturity might not receive 100% of the principal amount invested.

2. Know your client and suitability obligations — Any registrant that sells a security, including a PPN that is sold under a prospectus and registration exemption, must comply with the know your client (KYC) and suitability obligations. Additionally, the registrant must understand the PPN well enough to be able to assess its suitability for a client.[4] We are concerned that some sellers of PPNs are not meeting these requirements.

3. Retailization of alternative investment products — We are concerned that some PPNs are being used as vehicles for retail distribution of, or exposure to, complex alternative investment products like hedge funds, funds of funds, or managed futures, without the general protections Canadian securities laws provide or sufficient disclosure to permit an investor to make an informed investment decision.

4. Referral Arrangements — Securities laws in some jurisdictions and some self-regulatory organizations have specific requirements for how registrants handle referrals to and from registrants. Even where specific requirements do not exist, registrants are still bound by their general obligation to act in the best interests of their clients. We are concerned that some registrants may be making a referral to purchase a PPN without concluding that the referral is in the best interests of their clients.

What is our proposed course of action?

We propose to consult with industry and other stakeholders about the structuring and marketing of PPNs. These consultations will include discussions about how issuers are using the existing prospectus and registration exemptions for PPNs, how they are interpreting the scope of these exemptions and the types of products they are selling under the existing exemptions.

Based on the results of our consultation process and our ongoing monitoring activities, we will determine the form and content of any new regulatory requirements or guidance needed to regulate the offering and sale of PPNs. We will provide notice of any further course of action we propose to take. CSA members may also take appropriate action at any time if they become aware of non-compliance with Canadian securities laws or activities that threaten investors or the integrity of the capital markets.

What should issuers and dealers do now?

Any issuer that plans to offer a PPN should ensure that the accompanying disclosure documents and any sales and marketing materials are clear, comprehensive, balanced, and provide sufficient information for investors and their advisers to make informed investment decisions or recommendations.

Any person planning to sell PPNs should satisfy itself whether its representatives need to be registered and, if so, are properly registered to sell those products. Any registered dealer should also ensure that its representatives have the appropriate training and that they have a thorough enough understanding of the PPN to be able to assess its suitability for a particular client. Any registered dealer and its representatives should assess their policies for ensuring that any PPNs they recommend to clients are suitable.

Policies and Orders: CSAN 46-304, 46-306.

CSA Notice 46-304 — Update on Principal Protected Notes

Issue: July 27, 2007

30 O.S.C.B. 6651

What is the purpose of this notice?

This notice provides an update on the Canadian Securities Administrators' (CSA) consideration of Principal Protected Notes (PPNs).

---

[4]The Mutual Fund Dealers Association Notice #MR 0048 *Know-Your-Product* describes the MFDA's views on this issue as it applies to mutual fund dealers.

What is a PPN?

A PPN is an investment product that offers an investor potential returns based on the performance of an underlying investment and a guarantee that the investor will receive, on maturity of the PPN, not less than the principal amount invested. For the purpose of this notice, PPNs include the instruments commonly described as market-linked GICs and market-linked notes.

Background

On July 7, 2006, the CSA published CSA Notice 46-303 — *Principal Protected Notes* (CSA Notice 46-303) and an Investor Watch which identified a number of the CSA's concerns about PPNs. The key concerns related to four main areas:

1. Inadequate, overly complex and inappropriate disclosure in PPN information statements and marketing materials.

2. Compliance with know your client (KYC) and suitability obligations by registrants in connection with sales of PPNs.

3. Use of PPNs as a vehicle for selling alternative investment products to retail investors.

4. Registrant referrals to purchase PPNs without a determination by a registrant that the referral is in the best interests of the client.

CSA Consultations and Market Analysis

Since the publication of CSA Notice 46-303, the CSA has engaged in extensive consultations with industry stakeholders about the distribution and regulation of PPNs.

The CSA's consultations included meetings with representatives of:

- PPN issuers

- PPN manufacturers and distributors

- the Investment Dealers Association of Canada (IDA)

- the Mutual Fund Dealers Association of Canada (MFDA)

- the *Chambre de la sécurité financière* (CSF)

- law firms

- the federal Department of Finance

PPN Market

According to the October 2006 Investor Economics Report on Market-Linked Instruments, as of June 30, 2006, the total PPN market in Canada represented approximately $30.9 billion in assets, comprised of $13.8 billion of linked notes and $17.1 billion of linked GICs. Based on information contained in the report, as of June 30, 2006:

- Approximately 88% of all issued and outstanding linked notes had been issued by banks listed in Schedule I or Schedule II to the *Bank Act* (Canada);

- Approximately 42% of linked GICs had been issued by banks and trust companies and another 53.5% had been issued by caisses populaires/credit unions.

Based on our consultations and the figures cited in the report, we understand that a majority of PPNs are issued by federally regulated financial institutions, primarily Schedule I and Schedule II banks. We also understand that caisses populaires based in Québec issue the vast majority of the linked GICs that are issued by caisses populaires/credit unions.

Through our consultations, we also understand that approximately 70–80% of linked notes are sold by IDA registrants and another 10% of linked notes are sold by MFDA members and their representatives.

Proposed Federal PPN Regulations

On March 19, 2007, the federal government released its *Budget Plan 2007*. In a companion document to the *Budget Plan 2007* entitled *Creating a Canadian Advantage in Global Capital Markets*, the federal government announced that it will "soon release for comment principles-based regulations for banks that issue [PPNs]...".[1] The Budget companion document includes the following statements about the proposed federal PPN regulations:

- The regulations will ensure that consumers are informed of the fees, returns, risks, and cancellation and redemption rights associated with PPNs;

- The regulations will require information to be clearly disclosed by qualified individuals in order to ensure that investors have the information they need to make more informed investment decisions;

- The regulations will require disclosure after purchase to aid investors in monitoring and tracking their investments.

The CSA is consulting with the federal Department of Finance about the proposed federal PPN regulations and has provided comments on drafts of those regulations. We understand that the proposed regulations will apply to all PPNs (whether linked notes or linked GICs) issued by federally regulated financial institutions, including banks and authorized foreign banks under the *Bank Act* (Canada), retail associations under

---

[1]See page 39.

the *Cooperative Credit Associations Act* (Canada) and companies under the *Trust and Loan Companies Act* (Canada). We further understand that the Financial Consumer Agency of Canada (FCAC) will be responsible for compliance and enforcement of the proposed federal PPN regulations.

CSA's Proposed Course of Action

Full Review of Pending Proposed Federal PPN Regulations

Based on the statements made in the Budget companion document and our discussions with federal Department of Finance staff, we expect that the proposed federal PPN regulations will address our key disclosure concerns about PPNs identified in CSA Notice 46-303. Based on the market data that shows federal financial institutions issue a majority of PPNs, the proposed regulations will provide protection for a large proportion of PPN investors. The CSA will fully review the final form of the proposed regulations when the regulations are adopted. The CSA understands that the proposed regulations will be published for comment in the Fall of this year.

A significant portion of PPNs are issued by Québec-based caisses populaires that would not be subject to the proposed federal PPN regulations. Pending publication of those regulations, the *Autorité des marchés financiers* (AMF) will consider the appropriateness of regulating PPNs issued by these entities.

KYC and Suitability Obligations

As discussed above, registrants currently sell a substantial portion of linked notes. We think that compliance with KYC and suitability obligations are a critical aspect of investor protection and should apply to sales of all PPNs by registrants (except where a specific exemption exists). The IDA has confirmed that its regulations and by-laws that concern KYC and suitability obligations apply in respect of all dealings by its members, without limitation as to the type of investment product being sold. The CSA has initiated discussions with the MFDA regarding changes to MFDA rules that would confirm the application of KYC and suitability obligations to dealings in PPNs by MFDA members and their representatives. In Québec, mutual funds dealers are members of the CSF and are subject to the *Regulation respecting the rules and ethics in the securities sector* which provides that KYC and suitability obligations apply without limitation as to the type of investment being sold.

Conclusion

The CSA will continue to monitor the issue and sale of PPNs, but we believe that the regulatory initiatives described above will substantially address the key concerns identified in CSA Notice 46-303. In particular:

- the proposed federal PPN regulations contemplate disclosure enhancements for PPNs issued by federal financial institutions, which comprise a majority of the PPN market;

- the proposal for changes to be made to the MFDA rules (as discussed above), along with existing IDA and CSF standards, to ensure that KYC and suitability requirements apply when MFDA, IDA and CSF member registrants (or their representatives) sell PPNs;

- the concerns associated with the sale of PPNs as a vehicle for selling alternative investment products to retail investors will be substantially addressed by the improved disclosure and sales practices that should result from the changes contemplated above;

- finally, proposed National Instrument 31-103 — *Registration Requirements* (NI 31-103) includes provisions dealing with referral arrangements and practices by registrants relating to investment products, which would include PPNs.[2]

CSA Notice 46-305 — Second Update on Principal Protected Notes

Date: **August 29, 2008**

31 O.S.C.B. 8298

This notice provides an update on the Canadian Securities Administrators' (CSA) review of Principal Protected Notes (PPNs) and the recent coming into force of federal regulations applicable to PPNs (the Federal PPN Regulations).

What is a PPN?

A PPN is an investment product that offers an investor potential returns based on the performance of an underlying investment and a guarantee that the investor will receive, on maturity of the PPN, not less than the principal amount invested. For the purpose of this notice, PPNs include the instruments commonly described as market-linked GICs and market-linked notes.

Background

Identification of Concerns with PPNs

On July 7, 2006, the CSA published CSA Notice 46-303 — *Principal Protected Notes* (the 2006 Notice) and an Investor Watch which identified a number of the CSA's concerns about PPNs. The key concerns related to four main areas:

1. Inadequate, overly complex and inappropriate disclosure in PPN information statements and marketing materials.

2. Compliance with know your client (KYC) and suitability obligations by registrants in connection with sales of PPNs.

---

[2]The CSA published NI 31-103 for comment on February 20, 2007. See Part 6 of NI 31-103.

3. Use of PPNs as a vehicle for selling alternative investment products to retail investors.

4. Registrant referrals to purchase PPNs without a determination by a registrant that the referral is in the best interests of the client.

CSA Consultations and Market Analysis

Following publication of the 2006 Notice, the CSA's review of PPNs included:

- extensive consultations with industry stakeholders about the distribution and regulation of PPNs;

- an analysis of the issuer and distribution channels for the PPN market; and

- discussions with the federal Department of Finance about the proposed Federal PPN Regulations.

As a result of its consultations and market analysis, the CSA determined that the majority of PPNs (comprised of linked notes and linked GICs) are issued by federally-regulated financial institutions, primarily Schedule I and Schedule II banks. The CSA also notes that 70-80% of linked note PPNs are sold by members of the Investment Industry Regulatory Organization of Canada (IIROC) (formerly the Investment Dealers Association of Canada (IDA)) and another 10% of linked note PPNs are sold by members of the Mutual Fund Dealers Association of Canada (MFDA). The majority of linked GICs are issued by caisses populaires based in the province of Québec.

Previous Update on CSA's Review of PPNs and Proposed Course of Action

On July 28, 2007, the CSA provided an update on its review of PPNs in CSA Notice 46-304 *Update on Principal Protected Notes* (the 2007 Notice). In the 2007 Notice, we reviewed the data on issuer and distribution channels for the PPN market and noted that we were consulting with the federal Department of Finance regarding proposed Federal PPN Regulations. We also described our intention to review the final form of the proposed Federal PPN Regulations to determine whether they addressed our key disclosure concerns for PPNs issued by federally-regulated financial institutions. The 2007 Notice further noted that the CSA had initiated discussions with the MFDA regarding changes to MFDA rules that would confirm the application of KYC and suitability obligations to dealings in PPNs by MFDA members and their representatives.

Federal PPN Regulations

On July 1, 2008, the Federal PPN Regulations came into force. The regulations apply to all PPNs (whether linked notes or linked GICs) issued by federally-regulated financial institutions, including banks and authorized foreign banks under the *Bank Act* (Canada), retail associations under the *Cooperative Credit Associations Act* (Canada) and companies under the *Trust and Loan Companies Act* (Canada) (Federal Financial Institutions). The Federal PPN Regulations specify requirements for the content, manner and timing of disclosure for PPNs issued by Federal Financial Institutions. The Financial Consumer Agency of Canada (FCAC) will be responsible for compliance and enforcement of the Federal PPN Regulations.

A copy of the Federal PPN Regulations can be found at:

- http://laws.justice.gc.ca/en/showtdm/cr/SOR-2008-180

Prior to their publication in final form, the CSA consulted with the federal Department of Finance about the Federal PPN Regulations. We have reviewed the Federal PPN Regulations and think that they impose significant disclosure obligations for PPNs issued by Federal Financial Institutions. Further, in light of the market data that shows Federal Financial Institutions issue a majority of PPNs, the disclosure required by the Federal PPN Regulations could assist a large proportion of PPN investors.

KYC and Suitability Obligations

Compliance with KYC and suitability obligations is a critical aspect of investor protection and should apply to sales of all PPNs by registrants (except where a specific exemption exists).

As explained in the 2007 Notice, the IDA (now IIROC) has confirmed that its regulations and by-laws that impose KYC and suitability obligations apply to all its members' dealings without limitation as to the type of investment product being sold. The MFDA has recently issued suitability guidelines confirming that its members are responsible for assessing the suitability of recommendations made with respect to all business of the member, including investment advice or recommendations relating to PPNs.[3] The CSA continues to support the further objective of ensuring that KYC and suitability obligations also apply to all dealings in PPNs by representatives of IIROC and MFDA members. The CSA is discussing this objective with IIROC and the MFDA.

In Québec, representatives of mutual funds dealers are members of the *Chambre de la sécurité financière* and are subject to the *Regulation respecting the rules of ethics in the securities sector* which provides that KYC and suitability obligations apply without limitation as to the type of investment being sold.

Conclusion

The Federal PPN Regulations, together with our regulatory initiatives, substantially address our key concerns with PPNs identified in the 2006 Notice. In particular:

- the Federal PPN Regulations prescribe disclosure enhancements for PPNs issued by Federal Financial Institutions, which comprise a majority of the PPN market;

---

[3]Member Regulation Notice MR-0069 — *Suitability Guidelines* published by the MFDA on April 14, 2008.

- we continue to discuss with IIROC and the MFDA how best to ensure that KYC and suitability obligations apply to all dealings in PPNs by representatives of IIROC and MFDA members;

- the improved disclosure and sales practices that should result from the changes contemplated above substantially address the concerns associated with the sale of PPNs as a vehicle for selling alternative investment products to retail investors;

- proposed National Instrument 31-103 — *Registration Requirements* (NI 31-103) has specific requirements relating to registrant referral arrangements.[4]

In addition, the Autorité des marchés financiers intends to establish guidelines relating to disclosure, sales and sound business practices for PPNs sold by financial institutions authorized to carry on business in Québec. The majority of linked GICs are issued by caisses populaires based in the province of Québec.

The CSA will continue to monitor the issue and sale of PPNs.

CSA Multilateral Staff Notice 46-306 — Third Update on Principal Protected Notes

Date: August 30, 2013

35 O.S.C.B. 8064

August 30, 2012

This CSA Multilateral Staff Notice is being published by staff of all members of the Canadian Securities Administrators, except the securities regulator in Québec (the *CSA* or *we*).

Substance and Purpose

This notice provides an update on the CSA's consideration of Principal Protected Notes (*PPNs*), and serves as a supplement to the following previous CSA Notices:

- CSA Notice 46-303 *Principal Protected Notes* dated July 7, 2006 (*Notice 46-303*)

- CSA Notice 46-304 *Update on Principal Protected Notes* dated July 27, 2007 (*Notice 46-304*)

- CSA Notice 46-305 *Second Update on Principal Protected Notes* dated August 29, 2008 (*Notice 46-305*).

In Notice 46-305, the CSA communicated that the one remaining initiative to address our concerns about PPNs was to work with the Investment Industry Regulatory Organization of Canada and the Mutual Fund Dealers Association of Canada (the *SROs*) to ensure that know-your-client (*KYC*) and suitability obligations apply to all dealings in PPNs by individual registered representatives of their member firms (*SRO representatives*). This notice reports on the course being taken by the SROs to pursue that objective.

This Notice also sets out our expectation that banks and other federal and provincial deposit-taking institutions will use registered dealers (and registered individuals acting on behalf of those dealers) to distribute PPNs that do not fall within a limited class.

What is a PPN?

A PPN is an investment product that offers an investor potential returns based on the performance of an underlying investment and a guarantee that the investor will receive, on maturity of the PPN, not less than the principal amount invested. For the purposes of this notice, PPNs include, but are not limited to, instruments commonly described as market-linked or index-linked GICs and linked notes.

KYC and Suitability Obligations for SRO Members

In Notice 46-304, we stated that compliance with KYC and suitability obligations is a critical aspect of investor protection and should apply to sales of all PPNs by registrants (except where a specific exemption from these obligations exist). The SROs have confirmed that their KYC and suitability rules apply to all dealings in PPNs by SRO representatives that are transacted through their member firms.

However, if SRO representatives deal in PPNs outside of their member firms (and not in their capacity as an employee or agent of the member firm), the SRO's rules may not apply.

Application of KYC and Suitability Obligations to all Dealings in PPNs by SRO Representatives

The CSA want to ensure that SRO representatives who sell PPNs only do so in their capacity as an employee or agent of their member firm, so that the usual KYC and suitability obligations in the SRO rules apply to these sales.[5]

To achieve this objective, the recognizing regulators asked the SROs to take appropriate actions to clarify the applicability of these obligations to all dealings in PPNs by SRO representatives. To this end, each of the SROs will soon be issuing a notice to their members setting out their expectation that all dealings in PPNs by SRO representatives must be transacted by these individuals in their capacity as an employee or agent of their member firm.

---

[4]The CSA published NI 31-103 for comment on February 29, 2008. See Part 6 of NI 31-103.

[5]Except where the PPN is itself a contract of insurance that is required by applicable insurance legislation to be distributed through a licensed insurance agent.

PPN Distribution Channels and CSA Expectations

CSA Consultations and Market Analysis

Following publication of Notice 46-303, the CSA undertook extensive consultations with industry stakeholders about the distribution and regulation of PPNs, and analyzed the issuers and distribution channels for the PPN market. As a result of our consultations and market analysis, we determined that the majority of PPNs are issued by federally-regulated financial institutions, primarily Schedule I and Schedule II banks.

We understand that

- Schedule I and Schedule II banks are still the major issuers of PPNs

- a substantial portion of the PPNs issued by provincially-regulated financial institutions are issued by financial services cooperatives based in the province of Québec.

We also understand that while some PPNs are distributed directly by banks or other federal or provincial deposit-taking institutions, those PPNs that are not distributed through registered dealers are generally limited to circumstances where the PPN (a Specified PPN) has the following features:

- a term to maturity of five years or less, and

- eligibility for coverage by the Canada Deposit Insurance Corporation (or a provincial equivalent).

CSA Expectations for Distribution of PPNs by Banks and other Federal and Provincial Deposit-Taking Institutions

The CSA expect that these institutions will distribute PPNs that are not Specified PPNs only through registered dealers in order to ensure the application of the usual KYC and suitability obligations.

Compliance with CSA Expectations

We will continue to monitor the distribution of PPNs. If we become aware that the sales practices of any deposit-taking institution do not accord with our above-noted expectation, we will take appropriate action.

OSC Rule 46-501 — Self-Directed Registered Education Savings Plans

Date: June 27, 1997

Rule 46-501 was revoked by Rule 45-802, and replaced by s. 2.7 of Rule 45-501, effective September 14, 2005. [September 9, 2005: 28 O.S.C.B. (Supp-4)]

4.7 — Advertising and Marketing

See also NPS 42.

National Policy 47-201 — Trading Securities Using the Internet and Other Electronic Means

Date: December 17, 1999, amended effective August 13, 2013

22 O.S.C.B. 8173; 36 O.S.C.B. 8040

Table of Contents

PART 1 — GENERAL

1.1 Definitions — In this Policy

"securities legislation" means the statutes and other instruments listed in Appendix B of National Instrument 14-101 Definitions;

"securities regulatory authorities" means the securities commissions and similar authorities listed in Appendix C of National Instrument 14-101 Definitions;

1.2 Purpose of this Policy — (1) In recent years, market participants have begun using the Internet and other electronic means of communication to offer and sell securities and to facilitate distributions of securities. While the use of these methods of communication can be beneficial to market participants, enabling them to provide and access information in a timely, cost-efficient and user-friendly manner, the securities regulatory authorities recognize that the use of the Internet and other electronic means of communication in this context can raise investor protection concerns and issues concerning the application of securities legislation.

(2) The purpose of this Policy is to state the views of the securities regulatory authorities on a number of matters relating to the use of the Internet and other electronic means of communication in connection with trades and distributions of securities.

1.3 National Policy 11-201 — Market participants are referred to National Policy 11-201 Delivery of Documents by Electronic Means for a discussion of the views of the securities regulatory authorities concerning the use of electronic means to satisfy the delivery requirements of securities legislation.

PART 2 — USE OF THE INTERNET FOR TRADING IN SECURITIES

2.1 General Jurisdictional Issue — Information on the Internet may reach both intended recipients and anyone else in the world who has access to the Internet. The interjurisdictional nature of the Internet makes it important for issuers and other market participants to consider how they will satisfy the registration and prospectus requirements contained in securities legislation and similar requirements under the securities laws of foreign jurisdictions.

2.2 Trading in a Jurisdiction — (1) The securities regulatory authorities generally consider a person or company to be trading in securities in a local jurisdiction if that person or company posts on the Internet a document that offers or solicits trades of securities, and if that document is accessible to persons or companies in that local jurisdiction.

(2) Despite subsection (1), the securities regulatory authorities consider the posting of a document on the Internet that offers or solicits trades of securities not to be a trade or, if applicable, a distribution, in a local jurisdiction if

(a) the document contains a prominently displayed disclaimer that expressly identifies the local jurisdictions and/or foreign jurisdictions in which the offering or solicitation is qualified to be made, and that identification does not include the local jurisdiction; and

(b) reasonable precautions are taken by all persons or companies offering or soliciting trades of securities through the document posted on the Internet not to sell to anyone resident in the local jurisdiction.

(3) Market participants are reminded that the registration requirements of securities legislation apply in connection with the posting of a prospectus or other offering document on the Internet for use in connection with a distribution in a local jurisdiction. The act of posting a prospectus or offering document in those circumstances is an act in furtherance of a trade in that local jurisdiction, and the person or company posting the prospectus or offering document must, in order to comply with the registration requirements

(a) be registered to trade in the local jurisdiction;

(b) have the benefit of an exemption from the registration requirements in connection with the distribution in the local jurisdiction; or

(c) refer all inquiries concerning the document to a registered dealer in the local jurisdiction.

2.3 Trading from a Jurisdiction — A person or company located in British Columbia, Alberta or Quebec that is distributing securities entirely outside of those jurisdictions through the Internet is considered to be trading within those jurisdictions and is therefore subject to applicable registration and prospectus requirements in those jurisdictions. The securities regulatory authorities in those jurisdictions may provide relief from those provisions in appropriate circumstances. The securities regulatory authorities in the remaining jurisdictions will assert jurisdiction over market participants on a case by case basis, with due regard to the legal tests ordinarily applied in such circumstances.

2.4 Application of Securities Laws of Foreign Jurisdictions — Canadian issuers and other market participants are reminded that foreign securities regulators may take the view that documents posted on a website that is accessible by persons or companies in their jurisdiction may constitute an offering of securities in that foreign jurisdiction. In some foreign jurisdictions, securities regulators have informed the market as to the steps that should be taken to ensure that such regulators do not take the view that a document posted on a website constitutes an offering of securities in that foreign jurisdiction. Some of those steps could include the use of disclaimers in the document and/or measures that restrict access to the document. Issuers and other market participants are urged to inform themselves of any relevant guidelines in this regard. Reference is made to a report of the Technical Committee of the International Organization of Securities Commissions (IOSCO) dated September 1998 entitled "Securities Activity on the Internet", which is available on the website of IOSCO at www.iosco.org. The annex to that report refers market participants to the rules, policies and guidelines of various international securities regulators on these matters.

2.5 Distribution Lists — (1) Securities legislation requires certain persons or companies distributing securities under a prospectus to record the names and addresses of all persons or companies that have received a copy of the preliminary prospectus. Issuers and registrants are reminded that this requirement applies whether a preliminary prospectus is distributed in paper form or by electronic means.

(2) The securities regulatory authorities are of the view that no relief from this requirement is necessary or warranted in connection with the electronic distribution of prospectuses, since current technology makes it feasible for a person or company either to monitor who has had access to a preliminary prospectus or to require a written or electronic consent form from each recipient of a preliminary prospectus.

(3) In order to comply with securities legislation, a person or company should therefore record the names and addresses of all recipients of a preliminary prospectus by electronic means from such person or company, including those recipients who merely view a preliminary prospectus by electronic means.

2.6 Advertising — Persons or companies should be aware that the posting of new information on a website during a period of distribution may be construed as advertising, which is subject to restrictions in certain jurisdictions.

2.7 Road Shows — (1) For the purposes of this Policy, "road show" has the meaning assigned in National Instrument 41-101 *General Prospectus Requirements*.

(2) National Instrument 41-101 and other prospectus rules set out the circumstances in which an investment dealer may hold a road show in connection with a distribution of securities, including a road show held on the internet or by other electronic means.

(3) Subsections 13.9(3) and 13.10(3) of National Instrument 41-101, subsection 7.7(3) of National Instrument 44-101 *Short Form Prospectus Distributions*, subsection 9A.4(3) of National Instrument 44-102 *Shelf Distributions* and subsection 4A.4(3) of National Instrument 44-103 *Post-Receipt Pricing* provide that the investment dealer conducting the road show must establish and follow reasonable procedures to:

- ask any investor attending the road show in person, by telephone conference call, on the internet or by other electronic means to provide their name and contact information;
- keep a record of any information provided by the investor; and
- provide the investor with a copy of the relevant prospectus and any amendment.

(4) In this connection, the following procedures are recommended for a road show held on the internet or by other electronic means:

(a) Pursuant to securities legislation, a copy of the filed prospectus is required to be made available to each viewer before each road show transmission, and each transmission should contain visual statements emphasizing that the information conveyed through the road show does not contain all of the information in the prospectus, which should be reviewed for complete information. A copy of the prospectus could be sent electronically to viewers in accordance with the guidelines contained in National Policy 11-201.

(b) Electronic access to the transmission of a road show on the internet or by other electronic means should be controlled by the investment dealer conducting the road show, using such means as password protection or a similar mechanism, in order to ensure that all viewers are identified and have been offered a prospectus.

PART 3 — EFFECTIVE DATE

3.1 Effective Date — This National Policy comes into force on January 1, 2000.

Adoption by OSC: (1999) 22 O.S.C.B. 8170; Request for Comments: (1998) 21 O.S.C.B. 7782 and (1997) 21 O.S.C.B. 3075.

Policies and Orders: NPS 11-201.

CSA Staff Notice 47-302 — Pre-Marketing of Underwriters' Options of Bought Deals

Date: April 21, 2006

29 O.S.C.B. 3334

[Not reproduced]

OSC Policy 47-601 — Advertising During Waiting Period Between Preliminary and Final Prospectuses

[Rescinded 30 O.S.C.B. (Supp. 7) 325 (Dec. 21, 2007)]

(Renumbered as OSC Policy 47-601: (2003) 26 O.S.C.B. 2318; previously Uniform Act Policy 2-13)

4.8 — Distribution Restrictions

OSC Rule 48-501 — Trading during Distributions, Formal Bids and Share Exchange Transactions

Date: May 9, 2005, as amended effective September 28, 2009, November 2, 2015 and May 9, 2016

28 O.S.C.B. 3998, 32 O.S.C.B. (Supp. 5) 184, 38 O.S.C.B. 7243 and 39 O.S.C.B. 4288.

Table of Contents

Part 4:
DISTRIBUTIONS

PART 6 EFFECTIVE DATE

    6.1 Effective Date

PART 1 — DEFINITIONS

1.1 Definitions — In this Rule

"connected security" means, in respect of an offered security,

> (a) a security into which the offered security is immediately convertible, exchangeable or exercisable unless the security is a listed security or quoted security and the price at which the offered security is convertible, exchangeable or exercisable is greater than 110% of the best ask price of the security at the commencement of the restricted period,

> (b) a security of the issuer of the offered security or another issuer that, according to the terms of the offered security, may significantly determine the value of the offered security,

> (c) if the offered security is a special warrant, the security which would be issued on the exercise of the special warrant, and

> (d) if the offered security is an equity security, any other equity security of the issuer,

where the security trades on a marketplace or a market where there is mandated transparency of orders or trade information;

"dealer-restricted period" means, for a dealer-restricted person, the period,

> (a) in connection with a prospectus distribution or a restricted private placement of an offered security, commencing on the later of

>> (i) the date two trading days prior to the day the offering price of the offered security is determined, and

>> (ii) the date on which a dealer enters into an agreement or reaches an understanding to participate in the prospectus distribution or restricted private placement of securities, whether or not the terms and conditions of such participation have been agreed upon, and

> ending on the date the selling process ends and all stabilization arrangements relating to the offered security are terminated,

> (b) in connection with a securities exchange take-over bid or issuer bid, commencing on the date of dissemination of the take-over bid circular, issuer bid circular or similar document and ending with the termination of the period during which securities may be deposited under such bid, including any extension thereof, or the withdrawal of the bid, and

> (c) in connection with an amalgamation, arrangement, capital reorganization or similar transaction, commencing on the date of dissemination of the information circular for such transaction and ending on the date of approval of the transaction by the security holders that will receive the offered security or the termination of the transaction by the issuer or issuers;

"dealer-restricted person" means, in respect of a particular offered security,

> (a) a dealer that

>> (i) is an underwriter, as defined in the Act, in a prospectus distribution or a restricted private placement,

>> (ii) is participating, as agent but not as an underwriter, in a restricted private placement, and

>>> (A) the number of securities to be issued under the restricted private placement would constitute more than 10% of the issued and outstanding offered securities, and

>>> (B) the dealer has been allotted or is otherwise entitled to sell more than 25% of the securities to be issued under the restricted private placement,

>> (iii) has been appointed by an offeror to be the dealer-manager, manager, soliciting dealer or adviser in respect of a securities exchange take-over bid or issuer bid, or

>> (iv) has been appointed by an issuer to be the soliciting dealer or adviser in respect of obtaining security holder approval for an amalgamation, arrangement, capital reorganization or similar transaction that would result in the issuance of securities that would be a distribution exempt from prospectus requirements in accordance with applicable securities law,

> where, in each case, adviser means an adviser whose compensation depends on the outcome of the transaction,

> (b) a related entity of the dealer referred to in clause (a) but does not include such related entity, or any separate and distinct department or division of a dealer referred to in clause (a) where,

>> (i) the dealer

>>> (A) maintains and enforces written policies and procedures reasonably designed to prevent the flow of information regarding any prospectus distribution, private placement or transaction referred to in clause (a) to or from the related entity, department or division, and

>>> (B) obtains an annual assessment of the operation of such policies and procedures,

>> (ii) the dealer has no officers or employees that solicit orders or recommend transactions in securities in common with the related entity, department or division, and

>> (iii) the related entity, department or division does not during the dealer-restricted period, in connection with the restricted security,

>>> (A) act as a market maker (other than to meet its obligations under the rules of a recognized exchange),

>>> (B) solicit orders from clients, or

>>> (C) engage in proprietary trading,

> (c) a partner, director, officer, employee or a person holding a similar position or acting in a similar capacity for the dealer referred to in clause (a) or for a related entity of the dealer referred to in clause (b), or

> (d) any person or company acting jointly or in concert with a person or company described in clause (a), (b) or (c) for a particular transaction;

"exchange-traded fund" means a mutual fund, the units of which are

> (a) listed securities or quoted securities, and

> (b) in continuous distribution in accordance with applicable securities legislation;

"highly-liquid security" means a listed security or quoted security that,

    (a) has traded, in total, on one or more marketplaces as reported on a consolidated market display during a 60-day period ending not earlier than 10 days prior to the commencement of the restricted period,

        (i) an average of at least 100 times per trading day, and

        (ii) with an average trading value of at least $1,000,000 per trading day, or

    (b) is subject to Regulation M under the 1934 Act and is considered to be an "actively-traded security" thereunder;

"issuer-restricted period" means, for an issuer-restricted person, the period,

    (a) in connection with a prospectus distribution or a restricted private placement of an offered security, commencing on the date two trading days prior to the day the offering price of the offered security is determined, and ending on the date the selling process ends and all stabilization arrangements relating to the offered security are terminated,

    (b) in connection with a securities exchange take-over bid or issuer bid, commencing on the date of the dissemination of the take-over bid circular, issuer bid circular or similar document and ending with the termination of the period during which securities may be deposited under such bid, including any extension thereof, or the withdrawal of the bid, and

    (c) in connection with an amalgamation, arrangement, capital reorganization or other similar transaction, commencing on the date of dissemination of the information circular for such transaction and ending on the date of approval of the transaction by the security holders that will receive the offered security or the termination of the transaction by the issuer or issuers;

"issuer-restricted person" means, in respect of a particular offered security,

    (a) the issuer of the offered security,

    (b) a selling security holder of the offered security in connection with a prospectus distribution or restricted private placement,

    (c) an affiliated entity, associated entity or insider of the issuer of the offered security or a selling security holder but does not include a person who is an insider by virtue of clause (c) of the definition of "insider" under the Act so long as that person:

        (i) does not have, and has had not in the previous 12 months, any board or management representation in respect of the issuer or selling security holder; and

        (ii) does not have knowledge of any material information concerning the issuer or its securities that has not been generally disclosed; or

    (d) any person or company acting jointly or in concert with the person or company described in clause (a), (b) or (c) for a particular transaction;

"last independent sale price" means the last sale price of a trade on a market, other than a trade that a dealer-restricted person knows or ought reasonably to know was made by or on behalf of a person or company that is a dealer-restricted person or an issuer-restricted person;

"offered security" means all securities, that trade on a marketplace or a market where there is mandated transparency of orders or trade information, of the class of security that

    (a) is offered pursuant to a prospectus distribution or a restricted private placement,

    (b) is offered by an offeror in a securities exchange take-over bid in respect of which a take-over bid circular or similar document is required to be filed under securities legislation,

    (c) is offered by an issuer in an issuer bid in respect of which an issuer bid circular or similar document is required to be filed under securities legislation, or

    (d) would be issuable to a security holder pursuant to an amalgamation, arrangement, capital reorganization or similar transaction in relation to which proxies are being solicited from security holders that will receive the offered security in such circumstances that the issuance would be a distribution exempt from prospectus requirements in accordance with applicable securities legislation,

provided that, if the security referred to in clauses (a) to (d) is a unit comprised of more than one type or class, each security comprising the unit shall be considered an offered security;

"restricted private placement" means a distribution of offered securities made pursuant to sections 2.3 or 2.30 of National Instrument 45-106 *Prospectus Exemptions*; and"

"restricted security" means the offered security or any connected security.

1.2 Interpretation — (1) Affiliated Entity — The term "affiliated entity" has the meaning ascribed to that term in section 1.3 of National Instrument 21-101 — *Marketplace Operation*.

(2) Associated Entity — Where used to indicate a relationship with an entity, associated entity has the meaning ascribed to the term "associate" in subsection 1(1) of the Act and also includes any person or company of which the entity beneficially owns voting securities carrying more than 10 per cent of the voting rights attached to all outstanding voting securities of the person or company.

(3) Equity Security — An equity security is any security of an issuer that carries a residual right to participate in the earnings of the issuer and, upon liquidation or winding up of the issuer, in its assets.

(4) Related Entity — In respect of a dealer, a related entity is an affiliated entity of the dealer that carries on business in Canada and is registered as a dealer or adviser in accordance with applicable securities legislation.

(5) For the purposes of the definitions of "dealer-restricted period" and "issuer-restricted period":

    (a) the selling process shall be considered to end,

        (i) in the case of a prospectus distribution, if a receipt has been issued for the final prospectus, the dealer has allocated all of its portion of the securities to be distributed under the prospectus and all selling efforts have ceased, and

        (ii) in the case of a restricted private placement, the dealer has allocated all of its portion of the securities to be distributed under the offering; and

    (b) stabilization arrangements shall be considered to have terminated in the case of a syndicate of underwriters or agents when, in accordance with the syndication agreement, the lead underwriter or agent determines that the syndication agreement has been terminated such that any purchase or sale of a restricted security by a dealer after the time of termination is not subject to the stabilization arrangements or otherwise made jointly for the dealers that were party to the stabilization arrangements.

PART 2 — RESTRICTIONS

2.1 Dealer-restricted Person — Except as permitted under sections 3.1, 4.1 and 4.2, a dealer-restricted person shall not at any time during the dealer-restricted period,

(a) bid for or purchase a restricted security for an account of a dealer-restricted person, an account over which the dealer-restricted person exercises direction or control, or, except in accordance with section 3.2, an account which the dealer-restricted person knows or reasonably ought to know, is an account of an issuer-restricted person; or

(b) attempt to induce or cause any person or company to purchase any restricted security.

2.2 Issuer-restricted Person — Except as permitted under section 3.2, an issuer-restricted person shall not at any time during the issuer-restricted period,

(a) bid for or purchase a restricted security for an account of an issuer-restricted person or an account over which the issuer-restricted person exercises direction or control; or

(b) attempt to induce or cause any person or company to purchase any restricted security.

2.3 Deemed Re-commencement of a Restricted Period — If a dealer appointed to be an underwriter in a prospectus distribution or a restricted private placement receives a notice or notices of the exercise of statutory rights of withdrawal or rights of rescission from purchasers of, in the aggregate, not less than 5% of the offered securities allotted to or acquired by the dealer in connection with the prospectus distribution or the restricted private placement then a dealer-restricted period and issuer-restricted period shall be deemed to have re-commenced upon receipt of such notice or notices and shall be deemed to have ended at the time the dealer has distributed its participation, including the securities that were the subject of the notice or notices of the exercise of statutory rights of withdrawal or rights of rescission.

PART 3 — PERMITTED ACTIVITIES AND EXEMPTIONS

3.1 Exemptions — Dealer-restricted Persons — (1) Section 2.1 does not apply to a dealer-restricted person in connection with,

(a) market stabilization or market balancing activities on a marketplace where the bid for or purchase of a restricted security is for the purpose of maintaining a fair and orderly market in the offered security by reducing the price volatility of or addressing imbalances in buying and selling interests for the restricted security, provided that the bid or purchase is at a price which does not exceed the lesser of

(i) in the case of an offered security

(A) the price at which the offered security will be issued in a prospectus distribution or restricted private placement, if that price has been determined, and

(B) the last independent sale price at the time of the entry of the bid or order to purchase, or

(ii) in the case of a connected security

(A) the last independent sale price at the commencement of the dealer-restricted period, and

(B) the last independent sale price at the time of the entry of the bid or order to purchase,

provided that if the restricted security has not previously traded on a marketplace, the price also does not exceed the price of the last trade of the security executed on an exchange or organized regulated market outside of Canada that publicly disseminates details of trades executed on that market other than a trade that the dealer-restricted person knows or ought reasonably to know has been entered by or on behalf of a person or company that is a dealer-restricted person or an issuer-restricted person;

(b) a restricted security that is

(i) a highly-liquid security,

(ii) a unit or share of an exchange-traded fund, other than an exchange-traded fund that the Investment Industry Regulatory Organization of Canada has designated as subject to section 7.7 of the Universal Market Integrity Rules, or

(iii) a connected security of a security referred to in subclause (i) or (ii);

(c) a bid or purchase by a dealer-restricted person on behalf of a client, other than a client that the dealer-restricted person knows or ought reasonably to know is a person or company that is an issuer-restricted person, provided that

(i) the client's order was not solicited by the dealer-restricted person, or

(ii) if the client's order was solicited, the solicitation occurred before the commencement of the dealer-restricted period;

(d) the exercise of an option, right, warrant or a similar contractual arrangement held or entered into by the dealer-restricted person prior to the commencement of the dealer-restricted period;

(e) a bid for or purchase of a restricted security pursuant to a Small Securityholder Selling and Purchase Arrangement made in accordance with National Instrument 32-101 or similar rules applicable to any marketplace on which the bid or purchase is entered or executed;

(f) the solicitation of the tender of securities to a securities exchange take-over bid or issuer bid;

(g) a subscription for or purchase of an offered security pursuant to a prospectus distribution or restricted private placement;

(h) a bid for or purchase of a restricted security to cover a short position entered into prior to the commencement of the dealer-restricted period; or

(i) a bid for or purchase of a restricted security if the bid or purchase is made through the facilities of a marketplace in accordance with applicable marketplace rules.

(2) Where a dealer-restricted person is also an issuer-restricted person the exemptions in subsection (1) and sections 4.1 and 4.2 continue to be available to the dealer-restricted person.

3.2 Exemptions — Issuer-restricted Persons — Section 2.2 does not apply to an issuer-restricted person in connection with,

(a) the exercise of an option, right, warrant, or a similar contractual arrangement held or entered into by the issuer-restricted person prior to the commencement of the issuer-restricted period;

(b) a bid or purchase of a restricted security pursuant to a Small Securityholder Selling and Purchase Arrangement made in accordance with National Instrument 32-101 or similar rules applicable to any marketplace on which the bid or purchase is entered or executed;

(c) an issuer bid described in sections 4.6 and 4.7 of National Instrument 62-104 *Take-Over Bids and Issuer Bids* if the issuer did not solicit the sale of the securities sold under those clauses;

(d) the solicitation of the tender of securities to a securities exchange take-over bid or issuer bid; or

(e) a subscription for or purchase of an offered security pursuant to a prospectus distribution or restricted private placement.

PART 4 — RESEARCH REPORTS

4.1 Compilations and Industry Research — Despite section 53 of the Act and section 2.1, a dealer-restricted person may publish or disseminate any information, opinion, or recommendation relating to the issuer of a restricted security provided that such information, opinion or recommendation,

(a) is contained in a publication which:

(i) is disseminated with reasonable regularity in the normal course of business of the dealer-restricted person, and

(ii) includes similar coverage in the form of information, opinions or recommendations with respect to a substantial number of companies in the issuer's industry or contains a comprehensive list of securities currently recommended by the dealer-restricted person; and

(b) is given no materially greater space or prominence in such publication than that given to other securities or issuers.

4.2 Issuers of Highly-liquid Securities — Despite section 53 of the Act and section 2.1, a dealer-restricted person may publish or disseminate any information, opinion, or recommendation relating to the issuer of a restricted security that is a highly-liquid security provided that such information, opinion, or recommendation is contained in a publication which is disseminated with reasonable regularity in the normal course of the business of the dealer-restricted person.

PART 5 — EXEMPTION

5.1 Exemption — The Director may grant an exemption to this Rule, in whole or in part, subject to such conditions or restrictions as may be imposed in the exemption.

PART 6 — EFFECTIVE DATE

6.1 Effective Date — This Rule shall come into force on May 9, 2005.

Companion Policy 48-501CP — To Rule 48-501 Trading During Distributions, Formal Bids and Share Exchange Transactions

PART 1 — INTRODUCTION

1.1 Purpose — Ontario Securities Commission Rule 48-501 Trading during Distributions, Formal Bids and Share Exchange Transactions (the "Rule") imposes trading restrictions on dealers, issuers and certain related parties involved in a distribution of securities, take-over bids and certain other transactions. The Rule generally prohibits purchases of or bids for restricted securities in circumstances where there is heightened concern over the possibility of manipulation by those with an interest in the outcome of the distribution or transaction. This Companion Policy sets out the views of the Ontario Securities Commission (the "Commission") as to the interpretation of various terms and provisions in the Rule.

PART 2 — DEFINITIONS AND INTERPRETATIONS

2.1 "connected security" — The definition of "connected security" in section 1.1 of the Rule includes, among other things, a security of the issuer of the offered security or another issuer that, according to the terms of the offered security, may *significantly determine* the value of the offered security. The Commission takes the view that, absent other mitigating factors, a connected security "significantly determines" the value of the offered security, if, in whole or in part, it accounts for more than 25% of the value of the offered security.

2.2 [Repealed.]

2.3 End of "dealer-restricted period" and "issuer-restricted period" — distribution of securities and exercise of over-allotment option — The definitions of "dealer-restricted period" and "issuer-restricted period", with respect to a prospectus distribution and a "restricted private placement", refer to the end of the period as the date that the selling process ends and all stabilization arrangements relating to the offered security are terminated. Paragraph (a) of subsection 1.2(5) provides interpretation as to when the selling process is considered to end. As further clarification, the selling process is considered to end for a prospectus distribution when the receipt for the prospectus has been issued, the dealer has distributed all securities allocated to it and is no longer stabilizing, all selling efforts have ceased and the syndicate is broken. Selling efforts have ceased when the dealer is no longer making efforts to sell, and there is no intention to exercise an over-allotment option other than to cover the syndicate's short position. If the dealer or syndicate subsequently exercises an over-allotment option in an amount that exceeds the syndicate short position, the selling efforts would not be considered to have ceased. Securities allocated to a dealer that are held and transferred to their inventory account at the end of the distribution are considered distributed. Subsequent sales of such securities are secondary market transactions and should occur on a marketplace subject to any applicable exemptions (unless the subsequent sale transaction is a distribution by prospectus). To provide certainty around when the distribution has ended, appropriate steps should be taken to move the securities from the syndication account to the dealer's inventory account.

PART 3 — RESTRICTED PERSONS

3.1 Meaning of "acting jointly or in concert" — The definitions of "dealer-restricted person" and "issuer-restricted person" in section 1.1 of the Rule include a person or company acting jointly or in concert with a person or company that is also a dealer-restricted person or an issuer-restricted person for a particular transaction. For the purposes of the Rule, "acting jointly or in concert" has a similar meaning to that phrase as defined in section 91 of the Act, with necessary modifications. In the context of this Rule only, it is a question of fact whether a person or company is acting jointly or in concert with a dealer- or issuer-restricted person and, without limiting the generality of the foregoing, every person or company who, as a result of an agreement, commitment or understanding, whether formal or informal, with a dealer-restricted person or an issuer-restricted person, bids for or purchases a restricted security will be presumed to be acting jointly or in concert with such dealer-restricted person or issuer-restricted person.

3.2 Exclusion of "related party" — The definition of "dealer-restricted person" in clause 1.1(b) excludes a related entity where certain conditions are met. Subclause (i)(B) requires the dealer to obtain an annual assessment of the operation of the policies and procedures referred to in subclause (i)(A). In the Commission's view, this assessment may be conducted as part of the annual policy and procedure review of the supervision system as required by Policy 7.1 of the Universal Market Integrity Rules.

PART 4 — MARKETPLACE AND MARKETPLACE RULES

4.1 Meaning of "marketplace" — In this Rule, marketplace means all marketplaces as defined in section 1.1 of National Instrument 21-101 — *Marketplace Operation.*

4.2 Meaning of "marketplace rules" — Marketplace rules refer to the rules, policies and other similar instruments adopted by a recognized stock exchange or recognized quotation and trade reporting system as approved by the applicable securities regulatory authority but not including any rules, policies or other similar instruments relating solely to the listing of securities on a stock exchange or to the quoting of securities on a quotation and trade reporting system.

PART 5 — EXEMPTIONS

5.1 Fraud and Manipulation — Provisions against manipulation and fraud are found in securities legislation, specifically, Part 3 of National Instrument 23-101 — *Trading Rules* (NI 23-101) and section 126.1 of the *Securities Act* (Ontario) (when that provision comes into force). NI 23-101 prohibits manipulative or deceptive trading, including activities that may create misleading pricing or trading activity that is detrimental to investors and the integrity of the markets. The Rule specifically prohibits certain trading activities in circumstances where there is heightened concern over the possibility of manipulation by those with an interest in the outcome of the distribution or transaction. The Rule also provides certain exemptions to permit purchases and bids in situations where there is no, or a very low, possibility of manipulation. However, the Commission is of the view that notwithstanding that certain trading activities are permitted under the Rule these activities continue to be subject to the general provisions relating to manipulation and fraud found in securities legislation such that any activities carried out in accordance with the Rule must still meet the spirit of the general anti-manipulation and anti-fraud provisions.

5.2 Market Stabilization and Market Balancing — Subsection 3.1(1) of NI 23-101 prohibits manipulation or fraud which includes, among other things, a transaction or series of transactions that a person or company knows, or ought reasonably to have known, would contribute to a misleading appearance of trading activity or an artificial price for a security. Companion Policy 23-101CP to NI 23-101 states that the Canadian securities regulatory authorities do not consider market stabilization activities carried out in connection with a distribution of securities to be activities in breach of subsection 3.1(1) provided such activities are carried out in accordance with applicable marketplace rules or provisions of securities legislation that permit market stabilization activities. Clause 3.1(1)(a) of the Rule provides dealer-restricted persons with an exemption for market stabilization and market balancing activities subject to price limitations. Market stabilization and market balancing activities should be engaged in for the purpose of maintaining a fair and orderly market in the offered security by reducing the price volatility of or addressing imbalances in buying and selling interest for the restricted security.

The Commission considers it to be inappropriate for a dealer to engage in market stabilization activities in circumstances where the dealer knows or should reasonably know that the market price is not fairly and properly determined by supply and demand. This might exist where, for example, the dealer is aware that the market price is a result of inappropriate activity by a market participant or that there is undisclosed material information regarding the issuer.

Market balancing activities should contribute to a fair and orderly market by contributing to price continuity and depth and by minimizing supply-demand disparity. Market balancing does not seek to prevent or unduly retard any price movements, but merely to prevent erratic or disorderly changes in price.

5.2.1 Exchange-traded funds — Section 1.1 of the Rule defines an "exchange-traded fund" as an open-ended mutual fund, the units of which are listed or quoted securities. Generally trading in exchange-traded funds has not given rise to concerns of a misleading appearance of trading activity or artificial price and the Rule exempts trading in exchange-traded funds. However, if the Investment Industry Regulatory Organization of Canada makes a designation that trading in a particular fund is subject to the corresponding provisions of the Universal Market Integrity Rules because it is concerned that trading in units of the fund may be susceptible to manipulation, trading in that exchange-traded fund will be subject to the Rule.

5.3 Short-position Exemption — Subclause 3.1(1)(h) provides an exemption from the Rule for a dealer-restricted person in connection with a bid for or purchase to cover a short position provided it was entered into before the commencement of the dealer-restricted period. Short positions entered into during the dealer-restricted period may be covered by purchases made in reliance upon the market stabilization exemption in clause 3.1(1)(a), subject to the price limits set out in that exemption.

PART 6 — RESEARCH

6.1 Section 53 of the Act — Part 4 of the Rule provides exemptions from section 53 of the Act which prohibits providing research that in the Commission's view constitutes an act, advertisement, solicitation, conduct or negotiation directly or indirectly in furtherance of a trade prior to the filing and receipt of the preliminary prospectus and prospectus. The Commission is of the view that although sections 4.1 and 4.2 do permit dealer-restricted persons to disseminate research reports, this dissemination continues to be subject to the usual restrictions applicable to dealer-restricted persons when they are in possession of material inside information regarding the issuer.

6.2 Meaning of "reasonable regularity" — Sections 4.1 and 4.2 of the Rule provides circumstances where a dealer-restricted person may publish or disseminate information, an opinion, or a recommendation relating to the issuer of a restricted security. Clause 4.1(a) and section 4.2 require that the information, opinion or recommendation is contained in a publication which is disseminated with reasonable regularity in the normal course of business of the dealer-restricted person. The Commission considers that it is a question of fact whether a publication was disseminated "with reasonable regularity" and whether it was in the "normal course of business". A research publication would not likely be considered to have been published with reasonable regularity if it had not been published within the previous twelve month period or there had been no coverage of the issuer within the previous twelve month period. The nature and extent of the published information should also be consistent with prior publications and the dealer should not undertake new initiatives in the context of the distribution. For example, the inclusion of projections of issuers' earnings and revenues would likely only be permitted if they had previously been included on a regular basis. In considering whether it was "in the normal course of business", the Commission may consider the distribution channels. The research should be distributed through the dealer-restricted person's usual research distribution channels and should not be targeted or distributed specifically to prospective investors in the distribution as part of a marketing effort. However, the research may be distributed to a prospective investor if that investor was previously on the mailing list for the research publication.

6.3 Meaning of "similar coverage" and of "substantial number of companies" — Clause 4.1(b) of the Rule requires that the information, opinion or recommendation includes similar coverage in the form of information, opinions or recommendations with respect to a substantial number of issuers in the issuer's industry. This should not be interpreted as requiring that the opinions and recommendations relating to the issuer and other issuers in the issuer's industry must be similar or the same. In this context, in determining what is a "substantial number of issuers", reference should be made to the relevant industry. Generally, the Commission would consider a minimum of six issuers to be a sufficient number. However, where there are less than six issuers in an industry, then all issuers should be included in the research report. In any event the number of issuers should not be less than three.

Companion Policy 48-701 — Notice of Lapse of SEC No-Action Letter Regarding US Trading Rules and MJDS Transactions

Date: **June 27, 1997**
20 O.S.C.B. 3307

An exemption letter was received by the Ontario Securities Commission (the "OSC") and Commission des Valeurs Mobilières du Québec (the "CVMQ" dated August 22, 1991 (SEC File Number TP91-10)("1991 Exemption Letter") from the U.S. Securities and Exchange Commission (the "SEC"), regarding the application of certain SEC trading practices rules to distributions of certain Canadian securities pursuant to the Multijurisdictional Disclosure System (the "MJDS"), a reciprocal arrangement between the SEC and the jurisdictions of the Canadian Securities Administrators.

The SEC recently adopted a new Regulation M which replaced rules 10b-6, 10b-7 and 10b-8 (the subject matter of the 1991 Exemption Letter). *See* SEC Release No. 33-7375, 37-38067 (December 23, 1996). The December 20, 1996 release of the final rules regarding Regulation M indicated that the Exemption granted under the prior rules will no longer be in effect as of the effective date of Regulation M which was March 4, 1997. The final release further suggested that if a recipient of an exemption or no-action letter issued under the former trading practices rules believes that the relief granted by such letter continues to be necessary under Regulation M, that party may wish to contact the Office of Risk Management and Control, the SEC Division of Market Regulation.

Although the OSC and CVMQ are currently considering on what terms to make a request for an Exemption letter regarding the application of Regulation M with respect to certain market activities effected during distributions under MJDS transactions, *market participants should be aware that they cannot rely on the 1991 Exemption Letter and should consider whether and how Regulation M applies to those transactions.*

PART V — ONGOING REQUIREMENTS FOR ISSUERS AND INSIDERS

5.1 — Disclosure — General

National Instrument 51-101 — Standards of Disclosure for Oil and Gas Activities

Date: September 30, 2003, as amended effective September 15, 2005, December 30, 2005, December 28, 2007, December 30, 2010 and July 9, 2015

26 O.S.C.B. 6615, 28 O.S.C.B. 7181, 28 O.S.C.B. 10461, 31 O.S.C.B. 419, 33 O.S.C.B. 11945, 37 O.S.C.B. 10771, 38 O.S.C.B. 2093 and 38 O.S.C.B. 6143

Table of Contents

PART 7 OTHER INFORMATION

7.1 Information to be Furnished on Request

PART 8 EXEMPTIONS

8.1 Authority to Grant Exemption

8.2 Exemption for Certain Exchangeable Issues

PART 9 INSTRUMENT IN FORCE

9.1 Coming Into Force

PART 1 — APPLICATION AND TERMINOLOGY[1]

1.1 **Definitions** — In this *Instrument*:

"abandonment and reclamation costs" means all costs associated with the process of restoring a *reporting issuer's property* that has been disturbed by oil and gas activities to a standard imposed by applicable government or regulatory authorities;

"alternate reference point" means a location at which quantities and values of a *product type* are measured before the *first point of sale*;

"annual information form" has the same meaning as "AIF" in *NI 51-102*;

"analogous information" means information about an area outside the area in which the *reporting issuer* has an interest or intends to acquire an interest, which is referenced by the *reporting issuer* for the purpose of drawing a comparison or conclusion to an area in which the *reporting issuer* has an interest or intends to acquire an interest, which comparison or conclusion is reasonable, and includes:

(i) historical information concerning *reserves*;

(ii) estimates of the volume or value of *reserves*;

(iii) historical information concerning *resources*;

(iv) estimates of the volume or value of *resources*;

(v) historical *production* amounts;

(vi) *production* estimates; or

(vii) information concerning a *field*, well, basin or *reservoir*;

"anticipated results" means information that may, in the opinion of a reasonable person, indicate the potential value or quantities of *resources* in respect of the *reporting issuer's resources* or a portion of its *resources* and includes:

(i) estimates of volume;

(ii) estimates of value;

(iii) areal extent;

(iv) pay thickness;

(v) flow rates; or

(vi) hydrocarbon content;

"bitumen" means a naturally occurring solid or semi-solid *hydrocarbon*

(a) consisting mainly of heavier *hydrocarbons*, with a viscosity greater than 10,000 millipascal-seconds (mPa•s) or 10,000 centipoise (cP) measured at the *hydrocarbon's* original temperature in the *reservoir* and at atmospheric pressure on a gas-free basis, and

"BOEs" means barrels of *oil* equivalent;

"by-product" means a substance that is recovered as a consequence of *producing* a *product type*

"coal bed methane" means *natural gas* that

(a) primarily consists of methane, and

(b) is contained in a coal deposit;

"COGE Handbook" means the "Canadian Oil and Gas Evaluation Handbook" maintained by the Society of Petroleum Evaluation Engineers (Calgary Chapter), as amended from time to time;

"contingent resources data" means

(a) an estimate of the volume of *contingent resources*, and

(b) the *risked* net present value of *future net revenue* of *contingent resources*;

"conventional natural gas" means *natural gas* that has been generated elsewhere and has migrated as a result of hydrodynamic forces and is trapped in discrete *accumulations* by seals that may be formed by localized structural, depositional or erosional geological features;

"effective date", in respect of information, means the date as at which, or for the period ended on which, the information is provided;

"first point of sale" means the first point after initial *production* at which there is a transfer of ownership of a *product type*;

"forecast prices and costs" means future prices and costs that are:

(i) generally accepted as being a reasonable outlook of the future;

---

[1]For the convenience of readers, CSA Staff Notice 51-324 Glossary to NI 51-101 *Standards of Disclosure for Oil and Gas Activities* sets out the meanings of terms, including those defined in this Part, that are printed in italics in this *Instrument*, *Form 51-101F1*, *Form 51-101F2*, *Form 51-101F3* or Companion Policy 51-101CP.

(ii) if, and only to the extent that, there are fixed or presently determinable future prices or costs to which the *reporting issuer* is legally bound by a contractual or other obligation to supply a physical product, including those for an extension period of a contract that is likely to be extended, those prices or costs rather than the prices and costs referred to in subparagraph (i).

"foreign geographic area" means a geographic area outside North America within one country or including all or portions of a number of countries;

"Form 51-101F1" means Form 51-101F1 *Statement of Reserves Data and Other Oil and Gas Information*;

"Form 51-101F2" means Form 51-101F2 *Report on Reserves Data by Independent Qualified Reserves Evaluator or Auditor*;

"Form 51-101F3" means Form 51-101F3 *Report of Management and Directors on Oil and Gas Disclosure*;

"Form 51-101F4" means Form 51-101F4 *Notice of Filing of 51-101F1 Information*;

"Form 51-101F5" means Form 51-101F5 *Notice of Ceasing to Engage in Oil and Gas Activities*;

"future net revenue" means a forecast of revenue, estimated using *forecast prices and costs* or *constant prices and costs*, arising from the anticipated development and production of *resources*, net of the associated royalties, *operating costs, development costs*, and *abandonment and reclamation costs*;

"gas hydrate" means a naturally occurring crystalline substance composed of water and *gas* in an ice-lattice structure;

"heavy crude oil" means *crude oil* with a relative density greater than 10 degrees API gravity and less than or equal to 22.3 degrees API gravity;

"hydrocarbon" means a compound consisting of hydrogen and carbon, which, when naturally occurring, may also contain other elements such as sulphur;

"independent", in respect of the relationship between a *reporting issuer* and person or company, means a relationship between the *reporting issuer* and that person or company in which there is no circumstance that could, in the opinion of a reasonable person aware of all relevant facts, interfere with that person's or company's exercise of judgment regarding the preparation of information which is used by the *reporting issuer*;

"light crude oil" means *crude oil* with a relative density greater than 31.1 degrees API gravity;

"McfGEs" means thousand cubic feet of *gas* equivalent;

"medium crude oil" means *crude oil* with a relative density greater than 22.3 degrees API gravity and less than or equal to 31.1 degrees API gravity;

"natural gas" means a naturally occurring mixture of *hydrocarbon* gases and other gases;

"natural gas liquids" means those *hydrocarbon* components that can be recovered from *natural gas* as a liquid including, but not limited to, ethane, propane, butanes, pentanes plus, and condensates;

"NI 14-101" means National Instrument 14-101 *Definitions*;

"NI 51-102" means National Instrument 51-102 *Continuous Disclosure Obligations*;

"oil and gas activities" includes the following:

(a) searching for a *product type* in its natural location;

(b) acquiring *property* rights or a *property* for the purpose of exploring for or removing *product types* from their natural locations;

(c) any activity necessary to remove *product types* from their natural locations, including construction, drilling, mining and production, and the acquisition, construction, installation and maintenance of *field* gathering and storage systems including treating, *field* processing and *field* storage;

(d) producing or manufacturing of *synthetic crude oil* or *synthetic gas*;

but does not include any of the following:

(e) any activity that occurs after the *first point of sale*;

(f) any activity relating to the extraction of a substance other than a *product type* and their *by-products*;

(g) extracting *hydrocarbons* as a consequence of the extraction of geothermal steam;

"oil and gas metric" means a numerical measure of a *reporting issuer's oil and gas activities*;

"preparation date", in respect of written disclosure, means the most recent date to which information relating to the period ending on the *effective date* was considered in the preparation of the disclosure;

"product type" means any of the following:

(a) bitumen;

(b) coal bed methane;

(c) conventional natural gas;

(d) gas hydrates;

(e) heavy crude oil;

(f) light crude oil and medium crude oil combined;

(g) natural gas liquids;

(h) shale gas;

(i) synthetic crude oil;

(j) synthetic gas;

(k) tight oil;

"professional organization" means a self-regulatory organization of engineers, geologists, other geoscientists or other professionals whose professional practice includes *reserves evaluations* or *reserves audits*, that:

(i) admits members primarily on the basis of their educational qualifications;

(ii) requires its members to comply with the professional standards of competence and ethics prescribed by the organization that are relevant to the estimation, *evaluation, review* or *audit* of *reserves data*;

(iii) has disciplinary powers, including the power to suspend or expel a member; and

(iv) is either:

(A) given authority or recognition by statute in a jurisdiction of Canada; or

(B) accepted for this purpose by the *securities regulatory authority* or the *regulator*;

"prospective resources data" means

(a) an estimate of the volume of *prospective resources*, and

(b) the *risked* net present value of *future net revenue* of *prospective resources*;

"qualified reserves auditor" means an individual who:

(i) in respect of particular *reserves data, resources* or related information, possesses professional qualifications and experience appropriate for the estimation, *evaluation, review* and *audit* of the *reserves data, resources* and related information; and

(ii) is a member in good standing of a *professional organization*;

"qualified reserves evaluator" means an individual who:

(i) in respect of particular *reserves data, resources* or related information, possesses professional qualifications and experience appropriate for the estimation, *evaluation* and *review* of the *reserves data, resources* and related information; and

(ii) is a member in good standing of a *professional organization*;

"qualified reserves evaluator or auditor" means a *qualified reserves auditor* or a *qualified reserves evaluator*;

"reserves" means *proved, probable* or *possible reserves*;

"reserves data" means an estimate of *proved reserves* and *probable reserves* and related *future net revenue*, estimated using *forecast prices and costs*;

"risked" means adjusted for the probability of loss or failure in accordance with the *COGE Handbook*;

"shale gas" means *natural gas*

(a) contained in dense organic-rich rocks, including low-permeability shales, siltstones and carbonates, in which the *natural gas* is primarily adsorbed on the kerogen or clay minerals, and

(b) that usually requires the use of hydraulic fracturing to achieve economic production rates;

"supporting filing" means a document filed by a *reporting issuer* with a *securities regulatory authority*;

"synthetic crude oil" means a mixture of liquid *hydrocarbons* derived by upgrading *bitumen, kerogen* or other substances such as coal, or derived from *gas* to liquid conversion and may contain sulphur or other compounds;

(a) generated as a result of the application of an in-situ transformation process to coal or other *hydrocarbon*-bearing rock; and

(b) comprised of not less than 10% by volume of methane;

"tight oil" means *crude oil*

(a) contained in dense organic-rich rocks, including low-permeability shales, siltstones and carbonates, in which the *crude oil* is primarily contained in microscopic pore spaces that are poorly connected to one another, and

(b) that typically requires the use of hydraulic fracturing to achieve economic production rates.

1.2 COGE Handbook Definitions — (1) Terms used in this *Instrument* but not defined in this *Instrument*, *NI 14-101* or the securities statute in the *jurisdiction*, and defined or interpreted in the *COGE Handbook*, have the meaning or interpretation ascribed to those terms in the *COGE Handbook*.

(2) In the event of a conflict or inconsistency between the definition of a term in this *Instrument*, *NI 14-101* or the securities statute in the *jurisdiction* and the meaning ascribed to the term in the *COGE Handbook*, the definition in this *Instrument*, *NI 14-101* or the securities statute in the *jurisdiction*, as the case may be, applies.

1.3 Applies to Reporting Issuers Only — This *Instrument* applies only to *reporting issuers* engaged, directly or indirectly, in *oil and gas activities*.

1.4 Materiality Standard — (1) This *Instrument* applies only in respect of information that is *material* in respect of a *reporting issuer*.

(2) For the purpose of subsection (1), information is *material* in respect of a *reporting issuer* if it would be likely to influence a decision by a reasonable investor to buy, hold or sell a security of the *reporting issuer*.

PART 2 — ANNUAL FILING REQUIREMENTS

2.1 Reserves Data and Other Oil and Gas Information — A *reporting issuer* must, not later than the date on which it is required by *securities legislation* to file audited financial statements for its most recent financial year, file with the *securities regulatory authority* the following:

1. Statement of Reserves Data and Other Information — a statement of the *reserves data* and other information specified in *Form 51-101F1*, as at the last day of the *reporting issuer's* most recent financial year and for the financial year then ended;

2. Report of Independent Qualified Reserves Evaluator or Auditor — a report in accordance with *Form 51-101F2* that is:

(a) included in, or filed concurrently with, the document filed under item 1; and

(b) executed by one or more *qualified reserves evaluators or auditors* each of whom is *independent* of the *reporting issuer* and who must have,

(i) in the aggregate,

(A) *evaluated* or *audited* at least 75 percent of the *future net revenue*, calculated using a discount rate of 10 percent, attributable to *proved* plus *probable reserves*, as reported in the statement filed or to be filed under item 1, and

(B) *reviewed* the balance of that *future net revenue*, and

(ii) *evaluated* or *audited* the *contingent resources data* or *prospective resources data* reported in the statement filed or to be filed under item 1.

3. Report of Management and Directors — a report in accordance with *Form 51-101F3* that

    (a) refers to the information filed or to be filed under items 1 and 2;

    (b) confirms the responsibility of management of the *reporting issuer* for the content and filing of the statement referred to in item 1 and for the filing of the report referred to in item 2;

    (c) confirms the role of the board of directors in connection with the information referred to in paragraph (b);

    (d) is contained in, or filed concurrently with, the statement filed under item 1; and

    (e) is executed

        (i) *two officers* of the *reporting issuer*, one of whom is the chief executive officer, and

        (ii) on behalf of the board of directors, by

            (A) any two directors of the *reporting issuer*, other than the persons referred to in subparagraph (i) above, or

            (B) if the *reporting issuer* has only three directors, two of whom are the persons referred to in subparagraph (i), all of the directors of the *reporting issuer*.

2.2 [repealed]

2.3 Inclusion in Annual Information Form — (1) The requirements of section 2.1 may be satisfied by including the information specified in section 2.1 in an *annual information form* filed within the time specified in section 2.1.

(2) A *reporting issuer* that adopts the approach described in subsection (1) must, concurrently with filing its *annual information form*, file with the *securities regulatory authority* a notice of filing in accordance with *Form 51-101F4*.

2.4 Reservation in Report of Qualified Reserves Evaluator or Auditor — (1) If a *qualified reserves evaluator or auditor* cannot report without *reservation*, on *reserves data, contingent resources data* or *prospective resources data* the *reporting issuer* must ensure that the report of the *qualified reserves evaluator or auditor* prepared for the purpose of item 2 of section 2.1 sets out the cause of the *reservation* and the effect, if known to the *qualified reserves evaluator or auditor*, on the *reserves data, contingent resources data*, or *prospective resources data*.

(2) A report containing a *reservation*, the cause of which can be removed by the *reporting issuer*, does not satisfy the requirements of item 2 of section 2.1.

PART 3 — RESPONSIBILITIES OF REPORTING ISSUERS AND DIRECTORS

3.1 Interpretation — A reference to a board of directors in this Part means, for a *reporting issuer* that does not have a board of directors, those individuals whose authority and duties in respect of that *reporting issuer* are similar to those of a board of directors.

3.2 Reporting Issuer to Appoint Independent Qualified Reserves Evaluator or Independent Qualified Reserves Auditor — (1) A *reporting issuer* must appoint one or more *qualified reserves evaluators*, or *qualified reserves auditors*, each of whom is *independent* of the *reporting issuer*, and must direct each appointed evaluator or auditor to report to the board of directors of the *reporting issuer* on the *reserves data* disclosed in the statement prepared for the purpose of item 1 of section 2.1.

(2) If a *reporting issuer* discloses *contingent resources data* or *prospective resources data* in a statement prepared for the purpose of item 1 of section 2.1, the *reporting issuer* must appoint one or more *qualified reserves evaluators* or *qualified reserves auditors* and must direct each appointed evaluator or auditor to report to the board of directors of the *reporting issuer* on all *contingent resources data* and *prospective resources data* included in the statement.

3.2 Reporting Issuer to Appoint Independent Qualified Reserves Evaluator or Auditor — A *reporting issuer* must appoint one or more *qualified reserves evaluators or auditors*, each of whom is *independent* of the *reporting issuer*, to report to the board of directors of the *reporting issuer* on its *reserves data*.

3.3 Reporting Issuer to Make Information Available to Qualified Reserves Evaluator or Auditor — A *reporting issuer* must make available to the *qualified reserves evaluators or auditors* that it appoints under section 3.2 all information reasonably necessary to enable the *qualified reserves evaluators or auditors* to provide a report that will satisfy the applicable requirements of this Instrument.

3.4 Certain Responsibilities of Board of Directors — The board of directors of a *reporting issuer* must

    (a) review, with reasonable frequency, the *reporting issuer's* procedures relating to the disclosure of information with respect to *oil and gas activities*, including its procedures for complying with the disclosure requirements and restrictions of this *Instrument*;

    (b) review each appointment under section 3.2 and, in the case of any proposed change in such appointment, determine the reasons for the proposal and whether there have been disputes between the appointed qualified reserves evaluator or auditor and management of the reporting issuer;

    (c) review, with reasonable frequency, the reporting issuer's procedures for providing information to the qualified reserves evaluators or auditors who report on *reserves data, contingent resources data or prospective resources data* for the purposes of this Instrument;

    (d) before approving the filing of *reserves data, contingent resources data or prospective resources data* and the report of the qualified reserves evaluators or auditors thereon referred to in section 2.1, meet with management and each qualified reserves evaluator or auditor appointed under section 3.2, to

        (i) determine whether any restrictions affect the ability of the *qualified reserves evaluator or auditor* to report on *reserves data, contingent resources data or prospective resources data* without *reservation*; and

        (ii) review the *reserves data, contingent resources data or prospective resources data* and the report of the *qualified reserves evaluator or auditor* thereon; and

    (e) review and approve

        (i) the content and filing, under section 2.1, of the statement referred to in item 1 of section 2.1;

        (ii) the filing, under section 2.1, of the report referred to in item 2 of section 2.1; and

        (iii) the content and filing, under section 2.1, of the report referred to in item 3 of section 2.1.

3.5 Reserves Committee — (1) The board of directors of a *reporting issuer* may, subject to subsection (2), delegate the responsibilities set out in section 3.4 to a committee of the board of directors, provided that a majority of the members of the committee

    (a) are individuals who are not and have not been, during the preceding 12 months;

        (i) an officer or employee of the *reporting issuer* or of an affiliate of the *reporting issuer*;

        (ii) a person who beneficially owns 10 percent or more of the outstanding voting securities of the *reporting issuer*; or

        (iii) a relative of a person referred to in subparagraph (a)(i) or (ii), residing in the same home as that person; and

    (b) are free from any business or other relationship which could reasonably be seen to interfere with the exercise of their independent judgement.

(2) Despite subsection (1), a board of directors of a *reporting issuer* must not delegate its responsibility under paragraph 3.4(e) to approve the content or the filing of information.

(3) A board of directors that has delegated responsibility to a committee pursuant to subsection (1) must solicit the recommendation of that committee as to whether to approve the content and filing of information for the purpose of paragraph 3.4(e).

PART 4 — MEASUREMENT

4.1 [repealed]

4.2 Consistency in Dates — The date or period with respect to which the effects of an event or transaction are recorded in a *reporting issuer's* annual financial statements must be the same as the date or period with respect to which they are first reflected in the *reporting issuer's* annual *reserves data* disclosure under Part 2.

PART 5 — REQUIREMENTS APPLICABLE TO ALL DISCLOSURE

5.1 Application of Part 5 — This Part applies to disclosure made by or on behalf of a *reporting issuer*

    (a) to the public;

    (b) in any document filed with a *securities regulatory authority*; or

    (c) in other circumstances in which, at the time of making the disclosure, the *reporting issuer* knows, or ought reasonably to know, that the disclosure is or will become available to the public.

5.2 Disclosure of Reserves and Other Information — (1) If a *reporting issuer* makes disclosure of *reserves* or other information of a type that is specified in Form 51-101F1, the *reporting issuer* must ensure that the disclosure satisfies the following requirements:

    (a) estimates of reserves or future net revenue must

        (i) disclose the effective date of the estimate;

        (ii) have been prepared or audited by a qualified reserves evaluator or auditor;

        (iii) have been prepared or audited in accordance with the COGE Handbook;

        (iv) have been made assuming that development of each property in respect of which the estimate is made will occur, without regard to the likely availability to the reporting issuer of funding required for that development; and

        (v) in the case of estimates of possible reserves or related future net revenue disclosed in writing, also include a cautionary statement that is proximate to the estimate to the following effect:

            Possible reserves are those additional reserves that are less certain to be recovered than probable reserves. There is a 10% probability that the quantities actually recovered will equal or exceed the sum of proved plus probable plus possible reserves.;

    (b) for the purpose of determining whether reserves should be attributed to a particular undrilled property, reasonably estimated future abandonment and reclamation costs related to the property must have been taken into account;

    (c) in disclosing aggregate *future net revenue* the disclosure must comply with the requirements for the determination of *future net revenue* specified in Form 51-101F1; and

    (d) the disclosure must be consistent with the corresponding information, if any, contained in the statement most recently filed by the *reporting issuer* with the *securities regulatory authority* under item 1 of section 2.1, except to the extent that the statement has been supplemented or superseded by a report of a material change filed by the *reporting issuer* with the *securities regulatory authority*.

(2) Disclosure referred to under subsection (1) must indicate whether the estimates of *reserves* or *future net revenue* were prepared by an *independent qualified reserves evaluator* or *qualified reserves auditor*.

5.3 Classification of Reserves and of Resources Other than Reserves — (1) Reserves or *resources* other than *reserves* must be disclosed using the applicable terminology and category set out in the *COGE Handbook* and must be classified in the most specific category of *reserves* or *resources* other than *reserves* in which the *reserves* or *resources* other than *reserves* can be classified.

(2) Despite subsection (1), where the applicable terminology set out in the *COGE Handbook* for the disclosure of *resources* is *total petroleum initially-in-place*, *discovered petroleum initially-in-place* or *undiscovered petroleum initially-in-place*, the *reporting issuer* may depart from the applicable terminology by substituting, for the word "*petroleum*", reference to the specific *product type* of the *resource*.

5.4 Oil and Gas Reserves and Sales — (1) Disclosure of *resources* or of sales of *product types* or associated *by-products* must be made with respect to the *first point of sale*.

(2) Despite subsection (1), a *reporting issuer* may disclose *resources* or sales of *product types* or associated *by-products* with respect to an *alternate reference point* if, to a reasonable person, the *resources, product types* or associated *by-products* would be marketable at the *alternate reference point*.

(3) If a *reporting issuer* discloses *resources* or sales of *product types* or associated *by-products* with respect to an *alternate reference point*, the *reporting issuer* must

    (a) state that the disclosure is made with respect to an *alternate reference point*,

    (b) disclose the location of the *alternate reference point*, and

Part 5: ONGOING REQUIREMENTS

(c) explain why disclosure is not being made with respect to the *first point of sale*.

5.5 Natural Gas By-Products — Disclosure of *product types* or *by-products*, including *natural gas liquids* and sulphur must be made in respect only of volumes that have been or are to be recovered prior to the *first point of sale*, or an *alternate reference point*, as applicable.

5.6 Future Net Revenue Not Fair Market Value — Disclosure of an estimate of *future net revenue*, whether calculated without discount or using a discount rate, must include a statement to the effect that the estimated values disclosed do not represent fair market value.

5.7 [Repealed.]

5.8 Disclosure of Less Than All Reserves — If a *reporting issuer* that has more than one *property* makes written disclosure of any *reserves* attributable to a particular *property*

    (a) the disclosure must include a cautionary statement to the effect that

        "The estimates of reserves and future net revenue for individual properties may not reflect the same confidence level as estimates of reserves and future net revenue for all properties, due to the effects of aggregation"; and

    (b) the document containing the disclosure of any *reserves* attributable to one *property* must also disclose total *reserves* of the same classification for all *properties* of the *reporting issuer* in the same country (or, if appropriate and not misleading, in the same *foreign geographic area*).

5.9 Disclosure of Resources Other than Reserves — (1) If a *reporting issuer* discloses *anticipated results* from *resources* which are not currently classified as reserves, the *reporting issuer* must also disclose in writing, in the same document or in a *supporting filing*:

    (a) the *reporting issuer's* interest in the *resources*;

    (b) the location of the *resources*;

    (c) the *product types* reasonably expected;

    (d) the risks and the level of uncertainty associated with recovery of the *resources*; and

    (e) in the case of *unproved property*, if its value is disclosed,

        (i) the basis of the calculation of its value; and

        (ii) whether the value was prepared by an *independent* party.

(2) If disclosure referred to in subsection (1) includes an estimate of a quantity of *resources* other than reserves in which the *reporting issuer* has an interest or intends to acquire an interest, or an estimated value attributable to an estimated quantity, the estimate must:

    (a) have been prepared or audited by a *qualified reserves evaluator or auditor*;

    (b) have been prepared or audited in accordance with the *COGE Handbook*;

    (c) be classified in the most specific category of resources other than *reserves* as required by section 5.3; and

    (d) be accompanied by the following information:

        (i) a definition of the *resources* category used for the estimate;

        (ii) the *effective date* of the estimate;

        (iii) the significant positive and negative factors relevant to the estimate;

        (iii.1) a description of the applicable project or projects including the following:

            (A) the estimated total cost required to achieve *commercial* production;

            (B) the general timeline of the project, including the estimated date of first *commercial production*;

            (C) the recovery technology;

            (D) whether the project is based on a *conceptual or pre-development study*;

        (iv) in respect of *contingent resources*, the specific contingencies which prevent the classification of the *resources* as *reserves*; and

        (v) a cautionary statement that is proximate to the estimate to the effect that:

            (A) in the case of *discovered resources* or a subcategory of *discovered resources* other than *reserves*:

            "There is uncertainty that it will be commercially viable to produce any portion of the resources."; or

            (B) in the case of *undiscovered resources* or a subcategory of *undiscovered resources*:

            "There is no certainty that any portion of the resources will be discovered. If discovered, there is no certainty that it will be commercially viable to produce any portion of the resources."

(3) Paragraphs (1)(d) and (e) and subparagraphs (2)(d)(iii), (iii.1) and (iv) do not apply if:

    (a) the *reporting issuer* includes in the written disclosure a reference to the title and date of a previously filed document that complies with those requirements; and

    (b) the *resources* in the written disclosure, taking into account the specific *properties* and interests reflected in the *resources* estimate or other *anticipated result*, are *materially* the same *resources* addressed in the previously filed document.

(4) Any disclosure made under subsection (1) or (2) must indicate whether the *anticipated results* from resources which are not currently classified as *reserves* or the estimate of a quantity of *resources* other than *reserves* were prepared by an *independent qualified reserves evaluator or auditor*.

5.10 Analogous Information — (1) Sections 5.2, 5.3, 5.9 and 5.16 do not apply to the disclosure of *analogous information* provided that the *reporting issuer* discloses the following:

    (a) the source and date of the *analogous information*;

    (b) whether the source of the *analogous information* was *independent*;

    (c) if the *reporting issuer* is unable to confirm that the *analogous information* was prepared by a *qualified reserves evaluator or auditor* or in accordance with the *COGE Handbook*, a cautionary statement to that effect proximate to the disclosure of the *analogous information*; and

(d) the relevance of the *analogous information* to the *reporting issuer's oil and gas activities*.

(2) For greater certainty, if a *reporting issuer* discloses information that is an *anticipated result*, an estimate of a quantity of *reserves* or *resources*, or an estimate of value attributable to an estimated quantity of *reserves* or *resources* for an area in which it has an interest or intends to acquire an interest, that is based on an extrapolation from *analogous information*, sections 5.2, 5.3, 5.9 and 5.16 apply to the disclosure of the information.

5.11 [Repealed.]

5.12 [Repealed.]

5.13 [Repealed.]

5.14 Disclosure Using Oil and Gas Metrics — (1) If a *reporting issuer* discloses an *oil and gas metric*, other than an estimate of the volume or value of *resources* prepared in accordance with section 5.2, 5.9 or 5.18 or a comparative or equivalency measure under Part 2, 3, 4, 5, 6 or 7 of *Form 51-101F1*, the *reporting issuer* must include disclosure that

(a) identifies the standard and source of the *oil and gas metric*, if any,

(b) provides a brief description of the method used to determine the *oil and gas metric*,

(c) provides an explanation of the meaning of the *oil and gas metric*, and

(d) cautions readers as to the reliability of the *oil and gas metric*.

(2) If there is no identifiable standard for an *oil and gas metric*, the *reporting issuer* must also include disclosure that

(a) provides a brief description of the parameters used in the calculation of the *oil and gas metric*, and

(b) states that the *oil and gas metric* does not have any standardized meaning and should not be used to make comparisons.

5.15 [Repealed.]

5.16 Restricted Disclosure: Summation of Resource Categories — (1) A *reporting issuer* must not disclose a summation of an estimated quantity, or estimated value, of two or more of the following:

(a) *reserves*;

(b) *contingent resources*;

(c) *prospective resources*;

(d) the unrecoverable portion of *discovered petroleum initially-in-place*;

(e) the unrecoverable portion of *undiscovered petroleum initially-in-place*;

(f) *discovered petroleum initially-in-place*; and

(g) *undiscovered petroleum initially-in-place*.

(2) Despite subsection (1), a *reporting issuer* may disclose an estimate of *total petroleum initially-in-place*, *discovered petroleum initially-in-place* or *undiscovered petroleum initially-in-place* if the *reporting issuer* includes, proximate to that disclosure, an estimate of each of the following, as applicable:

(a) *reserves*;

(b) *contingent resources*;

(c) *prospective resources*;

(d) the commercial portion of *discovered petroleum initially-in-place*;

(e) the sub-commercial portion of *discovered petroleum initially-in-place*;

(f) the unrecoverable portion of *discovered petroleum initially-in-place*;

(g) the unrecoverable portion of *undiscovered petroleum initially-in-place*;

(h) *discovered petroleum initially-in-place*; and

(i) *undiscovered petroleum initially-in-place*.

(3) A *reporting issuer* may disclose an estimate of *total petroleum initially-in-place*, *discovered petroleum initially-in-place* or *undiscovered petroleum initially-in-place* as the most specific category that it can assign to its resources if, proximate to its disclosure, the *reporting issuer*

(a) explains why *total petroleum initially-in-place*, *discovered petroleum initially-in-place* or *undiscovered petroleum initially-in-place*, as the case may be, is the most specific assignable category; and

(b) includes

(i) in the case of disclosure of *discovered petroleum initially-in-place*, the cautionary statement required by clause 5.9(2)(d)(v)(A), or

(ii) in the case of disclosure of *total petroleum initially-in-place* or *undiscovered petroleum initially-in-place*, the cautionary statement required by clause 5.9(2)(d)(v)(B).

5.17 Disclosure of High-Case Estimates of Reserves and of Resources other than Reserves — (1) If a *reporting issuer* discloses an estimate of *proved* plus *probable* plus *possible reserves*, the *reporting issuer* must also disclose the corresponding estimates of *proved* and *proved* plus *probable reserves* or of *proved* and *probable reserves*.

(2) If a *reporting issuer* discloses a high-case estimate of *resources* other than *reserves*, the *reporting issuer* must also disclose the corresponding low and best-case estimates.

5.18 Supplementary Disclosure of Resources Using Evaluation Standards other than the COGE Handbook — (1) A *reporting issuer* may supplement disclosure provided in accordance with section 5.2, 5.3 or 5.9 with an estimate of the volume or the value of *resources* prepared in accordance with an alternative *resources* evaluation standard that

(a) has a comprehensive framework for the evaluation of *resources*,

(b) defines *resources* using terminology and categories in a manner that is consistent with the terminology and categories of the *COGE Handbook*,

(c) has a scientific basis, and

(d) requires that estimates of volume and value of *resources* be based on reasonable assumptions.

(2) If disclosure is made under subsection (1) and that disclosure is required under the laws of or by a *foreign jurisdiction*, the *reporting issuer* must, proximate to the disclosure,

(a) disclose the *effective date* of the estimate,

(b) describe any significant differences, and the reasons those differences exist, between the estimate prepared in accordance with the alternative *resources* evaluation standard and the estimate prepared in accordance with the *COGE Handbook*, and

(i) in accordance with section 5.2, 5.3 or 5.9, as applicable, and

(ii) at the same effective date as the alternative disclosure.

(3) If disclosure is made under subsection (1) and the disclosure is not required by a foreign jurisdiction, the *reporting issuer* must, proximate to the disclosure,

(a) disclose the effective date of the estimate,

(b) provide a description of the alternative *resources* evaluation standard,

(c) describe any significant differences, and the reasons those differences exist, between the estimate prepared in accordance with the alternative *resources* evaluation standard and the estimate prepared in accordance with the *COGE Handbook*, and

(d) disclose the estimate prepared

(i) in accordance with section 5.2, 5.3 or 5.9, as applicable, and

(ii) at the same *effective date* as the disclosure provided under subsection (1).

(4) An estimate under subsection (1) must have been prepared or *audited by* a *qualified reserves evaluator or auditor*.

PART 6 — MATERIAL CHANGE DISCLOSURE AND CEASING TO ENGAGE IN OIL AND GAS ACTIVITIES

6.1 Material Change from Information Filed under Part 2 — (1) This section applies in respect of a material change that, had it occurred on or before the *effective date* of information included in the statement most recently filed by a *reporting issuer* under item 1 of section 2.1, would have resulted in a significant change in the information contained in the statement.

(2) In addition to any other requirement of *securities legislation* governing disclosure of a material change, disclosure of a material change referred to in subsection (1) must discuss the *reporting issuer's* reasonable expectation of how the material change has affected its *reserves data* or other information.

6.2 Ceasing to Engage in Oil and Gas Activities — A *reporting issuer* must file with the *securities regulatory authority* a notice prepared in accordance with *Form 51-101F5* not later than 10 days after ceasing to be engaged, directly or indirectly, in *oil and gas activities*.

PART 7 — OTHER INFORMATION

7.1 Information to be Furnished on Request — A *reporting issuer* must, on the request of the *regulator*, deliver additional information with respect to the content of a document filed under this *Instrument*.

PART 8 — EXEMPTIONS

8.1 Authority to Grant Exemption — (1) The *regulator* or the *securities regulatory authority* may grant an exemption from this *Instrument*, in whole or in part, subject to such conditions or restrictions as may be imposed in the exemption.

(2) Despite subsection (1), in Ontario only the *regulator* may grant an exemption.

(3) Except in Ontario, an exemption referred to in subsection (1) is granted under the statute referred to in Appendix B of National Instrument 14-101 *Definitions*, opposite the name of the local jurisdiction.

8.2 Exemption for Certain Exchangeable Security Issuers — (1) An exchangeable security issuer, as defined in subsection 13.3(1) of *NI 51-102*, is exempt from this *Instrument* if all of the requirements of subsection 13.3(2) of *NI 51-102* are satisfied;

(2) For the purposes of subsection (1), the reference to "continuous disclosure documents" in clause 13.3(2)(d)(ii)(A) of *NI 51-102* includes documents filed under this *Instrument*.

PART 9 — INSTRUMENT IN FORCE

9.1 Coming Into Force — This *Instrument* comes into force on September 30, 2003.

9.2 [repealed]

Final Rule: (2003) 26 O.S.C.B. 6615; Approval by OSC: (2003) 26 O.S.C.B. 5517; Request for Comments: (2003) 26 O.S.C.B. 587 and (2002) 25 O.S.C.B. 505.

Approval of amendment to Rule by OSC: (2005) 28 O.S.C.B. 7181.

Amendment: (2005) 28 O.S.C.B. 10461; Approval by OSC: 28 O.S.C.B. 8569; Request for Comments: 28 O.S.C.B. 228.

Amendment: 31 O.S.C.B. 419; Approval by OSC: 30 O.S.C.B. (Supp-5) 1 (October 12, 2007); Request for Comments: 30 O.S.C.B. 551.

Amendments: (2010) 33 O.S.C.B. 11945; Approval by OSC: (2010) 33 O.S.C.B. 9503; Request for Comments: (2009) 32 O.S.C.B. 10523.

Policies and Orders: CSAN 51-309, 51-313, 51-317, 51-324, 51-327, 51-336; OPS 51-601.

Form 51-101F1 — Statement of Reserves Data and Other Oil and Gas Information

This is the form referred to in item 1 of section 2.1 of National Instrument 51-101 *Standards of Disclosure for Oil and Gas Activities* **("NI 51-101").**

General Instructions

(1) *Terms for which a meaning is given in NI 51-101 have the same meaning in this Form 51-101F1.*

(2) *Unless otherwise specified in this Form 51-101F1, information under item 1 of section 2.1 of NI 51-101 must be provided as at the last day of the reporting issuer's most recent financial year or for the financial year then ended.*

(3) *It is not necessary to include the headings or numbering, or to follow the ordering of Items, in this Form 51-101F1. Information may be provided in tables.*

(4) *To the extent that any Item or any component of an Item specified in this Form 51-101F1 does not apply to a reporting issuer and its activities and operations, or is not material, no reference need be made to that Item or component. It is not necessary to state that such an Item or component is "not applicable" or "not material". Materiality is discussed in NI 51-101 and Companion Policy 51-101CP.*

(5) *This Form 51-101F1 sets out minimum requirements. A reporting issuer may provide additional information not required in this Form 51-101F1 provided that it is not misleading and not inconsistent with the requirements of NI 51-101, and provided that material information required to be disclosed is not omitted, and that contingent resource data and prospective resource data only appears in an appendix to Form 51-101F1.*

(6) *A reporting issuer may satisfy the requirement of this Form 51-101F1 for disclosure of information "by country" by instead providing information by foreign geographic area in respect of countries outside North America as may be appropriate for meaningful disclosure in the circumstances.*

(7) **A reporting issuer** *disclosing financial information in a currency other than the Canadian dollar must, clearly and as frequently as is necessary to avoid confusing or misleading readers, disclose the currency in which the financial information is disclosed.*

(8) *The* **COGE Handbook** *provides guidance about reporting using units of measurement.* **Reporting issuers** *should not, without compelling reason, switch between imperial units of measure (such as barrels) and Système International (SI) units of measurement (such as tonnes) within or between disclosure documents.*

Part 1 — Date of Statement

Item 1.1 — Relevant Dates

1. Date the statement.

2. Disclose the *effective date* of the information being provided.

3. Disclose the *preparation date* of the information being provided.

Instructions

(1) For the purpose of Part 2 of NI 51-101, and consistent with General Instruction (2) of this Form 51-101F1, the effective date to be disclosed under section 2 of Item 1.1 is the last day of the reporting issuer's most recent financial year.

(2) The same effective date applies to reserves of each category reported and to related future net revenue. References to a change in an item of information, such as changes in production or a change in reserves, mean changes in respect of that item during the year ended on the effective date.

(3) The preparation date, in respect of written disclosure, means the most recent date to which information relating to the period ending on the effective date was considered in the preparation of the disclosure. The preparation date is a date subsequent to the effective date because it takes time after the end of the financial year to assemble the information for that completed year that is needed to prepare the required disclosure as at the end of the financial year.

(4) Because of the interrelationship between certain of the reporting issuer's reserves data and other information referred to in this Form 51-101F1 and certain of the information included in its financial statements, the reporting issuer should ensure that its financial statement auditor and its qualified reserves evaluators or auditors are kept apprised of relevant events and transactions, and should facilitate communication between them.

(5) If the reporting issuer provides information as at a date more recent than the effective date, in addition to the information required as at the effective date, also disclose the date as at which that additional information is provided. The provision of such additional information does not relieve the reporting issuer of the obligation to provide information as at the effective date.

Part 2 — Disclosure of Reserves Data

Item 2.1 — *Reserves Data (Forecast Prices and Costs)*

1. *Breakdown of Reserves (Forecast Case)* — Disclose, by country and in the aggregate, *reserves*, *gross* and *net*, estimated using *forecast prices and costs*, for each product type, in the following categories:

    (a) *proved developed producing reserves*;

    (b) *proved developed non-producing reserves*;

    (c) *proved undeveloped reserves*;

    (d) *proved reserves* (in total);

    (e) *probable reserves* (in total);

    (f) *proved plus probable reserves* (in total); and

    (g) if the *reporting issuer* discloses an estimate of *possible reserves* in the statement:

        (i) *possible reserves* (in total); and

        (ii) *proved* plus *probable* plus *possible reserves* (in total).

2. *Net Present Value of Future Net Revenue (Forecast Case)* — Disclose, by country and in the aggregate, the net present value of *future net revenue* attributable to the *reserves* categories referred to in section 1 of this Item, estimated using *forecast prices and costs*, before and after deducting *future income tax expenses*, calculated without discount and using discount rates of 5 percent, 10 percent, 15 percent and 20 percent. Also disclose the same information on a unit value basis (e.g., $/Mcf or $/bbl using net reserves) using a discount rate of 10 percent and calculated before deducting future income tax expenses. This unit value disclosure requirement may be satisfied by including the unit value disclosure for each category of *proved reserves* and for *probable reserves* in the disclosure referred to in paragraph 3(c) of Item 2.1.

3. *Additional Information Concerning Future Net Revenue (Forecast Case)*

    (a) This section 3 applies to *future net revenue* attributable to each of the following *reserves* categories estimated using *forecast prices and costs*:

        (i) *proved reserves* (in total);

        (ii) *proved* plus *probable reserves* (in total); and

        (iii) if paragraph 1(g) of this Item applies, *proved* plus *probable* plus *possible* reserves (in total).

    (b) Disclose, by country and in the aggregate, the following elements of *future net revenue* estimated using *forecast prices and costs* and calculated without discount:

        (i) revenue;

        (ii) royalties;

        (iii) *operating costs*;

        (iv) *development costs*;

        (v) abandonment and reclamation costs;

        (vi) *future net revenue* before deducting *future income tax expenses*;

        (vii) *future income tax expenses*; and

        (viii) *future net revenue* after deducting *future income tax expenses*.

    (c) Disclose, by *product type*, in each case with associated *by-products*, and on a unit value basis for each *product type*, in each case with associated *by-products* (e.g., $/Mcf or $/bbl using *net reserves*), the net present value of *future net revenue* (before deducting *future income tax expenses*) estimated using *forecast prices and costs* and calculated using a discount rate of 10 percent.

Instructions

(1) Disclose all of the reserves in respect of which the reporting issuer has a direct or indirect ownership, working or royalty interest. These concepts are explained in sections 5.5.4(a) "Ownership Considerations" and 7.5 "Interests" of volume 1 of the COGE Handbook, section 5.2 "Ownership Considerations" of volume 2 of the COGE Handbook and, with respect to an entitlement to share production under a production sharing agreement, section 4.0 "Fiscal Regimes" of the chapter entitled "Reserves Recognition For International Properties" of volume 3 of the COGE Handbook.

(2) Do not include, in the reserves data a product type that is subject to purchase under a long-term supply, purchase or similar agreement. However, if the reporting issuer is a party to such an agreement with a government or governmental authority, and participates in the operation of the properties

in which the product type is situated or otherwise serves as producer of the reserves (in contrast to being an independent purchaser, broker, dealer or importer), disclose separately the reporting issuer's interest in the reserves that are subject to such agreements at the effective date and the net quantity of the product type received by the reporting issuer under the agreement during the year ended on the effective date.

(3) Future net revenue includes the portion attributable to the reporting issuer's interest under an agreement referred to in Instruction (2).

(4) If the reporting issuer's disclosure of reserves would, to a reasonable person, be misleading, if stated without an explanation of the reporting issuer's ownership of or control over those reserves, explain the nature of the reporting issuer's ownership of or control over reserves disclosed in the statement filed or to be filed under item 1 of section 2.1 of NI 51-101.

Item 2.2 — Supplementary Disclosure (Constant Prices and Costs)

The *reporting issuer* may supplement its disclosure of *reserves data* under Item 2.1 by also disclosing estimates of *reserves*, *resources* other than *reserves*, or both, together with estimates of associated *future net revenue*, determined using constant prices and costs rather than *forecast prices and costs* for each applicable product type.

INSTRUCTION

For this purpose,

    (a) a constant price is,

        i) if the **reporting issuer** *is legally bound to supply the product at a particular price, that price; or*

        ii) in every other case, the price that is the unweighted arithmetic average of the first-day-of-the-month price for that product for each of the 12 months preceding the effective date; and

    (b) the costs to be used are to be reasonably estimated on the basis of existing economic conditions without escalation or adjustment for inflation..

Part 3 — Pricing Assumptions

Item 3.1 — Constant Prices Used in Supplementary Estimates

If supplementary disclosure under Item 2.2 is made, the *reporting issuer* must disclose, for each *product type*, the constant price used.

Item 3.2 — Forecast Prices Used in Estimates

1. For each *product type*, disclose:

    (a) the pricing assumptions used in estimating *reserves data* disclosed in response to Item 2.1:

        (i) for each of at least the following five financial years; and

        (ii) generally, for subsequent periods; and

    (b) the *reporting issuer's* weighted average historical prices for the most recent financial year.

2. The disclosure in response to section 1 must include the benchmark reference pricing schedules for the countries or regions in which the *reporting issuer* operates, and inflation and other forecast factors used.

Instructions

(1) *Benchmark reference prices may be obtained from sources such as public product trading exchanges or prices posted by purchasers.*

(2) *The defined term "forecast prices and costs" includes any fixed or presently determinable future prices or costs to which the reporting issuer is legally bound by a contractual or other obligation to supply a physical product, including those for an extension period of a contract that is likely to be extended. In effect, such contractually committed prices override benchmark reference prices for the purpose of estimating reserves data. To ensure that disclosure under this Part is not misleading, the disclosure should reflect such contractually committed prices.*

(3) *Under subsection 5.7(1) of NI 51-101, the reporting issuer must obtain the written consent of the qualified reserves evaluator or auditor to disclose his or her identity in response to section 3 of this Item.*

Part 4 — Reconciliation of Changes in Reserves

Item 4.1 — Reserves Reconciliation

1. Provide the information specified in section 2 of this Item in respect of the following *reserves* categories:

    (a) *gross proved reserves* (in total);

    (b) *gross probable reserves* (in total); and

    (c) *gross proved* plus *probable reserves* (in total).

2. Disclose changes between the *reserves* estimates made as at the *effective date* and the corresponding estimates ("prior-year estimates") made as at the last day of the preceding financial year of the *reporting issuer*:

    (a) by country;

    (b) for each of the following:

        (i) *bitumen*;

        (ii) *coal bed methane*;

        (iii) *conventional natural gas*;

        (iv) *gas hydrates*;

        (v) *heavy crude oil*;

        (vi) *light crude oil* and *medium crude oil* combined;

        (vii) *natural gas liquids*;

        (viii) *shale gas*;

          (ix) *synthetic crude oil*;

          (x) *synthetic gas*;

          (xi) *tight oil*;

    (c) separately identifying and explaining each of the following:

          (i) extensions and improved recovery;

          (ii) technical revisions;

          (iii) discoveries;

          (iv) acquisitions;

          (v) dispositions;

          (vi) economic factors;

          (vii) *production*.

Instructions

(1) *The reconciliation required under this Item 4.1 must be provided in respect of reserves estimated using forecast prices and costs, with the price and cost case indicated in the disclosure.*

(2) *For the purpose of this Item 4.1, it is sufficient to provide the information in respect of the products specified in paragraph 2(b), excluding solution gas, natural gas liquids and other associated by-products.*

(3) *The COGE Handbook provides guidance on the preparation of the reconciliation required under this Item 4.1.*

(4) ***Reporting issuers*** *must not include infill drilling* ***reserves*** *in the category of technical revisions specified in clause 2(c)(ii).* ***Reserves*** *additions from infill drilling must be included in the category of extensions and improved recovery in clause 2(c)(i) (or, alternatively, in an additional separate category under paragraph 2(c) labelled "infill drilling").*

(5) *If the* ***reporting issuer*** *first became engaged in* **oil and gas activities** *only after the last day of its preceding financial year and no evaluation report in respect of its reserves as at that date is available to the* ***reporting issuer****, so that there is no opening data to be reconciled, the* ***reporting issuer*** *need not provide the reconciliation otherwise required under this Part but must disclose the reason for its absence.*

Part 5 — Additional Information Relating to Reserves Data

Item 5.1 — Undeveloped Reserves

1. For *proved undeveloped reserves*:

    (a) disclose for each *product type* the volumes of *proved undeveloped reserves* that were first attributed in each of the most recent three financial years; and

    (b) discuss generally the basis on which the *reporting issuer* attributes *proved undeveloped reserves*, its plans (including timing) for developing the *proved undeveloped reserves* and, if applicable, its reasons for deferring the development of particular *proved undeveloped reserves* beyond two years.

2. For *probable undeveloped reserves*:

    (a) disclose for each *product type* the volumes of *probable undeveloped reserves* that were first attributed in each of the most recent three financial years; and

    (b) discuss generally the basis on which the *reporting issuer* attributes *probable undeveloped reserves*, its plans (including timing) for developing the *probable undeveloped reserves* and, if applicable, its reasons for deferring the development of particular *probable undeveloped reserves* beyond two years.

Instructions

(1) *The phrase "first attributed" refers to the initial allocation of an undeveloped volume of oil or gas reserves by a reporting issuer. Only previously unassigned undeveloped volumes of oil or gas reserves may be included in the first attributed volumes for the applicable financial year. For example, if in 2011 a reporting issuer allocated by way of acquisition, discovery, extension and improved recovery 300 MMcf of proved undeveloped conventional natural gas reserves, that would be the first attributed volume for 2011.*

(2) *The discussion of a reporting issuer's plans for developing undeveloped reserves, or the reporting issuer's reasons for deferring the development of undeveloped reserves, must enable a reasonable investor to assess the efforts made by the reporting issuer to convert undeveloped reserves to developed reserves.*

Item 5.2 — Significant Factors or Uncertainties Affecting Reserves Data

Identify and discuss significant economic factors or significant uncertainties that affect particular components of the *reserves data*.

Instructions

(1) *A reporting issuer must, under this Item, include a discussion of any significant abandonment and reclamation costs, unusually high expected development costs or operating costs, or contractual obligations to produce and sell a significant portion of production at prices substantially below those which could be realized but for those contractual obligations.*

(2) *If the information required by this Item is presented in the reporting issuer's financial statements and notes thereto for the most recent financial year ended, the reporting issuer satisfies this Item by directing the reader to that presentation.*

Item 5.3 — Future Development Costs

1. (a) Provide the information specified in paragraph 1(b) in respect of *development costs* deducted in

    the estimation of *future net revenue* attributable to each of the following *reserves* categories:

       (i) *proved reserves* (in total) estimated using *forecast prices and costs*; and

       (ii) *proved* plus *probable reserves* (in total) estimated using *forecast prices and costs*.

(b) Disclose, by country, the amount of *development costs* estimated:

    (i) in total, calculated using no discount; and

    (ii) by year for each of the first five years estimated.

2. Discuss the *reporting issuer's* expectations as to:

    (a) the sources (including internally-generated cash flow, debt or equity financing, farm-outs or similar arrangements) and costs of funding for estimated future *development costs*; and

    (b) the effect of those costs of funding on disclosed *reserves* or *future net revenue*.

3. If the *reporting issuer* expects that the costs of funding referred to in section 2, could make development of a *property* uneconomic for that *reporting issuer*, disclose that expectation and its plans for the *property*.

Part 6 — Other Oil and Gas Information

Item 6.1 — Oil and Gas Properties and Wells

1. Identify and describe generally the *reporting issuer's* important *properties*, plants, facilities and installations:

    (a) identifying their location (province, territory or state if in Canada or the United States, and country otherwise);

    (b) indicating whether they are located onshore or offshore;

    (c) in respect of *properties* to which *reserves* have been attributed and which are capable of *producing* but which are not *producing*, disclosing how long they have been in that condition and discussing the general proximity of pipelines or other means of transportation; and

    (d) describing any statutory or other mandatory relinquishments, surrenders, back-ins or changes in ownership.

2. State, separately for *oil* wells and *gas* wells, the number of the *reporting issuer's* producing wells and non-producing wells, expressed in terms of both *gross* wells and *net* wells, by location (province, territory or state if in Canada or the United States, and country otherwise).

Item 6.2 — Properties With No Attributed Reserves

1. For *unproved properties* disclose:

    (a) the *gross* area (acres or hectares) in which the *reporting issuer* has an interest;

    (b) the interest of the *reporting issuer* therein expressed in terms of net area (acres or hectares);

    (c) the location, by country; and

    (d) the existence, nature (including any bonding requirements), timing and cost (specified or estimated) of any work commitments.

2. Disclose, by country, the *net* area (acres or hectares) of *unproved property* for which the *reporting issuer* expects its rights to explore, develop and exploit to expire within one year.

Instruction

If the **reporting issuer** *holds interests in different formations under the same surface area pursuant to separate leases, disclose the method of calculating the* **gross** *and* **net** *area. A general description of the method of calculating the disclosed area will suffice.*

Item 6.2.1 — Significant Factors or Uncertainties Relevant to Properties with No Attributed Reserves

Identify and discuss significant economic factors or significant uncertainties that have affected or are reasonably expected to affect the anticipated development or production activities on *properties* with no attributed *reserves*.

Instructions

(1) *A reporting issuer must, under this Item, include a discussion of any significant abandonment and reclamation costs, unusually high expected development costs or operating costs, or contractual obligations to produce and sell a significant portion of production at prices substantially below those which could be realized but for those contractual obligations.*

(2) *If the information required by this Item is presented in the reporting issuer's financial statements and notes thereto for the most recent financial year ended, the reporting issuer satisfies this Item by directing the reader to that presentation.*

Item 6.3 — Forward Contracts

1. If the *reporting issuer* is bound by an agreement (including a transportation agreement), directly or through an aggregator, under which it may be precluded from fully realizing, or may be protected from the full effect of, future market prices for *oil* or *gas*, describe generally the agreement, discussing dates or time periods and summaries or ranges of volumes and contracted or reasonably estimated values.

2. A *reporting issuer* may satisfy the requirement in section 1 by including the information required by that section in its financial statements for the financial year ended on the *effective date*.

3. If the *reporting issuer's* transportation obligations or commitments for future physical deliveries of *oil* or *gas* exceed the *reporting issuer's* expected related future *production* from its *proved reserves*, estimated using *forecast prices and costs* and disclosed under Part 2, discuss such excess, giving information about the amount of the excess, dates or time periods, volumes and reasonably estimated value.

Item 6.4

[Repealed.]

Item 6.5 — Tax Horizon

If the *reporting issuer* is not required to pay income taxes for its most recently completed financial year, discuss its estimate of when income taxes may become payable.

Item 6.6 — Costs Incurred

Disclose by country for the most recent financial year ended each of the following:

    (a) *property acquisition costs*, separately for *proved properties* and *unproved properties*;

(b) *exploration costs*;

(c) *development costs*.

Instruction

If the costs specified in paragraphs (a), (b) and (c) are presented in the reporting issuer's financial statements and the notes to those statements for the most recent financial year ended, the reporting issuer satisfies this Item by directing the reader to that presentation.

Item 6.7 — Exploration and Development Activities

1. Disclose, by country and separately for *exploratory wells* and *development wells*:

    (a) the number of *gross* wells and *net* wells completed in the *reporting issuer's* most recent financial year; and

    (b) for each category of wells for which information is disclosed under paragraph (a), the number completed as *oil* wells, *gas* wells, *service wells* and *stratigraphic test wells* and the number that were dry holes.

2. Describe generally the *reporting issuer's* most important current and likely exploration and development activities, by country.

Item 6.8 — Production Estimates

1. Disclose, by country, for each *product type*, the volume of *production* estimated for the first year reflected in the estimates of *gross proved reserves* and *gross probable reserves* disclosed under Item 2.1.

2. If one *field* accounts for 20 percent or more of the estimated *production* disclosed under section 1, identify that *field* and disclose the volume of *production* estimated for the *field* for that year.

Item 6.9 — Production History

1. Disclose, for each quarter of its most recent financial year, by country for each *product type*:

    (a) the *reporting issuer's* share of average gross daily *production* volume; and

    (b) as an average per unit of volume (for example, $ / *bbl* or $ / *Mcf*):

        (i) the prices received;

        (ii) royalties paid;

        (iii) *production costs*; and

        (iv) the resulting netback.

2. For each important *field*, and in total, disclose the *reporting issuer's production* volumes for the most recent financial year, for each *product type*.

Instruction

In providing information for each product type for the purpose of Item 6.9, it is not necessary to allocate among multiple product types attributable to a single well, reservoir or other reserves entity. It is sufficient to provide the information in respect of the principal product type attributable to the well, reservoir or other reserves entity.

*Resulting netbacks may be disclosed on the basis of units of equivalency between **oil** and **gas** (e.g. **BOE**) but if so that must be made clear and disclosure must comply with section 5.14 of **NI 51-101**.*

Part 7 — Optional Disclosure of Contingent Resources Data and Prospective Resources Data

Instructions

(1) *A reporting issuer may disclose contingent resources data or prospective resources data in a statement of the reserves data and other information filed under item 1 of section 2.1 of NI 51-101, however, that data must only be disclosed as an appendix to that statement.*

(2) *The following cautionary statement must be included in bold font and appear proximate to the risked net present value of future net revenue associated with contingent resources or prospective resources:*

    An estimate of risked net present value of future net revenue of [contingent resources][and][prospective resources] is preliminary in nature and is provided to assist the reader in reaching an opinion on the merit and likelihood of the company proceeding with the required investment. It includes [contingent resources][and][prospective resources] that are considered too uncertain with respect to the [chance of development][and][chance of discovery] to be classified as reserves. There is uncertainty that the risked net present value of future net revenue will be realized.

(3) *A reporting issuer may not rely on subsection 5.9(3) of NI 51-101 for disclosure required to be included in this Part.*

(4) *If a reporting issuer's disclosure of contingent resources or prospective resources would, to a reasonable person, be misleading if not accompanied by an explanation of the reporting issuer's ownership of or control over those resources, explain the nature of the reporting issuer's ownership of or control over all contingent resources and prospective resources disclosed in the statement filed or to be filed under item 1 of section 2.1 of NI 51-101.*

(5) *A reporting issuer's disclosure respecting the value of prospective resources or contingent resources that are not in the development pending project maturity sub-class must be risked and must include an explanation of the factors considered respecting the chance of commerciality, which includes both chance of discovery and chance of development in the case of prospective resources and chance of development in the case of contingent resources.*

Guidance

(1) *A reporting issuer is subject to sections 5.9 and 5.17 of NI 51-101 when providing disclosure of contingent resources data or prospective resources data in this Form.*

(2) *A reporting issuer providing disclosure of contingent resources data or prospective resources data in this Form must have an evaluation process for contingent resources or prospective resources that*

    is at least as rigorous as would be the case for reserves data, and

    is recognized as well-established in the oil and gas industry.

(3) *An evaluation process described in subsection (2) is not needed if a reasonable qualified evaluator or auditor would conclude that it is not necessary in the circumstances.*

(4) *All public disclosure by reporting issuers is subject to the general prohibition against misleading statements. The disclosure of development on-hold, development unclarified or development not viable contingent resources, or prospective resources, in the statement of reserves data and other oil and gas information might be misleading where there is a significant degree of uncertainty and risk associated with those estimates.*

7.1 — Contingent Resources Data

1. If a *reporting issuer* discloses *contingent resources* in the statement filed under item 1 of section 2.1 of *NI 51-101*, the *reporting issuer* must disclose all of the following:

    (a) the *risked* 2C *contingent resources volumes, gross* and *net*, for each *product type*, and classified in each applicable *project maturity sub-class*;

    (b) if *contingent resources* in the *development pending project maturity sub-class* are disclosed, the *risked* net present value of *future net revenue* of the 2C *contingent resources* in the *development pending* project maturity *sub-class*, calculated using *forecast prices and costs* for each *product type*, before deducting *future income taxes* and using discount rates of 0 percent, 5 percent, 10 percent, 15 percent and 20 percent.

2. Disclose the numeric value of the chance of development risk and describe the method of all of the following:

    (a) quantifying the *chance of development* risk;

    (b) estimating the *contingent resources* adjusted for *chance of development* risk and the associated *risked* net present value of *future net revenue*.

7.2 — Prospective Resources Data

1. If a *reporting issuer* discloses *prospective resources* in the statement filed under item 1 of section 2.1 of *NI 51-101*, disclose the best estimate *prospective resources, gross* and *net*, for each *product type*.

2. Disclose the numeric value of the *chance of discovery* and *chance of development* and describe the method of all of the following:

    (a) quantifying the *chance of discovery* and *chance of development*;

    (b) estimating the *prospective resources* adjusted for *chance of discovery* and *chance of development*.

7.3 — Forecast Prices Used in Estimates

1. For each *product type*, disclose the pricing assumptions used in estimating *contingent resources data* and *prospective resources data* disclosed in response to Item 7.1 for each of the five years following the most recently completed financial year.

2. The disclosure in response to section 1 must include the benchmark reference pricing schedules for the countries or regions in which the *reporting issuer* operates, and inflation and other forecast factors used.

3. The pricing assumptions included in section 1 must be the same as the pricing assumptions disclosed in response to Part 3 of this *Form 51-101F1*.

Instructions

(1) Benchmark reference prices may be obtained from sources such as public product trading exchanges or prices posted by purchasers.

(2) The defined term "forecast prices and costs" includes any fixed or presently determinable future prices or costs to which the reporting issuer is legally bound by a contractual or other obligation to supply a physical product, including those for an extension period of a contract that is likely to be extended. Such contractually committed prices must be used, instead of benchmark reference prices for the purpose of estimating contingent resources data and prospective resources data, unless a reasonable investor would find the use those contractually committed prices misleading.

7.4 — Supplemental Contingent Resources Data

The *reporting issuer* may supplement its disclosure of *contingent resources data* under Item 7.1 by also disclosing estimates of *contingent resources* together with estimates of associated *risked* net present value of *future net revenue*, determined using *constant prices and costs* rather than *forecast prices and costs* for each applicable *product type*.

Form 51-101F2 — Report on [Reserves Data] [,] [Contingent Resources Data] [and] [Prospective Resources Data] By Independent Qualified Reserves Evaluator or Auditor

This is the form referred to in item 2 of section 2.1 of National Instrument 51-101 *Standards of Disclosure for Oil and Gas Activities* **("NI 51-101").**

1. Terms to which a meaning is ascribed in *NI 51-101* have the same meaning in this form.

2. The report on *reserves data, contingent resources data* or *prospective resources data*, if applicable, referred to in item 2 of section 2.1 of *NI 51-101*, to be executed by one or more *qualified reserves evaluators or auditors independent* of the *reporting issuer*, must in all *material* respects be in the following form:

Report on [Reserves Data][,] [Contingent Resources Data] [and] [Prospective Resources Data] by Independent Qualified Reserves Evaluator or Auditor

To the board of directors of [name of reporting issuer] (the "Company"):

    1. We have [audited][,] [and] [evaluated] [or reviewed] the Company's [reserves data][,] [contingent resources data] [and] [prospective resources data] as at [last day of the reporting issuer's most recently completed financial year]. *[If the Company has reserves, include the following sentence:* The reserves data are estimates of proved reserves and probable reserves and related future net revenue as at [last day of the reporting issuer's most recently completed financial year], estimated using forecast prices and costs.] *[If the Company has disclosed contingent resources data or prospective resources data, include the following sentence:* The [contingent resources data] [and] [prospective resources data] are risked estimates of volume of [contingent resources] [and] [prospective resources] and related risked net present value of future net revenue as at [last day of the reporting issuer's most recently completed financial year], estimated using forecast prices and costs.]

2. The [reserves data][,] [contingent resources data] [and] [prospective resources data] are the responsibility of the Company's management. Our responsibility is to express an opinion on the [reserves data][,] [contingent resources data] [and] [prospective resources data] based on our [audit][,] [and] [evaluation] [and review].

3. We carried out our [audit][,] [and] [evaluation] [and review] in accordance with standards set out in the Canadian Oil and Gas Evaluation Handbook as amended from time to time (the "COGE Handbook") maintained by the Society of Petroleum Evaluation Engineers (Calgary Chapter).

4. Those standards require that we plan and perform an [audit][,] [and] [evaluation] [and review] to obtain reasonable assurance as to whether the [reserves data][,] [contingent resources data] [and] [prospective resources data] are free of material misstatement. An [audit][,] [and] [evaluation] [and review] also includes assessing whether the [reserves data][,] [contingent resources data] [and] [prospective resources data] are in accordance with principles and definitions presented in the COGE Handbook.

5. [*If the Company has reserves, include this paragraph:*] The following table shows the net present value of future net revenue (before deduction of income taxes) attributed to proved plus probable reserves, estimated using forecast prices and costs and calculated using a discount rate of 10 percent, included in the reserves data of the Company [audited][,][and][evaluated][and reviewed] for the year ended [last day of the reporting issuer's most recently completed financial year], and identifies the respective portions thereof that we have [audited][,][and] [evaluated] [and reviewed] and reported on to the Company's [management/board of directors]:

Independent Qualified Reserves Evaluator or Auditor	Effective Date of [Audit/ Evaluation/ Review] Report	Location of Reserves (Country or Foreign Geographic Area)	Net Present Value of Future Net Revenue (before income taxes, 10% discount rate)			
			Audited	Evaluated	Reviewed	Total
Evaluator A	xxx xx, 20xx	Xxxx	$xxx	$xxx	$xxx	$xxx
Evaluator B	xxx xx, 20xx	Xxxx	xxx	$xxx	$xxx	$xxx
Totals			$xxx	$xxx	$xxx	$xxx

6. [*If the Company has disclosed contingent resources data or prospective resources data, include this paragraph and the tables:*] The following tables set forth the risked volume and risked net present value of future net revenue of [contingent resources] [and] [prospective resources] (before deduction of income taxes) attributed to [contingent resources] [and] [prospective resources], estimated using forecast prices and costs and calculated using a discount rate of 10%, included in the Company's statement prepared in accordance with Form 51-101F1 and identifies the respective portions of the [contingent resources data] [and] [prospective resources data] that we have [audited] [and] [evaluated] and reported on to the Company's [management/board of directors]:

Classification	Independent Qualified Reserves Evaluator or Auditor	Effective Date of [Audit/ Evaluation] Report	Location of Resources Other than Reserves (Country or Foreign Geographic Area)	Risked Net Present Value of Revenue (before income taxes, 10% discount rate)			
				Risked Volume	Audited	Evaluated	Total
Development Pending Contingent Resources (2C)	Evaluator	xxx xx, 20xx	xxxx	xxx	$xxxx	$xxxx	$xxxx

Classification	Independent Qualified Reserves Evaluator or Auditor	Effective Date of [Audit/ Evaluation] Report	Location of Resources Other than Reserves (Country or Foreign Geographic Area)	Risked Volume
Prospective Resources	Evaluator	xxx xx, 20xx	xxxx	xxxx
Contingent Resources [project maturity sub-classes other than Development Pending]	Evaluator	xxx xx, 20xx	xxxx	xxxx

7. In our opinion, the [reserves data][,][contingent resources data][and][prospective resources data] respectively [audited][and][evaluated] by us have, in all material respects, been determined and are in accordance with the COGE Handbook, consistently applied. We express no opinion on the [reserves data][,][contingent resources data][and] [prospective resources data] that we reviewed but did not audit or evaluate.

8. We have no responsibility to update our reports referred to in paragraph[s] [5] [and] [6] for events and circumstances occurring after the effective date of our reports.

9. Because the [reserves data][,][contingent resources data][and][prospective resources data] are based on judgements regarding future events, actual results will vary and the variations may be material.

Executed as to our report referred to above:

Evaluator A, City, Province or State / Country, Execution Date . . . . [signed]

Evaluator B, City, Province or State / Country, Execution Date . . . . [signed]

Form 51-101F3 — Report of Management and Directors on Oil and Gas Disclosure

This is the form referred to in item 3 of section 2.1 of National Instrument 51-101 *Standards of Disclosure for Oil and Gas Activities* **("NI 51-101").**

1. Terms to which a meaning is ascribed in *NI 51-101* have the same meaning in this form.

2. The report referred to in item 3 of section 2.1 of *NI 51-101* must in all *material* respects be in the following form:

Report of Management and Directors on Reserves Data and Other Information

Management of [name of reporting issuer] (the "Company") are responsible for the preparation and disclosure of information with respect to the Company's oil and gas activities in accordance with securities regulatory requirements. This information includes reserves data [and includes, if disclosed in the statement required by item 1 of section 2.1 of *NI 51-101*, other information such as contingent resources data or prospective resources data].

[Alternative A: Reserves Data to Report or Contingent Resources Data or Prospective Resources Data to Report]

[An] independent [qualified reserves evaluator[s] or qualified reserves auditor[s]] [has/have] [audited][,] [and] [evaluated] [and reviewed] the Company's [reserves data][,] [contingent resources data] [and] [prospective resources data]. The report of the independent [qualified reserves evaluator[s] or qualified reserves auditor[s]] [is presented below / will be filed with securities regulatory authorities concurrently with this report].

The [Reserves Committee of the] board of directors of the Company has

(a) reviewed the Company's procedures for providing information to the independent [qualified reserves evaluator[s] or qualified reserves auditor[s]];

(b) met with the independent [qualified reserves evaluator[s] or qualified reserves auditor[s]] to determine whether any restrictions affected the ability of the independent [qualified reserves evaluator[s] or qualified reserves auditor[s]] to report without reservation [and, in the event of a proposal to change the independent [qualified reserves evaluator[s] or qualified reserves auditor[s]], to inquire whether there had been disputes between the previous independent [qualified reserves evaluator[s] or qualified reserves auditor[s] and management]]; and

(c) reviewed the [reserves data][,] [contingent resources data] [and] [prospective resources data] with management and the independent [qualified reserves evaluator[s] or qualified reserves auditor[s]].

The [Reserves Committee of the] board of directors has reviewed the Company's procedures for assembling and reporting other information associated with oil and gas activities and has reviewed that information with management. The board of directors has [, on the recommendation of the Reserves Committee,] approved

> (a) the content and filing with securities regulatory authorities of Form 51-101F1 containing [reserves data][,][contingent resources data][and][prospective resources data] and other oil and gas information;

> (b) the filing of Form 51-101F2 which is the report of the independent [qualified reserves evaluator[s] or qualified reserves auditor[s]] on the reserves data, contingent resources data, or prospective resources data; and

> (c) the content and filing of this report.

Because the [reserves data][,] [contingent resources data] [and] [prospective resources data] are based on judgements regarding future events, actual results will vary and the variations may be material.

[Alternative B: No Reserves to Report and No Resources Other than Reserves to Report]

The [Reserves Committee of the] board of directors of the Company has reviewed the oil and gas activities of the Company and has determined that the Company had no reserves as of [last day of the reporting issuer's most recently completed financial year].

An independent qualified reserves evaluator or qualified reserves auditor has not been retained to evaluate the Company's reserves data. No report of an independent qualified reserves evaluator or qualified reserves auditor will be filed with securities regulatory authorities with respect to the financial year ended on [last day of the reporting issuer's most recently completed financial year].

The [Reserves Committee of the] board of directors has reviewed the Company's procedures for assembling and reporting other information associated with oil and gas activities and has reviewed that information with management. The board of directors has[, on the recommendation of the Reserves Committee,] approved

> (a) the content and filing with securities regulatory authorities of Form 51-101F1 containing information detailing the Company's oil and gas activities; and

> (b) the content and filing of this report.

....
[signature, name and title of chief executive officer]

....
[signature, name and title of an officer other than the chief executive officer]

....
[signature, name of a director]

....
[signature, name of a director]

....
[Date]

Form 51-101F4 — Notice of Filing of 51-101F1 Information

This is the form referred to in section 2.3 of National Instrument 51-101 Standards of Disclosure for Oil and Gas Activities ("NI 51-101").

> On [date of SEDAR Filing], [name of reporting issuer] filed its reports under section 2.1 of NI 51-101, which can be found [describe where a copy of the filed information can be found for viewing by electronic means (for example, in the company's *annual information form* under the company's profile on SEDAR at www.sedar.com)].

51-101F5 — Notice of Ceasing to Engage in Oil and Gas Activities

This is the form referred to in section 6.2 of National Instrument 51-101 Standards of Disclosure for Oil and Gas Activities ("NI 51-101").

1. Terms to which a meaning is ascribed in NI 51-101 have the same meaning in this form.

2. The notice referred to in section 6.2 of NI 51-101 must in all *material* respects be in the following form:

Notice of Ceasing to Engage in Oil and Gas Activities

Management and the board of directors of [name of reporting issuer] (the "Company") have determined that as of [date] the Company is no longer engaged, directly or indirectly, in oil and gas activities.

....
[signature, name and title of chief executive officer]

_____

[signature, name and title of an officer other than the chief executive officer]

_____

[signature, name of a director]

_____

[signature, name of a director]

_____

[Date]

Companion Policy 51-101 Companion Policy — To NI 51-101 Standards of Disclosure for Oil and Gas Activities

Date: September 30, 2003, as amended effective January 6, 2004, December 30, 2005, December 30, 2010 and July 1, 2015

26 O.S.C.B. 6645, 27 O.S.C.B. 1129, 28 O.S.C.B. 10462, 33 O.S.C.B. 9547 and 37 O.S.C.B. 10771

Table of Contents

APPENDIX 1 – SAMPLE RESERVES DATA DISCLOSURE

This Companion Policy sets out the views of the Canadian Securities Administrators (*CSA*) as to the interpretation and application of National Instrument 51-101 *Standards of Disclosure for Oil and Gas Activities* (*NI 51-101*) and related forms.

NI 51-101 supplements other continuous disclosure requirements of *securities legislation* that apply to *reporting issuers* in all business sectors.

The requirements under *NI 51-101* for the filing with *securities regulatory authorities* of information relating to *oil and gas activities* are designed in part to assist capital market participants in making investment decisions and recommendations.

The *CSA* encourage registrants and other persons and companies that wish to make use of information concerning *oil and gas activities* of a *reporting issuer*, including *reserves data*, to review the information filed on *SEDAR* under *NI 51-101* by the *reporting issuer* and, if they are summarizing or referring to this information, to use the applicable terminology consistent with *NI 51-101* and the *COGE Handbook*.

PART 1 — APPLICATION AND TERMINOLOGY

1.1 **Definitions** — (1) **General** — Several terms relating to *oil and gas activities* are defined in section 1.1 of *NI 51-101*. If a term is not defined in *NI 51-101*, *NI 14-101* or the securities statute in the *jurisdiction*, it will have the meaning or interpretation given to it in the *COGE Handbook* if it is defined or interpreted there, pursuant to section 1.2 of *NI 51-101*.

For the convenience of readers, CSA Staff Notice 51-324 *Glossary to NI 51-101 Standards of Disclosure for Oil and Gas Activities* (the NI 51-101 Glossary) as amended, restated or replaced from time to time, sets out the meaning of terms, including those defined in *NI 51-101* and several terms which are derived from the *COGE Handbook*.

The terms set out in the *NI 51-101 Glossary* are printed in italics in *NI 51-101*, *Form 51-101F1*, *Form 51-101F2*, *Form 51-101F3*, *Form 51-101F4*, *Form 51-101F5* or in this Companion Policy for the convenience of readers.

(2) **Forecast Prices and Costs** — The term *forecast prices and costs* is defined in section 1.1 of *NI 51-101* and discussed in the *COGE Handbook*. Except to the extent that the *reporting issuer* is legally bound by fixed or presently determinable future prices or costs, *forecast prices and costs* are future prices and costs "generally accepted as being a reasonable outlook of the future".

The *CSA* do not consider that future prices or costs would satisfy this requirement if they fall outside the range of forecasts of comparable prices or costs used, as at the same date, for the same future period, by major *independent qualified reserves evaluators or auditors* or by other reputable sources appropriate to the evaluation.

(3) **Independent** — The term *independent* is defined in section 1.1 of *NI 51-101*. Applying this definition, the following are examples of circumstances in which the CSA would consider that a *qualified reserves evaluator or auditor* (or other expert) is not *independent*. We consider a *qualified reserves evaluator or auditor* is not *independent* when the *qualified reserves evaluator or auditor*:

> (a) is an employee, insider, or director of the *reporting issuer*;

> (b) is an employee, insider, or director of a related party of the *reporting issuer*;

> (c) is a partner of any person or company in paragraph (a) or (b);

> (d) holds or expects to hold securities, either directly or indirectly, of the *reporting issuer* or a related party of the *reporting issuer*;

> (e) holds or expects to hold securities, either directly or indirectly, in another *reporting issuer* that has a direct or indirect interest in the property that is the subject of the technical report or an adjacent property;

> (f) has or expects to have, directly or indirectly, an ownership, royalty, or other interest in the property that is the subject of the technical report or an adjacent property; or

> (g) has received the majority of their income, either directly or indirectly, in the three years preceding the date of the technical report from the *reporting issuer* or a related party of the reporting issuer.

For the purpose of paragraphs (b) and (d) above, "related party of the *reporting issuer*" means an affiliate, associate, subsidiary, or control person of the *reporting issuer* as those terms are defined under securities legislation.

There may be instances in which it would be reasonable to consider that the independence of a *qualified reserves evaluator or auditor* would not be compromised even though the *qualified reserves evaluator or auditor* holds an interest in the *reporting issuer's* securities. The *reporting issuer* needs to determine whether a reasonable person would consider that such interest would interfere with the *qualified reserves evaluator's or auditor's* judgement regarding the preparation of the technical report.

There may be circumstances in which the *securities regulatory authorities* question the objectivity of the *qualified reserves evaluator or auditor*. In order to ensure the requirement for independence of the *qualified reserves evaluator or auditor* has been preserved, the *reporting issuer* may be asked to provide further information, additional disclosure or the opinion of another *qualified reserves evaluator or auditor* to address concerns about possible bias or partiality on the part of the *qualified reserves evaluator or auditor*.

(4) **Additional Disclosure** — The *CSA* encourage *reporting issuers* engaged in oil and gas activities that may require additional explanation to supplement the disclosure prescribed in NI 51-101 and Form 51-101F1, with information specific to those activities that can assist investors and others in understanding the business and results of the reporting issuer.

A *reporting issuer* should choose the closest *product type* if the substance produced does not exactly match one of the *product types* or if it matches more than one of the product types listed in NI 51-101. For example, *shale gas projects* may not strictly adhere to the formal lithological-based definition of "shale". The produced *gas* can come from intervals that contain clay, carbonates, siltstone and minor amounts of very fine-grained sandstone laminations. Despite coming from intervals that may not meet the technical definition of "shale", gas to which fracturing techniques have been applied, when intermingled with *gas* that comes from "shale", may be reported as being *shale gas*.

A *reporting issuer* must ensure that its disclosure is not misleading and will have to consider whether additional explanation is required to provide the necessary context.

(5) **Professional Organization** —

> (a) **Recognized Professional Organizations** — For the purposes of the *Instrument*, a *qualified reserves evaluator or auditor* must also be a member in good standing with a self-regulated *professional organization* of engineers, geologists, geoscientists or other *oil* and *gas* professionals.

The definition of "*professional organization*" (in section 1.1 of *NI 51-101* and in the NI 51-101 Glossary) has four elements, three of which deal with the basis on which the organization accepts members and its powers and requirements for continuing membership. The fourth element requires either authority or recognition given to the organization by a statute in Canada, or acceptance of the organization by the *securities regulatory authority* or *regulator*.

(a.1) Canadian Professional Organizations — As at December 4, 2014, each of the following organizations in Canada is a *professional organization* for the purposes of *NI 51-101*:

- Association of Professional Engineers and Geoscientists of Alberta (APEGA)
- Association of Professional Engineers and Geoscientists of the Province of British Columbia (APEGBC)
- Association of Professional Engineers and Geoscientists of Saskatchewan (APEGS)
- Association of Professional Engineers and Geoscientists of the Province Manitoba (APEGM)
- Association of Professional Geoscientists of Ontario (APGO)
- Professional Engineers Ontario (PEO)
- Ordre des ingénieurs du Québec (OIQ)
- Ordre des géologues du Québec (OGQ)
- Association of Professional Engineers of Prince Edward Island (APEPEI)
- Association of Professional Engineers and Geoscientists of New Brunswick (APEGNB)
- Association of Professional Engineers of Nova Scotia (APENS)
- Association of Professional Geoscientists of Nova Scotia (APGNS)
- Association of Professional Engineers and Geoscientists of Newfoundland and Labrador (APEGNL)
- Association of Professional Engineers of Yukon (APEY)
- Northwest Territories and Nunavut Association of Professional Engineers and Geoscientists (NAPEG)

(b) Other Professional Organizations — The *CSA* are willing to consider whether particular foreign professional bodies should be accepted as "*professional organizations*" for the purposes of *NI 51-101*. A *reporting issuer*, foreign professional body or other interested person can apply to have a self-regulatory organization that satisfies the first three elements of the definition of "*professional organization*" accepted for the purposes of NI 51-101.

In considering any such application for acceptance, the *securities regulatory authority* or *regulator* is likely to take into account the degree to which a foreign professional body's authority or recognition, admission criteria, standards and disciplinary powers and practices are similar to, or differ from, those of organizations listed above.

As at December 4, 2014, each of the following foreign organizations has been recognized as a *professional organization* for the purposes of *NI 51-101*:

- California Board for Professional Engineers Land Surveyors, and Geologists
- Colorado State Board of Licensure for Architects Professional Engineers and Professional Land Surveyors
- Louisiana Professional Engineering and Land Surveying Board (LAPELS)
- Oklahoma State Board of Licensure for Professional Engineers and Land Surveyors
- Texas Board of Professional Engineers
- American Association of Petroleum Geologists (AAPG) but only in respect of Certified Petroleum Geologists who are members of the AAPG's Division of Professional Affairs
- American Institute of Professional Geologists (AIPG), in respect of the AIPG's Certified Professional Geologists (CPG)
- Energy Institute (EI) but only for those members of the Energy Institute who are Members and Fellows
- Society of Petroleum Evaluation Engineers (SPEE), but only in respect of Members, Honorary Life Members and Life Members

(c) No Professional Organization — A *reporting issuer* or other person may apply for an exemption under Part 8 of *NI 51-101* to enable a *reporting issuer* to appoint, in satisfaction of its obligation under section 3.2 of *NI 51-101*, an individual who is not a member of a *professional organization*, but who has other satisfactory qualifications and experience. Such an application might refer to a particular individual or generally to members and employees of a particular foreign *reserves evaluation* firm. In considering any such application, the *securities regulatory authority* or *regulator* is likely to take into account the individual's professional education and experience or, in the case of an application relating to a firm, to the education and experience of the firm's members and employees, evidence concerning the opinion of a *qualified reserves evaluator or auditor* as to the quality of past work of the individual or firm, and any prior relief granted or denied in respect of the same individual or firm.

(d) Renewal Applications Unnecessary — A successful applicant would likely have to make an application contemplated in this subsection 1.1(5) only once, and not renew it annually.

(6) Qualified Reserves Evaluator or Auditor — The definitions of *qualified reserves evaluator* and *qualified reserves auditor* are set out in section 1.1 of *NI 51-101* and again in the NI 51-101 Glossary.

The defined terms "*qualified reserves evaluator*" and "*qualified reserves auditor*" have a number of elements. A *qualified reserves evaluator* or *qualified reserves auditor* must

- possess professional qualifications and experience appropriate for the tasks contemplated in the Instrument, and
- be a member in good standing of a professional organization.

Reporting issuers should satisfy themselves that any person they appoint to perform the tasks of a *qualified reserves evaluator or auditor* for the purpose of the *Instrument* satisfies each of the elements of the appropriate definition.

In addition to having the relevant professional qualifications, a *qualified reserves evaluator or auditor* must also have sufficient practical experience relevant to the *reserves data* to be reported on. In assessing the adequacy of practical experience, reference should be made to section 3 of volume 1 of the *COGE Handbook* — "Qualifications of Evaluators and Auditors, Enforcement and Discipline".

1.2 COGE Handbook — Pursuant to section 1.2 of *NI 51-101*, definitions and interpretations in the *COGE Handbook* apply for the purposes of *NI 51-101* if they are not defined in *NI 51-101*, *NI 14-101* or the securities statute in the *jurisdiction* (except to the extent of any conflict or inconsistency with *NI 51-101*, *NI 14-101* or the securities statute).

Section 1.1 of *NI 51-101* and the NI 51-101 Glossary set out definitions and interpretations, many of which are derived from the *COGE Handbook*. *Reserves* and *resources* definitions and categories are incorporated in the *COGE Handbook* and are also set out, in part, in the NI 51-101 Glossary.

Subparagraph 5.2(1)(a)(iii) of *NI 51-101* requires that all estimates of *reserves* or *future net revenue* be prepared or audited in accordance with the *COGE Handbook*. Under sections 5.2, 5.3 and 5.9 of *NI 51-101*, all types of public *oil* and *gas* disclosure, including disclosure of *reserves* and of *resources* other than *reserves* must be prepared in accordance with the *COGE Handbook* subject to the exception pursuant to section 5.18 of *NI 51-101*.

1.3 Applies to Reporting Issuers Only — *NI 51-101* applies to *reporting issuers* engaged in *oil and gas activities*. The definition of *oil and gas activities* is broad. For example, a *reporting issuer* with no *reserves*, but with *prospects*, unproved *properties* or *resources* other than *reserves*, may be deemed to be engaged in *oil and gas activities* because such activities include exploration and development of unproved *properties*.

NI 51-101 will also apply to an issuer that is not yet a *reporting issuer* if it files a prospectus or other disclosure document that incorporates prospectus requirements. Pursuant to the long-form prospectus requirements, the *reporting issuer* must disclose the information contained in *Form 51-101F1*, as well as the reports set out in *Form 51-101F2* and *Form 51-101F3*.

1.4 Materiality Standard — Section 1.4 of *NI 51-101* states that *NI 51-101* applies only in respect of information that is material.

NI 51-101 does not require disclosure or filing of information that is not material. If information is not required to be disclosed because it is not material, it is unnecessary to disclose that fact.

Materiality for the purposes of *NI 51-101* is a matter of judgement to be made in light of the circumstances, taking into account both qualitative and quantitative factors, assessed in respect of the *reporting issuer* as a whole.

The reference in subsection 1.4(2) of *NI 51-101* to a "reasonable investor" denotes an objective test: would a notional investor, broadly representative of investors generally and guided by reason, be likely to be influenced, in making an investment decision to buy, sell or hold a security of a *reporting issuer*, by an item of information or an aggregate of items of information? If so, then that item of information, or aggregate of items, is "material" in respect of that *reporting issuer*. An item that is immaterial alone may be material in the context of other information, or may be necessary to give context to other information. For example, a large number of small interests in *oil* and *gas properties* may be material in aggregate to a *reporting issuer*. Alternatively, a small interest in an *oil* and *gas property* may be material to a *reporting issuer*, depending on the size of the *reporting issuer* and its particular circumstances.

PART 2 — ANNUAL FILING REQUIREMENTS

2.1 Annual Filings on SEDAR — The information required under section 2.1 of *NI 51-101* must be filed electronically on *SEDAR*. Consult National Instrument 13-101 System for Electronic Document Analysis and Retrieval (*SEDAR*) and the current *CSA* "*SEDAR* Filer Manual" for information about filing documents electronically. The information required to be filed under item 1 of section 2.1 of *NI 51-101* is usually derived from a much longer and more detailed oil and gas report prepared by a *qualified reserves evaluator or auditor*. These long and detailed reports should not be filed electronically on SEDAR. The filing of an oil and gas report, or a summary of an oil and gas report, does not satisfy the requirements of the annual filing under *NI 51-101*.

2.2 Inapplicable or Immaterial Information — Section 2.1 of *NI 51-101* does not require the filing of any information, even if specified in *NI 51-101* or in a form referred to in *NI 51-101*, if that information is inapplicable or not material in respect of the *reporting issuer*. See section 1.4 of this Companion Policy for a discussion of *materiality*.

If an item of prescribed information is not disclosed because it is inapplicable or immaterial, it is unnecessary to state that fact or to make reference to the disclosure requirement.

2.3 Use of Forms — Section 2.1 of *NI 51-101* requires the annual filing of information set out in *Form 51-101F1* and reports in accordance with *Form 51-101F2* and *Form 51-101F3*. Appendix 1 to this Companion Policy provides an example of how certain of the *reserves data* might be presented. While the format presented in Appendix 1 in respect of *reserves data* and other oil and gas information is not mandatory, we encourage *reporting issuers* to use this format.

The information specified in all three forms, or any two of the forms, can be combined in a single document. A *reporting issuer* may wish to include statements indicating the relationship between documents or parts of one document. For example, the *reporting issuer* may wish to accompany the report of the *independent qualified reserves evaluator or auditor* (Form 51-101F2) with a reference to the *reporting issuer's* disclosure of the *reserves data* (Form 51-101F1), and vice versa.

A *reporting issuer* may supplement the annual disclosure required under *NI 51-101* with additional information corresponding to that prescribed in *Form 51-101F1*, *Form 51-101F2* and *Form 51-101F3*, but as at dates, or for periods, subsequent to those for which annual disclosure is required. However, to avoid confusion, such supplementary disclosure should be clearly identified as being interim disclosure and distinguished from the annual disclosure (for example, if appropriate, by reference to a particular interim period). Supplementary interim disclosure does not satisfy the annual disclosure requirements of section 2.1 of *NI 51-101*.

2.4 Annual Information Form — Section 2.3 of *NI 51-101* permits *reporting issuers* to satisfy the requirements of section 2.1 of *NI 51-101* by presenting the information required under section 2.1 in an *annual information form*. If a *reporting issuer* adopting this approach provides optional disclosure of *contingent resources data* and *prospective resources data* in its statement of reserves data and other oil and gas information required under section 2.1, that disclosure must be included as an appendix to the *reporting issuer's annual information form*.

(1) Meaning of "Annual Information Form" — *Annual information form* has the same meaning as "AIF" in National Instrument 51-102 Continuous Disclosure Obligations. Therefore, as set out in that definition, an *annual information form* can be a completed Form 51-102F2 *Annual Information Form* or, in the case of an *SEC* issuer (as defined in NI 51-102), a completed Form 51-102F2 or an annual report or transition report under the *1934 Act* on Form 10-K, Form 10-KSB or Form 20-F.

(2) Option to Set Out Information in Annual Information Form — Form 51-102F2 *Annual Information Form* allows the information required by section 2.1 of *NI 51-101* to be included in the *annual information form*. That information may be included either by setting out the text of the information in the *annual information form* or by incorporating it, by reference to the separately filed documents. The option offered by section 2.3 of

NI 51-101 enables a *reporting issuer* to satisfy its obligations under section 2.1 of *NI 51-101*, as well as its obligations in respect of *annual information form* disclosure, by setting out the information required under section 2.1 only once, in the *annual information form*. If the *annual information form* is on Form 10-K, this can be accomplished by including the information in a supplement (often referred to as a "wrapper") to the Form 10-K.

However, a *reporting issuer* that elects to follow this approach must file, at the same time and on *SEDAR*, in the appropriate *SEDAR* category, a notice in accordance with *Form 51-101F4* (see subsection 2.3(2) of *NI 51-101*).

This notification will assist other SEDAR users in finding that information. It is not necessary to make a duplicate filing of the *annual information form* itself under the SEDAR *NI 51-101 oil and gas* disclosure category.

2.5 Reporting Issuer With No Reserves or Ceasing to Engage in Oil and Gas Activities — The requirement to make annual *NI 51-101* filings is not limited to only those *reporting issuers* that have *reserves* and related *future net revenue*. A *reporting issuer* with no *reserves* but with *prospects*, unproved *properties* or *resources* may be engaged in *oil and gas activities* (see section 1.3 above) and therefore subject to NI 51-101. That means the *reporting issuer* must still make annual *NI 51-101* filings and ensure that it complies with other *NI 51-101* requirements. The following is guidance on the preparation of *Form 51-101F1*, *Form 51-101F2*, *Form 51-101F3*, *Form 51-101F5* and other *oil and gas* disclosure if the *reporting issuer* has no *reserves*.

(1) **Form 51-101F1** — Section 1.4 of *NI 51-101* states that the *Instrument* applies only in respect of information that is material in respect of a *reporting issuer*. If indeed a *reporting issuer* has no *reserves*, we would consider that fact alone material. The *reporting issuer's* disclosure, under Part 2 of *Form 51-101F1*, should make clear that it has no *reserves* and hence is not reporting related *future net revenue*.

Supporting information regarding *reserves data* required under Part 2 (e.g., price estimates) that are not material to the *reporting issuer* may be omitted. However, if the *reporting issuer* had disclosed *reserves* and related *future net revenue* in the previous year, and has no *reserves* as at the end of its current financial year, the *reporting issuer* is still required by Part 4 of Form 51-101F1 to present a reconciliation to the prior-year's estimates of *reserves*.

The *reporting issuer* is also required to disclose information required under Part 6 of *Form 51-101F1*. Those requirements apply irrespective of the quantum of *reserves*. This would include information about *properties* (items 6.1 and 6.2), costs (item 6.6), and exploration and development activities (item 6.7). The disclosure should make clear that the *reporting issuer* had no *production*, as that fact would be material.

(2) **Form 51-101F2** — *NI 51-101* requires a *reporting issuer* to retain an *independent qualified reserves evaluator or auditor* to *evaluate* or *audit* its *reserves data, contingent resources data* or *prospective resources data*, if that data is included in the statement required under item 1 of section 2.1 of *NI 51-101*, and to have that evaluator or auditor report to the board of directors.

If the *reporting issuer* had no *reserves* during the year it would not need to retain an evaluator or auditor just to file a (nil) report of the *independent* evaluators on the *reserves data* in the form of *Form 51-101F2*. If, however, the issuer did retain an evaluator or auditor to evaluate *reserves*, and the evaluator or auditor concluded that they could not be so categorized, or reclassified those *reserves* to *resources*, the issuer would have to file a report of the *qualified reserves evaluator* because the evaluator has, in fact, evaluated the *reserves* and expressed an opinion.

(3) **Form 51-101F3** — Irrespective of whether the *reporting issuer* has *reserves* or resources other than reserves to report, the requirement to file a report of management and directors in the form of *Form 51-101F3* applies.

(4) **Form 51-101F5** — Section 6.2 of *NI 51-101* requires *reporting issuers* that cease to be engaged in *oil and gas activities* to file a notice in the form of *Form 51-101F5*.

(5) **Other NI 51-101 Requirements** — *NI 51-101* does not require *reporting issuers* to disclose *anticipated results* from, or estimates of a quantity or an estimated value attributable to an estimated quantity of, their *contingent resources* or *prospective resources*. However, if a *reporting issuer* chooses to disclose that type of information, sections 5.9, 5.16 and 5.17 of *NI 51-101* apply to that disclosure. If disclosed in the statement required under item 1 of section 2.1 of *NI 51-101*, Part 7 of *Form 51-101F1* also applies to that disclosure.

Section 5.3 of *NI 51-101* requires *reserves* and *resources* other than *reserves* to be disclosed using the applicable terminology and categories set out in the *COGE Handbook*.

2.6 Reservation in Report of Independent Qualified Reserves Evaluator or Auditor — A report of an *independent qualified reserves evaluator or auditor* on *reserves data* will not satisfy the requirements of item 2 of section 2.1 of *NI 51-101* if the report contains a *reservation*, which can be removed by the *reporting issuer* (subsection 2.4(2) of *NI 51-101*).

The *CSA* do not generally consider time and cost considerations to be causes of a *reservation* that cannot be removed by the *reporting issuer*.

A report containing a *reservation* may be acceptable if the *reservation* is caused by a limitation in the scope of the *evaluation* or audit resulting from an event that clearly limits the availability of necessary records and which is beyond the control of the *reporting issuer*. This could be the case if, for example, necessary records have been inadvertently destroyed and cannot be recreated or if necessary records are in a country at war and access is not practicable.

One potential source of *reservations*, which the *CSA* consider can and should be addressed in a different way, is reliance by a *qualified reserves evaluator or auditor* on information derived or obtained from a *reporting issuer's independent* financial auditors or reflected in their report. The *CSA* recommend that *qualified reserves evaluators or auditors* follow the procedures and guidance set out in both sections 4 and 12 of volume 1 of the *COGE Handbook* in respect of dealings with *independent* financial auditors. In so doing, the *CSA* expect that the quality of *reserves data* can be enhanced and a potential source of *reservations* can be eliminated.

2.7 Disclosure in Form 51-101F1 — (1) **Royalty Interest in Reserves** — *Net reserves* (or "company *net reserves*") of a *reporting issuer* include its royalty interest in *reserves*.

If a reporting *issuer* cannot obtain the information it requires to enable it to include a royalty interest in *reserves* in its disclosure of *net reserves*, it should, proximate to its disclosure of *net reserves*, disclose that fact and its corresponding royalty interest share of *oil* and *gas production* for the year ended on the *effective date*.

(2) **Government Restriction on Disclosure** — If, because of a restriction imposed by a government or governmental authority having jurisdiction over a *property*, a *reporting issuer* excludes *reserves* information from its *reserves data* disclosed under *NI 51-101*, the disclosure should include a statement that identifies the *property* or country for which the information is excluded and explains the exclusion.

(3) **Computation of Future Net Revenue** —

(a) **Tax** — *Reporting issuers* are required to disclose estimates of after-tax net present value of *proved* and *probable reserves* in the statement prepared in accordance with *Form 51-101F1*. In addition, *reporting issuers* may, but are not required to, disclose volumes and estimates of risked after-tax net present value of *future net revenue* of *contingent resources* and *prospective resources* in an appendix to the statement prepared in accordance with *Form 51-101F1*. In a separate disclosure document, a *reporting issuer* may also disclose its *reserves* or other information of a type that is specified in the *Form 51-101F1* in the aggregate or for a portion of its activities, subject to the requirements of subparagraph 5.2(1)(a)(iii) and paragraph 5.2(1)(c) of *NI 51-101*.

Estimates of after-tax net present value are dependent on a number of factors including, but not limited to, one or more of the following:

- forecast future capital expenditure required to achieve forecast *production*;
- interaction with, or deductibility of, government royalties or proportionate sharing rights;
- inclusion of existing tax pool balances of the *reporting issuer* (inclusion is prescribed for *reporting issuer-aggregate* estimates according to section 7 of volume 1 of the *COGE Handbook*);
- tax pool write-off rates;
- sequence of tax pool utilization;
- applicability of special tax incentives; and
- forecast *production* revenue and expenses.

Each of these can have a significant impact on the outcome, which could mislead investors if not considered in the *evaluation* or if the *reporting issuer's* disclosure does not provide sufficient accompanying information.

If a *reporting issuer* discloses after-tax net present value, it should generally include, as appropriate, one or more of the following:

- a general explanation of the method and assumptions used in the *reporting issuer's* calculation, worded to reflect its specific circumstance and the approach taken. This need not be detailed, but major aspects should be addressed, such as whether tax pools have been included in the *evaluation*;
- an explanatory statement to the following effect:

> The after-tax net present value of [the name of company]'s oil and gas properties here reflects the tax burden on the properties on a stand-alone basis. It does not consider any tax planning. It does not provide an estimate of the value at the reporting issuer's related business entity, which may be significantly different. The financial statements and the management's discussion & analysis (MD&A) of the [name of reporting issuer] should be consulted for information at the level of the reporting issuer.

Tax pools should be taken into account when computing *future net revenue* after income taxes. The definition of "future income tax expense" is set out in the *NI 51-101 Glossary*. Essentially, *future income tax expenses* represent estimated cash income taxes payable on the *reporting issuer's* future pre-tax cash flows. These cash income taxes payable should be computed by applying the appropriate year-end statutory tax rates, taking into account future tax rates already legislated, to future pre-tax *net* cash flows reduced by appropriate deductions of estimated unclaimed costs and losses carried forward for tax purposes and relating to *oil and gas activities* (i.e., tax pools). Such tax pools may include Canadian oil and gas property expense (COGPE), Canadian development expense (CDE), Canadian exploration expense (CEE), undepreciated capital cost (UCC) and unused prior year's tax losses. (*Reporting issuers* should be aware of limitations on the use of certain tax pools resulting from acquisitions of *properties* in situations where provisions of the Income Tax Act concerning successor corporations apply.)

(b) **Other Fiscal Regimes** — Other fiscal regimes, such as those involving *production* sharing contracts, should be adequately explained with appropriate allocations made to various categories of proved *reserves* and to *probable reserves*.

(4) **Supplementary Disclosure of Future Net Revenue Using Constant Prices and Costs** — *Form 51-101F1* gives *reporting issuers* the option of disclosing *future net revenue*, together with associated estimates of *reserves* or *resources* other than *reserves*, calculated using constant prices and costs. Constant prices and costs are assumed not to change throughout the life of a *property*, except to the extent of certain fixed or presently determinable future prices or costs to which the *reporting issuer* is legally bound by a contractual or other obligation to supply a physical product (including those for an extension period of a contract that is likely to be extended).

(4.1) **Estimates of Contingent Resources and Prospective Resources** — Estimates of *contingent resources* should be disclosed to the most specific category set out in the *COGE Handbook*, which includes *project maturity sub-classes* for *contingent resources*.

Since *contingent resources* and *prospective resources* are subject to risks that result in less than 100% *chance of commerciality*, the *qualified reserves evaluator or auditor* of a *reporting issuer* will need to address those risks in the estimation and classification of that *reporting issuer's* publicly disclosed *contingent resources* and *prospective resources*. There are many methods to accomplish this and no particular method is being prescribed. Expected Value Theory is one of the methods which can be used to quantify the risked volumes and values of the *resources*. The expected value is the sum of all the possible outcomes of a *project*, such as volumes and values of the resources, multiplied by their respective estimated probabilities of occurrence. The expected value is not the actual value of the *contingent resources* or *prospective resources* for a particular *project* but an average of the outcomes weighted by probabilities of the outcomes. If a *reporting issuer* has a large number of similar *projects* and they are executed many times, the actual value obtained may approach the expected value. Expected value is a decision tool to decide if a *project* will go ahead.

If the expected value is in monetary terms, the calculated expected value is termed Expected Monetary Value (EMV) and it is one applicable method that can be used to estimate a risked net present value of *future net revenue*. One occurrence of a single *project* is unlikely to achieve the calculated EMV. In theory, by always choosing *projects* with the greatest positive EMV, the *reporting issuer* may achieve better results than by making more random decisions. The *COGE Handbook* states that EMV is not a projection of revenue but a tool for companies to determine whether it makes sense to proceed with a *project* to develop potential sales volumes. *Reporting issuers* will need to explain how those volumes and values were determined if included under Item 7.1 or 7.2 of *Form 51-101F1*.

Contingent resources in the *development pending project maturity sub-class* have the highest chance of development and *commerciality* of all *resources* other than *reserves*. Because there is additional uncertainty with the other *project maturity sub-classes* of *contingent resources* and *prospective resources*, disclosure of the risked net present value of *prospective resources* and *contingent resources* other than in the *development pending project maturity sub-class* should be accompanied by a detailed explanation of *chance of commerciality*, which includes both the *chance of discovery* and the *chance of development* based on economic and development-related factors (such as development plans, production forecasts, markets, facilities, capital and operating costs, product prices and approvals) in the case of *prospective resources* and *chance of development* in the case of *contingent resources*. Without disclosure relating to the *chance of discovery* and *chance of development*, disclosure of the risked net present value of *prospective resources* and *contingent resources* other than in the *development pending project maturity sub-class* may be misleading.

(5) [Repealed.]

(6) Reserves Reconciliation —

(a) If the *reporting issuer* reports *reserves*, but had no *reserves* to report at the start of the reconciliation period, a reconciliation of *reserves* must be carried out if any *reserves* added during the previous year are material. Such a reconciliation will have an opening balance of zero.

(b) The reserves reconciliation is prepared on a *gross reserves*, not *net reserves*, basis. For some *reporting issuers* with significant royalty interests, such as royalty trusts, the *net reserves* may exceed the *gross reserves*. In order to provide adequate disclosure given the distinctive nature of its business, the *reporting issuer* may also disclose its *reserves* reconciliation on a *net reserves* basis. The *reporting issuer* is not precluded from providing this additional information with its disclosure prescribed in *Form 51-101F1* provided that the *net reserves* basis for the reconciliation is clearly identified in the additional disclosure to avoid confusion.

(c) Clause 2(c)(ii) of item 4.1 of *Form 51-101F1* requires reconciliations of *reserves* to separately identify and explain reserves changes, including technical revisions. Technical revisions show changes in existing *reserves* estimates, in respect of carried-forward *properties*, over the period of the reconciliation (i.e., between estimates as at the *effective date* and the prior year's estimate) and are the result of new technical information, not the result of capital expenditure. With respect to making technical revisions, the following should be noted:

- *Infill Drilling*: It would not be acceptable to include infill drilling results as a technical revision. *Reserves* additions derived from infill drilling during the year are not attributable to revisions to the previous year's *reserves* estimates. Infill drilling *reserves* must either be included in the "extensions and improved recovery" reserve change category or in an additional stand-alone reserve change category in the reserves reconciliation labelled "infill drilling".

- *Acquisitions*: If an acquisition is made during the year, (i.e., in the period between the *effective date* and the prior year's estimate), the *reserves* estimate to be used in the reconciliation is the estimate of *reserves* at the *effective date*, not at the acquisition date, plus any *production* since the acquisition date. This *production* must be included as *production* in the reconciliation. If there has been a change in the *reserves* estimate between the acquisition date and the *effective date* other than that due to *production*, the *reporting issuer* should explain this as part of the reconciliation in a footnote to the reconciliation table.

(7) Significant Factors or Uncertainties — Item 5.2 of *Form 51-101F1* requires a *reporting issuer* to identify and discuss important economic factors or significant uncertainties that affect particular components of the *reserves data*.

Important economic factors or significant uncertainties may include *abandonment and reclamation costs*, unusually high expected *development costs* or *operating costs*, or contractual obligations to produce and sell a significant portion of *production* at prices substantially below those which could be realized but for those contractual obligations.

Incidents that lead to a significant decrease in the volume of *production* from business operations should be disclosed. This may include *production* losses due to theft and sabotage. In order to not be misleading, the decrease in the volume of *production* should be considered for disclosure when a *reporting issuer* sets out first-year *production* estimates under *Form 51-101F1* requirements.

If events subsequent to the *effective date* but prior to the preparation date have resulted in significant changes in expected future prices, such that the forecast prices reflected in the *reserves data* differ significantly from those that would be considered to be a reasonable outlook on the future around the date of the company's "statement of *reserves data* and other information", then the *reporting issuer's* statement might include, pursuant to item 5.2, a discussion of that change and its effect on the disclosed *future net revenue* estimates. It may be misleading to omit this information. Refer to subsection 2.8(3) of this Companion Policy respecting the related commentary relating to *qualified reserves evaluators or auditors*.

(8) Additional Information — As discussed in section 2.3 above and in the instructions to *Form 51-101F1*, *NI 51-101* offers flexibility in the use of the prescribed forms and the presentation of required information.

The disclosure prescribed in *Form 51-101F1* is the minimum disclosure required, subject to the *materiality* standard. *Reporting issuers* may provide additional disclosure that is not inconsistent with *NI 51-101* and not misleading.

To the extent that additional, or more detailed, disclosure can be expected to assist readers in understanding and assessing the mandatory disclosure, it is encouraged. Indeed, to the extent that additional disclosure of *material* facts is necessary in order to make mandated disclosure not misleading, a failure to provide that additional disclosure would amount to a misrepresentation.

(9) Sample Reserves Data Disclosure — Appendix 1 to this Companion Policy sets out an example of how certain of the *reserves data*, *contingent resources data* and *prospective resources data* might be presented in a manner which the *CSA* consider to be consistent with *NI 51-101* and *Form 51-101F1*. The CSA encourages *reporting issuers* to use the format presented in Appendix 1.

The sample presentation in Appendix 1 also illustrates how certain additional information not mandated under *Form 51-101F1* might be incorporated in an annual filing.

2.8 Form 51-101F2 — (1) Negative Assurance by Qualified Reserves Evaluator or Auditor — A *qualified reserves evaluator or auditor* conducting a review may wish to express only negative assurance — for example, in a statement such as "Nothing has come to my attention which would indicate that the *reserves data* have not been prepared in accordance with principles and definitions presented in the Canadian Oil and Gas Evaluation Handbook". This can be contrasted with a positive statement such as an opinion that "The *reserves data* have, in all material respects, been determined and presented in accordance with the Canadian Oil and Gas *Evaluation* Handbook and are, therefore, free of material misstatement".

The *CSA* are of the view that statements of negative assurance can be misinterpreted as providing a higher degree of assurance than is intended or warranted.

The *CSA* believe that a statement of negative assurance would constitute so *material* a departure from the report prescribed in *Form 51-101F2* as to fail to satisfy the requirements of item 2 of section 2.1 of *NI 51-101*.

In the rare case, if any, in which there are compelling reasons for making such disclosure (e.g., a prohibition on disclosure to external parties), the *CSA* believe that, to avoid providing information that could be misleading, the *reporting issuer* should include in such disclosure useful explanatory and cautionary statements. Such statements should explain the limited nature of the work undertaken by the *qualified reserves evaluator or auditor* and the limited scope of the assurance expressed, noting that it does not amount to a positive opinion.

(2) Variations in Estimates — The report prescribed by *Form 51-101F2* contains statements to the effect that variations between *reserves data*, *contingent resources data* and *prospective resources data* and actual results may be material but those estimates have been determined in accordance with the *COGE Handbook*, which has been consistently applied.

Reserves and *resources* other than *reserves* estimates are made at a point in time, being the *effective date*. A reconciliation of a *reserves* estimate to actual results is likely to show variations and the variations may be material. This variation may arise from factors such as exploration discoveries, acquisitions, divestments and economic factors that were not considered in the initial *reserves* estimate. Variations that occur with respect to *properties* that were included in both the *reserves* estimate and the actual results may be due to technical or economic factors. Any variations arising due to technical factors must be consistent with the fact that *reserves* and *resources* other than *reserves* are categorized according to the probability of their recovery.

(3) **Effective date of Evaluation** — A *qualified reserves evaluator or auditor* cannot prepare an *evaluation* using information that relates to events that occurred after the *effective date*, being the financial year-end. Information that relates to events that occurred after the year-end should not be incorporated into the forecasts. For example, information about drilling results from wells drilled in January or February, or changes in *production* that occurred after year-end date of December 31, should not be used. Even though this more recent information is available, the evaluator or auditor should not go back and change the forecast information for disclosure purposes. The forecast is to be based on the evaluator's or auditor's perception of the future as of December 31, the *effective date* of the report. Refer to subsection 2.7(4.1)(7) of this Companion Policy respecting the related commentary relating to *reporting issuers*.

2.9 Chief Executive Officer — Paragraph 2.1(3)(e) of *NI 51-101* requires a *reporting issuer* to file a report in accordance with *Form 51-101F3* that is executed by the chief executive officer. The term "chief executive officer" should be read to include the individual who has the responsiblities normally associated with this position or the person who acts in a similar capacity. This determination should be made irrespective of an individual's corporate title and whether that individual is employed directly or acts pursuant to an agreement or understanding.

2.10 Reporting Issuer Not a Corporation — If a *reporting issuer* is not a corporation, a report in accordance with *Form 51-101F3* must be executed by the persons who, in relation to the *reporting issuer*, are in a similar position or perform similar functions to the persons required to execute under paragraph 2.1(3)(e) of *NI 51-101.*.

PART 3 — RESPONSIBILITIES OF REPORTING ISSUERS AND DIRECTORS

3.1 Reserves Committee — Section 3.4 of *NI 51-101* enumerates certain responsibilities of the board of directors of a *reporting issuer* in connection with the preparation of *oil* and *gas* disclosure.

The *CSA* believe that certain of these responsibilities can in many cases more appropriately be fulfilled by a smaller group of directors who bring particular experience or abilities and an *independent* perspective to the task.

Subsection 3.5(1) of *NI 51-101* permits a board of directors to delegate responsibilities (other than the responsibility to approve the content or filing of certain documents) to a committee of directors, a majority of whose members are *independent* of management. Although subsection 3.5(1) is not mandatory, the *CSA* encourage *reporting issuers* and their directors to adopt this approach.

3.2 Responsibility for Disclosure — *NI 51-101* requires the involvement of an *independent qualified reserves evaluator or auditor* in preparing or reporting on certain *oil* and *gas* information disclosed by a *reporting issuer*, and in section 3.2 mandates the appointment of an *independent qualified reserves evaluator or auditor* to report on *reserves data* and *resources* other than *reserves* data.

The *CSA* do not intend or believe that the involvement of an *independent qualified reserves evaluator or auditor* relieves the *reporting issuer* of responsibility for information disclosed by it for the purposes of *NI 51-101*.

PART 4 — MEASUREMENT

4.1 Consistency in Dates — Section 4.2 of *NI 51-101* requires consistency in the timing of recording the effects of events or transactions for the purposes of both annual financial statements and annual *reserves data* disclosure.

To ensure that the effects of events or transactions are recorded, disclosed or otherwise reflected consistently (in respect of timing) in all public disclosure, a *reporting issuer* will wish to ensure that both its financial auditors and its *qualified reserves evaluators or auditors*, as well as its directors, are kept apprised of relevant events and transactions, and to facilitate communication between its financial auditors and its *qualified reserves evaluators or auditors*.

Sections 4 and 12 of volume 1 of the *COGE Handbook* set out procedures and guidance for the conduct of *reserves evaluations* and *reserves* audits, respectively. Section 12 deals with the relationship between a *reserves* auditor and the client's financial auditor. Section 4, in connection with *reserves evaluations*, deals somewhat differently with the relationship between the *qualified reserves evaluator or auditor* and the client's financial auditor. The *CSA* recommend that *qualified reserves evaluators or auditors* carry out the procedures discussed in both sections 4 and 12 of volume 1 of the *COGE Handbook*, whether conducting a *reserves evaluation* or a *reserves* audit.

PART 5 — REQUIREMENTS APPLICABLE TO ALL DISCLOSURE

5.1 Application of Part 5 — (1) **Genreal** — Part 5 of *NI 51-101* imposes requirements and restrictions that apply to all "disclosure" (or, in some cases, all written disclosure) of a type described in section 5.1 of NI 51-101. Section 5.1 refers to disclosure that is either

- filed by a *reporting issuer* with the *securities regulatory authority*, or
- if not filed, otherwise made available to the public or made in circumstances in which, at the time of making the disclosure, the *reporting issuer* expects, or ought reasonably to expect, the disclosure to become available to the public.

As such, Part 5 applies to a broad range of disclosure including

- the annual filings required under Part 2 of *NI 51-101*,
- other continuous disclosure filings, including material change reports (which themselves may also be subject to Part 6 of *NI 51-101*),
- public disclosure documents, whether or not filed, including news releases,
- public disclosure made in connection with a distribution of securities, including a prospectus, and
- except in respect of provisions of Part 5 that apply only to written disclosure, public speeches and presentations made by representatives of the *reporting issuer* on behalf of the *reporting issuer*.

For these purposes, the *CSA* consider written disclosure to include any writing, map, plot or other printed representation whether produced, stored or disseminated on paper or electronically. For example, if material distributed at a company presentation refers to *BOE*s, the material should be prepared in accordance with section 5.14 of *NI 51-101*.

To ensure compliance with the requirements of Part 5, the *CSA* encourage *reporting issuers* to involve a *qualified reserves evaluator or auditor*, or other person who is familiar with *NI 51-101* and the *COGE Handbook*, in the preparation, review or approval of all such *oil* and *gas* disclosure.

(2) Supplementary Resources Disclosure — All public disclosure of *reserves* or *resources* other than *reserves* made by a *reporting issuer* must be made in accordance with Part 5 of *NI 51-101*. This means that *reserves* and *resources* other than *reserves* disclosed publicly by a *reporting issuer* must be evaluated in accordance with the *COGE Handbook*. A *reporting issuer* may supplement its disclosure of *reserves* or *resources* other than *reserves* *evaluated* in accordance with an alternative *resources* evaluation standard under section 5.18 of *NI 51-101*, to the extent that such disclosure is not contrary to section 5.18 of *NI 51-101*. Alternative *resources* evaluation standards that the *CSA* considers acceptable include the *SEC*'s oil and gas disclosure framework and the Petroleum Resource Management System prepared by the Society of Petroleum Engineers.

The CSA are of the view that disclosure is "required under the laws of or by a foreign jurisdiction" when, in order to access the capital markets of a foreign jurisdiction, a *reporting issuer* is required by that jurisdiction to present *reserves* or *resources* other than *reserves* disclosure in accordance with that jurisdiction's resources evaluation standard.

If a reporting issuer re-discloses a *reserves* or *resources* other than *reserves* estimate that has been provided in response to the laws of a foreign jurisdiction in public disclosure that has not been required by a foreign jurisdiction (for example, in a news release), a *reporting issuer* will need to consider whether there is sufficient context in the non-required disclosure to allow a reader of that document to appreciate the nature of the alternative *resources* evaluation standard and the differences between the estimate prepared under NI 51-101 and the alternative *resources* evaluation standard.

Paragraphs 5.18(2)(b) and (3)(c) of NI 51-101 require a description of the differences between an estimate prepared under an alternative *resources* evaluation standard and an estimate prepared under *NI 51-101* and the *COGE Handbook*, and the reasons for those differences, but does not require an actual reconciliation of those estimates.

5.2 Disclosure of Reserves and Other Information — (1) General — A *reporting issuer* must comply with the requirements of section 5.2 of *NI 51-101* in its disclosure, to the public, of *reserves* estimates and other information of a type specified in *Form 51-101F1*. This would include, for example, disclosure of such information in a news release.

(2) Reserves — *NI 51-101* does not prescribe any particular methods of estimation but it does require that a *reserves* estimate be prepared in accordance with the *COGE Handbook*.

(3) Possible Reserves — A *possible reserves* estimate — either alone or as part of a sum — is often a relatively large number that, by definition, has a low probability of actually being recovered. For this reason, the cautionary language prescribed in subparagraph 5.2(1)(a)(v) of *NI 51-101* must accompany the written disclosure of a *possible reserves* estimate.

(4) Probabilistic and Deterministic Evaluation Methods — Section 5 of volume 1 of the *COGE Handbook* states that "In principle, there should be no difference between estimates prepared using probabilistic or deterministic methods".

When deterministic methods are used, in the absence of a "mathematically derived quantitative measure of probability", the classification of *reserves* is based on professional judgment as to the quantitative measure of certainty attained.

When probabilistic methods are used in conjunction with good engineering and geological practice, they will provide more statistical information than the conventional deterministic method. The following are a few critical criteria that an evaluator must satisfy when applying probabilistic methods:

- The evaluator must still estimate the *reserves* and *resources* other than *reserves* applying the definitions and using the guidelines set out in the *COGE Handbook*.
- Entity level probabilistic *reserves* and *resources* other than *reserves* estimates should be aggregated arithmetically to provide reported level *reserves* and *resources* other than *reserves*.
- If the evaluator also prepares aggregate *reserves* and *resources* other than *reserves* estimates using probabilistic methods, the evaluator should explain in the *evaluation* report the method used. In particular with respect to *reserves*, the evaluator should specify what confidence levels were used at the entity, *property*, and reported (i.e., total) levels for each of proved, proved + *probable* and proved + *probable* + *possible* (if reported) *reserves*.
- If the *reporting issuer* discloses the aggregate *reserves* and *resources* other than *reserves* that the evaluator prepared using probabilistic methods, the *reporting issuer* should provide a brief explanation, near that disclosure, about the *reserves* and *resources* other than *reserves* definitions used for estimating the *reserves* and *resources* other than *reserves*, about the method that the evaluator used, and the underlying confidence levels that the evaluator applied.

(5) Availability of Funding — In assigning *reserves* to an undeveloped *property*, the *reporting issuer* is not required to have the funding available to develop the *reserves*, since they may be developed by means other than the expenditure of the *reporting issuer's* funds (for example by a farm-out or sale). *Reserves* must be estimated assuming that development of the *properties* will occur without regard to the likely availability of funding required for that *property*. See section 7 of volume 1 of the *COGE Handbook* and subparagraph 5.2(a)(iv) of *NI 51-101*.

However, item 5.3 of *Form 51-101F1* requires a *reporting issuer* to discuss its expectations as to the sources and costs of funding for estimated future *development costs*. If the costs of funding would make development of a *property* unlikely, then even if *reserves* were assigned, the *reporting issuer* must also discuss that expectation and its plans for the *property*.

Disclosure of an estimate of *reserves*, *contingent resources* or *prospective resources* in respect of which timely availability of funding for development is not assured may be misleading if that disclosure is not accompanied, proximate to it, by a discussion (or a cross-reference to such a discussion in other disclosure filed by the *reporting issuer* on *SEDAR*) of funding uncertainties and their anticipated effect on the timing or completion of such development (or on any particular stage of multi-stage development such as often observed in oil sands developments).

(6) Proved or Probable Undeveloped Reserves — Proved or probable *undeveloped reserves* must be reported in the year in which they are recognized. If the *reporting issuer* does not disclose the proved or probable *undeveloped reserves*, it may be omitting *material* information, thereby causing the *reserves* disclosure to be misleading. If the proved or probable *undeveloped reserves* are not disclosed to the public, then those who have a special relationship with the *reporting issuer* and know about the existence of these *reserves* would not be permitted to purchase or sell the securities of the *reporting issuer* until that information has been disclosed. If the *reporting issuer* has filed or intends to file a prospectus, the prospectus might not contain "full true and plain disclosure" of all *material* facts if it does not contain information about these proved or probable *undeveloped reserves*. *Reporting issuers* should review section 10.3 of volume 1 of the *COGE Handbook* for a discussion on what information is to be included in disclosure about these *reserves*.

(7) Mechanical Updates — So-called "mechanical updates" of *reserves* and *resources* other than *reserves* reports are sometimes created, often by rerunning previous *evaluations* with a new price deck. This is problematic since there may have been material changes other than price that may result in the report being misleading. If a *reporting issuer* discloses the results of the mechanical update it should ensure that all relevant material changes are also disclosed so that the information is not misleading.

5.3 Classification of Reserves and of Resources Other Than Reserves — Section 5.3 of *NI 51-101* requires that any disclosure of *reserves* or of *resources* other than *reserves* must apply the applicable categories and terminology set out in the *COGE Handbook*. The definitions of *resource* categories, derived from the *COGE Handbook*, are provided in the NI 51-101 Glossary. In addition, section 5.3 of *NI 51-101* requires that disclosure of *reserves* or of *resources* other than *reserves* must relate to the most specific category of *reserves* or of *resources* other than *reserves* in which the *reserves* or *resources* other than *reserves* can be classified. For instance, there are several *project maturity sub-classes* of *contingent resources* including *development pending*, *development on-hold*, *development unclarified* and *development not viable*.

Reserves can be characterized as *proved*, *probable* or *possible*, according to the probability that such quantities will actually be produced. As described in the *COGE Handbook*, *proved*, *probable* and *possible reserves* represent conservative, realistic and optimistic estimates of *reserves*, respectively. Therefore, any disclosure of *reserves* must indicate whether they are *proved*, *probable* or *possible reserves*.

Reporting issuers that disclose *resources* other than *reserves* must identify those *resources* as *discovered* or *undiscovered* except in exceptional circumstances where the most specific category is *total petroleum initially-in-place*, *discovered petroleum initially-in-place* or *undiscovered petroleum initially-in-place*, in which case the *reporting issuer* must comply with subsection 5.16(3) of *NI 51-101*.

For further guidance on disclosure of *reserves* and of *resources* other than *reserves*, see sections 5.2 and 5.5 of this Companion Policy.

5.4 Natural Gas By-Products — Section 5.5 of *NI 51-101* does not allow *natural gas liquids reserves* (*NGLs*) to be assigned prior to the *first point of sale* unless the NGLs have been extracted from the natural gas stream. If the NGLs will be extracted prior to the first point of sale, it may be appropriate to disclose NGLs reserves if there is a contract in place that explicitly provides for alternate delivery or marketing arrangements.

5.5 Future Net Revenue Not Fair Market Value — A risked or unrisked net present value of *future net revenue* is not a measure of fair market value.

5.6 Disclosure of Resources Other than Reserves — Section 4.4 of volume 1 of the *COGE Handbook* recommends the preparation of an engagement letter that specifies a "project description confirming the scope and objective of the [evaluation] project". An *evaluation* report is typically prepared for a particular purpose. *CSA* staff recommend that *reporting issuers* seek the consent of the evaluator prior to disclosing information from a report for a purpose other than which the report was prepared, or for selective disclosure from any report. A requirement for the evaluator's consent to disclose part or all of an *evaluation* is often part of this engagement letter.

5.7 Disclosure of Resources Other than Reserves — **(1) Disclosure of Resources Generally** — The disclosure of *resources*, excluding *proved* and *probable reserves*, is not mandatory under *NI 51-101*, except that a *reporting issuer* must make disclosure concerning its *unproved properties* and *resource activities* in its annual filings as described in Part 6 of Form *51-101F1*. Additional disclosure beyond this is voluntary and must comply with section 5.9 of *NI 51-101* if *anticipated results* from the *resources* other than *reserves* are voluntarily disclosed.

For prospectuses, the general securities disclosure obligation of "full, true and plain" disclosure of all *material* facts would require the disclosure of *reserves* or of *resources* other than *reserves* that are *material* to the *reporting issuer*, even if the disclosure is not mandated by *NI 51-101*. Any such disclosure should be based on supportable analysis.

Disclosure of resources other than reserves may involve the use of statistical measures that may be unfamiliar to a user. It is the responsibility of the evaluator and the reporting issuer to be familiar with these measures and for the reporting issuer to be able to explain them to investors. Information on statistical measures may be found in the COGE Handbook (section 9 of volume 1 and section 4 of volume 2) and in the extensive technical literature[1] on the subject.

(2) Disclosure of Anticipated Results under Subsection 5.9(1) of NI 51-101 — If a *reporting issuer* voluntarily discloses *anticipated results* from *resources* that are not classified as *reserves*, it must disclose certain basic information concerning the *resources*, which is set out in subsection 5.9(1) of *NI 51-101*. Additional disclosure requirements arise if the *anticipated results* disclosed by the *reporting issuer* include an estimate of a *resource* quantity or associated value, as set out below in subsection 5.7(3).

If a *reporting issuer* discloses *anticipated results* relating to numerous aggregated *properties*, *prospects* or *resources*, the *reporting issuer* may, depending on the circumstances, satisfy the requirements of subsection 5.9(1) by providing summarized information in respect of each prescribed requirement. The *reporting issuer* must ensure that its disclosure is reasonable, meaningful and at a level appropriate to its size.

For a *reporting issuer* with a few *properties*, it may be appropriate to make the disclosure for each *property*. For a *reporting issuer* with many *properties*, and it may be more appropriate to summarize the information by major areas or for major *projects*. However, the convenience of aggregating *properties* will not justify disclosure of *resources* in a category specific than required to be disclosed by subsection 5.3 of *NI 51-101*.

Section 9 of volume 1 of the *COGE Handbook* provides the following definition of uncertainty:

"Uncertainty is used to describe the range of possible outcomes of a reserves estimate."

However, the concept of uncertainty is generally applicable to any estimate, including not only *reserves*, but also to all other categories of *resources*.

In satisfying the requirement of paragraph 5.9(1)(d) of *NI 51-101*, a *reporting issuer* should ensure that their disclosure includes the risks and uncertainties that are appropriate and meaningful for their activities. This may be expressed quantitatively as probabilities or qualitatively by appropriate description. If the *reporting issuer* chooses to express the risks and level of uncertainty qualitatively, the disclosure must be meaningful and not in the nature of a general disclaimer.

If the *reporting issuer* discloses the estimated value of an *unproved property* other than a value attributable to an estimated *resource* quantity, then the *reporting issuer* must disclose the basis of the calculation of the value, in accordance with paragraph 5.9(1)(e) of *NI 51-101*. This type of value is typically based on *petroleum* land management practices that consider activities and land prices in nearby areas. If done *independently*, it would be done by a valuator with petroleum land management expertise who would generally be a member of a *professional organization* such as the Canadian Association of Petroleum Landmen. This is distinguishable from the determination of a value attributable to an estimated *resource* quantity, as contemplated in subsection 5.9(2) of *NI 51-101*. This latter type of value estimate must be prepared by a *qualified reserves evaluator or auditor*.

---

[1]For example, Determination of Oil and Gas Reserves, Monograph No. 1, Chapter 22, Petroleum Society of CIM, Second Edition 2004. (ISBN 0-9697990-2-0) Newendorp, P., & Schuyler, J., 2000, Decision Analysis for Petroleum Exploration, Planning Press, Aurora, Colorado (ISBN 0-9664401-1-0). Rose, P. R., Risk Analysis and Management of Petroleum Exploration Ventures, AAPG Methods in Exploration Series No. 12, AAPG (ISBN 0-89181-062-1).

The calculation of an estimated value described in paragraph 5.9(1)(e) of *NI 51-101* may be based on one or more of the following factors

- the acquisition cost of the *unproved property* to the *reporting issuer*, provided there have been no *material* changes in the *unproved property*, the surrounding *properties*, or the general *oil* and *gas* economic climate since acquisition;
- recent sales by others of interests in the same *unproved property*;
- terms and conditions, expressed in monetary terms, of recent farm-in agreements related to the *unproved property*;
- terms and conditions, expressed in monetary terms, of recent work commitments related to the *unproved property*;
- recent sales of similar *properties* in the same general area;
- recent exploration and discovery activity in the general area;
- the remaining term of the *unproved property*; or
- burdens (such as overriding royalties) that impact on the value of the *property*.

The *reporting issuer* must disclose the basis of the calculation of the value of the *unproved property*, which may include one or more of the above-noted factors.

The *reporting issuer* must also disclose whether the value was prepared by an *independent* party. In circumstances in which paragraph 5.9(1)(e) of *NI 51-101* applies and where the value is prepared by an *independent* party, in order to ensure that the *reporting issuer* is not making public disclosure of misleading information, the *CSA* expect the *reporting issuer* to provide all relevant information to the valuator to enable the valuator to prepare the estimate.

(3) Disclosure of an Estimate of Quantity or Associated Value of a Resource under Subsection 5.9(2) of NI 51-101 —

(a) Pursuant to subsection 5.9(2) of *NI 51-101*, if a *reporting issuer* discloses an estimate of a *resource* quantity or an associated value, the estimate must have been prepared by a *qualified reserves evaluator or auditor*. *Contingent resources data* and *prospective resources data* disclosed as an appendix (see Instruction 1 of Part 7 of *Form 51-101F1*) to the statement required under item 1 of section 2.1 of *NI 51-101* must have been prepared by an *independent qualified reserves evaluator or auditor*.

If a *reporting issuer* provides disclosure of *reserves data*, *contingent resources data* or *prospective resources data* outside of its annual required filings under section 2.1 of *NI 51-101* and wishes to file or disseminate a report in a format comparable to that prescribed in *Form 51-101F2*, it may do so. However, the title of such a form should not contain the term "*Form 51-101 F2*" as this form is specific to the report required by item 2 of section of 2.1 of *NI 51-101*. A heading such as "Report on Resource Estimate by Independent Qualified Reserves Evaluator or Auditor" may be appropriate. Although such an evaluation is required to be carried out by a *qualified reserves evaluator or auditor*, there is no requirement that it be *independent*. If an *independent* party does not prepare the report, *reporting issuers* should consider amending the title or content of the report to make it clear that the report has not been prepared by an *independent* party and the *resources* estimate is not an independent *resources* estimate.

Pursuant to section 5.3 of *NI 51-101*, the *reporting issuer* must ensure that the estimated *resources* relate to the most specific applicable category of *resources* in which the resources can be classified. As discussed above in subsection 5.7(2) of this Companion Policy, if a *reporting issuer* wishes to disclose an aggregate *resources* estimate which involves the aggregation of numerous *properties*, *prospects* or *resources*, it must ensure that the disclosure does not result in a contravention of the requirement in subsection 5.3(1) of *NI 51-101*. A *reporting issuer* should be aware that the disclosure of the summation of volumes from an economic *project* with an un-economic *project* may be misleading.

Subsection 5.9(2) of *NI 51-101* requires the *reporting issuer* to disclose certain information in addition to that prescribed in subsection 5.9(1) of *NI 51-101* to assist recipients of the disclosure in understanding the nature of risks associated with the estimate. This information includes a definition of the *resource* category used for the estimate, disclosure of factors relevant to the estimate and cautionary language.

(b) Definitions of Resource Categories — For the purpose of complying with the requirement of defining the *resource* category, the *reporting issuer* must ensure that disclosure of the definition is consistent with the *resource* categories and terminology set out in the *COGE Handbook*, pursuant to section 5.3 of *NI 51-101* and the *NI 51-101 Glossary*. Section 5 of volume 1 and section 2 of volume 2 of the COGE Handbook and the NI 51-101 Glossary identify and define the various classes, *sub-classes* and *categories* of *resources*.

By definition, *reserves* of any type, *contingent resources* and *prospective resources* are estimates of volumes that are recoverable or potentially recoverable . Terms such as "potential *reserves*", "undiscovered *reserves*", "*reserves* in place", "in-place *reserves*" or similar terms must not be used because they are incorrect and misleading. The disclosure of *reserves* or of *resources* other than *reserves* must be consistent with the terminology and categories set out in the *COGE Handbook*, pursuant to section 5.3 of *NI 51-101*.

In addition to disclosing the most specific applicable category of *resources*, the *reporting issuer* may disclose *total petroleum initially-in-place*, *discovered petroleum initially-in-place* or *undiscovered petroleum initially-in-place* estimates provided that the additional disclosure required by subsection 5.16(3) of *NI 51-101* is included.

(c) Application of Subsection 5.9(2) of NI 51-101 — *Reporting issuers* are required to disclose significant positive and negative factors relevant to the estimate pursuant to subparagraph 5.9(2)(d)(iii) of *NI 51-101*. For example, if there is no infrastructure in the region to transport the *resources*, this may constitute a significant negative factor relevant to the estimate. Other examples would include *abandonment and reclamation costs*, a significant lease expiry, theft and sabotage as discussed in section 2.7(7) of this Companion Policy, or any legal, capital, political, technological, business or other factor that is highly relevant to the estimate. To the extent that the *reporting issuer* discloses an estimate for numerous properties that are aggregated, it may disclose significant positive and negative factors relevant to the aggregate estimate, unless discussion of a particular *material property* or *resources* is warranted in order to provide adequate disclosure to investors.

The cautionary language in subparagraph 5.9(2)(d)(v) of *NI 51-101* includes a prescribed disclosure that there is no certainty that it will be *commercially* viable to produce any portion of the *resources*. The concept of *commercial* viability would incorporate the criteria for determining *commerciality* provided in section 5.3 of volume 1 of the *COGE Handbook*.

5.8 Analogous Information — A *reporting issuer* may wish to base an estimate on, or include comparative *analogous information* for their area of interest, such as *reserves*, *resources*, and *production*, from fields or wells, in nearby or geologically similar areas. Particular care must be taken in using and presenting this type of information. For the purposes of *NI 51-101*, *CSA* staff interpret a field to be limited to a single pool or a grouping of several pools within the geographic area or administrative unit from which *product types* can reasonably be recovered. Using only the best wells or fields in an area, or ignoring dry holes, for instance, may be particularly misleading. It is important to present a factual and balanced view of the information being provided.

The *reporting issuer* must comply with the disclosure requirements of section 5.10 of *NI 51-101*, when it discloses *analogous information*, as that term is broadly defined in *NI 51-101*, for an area which includes the *reporting issuer's* area of interest. Pursuant to subsection 5.10(2) of *NI 51-101*, if the *reporting issuer* discloses an estimate of its own *reserves* or *resources* other than *reserves* based on an extrapolation from the *analogous information*, or if the *analogous information* itself is an estimate of its own *reserves* or *resources*, the *reporting issuer* must ensure the estimate is prepared in accordance with the *COGE Handbook* and disclosed in accordance with *NI 51-101* generally. For example, in respect of a *reserves* or *resources* other than *reserves* estimate, the estimate must be classified and prepared in accordance with the *COGE Handbook* by a *qualified reserves evaluator or auditor* and must otherwise comply with the requirements of section 5.2 of *NI 51-101*.

5.8.1 Consistent Use of Units of Measurement — *Reporting issuers* should be consistent in their use of units of measurement within and between disclosure documents, to facilitate understanding and comparison of the disclosure. For example, *reporting issuers* should not, without compelling reason, switch between imperial units of measure (such as barrels) and Système International (SI) units of measurement (such as tonnes) within or between disclosure documents. *Reporting issuers* should refer to appendices B and C of volume 1 of the *COGE Handbook* for the proper reporting of units of measurement

In all cases, in accordance with subparagraph 5.2(1)(a)(iii) and section 5.3 of *NI 51-101*, *reporting issuers* should apply the relevant terminology and unit prefixes set out in the *COGE Handbook*.

5.8.2 Oil and Gas Metrics — BOEs and McfGEs — Section 5.14 of *NI 51-101* sets out requirements that apply to all *oil and gas metrics*, including the disclosure of *reserves* or *resources* other than *reserves* by a *reporting issuer* using units of equivalency such as *BOEs* or *McfGEs*. A commonly used conversion ratio in the *oil* and *gas* industry is 6 *Mcf* of *gas* to 1 *bbl* of *oil*. If a *reporting issuer* uses a 6 *Mcf* to 1 *bbl* ratio, in order to satisfy paragraph 5.14(1)(d) of *NI 51-101*, the *reporting issuer* should provide a cautionary statement to the following effect:

BOEs [or *McfGEs* or other applicable units of equivalency] may be misleading particularly if used in isolation. A BOE conversion ratio of 6 Mcf: 1 *bbl* [or "A McfGE conversion ratio of 1 *bbl*: 6 Mcf"] is based on an energy equivalency conversion method primarily applicable at the burner tip and does not represent a value equivalency at the wellhead.

When the value ratio is significantly different from the energy equivalency of 6:1; the disclosure may be misleading without additional information.

Results using conversion ratios other than 6:1 may be disclosed, provided an explanation is given. Section 13 of volume 1 of the *COGE Handbook*, under the heading "Barrels of Oil Equivalent", provides additional guidance.

Net Asset Value, Reserve Replacement and Netbacks — If a *reporting issuer* discloses net asset value, *reserves* replacement or netbacks, additional disclosure will be required by paragraphs 5.14(1)(b) and 5.14(2)(a) of *NI 51-101*. For example, if a *reporting issuer* discloses

(a) net asset value or net asset value per share, it would be required to include a description of the methods used to value assets and liabilities and the number of shares used in the calculation,

(b) *reserves* replacement, it would be required to include an explanation of the method of calculation applied, or

(c) netback, it would be required to reflect netbacks calculated by subtracting royalties and operating costs from revenues and state the method of calculation.

5.9 Finding and Development Costs — Section 5.14 of *NI 51-101* sets out requirements that would apply if a *reporting issuer* discloses finding and *development costs*.

If a *reporting issuer* discloses finding and *development costs*, it must, pursuant to paragraphs 5.14(1)(b) and 5.14(2)(a) of *NI 51-101* include the method of calculation, the results of the calculation and if the disclosure also includes a result derived using any other method of calculation, a description of that method and the reason for its use.

5.9.1 Summation of Resource Categories — An estimate of quantity or an estimate of value constitutes a summation, disclosure of which is prohibited by subsection 5.16(1) of NI 51-101, if that estimate reflects a combination of estimates, known or available to the *reporting issuer*, for two or more of the subcategories enumerated in that provision. There may be circumstances in which a disclosed estimate was arrived at in accordance with the *COGE Handbook* without combining, and without the *reporting issuer* knowing or having access to, estimates in two or more of those enumerated categories. Disclosure of such an estimate would not generally be considered to constitute a summation for purposes of that provision.

5.10 Prospectus Disclosure — In addition to the general disclosure requirements in *NI 51-101* which apply to prospectuses, the following commentary provides additional guidance on topics of frequent enquiry.

(1) **Significant Acquisitions** — To the extent that a *reporting issuer* engaged in *oil and gas activities* discloses a significant acquisition in its prospectus, it must disclose sufficient information for a reader to determine how the acquisition affected the *reserves data* and other information previously disclosed in the *reporting issuer's Form 51-101F1*. This requirement stems from Part 6 of *NI 51-101* with respect to material changes. This is in addition to specific prospectus requirements for financial information satisfying significant acquisitions.

(2) **Disclosure of Resources** — The disclosure of *resources*, excluding proved and *probable reserves*, is generally not mandatory under *NI 51-101*, except for certain disclosure concerning the *reporting issuer's* unproved *properties* and *resource* activities as described in Part 6 of *Form 51-101F1*, which information would be incorporated into the prospectus. Additional disclosure beyond this is voluntary and must comply with Part 5 of *NI 51-101*, as applicable. However, the general securities disclosure obligation of "full, true, and plain" disclosure of all *material* facts in a prospectus would require the disclosure of *resources* that are *material* to the *reporting issuer*, even if the disclosure is not mandated by *NI 51-101*.

(3) **Proved or Probable Undeveloped Reserves** — Further to the guidance provided in subsection 5.2(6) of this Companion Policy, proved or probable *undeveloped reserves* must be reported in the year in which they are recognized. If the *reporting issuer* does not disclose the proved or probable *undeveloped reserves* just because it has not yet spent the capital to develop these *reserves*, it may be omitting *material* information, thereby causing the *reserves* disclosure to be misleading. If the *reporting issuer* has filed or intends to file a prospectus, the prospectus might not contain "full, true and plain disclosure" of all *material* facts if it does not contain information about these *proved undeveloped reserves*.

(4) **Reserves Reconciliation in an Initial Public Offering** — In an initial public offering, if the *reporting issuer* does not have a *reserves* report as at its prior year-end, or if this report does not provide the information required to carry out a *reserves* reconciliation pursuant to item 4.1 of *Form 51-101F1*, the *CSA* may consider granting relief from the requirement to provide the *reserves* reconciliation. A condition of the relief may include a description in the prospectus of relevant changes in any of the *reserve* change categories of the *reserves* reconciliation.

(5) **Relief to Provide More Recent Form 51-101F1 Information in a Prospectus** — If a *reporting issuer* is filing a preliminary prospectus and wishes to disclose *reserves data* and other *oil* and *gas* information as at a more recent date than its applicable year-end date, the *CSA* may consider relieving the *reporting issuer* of the requirement to disclose the *reserves data* and other information as at year-end.

A *reporting issuer* may determine that its obligation to provide "full, true and plain disclosure" obliges it to include in its prospectus *reserves data* and other *oil* and *gas* information as at a date more recent than specified in the prospectus requirements. The prospectus requirements state that the information must be as at the *reporting issuer's* most recent financial year-end in respect of which the prospectus includes financial statements.

CSA staff may consider granting relief on a case-by-case basis to permit a *reporting issuer* in these circumstances to include in its prospectus the *oil* and *gas* information prepared with an *effective date* more recent than the financial year-end date, without also including the corresponding information effective as at the year-end date. A consideration for granting this relief may include disclosure of *Form 51-101F1* information with an *effective date* that coincides with the date of interim financial statements. The *reporting issuer* should request such relief in the covering letter accompanying its preliminary prospectus. The grant of the relief would be evidenced by the prospectus receipt.

PART 6 — MATERIAL CHANGE DISCLOSURE

6.1 Changes from Filed Information — Part 6 of *NI 51-101* requires the inclusion of specified information in disclosure of certain material changes.

The information to be filed each year under Part 2 of *NI 51-101* is prepared as at, or for a period ended on, the *reporting issuer's* most recent financial year-end. That date is the *effective date* referred to in subsection 6.1(1) of *NI 51-101*. When a material change occurs after that date, the filed information may no longer, as a result of the material change, convey meaningful information, or the original information may have become misleading in the absence of updated information.

Part 6 of *NI 51-101* requires that the disclosure of the material change include a discussion of the *reporting issuer's* reasonable expectation of how the material change has affected the *reporting issuer's reserves data* and other information contained in its filed disclosure. This would not necessarily require that an *evaluation* be carried out. However, the *reporting issuer* should ensure it complies with the general disclosure requirements set out in Part 5, as applicable. For example, if the material change report discloses an updated *reserves* estimate, this should be prepared in accordance with the *COGE Handbook* and by a qualified reserves evaluator or auditor. The continuity of ongoing disclosure, including the disclosure of material changes as they happen, is an important factor in keeping investors informed of a *reporting issuer's* business.

This *material* change disclosure can reduce the likelihood of investors being misled, and maintain the usefulness of the original filed *oil* and *gas* information when the two are read together.

APPENDIX 1

Appendix 1 to Companion Policy 51-101 Standards of Disclosure for Oil and Gas Activities — Sample Reserves Data Disclosure

Format of Disclosure

NI 51-101 and *Form 51-101F1* do not mandate the format of the disclosure of *reserves data* and related information by *reporting issuers*. However, the *CSA* encourages *reporting issuers* to use the format presented in this Appendix.

Whatever format and level of detail a *reporting issuer* chooses to use in satisfying the requirements of *NI 51-101*, the objective should be to enable reasonable investors to understand and assess the information, and compare it to corresponding information presented by the *reporting issuer* for other reporting periods or to similar information presented by other *reporting issuers*, in order to be in a position to make informed investment decisions concerning securities of the *reporting issuer*.

A logical and legible layout of information, use of descriptive headings, and consistency in terminology and presentation from document to document and from period to period, are all likely to further that objective.

Reporting issuers and their advisers are reminded of the *materiality* standard under section 1.4 of *NI 51-101*, and of the instructions in *Form 51-101F1*.

See also sections 1.4, 2.2 and 2.3 and subsections 2.7(8) and 2.7(9) of Companion Policy 51-101.

Sample Tables

The following sample tables provide an example of how certain of the *reserves data* might be presented in a manner consistent with *NI 51-101*.

These sample tables do not reflect all of the information required by *Form 51-101F1*, and they have been simplified to reflect reserves in one country only. For the purpose of illustration, the sample tables also incorporate information not mandated by *NI 51-101* but which *reporting issuers* might wish to include in their disclosure; shading indicates this non-mandatory information.

SUMMARY OF OIL AND GAS RESERVES
as of December 31, 2015
FORECAST PRICES AND COSTS

RESERVES CATEGORY	RESERVES[(1)]							
	LIGHT CRUDE OIL AND MEDIUM CRUDE OIL		HEAVY CRUDE OIL		CONVENTIONAL NATURAL GAS		NATURAL GAS LIQUIDS	
	Gross (Mbbl)	Net (Mbbl)	Gross (Mbbl)	Net (Mbbl)	Gross (MMcf)	Net (MMcf)	Gross (Mbbl)	Net (Mbbl)
PROVED								
Developed Producing	xx	xx	xx	xx	xx	xx	xx	xx
Developed Non-Producing	xx	xx	xx	xx	xx	xx	xx	xx
Undeveloped	xx	xx	xx	xx	xx	xx	xx	xx
TOTAL PROVED	xxx	xxx	xxx	xxx	xxx	xxx	xxx	xxx
PROBABLE	xx	xx	xx	xx	xx	xx	xx	xx
TOTAL PROVED PLUS PROBABLE	xxx	xxx	xxx	xxx	xxx	xxx	xxx	xxx

(1) Other *product types* must be added if *material*.

SUMMARY OF NET PRESENT VALUE OF FUTURE NET REVENUE
as of December 31, 2015
FORECAST PRICES AND COSTS

RESERVES CATEGORY	NET PRESENT VALUE OF FUTURE NET REVENUE										UNIT VALUE BEFORE INCOME TAXES DISCOUNTED AT 10%/year	
	BEFORE INCOME TAXES DISCOUNTED AT (%/year)					AFTER INCOME TAXES DISCOUNTED AT (%/year)						
	0 (MM$)	5 (MM$)	10 (MM$)	15 (MM$)	20 (MM$)	0 (MM$)	5 (MM$)	10 (MM$)	15 (MM$)	20 (MM$)	($/Mcf)	($/bbl)
PROVED												
Developed Producing	xx	xx	xx	xx	xx	xx	xx	xx	xx	xx	xx	
Developed Non-Producing	xx	xx	xx	xx	xx	xx	xx	xx	xx	xx	xx	
Undeveloped	xx	xx	xx	xx	xx	xx	xx	xx	xx	xx	xx	
TOTAL PROVED	xxx	xxx	xxx	xxx	xxx	xxx	xxx	xxx	xxx	xxx	xx	
PROBABLE	xx	xx	xx	xx	xx	xx	xx	xx	xx	xx	xx	
TOTAL PROVED PLUS PROBABLE	xxxx	xxxx	xxxx	xxxx	xxxx	xxxx	xxxx	xxxx	xxxx	xxxx	xxx	

(1) A *reporting issuer* may wish to satisfy its requirement to disclose these unit values by inserting this disclosure for each category of *proved reserves* and *probable reserves*, by *product type*, in the chart for item 2.1(3)(c) of *Form 51-101F1* (see sample chart below entitled Future Net Revenue by Product Type).
(2) The unit values are based on *net reserves* volumes.

Reference: Item 2.1(1) and (2) of *Form 51-101F1*

TOTAL FUTURE NET REVENUE
(UNDISCOUNTED)
as of December 31, 2015
FORECAST PRICES AND COSTS

RESERVES CATEGORY	REVENUE (M$)	ROYALTIES (M$)	OPERATING COSTS (M$)	DEVELOPMENT COSTS (M$)	ABANDONMENT AND RECLAMATION COSTS (M$)	FUTURE NET REVENUE BEFORE INCOME TAXES (M$)	INCOME TAXES (M$)	FUTURE NET REVENUE AFTER INCOME TAXES (M$)
Proved Reserves	xxx	xxx	xxx	xxx	xxx	xxx	xxx	xxx
Proved Plus Probable Reserves	xxx	xxx	xxx	xxx	xxx	xxx	xxx	xxx

Reference: Item 2.1(3)(b) of *Form 51-101F1*

FUTURE NET REVENUE
BY PRODUCT TYPE as of December 31, 2015
FORECAST PRICES AND COSTS

RESERVES CATEGORY	PRODUCT TYPE	FUTURE NET REVENUE BEFORE INCOME TAXES (discounted at 10%/year) (M$)	UNIT VALUE ($/Mcf) ($/bbl)
Proved Reserves	Bitumen	xxx	xxx
	Coal Bed Methane	xxx	xxx
	Conventional Natural Gas (including by-products but excluding solution gas and by-products from oil wells)	xxx	xxx
	Gas Hydrates	xxx	xxx
	Heavy Crude Oil (including solution gas and other by-products)	xxx	xxx
	Light Crude Oil and Medium Crude Oil (including solution gas and other by-products)	xxx	xxx
	Natural Gas Liquids	xxx	xxx
	Shale Gas	xxx	xxx
	Synthetic Crude Oil	xxx	xxx
	Synthetic Gas	xxx	xxx
	Tight Oil	xxx	xxx
	Total	xxx	xxx
Proved Plus Probable Reserves	Bitumen	xxx	xxx
	Coal Bed Methane	xxx	xxx
	Conventional Natural Gas (including by-products but excluding solution gas and by-products from oil wells)	xxx	xxx
	Gas Hydrates	xxx	xxx
	Heavy Crude Oil (including solution gas and other by-products)	xxx	xxx
	Light Crude Oil and Medium Crude Oil (including solution gas and other by-products)	xxx	xxx
	Natural Gas Liquids	xxx	xxx
	Shale Gas	xxx	xxx
	Synthetic Crude Oil	xxx	xxx
	Synthetic Gas	xxx	xxx
	Tight Oil	xxx	xxx
	Total	xxx	xxx

Reference: Item 2.1(3)(c) of Form 51-101F1

SUMMARY OF PRICING ASSUMPTIONS
as of December 31, 2015
CONSTANT PRICES AND COSTS[1]

Year	OIL[2]				NATURAL GAS[2] AECO Gas Price ($Cdn/MMBtu)	NATURAL GAS LIQUIDS FOB Field Gate ($Cdn/bbl)	EXCHANGE RATE[3] ($US/$Cdn)
	WTI Cushing Oklahoma ($US/bbl)	Edmonton Par/Mixed Sweet Blend Price 40° API ($Cdn/bbl)	Hardisty Heavy 12° API ($Cdn/bbl)	Cromer Medium 29.3° API ($Cdn/bbl)			
Historical (Year End)							
2012	xx	xx	xx	xx	xx	xx	xx
2013	xx	xx	xx	xx	xx	xx	xx
2014	xx	xx	xx	xx	xx	xx	xx
2015 (Year End)	xx	xx	xx	xx	xx	xx	xx

(1) This disclosure is triggered by optional supplementary disclosure of item 2.2 of *Form 51-101F1*.
(2) This summary table identifies benchmark reference pricing schedules that might apply to a *reporting issuer*.
(3) The exchange rate used to generate the benchmark reference prices in this table.

Reference: Item 3.1 of *Form 51-101 F1*

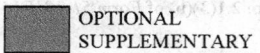 OPTIONAL SUPPLEMENTARY

SUMMARY OF PRICING AND INFLATION RATE ASSUMPTIONS
as of December 31, 2015
FORECAST PRICES AND COSTS

Year	OIL[1]				NATURAL GAS[1] AECO Gas Price ($Cdn/MMBtu)	NATURAL GAS LIQUIDS FOB Field Gate ($Cdn/bbl)	INFLATION RATES[2] %/Year	EXCHANGE RATE[3] $US/$Cdn
	WTI Cushing Oklahoma $US/bbl	Edmonton Par Price 40° API $Cdn/bbl	Hardisty Heavy 12° API $Cdn/bbl	Cromer Medium 29.3° API $Cdn/bbl				
Historical[4]								
2012	xx	xx	xx	xx	xx	xx	xx	xx
2013	xx	xx	xx	xx	xx	xx	xx	xx
2014	xx	xx	xx	xx	xx	xx	xx	xx
2015	xx	xx	xx	xx	xx	xx	xx	xx
Forecast								
2016	xx	xx	xx	xx	xx	xx	xx	xx
2017	xx	xx	xx	xx	xx	xx	xx	xx
2018	xx	xx	xx	xx	xx	xx	xx	xx
2019	xx	xx	xx	xx	xx	xx	xx	xx
2020	xx	xx	xx	xx	xx	xx	xx	xx
Thereafter	xx	xx	xx	xx	xx	xx	xx	xx

(1) This summary table identifies benchmark reference pricing schedules that might apply to a *reporting issuer*.
(2) Inflation rates for forecasting prices and costs.
(3) Exchange rates used to generate the benchmark reference prices in this table
(4) Item 3.2 (1)(b) of *Form 51-101F1* also requires disclosure of the *reporting issuer's* weighted average historical prices for the most recent financial year (2014, in this example).

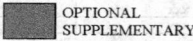 OPTIONAL SUPPLEMENTARY

Reference: Item 3.2 of *Form 51-101 F1*

**RECONCILIATION OF
COMPANY GROSS RESERVES
BY PRODUCT TYPE[1]
FORECAST PRICES AND COSTS**

FACTORS	LIGHT CRUDE OIL AND MEDIUM CRUDE OIL			HEAVY CRUDE OIL			CONVENTIONAL NATURAL GAS		
	Gross Proved (Mbbl)	Gross Probable (Mbbl)	Gross Proved Plus Probable (Mbbl)	Gross Proved (Mbbl)	Gross Probable (Mbbl)	Gross Proved Plus Probable (Mbbl)	Gross Proved (MMcf)	Gross Probable (MMcf)	Gross Proved Plus Probable (MMcf)
December 31, 2014	xxx	xxx	xxx	xxx	xxx	xxx	xxx	xxx	xxx
Extensions & Improved Recovery	xx	xx	xx	xx	xx	xx	xx	xx	xx
Technical Revisions	xx	xx	xx	xx	xx	xx	xx	xx	xx
Discoveries	xx	xx	xx	xx	xx	xx	xx	xx	xx
Acquisitions	xx	xx	xx	xx	xx	xx	xx	xx	xx
Dispositions	xx	xx	xx	xx	xx	xx	xx	xx	xx
Economic Factors	xx	xx	xx	xx	xx	xx	xx	xx	xx
Production	xx	xx	xx	xx	xx	xx	xx	xx	xx
December 31, 2015	xxx	xxx	xxx	xxx	xxx	xxx	xxx	xxx	xxx

(1) The *reserves* reconciliation must include other *product types*, including *bitumen, natural gas liquids, synthetic crude oil, coal bed methane, gas hydrates, shale gas* and *synthetic gas*, if *material* for the *reporting issuer*.

Reference: Item 4.1 of *Form 51-101F1*

**SUMMARY OF RISKED OIL AND GAS CONTINGENT RESOURCES[1]
as of December 31, 2015
FORECAST PRICES AND COSTS**

RESOURCES PROJECT MATURITY SUB-CLASS	CONTINGENT RESOURCES[2]							
	LIGHT CRUDE OIL AND MEDIUM CRUDE OIL		HEAVY CRUDE OIL		CONVENTIONAL NATURAL GAS		NATURAL GAS LIQUIDS	
	Gross (Mbbl)	Net (Mbbl)	Gross (Mbbl)	Net (Mbbl)	Gross (MMcf)	Net (MMcf)	Gross (Mbbl)	Net (Mbbl)
CONTINGENT (2C) Development Pending	xx	xx	xx	xx	xx	xx	xx	xx

(1) This disclosure is triggered by optional disclosure of *contingent resources* in the statement prepared in accordance with item 1 of section 2.1 of *NI 51-101*. Disclosure of risked estimates of volume are required under item 7.1(1)(a) of *Form 51-101F1*.
(2) Other *product types* must be added if *material*.
(3) The disclosure in this table must comply with and include the disclosure required by section 5.9 of *NI 51-101*, including section 5.9(2)(d).
(4) A *reporting issuer* should consider whether the disclosure of *development unclarified* or *development not viable sub-classes contingent resources* in the statement of *reserves data* and other *oil* and *gas* information would be misleading given the uncertainty and risk associated with those estimates. Section 2 of volume 2 of the *COGE Handbook* details *commerciality* factors.

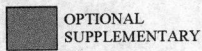 OPTIONAL SUPPLEMENTARY

Reference: Item 7.1(a) of *Form 51-101F1*

SUMMARY OF RISKED NET PRESENT VALUE OF FUTURE NET REVENUE[1]
(CONTINGENT RESOURCES)
as of December 31, 2015
FORECAST PRICES AND COSTS

An estimate of risked net present value of *future net revenue* of *contingent resources* is preliminary in nature and is provided to assist the reader in reaching an opinion on the merit and likelihood of the company proceeding with the required investment. It includes *contingent resources* that are considered too uncertain with respect to the *chance of development* to be classified as *reserves*. There is no certainty that the estimate of risked net present value of *future net revenue* will be realized.

RESOURCES PROJECT MATURITY SUB-CLASS	RISKED NET PRESENT VALUE OF FUTURE NET REVENUE									
	BEFORE INCOME TAXES DISCOUNTED AT (%/year)					AFTER INCOME TAXES DISCOUNTED AT (%/year)				
	0 (MM$)	5 (MM$)	10 (MM$)	15 (MM$)	20 (MM$)	0 (MM$)	5 (MM$)	10 (MM$)	15 (MM$)	20 (MM$)
CONTINGENT (2C) Development Pending	xx	xx	xx	xx	xx	xx	xx	xx	xx	xx

(1) This disclosure is triggered by optional disclosure of *contingent resources* in the statement prepared in accordance with item 1 of section 2.1 of *NI 51-101*.
(2) The disclosure in this table must comply with and include the disclosure required by section 5.9 of *NI 51-101*.

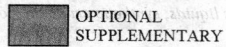 OPTIONAL SUPPLEMENTARY

Reference: Item 7.1(b) of *Form 51-101F1*

SUMMARY OF RISKED OIL AND GAS PROSPECTIVE RESOURCES[1]
as of December 31, 2015
VOLUMES

RESOURCES	PROSPECTIVE RESOURCES [2]							
	LIGHT CRUDE OIL AND MEDIUM CRUDE OIL		HEAVY CRUDE OIL		CONVENTIONAL NATURAL GAS		NATURAL GAS LIQUIDS	
	Gross (Mbbl)	Net (Mbbl)	Gross (Mbbl)	Net (Mbbl)	Gross (MMcf)	Net (MMcf)	Gross (Mbbl)	Net (Mbbl)
PROSPECTIVE (Best Estimate)	xx	xx	xx	xx	xx	xx	xx	xx

(1) This disclosure is triggered by optional disclosure of *prospective resources* in the statement prepared in accordance with item 1 of section 2.1 of *NI 51-101*. Disclosure of risked estimates of volume are required under Item 7.2(1) of *Form 51-101F1*
(2) Other *product types* must be added if *material*.
(3) The disclosure in this table must comply with and include the disclosure required by section 5.9 of *NI 51-101*
(4) A *reporting issuer* should consider whether the disclosure of *prospective resources* in the statement of *reserves data* and other *oil* and *gas* information would be misleading given the uncertainty and risk associated with those estimates.

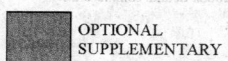 OPTIONAL SUPPLEMENTARY

Reference: Item 7.2(a) of *Form 51-101F1*

Adoption by OSC: (2003) 26 O.S.C.B. 6645 and (2003) 26 O.S.C.B. 5517; Request for Comments: (2003) 26 O.S.C.B. 587 and (2002) 25 O.S.C.B. 505.

Adoption of Amendment by OSC: (2005) 28 O.S.C.B. 10462 and 8569; Request for Comments: 28 O.S.C.B. 228.

Adoption of Revised Policy by OSC: 30 O.S.C.B. (Supp-5) 1 (October 12, 2007) and 31 O.S.C.B. 419; Request for Comments: 30 O.S.C.B. 551.

Adoption of Amendment by OSC: (2014) 37 O.S.C.B. 10771

Policies and Orders: CSAN 51-309.

National Instrument 51-102 — Continuous Disclosure Obligations

Date: March 30, 2004, as amended effective June 1, 2005, December 30, 2005, December 29, 2006, December 31, 2007, March 17, 2008, July 4, 2008, December 15, 2008, September 28, 2009, January 1, 2011, June 30, 2011, October 31, 2011, April 20, 2012, February 11, 2013, May 14, 2013, May 31, 2013, September 30, 2014, May 5, 2015, June 30, 2015 and November 17, 2015

27 O.S.C.B. 3439, 28 O.S.C.B. 4975, 28 O.S.C.B. 10384, 28 O.S.C.B. 10463, 30 O.S.C.B. (Supp. 1) 1, 30 O.S.C.B. 10499 and 10513, 31 O.S.C.B. (Supp. 2) 227, 31 O.S.C.B. 6571, 31 O.S.C.B. 10455, 31 O.S.C.B. 12047, 32 O.S.C.B. (Supp. 5) 159, 33 O.S.C.B. (Supp. 5) 43, 34 O.S.C.B. 7084, 34 O.S.C.B. 11499, 35 O.S.C.B. 2383, 35 O.S.C.B. 10709, 36 O.S.C.B. 4939, 36 O.S.C.B. 2619, 37 O.S.C.B. 6753, 38 O.S.C.B. (Supp. 1) 164, 38 O.S.C.B. 3415 and 38 O.S.C.B. 9330

[Editor's note: The following version of 51-102 reflects amendments that will come into force on June 30, 2015. For a version of this instrument without these amendments see the 57th edition of this book.]

Table of Contents

PART 1 — DEFINITIONS AND INTERPRETATION

1.1 Definitions and Interpretation — (1) In this Instrument:

"acquisition date" has the same meaning as in the issuer's GAAP;

"AIF" means a completed Form 51-102F2 *Annual Information Form* or, in the case of an SEC issuer, a completed Form 51-102F2 or an annual report or transition report under the 1934 Act on Form 10-K or Form 20-F;

"asset-backed security" means a security that is primarily serviced by the cash flows of a discrete pool of mortgages, receivables or other financial assets, fixed or revolving, that by their terms convert into cash within a finite period and any rights or other assets designed to assure the servicing or the timely distribution of proceeds to securityholders;

"board of directors" means, for a person or company that does not have a board of directors, an individual or group that acts in a capacity similar to a board of directors;

"business acquisition report" means a completed Form 51-102F4 *Business Acquisition Report*;

"class" includes a series of a class;

"common share" means an equity security to which are attached voting rights exercisable in all circumstances, irrespective of the number or percentage of securities owned, that are not less, per security, than the voting rights attached to any other outstanding securities of the reporting issuer;

"corporate law" has the same meaning as in section 1.1 of NI 54-101;

"date of transition to IFRS" means the date of transition to IFRSs as that term is defined in Canadian GAAP applicable to publicly accountable enterprises;

"designated rating organization" means

    (a) each of DBRS Limited, Fitch, Inc., Moody's Canada Inc., Standard & Poor's Ratings Services (Canada), including their DRO affiliates; or

    (b) any other credit rating organization that has been designated under securities legislation;

"DRO affiliate" has the same meaning as in section 1 of National Instrument 25-101 *Designated Rating Organizations*;

"electronic format" has the same meaning as in National Instrument 13-101 *System for Electronic Document Analysis and Retrieval (SEDAR)*;

"equity investee" means a business that the issuer has invested in and accounted for using the equity method;

"exchange-traded security" means a security that is listed on a recognized exchange or is quoted on a recognized quotation and trade reporting system or is listed on an exchange or quoted on a quotation and trade reporting system that is recognized for the purposes of National Instrument 21-101 *Marketplace Operation* and National Instrument 23-101 *Trading Rules*;

"executive officer" means, for a reporting issuer, an individual who is

    (a) a chair, vice-chair or president;

    (a.1) a chief executive officer or chief financial officer;

    (b) a vice-president in charge of a principal business unit, division or function including sales, finance or production; or

    (c) performing a policy-making function in respect of the issuer;

"financial outlook" means forward-looking information about prospective financial performance, financial position or cash flows that is based on assumptions about future economic conditions and courses of action and that is not presented in the format of a historical statement of financial position, statement of comprehensive income or statement of cash flows;

"financial statements" includes interim financial reports;

"first IFRS financial statements" has the same meaning as in Canadian GAAP applicable to publicly accountable enterprises;

"FOFI", or "future-oriented financial information", means forward-looking information about prospective financial performance, financial position or cash flows, based on assumptions about future economic conditions and courses of action, and presented in the format of a historical statement of financial position, statement of comprehensive income or statement of cash flows.

"form of proxy" means a document containing the information required under section 9.4 that, on completion and execution by or on behalf of a securityholder, becomes a proxy;

"forward-looking information" means disclosure regarding possible events, conditions or financial performance that is based on assumptions about future economic conditions and courses of action and includes future-oriented financial information with respect to prospective financial performance, financial position or cash flows that is presented either as a forecast or a projection;

"information circular" means a completed Form 51-102F5 *Information Circular*;

"informed person" means

    (a) a director or executive officer of a reporting issuer;

    (b) a director or executive officer of a person or company that is itself an informed person or subsidiary of a reporting issuer;

    (c) any person or company who beneficially owns, or controls or directs, directly or indirectly, voting securities of a reporting issuer or a combination of both carrying more than 10 percent of the voting rights attached to all outstanding voting securities of the reporting issuer other than voting securities held by the person or company as underwriter in the course of a distribution; and

    (d) a reporting issuer that has purchased, redeemed or otherwise acquired any of its securities, for so long as it holds any of its securities;

"inter-dealer bond broker" means a person or company that is approved by the Investment Industry Regulatory Organization of Canada under its Rule 36 *Inter-Dealer Bond Brokerage Systems*, as amended, and is subject to its Rule 36 and its Rule 2100 *Inter-Dealer Bond Brokerage Systems*, as amended;

"interim period" means,

    (a) in the case of a year other than a non-standard year or a transition year, a period commencing on the first day of the financial year and ending nine, six or three months before the end of the financial year;

    (a.1) in the case of a non-standard year, a period commencing on the first day of the financial year and ending within 22 days of the date that is nine, six or three months before the end of the financial year; or

    (b) in the case of a transition year, a period commencing on the first day of the transition year and ending

        (i) three, six, nine or twelve months, if applicable, after the end of the old financial year; or

        (ii) twelve, nine, six or three months, if applicable, before the end of the transition year;

"issuer's GAAP" has the same meaning as in National Instrument 52-107 *Acceptable Accounting Principles and Auditing Standards*;

"MD&A" means a completed Form 51-102F1 *Management's Discussion & Analysis* or, in the case of an SEC issuer, a completed Form 51-102F1 or management's discussion and analysis prepared in accordance with Item 303 of Regulation S-K under the 1934 Act;

"marketplace" means

    (a) an exchange;

    (b) a quotation and trade reporting system;

(c) a person or company not included in paragraph (a) or (b) that

    (i) constitutes, maintains or provides a market or facility for bringing together buyers and sellers of securities;

    (ii) brings together the orders for securities of multiple buyers and sellers; and

    (iii) uses established, non-discretionary methods under which the orders interact with each other, and the buyers and sellers entering the orders agree to the terms of a trade; or

(d) a dealer that executes a trade of an exchange-traded security outside of a marketplace,

but does not include an inter-dealer bond broker;

"material change" means

(a) a change in the business, operations or capital of the reporting issuer that would reasonably be expected to have a significant effect on the market price or value of any of the securities of the reporting issuer; or

(b) a decision to implement a change referred to in paragraph (a) made by the board of directors or other persons acting in a similar capacity or by senior management of the reporting issuer who believe that confirmation of the decision by the board of directors or any other persons acting in a similar capacity is probable;

"material contract" means any contract that an issuer or any of its subsidiaries is a party to, that is material to the issuer.

"mineral project" has the same meaning as in National Instrument 43-101 *Standards of Disclosure for Mineral Projects.*

"new financial year" means the financial year of a reporting issuer that immediately follows a transition year;

"NI 54-101" means National Instrument 54-101 *Communication with Beneficial Owners of Securities of a Reporting Issuer*;

"non-standard year" means a financial year, other than a transition year, that does not have 365 days, or 366 days if it includes February 29;

"non-voting security" means a restricted security that does not carry the right to vote generally, except for a right to vote that is mandated, in special circumstances, by law;

"notice-and-access" has the same meaning as in section 1.1 of NI 54-101;

"old financial year" means the financial year of a reporting issuer that immediately precedes a transition year;

"operating income" means gross revenue minus royalty expenses and production costs;

"preference share" means a security to which is attached a preference or right over the securities of any class of equity securities of the reporting issuer, but does not include an equity security;

"principal obligor" means, for an asset-backed security, a person or company that is obligated to make payments, has guaranteed payments, or has provided alternative credit support for payments, on financial assets that represent onethird or more of the aggregate amount owing on all of the financial assets servicing the asset-backed security;

"private enterprise" has the same meaning as in Part 3 of National Instrument 52-107 *Acceptable Accounting Principles and Auditing Standards*;

"profit or loss attributable to owners of the parent" has the same meaning as in Canadian GAAP applicable to publicly accountable enterprises;

"profit or loss from continuing operations attributable to owners of the parent" has the same meaning as in Canadian GAAP applicable to publicly accountable enterprises";

"proxy" means a completed and executed form of proxy by which a securityholder has appointed a person or company as the securityholder's nominee to attend and act for the securityholder and on the securityholder's behalf at a meeting of securityholders;

"proxy-related materials" means securityholder material relating to a meeting of securityholders that a person or company that solicits proxies is required under corporate law or securities legislation to send to the registered holders or beneficial owners of the securities;

"publicly accountable enterprise" has the same meaning as in Part 3 of National Instrument 52-107 *Acceptable Accounting Principles and Auditing Standards*;

"recognized exchange" means

(a) in Ontario, an exchange recognized by the securities regulatory authority to carry on business as a stock exchange;

(a.1) in Québec, a person or company authorized by the securities regulatory authority to carry on business as an exchange; and

(b) in every other jurisdiction, an exchange recognized by the securities regulatory authority as an exchange, selfregulatory organization or self-regulatory body;

"recognized quotation and trade reporting system" means

(a) in every jurisdiction other than British Columbia, a quotation and trade reporting system recognized by the securities regulatory authority under securities legislation to carry on business as a quotation and trade reporting system; and

(b) in British Columbia, a quotation and trade reporting system recognized by the securities regulatory authority under securities legislation as a quotation and trade reporting system or as an exchange;

"restricted security" means an equity security of a reporting issuer if any of the following apply:

(a) there is another class of securities of the reporting issuer that, to a reasonable person, appears to carry a greater number of votes per security relative to the equity security;

(b) the conditions of the class of equity securities, the conditions attached to another class of securities of the reporting issuer, or the reporting issuer's constating documents have provisions that nullify or, to a reasonable person, appear to significantly restrict the voting rights of the equity securities; or

(c) the reporting issuer has issued another class of equity securities that, to a reasonable person, appears to entitle the owners of securities of that other class to participate in the earnings or assets of the reporting issuer to a greater extent, on a per security basis, than the owners of the first class of equity securities;

"restricted security term" means each of the terms "non-voting security", "subordinate voting security" and "restricted voting security";

"restricted voting security" means a restricted security that carries a right to vote subject to a restriction on the number or percentage of securities that may be voted by one or more persons or companies, unless the restriction is

(a) permitted or prescribed by statute; and

(b) is applicable only to persons or companies that are not citizens or residents of Canada or that are otherwise considered as a result of any law applicable to the reporting issuer to be non-Canadians;

"restructuring transaction" means

(a) a reverse takeover;

(b) an amalgamation, merger, arrangement or reorganization;

(c) a transaction or series of transactions involving a reporting issuer acquiring assets and issuing securities that results in

(i) new securityholders owning or controlling more than 50% of the reporting issuer's outstanding voting securities; and

(ii) a new person or company, a new combination of persons or companies acting together, the vendors of the assets, or new management

(A) being able to materially affect the control of the reporting issuer; or

(B) holding more than 20% of the outstanding voting securities of the reporting issuer, unless there is evidence showing that the holding of those securities does not materially affect the control of the reporting issuer; and

(d) any other transaction similar to the transactions listed in paragraphs (a) to (c),

but does not include a subdivision, consolidation, or other transaction that does not alter a securityholder's proportionate interest in the issuer and the issuer's proportionate interest in its assets;

"retrospective" has the same meaning as in Canadian GAAP applicable to publicly accountable enterprises;

"retrospectively" has the same meaning as in Canadian GAAP applicable to publicly accountable enterprises;

"reverse takeover" means

(a) a reverse acquisition, which has the same meaning as in Canadian GAAP applicable to publicly accountable enterprises; or

(b) a transaction where an issuer acquires a person or company by which the securityholders of the acquired person or company, at the time of the transaction, obtain control of the issuer, where, for purposes of this paragraph, "control" has the same meaning as in Canadian GAAP applicable to publicly accountable enterprises;

"reverse takeover acquiree" means the legal parent in a reverse takeover;

"reverse takeover acquirer" means the legal subsidiary in a reverse takeover;

"SEC issuer" means an issuer that

(a) has a class of securities registered under section 12 of the 1934 Act or is required to file reports under section 15(d) of the 1934 Act; and

(b) is not registered or required to be registered as an investment company under the *Investment Company Act of 1940* of the United States of America, as amended;

"solicit", in connection with a proxy, includes

(a) requesting a proxy whether or not the request is accompanied by or included in a form of proxy;

(b) requesting a securityholder to execute or not to execute a form of proxy or to revoke a proxy;

(c) sending a form of proxy or other communication to a securityholder under circumstances that to a reasonable person will likely result in the giving, withholding or revocation of a proxy; or

(d) sending a form of proxy to a securityholder by management of a reporting issuer;

but does not include

(e) sending a form of proxy to a securityholder in response to a unsolicited request made by or on behalf of the securityholder;

(f) performing ministerial acts or professional services on behalf of a person or company soliciting a proxy;

(g) sending, by an intermediary as defined in NI 54-101, of the documents referred to in NI 54-101;

(h) soliciting by a person or company in respect of securities of which the person or company is the beneficial owner;

(i) publicly announcing, by a securityholder, how the securityholder intends to vote and the reasons for that decision, if that public announcement is made by

(i) a speech in a public forum; or

(ii) a press release, an opinion, a statement or an advertisement provided through a broadcast medium or by a telephonic, electronic or other communication facility, or appearing in a newspaper, a magazine or other publication generally available to the public;

(j) communicating for the purposes of obtaining the number of securities required for a securityholder proposal under the laws under which the reporting issuer or business is incorporated, organized or continued or under the reporting issuer's constating or establishing documents; or

(k) communicating, other than a solicitation by or on behalf of the management of the reporting issuer, to securityholders in the following circumstances:

(i) by one or more securityholders concerning the business and affairs of the reporting issuer, including its management or proposals contained in a management information circular, and no form of proxy is sent to those securityholders by the securityholder or securityholders making the communication or by a person or company acting on their behalf, unless the communication is made by

(A) a securityholder who is an officer or director of the reporting issuer if the communication is financed directly or indirectly by the reporting issuer;

(B) a securityholder who is a nominee or who proposes a nominee for election as a director, if the communication relates to the election of directors;

(C) a securityholder whose communication is in opposition to an amalgamation, arrangement, consolidation or other transaction recommended or approved by the board of directors of the reporting issuer and who is proposing or intends to propose an alternative transaction to which the securityholder or an affiliate or associate of the securityholder is a party;

(D) a securityholder who, because of a material interest in the subject-matter to be voted on at a securityholder's meeting, is likely to receive a benefit from its approval or non-approval, which benefit would not be shared *pro rata* by all other holders of the same class of securities, unless the benefit arises from the securityholder's employment with the reporting issuer; or

(E) any person or company acting on behalf of a securityholder described in any of clauses (A) to (D);

(ii) by one or more securityholders and concerns the organization of a dissident's proxy solicitation, and no form of proxy is sent to those securityholders by the securityholder or securityholders making the communication or by a person or company acting on their behalf;

(iii) as clients, by a person or company who gives financial, corporate governance or proxy voting advice in the ordinary course of business and concerns proxy voting advice if

(A) the person or company discloses to the securityholder any significant relationship with the reporting issuer and any of its affiliates or with a securityholder who has submitted a matter to the reporting issuer that the securityholder intends to raise at the meeting of securityholders and any material interests the person or company has in relation to a matter on which advice is given;

(B) the person or company receives any special commission or remuneration for giving the proxy voting advice only from the securityholder or securityholders receiving the advice; and

(C) the proxy voting advice is not given on behalf of any person or company soliciting proxies or on behalf of a nominee for election as a director; or

(iv) by a person or company who does not seek directly or indirectly the power to act as a proxyholder for a securityholder;

"special meeting" has the same meaning as in section 1.1 of NI 54-101;

"special resolution" has the same meaning as in section 1.1 of NI 54-101;

"stratification" has the same meaning as in section 1.1 of NI 54-101;

"subordinate voting security" means a restricted security that carries a right to vote, if there are securities of another class outstanding that carry a greater right to vote on a per security basis;

"transition year" means the financial year of a reporting issuer or business in which the issuer or business changes its financial year-end;

"U.S. AICPA GAAS" has the same meaning as in National Instrument 52-107 *Acceptable Accounting Principles and Auditing Standards*;

"U.S. GAAP" has the same meaning as in National Instrument 52-107 *Acceptable Accounting Principles and Auditing Standards*;

"U.S. laws" means the 1933 Act, the 1934 Act, all enactments made under those Acts and all SEC releases adopting the enactments, as amended;

"U.S. marketplace" means an exchange registered as a "national securities exchange" under section 6 of the 1934 Act, or the Nasdaq Stock Market; and

"U.S. PCAOB GAAS" has the same meaning as in National Instrument 52-107 *Acceptable Accounting Principles and Auditing Standards*;

"venture issuer" means a reporting issuer that, as at the applicable time, did not have any of its securities listed or quoted on any of the Toronto Stock Exchange, Aequitas NEO Exchange Inc., a U.S. marketplace, or a marketplace outside of Canada and the United States of America other than the Alternative Investment Market of the London Stock Exchange or the PLUS markets operated by PLUS Markets Group plc; where the "applicable time" in respect of

(a) Parts 4 and 5 of this Instrument and Form 51-102F1, is the end of the applicable financial period;

(b) Parts 6 and 9 of this Instrument and Form 51-102F6, is the end of the most recently completed financial year;

(c) Part 8 of this Instrument and Form 51-102F4, is the acquisition date; and

(d) section 11.3 of this Instrument, is the date of the meeting of the securityholders.

(2) **Affiliate** — In this Instrument, an issuer is an affiliate of another issuer if

(a) one of them is the subsidiary of the other, or

(b) each of them is controlled by the same person.

(3) **Control** — For the purposes of subsection (2), a person (first person) is considered to control another person (second person) if

(a) the first person beneficially owns, or controls or directs, directly or indirectly, securities of the second person carrying votes which, if exercised, would entitle the first person to elect a majority of the directors of the second person, unless that first person holds the voting securities only to secure an obligation,

(b) the second person is a partnership, other than a limited partnership, and the first person holds more than 50% of the interests of the partnership, or

(c) the second person is a limited partnership and the general partner of the limited partnership is the first person.

PART 2 — APPLICATION

2.1 **Application** — This Instrument does not apply to an investment fund.

PART 3 — LANGUAGE OF DOCUMENTS

3.1 **French or English** — (1) A person or company must file a document required to be filed under this Instrument in French or in English.

(2) Despite subsection (1), if a person or company files a document only in French or only in English but delivers to securityholders a version of the document in the other language, the person or company must file that other version not later than when it is first delivered to securityholders.

(3) In Québec, a reporting issuer must comply with linguistic obligations and rights prescribed by Québec law.

3.2 Filings Translated into French or English — If a person or company files a document under this Instrument that is a translation of a document prepared in a language other than French or English, the person or company must

    (a) attach a certificate as to the accuracy of the translation to the filed document; and

    (b) make a copy of the document in the original language available to a registered holder or beneficial owner of its securities, on request.

PART 4 — FINANCIAL STATEMENTS

4.1 Comparative Annual Financial Statements and Audit — (1) Subject to subsection 4.8(6), a reporting issuer must file annual financial statements that include

    (a) a statement of comprehensive income, a statement of changes in equity, and a statement of cash flows for

        (i) the most recently completed financial year; and

        (ii) the financial year immediately preceding the most recently completed financial year, if any;

    (b) a statement of financial position as at the end of each of the periods referred to in paragraph (a);

    (c) in the following circumstances, a statement of financial position as at the beginning of the financial year immediately preceding the most recently completed financial year:

        (i) the reporting issuer discloses in its annual financial statements an unreserved statement of compliance with IFRS, and

        (ii) the reporting issuer

            (A) applies an accounting policy retrospectively in its annual financial statements,

            (B) makes a retrospective restatement of items in its annual financial statements, or

            (C) reclassifies items in its annual financial statements;

    (d) in the case of the reporting issuer's first IFRS financial statements, the opening IFRS statement of financial position at the date of transition to IFRS; and

    (e) notes to the annual financial statements.

(2) Annual financial statements filed under subsection (1) must be audited.

(3) If a reporting issuer presents the components of profit or loss in a separate income statement, the separate income statement must be displayed immediately before the statement of comprehensive income filed under subsection (1).

4.2 Filing Deadline for Annual Financial Statements — The audited annual financial statements required to be filed under section 4.1 must be filed

    (a) in the case of a reporting issuer other than a venture issuer, on or before the earlier of

        (i) the 90th day after the end of its most recently completed financial year; and

        (ii) the date of filing, in a foreign jurisdiction, annual financial statements for its most recently completed financial year; or

    (b) in the case of a venture issuer, on or before the earlier of

        (i) the 120th day after the end of its most recently completed financial year; and

        (ii) the date of filing, in a foreign jurisdiction, annual financial statements for its most recently completed financial year.

4.3 Interim Financial Report — (1) Subject to sections 4.7 and 4.10, a reporting issuer must file an interim financial report for each interim period ended after it became a reporting issuer.

(2) Subject to subsections 4.7(4), 4.8(7), 4.8(8) and 4.10(3), the interim financial report required to be filed under subsection (1) must include

    (a) a statement of financial position as at the end of the interim period and a statement of financial position as at the end of the immediately preceding financial year, if any;

    (b) a statement of comprehensive income, a statement of changes in equity and a statement of cash flows, all for the year-to-date interim period, and comparative financial information for the corresponding interim period in the immediately preceding financial year, if any;

    (c) for interim periods other than the first interim period in a reporting issuer's financial year, a statement of comprehensive income for the three month period ending on the last day of the interim period and comparative financial information for the corresponding period in the immediately preceding financial year, if any;

    (d) in the following circumstances, a statement of financial position as at the beginning of the immediately preceding financial year:

        (i) the reporting issuer discloses in its interim financial report an unreserved statement of compliance with International Accounting Standard 34 *Interim Financial Reporting,* and

        (ii) the reporting issuer

            (A) applies an accounting policy retrospectively in its interim financial report,

            (B) makes a retrospective restatement of items in its interim financial report, or

            (C) reclassifies items in its interim financial report;

    (e) in the case of the reporting issuer's first interim financial report required to be filed in the year of adopting IFRS, the opening IFRS statement of financial position at the date of transition to IFRS; and

    (f) notes to the interim financial report.

(2.1) If a reporting issuer presents the components of profit or loss in a separate income statement, the separate income statement must be displayed immediately before the statement of comprehensive income filed under subsection (2).

(3) Disclosure of Auditor Review of an Interim Financial Report —

    (a) If an auditor has not performed a review of an interim financial report required to be filed under subsection (1), the interim financial report must be accompanied by a notice indicating that an interim financial report has not been reviewed by an auditor.

(b) If a reporting issuer engaged an auditor to perform a review of an interim financial report required to be filed under subsection (1) and the auditor was unable to complete the review, the interim financial report must be accompanied by a notice indicating that the auditor was unable to complete a review of the interim financial report and the reasons why the auditor was unable to complete the review.

(c) If an auditor has performed a review of the interim financial report required to be filed under subsection (1) and the auditor has expressed a reservation of opinion in the auditor's interim review report, the interim financial report must be accompanied by a written review report from the auditor.

(4) SEC Issuer — Restatement of Interim Financial Report — If an SEC issuer that is a reporting issuer

(a) has filed an interim financial report prepared in accordance with Canadian GAAP applicable to publicly accountable enterprises for one or more interim periods since its most recently completed financial year for which annual financial statements have been filed; and

(b) prepares its annual financial statements or an interim financial report for the period immediately following the periods referred to in paragraph (a) in accordance with U.S. GAAP,

the SEC issuer must

(c) restate the interim financial report for the periods referred to in paragraph (a) in accordance with U.S. GAAP; and

(d) file the restated interim financial report referred to in paragraph (c) by the filing deadline for the financial statements referred to in paragraph (b).

4.4 Filing Deadline for an Interim Financial Report — An interim financial report required to be filed under subsection 4.3(1) must be filed

(a) in the case of a reporting issuer other than a venture issuer, on or before the earlier of

(i) the 45th day after the end of the interim period; and

(ii) the date of filing, in a foreign jurisdiction, an interim financial report for a period ending on the last day of the interim period; or

(b) in the case of a venture issuer, on or before the earlier of

(i) the 60th day after the end of the interim period; and

(ii) the date of filing, in a foreign jurisdiction, an interim financial report for a period ending on the last day of the interim period.

4.5 Approval of Financial Statements — (1) The annual financial statements a reporting issuer is required to file under section 4.1 must be approved by the board of directors before the statements are filed.

(2) The interim financial report a reporting issuer is required to file under section 4.3 must be approved by the board of directors before the report is filed.

(3) In fulfilling the requirement in subsection (2), the board of directors may delegate the approval of the interim financial report to the audit committee of the board of directors.

4.6 Delivery of Financial Statements — (1) Subject to subsection (2), a reporting issuer must send annually a request form to the registered holders and beneficial owners of its securities, other than debt instruments, that the registered holders and beneficial owners may use to request any of the following:

(a) a paper copy of the reporting issuer's annual financial statements and MD&A for the annual financial statements;

(b) a copy of the reporting issuer's interim financial reports and MD&A for the interim financial reports.

(2) For the purposes of subsection (1), the reporting issuer must, applying the procedures set out in NI 54-101, send the request form to the beneficial owners of its securities who are identified under that Instrument as having chosen to receive all securityholder materials sent to beneficial owners of securities.

(3) If a registered holder or beneficial owner of securities, other than debt instruments, of a reporting issuer requests the reporting issuer's annual financial statements or interim financial reports, the reporting issuer must send a copy of the requested financial statements to the person or company that made the request, without charge, by the later of

(a) in the case of a reporting issuer other than a venture issuer, 10 calendar days after the filing deadline in subparagraph 4.2(a)(i) or 4.4(a)(i), section 4.7, or subsection 4.10(2), as applicable, for the financial statements requested;

(b) in the case of a venture issuer, 10 calendar days after the filing deadline in paragraph 4.2(b)(i) or 4.4(b)(i), section 4.7, or subsection 4.10(2), as applicable, for the financial statements requested; and

(c) 10 calendar days after the issuer receives the request.

(4) A reporting issuer is not required to send copies of annual financial statements or interim financial reports under subsection (3) that were filed more than one year before the issuer receives the request.

(5) Subsection (1) and the requirement to send annual financial statements under subsection (3) do not apply to a reporting issuer that sends its annual financial statements to its securityholders, other than holders of debt instruments, within 140 days of the issuer's financial year-end and in accordance with NI 54-101.

(6) If a reporting issuer sends financial statements under this section, the reporting issuer must also send, at the same time, the annual or interim MD&A relating to the financial statements.

4.7 Filing of Financial Statements After Becoming a Reporting Issuer — (1) Despite any provisions of this Part other than subsections (2), (3) and (4) of this section, the first annual financial statements and interim financial reports that a reporting issuer must file under sections 4.1 and 4.3 are the financial statements for the financial year and interim periods immediately following the periods for which financial statements of the issuer were included in a document filed

(a) that resulted in the issuer becoming a reporting issuer; or

(b) in respect of a transaction that resulted in the issuer becoming a reporting issuer.

(2) If, under subsection (1), a reporting issuer is required to file annual financial statements for a financial year that ended before the issuer became a reporting issuer, those annual financial statements must be filed on or before the later of

(a) the 20th day after the issuer became a reporting issuer; and

(b) the filing deadline in section 4.2.

(3) If, under subsection (1), a reporting issuer is required to file an interim financial report for an interim period that ended before the issuer became a reporting issuer, that interim financial report must be filed on or before the later of

(a) the 10th day after the issuer became a reporting issuer; and

(b) the filing deadline in section 4.4.

(4) A reporting issuer is not required to provide comparative interim financial information for periods that ended before the issuer became a reporting issuer if

(a) to a reasonable person it is impracticable to present prior-period information on a basis consistent with subsection 4.3(2);

(b) the prior-period information that is available is presented; and

(c) the notes to the interim financial report disclose the fact that the prior-period information has not been prepared on a basis consistent with the most recent interim financial information.

4.8 Change in Year-End — (1) Exemption from Change in Year-End Requirements — An SEC issuer satisfies this section if

(a) it complies with the requirements of U.S. laws relating to a change of fiscal year; and

(b) it files a copy of all materials required by U.S. laws relating to a change of fiscal year at the same time as, or as soon as practicable after, they are filed with or furnished to the SEC and, in the case of financial statements, no later than the filing deadlines prescribed under sections 4.2 and 4.4.

(2) Notice of Change — If a reporting issuer decides to change its financial year-end by more than 14 days, it must file a notice containing the information set out in subsection (3) as soon as practicable, and, in any event, not later than the earlier of

(a) the filing deadline, based on the reporting issuer's old financial year-end, for the next financial statements required to be filed, either annual or interim, whichever comes first; and

(b) the filing deadline, based on the reporting issuer's new financial year-end, for the next financial statements required to be filed, either annual or interim, whichever comes first.

(3) The notice referred to in subsection (2) must state

(a) that the reporting issuer has decided to change its year-end;

(b) the reason for the change;

(c) the reporting issuer's old financial year-end;

(d) the reporting issuer's new financial year-end;

(e) the length and ending date of the periods, including the comparative periods, of each interim financial report and the annual financial statements to be filed for the reporting issuer's transition year and its new financial year; and

(f) the filing deadlines, prescribed under sections 4.2 and 4.4, for the annual financial statements and interim financial reports for the reporting issuer's transition year.

(4) Maximum Length of Transition Year — For the purposes of this section,

(a) a transition year must not exceed 15 months; and

(b) the first interim period after an old financial year must not exceed four months.

(5) Interim Period Ends Within One Month of Year-End — Despite subsection 4.3(1), a reporting issuer is not required to file an interim financial report for any period in its transition year that ends not more than one month

(a) after the last day of its old financial year; or

(b) before the first day of its new financial year.

(6) Comparative Financial Information in Annual Financial Statements for New Financial Year — If a transition year is less than nine months in length, the reporting issuer must include as comparative financial information to its annual financial statements for its new financial year

(a) a statement of financial position, a statement of comprehensive income, a statement of changes in equity, a statement of cash flows, and notes to the financial statements for its transition year;

(b) a statement of financial position, a statement of comprehensive income, a statement of changes in equity, a statement of cash flows and notes to the financial statements for its old financial year;

(c) in the following circumstances, a statement of financial position as at the beginning of the old financial year:

(i) the reporting issuer discloses in its annual financial statements an unreserved statement of compliance with IFRS, and

(ii) the reporting issuer

(A) applies an accounting policy retrospectively in its annual financial statements,

(B) makes a retrospective restatement of items in its annual financial statements, or

(C) reclassifies items in its annual financial statements; and

(d) in the case of the reporting issuer's first IFRS financial statements, the opening IFRS statement of financial position at the date of transition to IFRS.

(7) Comparative Financial Information in each Interim Financial Report if Interim Periods Not Changed in Transition Year — If interim periods for the reporting issuer's transition year end three, six, nine or twelve months after the end of its old financial year, the reporting issuer must include

(a) as comparative financial information in each interim financial report during its transition year, the comparative financial information required by subsection 4.3(2), except if an interim period during the transition year is 12 months in length and the reporting issuer's transition year is longer than 13 months, the comparative financial information must be the statement of financial position, statement of comprehensive income, statement of changes in equity and statement of cash flows for the 12 month period that constitutes its old financial year;

(b) as comparative financial information in each interim financial report during its new financial year

    (i) a statement of financial position as at the end of its transition year; and

    (ii) the statement of comprehensive income, statement of changes in equity and statement of cash flows for the periods in its transition year or old financial year, for the same calendar months as, or as close as possible to, the calendar months in the interim period in the new financial year;

(c) in the following circumstances, a statement of financial position as at the beginning of the earliest comparative period:

    (i) the reporting issuer discloses in its interim financial report an unreserved statement of compliance with International Accounting Standard 34 *Interim Financial Reporting*, and

    (ii) the reporting issuer

        (A) applies an accounting policy retrospectively in its interim financial report,

        (B) makes a retrospective restatement of items in its interim financial report, or

        (C) reclassifies items in its interim financial report; and

(d) in the case of the reporting issuer's first interim financial report required to be filed in the year of adopting IFRS, the opening IFRS statement of financial position at the date of transition to IFRS.

(8) Comparative Financial Information in Interim Financial Reports if Interim Periods Changed in Transition Year — If interim periods for a reporting issuer's transition year end twelve, nine, six or three months before the end of the transition year, the reporting issuer must include

(a) as comparative financial information in each interim financial report during its transition year

    (i) a statement of financial position as at the end of its old financial year; and

    (ii) the statement of comprehensive income, statement of changes in equity and statement of cash flows for periods in its old financial year, for the same calendar months as, or as close as possible to, the calendar months in the interim period in the transition year;

(b) as comparative financial information in each interim financial report during its new financial year

    (i) a statement of financial position as at the end of its transition year; and

    (ii) the statement of comprehensive income, statement of changes in equity and statement of cash flows in its transition year or old financial year, or both, as appropriate, for the same calendar months as, or as close as possible to, the calendar months in the interim period in the new financial year;

(c) in the following circumstances, a statement of financial position as at the beginning of the earliest comparative period:

    (i) the reporting issuer discloses in its interim financial report an unreserved statement of compliance with International Accounting Standard 34 *Interim Financial Reporting*, and

    (ii) the reporting issuer

        (A) applies an accounting policy retrospectively in its interim financial report,

        (B) makes a retrospective restatement of items in its interim financial report, or

        (C) reclassifies items in its interim financial report; and

(d) in the case of the reporting issuer's first interim financial report required to be filed in the year of adopting IFRS, the opening IFRS statement of financial position at the date of transition to IFRS.

4.9 Change in Corporate Structure — If an issuer is party to a transaction that resulted in,

(a) the issuer becoming a reporting issuer other than by filing a prospectus; or

(b) if the issuer was already a reporting issuer, in

    (i) the issuer ceasing to be a reporting issuer,

    (ii) a change in the reporting issuer's financial year end, or

    (iii) a change in the name of the reporting issuer;

the issuer must, as soon as practicable, and in any event not later than the deadline for the first filing required under this Instrument following the transaction, file a notice stating

(c) the names of the parties to the transaction;

(d) a description of the transaction;

(e) the effective date of the transaction;

(f) the name of each party, if any, that ceased to be a reporting issuer after the transaction and of each continuing entity;

(g) the date of the reporting issuer's first financial year-end after the transaction if paragraph (a) or subparagraph (b)(ii) applies;

(h) the periods, including the comparative periods, if any, of the interim financial reports and the annual financial statements required to be filed for the reporting issuer's first financial year after the transaction, if paragraph (a) or subparagraph (b)(ii) applies; and

(i) what documents were filed under this Instrument that described the transaction and where those documents can be found in electronic format, if paragraph (a) or subparagraph (b)(ii) applies.

4.10 Reverse Takeovers — (1) **Change in Year End** — If a reporting issuer must comply with section 4.9 because it was a party to a reverse takeover, the reporting issuer must comply with section 4.8 unless

(a) the reporting issuer had the same year-end as the reverse takeover acquirer before the transaction; or

(b) the reporting issuer changes its year-end to be the same as that of the reverse takeover acquirer.

(2) Financial Statements of the Reverse Takeover Acquirer for Periods Ending Before a Reverse Takeover — If a reporting issuer completes a reverse takeover, it must

    (a) file the following financial statements for the reverse takeover acquirer, unless the financial statements have already been filed:

        (i) financial statements for all annual and interim periods ending before the date of the reverse takeover and after the date of the financial statements included in an information circular or similar document, or under Item 5.2 of the Form 51-102F3 Material Change Report, prepared in connection with the transaction; or

        (ii) if the reporting issuer did not file a document referred to in subparagraph (i), or the document does not include the financial statements for the reverse takeover acquirer that would be required to be included in a prospectus, the financial statements prescribed under securities legislation and described in the form of prospectus that the reverse takeover acquirer was eligible to use prior to the reverse takeover for a distribution of securities in the jurisdiction;

    (b) file the annual financial statements required by paragraph (a) on or before the later of

        (i) the 20th day after the date of the reverse takeover;

        (ii) the 90th date after the end of the financial year; and

        (iii) the 120th day after the end of the financial year if the reporting issuer is a venture issuer; and

    (c) file teach interim financial report required by paragraph (a) on or before the later of

        (i) the 10th day after the date of the reverse takeover;

        (ii) the 45th day after the end of the interim period;

        (iii) the 60th day after the end of the interim period if the reporting issuer is a venture issuer; and

        (iv) the filing deadline in paragraph (b).

(3) Comparative Financial Information in each Interim Financial Report after a Reverse Takeover — A reporting issuer is not required to provide comparative interim financial information for the reverse takeover acquirer for periods that ended before the date of a reverse takeover if

    (a) to a reasonable person it is impracticable to present prior-period information on a basis consistent with subsection 4.3(2);

    (b) the prior-period information that is available is presented; and

    (c) the notes to the interim financial report disclose the fact that the prior-period information has not been prepared on a basis consistent with the most recent interim financial information.

4.11 Change of Auditor — **(1) Definitions** — In this section

"appointment" means, in relation to a reporting issuer, the earlier of

    (a) the appointment as its auditor of a different person or company than its predecessor auditor; and

    (b) the decision by the board of directors of the reporting issuer to propose to holders of qualified securities to appoint as its auditor a different person or company than its predecessor auditor;

"consultation" means advice provided by a successor auditor, whether or not in writing, to a reporting issuer during the relevant period, which the successor auditor concluded was an important factor considered by the reporting issuer in reaching a decision concerning

    (a) the application of accounting principles or policies to a transaction, whether or not the transaction is completed;

    (b) a report provided by an auditor on the reporting issuer's financial statements;

    (c) scope or procedure of an audit or review engagement; or

    (d) financial statement disclosure;

"disagreement" means a difference of opinion between personnel of a reporting issuer responsible for finalizing the reporting issuer's financial statements and the personnel of a predecessor auditor responsible for authorizing the issuance of audit reports on the reporting issuer's financial statements or authorizing the communication of the results of the auditor's review of the reporting issuer's interim financial report, if the difference of opinion

    (a) resulted in a modified opinion in the predecessor auditor's audit report on the reporting issuer's financial statements for any period during the relevant period;

    (b) would have resulted in a modified opinion in the predecessor auditor's audit report on the reporting issuer's financial statements for any period during the relevant period if the difference of opinion had not been resolved to the predecessor auditor's satisfaction, not including a difference of opinion based on incomplete or preliminary information that was resolved to the satisfaction of the predecessor auditor upon the receipt of further information;

    (c) resulted in a qualified or adverse communication or denial of assurance in respect of the predecessor auditor's review of the reporting issuer's interim financial report for any interim period during the relevant period; or

    (d) would have resulted in a qualified or adverse communication or denial of assurance in respect of the predecessor auditor's review of the reporting issuer's interim financial report for any interim period during the relevant period if the difference of opinion had not been resolved to the predecessor auditor's satisfaction, not including a difference of opinion based on incomplete or preliminary information that was resolved to the satisfaction of the predecessor auditor upon the receipt of further information;

"former auditor" means the auditor of a reporting issuer that is the subject of the most recent termination or resignation;

"predecessor auditor" means the auditor of a reporting issuer that is the subject of the most recent termination or resignation;

"qualified securities" means securities of a reporting issuer that carry the right to participate in voting on the appointment or removal of the reporting issuer's auditor;

"relevant information circular" means

    (a) if a reporting issuer's constating documents or applicable law require holders of qualified securities to take action to remove the reporting issuer's auditor or to appoint a successor auditor

        (i) the information circular required to accompany or form part of every notice of meeting at which that action is proposed to be taken; or

(ii) the disclosure document accompanying the text of the written resolution provided to holders of qualified securities; or

(b) if paragraph (a) does not apply, the information circular required to accompany or form part of the first notice of meeting to be sent to holders of qualified securities following the preparation of a reporting package concerning a termination or resignation;

"relevant period" means the period

(a) commencing at the beginning of the reporting issuer's two most recently completed financial years and ending on the date of termination or resignation; or

(b) during which the predecessor auditor was the reporting issuer's auditor, if the predecessor auditor was not the reporting issuer's auditor throughout the period described in paragraph (a);

"reportable event" means a disagreement, a consultation, or an unresolved issue;

"reporting package" means

(a) the documents referred to in subparagraphs (5)(a)(i) and (6)(a)(i);

(b) the letter referred to in clause (5)(a)(ii)(B), if received by the reporting issuer, unless an updated letter referred to in clause (6)(a)(iii)(B) has been received by the reporting issuer;

(c) the letter referred to in clause (6)(a)(ii)(B), if received by the reporting issuer; and

(d) any updated letter referred to in clause (6)(a)(iii)(B) received by the reporting issuer;

"resignation" means notification from an auditor to a reporting issuer of the auditor's decision to resign or decline to stand for reappointment;

"successor auditor" means the person or company

(a) appointed;

(b) that the board of directors have proposed to holders of qualified securities be appointed; or

(c) that the board of directors have decided to propose to holders of qualified securities be appointed,

as the reporting issuer's auditor after the termination or resignation of the reporting issuer's predecessor auditor;

"termination" means, in relation to a reporting issuer, the earlier of

(a) the removal of its auditor before the expiry of the auditor's term of appointment, the expiry of its auditor's term of appointment without reappointment, or the appointment of a different person or company as its auditor upon expiry of its auditor's term of appointment; and

(b) the decision by the board of directors of the reporting issuer to propose to holders of its qualified securities that its auditor be removed before, or that a different person or company be appointed as its auditor upon, the expiry of its auditor's term of appointment;

"unresolved issue" means any matter that, in the predecessor auditor's opinion, has, or could have, a material impact on the financial statements, or reports provided by the auditor relating to the financial statements, for any financial period during the relevant period, and about which the predecessor auditor has advised the reporting issuer if

(a) the predecessor auditor was unable to reach a conclusion as to the matter's implications before the date of termination or resignation;

(b) the matter was not resolved to the predecessor auditor's satisfaction before the date of termination or resignation; or

(c) the predecessor auditor is no longer willing to be associated with any of the financial statements;

(2) Meaning of "Material" — For the purposes of this section, the term "material" has a meaning consistent with the discussion of the term "materiality" in the issuer's GAAP.

(3) Exemption from Change of Auditor Requirements — This section does not apply if

(a) the following three conditions are met:

(i) a termination, or resignation, and appointment occur in connection with an amalgamation, arrangement, takeover or similar transaction involving the reporting issuer or a reorganization of the reporting issuer;

(ii) the termination, or resignation, and appointment have been disclosed in a news release that has been filed or in a disclosure document that has been delivered to holders of qualified securities and filed; and

(iii) no reportable event has occurred;

(b) the change of auditor is required by the legislation under which the reporting issuer exists or carries on its activities; or

(c) the change of auditor arises from an amalgamation, merger or other reorganization of the auditor.

(4) Exemption From Change of Auditor Requirements — SEC Issuers — An SEC issuer satisfies this section if it

(a) complies with the requirements of U.S. laws relating to a change of auditor;

(b) files a copy of all materials required by U.S. laws relating to a change of auditor at the same time as, or as soon as practicable after, they are filed with or furnished to the SEC;

(c) issues and files a news release describing the information disclosed in the materials referred to in paragraph (b), if there are any reportable events; and

(d) includes the materials referred to in paragraph (b) with each relevant information circular.

(5) Requirements Upon Auditor Termination or Resignation — Upon a termination or resignation of its auditor, a reporting issuer must

(a) within 3 days after the date of termination or resignation

(i) prepare a change of auditor notice in accordance with subsection (7) and deliver a copy of it to the former auditor; and

(ii) request the former auditor to

(A) review the reporting issuer's change of auditor notice;

(B) prepare a letter, addressed to the regulator or securities regulatory authority, stating, for each statement in the change of auditor notice, whether the auditor

(I) agrees,

(II) disagrees, and the reasons why, or

(III) has no basis to agree or disagree; and

(C) deliver the letter to the reporting issuer within 7 days after the date of termination or resignation;

(b) within 14 days after the date of termination or resignation

(i) have the audit committee of its board of directors or its board of directors review the letter referred to in clause (5)(a)(ii)(B) if received by the reporting issuer, and approve the change of auditor notice;

(ii) file a copy of the reporting package with the regulator or securities regulatory authority;

(iii) deliver a copy of the reporting package to the former auditor;

(iv) if there are any reportable events, issue and file a news release describing the information in the reporting package; and

(c) include with each relevant information circular

(i) a copy of the reporting package as an appendix; and

(ii) a summary of the contents of the reporting package with a cross-reference to the appendix.

(6) **Requirements upon Auditor Appointment** — Upon an appointment of a successor auditor, a reporting issuer must

(a) within 3 days after the date of appointment

(i) prepare a change of auditor notice in accordance with subsection (7) and deliver it to the successor auditor and to the former auditor;

(ii) request the successor auditor to

(A) review the reporting issuer's change of auditor notice;

(B) prepare a letter addressed to the regulator or securities regulatory authority, stating, for each statement in the change of auditor notice, whether the auditor

(I) agrees,

(II) disagrees, and the reasons why, or

(III) has no basis to agree or disagree; and

(C) deliver that letter to the reporting issuer within 7 days after the date of appointment; and

(iii) request the former auditor to, within 7 days after the date of appointment,

(A) confirm that the letter referred to in clause (5)(a)(ii)(B) does not have to be updated; or

(B) prepare and deliver to the reporting issuer an updated letter to replace the letter referred to in clause (5)(a)(ii)(B);

(b) within 14 days after the date of appointment,

(i) have the audit committee of its board of directors or its board of directors review the letters referred to in clauses (6)(a)(ii)(B) and (6)(a)(iii)(B) if received by the reporting issuer, and approve the change of auditor notice;

(ii) file a copy of the reporting package with the regulator or securities regulatory authority;

(iii) deliver a copy of the reporting package to the successor auditor and to the former auditor; and

(iv) if there are any reportable events, issue and file a news release disclosing the appointment of the successor auditor and describing the information in the reporting package or referring to the news release required under subparagraph (5)(b)(iv).

(7) **Change of Auditor Notice Content** — A change of auditor notice must state

(a) the date of termination or resignation;

(b) whether the former auditor

(i) resigned on the former auditor's own initiative or at the reporting issuer's request;

(ii) was removed or is proposed to holders of qualified securities to be removed during the former auditor's term of appointment; or

(iii) was not reappointed or has not been proposed for reappointment;

(c) whether the termination or resignation of the former auditor and any appointment of the successor auditor were considered or approved by the audit committee of the reporting issuer's board of directors or the reporting issuer's board of directors;

(d) whether the former auditor's report on any of the reporting issuer's financial statements relating to the relevant period expressed a modified opinion and, if so, a description of each modification;

(e) if there is a reportable event, the following information:

(i) for a disagreement,

(A) a description of the disagreement;

(B) whether the audit committee of the reporting issuer's board of directors or the reporting issuer's board of directors discussed the disagreement with the former auditor; and

(C) whether the reporting issuer authorized the former auditor to respond fully to inquiries by any successor auditor concerning the disagreement and, if not, a description of and reasons for any limitation;

(ii) for a consultation,

(A) a description of the issue that was the subject of the consultation;

(B) a summary of the successor auditor's oral advice, if any, provided to the reporting issuer concerning the issue;

(C) a copy of the successor auditor's written advice, if any, received by the reporting issuer concerning the issue; and

(D) whether the reporting issuer consulted with the former auditor concerning the issue and, if so, a summary of the former auditor's advice concerning the issue; and

(iii) for an unresolved issue,

(A) a description of the issue;

(B) whether the audit committee of the reporting issuer's board of directors or the reporting issuer's board of directors discussed the issue with the former auditor; and

(C) whether the reporting issuer authorized the former auditor to respond fully to inquiries by any successor auditor concerning the issue and, if not, a description of and reasons for any limitation; and

(f) if there are no reportable events, a statement to that effect.

(8) **Predecessor Auditor's Obligations to Report Non-Compliance** — If a reporting issuer does not file the reporting package required to be filed under subparagraph (5)(b)(ii) or the news release required to be filed under subparagraph (5)(b)(iv), the predecessor auditor must, within 3 days of the required filing date, advise the reporting issuer in writing of the failure and deliver a copy of the letter to the regulator or, in Quebec, the securities regulatory authority.

(9) **Successor Auditor's Obligations to Report Non-Compliance** — If a reporting issuer does not file the reporting package required to be filed under subparagraph (6)(b)(ii) or the news release required to be filed under subparagraph (6)(b)(iv), the successor auditor must, within 3 days of the required filing date, advise the reporting issuer in writing of the failure and deliver a copy of the letter to the regulator or, in Quebec, the securities regulatory authority.

PART 4A — FORWARD-LOOKING INFORMATION

4A.1 Application — This Part applies to forward-looking information that is disclosed by a reporting issuer other than forward-looking information contained in oral statements.

4A.2 Reasonable Basis — A reporting issuer must not disclose forward-looking information unless the issuer has a reasonable basis for the forward-looking information.

4A.3 Disclosure — A reporting issuer that discloses material forward-looking information must include disclosure that

(a) identifies forward-looking information as such;

(b) cautions users of forward-looking information that actual results may vary from the forward-looking information and identifies material risk factors that could cause actual results to differ materially from the forward-looking information;

(c) states the material factors or assumptions used to develop forward-looking information; and

(d) describes the reporting issuer's policy for updating forward-looking information if it includes procedures in addition to those described in subsection 5.8(2).

PART 4B — FOFI AND FINANCIAL OUTLOOKS

4B.1 Application — (1) Subject to subsection (2), this Part applies to FOFI or a financial outlook that is disclosed by a reporting issuer.

(2) This Part does not apply to disclosure that is

(a) subject to requirements in National Instrument 51-101 *Standards of Disclosure for Oil and Gas Activities* or National Instrument 43-101 *Standards of Disclosure for Mineral Projects*;

(b) made to comply with the conditions of any exemption from the requirements referred to in paragraph (a) that a reporting issuer received from a regulator or securities regulatory authority unless the regulator or securities regulatory authority orders that this Part applies to disclosure made under the exemption; or

(c) contained in an oral statement.

4B.2 Assumptions — (1) A reporting issuer must not disclose FOFI or a financial outlook unless the FOFI or financial outlook is based on assumptions that are reasonable in the circumstances.

(2) FOFI or a financial outlook that is based on assumptions that are reasonable in the circumstances must, without limitation,

(a) be limited to a period for which the information in the FOFI or financial outlook can be reasonably estimated; and

(b) use the accounting policies the reporting issuer expects to use to prepare its historical financial statements for the period covered by the FOFI or the financial outlook.

4B.3 Disclosure — In addition to the disclosure required by section 4A.3, if a reporting issuer discloses FOFI or a financial outlook, the issuer must include disclosure that

(a) states the date management approved the FOFI or financial outlook, if the document containing the FOFI or financial outlook is undated; and

(b) explains the purpose of the FOFI or financial outlook and cautions readers that the information may not be appropriate for other purposes.

PART 5 — MANAGEMENT'S DISCUSSION & ANALYSIS

5.1 Filing of MD&A — (1) A reporting issuer must file MD&A relating to its annual financial statements and each interim financial report required under Part 4.

(1.1) Despite subsection (1), a reporting issuer does not have to file MD&A relating to the annual financial statements and interim financial reports required under sections 4.7 and 4.10 for financial years and interim periods that ended before the issuer became a reporting issuer.

(2) Subject to section 5.2, the MD&A required to be filed under subsection (1) must be filed on or before the earlier of

(a) the filing deadlines for the annual financial statements and each interim financial report set out in sections 4.2 and 4.4, as applicable; and

(b) the date the reporting issuer files the financial statements under subsections 4.1(1) or 4.3(1), as applicable.

5.2 Filing of MD&A for SEC Issuers — If an SEC issuer that is a reporting issuer is filing its annual or interim MD&A prepared in accordance with Item 303 of Regulation S-K under the 1934 Act, the SEC issuer must file that document on or before the earlier of

(a) the date the SEC issuer would be required to file that document under section 5.1; and

(b) the date the SEC issuer files that document with the SEC.

5.3 Additional Disclosure for Venture Issuers Without Significant Revenue — (1) A venture issuer that has not had significant revenue from operations in either of its last two financial years, must disclose in its MD&A, for each period referred to in subsection (2), a breakdown of material components of

(a) exploration and evaluation assets or expenditures;

(b) expensed research and development costs;

(c) intangible assets arising from development;

(d) general and administration expenses; and

(e) any material costs, whether expensed or recognized as assets, not referred to in paragraphs (a) through (d);

and if the venture issuer's business primarily involves mining exploration and development, the analysis of exploration and evaluation assets or expenditures must be presented on a property-by-property basis.

(2) The disclosure in subsection (1) must be provided for the following periods:

(a) in the case of annual MD&A, for the two most recently completed financial years; and

(b) in the case of interim MD&A for an issuer that is not providing disclosure in accordance with section 2.2.1 of Form 51-102F1, for the most recent year-to-date interim period and the comparative year-to-date period presented in the interim financial report.

(3) Subsection (1) does not apply if the information required under that subsection has been disclosed in the financial statements to which the MD&A relates.

5.4 Disclosure of Outstanding Share Data — (1) A reporting issuer must disclose in its annual MD&A and, if the issuer is not providing disclosure in accordance with section 2.2.1 of Form 51-102F1, its interim MD&A, the designation and number or principal amount of

(a) each class and series of voting or equity securities of the reporting issuer for which there are securities outstanding;

(b) each class and series of securities of the reporting issuer for which there are securities outstanding if the securities are convertible into, or exercisable or exchangeable for, voting or equity securities of the reporting issuer; and

(c) subject to subsection (2), each class and series of voting or equity securities of the reporting issuer that are issuable on the conversion, exercise or exchange of outstanding securities of the reporting issuer.

(2) If the exact number or principal amount of voting or equity securities of the reporting issuer that are issuable on the conversion, exercise or exchange of outstanding securities of the reporting issuer is not determinable, the reporting issuer must disclose the maximum number or principal amount of each class and series of voting or equity securities that are issuable on the conversion, exercise or exchange of outstanding securities of the reporting issuer and, if that maximum number or principal amount is not determinable, the reporting issuer must describe the exchange or conversion features and the manner in which the number or principal amount of voting or equity securities will be determined.

(3) The disclosure under subsections (1) and (2) must be prepared as of the latest practicable date.

5.5 Approval of MD&A — (1) The annual MD&A that a reporting issuer is required to file under this Part must be approved by the board of directors before being filed.

(2) The interim MD&A that a reporting issuer is required to file under this Part must be approved by the board of directors before being filed.

(3) In fulfilling the requirement in subsection (2), the board of directors may delegate the approval of the interim MD&A required to be filed under this Part to the audit committee of the board of directors.

5.6 Delivery of MD&A — (1) If a registered holder or beneficial owner of securities, other than debt instruments, of a reporting issuer requests the reporting issuer's annual or interim MD&A, the reporting issuer must send a copy of the requested MD&A to the person or company that made the request, without charge, by the delivery deadline set out in subsection 4.6(3) for the annual financial statements or interim financial report to which the MD&A relates.

(2) A reporting issuer is not required to send copies of any MD&A under subsection (1) that was filed more than two years before the issuer receives the request.

(3) The requirement to send annual MD&A under subsection (1) does not apply to a reporting issuer that sends its annual MD&A to its securityholders, other than holders of debt instruments, within 140 days of the issuer's financial year-end and in accordance with NI 54-101.

(4) If a reporting issuer sends MD&A under this section, the reporting issuer must also send, at the same time, the annual financial statements or interim financial report to which the MD&A relates.

5.7 Additional Disclosure for Reporting Issuers with Significant Equity Investees — (1) A reporting issuer that has a significant equity investee must disclose in its MD&A for each period referred to in subsection (2),

(a) summarized financial information of the equity investee, including the aggregated amounts of assets, liabilities, revenue and profit or loss; and

(b) the reporting issuer's proportionate interest in the equity investee and any contingent issuance of securities by the equity investee that might significantly affect the reporting issuer's share of profit or loss.

(2) The disclosure in subsection (1) must be provided for the following periods:

(a) in the case of annual MD&A, for the two most recently completed financial years; and

(b) in the case of interim MD&A for an issuer that is not providing disclosure in accordance with section 2.2.1 of Form 51-102F1, for the most recent year-to-date interim period and the comparative year-to-date period presented in the interim financial report.

(3) **Subsection (1) does not apply if**

    (a) the information required under that subsection has been disclosed in the financial statements to which the MD&A relates; or

    (b) the issuer files separate financial statements of the equity investee for the periods referred to in subsection (2).

5.8 Disclosure Relating to Previously Disclosed Material Forward-Looking Information — (1) Application — This section applies to material forward-looking information that is disclosed by a reporting issuer other than

    (a) forward-looking information contained in an oral statement; or

    (b) disclosure that is

        (i) subject to the requirements in National Instrument 51-101 *Standards of Disclosure for Oil and Gas Activities* or National Instrument 43-101 *Standards of Disclosure for Mineral Projects*; or

        (ii) made to comply with the conditions of any exemption from the requirements referred to in subparagraph (i) that a reporting issuer received from a regulator or securities regulatory authority unless the regulator or securities regulatory authority orders that this Part applies to disclosure made under the exemption.

(2) **Update —** A reporting issuer must discuss in its MD&A

    (a) events and circumstances that occurred during the period to which the MD&A relates that are reasonably likely to cause actual results to differ materially from material forward-looking information for a period that is not yet complete that the reporting issuer previously disclosed to the public; and

    (b) the expected differences referred to in paragraph (a).

(3) **Exemption —** Subsection (2) does not apply if the reporting issuer

    (a) includes the information required by subsection (2) in a news release issued and filed by the reporting issuer before the filing of the MD&A referred to in subsection (2); and

    (b) includes disclosure in the MD&A referred to in subsection (2) that

        (i) identifies the news release referred to in paragraph (a);

        (ii) states the date of the news release; and

        (iii) states that the news release is available at www.sedar.com.

(4) **Comparison to Actual —** A reporting issuer must disclose and discuss in its MD&A material differences between

    (a) actual results for the annual or interim period to which the MD&A relates; and

    (b) any FOFI or financial outlook for the period referred to in paragraph (a) that the reporting issuer previously disclosed.

(5) **Withdrawal —** If during the period to which its MD&A relates, a reporting issuer decides to withdraw previously disclosed material forward-looking information,

    (a) the reporting issuer must disclose in its MD&A the decision and discuss the events and circumstances that led the reporting issuer to that decision, including a discussion of the assumptions underlying the forward-looking information that are no longer valid; and

    (b) subsection (4) does not apply to the reporting issuer with respect to the MD&A

        (i) if the reporting issuer complies with paragraph (a); and

        (ii) the MD&A is filed before the end of the period covered by the forward-looking information.

(6) **Exemption —** Paragraph 5(a) does not apply if the reporting issuer

    (a) includes the information required by paragraph (5)(a) in a news release issued and filed by the reporting issuer before the filing of the MD&A referred to in subsection (5); and

    (b) includes disclosure in the MD&A referred to in subsection (5) that

        (i) identifies the news release referred to in paragraph (a);

        (ii) states the date of the news release; and

        (iii) states that the news release is available at www.sedar.com.

PART 6 — ANNUAL INFORMATION FORM

6.1 Requirement to File an AIF — A reporting issuer that is not a venture issuer must file an AIF.

6.2 Filing Deadline for an AIF — An AIF required to be filed under section 6.1 must be filed,

    (a) subject to paragraph (b), on or before the 90th day after the end of the reporting issuer's most recently completed financial year; or

    (b) in the case of a reporting issuer that is an SEC issuer filing its AIF on Form 10-K or Form 20-F, on or before the earlier of

        (i) the 90th day after the end of the reporting issuer's most recently completed financial year; and

        (ii) the date the reporting issuer files its Form 10-K or Form 20-F with the SEC.

PART 7 — MATERIAL CHANGE REPORTS

7.1 Publication of Material Change — (1) Subject to subsection (2), if a material change occurs in the affairs of a reporting issuer, the reporting issuer must

    (a) immediately issue and file a news release authorized by an executive officer disclosing the nature and substance of the change; and

    (b) as soon as practicable, and in any event within 10 days of the date on which the change occurs, file a Form 51-102F3 Material Change Report with respect to the material change.

(2) Subsection (1) does not apply if,

(a) in the opinion of the reporting issuer, and if that opinion is arrived at in a reasonable manner, the disclosure required by subsection (1) would be unduly detrimental to the interests of the reporting issuer; or

(b) the material change consists of a decision to implement a change made by senior management of the reporting issuer who believe that confirmation of the decision by the board of directors is probable, and senior management of the reporting issuer has no reason to believe that persons with knowledge of the material change have made use of that knowledge in purchasing or selling securities of the reporting issuer,

and the reporting issuer immediately files the report required under paragraph (1)(b) marked so as to indicate that it is confidential, together with written reasons for non-disclosure.

(3) [Repealed]

(4) [Repealed]

(5) If a report has been filed under subsection (2), the reporting issuer must advise the regulator or securities regulatory authority in writing if it believes the report should continue to remain confidential, within 10 days of the date of filing of the initial report and every 10 days thereafter until the material change is generally disclosed in the manner referred to in paragraph (1)(a), or, if the material change consists of a decision of the type referred to in paragraph (2)(b), until that decision has been rejected by the board of directors of the reporting issuer.

(6) Despite subsection (5), in Ontario, the reporting issuer must advise the securities regulatory authority.

(7) If a report has been filed under subsection (2), the reporting issuer must promptly generally disclose the material change in the manner referred to in subsection (1) upon the reporting issuer becoming aware, or having reasonable grounds to believe, that persons or companies are purchasing or selling securities of the reporting issuer with knowledge of the material change that has not been generally disclosed.

PART 8 — BUSINESS ACQUISITION REPORT

8.1 Interpretation and Application — (1) In this Part,

"acquisition" includes an acquisition of an interest in a business that is consolidated for accounting purposes or accounted for by another method, such as the equity method;

"acquisition of related businesses" means the acquisition of two or more businesses if

(a) the businesses were under common control or management before the acquisitions were completed;

(b) each acquisition was conditional upon the completion of each other acquisition; or

(c) the acquisitions were contingent upon a single common event;

"business" includes an interest in an oil and gas property to which reserves, as defined in National Instrument 51-101 *Standards of Disclosure for Oil and Gas Activities*, have been specifically attributed.

"specified profit or loss" means profit or loss from continuing operations attributable to owners of the parent, adjusted to exclude income taxes.

(2) This Part does not apply to a transaction that is a reverse takeover.

8.2 Obligation to File a Business Acquisition Report and Filing Deadline — (1) If a reporting issuer completes a significant acquisition, as determined under section 8.3, it must file a business acquisition report within 75 days after the acquisition date.

(2) Despite subsection (1), if the most recently completed financial year of the acquired business ended 45 days or less before the acquisition date, a reporting issuer must file a business acquisition report

(a) within 90 days after the acquisition date, in the case of an issuer other than a venture issuer, or

(b) within 120 days after the acquisition date, in the case of a venture issuer.

8.3 Determination of Significance — (1) Significant Acquisitions — Subject to subsection (3), and subsections 8.10(1) and 8.10(2), an acquisition of a business or related businesses is a significant acquisition,

(a) for a reporting issuer that is not a venture issuer, if the acquisition satisfies any of the three significance tests set out in subsection (2); and

(b) for a venture issuer, if the acquisition satisfies either of the significance tests set out in paragraphs (2)(a) or (b) if "20 percent" is read as "100 percent".

(2) Required Significance Tests — For the purposes of subsection (1) and subject to subsections (4.1) and (4.2), the significance tests are:

(a) The Asset Test — The reporting issuer's proportionate share of the consolidated assets of the business or related businesses exceeds 20 percent of the consolidated assets of the reporting issuer calculated using the audited annual financial statements of each of the reporting issuer and the business or the related businesses for the most recently completed financial year of each that ended before the acquisition date.

(b) The Investment Test — The reporting issuer's consolidated investments in and advances to the business or related businesses as at the acquisition date exceeds 20 percent of the consolidated assets of the reporting issuer as at the last day of the most recently completed financial year of the reporting issuer ended before the acquisition date, excluding any investments in or advances to the business or related businesses as at that date.

(c) The Profit or Loss Test — The reporting issuer's proportionate share of the consolidated specified profit or loss of the business or related businesses exceeds 20 percent of the consolidated specified profit or loss of the reporting issuer calculated using the audited annual financial statements of each of the reporting issuer and the business or related businesses for the most recently completed financial year of each ended before the acquisition date.

(3) Optional Significance Tests — Despite subsection (1) and subject to subsections 8.10(1) and 8.10(2), if an acquisition of a business or related businesses is significant based on the significance tests in subsection (2),

(a) a reporting issuer that is not a venture issuer may re-calculate the significance using the optional significance tests in subsection (4); and

(b) a venture issuer may re-calculate the significance using the optional significance tests in paragraphs (4)(a) or (b) if "20 percent" is read as "100 percent".

(4) For the purposes of subsection (3) and subject to subsections (4.1) and (4.2), the optional significance tests are:

    (a) **The Asset Test** — The reporting issuer's proportionate share of the consolidated assets of the business or related businesses exceeds 20 percent of the consolidated assets of the reporting issuer, calculated using the financial statements of each of the reporting issuer and the business or the related business for the most recently completed interim period or financial year of each, without giving effect to the acquisition.

    (b) **The Investment Test** — The reporting issuer's consolidated investments in and advances to the business or related businesses as at the acquisition date exceeds 20 percent of the consolidated assets of the reporting issuer as at the last day of the most recently completed interim period or financial year of the reporting issuer, excluding any investments in or advances to the business or related businesses as at that date.

    (c) **The Profit or Loss Test** — The specified profit or loss calculated under the following subparagraph (i) exceeds 20 percent of the specified profit or loss calculated under the following subparagraph (ii):

        (i) the reporting issuer's proportionate share of the consolidated specified profit or loss of the business or related businesses for the later of

            (A) the most recently completed financial year of the business or related businesses; or

            (B) the 12 months ended on the last day of the most recently completed interim period of the business or related businesses;

        (ii) the reporting issuer's consolidated specified profit or loss for the later of

            (A) the most recently completed financial year, without giving effect to the acquisition; or

            (B) the 12 months ended on the last day of the most recently completed interim period of the reporting issuer, without giving effect to the acquisition.

(4.1) For the purposes of subsections (2) and (4), the reporting issuer must not remeasure its previously held equity interest in the business or related businesses.

(4.2) For the purposes of paragraphs (2)(b) and (4)(b), the reporting issuer's investments in and advances to the business or related businesses must include

    (a) the consideration transferred for the acquisition, measured in accordance with the issuer's GAAP,

    (b) payments made in connection with the acquisition which do not constitute consideration transferred but which would not have been paid unless the acquisition had occurred, and

    (c) contingent consideration for the acquisition measured in accordance with the issuer's GAAP.

(5) If an acquisition does not meet any of the significance tests under subsection (4), the acquisition is not a significant acquisition.

(6) Despite subsection (3), the significance of an acquisition of a business or related businesses may be re-calculated using financial statements for periods that ended after the acquisition date only if, after the acquisition date, the business or related businesses remained substantially intact and were not significantly reorganized, and no significant assets or liabilities were transferred to other entities.

(7) **Application of the Profit or Loss Test if a Loss Occurred** — For the purposes of paragraphs (2)(c) and (4)(c), if any of the reporting issuer, the business or the related businesses has incurred a loss, the significance test must be applied using the absolute value of the loss from continuing operations attributable to owners of the parent, adjusted to exclude income taxes.

(8) **Application of the Profit or Loss Test if Lower Than Average Profit or Loss for the Most Recent Year** — For the purposes of paragraph (2)(c) and clause (4)(c)(ii)(A), if the reporting issuer's consolidated specified profit or loss for the most recently completed financial year was lower by 20 percent or more than its average consolidated specified profit or loss for the three most recently completed financial years, the issuer may, subject to subsection (10), substitute the average consolidated specified profit or loss for the three most recently completed financial years in determining whether the significance test set out in paragraph (2)(c) or (4)(c) is satisfied.

(9) **Application of the Optional Profit or Loss Test if Lower Than Average Profit or Loss for the Most Recent Year** — For the purpose of clause (4)(c)(ii)(B) if the reporting issuer's consolidated specified profit or loss for the most recently completed 12-month period was lower by 20 percent or more than its average consolidated specified profit or loss for the three most recently completed 12-month periods, the issuer may, subject to subsection (10), substitute the average consolidated specified profit or loss for the three most recently completed 12-month periods in determining whether the significance test set out in paragraph (4)(c) is satisfied.

(10) **Lower than Average Profit or Loss of the Issuer if a Loss Occurred** — If the reporting issuer's consolidated specified profit or loss for either of the two earlier financial periods referred to in subsections (8) and (9) is a loss, the reporting issuer's specified profit or loss for that period is considered to be zero for the purposes of calculating the average consolidated specified profit or loss for the three financial periods.

(11) **Application of Significance Tests — Multiple Investments in the Same Business** — If a reporting issuer has made multiple investments in the same business, then for the purposes of applying subsections (2) and (4),

    (a) if the initial investment and one or more incremental investments were made during the same financial year, the investments must be aggregated and tested on a combined basis;

    (b) if one or more incremental investments were made in a financial year subsequent to the financial year in which an initial or incremental investment was made and the initial or previous incremental investments are reflected in audited annual financial statements of the reporting issuer previously filed, the reporting issuer must apply the significance tests set out in subsections (2) and (4) on a combined basis to the incremental investments not reflected in audited financial statements of the reporting issuer previously filed; and

    (c) if one or more incremental investments were made in a financial year subsequent to the financial year in which the initial investment was made and the initial investment is not reflected in audited annual financial statements of the reporting issuer previously filed, the reporting issuer must apply the significance tests set out in subsections (2) and (4) to the initial and incremental investments on a combined basis.

(11.1) **Application of the Optional Profit or Loss Test based on Pro Forma Financial Information** — For the purposes of calculating the optional profit or loss test under clause (4)(c)(ii)(A), a reporting issuer may use pro forma consolidated specified profit or loss for its most recently completed financial year that was included in a previously filed document if

    (a) the reporting issuer has made a significant acquisition of a business after its most recently completed financial year; and

    (b) the previously filed document included

        (i) audited annual financial statements of that acquired business for the periods required by this Part; and

        (ii) the pro forma financial information required by subsection 8.4(5) or (6).

(12) **Application of Significance Tests — Related Businesses** — In determining whether an acquisition of related businesses is a significant acquisition, related businesses acquired after the ending date of the most recently filed audited annual financial statements of the reporting issuer must be considered on a combined basis.

(13) **Application of Significance Tests — Accounting Principles and Currency** — For the purposes of calculating the significance tests in subsections (2) and (4), the amounts used for the business or related businesses must

(a) subject to subsection (13.1), be based on the issuer's GAAP, and

(b) be translated into the same presentation currency as that used in the reporting issuer's financial statements.

(13.1) **Application of Significance Tests — Exemption — Canadian GAAP Applicable to Private Enterprises** — Paragraph 8.3(13)(a) does not apply to a venture issuer if

(a) the financial statements for the business or related businesses referred to in subsections 8.3(2) and (4)

(i) are prepared in accordance with Canadian GAAP applicable to private enterprises, and

(ii) are prepared in a manner that consolidates any subsidiaries and accounts for significantly influenced investees and joint ventures using the equity method; and

(b) none of the accounting principles described in paragraphs 3.11(1)(a) through (e) of National Instrument 52-107 *Acceptable Accounting Principles and Auditing Standards* were used to prepare financial statements for the business or related businesses referred to in subsections 8.3(2) and (4).

(14) **Application of Significance Tests — Use of Unaudited Financial Statements** — Despite subsections (2) and (4), the significance of an acquisition of a business or related businesses may be calculated using unaudited financial statements of the business or related businesses that comply with section 3.11 of National Instrument 52-107 *Acceptable Accounting Principles and Auditing Standards* if the financial statements of the business or related businesses for the most recently completed financial year have not been audited.

(15) **Application of Significance Tests — Use of Previous Audited Financial Statements** — Despite subsections (2) and (4), the significance of an acquisition of a business or related businesses may be calculated using the audited financial statements for the financial year immediately preceding the reporting issuer's most recently completed financial year if the reporting issuer has not been required to file, and has not filed, audited financial statements for its most recently completed financial year.

8.4 Financial Statement Disclosure for Significant Acquisitions — (1) **Comparative Annual Financial Statements** — If a reporting issuer is required to file a business acquisition report under section 8.2, subject to sections 8.6 through 8.11, the business acquisition report must include the following for each business or related businesses:

(a) a statement of comprehensive income, a statement of changes in equity and a statement of cash flows for the following periods:

(i) if the business has completed one financial year,

(A) the most recently completed financial year ended on or before the acquisition date; and

(B) the financial year immediately preceding the most recently completed financial year, if any; or

(ii) if the business has not completed one financial year, the financial period commencing on the date of formation and ending on a date not more than 45 days before the acquisition date;

(b) a statement of financial position as at the end of each of the periods specified in paragraph (a); and

(c) notes to the financial statements.

(2) **Audit** — The most recently completed financial period referred to in subsection (1) must be audited.

(3) **Interim Financial Report** — Subject to subsection (4) and sections 8.6 through 8.11, if a reporting issuer is required to include financial statements in a business acquisition report under subsection (1), the business acquisition report must include financial statements for

(a) the most recently completed interim period or other period that started the day after the date of the statement of financial position specified in paragraph (1)(b) and ended,

(i) in the case of an interim period, before the acquisition date; or

(ii) in the case of a period other than an interim period, after the interim period referred to in subparagraph (i) and on or before the acquisition date; and

(b) a comparable period in the preceding financial year of the business.

(3.1) **Contents of Interim Financial Report — Canadian GAAP Applicable to Private Enterprises** — If a reporting issuer is required under subsection (3) to include an interim financial report in a business acquisition report and the financial statements for the business or related businesses acquired are prepared in accordance with Canadian GAAP applicable to private enterprises, as permitted under National Instrument 52-107 *Acceptable Accounting Principles and Auditing Standards*, the interim financial report must include

(a) a balance sheet as at the end of the interim period and a balance sheet as at the end of the immediately preceding financial year, if any;

(b) an income statement, a statement of retained earnings and a cash flow statement, all for the year-to-date interim period, and comparative financial information for the corresponding interim period in the immediately preceding financial year, if any; and

(c) notes to the financial statements.

(4) **Earlier Financial Statements Permitted** — Despite subsection (3), the business acquisition report may include financial statements for a period ending not more than one interim period before the period referred to in subparagraph (3)(a)(i) if

(a) the business does not, or related businesses do not, constitute a material departure from the business or operations of the reporting issuer immediately before the acquisition; and

(b) [repealed]

(c) either

(i) the acquisition date is, and the reporting issuer files the business acquisition report, within the following time after the business's or related businesses' most recently completed interim period:

(A) 45 days, if the reporting issuer is not a venture issuer; or

(B) 60 days, if the reporting issuer is a venture issuer; or

(ii) the reporting issuer filed a document before the acquisition date that included financial statements for the business or related businesses that would have been required if the document were a prospectus, and those financial statements are for a period ending not more than one interim period before the interim period referred to in subparagraph (3)(a)(i).

(5) Pro Forma Financial Statements Required in a Business Acquisition Report — If a reporting issuer other than a venture issuer is required to include financial statements in a business acquisition report under subsection (1) or (3), the business acquisition report must include

(a) a pro forma statement of financial position of the reporting issuer,

(i) as at the date of the reporting issuer's most recent statement of financial position filed, that gives effect, as if they had taken place as at the date of the pro forma statement of financial position, to significant acquisitions that have been completed, but are not reflected in the reporting issuer's most recent statement of financial position for an annual or interim period; or

(ii) if the reporting issuer has not filed a statement of financial position for any annual or interim period, as at the date of the acquired business's most recent statement of financial position, that gives effect, as if they had taken place as at the date of the pro forma statement of financial position, to significant acquisitions that have been completed;

(b) a pro forma income statement of the reporting issuer that gives effect to significant acquisitions completed since the beginning of the financial year referred to in clause (i)(A) or (ii)(A), as applicable, as if they had taken place at the beginning of that financial year, for each of the following financial periods:

(i) the reporting issuer's

(A) most recently completed financial year for which it has filed financial statements; and

(B) interim period for which it has filed interim financial report that started after the period in clause (A) and ended immediately before the acquisition date or, in the reporting issuer's discretion, after the acquisition date; or

(ii) if the reporting issuer has not filed a statement of comprehensive income for any annual or interim period, for the business's or related businesses'

(A) most recently completed financial year that ended before the acquisition date; and

(B) period for which financial statements are included in the business acquisition report under paragraph (3)(a); and

(c) pro forma earnings per share based on the pro forma financial statements referred to in paragraph (b).

(6) Pro Forma Financial Statements based on Earlier Financial Statements Permitted — Despite paragraph (5)(a) and clauses (5)(b)(i)(B) and (5)(b)(ii)(B), if the reporting issuer relies on subsection (4), the business acquisition report may include

(a) a pro forma statement of financial position as at the date of the statement of financial position filed immediately before the reporting issuer's most recent statement of financial position filed; and

(b) a pro forma income statement for the period ending not more than one interim period before the interim period referred to in clause (5)(b)(i)(B) or (5)(b)(ii)(B), as applicable.

(7) Preparation of Pro Forma Financial Statements — If a reporting issuer is required to include pro forma financial statements in a business acquisition report under subsection (5),

(a) the reporting issuer must identify in the pro forma financial statements each significant acquisition, if the pro forma financial statements give effect to more than one significant acquisition;

(b) the reporting issuer must include in the pro forma financial statements

(i) adjustments attributable to each significant acquisition for which there are firm commitments and for which the complete financial effects are objectively determinable,

(ii) adjustments to conform amounts for the business or related businesses to the issuer's accounting policies, and

(iii) a description of the underlying assumptions on which the pro forma financial statements are prepared, cross-referenced to each related pro forma adjustment;

(c) if the financial year-end of the business differs from the reporting issuer's year-end by more than 93 days, for the purpose of preparing the pro forma income statement for the reporting issuer's most recently completed financial year, the reporting issuer must construct an income statement of the business for a period of 12 consecutive months ending no more than 93 days before or after the reporting issuer's year-end, by adding the results for a subsequent interim period to a completed financial year of the business and deducting the comparable interim results for the immediately preceding year;

(d) if a constructed income statement is required under paragraph (c), the pro forma financial statements must disclose the period covered by the constructed income statement on the face of the pro forma financial statements and must include a note stating that the financial statements of the business used to prepare the pro forma financial statements were prepared for the purpose of the pro forma financial statements and do not conform with the financial statements for the business included elsewhere in the business acquisition report;

(e) if a reporting issuer is required to prepare a pro forma income statement for an interim period required by paragraph (5)(b), and the pro forma income statement for the most recently completed financial year includes results of the business which are also included in the pro forma income statement for the interim period, the reporting issuer must disclose in a note to the pro forma financial statements the revenue, expenses and profit or loss from continuing operations included in each pro forma income statement for the overlapping period; and

(f) a constructed period referred to in paragraph (c) does not have to be audited.

(8) Financial Statements of Related Businesses — If a reporting issuer is required under subsection (1) to include financial statements for more than one business because the significant acquisition involves an acquisition of related businesses, the financial statements required under subsection (1) must be presented separately for each business, except for the periods during which the businesses have been under common control or management, in which case the reporting issuer may present the financial statements of the businesses on a combined basis.

8.5 [repealed]

8.6 Exemption for Significant Acquisitions Accounted for Using the Equity Method — A reporting issuer is exempt from the requirements in section 8.4 if

(a) the acquisition is, or will be, of an equity investee;

(b) the business acquisition report includes disclosure for the periods for which financial statements are otherwise required under subsection 8.4(1) that

(i) summarizes financial information of the equity investee, including the aggregated amounts of assets, liabilities, revenue and profit or loss; and

(ii) describes the reporting issuer's proportionate interest in the equity investee and any contingent issuance of securities by the equity investee that might significantly affect the reporting issuer's share of profit or loss;

(c) the financial information provided under paragraph (b) for the most recently completed financial year

(i) has been derived from audited financial statements of the equity investee; or

(ii) has been audited; and

(d) the business acquisition report

(i) identifies the financial statements referred to in subparagraph (c)(i) from which the disclosure provided under paragraph (b) has been derived; or

(ii) discloses that the financial information provided under paragraph (b), if not derived from audited financial statements, has been audited; and

(iii) discloses that the auditor expressed an unmodified opinion with respect to the financial statements referred to in subparagraph (i) or the financial information referred to in subparagraph.

8.7 [repealed]

8.8 Exemption for Significant Acquisitions if Financial Year End Changed — If under section 8.4 a reporting issuer is required to provide financial statements for a business acquired and the business changed its financial year end during either of the financial years required to be included, the reporting issuer may include financial statements for the transition year in satisfaction of the financial statements for one of the years, provided that the transition year is at least nine months.

8.9 Exemption from Comparatives if Financial Statements Not Previously Prepared — A reporting issuer is not required to provide comparative information for an interim financial report required under subsection 8.4(3) for a business acquired if

(a) to a reasonable person it is impracticable to present prior-period information on a basis consistent with the most recently completed interim period of the acquired business;

(b) the prior-period information that is available is presented; and

(c) the notes to the interim financial report disclose the fact that the prior-period information has not been prepared on a basis consistent with the most recent interim financial information.

8.10 Acquisition of an Interest in an Oil and Gas Property — (1) **Asset Test** — Despite subsections 8.3(2) and 8.3(4), the asset tests in paragraphs 8.3(2)(a) and 8.3(4)(a) do not apply to an acquisition

(a) of a business that is an interest in an oil and gas property or related businesses that are interests in oil and gas properties; and

(b) that is not of securities of another issuer, unless the vendor transferred the business referenced in paragraph (1)(a) to the other issuer and that other issuer

(i) was created for the sole purpose of facilitating the acquisition; and

(ii) other than assets or operations relating to the transferred business, has no

(A) substantial assets; or

(B) operating history.

(2) **Profit or Loss Test** — Despite subsections 8.3(2), 8.3(4), 8.3(8), 8.3(9), 8.3(10) and 8.3(11.1), a reporting issuer must substitute "operating income" for "specified profit or loss" for the purposes of the profit or loss test in paragraphs 8.3(2)(c) and 8.3(4)(c) if the acquisition is one described in subsection (1).

(3) **Exemption from Financial Statement Disclosure** — A reporting issuer is exempt from the requirements in section 8.4 if

(a) the significant acquisition is an acquisition described in subsection (1);

(b) the reporting issuer is unable to provide the financial statements in respect of the significant acquisition otherwise required under this Part because those financial statements do not exist or because the reporting issuer does not have access to those financial statements;

(c) the acquisition does not constitute a reverse takeover;

(d) [repealed]

(e) subject to subsection (4) in respect of the business or related businesses, for each of the financial periods for which financial statements would, but for this section, be required under section 8.4, the business acquisition report includes

(i) an operating statement for the business or related businesses prepared in accordance with subsection 3.11(5) of National Instrument 52-107 *Acceptable Accounting Principles and Auditing Standards*;

(ii) a pro forma operating statement of the reporting issuer that gives effect to significant acquisitions completed since the beginning of the reporting issuer's most recently completed financial year for which financial statements are required to have been filed, as if they had taken place at the beginning of that financial year, for each of the financial periods referred to in paragraph 8.4(5)(b);

(iii) a description of the property or properties and the interest acquired by the reporting issuer; and

(iv) disclosure of the annual oil and gas production volumes from the business or related businesses;

(f) the operating statement for the most recently completed financial period referred to in subsection 8.4(1) is audited; and

(g) the business acquisition report discloses

(i) the estimated reserves and related future net revenue attributable to the business or related businesses, the material assumptions used in preparing the estimates and the identity and relationship to the reporting issuer or to the vendor of the person who prepared the estimates; and

(ii) the estimated oil and gas production volumes from the business or related businesses for the first year reflected in the estimates disclosed under subparagraph (i).

(4) **Exemption from Alternative Disclosure** — A reporting issuer is exempt from the requirements of subparagraphs (3)(e)(i), (ii) and (iv), if

(a) production, gross sales, royalties, production costs and operating income were nil for the business or related businesses for each financial period; and

(b) the business acquisition report discloses this fact.

8.11 Exemption for Multiple Investments in the Same Business — Despite section 8.4, a reporting issuer is exempt from the requirements to file financial statements for an acquired business, other than the pro forma financial statements required by subsection 8.4(5), in a business acquisition report if the reporting issuer has made multiple investments in the same business and the acquired business has been consolidated in the reporting issuer's most recent annual financial statements that have been filed.

PART 9 — PROXY SOLICITATION AND INFORMATION CIRCULARS

9.1 Sending of Proxies and Information Circulars — (1) If management of a reporting issuer gives notice of a meeting to its registered holders of voting securities, management must, at the same time as or before giving that notice, send to each registered holder of voting securities who is entitled to notice of the meeting a form of proxy for use at the meeting.

(2) Subject to section 9.2, a person or company that solicits proxies from registered holders of voting securities of a reporting issuer must,

(a) in the case of a solicitation by or on behalf of management of a reporting issuer, send an information circular with the notice of meeting to each registered securityholder whose proxy is solicited; or

(b) in the case of any other solicitation, concurrently with or before the solicitation, send an information circular to each registered securityholder whose proxy is solicited.

9.1.1 Notice-and-Access — (1) A person or company soliciting proxies may use notice-and-access to send proxy-related materials to a registered holder of voting securities of a reporting issuer if all of the following apply:

(a) the registered holder of voting securities is sent a notice that contains the following information and no other information:

(i) the date, time and location of the reporting issuer's meeting for which the proxy-related materials are being sent;

(ii) a description of each matter or group of related matters identified in the form of proxy to be voted on, unless that information is already included in a form of proxy that is being sent to the registered holder of voting securities under paragraph (b);

(iii) the website addresses for SEDAR and the non-SEDAR website where the proxy-related materials are posted;

(iv) a reminder to review the information circular before voting;

(v) an explanation of how to obtain a paper copy of the information circular and, if applicable, the documents in paragraph (2)(b) from the person or company;

(vi) a plain-language explanation of notice-and-access that includes the following information:

(A) if the person or company is using stratification, a list of the types of registered holders or beneficial owners who will receive paper copies of the information circular and, if applicable, the documents in paragraph (2)(b);

(B) the estimated date and time by which a request for a paper copy of the information circular and, if applicable, the documents in paragraph (2)(b), is to be received in order for the requester to receive the paper copy in advance of any deadline for the submission of the proxy and the date of the meeting;

(C) an explanation of how the registered holder is to return the proxy, including any deadline for return of the proxy;

(D) the sections of the information circular where disclosure regarding each matter or group of related matters identified in the notice can be found;

(E) a toll-free telephone number the registered holder can call to get information about notice-and-access;

(b) the registered holder of voting securities is sent, by prepaid mail, courier or the equivalent, the notice required by paragraph (a) and a form of proxy for use at the meeting and, in the case of a solicitation by or on behalf of management of the reporting issuer, the notice and form of proxy are sent at least 30 days before the date of the meeting;

(c) in the case of a solicitation by or on behalf of management of the reporting issuer, the reporting issuer files on SEDAR the notification of meeting and record dates in the manner and within the time specified by NI 54-101;

(d) public electronic access to the information circular, form of proxy and the notice in paragraph (a) is provided on or before the date that the person or company soliciting proxies sends the notice in paragraph (a) to registered holders in the following manner:

(i) the documents are filed on SEDAR as required by section 9.3;

(ii) the documents are posted until the date that is one year from the date that the documents are posted, on a website other than the website for SEDAR;

(e) a toll-free telephone number is provided for use by the registered holder of voting securities to request a paper copy of the information circular and, if applicable, the documents in paragraph (2)(b), at any time from the date that the person or company soliciting proxies sends the notice in paragraph (a) to the registered holder up to and including the date of the meeting, including any adjournment;

(f) if a request for a paper copy of the information circular and, if applicable, the documents in paragraph (2)(b), is received at the toll-free telephone number provided under paragraph (e) or by any other means, a paper copy of any such document requested is sent free of charge by the person or company soliciting proxies to the requester at the address specified in the request in the following manner:

(i) in the case of a request received prior to the date of the meeting, within 3 business days after receiving the request, by first class mail, courier or the equivalent;

(ii) in the case of a request received on or after the date of the meeting, and within one year of the information circular being filed, within 10 calendar days after receiving the request, by prepaid mail, courier or the equivalent.

(2) Unless an information circular is included with the proxy-related materials, a reporting issuer that sends proxy-related materials to a registered holder of voting securities using notice-and-access must not include with the proxy-related materials any information or document that relates to the particulars of any matter to be submitted to the meeting, except for the following:

(a) the information required to be included in the notice under paragraph (1)(a);

(b) financial statements of the reporting issuer to be approved at the meeting and MD&A related to those financial statements, which may be part of an annual report.

(3) A notice under paragraph (1)(a) and the form of proxy may be combined in a single document.

9.1.2 **Posting materials on non-SEDAR website** — (1) A person or company that posts proxy-related materials in the manner referred to in subparagraph 9.1.1(1)(d)(ii) must also post on the website the following documents:

(a) any disclosure material regarding the meeting that the person or company has sent to registered holders or beneficial owners of voting securities;

(b) any written communications the person or company soliciting proxies has made available to the public regarding each matter or group of matters to be voted upon at the meeting, whether or not they were sent to registered holders or beneficial owners of voting securities.

(2) Proxy-related materials that are posted under subparagraph 9.1.1(1)(d)(ii) must be posted in a manner and be in a format that permit an individual with a reasonable level of computer skill and knowledge to do all of the following easily:

(a) access, read and search the documents on the website;

(b) download and print the documents.

9.1.3 **Consent to other delivery methods** — For greater certainty, section 9.1.1 does not

(a) prevent a registered holder of voting securities from consenting to a person or company's use of other delivery methods to send proxy-related materials,

(b) terminate or modify a consent that a registered holder of voting securities previously gave to a person or company regarding the use of other delivery methods to send proxy-related materials, or

(c) prevent a person or company from sending proxy-related materials using a delivery method to which a registered holder has consented prior to February 11, 2013.

9.1.4 **Instructions to receive paper copies** — (1) Despite section 9.1.1, a reporting issuer may obtain standing instructions from a registered holder of voting securities that a paper copy of the information circular and, if applicable, the documents in paragraph 9.1.1(2)(b), be sent to the registered holder in all cases when the reporting issuer uses notice-and-access.

(2) If a reporting issuer has obtained standing instructions from a registered holder under subsection (1), the reporting issuer must do both of the following:

(a) include with the notice required by paragraph 9.1.1(1)(a) any paper copies of information circulars and, if applicable, the documents in paragraph 9.1.1(2)(b), required to comply with standing instructions obtained under subsection (1);

(b) include with the notice under paragraph (a) a description, or otherwise inform the registered holder of, the means by which the registered holder may revoke the registered holder's standing instructions.

9.1.5 **Compliance with SEC Notice-and-Access Rules** — A reporting issuer that is an SEC issuer can send proxy-related materials to registered holders under section 9.1 using a delivery method permitted under U.S. federal securities law, if both of the following apply:

(a) the SEC issuer is subject to, and complies with Rule 14a-16 under the 1934 Act;

(b) residents of Canada do not own, directly or indirectly, outstanding voting securities carrying more than 50% of the votes for the election of directors, and none of the following apply:

(i) the majority of the executive officers or directors of the issuer are residents of Canada;

(ii) more than 50% of the consolidated assets of the issuer are located in Canada;

(iii) the business of the issuer is administered principally in Canada.

9.2 **Exemptions from Sending Information Circular** — (1) Subsection 9.1(2) does not apply to a solicitation by a person or company in respect of securities of which the person or company is the beneficial owner.

(2) Paragraph 9.1(2)(b) does not apply to a solicitation if the total number of securityholders whose proxies are solicited is not more than 15.

(3) For the purposes of subsection (2), two or more persons or companies who are joint registered owners of one or more securities are considered to be one securityholder.

(4) Despite paragraph 9.1(2)(b), a person or company, other than management of a reporting issuer or a person or company acting on behalf of management, may solicit proxies from registered securityholders of a reporting issuer without sending an information circular, if

(a) the solicitation is made to the public by broadcast, speech or publication;

(b) soliciting proxies by broadcast, speech or publication is permitted by the laws under which the reporting issuer is incorporated, organized or continued and the person or company making the solicitation complies with the requirements, if any, of those laws relating to the broadcast, speech or publication;

(c) the person or company has filed the following information:

(i) the name and address of the reporting issuer to which the solicitation relates,

(ii) the information required under item 2, sections 3.2, 3.3 and 3.4 and paragraphs (b) and (d) of item 5 of Form 51-102F5 *Information Circular*,

(iii) any information required to be disclosed in respect of the broadcast, speech or publication by the laws under which the reporting issuer is incorporated, organized or continued, and

(iv) a copy of any communication intended to be published; and

(d) the broadcast, speech or publication contains the information referred to in paragraphs (c)(i) to (iii).

(5) Subsection (4) does not apply to a person or company that is proposing, at the time of the solicitation, a significant acquisition or restructuring transaction involving the reporting issuer and the person or company, under which securities of the person or company, or securities of an affiliate of the person or company, are to be changed, exchanged, issued or distributed, unless

(a) the person or company has filed an information circular or other document containing the information required by section 14.4 of Form 51-102F5 *Information Circular*; and

(b) the solicitation refers to that information circular or other document and discloses that the circular or other document is on SEDAR.

(6) Subsection (4) does not apply to a person or company that is nominating or proposing to nominate, at the time of the solicitation, an individual, including himself or herself, for election as a director of the reporting issuer, unless

(a) the person or company has filed an information circular or other document containing the information required by Form 51-102F5 *Information Circular* in respect of the proposed nominee; and

(b) the solicitation refers to that information circular or other document and discloses that the circular or other document is on SEDAR.

9.3 Filing of Information Circulars and Proxy-Related Material — A person or company that is required under this Instrument to send an information circular or form of proxy to registered securityholders of a reporting issuer must promptly file a copy of the information circular, form of proxy and all other material required to be sent by the person or company in connection with the meeting to which the information circular or form of proxy relates.

9.3.1 Content of Information Circular — (1) Subject to Item 8 of Form 51-102F5, if a reporting issuer is required to send an information circular to a securityholder under paragraph 9.1(2)(a), the issuer must

(a) disclose all compensation paid, payable, awarded, granted, given, or otherwise provided, directly or indirectly, by the issuer, or a subsidiary of the issuer, to each NEO and director, in any capacity, including, for greater certainty, all plan and non-plan compensation, direct or indirect pay, remuneration, economic or financial award, reward, benefit, gift or perquisite paid, payable, awarded, granted, given, or otherwise provided to the NEO or director for services provided, directly or indirectly, to the issuer or a subsidiary of the issuer, and

(b) include detail and discussion of the compensation, and the decision-making process relating to compensation, presented in such a way that it provides a reasonable person an understanding of

(i) how decisions about NEO and director compensation are made,

(ii) the compensation paid, made payable, awarded, granted, given or otherwise provided to each NEO and director, and

(iii) how specific NEO and director compensation relates to the overall stewardship and governance of the reporting issuer.

(2) The disclosure required under subsection (1) must be provided for the periods set out in and in accordance with Form 51-102F6 *Statement of Executive Compensation*.

(2.1) Despite subsection (2), a venture issuer may provide the disclosure required by subsection (1) for the periods set out in and in accordance with Form 51-102F6V *Statement of Executive Compensation – Venture Issuers*.

(2.2) The disclosure required under subsection (1) must be filed

(a) not later than 140 days after the end of the issuer's most recently completed financial year, in the case of an issuer other than a venture issuer, or

(b) not later than 180 days after the end of the issuer's most recently completed financial year, in the case of a venture issuer.

(3) For the purposes of this section, "NEO" and "plan" have the meaning ascribed to those terms in Form 51-102F6 *Statement of Executive Compensation* or, for a venture issuer relying on subsection (2.1), in Form 51-102F6V *Statement of Executive Compensation – Venture Issuers*

(4) [Repealed.]

(5) Subsection (2.2) applies to an issuer in respect of a financial year beginning on or after July 1, 2015.

9.4 Content of Form of Proxy — (1) A form of proxy sent to securityholders of a reporting issuer by a person or company soliciting proxies must indicate in bold-face type whether or not the proxy is solicited by or on behalf of the management of the reporting issuer, provide a specifically designated blank space for dating the form of proxy and specify the meeting in respect of which the proxy is solicited.

(2) An information circular sent to securityholders of a reporting issuer or the form of proxy to which the information circular relates must

(a) indicate in bold-face type that the securityholder has the right to appoint a person or company to represent the securityholder at the meeting other than the person or company if any, designated in the form of proxy; and

(b) contain instructions as to the manner in which the securityholder may exercise the right referred to in paragraph (a).

(3) If a form of proxy sent to securityholders of a reporting issuer contains a designation of a named person or company as nominee, it must provide an option for the securityholder to designate in the form of proxy some other person or company as the securityholder's nominee.

(4) A form of proxy sent to securityholders of a reporting issuer must provide an option for the securityholder to specify that the securities registered in the securityholder's name will be voted for or against each matter or group of related matters identified in the form of proxy, in the notice of meeting or in an information circular, other than the appointment of an auditor and the election of directors.

(5) A form of proxy sent to securityholders of a reporting issuer may confer discretionary authority with respect to each matter referred to in subsection (4) as to which a choice is not specified if the form of proxy or the information circular states in bold-face type how the securities represented by the proxy will be voted in respect of each matter or group of related matters.

(6) A form of proxy sent to securityholders of a reporting issuer must provide an option for the securityholder to specify that the securities registered in the name of the securityholder must be voted or withheld from voting in respect of the appointment of an auditor or the election of directors.

(7) An information circular sent to securityholders of a reporting issuer or the form of proxy to which the information circular relates must state that

(a) the securities represented by the proxy will be voted or withheld from voting in accordance with the instructions of the securityholder on any ballot that may be called for; and

(b) if the securityholder specifies a choice under subsection (4) or (6) with respect to any matter to be acted upon, the securities will be voted accordingly.

(8) A form of proxy sent to securityholders of a reporting issuer may confer discretionary authority with respect to

(a) amendments or variations to matters identified in the notice of meeting; and

(b) other matters which may properly come before the meeting,

if,

(c) the person or company by whom or on whose behalf the solicitation is made is not aware within a reasonable time before the time the solicitation is made that any of those amendments, variations or other matters are to be presented for action at the meeting; and

(d) a specific statement is made in the information circular or in the form of proxy that the proxy is conferring such discretionary authority.

(9) A form of proxy sent to securityholders of a reporting issuer must not confer authority to vote

(a) for the election of any person as a director of a reporting issuer unless a bona fide proposed nominee for that election is named in the information circular or, in the case of a solicitation under subsection 9.2(4), the document required under paragraph 9.2(6)(a); or

(b) at any meeting other than the meeting specified in the notice of meeting or any adjournment of that meeting.

9.5 Exemption — Sections 9.1 to 9.4 do not apply to a reporting issuer, or a person or company that solicits proxies from registered holders of voting securities of a reporting issuer, if

(a) the reporting issuer or other person or company complies with the requirements of the laws relating to the solicitation of proxies under which the reporting issuer is incorporated, organized or continued;

(b) the requirements referred to in subsection (a) are substantially similar to the requirements of this Part; and

(c) the reporting issuer or other person or company files a copy of any information circular and form of proxy, or other documents that contain substantially similar information, promptly after the reporting issuer or other person or company sends the circular, form or other document in connection with the meeting.

PART 10 — RESTRICTED SECURITY DISCLOSURE

10.1 Restricted Security Disclosure — (1) Except as otherwise provided in section 10.3, if a reporting issuer has outstanding restricted securities, or securities that are directly or indirectly convertible into or exercisable or exchangeable for restricted securities or securities that will, when issued, result in an existing class of outstanding securities being considered restricted securities, each document referred to in subsection (2) must

(a) refer to restricted securities using a term that includes the appropriate restricted security term;

(b) not refer to securities by a term that includes "common", or "preference" or "preferred", unless the securities are common shares or preference shares, respectively;

(c) describe any restrictions on the voting rights of restricted securities;

(d) describe the rights to participate, if any, of holders of restricted securities if a takeover bid is made for securities of the reporting issuer with voting rights superior to those attached to the restricted securities;

(e) state the percentage of the aggregate voting rights attached to the reporting issuer's securities that are represented by the class of restricted securities; and

(f) if holders of restricted securities have no right to participate if a takeover bid is made for securities of the reporting issuer with voting rights superior to those attached to the restricted securities, contain a statement to that effect in bold-face type.

(2) Subsection (1) applies to the following documents except as provided in subsections (3) and (6):

(a) an information circular;

(b) a document required by this Instrument to be delivered upon request by a reporting issuer to any of its securityholders; and

(c) an AIF prepared by a reporting issuer.

(3) Despite subsection (2), annual financial statements, an interim financial report and MD&A or other accompanying discussion by management of those financial statements are not required to include the details referred to in paragraphs (1)(c), (d), (e) and (f).

(4) Each reference to restricted securities in any document not referred to in subsection (2) that a reporting issuer sends to its securityholders must include the appropriate restricted security term.

(5) A reporting issuer must not refer, in any of the documents described in subsection (4), to securities by a term that includes "common" or "preference" or "preferred", unless the securities are common shares or preference shares, respectively.

(6) Despite paragraph (1)(b) and subsection (5), a reporting issuer may, in one place only in a document referred to in subsection (2) or (4), describe the restricted securities by the term used in the constating documents of the reporting issuer, to the extent that term differs from the appropriate restricted security term, if the description is not on the front page of the document and is in the same type face and type size as that used generally in the document.

10.2 Dissemination of Disclosure Documents to Holder of Restricted Securities — (1) If a reporting issuer sends a document to all holders of any class of its equity securities the document must also be sent by the reporting issuer at the same time to the holders of its restricted securities.

(2) A reporting issuer that is required by this Instrument to arrange for, or voluntarily makes arrangements for, delivery of the documents referred to in subsection (1) to the beneficial owners of any securities of a class of equity securities registered in the name of a registrant, must make similar arrangements for delivery of the documents to the beneficial owners of securities of a class of restricted securities registered in the name of the registrant.

10.3 Exemptions for Certain Reporting Issuers — The provisions of sections 10.1 and 10.2 do not apply to

(a) securities that carry a right to vote subject to a restriction on the number or percentage of securities that may be voted or owned by persons or companies that are not citizens or residents of Canada or that are otherwise considered as a result of any law applicable to the reporting issuer to be non-Canadians, but only to the extent of the restriction; and

(b) securities that are subject to a restriction, imposed by any law governing the reporting issuer, on the level of ownership of the securities by any person, company or combination of persons or companies, but only to the extent of the restriction.

PART 11 — ADDITIONAL DISCLOSURE REQUIREMENTS

11.1 Additional Filing Requirements — (1) A reporting issuer must file a copy of any disclosure material

(a) that it sends to its securityholders;

(b) in the case of an SEC issuer, that it files with or furnishes to the SEC under the 1934 Act, including material filed as exhibits to other documents, if the material contains information that has not been included in disclosure already filed in a jurisdiction by the SEC issuer; or

(c) that it files with another provincial or territorial securities regulatory authority or regulator other than in connection with a distribution.

(2) A reporting issuer must file the material referred to in subsection (1) on the same date as, or as soon as practicable after, the earlier of

(a) the date on which the reporting issuer sends the material to its securityholders;

(b) the date on which the reporting issuer files or furnishes the material to the SEC; and

(c) the date on which the reporting issuer files that material with the other provincial or territorial securities regulatory authority or regulator.

11.2 Change of Status Report — A reporting issuer must file a notice promptly after the occurrence of either of the following:

(a) the reporting issuer becomes a venture issuer; or

(b) the reporting issuer ceases to be a venture issuer.

11.3 Voting Results — A reporting issuer that is not a venture issuer must, promptly following a meeting of securityholders at which a matter was submitted to a vote, file a report that discloses, for each matter voted upon

(a) a brief description of the matter voted upon and the outcome of the vote; and

(b) if the vote was conducted by ballot, including a vote on a matter in which votes are cast both in person and by proxy, the number or percentage of votes cast for, against or withheld from the vote.

11.4 Financial Information — A reporting issuer must file a copy of any news release issued by it that discloses information regarding its historical or prospective financial performance or financial condition for a financial year or interim period.

11.5 Re-filing Documents — If a reporting issuer decides it will

(a) re-file a document filed under this Instrument, or

(b) re-state financial information for comparative periods in financial statements for reasons other than retrospective application of a change in an accounting standard or policy or a new accounting standard,

and the information in the re-filed document, or re-stated financial information, will differ materially from the information originally filed, the issuer must immediately issue and file a news release authorized by an executive officer disclosing the nature and substance of the change or proposed changes.

11.6 Executive Compensation Disclosure for Certain Reporting Issuers — (1) A reporting issuer that is not required to send to its securityholders an information circular and does not send an information circular that includes the disclosure required by Item 8 of Form 51-102F5 and that does not file an AIF that includes the executive compensation disclosure required by Item 18 of Form 51-102F2 must

(a) disclose all compensation paid, payable, awarded, granted, given, or otherwise provided, directly or indirectly, by the issuer, or a subsidiary of the issuer, to each NEO and director, in any capacity, including, for greater certainty, all plan and non-plan compensation, direct or indirect pay, remuneration, economic or financial award, reward, benefit, gift or perquisite paid, payable, awarded, granted, given, or otherwise provided to the NEO or director for services provided, directly or indirectly, to the issuer or a subsidiary of the issuer, and

(b) include detail and discussion of the compensation, and the decision-making process relating to compensation, presented in such a way that it provides a reasonable person an understanding of

(i) how decisions about NEO and director compensation are made,

(ii) the compensation paid, made payable, awarded, granted, given or otherwise provided to each NEO and director, and

(iii) how specific NEO and director compensation relates to the overall stewardship and governance of the reporting issuer.

(2) The disclosure required under subsection (1) must be provided for the periods set out in, and in accordance with, Form 51-102F6 *Statement of Executive Compensation.*

(2.1) Despite subsection (2), a reporting issuer that is a venture issuer may provide the disclosure required under subsection (1) for the periods set out in and in accordance with Form 51-102F6V *Statement of Executive Compensation – Venture Issuers.*

(3) The disclosure required under subsection (1) must be filed not later than 140 days after the end of the reporting issuer's most recently completed financial year.

(4) For the purposes of this section, "NEO" and "plan" have the meaning ascribed to those terms in Form 51-102F6 *Statement of Executive Compensation* or, for a venture issuer relying on subsection (2.1), in Form 51-102F6V *Statement of Executive Compensation – Venture Issuers.*

(5) This section does not apply to an issuer that satisfies securities legislation requirements relating to information circulars, proxies and proxy solicitation under section 4.6 or 5.7 of National Instrument 71-102 *Continuous Disclosure and Other Exemptions Relating to Foreign Issuers*.

Part 12 — Filing of Certain Documents

12.1 Filing of Documents Affecting the Rights of Securityholders — (1) A reporting issuer must file copies of the following documents, and any material amendments to the following documents, unless previously filed:

(a) articles of incorporation, amalgamation, continuation or any other constating or establishing documents of the issuer, unless the constating or establishing document is a statutory or regulatory instrument;

(b) by-laws or other corresponding instruments currently in effect;

(c) any securityholder or voting trust agreement that the reporting issuer has access to and that can reasonably be regarded as material to an investor in securities of the reporting issuer;

(d) any securityholders' rights plans or other similar plans; and

(e) any other contract of the issuer or a subsidiary of the issuer that creates or can reasonably be regarded as materially affecting the rights or obligations of its securityholders generally.

(2) A document required to be filed under subsection (1) may be filed in paper format if

(a) it is dated before March 30, 2004; and

(b) it does not exist in an acceptable electronic format.

12.2 Filing of Material Contracts — (1) Unless previously filed, a reporting issuer must file a material contract entered into

(a) within the last financial year; or

(b) before the last financial year if that material contract is still in effect.

(2) Despite subsection (1), a reporting issuer is not required to file a material contract entered into in the ordinary course of business unless the material contract is

(a) a contract to which directors, officers, or promoters are parties other than a contract of employment;

(b) a continuing contract to sell the majority of the reporting issuer's products or services or to purchase the majority of the reporting issuer's requirements of goods, services, or raw materials;

(c) a franchise or licence or other agreement to use a patent, formula, trade secret, process or trade name;

(d) a financing or credit agreement with terms that have a direct correlation with anticipated cash distributions;

(e) an external management or external administration agreement; or

(f) a contract on which the reporting issuer's business is substantially dependent.

(3) A provision in a material contract filed pursuant to subsections (1) or (2) may be omitted or marked to be unreadable if an executive officer of the reporting issuer reasonably believes that disclosure of that provision would be seriously prejudicial to the interests of the reporting issuer or would violate confidentiality provisions.

(4) Subsection (3) does not apply if the provision relates to

(a) debt covenants and ratios in financing or credit agreements;

(b) events of default or other terms relating to the termination of the material contract; or

(c) other terms necessary for understanding the impact of the material contract on the business of the reporting issuer.

(5) If a provision is omitted or marked to be unreadable under subsection (3), the reporting issuer must include a description of the type of information that has been omitted or marked to be unreadable immediately after the provision in the copy of the material contract filed by the reporting issuer.

(6) Despite subsections (1) and (2), a reporting issuer is not required to file a material contract entered into before January 1, 2002.

12.3 Time for Filing of Documents — The documents required to be filed under sections 12.1 and 12.2 must be filed no later than the time the reporting issuer files a material change report in Form 51-102F3, if the making of the document constitutes a material change for the issuer, and

(a) no later than the time the reporting issuer's AIF is filed under section 6.1, if the document was made or adopted before the date of the issuer's AIF; or

(b) if the reporting issuer is not required to file an AIF under section 6.1, within 120 days after the end of the issuer's most recently completed financial year, if the document was made or adopted before the end of the issuer's most recently completed financial year.

Part 13 — Exemptions

13.1 Exemptions from this Instrument — (1) The regulator or securities regulatory authority may grant an exemption from this Instrument, in whole or in part, subject to such conditions or restrictions as may be imposed in the exemption.

(2) Despite subsection (1), in Ontario only the regulator may grant such an exemption.

(3) Except in Ontario, an exemption referred to in subsection (1) is granted under the statute referred to in Appendix B of National Instrument 14-101 *Definitions* opposite the name of the local jurisdiction.

13.2 Existing Exemptions — (1) A reporting issuer that was entitled to rely on an exemption, waiver or approval granted to it by a regulator or securities regulatory authority relating to continuous disclosure requirements of securities legislation or securities directions existing immediately before this Instrument came into force is exempt from any substantially similar provision of this Instrument to the same extent and on the same conditions, if any, as contained in the exemption, waiver or approval.

(2) A reporting issuer must, at the time that it first intends to rely on subsection (1) in connection with a filing requirement under this Instrument, inform the securities regulatory authority in writing of

(a) the general nature of the prior exemption, waiver or approval and the date on which it was granted; and

(b) the requirement under prior securities legislation or securities directions in respect of which the prior exemption, waiver or approval applied and the substantially similar provision of this Instrument.

13.3 Exemption for Certain Exchangeable Security Issuers — (1) In this section:

"designated Canadian jurisdiction" means Alberta, British Columbia, Manitoba, New Brunswick, Nova Scotia, Ontario, Québec, or Saskatchewan;

"designated exchangeable security" means an exchangeable security which provides the holder of the security with economic and voting rights which are, as nearly as possible except for tax implications, equivalent to the underlying securities;

"exchangeable security" means a security of an issuer that is exchangeable for, or carries the right of the holder to purchase, or of the parent issuer to cause the purchase of, an underlying security;

"exchangeable security issuer" means a person or company that has issued an exchangeable security;

"parent issuer", when used in relation to an exchangeable security issuer, means the person or company that issues the underlying security; and

"underlying security" means a security of a parent issuer issued or transferred, or to be issued or transferred, on the exchange of an exchangeable security.

(2) Except as provided in this subsection, an exchangeable security issuer satisfies the requirements in this Instrument if

    (a) the parent issuer is the beneficial owner of all the issued and outstanding voting securities of the exchangeable security issuer;

    (b) the parent issuer is either

        (i) an SEC issuer with a class of securities listed or quoted on a U.S. marketplace that has filed all documents it is required to file with the SEC; or

        (ii) a reporting issuer in a designated Canadian jurisdiction that has filed all documents it is required to file under this Instrument;

    (c) the exchangeable security issuer does not issue any securities, and does not have any securities outstanding, other than

        (i) designated exchangeable securities;

        (ii) securities issued to and held by the parent issuer or an affiliate of the parent issuer;

        (iii) debt securities issued to and held by banks, loan corporations, loan and investment corporations, savings companies, trust corporations, treasury branches, savings or credit unions, financial services cooperatives, insurance companies or other financial institutions; or

        (iv) securities issued under exemption from the prospectus requirement in section 2.35 of National Instrument 45-106 *Prospectus Exemptions*;

    (d) the exchangeable security issuer files in electronic format,

        (i) if the parent issuer is not a reporting issuer in a designated Canadian jurisdiction, copies of all documents the parent issuer is required to file with the SEC under the 1934 Act, at the same time as, or as soon as practicable after, the filing by the parent issuer of those documents with the SEC; or

        (ii) if the parent issuer is a reporting issuer in a designated Canadian jurisdiction,

            (A) a notice indicating that the exchangeable security issuer is relying on the continuous disclosure documents filed by its parent issuer and setting out where those documents can be found in electronic format, if the parent issuer is a reporting issuer in the local jurisdiction; or

            (B) copies of all documents the parent issuer is required to file under securities legislation, other than in connection with a distribution, at the same time as the filing by the parent issuer of those documents with a securities regulatory authority or regulator;

    (e) the exchangeable security issuer concurrently sends to all holders of designated exchangeable securities all disclosure materials that are sent to holders of the underlying securities in the manner and at the time required by

        (i) U.S. laws and any U.S. marketplace on which securities of the parent issuer are listed or quoted, if the parent issuer is not a reporting issuer in a designated Canadian jurisdiction; or

        (ii) securities legislation, if the parent issuer is a reporting issuer in a designated Canadian jurisdiction;

    (f) the parent issuer

        (i) complies with U.S. laws and the requirements of any U.S. marketplace on which the securities of the parent issuer are listed or quoted if the parent issuer is not a reporting issuer in a designated Canadian jurisdiction, or securities legislation if the parent issuer is a reporting issuer in a designated Canadian jurisdiction, in respect of making public disclosure of material information on a timely basis; and

        (ii) immediately issues in Canada and files any news release that discloses a material change in its affairs;

    (g) the exchangeable security issuer issues in Canada a news release and files a material change report in accordance with Part 7 of this Instrument for all material changes in respect of the affairs of the exchangeable security issuer that are not also material changes in the affairs of its parent issuer; and

    (h) the parent issuer includes in all mailings of proxy solicitation materials to holders of designated exchangeable securities a clear and concise statement that

        (i) explains the reason the mailed material relates solely to the parent issuer;

        (ii) indicates that the designated exchangeable securities are the economic equivalent to the underlying securities; and

        (iii) describes the voting rights associated with the designated exchangeable securities.

(3) The insider reporting requirement and the requirement to file an insider profile under National Instrument 55-102 *System for Electronic Disclosure by Insiders* does not apply to any insider of an exchangeable security issuer in respect of securities of the exchangeable security issuer so long as,

    (a) if the insider is not the parent issuer,

        (i) the insider does not receive, in the ordinary course, information as to material facts or material changes concerning the parent issuer before the material facts or material changes are generally disclosed; and

        (ii) the insider is not an insider of the parent issuer in any capacity other than by virtue of being an insider of the exchangeable security issuer;

(b) the parent issuer is the beneficial owner of all of the issued and outstanding voting securities of the exchangeable security issuer;

(c) if the insider is the parent issuer, the insider does not beneficially own any designated exchangeable securities other than securities acquired through the exercise of the exchange right and not subsequently traded by the insider;

(d) the parent issuer is an SEC issuer or a reporting issuer in a designated Canadian jurisdiction; and

(e) the exchangeable security issuer has not issued any securities and does not have any securities outstanding, other than

    (i) designated exchangeable securities;

    (ii) securities issued to and held by the parent issuer or an affiliate of the parent issuer;

    (iii) debt securities issued to and held by banks, loan corporations, loan and investment corporations, savings companies, trust corporations, treasury branches, savings or credit unions, financial services cooperatives, insurance companies or other financial institutions; and

    (iv) securities issued under exemption from the prospectus requirement in section 2.35 of National Instrument 45-106 *Prospectus Exemptions*.

13.4 Exemption for Certain Credit Support Issuers — (1) In this section:

"alternative credit support" means support, other than a guarantee, for the payments to be made by the issuer, as stipulated in the terms of the securities or in an agreement governing rights of, or granting rights to, holders of the securities that

(a) obliges the person or company providing the support to provide the issuer with funds sufficient to enable the issuer to make the stipulated payments, or

(b) entitles the holder of the securities to receive, from the person or company providing the support, payment if the issuer fails to make a stipulated payment;

"credit support issuer" means an issuer of securities for which a credit supporter has provided a guarantee or alternative credit support;

"credit supporter" means a person or company that provides a guarantee or alternative credit support for any of the payments to be made by an issuer of securities as stipulated in the terms of the securities or in an agreement governing rights of, or granting rights to, holders of the securities;

"designated Canadian jurisdiction" means Alberta, British Columbia, Manitoba, New Brunswick, Nova Scotia, Ontario, Québec or Saskatchewan;

"designated credit support securities" means

(a) non-convertible debt securities or convertible debt securities that are convertible into non-convertible securities of the credit supporter; or

(b) non-convertible preferred shares or convertible preferred shares that are convertible into securities of the credit supporter,

in respect of which a parent credit supporter has provided

(c) alternative credit support that

    (i) entitles the holder of the securities to receive payment from the credit supporter, or enables the holder to receive payment from the credit support issuer, within 15 days of any failure by the credit support issuer to make a payment; and

    (ii) results in the securities receiving the same credit rating as, or a higher credit rating than, the credit rating they would have received if payment had been fully and unconditionally guaranteed by the credit supporter, or would result in the securities receiving such a rating if they were rated; or

(d) a full and unconditional guarantee of the payments to be made by the credit support issuer, as stipulated in the terms of the securities or in an agreement governing the rights of holders of the securities, that results in the holder of such securities being entitled to receive payment from the credit supporter within 15 days of any failure by the credit support issuer to make a payment;

"parent credit supporter" means a credit supporter of which the reporting issuer is a subsidiary;

"subsidiary credit supporter" means a credit supporter that is a subsidiary of the parent credit supporter;

"summary financial information" includes the following line items:

(a) revenue;

(b) profit or loss from continuing operations attributable to owners of the parent;

(c) profit or loss attributable to owners of the parent; and

(d) unless the accounting principles used to prepare the financial statements of the person or company permits the preparation of the person or company's statement of financial position without classifying assets and liabilities between current and non-current and the person or company provides alternative meaningful financial information which is more appropriate to the industry,

    (i) current assets;

    (ii) non-current assets;

    (iii) current liabilities; and

    (iv) non-current liabilities.

[**Note:** See section 1.1 of the Instrument for the definitions of "profit or loss attributable to owners of the parent" and "profit or loss from continuing operations attributable to owners of the parent".]

(1.1) For the purposes of subparagraph (2)(g)(ii), consolidating summary financial information must be prepared on the following basis:

(a) an entity's annual or interim summary financial information must be derived from the entity's financial information underlying the corresponding consolidated financial statements of the parent credit supporter for the corresponding period;

(b) the parent credit supporter column must account for investments in all subsidiaries under the equity method; and

(c) all subsidiary entity columns must account for investments in non-credit supporter subsidiaries under the equity method.

(2) Except as provided in this section, a parent credit support issuer satisfies the requirements in this Instrument if

(a) the parent credit supporter is the beneficial owner of all the outstanding voting securities of the credit support issuer;

(b) the parent credit supporter is either

    (i) an SEC issuer that is incorporated or organized under the laws of the United States of America or any state or territory of the United States of America or the District of Columbia and that has filed all documents it is required to file with the SEC; or

    (ii) subject to subsection (4), a reporting issuer in a designated Canadian jurisdiction that has filed all documents it is required to file under this Instrument;

(c) the credit support issuer does not issue any securities, and does not have any securities outstanding, other than

    (i) designated credit support securities;

    (ii) securities issued to and held by the parent credit supporter or an affiliate of the parent credit supporter;

    (iii) debt securities issued to and held by banks, loan corporations, loan and investment corporations, savings companies, trust corporations, treasury branches, savings or credit unions, financial services cooperatives, insurance companies or other financial institutions; or

    (iv) securities issued under exemption from the prospectus requirement in section 2.35 of National Instrument 45-106 *Prospectus Exemptions*;

(d) the credit support issuer files in electronic format,

    (i) if the parent credit supporter is not a reporting issuer in a designated Canadian jurisdiction, copies of all documents the parent credit supporter is required to file with the SEC under the 1934 Act, at the same time or as soon as practicable after the filing by the parent credit supporter of those documents with the SEC; or

    (ii) if the parent credit supporter is a reporting issuer in a designated Canadian jurisdiction,

        (A) a notice indicating that the credit support issuer is relying on the continuous disclosure documents filed by the parent credit supporter and setting out where those documents can be found for viewing in electronic format, if the credit support issuer is a reporting issuer in the local jurisdiction; or

        (B) copies of all documents the parent credit supporter is required to file under securities legislation, other than in connection with a distribution, at the same time as the filing by the parent credit supporter of those documents with a securities regulatory authority or regulator;

(e) if the parent credit supporter is not a reporting issuer in a designated Canadian jurisdiction, the parent credit supporter

    (i) complies with U.S. laws and the requirements of any U.S. marketplace on which securities of the parent credit supporter are listed or quoted in respect of making public disclosure of material information on a timely basis; and

    (ii) immediately issues in Canada and files any news release that discloses a material change in its affairs;

(f) the credit support issuer issues in Canada a news release and files a material change report in accordance with Part 7 for all material changes in respect of the affairs of the credit support issuer that are not also material changes in the affairs of the parent credit supporter;

(g) the credit support issuer files, in electronic format, in the notice referred to in clause (d)(ii)(A) or in or with the copy of each consolidated interim financial report and consolidated annual financial statements filed under subparagraph (d)(i) or clause (d)(ii)(B), either

    (i) a statement that the financial results of the credit support issuer are included in the consolidated financial results of the parent credit supporter, if at that time,

        (A) the credit support issuer has minimal assets, operations, revenue or cash flows other than those related to the issuance, administration and repayment of the securities described in paragraph (c), and

        (B) each item of the summary financial information of the subsidiaries of the parent credit supporter on a combined basis, other than the credit support issuer, represents less than 3% of the corresponding items on the consolidated financial statements of the parent credit supporter being filed or referred to under paragraph (d), or

    (ii) for the periods covered by the consolidated interim financial report or consolidated annual financial statements of the parent credit supporter filed, consolidating summary financial information for the parent credit supporter presented with a separate column for each of the following:

        (A) the parent credit supporter;

        (B) the credit support issuer;

        (C) any other subsidiaries of the parent credit supporter on a combined basis;

        (D) consolidating adjustments; and

        (E) the total consolidated amounts;

(h) the credit support issuer files a corrected notice under clause (d)(ii)(A) if the credit support issuer filed the notice with the statement contemplated in subparagraph (g)(i) and the credit support issuer can no longer rely on subparagraph (g)(i);

(i) in the case of designated credit support securities that include debt, the credit support issuer concurrently sends to all holders of such securities all disclosure materials that are sent to holders of similar debt of the parent credit supporter in the manner and at the time required by

    (i) U.S. laws and any U.S. marketplace on which securities of the parent credit supporter are listed or quoted, if the parent credit supporter is not a reporting issuer in a designated Canadian jurisdiction; or

    (ii) securities legislation, if the parent credit supporter is a reporting issuer in a designated Canadian jurisdiction;

(j) in the case of designated credit support securities that include preferred shares, the credit support issuer concurrently sends to all holders of such securities all disclosure materials that are sent to holders of similar preferred shares of the parent credit supporter in the manner and at the time required by

    (i) U.S. laws and any U.S. marketplace on which securities of the parent credit supporter are listed or quoted, if the parent credit supporter is not a reporting issuer in a designated Canadian jurisdiction; or

    (ii) securities legislation, if the parent credit supporter is a reporting issuer in a designated Canadian jurisdiction; and

(k) no person or company other than the parent credit supporter has provided a guarantee or alternative credit support for the payments to be made under any issued and outstanding securities of the credit support issuer.

(2.1) A credit support issuer satisfies the requirements of this Instrument where there is a parent credit supporter and one or more subsidiary credit supporters if

(a) the conditions in paragraphs (2)(a) to (f), (i), and (j) are complied with;

(b) the parent credit supporter controls each subsidiary credit supporter and the parent credit supporter has consolidated the financial statements of each subsidiary credit supporter into the parent credit supporter's financial statements that are filed or referred to under paragraph (2)(d);

(c) the credit support issuer files, in electronic format, in the notice referred to in clause (2)(d)(ii)(A) or in or with the copy of each consolidated interim financial report and the consolidated annual financial statements filed under subparagraph (2)(d)(i) or clause (2)(d)(ii)(B), for a period covered by any consolidated interim financial report or consolidated annual financial statements of the parent credit supporter filed by the parent credit supporter, consolidating summary financial information for the parent credit supporter presented with a separate column for each of the following:

(i) the parent credit supporter;

(ii) the credit support issuer;

(iii) each subsidiary credit supporter on a combined basis;

(iv) any other subsidiaries of the parent credit supporter on a combined basis;

(v) consolidating adjustments; and

(vi) the total consolidated amounts;

(d) no person or company, other than the parent credit supporter or a subsidiary credit supporter has provided a guarantee or alternative credit support for the payments to be made under the issued and outstanding designated credit support securities; and

(e) the guarantees or alternative credit supports are joint and several.

(2.2) Despite paragraph (2.1)(c), the information set out in a column in accordance with

(a) subparagraph (2.1)(c)(iv), may be combined with the information set out in accordance with any of the other columns in paragraph (2.1)(c) if each item of the summary financial information set out in a column in accordance with subparagraph (2.1)(c)(iv) represents less than 3% of the corresponding items on the consolidated financial statements of the parent credit supporter being filed or referred to under paragraph (2)(d),

(b) subparagraph (2.1)(c)(ii) may be combined with the information set out in accordance with any of the other columns in paragraph (2.1)(c) if the credit support issuer has minimal assets, operations, revenue or cash flows other than those related to the issuance, administration and repayment of the securities described in paragraph (2)(c).

(3) The insider reporting requirement and the requirement to file an insider profile under National Instrument 55-102 *System for Electronic Disclosure by Insiders* do not apply to an insider of a credit support issuer in respect of securities of the credit support issuer so long as,

(a) the conditions in paragraphs (2)(a) to (c) are complied with;

(b) if the insider is not a credit supporter,

(i) the insider does not receive, in the ordinary course, information as to material facts or material changes concerning a credit supporter before the material facts or material changes are generally disclosed, and

(ii) the insider is not an insider of a credit supporter in any capacity other than by virtue of being an insider of the credit support issuer; and

(c) if the insider is a credit supporter, the insider does not beneficially own any designated credit support securities.

(4) A parent credit supporter is not a reporting issuer in a designated Canadian jurisdiction for the purposes of subparagraph (2)(b)(ii) if the parent credit supporter complies with a requirement of this Instrument by relying on a provision of National Instrument 71-102 *Continuous Disclosure and Other Exemptions Relating to Foreign Issuers*.

PART 14 — EFFECTIVE DATE AND TRANSITION

14.1 Effective Date — This Instrument comes into force on March 30, 2004.

14.2 Transition — Despite section 14.1, section 5.7 applies for financial years of the reporting issuer beginning on or after January 1, 2007.

14.3 Transition — Interim Financial Report — (1) Despite section 4.4 and paragraph 4.10(2)(c), the first interim financial report required to be filed in the year of adopting IFRS in respect of an interim period beginning on or after January 1, 2011 may be filed

(a) in the case of a reporting issuer other than a venture issuer, on or before the earlier of

(i) the 75th day after the end of the interim period; and

(ii) the date of filing, in a foreign jurisdiction, an interim financial report for a period ending on the last day of the interim period; or

(b) in the case of a venture issuer, on or before the earlier of

(i) the 90th day after the end of the interim period; and

(ii) the date of filing, in a foreign jurisdiction, an interim financial report for a period ending on the last day of the interim period.

(2) Despite subsection 5.1(2), the MD&A required to be filed under subsection 5.1(1) relating to the first interim financial report required to be filed in the year of adopting IFRS in respect of an interim period beginning on or after January 1, 2011 may be filed on or before the earlier of

(a) the filing deadline for the interim financial report set out in subsection (1); and

(b) the date the reporting issuer files the interim financial report under subsections (1) or 4.3(1), as applicable.

(3) Despite subsection 4.6(3), if a registered holder or beneficial owner of securities, other than debt instruments, of a reporting issuer requests the issuer's first interim financial report required to be filed in the year of adopting IFRS in respect of an interim period beginning on or after January 1, 2011, the reporting issuer may send a copy of the required interim financial report and the interim MD&A relating to the interim financial report to the person or company that made the request, without charge, by the later of,

(a) in the case of a reporting issuer relying on subsection (1), 10 calendar days after the filing deadline set out in subsection (1), for the financial statements requested;

(b) in the case of a reporting issuer not relying on subsection (1), 10 calendar days after the filing deadline in subparagraph 4.4(a)(i) or 4.4(b)(i), subsection 4.10(2) or subsection 14.3(1), as applicable, for the financial statements requested; and

(c) 10 calendar days after the issuer receives the request.

(4) Subsections (1), (2) and (3) do not apply unless the reporting issuer

(a) is disclosing, for the first time, a statement of compliance with International Accounting Standard 34 *Interim Financial Reporting*; and

(b) did not previously file financial statements that disclosed compliance with IFRS.

(5) Subsections (1), (2) and (3) do not apply if the first interim financial report is in respect of an interim period ending after March 30, 2012.

Final Rule: (2004) 27 O.S.C.B. 3439; Approval by OSC: (2003) 26 O.S.C.B. (Supp-3) 1 (December 19, 2003); Request for Comments: (2003) 26 O.S.C.B. 4577 and (2002) 25 O.S.C.B. 3701.

Amendment to Rule: (2005) 28 O.S.C.B. 4975; Approval by OSC: (2005) 28 O.S.C.B. (Supp-1) 52.

Amendment to Rule: (2005) 28 O.S.C.B. 10384; Approval by OSC: 28 O.S.C.B. 8117; Request for Comments: 27 O.S.C.B. 7699.

Amendment to Rule: (2005) 28 O.S.C.B. 10463; Approval by OSC: 28 O.S.C.B. 8569; Request for Comments: 28 O.S.C.B. 228.

Amendment to Rule: 30 O.S.C.B. (Supp-1) 1; Approval by OSC: 29 O.S.C.B. (Supp-2) 1; Request for Comments: 28 O.S.C.B. 9845.

Amendment to Rule: 30 O.S.C.B. 10499; Approval by OSC: 30 O.S.C.B. 8570; Request for Comments: 30 O.S.C.B. 2969.

Amendment to Rule: 30 O.S.C.B. 10513; Approval by OSC: 30 O.S.C.B. 8539; Request for Comments: 29 O.S.C.B. 9339.

Amendment to Rule: 31 O.S.C.B. (Supp. 2) 227 (March 7, 2008); Approval by OSC: 30 O.S.C.B. (Supp 7) 1 (Dec. 21, 2007); Request for Comments: 29 O.S.C.B. (Supp 3) 1 (Dec. 22, 2006).

Amendment to Rule: 31 O.S.C.B. 6571; Approval by OSC: 31 O.S.C.B. 4261; Request for Comments: 30 O.S.C.B. 8570.

Amendment to Rule: 31 O.S.C.B. 10455; Approval by OSC: 31 O.S.C.B. 7949; Request for Comments: 31 O.S.C.B. (Supp. 3) 1 (April 18, 2008).

Amendment to Rule: 31 O.S.C.B. 12047; Approval by OSC: 31 O.S.C.B. 8931; Request for Comments: 31 O.S.C.B. 2015 and 30 O.S.C.B. 2969.

Amendment to Rule: (2009) 32 O.S.C.B. (Supp. 5) 159; Approval by OSC: (2009) 32 O.S.C.B. (Supp. 3) 1; Request for Comments: (2009) 32 O.S.C.B. 4233 and (2008) 31 O.S.C.B. (Supp. 1) 1.

Amendment to Rule: (2010) 33 O.S.C.B. (Supp. 5) 43; Approval by OSC: (2010) 33 O.S.C.B. (Supp. 3) 113; Request for Comments: (2009) 32 O.S.C.B. (Supp. 6) 1.

Amendment to Rule: (2011) 34 O.S.C.B. 7084; Approval by OSC: (2011) 34 O.S.C.B. (Supp. 2) 1; Request for Comments: (2010) 33 O.S.C.B. 3703.

Amendment to Rule: (2011) 34 O.S.C.B. 11499; Approval by OSC: (2011) 34 O.S.C.B. 8047; Request for Comments: (2010) 33 O.S.C.B. 10723.

Amendment to Rule: (2012) 35 O.S.C.B. 3294; Approval by OSC: (2012) 35 O.S.C.B. 2383 and 913; Request for Comments: (2011) 34 O.S.C.B. 3249 and (2010) 33 O.S.C.B. 6353.

Amendment to Rule: Approval by OSC: (2013) 35 O.S.C.B. 10709; Request for Comments: (2011) 34 O.S.C.B. 6799 and (2010) 33 O.S.C.B. 3109.

Amendment to Rule: (2013) 36 O.S.C.B. 4939; Approval by OSC: (2013) 36 O.S.C.B. (Supp. 2) 1; Request for Comments: (2011) 34 O.S.C.B. (Supp. 4) 1.

Amendment to Rule: Approval by OSC: (2013) 36 O.S.C.B. 2619; Request for Comments: (2012) 35 O.S.C.B. 6887.

Amendment to Rule: Approval by OSC: (2014) 37 O.S.C.B. 6753; Request for Comments: (2013) 36 O.S.C.B. 10147.

Amendment to Rule: (2015) 38 O.S.C.B. (Supp. 1) 164.

Amendment to Rule: (2015) 38 O.S.C.B. 3415.

Rules: NI 71-102, 52-107, 81-106, 52-110, 58-101; NI 52-109; Rule 51-801.

Policies and Orders: NPS 51-102CP; OPS 51-801CP; CSAN 51-308, 51-311, 51-312, 51-316, 51-319, 51-328, 51-330, 51-331, 51-332, 51-333, 51-334, 51-338, 52-320, 52-326, 52-328; OSCN 51-706, 51-717, 51-718, 51-720, 51-721, 52-718, 52-719, 52-720, 52-711.

Form 51-102F1 — Management's Discussion & Analysis

Table of Contents

(h) Reverse Takeover Transactions

(i) [repealed]

(j) Resource Issuers

(l) Numbering and Headings

(l) Omitting Information

(m) Defined Terms

(n) Plain Language

(o) Available Prior Period Information

(p) Use of "Financial Condition"

PART 2 CONTENT OF MD&A

Item 1 Annual MD&A

    1.1 Date

    1.2 Overall Performance

    1.3 Selected Annual Information

    1.4 Results of Operations

    1.4 Discussion of Operations

    1.5 Summary of Quarterly Results

    1.6 Liquidity

    1.7 Capital Resources

    1.8 Off-Balance Sheet Arrangements

    1.9 Transactions between Related Parties

    1.10 Fourth Quarter

    1.11 Proposed Transactions

    1.12 Critical Accounting Estimates

    1.13 Changes in Accounting Policies including Initial Adoption

    1.14 Financial Instruments and Other Instruments

    1.15 Other MD&A Requirements

Item 2 Interim MD&A

    2.1 Date

    2.2 Interim MD&A

    2.3 Other Interim MD&A Requirements

Part 1 — General Provisions

(a) — What is MD&A?

MD&A is a narrative explanation, through the eyes of management, of how your company performed during the period covered by the financial statements, and of your company's financial condition and future prospects. MD&A complements and supplements your financial statements, but does not form part of your financial statements.

Your objective when preparing the MD&A should be to improve your company's overall financial disclosure by giving a balanced discussion of your company's financial performance and financial condition including, without limitation, such considerations as liquidity and capital resources — openly reporting bad news as well as good news. Your MD&A should

- help current and prospective investors understand what the financial statements show and do not show;

- discuss material information that may not be fully reflected in the financial statements, such as contingent liabilities, defaults under debt, off-balance sheet financing arrangements, or other contractual obligations;

- discuss important trends and risks that have affected the financial statements, and trends and risks that are reasonably likely to affect them in the future; and

- provide information about the quality, and potential variability, of your company's profit or loss and cash flow, to assist investors in determining if past performance is indicative of future performance.

(b) — Date of Information

In preparing the MD&A, you must take into account information available up to the date of the MD&A. If the date of the MD&A is not the date it is filed, you must ensure the disclosure in the MD&A is current so that it will not be misleading when it is filed.

(c) — Use of "Company"

Wherever this Form uses the word "company", the term includes other types of business organizations such as partnerships, trusts and other unincorporated business entities.

(d) — Explain Your Analysis

Explain the nature of, and reasons for, changes in your company's performance. Do not simply disclose the amount of change in a financial statement item from period to period. Avoid using boilerplate language. Your discussion should assist the reader to understand trends, events, transactions and expenditures.

(e) — Focus on Material Information

Focus your MD&A on material information. You do not need to disclose information that is not material. Exercise your judgment when determining whether information is material.

(f) — What is Material?

Would a reasonable investor's decision whether or not to buy, sell or hold securities in your company likely be influenced or changed if the information in question was omitted or misstated? If so, the information is likely material.

(g) — Venture Issuers

If your company is a venture issuer, you have the option of meeting the requirement to provide interim MD&A under section 2.2 by instead providing quarterly highlights disclosure. Refer to Companion Policy 51-102CP for guidance on quarterly highlights.

If your company is a venture issuer without significant revenue from operations, in your MD&A including any quarterly highlights, focus your discussion and analysis of financial performance on expenditures and progress towards achieving your business objectives and milestones.

(h) — Reverse Takeover Transactions

If an acquisition is a reverse takeover, the MD&A should be based on the reverse takeover acquirer's financial statements.

(i) — [repealed]

(j) — Resource Issuers

If your company has mineral projects, your disclosure must comply with National Instrument 43-101 *Standards of Disclosure for Mineral Projects*, including the requirement that all scientific and technical disclosure be based on a technical report or other information prepared by or under the supervision of a qualified person.

If your company has oil and gas activities, your disclosure must comply with National Instrument 51-101 *Standards of Disclosure for Oil and Gas Activities*.

(k) — Numbering and Headings

The numbering, headings and ordering of items included in this Form are guidelines only. You do not need to include the headings or numbering or follow the order of items in this Form. Disclosure provided in response to any item need not be repeated elsewhere.

(l) — Omitting Information

You do not need to respond to any item in this Form that is inapplicable.

(m) — Defined Terms

If a term is used but not defined in this Form, refer to Part 1 of National Instrument 51-102 and to National Instrument 14-101 *Definitions*. If a term is used in this Form and is defined in both the securities statute of the local jurisdiction and in National Instrument 51-102, refer to section 1.4 of Companion Policy 51-102CP for further guidance.

This Form also uses accounting terms that are defined or used in Canadian GAAP applicable to publicly accountable enterprises. For further guidance, see subsections 1.4(7) and (8) of Companion Policy 51-102CP.

(n) — Plain Language

Write the MD&A so that readers are able to understand it. Refer to the plain language principles listed in section 1.5 of Companion Policy 51-102CP for further guidance. If you use technical terms, explain them in a clear and concise manner.

(o) — Available Prior Period Information

If you have not presented comparative financial information in your financial statements, in your MD&A you must provide prior period information relating to financial performance that is available.

(p) — Use of "Financial Condition"

This Form uses the term "financial condition". Financial condition reflects the overall health of the company and includes your company's financial position (as shown on the statement of financial position) and other factors that may affect your company's liquidity, capital resources and solvency.

Part 2 — Content of MD&A

Item 1 — Annual MD&A

1.1 — Date

Specify the date of your MD&A. The date of the MD&A must be no earlier than the date of the auditor's report on the annual financial statements for your company's most recently completed financial year.

1.2 — Overall Performance

Provide an analysis of your company's financial condition, financial performance and cash flows. Discuss known trends, demands, commitments, events or uncertainties that are reasonably likely to have an effect on your company's business. Compare your company's performance in the most recently completed financial year to the prior year's performance. Your analysis should address at least the following:

    (a) operating segments that are reportable segments as those terms are described in the issuer's GAAP;

    (b) other parts of your business if

        (i) they have a disproportionate effect on revenue, profit or loss or cash needs; or

        (ii) there are any legal or other restrictions on the flow of funds from one part of your company's business to another;

    (c) industry and economic factors affecting your company's performance;

    (d) why changes have occurred or expected changes have not occurred in your company's financial condition and financial performance; and

    (e) the effect of discontinued operations on current operations.

Instructions

(i) When explaining changes in your company's financial condition and results, include an analysis of the effect on your continuing operations of any acquisition, disposition, write-off, abandonment or other similar transaction.

(ii) A discussion of financial condition should include important trends and risks that have affected the financial statements, and trends and risks that are reasonably likely to affect them in the future.

(iii) Include information for a period longer than two financial years if it will help the reader to better understand a trend.

1.3 — Selected Annual Information

(1) Provide the following financial data derived from your company's annual financial statements for each of the three most recently completed financial years:

    (a) total revenue;

    (b) profit or loss from continuing operations attributable to owners of the parent, in total and on a per-share and diluted per-share basis;

    (c) profit or loss attributable to owners of the parent, in total and on a per-share and diluted per-share basis;

    (d) total assets;

    (e) total non-current financial liabilities; and

    (f) distributions or cash dividends declared per-share for each class of share.

(2) Discuss the factors that have caused period to period variations including discontinued operations, changes in accounting policies, significant acquisitions or dispositions and changes in the direction of your business, and any other information your company believes would enhance an understanding of, and would highlight trends in, financial position and financial performance.

Instructions

(i) For each of the three most recently completed financial years, indicate the accounting principles that the financial data has been prepared in accordance with, the presentation currency and the functional currency if different from the presentation currency.

(ii) If the financial data provided was not prepared in accordance with the same accounting principles for all three years, focus the discussion on the important trends and risks that have affected the business.

1.4 — Discussion of Operations

Discuss your analysis of your company's operations for the most recently completed financial year, including

    (a) total revenue by reportable segment, including any changes in such amounts caused by selling prices, volume or quantity of goods or services being sold, or the introduction of new products or services;

    (b) any other significant factors that caused changes in total revenue;

    (c) cost of sales or gross profit;

(d) for issuers that have significant projects that have not yet generated revenue, describe each project, including your company's plan for the project and the status of the project relative to that plan, and expenditures made and how these relate to anticipated timing and costs to take the project to the next stage of the project plan;

(e) for resource issuers with producing mines or mines under development, identify any milestone, including, without limitation, mine expansion plans, productivity improvements, plans to develop a new deposit, or production decisions, and whether the milestone is based on a technical report filed under National Instrument 43-101 *Standards of Disclosure for Mineral Projects*;

(f) factors that caused a change in the relationship between costs and revenue, including changes in costs of labour or materials, price changes or inventory adjustments;

(g) commitments, events, risks or uncertainties that you reasonably believe will materially affect your company's future performance including total revenue and profit or loss from continuing operations attributable to owners of the parent;

(h) effect of inflation and specific price changes on your company's total revenue and on profit or loss from continuing operations attributable to owners of the parent;

(i) a comparison in tabular form of disclosure you previously made about how your company was going to use proceeds (other than working capital) from any financing, an explanation of variances and the impact of the variances, if any, on your company's ability to achieve its business objectives and milestones; and

(j) unusual or infrequent events or transactions.

Instruction

Your discussion under paragraph 1.4(d) should include

(i) whether or not you plan to expend additional funds on the project; and

(ii) any factors that have affected the value of the project(s) such as change in commodity prices, land use or political or environmental issues.

1.5 — Summary of Quarterly Results

Provide the following information in summary form, derived from your company's financial statements, for each of the eight most recently completed quarters:

(a) total revenue;

(b) profit or loss from continuing operations attributable to owners of the parent, in total and on a per-share and diluted per-share basis; and

(c) profit or loss attributable to owners of the parent, in total and on a per-share and diluted per-share basis.

Discuss the factors that have caused variations over the quarters necessary to understand general trends that have developed and the seasonality of the business.

Instructions

(i) In the case of the annual MD&A, your most recently completed quarter is the quarter that ended on the last day of your most recently completed financial year.

(ii) You do not have to provide information for a quarter prior to your company becoming a reporting issuer if your company has not prepared financial statements for those quarters.

(iii) For sections 1.2, 1.3, 1.4 and 1.5 consider identifying, discussing and analyzing the following factors:

(A) changes in customer buying patterns, including changes due to new technologies and changes in demographics;

(B) changes in selling practices, including changes due to new distribution arrangements or a reorganization of a direct sales force;

(C) changes in competition, including an assessment of the issuer's resources, strengths and weaknesses relative to those of its competitors;

(D) the effect of exchange rates;

(E) changes in pricing of inputs, constraints on supply, order backlog, or other input-related matters;

(F) changes in production capacity, including changes due to plant closures and work stoppages;

(G) changes in volume of discounts granted to customers, volumes of returns and allowances, excise and other taxes or other amounts reflected on a net basis against revenue;

(H) changes in the terms and conditions of service contracts;

(I) the progress in achieving previously announced milestones;

(J) for resource issuers with producing mines, identify changes to cash flows caused by changes in production throughput, head-grade, cut-off grade, metallurgical recovery and any expectation of future changes; and

(K) if you have an equity investee that is significant to your company, the nature of the investment and significance to your company.

(iv) For each of the eight most recently completed quarters, indicate the accounting principles that the financial data has been prepared in accordance with, the presentation currency and the functional currency if different from the presentation currency.

(v) If the financial data provided was not prepared in accordance with the same accounting principles for all eight quarters, focus the discussion on the important trends and risks that have affected the business.

1.6 — Liquidity

Provide an analysis of your company's liquidity, including

(a) its ability to generate sufficient amounts of cash and cash equivalents, in the short term and the long term, to maintain your company's capacity, to meet your company's planned growth or to fund development activities;

(b) trends or expected fluctuations in your company's liquidity, taking into account demands, commitments, events or uncertainties;

(c) its working capital requirements;

(d) liquidity risks associated with financial instruments;

(e) if your company has or expects to have a working capital deficiency, discuss its ability to meet obligations as they become due and how you expect it to remedy the deficiency;

(f) statement of financial position conditions or profit or loss attributable to owners of the parent or cash flow items that may affect your company's liquidity;

(g) legal or practical restrictions on the ability of subsidiaries to transfer funds to your company and the effect these restrictions have had or may have on the ability of your company to meet its obligations; and

(h) defaults or arrears or significant risk of defaults or arrears on

(i) distributions or dividend payments, lease payments, interest or principal payment on debt;

(ii) debt covenants; and

(iii) redemption or retraction or sinking fund payments,

and how your company intends to cure the default or arrears or address the risk.

Instructions

(i) In discussing your company's ability to generate sufficient amounts of cash and cash equivalents you should describe sources of funding and the circumstances that could affect those sources that are reasonably likely to occur. Examples of circumstances that could affect liquidity are market or commodity price changes, economic downturns, defaults on guarantees and contractions of operations.

(ii) In discussing trends or expected fluctuations in your company's liquidity and liquidity risks associated with financial instruments you should discuss

(A) provisions in debt, lease or other arrangements that could trigger an additional funding requirement or early payment. Examples of such situations are provisions linked to credit rating, profit or loss, cash flows or share price; and

(B) circumstances that could impair your company's ability to undertake transaction considered essential to operations. Examples of such circumstances are the inability to maintain investment grade credit rating, profit or loss per-share, cash flow or share price.

(iii) In discussing your company's working capital requirements you should discuss situations where your company must maintain significant inventory to meet customers' delivery requirements or any situations involving extended payment terms.

(iv) In discussing your company's statement of financial position conditions or profit or loss or cash flow items you should present a summary, in tabular form, of contractual obligations including payments due for each of the next five years and thereafter. The summary and table do not have to be provided if your company is a venture issuer. An example of a table that can be adapted to your company's particular circumstances follows:

Payments Due by Period

Contractual Obligations	Total	Less than 1 year	1–3 years	4 - 5 years	After 5 years
Debt	....	....	....		....
Finance Lease Obligations	....	....	....	....	....
Operating Leases	....	....	....	....	....
Purchase Obligations[1]	....	....	....	....	....
Other Obligations[2]	....	....		....	....
Total Contractual Obligations	....	....	....	....	....

Notes:

1   "Purchase Obligation" means an agreement to purchase goods or services that is enforceable and legally binding on your company that specifies all significant terms, including: fixed or minimum quantities to be purchased; fixed, minimum or variable price provisions; and the approximate timing of the transaction.

2   "Other Obligations" means other financial liabilities reflected on your company's statement of financial position.

1.7 — Capital Resources

Provide an analysis of your company's capital resources, including

(a) commitments for capital expenditures as of the date of your company's financial statements including

(i) the amount, nature and purpose of these commitments;

(ii) the expected source of funds to meet these commitments; and

(iii) expenditures not yet committed but required to maintain your company's capacity, to meet your company's planned growth or to fund development activities;

(b) known trends or expected fluctuations in your company's capital resources, including expected changes in the mix and relative cost of these resources; and

(c) sources of financing that your company has arranged but not yet used.

Instructions

(i) Capital resources are financing resources available to your company and include debt, equity and any other financing arrangements that you reasonably consider will provide financial resources to your company.

(ii) In discussing your company's commitments you should discuss any exploration and development, or research and development expenditures required to maintain properties or agreements in good standing.

1.8 — Off-Balance Sheet Arrangements

Discuss any off-balance sheet arrangements that have, or are reasonably likely to have, a current or future effect on the financial performance or financial condition of your company including, without limitation, such considerations as liquidity and capital resources.

In your discussion of off-balance sheet arrangements you should discuss their business purpose and activities, their economic substance, risks associated with the arrangements, and the key terms and conditions associated with any commitments. Your discussion should include

(a) a description of the other contracting party(ies);

(b) the effects of terminating the arrangement;

(c) the amounts receivable or payable, revenue, expenses and cash flows resulting from the arrangement;

(d) the nature and amounts of any other obligations or liabilities arising from the arrangement that could require your company to provide funding under the arrangement and the triggering events or circumstances that could cause them to arise; and

(e) any known event, commitment, trend or uncertainty that may affect the availability or benefits of the arrangement (including termination) and the course of action that management has taken, or proposes to take, in response to any such circumstances.

Instructions

(i) Off-balance sheet arrangements include any contractual arrangement with an entity not reported on a consolidated basis with your company, under which your company has

(A) any obligation under certain guarantee contracts;

(B) a retained or contingent interest in assets transferred to an unconsolidated entity or similar arrangement that serves as credit, liquidity or market risk support to that entity for the assets;

(C) any obligation under certain derivative instruments; or

(D) any obligation held by your company in an unconsolidated entity that provides financing, liquidity, market risk or credit risk support to your company, or engages in leasing, hedging activities or, research and development services with your company.

(ii) Contingent liabilities arising out of litigation, arbitration or regulatory actions are not considered to be off-balance sheet arrangements.

(iii) Disclosure of off-balance sheet arrangements should cover the most recently completed financial year. However, the discussion should address changes from the previous year where such discussion is necessary to understand the disclosure.

(iv) The discussion need not repeat information provided in the notes to the financial statements if the discussion clearly cross-references to specific information in the relevant notes and integrates the substance of the notes into the discussion in a manner that explains the significance of the information not included in the MD&A.

1.9 — Transactions Between Related Parties

Discuss all transactions between related parties as defined by the issuer's GAAP.

Instruction

In discussing your company's transactions between related parties, your discussion should include both qualitative and quantitative characteristics that are necessary for an understanding of the transactions' business purpose and economic substance. You should discuss

(A) the relationship and identify the related person or entities;

(B) the business purpose of the transaction;

(C) the recorded amount of the transaction and describe the measurement basis used; and

(D) any ongoing contractual or other commitments resulting from the transaction.

1.10 — Fourth Quarter

Discuss and analyze fourth quarter events or items that affected your company's financial condition, financial performance or cash flows, year-end and other adjustments, seasonal aspects of your company's business and dispositions of business segments. If your company has filed separate MD&A for its fourth quarter, you may satisfy this requirement by incorporating that MD&A by reference.

1.11 — *Proposed Transactions*

Discuss the expected effect on financial condition, financial performance and cash flows of any proposed asset or business acquisition or disposition if your company's board of directors, or senior management who believe that confirmation of the decision by the board is probable, have decided to proceed with the transaction. Include the status of any required shareholder or regulatory approvals.

Instruction

You do not have to disclose this information if, under section 7.1 of National Instrument 51-102, your company has filed a Form 51-102F3 Material Change Report *regarding the transaction on a confidential basis and the report remains confidential.*

1.12 — *Critical Accounting Estimates*

If your company is not a venture issuer, provide an analysis of your company's critical accounting estimates. Your analysis should

    (a) identify and describe each critical accounting estimate used by your company including

        (i) a description of the accounting estimate;

        (ii) the methodology used in determining the critical accounting estimate;

        (iii) the assumptions underlying the accounting estimate that relate to matters highly uncertain at the time the estimate was made;

        (iv) any known trends, commitments, events or uncertainties that you reasonably believe will materially affect the methodology or the assumptions described; and

        (v) if applicable, why the accounting estimate is reasonably likely to change from period to period and have a material impact on the financial presentation;

    (b) explain the significance of the accounting estimate to your company's financial position, changes in financial position and financial performance and identify the financial statement line items affected by the accounting estimate;

    (c) [repealed]

    (d) discuss changes made to critical accounting estimates during the past two financial years including the reasons for the change and the quantitative effect on your company's overall results of operations and financial statement line items; and

    (e) identify the reportable segments of your company's business that the accounting estimate affects and discuss the accounting estimate on a reportable segment basis, if your company operates in more than one reportable segment.

Instructions

(i) An accounting estimate is a critical accounting estimate only if

    (A) it requires your company to make assumptions about matters that are highly uncertain at the time the accounting estimate is made; and

    (B) different estimates that your company could have used in the current period, or changes in the accounting estimate that are reasonably likely to occur from period to period, would have a material impact on your company's financial condition, changes in financial condition or financial performance.

(ii) As part of your description of each critical accounting estimate, in addition to qualitative disclosure, you should provide quantitative disclosure when quantitative information is reasonably available and would provide material information for investors. Similarly, in your discussion of assumptions underlying an accounting estimate that relates to matters highly uncertain at the time the estimate was made, you should provide quantitative disclosure when it is reasonably available and it would provide material information for investors. For example, quantitative information may include a sensitivity analysis or disclosure of the upper and lower ends of the range of estimates from which the recorded estimate was selected.

1.13 — *Changes in Accounting Policies including Initial Adoption*

Discuss and analyze any changes in your company's accounting policies, including

    (a) for any accounting policies that you have adopted or expect to adopt subsequent to the end of your most recently completed financial year, including changes you have made or expect to make voluntarily and those due to a change in an accounting standard or a new accounting standard that you do not have to adopt until a future date, you should

        (i) describe the new standard, the date you are required to adopt it and, if determined, the date you plan to adopt it;

        (ii) disclose the methods of adoption permitted by the accounting standard and the method you expect to use;

        (iii) discuss the expected effect on your company's financial statements, or if applicable, state that you cannot reasonably estimate the effect; and

        (iv) discuss the potential effect on your business, for example technical violations or default of debt covenants or changes in business practices; and

    (b) for any accounting policies that you have initially adopted during the most recently completed financial year, you should

        (i) describe the events or transactions that gave rise to the initial adoption of an accounting policy;

        (ii) describe the accounting policy that has been adopted and the method of applying that policy;

        (iii) discuss the effect resulting from the initial adoption of the accounting policy on your company's financial position, changes in financial position and financial performance;

(iv) if your company is permitted a choice among acceptable accounting policies,

    (A) state that you made a choice among acceptable alternatives;

    (B) identify the alternatives;

    (C) describe why you made the choice that you did; and

    (D) discuss the effect, where material, on your company's financial position, changes in financial position and financial performance under the alternatives not chosen; and

(v) if no accounting literature exists that covers the accounting for the events or transactions giving rise to your initial adoption of the accounting policy, explain your decision regarding which accounting policy to use and the method of applying that policy.

Instruction

You do not have to present the discussion under paragraph 1.13(b) for the initial adoption of accounting policies resulting from the adoption of new accounting standards.

1.14 — Financial Instruments and Other Instruments

For financial instruments and other instruments,

    (a) discuss the nature and extent of your company's use of, including relationships among, the instruments and the business purposes that they serve;

    (b) describe and analyze the risks associated with the instruments;

    (c) describe how you manage the risks in paragraph (b), including a discussion of the objectives, general strategies and instruments used to manage the risks, including any hedging activities;

    (d) disclose the financial statement classification and amounts of income, expenses, gains and losses associated with the instrument; and

    (e) discuss the significant assumptions made in determining the fair value of financial instruments, the total amount and financial statement classification of the change in fair value of financial instruments recognized in profit or loss for the period, and the total amount and financial statement classification of deferred or unrecognized gains and losses on financial instruments.

Instructions

(i) "Other instruments" are instruments that may be settled by the delivery of non-financial assets. A commodity futures contract is an example of an instrument that may be settled by delivery of non-financial assets.

(ii) Your discussion under paragraph 1.14(a) should enhance a reader's understanding of the significance of recognized and unrecognized instruments on your company's financial position, financial performance and cash flows. The information should also assist a reader in assessing the amounts, timing, and certainty of future cash flows associated with those instruments. Also discuss the relationship between liability and equity components of convertible debt instruments.

(iii) For purposes of paragraph 1.14(c), if your company is exposed to significant price, credit or liquidity risks, consider providing a sensitivity analysis or tabular information to help readers assess the degree of exposure. For example, an analysis of the effect of a hypothetical change in the prevailing level of interest or currency rates on the fair value of financial instruments and future profit or loss and cash flows may be useful in describing your company's exposure to price risk.

(iv) For purposes of paragraph 1.14(d), disclose and explain the revenue, expenses, gains and losses from hedging activities separately from other activities.

1.15 — Other MD&A Requirements

(a) Your MD&A must disclose that additional information relating to your company, including your company's AIF if your company files an AIF, is on SEDAR at www.sedar.com.

(b) Your MD&A must also provide the information required in the following sections of National Instrument 51-102, if applicable:

    (i) Section 5.3 — Additional Disclosure for Venture Issuers without Significant Revenue;

    (ii) Section 5.4 — Disclosure of Outstanding Share Data; and

    (iii) Section 5.7 — Additional Disclosure for Reporting Issuers with Significant Equity Investees.

(c) Your MD&A must include the MD&A disclosure required by National Instrument 52-109 *Certification of Disclosure in Issuers' Annual and Interim Filings* and, as applicable, Form 52-109F1 *Certification of Annual Filings — Full Certificate*, Form 52-109F1R *Certification of Refiled Annual Filings*, or Form 52-109F1 *AIF Certification of Annual Filings in Connection with Voluntarily Filed AIF*.

Item 2 — Interim MD&A

2.1 — Date

Specify the date of your interim MD&A.

2.2 — Interim MD&A

Interim MD&A must update your company's annual MD&A for all disclosure required by Item 1 except section 1.3. This disclosure must include

(a) a discussion of your analysis of

(i) current quarter and year-to-date results including a comparison of financial performance to the corresponding periods in the previous year;

(i.1) a comparison of cash flows to the corresponding period in the previous year;

(ii) changes in financial performance and elements of profit or loss attributable to owners of the parent that are not related to ongoing business operations;

(iii) any seasonal aspects of your company's business that affect its financial position, financial performance or cash flows; and

(b) a comparison of your company's interim financial condition to your company's financial condition as at the most recently completed financial year-end.

Instruction

(i) If the first MD&A you file in this Form (your first MD&A) is an interim MD&A, you must provide all the disclosure called for in Item 1 in your first MD&A. Base the disclosure, except the disclosure for section 1.3, on your interim financial report. Since you do not have to update the disclosure required in section 1.3 in your interim MD&A, your first MD&A will provide disclosure under section 1.3 based on your annual financial statements. Your subsequent interim MD&A for that year will update your first interim MD&A.

(ii) For the purposes of paragraph 2.2(b), you may assume the reader has access to your annual MD&A or your first MD&A. You do not have to duplicate the discussion and analysis of financial condition in your annual MD&A or your first MD&A. For example, if economic and industry factors are substantially unchanged you may make a statement to this effect.

(iii) For the purposes of subparagraph 2.2(a)(i), you should generally give prominence to the current quarter.

(iv) In discussing your company's statement of financial position conditions or profit or loss or cash flow items for an interim period, you do not have to present a summary, in tabular form, of all known contractual obligations contemplated under section 1.6. Instead, you should disclose material changes in the specified contractual obligations during the interim period.

(v) Interim MD&A prepared in accordance with Item 2 is not required for your company's fourth quarter as relevant fourth quarter content will be contained in your company's annual MD&A prepared in accordance with Item 1 (see section 1.10).

(vi) In your interim MD&A, update the summary of quarterly results in section 1.5 by providing summary information for the eight most recently completed quarters.

(vii) Your annual MD&A may not include all the information in Item 1 if you were a venture issuer as at the end of your last financial year. If you ceased to be a venture issuer during your interim period, you do not have to restate the MD&A you previously filed. Instead, provide the disclosure for the additional sections in Item 1 that you were exempt from as a venture issuer in the next interim MD&A you file. Base your disclosure for those sections on your interim financial report.

2.2.1 — Quarterly Highlights

If your company is a venture issuer, you have the option of meeting the requirement to provide interim MD&A under section 2.2 by instead providing a short discussion of all material information about your company's operations, liquidity and capital resources. Include in your discussion:

- an analysis of your company's financial condition, financial performance and cash flows and any significant factors that have caused period to period variations in those measures;

- known trends, risks or demands;

- major operating milestones;

- commitments, expected or unexpected events, or uncertainties that have materially affected your company's operations, liquidity and capital resources in the interim period or are reasonably likely to have a material effect going forward;

- any significant changes from disclosure previously made about how the company was going to use proceeds from any financing and an explanation of variances;

- any significant transactions between related parties that occurred in the interim period.

Instructions

(i) If the first MD&A you file in this Form (your first MD&A) is an interim MD&A, you cannot use quarterly highlights. Rather, you must provide all the disclosure called for in Item 1 in your first MD&A Base the disclosure, except the disclosure for section 1.3, on your interim financial report. Since you do not have to update the disclosure required in section 1.3 in your interim MD&A, your first MD&A will provide disclosure under section 1.3 based on your annual financial statements.

(ii) Provide a short, focused discussion that gives a balanced and accurate picture of the company's business activities during the interim period. The purpose of the quarterly highlights reporting is to provide a brief narrative update about the business activities, financial condition, financial performance and cash flow of the company. While summaries are to be clear and concise, they are subject to the normal prohibitions against false and misleading statements.

(iii) Quarterly highlights prepared in accordance with section 2.2.1 are not required for your company's fourth quarter as relevant fourth quarter content will be contained in your company's annual MD&A prepared in accordance with Item 1 (see section 1.10).

(iv) You must title your quarterly highlights "Interim MD& – Quarterly Highlights".

(v) If there was a change to the company's accounting policies during the interim period, include a description of the material effects resulting from the change.

2.2.2 — Quarterly Highlights – Transition

Section 2.2.1 applies to an issuer in respect of a financial year beginning on or after July 1, 2015.

2.3 — Other Interim MD&A Requirements

Your interim MD&A must include the interim MD&A disclosure required by National Instrument 52-109 *Certification of Disclosure in Issuers' Annual and Interim Filings* and, as applicable, Form 52-109F2 *Certification of Interim Filings — Full Certificate* or Form 52-109F2R *Certification of Refiled Interim Filings.*

Form 51-102F2 — Annual Information Form

Table of Contents

Part 1 — General Provisions

(a) — What is an AIF?

An AIF (annual information form) is required to be filed annually by certain companies under Part 6 of National Instrument 51-102. An AIF is a disclosure document intended to provide material information about your company and its business at a point in time in the context of its historical and possible future development. Your AIF describes your company, its operations and prospects, risks and other external factors that impact your company specifically.

This disclosure is supplemented throughout the year by subsequent continuous disclosure filings including news releases, material change reports, business acquisition reports, financial statements and management discussion and analysis.

(b) — Date of Information

Unless otherwise specified in this Form, the information in your AIF must be presented as at the last day of your company's most recently completed financial year. If necessary, you must update the information in the AIF so it is not misleading when it is filed. For information presented as at any date other than the last day of your company's most recently completed financial year, specify the relevant date in the disclosure.

(c) — Use of "Company"

Wherever this Form uses the word "company", the term includes other types of business organizations such as partnerships, trusts and other unincorporated business entities.

All references to "your company" in Items 4, 5, 6, 12, 13, 15 and 16 of this Form apply collectively to your company, your company's subsidiaries, joint ventures to which your company is a party and entities in which your company has an investment accounted for by the equity method.

(d) — Focus on Material Information

Focus your AIF on material information. You do not need to disclose information that is not material. Exercise your judgment when determining whether information is material. However, you must disclose all corporate and individual cease trade orders, bankruptcies, penalties and sanctions in accordance with Item 10 and section 12.2 of this Form.

(e) — What is Material?

Would a reasonable investor's decision whether or not to buy, sell or hold securities in your company likely be influenced or changed if the information in question was omitted or misstated? If so, the information is likely material.

(f) — Incorporating Information by Reference

You may incorporate information required to be included in your AIF by reference to another document, other than a previous AIF. Clearly identify the referenced document or any excerpt of it that you incorporate into your AIF. Unless you have already filed the referenced document or excerpt, including any documents incorporated by reference into the document or excerpt, under your SEDAR profile, you must file it with your AIF. You must also disclose that the document is on SEDAR at www.sedar.com.

(g) — Defined Terms

If a term is used but not defined in this Form, refer to Part 1 of National Instrument 51-102 and to National Instrument 14-101 Definitions. If a term is used in this Form and is defined in both the securities statute of a local jurisdiction and in National Instrument 51-102, refer to section 1.4 of Companion Policy 51-102CP for further guidance.

This Form also uses accounting terms that are defined or used in Canadian GAAP applicable to publicly accountable enterprises. For further guidance, see subsections 1.4(7) and (8) of Companion Policy 51-102CP.

(h) — Plain Language

Write the AIF so that readers are able to understand it. Refer to the plain language principles listed in section 1.5 of Companion Policy 51-102CP for further guidance. If you use technical terms, explain them in a clear and concise manner.

(i) — Special Purpose Entities

If your company is a special purpose entity, you may have to modify the disclosure items in this Form to reflect the special purpose nature of your company's business.

(j) — Numbering and Headings

The numbering, headings and ordering of items included in this Form are guidelines only. You do not need to include the headings or numbering or follow the order of items in this Form. Disclosure provided in response to any item need not be repeated elsewhere.

(k) — Omitting Information

You do not need to respond to any item in this Form that is inapplicable and you may omit negative answers.

Part 2 — Content of AIF

Item 1 — Cover Page

1.1 — Date

Specify the date of your AIF. The date must be no earlier than the date of the auditor's report on the financial statements for your company's most recently completed financial year.

You must file your AIF within 10 days of the date of the AIF.

1.2 — Revisions

If you revise your company's AIF after you have filed it, identify the revised version as a "revised AIF".

Item 2 — Table of Contents

2.1 — Table of Contents

Include a table of contents.

Item 3 — Corporate Structure

3.1 — Name, Address and Incorporation

(1) State your company's full corporate name or, if your company is an unincorporated entity, the full name under which it exists and carries on business, and the address(es) of your company's head and registered office.

(2) State the statute under which your company is incorporated, continued or organized or, if your company is an unincorporated entity, the laws of the jurisdiction or foreign jurisdiction under which it is established and exists. Describe the substance of any material amendments to the articles or other constating or establishing documents of your company.

3.2 — Intercorporate Relationships

Describe, by way of a diagram or otherwise, the intercorporate relationships among your company and its subsidiaries. For each subsidiary state:

(a) the percentage of votes attaching to all voting securities of the subsidiary beneficially owned, or controlled or directed, directly or indirectly, by your company;

(b) the percentage of each class of restricted securities of the subsidiary beneficially owned, or controlled or directed, directly or indirectly, by your company by your company; and

(c) where it was incorporated, continued, formed or organized.

Instruction

You may omit a particular subsidiary if, at the most recent financial year-end of your company,

    (i) the total assets of the subsidiary do not exceed 10 per cent of the consolidated assets of your company;

    (ii) the revenue of the subsidiary does not exceed 10 per cent of the consolidated revenue of your company; and

    (iii) the conditions in paragraphs (i) and (ii) would be satisfied if you

        (A) aggregated the subsidiaries that may be omitted under paragraphs (i) and (ii), and

        (B) changed the reference in those paragraphs from 10 per cent to 20 per cent.

Item 4 — General Development of the Business

4.1 — Three Year History

Describe how your company's business has developed over the last three completed financial years. Include only events, such as acquisitions or dispositions, or conditions that have influenced the general development of the business. If your company produces or distributes more than one product or provides more than one kind of service, describe the products or services. Also discuss changes in your company's business that you expect will occur during the current financial year.

4.2 — Significant Acquisitions

Disclose any significant acquisition completed by your company during its most recently completed financial year for which disclosure is required under Part 8 of National Instrument 51-102, by providing a brief summary of the significant acquisition and stating whether your company has filed a Form 51-102F4 in respect of the acquisition.

Item 5 — Describe the Business

5.1 — General

(1) Describe the business of your company and its operating segments that are reportable segments as those terms are described in the issuer's GAAP. For each reportable segment include:

    (a) *Summary* — For products or services,

        (i) their principal markets;

        (ii) distribution methods;

        (iii) for each of the two most recently completed financial years, as dollar amounts or as percentages, the revenue for each category of products or services that accounted for 15 per cent or more of total consolidated revenue for the applicable financial year derived from

            A. sales or transfers to joint ventures in which your company is a participant or to entities in which your company has an investment accounted for by the equity method,

            B. sales to customers, other than those referred to in clause A, outside the consolidated entity, and

            C. sales or transfers to controlling shareholders;

        (iv) if not fully developed, the stage of development of the products or services and, if the products are not at the commercial production stage

            A. the timing and stage of research and development programs,

            B. whether your company is conducting its own research and development, is subcontracting out the research and development or is using a combination of those methods, and

            C. the additional steps required to reach commercial production and an estimate of costs and timing.

    (b) *Production and Services* — The actual or proposed method of production and, if your company provides services, the actual or proposed method of providing services.

    (c) *Specialized Skill and Knowledge* — A description of any specialized skill and knowledge requirements and the extent to which the skill and knowledge are available to your company.

    (d) *Competitive Conditions* — The competitive conditions in your company's principal markets and geographic areas, including, if reasonably possible, an assessment of your company's competitive position.

    (e) *New Products* — If you have publicly announced the introduction of a new product, the status of the product.

    (f) *Components* — The sources, pricing and availability of raw materials, component parts or finished products.

    (g) *Intangible Properties* — The importance, duration and effect of identifiable intangible properties, such as brand names, circulation lists, copyrights, franchises, licences, patents, software, subscription lists and trademarks, on the segment.

    (h) *Cycles* — The extent to which the business of the reportable segment is cyclical or seasonal.

    (i) *Economic Dependence* — A description of any contract upon which your company's business is substantially dependent, such as a contract to sell the major part of your company's products or services or to purchase the major part of your company's requirements for goods, services or raw materials, or any franchise or licence or other agreement to use a patent, formula, trade secret, process or trade name upon which your company's business depends.

(j) *Changes to Contracts* — A description of any aspect of your company's business that you reasonably expect to be affected in the current financial year by renegotiation or termination of contracts or sub-contracts, and the likely effect.

(k) *Environmental Protection* — The financial and operational effects of environmental protection requirements on the capital expenditures, profit or loss and competitive position of your company in the current financial year and the expected effect in future years.

(l) *Employees* — The number of employees as at the most recent financial year-end or the average number of employees over the year, whichever is more meaningful to understand the business.

(m) *Foreign Operations* — Describe the dependence of your company and any reportable segment upon foreign operations.

(n) *Lending* — With respect to your company's lending operations, disclose the investment policies and lending and investment restrictions.

(2) *Bankruptcy and Similar Procedures* — Disclose the nature and results of any bankruptcy, receivership or similar proceedings against your company or any of its subsidiaries, or any voluntary bankruptcy, receivership or similar proceedings by your company or any of its subsidiaries, within the three most recently completed financial years or during or proposed for the current financial year.

(3) *Reorganizations* — Disclose the nature and results of any material reorganization of your company or any of its subsidiaries within the three most recently completed financial years or completed during or proposed for the current financial year.

(4) *Social or Environmental Policies* — If your company has implemented social or environmental policies that are fundamental to your operations, such as policies regarding your company's relationship with the environment or with the communities in which it does business, or human rights policies, describe them and the steps your company has taken to implement them.

5.2 — Risk Factors

Disclose risk factors relating to your company and its business, such as cash flow and liquidity problems, if any, experience of management, the general risks inherent in the business carried on by your company, environmental and health risks, reliance on key personnel, regulatory constraints, economic or political conditions and financial history and any other matter that would be most likely to influence an investor's decision to purchase securities of your company. If there is a risk that securityholders of your company may become liable to make an additional contribution beyond the price of the security, disclose that risk.

Instructions

(i) *Disclose the risks in order of seriousness from the most serious to the least serious.*

(ii) *A risk factor must not be de-emphasized by including excessive caveats or conditions.*

5.3 — Companies with Asset-backed Securities Outstanding

If your company had asset-backed securities outstanding that were distributed under a prospectus, disclose the following information:

(1) *Payment Factors* — A description of any events, covenants, standards or preconditions that may reasonably be expected to affect the timing or amount of any payments or distributions to be made under the asset-backed securities.

(2) *Underlying Pool of Assets* — For the three most recently completed financial years of your company or the lesser period commencing on the first date on which your company had asset-backed securities outstanding, financial disclosure that described the underlying pool of financial assets servicing the asset-backed securities relating to

(a) the composition of the pool as of the end of each financial year or partial period;

(b) profit and losses from the pool on at least an annual basis or such shorter period as is reasonable given the nature of the underlying pool of assets;

(c) the payment, prepayment and collection experience of the pool on at least an annual basis or such shorter period as is reasonable given the nature of the underlying pool of assets;

(d) servicing and other administrative fees; and

(e) any significant variances experienced in the matters referred to in paragraphs (a) through (d).

(2.1) If any of the financial disclosure disclosed in accordance with subsection (2) has been audited, disclose the existence and results of the audit.

(3) *Investment Parameters* — The investment parameters applicable to investments of any cash flow surpluses.

(4) *Payment History* — The amount of payments made during the three most recently completed financial years or the lesser period commencing on the first date on which your company had asset-backed securities outstanding, in respect of principal and interest or capital and yield, each stated separately, on asset-backed securities of your company outstanding.

(5) *Acceleration Event* — The occurrence of any event that has led to, or with the passage of time could lead to, the accelerated payment of principal, interest or capital of asset-backed securities.

(6) *Principal Obligors* — The identity of any principal obligors for the outstanding asset-backed securities of your company, the percentage of the pool of financial assets servicing the asset-backed securities represented by obligations of each principal obligor and whether the principal obligor has filed an AIF in any jurisdiction or a Form 10-K or Form 20-F in the United States.

Instructions

(i) Present the information requested under subsection (2) in a manner that enables a reader to easily determine the status of the events, covenants, standards and preconditions referred to in subsection (1).

(ii) If the information required under subsection (2)

    (A) is not compiled specifically on the pool of financial assets servicing the asset-backed securities, but is compiled on a larger pool of the same assets from which the securitized assets are randomly selected so that the performance of the larger pool is representative of the performance of the pool of securitized assets, or

    (B) in the case of a new company, where the pool of financial assets servicing the asset-backed securities will be randomly selected from a larger pool of the same assets so that the performance of the larger pool will be representative of the performance of the pool of securitized assets to be created, a company may comply with subsection (2) by providing the information required based on the larger pool and disclosing that it has done so.

5.4 — Companies With Mineral Projects

If your company had a mineral project, provide the following information, by summary if applicable, for each project material to your company:

(1) *Current Technical Report* — The title, author(s), and date of the most recent technical report on the property filed in accordance with National Instrument 43-101 *Standards of Disclosure for Mineral Projects*.

(2) *Project Description, Location, and Access*

    (a) The location of the project and means of access.

    (b) The nature and extent of your company's title to or interest in the project, including surface rights, obligations that must be met to retain the project, and the expiration date of claims, licences and other property tenure rights.

    (c) The terms of any royalties, overrides, back-in rights, payments or other agreements and encumbrances to which the project is subject.

    (d) To the extent known, any significant factors or risks that might affect access or title, or the right or ability to perform work on the property, including permitting and environmental liabilities to which the project is subject.

(3) *History*

    (a) To the extent known, the prior exploration and development of the property, including the type, amount, and results of any exploration work undertaken by previous owners, any significant historical estimates, and any previous production on the property.

(4) *Geological Setting, Mineralization, and Deposit Types* — The regional, local and property geology.

    (a) The regional, local, and property geology.

    (b) The significant mineralized zones encountered on the property, the surrounding rock types and relevant geological controls, and the length, width, depth and continuity of the mineralization together with a description of the type, character and distribution of the mineralization.

    (c) The mineral deposit type or geological model or concepts being applied.

(5) *Exploration* — The nature and extent of all relevant exploration work other than drilling, conducted by or on behalf of your company, including a summary and interpretation of the relevant results.

(6) *Drilling* — The type and extent of drilling and a summary and interpretation of all relevant results.

(7) *Sampling, Analysis, and Data Verification* — The sampling and assaying including, without limitation,

    (a) sample preparation methods and quality control measures employed before dispatch of samples to an analytical or testing laboratory,

    (b) the security measures taken to ensure the validity and integrity of samples taken,

    (c) assaying and analytical procedures used and the relationship, if any, of the laboratory to your company, and

    (d) quality control measures and data verification procedures, and their results.

(8) *Mineral Processing and Metallurgical Testing* — If mineral processing or metallurgical testing analyses have been carried out, describe the nature and extent of the testing and analytical procedures, and provide a summary of the relevant results and, to the extent known, provide a description of any processing factors or deleterious elements that could have a significant effect on potential economic extraction.

(9) *Mineral Resource and Mineral Reserve Estimates* — The mineral resources and mineral reserves, if any, including, without limitation,

    (a) the effective date of the estimates,

    (b) the quantity and grade or quality of each category of mineral resources and mineral reserves,

    (c) the key assumptions, parameters, and methods used to estimate the mineral resources and mineral reserves, and

    (d) the extent to which the estimate of mineral resources and mineral reserves may be materially affected by metallurgical, environmental, permitting, legal, title, taxation, socio-economic, marketing, political, and other relevant issues.

(10) *Mining Operations* — For advanced properties, the current or proposed mining methods, including a summary of the relevant information used to establish the amenability or potential amenability of the mineral resources or mineral reserves to the proposed mining methods.

(11) *Processing and Recovery Operations* — For advanced properties, a summary of current or proposed processing methods and reasonably available information on test or operating results relating to the recoverability of the valuable component or commodity.

(12) *Infrastructure, Permitting, and Compliance Activities* — For advanced properties,

    (a) the infrastructure and logistic requirements for the project, and

    (b) the reasonably available information on environmental, permitting, and social or community factors related to the project.

(13) *Capital and Operating Costs* — For advanced properties,

    (a) a summary of capital and operating cost estimates, with the major components set out in tabular form, and

    (b) an economic analysis with forecasts of annual cash flow, net present value, internal rate of return, and payback period, unless exempted under Instruction (2) to Item 22 of Form 43-101F1.

(14) *Exploration, Development, and Production* — A description of your company's current and contemplated exploration, development or production activities.

Instructions

(i) Disclosure regarding mineral exploration, development or production activities on material projects must comply with National Instrument 43-101 Standards of Disclosure for Mineral Projects, including the limitations set out in it. You must use the appropriate terminology to describe mineral reserves and mineral resources. You must base your disclosure on information prepared by, under the supervision of, or approved by, a qualified person.

(ii) You are permitted to satisfy the disclosure requirements in section 5.4 by reproducing the summary from the technical report on the material property and incorporating the detailed disclosure in the technical report into the AIF by reference.

5.5 — Companies with Oil and Gas Activities

If your company is engaged in oil and gas activities as defined in National Instrument 51-101 *Standards of Disclosure for Oil and Gas Activities*, disclose the following information:

(1) *Reserves Data and Other Information*

    (a) In the case of information that, for purposes of Form 51-101F1 *Statement of Reserves Data and Other Oil and Gas Information*, is to be prepared as at the end of a financial year, disclose that information as at your company's most recently completed financial year-end.

    (b) In the case of information that, for purposes of Form 51-101F1, is to be prepared for a financial year, disclose that information for your company's most recently completed financial year.

(2) *Report of Independent Qualified Reserves Evaluator or Auditor* — Include with the disclosure under subsection (1) a report in the form of Form 51-101F2 *Report on Reserves Data by Independent Qualified Reserves Evaluator or Auditor*, on the reserves data included in the disclosure required under subsection (1).

(3) *Report of Management* — Include with the disclosure under subsection (1) a report in the form of Form 51-101F3 *Report of Management and Directors on Oil and Gas Disclosure* that refers to the information disclosed under subsection (1).

(4) *Material Changes* — To the extent not reflected in the information disclosed in response to subsection (1), disclose the information contemplated by Part 6 of National Instrument 51-101 *Standards of Disclosure for Oil and Gas Activities* in respect of material changes that occurred after your company's most recently completed financial year-end.

Instruction

The information presented in response to section 5.5 must be in accordance with National Instrument 51-101 Standards of Disclosure for Oil and Gas Activities.

Item 6 — Dividends and Distributions

6.1 — Dividends and Distributions

(1) Disclose the amount of cash dividends or distributions declared per security for each class of your company's securities for each of the three most recently completed financial years.

(2) Describe any restriction that could prevent your company from paying dividends or distributions.

(3) Disclose your company's current dividend or distribution policy and any intended change in dividend or distribution policy.

Item 7 — Description of Capital Structure

7.1 — General Description of Capital Structure

Describe your company's capital structure. State the description or the designation of each class of authorized security, and describe the material characteristics of each class of authorized security, including voting rights, provisions for exchange, conversion, exercise, redemption and retraction, dividend rights and rights upon dissolution or winding-up.

Instruction

This section requires only a brief summary of the provisions that are material from a securityholder's standpoint. The provisions attaching to different classes of securities do not need to be set out in full. This summary should include the disclosure required in subsection 10.1(1) of National Instrument 51-102.

7.2 — Constraints

If there are constraints imposed on the ownership of securities of your company to ensure that your company has a required level of Canadian ownership, describe the mechanism, if any, by which the level of Canadian ownership of the securities is or will be monitored and maintained.

7.3 — Ratings

(1) If you have asked for and received a credit rating, or if you are aware that you have received any other kind of rating, including a stability rating or a provisional rating, from one or more credit rating organizations for securities of your company that are outstanding, or will be outstanding, and the rating or ratings continue in effect, disclose

   (a) each rating received from a credit rating organization;

   (b) for each rating disclosed under paragraph (a), the name of the credit rating organization that has assigned the rating;

   (c) a definition or description of the category in which each credit rating organization rated the securities and the relative rank of each rating within the organization's overall classification system;

   (d) an explanation of what the rating addresses and what attributes, if any, of the securities are not addressed by the rating;

   (e) any factors or considerations identified by the credit rating organization as giving rise to unusual risks associated with the securities;

   (f) a statement that a credit rating or a stability rating is not a recommendation to buy, sell or hold securities and may be subject to revision or withdrawal at any time by the credit rating organization; and

   (g) any announcement made by, or any proposed announcement known to your company that is to be made by, a credit rating organization to the effect that the organization is reviewing or intends to revise or withdraw a rating previously assigned and required to be disclosed under this section.

(2) If payments were, or reasonably will be, made to a credit rating organization that provided a rating described in subsection (1), state that fact and state whether any payments were made to the credit rating organization in respect of any other service provided to your company by the credit rating organization during the last two years.

Instructions

There may be factors relating to a security that are not addressed by a credit rating organization when they give a rating. For example, in the case of cash settled derivative instruments, factors in addition to the creditworthiness of the issuer, such as the continued subsistence of the underlying interest or the volatility of the price, value or level of the underlying interest may be reflected in the rating analysis. Rather than being addressed in the rating itself, these factors may be described by a credit rating organization by way of a superscript or other notation to a rating. Any such attributes must be discussed in the disclosure under section 7.3.

A provisional rating received before the company's most recently completed financial year is not required to be disclosed under section 7.3.

[Editor's note: The foregoing version of section 7.3 applies only to documents required to be prepared, filed, delivered or sent under National Instrument 51-102 Continuous Disclosure Obligations *for periods relating to a financial year ending on or after April 20, 2012. For the previous version, see the 51st edition of this work.]*

Item 8 — Market for Securities

8.1 — Trading Price and Volume

(1) For each class of securities of your company that is traded or quoted on a Canadian marketplace, identify the marketplace and the price ranges and volume traded or quoted on the Canadian marketplace on which the greatest volume of trading or quotation generally occurs.

(2) If a class of securities of your company is not traded or quoted on a Canadian marketplace, but is traded or quoted on a foreign marketplace, identify the foreign marketplace and the price ranges and volume traded or quoted on the foreign marketplace on which the greatest volume of trading or quotation generally occurs.

(3) Provide the information required under subsections (1) and (2) on a monthly basis for each month or, if applicable, partial months of the most recently completed financial year.

8.2 — Prior Sales

For each class of securities of your company that is outstanding but not listed or quoted on a marketplace, state the price at which securities of the class have been issued during the most recently completed financial year by your company, the number of securities of the class issued at that price, and the date on which the securities were issued.

Item 9 — Escrowed Securities and Securities Subject to Contractual Restriction on Transfer

9.1 — Escrowed Securities and Securities Subject to Contractual Restriction on Transfer

(1) State, in substantially the following tabular form, the number of securities of each class of your company held, to your company's knowledge, in escrow or that are subject to a contractual restriction on transfer and the percentage that number represents of the outstanding securities of that class for your company's most recently completed financial year.

ESCROWED SECURITIES AND SECURITIES SUBJECT TO CONTRACTUAL RESTRICTION ON TRANSFER

Designation of class	Number of securities held in escrow or that are subject to a contractual restriction on transfer	Percentage of class

(2) In a note to the table disclose the name of the depository, if any, and the date of and conditions governing the release of the securities from escrow or the date the contractual restriction on transfer ends, as applicable.

Instructions

(i) For the purposes of this section, escrow includes securities subject to a pooling agreement.

(ii) For the purposes of this section, securities subject to contractual restrictions on transfer as a result of pledges made to lenders are not required to be disclosed.

Item 10 — Directors and Officers

10.1 — Name, Occupation and Security Holding

(1) List the name, province or state, and country of residence of each director and executive officer of your company and indicate their respective positions and offices held with your company and their respective principal occupations during the five preceding years.

(2) State the period or periods during which each director has served as a director and when his or her term of office will expire.

(3) State the number and percentage of securities of each class of voting securities of your company or any of its subsidiaries beneficially owned, or controlled or directed, directly or indirectly, by all directors and executive officers of your company as a group.

(4) Identify the members of each committee of the board.

(5) If the principal occupation of a director or executive officer of your company is acting as an officer of a person or company other than your company, disclose that fact and state the principal business of the person or company.

Instruction

For the purposes of subsection (3), securities of subsidiaries of your company that are beneficially owned, or controlled or directed, directly or indirectly, by directors or executive officers through ownership, or control or direction, directly or indirectly, over securities of your company, do not need to be included.

10.2 — Cease Trade Orders, Bankruptcies, Penalties or Sanctions

(1) If a director or executive officer of your company is, as at the date of the AIF, or was within 10 years before the date of the AIF, a director, chief executive officer or chief financial officer of any company (including your company), that:

    (a) was subject to an order that was issued while the director or executive officer was acting in the capacity as director, chief executive officer or chief financial officer, or

    (b) was subject to an order that was issued after the director or executive officer ceased to be a director, chief executive officer or chief financial officer and which resulted from an event that occurred while that person was acting in the capacity as director, chief executive officer or chief financial officer,

state the fact and describe the basis on which the order was made and whether the order is still in effect.

(1.1) For the purposes of subsection (1), "order" means

    (a) a cease trade order;

    (b) an order similar to a cease trade order; or

    (c) an order that denied the relevant company access to any exemption under securities legislation,

that was in effect for a period of more than 30 consecutive days.

(1.2) If a director or executive officer of your company, or a shareholder holding a sufficient number of securities of your company to affect materially the control of your company

    (a) is, as at the date of the AIF, or has been within the 10 years before the date of the AIF, a director or executive officer of any company (including your company) that, while that person was acting in that capacity, or within a year of that person ceasing to act in that capacity, became bankrupt, made a proposal under any legislation relating to bankruptcy or insolvency or was subject to or instituted any proceedings, arrangement or compromise with creditors or had a receiver, receiver manager or trustee appointed to hold its assets, state the fact; or

(b) has, within the 10 years before the date of the AIF, become bankrupt, made a proposal under any legislation relating to bankruptcy or insolvency, or become subject to or instituted any proceedings, arrangement or compromise with creditors, or had a receiver, receiver manager or trustee appointed to hold the assets of the director, executive officer or shareholder, state the fact.

(2) Describe the penalties or sanctions imposed and the grounds on which they were imposed, or the terms of the settlement agreement and the circumstances that gave rise to the settlement agreement, if a director or executive officer of your company, or a shareholder holding a sufficient number of securities of your company to affect materially the control of your company, has been subject to

(a) any penalties or sanctions imposed by a court relating to securities legislation or by a securities regulatory authority or has entered into a settlement agreement with a securities regulatory authority; or

(b) any other penalties or sanctions imposed by a court or regulatory body that would likely be considered important to a reasonable investor in making an investment decision.

(3) Despite subsection (2), no disclosure is required of a settlement agreement entered into before December 31, 2000 unless the disclosure would likely be important to a reasonable investor in making an investment decision.

Instructions

(i) The disclosure required by subsections (1), (1.2) and (2) also applies to any personal holding companies of any of the persons referred to in subsections (1), (1.2) and (2).

(ii) A management cease trade order which applies to directors or executive officers of a company is an "order" for the purposes of paragraph 10.2(1)(a) and must be disclosed, whether or not the director, chief executive officer or chief financial officer was named in the order.

(iii) A late filing fee, such as a filing fee that applies to the late filing of an insider report, is not a "penalty or sanction" for the purposes of section 10.2.

(iv) The disclosure in paragraph 10.2(1)(a) only applies if the director or executive officer was a director, chief executive officer or chief financial officer when the order was issued against the company. You do not have to provide disclosure if the director or executive officer became a director, chief executive officer or chief financial officer after the order was issued.

10.3 — Conflicts of Interest

Disclose particulars of existing or potential material conflicts of interest between your company or a subsidiary of your company and any director or officer of your company or of a subsidiary of your company.

Item 11 — Promoters

11.1 — Promoters

For a person or company that has been, within the two most recently completed financial years or during the current financial year, a promoter of your company or of a subsidiary of your company, state

(a) the person or company's name;

(b) the number and percentage of each class of voting securities and equity securities of your company or any of its subsidiaries beneficially owned, or controlled or directed, directly or indirectly;

(c) the nature and amount of anything of value, including money, property, contracts, options or rights of any kind received or to be received by the promoter directly or indirectly from your company or from a subsidiary of your company, and the nature and amount of any assets, services or other consideration received or to be received by your company or a subsidiary of your company in return; and

(d) for an asset acquired within the two most recently completed financial years or during the current financial year, or an asset to be acquired, by your company or by a subsidiary of your company from a promoter

(i) the consideration paid or to be paid for the asset and the method by which the consideration has been or will be determined;

(ii) the person or company making the determination referred to in subparagraph (i) and the person or company's relationship with your company, the promoter, or an associate or affiliate of your company or of the promoter; and

(iii) the date that the asset was acquired by the promoter and the cost of the asset to the promoter.

Item 12 — Legal Proceedings and Regulatory Actions

12.1 — Legal Proceedings

(1) Describe any legal proceedings your company is or was a party to, or that any of its property is or was the subject of, during your company's financial year.

(2) Describe any such legal proceedings your company knows to be contemplated.

(3) For each proceeding described in subsections (1) and (2), include the name of the court or agency, the date instituted, the principal parties to the proceeding, the nature of the claim, the amount claimed, if any, whether the proceeding is being contested, and the present status of the proceeding.

Instruction

You do not need to give information with respect to any proceeding that involves a claim for damages if the amount involved, exclusive of interest and costs, does not exceed ten per cent of the current assets of your company. However, if any proceeding presents in large degree the same legal and factual issues as other proceedings pending or known to be contemplated, you must include the amount involved in the other proceedings in computing the percentage.

12.2 — Regulatory Actions

Describe any

(a) penalties or sanctions imposed against your company by a court relating to securities legislation or by a securities regulatory authority during your financial year,

(b) any other penalties or sanctions imposed by a court or regulatory body against your company that would likely be considered important to a reasonable investor in making an investment decision, and

(c) settlement agreements your company entered into before a court relating to securities legislation or with a securities regulatory authority during your financial year.

Item 13 — Interest of Management and Others in Material Transactions

13.1 — Interest of Management and Others in Material Transactions

Describe, and state the approximate amount of, any material interest, direct or indirect, of any of the following persons or companies in any transaction within the three most recently completed financial years or during the current financial year that has materially affected or is reasonably expected to materially affect your company:

(a) a director or executive officer of your company;

(b) a person or company that beneficially owns, or controls or directs, directly or indirectly, more than 10 percent of any class or series of your outstanding voting securities; and

(c) an associate or affiliate of any of the persons or companies referred to in paragraphs (a) or (b).

Instructions

(i) The materiality of the interest is to be determined on the basis of the significance of the information to investors in light of all the circumstances of the particular case. The importance of the interest to the person having the interest, the relationship of the parties to the transaction with each other and the amount involved are among the factors to be considered in determining the significance of the information to securityholders.

(ii) This Item does not apply to any interest arising from the ownership of securities of your company if the securityholder receives no extra or special benefit or advantage not shared on an equal basis by all other holders of the same class of securities or all other holders of the same class of securities who are resident in Canada.

(iii) Give a brief description of the material transactions. Include the name of each person or company whose interest in any transaction is described and the nature of the relationship to your company.

(iv) For any transaction involving the purchase of assets by or sale of assets to your company or a subsidiary of your company, state the cost of the assets to the purchaser, and the cost of the assets to the seller if acquired by the seller within three years before the transaction.

(v) You do not need to give information under this Item for a transaction if

(A) the rates or charges involved in the transaction are fixed by law or determined by competitive bids,

(B) the interest of a specified person or company in the transaction is solely that of a director of another company that is a party to the transaction,

(C) the transaction involves services as a bank or other depository of funds, a transfer agent, registrar, trustee under a trust indenture or other similar services, or

(D) the transaction does not involve remuneration for services and the interest of the specified person or company arose from the beneficial ownership, direct or indirect, of less than ten per cent of any class of equity securities of another company that is party to the transaction and the transaction is in the ordinary course of business of your company or your company's subsidiaries.

(vi) Describe all transactions not excluded above that involve remuneration (including an issuance of securities), directly or indirectly, to any of the specified persons or companies for services in any capacity unless the interest of the person or company arises solely from the beneficial ownership, direct or indirect, of less than ten per cent of any class of equity securities of another company furnishing the services to your company or your company's subsidiaries.

Item 14 — Transfer Agents and Registrars

14.1 — Transfer Agents and Registrars

State the name of your company's transfer agent(s) and registrar(s) and the location (by municipalities) of the register(s) of transfers of each class of securities.

Item 15 — Material Contracts

15.1 — Material Contracts

Give particulars of any material contract

(a) required to be filed under section 12.2 of the Instrument at the time this AIF is filed, as required under section 12.3 of the Instrument, or

(b) that would be required to be filed under section 12.2 of the Instrument at the time this AIF is filed, as required under section 12.3 of the Instrument, but for the fact that it was previously filed.

Instructions

(i) You must give particulars of any material contract that was entered into within the last financial year or before the last financial year but is still in effect, and that is required to be filed under section 12.2 of the Instrument or would be required to be filed under section 12.2 of the Instrument but for the fact that it was previously filed. You do not need to give particulars of a material contract that was entered into before January 1, 2002 because these material contracts are not required to be filed under section 12.2 of the Instrument.

(ii) Set out a complete list of all contracts for which particulars must be given under this section, indicating those that are disclosed elsewhere in the AIF. Particulars need only be provided for those contracts that do not have the particulars given elsewhere in the AIF.

(iii) Particulars of contracts must include the dates of, parties to, consideration provided for in, and general nature and key terms of, the contracts.

Item 16 — Interests of Experts

16.1 — Names of Experts

Name each person or company

    (a) who is named as having prepared or certified a report, valuation, statement or opinion described or included in a filing, or referred to in a filing, made under National Instrument 51-102 by your company during, or relating to, your company's most recently completed financial year; and

    (b) whose profession or business gives authority to the report, valuation, statement or opinion made by the person or company.

16.2 — Interests of Experts

(1) Disclose all registered or beneficial interests, direct or indirect, in any securities or other property of your company or of one of your associates or affiliates

    (a) held by an expert named in section 16.1 and, if the expert is not an individual, by the designated professionals of that expert, when that expert prepared the statement, report, or valuation referred to in paragraph 16.1(a);

    (b) received by an expert named in section 16.1 and, if the expert is not an individual, by the designated professionals of that expert after the time specified in paragraph 16.2(1)(a); or

    (c) to be received by an expert named in section 16.1.

(1.1) For the purposes of subsection (1), a "designated professional" means, in relation to an expert named in section 16.1,

    (a) each partner, employee or consultant of the expert who participated in and who was in a position to directly influence the preparation of the statement, report or valuation referred to in paragraph 16.1(a); and

    (b) each partner, employee or consultant of the expert who was, at any time during the preparation of the statement, report or valuation referred to in paragraph 16.1(a), in a position to directly influence the outcome of the preparation of the statement, report or valuation, including, without limitation

        (i) any person who recommends the compensation of, or who provides direct supervisory, management or other oversight of, the partner, employee or consultant in the performance of the preparation of the statement, report or valuation referred to in paragraph 16.1(a), including those at all successively senior levels through to the expert's chief executive officer;

        (ii) any person who provides consultation regarding technical or industry-specific issues, transactions or events for the preparation of the statement, report or valuation referred to in paragraph 16.1(a); and

        (iii) any person who provides quality control for the preparation of the statement, report or valuation referred to in paragraph 16.1(a).

(2) For the purposes of subsection (1), if the person's or company's interest in the securities represents less than one per cent of your outstanding securities of the same class, a general statement to that effect is sufficient.

(2.1) Despite subsection (1), an auditor who is independent in accordance with the auditor's rules of professional conduct in a jurisdiction of Canada or who has performed an audit in accordance with U.S. PCAOB GAAS or U.S. AICPA GAAS is not required to provide the disclosure in subsection (1) if there is disclosure that the auditor is independent in accordance with the auditor's rules of professional conduct in a jurisdiction of Canada or that the auditor has complied with the SEC's rules on auditor independence.

(3) If a person or a director, officer or employee of a person or company referred to in subsection (1) is or is expected to be elected, appointed or employed as a director, officer or employee of your company or of any associate or affiliate of your company, disclose the fact or expectation.

Instructions

(i) [repealed]

(ii) Section 16.2 does not apply to

    (A) auditors of a business acquired by your company provided they have not been or will not be appointed as your company's auditor subsequent to the acquisition, and

    (B) your company's predecessor auditors, if any, for periods when they were not your company's auditor.

(iii) Section 16.2 does not apply to registered or beneficial interests, direct or indirect, held through mutual funds.

Item 17 — Additional Information

17.1 — Additional Information

(1) Disclose that additional information relating to your company may be found on SEDAR at www.sedar.com.

(2) If your company is required to distribute a Form 51-102F5 to any of its securityholders, include a statement that additional information, including directors' and officers' remuneration and indebtedness, principal holders of your company's securities and securities authorized for issuance under equity compensation plans, if applicable, is contained in your company's information circular for its most recent annual meeting of securityholders that involved the election of directors.

(3) Include a statement that additional financial information is provided in your company's financial statements and MD&A for its most recently completed financial year.

Instruction

Your company may also be required to provide additional information in its AIF as set out in Form 52-110F1 Audit Committee Information Required in an AIF.

Item 18 — Additional Disclosure for Companies Not Sending Information Circulars

18.1 — Additional Disclosure

For companies that are not required to send a Form 51-102F5 to any of their securityholders, disclose the information required under Items 6 to 10, 12 and 13 of Form 51-102F5, as modified below, if applicable:

Form 51-102F5 Reference	Modification
Item 6 — Voting Securities and Principal Holders of Voting Securities	Include the disclosure specified in section 6.1 without regard to the phrase "entitled to be voted at the meeting". Do not include the disclosure specified in sections 6.2, 6.3 and 6.4. Include the disclosure specified in section 6.5.
Item 7 — Election of Directors	Disregard the preamble of section 7.1. Include the disclosure specified in section 7.1 without regard to the word "proposed" throughout. Do not include the disclosure specified in section 7.3.
Item 8 — Executive Compensation	Disregard the preamble and paragraphs (a), (b) and (c) of Item 8. A company that does not send a management information circular to its securityholders must provide the disclosure required by Form 51-102F6.
Item 9 — Securities Authorized for Issuance under Equity Compensation Plans	Disregard subsection 9.1(1).
Item 10 — Indebtedness of Directors and Executive Officers	Include the disclosure specified throughout; however, replace the phrase "date of the information circular" with "date of the AIF" throughout. Disregard paragraph 10.3(a).
Item 12 — Appointment of Auditor	Name the auditor. If the auditor was first appointed within the last five years, state the date when the auditor was first appointed.

Form 51-102F3 — Material Change Report

Part 1 — General Provisions

(a) — Confidentiality

If this Report is filed on a confidential basis, state in block capitals "CONFIDENTIAL" at the beginning of the Report.

(b) — Use of "Company"

Wherever this Form uses the word "company" the term includes other types of business organizations such as partnerships, trusts and other unincorporated business entities.

(c) — Numbering and Headings

The numbering, headings and ordering of the items included in this Form are guidelines only. You do not need to include the headings or numbering or follow the order of items in this Form. Disclosure provided in response to any item need not be repeated elsewhere.

(d) — Defined Terms

If a term is used but not defined in this Form, refer to Part 1 of National Instrument 51-102 and to National Instrument 14-101 Definitions. If a term is used in this Form and is defined in both the securities statute of a local jurisdiction and in National Instrument 51-102, refer to section 1.4 of Companion Policy 51-102CP.

(e) — Plain Language

Write the Report so that readers are able to understand it. Consider both the level of detail provided and the language used in the document. Refer to the plain language principles listed in section 1.5 of Companion Policy 51-102CP. If you use technical terms, explain them in a clear and concise manner.

Part 2 — Content of Material Change Report

Item 1 — Name and Address of Company

State the full name of your company and the address of its principal office in Canada.

Item 2 — Date of Material Change

State the date of the material change.

Item 3 — News Release

State the date and method(s) of dissemination of the news release issued under section 7.1 of National Instrument 51-102.

Item 4 — Summary of Material Change

Provide a brief but accurate summary of the nature and substance of the material change.

Item 5 — Full Description of Material Change

5.1 — Full Description of Material Change

Supplement the summary required under Item 4 with sufficient disclosure to enable a reader to appreciate the significance and impact of the material change without having to refer to other material. Management is in the best position to determine what facts are significant and must disclose those facts in a meaningful manner. See also Item 7.

Some examples of significant facts relating to the material change include: dates, parties, terms and conditions, description of any assets, liabilities or capital affected, purpose, financial or dollar values, reasons for the change, and a general comment on the probable impact on the issuer or its subsidiaries. Specific financial forecasts would not normally be required.

Other additional disclosure may be appropriate depending on the particular situation.

5.2 — Disclosure for Restructuring Transactions

This item applies to a material change report filed in respect of the closing of a restructuring transaction under which securities are to be changed, exchanged, issued or distributed. This item does not apply if, in respect of the transaction, your company sent an information circular to its securityholders or filed a prospectus or a securities exchange takeover bid circular.

Include the disclosure for each entity that resulted from the restructuring transaction, if your company has an interest in that entity, required by section 14.2 of Form 51-102F5. You may satisfy the requirement to include this disclosure by incorporating the information by reference to another document.

Instructions

(i) If your company is engaged in oil and gas activities, the disclosure under Item 5 must also satisfy the requirements of Part 6 of National Instrument 51-101 Standards of Disclosure for Oil and Gas Activities.

(ii) If you incorporate information by reference to another document, clearly identify the referenced document or any excerpt from it. Unless you have already filed the referenced document or excerpt, you must file it with the material change report. You must also disclose that the document is on SEDAR at www.sedar.com.

Item 6 — Reliance on subsection 7.1(2) of National Instrument 51-102

If this Report is being filed on a confidential basis in reliance on subsection 7.1(2) of National Instrument 51-102, state the reasons for such reliance.

Instruction

Refer to subsections 7.1 (5), (6) and (7) of National Instrument 51-102 concerning continuing obligations in respect of reports filed under subsection 7.1(2) of National Instrument 51-102.

Item 7 — Omitted Information

State whether any information has been omitted on the basis that it is confidential information.

In a separate letter to the applicable regulator or securities regulatory authority marked "Confidential" provide the reasons for your company's omission of confidential significant facts in the Report in sufficient detail to permit the applicable regulator or securities regulatory authority to determine whether to exercise its discretion to allow the omission of these significant facts.

Part 5: ONGOING REQUIREMENTS

Instructions

In certain circumstances where a material change has occurred and a Report has been or is about to be filed but subsection 7.1(2) or (5) of National Instrument 51-102 is not or will no longer be relied upon, your company may nevertheless believe one or more significant facts otherwise required to be disclosed in the Report should remain confidential and not be disclosed or not be disclosed in full detail in the Report.

Item 8 — Executive Officer

Give the name and business telephone number of an executive officer of your company who is knowledgeable about the material change and the Report, or the name of an officer through whom such executive officer may be contacted.

Item 9 — Date of Report

Date the Report.

Form 51-102F4 — Business Acquisition Report

Part 1 — General Provisions

(a) — What is a Business Acquisition Report?

Your company must file a Business Acquisition Report after completing a significant acquisition. See Part 8 of National Instrument 51-102. The Business Acquisition Report describes the significant businesses acquired by your company and the effect of the acquisition on your company.

(b) — Use of "Company"

Wherever this Form uses the word "company", the term includes other types of business organizations such as partnerships, trusts and other unincorporated business entities.

(c) — Focus on Relevant Information

When providing the disclosure required by this Form, focus your discussion on information that is relevant to an investor, analyst or other reader.

(d) — Incorporating Material By Reference

You may incorporate information required by this Form, by reference to another document. Clearly identify the referenced document, or any excerpt of it, that you incorporate into this Report. Unless you have already filed the referenced document or excerpt, including any documents incorporated by reference into the document or excerpt, you must file it with this Report. You must also disclose that the document is on SEDAR at www.sedar.com.

(e) — Defined Terms

If a term is used but not defined in this Form, refer to Part 1 of National Instrument 51-102 and to National Instrument 14-101 Definitions. If a term is used in this Form and is defined in both the securities statute of a local jurisdiction and in National Instrument 51-102, refer to section 1.4 of Companion Policy 51-102CP for further guidance.

This Form also uses accounting terms that are defined or used in Canadian GAAP applicable to publicly accountable enterprises. For further guidance, see subsections 1.4(7) and (8) of Companion Policy 51-102CP.

(f) — Plain Language

Write this Report so that readers are able to understand it. Consider both the level of detail provided and the language used in the document. Refer to the plain language principles listed in section 1.5 of Companion Policy 51-102CP for further guidance. If you use technical terms, explain them in a clear and concise manner.

(g) — Numbering and Headings

The numbering, headings and ordering of items included in this Form are guidelines only. You do not need to include the headings or numbering or follow the order of items in this Form. Disclosure provided in response to any item need not be repeated elsewhere in the Report.

Part 2 — Content of Business Acquisition Report

Item 1 — Identity of Company

1.1 — Name and Address of Company

State the full name of your company and the address of its principal office in Canada.

1.2 — Executive Officer

Give the name and business telephone number of an executive officer of your company who is knowledgeable about the significant acquisition and the Report, or the name of an officer through whom such executive officer may be contacted.

Item 2 — Details of Acquisition

2.1 — Nature of Business Acquired

Describe the nature of the business acquired.

2.2 — Acquisition Date

State the acquisition date used for accounting purposes.

2.3 — Consideration

Disclose the type and amount of consideration, both monetary and non-monetary, paid or payable by your company in connection with the significant acquisition, including contingent consideration. Identify the source of funds used by your company for the acquisition, including a description of any financing associated with the acquisition.

2.4 — Effect on Financial Position

Describe any plans or proposals for material changes in your business affairs or the affairs of the acquired business which may have a significant effect on the financial performance and financial position of your company. Examples include any proposal to liquidate the business, to sell, lease or exchange all or a substantial part of its assets, to amalgamate the business with any other business organization or to make any material changes to your business or the business acquired such as changes in corporate structure, management or personnel.

2.5 — Prior Valuations

Describe in sufficient detail any valuation opinion obtained within the last 12 months by the acquired business or your company required by securities legislation or a Canadian exchange or market to support the consideration paid by your company or any of its subsidiaries for the business, including the name of the author, the date of the opinion, the business to which the opinion relates, the value attributed to the business and the valuation methodologies used.

2.6 — Parties to Transaction

State whether the transaction is with an informed person, associate or affiliate of your company and, if so, the identity and the relationship of the other parties to your company.

2.7 — Date of Report

Date the Report.

Item 3 — Financial Statements and Other Information

Include the financial statements or other information required by Part 8 of National Instrument 51-102. If applicable, disclose that the auditors have not given their consent to include their audit report in this Report.

Form 51-102F5 — Information Circular

Table of Contents

Item 9 Securities Authorized for Issuance Under Equity Compensation Plans

Item 10 Indebtedness of Directors and Executive Officers

Item 11 Interest of Informed Persons in Material Transactions

Item 12 Appointment of Auditor

Item 13 Management Contracts

Item 14 Particulars of Matters to be Acted Upon

Item 15 Restricted Securities

Item 16 Additional Information

Part 1 — General Provisions

(a) — Timing of Information

The information required by this Form 51-102F5 must be given as of a specified date not more than thirty days prior to the date you first send the information circular to any securityholder of the company.

(b) — Use of "Company"

Wherever this Form uses the word "company", the term includes other types of business organizations such as partnerships, trusts and other unincorporated business entities.

(c) — Incorporating Information by Reference

You may incorporate information required to be included in your information circular by reference to another document. Clearly identify the referenced document or any excerpt of it that you incorporate into your information circular. Unless you have already filed the referenced document or excerpt, including any documents incorporated by reference into the document or excerpt, you must file it with your information circular. You must also disclose that the document is on SEDAR at www.sedar.com and that, upon request, you will promptly provide a copy of any such document free of charge to a securityholder of the company. However, you may not incorporate information required to be included in Form 51-102F6 *Statement of Executive Compensation* or Form 51-102F6V *Statement of Executive Compensation – Venture Issuers* by reference into your information circular.

(d) — Defined Terms

If a term is used but not defined in this Form, refer to Part 1 of National Instrument 51-102 and to National Instrument 14-101 *Definitions*. If a term is used in this Form and is defined in both the securities statute of the local jurisdiction and in National Instrument 51-102, refer to section 1.4 of Companion Policy 51-102CP for further guidance.

This Form also uses accounting terms that are defined or used in Canadian GAAP applicable to publicly accountable enterprises. For further guidance, see subsections 1.4(7) and (8) of Companion Policy 51-102CP.

(e) — Plain Language

Write this document so that readers are able to understand it. Refer to the plain language principles listed in section 1.5 of Companion Policy 51-102CP for further guidance. If you use technical terms, explain them in a clear and concise manner.

(f) — Numbering and Headings

The numbering, headings and ordering of items included in this Form are guidelines only. You do not need to include the headings or numbering or follow the order of items in this Form. Disclosure provided in response to any item need not be repeated elsewhere.

(g) — Tables and Figures

Where it is practicable and appropriate, present information in tabular form. State all amounts in figures.

(h) — Omitting Information

You do not need to respond to any item in this Form that is inapplicable. You may also omit information that is not known to the person or company on whose behalf the solicitation is made and that is not reasonably within the power of the person or company to obtain, if you briefly state the circumstances that render the information unavailable.

You may omit information that was contained in another information circular, notice of meeting or form of proxy sent to the same persons or companies whose proxies were solicited in connection with the same meeting, as long as you clearly identify the particular document containing the information.

Part 2 — Content

Item 1 — Date

Specify the date of the information circular.

Item 2 — Revocability of Proxy

State whether the person or company giving the proxy has the power to revoke it. If any right of revocation is limited or is subject to compliance with any formal procedure, briefly describe the limitation or procedure.

Item 3 — Persons Making the Solicitation

3.1 If a solicitation is made by or on behalf of management of the company, state this. Name any director of the company who has informed management in writing that he or she intends to oppose any action intended to be taken by management at the meeting and indicate the action that he or she intends to oppose.

3.2 If a solicitation is made other than by or on behalf of management of the company, state this and give the name of the person or company by whom, or on whose behalf, it is made.

3.3 If the solicitation is to be made other than by mail, describe the method to be employed. If the solicitation is to be made by specially engaged employees or soliciting agents, state,

    (a) the parties to and material features of any contract or arrangement for the solicitation; and

    (b) the cost or anticipated cost thereof.

3.4 State who has borne or will bear, directly or indirectly, the cost of soliciting.

Item 4 — Proxy Instructions

4.1 The information circular or the form of proxy to which the information circular relates must indicate in bold-face type that the securityholder has the right to appoint a person or company to represent the securityholder at the meeting other than the person or company, if any, designated in the form of proxy and must contain instructions as to the manner in which the securityholder may exercise the right.

4.2 The information circular or the form of proxy to which the information circular relates must state that the securities represented by the proxy will be voted or withheld from voting in accordance with the instructions of the securityholder on any ballot that may be called for and that, if the securityholder specifies a choice with respect to any matter to be acted upon, the securities will be voted accordingly.

4.3 The information circular must include the following, if applicable:

    (a) a statement that the reporting issuer is sending proxy-related materials to registered holders or beneficial owners using notice-and-access and, if stratification will be used, a description of the types of registered holders or beneficial owners who will receive paper copies of the information circular and, if applicable, the documents in paragraph 9.1.1(2)(b);

    (b) a statement that the reporting issuer is sending proxy-related materials directly to non-objecting beneficial owners under NI 54-101;

    (c) a statement that management of the reporting issuer does not intend to pay for intermediaries to forward to objecting beneficial owners under NI 54-101 the proxy-related materials and Form 54-101F7 — Request for Voting Instructions Made by Intermediary, and that in the case of an objecting beneficial owner, the objecting beneficial owner will not receive the materials unless the objecting beneficial owner's intermediary assumes the cost of delivery.

Item 5 — Interest of Certain Persons or Companies in Matters to be Acted Upon

Briefly describe any material interest, direct or indirect, by way of beneficial ownership of securities or otherwise, of each of the following persons or companies in any matter to be acted upon other than the election of directors or the appointment of auditors:

    (a) if the solicitation is made by or on behalf of management of the company, each person who has been a director or executive officer of the company at any time since the beginning of the company's last financial year;

    (b) if the solicitation is made other than by or on behalf of management of the company, each person or company by whom, or on whose behalf, directly or indirectly, the solicitation is made;

    (c) each proposed nominee for election as a director of the company; and

    (d) each associate or affiliate of any of the persons or companies listed in paragraphs (a) to (c).

Instructions

(i) The following persons and companies are deemed to be persons or companies by whom or on whose behalf the solicitation is made (collectively, "solicitors" or individually a "solicitor"):

    (A) any member of a committee or group that solicits proxies, and any person or company whether or not named as a member who, acting alone or with one or more other persons or companies, directly or indirectly takes the initiative or engages in organizing, directing or financing any such committee or group;

    (B) any person or company who contributes, or joins with another to contribute, more than $250 to finance the solicitation of proxies; or

    (C) any person or company who lends money, provides credit, or enters into any other arrangements, under any contract or understanding with a solicitor, for the purpose of financing or otherwise inducing the purchase, sale, holding or voting of securities of the company but not including a bank or other lending institution or a dealer that, in the ordinary course of business, lends money or executes orders for the purchase or sale of securities.

(ii) Subject to paragraph (i), the following persons and companies are deemed not to be solicitors:

    (A) any person or company retained or employed by a solicitor to solicit proxies or any person or company who merely transmits proxy-soliciting material or performs ministerial or clerical duties;

(B) any person or company employed or retained by a solicitor in the capacity of lawyer, accountant, or advertising, public relations, investor relations or financial advisor and whose activities are limited to the performance of their duties in the course of the employment or retainer;

(C) any person regularly employed as an officer or employee of the company or any of its affiliates; or

(D) any officer or director of, or any person regularly employed by, any solicitor.

Item 6 — Voting Securities and Principal Holders of Voting Securities

6.1 For each class of voting securities of the company entitled to be voted at the meeting, state the number of securities outstanding and the particulars of voting rights for each class.

6.2 For each class of restricted securities, provide the information required in subsection 10.1(1) of National Instrument 51-102.

6.3 Give the record date as of which the securityholders entitled to vote at the meeting will be determined or particulars as to the closing of the security transfer register, as the case may be, and, if the right to vote is not limited to securityholders of record as of the specified record date, indicate the conditions under which securityholders are entitled to vote.

6.4 If action is to be taken with respect to the election of directors and if the securityholders or any class of securityholders have the right to elect a specified number of directors or have cumulative or similar voting rights, include a statement of such rights and state briefly the conditions precedent, if any, to the exercise thereof.

6.5 If, to the knowledge of the company's directors or executive officers, any person or company beneficially owns, or controls or directs, directly or indirectly, voting securities carrying 10 per cent or more of the voting rights attached to any class of voting securities of the company, name each person or company and state

    (a) the approximate number of securities beneficially owned, or controlled or directed, directly or indirectly, by each such person or company; and

    (b) the percentage of the class of outstanding voting securities of the company represented by the number of voting securities so owned, controlled or directed, directly or indirectly.

Item 7 — Election of Directors

7.1 If directors are to be elected, provide the following information, in tabular form to the extent practicable, for each person proposed to be nominated for election as a director (a "proposed director") and each other person whose term of office as a director will continue after the meeting:

    (a) State the name, province or state, and country of residence, of each director and proposed director.

    (b) State the period or periods during which each director has served as a director and when the term of office for each director and proposed director will expire.

    (c) Identify the members of each committee of the board.

    (d) State the present principal occupation, business or employment of each director and proposed director. Give the name and principal business of any company in which any such employment is carried on. Furnish similar information as to all of the principal occupations, businesses or employments of each proposed director within the five preceding years, unless the proposed director is now a director and was elected to the present term of office by a vote of securityholders at a meeting, the notice of which was accompanied by an information circular.

    (e) If a director or proposed director has held more than one position in the company, or a parent or subsidiary, state only the first and last position held.

    (f) State the number of securities of each class of voting securities of the company or any of its subsidiaries beneficially owned, or controlled or directed, directly or indirectly, by each proposed director.

    (g) If securities carrying 10 per cent or more of the voting rights attached to all voting securities of the company or of any of its subsidiaries are beneficially owned, or controlled or directed, directly or indirectly, by any proposed director and the proposed director's associates or affiliates,

        (i) state the number of securities of each class of voting securities beneficially owned, or controlled or directed, directly or indirectly, by the associates or affiliates; and

        (ii) name each associate or affiliate whose security holdings are 10 per cent or more.

7.2 If a proposed director

    (a) is, as at the date of the information circular, or has been, within 10 years before the date of the information circular, a director, chief executive officer or chief financial officer of any company (including the company in respect of which the information circular is being prepared) that,

        (i) was subject to an order that was issued while the proposed director was acting in the capacity as director, chief executive officer or chief financial officer; or

        (ii) was subject to an order that was issued after the proposed director ceased to be a director, chief executive officer or chief financial officer and which resulted from an event that occurred while that person was acting in the capacity as director, chief executive officer or chief financial officer,

    state the fact and describe the basis on which the order was made and whether the order is still in effect; or

(b) is, as at the date of the information circular, or has been within 10 years before the date of the information circular, a director or executive officer of any company (including the company in respect of which the information circular is being prepared) that, while that person was acting in that capacity, or within a year of that person ceasing to act in that capacity, became bankrupt, made a proposal under any legislation relating to bankruptcy or insolvency or was subject to or instituted any proceedings, arrangement or compromise with creditors or had a receiver, receiver manager or trustee appointed to hold its assets, state the fact; or

(c) has, within the 10 years before the date of the information circular, become bankrupt, made a proposal under any legislation relating to bankruptcy or insolvency, or become subject to or instituted any proceedings, arrangement or compromise with creditors, or had a receiver, receiver manager or trustee appointed to hold the assets of the proposed director, state the fact.

7.2.1 Describe the penalties or sanctions imposed and the grounds on which they were imposed, or the terms of the settlement agreement and the circumstances that gave rise to the settlement agreement, if a proposed director has been subject to

(a) any penalties or sanctions imposed by a court relating to securities legislation or by a securities regulatory authority or has entered into a settlement agreement with a securities regulatory authority; or

(b) any other penalties or sanctions imposed by a court or regulatory body that would likely be considered important to a reasonable securityholder in deciding whether to vote for a proposed director.

7.2.2 Despite section 7.2.1, no disclosure is required of a settlement agreement entered into before December 31, 2000 unless the disclosure would likely be important to a reasonable securityholder in deciding whether to vote for a proposed director.

INSTRUCTIONS

(i) The disclosure required by sections 7.2 and 7.2.1 also applies to any personal holding companies of the proposed director.

(ii) A management cease trade order which applies to directors or executive officers of a company is an "order" for the purposes of paragraph 7.2(a)(i) and so must be disclosed, whether or not the proposed director was named in the order.

(iii) A late filing fee, such as a filing fee that applies to the late filing of an insider report, is not a "penalty or sanction" for the purposes of section 7.2.1.

(iv) The disclosure in paragraph 7.2(a)(i) only applies if the proposed director was a director, chief executive officer or chief financial officer when the order was issued against the company. You do not have to provide disclosure if the proposed director became a director, chief executive officer or chief financial officer after the order was issued.

7.2.3 For the purposes of subsection 7.2(a), "order" means

(a) a cease trade order;

(b) an order similar to a cease trade order; or

(c) an order that denied the relevant company access to any exemption under securities legislation,

that was in effect for a period of more than 30 consecutive days.

7.3 If any proposed director is to be elected under any arrangement or understanding between the proposed director and any other person or company, except the directors and executive officers of the company acting solely in such capacity, name the other person or company and describe briefly the arrangement or understanding.

Item 8 — Executive Compensation

If you are sending this information circular in connection with a meeting

(a) that is an annual general meeting,

(b) at which the company's directors are to be elected, or

(c) at which the company's securityholders will be asked to vote on a matter relating to executive compensation,

include a completed Form 51-102F6 *Statement of Executive Compensation* or, in the case of a venture issuer, a completed Form 51-102F6 *Statement of Executive Compensation* or a completed Form 51-102F6V *Statement of Executive Compensation – Venture Issuers.*

Item 9 — Securities Authorized for Issuance Under Equity Compensation Plans

9.1 Equity Compensation Plan Information — (1) Provide the information in subsection (2) if you are sending this information circular in connection with a meeting

(a) that is an annual general meeting,

(b) at which the company's directors are to be elected, or

(c) at which the company's securityholders will be asked to vote on a matter relating to executive compensation or a transaction that involves the company issuing securities.

(2) In the tabular form under the caption set out, provide the information specified in section 9.2 as of the end of the company's most recently completed financial year with respect to compensation plans under which equity securities of the company are authorized for issuance, aggregated as follows:

(a) all compensation plans previously approved by securityholders; and

(b) all compensation plans not previously approved by securityholders.

Equity Compensation Plan Information

Plan Category	Number of securities to be issued upon exercise of outstanding options, warrants and rights (a)	Weighted-average exercise price of outstanding options, warrants and rights (b)	Number of securities remaining available for future issuance under equity compensation plans (excluding securities reflected in column (a)) (c)
Equity compensation plans approved by securityholders	....	....	....
Equity compensation plans not approved by securityholders	....	....	....
Total	....	....	....

9.2 Include in the table the following information as of the end of the company's most recently completed financial year for each category of compensation plan described in section 9.1:

(a) the number of securities to be issued upon the exercise of outstanding options, warrants and rights (column (a));

(b) the weighted-average exercise price of the outstanding options, warrants and rights disclosed under subsection 9.2(a) (column (b)); and

(c) other than securities to be issued upon the exercise of the outstanding options, warrants and rights disclosed in subsection 9.2(a), the number of securities remaining available for future issuance under the plan (column (c)).

9.3 For each compensation plan under which equity securities of the company are authorized for issuance and that was adopted without the approval of securityholders, describe briefly, in narrative form, the material features of the plan.

Instructions

(i) The disclosure under Item 9 relating to compensation plans must include individual compensation arrangements.

(ii) Provide disclosure with respect to any compensation plan of the company (or parent, subsidiary or affiliate of the company) under which equity securities of the company are authorized for issuance to employees or non-employees (such as directors, consultants, advisors, vendors, customers, suppliers or lenders) in exchange for consideration in the form of goods or services. You do not have to provide disclosure regarding any plan, contract or arrangement for the issuance of warrants or rights to all securityholders of the company on a pro rata basis (such as a rights offering).

(iii) If more than one class of equity security is issued under the company's compensation plans, disclose aggregate plan information for each class of security separately.

(iv) You may aggregate information regarding individual compensation arrangements with the plan information required under subsections 9.1(a) and (b), as applicable.

(v) You may aggregate information regarding a compensation plan assumed in connection with a merger, consolidation or other acquisition transaction pursuant to which the company may make subsequent grants or awards of its equity securities with the plan information required under subsections 9.1(a) and (b), as applicable. Disclose on an aggregated basis in a footnote to the table the information required under subsections 9.2(a) and (b) with respect to any individual options, warrants or rights outstanding under the compensation plan assumed in connection with a merger, consolidation or other acquisition transaction.

(vi) To the extent that the number of securities remaining available for future issuance disclosed in column (c) includes securities available for future issuance under any compensation plan other than upon the exercise of an option, warrant or right, disclose the number of securities and type of plan separately for each such plan in a footnote to the table.

(vii) If the description of a compensation plan set forth in the company's financial statements contains the disclosure required by section 9.3, a cross-reference to the description satisfies the requirements of section 9.3.

(viii) If an equity compensation plan contains a formula for calculating the number of securities available for issuance under the plan, including, without limitation, a formula that automatically increases the number of securities available for issuance by a percentage of the number of outstanding securities of the company, describe this formula in a footnote to the table.

Item 10 — Indebtedness of Directors and Executive Officers

10.1 Aggregate Indebtedness

Purpose (a)	AGGREGATE INDEBTEDNESS ($) To the Company or its Subsidiaries (b)	To Another Entity (c)
Share purchases	....	....
Other	....	....

(1) Complete the above table for the aggregate indebtedness outstanding as at a date within thirty days before the date of the information circular entered into in connection with:

  (a) a purchase of securities; and

  (b) all other indebtedness.

(2) Report separately the indebtedness to

  (a) the company or any of its subsidiaries (column (b)); and

  (b) another entity if the indebtedness is the subject of a guarantee, support agreement, letter of credit or other similar arrangement or understanding provided by the company or any of its subsidiaries (column (c)),

of all executive officers, directors, employees and former executive officers, directors and employees of the company or any of its subsidiaries.

(3) "Support agreement" includes, but is not limited to, an agreement to provide assistance in the maintenance or servicing of any indebtedness and an agreement to provide compensation for the purpose of maintaining or servicing any indebtedness of the borrower.

10.2 Indebtedness of Directors and Executive Officers under (1) Securities Purchase and (2) Other Programs

INDEBTEDNESS OF DIRECTORS AND EXECUTIVE OFFICERS UNDER (1) SECURITIES PURCHASE AND (2) OTHER PROGRAMS

Name and Principal Position	Involvement of Company or Subsidiary	Largest Amount Outstanding During [Most Recently Completed Financial Year] ($)	Amount Outstanding as at [Date within 30 days] ($)	Financially Assisted Securities Purchases During [Most Recently Completed Financial Year] (#)	Security for Indebtedness	Amount Forgiven During [Most Recently Completed Financial Year] ($)
(a)	(b)	(c)	(d)	(e)	(f)	(g)
Securities Purchase Programs						
....	....	....	....	....	....	....
....	....	....	....			....
Other Programs						
....	....	....	....	....	....	....
....	....	....	....			....

(1) Complete the above table for each individual who is, or at any time during the most recently completed financial year was, a director or executive officer of the company, each proposed nominee for election as a director of the company, and each associate of any such director, executive officer or proposed nominee,

  (a) who is, or at any time since the beginning of the most recently completed financial year of the company has been, indebted to the company or any of its subsidiaries, or

  (b) whose indebtedness to another entity is, or at any time since the beginning of the most recently completed financial year has been, the subject of a guarantee, support agreement, letter of credit or other similar arrangement or understanding provided by the company or any of its subsidiaries,

and separately disclose the indebtedness for security purchase programs and all other programs.

(2) Note the following:

  Column (a) — disclose the name and principal position of the borrower. If the borrower was, during the most recently completed financial year, but no longer is a director or executive officer, state that fact. If the borrower is a proposed nominee for election as a director, state that fact. If the borrower is included as an associate, describe briefly the relationship of the borrower to an individual who is or, during the financial year, was a director or executive officer or who is a proposed nominee for election as a director, name that individual and provide the information required by this subparagraph for that individual.

  Column (b) — disclose whether the company or a subsidiary of the company is the lender or the provider of a guarantee, support agreement, letter of credit or similar arrangement or understanding.

  Column (c) — disclose the largest aggregate amount of the indebtedness outstanding at any time during the most recently completed financial year.

  Column (d) — disclose the aggregate amount of indebtedness outstanding as at a date within thirty days before the date of the information circular.

  Column (e) — disclose separately for each class or series of securities, the sum of the number of securities purchased during the most recently completed financial year with the financial assistance (security purchase programs only).

  Column (f) — disclose the security for the indebtedness, if any, provided to the company, any of its subsidiaries or the other entity (security purchase programs only).

  Column (g) — disclose the total amount of indebtedness that was forgiven at any time during the most recently completed financial year.

(3) Supplement the above table with a summary discussion of

    (a) the material terms of each incidence of indebtedness and, if applicable, of each guarantee, support agreement, letter of credit or other similar arrangement or understanding, including

        (i) the nature of the transaction in which the indebtedness was incurred;

        (ii) the rate of interest;

        (iii) the term to maturity;

        (iv) any understanding, agreement or intention to limit recourse; and

        (v) any security for the indebtedness;

    (b) any material adjustment or amendment made during the most recently completed financial year to the terms of the indebtedness and, if applicable, the guarantee, support agreement, letter of credit or similar arrangement or understanding. Forgiveness of indebtedness reported in column (g) of the above table should be explained; and

    (c) the class or series of the securities purchased with financial assistance or held as security for the indebtedness and, if the class or series of securities is not publicly traded, all material terms of the securities, including the provisions for exchange, conversion, exercise, redemption, retraction and dividends.

10.3 You do not need to disclose information required by this Item

    (a) if you are not sending this information circular in connection with a meeting

        (i) that is an annual general meeting,

        (ii) at which the company's directors are to be elected, or

        (iii) at which the company's securityholders will be asked to vote on a matter relating to executive compensation,

    (b) for any indebtedness that has been entirely repaid on or before the date of the information circular, or

    (c) for routine indebtedness.

"Routine indebtedness" means indebtedness described in any of the following clauses:

    (i) If the company or its subsidiary makes loans to employees generally,

        (A) the loans are made on terms no more favourable than the terms on which loans are made by the company or its subsidiary to employees generally, and

        (B) the amount, at any time during the last completed financial year, remaining unpaid under the loans to the director, executive officer or proposed nominee, together with his or her associates, does not exceed $50,000.

    (ii) A loan to a person or company who is a full-time employee of the company,

        (A) that is fully secured against the residence of the borrower, and

        (B) the amount of which in total does not exceed the annual salary of the borrower.

    (iii) If the company or its subsidiary makes loans in the ordinary course of business, a loan made to a person or company other than a full-time employee of the company

        (A) on substantially the same terms, including those as to interest rate and security, as are available when a loan is made to other customers of the company or its subsidiary with comparable credit, and

        (B) with no more than the usual risks of collectibility.

    (iv) A loan arising by reason of purchases made on usual trade terms or of ordinary travel or expense advances, or for similar reasons, if the repayment arrangements are in accord with usual commercial practice.

Item 11 — Interest of Informed Persons in Material Transactions

Describe briefly and, where practicable, state the approximate amount of any material interest, direct or indirect, of any informed person of the company, any proposed director of the company, or any associate or affiliate of any informed person or proposed director, in any transaction since the commencement of the company's most recently completed financial year or in any proposed transaction which has materially affected or would materially affect the company or any of its subsidiaries.

Instructions:

(i) Briefly describe the material transaction. State the name and address of each person or company whose interest in any transaction is described and the nature of the relationship giving rise to the interest.

(ii) For any transaction involving the purchase or sale of assets by or to the company or any subsidiary, other than in the ordinary course of business, state the cost of the assets to the purchaser and the cost of the assets to the seller, if acquired by the seller within two years prior to the transaction.

(iii) This Item does not apply to any interest arising from the ownership of securities of the company where the securityholder receives no extra or special benefit or advantage not shared on a proportionate basis by all holders of the same class of securities or by all holders of the same class of securities who are resident in Canada.

(iv) Include information as to any material underwriting discounts or commissions upon the sale of securities by the company where any of the specified persons or companies was or is to be an underwriter in a contractual relationship with the company with respect to securities or is an associate or affiliate of a person or company that was or is to be such an underwriter.

(v) You do not need to disclose the information required by this Item for any transaction or any interest in that transaction if

    (A) the rates or charges involved in the transaction are fixed by law or determined by competitive bids,

    (B) the interest of the specified person in the transaction is solely that of director of another company that is a party to the transaction,

    (C) the transaction involves services as a bank or other depositary of funds, transfer agent, registrar, trustee under a trust indenture or other similar services, or

    (D) the transaction does not directly or indirectly, involve remuneration for services, and

        (I) the interest of the specified person or company arose from the beneficial ownership, direct or indirect, of less than 10 per cent of any class of voting securities of another company that is a party to the transaction,

        (II) the transaction is in the ordinary course of business of the company or its subsidiaries, and

        (III) the amount of the transaction or series of transactions is less than 10 per cent of the total sales or purchases, as the case may be, of the company and its subsidiaries for the most recently completed financial year.

(vi) Provide information for transactions not excluded above which involve remuneration, directly or indirectly, to any of the specified persons or companies for services in any capacity unless the interest of the person arises solely from the beneficial ownership, direct or indirect, of less than 10 per cent of any class of voting securities of another company furnishing the services to the company or its subsidiaries.

Item 12 — Appointment of Auditor

Name the auditor of the company. If the auditor was first appointed within the last five years, state the date when the auditor was first appointed.

If action is to be taken to replace an auditor, provide the information required under section 4.11 of National Instrument 51-102.

Item 13 — Management Contracts

If management functions of the company or any of its subsidiaries are to any substantial degree performed other than by the directors or executive officers of the company or subsidiary,

    (a) give details of the agreement or arrangement under which the management functions are performed, including the name and address of any person or company who is a party to the agreement or arrangement or who is responsible for performing the management functions;

    (b) give the names and provinces of residence of any person that was, during the most recently completed financial year, an informed person of any person or company with which the company or subsidiary has any such agreement or arrangement and, if the following information is known to the directors or executive officers of the company, give the names and provinces of residence of any person or company that would be an informed person of any person or company with which the company or subsidiary has any such agreement or arrangement if the person were an issuer;

    (c) for any person or company named under paragraph (a) state the amounts paid or payable by the company and its subsidiaries to the person or company since the commencement of the most recently completed financial year and give particulars; and

    (d) for any person or company named under paragraph (a) or (b) and their associates or affiliates, give particulars of,

        (i) any indebtedness of the person, company, associate or affiliate to the company or its subsidiaries that was outstanding, and

        (ii) any transaction or arrangement of the person, company, associate or affiliate with the company or subsidiary,

at any time since the start of the company's most recently completed financial year.

Instructions:

(i) Do not refer to any matter that is relatively insignificant.

(ii) In giving particulars of indebtedness, state the largest aggregate amount of indebtedness outstanding at any time during the period, the nature of the indebtedness and of the transaction in which it was incurred, the amount of the indebtedness presently outstanding and the rate of interest paid or charged on the indebtedness.

(iii) Do not include as indebtedness amounts due from the particular person for purchases subject to usual trade terms, for ordinary travel and expense advances and for other similar transactions.

Item 14 — Particulars of Matters to be Acted Upon

14.1 If action is to be taken on any matter to be submitted to the meeting of securityholders other than the approval of annual financial statements, briefly describe the substance of the matter, or related groups of matters, except to the extent described under the foregoing items, in sufficient detail to enable reasonable securityholders to form a reasoned judgment concerning the matter. Without limiting the generality of the foregoing, such matters include alterations of share capital, charter amendments, property acquisitions or dispositions, reverse takeovers, amalgamations, mergers, arrangements or reorganizations and other similar transactions.

14.2 If the action to be taken is in respect of a significant acquisition as determined under Part 8 of National Instrument 51-102 under which securities of the acquired business are being exchanged for the company's securities, or in respect of a restructuring transaction under which securities are to be changed, exchanged, issued or distributed, include disclosure for

    (a) the company, if the company has not filed all documents required under National Instrument 51-102,

    (b) the business being acquired, if the matter is a significant acquisition,

(c) each entity, other than the company, whose securities are being changed, exchanged, issued or distributed, if

(i) the matter is a restructuring transaction, and

(ii) the company's current securityholders will have an interest in that entity after the restructuring transaction is completed, and

(d) each entity that would result from the significant acquisition or restructuring transaction, if the company's securityholders will have an interest in that entity after the significant acquisition or restructuring transaction is completed.

The disclosure for the company, business or entity must be the disclosure (including financial statements) prescribed under securities legislation and described in the form of prospectus that the company, business or entity, respectively, would be eligible to use immediately prior to the sending and filing of the information circular in respect of the significant acquisition or restructuring transaction, for a distribution of securities in the jurisdiction.

14.3 If the matter is one that is not required to be submitted to a vote of securityholders, state the reasons for submitting it to securityholders and state what action management intends to take in the event of a negative vote by the securityholders.

14.4 Section 14.2 does not apply to an information circular that is sent to holders of voting securities of a reporting issuer soliciting proxies otherwise than on behalf of management of the reporting issuer (a "dissident circular"), unless the sender of the dissident circular is proposing a significant acquisition or restructuring transaction involving the reporting issuer and the sender, under which securities of the sender, or an affiliate of the sender, are to be distributed or transferred to securityholders of the reporting issuer. However, a sender of a dissident circular shall include in the dissident circular the disclosure required by section 14.2 if the sender of the dissident circular is proposing a significant acquisition or restructuring transaction under which securities of the sender or securities of an affiliate of the sender are to be changed, exchanged, issued or distributed.

14.5 A company satisfies section 14.2 if it prepares an information circular in connection with a Qualifying Transaction, for a company that is a CPC or in connection with a Reverse Take-Over (as Qualifying Transaction, CPC and Reverse Take-Over are defined in the TSX Venture Exchange policies) provided that the company complies with the policies and requirements of the TSX Venture Exchange in respect of that Qualifying Transaction or Reverse Take-Over.

INSTRUCTION

For the purposes of section 14.2, a securityholder will not be considered to have an interest in an entity after an acquisition or restructuring transaction is completed if the securityholder will only hold a redeemable security that is immediately redeemed for cash.

Item 15 — Restricted Securities

15.1 If the action to be taken involves a transaction that would have the effect of converting or subdividing, in whole or in part, existing securities into restricted securities, or creating new restricted securities, the information circular must also include, as part of the minimum disclosure required, a detailed description of:

(a) the voting rights attached to the restricted securities that are the subject of the transaction or that will result from the transaction either directly or following a conversion, exchange or exercise, and the voting rights, if any, attached to the securities of any other class of securities of the company that are the same or greater on a per security basis than those attached to the restricted securities that are the subject of the transaction or that will result from the transaction either directly or following a conversion, exchange or exercise;

(b) the percentage of the aggregate voting rights attached to the company's securities that are represented by the class of restricted securities;

(c) any significant provisions under applicable corporate and securities law, in particular whether the restricted securities may or may not be tendered in any takeover bid for securities of the reporting issuer having voting rights superior to those attached to the restricted securities, that do not apply to the holders of the restricted securities that are the subject of the transaction or that will result from the transaction either directly or following a conversion, exchange or exercise, but do apply to the holders of another class of equity securities, and the extent of any rights provided in the constating documents or otherwise for the protection of holders of the restricted securities; and

(d) any rights under applicable corporate law, in the constating documents or otherwise, of holders of restricted securities that are the subject of the transaction either directly or following a conversion, exchange or exercise, to attend, in person or by proxy, meetings of holders of equity securities of the company and to speak at the meetings to the same extent that holders of equity securities are entitled.

15.2 If holders of restricted securities do not have all of the rights referred to in section 15.1, the detailed description referred to in section 15.1 must include, in bold-face type, a statement of the rights the holders do not have.

Item 16 — Additional Information

16.1 Disclose that additional information relating to the company is on SEDAR at www.sedar.com. Disclose how securityholders may contact the company to request copies of the company's financial statements and MD&A.

16.2 Include a statement that financial information is provided in the company's comparative annual financial statements and MD&A for its most recently completed financial year.

Form 51-102F6 — Statement of Executive Compensation (in respect of financial years ending on or after December 31, 2008)

Table of Contents
Item 1 General Provisions
    1.1 Objective

Item 1 — General Provisions

1.1 — Objective

All direct and indirect compensation provided to certain executive officers and directors for, or in connection with, services they have provided to the company or a subsidiary of the company must be disclosed in this form.

The objective of this disclosure is to communicate the compensation the company paid, made payable, awarded, granted, gave or otherwise provided to each NEO and director for the financial year and the decision-making process relating to compensation. This disclosure will provide insight into executive compensation as a key aspect of the overall stewardship and governance of the company and will help investors understand how decisions about executive compensation are made.

A company's executive compensation disclosure under this form must satisfy this objective and subsections 9.3.1(1) or 11.6(1) of the Instrument.

1.2 — Definitions

If a term is used in this form but is not defined in this section, refer to subsection 1.1(1) of the Instrument or to National Instrument 14-101 *Definitions.*

In this form,

  "*CEO*" means an individual who acted as chief executive officer of the company, or acted in a similar capacity, for any part of the most recently completed financial year;

  "*CFO*" means an individual who acted as chief financial officer of the company, or acted in a similar capacity, for any part of the most recently completed financial year;

"closing market price" means the price at which the company's security was last sold, on the applicable date,

(a) in the security's principal marketplace in Canada, or

(b) if the security is not listed or quoted on a marketplace in Canada, in the security's principal marketplace;

"company" includes other types of business organizations such as partnerships, trusts and other unincorporated business entities;

"equity incentive plan" means an incentive plan, or portion of an incentive plan, under which awards are granted and that falls within the scope of IFRS 2 *Share-based Payment*;

"external management company" includes a subsidiary, affiliate or associate of the external management company;

"grant date" means a date determined for financial statement reporting purposes under IFRS 2 *Share-based Payment*;

"incentive plan" means any plan providing compensation that depends on achieving certain performance goals or similar conditions within a specified period;

"incentive plan award" means compensation awarded, earned, paid, or payable under an incentive plan;

"NEO" or *"named executive officer"* means each of the following individuals:

(a) a CEO;

(b) a CFO;

(c) each of the three most highly compensated executive officers of the company, including any of its subsidiaries, or the three most highly compensated individuals acting in a similar capacity, other than the CEO and CFO, at the end of the most recently completed financial year whose total compensation was, individually, more than $150,000, as determined in accordance with subsection 1.3(6), for that financial year; and

(d) each individual who would be an NEO under paragraph (c) but for the fact that the individual was neither an executive officer of the company or its subsidiaries, nor acting in a similar capacity, at the end of that financial year;

"non-equity incentive plan" means an incentive plan or portion of an incentive plan that is not an equity incentive plan;

"option-based award" means an award under an equity incentive plan of options, including, for greater certainty, share options, share appreciation rights, and similar instruments that have option-like features;

"plan" includes any plan, contract, authorization, or arrangement, whether or not set out in any formal document, where cash, securities, similar instruments or any other property may be received, whether for one or more persons;

"replacement grant" means an option that a reasonable person would consider to be granted in relation to a prior or potential cancellation of an option;

"repricing" means, in relation to an option, adjusting or amending the exercise or base price of the option, but excludes any adjustment or amendment that equally affects all holders of the class of securities underlying the option and occurs through the operation of a formula or mechanism in, or applicable to, the option;

"share-based award" means an award under an equity incentive plan of equity-based instruments that do not have option-like features, including, for greater certainty, common shares, restricted shares, restricted share units, deferred share units, phantom shares, phantom share units, common share equivalent units, and stock.

1.3 — Preparing the form

(1) — All compensation to be included

(a) When completing this form, the company must disclose all compensation paid, payable, awarded, granted, given, or otherwise provided, directly or indirectly, by the company, or a subsidiary of the company, to each NEO and director, in any capacity, including, for greater certainty, all plan and non-plan compensation, direct and indirect pay, remuneration, economic or financial award, reward, benefit, gift or perquisite paid, payable, awarded, granted, given, or otherwise provided to the NEO or director for services provided and for services to be provided, directly or indirectly, to the company or a subsidiary of the company.

(b) Despite paragraph (a), in respect of the Canada Pension Plan, similar government plans, and group life, health, hospitalization, medical reimbursement and relocation plans that do not discriminate in scope, terms or operation and are generally available to all salaried employees, the company is not required to disclose as compensation

(i) any contributions or premiums paid or payable by the company on behalf of an NEO, or of a director, under these plans, and

(ii) any cash, securities, similar instruments or any other property received by an NEO, or by a director, under these plans.

(c) For greater certainty, the plans described in paragraph (b) include plans that provide for such benefits after retirement.

(d) If an item of compensation is not specifically mentioned or described in this form, it is to be disclosed in column (h) ("All other compensation") of the summary compensation table in section 3.1.

(2) — Departures from format

(a) Although the required disclosure must be made in accordance with this form, the disclosure may

(i) omit a table, column of a table, or other prescribed information, if it does not apply, and

(ii) add a table, column, or other information if

(A) necessary to satisfy the objective in section 1.1, and

(B) to a reasonable person, the table, column, or other information does not detract from the prescribed information in the summary compensation table in section 3.1.

(b) Despite paragraph (a), a company must not add a column in the summary compensation table in section 3.1.

(3) — Information for full financial year

If an NEO acted in that capacity for the company during part of the financial year for which disclosure is required in the summary compensation table, provide details of all of the compensation that the NEO received from the company for that financial year. This includes compensation the NEO earned in any other position with the company during the financial year.

Do not annualize compensation in a table for any part of a year when an NEO was not in the service of the company. Annualized compensation may be disclosed in a footnote.

(4) — External management companies

(a) If one or more individuals acting as an NEO of the company are not employees of the company, disclose the names of those individuals.

(b) If an external management company employs or retains one or more individuals acting as NEOs or directors of the company and the company has entered into an understanding, arrangement or agreement with the external management company to provide executive management services to the company directly or indirectly, disclose any compensation that:

(i) the company paid directly to an individual employed, or retained by the external management company, who is acting as an NEO or director of the company; and

(ii) the external management company paid to the individual that is attributable to the services they provided to the company directly or indirectly.

(c) If an external management company provides the company's executive management services and also provides executive management services to another company, disclose the entire compensation the external management company paid to the individual acting as an NEO or director, or acting in a similar capacity, in connection with services the external management company provided to the company, or the parent or a subsidiary of the company. If the management company allocates the compensation paid to an NEO or director, disclose the basis or methodology used to allocate this compensation.

Commentary

An NEO may be employed by an external management company and provide services to the company under an understanding, arrangement or agreement. In this case, references in this form to the CEO or CFO are references to the individuals who performed similar functions to that of the CEO or CFO. They are generally the same individuals who signed and filed annual and interim certificates to comply with National Instrument 52-109 Certification of Disclosure in Issuers' Annual and Interim Filings.

(5) — Director and NEO compensation

Disclose any compensation awarded to, earned by, paid to, or payable to each director and NEO, in any capacity with respect to the company. Compensation to directors and NEOs must include all compensation from the company and its subsidiaries.

Disclose any compensation awarded to, earned by, paid to, or payable to, an NEO, or director, in any capacity with respect to the company, by another person or company.

(6) — Determining if an individual is an NEO

For the purpose of calculating total compensation awarded to, earned by, paid to, or payable to an individual under paragraph (c) of the definition of NEO,

(a) use the total compensation that would be reported under column (i) of the summary compensation table required by section 3.1 for each executive officer, as if that executive officer were an NEO for the company's most recently completed financial year, and

(b) exclude from the calculation,

(i) any compensation that would be reported under column (g) of the summary compensation table required by section 3.1,

(ii) any incremental payments, payables, and benefits to an executive officer that are triggered by, or result from, a scenario listed in section 6.1 that occurred during the most recently completed financial year, and

(iii) any cash compensation that relates to foreign assignments that is specifically intended to offset the impact of a higher cost of living in the foreign location, and is not otherwise related to the duties the executive officer performs for the company.

Commentary

The $150,000 threshold in paragraph (c) of the definition of NEO only applies when determining who is an NEO in a company's most recently completed financial year. If an individual is an NEO in the most recently completed financial year, disclosure of compensation in prior years must be provided if otherwise required by this form even if total compensation in a prior year is less than $150,000 in that year.

(7) — Compensation to associates

Disclose any awards, earnings, payments, or payables to an associate of an NEO, or of a director, as a result of compensation awarded to, earned by, paid to, or payable to the NEO or the director, in any capacity with respect to the company.

(8) — New reporting issuers

(a) Subject to paragraph (b) and subsection 3.1(1), disclose information in the summary compensation table for the three most recently completed financial years since the company became a reporting issuer.

(b) Do not provide information for a completed financial year if the company was not a reporting issuer at any time during the most recently completed for any part of that financial year, unless the company became a reporting issuer as a result of a restructuring transaction.

(c) If the company was not a reporting issuer at any time during the most recently completed financial year and the company is completing the form because it is preparing a prospectus, discuss all significant elements of the compensation to be awarded to, earned by, paid to, or payable to NEOs of the company once it becomes a reporting issuer, to the extent this compensation has been determined.

Commentary

1. Unless otherwise specified, information required to be disclosed under this form may be prepared in accordance with the accounting principles the company uses to prepare its financial statements, as permitted by National Instrument 52-107 Acceptable Accounting Principles and Auditing Standards.

2. The definition of "director" under securities legislation includes an individual who acts in a capacity similar to that of a director.

(9) — Currencies

Companies must report amounts required by this form in Canadian dollars or in the same currency that the company uses for its financial statements. A company must use the same currency in the tables in sections 3.1, 4.1, 4.2, 5.1, 5.2 and 7.1 of this form.

If compensation awarded to, earned by, paid to, or payable to an NEO was in a currency other than the currency reported in the prescribed tables of this form, state the currency in which compensation was awarded, earned, paid, or payable, disclose the currency exchange rate and describe the methodology used to translate the compensation into Canadian dollars or the currency that the company uses in its financial statements.

(10) — Plain language

Information required to be disclosed under this form must be clear, concise, and presented in such a way that it provides a reasonable person an understanding of,

(a) how decisions about NEO and director compensation are made; and

(b) how specific NEO and director compensation relates to the overall stewardship and governance of the company.

Commentary

Refer to the plain language principles listed in section 1.5 of Companion Policy 51-102CP Continuous Disclosure Obligations for further guidance.

Item 2 — Compensation Discussion and Analysis

2.1 — Compensation discussion and analysis

(1) Describe and explain all significant elements of compensation awarded to, earned by, paid to, or payable to NEOs for the most recently completed financial year. Include the following:

(a) the objectives of any compensation program or strategy;

(b) what the compensation program is designed to reward;

(c) each element of compensation;

(d) why the company chooses to pay each element;

(e) how the company determines the amount (and, where applicable, the formula) for each element; and

(f) how each element of compensation and the company's decisions about that element fit into the company's overall compensation objectives and affect decisions about other elements.

(2) If applicable, describe any new actions, decisions or policies that were made after the end of the most recently completed financial year that could affect a reasonable person's understanding of an NEO's compensation for the most recently completed financial year.

(3) If applicable, clearly state the benchmark and explain its components, including the companies included in the benchmark group and the selection criteria.

(4) If applicable, disclose performance goals or similar conditions that are based on objective, identifiable measures, such as the company's share price or earnings per share. If performance goals or similar conditions are subjective, the company may describe the performance goal or similar condition without providing specific measures.

If the company discloses performance goals or similar conditions that are non-GAAP financial measures, explain how the company calculates these performance goals or similar conditions from its financial statements.

Exemption

The company is not required to disclose performance goals or similar conditions in respect of specific quantitative or qualitative performance-related factors if a reasonable person would consider that disclosing them would seriously prejudice the company's interests.

For the purposes of this exemption, a company's interest's are not considered to be seriously prejudiced solely by disclosing performance goals or similar conditions if those goals or conditions are based on broad corporate-level financial performance metrics which include earnings per share, revenue growth, and earnings before interest, taxes, depreciation and amortization.

This exemption does not apply if it has publicly disclosed the performance goals or similar conditions.

If the company is relying on this exemption, state this fact and explain why disclosing the performance goals or similar conditions would seriously prejudice the company's interests.

If the company does not disclose specific performance goals or similar conditions, state what percentage of the NEO's total compensation relates to this undisclosed information and how difficult it could be for the NEO, or how likely it will be for the company, to achieve the undisclosed performance goal or similar condition.

(5) Disclose whether or not the board of directors, or a committee of the board, considered the implications of the risks associated with the company's compensation policies and practices. If the implications were considered, disclose the following:

(a) the extent and nature of the board of directors' or committee' role in the risk oversight of the company's compensation policies and practices;

(b) any practices the company uses to identify and mitigate compensation policies and practices that could encourage an NEO or individual at a principal business unit or division to take inappropriate or excessive risks;

(c) any identified risks arising from the company's compensation policies and practices that are reasonably likely to have a material adverse effect on the company.

(6) Disclose whether or not an NEO or director is permitted to purchase financial instruments, including, for greater certainty, prepaid variable forward contracts, equity swaps, collars, or units of exchange funds, that are designed to hedge or offset a decrease in market value of equity securities granted as compensation or held, directly or indirectly, by the NEO or director.

Commentary

1. The information disclosed under section 2.1 will depend on the facts. Provide enough analysis to allow a reasonable person to understand the disclosure elsewhere in this form. Describe the significant principles underlying policies and explain the decisions relating to compensation provided to an NEO. Disclosure that merely describes the process for determining compensation or compensation already awarded, earned, paid, or payable is not adequate. The information contained in this section should give readers a sense of how compensation is tied to the NEO's performance. Avoid boilerplate language.

2. If the company's process for determining executive compensation is very simple, for example, the company relies solely on board discussion without any formal objectives, criteria and analysis, then make this clear in the discussion.

3. If the company used any benchmarking in determining compensation or any element of compensation, include the benchmark group and describe why the benchmark group and selection criteria are considered by the company to be relevant.

4. The following are examples of items that will usually be significant elements of disclosure concerning compensation:

- *contractual or non-contractual arrangements, plans, process changes or any other matters that might cause the amounts disclosed for the most recently completed financial year to be misleading if used as an indicator of expected compensation levels in future periods;*

- *the process for determining perquisites and personal benefits;*

- *policies and decisions about the adjustment or recovery of awards, earnings, payments, or payables if the performance goal or similar condition on which they are based are restated or adjusted to reduce the award, earning, payment, or payable;*

- *the basis for selecting events that trigger payment for any arrangement that provides for payment at, following or in connection with any termination or change of control;*

- *any waiver or change to any specified performance goal or similar condition to payout for any amount, including whether the waiver or change applied to one or more specified NEOs or to all compensation subject to the performance goal or similar condition;*

- *whether the board of directors can exercise a discretion, either to award compensation absent attainment of the relevant performance goal or similar condition or to reduce or increase the size of any award or payout, including if they exercised discretion and whether it applied to one or more named executive officers;*

- *whether the company will be making any significant changes to its compensation policies and practices in the next financial year;*

- *the role of executive officers in determining executive compensation; and*

- *performance goals or similar conditions in respect of specific quantitative or qualitative performance-related factors for NEOs.*

5. The following are examples of situations that could potentially encourage an executive officer to expose the company to inappropriate or excessive risks:

- *compensation policies and practices at a principal business unit of the company or a subsidiary of the company that are structured significantly differently than others within the company;*

- *compensation policies and practices for certain executive officers that are structured significantly differently than other executive officers within the company;*

- *compensation policies and practices that do not include effective risk management and regulatory compliance as part of the performance metrics used in determining compensation;*

- *compensation policies and practices where the compensation expense to executive officers is a significant percentage of the company's revenue;*

- *compensation policies and practices that vary significantly from the overall compensation structure of the company;*

- *compensation policies and practices where incentive plan awards are awarded upon accomplishment of a task while the risk to the company from that task extends over a significantly longer period of time;*

- *compensation policies and practices that contain performance goals or similar conditions that are heavily weighed to short-term rather than long-term objectives;*

- *incentive plan awards that do not provide a maximum benefit or payout limit to executive officers.*

The examples above are not exhaustive and the situations to consider will vary depending upon the nature of the company's business and the company's compensation policies and practices.

2.2 — Performance graph

(a) This section does not apply to

(i) venture issuers,

(ii) companies that have distributed only debt securities or non-convertible, non-participating preferred securities to the public, and

(iii) companies that were not reporting issuers in any jurisdiction in Canada for at least 12 calendar months before the end of their most recently completed financial year, other than companies that became new reporting issuers as a result of a restructuring transaction.

(b) Provide a line graph showing the company's cumulative total shareholder return over the five most recently completed financial years. Assume that $100 was invested on the first day of the five-year period. If the company has been a reporting issuer for less than five years, use the period that the company has been a reporting issuer.

Compare this to the cumulative total return of at least one broad equity market index that, to a reasonable person, would be an appropriate reference point for the company's return. If the company is included in the S&P/TSX Composite Total Return Index, use that index. In all cases, assume that dividends are reinvested.

Discuss how the trend shown by this graph compares to the trend in the company's compensation to executive officers reported under this form over the same period.

Commentary

For section 2.2, companies may also include other relevant performance goals or similar conditions.

2.3 — Share-based and option-based awards

Describe the process the company uses to grant share-based or option-based awards to executive officers. Include the role of the compensation committee and executive officers in setting or amending any equity incentive plan under which a share-based or option-based award is granted. State whether previous grants of are taken into account when considering new grants.

2.4 — Compensation governance

(1) Describe any policies and practices adopted by the board of directors to determine the compensation for the company's directors and executive officers.

(2) If the company has established a compensation committee

(a) disclose the name of each committee member and, in respect of each member, state whether or not the member is independent or not independent;

(b) disclose whether or not one or more of the committee members has any direct experience that is relevant to his or her responsibilities in executive compensation;

(c) describe the skills and experience that enable the committee to make decisions on the suitability of the company's compensation policies and practices; and

(d) describe the responsibilities, powers and operation of the committee.

(3) If a compensation consultant or advisor has, at any time since the company's most recently completed financial year, been retained to assist the board of directors or the compensation committee in determining compensation for any of the company's directors or executive officers

(a) state the name of the consultant or advisor and a summary of the mandate the consultant or advisor has been given;

(b) disclose when the consultant or advisor was originally retained; and

(c) if the consultant or advisor has provided any services to the company, or to its affiliated or subsidiary entities, or to any of its directors or members of management, other than or in addition to compensation services provided for any of the company's directors or executive officers,

(i) state this fact and briefly describe the nature of the work,

(ii) disclose whether the board of directors or compensation committee must pre-approve other services the consultant or advisor, or any of its affiliates, provides to the company at the request of management, and

(d) For each of the two most recently completed financial year, disclose,

(i) under the caption "Executive Compensation-Related Fees", the aggregate fees billed by each consultant or advisor, or any of its affiliates, for services related to determining compensation for any of the company's directors and executive officers, and

(ii) under the caption "All Other Fees", the aggregate fees billed for all other services provided by each consultant or advisor, or any of its affiliates, that are not reported under subparagraph (i) and include a description of the nature of the services comprising the fees disclosed under this category.

Commentary

For section 2.4, a director is independent if he or she would be independent within the meaning of section 1.4 of NI 52-110 Audit Committees.

Item 3 — Summary Compensation Table

3.1 — Summary compensation table

(1) For each NEO in the most recently completed financial year, complete this table for each of the company's three most recently completed financial years that end on or after December 31, 2008.

Name and principal position (a)	Year (b)	Salary ($) (c)	Share-based awards ($) (d)	Option-based awards ($) (e)	Non-equity incentive plan compensation ($) (f)		Pension value ($) (g)	All other compensation ($) (h)	Total compensation ($) (i)
					Annual incentive plans (f1)	Long-term incentive plans (f2)			
CEO									
CFO									
A									
B									
C									

Commentary

Under subsection (1), a company is not required to disclose comparative period disclosure in accordance with the requirements of either Form 51-102F6 Statement of Executive Compensation, which came into force on March 30, 2004, as amended, or this form, in respect of a financial year ending before December 31, 2008.

(2) In column (c), include the dollar value of cash and non-cash base salary an NEO earned during a financial year covered in the table (a covered financial year). If the company cannot calculate the amount of salary earned in a financial year, disclose this in a footnote, along with the reason why it cannot be determined. Restate the salary figure the next time the company prepares this form, and explain what portion of the restated figure represents an amount that the company could not previously calculate.

(3) In column (d), disclose the dollar amount based on the fair value of the award on the grant date for a covered financial year.

(4) In column (e), disclose the dollar amount based on the fair value of the award on the grant date for a covered financial year. Include option-based awards both with or without tandem share appreciation rights.

(5) For an award disclosed in column (d) or (e), in a narrative after the table,

(a) describe the methodology used to calculate the fair value of the award on the grant date, disclose the key assumptions and estimates used for each calculation, and explain why the company chose that methodology, and

(b) if the fair value of the award on the grant date is different from the fair value determined in accordance with IFRS 2 *Share-based Payment* (accounting fair value), state the amount of the difference and explain the reasons for the difference.

Commentary

1. This commentary applies to subsections (3), (4) and (5).

2. The value disclosed in columns (d) and (e) of the summary compensation table should reflect what the company paid, made payable, awarded, granted, gave or otherwise provided as compensation on the grant date (fair value of the award) as set out in comment 3, below. This value might differ from the value reported in the issuer's financial statements.

3. While compensation practices vary, there are generally two approaches that boards of directors use when setting compensation. A board of directors may decide the value in securities of the company to be awarded or paid as compensation. Alternatively, a board of directors may decide the portion of the potential ownership of the company to be transferred as compensation. A fair value ascribed to the award will normally result from these approaches.

A company may calculate this value either in accordance with a valuation methodology identified in IFRS 2 Share-based Payment or in accordance with another methodology set out in comment 5 below.

4. In some cases, the fair value of the award disclosed in columns (d) and (e) might differ from the accounting fair value. For financial statement purposes, the accounting fair value amount is amortized over the service period to obtain an accounting cost (accounting compensation expense), adjusted at year end as required.

5. While the most commonly used methodologies for calculating the value of most types of awards are the Black-Scholes-Merton model and the binomial lattice model, companies may choose to use another valuation methodology if it produces a more meaningful and reasonable estimate of fair value.

6. The summary compensation table requires disclosure of an amount even if the accounting compensation expense is zero. The amount disclosed in the table should reflect the fair value of the award following the principles described under comments 2 and 3, above.

7. Column (d) includes common shares, restricted shares, restricted share units, deferred share units, phantom shares, phantom share units, common share equivalent units, stock, and similar instruments that do not have option-like features.

(6) In column (e), include the incremental fair value if, at any time during the covered financial year, the company has adjusted, amended, cancelled, replaced or significantly modified the exercise price of options previously awarded to, earned by, paid to, or payable to, an NEO. The repricing or modification date must be determined in accordance with IFRS 2 *Share-based Payment*. The methodology used to calculate the incremental fair value must be the same methodology used to calculate the initial grant.

This requirement does not apply to any repricing that equally affects all holders of the class of securities underlying the options and that occurs through a pre-existing formula or mechanism in the plan or award that results in the periodic adjustment of the option exercise or base price, an antidilution provision in a plan or award, or a recapitalization or similar transaction.

(7) Include a footnote to the table quantifying the incremental fair value of any adjusted, amended, cancelled, replaced or significantly modified options that are included in the table.

(8) In column (f), include the dollar value of all amounts earned for services performed during the covered financial year that are related to awards under non-equity incentive plans and all earnings on any such outstanding awards.

(a) If the relevant performance goal or similar condition was satisfied during a covered financial year (including for a single year in a plan with a multi-year performance goal or similar condition), report the amounts earned for that financial year, even if they are payable at a later date. The company is not required to report these amounts again in the summary compensation table when they are actually paid to an NEO.

(b) Include a footnote describing and quantifying all amounts earned on non-equity incentive plan compensation, whether they were paid during the financial year, were payable but deferred at the election of an NEO, or are payable by their terms at a later date.

(c) Include any discretionary cash awards, earnings, payments, or payables that were not based on pre-determined performance goals or similar conditions that were communicated to an NEO. Report any performance-based plan awards that include pre-determined performance goals or similar conditions in column (f).

(d) In column (f1), include annual non-equity incentive plan compensation, such as bonuses and discretionary amounts. For column (f1), annual non-equity incentive plan compensation relates only to a single financial year. In column (f2), include all non-equity incentive plan compensation related to a period longer than one year.

(9) In column (g), include all compensation relating to defined benefit or defined contribution plans. These include service costs and other compensatory items such as plan changes and earnings that are different from the estimated earnings for defined benefit plans and above-market earnings for defined contribution plans.

This disclosure relates to all plans that provide for the payment of pension plan benefits. Use the same amounts included in column (e) of the defined benefit plan table required by Item 5 for the covered financial year and the amounts included in column (c) of the defined contribution plan table as required by Item 5 for the covered financial year.

(10) In column (h), include all other compensation not reported in any other column of this table. Column (h) must include, but is not limited to:

(a) perquisites, including property or other personal benefits provided to an NEO that are not generally available to all employees, and that in aggregate are worth $50,000 or more, or are worth 10% or more of an NEO's total salary for the financial year. Value these items on the basis of the aggregate incremental cost to the company and its subsidiaries. Describe in a footnote the methodology used for computing the aggregate incremental cost to the company.

State the type and amount of each perquisite the value of which exceeds 25% of the total value of perquisites reported for an NEO in a footnote to the table. Provide the footnote information for the most recently completed financial year only;

(b) other post-retirement benefits such as health insurance or life insurance after retirement;

(c) all "gross-ups" or other amounts reimbursed during the covered financial year for the payment of taxes;

(d) the incremental payments, payables, and benefits to an NEO that are triggered by, or result from, a scenario listed in section 6.1 that occurred before the end of the covered financial year;

(e) the dollar value of any insurance premiums paid or payable by, or on behalf of, the company during the covered financial year for personal insurance for an NEO if the estate of the NEO is the beneficiary;

(f) the dollar value of any dividends or other earnings paid or payable on share-based or option-based awards that were not factored into the fair value of the award on the grant date required to be reported in columns (d) and (e);

(g) any compensation cost for any security that the NEO bought from the company or its subsidiaries at a discount from the market price of the security (through deferral of salary, bonus or otherwise). Calculate this cost at the date of purchase and in accordance with IFRS 2 *Share-based Payment*; and

(h) above-market or preferential earnings on compensation that is deferred on a basis that is not tax exempt other than for defined contribution plans covered in the defined contribution plan table in Item 5. Above-market or preferential applies to non-registered plans and means a rate greater than the rate ordinarily paid by the company or its subsidiary on securities or other obligations having the same or similar features issued to third parties;

(i) any company contribution to a personal savings plan like a registered retirement savings plan made on behalf of the NEO.

Commentary

1. Generally, there will be no incremental payments, payables, and benefits that are triggered by, or result from, a scenario described in section 6.1 that occurred before the end of a covered financial year for compensation that has been reported in the summary compensation table for the most recently completed financial year or for a financial year before the most recently completed financial year.

If the vesting or payout of the previously reported compensation is accelerated, or a performance goal or similar condition in respect of the previously reported compensation is waived, as a result of a scenario described in section 6.1, the incremental payments, payables, and benefits should include the value of the accelerated benefit or of the waiver of the performance goal or similar condition.

2. Generally, an item is not a perquisite if it is integrally and directly related to the performance of an executive officer's duties. If something is necessary for a person to do his or her job, it is integrally and directly related to the job and is not a perquisite, even if it also provides some amount of personal benefit.

If the company concludes that an item is not integrally and directly related to performing the job, it may be a perquisite if the item provides an NEO with any direct or indirect personal benefit. If it does provide a personal benefit, the item is a perquisite, whether or not it is provided for a business reason or for the company's convenience, unless it is generally available on a non-discriminatory basis to all employees.

Companies must conduct their own analysis of whether a particular item is a perquisite. The following are examples of things that are often considered perquisites or personal benefits. This list is not exhaustive:

- *Cars, car lease and car allowance;*
- *Corporate aircraft or personal travel financed by the company;*
- *Jewellery;*
- *Clothing;*
- *Artwork;*
- *Housekeeping services;*
- *Club membership;*
- *Theatre tickets;*
- *Financial assistance to provide education to children of executive officers;*
- *Parking;*
- *Personal financial or tax advice;*
- *Security at personal residence or during personal travel; and*
- *Reimbursements of taxes owed with respect to perquisites or other personal benefit.*

(11) In column (i), include the dollar value of total compensation for the covered financial year. For each NEO, this is the sum of the amounts reported in columns (c) through (h).

(12) Any deferred amounts must be included in the appropriate column for the covered financial year in which they are earned.

(13) If an NEO elected to exchange any compensation awarded to, earned by, paid to, or payable to the NEO in a covered financial year under a program that allows the NEO to receive awards, earnings, payments, or payables in another form, the compensation the NEO elected to exchange must be reported as compensation in the column appropriate for the form of compensation exchanged: Do not report it in the form in which it was or will be received by the NEO. State in a footnote the form of awards, earnings, payments, or payables substituted for the compensation the NEO elected to exchange.

3.2 — Narrative discussion

Describe and explain any significant factors necessary to understand the information disclosed in the summary compensation table required by section 3.1.

Commentary

The significant factors described in section 3.2 will vary depending on the circumstances of each award but may include:

- *the significant terms of each NEO's employment agreement or arrangement;*
- *any repricing or other significant changes to the terms of any share-based or option-based award program during the most recently completed financial year; and*
- *the significant terms of any award reported in the summary compensation table, including a general description of the formula or criterion to be applied in determining the amounts payable and the vesting schedule. For example, if dividends will be paid on shares, state this, the applicable dividend rate and whether that rate is preferential.*

3.3 — [deleted]

3.4 — Officers who also act as directors

If an NEO is also a director who receives compensation for services as a director, include that compensation in the summary compensation table and include a footnote explaining which amounts relate to the director role. Do not provide disclosure for that NEO under Item 7.

Item 4 — Incentive Plan Awards

4.1 — Outstanding share-based awards and option-based awards

(1) Complete this table for each NEO for all awards outstanding at the end of the most recently completed financial year. This includes awards granted before the most recently completed financial year. For all awards in this table, disclose the awards that have been transferred at other than fair market value.

Name	Option-based Awards				Share-based Awards		
	Number of securities underlying unexercised options (#)	Option exercise price ($)	Option expiration date	Value of unexercised in-the-money options ($)	Number of shares or units of shares that have not vested (#)	Market or payout value of share-based awards that have not vested ($)	Market or payout value of vested share-based awards not paid out or distributed ($)
(a)	(b)	(c)	(d)	(e)	(f)	(g)	(h)
CEO	………	………	………	………	………	………	………
CFO	………	………	………	………	………	………	………
A	………	………	………				
B	………	………	………				
C	………	………	………		………	………	………

(2) In column (b), for each award, disclose the number of securities underlying unexercised options.

(3) In column (c), disclose the exercise or base price for each option under each award reported in column (b). If the option was granted in a different currency than that reported in the table, include a footnote describing the currency and the exercise or base price.

(4) In column (d), disclose the expiration date for each option under each award reported in column (b).

(5) In column (e), disclose the aggregate dollar amount of in-the-money unexercised options held at the end of the year. Calculate this amount based on the difference between the market value of the securities underlying the instruments at the end of the year, and the exercise or base price of the option.

(6) In column (f), disclose the total number of shares or units that have not vested.

(7) In column (g), disclose the aggregate market value or payout value of share-based awards that have not vested.

If the share-based award provides only for a single payout on vesting, calculate this value based on that payout.

If the share-based award provides for different payouts depending on the achievement of different performance goals or similar conditions, calculate this value based on the minimum payout. However, if the NEO achieved a performance goal or similar condition in a financial year covered by the share-based award that on vesting could provide for a payout greater than the minimum payout, calculate this value based on the payout expected as a result of the NEO achieving this performance goal or similar condition.

(8) In column (h), disclose the aggregate market value or payout value of vested share-based awards that have not yet been paid out or distributed.

4.2 — Incentive plan awards — value vested or earned during the year

(1) Complete this table for each NEO for the most recently completed financial year.

Name	Option-based awards — Value vested during the year ($)	Share-based awards — Value vested during the year ($)	Non-equity incentive plan compensation — Value earned during the year ($)
(a)	(b)	(c)	(d)
CEO	………	………	………
CFO	………		………	………
A	………	………	………
B	………	………	………
C	………	………	………

(2) In column (b), disclose the aggregate dollar value that would have been realized if the options under the option-based award had been exercised on the vesting date. Compute the dollar value that would have been realized by determining the difference between the market price of the underlying securities at exercise and the exercise or base price of the options under the option-based award on the vesting date. Do not include the value of any related payment or other consideration provided (or to be provided) by the company to or on behalf of an NEO.

(3) In column (c), disclose the aggregate dollar value realized upon vesting of share-based awards. Compute the dollar value realized by multiplying the number of shares or units by the market value of the underlying shares on the vesting date. For any amount realized upon vesting for which receipt has been deferred, include a footnote that states the amount and the terms of the deferral.

4.3 — Narrative discussion

Describe and explain the significant terms of all plan-based awards, including non-equity incentive plan awards, issued or vested, or under which options have been exercised, during the year, or outstanding at the year end, to the extent not already discussed under sections 2.1, 2.3 and 3.2. The company may aggregate information for different awards, if separate disclosure of each award is not necessary to communicate their significant terms.

Commentary

The items included in the narrative required by section 4.3 will vary depending on the terms of each plan, but may include:

- *the number of securities underlying each award or received on vesting or exercise;*
- *general descriptions of formulae or criteria that are used to determine amounts payable;*
- *exercise prices and expiry dates;*
- *dividend rates on share-based awards;*
- *whether awards are vested or unvested;*
- *performance goals or similar conditions, or other significant conditions;*
- *information on estimated future payouts for non-equity incentive plan awards (performance goals or similar conditions and maximum amounts); and*
- *the closing market price on the grant date, if the exercise or base price is less than the closing market price of the underlying security on the grant date.*

Item 5 — Pension Plan Benefits

5.1 — Defined benefit plans table

(1) Complete this table for all pension plans that provide for payments or benefits at, following, or in connection with retirement, excluding defined contribution plans. For all disclosure in this table, use the same assumptions and methods used for financial statement reporting purposes under the accounting principles used to prepare the company's financial statements, as permitted by National Instrument 52-107 *Acceptable Accounting Principles and Auditing Standards.*

Name	Number of years credited service (#)	Annual benefits payable ($)		Opening present value of defined benefit obligation ($)	Compensatory change ($)	Non-compensatory change ($)	Closing present value of defined benefit obligation ($)
(a)	(b)	(c)		(d)	(g)	(e)	(f)
		At year end (c1)	At age 65 (c2)				
CEO	....	....	....	....	....	....	....
CFO	....	....	....	....	....	....	....
A	....	....	....	....	....	....	....
B	....	....	....	....	....	....	....
C	....	....	....	....	....	....	....

(2) In columns (b) and (c), the disclosure must be as of the end of the company's most recently completed financial year. In columns (d) through (g), the disclosure must be as of the reporting date used in the company's audited annual financial statements for the most recently completed financial year.

(3) In column (b), disclose the number of years of service credited to an NEO under the plan. If the number of years of credited service in any plan is different from the NEO's number of actual years of service with the company, include a footnote that states the amount of the difference and any resulting benefit augmentation, such as the number of additional years the NEO received.

(4) In column (c), disclose

(a) the annual lifetime benefit payable at the end of the most recently completed financial year in column (c1) based on years of credited service reported in column (b) and actual pensionable earnings as at the end of the most recently completed financial year. For purposes of this calculation, the company must assume that the NEO is eligible to receive payments or benefits at year end, and

(b) the annual lifetime benefit payable at age 65 in column (c2) based on years of credited service as of age 65 and actual pensionable earnings through the end of the most recently completed financial year, as per column (c1).

Commentary

For purposes of quantifying the annual lifetime benefit payable at the end of the most recently completed financial year in column (c1), the company may calculate the annual lifetime benefit payable as follows:

$$\text{annual benefits payable at the presumed} \quad \times \quad \frac{\text{years of credited service}}{\text{at year end}}$$

retirement age used to calculate the closing present value of the defined benefit obligation	years of credited service at the presumed retirement age

The company may calculate the annual lifetime benefit payable in accordance with another formula if the company reasonably believes that it produces a more meaningful calculation of the annual lifetime benefit payable at year end.

(5) In column (d), disclose the present value of the defined benefit obligation at the start of the most recently completed financial year.

(6) In column (e), disclose the compensatory change in the present value of the defined benefit obligation for the most recently completed financial year. This includes service cost net of employee contributions plus plan changes and differences between actual and estimated earnings, and any additional changes that have retroactive impact, including, for greater certainty, a change in valuation assumptions as a consequence of an amendment to benefit terms.

Disclose the valuation method and all significant assumptions the company applied in quantifying the closing present value of the defined benefit obligation. The company may satisfy all or part of this disclosure by referring to the disclosure of assumptions in its financial statements, footnotes to the financial statements or discussion in its management's discussion and analysis.

(7) In column (f), disclose the non-compensatory changes in the present value of the defined benefit obligation for the company's most recently completed financial year. Include all items that are not compensatory, such as changes in assumptions other than those already included in column (e) because they were made as a consequence of an amendment to benefit terms, employee contributions and interest on the present value of the defined benefit obligation at the start of the most recently completed financial year.

(8) In column (g), disclose the present value of the defined benefit obligation at the end of the most recently completed financial year.

5.2 — Defined contribution plans table

(1) Complete this table for all pension plans that provide for payments or benefits at, following or in connection with retirement, excluding defined benefit plans. For all disclosure in this table, use the same assumptions and methods used for financial statement reporting purposes under the accounting principles used to prepare the company's financial statements, as permitted by National Instrument 52-107 *Acceptable Accounting Principles and Auditing Standards.*

Name (a)	Accumulated value at start of year ($) (b)	Compensatory ($) (c)	Accumulated value at year end ($) (d)
CEO	....	....	....
CFO	....	....	....
A	....	....	....
B	....	....	....
C	....	....	....

(2) In column (c), disclose the employer contribution and above-market or preferential earnings credited on employer and employee contributions. Above-market or preferential earnings applies to non-registered plans and means a rate greater than the rate ordinarily paid by the company or its subsidiary on securities or other obligations having the same or similar features issued to third parties.

(3) [deleted]

(4) In column (d), disclose the accumulated value at the end of the most recently completed financial year.

Commentary

1. For pension plans that provide the maximum of: (i) the value of a defined benefit pension; and (ii) the accumulated value of a defined contribution pension, companies should disclose the global value of the pension plan in the defined benefit plans table under section 5.1.

For pension plans that provide the sum of a defined benefit component and a defined contribution component, companies should disclose the respective components of the pension plan. The defined benefit component should be disclosed in the defined benefit plans table under section 5.1 and the defined contribution component should be disclosed in the defined contribution plans table under section 5.2.

2. Any contributions by the company or a subsidiary of the company to a personal savings plan like a registered retirement savings plan made on behalf of the NEO must still be disclosed in column (h) of the summary compensation table, as required by paragraph 3.1(10)(i).

5.3 — Narrative discussion

Describe and explain for each retirement plan in which an NEO participates, any significant factors necessary to understand the information disclosed in the defined benefit plan table in section 5.1 and the defined contribution plan table in section 5.2.

Commentary

Significant factors described in the narrative required by section 5.3 will vary, but may include:

- *the significant terms and conditions of payments and benefits available under the plan, including the plan's normal and early retirement payment, benefit formula, contribution formula, calculation of interest credited under the defined contribution plan and eligibility standards;*

- *provisions for early retirement, if applicable, including the name of the NEO and the plan, the early retirement payment and benefit formula and eligibility standards. Early retirement means retirement before the normal retirement age as defined in the plan or otherwise available under the plan;*

- *the specific elements of compensation (e.g., salary, bonus) included in applying the payment and benefit formula. If a company provides this information, identify each element separately; and*

- *company policies on topics such as granting extra years of credited service, including an explanation of who these arrangements relate to and why they are considered appropriate.*

5.4 — Deferred compensation plans

Describe the significant terms of any deferred compensation plan relating to each NEO, including:

(a) the types of compensation that can be deferred and any limitations on the extent to which deferral is permitted (by percentage of compensation or otherwise);

(b) significant terms of payouts, withdrawals and other distributions; and

(c) measures for calculating interest or other earnings, how and when these measures may be changed, and whether an NEO or the company chose these measures. Quantify these measures wherever possible.

Item 6 — Termination and Change of Control Benefits

6.1 — Termination and change of control benefits

(1) For each contract, agreement, plan or arrangement that provides for payments to an NEO at, following or in connection with any termination (whether voluntary, involuntary or constructive), resignation, retirement, a change in control of the company or a change in an NEO's responsibilities, describe, explain, and where appropriate, quantify the following items:

(a) the circumstances that trigger payments or the provision of other benefits, including perquisites and pension plan benefits;

(b) the estimated incremental payments, payables, and benefits that are triggered by, or result from, each circumstance, including timing, duration and who provides the payments and benefits;

(c) how the payment and benefit levels are determined under the various circumstances that trigger payments or provision of benefits;

(d) any significant conditions or obligations that apply to receiving payments or benefits. This includes but is not limited to, non-compete, non-solicitation, non-disparagement or confidentiality agreements. Include the term of these agreements and provisions for waiver or breach; and

(e) any other significant factors for each written contract, agreement, plan or arrangement.

(2) Disclose the estimated incremental payments, payables, and benefits even if it is uncertain what amounts might be paid in given circumstances under the various plans and arrangements, assuming that the triggering event took place on the last business day of the company's most recently completed financial year. For valuing share-based awards or option-based awards, use the closing market price of the company's securities on that date.

If the company is unsure about the provision or amount of payments or benefits, make a reasonable estimate (or a reasonable estimate of the range of amounts) and disclose the significant assumptions underlying these estimates.

(3) Despite subsection (1), the company is not required to disclose the following:

(a) Perquisites and other personal benefits if the aggregate of this compensation is less than $50,000. State the individual perquisites and personal benefits as required by paragraph 3.1(10)(a).

(b) Information about possible termination scenarios for an NEO whose employment terminated in the past year. The company must only disclose the consequences of the actual termination.

(c) Information in respect of a scenario described in subsection (1) if there will be no incremental payments, payables, and benefits that are triggered by, or result from, that scenario.

Commentary

1. Subsection (1) does not require the company to disclose notice of termination without cause, or compensation in lieu thereof, which are implied as a term of an employment contract under common law or civil law.

2. Item 6 applies to changes of control regardless of whether the change of control results in termination of employment.

3. Generally, there will be no incremental payments, payables, and benefits that are triggered by, or result from, a scenario described in subsection (1) for compensation that has been reported in the summary compensation table for the most recently completed financial year or for a financial year before the most recently completed financial year.

If the vesting or payout of the previously reported compensation is accelerated, or a performance goal or similar condition in respect of the previously reported compensation is waived, as a result of a scenario described in subsection (1), the incremental payments, payables, and benefits should include the value of the accelerated benefit or of the waiver of the performance goal or similar condition.

4. A company may disclose estimated incremental payments, payables and benefits that are triggered by, or result from, a scenario described in subsection (1), in a tabular format.

Item 7 — Director Compensation

7.1 — Director compensation table

(1) Complete this table for all amounts of compensation provided to the directors for the company's most recently completed financial year.

Name	Fees earned ($)	Share-based awards ($)	Option-based awards ($)	Non-equity incentive plan compensation ($)	Pension value ($)	All other compensation ($)	Total ($)
(a)	(b)	(c)	(d)	(e)	(f)	(g)	(h)
A	....	....	....	....	....	....	....
B	....	....	....	....	....	....	....
C	....	....	....	....	....	....	....
D	....	....	....	....	....	....	....
E	....	....	....	....	....	....	....

(2) All forms of compensation must be included in this table.

(3) Complete each column in the manner required for the corresponding column in the summary compensation table in section 3.1, in accordance with the requirements of Item 3, as supplemented by the commentary to Item 3, except as follows:

(a) In column (a), do not include a director who is also an NEO if his or her compensation for service as a director is fully reflected in the summary compensation table and elsewhere in this form. If an NEO is also a director who receives compensation for his or her services as a director, reflect the director compensation in the summary compensation table required by section 3.1 and provide a footnote to this table indicating that the relevant disclosure has been provided under section 3.4.

(b) In column (b), include all fees awarded, earned, paid, or payable in cash for services as a director, including annual retainer fees, committee, chair, and meeting fees.

(c) In column (g), include all compensation paid, payable, awarded, granted, given, or otherwise provided, directly or indirectly, by the company, or a subsidiary of the company, to a director in any capacity, under any other arrangement. This includes, for greater certainty, all plan and non-plan compensation, direct and indirect pay, remuneration, economic or financial award, reward, benefit, gift or perquisite paid, payable, awarded, granted, given, or otherwise provided to the director for services provided, directly or indirectly, to the company or a subsidiary of the company. In a footnote to the table, disclose these amounts and describe the nature of the services provided by the director that are associated with these amounts.

(d) In column (g), include programs where the company agrees to make donations to one or more charitable institutions in a director's name, payable currently or upon a designated event such as the retirement or death of the director. Include a footnote to the table disclosing the total dollar amount payable under the program.

7.2 — Narrative discussion

Describe and explain any factors necessary to understand the director compensation disclosed in section 7.1.

Commentary

Significant factors described in the narrative required by section 7.2 will vary, but may include:

- *disclosure for each director who served in that capacity for any part of the most recently completed financial year;*

- *standard compensation arrangements, such as fees for retainer, committee service, service as chair of the board or a committee, and meeting attendance;*

- *any compensation arrangements for a director that are different from the standard arrangements, including the name of the director and a description of the terms of the arrangement; and*

- *any matters discussed in the compensation discussion and analysis that do not apply to directors in the same way that they apply to NEOs such as practices for granting option-based awards.*

7.3 — Share-based awards, option-based awards and non-equity incentive plan compensation

Provide the same disclosure for directors that is required under Item 4 for NEOs.

Item 8 — Companies Reporting in the United States

8.1 — Companies reporting in the United States

(1) Except as provided in subsection (2), SEC issuers may satisfy the requirements of this form by providing the information they are required to disclose in the United States under Item 402 "Executive compensation" of Regulation S-K under the 1934 Act.

(2) Subsection (1) does not apply to a company that, as a foreign private issuer, satisfies Item 402 of Regulation S-K by providing the information required by Items 6.B "Compensation" and 6.E.2 "Share Ownership" of Form 20-F under the 1934 Act.

Item 9 — Effective Date and Transition

9.1 — Effective date

(1) This form comes into force on December 31, 2008.

(2) This form applies to a company in respect of a financial year ending on or after December 31, 2008.

9.2 — Transition

(1) The form entitled Form 51-102F6 *Statement of Executive Compensation*, which came into force on March 30, 2004, as amended,

    (a) does not apply to a company in respect of a financial year ending on or after December 31, 2008, and

    (b) for greater certainty, applies to a company that is required to prepare and file executive compensation disclosure because

        (i) the company is sending an information circular to a securityholder under paragraph 9.1(2)(a) of National Instrument 51-102 *Continuous Disclosure Obligations*, the information circular includes the disclosure required by Item 8 of Form 51-102F5, and the information circular is in respect of a financial year ending before December 31, 2008, or

        (ii) the company is filing an AIF that includes the disclosure required by Item 8 of Form 51-102F5, in accordance with Item 18 of Form 51-102F2, and the AIF is in respect of a financial year ending before December 31, 2008.

(2) A company that is required to prepare and file executive compensation disclosure for a reason set out in paragraph (1)(b) may satisfy that requirement by preparing and filing the disclosure required by this form.

Form 51-102F6V — Statement of Executive Compensation — Venture Issuers

Table of Contents

Item 1 — General Provisions

1.1 — Objective

All direct and indirect compensation provided to certain executive officers and directors for, or in connection with, services they have provided to the company or a subsidiary of the company must be disclosed in this form.

The objective of this disclosure is to communicate the compensation the company paid, made payable, awarded, granted, gave or otherwise provided to each named executive officer and director for the financial year, and the decision-making process relating to compensation. This disclosure will provide insight into executive compensation as a key aspect of the overall stewardship and governance of the company and will help investors understand how decisions about executive compensation are made.

A company's executive compensation disclosure under this form must satisfy this objective and subsections 9.3.1(1) or 11.6(1) of the Instrument.

While the objective of this disclosure is the same as the objective in section 1.1 of Form 51-102F6, this form is to be used by venture issuers only. Reporting issuers that are not venture issuers must complete Form 51-102F6.

1.2 — Definitions

If a term is used in this form but is not defined in this section, refer to subsection 1.1(1) of the Instrument or to National Instrument 14-101 *Definitions*.

In this form,

    *"company"*includes other types of business organizations such as partnerships, trusts and other unincorporated business entities;

    *"compensation securities"*includes stock options, convertible securities, exchangeable securities and similar instruments including stock appreciation rights, deferred share units and restricted stock units granted or issued by the company or one of its subsidiaries for services provided or to be provided, directly or indirectly, to the company or any of its subsidiaries;

    *"external management company"*includes a subsidiary, affiliate or associate of the external management company;

    "named executive officer" or *"NEO"*means each of the following individuals:

        (a) each individual who, in respect of the company, during any part of the most recently completed financial year, served as chief executive officer, including an individual performing functions similar to a chief executive officer;

        (b) each individual who, in respect of the company, during any part of the most recently completed financial year, served as chief financial officer, including an individual performing functions similar to a chief financial officer;

(c) in respect of the company and its subsidiaries, the most highly compensated executive officer other than the individuals identified in paragraphs (a) and (b) at the end of the most recently completed financial year whose total compensation was more than $150,000, as determined in accordance with subsection 1.3(5), for that financial year;

(d) each individual who would be a named executive officer under paragraph (c) but for the fact that the individual was not an executive officer of the company, and was not acting in a similar capacity, at the end of that financial year;

"plan" includes any plan, contract, authorization, or arrangement, whether or not set out in any formal document, where cash, compensation securities or any other property may be received, whether for one or more persons;

"underlying securities" means any securities issuable on conversion, exchange or exercise of compensation securities.

1.3 — Preparing the form

(1) — All compensation to be included

(a) When completing this form, the company must disclose all compensation paid, payable, awarded, granted, given, or otherwise provided, directly or indirectly, by the company, or a subsidiary of the company, to each named executive officer and director, in any capacity, including, for greater certainty, all plan and non-plan compensation, direct and indirect pay, remuneration, economic or financial award, reward, benefit, gift or perquisite paid, payable, awarded, granted, given, or otherwise provided to the named executive officer or director for services provided and for services to be provided, directly or indirectly, to the company or a subsidiary of the company.

(b) If an item of compensation is not specifically mentioned or described in this form, disclose it in the column "Value of all other compensation" of the table in section 2.1.

Commentary

1. Unless otherwise specified, information required to be disclosed under this form may be prepared in accordance with the accounting principles the company uses to prepare its financial statements, as permitted by National Instrument 52-107 Acceptable Accounting Principles and Auditing Standards.

2. The definition of "director" under securities legislation includes an individual who acts in a capacity similar to that of a director.

(2) — Departures from format

(a) Although the required disclosure must be made in accordance with this form, the disclosure may

    (i) omit a table, column of a table, or other prescribed information, if it does not apply, and

    (ii) add a table, column, or other information if

        (A) necessary to satisfy the objective in section 1.1, and

        (B) to a reasonable person, the table, column, or other information does not detract from the prescribed information in the table in section 2.1.

(b) Despite paragraph (a), a company must not add a column to the table in section 2.1.

(3) — Information for full financial year

(a) If a named executive officer acted in that capacity for the company during part of a financial year for which disclosure is required in the table in section 2.1, provide details of all of the compensation that the named executive officer received from the company for that financial year. This includes compensation the named executive officer earned in any other position with the company during the financial year.

(b) Do not annualize compensation in a table for any part of a year when a named executive officer was not in the service of the company. Annualized compensation may be disclosed in a footnote.

(4) — Director and named executive officer compensation

(a) Disclose any compensation awarded to, earned by, paid to, or payable to each director and named executive officer, in any capacity with respect to the company. Compensation to directors and named executive officers must include all compensation from the company and its subsidiaries.

(b) Disclose any compensation awarded to, earned by, paid to, or payable to, a named executive officer, or director, in any capacity with respect to the company, by another person or company.

(5) — Determining if an individual is a named executive officer

For the purpose of calculating total compensation awarded to, earned by, paid to, or payable to an executive officer under paragraph (c) of the definition of named executive officer,

    (a) use the total compensation that would be reported for that executive officer in the table in section 2.1, as if the executive officer were a named executive officer for the company's most recently completed financial year, and

    (b) exclude any compensation disclosed in the column "Value of all other compensation" of the table in section 2.1.

Commentary

The $150,000 threshold in paragraph (c) of the definition of named executive officer only applies when determining who is a named executive officer in a company's most recently completed financial year. If an individual is a named executive officer in the most recently completed financial year, disclosure of compensation in the prior years must be provided even if total compensation in a prior year is less than $150,000.

(6) — Compensation to associates

Disclose any awards, earnings, payments, or payables to an associate of a named executive officer, or of a director, as a result of compensation awarded to, earned by, paid to, or payable to the named executive officer or the director, in any capacity with respect to the company.

(7) — Currencies

(a) Companies must report amounts required by this form in Canadian dollars or in the same currency that the company uses for its financial statements. A company must use the same currency in all of the tables of this form.

(b) If compensation awarded to, earned by, paid to, or payable to a named executive officer or director was in a currency other than the currency reported in the prescribed tables of this form, state the currency in which compensation was awarded, earned, paid, or payable, disclose the currency exchange rate and describe the methodology used to translate the compensation into Canadian dollars or the currency that the company uses in its financial statements.

(8) — New reporting issuers

(a) A company is not required to provide information for a completed financial year if the company was not a reporting issuer at any time during the most recently completed financial year, unless the company became a reporting issuer as a result of a restructuring transaction.

(b) If the company was not a reporting issuer at any time during the most recently completed financial year and the company is completing this form because it is preparing a prospectus, discuss all significant elements of the compensation to be awarded to, earned by, paid to, or payable to named executive officers and directors of the company once it becomes a reporting issuer, to the extent this compensation has been determined.

(9) — Plain language

Information required to be disclosed under this form must be clear, concise, and presented in such a way that it provides a person, applying reasonable effort, an understanding of

(a) how decisions about named executive officer and director compensation are made, and

(b) how specific named executive officer and director compensation relates to the overall stewardship and governance of the company.

Commentary

Refer to the plain language principles listed in section 1.5 of Companion Policy 51-102CP Continuous Disclosure Obligations for further guidance.

Item 2 — Director and Named Executive Officer Compensation

2.1 — Director and named executive officer compensation, excluding compensation securities

(1) Using the following table, disclose all compensation referred to in subsection 1.3(1) of this form for each of the two most recently completed financial years, other than compensation disclosed under section 2.3.

Commentary

For venture issuers, compensation includes payments, grants, awards, gifts and benefits including, but not limited to,

- *salaries,*
- *consulting fees,*
- *management fees,*
- *retainer fees,*
- *bonuses,*
- *committee and meeting fees,*
- *special assignment fees,*
- *pensions and employer paid RRSP contributions,*
- *perquisites such as*
  - *car, car lease, car allowance or car loan,*
  - *personal insurance,*
  - *parking,*
  - *accommodation, including use of vacation accommodation,*
  - *financial assistance,*
  - *club memberships,*
  - *use of corporate motor vehicle or aircraft,*
  - *reimbursement for tax on perquisites or other benefits, and*
  - *investment-related advice and expenses.*

Table of compensation excluding compensation securities							
Name and position	Year	Salary, consulting fee, retainer or commission ($)	Bonus ($)	Committee or meeting fees ($)	Value of perquisites ($)	Value of all other compensation ($)	Total compensation ($)

(2) In the table required under subsection (1), disclose compensation of each named executive officer first, followed by compensation of any director who is not a named executive officer.

(3) If the individual is a named executive officer and a director, state both positions in the column entitled "Name and position". In a footnote to the table, identify how much compensation the NEO received for each position.

(4) In the column entitled "Value of perquisites", include perquisites provided to an NEO or director that are not generally available to all employees and that, in aggregate, are greater than

(a) $15,000, if the NEO or director's total salary for the financial year is $150,000 or less,

(b) 10% of the NEO or director's salary for the financial year, if the NEO or director's total salary for the financial year is greater than $150,000 but less than $500,000, or

(c) $50,000, if the NEO or director's total salary for the financial year is $500,000 or greater.

Value these items on the basis of the aggregate incremental cost to the company and its subsidiaries. Describe in a footnote the methodology used for computing the aggregate incremental cost to the company.

Provide a note to the table to disclose the nature of each perquisite provided that equals or exceeds 25% of the total value of perquisites provided to that named executive officer or director, and how the value of the perquisite was calculated, if it is not provided in cash.

Commentary

For the purposes of the column entitled "Value of perquisites", an item is generally a perquisite if it is not integrally and directly related to the performance of the director or named executive officer's duties. If something is necessary for a person to do his or her job, it is integrally and directly related to the job and is not a perquisite, even if it also provides some amount of personal benefit.

(5) If non-cash compensation, other than compensation required to be disclosed in section 2.3, was provided or is payable, disclose the fair market value of the compensation at the time it was earned or, if it is not possible to calculate the fair market value, disclose that fact in a note to the table and the reasons why.

(6) In the column entitled "Value of all other compensation", include all of the following:

(a) any incremental payments, payables and benefits to a named executive officer or director that were triggered by, or resulted from, a scenario listed in subsection 2.5(2) that occurred before the end of the applicable financial year,

(b) all compensation relating to defined benefit or defined contribution plans including service costs and other compensatory items such as plan changes and earnings that are different from the estimated earnings for defined benefit plans and above market earnings for defined contribution plans.

Commentary

The disclosure of defined benefit or defined contribution plans relates to all plans that provide for the payment of pension plan benefits. Use the same amounts indicated in column (e) of the defined benefit plan table required by section 2.7 for the applicable financial year and the amounts included in column (c) of the defined contribution plan table required by section 2.7 for the applicable financial year.

(7) Despite subsection (1), it is not necessary to disclose Canada Pension Plan, similar government plans and group life, health, hospitalization, medical reimbursement and relocation plans that do not discriminate in scope, terms or operation that are generally available to all salaried employees.

(8) If a director or named executive officer has served in that capacity for only part of a year, indicate the number of months he or she has served; do not annualize the compensation.

(9) Provide notes to the table to disclose each of the following for the most recently completed financial year only:

(a) compensation paid or payable by any person or company other than the company in respect of services provided to the company or its subsidiaries, including the identity of that other person or company;

(b) compensation paid or payable indirectly to the director or named executive officer and, in such case, the amount of compensation, to whom it is paid or payable and the relationship between the director or named executive officer and such other person or company;

(c) for the column entitled "Value of all other compensation", the nature of each form of other compensation paid or payable that equals or exceeds 25% of the total value of other compensation paid or payable to that director or named executive officer, and how the value of such other compensation was calculated, if it is not paid or payable in cash.

2.2 — External management companies

(1) If one or more individuals acting as named executive officers of the company are not employees of the company, disclose the names of those individuals.

(2) If an external management company employs or retains one or more individuals acting as named executive officers or directors of the company and the company has entered into an understanding, arrangement or agreement with the external management company to provide executive management services to the company, directly or indirectly, disclose any compensation that

(a) the company paid directly to an individual employed, or retained by the external management company, who is acting as a named executive officer or director of the company;

(b) the external management company paid to the individual that is attributable to the services they provided to the company, directly or indirectly.

(3) If an external management company provides the company's executive management services and also provides executive management services to another company, disclose the entire compensation the external management company paid to the individual acting as a named executive officer or director, or acting in a similar capacity, in connection with services the external management company provided to the company, or the parent or a subsidiary of the company. If the management company allocates the compensation paid to a named executive officer or director, disclose the basis or methodology used to allocate this compensation.

Commentary

A named executive officer may be employed by an external management company and provide services to the company under an understanding, arrangement or agreement. In this case, references in this form to the chief executive officer or chief financial officer are references to the individuals who performed similar functions to that of the chief executive officer or chief financial officer. They are typically the same individuals who signed and filed annual and interim certificates to comply with National Instrument 52-109 Certification of Disclosure in Issuers' Annual and Interim Filings.

2.3 — Stock options and other compensation securities

(1) Using the following table, disclose all compensation securities granted or issued to each director and named executive officer by the company or one of its subsidiaries in the most recently completed financial year for services provided or to be provided, directly or indirectly, to the company or any of its subsidiaries.

Compensation Securities							
Name and position	Type of compensation security	Number of compensation securities, number of underlying securities, and percentage of class	Date of issue or grant	Issue, conversion or exercise price ($)	Closing price of security or underlying security on date of grant ($)	Closing price of security or underlying security at year end ($)	Expiry date

(2) Position the tables prescribed in subsections (1) and (4) directly after the table prescribed in section 2.1.

(3) Provide notes to the table to disclose each of the following:

(a) the total amount of compensation securities, and underlying securities, held by each named executive officer or director on the last day of the most recently completed financial year end;

(b) any compensation security that has been re-priced, cancelled and replaced, had its term extended, or otherwise been materially modified, in the most recently completed financial year, including the original and modified terms, the effective date, the reason for the modification, and the name of the holder;

(c) any vesting provisions of the compensation securities;

(d) any restrictions or conditions for converting, exercising or exchanging the compensation securities.

(4) Using the following table, disclose each exercise by a director or named executive officer of compensation securities during the most recently completed financial year.

Exercise of Compensation Securities by Directors and NEOs							
Name and position	Type of compensation security	Number of underlying securities exercised	Exercise price per security ($)	Date of exercise	Closing price per security on date of exercise ($)	Difference between exercise price and closing price on date of exercise ($)	Total value on exercise date ($)

(5) For the tables prescribed in subsections (1) and (4), if the individual is a named executive officer and a director, state both positions in the columns entitled "Name and position".

Commentary

For the purposes of the column entitled "Total value on exercise date" multiply the number in the column entitled "Number of underlying securities exercised" by the number in the column entitled "Difference between exercise price and closing price on date of exercise".

2.4 — *Stock option plans and other incentive plans*

(1) Describe the material terms of each stock option plan, stock option agreement made outside of a stock option plan, plan providing for the grant of stock appreciation rights, deferred share units or restricted stock units and any other incentive plan or portion of a plan under which awards are granted.

Commentary

Examples of material terms are vesting provisions, maximum term of options granted, whether or not a stock option plan is a rolling plan, the maximum number or percentage of options that can be granted, method of settlement.

(2) Indicate for each such plan or agreement whether it has previously been approved by shareholders and, if applicable, when it is next required to be approved.

(3) Disclosure is not required of plans, such as shareholder rights plans, that involve issuance of securities to all securityholders.

2.5 — *Employment, consulting and management agreements*

(1) Disclose the material terms of each agreement or arrangement under which compensation was provided during the most recently completed financial year or is payable in respect of services provided to the company or any of its subsidiaries that were

(a) performed by a director or named executive officer, or

(b) performed by any other party but are services typically provided by a director or a named executive officer.

(2) For each agreement or arrangement referred to in subsection (1), disclose each of the following:

(a) the provisions, if any, with respect to change of control, severance, termination or constructive dismissal;

(b) the estimated incremental payments that are triggered by, or result from, change of control, severance, termination or constructive dismissal;

(c) any relationship between the other party to the agreement and a director or named executive officer of the company or any of its subsidiaries.

2.6 — *Oversight and description of director and named executive officer compensation*

(1) Disclose who determines director compensation and how and when it is determined.

(2) Disclose who determines named executive officer compensation and how and when it is determined.

(3) For each named executive officer, disclose each of the following:

(a) a description of all significant elements of compensation awarded to, earned by, paid or payable to the named executive officer for the most recently completed financial year, including at a minimum each element of compensation that accounts for 10% or more of the named executive officer's total compensation;

(b) whether total compensation or any significant element of total compensation is tied to one or more performance criteria or goals, including for example, milestones, agreements or transactions and, if so,

(i) describe the performance criteria and goals, and

(ii) indicate the weight or approximate weight assigned to each performance criterion or goal;

(c) any significant events that have occurred during the most recently completed financial year that have significantly affected compensation including whether any performance criterion or goal was waived or changed and, if so, why;

(d) how the company determines the amount to be paid for each significant element of compensation referred to in paragraph (a), including whether the process is based on objective, identifiable measures or a subjective decision;

(e) whether a peer group is used to determine compensation and, if so, describe the peer group and why it is considered appropriate;

(f) any significant changes to the company's compensation policies that were made during or after the most recently completed financial year that could or will have an effect on director or named executive officer compensation.

(4) Despite subsection (3), if a reasonable person would consider that disclosure of a previously undisclosed specific performance criterion or goal would seriously prejudice the company's interests, the company is not required to disclose the criterion or goal provided that the company does each of the following:

(a) discloses the percentage of the named executive officer's total compensation that relates to the undisclosed criterion or goal;

(b) discloses the anticipated difficulty in achieving the performance criterion or goal;

(c) states that it is relying on this exemption from the disclosure requirement;

(d) explains why disclosing the performance criterion or goal would seriously prejudice its interests.

(5) For the purposes of subsection (4), a company's interests are considered not to be seriously prejudiced solely by disclosing a performance goal or criterion if that criterion or goal is based on broad corporate-level financial performance metrics such as earnings per share, revenue growth, or earnings before interest, taxes, depreciation and amortization (EBITDA).

2.7 — *Pension disclosure*

If the company provides a pension to a director or named executive officer, provide for each such individual the additional disclosure required by Item 5 of Form 51-102F6.

2.8 — Companies reporting in the United States

(1) Except as provided in subsection (2), SEC issuers may satisfy the requirements of this form by providing the information that they disclose in the United States pursuant to item 402 "Executive compensation" of Regulation S-K under the 1934 Act.

(2) Subsection (1) does not apply to a company that, as a foreign private issuer, satisfies Item 402 of Regulation S-K by providing the information required by Items 6.B "Compensation" and 6.E.2 "Share Ownership" of Form 20-F under the 1934 Act.

Companion Policy 51-102CP — Continuous Disclosure Obligations

Table of Contents

PART 1 — INTRODUCTION AND DEFINITIONS

1.1 Introduction and Purpose — (1) National Instrument 51-102 *Continuous Disclosure Obligations* (the "Instrument") sets out disclosure requirements for all issuers, other than investment funds, that are reporting issuers in one or more jurisdictions in Canada.

(2) The purpose of this Companion Policy (the "Policy") is to help you understand how the provincial and territorial regulatory authorities interpret or apply certain provisions of the Instrument. This Policy includes explanations, discussion and examples of various parts of the Instrument.

1.2 Filing Obligations — (1) Reporting issuers must file continuous disclosure documents under the Instrument only in the local jurisdictions in which they are a reporting issuer.

(2) In some circumstances, the Instrument permits an issuer to satisfy a filing requirement by filing a different document instead. If an issuer is relying on one of these sections, the issuer must file the substitute document in the appropriate filing category and type on SEDAR. For example, an exchangeable share issuer relying on section 13.3(2) that must file a copy of its parent issuer's annual financial statements must file those financial statements under the exchangeable share issuer's SEDAR profile in the "Annual Financial Statement" filing type.

1.3 Corporate Law Requirements — Reporting issuers are reminded that they may be subject to requirements of corporate law that address matters similar to those addressed by the Instrument, and which may impose additional or more onerous requirements. For example, applicable corporate law may require the delivery of annual financial statements to shareholders or may require the board of directors to approve interim financial reports.

1.4 Definitions — (1) **General** — Many of the terms for which the Instrument or Forms prescribed by the Instrument provide definitions are defined somewhat differently in the applicable securities legislation of several local jurisdictions. A term used in the Instrument and defined in the securities statute of a local jurisdiction has the meaning given to it in the statute unless: (a) the definition in that statute is restricted to a specific portion of the statute that does not govern continuous disclosure; or (b) the context otherwise requires.

For instance, the terms "form of proxy", "material change", "proxy" and "recognized quotation and trade reporting system" are defined in local securities legislation of most jurisdictions. The provincial and territorial regulatory authorities consider the meanings given to these terms in securities legislation to be substantially similar to the definitions set out in the Instrument.

(2) **Asset-backed security** — Section 1.8 of Companion Policy 44-101CP provides guidance for the definition of "asset-backed security".

(3) **Directors and Executive Officers** — Where the Instrument or any of the Forms use the term "directors" or "executive officers", a reporting issuer that is not a corporation must refer to the definitions in securities legislation of "director". The definition of "director" typically includes a person acting in a capacity similar to that of a director of a company. Therefore, non-corporate issuers must determine in light of the particular circumstances which individuals or persons are acting in such capacities for the purposes of complying with the Instrument and the Forms. Further, in considering paragraph (c) of the definition of "executive officer", we would consider an individual that is employed by an entity separate from the reporting issuer, but that performs a policy-making function in respect of the reporting issuer through that separate entity or otherwise, to fit within this definition.

Similarly, the terms chief executive officer and chief financial officer should be read to include the individuals who have the responsibilities normally associated with these positions or act in a similar capacity. This determination should be made irrespective of an individual's corporate title or whether that individual is employed directly or acts pursuant to an agreement or understanding.

(4) **Investment Fund** — Generally, the definition of "investment fund" would not include a trust or other entity that issues securities which entitle the holder to substantially all of the net cash flows generated by: (i) an underlying business owned by the trust or other entity, or (ii) the income-producing properties owned by the trust or other entity. Examples of trusts or other entities that are not included in the definition are business income trusts, real estate investment trusts and royalty trusts.

(5) **Reverse Takeover** — The definition of reverse takeover includes reverse acquisitions as defined or interpreted in Canadian GAAP applicable to publicly accountable enterprises and any other transaction in which an issuer issues enough voting securities as consideration for the acquisition of an entity such that control of the issuer passes to the securityholders of the acquired entity (such as a Qualifying Transaction, as that term is defined in the TSX Venture Exchange policies). In a reverse acquisition, although legally the entity (the legal parent) that issued the securities is regarded as the parent, the entity (the legal subsidiary) whose former securityholders now control the combined entity is treated as the acquirer for accounting purposes. As a result, for accounting purposes, the issuing entity (the legal parent) is deemed to be a continuation of the acquirer and the acquirer is deemed to have acquired control of the assets and business of the issuing entity in consideration for the issue of capital.

(6) **Restructuring transaction** — A "restructuring transaction" includes a transaction in which a reporting issuer acquires assets, which may include assets that constitute a business, and issues securities resulting in

- new securityholders owning or controlling more than 50% of the reporting issuer's outstanding voting securities, and

- a new control person or company, or new control group.

The acquisition and issuance may be in a single transaction, or a series of transactions. To be a "series of transactions", the transactions must be related to each other.

The phrase "new securityholders" includes both beneficial owners who did not hold any of the reporting issuer's securities before the restructuring transaction, and beneficial owners that held some securities in the reporting issuer before the transaction, but who now, as a result of the transaction, own more than 50% of the outstanding voting securities.

(7) **Accounting terms** — The Instrument uses accounting terms that are defined or used in Canadian GAAP applicable to publicly accountable enterprises. In certain cases, some of those terms are defined differently in securities legislation. In deciding which meaning applies, you should consider that National Instrument 14-101 *Definitions* provides that a term used in the Instrument and defined in the securities statute of a local jurisdiction has the meaning given to it in the statute unless: (a) the definition in that statute is restricted to a specific portion of the statute that does not govern continuous disclosure; or (b) the context otherwise requires.

For example, the term "associate" is defined in local securities statutes and Canadian GAAP applicable to publicly accountable enterprises. Securities regulatory authorities are of the view that the references to the term "associate" in the Instrument and its forms (e.g., item 7.1(g) of Form 51-102F5 *Information Circular*) should be given the meaning of the term under local securities statutes since the context does not indicate that the accounting meaning of the term should be used.

(8) **Acceptable accounting principles other than Canadian GAAP applicable to publicly accountable enterprises** — If an issuer is permitted under National Instrument 52-107 *Acceptable Accounting Principles and Auditing Standards* to file financial statements in accordance with acceptable accounting principles other than Canadian GAAP applicable to publicly accountable enterprises, then the issuer may interpret any reference in the Instrument to a term or provision defined or used in Canadian GAAP applicable to publicly accountable enterprises as a reference to the corresponding term or provision in the other acceptable accounting principles.

(9) **Rate-regulated activities** — If a qualifying entity is relying on the exemption in paragraph 5.4(1)(a) of National Instrument 52-107 *Acceptable Accounting Principles and Auditing Standards*, then the qualifying entity may interpret any reference in the Instrument to a term or provision defined or used in Canadian GAAP applicable to publicly accountable enterprises as a reference to the corresponding term or provision in Part V of the Handbook.

1.5 Plain Language Principles — You should apply plain language principles when you prepare your disclosure including:

- using short sentences

- using definite everyday language

- using the active voice

- avoiding superfluous words

- organizing the document in clear, concise sections, paragraphs and sentences

- avoiding jargon

- using personal pronouns to speak directly to the reader

- avoiding reliance on glossaries and defined terms unless it facilitates understanding of the disclosure

- not relying on boilerplate wording

- avoiding abstract terms by using more concrete terms or examples

- avoiding multiple negatives

- using technical terms only when necessary and explaining those terms

- using charts, tables and examples where it makes disclosure easier to understand.

Question and answer bullet point formats are consistent with the disclosure requirements of the Instrument.

1.6 Signature and Certificates — Reporting issuers are not required by the Instrument to sign or certify documents filed under the Instrument. Certification requirements apply to some documents under National Instrument 52-109 *Certification of Disclosure in Companies' Annual and Interim Filings*. Whether or not a document is signed or certified, it is an offence under securities legislation to make a false or misleading statement in any required document.

1.7 Audit Committees — Reporting issuers are reminded that their audit committees must fulfill their responsibilities set out in other securities legislation. For example, the responsibilities of audit committees are set out in National Instrument 52-110 *Audit Committees*.

1.8 Acceptable Accounting Principles and Auditing Standards — An issuer filing any of the following items under the Instrument must comply with National Instrument 52-107 *Acceptable Accounting Principles and Auditing Standards*:

    (a) financial statements;

    (b) an operating statement for an oil and gas property as referred to in section 8.10 of the Instrument;

    (c) summarized financial information, including the aggregated amounts of assets, liabilities, revenue and profit or loss of a business as referred to in section 8.6 of the Instrument; or

    (d) financial information derived from a credit support issuer's financial statements as referred to in section 13.4 of the Instrument.

National Instrument 52-107 *Acceptable Accounting Principles and Auditing Standards* sets out, among other things, the use of accounting principles other than Canadian GAAP applicable to publicly accountable enterprises or auditing standards other than Canadian GAAS in preparing or auditing financial statements.

1.9 Ordinary Course of Business — Whether a contract has been entered into in the ordinary course of business is a question of fact. It must be considered in the context of the reporting issuer's business and the industry in which it operates.

1.10 Material Deficiencies — After filing a document under the Instrument, a reporting issuer may determine that the document was materially deficient in some respect and, as a result, the filing does not comply with the requirements of the Instrument. In this situation, the reporting issuer is expected to comply with the Instrument by filing an amended version of the materially deficient document.

PART 2 — FOREIGN ISSUERS AND INVESTMENT FUNDS

2.1 Foreign Issuers — National Instrument 71-102 *Continuous Disclosure and Other Exemptions Relating to Foreign Issuers* provides relief for foreign reporting issuers from certain continuous disclosure and other obligations, including certain obligations contained in the Instrument.

2.2 Investment Funds — Section 2.1 of the Instrument states that the Instrument does not apply to an investment fund. Investment funds should look to securities legislation of the local jurisdiction including, National Instrument 81-106 *Investment Fund Continuous Disclosure* to find the continuous disclosure requirements applicable to them.

PART 3 — FINANCIAL STATEMENTS

3.1 Financial Year — (1) **Length of Financial Year** — For the purposes of the Instrument, unless otherwise expressly provided, references to a financial year apply irrespective of the length of that year. The first financial year of a reporting issuer commences on the date of its incorporation or organization and ends at the close of that year.

(2) **Non-Standard Year** — An issuer with a non-standard year should advise the regulator or securities regulatory authority how it calculates its interim and annual periods before its first financial statements are due under the Instrument.

3.2 Audit of Comparative Annual Financial Statements — Section 4.1 of the Instrument requires a reporting issuer to file annual financial statements that include comparative information for the immediately preceding financial year and that are audited. The auditor's report must cover both the most recently completed financial year and the comparative period, except if the issuer changed its auditor during the periods presented in the annual financial statements and the new auditor has not audited the comparative period. In this situation, the auditor's report would normally refer to the predecessor auditor's report unless the predecessor auditor's report on the prior period's annual financial statements is reissued with the financial statements. This is consistent with Canadian Auditing Standard 710 *Comparative Information — Corresponding Figures and Comparative Financial Statements*.

3.3 Filing Deadline for Annual Financial Statements and Auditor's Report — Section 4.2 of the Instrument sets out filing deadlines for annual financial statements. While section 4.2 of the Instrument does not address the auditor's report date, reporting issuers are encouraged to file their annual financial statements as soon as practicable after the date of the auditor's report. The delivery obligations set out in section 4.6 of the Instrument are not tied to the filing of the annual financial statements.

3.4 Auditor Involvement with an Interim Financial Report — (1) The board of directors of a reporting issuer, in discharging its responsibilities for ensuring the reliability of an interim financial report, should consider engaging an external auditor to carry out a review of the interim financial report.

(2) Subsection 4.3(3) of the Instrument requires a reporting issuer to disclose if an auditor has not performed a review of the interim financial report, to disclose if an auditor was unable to complete a review and why, and to file a written report from the auditor if the auditor has performed a review and expressed a reservation in the auditor's interim review report. No positive statement is required when an auditor has performed a review and provided an unqualified communication. If an auditor was engaged to perform a review on an interim financial report applying review standards set out in the

Handbook, and the auditor was unable to complete the review, the issuer's disclosure of the reasons why the auditor was unable to complete the review would normally include a discussion of

    (a) inadequate internal control;

    (b) a limitation on the scope of the auditor's work; or

    (c) the failure of management to provide the auditor with the written representations the auditor believes are necessary.

(3) If a reporting issuer's annual financial statements are audited in accordance with Canadian GAAS, the terms "review" and "interim review report" used in subsection 4.3(3) of the Instrument refer to the auditor's review of, and report on, an interim financial report applying standards for a review of an interim financial report by the auditor as set out in the Handbook. However, if the reporting issuer's financial statements are audited in accordance with auditing standards other than Canadian GAAS, the corresponding review standards should be applied.

3.5 Delivery of Financial Statements and Paper Copies of Information Circulars — (1) Subsection 4.6(1) of the Instrument requires reporting issuers to send a request form to the registered holders and beneficial owners of their securities, other than debt instruments. The registered holders and beneficial owners may use the request form to request a paper copy of the reporting issuer's annual financial statements and related MD&A, interim financial reports and related MD&A, or both.

In addition, the request form also may (but is not required to) be used to request a paper copy of the information circular and annual financial statements and related MD&A where a reporting issuer uses notice-and-access to deliver proxy-related materials.

Reporting issuers are only required to deliver financial statements and MD&A to the person or company that requests them. As a result, if a beneficial owner requests financial statements and MD&A through its intermediary, the issuer is only required to deliver the requested documents to the intermediary.

Failing to return the request form or otherwise specifically request a copy of the financial statements or MD&A from the reporting issuer will override the beneficial owner's standing instructions under NI 54-101 in respect of the financial statements.

The Instrument does not prescribe when the request form must be sent, or how it must be returned to the reporting issuer.

(2) Subsection 4.6(5) provides that subsection 4.6(1) and the requirement to send annual financial statements under subsection 4.6(3) do not apply to a reporting issuer that sends its annual financial statements to its securityholders, other than holders of debt instruments, within 140 days of the issuer's financial year-end and in accordance with NI 54-101. Notice-and-access can be used to send the annual financial statements and related MD&A under subsection 4.6(5). Notice-and-access is consistent with the principles for electronic delivery set out in National Policy 11-201 Electronic Delivery of Documents.

Failing to return the request form or otherwise specifically request a copy of the financial statements or MD&A from the reporting issuer will override the beneficial owner's standing instructions under NI 54-101 in respect of the financial statements.

The Instrument does not prescribe when the request form must be sent, or how it must be returned to the reporting issuer.

3.6 Comparative Interim Financial Information After Becoming a Reporting Issuer — Section 4.7(4) of the Instrument provides that a reporting issuer does not have to provide comparative financial information when it first becomes a reporting issuer if it complies with specific requirements. Section 4.10(3) of the Instrument provides a similar exemption for comparative financial information for a reverse takeover acquirer. These exemptions may, for example, apply to an issuer that was, before becoming a reporting issuer or before the reverse takeover, a private entity and that is unable to prepare the comparative financial information because it is impracticable to do so. The test of whether "to a reasonable person it is impracticable to present prior-period information on a basis consistent with subsection 4.3(2)" is objective, rather than subjective. Securities regulatory authorities are of the view that a reporting issuer can rely on the exemption only if it has made every reasonable effort to present prior-period information on a basis consistent with subsection 4.3(2) of the Instrument. We are of the view that an issuer should only rely on this exemption in unusual circumstances and generally not related solely to the cost or the time involved in preparing the financial statements.

3.7 Change in Year-End — Appendix A to this Policy is a chart outlining the financial statement filing requirements under section 4.8 of the Instrument if a reporting issuer changes its financial year-end.

3.8 Reverse Takeovers — (1) Following a reverse takeover, although the reverse takeover acquiree is the reporting issuer, from an accounting perspective, the financial statements will be those of the reverse takeover acquirer. Those financial statements must be prepared and filed as if the reverse takeover acquirer had always been the reporting issuer.

(2) The reverse takeover acquiree must file its own financial statements required by sections 4.1 and 4.3 and the related MD&A for all interim and annual periods ending before the date of the reverse takeover, even if the filing deadline for those financial statements is after the date of the reverse takeover.

3.9 Change in Corporate Structure — (1) Section 4.9 of the Instrument requires a reporting issuer to file a notice if the issuer has been party to certain transactions. The reporting issuer may satisfy this requirement by filing a copy of its material change report or news release, provided that

    (a) the material change report or news release contains all the information required in the notice; and

    (b) the reporting issuer files the material change report or news release with the securities regulatory authority or regulator

        (i) under the Change in Corporate Structure category on SEDAR, or

        (ii) if the issuer is not an electronic filer, as a notice under section 4.9.

(2) If the transaction was a reverse takeover, the notice should state that fact and who the reverse takeover acquirer was.

(3) Under paragraph 4.9(h) of the Instrument, the issuer must state the periods of the interim financial reports and the annual financial statements it has to file for its first financial year. Issuers should explain how they determined the periods, particularly if section 4.7 of the Instrument applies.

3.10 Change of Auditor — The term "disagreement" defined in subsection 4.11(1) should be interpreted broadly. A disagreement may not involve an argument, but rather, a mere difference of opinion. Also, where a difference of opinion occurs that meets the criteria in item (b) of the definition of "disagreement", and the issuer reluctantly accepts the auditor's position in order to obtain an unqualified report, a reportable disagreement may still exist. The subsequent rendering of an unqualified report does not, by itself, remove the necessity for reporting a disagreement.

Subsection 4.11(5) of the Instrument requires a reporting issuer, upon a termination or resignation of its auditor, to prepare a change of auditor notice, have the audit committee or board of directors approve the notice, file the reporting package with the regulator or securities regulatory authority in each jurisdiction where it is a reporting issuer, and if there are any reportable events, issue and file a news release describing the information in the reporting

Part 5: ONGOING REQUIREMENTS

package. Subsection 4.11(6) of the Instrument requires the reporting issuer to perform these procedures upon an appointment of a successor auditor. If a termination or resignation of a former auditor and appointment of a successor auditor occur within a short period of time, it may be possible for a reporting issuer to perform the procedures described above required by both subsections 4.11(5) and 4.11(6) concurrently and meet the timing requirements set out in those subsections. In other words, the reporting issuer would prepare only one comprehensive notice and reporting package.

PART 4 — DISCLOSURE AND PRESENTATION OF FINANCIAL INFORMATION

4.1 Disclosure of Financial Information — (1) Subsection 4.5(1) of the Instrument requires that annual financial statements be approved by the board of directors before filing. Subsections 4.5 (2) and 4.5(3) of the Instrument require that each interim financial report be approved by the board of directors or by the company's audit committee before filing. We believe that extracting information from financial statements that have not been approved as required by those provisions and releasing that information to the marketplace in a news release is inconsistent with the prior approval requirement. Also see National Policy 51-201 *Disclosure Standards*.

(2) Reporting issuers that intend to disclose financial information to the marketplace in a news release should consult National Instrument 52-107 *Acceptable Accounting Principles and Auditing Standards*. We believe that disclosing financial information in a news release without disclosing the accounting principles used is inconsistent with the requirement in National Instrument 52-107 *Acceptable Accounting Principles and Auditing Standards* to identify the accounting principles used in the financial statements.

4.2 Non-GAAP Financial Measures — Reporting issuers that intend to publish financial measures other than those prescribed by Canadian GAAP applicable to publicly accountable enterprises should refer to CSA Staff Notice 52-306 *Non-GAAP Financial Measures* for a discussion of staff expectations concerning the use of non-GAAP measures.

4.3 Presentation of Financial Information — Canadian GAAP applicable to publicly accountable enterprises provides an issuer two alternatives in presenting its income: (a) in one single statement of comprehensive income, or (b) in a statement of comprehensive income with a separate income statement. If an issuer presents its income using the second alternative, both statements must be filed to satisfy the requirements of this Instrument. (See subsections 4.1(3) and 4.3(2.1) of the Instrument).

4.4 Predecessor and successor auditor reporting of non-compliance with change of auditor requirements — Subsections 4.11(8) and 4.11(9) of the Instrument require a predecessor and successor auditor to deliver to the regulator or, in Quebec, the securities regulatory authority, a copy of a letter sent to a reporting issuer advising a reporting issuer of its failure to comply with the change of auditor reporting requirements. "Regulator" and "securities regulatory authority" are defined in NI 14-101 — *Definitions*. The securities regulatory authorities will consider the notice requirement in each of these provisions of the Instrument to have been satisfied if the notice is sent to auditor.notice@acvm-csa.ca.

PART 4A — FORWARD-LOOKING INFORMATION

4A.1 Application — Section 4A.1 of the Instrument indicates that Part 4A applies to forward-looking information that is disclosed by a reporting issuer other than forward-looking information contained in oral statements. Reporting issuers should consider broadly the various instances of forward-looking information made available to the public in considering the scope of forward-looking information that is disclosed. This includes, but is not limited to:

- Information that a reporting issuer files with securities regulators
- Information contained in news releases issued by a reporting issuer
- Information published on a reporting issuer's website
- Information published in marketing materials or other similar materials prepared by a reporting issuer or distributed to the public by a reporting issuer.

4A.2 Reasonable Basis — Section 4A.2 of the Instrument requires a reporting issuer to have a reasonable basis for any forward-looking information it discloses. When interpreting "reasonable basis", reporting issuers should consider:

(a) the reasonableness of the assumptions underlying the forward-looking information; and

(b) the process followed in preparing and reviewing forward-looking information.

4A.3 Material Forward-Looking Information — Section 4A.3 and section 5.8 of the Instrument require a reporting issuer to include specified disclosure in material forward-looking information it discloses. Reporting issuers should exercise judgement when determining whether information is material. If a reasonable investor's decision whether or not to buy, sell or hold securities of the reporting issuer would be influenced or changed if the information were omitted or misstated, then the information is likely material.

Section 1.1 contains definitions of the terms "financial outlook" and "FOFI." We consider FOFI and most financial outlooks to be material forward-looking information. Examples of financial outlooks include expected revenue, profit or loss, earnings per share and R&D spending. A financial outlook relating to profit or loss is commonly referred to as "earnings guidance."

An example of forward-looking information that is not a financial outlook or FOFI would be an estimate of future store openings by an issuer in the retail industry. This type of information may or may not be material, depending on whether a reasonable investor's decision whether or not to buy, sell or hold securities of that issuer would be influenced or changed if the information were omitted or misstated.

4A.4 Location of Disclosure — Section 4A.3 of the Instrument requires that any material forward-looking information include specified disclosure. This disclosure should be presented in a manner that allows an investor who reads the document or other material containing the forward-looking information to be able to readily:

(a) understand that the forward-looking information is being provided in the document or other material;

(b) identify the forward-looking information; and

(c) inform himself or herself of the material assumptions underlying the forward-looking information and the material risk factors associated with the forward-looking information.

4A.5 Disclosure of Cautionary Language and Material Risk Factors — (1) Paragraph 4A.3(b) of the Instrument requires a reporting issuer to accompany any material forward-looking information with disclosure that cautions users that actual results may vary from the forward-looking information and identifies material risk factors that could cause material variation. The material risk factors identified in the cautionary language should be relevant to the forward-looking information and the disclosure should not be boilerplate in nature.

(2) The cautionary statements required by paragraph 4A.3(b) of the Instrument should identify significant and reasonably foreseeable factors that could reasonably be expected to cause results to differ materially from those projected in the material forward-looking statement. Reporting issuers should not interpret this as requiring a reporting issuer to anticipate and discuss everything that could conceivably cause results to differ.

4A.6 Disclosure of Material Factors or Assumptions

Paragraph 4A.3(c) of the Instrument requires a reporting issuer to disclose the material factors or assumptions used to develop material forward-looking information. The factors or assumptions should be relevant to the forward-looking information. Disclosure of material factors or assumptions does not require an exhaustive statement of every factor or assumption applied — a materiality standard applies.

4A.7 Date of Assumptions

Management of a reporting issuer that discloses material forward-looking information should satisfy itself that the assumptions are appropriate as of the date management discloses the material forward-looking information even though the material forward-looking information may have been prepared at an earlier time, and may be based on information accumulated over a period of time.

4A.8 Time Period

Paragraph 4B.2(2)(a) of the Instrument requires a reporting issuer to limit the period covered by FOFI or a financial outlook to a period for which the information can be reasonably estimated. In many cases that time period will not go beyond the end of the reporting issuer's next fiscal year. Some of the factors a reporting issuer should consider include the reporting issuer's ability to make appropriate assumptions, the nature of the reporting issuer's industry, and the reporting issuer's operating cycle.

PART 5 — MD&A

5.1 Delivery of MD&A

Reporting issuers are not required to send a request form to their securityholders under Part 5 of the Instrument. This is because the request form that must be delivered under section 4.6 of the Instrument relates to both a reporting issuer's financial statements, and the MD&A applicable to those financial statements.

5.2 Additional Information for Venture Issuers Without Significant Revenue

Section 5.3 of the Instrument requires certain venture issuers to provide in their annual or interim MD&A (unless the information is included in their annual financial statements or interim financial report), a breakdown of material costs whether expensed or recognized as assets. A component of cost is generally considered to be a material component if it exceeds the greater of

    (a) 20% of the total amount of the class; and

    (b) $25,000.

5.3 Disclosure of Outstanding Share Data

Section 5.4 of the Instrument requires disclosure of information relating to the outstanding securities of the reporting issuer as of the latest practicable date. The "latest practicable date" should be current, as close as possible, to the date of filing of the MD&A. Disclosing the number of securities outstanding at the period end is generally not sufficient to meet this requirement.

5.4 Additional Disclosure for Equity Investees

Section 5.7 of the Instrument requires issuers with significant equity investees to provide in their annual or, if the issuer is an issuer that is not providing disclosure in accordance with section 2.2.1 of Form 51-102F1, their interim MD&A (unless the information is included in their annual financial statements or interim financial report), summarized information about the equity investee. Generally, we will consider that an equity investee is significant if, using the financial statements of the equity investee and the issuer as at the issuer's financial year-end, either of the following apply:

    (a) for a reporting issuer that is not a venture issuer, the equity investee would meet the thresholds for the significance tests in Part 8;

    (b) for a venture issuer, the equity investee would meet the thresholds for the significance tests in Part 8 if "100 percent" is read as "40 percent".

5.5 Previously disclosed material forward-looking information

(1) Subsection 5.8(2) of the Instrument requires a reporting issuer to discuss certain events and circumstances that occurred during the period to which its MD&A relates. The events to be discussed are those that are reasonably likely to cause actual results to differ materially from material forward-looking information for a period that is not yet complete. This discussion is only required if the reporting issuer previously disclosed the forward-looking information to the public. Subsection 5.8(2) also requires a reporting issuer to discuss the expected differences.

For example, assume that a reporting issuer published FOFI for the current year assuming no change in the prime interest rate, but by the end of the second quarter the prime interest rate went up by 2%. In its MD&A for the second quarter, the reporting issuer should discuss the interest rate increase and its expected effect on results compared to those indicated in the FOFI.

A reporting issuer should consider whether the events and circumstances that trigger MD&A disclosure under subsection 5.8(2) of the Instrument might also trigger material change reporting requirements under Part 7 of the Instrument.

(2) Subsection 5.8(4) of the Instrument requires a reporting issuer to disclose and discuss material differences between actual results for the annual or interim period to which its MD&A relates and any FOFI or financial outlook for that period that the reporting issuer previously disclosed to the public. A reporting issuer should disclose and discuss material differences for material individual items included in the FOFI or financial outlook, including assumptions.

For example, if the actual dollar amount of revenue approximates forecasted revenue but the sales mix or sales volume differs materially from what the reporting issuer expected, the reporting issuer should explain the differences.

(3) Subsection 5.8(5) of the Instrument addresses a reporting issuer's decision to withdraw previously disclosed material forward-looking information. The subsection requires the reporting issuer to disclose that decision and discuss the events and circumstances that led the reporting issuer to the decision to withdraw the material forward-looking information, including a discussion of the assumptions included in the material forward-looking information that are no longer valid. A reporting issuer should consider whether the events and circumstances that trigger MD&A disclosure under subsection 5.8(5) of the Instrument might also trigger material change reporting requirements under Part 7 of the Instrument. We encourage all reporting issuers to promptly communicate to the market a decision to withdraw material forward-looking information, even if the material change reporting requirements are not triggered.

5.6 Venture Issuers — Quarterly Highlights

(1) A venture issuer that provides quarterly highlights is not required to update its annual MD&A in the quarterly highlights. However, to meet the requirements of section 2.2.1 of Form 51-102F1, the venture issuer should disclose in its quarterly highlights any change, if material, from plans disclosed in the annual MD&A. For example, if a mining issuer discloses a drill program in its annual

MD&A and decides to make a change to that drill program in a subsequent interim period, that change, if material, should be disclosed in the quarterly highlights for that period.

(2) Although all venture issuers have the option of providing quarterly highlights, there are some instances where a venture issuer may want to consider providing full interim MD&A instead of quarterly highlights. We believe the option to use quarterly highlights will likely satisfy the needs of investors in smaller venture issuers. However, investors in larger venture issuers, including those with significant revenue, may want full interim MD&A to assist them in making informed investment decisions. Issuers will likely take the needs of their investors into consideration when determining whether to provide quarterly highlights or full interim MD&A.

(3) For greater certainty, a reference to interim MD&A is a reference to the quarterly highlights a venture issuer has the option of providing in accordance with section 2.2.1 of Form 51-102F1. As such, any requirements in National Instrument 52-109 *Certification of Disclosure in Issuer's Annual and Interim Filings* that apply to interim MD&A will apply to the quarterly highlights

PART 6 — AIF

6.1 Additional and Supporting Documentation — Any material incorporated by reference in an AIF is required to be filed with the AIF unless the material has been previously filed. When a reporting issuer using SEDAR files a previously unfiled document with its AIF, the reporting issuer should ensure that the document is filed under the appropriate SEDAR filing type and document type specifically applicable to the document, rather than generic type "Documents Incorporated by Reference". For example, a reporting issuer that has incorporated by reference an information circular in its AIF and has not previously filed the circular should file the circular under the "Management Proxy Materials" filing subtype and the "Management proxy/information circular" document type.

If the reporting issuer incorporates a document, or a portion of a document, by reference into its AIF, and that document, or that portion of the document, as applicable, incorporates another document by reference, the issuer must also file the underlying document with its AIF.

6.2 AIF Disclosure of Asset-backed Securities — (1) **Factors to consider** — Issuers that have distributed asset-backed securities under a prospectus are required to provide disclosure in their AIF under section 5.3 of Form 51-102F2. Issuers of asset-backed securities must determine which other prescribed disclosure is applicable and ought to be included in the AIF. Disclosure for a special purpose issuer of asset-backed securities will generally explain

- the nature, performance and servicing of the underlying pool of financial assets;
- the structure of the securities and dedicated cash flows; and
- any third party or internal support arrangements established to protect holders of the asset-backed securities from losses associated with non-performance of the financial assets or disruptions in payment.

The nature and extent of required disclosure may vary depending on the type and attributes of the underlying pool and the contractual arrangements through which holders of the asset-backed securities take their interest in such assets.

An issuer of asset-backed securities should consider the following factors when preparing its AIF:

1. The extent of disclosure respecting an issuer will depend on the extent of the issuer's on-going involvement in the conversion of the assets comprising the pool to cash and the distribution of cash to securityholders; this involvement may, in turn, vary dramatically depending on the type, quality and attributes of the assets comprising the pool and on the overall structure of the transaction.

2. Disclosure about the business and affairs of the issuer should relate to the financial assets underlying the asset-backed securities.

3. Disclosure about the originator or the seller of the underlying financial assets will often be relevant to investors in the asset-backed securities particularly where the originator or seller has an on-going involvement with the financial assets comprising the pool. For example, if asset-backed securities are serviced with the cash flows from a revolving pool of receivables, an evaluation of the nature and reliability of the future origination or the future sales of underlying assets by the seller to or through the issuer may be a critical aspect of an investor's investment decision.

To address this, the focus of disclosure respecting an originator or seller of the underlying financial assets should deal with whether there are current circumstances that indicate that the originator or seller will not generate adequate assets in the future to avoid an early liquidation of the pool and, correspondingly, an early payment of the asset-backed securities. Summary historical financial information respecting the originator or seller will ordinarily be adequate to satisfy the disclosure requirement applicable to the originator or seller in circumstances where the originator or seller has an ongoing relationship with the assets comprising the pool.

Financial information respecting the pool of assets to be described and analyzed in the AIF will consist of information commonly set out in servicing reports prepared to describe the performance of the pool and the specific allocations of profit, loss and cash flows applicable to outstanding asset-backed securities made during the relevant period.

(2) **Underlying pool of assets** — Paragraph 5.3(2)(a) of Form 51-102F2 requires issuers of asset-backed securities that were distributed by way of prospectus to include financial disclosure relating to the composition of the underlying pool of financial assets, the cash flows from which service the asset-backed securities. Disclosure respecting the composition of the pool will vary depending upon the nature and number of the underlying financial assets. For example, in a geographically dispersed pool of financial assets, it may be appropriate to provide a summary disclosure based on the location of obligors. In the context of a revolving pool, it may be appropriate to provide details relating to aggregate outstanding balances during a year to illustrate historical fluctuations in asset origination due, for example, to seasonality. In pools of consumer debt obligations, it may be appropriate to provide a breakdown within ranges of amounts owing by obligors in order to illustrate limits on available credit extended.

PART 7 — MATERIAL CHANGE REPORTS

7.1 Publication of News Release — Section 7.1 of the Instrument requires reporting issuers to immediately issue and file a news release disclosing the nature of a material change. This requirement is substantively the same as the material change reporting requirements in some securities legislation for the news release to be issued forthwith.

PART 8 — BUSINESS ACQUISITION REPORTS

8.1 Obligations to File a Business Acquisition Report — (1) **Filing of a Material Change Report** — The requirement in the Instrument for a reporting issuer to file a business acquisition report is in addition to the reporting issuer's obligation to file a material change report, if the significant acquisition constitutes a material change.

(2) Filing of a Business Acquisition Report by SEC Issuers — If a document or a series of documents that an SEC issuer files with or furnishes to the SEC in connection with a business acquisition contains all of the information, including financial statements, required to be included in a business acquisition report under the Instrument, the SEC issuer may file a copy of the documents as its business acquisition report.

(3) Financial Statement Disclosure of Significant Acquisitions — Reporting issuers are reminded that National Instrument 52-107 *Acceptable Accounting Principles and Auditing Standards* prescribes the accounting principles and auditing standards that must be used to prepare and audit the financial statements required by Part 8 of the Instrument.

(4) Acquisition of a Business — A reporting issuer that has made a significant acquisition must include in its business acquisition report certain financial statements of each business acquired. The term "business" should be evaluated in light of the facts and circumstances involved. We generally consider that a separate entity, a subsidiary or a division is a business and that in certain circumstances a smaller component of a company may also be a business, whether or not the business previously prepared financial statements. In determining whether an acquisition constitutes the acquisition of a business, a reporting issuer should consider the continuity of business operations, including the following factors:

(a) whether the nature of the revenue producing activity or potential revenue producing activity will remain generally the same after the acquisition; and

(b) whether any of the physical facilities, employees, marketing systems, sales forces, customers, operating rights, production techniques or trade names are acquired by the reporting issuer instead of remaining with the vendor after the acquisition.

(5) Acquisition by a Subsidiary — If a reporting issuer's subsidiary, which is also a reporting issuer, has acquired a business, both the parent and subsidiary must test the significance of the acquisition. Even if the subsidiary files a business acquisition report, the parent must also file a business acquisition report if the acquisition is also significant for the parent.

8.2 Significance Tests — (1) Nature of Significance Tests — Subsection 8.3(2) of the Instrument sets out the required significance tests for determining whether an acquisition of a business by a reporting issuer is a "significant acquisition". The first test measures the assets of the acquired business against the assets of the reporting issuer. The second test measures the reporting issuer's investments in and advances to the acquired business against the assets of the reporting issuer. The third test measures the specified profit or loss of the acquired business against the specified profit or loss of the reporting issuer. If any one of these three tests is satisfied at the prescribed level, the acquisition is considered "significant" to the reporting issuer. The test must be applied as at the acquisition date using the most recent audited annual financial statements of the reporting issuer and the business. These tests are similar to requirements of the SEC and provide issuers with certainty that if an acquisition is not significant at the acquisition date, then no business acquisition report will be required to be filed.

(2) Business Using Accounting Principles Other Than Those Used by the Reporting Issuer — Subsection 8.3(13) of the Instrument provides that, for the purposes of calculating the significance tests, the amounts used for the business or related businesses must, subject to subsection 8.3(13.1) of the Instrument, be based on the issuer's GAAP, and translated into the same presentation currency as that used in the reporting issuer's financial statements. This means that in some cases the amounts must be converted to the issuer's GAAP and translated into the same presentation currency as that used in the reporting issuer's financial statements.

Subsection 8.3(13.1) of the Instrument exempts venture issuers from the requirement in paragraph 8.3(13)(a) that, for the purposes of calculating the significance tests, the amounts used for the business or related businesses must be based on the issuer's GAAP, but only where the financial statements for the business or related businesses were prepared in accordance with Canadian GAAP applicable to private enterprises and certain other conditions are met.

National Instrument 52-107 *Acceptable Accounting Principles and Auditing Standards* permits financial statements for a business or related businesses to be prepared in accordance with U.S. GAAP without reconciliation to the issuer's GAAP. This does not impact the application of paragraph 8.3(13)(a) of the Instrument. Thus, if the issuer's GAAP is not U.S. GAAP, paragraph 8.3(13)(a) of the Instrument requires, for the purposes of calculating the significance tests, that the amounts used for the business or related businesses be based on the issuer's GAAP.

Paragraph 8.3(13)(b) of the Instrument applies to all issuers and requires, for the purpose of calculating the significance tests, that the amounts used for the business or related businesses be translated into the same presentation currency as that used in the reporting issuer's financial statements.,

(3) Acquisition of a Previously Unaudited Business — Subsections 8.3(2) and 8.3(4) of the Instrument require the significance of an acquisition to be determined using the most recent audited annual financial statements of the reporting issuer and the business acquired. However, if the annual financial statements of the business or related businesses for the most recently completed financial year were not audited, subsection 8.3(14) of the Instrument permits use of the unaudited annual financial statements for the purpose of applying the significance tests. If the acquisition is determined to be significant, then the annual financial statements required by subsection 8.4(1) of the Instrument must be audited.

(3.1) Application of Significance Tests for Business Combinations Achieved in Stages — IFRS 3 *Business Combinations*, requires that when a business combination is achieved in stages the acquirer's previously held equity interest in the acquiree is remeasured at its acquisition date fair value with any resulting gain or loss recognized in profit or loss. The remeasurement of the previously held equity interest should not be included in the asset or the investment test and the resulting gain or loss from remeasurement should not be included in the profit or loss test. (See subsection 8.3(4.1) of the Instrument).,

(4) Application of Investment Test for Significance of an Acquisition — One of the significance tests set out in subsections 8.3(2) and (4) of the Instrument is whether the reporting issuer's consolidated investments in and advances to the business or related businesses exceed a specified percentage of the consolidated assets of the reporting issuer. In applying this test, the "investments in" the business should be determined using the consideration transferred, measured in accordance with the issuer's GAAP, including any contingent consideration. In addition, any payments made in connection with the acquisition which would not constitute consideration transferred but which would not have been paid unless the acquisition had occurred, should be considered part of investments in and advances to the business for the purpose of applying the significance tests. Examples of such payments include loans, royalty agreements, lease agreements and agreements to provide a pre-determined amount of future services. For purposes of the investment test, "consideration transferred" should be adjusted to exclude the carrying value of assets transferred by the reporting issuer to the business or related businesses that will remain with the business or related businesses after the acquisition.

(5) Application of the Significance Tests When the Financial Year Ends are Non-Coterminous — Subsection 8.3(2) of the Instrument requires the significance of a business acquisition to be determined using the most recent audited annual financial statements of both the reporting issuer and the acquired business. For the purpose of applying the tests under this subsection, the year-ends of the reporting issuer and the acquired business need not be coterminous. Accordingly, neither the audited annual financial statements of the reporting issuer nor those of the business should be adjusted for the purposes of applying the significance tests. However, if the acquisition of a business is determined to be significant and pro forma income statements are required by subsection 8.4(3) of the Instrument and, if the business' year-end is more than 93 days before the reporting issuer's year-end, the

business' reporting period required under paragraph 8.4(4)(c) of the Instrument should be adjusted to reduce the gap to 93 days or less. Refer to subsection 8.7(3) of this Policy for further guidance.

8.3 Optional Significance Tests — (1) Optional Significance Tests — Decrease in Significance — If an acquisition is determined under subsection 8.3(2) of the Instrument to be significant, a reporting issuer has the option under subsections 8.3(3) and (4) of the Instrument of applying optional significance tests using more recent financial statements than those used for the required significance tests in subsection 8.3(2). The optional significance tests under subsections 8.3(3) and (4) have been included to recognize the possible growth of a reporting issuer between the date of its most recently completed year-end and the date of filing a business acquisition report and the corresponding potential decline in significance of the acquisition to the reporting issuer.

(2) Availability of the Optional Significance Tests — The optional significance tests permitted under subsections 8.3(4) and (6) of the Instrument are available to all reporting issuers. However, depending on how or when a reporting issuer integrates the acquired business into its existing operations and the nature of post-acquisition financial records it maintains for the acquired business, it may not be possible for a reporting issuer to apply the optional significance test under subsection 8.3(6).

(3) Optional Investment Test — For the purpose of applying the optional investment test under paragraph 8.3(4)(b) of the Instrument, the reporting issuer's investments in and advances to the business should be as at the acquisition date and not as at the date of the reporting issuer's financial statements used to determine its consolidated assets for the optional investment test.

(4) Optional Profit or Loss Test based on Pro Forma Information — A reporting issuer may apply the optional profit or loss test in subsection 8.3(11.1) of the Instrument based on more recent pro forma consolidated specified profit or loss. By permitting reporting issuers to base the optional profit or loss test on pro forma consolidated specified profit or loss, this test recognizes the possible growth of a reporting issuer as a result of acquisitions completed between its most recently completed year end and the date of filing a business acquisition report and the corresponding potential decline in significance of the acquisition to the reporting issuer.

8.4 Financial Statements of Related Businesses — Subsection 8.4(8) of the Instrument requires that if a reporting issuer includes in its business acquisition report financial statements for more than one related business, separate financial statements must be presented for each business except for the periods during which the businesses were under common control or management, in which case the reporting issuer may present the financial statements on a combined basis. Although one or more of the related businesses may be insignificant relative to the others, separate financial statements of each business for the same number of periods required must be presented. Relief from the requirement to include financial statements of the least significant related business or businesses may be granted depending on the facts and circumstances.

8.5 Application of the Significance Tests for Multiple Investments in the Same Business — Subsection 8.3(11) of the Instrument explains how the significance test should be applied when the reporting issuer has made multiple investments in the same business. If the reporting issuer acquired an interest in the business in a previous year and that interest is reflected in the most recent audited annual financial statements of the reporting issuer filed, then the issuer should determine the significance of only the incremental investment in the business which is not reflected in the reporting issuer's most recent audited annual financial statements filed.

8.6 Preparation of Divisional and Carve-out Financial Statements — (1) Interpretations — In this section of this Policy, unless otherwise stated,

    (a) a reference to "a business" includes a division or some lesser component of another business acquired by a reporting issuer that constitutes a significant acquisition; and

    (b) the term "parent" refers to the vendor from whom the reporting issuer purchased a business.

(2) Acquisition of a Division — As discussed in subsection 8.1(4) of this Policy, the acquisition of a division of a business and in certain circumstances, a lesser component of a person or company, may constitute an acquisition of a business for purposes of the Instrument, whether or not the subject of the acquisition previously prepared financial statements. To determine the significance of the acquisition and comply with the requirements for financial statements in a business acquisition report under Part 8 of the Instrument, financial statements for the business must be prepared. This section provides guidance on preparing these financial statements.

(3) Divisional and Carve-Out Financial Statements — The terms "divisional" and "carve-out" financial statements are often used interchangeably although a distinction is possible. Some companies maintain separate financial records and financial statements for a business activity or unit that is operated as a division. Financial statements prepared from these financial records are often referred to as "divisional" financial statements. In other circumstances, no separate financial records for a business activity are maintained; they are simply consolidated with the parent's records. In these cases, if the parent's financial records are sufficiently detailed, it is possible to extract or "carve-out" the information specific to the business activity in order to prepare separate financial statements of that business. Financial statements prepared in this manner are commonly referred to as "carve-out" financial statements. The guidance in this section applies to the preparation of both divisional and carve-out financial statements unless otherwise stated.

(4) Preparation of Divisional and Carve-Out Financial Statements —

    (a) When complete financial records of the business acquired have been maintained, those records should be used for preparing and auditing the financial statements of the business. For the purposes of this section, it is presumed that the parent maintains separate financial records for its divisions.

    (b) When complete financial records of the business acquired do not exist, carve-out financial statements must be prepared in accordance with subsection 3.11(6) of National Instrument 52-107 *Acceptable Accounting Principles and Auditing Standards*.

(5) Statements of Assets Acquired, Liabilities Assumed and Statements of Operations — When it is impracticable to prepare carve-out financial statements of a business, a reporting issuer may be required to include in its business acquisition report an audited statement of assets acquired and liabilities assumed and a statement of operations of the business. The statement of operations should exclude only those indirect operating costs not directly attributable to the business, such as corporate overhead. If indirect operating costs were previously allocated to the business and there is a reasonable basis of allocation, they should not be excluded.

8.7 Preparation of Pro Forma Financial Statements Giving Effect to Significant Acquisitions — (1) Objective and Basis of Preparation — The objective of pro forma financial statements is to illustrate the impact of a transaction on a reporting issuer's financial position and financial performance by adjusting the historical financial statements of the reporting issuer to give effect to the transaction. Accordingly, the pro forma financial statements should be prepared on the basis of the reporting issuer's financial statements as already filed. No adjustment should be made to eliminate discontinued operations.

(2) Pro Forma Statement of Financial Position — Subsection 8.4(3) of the Instrument does not require a pro forma statement of financial position to be prepared to give effect to significant acquisitions that are reflected in the reporting issuer's most recent annual or interim statement of financial position filed under the Instrument.

(3) Non-coterminous Year-ends — Where the financial year-end of a business differs from the reporting issuer's year-end by more than 93 days, paragraph 8.4(7)(c) requires a statement of comprehensive income for the business to be constructed for a period of 12 consecutive months. For example, if the constructed reporting period is 12 months and ends on June 30, the 12 months should commence on July 1 of the immediately preceding year; it should not begin on March 1st of the immediately preceding year with three of the following 15 months omitted, such as the period from October 1 to December 31, since this would not be a consecutive 12 month period.

(4) Effective Date of Adjustments — For the pro forma income statements included in a business acquisition report, the acquisition and the adjustments should be computed as if the acquisition had occurred at the beginning of the reporting issuer's most recently completed financial year and carried through the most recent interim period presented, if any. However, one exception to the preceding is that adjustments related to the allocation of the purchase price, including the amortization of fair value increments and intangibles, should be based on the acquisition date amounts of assets acquired and liabilities assumed as if the acquisition occurred on the date of the reporting issuer's most recent statement of financial position filed.

(5) Acceptable Adjustments — Pro forma adjustments are generally limited to the following two types of adjustments required by paragraph 8.4(7)(b) of the Instrument:

(a) those directly attributable to the specific acquisition transaction for which there are firm commitments and for which the complete financial effects are objectively determinable; and

(b) adjustments to conform amounts for the business or related businesses to the issuer's accounting policies.

If financial statements for a business or related businesses are prepared in accordance with accounting principles that differ from the issuer's GAAP and the financial statements do not include a reconciliation to the issuer's GAAP, pro forma adjustments as described in item (b) above will often be necessary. For example, financial statements for a business or related businesses may be prepared in accordance with U.S. GAAP, or in the case of a venture issuer, in accordance with Canadian GAAP applicable to private enterprises, in each case without a reconciliation to the issuer's GAAP. Even if financial statements for a business or related businesses are prepared in accordance with the issuer's GAAP, pro forma adjustments as described in item (b) may be necessary to conform amounts for the business or related businesses to the issuer's accounting policies, including, for example, the issuer's revenue recognition policy where the revenue recognition policy of the business or related businesses differs from the issuer's policy.

If the presentation currency used in financial statements for a business or related businesses differs from the presentation currency used in the issuer's financial statements, the pro forma financial statements must present amounts for the business or related businesses in the presentation currency of the issuer's financial statements. The pro forma financial statements should explain any adjustments to conform presentation currency.

(6) Multiple Acquisitions — If a reporting issuer has completed multiple acquisitions then, under subsection 8.4(5) of the Instrument, the pro forma financial statements must give effect to each acquisition completed since the beginning of the most recently completed financial year. The pro forma adjustments may be grouped by line item on the face of the pro forma financial statements provided the details for each transaction are disclosed in the notes.

(7) Pro Forma Financial Statements Based on an Earlier Interim Financial Report — The pro forma financial statements are prepared on the basis of the financial statements included in the business acquisition report. As a result, if the reporting issuer relies on subsection 8.4(4) of the Instrument to include financial statements for an earlier interim period of the acquired business than would otherwise be required under subsection (3), the issuer uses its comparable interim period to prepare the pro forma statements.

(8) Indirect Acquisitions — Under the securities legislation of certain jurisdictions, it is generally an offence to make a statement in a document that is required to be filed under securities legislation, and that does not state a fact that is necessary to make the statement not misleading. When a reporting issuer acquires a business that has itself recently acquired another business or related businesses (an "indirect acquisition"), the reporting issuer should consider whether it needs to provide disclosure of the indirect acquisition in the business acquisition report, including historical financial statements, and whether the omission of these financial statements would cause the business acquisition report to be misleading, untrue or substantially incomplete. In making this determination, the reporting issuer should consider the following factors:

- if the indirect acquisition would meet any of the significance tests in section 8.3 of the Instrument when the reporting issuer applies each of those tests to its proportionate interest in the indirect acquisition of the business, and

- if the amount of time between the separate acquisitions is such that the effect of the first acquisition is not adequately reflected in the results of the business or related businesses the reporting issuer is acquiring.

(9) Pro Forma Financial Statements where Financial Statements of a Business or Related Businesses are Prepared using Accounting Principles that Differ from the Issuer's GAAP — Section 3.11 of National Instrument 52-107 *Acceptable Accounting Principles and Auditing Standards* permits reporting issuers to include in a business acquisition report financial statements of a business or related businesses prepared in accordance with U.S. GAAP and without a reconciliation to the issuer's GAAP. That section also permits, subject to specified conditions, a venture issuer to include in a business acquisition report financial statements of a business or related businesses prepared in accordance with Canadian GAAP applicable to private enterprises and without a reconciliation to the issuer's GAAP. However, section 3.14 of National Instrument 52-107 *Acceptable Accounting Principles and Auditing Standards* requires that pro forma financial statements be presented using accounting principles that are permitted by the issuer's GAAP and would apply to the information presented in the pro forma financial statements if that information were included in the issuer's financial statements for the same time period as that of the pro forma financial statements. As well, subsection 8.4(7) of the Instrument requires pro forma financial statements to include a description of the underlying assumptions on which the pro forma financial statements are prepared, cross-referenced to each related pro forma adjustment. Therefore, the pro forma financial statements must describe the adjustments presented in the pro forma income statement relating to the business or related businesses to adjust amounts to the issuer's GAAP and accounting policies.

The pro forma statement of financial position should present the following information:

(i) the statement of financial position of the reporting issuer;

(ii) the statement of financial position of the business or related businesses;

(iii) pro forma adjustments attributable to each significant acquisition that reflect the reporting issuer's accounting for the acquisition and include new values for the business' assets and liabilities; and

(iv) a pro forma statement of financial position combining items (i) through (iii).

The pro forma income statement should present the following information:

(i) the income statement of the reporting issuer;

(ii) the income statement of the business or related businesses;

(iii) pro forma adjustments attributable to each significant acquisition and other adjustments relating to the business or related businesses to conform amounts to the issuer's GAAP and accounting policies; and

(iv) a pro forma income statement combining items (i) through (iii).

8.7.1 Financial Year End Changed — If the transition year of the acquired business is less than 9 months, the issuer may be required to include financial statements for the transition year of the acquired business in addition to financial statements for the two financial years required by subsection 8.4(1) of the Instrument. The transition year may or may not be audited, but at minimum, the most recently completed financial year must be audited in accordance with subsection 8.4(2).

8.8 Relief from the Requirement to Audit Operating Statements of an Oil and Gas Property — The securities regulatory authority or regulator may exempt a reporting issuer from the requirement to audit the operating statements referred to in section 8.10 of the Instrument if, during the 12 months preceding the acquisition date, the average daily production of the property is less than 20 percent of the total average daily production of the vendor for the same or similar periods, and

(a) the reporting issuer provides written submissions prior to the deadline for filing the business acquisition report which establishes to the satisfaction of the appropriate regulator, that despite reasonable efforts during the purchase negotiations, the reporting issuer was prohibited from including in the purchase agreement the rights to obtain an audited operating statement of the property;

(b) the purchase agreement includes representations and warranties by the vendor that the amounts presented in the operating statement agree to the vendor's books and records; and

(c) the reporting issuer discloses in the business acquisition report its inability to obtain an audited operating statement, the reasons therefor, the fact that the representations and warranties referred to in paragraph (b) have been obtained, and a statement that the results presented in the operating statement may have been materially different if the statement had been audited.

For the purpose of determining average daily production when production includes both oil and natural gas, production may be expressed in barrels of oil equivalent using the conversion ratio of 6000 cubic feet of gas to one barrel of oil.

8.9 Exemptions From Requirement for Financial Statements in a Business Acquisition Report — (1) **Exemptions** — We are of the view that relief from the financial statement requirements of Part 8 of the Instrument should be granted only in unusual circumstances and generally not related solely to cost or the time involved in preparing and auditing the financial statements. Reporting issuers seeking relief from the financial statement or audit requirements of Part 8 must apply for the relief before the filing deadline for the business acquisition report and before the closing date of the transaction, if applicable. Reporting issuers are reminded that many securities regulatory authorities and regulators do not have the power to grant retroactive relief.

(2) **Conditions to Exemptions** — If relief is granted from the requirements of Part 8 of the Instrument to include audited annual financial statements of an acquired business or related businesses, conditions will likely be imposed, such as a requirement to include audited divisional or partial statements of comprehensive income or divisional statements of cash flows, or an audited statement of operations.

(3) **Exemption from Comparatives if Financial Statements Not Previously Prepared** — Section 8.9 of the Instrument provides that a reporting issuer does not have to provide comparative financial information for an acquired business in a business acquisition report if it complies with specific requirements. This exemption may, for example, apply to an acquired business that was, before the acquisition, a private entity and that the reporting issuer is unable to prepare the comparative financial information for because it is impracticable to do so.

(4) Relief may be granted from the requirement to include certain financial statements of an acquired business or related businesses in a business acquisition report in some situations that may include the following:

(a) the business's historical accounting records have been destroyed and cannot be reconstructed. In this case, as a condition of granting the exemption, the reporting issuer may be requested by the securities regulatory authority or regulator to

(i) represent in writing to the securities regulatory authority or regulator, no later than the time the business acquisition report is required to be filed, that the reporting issuer made every reasonable effort to obtain copies of, or reconstruct the historical accounting records necessary to prepare and audit the financial statements, but such efforts were unsuccessful; and

(ii) disclose in the business acquisition report the fact that the historical accounting records have been destroyed and cannot be reconstructed; or

(b) the business has recently emerged from bankruptcy and current management of the business and the reporting issuer is denied access to the historical accounting records necessary to audit the financial statements. In this case, as a condition of granting the exemption, the reporting issuer may be requested by the securities regulatory authority or regulator to

(i) represent in writing to the securities regulatory authority or regulator, no later than the time the business acquisition report is required to be filed that the reporting issuer has made every reasonable effort to obtain access to, or copies of, the historical accounting records necessary to audit the financial statements but that such efforts were unsuccessful; and

(ii) disclose in the business acquisition report the fact that the business has recently emerged from bankruptcy and current management of the business and the reporting issuer are denied access to the historical accounting records.

8.10 Audits and Auditor Review of Financial Statements of an Acquired Business — (1) **Unaudited Comparatives in Annual Financial Statements of an Acquired Business** — Subsection 8.4(1) requires a reporting issuer to include comparative financial information of the business in the business acquisition report. This comparative financial information may be unaudited.

(2) **Auditor Review of an Interim Financial Report of an Acquired Business** — An issuer does not have to engage an auditor to review the interim financial report of an acquired business included in a business acquisition report. However, if the issuer later incorporates the business acquisition report into a prospectus, the interim financial report will have to be reviewed in accordance with the requirements relating to financial statements included in a prospectus.

PART 9 — PROXY SOLICITATION AND INFORMATION CIRCULARS

9.1 Beneficial Owners of Securities — Reporting issuers are reminded that NI 54-101 prescribes certain procedures relating to the delivery of materials, including forms of proxy, to beneficial owners of securities and related matters. It also prescribes certain disclosure that must be included in the proxy-related materials sent to beneficial owners.

9.2 Prospectus-level Disclosure in Certain Information Circulars — Section 14.2 of Form 51-102F5 *Information Circular* requires an issuer to provide prospectus-level disclosure about certain entities if securityholder approval is required in respect of a significant acquisition under which securities of the acquired business are being exchanged for the issuer's securities or in respect of a restructuring transaction under which securities are to be changed, exchanged, issued or distributed.

Section 14.2 provides that the disclosure must be the disclosure (including financial statements) prescribed by the form of prospectus that the entity would be eligible to use immediately prior to the sending and filing of the information circular in respect of the significant acquisition or restructuring transaction, for a distribution of securities in the jurisdiction.

For example, if disclosure was required in an information circular of Company A for both Company A (an issuer that was only eligible to file a long form prospectus) and Company B (an issuer that was eligible to file a short form prospectus), the disclosure for Company A would be that required by the long form prospectus rules and the disclosure for Company B would be that required by the short form prospectus rules. Any information incorporated by reference in the information circular of Company A would have to comply with paragraph (c) of Part 1 of Form 51-102F5 and be filed under Company A's profile on SEDAR.

9.3 Proxy Solicitations Made to the Public by Broadcast, Speech or Publication — Subsection 9.2(4) of the Instrument provides an exemption from the proxy solicitation and information circular requirements for certain proxy solicitations made to the public by broadcast, speech or publication. The exemption permits securityholders to solicit proxies by public means, including a speech or broadcast, through a newspaper advertisement or over the Internet (provided that the solicitation contains certain information and that information is filed on SEDAR).

The exemption will only apply if the proxy solicitation is made to the public. Securities regulatory authorities generally consider a solicitation to be made to the public if it is disseminated in a manner calculated to effectively reach the marketplace. A solicitation to the public would generally include a solicitation that is made by:

(a) a speech in a public forum; or

(b) a press release, a statement or an advertisement provided through a broadcast medium or by a telephone conference call or electronic or other communication facility generally available to the public, or appearing in a newspaper, a magazine, a website or other publication generally available to the public.

A proxy solicitation to the public would generally not include a solicitation made by phone, mail or email to only a select group of securityholders of a reporting issuer.

PART 10 — ELECTRONIC DELIVERY OF DOCUMENTS

10.1 Electronic Delivery of Documents — Generally, any documents required to be sent under the Instrument may be sent by electronic delivery, as long as such delivery is consistent with the guidance in National Policy 11-201 *Electronic Delivery of Documents*. However, if a reporting issuer is using notice-and-access to deliver proxy-related materials, it should refer to the specific guidance in section 10.3 of the Policy.

10.2 Delivery of Proxy-Related Materials — (1) This section provides guidance on delivery of proxy-related materials. Reporting issuers should also review any other applicable legislation, such as corporate legislation.

(2) Paper copies of proxy-related materials must be sent using prepaid mail, courier or an equivalent delivery method. An equivalent delivery method is any delivery method where the registered holder receives paper copies in a similar time frame as prepaid mail or courier. For example, a reporting issuer that sponsors an employee share purchase plan could arrange for the proximate intermediary to deliver proxy-related materials to registered holder employees through the reporting issuer's internal mail system.

10.3 Notice-and-access — (1) This Instrument permits a reporting issuer to use notice-and-access to send proxy-related materials to registered holders.

(2) With respect to matters to be voted on at the meeting, the notice must only contain a description of each matter or group of related matters identified in the form of proxy, unless such information is already included in the form of proxy. We expect that reporting issuers who use notice-and-access will state each matter or group of related matters in the proxy in a reasonably clear and user-friendly manner. For example, it would be inappropriate to identify the matter to be voted on solely by referring to disclosure contained in the information circular as follows: "To vote For or Against the resolution in Schedule A of management's information circular".

The notice must contain a plain-language explanation of notice-and-access. The explanation also can address other aspects of the proxy voting process. However, there should not be any substantive discussion of the matters to be considered at the meeting.

(3) Paragraph 9.1.1(1)(b) of the Instrument requires the registered holder to be sent the form of proxy as part of the notice package. The notice package must be sent by prepaid mail, courier or the equivalent; however, section 9.1.3 permits an alternate delivery method (e.g., email) to be used if the registered holder's consent has been or is obtained. In the case of a solicitation by reporting issuer management, the notice package must be sent at least 30 days before the date fixed for the meeting.

(4) Paragraph 9.1.1(1)(c) of the Instrument requires the reporting issuer to file the notification of meeting and record dates required by subsection 2.2(1) of NI 54-101 in the manner and within the time specified by NI 54-101. See the guidance in Companion Policy 54-101CP to NI 54-101.

(5) Paragraph 9.1.1(1)(d) of the Instrument requires the notice, information circular and form of proxy to be filed on SEDAR and posted on a website other than SEDAR. The non-SEDAR website can be the website of the person or company soliciting proxies (e.g., the reporting issuer's website) or the website of a service provider.

(6) Paragraph 9.1.1(1)(e) of the Instrument requires the person or company soliciting proxies to establish a toll-free telephone number for the registered holder to request a paper copy of the information circular. A person or company soliciting proxies may choose to, but is not required to, provide additional methods for requesting a paper copy of the information circular. If a person or company soliciting proxies does so, it must still comply with the fulfillment timelines in paragraph 9.1.1(1)(f) of the Instrument.

(7) Subsection 9.1.2(2) of the Instrument is intended to allow registered holders to access the posted proxy-related materials in a user-friendly manner. For example, requiring the registered holder to navigate through several web pages to access the proxy-related materials would not be user-friendly. Providing the registered holder with the specific URL where the documents are posted would be more user-friendly. We encourage reporting issuers and their service providers to develop best practices in this regard.

(8) Where a reporting issuer uses notice-and-access, it generally must send the same basic notice package to all registered holders. However, the following are exceptions to this general principle:

- Section 9.1.3 of the Instrument provides that where a reporting issuer uses notice-and-access, a registered holder still can be sent proxy-related materials using an alternate method to which the registered holder has previously consented. For example, service providers acting on behalf of reporting issuers or intermediaries may have previously obtained (and continue to obtain) consents from registered holders for proxy-related materials to be sent by email. This delivery method would still be available.

- Section 9.1.4 of the Instrument permits a reporting issuer to obtain standing instructions from a registered holder to be sent a paper copy of the information circular and if applicable, annual financial statements and annual MD&A in all cases where the reporting issuer uses notice-and-access. Where such standing instructions have been obtained, the notice package for the registered holder will contain a paper copy of the relevant documents.

(9) The addition of a paper information circular to the notice package sent to some registered holders is referred to as "stratification" and is a term defined in section 1.1 of the Instrument and in NI 54-101.

We do not mandate the use of stratification, except if it is necessary to comply with standing instructions or other requests for paper copies of information circulars that reporting issuers or intermediaries have chosen to obtain from registered holders or beneficial owners. We expect that any additional stratification criteria will develop and evolve through market demand and practice. However, we expect that a reporting issuer that uses stratification for purposes other than complying with registered holder instructions does so in order to enhance effective communication, and not to disenfranchise registered holders. We require reporting issuers to disclose whether they are using stratification, and what criteria they are applying to determine which types of registered holders will receive a copy of the information circular.

PART 11 — ADDITIONAL DISCLOSURE REQUIREMENTS

11.1 Additional Filing Requirements — Paragraph 11.1(1)(b) of the Instrument requires a document to be filed only if it contains information that has not been included in disclosure already filed by the reporting issuer. For example, if a reporting issuer has filed a material change report under the Instrument and the Form 8-K filed by the reporting issuer with the SEC discloses the same information, whether in the same or a different format, there is no requirement to file the Form 8-K under the Instrument.

11.2 Re-filing Documents or Re-stating Financial Information — If a reporting issuer decides to re-file a document, or re-state financial information for comparative periods in financial statements for reasons other than retroactive application of a change in an accounting standard or policy or a new accounting standard, and the re-filed or re-stated information is likely to differ materially from the information originally filed, the issuer should disclose in the news release required by section 11.5 of the Instrument when it makes that decision

    (a) the facts underlying the changes,

    (b) the general impact of the changes on previously filed information, and

    (c) the steps the issuer would take before filing an amended document, or filing re-stated financial information, if the issuer is not filing amended information immediately.

PART 12 — FILING OF CERTAIN DOCUMENTS

12.1 Statutory or Regulatory Instruments — Paragraph 12.1(1)(a) of the Instrument requires reporting issuers to file copies of their articles of incorporation, amalgamation, continuation or any other constating or establishing documents, unless the document is a statutory or regulatory instrument. This carve out for a statutory or regulatory instrument is very narrow. For example, the carve out would apply to Schedule I or Schedule II banks under the Bank Act, whose charter is the Bank Act. It would not apply when only the form of the constating document is prescribed under statute or regulation, such as articles under the Canada Business Corporations Act.

12.2 Contracts that Affect the Rights or Obligations of Securityholders — Paragraph 12.1(1)(e) of the Instrument requires reporting issuers to file copies of contracts that can reasonably be regarded as materially affecting the rights of their securityholders generally. A warrant indenture is one example of this type of contract. We would expect that contracts entered into in the ordinary course of business would not usually affect the rights of securityholders generally, and so would not have to be filed under this paragraph.

12.3 Material Contracts — (1) **Definition** — Under subsection 1.1(1) of the Instrument, a material contract is defined as a contract that a reporting issuer or any of its subsidiaries is a party to, that is material to the reporting issuer. A material contract generally includes a schedule, side letter or exhibit referred to in the material contract and any amendment to the material contract. The redaction and omission provisions in subsections 12.2(3) and (4) of the Instrument apply to these schedules, side letters, exhibits or amendments.

(2) **Filing Requirements** — Subject to the exceptions in paragraphs 12.2(2)(a) through (f) of the Instrument, subsection 12.2(2) of the Instrument provides an exemption from the filing requirement for a material contract entered into in the ordinary course of business. Whether a reporting issuer entered into a contract in the ordinary course of business is a question of fact that the reporting issuer should consider in the context of its business and industry.

Paragraphs 12.2(2)(a) through (f) of the Instrument describe specific types of material contracts that are not eligible for the ordinary course of business exemption. Accordingly, if subsection 12.2(1) of the Instrument requires a reporting issuer to file a material contract of a type described in these paragraphs, the reporting issuer must file that material contract even if the reporting issuer entered into it in the ordinary course of business.

(3) **Contract of Employment** — Paragraph 12.2(2)(a) of the Instrument provides that a material contract with certain individuals is not eligible for the ordinary course of business exemption, unless it is a "contract of employment". One way for reporting issuers to determine whether a contract is a contract of employment is to consider whether the contract contains payment or other provisions that are required disclosure under Form 51-102F6 as if the individual were a named executive officer or director of the reporting issuer.

(4) **External Management and External Administration Agreements** — Under paragraph 12.2(2)(e) of the Instrument, external management and external administration agreements are not eligible for the ordinary course of business exemption. External management and external administration

agreements include agreements between the reporting issuer and a third party, the reporting issuer's parent entity, or an affiliate of the reporting issuer, under which the latter provides management or other administrative services to the reporting issuer.

(5) Material Contracts on which the Reporting Issuer's Business is Substantially Dependent — Paragraph 12.2(1)(f) of the Instrument provides that a material contract on which the "reporting issuer's business is substantially dependent" is not eligible for the ordinary course of business exemption. Generally, a contract on which the reporting issuer's business is substantially dependent is a contract so significant that the reporting issuer's business depends on the continuance of the contract. Some examples of this type of contract include:

(a) a financing or credit agreement providing a majority of the reporting issuer's capital requirements for which alternative financing is not readily available at comparable terms;

(b) a contract calling for the acquisition or sale of substantially all of the reporting issuer's property, plant and equipment, long-lived assets, or total assets; and

(c) an option, joint venture, purchase or other agreement relating to a mining or oil and gas property that represents a majority of the reporting issuer's business.

(6) Confidentiality Provisions — Under subsection 12.2(3) of the Instrument, a reporting issuer may omit or redact a provision of a material contract that is required to be filed if an executive officer of the reporting issuer has reasonable grounds to believe that disclosure of the omitted or redacted provision would violate a confidentiality provision. A provision of the type described in paragraphs 12.2(4)(a), (b) or (c) of the Instrument may not be omitted or redacted even if disclosure would violate a confidentiality provision, including a blanket confidentiality provision covering the entire material contract.

When negotiating material contracts with third parties, reporting issuers should consider their disclosure obligations under securities legislation. A regulator or securities regulatory authority may consider granting an exemption to permit a provision of the type listed in subsection 12.2(4) of the Instrument to be redacted if:

(a) the disclosure of that provision would violate a confidentiality provision; and

(b) the material contract was negotiated before the adoption of the exceptions in subsection 12.2(4) of the Instrument.

The regulator may consider the following factors, among others, in deciding whether to grant an exemption:

(c) whether an executive officer of the reporting issuer reasonably believes that the disclosure of the provisions would be prejudicial to the interests of the reporting issuer; and

(d) whether the reporting issuer is unable to obtain a waiver of the confidentiality provision from the other party.

(7) Disclosure Seriously Prejudicial to Interests of Reporting Issuer — Under subsection 12.2(3) of the Instrument, a reporting issuer may omit or redact certain provisions of a material contract that is required to be filed if an executive officer of the reporting issuer reasonably believes that disclosure of the omitted or redacted provision would be seriously prejudicial to the interests of the reporting issuer. One example of disclosure that may be seriously prejudicial to the interests of the reporting issuer is disclosure of information in violation of applicable Canadian privacy legislation. However, in situations where securities legislation requires disclosure of the particular type of information, applicable privacy legislation generally provides an exemption for the disclosure. Generally, disclosure of information that a reporting issuer or other party has already publicly disclosed is not seriously prejudicial to the interests of the reporting issuer.

(8) Terms Necessary for Understanding Impact on Business of Reporting Issuer — A reporting issuer may not omit or redact a provision of a type described in paragraph 12.2(4)(a), (b), or (c) of the Instrument. Paragraph 12.2(4)(c) of the Instrument provides that a reporting issuer may not omit or redact "terms necessary for understanding the impact of the material contract on the business of the reporting issuer". Terms that may be necessary for understanding the impact of the material contract on the business of the reporting issuer include the following:

(a) the duration and nature of a patent, trademark, license, franchise, concession, or similar agreement;

(b) disclosure about related party transactions; and

(c) contingency, indemnification, anti-assignability, take-or-pay clauses, or change-of-control clauses.

(9) Summary of Omitted or Redacted Provisions — Under subsection 12.2(5) of the Instrument, a reporting issuer must include a description of the type of information that has been omitted or redacted in the copy of the material contract filed by the reporting issuer. A brief one-sentence description immediately following the omitted or redacted information is generally sufficient.

PART 13 — EXEMPTIONS

13.1 Prior Exemptions and Waivers — Section 13.2 of the Instrument essentially allows a reporting issuer, in certain circumstances, to continue to rely upon an exemption or waiver from continuous disclosure obligations obtained prior to the Instrument coming into force if the exemption or waiver relates to a substantially similar provision in the Instrument and the reporting issuer provides written notice to the securities regulatory authority or regulator of its reliance on such exemption or waiver. Upon receipt of such notice, the securities regulatory authority or regulator, as the case may be, will review it to determine if the provision of the Instrument referred to in the notice is substantially similar to the provision from which the prior exemption or waiver was granted. The written notice should be sent to each jurisdiction where the prior exemption or waiver is relied upon. Contact addresses for these notices are:

Alberta Securities Commission

4th Floor

300-5th Avenue S.W.

Calgary, Alberta

T2P 3C4

Attention: Director, Corporate Finance

British Columbia Securities Commission

P.O. Box 10142, Pacific Centre

701 West Georgia Street

Vancouver, British Columbia

V7Y 1L2

Attention: Financial Reporting

Manitoba Securities Commission

500 — 400 St. Mary Avenue

Winnipeg, Manitoba

R3C 4K5

Attention: Corporate Finance

New Brunswick Securities Commission

85 Charlotte Street, Suite 300

Saint John, N.B.

E2L 2J2

Attention: Corporate of Finance

Securities Commission of Newfoundland and Labrador

P.O. Box 8700

2nd Floor, West Block

Confederation Building

75 O'Leary Avenue

St. John's, NFLD

A1B 4J6

Attention: Director of Securities

Department of Justice, Northwest Territories

Securities Office

P.O. Box 1320

1st Floor, 5009-49th Street

Yellowknife, NWT X1A 2L9

Attention: Superintendent of Securities

Nova Scotia Securities Commission

2nd Floor, Joseph Howe Building

1690 Hollis Street

Halifax, Nova Scotia B3J 3J9

Attention: Corporate Finance

Department of Justice, Nunavut

Legal Registries Division

P.O. Box 1000 — Station 570

1st Floor, Brown Building

Iqaluit, NT X0A 0H0

Attention: Superintendent of Securities

Ontario Securities Commission

Suite 1903, Box 55

20 Queen Street West

Toronto, ON M5H 3S8

Attention: Manager, Team 3, Corporate Finance

Registrar of Securities, Prince Edward Island

P.O. Box 2000

95 Rochford Street, 5th Floor,

Charlottetown, PEI

C1A 7N8

Attention: Registrar of Securities

Autorité des marchés financiers

800 Square Victoria, 22nd Floor

P.O. Box 246, Tour de la Bourse

Montréal, Québec

H4Z 1G3

Attention: Direction des marchés des capitaux

Saskatchewan Financial Services Commission — Securities Division

Suite 601
1919 Saskatchewan Drive
Regina, SK S4P 4H2
Attention: Deputy Director, Corporate Finance

Superintendent of Securities, Government of Yukon
Corporate Affairs J-9
P.O. Box 2703
Whitehorse, Yukon
Y1A 5H3
Attention: Superintendent of Securities

PART 14 — TRANSITION

14.1 Transition — Application of Amendments — The amendments to the Instrument and this Policy which came into effect on January 1, 2011 only apply to documents required to be prepared, filed, delivered or sent under the Instrument for periods relating to financial years beginning on or after January 1, 2011.

APPENDIX A — EXAMPLES OF FILING REQUIREMENTS FOR CHANGES IN THE YEAR END

The following examples assume the old financial year ended on December 31, 20X0

Transition Year	Comparative Annual Financial Statements to Transition Year	New Financial Year	Comparaive Annual Financial Statements to New Financial Year	Interim Periods for Transition Year	Comparative Interim Periods to Interim Periods in Transition Year	Interim Periods for New Financial Year	Comparative Interim Periods to Interim Periods in New Financial Year
Financial year end changed by up to 3 months							
2 months ended 2/28/X1	12 months ended 12/31/X0	2/28/X2	2 months ended 2/28/X1 and 12 months ended 12/31/X0*	Not applicable	Not applicable	3 months ended 5/31/X1 6 months ended 8/31/X1 9 months ended 11/30/X1	3 months ended 6/30/X0 6 months ended 9/30/X0 9 months ended 12/31/X0
Or							
14 months ended 2/28/X2	12 months ended 12/31/X0	2/28/X3	14 months ended 2/28/X2	3 months ended 3/31/X1 6 months ended 6/30/X1 9 months ended 9/30/X1 12 months ended 12/31/X1	3 months ended 3/31/X0 6 months ended 6/30/X0 9 months ended 9/30/X0 12 months ended 12/31/X0	3 months ended 5/31/X2 6 months ended 8/31/X2 9 months ended 11/30/X2	3 months ended 6/30/X1 6 months ended 9/30/X1 9 months ended 12/31/X1
				or			
				2 months ended 2/28/X1 5 months ended 5/31/X1 8 months ended 8/31/X1 11 months ended 11/30/X1	3 months ended 3/31/X0 6 months ended 6/30/X0 9 months ended 9/30/X0 12 months ended 12/31/X0	3 months ended 5/31/X2 6 months ended 8/31/X2 9 months ended 11/30/X2	3 months ended 6/30/X1 6 months ended 9/30/X1 9 months ended 12/31/X1
Financial year end changed by 4 to 6 months							
6 months ended 6/30/X1	12 months ended 12/31/X0	6/30/X2	6 months ended 6/30/X1 and 12 months ended 12/31/X0*	3 months ended 3/31/X1	3 months ended 3/31/X0	3 months ended 9/30/X1 6 months ended 12/31/X1 9 months ended 3/31/X2	3 months ended 9/30/X0 6 months ended 12/31/X0 9 months ended 3/31/X1
Financial year end changed by 7 or 8 months							
7 months ended 7/31/X1	12 months ended 12/31/X0	7/31/X2	7 months ended 7/31/X1 and 12 months ended 12/31/X0*	3 months ended 3/31/X1	3 months ended 3/31/X0	3 months ended 10/31/X1 6 months ended 1/31/X2 9 months ended 4/30/X1	3 months ended 9/30/X0 6 months ended 12/31/X0 9 months ended 3/31/X1

Or

Transition Year	Comparative Annual Financial Statements to Transition Year	New Financial Year	Comparaive Annual Financial Statements to New Financial Year	Interim Periods for Transition Year	Comparative Interim Periods to Interim Periods in Transition Year	Interim Periods for New Financial Year	Comparative Interim Periods to Interim Periods in New Financial Year
				4 months ended 4/30/X1	3 months ended 3/31/X0	3 months ended 10/31/X1 6 months ended 1/31/X2 9 months ended 4/30/X1	3 months ended 9/30/X0 6 months ended 12/31/X0 10 months ended 4/30/X1

Financial year end changed by 9 to 11 months

Transition Year	Comparative Annual Financial Statements to Transition Year	New Financial Year	Comparaive Annual Financial Statements to New Financial Year	Interim Periods for Transition Year	Comparative Interim Periods to Interim Periods in Transition Year	Interim Periods for New Financial Year	Comparative Interim Periods to Interim Periods in New Financial Year
10 months ended 10/31/X1	12 months ended 12/31/X0	10/31/X2	10 months ended 10/31/X1	3 months ended 3/31/X1 6 months ended 6/30/X1	3 months ended 3/31/X0 6 months ended 6/30/X0	3 months ended 1/31/X2 6 months ended 4/30/X2 9 months ended 7/31/X2	3 months ended 12/31/X0 6 months ended 3/31/X1 9 months ended 6/30/X1
				or			
				4 months ended 4/30/X1 7 months ended 7/31/X1	3 months ended 3/31/X0 6 months ended 6/30/X0	3 months ended 1/31/X2 6 months ended 4/30/X2 9 months ended 7/31/X2	3 months ended 12/31/X0 6 months ended 3/31/X1 9 months ended 6/30/X1

* Statement of financial position required only at the transition year end date

Notes:

1 This decision chart provides general guidance and should be read in conjunction with National Instrument 51-102 and Companion Policy 51-102CP.

2 If an acquisition of related businesses constitutes a significant acquisition when the results of the related businesses are combined, the required financial statements shall be provided for each of the related businesses, except for the periods during which the businesses have been under common control or management, in which case the reporting issuer may present the financial statements of the businesses on a combined basis.

3 As an alternative to the most recent interim period, financial statements for the acquired business may be provided for the period that started the day after the business' most recent annual Statement of financial position and ended on a day that is more recent than the ending date of the most recent interim period otherwise required and is not later than the date of acquisition.

Adoption by OSC: (2004) 27 O.S.C.B. 3476 and (2003) 26 O.S.C.B. (Supp-3) 1 (December 19, 2003); Request for Comments: (2003) 26 O.S.C.B. 4577 and (2002) 25 O.S.C.B. 3701.

Adoption of Amendment by OSC: (2007) 30 O.S.C.B. (Supp-1) 143; (2006) 29 O.S.C.B. (Supp-2) 1; Request for Comments: (2008) 28 O.S.C.B. 9845.

Adoption of Amendment by OSC: 30 O.S.C.B. 10499 and 8570; Request for Comments: 30 O.S.C.B. 2969.

Adoption of Amendment by OSC: 30 O.S.C.B. 10512 and 8539; Request for Comments: 29 O.S.C.B. 9339.

Adoption of Amendment by OSC: 31 O.S.C.B. (Supp. 2) 235 (March 7, 2008) and 30 O.S.C.B. (Supp 7) 1 (Dec. 21, 2007); Request for Comments: 29 O.S.C.B. (Supp 3) 1 (Dec. 22, 2006).

Adoption of Amendment by OSC: 31 O.S.C.B. 6571 and 4261; Request for Comments: 30 O.S.C.B. 8570.

Adoption of Amendment by OSC: 32 O.S.C.B. 11350.

Adoption of Amendment to Policy: 33 O.S.C.B. (Supp. 5) 67 and (Supp. 3) 113; Request for Comments: 32 O.S.C.B. (Supp. 6) 1.

Adoption of Amendment by OSC: (2012) 35 O.S.C.B. 10709; Request for Comments: (2011) 34 O.S.C.B. 6769 and (2010) 33 O.S.C.B. 3109.

Adoption of Amendment by OSC: (2014) 37 O.S.C.B. 6753; Request for Comments: (2013) 36 O.S.C.B. 10147.

Adoption of Amendment by OSC: (2015) 38 O.S.C.B. 3431.

Rules: NI 51-102, 81-106; Rule 51-801.

Policies and Orders: OPS 51-601, 51-801CP; CSAN 51-304, 51-310, 51-312, 51-316, 52-312; OSCN 51-706.

National Policy 51-201 — Disclosure Standards

Date: July 12, 2002, as amended effective December 31, 2007 and May 31, 2013

25 O.S.C.B. 4492, 30 O.S.C.B. 10524 and 36 O.S.C.B. 2619

Table of Contents

PART I — INTRODUCTION

1.1 Purpose — (1) It is fundamental that everyone investing in securities have equal access to information that may affect their investment decisions. The Canadian Securities Administrators ("the CSA" or "We") are concerned about the selective disclosure of material corporate information by companies to analysts, institutional investors, investment dealers and other market professionals. Selective disclosure occurs when a company discloses material nonpublic information to one or more individuals or companies and not broadly to the investing public. Selective disclosure can create opportunities for insider trading and also undermines retail investors' confidence in the marketplace as a level playing field.

(2) This policy provides guidance on "best disclosure" practices in a difficult area involving competing business pressures and legislative requirements. Our recommendations are not intended to be prescriptive. We encourage companies to adopt the suggested measures, but they should be implemented flexibly and sensibly to fit the situation of individual companies.

(3) The timely disclosure requirements and prohibitions against selective disclosure are substantially similar everywhere in Canada, but there are differences among the provinces and territories, so companies should carefully review the legislation which is applicable to them for the details.

PART II — TIMELY DISCLOSURE

2.1 Timely Disclosure — (1) Companies are required by law to immediately disclose a "material change"[1] in their business. For changes that a company initiates, the change occurs once the decision has been made to implement it. This may happen even before a company's directors approve it,

---

[1]Securities legislation defines the term material change as "a change in the business, operations or capital of the issuer that would reasonably be expected to have a significant effect on the market price or value of any of the securities of the issuer and includes a decision to implement such a change made by the board

if the company thinks it is probable they will do so. A company discloses a material change by issuing and filing a press release describing the change. A company must also file a material change report as soon as practicable, and no later than 10 days after the change occurs. This policy statement does not alter in any way the timely disclosure obligations of companies.

(2) Announcements of material changes should be factual and balanced. Unfavourable news must be disclosed just as promptly and completely as favourable news. Companies that disclose positive news but withhold negative news could find their disclosure practices subject to scrutiny by securities regulators. A company's press release should contain enough detail to enable the media and investors to understand the substance and importance of the change it is disclosing. Avoid including unnecessary details, exaggerated reports or promotional commentary.

2.2 Confidentiality — (1) Securities legislation permits a company to delay disclosure of a material change and to keep it confidential temporarily where immediate release of the information would be unduly detrimental to the company's interests.[2] For example, immediate disclosure might interfere with a company's pursuit of a specific objective or strategy, with ongoing negotiations, or with its ability to complete a transaction. If the harm to a company's business from disclosing outweighs the general benefit to the market of immediate disclosure, withholding disclosure is justified. In such cases a company may withhold public disclosure, but it must make a confidential filing with the securities commission.[3] Certain jurisdictions also require companies to renew the confidential filing every 10 days should they want to continue to keep the information confidential.

(2) We discourage companies from delaying disclosure for a lengthy period of time as it becomes less likely that confidentiality can be maintained beyond the short term.

2.3 Maintaining Confidentiality — (1) Where disclosure of a material change is delayed, a company must maintain complete confidentiality. During the period before a material change is disclosed, market activity in the company's securities should be carefully monitored. Any unusual market activity may mean that news of the matter has been leaked and that certain persons are taking advantage of it. If the confidential material change, or rumours about it, have leaked or appear to be impacting the share price, a company should take immediate steps to ensure that a full public announcement is made. This would include contacting the relevant exchange and asking that trading be halted pending the issuance of a news release.[4]

(2) Where a material change is being kept confidential, the company is under a duty to make sure that persons with knowledge of the material change have not made use of such information in purchasing or selling its securities. Such information should not be disclosed to any person or company, except in the necessary course of business.

PART III — OVERVIEW OF THE STATUTORY PROHIBITIONS AGAINST SELECTIVE DISCLOSURE

3.1 Tipping and Insider Trading — (1) Securities legislation prohibits a reporting issuer and any person or company in a *special relationship* with a reporting issuer from informing, other than in the *necessary course of business*[5], anyone of a *"material fact"*[6] or a *"material change"* (or *"privileged information"* in the case of Québec)[7] before that material information[8] has been *generally disclosed*.[9] This prohibited activity is commonly known as "tipping".

(2) Securities legislation also prohibits anyone in a special relationship with a reporting issuer from purchasing or selling securities of the reporting issuer[10] with knowledge of a material fact or material change about the issuer that has not been generally disclosed.[11] This prohibited activity is commonly known as "insider trading".

(3) Securities legislation prohibits any person or company who is proposing:

> to make a take-over bid;
>
> to become a party to a reorganization, amalgamation, merger, arrangement or similar business combination; or

---

of directors of the issuer or by senior management of the issuer who believe that confirmation of the decision by the board of directors is probable". The Québec Securities Act does not define the term "material change" and provides that "where a material change occurs that is likely to have a significant influence on the value or the market price of the securities of a reporting issuer and is not generally known, the reporting issuer shall immediately prepare and distribute a press release disclosing the substance of the change". See also *Pezim v. British Columbia (Superintendent of Brokers)*, [1994] 2 S.C.R. 557, where the Supreme Court held that a change in assay and drilling results was a material change in the company's assets.

[2]Confidentiality is also permitted in situations where the material change consists of a decision to implement a change made by the company's senior management, who believe that confirmation of the decision by the company's board of directors is probable.

[3]While the Québec Securities Act does not require a confidential filing, it does relieve a company from the obligation to disclose a material change if senior management reasonably believes that (i) disclosure would be seriously prejudicial to it; and (ii) no one has purchased or sold, or will purchase and sell its securities based on the undisclosed information. A company must issue and file a press release once the reasons for not disclosing no longer exist.

[4]See The Toronto Stock Exchange Statement on Timely Disclosure and Related Guidelines and the TSX Venture Exchange Policy 3.3 Timely Disclosure.

[5]The Alberta and British Columbia Securities Acts use the phrase "is necessary in the course of business". The Québec Securities Act uses the phrase in the "course of business".

[6]Securities legislation defines a "material fact" as follows: "material fact, where used in relation to securities issued or proposed to be issued means a fact that significantly affects, or would reasonably be expected to have a significant effect on, the market price or value of such securities".

[7]"Privileged information" is defined under the Québec Securities Act as "any information that has not been disclosed to the public and that could affect the decision of a reasonable investor".

[8]Material facts and material changes are collectively referred to as "material information." When used in the Policy, material information means both "material facts" and "material changes."

[9]The Québec Securities Act uses the term "generally known".

[10]For the purposes of the prohibition against illegal insider trading, a "security of the reporting issuer" is deemed to include a security, the market price of which varies materially with the market price of the securities of the issuer (see subsection 76(6)(b) of the Ontario Securities Act).

[11]Section 187 of the Québec Securities Act provides that "no insider of a reporting issuer having privileged information relating to securities of the issuer may trade in such securities except in the following cases: (i) he is justified in believing that the information is generally known or known to the other party; (ii) he avails himself of an automatic dividend reinvestment plan, automatic subscription plan or any other automatic plan established by a reporting issuer, according to conditions set down in writing, before he learned the information". Section 189 further expands the number of persons who are subject to the prohibition in section 187.

to acquire a substantial portion of a company's property

from informing anyone of material information that has not been generally disclosed. An exception to this disclosure prohibition is provided where the material information is given in the "necessary course of business" to effect the take-over bid, business combination or acquisition.

(4) It is important to remember that the tipping and insider trading provisions apply to both material facts and material changes. A company's timely disclosure obligations generally only apply to material changes. This means that a company does not have to disclose all material facts on a continuous basis. However, if a company chooses to selectively disclose a material fact, other than in the necessary course of business, this would be in breach of securities legislation.

3.2 Persons Subject to Tipping Provisions — (1) The tipping provisions generally apply to anyone in a "special relationship" with a reporting issuer.[12] Persons in a special relationship include, but are not limited to:

(a) insiders as defined under securities legislation;

(b) directors, officers and employees;

(c) persons engaging in professional or business activities for or on behalf of the company; and

(d) anyone (a "tippee") who learns of material information from someone that the tippee knows or should know is a person in a special relationship with the company.

(2) The "special relationship" definition is broad. The tipping prohibition is not limited to communications made by senior management, investor relations professionals and others who regularly communicate with analysts, institutional investors and market professionals. The tipping prohibition applies, for example, to unauthorized disclosures by non-management employees.

(3) There is a potentially infinite chain of tippees who are caught by the prohibitions against tipping and insider trading. Because tippees are themselves considered to be in a special relationship with a reporting issuer, material information may be third or fourth hand and still be subject to the prohibitions.

(4) Because the "special relationship" definition is so broad, it is important that companies establish corporate disclosure policies and clearly define who within the company has responsibility for corporate communications.

3.3 Necessary Course of Business — (1) The "tipping" provision allows a company to make a selective disclosure if doing so is in the "necessary course of business". The question of whether a particular disclosure is being made in the necessary course of business is a mixed question of law and fact that must be determined in each case and in light of the policy reasons for the tipping provisions. Tipping is prohibited so that everyone in the market has equal access to, and opportunity to act upon, material information. Insider trading and tipping prohibitions are designed to ensure that anyone who has access to material undisclosed information does not trade or assist others in trading to the disadvantage of investors generally.

(2) Different interpretations are being applied, in practice, to the phrase "necessary course of business".[13] As a result, we believe interpretive guidance in this regard is necessary. The "necessary course of business" exception exists so as not to unduly interfere with a company's ordinary business activities. For example, the "necessary course of business" exception would generally cover communications with:

(a) vendors, suppliers, or strategic partners on issues such as research and development, sales and marketing, and supply contracts;

(b) employees, officers, and board members;

(c) lenders, legal counsel, auditors, underwriters, and financial and other professional advisors to the company;

(d) parties to negotiations;

(e) labour unions and industry associations;

(f) government agencies and non-governmental regulators; and

(g) credit rating agencies (provided that the information is disclosed for the purpose of assisting the agency to formulate a credit rating and the agency's ratings generally are or will be publicly available).

(3) Securities legislation prohibits any person or company that is proposing to make a take-over bid, become a party to a reorganization, amalgamation, merger, arrangement or similar business combination or acquire a substantial portion of a company's property from informing anyone of material information that has not been generally disclosed. An exception to this prohibition is provided where the material information is given in the "necessary course of business" to effect the take-over bid, business combination or acquisition.

(4) Disclosures by a company in connection with a private placement may be in the "necessary course of business" for companies to raise financing. The ability to raise financing is important. We recognize that select communications between the parties to a private placement of material information may be necessary to effect the private placement.[14] Communications to controlling shareholders may also, in certain circumstances, be considered in

---

[12]The tipping prohibition in Québec applies to insiders and persons listed in section 189 of the Québec Securities Act. Québec securities legislation extends the prohibition to communications by persons having privileged information that, to their knowledge, was disclosed by an insider, affiliate, associate or by any other person having acquired privileged information in the course of his relations with the reporting issuer and by persons having acquired privileged information that these persons know to be such.

[13]See *Re Royal Trustco Ltd. et al. and Ontario Securities Commission* (1983), 42 O.R. (2d) 147 (Div. Ct.) affirming (1981), 2 O.S.C.B. 322C. In Royal Trustco, it was alleged that two officers had revealed to a major shareholder, other than in the "necessary course of business" certain material facts in relation to the affairs of Royal Trustco that had not been generally disclosed including: (i) that approximately 60% of the shares of Royal Trustco were owned by persons or companies who the officers knew or had reason to believe would not tender pursuant to a bid; and (ii) that Royal Trustco management was considering recommending to the board that the dividends payable on the Royal Trustco shares be increased. The Court held that the information disclosed fell within the category of material facts and that such material facts had been made available to such shareholder not "in the necessary course of business" from Royal Trustco's perspective.

[14]Securities legislation provides an exemption from the insider trading and selective disclosure prohibition where the person or company who trades with material undisclosed information or tips it proves that they reasonably believed that the other party to the trade or the tippee had knowledge of the information. Under the Québec Securities Act, the person or company must be justified in believing that the information is known to the other party.

the "necessary course of business."[15] Nevertheless, we believe that in these situations, material information that is provided to private placees and controlling shareholders should be generally disclosed at the earliest opportunity.

(5) The "necessary course of business" exception would not generally permit a company to make a selective disclosure of material corporate information to an analyst, institutional investor or other market professional.[16]

(6) There may be situations where an analyst will be "brought over the wall" to act as an advisor in a specific transaction involving a reporting issuer they would normally issue research about. In these situations, the analyst becomes a "person in a special relationship" with the reporting issuer and is subject to the prohibitions against tipping and insider trading. This means that the analyst is prohibited from further informing anyone of material undisclosed information they learn in this advisory capacity, including issuing any research recommendations or reports.[17]

(7) We draw a distinction between disclosures to credit rating agencies, which would generally be regarded as being in the "necessary course of business," and disclosures to analysts, which would not be. This distinction is based on differences in the nature of the business they are engaged in and in how they use the information. The credit ratings generated by rating agencies are either confidential (disclosed only to the company seeking the rating) or directed at a wide public audience. Generally, the objective of the rating process is a widely available publication of the rating.[18] The reports generated by analysts are targeted, first and foremost, to an analyst's firm's clients. Also, rating agencies are not in the business of trading in the securities they rate. Sell-side analysts are typically employed by investment dealers that are in the business of buying and selling, underwriting, and advising with respect to securities. Further, securities legislation requires specified ratings from designated rating organizations in certain circumstances.[19] Consequently, ratings form part of the statutory framework of provincial securities legislation in a way that analysts' reports do not.

(8) When companies communicate with the media, they should be mindful not to selectively disclose material information that has not been generally disclosed. The "necessary course of business" exception would not generally permit a company to make a selective disclosure of material undisclosed information to the media. However, we are not suggesting that companies should stop speaking to the media. We recognize that the media can play an important role in informing and educating the marketplace.

3.4 Necessary Course of Business Disclosures and Confidentiality — (1) If a company discloses material information under the "necessary course of business" exception, it should make sure those receiving the information understand that they cannot pass the information onto anyone else (other than in the necessary course of business), or trade on the information, until it has been generally disclosed.

(2) We understand that companies sometimes disclose material information pursuant to a confidentiality agreement with the recipient, so that the recipient is prevented from further informing anyone of the material information. Obtaining a confidentiality agreement in these circumstances can be a good practice and may help to safeguard the confidentiality of the information. However, there is no exception to the prohibition against "tipping" for disclosures made pursuant to a confidentiality agreement. The only exception is for disclosures made in the "necessary course of business." Consequently, there must still be a determination, prior to disclosure supported by a confidentiality agreement, that such disclosure is in the "necessary course of business."

3.5 Generally Disclosed — (1) The tipping prohibition does not require a company to release all material information to the marketplace.[20] Instead, it prohibits a company from disclosing nonpublic material information to anyone (other than in the "necessary course of business") before the company generally discloses the information to the marketplace.

(2) Securities legislation does not define the term "generally disclosed". Insider trading court decisions state that information has been generally disclosed if:

(a) the information has been disseminated in a manner calculated to effectively reach the marketplace; and

(b) public investors have been given a reasonable amount of time to analyze the information.[21]

---

[15]For example, a company may need to share sensitive strategic information with a controlling shareholder when preparing consolidated financial statements.

[16]See *In the Matter of Gary George* (1999), 22 OSCB 717, where the Ontario Securities Commission addressed in obiter the issue of a selective disclosure made by an issuer's chief executive officer to an analyst and the subsequent disclosure by the analyst to other members of his firm. We agree with the principles expressed by the Ontario Securities Commission:

It would appear that some corporate officers see the maintenance of good relations with analysts as being more important than ensuring equality of material information among shareholders. The fact that it was thought that [the analyst] was about to come out with a report as to [the issuer] which would overvalue its shares would in no way justify [the President] giving the information to [the analyst] rather than publicly disseminating it. If the information was material enough to cause [the analyst] to change his projections, it should have been publicly disseminated. In general, we view one-on-one discussions between an officer of a reporting issuer and an analyst as being fraught with difficulties.

Also see *In the Matter of Air Canada*, where employees of the company disclosed information about third quarter earnings per share results and a revised forecast for the next quarter to 13 analysts who covered the company but not to the marketplace generally. In the Excerpt from the Settlement Hearing Containing the Oral Reasons for Decision, the Ontario Securities Commission said:

Communication by a corporation with analysts is not covered under some exception; so what is disclosed to analysts, if it is material and will significantly affect the market price, or reasonably may be expected to significantly affect the market price of the shares of the issuer, should not be selectively disclosed.

[17]Parties to a transaction in which an analyst is "brought over the wall" should be mindful that bringing an analyst over the wall can be a risky practice and may in itself be a signal to others of a significant development involving a reporting issuer.

[18]This is consistent with the reasoning of the SEC in excluding ratings organizations from Regulation FD. As the SEC indicated in paragraph II.B.1.a., of the implementing release, "[r]atings organizations...have a mission of public disclosure; the objective and result of the ratings process is a widely available publication of the rating when it is completed."

[19]For example, under National Instrument 44-101 — Short Form Prospectus Distributions, alternative eligibility requirements allow companies without the requisite public float to issue "designated rating" non-convertible debt, preferred shares or cash-settled derivatives under a short form prospectus.

[20]See, however, section 2.1 regarding an issuer's timely disclosure obligations.

[21]*Green v. Charterhouse Group Can. Ltd.* (1976), 12 O.R. (2d) 280. *In the Matter of Harold P. Connor et al.* (1976) Volume II OSCB 149. Existing case law does not establish a firm rule as to what would be a reasonable amount of time for investors to be given to analyze information. The time period will depend on a number of factors including the circumstances in which the event arises, the nature and complexity of the information, the nature of the market for the com-

(3) Except for "material changes," which must be disclosed by news release, securities legislation does not generally require a particular method of disclosure to satisfy the "generally disclosed" requirement. In determining whether material information has been generally disclosed, we will consider all of the relevant facts and circumstances, including the company's traditional practices for publicly disclosing information and how broadly investors and the investment community follow the company. We recognize that the effectiveness of disclosure methods varies between companies. Whatever disclosure method is used to release information, we encourage consistency in a company's disclosure practices.[22]

(4) Companies may satisfy the "generally disclosed" requirement by using one or a combination of the following disclosure methods:

(a) News releases distributed through a widely circulated news or wire service.[23]

(b) Announcements made through press conferences or conference calls that interested members of the public may attend or listen to either in person, by telephone, or by other electronic transmission (including the Internet). A company needs to provide the public with appropriate notice of the conference or call by news release.[24] The notice should include the date and time of the conference or call, a general description of what is to be discussed, and the means of accessing the conference or call.[25] The notice should also indicate for how long the company will make a transcript or replay of the call available over its Web site.

(5) We recognize that many companies prefer news release disclosure as the safest means of satisfying the "generally disclosed" requirement. In section 6.6 of the Policy, we recommend as a "best practice" a disclosure model centred around news release disclosure of material information, followed by an open and accessible conference call to discuss the information contained in the news release. However, we believe that alternative methods may also be appropriate. We believe it is important to preserve for companies the flexibility to develop a disclosure model that suits their circumstances and disseminates material information in the manner best calculated to effectively reach the marketplace.

(6) Posting information to a company's Web site will not, by itself, be likely to satisfy the "generally disclosed" requirement. Investors' access to the Internet is not yet sufficiently widespread such that a Web site posting alone would be a means of dissemination "calculated to effectively reach the marketplace." Further, effective dissemination involves the "pushing out" of information into the marketplace. Notwithstanding the ability of some issuers' Web sites to alert interested parties to new postings, Web sites by and large do not push information out into the marketplace. Instead, investors would be required to seek out this information from a company's Web site. Active and effective dissemination of information is central to satisfying the "generally disclosed" requirement.

(7) We support the use of technology in the disclosure process and believe that companies' Web sites can be an important and useful tool in improving communications to the marketplace. As technology evolves and as more investors gain access to the Internet, it may be that postings to certain companies' Web sites alone could satisfy the "generally disclosed" requirement. At such time, we will revisit this policy statement and reconsider the guidance provided on this issue. In the meantime, we strongly encourage companies to utilize their Web sites to improve investor access to corporate information.[26]

3.6 Unintentional Disclosure — Securities legislation does not provide a safe harbour which allows companies to correct an unintentional selective disclosure of material information. If a company makes an unintentional selective disclosure it should take immediate steps to ensure that a full public announcement is made. This includes contacting the relevant stock exchange and requesting that trading be halted pending the issuance of a news release. Pending the public release of the material information, the company should also tell those parties who have knowledge of the information that the information is material and that it has not been generally disclosed.

3.7 Administrative Proceedings — (1) We may consider any number of mitigating factors in a selective disclosure enforcement proceeding including:

(a) whether and to what extent a company has implemented, maintained and followed reasonable policies and procedures to prevent contraventions of the tipping provisions;

(b) whether any selective disclosure was unintentional; and

(c) what steps were taken to disseminate information that had been unintentionally disclosed (including how quickly the information was disclosed).

If a company's disclosure record shows a pattern of "unintentional selective disclosures", it will be harder to show that a particular selective disclosure was truly unintentional.

(2) Nothing in this policy statement limits our discretion to request information relating to a possible selective disclosure violation or to take enforcement proceedings within our jurisdiction where there has been a breach of the tipping provisions.

PART IV — MATERIALITY

4.1 Materiality Standard — (1) The definitions of "material fact" and "material change" under securities legislation are based on a market impact test. The definition of "privileged information" contained in the "tipping" provision of the securities legislation of Québec is based on a reasonable investor test. Despite these differences, the two materiality standards are likely to converge, for practical purposes, in most cases.

---

pany's securities, and the manner used to release the information. We recognize that the case law is dated in this respect and that, if the courts were to revisit these decisions today, they may not find the time parameters set out in the decisions appropriate for modern technology.

[22] A sudden change from the usual method of generally disclosing material information may attract regulatory attention in certain circumstances; for example, a last minute webcast of poor quarterly results without advance notice when positive quarterly results are generally released in advance of a subsequently scheduled discussion of the results.

[23] We encourage companies to file their news releases on SEDAR. Filing a news release on SEDAR alone will not constitute "general disclosure".

[24] This is based on guidance provided by the U.S. Securities and Exchange Commission (the "SEC") in the adopting release to Regulation FD.

[25] This might include a Web site link to any software that is necessary to access the webcast.

[26] See also The Toronto Stock Exchange's Electronic Communications Disclosure Guidelines.

(2) The definition of a "material fact" includes a two part materiality test. A fact is material when it (i) significantly affects the market price or value of a security; or (ii) would reasonably be expected to have a significant effect on the market price or value of a security.[27]

4.2 Materiality Determinations — (1) In making materiality judgements, it is necessary to take into account a number of factors that cannot be captured in a simple bright-line standard or test. These include the nature of the information itself, the volatility of the company's securities and prevailing market conditions. The materiality of a particular event or piece of information may vary between companies according to their size, the nature of their operations and many other factors. An event that is "significant" or "major" for a smaller company may not be material to a larger company. Companies should avoid taking an overly technical approach to determining materiality.[28] Under volatile market conditions, apparently insignificant variances between earnings projections and actual results can have a significant impact on share price once released. For example, information regarding a company's ability to meet consensus earnings[29] published by securities analysts should not be selectively disclosed before general public release.

(2) We encourage companies to monitor the market's reaction to information that is publicly disclosed. Ongoing monitoring and assessment of market reaction to different disclosure will be helpful when making materiality judgements in the future. As a guiding principle, if there is any doubt about whether particular information is material, we encourage companies to err on the side of materiality and release information publicly.[30]

4.3 Examples of Potentially Material Information — The following are examples of the types of events or information which may be material. This list is not exhaustive and is not a substitute for companies exercising their own judgement in making materiality determinations.

Changes in Corporate Structure
- changes in share ownership that may affect control of the company
- major reorganizations, amalgamations, or mergers
- take-over bids, issuer bids, or insider bids

Changes in Capital Structure
- the public or private sale of additional securities
- planned repurchases or redemptions of securities
- planned splits of common shares or offerings of warrants or rights to buy shares
- any share consolidation, share exchange, or stock dividend
- changes in a company's dividend payments or policies
- the possible initiation of a proxy fight
- material modifications to rights of security holders

Changes in Financial Results
- a significant increase or decrease in near-term earnings prospects
- unexpected changes in the financial results for any periods
- shifts in financial circumstances, such as cash flow reductions, major asset write-offs or write-downs
- changes in the value or composition of the company's assets
- any material change in the company's accounting policy

Changes in Business and Operations
- any development that affects the company's resources, technology, products or markets
- a significant change in capital investment plans or corporate objectives
- major labour disputes or disputes with major contractors or suppliers
- significant new contracts, products, patents, or services or significant losses of contracts or business
- significant discoveries by resource companies
- changes to the board of directors or executive management, including the departure of the company's CEO, CFO, COO or president (or persons in equivalent positions)
- the commencement of, or developments in, material legal proceedings or regulatory matters
- waivers of corporate ethics and conduct rules for officers, directors, and other key employees
- any notice that reliance on a prior audit is no longer permissible

---

[27]Section 13 of the Québec Securities Act provides that a prospectus must disclose all material facts likely to affect the value of the market price of the securities to be distributed.

[28]See also *Re Royal Trustco Ltd. et al. and Ontario Securities Commission* (1983), 42 O.R. (2d) 147 (Div. Ct.), affirming (1981), 2 OSCB 322C, where the Ontario Securities Commission issued a denial of exemption order against two senior officers of Royal Trustco who disclosed to officers of a Canadian chartered bank that certain shareholders of Royal Trustco did not intend to tender their Royal Trustco shares to a hostile take-over bid by Campeau Corporation. The Ontario Securities Commission held that the disclosure constituted illegal "tipping". On appeal the Divisional Court stated that the term "fact" should not be read "super-critically" and that "information" that shareholders of Royal Trustco did not intend to tender to a hostile take-over bid by Campeau Corporation "was sufficiently factual or a sufficient alteration of circumstances to be a material "change" to fall within the [tipping provision]."

[29]The range of earnings estimates issued by analysts following a company.

[30]See also Canadian Investor Relations Institute, "*Model Disclosure Policy*", (February 2001) where CIRI noted in its explanatory notes that "Determining the materiality of information is clearly an area where judgement and experience are of great value. If it is a borderline decision, the information should probably be considered material and released using a broad means of dissemination. Similarly, if several company officials have to deliberate extensively over whether information is material, they should err on the side of materiality and release it publicly".

- de-listing of the company's securities or their movement from one quotation system or exchange to another

Acquisitions and Dispositions

- significant acquisitions or dispositions of assets, property or joint venture interests
- acquisitions of other companies, including a take-over bid for, or merger with, another company

Changes in Credit Arrangements

- the borrowing or lending of a significant amount of money
- any mortgaging or encumbering of the company's assets
- defaults under debt obligations, agreements to restructure debt, or planned enforcement procedures by a bank or any other creditors
- changes in rating agency decisions
- significant new credit arrangements

4.4 External Political, Economic and Social Developments — Companies are not generally required to interpret the impact of external political, economic and social developments on their affairs. However, if an external development will have or has had a direct effect on the business and affairs of a company that is both material and uncharacteristic of the effect generally experienced by other companies engaged in the same business or industry, the company is urged to explain, where practical, the particular impact on them. For example, a change in government policy that affects most companies in a particular industry does not require an announcement, but if it affects only one or a few companies in a material way, such companies should make an announcement.

4.5 Exchange Policies — (1) The Toronto Stock Exchange Inc. (the "TSX") and the TSX Venture Exchange Inc. ("TSX Venture") each have adopted timely disclosure policy statements which include many examples of the types of events or information which may be material. Companies should also refer to the guidance provided in these policies when trying to assess the materiality of a particular fact, change or piece of information.

(2) The TSX and TSX Venture policies require the timely disclosure of "material information". Material information includes both material facts and material changes relating to the business and affairs of a company. The timely disclosure obligations in the exchanges' policies exceed those found in securities legislation. It is not uncommon, or inappropriate, for exchanges to impose requirements on their listed companies which go beyond those imposed by securities legislation.[31] We expect listed companies to comply with the requirements of the exchange they are listed on. Companies who do not comply with an exchange's requirements could find themselves subject to an administrative proceeding before a provincial securities regulator.[32]

PART V — RISKS ASSOCIATED WITH CERTAIN DISCLOSURES

5.1 Private Briefings with Analysts, Institutional Investors and other Market Professionals — (1) The role that analysts play in seeking out information, analyzing and interpreting it and making recommendations can contribute to a more efficient marketplace. Companies should be sensitive though to the risks involved in private meetings with analysts. We are not suggesting that companies should stop having private briefings with analysts or that these private meetings are somehow illegal. Companies should have a firm policy of providing only non-material information and publicly disclosed information to analysts.

(2) Companies should not disclose significant data, and in particular financial information such as sales and profit figures, to analysts, institutional investors and other market professionals selectively rather than to the market as a whole. Earnings forecasts are in the same category. Even within these constraints there is plenty of scope to hold a useful dialogue with analysts and other interested parties about a company's prospects, business environment, management philosophy and long term strategy.

(3) Another way to avoid selective disclosure is to include, in the company's regular periodic disclosures, details about topics of interest to analysts. For example, companies should expand the scope of their interim management's discussion and analysis disclosure ("MD&A"). More comprehensive MD&A can have practical benefits including: greater analyst following; more accurate forecasts with fewer revisions; a narrower range between analysts' forecasts; and increased investor interest.

(4) A company cannot make material information immaterial simply by breaking the information into seemingly non-material pieces. At the same time, a company is not prohibited from disclosing non-material information to analysts, even if these pieces help the analyst complete a "mosaic" of information that, taken together, is material undisclosed information about the company.[33]

5.2 Analyst Reports — (1) It is not unusual for analysts to ask corporate officers to review earnings estimates that they are preparing. A company takes on a high degree of risk of violating securities legislation if it selectively confirms that an analyst's estimate is "on target" or that an analyst's estimate is "too high" or "too low", whether directly or indirectly through implied "guidance".[34]

(2) Even when confirming information previously made public, a company needs to consider whether the selective confirmation itself communicates information above and beyond the initial forecast and whether the additional information is material. This will depend in large part on how much time has passed between the original statement and the company's confirmation, as well as the timing of the two statements relative to the end of the company's fiscal period. For example, a selective confirmation of expected earnings near the end of a quarter is likely to represent guidance (as it may well be based on how the company actually performed). Materiality of a confirmation may also depend on intervening events.[35]

---

[31]For example, securities legislation provides that a recognized stock exchange may impose additional requirements within its jurisdiction.

[32]See *In the Matter of Air Canada, supra*, note 16. In this case, the parties to the settlement agreed that by disclosing earnings information to 13 analysts and not generally disclosing the information, the company failed to comply with the provisions of the TSX Company Manual and thereby acted contrary to the public interest. In the Excerpt from the Settlement Hearing Containing the Oral Reasons for Decision, the Ontario Securities Commission said, "[w]e feel that it will help foster confidence in the financial markets to know that the law requires, and that good corporations will comply with the requirement for, full disclosure of all material information on a timely basis as required by ... the Toronto Stock Exchange's listing agreement and listing requirements."

[33]See also SEC's adopting release to Regulation FD.

[34]This position follows the position adopted by the SEC in the adopting release to Regulation FD and the position taken by the Australian Securities & Investments Commission in its guidance note "Better Disclosure for Investors" (http://www.asic.gov.au).

[35]The guidance with respect to the materiality of confirming information previously made public is based on SEC Staff interpretive guidance on Regulation FD.

(3) One way companies can try to ensure that analysts' estimates are in line with their own expectations is through the regular and timely public dissemination of qualitative and quantitative information. The better the marketplace is informed, the less likely it is that analysts' estimates will deviate significantly from a company's own expectations.

(4) A company that redistributes an analyst's report to people outside the company risks being seen as endorsing that report. Companies should avoid redistributing analysts' reports to their employees or to people outside the company.[36] If a company elects to post to its Web site or otherwise publish the names of analysts who cover the company and/or their recommendations, the names and/or recommendations of all analysts who cover the company should be similarly posted or published.

5.3 Confidentiality Agreements with Analysts — While we recognize that relying on a confidentiality agreement to safeguard the continued confidentiality of material information can be a prudent practice, there is no exception to the tipping prohibition for disclosures made to an analyst under a confidentiality agreement.[37] If a company discloses material undisclosed information to an analyst, it has violated the prohibition, with or without a confidentiality agreement (unless the disclosure is made in the necessary course of business). Analysts who get an advance private briefing have an advantage. They have more time to prepare and can therefore brief their firm members and clients sooner than those who did not have access to the information.

5.4 Analysts as "Tippees" — (1) Analysts, institutional investors, investment dealers and other market professionals who receive material undisclosed information from a company are "tippees". It is against the law for a tippee to trade or further inform anyone about such information, other than in the necessary course of business.

(2) We recommend that analysts, institutional investors and other market professionals adopt internal review procedures to help them identify situations where they may have received nonpublic material information and set up guidelines for dealing with such situations.

5.5 Selective Disclosure Violations Can Occur in a Variety of Settings — Selective disclosure most often occurs in one-on-one discussions (like analyst meetings) and in industry conferences and other types of private meetings and break-out sessions. But it can occur elsewhere. For example, a company should not disclose material nonpublic information at its annual shareholders meeting unless all interested members of the public may attend the meeting and the company has given adequate public notice of the meeting (including a description of what will be discussed at the meeting). Alternatively, a company can issue a news release at or before the time of the meeting.

PART VI — BEST DISCLOSURE PRACTICES

6.1 General — (1) There are some practical measures that companies can adopt to help ensure good disclosure practices. The consistent application of "best practices" in the disclosure of material information will enhance a company's credibility with analysts and investors, contribute to the fairness and efficiency of the capital markets and investor confidence in those markets, and minimize the risk of non-compliance with securities legislation.

(2) The measures recommended in this policy statement are not intended to be prescriptive. We recognize that many large listed companies have specialist investor relations staff and devote considerable resources to disclosure, while in smaller companies this is often just one of the many roles of senior officers. We encourage companies to adopt the measures suggested in this policy statement, but they should be implemented flexibly and sensibly to fit the situation of each individual company.

6.2 Establishing a Corporate Disclosure Policy — (1) Establish a written corporate disclosure policy. A disclosure policy gives you a process for disclosure and promotes an understanding of legal requirements among your directors, officers and employees. The process of creating it is itself a benefit, because it forces a critical examination of your current disclosure practices.

(2) You should design a policy that is practical to implement. Your policy should be reviewed and approved by your board of directors and widely distributed to your officers and employees. Directors, officers and those employees who are, or may be, involved in making disclosure decisions should also be trained so that they understand and can apply the disclosure policy. Your policy should be periodically reviewed and updated, as necessary, and responsibility for these functions (i.e., review and update of the policy and education of appropriate employees and company officials) should be clearly assigned within your company.

(3) The focus of your disclosure policy should be on promoting consistent disclosure practices aimed at informative, timely and broadly disseminated disclosure of material information to the market. Every disclosure policy should generally include the following:

    (a) how to decide what information is material;

    (b) policy on reviewing analyst reports;

    (c) how to release earnings announcements and conduct related analyst calls and meetings;

    (d) how to conduct meetings with investors and the media;

    (e) what to say or not to say at industry conferences;

    (f) how to use electronic media and the corporate Web site;

    (g) policy on the use of forecasts and other forward-looking information (including a policy regarding issuing updates);

    (h) procedures for reviewing briefings and discussions with analysts, institutional investors and other market professionals;

    (i) how to deal with unintentional selective disclosures;

    (j) how to respond to market rumours;

    (k) policy on trading restrictions; and

    (l) policy on "quiet periods".

6.3 Overseeing and Coordinating Disclosure — Establish a committee of company personnel or assign a senior officer to be responsible for:

    (a) developing and implementing your disclosure policy;

---

[36]Companies should also avoid redistributing third party newsletters or tip sheets that contain earnings-related information.

[37]By comparison, Regulation FD allows an issuer to make a disclosure of material nonpublic information to an analyst if the analyst enters into a confidentiality agreement with the issuer.

(b) monitoring the effectiveness of and compliance with your disclosure policy;

(c) educating your directors, officers and certain employees about disclosure issues and your disclosure policy;

(d) reviewing and authorizing disclosure (including electronic, written and oral disclosure) in advance of its public release; and

(e) monitoring your Web site.

6.4 Board and Audit Committee Review of Certain Disclosure — (1) Have your board of directors or audit committee review the following disclosures in advance of their public release by the company:

> financial outlooks and FOFI, as defined in National Instrument 51-102 Continuous Disclosure Obligations; and
> news releases containing financial information based on a company's financial statements prior to the release of such statements.[38]

You should also indicate at the time such information is publicly released whether your board or audit committee has reviewed the disclosure. Having your board or audit committee review such disclosure in advance of its public release acts as a good discipline on management and helps to increase the quality, credibility and objectivity of such disclosures. This review process also helps to force a critical examination of all issues related to the disclosure and reduces the risk of having to make subsequent adjustments or amendments to the information it contains.

(2) Where feasible, issue your earnings news release[39] concurrently with the filing of your quarterly or annual financial statements. This will help to ensure that a complete financial picture is available to analysts and investors at the time the earnings release is provided. Coordinating the release of a company's earnings information with the filing of its quarterly or annual financial statements will also facilitate review of these disclosures by the board or audit committee of the company.[40]

6.5 Authorizing Company Spokespersons — Limit the number of people who are authorized to speak on behalf of your company to analysts, the media and investors. Ideally, your spokesperson should be a member(s) of senior management. Spokespersons should be knowledgeable about your disclosure record and aware of analysts' reports relating to your company. Everyone in your company should know who the company spokespersons are and refer all inquiries from analysts, investors and the media to them. Having a limited number of company spokespersons helps to reduce the risk of:

(a) unauthorized disclosures;

(b) inconsistent statements by different people in the company; and

(c) statements that are inconsistent with the public disclosure record of the company.[41]

6.6 Recommended Disclosure Model — (1) You should consider using the following disclosure model when making a planned disclosure of material corporate information, such as a scheduled earnings release:

(a) issue a news release containing the information (for example, your quarterly financial results) through a widely circulated news or wire service;

(b) provide advance public notice by news release of the date and time of a conference call to discuss the information, the subject matter of the call and the means for accessing it;

(c) hold the conference call in an open manner, permitting investors and others to listen either by telephone or through Internet webcasting; and

(d) provide dial-in and/or web replay or make transcripts of the call available for a reasonable period of time after the analyst conference call.[42]

(2) The combination of news release disclosure of the material information and an open and accessible conference call to subsequently discuss the information should help to ensure that the information is disseminated in a manner calculated to effectively reach the marketplace and minimize the risk of an inadvertent selective disclosure during the follow-up call.

6.7 Analyst Conference Calls and Industry Conferences — (1) Hold analyst conference calls and industry conferences in an open manner, allowing any interested party to listen either by telephone and/or through a webcast. This helps to reduce the risk of selective disclosure.

(2) Company officials should meet before an analyst conference call, private analyst meeting or industry conference. Where practical, statements and responses to anticipated questions should be scripted in advance and reviewed by the appropriate people within your company. Scripting will help to identify any material corporate information that may need to be publicly disclosed through a news release.

(3) Keep detailed records and/or transcripts of any conference call, meeting or industry conference. These should be reviewed to determine whether any unintentional selective disclosure has occurred. If so, you should take immediate steps to ensure that a full public announcement is made, including contacting the relevant stock exchange and asking that trading be halted pending the issuance of a news release.

6.8 Analyst Reports — Establish a policy for reviewing analyst reports. As noted in section 5.2 of the Policy, there is a serious risk of violating the tipping prohibition if you express comfort with or provide guidance on an analyst's report, earnings model or earnings estimates. There is also a risk of selectively disclosing material non-financial information in the course of reviewing an analyst's report. If your policy allows for the review of analyst reports, your review should be limited to identifying publicly disclosed factual information that may affect an analyst's model or to pointing out inaccuracies or omissions with reference to publicly available information about your company.

---

[38]Some provinces require that annual financial statements be reviewed by a company's audit committee (if the company has an audit committee) before board approval. A board of directors must also review interim financial statements before they are filed and distributed. In the case of interim financial statements, boards are permitted to delegate this review function to the audit committee (see for example, OSC Rule 52-501 Financial Statements). Where such a requirement exists at law, we believe that extracting information from financial statements that have not been reviewed by the board or audit committee and releasing that information to the marketplace in a news release is inconsistent with the prior review requirement.

[39]Companies often issue news releases announcing corporate earnings which highlight major items and may include *pro forma* results.

[40]Certain jurisdictions impose a requirement to concurrently deliver to shareholders financial statements that are filed. This may militate against the early filing of annual financial statements to avoid the cost of mailing them twice, once at the time of early filing and subsequently as part of the company's annual report. The CSA is considering eliminating this concurrent delivery obligation in the context of harmonizing continuous disclosure requirements across the country.

[41]In some circumstances a company's designated spokesperson will not be informed of developing mergers and acquisitions until necessary, to avoid leakage of the information.

[42]This model disclosure policy was recommended by the SEC in the adopting release to Regulation FD.

6.9 Quiet Periods — Observe a quarterly quiet period, during which no earnings guidance or comments with respect to the current quarter's operations or expected results will be provided to analysts, investors or other market professionals. The quiet period should run between the end of the quarter and the release of a quarterly earnings announcement although, in practice, quiet periods vary by company.[43] Companies need not stop all communications with analysts or investors during the quiet period. However, communications should be limited to responding to inquiries concerning publicly available or non-material information.

6.10 Insider Trading Policies and Blackout Periods — Adopt an insider trading policy that provides for a senior officer to approve and monitor the trading activity of all your insiders, officers, and senior employees. Your insider trading policy should prohibit purchases and sales at any time by insiders and employees who are in possession of material nonpublic information. Your policy should also provide for trading "blackout periods" when trading by insiders, officers and employees may typically not take place (for example a blackout period which surrounds regularly scheduled earnings announcements). However, insiders, officers and employees should have the opportunity to apply to the company's trading officer for approval to trade the company's securities during the blackout period. A company's blackout period may mirror the quiet period described above.

6.11 Electronic Communications — (1) Establish a team responsible for creating and maintaining the company Web site. The Web site should be up to date and accurate. You should date all material information when it is posted or modified. You should also move outdated information to an archive. Archiving allows the public to continue accessing information that may have historical or other value even though it is no longer current. You should establish minimum retention periods for information that is posted to and archived on your Web site. Retention periods may vary depending on the kind of information posted.[44] You should also explain how your Web site is set up and maintained. You should remember that posting material information on your Web site is not acceptable as the sole means of satisfying legal requirements to "generally disclose" information.

(2) Use current technology to improve investor access to your information. You should concurrently post to your Web site, if you have one, all documents that you file on SEDAR. You should also post on the investor relations part of your Web site all supplemental information that you give to analysts, institutional investors and other market professionals. This would include data books, fact sheets, slides of investor presentations and other materials distributed at analyst or industry presentations.[45] When you make a presentation at an industry sponsored conference try to have your presentation and "question and answer" session webcast.

6.12 Chat Rooms, Bulletin Boards and e-mails — Do not participate in, host or link to chat rooms or bulletin boards. Your disclosure policy should prohibit your employees from discussing corporate matters in these forums. This will help to protect your company from the liability that could arise from the well-intentioned, but sporadic, efforts of employees to correct rumours or defend the company. You should consider requiring employees to report to a designated company official any discussion pertaining to your company which they find on the Internet. If your Web site allows viewers to send you e-mail messages, remember the risk of selective disclosure when responding.

6.13 Handling Rumours: — Adopt a "no comment" policy with respect to market rumours and make sure that the policy is applied consistently.[46] Otherwise, an inconsistent response may be interpreted as "tipping". You may be required by your exchange to make a clarifying statement where trading in your company's securities appears to be heavily influenced by rumours. If material information has been leaked and appears to be affecting trading activity in your company's securities, you should take immediate steps to ensure that a full public announcement is made. This includes contacting your exchange and asking that trading be halted pending the issuance of a news release.[47]

Adopted: (2002) 25 O.S.C.B. 4492; Request for Comments: (2001) 24 O.S.C.B. 3301. Replaced NPS 40.

Amendment to Policy Adopted by OSC: (2007) 30 O.S.C.B. 10524 and 8539; Request for Comments: (2007) 30 O.S.C.B. 2969.

Amendment to Policy Adopted by OSC: (2013) 36 O.S.C.B. 2619; Request for Comments: (2012) 35 O.S.C.B. 6887.

CSA Staff Notice 51-309 — National Instrument 51-101 Standards of Disclosure for Oil and Gas Activities — Acceptance of Certain Foreign Professional Boards as a "Professional Organization"

Date: January 19, 2004, June 11, 2004 and March 9, 2007

27 O.S.C.B. 1128 and amended 27 O.S.C.B. 5621 and 30 O.S.C.B. 2029

Updated March 9, 2007

This notice updates and replaces the information in CSA Staff Notice 51-309 originally dated January 19, 2004, and updated June 8, 2004 and October 4, 2004.

Introduction

In January 2004 (February 2007 in Québec)[1], we added the following professional boards to the list of professional organizations accepted for the purposes of National Instrument 51-101 *Standards of Disclosure for Oil and Gas Activities* (NI 51-101):

- California Board for Professional Engineers and Land Surveyors,

---

[43]Some companies adopt a quiet period beginning at the start of the third month of the quarter, and ending upon issuance of the earnings release. Other companies wait until two weeks before the end of the quarter or even the first day of the month following the end of the quarter to start the quiet period.

[44]See the TSX's Electronic Communications Disclosure Guidelines.

[45]This recommendation is based on the recommendations contained in The Toronto Stock Exchange Committee on Corporate Disclosure's final report issued in March 1997 and in the TSX's Electronic Communications Disclosure Guidelines. See also the guidance note "Better Disclosure for Investors" issued by the Australian Securities & Investments Commission (http://www.asic.gov.au).

[46]A "no comment" policy means that you respond with a statement to the effect that "it is our policy not to comment on market rumours or speculation".

[47]If the rumour relates to a material change in the company's affairs that has, in fact, occurred, you have a legal obligation to make timely disclosure of the change.

[1]MRRS Decision Document dated January 6, 2004 *In the Matter of ... National Instrument 51-101 Standards of Disclosure for Oil and Gas Activities (NI 51-101) ... and ...*[the professional boards named in this CSA notice].

- State of Colorado Board of Registration for Professional Engineers and Professional Land Surveyors,
- Louisiana State Board of Registration for Professional Engineers and Land Surveyors,
- Oklahoma State Board of Registration for Professional Engineers and Land Surveyors, and
- Texas Board of Professional Engineers.

On June 8, 2004[2], we added the *American Association of Petroleum Geologists* (AAPG) to that list. At its request, on March 1, 2007[3], we revoked the June 8, 2004 MRRS Decision Document and accepted the AAPG as a "professional organization" under NI 51-101, but only for Certified Petroleum Geologists within the AAPG's Division of Professional Affairs.

On October 4, 2004 (February 2007 in Québec)[4], we added to that list the *American Institute of Professional Geologists* (AIPG), but only for the AIPG's Certified Professional Geologists.

On March 1, 2007[5], we added the United Kingdom's *Energy Institute* to that list.

Accompanying this notice is an updated list of all accepted professional organizations under NI 51-101.

Background

NI 51-101 requires reporting issuers to appoint one or more qualified reserves evaluators or reserves auditors to report to its board of directors on its reserves data (section 3.2). To be "qualified", a reserves evaluator or reserves auditor must possess appropriate professional qualifications and experience, and be a member in good standing of a "professional organization" (subsections 1.1(x) and (y)).

The definition of "professional organization" in subsection 1.1(w) has four elements:

(w) "professional organization" means a self-regulatory organization of engineers, geologists, other geoscientists or other professionals whose professional practice includes *reserves evaluations* or *reserves audits*, that:

(i) admits members primarily on the basis of their educational qualifications;

(ii) requires its members to comply with the professional standards of competence and ethics prescribed by the organization that are relevant to the estimation, *evaluation*, *review* or *audit* of *reserves data*;

(iii) has disciplinary powers, including the power to suspend or expel a member; and

(iv) is either:

A. given authority or recognition by statute in a Canadian jurisdiction; or

B. accepted for this purpose by the *securities regulatory authority* or the *regulator*.

CSA staff reviewed relevant documentation concerning each of the professional organizations' authority and recognition, membership requirements and disciplinary powers. We concluded that acceptance of each would not be contrary to the public interest and would facilitate compliance with NI 51-101 by enabling reporting issuers active in the United States and the United Kingdom to continue the traditional, and acceptable, practice of engaging US and UK professionals whose qualifications are consistent with the objectives of NI 51-101.

Acceptance of Professional Organizations does not Supersede Other Requirements

Membership in one of the accepted professional organizations does not automatically mean that a person is a "qualified reserves evaluator" or "qualified reserves auditor" under NI 51-101. To be qualified under NI 51-101, the person must also have the requisite professional experience to carry out reserves evaluations or reserves audits in accordance with the requirements of NI 51-101 and the standards of the Canadian Oil and Gas Evaluation Handbook.

The CSA's acceptance of the professional organizations under NI 51-101 is only for the purposes of NI 51-101. NI 51-101 does not supersede or alter local regulations or requirements regarding professional membership, practice or proficiency.

National Instrument 51-101 — Standards of Disclosure for Oil and Gas Activities Professional Organizations

This list, updated March 9, 2007, supersedes the list of organizations set out in section 1.5(b) of Companion Policy 51-101CP.

Each of the following organizations is a *professional organization* for the purposes of NI 51-101:

Canada

Association of Professional Engineers, Geologists and Geophysicists of Alberta (APEGGA)

Association of Professional Engineers and Geoscientists of the Province of British Columbia (APEGBC)

Association of Professional Engineers and Geoscientists of Saskatchewan (APEGS)

Association of Professional Engineers and Geoscientists of Manitoba (APEGM)

---

[2]MRRS Decision Document dated June 8, 2004 *In the Matter of ... National Instrument 51-101 Standards of Disclosure for Oil and Gas Activities (NI 51-101) ... and ... the American Association of Petroleum Geologists (AAPG).*

[3]MRRS Decision Document dated March 1, 2007 *In the Matter of ... National Instrument 51-101 Standards of Disclosure for Oil and Gas Activities (NI 51-101) ... and ... the American Association of Petroleum Geologists (AAPG) but only members of the AAPG's Division of Professional Affairs.*

[4]MRRS Decision Document dated October 4, 2004 *In the Matter of ... National Instrument 51-101 Standards of Disclosure for Oil and Gas Activities (NI 51-101) ... and ... the American Institute of Professional Geologists (AIPG). In Québec, Decision No 2007-PDG-0050 dated February 16, 2007.*

[5]MRRS Decision Document dated March 1, 2007 *In the Matter of ... National Instrument 51-101 Standards of Disclosure for Oil and Gas Activities (NI 51-101) ... and ... the Energy Institute of the United Kingdom.*

Association of Professional Geoscientists of Ontario (APGO)

Professional Engineers of Ontario (PEO)

Ordre des ingénieurs du Québec (OIQ)

Ordre des Géologues du Québec (OGQ)

Association of Professional Engineers of Prince Edward Island (APEPEI)

Association of Professional Engineers and Geoscientists of New Brunswick (APEGNB)

Association of Professional Engineers of Nova Scotia (APENS)

Association of Professional Engineers and Geoscientists of Newfoundland (APEGN)

Association of Professional Engineers of Yukon (APEY)

Association of Professional Engineers, Geologists & Geophysicists of the Northwest Territories (NAPEGG) (representing the Northwest Territories and Nunavut Territory)

United States

American Association of Petroleum Geologists (AAPG), but only for its Certified Petroleum Geologists within the AAPG's Division of Professional Affairs

American Institute of Professional Geologists (AIPG), but only for its Certified Professional Geologists, as defined in AIPG's by-laws

California Board for Professional Engineers and Land Surveyors

Louisiana State Board of Registration for Professional Engineers and Land Surveyors

Oklahoma State Board of Registration for Professional Engineers and Land Surveyors

State of Colorado Board of Registration for Professional Engineers and Professional Land Surveyors

Texas Board of Professional Engineers

United Kingdom

Energy Institute, but only for its Fellows and Members

CSA Multilateral Staff Notice 51-310 — Report on Staff's Continuous Disclosure Review of Income Trust Issuers

Date: February 13, 2004

27 O.S.C.B. 1847

Purpose of Notice

This notice reports the findings and comments of staff of the British Columbia Securities Commission, Manitoba Securities Commission, Ontario Securities Commission and Commission des valeurs mobilières du Québec (collectively, staff or we) arising from a review of the continuous disclosure records of 40 income trust issuers.

Objective and Scope of Review

The income trust structure has become a popular vehicle for public offerings. In an effort to further understand and evaluate the financial disclosure practices of income trusts, staff conducted a coordinated project to review the continuous disclosure records of 40 income trusts. The income trusts were in various industries and eleven of the 40 trusts had existed for more than one year when we began our review. Based on our review of the continuous disclosure records of these trusts, six specific issues emerged that we comment on in this notice:

- Distributable cash

- Comparative figures

- Unitholders' equity

- Future oriented financial information

- Non-GAAP financial measures

- Goodwill and intangibles

We started our reviews in early 2003 and completed them by September 2003.

Summary of Findings

Our findings suggest that many income trust issuers need to improve the quality of their disclosure.

Twenty-nine of the income trusts committed to change disclosure in future Management Discussion & Analysis (MD&A) filings, annual and interim financial statements and press releases.

Two of the income trusts were required to re-file their disclosure documents as a result of our review.

Nine of the income trusts reviewed were not required to change their previously filed disclosure documents or to commit to prospective changes.

Findings for Specific Issues Identified

1. — Distributable Cash

Distributable cash generally refers to the net cash generated by an income trust's business or assets that is available for distribution, at the discretion of the income trust, to the income trust's unitholders.

We reviewed the disclosure of the income trusts for the following aspects of distributable cash disclosure:

- Location of information about distributable cash — presented as a separate financial statement, in the notes to the financial statements or within MD&A.

- Reconciliation of distributable cash figures to the financial statements.

- Starting point in GAAP financial statements for the reconciliation of distributable cash — net income from operations, or cash flow from operations.

- MD&A discussion of discretionary amounts such as reserves.

Distributable cash information was presented in a variety of locations. Of the 40 income trusts reviewed:

- Eighteen trusts included a statement of distributable cash in the MD&A

- Sixteen trusts presented distributable cash information in a note to the financial statements

- Three trusts presented distributable cash as a separate statement within the financial statements

- Three trusts did not present distributable cash information

Of the 40 income trusts reviewed, nine trusts presented distributable cash figures without a reconciliation to the audited financial statements. Presentation of distributable cash without a reconciliation to GAAP measures may confuse readers as to the source of the amounts and may mislead them into erroneous conclusions about what the distributable cash presentation communicates. For example, in one occurrence, the income trust presented a statement of distributable cash that covered a different period than the audited financial statements.

Twenty-six of the 40 income trusts provided a reconciliation between distributable cash and net earnings. The remainder of the income trusts provided a reconciliation between distributable cash and some other financial measure such as earnings before interest, taxes, depreciation and amortization (EBITDA), net cash from operations, net sales or cash and cash equivalents.

Fifteen of the 40 income trusts disclosed some type of reserve to arrive at distributable cash. However, in most cases the calculation of the reserve amounts and the reasons for any changes to the reserve amounts were not discussed in the MD&A.

We remind income trust issuers to refer to the disclosure guidance of CSA Staff Notice 52-306 *Non-GAAP Financial Measures* when presenting distributable cash. Specifically, distributable cash should be reconciled to the most directly comparable measure calculated in accordance with GAAP which staff believes is generally cash flow from operations. Income trust issuers should also discuss all reconciling items, especially those items of a discretionary nature, and explain the implications of any difference between distributable cash and cash distributions made.

2. — Comparative Figures

Most income trusts continue an existing business that was previously operated under a different legal form. The operating assets or shares of an operating business initially acquired by the income trust may be accounted for at their previous carrying value or at fair value using the purchase method.

For the purpose of our review, we focussed on the presentation of comparative information for the business for periods prior to its transfer to the income trust. Specifically, we reviewed the selected income trusts for the following:

- Presentation of comparative figures in the financial statements when the initial acquisition of the operating business was recorded at previous carrying values.

- Presentation of comparative figures in the MD&A when the initial acquisition of the operating business was recorded using the purchase method.

We reviewed 29 of the 40 income trusts for the inclusion of comparative information in the issuer's first fiscal year. The remaining eleven income trusts had existed for more than one year and therefore were not reviewed for this issue.

Six of the twenty-nine income trusts accounted for the initial acquisition of the operating company using previous carrying values. After being requested by staff, five of the six income trusts included comparative figures in their financial statements, and discussed in their notes to the financial statements the basis of presentation (one issuer restated its quarterly financial statements and the other five included comparatives on a prospective basis). The remaining income trust agreed to include comparative financial information along with a comparative discussion in future MD&A filings; this approach was considered appropriate given certain unique features of the operating business' history.

The remaining twenty-three income trusts accounted for the initial acquisition using the purchase method. Of these, eight income trusts included some comparative information and discussion in the MD&A, with the remaining fifteen trusts omitting any comparative figures or discussion in both the financial statements and MD&A. In response to staff's comments, each of the fifteen income trusts agreed to include comparative financial information along with a comparative discussion in future MD&A filings.

We direct income trust issuers to proposed National Policy 41-201 *Income Trusts and Other Indirect Offerings* that discusses staff's expectations for the provision of comparative information.

3. — Unitholders' Equity

Income trusts present surplus in the financial statements as "unitholders' equity". Total unitholders' equity represents the sum of contributed capital and retained earnings (undistributed earnings). We reviewed the income trusts included in this review project to identify the level of detail provided for unitholders' equity.

Only nine income trusts provided a breakdown of unitholders' equity into each of the main components of capital contributions, income earned, and distributions on a cumulative basis.

For those income trusts that existed for more than one year that did not provide a breakdown of the components of unitholders' equity, it was difficult to determine whether any distributions paid had been distributed from equity contributed from the original issuance of trust units. In one instance, if provided, the breakdown of unitholders' equity would have shown that the income trust had distributed 60% more than its cumulative earnings and that some portion of the distributions were being paid as a return of capital.

We remind income trust issuers that CICA Handbook Section 3250.07 requires that items of surplus be segregated so as to distinguish between those derived from earnings and those derived from contributions.

4. — Future Oriented Financial Information

Future Oriented Financial Information (FOFI) portrays prospective results of operations and financial position. We reviewed the income trusts included in this review project for their disclosure of FOFI and consistency with the guidance of National Policy 48 *Future — Oriented Financial Information* (NP48).

Thirteen of the income trusts reviewed provided some form of future oriented information. In eleven of the instances, we did not identify any consistency issues with the disclosure guidance of NP 48. The remaining two income trusts were not consistent with the guidance of NP48, as they originally included a forecast in their prospectus and did not discuss or compare actual results to the forecast in any of the quarters filed after the prospectus even though variances were considered material. In both instances, at staff's request, the income trusts discussed the variances in the annual MD&A.

5. — Non-GAAP Financial Measures

Many income trusts publish non-GAAP financial measures in press releases, MD&A and prospectus filings. Many non-GAAP financial measures are derived from net income determined in accordance with GAAP and, by omission of selected items, present a more positive picture of financial performance. Non-GAAP financial measures may be identified as "pro forma earnings", "operating earnings", "cash earnings", "free cash flow", "distributable cash", "EBITDA", "adjusted earnings", and "earnings before one-time charges".

We reviewed the income trusts included in this review project for their disclosure of non-GAAP financial measures and consistency with the disclosure guidance of CSA Staff Notice 52-303 *Non-GAAP Earnings Measures* (or its successor CSA Staff Notice 52-306 *Non-GAAP Financial Measures*).

All of the income trusts reviewed disclosed some type of Non-GAAP financial measure. The majority of income trusts reviewed did not fully comply with disclosure guidance contained in CSA Staff Notice 52-303 *Non-GAAP Earnings Measures* (or its successor CSA Staff Notice 52-306 *Non-GAAP Financial Measures*). Each of these income trusts confirmed that prospective presentation would be in accordance with the Notice.

6. — Goodwill and Intangibles

In many business combinations, some portion of the purchase price should be assigned to intangible assets. Given that income trusts usually acquire mature businesses with a history of operations, it is likely that intangible assets exist and should be recognized in the allocation of the purchase price.

In the course of this review project, we did not identify any specific issues relating to goodwill and intangibles. However, during previous prospectus reviews of several of the income trusts included in this review project, we identified failures to properly record intangible assets. In several instances, income trusts initially did not allocate any fair value to intangibles. When asked to justify this position given contrary evidence detailed in the preliminary prospectus (such as customer contracts, proprietary processes, trademarks), in all instances the issuer agreed to assign value to intangible assets.

As an example, one income trust had recognized minimal intangible assets and significant goodwill on the initial acquisition of the business. In their marketing material, the income trust made various references to established relationships with customers. Although the income trust argued that they did not have long-term contracts with these customers, these customers placed frequent and significant purchase orders. The income trust made minimal solicitation efforts and enjoyed low customer turnover. Staff concluded that these customer relationships justified the recognition of an intangible asset.

We remind income trust issuers of the requirements of CICA Handbook Section 1581, including the examples of intangible assets included in Appendix A of that section, as well as the guidance contained in EIC-137 *Recognition of Customer Relationship Intangible Assets Acquired in a Business Combination.*

Conclusion

Our findings suggest that many income trust issuers need to improve the quality of their disclosure.

We remind income trust issuers of existing requirements and guidance including, but not limited to:

- CSA Staff Notice 52-306 *Non-GAAP Financial Measures*
- Proposed National Policy 41-201 *Income Trusts and Other Indirect Offerings*
- National Policy 48 *Future — Oriented Financial Information*
- CICA Handbook Section 3250 *Surplus*
- CICA Handbook Section 1581 *Business Combinations*
- EIC-137 *Recognition of Customer Relationship Intangible Assets Acquired in a Business Combination*

We intend to continue monitoring the continuous disclosure provided by income trusts, including disclosure for the six specific issues addressed in this memo.

Policies and Orders: NPS 41-201; CSAN 51-319, 52-306.

CSA Staff Notice 51-311 — Frequently Asked Questions Regarding National Instrument 51-102 Continuous Disclosure Obligations

Date: March 26, 2004, revised April 23, 2004, June 18, 2004, February 11, 2005 and May 4, 2007

27 O.S.C.B. 3137, 4148, 5781, 28 O.S.C.B. 1527 and 30 O.S.C.B. 4119

Background

The framework set out in National Instrument 51-102 *Continuous Disclosure Obligations* (NI 51-102) has been applicable since March 30, 2004. The most recent amendments to NI 51-102 came into effect on December 29, 2006. Those amendments clarify some provisions, address additional areas and streamline requirements.

Frequently asked questions on NI 51-102

Users of NI 51-102 should first consult NI 51-102 itself, its companion policy (51-102CP), and the instructions to the forms for answers to their questions about NI 51-102. To assist persons and companies that use NI 51-102, we have compiled a list of frequently asked questions (FAQs).

This list is not exhaustive, but does broadly represent the types of inquiries we have received.

Some terms we have used in these FAQs are defined in NI 51-102 or in National Instrument 14-101 *Definitions*.

We have divided the FAQs into the following categories:

A. Definitions
B. Financial statements
C. MD&A
D. Annual information forms (AIFs)
E. Business acquisition reports (BAR)
F. Information circulars and proxy solicitations
G. Filing material documents
H. Transition
I. Other

A. — Definitions

A-1 Q: I am a scholarship plan. Am I an *investment fund*, and so not subject to NI 51-102?

A: A scholarship plan is an investment fund as defined in NI 51-102. As a result, you are not subject to NI 51-102, but you should instead refer to National Instrument 81-106 *Investment Fund Continuous Disclosure*. [Amended May 4, 2007]

A-2 [Deleted May 4, 2007]

A-3 Q: I am a large debt issuer, but none of my securities are listed or quoted on a marketplace. Am I still a *venture issuer*?

A: Yes, any issuer without securities listed or quoted on a marketplace is a venture issuer. However, we published proposed amendments to NI 51-102 on March 29, 2007 that would amend the definition of venture issuer to remove debt-only issuers with total assets of over $25 million from the definition. If we adopt those amendments, then large debt-only issuers would be classified as non-venture issuers. [Amended May 4, 2007]

A-4 Q: I have securities listed on the TSX Venture Exchange (TSXV), and quoted on the Over-the-Counter Bulletin Board in the United States. Am I still a *venture issuer*?

A: You are still a venture issuer. As long as none of the marketplaces on which you are listed or quoted are identified in the definition of *venture issuer* in section 1.1 of NI 51-102, you are a venture issuer, regardless of how many marketplaces your securities are listed or quoted on. [Amended May 4, 2007]

A-5 Q: If I have securities listed on a junior exchange in Europe, am I a *venture issuer*?

A: You are not a venture issuer if you have securities listed or quoted on any marketplace outside of Canada and the United States other than the Alternative Investment Market of the London Stock Exchange or the market formerly known as OFEX (now the PLUS markets — see Question A-8). You must first determine if your securities are listed or quoted (instead of just admitted to trading), and if the facility is a marketplace as defined in NI 51-102.

When NI 51-102 was first implemented, we received inquiries regarding the Regulated Unofficial Market of the Frankfurt Stock Exchange (RUM) and the Unofficial Regulated Market of the Berlin-Bremen Stock Exchange (URM). While we were investigating those facilities, and to give certainty to industry, some jurisdictions issued blanket exemption orders so that issuers with securities traded on those facilities would be treated as venture issuers for the purposes of NI 51-102. Other jurisdictions issued discretionary orders, on a case-by-case basis. We later completed our review, and determined that trading on the RUM (now known as the Open Market) or URM does not constitute a listing or quotation. As a result, issuers that otherwise meet the definition of "venture issuer" with securities traded on those facilities are venture issuers for the purposes of NI 51-102. [Amended April 23, 2004, February 11, 2005 and May 4, 2007]

A-6 *Q:* According to the definition of *venture issuer* in section 1.1 of NI 51-102, if I am listed on an exchange registered as a "national securities exchange" under section 6 of the 1934 Act, I am not a *venture issuer*. How do I find out what exchanges are registered as national securities exchanges?

A: The SEC publishes the names of the registered national securities exchanges on its website at www.sec.gov/answers/exchanges.htm. [Amended May 4, 2007]

A-7 *Q:* When do I make the determination of whether or not I am a *venture issuer* in section 1.1 of NI 51-102 for the purposes of NI 51-102?

A: The definition of *venture issuer* in section 1.1 of NI 51-102 sets out the times at which you determine if you are a venture issuer for the various requirements in NI 51-102. That time differs depending on the part of NI 51-102 you are applying. [Amended May 4, 2007]

A-8 *Q:* According to the definition of *venture issuer*, I will not lose my status as a venure issuer if I have securities quoted on the market known as OFEX. However, OFEX recently changed its name to PLUS. Will I still be a *venture issuer* if my securities are quoted on PLUS? [Added May 4, 2007]

A: Yes. We interpret the reference to "the market known as OFEX" in the definition of *venture issuer* as a reference to the PLUS markets operated by PLUS Markets Group plc. The proposed amendments to NI 51-102 that were published for comment on March 29, 2007 included "housekeeping" amendments to the definition of *venture issuer* to reflect the change of name of OFEX to the PLUS markets.

A-9 *Q:* We have recently completed a transaction that involves an operating non-public enterprise and a non-operating public enterprise (i.e. a shell company). The transaction resulted in the owners and management of the operating non-public enterprise acquiring control of the combined enterprise. The accounting principles applicable to the issuer refer to this transaction as a reverse takeover or a reverse acquisition, even though the accounting principles specify that this type of transaction is not a business combination because the non-operating public enterprise does not meet the definition of a business. Would this type of transaction be included in the definition of a reverse takeover under NI 51-102? [Added May 4, 2007]

A: Yes. Although these reverse takeover transactions are accounted for as capital transactions (because they are not business combinations), they are still considered to be reverse takeovers under accounting principles and are included in the definition of reverse takeover under NI 51-102.

B. — Financial statements

B-1 *Q:* My auditors did not review my interim financial statements. As a result, under NI 51-102 my interim financial statements must be accompanied by a notice. What form should this notice take?

A: NI 51-102 does not specify the form of notice that should accompany the financial statements. The notice accompanies, but does not form part of, the financial statements. We expect that the notice will normally be provided on a separate page appearing immediately before the financial statements, in a manner similar to an audit report that accompanies annual financial statements.

B-2 *Q:* Do I have to file a notice indicating that my interim financial statements have not been reviewed by my auditor, if a public accountant that is not my auditor, reviews them?

A: Yes. If your auditor does not review your interim financial statements, you must file the notice, even if a public accountant reviews the statement. Refer to subsection 3.4(3) of 51-102CP for a discussion of what is meant by "review" if your annual financial statements are audited in accordance with Canadian GAAS, or auditing standards other than Canadian GAAS. If your annual financial statements are audited in accordance with Canadian GAAS, the relevant requirements for a review of interim financial statements by the auditor are set out in the Handbook section 7050. [Amended May 4, 2007]

B-3 *Q:* Do I have to file a notice indicating that my interim financial statements have not been reviewed if only the current period, and not the comparative interim period, have been reviewed by my auditor?

A: Yes. The review of the interim financial statements must cover all periods presented in the statements (subsection 4.3(3) of NI 51-102). [Amended May 4, 2007]

B-4 *Q:* When does the annual request form under section 4.6 have to be sent?

A: Once a year — at any time during the year.

B-5 *Q:* If I send my annual financial statements to all my securityholders, do I still have to send a request form under subsection 4.6(1) in respect of my interim financial statements?

A: No. Subsection 4.6(5) is a complete exemption from having to send an annual request form, if you send your annual financial statements to your securityholders (other than holders of debt securities) within 140 days of year-end and in accordance with National Instrument 54-101 *Communication with Beneficial Owners of Securities of a Reporting Issuer* (NI 54-101). You will still have to send a copy of your interim financial statements to any securityholder that requests a copy (subsection 4.6(3) of NI 51-102). [Amended May 4, 2007]

B-6 *Q:* My current auditor does not intend to register with the Canadian Public Accountability Board. As a result, I am changing my auditor in order to comply with National Instrument 52-108 *Auditor Oversight*. Do I have to comply with the change of auditor requirements?

A: Yes, you must comply with the change of auditor requirements, even if the change in your auditor is only to comply with NI 52-108.

B-7 *Q:* Does the filing deadline in NI 51-102 for our annual financial statements and MD&A affect when we must hold our annual meeting and send our proxy-related materials? [Added February 11, 2005, amended May 4, 2007]

A: Under subsections 4.6(3) and 5.6(1) of NI 51-102, you must send your annual financial statements and MD&A by 10 calendar days after the filing deadline (a maximum of 100 days after your financial year end if you are a non-venture issuer, 130 days if you are a venture issuer) to all your securityholders who have previously requested these documents by either returning the request form or otherwise making a request. (If you receive a request after the filing deadline, the delivery deadline is 10 calendar days after you receive the request.)

As a result, the annual filing deadlines in NI 51-102 will, in effect, require you to either

- send your annual financial statements and MD&A within 10 days after the filing deadline for your financial year end, to securityholders who previously requested them (if any). If the proxy-related materials are not available at that time, send those materials later, in a second mailing, in time for your annual meeting; or

- if you want to do only one mailing, rely on the exemption in subsections 4.6(5) and 5.6(3) from the requirement to send a request form and send financial statements and MD&A on request, by mailing your annual financial statements and MD&A with your proxy-related materials to your securityholders (other than holders of debt instruments) within 140 days after your financial year end and in accordance with NI 54-101.

B-8 [Deleted May 4, 2007]

B-9 *Q:* I am required to file financial statements for a reverse takeover acquirer under section 4.10 of NI 51-102. How do I file those documents on SEDAR? [Added May 4, 2007]

A: Financial statements required under section 4.10 of NI 51-102 for the reverse takeover acquirer are filed on SEDAR under the profile of the reporting issuer. You should file the financial statements within the same project that relates to the corresponding interim or annual period of the reporting issuer. You should attach the financial statements to the document type "Financial statements of operating entity".

B-10 *Q:* We are changing our year-end from February 28 to December 31. Our transition year will be the 10 months ending December 31, 2007 and our interim periods in the transition year will end on May 31, August 31 and November 30, 2007. Does subsection 4.8(5) of NI 51-102 require the filing of interim financial statements for the 3 months ending November 30, 2007? [Added May 4, 2007]

A: No, you are not required to file financial statements for the interim period ending on November 30, 2007.

C. — MD&A

General

C-1 *Q:* Since my MD&A is filed with my financial statements, do my auditors have to review my MD&A before I file it?

A: NI 51-102 does not include a direct requirement for MD&A to be reviewed by an issuer's auditor. However, under CICA Handbook section 7500 *Auditor association with annual reports, interim reports and other public documents*, an auditor is deemed to be associated with MD&A corresponding to annual financial statements on which the auditor has issued an auditor's report. Also, an auditor is deemed to be associated with interim MD&A if the auditor has been engaged to audit or review the corresponding interim financial statements.

If an auditor is deemed to be associated with MD&A, the auditor must perform the procedures specified in section 7500 of the Handbook. The auditor's specific aims when performing those procedures are to: (a) determine whether the financial statements, and when applicable, the report of the auditor, have been accurately reproduced; and (b) consider whether any of the other information in the document raises questions regarding, or appears to be otherwise inconsistent with, the financial statements.

Handbook section 7500 specifies that the auditor should arrange to obtain the MD&A prior to its release and perform the procedures set out in the section. Further, when circumstances prevent the auditor from obtaining the MD&A prior to its release, the auditor should perform the procedures required by Handbook as soon as possible after its release, and consider advising the audit committee of the circumstances.

If the reporting issuer's annual financial statements are audited in accordance with auditing standards other than Canadian GAAS, then the auditor's association with, and the requirement for procedures relating to, annual and interim MD&A would be determined by those other auditing standards.

Form

C-2 *Q:* Do I have to duplicate in my MD&A information already included in the notes to the financial statements?

A: Information specifically required by Form 51-102F1 must be included in the MD&A, and simply cross-referencing to a note in the financial statements would not be sufficient. For example, although the various notes to the financial statements may include information about contractual obligations, Form 51-102F1 requires an issuer that is not a venture issuer to include in the MD&A a summary, in tabular form, of contractual obligations. In this example a cross-reference would not meet the Form 51-102F1 requirement.

Issuers should use their judgment to ensure the MD&A complements and supplements the financial statements. This may include a discussion and analysis, but not a repetition of details disclosed in notes to the financial statements that are not specifically required by Form 51-102F1.

C-3 [Deleted May 4, 2007]

C-4 [Deleted May 4, 2007]

C-5 [Deleted May 4, 2007]

C-6 [Deleted May 4, 2007]

D. — Annual information forms (AIFs)

General

D-1 *Q:* Are there situations when a venture issuer may have to file an AIF?

A: Venture issuers do not have to file an AIF under NI 51-102. There are other policies or rules that require the filing of an AIF to benefit from those instruments. For example, to use the short form prospectus system under National Instrument 44-101 *Short Form Prospectus Distributions* (NI 44-101), an issuer must file an AIF. Similarly, if a TSXV listed issuer intends to complete a public offering by short form offering document under TSXV Policy 4.6, or an issuer wants to use the offering memorandum for qualifying issuers under National Instrument 45-106 *Prospectus and Registration Exemptions*, the issuer must file an AIF. [Amended May 4, 2007]

D-2 [Deleted May 4, 2007]

Form

D-3 *Q:* Can I use my information circular in connection with an arrangement or reverse takeover as an alternative form of AIF?

A: No. The acceptable alternative forms of annual information forms are set out in the definition of AIF in section 1.1 of NI 51-102. They include a Form 10-K, Form 10-KSB or Form 20-F for SEC issuers, as defined in NI 51-102. Information circulars are not acceptable alternative forms of AIFs. [Amended May 4, 2007]

E. — Business acquisition reports (BAR)

E-1 *Q:* The optional significance tests in section 8.3(4) of NI 51-102 are based on financial information relating to my most recently completed interim period or financial year. In calculating the optional significance tests, can I use financial information relating to financial statements for a completed interim period or financial year that have not yet been approved by my board of directors or audit committee, and have not yet been filed?

A: Yes. However, you would want to consider the possibility that adjustments to the financial statements from subsequent review by your external auditors, audit committee or board of directors may change the results of the calculation. For example, the acquisition may be a significant acquisition based on the adjusted financial statements, when it initially did not meet the significance thresholds, in which case you may be in default of the BAR requirements. [Amended May 4, 2007]

E-2 *Q:* If I am acquiring a business, there are no financial statements, and confidentiality provisions prevent disclosure of certain information about the business, how do I file a BAR?

A: Paragraph 8.1(4) of NI 51-102CP discusses the term "business" and indicates that whether or not the business previously prepared financial statements, an acquisition may be considered a business and trigger the requirement for financial statements in a BAR. As well, section 8.6 of NI 51-102CP provides guidance on the preparation of divisional and carve-out financial statements. If an issuer is considering the acquisition of a business, it must consider its obligations under NI 51-102 to file a BAR and the issuer must plan its acquisition in a manner that will ensure it can meet those obligations.

E-2.1 *Q:* Is an investment in equity securities of another company that is accounted for by the issuer using the cost method considered an acquisition of a business under subsection 8.1(1) of NI 51-102?

A: No. An investment accounted for by the cost method is not considered an acquisition of a business under subsection 8.1(1) of NI 51-102. However, investments that are consolidated or are accounted for by the equity method or by proportionate consolidation are considered acquisitions of a business as discussed in subsection 8.1(1). [Added June 18, 2004]

E-3 *Q:* If I acquire a business that will be accounted for by the equity method and the acquisition qualifies for the exemption in section 8.6, does my BAR have to name the auditor of the investee and indicate that the auditor of the investee has not consented?

A: Section 8.6 of the NI 51-102 does not require an issuer to name the auditor of the financial information or underlying financial statements or to include the auditor's report on the financial information or underlying financial statements. As a result, the issuer does not have to disclose the absence of consent from the auditor of the investee.

E-4 *Q:* If an issuer's subsidiary acquires shares in itself from interests outside the consolidated group, is that acquisition subject to the "step-by-step" provisions in Part 8 of NI 51-102?

A: Yes, the acquisition by the subsidiary of shares in itself increases the issuer's proportionate interest in the subsidiary and so should be considered a step acquisition by the issuer. The provisions in section 8.11 for step-by-step acquisitions apply if the acquisition is a significant acquisition. [Added June 18, 2004]

F. — Information circulars and proxy solicitations

F-1 [Deleted May 4, 2007]

G. — Filing material documents

G-1 *Q:* Do material documents, such as constating documents or material contracts, dated before March 30, 2004 have to be filed under the new filing requirements? When do they have to be filed?

A: Any constating documents, including articles of incorporation, that are dated before March 30, 2004 must be filed under the filing requirements, as long as they are still effective (Part 12 of NI 51-102). The documents must be filed no later than when you first file an AIF under NI 51-102, if you are not a venture issuer (section 12.3 of NI 51-102). If you are a venture issuer, you must file the document within 120 days of the end of your first financial year beginning on or after January 1, 2004 (clause 12.3(b) of NI 51-102). However, if the making of the document constitutes a material change for the issuer, the document must be filed no later than the time of filing a material change report (section 12.3 of NI 51-102). [Amended May 4, 2007]

G-2 *Q:* Do the original forms of constating documents or material contracts that have been amended before March 30, 2004 have to be filed under the new filing requirements?

A: Only the current versions of documents have to be filed — that is, the documents, as amended, not the original forms that are no longer applicable.

G-3 *Q:* Will material contracts be public documents?

A: Yes.

H. — Transition

Financial statements

H-1 [Deleted May 4, 2007]

H-2 [Deleted May 4, 2007]

H-3 [Deleted May 4, 2007]

H-4 [Deleted May 4, 2007]

H-5 [Deleted May 4, 2007]

MD&A

H-6 [Deleted May 4, 2007]

H-7 [Deleted May 4, 2007]

H-7.1 [Deleted May 4, 2007]

AIFs

H-8 [Deleted May 4, 2007]

H-9 [Deleted May 4, 2007]

General

H-10 [Deleted May 4, 2007]

H-11 [Deleted May 4, 2007]

H-12 *Q:* Effective June 1, 2004, NI 51-102 has replaced the current form of executive compensation disclosure in Ontario — Form 40 — with Form 51-102F6. However, Item 17.1 of the Ontario long form prospectus — Form 41-501F1 — requires executive compensation disclosure in Form 40. What form of executive compensation disclosure do I give in my Ontario long form prospectuses?

A: You should provide disclosure of executive compensation in your Form 41-501F1 using Form 51-102F6. [Added June 18, 2004, Amended May 4, 2007]

I. — Other

I-1 [Deleted May 4, 2007]

I-2 [Deleted May 4, 2007]

I-3 [Deleted May 4, 2007]

I-4 [Deleted May 4, 2007]

CSA Staff Notice 51-312 — Harmonized Continuous Disclosure Review Program

Date: July 16, 2004; replaced July 24, 2009

27 O.S.C.B. 6475 and O.S.C.B. 5878

Purpose

In 2004, staff (we) of the Canadian Securities Administrators (CSA) established a harmonized program for continuous disclosure reviews (the CDR program). The goal of the program is to improve the completeness, quality and timeliness of continuous disclosure (CD) by reporting issuers in Canada.

In July 2004, we issued CSA Staff Notice 51-312, which described the new program. This revised notice updates issuers, investors and other market participants on the CDR program. It also gives an overview of how the CDR program works.

Background

Under Canadian securities law, reporting issuers must provide timely CD about their businesses and affairs. Market participants, including investors, rely on this information to make informed investment decisions.

Most of the continuous disclosure requirements are in the following rules or regulations (the CD rules):

- National Instrument 51-102 *Continuous Disclosure Obligations* (NI 51-102)
- National Instrument 51-101 *Standards of Disclosure for Oil and Gas Activities*
- National Instrument 52-109 *Certification of Disclosure in Issuer's Annual and Interim Filing*
- National Instrument 52-110 *Audit Committees*
- National Instrument 58-101 *Disclosure of Corporate Governance Practices*
- National Instrument 43-101 *Standards of Disclosure for Mineral Projects*

The CD rules are intended to ensure that Canadian investors receive a uniformly high level of CD across the country. Through the CDR program, we are working to ensure that the scope and level of CD reviews carried out by staff across Canada are consistent.

Under the CDR program, the CSA regulators generally follow principles of mutual reliance. That means issuers deal only with staff of their principal regulator. Staff of the other regulators rely on the staff of the principal regulator on matters related to CD reviews.

Objectives of the CDR program

The CDR program helps ensure that issuers understand and comply with their obligations under the CD rules. Accordingly, the CDR program has two fundamental objectives: education and compliance.

Education

Issuers should understand the nature and extent of their disclosure obligations under the CD rules. We educate issuers through our interaction with them during our CD reviews. We also provide guidance through our publications, seminars, webcasts and other forums that address specific aspects of the CD rules.

Compliance

The CD review process helps us determine whether issuers are complying with their disclosure obligations under the CD rules. The CDR program is designed to identify material disclosure deficiencies and questionable transactions that affect the reliability and accuracy of an issuer's disclosure record.

Role of the principal regulator

The principal regulator is responsible for reviewing an issuer's CD information and taking any necessary steps to ensure that the issuer complies with its CD obligations. An issuer's principal regulator is determined by the principles set out in Part 3 of National Policy 11-202 *Process for Prospectus Reviews in Multiple Jurisdictions*.

The principal regulator is usually the regulator in the jurisdiction where the reporting issuer's head office is located. As a result, an issuer will generally only have to deal with staff of a single regulator on CD-related matters. It also allows staff in each jurisdiction to develop a greater understanding of their respective issuers, which helps enhance the efficiency and quality of CD reviews.

Selecting issuers for review

In general, we use a risk-based approach to select issuers for review and to determine the type of reviews to conduct. This approach takes into account the potential harm to Canadian capital markets if an issuer fails to provide complete, accurate and timely disclosure about its business and affairs.

We apply risk-based criteria to select issuers for review. We also consider specific issues and concerns affecting each industry. The selection criteria may change, for example, if certain disclosure-related issues gain greater public prominence, or the CSA develops a consensus or has concerns about particular accounting issues or disclosure practices. In addition to the risk-based criteria, individual jurisdictions may use criteria specific to their jurisdiction.

The CDR program has continued to evolve and we have now established industry discussion groups to facilitate the sharing of information. These discussion groups allows us to expand our knowledge and identify risks particular to specific industries. This approach also allows us to conduct CD reviews more efficiently and address the key risk areas, accounting issues and general disclosure issues affecting each industry.

Types of review

In general, we will conduct either a "full" review or an "issue-oriented" review.

Full review

A full review is broad in scope and covers many types of disclosure. A full review covers the issuer's most recent annual and interim financial statements and MD&A filed before the start of the review. For all other disclosure, the review covers a 12- to 15-month period before the start of the review. In certain cases, we may extend the scope of the review to cover prior periods. We monitor a reporting issuer's CD until we complete the review. Among other things, we usually review the issuer's:

- annual financial statements and management's discussion and analysis (MD&A)
- interim financial statements and MD&A

- technical disclosure, including technical reports for oil and gas, and mining issuers

- annual information forms (AIF)

- annual reports

- information circulars

- press releases, material change reports and business acquisition reports (BARs)

- website

- CFO and CEO certifications

- material contracts

We may also review media coverage and analysts' reports, if warranted.

Issue-oriented review

An issue-oriented review is an in-depth review focusing on a specific accounting, legal or regulatory issue that we believe warrants regulatory scrutiny. Issue-oriented reviews may be conducted locally by individual jurisdictions or co-ordinated across the CSA. The nature of the issue or issues identified determines the period we will review.

Review process

The primary focus of a CD review is to ensure an issuer's compliance with securities legislation. This includes compliance of its financial statements to generally accepted accounting principles.

We examine the consistency of disclosure in the issuer's CD record and the overall quality of the disclosure. In particular, we assess whether there is sufficient information for the reader to understand the issuer's financial performance, financial position, business risks and future prospects.

If we do not identify any issues, we close the CD review file. If we identify issues, we communicate them to the issuer, usually through a comment letter. We also ask the issuer to provide its audit committee and its auditors with a copy of all correspondence between the issuer and the principal regulator during the review.

In general, we expect issuers to provide a written response within two weeks of the date of the comment letter. The more complete and comprehensive the response is, the faster and more efficiently we can conclude the review. It will also reduce the need for additional follow up.

While the objective of a CD review is to improve the overall quality of an issuer's disclosure, the fact that an issuer has been the subject of a CD review does not guarantee the accuracy of its disclosure.

Resolving issues

We work with issuers to ensure that the issues identified during the review are resolved in a timely and appropriate manner.

When material deficiencies or errors are identified, we expect issuers to correct them by restating and re-filing the document. In some circumstances, we may ask the issuer to restate comparative information in financial statements in subsequent filings.

Under section 11.5 of NI 51-102, if an issuer has to restate or re-file a CD document because of a material deficiency or error, it must promptly issue and file a news release disclosing:

- the nature and substance of the change or proposed changes

- the general impact of the changes on previously filed information, and

- the steps the issuer will take before amending or filing restated CD document.

In certain situations, where we have identified a material deficiency or error during the CD review, we may place the issuer on our default lists or issue a cease-trade order.

If we identify a material breach of securities legislation and cannot resolve it with the issuer, we may consider recommending enforcement action against the issuer. If the issuer corrects the disclosure problem in the meantime, we may still pursue enforcement action. However, the correction will minimize the harm to investors and will generally be taken into account in considering whether any action is necessary.

Policies and Orders: CSAN 51-332, 51-334, 52-315, 52-325.

CSA Staff Notice 51-316 — Continuous Disclosure Review of Smaller Issuers

Date: December 9, 2005

28 O.S.C.B. 9808

Purpose of Notice

Staff in the jurisdictions represented by the Canadian Securities Administrators (CSA or we) are publishing this notice to summarize some of the deficiencies we see most frequently when we review the continuous disclosure (CD) record of smaller issuers. By alerting issuers to some of these problems, we hope they will avoid some common disclosure deficiencies.

For the purpose of the notice, we focused on those issuers with assets under $5 million; however, we believe the guidance in this notice may be useful to larger issuers.

Overview

This notice addresses common deficiencies we found within the following four CD areas:

1. — Financial Statements

This notice focuses on the most common financial statement deficiencies arising from a failure to comply with the following Generally Accepted Accounting Principles (GAAP):

- Enterprises in the Development Stage (Accounting Guideline (AcG)-11)

- Revenue Recognition (Emerging Issues Committee Abstract (EIC)-141)

- Interim Financial Statements (CICA Handbook (HB) 1751)

- Related Party Transactions (CICA HB 3840)

- Cash Flow Statements (CICA HB 1540)

- New GAAP Requirements

2. — Management's Discussion & Analysis (MD&A)

Frequently, the MD&A of smaller issuers contains superficial analyses that merely repeat the information in the accompanying financial statements. This notice describes the most commonly noted deficiencies on the following MD&A topics:

- Operational Analysis

- Liquidity and Capital Resources

- Projects Under Development

- Related Party Transactions

3. — Mining and Oil & Gas Industries

This notice discusses the most common non-technical disclosure deficiencies made by issuers in the extractive industries.

4. — Other Disclosure Issues

- SEDI — Issuer and Insider filing requirements

- Timely Disclosure — The requirement for issuers to maintain an ongoing communication with the capital markets

- Audit Committees — The mandatory role of audit committees and their involvement with corporate disclosure

- Certification — CEO and CFO certifications of their issuer's annual and interim filings

This staff notice is not an exhaustive summary of all smaller issuer CD compliance issues. We remind issuers their CD record must comply with all relevant securities legislation. Addressing only the issues we raise in this staff notice may not satisfy all the obligations a smaller issuer has under securities law.

As explained in CSA Staff Notice 51-312 Harmonized Continuous Disclosure Review Program, we expect issuers to correct material deficiencies or errors by restating and re-filing the CD document.

Financial Statements

Financial statements form the foundation of an issuer's CD record. Management is responsible for accurately recording transactions and preparing financial statements. GAAP provides a framework for this disclosure, however we frequently observe the following GAAP deficiencies within smaller issuers' financial statements.

Enterprises in the Development Stage

Paragraphs 29 to 35 of AcG-11 specify additional disclosures that enterprises in the development stage must provide (paragraphs 2 to 6 of AcG-11 explain when an issuer is in the development stage). Examples of insufficient disclosure include:

- failure to discuss the nature of development activities and the planned principal operations of the enterprise

- insufficient disclosures about projects under development

This disclosure should be current and reflect the project's state of development. The Appendix to AcG-11 contains examples of the disclosure issuers should provide.

CICA HB 3063 *Impairment of Long-Lived Assets* (CICA HB 3063) contains requirements for the write-down of long-lived assets. EIC-126 *Accounting by Mining Enterprises for Exploration Costs* provides additional information on the application of certain aspects of CICA HB 3063. We also remind issuers in the development stage to consider the additional asset impairment guidance in paragraphs 12 to 20 of AcG-11.

We have found that some smaller issuers in the extractive industries have not written down long-lived assets even though certain asset impairment triggers in AcG-11 are present. Some examples of asset impairment triggers in paragraphs 16 to 18 of AcG-11 include:

- unfavourable changes to project economics

- inability to access the site

- political instability in the region in which the property is located

- delay in development activity extending beyond three years (the general presumption being that a write-down is necessary)

- exploration results are not promising and no more work is being planned in the foreseeable future

If an asset's value is impaired, the issuer should write down the value of the asset immediately, which may be before the project is abandoned.

"Enterprises in the development stage ... have, by their nature, only limited information on past performance. The absence of a track record for these enterprises removes one important means of predicting how well the enterprise will do in the future. In order to make these assessments, users of financial statements of enterprises in the development stage are interested in information regarding the significant projects being undertaken."[1]

Revenue Recognition

Revenue and revenue growth are often important elements for investors to consider when reviewing an issuer's financial statements.

It is important for investors to be able to understand an issuer's sources of revenue. EIC-141 requires issuers to disclose their revenue recognition policy. The revenue recognition policy should address each material source of revenue and alternative methods of delivery of the same good or service. Some issuers omit this disclosure, or include disclosure that does not meaningfully describe their policy. For example, we commonly encounter revenue recognition policies that say, "Revenue is recorded when earned". An example of a better revenue recognition policy might say,

> *The Company recognizes contract revenues under the percentage-of-completion method using milestones or engineering approvals to determine the percentage complete. The Company makes a complete provision for contract losses as soon as such losses are estimable. The timing of revenue recognition may differ from the contract payment schedules, resulting in revenues that have been earned but not billed. Billings are applied against construction in process for financial statement presentation. The Company recognizes maintenance service revenues when it renders the services. When the Company recognizes revenue, it also records a provision for potential warranty claims. It bases the provision on warranty terms and claims experience.*

Issuers should consult EIC-141 for guidance on revenue recognition timing issues (such as those transactions involving upfront fee payments) and revenue measurement issues (most notably for those transactions involving a right of return), to ensure their revenue recognition policies comply with GAAP.

Interim Financial Statements

Interim financial statements are an essential source of information about an issuer's activities. However, many smaller issuers' financial statements omit proper note disclosure, or contain material measurement errors. Both of these deficiencies result in financial statements that do not comply with GAAP.

Some common deficiencies are:

- not presenting the financial periods required by paragraph 16 of CICA HB 1751 in the interim financial statements

- omitting the mandatory financial statement note disclosures required by paragraph 14 of CICA HB 1751

- failing to adjust accruals and estimates throughout the year. For example, some issuers are not updating their accounting for future tax liabilities, amortization, or possible asset impairment until they produce their next annual financial statements. Making such adjustments only on an annual basis can result in a misleading depiction of an issuer's current financial condition at interim reporting periods.

If an auditor has not performed a review of the interim financial statements, National Instrument 51-102 Continuous Disclosure Obligations requires the issuer to attach a notice stating this fact, to the interim financial statements.

Related Party Transactions

To comply with CICA HB 3840, issuers with related party transactions must provide complete and transparent information about the transaction in question. In some cases, issuers used the exchange amount to record the transaction, but did not disclose how the exchange amount was determined.

We frequently see smaller issuers account for a transfer of a business between enterprises under common control as a "business combination", and provide inadequate disclosure of the transaction and the relationship between the parties. Such transactions are not business combinations and CICA HB 1581 *Business Combinations* does not apply. Instead, CICA HB 3840 provides the relevant guidance as to the use of the exchange amount or carrying amount for such related party transfers. EIC-66 *Transfer of a Business Between Enterprises Under Common Control* discusses how to account for these transactions using the exchange amount to determine the cost of the purchase. If enterprises under common control account for a transfer of a business using the carrying amounts, EIC-89 *Exchanges of Ownership Interests Between Enterprises Under Common Control — Wholly and Partially-Owned Subsidiaries* indicates that "continuity-of-interests" accounting is appropriate,

---

[1]Accounting Guideline AcG-11, *Enterprises in the Development Stage.*

and the financial statements for all prior periods of the combining entities will be presented as though they were one issuer since their inception.

Cash Flow Statement

Smaller issuers often make these mistakes when preparing their cash flow statement:

- offsetting transactions such as capital asset purchases and disposals

- including investing and financing activities in operating activities (or vice-versa)

- including non-monetary transactions (such as converting debt to equity) in the cash flow statement rather than note disclosure

Issuers should remember that cash flow statements are more than a reproduction of information in the income statement and changes in balance sheet accounts. Correctly prepared, a cash flow statement can provide users with information about an issuer's ability to meet its liquidity commitments and finance its capital resource investments. Issuers should complement this disclosure through their liquidity discussion under item 1.6 of Form 51-102F1 in their MD&A.

"Information about the cash flows of an enterprise enables users of financial statements to assess the capacity of the enterprise to generate cash and cash equivalents and the needs of the enterprise for cash resources."[2]

New GAAP Requirements

In many cases, smaller issuers have not adopted new accounting requirements. For example, we found many did not account for their stock option expenses and did not provide the disclosures required by CICA HB 3870 *Stock-Based Compensation and Other Stock-Based Payments.* We expect issuers to maintain a current knowledge of GAAP and, if an issuer seeks assistance from professional advisors when preparing its financial statements, the issuer should ensure these advisors possess a current knowledge of GAAP. Issuers are ultimately responsible for their financial statements.

The CICA Accounting Standards Board's FYI newsletters, in particular the annual special editions, summarize recent accounting pronouncements issuers should consider when they prepare financial statements. Issuers can find copies of the FYI newsletter on the Accounting Standards Board's website at www.acsbcanada.org.

MD&A

If financial statements provide the foundation for an issuer's CD record, then MD&A completes the picture by going beyond the numbers to provide a greater understanding of an issuer's business. For many smaller issuers, the requirement to prepare and file MD&A is relatively new. Many MD&A filings we have reviewed provide limited information or only focus on the positive aspects of the business.

An MD&A's quality is not measured by its length, but in the breadth and depth of its analysis. Reproducing information from financial statements provides little, if any, meaningful information alone.

Operational Analysis

An MD&A's discussion and analysis of operating results should explain what factors contributed to changes in an issuer's operations. A common deficiency we see with smaller issuers is that they reproduce information from the income statement in their MD&A, without explaining what caused the changes reflected in the income statement. For example,

> *Revenues increased from $900,000 to $1,080,000, a 20% increase. Gross Margin increased from $400,000 to $408,000, a 2% increase.*

Part 1.4 of Form 51-102F1 *MD&A* (Form 51-102F1) indicates that MD&A should quantify how volume and price changes affected revenues, and discuss why changes occurred. If other elements affected revenues, such as the introduction of a new product or new competitors, the MD&A should also address those factors. Issuers should not limit the operational analysis to revenues; if the issuer experienced a change in its gross margin percentage, the MD&A should discuss the factors behind the change. If an issuer's financial statements present information from more than one operating segment, the MD&A should discuss the results of each segment. Finally, if an issuer's other expenses differ significantly from a prior period, the MD&A should discuss the reasons behind those changes. An example of a more thorough analysis of one aspect of an issuer's operations might say,

> *Three factors caused a net revenue increase of $180,000:*
>
> - *increased sales volume of Product X — $60,000*
>
> - *decreased unit price of Product X — ($30,000), and*
>
> - *the introduction of a new product during the fourth quarter, Product Y — $150,000*
>
> *In late 2004, we anticipated new competition entering our market, so we discounted our remaining Product X units to encourage their sale and to allow us to focus on its replacement, Product Y. Discounts on Product X caused the reduced gross margin percentage. We expect to continue discounting Product X in the first quarter, but expect our Gross Margin to improve as Product Y replaces Product X.*

This analysis is a discussion of a fictitious issuer's operating results. Depending on the circumstances, issuers should also discuss other factors relevant to their operations, such as the introduction of the new product (projections, or results to date vs. expectations).

For more information on drafting better MD&A, refer to the British Columbia Securities Commission's Continuous Disclosure update 5 and 5R, and the Ontario Securities Commission Staff Notice 51-713 Report on Staff's Review of MD&A. Each of these documents is available on

---

[2]CICA Handbook — Accounting, Section 1540 *Cash Flow Statements.*

the respective commission's website. Further MD&A guidance and a MD&A self-assessment checklist is available on the CICA's website at www.cica.ca.

Liquidity and Capital Resources

Smaller issuers often focus on expanding their operations or completing a project. In order to comply with Parts 1.6 and 1.7 of Form 51-102F1, MD&A should discuss the issuer's working capital requirements and any expenditure the issuer is committed to make. We often find MD&A that reproduces information from the balance sheet and cash flow statement as a substitute for liquidity analysis, for example,

> *As at year-end, the Company had cash of $9,000 and accounts receivable of $50,000. Current assets amounted to $150,000 with current liabilities of $400,000 resulting in a working capital deficit of $250,000. The Company believes that it has sufficient capital on hand to satisfy working capital requirements for the next 12 months.*

The MD&A should explain how the issuer will fund its working capital and capital resource requirements. If the issuer has a working capital deficiency, the MD&A should explain how the issuer will meet its obligations as they become due and remedy the deficiency. The MD&A should discuss provisions in debt agreements that could affect the issuer's cash flow. If there is a default under such an agreement, the MD&A should explain how the issuer will rectify the default. An example of a more thorough analysis of an issuer's liquidity and capital resources might say,

> *As of year-end, the Company's debt to equity ratio was in breach of a covenant in its loan agreement. Subsequent to year-end, the Company:*
>
> - *renegotiated the covenants in the loan agreement to cure the default; and*
>
> - *borrowed an additional $300,000 to meet current and future working capital requirements.*
>
> *New terms under the loan agreement restrict repayment of existing debt payable to related parties. We estimate that the Company will need $500,000 over the next two years to complete its exploration project. In the short-term, the Company will rely on advances from shareholders and the exercise of options and share purchase warrants to fund exploration costs. We expect to fund the balance of exploration costs with an announced private placement for proceeds up to $300,000.*

Depending on the circumstances, issuers may need to discuss other aspects of their liquidity, such as the loan covenant(s) breached, the terms of the new debt, or reasons for the changes in the their working capital balances (e.g. accounts receivable).

Projects Under Development

When an issuer's operations are not producing significant revenue, the MD&A should focus on the issuer's expenses and business objectives, as stated in general instruction (h) and Item 1.4 (d) of Form 51-102F1. The MD&A should discuss:

- the issuer's plans

- its progress to date against those plans

- the additional costs and time it will require to complete its plans

Although the instructions in Form 51-102F1 do not state it, if applicable, issuers should also discuss the reasons why they did not achieve the plan's milestones.

An MD&A's discussion of the above might say,

> *The Company is developing a medical device to treat burn victims. The product will accelerate the victim's healing process, while reducing pain and scarring. The Company expects this technology will have other applications such as in cosmetic surgery. The Company intends to market the product to hospitals and large care centres, and license the product for use internationally.*

> *Before the Company can market the product, it must receive regulatory approval. In this past year, the Company successfully completed the preliminary testing of its technology. In August of this year, the Company began clinical trials to obtain FDA approval. Initial test results are positive, and the Company has provided additional information to the FDA. The Company does not expect to receive FDA approval for at least 2 years. The Company expects to begin shipping the product 4 months after receiving FDA approval. The Company has spent approximately $1.2 million to date developing and testing the technology, and will require an additional $1.3 million to complete testing and receive FDA approval. Following FDA approval, the Company expects to incur $2 million in production and marketing costs to bring this product to market.*

> *As disclosed in previous MD&A, initial test results required the Company to modify its prototype. As a result, the Company is currently $500,000 over budget and 6 months behind schedule. Since this initial setback, the Company has experienced no additional delays or unexpected costs.*

In addition, the MD&A would usually discuss the project's liquidity and capital resource requirements. Depending on the circumstances, issuers may need to expand their discussion of a project's development.

To provide an understanding of the operational cash demands, the MD&A should also discuss any significant costs aggregated within financial statement line items.

Related Party Transactions

It is common for issuers to reproduce their financial statements' related party disclosure in their MD&A. This does not meet the requirement in Part 1.9 of Form 51-102F1, which requires a discussion of the business purpose of the related party transaction. A discussion of an issuer's related party transactions might say,

> *During the year, the Company paid $60,000 in interest on a loan payable to the majority shareholder. The unsecured loan bears interest at 14% per annum, and matures in two years with an option by the Company to extinguish the debt at any time without penalty. The Company consummated this related party transaction because alternate sources of financing were unavailable due to the Company's limited operating history and lack of collateral. The Company also paid $45,000 ($15,000 per month) in rent to a company controlled by the CEO. The Company had outgrown its previous location and opted not to renew its lease. The Company entered into this month-to-month lease until the Company constructs its new premises, (presently estimated to be April next year).*

Depending on the circumstances, issuers may need to discuss other elements of the related party transaction, such as its fair value.

Industry Specific Concerns

Oil & Gas Industry

Many smaller issuers are not meeting the requirements of National Instrument 51-101 *Standards of Disclosure for Oil and Gas Activities* (NI 51-101) and its related forms. Examples include failing to issue a news release disclosing that they have made the required filings, and failing to sign and date the required filings.

Smaller issuers frequently aggregate data in their filings despite the fact that Form 51-101F1 *Statement of Reserves Data and Other Oil and Gas Information* (Form 51-101F1) requires issuers to present specified reserves data by "product type" (as defined in section 1.1 of NI 51-101). Issuers should present specified data regarding crude oil separately from data regarding natural gas liquids, and present data regarding light and medium crude oil separately from data regarding heavy oil. Form 51-101F1 filings should also include reconciliations of changes in reserves, and future net revenue (discounted at 10%). Issuers' Form 51-101F1 filings should use a format consistent with the objectives of understandability and comparability expressed in Appendix 2 of NI 51-101's companion policy.

For guidance on the technical disclosure required by NI 51-101, issuers should review CSA Staff Notice 51-313 — *Frequently Asked Questions National Instrument 51-101 Standards of Disclosure for Oil and Gas Activities* and the Alberta Securities Commission's *Consolidated Oil and Gas Review Report* on 2004 NI 51-101 filings. The latter report is available on the ASC's website; the ASC will report on 2005 NI 51-101 filings in early 2006.

Some smaller issuers continue to file a summary of the oil and gas report prepared by an external engineer (as described in Item 2.3(1)(3) of NI 13-101(1)). This summary report is not a substitute for the disclosure required by Form 51-101F1. NI 51-101, the related forms and companion policy are available on the securities commission websites provided at the end of this notice.

Mining Industry

We have amended National Instrument 43-101 *Standards of Disclosure for Mineral Projects* (NI 43-101) and its related form. We expect the amendments to come into force on December 30, 2005. Additional guidance on complying with the amended NI 43-101 is available within its accompanying companion policy.

When smaller issuers discuss mining properties, particularly after an acquisition, they must clearly identify whether the resource estimates on the material property are historical in nature, or are recent estimates based on standards established by the Canadian Institute of Mining, Metallurgy and Petroleum. Many smaller issuers fail to comply with the non-technical requirements of NI 43-101, such as filing a NI 43-101 technical report within the prescribed time limit and failing to name the Qualified Person associated with written disclosure of a scientific or technical nature.

We remind issuers in the mining industry to consider the asset impairment guidance referred to above under the heading "Enterprises in the Development Stage".

Other Disclosure Issues

SEDI

SEDI exists primarily to facilitate timely disclosure of material information about trading by insiders. National Instrument 55-102 *System for Electronic Disclosure by Insiders (SEDI)* requires issuers to establish and maintain issuer profile supplements. It also requires their insiders who own (or exercise control or direction over) securities of the issuer to establish and maintain insider profiles. We often find issuers with at least one insider who failed to maintain a current insider profile or who failed to file accurate insider reports. We recognize the responsibility to file insider reports rests with each individual insider. However, we believe it is in issuers' best interests to monitor their insiders' compliance with SEDI, as errors and omissions may reflect negatively on an issuer.

To avoid late filing fees, insiders should report grant of options within ten calendar days of the date they are notified of the grant (rather than the date the board of directors authorized the grant). If the grant is subject to approval of a stock exchange, then the date of grant can be no earlier than the date of the stock exchange's approval.

Do you have a SEDI filing question or difficulty? For technical problems, contact the SEDI operator (CDS Inc.) at 1-800-219-5381. For SEDI compliance or filing questions, contact your securities regulatory authority listed in Appendix "A" of CSA Staff Notice 55-310 Questions and Answers on SEDI.

Timely disclosure

Part IV of National Policy 51-201 *Disclosure Standards* (NP 51-201) provides examples of situations that normally warrant disclosure via news release and material change report. Disclosure obligations apply to both positive and negative information. We noted instances when issuers have not filed news releases for an extended length of time. As a result, the issuer's only disclosures were its quarterly filings. Disclosing the existence of significant events up to 90 days after their occurrence is not timely disclosure.

We expect the disclosure on issuers' websites to be up-to-date and accurate. For example, issuers should base website content concerning a mining project on information from the most recent technical report. Issuers should also consider including on their websites either all documents they file on SEDAR, or a link to their SEDAR profile.

A corporate disclosure policy can help issuers avoid disclosure transgressions. As noted in National Policy 58-201 *Corporate Governance Guidelines*, a board of directors' mandate should include responsibility for adopting a communication policy for its issuer. The process of drafting a corporate disclosure policy can help an issuer's directors, officers and employees understand the issuer's legal requirements. We encourage issuers to review their corporate disclosure policies against the best practice disclosure guidelines in NP 51-201. A comprehensive disclosure policy can help issuers balance their business pressures and legal requirements and minimize the risk of non-compliance with securities laws.

Audit Committees

Multilateral Instrument 52-110 *Audit Committees* (MI 52-110) and BC Instrument 52-509 *Audit Committees* (BCI 52-509) (collectively, the Instruments) require all issuers to have an audit committee (or a board of directors performing the audit committee's functions, if the issuer qualifies for BCI 52-509's exemption). MI 52-110 requires the audit committee to be satisfied its issuer has adequate procedures in place to ensure the quality of the issuer's financial disclosure, and to review its issuer's financial statements, MD&A, and annual and interim earnings press releases prior to public distribution. The Instruments require the audit committee to oversee the work of the external auditor, and have the external auditor report directly to the audit committee. The Instruments also require the audit committee to play a greater role in ensuring the independence of the external auditor and create additional disclosure obligations for issuers relating to the function and composition of their audit committee. Each issuer should review the Instrument applicable to its jurisdiction for further details on these requirements.

Certification

Multilateral Instrument 52-109 *Certification of Disclosure in Issuers' Annual and Interim Filings* (MI 52-109) requires issuers' CEOs and CFOs to certify that their periodic filings "fairly present in all material respects the financial condition, results of operations and cash flows of the issuer". To effectively certify, the CEO and CFO should consider the content and quality of the filings as a whole, rather than as a collection of unrelated documents prepared to a minimum standard. As discussed in Part 8 of MI 52-109's companion policy, if an issuer's financial statements fail to portray an aspect of an issuer's financial condition, the issuer should supplement the financial statements with additional disclosure in its MD&A.

Conclusion

We expect issuers to consider the guidance in this notice when reviewing their CD records to ensure their disclosure documents comply with securities regulations. Issuers should be aware that some securities legislation provides a statutory right of action for damages for misrepresentation in CD documents. A misrepresentation can arise by providing erroneous information or failing to provide complete information in a timely manner.

Obligations aside, issuers should see timely disclosure as an opportunity to reach investors. Ongoing communication can remove perceived uncertainties relating to an issuer's operations, lowering its cost of capital and increasing its access to capital markets.

You can find the securities regulation literature referred to in this notice, as well as other securities regulation documents, on the following securities commission websites:

- British Columbia Securities Commission; www.bcsc.bc.ca
- Alberta Securities Commission; www.albertasecurities.com
- Saskatchewan Financial Services Commission; www.sfsc.gov.sk.ca
- Manitoba Securities Commission; www.msc.gov.mb.ca
- Ontario Securities Commission; www.osc.gov.on.ca
- Autorité des marchés financiers; www.lautorite.qc.ca
- New Brunswick Securities Commission; www.nbsc-cvmnb.ca
- Nova Scotia Securities Commission; www.gov.ns.ca/nssc
- Newfoundland & Labrador, Dept. of Government Services, Financial Services Regulation Division; www.gs.gov.nl.ca/cca/scon
- Northwest Territories, Dept. of Justice, Securities Registry; www.justice.gov.nt.ca/SecuritiesRegistry/SecuritiesRegistry.htm

CSA Notice 51-319 — Report on Staff's Second Continuous Disclosure Review of Income Trust Issuers

Date: August 4, 2006
29 O.S.C.B. 6272

1. — Purpose

This notice reports the findings and recommendations of staff at the British Columbia, Alberta, Manitoba, Ontario and Nova Scotia securities commissions and the Autorité des marchés financiers (collectively, we or staff) arising from a targeted review of business income trust issuers. This notice supplements the guidance and interpretations provided in National Policy 41-201 *Income Trusts and Other Indirect Offerings* (NP 41-201), Multilateral Staff Notice 51-310 — *Report on Staff's Continuous Disclosure Review of Income Trust Issuers*, CSA Staff Notice 52-306 *Non-GAAP Financial Measures* (SN 52-306) and CSA Staff Notice 41-304 *Income Trusts: Prospectus Disclosure of Distributable Cash*, and the requirements in NI 51-102 *Continuous Disclosure Obligations* (NI 51-102).

2. — Objective and Scope

The income trust structure continues to be a preferred vehicle for a diverse range of businesses to complete initial public offerings. As part of our continuous disclosure review program, we periodically assess income trusts for regulatory compliance in their on-going disclosure. Recently, staff selected 45 business income trust issuers, with head-offices throughout Canada, for a full review of their continuous disclosure.

3. — Summary of Findings and Comments

The results of our review suggest that, in order to fully comply with the continuous disclosure requirements, income trust issuers need to significantly improve the nature and extent of their disclosure. In particular, they need to improve the distributable cash disclosure in Management's Discussion and Analysis (MD&A).

Of the 45 income trust issuers reviewed:

7 issuers had to re-file disclosure documents or file disclosure documents that they did not previously file;

31 issuers committed to provide disclosure enhancements in future MD&A, financial statements, AIF or press releases; and

7 issuers had no identifiable deficiencies in their continuous disclosure.

4. — Significant Disclosure Issues

A. — MD&A Disclosure

The presentation of distributable cash continues to cause considerable confusion. This figure, which represents the expected net cash to be generated by the income trust's businesses or assets often contains significant estimates and assumptions. The amount the trust actually distributes is at its discretion.

To satisfy the requirements of Form 51-102F1 — *Management's Discussion and Analysis* (Form 51-102F1), income trusts should supplement the distributable cash presentation in their MD&A with comprehensive disclosure of the assumptions, risks and uncertainties, working capital requirements and financing decisions related to the trust. This information helps investors determine whether the amount of estimated distributable cash is reasonable and sustainable.

Of the 45 trusts reviewed, 18 income trust issuers committed to providing disclosure enhancements relating to distributable cash disclosures in future MD&A.

In addition to their deficient distributable cash disclosures, two income trust issuers were required to re-file previously filed MD&A because they had other significant disclosure deficiencies and four issuers committed to prospective overall disclosure enhancements.

During our review, we concluded that distributable cash disclosures in MD&A were significantly deficient in one or more of the three specific areas required by Form 51-102F1, (i) liquidity; (ii) risks and uncertainties; and (iii) overall performance and results of operations.

(i) — Liquidity[1]

Form 51-102F1 requires that an issuer discuss in its interim and annual MD&A the issuer's ability to generate sufficient amounts of cash and cash equivalents to meet its planned growth including a description of the sources of funding and the circumstances that could affect those sources that are reasonably likely to occur. In many cases, income trust issuers did not provide sufficient disclosure about their sources of funding relating to current and future cash distributions. To fully comply with the continuous disclosure requirements, there should be a comprehensive discussion of the sources of funding relating to current and future cash distributions. This discussion helps unitholders form a reasoned judgment about a trust's ability to sustain distributions over the long-term.

While income trusts intend to make distributions of their available cash to unitholders, the actual amount distributed depends on numerous factors, including the operating entity's financial performance, working capital requirements and future capital requirements. In many trusts we reviewed, the consolidated financial statements revealed that some portion of distributions to unitholders was funded from sources other than cash flows from operations. For example, in some instances, a portion of distributions were funded from operating lines, long-term credit facilities, reserves held-back from prior periods, or a return of unitholder's capital.

Many trusts either provided a "boilerplate" discussion with minimal or no quantification of the sources of cash flows or provided no discussion at all. Here is an example of a liquidity discussion that is not acceptable:

> *The shortfall between 'Cash available for distribution' and 'Distributions to unitholders' has been funded primarily by working capital. Should any further shortfall arise, Management expects to be able to cover the difference between cash generated and cash distributed through working capital, cash on hand or its credit facility. Working capital has been built up over time from public offerings.*

The above discussion provides limited information to investors. Although this trust may have made distributions in excess of its cash flows from operations, it is unclear from the discussion how the trust is funding distributions. The disclosure provides no meaningful information to investors to determine the long-term sustainability of distributions and implies that the trust is paying distributions from proceeds of equity offerings.

Although the instructions in Form 51-102F1 do not specifically state it, to meet the disclosure requirements for liquidity in Form 51-102F1, income trusts should provide sufficient disclosure about their sources of funding relating to current and future cash distributions so unitholders can understand what portion, if any, of the distributions they received were funded by non-operational cash flows. Also, income trusts should quantify these amounts and discuss the impact on the trust's long-term ability to sustain distributions if non-operational cash flows are being used to fund distributable cash.

---

[1]Part 2, Item 1.6 of Form 51-102F1.

(ii) — Risks and Uncertainties[2]

MD&A provides information to investors to help them assess the potential risks and uncertainties that may materially affect the underlying entity's (the operating entity) performance and, in turn, impact current and future distributions. All of the income trust issuers reviewed provided some disclosure on risks and uncertainties relating to the trust structure, taxation, regulation, and industry specific risk factors. However, 13 of them provided only a "boilerplate" discussion of these commitments, events, risks or uncertainties. Boilerplate discussions generally provide little or no useful information for investors and, in some cases, do not comply with the requirements of the form.

The operating entities are in a diverse range of businesses. Each operating entity has unique risks and commitments that may significantly impact the amount of cash flows that it can indirectly pass on to unitholders through the trust. Our reviews indicate that some of these risks include exposure to fluctuations in commodity price, foreign exchange, working capital commitments, credit risk, economic dependence, and overall economic factors. Under Form 51-102F1, an income trust must discuss known trends and risks that have affected the operating entity's financial statements, and trends and risks that are reasonably likely to affect them in the future. Here are two examples of "boilerplate" risks and uncertainties discussions that would not comply with the requirements in Form 51-102F1:

Example 1

The timing and amount of capital expenditures by Trust A will indirectly affect the amount of cash available for distribution to Unitholders. Distributions may be reduced, or even eliminated, at times when Trust A deems it necessary to make significant capital or other expenditures.

This example provides limited information to investors. The risk associated with the maintenance and replacement of the operating entity's capital assets is a significant and primary risk for most income trusts. The cash commitment required to maintain and replace its capital asset base is information an investor needs to assess a trust's ability to sustain distributions over the long-term. The operating entity's capital assets generate the cash flows to pay distributions. Therefore, an adverse change in their composition is likely to have a significant impact on distributions.

Although the instructions in Form 51-102F1 do not specifically state it, to meet the requirement to disclose risks, income trusts should provide a detailed risk factor discussion about the potential commitment to replace and maintain capital assets, including a quantitative discussion about expected annual capital maintenance levels relative to current levels, and the expected effect on distributions.

Example 2

Trust B's profitability is sensitive to fluctuations in wholesale prices of 'commodity X' caused by changes in supply, taxes, price controls and/or other market conditions affecting the 'commodity X' industry generally. Many of these factors are beyond Trust B's control and thus, when there are sudden and sharp increases in the wholesale price of 'commodity X', Trust B may not be able to pass through these price increases to customers through retail sales prices. In addition, the timing of price pass-throughs can significantly affect margins. Wholesale price increases could reduce Trust B's gross profits and could, if continued over an extended period of time, reduce demand by providing economic incentive to consumers to reduce consumption or convert to alternative energy sources.

Again, this example provides limited information in assessing the trust's future prospects and the potential impact that this risk might have on distributions. To comply with Form 51-102F1, income trusts should quantify, if possible, the past and expected future impact of each risk to facilitate the analysis of each risk's relative impact. For some trusts, this might best be presented as a sensitivity analysis of potential fluctuations in the price of the commodity and its impact on distributions. This would provide unitholders with more meaningful information to assess this risk factor. It would also assist investors in further understanding the relationship between specific risks and their impact on operations. Also, although some of the instructions in Form 51-102F1 do not specifically state it, to accurately describe a risk, an income trust should disclose any steps it has taken, or plans to take, to mitigate the impact of any risk.

(iii) — Overall performance and results of operations[3]

Item 1.2 of Form 51-102F1 requires an issuer to provide in its MD&A an analysis of its financial condition, results of operations and cash flows. This required analysis includes a comparison of the performance in the most recently completed financial period to the prior period's performance and an explanation of why changes have occurred or expected changes have not occurred. This discussion should also describe and quantify material variances.

Ten of the income trust issuers we reviewed did not provide an adequate discussion of events in the year that caused variances in specific financial statement line items. In these instances, the trusts did not quantify factors used to explain material variances. A quantification of specific factors causing variances assists investors in understanding the impact of the factor on results for the period. Many trusts simply provided a superficial discussion rather than providing a detailed analysis of overall performance. Here is an example of MD&A with a deficient financial statement analysis (details have been changed):

Revenues

Sales of $13.7 million for the three months ended June 30, 2005 increased by $2.2 million, or 19%, from $11.5 million for the three months ended June 30, 2004. Gross profit percentage in the second quarter was 39.1% compared to 42.2% during the same period last year. Factors causing the decline in gross profit percentage included: 1) freight used to import materials to meet aggressive lead times from customers; 2) more production outsourced than in the prior year in order to satisfy anticipated inventory demands from retailers; and 3) the sales mix in the prior period was heavily weighted in certain items which carry higher margins.

In this example, the trust did not provide information for changes in sales, other than what was readily available from its financial statements. Although the trust listed factors causing decreases in gross profit percentage for the period, these individual factors are not quantified or

---

[2]Part 2, Item 1.2 of Form 51-102F1.

[3]Part 2, Items 1.2 and 1.4 of Form 51-102F1.

meaningfully discussed. To comply with Form 51-102F1, an income trust should discuss the individual factors so that investors can assess the relative significance of each factor.

B. — Non-GAAP financial measures

Most income trusts present non-GAAP financial measures. The number of non-GAAP measures presented and the consistency in presentation vary considerably from trust to trust. In some instances, income trusts rely solely on non-GAAP measures as a means of discussing the trust's financial results for a period in earnings releases and for the purposes of MD&A. However, in many instances, the presentation of non-GAAP measures by income trusts issuers does not meet the minimum standards set out in SN 52-306.

(i) — Reconcile to GAAP measure

When non-GAAP measures such as distributable cash or EBITDA are presented by income trust issuers, under SN 52-306, the trust should reconcile the non-GAAP measure to the most directly comparable GAAP measure. For distributable cash, we interpret the most directly comparable GAAP measure to be cash flows from operating activities as presented in the issuer's financial statements. Instead, many income trusts reviewed began their GAAP reconciliation with earnings or EBITDA. This leads to many adjustments appearing in the distributable cash reconciliation which provide limited information and are increasingly confusing. In some cases, these adjustments have limited cash flow impact, and therefore may lead to distributable cash amounts that do not accurately reflect the amount of cash that was available for distribution. For example, one trust issuer included an adjustment for "elimination of purchase accounting impact" which increased distributable cash but did not show any cash flow impact.

As stated in SN 52-306, income trust issuers should ensure that when they present distributable cash, the reconciliation to the most directly comparable GAAP measure begins with cash flows from operations from the issuer's financial statements, including changes during the period in non-cash working capital balances.

(ii) — Equal Prominence

SN 52-306 also states that when non-GAAP measures are presented, the most directly comparable GAAP measure should also be presented in equal or greater prominence than the non-GAAP measure. In our review, many trusts did not provide this level of equal prominence, and in some instances, did not even disclose a GAAP measure. We required two trust issuers to re-file disclosure documents because the original disclosure gave greater prominence to a non-GAAP measure than to the most directly comparable GAAP measure.

Here is an example of an unacceptable earnings release (details have been changed):

> Trust A income fund commented today on its results for the third quarter ended September 30, 2005. On a preliminary basis, sales during the quarter for the Fund were approximately $21.7 million, up from $20.6 million in the comparable period last year. As a result of the sales increase, adjusted earnings before interest, taxes, depreciation and amortization ("Adjusted EBITDA") for the period are estimated to have increased to $4.4 million from approximately $3.3 million for the comparable period last year. Based on these preliminary results, the Fund estimates that Distributable Cash was approximately $1,750,000 in the quarter, resulting in an increase of $725,000 as the Fund paid cash distributions to Unitholders of $1.9 million during the period. The financial results for the third quarter of 2005 reflect an increase in sales in the United States and a decline in sales in Western Canada which, when combined with the carryover of large dealer inventories resulted in a 18% increase in consolidated sales in the period compared with last year's third quarter.

In this example, the trust only later revealed in its financial statements that it experienced a net loss in the period as opposed to the prior period when the income trust experienced a positive net income. This result is not evident from the earnings release. We find this type of presentation to be misleading. The exclusion or minimal prominence of the relevant GAAP measure does not provide investors with an accurate standardized representation of the issuer's current financial results. As stated in SN 52-306, income trusts should prominently disclose and discuss the most directly comparable GAAP measure whenever presenting non-GAAP financial measures.

C. — Goodwill

Our review identified some instances where it appears that the goodwill impairment testing required by CICA Handbook Section 3062 *Goodwill and Other Intangible Assets* (S. 3062)[4] was not done in an appropriate timeframe. Generally, S. 3062 requires that goodwill should be tested for impairment on an annual basis. However, S. 3062 also states that goodwill should be tested for impairment between annual tests when an event or circumstance occurs that more likely than not reduces the fair value of a reporting unit below its carrying amount.

Many businesses enjoyed considerable increases in their value on completion of their income trust IPO or through conversion to a trust. The excess of the fair value of the business over the carrying value of the assets has led to significant amounts of goodwill being recorded in the financial statements of many income trusts.

In some cases, income trusts determined that no impairment testing was necessary even though there were a number of factors that suggest the trust had a potential impairment. Specifically, events such as the deterioration in the underlying entity's business climate or the loss of significant customers, suggested that impairment testing was necessary.

---

[4]Section 3.1 of NI 52-107 *Acceptable Accounting Principles, Auditing Standards and Reporting Currency* requires issuers to prepare their financial statements in accordance with Canadian GAAP, which is defined in NI 14-101 *Definitions* as generally accepted accounting principles determined with reference to the Handbook.

As stated in OSC Staff Notice 51-706 *Corporate Finance Report (2005)*[5], income trusts should use multiple valuation methods to assess the fair value of reporting units whenever goodwill impairment testing is performed, especially when an approach based on quoted market prices does not appear to generate results consistent with indications from external factors.

D. — Executive Compensation

Form 51-102F6 *Statement of Executive Compensation* (Form 51-102F6) sets out the disclosure a reporting issuer must make about the compensation paid to its executive officers. Some income trust issuers use an external management company to provide executive management services to the trust and or operating entity. In some instances that we reviewed, due to this external management structure, compensation paid to these executive officers was not fully disclosed in accordance with Form 51-102F6.

The definition of "senior officer" in securities legislation includes any individual who performs functions for an issuer similar to those normally performed by certain named senior positions. The definition of "executive officer" in NI 51-102 includes an individual who is performing a policy-making function in respect of an issuer. The definitions of "CEO" and "CFO", for the purposes of Form 51-102F6 include each individual who acted in a similar capacity. As stated in OSC Staff Notice 51-706[6], we generally consider the officers of the external management company to be persons performing functions in respect of the trust and the operating company similar to those normally performed by senior officers of a company, including policy-making functions. Consequently, any requirements of securities legislation that apply to senior officers or executive officers of a reporting issuer would usually apply to the executive officers of the external management company.

In particular, as stated in OSC SN 51-706, in addition to disclosing any management fee, incentive fee or other amounts payable by the income trust to the external management company, income trusts should include the executive compensation disclosure required by Form 51-102F6 for the executive officers of the external management company. This disclosure should include any compensation payable directly by the income trust to the executive officers, as well as any compensation payable by the external management company to its executive officers that can be attributed to the management fee or other payments from the income trust (e.g. any salary, bonus, dividends, distributions or other payments).

E. — Timely disclosure

We identified some events at the operating entity level that appeared to meet the definition of a "material change"[7] for the trust issuers but for which the trusts did not file material change reports. For example, in three instances, a trust's operating entity breached financial covenants under its credit facilities. As a result, in each instance, the trust issuer either suspended or significantly reduced distributions to its unitholders. Although, the filing of the press release announcing the change in distributions had a significant effect on the market price of the trust's units, the issuers argued that these events do not meet the definition of a material change.

For an income trust, a "material change", as it is defined in NI 51-102, includes an event at the operating entity level that results in a change in the business, operations, or capital of the trust that would reasonably be expected to have a significant effect on the trust's unit price. To comply with the material change disclosure requirements in NI 51-102, a trust must therefore assess events that occur at the operating entity level as they affect the trust, particularly if the events impact distributions to unitholders.

F. — Material Contracts[8]

We identified three income trust issuers that obtained waivers for financial covenants and made amendments to their credit facilities, but did not file the amended credit agreements on SEDAR. In one instance, the trust issuer did not file the original credit facility agreement and subsequently did not file amendments to that agreement. Since most credit facility arrangements entered into by income trust issuers include restrictive financial covenants over the amount of cash the trust may distribute, the material terms of these arrangements should always be available to investors.

Section 12.2 of NI 51-102 requires an issuer to file all material contracts on SEDAR, except contracts that are made in the ordinary course of business. NP 41-201 advises income trust issuers to consider any contract that has a direct correlation with the anticipated cash distributions of the trust to be a material contract that the trust must file with its prospectus. While NP 41-201 does not specifically state this, income trusts should file any changes to these contracts on SEDAR as well as filing any new contracts of this type.

Conclusion

Our findings suggest that, to meet the requirements of NI 51-102, many income trust issuers need to improve the nature and extent of their disclosure, particularly as it relates to distributable cash disclosures in MD&A. MD&A provided by income trust issuers is critical disclosure for unitholders. It assists them to understand a trust's financial statements and, most importantly, to assess the value of their investments which, for income trusts, depends on the sustainability of distributions.

Policies and Orders: CSAN 51-310.

---

[5]Part 2, Item A of OSC Staff Notice 51-706. Not all jurisdictions have issued a similar staff notice, however most income trust issuers are reporting issuers in multiple jurisdictions, including Ontario.

[6]Part 2, Item H of OSC Staff Notice 51-706. Not all jurisdictions have issued a similar staff notice, however most income trust issuers are reporting issuers in multiple jurisdictions, including Ontario.

[7]Subsection 1.1 of NI 51-102.

[8]Part 2, item C, section 2.8 of NP 41-201.

CSA Staff Notice 51-320 — Options Backdating

Date: September 8, 2006

29 O.S.C.B. 7190

As a result of recent media attention about the apparent backdating of options in the US, Canadian market participants have expressed interest in the dating of stock options granted by reporting issuers in Canada. Staff in the jurisdictions represented by the Canadian Securities Administrators (CSA), are publishing this notice to communicate our understanding of this issue in the Canadian context.

It has been suggested that some US-based companies granted options to executives and then claimed that they issued them at an earlier date than they actually did. This enabled them to base the exercise price of the options on a lower market price for the issuer's shares. There are also broader concerns in the US that issuers may have timed the granting of stock options using their expectations of stock price movements.

There are some historically different regulatory requirements in Canada that may reduce the opportunity for Canadian companies to backdate or time option grants, for example:

- The Toronto Stock Exchange (TSX) imposes the following rules for its listed companies:

    (i) the exercise price for options granted by listed issuers must not be less than the market price of the underlying securities when the options are granted;

    (ii) the exercise price must not be based on market prices that do not reflect undisclosed material information; and

    (iii) all option grants must be reported to the TSX within ten days of the end of the month in which the grant was made.

- The TSX Venture Exchange (TSX-V) imposes similar rules, though it allows an issuer to set the exercise price at a discount (ranging from 15% to 25%) from the market price, which is specified by the TSX-V.

- Securities legislation generally requires insiders of reporting issuers to file a report on SEDI within ten days of any change in their direct or indirect beneficial ownership of or control or direction over securities of the issuer, including options.

The board of directors of an issuer is responsible for ensuring that the issuer prices options appropriately and discloses them properly. The following guidance may reduce concerns about the timing of option grants and the risk of non-compliance with securities legislation:

- establish a compensation committee that follows the guidance contained in National Policy 58-201 — *Corporate Governance Guidelines*;

- consider the guidance in National Policy 51-201 — *Disclosure Standards* including adopting a corporate disclosure policy, adopting an insider trading policy, and establishing "blackout periods" around earnings announcements; and

- ensure that, following a grant of options to insiders, the issuer provides them with details of their grants so that they can comply with their legal obligation to file insider reports on SEDI within 10 days.

CSA staff recommend that all issuers assess current policies, procedures and controls for option grants and equity-based awards to ensure that they comply with relevant stock exchange rules and securities legislation. If CSA staff become aware, through disclosure reviews, tips, or otherwise, of abuses by reporting issuers, they may take enforcement action against the issuers or their directors and officers. In considering the appropriate course of action, CSA staff may take into account what steps, if any, such issuers took to ensure their policies and controls complied with regulatory requirements.

CSA Notice 51-322 — Reporting Issuer Defaults

Date: January 5, 2007

30 O.S.C.B. 4

Purpose of notice

The Canadian securities regulatory authorities have developed a harmonized list of deficiencies that will generally result in a reporting issuer being noted in default of the securities laws of a particular jurisdiction. This notice describes those deficiencies.

Categories of default

The circumstances under which the securities regulatory authorities will consider a reporting issuer to be in default are:

1. The reporting issuer has failed to file the following continuous disclosure prescribed by securities laws:

    (a) annual financial statements;

    (b) interim financial statements;

    (c) annual or interim management's discussion and analysis (MD&A) or annual or interim management report of fund performance (MRFP);

    (d) annual information form (AIF);

    (e) certification of annual or interim filings under Multilateral Instrument 52-109 *Certification of Disclosure in Issuers' Annual and Interim Filings* (MI 52-109);

    (f) proxy materials or a required information circular;

    (g) issuer profile supplement on the System for Electronic Disclosure By Insiders (SEDI);

    (h) material change report;

(i) written update after filing a confidential report of a material change;

(j) business acquisition report;

(k) annual oil and gas disclosure prescribed by National Instrument 51-101 *Standards of Disclosure for Oil and Gas Activities* (NI 51-101) or technical reports for a mineral project required under National Instrument 43-101 *Standards of Disclosure for Mineral Projects* (NI 43-101);

(l) mandatory news release;

(m) corporate governance disclosure as required by National Instrument 58-101 *Disclosure of Corporate Governance Practices*;

(n) audit committee disclosure as required by Multilateral Instrument 52-110 *Audit Committees* or BC Instrument 52-509 *Audit Committees*; or

(o) disclosure in an issuer's MD&A relating to disclosure controls and procedures and their effectiveness that is referred to in a certificate filed under MI 52-109.

2. The reporting issuer's continuous disclosure is deficient because:

(a) the financial statements of the reporting issuer, or the auditor's report accompanying the financial statements, do not comply with the requirements of National Instrument 51-102 *Continuous Disclosure Obligations* (NI 51-102), National Instrument 81-106 *Investment Fund Continuous Disclosure* (NI 81-106) or National Instrument 52-107 *Acceptable Accounting Principles, Auditing Standards and Reporting Currency*;

(b) the reporting issuer has acknowledged that its financial statements, or the auditor's report accompanying the financial statements, may no longer be relied upon;

(c) the reporting issuer's AIF, MD&A, MRFP, information circular or business acquisition reports do not contain information for each of the content items required by NI 51-102 or NI 81-106; or

(d) the reporting issuer's technical disclosure or other reports do not comply with the disclosure requirements of NI 43-101 or NI 51-101.

3. The reporting issuer has failed to pay a fee required by securities laws.

4. The reporting issuer has failed to comply with any other requirement related to continuous disclosure.

Lists of defaulting reporting issuers

Certain securities regulatory authorities maintain lists that identify those reporting issuers that have been noted in default in the relevant jurisdiction. The lists identify the name of the reporting issuer, and the nature and description of the default. The lists, together with the harmonized categories of default and nomenclature used to identify each category, can be found on the following websites:

www.bcsc.bc.ca

www.albertasecurities.com

www.sfsc.gov.sk.ca

www.msc.gov.mb.ca

www.osc.gov.on.ca

www.lautorite.qc.ca

www.nbsc-cvmnb.ca

www.gov.ns.ca/nssc

Certain securities regulatory authorities have also published policies or notices containing information relating to defaults by reporting issuers. These local polices or notices are:

Alberta: Alberta Securities Commission Policy 51-601 — *Reporting Issuers List*

Saskatchewan: Saskatchewan Policy Statement 51-601 — *Reporting Issuers in Default*

Manitoba: Manitoba Securities Commission Local Policy 51-601 — *Reporting Issuers List*

Ontario: Ontario Securities Commission Policy 51-601 — *Reporting Issuer Defaults*

Quebec: AMF Notice on Reporting Issuer Defaults

New Brunswick: New Brunswick Securities Commission Policy 51-601 — *Reporting Issuers List*

Policies and Orders: NPS 12-203.

CSA Notice 51-323 — XBRL Filing Program and Request for Volunteers

Date: **January 19, 2007**

30 O.S.C.B. 510

Introduction

The Canadian Securities Administrators (CSA or we) are establishing a program that will allow issuers to voluntarily file financial statements in eXtensible Business Reporting Language (XBRL) format.

Reporting issuers participating in the voluntary program will file financial statements in XBRL format on SEDAR. Under the current continuous disclosure requirements, these issuers must also continue filing their official financial statements in PDF format on SEDAR. The CSA will make the XBRL financial statements available to the public through the SEDAR website at www.sedar.com.

The purpose of the voluntary program is to help the Canadian marketplace gain practical knowledge and experience in preparing, filing and using XBRL information. It will also help the CSA assess the usefulness of XBRL as it considers whether to make filing in this format a requirement.

The voluntary program

Beginning in May 2007, reporting issuers participating in the voluntary program will file financial statements in XBRL format on SEDAR. They can prepare their financial statements in XBRL by purchasing off-the-shelf XBRL preparation software or hiring third-party service providers to prepare XBRL financial statements.

We will obtain feedback from participants in the voluntary program and from other stakeholders to determine the challenges, benefits and usefulness of the XBRL financial statements.

Request for volunteers

The CSA is looking for reporting issuers to participate in the voluntary program. Please contact one of the CSA staff members listed at the end of this notice if you are interested in volunteering.

Background

What is XBRL?

XBRL is a business reporting language that organizations can use to share financial information and investors can use to analyze data. Instead of treating financial information as a block of text, XBRL assigns an identifying tag to each item of data. For example, XBRL assigns tags to individual financial statement items, such as "revenue" or "cost of sales". These tags allow systems and analysis tools to process the information automatically. For example, XBRL-enabled software can perform automated financial analysis for multiple companies over multiple years with XBRL data, eliminating labour-intensive manual data re-entry and verification. As a result, XBRL can increase the speed of handling of financial data, reduce errors and make it easier to analyze information.

Survey results

On June 29, 2006, the CSA issued CSA Notice 52-314 *Securities Regulators Want Your Feedback on XBRL*. This notice provided information about XBRL and introduced a CSA survey to help us understand the awareness level of XBRL in the marketplace.

The CSA conducted its XBRL survey from June 29 to September 30, 2006. We received 150 responses from various stakeholders, including accountants, investors and analysts.

The results of the survey confirmed our impressions about the lack of practical knowledge and experience with XBRL in the Canadian marketplace. The results also suggested that a voluntary filing program would be a reasonable next step to help the marketplace gain a greater understanding of the functionality and usability of XBRL data.

The following are some highlights from the survey:

- 83% of respondents are in favour of the CSA introducing either a voluntary or a mandatory XBRL filing program.

- 53% of respondents were aware of XBRL before they received our notice and survey.

- 96% of respondents who are users of financial information had never used XBRL in their analysis and virtually no respondents who are preparers of financial information had prepared information in XBRL format.

Both users and preparers of financial information believe that the time and effort needed to learn about XBRL was a significant barrier to adopting this format.

For more information about XBRL

Please see CSA Notice 52-314 *Securities Regulators Want Your Feedback on XBRL*.

You can find more information about XBRL on the following sites:

www.xbrl.org

www.xbrl.ca

www.sec.gov/spotlight/xbrl.htm

CSA Notice 51-324 — (Revised) Glossary to NI 51-101 Standards of Disclosure for Oil and Gas Activities

Date: December 28, 2007 as revised effective December 30, 2010 and December 4, 2014

31 O.S.C.B. 6, 33 O.S.C.B. 11927

Section 1.1 of National Instrument 51-101 *Standards of Disclosure for Oil and Gas Activities* (*NI 51-101*) defines a number of terms used in *NI 51-101*, *Form 51-101F1*, *Form 51-101F2*, *Form 51-101F3* and Companion Policy 51-101CP.[1] Section 1.2 of *NI 51-101* provides that terms used in the *Instrument* but not defined in the *Instrument*, National Instrument 14-101 *Definitions* (*NI 14-101*) or the securities statute in the *jurisdiction* have the meaning or interpretation, if any, set out in the *COGE Handbook*.

Part 1 of this Glossary explains much of the terminology used in *NI 51-101* and its accompanying documents. It is provided only as a convenience to users of *NI 51-101*, to assist them in better understanding the purpose and application of *NI 51-101*. Part 2 of the Glossary focuses on the definition of *reserves* and is derived from Section 5 of Volume 1 of the *COGE Handbook*.

The explanations in Part 1 of this Glossary are derived from a number of sources, including section 1.1 of *NI 51-101*, *NI 14-101* and the *COGE Handbook*. Where applicable, the source document for the explanation is indicated in square brackets after the explanation (even if the explanation is not verbatim to the source document). These explanations may change from time to time. Readers are cautioned to consult a current edition of the source document for updated explanations.

Background or further guidance may be found in the source documents:

- The *COGE Handbook* can be obtained from the Society of Petroleum Engineers, Calgary Section (Telephone 403-237-5112; email specal@spe.org; website www.speca.ca).

- *NI 14-101* can be viewed on the websites of a number of *securities regulatory authorities*.

Part 1 of this Glossary includes definitions of the various categories of *resources* that are identified and defined in the *COGE Handbook*. At the present time, these *resource* categories are as follows:

- *total petroleum initially-in-place* (equivalent to *total resources*);
- *discovered petroleum initially-in-place* (equivalent to *discovered resources*);
- *discovered unrecoverable petroleum initially-in-place* (equivalent to *discovered unrecoverable resources*);
- *contingent resources*;
- *undiscovered petroleum initially-in-place* (equivalent to *undiscovered resources*);
- *undiscovered unrecoverable petroleum initially-in-place* (equivalent to *undiscovered unrecoverable resources*); and
- *prospective resources*.

Readers are cautioned to consult a current edition of the *COGE Handbook* for updated *resource* categories and definitions.

Part 1 — Definitions

The terms (and plural, singular or other grammatical variants thereof) set out in the left column below have the meanings respectively set out in the right column.

Defined Term	Meaning
1934 Act	The Securities Exchange Act of 1934 of the United States of America, as amended from time to time. [*NI 14-101*]
Abandonment and reclamation costs	All costs associated with the process of restoring a *reporting issuer's property* that has been disturbed by *oil and gas activities* to a standard imposed by applicable government or regulatory authorities. [*NI 51-101*]
Accumulation	An individual body of *petroleum* in a *reservoir*. [*COGE Handbook*]
Adsorption	The adhesion of molecules to a surface. This may occur as physisorption, due to weak van der Waals forces, chemisorption, the result of covalent bonding, or to electrostatic attraction. [*COGE Handbook*]
Alternate reference point	A location at which quantities and values of a product type are measured before the first point of sale. [*NI 51-101*]
Amenable volumes	A subsurface stratigraphic interval containing a certain minimum thickness of continuous, predominantly *bitumen*-saturated sand, net of non-*reservoir*, with porosity and mass *bitumen* content (ratio of *bitumen* to water and mineral matter) meeting specific criteria (typically, a minimum of 27 and 7–8 percent, respectively).
	This is the volume of *bitumen* that it is estimated could be physically extracted from an *accumulation* being evaluated after the application of *reservoir* cut-offs and project technical considerations, but before consideration of regulatory aspects, and surface limitations such as access. [*COGE Handbook*]

---

[1]Terms italicized in this notice are defined in Part 1 of the Glossary of this notice.

Defined Term	Meaning
Annual information form	A completed Form 51-102F2 *Annual Information Form*, or in the case of an *SEC* issuer (as defined in National Instrument 51-102 Continuous Disclosure Obligations) a completed Form 51-102F2 or an annual report or transition report under the 1934 Act on Form 10-K, Form 10-KSB or Form 20-F. [*NI 51-102*]
Analogous information	Information about an area outside the area the *reporting issuer* has an interest or intends to acquire an interest, which is referenced by the *reporting issuer* for the purpose of drawing a comparison or conclusion to an area in which the *reporting issuer* has an interest or intends to acquire an interest, which comparison or conclusion is reasonable, and includes without limitation:

- historical information concerning *reserves*;
- estimates of the volume or value of *reserves*;
- historical information concerning *resources*;
- estimates of the volume or value of *resources*;
- historical *production* amounts;
- *production* estimates; or
- information concerning a *field*, well, basin or *reservoir*.

[*NI 51-101*]

Analogy	The process of transferring information on a subject *accumulation* or *reservoir* (the analogue or source) to another *accumulation* or *reservoir* (the target or subject). (See also reservoir analogue and recovery process analogue.) [*COGE Handbook*]
Anticipated results	Information that may, in the opinion of a reasonable person, indicate the potential value or quantities of resources in respect of the reporting issuer's resources or a portion of its resources and includes:

- estimates of volume;
- estimates of value;
- areal extent;
- pay thickness;
- flow rates; or
- *hydrocarbon* content.

[*NI 51-101*]

Audit	In relation to *reserves data*, the process whereby an *independent qualified reserves auditor* carries out procedures designed to allow the *independent qualified reserves auditor* to provide reasonable assurance, in the form of an opinion that the *reporting issuer's* reserves data (or specific parts thereof) have, in all *material* respects, been determined and presented in accordance with the *COGE Handbook* and are, therefore, free of *material* misstatement.

Because of

(a)   the nature of the subject matter (estimates of future results with many uncertainties);

(b)   the fact that the *independent qualified reserves auditor* assesses the qualifications and experience of the *reporting issuer's* staff, assesses the *reporting issuer's* systems, procedures and controls and relies on the competence of the *reporting issuer's* staff and the appropriateness of the *reporting issuer's* systems, procedures and controls; and

(c)   the fact that tests and samples (involving examination of underlying documentation supporting the determination of the *reserves* and *future net revenue*) as opposed to complete *evaluations*, are involved; the level of assurance is designed to be high, though not absolute.

The level of assurance cannot be described with numeric precision. It will usually be less than, but reasonably close to, that of an independent evaluation and considerably higher than that of a *review*. [*COGE Handbook*]

Bbl	Barrel. [*COGE Handbook*]
Bitumen	A naturally occurring solid or semi-solid hydrocarbon

(a)   consisting mainly of heavier hydrocarbons, with a viscosity greater than 10,000 millipascal-seconds (mPa•s) or 10,000 centipoise (cP) measured at the *hydrocarbons'* original temperature in the *reservoir* and at atmospheric pressure on a gas-free basis, and

Defined Term	Meaning
	(b) that is not primarily recoverable at economic rates through a well without the implementation of enhanced recovery methods. [*NI 51-101*]
BOE	Barrels of *oil* equivalent. [*NI 51-101* and *COGE Handbook*]
By-product	A substance that is recovered as a consequence of producing a *product type*. [*NI 51-101*]
Chance of commerciality	The product of the *chance of discovery* and the *chance of development*. [*COGE Handbook*]
Chance of discovery	The estimated probability that exploration activities will confirm the existence of a significant *accumulation* of potentially recoverable petroleum. [*COGE Handbook*]
Coal bed methane	*Natural gas* that (a) primarily consists of methane, and (b) is contained in a coal deposit. [*NI 51-101*]
Commercial	When a *project* is commercial this implies that the essential social, environmental, and economic conditions are met, including political, legal, regulatory, and contractual conditions. Considerations with regard to determining commerciality include <ul><li>economic viability of the related development project;</li><li>a reasonable expectation that there will be a market for the expected sales quantities of *production* required to justify development;</li><li>evidence that the necessary *production* and transportation facilities are available or can be made available;</li><li>evidence that legal, contractual, environmental, governmental, and other social and economic concerns will allow for the actual implementation of the recovery *project* being *evaluated*;</li><li>a reasonable expectation that all required internal and external approvals will be forthcoming. Evidence of this may include items such as signed contracts, budget approvals, and approvals for expenditures, etc.</li><li>evidence to support a reasonable timetable for development. A reasonable time frame for the initiation of development depends on the specific circumstances and varies according to the scope of the project. Although five years is recommended as a maximum time frame for classification of a project as commercial, a longer time frame could be applied where, for example, development of economic projects are deferred at the option of the producer for, among other things, market-related reasons or to meet contractual or strategic objectives.</li></ul> [*COGE Handbook*]
Conceptual (scoping) study	The initial stage of the development of a project scenario, with limited detail and typically based on limited information. [*COGE Handbook*]
Contingency	A condition that must be satisfied for a portion of *contingent resources* to be classified as *reserves* that is: (a) specific to the *project* being *evaluated*; and (b) expected to be resolved within a reasonable timeframe. For additional information, see section 2.5 of the *ROTR Guidelines*. Note that the Petroleum Resources Management System equates contingency with conditions, which are defined as follows: "the economic, marketing, legal, environmental, social, and governmental factors forecast to exist and impact the project during the time period being evaluated." Contingency was not defined in the *COGE Handbook* before the *ROTR Guidelines* was published, although a similar list is provided. The term "condition" is purely descriptive and does not imply that that any action is required, whereas a "contingency" is a factor that must be resolved in order to reclassify a resource. The Petroleum Resources Management System Guidelines use the term "critical contingency" and, although some contingencies may be more easily resolved than others, they are all go/no-go decision gates that must be resolved. (See also technical contingency.)

Part 5: ONGOING REQUIREMENTS

Defined Term	**Meaning**

Contingent resources

Those quantities of *petroleum* estimated, as of a given date, to be potentially recoverable from *known accumulations* using *established technology* or *technology under development*, but which are not currently considered to be *commercially* recoverable due to one or more *contingencies*. (See also economic contingent resources, and sub-economic contingent resources.)

[*COGE Handbook*]

Contingent resources data

Means

(a)   an estimate of the volume of *contingent resources*, and

(b)   the *risked* net present value of *future net revenue of contingent resources*.

[*NI 51-101*]

Conventional natural gas

Natural gas that has been generated elsewhere and has migrated as a result of hydrodynamic forces and is trapped in discrete *accumulations* by seals that may be formed by localized structural, depositional or erosional geological features.

[*NI 51-101*]

Crude oil

A mixture consisting mainly of pentanes and heavier *hydrocarbons* that exists in the liquid phase in *reservoirs* and remains liquid at atmospheric pressure and temperature. *Crude oil* may contain small amounts of sulphur and other non-*hydrocarbons* but does not include liquids obtained from the processing of *natural gas*.

[*COGE Handbook*]

CSA

The Canadian Securities Administrators, an association consisting of the thirteen *securities regulatory authorities* in Canada.

Cut-off

A limiting value of a *reservoir* parameter that removes non-contributing intervals from *resource* calculations. The *petroleum* contained in the *reservoir* below a cut-off is classified as *unrecoverable*.

[*COGE Handbook*]

Developed non-producing reserves

See Part 2 of this Glossary. [*COGE Handbook*]

Developed producing reserves

See Part 2 of this Glossary. [*COGE Handbook*]

Developed reserves

See Part 2 of this Glossary. [*COGE Handbook*]

Development costs

Costs incurred to obtain access to *reserves* and to provide facilities for extracting, treating, gathering and storing the *oil* and *gas* from the *reserves*.

More specifically, *development costs*, including applicable *operating costs* of *support equipment and facilities* and other costs of development activities, are costs incurred to:

(a)   gain access to and prepare well locations for drilling, including surveying well locations for the purpose of determining specific development drilling sites, clearing ground, draining, road building, and relocating public roads, *gas* lines and power lines, to the extent necessary in developing the *reserves*;

(b)   drill and equip *development wells*, development type *stratigraphic test wells* and *service wells*, including the costs of platforms and of well equipment such as casing, tubing, pumping equipment and the wellhead assembly;

(c)   acquire, construct and install *production* facilities such as flow lines, separators, treaters, heaters, manifolds, measuring devices and *production* storage tanks, *natural gas* cycling and processing plants, and central utility and waste disposal systems; and

(d)   provide improved recovery systems.

Development well

A well drilled inside the established limits of an *oil* or *gas reservoir*, or in close proximity to the edge of the *reservoir*, to the depth of a stratigraphic horizon known to be productive.

Defined Term	Meaning
Discovered petroleum initially-in-place	That quantity of *petroleum* that is estimated, as of a given date, to be contained in *known accumulations* prior to *production*.
	The recoverable portion of *discovered petroleum initially-in-place* includes *production, reserves* and *contingent resources*; the remainder is unrecoverable.
	[*COGE Handbook*]
Discovered resources	Refer to *discovered petroleum initially-in-place* as both terms are equivalent. [*COGE Handbook*]
Discovered unrecoverable petroleum initially-in-place	That portion of *discovered petroleum initially-in-place* which is estimated, as of a given date, not to be recoverable by future development *projects*.
	A portion of these quantities may become recoverable in the future as *commercial* circumstances change or technological developments occur; the remaining portion may never be recovered due to the physical/chemical constraints represented by subsurface interaction of fluids and *reservoir* rocks.
	[*COGE Handbook*]
Discovered unrecoverable resources	Refer to *discovered unrecoverable petroleum initially-in-place* as both terms are equivalent.
	[*COGE Handbook*]
Discovery	The confirmation of the existence of an *accumulation* of a significant quantity of potentially recoverable *petroleum*. For additional information, see section 2.2.2 of the *COGE Handbook*, vol. 2 Definitions. [*COGE Handbook*]
Economic contingent resources	Those *contingent resources* that are currently economically recoverable. [*COGE Handbook*]
Effective date	In respect of information, the date as at which, or for the period ended on which, the information is provided. [*NI 51-101*]
Established technology	Methods that have been proven to be successful in *commercial* applications. [*COGE Handbook*]
Evaluation	In relation to *reserves data* or *resources other than reserves*, the process whereby an economic analysis is made of a property to arrive at an estimate of a range of net present values of the estimated *future net revenue* resulting from the *production* of the *reserves* or *resources other than reserves* associated with the property. [*COGE Handbook*]
Experimental technology	A technology that is being field tested to determine the technical viability of applying a recovery process to *unrecoverable discovered petroleum initially-in-place* in a subject *reservoir*. It cannot be used to assign any class of recoverable *resources* (i.e., *reserves, contingent resources, prospective resources*). [*COGE Handbook*]
Exploitable bitumen in-place (EBIP)	This is the volume of accessible *bitumen* that is estimated could be extracted from a volume considered to be amenable to exploitation, after the application of regulatory factors and surface limitations. [*COGE Handbook*]
Exploration costs	Costs incurred in identifying areas that may warrant examination and in examining specific areas that are considered to have *prospects* that may contain *oil* and *gas reserves*, including costs of drilling *exploratory wells* and exploratory type *stratigraphic test wells*.
	Exploration costs may be incurred both before acquiring the related *property* (sometimes referred to in part as "prospecting costs") and after acquiring the *property*. *Exploration costs*, which include applicable *operating costs of support equipment and facilities* and other costs of exploration activities, are:

Defined Term	Meaning

(a) costs of topographical, geochemical, geological and geophysical studies, rights of access to *properties* to conduct those studies, and salaries and other expenses of geologists, geophysical crews and others conducting those studies (collectively sometimes referred to as "geological and geophysical costs");

(b) costs of carrying and retaining *unproved properties*, such as delay rentals, taxes (other than income and capital taxes) on *properties*, legal costs for title defence, and the maintenance of land and *lease* records;

(c) dry hole contributions and bottom hole contributions;

(d) costs of drilling and equipping *exploratory wells*; and

(e) costs of drilling exploratory type *stratigraphic test wells*.

Exploratory well — A well that is not a *development well*, a *service well* or a *stratigraphic test well*.

First point of sale — The first point after initial production at which there is a transfer of ownership of a product type. [*NI 51-101*]

Forecast prices and costs — Future prices and costs that are:

(a) generally accepted as being a reasonable outlook of the future;

(b) if, and only to the extent that, there are fixed or presently determinable future prices or costs to which the *reporting issuer* is legally bound by a contractual or other obligation to supply a physical product, including those for an extension period of a contract that is likely to be extended, those prices or costs rather than the prices and costs referred to in paragraph (a). [*NI 51-101*]

Foreign geographic area — A geographic area outside North America within one country or including all or portions of a number of countries.

Form 51-101F1 — Form 51-101F1 *Statement of Reserves Data and Other Oil and Gas Information*.

Form 51-101F2 — Form 51-101F2 Report on *[Reserves Data]][,] [Contingent Resources Data] [and] [Prospective Resources Data] by Independent Qualified Reserves Evaluator or Auditor*.

Form 51-101F3 — Form 51-101F3 *Report of Management and Directors on Oil and Gas Disclosure*.

Form 51-101F4 — Form 51-101F4 *Notice of Filing of 51-101F1 Information*.

Form 51-101F5 — Form 51-101F5 *Notice of Ceasing to Engage in Oil and Gas Activities*.

Future income tax expenses — *Expenses* estimated (generally, year-by-year):

(a) making appropriate allocations of estimated unclaimed costs and losses carried forward for tax purposes, between *oil and gas activities* and other business activities;

(b) without deducting estimated future costs (for example, Crown royalties) that are not deductible in computing taxable income;

(c) taking into account estimated tax credits and allowances (for example, royalty tax credits); and

(d) applying to the future pre-tax net cash flows relating to the *reporting issuer's oil and gas activities* the appropriate year-end statutory tax rates, taking into account future tax rates already legislated.

Future net revenue — A forecast of revenue, estimated using *forecast prices and costs* or constant prices and costs, arising from the anticipated development and production of *resources*, net of the associated royalties, *operating costs, development costs*, and *abandonment and reclamation costs*. [*NI 51-101*]

Cas — Includes *natural gas, conventional natural gas, coal bed methane, gas hydrates, shale gas*, and *synthetic gas*.

Gas hydrate — A naturally occurring crystalline substance composed of water and *gas* in an ice-lattice structure. [*NI 51-101*]

Gross —

(a) In relation to a *reporting issuer's* interest in *production* or *reserves*, its "company *gross reserves*", which are the *reporting issuer's* working interest (operating or non-operating) share before deduction of royalties and without including any royalty interests of the *reporting issuer*.

(b) In relation to wells, the total number of wells in which a *reporting issuer* has an interest.

Defined Term	Meaning
	(c) In relation to *properties*, the total area of properties in which a *reporting issuer* has an interest.
Heavy crude oil	*Crude oil* with a relative density greater than 10 degrees API gravity and less than or equal to 22.3 degrees API gravity. [*NI 51-101*]
Hydrocarbons	A compound consisting of hydrogen and carbon, which, when naturally occurring, may also contain other elements such as sulphur. [*NI 51-101*]
Independent	In respect of the relationship between a *reporting issuer* and a person or company, the relationship between the *reporting issuer* and that person or company in which there is no circumstance that could, in the opinion of a reasonable person aware of all relevant facts, interfere with that person's or company's exercise of judgment regarding the preparation of information which is used by the *reporting issuer*. [*NI 51-101*]
Instrument (or NI 51-101)	National Insrument 51-101 *Standards of Disclosure for Oil and Gas Activities.*
Jurisdiction	For the purposes of *NI 51-101*, a province or territory of Canada. [*NI 14-101*]
Kerogen	A solid organic substance, insoluble in organic solvents, that results from the degradation of algae and woody plant material. [*COGE Handbook*]
Kerogenous shale (oil shale)	Shale that contains the solid *hydrocarbon kerogen*, which can sometimes be burned without processing or can be converted to liquid *petroleum* by a pyrolysis process, either in situ or at surface after mining. [*COGE Handbook*]
Known accumulation	An *accumulation* that has been penetrated by a well that has demonstrated the existence of a significant quantity of potentially recoverable *petroleum*, preferably by flow testing that demonstrates that the *petroleum* is moveable. If there is no flow test, log and/or core data may suffice, provided a good *commercial* analogue is available to justify the assumption that the *petroleum* is moveable. Where log and/or core data demonstrate the existence of an *accumulation* but recovery potential can only be justified through extensive testing or *experimental technology*, the associated *petroleum initially-in-place* must be classified as *discovered unrecoverable* until a technically viable recovery technology can be demonstrated. [*COGE Handbook*]
Lead	A potential *accumulation* within a play that requires more data acquisition and/or evaluation in order to be classified as a prospect. [*COGE Handbook*]
Lease	An agreement granting to the lessee rights to explore, develop and exploit a *property*.
Light crude oil	*Crude oil* with a relative density greater than 31.1 degrees API gravity. [*NI 51-101*]
Marketable	In respect of *reserves* or sales of *oil*, *gas* or associated *by-products*, the volume of oil, gas or associated by-products measured at the point of sale to a third party, or of transfer to another division of the issuer for treatment prior to sale to a third party. For *gas*, this may occur either before or after the removal of *natural gas liquids*. For *heavy crude oil* or *bitumen*, this is before the addition of diluent.
Material (or materiality)	For the purposes of *NI 51-101*, information is *material*, in respect of a *reporting issuer*, if it would be likely to influence a decision by a reasonable investor to buy, hold or sell a security of the *reporting issuer*. This meaning differs from the definitions of "material change" and "material fact" in *securities legislation*. [*NI 51-101*]
Mcf	Thousand cubic feet. [*COGE Handbook*]
McfGE	Thousand cubic feet of *gas* equivalent. [*NI 51-101* and *COGE Handbook*]
Natural gas	A naturally occurring mixture of *hydrocarbon gases* and other gases. [*NI 51-101*]

Defined Term	Meaning
Natural Gas liquids (or NGLs)	Those *hydrocarbon* components that can be recovered from *natural gas* as a liquid including, but not limited to, ethane, propane, butanes, pentanes plus, and condensates. [*NI 51-101*]
Net	(a) In relation to a *reporting issuer's* interest in *production* or *reserves*, the *reporting issuer's* working interest (operating or non-operating) share after deduction of royalty obligations, plus the *reporting issuer's* royalty interests in *production* or *reserves*.
	(b) In relation to a *reporting issuer's* interest in wells, the number of wells obtained by aggregating the *reporting issuer's* working interest in each of its *gross* wells.
	(c) In relation to a *reporting issuer's* interest in a *property*, the total area in which the *reporting issuer* has an interest multiplied by the working interest owned by the *reporting issuer*.
Net pay	That portion of the thickness of a *reservoir* from which *petroleum* can be produced or extracted. [*COGE Handbook*]
NI 14-101	National Instrument 14-101 *Definitions*.
NI 51-101 or the Instrument	National Instrument 51-101 *Standards of Disclosure for Oil and Gas Activities*.
NI 51-102	National Instrument 51-102 *Continuous Disclosure Obligations*.
Oil	Includes *crude oil*, *bitumen*, *tight oil* and *synthetic crude oil*.
Oil and gas activities	Includes the following:
	(a) searching for a *product type* in its natural location;
	(b) acquiring *property* rights or a *property* for the purpose of exploring for or removing *product types* from their natural locations;
	(c) any activity necessary to remove *product types* from their natural locations, including construction, drilling, mining and production, and the acquisition, construction, installation and maintenance of *field* gathering and storage systems including treating, *field* processing and field storage;
	(d) producing or manufacturing of *synthetic crude oil* or *synthetic gas*;
	but does not include any of the following:
	(e) any activity that occurs after the *first point of sale*;
	(f) any activity relating to the extraction of a substance other than a *product type* and their *by-products*;
	(g) extracting *hydrocarbons* as a consequence of the extraction of geothermal steam. [*NI 51-101*]
Oil and gas metric	A numerical measure of a *reporting issuer's* oil and gas activities.
Operating costs	*Production costs*.
Ore	Ore is a mining term describing oil sand with a minimum thickness that can be technically removed with current mining equipment and contains a minimum *bitumen* content required for anticipated extraction technology. [*COGE Handbook*]
Petroleum	A naturally occurring mixture consisting predominantly of *hydrocarbons* in the gaseous, liquid, or solid phase. [*COGE Handbook*]
Play	A family of geologically similar fields, discoveries, prospects, and leads. [*COGE Handbook*]
Possible reserves	See Part 2 of this Glossary. [*COGE Handbook*]

Defined Term	Meaning
Pre-development study	An intermediate step in the development of a project evaluation scenario. The amount of information that is available for the *reservoir* of interest is greater than for a *conceptual study*. In particular, the *petroleum initially-in-place* has been reasonably well defined and the remaining uncertainty lies largely in the recovery factor and the economic viability. The level of economic analysis is sufficient to assess development options and overall *project* viability, but is insufficient for a final investment decision or for seeking outside major financing. [*COGE Handbook*]
Preparation date	In respect of written disclosure, the most recent date to which information relating to the period ending on the *effective date* was considered in the preparation of the disclosure. [*NI 51-101*]
Probable reserves	See Part 2 of this Glossary. [*COGE Handbook*]
Product type	Any of the following: (a) *bitumen*; (b) *coal bed methane*; (c) *conventional natural gas*; (d) *gas hydrates*; (e) *heavy crude oil*; (f) *light crude oil* and *medium crude oil* combined; (g) *shale gas*; (h) *shale gas*; (i) *synthetic crude oil*; (j) *synthetic gas*; or (k) *tight oil*. [*NI 51-101*]
Production	The cumulative quantity of *petroleum* that has been recovered at a given date. [*COGE Handbook*] Recovering, gathering, treating, field or plant processing (for example, processing gas to extract *natural gas liquids*) and field storage of *oil* and *gas*. The *oil* production function is usually regarded as terminating at the outlet valve on the *lease* or field production storage tank. The *gas* production function is usually regarded as terminating at the plant gate. In some circumstances, it may be more appropriate to regard the production function as terminating at the first point at which *oil*, *gas* or their by-products are delivered to a main pipeline, a common carrier, a refinery or a marine terminal.
Production costs (or Operating costs)	Costs incurred to operate and maintain wells and related equipment and facilities, including applicable *operating costs* of *support equipment and facilities* and other costs of operating and maintaining those wells and related equipment and facilities. Lifting costs become part of the cost of *oil* and *gas* produced. Examples of *production costs* are: (a) costs of labour to operate the wells and related equipment and facilities; (b) costs of repairs and maintenance; (c) costs of materials, supplies and fuel consumed, and supplies utilized, in operating the wells and related equipment and facilities; (d) costs of workovers; (e) *property* taxes and insurance costs applicable to *properties* and wells and related equipment and facilities; and (f) taxes, other than income and capital taxes.
Professional organization	A self-regulatory organization of engineers, geologists, other geoscientists or other professionals whose professional practice includes *reserves evaluations* or *reserves audits*, that: (a) admits members primarily on the basis of their educational qualifications;

Defined Term	Meaning

(b) requires its members to comply with the professional standards of competence and ethics prescribed by the organization that are relevant to the estimation, *evaluation*, review or *audit* of *reserves data*;

(c) has disciplinary powers, including the power to suspend or expel a member; and

(d) is either:

  (i) given authority or recognition by statute in a Canadian *jurisdiction*; or

  (ii) accepted for this purpose by the *securities regulatory authority* or the *regulator*.[NI 51-101]

Project A defined activity, or set of activities, that provides the basis for the assessment and classification of resources. [*COGE Handbook*]

Project Evaluation Scenario Status The degree to which the project scenario has been developed. Three levels of development are identified — conceptual, pre-development, and development. For additional information, see section 2.4.7 Recovery Project Evaluation Scenario Status in section 2 of volume 2 of the *COGE Handbook*. (See also *conceptual (scoping) study*, *pre-development study*, and *development study*.) [*COGE Handbook*]

Project Maturity Sub-Classes for Contingent Resources See also *development unclarified*, *development pending*, *development on hold*, and *development not viable*. [*COGE Handbook*]

Property Includes:

(a) fee ownership or a *lease*, concession, agreement, permit, licence or other interest representing the right to extract *oil* or *gas* subject to such terms as may be imposed by the conveyance of that interest;

(b) royalty interests, *production* payments payable in *oil* or *gas*, and other non-operating interests in *properties* operated by others; and

(c) an agreement with a foreign government or authority under which a *reporting issuer* participates in the operation of *properties* or otherwise serves as "producer" of the underlying *reserves* (in contrast to being an *independent* purchaser, broker, dealer or importer).

A *property* does not include supply agreements, or contracts that represent a right to purchase, rather than extract, *oil* or *gas*.

Property acquisition costs Costs incurred to acquire a *property* (directly by purchase or *lease*, or indirectly by acquiring another corporate entity with an interest in the *property*), including:

(a) costs of *lease* bonuses and options to purchase or *lease* a *property*;

(b) the portion of the costs applicable to *hydrocarbons* when land including rights to *hydrocarbons* is purchased in fee;

(c) brokers' fees, recording and registration fees, legal costs and other costs incurred in acquiring *properties*.

Prospect A geographic or stratigraphic area, in which the *reporting issuer* owns or intends to own one or more *oil* and *gas* interests, which is geographically defined on the basis of geological data and which is reasonably anticipated to contain at least one *reservoir* or part of a *reservoir* of *oil* and *gas*.

Prospective resources Those quantities of *petroleum* estimated, as of a given date, to be potentially recoverable from undiscovered *accumulations* by application of future development projects.

Prospective resources have both an associated *chance of discovery* and a *chance of development*. [*COGE Handbook*]

Prospective resources data Means

(a) an estimate of the volume of *prospective resources*, and

(b) the *risked* net present value of *future net revenue* of *prospective resources*; [NI 51-101]

Proved property A *property* or part of a *property* to which *reserves* have been specifically attributed.

Defined Term	Meaning
Proved reserves	See Part 2 of this Glossary. [*COGE Handbook*]
Qualified reserves auditor	An individual who:
	(a) in respect of particular *reserves data*, *resources* or related information, possesses professional qualifications and experience appropriate for the estimation, *evaluation*, *review* and *audit* of the *reserves data*, *resources* and related information; and
	(b) is a member in good standing of a *professional organization*.
	[*NI 51-101*]
Qualified reserves evaluator	An individual who:
	(a) in respect of particular *reserves data* or related information, possesses professional qualifications and experience appropriate for the estimation, *evaluation* and review of the *reserves data* and related information; and
	(b) is a member in good standing of a *professional organization*.
	[*NI 51-101*]
Qualified reserves evaluator or auditor	A *qualified reserves evaluator* or a *qualified reserves auditor*. [*NI 51-101*]
Recovery process analogue	A recovery process that is an *established technology* or *technology under development* in the analogue *reservoir* that can be applied to the subject *reservoir* being evaluated. [*COGE Handbook*]
Recovery technology status	See *established technology*, *technology under development*, and *experimental technology*. [*COGE Handbook*]
Refinery	A refinery (depending on the processes in the facility) can use different *crude oils*, conventional (unprocessed) or synthetic (already *upgraded* once) including heavy *crude oil* and *bitumen*, to make final products for the market or specialized products for further processing, like petrochemicals. [*COGE Handbook*]
Regulator	The *securities regulatory authority* or a person who holds a specified position with the *securities regulatory authority* (in several instances, its Executive Director or Director) in each *jurisdiction*.
	[*NI 14-101*]
Reporting issuer	(a) A "*reporting issuer*" as defined in *securities legislation*; or
	(b) in a *jurisdiction* in which the term is not defined in *securities legislation*, an issuer of securities that is required to file financial statements with the *securities regulatory authority*.
Reservation	In relation to a report on *reserves data* or *resources* (if applicable), a modification of the standard report of an *independent qualified reserves evaluator* or *auditor on reserves data* or *resources* set out in *Form 51-101F2*, caused by a departure from the *COGE Handbook* or by a limitation in the scope of work that the *independent qualified reserves evaluator* or *auditor* considers necessary. A modification may take the form of a qualified or adverse opinion or a denial of opinion.
Reserves	See Part 2 of this Glossary. [*COGE Handbook*]
Reserves data	Estimates of *proved reserves* and *probable reserves* and related *future net revenue* estimated using *forecast prices* and *costs*. [*NI 51-101*]
Reservoir	subsurface rock unit that contains an *accumulation* of *petroleum*. [*COGE Handbook*]
Reservoir Analogue	A *reservoir* with similar rock properties (lithological, depositional, diagenetic, and structural), fluid properties (*hydrocarbon* type, composition, density, and viscosity), *reservoir* conditions (depth, temperature, and pressure) and drive mechanisms that can be used as a model for the subject *reservoir* being evaluated. [*COGE Handbook*]

Part 5: ONGOING REQUIREMENTS

Defined Term	Meaning
Resource Type	Describes the *accumulation* and is determined by the combination of the type of *hydrocarbon* and the rock in which it occurs. For additional information, see section 2.1.3 Resource Types of section 2 of volume 2 of the COGE Handbook. [*COGE Handbook*]
Resources	*Petroleum* quantities that originally existed on or within the earth's crust in naturally occurring *accumulations*, including discovered and undiscovered (recoverable and *unrecoverable*) plus quantities already produced. *Total resources* is equivalent to *total petroleum initially-in-place*. [*COGE Handbook*]
Review	In relation to the role of a *qualified reserves evaluator or auditor* in respect of reserves data, steps carried out by the *qualified reserves evaluator or auditor*, consisting primarily of enquiry, analytical procedures, analysis, review of historical *reserves* performance and discussion with *reserves* management staff related to a *reporting issuer's reserves data*, with the limited objective of assessing whether the *reserves* data is "plausible" in the sense of appearing to be worthy of belief based on the information obtained by the *qualified reserves evaluator or auditor* as a result of carrying out such steps. Examination of documentation is not required unless the information does not appear to be plausible.
	A *reserves* review, due to the limited nature of the investigation involved, does not provide the level of assurance provided by a *reserves audit*. Although *reserves* reviews can be done for specific applications, they are not a substitute for an *audit*. [*COGE Handbook*]
Risked	Adjusted for the probability of loss or failure in accordance with the *COGE Handbook*. [*NI 51-101*]
SEC	The Securities and Exchange Commission of the United States of America. [*NI 14-101*]
Securities legislation	The statute (in most cases entitled the "Securities Act") and subordinate legislation (in most cases including regulations or rules) specified, for each *jurisdiction*, in *NI 14-101*.
	References in *NI 51-101* to *securities legislation* are to be read as references to *securities legislation* in the particular *jurisdiction*.
Securities regulatory authority	The securities commission or comparable body specified, for each *jurisdiction*, in *NI 14-101*.
	References in *NI 51-101* to the *securities regulatory authority* are to be read as references to the *securities regulatory authority* in the particular *jurisdiction*.
SEDAR	The System for Electronic Document Analysis and Retrieval referred to in National Instrument 13-101 *System for Electronic Document Analysis and Retrieval* (*SEDAR*).
Service well	A well drilled or completed for the purpose of supporting *production* in an existing *field*. Wells in this class are drilled for the following specific purposes: gas injection (*natural gas*, propane, butane or flue *gas*), water injection, steam injection, air injection, salt-water disposal, water supply for injection, observation, or injection for combustion.
Shale gas	*Natural gas*: (a) contained in dense organic-rich rocks, including low-permeability shales, siltstones and carbonates, in which the *natural gas* is primarily adsorbed on the kerogen or clay minerals, and (b) that usually requires the use of hydraulic fracturing to achieve economic production rates. [*NI 51-101*]
Solution gas	*Gas* dissolved in *crude oil*.
Stratigraphic test well	A drilling effort, geologically directed, to obtain information pertaining to a specific geologic condition. Ordinarily, such wells are drilled without the intention of being completed for *hydrocarbon production*. They include wells for the purpose of core tests and all types of expendable holes related to *hydrocarbon* exploration.
	Stratigraphic test wells are classified as

Defined Term	Meaning

| | (a)   "exploratory type" if not drilled into a proved *property*; or |
| | (b)   "development type", if drilled into a proved *property*. Development type stratigraphic wells are also referred to as "*evaluation* wells". |

Sub-economic contingent resources	Those *contingent resources* that are not currently economically recoverable. There should be a reasonable expectation of a change in economic conditions within the near future that will result in them becoming economically viable. [*COGE Handbook*]
Support equipment and facilities	Equipment and facilities used in *oil and gas activities*, including seismic equipment, drilling equipment, construction and grading equipment, vehicles, repair shops, warehouses, supply points, camps, and division, district or *field* offices.
Supporting filing	A document filed by a *reporting issuer* with a *securities regulatory authority*. [*NI 51-101*]
Synthetic crude oil	A mixture of liquid *hydrocarbons* derived by upgrading *bitumen*, *kerogen* or other substances such as coal, or derived from *gas* to liquid conversion and may contain sulphur or other compounds. [*NI 51-101*]
Synthetic gas	A gaseous fluid
	(a) generated as a result of the application of an in-situ transformation process to coal or other h*ydrocarbon*-bearing rock; and
	(b) comprised of not less than 10% by volume of methane. [*NI 51-101*]
Technical contingency	A technical issue that must be resolved to allow the *commercial* application of a recovery process technology to a specific *reservoir*. [COGE Handbook]
Technology under development	A recovery process that has been determined to be technically viable via field test and is being field tested further to determine its economic viability in the subject *reservoir*. *Contingent resources* may be assigned if the *project* provides information that is sufficient and of a quality to meet the requirements for this *resource class*. (Note: this replaces the definition in the *COGE Handbook* volume 1, Appendix A — Glossary.) [*COGE Handbook*]
Tight Oil	*Crude oil*
	(a) contained in dense organic-rich rocks, including low-permeability shales, siltstones and carbonates, in which the *crude oil* is primarily contained in microscopic pore spaces that are poorly connected to one another, and
	(b) that typically requires the use of hydraulic fracturing to achieve economic *production* rates. [*NI 51-101*]
Total petroleum initially-in-place	That quantity of *petroleum* that is estimated to exist originally in naturally occurring *accumulations*.
	It includes that quantity of *petroleum* that is estimated, as of a given date, to be contained in *known accumulations*, prior to *production*, plus those estimated quantities in *accumulations* yet to be discovered. [*COGE Handbook*]
Total resources	Refer to *total petroleum initially-in-place* as both terms are equivalent. [*COGE Handbook*]
Total volume (m³): bitumen in-place (m³) (TV:BIP)	The ratio of the total volume of material under consideration for mining to the total contained *bitumen* within the ore component of that volume. The in-place *bitumen* content is derived exclusively from the component model blocks or zones, which have been determined to be ore, through an ore-waste discrimination process. [*COGE Handbook*]
Undeveloped reserves	See Part 2 of this Glossary. [*COGE Handbook*]
Undiscovered petroleum initially-in-place	That quantity of *petroleum* that is estimated, on a given date, to be contained in *accumulations* yet to be discovered.

Part 5: ONGOING REQUIREMENTS

Defined Term	Meaning
	The recoverable portion of *undiscovered petroleum initially-in-place* is referred to as *prospective resources*; the remainder is unrecoverable. [*COGE Handbook*]
Undiscovered resources	Refer to *undiscovered petroleum initially-in-place* as both terms are equivalent. [*COGE Handbook*]
Undiscovered unrecoverable petroleum initially-in-place	That portion of *undiscovered petroleum initially-in-place* which is estimated, as of a given date, not to be recoverable by future development projects. A portion of these quantities may become recoverable in the future as *commercial* circumstances change or technological developments occur; the remaining portion may never be recovered due to the physical/chemical constraints represented by subsurface interaction of fluids and *reservoir* rocks. [*COGE Handbook*]
Undiscovered unrecoverable resources	Refer to *undiscovered unrecoverable petroleum initially-in-place* as both terms are equivalent.
Unproved property	A *property* or part of a *property* to which no *reserves* have been specifically attributed.
Unrecoverable	That portion of discovered or undiscovered *petroleum initially-in-place* quantities which is estimated, as of a given date, not to be recoverable by future development *projects*. A portion of these quantities may become recoverable in the future as commercial circumstances change or technological developments occur; the remaining portion may never be recovered due to the physical/chemical constraints represented by subsurface interaction of fluids and reservoir rocks. [*COGE Handbook*]
Upgrader	An upgrader is a facility that processes either *heavy crude oil* or *bitumen* into products that can either flow without diluent being added or other blends of crude with properties that are now desirable in a typical *refinery*. Many different blends can be made at an upgrader for the final user. One of the most common (sweet synthetic) is the premium *crude*, which is made from a blend of treated naphtha, kerosene (distillate) and gas oil. This product has been sold in the market place since the late 1960s. It is also possible to make untreated blends of upgraded *crude oils* and final products like diesel fuel. Typically, gasoline is not made at an upgrader. [*COGE Handbook*]
Upgrading	Upgrading is a term used to describe the process of changing the structure or improving the quality of a *heavy crude oil* or *bitumen* to allow either further use as a final product or feedstock to a *refinery*. Typically, *heavy oils* and *bitumen* contain large amounts of asphaltenes, metals, sulphur, and nitrogen components. Removal of these components or impurities will usually result in a higher price for the upgraded *oil*. Constituents like asphaltenes are long chain aromatic ring type hydrocarbons that are prone to coking (a term which results in these long chain molecules breaking and then rejoining to form even longer chain molecules), which will plug or foul equipment and catalyst. [*COGE Handbook*]
U.S. federal securities laws	The federal statutes of the United States of America concerning the regulation of securities markets and trading in securities and the regulations, rules, forms and schedules under those statues, all as amended from time to time. [*NI 14-101*]

Part 2 — Definitions of Reserves

This Part is derived from Section 5 of Volume 1 of the COGE Handbook (Second Edition, September 1, 2007). Consult a current edition of the COGE Handbook for updates and for additional explanation and guidance.

The following *reserves* definitions and guidelines are designed to assist evaluators in making *reserves* estimates on a reasonably consistent basis, and assist users of evaluation reports in understanding what such reports contain and, if necessary, in judging whether evaluators have followed generally accepted standards.

The guidelines outline

- general criteria for classifying *reserves*,

- procedures and methods for estimating *reserves*,

- confidence levels of individual entity and aggregate *reserves* estimates,
- verification and testing of *reserves* estimates.

The determination of *oil* and *gas reserves* involves the preparation of estimates that have an inherent degree of associated uncertainty. Categories of *proved*, probable, and *possible reserves* have been established to reflect the level of these uncertainties and to provide an indication of the probability of recovery.

The estimation and classification of reserves requires the application of professional judgement combined with geological and engineering knowledge to assess whether or not specific *reserves* classification criteria have been satisfied. Knowledge of concepts including uncertainty and risk, probability and statistics, and deterministic and probabilistic estimation methods is required to properly use and apply *reserves* definitions. These concepts are presented and discussed in greater detail within the guidelines in Section 5.5 [of the *COGE Handbook*].

The following definitions apply to both estimates of individual reserves entities and the aggregate of reserves for multiple entities.

Reserves Categories

Reserves are estimated remaining quantities of *oil* and *natural gas* and related substances anticipated to be recoverable from *known accumulations*, as of a given date, based on

- analysis of drilling, geological, geophysical and engineering data;
- the use of established technology;
- specified economic conditions, which are generally accepted as being reasonable, and shall be disclosed.

Reserves are classified according to the degree of certainty associated with the estimates.

(a) *Proved reserves* are those *reserves* that can be estimated with a high degree of certainty to be recoverable. It is likely that the actual remaining quantities recovered will exceed the estimated proved *reserves*.

(b) *Probable reserves* are those additional reserves that are less certain to be recovered than *proved reserves*. It is equally likely that the actual remaining quantities recovered will be greater or less than the sum of the estimated *proved* plus *probable reserves*.

(c) *Possible reserves* are those additional *reserves* that are less certain to be recovered than *probable reserves*. It is unlikely that the actual remaining quantities recovered will exceed the sum of the estimated *proved* plus *probable* plus *possible reserves*.

Other criteria that must also be met for the classification of reserves are provided in [Section 5.5.4 of the *COGE Handbook*].

Development and *Production* Status

Each of the *reserves* categories (*proved*, *probable* and *possible*) may be divided into *developed* and *undeveloped* categories:

(a) *Developed reserves* are those reserves that are expected to be recovered from existing wells and installed facilities or, if facilities have not been installed, that would involve a low expenditure (e.g., when compared to the cost of drilling a well) to put the *reserves* on production. The *developed* category may be subdivided into producing and non-producing.

  Developed producing reserves are those reserves that are expected to be recovered from completion intervals open at the time of the estimate. These *reserves* may be currently producing or, if shut-in, they must have previously been on *production*, and the date of resumption of *production* must be known with reasonable certainty.

  Developed non-producing reserves are those *reserves* that either have not been on *production*, or have previously been on production but are shut-in and the date of resumption of *production* is unknown.

(b) *Undeveloped reserves* are those reserves expected to be recovered from *known accumulations* where a significant expenditure (e.g., when compared to the cost of drilling a well) is required to render them capable of *production*. They must fully meet the requirements of the reserves category (*proved*, *probable*, *possible*) to which they are assigned.

  In multi-well pools it may be appropriate to allocate total pool *reserves* between the *developed* and *undeveloped* categories or to subdivide the *developed reserves* for the pool between *developed producing* and *developed non-producing*. This allocation should be based on the estimator's assessment as to the reserves that will be recovered from specific wells, facilities, and completion intervals in the pool and their respective development and *production* status.

Levels of Certainty for Reported *Reserves*

The qualitative certainty levels referred to in the definitions above are applicable to "individual reserves entities", which refers to the lowest level at which reserves calculations are performed, and to "reported *reserves*", which refers to the highest level sum of individual entity estimates for which *reserves* estimates are presented. Reported *reserves* should target the following levels of certainty under a specific set of economic conditions:

- at least a 90 percent probability that the quantities actually recovered will equal or exceed the estimated *proved reserves*;
- at least a 50 percent probability that the quantities actually recovered will equal or exceed the sum of the estimated *proved* plus *probable reserves*; and
- at least a 10 percent probability that the quantities actually recovered will equal or exceed the sum of the estimated *proved* plus *probable* plus *possible reserves*.

A quantitative measure of the certainty levels pertaining to estimates prepared for the various *reserves* categories is desirable to provide a clearer understanding of the associated risks and uncertainties. However, the majority of reserves estimates are prepared using deterministic methods that do not provide a mathematically derived quantitative measure of probability. In principle, there should be no difference between estimates prepared using probabilistic or deterministic methods.

Additional clarification of certainty levels associated with *reserves* estimates and the effect of aggregation is provided in Section 5 [of the *COGE Handbook*].

Questions

Please refer questions to any of the following:

[Omitted.]

CSA Staff Notice 51-327 (Revised) — Guidance on Oil and Gas Disclosure

Date: February 27, 2009 as revised effective December 30, 2010, December 29, 2011 and December 4, 2014

    32 O.S.C.B. 1774, 33 O.S.C.B. 11920, 35 O.S.C.B. 616 and 37 O.S.C.B. 10695

1. — Introduction

This revised Canadian Securities Administrators (**CSA**) Staff Notice (**Notice**) provides guidance on compliance with aspects of National Instrument 51-101 *Standards of Disclosure for Oil and Gas Activities* (**NI 51-101**).

NI 51-101 applies to reporting issuers that are directly or indirectly engaged in oil and gas activities (Oil and Gas Issuers). Central to the NI 51-101 disclosure regime is mandatory disclosure of prescribed reserves data, which includes estimates of proved reserves and probable reserves and related future net revenues. NI 51-101 also establishes standards for certain non-mandatory disclosure that Oil and Gas Issuers may choose to make regarding oil and gas activities.[1]

When first issued on 27 February 2009 under the title *Oil and Gas Disclosure: Resources Other Than Reserves Data*, this Notice was designed to address observations by CSA staff of issues arising as a result of an increase in non-mandatory disclosure of possible reserves and other resource classes, especially for unconventional resources. This Notice was revised as of 30 December 2010 to address additional issues relating to oil and gas disclosure and to remove guidance on certain issues that we addressed by amendments to NI 51-101.[2] This Notice was again revised as of 29 December 2011 to discuss observations by CSA staff in reviewing disclosure in light of amendments to NI 51-101 in 2010 and to re-emphasize or expand guidance on some issues discussed in previous versions of this Notice.

This Notice is now being revised in connection with the publication of amendments to NI 51-101 on December 4, 2014, the adoption of the detailed guidelines for estimation and classification of bitumen resources (Bitumen Guidelines) into volume 3 of the Canadian Oil and Gas Evaluation Handbook (COGE Handbook) on April 1, 2014, and the adoption of the guidelines for estimation and classification of resources other than reserves (ROTR Guidelines) into section 2 of volume 2 of the COGE Handbook on July 17, 2014.

Context and Cautions

- *Suggested Wording* — We recommend, at various points in this Notice, that non-mandatory disclosure be accompanied by cautionary statements, and we suggest wording that may be helpful. We recommend cautionary statements based on our view that disclosure of resources other than proved and probable reserves may mislead if the disclosure lacks context; we intend the cautionary statements to provide appropriate context. Adequate disclosure will provide explanation and, where appropriate, cautionary information. An Oil and Gas Issuer may use cautionary wording other than what we recommend by this Notice where necessary to provide complete and accurate disclosure.

- *General Guidance with Examples* — We have chosen specific disclosure topics for discussion in this Notice as examples of how general principles apply to specific situations, the topics chosen reflecting recurring concerns arising from observations of CSA staff in reviewing disclosure. This Notice is not a checklist - we intend that Oil and Gas Issuers, and their evaluators and auditors, will use this Notice to guide them in preparing oil and gas disclosure. The themes illustrated in that discussion of professional responsibility and careful choices in formulating disclosure apply also to other topics not mentioned here.

Notes on Terminology

- *Terminology References* — Clarity and consistency in the use of terminology is essential to good disclosure by Oil and Gas Issuers. Important terminological sources include:

  - COGE Handbook — refer to section 5 of Volume 1[3] of the Canadian Oil and Gas Evaluation Handbook (the **COGE Handbook**), titled "*Definitions of Resources and Reserves*", notably Figure 5-1; and

  - CSA Staff Notice 51-324 *Glossary to NI 51-101 Standards of Disclosure for Oil and Gas Activities* (the **CSA Glossary**).

- *Specific Terms* — The classification and categorization of resources is a vital aspect of disclosure under NI 51-101. Although there is now broad alignment between the COGE Handbook and the Society for Petroleum Engineers — Petroleum Resource Management System (SPE-PRMS), some differences remain.[4] Terms in this Notice, unless otherwise defined, have the meaning as set out in NI 51-101,

---

[1]See NI 51-101, section 5.9.

[2]See CSA Notice of Amendments to National Instrument 51-101 *Standards of Disclosure for Oil and Gas Activities* and related and consequential amendments, published 15 October 2010.

[3]Available   on   the   Alberta   Securities   Commission   website   at: http://www.albertasecurities.com/securitiesLaw/Regulatory%20Instruments/5/2232/COGEHs.5DefinitionsofOiland GasResourcesandReserves.pdf

[4]See section 5.1.1 of Volume 1 of the COGE Handbook.

which incorporates defined terms from the COGE Handbook (including the latest additions of the Bitumen Guidelines and the ROTR Guidelines). For clarity, NI 51-101 and this Notice use terminology as follows:

category — In colloquial usage, the term "category" includes both "class" and "category". As a result, volume 1 (2nd Edition 2007) and volume 2 (2005) of the COGE Handbook use the terms "class" and "category" interchangeably. The ROTR Guidelines (July 17, 2014) have adopted the usage in the SPE-PRMS (see Figure 2-1 Resources Classification Framework) as follows:

"Class" describes the chance of commerciality (reserves, contingent resources, etc.) as expressed on the vertical axis of the SPE-PRMS matrix.

"Category" describes the range of uncertainty within a class as expressed on the horizontal axis of the SPE-PRMS matrix. For example, within the class of "reserves" are the categories of "proved", "probable" and "possible", and for other classes the estimation categories of "low estimate", "best estimate" and "high case".

In view of the fact that the COGE Handbook (other than ROTR Guidelines) generally uses the term category to mean both "class" and "category", for the purpose of NI 51-101, the term "category" includes, but is not limited to, both the concepts of "class" and "category" as described above.

resources — In colloquial usage, the term "resources" may or may not include reserves volumes. We refer to "resources", consistent with the CSA Glossary, as a general term that may refer to all or a portion of total resources, with "total resources" as equivalent to "total petroleum initially-in-place" as defined in the COGE Handbook.

reserves data — We refer to "reserves data" as defined in NI 51-101 as an estimate of proved reserves and probable reserves and related future net revenue. The phrase "resources other than proved or probable reserves" refers to all other classes of resources as classified in the COGE Handbook, including possible reserves.

2. — Responsibility for Disclosure of Oil and Gas Information

All who are involved in Oil and Gas Issuers' disclosure — the issuers themselves, their management and directors, and those individuals or firms who provide professional services to them — should be mindful of both (i) the fundamental objectives of Canadian securities legislation, and (ii) the various sources of requirements, restrictions and standards that may apply to formulating disclosure. To protect investors and foster fair and efficient capital markets, Canadian securities legislation is designed to provide the investing public with timely, useful and reliable information from reporting issuers. Those involved in providing such information should give thought to those key objectives. Such individuals must also take note of applicable rules and requirements of relevant professional associations and applicable requirements and restrictions of Canadian securities legislation, which include but are not entirely limited to NI 51-101, which mandates compliance with the COGE Handbook.

(a) — Oil and Gas Issuers — General Standards and Responsibilities

Disclosure relating to oil and gas activities of an Oil and Gas Issuer is subject to the specific requirements and restrictions of NI 51-101, but disclosure requirements are not limited to NI 51-101. Oil and Gas Issuers must make their disclosure within the larger context of Canadian securities legislation and make appropriate use of instructional guides in developing and reporting disclosure.

(i) — Canadian Securities Legislation, Generally

Disclosure relating to oil and gas activities is subject not only to the specific requirements and restrictions of NI 51-101 but also to applicable requirements and prohibitions of other elements of Canadian securities legislation. Not every topic of disclosure is discussed specifically in NI 51-101 or elsewhere in Canadian securities legislation. Oil and Gas Issuers must also give attention to the broader purposes, principles and prohibitions of Canadian securities legislation. Following are discussions of a few examples.

A. — Misrepresentations or Misleading Statements

Among the broad prohibitions of Canadian securities legislation is the ban on misrepresentations — that is (broadly speaking), false, untrue or misleading statements (or omissions from statements) of facts that are material in the sense of being reasonably likely to significantly affect the market price or value of a security. Such materially misleading disclosure is improper and illegal. All responsible for an Oil and Gas Issuer's disclosure should, therefore, give close attention to its quality, ensuring that it does not — expressly, or by omission — mislead. In assessing the quality and sufficiency of disclosure or proposed disclosure, they should bear in mind not only specific disclosure requirements (if applicable) but also, more broadly, the key purposes of Canadian securities legislation, mentioned above.

The following are examples of disclosure that, in the view of CSA staff, could be materially misleading or untrue:

- disclosure of a contingent resource for which there is no flow test or good analog;

- the results of an evaluation for a reservoir based on a production process that has never been used in that type of reservoir;

- inappropriate analog — that is, use of information that is not truly analogous to the reported reserves; and

- disclosure of unconventional resources using a project scenario that is not reasonable with regard to timing or cost and may result in misleading disclosure with respect to the value of a project.[5]

---

[5]Further, it may be misleading for an Oil and Gas Issuer to disclose the result of an evaluation for a project that the Oil and Gas Issuer may not be able, or does not intend, to carry out without disclosing this fact and providing a discussion of how the disclosed value of the project could be realized.

Similarly, the following are examples of disclosure that CSA staff consider could be materially misleading or untrue by reason of omissions — failures to state facts that may be required or necessary to be stated to avoid what is stated being misleading:

- disclosure of petroleum initially-in-place (PIIP) without clarifying whether it is discovered or undiscovered;

- disclosure of a contingent resource without providing information as to its economic viability;

- disclosure of a resource of any class or category without adequate disclosure of the associated significant economic factors or significant uncertainties that are specific to the Oil and Gas Issuer that may affect any associated project;

- disclosure of a contingent resource with only general or vague mention of the contingencies — for example, using wording commonly used by other Oil and Gas Issuers that may not fully or accurately describe the contingencies that apply in the particular circumstances; and

- disclosure of a short-term peak rate for a well test without providing additional disclosure on the test, including that the reported rate is a short-term peak rate.

B. — Material Changes

As one example of a specific disclosure requirement arising outside NI 51-101, Canadian securities legislation requires prompt public disclosure of any "material change".[6] A reporting issuer satisfies this important disclosure obligation by issuing and filing a news release and filing a material change report; it is not satisfied merely by including information in an Oil and Gas Issuer's annual statement of reserves data filed under NI 51-101 or issuing a news release alone.

C. — Requirements Applicable to Disclosure of Oil and Gas Activities

NI 51-101 imposes standards and restrictions that apply to disclosure of oil and gas activities, whether or not such disclosure is restricted to proved and probable reserves and related future net revenue. That is, an Oil and Gas Issuer must consider whether disclosure of oil and gas activities, in any form, and whether made voluntarily or in response to any specific provision of NI 51-101, adheres to applicable provisions of Part 5 of NI 51-101.

It is not possible to identify in advance for all issuers all potentially sound — or improper — disclosure. Oil and Gas Issuers and those involved in preparing, authorizing and disseminating their disclosure must assess their particular facts and circumstances and make judgements on such matters as materiality, taking into account express legal requirements and restrictions, as well as broader principles and prohibitions. That said, CSA staff believe that the observations and recommendations in this Notice will assist Oil and Gas Issuers and those involved in preparing, authorizing and disseminating their disclosure.

(ii) — COGE Handbook and Other Guides

The COGE Handbook is a useful reference for preparing and issuing disclosure required by Canadian securities legislation. It is not, however, an exhaustive guide. Oil and Gas Issuers should bear in mind relevant general principles when formulating disclosure.

When using the COGE Handbook in the preparation and review of information for securities disclosure, Oil and Gas Issuers must interpret it in a manner that is consistent with all applicable Canadian securities legislation including, but not limited to, the principles and specific requirements and restrictions of NI 51-101.

Volume 1 (2nd edition, 2007) and volume 2 (2005) of the COGE Handbook contains general guidance on the evaluation and classification of resources, but the focus is on the evaluation of conventional reserves. For this reason, it has been necessary to supplement this guidance with material on the evaluation of "non-conventional" reserves and resources other than reserves.

The recent addition of the Bitumen Guidelines to volume 3 (2007) of the COGE Handbook addresses the evaluation and classification of the volumes of heavy oil or bitumen existing in, and recoverable from, formations that are suitable for exploitation using in-situ or mining recovery methods. An objective of these guidelines is to ensure that, regardless of the recovery method, the estimate satisfies a single set of classification criteria.

The further addition of the ROTR Guidelines in section 2 of volume 2 of the COGE Handbook address other resources classes. The ROTR Guidelines progress from the estimation of petroleum initially in place, through classification as discovered/undiscovered, identification and characterization of recovery technologies and projects, and to the estimation and economic status of recoverable volumes and description of contingencies and project maturity.

The ROTR Guidelines cover topics that are already addressed to some extent in other sections of the COGE Handbook. There are some differences between the ROTR Guidelines and the guidance in other volumes and sections of the COGE Handbook. Where there is a conflict between the ROTR Guidelines and other parts of the COGE Handbook, the ROTR Guidelines take precedence with respect to the evaluation of resources other than reserves. Those differences may be addressed in future revisions to the COGE Handbook.

(iii) — Specific Description Rather than Commonly-used Wording

To avoid misleading disclosure, Oil and Gas Issuers should tailor their disclosure to their particular circumstances. We have observed the use, verbatim, of wording that appears in other issuers' disclosure. Boilerplate disclosure is unhelpful for an investor; it may also be misleading.

As an example, the long standing requirement found in item 5.2 of Form 51-101F1 *Statement of Reserves Data and Other Oil and Gas Information* (Form 51-101F1) that requires an Oil and Gas Issuer to discuss company-applicable significant factors or uncertainties with respect to reserves data has been extended to other resource categories. Section 5.9 of NI 51-101 and item 6.2.1 of Form 51-101F1 detail these

---

[6]See National Instrument 51-102 *Continuous Disclosure Obligations* (**NI 51-102**), section 7.1.

requirements. In order to comply with NI 51-101, the disclosure should clearly address the factors and uncertainties that are specific to the Oil and Gas Issuer's properties and not simply repeat boilerplate discussion or repeat other Oil and Gas Issuers' disclosure.

(iv) — Use of NI 51-101 Forms for Other Purposes

Forms 51-101F1, 51-101F2 *Report on [Reserves Data][,][Contingent Resources Data][and][Prospective Resources Data] by Independent Qualified Reserves Evaluator or Auditor* (Form 51-101F2) and 51-101F3 *Report of Management and Directors on Oil and Gas Disclosure* (Form 51-101F3) are intended to be used for annual disclosure of reserves data and other specific information. An Oil and Gas Issuer may use such forms as templates for other disclosure purposes, but those documents that offer additional disclosure should not be identified as "*Form 51-101F1*", "*Form 51-101F2*" or "*Form 51-101F3*", and the headings should be modified to describe the actual contents of the disclosure.

(b) — Evaluators and Auditors — General Standards and Responsibilities

An independent qualified reserves evaluator or auditor who signs a report in Form 51-101F2 is representing that the disclosed information is not misleading and that the reserves data and resources data (if disclosed) are free of material misstatement. Therefore, by signing those forms, qualified reserves evaluators and auditors are taking on a professional responsibility that reflects on their individual professionalism and the integrity of their profession. This section provides guidance using, as an example, representations about the net present value of future net revenue of an Oil and Gas Issuer's estimated proved and probable reserves.

(i) — Professional Responsibility

One of the requirements of NI 51-101 is that a qualified reserves evaluator or auditor must be a member of a professional organisation as defined in section 1.1 of NI 51-101.[7]

Oil and Gas Issuers and evaluators must be aware of section 4.8 of volume 1 of the COGE Handbook, titled "Independence, Objectivity and Confidentiality". It may, for instance, be inappropriate for an evaluator to provide an evaluation of a project on which the evaluator has also provided significant engineering advice.

(ii) — Misrepresentations or Misleading Statements

The guidance regarding misrepresentations or misleading statements discussed above[8] applies equally to a qualified reserves evaluator or auditor who signs a statement in Form 51-102F2. In particular, professionals must represent that evaluated projects of the Oil and Gas Issuer provide a net present value of future net revenue that is not misleading.

The evaluation of oil and gas resources is based on a defined scenario or project.[9] Many unconventional resources are developed through large projects, often with long timelines and a net present value that captures the time-discounted value of expenditures and revenues. A project scenario that is not reasonable with regard to timing or cost could result in misleading disclosure with respect to the value of a project.

An evaluation scenario, whether provided to the evaluator for review by the Oil and Gas Issuer or developed by the evaluator, should be reasonable with regard to timing and cost. Oil and Gas Issuers may consider providing a description of key factors in a major project scenario in order to avoid misleading disclosure.

(iii) — Use of COGE Handbook and Other Guides

The guidance provided above in subparagraph 2(a)(ii) of this Notice similarly applies to activities of qualified reserves evaluators and auditors in reviewing Oil and Gas Issuers' disclosure. Technical manuals and reference materials are valuable tools, and in some cases required, to aid in developing disclosure. They should be used appropriately in the exercise of fulfilling the general, as well as specific, obligations of Canadian securities legislation.

(iv) — Expertise Required to Perform Evaluation

When evaluators or auditors sign a report prepared in accordance with Form 51-101F2 they are representing that they possess the expertise to carry out the evaluation that is being reported. NI 51-101 requires that such professionals possess the professional qualifications and experience appropriate to carry out the required review.[10] In addition to the NI 51-101 requirements that evaluators and auditors be qualified professionals, obligations and standards of their profession will apply.[11]

As an example, where an evaluator assigns a net present value or confirms a net present value that has been assigned on the basis of such things as a novel recovery technology or upgrading, the evaluator must be certain as a professional that they possess adequate qualifications and experience to make that professional judgement.

---

[7] An example of such a professional organisation is the Association of Professional Engineers and Geoscientists of Alberta (APEGA), which recognises the COGE Handbook as the practice standard for oil and gas evaluation. Each evaluator, whether independent or an employee of an Oil and Gas Issuer, must be mindful at all times of obligations imposed on them as an individual member of a professional organization. A particular example of such professional obligation is the adherence to the APEGA Guideline for Ethical Practice. Another example of such a professional organisation is the Association of Professional Engineers and Geoscientists of British Columbia.

[8] See clause 2(a)(i)(A) of this Notice.

[9] See section 5.3.3 of Volume 1 of the COGE Handbook.

[10] NI 51-101, paragraphs 1.1(x) and (y).

[11] For example, Rule 2 of the Guideline for Ethical Practice of APEGGA states, "professional engineers, geologists and geophysicists shall undertake only work that they are competent to perform by virtue of their training and experience."

3. — Specific Disclosure Topics

The following discussion topics should not be viewed or treated as an exhaustive list of potential issues related to oil and gas disclosure. The following serve as examples that incorporate some of the general concepts discussed in section 2 above.

(a) — Disclosure of Well-Flow Test Results

Disclosure of well-flow test results can have a significant effect on the market price or value of an Oil and Gas Issuer. Additional information is often necessary in order to avoid misleading readers with such disclosure.[12] Disclosing the results of short-term tests, "rates up to", or short-term peak rates as daily rates, for example, would be misleading without additional explanation.

Oil and Gas Issuers should include information about all of the following when disclosing well-flow test results:

- the geological formation(s) for which test results are being disclosed;
- the type of test (examples include wireline, drillstem testing (DST), or production test);
- duration of the test;
- average rate of oil- or gas-flow during the test;
- recovered fluid types and volumes (reporting the recovery of load fluid without stating that it is load fluid would be regarded as misleading);
- significant production or pressure decline during the test;
- if a pressure transient analysis or well-test interpretation has not been carried out, a cautionary statement should be made to the effect that the data should be considered to be preliminary until such analysis or interpretation has been done; and
- a cautionary statement that the test results are not necessarily indicative of long-term performance or of ultimate recovery.

In addition to the disclosure of the above information on a well-flow test, further disclosure may be necessary to avoid being misleading to readers, especially when high initial decline rates or a short production life are anticipated. Such additional disclosure could include expected duration of production.

Canadian securities legislation requires an Oil and Gas Issuer to make timely disclosure — notably when the result of a test and its implications could amount to a material change.

(b) — Classification to Most Specific Class and Category of Reserves and of Resources Other than Reserves

Section 5.3 of Companion Policy 51-101 *Standards of Disclosure for Oil and Gas Activities* (51-101CP) contemplates as "exceptional circumstances" a situation in which an Oil and Gas Issuer is unable to classify a discovered resource into one of the sub-categories of discovered resources. The guidance in 51-101CP originally reflected established mining practice, which requires a pre-feasibility or a feasibility study before reserves are assigned to mining operations. In that case, the recovery technology is well established but commerciality requires confirmation. The applicability of "exceptional circumstances" for recovery of hydrocarbons by means other than mining would be limited to situations in which it is not possible to define a project[13] for the recovery of a resource from a petroleum accumulation. Subsection 5.16(3) of NI 51-101 provides for this by allowing the disclosure of discovered PIIP without disclosure of reserves or contingent resources. However, subsection 5.16(3) of NI 51-101 only applies when the Oil and Gas Issuer cannot disclose the more specific class, and is not an option that may be exercised to avoid disclosure of the most specific class and category, including the fact that the resources are currently unrecoverable, when the information is or can be made available.

If Oil and Gas Issuers can develop projects using several recovery processes but no decision has been made among them, one or more of such possible processes may be reflected in an evaluation as the basis of disclosure, and the results disclosed in an appropriate class (most likely contingent resources) with relevant discussion.

The definition of discovered PIIP includes the following statement: "the recoverable portion of discovered petroleum initially-in-place includes production, reserves, and contingent resources; the remainder is unrecoverable". Therefore, any volume for which a project cannot be defined and evaluated for classification of production, reserves, contingent resources or, in the case of undiscovered PIIP, prospective resources, at the evaluation date, is by definition, unrecoverable at the time of the evaluation.

Oil and Gas Issuers with volumes currently classified as unrecoverable but who are developing recovery projects, possibly at an experimental level, may describe their activities in the disclosure, provided it is accompanied by a discussion of significant positive and negative factors.[14]

---

[12]See subparagraph 2(a)(i)(A) of this Notice.

[13]For this purpose, a project is a program of work that can be evaluated to demonstrate its commercial viability using established technology or technology under development (refer to subparagraph 3(d)(vi)(C) of this Notice). The level of detail in a project and the sophistication of an evaluation will generally increase from prospective, to contingent resources, to reserves.

[14]See subparagraph 5.9(2)(d)(iii) of NI 51-101.

(c) — Stand-Alone Possible Reserves

Stand-alone possible reserves are possible reserves that are assigned to a property for which no proved or probable reserves volumes have been assigned. We think it is potentially misleading to disclose possible reserves on a stand-alone basis. Situations in which it might be appropriate to disclose possible reserves on a stand-alone basis are rare, but could include any one or more of the following:

- project economics are such that no proved or probable reserves can be assigned, but on a proved + probable + possible reserves basis the project is economically viable, and a development decision has been made (e.g., adding compression, expanding facilities, offshore development of a structure delineated mainly with seismic with only limited well control);

- only minor expenditure is required to develop the possible reserves and development is likely to proceed in the near future (e.g., behind-pipe zones in a well which has proved or probable reserves in another interval);

- possible reserves may be assigned to that part of an accumulation for which an Oil and Gas Issuer has the rights when proved or probable reserves have been assigned to adjacent parts of the same accumulation for which the Oil and Gas Issuer does not have rights.

In all of these situations, there should be an intention to develop the stand-alone possible reserves within a reasonable time.

In these situations, an Oil and Gas Issuer that includes material stand-alone possible reserves in its disclosure should also disclose the fact that such reserves are classified as stand-alone possible reserves, provide a clear proximate explanation as to why the possible reserves have been disclosed on a stand-alone basis and also include the cautionary statement required by subparagraph 5.2(1)(a)(v) of NI 51-101 regarding possible reserves.

(d) — Aggregation of Resource Estimates for Several Properties

Oil and Gas Issuers may aggregate volumes of the same class, but not of different classes.

Current guidance on the aggregation of resource estimates is provided in subsection 5.2(4) of 51-101CP, titled "Probabilistic and Deterministic Evaluation Methods" and in sections 5.5.3, 9.6 of volume 1 and in section 4.4 of volume 2 of the COGE Handbook. Although the general principles discussed in those publications are relevant to the aggregation of all resource classes, the guidance in 51-101CP and the COGE Handbook was written primarily to address the aggregation of reserves data (i.e., of proved and of proved + probable reserves). Section 2.8 of volume 2 of the COGE Handbook provides specific guidance on the aggregation of estimates of contingent resources and of estimates of prospective resources. Below we provide additional guidance on the public disclosure of aggregated estimates that include resources other than reserves data.

(i) — Probabilistic Aggregation of Resource Estimates for Several Properties

Guidance found in subsection 5.2(4) of 51-101CP on the probabilistic aggregation of reserves titled "Probabilistic and Deterministic Evaluation Methods" and in section 5.5.3 of volume 1 of the COGE Handbook, titled "Aggregation of Reserves Estimates" is also applicable to disclosure of estimates of resources other than reserves data. Although section 2.8.1 of volume 2 of the COGE Handbook discourages aggregating probabilistically above the field or property level, the authors suggest that where "aggregations are externally disclosed there must be an explanation of the methods and assumptions employed."

(ii) — Arithmetic Aggregation of Resource Estimates for Several Properties

Proved, proved + probable and proved + probable + possible reserves estimates and high, best, and low estimates of other resource classes are measures of the probability that actual remaining recovered quantities will exceed the disclosed volumes. Disclosure of the arithmetic sum of low estimates or high estimates of multiple properties may be misleading.

Proved + probable reserves, and best estimates of other resource classes, are generally considered to be approximations to a mean estimate[15] and, as such, their summation provides meaningful information and may be disclosed without misleading readers.

However, when other estimates are aggregated (e.g., multiple estimates of proved + probable + possible reserves or multiple high estimates of other resource classes) statistical principles indicate that the resulting sums will lie beyond a reasonable range of expected actual outcomes and, therefore, will potentially mislead readers.

Accordingly, where an Oil and Gas Issuer discloses an arithmetic aggregation of several proved + probable + possible reserves estimates or of several high estimates of other resource classes, the Oil and Gas Issuer should consider (in addition to applying the guidance set out in subsection 5.2(4) of 51-101CP) accompanying the disclosure with a clear cautionary statement to the following effect:

> This volume is an arithmetic sum of multiple estimates of [identify reserves or resource classes], which statistical principles indicate may be misleading as to volumes that may actually be recovered. Readers should give attention to the estimates of individual classes of [reserves or resources] and appreciate the differing probabilities of recovery associated with each class as explained [indicate where disclosed and explained].

Example: Arithmetic Aggregation

Reserves in Bcf	Proved (circa P90)	Proved + Probable (circa P50)	Proved + Probable + Possible (circa P10)
Property 1	10	20	50
Property 2	12	18	30

---

[15]This will not always be the case, especially for estimates made for frontier areas or for unconventional hydrocarbons. The implications of this should be considered when adding estimates of this nature.

Reserves in Bcf	Proved (circa P90)	Proved + Probable (circa P50)	Proved + Probable + Possible (circa P10)
Property 3	5	12	25
Property 4	25	40	75
Property 5	32	50	80
Total	84	140	260

Probability of getting:

More than	84 Bcf	>> 90% (much greater than 90%)
About	140 Bcf	~ 50% (equal likelihood of getting more or less)
More than	260 Bcf	<< 10% (much less than 10%)

That is, the probability that the combined production from all properties will exceed 260 Bcf is much lower (perhaps 1%) than the criterion for proved + probable + possible reserves (i.e., a 10% probability of recovering a greater volume). Conversely, the probability that actual production will exceed 84 Bcf is considerably greater (perhaps 98%).

This example uses P90, P50, and P10 criteria, but the same argument applies for any estimates that are greater or less than a mean, whether they have been determined using deterministic or probabilistic methods.

(e) — Use of the Term "Best Estimate"

The term "best estimate" is defined in Appendix A of volume 1 of the COGE Handbook with respect to entity-level estimates as follows:

> . . .the value derived by an evaluator using deterministic methods that best represents the expected outcome with no optimism or conservatism. . . If probabilistic methods are used, there should be at least a 50 percent probability (P_{50}) that the quantities actually recovered will equal or exceed the best estimate.

The term "best estimate" should not be used to describe the results of arithmetic or probabilistic aggregation of resource estimates, unless these are risked in the aggregation process in such a manner that the aggregated value is strictly in accord with the definition of "best estimate" (refer to section 5.3.5 of volume 1 of the COGE Handbook, titled "Uncertainty Categories").

Questions

Please refer questions to any of the following:

[Omitted.]

CSA Staff Notice 51-328 — Continuous Disclosure Considerations Related to Current Economic Conditions

Date: **January 8, 2009**

32 O.S.C.B. 275

Purpose of Notice

Current economic conditions present more than normal challenges for many issuers in preparing their financial statements and Management's Discussion and Analysis (MD&A). Because of the unusual economic conditions, the Canadian Securities Administrators (CSA or we) are highlighting some specific areas for which disclosure will likely be important to help investors understand the risks and circumstances facing issuers.

A detailed discussion of the specific areas can be found in Appendix A which is in the form of an illustrative continuous disclosure letter to the issuer. As part of our continuous disclosure review program, we examine disclosure and financial reporting and provide specific comment letters for individual issuers selected for review (refer to CSA Staff Notice 51-312 *Harmonized Continuous Disclosure Review Program*).

Overview

This notice addresses the following topics:

- MD&A, including:
  - general considerations
  - liquidity and capital resources
  - distributed cash
  - critical accounting estimates
  - forward-looking information
- going concern
- impairment of goodwill, intangible assets and long-lived assets
- financial instruments
- capital disclosures

- defined benefit pension plans

- non-GAAP financial measures

- additional considerations for junior resource companies

Although this notice discusses topics likely to affect many issuers, it does not provide an exhaustive list of all requirements. Each reporting issuer should consider the accounting and disclosure issues specific to its circumstances in the current economic environment.

Appendix A

January 2009

Name

Chief Financial Officer

ABC Issuer

Address

Dear Chief Financial Officer:

The current economic uncertainty and financial market volatility make it especially important for your company[1] to disclose clearly the current and anticipated impacts of market conditions on your company's operations, financial condition, liquidity and future prospects. Below, we have provided examples of the accounting and disclosure areas that the CSA are focusing on when reviewing continuous disclosure filings. Your company should ensure compliance with these existing accounting and regulatory requirements, where applicable, when preparing continuous disclosure filings.

I. — MD&A

A. — General Considerations

MD&A should identify and evaluate information that would give investors an accurate understanding of your company's current and prospective financial position and operating results. This would include the potential effects of known trends, commitments and uncertainties that have arisen due to the current market conditions.

Items 1.2 *Overall Performance* and 1.4 *Results of Operations of* Form 51-102F1 *Management's Discussion & Analysis* of National Instrument 51-102 *Continuous Disclosure Obligations* require a detailed discussion of the specific economic factors currently affecting or anticipated to affect your company's industry and performance. Disclosures should provide a qualitative and quantitative discussion of how market conditions have affected:

- the demand for products and services, including any changes or expected changes to volume, selling prices or other revenue drivers;

- costs, including changes in prices or constraints on supply, volume discounts, inventory adjustments or other factors that alter the relationship between costs and revenues;

- revenue and expenses, due to changes in interest rates, borrowing costs, foreign exchange rates and commodity prices;

- financial results, due to unusual transactions or events including charges, gains or losses that have not been typically reflected in historical results;

- the company's overall strategy or changes to strategies, including cost saving measures, restructuring initiatives or a realignment of operational and financial resources; and

- any other relevant factors not mentioned above.

Provide this discussion for any operating segments or other parts of the business that have a significant impact on revenues, income or cash needs in the current environment. Part 1(b) *Date of Information* of Form 51-102F1 also requires that, in preparing MD&A, you take into account information available up to the date of the MD&A and that you ensure the disclosure is current so that it will not be misleading when it is filed.

B. — Liquidity and Capital Resources

Items 1.6 *Liquidity* and 1.7 *Capital Resources* of Form 51-102F1 require an analysis of your company's ability to generate sufficient cash and to access financial resources to meet operating needs in the current market environment. This discussion should not include "boilerplate" statements. It should disclose and quantify the following in sufficient detail for investors to understand the company's financial circumstances:

- cash necessary to fund current operations and the ability to satisfy obligations including debt maturities;

- commitments or planned expenditures necessary to maintain growth objectives and performance targets such as acquisition targets, new product launches or project milestones;

- future cash requirements associated with known trends and uncertainties due to current market conditions;

---

[1]Whenever this illustrative letter uses the word "company", the term includes other types of business organizations such as partnerships, trusts and other unincorporated business entities.

- additional liquidity risks associated with financial instruments where trading volumes have declined;

- significant risks of default on dividend payments, debt payments, debt covenants or other contractual obligations;

- movements in working capital accounts such as accounts receivable, inventory and accounts payable explaining any changes in terms or internal policies contributing to these movements;

- past and future funding sources from credit facilities, public offerings, related parties and other sources including what may impact the availability of such funding; and

- for an existing or expected working capital deficiency, the ability to meet obligations as they come due and how the deficiency is expected to be remedied.

C. — Discussion of Distributed Cash

As set out in Part 6.5.2 of National Policy 41-201 *Income Trusts and Other Indirect Offerings*, income trust issuers should provide disclosure that compares cash distributions paid to cash flow from operating activities and net income. Where cash distributions paid exceeds cash flow from operating activities and net income, a discussion of how the resulting shortfall will be funded and whether cash distributions will continue to exceed net income or cash flow from operating activities in the foreseeable future is required. Income trust issuers must also discuss whether this level of cash distribution is sustainable or whether cash distributions are anticipated to be suspended in the foreseeable future.

D. — Critical Accounting Estimates

If your company is not a venture issuer, the current market conditions may result in a requirement for you to disclose additional critical accounting estimates from the prior year. The MD&A should discuss the specific impact of current market conditions on critical accounting estimates such as allowance for credit losses, fair value of financial instruments, inventory, revenue recognition, contingencies, goodwill and asset impairments, pensions, future income tax assets and stock-based compensation.

Disclosure under Item 1.12 *Critical Accounting Estimates* of Form 51-102F1 does not end with a discussion of the methodology and assumptions used in determining critical accounting estimates. Item 1.12 also requires insightful information on:

- your company's assessment of trends, events or uncertainties that may affect the methods and assumptions used to determine critical accounting estimates;

- how sensitive the estimate is to a change in assumptions;

- the likelihood that estimates might change with evolving economic conditions; and

- the impact of and rationale for changes made to critical accounting estimates during the period.

MD&A disclosure should supplement and build on the financial statement disclosure and not simply reiterate the accounting policy disclosed in the financial statements.

E. — Forward-Looking Information

Recent economic and market events will cause actual results for many issuers to differ significantly from previously disclosed material forward-looking information. If this has happened to your company, you are required under Part 5.8 *Disclosure Relating to Previously Disclosed Material Forward-Looking Information* of NI 51-102 to discuss in the MD&A or in a press release these events and circumstances and the expected differences between actual and forecasted results.

II. — Going Concern

In light of current economic conditions, you should consider the recent amendments to CICA HB Section 1400.08A-08C *General Standards of Financial Statement Presentation*. The amendments apply to interim and annual financial statements for fiscal years beginning on or after January 1, 2008 and require a company to carefully assess and disclose in the financial statements the material uncertainties that may put into question its ability to continue as a going concern. Examples of material uncertainties include: continued and expected operating losses, negative operating cash flows, a failure to obtain or renew financing, a significant decline in the demand for a company's products, declining prices, substantial refinancing requirements and an inability to make scheduled payments on debt.

If your company faces material uncertainties about its ability to continue as a going concern, your MD&A should (as set out in Instruction (ii) of Item 1.2 *Overall Performance* of Form 51-102F1) supplement the financial statement disclosure and provide further insight into:

- management's reasons for determining the ability of the company to continue as a going concern in light of these uncertainties; and

- planned strategies or known events that may mitigate the uncertainties.

III. — Impairment of Goodwill, Intangible Assets and Long-Lived Assets

Accounting guidance for impairment testing of goodwill, intangible assets and long-lived assets can be found in the following CICA HB Sections: Section 3062 *Goodwill and other Intangible Assets* (replaced by Section 3064 *Goodwill and Intangible Assets* for annual and interim financial statements relating to fiscal years beginning on or after October 1, 2008) and Section 3063 *Impairment of Long-lived Assets*.

In our view, the current economic and market conditions represent circumstances that are likely to affect the carrying amount of assets. Examples of impairment indicators to consider when testing goodwill, intangible assets and long-lived assets include:

- a significant decrease in the company's share price;

- a significant adverse change in the business climate and/or the industry your company operates in;
- a current-period operating or cash flow loss combined with a history of operating or cash flow losses, or a projection or forecast that demonstrates continuing losses; and
- an accumulation of costs significantly in excess of the amount originally expected for its acquisition or construction.

If your company incurs an impairment charge, your MD&A should not only discuss the financial impact of the charge but also provide meaningful insight into the reasons and business circumstances surrounding the impairment as required by Item 1.2 *Overall Performance* of Form 51-102F1.

IV. — Financial Instruments

There has been additional guidance issued in recent months by regulators and accounting standard setters in Canada, the United States and at the international level on the determination of fair value and disclosures relating to financial instruments in the absence of an active market. You should assess the valuation techniques for your financial instruments to ensure that they are based on assumptions that are appropriate in the current market conditions. The valuation methods you apply now may differ significantly from the methods you used to value financial instruments when you purchased them.

The requirements for financial instrument disclosure are found in CICA HB Section 3862 *Financial Instruments — Disclosures* and Item 1.14 *Financial Instruments and Other Instruments* of Form 51-102F1. It is important to provide disclosure in enough detail to help investors understand the significance, impact and risks of financial instruments to the company's financial position, operations and cash flows. Disclosures for financial instruments should include a detailed discussion of:

- the credit, liquidity and market risks associated with financial instruments, highlighting any changes in these risks given current market conditions;
- financial assets that are past due at the balance sheet date but are not treated as impaired;
- the methodology and assumptions used to determine fair market value including:
  - the observable and unobservable inputs used for the calculations
  - any adjustments made for credit, liquidity and other risks and how adjustments were determined
  - how transaction prices in inactive markets were taken into account in valuation techniques and how the company decided that the market was inactive
- the impact on fair value assessments (sensitivity analysis) if other reasonable assumptions relating to unobservable inputs are used in valuation techniques;
- the nature, impact and rationale of any significant changes made to valuation techniques or assumptions from prior periods;
- the financial statement impact of any reclassification of financial instruments your company chooses to make under the recent amendments to CICA HB Section 3855 *Financial Instruments — Recognition and Measurement;* and
- the factors considered in determining impairment including any trends or uncertainties that are reasonably believed to affect these factors over time.

V. — Capital Disclosures

In respect of CICA HB Section 1535 *Capital Disclosures*, disclosure should include a detailed discussion of how current economic conditions have affected your company's objectives, policies and processes for managing capital. As indicated earlier, Item 1.7 *Capital Resources* of Form 51-102F1 requires an analysis of your company's capital resources in the MD&A.

VI. — Defined Benefit Pension Plans

If your company has a material defined benefit pension plan, the MD&A should discuss:

- the anticipated impact of the funding status on future contributions, cash flows and pension expense as contemplated by Item 1.6 *Liquidity* of Form 51-102F1; and
- the risks associated with the pension plan, which may include:
  - the ability of the plan to earn the assumed rate of return
  - any expected increase in future contributions that results from market conditions and differs significantly from previous estimates
  - the measurement uncertainty reflected in the actuarial valuation process.

VII. — Non-GAAP Financial Measures

The CSA continues to monitor the use of non-GAAP financial measures. We have set out in CSA Staff Notice 52-306 (Revised) *Non-GAAP Financial Measures* our view of the steps issuers should take, if they choose to publish non-GAAP financial measures, to ensure that their disclosure is not misleading. If your company discloses a measure like "adjusted earnings" or "earnings before one-time charges," you should consider the guidance set out in the staff notice. In particular you should:

- disclose with the non-GAAP measure the most directly comparable measure calculated in accordance with GAAP, in equal prominence, together with a quantitative reconciliation to the GAAP measure; and

- explain in detail why the non-GAAP financial measure is relevant to investors.

You should also consider carefully the validity of any representation you intend to make, either explicitly or implicitly through a non-GAAP measure, that a charge is non-recurring. For example, it would normally not be appropriate to adjust earnings for a charge identified as non-recurring if a similar charge is likely to occur within the next two years or has occurred during the prior two years.

VIII. — Additional Considerations for Junior Resources Companies

A. — Asset Impairments

If your company is a resource exploration company in the development stage, you need to consider the additional asset impairment guidance in CICA HB Accounting Guideline 11 *Enterprises in the Development Stage* (paragraphs 12 to 20) and in CICA HB EIC-126 *Accounting by Mining Enterprises for Exploration Costs* for capitalized exploration costs. Factors that may indicate the need for a write-down of a capital asset held by an enterprise in the development stage engaged in extractive operations include:

- unfavourable changes in the project economics such as declining metal or oil and gas prices;

- delay in development activity extending beyond three years; and

- poor exploration results and no planned work in the foreseeable future.

These factors would suggest that future benefits are uncertain. Similarly, declining metal or oil and gas prices could result in goodwill being impaired. If an asset's value is impaired, it should be written down immediately, which may be before the project is abandoned.

B. — MD&A Considerations

When operations are not producing significant revenue, the MD&A should focus on the company's expenses and business objectives, as stated in Part 1(g) *Venture Issuers Without Significant Revenues* and paragraph (d) of Item 1.4 *Results of operations* of Form 51-102F1.
The MD&A should discuss:

- mining or oil and gas property plans including the impact of falling commodity prices on plans or property values;

- progress to date against those plans and remaining expenditures needed to acquire ownership or additional working interest in a property;

- the additional costs and time the company will require to complete plans and the reasons why any plan milestones were not met; and

- the factors that may affect the value of mineral or oil and gas projects and adversely affect estimates of resources or reserves (if price assumptions used to determine estimates are materially different from current prices, discuss in general terms the potential impact).

The following disclosures should be provided when discussing Items 1.6 *Liquidity* and 1.7 *Capital Resources* of Form 51-102F1:

- a quantified and analytical discussion of the company's financial resources and financial requirements, distinguishing those requirements that are committed versus discretionary in nature; and

- a discussion of any difficulties in obtaining financing and how this will affect exploration and development projects.

C. — Specific Oil and Gas Disclosures

In addition to the disclosure identified above, an oil and gas issuer, where applicable, should provide the following disclosure:

- benchmark prices used for each of the first five years for applying the impairment test and any adjustments to prices made to arrive at revenue, as set out in CICA HB Accounting Guideline 16 *Oil and Gas Accounting — Full Cost*;

- the implications of the current economic environment on the company's plans (including timing) for developing proved and probable undeveloped reserves, as set out in Item 5.1(1) and (2) *Undeveloped Reserves* of Form 51-101F1 *Statement of Reserves Data and Other Oil and Gas Information* of National Instrument 51-101 *Standards of Disclosure for Oil and Gas Activities*;

- the expectations as to the sources and costs of funding for estimated future development costs and the effect of those costs of funding on disclosed reserves or future net revenue as required under Item 5.3(2)*Future Development Costs* of Form 51-101F1; and

- if the company expects that the cost of funding could make development of a property uneconomic, the company should disclose that expectation and its plans for the property as required under Item 5.3(2) and (3) *Future Development Costs* of Form 51-101F1.

IX. — Other

The topics covered in this letter do not include all accounting and disclosure issues. Your company should consider the accounting and disclosure issues specific to its circumstances in the current economic environment.

CSA Staff Notice 51-330 — Guidance Regarding the Application of Forward-looking Information Requirements under NI 51-102 Continuous Disclosure Obligations

Date: **November 20, 2009**

32 O.S.C.B. 9607

Purpose

The Canadian Securities Administrators (collectively, we or staff) recently conducted continuous disclosure reviews on the application of the forward-looking information (FLI) requirements in National Instrument 51-102 *Continuous Disclosure Obligations* (NI 51-102 or the Rule) that came into effect on December 31, 2007 (New FLI Requirements). We looked at various documents during the course of our reviews including Annual Information Forms, Management Discussion and Analyses, news releases and investor presentations archived on company websites. Although staff requested a number of issuers to improve their disclosure in future filings, our reviews did not result in issuers having to re-file documents in order to correct identified deficiencies.

This notice focuses on areas where we identified deficiencies, as well as areas where we think disclosure of FLI can be enhanced. In addition, we also provide a reminder to issuers of the potential impact of the transition to International Financial Reporting Standards (IFRS) on disclosure of future-oriented financial information (FOFI) and "financial outlooks".

1. — Identification of FLI

Section 4A.3 of NI 51-102 requires reporting issuers to identify material FLI as such. The Rule does not prescribe the manner in which an issuer is required to identify material FLI. Section 4A.4 of the Companion Policy to NI 51-102 (51-102CP) provides guidance that the disclosure should be presented in a manner that allows an investor who reads the document or other material containing the FLI to be able to readily identify the material FLI.

Issuers that we reviewed took different approaches to identification. Many issuers identified the material FLI solely through a cautionary paragraph at the beginning or end of the disclosure document. Some issuers included disclosure throughout the document identifying material FLI as it was used. In some cases, issuers consolidated most of their FLI in a particular section such as an "Outlook" section or in a table and then included, in the introduction to this section or table, disclosure identifying the material FLI as such.

Where issuers identify material FLI through a cautionary paragraph at the beginning or end of a disclosure document, we encourage issuers to give readers an indication of the nature of the material FLI covered in the document. In staff's view, this type of disclosure allows an investor to more readily identify material FLI when it is encountered in the document.

To illustrate this point, some issuers simply identified FLI by referring to the types of words that could potentially be found in a forward-looking statement. For example[1]:

> *This document may contain forward-looking statements. Forward-looking statements are often, but not always, identified by words such as "believes", "may", "likely", "plans" or similar words.*

Other issuers identified FLI as, essentially, any disclosure relating to the future. For example:

> *All statements, other than statements of historical fact, that address activities, events, or developments that Company X expects or anticipates will or may occur in the future are forward-looking statements.*

In staff's view, disclosure such as that identified in the above two examples generally would not enable a reader to readily identify material FLI included in the document or other disclosure, if the disclosure does not also include additional more specific information identifying the material FLI.

In contrast, the following is an example of a more effective method of identifying material FLI in that it identifies the nature of the material FLI included in the document:

> *Forward-looking statements included or incorporated by reference in this document include statements with respect to:*
>
> - *the Company's acquisition strategy, including acquisition criteria and acquisition benefits;*
> - *the Company's goal to sustain or grow production and reserves through prudent management and acquisitions;*
> - *expectations regarding the ability to raise capital and continually add to reserves through acquisition and development;*

In other circumstances, issuers stated that FLI was included in a particular disclosure document when in fact no FLI was included. We encourage issuers to avoid including statements that a document contains FLI when to the issuer's knowledge that is not the case.

2. — Disclosure regarding material risk factors and material factors or assumptions

a) — Identification of material risk factors and material factors or assumptions

Section 4A.3 of NI 51-102 requires reporting issuers that disclose material FLI to include disclosure that identifies material risk factors that could cause actual results to differ materially from the FLI. The disclosure must also include material factors or assumptions used to develop material FLI. Section 4A.4 of 51-102CP provides guidance that this disclosure should allow an investor who reads the document or other material containing the FLI to be able to readily inform himself or herself of the material assumptions underlying the FLI and the material risk factors associated with it.

In various instances, issuers either neglected to discuss the underlying factors or assumptions or stated that there were factors or assumptions without identifying them. In our view, this practice does not comply with section 4A.3 of the Rule.

---

[1]Please note that the examples are based on, but are not actual examples of, disclosure we reviewed.

b) — Incorporation by reference of relevant material risk factors and material factors or assumptions

The New FLI Requirements do not preclude an issuer from incorporating by reference material risk factors and material factors or assumptions contained in another document. However, issuers should consider whether incorporation by reference, in the circumstances, enables a reader to readily inform himself or herself of the material risk factors, and material factors or assumptions, associated with the material FLI.

c) — Avoiding "boilerplate" disclosure

During the course of our reviews we noted that issuers often included identical or nearly identical risk factor/factors and assumptions disclosure in each of their disclosure documents or other material despite differences in the nature of the FLI contained in the particular document or material. Issuers should avoid "boilerplate" disclosure and should disclose material risk factors and material factors and assumptions that are relevant to the FLI (see sections 4A.5(1) and 4A.6 of 51-102CP).

d) — User-friendly presentation

We encourage issuers to consider using tables and other methods of presentation that clearly link specific material risk factors and material factors and assumptions to the particular FLI. For example:

The following table outlines forward-looking information included in this MD&A:

Forward-looking Information	*Key Assumptions*	*Most Relevant Risk Factors*
2009 capital spending program		
Ability to finance announced projects		
...	*...*	*...*

3. — Updating practices

Some issuers included a statement similar to the following in their disclosure:

The Company does not assume any obligation to update forward-looking statements if management beliefs, expectations or opinions should change.

This type of statement is inappropriate as section 5.8(2) of NI 51-102 provides that issuers must update previously disclosed FLI in certain circumstances. Issuers should ensure that their policy for updating FLI is in compliance with the New FLI Requirements.

4. — Explanation of purpose of, and cautionary language related to, financial outlook or FOFI

Section 4B.3(b) of NI 51-102 requires reporting issuers that disclose FOFI or a financial outlook, to also disclose the purpose of the information and caution readers that the information may not be appropriate for other purposes. We remind issuers that this requirement is in addition to the material risk factors and material factors or assumptions disclosure required by section 4A.3 of the Rule. Disclosure of material risk factors and material factors or assumptions contained in a cautionary paragraph at the beginning or end of a document generally will not satisfy this requirement.

5. — Disclosure regarding goals or targets

During our reviews, staff considered whether disclosure regarding a goal or target constitutes FLI as defined in securities legislation.

Under securities legislation in all Canadian[2] jurisdictions, FLI means:

disclosure regarding possible events, conditions or results of operations that is based on assumptions about future economic conditions and courses of action, and includes future-oriented financial information with respect to prospective results of operations, financial position or cash flows that is presented either as a forecast or a projection.

In order to constitute FLI, the achievement of the target or goal would have to be "possible" based on assumptions about future economic conditions and courses of action. We would generally expect a reporting issuer to disclose a target or goal only if it is "possible" to achieve. Consequently, in staff's view, a disclosed target or goal can constitute FLI and, if material, the document containing the FLI should include disclosure regarding this goal or target that complies with the New FLI Requirements. This would include disclosure required under Part 4B of NI 51-102 in the circumstances that a disclosed target or goal also constitutes a financial outlook.

If management determines that a material target or goal that is disclosed does not constitute material FLI, management should consider including additional disclosure explaining the purpose of the information.

6. — Impact of the transition to IFRS on FOFI or financial outlooks

Section 4B.2(2)(b) of NI 51-102 requires that FOFI or a financial outlook be based on the accounting policies that the reporting issuer expects to use to prepare its historical financial statements for the period covered by the FOFI or the financial outlook. In light of the fact that the Canadian Accounting Standards Board has confirmed that IFRS will replace Canadian Generally Accepted Accounting Principles for publicly accountable enterprises for fiscal years beginning on or after January 1, 2011, issuers should ensure that FOFI or financial outlooks that cover their 2011 fiscal year are based on the appropriate accounting policies.

---

[2]In Québec, the wording of the definition of "forward-looking information" differs slightly, but in substance this definition is harmonized in all jurisdictions.

CSA Staff Notice 51-331 — Report on Staff's Review of Executive Compensation Disclosure

Date: **November 20, 2009**

32 O.S.C.B. 9599

I. — Introduction

On September 18, 2008, the Canadian Securities Administrators (**CSA**) announced the adoption of revised Form 51-102F6 *Statement of Executive Compensation (in respect of financial years ending on or after December 31, 2008)* (the **Form**). The Form became effective across all CSA jurisdictions on December 31, 2008.

The CSA generally monitors new rules in the first year after implementation to ensure they are working as intended. This process often includes conducting targeted compliance reviews.

In Spring of 2009, staff of the British Columbia Securities Commission, the Alberta Securities Commission, the Ontario Securities Commission and the Autorité des marchés financiers (**we**) launched targeted reviews of executive compensation disclosure to assess compliance with the disclosure requirements in the Form. We reviewed a total of 70 reporting issuers. This CSA staff notice (the **Staff Notice**) reports our findings from these reviews.

II. — Objective and Scope

Our reviews focused on companies' executive compensation disclosure for their financial years ending on or after December 31, 2008. Our main objectives were to:

- assess compliance with the executive compensation disclosure requirements;

- use the results of the reviews to educate companies about the new requirements; and

- identify any requirements that need clarification or further explanation to assist companies in fulfilling their disclosure obligations.

In setting these objectives, we designed our reviews to help us understand if companies are providing investors with improved executive compensation disclosure. Improved disclosure should provide investors insight into executive compensation as a key aspect of the overall stewardship and governance of a company and allow investors to understand how boards of directors make decisions about executive compensation.

III. — General Observations

Sixty-two of the 70 companies we reviewed filed executive compensation disclosure that generally met the requirements of the Form. Nevertheless, we asked most of these companies to improve their disclosure in future filings, specifically, in respect of the significant disclosure issues discussed in this Staff Notice. Eight of the companies we reviewed provided disclosure that did not meet minimum acceptable standards. We instructed these companies to file supplemental executive compensation disclosure in their timely disclosure documents.

A number of companies we reviewed did not explain sufficiently in the Compensation Discussion and Analysis (**CD&A**) how each element of compensation is tied to each named executive officer's (**NEO**) performance. We frequently found that the CD&A did not fully or accurately describe the process of making executive compensation decisions. We were often unable to tie the discussion in the CD&A to the rest of the company's executive compensation disclosure, including the Summary Compensation Table (**SCT**). This was of particular concern with respect to performance goals and similar conditions.

A number of companies did not provide complete disclosure regarding the use of benchmarks and the determination of performance goals.

A significant number of companies subject to the performance graph requirement did not fully discuss how the trend shown in the performance graph compared to the trend in the compensation of executive officers.

Though most companies were generally in compliance with the SCT disclosure requirements, a number of companies did not satisfy specific requirements under Item 3 of the Form.

We also found significant issues in connection with the disclosure of pension plan benefits and the disclosure of termination and change of control benefits.

We have highlighted most of the significant disclosure issues discussed in Part IV, below, because we found them to be the most common. We have highlighted others, even though we found them only in isolated cases, because they relate to a requirement that is fundamental to the objective of executive compensation disclosure.

In addition to the significant disclosure issues, we identified, in our reviews, a number of other issues. We have included a brief discussion of them in Part V, below.

We do not intend this Staff Notice to be an exhaustive summary of all our concerns regarding executive compensation disclosure.

IV. — Significant Disclosure Issues

The following table summarizes the significant disclosure issues we identified in our reviews. Each of these issues is discussed in the narrative sections following the table. These observations emphasize principles that all companies should consider when preparing their executive compensation disclosure.

Table 1

Area	Significant Disclosure Issue	Number of Companies with a Significant Disclosure Issue
Compensation discussion and analysis	Performance goals or similar conditions	45
	Benchmarking	42
	Performance graph	16
Summary compensation table	Grant date fair value of multi-year awards	3
	Reconciliation of grant date fair value and accounting fair value	15
Pension plan benefits	Annual lifetime benefit payable at the end of the most recently completed financial year	1
Termination and change of control benefits	Quantification	13

A. — Performance goals or similar conditions

Subsection 2.1(4) of the Form requires disclosure of performance goals or similar conditions. We found more significant disclosure issues regarding performance goals than for any other disclosure item.

1. — Tie to other executive compensation disclosure

A number of companies did not tie the discussion on performance goals in the CD&A to the disclosure in the SCT, and vice versa.

> *Example 1*
>
> *A company discloses a grant of a bonus to an NEO but the CD&A does not explain that the company granted the bonus because performance goals were met. Conversely, another company discloses in the CD&A that performance goals were met but the SCT discloses that no bonuses were earned.*

These companies should have explicitly linked the discussion about performance goals in the CD&A with their NEOs' compensation as reported in their SCTs. For example, if a company disclosed a performance goal based on an objective measure in its CD&A and the SCT disclosed a bonus was actually earned, the CD&A should also disclose the actual objective measure achieved in explaining why the company paid the bonus.

2. — Corporate goals versus individual performance

A number of companies did not fully and accurately describe the relative importance between corporate-level goals and individual performance objectives in making executive compensation decisions.

> *Example 2*
>
> *A company provides meaningful disclosure regarding corporate-level performance goals and goes on to state that individual performance was also evaluated based on other performance goals. The company does not clarify the relative importance of the corporate-level performance goals and an NEO's individual performance in determining the NEO's reported compensation.*

The company should have provided this clarification in its CD&A.

3. — Use of discretion

A number of companies applied discretion to either increase or decrease compensation following the initial setting of objective performance goals but did not fully explain the discretionary process in their CD&A.

> *Example 3*
>
> *A company discloses that it established performance goals based on objective measures at the beginning of the financial year but does not quantify those measures in the CD&A. The company believes that the objective measures were only intended to be guidelines and that the payment of bonuses and the criteria for the payment of bonuses remain at the discretion of the board of directors.*

The company should have clarified in the CD&A that the objective measures were only intended to be guidelines and explained the importance of board discretion in determining the actual bonus paid to each NEO.

4. — Objective measures

A number of companies did not quantify performance goals that were based on objective measures, such as earnings per share, EBITDA, growth in net sales, and operational targets. The requirement to quantify the objective measures applies regardless of whether the objective measures are guidelines or hard targets.

In Example 3, above, the company does not quantify the performance goals that were based on objective measures. Despite the fact that the objective measures were only intended to be guidelines, the company should have quantified them in the CD&A. As discussed above, the clarification that the payment of bonuses ultimately remained at the discretion of the board of directors should also have been included in the CD&A to place the quantification of the objective measures in context.

5. — "Seriously prejudice" exemption

Subsection 2.1(4) of the Form provides an exemption from the requirement to disclose specific performance goals on the basis that disclosure would seriously prejudice the interests of the company. Some companies improperly attempted to rely on this exemption.

> ### Example 4
> *A company discloses that NEO bonuses are based, in part, on the company achieving an EBITDA target in the financial year. However, the company does not quantify the EBITDA target in reliance on the "seriously prejudice" exemption.*

Generally, we think that disclosing past performance metrics based on broad corporate-level financial performance measures like earnings per share, revenue growth, and EBITDA, would not seriously prejudice the company's interests. These measures are generally publicly available in other disclosure documents. Thus, the company should have quantified the historical EBITDA target.

> ### Example 5
> *A company discloses that NEO bonuses are based, in part on the company achieving target growth in square footage of leasing and building opportunities in the financial year. However, the company does not quantify the growth target in reliance on the exemption.*

Reliance on the exemption may be appropriate in respect of performance goals based on historical operational targets. In this example, reliance on the exemption would be appropriate if quantification of the growth target would adversely impact a company's competitive position by compromising the company's ability to negotiate competitive lease rates with prospective tenants or affecting its ability to acquire assets at the lowest cost.

For the purpose of these reviews, we asked each company that relied on this exemption to provide us with analysis of the reasons why it believes disclosure of a performance goal would seriously prejudice the company's interests. Companies should be prepared to provide such an analysis to us in the context of a continuous disclosure review whenever they rely on this exemption.

6. — Undisclosed performance goals

Companies that did not disclose specific performance goals often neglected to state what percentage of the NEO's total compensation relates to the undisclosed information and how difficult it would be for the NEO, or how likely it would be for the company, to achieve the undisclosed performance goal.

> ### Example 6
> *A company does not disclose specific performance goals because disclosure would seriously prejudice the company's interests. The company does not disclose that 50% of the NEO's bonus was subject to the undisclosed performance goal. The company only states that achieving the undisclosed performance goal would be "challenging".*

The company should have disclosed that 50% of the NEO's bonus was subject to the undisclosed performance goal.

The company should also have provided contextual disclosure regarding the meaning of the term "challenging". Merely disclosing that achieving an undisclosed performance goal would be "challenging" does not help investors understand how decisions about executive compensation are made. To add context, the company could disclose whether the undisclosed performance goal was achieved in the past. Moreover, if the undisclosed performance goal is incrementally more difficult to achieve based on prior year results, then the CD&A could emphasize that these are "stretch" targets and are intended to promote enhanced performance year over year.

B. — Benchmarking

Subsection 2.1(3) of the Form requires that the CD&A disclose any benchmark and explain its components. We found a significant number of disclosure issues in this area.

1. — Explanation of methodology

A number of companies did not clearly explain their benchmarking methodologies. Though these companies disclosed that they reviewed the compensation practices of a peer group and listed the components of that group, they did not fully explain how they used that information in decisions about executive compensation.

We note that benchmarks may differ among elements of compensation. For example, a company could benchmark against one peer group for base salaries and another peer group for share-based awards. Similarly, benchmarks may differ among different NEOs. For example, a company may use a U.S. peer group to benchmark for U.S. based executives and a Canadian peer group to benchmark for Canadian executives.

If a company uses different peer groups for different components of compensation or for different NEOs, the company should clearly describe which peer group it used for each component or NEO. The company should also disclose how the benchmark is used.

2. — Benchmark group

A number of companies did not fully comply with the requirement to disclose the components of a benchmark group.

> *Example 7*
>
> *A company discloses that it based compensation in part on the "market practices of companies in similar industries", and "companies of similar size and revenues" but does not identify the peer companies.*

The company should disclose the composition of the benchmark group. A complete list of the benchmark group will provide meaningful disclosure to investors, even if the list is extensive.

The use of compensation data collected from a peer group of companies as a guideline (and not to set hard targets) for compensation constitutes benchmarking and companies should disclose the peer group components. Clarification in the CD&A that the compensation data is only used as a guidepost may be appropriate.

C. — Performance graph

Paragraph 2.2(b) of the Form requires certain companies to provide a line graph showing the company's cumulative total shareholder return over the five most recently completed financial years. Companies are also required to discuss how the trend shown by this graph compares to the trend in the company's compensation to executive officers over the same period.

A number of companies did not fully satisfy this comparison requirement.

> *Example 8*
>
> *A company merely states that there is no specific relationship between executive compensation and the cumulative total shareholder return over the time period in the performance graph without any further disclosure.*

The company should have specifically described the trend in executive compensation and described how that trend compared to the trend in cumulative total shareholder return before indicating that the two trends were not related.

We also found that some companies only compared the trends shown by the performance graph for the three most recently completed financial years (i.e. as if to conform with the SCT disclosure). Despite the three-year disclosure period in the SCT, the performance graph requirement is for a five-year period and the comparison must be over that longer period.

While not a requirement, we found that some companies provided an additional line in the performance graph showing the trend of the NEOs total compensation over the same period. We found this to be an effective and meaningful way of comparing compensation trends with total shareholder performance, when combined with a narrative discussion.

D. — Summary Compensation Table

1. — Grant date fair value of multi-year awards

Subsections 3.1(3) and (4) of the Form requires companies to disclose the grant date fair value of share-based awards and option-based awards in the appropriate columns in the SCT.

Under these requirements, the grant date fair value of these types of awards must be reported in the SCT in the year of grant irrespective of whether part or all of the award relates to multiple financial years and payout is subject to performance goals and similar conditions, including vesting, to be applied in future financial years.

If payout of an award granted in a financial year is subject to conditions being satisfied in future financial years, the grant date fair value methodology used will typically take these conditions into account. As a result, companies cannot defer reporting a value in the SCT for an award until the conditions have been satisfied in the future or on the basis that the board of directors intended to pay part of that award in a future financial period. The financial year in which the value of an equity incentive plan award is reported in the SCT is determined by the grant date of the award. Likewise, the disclosure of the grant date fair value of share-based and option-based awards in a separate table does not comply with the requirements of section 3.1 of the Form.

> *Example 9*
>
> *In 2008, a company grants restricted share units (RSUs) to an NEO. Under the terms of the award, the NEO will be entitled to payout of 1,000 RSUs in each of 2008, 2009, and 2010 if certain performance goals, including vesting, are satisfied in those years. The performance goals, including vesting, in respect of the 2008 part of the award have been satisfied and the company reports the grant date fair value of that part of the award in the 2008 SCT but decides to defer reporting the part of the award related to 2009 and 2010 to the SCT for those years.*

The company should have reported the grant date fair value of the entire award, including the parts related to 2009 and 2010, in the 2008 SCT. The grant date fair value methodology used should have taken into account the fact that the NEO will not receive those RSUs unless the performance goals, including vesting, for 2009 and 2010 are satisfied.

2. — Reconciliation to "accounting fair value"

Subsection 3.1(5) of the Form requires companies to reconcile any difference between the grant date fair value reported in the SCT and the accounting fair value of share-based and option-based awards. Under this requirement, companies must both state and explain the difference and include a description of the methodology used to calculate the grant date fair value, a description of the key assumptions and estimates used for each calculation, and an explanation of why the company chose that methodology.

A few companies did not satisfy this requirement.

> *Example 10*

A company reports the grant date fair value of an option-based award by discounting the accounting fair value to reflect the fact that a substantial part of the award is subject to performance goals associated with future financial periods. However, the company does not quantify and explain the difference between the grant date fair value and the accounting fair value (e.g. in a footnote to the SCT).

The company should have quantified the difference and provided a footnote explaining the difference in methodology, including the fact that it applied a discount factor to the accounting fair value to reflect that payout of the award is subject to the satisfaction of future performance goals.

Note that in the example described above, the amount actually received by the NEO in the future period will not be reported in the SCT for that future period.

3. — Format

Subsection 1.3(2) of the Form permits companies to add tables, columns, and other information, if necessary to communicate the compensation the board of directors intended the company to pay, make payable, award, grant, give or otherwise provide to each NEO and director for the financial year.

We found some companies relied on this subsection to present the SCT in a format different from that required by subsection 3.1(1) of the Form. Though the companies we reviewed appropriately relied on subsection 1.3(2), our consideration of this issue alerted us to the question of when this subsection would not permit alternative presentation. For example, a company cannot rely on subsection 1.3(2) to deemphasize the total compensation column. Such a revision is not necessary to satisfy the objective of executive compensation disclosure.

> *Example 11*
>
> *A company's SCT includes a column at the far right (to the immediate right of the total compensation column). The column is titled "adjusted compensation" and discloses total compensation less a one-time share-based award granted to the NEOs. The column is highlighted and presented more prominently than the total compensation column.*
>
> *The company also provides narrative disclosure in the CD&A, and footnote disclosure in the SCT, of the one-time award, including an explanation of why the company granted the award.*

The company should not have added the column to the SCT. Narrative disclosure in the CD&A, and footnote disclosure in the SCT, of the one-time share-based award provide investors with sufficient information to understand why the one-time award was granted and how it fits into the company's overall executive compensation decisions.

E. — Pension plan benefits — annual lifetime benefit payable at the end of the most recently completed financial year

Paragraph 5.1(4)(a) of the Form relating to the defined benefit plan table requires companies to disclose the annual lifetime benefit payable at the end of the most recently completed financial year based on years of credited service and actual pensionable earnings.

For purposes of quantifying the annual lifetime benefit payable at the end of the most recently completed financial year, companies should assume at year end that the NEO is eligible to receive pension benefits.

For example, an NEO has not reached the minimum required age of 55 as prescribed by the pension plan to be eligible to receive pension benefits at year end. In this case, the company should calculate the annual lifetime benefit payable as follows:

$$\text{annual benefits payable at the presumed retirement age used to calculate the accrued obligation at year end} \times \frac{\text{years of credited service at year end}}{\text{years of credited service at the presumed retirement age}}$$

The value disclosed as an annual lifetime benefit payable at the end of the most recently completed financial year should have a value other than nil.

F. — Termination and change in control benefits — quantification

Subsection 6.1(1) of the Form requires companies, among other things, to describe, explain and where appropriate, quantify, the estimated incremental payments, payables and benefits that are triggered by a termination, resignation, a change in control of the company or a change in an NEO's responsibilities.

A number of companies described in narrative format the payments and entitlements of the NEOs but did not quantify the estimated incremental payments and benefits.

> *Example 12*
>
> *A company discloses that if the CEO was terminated without cause, the CEO would be entitled to a payment equal to three years salary and bonus under an employment contract. However, the company does not quantify this amount.*

Though investors might be able to estimate those amounts based on the current year's SCT disclosure of the CEO's salary and bonus, the Form requires the company to quantify those amounts in its disclosure of termination and change of control benefits.

We also found that some companies simply disclosed an aggregate amount for all NEOs. Providing an aggregate amount for all NEOs does not satisfy the quantification requirement.

While the Form does not require tabular disclosure of potential post-employment payments, we found the tabular presentation used by some companies to be an effective and meaningful way of disclosing this information.

V. — Other Issues

A. — Definition of "grant date"

Under section 1.2 of the Form, "grant date" means a date determined for financial statement reporting purposes under Section 3870 of the Handbook. The requirements under subsections 3.1(3) and (4) of the Form to disclose the grant date fair value of equity incentive plan awards do not apply to commitments to grant such awards in future periods if the date the commitment is made is not the grant date.

B. — Long-term non-equity incentive plan compensation

Subsection 3.1(8) of the Form requires companies to disclose all amounts earned that are related to awards under non-equity incentive plans and all earnings on any such outstanding awards. Under this requirement, companies must disclose long-term non-equity incentive plans in column (f2) of the SCT only in the year earned, which typically would be the year in which the award vests or is paid out.

C. — Non-equity incentive plan compensation — Value earned during the year

Subsection 4.2(1) of the Form requires companies to disclose the value for non-equity incentive plan compensation earned during the year. This value should be the same as the value for non-equity incentive plan compensation earned during the year required to be disclosed in column (f) of the SCT.

D. — Defined contribution plans

Section 5.2 of the Form requires companies to disclose the information on all pension plans other than defined benefits plans. The requirement includes disclosure of both compensatory amounts and non-compensatory amounts. For example, companies cannot claim that the information on non-compensatory items such as the NEO's contributions is personal in order to avoid disclosing the amounts. For the same reason, companies cannot choose to include the compensatory elements of the plan under column (h) "all other compensation" of the SCT.

E. — Director compensation

In accordance with subsection 7.1(3) of the Form, the director compensation table must be completed in the same manner as the SCT. Similarly, section 7.3 of the Form requires companies to provide the same incentive plan awards disclosure for directors as required under Item 4 for NEOs, including the "Outstanding share-based awards and option-based awards" table and the "Incentive plan awards — value vested or earned during the year" table.

To comply with section 7.2 of the Form, companies must describe and explain any significant factors necessary to understand the compensation disclosed in the directors compensation table.

VI. — Conclusion

While only eight of the 70 companies we reviewed were instructed to file supplemental disclosure to cure deficiencies in their executive compensation disclosure, our overall observation is that there remains room for improvement. In particular, we asked most of the companies we reviewed to make varying levels of prospective improvements to their disclosure, specifically, in respect of the significant disclosure issues discussed in this Staff Notice.

We will continue to review executive compensation disclosure as part of our continuous disclosure review programs, focusing in particular on:

- CD&A disclosure, including the need to tie the disclosure of performance goals to NEO compensation, the disclosure of performance goals generally, and the disclosure of benchmarking;

- SCT disclosure, including the recognition of grant date fair value of multi-year awards, descriptions of any differences between the grant date fair value reported in the SCT and the accounting fair value for equity incentive plan awards, and SCT presentation; and

- termination and change in control benefits disclosure.

We encourage companies to review the Form carefully and to use this Staff Notice to assist them in the preparation of their executive compensation disclosure.

CSA Staff Notice 51-332 — Continuous Disclosure Review Program Activities for the Fiscal Year Ended March 31, 2010

Date: July 9, 2010

33 O.S.C.B. 6145

Purpose of this Notice

The Canadian Securities Administrators (CSA) continuous disclosure (CD) program is designed to identify material disclosure deficiencies that affect the reliability and accuracy of a reporting issuer's (issuers) disclosure record. Reliable and accurate information is critical to strengthen investor confidence and efficient capital markets. In any given year, issuers are affected by new accounting standards and regulatory changes and these are areas that we generally emphasize in our CD review program. The CD review program has two fundamental objectives: education and compliance. See CSA Staff Notice 51-312 — *(Revised) Harmonized Continuous Disclosure Review Program* for further details on the program.

This notice summarizes the results of the CD review program of issuers other than investment funds for the fiscal year ended March 31, 2010 (fiscal 2010).

Results for fiscal 2010

There are approximately 4,200 reporting issuers (excluding issuers that have been cease-traded) other than investment funds in Canada. Staff of the jurisdictions of the CSA (we) use a risk-based approach to select issuers for review and to determine the type of review to conduct (full or issue-oriented). This allows us to address areas of particular concern and apply both qualitative and quantitative criteria in determining the level of review required. As market conditions change, our program adapts to incorporate new risk factors. Our risk-based approach focuses on accounting issues and disclosure areas where either non-compliance is probable or we foresee a need for increased compliance.

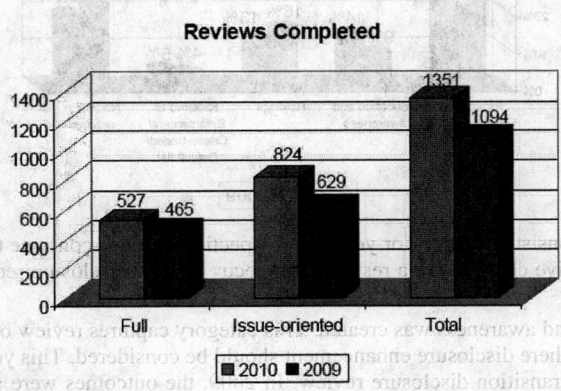

The above chart illustrates the composition of the type of reviews we conducted in fiscal 2010 compared to fiscal 2009. The number of full reviews conducted in fiscal 2010 increased by 13% from the previous year. The number of issue-oriented reviews increased by 31%. The majority of the increase in issue-oriented reviews is a result of International Financial Reporting Standards (IFRS) transition disclosure reviews and regulatory compliance reviews, including National Instrument 52-109 *Certification of Disclosure in Issuers' Annual and Interim Filings* (Certification) and Form 51-102F6 (new) — *Statement of Executive Compensation (in respect of financial years ending on or after December 31, 2008)* of National Instrument 51-102 *Continuous Disclosure Obligations* (NI 51-102) (Executive Compensation).

Outcomes for fiscal 2010

Given our risk-based approach to the selection of issuers, we generally select issuers at higher risk of non-compliance. In 2010, 72% of issuers reviewed were required to take action to improve disclosure, compared to 80% in 2009.

We classify the outcomes of the full and issue-oriented reviews into the five categories identified below. A CD review could have more than one category of outcome. For example, an issuer could be required to refile certain documents as well as make certain changes on a prospective basis.

Prospective Changes

The issuer was informed that certain changes or enhancements are required in its next filing as a result of deficiencies identified.

Education and Awareness

The issuer was selected based on its particular risk profile and has received a proactive letter alerting it to certain disclosure enhancements that should be considered in its next filing.

Refiling

The issuer must amend and refile certain CD documents.

Enforcement referral / Default list / Cease trade order

If the issuer has critical CD deficiencies, we may add the issuer to our default lists, issue a cease trade order or refer the issuer to Enforcement.

No action required

The issuer does not need to make any changes or additional filings.

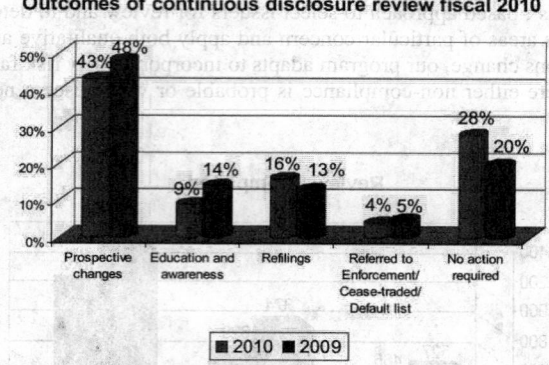

Outcomes of continuous disclosure review fiscal 2010

Generally, the outcomes have remained consistent with prior years as prospective changes continue to be the most dominant outcome (43% in 2010, 48% in 2009). Most of the prospective changes are a result of our focus on new disclosure requirements and our objective of educating issuers about those requirements.

In fiscal 2009, the category of education and awareness was created. This category captures review outcomes where issuers are contacted prior to their next CD filing to highlight areas where disclosure enhancement should be considered. This year the outcomes captured in this category were generally associated with the IFRS transition disclosure review. In 2009, the outcomes were associated with reviews related to market conditions.

Common deficiencies identified in Full Reviews

To assist issuers in avoiding the common pitfalls that we continue to see in disclosure documents, we have provided some examples of the more common deficiencies found in financial statements, Management's Discussion and Analysis (MD&A) and oil and gas disclosure. This is not an exhaustive list of examples of all common deficiencies, and issuers should be reminded that their CD record must comply with all relevant securities legislation.

Financial statement deficiencies

Common problems identified within the financial statements generally relate to disclosure of accounting policies and measurement issues. A clear and concise description of the significant accounting policies of an issuer is considered an integral part of their financial statements as the policies provide a roadmap to investors for understanding the financial results.

There are four areas in which we continue to find measurement issues and see deficient disclosure in financial statements: financial instruments, revenue recognition, goodwill, and capital disclosure. For each area we provide examples of deficient disclosure contrasted against more robust, entity-specific disclosure.

Financial instruments

Many issuers continue to incorrectly measure financial instruments in accordance with appropriate standards and many issuers continue to omit disclosure of the following:

- methods and, when a valuation technique is used, the assumptions applied in determining fair values of each class of financial assets or financial liabilities;

- complete information on credit and liquidity risk;

- aging analysis of past due accounts receivable balances; and

- sensitivity analysis related to market risks.

Issuers should assess the valuation techniques used to measure financial instruments (e.g., fair value) to ensure that they are based on factors and assumptions appropriate in the current economic climate.

Appropriate measurement and disclosure about financial instruments enables investors to evaluate the significance of financial instruments for the issuer's financial position and performance and to evaluate the nature and extent of risks arising from financial instruments.

Example of Deficient Disclosure — Financial instruments

Carrying value approximates fair value given the short term nature of financial assets held.

Example of Entity-Specific Disclosure — Financial instruments

The Company has used a discounted cash flow approach to determine the fair value of investments, taking into account the expected risk and return profile of the notes in comparison to market returns. The Company also used a discount factor appropriate for a high yield instrument for Investment C. The Company used the following expected rates and discount factors at year end:

Restructured Notes	Return	Market Discount Factor
Investment A	BAs minus 50 basis points	BAs plus 545 basis points
Investment B	Nil	100% Provision
Investment C	BAs plus 30 basis points	BAs plus 1,183 basis points

The Company believes that the market discount factors shown above are reflective of functioning market returns for products with similar maturities and risk profiles to the investments.

Sensitivity

The use of the discounted cash flow approach described above resulted in a carrying value for total investments of $50 million on notes with a face value of $100 million. The difference of $50 million is composed of fair value adjustments due to the discounting of cash flows at market rates of $40 million and an estimate of credit losses, net of the benefits of the agreement with a financial institution of $10 million. A change of 50 basis points in the market discount factors would impact the fair value adjustment by approximately $2 million. There is no assurance that the fair value of the Company's investments will not decline further. Accordingly, the estimated fair value of the Company's investments, including the estimate of expected credit losses, may change in subsequent periods. Any such changes could be material and would be reflected in the statement of operations as they occur.

Revenue recognition

An issuer's revenue recognition policy disclosure should be clear and concise. Revenue recognition generally has a significant impact on the financial results of an issuer. It is therefore important for investors to know how and when revenue is being recognized. Disclosure should clearly set out triggers for recognition and the basis for revenue from each product or service, including disclosure of any credit terms, rights of return, or conditions.

Example of Deficient Disclosure — Revenue recognition

The company recognizes revenue at the time persuasive evidence of an agreement exists, price is fixed and the product is delivered.

Example of Entity-Specific Disclosure — Revenue recognition

The Company recognizes revenue on the sale of merchandise. The Company also earns revenue on maintenance services provided for merchandise. The sale of merchandise and maintenance services are sold as separate arrangements and therefore do not require arrangements with multiple deliverables.

The Company enters into contracts for the sale of its merchandise with its customers. Revenue is recognized when a contract has been established with a customer, delivery has occurred or services have been rendered, the sales price is fixed or determinable, collection is reasonably assured and there are no remaining performance obligations.

The Company's policy is to bill the customer once the contract has been established with the customer. Billings are received prior to shipment or provision of services and are recorded as deferred revenue and recognized once the merchandise is shipped or service has been provided. There is no general right of return.

Revenue from the sale of merchandise is recognized upon delivery and title of the merchandise passes to the customer. Once the merchandise is delivered and the title passes to the customer, the Company has satisfied its performance obligations.

Revenues earned on maintenance service is recognized when the Company provides service to the customer and the Company has no further obligations to the customer.

Goodwill

Inadequate disclosure of the methodology used to conduct goodwill impairment testing is an ongoing issue. Impairment testing and the disclosure of the methodology used allow investors to consider the methodology and assumptions used. Current economic and market conditions are circumstances likely to affect the carrying value of assets.

Example of Deficient Disclosure — Goodwill

Goodwill is not amortized and is generally tested annually for impairment or more frequently if an event or circumstance occurs that more likely than not reduces the fair value of a reporting unit below its carrying amount.

Example of Entity-Specific Disclosure — Goodwill

During the fourth quarter, we performed our annual goodwill impairment assessment. Our goodwill balance prior to the impairment charge was $100 million and was established primarily as a result of the acquisition in Subsidiary A.

We completed our step one analysis using a combination of valuation approaches including a market capitalization approach, a multiples approach and discounted cash flow. The market capitalization approach uses our publicly traded stock price to determine fair value. The multiples approach uses comparable market multiples to arrive at a fair value and the discounted cash flow method uses revenue and expense projections and risk-adjusted discount rates.

The process of determining fair value is subjective and requires management to exercise a significant amount of judgment in determining future growth rates, discount and tax rates and other factors. The current economic environment has impacted our ability to forecast future demand and has in turn resulted in our use of higher discount rates, reflecting the risk and uncertainty in current markets. The results of our step one analysis indicated potential impairment in our Location X reporting unit, which was corroborated by a combination of factors including a significant and sustained decline in our market capitalization, which is significantly below our book value, and the deteriorating macro environment, which has resulted in a decline in expected future demand.

We therefore performed the second step of the goodwill impairment assessment to quantify the amount of impairment. This involved calculating the implied fair value of goodwill, determined in a manner similar to a purchase price allocation, and comparing the residual amount to the carrying amount of goodwill. Based on our analysis incorporating the declining market capitalization, as well as the significant end market deterioration and economic uncertainties impacting expected future demand, we concluded that the entire goodwill balance was impaired.

Capital disclosure

Issuers are required to disclose information that enables investors to evaluate their objectives, policies and processes for managing capital. Issuers often fail to provide summary quantitative data about what they manage as capital and fail to discuss if they specifically have met their objectives for managing capital.

Example of Deficient Disclosure — Capital disclosure

The Company manages the capital structure and makes adjustments to it in light of changes in economic condition and the risk characteristics of the underlying assets. The capital structure of the Company consists of common shares, contributed surplus, warrants, deficits and accumulated other comprehensive income. The Company's objectives when managing capital are to: (i) preserve capital, and (ii) maintain liquidity. The Company may attempt to issue new shares, issue new debt, acquire or dispose of assets or adjust the amount of cash and cash equivalents and investments.

Example of Entity-Specific Disclosure — Capital disclosure

The Company manages its capital with the following objectives:

- to ensure sufficient financial flexibility to achieve the ongoing business objectives including replacement of production, funding of future growth opportunities, and pursuit of accretive acquisitions; and

- to maximize shareholder return through enhancing the share value.

The Company monitors its capital structure and makes adjustments according to market conditions in an effort to meet its objectives given the current outlook of the business and industry in general. The Company may manage its capital structure by issuing new shares, repurchasing outstanding shares, obtaining additional financing either through bank indebtedness or convertible debenture issuances, refinancing current debt, issuing other financial or equity-based instruments, declaring a dividend or adjusting the amount of dividends paid, implementing a dividend reinvestment plan, adjusting capital spending, or disposing of assets. The capital structure is reviewed by Management and the Board of Directors on an ongoing basis.

The Company's capital structure as at December 31, 2009 is as follows:

	($000s)
Bank indebtedness (long-term)	$300
Working capital deficit	100
Net debt	400
Shares outstanding market value	1,200
Convertible debentures maturity value (long-term)	150
Capital lease obligations (long-term)	8
Total capitalization	$1,758
Debt to total capitalization	22%

The Company's bank indebtedness is governed by a $525 million credit facility agreement that contains standard commercial covenants for facilities of this nature. The only financial covenant is a requirement for the Company to maintain a minimum cash flow to interest expense ratio of 3.5:1, determined on a rolling four quarter basis. This covenant was met at December 31, 2009. The Company is in compliance with all other credit facility covenants.

The Company manages capital on the basis of the proportion of net debt to total capitalization, and targets to maintain the proportion to be in the range of 20–25%. In addition, management of the Company's capital structure is facilitated through its financial and operational forecasting processes. The forecast of the Company's future cash flows is based on estimates of production, commodity prices, forecast capital and operating expenditures, and other investing and financing activities. The forecast is regularly updated based on new commodity prices and other changes, which the Company views as critical in the current environment. Selected forecast information is frequently provided to the Board of Directors. The Company's capital management objectives, policies and processes have remained unchanged during the year ended December 31, 2009.

MD&A deficiencies

MD&A remains the area with the most compliance issues. The MD&A is a critical disclosure document for investors and should provide clear and concise disclosure of important risks and trends in addition to material information that may not be fully reflected in the financial statements. We often find boilerplate disclosure rather than entity-specific disclosure that would enable a reader to assess the current financial condition of the issuer and its future prospects.

There are five critical areas where we continue to see generic disclosure in the MD&A: operations, liquidity, risk, related parties, and critical accounting estimates. For each, we provide examples of deficient disclosure contrasted against more robust, entity-specific disclosure.

Operations

Common deficiencies in the MD&A continue to result from a lack of meaningful analysis and discussion of operating results, financial condition, and liquidity. In some circumstances issuers fail to provide a quantitative and qualitative explanation of material movements in the income statement. Issuers should describe the reasons behind material variances to assist investors in determining if past performance is indicative of future performance.

Example 1: Deficient Disclosure — Results of operations

Revenue increased from $900,000 to $1,080,000, a 20% increase. Gross margin increased from $400,000 to $408,000, a 2% increase.

Example 1: Entity-Specific Disclosure — Results of operations

Revenue increased by $180,000 during the period due to several factors:

- increased sales volume of Product A — $60,000;

- decreased unit price of Product A — ($30,000); and

- the introduction of a new product during the quarter, Product B — $150,000

In late 2009, we anticipated increased market competition for Product A and reduced the selling price to encourage the sale of Product A. The discounts on Product A resulted in reduced gross margin. In the current quarter, we expect to continue discounting Product A and expect the gross margin to improve as Product B replaces Product A.

Example 2: Deficient Disclosure — Results of operations

In fiscal 2009, the Company completed the first phase of its drilling program on the XYZ Lake property and the results suggested the existence of significant gold mineralization on the property. Additional drilling is necessary to fully test the potential of this property.

Example 2: Entity-Specific Disclosure — Results of operations

In fiscal 2009, the Company completed the first phase of its drilling program on the XYZ Lake property and the results suggested the existence of significant gold mineralization on the property. In the second half of 2010, the Company plans to complete additional 20 drill holes and further geological mapping. The Company has spent $1,000,000 to date and will require $2,000,000 to complete the additional work in 2010. The Company intends to obtain the funds from its recently negotiated undrawn revolving credit facility, which has an authorized limit of $3,000,000.

Liquidity — Working capital deficiency

Issuers who have or expect to have a working capital deficiency are required to discuss their ability to meet obligations as they become due and how they expect to remedy the deficiency. The MD&A should provide an analysis of the ability to generate sufficient cash to allow investors to determine if adequate financial resources are available to meet operating needs. Many issuers who have a working capital deficiency fail to provide plans to remedy this deficiency.

Example of Deficient Disclosure — Working capital deficiency

At year end, the Company had cash of $10,000, total current assets of $200,000 and total current liabilities of $500,000. This resulted in a working capital deficiency of $300,000. The Company is actively seeking alternative sources of financing.

Example of Entity-Specific Disclosure — Working capital deficiency

At year end, the Company had cash of $10,000, total current assets of $200,000 and total current liabilities of $500,000. This resulted in a working capital deficiency of $300,000. Subsequent to year end, the Company has entered into discussions to borrow an additional $350,000 from both private investors and shareholders to meet current and future working capital requirements. The Company is also exploring other financing alternatives, such as factoring accounts receivables and sale and leaseback of capital assets. In the short term, the Company will rely on advances from shareholders and the exercise of options to fund operating costs.

Risks

Issuers are required to disclose material risks and uncertainties that could cause reported financial information to not be indicative of future operating results or future financial position. This information enables investors to analyze important trends and risks that are reasonably likely to impact an issuer. Issuers should include a discussion of the effects of the current economic environment on financial condition, operations and liquidity.

Example of Deficient Disclosure — Risks

The Company faces significant competition for Product A and B, both locally and internationally, including competition from other retail companies in the industry.

Example of Entity-Specific Disclosure — Risks

The Company faces significant competition for Product A and B in Canada, including competition from other companies in the industry. Competition is based mainly on price and product quality. The product offerings of our competitors could impact our competitive position and may materially affect our business, operations and earnings. To mitigate competition risk, processes are in place to actively monitor and analyze demographic, consumer behaviour and competitive developments in Canada. On a monthly basis, executives from each product division meet to discuss and analyze the developments and adjust the Company's strategic, operational and investment plans. The Board of Directors has an oversight role in ensuring the Company's strategy takes into account shifts in competitive factors.

Related party transactions

Many issuers do not disclose the business purpose of related party transactions as required in the MD&A, which is incremental to the disclosure requirements under Canadian generally accepted accounting principles. Disclosure of both the quantitative and qualitative aspects of related party transactions in the MD&A is necessary for investors to understand the economic substance and business purposes of the transactions.

Example of Deficient Disclosure — Related party transactions

During the year, the Company paid $200,000 in interest on a loan payable to a majority shareholder.

Example of Entity-Specific Disclosure — Related party transactions

During the year, the Company paid $200,000 in interest on a loan of $2,000,000 received from the CEO, who is a majority shareholder. The unsecured loan bears interest at 10% per annum, and matures in five years with an option by the Company to extinguish the debt at any time without penalty. The Company entered into this related party transaction because alternate sources of financing were unavailable due to the Company's limited operating history, lack of collateral and limited access to public financing due to current global financial conditions.

Critical accounting estimates

The MD&A should provide a discussion of the methodology and assumptions used in determining critical accounting estimates. This includes information such as assumptions underlying accounting estimates that relate to highly uncertain matters at the time the estimate was made, known trends, commitments, events or uncertainties that will materially affect the methodology or the assumptions used, why the accounting estimate is reasonably likely to change from period to period and why it may have a material impact on the financial presentation. This information allows investors to evaluate the significance of the critical accounting estimates.

Example of Deficient Disclosure — Critical accounting estimates (asset retirement obligation)

Management calculates the asset retirement obligation based on estimated costs to abandon and reclaim its net ownership interest in all wells and facilities and the estimated timing of the costs to be incurred in future periods. The fair value estimate is capitalized to PP&E as part of the cost of the related asset and amortized over its useful life.

Example of Entity-Specific Disclosure — Critical accounting estimates (asset retirement obligation)

The asset retirement obligation is estimated based on existing laws, contracts or other policies and current technology and conditions. The fair value of the obligation is based on estimated future costs for abandonment and reclamation, discounted at a credit-adjusted risk-free rate. The costs are included in property, plant and equipment and amortized over their useful life. The liability is adjusted each reporting period to reflect the passage of time, with the accretion charged to earnings and for revisions to the estimated future cash flows. The estimates or assumptions required to calculate asset retirement obligation includes, among other items, abandonment and reclamation amounts, inflation rates, credit-adjusted discount rates and timing of retirement of assets. By their nature, these estimates are subject to measurement uncertainty and the impact on the financial statements could be material.

The following significant assumptions were assumed for the purpose of estimating asset retirement obligation:

	2009	2008
Undiscounted abandonment costs ($000s)	$ 60,640	$ 52,960
Credit-adjusted risk-free rate	6.50%	6.80%
Inflation rate	2%	2.20%
Average years to reclamation	11	12

Oil and Gas disclosure deficiencies

Oil and gas terminology

We commonly see disclosure of in-place volumes described as Original Oil in Place (OOIP) or Original Gas in Place (OGIP). OOIP and OGIP are not terms recognized by the Canadian Oil and Gas Evaluation Handbook (COGEH) and should not be used for disclosure purposes by issuers. Total Petroleum Initially in Place, Discovered Petroleum Initially in Place or Undiscovered Petroleum Initially in Place are terms recognized by COGEH that could be used to disclose in place volumes, as appropriate.

Another common problem we see is the combining of terms which results in potentially misleading disclosure such as volumes described as contingent reserves or prospective reserves. It is important to use terminology and categories as presented in Section 5 of COGEH and to not modify these terms. It should also be noted that using the term reserve when describing resource volumes other than reserves is inappropriate and potentially misleading.

Issue-oriented reviews

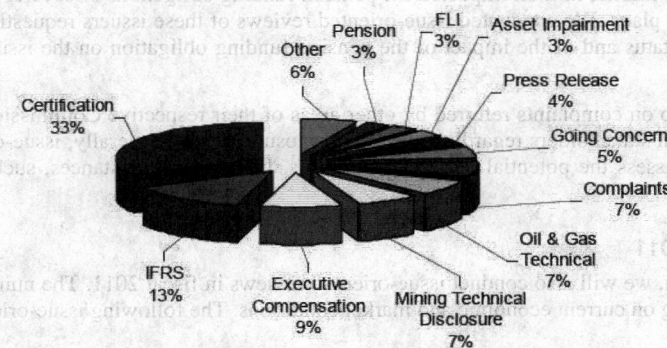

Of the 1,351 reviews that were completed in fiscal 2010, 61% of the reviews (as compared to 57% of the reviews last year) were issue-oriented reviews completed either as a CSA coordinated initiative or by local jurisdictions. Some jurisdictions did not conduct certain issue-oriented reviews but incorporated specific procedures in their full reviews to address topics or concerns identified in the issue-oriented reviews. The following issue-oriented reviews were completed this year by one or more of the jurisdictions:

- *Certification* — see CSA Staff Notice 52-325 *Certification Compliance Review* issued September 11, 2009.

- *IFRS Transition Disclosure* — see OSC Staff Notice 52-718 *IFRS Transition Disclosure Review* and *Notice of Autorité des marchés financiers related to disclosure by reporting issuers on changeover to international financial reporting standards* issued February 5, 2010.

- *Executive Compensation* — see CSA Staff Notice 51-331 *Report on Staff's Review of Executive Compensation Disclosure* issued on November 20, 2009.

- *Mining Technical Disclosure* — Issue-oriented reviews are regularly conducted on mining technical disclosure. The following problem areas remain consistent with prior years:

  - the name of the qualified person was not always included in documents containing scientific and technical information;

  - required disclosure for historical estimates, such as the source and date of the estimate was not included;

  - certificates or consents for the qualified person were not included; and

  - corporate presentations or other content on the website did not comply with National Instrument 43-101 *Standards of Disclosure for Mineral Projects*.

- *Oil and Gas Technical Disclosure* — We conducted reviews on issuers engaged in oil and gas activities to assess compliance with requirements set out in National Instrument 51-101 *Standards of Disclosure for Oil and Gas Activities* (NI 51-101). While there was general compliance among issuers, common issues identified include:

  - all of the information required under NI 51-101 was not provided and the information provided was not consistent throughout the oil and gas disclosure;

  - terminology set out in the COGEH was not properly used; and

  - disclosure of important economic factors or significant uncertainties that affect particular components of the reserves data was not provided.

- *Going Concern* — We conducted a review to assess disclosure in financial statements and MD&A of the risk that an issuer will not be able to continue as a going concern. The majority of issuers reviewed did not provide complete disclosure of this risk in their financial statements and MD&A. The review was extended to examine the going concern disclosure of issuers that recently went bankrupt and similar rates of non-compliance were found.

- *Asset Impairment* — In light of market conditions at the time, we completed a targeted review of issuers in certain industries with a higher risk of triggering an asset impairment. The review focused on the timing of recording impairments, the completeness of the methodology used in the impairment analysis, and disclosure of accounting policies relating to impairment. Generally we found that issuers complied with the requirements. The main deficiency identified was insufficient disclosure of asset impairments, specifically disclosure of critical accounting estimates used in the impairment analysis.

- *Forward-Looking Information (FLI)* — see CSA Staff Notice 51-330 *Guidance Regarding the Application of Forward-looking Information Requirements under NI 51-102 Continuous Disclosure Obligations* issued November 20, 2009 (the FLI notice).

- *Press Releases* — Press releases, websites, corporate presentations and other promotional materials are regularly reviewed to assess compliance with NI 51-101 and COGEH disclosure requirements, FLI requirements NI 51-102 and the press release requirement in section 11.5 of NI 51-102 announcing a refiling or restatement. Common issues identified include non-compliant reserve and resource classification and disclosure, non-compliant use of oil and gas terminology and the common FLI issues identified in the FLI notice.

- *Defined Benefit Pension Plans* — These reviews were conducted as a response to the market turmoil that impacted the pension funding obligations of many issuers. The market turmoil impacted the pension funding obligations of several issuers that we identified as having material defined benefit pension plans. We conducted issue-oriented reviews of these issuers requesting enhanced disclosure of the risks related to the issuer's funding status and of the impact of the pension funding obligation on the issuer's capital, liquidity and financial position.

- *Complaints* — Staff followed up on complaints referred by other areas of their respective Commissions. Complaints were also received from investors and other external stakeholders regarding specific disclosure issues. Generally, issue-oriented reviews were conducted to consider the issues raised and assess the potential impact to investors. In some circumstances, such complaints lead to further action being taken against an issuer.

Areas of focus for fiscal year 2011

In addition to our full review program, we will also conduct issue-oriented reviews in fiscal 2011. The number and type of reviews conducted during the year may change depending on current economic and market conditions. The following issue-oriented reviews are currently planned for 2011:

- IFRS transition disclosure;
- Material contracts;
- Corporate governance; and
- Follow-up review of Certification.

Results by jurisdiction

The Alberta Securities Commission, the Ontario Securities Commission and the Autorité des marchés financiers publish reports summarizing the results of the CD review program in their jurisdictions. See the individual regulator's website for a copy of its report:

- www.albertasecurities.com
- www.osc.gov.on.ca
- www.lautorite.qc.ca

CSA Staff Notice 51-333 — Environmental Reporting Guidance

Date: October 27, 2010

33 O.S.C.B. 9951

Contents

1. Introduction

1.1 Developments in the marketplace
- Impact of environmental matters on issuers
- Changing regulatory landscape
- Investor interest in environmental matters

2. Environmental information required to be disclosed

2.1 Material information
- Test for materiality
- Materiality determinations

2.2 Environmental risks and related matters
- Environmental risks
- Trends and uncertainties
- Environmental liabilities
- Asset retirement obligations
- Financial and operational effects of environmental protection requirements

2.3 Risk oversight and management

- Environmental policies fundamental to operations

- Board mandate and committees

2.4 Impact of adoption of IFRS

2.5 Forward-looking information requirements

3. Governance structures around environmental disclosure

3.1 Review, approval and certification of disclosure

3.2 Controls and procedures

3.3 Integration of financial and voluntary reporting

4. Conclusion

Appendix – Examples of entity-specific disclosure

1. — Introduction

The purpose of this notice is to provide guidance to reporting issuers (other than investment funds) on existing continuous disclosure (CD) requirements relating to environmental matters under securities legislation.

This notice clarifies existing disclosure requirements relating to environmental matters and does not create any new legal requirements or modify existing ones. It is intended to assist issuers in: (1) determining what information about environmental matters needs to be disclosed, and (2) enhancing or supplementing their disclosure regarding environmental matters, as necessary.

Environmental matters include a broad range of issues, including issues related to air, land, water and waste. This notice applies to all issuers but may be more relevant to certain issuers given their particular circumstances.

1.1 — Developments in the marketplace

The issuance of this notice has been motivated by three key developments: the impact of environmental matters on issuers, the changing regulatory landscape and increasing investor interest in environmental matters.

Impact of environmental matters on issuers

Issuers are increasingly recognizing the current and potential effects on their performance and operations, both positive and negative, that are associated with environmental matters. For example, environmental matters can impact an issuer by:

- interrupting operations (including supply and distribution chains, personnel and physical assets)

- resulting in material unplanned costs, such as costs to address an environmental accident

- affecting the issuer's license to operate

- affecting capital expenditure decisions and the viability of projects

- changing consumer preferences

- affecting the issuer's reputation

- altering access to and the cost of capital

- affecting the affordability and availability of insurance, and

- providing new business opportunities.

Changing regulatory landscape

The environmental regulatory landscape is constantly changing. Issuers need to regularly assess their disclosure obligations in light of ongoing environmental regulatory developments domestically and abroad, to the extent they may affect an issuer's operations, assets, supply chain or markets.

Investor interest in environmental matters

A number of investors are increasingly interested in how environmental matters affect issuers and have been requesting information about these matters from issuers through a number of avenues, such as shareholder resolutions and the issuance of surveys.

Investor concerns regarding inadequate environmental disclosure

Investors and other stakeholders consulted during the Ontario Securities Commission's 2009 corporate sustainability reporting initiative expressed concerns regarding the adequacy of disclosure about environmental matters. In particular, they think that, in some cases:

- material information regarding environmental matters is found in voluntary reports and not in securities regulatory filings

- the information provided is not necessarily complete, reliable or comparable among issuers, and is boilerplate disclosure that does not provide meaningful information to investors

- if the information is not included in securities regulatory filings, it is not necessarily provided in a timely manner as the prescribed timelines for CD documents under securities legislation do not apply to voluntary reporting, and

- the information is not integrated into financial reporting.

2. — Environmental Information Required to be Disclosed

National Instrument 51-102 *Continuous Disclosure Obligations* (NI 51-102) contains a number of disclosure requirements relating to environmental matters. In addition, National Instrument 58-101 *Disclosure of Corporate Governance Practices* (NI 58-101) and National Instrument 52-110 *Audit Committees* (NI 52-110) contain relevant disclosure requirements.

These disclosure requirements can be considered in the following groups:

- risks and related matters

- risk oversight and management

- forward-looking information (FLI) requirements, and

- impact of adoption of International Financial Reporting Standards (IFRS) on disclosure provided under NI 51-102.

To help issuers comply with these disclosure requirements, we have provided guidance below and included examples of disclosure in the Appendix.

2.1 — Material information

In considering whether information is required to be disclosed, the determining factor is materiality. As provided in Part 1(e) of Form 51-102F1 *Management's Discussion & Analysis* (Form 51-102F1) and Part 1(d) of Form 51-102F2 *Annual Information Form* (Form 51-102F2), only material information needs to be included in CD documents.

Test for materiality for CD documents

The test for materiality is objective. Information relating to environmental matters is likely material if a reasonable investor's decision whether or not to buy, sell or hold securities of the issuer would likely be influenced or changed if the information was omitted or misstated. See Part 1(f) of Form 51-102F1 and Part 1(e) of Form 51-102F2.

As noted in Form 51-102F1 and Form 51-102F2, this concept of materiality is consistent with the financial reporting notion of materiality contained in the Canadian Institute of Chartered Accountants (CICA) Handbook.

Materiality determinations

Process for assessing material information

A TSX-listed issuer[1] is required to establish and maintain disclosure controls and procedures under National Instrument 52-109 *Certification of Disclosure in Issuers' Annual and Interim Filings* (NI 52-109). These controls and procedures include those that are designed to ensure that information required to be disclosed by an issuer in its annual filings, interim filings or other reports filed or submitted under securities legislation is accumulated and communicated to the issuer's management, including its certifying officers, as appropriate to allow timely decisions regarding required disclosure.

While materiality determinations may limit what is actually disclosed by the issuer, they should not limit the information that management considers in making its determinations.

Considerations for determining materiality

The key question for an issuer is whether a particular environmental matter under consideration is material and requires disclosure.

We have been advised that some issuers in the past have found determining materiality in the environmental context to be challenging. To assist issuers, we have set out below some guiding principles to consider when making materiality determinations regarding environmental matters. We note that the guiding principles may assist issuers in making materiality determinations in other contexts.

Some of the guiding principles are derived from National Policy 51-201 *Disclosure Standards* (NP 51-201), which came into force on July 12, 2002. In addition, the guiding principles are derived from decisions of the Canadian securities regulatory authorities rendered after NP 51-201 came into force, such as the Ontario Securities Commission's decision, *Re YBM Magnex International Inc* (2003), 26 OSCB 5285 (the YBM decision). We also reviewed discussions of materiality in the environmental context in sources such as:

- the CICA publication, *Executive Briefing — Climate Change and Related Disclosures* (March 2008)

- the CICA publication, *Building A Better MD&A: Climate Change Disclosures* (November 2008)

- the CICA publication, *Climate Change Briefing* (July 2009)

- the CICA publication, *Environmental, Social and Governance (ESG) Issues in Institutional Investor Decision Making* (August 2010)

- the May 2009 exposure draft of the Climate Disclosure Standards Board Reporting Framework, and

---

[1]References to TSX-listed issuers in this notice include references to all reporting issuers that are not venture issuers (as defined in NI 51-102).

- the U.S. Securities and Exchange Commission's guidance, *Commission Guidance Regarding Disclosure Related to Climate Change* (effective February 2, 2010).

The guiding principles below are not an exhaustive list of the factors to be considered when making materiality determinations. They are intended as a general guide, and are not meant as legal or other advice on whether a particular environmental matter is material for a particular issuer. Issuers should refer to securities legislation and NP 51-201, and as noted in Part 1(e) of Form 51-102F1 and Part 1(d) of Form 51-102F2, should exercise their judgement when determining whether information is material.

- **No bright-line test** — There is no uniform quantitative threshold at which a particular type of information becomes material. The materiality of certain information may vary between industries and even between issuers within an industry according to their particular circumstances. An event that is "significant" or "major" for a smaller issuer may not be material to a larger issuer. In our view, issuers should consider both quantitative and qualitative factors in determining materiality.[2]

- **Context** — Materiality depends on the nature and amount of the item judged in the particular circumstances of its omission or misstatement. Some facts are material on their own. When one or more facts do not appear to be material on their own, materiality must be considered in light of all the facts available. An issuer should not "lose sight of the forest for the trees" by assessing the materiality of individual facts piecemeal.[3]

- **Timing** — Determining whether information is material is a dynamic process that depends on the prevailing relevant conditions at the time of reporting. In assessing materiality, an issuer should consider whether the impact of an environmental matter might reasonably be expected to grow over time, in which case early disclosure of the matter might be important to reasonable investors. This would be particularly relevant where the issuer is in an industry with a longer operation or investment cycle or where new technologies are going to be required.[4]

- **Trends, demands, commitments, events and uncertainties** — Generally, the time horizon of a known trend, demand, commitment, event or uncertainty may be relevant to an issuer's assessment of materiality. As with other types of disclosure, materiality in cases of a known environmental trend, demand, commitment, event or uncertainty turns on an analysis of:
  - the probability that the trend, demand, commitment, event or uncertainty will occur, and
  - the anticipated magnitude of its effect.[5]

- **Err on side of materiality** — If there is any doubt about whether particular information is material, we encourage issuers to err on the side of materiality and disclose the information.[6]

2.2 — Environmental risks and related matters

There are five key disclosure requirements in NI 51-102 that relate to environmental matters:

- environmental risks
- trends and uncertainties
- environmental liabilities
- asset retirement obligations, and
- financial and operational effects of environmental protection requirements.

Disclosure about these matters, if material, is important as each provides insight into an issuer's risk profile.

Environmental risks

Item 5.2 of Form 51-102F2 requires an issuer to disclose risk factors relating to the issuer and its business. The annual information form (AIF) should provide insight into what the issuer believes are the risks relating to the issuer and its business so that investors can assess the effect of these risks on the issuer's operations and/or financial performance. This includes environmental risks and any other matters that would be most likely to influence an investor's decision to purchase the issuer's securities.

Comments

An issuer should assess whether, due to the nature of its operations, it needs to address environmental risks in its CD documents. All relevant environmental risks should be considered in deciding what to disclose. Generally, risks that may impact an issuer's business and operations can be divided into five categories: litigation, physical, regulatory, reputation and business model.

---

[2]This guiding principle has been derived from sources such as subsection 4.2(1) of NP 51-201, OSC Staff Notice 51-716 *Environmental Reporting* (February 27, 2008) and Form 41-101F1 *Information Required in a Prospectus*, General Instruction 3.

[3]This guiding principle has been derived from sources such as paragraphs 94 and 101 of the YBM decision.

[4]This guiding principle has been derived from sources such as the CICA publication, *Building A Better MD&A: Climate Change Disclosures* (November 2008) and the May 2009 exposure draft of the Climate Disclosure Standards Board Reporting Framework.

[5]This guiding principle has been derived from sources such as paragraph 92 of the YBM decision and item 1.2 of Form 51-102F1.

[6]This guiding principle has been derived from sources such as subsection 4.2(2) of NP 51-201.

Part 5: ONGOING REQUIREMENTS

As with any other type of disclosure, material risks should be disclosed in a meaningful way, avoiding boilerplate disclosure. An issuer needs to disclose both the risk and the factual basis for it. The issuer should consider the following questions when identifying the material risks it faces.

Type of risk	Questions for issuers to consider
Litigation risks	• Is the issuer a party to any environmental litigation? What is the anticipated liability exposure under those claims? What is the likelihood of those claims succeeding?
	• Are there any such legal proceedings known to be contemplated?
Physical risks	• How is the issuer likely to be affected by physical risks of environmental matters, such as the impacts of industrial contamination, changing weather patterns and water availability?
	• Impacts could include:
	• property damage
	• health and safety issues for employees and to members of the public
	• disruptions to operations, including manufacturing operations or the transport of manufactured products
	• disruptions to operations of major customers or suppliers
	• increased insurance claims and liabilities for insurance and reinsurance issuers, and
	• increased insurance premiums and deductibles, or a decrease in the availability or loss of coverage.
	• What risk management, adaptation and mitigation strategies has the issuer adopted, or is the issuer planning to adopt in the near future? What are the expected costs of those strategies?
Regulatory risks	• What are the actual and expected impacts of current and likely environmental regulation on the issuer's business and strategy? Regulations may include environmental permits, reporting requirements, carbon pricing systems, carbon limits and trading systems, energy efficiency standards and building codes. They can include both applicable domestic and foreign requirements. The issuer should consider specific risks it faces as a result of environmental legislation or regulation, and avoid generic risk factor disclosure. Where the exact limits or targets are uncertain, an assumption of ranges may be used to determine how certain requirements might reasonably be expected to affect an issuer.
	• What are the applicable and anticipated environmental regulatory requirements? Is the issuer currently in material compliance with those requirements? What are the current and anticipated future costs of compliance (and can these costs be broken down by category such as the rehabilitation of contaminated sites or the disposal of hazardous materials)? Where quantification of a risk or cost is uncertain, the disclosure of the factual basis for the risk will help investors in understanding it.
Reputational risks	• How is the issuer addressing environmental matters? How an issuer addresses environmental matters can have a positive or negative impact on core intangible assets such as brand value, consumer confidence, employee loyalty, ability to attract financial capital and obtaining regulatory approval of projects.
	• What is the impact on the issuer's results and operations arising from its interaction on environmental matters with local communities and other parties affected by the issuer's operations? An issuer's relationship with local communities can affect an issuer's ability to operate and the costs of doing so.
Risks relating to business model	• Have legal, technological, political and scientific developments regarding environmental matters created new material opportunities or risks for the issuer? For example, possible indirect consequences or opportunities may include:
	• changes to production practices
	• changes due to emerging technologies
	• decreased demand for goods that have a negative impact on the environment or fail to meet customer standards

Type of risk	Questions for issuers to consider
	• increased demand for goods that have less of an impact on the environment than competing products
	• changes to tax incentives and subsidies
	• increased competition to develop innovative products
	• increased demand for generation and transmission of energy from alternative energy sources, and
	• decreased demand for services related to carbon-based energy sources, such as drilling services or equipment maintenance services.

Trends and uncertainties

As provided in Part 1(a) of Form 51-102F1, MD&A is a narrative explanation, through the eyes of management, of how an issuer performed during the period covered by the financial statements, and of the issuer's financial condition and future prospects. MD&A should, among other things, discuss: (i) material information that may not be fully reflected in the financial statements, such as contingent liabilities or other contractual obligations, and (ii) important trends and risks that have affected the financial statements, and trends and risks that are reasonably likely to affect them in the future.

Item 1.4(g) of Form 51-102F1 requires the issuer to discuss its analysis of its operations for the most recently completed financial year, including commitments, events, risks or uncertainties that it reasonably believes will materially affect the issuer's future performance.

Comments

An issuer should examine to what extent trends and uncertainties regarding environmental matters materially impact its financial performance and future prospects. Disclosure decisions concerning these trends and uncertainties should generally involve:

- consideration of financial, operational and other information known to the issuer

- identification of known trends and uncertainties, and

- an assessment of whether these trends and uncertainties will have, or are reasonably likely to have, a material impact on the issuer's liquidity, capital resources or results of operations.

There is no specified future time period that must be considered in assessing the impact of a known trend or uncertainty that is reasonably likely to occur. The necessary time period will depend on an issuer's particular circumstances and the particular trend or uncertainty under consideration. Furthermore, the time horizon of a known trend or uncertainty may be relevant to an issuer's assessment of its materiality and whether or not the impact is reasonably likely.

An issuer should disclose:

- what has been, and is reasonably likely to be, the impact of environmental trends or uncertainties on revenues, expenditures and cash flows, and

- the impact environmental trends or uncertainties have on its financial condition and liquidity, if any.

Examples of how revenues and expenses may be impacted by environmental matters

Revenues	• changes in consumer preference or demand for goods and services due, in whole or in part, to environmental matters or trends
	• changes in supply chain requirements related to environmental matters
	• new rules requiring design changes to products
	• the sale of, or royalties on, innovative technologies
	• delayed or denied regulatory environmental approvals
	• the availability and price of emissions credits or offsets
Expenses	• the need to retrofit existing facilities to address physical, health and safety, or regulatory constraints
	• research and development activities related to more environmentally efficient operations and processes
	• purchase and implementation of new information systems to measure and record natural resource impacts (including, for example, greenhouse gas emissions and water and energy usage)
	• increased or new insurance coverage or premiums
	• purchases of allowances or offsets to meet regulatory emissions requirements
	• penalties for failure to meet government-mandated reduction targets
	• repairing or rebuilding facilities impacted by adverse weather events
	• investments in productive capacity that embody new "green" or more energy-efficient technologies
	• investments in projects to generate offsets
	• financing costs related to expenditures

Environmental liabilities

An environmental liability can include a legal obligation to make a future expenditure due to the past or ongoing manufacture; use, release or threatened release of a particular substance, or other activities that adversely impact the environment.

Similarly, a potential environmental liability can include a potential legal obligation to make a future expenditure due to the ongoing or future manufacture; use, release or threatened release of a particular substance, or other activities that adversely impact the environment. An obligation is potential when it depends on future events or when a law or regulation creating the liability is not yet in force. With a potential environmental liability, an issuer may have the opportunity to prevent the liability from occurring by altering its own practices or adopting new practices to avoid or reduce the adverse effect on the environment.

Examples of environmental liabilities

- compliance obligations related to laws and regulations or other binding requirements that apply to the manufacture, use, disposal and release of substances, and other activities that may adversely affect the environment
- existing and future site remediation obligations
- obligations to pay civil, administrative and criminal fines and penalties for statutory or regulatory non-compliance
- obligations to compensate private parties for personal injury, property damage and economic loss
- obligations to pay punitive or special damages, or make or maintain specific reserves for those damages
- obligations to pay for natural resource damages

Comments

There are two broad categories of environmental liabilities that are to be considered for disclosure: those that are reflected in the issuer's financial statements and those that are not.

Estimates reflected in financial statements

Where measurement of an environmental liability involves a critical accounting estimate (as defined in Form 51-102F1), certain disclosure is required. Specifically, item 1.12 of Form 51-102F1 requires management of TSX-listed issuers to include an analysis of critical accounting estimates in their MD&A.

We are of the view that in order for a TSX-listed issuer to meet the requirements of item 1.12 of Form 51-102F1, the issuer should quantify the accounting estimate where quantitative information is reasonably available and would provide material information to investors. Quantitative disclosure could include matters such as the amount claimed by a plaintiff, if publicly disclosed. It should also identify and explain that the estimate was highly uncertain at the time it was made and provide a detailed discussion of the estimate, which may include a sensitivity analysis or disclosure of the upper and lower ends of the range of estimates from which the recorded estimate was selected.

Potential environmental liabilities not reflected in financial statements

Part 1(a) of Form 51-102F1 states that an issuer's MD&A should discuss:

- material information that may not be fully reflected in the issuer's financial statements, and
- important trends and risks that have affected the financial statements, and trends and risks that are reasonably likely to affect them in the future.

An issuer may have potential environmental liabilities that are not reflected in the financial statements because their long-term or contingent nature can make them particularly difficult to quantify. In addition, an issuer may have several potential environmental liabilities that have not been recognized because they are not individually material, but it is possible that together they may indicate an underlying risk or trend that could be material to the issuer over the long-term.

We are of the view that a discussion of material potential environmental liabilities should be included in an issuer's CD documents whether or not the liability has been accrued in the financial statements or has been disclosed in the notes to the financial statements. The objective of this disclosure is to help investors understand the nature of potential liabilities, their likely timing and magnitude, and their probability of occurring.

Asset retirement obligations

An issuer is required to include certain disclosure about asset retirement obligations (AROs) in its financial statements, if applicable.

Item 1.2 of Form 51-102F1 requires an analysis of an issuer's financial condition, results of operations and cash flows, which includes a discussion of commitments, events or uncertainties that are reasonably likely to have an effect on the issuer's business. Item 1.6 of Form 51-102F1, and the corresponding instructions for this item, require TSX-listed issuers to provide a summary, in a table, of contractual obligations for the issuer's balance sheet conditions or income or cash flow, including payments due for each of the next five years and thereafter. Other long-term obligations must be disclosed in the table. In addition, as noted above, item 1.12 of Form 51-102F1 requires an analysis of critical accounting estimates for TSX-listed issuers.

Comments

Assets are considered retired if they are sold, abandoned, recycled or disposed of, but do not include assets temporarily removed from service. An ARO is a requirement to perform certain procedures, rather than a promise to pay cash. Legal obligations resulting from the retirement of an asset could include:

- government actions, such as laws or regulations

- written or oral agreements between entities, and

- a promise to a third party that imposes a reasonable expectation of performance.

We are of the view that if an ARO is material to an issuer, in addition to providing the required financial statement disclosure, the issuer should provide supplemental disclosure in its MD&A. Specifically, an issuer should include in its MD&A a comprehensive discussion of commitments, events or uncertainties, including AROs, that are reasonably likely to have an effect on the issuer's business. AROs are generally incurred over more than one reporting period, and information should be provided for all periods that may be materially impacted.

A discussion of AROs should indicate the associated asset to be reclaimed or restored. If environmental remediation costs are applicable, material, and information about these costs is reasonably available, that information should be disclosed. This discussion should set out the costs of compliance with environmental legislation, including:

- the costs associated with the disposal of hazardous materials, and

- the costs associated with the implementation of reclamation technologies.

The discussion should also set out the current and estimated future impact of those costs on the issuer's financial results.

Issuers should recognize that laws differ from one jurisdiction to another, and evolve from time to time within jurisdictions. Issuers should be aware that a new law or regulation could give rise to a new ARO as a result of its past activities.

An issuer should also evaluate whether AROs are material long-term obligations. If so, we are of the view that TSX-listed issuers should include these AROs in the summary contractual obligations table in their MD&A as required under item 1.6 of Form 51-102F1. The payments due for each of the next five years and thereafter in respect of these AROs would need to be quantified in the table.

We are of the view that in most cases AROs are critical accounting estimates, and TSX-listed issuers should include an analysis of these estimates in their MD&A as required by item 1.12 of Form 51-102F1.

Financial and operational effects of environmental protection requirements

Item 5.1(1)(k) of Form 51-102F2 requires an issuer to disclose the financial and operational effects of environmental protection requirements on the issuer's capital expenditures, earnings and competitive position in the current financial year and the expected effect in future years.

Comments

In discussing the financial and operational effects of environmental protection requirements, an issuer should disclose the costs associated with these requirements. This discussion should include:

- a quantification of the costs, where this information is reasonably available and would provide material information to investors

- anticipated trends in respect of these costs, and

- the potential impact of these costs on the issuer's financial and operational results.

For example, with respect to existing provisions relating to new or current environmental laws and regulations, an issuer should disclose material estimated capital expenditures for environmental control facilities for the remainder of the issuer's current fiscal year and its succeeding fiscal year and for such future periods as the issuer may deem material.

2.3 — Risk oversight and management

Investors have indicated that they would like information to assess whether directors are appropriately focusing on risk management, including environmental risk management. There is no single model for risk oversight and management and the structures and practices that are most appropriate will vary among issuers.

Two key sets of disclosure requirements provide insight into an issuer's oversight and management of environmental risks: environmental policies implemented by the issuer and board governance.

Environmental policies fundamental to operations

If an issuer has implemented environmental policies that are fundamental to its operations, item 5.1(4) of Form 51-102F2 requires the issuer to describe these policies and the steps it has taken to implement them.

Comments

In our view, the term "policy" should be broadly construed. It may include policies for sustainable development, community relations, the use and disposal of toxic or otherwise hazardous materials, prevention of spills, recycling, conservation of water and the reduction of greenhouse gas emissions.

When discussing environmental policies fundamental to its operations, an issuer should evaluate and describe the impact or potential impact these policies may have on its operations. This discussion may include a quantification of the costs associated with these policies, where quantitative information is reasonably available and would provide meaningful information to investors.

The issuer should also explain the purpose of these environmental policies, including the risks the policies are designed to address. This may include a discussion of the policy's effectiveness in meeting that purpose, as well as how the issuer is monitoring and updating the policy.

Environmental policies can be a tool used by issuers to manage risks associated with environmental matters. As noted above, an issuer is required to disclose its environmental risks and disclosure of environmental policies can explain how the issuer is managing those risks. This information may be of interest to investors, who may want to assess whether the risk management strategies employed by the issuer are adequate and appropriate for the types of risk in question and the issuer's risk tolerance.

Board mandate and committees

Understanding how the board manages risk, including environmental risk, is useful for investors.

Board mandate

Section 3.4 of National Policy 58-201 *Corporate Governance Guidelines* states that the board should adopt a written mandate in which it explicitly acknowledges responsibility for, among other things:

- adopting a strategic planning process and approving, on at least an annual basis, a strategic plan which takes into account, among other things, the opportunities and risks of the business, and

- identifying the principal risks of the issuer's business and ensuring the implementation of appropriate systems to manage those risks.

Item 2 of Form 58-101F1 *Corporate Governance Disclosure* (Form 58-101F1) requires TSX-listed issuers to disclose the text of the board's written mandate, or if the board does not have a written mandate, to describe how the board delineates its role and responsibilities.

Board committees

There are two relevant disclosure requirements relating to board standing committees and audit committees.

Board structure	Related disclosure requirement
Board standing committees	Item 8 of Form 58-101F1 requires TSX-listed issuers to disclose if their boards have standing committees other than the audit, compensation and nominating committees, and if so, to identify the committees and describe their function. These committees may include environmental or health and safety board committees. The mandate of those committees may include responsibility for environmental risk management.
Audit committees	Item 1 of Form 52-110F1 *Audit Committee Information Required in an AIF* and Form 52-110F2 *Disclosure by Venture Issuers* requires issuers to disclose the text of the audit committee's charter in the AIF. The audit committee may have responsibility for risk management, including environmental risk management.

Comments

Disclosure regarding oversight and management of environmental risks should indicate:

- the board's responsibility for oversight and management of risks, including environmental risks, if applicable, and

- any board and management-level committee to which responsibility for oversight and management of risks, including environmental risks, has been delegated.

The disclosure should provide insight into:

- the development and periodic review of the issuer's risk profile

- the integration of risk oversight and management into the issuer's strategic plan

- the identification of significant elements of risk management, including policies and procedures to manage risk, and

- the board's assessment of the effectiveness of risk management policies and procedures, where applicable.

2.4 — Impact of adoption of IFRS

Most Canadian publicly accountable enterprises, which include reporting issuers, will be required to use IFRS as issued by the IASB for financial years beginning on or after January 1, 2011 (the changeover).

The changeover to IFRS from existing Canadian GAAP may have a significant impact on financial reporting and other business activities of reporting issuers. IFRS contain some important differences from Canadian GAAP for recognition and measurement of provisions, including environmental provisions. Under IFRS, issuers may be required to accrue more environmental liabilities, at higher amounts, and provide more disclosure regarding these liabilities.

Key differences under IFRS (as of the date of this notice)

- **When a provision exists**. A liability exists under Canadian GAAP if there is a legal, equitable or constructive obligation arising as a result of a transaction or event. Under Canadian GAAP, an equitable obligation is a duty based on ethical or moral considerations, and a constructive obligation is one that can be inferred from the facts in a particular situation. Under IFRS, a provision is recorded if there is a present (legal or constructive) obligation as a result of a past event. A constructive obligation arises when an entity creates a valid expectation to other parties that it will discharge certain responsibilities based on an established pattern of past practice, published policies, or has indicated to other parties that it will accept certain responsibilities. Since IFRS provide a more precise definition and specific examples of a constructive obligation, a provision may be recognized at a different point in time depending on past practice of determining when an equitable or contractual obligation exists under Canadian GAAP.

- **Recognition threshold.** Under Canadian GAAP, a contingent liability is recognized when it is likely that a future event will confirm a liability has been incurred and the amount of the loss can be reasonably estimated. Under IFRS, a provision is recognized when there is a present obligation, it is more likely than not that an outflow of resources will be required to settle the obligation and a reliable estimate can be made of the amount of the obligation. This could potentially lead to situations where a provision may be recognized under IFRS, but was not previously recognized under Canadian GAAP.

- **Amount to be accrued.** When measuring provisions, Canadian GAAP allows issuers to accrue provisions at the low end of the range of estimates when no outcome is more likely than the others. Under IFRS, the mid-point of the range is used to measure the provision when each outcome in a range is as likely as any other. This could potentially lead to provisions being accrued at higher amounts under IFRS.

- **Note disclosure requirement.** IFRS disclosure requirements of provisions and contingent liabilities will be significant compared to current Canadian GAAP disclosure requirements. Under IFRS, issuers will be required to disclose a provision continuity schedule for each class of provision, disclosing the beginning and ending carrying amounts, additional provisions made in the period, amounts used in the period, unused amounts reversed during the period and changes resulting from the passage of time and any revisions to the discount rate. Issuers will also have to disclose a description of the nature of the obligation, the expected timing of any resulting outflows of economic benefits and an indication of the uncertainties about the amount or timing of those outflows and where necessary, they will have to disclose the major assumptions made concerning future events.

2.5 — Forward-looking information requirements

Forward-looking information (FLI) is defined in securities legislation to include disclosure regarding possible events, conditions or results of operations that is based on assumptions about future economic conditions and courses of action. It includes future oriented financial information (FOFI) with respect to prospective results of operations, financial position or cash flows that is presented either as a forecast or a projection.

There are disclosure requirements regarding FLI in Part 4A and regarding FOFI and financial outlooks in Part 4B of NI 51-102. These requirements apply to CD documents (subject to certain exceptions as set out in NI 51-102), voluntary reports and websites, but do not apply to oral statements.

Comments

Some issuers disclose goals or targets regarding environmental matters in their CD documents, in voluntary reports or on their websites. Examples include:

- The issuer plans to reduce its greenhouse gas emissions by X by 20XX.
- The issuer's goal is to reduce its water usage by x% by 20XX. This reduction may lead to an increase in expenses by $X in the short-term as alternative production methods are developed.

These disclosed targets or goals may or may not be labelled as a "target", "goal", "forecast" or "projection".

In considering whether these disclosed goals and targets can be FLI, the issuer should make the following assessments:

- Is the target or goal "possible" to achieve based on assumptions about future economic conditions and courses of actions?
- If yes, is the target or goal material information?

If the target or goal is material information, the document containing the target or goal must comply with the FLI requirements in Part 4A of NI 51-102. If the disclosed target or goal also is FOFI or a financial outlook, the document must comply with the FOFI requirements in Part 4B of NI 51-102.

Additional guidance regarding these requirements is set out in CSA Staff Notice 51-330 *Guidance Regarding the Application of Forward-Looking Information Requirements under NI 51-102 Continuous Disclosure Obligations.* Issuers and their directors and officers also should refer to policies and other statements regarding defence for misrepresentations in FLI, such as OSC Policy 51-604 *Defence for Misrepresentations in Forward-Looking Information.*

Impact of adoption of IFRS

Where these goals and targets are FOFI or financial outlooks, they must be based on the accounting policies that the issuer expects to use to prepare its historical financial statements for the period covered by the FOFI or the financial outlooks. In light of the changeover to IFRS, where an issuer provides FOFI or financial outlooks for periods that extend into 2011 and beyond, the impact of the conversion to IFRS should be considered.

3. — Governance Structures Around Environmental Disclosure

3.1 — Review, approval and certification of disclosure

An issuer's environmental disclosure in CD documents is subject to three levels of oversight: review by the audit committee, approval by the board of directors and certification by the CEO and CFO.

Persons responsible	Oversight function
Audit committee review	Under NI 52-110, an audit committee is required to review an issuer's financial statements and MD&A before the issuer publicly discloses this information.
Board approval	Under NI 51-102, the board must approve the annual and interim financial statements and MD&A. The board may delegate approval of interim financial statements and MD&A to its audit committee.
CEO and CFO certification	NI 52-109 requires certifying officers to certify, among other things, that the issuer's financial statements and the other financial information included in the issuer's MD&A and AIF, if applicable, fairly present, in all material respects, the issuer's financial condition, results of operations and cash flows.

Comments

In our view, meaningful discussion of material environmental matters, where applicable, in an issuer's MD&A and AIF is important to achieve fair presentation of the issuer's financial condition in all material respects and for CEOs and CFOs to be able to certify that the issuer's filings do not contain any misrepresentations.

In fulfilling their oversight functions relating to environmental disclosure, audit committees, boards and certifying officers should consider:

- what environmental matters are reasonably likely to impact the issuer's business and operations in the foreseeable future

- what are the magnitude, sources and nature of the issuer's current and anticipated environmental risks and liabilities

- what has been, and is likely to be, the impact of environmental matters on revenues, expenditures and cash flows

- what impact, if any, could environmental matters have on the issuer's financial condition and liquidity, and

- what assessment has management made regarding the materiality to investors about the information on environmental matters, and are the disclosures made in the financial statements, MD&A and AIF consistent with this assessment.

3.2 — Controls and procedures

To support the review, approval and certification process, an issuer must have adequate controls and procedures in place to provide rigour around its disclosure of environmental matters. Both the audit committee and certifying officers have responsibilities in establishing these underlying controls and procedures.

Persons responsible	Controls and procedures
Audit committee responsibilities	Under NI 52-110, the audit committee must be satisfied that adequate procedures are in place for the review of the issuer's public disclosure of financial information extracted or derived from the issuer's financial statements (other than the issuer's financial statements, MD&A and annual and interim earnings press releases), and must periodically assess the adequacy of those procedures.
Disclosure controls and procedures	Under NI 52-109, certifying officers of TSX-listed issuers must certify that they are responsible for establishing and maintaining:

- disclosure controls and procedures, and
- internal control over financial reporting.

In addition, certifying officers of TSX-listed issuers must certify that they have:

- subject to disclosed limitations, designed these controls and procedures, or caused them to be designed, and
- evaluated their effectiveness, or caused them to be evaluated under their supervision.

Comments

Directors and certifying officers need to know that management has implemented systems, procedures and controls to gather reliable and timely environmental information for both management analysis and decision-making purposes and disclosure to investors, regulators and other stakeholders. Consideration should also be given to whether the information about environmental matters is subject to the same governance processes and controls and procedures as financial reporting.

The establishment of appropriate data collection and reporting systems, and related controls and procedures, requires a decision on the part of management and dedication of appropriate resources. Some issuers have invested significantly in establishing reliable measurement and reporting systems related to environmental information, but as yet many have not. The reliability of these systems and controls is a necessary underpinning for securities regulatory filings, including CEO and CFO certifications under NI 52-109.

3.3 — Integration of financial and voluntary reporting

Some issuers choose to provide information regarding environmental matters in voluntary reports[7], in responses to surveys[8] and on their websites. Voluntary reporting can provide important information to investors outside of issuers' CD documents.

Completeness of CD documents

Issuers should be aware that some of the information they may be reporting pursuant to these voluntary mechanisms also may be required to be disclosed in their CD documents if that information is material under securities legislation. It is not sufficient for issuers to discuss material environmental matters required by securities legislation solely on their website, or in voluntary reports and responses to surveys.

Reliability of voluntary reporting

Issuers should ensure that their websites, voluntary reports and responses to surveys do not contain any misrepresentations. While these documents and other written communications are not required to be filed with the securities regulatory authorities, they may be subject to the provisions under securities legislation regarding FLI and civil liability for secondary market disclosure. In addition, issuers should ensure that the disclosure in these documents and on their websites is consistent with the disclosure in their CD documents.

Guidance for board and management on voluntary reports

Boards should ask questions such as:

- What assessment has management made of the materiality to investors of information about environmental matters? Are disclosures made in CD documents consistent with this assessment?

- Is the material information in voluntary reports also disclosed on a timely basis in securities regulatory filings?

- How has management ensured that information reported on corporate websites or in voluntary reports is consistent with that provided in their CD documents?

- Does any FLI in the voluntary reports comply with FLI requirements under securities legislation?

4. — Conclusion

Issuers should consider the guidance in this notice when preparing their CD documents to ensure that their disclosure of environmental matters complies with securities legislation and provides investors with meaningful information for making investment decisions. We will continue to monitor disclosure of environmental matters as part of our ongoing CD review program.

Appendix Examples of Entity-Specific Disclosure

Introduction

To assist issuers in meeting the existing disclosure requirements relating to environmental matters, we have provided some examples of entity-specific disclosure. The examples are for illustration purposes only and are based on assumed facts. They should not be viewed as an exhaustive list of environmental matters required to be disclosed, nor are they applicable to all issuers or comprehensive in all cases. The examples assume that the information disclosed is material in the particular case.

Issuers are reminded that their disclosure should be tailored to their particular circumstances, and that their CD documents must comply with all applicable disclosure requirements.

The examples of entity-specific disclosure are set out under the following headings:

- environmental risks

---

[7]Voluntary reports can be prepared in accordance with a number of sustainability reporting frameworks, such as the framework developed by the Global Reporting Initiative (GRI). The GRI framework sets out the principles and indicators that issuers can use to measure and report their economic, environmental and social performance.

[8]One example of a survey is the questionnaire requesting carbon and climate change information circulated by the Carbon Disclosure Project (CDP) to large issuers. CDP is an investor coalition that includes 534 signatory investors with assets under management of US$64 trillion. CDP's request for information covers management's views on the risks and opportunities related to climate change, greenhouse gas emissions accounting, management's strategy to reduce emissions/minimize risk and capitalize on opportunity, and corporate governance with regard to climate change.

Part 5: ONGOING REQUIREMENTS

- trends and uncertainties
- environmental liabilities
- asset retirement obligations
- financial and operational effects of environmental protection requirements
- environmental policies fundamental to operations, and
- board mandate and committees.

Forward-looking information

Some of the examples below contain forward-looking information, future oriented financial information and financial outlooks. Refer to section 2.5 of the notice and CSA Staff Notice 51-330 *Guidance Regarding the Application of Forward-Looking Information Requirements under NI 51-102 Continuous Disclosure Obligations* for guidance on the applicable disclosure requirements.

Environmental risks

Example 1 — Litigation risk

The company is currently subject to litigation regarding environmental matters, and may be involved in disputes regarding environmental matters which may result in litigation. The results of litigation cannot be predicted. If the company is not able to resolve the litigation and disputes favourably, there may be a material adverse impact on its financial condition, cash flows and results of operations.

Below is a summary of potentially material environmental litigation to which the company is a party.

[Insert name of advanced civil litigation matter]

As noted below, the company has recorded a provision in respect of [insert name of advanced litigation]. Please see the discussion under x for more information [see Example 1 for Environmental Liabilities].

[Insert name of early stage civil litigation matter]

The company has been named as a defendant in an action filed in Province X, where the plaintiffs have alleged that the company's operations have contaminated the local water supply, resulting in health and economic damages to local fisheries. The statement of claim seeks damages in the amount of $x and punitive damages in the amount of $x. The company filed a statement of defence on x, 20xx. It believes this action lacks legal or factual merit and intends to vigorously defend this action. No amounts have been accrued in the financial statements for any potential loss under this action.

No trial date has been set at this time. While the company believes the action is without merit, an adverse outcome could result in payment of significant damages or penalties and significant capital expenditures which cannot be determined at this time. Defence costs associated with the action could also be significant, and may not be completely covered by the company's insurance. These payments or expenditures could significantly affect the company's financial condition, cash flows and results of operations.

[Insert name of regulatory proceeding]

On x, 20xx, the government in Province X charged the company under Act X, which includes the following prohibition: X. The charge was laid under section x of Act X. The Crown alleged that the company's operations damaged the environmental habitat of wildlife.

The trial commenced on x and is ongoing. The company has pleaded not guilty and plans to continue to vigorously defend the action over the course of the trial, which is scheduled to conclude in x, 20xx. At this stage, the company continues to believe that it is not in violation of the requirements of Act X.

The charges brought could have significant consequences for the company because it questions the legality of certain aspects of the company's operations, and may expose the company to civil lawsuits and uncertainty regarding its operations.

At this stage, the likelihood of a guilty verdict and the materiality of a conviction are not reasonably determinable. As a result, no amounts have been accrued in the company's financial statements in respect of this action. If the company is found guilty, the penalties range from $x to $x under Act X.

Except as noted above, the issuer is not aware of any environmental litigation outstanding, threatened or pending against it as of the date hereof that would be material to its financial condition, cash flows and results of operations.

Example 2 — Physical risk

The company's supply chain is based on agricultural commodities produced in Countries X, Y and Z. In particular, product X is a key component of the company's business. Sales of product X represent x% of the company's total revenues in its most recently completed financial year. Forty-five percent of the company's supply of product X is grown in Country X.

Country X is highly susceptible to hurricanes and other extreme weather events. In x of the last x years, Country X has experienced hurricanes that have resulted in significant damages to its crops of product x.

Extreme weather events, such as hurricanes, can impact the overall availability and quality of product X. This in turn may impact:

- the company's ability to buy sufficient quantities of product X, or

• the price the company pays for product X.

Any interruptions to the company's supply of product X or changes in the price that the company pays for product X could lower the company's revenues, increase its operating costs and impact its overall financial results. For example, the company currently estimates that a 1% increase in the price of product X will lead to an increase in the company's costs by $x. During 20xx, the company's costs associated with product X increased by x% in the x months following Hurricane X in Country X. This led to a corresponding decrease in the company's revenues, as it was not able to fully recover the increase in its costs through higher sales revenues.

Example 3 — Regulatory risk

The company is subject to a variety of environmental and land use laws and regulations in Provinces X and Y, as well as the laws and regulations of the Canadian federal government. These laws and regulations mandate, among other things:

• the maintenance of air and water quality standards

• land reclamation

• regulation of greenhouse gas (GHG) emissions, and

• energy efficiency standards.

The laws and regulations require the company to obtain various environmental registrations, licenses, permits, inspections and other approvals in order to operate. They impose certain standards and controls on the company's activities.

The company operates x number of manufacturing facilities in Provinces X and Y. X per cent of these facilities emit more than 25,000 tonnes of carbon, and x% of these facilities emit more than 50,000 tonnes of carbon. The following is a discussion of GHG regulation that has, or the company anticipates will have, a significant impact on its operations.

Current regulation in Province X

In Province X, the government has announced Act X, which imposes GHG emissions limits on facilities emitting greater than x tonnes of carbon dioxide equivalent per year. Act X calls for emission reductions of x% beginning in 20xx. The company must file compliance reports that describe the actions the company took during the year to meet its emissions target for the year. To date, the company is in compliance with all GHG emission reductions required under Act X and compliance with these requirements has not had a material effect on the company's financial condition, cash flows and results of operations. The company anticipates that the future costs associated with compliance with Act X to be incurred through 20xx will be in the range of $x to $x, which includes $x spent to date. In planning its activities, the company has assumed a carbon price of $x, and has conducted scenario analysis based on carbon prices within the range of $x to $x.

Future regulation contemplated

In addition to the requirements of Act X, the company's facilities and operations will be subject to future changes to environmental legislation at the provincial and federal levels. The company expects the imposition of additional regulations, including X legislation for air pollution and further GHG regulations. The following discussion is a summary of anticipated future developments to environmental legislation that are expected to have a significant impact on the company.

In 20xx, Province Y joined the X Climate Initiative, committing to implement a GHG emissions or cap-and-trade regime by 20xx. In 20xx, Regulation Y was enacted under the Environmental Act Y in Province Y. Regulation Y requires facilities that emit x tonnes of carbon dioxide equivalent or more per year to monitor, measure and report emissions on an annual basis. The purpose of Regulation Y is to support the implementation in Province Y of a cap-and-trade system for emissions trading. Province Y will continue to work with the Canadian federal government and other members of the X Climate Initiative to harmonize emissions reporting requirements. In the event that Province Y establishes a cap-and-trade system, the company may need to purchase GHG allowances via auction to offset the amount of GHG they will emit into the atmosphere. The company currently does not believe that its operations will be adversely affected by Regulation Y.

The company is currently developing and implementing GHG emissions reduction programs to both reduce GHG emissions and generate GHG emissions reduction credits or offsets for use by the company. The company is committed to reducing GHG emissions within a range of x% to x% from 20xx to 20xx.[1] There is no guarantee that the company will be successful in developing and implementing these programs, and it is too early to predict the exact costs of compliance.

There is uncertainty around the impact of environmental laws and regulations, including those currently in force and proposed laws and regulations. It is not possible to predict the outcome and nature of certain of these requirements on the company and its business at the current time. However, failure to comply with current and proposed regulations can have a material adverse impact on the company's business and results of operations by substantially increasing its capital expenditures and compliance costs, its ability to meet its financial obligations, including debt payments and the payment of dividends. It may also lead to the modification or cancellation of operating licenses and permits, penalties and other corrective actions.

Example 4 — Regulatory risk

The company manufactures chemical x at Facility X in Country X. Chemical x is used in the production of chemical y, which is manufactured at the company's Facility Y in Country Y. The company plans to expand its production of chemical y, which requires an increase in the production of chemical x and an expansion to Facility X and Facility Y. Pending regulatory approval, the company expects the expansions to

---

[1]This target constitutes forward-looking information. See the introduction above for guidance on the applicable disclosure requirements.

Facility X and Facility Y to become operational in 20xx. The increased production of chemical y is expected to generate earnings before interest, taxes, depreciation and amortization of approximately $x to $x in the first fiscal year that the expansions to Facility X and Facility Y become operational.

The company has filed the necessary regulatory applications in Countries X and Y for approval to construct and operate the expansions to Facility X and Facility Y. In January 20xx, the company was granted approval from Authority X in Country X to construct and operate the expansion to Facility X. The company expects a decision on its application for the necessary permits from Authority Y in Country Y regarding the expansion of Facility Y in the next x months.

There is a significant risk that regulatory approval for the extension of Facility Y will not be granted or will be significantly delayed by Authority Y in Country Y. In recent months, environmental groups and prominent politicians in Country Y have publicly opposed the expansion of Facility Y due to its location beside public water sources and have called on Authority Y and the government of Country Y to re-examine the potential impact of chemical production on the environment generally. A number of environmental, public health and indigenous activists, as well as landowners whose property are located adjacent to the water sources, have organized large protests outside government offices in Country Y. If regulatory approval for the expansion of Facility Y is not granted by Authority Y, the company will not be able to increase the total commercial capacity of Facility Y or recover the capital cost of the extensions to Facility X and Facility Y ($x has been spent to date), which could have a material adverse impact on the financial results of the company.

Example 5 — Reputational risk

The company faces strong competition in the retail industry. The industry is driven primarily by consumer demand, which is impacted by matters such as economic trends, changing demographics and environmental awareness. A recent consumer trend that is dominating the industry is an increasing demand that retailers source products in a way that demonstrates care for the environment, and otherwise follow environmentally responsible business practices.

The company endeavours to be environmentally responsible and recognizes that the competitive pressures for economic growth and cost efficiency must be integrated with sound sustainability management, including environmental stewardship. The company has adopted sourcing and other business practices to address the environmental concerns of its customers. Despite these efforts, evolving customer concerns could negatively affect the company's reputation and financial performance.

The company's brand image is driven by the development and delivery of high quality products while maintaining the highest level of environmental responsibility. Claims of environmentally irresponsible practices could harm the reputation of the company.

The company establishes and monitors compliance with operating guidelines both internally and for the company's independent suppliers. These guidelines require environmentally responsible business practices, including x, x and x. Although the company requires its suppliers to certify compliance with these guidelines and periodically requests documentation in support of the certificates, there is no guarantee that these suppliers will not take actions that hurt the company's reputation, as they are independent third parties that the company does not control. However, if there is a lack of apparent compliance, it may lead the company to search for alternative suppliers. This may have an adverse effect on the company's financial results, by increasing costs, potentially causing shortages in products, delays in delivery or other disruptions in operations.

Adverse publicity resulting from actual or perceived violations of environmental laws and regulations, from business practices considered environmentally irresponsible, or from damage to the environmental reputation of the company's suppliers, may weaken the value of the company's brand image, negatively impact customer attitudes and decrease demand for the company's products. This may lead to a decrease in results of operations and the company's share price. These impacts may occur even if the allegations are not directed against the company or are not valid, and even if the company is not found liable. Other companies in the industry have encountered these issues, resulting in reduced demand for, or boycotts of, their products.

Example 6 — Risks relating to business model

Wind energy products are at an early stage of market acceptance and have been developed through technologies that may not be proven or whose commercial application is limited. The company's products may not gain sufficient commercial acceptance or success for the company's business plan to succeed. The alternative power market is also highly competitive and characterized by rapidly evolving technology and changes in pricing strategy. If the company fails to continually improve and refine its technology, the company's products could become uncompetitive or obsolete. There is also the risk that the company's competitors could attempt to reverse engineer or copy the company's product, which could draw business away from the company.

The company's business is dependant on the availability of government subsidies and incentives to support the development of the wind energy market. The cost of wind, solar and other alternative power currently exceeds retail electric rates in many jurisdictions. As a result, governments in Countries X, Y and Z have provided subsidies and incentives in the form of rebates, tax credits and other incentives to end-users, distributors, system integrators and manufacturers of alternative power products to promote the use of renewable energy sources. There is significant uncertainty about the extent to which such favourable government subsidies and incentives will be available to the company in the future. The reduction, expiration or elimination of these government subsidies and incentives could result in lower revenues and greater expenses for the company, which could have a material adverse effect on the company's business.

The company's electricity generation levels are directly dependent on wind intensity and duration, both of which vary relative to facility location and time of year. Due to climate change, wind regimes may change within regions where turbines are located, which in the longer term could affect changes in electricity generation capacity. This may lead to volatility in production levels and profitability.

Demand for wind energy technology may be affected by the following factors:

- the performance, reliability and cost-effectiveness of wind energy technology compared to conventional energy sources and products

- the success of other renewable energy generation technologies (e.g. geothermal and solar)

- fluctuations in capital expenditures by utilities and independent power producers
- the development of new and profitable applications requiring the remote electric power provided by wind energy systems, and
- overall growth in the renewable energy market.

Trends and uncertainties

Example

The company is unable to predict market conditions and the fares the company may be able to charge. . . Factors that may reduce demand for air travel include concerns about the environmental impacts of air travel and a growing movement towards "green" travel initiatives where consumers reduce their air travel.

The company operates in various jurisdictions where there are legislative initiatives relating to greenhouse gas (GHG) emissions being considered or adopted. Jurisdictions that have proposed to regulate GHG emissions include Countries X, Y and Z. Although these jurisdictions have not yet published details of their proposed regulations or their compliance mechanisms, the company will likely face increased capital and operating costs to comply with these regulations and these costs could be material. Notwithstanding the current regulatory uncertainty in these jurisdictions, the company has assumed a carbon price of $x, and has conducted scenario analysis based on carbon prices within the range of $x to $x. The company has incorporated a range of potential carbon prices and regulatory outcomes into future capital planning.

While there is no GHG emissions legislation in place in Country X, the company is a signatory to a voluntary agreement with the government of Country X to reduce GHG emissions. Under the voluntary agreement, the company is committed to a fuel efficiency improvement target of x% from 19xx levels by 20xx. The company has surpassed this fuel efficiency target and in 20xx, set its own new target to improve the fuel efficiency of its fleet operations by a further x% from 20xx to 20xx.[1] In 20xx, this program reduced emission by x tonnes compared to what the company would have otherwise consumed.

Environmental liabilities

Example 1 — Environmental estimates reflected in financial statements

The company is subject to environmental laws and regulations that affect aspects of the company's past, present and future operations, including air emissions, water quality, wastewater discharges and the generation, transport and disposal of waste and hazardous substances. The company's activities have the potential to impair natural habitat, damage plant and wildlife, or cause contamination to land or water that may require remediation under applicable laws and regulations. These laws and regulations require the company to obtain and comply with a variety of environmental registrations, licenses, permits and other approvals. Both public officials and private individuals may seek to enforce environmental laws and regulations against the company.

Environmental liabilities are recorded when it is considered likely that a liability has been incurred at the date of the financial statements and the amount of the liability can be reasonably estimated. As at December 31, 20xx, the company had a provision of $x million for environmental, remedial and similar obligations. The primary component of this provision was an amount for a legal action brought in Country X against the company and other defendants for damage to the environment. The plaintiffs, who are residents of lands surrounding one of the company's former facilities, are seeking damages of $x million for wrongful death claims and to fund environmental remediation of the alleged environmental harm.

An expert appointed by the court in Country X to assess and determine the cause of the environmental damage released a report recommending that the court assess damages of $x million against the company. The court is expected to render a judgment within the next x months. The company intends to vigorously defend any attempted imposition of liability.

In estimating the amount to be included in the provision for the legal action in Country X, the company conducted an assessment of the possible outcomes and range of loss, based on considerations such as the company's past experiences with environmental lawsuits and the recommendations of legal counsel. The estimate is based on the following assumptions:

- the court will find against the issuer
- the court will award damages of x% of the total amount claimed
- the court will not award punitive damages, and
- the proportionate liability of the company is x% of the claim.

The company also estimated the costs of remediation based on an assessment of the existing remediation technology available. However, although the company expects to incur a liability of $x million (as reflected in the line item "environmental, remedial and similar obligations" in the 20xx financial statements), the actual liability remains highly uncertain and can vary from the company's estimate due to factors such as:

- differing interpretations of laws, opinions on culpability and assessments on the amount of damages
- the length and outcome of the appeal process (in the event of an adverse judgment)
- the unknown timing and extent of the remediation and other corrective actions that may be required, and

---

[1]This target constitutes forward-looking information. See the introduction above for guidance on the applicable disclosure requirements.

- the determination of the company's liability in proportion to other responsible parties and the extent to which such costs are recoverable from third parties.

The estimated liability will be regularly adjusted as the case proceeds. As a result of recommendations from legal counsel, the estimated amount of the liability has increased by $x million since the last financial statements were issued.

Example 2 — Potential environmental liabilities not reflected in financial statements

The company may be subject to remedial environmental and litigation costs resulting from potential unknown and unforeseeable environmental impacts arising from the company's operations. While these costs have not been material to the company in the past, there is no guarantee that this will continue to be the case in the future as the company carries on with the development of the complex technologies necessary to differentiate the company from its competitors and meet market demand.

Given the nature of the company's business, there are inherent risks of oil spills occurring at the company's drilling sites. Large spills of oil and oil products can result in significant clean-up costs. Oil spills can occur from operational issues, such as operational failure, accidents and deterioration and malfunctioning of equipment. In certain countries where the company operates, oil spills can also occur as a result of sabotage and damage to the pipelines. If the company experiences operational spills, this may impact the company's ability to maintain its licence to operate and may harm its reputation. In 20xx, the number of spills "increased/decreased" by x%, totalling a volume of x tonnes (compared to x spills totaling x tonnes in the previous year of 20xx).

Although unlikely and not estimable or quantifiable at this time, if an oil spill occurred at the company's offshore drilling rig X, potential impacts could include employee injuries and loss of life, harm to the surrounding environment and wildlife, and disruption or cessation of the company's activities. These may lead to significant potential environmental liabilities, such as clean-up and litigation costs, which may materially affect the company's financial condition, cash flows and results of operations. Depending on the cause and severity of the oil spill, the company's reputation may also be adversely affected, which could limit the company's ability to obtain permits and affect its future operations.

To prevent and/or mitigate potential environmental liabilities from occurring, the company has policies and procedures designed to prevent and contain oil spills. The company works to minimize spills through a program of well designed facilities that are safely operated, effective operations integrity management, continuous employee training, regular upgrades to facilities and equipment and implementation of a comprehensive inspection and surveillance system. The company also has a rigorously tested oil spill emergency response capability. The company plans, prepares and practices its emergency response to help effectively mitigate the environmental, operational and financial consequences of an oil spill.

Asset retirement obligations

Example

Asset retirement obligations (AROs) result from the acquisition, development, construction and ordinary operation of mining property, plant and equipment, and from environmental regulations set by regulatory authorities. AROs include costs related to tailings pond, tailings dam, heaps and heap leach pad reclamation and/or closure (i.e. ongoing monitoring of ground water quality; tailings dam and/or leach pad integrity; heap washing; closing of portals, shafts and tunnels, recontouring, revegetation etc.), and removal and/or demolition of mine and processing equipment (i.e. crushers, conveyors, mills, flotation tanks etc.), buildings and other infrastructure.

The company estimates the fair value of AROs to range between $x million and $x million. As at December 31, 20xx, the company recognized a liability of $x million for AROs. The fair value of AROs are estimated using a present value technique and is based on existing laws, contracts or other policies and current technology and conditions. The estimates or assumptions required to calculate the fair value of AROs include, among other items, abandonment and reclamation amounts, inflation rates, credit-adjusted risk free rates and timing of retirement of assets. The following significant assumptions were made for the purpose of estimating AROs:

Assumption	20xx	20xx[•]
Undiscounted abandonment costs ($$$)	x	x
Credit adjusted risk free rate	x	x
Inflation rate	x	x
Average years to reclamation	x	x

Notes:

{•}   Year-on-year comparison

AROs are considered critical accounting estimates for the company. There are significant uncertainties related to AROs and the impact on the financial statements could be material. The eventual timing of and costs for these AROs could differ from current estimates. The main factors that can cause expected cash flows to change are:

- changes to laws and legislation

- construction of new facilities

- changes in the quality of water that affect the extent of water treatment required

- change in the reserve estimate and the resulting amendment to the life of the mine, and

- changes in technology.

In general, as the life of a mine ends, the expected cash flows become more reliable but the estimate of an ARO at the beginning of the mine life, is primarily more subjective. Any future changes to the estimated or actual costs for reclamation and mine closure and for removal and/or demolition of mine and processing equipment, buildings and other infrastructure, could have a material and adverse effect on the company's future operating results.

The company does not strictly reserve cash or assets for the purpose of settling AROs. As a result, at the time of closure and restoration of the mine sites, the company will have a significant cash outlay that may affect its ability to satisfy its debt and other contractual obligations. The costs associated with the AROs may be significant and the company may not have sufficient or available resources to fund the costs. If the company is unable to make these payments, regulatory authorities may take further corrective action with respect to these obligations, including issuing clean-up orders and laying charges. Currently the company has secured its obligations under its AROs and obtained letters of credit.

The following is a breakdown of the ARO by category:

Category	20xx	20xx[•]
Open Mines	x	x
Closed Mines	x	x
Development Projects	x	x
Total AROs	x	x

Notes:

{•} Year-on-year comparison

The following is a breakdown of ARO by significant mine/property:

Mine	20xx	20xx[•]
Mine 1	x	x
Mine 2	x	x
Mine 3	x	x
Other[••]	x	x
Total AROs	x	x

Notes:

{•} Year-on-year comparison

{••} Aggregate of remaining mines determined to be insignificant on an individual basis

Summary Contractual Obligations Table

Provide asset retirement obligations for the current year and the following 5 years and thereafter.

	2010	2011	2012	2013	2014	thereafter	Total
AROsx	x	x	x	x	x	x	x

AROs — Amounts presented in the table represent the undiscounted future payments for the expected cost of asset retirement obligations.

Financial and operational effects of environmental protection requirements

Example 1

In Country X where the company operates, the company is currently obligated to comply with environmental protection Regulation X relating to water pollution and conservation. To comply with Regulation X, the company began construction of a new water treatment plant in 20xx to collect and treat contaminated water from its facilities in Country X. In 20xx, the company's aggregate expenditures (both capital and operating) to construct and maintain the new water treatment plant were $x million, compared to $x million in 20xx. The company estimates that total environmental expenditures in Country X for the next year will be approximately $x million in capital expenditures and $x in operating expenditures. If environmental protection regulations relating to water pollution and conservation in Country X change, or the enforcement of Regulation X becomes more rigorous, the company may be required to incur additional, significant capital and operating expenditures to comply, which could have a material adverse effect on the company's financial condition and competitive position.

Example 2

In Province X where the company has x facilities, contaminated sites legislation came into effect in 20xx. The legislation specifies the circumstances in which a "site profile" must be prepared in respect of any property that has been used for certain industrial or commercial purposes. A particular site is determined to be a "contaminated site" if concentrations of certain substances in soil and groundwater exceed prescribed levels. If a site is determined to be contaminated, remediation will normally be required under government supervision. The company is not aware of any of its sites being considered contaminated under the legislation, and compliance with the legislation has not resulted in any material costs to the company in 20xx. However, there is no guarantee that material costs will not be incurred in the future due to the discovery of unknown conditions or changes in enforcement policies.

Environmental policies fundamental to operations

Example

The company established an environmental policy (the Policy) in 20xx. The Policy is updated periodically and was last updated in 20xx. The Policy affirms the company's commitment to environmental protection, which the company believes is an integral part of doing business and needs to be managed systemically under a continuous improvement process. The Policy contains principles which range from exercising due diligence to meet or exceed requirements under applicable environmental legislation, to preventing pollution and promoting initiatives that minimize resource use and waste generation. The company has instructed its subsidiaries to support these principles, and has established a management-level committee, Committee X, to oversee the implementation of the Policy.

In 20xx, the company spent $x million on environmental policy compliance (x% of this was expensed and x% was for capital expenditures). For the next fiscal year, the company has budgeted $x million (x% for expenses and x% for capital expenditures) to seek to ensure that the Policy is applied properly and its environmental risks are minimized.

Consistent with the Policy, the company regularly procures, installs and operates pollution control devices, including wastewater treatment plants, groundwater monitoring devices and air strippers or separators.

The company monitors its operations to seek to ensure that it complies with all applicable environmental requirements and standards, and takes action to prevent and correct problems if needed. The company has had an environmental management system in place since 20xx that:

- provides early warning of potential problems

- identifies management and cost-saving opportunities

- establishes a course of action, and

- ensures ongoing improvement through regular monitoring and reporting.

The company also analyzes changes to environmental laws and regulations on a regular basis. In 20xx, the company obtained the ISO 140001 certification for its environmental management system.

Board mandate and committees

Example

The Audit Committee's responsibilities include approving a formalized and integrated enterprise risk management process that is developed by senior management and, as appropriate, the company's X Committee (e.g. Environmental, Health and Safety Committee), to monitor, manage and report risks and opportunities, including those relating to environmental matters, litigation and regulation. At least semi-annually, the Audit Committee is responsible for obtaining from senior management and, as appropriate, the X Committee, a report specifying the management of the company's principal risks, including compliance with the company's enterprise risk management policy and other policies used to manage risks.

The purpose of the X Committee is to:

- review the company's environmental, health, safety and sustainable development (EHSSD) policies and programs

- assess the performance and effectiveness of the company's EHSSD policies and programs

- monitor current and future regulatory issues relating to EHSSD matters

- review quarterly management stewardship reports

- examine the findings of significant external and internal EHSSD investigations, assessments, reviews and audits

- review the company's public sustainability report, which includes reporting on the company's EHSSD progress, plans and performance objectives, and

- make recommendations, where appropriate, on significant matters relating to EHSSD matters to the Board.

The X Committee holds regular *in camera* sessions where it meets in the absence of management.

CSA Staff Notice 51-334 — Continuous Disclosure Review Program Activities for the fiscal year ended March 31, 2011

Date: July 15, 2011

34 O.S.C.B. 7763

Purpose of this Notice

Reliable and accurate information by reporting issuers is critical to strengthen investor confidence and promote efficient capital markets. CSA's continuous disclosure (CD) review program is designed to identify material disclosure deficiencies that affect the reliability and accuracy of a reporting issuer's disclosure record, and has two fundamental objectives: education and compliance. This notice:

- helps issuers understand and comply with their obligations,

- summarizes the results of the CD review program for the fiscal year ended March 31, 2011 (fiscal 2011), and

- provides examples of areas of common deficiencies.

In any given year, issuers are affected by new accounting standards and regulatory changes and these are areas that we generally emphasize in our CD review program. See *CSA Staff Notice 51-312 — (Revised) Harmonized Continuous Disclosure Review Program* for further details on the program.

Year in Review — Fiscal 2011

There are approximately 4,100 issuers in Canada, excluding investment funds and issuers that have been cease-traded. Staff of the jurisdictions of the CSA (we) use a risk based approach combined with a high level screening system to select issuers for review and to determine the type of review to conduct (full or issue-oriented). This approach allows us to address areas of particular concern. We apply both qualitative and quantitative criteria in determining the level of review required. The criteria are updated as market conditions change. We focus on accounting issues and disclosure areas where either non-compliance is probable or we foresee a need for increased compliance.

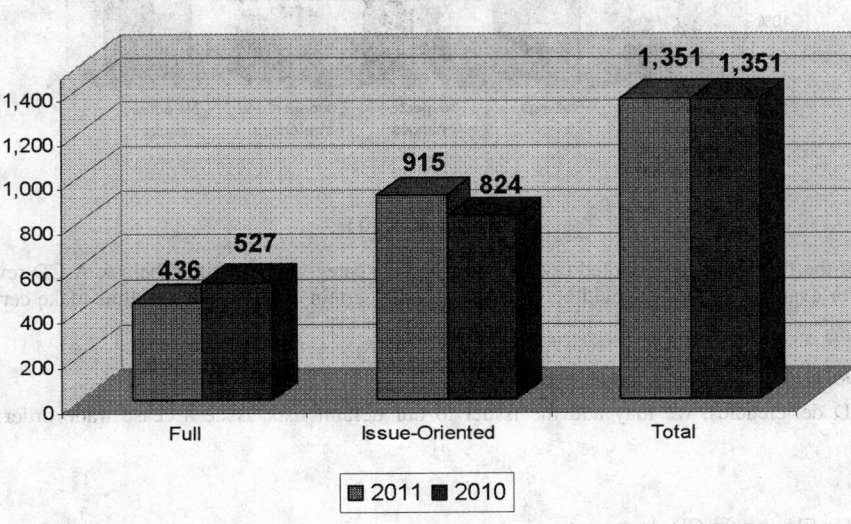

The above chart illustrates the composition of the type of reviews we conducted in fiscal 2011 compared to fiscal 2010. The number of full reviews conducted in fiscal 2011 decreased by 17% from the previous year. The number of issue-oriented reviews increased by 11%. The majority of the increase in issue-oriented reviews is a result of International Financial Reporting Standards (IFRS) transition disclosure reviews, material contract filing requirement reviews, and oil and gas technical disclosure reviews under *National Instrument 51-101 Standards of Disclosure for Oil and Gas Activities* (NI 51-101).

Outcomes for Fiscal 2011

Given our risk based approach combined with a high level screening system to the selection of issuers, we generally select issuers at higher risk of non-compliance. In 2011, 70% of issuers reviewed were required to take action to improve disclosure, compared to 72% in 2010.

In any given year, issuers are affected by new accounting standards and regulatory changes and those are areas that we generally emphasize in our CD review program. See CSA Staff Notice 51-312 — (Revised) Harmonized Continuous Disclosure Review Program for further details on the program.

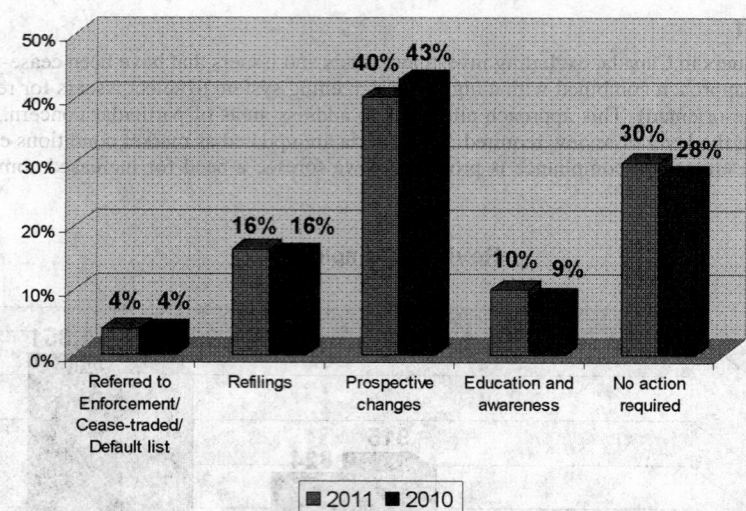

Review Outcomes 2011

We classify the outcomes of the full and issue-oriented reviews into the five categories identified below. A CD review could have more than one category of outcome. For example, an issuer could be required to refile certain documents as well as make certain changes on a prospective basis.

Enforcement referral/ Default list/ Cease trade order

If the issuer has critical CD deficiencies, we may add the issuer to our default lists, issue a cease trade order and/or refer the issuer to Enforcement.

Refiling

The issuer must amend and refile certain CD documents.

Prospective Changes

The issuer is informed that certain changes or enhancements are required in its next filing as a result of deficiencies identified.

Education and Awareness

The issuer receives a proactive letter alerting it to certain disclosure enhancements that should be considered in its next filing.

No action required

The issuer does not need to make any changes or additional filings.

Full Reviews

A full review is broad in scope and covers many types of disclosure. A full review covers the issuer's most recent annual and interim financial statements, Management Discussion and Analysis (MD&A), and other disclosure documents such as:

- technical disclosure, including technical reports for oil and gas, and mining issuers;

- annual information forms (AIF);

- annual reports;

- information circulars;

- press releases, material change reports and business acquisition reports (BARs);

- website;

- CFO and CEO certifications; and

- material contracts.

Issue-Oriented Reviews

An issue-oriented review is an in-depth review focusing on a specific accounting, legal or regulatory issue that we believe warrants regulatory scrutiny. The nature of the issue or issues identified determines the periods we will review.

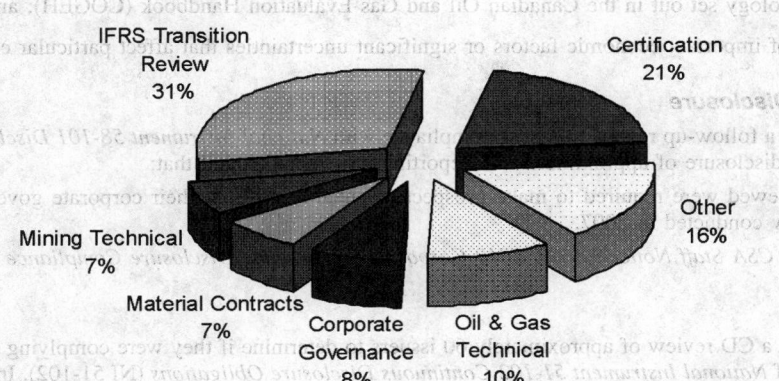

Issue-Oriented Reviews 2011

- IFRS Transition Review 31%
- Certification 21%
- Mining Technical 7%
- Material Contracts 7%
- Corporate Governance 8%
- Oil & Gas Technical 10%
- Other 16%

Of the 1,351 reviews that were completed in fiscal 2011, 68% of the reviews (as compared to 61% of the reviews last year) were issue-oriented reviews completed either as a CSA coordinated initiative or by local jurisdictions. Some jurisdictions did not conduct certain issue-oriented reviews but incorporated specific procedures in their full reviews to address topics or concerns identified in the issue-oriented reviews. The following issue-oriented reviews were completed this year by one or more of the jurisdictions:

IFRS Transition Disclosure

We conducted a review to assess the extent and quality of IFRS transition disclosure made by issuers in 2009 annual MD&A. We compared the disclosure of 196 issuers to the disclosure guidance provided in *CSA Staff Notice 52-320 Disclosure of Expected Accounting Policies Related to the Changeover to International Financial Reporting Standards* (SN 52-320). Based on the expectations of SN 52-320, 2009 annual MD&A should have provided a progress update to the issuer's changeover plan and a description of the identified accounting policy differences between the issuer's current Canadian GAAP financial statements and the IFRS policies they intended to adopt after transition. Sufficient IFRS transition disclosure would reduce investor uncertainty about transition readiness and inform users of the potential for volatility in future reported results.

Our review found that:

- 60% of issuers provided details of the key elements of their IFRS changeover plan;

- 82% of issuers provided a description of the identified accounting policy differences between the issuer's current Canadian GAAP financial statements and the IFRS policies they intend to adopt after transition; and

- issuers discussed their changeover plans and identified accounting policy differences but the discussion was often generic and did not provide the specific anticipated impact to the issuer's own financial statements and operations.

For additional reference, see *CSA Staff Notice 52-326 IFRS Transition Disclosure Review*.

Certification

During fiscal 2011 we conducted a follow-up review of issuers to evaluate the level of improvement in compliance with the provisions of *National Instrument 52-109 Certification of Disclosure in Issuers' Annual and Interim Filings (NI 52-109)*. The fiscal 2011 review included the review of issuers identified in the previous fiscal year's review as not fully compliant and included the review of issuers that re-filed financial statements to correct accounting errors. Staff also reviewed the MD&A disclosure relating to the impact of the IFRS on Internal Control over Financial Reporting (ICFR) and Disclosure Control and Procedures (DC&P). The results of the fiscal 2011 review indicated moderate improvement in the level of issuers' compliance as compared to the results of the previous fiscal year's review. For the fiscal 2011 review, 22% of issuers reviewed were required to re-file their MD&A and/or the certificates compare to 30% of issuers in the previous fiscal year review. Common issues identified during this year's review include the following:

- issuers did not disclose or did not fully disclose the certifying officers' conclusion about the effectiveness of ICFR or DC&P in their MD&A or they qualified the conclusions;

- the wording on forms were amended; and

- venture issuers that filed basic certificates voluntarily discussed ICFR or DC&P in their annual MD&A but did not include cautionary language as discussed in part 15.3 of Companion Policy NI 52-109CP.

For additional reference, see *CSA Staff Notice 52-327 Certification Compliance Update*.

Oil and Gas Technical Disclosure

We conducted reviews on issuers engaged in oil and gas activities to assess compliance with requirements set out in NI 51-101. While there was general compliance among issuers, common issues identified include:

- Omitting some of the information required under Form 51-101F1 and disclosing units inconsistently throughout the oil and gas disclosure;

- Improper use of terminology set out in the Canadian Oil and Gas Evaluation Handbook (COGEH); and

- Boilerplate disclosure of important economic factors or significant uncertainties that affect particular components of the reserves data.

Corporate Governance Disclosure

In fiscal 2011, we conducted a follow-up review to assess compliance with *National Instrument 58-101 Disclosure of Corporate Governance Practices*. We reviewed the disclosure of approximately 75 reporting issuers and found that:

- 55% of the issuers reviewed were required to make prospective enhancements to their corporate governance disclosure, compared to 36% in a similar review conducted in 2007.

For additional reference, see *CSA Staff Notice 58-306 2010 Corporate Governance Disclosure Compliance Review*.

Material Contracts

In fiscal 2011, we completed a CD review of approximately 60 issuers to determine if they were complying with the material contract filing requirements under Part 12 of *National Instrument 51-102 Continuous Disclosure Obligations* (NI 51-102). In 2008, significant changes were made to the filing requirements of material contracts. Prior to the changes, issuers were not required to file material contracts if they were entered into in the ordinary course of business. The changes do not permit the ordinary course exclusion in certain circumstances. Generally these are situations where it is determined the contract is important to understanding the issuer's business. There were also limits placed upon redaction of material contracts, where previously an issuer could redact any portion of the contract that an executive officer felt would be seriously prejudicial to the interests of the issuer or would violate confidentiality provisions. If the terms and conditions of the contract are necessary for understanding the impact of the material contract on the business of the issuer omission or redaction is not permitted.

Our review found that:

- 16% of issuers reviewed were required to file missing material contracts

- 3% of issuers reviewed were required to revise redacted provisions to comply with our requirements

Issuers should carefully consider the material contract filing rules in NI 51-102 and the related companion policy guidance. In particular, issuers should be aware that they must continually assess whether or not a given contract is material. For example, a contract that was not previously material to an issuer may become material if, due to changes in the issuer's business or other contracts, the issuer becomes substantially dependent on that contract.

Mining Technical Disclosure

Issue-oriented reviews are regularly conducted on mining technical disclosure. The following problem areas remain consistent with prior years:

- the name of the qualified person was not always included in documents containing scientific and technical information;

- required disclosure for historical estimates, such as the source and date of the estimate was not included;

- certificates or consents for the qualified person were not included; and

- corporate presentations or other content on the website did not comply with *National Instrument 43-101 Standards of Disclosure for Mineral Projects*.

Other

- **Press Releases**

 Press releases, websites, corporate presentations and other promotional materials are regularly reviewed to assess compliance with NI 51-101 and COGEH disclosure requirements, and Forward-Looking Information (FLI) requirements in NI 51-102. Press releases are also reviewed to assess compliance with section 11.5 of NI 51-102 announcing a refiling or restatement (11.5 Press Release). Common issues identified include:

 - non-compliant reserve and resource classification and disclosure;

 - non-compliant use of oil and gas terminology;

 - failure to file an 11.5 Press Release in a timely manner; and

- the common issues relating to FLI requirements identified in *CSA Staff Notice 51-330 Guidance Regarding the Application of Forward-Looking Information Requirements under NI 51-102 Continuous Disclosure Obligations* (SN 51-330).

- **Complaints**

  Staff followed up on complaints referred by other areas of our respective Commissions. Complaints were also received from investors and other external stakeholders regarding specific disclosure issues. Generally, issue-oriented reviews were conducted to consider the issues raised and assess the potential impact to investors. In some circumstances, such complaints lead to further action being taken against an issuer.

Common Deficiencies Identified

Our reviews continue to focus on identifying material deficiencies and disclosure enhancements. To help issuers better understand their disclosure obligations we have provided guidance and examples of common deficiencies in the following appendices:

Appendix A: MD&A Deficiencies
1. Non-GAAP Financial Measures
2. Forward-Looking Information
3. Discussion of Operations
4. Liquidity
5. Fourth Quarter and Quarterly Discussion
6. Venture Issuer

Appendix B: Financial Statements Deficiencies
1. Inventory
2. Related Party Transactions

Appendix C: Regulatory Compliance Deficiencies
1. Statement of Executive Compensation (Form 51-102F6)

This is not an exhaustive list of deficiencies noted in our reviews, and issuers should be reminded that their CD record must comply with all relevant securities legislation.

Areas of Focus for Fiscal Year 2012

IFRS

For fiscal 2012, our main focus will be on IFRS transition. We will continue to use a risk based approach combined with a high level screening system to determine the issuers we will select for review and the type of review required. In addition, we will continue to be responsive to any market condition changes and address particular areas of concern in a timely manner.

Results by jurisdiction

The Alberta Securities Commission, the Ontario Securities Commission and the Autorité des marchés financiers publish reports summarizing the results of the CD review program in their jurisdictions. See the individual regulator's website for a copy of its report:

- www.albertasecurities.com
- www.osc.gov.on.ca
- www.lautorite.qc.ca

Appendix A — MD&A Deficiencies

The quality of MD&A disclosure continues to be an area where we see deficiencies. MD&A is a narrative explanation through the eyes of management of how the issuer performed during the period covered by the financial statements, and what the issuer's financial condition and future prospects are. We often find boilerplate disclosure that does not change from period to period. Issuers frequently replicate disclosure from the financial statements without any analysis. Entity-specific disclosure provides investors with information that complements the financial statements so they are able to assess the current financial condition of the issuer and its future prospects.

There are six important areas where we continue to see boilerplate disclosure in the MD&A: non-GAAP financial measures, forward looking information (FLI), discussion of operations, liquidity, 4th quarter discussion, and venture issuer disclosure. For each, we have provided examples of deficient disclosure contrasted against more robust, entity-specific disclosure.

1. — Non-GAAP Financial Measures

Issuers often provide key performance measures in continuous disclosure documents. If these measures are not permitted by an issuer's GAAP they constitute non-GAAP financial measures per *CSA Staff Notice 52-306 Non-GAAP Financial Measures* (SN 52-306). Note that SN 52-306 was amended in November 2010 to reflect the changeover to IFRS.

Part 5: ONGOING REQUIREMENTS

Non-GAAP financial measures are often provided in MD&A without the additional disclosure prescribed by SN 52-306. Issuers frequently omit the following disclosure:

- an explanation of why the non-GAAP financial measure is meaningful to investors and the additional purpose, if any, for which management uses the non-GAAP financial measure; and

- a clear quantitative reconciliation from the non-GAAP financial measure to the most directly comparable measure calculated in accordance with the issuer's GAAP presented in the financial statements.

In addition, issuers are reminded of their responsibility to ensure that information provided is not misleading. Therefore, adjustments should not be described as non-recurring or unusual if they are reasonably likely to occur within the next two years or have occurred in the previous two years.

Example of deficient disclosure

Our operating income before specific items rose 31%, reaching a new peak of $101 million.

Example of entity-specific disclosure

Our profit for the fiscal year was $50 million compared to $31 million in the previous fiscal year. Operating income before specific items (OIBI) rose 31%, reaching a new peak of $101 million. OIBI of the previous fiscal year was $77 million.

OIBI is mainly derived from the consolidated financial statements but does not have any standardized meaning prescribed by Canadian GAAP. Therefore it is unlikely to be comparable to similar measures presented by other companies.

OIBI is used by management to evaluate the performance of its operations based on a comparable basis which excludes specific items that are non-recurring. When a specific item occurs in more than two consecutives fiscal years, it is no longer considered to be non-recurring by management.

We believe that a significant number of users of our MD&A analyze our results based on OIBI since it is a yearly comparable measure of the performance of the Company.

Reconciliation of OIBI to profit in thousands of dollars:

OIBI	$101	$77
Restructuring of distribution network	($6)	$0
Relocation of production	$0	($9)
Gross income as per financial statements	$95	$68
Sales and admini s trative expenses.	$23	$19
Financial expenses	$12	$9
Tax expenses	$10	$9
Profit as per financial statements	$50	$31

2. — Forward Looking Information (FLI)

Part 4A.3 of NI 51-102 sets out the disclosure requirements for FLI. Many issuers do not identify material FLI in their disclosure. Identification of material FLI is important to investors in order for them to understand that FLI is being provided. Disclosure of both the material factors or assumptions including material risk factors underlying the FLI is necessary for investors to understand that actual results may vary from FLI. Issuers continue to provide boilerplate disclosure and are reminded that the material factors or assumptions used to develop the FLI should be disclosed. Also, in light of the current transition to IFRS, issuers are reminded that Part 4B.2(2)(b) of NI 51-102 requires that FLI be based on the accounting policies that the issuer expects to use to prepare its historical financial statement for the period covered by the FLI.

Example of deficient disclosure

In order to attain its profitability objectives and ensure its continued operation, the Company must continue to increase cash flows from day-to-day operation. To do so, the Company expects sales to increase in 2011.

Example of entity-specific disclosure

In order to attain its profitability objectives and ensure its continued operation, the Company must continue to increase cash flows from day-to-day operation. To do so, the Company expects that the level of sales in 2011 will increase.

The following factors support management assessment about increase of sales:

- Economic recovery
- Seller network completed in the course of 2011
- Restructuration of some sale territories based on market sectors
- Customer development for private label.

Unknown risks and uncertainties could impact our expectation on sale increase such as, increase competition, pressure on sales prices and failure in launching new products. We will update our forward-looking statement for any adverse events that could materially impact management expectation of increase of sales.

For additional reference, see SN 51-330.

3. — Discussion of Operations

Issuers are required to analyze their operations in the most recently completed financial year, including a comparison against the previous completed financial year. The analysis should discuss and quantify all material variances. Common deficiencies include discussion of immaterial information without inclusion of information that maybe material to investors and insufficient analysis of why changes have occurred. Issuers are reminded that the MD&A should contain a balanced discussion of their operations. In the example below we highlight an element to be considered in the discussion of operations, the gross profit.

Example of Deficient Disclosure

Gross profit was $75 million, compared with $100 million the preceding year.

Example of entity-specific disclosure

Gross profit for the fiscal year ended April 30, 2010 decreased by 25 percent to $75 million from $100 million for the corresponding period last year. The first eight months of the year were marked by contract cancellations and delays due to the prevailing economic situation. The unfavourable foreign exchange translation impact on gross profit for the year, when compared to the effective rates for the same period last year, is estimated at $5 million.

Canada-U.S.

Gross profit in Canada-U.S. decreased by approximately 10 million year-over-year as competitive pressures negatively affected pricing and margins. This was offset by an increase in gross profit of approximately $2 million as a result of cost cutting measures.

South and Central America

Gross profit in this geographic segment decreased significantly due to competitive pressures on pricing and higher repair costs relating to the ramp up near year end to fulfill new contracts. The impact on gross profit of each element was approximately $7 million and $1 million respectively.

4. — Liquidity

The MD&A should identify and discuss any known or expected fluctuations and trends in an issuer's liquidity, taking into account demands, commitments, events or uncertainties. Where applicable the discussion should also include disclosure of any defaults or risk of defaults on debt covenants and how the issuer intends to cure the default or otherwise address the risk as set out in the example below. The disclosure relating to expected liquidity fluctuations is required for all issuers but it is especially important when issuers have negative cash flows from operations, a negative working capital position or have breached their debt covenants.

Example of deficient disclosure

The Company's credit facility contains certain covenants that the Company must comply with. Otherwise the amounts outstanding are payable on demand. As at December 31, 2010 the Company violated such covenants.

Example of entity-specific disclosure

The Company's share capital is not subject to any external restrictions; however its credit facility is subject to periodic reviews. The credit facility also contains certain covenants, such that the Company cannot, without prior approval of the bank, hedge or contract petroleum or natural gas volumes, on a fixed price basis, exceeding 50 per cent of production volumes, nor can it monetize or settle any fixed price financial hedge or contract. The credit facility also contains a financial covenant that requires the Company to maintain a working capital ratio of at least 1:1. As at December 31, 2010, this ratio was 0.5:1. The bank has waived the breach and has allowed the Company six months to remedy the deficiency. The Company intends to acquire additional financing through private placements to fund current working capital needs and remedy the deficiency.

5. — Fourth Quarter and Quarterly Discussion

Issuers must discuss and analyze items or events that have had a material impact in the fourth quarter. Many issuers tend to overlook this area. Some issuers file a separate fourth-quarter MD&A and use the exemption available under section 1.10 of NI 51-102F1, however do not make appropriate reference to the separate quarterly MD&A.

Example of deficient disclosure

During August 2010, the Company reactivated exploration activities, initiating a drill program on its XYZ property. Also, during the fourth quarter of fiscal 2009, the Company incurred a write-down of resource properties of $1.1 million relating to the GHI property. Operating costs, excluding property write-downs, for the quarter totalled $0.2 million and consisted primarily of management salaries, management services and non-cash stock-based compensation expense.

Example of entity-specific disclosure

The Company recorded a net loss of $400,000 in the quarter compared to a net loss of $900,000 in the prior quarter. Operating expenses increased during the quarter, which was offset by foreign exchange gains of $300,000 and a tax recovery of $700,000. The increase in operating expenses is largely attributable to an increase in advisory fees and salaries of approximately $500,000. The increase in advisory fees is related to strategic alternatives that would enable financing of the ABC Project. The increase in salaries is attributable to the advancement of the ABC Project during the quarter. The Company will continue to incur operating losses until such time as the commercial development of the ABC Project results in positive earnings.

6. — Venture Issuer Disclosure

Section 5.3 of NI 51-102 requires venture issuers that have not had significant revenue from operations to provide a breakdown of material components of capitalized or expensed exploration costs. In staff's view the description of the component should be specific enough for a reader to understand its nature. For example, the descriptor "Consultant" is not specific enough for a reader to understand the nature of the costs incurred.

Furthermore, if the venture issuer's business primarily involves mining exploration, the analysis must be presented on a property-by-property basis. In some cases we have observed that venture mining issuers have not presented the required disclosure on a property by property basis.

Appendix B — Financial Statement Deficiencies

Common problems identified within the financial statements generally relate to note disclosure and measurement issues. A clear and concise description of the significant accounting policies of an issuer is considered an integral part of their financial statements as the policies provide a roadmap to investors for understanding the financial results.

Inventory and Related Party disclosure continues to be an area where we commonly see insufficient disclosure. Discussion in these areas tends to be boilerplate. In order for investors to understand the significance to the issuer's financial condition and operations we expect issuers to provide all the required disclosure. For each area we provide examples of deficient disclosure contrasted against more robust, entity-specific disclosure.

1. — Inventory

The financial statement inventory note disclosure required by Part V of the CICA Handbook — Canadian GAAP (Pre-changeover Canadian GAAP) is now harmonized with IFRS. IFRS allows fewer alternatives for the measurement of inventories. It also permits reversal of write-downs, requires impairment testing at each reporting period, and has increased disclosure requirements. Issuers generally comply with the measurement of inventories but frequently do not provide all of the required disclosure.

Example of deficient disclosure

For the year ended December 31, 2010, the cost of sales was $1,032,485 ($984,502 in 2009). The cost of sale includes an inventory impairment reversal of $165,242 ($0 in 2009).

Paragraph 3031.36(g) of Pre-changeover Canadian GAAP and paragraph 36(f) and (g) of IAS 2 *Inventories* requires the disclosure of the circumstances or events that led to the reversal of a write-down of inventories. In the above example, the disclosure was not provided.

Example of deficient disclosure

Raw materials and finished goods are recorded at the lower of average cost and net realizable value. The cost of inventory is recognized as an expense when the inventory is sold. Previous write-downs to net realizable value are reversed if there is a subsequent increase in the value of the related inventories.

In the above example the issuer did not provide the cost formula to measure inventory as required by paragraph 3031.36(a) of Pre-changeover Canadian GAAP and paragraph 36(a) of IAS 2 *Inventories*.

Example of entity-specific disclosure

Inventories of finished products, converted products, raw materials and materials & supplies are valued at the lower of cost and net realizable value. Costs are allocated to inventory using the weighted average cost method and include direct costs related to units of production as well as a systematic allocation of fixed and variable production overhead. Net realizable value for finished products, converted products and raw materials is considered to be the selling price of the finished product in the ordinary course of business less the estimated costs of completion and estimated costs to complete the sale. In certain circumstances, particularly pertaining to the company's materials & supplies inventories, replacement cost is considered to be the best available measure of net realizable value. Inventory is reviewed monthly to ensure the carrying value does not exceed net realizable value. If carrying value does not exceed net realizable value, a write-down is recognized immediately. The write-down may be reversed in a subsequent period if the circumstances which caused it no longer exist.

---

2. — Related Party Transactions

Issuers tend to be too generic in disclosure of related party transactions. Frequently, disclosure of the nature of the transaction and description of the relationship with the related party is omitted. In addition, when issuers have significant balances owing to related parties details provided in the financial statements notes do not contain all the required disclosure.

Example of deficient disclosure

Selling and administrative expenses includes $750,000 paid to directors and officers of the Corporation. Included in professional fees is $200,000 in fees paid and accrued to directors and officers of the Corporation. The due to related parties balance of $900,000 includes amounts owing to directors and officers of the Corporation for services rendered. The amounts owing to related parties are non-interest bearing.

Example of entity-specific disclosure

The related party payable of $900,000 at year end includes $400,000 of consulting services rendered by the Chief Information Officer in the current year for technical feasibility studies in relation to product XYZ. The remaining balance of $500,000 pertains to rent owing to an entity controlled by the Vice-President of Marketing for last 4 fiscal years. Given the Corporation's financial status, the related parties and the Corporation agreed to no fixed term for repayment.

Selling and administrative expenses includes $750,000 paid to directors and officers of the Corporation. Consulting services provided by the Chief Information Officer represents $550,000 of this expense and the balance is comprised of $200,000 in rent paid to the Vice-President of Marketing. Included in professional fees is $200,000 is fees paid to a director of the Corporation for legal services in connection with the litigation disclosed in Note 14. These related party transactions are considered to be in the normal course of business and are recorded at the exchange amount, which is considered to be equal to amounts agreed upon by the related parties.

Issuers will have to revisit their related party transaction disclosure as part of their transition to IFRS, as the requirements differ from Pre-changeover Canadian GAAP. One of the major differences for issuers to consider is that Pre-changeover Canadian GAAP addresses both the measurement and disclosure of related party transactions, while IAS 24 *Related Party Disclosures* only addresses disclosure requirements. Other differences between IFRS and Pre-changeover Canadian GAAP include the following areas:

- the definition of related parties is broader under IFRS than under Pre-changeover Canadian GAAP; and

- compensation for key management personnel is a related party disclosure under IFRS, whereas executive compensation arrangements are generally not considered related party transactions under Pre-changeover Canadian GAAP but are governed by securities legislation.

Appendix C — Regulatory Compliance Deficiencies

The CD review program assesses issuer compliance with requirements in our securities laws. Our objective is to promote clear and informative disclosure that will allow investors to make informed investment decisions. We have identified the following areas where we continue to see lack of compliance: executive compensation and material contracts.

1. — Statement of Executive Compensation (Form 51-102F6)

All direct and indirect compensation provided to certain executive officers and directors for, or in connection with, services they have provided to the issuer or subsidiary of the issuer must be disclosed. The objective of this requirement is to provide insight into executive compensation as a key aspect of the overall stewardship and governance of issuers and to help investors understand how decisions about executive compensation are made. Many issuers continue to provide insufficient disclosure of performance goals or similar conditions, as well as the benchmark group used for specific levels of compensation.

Benchmarking

Generally, benchmarking is the process of setting a target for executive compensation at a level relative to the issuer's peers. If an issuer benchmarks, it must: (i) disclose the name of all of the individual companies included in the benchmark group; and (ii) discuss why those companies were selected to be part of the peer group.

Example of deficient disclosure

Compensation for the named executive officers (NEOs) is composed primarily of three components: base fees, performance bonuses and stock based compensation. The determination of each component is based on industry standards. In establishing compensation, the Company takes into consideration levels of compensation provided by industry competitors.

Example of entity-specific disclosure

In order to promote competitive compensation practices, the board evaluates compensation of the NEOs, relative to a peer group of 10 publicly traded Canadian companies (the "Canadian Group"). These companies are selected on the basis of a number of factors, including similar industry characteristics, revenue and market capitalization. The objective of the executive compensation policy is to position the total compensation package at the median of the Canadian Group. Each of the elements of the compensation package (base salary, short-term incentives and long-term incentives) is separately considered in the benchmarking in order to be consistent with general market practices. The 10 companies included in the Canadian Group in 2010 were: [List of companies].

The Canadian Group is reviewed on an annual basis to ensure that the inclusion criteria and companies on the list are still pertinent. Changes may be made, if necessary.

Performance goals or similar conditions

Issuers should provide disclosure of a performance goal or similar condition that is either a quantitative or qualitative performance target achieved by the issuer on which the issuer has based its decision to award compensation. For subjective targets, the issuer may describe the target without providing specific measures. In this situation, the issuer's compensation, analysis and disclosure should clearly disclose that compensation decisions are not based on objective identifiable measures. For targets that are based on objective identifiable measures, issuers must disclose them unless a reasonable person would consider that disclosing them would seriously prejudice the issuer's interests.

Example of deficient disclosure

To determine short term incentive compensation, the Board of Directors reviews the performance of the NEOs and considers a variety of factors, both objective and subjective, when determining compensation levels. These factors include the long-term interests of the Company and its shareholders, the financial and operating performance of the Company and each NEO's individual per-formance, contribution towards meeting corporate objectives, responsibilities and length of service.

Example 1 of entity-specific disclosure

The compensation paid to directors and NEOs of the Company is determined on a case-by-case basis with reference to the role that each director and NEO provides to the Company. The Company does not currently prescribe a set of formal objective measures to determine discretionary bonus entitlements. Rather, the Company uses informal goals typical for development and early production stage companies such as strategic acquisitions, advancement of exploration and other transactions that serve to increase the Company's valuation. Precise goals or milestones are not pre-set by the board of directors of the Company.

Example 2 of entity-specific disclosure

Bonuses paid pursuant to the short term incentive compensation program depend on the level of achievement of financial objectives of the Company. The Company attributes to each NEO, depending on his hierarchic level, a bonus target level set as a percentage of his salary, representing the amount which will be paid if all objectives are achieved according to the targets set. Depending on the performance, actual bonuses may vary between zero and twice the target bonus, based on the level of achievement of the objectives set out at the beginning of the fiscal year.

For the fiscal year ended October 31, 2010, the financial objectives used for purposes of the short term incentive compensation were earnings per share and earnings before interest and taxes of the sector. These objectives are meant to tie the performance of the executive with the financial performance of the Company.

The following table presents the objectives for 2010 approved by the Board of Directors and the results achieved by the Company:

Performance measure	Objectives	Results
Earnings per share	$1.32	$1.50
Earnings before interest and taxes sector A (millions of dollars)	$162	$189
Earnings before interest and taxes sector B (millions of dollars)	$79	$98
Earnings before interest and taxes sector C (millions of dollars)	$83	$91

Incentive compensation as a percentage of salary:					
	NEO-1	**NEO-2**	**NEO-3**	**NEO-4**	**NEO-5**
Minimum	0%	0%	0%	0%	0%
Target	100%	100%	50%	75%	50%
Maximum	200%	200%	100%	100%	75%

For additional reference, see *CSA Staff Notice 51-331 Report on Staff's Review of Executive Compensation Disclosure*.

Policies and Orders: CSAN 51-312.

CSA Multilateral Staff Notice 51-336 — Issuers Using Mass Advertising

Date: September 13, 2011

34 O.S.C.B. 9528

This notice sets out the views of staff (staff or we) of the participating CSA Jurisdictions (Alberta, Ontario, Québec, Nova Scotia, New Brunswick and Northwest Territories, collectively, the "Jurisdictions") with respect to companies (issuers) using television advertising in an apparent effort to promote interest in an issuer's securities.

The concerns highlighted in this notice with respect to television advertising apply equally to advertising through other means such as radio, internet, social media or print.

Observed Practice

Staff have observed a practice, primarily used by junior issuers in various industries, whereby they are using television advertisements that are generally 15 to 30 seconds in length and focus mainly on positive aspects of the issuer's business or its prospects. In the case of an issuer listed on a stock exchange, the issuer's stock symbol figures prominently in the communication. In the case of an unlisted issuer, contact information is generally provided for investment enquiries. These advertisements appear to be for the specific purpose of promoting interest in the issuer's securities.

Staff's View

We are of the view that these advertisements may fail to comply with disclosure requirements under the securities legislation in the Jurisdictions (as discussed more fully below) and/or may be misleading to investors.

General comments on advertisements

We think that advertisements of the nature described above may be contrary to securities legislation and misleading to investors. These types of advertisements do not appear to be aimed at selling the products or services of the issuer or raising public awareness of the issuer. This notice is not directed towards advertising or publicity campaigns that are legitimately aimed at such purposes.

In addition to the specific compliance issues relating to the advertisements and the investor protection concerns that they raise, we think that advertising apparently intended to promote trading in an issuer's securities does not reflect positively on issuers or the Canadian capital markets.

Restrictions on advertising during prospectus distributions

Advertising or marketing activities undertaken during a period of distribution of securities or in furtherance of a distribution are subject to restrictions in the Jurisdictions. Restricted advertising or marketing activities may be oral, written or electronic and include television advertisements. For more information, please refer to National Instrument 41-101 *General Prospectus Requirements* and Companion Policy 41-101CP *Companion Policy to National Instrument 41-101 General Prospectus Requirements.*

Requirements applicable to mining and oil and gas disclosure

A number of these advertisements contain scientific and technical disclosure regarding mineral or oil and gas projects. Disclosure by an issuer related to mineral projects must comply with National Instrument 43-101 *Standards of Disclosure for Mineral Projects* (NI 43-101). Part 2 of NI 43-101 requires that all disclosure made by an issuer of scientific or technical information (including disclosure of mineral resource or mineral reserve) concerning a mineral project on a property material to the issuer must be based upon information prepared by or under the supervision of a qualified person or approved by a qualified person. Similarly, the specific disclosure requirements under Part 5 of National Instrument 51-101 *Standards of Disclosure for Oil and Gas Activities* apply to disclosure of reserves and other information made by an issuer engaged in oil and gas activities.

Future action

We will continue to monitor advertisements by issuers. If an issuer's advertisement breaches securities legislation (including the relevant National Instruments), or appears to be misleading to investors or contrary to the public interest, the issuer should anticipate that staff will take appropriate regulatory action which may include a review of the issuer's overall disclosure or issuances of securities.

CSA Staff Notice 51-337 — Continuous Disclosure Review Program Activities for the fiscal year ended March 31, 2012

Date: **July 19, 2012**

35 O.S.C.B. 7595

Purpose of this Notice

Reliable and accurate information by reporting issuers (issuers) is critical for investor confidence and to promote efficient capital markets. The CSA's continuous disclosure (CD) review program is designed to identify material disclosure deficiencies that affect the reliability and accuracy of an issuer's disclosure record, and has two fundamental objectives: education and compliance. The objectives of this notice are to:

- help issuers understand and comply with their obligations;

- summarize the results of the CD review program for the fiscal year ended March 31, 2012 (fiscal 2012); and

- provide examples of areas of common deficiencies.

To assist issuers in better understanding their continuous disclosure obligations, we have provided guidance and examples of common deficiencies in the following areas:

- Appendix A — Financial Statement Deficiencies

- Appendix B — Management's Discussion and Analysis (MD&A) Deficiencies

- Appendix C — Other Regulatory Deficiencies

For further details on the program, see *CSA Staff Notice 51-312 — (Revised) Harmonized Continuous Disclosure Review Program.*

International Financial Reporting Standards

Most issuers are now required to prepare financial statements in accordance with International Financial Reporting Standards (IFRS) as issued by the International Accounting Standards Board (IASB) for fiscal years beginning on or after January 1, 2011.

Bulletins and IFRS-related content were provided on many jurisdictions' websites to assist issuers in their transition to IFRS. These jurisdictions updated this IFRS-related content during the year by proactively communicating with issuers and their advisors on IFRS-related securities law changes and transition issues.

In fiscal 2012, we conducted reviews that focused on issuers' first IFRS interim financial reports. The results of the IFRS transition reviews were generally positive. Compliance was better than expected based upon the results of earlier IFRS targeted reviews. Approximately 5% of issuers were required to refile financial statements due to basic transition issues.

Year in Review — fiscal 2012

There are approximately 4,200 issuers in Canada[1]. We use a high level screening system that considers risk factors to select issuers for review and to determine the type of review to conduct (full or issue-oriented). We apply both qualitative and quantitative criteria in determining the level of review required. The criteria are updated as market conditions change. We focus on accounting and disclosure issues where either non-compliance is probable or a need for increased compliance is foreseen.

---

[1]Excluding investment funds and issuers that have been cease-traded.

Part 5: ONGOING REQUIREMENTS

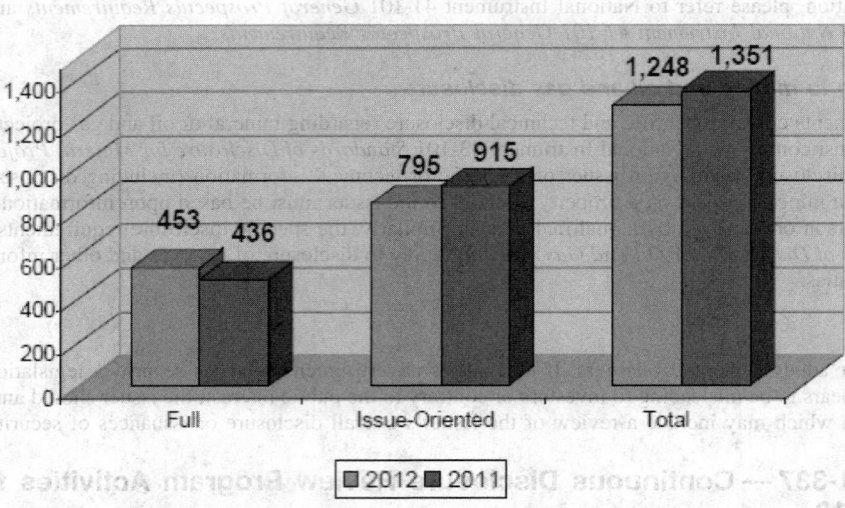

Reviews Completed

The above chart illustrates the composition of the type of reviews we conducted in fiscal 2012 compared to fiscal 2011. The number of full reviews conducted in fiscal 2012 increased by 4% from the previous year. The number of issue-oriented reviews decreased by 13%. The decrease in issue-oriented reviews is primarily the result of the fact that we concentrated our resources on IFRS by:

- conducting full reviews;

- focusing on IFRS issue-oriented reviews that were more complex and comprehensive than those done in fiscal 2011; and

- communicating more frequently with issuers to assist them in their IFRS transition.

Outcomes for fiscal 2012

Given our high level screening system that considers risk factors for the selection of issuers, we select issuers with higher risk of non-compliance. In fiscal 2012, 56% of our review outcomes required issuers to take action to improve disclosure, compared to 70% in fiscal 2011.

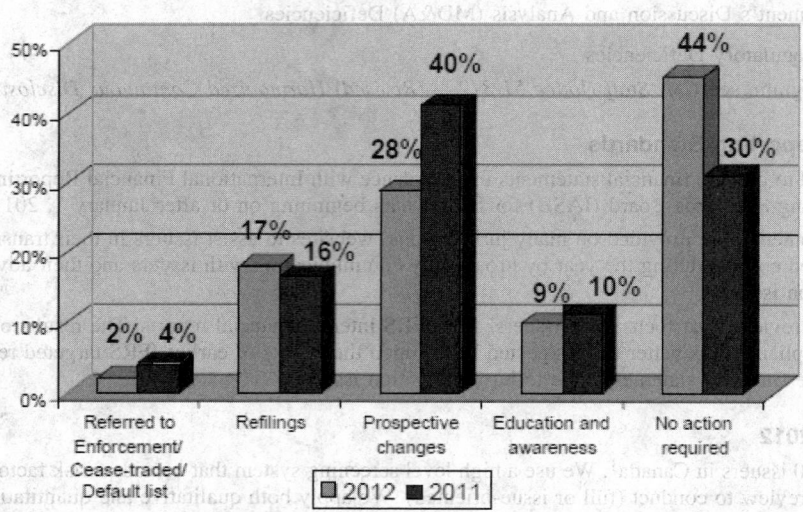

Review Outcomes 2012

The increase of outcomes in the no action required category is mainly due to the increase in the number of issue-oriented reviews conducted that did not result in a letter being sent to the issuer. These issue-oriented reviews were completed to gather information on the IFRS transition, to identify industry trends and to identify differences between pre-changeover Canadian Generally Accepted Accounting Principles (GAAP) and IFRS that resulted in adjustments to reported results and disclosures.

We classified the outcomes of the full and issue-oriented reviews in the five categories described in Appendix D. More than one category of outcome could have been generated by a CD review. For example, an issuer could be required to refile certain documents as well as make certain changes on a prospective basis.

Issue-oriented reviews

An issue-oriented review is an in-depth review focusing on a specific accounting, legal or regulatory issue that we believe warrants regulatory scrutiny.

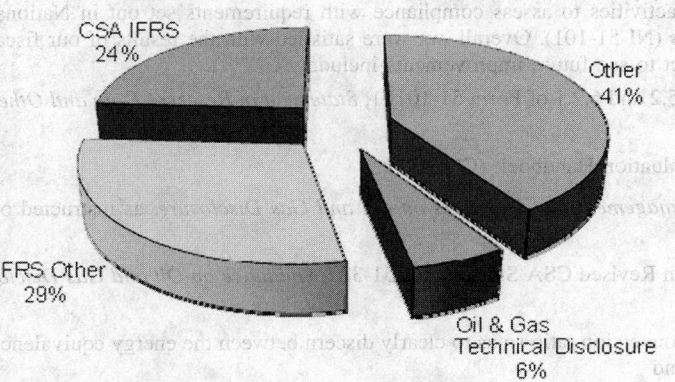

Issue-Oriented Reviews 2012

- CSA IFRS 24%
- Other 41%
- IFRS Other 29%
- Oil & Gas Technical Disclosure 6%

The "Other" category includes reviews of:
- Auditor Review of Interim Reports;
- Complaints;
- Environmental disclosure;
- Press releases;
- Executive compensation;
- Audit Committee;
- Certification;
- MD&A; and
- Cash Flow.

Part 5: ONGOING REQUIREMENTS

In fiscal 2012, 64% of the reviews (as compared to 68% of the reviews in fiscal 2011) were issue-oriented reviews. The following issue-oriented reviews were completed by one or more of the jurisdictions:

CSA IFRS Issue-oriented Review

The CSA conducted a CSA IFRS issue-oriented review. We reviewed the financial statements of selected issuers in addition to their MD&A. We examined these reports to determine whether the issuers provided information to enable readers to analyze and understand how the transition to IFRS affected the issuers' financial position, financial performance and cash flow.

We reviewed 164 issuers and noted that compliance was generally positive.

- 72% of reviews required no action.

- When we noted deficiencies, we sent comment letters asking issuers for clarification.

- The most common MD&A deficiency was issuers not clearly labelling and identifying the accounting principles used when they presented a mix of financial information in accordance with pre-changeover Canadian GAAP and IFRS. We reminded issuers of this requirement and asked them to comply in future MD&A.

- We found that issuers commonly did not include a statement of changes in equity for the comparative interim periods as required by subsection 4.3(2)(b) of National Instrument 51-102, *Continuous Disclosure Obligations*.

IFRS Other Issue-oriented Reviews

a. — Education IFRS Transition

In early fiscal 2012, we continued conducting education reviews to assess the level of readiness of issuers to file their first IFRS interim financial report. We reviewed the IFRS transition disclosure provided by issuers in their third interim and/or last annual MD&A before their first IFRS filings. Only a few issuers needed to be followed up with due to their risk of not being ready to file their first IFRS interim financial report on time.

b. — IFRS Transition Disclosure

In addition to the CSA IFRS issue-oriented reviews performed, certain jurisdictions carried out further reviews of disclosure provided by issuers in their first IFRS interim financial report, including both the financial statements and the MD&A. The objective of the review was to gather insights on the extent and nature of the disclosures provided by issuers. Information was tracked to provide insight on industry trends, differences between pre-changeover Canadian GAAP and IFRS that resulted in adjustments to reported results, and disclosures. No letters were sent to issuers as a result of this review.

c. — Decommissioning Provision

Staff conducted a review of issuers engaged in oil and gas activities to assess appropriate compliance with recognition, measurement and disclosure rules for decommissioning provisions under IAS 37, *Provisions, contingent liabilities and contingent assets* (IAS 37). Based on differences between pre-changeover GAAP and IAS 37, we expected to see IFRS transition adjustments in most cases. While a few issuers failed to appropriately recognize a provision, most complied with the recognition and measurement rules. We did note some general disclosure deficiencies in the following areas:

- inappropriate disclosure of material estimates and assumptions (e.g. discount rate, expected timing of outflows);

- over 50% of issuers reviewed did not disclose the requirement to re-measure the provision at each reporting period in order to reflect rates in effect at the time; and

- over 50% of issuers reviewed provided no disclosure of the discount rates applied on transition to IFRS or in the comparative quarter.

Oil and Gas Technical Disclosure Issue-oriented Review

Annually, staff conducts reviews on issuers engaged in oil and gas activities to assess compliance with requirements set out in National Instrument 51-101, *Standards of Disclosure for Oil and Gas Activities* (NI 51-101). Overall, we were satisfied with the results of our fiscal 2012 reviews. However, areas where we noted deficiencies and expect to see future improvements include:

- disclosure on significant factors and uncertainties as per sections 5.2 and 6.2.1 of Form 51-101F1, *Statement of Reserves Data and Other Oil and Gas Information*;

- use proper terminology set out in the Canadian Oil and Gas Evaluation Handbook (COGEH);

- include all required signatures on Form 51-101F3, *Report of Management and Directors on Oil and Gas Disclosure*, as instructed on subsection 2.1.3(e) of NI 51-101;

- consistently comply with section 5.9 of NI 51-101 and guidance in Revised CSA Staff Notice 51-327, *Guidance on Oil and Gas Disclosure*, concerning the disclosure of resources other than reserves;

- provide appropriate cautionary language concerning the 6:1 boe conversion ratio so as to clearly discern between the energy equivalency and the market price equivalency between natural gas and oil; and

- be consistent and accurate in the use of units of measurement and disclosure of reserves within and between disclosure documents.

Full Reviews

A full review is broad in scope and covers many types of disclosure. It covers the issuer's most recent annual financial statements and interim financial reports (pre-changeover Canadian GAAP) or at least the issuer's first IFRS interim financial reports (IFRS), MD&A, and other disclosure documents[1].

The following table provides a breakdown of these full reviews that have been conducted in fiscal 2012.

Type of review	Total 2012	Total 2011
Full — pre-changeover Canadian GAAP	120	436
Full — IFRS	333	—
Total Full	**453**	**436**

Common deficiencies identified

Our reviews focus on identifying material deficiencies and disclosure enhancements. To help issuers better understand their disclosure obligations, we have provided guidance and examples of common deficiencies:

    Appendix A: Financial Statement Deficiencies

        1. First-time adoption of International Financial Reporting Standards

            a. Reconciliations

            b. Explanations of material adjustments

            c. Accounting policies

        2. Classification of a liability as current

        3. Business combinations

        4. Flow-through shares

    Appendix B: MD&A Deficiencies

        1. Discussion of Operations

        2. Liquidity

---

[1]Other disclosure documents are: technical disclosures, including technical reports for oil and gas, and mining issuers; annual information forms (AIF); annual reports; information circulars; press releases, material change reports and business acquisition reports (BARs); websites; certifications; and material contracts.

3. General Provisions

Appendix C: Other Regulatory Deficiencies

    1. Standards of Disclosure for Mineral Projects

    2. Statement of Executive Compensation

        a. Summary compensation table

        b. Compensation discussion and analysis

    3. Disclosure of corporate governance practices

This is not an exhaustive list of deficiencies noted in our reviews, issuers should be reminded that their CD record must comply with all relevant securities legislation and lengthy disclosure does not necessarily equal full compliance. Examples do not include all requirements that could apply to a particular issuer's situation.

Areas of focus for fiscal year 2013

During fiscal 2013, our focus will be on the first annual IFRS report. We will continue to use a high level screening system that considers risk factors to determine the issuers we will select for review and the type of review required. Some of the topics that may receive greater attention by our CD program include:

- judgments and sources of estimation uncertainty disclosure;

- asset impairments; and

- business combinations.

Results by jurisdiction

The Alberta Securities Commission, the Ontario Securities Commission and the Autorité des marchés financiers publish reports summarizing the results of the CD review program in their jurisdictions. See the individual regulator's website for a copy of its report:

- www.albertasecurities.com

- www.osc.gov.on.ca

- www.lautorite.qc.ca

Appendix A — Financial Statement Deficiencies

We provided examples of deficient disclosure and presentation contrasted against more robust, entity-specific disclosure and presentation. The most notable financial statement deficiencies concerned requirements for first-time adoption of IFRS (IFRS 1, *First-time adoption of International Financial Reporting Standards* (IFRS 1)), presentation of financial statements (IAS 1, *Presentation of financial statements* (IAS 1)), business combinations (IFRS 3, *Business combinations* (IFRS 3)) and flow-through shares.

1. — First-time adoption of International Financial Reporting Standards

In the first annual report and each interim financial report in the period covered by its first financial statements prepared in accordance with IFRS, issuers are required to apply IFRS 1. In accordance with IFRS 1, issuers must provide reconciliations and explain the effect of identified differences or changes in accounting policies resulting from the transition from their pre-changeover GAAP to IFRS.

a. — Reconciliations

Some issuers omitted to provide all required reconciliations.

b. — Explanations of material adjustments

Many issuers did not provide explanations for all material adjustments (including cash flows), or did not sufficiently explain the nature of the adjustment.

c. — Accounting policies

We noted that some issuers did not change all their accounting policies to comply with IFRS, or that no reconciling items were identified for changes in accounting policies. Issuers must present coherent and complete information in their financial statements.

We also noted that some issuers provided boilerplate and nonspecific accounting policy disclosure. Users are faced with new accounting standards and in certain cases there may be accounting policy choices. Issuers must ensure they provide clear and entity-specific accounting policy disclosure.

For information about the disclosure of accounting policies used in the interim and annual MD&As in the changeover year to IFRS, see *CSA Staff Notice 52-328 — Disclosures about Accounting Policies in the Year of Changeover to International Financial Reporting Standards (IFRS)*.

2. — Classification of a liability as current

Liability classification under IFRS differs from pre-changeover Canadian GAAP. In accordance with paragraph 69 of IAS 1, an issuer shall classify a liability as current only when it expects to settle the liability in its normal operating cycle; it holds the liability primarily for the purpose of trading; or the liability is due to be settled within twelve months after the reporting period or it does not have an unconditional right to defer settlement of the liability for at least twelve months after the reporting period. Some issuers were required to reclassify debt that was classified as non-current under pre-changeover Canadian GAAP to current under IFRS. However, when a refinancing or rolling over of the obligation is not at the discretion of the issuer (for example, when there is no arrangement for refinancing at the reporting date), many issuers incorrectly classified the obligation as non-current.

Example of incorrect classification (Long-term debt classified as non-current instead of current)

Consolidated Statements of Financial Position filed on March 19, 2012

IFRS line items	December 31 2011	December 31 2010	January 1 2010
Assets	25,561	24,372	25,269
Liabilities			
Current liabilities:			
Trade and other payables	3,772	11,908	4,046
Current portion of long-term debt	1,515	838	1,390
	5,287	12,746	5,436
Long-term debt (note 10)	8,302	326	9,060
Shareholders' Equity	11,972	11,300	10,773
	25,561	24,372	25,269

Note 10:

As at December 31, 2011, the Company did not meet a financial ratio on the long-term debt. In February 2012, a waiver was obtained allowing the Company to not meet this financial ratio for more than twelve months. Therefore, no reclassification has been made.

Example of entity-specific classification

Consolidated Statements of Financial Position filed on March 19, 2012

IFRS line items	December 31 2011	December 31 2010	January 1 2010
Assets	25,561	24,372	25,269
Liabilities			
Current liabilities:			
Trade and other payables	3,772	11,908	4,046
Current portion of long-term debt	9,817	838	1,390
	13,589	12,746	5,436
Long-term debt (note 10)	—	326	9,060
Shareholders' Equity	11,972	11,300	10,773
	25,561	24,372	25,269

Note 10:

As at December 31, 2011, the Company did not meet a financial ratio on the long-term debt. In February 2012, a waiver was obtained allowing the Company to not meet this financial ratio for more than twelve months. Thus, in accordance with IAS 1, the Company has reclassified an amount of $8,302 of long-term debt to current liabilities as the waiver was not obtained before the reporting date.

3. — Business combinations

The adoption of IFRS 3 introduced a number of changes in accounting for business combinations. This has impacted the amount of goodwill recognized, the results in the period that an acquisition occurs and subsequent periods. Also, there are significant disclosure requirements concerning business acquisitions in annual financial statements and interim financial reports. In particular, we noted that some issuers have omitted the following required information:

- the amounts of revenue and profit or loss of the acquiree since the acquisition date included in the consolidated statement of comprehensive income for the reporting period (paragraph B64(q)(i));

- the revenue and profit or loss of the combined entity for the current reporting period as though the acquisition date for all business combinations that occurred during the year had been as of the beginning of the annual reporting period (paragraph B64(q)(ii));

- for a business combination done after the end of the reporting period but before the financial statements are authorized for issue, the information required by paragraph B64 of IFRS 3 unless the initial accounting for the business combination is incomplete at the time the financial statements are authorized for issue (paragraph B66);

- the primary reasons for the business combination and a description of how the acquirer obtained control of the acquiree (paragraph B64(d));

- a qualitative description of the factors that make up the goodwill recognized, such as expected synergies from combining operations of the acquiree and the acquirer, intangible assets that do not qualify for separate recognition or other factors (paragraph B64(e));

- for each contingent liability recognized, the information required in paragraphs 85 and 86 of IAS 37 (paragraph B64(j));

- in a bargain purchase, a description of the reasons why the transaction resulted in a gain (paragraph B64(n)(ii)); and

- for acquired receivables, the gross contractual amounts receivable and the best estimate at the acquisition date of the contractual cash flows not expected to be collected.

Furthermore, we have noted that some issuers have not disclosed the required information separately for each significant business combination or did not aggregate the required information for individually immaterial business combinations that are material collectively.

Example of deficient disclosure

On February 28, 2011, the Company acquired ABC Ltd. for an amount of $1.6 million which was funded from cash generated from the Company's operations. The acquisition has been accounted for using the purchase method with operating results included in the Company's earnings from the date of acquisition. The purchase price allocation is as follows:

Accounts receivable	578
Inventories	483
Prepaid expenses	27
Property, plant and equipment	620
Goodwill	250
Accounts payable and accrued liabilities	(328)
Net assets acquired	**1,630**
Consideration	
Cash	1,239
Contingent consideration and distributions	500
Balance of sale receivable	(109)
	1,630

Example of entity-specific disclosure

On February 28, 2011, the Company acquired 100% of the shares and voting interests in ABC Ltd., a leading manufacturer and erector of structural steel products operating across Canada, for an amount of $1.6 million using cash generated from the Company's operations. The acquisition costs related to this transaction amounted to $152,070 and have been accounted as such in the consolidated statement of earnings in 2011 under "General and Administrative expenses". The acquisition has been accounted for using the acquisition method with operating results included in the Company's earnings from the date of acquisition. The purchase price allocation is as follows:

At fair value	(in 000's)
Accounts receivable	578
Inventories	483
Prepaid expenses	27
Property, plant and equipment	620
Goodwill	250
Accounts payable and accrued liabilities	(328)
Net assets acquired	**1,630**
Consideration	
Cash	1,239
Contingent consideration	500
Balance of sale receivable	(109)
	1,630

The acquisition of ABC Ltd. is consistent with the Company's acquisition strategy of identifying strategic opportunities within its existing core business segment and acquiring well-established companies with complementary strengths to achieve meaningful synergies. The synergies are expected to consist primarily of cost savings relating to raw materials and reduction of overhead expenses, and represent the goodwill. Goodwill from this business combination is not expected to be deductible for tax purposes.

Since the acquisition, the acquired company has contributed a total of $200,341 to the Company's sales of goods and $3,546 to earnings. Management estimates that, if the acquisition had occurred on January 1, 2011, additional sales of goods would have been $40,743 and additional operating earnings would have been $785 from January 1, 2011 to February 28, 2011.

The gross contractual amount of accounts receivable amounts to $600,058. At the acquisition date, the best estimate of contractual cash flows that is not expected be recovered is $22,111. An initial amount of $50,000 was withheld as a provision for adjustments, of which $25,000 was paid on September 1, 2011 and $25,000 on February 2, 2012.

At the acquisition date, the amount recognized as contingent consideration represent the fair value which was the discounted maximum amount indicated in the purchase agreement based on ABC's financial projections (see note 4 for disclosure on business acquisition significant estimates and the range of estimated amounts).

4. — Flow-through shares

IFRS do not specifically address the accounting for flow-through shares or the related tax consequences arising from such transactions. Pre-changeover Canadian GAAP, however, addressed the accounting for flow-through shares in Section 3465, *Income taxes* and EIC-146, *Flow-through shares*, that cannot anymore be used. We have noted that many issuers have not identified any IFRS transition impact in their reconciliations from pre-changeover Canadian GAAP to IFRS. We expected that issuers would have made some changes in their flow-through shares accounting policy.

Example of deficient disclosure

Flow-through shares:

Proceeds received upon the issue of common shares that transfer the exploratory expense deductions to investors are credited to the share capital and the related exploration costs are charged to deferred exploration costs. The estimated tax benefits transferred to shareholders are recorded as a future income tax liability at the time of filing of the renouncement documents with the tax authorities with a corresponding reduction in share capital.

Example of entity-specific disclosure

Flow-through shares[1]:

Issuance of flow-through shares represents in substance an issue of common shares and the sale of right to tax deductions to the investors when the flow-through shares are issued. The sale of the right to tax deductions is deferred and presented as other liabilities in the statement of financial position. The proceeds received from flow-through placements are allocated between share capital and any warrants issued and liability using the residual method which means that the shares are valued at the fair value of existing shares at the time of issuance and the residual proceeds are allocated between warrants and other liability. The liability component recorded initially on the issuance of shares is reversed on renouncement of the right to the tax deductions to the investors and when admissible expenses are incurred and recognized in profit or loss as a reduction of deferred income tax expense and a deferred tax liability is recognized for the taxable temporary difference that arises from the difference between the carrying amount of admissible expenditures capitalized as an asset and its tax basis.

Appendix B — MD&A Deficiencies

The quality of MD&A disclosure continues to be an area where we see deficiencies. MD&A is a narrative explanation through the eyes of management of how the issuer performed during the period covered by the financial statements, and what the issuer's financial condition and future prospects are. We often find boilerplate disclosure that does not change from period to period. Issuers frequently replicate disclosure from the financial statements without any analysis. Entity-specific disclosure provides investors with information that complements the financial statements so they are able to assess the current financial condition of the issuer and its future prospects. Under the requirements, the MD&A should:

- help current and prospective investors understand what the financial statements show and do not show;

- discuss important trends and risks that have affected the financial statements, and trends and risks that are reasonably likely to affect them in the future; and

- provide information about the quality, and potential variability, of the issuer's earnings and cash flow, to assist investors in determining whether past performance is indicative of future performance.

There are three important areas where we continue to see boilerplate disclosure in the MD&A: discussion of operations, liquidity, and general provisions. For each, we have provided examples of deficient disclosure contrasted against more robust entity-specific disclosure.

1. — Discussion of Operations

Issuers are required to analyze their operations during the most recently completed financial year, including a comparison against the previously completed financial year. The analysis should discuss and quantify all material variances. Common deficiencies include: discussion of immaterial information without inclusion of information that may be material to investors; and insufficient analysis of why changes have occurred. Issuers are reminded that the MD&A should contain a balanced discussion of their operations. Issuers should quantify how volume and price changes affected revenue, and discuss why changes occurred. If other elements affected revenue, such as the introduction of a new

---

[1]The entity-specific disclosure for flow-through shares is not the only allowable treatment.

product or new competitors, the MD&A should also address these factors. Issuers should not limit the operational analysis to revenue; if issuers experienced a change in their gross profit percentage, the MD&A should discuss the factors behind the change.

Example of Deficient Disclosure

Revenue increased from $900,000 to $1,080,000, a 20% increase. Gross profit increased from $400,000 to $408,000, a 2% increase.

Example of entity-specific disclosure

Revenue increased from $900,000 to $1,080,000, a 20% increase. Gross profit increased from $400,000 to $408,000, a 2% increase. Three factors caused revenue to increase by $180,000:

- increased sales volume of Product X-$60,000;
- decreased unit price of Product X-($30,000); and
- the introduction of a new product during the fourth quarter, Product Y-$150,000.

In late 2011, we anticipated new competition entering our market, so we discounted our remaining Product X units to encourage their sale and to allow us to focus on its replacement, Product Y. Discounts on Product X caused the reduced gross profit percentage. We expect to continue discounting Product X in the first quarter, but expect our gross profit to improve as Product Y replaces Product X.

---

2. — Liquidity

The MD&A should identify and discuss any known or expected fluctuations and trends in an issuer's liquidity, taking into account demands, commitments, events or uncertainties. Where applicable, the discussion should also include disclosure of any defaults or risk of defaults on debt covenants and how the issuer intends to cure the default or otherwise address the risk as set out in the example below. The disclosure relating to expected liquidity fluctuations is required for all issuers, but it is especially important when issuers have negative cash flows from operations, a negative working capital position or have breached or expect to breach their debt covenants.

Example of deficient disclosure

As at year-end, the Company had cash of $100,000 and accounts receivable of $50,000. Current assets amounted to $150,000 with current liabilities of $400,000 resulting in a working capital deficit of $250,000. The Company believes that it has sufficient capital on hand to satisfy working capital requirements for the next 12 months.

Example of entity-specific disclosure

As of year-end, the Company's debt to equity ratio was in breach of a covenant in its loan agreement. Subsequent to year-end, the Company:

- renegotiated the covenants in the loan agreement to cure the default; and
- borrowed an additional $300,000 to meet current and future working capital requirements.

New terms under the loan agreement restrict repayment of existing debt payable to related parties. We estimate that the Company will need $500,000 over the next two years to complete its exploration project. In the short-term, the Company will rely on advances from shareholders and the exercise of options and share purchase warrants to fund exploration costs.

---

3. — General Provisions

Issuers must endeavour to improve MD&A disclosure. In particular, many issuers operating in a specialized industry or high-tech sector do not sufficiently describe their operations, thereby restricting the usefulness of their MD&As. We would like to remind issuers of the requirements under Part 1(a) of Form 51-102F1, *Management's Discussion & Analysis*.

Example of deficient disclosure
Strategy
The Corporation (ABC) expects to generate revenue from its product candidates in the form of royalties. ABC sold its interest in its joint venture to its partner, XYZ Inc. (XYZ) on June 30, 2011. Following this transaction, ABC manages its relationship with its two major partners to maximize value from the products that will generate royalties on a going-forward basis. The main assets of ABC are the patent portfolio licensed to NMO Inc. and the royalty agreement with XYZ.

Example of entity-specific disclosure
Strategy
We have implemented a business strategy with intent to reacquire growth in revenue and improve our operations. We continue to invest in order to transform from a print directory business to a digital media and marketing solutions company.

Our strategy remains to leverage our multiplatform media and marketing solutions, to enhance services to our advertisers, build traffic to our network of properties and improve user experience. Our goal is to serve the advertising needs of small and medium enterprises across Canada, by providing the right services and tools to manage and grow their businesses.

We are focusing on key areas, such as:

- Improving our operations with increased focus on sales effectiveness, product fulfillment, billing and customer support;
- Provisioning of new services for our customers with the objective of offering an overall better customer experience and return on investment by driving more quality leads through calls, clicks, forms and emails;
- Improving our value proposition for the consumer by enhancing our content on our online and mobile properties;
- Creating partnerships in traffic and distribution to augment leads to our advertisers; and

- Branding and promotion to raise awareness on our product portfolio and accelerate our brand transformation.

We achieve profitability by maximizing our operating efficiency and constantly reviewing all of our operations with a view to ensuring we maintain a competitive cost structure. Improving our cost structure remains a key priority and will continue to be achieved through:

- Business process redesign;
- Cost containment initiatives; and
- Investment in technology to better support our operations and our transformation.

Our key priorities for 2012 are to:

- Execute our sales approach;
- Deliver superior customer value; and
- Lead our industry transformation.

Appendix C — Other Regulatory Deficiencies

CSA Staff assess issuer compliance with requirements of our securities laws. Our objective is to promote clear and informative disclosure that will allow investors to make informed investment decisions. We have identified the following areas where we continue to see lack of compliance: mineral projects, executive compensation and governance practices.

1. — Standards of Disclosure for Mineral Projects

National Instrument 43-101, *Standards of Disclosure for Mineral Projects* (NI 43-101), sets out the requirements when a mining company discloses scientific or technical information on mineral projects. Under these requirements, the disclosure must be based on information prepared by a qualified person. Deficiencies identified include:

- incomplete or inadequate disclosure of preliminary economic assessments, mineral resources and mineral reserves;

- non-compliant certificates and consents of qualified persons for technical reports;

- incomplete or inadequate disclosure of historical estimates and exploration targets; and

- name of the qualified person omitted in documents containing scientific and technical information.

We remind issuers that the amendments to NI 43-101 came in force on June 30, 2011.

2. — Statement of Executive Compensation

All direct and indirect compensation provided to certain executive officers and directors for, or in connection with, services they have provided to the issuer or subsidiary of the issuer must be disclosed. The objective of this requirement is to provide insight into executive compensation as a key aspect of the overall stewardship and governance of issuers and to help investors understand how decisions about executive compensation are made. Many issuers continue to provide insufficient disclosure related to the summary compensation table, as well as in their compensation discussion and analysis.

a. — Summary compensation table

Section 3.1 of Form 51-102F6, *Statement of executive compensation* (Form 51-102F6), requires issuers to provide a summary compensation table (SCT). We noted that some issuers did not disclose in the SCT the grant date fair value of share-based awards and option-based awards. We remind issuers that the grant date fair value of these types of awards must be reported in the SCT in the year of grant irrespective of whether part or the entire award relates to multiple financial years or payout is subject to performance goals and similar conditions. We also remind issuers that they must disclose key assumptions and estimates used to calculate the fair value of the grant.

Example of deficient application

In 2011, a company grants restricted share units (RSUs) to a named executive officer (NEO). Under the terms of the award, the NEO will be entitled to a payout of 1,000 RSUs in each of 2011, 2012, and 2013 if certain performance goals, including vesting, are satisfied in those years. The performance goals, including vesting, in respect of the 2011 part of the award have been satisfied and the company reports the grant date fair value of that part of the award in the 2011 SCT but decides to defer reporting the part of the award related to 2012 and 2013.

What should have been done

The company should have reported the grant date fair value of the entire award, including the parts related to 2012 and 2013, in the 2011 SCT. The grant date fair value methodology used should have taken into account the fact that the NEO will not receive those RSUs unless the performance goals, including vesting, for 2012 and 2013 are satisfied.

b. — Compensation discussion and analysis

Section 2.1 of Form 51-102F6 requires issuers to describe and explain all significant elements of compensation awarded to, earned by, paid to, or payable to NEOs. The compensation discussion and analysis must include the following:

(a) the objectives of any compensation program or strategy;

(b) what the compensation program is designed to reward;

(c) each element of compensation;

(d) why the company chooses to pay each element;

(e) how the company determines the amount (and, where applicable, the formula) for each element; and

(f) how each element of compensation and the company's decisions about that element fit into the company's overall compensation objectives and affect decisions about other elements.

A number of issuers did not provide the required disclosure. Many issuers provided an analysis expressed in boilerplate language; others did not fully and accurately explain significant elements of compensation awarded to NEOs.

Example of deficient disclosure

The objective of the Corporation's compensation is to: (i) compensate management in a manner that encourages and rewards a high level of performance with a view to increasing long-term shareholder value; (ii) align management's interests with the long term interests of shareholders; and (iii) provide a compensation package that is commensurate with other junior companies in order to enable the Corporation to attract and retain talent.

Example of entity-specific disclosure

The Compensation Discussion and Analysis section explains the pay program for the financial year ended December 31, 2011 for our NEOs, which include our President and Chief Executive Officer, Executive Vice President and Chief Financial Officer, and our three other most highly compensated executive officers as follows: [list of names].

Executive Compensation Philosophy and Policy

Executive compensation at XYZ Inc. (XYZ) is aligned in several ways with our strategic business plan. Our key long-term objective is to motivate executives to achieve targets that are aligned with the Corporation's strategic goals and that are expected to enhance shareholder value over the long term. Our shorter-term corporate goals, business unit objectives, and individual contributions to business success are reflected in the annual incentive plan. A significant portion of the executive pay program consists of "at-risk" pay meaning that compensation is dependent on achieving corporate, business unit and individual performance objectives both in the short and long term.

XYZ's executive pay program is also designed to attract and retain experienced executives who have the skills required to help the Corporation achieve its strategic and organizational goals. XYZ is committed to providing compensation plans that are consistent with best practices in corporate governance.

The Corporation's executive compensation policy is to provide total compensation that is generally competitive with the median of its peer group, taking into consideration additional Corporation-specific issues such as the achievement of financial and operational objectives, and the specific roles and responsibilities of different executive positions. Total compensation plans are structured to provide compensation that is above market median when results exceed the Corporation's business objectives and below market median when results are below target.

Executive Compensation Components

The following describes the different compensation components, which together provide compensation packages that meet the objectives of XYZ's compensation philosophy.

Base Salary: Market-competitive fixed rate of pay to attract and retain executives with experience and skills required to achieve strategic and organizational goals.

Annual Incentive Plan (AIP): Annual cash bonus with target awards established for each NEO as a percentage of base salary to motivate executives to drive superior short-term performance through Corporation, business unit and individual objectives.

Long-term Incentive Plan (LTIP): Option grant levels are based on individual performance and options are time-vested rateably over 4 years with a 10-year term to promote retention and encourage executives to pursue opportunities that will increase shareholder value over the long term.

To achieve the objectives described above, each element of pay is targeted at the market median with adjustments based on meeting specific performance goals as follows:

- Base salary is adjusted above and below the median to reflect specific circumstances such as experience, individual performance and changes in responsibility;

- AIP payouts may exceed market median target levels when results exceed objectives and may be below median levels (down to zero) when results are below targets; and

- LTIP grants of stock options can be adjusted from 0% to 200% of target levels based on each individual's performance and contribution to the Corporation's overall results.

The Corporation has chosen to reward achievement of overall Corporation performance goals defined as earnings before income taxes and non-controlling interest (adjusted EBT). The Corporation believes that adjusted EBT is the most appropriate indicator of the operational and financial performance of the business. For 2011, there was no payout in respect of the corporate objective of the AIP and LTIP, as the minimum performance threshold of $3.5 M in respect of adjusted EBT was not achieved.

For more information and guidance about the compensation discussion and analysis, see *CSA Staff Notice 51-331 — Report on Staff's Review of Executive Compensation Disclosure.* Although, we remind issuers that new amendments to Form 51-102F6 came in force on October 31, 2011.

3. — Disclosure of corporate governance practices

Issuers must adequately disclose their corporate governance practices. For example, Item 6 of Form 58-101F1, *Corporate Governance Disclosure,* and Item 5 of Form 58-101F2, *Corporate Governance Disclosure (Venture Issuers),* require issuers to describe the process by which the board identifies new candidates for board nomination. Disclosure by issuers reviewed was often deficient.

Some issuers simply indicated that the nominating committee or another board committee was responsible for identifying candidates. Others merely stated that the nominee committee was responsible for recommending candidates for board nomination. This type of disclosure is insufficient, as it does not explain the process for identifying new board nominees.

Example of deficient disclosure

Members of the Human Resources, Corporate Governance and Nomination Committee, the Board and management are responsible to determine the nomination of new candidates for Board nomination.

The following example illustrates full disclosure of the board nominee selection process.

Example of entity-specific disclosure

The board of directors has conferred on the Corporate Governance Committee responsibility for identifying new candidates for director positions and for proposing these candidates to the board of directors. The process by which the Corporate Governance Committee identifies new candidates for director positions begins with the approval by the board of a statement of competencies and experience sought with respect to each new candidate. The board of directors or management may propose candidates to the committee. On occasion, the services of a recruitment adviser may be used. Potential candidates are interviewed by the chairman of the board of directors and the lead director as well as by the other members of the board, as necessary. An invitation to join the board is made only where board consensus regarding the proposed candidate is obtained.

Appendix D — Categories of Outcomes

Enforcement referral/ Default list/ Cease trade order

If the issuer has critical CD deficiencies, we may add the issuer to our default lists, issue a cease trade order and/or refer the issuer to Enforcement.

Refiling

The issuer must amend and refile certain CD documents.

Prospective Changes

The issuer is informed that certain changes or enhancements are required in its next filing as a result of deficiencies identified.

Education and Awareness

The issuer receives a proactive letter alerting it to certain disclosure enhancements that should be considered in its next filing.

No action required

The issuer does not need to make any changes or additional filings.

Multilateral CSA Staff Notice 51-338 — Continuous Disclosure and Prospectus Requirements Relating to Documents Prepared under the U.S. *Securities and Exchange Act of 1934*

Date: March 7, 2013

36 O.S.C.B. 2243

Purpose

This CSA staff notice is published by the following jurisdictions: Saskachewan, Manitoba, Ontario, Québec, New Brunswick, Prince Edward Island, Nova Scotia, Newfoundland and Labrabor, Yukon, Northwest Territories and Nunavut. This notice provides information about continuous disclosure and prospectus requirements applicable to documents that are schedules or exhibits to, or incorporated by reference in, disclosure documents prepared in accordance with the United States *Securities and Exchange Act of 1934* (the 1934 Act) and filed in Canada.

Filing requirements under continous disclosure rules

National Instrument 51-102

National Instrument 51-102 *Continuous Disclosure Obligations* (NI 51-102) has certain provisions that apply to reporting issuers that are SEC issuers (as defined in that rule).

In particular, the definition of annual information form (AIF) in NI 51-102 allows SEC issuers to file as an AIF an annual report under the 1934 Act on Form 10-K or Form 20-F (a 1934 annual report). A 1934 annual report may contain various schedules and exhibits, as well as documents incorporated by reference, all of which form part of the 1934 annual report.

- Staff have noted that certain SEC issuers filing a 1934 annual report in Canada do not include in their SEDAR filings all schedules and exhibits to, or documents incorporated by reference in, the 1934 annual report.

- An SEC issuer filing a 1934 annual report in Canada as its AIF must also file all schedules and exhibits to, and documents incorporated by reference in, the 1934 annual report.

Furthermore, section 11.1 of NI 51-102 requires a reporting issuer that is an SEC issuer to file a copy of any disclosure material that it files with, or furnishes to, the U.S. Securities and Exchange Commission (SEC) under the 1934 Act. This includes material filed as exhibits to other documents, if the material contains information that has not been included in disclosure already filed in Canada by the SEC issuer. Staff have noted that certain SEC issuers do not comply with this requirement.

National Instrument 71-102

Part 4 of National Instrument 71-102 *Continuous Disclosure and Other Exemptions Relating to Foreign Issuers* (NI 71-102) contains certain exemptions that apply to reporting issuers that are SEC foreign issuers (as defined in that rule).

In particular, Part 4 of NI 71-102 allows an SEC foreign issuer to satisfy certain continuous disclosure obligations under NI 51-102 by filing in Canada a copy of certain disclosure documents that it files with, or furnishes to, the SEC.

- Staff have noted that certain SEC foreign issuers filing a U.S. disclosure document in reliance on an exemption in Part 4 do not include in their SEDAR filings all schedules and exhibits to, or documents incorporated by reference in, the U.S. disclosure document.

- An SEC foreign issuer filing a U.S. disclosure document in Canada in reliance on an exemption in Part 4 must also file all schedules and exhibits to, and documents incorporated by reference in, the U.S. disclosure document.

Incorporation by reference requirements under short form prospectus rule

If an SEC issuer uses its 1934 annual report as an AIF in Canada, the 1934 annual report must be incorporated by reference in any short form prospectus filed under National Instrument 44-101 *Short Form Prospectus Distributions* (NI 44-101), as required by item 11 of Form 44-101F1 *Short Form Prospectus*.

- Staff have received questions from issuers as to whether it is possible not to incorporate by reference certain portions of, or schedules and exhibits to, a 1934 annual report that are not required in an AIF prepared under Form 51-102F2 *Annual Information Form*.

- The requirement to incorporate a document by reference under item 11 of Form 44-101F1 applies to the entire document, including schedules and exhibits to, and documents incorporated by reference in, the document.

Filing schedules, exhibits and documents incorporated by reference on SEDAR

When an SEC issuer files a 1934 annual report or other U.S. disclosure document on SEDAR, the issuer may comply with the above requirements by filing the schedules, exhibits and documents incorporated by reference as:

- attachments to the version of the 1934 annual report or other disclosure document that is filed on SEDAR (i.e., as one single document under the appropriate document type),

- a single filing under the document type "Other" in the same SEDAR project, or

- separate filings under the document type "Other" in the same SEDAR project.

However, if annual financial statements, annual MD&A, a management information circular, a material contract or other specific continuous disclosure document required by NI 51-102 has already been filed under the appropriate document type in the "Continuous Disclosure" category on SEDAR, it is not necessary to re-file them with the 1934 annual report if they are incorporated by reference into that 1934 annual report.

Furthermore, an SEC issuer that files a 1934 annual report may incorporate by reference all or part of a document that was previously filed on SEDAR as part of a 1934 annual report for a previous year.

Regardless of which of the above methods is followed for a 1934 annual report or other U.S. disclosure document filed on SEDAR, we suggest that SEC issuers file a "notice to public" under the document type "Cover Letter" in the same SEDAR submission indicating where the schedules, exhibits and documents incorporated by reference can be found (e.g., by referring to the date of filing on SEDAR).

Exemptive relief

We have granted exemptive relief to certain SEC issuers that made submissions on why they should not be required to:

- file in Canada certain schedules and exhibits to, or documents incorporated by reference in, a U.S. disclosure document, or

- incorporate those materials by reference into a short form prospectus.

Staff will consider applications for exemptive relief on a case-by-case basis. If an SEC issuer seeks exemptive relief in respect of certain schedules or exhibits required to be filed with or furnished to the SEC, staff will consider a number of factors, including whether the schedules and exhibits:

- consist of documents that only have to be filed under a specific requirement of U.S. securities legislation that has no equivalent in Canada, or

- contain material information that the issuer is required to disclose under Canadian securities legislation, including NI 51-102 or NI 44-101.

French language requirements under Québec legislation

If an issuer files a short form prospectus in Québec, section 40.1 of the *Securities Act* (Québec) requires that the prospectus, as well as any document required to be incorporated by reference in the prospectus, be drawn up in French or in French and English. Accordingly, any 1934 annual report or other document prepared in accordance with the 1934 Act that is incorporated by reference in a short form prospectus filed in Québec (including all schedules and exhibits to, and documents incorporated by reference in, the 1934 annual report or other document), must

Part 5: ONGOING REQUIREMENTS

be drawn up in French or in French and English, unless exemptive relief from section 40.1 is granted by the Autorité des marchés financiers (AMF).

OSC Staff Notice 51-339 — Continuous Disclosure Review Program Activities for the fiscal year ended March 31, 2013

Date: July 18, 2013

36 O.S.C.B. 7358

Introduction

This notice contains the results of the reviews conducted by the Canadian Securities Administrators (**CSA**) within the scope of their Continuous Disclosure (**CD**) Review Program. This program was established to review the compliance of the CD documents of reporting issuers[1] (**issuers**) to ensure they are reliable and accurate. The CSA seek to ensure that Canadian investors receive high quality disclosure from issuers.

In this notice, we summarize the results of the CD Review Program for the fiscal year ended March 31, 2013 (**fiscal 2013**). To raise awareness about the importance of filing compliant CD documents, we also discuss certain areas where common deficiencies were noted and provide examples to help issuers address these deficiencies in the following appendices:

- Appendix A — Financial Statements Deficiencies

- Appendix B — Management's Discussion and Analysis (**MD&A**) Deficiencies

- Appendix C — Other Regulatory Disclosure Deficiencies

For further details on the CD Review Program, see CSA Staff Notice 51-312 (revised) *Harmonized Continuous Disclosure Review Program*.

Results for Fiscal 2013

During fiscal 2013, a total of 1,336 CD reviews (368 full reviews and 968 issue-oriented reviews) were conducted. This is a 7% increase compared to the 1,248 CD reviews (453 full reviews and 795 issue-oriented reviews) completed during fiscal 2012.

Reviews Completed

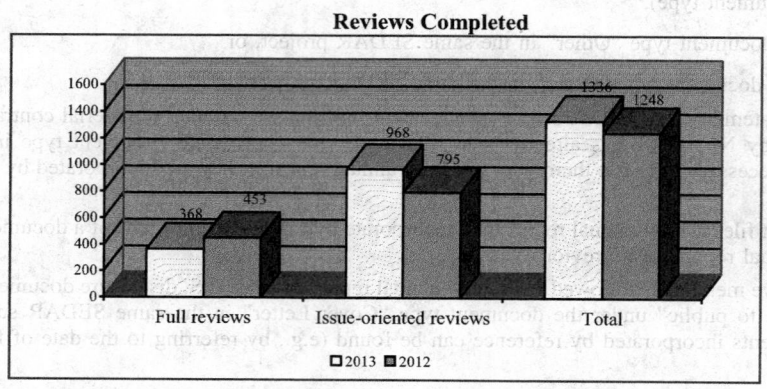

The increased number of total reviews during fiscal 2013 reflects a slightly greater emphasis on issue-oriented reviews which increased due to certain CSA jurisdictions examining technical disclosure and IFRS specific topics on a larger sample of issuers. Technical issue-oriented reviews focused on compliance with National Instrument 43-101 *Standards of Disclosure for Mineral Projects* (**NI 43-101**), and National Instrument 51-101 *Standards of Disclosure for Oil and Gas Activities* (**NI 51-101**). Specific topic issue-oriented reviews were conducted to determine issuers' compliance with a specific IFRS and to determine if the MD&A disclosure on a specific subject was compliant with Form 51-102F1 *Management's Discussion & Analysis* of National Instrument 51-102 *Continuous Disclosure Obligations* (**Form 51-102F1**).

Outcomes for Fiscal 2013

In fiscal 2013, 47% of our review outcomes required issuers to take action to improve their disclosure, compared to 56% in fiscal 2012.

---

[1]In this notice "issuers" means those reporting issuers contemplated in National Instrument 51-102 *Continuous Disclosure Obligations*.

Review outcomes

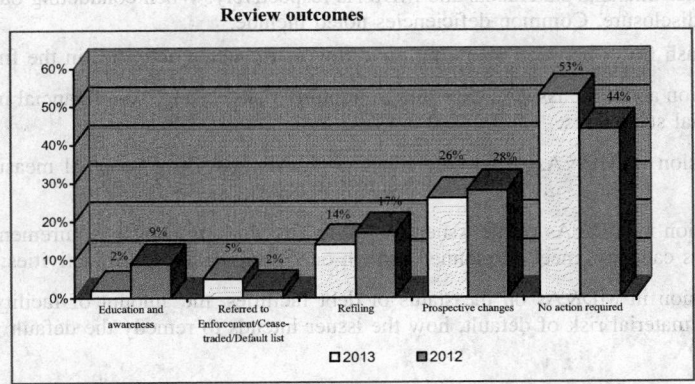

Review outcomes

We classified the outcomes of the full and issue-oriented reviews in the five categories described in Appendix D. Some CD reviews generated more than one category of outcome. For example, an issuer may have been required to refile certain documents and also make certain changes on a prospective basis.

The largest review outcome was in the "no action required" category (53%). This category is made up primarily from the results of issue-oriented reviews on specific IFRS topics and Form 51-102F1 disclosures. These reviews generally did not result in issuing comment letters. Our main objective was to monitor overall quality of disclosure, observe trends and conduct research. Our learning from these findings will be incorporated into our CD review program going forward. These reviews included reviews of cash flow and operating segments.

The "prospective changes" category (26%) continues to represent a large portion of our outcomes. If material deficiencies or errors are identified, we expect issuers to correct them by restating and refiling the CD documents. However, when enhancements are required as a result of deficiencies identified, we request that amendments be made when the issuer next files CD documents. We aim to educate issuers by providing future filing comments. Some of the common examples of the "prospective changes" include enhancement of:

- financial statement disclosure for critical judgements, sources of estimation uncertainty disclosure and going concern disclosure, consistent with IFRS requirements;

- MD&A to comply with Form 51-102F1, including discussion of operations, liquidity and transactions between related parties;

- executive compensation disclosure to comply with Form 51-102F6 *Statement of Executive Compensation*, with emphasis on compensation discussion and analysis.

Issue-Oriented Reviews

An issue-oriented review focuses on a specific accounting, legal or regulatory issue that we believe warrants scrutiny. In fiscal 2013, a total of 72% of the reviews were issue-oriented reviews (as compared to 64% of the reviews in fiscal 2012).

Issue-Oriented reviews 2013

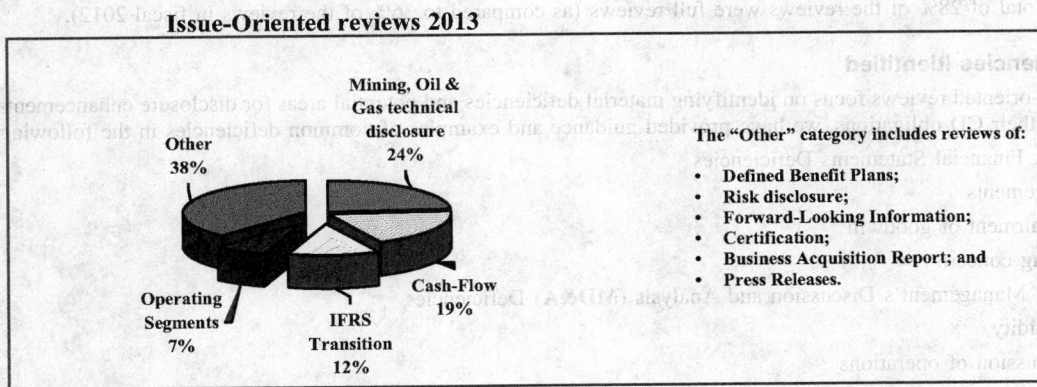

Issue-Oriented reviews 2013

The "Other" category includes reviews of:
- Defined Benefit Plans;
- Risk disclosure;
- Forward-Looking Information;
- Certification;
- Business Acquisition Report; and
- Press Releases.

You will find below the results of certain issue-oriented reviews conducted during fiscal 2013 and the common deficiencies noted. Please refer to Appendix C for "Mining, Oil & Gas technical disclosure" common deficiencies.

Cash flow disclosure

Issuers must comply with the disclosure obligations set out in IAS 7 *Statement of cash flows*, and sections 1.6 and 1.7 of Form 51-102F1 when addressing cash flow reporting in theirfinancial statements and MD&As respectively. When conducting our reviews, we focused oncash flow presentation, liquidity and capital disclosure. Common deficiencies noted include:

- inadequate classification of cash flows between operating, investing or financing activities in the financial statements;

- incomplete or unclear discussion about the issuer's exposure to liquidity risks arising from financial instruments, such as short and long-term borrowing in the financial statements;

- incomplete or unclear discussion in MD&As of why certain non-GAAP cash flow financial measures provide useful information to investors;

- incomplete or unclear discussion in MD&As of the issuer's liquidity, its working capital requirements, its ability to generate sufficient amount of cash to maintain its capacity, meet its planned growth or to fund development activities; and

- incomplete or unclear discussion in MD&As on the status of debt facilities, the amount of facility drawn and remaining, details of covenants, and when there is material risk of default, how the issuer intends to remedy the default or address the risk.

IFRS transition

During fiscal 2013 we reviewed the first IFRS interim financial reports of issuers with noncalendar year ends. When conducting our reviews, we focused on IFRS transition disclosures.

Common deficiencies noted include:

- insufficient or unclear description of the effect of the transition; and

- omission of certain reconciliations with previous Canadian GAAP — Part V.

Operating segments

Issuers must comply with the disclosure obligations set out in IFRS 8 *Operating segments*, and section 1.2 of Form 51-102F1 when addressing operating segments in their financial statements and MD&As. Common deficiencies noted include:

- incomplete or omitted information about geographic areas and major customers in financial statements;

- failure to combine and disclose in an "all other segments" category information about other business activities and operating segments that are not reportable, i.e. disclosed separately from other reconciling items in the reconciliations required in financial statements;

- failure to provide restated comparative period segment data reflecting a change in reportable segments in financial statements; and

- incomplete analysis of operating segments that are reportable segments in MD&As.

Full Reviews

A full review is broad in scope and covers many types of disclosure. A full review covers the selected issuer's most recent annual and interim financial reports and MD&A filed before the start of the review. For all other CD disclosure documents, the review covers a period of approximately 12 to 15 month. In certain cases, the scope of the review may be extended in order to cover prior periods. The issuer's CD documents are monitored until the review is completed. A full review includes an issuer's technical disclosure (i.e. technical reports for oil and gas and mining issuers), annual information form, annual report, information circulars, press releases, material change reports, business acquisition reports, websites, certifying officers' certifications and material contracts.

In fiscal 2013, a total of 28% of the reviews were full reviews (as compared to 36% of the reviews in fiscal 2012).

Common Deficiencies Identified

Our full and issue-oriented reviews focus on identifying material deficiencies and potential areas for disclosure enhancements. To help issuers better understand their CD obligations, we have provided guidance and examples of common deficiencies in the following appendices:

    Appendix A: Financial Statements Deficiencies

        1. Judgements

        2. Impairment of goodwill

        3. Going concern

    Appendix B: Management's Discussion and Analysis (**MD&A**) Deficiencies

        1. Liquidity

        2. Discussion of operations

        3. Related party transactions

    Appendix C: Other Regulatory Disclosure Deficiencies

        1. Mineral projects

        2. Oil and gas activities

        3. Disclosure controls and procedures and internal control over financial reporting in venture issuers' MD&A

4. Executive compensation

This is not an exhaustive list of disclosure deficiencies noted in our reviews. We remind issuers that their CD record must comply with all relevant securities legislation and lengthy disclosure does not necessarily equal full compliance. Examples do not include all requirements that could apply to a particular issuer's situation.

Results by jurisdiction

The Alberta Securities Commission and the *Autorité des marchés financiers* publish reports summarizing the results of the CD review program in their jurisdictions. See the individual regulator's website for a copy of its report:

- www.albertasecurities.com
- www.lautorite.qc.ca

Appendix A — Financial Statements Deficiencies

This Appendix provides some examples of deficient disclosure contrasted against more robust entity-specific disclosure for three areas of IFRS requirements. Many issuers could improve compliance in these areas.

1. — Judgements

In accordance with paragraph 122 of IAS 1 *Presentation of Financial Statements* (**IAS 1**), an issuer shall disclose in the summary of significant accounting policies or other notes, the judgements, apart from those involving estimations, that management has made in the process of applying the entity's accounting policies and that have the most significant effect on the amounts recognised in the financial statements.

We found that the disclosure about judgements that have the most significant effect on the amounts recognised in the financial statements is generally deficient and boilerplate. We noted that some issuers did not disclose any information about judgements. In some instances, issuers included a note with a title referring to judgements and estimates in the financial statements, but the note only included information about estimates. In other instances, issuers listed the financial statements items involving judgements, but they did not disclose the judgements made.

Example of deficient disclosure

Use of estimates and judgements

The preparation of financial statements in compliance with IFRS requires management to make judgements, estimates and assumptions that affect the application of accounting policies and the reported amounts of assets, liabilities, income and expenses. Actual results may differ from these estimates.

Estimates are based on management's best knowledge of current events and actions that the Company may undertake in the future. Estimates and underlying assumptions are reviewed on an on-going basis.

Critical judgements in applying accounting policies that have the most significant effect on the amounts recognized in the financial statements include assessing when depletion of capitalized costs for mining properties begins.

Example of entity-specific disclosure

Judgements

In applying the Company's accounting policies, management used its judgement in areas which have the most significant effect on the amounts recognized in the consolidated financial statements, including:

Determining Production Stage of a Mine

The Company capitalizes costs incurred in exploration, evaluation and development as part of mining properties prior to a mine being capable of operating at levels intended by management. Depletion of capitalized costs for mining properties begins upon the mine entering into production stage, which requires significant judgement in its determination. Management considers various factors to determine when a mine is substantially complete and ready for its intended use. These factors include: 1) level of capital expenditures compared to construction cost estimates; 2) completion of a reasonable period of testing of major mine and plant components; 3) achievement of consistent operational results over a reasonable period of time; 4) achievement of planned production capacity for plant and mill; and 5) ability to sustain ongoing production. The Company determined that the ABC mine was capable of operating at levels intended by management and moved into production stage on March 1, 2013.

2. — Impairment of goodwill

In accordance with paragraph 134 of IAS 36 *Impairment of Assets* (**IAS 36**), an issuer must disclose information on each cash-generating unit (**CGU**) or group of CGUs for which the carrying amount of goodwill or intangible assets with indefinite useful lives allocated to that CGU or group of CGUs is significant in comparison with the entity's total carrying amount of goodwill or intangible assets with indefinite useful lives. If the CGU or group of CGUs' recoverable amount is based on value in use, this information includes a description of each key assumption on which management has based its cash flow projections for the period covered by the most recent budgets/forecasts. Key assumptions are those to which the CGU or group of CGUs' recoverable amount is most sensitive.

Some issuers did not disclose all the information required by paragraph 134 of IAS 36.

Example of deficient disclosure

Goodwill is tested at least annually for impairment. The Corporation performed its impairment test as at December 31, 2012. For the purpose of impairment testing, goodwill is tested for impairment at the CGU level. The recoverable amount of the CGUs is based on value in use. If the carrying value exceeds the recoverable amount, an impairment charge is recognized to the extent that the carrying value exceeds the recoverable amount.

The recoverable amount of all CGUs has been determined based on cash flow projections on financial budgets approved by management covering a five-year period. Cash flows beyond the five-year period are extrapolated using estimated growth rates of 2%.

The discount rates used are pre-tax and reflect specific risks relating to the relevant CGUs. The pre-tax discount rate used for the value in use calculation was 16%.

No impairment charge has arisen as a result of the review performed as at December 31, 2012. Reasonably possible changes in key assumptions would not cause the recoverable amount of CGUs to fall below the carrying value.

In the above example, the issuer did not provide:

- the carrying amount of goodwill allocated to the CGU or group of CGUs for which the carrying amount of goodwill is significant in comparison with the issuer's total carrying amount of goodwill (Paragraph 134 (a) of IAS 36);

- a complete description, by CGU or group of CGUs, of each key assumption on which management has based its cash flow projections for the period covered by the most recent budgets/forecasts. Key assumptions are those to which the CGU or group of CGUs' recoverable amount is most sensitive (Paragraph 134 (d) (i) of IAS 36). Examples may include revenue growth or gross margin percentage assumptions; and

- a description of management's approach in determining the value (or values) assigned to each key assumption, whether these values reflect past experience or, if appropriate, are consistent with external sources of information, and, if not, how and why they differ from past experience or external sources of information (Paragraph 134 (d) (ii) of IAS 36). For example, if the gross margin percentage for a specific CGU or group of CGUs is higher in the cash flow projection than what has been experienced, it would be important for users to be alerted to this and to understand why.

Example of entity-specific disclosure for paragraph 134 (a) of IAS 36

For the purpose of annual impairment testing, goodwill is allocated to the following CGUs which are the units expected to benefit from the synergies of the business combinations in which the goodwill arises.

CGU A: $300,000	Note 1 : Assumes that CGU A, B, C and D are adequately described in another note. Also assumes that all other information required by paragraph 134 of IAS 36 is disclosed.
CGU B: $150,000	
CGU C: $95,000	
CGU D: $80,000	

3. — Going concern

Under IAS 1, when management is aware of material uncertainties related to events or conditions that may cast significant doubt upon the issuer's ability to continue as a going concern, the issuer must disclose these uncertainties.

Under paragraph 19 of the Canadian Auditing Standards 570 *Going Concern*, if adequate disclosure is made in the financial statements, the auditor shall express an unmodified opinion and include an "Emphasis of Matter" paragraph in the auditor's report to highlight the existence of a material uncertainty relating to the event or condition that may cast significant doubt on the entity's ability to continue as a going concern and draw attention to the note in the financial statements that discloses the matters set out in this paragraph.

We sometimes see inconsistent information between the going concern disclosure provided in an issuer's financial statements and the going concern disclosure included in the auditor's report.

Some issuers provide indications of financial difficulty, sometimes under a going concern heading, without explicitly stating that the disclosed uncertainties may cast significant doubt upon the issuer's ability to continue as a going concern despite the fact that the auditor's report highlights the existence of a material uncertainty relating to the event or condition that may cast significant doubt on the issuer's ability to continue as a going concern.

Example of deficient disclosure

Extract from the auditor's report

Emphasis of Matter paragraph

We draw attention to Note 2 to the financial statements that highlights the existence of a material uncertainty relating to the event or condition that may cast significant doubt on the entity's ability to continue as a going concern. Our opinion is not qualified in respect of this matter.

Extract from the financial statements

Note 2 — Going concern assumption

At year-end the Company had minimal cash and a working capital deficiency. While the Company has prepared its financial statements on the going concern basis, it is dependent on its ability to obtain additional financing from related parties and external financing to sustain operations and fund its expenditures.

Management is actively pursuing such additional sources of financing, and while it has been successful in doing so in the past, there can be no assurance it will be able to do so in the future.

Example of entity-specific disclosure

Extract from the auditor's report

Emphasis of Matter paragraph

We draw attention to Note 2 to the financial statements that highlights the existence of a material uncertainty relating to the event or condition that may cast significant doubt on the entity's ability to continue as a going concern. Our opinion is not qualified in respect of this matter.

Extract from the financial statements

Note 2 — Going concern assumption

The financial statements were prepared on a going concern basis. The going concern basis assumes that the Company will continue to operate in the foreseeable future and will be able to realize its assets and discharge its liabilities and commitments in the normal course of business.

For the year ended December 31, 2012, the Company had a net loss from operations of $3 million, a negative cash flow from operations of $2 million. As at year-end, the Company had a working capital deficiency of $1.5 million and cash on hand of $2 million.

The Company has a history of operating losses. In recent years, it had negative cash flows from operations and working capital deficiencies. The Company's credit facility contains certain financial covenants that are subject to periodic reviews. As part of its debt agreement, the Company must maintain a working capital ratio of at least 1:1. As at December 31, 2012, this ratio was 0.5:1. Given the breach, the lender has the right to demand full repayment at any time. As a result, the bank debt has been reclassified to short term liabilities resulting in a higher working capital deficiency. The Company is currently in negotiations with the lender to waive the covenant violations.

Whether and when the Company can attain profitability and positive cash flows is uncertain. These uncertainties cast significant doubt upon the Company's ability to continue as a going concern.

The Company will need to complete a short term financing to make the payment for the credit facility, raise sufficient working capital to maintain operations, reduce operating expenses and increase revenues. Subsequent to year end, the Company completed a private placement of $3 million to fund ongoing operations and to pay off the credit facility in the event the waiver cannot be obtained.

We remind issuers, that when there are uncertainties that cast doubt on the issuer's ability to continue as going concern, the MD&A should also provide a discussion and analysis on how the issuer expects to resolve the uncertainty event or condition.

Appendix B — Management's Discussion and Analysis (MD&A) Deficiencies

As in prior years, deficiencies were noted in the MD&A disclosure. As stated in Part 1(a) of Form 51-102F1 *Management's Discussion and Analysis* of National Instrument 51-102 *Continuous disclosure obligations* (**Form 51-102F1**), the MD&A should include balanced discussions of the issuer's financial performance and financial condition, including, without limitation, such considerations as liquidity and capital resources. The MD&A should help current and prospective investors to understand what the financial statements show and do not show. It should also discuss material information that may not be fully reflected in the financial statements.

There are three important areas of the MD&A where deficient disclosures were noted:

> 1) liquidity; 2) discussion of operations; and 3) related party transactions. For each area, we have provided examples of deficient disclosure contrasted against more robust entity-specific disclosure.

1. — Liquidity

Many smaller issuers focus their resources on completing a project or on expanding their operations. In accordance with section 1.6 of Form 51-102F1, the MD&A should focus on the issuer's ability to generate sufficient liquidity in the short term and in the long term to fund development activities or to meet planned growth. Moreover, the MD&A should explain how an issuer will meet its obligations as they become due and how they will address working capital deficiencies. We often find issuers reproduce in their MD&A information that is readily available from the financial statements without ensuring compliance with section 1.6 of Form 51-102F1.

Example of deficient disclosure

Liquidity

Year ended	December 31, 2012 $	December 31, 2011 $	Difference $
Cash flows from operating activities	(270,000)	102,000	(372,000)
Cash flows from investing activities	(350,000)	(340,000)	(10,000)
Cash flows from financing activities	520,000	425,000	95,000
Increase (decrease) of cash flows	(100,000)	187,000	(287,000)

Operating activities

The cash flows used in operating activities totalled $270,000. For the same period last year, the cash flow from operating totalled $102,000.

Investing activities

The cash flows used in investing activities increased by $10,000.

Financing activities

The cash flows from financing activities totalled $520,000. For the same period last year, the cash flows from financing totalled $425,000.

	December 31, 2012 $	December 31, 2011 $	Increase (decrease in working capital) $
Cash	51,000	151,000	(100,000)
Accounts receivable	789,000	852,000	(63,000)
Inventory	800,000	942,000	(142,000)
Prepaid expenses	30,000	28,000	2,000
Bank indebtedness	350,000	0	(350,000)
Loan — Investment tax credits	120,000	0	(120,000)
Accounts payable	1,035,000	877,000	(158,000)
Current portion of long term debt	150,000	100,000	(50,000)
Total working capital	15,000	996,000	(981,000)

The company's working capital decreased by $981,000.

Example of entity-specific disclosure

At the end of fiscal 2012, the Company had $51,000 of cash on hand and working capital of $15,000.

Given the various projects the Company is handling in the short and medium terms, management still considers the current cash balance and forecast net cash flows from operating activities for the next 12 months to be below the $300,000 desirable for its planned business development activities.

The success of development projects depends greatly on the Company's ability to generate sufficient cash to meet its needs. In fiscal 2012, the Company renegotiated the terms of its financing agreement with its financial institution and obtained an operating line of credit of $500,000 to continue development of its X products distribution activities and to finance growth. As at the end of fiscal 2012, $150,000 was available on the line of credit. Also in 2012, the Company contracted new financing of $120,000, secured by investment tax credits, to continue research and development work on its Y project. This financing was used at the end of fiscal 2012.

Hence, as of the end of fiscal 2012, management was still considering various sources of financing available on the market to increase the Company's liquidity. At year end, management was negotiating a private placement of $500,000 that was completed after year end.

2. — Discussion of operations

An MD&A should explain what factors contributed to changes in an issuer's operations. Issuers often reproduce information from the statement of profit or loss and other comprehensive income in their MD&A, without explaining what caused the changes.

In accordance with section 1.4 of Form 51-102F1, the revenue analysis included in an issuer's MD&A should discuss any change caused by selling prices, volume or quantity of goods or services being sold, or the introduction of new products or services. It is useful to investors if the issuer quantifies each of these elements. If other elements affected revenue, such as the introduction of a new competitor, the issuer's MD&A should also address these factors. If an issuer's financial statements present information from more than one reportable segment, the issuer must discuss the results of each segment in its MD&A.

Example of deficient disclosure

The Company reported revenue of $7,666,000 for the year ended December 31, 2012, compared with $7,098,000 a year earlier, an increase of 8%. The growth is mainly due to the sales of L products.

Example of entity-specific disclosure

During fiscal 2012, the Company's sales increased by 8%. The Company undertook a new activity, namely the distribution of L product in the Canadian manufacturing sector. As at year end, because of a delay in the manufacturing of L products, this activity had not yet reached the level that management had anticipated. The sales of L products increased sales by 7%.

Since 30% of sales are made in US dollars, the depreciation of the Canadian dollar had a positive impact on sales.

This impact was a 3% increase in sales. Despite the positive effect of the introduction of L product and of the exchange rate, the arrival of a new competitor forced the Company to decrease its sale price on product V. With this decrease, the Company was able to maintain the sale volume of product V. Due to the quality reputation of product V, management believes that no other decrease of the sale price will be necessary to maintain the sale volume of product V in the future. The decrease in the sale price caused a 2% decrease in sales.

3. — Related party transactions

Under section 1.9 of Form 51-102F1, issuers are required to identify the related person or entities, to discuss the business purpose of the transaction, to describe the measurement basis used and to discuss ongoing commitments resulting from the transaction. It is common for issuers to reproduce the related party transactions note provided in their financial statements or to simply refer to that note. However, IAS 24 *Related Party Disclosures* does not require the same level of information as section 1.9 of Form 51-102F1.

Example of deficient disclosure

The Company paid $150,000 to a company controlled by a director for consulting services.

Example of entity-specific disclosure

During the year, the Company paid $150,000 to Orange Inc., which is controlled by Mr. Smith, Chief Executive Officer and director of the Company. The $150,000 fee was paid for programming services relating to the implementation of new inventory software. The fee is based on what Orange Inc. usually charges its regular clients less a 10% discount. The Company expects to continue to use Orange Inc.'s programming services until the implementation of the new inventory software is completed.

Appendix C — Other Regulatory Disclosure Deficiencies

CSA Staff assess issuer compliance with securities laws. Our objective is to promote clear and informative disclosure that will allow investors to make informed investment decisions. The areas where compliance issues persist include disclosure about: 1) mineral projects; 2) oil and gas activities; 3) disclosure controls and procedures and internal control over financial reporting in venture issuers' MD&A; and 4) executive compensation.

1. — Mineral projects

Issuers engaged in mining activities have to comply with the requirements set out in National Instrument 43-101 *Standards of Disclosure for Mineral Projects*. Common deficiencies noted include:

- incomplete or inadequate disclosure of preliminary economic assessments, mineral resources and mineral reserves;
- non-compliant certificates and consents of qualified persons for technical reports;
- incomplete or inadequate disclosure of historical estimates and exploration targets; and
- name of the qualified person omitted in documents containing scientific and technical information.

2. — Oil and gas activities

Issuers engaged in oil and gas activities must comply with the requirements set out in National Instrument 51-101 *Standards of Disclosure for Oil and Gas Activities* (**NI 51-101**). Common deficiencies noted include:

- failure to adapt to current requirements of Form 51-101F1 *Statement of Reserves Data and Other Oil and Gas Information* (**Form 51-101F1**), Form 51-101F2 *Report on Reserves Data by Independent Qualified Reserves Evaluator or Auditor*, and Form 51-101F3 *Report of Management and Directors on Oil and Gas Disclosure*;

- non-compliance with sections 5.9, 5.16 and 5.17 of NI 51-101 concerning disclosure of resources other than reserves, classification to the most specific category of resources, summation across resource categories and disclosure of high case estimates of resources;

- inadequate disclosure of the meaning of, and method of calculating, the metrics used by issuers to measure and compare oil and gas activities;

- deficiencies in reserves reconciliation disclosure, including, for example, opening balances for the reserves reconciliation required under item 4.1 of Form 51-101F1 that do not agree with the prior year's closing balances; and

- insufficient and boilerplate disclosure of significant factors and uncertainties as per items 5.2 and 6.2.1 of Form 51-101F1, regarding the issuer's proved and probable undeveloped reserves and plans for developing those reserves under item 5.1 of Form 51-101F1.

3. — Disclosure controls and procedures (DC&P) and internal control over financial reporting (ICFR) in venture issuers' MD&A

Some venture issuers discussed DC&P or ICFR in their MD&As, but did not include cautionary language. In accordance with section 15.3 of the Companion Policy to National Instrument 52-109 *Certification of Disclosure in Issuers' Annual and Interim Filings* (**52-109 CP**), if a venture issuer and its certifying officers file Forms 52-109FV1 or 52-109FV2 (**Venture Issuers Basic Certificates**) and choose to discuss the design or operation of one or more components of their ICFR and DC&P in the MD&A or other regulatory filings, they should also consider disclosing in the same document that:

(a) the venture issuer is not required to certify the design and evaluation of its DC&P and ICFR and has not completed such an evaluation; and

(b) inherent limitations on the ability of the certifying officers to design and implement on a cost-effective basis DC&P and ICFR for the issuer may result in additional risks to the quality, reliability, transparency and timeliness of interim and annual filings and other reports provided under securities legislation.

Venture Issuers Basic Certificates provided in National Instrument 52-109 *Certification of Disclosure in Issuers' Annual and Interim Filings* (**NI 52-109**) include a "Note to Reader" that the certifying officers are not making any representations relating to the establishment and maintenance of:

i) controls and other procedures designed to provide reasonable assurance that information required to be disclosed by the issuer in its annual filings, interim filings or other reports filed or submitted under securities legislation is recorded, processed, summarized and reported within the time periods specified in securities legislation; and

ii) a process to provide reasonable assurance regarding the reliability of financial reporting and the preparation of financial statements for external purposes in accordance with the issuer's GAAP.

In the following example, the venture issuer used Venture Issuers Basic Certificates.

Example of deficient disclosure

Disclosure controls and procedures

The Company's Chief Executive Officer (CEO) and the Chief Financial Officer (CFO) are responsible for establishing and maintaining the Company's disclosure controls and procedures. These controls and procedures have been evaluated as at December 31, 2012 and have been determined to be effective.

Internal controls over financial reporting

The Company's CEO and the CFO are responsible for establishing and maintaining the Company's internal controls over financial reporting.

The internal control system pertaining to financial reporting gives a reasonable assurance as to the reliability of the financial information reported and the preparation of the financial statements in accordance with IFRS.

In the above example, to avoid confusion, it would have been more appropriate for the venture issuer to use Forms 52-109F1 or 52-109F2 (**Full Certificates**) as allowed by subsections 4.2(2) and 5.2(2) of NI 52-109. However, if the venture issuer does use Full Certificates, it must use a control framework for the design of ICFR, as required by subsection 3.4(2) of NI 52-109. The guidance in Parts 6 and 7 of 52-109 CP regarding establishing and evaluating DC&P and ICFR would also apply.

If in the above example, the venture issuer intends to use only a Venture Issuers Basic Certificate then it could have discussed only one or a few discrete components of DC&P or ICFR. In addition, the MD&A disclosure should be clear and should not include assertions about the design or evaluation of all aspects of DC&P or ICFR, and should not include any conclusions on the effectiveness of DC&P or ICFR. In addition, the cautionary language set out in section 15.3 of 52-109 CP would ensure transparent disclosure.

For additional guidance on NI 52-109, please see CSA Staff Notice 52-325 *Certification Compliance Review* and CSA Staff Notice 52-327 *Certification Compliance Update*.

4. — Executive compensation

Issuers must provide the executive compensation disclosure for the periods set out in, and in accordance with Form 51-102F6 *Statement of Executive Compensation* of National Instrument 51-102 *Continuous disclosure obligations*. This disclosure can be included in an information circular, an annual information form (**AIF**) or as a stand-alone document.

The executive compensation disclosure must be filed not later than 140 days after the end of the issuer's most recently completed financial year pursuant to subsection 11.6(3) of National Instrument 51-102 *Continuous Disclosure Obligations*. We noted that some issuers failed to file the executive compensation disclosure within 140 days. We remind issuers, that if they are not planning to send an information circular to their securityholders within 140 days after the end of their most recently completed financial year, they must include the executive compensation disclosure in either the AIF or as a stand-alone document, and file it within the 140 days.

Appendix D — Categories of Outcomes

Enforcement referral/ Default list/ Cease trade order

If the issuer has critical CD deficiencies, we may add the issuer to our default list, issue a cease trade order and/or refer the issuer to Enforcement.

Refiling

The issuer must amend and refile certain CD documents.

Prospective Changes

The issuer is informed that certain changes or enhancements are required in its next filing as a result of deficiencies identified.

Education and Awareness

The issuer receives a proactive letter alerting it to certain disclosure enhancements that should be considered in its next filing.

No action required

The issuer does not need to make any changes or additional filings. The issuer could have been selected in order to monitor overall quality disclosure of a specific topic, observe trends and conduct research.

CSA Notice 51-340 — Update on Proposed National Instrucment 51-103 — Ongoing Governance and Disclosure Requirements for Venture Issues

Date: July 25, 2013

36 O.S.C.B. 7356

[Not reproduced]

CSA Staff Notice 51-341 — Continuous Disclosure Review Program Activities for the Fiscal Year Ended March 31, 2014

Date: July 17, 2014

37 O.S.C.B. 661

Introduction

This notice contains the results of the reviews conducted by the Canadian Securities Administrators (**CSA**) within the scope of their Continuous Disclosure (**CD**) Review Program. This program was established to review the compliance of the CD documents of reporting issuers[1] (**issuers**) to ensure they are reliable and accurate. The CSA seek to ensure that Canadian investors receive high quality disclosure from issuers.

In this notice, we summarize the results of the CD Review Program for the fiscal year ended March 31, 2014 (**fiscal 2014**). To raise awareness about the importance of filing compliant CD documents, we also discuss certain areas where common deficiencies were noted and provide examples to help issuers address these deficiencies in the following appendices:

- Appendix A — Financial Statement Deficiencies
- Appendix B — Management's Discussion and Analysis (**MD&A**) Deficiencies
- Appendix C — Other Regulatory Disclosure Deficiencies

For further details on the CD Review Program, see CSA Staff Notice 51-312 (revised) *Harmonized Continuous Disclosure Review Program.*

---

[1]In this notice "issuers" means those reporting issuers contemplated in National Instrument 51-102 *Continuous Disclosure Obligations*.

Results for Fiscal 2014

CD Activity Levels

During fiscal 2014, a total of 991 reviews (221 full reviews and 770 issue oriented reviews (**IOR**)) were conducted. This is a 26% decrease from the 1,336 CD reviews (368 full reviews and 968 IORs) completed during fiscal 2013.

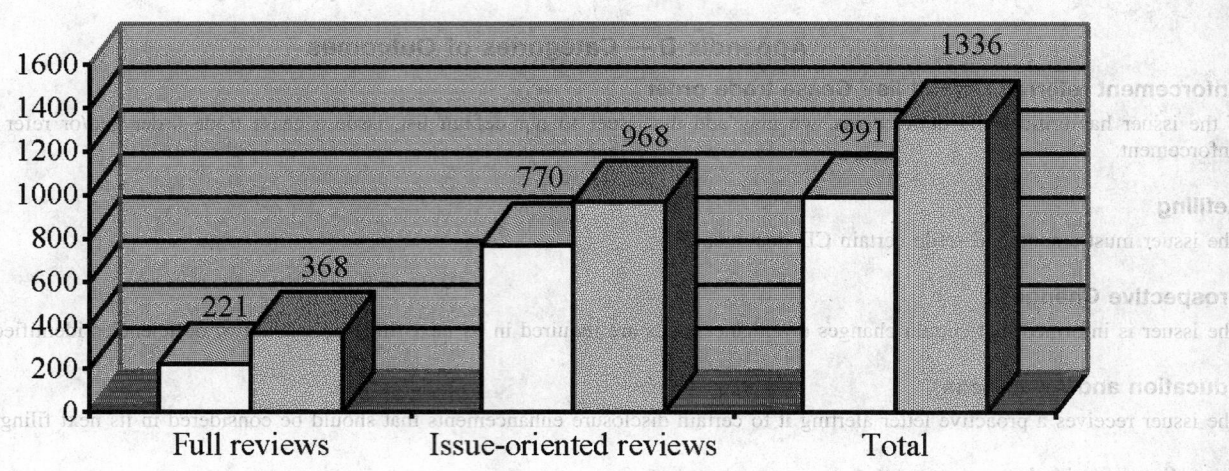

Reviews Completed

The decrease in the number of reviews can be primarily attributed to a change in our review focus. A higher number of IORs were conducted in fiscal 2013, where the main objective was to monitor quality of disclosure, observe trends and conduct research. In fiscal 2014, we focused on obtaining more substantive outcomes, as evidenced by the review outcomes chart below. We applied both qualitative and quantitative criteria in determining the level of review and type of review required. Some jurisdictions have also devoted additional resources to communicating results and findings to the public by issuing local staff notices and reports, where applicable, and holding education and outreach seminars to help issuers better understand their CD obligations.

CD Outcomes for Fiscal 2014

In fiscal 2014, 76% of our review outcomes required issuers to take action to improve their disclosure or resulted in the issuer being referred to enforcement, ceased traded or placed on the default list, compared to 47% in fiscal 2013.

Review Outcomes

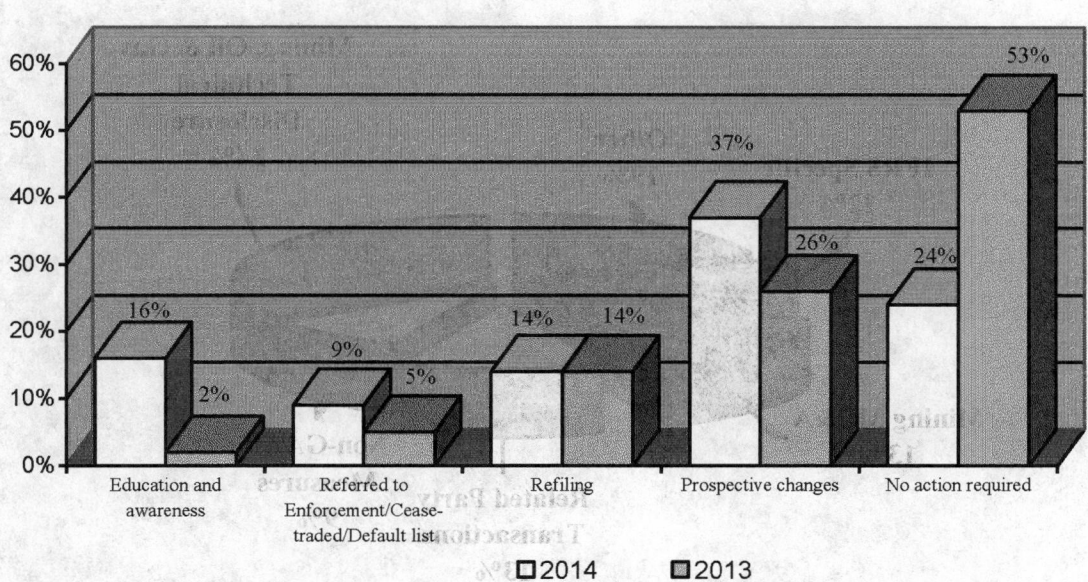

We classified the outcomes of the full reviews and IORs into five categories as described in Appendix D. Some CD reviews generated more than one category of outcome. For example, an issuer may have been required to refile certain documents and also make certain changes on a prospective basis.

Although the number of reviews conducted in fiscal 2014 decreased, the total number of review outcomes resulting from our reviews has remained fairly consistent with fiscal 2013. These results reflect our focused approach on obtaining more substantive outcomes. As noted in the review outcomes chart above, the significant changes were a decrease in the "No action required" category offset by increases in the "Prospective changes" and "Referred to Enforcement/Cease traded/Default list" categories. There was also a significant increase in the "Education and awareness" category and a consistent number of outcomes in the "Refiling" category.

For fiscal 2014, the largest review outcome was in the "Prospective changes" category. If material deficiencies or errors are identified, we generally expect issuers to correct them by restating and refiling the related CD documents. However, when enhancements are required as a result of deficiencies identified, we request that amendments be made when the issuer next files its CD documents.

Some of the observed deficiencies requiring prospective changes and/or refiling, included:

- financial statement measurement and disclosure, which may include going concern, accounting policies, critical judgements, sources of estimation uncertainty and fair value measurement;
- MD&A compliance with Form 51-102F1 of National Instrument 51-102, *Continuous Disclosure Obligations* (**Form 51-102F1**), which may include non-GAAP measures, forward looking information, discussion of operations, liquidity, related party transactions, etc.;
- executive compensation disclosure compliance with Form 51-102F6 *Statement of Executive Compensation*, particularly the compensation discussion and analysis; and
- business acquisition reports in compliance with Part 8 of National Instrument 51-102 *Continuous Disclosure Obligations* (**NI 51-102**).

Issue-Oriented Reviews

An IOR focuses on a specific accounting, legal or regulatory issue. IORs may focus on emerging issues, implementation of recent rules or when we want to narrow the scope of our review and focus on specific issues. In fiscal 2014, a total of 78% of all CD reviews were IORs (fiscal 2013 — 72%). The following are some of the IORs conducted by one or more jurisdictions:

Issue-Oriented reviews 2014

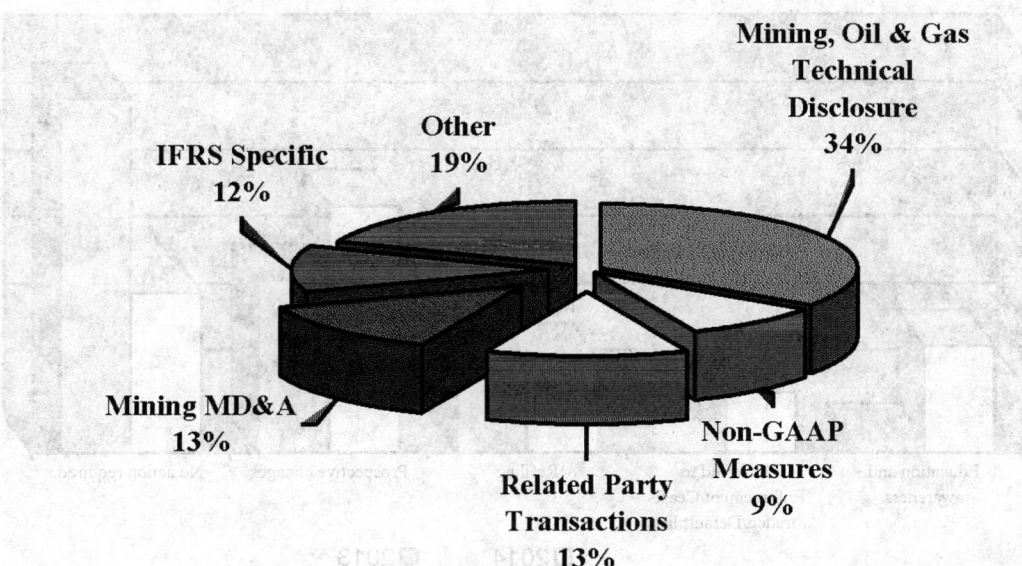

The "Other" category includes reviews of:

- Social Media

- Business Acquisition Reports

- Certifications

- Operating Segments

- Timely Disclosure

- Management Information Circular

The "Other" category of IORs noted above is not an exhaustive list. We may undertake an IOR for various other subject matters during the year. Refer to the Appendices for some common deficiencies identified as a result of our IORs.

Full Reviews

A full review is broad in scope and covers many types of disclosure. A full review covers the selected issuer's most recent annual and interim financial reports and MD&A filed before the start of the review. For all other CD disclosure documents, the review covers a period of approximately 12 to 15 months. In certain cases, the scope of the review may be extended in order to cover prior periods. The issuer's CD documents are monitored until the review is completed. A full review also includes an issuer's technical disclosure (e.g. technical reports for oil and gas and mining issuers), annual information form (**AIF**), annual report, information circulars, news releases, material change reports, business acquisition reports, corporate websites, certifying officers' certifications and material contracts.

In fiscal 2014, a total of 22% of the reviews were full reviews (fiscal 2013 — 28%).

Common Deficiencies Identified

Our full reviews and IORs focus on identifying material deficiencies and potential areas for disclosure enhancements. To help issuers better understand their CD obligations, we have provided guidance and examples of common deficiencies in the following appendices:

Appendix A: Financial Statement Deficiencies

   1. Disclosure of Interests in Other Entities

   2. Revenue Recognition

   3. Impairment of Assets

Appendix B: Management's Discussion and Analysis (**MD&A**) Deficiencies

   1. Non-GAAP Measures

   2. Forward Looking Information

   3. Additional Disclosure for Venture Issuers Without Significant Revenue

Appendix C: Other Regulatory Disclosure Deficiencies

1. Mineral Projects

2. Executive Compensation

3. Filing of News Releases and Material Change Reports (**MCRs**)

This is not an exhaustive list of disclosure deficiencies noted in our reviews. We remind issuers that their CD record must comply with all relevant securities legislation and lengthy disclosure does not necessarily result in full compliance. The examples in the appendices do not include all requirements that could apply to a particular issuer's situation and are only provided for illustrative purposes.

Results by Jurisdiction

All jurisdictions participate in the CD review program and some local jurisdictions may publish staff notices and reports summarizing the results of the CD reviews conducted in their jurisdictions. Refer to the individual regulator's website for copies of these notices and reports:

- www.bcsc.bc.ca

- www.albertasecurities.com

- www.osc.gov.on.ca

- www.lautorite.qc.ca

Appendix A — Financial Statement Deficiencies

This Appendix provides some examples of deficient disclosure contrasted against more robust entity-specific disclosure for three areas of IFRS requirements. Many issuers could improve compliance in these areas.

1. — Disclosure of Interests in Other Entities

IFRS 10 *Consolidated Financial Statements* (**IFRS 10**), IFRS 11 *Joint Arrangements* (**IFRS 11**) and IFRS 12 *Disclosure of Interests in Other Entities* (**IFRS 12**) came into effect for annual periods beginning on or after January 1, 2013. IFRS 10 and IFRS 11 changed the definition of control and joint control as well as the classification of, and in some cases the accounting for, joint arrangements. IFRS 12 resulted in additional disclosure requirements for all entities with subsidiaries, joint arrangements, associates and structured entities.

For the majority of issuers, the adoption of these standards did not have a material impact on comprehensive income and the statement of financial position. For those issuers where adoption of the standards led to significant changes, such as from joint control to control, we observed many examples of insufficient disclosure in the financial statements to explain the basis for the change. In these instances, it was not apparent what factor(s) when considered in the context of the new standards led to the changes, such as the underlying structure, the agreements in place and/or the relevant activities. In many of these circumstances, we noted that the issuer only disclosed what the change was and how it was accounted for, but did not explain the significant judgements and assumptions made in arriving at management's conclusion.

The following is an example of good disclosure of the significant judgements and assumptions made where the issuer changed their assessment from joint control to control (Paragraphs 7(a) and (b) of IFRS 12). In this instance, while the issuer had lengthy disclosure, all information presented appeared relevant. For ease of presentation, we have provided only a summary of the key disclosure.

Example of Entity-Specific Disclosure

Critical Accounting Estimates and Judgements

The Company owns 85% of Entity B, with the remaining 15% owned by a third party. Under the shareholder agreement, majority shareholder approval (greater than 50%) is required for certain items such as commissioning feasibility studies and approving projects based on these studies, signing new operating agreements and voting on expansion activities that do not represent activities outside of the core business.

However, other items require the unanimous approval of all shareholders, such as entering into new credit financing, approval of operating and capital budgets and expansion outside of the ordinary course of business.

Under IAS 27 and IAS 31[2], the Company determined that it did not have control as it did not have the power to govern the financial and operating policies so as to benefit from the activities based on the items which required unanimous approval.

On adoption of IFRS 10, the Company assessed the power to direct the relevant activities of Entity B. The Company assessed that the relevant activities of Entity B were only those requiring majority approval under the shareholder agreement.

In assessing the relevant activities, management used significant judgement to determine that the ability to unilaterally undertake feasibility studies and acting on these studies, as well as signing new operating agreements, meant that the Company, in addition to being exposed to variable returns through their 85% interest, had the ability to use its power to affect the potential returns from Entity B, and therefore these relevant activities supported the determination that the Company now controlled Entity B.

Example of Entity-Specific Disclosure

Critical Accounting Estimates and Judgements

Furthermore, as Entity B does not currently have or intend to have external debt, and does not plan to undertake any projects outside of the ordinary course of business, these were not deemed to be relevant activities.

Notes:

2   IAS 27 *Separate Financial Statements* and IAS 31 *Interests in Joint Ventures*. IAS 31 was superseded by IFRS 11 and IFRS 12 with effect from annual periods beginning on or after 1 January 2013.

The above example is specific to the facts of one issuer, and issuers are reminded that the disclosure should clearly discuss all relevant factors and significant judgements made by the issuer.

2. — Revenue Recognition

IAS 18 *Revenue* (**IAS 18**) defines revenue as income that arises in the course of ordinary activities of an entity, and sets out a framework for recognizing revenue. One of the key determinations that needs to be made when recording revenue, is whether the issuer is acting as principal or agent. When an agency relationship exists an issuer collects amounts on behalf of a third party rather than on their own behalf. Therefore, in agency relationships the issuer can only recognize the fee, commission or mark-up that will be paid to the issuer as revenue.

The determination as to whether the issuer is acting as principal or agent is based on the specific facts and circumstances of the transactions, and the role of each party to the arrangements. Whether revenue is generated from the sale of goods, the rendering of services or the receipt of interest, royalties or dividends will also need to be factored into the assessment, and the specific conditions to recognize revenue in these circumstances are outlined in IAS 18, paragraphs 14, 20 and 29, respectively. Examples have been noted whereby an issuer recognized revenue as either principal or agent but their disclosure documents (e.g. financial statements, MD&A, AIF) contradicted or did not support the accounting treatment. We expect issuers to provide sufficient disclosure of their accounting policies and judgements applied in determining those policies.

In the following example, the issuer recognized the revenue as principal.

Example of Deficient Disclosure

Significant Accounting Policies

The sub-contract revenue is recognized when the service has been performed, the related costs are incurred, the revenue can be reliably measured and when collectability is reasonably assured. There are no post-service obligations.

For the above example, the only additional disclosure in the MD&A was that sub-contracting revenues are generated by sub-contractors who own and operate their own vehicles, suggesting an agency relationship.

Based on this limited and potentially conflicting disclosure, we questioned the issuer's rationale for recognizing the revenue as principal. In particular, the issuer did not provide:

- entity-specific disclosure in the policy note;

- discussion of the significant judgements, if any, that management has made in the process of applying the issuer's accounting policies (paragraph 122 of IAS 1 *Presentation of Financial Statements*); and

- disclosure of the factors that were assessed in the determination of recognizing revenue on a gross basis as principal (paragraph 122 of IAS 1 *Presentation of Financial Statements*). Indicators that suggest the issuer is acting as principal include if the issuer (paragraph 21 of IAS 18 Illustrative Examples):

  - has the primary responsibility for providing the goods or services to the customer;

  - assumes the risk of inventory before or after the customer order, during shipping or on return;

  - has latitude in establishing prices either directly or indirectly; and

  - assumes the credit risk on the receivable due from the customer.

Example of Entity-Specific Disclosure

Significant Accounting Policies

The Company evaluates whether it is appropriate to record the gross amount of its revenues and related costs by considering a number of factors, including, among other things, whether the Company is the primary obligor under the arrangement and has latitude in establishing prices. Sub-contract revenue is derived from lease operators providing services to customers operating under the Company banner. Management has reviewed the primary indicators of the lease operator transactions such as:

-       The sub-contractor provides the service to the customer operating on behalf of the Company;

- The Company has control over who performs the service;

Example of Entity-Specific Disclosure (cont'd)

- The Company is responsible for all billing and collecting of revenues;

- The Company is responsible for setting all rates; and

- The lease operator receives a set percentage of lease operator revenues generated.

Taking all of the above into consideration, management has made the judgement that the Company is the primary obligor in these transactions and has sole latitude in establishing prices. Accordingly, revenue is recorded on a gross basis, excluding any taxes, when the service has been performed, the related costs are incurred, the revenues can be reliably measured and when collectability is reasonably assured.

3. — Impairment of Assets

In accordance with paragraph 130 of IAS 36 *Impairment of Assets* (**IAS 36**), an issuer must disclose information about the events and circumstances that led to the recognition or reversal of an impairment loss, and the amount of impairment loss recognized or reversed during the period. An issuer must disclose whether the recoverable amount of the asset (cash-generating unit) is its fair value less costs of disposal or its value in use. For level 2 and level 3 fair value measurements, if the recoverable amount is fair value less costs of disposal, an issuer must disclose the valuation technique used to measure fair value less costs of disposal. If recoverable amount is value in use, an issuer must disclose the discount rate(s) used in the current estimate and previous estimate (if any) of value in use. Some issuers did not disclose all the information required by paragraph 130 of IAS 36.

Example of Deficient Disclosure

The recoverable amount of the Company's cash generating unit A (CGU A), which includes oil and natural gas assets, is determined at each reporting period end, or where facts and circumstances provide impairment indicators. During the year ended December 31, 2013, the Company performed an impairment test on CGU A and identified that the carrying amount of CGU A of approximately $140 million exceeded its recoverable amount of approximately $85 million, and accordingly recognized an impairment expense of approximately $55 million. The impairment test was conducted by management based on information provided by an independent reserves evaluator.

In the above example, the issuer did not disclose:

- the events and circumstances that led to the recognition of the impairment loss (paragraph 130(a) of IAS 36);

- whether the recoverable amount of the assets is its fair value less costs of disposal or its value in use (paragraph 130(e) of IAS 36);

- if the recoverable amount is fair value less costs of disposal, how fair value is determined, and the valuation technique used to measure fair value less costs of disposal (paragraph 130(f) of IAS 36); and

- if the recoverable amount is value in use, the discount rate(s) used in the current estimate and previous estimate (if any) of value in use (paragraph 130(g) of IAS 36).

Example of Entity-Specific Disclosure

During the year ended December 31, 2013, the Company performed an impairment test on its cash generating unit A (CGU A), which includes oil and natural gas assets. The Company determined that the carrying amount of CGU A of approximately $140 million exceeded its recoverable amount of approximately $85 million due to a decline in estimated reserve volumes, and accordingly recognized an impairment expense of approximately $55 million.

The recoverable amount of CGU A was based on the higher of value in use and fair value less costs of disposal. The fair value measurement of CGU A is categorized within level 3 of the fair value hierarchy. The estimate of the fair value less costs of disposal was determined using forecasted cash flows based on proved plus probable reserves, forecasted commodity prices, and an after-tax discount rate of 5% which represents the Company's weighted average cost of capital and which includes estimates for risk-free interest rates, market value of the Company's equity, market return on equity and share volatility. The key input estimates used to determine cash flows from oil and gas reserves, which are subject to significant changes, include:

reserves at the time of reserve estimation, forward oil and natural gas prices, and the discount rate. See table below for the values of these input estimates (*table not provided in this illustrative example*).

Appendix B — Management's Discussion and Analysis Deficiencies

As in prior years, deficiencies were also noted in the MD&A disclosure. As stated in Part 1(a) of Form 51-102F1, the MD&A should include balanced discussions of the issuer's financial performance and financial condition, including, without limitation, such considerations as liquidity and capital resources. The MD&A should help current and prospective investors to understand what the financial statements show and do not show. It should also discuss material information that may not be fully reflected in the financial statements.

In fiscal 2014, we identified three areas of the MD&A where deficient disclosure was noted: 1) non-GAAP measures; 2) forward looking information; and 3) additional disclosure for venture issuers without significant revenue. For each area, we have provided examples of deficient disclosure contrasted against more robust entity-specific disclosure.

1. — Non-GAAP Measures

CSA Staff Notice 52-306 (Revised) *Non-GAAP Financial Measures and Additional GAAP Measures* (**SN 52-306**)provides issuers with guidance on non-GAAP financial measures and additional GAAP measures. A non-GAAP financial measure is a numerical measure of an issuer's historical or future financial performance, financial position or cash flows that does not meet one or more of the criteria of an issuer's GAAP for presentation in financial statements, and that either:

    i. excludes amounts that are included in the most directly comparable measure calculated and presented in accordance with the issuer's GAAP, or

    ii. includes amounts that are excluded from the most directly comparable measure calculated and presented in accordance with the issuer's GAAP.

Non-GAAP financial measures are often found in public documents, such as the MD&A, news releases, prospectus filings, corporate websites and marketing materials. Earnings before interest, taxes, depreciation and amortization (**EBITDA**) is a commonly used non-GAAP financial measure. We note that while EBITDA is generally a non-GAAP measure presented outside the financial statements, in some cases it may be an additional GAAP measure if it is presented in the financial statements (e.g. as a subtotal in the statement of comprehensive income).

Based on our reviews, we noted that the composition of EBITDA is often inconsistent with this commonly understood meaning. We noted that additional adjustments are often made to EBITDA to make the metric look more positive. When additional adjustments are included in the EBITDA calculation, the measure could be seen as potentially misleading or confusing to investors.

In the following example, adjustments for impairment, restructuring and foreign exchange charges have been made to EBITDA, which makes the non-GAAP measure potentially misleading, as it is unlikely to be comparable to similar measures presented by other issuers.

Example of Deficient Disclosure	2013	2012
Net earnings	$3,453	$2,768
Interest expense	335	326
Current and deferred taxes	522	468
Depreciation and amortization	45	48
Impairment charges	350	520
Restructuring charges	240	120
Foreign exchange loss	85	65
EBITDA	**5,030**	**4,315**

The following example illustrates better and more transparent disclosure where the impairment, restructuring and foreign exchange charges are not included as part of the EBITDA calculation, rather applied to EBITDA to arrive at Adjusted EBITDA.

Example of Entity-Specific Disclosure	2013	2012
Net earnings	$3,453	$2,768
Interest expense	335	326
Current and deferred taxes	522	468
Depreciation and amortization	45	48
EBITDA	**4,355**	**3,610**
Impairment charges	350	520
Restructuring charges	240	120
Foreign exchange loss	85	65
Adjusted EBITDA	**5,030**	**4,315**

In addition to the table above, in order to ensure the disclosure is not misleading, the issuer should include all material disclosures set out in SN 52-306.

2. — Forward Looking Information

Section 4A.3 of NI 51-102 states that a reporting issuer that discloses material forward-looking information (**FLI**) must include disclosure that:

a) identifies the FLI as such;

b) cautions users of FLI that actual results may vary from the FLI and identifies material risk factors that could cause actual results to differ materially from the FLI;

c) states the material factors or assumption used to develop FLI; and

d) describes the reporting issuer's policy for updating FLI if it includes procedures in addition to those described in subsection 5.8(2) of NI 51-102.

FLI is a key area of interest for investors. Most issuers include some FLI in a continuous disclosure document, a news release or on their website. When prepared properly, FLI can be used to enhance transparency and increase an investor's understanding of a reporting issuer's business and future prospects.

Our reviews identified four common areas where improvement is needed:

- clear identification of FLI;

- disclosure of material factors or assumptions used to develop FLI;

- updating previously disclosed FLI; and

- comparison of actual results to the future oriented financial information or financial outlook previously disclosed.

The most significant area of required improvement is disclosure of the material factors or assumptions used to develop FLI. Material factors and assumptions should be disclosed and should be reasonable, supportable, entity specific, and tied to FLI. Reporting issuers continue to provide general boilerplate disclosure that does not adequately describe the key assumptions used and how primary risks may impact future performance.

Example of Deficient Disclosure

In fiscal 2013, the Company anticipates that total sales will increase by 5.0% to 6.0%.

The following entity-specific disclosure example includes detailed factors and assumptions specific to the issuer's business. This is an example of clear disclosure which will assist an investor in understanding the issuer's business.

Example of Entity-Specific Disclosure

The following represents forward-looking information and users are cautioned that actual results may vary. In fiscal 2013, the Company expects total sales to increase by 5.0% to 6.0%. This expectation is based on same-store sales growth of between 3.0% and 4.0% and the introduction of new brands to our centre stores. It is expected that new brands will contribute to the increase in sales and will be offset by increased competition from U.S. retailers. A key performance indicator for the Company includes retail sales per square foot. This target assumes an average sale per square foot of $45. An increase of 25 basis points in interest rates may cause the sales target to decrease by 1.0% to 2.0%.

3. — Additional Disclosure for Venture Issuers Without Significant Revenue

Section 5.3 of NI 51-102 and Item 1.15 of Form 51-102F1, require a venture issuer that has not had significant revenue from operations in either of its last two financial years, to disclose in its MD&A, on a comparative basis, a breakdown of material components of:

a) exploration and evaluation (**E&E**) assets or expenditures;

b) expensed research and development costs;

c) intangible assets arising from development;

d) general and administration expenses; and

e) any material costs, whether expensed or recognized as assets, not referred to in paragraphs (a) through (d);

and if the venture issuer's business primarily involves mining exploration and development, the analysis of E&E assets or expenditures must be presented on a property-by-property basis.

We often find disclosure, as presented in the example below, where the issuer presents its exploration expenditures on a property-by-property basis without giving a breakdown by material components. This disclosure does not allow an investor to understand where and how the money was spent.

Example of Deficient Disclosure

	Property A	Property B	Total
Balance, as at December 31, 2011	$ 3,000,000	$ 1,000,000	$ 4,000,000
Additions	1,812,910	175,620	1,988,530
Balance, as at December 31, 2012	**4,812,910**	**1,175,620**	**5,988,530**

Example of Deficient Disclosure

	Property A	Property B	Total
Additions	775,220	469,840	1,245,060
Balance, as at December 31, 2013	**5,588,130**	**1,645,460**	**7,233,590**

In the following entity-specific example, the issuer has disclosed its E&E expenditures by material components and has provided the information for both of its material properties. The example assumes that the issuer's accounting policy is to expense E&E expenditures, however we would expect similar disclosure, along with a reconciliation of opening and closing balances if the issuer capitalized the amounts. In addition to such presentation, we would expect relevant qualitative discussion.

Example of Entity-Specific Disclosure

	Property A		Property B		Total		Total
	December 31, 2013	December 31, 2012	December 31, 2013	December 31, 2012	December 31, 2013	December 31, 2012	
Exploration Expenditures							
Assays and geochemistry	$ 41,050	$ 145,730	$ 27,390	—	$ 68,440	$ 145,730	
Camp costs	25,550	57,400	5,410	—	30,960	57,400	
Consulting	15,490	6,400	7,650	28,880	23,140	35,280	
Drilling	466,820	1,248,500	330,390	—	797,210	1,248,500	
Geology	38,690	19,400	17,420	—	56,110	19,400	
Geophysics	25,990	42,200	—	92,480	25,990	134,680	
Travel and lodging	77,260	124,880	36,120	21,660	113,380	146,540	
Salaries and labour	84,370	168,400	45,460	32,600	129,830	201,000	
Total exploration expenditures	**775,220**	1,812,910	**469,840**	175,620	**1,245,060**	1,988,530	
Cumulative E&E since inception	$ **5,588,130**	$ 4,812,910	$ **1,645,460**	$ 1,175,620	$ **7,233,590**	$ 5,988,530	

Appendix C — Other Regulatory Disclosure Deficiencies

CSA Staff assess issuer compliance with securities laws. Our objective is to promote clear and informative disclosure that will allow investors to make informed investment decisions. Some of the areas where compliance issues persist include disclosure or filings related to: 1) mineral projects; 2) executive compensation; and 3) news releases and material change reports.

1. — Mineral Projects

Issuers engaged in mineral exploration and mining activities have to comply with the requirements set out in National Instrument 43-101 *Standards of Disclosure for Mineral Projects* (**NI 43-101**) which includes Form 43-101F1 *Technical Report* (**Form 43-101F1**). Common deficiencies noted in complying with Form 43-101F1 include the following:

- lack of clearly disclosing how "reasonable prospects for economic extraction" were established for projects with mineral resource estimates, including the key assumptions, parameters and methods;

- insufficient discussion of any potential social or community related requirements and plans for advanced properties and the status of any negotiations or agreements with local communities;

- failure to provide the required context and justification for capital and operating cost estimates for advanced properties;

- inadequate information related to economic analysis information for advanced properties, particularly disclosing only pre-tax cash flows or only up-side sensitivity analysis;

- lack of disclosure related to project-specific risks and uncertainties that could reasonably be expected to affect the reliability or confidence in the information presented;

- incomplete disclosure of the "key findings" about the mineral property in the summary section; and

- missing statements required under section 8.1(2) of NI 43-101 in the qualified person's certificate.

Given the significance of the mining sector in Canadian capital markets, compliance with NI 43-101 and Form 43-101F1 for issuers with mineral projects is critical.

2. — Executive Compensation

Issuers must provide, in accordance with Form 51-102F6 *Statement of Executive Compensation* of NI 51-102 (**Form 51-102F6**) a Compensation Discussion and Analysis (**CD&A**) that describes and explains all significant elements of compensation awarded to, earned by, paid to, or payable to named executive officers (**NEO**).

A number of issuers that were reviewed did not include sufficient explanation in their CD&A as to how each element of compensation is tied to each NEO's performance. In many cases, the CD&A did not fully describe how executive compensation decisions were made. This was of particular concern with regard to performance goals and similar conditions.

We remind issuers that subsection 2.1(4) of Form 51-102F6 requires that if applicable, performance goals or similar conditions that are based on objective, identifiable measures, such as the company's share price or earnings per share, be disclosed. When an issuer discloses the grant of a bonus to an NEO, the issuer also has to explain in the CD&A that it granted the bonus because the performance goals were met and explicitly link this discussion with its NEO's compensation, as reported in the summary compensation table. If the payment of a bonus ultimately remained at the discretion of the board of directors, this fact should also be included in the CD&A to place the quantification of the objective measures in context.

We also remind issuers that, if they disclose performance goals that are non-GAAP financial measures, for example EBITDA, they have to explain how the issuer calculates these performance goals and similar conditions from its financial statements.

3. — Filing of News Releases and Material Change Reports (MCRs)

In accordance with National Policy 51-201 *Disclosure Standards*, news releases and announcements of material changes should be factual and balanced. In particular, an issuer's disclosure should contain enough detail to enable the media and investors to understand the substance and importance of the change it is disclosing. Issuers should avoid including unnecessary details, exaggerated reports or promotional commentary. Over the past fiscal year, we have seen many issuers filing news releases and/or MCRs when the timing of the release may be inappropriate and/or the content of the report is inadequate.

For example, if the issuer is changing the focus of their business to a different industry, the issuer should consider whether they have done sufficient due diligence prior to deciding whether they should file a news release and/or issue a MCR. This may include, but is not limited to, obtaining the appropriate licenses and/or meeting regulations, determining whether the issuer has sufficient capital or other resources to implement the changes, etc. The issuer would then need to consider the level of disclosure to be included in the news release and MCR, which should include, among other things, information about the time and resources required for the change in business as well as the barriers and obligations involved in realizing the change.

We also continue to see issuers who either do not file their news releases and/or MCRs or fail to do so on a timely basis in accordance with Part 7 of NI 51-102. We have also noted several issuers are inconsistent with their filings of news releases and/or MCRs. The following are some examples of these types of situations:

- Announcement of directors and officers appointments or resignations. We note issuers file news releases and/or MCRs announcing new appointments but do not file similar announcements of resignations. We have also observed several instances where issuers' disclosure of the appointments/resignations of directors and officers is buried within lengthy news releases, often after positive earnings and production activity.

- Breach and/or waiver of financial covenants. We note issuers do not file news releases and/or MCRs for a breach and/or waiver of financial covenant in a timely manner. In several instances we have observed issuers that have breached and/or received a waiver but wait until the filing of their next interim or annual filings before this information is disseminated.

We will continue to monitor these types of filings going forward.

Appendix D — Categories of Outcomes

Referred to Enforcement/Cease-Traded/Default List

If the issuer has critical CD deficiencies, we may add the issuer to our default list, issue a cease trade order and/or refer the issuer to enforcement.

Refiling

The issuer must amend and refile certain CD documents.

Prospective Changes

The issuer is informed that certain changes or enhancements are required in its next filing as a result of deficiencies identified.

Education and Awareness

The issuer receives a proactive letter alerting it to certain disclosure enhancements that should be considered in its next filing or when staff of local jurisdictions publish staff notices and reports on a variety of continuous disclosure subject matters reflecting best practices and expectations.

No Action Required

The issuer does not need to make any changes or additional filings. The issuer could have been selected in order to monitor overall quality disclosure of a specific topic, observe trends and conduct research.

Questions — Please refer your questions to any of the following:

[Omitted.]

CSA Staff Notice 51-342 — Staff Review of Issuers Entering Into Medical Marijuana Business Opportunities

Date: February 26, 2015
 38 O.S.C.B. 1843

[Not reproduced]

CSA Staff Notice 51-344 — Continuous Disclosure Review Program Activities for the fiscal year ended March 31, 2015

Date: July 16, 2015
 38 O.S.C.B. 6343

Introduction

This notice contains the results of the reviews conducted by the Canadian Securities Administrators (**CSA**) within the scope of their Continuous Disclosure Review Program (**CD Review Program**). The goal of the program is to improve the completeness, quality and timeliness of continuous disclosure provided by reporting issuers[1] (**issuers**) in Canada. This program was established to assess the compliance of continuous disclosure (**CD**) documents and to help issuers understand and comply with their obligations under the CD rules so that investors receive high quality disclosure.

In this notice, we summarize the results of the CD Review Program for the fiscal year ended March 31, 2015 (**fiscal 2015**). To raise awareness about the importance of filing compliant CD documents, Appendix A includes information about areas where common deficiencies were noted, with examples in certain instances, to help issuers address these deficiencies as well as best practices.

For further details on the CD Review Program, see CSA Staff Notice 51-312 (revised) *Harmonized Continuous Disclosure Review Program.*

Results for Fiscal 2015

CD Activity Levels

During fiscal 2015, a total of 1,058 CD reviews (280 full reviews and 778 issue oriented reviews (**IOR**)) were conducted. This represents a 7% increase from the 991 CD reviews (221 full reviews and 770 IORs) completed during fiscal 2014.

---

[1]In this notice "issuers" means those reporting issuers contemplated in National Instrument 51-102 *Continuous Disclosure Obligations* (**NI 51-102**).

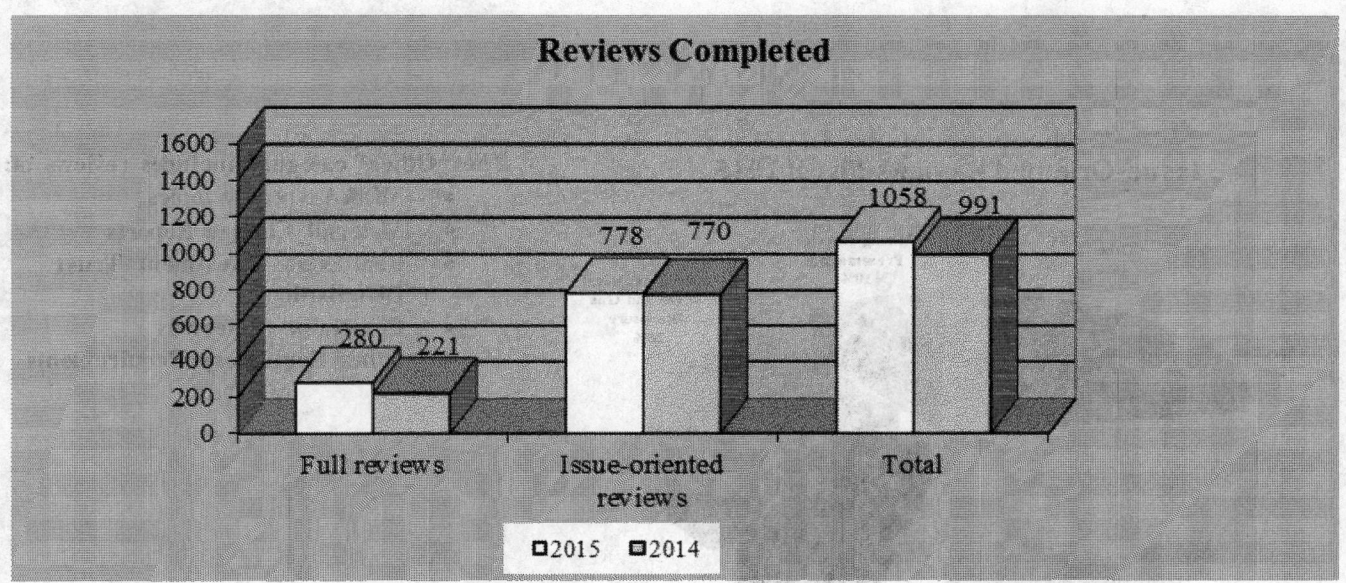

Issuers annually selected for a full CD review are identified using a risk based approach. Issuers selected for an IOR are identified based on the targeted objective or subject matter of the review.

We apply both qualitative and quantitative criteria in determining the level of review and type of review required. Some CSA jurisdictions also devote additional resources to communicating results and findings to market participants by issuing local staff notices and reports, where applicable, and holding education and outreach seminars to help issuers better understand their CD obligations.

Issue-Oriented Reviews

An IOR focuses on a specific accounting, legal or regulatory issue. IORs may focus on emerging issues, implementation of recent rules or on matters where we believe there may be a heightened risk of investor harm. In fiscal 2015, a total of 74% of all CD reviews completed were IORs (fiscal 2014 — 78%). The following are some of the IORs conducted by one or more jurisdictions:

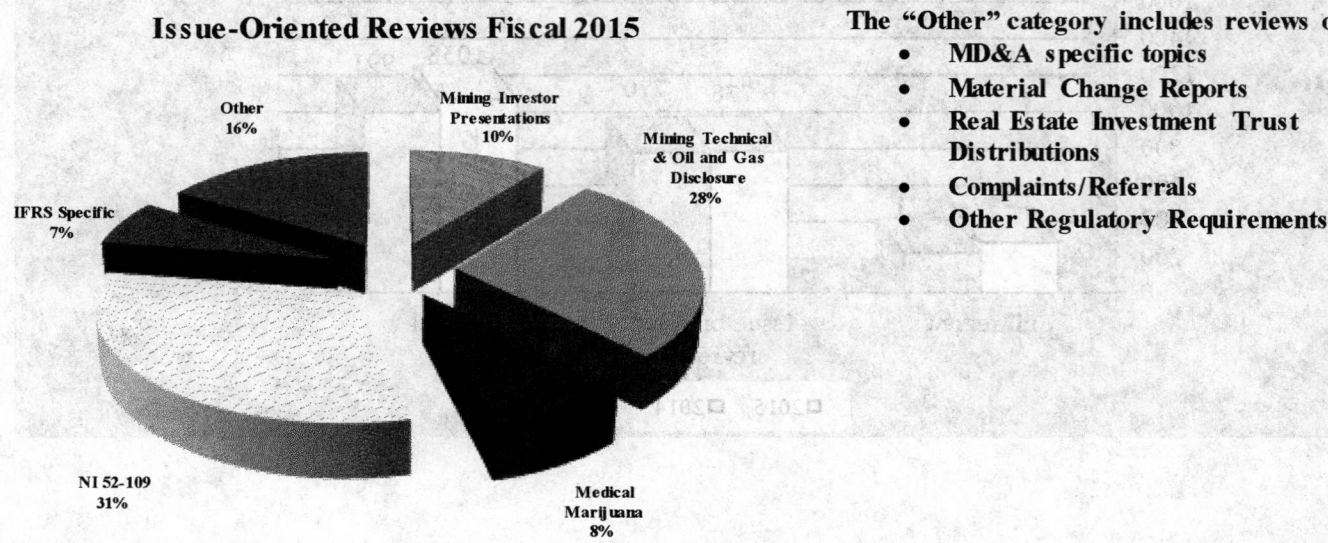

Issue-Oriented Reviews Fiscal 2015

- Other 16%
- Mining Investor Presentations 10%
- Mining Technical & Oil and Gas Disclosure 28%
- IFRS Specific 7%
- NI 52-109 31%
- Medical Marijuana 8%

The "Other" category includes reviews of:
- **MD&A specific topics**
- **Material Change Reports**
- **Real Estate Investment Trust Distributions**
- **Complaints/Referrals**
- **Other Regulatory Requirements**

The "Other" category of IORs noted above is not an exhaustive list. We may undertake an IOR for various other subject matters during the year. Refer to Appendix A — *Financial Statements, MD&A and Other Regulatory Deficiencies* (**Appendix A**) for some common deficiencies identified as a result of our IORs.

Full Reviews

A full review is broad in scope and covers many types of disclosure. A full review covers the selected issuer's most recent annual and interim financial reports and MD&A filed before the start of the review. For all other CD disclosure documents, the review covers a period of approximately 12 to 15 months. In certain cases, the scope of the review may be extended in order to cover prior periods. The issuer's CD documents are monitored until the review is completed. A full review also includes an issuer's technical disclosure (e.g. technical reports for oil and gas and mining issuers), annual information form (**AIF**), annual report, information circulars, news releases, material change reports, business acquisition reports, corporate websites, certifying officers' certifications and material contracts. In fiscal 2015, a total of 26% of the CD reviews were full reviews (fiscal 2014 — 22%).

CD Outcomes for Fiscal 2015

In fiscal 2015, 59% of our review outcomes required issuers to take action to improve and/or amend their disclosure or resulted in the issuer being referred to enforcement, ceased traded or placed on the default list. In fiscal 2014, 60% of the reviews resulted in a similar outcome.

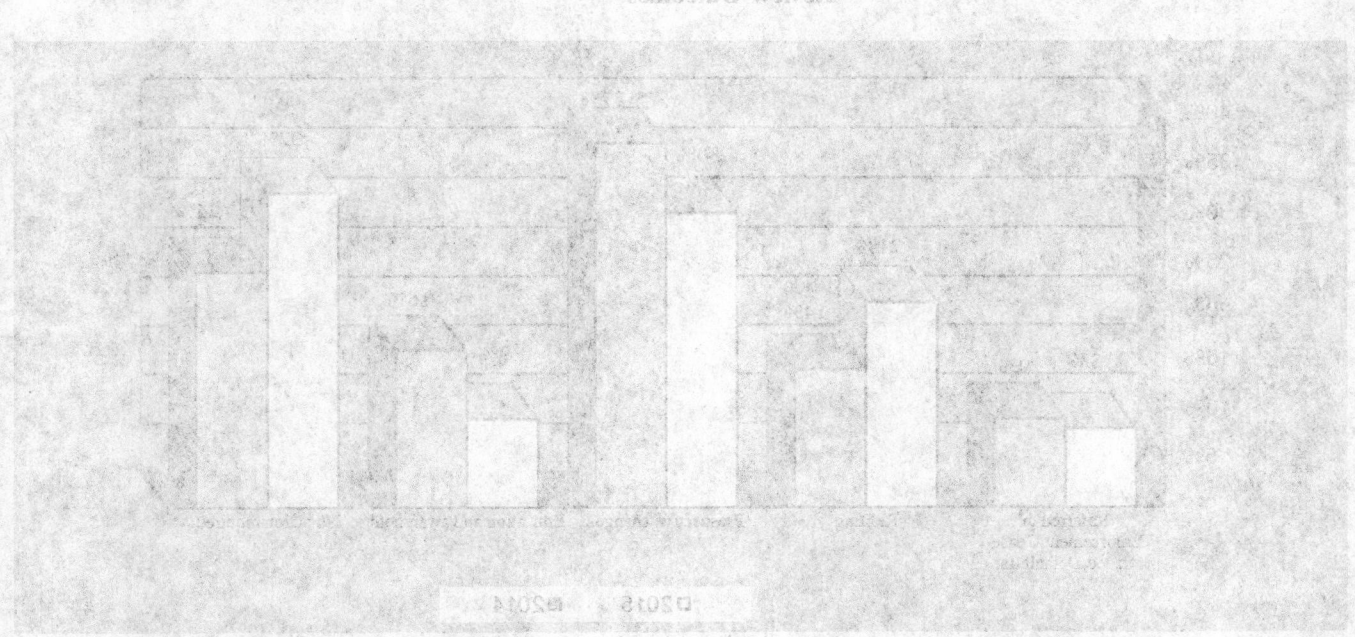

The "Other" category of IORs noted above is not an exhaustive list. We may undertake an IOR for various other subject matters during the year. Refer to Appendix A — Financial Statements, MD&A and Other Regulatory Deficiencies (Appendix A) for some common deficiencies identified as a result of our IOR.

Full Reviews

A full review is broad in scope and covers many types of disclosure. A full review covers the selected issuer's most recent annual and interim financial reports and MD&A filed before the start of the review. For all classes of documents, the review covers a period of approximately 12 to 15 months. In certain cases, the scope of the review may be extended in order to cover prior periods. The issuer's CD documents are monitored until the review is completed. A full review also includes an issuer's technical disclosure (e.g. technical reports for oil and gas and mining issuers), annual information form (AIF), annual report, information circulars, news releases, material change reports, business acquisition reports, corporate web-sites, certifying officers' certifications and material contracts. In fiscal 2015, a total of 20% of the CD reviews were full reviews (fiscal 2014 — 23%).

CD Outcomes for Fiscal 2015

In fiscal 2015, 59% of our review outcomes required issuers to take action to improve and/or amend their disclosure or resulted in the issuer being referred to enforcement, cease traded or placed on the default list. In fiscal 2014, 60% of the reviews resulted in a similar outcome.

Review Outcomes

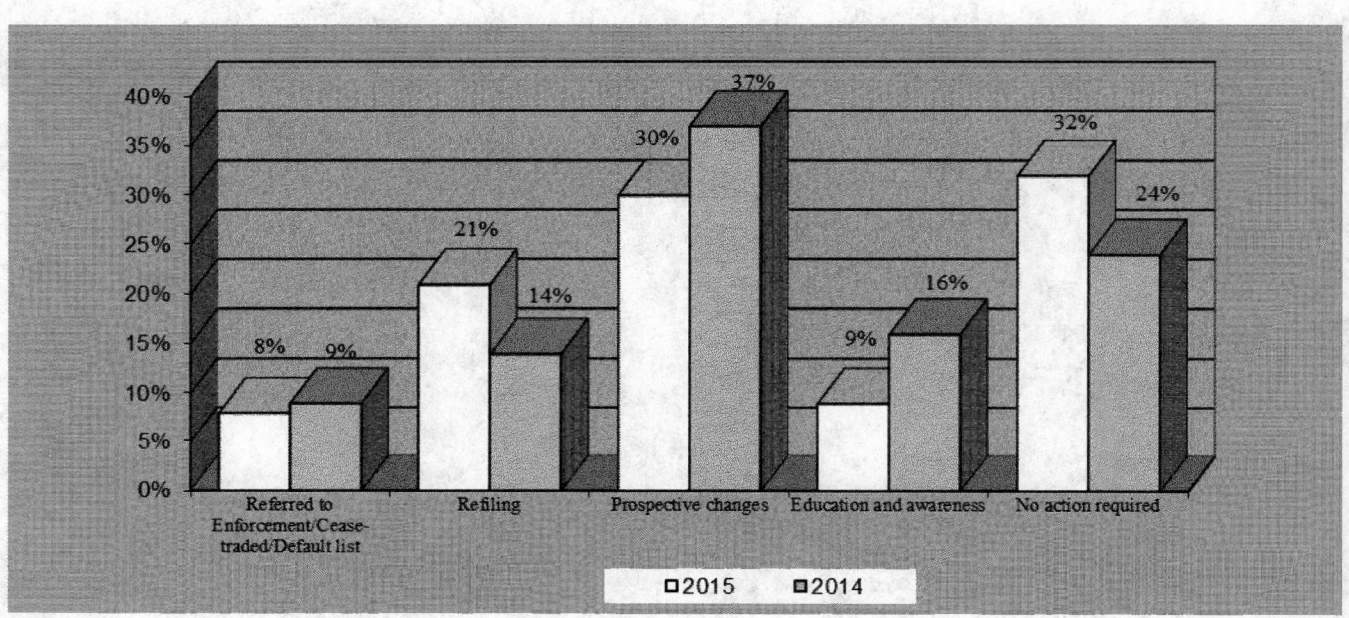

We classify the outcomes of the full reviews and IORs into five categories as described in Appendix B. Some CD reviews may generate more than one category of outcome. For example, an issuer may have been required to refile certain documents and also make certain changes on a prospective basis.

Where possible, we have attempted to identify trends we observed when reviewing comparative results. However, given our risk based approach noted above, the outcomes on a year to year basis may vary and cannot be interpreted as an emerging trend. Issues and issuers reviewed each year might be different. The result in fiscal 2015 is that we continued to see substantive outcomes being obtained as a result of our reviews as noted in the refilings and referred to enforcement/default list/cease traded categories.

The refilings of issuers' CD record included some of the following areas:

- **Financial Statements**: compliance with recognition, measurement and disclosure requirements in IFRS, which included, but was not limited to, impairment, revenue, accounting policies, significant judgements and auditors' reports;

- **Management's Discussion and Analysis (MD&A)**: compliance with Form 51-102F1 of NI 51-102 (**Form 51-102F1**), which included, but was not limited to, non-GAAP measures, discussion of operations, liquidity, related party transactions, disclosure controls and procedures (**DC&P**) and internal controls over financial reporting (**ICFR**);

- **Other Regulatory Requirements**: compliance with other regulatory matters, which included, but was not limited to, mining technical reports and investor presentations for content deficiencies, business acquisition reports, certificates, and filing of previously unfiled documents, such as material contracts, or clarifying news releases to address concerns around unbalanced disclosure.

Refilings are significant events that should be clearly and broadly disclosed to the market in a timely manner. Please refer to "News Release upon Refiling of CD Documents" in Appendix A to this Notice for further discussion.

Common Deficiencies Identified

Our full reviews and IORs focus on identifying material deficiencies and potential areas for disclosure enhancements. We have provided guidance and examples of common deficiencies in Appendix A.

This is not an exhaustive list of disclosure deficiencies noted in our reviews. Issuers must ensure that their CD record complies with all relevant securities legislation. The volume of disclosure filed does not necessarily equate to full compliance. The examples in Appendix A do not include all requirements that could apply to a particular issuer's situation and are provided for illustrative purposes only.

Results by Jurisdiction

All CSA jurisdictions participate in the CD Review Program and some local jurisdictions may publish staff notices and reports summarizing the results of the CD reviews conducted in their jurisdictions. Refer to the individual regulator's website for copies of these notices and reports:

- www.bcsc.bc.ca

- www.albertasecurities.com

- www.osc.gov.on.ca

- www.lautorite.qc.ca

Appendix A — Financial Statement, MD&A and Other Regulatory Deficiencies

Our CD reviews identified several financial statement, MD&A and other regulatory deficiencies that resulted in issuers enhancing their disclosure and/or refiling their CD documents. To help issuers better understand and comply with their CD obligations, we present the key observations from our reviews in both a hot buttons chart as well as detailed discussions. The hot buttons section includes observations along with considerations for issuers including the relevant authoritative guidance. The discussion that follows each chart includes examples of deficient disclosure contrasted against more robust entity-specific disclosure or a more in-depth explanation of the matters we observed.

Please note that the following observations do not constitute an exhaustive list.

Financial Statement Deficiencies

Hot Buttons

	Observations	Considerations
Financial Statements		
Operating Segments	• We continue to see issuers that fail to disclose certain information about geographic areas, in particular revenues from external customers. • We also see issuers that fail to disclose information about major customers, in particular when revenues from transactions with a single external customer amount to 10% or more of the issuer's revenues.	• Issuers must disclose information about operating segments so that investors are able to evaluate the nature and financial effects of the business activities in which they engage and the economic environments in which they operate. • Disclosure about major customers may assist users in determining if there is economic dependence. *Reference: Paragraph 33 and 34 of IFRS 8 Operating Segments*

Observations	Considerations
Financial Statements	
Business Combinations • Upon acquisition of a business, issuers are reporting a significant portion of the purchase price in goodwill without separately identifying and assigning a value to other intangible assets, such as customer lists, intellectual property, etc.	• The allocation to the appropriate identifiable assets is important as it may impact an issuer's accounting for intangibles in its financial statements. For example, definite life intangibles require amortization into the statement of profit or loss and will therefore impact income in subsequent periods. • The measurement period shall not exceed one year from the acquisition date. *Reference: Paragraph 10 to 13 and 45 and Appendix B of IFRS 3 Business Combinations*
Fair Value Measurement • We continue to see issuers that fail to disclose a description of the valuation technique and inputs used for fair value measurements categorized within Level 3 of the fair value hierarchy.	• For Level 3 fair value measurements, issuers must describe the valuation technique used in the fair value measurement. • Issuers must also describe and provide *quantitative* information about *all* significant unobservable inputs used. • These disclosures will assist users to understand the measurement uncertainty inherent in fair value measurements. *Reference: Paragraph 93(d) to (h) of IFRS 13 Fair Value Measurement*

Disclosure Example

1. — Impairment of Assets

In the prior year, we noted that some issuers did not disclose how they determined the amount of impairment loss in accordance with paragraph 130 of IAS 36 *Impairment of Assets* (**IAS 36**). Given the current economic conditions, we continue to note this issue.

In accordance with paragraph 130 of IAS 36, if an impairment loss has been recognized or reversed for an individual asset, or a cash-generating unit (**CGU**), an issuer must disclose whether the recoverable amount of the asset or CGU is its fair value less costs of disposal or its value in use. If the recoverable amount is fair value less costs of disposal, an issuer must disclose the level of the fair value hierarchy within which the fair value measurement of the asset or CGU is categorized. In the case of Level 2 and Level 3 of the fair value hierarchy, an issuer must also describe the valuation technique and key assumptions used. If the recoverable amount is value in use, an issuer must disclose the discount rate(s) used in the current estimate and previous estimate (if any) of value in use.

Some issuers who measured the recoverable amount of an asset or a CGU as value in use did not base cash flow projections on reasonable and supportable assumptions that represent management's best estimate of the range of economic conditions that will exist over the remaining useful life of the asset or CGU, as required by paragraph 33(a) of IAS 36. Some issuers inappropriately based cash flow projections on forecasts for periods longer than five years where management could not demonstrate its experience to forecast over such periods, as discussed in paragraph 35 of IAS 36.

Additionally, some issuers did not disclose the significant judgements and the uncertainties involved in estimating the recoverable amount of the asset or the CGU, where such judgements and sources of estimation uncertainty met the criteria for disclosure under IAS 1 *Presentation of Financial Statements* (**IAS 1**).

Issuers should assess at the end of each reporting period whether there is any indication that an asset or CGU may be impaired in accordance with paragraphs 8 — 17 of IAS 36, or paragraph 18–20 of IFRS 6 as applicable to exploration for and evaluation of mineral resources. If any such indication exists, the entity must estimate the recoverable amount of the asset in accordance with paragraphs 18–57 of IAS 36. At the end of each reporting period, issuers must assess the need to reverse an impairment loss recognized for an asset or a CGU in prior periods as required by paragraphs 109–123 of IAS 36. We caution issuers that an improper impairment test and impairment charge may result in misstatements in profit or loss in the current and future periods.

Example of Deficient Disclosure — Impairment of Assets (exploration stage mining company)

Due to poor market conditions, the Company considered the likelihood of obtaining suitable financing in the foreseeable future in order to conduct further exploration on Property Y was unlikely. Therefore, it determined that Property Y is impaired and recognized an impairment loss of $5 million to write down the carrying value of Property Y from $7.5 million to $2.5 million in the year ended December 31, 2014.

Example of Deficient Disclosure — Impairment of Assets (exploration stage mining company)

In the above example, the issuer did not disclose how it measured the recoverable amount of Property Y and the associated judgements and estimation uncertainty including:

- Whether the recoverable amount of $2.5 million is value in use or fair value less costs of disposal;

- If the recoverable amount is value in use, the discount rate(s) used in the current and previous estimate (if any) of value in use (IAS 36, paragraph 130(g));

- If the recoverable amount is fair value less costs of disposal, the applicable level of the fair value hierarchy, and in the case of Level 2 and Level 3 of the hierarchy, the valuation technique and key assumptions used (IAS 36, paragraph 130(f)); and

- Judgements made and the uncertainties involved in estimating the recoverable amount of the property (IAS 1, paragraph 125).

Entity-Specific Disclosure Example — Impairment of Assets (exploration stage mining company)

Due to the lack of suitable financing, the Company has determined that it does not have adequate resources to conduct further exploration on Property Y for the foreseeable future. Therefore, the Company suspended the exploration program at Property Y in the year ended December 31, 2014, wrote down the carrying value of Property Y from $7.5 million to $2.5 million, and recognized an impairment loss of $5 million. The recoverable amount of $2.5 million is based on Property Y's fair value less

costs of disposal. In estimating the fair value less costs of disposal, the Company used a market approach. The Company used sale prices of adjacent properties obtained from the local Ministry of Mines, and adjusted this to consider market capitalization declines of comparable companies with comparable properties over the past year. The Company also discussed with its external technical consultants the drilling activities and exploration program conducted on Property Y and the uncertainty regarding future prospects in the mining industry. As this valuation technique requires the use of unobservable inputs including the Company's data about the property and management's interpretation of that data, it is classified within Level 3 of the fair value hierarchy. A value in use calculation is not applicable as the Company does not have any expected cash flows from using the property at this stage of operations.

In estimating fair value less costs of disposal, management's judgement was involved in identifying comparable properties with characteristics similar to Property Y (e.g. nature and amount of resources, size and accessibility). The comparable properties are in the same mineral district, with exploration directed for the same commodity using the same mineral deposit model. The comparable properties are also at a similar stage of development in terms of the existence, quantity and quality of mineral resources and availability of critical infrastructure.

The above example is specific to the facts of this issuer. The nature and extent of the information provided by issuers may vary depending on facts and circumstances; however, the information provided must help users of financial statements understand the judgements that management made about the future and other sources of estimation uncertainty. This may include more qualitative and quantitative information about the assumptions used.

MD&A Deficiencies

Hot Buttons

	Observations	Considerations
MD&A		
Liquidity and Capital Resources	- We continue to see issuers that fail to provide sufficient analysis of their liquidity and capital resources. - Issuers often reproduce information in the MD&A that is readily available from the financial statements. For example, repeating the balances of cash flows from operating, investing and financing activities.	- This section of the MD&A should focus on an issuer's ability to generate sufficient liquidity in the short term and long term in order to fund planned growth, development activities or expenditures necessary to maintain capacity. - In addition, the MD&A should provide an analysis of an issuer's capital resources, including the amount, nature and purpose of commitments and the expected source of funds to meet these commitments.

Part 5: ONGOING REQUIREMENTS

	Observations	Considerations
MD&A		
		• While these disclosures are required for all issuers, they are especially important when issuers have negative cash flows from operations, a negative working capital position or a deteriorating financial condition. • This disclosure enables users to assess how the issuer will meet its obligations and its short and long term objectives. *Reference: Item 1.6 and 1.7 of Form 51-102F1*
Results of Operations	• We continue to see issuers that provide boilerplate disclosure when discussing their results of operations. Issuers simply repeat information that is readily available in the financial statements. • Issuers provide the year over year change in the balance without explaining, in sufficient detail, the key drivers and reasons contributing to the change.	• This section of the MD&A should provide a narrative explanation of how the issuer performed during the period, along with trends, commitments, risk and uncertainties that will impact the company. • Trend analysis should include a discussion of the significant factors that caused the change in the financial statement balance. For example, revenues, expenses, gross profit, etc. • In certain instances, for example general and administrative expenses, it may be helpful to quantify each material component of the balance to better explain the movement in the total balance. • This disclosure provides users the ability to assess the business of the issuer and to identify and understand trends. *Reference: Item 1.4 of Form 51-102F1*
Forward Looking Information (FLI) / Non-GAAP Measures (NGM)	• We continue to see issuers that use FLI and NGM in the MD&A, news releases, websites, marketing materials and other documents without clearly identifying them as such or including the appropriate disclosures.	• The disclosure requirements for FLI and the disclosure guidance provided for NGM apply regardless of whether FLI and NGM are used in the MD&A or on a website, news release or other public document. • If the above-noted disclosure of FLI and/or NGM are made in another document, such as the MD&A, the information should be cross referenced or re-produced. • Users may be misled if these disclosures are not provided. *Reference:* *FLI — Part 4A and 4B of NI 51-102* *NGM — CSA Staff Notice 52-306*
Real Estate Investment Trust (REIT) Distributions	• We note that some REITs declare distributions which exceed the cash they generate from operating their own underlying properties (cash flow from operations) but do not provide the relevant disclosure in their MD&A and AIF.	• The disclosure should signal to investors that excess distributions occurred, how they were financed, and that they represented a return of capital, amongst other things. • Investors may be misled if such excess distributions, in addition to risks about their sustainability, are not appropriately disclosed. *Reference:* *Section 6.5.2 of National Policy 41-201 Income Trusts and Other Indirect Offerings*

Disclosure Examples

1. — Related Party Transactions

While many of the MD&A requirements for related party transactions in Form 51-102F1 are similar to the requirements under IAS 24 *Related Party Disclosures*, Form 51-102F1 specifically requires an issuer to identify the related person or entity, as well as to discuss the business purpose of the transaction.

MD&A disclosure of related party transactions is intended to provide both qualitative and quantitative information that is necessary for an understanding of the business purpose and economic substance of a transaction. To meet this requirement, the disclosure should be specific and detailed, rather than simply repeat disclosure from the financial statements.

The disclosure below is an example of boilerplate disclosure for a related party transaction:

Example of Deficient Disclosure — Related Party Transactions

For the years ended December 31, 2014 and 2013 the Company paid a related party $43 million and $40 million, respectively, for management and administrative fees. As of December 31, 2014 and 2013 outstanding balance amounted to $4 million and $5 million, respectively.

In the above example, the issuer does not disclose the identity of the related party and the business purpose of the transaction. A better example of disclosure for related party transactions would be as follows:

Example of Entity-Specific Disclosure — Related Party Transactions

The Company does not directly employ any of the individuals responsible for managing and operating the business. XYZ Corp., a major stockholder, provides management and administrative workforce to the Company under the terms of the Agreement. The costs of all compensation, benefits and employer expenses are invoiced by XYZ Corp. based on actual costs incurred and are settled on a monthly basis. The Company presents these charges as general and administrative costs and costs incurred under administrative services agreements. For the years ended December 31, 2014 and 2013, the Company incurred $43 million and $40 million, respectively, under this Agreement. As of December 31, 2014 and 2013, outstanding balance payable to XYZ Corp. amounted to $4 million and $5 million, respectively.

---

2. — NI 52-109 Certification of Disclosure in Non-Venture Issuers' Annual and Interim Filings

NI 52-109 *Certification of Disclosure in Issuers' Annual and Interim Filings* (**NI 52-109**) requires both non-venture and venture issuers to file certificates of annual and interim filings signed by an issuer's Chief Executive Officer and Chief Financial Officer (**Certifying Officers**). In addition, non-venture issuers must establish and maintain DC&P and ICFR.

Forms 52-109F1 *Certificate of Annual Filings-Full Certificate* (**Annual Certificate**) and 52-109F2 *Certification of Interim Filings-Full Certificate* (**Interim Certificate**), which NI 52-109 requires non-venture issuers to file, state that the Certifying Officers have designed, or caused to be designed, DC&P and ICFR. Furthermore, Annual Certificates indicate that the Certifying Officers have evaluated or caused to be evaluated, under their supervision, the effectiveness of DC&P and ICFR, and that the issuer has disclosed in its annual MD&A the Certifying Officers' conclusions about the effectiveness of DC&P and ICFR. When the Certifying Officers determine there is a material weakness relating to the design or operations of ICFR, or when there has been a limitation on the scope of design, issuers must include paragraphs 5.2, 5.3 and/or 6(b)(ii) in an Annual Certificate or paragraph 5.2 or 5.3 in an Interim Certificate, and include disclosure in the MD&A describing the material weakness or summary financial information relating to the entities subject to the scope limitation.

Our reviews identified three common areas of deficiencies: (i) inconsistency between a certificate and MD&A disclosure; (ii) material weakness disclosure; and (iii) limitations on scope of design relating to an acquired business.

(i) — Inconsistency between a certificate and MD&A disclosure

We observed inconsistency between conclusions in a certificate about the effectiveness of ICFR and the related disclosure in an issuer's MD&A. This inconsistency caused uncertainty as to whether the Certifying Officers were concluding ICFR were effective. The two most common deficiencies were:

- Certifying Officers specified the existence of a material weakness in paragraph 5.2 and/or 6(b)(ii) of their Annual Certificate. However, the MD&A did not include any discussion of a material weakness.

- paragraph 6(b)(i) of an issuer's Annual Certificate stated that the Certifying Officers' conclusion about effectiveness of the issuer's ICFR was disclosed in the MD&A. However, the MD&A conclusions were incomplete or qualified.

(ii) — Material Weakness

When Certifying Officers identify a material weakness in the design or operations of ICFR at the period-end date, the Certifying Officers cannot conclude ICFR is effective. If a non-venture issuer determines that it has a material weakness, section 3.2 of NI 52-109 requires the issuer to disclose in its annual or interim MD&A a description of the weakness, the impact of the material weakness on the issuer's financial reporting and its ICFR, and the issuer's current plans, if any, or any actions already undertaken, for remediating the material weakness. A material weakness may relate to the design or operation of an issuer's ICFR. The MD&A disclosure should clearly describe the nature of the material weakness.

We observed issuers that identified a material weakness, provided a vague description of the material weakness and gave little insight about the impact on the issuer's financial reporting. We also noted a few issuers identified the same material weakness for a number of consecutive years, and during that same time period had experienced significant growth in their operations. While NI 52-109 does not require an issuer to remediate an identified weakness, section 9.7 of Companion Policy 52-109CP (**52-109CP**) notes that MD&A disclosure will be useful to investors if it discusses whether the issuer has committed, or will commit, to a plan to remediate an identified material weakness, and whether there are any mitigating procedures that reduce the risks that have not been addressed as a result of the identified material weakness. A meaningful discussion of an un-remediated material weakness should be updated in each MD&A to ensure the impact of the material weakness continues to be properly reflected as the company grows or experiences other changes in operations.

Example of Deficient Disclosure — NI 52-109 Certification

The Company's Chief Executive Officer (**CEO**) and Chief Financial Officer (**CFO**) have designed an internal control framework to provide reasonable assurance regarding the reliability of financial reporting and the preparation of financial statements for external purposes in accordance with IFRS. The control framework used to design the Company's Internal Control over Financial Reporting (**ICFR**) is Risk Management and Governance — Guidance on Control, published by the Canadian Institute of Chartered Accountants. The CEO and CFO have concluded that the design and operation of the Company's disclosure controls and procedures were not effective as of December 31, 2014 due to the deficiencies noted in the following paragraph.

The Company identified internal control deficiencies that are common for a company of this size including lack of segregation of duties due to a limited number of employees dealing with accounting and financial matters. However, management believes that at this time, the potential benefits of adding employees to clearly segregate duties do not justify the costs associated with such an increase. The risk of material misstatement is mitigated by the direct involvement of senior management in the day-to-day operations of the Company and review of the financial statements and disclosures by senior management, the members of Audit Committee and the Board of Directors. These mitigating procedures are not considered sufficient to reduce the likelihood that a material misstatement would not be prevented or detected.

There were no material changes in ICFR during 2014.

The above example includes the following deficiencies:

i. *Inconsistency between the certificate and MD&A disclosure.* The issuer filed its annual certificate and included the paragraphs 5.2 and 6(b)(ii); however, the issuer only concluded that the DC&P was ineffective in its MD&A disclosure.

ii. *Material weakness.* The MD&A disclosure did not sufficiently describe the material weakness, the impact of the material weakness on the issuer's financial reporting and its ICFR, or the issuer's plans, if any, to remediate as follows:

- the second paragraph refers to more than one internal control deficiency but only describes one deficiency (a lack of segregation of duties);

- the disclosure does not clearly identify the deficiency as a material weakness;

- the meaning of the term "financial matters" used in the description of the deficiency relating to segregation of duties is unclear and insufficient; and

- the issuer has a market capitalization of over $300 million, assets greater than one billion and net income greater than $60 million; however, the disclosure states that lack of segregation of duties is common for an issuer of this size. Staff have not observed this to be the case and have requested issuers provide clarification.

(iii) — Limitations on Scope in Design

Section 3.3 of NI 52-109 permits limitations on the scope of design of DC&P and ICFR to exclude controls, policies, and procedures of a business the issuer acquired not more than 365 day before issuer's financial year end, for an allowed period of time as set out in 3.3(4) of NI 52-109. When issuers limit the scope of their design, subsection 3.3(2)(b) requires that they disclose the scope limitation and provide meaningful summary financial information about each underlying entity in the MD&A. Certain issuers had a scope limitation relating to two or more unrelated entities but presented combined financial summary information instead of disclosing information for each entity separately. Section 14.2 of 52-109CP allows for the presentation of combined financial information only in instances where the businesses are related.

Other Regulatory Disclosure Deficiencies

Hot Buttons

	Observations		Considerations
		Regulatory	
Material Contracts	• We continue to see issuers that fail to file material contracts.	•	Subsection 12.2(2) of NI 51-102 provides a list of contracts required to be filed even if entered into in the ordinary course of business. These may include a financing or credit agreement with terms that have a direct correlation with anticipated cash distributions or a contract on which the issuer's business is substantially dependent.
		•	Material contracts must be filed no later than the time the issuer files a material change report if the making of the document constitutes a material change for the issuer, or when the AIF is filed within 120 days after the end of the issuer's most recently completed financial year.
			Reference: Sections 12.2 and 12.3 of NI 51-102
Material Change Reports (MCRs)	• We continue to see situations where it appears that a material change has occurred and issuers do not file a MCR as soon as practicable, or within 10 days of the date of which the change occurs. For example, in situations where the issuer has eliminated or significantly reduced its dividend payments or the issuer has experienced a significant increase or decrease in near-term earnings prospects.	•	Announcements of material changes should be factual and balanced. Unfavourable news must be disclosed just as promptly and completely as favourable news.
		•	National Policy 51-201, *Disclosure Standards* (**NP 51-201**) lays out examples of potentially material information, including changes in a company's dividend payments or policies.
		•	Part 7 of NI 51-102 requires an issuer to file a MCR within 10 days of the occurrence of a material change.
			Reference: Section 4.3 of NP 51-201 and Part 7 of NI 51-102
Selective Disclosure	• Selective disclosure occurs when a company discloses material non-public information to one or more individuals or companies and not broadly to the investing public.	•	Issuers holding private meetings with analysts, industry conferences etc., must ensure that selective disclosure is not provided in these meetings.
		•	If unintentional selective disclosure has occurred, issuers must make a full public announcement including contacting the relevant stock exchange and asking that trading be halted.
		•	Keeping detailed meeting notes and/or transcripts may be useful to determine if unintentional selective disclosure has occurred.
			Reference: Section 5.1 of NP 51-201

Part 5: ONGOING REQUIREMENTS

Discussion of other regulatory deficiencies

1. — Mineral Projects

Mining issuers' disclosure must comply with National Instrument 43-101 *Standard of Disclosure for Mineral Projects* (**NI 43-101**) including written disclosure contained on an issuer's website such as investor presentations, fact sheets, media articles, and links to third party content. A review of mining issuers' investor presentations identified several areas where issuers need to improve their disclosure in order to better comply with NI 43-101 including:

• Naming the qualified person: naming the individual who approved technical information and noting their relationship to the issuer;

- Preliminary economic assessments: providing required cautionary statements so investors can understand the limitations of study's results;

- Mineral resources and mineral reserves: including a clear statement on whether mineral resources include or exclude mineral reserves;

- Exploration targets: expressing potential quantity and grade as a range and including the required statements outlining the target limitations;

- Historical estimates: including source, date, reliability, and key assumptions along with the required cautionary statements rather than simply stating "*not NI 43-101 compliant*"; and

- Avoiding overly promotional terms and potentially misleading information especially exploration stage and mineral resource stage issuers: securities legislation prohibits misleading disclosure and misrepresentation. Terms which may be used inappropriately in certain circumstances include: *"world-class", "spectacular and exceptional results", "production ready"*.

Refer to CSA Staff Notice 43-309 *Review of Website Investor Presentations by Mining Issuers* for further information.

Given the significance of the mining sector in Canadian capital markets, compliance with NI 43-101 and Form 43-101F1 for issuers with mineral projects is critical. We will continue to review mining issuers' website disclosure as part of our overall CD Review Program.

2. — Filing of News Releases

Unbalanced and Promotional Disclosure

We continue to see news releases filed by issuers that contain unbalanced and promotional disclosure. In fiscal 2015, staff from certain CSA jurisdictions reviewed the disclosure provided by issuers that publicly announced their intention to enter into Canada's medical marijuana industry. As a result of our review, we published CSA Staff Notice 51-342 *Staff Review of Issuers Entering Into Medical Marijuana Business Opportunities* (**SN 51-342**).

The guidance in SN 51-342 is applicable to all industries, particularly companies thinking about material changes to their primary business or where an event has or will have an impact on future prospects.

In general, staff found that issuers' news releases were unbalanced and promotional in nature. While the benefits associated with involvement in the medical marijuana industry were often discussed, these discussions were not consistently accompanied by disclosures about the necessary approvals required to enter the industry, risks, uncertainties, cost implications and time required before the issuer can begin licensed operations. Additionally, a discussion of barriers and obligations to enter the industry was often not provided. Issuers that did not provide sufficient disclosure in their news releases were required to file a clarifying disclosure document as a result of our review. All issuers should provide investors comprehensive, factual and balanced disclosure and avoid promotional commentary.

Issuers should refer to the guidance on best disclosure practices in National Policy 51-201 as well as the disclosure requirements in Part 1(a) of Form 51-102F1.

News Release upon Refiling of CD Documents

We note that certain issuers failed to issue and file a news release on a timely basis after deciding to refile a CD document or restate financial information for comparative periods in financial statements. In certain instances, issuers indicated that the delay to issue a news release was due to the fact that there were no scheduled Audit Committee and/or Board meetings where the news release would be approved. As a result, issuers waited to issue a news release until the next scheduled meeting and in many cases until the actual refiling of the CD documents. In our view, it is not appropriate for issuers to delay the filing of a new release for these reasons.

Section 11.5 of NI 51-102 indicates that if the issuer decides it will re-file a document under NI 51-102 and the information in the refiled document or restated financial information will differ materially from the information originally filed, the issuer must *immediately* issue and file a news release authorized by an executive officer disclosing the nature and substance of the change or proposed changes. This may involve engaging Audit Committee and/or Board members prior to their next scheduled meeting. This will ensure timely issuance of a news release.

Certain CSA jurisdictions have published a staff notice that provides guidance on their expectations related to refiling of documents by issuers and the associated news releases. We note that certain jurisdictions also maintain a list on their website that includes issuers that amend and refile continuous disclosure documents pursuant to staff's review.

We will continue to monitor issuers' compliance with these requirements.

Appendix B — Categories of outcomes

Referred to Enforcement/Cease-Traded/Default List

If the issuer has substantive CD deficiencies, we may add the issuer to our default list, issue a cease trade order and/or refer the issuer to enforcement.

Refiling

The issuer must amend and refile certain CD documents or must file a previously unfiled document.

Prospective Changes

The issuer is informed that certain changes or enhancements are required in its next filing as a result of deficiencies identified.

Education and Awareness

The issuer receives a proactive letter alerting it to certain disclosure enhancements that should be considered in its next filing or when staff of local jurisdictions publish staff notices and reports on a variety of continuous disclosure subject matters reflecting best practices and expectations.

No Action Required

The issuer does not need to make any changes or additional filings. The issuer could have been selected in order to monitor overall quality disclosure of a specific topic, observe trends and conduct research.

Questions — Please refer your questions to any of the following:

Sonny Randhawa Manager, Corporate Finance Ontario Securities Commission 416-204-4959 srandhawa@osc.gov.on.ca	Allan Lim Manager British Columbia Securities Commission 604-899-6780 Toll-free 800-373-6393 alim@bcsc.bc.ca
Christine Krikorian Senior Accountant, Corporate Finance Ontario Securities Commission 416-593-2313 ckrikorian@osc.gov.on.ca	Sabina Chow Senior Securities Analyst British Columbia Securities Commission 604-899-6797 Toll-free 800-373-6393 schow@bcsc.bc.ca
Oujala Motala Accountant, Corporate Finance Ontario Securities Commission 416-263-3770 omotala@osc.gov.on.ca	
Cheryl McGillivray Manager, Corporate Finance Alberta Securities Commission 403-297-3307 cheryl.mcgillivray@asc.ca	Tony Herdzik Deputy Director, Corporate Finance Financial and Consumer Affairs Authority of Saskatchewan 306-787-5849 tony.herdzik@gov.sk.ca
Froshell Saure Securities Analyst, Corporate Finance Alberta Securities Commission 403-355-3885 froshell.saure@asc.ca	
Patrick Weeks Analyst, Corporate Finance Manitoba Securities Commission 204-945-3326 patrick.weeks@gov.mb.ca	Nadine Gamelin Analyst, Continuous Disclosure Autorité des marchés financiers 514-395-0337, ext. 4417 Toll-free: 1-877-525-0337, ext. 4417 nadine.gamelin@lautorite.qc.ca
To-Linh Huynh Senior Analyst Financial and Consumer Services Commission (New Brunswick) 506-643-7856 To-Linh.Huynh@fcnb.ca	Kevin Redden Director, Corporate Finance Nova Scotia Securities Commission 902-424-5343 Kevin.redden@novascotia.ca
John Paixao Compliance Officer Financial and Consumer Services Commission (New Brunswick) 506-658-3116	Junjie (Jack) Jiang Securities Analyst, Corporate Finance Nova Scotia Securities Commission 902-424-7059 Jack.jiang@novascotia.ca

CSA Staff Notice 51-345 — Disclosure of Abandonment and Reclamation Costs in National Instrument 51-101 Standards of Disclosure for Oil and Gas Activities and Related Forms

Date: November 5, 2015

38 O.S.C.B. 9255

This Staff Notice is published in response to numerous inquiries concerning disclosure requirements for abandonment and reclamation costs in National Instrument 51-101 *Standards of Disclosure for Oil and Gas Activities* (**NI 51-101**) and its related forms. Some of these inquiries relate to amendments to NI 51-101 and its related forms that were effective July 1, 2015 (**Amendments**). Reporting issuers engaged in oil and gas activities are reminded that publicly disclosed estimates of future net revenue must be net of abandonment and reclamation costs.

With the Amendments, definitions for future net revenue and abandonment and reclamation costs were added to section 1.1 of NI 51-101.

> **Future net revenue** — A forecast of revenue, estimated using forecast prices and costs or constant prices and costs, arising from the anticipated development and production of resources, net of the associated royalties, operating costs, development costs and abandonment and reclamation costs.

> **Abandonment and reclamation costs** — All costs associated with the process of restoring a reporting issuer's property that has been disturbed by oil and gas activities to a standard imposed by applicable government or regulatory authorities.

Item 2.1(2) of Form 51-101F1 *Statement of Reserves Data and Other Oil and Gas Information* (**Form 51-101F1**) mandates disclosure of future net revenue. Disclosure is required in aggregate by country and product type for the reserves categories specified in Item 2.1(1). Item 2.1(3) details specific disclosure of abandonment and reclamation costs. New Part 7 of Form 51-101F1 provides requirements regarding the optional disclosure of resources other than reserves.

Form 51-101F1 requires additional disclosure concerning significant abandonment and reclamation costs. In particular, Item 5.2 addresses instances where these costs affect particular components of reserves data and Item 6.2.1, in situations where they have affected or are reasonably expected to affect activities on properties with no attributed reserves.

Reporting issuers and their independent qualified reserves evaluators or auditors are reminded of their responsibilities, as described in Form 51-101F3 *Report of Management and Directors on Oil and Gas Disclosure* and Form 51-101F2 *Report on [Reserves Data][,] [Contingent Resources Data] [and] [Prospective Resources Data] by Independent Qualified Reserves Evaluator or Auditor*, respectively.

Questions

Please refer your questions to any of the following:

Craig Burns
Manager, Petroleum
Alberta Securities Commission
403-355-9029
craig.burns@asc.ca

Floyd Williams
Senior Petroleum Evaluation Engineer
Alberta Securities Commission
403-297-4145
floyd.williams@asc.ca

Gordon Smith
Senior Legal Counsel, Corporate Finance
British Columbia Securities Commission
604-899-6656 or 800-373-6393 (toll free across Canada)
gsmith@bcsc.bc.ca

Darin Wasylik
Senior Geologist
British Columbia Securities Commission
604-899-6517 or 800-373-6393 (toll free across Canada)
dwasylik@bcsc.bc.ca

James Whyte
Senior Geologist
Ontario Securities Commission
416-593-2168
jwhyte@osc.gov.on.ca

Jason Alcorn
Legal Counsel
Financial and Consumer Services Commission, New Brunswick
506-643-7857
jason.alcorn@fcnb.ca

Luc Arsenault
Géologue
Autorité des marchés financiers
514-395-0337 ext. 4373 or 877-525-0337 (toll free across Canada)
luc.arsenault@lautorite.qc.ca

OSC Rule 51-501 — AIF and MD&A

Date: December 15, 2000 as amended effective December 31, 2001, March 30, 2004 (by Rule 51-801) and May 16, 2005
23 O.S.C.B. 8365; 24 O.S.C.B. 7417; 25 O.S.C.B. 4559

[Revoked]
Final Rule: (2000) 23 O.S.C.B. 8365; Approval by OSC: (2000) 23 O.S.C.B. 7283; Request for Comments: (2000) 23 O.S.C.B. 1783. Replaced ON LPS 5.10.
Amendment to Rule: (2001) 24 O.S.C.B. 7417 (December 14, 2001); Approval by OSC: (2001) 24 O.S.C.B. 6051 (October 12, 2001).
Amendment to Rule: (2005) 28 O.S.C.B. 4559; Approval by OSC: (2005) 28 O.S.C.B. 2234.

Companion Policy 51-501CP — To OSC Rule 51-501 AIF and MD&A

[Revoked]
Adoption by OSC: (2000) 23 O.S.C.B. 8365 and 7283; Request for Comments: (2000) 23 O.S.C.B. 1783.
Adoption of Amendment: (2003) 26 O.S.C.B. (Supp-3) 184.

OSC Policy 51-601 — Reporting Issuer Defaults

Date: November 2, 2001, May 27, 2005, as replaced effective January 5, 2007, as amended effective January 1, 2011
24 O.S.C.B. 6587, 28 O.S.C.B. 4745, 30 O.S.C.B. 31 and 33 O.S.C.B. (Supp. 5) 41

Part 1 — Purpose

1.1 Purpose of this Policy — This Policy describes the Commission's list of reporting issuers, outlines the key deficiencies resulting in an issuer being noted in default and indicates how the Commission determines whether a reporting issuer is in default of any requirement of the Act or the regulations.

Part 2 — List of Reporting Issuers

2.1 General — The Commission maintains a list of Ontario reporting issuers that identifies those reporting issuers that are in default. The list is available for public inspection at the Commission's offices during normal business hours and is on the Commission's website at http://www.osc.gov.on.ca/en/Companies index.htm.

2.2 Completeness of the List

(1) Given the breadth of the definition of "reporting issuer", the Commission does not represent that this is a complete list of Ontario reporting issuers. For example, there may be corporations subject to the *Business Corporations Act* that have offered securities to the public within the meaning of that statute but have not filed material with the Commission. They would fall within the definition of "reporting issuer", but would not be on the list. Also, since the Commission does not continuously review the corporate status of issuers, corporations that have been dissolved may still be on the list.

(2) The absence of a default notation on the list of reporting issuers does not necessarily mean that the reporting issuer is in full compliance with all of its obligations under the Act or the regulations. There may be situations where an issuer is in default of a continuous disclosure requirement but the default is not reflected in the list.

These situations may arise for the following reasons. First, the list will not reflect undetected deficiencies. For example, if an issuer fails to make a required filing relating to a non-periodic event, such as a material change report or a business acquisition report, this deficiency may not be immediately apparent to staff responsible for maintaining the list. Secondly, a deficiency may be detected, but the issuer may disagree with staff as to whether the issuer is in default. As described in subsection 3.2(2) below, if the issuer and staff disagree about whether the issuer is in default, the issuer will generally not be noted in default pending a determination of the issue by the Commission. Thirdly, where an issuer has been noted in default, the default notation may subsequently be removed if it is determined that the default has ceased to be material. For example, an issuer may be noted in default for failing to file an interim financial report and related MD&A, and then remain in default for an extended period of time. In these circumstances, the Commission may be prepared to remove the default notation, and revoke a cease trade order if one has been issued, where the Commission is satisfied that the issuer has substantially brought its filings up to date. The Commission will generally consider this to be the case where the issuer files audited annual financial statements and related MD&A for the three most recently completed financial years and interim financial reports and related MD&A for the current financial year. In these circumstances, the Commission may, depending upon its review of all relevant factors, accept that the issuer should no longer be considered in default of a current material continuous disclosure requirement and remove the default notation. As a technical matter, the issuer remains in default of those filing requirements that have not been met.

Market participants should consider these limitations and make their own investigations as appropriate before relying on the list.

2.3 *Categories of Default* — If a reporting issuer is in default, beside the issuer's name on the reporting issuer list will appear the words "In default" and one or more letters indicating the nature of the default. These categories of default occasionally change to reflect amendments to the Act or regulations. At the issue date of this policy, the key continuous disclosure deficiencies resulting in default are those listed in Appendix A.

Part 3 — Determining Whether a Reporting Issuer is in Default

3.1 *The Test* — The Commission will generally not consider a reporting issuer to be in default unless it is in default of a material requirement of the Act or the regulations. While the categories set out in Appendix A identify a number of material requirements, they are not an exhaustive description of the circumstances in which a reporting issuer may be considered to be in default.

3.2 *The Process*

(1) Subject to subsection (2), staff will notify a reporting issuer when noting an the issuer in default. If an issuer is notified by staff, it may either remedy the default within the time specified by staff or provide information to staff to demonstrate that it is not in default. If an issuer remedies the default within the time period specified by staff or satisfies staff that it is not in default, staff will remove the default notation.

(2) If staff is of the view that a reporting issuer is in default based on a content deficiency in the issuer's continuous disclosure record, staff will notify the issuer before noting the issuer in default. If the issuer and staff disagree about whether the issuer is in default, the issuer will generally not be noted in default at that time. Staff may seek an order from the Commission under paragraph 127(1)5 that the issuer's continuous disclosure record be amended in whatever manner is necessary to address the issues identified. At the same time, staff may seek any other orders from the Commission under subsection 127(1) that the Commission considers appropriate. Subsection 127(4) of the Act provides that the Commission will not make any such orders without a hearing.

(3) National Policy 12-203 *Cease Trade Orders for Continuous Disclosure Defaults* describes how the Canadian Securities Administrators will generally respond to certain types of continuous disclosure defaults by reporting issuers.

3.3 *Removal of Default Notation* — A reporting issuer will no longer be identified as being in default once it has remedied the default by filing the required document, correcting the deficiency in its continuous disclosure record, remitting the applicable fee or otherwise demonstrating that it is not in default.

3.4 *Filing Considerations*

(1) An issuer may become a defaulting reporting issuer if it does not file a document when it is due.

(2) National Instrument 13-101 *System for Electronic Document Analysis and Retrieval (SEDAR)* (NI 13-101) provides that a document filed through SEDAR is filed on the day that the transmission of the document is completed, so long as it is completed by 5:00 p.m. A temporary hardship exemption is available under NI 13-101 to an issuer that encounters unanticipated technical difficulties when attempting to file through SEDAR.

(3) A document that is not filed through SEDAR is filed when the Commission receives it, not when the issuer sends it. A reporting issuer that relies on the postal system may become a defaulting reporting issuer if the mail is delayed or the document is lost in the mail. A reporting issuer that sends a document to the Commission by facsimile should retain the facsimile verification as evidence that the Commission received the document.

Part 4 — Certificate of No Default

Intentionally deleted

Part 5 — Form of Certificate of No Default

Intentionally deleted

Appendix A — Key Deficiencies Resulting in Default

1. *Failure to file the following continuous disclosure prescribed by Ontario securities laws:*

(a) annual financial statements;

(b) interim financial report;

(c) annual or interim management's discussion and analysis (MD&A) or annual or interim management report of fund performance (MRFP);

(d) annual information form (AIF);

(e) certification of annual or interim filings under National Instrument 52-109 *Certification of Disclosure in Issuers' Annual and Interim Filings* (NI 52-109);

(f) proxy materials or a required information circular;

(g) issuer profile supplement on the System for Electronic Disclosure By Insiders (SEDI);

(h) material change report;

(i) written update as required after filing a confidential report of a material change;

(j) business acquisition report;

(k) annual oil and gas disclosure prescribed by National Instrument 51-101 *Standards of Disclosure for Oil and Gas Activities* (NI 51-101) or technical reports for a mineral project required under National Instrument 43-101 *Standards of Disclosure for Mineral Projects* (NI 43-101);

(l) mandatory news release;

(m) corporate governance disclosure as required by National Instrument 58-101 *Disclosure of Corporate Governance Practices*;

(n) audit committee disclosure as required by National Instrument 52-110 *Audit Committees*; or

(o) disclosure in an issuer's MD&A relating to disclosure controls and procedures and their effectiveness that is referred to in a certificate filed under NI 52-109.

2. *Continuous disclosure that is deficient because:*

(a) financial statements of the reporting issuer, or the auditor's report accompanying the financial statements, do not comply with the requirements of National Instrument 51-102 *Continuous Disclosure Obligations* (NI 51-102), National Instrument 81-106 *Investment Fund Continuous Disclosure* (NI 81-106) or National Instrument 52-107 *Acceptable Accounting Principles and Auditing Standards*;

(b) the reporting issuer has acknowledged that its financial statements, or the auditor's report accompanying the financial statements, may no longer be relied upon;

(c) the reporting issuer's AIF, MD&A, MRFP, information circular, or business acquisition reports do not contain information for each of the content items required by NI 51-102 or NI 81-106; or

(d) the reporting issuer's technical disclosure or other reports do not comply with the disclosure requirements of NI 43-101 or NI 51-101.

3. *Failure to pay a fee required by Ontario securities laws.*

4. *Failure to comply with any other requirement related to continuous disclosure.*

Adoption of Replacement Policy by OSC: (2007) 30 O.S.C.B. 31.

Adoption of Amendment to Policy: (2010) 33 O.S.C.B. (Supp. 5) 41 and (Supp. 3) 1.

Policies and Orders: OPS 57-603; OSCN 51-711.

OSC Policy 51-604 — Defence for Misrepresentations in Forward-Looking Information

Date: October 3, 2008 as amended effective January 1, 2011

31 O.S.C.B. 9543 and 33 O.S.C.B. (Supp. 5) 41

Part I — Introduction

1.1 Background —

(1) Ontario securities law provides public issuers, directors, officers and other parties with a defence from statutory civil liability for misrepresentations in forward-looking information. The defence for misrepresentations in forward-looking information was first introduced into Ontario securities law in December 2002 and came into force on December 31, 2005 as part of the introduction of a statutory civil liability regime in favour of secondary market investors.[1] A similar defence exists in those parts of the *Securities Act* that provide a statutory right of action for damages for misrepresentations in primary market offering documents.[2] The defence contained in the *Securities Act* is based on draft legislation that the Commission, together with certain members of the Canadian Securities Administrators, proposed for public comment.

(2) Ontario securities law defines forward-looking information as disclosure about possible events, conditions or financial performance that is based on assumptions about future economic conditions and courses of action.[3] Forward-looking information includes, but is not limited to, future-oriented financial information with respect to prospective results of operations, financial position and/or cash flows that is presented as either a forecast or a projection. Earnings guidance is an example of forward-looking information. MD&A may also contain forward-looking information.

(3) Forward-looking information is, by its very nature, information that carries with it a level of uncertainty. There is a concern that attaching statutory civil liability to information that contains inherent uncertainties will discourage issuers from disclosing or providing forward-looking information. Such a "disclosure chill" would not be desirable. Understanding management's assessment of the future prospects and potential of a company is valuable to shareholders and prospective investors. Indeed, some forward-looking information, for example in the form of MD&A, is required. The policy objective behind the defence applicable to forwarding-looking information is to facilitate responsible and balanced disclosure about an issuer's anticipated future prospects.

(4) This policy statement expresses the Commission's views on some of the policy considerations underlying the defence for misrepresentations in forward-looking information and explains how the Commission approaches the interpretation of certain aspects of the defence. It is being issued under subsection 143.8(1)(b) of the *Securities Act*.

This policy statement represents the views of the Commission which do not have the force of law. These views are also not legal advice and should not be relied on as such.

We expect that disclosure practices in this area will vary among issuers and will evolve over time.

---

[1] See paragraphs (9), (9.1), (9.2) and (10) of section 138.4 of the *Securities Act*.

[2] See section 132.1 of the *Securities Act*.

[3] See subsection 1(1) of the *Securities Act*.

Part II — Defence for Misrepresentations in Forward-Looking Information

2.1 Legislative scheme — Written and oral forward-looking information is protected from statutory civil liability if:

(a) the document or public oral statement contains:

(i) reasonable cautionary language identifying the forward-looking information as such (the "identifier");

(ii) reasonable cautionary language identifying material factors that could cause actual results to differ materially from a conclusion, forecast or projection in the forward-looking information ("risk factors"); and

(iii) a statement of the material factors or assumptions that were applied in drawing a conclusion or in making a forecast or projection set out in the forward-looking information ("assumptions");

(b) the identifier and disclosure of risk factors and assumptions appear proximate to the forward-looking information; and

(c) the person or company had a reasonable basis for drawing the conclusions or making the forecast or projection.[4]

2.2 Animating Principles — The principles animating the defence for forward-looking information include:

(a) an investor who reads a disclosure document or listens to an oral statement containing forward-looking information should be able to readily:

(i) understand that forward-looking information is being provided in the document or statement;

(ii) identify the forward-looking information; and

(iii) inform himself or herself of the material assumptions underlying the forward-looking information and the material risk factors associated with a particular conclusion, forecast or projection; and

(b) effective disclosure is based on clarity of presentation and simplicity of language and style.

2.3 The "proximate" requirement —

(1) Concerns have been expressed that the word "proximate" may be interpreted so as to require immediate juxtaposition of information in every instance. If this were the case, each statement of forward-looking information would need to be individually identified as such and all of the material risk factors and assumptions applicable to the statement immediately included, irrespective of the fact that these risk factors and assumptions may apply to various statements of forward-looking information in the same disclosure. The Commission does not interpret the "proximate" requirement to require immediate juxtaposition.

(2) MD&A, for example, frequently has threads of forward-looking information throughout. These threads of forward-looking information may be subject to common assumptions and risk factors. Breaking the flow of the discussion to indicate each time that a particular statement is forward-looking and to identify in a meaningful way the factors that could affect its outcome introduces complexity in presentation that could frustrate an investor's ability to readily follow the MD&A discussion and appreciate the nature of the forward-looking information. A reader may be better served by a single broader reference prefacing or following, as appropriate, the MD&A identifying and setting out the applicable assumptions and risk factors. The Commission believes that such placement should generally satisfy the "proximate" requirement of the defence.

(3) There may be situations where particular assumptions and risk factors apply equally to multiple instances of forward-looking information in a single document. In the Commission's view, the use of cross-referencing in a manner that supports user friendliness and the principles animating the defence is consistent with the "proximate" requirement of the defence. We recognise that practices with respect to the use and extent of cross-referencing will vary among issuers depending on the circumstances and the nature of the particular disclosure.

(4) In the Commission's view, the animating principles underlying the defence suggest that, as a general principle, the more closely-tied a particular risk factor or assumption is to a particular conclusion, forecast or projection, the more "proximate" it should be to the forward-looking information. For example, where the disclosure of risk factors and assumptions is particularly tied to a forward-looking statement but does not immediately precede or follow the forward-looking statement, it may be necessary to provide a cross-reference or footnote that ties the risk factor or assumption to the specific conclusion, forecast or projection.

2.4 Risk factor disclosure —

(1) The defence for misrepresentations in forward-looking information requires the material factors that could cause actual results to differ materially from a conclusion, forecast or projection in the forward-looking information to be identified ("risk factors"). The risk factors identified in the cautionary language should be relevant to the conclusion, forecast or projection and should not be boilerplate in nature.

(2) The use of the word "material" underscores, in the Commission's view, that the cautionary statements should identify significant and reasonably foreseeable factors that could reasonably cause results to differ materially from those projected in the forward-looking statement. We do not believe that the defence should be interpreted as requiring an issuer to anticipate and discuss everything that could conceivably cause results to differ. It follows that failure to include the particular factor that ultimately causes the forward-looking statement not to materialize as predicted should not necessarily mean that the defence is not available. The defence does not, in the Commission's view, require companies to warn of every risk factor that, with the benefit of hindsight, ultimately could or might cause the forward-looking information not to come true. Similarly, the failure to include disclosure of the particular assumption that ultimately causes the forward-looking statement not to materialize as predicted should not necessarily mean that the defence is not available.

2.5 Assumption disclosure — The defence for misrepresentations in forward-looking information requires a statement to be included of the material factors or assumptions that were applied in drawing a conclusion or making a forecast or projection set out in the forward-looking

---

[4]See subsection 138.4(9) of the *Securities Act*.

information. The requirement for a statement of the material factors or assumptions that were applied requires, in the Commission's view, the factors or assumptions to be relevant to the conclusion, forecast or projection. The use of the word "material" underscores, in the Commission's view, that the defence does not require an exhaustive statement of every factor or assumption applied — a materiality standard applies.

2.6 Reasonable Basis — In order to benefit from the defence, a company must have a reasonable basis for drawing the conclusion or making the forecast or projection set out in the forward-looking information. When interpreting "reasonable basis", we believe that relevant factors would generally include the reasonableness of the assumptions applied in drawing the conclusion or making the forecast or projection; and the inquiries made and the process followed in preparing and reviewing the forward-looking information.

III — Defence for Misrepresentations in Oral Statements Containing Forward-Looking Information

3.1 Legislative Scheme — The *Securities Act* provides that in the case of a public oral statement containing forward-looking information, a person or company is deemed to have satisfied the requirements of the defence in paragraph 1 of subsection 138.4(9) (which are discussed in Part II of this Policy) if the person making the public oral statement states that:

a) the oral statement contains forward-looking information;

b) actual results could differ materially from a conclusion, forecast or projection in the oral forward-looking information;

c) certain material factors or assumptions were applied in drawing the conclusions or making the forecasts or projections included in the oral forward-looking information; and

d) additional information about the applicable risk factors and assumptions are contained in a "readily available" document and identifies that document.[5]

For purposes of the defence, a document filed with the Commission or otherwise generally disclosed is deemed to be "readily available".[6]

3.2 A more flexible approach —

(1) The *Securities Act* recognizes that it may be unwieldy to make oral disclosures containing forward-looking information that satisfy all of the requirements of the defence contained in subsection 138.4(9). Instead, the Securities Act provides for a more flexible approach for oral statements containing forward-looking information that facilitates these types of oral communications by an issuer while still providing the information that would have been received if the forward-looking information had been contained in a written disclosure document.

(2) The deeming provision in subsection 138.4 (9.1) specifically refers to the requirements of the defence being satisfied in the case of public oral statements when the person making the public oral statement makes the required cautionary statements. In the Commission's view, subsection 138.4 (9.1) should not be interpreted as exhaustive; the requirements of the defence may be satisfied in appropriate circumstances by one person making the required cautionary statements on behalf of another person who is making the forward-looking statement. The animating principles underlying the defence support a pragmatic interpretation.

IV — Duty to Update

4.1 We do not interpret the defence for misrepresentations in forward-looking information as imposing upon any person or company a duty to update forward-looking information beyond any duty imposed under Ontario securities law or otherwise.

Adoption of Policy: (2008) 31 O.S.C.B. 9543; Request for Comments: (2006) 29 O.S.C.B. 4571.

Policies and Orders: CSAN 51-330.

OSC Staff Notice 51-706 (2001) — Corporate Finance Report

Date: November 16, 2001, August 16, 2002 (originally published as OSCN 51-708), August 29, 2003 (originally published as OSCN 51-712), October 22, 2004 (originally published as OSCN 51-715), December 16, 2005, October 27, 2006, November 2, 2007, September 12, 2008, December 4, 2009 and October 22, 2010

24 O.S.C.B. 6842, 25 O.S.C.B. 5555, 26 O.S.C.B. 6123, 27 O.S.C.B. 8653, 28 O.S.C.B. 10074, 29 O.S.C.B. 8365, 30 O.S.C.B. 9049, 31 O.S.C.B. 8692, 31 O.S.C.B. 9125 (correction), 32 O.S.C.B. 9981 and 33 O.S.C.B. 9802

[Not reproduced]

OSC Staff Notice 51-706 (2002) — Corporate Finance Report

[Not reproduced]

OSC Staff Notice 51-706 (2003) — Corporate Finance Report

[Not reproduced]

---

[5]See subsection 138.4(9.1) of the *Securities Act*.

[6]See subsection 138.4(9.2) of the *Securities Act*.

OSC Staff Notice 51-706 (2004) — Corporate Finance Report

[Not reproduced]

OSC Staff Notice 51-706 (2005) — Corporate Finance Report

[Not reproduced]

OSC Staff Notice 51-706 (2006) — Corporate Finance Report

[Not reproduced]

OSC Staff Notice 51-706 (2007) — Corporate Finance Branch Report

[Not reproduced]

OSC Staff Notice 51-706 (2008) — Corporate Finance Branch Report

[Not reproduced]

OSC Staff Notice 51-706 (2009) — Corporate Finance Branch Report

[Not reproduced]

OSC Staff Notice 51-706 (2010) — Corporate Finance Branch Report

Date: October 22, 2010
33 O.S.C.B. 9802

Contents

1. Introduction

2. Disclosure to investors

3. IFRS reporting and communication

4. Shareholder empowerment and board governance

5. Exempt market financing and novel, complex products

6. Questions and additional resources

Appendix – Corporate Finance Branch contact information

1. — Introduction

This report is a summary of the key activities and initiatives of the Corporate Finance Branch (the Branch or we) of the Ontario Securities Commission (the OSC or the Commission) for fiscal 2010 (April 1, 2009 to March 31, 2010).

1.1 — Role of the Corporate Finance Branch

The Branch is responsible for regulating approximately 4,200 reporting issuers in Ontario, of which approximately 1,400 are based in Ontario. This includes public companies and other issuers of securities, other than investment funds (referred to in this report as issuers or reporting issuers).

The cornerstone of our regulation of issuers is disclosure. We require issuers to provide information to the marketplace about the securities they are selling, their business and the activities or knowledge of their insiders. Complete, accurate and timely information is critical to maintaining and strengthening investor confidence and efficient capital markets. Our review program for continuous disclosure (CD), prospectus and other filings is focused on upholding high standards of disclosure by issuers.

We also regulate issuers by:

- prohibiting certain activities such as insider trading and certain types of pre-marketing that we think can be harmful to investors and the markets

- applying measures to protect investors in take-over bids and significant conflict of interest transactions, and

- issuing guidance and mandating procedures to make voting rights more effective for investors.

You can find more information on the Branch in the About the OSC section of the OSC website (found at: http://www.osc.gov.on.ca/en/About_cf_index.htm).

1.2 — Purpose of this report

During fiscal 2010, we remained focused on providing protection to investors and fostering fair and efficient capital markets as the markets continued to undergo significant change. In doing so, we undertook several initiatives that were designed to:

- proactively address continuing market conditions

- improve disclosure provided to investors for the purpose of making investment decisions

- preserve and enhance investor rights

- respond to feedback from investors, issuers and other market participants regarding the securities regulatory framework for reporting issuers, and

- keep pace with global developments.

This report is intended to help issuers improve their understanding of securities law requirements. It may also be of interest to investors and investor advocacy groups. This report is intended to supplement the information in various Commission and Staff Notices on specific topics applicable to these issuers. It summarizes the Branch's key initiatives during fiscal 2010 relating to:

- disclosure to investors

- International Financial Reporting Standards (IFRS) reporting and communication

- shareholder empowerment and board governance, and

- exempt market financing and novel, complex products.

We also discuss developing issues and some aspects of the Branch's plans for fiscal 2011 (April 1, 2010 to March 31, 2011) that we believe will be of particular interest to issuers and their investors.

1.3 — Ontario's capital markets

We are the principal regulator and generally have responsibility for all 1,429 reporting issuers with head offices in Ontario that represent approximately $702 billion or 37% of Canada's $1.9 trillion market capitalization (as of March 31, 2010).

The number of reporting issuers in Ontario for which the OSC is the principal regulator has remained relatively consistent over the past three years.

	Fiscal 2008	Fiscal 2009	Fiscal 2010
Reporting issuers	1,466	1,482	1,429

The issuers that we regulate span a variety of industries. The three largest industry groups in Ontario's capital markets by percentage of market capitalization are banking and insurance, mining, and manufacturing and retail. The three largest industry groups by number of reporting issuers are mining, technology and biotechnology, and financial services.

Part 5: ONGOING REQUIREMENTS

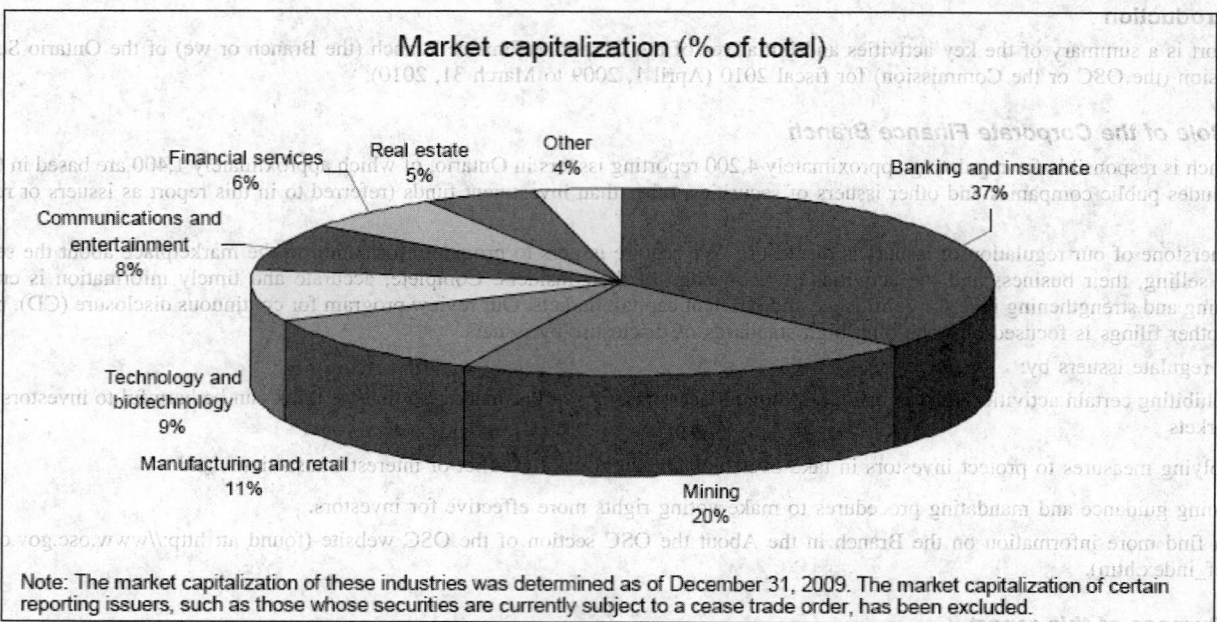

Market capitalization (% of total)

- Financial services 6%
- Real estate 5%
- Other 4%
- Banking and insurance 37%
- Communications and entertainment 8%
- Technology and biotechnology 9%
- Manufacturing and retail 11%
- Mining 20%

Note: The market capitalization of these industries was determined as of December 31, 2009. The market capitalization of certain reporting issuers, such as those whose securities are currently subject to a cease trade order, has been excluded.

Given the diversity in Ontario's capital markets and the scope of the Branch's activities, we deal with a variety of regulatory issues. We focus many of our reviews along industry lines in order to enable us to gain a greater understanding of the specific issues and concerns of each industry. Doing so allows us to address accounting and general disclosure issues affecting these industries.

Highlights of our two largest industry specializations

- **Banking and insurance issuers:** Ontario's banking and insurance industry, although small in number of issuers, represents 37% of Ontario's market capitalization. In assessing a bank or insurance issuer's business, it is imperative to understand the nature and extent of risks arising from financial instruments that an issuer is exposed to and how these risks are managed. Our reviews often focus on the adequacy of the disclosure of the risks and uncertainties, including how these risks impact the valuation of financial instruments and disclosure in the financial statements and management's discussion and analysis (MD&A).

- **Mining issuers:** The OSC is the principal regulator of approximately 350 reporting issuers operating in the mining industry. These issuers have a combined market capitalization of more than $135 billion, representing 20% of Ontario's market capitalization. The stage of development of a mining company largely determines its risk profile. Mining issuers can range from start-up companies that conduct a single grass-roots exploration program to multinational companies that develop and operate producing mines throughout the world. We factor a mining issuer's stage of development into how we design and conduct our review.

2. — Disclosure to investors

In this section of the report, we explain how we focus our Branch operations on our disclosure review programs. Issuers need to provide complete, accurate and timely information to allow investors to make informed investment decisions to buy, sell or hold securities or to participate in a change of control. We are seeking and getting enhanced disclosure through our comments on CD, prospectus and rights offering reviews. We also get longer term enhancements to disclosure by reviewing and updating our rules, policies and notices.

During fiscal 2010, the Branch continued its focus on holding issuers to high standards of disclosure. This involved:

- reviewing CD, prospectuses and rights offering circulars to assess issuer's compliance with disclosure obligations (discussed in section 2.1 *Review program for CD and offering documents*), and

- proposing changes or issuing additional guidance to facilitate enhanced disclosure to investors in a number of important areas (discussed in section 2.2 *Enhancing disclosure by reporting issuers and insiders*).

2.1 — Review program for CD and offering documents

Our review programs for CD and offering documents are risk-based and outcome focused. They have two main objectives:

Compliance	Issuer education and outreach
• to assess whether issuers are complying with their disclosure obligations.	• to help issuers better understand their disclosure obligations.

Risk-based approach

Generally, we use risk-based criteria to determine (1) the issuers whose disclosure we will select for review and (2) the level of review required. The criteria are designed to identify issuers whose disclosure is most likely to be materially improved or brought into compliance with Ontario securities law or accounting standards as a result of our review. Based on our previous experience, data analysis and awareness of best practices, we have found that certain criteria are useful in predicting where compliance problems may exist. The criteria used include both qualitative and quantitative factors, and are regularly reviewed and updated as market conditions change. This allows us to address particular areas of concern in a timely manner.

Notwithstanding our risk-based approach, some issuers are selected for review on a random basis.

Types of reviews

In general, we will conduct either a "full" review or an "issue-oriented" review. A full review is broad in scope and generally encompasses a review of the full prospectus or a review of an issuer's CD record for a period of at least 12 months. An issue-oriented review is an in-depth review focusing on one or more specific accounting, legal or regulatory issue(s) that we believe warrant regulatory scrutiny. Full and issue-oriented reviews allow us to:

- assess compliance with new requirements and accounting standards, and

- communicate our interpretation of securities law requirements and areas of concern.

In addition, issue-oriented reviews allow us to quickly address specific areas of risk.

Outcomes for fiscal 2010

Through our reviews, we strive to foster a culture of compliance with our disclosure regime. Compliance is an important part of our regulatory oversight. Enhanced compliance can lead to more complete, accurate and timely disclosure for investors, which in turn enables them to make better informed investment decisions.

In fiscal 2010, a significant number of our compliance reviews resulted in either enhanced compliance by reporting issuers or commitments to improve compliance going forward.

Program	Percentage of files that resulted in an outcome	Dominant outcome
CD reviews	72% of reviews	Prospective disclosure enhancements (63% of outcomes)
Prospectus reviews	57% of reviews	Material disclosure enhancements (57% of outcomes)

The outcomes of our CD and prospectus review programs are discussed in more detail below.

A. — CD reviews

A critical component of the Branch's focus on compliance with disclosure requirements is our CD program. This program is designed to monitor and enhance compliance with accounting standards and disclosure requirements under securities law. Our reviews focus on critical disclosures that are important to investors and areas where material changes and enhancements are required. This program also contributes to the culture of compliance in our marketplace, as reporting issuers are aware that we review a significant number of issuers each year and that their disclosure may be reviewed at any point. Having high quality, transparent information allows investors to have confidence in the credibility of the information provided by reporting issuers.

Results for fiscal 2010

The overall number and composition of CD reviews undertaken each year depends on market conditions and risks identified. Given continuing market conditions and the importance for investors of having a reliable CD record to use when making their investment decisions, we increased our focus on CD reviews in fiscal 2010. Specifically, the number of full reviews conducted in fiscal 2010 increased by 33% from the previous year. The number of issue-oriented reviews also increased by 6% from the prior year.

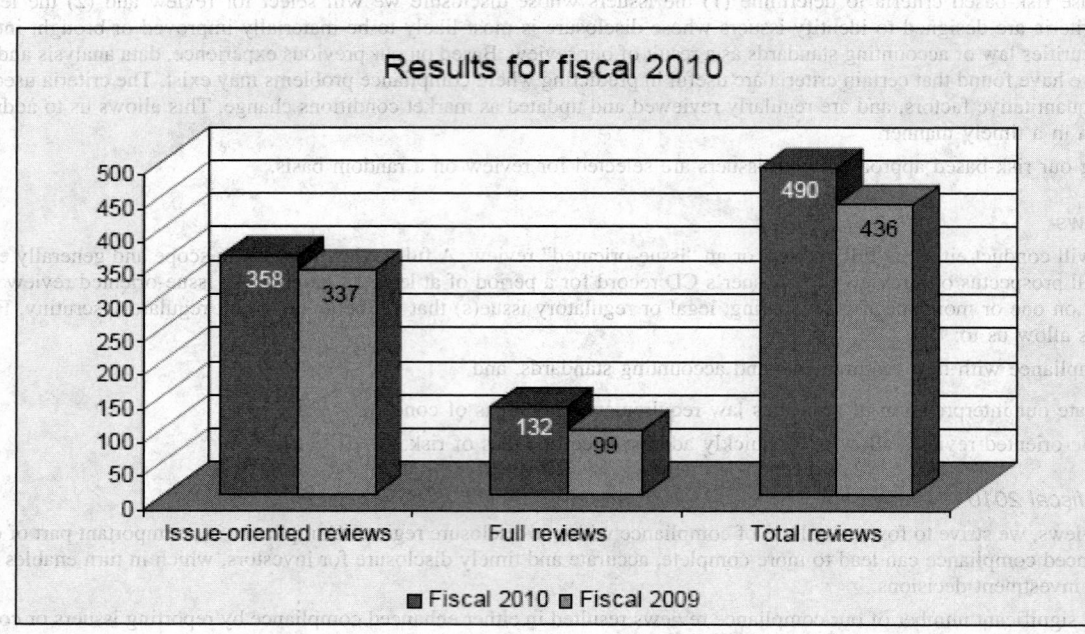

Outcomes for fiscal 2010

We generally select for review issuers at higher risk of non-compliance. In fiscal 2010, 72% of our CD reviews resulted in an outcome, compared to 80% in fiscal 2009. While we have seen efforts from issuers to improve their disclosure, we believe that further enhancements to their disclosure are needed.

We classify the outcomes of CD reviews into three categories:

- prospective disclosure enhancements
- issuer education and outreach, and
- refilings and other regulatory actions.

A CD review can have more than one category of outcome. For example, an issuer may be required to refile certain CD documents as well as make changes on a prospective basis. The chart below shows the range of review outcomes for fiscal 2010 compared to fiscal 2009.

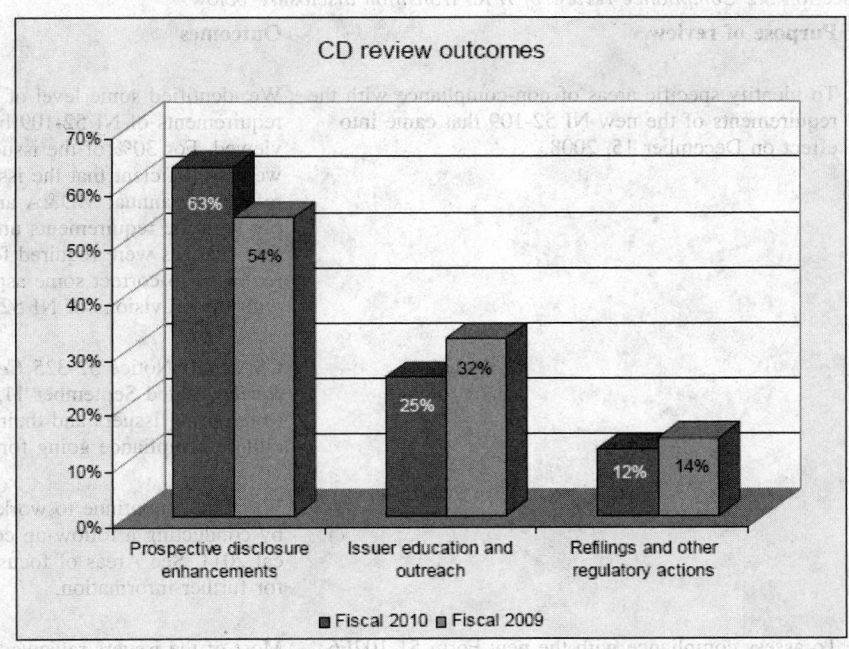

CD review outcomes

Generally, the outcomes have remained consistent with prior years as prospective changes continue to be the most dominant outcome.

Summary of CD review outcomes

- **Prospective disclosure enhancements:** In fiscal 2010, the majority of the outcomes involved informing the issuer that certain enhancements were required in its next CD filing as a result of deficiencies identified. For example, issuers agreed to make prospective enhancements to executive compensation, forward-looking information and asset impairment, as well as disclosure related to the certification requirements set out in National Instrument 52-109 *Certification of Disclosure in Issuers' Annual and Interim Filings* (NI 52-109).

- **Issuer education and outreach about specific disclosure risks:** A newer area of focus has been issuer education and outreach. We selected issuers based on a particular risk profile and proactively alerted them to certain disclosure enhancements that should be considered in their next CD filing. In fiscal 2010, issuer education and outreach were mainly focused around IFRS.

- **Refilings and other regulatory actions:** Another area of outcomes involved the identification of significant deficiencies that led to a refiling of a CD document, such as MD&A and certificates filed under NI 52-109, or another regulatory action, such as adding the issuer to the default list, issuing a cease trade order or referring the issuer to the OSC's Enforcement Branch.

Refer to CSA Staff Notice 51-332 *Continuous Disclosure Review Program Activities for the fiscal year ended March 31, 2010* (dated July 9, 2010) for a discussion of the common deficiencies identified in CD reviews.

Issue-oriented CD reviews conducted in fiscal 2010

Of the 490 CD reviews completed in fiscal 2010, 73% of the reviews were issue-oriented reviews. Issue-oriented reviews are an effective way to:

- assess issuers' understanding of new accounting standards, such as IFRS, or regulatory requirements such as certification, forward-looking information and executive compensation, and

- focus on particular areas of risk, such as continuing market conditions.

During fiscal 2010, we conducted six issue-oriented reviews, five of which are summarized below. The sixth, relating to IFRS transition disclosure, is discussed in section 3.2 *Compliance review of IFRS transition disclosure* below.

Review	Purpose of review	Outcomes
Certification requirements under NI 52-109	To identify specific areas of non-compliance with the requirements of the new NI 52-109 that came into effect on December 15, 2008.	We identified some level of non-compliance with the requirements of NI 52-109 by 62% of the issuers reviewed. For 30% of the issuers reviewed, the filings were so deficient that the issuers were required to refile their annual MD&A and/or certificates to comply with the requirements under NI 52-109. Prospective changes were required for 32% of the issuers reviewed to correct some aspect of their compliance with the provisions of NI 52-109 going forward. CSA Staff Notice 52-325 *Certification Compliance Review* (dated September 11, 2009) provides guidance to reporting issuers and their certifying officers to facilitate compliance going forward. We plan to continue to work with issuers in this area by conducting a follow-up compliance review in fiscal 2011. See Areas of focus for fiscal 2011 below for further information.
Executive compensation disclosure	To assess compliance with the new Form 51-102F6 *Statement of Executive Compensation* that came into effect on December 31, 2008.	Most of the issuers reviewed were asked to make prospective enhancements to their executive compensation disclosure including: • disclosing performance goals or similar conditions along with the benchmark group used for specific levels of compensation • providing more information regarding the grant date fair value of share-based and option-based awards, and • quantifying the estimated benefits payable as a result of a termination or change of control. Issuers should review both the requirements in the form and the guidance in CSA Staff Notice 51-331 *Report on Staff's Review of Executive Compensation Disclosure* (dated November 20, 2009) to assist them in the preparation of their executive compensation disclosure going forward.
Forward-looking information (FLI)	To assess compliance with the FLI requirements under Parts 4A and 4B of National Instrument 51-102 *Continuous Disclosure Obligations* (NI 51-102) that came into effect on December 31, 2007.	We identified areas where FLI disclosure was either non-compliant, or where it could be made more readable and user-friendly. These include the disclosure regarding: • the identification of FLI • material risk factors and material factors and assumptions • the purpose of FLI • goals and targets, and • the impact of the transition to IFRS. CSA Staff Notice 51-330 *Guidance Regarding the Application of Forward-Looking Information Requirements under NI 51-102 Continuous Disclosure Obligations* (dated November 20, 2009) contains guidance for issuers on these areas.

Review	Purpose of review	Outcomes
Continuing market conditions — Asset impairment	To review how reporting issuers in industries with a higher risk of having an impairment of assets have dealt with the impairment of: • goodwill • intangible assets • long-lived assets • investments, and • future tax assets.	While our review did not find the accounting for the impairment to be a significant concern, we found disclosure to be generally deficient in management's discussion & analysis (MD&A) regarding the rationale and circumstances behind impairment charges and the methodology used in the impairment analysis. We required issuers to enhance their MD&A disclosure, especially with respect to their critical accounting estimates, to provide a greater link between the financial statements and the related MD&A disclosure.
Continuing market conditions — Going concern	To review reporting issuers' disclosure of their going concern uncertainty as required by section 1400 of the CICA Handbook and the disclosure requirements regarding financial condition, liquidity needs and risks in Form 51-102F1 *Management's Discussion & Analysis*.	We found that the issuers generally did not provide complete disclosure of this risk in the financial statements and MD&A. We required some issuers to provide prospective disclosure enhancements in the notes to their financial statements and their MD&A disclosure. In particular, the discussion of liquidity and capital resources did not provide an adequate analysis of the issuers' cash needs and was not linked to the going concern note in their financial statements.

Areas of focus for fiscal 2011

While the number and type of reviews may change depending on current economic conditions and market developments, the following issue-oriented reviews are currently planned for fiscal 2011:

Proposed issue-oriented reviews

- **Risk disclosure:** Disclosure of risk and risk management practices enables investors and other stakeholders to understand and evaluate risks and their potential impact on a reporting issuer's future prospects. We will conduct a review of this disclosure in MD&A, annual information forms, prospectuses and other documents filed in 2010. The objectives of the review will be to: (1) assess compliance with existing risk disclosure requirements which are mainly set out in NI 51-102, National Instrument 41-101 *General Prospectus Requirements* and National Instrument 44-101 *Short Form Prospectus Distributions*, (2) use the results of the review to educate reporting issuers about the requirements and promote best practices for risk disclosure, and (3) identify any requirements that need clarification or further explanation to assist issuers in fulfilling their risk disclosure requirements.

- **Corporate governance:** Some investors and other stakeholders have raised concerns about the corporate governance disclosure currently being provided by some reporting issuers. As a result, we are conducting a follow-up corporate governance disclosure review to assess compliance with the existing disclosure requirements set out in National Instrument 58-101 Disclosure of Corporate Governance Practices (NI 58-101). The review involves assessing the adequacy of corporate governance disclosure in information circulars (or annual information forms or annual MD&A, if applicable) filed by reporting issuers in spring 2010. It is intended to build on the CSA's 2007 review, described in CSA Staff Notice 58-303 Corporate Governance Disclosure Compliance Review. Following the review, we expect to issue a staff notice in 2010 that will summarize the results of the review and provide additional guidance for reporting issuers.

- **Follow-up review of NI 52-109 certification:** Certification of disclosure controls and procedures is meant to confirm that the information required to be included in the periodic reports filed with the OSC is not misleading and fairly presents the financial condition of an issuer. When we first looked at certification compliance in fiscal 2009, we found a high non-compliance rate (approximately 62%) with the requirements of NI 52-109 (see the discussion of the 2009 issue-oriented review on page 10). As a result, we are conducting a follow-up review. Our follow-up review focuses on two aspects: (1) assessing form compliance, including following up on issuers previously reviewed for which deficiencies were identified, and (2) reviewing issuers that refiled their financial statements in fiscal 2009. We expect to issue a staff notice in the fall of 2010 that will summarize the results of the review.

- **Material contracts:** The material contract filing requirements are an important aspect of our CD regime because they enable investors and potential investors to understand the terms and conditions of contracts that are of key significance to a particular issuer's business and/or operations. We plan to review compliance with material contract filing requirements under NI 51-102. The review will focus on whether issuers are: (1) filing all of their material contracts, (2) interpreting the exemption for contracts entered into in the "ordinary course of business" correctly, and (3) complying with provisions allowing for the omission and redaction of information from material contracts.

In addition, we plan to conduct a follow-up review of IFRS transition disclosure in fiscal 2011. Refer to section 3.2 *Compliance review of IFRS transition disclosure* for more information about the review.

B. — Prospectus reviews

Another key component of the Branch's disclosure compliance program focused on disclosure is our review of offering documents. When issuers seek to raise capital, they are required to meet a number of disclosure requirements considered important to assist investors in making informed investment decisions. We discuss below some of the results of our reviews of public offering documents in fiscal 2010.

Filings made in fiscal 2010

There was a 33% increase in the total number of offering documents (excluding investment fund offerings) reviewed by us in fiscal 2010 from the previous year. We believe this is largely a reflection of the general recovery of the Canadian and global economies, and the perception that raising capital in the public markets was more attractive than in fiscal 2009. The composition of the filings changed in fiscal 2010. In particular, we saw a 37% decrease in the number of initial public offerings (IPO) in fiscal 2010 and a 155% increase in the number of bought deals in fiscal 2010.

Issuers in a range of industries sought public financing. Fifty per cent of the offerings were made by issuers in the mining and oil & gas industries. Issuers in the real estate industry were also active in the public markets in fiscal 2010.

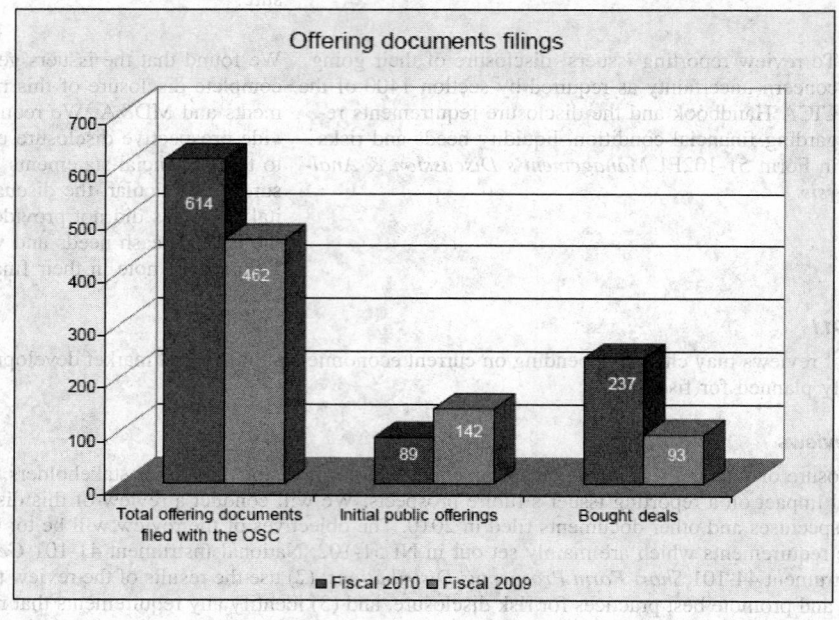

Results for fiscal 2010

The chart below shows the composition of the type of offering document reviews we conducted in fiscal 2010 compared to fiscal 2009.

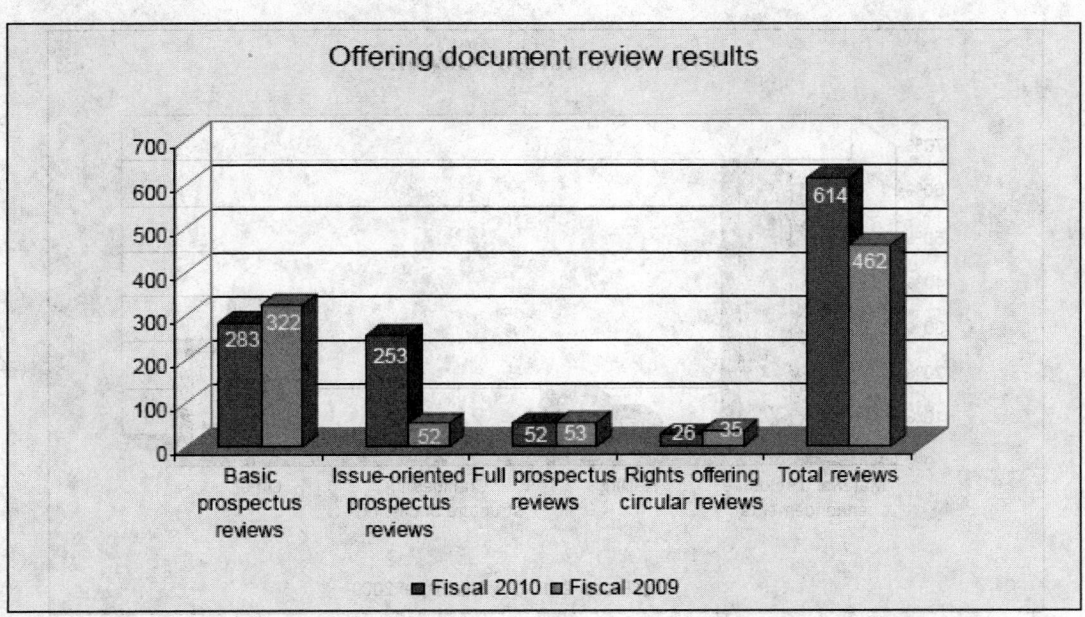

As with CD reviews, the overall number and composition of offering document reviews undertaken each year depends on market conditions and risks identified. The number of full prospectus reviews conducted in fiscal 2010 is consistent with the previous year. The significant increase in issue-oriented prospectus reviews in fiscal 2010 is a result of changes made to our risk-based selection criteria to respond to continuing market conditions and recent regulatory developments.

Outcomes for fiscal 2010

In addition to selecting all IPO prospectuses, we generally select issuers at higher risk of non-compliance for review. In fiscal 2010, 57% of the offering documents selected for review resulted in an outcome, compared to 75% in fiscal 2009. Due to regulatory changes in fiscal 2010, we started tracking outcomes from prospectus reviews where the OSC was not the principal regulator. Outcomes on these reviews were lower than for prospectuses filed with the OSC as principal regulator, as the OSC does not record an outcome for issues raised and resolved by the issuer's principal regulator.

We classify the outcomes of our full and issue-oriented prospectus reviews into four categories:

- material disclosure enhancements
- refilings
- changes in offering structure, and
- other outcomes.

The chart below shows the range of review outcomes for fiscal 2010 compared to fiscal 2009.

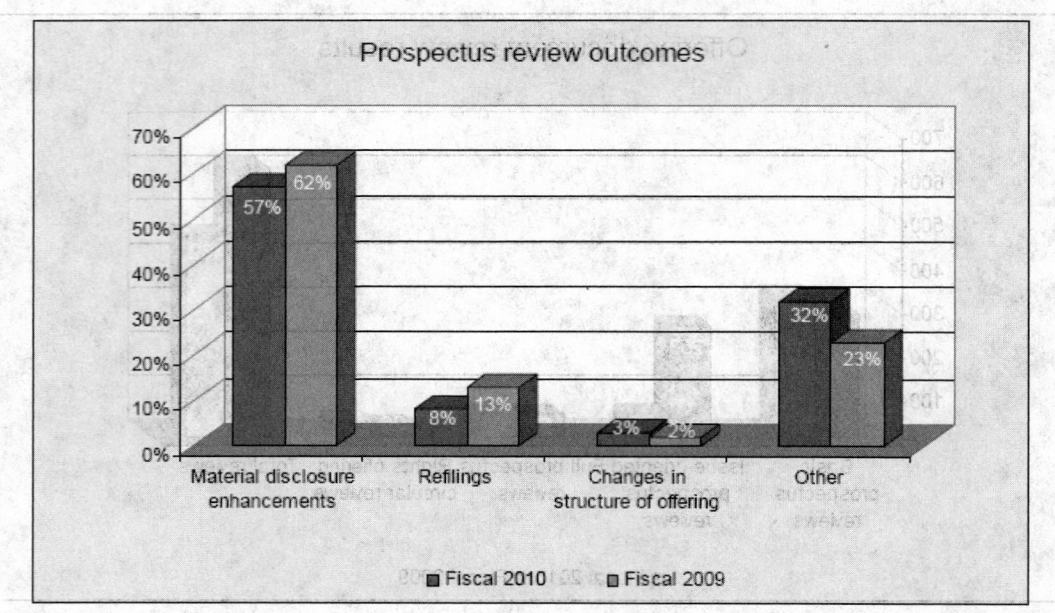

Consistent with prior years, material disclosure enhancements remained the most dominant outcome.

Summary of prospectus review outcomes

- **Material disclosure enhancements:** In fiscal 2010, more than half of our outcomes were material disclosure enhancements made by issuers. The key areas requiring enhancements were disclosure of qualified persons, technical mining information, use of proceeds, risk factors and executive compensation.

- **Refilings:** Less commonly, our reviews resulted in the refiling of a significantly deficient document or the filing of a required document that was not previously filed. Many of the deficiencies that led to a refiling in fiscal 2010 related to a failure to file technical reports and related consents.

- **Changes in structure of offering:** A few of the outcomes involved a change in the offering structure as a result of our review. The most common change was an increase in the minimum offering size to ensure that the issuer had sufficient funds to sustain its operations for a reasonable period of time and/or achieve the disclosed purposes of the offering.

- **Other:** This category includes outcomes that do not result in a change to a prospectus but are significant to our mandate in other ways. For example, it includes reviews where we have had substantive discussions with the issuer, exemptive relief was granted or procedural enhancements were implemented by the issuer. A significant number of these outcomes were undertakings filed by issuers under which they agreed to pre-clear the disclosure in prospectus supplements related to the issuance of convertible, exchangeable or complex securities.

2.2 — Enhancing disclosure by reporting issuers and insiders

A. — Disclosure by reporting issuers

In fiscal 2010, we continued to focus on investor protection by taking steps to improve the disclosure provided to investors by reporting issuers. In particular, we achieved milestones on two disclosure-related initiatives: the publication of the OSC's report on corporate sustainability reporting and the publication for comment of a new set of mining disclosure requirements. These initiatives are discussed below.

Corporate sustainability reporting

On April 9, 2009, the Ontario Legislature approved a non-binding resolution calling on the OSC to undertake a broad consultation to consider best practices in corporate social responsibility and environmental, social and governance disclosure. In response, the OSC published on December 18, 2009:

- OSC Corporate Sustainability Initiative Report to the Minister of Finance, and

- OSC Notice 51-717 *Corporate Governance and Environmental Disclosure.*

These documents summarize our plan to enhance compliance by reporting issuers with existing corporate governance and environmental disclosure requirements. Our plan involves:

- **Corporate governance disclosure compliance review:** During 2010, we are conducting a follow-up corporate governance disclosure review to assess compliance with the existing disclosure requirements. Refer to Areas of focus for fiscal 2011 in section 2.1 *Review program for CD and offering documents* for further information.

• **Environmental reporting guidance:** During 2010, we are developing additional staff guidance on disclosure of environmental matters. The staff guidance seeks to build on OSC Staff Notice 51-716 *Environmental Reporting* (dated February 27, 2008). In developing the staff guidance, we are consulting with stakeholders and experts in this area. We are also considering international developments, such as the SEC's interpretative release, *Commission Guidance Regarding Disclosure Related to Climate Change*, which became effective on February 8, 2010. We intend to publish the guidance in fall 2010 so that reporting issuers have sufficient time to consider the guidance when preparing their 2010 annual CD documents.

Both of these initiatives reflect the feedback received during our consultations in 2009. We consulted with various stakeholders, the OSC's advisory committees and the Prospectors & Developers Association of Canada. We also held a roundtable discussion on September 18, 2009, which was attended by representatives of investors, issuers and professional bodies, analysts, legal and accounting advisors and academics.

Updating of mining disclosure requirements

On April 23, 2010, the Canadian Securities Administrators (CSA) published for a 90-day public comment period a proposal to amend National Instrument 43-101 *Standards of Disclosure for Mineral Projects* (NI 43-101). The comment period closed on July 23, 2010 and the CSA received 50 written submissions.

NI 43-101 is generally regarded as a world standard for mining disclosure and it is important to Ontario's capital markets given the size of our mining industry. This is the first major proposal for amendments since NI 43-101 came into effect in 2001 and reflects nine years of regulatory experience with the instrument and broad industry consultation through focus groups and advisory committees.

The purposes of the proposed changes are to enhance the efficiency and effectiveness of the regulation of mining disclosure, reduce compliance costs for reporting issuers, and maintain internationally-leading standards for mining disclosure consistent with our mandate of investor protection.

The proposed changes include:

• updating the expert certificate and consent requirements to provide greater consistency and efficiency, and

• modifying the technical report disclosure requirements to enable the reports to better reflect the stage of development of a mineral property, and as a result, provide more useful information to investors.

In addition, the CSA has requested specific feedback on whether to keep, modify or eliminate the existing requirement to file a technical report with a short form prospectus. The feedback will likely confirm whether the time and costs of producing a technical report for a short form prospectus is a significant issue for the mining industry, and whether investors think they will be disadvantaged if new technical disclosure in a short form prospectus is not supported by a current technical report.

Issuers in the mining industry should monitor these changes to ensure their mining technical disclosure in their CD documents, including technical reports, and on their websites complies with all current disclosure requirements.

B. — Disclosure by insiders

During fiscal 2010, we finalized National Instrument 55-104 *Insider Reporting Requirements and Exemptions* (NI 55-104), which came into force on April 30, 2010.

The new instrument modernizes, harmonizes and streamlines insider reporting in Canada, and will benefit investors by:

• focusing the insider reporting requirement on a core group of insiders with the greatest access to material undisclosed information and the greatest influence over the issuer

• improving the consistency of the reporting requirements for stock-based compensation arrangements, and

• after a transition period, accelerating the filing deadline for reports of trading activity, which will make this important information available to the market sooner.

Reporting issuers and their advisors should familiarize themselves with the new insider reporting requirements to assist their reporting insiders in complying with their reporting obligation. In addition, reporting issuers should adopt appropriate policies and procedures relating to black-out periods, timely disclosure of material information, and monitoring and restricting of insider trading and tipping activities.

For further guidance on the new insider reporting regime, refer to:

• CSA Staff Notice 55-315 *Frequently Asked Questions (FAQs) about National Instrument 55-104 Insider Reporting Requirements and Exemptions* dated April 28, 2010

• CSA Staff Notice 55-312 *Insider Reporting Guidelines for Certain Derivative Transactions (Equity Monetization) (REVISED)* dated June 11, 2010, and

• CSA Staff Notice 55-316 *Questions and Answers on Insider Reporting and the System for Electronic Disclosure by Insiders (SEDI)* dated June 11, 2010.

3. — IFRS reporting and communication

Following a period of public consultation, the Canadian Accounting Standards Board adopted a strategic plan to move financial reporting for Canadian publicly accountable enterprises to IFRS as issued by the International Accounting Standards Board. For financial years beginning on or after January 1, 2011, Canadian GAAP for publicly accountable enterprises will be IFRS as incorporated into the CICA Handbook.

The OSC supports Canada's move to IFRS, a globally accepted, high quality set of accounting principles. With issuers increasingly making decisions in a global context, the move to IFRS places Canada with more than 100 other countries, including the United Kingdom, other

Part 5: ONGOING REQUIREMENTS

European Union nations and Australia, that have already adopted IFRS. Our objective is to facilitate a smooth transition from current Canadian GAAP to IFRS for reporting issuers. During fiscal 2010, we continued to educate reporting issuers and their advisors on IFRS changes and transitional issues as they prepare their first set of IFRS-compliant financial statements.

3.1 — Regulatory impacts of IFRS

On October 1, 2010, we published amendments to the CD, prospectus and certification rules that address the changes required to reflect the adoption of IFRS. Subject to receiving Ministerial approval, the amendments will come into force for issuers with financial years beginning on or after January 1, 2011.

The amendments include a list of changes to accounting terms and phrases, and transition changes that should assist issuers with the conversion to IFRS. The amendments will:

- replace existing Canadian GAAP terms and phrases with IFRS terms and phrases

- change disclosure requirements in instances where IFRS contemplates different financial statements than existing Canadian GAAP

- require the opening IFRS statement of financial position to be presented in an issuer's first IFRS interim financial report and first IFRS financial statements

- provide a 30-day extension to the filing deadline for the first IFRS interim financial report, and

- clarify, amend or delete existing provisions where the provision is no longer accurate or appropriate.

The amendments are intended to provide an efficient transition mechanism for issuers to reflect the changeover to IFRS and produce high quality financial reporting for the benefit of investors and other stakeholders.

3.2 — Compliance review of IFRS transition disclosure

It is likely that the conversion to IFRS will require a significant commitment of resources by reporting issuers and sufficient advance planning. IFRS transition disclosure is important to assist investors in assessing the readiness of a reporting issuer's transition to IFRS and the impact the adoption of IFRS may have on the issuer. Issuers that provide sufficient information about their conversion process and its effects prior to the IFRS changeover will reduce the level of investor uncertainty about their IFRS readiness. This disclosure should lead to a more stable and less disruptive transition to IFRS, which will be beneficial to both issuers and their investors.

During fiscal 2010, the Branch continued to work towards facilitating a smooth conversion to IFRS for reporting issuers and their investors. As part of this goal, we conducted targeted reviews of IFRS transition disclosures made by issuers in their 2008 and 2009 annual MD&A. Our review of the 2008 annual MD&A disclosures found that the issuers reviewed were not adequately disclosing information related to their IFRS transition efforts. A detailed discussion of the findings of this review can be found in OSC Staff Notice 52-718 *IFRS Transition Disclosure Review* dated February 5, 2010. We recently completed our review of 2009 annual MD&A. Overall, we found an improvement in the amount and quality of IFRS transition disclosure provided by issuers in their 2009 annual MD&A compared to the prior year. This improvement should be expected since we are closer to the changeover date of January 1, 2011 and issuers generally are farther along in implementing their changeover plans and assessing the impact of accounting policy differences. We issued CSA Staff Notice 52-326 *IFRS Transition Disclosure Review* on July 23, 2010 which details the findings of the review and provides additional guidance for issuers preparing future MD&A.

Issuers that provide sufficient information about their conversion process and its effects prior to the changeover date will reduce the level of investor uncertainty about IFRS readiness and inform investors and other stakeholders about the potential for volatility in future reported results. This disclosure should lead to a more stable and less disruptive transition to IFRS, which will be beneficial to both issuers and their investors.

Given the short time remaining before the changeover to IFRS, it is critical that issuers provide investors with sufficient information about their conversion process and the potential impact of IFRS on the expected financial results. We will continue to review IFRS transition disclosure provided by reporting issuers as part of our CD review program.

4. — Shareholder empowerment and board governance

During fiscal 2010, merger and acquisition (M&A) activity increased as issuers shifted their focus towards growth opportunities. This recent rise in M&A activity has also resulted in more contested transactions. The Branch continued to concentrate on the enhancement and protection of shareholder rights in the context of M&A transactions and the ability of shareholders to participate in director elections and other matters that are the subject of shareholder meetings. The measures we took include:

- intervening in mergers, acquisitions and significant related party transactions

- providing guidance to market participants about the take-over bid process

- improving shareholder access to proxy related materials, and

- addressing board governance.

4.1 — Overview of mergers and acquisition matters

We have a specialized transactional and policy team that regulates take-over bids, issuer bids, business combinations, related party transactions and early warning reporting. This regulation focuses on shareholder rights in change of control and conflict of interest transactions.

This past year, our regulatory efforts included:

- addressing non-compliance with disclosure requirements applicable to M&A transactions

- participating in Commission M&A hearings

- publishing CSA Staff Notice 62-305 *Varying the Terms of Take-Over Bids*, and

- coordinating with our CSA colleagues on major transactional and policy matters.

Compliance

We routinely address non-compliance with take-over bid and early warning requirements. We identify non-compliance through independent staff review, third party complaints and self-reporting. Non-compliance outcomes include:

- public disclosure of non-compliance

- applications for compliance or public interest orders made to the Commission

- remedial measures, such as requiring the orderly sale of shares acquired without an exemption to the take-over bid provisions, and

- preventative action to minimize the risk of future non-compliance.

Significant hearings

The Commission held two public interest hearings concerning related party transactions regulated by Multilateral Instrument 61-101 *Protection of Minority Security Holders in Special Transactions* (MI 61-101). Both transactions involved a controlling shareholder.

Magna International Inc.

On June 23 and 24, 2010, the Commission held a hearing concerning the proposed reorganization of Magna International Inc. (Magna) to collapse Magna's dual class structure (the Arrangement). In a statement of allegations, Staff asked the Commission to cease trade Magna's class B shares because:

- Magna's board of directors failed to provide a recommendation to shareholders and the management information circular (the Circular) in respect of the Arrangement did not contain sufficient information to allow shareholders to form a reasoned judgment, and

- the approval and review process followed by Magna's board was inadequate.

In its decision, the Commission concluded that while the Arrangement was not abusive of Magna's subordinate voting shareholders or the capital markets generally, the Circular contained serious and substantive deficiencies which precluded the subordinate voting shareholders from being able to make an informed voting decision in respect of the Arrangement.

The Commission took a contextual approach in reaching this conclusion. The Commission stated that the disclosure standard for a management information circular must be applied in the circumstances of the transaction. In the case of the Arrangement, the following circumstances were found to be relevant:

- The Arrangement was a material related party transaction between Magna and its controlling shareholder

- Neither the board nor special committee made any recommendation to the subordinate voting shareholders as to how to vote on the Arrangement

- Neither the board nor special committee gave their view as to the fairness of the Arrangement

- No fairness opinion was obtained with respect to the Arrangement, and

- The Arrangement was complex and some portions of the consideration to be paid were difficult to evaluate.

Given these circumstances, the Commission concluded that the Circular must provide the subordinate voting shareholders with substantially the same information and analysis received by the special committee.

The Commission ordered the Arrangement be cease traded until Magna provided extensive supplemental disclosure in the Circular.

The Commission stated that it had concerns about the process followed by the Magna board, the special committee and management in reviewing and submitting the Arrangement to the subordinate voting shareholders. The Commission stated its intention to discuss those concerns in its full reasons for the decision.

MI Developments Inc.

Staff was involved in a Commission hearing on whether MI Developments Inc. (MID) failed to comply with MI 61-101 in connection with certain related party transactions. On December 23, 2009, the Commission released its reasons. These are some of the significant aspects of the decision:

- Only staff has a right to bring an application under section 127 of the *Securities Act* (Ontario) (the Act).

- The Commission has discretion to permit a person other than staff to make an application under section 127 of the Act. The Commission cited the following reasons to support its decision to permit the applicants to bring their applications under section 127 of the Act in this case:

  - the applications involved past and possible future related party transactions, governed by MI 61-101

  - the applications involved breaches of MI 61-101, but were not purely enforcement in nature

  - the relief sought was future looking and was intended to prevent future related party transactions

- the Commission had the authority to impose an appropriate remedy, and

- the applicants, as substantial shareholders of MID, were directly affected by the past conduct of MID and would have been directly affected by future related party transactions.

- The Commission confirmed that issuers can arrange their affairs through *bona fide* transactions to qualify for exemptions from our conflict of interest regime, MI 61-101. However, the Commission emphasized that it would look to the substance and effect of the transaction to determine whether the issuer should be able to rely upon the exemption.

Policy initiatives

Varying the terms of a bid

We published CSA Staff Notice 62-305 *Varying the Terms of Take-Over Bids* on December 18, 2009 to address concerns over how the market was interpreting certain rules relating to formal take-over bids. Specifically, the notice sets out the views of CSA staff on the ability of an offeror to vary the terms of a formal bid in a manner that makes the bid less favourable to target security holders. The notice highlights that an offeror's conditions to a formal take-over bid should be *bona fide*, and should be interpreted in good faith since the bid creates an expectation among security holders that the bid will be completed at the price specified if the conditions are satisfied.

Shareholder rights plans

We, together with our CSA colleagues, are following recent developments in shareholder rights plan case law both in Ontario and across Canada. National Policy 62-202 *Take-Over Bids — Defensive Tactics* currently sets out the CSA's views on defensive tactics. In May 2009, the Commission dismissed an application by Pala Investments Holding Limited to cease trade the shareholder rights plan of Neo Material Technologies Inc. The plan was adopted by the target board and approved by the shareholders during the course of a hostile partial bid. Staff are reviewing the impact of this, and other recent CSA decisions, to determine whether there is a need for further guidance on shareholder rights plans.

4.2 — Communication with beneficial owners of securities

As part of our focus on shareholder rights, we want to improve the process through which beneficial owners of reporting issuer securities, as opposed to registered securityholders, receive proxy related materials and how their voting instructions are solicited. Our goal is to make it simpler for beneficial owners to understand what they are being asked to vote on and to cast their vote.

During fiscal 2010, the CSA finalized proposed amendments to National Instrument 54-101 *Communication with Beneficial Owners of Securities of a Reporting Issuer* (NI 54-101). The proposed amendments are intended to simplify and clarify aspects of the voting process for beneficial owners. They include:

- introduction of a voluntary "notice-and-access" method of informing registered holders and beneficial owners of reporting issuer securities that the proxy-related materials have been posted on a website that is not SEDAR, and explaining how to access them

- simplification of the process by which beneficial owners who hold securities through an intermediary are appointed as proxy holders

- enhanced disclosure by reporting issuers of the beneficial owner voting process, and

- restrictions designed to minimize the potential for misuse of certain beneficial owner information.

In developing the proposed amendments, CSA staff consulted with issuers, intermediaries, beneficial owners, a proxy advisory firm, proxy solicitors and service providers, as well as with the OSC's advisory committees. The proposed amendments reflect the feedback received during those consultations.

The proposed amendments were published for a 144-day comment period on April 9, 2010. The comment period ended on August 31, 2010 and the CSA received 25 written submissions.

Our policymaking in the area of beneficial owner communications reflects our commitment to the principles animating NI 54-101:

- all securityholders of a reporting issuer, whether registered holders or beneficial owners, should have the opportunity to be treated alike as far as is practicable

- efficiency should be encouraged, and

- the obligation of each party in the securityholder communication process should be equitable and clearly defined.

4.3 — Board governance

In addition to initiatives regarding shareholder rights, we continued our focus on disclosure surrounding the practices of those charged with "representing" shareholder interests, such as the board of directors. As part of our corporate sustainability reporting initiative, we reviewed the existing disclosure requirements regarding corporate governance matters during fiscal 2010. We heard feedback from stakeholders consulted that the existing disclosure requirements are adequate. However, they noted that compliance by reporting issuers with these requirements could be enhanced.

On December 18, 2009, the OSC announced its plan to conduct a review of compliance with the requirements of NI 58-101. Refer to Areas of focus for fiscal 2011 in section 2.1 *Review program for CD and offering documents* for a discussion of this review.

Consistent with our decision to focus on compliance with the existing requirements, CSA staff published CSA Staff Notice 58-305 *Status Report on the Proposed Changes to the Corporate Governance Regime* on November 13, 2009. The notice confirmed that the CSA did not intend to implement proposed changes to the corporate governance regime, including the related disclosure requirements, published for comment on December 19, 2008. The CSA's decision was in response to comments received on the proposed changes. A majority of commenters expressed the view that it was not the appropriate time to introduce significant changes to the corporate governance regime in Canada, and in particular, they expressed concerns about moving towards a principles-based corporate governance regime. They also noted that issuers were currently focused on business sustainability issues in a challenging economic climate and on the transition to IFRS.

5. — Exempt market financing and novel, complex products

Canadian investors increasingly are being offered, on an exempt basis as well as through prospectuses, a variety of novel and complex financial products. In fiscal 2010, we continued to work on initiatives intended to permit financial innovation without compromising investor protection. This work will continue into fiscal 2011.

5.1 — Regulation of credit rating organizations

Credit rating organizations (CROs) play an important role in the financial markets. CRO ratings are referred to in a number of rules made under securities legislation. The importance of credit ratings, and their role in the recent global financial crisis and 2007 Canadian asset-backed commercial paper (ABCP) market turmoil, has resulted in a consensus in Canada and internationally that CROs must be subject to appropriate regulation.

During fiscal 2010, we continued to develop a framework for regulating CROs that will be complementary to international regulatory regimes. The CSA published proposed National Instrument 25-101 *Designated Rating Organizations* for a 90-day public comment period on July 16, 2010. The comment period closes on October 25, 2010. We encourage interested stakeholders to provide written submissions on the proposal.

Under the proposed instrument, a credit rating organization will be able to apply for designation as a "designated rating organization" by filing an application containing prescribed information. The central requirement of the proposed instrument is that, once designated, a rating organization must establish, maintain and ensure compliance with a code of conduct that is substantially the same as the Code of Conduct Fundamentals for Credit Rating Agencies published by the International Organization of Securities Commissions (IOSCO). A designated rating organization would also be required to establish policies and procedures to manage conflicts of interest, prevent inappropriate use of information, appoint a compliance officer and make an annual filing. While the CSA intends to appropriately regulate CROs, they are not proposing to direct or regulate the content of credit ratings or the methodologies used to determine credit ratings.

5.2 — Offerings of novel and complex products

We continue to monitor how novel, complex products are sold in both the exempt markets as well as through prospectuses, and to develop appropriate regulatory responses.

Internet offerings of over-the-counter derivatives

The internet has increased the opportunities for Ontario residents to invest in securities, including over-the-counter derivatives such as contracts for difference (CFDs) and foreign exchange contracts. We became concerned that certain internet offerings were being made by unregistered, offshore entities to retail investors in Ontario. To address these investor protection concerns, we issued OSC Staff Notice 91-702 *Offerings of Contracts for Difference and Foreign Exchange Contracts to Investors in Ontario* on October 30, 2009. The notice gives general guidance to market participants on CFDs, as well as foreign exchange contracts and similar over-the-counter derivatives.

Market participants must comply with the registration and prospectus requirements of Ontario securities law, or obtain exemptive relief, when offering these products to Ontario investors. This means investors will receive prospectus-level disclosure and registrants selling these products will need to fulfill their know-your-client and suitability obligations, unless exemptive relief has been granted.

Securitized products

Securitized products are securities whose payments are supported by an underlying pool of cash-generating financial assets collected in a bankruptcy-remote special purpose vehicle. ABCP and collateralized debt obligations (CDOs) are types of securitized products. Examples of financial assets that are commonly securitized in this way include residential and commercial mortgages, credit card receivables, and automobile and agricultural equipment leases.

ABCP is generally issued in the exempt market. The majority of term asset-backed securities and other types of securitized products are prospectus qualified (often through a short form or shelf prospectus).

There is an international consensus that securitized products have unique features that require specific regulation. The 2007 Canadian ABCP crisis demonstrated the need to examine the regulation of securitized products, both on the disclosure side and the distribution side.

The CSA has been developing regulatory proposals to address these concerns in a manner that:

- balances investor protection with efficient capital markets, and

- facilitates transparency and a robust market infrastructure so that the securitization market can continue to function even in times of financial stress.

In developing proposals regarding securitization, we have considered international regulatory and industry developments, and are reviewing them against current Canadian requirements applicable to the distribution of securitized products. For example, we are reviewing the final recommendations of IOSCO's report, *Disclosure Principles for Public Offerings and Listings of Asset-Backed Securities,* and the SEC's notice of proposed rule-making relating to asset-backed securities and other structured finance products.

We expect to publish amendments to our rules relating to the sale of ABCP and other securitized products in the exempt market as well as through prospectuses later in 2010. Refer to CSA Staff Notice 45-307 *Regulatory Developments Regarding Securitization* (dated June 18, 2010) for further information.

These proposals are significant given the size of the Canadian securitization market. According to DBRS, as of March 31, 2010, the size of the Canadian securitization market was $104 billion. The securitization market is significant to Ontario capital markets and the OSC is the principal regulator for the majority of asset-backed securities issuers.

5.3 — Updating of exempt market regime

We continuously update our prospectus exemptions regime in response to market developments and related regulatory initiatives. On September 28, 2009, amended and restated versions of National Instrument 45-106 *Prospectus and Registration Exemptions* and OSC Rule 45-501 *Ontario Prospectus and Registration Exemptions*, and amendments to the related resale instrument, National Instrument 45-102 *Resale of Securities* came into effect. These amendments facilitate the implementation of our new registration regime, which was introduced at the same time through National Instrument 31-103 *Registration Requirements and Exemptions*, and amendments to the Act.

Our focus in fiscal 2011 will be on reviewing how products are sold to retail investors on a prospectus exempt basis. In particular, we are reviewing the accredited investor and $150,000 minimum amount investment prospectus exemptions to assess whether they continue to be appropriate, or whether amendments are needed.

6. — Questions and additional resources

6.1 — Questions about this report

If you have any questions about this report, please contact:

Leslie Byberg

Director, Corporate Finance

Phone: 416-593-2356

Email: lbyberg@osc.gov.on.ca

Jo-Anne Matear

Assistant Manager, Corporate Finance

Phone: 416-593-2323

Email: jmatear@osc.gov.on.ca

Sandra Heldman

Senior Accountant, Corporate Finance

Phone: 416-593-2355

Email: sheldman@osc.gov.on.ca

Frédéric Duguay

Legal Counsel, Corporate Finance

Phone: 416-593-3677

Email: fduguay@osc.gov.on.ca

6.2 — General questions

If you have any general questions about the Branch or any of its activities, please contact the OSC Inquiries and Contact Centre or Branch staff.

The OSC Inquiries and Contact Centre can be contacted by:

Phone: 416-593-8314 (Toronto area)/ 1-877-785-1555 (toll-free)/ 1-866-827-1295 (TTY)

E-mail: inquiries@osc.gov.on.ca

Fax: 416-593-8122

Appendix A contains the contact information for the professional and clerical staff in the Branch.

6.3 — Additional resources

A part of our Branch's mandate is to foster a culture of compliance through outreach and other initiatives. Although we cannot provide legal, financial accounting or other advice, we try to assist issuers in meeting their regulatory requirements in a number of ways.

Corporate Finance section of OSC website

During fiscal 2010, we updated the Corporate Finance section of the OSC website. This section of the website provides a basic outline for issuers on how to comply with Ontario securities law and file certain documents with the OSC. It describes the steps an issuer needs to take to:

- distribute and market securities

- disclose information on a timely and accurate basis, and

- apply for regulatory exemptions.

In particular, there is a page that contains links to information for smaller issuers (both reporting issuers and other issuers) that want to learn more about Ontario securities law.

The Information for Companies section of the OSC website can be found at: http://www.osc.gov.on.ca/en/Companies_index.htm.

Other outreach initiatives

We continued our efforts during fiscal 2010 to be transparent regarding the Branch's initiatives and practices and procedures in as timely a manner as possible. Our intent in doing so is to better enable issuers and their advisors to avoid potential regulatory issues before they undertake any transactions or make any regulatory filings. The primary tools that we use are staff notices (such as the notices referred to in this report) and public speaking engagements. We will continue to communicate regularly with our stakeholders about developing issues.

[Appendix omitted]

OSC Staff Notice 51-711 — List of Refilings and Corrections of Errors as a Result of Regulatory Reviews

Date: **January 3, 2003, as amended effective May 27, 2005**

26 O.S.C.B. 4 and 28 O.S.C.B. 4707

This is an amended version of Staff Notice 51-709, Refilings and Corrections of Errors as a Result of Regulatory Reviews, which has now been withdrawn.

This staff notice discusses our expectations for disclosure by issuers that have failed to comply with periodic and timely disclosure requirements, including issuers that identify errors in documents that they have filed with the Commission. It also describes how we maintain a public list of refilings and errors.

Company Disclosure

When an issuer, to correct an error in how it has complied with disclosure requirements

    (i) amends and refiles a document previously filed with the Commission,

    (ii) files a document that should have been filed at an earlier date, or

    (iii) implements an accounting or disclosure change on a retroactive basis in order to correct an error in a previously filed document

it is our view that these are significant events that should be clearly and broadly disclosed to the market in a timely manner. This responsibility is the same whether the correction is made in the context of a staff review or at any other time.

Specifically, when an issuer identifies a material error in a document that it has filed with the Commission, this will generally represent a material change that should be immediately communicated to the market place by way of a news release and report of the material change in accordance with section 75 of the Act. Even where the correction may not represent a material change, we take the view that investors should be informed immediately by way of a news release.

In our view, it is not appropriate to withhold disclosure of the error until the next required filing or the next earnings press release, even if the issuer requires more time to investigate and quantify all aspects of the error.

From the time the issuer identifies a material error until it is remedied, the issuer will generally be in default of its requirements under the Act and regulations. Under the guidance contained in OSC Policy 51-601, *Reporting Issuer Defaults*, such an issuer will be recorded on the list of defaulting reporting issuers until the default is remedied. OSC Policy 57-603 *Defaults by Reporting Issuers in Complying with Financial Statement Filing Requirements* sets out our expectations for disclosure by the issuer during the period of the default.

All news releases should be released in a way that ensures they are widely and publicly disseminated, and copies should be concurrently provided to the Commission. Any documents that are amended and refiled should be clearly labeled as "revised" or "restated", should identify and describe the nature of the revisions and should be filed under the applicable "amended" document type on SEDAR.

Also, in our view, the news release and the refiled document should be made prominent in the section of the Company's website where financial results are available, and a copy of the news release and the refiled document should be delivered to all shareholders who received a copy of the original document.

Any documents that are being filed for the first time to correct a non-filing at an earlier date should clearly label the document as remedying a previous non-filing and should describe the circumstances surrounding the late filing of the document.

Public List on OSC Website

On October 25, 2002, we started posting a *Refilings and Errors list* on the Commission's Web site (*http://www.osc.gov.on.ca*). This list includes issuers that, after a staff review,

    (1) restate and refile financial statements;

    (2) implement accounting or disclosure changes on a retroactive basis, where the changes represent the correction of an error in the information as originally filed;

    (3) amend and refile other continuous disclosure documents; or

    (4) file documents to correct a non-filing at an earlier date.

Any deficiency in an issuer's disclosure record that is identified during a staff review and that leads to one of these events will result in that issuer being placed on the *Refilings and Errors list*. In this regard, it makes no difference whether (i) the deficiency was identified by staff or by the issuer and its advisors during the review process, or (ii) the Commission ordered the filing or refiling or the issuer took this step voluntarily. A staff review is considered to begin when an issuer receives a comment letter from staff and ends when the issuer is notified that staff has completed its review.

Once placed on the *Refilings and Errors list*, an issuer's name will be kept on the list for a period of three years from the date of refiling or filing to correct an error. After the three-year period, the issuer's name will be archived.

OSC Staff Notice 51-713 — Report on Staff's Review of MD&A

Date: **January 16, 2004**
27 O.S.C.B. 715

The corporate collapses that have occurred around the world in recent years have highlighted the need for improved disclosure and transparency. In particular, attention worldwide has focused on the importance of greater transparency in disclosure of financial information, including both the financial statements and ... Management's Discussion and Analysis ....[1]

MD&A is a narrative explanation, through the eyes of management, of how your company performed during the period covered by the financial statements, and of your company's financial condition and future prospects. MD&A complements and supplements your financial statements, but does not form part of your financial statements.

Your objective when preparing the MD&A should be to improve your company's overall financial disclosure by giving a balanced discussion of your company's results of operations and financial condition including, without limitation, such considerations as liquidity and capital resources — openly reporting bad news as well as good news. Your MD&A should

- *help current and prospective investors understand what the financial statements show and do not show;*

- *discuss material information that may not be fully reflected in the financial statements, such as contingent liabilities, defaults under debt, off-balance sheet financing arrangements, or other contractual obligations;*

- *discuss important trends and risks that have affected the financial statements, and trends and risks that are reasonably likely to affect them in the future; and*

- *provide information about the quality, and potential variability, of your company's earnings and cash flow, to assist investors in determining if past performance is indicative of future performance.*[2]

I. — Purpose

On March 5, 2003, the Canadian Securities Administrators (the *CSA*) announced it had launched a review to assess how well publicly-traded companies comply with their management's discussion and analysis (*MD&A*) disclosure obligations. Under this initiative, a number of CSA jurisdictions reviewed a sample of the MD&A of companies in their local jurisdictions.

In April 2003, the British Columbia Securities Commission published a special edition of its Continuous Disclosure Update to provide MD&A guidance for junior resource and non-resource sector companies. On October 30, 2003, the Quebec Securities Commission (the *QSC*) published a report on Phase I of a program to review the continuous disclosure of major Quebec issuers. Included in the QSC program was a review of MD&A. The Alberta Securities Commission (the *ASC*) reviewed MD&A filed with the ASC as part of their review of issuers' continuous disclosure. The ASC expects to release their *2003 Report on the Review of Financial Statements, MD&A and Other Continuous Disclosure* in early 2004.

Concurrent with the reviews in other jurisdictions, staff of the Ontario Securities Commission (the *OSC*) reviewed the MD&A of forty-seven companies, primarily with head offices in Ontario. This staff notice reports our findings and comments arising from these reviews.

II. — Executive Summary

We have a number of general observations about how companies prepare their MD&A. We found that some companies:

- omit information that may be material to investors;

- disclose an excessive amount of immaterial information;

- disclose good news but not bad news;

- tend not to have a forward-looking orientation to their MD & A; and

- lack adequate internal policies and procedures for preparing, reviewing and approving their MD & A.

In Part IV, we discuss our views with respect to each of these observations.

Of the forty-seven companies reviewed, thirty-four (72%) filed their MD & A with one or more of the deficiencies set out in the following table. Of these thirty-four companies, three restated and refiled their MD&A and have been recorded on the Refilings and Errors list main-

---

[1]Technical Committee, the International Organization of Securities Commissions, *General Principles Regarding Disclosure of Management's Discussion and Analysis of Financial Condition and Results of Operations* (2003).

[2]Section 1(a), proposed Form 51-102F1 *Management's Discussion & Analysis.*

tained on the OSC's website (*http:/www.osc.gov.on.ca*). The remaining thirty-one companies committed to make prospective improvements to their MD&A.

Table 1

Area of Deficiency	Type of Deficiency	Number of Companies	Percentage of Total
Results of Operations and Financial Condition	Failure to quantify explanations of material variances or failure to analyze material variances.	21	45%
	Failure to disclose and analyze key value drivers.	8	17%
	Failure to analyze reportable segments.	6	13%
	Failure to analyze known trends that have had or that the company reasonably expects will have a favourable or unfavourable effect.	3	6%
	Failure to disclose and analyze items with a material impact in the fourth quarter.	1	2%
Risks and Uncertainties	Failure to disclose and analyze risks.	8	17%
	Failure to adequately analyze identified risks.	13	28%
Liquidity and Capital Resources	Failure to analyze liquidity, generally.	12	26%
	Failure to disclose and analyze breach of debt covenants.	1	2%
	Failure to disclose and analyze certain off-balance sheet arrangements.	1	2%
Selected Quarterly Financial Information	Failure to disclose and analyze selected quarterly financial information.	13	28%
Interim MD&A	Failure to comply with interim MD&A requirements.	9	19%

In Part V, we discuss each of these MD&A requirements, provide examples of how companies fail to meet these requirements, and provide our views on how companies should meet these requirements.

III. — Objective and Scope

Our main objective was to assess compliance with the MD&A requirements of Ontario Securities Commission Rule 51-501 *AIF and MD&A* (*Rule 51-501*). Rule 51-501 generally requires Ontario reporting issuers above certain size thresholds to file annual MD&A following the form requirements of Form 44-101F2 *MD&A* (*Form 44-101F2*), and interim MD&A following the requirements of section 4.2 of Rule 51-501.

We expect these size thresholds will be eliminated in 2004, and all Canadian reporting issuers will have to file their MD&A following the adoption of proposed National Instrument 51-102 *Continuous Disclosure Obligations* (*NI 51-102*). Proposed Form 51-102F1 *Management's Discussion & Analysis* (*Form 51-102F1*) sets out new MD&A form requirements. The new form will require additional disclosure above the form requirements of Form 44-101F2 but we believe the existing requirements will otherwise remain largely unchanged. All of the deficiencies against the Rule 51-501 requirements identified in this staff notice would also be deficiencies under NI 51-102.

Our review focused on annual and interim MD&A. To do this, we conducted reviews of the full continuous disclosure records of all selected issuers. Though other comments were raised, we limit our discussion in this staff notice to MD&A issues. Although the observations in this notice are based on a review of the MD&A filed as part of continuous disclosure, they are equally applicable to the MD&A included in prospectuses.

This staff notice is not intended to be an exhaustive summary of all our concerns regarding MD&A. We emphasize that companies will not necessarily comply with the MD&A requirements of Ontario securities law solely by following the guidance set out in this staff notice.

Companies may want to review the results of the MD&A reviews in other CSA jurisdictions, as well as the publications of other organizations like the Canadian Institute of Chartered Accountants (the *CICA*), the International Organization of Securities Commissions, and the U.S. Securities and Exchange Commission.[3]

IV. — General Observations

The following is a number of general observations we found in our reviews. We believe these observations emphasize principles that all companies should follow when preparing their MD&A. Specific deficiencies against the requirements of Rule 51-501 often reflect the failure to apply one or more of these underlying principles.

---

[3]*See e.g.*, Canadian Institute of Chartered Accountants, *Management's Discussion and Analysis, Guidance on Preparation and Disclosure* (2002); Commission Guidance Regarding Management's Discussion and Analysis of Financial Condition and Results of Operations, Exchange Act Release Nos. 33-8350, 34-48960, 68 Fed. Reg. 75,056 (December 29, 2003); U.S. Securities and Exchange Commission, *Summary by the Division of Corporation Finance of Significant Issues Addressed in the Review of the Periodic Reports of the Fortune 500 Companies* (2003); Management's Discussion and Analysis of Financial Condition and Results of Operations, Exchange Act Release Nos. 33-6835, 34-26,831, 54 Fed. Reg. 22,427 (May 24, 1989).

Part 5: ONGOING REQUIREMENTS

1. — *Materiality*

Instruction (4) of Form 44-101F2 generally describes materiality in an MD&A as follows:

> Materiality is a matter of judgement in particular circumstances and should generally be determined in relation to an item's significance to investors, analysts and other users of information. An item of information, or an aggregate of items, is considered material if it is probable that its omission or misstatement would influence or change an investment decision with respect to the issuer's securities.

Section 1(f) of Form 51-102F1 generally describes materiality in an MD&A as follows:

> Would a reasonable investor's decision whether or not to buy, sell or hold securities in your company likely be influenced or changed if the information in question was omitted or misstated? If so, the information is likely material.

We believe that these are objective tests. It is not sufficient for management to determine that it believes that certain information is immaterial, based solely on its own impressions and instincts. Management should determine materiality by asking whether a reasonable investor would believe in the circumstances that certain information was material.

We found that some companies omit information from their MD&A even when there may be some uncertainty as to whether the information would influence a reasonable investor's decision. Since omitting material information required to be disclosed under Rule 51-501 is a violation of Ontario securities law, we believe management should err on the side of caution when deciding what information is material. We are not suggesting that companies should disclose everything and allow readers to decide whether the disclosure is material but rather that management should exercise its judgement with a bent to caution.

This last point is important because we also found that some companies disclose an excessive amount of immaterial information. These companies tend to provide boilerplate explanations, provide explanations of immaterial changes, or simply repeat variances that can be easily calculated from the financial statements without any analysis. Companies should avoid disclosing information that users do not need or that does not provide insight into the company's past or future performance. Omitting repetitive and boilerplate information will permit companies to focus their MD&A on analyzing the material information that is most useful to investors.

2. — *Balance*

We found that companies tend to disclose good news and avoid discussing bad news. Companies should provide a balanced picture of their operations and financial conditions in their MD&A. By disclosing an excessive amount of positive information while failing to disclose negative information, companies create an overly optimistic and misleading picture of the company. Similarly, disclosing an excessive amount of negative information may create an overly pessimistic picture.

3. — *Forward-Looking Orientation*

We found that companies tend to focus on past variances in financial statement line items without considering future consequences. As set out in the Instructions of Form 44-101F2 and section 1(g) of Form 51-102F1, one important principle of the MD&A requirements is that disclosure should be forward looking. The discussion of historical results is more useful when it addresses items that are reasonably expected to have a material impact on future operations. A forward-looking orientation is also important in disclosing trends, risks, and other matters.

4. — *Adequate Internal Policies and Procedures*

We found many companies do not have adequate systems for preparing, reviewing, and approving their MD&A. A company's MD&A should be prepared by individuals with a detailed knowledge of the company's operations as well as a strategic view of the company as a whole. Senior management, the board of directors and the audit committee should review the MD&A. Senior management and the board of directors should perform a comprehensive review to ensure that the disclosure meets the letter and spirit of the MD&A requirements. Companies may also seek input from professional advisors who have specialized knowledge of evolving regulatory requirements.

The goal of these procedures should be to improve the overall quality of the MD&A and not just to meet the minimum requirements. These procedures should be integrated with the company's overall financial reporting process. Companies should specifically consider whether to incorporate these policies and procedures into their corporate disclosure policies.

V. — Specific Areas of Non-Compliance

The examples below are hypothetical and have been included only to emphasize some of our concerns.

1. — *Results of Operation and Financial Condition*

Twenty-four companies had one or more of the following deficiencies in their MD&A disclosure of results of operations or financial condition.

a. — *Material Variances*

Section 1(1) of Form 44-101F2 requires companies to analyze their results of operations and financial condition in the most recently completed financial year, including a comparison against the previously completed financial year and an explanation of why these changes occurred. Companies should describe and quantify explanations of material variances.[4] Twenty-one companies failed to meet this requirement.

---

[4]In most cases, we believe an explanation should be quantified in financial terms by stating the financial impact of the explanation on the material variance of the financial statement line item. For example, if a company explains an increase in overall sales by an increase in sales to two major customers, the company should quantify this explanation by comparing dollar sales to these two customers in each period. Furthermore, if the increase in sales to either of these two major customers is itself material, the company should further explain this increase. Thus, if sales increased $40, sales to Customer A increased $20, sales to

These companies either qualitatively explained a material variance without quantifying the impact of that explanation or completely failed to provide any analysis of a material variance.

Example 1

The company's year-to-year net sales increased X% to $X because sales of Product A and Product B increased. Both retail sales of Product A, and wholesale sales of Product A, increased because of an increase in unit sales of Product A due to a new marketing program. The annual increase in retail sales of Product A was partially offset by a decrease in fourth-quarter unit sales due to bad weather. Sales of Product B decreased marginally.

The company identifies a number of explanations for the increase in net sales but does not quantify any of these explanations. Without quantifying these explanations, investors would not be able to measure the relative impact of each explanation, understand and analyze the overall change in sales, or form an expectation of future results. The company should quantify the increases in retail and wholesale sales of Product A, and the decreases in fourth-quarter retail unit sales of Product A and sales of Product B. The company should also describe how the new marketing program increased unit sales of Product A, quantify the increase in unit sales due to the new marketing program, and quantify the cost of the new marketing program.

b. — Key Value Drivers

Section 4(3) of Form 44-101F2 requires companies to discuss the extent to which any changes in net sales or revenues are attributable to changes in selling prices, to changes in the volume or quantity of goods or services being sold, or to the introduction of new products or services. Companies should disclose their key value drivers and analyze any impact of changes in these key drivers on net sales or revenues. Eight companies failed to disclose and analyze key value drivers.

Example 2

The company operates divisions in two industries: retailing and telecommunications. Revenue of the company increased X% to $X because sales of the retail division increased X% to $X and revenue of telecommunications division increased X% to $X. The company acquired the telecommunications division in the prior year. The increase in revenue in the telecommunications division is the result of this division generating revenue for a full year.

The company identifies a number of explanations for the increase in overall revenue. The company also quantifies these explanations but fails to identify and analyze the key drivers of net sales and revenue in the retail and telecommunications divisions. The company should identify and analyze the key value drivers in both divisions. For example, the key value drivers in the retail division might include same store sales, gross margins, and market share; and the key value drivers in the telecommunications division might include competitive landscape, customer churn rate, and regulatory environment.

c. — Segments

Subsection 1(1)(b) of Form 44-101F2 requires companies to include an analysis and comparison of each reportable segment, as well as the company as a whole, if necessary to understand the analysis and comparison of the company's results of operations. Six companies failed to analyze material information about a reportable segment. Some of these companies had no disclosure in their MD&A, while others provided minimal disclosure that did not give readers a complete picture of how various segments contributed to the results or position of the overall company.

Example 3

The company has two reportable segments: Canada and the United States. Overall earnings before interest, taxes, depreciation and amortization (*EBITDA*) increased X% to $X.[5] The company expects EBITDA to increase next year due to expected volume increases in both reportable segments.

The company does not discuss each reportable segment's impact on EBITDA. The company should disclose EBITDA and explain the expected EBITDA increase, including the expected volume increases, for each of its reportable segments. This holds whether the company's reportable segments are based on geographic areas of operations, or on other factors relating to operations or management structure.

Customer B increased $10, and the increase in sales to Customer A is material but the increase in sales to Customer B is not, the company should further explain the increase in sales to Customer A. The company could further explain that sales to Customer A of Product A increased $10, and of Product B increased $10.

Alternatively, we believe an explanation may be quantified in non-financial terms. For example, if a company explains an increase in sales by an increase in its customer base, the company should quantify this explanation by comparing the average number of customers in each period.

We believe that companies should also identify and analyze known trends with respect to each explanation. For example, if sales to specific customers or if the average number of customers has been steadily increasing from prior periods and management expects this trend to continue, the company should say so. Alternatively, if the increase in sales to specific customers is an anomaly and is not expected to continue, the company should say so.

[5] As set out in Revised CSA Staff Notice 52-306 Non-GAAP Financial Measures (*CSA Staff Notice 52-306*), we are concerned about the use of financial measures, like EBITDA, that are not prescribed by Generally Accepted Accounting Principles (*GAAP*). Nevertheless, we acknowledge that discussion of non-GAAP financial measures in the MD&A may be a useful means of providing additional information to investors, so long as the disclosure of these measures in the MD&A is consistent with the expectations set out in CSA Staff Notice 52-306. Once a company decides to disclose a non-GAAP financial measure like EBITDA in its MD&A, the company should disclose the financial measure for each reportable segment.

d. — Trends

Section 4(2) of Form 44-101F2 requires companies to describe any known trends that have had or that they reasonably expect will have a favourable or unfavourable effect on results of operations and financial condition. Three companies failed to identify and adequately analyze these trends.

Example 4

The company has two divisions. Overall revenue decreased X% to $X. Division A revenue decreased $X and Division B revenue decreased $X. Revenue in both divisions is expected to improve next year.

The company does not explain why it expects revenue to improve next year. Given the decrease in revenue of both divisions, this expectation appears to be a reversal of a known trend. The company fails to describe and analyze this known trend. The company should identify and analyze the downward trend in revenue of each division, and explain why it expects revenue to improve in future periods despite this year's declines.

e. — Fourth Quarter

Section 1(2) of Form 44-101F2 requires companies to describe and quantify any events or items that have had a material impact on the issuer's results of operations or financial condition for the fourth quarter of their most recently completed financial year. Companies are not required to produce separate interim MD&A for the fourth quarter. When events or items that have had a material impact occur in the fourth quarter, the analysis required by this section may be the only disclosure investors receive. Accordingly, companies must include this disclosure in their annual MD&A. One company failed to disclose and analyze an item with a material impact in the fourth quarter.

2. — Risks and Uncertainties

Twenty-one companies had inadequate disclosure of risks and uncertainties.

Section 1(3) of Form 44-101F2 requires companies to disclose information on risks and uncertainties necessary to understand their financial condition, changes in financial condition and results of operations. Section 1(4) of Form 44-101F2 requires companies to analyze material risks, events, and uncertainties that could cause reported financial information to not necessarily be indicative of future operating results or of future financial position, including a qualitative and quantitative discussion of factors that could have an effect in the future but that have not had an effect in the past, and that have had an effect in the past but are not expected to have an effect in the future. Section 5.2 of proposed Form 51-102F2 *Annual Information Form* will require disclosure of general risk factors in the annual information form (the *AIF*) but we believe Form 51-102F1 will also require MD&A disclosure of risks and uncertainties necessary to make the MD&A complete and understandable. Companies will still be required to identify and analyze risks and uncertainties as discussed in this staff notice but this disclosure may be in the AIF, in the MD&A, or in both.

Eight companies failed to disclose any risks at all while thirteen failed to adequately analyze identified risks. Several of the latter simply disclosed a list of risks with no analysis. Some of these companies expressed the view that they only needed to disclose unusual business risks. We believe that companies are required to disclose all material risks and uncertainties that are reasonably expected to have a material impact on the company's financial condition, changes in financial condition, and results of operations.

Example 5

The company is a retailer. The retail industry is exposed to a wide range of risks that are reasonably expected to have a material impact on future operations. These risks include: occupancy risk, credit risk, foreign exchange exposure, bad debts exposure, interest rate risk, inventory in-stock and flow of goods risk, buying and pricing risk, and competitive risk. The company's competitors provide substantial disclosure of these risks in their MD&A.

The company does not identify any of these risks in its MD&A. The company believes that all retailers have similar risks, that these risks are known and understood by investors, are not considered unusual risks, and do not need to be disclosed in its MD&A.

The company should describe all material risks. The company should also explain how each risk has affected results of operations and financial condition in the past or how each risk is expected to affect future results of operations and financial condition. The company should also quantify, if possible, the past and expected future impact of each risk to facilitate the analysis of each risk's relative impact. Finally, the company should disclose any steps it has taken, or plans to take, to mitigate the impact of any risk.

3. — Liquidity and Capital Resources

Fourteen companies had inadequate disclosure of liquidity and capital resources.

a. — Generally

Subsection 3(1)(a) of Form 44-101F2 requires companies to discuss their ability to generate adequate amounts of cash and cash equivalents. Subsection 3(1)(b) requires companies to identify any known trends or expected fluctuations in their liquidity and if a short- or long-term deficiency is identified, to indicate the course of action that has been taken or is proposed to be taken to remedy the deficiency. This disclosure is required for all companies but is particularly important for companies with negative cash flow from operations (as defined in the Handbook of the CICA), with material declines in cash flow from operations, or with positive cash flow from operations only because of favourable working capital variances. Twelve companies failed to disclose and analyze potential liquidity problems.

Example 6

The company had $X of liquid investments, net of bank indebtedness. Cash of $X was deployed in operating activities. Cash of $X was deployed in capital expenditures. Cash of $X was raised from a private placement. The company's future obligations include a capital lease of $X and an amount due to shareholders of $X

The company's disclosure on liquidity mostly repeats information that investors could easily calculate themselves from the financial statements. The company should describe whether it expects negative cash flow from operations in the coming year and, if so, how it intends to finance its operations. The company also fails to discuss how it intends to reverse its negative cash flow from operations.

Example 7

The company's non-cash working capital increased $X. This was the result of a decrease in accounts receivable of $X and an increase in trade payables $X, offset by an increase in inventory $X. The increase in non-cash working capital, offset by losses from operations, resulted in net positive cash flow from operations of $X.

The company would have negative cash flow from operations if not for a favourable variance in non-cash working capital yet the company's disclosure of non-cash working capital merely repeats information that investors could easily calculate themselves from the financial statements. The company should analyze the changes in each of its non-cash working capital accounts.. For example, the company should explain why accounts receivable decreased, accounts payable increased, and inventory increased. If accounts receivable decreased because collections improved, the company should say so. If trade payables increased because the company has more overdue payables at year end, the company should say so. If ending inventory was higher because of a decline in fourth-quarter sales, the company should say so.

b. — Debt Covenants

Subsection 3(1)(f) of Form 44-101F2 requires companies to disclose information concerning any default on any debt covenants and the method or anticipated method of curing the default. Companies should also discuss the nature and duration of any waiver received from creditors with respect to the breach. One company failed to disclose and analyze a breach of a debt covenant.

c. — Off-Balance Sheet Arrangements

Subsection 3(1)(a) of Form 44-101F2 requires companies to discuss their ability to generate adequate amounts of cash and cash equivalents. Companies should disclose and analyze information about certain off-balance sheet arrangements, like pension obligations, minimum payments on operating leases, and encumbered assets, if these arrangements will likely have a material impact on the company's future liquidity. One company failed to disclose and analyze a material off-balance sheet arrangement. More detailed disclosure of off-balance sheet arrangements will be required under Item 1.8 of Form 51-102F1.

Example 8

The company funds a defined benefit pension plan for the benefit of its employees. The present value of expected future pension obligations (not necessarily the pension liability on the balance sheet) exceeds the value of plan assets. The difference is material and the company did not discuss or analyze the difference in its MD&A.

The company should identify the difference between pension obligations and plan assets and explain how and when the difference will be addressed in future periods. For example, if the company expects to fund the difference out of operating profits or expects that the difference will be addressed through return on plan assets, it should say so. It should also discuss the risk and uncertainty associated with this item as required by sections 1(3) and (4) of Form 44-101F2.

4. — Other Deficiencies

a. — Selected Quarterly Financial Information

Section 2(1) of Form 44-101F2 requires companies to disclose selected quarterly financial information for each of the past eight quarters. Selected quarterly financial information must be disclosed in the MD&A, notwithstanding that this information is also disclosed in the AIF. Thirteen companies failed to disclose this information in their MD&A. To the extent that a material trend can be identified in the selected quarterly information, companies should also identify and analyze the trend. Section 1.5 of Form 51-102F1 will require disclosure of selected quarterly financial information in the MD&A but NI 51-102 will not generally require this disclosure in the AIF.

b. — Interim MD&A

Companies that are required to file annual MD&A under Rule 51-501 are also required to file interim MD&A that complies with section 4.2 of Rule 51-501. Companies should update the analysis of their financial condition in the annual MD&A for the most recently completed financial year and analyze their results from operations and cash flows for the most recently completed interim period.[6] We also encourage companies to provide an update in their interim MD&A of their annual MD&A disclosure of known trends, and risks and uncertainties, as recommended by section 2.3 of Companion Policy 51-501CP *To Ontario Securities Commission Rule 51-501 AIF and MD&A*. Nine companies had deficient interim MD&A disclosure. The deficiencies were similar to the annual MD&A deficiencies discussed above.

---

[6]Interim MD&A was also reviewed in Ontario Securities Commission Staff Notice 52-713 *Report on Staffs Review of Interim Financial Statements and Interim Management's Discussion and Analysis — February 2002.*

Part 5: ONGOING REQUIREMENTS

VI. — Conclusion

We will continue to review MD&A as part of our continuous disclosure review program, focusing in particular on the new requirements of NI 51-102. These include disclosure of:

- certain off-balance sheet arrangements;

- transactions with related parties;

- tabular presentation of contractual obligations;

- for companies that are not venture issuers (as defined in NI 51-102), analysis of critical accounting estimates; and

- for venture issuers without significant revenues, additional matters.

We may also raise comments about:

- proposed transactions, including the impact of major acquisitions;

- changes in accounting policies including initial adoption;

- the impact of reversals of prior period accounting treatments (for example, material sales of previously written-off inventory);

- financial instruments;

- the use of pro-forma or non-GAAP financial information;

- the issuance of stock options or other securities that dilute shareholders' equity; and

- the impact of income taxes.

Proposed Multilateral Instrument 52-109 *Certification of Disclosure in Companies' Annual and Interim Filings (MI 52-109)* is scheduled to become effective on March 30, 2004. MI 52-109 will require reporting issuers, other than investment funds, to file separate annual and interim certificates signed by their chief executive officers and chief financial officers, or persons who perform similar functions.

Each certificate will state, among other things, that the certifying officer has reviewed the annual and interim filings (which include the MD&A), that the annual and interim filings do not contain misrepresentations, and that the filings fairly present the financial condition of the issuer. We believe that meaningful MD&A will be an important element of how an issuer achieves this fair presentation.

We believe that the MD&A requirements are clear. Nevertheless, our review suggests that many companies are not meeting these requirements. Though in this review we often accepted commitments to make prospective changes, it is increasingly likely that we will ask companies to restate and refile their MD&A if they fail to meet the MD&A requirements. We will provide further guidance as appropriate.

Policies and Orders: OSCN 51-715.

OSC Notice 51-714 — OSC Continuous Disclosure Advisory Committee

Date: May 14, 2006, as revised May 26, 2006 and May 30, 2008

29 O.S.C.B. 4629 and 4297 and 31 O.S.C.B. 5380

[Not reproduced]

OSC Staff Notice 51-716 — Environmental Reporting

Date: February 29, 2008

31 O.S.C.B. 2223

Introduction

National Instrument 51-102 *Continuous Disclosure Obligations* (NI 51-102) requires reporting issuers to disclose information about environmental matters in their continuous disclosure (CD) documents. This notice outlines the results of a targeted review of compliance with these requirements that staff of the Ontario Securities Commission (OSC) recently conducted. This review was announced in OSC Staff Notice 51-706 *Corporate Finance Branch Report 2007*, dated November 1, 2007.

Scope of Our Review

Issuer sample

We completed a review of 35 reporting issuers for whom the OSC is the principal regulator. Twenty-two were TSX-listed issuers and 13 were venture issuers[1]. Each of the issuers we reviewed operates in one of the following industries: environmental services, industrial products, mining, oil and gas, steel, transportation services, or utilities. This notice includes commentary that may be relevant to issuers operating in other industries.

---

[1]The commentary regarding disclosure obligations of TSX-listed issuers applies to all issuers that do not qualify as venture issuers. A "venture issuer" is defined in NI 51-102 as a reporting issuer that, as at the applicable time, did not have any of its securities listed or quoted on any of the Toronto Stock Exchange, a U.S. marketplace, or a marketplace outside of Canada and the United States of America other than the Alternative Investment Market of the London Stock Exchange or the PLUS markets operated by PLUS Markets Group plc.

Documents reviewed

We reviewed the CD documents of each issuer, which included the issuer's most recent annual financial statements, annual management's discussion and analysis (MD&A) and annual information form (AIF), if applicable.

We also reviewed each issuer's website for disclosure of information relating to environmental matters to determine if that disclosure was consistent with the disclosure in its CD documents.

Disclosure

We examined disclosure about the following matters:

- financial liabilities related to the environment (environmental liabilities)
- asset retirement obligations
- financial and operational effects of environmental protection requirements
- environmental policies fundamental to operations, and
- environmental risks

Focus on material information

As provided in Part 1(f) of Form 51-102F1 *Management's Discussion & Analysis* (Form 51-102F1) and Part 1(e) of Form 51-102F2 *Annual Information Form* (Form 51-102F2), materiality is the determining factor for including information in CD documents.

Information relating to environmental matters is likely material if a reasonable investor's decision whether or not to buy, sell or hold securities of the issuer would likely be influenced or changed if the information was omitted or misstated. As noted in Form 51-102F1 and Form 51-102F2, this concept of materiality is consistent with the financial reporting notion of materiality included in the Canadian Institute of Chartered Accountants Handbook (the Handbook).

We are of the view that issuers should consider both quantitative and qualitative factors in determining materiality generally, and particularly for disclosure relating to environmental matters.

Summary of Findings and Comments

A. — Environmental liabilities

Estimates reflected in financial statements

Under Section 3290 — Contingencies of the Handbook, a contingency is defined as an existing condition or situation involving uncertainty as to possible gain or loss to an issuer that will ultimately be resolved when one or more future events occur or fail to occur. For example, an issuer involved in litigation over environmental matters may include an estimated amount for a contingent environmental liability in its financial statements (including the related notes) at the date of its financial statements. The estimate may be selected from a range of possibilities. The estimate may change over time. Canadian generally accepted accounting principles (GAAP) allow the minimum estimate to be accrued if no estimate within the range is more probable than another. Prediction of the outcome of contingencies, including estimation of the financial effects, is a matter of judgment by those responsible for preparing financial statements, taking into account the particular circumstances.

Where the environmental liability involves a critical accounting estimate (as defined in Form 51-102F1), certain disclosure is required. Specifically, item 1.12 of Form 51-102F1 requires management of TSX-listed issuers to include an analysis of critical accounting estimates in their MD&A. This analysis should:

- identify and describe each critical accounting estimate, including:
  - a description of the accounting estimate
  - the methodology used in determining the critical accounting estimate
  - the assumptions underlying the accounting estimate that relate to matters highly uncertain at the time the estimate was made
  - any known trends, commitments, events or uncertainties that management reasonably believes will materially affect the methodology or assumptions described, and
  - if applicable, why the estimate is reasonably likely to change from period to period and have a material impact on the financial presentation
- explain the significance of the estimate to the issuer's financial condition, changes in financial condition and results of operations and identify the financial statement line items affected by the accounting estimate
- discuss changes made to critical accounting estimates during the past two financial years, including the reasons for the change and the quantitative effect on the issuer's overall financial performance and financial statement line items, and
- identify the segments of the issuer's business that the accounting estimate affects and discuss the accounting estimate on a segment basis, if the issuer operates in more than one segment

Findings

The MD&A of some of the TSX-listed issuers we reviewed included a detailed analysis of the issuer's environmental estimates. For example, in discussing reclamation costs, one issuer stated that its operations are subject to environmental laws in the various countries where it has closed mines and open mines. The issuer then stated that technical issues made the reclamation of closed mines uncertain, which, together with any future changes in environmental laws, made estimating reclamation costs difficult. Nevertheless, the issuer provided a breakdown of its estimated reclamation costs for its closed mines and its open mines, and provided the basis and methodology for making these estimates. The issuer concluded its analysis by noting that it recognized changes in its estimated reclamation costs immediately for closed mines and amortized any changes in its estimated reclamation costs over the life of its open mines.

In contrast, many of the other TSX-listed issuers we reviewed included boilerplate discussion of environmental estimates in their MD&A with minimal or no analysis, or did not discuss the environmental estimates at all. For example, in its MD&A, one issuer simply stated that it is responsible for its share of environmental costs and maintains insurance for environmental risks, but that there is no guarantee that the insurance will cover all environmental claims brought against the issuer.

Comments

We are of the view that in order for a TSX-listed issuer to meet the requirements of item 1.12 of Form 51-102F1, the issuer should quantify the accounting estimate where quantitative information is reasonably available and would provide material information to investors. They should also identify and explain that the estimate was highly uncertain at the time it was made and provide a detailed discussion of the estimate, which may include a sensitivity analysis or disclosure of the upper and lower ends of the range of estimates from which the recorded estimate was selected.

We are of the view that boilerplate disclosure is insufficient because it does not specifically identify how the estimate relates to that issuer, and therefore does not provide meaningful information to investors.

Potential environmental liabilities not reflected in financial statements

Findings

Many of the issuers we reviewed only discussed potential environmental liabilities in their MD&A if they had included these potential liabilities in their financial statements.

Eight issuers mentioned environmental contingencies and commitments in the notes to their financial statements. These included chemical spills, litigation resulting from a variety of environmental matters, arbitration in foreign jurisdictions concerning licences and permits, and soil remediation. However, only six of these issuers discussed these environmental contingencies and commitments in their MD&A.

Comments

Some issuers may have potential liabilities that are not reflected in the financial statements because their long-term or contingent nature can make them particularly difficult to quantify.

Some issuers may have several contingent environmental liabilities that have not been recognized because they are not individually material, but it is possible that together they may indicate an underlying risk or trend that could be material to the issuer in the long-term.

We are of the view that a discussion of material contingent environmental liabilities should be included in an issuer's MD&A and/or AIF whether or not the liability has been accrued in the financial statements or has been disclosed in the notes to the financial statements.

B. — Asset retirement obligations

In accordance with Section 3110 — Asset Retirement Obligations of the Handbook, issuers are required to include certain disclosure about asset retirement obligations (AROs) in their financial statements, if applicable.

Item 1.2 of Form 51-102F1 requires an analysis of an issuer's financial condition, results of operations and cash flows, which includes a discussion of commitments, events or uncertainties that are reasonably likely to have an effect on the issuer's business. In addition, item 1.6 of Form 51-102F1, and the corresponding instructions for item 1.6 included in Form 51-102F1, require TSX-listed issuers to provide a summary, in a table, of contractual obligations for the issuer's balance sheet conditions or income or cash flow, including payments due for each of the next five years and thereafter. Among other things, TSX-listed issuers must list other long-term obligations, which may include AROs.

Findings

Thirteen issuers, including two venture issuers, included AROs in their financial statements. Seven of these issuers also included AROs in the summary contractual obligations table in their MD&A.

Five issuers discussed the AROs in both their MD&A and their AIF, seven issuers discussed the AROs only in their MD&A and one issuer did not discuss the AROs in their MD&A or AIF.

Disclosure of AROs varied among issuers. For example, some issuers recognized, measured and disclosed liabilities for AROs associated with the retirement of long-lived assets in accordance with GAAP, but did not include a discussion of these liabilities in their MD&A and/or AIF.

Other issuers provided more useful information regarding AROs to investors. For example, one issuer accrued environmental remediation costs relating to certain mines in its annual financial statements in accordance with GAAP. The issuer also included a comprehensive discussion of these costs in its MD&A and AIF, separating the costs into categories such as the costs of compliance with environmental legislation and the costs associated with the disposal of hazardous materials, and also divided the costs among open mines, closed mines and development projects. The issuer then identified the current and future impact of the costs on financial results and noted that it would record a loss accrual if a contingent loss arose due to the improper use of an asset and the loss was probable and could be reasonably estimated.

Comments

A liability for an ARO should be recognized in the period when a reasonable estimate of fair value can be made. Once this estimate can be made, GAAP requires that the estimate be included in the issuer's financial statements.

We are of the view that if an ARO is material to an issuer, in addition to providing the required financial statement disclosure, the issuer should strive to enhance a reader's understanding by providing supplemental disclosure in its MD&A. Specifically, issuers should include in their MD&A a comprehensive discussion of material commitments, events or uncertainties, including AROs, that are reasonably likely to have an effect on the issuer's business.

Issuers should also evaluate whether AROs are material long-term obligations. If so, we are of the view that TSX-listed issuers should include these AROs in the summary contractual obligations table in their MD&A as required under item 1.6 of Form 51-102F1.

C. — Financial and operational effects of environmental protection requirements

Item 5.1(1)(k) of Form 51-102F2 requires issuers to disclose the financial and operational effects of environmental protection requirements on the issuer's capital expenditures, earnings and competitive position in the current financial year and the expected effect in future years.

Findings

Twenty-two of the issuers we reviewed were required to file an AIF. Fourteen of these issuers included disclosure about environmental protection requirements in their AIF. Eight issuers did not include any disclosure in their AIF about environmental protection requirements.

Most of the issuers that included disclosure in their AIF about environmental protection requirements provided only a qualitative discussion of environmental protection requirements. They did not quantify the costs or the impact or potential impact on financial and operational results. This qualitative disclosure was typically discussed in the context of a risk factor.

In addition, many of these issuers provided only a limited discussion of these requirements, again with no quantification on the results of the issuer's operations. For example, one issuer simply stated that future environmental changes could affect any aspect of its activities.

Some issuers did include a detailed discussion of the financial and operational effects of environmental protection requirements on their capital expenditures, earnings and competitive position in the current financial year and the expected effect in future years. For example, one issuer stated that it designs and operates in compliance with all applicable environmental requirements relating to the protection of the environment. The issuer also stated that it cannot predict the changes that could be made to environmental requirements in the future. The issuer concluded its discussion by stating that its capital and operating costs for environmental controls would likely increase in the future, but these increases were not expected to have a material effect on the earnings or competitive position of the issuer.

Comments

We are of the view that in order to meet the requirements of item 5.1(1)(k) of Form 51-102F2, the AIF should, where reasonably available, include a quantification of the costs associated with environmental protection requirements, and the impact or potential impact of these costs on financial and operational results. Boilerplate disclosure is insufficient to properly meet these requirements.

D. — Environmental policies fundamental to operations

If an issuer has implemented environmental policies that are fundamental to its operations (such as policies on the issuer's relationship with the environment), item 5.1(4) of Form 51-102F2 requires the issuer to describe these policies and the steps it has taken to implement them.

Findings

Disclosure of environmental policies varied significantly in the AIFs that we reviewed. Some issuers provided meaningful information to investors. For example, one issuer discussed its various programs to prevent and control spills and protect water quality, reuse and conserve water, and mitigate the dust produced by its operations for each of its properties. The issuer also addressed how harmful materials generated by its operations are removed and destroyed, and described its policy of performing regular environmental audits on all of its properties.

A number of issuers did not provide a meaningful discussion of their environmental policies and the actions they have taken to implement these policies, or they only provided generic boilerplate discussion of their environmental policies.

Comments

We are of the view that when discussing environmental policies fundamental to their operations, issuers should evaluate and describe the impact or potential impact these policies may have on their operations. This discussion may include a quantification of the costs associated with these environmental policies, where quantitative information is reasonably available and would provide meaningful information to investors. Boilerplate disclosure is insufficient to properly meet these requirements.

E. — Environmental risks

Item 5.2 of Form 51-102F2 requires an issuer to disclose risk factors relating to the issuer and its business. This includes environmental risks and any other matter that would be most likely to influence an investor's decision to buy the issuer's securities. The AIF should provide insight into what the issuer believes are the risks relating to the issuer and its business so that investors can assess the effect of these risks on the issuer's operations and/or financial performance.

Findings

Eighteen of the 22 issuers we reviewed that were required to file an AIF, provided disclosure about environmental risks. Four of the 22 issuers did not address environmental risks as a risk factor, despite being in an industry where environmental risks appear to be relevant.

Disclosure about environmental risks varied among issuers. For example, one issuer provided a detailed discussion of the foreign environmental laws and regulations that apply to it and quantified the costs of compliance with these laws and regulations in both the short- and long-term. The issuer also discussed how significant changes to these laws or regulations could materially impact its expenditures, which in turn could affect its business, financial results and financial condition.

In contrast, other issuers used boilerplate language, simply disclosing that they are subject to environmental laws and regulations, and that they have established general provisions for expenses associated with environmental obligations. There was no quantification of these expenses. For example, one issuer stated that it was subject to the risk of penalties if it did not comply with applicable environmental laws and indicated that there was no assurance that it could comply with these laws.

Comments

An issuer should assess whether, due to the nature of its operations, it should address environmental risks in its CD documents. If so, those risks should be disclosed in the issuer's AIF, if required to be filed. If the issuer is not required to file an AIF, those risks should be disclosed in the issuer's MD&A.

We are of the view that if any risks relating to environmental laws are material to an issuer's operations, whether national or international, the issuer should include a detailed discussion of these laws. This discussion should provide meaningful information to investors. For example, it may include whether or not the issuer is in compliance with these laws and any costs of compliance. Boilerplate disclosure is insufficient to properly meet these requirements.

Conclusion

General

Existing CD obligations require issuers to disclose material information, including material information about environmental matters. Issuers should consider the guidance in this notice when preparing their financial statements, MD&A and AIFs to ensure that the disclosure of environmental matters complies with securities legislation and provides investors with meaningful information for making investment decisions.

Website disclosure

All of the issuers we reviewed disclosed environmental information on their website that was consistent with their CD documents. We remind issuers that disclosure of material environmental matters should be set out in their CD documents filed with the securities regulatory authorities as required by GAAP and applicable securities legislation, and that it is insufficient to discuss environmental matters required by securities legislation solely on their website.

Certification and audit committee responsibilities

Multilateral Instrument 52-109 *Certification of Disclosure in Issuers' Annual and Interim Filings* requires that certifying officers certify, among other things, that an issuer's financial statements, together with the other financial information included in the issuer's MD&A and AIF, if applicable, fairly present, in all material respects, the issuer's financial condition. We are of the view that meaningful discussion of material environmental matters, where applicable, in an issuer's MD&A and AIF is important to achieve fair presentation of the issuer's financial condition in all material respects.

In addition, under Multilateral Instrument 52-110 *Audit Committees*, an audit committee is required to review an issuer's financial statements and MD&A before the issuer publicly discloses this information. The audit committee must also be satisfied that adequate procedures are in place for the review of the issuer's public disclosure of financial information extracted or derived from the issuer's financial statements, and must periodically assess the adequacy of these procedures. We are of the view that the audit committee's oversight of financial reporting related to material environmental matters, where applicable, in CD documents is an important aspect of meeting these responsibilities.

We will continue to monitor disclosure of environmental matters as part of our ongoing CD reviews.

Questions or Comments

We encourage issuers or their representatives to contact us with any questions or comments on these matters.

Policies and Orders: CSAN 51-333.

OSC Notice 51-717 — Corporate Governance and Environmental Disclosure

Date: December 18, 2009

32 O.S.C.B. 10459

Purpose of this notice

The purpose of this notice is to communicate the Ontario Securities Commission's (OSC) plans regarding disclosure of corporate governance and environmental matters by reporting issuers (other than investment funds).

Corporate governance disclosure review

During 2010, we will conduct a review of compliance with the requirements of National Instrument 58-101 *Disclosure of Corporate Govern-ance Practices*. The review will build on the results of our 2007 review, described in CSA Staff Notice 58-303 *Corporate Governance Disclosure Compliance Review*. Our review will involve assessing the adequacy of corporate governance disclosure in information circulars (or annual information forms or annual management's discussion & analysis, if applicable) filed by issuers in spring 2010.

Environmental disclosure guidance

During 2010, we intend to issue a staff notice providing guidance on compliance with existing environmental disclosure requirements under National Instrument 51-102 *Continuous Disclosure Obligations*. In developing the notice, we plan to consult with our advisory committees and other experts in this area. We intend to publish the notice by December 2010 so that reporting issuers will have sufficient time to consider the guidance when preparing their 2010 annual continuous disclosure documents.

Background

These actions are the outcome of our corporate sustainability reporting initiative, which was undertaken in response to a broad resolution introduced by MPP Laurel Broten and unanimously approved by the Ontario Legislature on April 9, 2009. The non-binding resolution called on the OSC to undertake a broad consultation to establish best practice corporate social responsibility and environmental, social and govern-ance reporting standards.

Following the approval of the resolution, the Ministry of Finance and the OSC agreed that the OSC would:

- review existing disclosure requirements under Ontario securities legislation for reporting issuers (other than investment funds) regarding corporate governance and environmental matters

- consult with investors, issuers, advisors and other stakeholders on these matters, and

- make recommendations to the Minister of Finance by January 1, 2010 regarding "next steps" to enhance disclosure of these matters, if determined necessary and appropriate.

In developing the mandate, a number of factors were considered, including the areas of concern expressed by investors and other stakeholders, various international developments and the relatively short timeline to complete this initiative. In light of those factors, the OSC and the Ministry of Finance agreed that the OSC should focus on the disclosure of corporate governance and environmental matters at this time. The Hennick Centre for Business and Law at York University (the Hennick Centre) is currently undertaking a review of disclosure requirements for social matters and will report to the Minister of Finance. As part of that initiative, the Hennick Centre and Jantzi-Sustainalytics hosted a roundtable on corporate social reporting on December 7, 2009, to which they invited representatives from government agencies (including the OSC), non-profit organizations and business.

As part of our initiative, we consulted with stakeholders, our Continuous Disclosure Advisory Committee, our Securities Advisory Committee and the Prospectors & Developers Association of Canada. We also held a roundtable discussion on September 18, 2009, to which we invited representatives of investors, issuers and professional bodies, analysts, legal and accounting advisors and academics. A consultation paper was distributed to the roundtable participants to seek their input on the initiative. An updated version of that paper is attached to our report to the Minister of Finance, which is being published concurrently with this notice.

The OSC's plans regarding disclosure of corporate governance and environmental matters as described in this notice and our report to the Minister of Finance reflect the feedback we received on this initiative during the consultation process.

The OSC will invite staff at other Canadian Securities Administrators to participate in the corporate governance compliance review and the development of the guidance for environmental disclosures.

OSC Staff Notice 51-718 — Key Considerations Relating to an Auditor's Involvement with Interim Financial Reports

Date: May 20, 2011

34 O.S.C.B. 5788

Introduction

Ontario Securities Commission (OSC) staff recently reviewed a sample of issuers to assess their compliance with the provisions relating to an auditor's involvement with interim financial reports as set out in subsection 4.3(3) of National Instrument 51-102 *Continuous Disclosure Obligations* (NI 51-102). While NI 51-102 does not require an issuer to engage its auditor to review its interim financial report, it does however require an issuer to disclose in an accompanying notice if an interim review has not been performed by its auditor. We found a significant level of non-compliance with this disclosure requirement and in these cases, issuers were requested to refile their interim financial statements with the required disclosure.

The purpose of this notice is to summarize the results of our review and to clarify the securities law requirements relating to an auditor's involvement with interim financial reports. As well, we have provided further guidance on the review requirements for an issuer's first interim financial report prepared following its transition to International Financial Reporting Standards (IFRS). Issuers and their advisors should take this notice into account when assessing the extent to which future disclosure meets the requirements of securities legislation and their inves-tors' need for transparent disclosure. Investors need to be properly informed about an auditor's level of involvement with an issuer's interim financial report given that auditor involvement levels will continue to vary amongst issuers.

Investor impact

When an issuer has not engaged its auditor to perform a review, it is critical that the issuer clearly disclose this fact in a notice accompanying its interim financial report. This disclosure is important as it alerts investors and other users of the financial statements that the issuer's auditor did not complete a review of the interim financial report. With this disclosure, users of financial statements are able to determine the amount of reliance they may place on an issuer's interim financial report when deciding to buy or sell investments throughout the year.

Review results

We reviewed a sample of 72 issuers, comprised of 28 non-venture and 44 venture issuers, where it appeared that the interim financial statements had been reviewed by its auditor. We asked these issuers to confirm that their interim financial statements had been reviewed in accordance with securities legislation and Section 7050 *auditor review of interim financial statements* (Section 7050) of the Canadian Institute of Chartered Accountants Handbook (the Handbook).

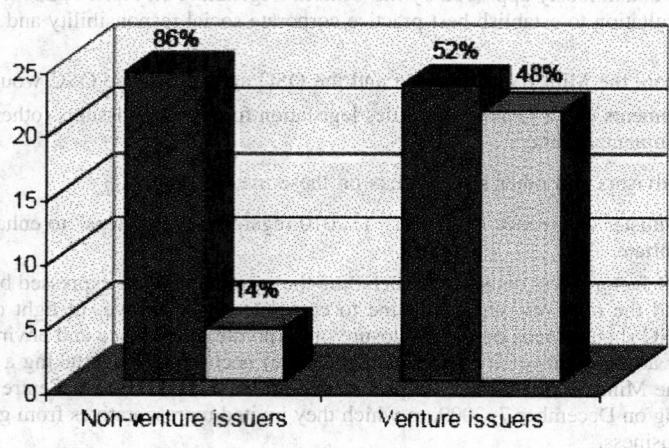

Overall, we found that 35% of the issuers reviewed, consisting of four non-venture and 21 venture issuers, did not comply with the disclosure requirements relating to an auditor's involvement with interim financial statements. Specifically, 48% of venture issuers and 14% of non-venture issuers selected, confirmed that an auditor did not perform a review of its interim financial statements and yet these statements were not accompanied by a notice indicating that fact. Given the importance of this information to investors, we requested that these issuers refile their third quarter interim financial statements with the disclosure that its previously filed interim financial statements were not reviewed by its auditor. The reasons cited for non-compliance by issuers included a general lack of awareness about their disclosure obligations or confusion about what would constitute a review under securities legislation and Section 7050 of the Handbook. To improve the level of compliance going forward, we have highlighted below the relevant securities law requirements relating to an auditor's involvement with interim financial reports.

Continuous disclosure obligations

An issuer is not required to engage its auditor to review its interim financial report for the purposes of fulfilling its continuous disclosure obligations under NI 51-102. As depicted in the chart below however, subsection 4.3(3) of NI 51-102 requires a reporting issuer to disclose if an auditor has not performed a review of the interim financial report, to disclose if an auditor was unable to complete a review and why, and to file a written report from the auditor if the auditor has performed a review and expressed a reservation in the auditor's interim review report,

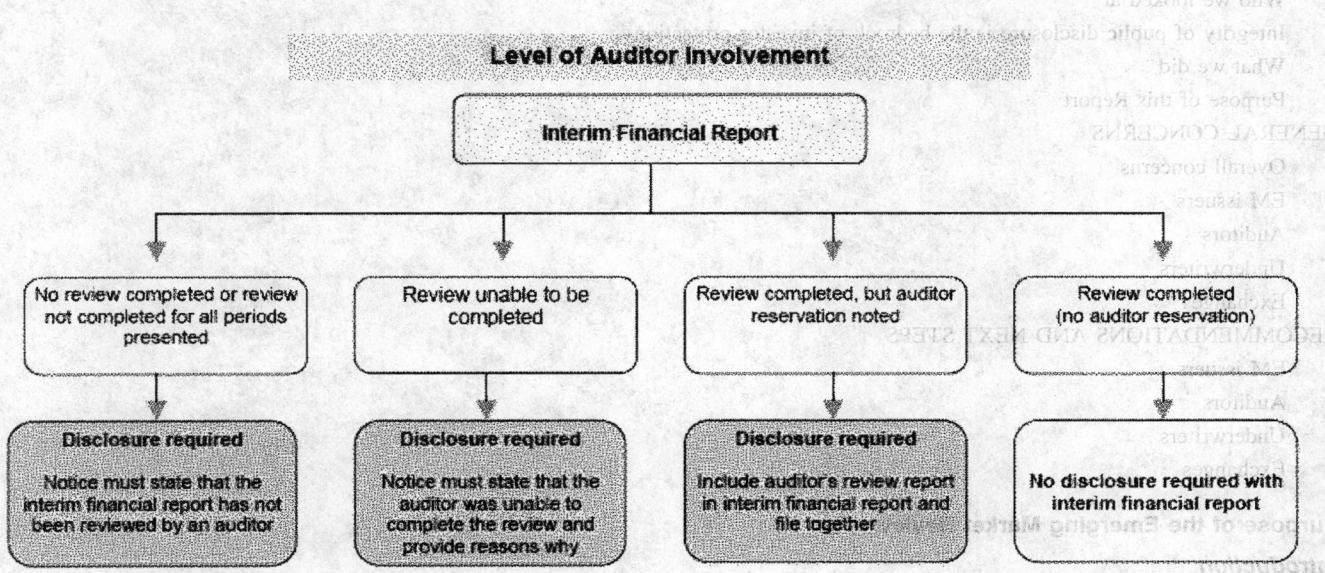

As the white box in the chart shows, the only time that disclosure is not required is when an auditor has performed a review and has not expressed a reservation in the auditor's interim review report. The term "*review*" refers to a review engagement where the auditor reports to the issuer's audit committee on the results of a review of the issuer's interim financial report for all of the periods presented in the report and in accordance with Section 7050 of the Handbook. (If a reporting issuer's financial statements are audited in accordance with auditing standards other than Canadian generally accepted auditing standards, the corresponding review standards should be applied.) Where an auditor has been retained to perform limited review procedures or to review only certain components of an issuer's interim financial report, this would not constitute a "review" and we would require disclosure of a notice indicating that the interim financial report has not been reviewed by the auditor. While NI 51-102 does not prescribe the format of this notice, issuers typically provide this disclosure on a separate page appearing immediately before the interim financial report.

Review of the first IFRS interim financial report

Issuers should note that we did not make any changes to the requirements for the level of auditor involvement with issuers' interim financial reports as part of our IFRS-related rule amendments to NI 51-102. However, if an issuer engages its external auditor to review its first IFRS interim financial report, we remind issuers and their auditors that all financial statements and notes presented are subject to that review. Therefore, for the first IFRS interim financial report this review will have to include, in addition to the current and comparative period results, the opening IFRS statement of financial position and all IFRS 1 *First-time Adoption of International Financial Reporting Standards* reconciliations presented in the notes. To the extent a review of all components of the interim financial report is not completed, the interim financial report will need to be accompanied by a notice indicating that it has not been reviewed by the issuer's auditor. Issuers should consider the extra time that may be needed by its auditor to review the additional information in the first IFRS interim financial report when coordinating the timing of the review.

Future action

We will continue to monitor issuers' compliance with the disclosure requirements relating to the auditor's involvement with interim financial reports as part of our overall continuous disclosure review program. We urge issuers and their audit committee members to consult with their auditor to confirm the scope of the auditor's review engagement, to establish whether the review of the interim financial report will be completed in accordance with Section 7050 of the Handbook and to determine whether a notice is required to be attached to its interim financial report. Auditors may also wish to consider how an issuer is communicating their level of involvement with the interim financial report given that an omission of disclosure implies that the report has been reviewed when a review engagement may not have been performed. We believe that investors need to be able to discern the level of auditor involvement in an issuer's interim financial report when making investment decisions, and as such, staff will continue to request re-filings of this report when an issuer has not met its disclosure obligations in this area.

OSC Staff Notice 51-719 — Emerging Markets Issuer Review

Date: March 30, 2012

35 O.S.C.B. 3004

Table of Contents

PURPOSE OF THE EMERGING MARKET REVIEW

Purpose of the Emerging Market Review

Introduction

On July 5, 2011, the OSC announced the commencement of a regulatory review (EMIR Review or the Review) of emerging market issuers (EM issuers) that would examine a targeted selection of Ontario reporting issuers that were listed on Canadian exchanges and had significant business operations in emerging market jurisdictions.

We conducted the Review in the face of notable concerns that began to surface involving some EM issuers that were listed for trading and raising capital in our markets. We also did this work in recognition of our increasingly globalized marketplace and the corresponding importance of remaining focused on investor protection and the integrity of our markets.

Given the importance of EM issuers in both the global and Canadian marketplace, we wanted to ensure that any systemic or specific issues that affect these issuers were identified and addressed. This is important to investors and for the integrity of the Canadian capital markets.

Several securities regulators in other jurisdictions had also been taking action in similar areas due to some concerns relating to information about title to assets and operations of issuers headquartered in foreign jurisdictions, as well as access to that information. In addition, the body responsible for the oversight of auditors in the U.S., the Public Company Accounting Oversight Board (PCAOB), focused on the fraud risks that auditors might encounter in audits of companies with operations in emerging market jurisdictions and published in October, 2011, a Staff Audit Practice Alert on auditors' responsibilities for addressing those risks, and certain other auditor responsibilities under PCAOB auditing standards. In Canada, the Canadian Public Accountability Board (CPAB) issued a special report in February, 2012, outlining its significant findings and recommendations following its review of audit files for Canadian public companies with their primary operations in China.

The purpose of the Review was to assess the quality and adequacy of selected EM issuers' disclosure and corporate governance practices, as well as the adequacy of the gatekeeper roles played by auditors, underwriters and the exchanges, to identify any broad policy issues and entity-specific concerns. In addition, the Review also examined the legal vehicles through which EM issuers have accessed the Ontario market. In undertaking the Review, staff contacted issuers and their advisors, and organizations such as Canadian exchanges, CPAB and other provincial securities regulators.

We understand the importance of Ontario's markets being attractive globally to quality issuers seeking capital investment. We want Ontario investors to have access to a wide variety of investment opportunities but also want to ensure that this access is balanced with the right level of investor protection. The Review was undertaken to determine if there are areas in the regulation of EM issuers that we can improve or strengthen, including the oversight of the performance of different entities that play a role in bringing these issuers to our market.

A snapshot of EM issuers in Canada

While the term 'emerging market' has different meanings in different contexts, for the purposes of conducting the Review, staff considered a number of criteria in determining whether a reporting issuer was an EM issuer. Staff focused on issuers with the following characteristics:

- whose mind and management are largely outside of Canada and

- whose principal active operations are outside of Canada, in regions such as Asia, Africa, South America and Eastern Europe

TMX Group issuers listed on the TSX and TSXV and CNSX issuers listed on the CNSX as at April 30, 2011, and having headquarters in jurisdictions other than Canada, the US, the UK, Western Europe, Australia and New Zealand, totalled 108.

At April 30, 2011, these 108 issuers had a total market capitalization of approximately $40 billion. This was in contrast to a total of nearly 4,000 exchange-listed reporting issuers in Canada, having a total market capitalization of $2.39 trillion.

EM Issuers — Canada

All data as at April 2011, as supplied by TMX Group and CNSX

	# Issuers	Market Cap. (CAD $ mill)
TSX	50	$37,108
TSXV	55	$3,228
CNSX	3	$33
Total	**108**	**$40,369**

EM issuers were present and operated in a variety of industries, primarily mining, as indicated in the chart below.

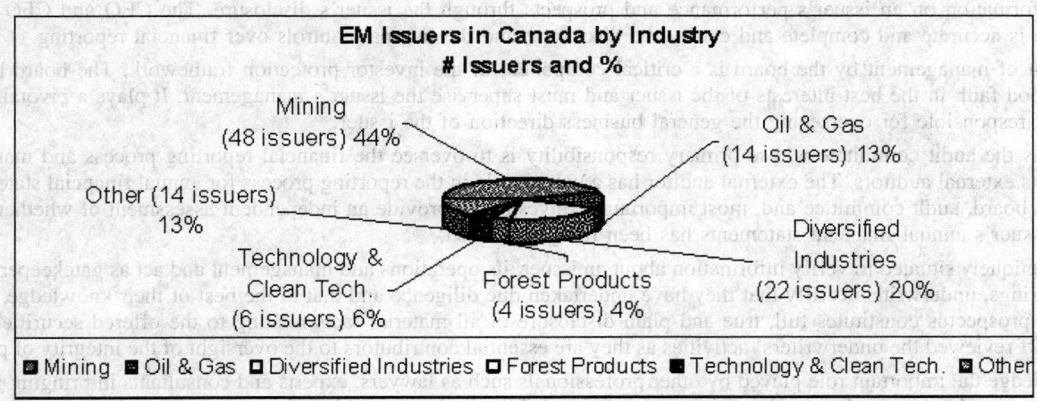

Of the 108 EM issuers in Canada, approximately 43% had the OSC as their principal regulator.

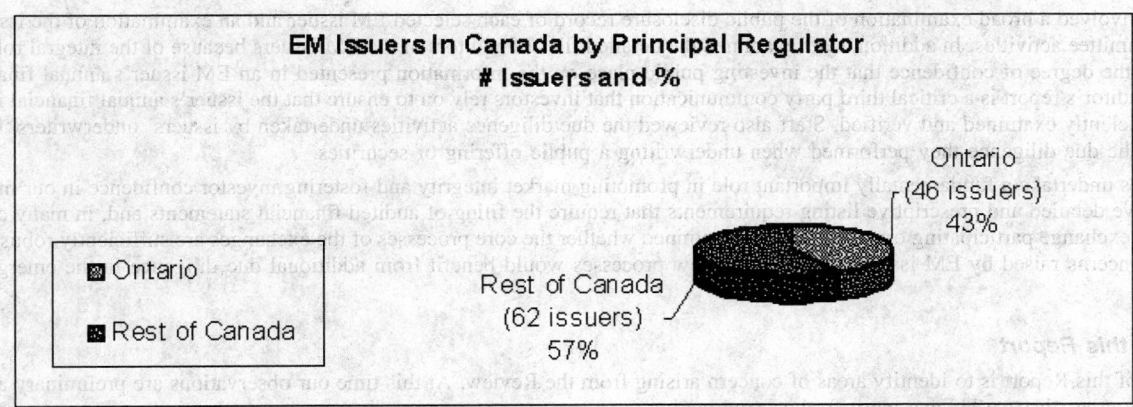

The number of EM issuers in Ontario is relatively small compared to the total number of reporting issuers in Ontario. However, staff wished to assess if investors in EM issuers could be exposed to any inappropriate risks or associated risks that were not fully understood. While we appreciate the importance of EM issuers to our markets, we thought it was important to determine if any issues existed that could impact the reputation and integrity of Ontario's market, either at home or abroad.

Who we looked at

Staff selected and reviewed 24 issuers, which represented more than 50% of the EM issuers for which Ontario is the principal regulator. All had operations in emerging market jurisdictions and were listed on Canadian exchanges. The issuers ranged across a number of industries, including mining, forestry, financial services, technology and clean energy, and diversified industries and operated in a variety of countries.

Integrity of public disclosure is the bedrock of investor protection

The integrity of public disclosure by reporting issuers, including financial reporting, is core to investor information and protection. This disclosure depends critically on each of the following performing their duties responsibly:

- the Chief Executive Officer (CEO)
- the Chief Financial Officer (CFO)
- the board of directors (board)
- the audit committee of the board
- the external auditor
- the underwriter
- the exchange

Integrity of public disclosure starts with management. The CEO and CFO are the key individuals that investors rely on to provide accurate and comprehensive information on an issuer's performance and prospects through the issuer's disclosure. The CEO and CFO must ensure the issuer's disclosure is accurate and complete and certify the disclosure and the internal controls over financial reporting.

Effective oversight of management by the board is a critical component of the investor protection framework. The board has a duty to act honestly and in good faith in the best interests of the issuer and must supervise the issuer's management. It plays a pivotal role in effective governance and is responsible for overseeing the general business direction of the issuer.

The board appoints the audit committee whose primary responsibility is to oversee the financial reporting process and manage the issuer's relationship with its external auditors. The external auditor has a unique role in the reporting process for annual financial statements which are relied upon by the board, audit committee and, most importantly, investors to provide an independent assessment of whether the information presented in the issuer's annual financial statements has been fairly presented.

Underwriters are uniquely situated to verify information about an issuer, its operations and management and act as gatekeepers to our markets. In prospectus offerings, underwriters certify that they have undertaken due diligence and that to the best of their knowledge, information and belief the issuer's prospectus constitutes full, true and plain disclosure of all material facts relating to the offered securities. As part of the EMIR Review, staff reviewed the underwriters' activities as they are essential contributors to the oversight of the integrity of public disclosure.

Staff also acknowledge the important role played by other professionals such as lawyers, experts and consultants in bringing issuers to market and confirming the completeness and accuracy of issuers' ongoing public disclosure. Although they were not the focus of the Review, staff also encourage these professionals to be cognizant of the role they play in the disclosure process, and of the importance of due diligence, professional scrutiny and full disclosure of the risks in their work on emerging market related matters.

What we did

The Review involved a broad examination of the public disclosure record of each selected EM issuer and an examination of the issuer's board and audit committee activities. In addition, staff examined the detailed files of auditors of the EM issuers because of the integral role they play in enhancing the degree of confidence that the investing public place on the information presented in an EM issuer's annual financial statements. The auditor's report is a critical third party communication that investors rely on to ensure that the issuer's annual financial information has been sufficiently examined and verified. Staff also reviewed the due diligence activities undertaken by issuers' underwriters, focusing on the depth of the due diligence they performed when underwriting a public offering of securities.

The exchanges undertake a fundamentally important role in promoting market integrity and fostering investor confidence in our markets. The exchanges have detailed and prescriptive listing requirements that require the filing of audited financial statements and, in many cases, sponsorship by an exchange participating organization. We examined whether the core processes of the exchanges are sufficiently robust to address the unique concerns raised by EM issuers and if the review processes would benefit from additional due diligence in the emerging market context.

Purpose of this Report

The purpose of this Report is to identify areas of concern arising from the Review. At this time our observations are preliminary and identify the key policy areas that we believe merit further examination.

The ultimate goals of the EMIR Review and Report are to identify areas of concern and recommend changes that will contribute to the protection of investors and strengthen the integrity of our markets.

Much of the information staff reviewed is protected by confidentiality provisions in the *Securities Act* (Ontario) and therefore cannot be publicly disclosed. As a result, this Report is general in its discussion, rather than citing specific instances or examples.

Where the Review resulted in significant staff concerns about an issuer's, auditor's or underwriter's apparent regulatory non-compliance, files were referred to the Enforcement Branch of the OSC for further assessment and, if warranted, the initiation of enforcement proceedings.

General Concerns

In this section of the Report, we identify four principal concerns arising from our EMIR Review including:

- the level of EM issuer governance and disclosure
- the adequacy of the audit function for an EM issuer's annual financial statements

- the adequacy of the due diligence process conducted by underwriters in offerings of securities by EM issuers
- the nature of the exchange listing approval process

For each of these four areas of concern, we have identified the main focus for additional examination and analysis. We anticipate that these concerns can be addressed by a combination of action by issuers, auditors, underwriters, exchanges, securities regulators, other oversight bodies and gatekeepers working together to strengthen our markets and protect investors.

Overall concerns

As noted, the regulatory framework for issuers involves a system of reliance and connection between different groups — the issuers themselves, their boards and audit committees, auditors, underwriters and exchanges. We found examples of practices in all of these areas that concerned us and we believe further work is warranted to improve compliance by all of these important groups of market participants with their regulatory obligations.

One of our central concerns was the apparent 'form over substance' approach to compliance with applicable standards for disclosure, issuer governance, board oversight, audit practices and due diligence practices. In our view, the level of rigor and independent-mindedness applied by boards, auditors and underwriters in doing their important jobs — management oversight, audit, due diligence on offerings — should have been more thorough.

The fact that the core operations and assets of many of the issuers were located in an emerging market jurisdiction, with very little presence in Canada in most cases, contributed to a separation between the issuer's Canadian governance and local management functions. It also contributed to challenges for both the audit process and the performance of due diligence by underwriters.

The need for a good understanding of local business practices, how the business operates in the emerging market jurisdiction, and the degree of reliance that can be placed on local members of management, should generally have been given more prominence in management oversight, audits and due diligence functions. Language barriers and translation issues also appeared to be important factors in how well those functions were performed.

EM issuers

Staff conducted in-depth reviews of the public disclosure record of the selected EM issuers and examined information concerning the function of each selected EM issuer's board and audit committee. Our principal concerns are set out below.

EM issuers, their management and boards are expected to discharge all of their responsibilities in a way that promotes the protection of Ontario investors and confidence in our markets. They are expected to do this on a basis that is fully informed by both the business and cultural practices of all of the jurisdictions in which the EM issuer operates.

Corporate governance practices

An issuer's board and audit committee must have a thorough understanding of the business and the operating environment of the issuer as this understanding is the foundation upon which the executives will execute all of their responsibilities. For Canadian reporting issuers whose businesses are based in Canada, the Canadian directors serving on their boards are expected to have a thorough understanding of the Canadian marketplace and its legal, business and political environment.

We recognize that board members of EM issuers may face a steeper learning curve to understand these same aspects of the EM issuer's business and operating environment. The time zone, language, location of key books and records and cultural differences may make communication especially complicated in these situations. Nevertheless, all board members of Canadian reporting issuers, regardless of where they are located and where the business operations are located, are required to adhere to Canadian regulatory requirements.

It appeared to us that the level of engagement by boards and audit committees in their oversight of management and sense of responsibility for the stewardship of an EM issuer with public investors was in certain cases deficient. For example, in some cases it appeared that the board had very little contact with senior management in the emerging market jurisdiction running the business.

We were concerned with the extent of knowledge of boards and audit committees of the cultural and business practices of the jurisdictions in which the issuer operated. In some situations, it appeared that the board was not aware of environmental factors that could have a significant impact on the issuer, such as banking practices, currency restrictions and the regulatory and legal environment specific to the industry in which the issuer operated. To the extent there was knowledge of relevant cultural and business practices, the manner of board oversight was not, in some situations, appropriately adjusted to reflect those practices. For instance, we observed situations in which it appeared that board members relied solely on a member of management to provide an overview of key business documents in a foreign language and did not obtain appropriate translations in order to read and assess the documents themselves.

Corporate structures

An issuer's structure should be designed to facilitate the conduct of its business. Emerging market jurisdictions may present additional challenges to issuers as they must navigate the political, legal and cultural realities of those markets and design an appropriate corporate structure. In some cases, the legal or regulatory system may present impediments to foreign ownership or control and may result in the need for specific structures to enable the issuer to do business in that market.

Complex structures may increase the risk profile of an issuer. These structures may be difficult to adequately describe to investors in disclosure, and they may impact the ability of the board to properly oversee management or understand the full extent of the issuer's operations. In particular, boards should consider the potential for complex structures to facilitate inappropriate activity, such as fraud or misappropriation of assets, or misrepresentations about an issuer's financial performance or condition.

In the Review, we observed structures that caused us to question their appropriateness and transparency, such as the presence of multiple legal entities supporting a single operating business. We were concerned that the complexity of certain corporate structures did not appear to be clear or necessary to support the EM issuer's underlying business model. The quality of controls in place to manage the risks arising from the complexity of the structure was also a concern in these cases.

Related party transactions

Related party transactions (RPTs) warrant careful scrutiny by investors so that they may evaluate the fairness of the transactions and the impact they may have on an issuer's operations and financial results. Although not unique to EM issuers, transactions with other issuers in the same group of issuers, or with parties linked to an issuer's shareholders, directors or management may represent a heightened risk for issuers conducting business in these markets. Some of this may be due to differences between local business practices and cultural norms and the legal requirements in North America. Nevertheless, they need to be understood and disclosed accurately.

While RPTs may provide the issuer with benefits that are not available from other arms-length parties or to other issuers on the same terms, they can also be abusive if they only benefit the related party and not the issuer. We are concerned about transactions of this nature as they can be detrimental to investors in the issuer and can undermine the integrity of our capital markets.

Boards and audit committees are expected to approach their oversight role with an appropriate degree of independent-mindedness. In the case of the RPTs involving some EM issuers we reviewed, we observed that this could have been done better. In these cases, we were particularly concerned with the extent and frequency of RPTs and the quality of the management and board processes in place to identify and approve RPTs. Our disclosure reviews also revealed deficiencies in the completeness and appropriate clarity of related party disclosures.

Risk management and internal controls

The board's responsibility for the stewardship of an issuer includes the identification of principal risks to the issuer's business and oversight of the implementation of appropriate systems to manage those risks. The board oversees management, which is responsible for identifying and quantifying an issuer's exposure to risks and for adopting suitable risk management systems to address those risks.

Boards of EM issuers should be particularly sensitive to the unique risks associated with operations in emerging market jurisdictions, especially those that could result in a serious disruption to business operations. Board members should ensure that they have a sufficient understanding of the political and cultural risks impacting the EM issuer and assess those risks in the context of the emerging market jurisdiction, and not only from a North American viewpoint. Risk analysis and mitigation techniques that may seem appropriate in a Canadian or North American business context may not be effective in emerging market jurisdictions. It is important that boards obtain a clear understanding of how the risks of operating in emerging market jurisdictions could impact the corporate structure, operations and material assets of the issuer.

Internal controls are an important way to manage risk. Boards should review and be satisfied that management has put in place appropriate internal controls to manage the risks facing the issuer. For example, effective internal controls help reduce the risks of inaccurate financial reporting. A breakdown of the integrity of financial reporting often stems from a lack of, or a circumvention of, internal controls. It is therefore important for board members to oversee the design and implementation of internal controls and to assess the appropriateness of the remediation of significant deficiencies and material weaknesses. Board members should also be aware of the risks if there is a material weakness in the issuer's internal controls.

Staff concerns with some EM issuers' internal controls related to the risks of doing business in emerging market jurisdictions, and linked to this, the quality and extent of work performed by the CEO and CFO to support their certification of annual and interim filings. We would have expected to see the internal controls adjusted to reflect the particular risks of having significant business operations located in an emerging market, including those associated with political, legal and cultural factors, as well as the location of books and records and language barriers. However, in certain cases, this was not what we observed.

For EM issuers, internal controls may be particularly important to assist in mitigating such risks. For example, it is particularly challenging for a board whose members principally reside in Canada to govern an issuer whose operations are located in a foreign jurisdiction. This challenge may further be magnified in circumstances where the CEO, being the principal decision-maker, resides in the emerging market, and the CFO resides in Canada.

In the Review, we noted risks that may not have been appropriately identified, understood or managed by the board including risks related to:

- political factors, such as government instability and changing governmental policy that may affect legal rights, such as property ownership

- the legal and regulatory framework, given that emerging market jurisdictions may have less developed legal or regulatory systems

- the movement and conversion of currency out of the foreign jurisdiction, which could hinder the repatriation of profits to Canadian investors

- legal title to assets

We also found that risk disclosures by the issuers were not as specific or relevant as they should have been to be helpful and informative to investors.

Auditors

In the course of the Review, we identified several areas of potential concern with respect to the way in which the external audit function was performed for EM issuers. We were concerned that auditors may not have performed sufficient procedures in some instances to understand and appropriately scrutinize the information provided to them by an issuer and/or foreign 'component' auditor. On February 21, 2012, CPAB issued a special report "Auditing in Foreign Jurisdictions" outlining its significant findings and recommendations following its review of audit files for Canadian public companies with their primary operations in China. The observations noted in CPAB's report are largely consistent with our principal concerns, as set out below.

Level of professional scepticism

The level of professional scepticism exhibited by auditors when examining the information gathered in the course of their audit was generally lacking. We were concerned that in some instances the auditor accepted management's representations at face value and did not perform sufficient alternative procedures to independently verify the information they received. There were also instances where, in our view, auditors should have been uncomfortable based on the work performed and information received — for example if responses received were unusual or unexpected, we would have expected an auditor to further challenge or examine the response to ensure they understood the situation.

In addition, we saw conclusions for areas of judgement that were not supported by an underlying analysis, for example, broad-based conclusions (i.e., a conclusion that no issues were noted) with no underlying analysis regarding the procedures or evidence obtained to support the general statement. This disconnect raised issues on what work, if any, was done to substantiate the auditor's conclusion or ensure that risks were sufficiently mitigated.

Degree of knowledge auditors had of the local cultural and business practices

It was unclear in some instances what was done to understand an issuer's business environment. For example, if checklists were prepared it was questionable that responses resulted in sufficient understanding of the cultural and business practices of the jurisdictions in which the issuer operated. Some auditors appeared to have an insufficient understanding of the legal environment (i.e. use of corporate seals) and/or procedures to obtain licenses and/or permits in the emerging market. In some cases auditors appeared to accept certain information provided by management at face value without performing any procedures to support those representations with independent external information.

Extent of delegation to a foreign 'component' auditor

Applicable auditing standards have no defined parameters for the extent of work that can be delegated to a component auditor, and we were concerned that this resulted in group auditors' insufficient involvement with the audit of underlying operations in some circumstances. This was particularly true in situations where an issuer's underlying operations were entirely in the emerging market and the foreign component auditor performed all audit procedures in the emerging market.

A key concern noted was that some component working paper files could not be removed from a foreign jurisdiction. This could prevent regulators (i.e., the Commission or CPAB) from reviewing files or group auditors from including key working papers from a component auditor in their files. It was also unclear to us the extent of review that group auditors were choosing to, or were able to, perform on audit files of component auditors or whether group auditors were visiting the foreign jurisdiction.

It appeared in some instances that group auditors asked component auditors to do the work to understand the business and environment but did not receive sufficient communication back to understand what the component auditor learned or understood. In fact, we do not believe there was enough communication in general between group and component auditors, particularly communication from the component auditor to the group auditor. We would expect to see more group auditor executives visiting foreign operations or interacting with members of issuers' management.

Inability to access audit working papers

We experienced difficulty in obtaining domestic auditor working papers voluntarily, so other means were generally needed to obtain audit working papers. When an auditor resided in a foreign jurisdiction, or a portion of the audit work was done by a component auditor, we were unable to obtain those working papers.

Language barriers

We observed that language barriers impacted an auditor's ability to communicate with management or examine documentation. We could not discern how audit executives addressed these language concerns in some audits or why this was not an issue for consideration in connection with the audit. For example, in some instances the communication between audit executives and key client executives appeared to be insufficient due to language differences. Perhaps more importantly, there also appeared to be insufficient translation of key documents despite audit engagement executives not being fluent in the local language. It was not clear from the Review how auditors addressed language barriers in client documents for audit executives who did not speak the local language.

Underwriters

Underwriters, as gatekeepers to our securities markets, are uniquely situated to verify information about an issuer, its operations and management. In prospectus offerings, underwriters must certify that to the best of their knowledge, information and belief, the prospectus constitutes full, true and plain disclosure of all material facts relating to the offered securities. In the listing process, the underwriters may act as sponsors. In this role, they conduct due diligence and may prepare reports on, among other things, the issuer's business and financial position, the issuer's directors and officers, and the issuer's qualifications for meeting all relevant listing criteria. The role of the sponsor in the listing process is a critical part of the listing review and approval.

Underwriters should participate in the offering process with a healthy amount of scepticism regarding management claims. Their due diligence must be designed to detect if there are material misstatements or omissions in prospectus disclosure. An underwriter must also develop a full understanding of an issuer's finances, management, operations, industry and country of origin, in order to be able to certify the prospectus. They should also document their findings in a clear and concise manner.

Staff reviewed the work of underwriters in the public offerings of securities by selected EM issuers. Our principal concerns are set out below.

Variations in due diligence practices

While there is some general guidance on due diligence practices for Canadian underwriters, there are no explicit, standard requirements for the conduct of due diligence by underwriters. As a result, it was evident during the Review that underwriters adopted a varied array of policies, procedures and practices. Some underwriters provided internal policies and due diligence checklists, while others had limited processes. Some of the reviews appeared to be thorough and some were not. We also noted that internal committee memoranda, due diligence committee meeting minutes and due diligence checklists were largely not provided to us. We observed in some cases that risks were not always documented, and if they were raised, there was little or no follow-up recorded or evident in the due diligence materials.

We reviewed transcripts of due diligence calls with issuers and observed a number of instances where several customers of a single issuer provided identical answers to questions posed by the underwriters. We think the similarity of these responses should have raised some degree of scepticism and further questioning by the underwriter, yet this did not occur. In addition, in some cases, questions posed during the course of due diligence calls were deflected, not answered or inadequately explained by the issuer's management and the questions were not pursued nor were satisfactory explanations provided. We also noted situations where site visits were attempted unsuccessfully and these were not rescheduled, nor were additional questions asked about the site's availability during the remainder of the due diligence process.

Level of professional scepticism and rigor

In the underwriter material we examined, we observed that the level of professional scepticism and rigor that appeared to be applied in the due diligence process was lacking. We noted several instances where 'red flags' (such as significant growth or a change in the issuer's business in the recent past, financial metrics that were superior to an industry average, unusual year-over-year growth results and a high degree of reliance on government relationships or the founder/CEO) should have prompted further probing or questions. Our review indicated little or no follow-up in these instances to either understand or analyze the concerns, or disclose them.

Approval process for offerings

We observed some cases where, due to a lack of documentation of due diligence meetings, site visits and bring-down calls (calls among the underwriter, issuer, auditors and legal counsel to reconfirm statements previously made during the due diligence investigation), it was not always evident that the approvals process called for by the underwriter's own internal process was followed.

Understanding of emerging market jurisdictions

The due diligence information and process we examined in connection with a number of EM issuer offerings contained little documentation or discussion of the risks associated with the issuer's operations. Even where the due diligence policies and procedures of a firm contemplated additional factors or steps that should be considered or taken in light of additional risks, it was evident from the documentation that these were not taken into account in performing the due diligence.

Due diligence documentation

In the Review, we noted that the amount and degree of due diligence documentation varied widely. In some circumstances, the documentation did not reflect the process by which due diligence was undertaken and completed nor the risks identified in connection with the offering (including those related to the issuer's industry group or market, if appropriate).

In terms of due diligence calls, while we found the lists of questions to be asked of the issuer were documented, in some cases the names of the participants on the calls were not provided and written transcripts were not provided.

Exchanges

The exchanges are important gatekeepers to our securities markets as they set standards for issuers seeking to list their securities on Canadian markets. The exchanges undertake a vigorous review process, including review and reliance on third party reports to determine if the issuer meets the listing requirements, which is a critical part of the access to public capital. As part of this process, when sponsorship is required, the sponsors conduct due diligence and prepare reports on the issuer's business and financial position, the issuer's directors and officers, and the issuer's qualifications for meeting all relevant listing criteria.

We examined the listing processes in place and the listing review that was undertaken for the EM issuers selected for this study. We considered whether the core processes of the exchanges are sufficiently robust to address the unique concerns raised by EM issuers that have come to light as a result of the EMIR Review and other recent events. We also considered whether the exchange review processes would benefit from additional due diligence in the emerging market context, particularly with respect to reliance on work performed by third parties and the quality of third parties' work.

We also examined the methods by which EM issuers selected for review accessed the Ontario market and raised capital from Ontario investors. An issuer can become a reporting issuer through different methods, including:

- an initial public offering (IPO), which involves the preparation of a prospectus to be filed with securities regulators and is often accompanied by an application for a public listing on an exchange
- a direct listing on a recognized Canadian exchange, which may be facilitated if the issuer is already listed on another exchange in a foreign jurisdiction
- a reverse take-over (RTO) (also known as a back door listing or reverse merger), which usually involves a transaction with an existing issuer that is already a reporting issuer. The form of transaction varies but typically involves an amalgamation or issuance of shares in exchange for other shares or assets.

The EM issuers in our review sample accessed our market through different methods, including IPOs, direct listings and RTOs. We did not identify any particular method of accessing the market and becoming a reporting issuer as being specifically problematic.

In conducting this work, we worked co-operatively with staff at the TSX and considered:

- how the issuers 'went public'

- the various parties involved in the listing of an EM issuer

- the inter-reliance of those parties and their interconnectivity with the exchange listing framework applicable to EM issuers

- the listing requirements and review processes of Canadian exchanges that generally apply to the types of reporting issuers selected for review

Our principal concerns are set out below.

Specific listing requirements for EM issuers

The exchanges have supplemental procedures and policies geared to EM issuers. However, a re-examination of the sufficiency of those procedures and policies may be warranted in light of our increased understanding of risks associated with emerging markets. There also does not appear to be a requirement for an EM issuer whose primary listing is in Canada to maintain a meaningful 'Canadian presence' (which could include having a combination of directors, key officers, employees, books and records and assets (such as cash) located in Canada).

Transparency when exchanges waive any listing requirements

In accordance with the exchanges' listing requirements, the exchanges have broad discretion in how they apply the listing requirements. The exchanges may, in their discretion, take into account any factors they consider relevant in assessing the merits of a listing application, resulting in the granting or denial of a listing application notwithstanding the published criteria. There does not generally appear to be any public disclosure that is made about waivers of listing requirements granted to specific issuers.

Strong reliance on third parties in conducting due diligence

The listing process involves the exchanges' review of various documents prepared for the issuer by outside experts, such as auditors, geologists or sponsors. In particular, the exchanges place significant reliance on the role of sponsors to conduct due diligence of prospective listings. Sponsors are expected to undertake a comprehensive review of the issuer being sponsored, including, potentially, site visits, reviewing all relevant documentation and evaluating past conduct of directors and officers, among other things. Notwithstanding the prescribed exchange requirements for a sponsorship report, the actual terms of a sponsorship report are generally negotiated between the sponsor and the issuer seeking a listing, and the sponsor is paid a fee for providing this service. In addition, there does not generally appear to be publicly available information regarding a particular sponsor's role in a new listing or the sponsor's due diligence report.

Recommendations and Next Steps

All issuers, including emerging market issuers, their management and boards are expected to discharge all of their responsibilities in a way that promotes the protection of Ontario investors and confidence in our markets. They are expected to do so on a basis that is fully informed by the business and cultural practices of all of the jurisdictions in which the EM issuer operates. Auditors, underwriters and all other advisors to issuers are also expected to discharge their responsibilities in a similar manner with a full appreciation of the reliance that Ontario investors place on them.

This Report raises particular issues associated with EM issuers coming to market. Emerging market issuers are an important growth market for Canadian investors and this Report identifies areas for improvement related to governance and the critical work of auditors, underwriters and other experts. We will continue to follow up with individual issuers and their advisors as appropriate, and will continue to refer matters to our Enforcement Branch as warranted. We will also continue to work with CPAB to address audit related concerns, with staff at the Canadian exchanges to address concerns related to the listing process and with the Investment Industry Regulatory Organization of Canada (IIROC) on the underwriter practices we observed in the Review.

The concerns we have identified in this Report are, to varying degrees, unfolding on a global basis. With that in mind, we will continue to engage in dialogue with other securities regulators within and outside of Canada to share perspectives and best practices to address areas of common concern.

Staff expect that EM issuers, their auditors, underwriters and their other advisors, as well as the exchanges, will address the concerns identified in this Report and will, where necessary, take immediate steps to improve their practices to effectively discharge their responsibilities to protect investors in Ontario.

What follows is a list of recommendations for further work needed to address the principal concerns in this Report. In most cases, these recommendations do not involve the creation of new policies or rules but instead involve the development of guidance, best practices or enhanced vigilance to support compliance with current requirements.

EM issuers

- establish guidance to improve corporate governance practices, particularly in the areas related to the responsibilities of the board and its committees to understand the business, operating environment and risks for issuers whose principal operations are in foreign jurisdictions

- clarify the regulatory expectations of CEOs and CFOs in conducting reasonable due diligence to support their certifications for companies whose principal operations are in foreign jurisdictions

- require better disclosure to investors of complex corporate structures and their purpose

- require better explanations of risk factors relevant to EM issuers

- raise investor awareness of risks associated with investments in issuers whose principal operations are in foreign jurisdictions

- ensure the maintenance of appropriate books and records in Canada

- consider a minimum language competency component for Canadian-resident board members in the applicable local language where the issuer's principal business operations are located

- consider minimum Canadian director residency requirements

Auditors

- facilitate access by the OSC to the audit working papers of Ontario reporting issuers

- determine what should be done to address situations where regulators are unable to access foreign audit files relating to reporting issuers

- work with CPAB to analyse whether securities rules can be enhanced to allow more information sharing in connection with the oversight of audit firms

- examine whether suitability standards for auditors of reporting issuers should be developed

- analyse whether auditors should be required to publicly disclose their resignation from a file, and to explain the reasons for that resignation

- develop greater cooperation among securities regulators and audit oversight bodies to monitor the quality of audits of public companies with operations in emerging markets

- continue to discuss the audit-related concerns in this Report with CPAB and audit firms

- bring these concerns to the attention of both the Canadian Audit and Assurance Standards Board and the International Auditing and Assurance Standards Board

Underwriters

- establish a consistent and transparent set of requirements for the conduct of due diligence by underwriters

- ensure these requirements include a process that addresses:

  - the issuer's operational structure

  - internal controls and risk management

  - translation and foreign language issues

  - business practices and business environment in which the issuer operates

  - government relationships

  - asset ownership

  - CEO/founder shareholdings and RPTs

  - cultural norms that affect the issuer's structure, operations, governance and the ability to do business

  - review of key documents

  - review of key members of management

  - review of customers, suppliers and others parties relevant to the issuer's business

  - reporting on results of site visits

- develop best practices around documentation of all aspects of an underwriter's due diligence

- develop best practices for due diligence calls and site visits

Exchanges

- assess whether additional listing requirements are needed for EM issuers to address specific risks associated with them, or if additional exchange review procedures are required to assess if significant risks are present and how those risks could be addressed

- provide greater transparency regarding waivers of any listing requirements

- assess whether the extent of reliance on third parties in conducting due diligence is appropriate in the listings process or whether additional due diligence steps are warranted

- review the role of sponsors (if applicable) in bringing EM issuers to market to ensure that there is adequate accountability placed on the sponsor and if there is an appropriate level of transparency regarding the sponsor's due diligence work

OSC staff will continue to work on the issues identified in this Report with other provincial securities regulators, CPAB, IIROC, the exchanges and other interested parties so that we can advance the work we have begun through the EMIR Review. We think it is also important to recognize that some of the policy issues we may pursue from the EMIR Review could have broader applications and a more general benefit to our markets.

We are focused on our markets remaining open and attractive to issuers from all jurisdictions. Fostering markets that are fair and efficient and that protect investors interests will continue to attract both domestic and foreign issuers.

OSC Staff Notice 51-720 — Issuer Guide for Companies Operating in Emerging Markets

Date: November 9, 2012

35 O.S.C.B. 10230

Table of Contents

Background

Purpose of this Guide

Eight Areas to Consider for Companies Operating in Emerging Markets

    1. Business and Operating Environment

    2. Language and Cultural Differences

    3. Corporate Structure

    4. Related Parties

    5. Risk Management and Disclosure

    6. Internal Controls

    7. Use of and Reliance on Experts

    8. Oversight of the External Auditor

Conclusion

BACKGROUND

Emerging Market Issuer Review

In response to public questions and concerns involving Canadian public companies with significant business operations in emerging markets[1] (referred to in this guidance as "emerging market issuers"), the OSC announced on July 5, 2011 the commencement of a regulatory review (EMIR Review or the Review) of selected emerging market issuers. We engaged in this review in recognition of our increasingly globalized marketplace and the need to protect Ontario investors and the integrity of our markets. The purpose of the Review was to assess the quality and adequacy of the issuers' compliance with disclosure and other regulatory requirements, as well as the adequacy of the gatekeeper roles played by their auditors and underwriters and the exchanges on which the issuers had listed. Our findings and recommendations were published in OSC Staff Notice 51-719 *Emerging Markets Issuer Review* dated March 20, 2012 (the EMIR Report).

As indicated in the EMIR Report, we selected 24 issuers to be subject to the EMIR Review, which represented more than 50% of the 46 emerging market issuers for which Ontario is the principal regulator. The issuers selected included all non-resource emerging market issuers (14) and approximately one-third of the resource issuers operating in emerging markets (10). Staff conducted in-depth reviews of the public disclosure record of the selected emerging market issuers and examined information concerning the function of each selected emerging market issuer's board and audit committee.

Our review identified the following main areas of concerns related to emerging market issuers:

- Corporate Governance Practices

    It appeared to us that the level of engagement by boards and audit committees in their oversight of management and sense of responsibility for the stewardship of an emerging market issuer with public investors was in certain cases deficient. We were also concerned with the extent of knowledge of boards and audit committees of the cultural and business practices of the jurisdictions in which the issuer operated.

- Corporate Structures

    We were concerned that the complexity of certain corporate structures did not appear to be either clear or necessary to support the emerging market issuer's underlying business model and that the quality of controls in place to manage the risks arising from the complexity of the structure was a concern.

---

[1]As indicated in OSC Staff Notice 51-719 *Emerging Markets Issuer Review*, while the term "emerging market" has different meanings in different contexts, staff focused on issuers with the following characteristics when conducting the review of selected emerging market issuers:

- issuers whose mind and management are largely outside of Canada; and

- issuers whose principal active operations are outside of Canada, in regions such as Asia, Africa, South America and Eastern Europe.

Part 5: ONGOING REQUIREMENTS

- **Related Party Transactions**

  We were particularly concerned with the extent and frequency of related party transactions and the quality of the management and board processes in place to identify and approve these transactions. Our disclosure reviews also revealed deficiencies in the completeness and appropriate clarity of these related party disclosures.

- **Risk Management and Internal Controls**

  Many risks were not appropriately identified, understood or managed by the board. We also found that risk disclosures by the issuers were not specific or relevant as they should have been to be informative to investors.

Our review identified material disclosure deficiencies in 15 of the 24 emerging market issuers reviewed. After this review, the disclosure deficiencies identified were corrected through restatements and refilings or prospective enhancements. Several issuers were referred to Enforcement for further investigation of additional issues.

Outcomes of the EMIR Review

The OSC has identified several changes required to address the concerns outlined in the review. These include:

OSC

We have adapted our continuous disclosure review issuer selection process to incorporate the key risk factors identified in the EMIR Review. The prospectus review process has also been enhanced to address both the risks and concerns that arise in emerging market issuers. We continue to look to improving the OSC oversight regime.

Issuers

We do recognize that board members of emerging market issuers may face a steeper learning curve to understand the emerging market issuer's business and operating environment. The time zone, language, location of key books and records and cultural differences may make communication especially complicated in these situations. Nevertheless, all board members of Canadian reporting issuers, regardless of where they are located and where the business operations are located, are required to adhere to Canadian regulatory requirements.

We believe specific guidance that highlights areas of risk that require particular focus and clearly articulates OSC staff's expectations regarding regulatory compliance will assist directors and management of emerging market issuers in meeting the level of standards that are expected in Ontario capital markets. This Guide has been prepared to provide such guidance, and is one of the steps the OSC is taking to address the principal concerns identified in the EMIR Report.

Other regulatory partners

Underwriters:

The OSC will work with the Investment Industry Regulatory Organization of Canada as it reviews underwriting due diligence standards with a view of promoting industry best practices and standards in this area.

Auditors:

The OSC is working closely with the Canadian Public Accountability Board (CPAB) on issues of common interest, including the opportunity to share information permitted by legislation. We have held discussions with the audit community, CPAB and international securities regulators to address concerns about the use, access and reliance on foreign component auditors' work products. The OSC will examine the need for changes in order to respond to other audit related concerns identified.

Exchanges:

Toronto Stock Exchange and TSX Venture Exchange are currently finalizing additional guidance to address risks associated with listing emerging market issuers. This includes clarification of the expectations of issuers and the advisory community. The Exchanges expect to publish the new requirements for comment in November.

PURPOSE OF THIS GUIDE

We believe directors and management of all market issuers will benefit from specific guidance that help them meet the regulatory and investor expectations in Ontario's capital markets. We are publishing this Guide to provide assistance to emerging market issuers and their directors and management on their governance and disclosure practices in light of the unique challenges they face.

Specifically, this Guide:

1. highlights to emerging market issuers and their directors and management potential areas of risk or red flags that may warrant further scrutiny;

2. sets out questions that directors and management of emerging market issuers should consider when deciding how to address risks of doing business in emerging markets; and

3. outlines our expectations regarding compliance with existing disclosure requirements.

This Guide is intended to help clarify the existing continuous disclosure requirements under securities legislation for emerging market issuers other than investment funds who are reporting issuers in Ontario. It should not be considered legal advice and is not intended to create new legal obligations or modify existing ones.

While this Guide is primarily directed at emerging market issuers and their directors and management, other issuers will find the discussion useful. We also anticipate that investors in emerging market issuers will find this Guide useful to help them understand and assess the operational, strategic and compliance performance of the companies in which they have either invested or are planning to invest.

EIGHTS AREAS TO CONSIDER FOR COMPANIES OPERATING IN EMERGING MARKETS

We have identified eight areas for consideration. In each of the areas we have highlighted matters to consider and disclosure tips to assist companies and their boards in assessing risks and complying with securities laws.

The eight areas are as follows:

1. Business and operating environment
2. Language and cultural differences
3. Corporate structure
4. Related parties
5. Risk management and disclosure
6. Internal controls
7. Use of and reliance on experts
8. Oversight of the external auditor

This is not an exhaustive list, and these issues may be considered along with the other matters the board and management determine to be appropriate.

1. — Business and Operating Environment

A company's board and management must have a thorough understanding of the political, cultural, legal and business environments of the company, as these are the foundation from which the executives will make decisions and carry out their responsibilities. Canadian directors on the boards of Canadian public companies are generally expected to have a thorough understanding of the Canadian marketplace and its legal and political framework from their experience doing business in this market. On the other hand, Canadian directors of an emerging market issuer may, with respect to the company's foreign operations, have limited knowledge and experience regarding its operating environment. They must therefore be cognizant of the need to exercise additional diligence to close any knowledge gap that might exist.

Regardless of the location of a company's operations, Canadian reporting issuers, their management and board are reminded that they are required to adhere to Canadian regulatory requirements. It is the responsibility of the company to ensure that its directors and management have the appropriate orientation and training on Canadian capital markets' requirements. Foreign directors and management of an emerging market issuer who are unfamiliar with Canadian regulatory requirements should also address any knowledge gap, including seeking assistance from Canadian directors and advisors, who may be in the best position to provide guidance.

Canadian reporting issuers, their management and board are reminded that they are required to adhere to Canadian regulatory requirements regardless of the location of the company's operations.

Matters to Consider

Boards of companies operating in emerging markets should enhance their knowledge of the business and operating environment of an emerging market by addressing the following questions:

- What role does the foreign government and regulatory authorities have in the foreign operations?

- Have restrictions or conditions been imposed, or can they be imposed, by the foreign government and regulatory authorities on the company's ability to operate in the foreign jurisdiction?

- Who in the company manages the relationship with the foreign government and regulatory authorities?

- What is the legal environment of the foreign jurisdiction? How does the legal system operate and how may it impact the company?

- What regulatory requirements is the company or its business or operations subject to in the foreign jurisdiction?

- Does the board have access to relevant expertise to ascertain the political, legal and cultural realities of the jurisdiction where the company's principal business operations are located, and the impact they may have on the company's business or operations?

- What are the banking customs in the foreign jurisdiction? How do they differ from Canadian customs?

- Are there any restrictions on the company's ability to transfer and/or verify the existence of funds in bank accounts located in foreign countries?

- What are the impacts of local laws and customs on ownership and rights to property?

- Who are the major suppliers and customers? How did the company establish relationship with them? Are these entities, or their executive officers or directors, related to the company or its officers?

- How frequently do Canadian board members and management visit operations in the foreign jurisdiction?

- Where are the company's books and records located and are there any access restrictions?

- Will an investor's ability to exercise and enforce statutory rights and remedies under Canadian securities law be impacted by the fact that all or substantially all of the issuer's assets are primarily located in a foreign jurisdiction?

Section 19 of the Ontario Securities Act requires reporting issuers to keep appropriate books and records. Boards are also reminded that they should have effective access as needed to these books and records, and should consider what mechanisms are in place to ensure this happens.

Disclosure Requirements

Securities legislation requires a company to describe its business and operations.

For example, a company's annual information form (AIF) must include, among other things, disclosure about the company's principal markets, competitive conditions, economic dependence on significant contracts, and dependence on foreign operations[2]. A company's management's discussion and analysis (MD&A) is also required to discuss events or uncertainties that are reasonably likely to have an effect on the company's business, and industry and economic factors affecting the company's business[3]. For companies operating in emerging markets, the disclosure should highlight the challenges and risks of operating in these markets. Meaningful disclosure for investors can only be provided when management and the board thoroughly understand the intricacies of the company's business.

Disclosure Tips

A company's disclosure should:

- sufficiently highlight those operating conditions that are applicable to the company as a result of operating in an emerging market

- capture issues, risks and characteristics unique to operating in the emerging market

- provide both a factual description and an analysis of these issues, risks and characteristics, and how they affect operations

- use understandable language and either refrain from including, or provide explanations for, industry jargon

The disclosure should allow an investor to understand the business model of the company and its unique characteristics.

2. — Language and Cultural Differences

Given that the environment in which emerging market issuers operate may be significantly different from that in Canadian markets, it is important that the board of an emerging market issuer includes members that have appropriate experience in the emerging market in addition to members with only Canadian or North American business expertise. This will assist the board in identifying the specific risks associated with the company or with the foreign jurisdiction in which the company operates, so that the board's governance and oversight responsibilities can be properly discharged.

One such challenge relates to language and/or culture of the emerging market being different from that of North America. Boards should devise appropriate policies such as the use of an independent translator to overcome these language and cultural barriers. They should also be mindful of placing full reliance on local management, or local board members who are not independent of the company, and should develop mechanisms to obtain independent input from other sources. In addition, companies should consider the inclusion on the board of independent board members with an understanding of carrying on business operations in the emerging market. Boards should also arrange for site visits to the foreign business operations to mitigate the geographic distance between the board and the local operations.

Matters to Consider

The board should consider the following questions when evaluating the language and cultural differences that may impact the issuer:

- Does the composition of the board provide the appropriate level of knowledge and expertise in the language and cultural practices of the emerging market?

- Is any board member fluent in the foreign language or does the board have access to an independent translator to overcome any language differences?

- How frequently should the board members visit the operations in the emerging market and meet with local management?

- Has the board engaged with local management to understand the manner in which business is conducted in the foreign jurisdiction?

- Have the books and records, including key documents such as material contracts or bank documents, been prepared in English or French or appropriately translated?

- Does the board have access to resources, beyond local management or local directors who are not independent, that can help overcome language and cultural issues?

3. — Corporate Structure

Emerging market issuers may face challenges associated with designing an appropriate structure that takes into consideration the political, legal and cultural realities of emerging markets. In some cases, the legal or regulatory system may present impediments to foreign ownership or control and may result in the need for complex structures to enable the company to do business in that market.

---

[2]Item 5 of Form 51-102 F2 *Annual Information Form.*

[3]Item 1 of Form 51-102 F1 *Management's Discussion and Analysis.*

While there may be important reasons for their establishment, complex structures may be difficult to understand and may present additional challenges for the board to effectively direct the decision making of the company. Boards should consider the risks that may flow from complex structures, such as obscuring the misappropriation of assets or other fraudulent activities, or conveying a false impression of financial performance or condition through distorted financial statements.

Boards should assess whether a simpler corporate structure could facilitate the conduct of the company's business and again with its operating environment.

Although complex corporate structures may take various forms, two types of structures are commonly used by companies operating in emerging markets: (i) those that have multiple layers of entities and numerous subsidiaries which are incorporated in various jurisdictions; and (ii) those that encompass "special purpose entities"[4].

(i) — Structures with multiple layers and numerous subsidiaries

Any structure that separates the board from its operating subsidiaries may present challenges for the board in effectively directing the decision making of the company. For example, key operating decisions may be made at lower levels of the corporate hierarchy without being communicated to the board for its consideration. The existence of numerous subsidiaries incorporated in various foreign jurisdictions may also make it more difficult for a board to fully understand the risks associated with each of the entities and the particular risks associated with their jurisdiction of incorporation.

(ii) — Control through a special purpose entity (SPE)

Some emerging market issuers may use one or more SPEs to provide an investor with a controlling interest in an entity that is not based on a majority of voting rights. Although the relationship may be similar to one established by majority voting rights, control will be established through a series of structural and contractual arrangements with the entity. For example, through an SPE structure, the foreign operating entities of an emerging market issuer may transfer their economic returns through multiple entities (which often include an offshore entity), and ultimately to the Canadian holding company. The foreign operating entities' operations would be included in the Canadian holding company's financial statements on a consolidated basis in the same way as the operations of a Canadian company with a majority voting right. This structure is often used to gain access to sectors of emerging market economies where foreign investment is restricted or prohibited. Where an SPE is used for this purpose, there is a risk that a company could nonetheless be deemed by the government of the relevant foreign jurisdiction not to be in compliance with the foreign investment restrictions of that jurisdiction, and the foreign government may consequently force the structure to be unwound. In addition, there are legal risks that need to be assessed related to enforceability of the contracts used to establish the SPE. The use of an SPE may therefore make it difficult to assess whether a Canadian reporting entity has effective continuing control and ownership over the foreign operating entities and their assets.

Matters to Consider

In assessing the risks of an emerging market issuer's corporate structure, its board should ask the following questions:

- Has the need for a complex structure been carefully assessed by management, including whether the company's objectives could be achieved through a simpler structure?

- Is the company's corporate structure consistent with its business model and the political, legal and cultural realities of the jurisdiction where its principal business operations are located?

- Where the company uses a structure that involves one or more SPEs, does it have effective control and ownership over the foreign operating entities and is the SPE structure compliant with relevant foreign investment restrictions?

- Does the board have the means to monitor legal and regulatory developments in the foreign jurisdiction relative to SPE structures?

- Does the corporate structure limit or inhibit the ability of the board to oversee and monitor management of the foreign operations?

- How does the board ensure that information from the local jurisdiction is communicated to the board in a timely manner?

- Can the Canadian parent company effectively change the board and management of the foreign operating entities?

- Have the risks associated with the company's corporate structure been identified and evaluated? Does management have appropriate controls in place to address those risks?

Disclosure Requirements

We expect a company's disclosure to contain a clear and understandable description of its corporate structure, together with an explanation of how that structure facilitates the company's business and aligns with the parameters of its operating environment. The disclosure should also describe the risks associated with the structure and how those risks are managed. Where a company files an AIF, we expect that companies with complex structures will address in their disclosure the matters described above in the course of discussing their inter-corporate relationships. (See additional guidance related to risk disclosure in section 5 of this Guide.)

---

[4]Emerging market issuers have customarily used the phrase *variable interest entities* to refer to the unique structure described herein. This phrase was used under Canadian generally accepted accounting principles — Part V, but not under International Financial Reporting Standards, which, instead, specify the accounting treatment for *special purpose entities*, a concept similar to, but broader than, *variable interest entities*. Readers should note that the discussions herein with respect to *special purpose entities* are on the implications and risks resulting from the use of such structures in general, and may include those structures usually termed *variable interest entities*.

The following example[5] illustrates disclosure that would be considered boilerplate with a comparison to enhanced disclosure that provides more useful information for investors. Issuers should consider including a diagram depicting the corporate structure with the narrative disclosure to facilitate readers' understanding.

Example of boilerplate disclosure:

Company A is incorporated in Country 1. Company A holds a 99% interest in Company B which is incorporated in Country 2. Company B, in turn, holds a 100% interest in each of Company C which is incorporated in Country 3 and Company D which is incorporated in Country 4.

Example of entity-specific disclosure:

Company A is incorporated in Country 1. Company A holds a 99% interest in Company B which is incorporated in Country 2. Company B, in turn, holds a 100% interest in each of Company C which is incorporated in Country 3 and Company D which is incorporated in Country 4.

Country 1 has experienced political and economic stability for many years and its legal system is based on the British common law system. Its banking system and standards for professional services are comparable to those in North America, at lower operating costs. In addition, Country 1 has a tax treaty with each of Countries 2, 3 and 4 that exempts payments from those countries from local tax.

Company B was the holding company of each of Company C and Company D at the time of the acquisition of those companies by Company A. The Company's manufacturing operations are conducted by Companies C and D which are incorporated in Countries 3 and Country 4, respectively. This structure is necessary for the Company's operations in these countries, as it allows the Company to comply with the laws of each of these countries and is conducive to maintaining positive relationships with local entities and government officials upon whom the Company's operations are substantively reliant. Operating through Companies C and D which are located in the same jurisdictions as its manufacturing operations also enables the Company to maintain more effective controls over those operations and financial reporting.

There are however risks associated with operating in Countries 3 and 4. These include. . . .

Disclosure Tips

A company's disclosure should:

- provide a description of the company's corporate structure, including a diagram of the structure where helpful

- explain how that structure facilitates (or hinders) the conduct of the company's business

- explain how that structure is necessary or desirable given the company's operating environment

- describe the risks associated with the corporate structure and how the board monitors and addresses those risks

4. — Related Parties

Transactions with other companies in the same group (i.e., the company's parent company and fellow subsidiaries) or with parties linked to its shareholders, directors or management, or other related party transactions (RPTs)[6] may represent a heightened risk for emerging market issuers. This is due to differences in local business practices, cultural norms, and legal requirements compared to North American standards. Investors must be able to understand how RPTs impact a company's operations and financial results.

RPTs may provide the company with benefits or better terms than those that are available from arms' length parties. Conversely, it is also possible that RPTs may benefit the related party while providing little or no benefit for the company. Non-related investors may also be harmed by an inappropriate transfer of corporate assets to related parties. Such transfers may occur on a one-off basis or could involve a series of continuous transfers via smaller operational expenditures that are cumulatively material. Transactions of this nature are often detrimental to the company and undermine the credibility of our capital markets.

In some cases, companies may be owned or controlled by a small group of individuals or a family. In family controlled companies, senior management and the board are often dominated by family members. The interests of a company's controlling shareholders may not fully align with those of its minority shareholders. In these circumstances, there is a heightened risk, which the board should manage, that the company may be operated in a manner that disproportionately advances the interests of its controlling shareholders at the expense of its minority shareholders.

Effective identification and monitoring of RPTs by management and the board is necessary to prevent potential abuse and protect investors. This requires appropriate policies, procedures and scrutiny for the identification, evaluation and approval of RPTs. In addition, boards should ensure that the company complies with requirements under generally accepted accounting principles and Form 51-102 F1 *Management's Discussion and Analysis* for the disclosure of RPTs (see further discussion below).

The board should ensure that policies and procedures are in place to identify and independently evaluate and approve related party transactions.

Issuers are further reminded that certain RPTs are subject to Multilateral Instrument 61-101 *Protection of Minority Security Holders in Special Transactions* (MI 61-101), which requires, among other things, a formal valuation and minority shareholder approval of the transaction.

---

[5]Examples in this Guide are provided for illustrative purposes only, and may have been simplified for ease of illustration.

[6]Please refer to paragraph 9 of IAS 24 *Related Party Disclosures* or section 1.1 of MI 61-101 for more precise definitions of a related party.

Companies are also required in these circumstances to disclose the review and approval process adopted by the board of directors and the special committee, if any, as well as the material factors on which the directors relied in assessing the fairness of the transaction.[7]

Matters to Consider

In assessing the risks of RPTs, the board should consider the following questions:

- Has management implemented effective policies and procedures to identify related parties and any transactions with such parties, evaluate the merits of such transactions, and require that the transactions be reported to the board and be subject to prior board approval?

- Are directors and senior management required to obtain board approval or the approval of independent or disinterested directors before entering into transactions in which they have an interest?

- Are RPTs evaluated by disinterested directors (i.e., as opposed to evaluation by directors who may be definitionally "independent" for purposes of securities regulation but would not be considered disinterested by a reasonable person)?

- Is the transaction subject to the minority shareholder approval and formal valuation requirements under MI 61-101?

- Are transactions that fall outside the normal course of business scrutinized to determine whether related parties have a direct or indirect interest in those transactions?

- Could the same or similar benefits derived by a company through an RPT be obtained at a lower cost or with less risk on an arm's length basis (including, for example, public tender)?

- What would the impact be on the company in the event the related party no longer supplied certain goods or its services?

- What is the track record of the related party in supplying the goods or services?

- Does the related party have the requisite skills, experience and/or financial capability to supply the good or service?

- Are balances due from related parties collectible?

- Are there tax risks that arise from RPTs?

- Can the business effectively continue to operate without the approval or participation of the related party or significant shareholder?

Disclosure Requirements

Comprehensive disclosure is essential for investors to understand and evaluate RPTs. Minimum disclosure requirements for RPTs are prescribed in both accounting standards and securities regulation. For example, International Financial Reporting Standards require that a company's financial statements contain the disclosures necessary to draw attention to the possibility that its financial position and profit or loss may have been affected by the existence of related parties and by transactions and outstanding balances, including commitments, with such parties[8].

Comprehensive disclosure of related party transactions is essential for investors to understand and evaluate those transactions.

The disclosure in a company's MD&A should contribute to an investor's understanding of an RPT's business purpose and economic substance, and not merely repeat the disclosure included in its financial statements[9]. It should be comprehensive in nature, encompassing both quantitative and qualitative information necessary to achieve that understanding. In fulfilling this objective, a company is required to disclose at least the following information:

- the relationship and identity of the related person or entities
- the business purpose of the transaction
- the recorded amount of the transaction and the measurement basis used
- any ongoing contractual or other commitments resulting from the transaction

We expect issuers to consider the materiality of RPTs. In making this determination we encourage all issuers to review and apply the discussion relating to the "Interest of Management and Others in Material Transactions" in Item 13 of Form 51-102 F2 *Annual Information Form*. The instructions for this item direct that the materiality of an interest is to be determined on the basis of the significance of the information to investors in light of all the circumstances of the particular case. The importance of an interest to the person that holds that interest, the relationship of the parties to the transaction with each other, and the amount involved are among the factors to be considered in determining the significance of the information to security holders. In other words, qualitative, in addition to quantitative, factors have to be considered.

Example of boilerplate disclosure:

---

[7]Issuers are also reminded to consider requirements under stock exchange rules, which require valuation and/or shareholder approval for certain related party transactions.

[8]Paragraph 1 IAS 24 *Related Party Disclosure*.

[9]Item 1.9 of Form 51-102F1 *Management's Discussion & Analysis*.

On September 24, 2011, the Company entered into an exploration contract in the amount of $5,800,000 with XYZ Exploration Ltd., a company controlled by the brother of an officer and director of the company. The contract was to conduct exploration on the ABC property. On December 12, 2011, the Company made a deposit of $3,900,000 under the contract.

Example of entity-specific disclosure:

On September 24, 2011, the Company entered into an exploration contract in the amount of $5,800,000 with XYZ Exploration Ltd., a company controlled by the brother of John X who is an officer, director and controlling shareholder of the company. The contract was to conduct sufficient exploration and drilling on the ABC property in order to determine an initial resource estimate. On December 12, 2011, the Company made a deposit of $3,900,000 under the contract.

The contract was put out for public tender and three bids were submitted. XYZ Exploration Ltd. was selected to undertake the exploration program as its bid was the lowest of the three bids that were received, and it was well qualified to undertake the exploration work, having conducted significant exploration in the area of the ABC property over the last several years.

In [name of country], it is customary for an exploration contractor to provide both a fixed price bid and a flexible price bid. Under a fixed price bid, a contractor undertakes to conduct a given project at the fixed price. Under a flexible price bid, a contractor undertakes to conduct a given project at an estimated price, which may ultimately be more or less than the actual cost of a given project. The actual cost of the project is the one that is ultimately charged to a company. The Company's board, which is required to pre-approve all related party transactions proposed to be entered into by the Company, determined that it was beneficial to accept a fixed price bid in order to avoid any unexpected costs. John X recused himself from the board's discussion of the contract as well as from the vote.to approve the transaction.

Disclosure Tips

A company's disclosure should:

- not merely repeat the disclosure included in its financial statements

- specifically identify the related parties and their relationship with the company

- include both quantitative and qualitative information that is necessary for an investor to understand the business purpose and economic substance of RPTs

- discuss the nature, role, impact, benefits and risks of RPTs in conducting business in the jurisdiction where the applicable business or operations are located

- discuss how the company's structure impacts on its use of RPTs in conducting its business

- describe the company's processes and procedures for identifying, evaluating and approving RPTs

5. — Risk Management and Disclosure

National Policy 58-201 *Corporate Governance Guidelines* states that the board should adopt a written mandate in which it explicitly acknowledges responsibility for, among other things, the identification of principal risks of the company's business and oversight of the implementation of appropriate systems to manage these risks[10]. The board oversees management, which is responsible for identifying and quantifying a company's exposure to risks and for adopting suitable risk management systems to address such risks.

Boards of companies whose principal operations are located in an emerging market should be particularly sensitive to the risks associated with operations in those markets, especially those that may result in serious disruption to, or significant adverse impact on, business operations. Board members should ensure that they have a sufficient understanding of the legal, regulatory, political and cultural risks impacting the company and evaluate these risks in the context of the particular emerging market, rather than through a North American lens. Risk analysis and mitigation techniques that may be appropriate in the Canadian or North American business context may be less effective in emerging markets. It is important that boards obtain an understanding of how the risks of operating in emerging markets impact the corporate structure, operations and material assets of the company.

Boards should obtain a clear understanding of any risks associated with operations in a particular emerging market and how they impact operations. Boards should consider that risk analysis and mitigation techniques that may be less effective in emerging markets.

Examples of some specific risks of operating in emerging markets may include risks related to:

- political factors, including political instability and arbitrary or sudden changes to laws

- the legal and regulatory framework in the foreign jurisdiction which may increase the likelihood that laws will not be enforced and judgments will not be upheld

- the movement and conversion of currency out of the foreign jurisdiction, which could hinder the payment of dividends or other distributions to Canadian investors

- corruption, bribery (including possible prosecution under the federal *Corruption of Foreign Public Officials Act*[11]), civil unrest and economic uncertainty, which may negatively impact and disrupt business operations

---

[10]Part 3.4(c) of National Policy 58-201 *Corporate Governance Guidelines*.

[11]Boards should be aware of the *Corruption of Foreign Public Officials Act* (Canada). Under this legislation, the federal government has jurisdiction over the bribery of foreign public officials and may prosecute an individual or a corporation for this offence and may also seize the property and proceeds obtained or

- factors that may affect the company's title to its assets
- potential expropriation or nationalization of assets
- access to assets

Matters to Consider

In assessing the quality of the risk management processes, the board should consider the following questions:

- Does the board have a full understanding of the risks facing the company and how those relate to the overall risk appetite of the company?

- Is there a strategy in place to ensure that significant risks related to operations in the emerging market are identified and managed by the board and management?

- Does the board regularly engage with management to review and update the risk identification and management strategy?

- Does the board ask probing questions and seek confirmations that decisions made by management are consistent with board-approved strategies and the company's overall risk appetite?

- Does the board obtain confirmation from management that risk exposures are in compliance with established limits?

- Do board members take appropriate steps to stay informed of key developments that could increase the company's risk exposure in the emerging market?

- Has the board established contacts in the foreign jurisdiction that may assist the board in staying abreast of developments that could impact the company's risk exposure and does the board regularly engage with these contacts?

- Does the board have a clear understanding of the internal controls and processes in place to respond to risk?

- Does the board review how disruptions to business operations caused by political, legal and cultural factors in the emerging market were dealt with by management?

Disclosure Requirements

A company's disclosures about the risks it faces are an important element of investor protection. Boards should ensure that investors are provided with sufficient information about the risks associated with operating in a particular emerging market.

Companies required to file an AIF under securities law must disclose the risks that would most likely influence an investor's decision to purchase securities of the company[12]. All companies are required to disclose in their MD&A those risks that have affected their financial statements and those that are reasonably likely to affect them in the future[13]. Further, all issuers must disclose risk factors in their prospectus filings[14].

Boards should ensure that disclosures relating to risks of operating in emerging markets are entity-specific.

Example of boilerplate disclosure:

The company is exposed to significant political risk resulting from operations in developing countries. These risks may have a significant impact on the ability of the Company to carry on business operations.

Example of entity-specific disclosure:

Risk Factors

The company is exposed to significant political risk resulting from operations in developing countries. In particular, operations in Country ABC may be severely impacted by the changing political landscape experienced in recent years as a result of the economic crisis which began two years ago. Significant changes to laws may be imposed by the Country ABC government and responses to similar changes in the past have resulted in civil unrest in Country ABC. The government of Country ABC has implemented restrictions on imports and exports of goods and services and has imposed restrictions on the conversion of Country ABC's currency.

Each of these factors may have a significant impact on the ability of the Company to carry on business operations in Country ABC. Currently, all of our widgets are only sold within Country ABC and any import of supplies in our production of widgets must be approved by Country ABC Import Agency. The Company currently has all required import permits and is in good standing with Country ABC Import Agency. Further, the Company has not experienced any labour stoppages as a result of the economic crisis and civil unrest that has recently occurred in Country ABC.

---

derived from bribing a foreign official. The OSC has the authority to share certain information on potential criminal matters, including possible violations under the *Corruption of Foreign Public Officials Act*, with the police.

[12]Item 5.2 of Form 51-102F2 *Annual Information Form*.

[13]Part 1 of Form 51-102F1 *Management's Discussion & Analysis*.

[14]Item 1.10 of Form 41-101F1 *Information Required in a Prospectus* and Item 17 of Form 44-101F1 *Short Form Prospectus*.

Risk Management Strategies

To manage the political risks of operating in Country ABC, processes are in place to actively monitor and analyze the political landscape in Country ABC. On a monthly basis, executives meet to discuss and analyze the political developments in Country ABC. The Company's strategic, operational and investment plans are adjusted accordingly where required. The Board of Directors has an oversight role in ensuring the Company's strategy takes into account shifts in political factors.

Disclosure Tips

A company's disclosure should:

- identify the company's specific risks of operating in an emerging market

- where the issuer or its operating entities are domiciled in a foreign jurisdiction, explain the risks and other implications on investors' ability to exercise statutory rights and remedies under Canadian securities law

- provide sufficient details for investors to understand the nature of the risks and what the risks mean to the company (i.e. how such risks could be detrimental to the company's business operations in the foreign market)

- indicate the board's responsibility for oversight and management of risks and any board and management-level committee to which responsibility for oversight and management of risks has been delegated

- describe the process used by the board to oversee the risk management process

- where appropriate describe the company's risk management strategy and the systems that management has in place to manage and mitigate the risks of operating in emerging markets

- be updated in each filing to reflect any new identified risks and the company's current risk management strategy

6. — Internal Controls

Effective internal controls (including internal control over financial reporting and disclosure controls and procedures) help reduce the risks of inaccurate financial reporting. A breakdown of the integrity of financial reporting may stem from a lack of or a circumvention of internal controls. It is therefore important for board members to consider the guidance in National Policy 58-201 *Corporate Governance Guidelines* in which it is recommended that boards adopt a written mandate explicitly acknowledging responsibility for the stewardship of the company, including responsibility for the company's internal control and management information systems[15].

The unique risks of operating in an emerging market magnifies the importance of strong internal controls. For example, it is particularly challenging for a board whose members principally reside in Canada to appropriately oversee a company whose operations are located in a foreign jurisdiction. The time zone, language, and cultural differences can make communication especially complicated and may hinder the accuracy and timeliness of financial reporting that properly reflects the business decisions made in the local jurisdiction. Appropriate internal controls can provide checks and balances on the local operations to reduce the risks of inaccurate financial reporting and ensure that appropriate information is reported on a timely basis.

The audit committee of the board, in particular, should actively oversee the monitoring of any identified weaknesses in internal controls, as well as the risks they create for the company. The audit committee, and the board more generally, should also oversee the timely remediation of weaknesses and, in the interim, the mitigation of the related risks. In our view, this responsibility is inherent in the audit committee's obligation under NI 52-110 *Audit Committees* (NI 52-110) to review the company's financial statements, MD&A and annual profit or loss press releases before they are publicly disclosed[16]. When the effectiveness of internal controls is in doubt or ongoing material weaknesses are present, audit committee members should exercise a higher degree of scepticism in their review of the company's filings.

Matters to Consider

At board and audit committee meetings, discussions with management should be interactive and probing. Moreover, remediation plans should be put in place to address internal control deficiencies. Board members should hold management accountable if the remediation of internal control deficiencies and weakness has not progressed according to plan.

Questions regarding internal controls that the audit committee should ask management include:

- What has management done to determine if the company has the proper internal controls in place to address each of the identified risks, in particular the risks associated with operating in an emerging market?

- What are the deficiencies and weaknesses in internal controls that have been identified? How material are these deficiencies or weaknesses?

- What potential risks flow from the identified deficiencies and weaknesses?

- What are the ways that such deficiencies and weaknesses can be remediated?

- Does management have a plan and timeframe for the remediation? Does the plan include immediate/ interim steps to manage the risks that have been identified? Is the timeframe proposed by management reasonable?

---

[15]Section 3.4(f) of National Policy 58-201 *Corporate Governance Guidelines*.

[16]Section 2.3(5) of NI 52-110 *Audit Committees*.

- What is the status of on-going remediation plans?

- Are there any interim measures that should be adopted before the remediation is complete?

- What are the auditor's views on the company's internal controls?

Companies that continue to have material weaknesses in internal controls in successive years may have heightened risks that need to be actively managed and controlled.

Disclosure Requirements

Certifying officers of a non-venture issuer are required to certify that they have established and evaluated, on an annual basis, the effectiveness of the issuer's internal controls. If material weaknesses in internal controls are identified, this fact must be disclosed in the issuer's MD&A pursuant to NI 52-109 *Certification of Disclosure in Issuer's Annual and Interim Filings*[17]. It is also advisable for venture issuers to disclose known material weaknesses in internal controls in their MD&As, if the material weaknesses give rise to a risk factor for the company.

The disclosure should be entity specific, and contain the information expected by regulators as discussed in the guidance in Companion Policy 52-109CP[18]. Transparency is particularly important to investors when a company has identified material weaknesses in its internal controls over financial reporting (ICFR), and sufficient information should be provided to investors to allow them to assess the nature and implications of those weaknesses.

Example of boilerplate disclosure: (Note)

Based on an evaluation of the Company's internal controls over financial reporting, the Company concluded that material weaknesses exist in the internal controls over the Company's process for recognizing sales and receivables. The material weaknesses were due to inadequate accounting systems and the lack of segregation of duties in this process. The Company will endeavour to remediate these material weaknesses in the near future.

Example of entity-specific disclosure: (Note)

Based on an evaluation of the Company's internal controls over financial reporting (ICFR), the Company concluded that there are material weaknesses relating to both the design and operating effectiveness of ICFR over the Company's process for recognizing sales and receivables.

Material weaknesses of ICFR over sales and receivables include the following:

- The use of manual spreadsheets to record sales transactions, and the lack of end-user computing controls to prevent unauthorized access to the spreadsheets.

- The lack of controls over management override with respect to the recording of sales transactions.

- The lack of segregation of duties in the authorization, recording and reconciliation of sales transactions.

- The lack of appropriate documentation for certain sales transactions that took place in the current fiscal year.

Due to these material weaknesses, there are risks related to whether the recorded sales transactions occurred and whether the recorded accounts receivable existed, and whether they were recorded at the appropriate amounts. Therefore, management concluded that the ICFR over the Company's process for recognizing sales and receivables is ineffective.

To mitigate these risks, management directed financial personnel other than those involved in the sales and receivables process to verify 100% of the Company's sales transactions in the year, and obtained appropriate independent verification for those sales transactions that lacked documentation. In addition, the audit committee of the Company independently reviewed the validity of individual sales transactions on a sample basis, and conducted interviews with the financial personnel involved to ascertain the process relied upon for recording and verification of sales transactions.

The Company is currently seeking to replace the manual spreadsheets with appropriate accounting applications, and to build in the proper controls to prevent or overcome management overrides and the lack of segregation of duties. A third-party provider has been engaged to assist in this process, and the Company expects to remediate these material weaknesses before the end of the second quarter in fiscal 2013.

Note: For simplicity, these examples have focused only on internal control over financial reporting, and have not included disclosure related to disclosure controls and procedures.

Disclosure Tips

The disclosure should be specific and should include sufficient details to allow a reader to understand:

- Each of the internal processes or functions that contain a material weakness

- The nature of each of the material weaknesses

- The implications of each of those material weaknesses on financial reporting, as well as on the company's internal controls over financial reporting

- Details of any mitigating factors that help to reduce the risks stemming from the material weaknesses

---

[17]Section 3.2 of NI 52-109 *Certification of Disclosure in Issuers' Annual and Interim Filings.*

[18]Sections 9.6 and 9.7 of 52-109 CP, in particular.

Part 5: ONGOING REQUIREMENTS

- Details of any remediation plan that management is carrying out to remediate the material weaknesses

- The timeline and status of the remediation plan

7. — Use of and Reliance on Experts

Companies need to bear in mind the risks associated with the use of and reliance on experts in emerging markets. Emerging market issuers should evaluate experts' credentials and specialized knowledge to asses whether they are similar to what would be expected in a Canadian context. When an expert is retained to assist in matters that are material to the company and could expose it to significant liability or result in a disruption of its business operations, boards should evaluate the level of diligence exercised by the expert in carrying out the task.

Boards should keep in mind that industry professionals in emerging markets may not be subject to the same rules of professional conduct as they would be in Canada.

Companies operating in emerging markets may hire industry professionals or experts with specialized knowledge to assist with complex matters arising in the foreign jurisdiction. Some examples of when companies may consider retaining experts in emerging market operations include:

- Tax professionals may be retained to assist with the intricacies of taxation laws for entities operating in emerging markets. Taxation laws developed in emerging markets may have specific rules for companies that are considered to be foreign-owned by the applicable local tax regulatory authority.

- Legal professionals may be retained for their expertise on various matters including the interpretation and application of laws in the emerging markets.

- Valuation professionals may be retained to provide certified valuation opinions on proposed acquisitions/sales within the foreign jurisdiction.

Industry professionals in the emerging market may not be subject to equivalent rules of professional conduct and standards of care as they would be in the Canadian market. Boards will therefore need to assess the quality of the advice provided and their ability to rely on the advice.

Matters to Consider

When using and relying on experts, the board should consider the following:

- Has the company considered the significance of the expert's work on the company's operations and the potential impact on the company of an error or inaccuracy in the expert's work?

- What are the expert's credentials? Have background checks on the expert been conducted, including whether the expert is in good standing with its relevant industry organization in the foreign jurisdiction?

- Does the board have systems in place to identify whether the expert is independent of the company, its management, directors, officers, significant shareholders, and other related parties?

- Has the company considered differences between local customs and practices in the emerging market compared to Canada, and the adequacy of the rules of professional conduct developed by the professional organization of the expert in the emerging market?

- Has the company evaluated the level of due diligence exercised by the expert? Was the expert's opinion fully substantiated by accurate facts and thorough analysis?

- Is a corroborating opinion (provided by Canadian experts, for example) necessary or desirable?

Disclosure Requirements

In certain circumstances, companies required to file an AIF under securities law must disclose the names of experts who have prepared or certified a report, valuation, statement of opinion referred to in a continuous disclosure filing and (subject to specified exceptions) must also disclose all of an expert's interests in the company[19]. As part of their oversight role, boards should ensure that disclosure of experts' interests is adequate and provides sufficient detail for investors.

Example of boilerplate disclosure:

The company has relied on the work of XYZ Valuations Inc. To the Company's knowledge, the employees and partners of XYZ Valuations Inc. beneficially own, directly or indirectly, less than 1% of the company's securities.

Example of entity-specific disclosure:

The company has relied on the work of XYZ Valuations Inc. to provide an independent valuation of the market value of Property A in Country ABC as referred to in our December 31, 2011 financial statements and related Management's Discussion and Analysis filed under NI 51-102.

XYZ Valuations Inc.'s independent valuation was prepared by Country ABC Valuation Standards governed by the Valuation Institute of Country ABC. XYZ Valuation Inc. is in good standing with the Valuation Institute of Country ABC.

---

[19]Item 16 of Form 51-102F2 *Annual Information Form*.

As of the current date and to the company's knowledge, the registered or beneficial interests, direct or indirect, in any of the company's securities or other property of the company held by, received by, and to be received by the "designated professionals" (as defined in NI 51-102) including the partners, employees or consultants of XYZ Valuations Inc., represent less than 1% of any class of shares issued by the company or of any of the company's associates or affiliates.

Disclosure Tips

A company's disclosure should:

- identify all experts, both in Canada and in the company's foreign operations, who have been named in or referred to in a continuous disclosure filing;

- identify the report prepared by or certified by the expert and make reference to the continuous disclosure document that contains the report;

- quantify all registered or beneficial interests held by, received by, or to be received by the expert in any securities or other property of the company.

8. — Oversight of the External Auditor

The external auditor is an important gatekeeper that investors rely on to ensure that a company's financial statements are fairly presented. As stated in NI 52-110, a company's audit committee is directly responsible for overseeing the work of the external auditor, including the resolution of any disagreements between management and the external auditor regarding financial reporting[20]. In order for the audit committee to discharge its responsibilities, it must determine if the company's external auditors have the appropriate expertise and experience to carry out the audit, and that the audit committee effectively oversees the external auditor's work.

Matters to Consider

The audit committee of an emerging market issuer should take into consideration factors relating to the auditor's competence, experience and qualifications in the foreign market when it recommends that the board of directors retain a particular external auditor. Similar considerations should apply where a company's domestic auditor delegates a portion of the audit to a foreign "component" auditor[21]. Additional questions for the audit committee to consider when selecting an auditor of an emerging market issuer include:

- Does the auditor have a presence or affiliation in the jurisdiction in which the company's overseas operations are located?

- Do any members of the audit team have the language, skills relevant to, and cultural knowledge of, the local jurisdiction?

- Does the auditor have sufficient experience in the accounting and tax rules of the foreign jurisdiction?

- Does the auditor understand the risks and challenges facing the emerging market issuer, and does it have sufficient appropriate audit procedures to address them?

- What are the responsibilities of the domestic auditor versus the component auditor?

- How does the domestic audit team oversee the component audit team?

- How can the audit committee ensure that it has sufficient access, directly or indirectly, to the component audit team to discharge its external auditor oversight responsibility?

Overseeing the external auditor's work

In order for an emerging market issuer's audit committee to discharge its responsibility in reviewing financial statements as required under NI 52-110, the audit committee should enquire about and evaluate the external auditor's approach in auditing the areas that present risks specific to the company, and understand how the auditor fulfilled its responsibility to obtain sufficient appropriate audit evidence in these areas of risk. This would include an understanding of how component auditors are used and the extent of audit evidence provided by the component auditor used by the domestic auditor to support its opinion.

In staff's view, it would be beneficial for the audit committee to maintain frequent informal communications with the audit engagement team and to obtain information regarding the audit on a real-time basis, in addition to formally meeting with the auditor at the audit planning and completion stages. The committee should pay particular attention to any signs of delays in the audit schedule or unusual management intervention in the audit process. We also believe it would be beneficial for the audit committee to hold "in-camera" sessions (meetings without the presence of management) with the auditor. The auditor can be a significant source of information, and a frequent and open dialogue with the auditor helps the audit committee to tap into that information.

The audit committee should maintain continuous communication with the auditor throughout the year and foster an environment for open and frank exchange of information.

---

[20]Section 2.3(3) of NI 52-110 *Audit Committees*.

[21]i.e., an auditor who performs work on financial information related to a component of the group audit. A component auditor may or may not belong to the same firm as the domestic auditor.

Disclosure Tips

When there is a change of auditor, a company needs to disclose (among other things) any "reportable event", i.e., a disagreement, a consultation, or an unresolved issue, with the former auditor, to comply with securities rules[22]. When an auditor resigns, we expect directors to further consider whether the reasons for the auditor's resignation should also be disclosed even if they do not represent a reportable event, so that investors have full access to pertinent information and risks about the company.

Conclusion

All reporting issuers, including emerging market issuers, their management and boards, are expected to discharge their responsibilities in a way that promotes the protection of Ontario investors and confidence in our markets. Boards, in particular, are expected to adopt appropriate corporate governance practices to facilitate the proper oversight of management. Faced with the unique challenges of operating in an emerging market, boards of emerging market issuers have to take extra measures to ensure investors' interests are protected.

This Guide is one of the steps that OSC staff are taking to help directors and management of emerging market issuers to more effectively discharge their responsibilities. We expect emerging market issuers to carefully consider the guidance provided in this Guide in evaluating and improving their corporate governance practices.

OSC Staff Notice 51-721 — Forward-Looking Information Disclosure

Date:　　**June 13, 2013**

36 O.S.C.B. 5907

Table of Contents

1. — Executive Summary

Forward-looking information ("FLI") is a key area of interest for investors. Investors want transparent and clear disclosure about present and future corporate operations and performance. When prepared properly, FLI can be used to enhance transparency and provide opportunities to increase an investor's understanding of a reporting issuer's business and future prospects. Staff of the Ontario Securities Commission ("we") recognize that FLI is a challenging area. Reporting issuers need to address investors' demands by providing reliable and relevant information. Disclosure must be both useful and understandable. Disclosure should include the most relevant information in a format that investors can understand.

FLI requirements have been in place for several years with the most recent changes coming into effect on December 31, 2007. We note that most reporting issuers include some FLI in either a continuous disclosure ("CD") document, a news release or on their website. We conducted FLI reviews (the "Review") of Ontario reporting issuers from several industries and the issues identified were consistent across all industries. Despite the fact that more than five years have passed since the most recent changes to the requirements, we note that for many reporting issuers there continues to be a need for improvement relating to the quality of the required FLI disclosure.

Our Review identified four common areas where improvement is needed:

- clear identification of FLI

- disclosure of the material factors or assumptions used to develop FLI

- updating previously disclosed FLI

- comparison of actual results to the future oriented financial information (FOFI) or financial outlook previously disclosed

The purpose of the Review was to assess the overall quality of FLI disclosure. This notice provides guidance and examples to assist reporting issuers in preparing FLI.

2. — Introduction

FLI is a key area of interest for investors. Investors want transparent and clear disclosure about present and future corporate operations and performance. When prepared properly, FLI can be used to enhance transparency and provide opportunities to increase the investor's understanding of a reporting issuer's business and future prospects. Reporting issuers need to address investors' demands by providing reliable and relevant information in a format that investors can understand.

---

[22]Section 4.11 of NI 51-102 *Continuous Disclosure Obligation*.

FLI should provide valuable insight about a reporting issuer's business and how that reporting issuer intends to attain its corporate objectives and targets. Clear, specific and relevant information allows investors to better understand the performance of a reporting issuer, enabling investors to make effective and efficient decisions in the capital markets.

Many reporting issuers find incorporating key performance indicators ("KPIs") into FLI disclosure provides investors with valuable and meaningful information about their company. Ongoing disclosure of KPIs demonstrates how a reporting issuer is progressing toward its objectives and targets. KPIs should be relevant and meaningful. Examples of KPIs include:

- customer retention
- capital expenditures
- same store sales
- exploration success rate

The purpose of this publication is to assist reporting issuers and management in understanding FLI securities requirements so that they provide more effective and relevant disclosure to investors. This notice:

- clarifies the disclosure requirements related to FLI, including FOFI and financial outlook
- provides disclosure examples
- highlights common areas of non-compliance

We reviewed the disclosure and presentation of FLI for 60 issuers, including FOFI and financial outlook, with a focus on the following main areas:

- clear identification of FLI
- disclosure of material factors and assumptions
- updating previously disclosed FLI (including expected differences)
- comparison of actual results to previously disclosed FOFI or financial outlook

What is Forward-Looking Information?

FLI is disclosure about possible events, conditions or financial performance that is based on assumptions about future economic conditions and courses of action. FLI includes two subcategories dealing with financial information: (a) FOFI and (b) financial outlook. Both FOFI and financial outlook are FLI about prospective financial performance, financial position or cash flows, based on assumptions about future economic conditions and courses of action. The difference between FOFI and financial outlook is the format in which the financial information is presented. In the case of FOFI, the information is presented in the format of a historical financial statement. Examples are provided in the chart below.

Part 5: ONGOING REQUIREMENTS

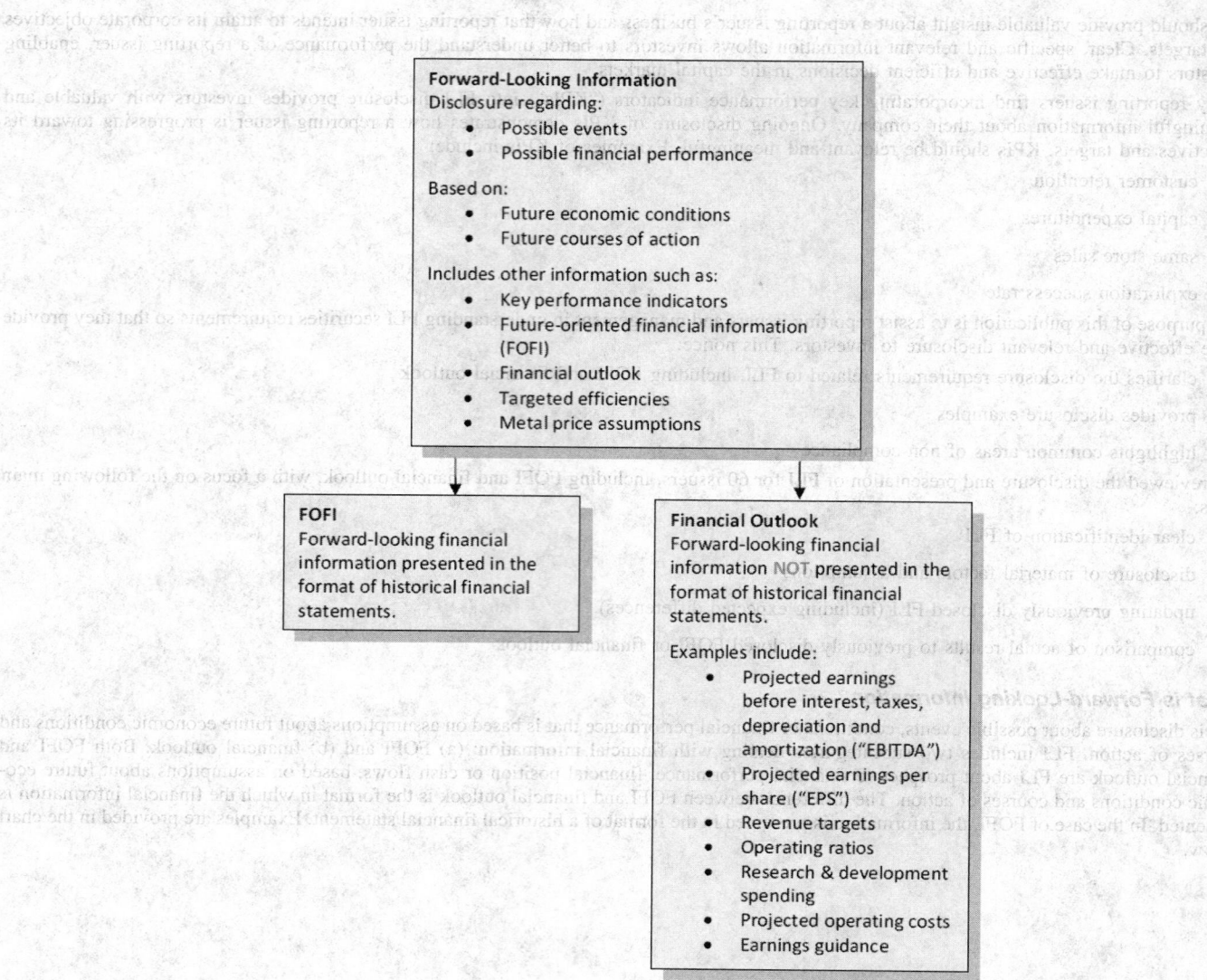

Forward-Looking Information
Disclosure regarding:
- Possible events
- Possible financial performance

Based on:
- Future economic conditions
- Future courses of action

Includes other information such as:
- Key performance indicators
- Future-oriented financial information (FOFI)
- Financial outlook
- Targeted efficiencies
- Metal price assumptions

FOFI
Forward-looking financial information presented in the format of historical financial statements.

Financial Outlook
Forward-looking financial information NOT presented in the format of historical financial statements.

Examples include:
- Projected earnings before interest, taxes, depreciation and amortization ("EBITDA")
- Projected earnings per share ("EPS")
- Revenue targets
- Operating ratios
- Research & development spending
- Projected operating costs
- Earnings guidance

3. — Requirements

Disclosure of FLI is not mandatory for reporting issuers. However, we recognize that many reporting issuers provide FLI, generally, in news releases, management's discussion and analysis ("MD&A"), annual information forms, marketing materials or on their website. FLI is by definition likely to be less reliable than historical information because it is based on management's best judgment and assumptions on how future trends will impact their business. As such, it is important that FLI be clearly identified so that readers understand the limitation of this information, are not confused and don't treat FLI as historical information. Further, it is critical that readers understand the basis on which the FLI was determined. This basis must be reasonable. In addition, material risk factors and related assumptions used to develop the FLI must accompany the disclosure. In determining what constitutes a "reasonable basis" for FLI, a reporting issuer should consider the reasonableness of the assumptions underlying the FLI and the process followed in preparing and reviewing the FLI. Updates on FLI help investors understand how actual results are reasonably likely to differ materially from previously disclosed FLI and how the reporting issuer is progressing towards the achievement of its disclosed targets and objectives.

The disclosure of FLI is subject to securities requirements under National Instrument 51-102 *Continuous Disclosure Obligations* (NI 51-102),[1] irrespective of where FLI is located within a document or the nature of the document where FLI is disclosed. Therefore, the rules apply regardless of whether FLI is on a website, in a news release or in the MD&A. The requirements can be divided in two parts: (a) requirements relating to the initial disclosure of FLI, and (b) requirements relating to the ongoing obligations to update, compare to actual results and, if appropriate, withdraw previously disclosed FLI. We have summarized these requirements in Appendix A *Requirements*.

---

[1]Part 4A — Forward-Looking Information, Part 4B — FOFI and Financial Outlook and Section 5.8 — Disclosure Relating to Previously Disclosed Material Forward-Looking Information.

Exceptions

Oral statements

The rules do not apply to FLI presented orally. However, if oral statements containing FLI are transcribed, for example, if the issuer transcribes the quarterly conference call with analysts where management of a reporting issuer discusses their results, these statements would be subject to the requirements under NI 51-102.

Disclosure for Oil and Gas Activities or for Mineral Projects

Part 4B and section 5.8 of NI 51-102 do not apply to disclosure of FOFI or financial outlook subject to requirements in National Instrument 51-101 *Standards of Disclosure for Oil and Gas Activities* or National Instrument 43-101 *Standards of Disclosure for Mineral Projects*. This disclosure is still subject to the requirements under Part 4A of NI 51-102, including identifying FLI, stating material factors and assumptions used, and providing the required disclaimers and cautionary language. We note that frequently, scientific and technical information about a mineral project includes or is based on FLI. Examples of FLI include metal price assumptions, cash flow forecasts, projected capital and operating costs, metal or mineral recoveries, mine life and production rates, and other assumptions used in preliminary economic assessments, pre-feasibility studies, and feasibility studies.

Update and withdrawal

Updating or notification that FLI is being withdrawn must be included in the MD&A or in a news release. Section 5.8 of NI 51-102 provides flexibility to allow the updated information to be included in a news release as long as it is filed prior to the MD&A. In this case, the MD&A must refer to the news release to satisfy the requirements. The disclosure and discussion of material differences between actual results and previously disclosed FOFI or financial outlook must be included in the MD&A; including this information in a news release instead of the MD&A is not permitted.

Audit Committee and Board of Directors

Section 5.5 of NI 51-102 requires the annual and interim MD&A to be approved by the board of directors before being filed[2] and National Instrument 52-110 *Audit Committees* requires that an audit committee review an issuer's financial statements, MD&A, and interim and annual profit or loss press releases before a reporting issuer publicly discloses this information. This includes FLI included in the MD&A or in a press release.

The audit committee and board of directors' role in the oversight of FLI helps ensure the dissemination of timely and transparent information to investors. As such, the audit committee and board of directors should consider reviewing and approving the initial FLI disclosure, determining whether updates are required, questioning management on the assumptions being used to develop FLI, and approving the targets before they are disclosed publicly.

4. — What We Found

In our review of 60 reporting issuers we identified four common areas where improvement is needed:

- clear identification of FLI
- material factors and assumptions
- updating previously disclosed FLI
- comparison of actual results to previously disclosed FOFI or financial outlook

To help reporting issuers improve their disclosure, in this section we provide examples of frequently identified boilerplate/non-compliant disclosure, along with suggestions to improve disclosure with entity-specific compliant FLI.

1. — Identification of FLI

Section 4A.3 of NI 51-102 requires reporting issuers to clearly identify material FLI. All but one reporting issuer that we reviewed included cautionary language which identified the existence of FLI in their financial reporting document. However, our review revealed that only 47% of reporting issuers clearly identified entity-specific FLI.

---

[2]The approval of the interim MD&A by the board of directors may be delegated to the audit committee.

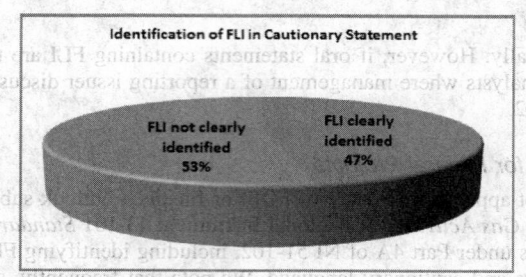

As indicated previously in this notice, it is important that FLI be clearly identified so that readers are not confused and treat it as historical information. The identification of material FLI in a generic and boilerplate manner does not allow users of the financial information to specifically identify and understand that a forward-looking statement is being provided by the reporting issuer in a document or website.

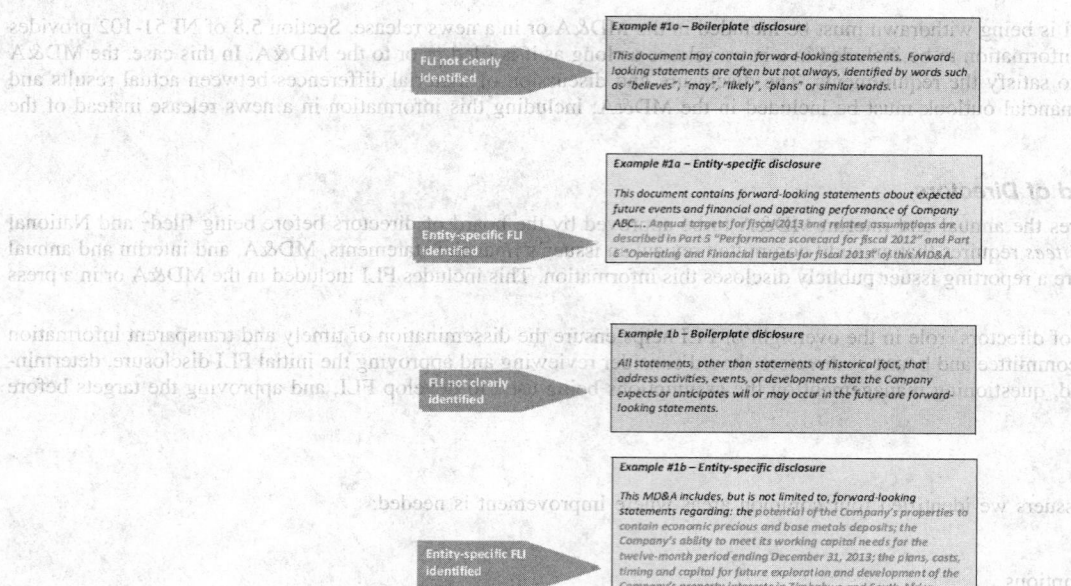

The boilerplate disclosure in the two examples above does not contain details that clearly identify the FLI relating to the issuer's business. As illustrated in the entity-specific examples, FLI is clearly identified allowing a user of the information to understand that it is FLI that is being disclosed and not historical information.

2. — Material Factors and Assumptions

Disclosure of specific relevant material factors or assumptions including material risk factors underlying the FLI is necessary for investors to understand how actual results may vary from FLI. Based on our review, 24% of reporting issuers did not disclose any material factors or assumptions used to develop their FLI. In addition, 19% of reporting issuers only provided generic factors and assumptions within the cautionary statement. Reporting issuers should carefully analyze the assumptions that underlie FLI. Assumptions should be reasonable, supportable and entity-specific. Whenever possible, assumptions should be quantified as this provides valuable information for investors.

Material factors and assumptions must be:

- reasonable
- supportable
- entity-specific
- tied to FLI
- disclosed

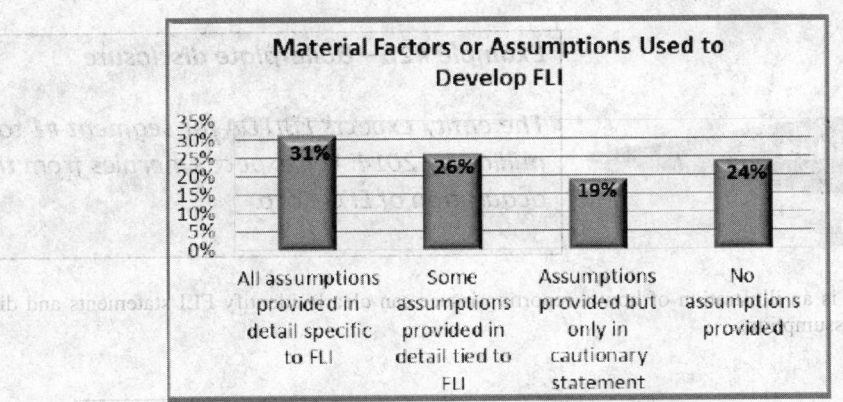

Material Factors or Assumptions Used to Develop FLI

- All assumptions provided in detail specific to FLI: 31%
- Some assumptions provided in detail tied to FLI: 26%
- Assumptions provided but only in cautionary statement: 19%
- No assumptions provided: 24%

The majority of issuers reviewed did not quantify their assumptions. Reporting issuers continue to provide general boilerplate disclosure that does not adequately describe the key assumptions used and how primary risks may impact future performance. Assumptions disclosed are not specific to the reporting issuers' business and do not tie directly to the disclosure being provided. Example 2a below, is a common example where assumptions supporting the sales target were not provided.

No assumptions provided

Example #2a – Boilerplate disclosure

In fiscal 2013, the Company anticipates meeting the following target:

- *Total sales to increase by 5.0% to 6.0%*

A description of key specific risks and uncertainties that may impact a reporting issuer's future performance will assist an investor's understanding of an issuer's business and will lead to better reporting. This is illustrated in the entity-specific example below. General risk factors and assumptions provide investors with limited information and do not provide insight on how they relate to and impact the FLI being disclosed.

Identification of FLI

Specific assumptions

Example #2a – Entity-specific disclosure

The following represents forward-looking information and users are cautioned that actual results may vary. In fiscal 2013, the Company expects total sales to increase by 5.0% to 6.0%. This expectation is based on same-store sales growth of between 3.0% and 4.0% and the introduction of new brands to our city centre stores. It is expected that new brands will contribute to the increase in sales and will be offset by increased competition from U.S. retailers. Key performance indicator for the Company includes retail sales per square foot; this target assumes an average sale per square foot of $45. An increase of 25 basis points in interest rates may cause the sales target to decrease by 1-2%.

In example 2b (boilerplate disclosure), the reporting issuer has provided targets for the fiscal year but has not provided assumptions that support the FLI provided. The statement about the issuer achieving synergies does not help an investor understand how these synergies will help the issuer attain EBITDA of $125 million for segment #1.

Example #2b – Boilerplate disclosure

The entity expects EBITDA for segment #1 to reach $125 million by 2014. We expect synergies from the acquisition of EFG Corp.

The entity-specific example below is an illustration of how a reporting issuer can clearly identify FLI statements and disclose relevant and specific material risk factors and assumptions.

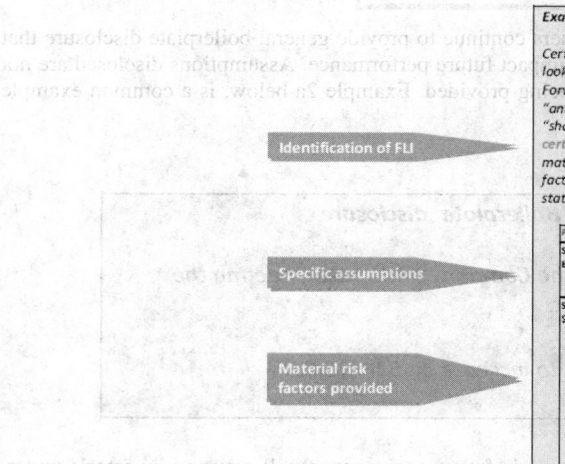

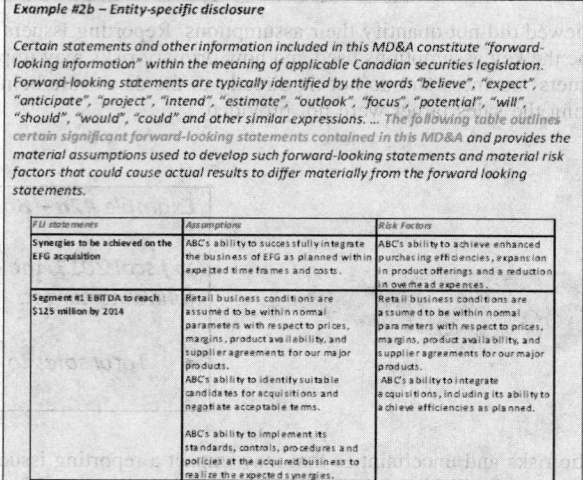

3. — Updating previously disclosed FLI

A reporting issuer is required under Section 5.8 of NI 51-102 to discuss in the MD&A or in a press release, events and circumstances that are reasonably likely to cause actual results to differ materially from previously disclosed FLI. The expected differences must also be disclosed. For example, economic and market events may cause actual results to differ materially from previously disclosed material FLI.

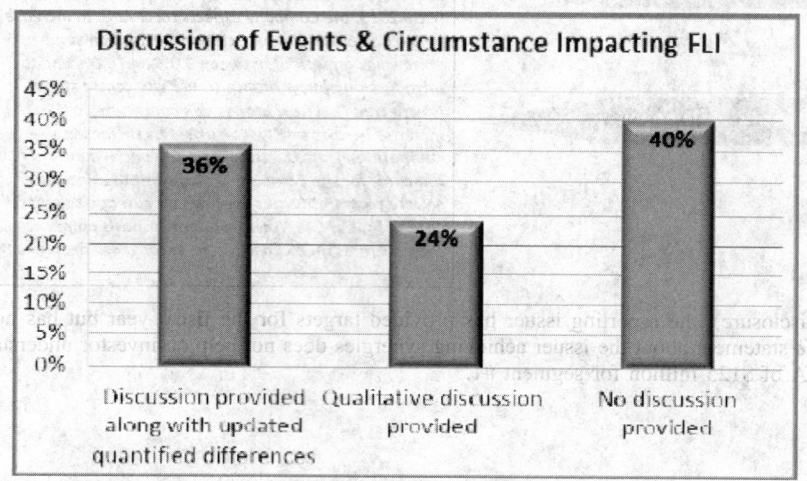

Forty percent of reporting issuers reviewed did not disclose the events and circumstances impacting their previously reported FLI that occurred during the period. Overall, only 36% of reporting issuers included a quantified discussion of events and circumstances that are reasonably likely to cause actual results to differ materially from previously reported FLI. Failure to provide disclosure of material differences in events and circumstances prevents investors from assessing how well the reporting issuer is progressing towards the achievement of its disclosed targets and objectives. For example, updated quantified data that relates to factors and assumptions that may impact the future performance of the issuer will clarify how and why these changes may impact future performance; this will lead to a clearer understanding of events and circumstances that occurred in the business environment in which the reporting issuer operates.

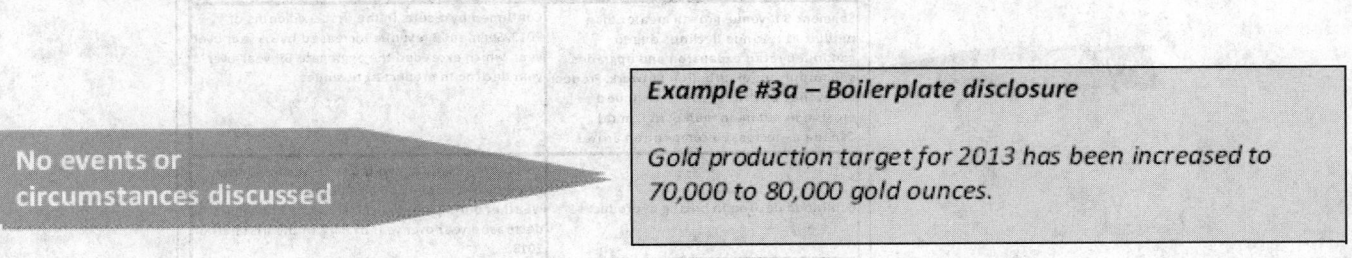

No events or circumstances discussed

Example #3a – Boilerplate disclosure

Gold production target for 2013 has been increased to 70,000 to 80,000 gold ounces.

In example 3a (boilerplate disclosure), the reporting issuer did not disclose events or circumstances that occurred during the period and how they impact previously disclosed FLI. Simply providing an update of previously disclosed FLI without the data that relates to the underlying factors and assumptions provides no insight on why and how the target has changed.

Updated FLI

Events and circumstances discussed

Updated assumptions

Example #3a – Entity-specific disclosure
Gold production was originally anticipated to be in the range of 40,000 to 50,000 gold ounces for 2013. Given the recent developments in Q2, the target for 2013 has increased to 70,000 to 80,000 gold ounces. The expansion and development of ABC mine was completed at the end of Q2 and will be contributing to the increased production. It is expected that weekly production will increase by approximately 1,400 ounces. The Company is in the process of hiring additional engineering staff to support the increased production. If we are unable to hire qualified personnel, the target may only increase to 60,000 to 70,000 gold ounces.

In the example above, the reporting issuer provides a discussion of the event that occurred during the period and the impact it has on the original target. Updated assumptions and risks are also included, which provides investors greater insight on the issuer's future performance.

Finally, we have included two examples on the following pages illustrating different approaches on how reporting issuers can clearly identify FLI and update previously disclosed FLI by explaining why the original assumptions changed with supporting numbers. Using tables is an effective approach to clearly communicate FLI and update the information.

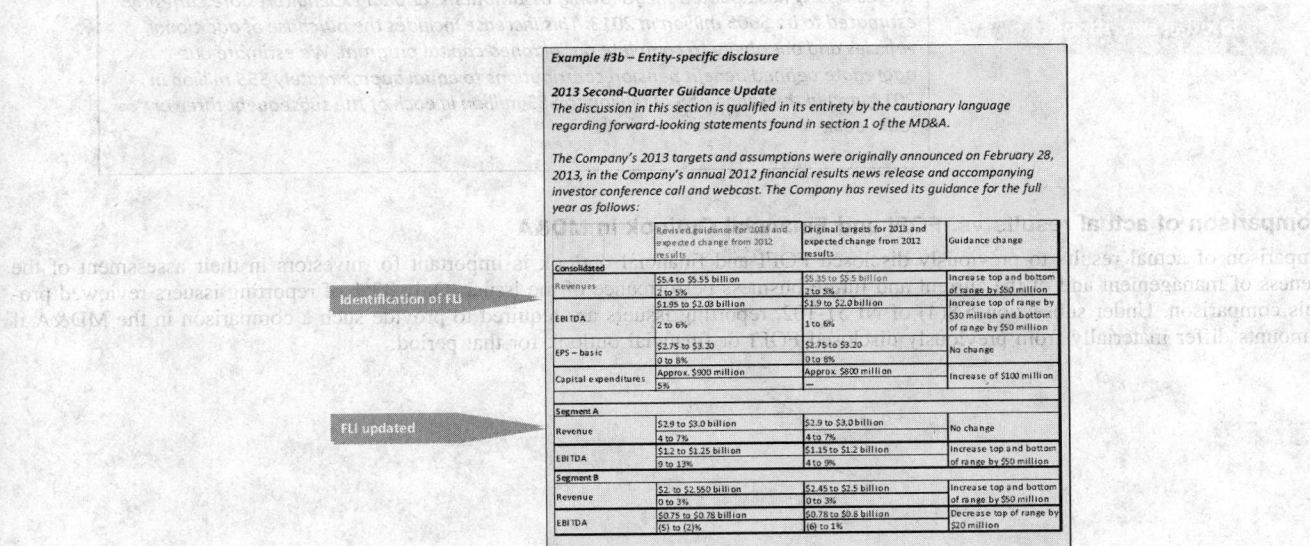

Identification of FLI

FLI updated

Example #3b – Entity-specific disclosure

2013 Second-Quarter Guidance Update
The discussion in this section is qualified in its entirety by the cautionary language regarding forward-looking statements found in section 1 of the MD&A.

The Company's 2013 targets and assumptions were originally announced on February 28, 2013, in the Company's annual 2012 financial results news release and accompanying investor conference call and webcast. The Company has revised its guidance for the full year as follows:

	Revised guidance for 2013 and expected change from 2012 results	Original targets for 2013 and expected change from 2012 results	Guidance change
Consolidated			
Revenues	$5.4 to $5.55 billion	$5.35 to $5.5 billion	Increase top and bottom of range by $50 million
	2 to 5%	2 to 5%	
EBITDA	$1.95 to $2.03 billion	$1.9 to $2.0 billion	Increase top of range by $30 million and bottom of range by $50 million
	2 to 6%	1 to 6%	
EPS – basic	$2.75 to $3.20	$2.75 to $3.20	No change
	0 to 8%	0 to 8%	
Capital expenditures	Approx. $900 million	Approx. $800 million	Increase of $100 million
	5%	—	
Segment A			
Revenue	$2.9 to $3.0 billion	$2.9 to $3.0 billion	No change
	4 to 7%	4 to 7%	
EBITDA	$1.2 to $1.25 billion	$1.15 to $1.2 billion	Increase top and bottom of range by $50 million
	9 to 13%	4 to 9%	
Segment B			
Revenue	$2. to $2.550 billion	$2.45 to $2.5 billion	Increase top and bottom of range by $50 million
	0 to 3%	0 to 3%	
EBITDA	$0.75 to $0.78 billion	$0.78 to $0.8 billion	Decrease top of range by $20 million
	(5) to (2)%	(6) to 1%	

Part 5: ONGOING REQUIREMENTS

Updated assumptions

Assumptions for 2013 original targets	Result to date or expectation for full year
Segment B revenue growth greater than product #1 revenue declines due to continued retail expansion and upgrades supporting our distribution network. Product #1 revenue declines reflect continued erosion in our main market in Central Canada as increased competition arrives.	Confirmed by results in the first six months of 2013. Segment B revenue increased by 9% year over year, which exceeded the aggregate 6% year-over-year decline in product #1 revenues.
Continued decline in pricing of product #1	Product #1 revenues continued to decline due to retail price competition and unfavourable weather during the quarter. Product #1 revenues decreased year over year by 6.0% in the first half of 2013.
Between $20 and $30 million in restructuring costs to support several operating and capital efficiency initiatives.	Different initiatives expected to impact restructuring costs are currently estimated at approximately $40 million for the full year. Restructuring costs of $15 million were recorded in the first half of 2013, of which $10 million was for employee-related initiatives and $5 million was related to sale of real estate.
.....	.....

Example #3c – Entity-specific disclosure

2013 Financial Assumptions
In the 2012 annual MD&A, the Company previously provided assumptions for 2013 which included capital expenditures estimated to range from $525 million to $550 million (discussed further in Section 3.5, Liquidity and Capital Resources). The Company expects its tax rate to be in the 23% to 28% range (discussed further in Section 2.9, Other Income Items). The 2013 pension contributions were estimated to be between $55 million and $70 million (discussed further in Section 3.9, Commitments and Future Trends). Undue reliance should not be placed on these assumptions and other forward-looking information.

Previously disclosed assumptions

2013 Third-Quarter Guidance
The Company has updated the following assumptions: Capital expenditures are currently estimated to be $605 million in 2013. This increase includes the purchase of additional vehicles and our ability to complete our planned capital program. We estimate our aggregate defined benefit pension contributions to equal approximately $55 million in 2013, and in the range of $70 million to $85 million in each of the subsequent three or four years.

Updated assumptions

4. — Comparison of actual results vs. FOFI and Financial Outlook in MD&A

The comparison of actual results to previously disclosed FOFI and financial outlook is important for investors in their assessment of the effectiveness of management and of the current and future business performance of the issuer. Only 33% of reporting issuers reviewed provided this comparison. Under subsection 5.8(4) of NI 51-102, reporting issuers are required to provide such a comparison in the MD&A if actual amounts differ materially from previously disclosed FOFI or financial outlook for that period.

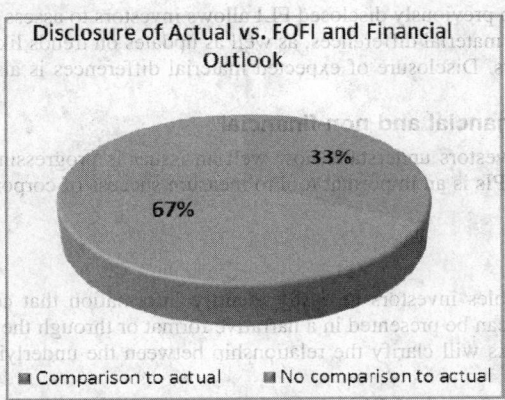

The disclosure in the example below does not provide a comparison between actual results and previously disclosed financial outlook. A comparison of the actual results to the FOFI or financial outlook originally disclosed in previous documents will allow investors the opportunity to assess the reasonableness of previous disclosure and adjust their expectations.

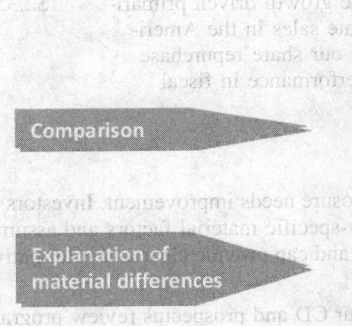

> ### Example #4a – Boilerplate disclosure
>
> *ABC Company achieved sales growth of 10.5% in 2012 and maintained capital expenditures at $15 million.*

The disclosure in the entity-specific example below provides a comprehensive discussion comparing actual results to previously disclosed financial outlook. The discussion includes a qualitative and quantitative explanation of the material differences. Investors will be able to clearly understand whether the targets were or were not achieved and why.

Example #4a – Entity-specific disclosure

2012 objectives	Accomplishments in 2012
Sales growth of 3-4%	Sales growth of 10.5% - A 6% increase in sales was achieved during fiscal 2012 due to the introduction of product X in Q4. - The remaining 4.5% of sales growth resulted from sales of product Y. The reduction of product Y's selling price drove an increase in sales volume for product Y.
Capital expenditure $25-35 million	Capital expenditure of $15 million. - Spending was substantially lower than anticipated due to lower information technology enhancement requirements ($8 million) and less equipment replacements ($7 million).

5. — Practice Points

Effective communication of FLI enables investors to have a better understanding of a reporting issuer's business, their long term objectives, and their progress in achieving those objectives. The following practice points will assist issuers and their advisors in promoting clear, transparent disclosure for FLI.

1. — Quality of assumptions

Assumptions should be reasonable and specific to a reporting issuer. Material factors and assumptions should be provided where FLI is disclosed. Qualitative, entity-specific and quantitative assumptions are informative and useful to investors.

2. — Timely updating of ongoing progress

Updating of ongoing progress as compared to previously disclosed FLI allows investors to assess corporate performance during the fiscal year. Affirmation of targets, disclosure of affected material differences, as well as updates on trends likely to impact future performance on a timely basis is informative information for investors. Disclosure of expected material differences is also important.

3. — Key Performance Indicators — financial and non-financial

KPIs can help both reporting issuers and investors understand how well an issuer is progressing towards their objectives. Disclosure of an issuer's objectives along with their related KPIs is an important tool to measure success of corporate performance. KPIs can be both quantitative and qualitative in nature.

4. — Separate Presentation

Having a separate section with all FLI enables investors to easily identify information that constitutes material FLI and what represents historical information. The FLI for an issuer can be presented in a narrative format or through the use of tables and charts. A table that sets out objectives, key specific assumptions and risks will clarify the relationship between the underlying key components and the FLI.

5. — Role of the Audit Committee and Board of Directors

The audit committee and board of directors play a key role in the oversight of FLI. As such, they should consider reviewing and approving all FLI disclosure before it is publicly disclosed, including the underlying assumptions being used to develop the FLI.

The following is an illustration of an entity-specific example where the reporting issuer provides comprehensive and understandable FLI disclosure. The table includes discussion of the original target for the KPI, a comparison to actual results, inclusion of entity-specific related assumptions and updated targets for the upcoming year.

Scorecard	What we targeted	How we did	Commentary	What we are targeting to do in 2013
Same store sales growth	3%–5%	6.30%	Our same-store sales growth was driven mainly by changes to our clothing lines with quality products introduced at targeted price points which contributed to positive product mix, and combined with pricing, resulted in a higher average sale per consumer. Additional advertising targeted at our core growth markets in Eastern U.S. also contributed favourably, and we believe was a significant factor in the strong performance during the period.	4%–6%
EPS (fully diluted)	$2.30–$2.40	$2.35	A combination of operating income growth driven primarily by continued strength in corporate sales in the Americas, a lower effective tax rate, and our share repurchase program contributed to our EPS performance in fiscal 2012.	$2.35–$2.45

6. — Conclusions

The findings of our review illustrate that the quality of FLI continues to be an area where disclosure needs improvement. Investors continue to demand forward-looking information. Clear identification of FLI, detailed disclosure of entity-specific material factors and assumptions, updating FLI, and providing comparisons is important, required information for reporting issuers and can provide clear and informative information to investors.

Given its importance to investors, this is an area of disclosure we will continue to assess in our CD and prospectus review programs. Issuers who have not complied with the FLI requirements will be expected to take corrective action.

7. — Questions and Additional Resources

[Omitted]

8. — Appendix A — Requirements

	Rule Reference & Subsection	Description	FLI	FOFI and financial outlook
Definitions	*1.1 of NI 51-102*	Definitions for FLI, FOFI and financial outlook	✓	✓
Reasonable Basis	*4A.2 of NI 51-102*	Reasonable basis for FLI required	✓	✓

	Rule Reference & Subsection	Description	FLI	FOFI and financial outlook
	4A.2 of NI 51-102CP			
Assumptions	4B.2 of NI 51-102	Reasonable assumptions in the circumstances supporting financial outlook or FOFI required		✓
		• Financial outlook or FOFI must		
		• be limited to a period for which information can be reasonably estimated (generally not more than a year)		
		• use the accounting policies the reporting issuer expects to use to prepare its historical F/S for the period covered by the FOFI or financial outlook		
Disclosure	4A.3(a) of NI 51-102	Information must be identified as FLI	✓	✓
	4A.3(b) of NI 51-102	Users must be cautioned that actual results may vary from FLI	✓	✓
	4A.3(b) of NI 51-102	Material risk factors that could cause actual results to differ materially from the FLI must be identified	✓	✓
	4A.5 of NI 51-102CP			
	4A.3(c) of NI 51-102	Material factors and assumptions used to develop FLI must be identified	✓	✓
	4A.6 of NI 51-102CP			
	4A.3(c) of NI 51-102	Description of the issuer's policy for updating FLI if it includes procedures in addition to those required under Section 5.8 of NI 51-102 (described below)	✓	✓
Additional disclosure for financial outlook and FOFI	4B.3(a) of NI 51-102	If the document containing the disclosure is not dated, include the date management approved the FOFI or financial outlook		✓
	4B.3(b) of NI 51-102	Purpose of financial outlook or FOFI must be explained		✓
	4B.3(b) of NI 51-102	Readers must be cautioned that information may not be appropriate for other purposes		✓

Part 5: ONGOING REQUIREMENTS

	Rule Reference & Subsection	Description	FLI	FOFI and financial outlook
Updating FLI in interim or annual MD&A	*5.8(2) of NI 51-102*	Disclose events or circumstances that have occurred in the period that are reasonably likely to cause actual results to differ materially from the previously publicly disclosed material FLI. Discuss the expected differences. This applies to FLI for a financial period that is not yet complete.	✓	✓
Comparison to Actual	*5.8(4) of NI 51-102*	Disclose material differences between actual annual or interim results and any FOFI or financial outlook previously disclosed for the period		✓
Withdrawal	*5.8(5) of NI 51-102*	Disclose any decision to withdraw previously disclosed FLI. The events and circumstances that led to this decision must be discussed as are the assumptions underlying the FLI that are no longer valid.	✓	✓

OSC Staff Notice 51-722 — Report on a Review of Mining Issuers' Management's Discussion and Analysis and Guidance

Date: February 6, 2014
37 O.S.C.B. 1361

Part A — Staff's Review of MD&A in the Mining Industry

1. — *Executive Summary*

Management's Discussion and Analysis (**MD&A**) is a key disclosure document for all reporting issuers as it gives investors the ability to look at an issuer through the eyes of management. The MD&A must be transparent and clear to be informative.

The MD&A requirements are set out in National Instrument 51-102 *Continuous Disclosure Obligations* (**NI 51-102**), specifically in Part 5 *Management's Discussion and Analysis* and in Form 51-102F1 *Management's Discussion and Analysis* (**Form 51-102F1**).

As a securities regulator, the Ontario Securities Commission (**OSC**) understands the challenges faced by small mining issuers in today's challenging market environment. Limited resources can make it difficult for small mining issuers to meet their regulatory obligations and comply with their reporting requirements.

Recognizing these challenges and the importance of smaller mining issuers in Ontario, staff of the OSC conducted a review (the **Review**) of the MD&A filed by mining issuers with a market capitalization of less than $100 million in an effort to understand the issues they face and to identify areas where regulatory guidance would assist the management of these companies in complying with their regulatory obligations. These issuers represent approximately 34% of the 1,105 reporting issuers for which the OSC is the principal regulator.

While the guidance provided in the Notice is specific to the mining issuers reviewed, the content of the Notice, including our disclosure examples, will benefit all issuers.

OSC Staff Notice 51-722 *Report on a Review of Mining Issuers' Management's Discussion and Analysis and Guidance* (the **Notice**):

- is meant to be an educational tool to assist issuers in complying with their MD&A disclosure obligations

- summarizes the results of the Review

- identifies areas for improvement

- provides concrete examples on how issuers can present their information in a relevant and meaningful manner

Our review focused on:

- venture issuer disclosure

- discussion of operations

- liquidity and capital resources disclosure

- disclosure of transactions between related parties

- disclosure of risk factors and uncertainties

- reporting on use of financing proceeds

Summary of Results

We identified specific areas for improvement:

- venture issuers without significant revenue from operations did not provide the breakdown of material components of exploration and evaluation (**E&E**) assets or expenditures

- issuers with exploration projects did not discuss and itemize their exploration expenditures

- issuers with a working capital deficiency provided very general discussion or no discussion about potential sources of financing and how they plan on continuing operations

- issuers did not appropriately disclose the identity of the party involved in the related party transaction

2. — Introduction

The MD&A is a summary written through the eyes of management which allows management to provide insights beyond the numbers found in the financial statements. As such, the MD&A should:

- provide a balanced discussion of an issuer's results, financial condition and future prospects — openly discussing bad news as well as good news

- help current and prospective investors understand what is presented in the financial statements

- discuss trends and risks that have affected or are reasonably likely to affect the financial statements in the future

- provide information about the quality and potential variability of an issuer's earnings, cash flow and operations

The current market environment is making it very difficult for mining issuers to raise capital, with the smaller mining issuers being particularly affected. We also understand such an environment can make complying with reporting requirements quite challenging for smaller issuers due to the lack of resources. To assist smaller mining issuers to better understand certain MD&A requirements and to foster regulatory compliance we have developed the guidance and examples found in Part B — *Guide to MD&A Disclosure for Mining Issuers* (**Part B**). We hope these examples will assist issuers to present clear, specific and relevant information about their financial condition and future prospects.

3. — Review Results

A. — Scope of Review

The OSC is the principal regulator for approximately 449 reporting issuers in the mining industry[1], which is a very important sector in the capital markets in Ontario. These issuers have a combined market capitalization of $90.2[1] billion, representing 11% of Ontario's overall market capitalization. There are 374 Ontario mining issuers with a market capitalization of less than $100 million. In our ongoing compliance efforts, we have realized that many smaller mining issuers continue to struggle to provide complete and meaningful MD&A disclosure and generally need more guidance.

To understand the issues, we focused the Review on a sample of 100 Ontario mining issuers with a market capitalization of less than $100 million and focused on compliance with various aspects of the MD&A requirements in NI 51-102, including:

- venture issuer disclosure

- discussion of operations

- liquidity and capital resources disclosure

- disclosure of transactions between related parties

- disclosure of risk factors and uncertainties

- reporting on use of financing proceeds

B. — Issuers Reviewed

Of the 100 Ontario mining issuers we reviewed, approximately 46% were non-venture issuers[2] and 54% were venture issuers[2]. Fifty-four percent of the issuers had a market capitalization of less than $25 million, with 28% having a market capitalization of less than $10 million. In terms of stage of development, the majority of issuers, 53%, were at the mineral resource stage, 23% were at the exploration stage and 24% were at the development or production stage.

[1] As at September 30, 2013.

[2] As defined in NI 51-102.

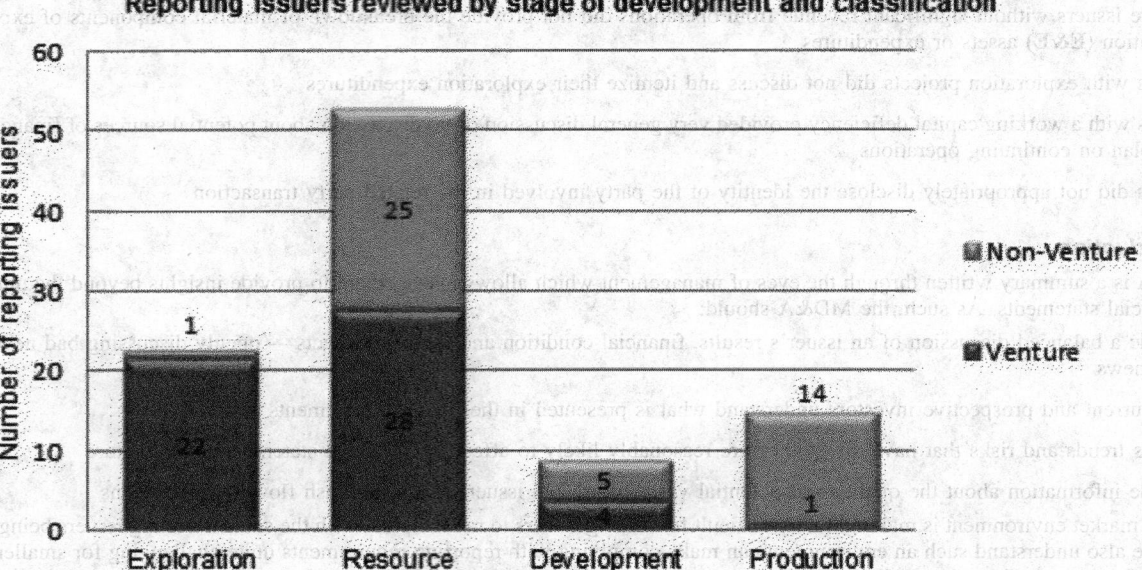

Reporting issuers reviewed by stage of development and classification

C. — Summary of Results

General

We found that many smaller mining issuers continue to struggle to provide complete and meaningful MD&A disclosure. The size of an issuer (as defined by market capitalization) was not a predictive factor as to whether an issuer met MD&A disclosure requirements. However, we note that issuers in the exploration stage generally need more guidance on appropriate entity-specific disclosure to be included in their MD&A than issuers in the development and production stages.

Venture Issuer Disclosure

Providing a breakdown of the material components of E&E, a presentation of E&E assets or expenditures on a property-by-property basis, general and administrative (**G&A**) expenses and other material costs incurred, helps investors understand the nature of the work being performed, how money is being spent and helps them evaluate the impact the expenses have in moving the exploration or developments of properties forward.

For venture issuers without significant revenue from operations, our Review found:

- 37% did not provide the breakdown of material components of E&E

- 20% presented the E&E on a property-by-property basis in their MD&A but failed to provide a further breakdown by material components

- 39% did not include a breakdown of material components of G&A expenses

Discussion of Operations

Issuers without producing mines — Beyond just the description of a project, it is important that investors receive essential information about an issuer's material mineral projects: work completed and expenses incurred during the period, current (and future) project plans and budgets. Providing this information will help investors follow and understand the progress of a project and measure how it is performing. It will also help investors connect the dots between initial plans and budgets and the time and costs required to take the project to the next stage.

Issuers with producing mines — The MD&A may be the principal document to inform shareholders and potential investors about the production and operations of a project. It is important that in the MD&A, issuers provide information on: production figures, production activities and milestones, operating and production costs, sales and revenue, explanations of any substantial changes to production and operation information, new developments and the impact each of these have on mineral resources and reserves.

Our Review found that:

- 70% of issuers without a producing mine provided limited disclosure about the plans or milestones for significant exploration and development projects, including anticipated costs to take the projects to the next stage of the project plan

- 44% of issuers with exploration projects did not discuss and itemize their exploration expenditures

Liquidity and Capital Resources

To better assess whether an issuer has sufficient funds to meet its business plans in the short-term and long-term, investors require meaningful information about an issuer's liquidity and ability to generate the cash needed to maintain operations. The MD&A provides an issuer with the opportunity to provide insight beyond the numbers and discuss material cash requirements, historical sources and uses of cash, material trends and uncertainties, and to explain and quantify working capital needs and how these needs relate to future business plans or milestones.

Of the 100 mining issuers reviewed:

- 27% clearly had significant current cash resources to meet their business needs

- 21% included a quantified discussion of how they intend to address in the short and long term their working capital requirements

- 52% provided either no disclosure or limited disclosure of their working capital requirements. This makes it difficult for a reader to assess whether the issuer has sufficient funds available to meet the issuer's business needs for the following 12 months

Disclosure of Working Capital Requirements

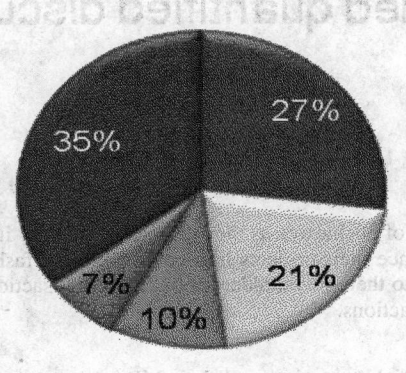

- No discussion but issuer has significant cash on hand to meet long term needs

- Short and long term working capital requirments quantified

- Short term requirements quantified, no long term information

- No working capital information provided

- General working capital discussion with no quantification

For issuers with a working capital deficiency:

- 26% included a detailed quantified plan of how they will meet their obligations as they come due and how they plan to rectify the deficiency

- 74% provided no discussion or a very general discussion about needing to access the capital markets in the future

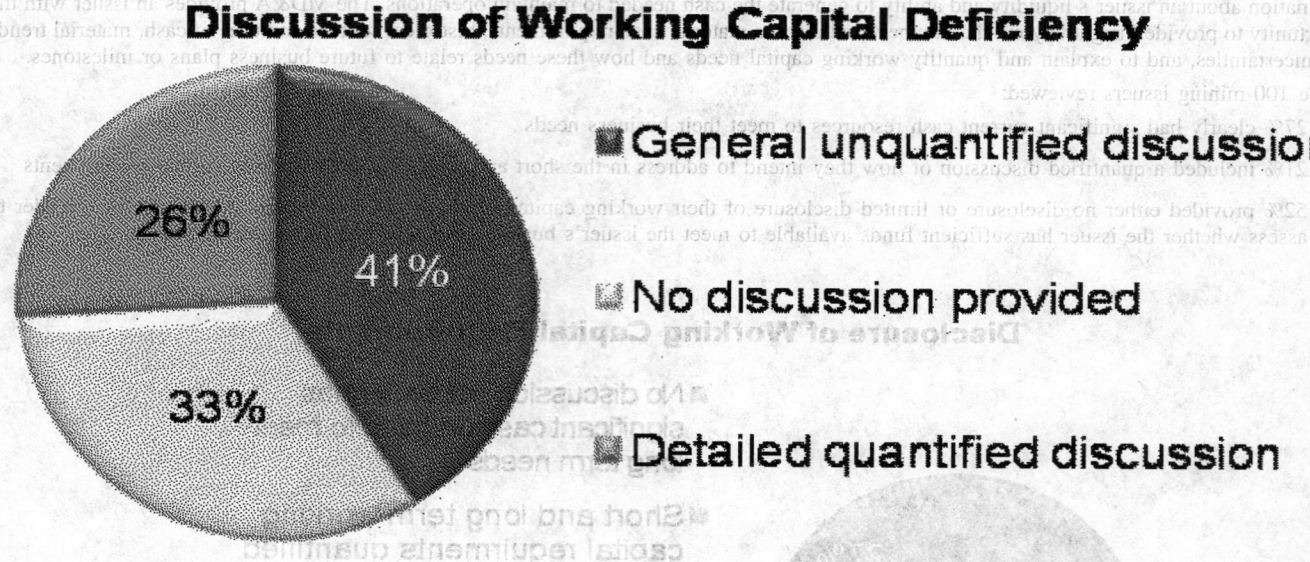

Discussion of Working Capital Deficiency

- General unquantified discussion — 41%
- No discussion provided — 33%
- Detailed quantified discussion — 26%

Transactions Between Related Parties

Related party transactions (**RPT**) often play a significant role in the operations of businesses as they grow and can vary in complexity. We are aware that many smaller issuers leverage their business relationships to advance their projects in a cost controlled fashion by entering into related party contracts or transactions. It is critical that issuers are transparent to their shareholders about these transactions in the MD&A, so investors can better understand the business purpose and value of these transactions.

We note that:

- 95% of the issuers had some form of RPT disclosed in both their financial statements and their MD&A
- 48% of the issuers did not appropriately disclose the identity of the related party involved in the transaction. Most commonly, the relationship was disclosed but the actual party involved in the transaction was not named
- 14% of the issuers reviewed did not quantify the RPT

Risk Factors and Uncertainties

Company risks can impact an investor's investment decision, so it is important that issuers provide specifics about the risks impacting an issuer's business. Where possible, issuers should quantify the risks and when listing or ranking potential risks, be clear about their severity and significance. To make the information more meaningful, issuers should update their risk disclosures when circumstances change.

All issuers reviewed included some form of risk disclosure.

For issuers with a going concern risk:

- 9% provided no discussion of their liquidity risks despite having going concern issues
- 86% provided a generic, unquantified discussion of liquidity risks

Disclosure of Risks for Issuers with a Going Concern

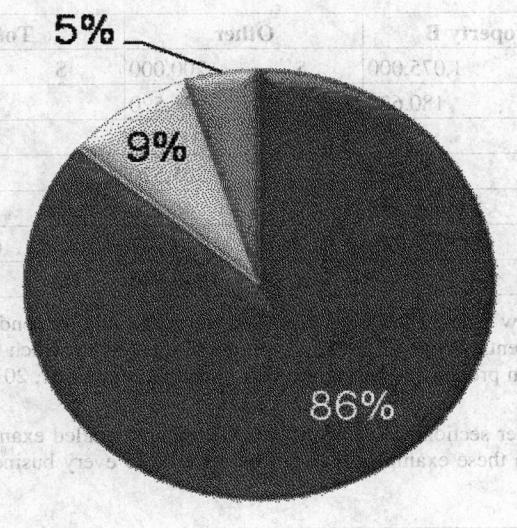

■ A general unquantified discussion of liquidity risks

▧ No discussion of liquidity risks despite going concern

■ Detailed quantified discussion of liquidity risks

5%

9%

86%

Use of Financing Proceeds

Our Review identified only four issuers that raised capital through a prospectus offering in the past fiscal year:

- two issuers included a tabular comparison without any explanations of the changes
- two issuers did not include any disclosure relating to how the proceeds were used

Summary

As a result of our Review, we identified specific areas where our issuers would benefit from some additional guidance. Using the guidance in Part B will assist issuers in preparing their MD&A. An accurate MD&A and a complete continuous disclosure (**CD**) record will help ensure the process for obtaining a prospectus receipt is not delayed. We will continue to monitor MD&A filed by Ontario mining issuers as part of our ongoing CD review program.

Part B — Guide to MD&A Disclosure for Mining Issuers

1. — MD&A Guidance for Mining Issuers

To assist mining issuers in complying with the disclosure requirements in both NI 51-102 and Form 51-102F1, we have set out guidance for the sections where we noted areas where disclosure could be improved. When referring to this guidance be aware that you do not need to disclose information that is not material or not relevant to your business. While the guidance in section A *Venture Issuer Disclosure* applies specifically to venture issuers, non-venture issuers may find the information useful in preparing their MD&A. The examples provided below are for illustrative purposes only and readers are reminded that these examples are only one of many possible approaches management could take to present the information. Management must consider the particular elements of the issuer's business and ensure that all material information relating to the business is reflected in the MD&A.

A. — Venture Issuer Disclosure

Disclosure requirement

Section 5.3 of NI 51-102 requires a venture issuer that has not had significant revenue from operations in either of its last two financial years to disclose in its MD&A on a comparative basis, a breakdown of material components of:

- E&E assets or expenditures
- G&A expenses
- other material costs

Further, the E&E assets or expenditures must be presented on a property-by-property basis.

Commentary

A breakdown of costs incurred helps investors understand the nature of the work that was performed and how an issuer is spending money. Further, a presentation of E&E assets or expenditures on a property-by-property basis helps investors evaluate the impact those expenditures have in moving the exploration or development of those properties forward.

Many issuers included disclosure similar to Example 1.

Example 1 — boilerplate disclosure

	Property A	Property B	Other	Total
Balance, as at December 31, 2011	$ 3,300,000	$ 1,075,000	$ 200,000	$ 4,575,000
Additions	1,812,910	180,620	36,520	2,030,050
Impairments	—	—	(35,000)	(35,000)
Balance, as at December 31, 2012	5,112,910	1,255,620	201,520	6,570,050
Additions	825.220	469,840	46,120	1,341,180
Impairments		(1,725,460)	—	(1,725,460)
Balance, as at December 31, 2013	**$ 5,938,130**	—	**$ 247,640**	**$ 6,185,770**

Example 1 is an example of disclosure frequently found during our Review where the issuer disclosed its exploration expenditures on a property-by-property basis without giving a breakdown by material components. While an investor will get a sense as to which property or project the issuer has moved forward, the fact that $825,220 was expended on property A during the year ended December 31, 2013 does not allow an investor to understand where and how the money was spent.

Examples 2a and 2b illustrate how an issuer can meet the requirements under section 5.3 of NI 51-102. These are detailed examples. Each issuer should assess the particulars of their business as the level of detail in these examples may not be material to every business.

Example 2a — entity-specific disclosure (E&E capitalized)

	Property A December 31, 2013	Property A December 31, 2012	Property B December 31, 2013	Property B December 31, 2012	Other December 31, 2013	Other December 31, 2012	Total December 31, 2013	Total December 31, 2012
Acquisition costs								
Balance, beginning of period	300,000	300,000	80,000	75,000	65,000	75,000	445,000	450,000
Incurred during period	50,000	—	—	5,000	15,000	—	65,000	5,000
Mineral properties abandoned	—	—	(80,000)	—	—	(10,000)	(80,000)	(10,000)
Balance, end of period	**350,000**	300,000	—	80,000	**80,000**	65,000	**430,000**	445,000
Exploration Expenditures								
Balance, beginning of period	4,812,910	3,000,000	1,175,620	1,000,000	136,520	125,000	6,125,053	4,125,000
Assays and geochemistry	41,050	145,730	27,390	—	5,880	2,990	74,320	148,720
Camp costs	25,550	57,400	5,410	—	—	—	30,960	57,400
Consulting	15,490	6,400	7,650	28,880	—	13,680	23,140	48,960
Drilling	466,820	1,248,500	330,390	—	—	—	797,210	1,248,500
Geology	38,690	19,400	17,420	—	12,770	6,750	68,880	26,150
Geophysics	25,990	42,200	—	92,480	—	—	25,990	134,680
Travel and lodging	77,260	124,880	36,120	21,660	4,990	9,600	118,370	156,140
Salaries and labour	84,370	168,400	45,460	32,600	7,480	3,500	137,310	204,500
Total exploration expenditures	775,220	1,812,910	469,840	175,620	31,120	36,520	**1,276,180**	2,025,050

	Property A		Property B		Other		Total	Total
	December 31, 2013	December 31, 2012	December 31, 2013	December 31, 2012	December 31, 2013	December 31, 2012	December 31, 2013	December 31, 2012
Mineral properties abandoned	—	—	(1,645,460)	—	—	(25,000)	(1,645,460)	(25,000)
Balance, end of period	**5,588,130**	4,812,910	—	1,175,620	**167,640**	136,520	**5,755,770**	6,125,053
Cumulative mineral property costs	**5,938,130**	5,112,910	—	1,255,620	**247,640**	201,520	**6,185,770**	6,570,050

Example 2a shows that the issuer has disclosed its E&E expenditures by material components and has provided the information for both of its material properties. The issuer has aggregated E&E for other non-material projects / properties in a separate column under "Other". The disclosure is also provided on a comparative basis. While the requirements in section 5.3 of NI 51-102 do not specifically require a qualitative discussion of the expenditures, staff is of the view that a discussion of the issuer's E&E assets or expenditures and G&A expenses should be included as part of the issuer's analysis of its operations under item 1.4 of Form 51-102F1. For example, we would expect a qualitative discussion on the increase in E&E on Property B in the year ended December 31, 2013, including drilling results and reasons supporting the decision to abandon the property. We would also expect a qualitative discussion about E&E on Property A decreasing during the year ended December 31, 2013 (e.g. the issuer is focusing on its main property due to budget constraints).

The information included in example 2a discloses "cumulative property costs" which allows an investor to reconcile the information included in the MD&A and the amount shown on the face of the statement of financial position under "property costs".

Example 2a assumes that the issuer's accounting policy is to capitalize E&E expenditures. Example 2b illustrates how an issuer that expenses its expenditures would present the information.

Example 2b — entity-specific disclosure (E&E expensed)

	Property A		Property B		Other		Total	Total
	December 31, 2013	December 31, 2012	December 31, 2013	December 31, 2012	December 31, 2013	December 31, 2012	December 31, 2013	December 31, 2012
Exploration Expenditures								
Assays and geochemistry	41,050	145,730	27,390	—	5,880	2,990	74,320	148,720
Camp costs	25,550	57,400	5,410	—	—	—	30,960	57,400
Consulting	15,490	6,400	7,650	28,880	—	13,680	23,140	48,960
Drilling	466,820	1,248,500	330,390	—	—	—	797,210	1,248,500
Geology	38,690	19,400	17,420	—	12,770	6,750	68,880	26,150
Geophysics	25,990	42,200	—	92,480	—	—	25,990	134,680
Travel and lodging	77,260	124,880	36,120	21,660	4,990	9,600	118,370	156,140
Salaries and labour	84,370	168,400	45,460	32,600	7,480	3,500	137,310	204,500
Total exploration expenditures	**775,220**	1,812,910	**469,840**	175,620	**31,120**	36,520	**1,276,180**	2,025,050
Cumulative E&E since inception	**5,588,130**	4,812,910	—	1,175,620	**167,640**	136,520	**5,755,770**	6,125,053

Reminder

Venture issuers without significant revenues must:

- disclose a breakdown of the material components of E&E assets or expenditures, G&A expenses, and other material costs on a comparative basis
- present E&E assets or expenditures on a property-by-property basis
- include a qualitative discussion of those expenditures

B. — Discussion of Operations — Issuers without producing mines

Disclosure requirement

Item 1.4 of Form 51-102F1 requires issuers to analyze their operations for the most recently completed period. The nature of the discussion should vary depending on the maturity of an issuer's operations. For example, Item 1.4 (d) of Form 51-102F1 requires issuers that have significant projects that have not yet generated revenue to describe each project including (a) the issuer's plan for each of its significant projects, (b) the status of each project relative to that plan, (c) expenditures made and (d) how the expenditures made relate to anticipated timing and costs to take the project to the next stage of the project plan.

Commentary

The annual MD&A for a mining issuer that is not at the production stage should provide the investor with information essential to understanding the issuer's material mineral projects. This would be more important for a venture issuer who chooses not to file an Annual Information Form[3] (**AIF**), and for issuers with early-stage exploration projects that may not have yet filed a technical report[4] on their projects. In these circumstances, the annual MD&A may be the only continuous disclosure document where management can summarize the project for investors and the interim MD&A allows that information to be updated.

To meet the requirements under Item 1.4 (d) of Form 51-102F1, issuers must include disclosure about the following items, on a property-by-property basis:

- description of the project
- work completed and expenditures made during the period
- current status — project plans and budgets
- explanation of how expenditures relate to anticipated timing and cost to take the project to the next stage of the project plan

We describe each of these items in further details on the following page.

Description of the project

- What are you looking for?
- Where are you looking?

The project description in the annual MD&A should provide investors with enough information to follow progress on the project as reported by the issuer in subsequent disclosures such as interim MD&A and news releases. That description should include the following information:

- location of the property
- property ownership, and the issuer's ongoing obligations to maintain its interest
- type of commodities
- geological setting — a brief description of the geology and known mineral occurrences
- exploration work to date — the work done and a summary of significant results
- any mineral resources or mineral reserves outlined on the property
- information required by Part 3 of National Instrument 43-101 *Standards of Disclosure for Mineral Properties* (**NI 43-101**). If this information is summarized in the MD&A, it can be referred to in later filings to comply with disclosure requirements of NI 43-101 as per section 3.5 of NI 43-101
- name of the qualified person for the technical information

If the issuer has filed an AIF or technical report with this information, a reference to that filing should be included.

Issuers do not need to repeat the history of a project in every MD&A. We noted many instances where issuers were merely repeating the information previously disclosed in an earlier MD&A without including information about the current period. While issuers without a current AIF may want to include more historical information to provide background information about their projects, the majority of the discussion should focus on what happened in the current year or interim period.

Work completed and expenditures made during the period

- What have you done?
- What did it cost you?

In this section, the issuer should provide information on the progress of the project to date. Repeating information found in the financial statements without explaining significant changes does not provide meaningful insight to an investor.

We note nearly half of issuers reviewed did not provide an itemized breakdown of historical and current period exploration expenditures on a property-by-property basis. As discussed in Section A, venture issuers without significant revenue are required to include the disclosure in

---

[3]Form 51-102F2 *Annual Information Form.*

[4]As defined in National Instrument 43-101 *Standards of Disclosures for Mineral Projects.*

section 5.3 of NI 51-102. However, for non-venture issuers that have significant projects not yet generating revenue, an itemized breakdown helps investors understand how the issuer performed during the period covered by the MD&A.

In the absence of significant revenues, the disclosure of itemized expenditures will help an issuer:

- explain the operations of the issuer and describe where progress has been made on the different projects / properties

- identify important trends and risks that have affected the financial statements (e.g. changes in the amount or type of exploration expenditures)

- provide information about the potential variability of the issuer's profit or loss and cash flow

Further, staff believe that answering the following questions in the MD&A provides useful disclosure to investors:

- What new exploration work (e.g. geophysical or geochemical surveys, mapping, sampling, or drilling) has the issuer done on the project?

- How much was spent on the work completed and is the amount substantially different from budgets disclosed in previous filings and offering documents?

Current status — Project plans and budgets

- What did the work accomplish?

- What are you planning next?

- How will you pay for it?

While issuers generally describe their significant projects and the work that has been completed during the period, MD&A would be improved by identifying how the accomplishments relate to the issuer's plans or next steps. For example:

- Is further work planned or has the issuer reached a decision on whether to advance the project further?

- What exploration or development milestones have been reached (for example, have all targets been tested or has a mineral resource been outlined)?

- Has the issuer met the requirements of an option or joint-venture agreement?

Issuers generally include some information about their plan for a significant project but the information is often vague and not meaningful. Issuers need to better explain the relationships or "connect the dots" between the current status of a project, their plan for the project, what they will spend on the project and when those expenditures will take place. This discussion is even more important when an issuer has liquidity or going concern issues so investors can understand the issuer's ability to meet cash requirements. The issuer must also discuss if sufficient resources are available to meet the projected capital commitments and, if not, disclose the expected source(s) of funds to meet those commitments. Further information on "liquidity and capital resources" can be found in Section D.

Investors are interested in understanding what the next phase of exploration or development is for the project by getting answers to questions such as:

- Is the issuer continuing to advance the project?

- Will the issuer be in a position to report a mineral resource estimate, and if so, when?

Example 3 is an example of disclosure commonly provided where an issuer fails to comply with the requirement. The disclosure is vague and lacks the details and quantification that would make it meaningful.

Example 3 — boilerplate example

In 2013, the Company continued its exploration efforts on the XYZ Lake property including additional drilling on the Fire Zone which continued to intersect significant zone of mineralization. In addition, geophysical surveys identified several targets for testing which may represent zones of mineralization similar to the Fire Zone.

In 2014, the Company expects to continue its drilling efforts to outline the Fire Zone mineralization and also drill test the geophysical targets. The Company anticipates it will be in a position to disclose an initial mineral resource estimate on the XYZ Lake property in 2014.

The following example illustrates better disclosure on how issuers can discuss their plans and expected expenditures for their projects.

Example 4 — entity-specific example

In 2013, the Company spent $873,100 on exploration expenses on the XYZ Lake property which consisted mainly of two phases of diamond drilling on the Fire Zone (totaling 25 holes for 4,820 metres) which were completed in February, 2013 and September, 2013. This drilling continued to outline significant zones of mineralization, the results of which were reported by the Company in news releases on May 30, 2013, June 24, 2013 and November 29, 2013. In addition, an airborne geophysical survey (703 line km) was completed in the summer which identified several targets for testing which may represent zones of mineralization similar to the Fire Zone.

In early 2014, the Company expects to spend approximately $800,000 conducting additional diamond drilling on the Fire Zone as well as follow-up drill testing of the high priority geophysical targets. It is expected that both drilling programs will consist of approximately 20 drill holes totaling about 5,000 metres. By the third quarter of 2014, the Company anticipates it will have completed a sufficient amount for drilling in order to commission an initial independent NI 43-101 mineral resource estimate on the Fire Zone which is expected to be disclosed by the end of 2014.

Example 5 is an example that provides limited information to investors.

Example 5 — boilerplate example

Due to the challenging economic environment, the Company does not plan to spend any funds on the ABC property until market conditions improve.

Example 6 clarifies what was spent in the current year as well as the issuer's future plans. Depending on the circumstances, the disclosure does not always need to be extensive to meet the requirements.

Example 6 — entity-specific example

In May, 2013 the Company spent $133,750 on exploration expenses related to the ABC property which consisted of an airborne geophysical survey (525 line km) to identify additional targets for drill testing. Four high priority targets were identified which may represent zones of mineralization similar to the Hill Zone discovered in the summer of 2012.

Due to the challenging economic environment, the Company does not plan to spend any additional funds on the ABC property until market conditions improve.

Example 7 illustrates how issuers can summarize and link the work completed on a specific project / property, the plans for that project / property, the status of the project relative to those plans and how the expenditures made relate to anticipated timing and costs to take the project to the next stage of the project plan.

Example 7 — entity-specific example

Property	Summary of Completed Activities (Jan 1, 2013–Dec 31, 2013)	Expenditures (Year ended Dec 31, 2013)	Plans for the Project for 2014	Planned Expenditures for 2014
A	• January to March 2013 — the Company completed 10 diamond drill holes (3,115 metres) testing for extensions of the Main Zone discovered in 2012. Five of these holes successfully intersected mineralization with similar gold grades and widths as observed in the Main Zone. These holes have traced the Main Zone for approximately 550 metres along strike and to a depth of 250 metres. One hole (A13-08) identified a new and potentially significant gold-bearing zone associated with a strong albite alteration.	$775,220 (total for the year)	• Conduct in-fill diamond drilling (approximately 15 holes totalling 4,500 metres) to provide sufficient data to support an initial NI 43-101 mineral resource estimate to be completed in Q3 or Q4 of 2014.	$750,000
	• Several of the 2013 drill holes were followed-up by downhole IP surveys which will be used to guide further exploration.		• Undertake initial metallurgical test work to determine potential gold recovery rates and processing method options.	$30,000
	• August 2013 — additional geological mapping and structural analysis was undertaken to better understand the complex nature of the Main Zone mineralization.		• Initial mineral resource estimate and independent NI 43-101 technical report.	$70,000
	• October to December 2013 — the Company compiled and assessed the exploration results obtained over the previous two drilling campaigns (25 drill holes totalling 11,440 metres) along with the geological, structural and geophysical data to assist with planning the next phase of work.			
B	• June to September 2013 — the Company completed 15	$469,840	• No further work is planned on the	—

Property	Summary of Completed Activities (Jan 1, 2013–Dec 31, 2013)	Expenditures (Year ended Dec 31, 2013)	Plans for the Project for 2014	Planned Expenditures for 2014
	diamond drill holes (2,750 metres) testing the most significant anomalies identified during the 2012 airborne VTEM electromagnetic and magnetic survey. Two holes (B13-04 and B13-12) intersected weakly mineralized zones associated with quartz veining which returned values ranging from 1-2 g/t gold over 1.5 metres. Although a number of other drill holes intersected several significant zones of sulphide mineralization and associated alteration, the assay results for these zones were disappointing.	(total for the year)	property and management has decided to return the property to the vendor.	
Other	• Fall 2013 — the Company completed several prospecting and soil geochemistry programs on non-material properties.	$31,120 (total for the year)	• Further work to be determined.	—

It is important to note that information included in the columns "Plans for the Project for 2014" and "Planned Expenditures for 2014" would be forward-looking information (**FLI**) subject to securities requirements.[5]

Reminder

Issuers with significant projects that have not yet generated revenue must disclose useful information for each material property or project that is not at the development or production stage including:

- description of the project
- work completed and expenditures made during the period
- current status of the project plans and budgets
- how expenditures relate to anticipated timing and cost to take the project to the next stage of the project plan

C. — Discussion of Operations — Issuers with producing mines

Disclosure requirement

Item 1.4 of Form 51-102F1 requires issuers to analyze their operations for the most recently completed period. As mentioned in Section B, the discussion should vary with the stage of development of an issuer's operations.

Commentary

When a mining issuer has mineral properties in production, it is likely those properties are material to the issuer's affairs. The MD&A may be the principal document to inform shareholders and potential investors about production figures, operating costs, new developments and the impact each of these has on mineral resources and mineral reserves. In addition to the general information applicable to mineral exploration properties, issuers with mines in production should inform the reader about the production activities.

To meet the requirements under Item 1.4 (e) of Form 51-102F1, issuers must include useful disclosure about the following items, on a property-by-property basis:

- development and production milestones
- mineral resources and mineral reserves
- operating and production information

Each of these items is described in further detail below.

Development and Production Milestones

Item 1.4(e) of Form 51-102F1 requires an issuer to discuss development milestones, which could include any of the following:

- mineral resource or mineral reserve estimates
- results of pre-feasibility or feasibility studies

---

[5]Forward-Looking Information requirements can be found in Part 4A — *Forward-Looking Information*, Part 4B — *FOFI and Financial Outlook* and Section 5.8 — *Disclosure Relating to Previously Disclosed Material Forward-Looking Information* of NI 51-102. We also refer issuers to OSC Staff Notice 51-721 *Forward-Looking Information Disclosure* issued on June 13, 2013 for guidance and examples on how to disclose FLI.

- exploration discoveries

- mineral resource or mineral reserve losses (for example, through ground failures)

- production decisions, expansion plans, or development of new resource zones

- expansions or changes to a processing plant

- name of the qualified person for the technical information

An issuer must also state whether there is a technical report supporting the disclosure of a mineral reserve, whether the technical report is the basis for any milestone and whether it forms the basis for a production decision. If the issuer has gone into production without a mineral reserve estimate based on at least a pre-feasibility study, the MD&A must disclose this information.

Mineral Resources and Mineral Reserves

Changes to a project's mineral resource base will usually be material information. In the MD&A, the issuer should:

- present the results of mine-area exploration programs and show their effect on mineral resource and mineral reserve estimates

- describe changes to mine plans, cut-off grades, process flow sheets, offtake or sales agreements or commodity prices, and their effect on mineral resource and mineral reserve estimates

Operating and Production Information

Both the annual and the interim MD&A should describe the results of operations including mine production, sales volume, and operating revenue. Some basic requirements for discussing an operating mine's results would include:

- mine production for the period

- mill throughput and head grades

- mill recovery and production of the mine's saleable commodities (for example, gold in doré or base metal in concentrate)

- operating cost, calculated using a recognized formula (e.g. all-in sustaining cash cost)

When production figures or operating costs change substantially from one interim period to the next or year to year, the MD&A should explain the reasons behind the change. The MD&A should describe:

- changes to mine plans, abandonment of uneconomic or inaccessible zones or accelerated production from parts of the mineral reserve

- development programs, particularly where those programs require the issuer to curtail production temporarily

- modifications to processes that affect production rates, mill throughput, head grade or recoveries

The MD&A should discuss the outlook for the operation for the forthcoming period (next year, in annual MD&A; next quarter, in interim MD&A):

- discuss any plans for significant capital expenditures, such as underground development, changes to plant capacity, or renewal of the mining fleet

- provide an outlook for expected production and operating costs

In example 8, the issuer does not include sufficient information to meet the requirements of item 1.4(e) of Form 51-102F1. While the issuer discloses the mine production for the period, the issuer does not state the gold grades, only that they improved, and does not explain why they changed. Further, there are no explanations about variances in production costs. We also note that the issuer does not explain the reasons leading to an impairment at Small Gold Mine. Finally, while the issuer includes an outlook, the information lacks sufficient details to be useful.

Example 8 — boilerplate example

Main Gold Mine

Total ore mined in the quarter ended June 30, 2013 was 102,200 tonnes at improved gold grades compared to last quarter's figures due to improvements made at the end of 2012. These improvements reduced the cash cost per ounce[6] to US$1,088 in the current quarter and the Company sold its increased gold production at an average price of US$1,404. Operations continued to focus on the Upper Vein.

Small Gold Mine

Higher than expected costs at Small Gold Mine resulted in an impairment charge of $10,345,956.

Outlook to September 30, 2013

- Continue to explore and develop Main Gold Mine.

---

[6]Examples 8 and 9 include non-GAAP financial measures such as "cash cost per ounce" and "all-in sustaining cash cost". For guidance on the disclosure of non-GAAP financial measures, please see CSA Staff Notice 52-306 (Revised) *Non-GAAP Financial Measures and Additional GAAP Measures* (**CSA SN 52-306**). To keep the examples shorter, guidance suggested in CSA SN 52-306 has not been included in Examples 8 and 9.

- Make improvements at Small Gold Mine.
- Obtain the required permits for other projects.

While example 9 is a simplified version of what an issuer would include in its MD&A, it illustrates how an issuer can provide meaningful information to investors by complying with the requirements. In this example, the issuer includes a comparative discussion of mine results with information about mine production for the period and reasons for the improvements, including figures for all-in sustaining cash costs. Operating decisions concerning Small Gold Mine are also described, including reasons leading to an impairment charge and its impact on the financial statements. Finally, plans for the issuer's two mines include specific information about what an investor can expect for the next interim period.

Example 9 — entity-specific example

Main Gold Mine

Total ore mined in the quarter ended June 30, 2013 was 102,200 tonnes at 6.47 g/t gold. The tonnage and grade is 36% and 11% above last quarter's figures, respectively, driven by productivity improvements at the mine and at the mill. The increased mining rate is attributable to a larger mechanized mining fleet suitably fitted to the mining method and improved underground infrastructure. The mill attained an average daily production rate of 920 tonnes at 94% gold recovery with improved performance attributable to the mill expansion completed at the end of 2012 with installation of a ball mill with twice the previous capacity. These improvements contributed to a significant year-over-year reduction in all-in sustaining cost per ounce of US$1,088 in the current quarter from US$1,242 last year. The Main Gold Mine sold a total of 14,686 ounces of gold at an average price of US$1,404 in the quarter compared to gold sales of 12,109 ounces at an average price of US$1,612 in the comparable period last year. Total capital development of underground workings during the quarter is 422 meters. Operations are focusing on the continued development of the Upper Vein which was identified by drilling in early 2012.

Small Gold Mine

Higher than expected costs at Small Gold Mine, that are now forecast to continue, prompted management to assess indicators of impairment related to the project and its associated assets. Management used a discounted cash flow model to calculate the recoverable amount. This resulted in an impairment charge of $10,345,956 to Small Gold Mine and its associated assets with $2,846,000 allocated to property, plant and equipment, and $7,499,956 to deferred development expenditure. Management is implementing several cost cutting measures related to mining and personnel to address the higher costs.

Outlook to September 30, 2013

- Continue to explore and develop the Upper Vein at Main Gold Mine.
- Implement cost cutting measures at Small Gold Mine while continuing to review and assess its continued viability.
- Work with local and federal governments to obtain the required permits to advance the Company's other gold projects.

Reminder

Issuers with producing mines or mines under development must include useful disclosure on a property — by-property basis about:

- development and production milestones
- mineral resources and mineral reserves
- operating and production information

D. — Liquidity and Capital Resources

Disclosure requirement

The MD&A should include a meaningful discussion of an issuer's liquidity including its ability to generate sufficient amounts of cash in the short and long term to maintain its operations. Items 1.6 and 1.7 of Form 51-102F1 require an issuer to disclose, among other things:

- its ability to meet planned growth or fund development activities
- its working capital requirements
- its capital expenditures, including an analysis of expenditures not yet committed but required to meet planned growth or to fund development activities

If an issuer has or expects to have a working capital deficiency, the issuer must discuss its ability in both the short and long term to meet its obligations as they come due. The issuer must also discuss how it plans to remedy the working capital deficiency.

Commentary

Meaningful analysis in an issuer's MD&A of material cash requirements, historical sources and uses of cash as well as material trends and uncertainties is important so investors can understand the issuer's ability to generate cash and meet cash requirements. A good analysis of liquidity position involves a meaningful discussion of cash flows from operations, investing, and financing, beyond stating balances from the financial statements. In particular, a detailed liquidity discussion is especially important for smaller non-producing issuers given the constant demands for financing to meet project milestones. The disclosure should explain why management believes it has sufficient resources. Issuers can improve their discussion of working capital requirements by better explaining and quantifying their working capital needs and how their working capital needs relate to their plan for the next fiscal year or up to the next business milestone. Having working capital in excess of last year's expenditures is not sufficient for investors to understand why the issuer has sufficient financial resources if the plan/outlook isn't also disclosed.

Rather than repeating items that are reported in the statement of cash flows, an issuer should concentrate on disclosing the primary drivers of cash flows and the reasons for material changes in major sub-items underlying the line items reported in the financial statements. Issuers should also consider whether they need to provide enhanced disclosures about significant debt instruments, guarantees, and covenants.

Without providing further details, including quantification, example 10 does not allow an investor to assess whether or not the issuer's statement that it has sufficient liquidity to meet its current working capital requirements and fund its development activities is reasonable.

Example 10 — boilerplate example

Management believes that the funds currently on hand are sufficient to meet the Company's short-term obligations.

Example 11 — entity-specific example

The Company's working capital requirements for the past year are discussed in detail in the Discussion of Operations section. Fixed costs to maintain operations, pay taxes and royalties and upkeep are about $60,000 per annum. Corporate and general costs to maintain the requirements of a listed company have been about $95,000 in both 2013 and 2012. Therefore, minimum working capital requirements are estimated at $155,000 per year.

Estimated Working Capital Requirements 2014

Complete preliminary economic assessment (PEA)	$ 300,000
Corporate & general	$ 155,000
Convertible note repayment	$ 1,200,000
Total	$ 1,655,000

As at December 31, 2013, the Company's cash and cash equivalents were $684,000. The Company has access to sufficient funds to meet its current overhead requirements. The Company also has sufficient cash to fund the PEA. The resulting PEA report will provide the basis of a decision to advance development, finance further exploration or consider other options. The Company does not currently have sufficient resources to repay the convertible notes in December 2014. The Company plans to complete an offering of new debt securities in the fall to fund the repayment.

Example 11 clearly illustrates the issuer's current financial position. Clear entity-specific disclosure is important so that investors can understand any anticipated funding shortfalls and financing resources available to meet spending commitments and continue key projects. It is important to focus on realistic solutions and providing an analysis that will let investors know how the issuer will carry on its business.

Disclosure is helpful, even when exploration has been put on hold. A complete discussion of the issuer's financial obligations and discretionary expenses helps an investor better understand how an issuer is meeting its obligations during a time when exploration is on hold. This is an opportunity for an issuer to explain to investors how it is controlling its costs, the minimum amount of funds it needs to get through the next period and how the issuer expects to finance it.

It is also important that the discussion in the liquidity section ties to the operating plan. In our Review, we noted instances where there was disclosure of a plan to spend significant amounts to develop a property. In some of these instances the liquidity section only discussed current working capital requirements which was inconsistent with the discussion of operations, and the plans to develop the property. The liquidity section should be a complete discussion including cash requirements for both operating and capital requirements planned for in the coming year. Obligations for payments with respect to flow through shares should also be included when discussing cash requirements. Example 12 shows how an issuer may want to provide an update of their obligations relating to flow-through shares.

Example 12 — entity-specific example

In January, the Company issued $3.5 million of flow-through shares. In addition to the amounts disclosed in the contractual obligations table, the Company is committed to spend $3.5 million in Canadian exploration expenses. As of March 31 the Company had spent $0.7 million in Canadian exploration expenses, the remaining balance of $2.8 million must be spent by December 31, 2014.

When disclosing capital requirements it is important that all obligations are discussed so that investors can understand what is required for the issuer to continue operating its business. Many issuers simply provide the contractual obligations table required by item 1.6 of Form 51-102F1 but neglect to provide a discussion of these obligations.

Reminder

To be meaningful, the discussion of liquidity and capital resources must address in detail all future cash requirements of an operating and capital nature and how they will be funded. Simply disclosing that management believes it has sufficient resources to fund currently planned exploration or development is not sufficient.

E. — Transactions between Related Parties

Disclosure requirement

For issuers that enter into transactions between related parties, item 1.9 of Form 51-102F1 requires the relationship be discussed and the related person or entity be identified in the MD&A. In addition to identifying the related party, the issuer must discuss the business purpose of the transaction, the recorded amount of the transaction and how it was measured. If there are any ongoing commitments related to the transaction, these must also be disclosed.

Commentary

RPTs often play a significant role in the operations of businesses as they grow. These transactions can vary from simple contracts for key management personnel to complex financing agreements. While RPTs may provide the issuer with benefits that are not available from other arms-length parties or to other issuers on the same terms, disclosure needs to insure there is transparency around these transactions so readers of the MD&A understand the business purpose of these transactions. In addition, the measurement basis used is important disclosure so the value of the transaction can be evaluated. Example 13 illustrates the type of RPT disclosure we frequently saw in our Review.

Example 13 — boilerplate example

During the year, the Company paid $148,541 for services to a firm in which a director is a partner.

Example 13 lacks detail as it does not explain the services provided, how they were valued or the business reason for entering into the transaction. In addition, a reader cannot tell from this statement which director was involved in the RPT. It is not sufficient to disclose that "the Company paid for services to a firm related to one of the directors"; rather one must clearly identify the specific person or entity.

Example 14 shows how the disclosure in example 13 could be improved to meet the requirements in item 1.9 of Form 51-102F1. In example 14, the name of the related party is included, the business purpose of the transaction is discussed and how the transaction was valued is described.

Example 14 — entity-specific example

During the year, the Company paid professional fees of $148,541 to Best Miner LLP, a law firm of which Joe Prospector, a director of the Board, is a partner. These services were incurred in the normal course of operations for general corporate matters, attendance at committee and board meetings, as well as evaluating business opportunities. All services were made on terms equivalent to those that prevail with arm's length transactions.

Example 15 is another instance of boilerplate disclosure relating to a RPT transaction.

Example 15 — boilerplate example

During the year, the Company paid $200,000 of interest on a loan payable to a majority shareholder.

Example 16 shows both the business purpose and the amount of the transaction.

Example 16 — entity-specific example

During the year, the Company paid $200,000 in interest on a loan of $2,000,000 received from the CEO, who is a majority shareholder. The unsecured loan bears interest at 10% per annum and matures in five years with an option by the Company to extinguish the debt at any time without penalty. The transaction was recorded in the Company's financial statements at the exchange amount. The Company entered into this related party transaction because alternate sources of financing were unavailable due to the Company's limited operating history, lack of collateral and limited access to public financing due to current global financial conditions.

For mining issuers, it is not uncommon for the acquisition of a property to come from a related party. Example 17 is an example of boilerplate disclosure relating to the acquisition of such a property.

Example 17 — boilerplate example

In March 2013, the Company closed an acquisition of the Golden Mine property with Mr. Striker, a director of the Company. The company issued 500,000 shares to Mr. Striker for a 100% interest in the property, subject to a 1.5% net smelter return retained by Mr. Striker.

In addition to disclosing the nature and relationship of the related party, it is also important to disclose the business purpose of the transaction so that investors can evaluate these services and the business purpose of the related party transaction. The following example highlights how the issuer disclosed the purpose of the transaction.

Example 18 — entity-specific example

In March 2013, the Company closed an acquisition of the Golden Mine property with Mr. Striker, a director of the Company. The transaction was approved by the board of directors with Mr. Striker abstaining from the vote. The Company issued 500,000 shares to Mr. Striker for a 100% interest in the property, subject to a 1.5% net smelter return retained by Mr. Striker. An independent valuation by ABC Consultants stated the transaction was within a range of fair values for a similar mineral property. The transaction gives the company a large land position near the Brilliant Mine discovery of DEF Minerals Limited.

Reminder

By virtue of their nature, transactions between related parties lack the independence inherent in arm's length transactions. Investors need to understand who are the specific parties involved, the business purpose and economic substance of RPTs, so they can understand the rationale for transactions and impact on the business.

F. — Risk Factors and Uncertainties
Disclosure requirement

To comply with item 1.4(g) of Form 51-102F1, the MD&A must include a discussion of risk factors and uncertainties the issuer believes will materially affect its future financial performance. This discussion should include entity specific information about risks that may affect or have affected the issuer and that would be most likely to influence an investor's decision to purchase its securities, risks that affect the issuer's financial statements or risks that are reasonably likely to affect them in the future. Where possible, the impact of the risk should be quantified.

Commentary

Investors need to understand the entity specific risks and how those risks may impact the issuer and its business, both of which may affect an investment decision or the value of its investment should the risks be realized. To avoid boilerplate disclosure, reporting issuers should be more specific on the potential consequences of risks to the company.

We noted that issuers often conclude an individual risk discussion by saying that if the risk was realized it "could have a material adverse impact on the Company", without stating what that specifically may be.

- Would it affect revenues, cash flows, costs?

- Would the impact potentially be isolated such that it could be managed swiftly or would it have a sweeping pervasive effect that could endanger the Company's solvency/viability, or would its effect lie somewhere in between?

- For how long can the issuer rely on existing sources of liquidity before additional financing is needed?

These risks should be quantified when possible.

When reviewing the MD&A, it is often difficult based on the disclosure provided to determine which are the most immediate or most serious risks to the issuer. The AIF requires issuers to disclose the risks in order of seriousness from the most serious to the least serious. Form 51-102F1 does not have a similar instruction but rather directs issuers to focus the MD&A on material information. We have found many issuers include a lengthy list of risks without any indication of the level of exposure or significance of the risks. When presented this way, key risk information may become lost amid less relevant information.

In addition to providing a detailed and quantified description of potential risks, to provide meaningful risk disclosures to investors, issuers should update their risk disclosures when circumstances change. It appears from our Review, that there is little to no updating of risk disclosures year over year or from annual to subsequent interim periods. Issuers should consider enhancing processes to monitor for changes in risks to ensure their disclosures are comprehensive and reflect current circumstances. A statement in the MD&A that the risks remain unchanged or a summary of the changes since the previous disclosures would help investors focus on new information. Issuers should also consider disclosing anticipated future changes in risk exposure.

Risk disclosure needs to be specific. As seen in the boilerplate example below, knowing that an issuer faces normal risks inherent to the mining industry does not inform investors of the issuer's specific operations.

Example 19 — boilerplate example

The Company's operations are located in Foreign Country X. The company is subject to the political risks and economic considerations of operating in Foreign Country X.

Knowing the specific risks an issuer faces helps a reader of the MD&A understand and evaluate the risk. The disclosure in example 19 is boilerplate and could apply to many issuers operating in foreign countries. By contrast, the disclosure in example 20 shows how the impact of the foreign operations could specifically impact the issuer.

Example 20 — entity-specific example

The Company's principal property is located in Region Y of Foreign Country X. Consequently, the Company is subject to certain risks associated with foreign ownership, including currency, inflation, political and property title risk. On January 13, 2013, a coup was initiated by members of the Region Y army, creating uncertainty within the area where the company operates. Currently, operations are continuing but travel and access to the property may be curtailed due to political instability or risks to personnel which may result in project delays. The Company is closely monitoring the situation and management will continue to provide updates.

Reminder

To be meaningful to investors, risk disclosure needs to be entity-specific and updated regularly.

G. — Use of Financing Proceeds

Disclosure requirement

Item 1.4(i) of Form 51-102F1 requires issuers that have raised capital in a prospectus offering to compare, in tabular form, any changes in the use of proceeds and to explain the impact of the changes on the issuer's ability to achieve its business objectives and milestones.

Commentary

In a prospectus offering an issuer must disclose the principle purposes for which the funds raised will be used. It is important that investors be updated on how the money raised has been spent as the funds raised for mining issuers are often earmarked for specific projects or stages of specific projects. This information allows investors to assess how an issuer is spending the proceeds raised in an offering document.

Answering the following questions in the MD&A provides useful disclosure to investors:

- How does the nature and amount of expenditures made by the issuer compare to the use of proceeds from previous financing?

- How do variances impact future operations?
- How will the variance affect the issuer's ability to achieve its business objective and milestones?
- Will the issuer require additional financing to meet its next milestone?

2. — How to Avoid Boilerplate Disclosure

Good public disclosure and comprehensive MD&A will help investors understand your business and will assist issuers in complying with the requirements in NI 51-102 and Form 51-102F1. Considering the following questions may assist issuers in preparing a meaningful and useful MD&A.

Venture Issuer Disclosure

Areas	Considerations

Additional disclosure for venture issuers without significant revenue	• Is there a breakdown of material components of:
	        • E&E assets or expenditures?
	        • General and administrative expenses?
	        • Other material costs?
	• Has the breakdown been provided for each of the last two financial years?
	Note: Considered to be a material component of cost if the cost exceeds greater that 20% of total amount of class or $25,000

Mining exploration and development issuers	• Have E&E assets or expenditures been presented on a property-by-property basis?

Discussion of Operations

Areas	Considerations

Exploration Projects	• Has the following disclosure been made for each material project:
	        • A description of the project?
	        • Plans for the project?
	        • Status of the project relative to that plan?
	        • Expenditures made to date and how these relate to anticipated timing and costs to take the project to the next stage of the project plan?

Availability of capital resources	• Are sufficient resources available to meet projected capital commitments? If not, is there disclosure about the expected source(s) of funds to meet those commitments? *Note: Refer to discussion on "liquidity and capital resources"*

Variance in use of prospectus proceeds	• If capital has been raised from a prospectus offering:
	        • Has any difference between the planned use of proceeds and their actual use, been explained?
	        • Has the issuer disclosed how these variances may impact the issuer's ability to take the project to the next stage of the project plan?

Liquidity and Capital Resources

Areas	Considerations

Ability to generate sufficient cash	• Has the issuer analyzed its ability to generate sufficient cash, in the short term and the long term to:
	    • Address working capital requirements?
	    • Maintain properties and agreements in good standing?
	    • Meet spending commitments?
	    • Finance new opportunities?

Working capital requirements	• Are the issuer's working capital requirements disclosed?
	• If a working capital deficiency exists, or is expected, has the issuer discussed and analyzed its:
	    • Ability to meet obligations as they become due?
	    • Plans, if any, to remedy the deficiency?

Spending requirements	• Is there disclosure and analysis about:
	    • Exploration and development expenditures required to maintain properties or agreements in good standing?
	    • Amount, nature and purpose of commitments?
	    • Expenditures that are not yet committed but are required to maintain the issuer's capacity or finance new opportunities?

Sources of financing	• Have the expected sources of financing been identified? • Has the issuer discussed known trends or expected fluctuations in capital resources, including changes in mix and relative cost of resources? • Has the issuer discussed how difficulties in obtaining financing could affect the issuer including status of projects, financing operations and ability to continue as going concern?

Transactions between Related Parties

Areas	Considerations
Disclosure of all RPTs	• Are all transactions between related parties disclosed and discussed?

Identity and relationship of related party	• Is there disclosure of:
	    • The name of the related party (not only the related party's position or relationship with the issuer)?
	    • The name of ultimate beneficiaries of the RPT, where the transaction is conducted through a corporate entity?
	    • The relationship between the issuer and the related party?

Business purpose and economic substance of transaction	• Are the reasons for entering into the RPTs disclosed and explained?
	    • Are the economic benefits to the issuer from each RPT disclosed and explained?
	    • Is there disclosure of the consideration that was paid?
	    • Is there an explanation as to why the issuer acquired assets or services from a related party as opposed to an arm's length party?
	    • Is the discussion quantified where possible?
	Note: Avoid generic descriptions such as "consulting" or "for services performed"

Areas	Considerations
Recorded amount of transaction and measurement basis used	• Is the recorded amount of the transaction and the measurement basis used disclosed?
Ongoing or contractual or other commitments	• Is there disclosure and discussion of ongoing contractual or other commitments arising out of RPTs?
Processes and procedures for identifying, evaluating and approving RPTs	• Is there a description of management and board processes and procedures for identifying, evaluating and approving RPTs?

Risk Factors Disclosure

Areas	Considerations
MD&A disclosure	• Is there a discussion of important trends and risks that have affected the issuer's financial statements? • Is there a discussion of trends and risks that are reasonably likely to affect the issuer's financial statements in the future? • Is there a discussion of commitments, events, risks or uncertainties that the issuer reasonably believes will materially affect its future performance? *Note: An issuer should not provide a "laundry list" of every conceivable risk*
Suggested risk management practices	• Does the board have a full understanding of the risks facing the issuer and how those relate to the overall risk appetite of the issuer? • Does the board take appropriate steps to stay informed of key developments that could increase the issuer's risk exposure? • Is there a strategy in place to ensure that significant risks are identified and managed by the board and management?

Part C — Conclusion

1. — Conclusion

The MD&A is a key disclosure document that provides information about an issuer's present and future operations and performance. A robust MD&A is necessary to meet the legal requirements of NI 51-102 and supports capital formation by providing investors with key information for investment purposes. Using the guidance in the Notice when preparing interim and annual MD&A will assist issuers in providing meaningful disclosure in their MD&A.

Given its importance to investors, this is an area of disclosure we will continue to assess in our ongoing CD and prospectus review programs. Further information about the CD review program can be found in CSA Staff Notice 51-312 *Harmonized Continuous Disclosure Review Program*. We remind issuers that they will be expected to take corrective action for instances of non-compliance with the MD&A requirements.

OSC Staff Notice 51-723 — Report on Staff's Review of Related Party Transaction Disclosure and Guidance on Best Practices

Date: January 29, 2015

38 O.S.C.B. 845

1. — Introduction

Related Party Transactions (**RPT**) are a regular feature of business and commerce and can be beneficial to a company. Many issuers, particularly smaller issuers, rely extensively on RPTs because RPTs enable issuers to advance their business on a cost-effective basis by leveraging their existing relationships. Under International Accounting Standards, a RPT is a transfer of resources, services or obligations between an issuer and a party related to the issuer or its executive officers or directors.[1] Under Multilateral Instrument 61-101 *Protection of Minority Security Holders in Special Transactions* (**MI 61-101**), a RPT is a transaction between the issuer and a related party of the issuer at the time the transaction is agreed to as a consequence of which the issuer directly or indirectly enters into specified transactions, including a purchase or sale of assets, issuing securities or subscribing for securities, borrowing or lending money, and forgiving debts or liabilities.

While RPTs can be beneficial, due to the inherent conflicts of interest, such transactions have the potential in certain circumstances to be unfair or abusive to the issuer or security holders.[2] Controlling shareholders, conflicted directors or others with influence may enter into transactions that are not beneficial to the issuer or may value RPTs in a manner that benefits the related party over the interests of the issuer and its security holders. Accordingly, it is essential, in connection with the disclosure, valuation, review and approval processes followed for RPTs that all security holders be treated in a manner that is fair and perceived to be fair.[3]

Fair treatment of security holders is essential to the protection of the public interest in maintaining capital markets that operate efficiently, fairly and with integrity.[4] In order to assess fairness, it is critical that issuers provide full and adequate disclosure to their shareholders about these transactions, so investors can better understand their business purpose and value. This is the case for ongoing transactions reflected in normal continuous disclosure filings as well as special transactions subject to MI 61-101.

We reviewed 100 issuers to assess RPT disclosure as described below. Our review found that almost all issuers engaged in some form of RPT and provided disclosure with respect to them. There is a general awareness of the need to provide information on RPTs in both the financial statements and the MD&A. However, our review found that in some instances the disclosure lacked an appropriate level of detail. This staff notice provides insight into areas where issuers can focus on improving their disclosure, including examples. In addition, boards can consider this guidance in developing policies for the identification and review of RPTs and ensuring that sufficient detail of the RPT is included in the issuers' public filings.

2. — Scope of Review

In Canada, financial statement disclosure requirements under International Financial Reporting Standards (**IFRS**) and disclosure requirements under Management's Discussion and Analysis (**MD&A**) in Form 51-102F1 *Management's Discussion & Analysis* (**Form 51-102F1**) serve to ensure that investors are provided with sufficient information to make informed investment decisions. In addition, MI 61-101 outlines the requirements for more significant RPTs to ensure fair treatment of security holders. The following table provides a high level overview of the disclosure requirements under these accounting and securities rules.

IAS 24	Form 51-102F1	MI 61-101
• Relationship of parents and subsidiaries • Nature of the related party relationship • Amount of RPT, including commitments	• Relationship of related parties • Identity of related parties • Business purpose of the RPT • Recorded amount and measurement basis used • Ongoing commitments	• Description of the RPT • Purpose and business reasons for RPT • Effect of RPT on issuer • Review and approval process followed • Description of the interest of every related party and interested party • Exemptions from the formal valuation and minority approval requirements relied upon

Staff of the Ontario Securities Commission (**OSC**) conducted a review of 100 Ontario reporting issuers with the following two objectives:

- assessing issuer compliance with RPT disclosure requirements under securities and financial statement rules; and
- understanding the range of practice around issuer's corporate governance including their disclosure and approval of RPTs.

The sample of 100 issuers was selected randomly across all industries.

---

[1]Section 9 of International Accounting Standard 24 *Related Party Disclosures,*

[2]Section 1.1 of Companion Policy 61-101CP *To Multilateral Instrument 61-101 Protection of Minority Security Holders in Special Transactions.*

[3]Section 1.1 of Companion Policy 61-101CP *To Multilateral Instrument 61-101 Protection of Minority Security Holders in Special Transactions.*

[4]Section 1.1 of Companion Policy 61-101CP *To Multilateral Instrument 61-101 Protection of Minority Security Holders in Special Transactions.*

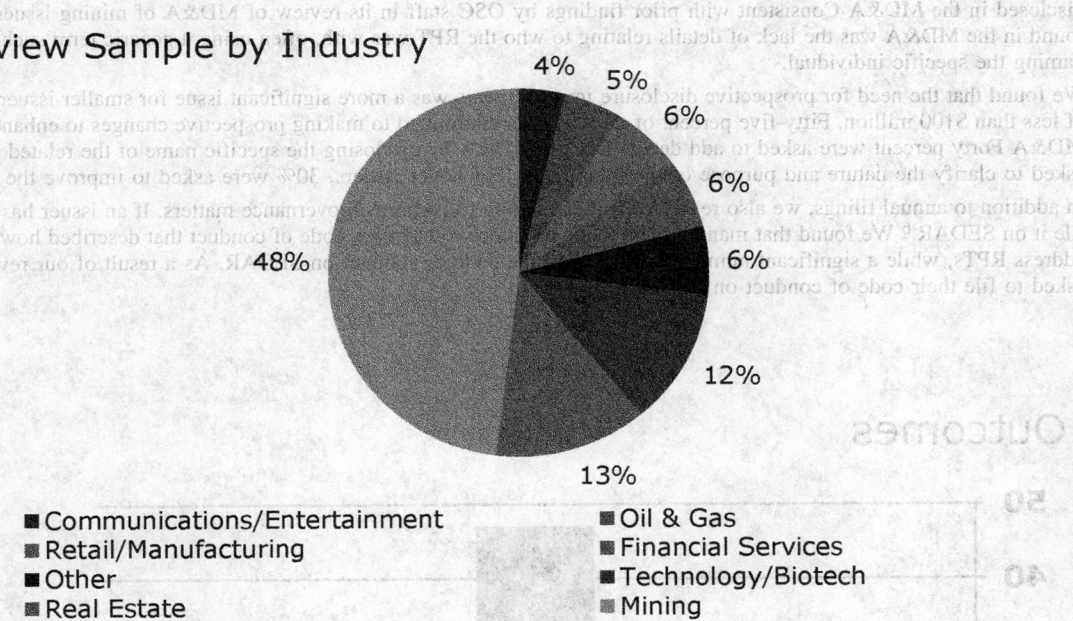

Review Sample by Industry

4%
5%
6%
6%
6%
12%
13%
48%

- ■ Communications/Entertainment
- ■ Retail/Manufacturing
- ■ Other
- ■ Real Estate
- ■ Oil & Gas
- ■ Financial Services
- ■ Technology/Biotech
- ■ Mining

Forty-seven percent of issuers selected were venture issuers and 53% were non-venture issuers. Those reviewed included issuers of various sizes based on market capitalization. Of the issuers selected, 25% had a market capitalization of less than $5 million and 33% had a market capitalization of greater than $100 million. The remaining 42% had a market capitalization between $5 million and $100 million.

3. — Summary of Results

We found that 96% of issuers disclosed RPTs in their financial statements and / or within their MD&A The most common types of RPTs found in our review were executive compensation, purchase of services or products from a related party, leases of property and loans to or from a related party. Other less common RPTs included sales of products or services to a related party.

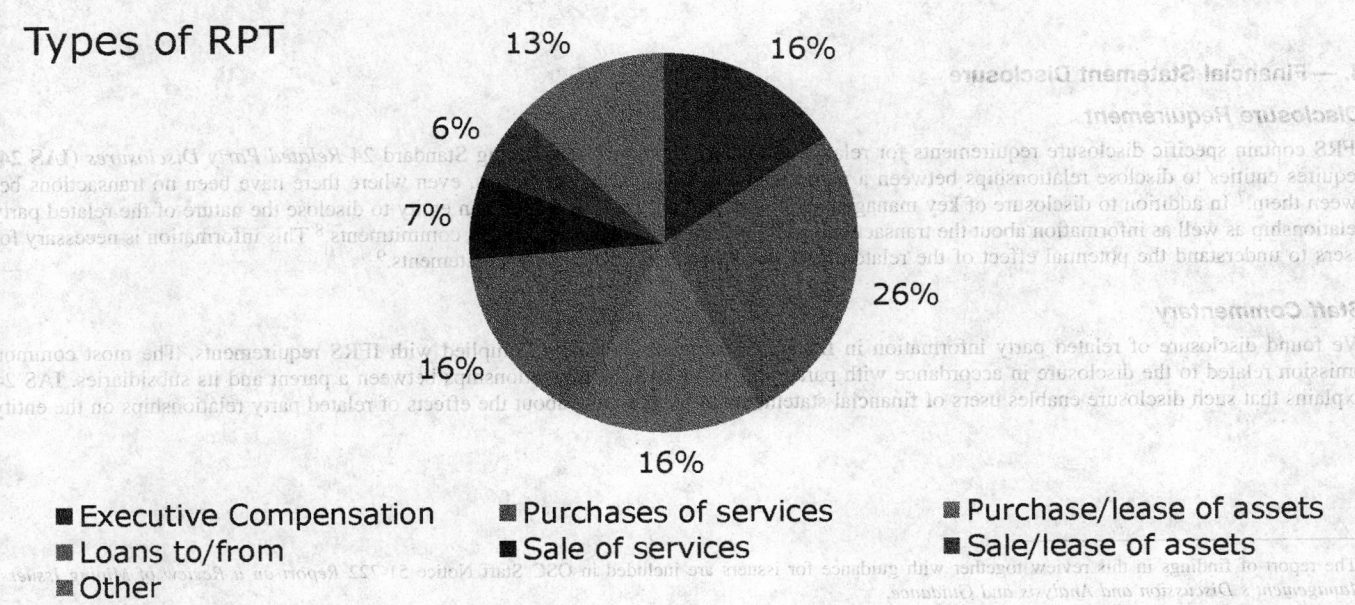

Types of RPT

13%
16%
6%
7%
26%
16%
16%
16%

- ■ Executive Compensation
- ■ Loans to/from
- ■ Other
- ■ Purchases of services
- ■ Sale of services
- ■ Purchase/lease of assets
- ■ Sale/lease of assets

Overall, financial statement and MD&A disclosure met most of the key disclosure requirements and there were no instances where we required restatements. In 17% of the financial statements reviewed, a prospective improvement in disclosure was requested, most frequently relating to disclosure of the relationship between an issuer and its parent or subsidiaries. In 47% percent of MD&A reviewed, the main issue related to disclosure that was overly generic and not specific to the issuer. Prospective changes were requested to improve clarity about RPTs disclosed in the MD&A Consistent with prior findings by OSC staff in its review of MD&A of mining issuers,[5] the most significant issue found in the MD&A was the lack of details relating to who the RPT was with, often using a generic term such as a "director" as opposed to naming the specific individual.

We found that the need for prospective disclosure improvements was a more significant issue for smaller issuers with a market capitalization of less than $100 million. Fifty-five percent of these issuers committed to making prospective changes to enhance the RPT disclosure in their MD&A Forty percent were asked to add details to their MD&A by disclosing the specific name of the related party involved and 33% were asked to clarify the nature and purpose of the transaction. For larger issuers, 30% were asked to improve the disclosure in their MD&A.

In addition to annual filings, we also reviewed filings relating to corporate governance matters. If an issuer has a code of conduct, they must file it on SEDAR.[6] We found that many issuers made reference to having a code of conduct that described how the board of directors should address RPTs, while a significant number had not filed the code of conduct on SEDAR. As a result of our review, 20% of the issuers were asked to file their code of conduct on SEDAR.

Outcomes

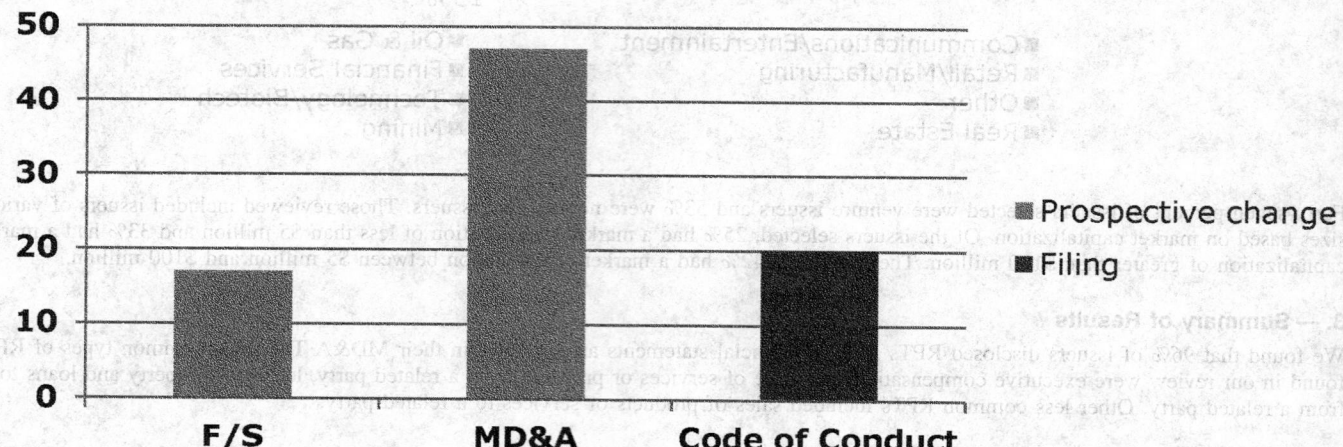

4. — Financial Statement Disclosure

Disclosure Requirement

IFRS contain specific disclosure requirements for related parties. International Accounting Standard 24 *Related Party Disclosures* (**IAS 24**) requires entities to disclose relationships between a parent and any subsidiaries it controls, even where there have been no transactions between them.[7] In addition to disclosure of key management compensation, IAS 24 requires an entity to disclose the nature of the related party relationship as well as information about the transactions and outstanding balances, including commitments.[8] This information is necessary for users to understand the potential effect of the related party relationship on the financial statements.[9]

Staff Commentary

We found disclosure of related party information in financial statements generally complied with IFRS requirements. The most common omission related to the disclosure in accordance with paragraph 13 of IAS 24 of relationships between a parent and its subsidiaries. IAS 24 explains that such disclosure enables users of financial statements to form a view about the effects of related party relationships on the entity

---

[5]The report of findings in this review together with guidance for issuers are included in OSC Staff Notice 51-722 *Report on a Review of Mining Issuers' Management's Discussion and Analysis and Guidance.*

[6]Section 2.3 of *National Instrument 58-101 Disclosure of Corporate Governance Practices.*

[7]Paragraph 13 of IAS 24.

[8]Paragraph 18 of IAS 24.

[9]Paragraph 14 of IAS 24.

and should be disclosed irrespective of whether there have been transactions between the parties.[10] Nine issuers agreed to prospectively include this disclosure.

In some circumstances, we found issuers disclosed only the existence of RPTs and outstanding amounts payable to, or receivable from, related parties, without providing further description of the nature and terms of the transactions. More descriptive disclosure provides transparency and clarity, which allows investors to better assess the merits of the transactions, especially when the transactions are material or not in the normal course. As a result of our review, four issuers were asked to prospectively provide more descriptive disclosure in their next set of financial statements.

Example — Entity-specific Disclosure

Disclosure of relationships between a company and both its parent and / or its subsidiaries is required regardless of whether there have been transactions between them. Some companies omit this disclosure. The following is an example of appropriate disclosure when this requirement is applicable:

The following lists the Company's corporate relationships:

Parent:

AA Parent P.L.C., a company incorporated in the United Kingdom and listed on the London Stock Exchange, is the Company's parent company. There were no transactions, other than dividends paid, between the Company and AA Parent P.L.C. during the financial year.

Subsidiaries:

Name	Country of Incorporation	% equity interest 2013	2012
X Limited	Canada	80.0	-
Y Limited	Canada	95.0	95.0
Z Inc.	United States	100.0	100.0

Joint venture in which the Company is a venturer:

The Company has a 50% interest in V Limited (2012: 50%). Please refer to note 10 for more disclosure related to this joint venture.

5. — MD&A

Disclosure Requirement

The MD&A should complement and supplement the financial statements. While many of the MD&A requirements for RPTs in Form 51-102F1 are similar to the requirements under IAS 24, Form 51-102F1 specifically requires an issuer to identify the related person or entity, as well as to discuss the business purpose of the transaction.[11]

Staff Commentary MD&A disclosure of RPTs is intended to provide both qualitative and quantitative information that is necessary for an understanding of the business purpose and economic substance of a transaction.[12] In order to meet this requirement, the disclosure should be specific and detailed. Overall, we found the disclosure in the MD&A often repeated the disclosure in the financial statements and did not provide the additional disclosure required in the MD&A Thirty-six percent of issuers reviewed did not provide details about the related party, often using generic terms such as an "officer" or "director" rather than specifically identifying the individual involved in the transaction. In addition, only 38% of the issuers reviewed provided the business purpose for all of their RPTs.

Example — Boilerplate Disclosure

The disclosure below is an example of boilerplate disclosure for RPTs that does not disclose the identity of the related party and the business purpose of the transaction:

During the year, the Company paid $120,000 to a director as lease payments. As at December 31, 2014, the amount outstanding to the director was $10,000.

Example — Entity-specific Disclosure

A better example of disclosure for RPTs would be as follows:

During the year, the Company paid $120,000 to Mr. John Smith, a director of the Company, as lease payments for leasing the space used as the Company's warehouse. The current lease expires on December 31, 2015. The terms of the lease were reviewed by disinterested directors of the Board, and were found to be comparable to market terms. The lease is to be reviewed by disinterested directors of the Board every two years and renewed on the condition that the terms are comparable to, or more favourable than, market terms. As at December 31, 2014, the amount outstanding to Mr. Smith was $10,000, which represents the amount for one month's rent.

---

[10]Paragraph 14 of IAS 24.

[11]Item 1.9 of Form 51-102F1.

[12]Item 1.9 of Form 51-102F1.

6. — Corporate Governance Practice Disclosure

Disclosure Requirement

While Canadian securities requirements do not mandate corporate governance practices, National Policy 58-201 *Corporate Governance Guidelines* (**NP 58-201**) contains recommended guidance on corporate governance practices. For example, section 3.8 of NP 58-201 states that the board should adopt a written code of business conduct and ethics that addresses, among other things, conflicts of interest, including transactions and agreements in respect of which a director or executive officer has a material interest. National Instrument 58-101 *Disclosure of Corporate Governance Practices* (**NI 58-101**) contains requirements for disclosure of corporate governance practices for non-venture and venture issuers. A non-venture issuer is required by item 5(b) of Form 58-101F1 *Corporate Governance Disclosure* (**Form 58-101F1**) to describe in its management information circular or annual information form any steps the board takes to ensure that directors exercise independent judgment in considering transactions and agreements in respect of which a director or executive officer has a material interest. Further, item 5(a) of Form 58-101F1 requires non-venture issuers to disclose whether or not the board has adopted a written code of business conduct and ethics for directors, officers and employees, and if so, to make certain disclosure related to the code.

While only non-venture issuers are subject to the requirements in Form 58-101F1, item 4 of Form 58-101F2 requires venture issuers to describe what steps, if any, the board takes to encourage and promote a culture of ethical business conduct. Venture issuers are encouraged to disclose whether the board has adopted a written code of business conduct and ethics to help investors to assess their corporate governance practices with respect to RPTs.

If an issuer has adopted a code, the issuer should file a copy of the code on SEDAR in accordance with section 2.3 of NI 58-101. This requirement applies to both venture and non-venture issuers.

Staff Commentary

The board of directors plays a key role in overseeing the identification of RPTs and ensuring all RPTs are disclosed. We encourage the board of a reporting issuer to adopt a written code of business conduct and ethics that establishes written standards reasonably designed to promote integrity and to deter wrongdoing. Effective codes apply to directors, officers and employees of the issuer and address, among other things, conflicts of interest and transactions and agreements where a director or officer has an interest, including RPTs. It is good practice to require directors, officers and employees to certify on an annual basis that they have complied with the code.

We also encourage issuers to consider providing more detailed disclosure about their process for identifying, evaluating and approving RPTs. This could include considering:

- whether the board or a committee of the board reviews and approves RPTs;
- whether a materiality threshold has been adopted to determine which RPTs are subject to independent review by the board or a committee of the board;
- whether the issuer has rules, guidelines or procedures for RPTs conducted in the normal course of business; and
- whether the issuer has rules, guidelines or processes to satisfy itself that a non-material RPT is transacted at fair value.

The review found that most non-venture issuers have generally complied with the requirement in item 5(b) of Form 58-101F1 to describe any steps the board takes to ensure that directors exercise independent judgment in considering conflicted transactions. However, twelve of the non-venture issuers in our sample either did not disclose whether they had a written code of business conduct and ethics in accordance with item 5(a) of Form 58-101F1, or did not file a code on SEDAR in accordance with section 2.3 of NI 58-101 where they indicated that they had one. At staff's request, the 12 issuers agreed to make the appropriate disclosure prospectively and, if applicable, file the code.

In the case where a venture issuer chooses to adopt a code of conduct, they must file it on SEDAR pursuant to section 2.3 of NI 58-101. Eight of the venture issuers in our sample made reference to a code of conduct that had not been filed on SEDAR. At staff's request, the issuers agreed to file their code of conduct.

Example — Boilerplate Disclosure

The following is a boilerplate example that does not provide details of the process that the audit committee or management undertakes in their review:

> The audit committee reviews and approves all material related party transactions in which the Company is involved or which the Company proposes to enter into.

Example — Entity-specific Disclosure

A better example would be as follows:

> The Company's management team discusses all related party transactions. In considering related party transactions, management will assess the materiality of related party transactions on a case-by-case basis with respect to both the qualitative and quantitative aspects of the proposed related party transaction. Related party transactions that are in the normal course are subject to the same processes and controls as other transactions, that is, they are subject to standard approval procedures and management oversight, but will also be considered by management for reasonability against fair value. Related party transactions that are found to be material are subject to review and approval by the Company's audit committee which is comprised of independent directors.

7. — Special Transactions

Requirement

MI 61-101 regulates significant RPTs including those transactions involving directors or senior management of a reporting issuer. When RPTs are undertaken, MI 61-101 requires the board of directors to play an important role in ensuring that all security holders are treated fairly and that the interests of the issuer and minority shareholders are protected. The board is responsible for ensuring that investors are provided with sufficient information to make an informed decision to approve or challenge the approval of a RPT.[13] The board, or an independent special committee appointed by the board, is responsible for overseeing RPTs by, among other things, supervising the preparation of a formal valuation,[14] unless specified exemptions apply,[15] and providing enhanced disclosure in information circulars and material change reports.[16] In addition, RPTs are subject to minority shareholder approval under MI 61-101,[17] unless specified exemptions are available.[18]

If a material change report is required to be filed with respect to a RPT, the material change report must include specific disclosure of the RPT, including:

> a description of the transaction and its material terms;
>
> the purpose and business reasons for the transaction;
>
> its effect on the issuer;
>
> the review and approval process followed by the issuer; a description of the interest of every interested party and related party; and
>
> if applicable, the formal valuation or minority approval exemptions relied upon.[19]

If the issuer files a material change report less than 21 days before the expected date of the closing of the transaction, the issuer must explain in the news release and in the material change report why the shorter period is reasonable or necessary in the circumstances.[20]

MI 61-101 also prescribes information that an issuer must include in an information circular prepared in connection with a meeting of the holders of affected securities if minority approval of the RPT is required.[21] The information required to be disclosed in an information circular is similar to what should be included in the material change report, discussed above. The disclosure must permit holders of affected securities to make an informed decision whether to approve the RPT.

Staff Commentary

When considering a RPT, consideration should also be given to the guidance provided by Companion Policy 61-101CP *To Multilateral Instrument 61-101 Protection of Minority Security Holders in Special Transactions* (**61-101CP**) to ensure that all security holders are treated fairly. In our view, providing sufficient information to security holders includes directors disclosing their reasonable beliefs as to the desirability or fairness of the proposed RPT and making useful recommendations regarding the RPT.[22] The disclosure should describe in reasonable detail the material factors on which beliefs regarding the RPT are based. The board should also fully discuss the background of deliberations by the directors and any analysis of expert opinions received.[23]

A statement that the directors are unable to make or are not making a recommendation about the RPT, a statement that the directors have no reasonable belief as to the desirability or fairness of the RPT, or a failure to indicate whether the directors consider the RPT to be fair, without more detailed reasons, would generally be viewed as insufficient disclosure.[24]

In addition, it is important for boards to put in place an appropriate review and approval process to safeguard against the potential that a related party would have an unfair advantage arising as a result of a conflict of interest or informational or other advantage in connection with a proposed RPT. A good practice, as set out in subsection 6.1(6) of 61-101CP, is to appoint a special committee of disinterested directors to carry out, review and report on the negotiation of the RPT. In Staff's view, the mandate of any special committee considering a RPT should generally give the special committee full authority to negotiate the terms of the transaction, consider other alternative transactions, and consider whether the RPT is in the interests of, or fair to, security holders.

In our review, the disclosure requirements in MI 61-101 for material change reports for RPTs were generally complied with. Approximately 9% of the issuers reviewed filed a material change report in relation to RPTs. No issuer reviewed was required to provide a formal valuation or obtain minority approval under MI 61-101 of a RPT. The two most commonly relied upon exemptions from the minority shareholder approval and formal valuation requirements of MI 61-101 were the 25% market capitalization exemption and the financial hardship exemption.[25]

In a few instances, issuers did not disclose in the material change report information about insider participation in a private placement where the private placement was a material change for the issuer. Although the insider participation in itself may not have been material in value, the

---

[13]Subsection 6.1(2) of Companion Policy 61-101CP *To Multilateral Instrument 61-101 Protection of Minority Security Holders in Special Transactions*.

[14]Section 5.4 of MI 61-101.

[15]Section 5.5 of MI 61-101.

[16]Sections 5.2 and 5.3 of MI 61-101.

[17]Section 5.6 of MI 61-101.

[18]Section 5.7 of MI 61-101.

[19]Subsection 5.2(1) of MI 61-101.

[20]Subsection 5.2(2) of MI 61-101.

[21]Subsection 5.2(3) of MI 61-101.

[22]Subsection 6.1(2) of 61-101CP.

[23]Subsection 6.1(3) of 61-101CP.

[24]Subsections 6.1(2) and 6.1(4) of 61-101CP.

[25]In the board's assessment of whether the issuer can avail itself of the financial hardship exemption, the board is encouraged to consider the guidance set out in the notice published by the TSX dated April 27, 2009 (the **TSX Staff Notice**) on the types of procedural and informational considerations it would expect from issuers seeking to establish financial hardship as a basis for reliance upon the financial hardship exemption in subsection 604(e) of the TSX Company Manual. As the TSX financial hardship considerations are similar to, and are based on, the financial hardship exemption in MI 61-101, the considerations set out in the TSX Staff Notice may be relevant to not only a TSX listed issuer, but also a venture issuer, that proposes to rely upon the financial hardship exemption in MI 61-101.

obligation to provide disclosure about a RPT is triggered when a material change report is required to be filed even if the transaction is exempt from minority approval under MI 61-101. In other words, when filing a material change report where there is any insider participation, the material change report should contain information about the insider participation in a RPT, including a description of the interest of every interested party and the review and approval process followed by the issuer, even if the insider participation may form only a small part of the private placement.

Example — Boilerplate Disclosure

The example below illustrates the kind of boilerplate disclosure that is occasionally found in a material change report describing RPT:

> The Company announced a non-brokered private placement offering of 5,000,000 shares (the **Offered Shares**) at a price of $0.50 per share for aggregate proceeds of $2,500,000. Insiders of the Company have subscribed for 20% of the Offered Shares.

Example — Entity-specific Disclosure

The example below illustrates better disclosure included in the material change report when there is a RPT:

> On January 21, 2014, the Company announced a non-brokered private placement offering of 5,000,000 shares (**the Offered Shares**) at a price of $0.50 per share for aggregate proceeds of $2,500,000. The Proposed Private Placement is expected to close on March 1, 2014. The net proceeds of this private placement will be used to advance the Company's exploration in the Company's Ottawa property, as well as for working capital and general administrative purposes.

> Insiders of the Company have subscribed for an aggregate of 1,000,000 shares at a price of $0.50 per share, for aggregate proceeds of $500,000, comprising 20% of the total amount raised.

> John Smith, the CEO and a director of the Company, subscribed for 600,000 shares for $300,000, increasing his holding from 2.0% to 4.0% of the issued and outstanding shares.

> Jane Doe, a director of the Company, subscribed for 400,000 shares for $200,000, increasing her holding from 0.5% to 2.0% of the issued and outstanding shares.

> The participation of Mr. Smith and Ms. Doe in the private placement constitutes a "related party transaction" as such terms are defined in Multilateral Instrument 61-101 *Protection of Minority Security Holders in Special Transactions* (**MI 61-101**). The Company is relying on the exemptions from the formal valuation and minority approval requirements set out in subsection 5.5(a) and paragraph 5.7(1)(a) of MI 61-101 because the fair market value of the consideration for the securities of the Company to be issued to the insiders does not exceed 25% of its market capitalization.

> The insider private placements were approved by the disinterested directors of the Company who concluded that the private placements were entered into on market terms and were fair to minority security holders.

8. — Conclusion

RPTs are a normal feature of commerce and business and such transactions by their very nature give rise to conflicts of interest and have the potential to be unfair or abusive to issuers and their securities holders. As part of a good governance regime, reporting issuers and their board of directors should consider the guidance and recommendations in this staff notice. Consideration should also be given to a company's policies and procedures for identifying, evaluating and approving RPTs. Once RPTs are identified, the board of directors should ensure that they are properly disclosed in accordance with accounting and securities rules.

This is a notice setting forth Staff's views which are not necessarily those of the Commission.

If you have questions or comments about this report, please contact:

[Editor's note: Names omitted.]

OSC Staff Notice 51-724 — Report on Staff's Review of REIT Distributions Disclosure

Date: January 29, 2015

38 O.S.C.B. 833

1. — Purpose

Real Estate Investment Trusts (REITs) are companies that own, and may also operate, income producing real estate assets. While many REITs may generate capital appreciation, the ability to receive a dividend or distribution is of most importance to investors. As flow through entities, REITs are required to distribute taxable income to unitholders and do not incur tax. As a result, a key attribute of the REIT structure as an investment vehicle is to provide investors with an expectation of a predictable cash flow stream.

Given the importance of distributions to investors, a REIT's continuous disclosure record should provide investors with transparent information to assess the source of funding for distributions paid and, in turn, the sustainability of those distributions.

National Policy 41-201 *Income Trusts and Other Indirect Offerings* (NP 41-201)[26] governs certain disclosure expectations for REITs. Staff of the Ontario Securities Commission (we) recently reviewed the disclosure provided by 30 Ontario head office REITs, to assess the quality and sufficiency of disclosure provided by those REITs relating to the sustainability of their distributions, in light of NP 41-201.

---

[26]Part 1.2 of NP 41-201 specifically states that REITs are included in the scope of this policy.

While REITs were generally fulsome in their disclosures, our review identified the following four areas where disclosure should be improved. These concerns were heightened in instances where REITs provided excess distributions (ie. when distributions paid exceeded the cash flows generated by the REIT's underlying real estate properties):

- The content of disclosure where excess distributions are paid.

- Consistency of disclosure about excess distributions.

- Timely disclosure where a reduction or termination of distributions occurs.

- Presentation of metrics common to the real estate industry such as adjusted funds from operations (AFFO).

2. — Introduction

The opportunity to receive stable and recurring distributions provides investors with an incentive to invest in REIT units. Investors may compare distribution yields across REITs in pursuit of the highest returns available in exchange for the level of risk assumed.

REITs are subject to a variety of risk factors which may negatively impact their distributions. Such risk factors include, but are not limited to, the following:

- Increases in market interest rates may eventually lead to a REIT's debt being refinanced at higher rates, placing downward pressure on the net operating cash flows used to finance distributions.

- Distributions financed by increasing levels of debt (as opposed to increases in underlying income or rents) are not sustainable.

- The population of potential investment properties which meet REIT investment objectives and strategy may be limited.

Since REIT distributions are typically characterized by a distribution of income, which exempt a REIT from the payment of income taxes as a flow through entity, investors will generally regard REIT distributions as a return on capital. In practice, a REIT which distributes more cash than it generated in the period from its operating activities may be using financing activities, such as the incurrence of additional debt, in order to provide distributions. Such distributions represent a return *of* capital, rather than a return *on* capital, since they ultimately decrease the value of the REIT's remaining net assets and therefore also decrease the value each unitholder will receive when they ultimately dispose of their units. REITs which consistently obtain cash flows from other financing sources aside from operations have a higher risk profile. For example, incurring additional debt to finance distributions creates additional interest expense, which further reduces a REIT's ability to pay ongoing distributions. Additionally, incremental sources of financing may not be available in the future.

As a result, REITs need to provide investors with sufficient information to help them evaluate how much cash is available for distribution and, if distributions exceed this amount, to provide clear disclosure acknowledging that a return of capital has occurred. Given the importance of distributions to investors, it is critical for investors to understand if the source for distributions is a REIT's own capital.

3. — Disclosure Expectations

Item 2.1 of NP 41-201 states that "*the amount of cash distributed by [a real estate investment trust] may sometimes be greater than what it can safely distribute without eroding its productive capacity and threatening the sustainability of its distributions . . . We are concerned that disclosure by [real estate investment trusts] has not always been sufficiently plain to allow an investor to assess whether a possible concern exists in this respect.*" The following is a summary of expected disclosure, as outlined in NP 41-201, which is intended to address this concern:

- Item 2.5 of NP 41-201 discusses disclosure expectations related to any non-GAAP measure that a REIT may use to describe the amount of net cash it has generated during the period which is available for distribution[27] . This may include distributable cash, funds from operations or adjusted funds from operations.

- Item 6.5.2 of NP 41-201 discusses additional disclosure expectations which are applicable only in circumstances where a REIT's distributions exceed its cash flow from operations.

The following chart summarizes the disclosure expectations presented by NP 41-201 in each of the two aforementioned areas:

Disclosure	Subtopic	Disclosure Expectation*
Disclosure expectations when distributions exceed cash flow from operations (Item 6.5.2)	Quantify 'excess' distributions	Quantify the amount of distributions which were funded by sources of cash other than operating activities.
	Discuss any implications of 'excess' distributions	Acknowledge that a return of capital has been provided and discuss why a decision was made to provide distributions partly representing a return of capital.
		Discuss the specific sources of cash, such as debt, mortgages or other financing instruments, which were used to finance distributions in excess of operating activities. Quantify the amount of distributions financed by each instrument and summarize the repayment terms of each instrument, if any.
		Disclose whether a material contract was amended in order to fund distributions in excess of cash flow from operations.

---

[27]Part 2.5 of NP 41-201 specifically refers to this non-GAAP measure as 'distributable cash' however part 2.1 of the policy further clarifies that disclosure expectations about distributable cash extend to any other non-GAAP measure which a REIT may use to describe the amount of net cash it has generated during the period which is available for distribution (such as funds from operations or adjusted funds from operations).

Disclosure	Subtopic	Disclosure Expectation*
		Disclose any risk factors related to providing distributions in excess of cash flow from operations and discuss whether such 'excess' distributions are expected to continue. Discuss any impact on the sustainability of distributions.
		Disclose whether cash distributions may be suspended in the foreseeable future.
Disclosure expectations regarding non-GAAP measures used to describe cash available for distribution (Item 2.5)	Purpose of the non-GAAP measure	Explain that the non-GAAP measure does not have a standard meaning and may not be comparable to other issuers.
		Explain why the non-GAAP measure provides useful information, and how management uses it as a financial measure.
	Reconciliation to the nearest GAAP measure	Reconcile the non-GAAP measure to the nearest GAAP measure, which is assumed to be cash flow from operations (not net income) since a non-GAAP measure which describes cash available for distribution is a cash flow measure.
		Present cash flow from operations (the nearest GAAP measure) with equal or greater prominence to the non-GAAP measure when providing any reconciliation to the non-GAAP measure.
	Changes in the non-GAAP measure	Explain any changes in the composition of the non-GAAP measure during the reporting period.

Notes:

*   The disclosure expectations outlined by NP 41-201 items 6.5.2 (including notes (i) through (vi)) and 2.5 (including subpoints (i) through (v)) are referred to in this column.

4. — What We Found

4.1 — Overall Results

We found generally that most REITs provide adequate disclosure about their distributions. However, our review did identify a significant number of REITs which distribute more than they generate in cash, without sufficiently highlighting this increased risk. Given the importance of maintaining distribution levels, we are concerned that management of REITs may face inherent pressure to hold or increase distribution yields over time, even if their ability to generate the cash needed to finance these distributions from underlying properties is not aligned. We are also concerned that investors may be potentially misled if these risks are not appropriately disclosed.

We sent comment letters to 50% of the REITs that we reviewed. The remaining REITs were not sent a letter because their distributions did not exceed cash flow from operating activities or because they provided adequate disclosures. Of the REITs that we sent comment letters to, staff requested 67% of these issuers to enhance their disclosure prospectively, which they did. None of the reviews identified the need to refile or restate continuous disclosure documents.

During the course of our review, we identified the following areas where improved disclosure is needed.

4.2 — The Content of Disclosure Where Excess Distributions Are Paid

When distributions exceed cash flow from operations, it is important that REITs adequately provide disclosures which are necessary for investors to understand risks relevant to a REIT and its distributions.[28]

Based on our review, 33% of REITs paid distributions which exceeded cash flow from operations. None of these REITs provided the expected disclosures in relation to their excess distributions, though some may have provided boilerplate disclosure. Distributions were in excess by more than 10% of annualized cash flows in 70% of the REITs whose total distributions (including both cash and non-cash distributions) exceeded cash flow from operations, signaling the magnitude by which other sources were used to finance distributions.

---

[28]Disclosure expectations in such instances are outlined by item 6.5.2 of NP 41-201.

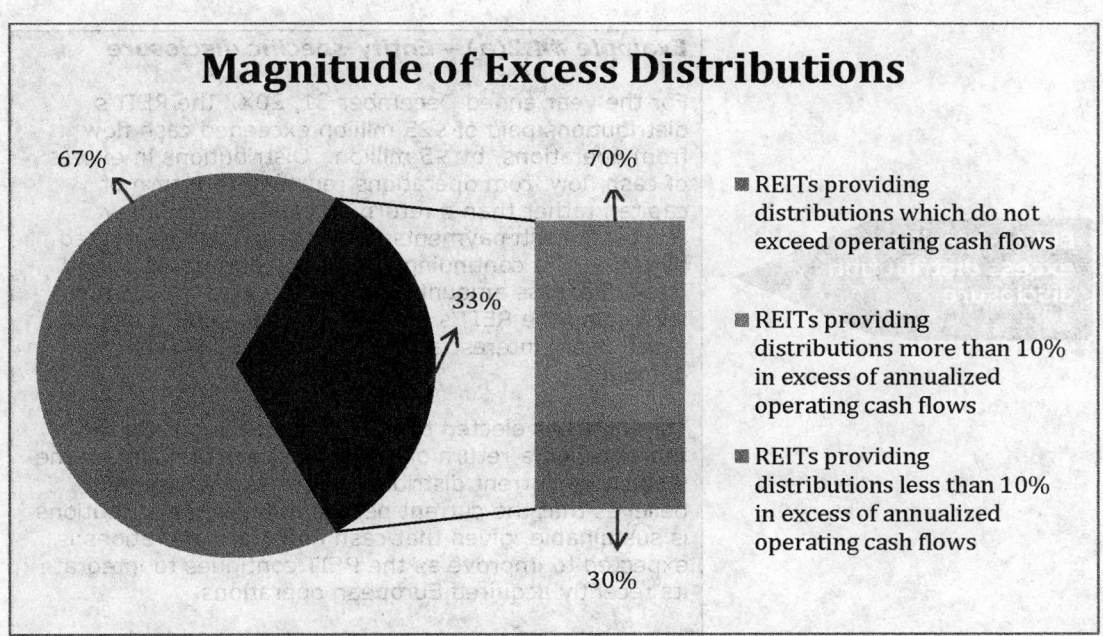

It is critical that investors receive prominent and transparent disclosure about the heightened risk profile which results from distributions in excess of cash flow from operations. REITs declaring distributions in excess of cash flow from operations should include relevant disclosure in their MD&A and in their Annual Information Form, in accordance with Part 1 *General Provisions* of Form 51-102F1 and Part 5.2 *Risk Factors* of Form 51-102F2 respectively.

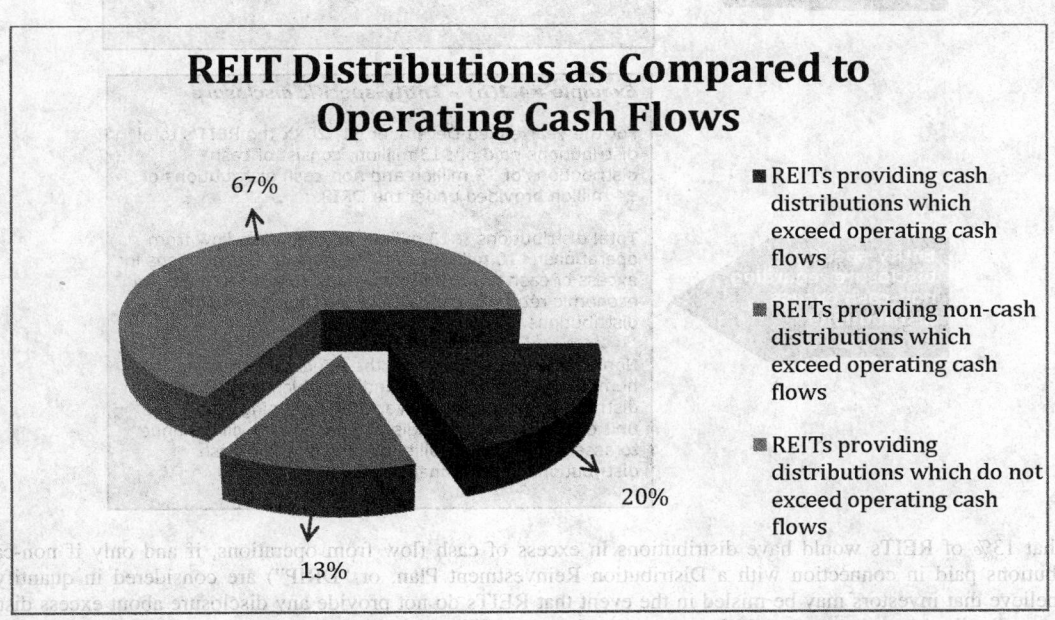

The following example illustrates the type of boilerplate disclosure which was observed during our review in situations where excess distributions were paid, along with suggestions to improve disclosure with entity specific information.

Entity-specific excess distribution disclosure

> **Example #4.2(a) – Entity-specific disclosure**
>
> For the year ended December 31, 20XX the REIT's distributions paid of $25 million exceeded cash flow from operations, by $5 million. Distributions in excess of cash flow from operations represent a return of capital, rather than a return on capital, since they represent cash payments in excess of cash generated by the REIT's continuing operations during the period. The full excess amount of $5 million was financed by leveraging the REIT's existing revolving credit facility, which bears interest at LIBOR + 3% and is repayable on demand.
>
> The REIT has elected to provide distributions partly representing a return of capital in order to maintain the stability of current distribution levels. Management believes that the current per share level of distributions is sustainable, given that cash flow from operations is expected to improve as the REIT continues to integrate its recently acquired European operations.

Boilerplate disclosure regarding non-cash excess distributions

> **Example #4.2(b) – Boilerplate disclosure**
>
> For the year ended December 31, 20XX the REIT's cash distributions of $9 million were lower than cash flow from operations of $10 million.

> **Example #4.2(b) – Entity-specific disclosure**
>
> For the year ended December 31, 20XX the REIT's total distributions paid of $13 million, consist of cash distributions of $9 million and non-cash distributions of $4 million provided under the DRIP.
>
> Total distributions ($13 million) exceed cash flow from operations ($10 million) over the period. Distributions in excess of cash flow from operations do not represent an economic return of capital because the excess portion of distributions is non-cash in nature.
>
> Non-cash distributions have the effect of increasing the number of REIT units outstanding, which will cause cash distributions to increase over time assuming stable per unit cash distribution levels. Management will continue to assess the sustainability of cash and non-cash distributions in each financial reporting period.

Entity-specific disclosure regarding non-cash excess distributions

We also noted that 13% of REITs would have distributions in excess of cash flow from operations, if and only if non-cash distributions (including distributions paid in connection with a Distribution Reinvestment Plan, or "DRIP") are considered in quantifying the amount distributed. We believe that investors may be misled in the event that REITs do not provide any disclosure about excess distributions, solely because such excess distributions were non-cash. Investors may be potentially misled into believing there is no liquidity impact by the issuance of a non-cash distribution, however, recurring non-cash distributions could have an effect on the sustainability of cash distributions over time.

Non-cash distributions have the effect of increasing the number of units outstanding and therefore increase the aggregate dollar amount of distributions over time, assuming a stable cash component of distributions on a per unit basis. The following example suggests how REITs may improve their disclosure in this area.

Boilerplate disclosure regarding non-cash excess distributions

Example #4.2(b) – Boilerplate disclosure

For the year ended December 31, 20XX the REIT's cash distributions of $9 million were lower than cash flow from operations of $10 million.

Example #4.2(b) – Entity-specific disclosure

For the year ended December 31, 20XX the REIT's total distributions paid of $13 million, consist of cash distributions of $9 million and non-cash distributions of $4 million provided under the DRIP.

Total distributions ($13 million) exceed cash flow from operations ($10 million) over the period. Distributions in excess of cash flow from operations do not represent an economic return of capital because the excess portion of distributions is non-cash in nature.

Non-cash distributions have the effect of increasing the number of REIT units outstanding, which will cause cash distributions to increase over time assuming stable per unit cash distribution levels. Management will continue to assess the sustainability of cash and non-cash distributions in each financial reporting period.

Entity-specific disclosure regarding non-cash excess distributions

4.3 — Consistency of Disclosure About Excess Distributions

Long term debt, as well as any related interest expense, is often material for REITs. In virtually all cases, investment properties held by REITs are leveraged against mortgages generating significant period to period interest expense. International Financial Reporting Standards ("IFRS") allow an accounting policy choice as to where borrowing costs are recorded on the statement of cash flows.[29] As a result, a REIT's cash flow from operations may include or exclude interest paid. The purpose of the cash flow from operations caption on a REIT's statement of cash flows is to illustrate the net amount of cash generated from, or used by, its principal revenue generating activities during the period.

---

[29]See paragraph 33 of International Accounting Standard 7 *Statement of Cash Flows*.

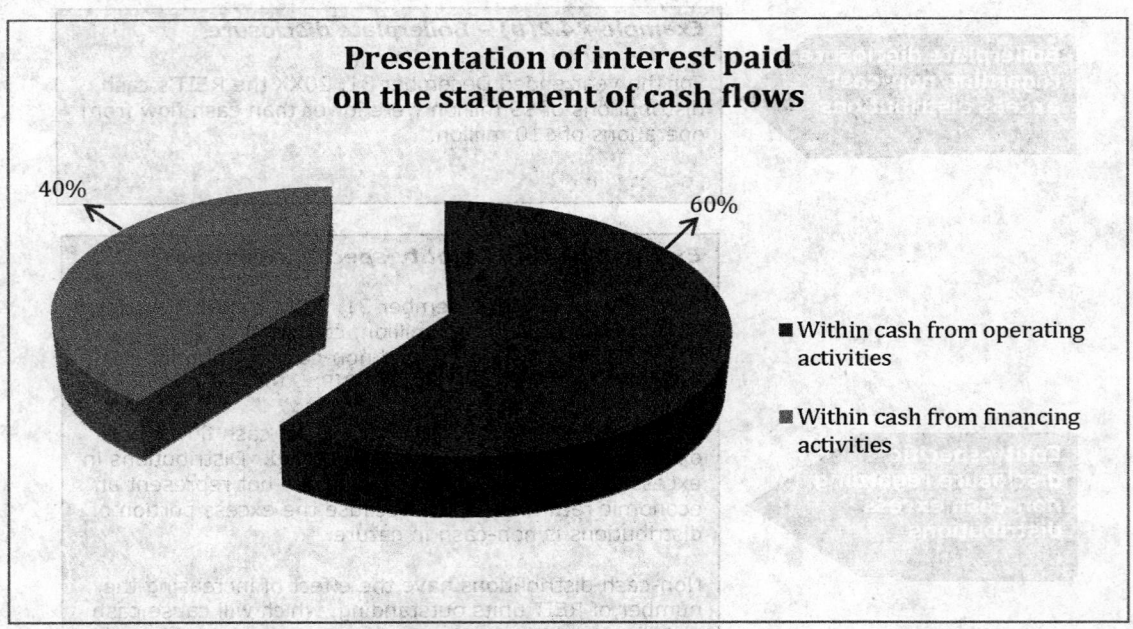

NP 41-201 outlines additional disclosure expectations for REITs whose distributions exceed their cash flow from operations (see item 4.2 of this notice). However, for 10% of REITs reviewed, distributions did not exceed cash flow from operations only because the REIT has made an accounting policy choice to classify interest paid as a financing activity on the statement of cash flows. If these REITs had instead elected to classify interest as an operating cash flow item, then their distributions would have exceeded cash flow from operations.

While IFRS permits REITs an accounting policy choice relating to the classification of interest paid on the statement of cash flows, we are concerned that investors may be misled if the disclosure expectations outlined by item 6.5.2 of NP 41-201 are not provided soley as a result of this accounting policy choice.

By way of background, this accounting policy choice under IFRS represents a change from Canadian GAAP which previously required interest paid to be included within cash flow from operations on the statement of cash flows. United States Generally Accepted Accounting Principals also state that cash flow from operations is generally considered to represent the cash effects of transactions and other events that enter into the determination of net income, specifically including cash payments to lenders and other creditors for interest.[30]

During the course of our review, we examined the financial statements of certain REITs prior to and during the year of conversion to IFRS. We confirmed that five REITs did change their classification of interest paid from operating activities to financing activities on transition from Canadian GAAP to IFRS. These REITs typically did not disclose a reason for the change in policy on transition, since such disclosure is not required by IFRS.

While an accounting policy choice is available to REITs, the principal intent of NP 41-201 was the inclusion of interest within cash flow from operations. Now that REITs have a policy choice for the classification of interest under IFRS, we are of the view that if interest were reclassified from a financing activity (as this was the policy choice made under IFRS) to an operating activity, and if distributions would now exceed cash flow from operations, then disclosure under item 6.5.2 of NP 41-201 should be provided. This was and continues to be the principal intent of NP 41-201.

The following example illustrates two different situations in which the 'excess distribution' disclosures outlined by item 6.5.2 of NP 41-201 should be presented in a manner consistent with item 4.2 of this notice. The only difference between the two situations is the classification of interest paid on the IFRS statement of cash flows which, as discussed, should have no bearing on whether or not excess distribution disclosures are expected.

Example #4.3(a) — Interest paid within operating activities

In the statement of cash flows shown, the REIT has made an accounting policy choice under IFRS to classify interest paid as an operating cash flow item. In this situation, distributions clearly exceed cash flow from operations (ie. the absolute value of [**B**] exceeds the absolute value of [**A**]) and therefore the 'excess distribution' disclosures outlined in item 4.2 of this notice should be provided in the REIT's AIF and MD&A.

---

[30]See FASB Accounting Standards Codification 230-10-20 and 230-10-45-17(d).

Part 5: ONGOING REQUIREMENTS

CASH FLOW FROM OPERATIONS	
Net income	1,000,000
Add (deduct) items not affecting cash	
Depreciation of property plant & equipment	150,000
Stock based compensation	100,000
Net change in non-cash working capital	(100,000)
Interest expense	500,000
Interest paid	(450,000)
Cash flow from (used in) operations	**1,200,000** A
CASH FLOW FROM INVESTING	
Purchase of property plant & equipment	(200,000)
Cash flow from (used in) investing	**(200,000)**
CASH FLOW FROM FINANCING	
Repayment of long term debt	(100,000)
Distributions paid	(1,500,000) B
Cash flow from (used in) financing	**(1,600,000)**
Net increase (decrease) in cash during the period	(600,000)
Cash, beginning of period	2,600,000
Cash, end of period	2,000,000

Summary:

Cash flow from operations (includes interest paid)	$1,200,000	**[A]**
Distributions paid	$1,500,000	**[B]**
Excess distributions	**($ 300,000)**	**[A] - [B]**

Example #4.3(a) — Interest paid within financing activities

In this statement of cash flows, the REIT has made an accounting policy choice under IFRS to classify interest paid as a financing item. Excluding the impact of that policy choice, the statement of cash flows shown in this example is identical to the previous example. However, in this example, cash flow from operating activities no longer exceeds distributions (ie. the absolute value of **[B]** no longer exceeds the absolute value of **[A]**). As discussed, we would still expect this REIT to present the 'excess distribution' disclosures outlined in item 4.2 of this notice because distributions would exceed cash flow from operations if those cash flows were adjusted to include a deduction for interest paid currently classified as a financing activity.

CASH FLOW FROM OPERATIONS		
Net income	1,000,000	
Add (deduct) items not affecting cash		
Depreciation of property plant & equipment	150,000	
Stock based compensation	100,000	
Net change in non-cash working capital	(100,000)	
Interest expense	500,000	
Cash flow from (used in) operations	**1,650,000**	**A**
CASH FLOW FROM INVESTING		
Purchase of property plant & equipment	(200,000)	
Cash flow from (used in) investing	**(200,000)**	
CASH FLOW FROM FINANCING		
Repayment of long term debt	(100,000)	
Interest paid	(450,000)	**C**
Distributions paid	(1,500,000)	**B**
Cash flow from (used in) financing	**(2,050,000)**	
Net increase (decrease) in cash during the period	(600,000)	
Cash, beginning of period	2,600,000	
Cash, end of period	2,000,000	

Summary:

Cash flow from operations	$1,650,000	[A]
Interest paid	($ 450,000)	[C]
Cash flow from operations, including interest paid	$1,200,000	[A] + [C] = [D]
Distributions paid	$1,500,000	[B]

Excess distributions   ($ 300,000)   [D] - [B]

4.4 — Timely Disclosure Where a Reduction or Termination of Distributions Occurs

The 'excess distribution' disclosures discussed in item 4.2 of this notice should be presented by a REIT in any period in which distributions exceed cash flow from operations. Such disclosures would include commentary about the sustainability of any excess distributions. However, there are other situations in which a REIT may need to provide disclosure about risks to the sustainability of distributions.

During our review we observed an instance where a REIT reduced or eliminated its distributions without providing sufficient advance notice to investors.

The timely disclosure policies outlined in part 2.1 of National Policy 51-201 — *Disclosure Standards* state that "*companies are required by law to immediately disclose a material change in their business. For changes that a company initiates, the change occurs once the decision has been made to implement it. This may happen even before a company's directors approve it, if the company thinks it is probable they will do so.*" We are of the view that the reduction or elimination of distributions may constitute a material change.

Form 51-102F1 *Management's Discussion & Analysis* also requires a REIT to openly discuss bad news as well as good news. REITs should discuss trends and risks that are reasonably likely to affect them in the future, including any risks or events which may result in a possible reduction or elimination of distributions.

Sufficient advance notice of any prospective distribution reduction, either to conserve capital for use in future projects or because current distribution levels have become unsustainable, should be provided to investors as soon as practicable. It is critical that investors receive information required in order to understand and assess any risks related to the sustainability of distributions on a timely basis.

4.5 — Presentation of Metrics Common to the Real Estate Industry Such As Adjusted Funds From Operations (AFFO)

Item 2.5 of NP 41-201 outlines disclosure expectations relating to distributable cash, however, distributable cash is infrequently used in practice by REITs today. We have observed that the REIT industry has moved towards the use of AFFO instead of distributable cash. These two terms, while not intended to be identical, in our view often both represent measures of the resources which have been generated by a REIT's operations and are available for distribution.

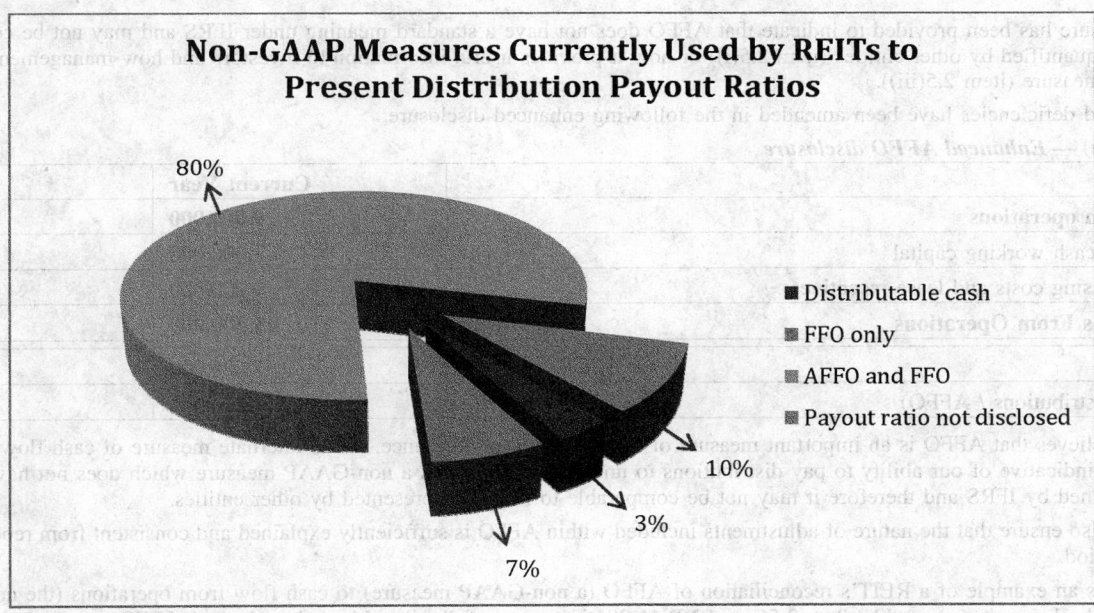

Non-GAAP Measures Currently Used by REITs to Present Distribution Payout Ratios

80%

- ■ Distributable cash
- ■ FFO only
- ■ AFFO and FFO
- ■ Payout ratio not disclosed

10%

3%

7%

While industry guidance exists for FFO[31] , there is currently no consensus in terms of what type of adjustments may or may not be included in the determination of AFFO. As a result there is diversity in practice amongst REITs as to what items are included in AFFO.

While NP 41-201 does not specifically mention AFFO, part 2.1 of the national policy does indicate that "*some issuers have refered to net cash available for distribution by a term other than distributable cash . . . Distributable cash includes all such other terms used to describe the amount available for distribution to . . . securityholders.*"

REITs routinely quantify their distributions as a percent of AFFO. During the course of our review we also noted that some REITs describe the nature and purpose of AFFO as:

- A measure of cash generated by operating activities, after providing for stabilized operating capital requirements.

---

[31]See 'White Paper on Funds From Operations for IFRS' dated April 2014 as issued by the Real Property Association of Canada.

- An alternative measure of cash generated from operations.

- Indicative of ability to pay distributions.

- An indicator of the sustainability of cash distributions.

When AFFO represents a cash flow measure because the adjustments used to arrive at AFFO encompass adjustments for non-cash items, we are of the view that AFFO would represent a measure of the net cash available for distribution to securityholders. In such situations, REITs should ensure that they are consistent with the disclosure expectations outlined in item 2.5 of NP 41-201 for distributable cash, related to any AFFO disclosure provided.

The following example illustrates deficient AFFO disclosure which is then revised to conform to the disclosure expectations of item 2.5 of NP 41-201 for distributable cash.

Example #4.5(a) — Deficient AFFO disclosure

	Current Year	Prior Year
Net income	1,000,000	700,000
Amortization and depreciation	200,000	100,000
Straight line rent adjustment	(300,000)	(200,000)
Fair value adjustments to investment properties	10,300,000	5,500,000
Adjusted Funds From Operations	**11,200,000**	**6,100,000**
Distributions	7,000,000	4,000,000
Payout ratio (distributions / AFFO)	62.5%	65.6%

This example contains the following areas where disclosure can be improved to meet the disclosure expectations of NP 41-201:

- The non-GAAP measure AFFO has been presented in bold font whereas the nearest GAAP measure (net income) has not. Item 2.5(ii) indicates that the nearest GAAP measure should be presented with equal or greater prominence to the non-GAAP measure.

- AFFO has been reconciled to net income. Item 2.5(iv) indicates that it should be reconciled to cash flow from operations.

- No disclosure has been provided to indicate that AFFO does not have a standard meaning under IFRS and may not be comparable to AFFO as quantified by other entities (item 2.5(i)) or how it provides useful information to investors and how management uses it as a financial measure (item 2.5(iii)).

The above noted deficiencies have been amended in the following enhanced disclosure.

Example #4.5(a) — Enhanced AFFO disclosure

	Current Year	Prior Year
Cash flow from operations	**10,000,000**	**8,000,000**
Change in non-cash working capital	1,000,000	(2,000,000)
Initial direct leasing costs and lease incentives	200,000	100,000
Adjusted Funds From Operations	**11,200,000**	**6,100,000**
Distributions	7,000,000	4,000,000
Payout ratio (distributions / AFFO)	62.5%	65.6%

Management believes that AFFO is an important measure of our economic performance. As an alternate measure of cash flow from operations, AFFO is indicative of our ability to pay distributions to unitholders. AFFO is a non-GAAP measure which does not have a standard meaning as defined by IFRS and therefore it may not be comparable to AFFO as presented by other entities.

REITs should also ensure that the nature of adjustments included within AFFO is sufficiently explained and consistent from reporting period to reporting period.

The following is an example of a REIT's reconciliation of AFFO (a non-GAAP measure) to cash flow from operations (the nearest GAAP measure). This disclosure is expected by item 2.5(iv) of NP 41-201 in respect of distributable cash and, since AFFO is a measure of amounts available for distribution to unitholders, we are of the view that such disclosure should be provided for AFFO.

Example #4.5(b) — Deficient AFFO disclosure

	Current Year	Prior Year
Cash flow from operations	**5,000,000**	**4,000,000**
Change in non-cash working capital	1,000,000	(2,000,000)
Normalized lease expenditures	900,000	-
Adjusted Funds From Operations	**6,900,000**	**2,000,000**

In this reconciliation, it is not clear whether a prior year impact of the normalized lease adjustment is applicable. The REIT may not have included an adjustment for normalized lease expenditures in the prior year as it may not have had a favourable impact to AFFO. REITs should ensure that adjustments included in the determination of AFFO are included consistently from year to year. If REITs identify a new reconciling item then they should ensure that the adjustment is reflected in the prior year comparative figures as well. Additionally, the nature of the normalized lease expenditure adjustment in this example has not been explained in sufficient detail for investors to be able to understand what it relates to and/or how it was determined.

In the enhanced disclosure provided, the prior year AFFO reconciliation included the impact of the normalized lease expenditure adjustment, even though the adjustment was not favourable to AFFO. Additional detail about the nature of the adjustment has also been provided in a footnote, including the factors and assumptions related to the adjustment.

Example #4.5(b) — Enhanced AFFO disclosure

	Current Year	Prior Year
Cash flow from operations	**5,000,000**	**4,000,000**
Change in non-cash working capital	1,000,000	(2,000,000)
Normalized lease expenditures*	900,000	(1,500,000)
Adjusted Funds From Operations	**6,900,000**	**500,000**

Notes:

* In the calculation of AFFO the REIT makes an adjustment to normalize lease expenditures incurred (such as tenant incentives and direct leasing costs) to 5% of net operating income. The 5% assumption is based on historical results and will continue to be reassessed in prospective reporting periods.

5. — Conclusions

Our review identified that the majority of REITs pay their distributions in alignment with cash generated from underlying properties. However, where distributions exceed cash flow from operations, the findings of our review indicate that the quality and consistency of disclosure for REIT distributions are areas which need improvement. In large part, guidance contained in NP 41-201 which was intended to guide staff disclosure expectations where excessive distributions have been paid has been absent in REIT continuous disclosure.

REITs are an important investment vehicle for many investors and we expect a REIT's disclosure to accurately represent its current risk profile, and its ability to sustain distributions at current levels. Wherever possible, this disclosure should be available to investors as soon as relevant information becomes available so that they may assess the sustainability of distributions well in advance of any actual reduction or termination of distributions. We expect the outcome of this review to improve the transparency and completeness of REIT distribution disclosure on a prospective basis.

Given the importance of this disclosure to investors, we will continue to assess these items in our continuous disclosure and prospectus review programs. REITs who have not complied with these disclosure expectations will be expected to take corrective action.

The OSC Inquiries & Contact Centre operates from 8:30 a.m. to 5:00 p.m. Eastern Time, Monday to Friday, and can be reached on the Contact Us page of osc.gov.on.ca

If you have questions or comments about this report, please contact:

[Editor's note: Names omitted.]

OSC Staff Notice 51-725 — Corporate Finance Branch — 2014-2015 Annual Report

Date: July 14, 2015

38 O.S.C.B. 6362

[Not reproduced]

OSC Staff Notice 51-726 — Report on Staff's Review of Insider Reporting and User Guides for Insiders and Issuers

Date: February 18, 2016

(2016), 39 OSCB 1461

Table of Contents

1. — Introduction

This notice reports the findings and comments of staff (collectively, **staff** or **we**) of the Ontario Securities Commission (**OSC**) arising from an issue-oriented review of the continuous disclosure (**CD**) records and insider filings of 100 reporting issuers whose principal regulator (**PR**) is Ontario. The purpose of the review was to assess compliance and assist reporting insiders with meeting insider reporting requirements.

The 100 Ontario PR reporting issuers selected for the review resulted in a corresponding review of approximately 1,500 reporting insiders. While approximately 85% of the reporting insiders we reviewed were materially compliant, we found material insider reporting deficiencies[1] in approximately 15% which resulted in approximately 200 reporting insiders filing new insider reports on the System for Electronic Disclosure by Insiders (**SEDI**) to address these deficiencies. Generally, these reporting insiders were charged late filing fees as contemplated in section 10.1(2) of Companion Policy 55-104CP *Insider Reporting Requirements and Exemptions* (**55-104CP**).

The compliance rate for insider reporting can be substantially improved, and this improvement needs to happen across all reporting issuers. We found material insider reporting deficiencies in approximately 70% of the issuers we reviewed. There was minimal correlation between the size of the reporting issuer and the occurrence of material insider reporting deficiencies. Our findings suggest that reporting insiders of issuers of all sizes need to improve the quality of their insider reporting for accuracy, completeness and timeliness.

To assist issuers and reporting insiders in meeting their reporting obligations, staff strongly recommend that issuers and reporting insiders take note of the guidance provided in this notice including the user guides for reporting insiders and reporting issuers attached as **Appendix B** and **Appendix C**, respectively. We will continue to monitor and review insider reporting as part of our normal course CD review program, with an emphasis on:

- educating issuers and their reporting insiders; and

- identifying reporting insiders who are failing to report and thereby compromising the integrity of our insider reporting regime.

2. — Background

The insider reporting requirements serve a number of functions, including deterring improper insider trading based on material undisclosed information and increasing market efficiency by providing investors with information concerning the trading activities of insiders, and, by inference, the insiders' views of the respective issuer's future prospects.

Insider reporting also discourages illegal or otherwise improper activities involving stock options and similar equity-based instruments, including stock option backdating, option repricing and opportunistic timing of grants since the requirement for timely disclosure and public scrutiny of such disclosure will generally limit opportunities for insiders to engage in such improper practices.

When insiders fail to comply with insider reporting requirements, this affects the integrity, reliability and effectiveness of the insider reporting regime, which in turn has a negative impact on market efficiency. As such, it is crucial for investors to have access to reliable trading

---

[1]"Material insider reporting deficiency" or "material deficiency" means a compliance deficiency with insider reporting requirements which requires a reporting insider to file one or more new insider reports on SEDI (**remedial filings**) in order to correct the deficiency.

information of insiders. All instances of inaccurate reporting can negatively impact the insider reporting regime. However, when an insider fails to file any report in connection with a trade in a security, our regime is significantly impacted.

3. — Regulatory Requirements and Guidance

The following represents a summary of the key regulatory requirements and guidance on insider reporting.

National Instrument 55-104

In Ontario, the general insider reporting requirements are found in the *Securities Act* (Ontario) (the **Act**). Certain insider reporting requirements in the Act have been varied by National Instrument 55-104 *Insider Reporting Requirements and Exemptions* (**NI 55-104**) which consolidated the principal insider reporting requirements and exemptions available in various Canadian jurisdictions in a single national instrument to make it easier for reporting issuers and reporting insiders to understand their obligations.

Reporting insiders are generally required to file an initial insider report within 10 calendar days of becoming a reporting insider. Any subsequent insider reports reflecting changes in their holdings must be filed within 5 calendar days of such change. "Reporting insider" is defined in NI 55-104, and generally includes persons who have routine access to material undisclosed information concerning a reporting issuer and/or significant influence over the reporting issuer.

National Instrument 55-102

National Instrument 55-102 *System for Electronic Disclosure by Insiders (SEDI)* (**NI 55-102**) sets out the process for filing insider reports. Reporting insiders are required to file insider reports containing securities trading information in electronic format at www.sedi.ca for public dissemination.

National Policy 51-201

National Policy 51-201 *Disclosure Standards* (**NP 51-201**) provides guidance on "best disclosure" practices for issuers to promote good disclosure, enhance their credibility with investors and minimize the risk of non-compliance with securities legislation. As part of the guidance, NP 51-201 includes a provision on insider trading policies and blackout periods.

Additional Guidance

There are numerous Canadian Securities Administrators (**CSA**) and OSC staff notices[2] which remind reporting issuers and their reporting insiders of their filing obligations and provide guidance on the process by which to file their insider reports.

4. — Review Objectives

The objectives of our review were as follows:

- to assess insider reporting compliance;
- to raise awareness for issuers and insiders on insider filing requirements; and
- to gather information about insider trading policies.

5. — Review Scope

For the purpose of this review, we selected 100 reporting issuers whose PR is Ontario. The issuers were randomly selected from across all industries in proportion to the total number of Ontario PR reporting issuers in each industry.[3] Sixty-five percent of the reporting issuers selected for review were non-venture issuers and the remaining 35% were venture issuers.[4] Each selected issuer had, on average, 15 active reporting insiders at the beginning of the review, for a combined total of approximately 1,500 reporting insiders.

---

[2]CSA Staff Notice 55-312 *Insider Reporting Guidelines for Certain Derivative Transactions (Equity Monetization)(Revised)*; CSA Staff Notice 55-315 *Frequently Asked Questions about National Instrument 55-104 Insider Reporting Requirements and Exemptions*; CSA Staff Notice 55-316 *Questions and Answers on Insider Reporting and the System for Electronic Disclosure by Insiders (SEDI)* (**Staff Notice 55-316**); OSC Staff Notice 55-701 *Automatic Securities Disposition Plans and Automatic Securities Purchase Plans*.

[3]As at March 31, 2015.

[4]"Venture issuer" has the same meaning given to the term in National Instrument 51-102 *Continuous Disclosure Obligations*.

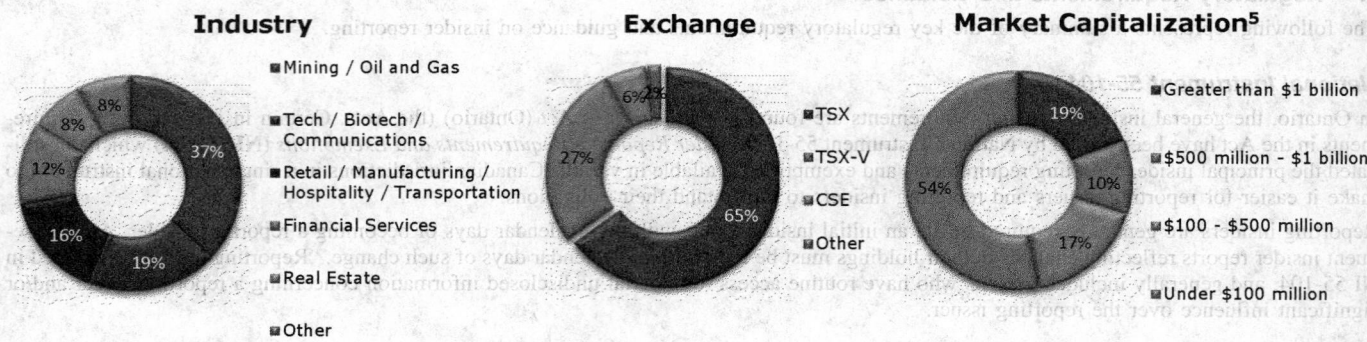

Industry	Exchange	Market Capitalization[5]

Industry
- Mining / Oil and Gas
- Tech / Biotech / Communications
- Retail / Manufacturing / Hospitality / Transportation
- Financial Services
- Real Estate
- Other

Exchange
- TSX
- TSX-V
- CSE
- Other

Market Capitalization[5]
- Greater than $1 billion
- $500 million – $1 billion
- $100 – $500 million
- Under $100 million

We compared the insider information contained in public CD documents of the issuers available on the System for Electronic Document Analysis and Retrieval (**SEDAR**) (including management information circulars, annual information forms, annual financial statements and prospectuses) with the insider information reported on SEDI to identify any discrepancies. We also reviewed insider trading policies requested from issuers to determine whether issuers have developed these policies in accordance with the best practices set out in NP 51-201.

As part of the review, we corresponded with all 100 reporting issuers. In addition, in order to address the matters noted during our review, we corresponded with approximately 530 reporting insiders or their filing agents about the reporting insiders' SEDI filings.

6. — Findings

Based on our review, we identified two main areas where improvement is needed:

Issues
1. The quality of insider reporting
2. Insider trading policies

Improvement in the Quality of Insider Reporting is Required

We found deficiencies in insider reports filed by reporting insiders of issuers of all sizes which resulted in reporting insiders or issuers, as applicable, having to make either remedial or correctional filings or other amendments on SEDI as described below.

a) — Material deficiencies leading to remedial filings

- *We found material insider reporting deficiencies in approximately 15% of the reporting insiders we reviewed, which resulted in approximately 200 reporting insiders making one or more remedial filings on SEDI to address these deficiencies.*

- *In approximately 70% of the issuers reviewed, at least one insider was required to file a remedial filing to address a material deficiency.*

These reporting insiders were generally charged late filing fees as contemplated in 55-104CP.

In general, we found material insider reporting deficiencies where there were:

i. — Missing reporting insider profiles

- *Approximately 30% of the issuers had at least one reporting insider that did not have an insider profile and failed to file insider reports on SEDI.*

The majority of these reporting insiders were either directors or senior officers of reporting issuers or significant shareholders of reporting issuers. In certain cases, the reporting insiders who failed to file were the issuers themselves (e.g., for acquisitions under a normal course issuer bid (**NCIB**)). In most cases, these reporting insiders failed to report their holdings in the respective issuers' common shares.

ii. — Balance discrepancy in SEDI filings vs. CD records

- *Approximately 65% of the issuers had at least one reporting insider that had a variance equal to or greater than 5% between the balances of securities holdings as reported on SEDI versus CD records of the respective issuer.*

---

[5]As at March 31, 2015.

The majority of these reporting insiders were directors or senior officers of reporting issuers. The variances were most common for holdings of common shares and stock options, followed by deferred share awards (**DSAs**), restricted share awards (**RSAs**) and performance share awards (**PSAs**) as shown in the chart below.

Balance Discrepancies by Security

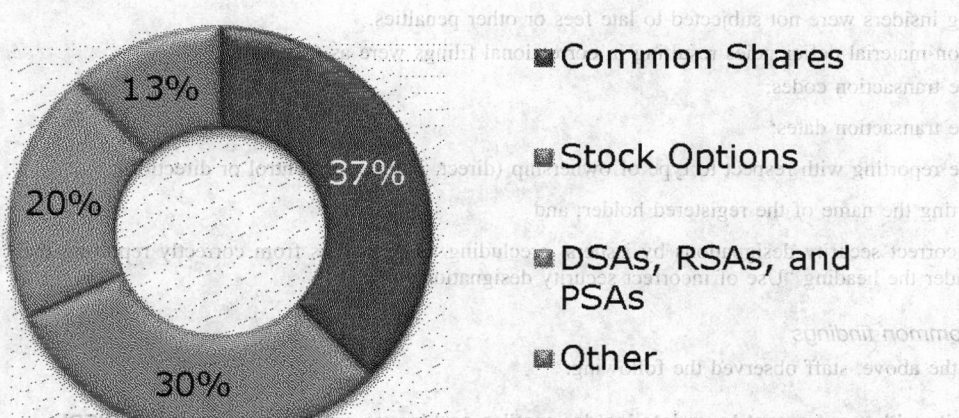

- Common Shares
- Stock Options
- DSAs, RSAs, and PSAs
- Other

37%, 13%, 20%, 30%

Some of the common reasons we noted in our review for the material discrepancies discussed above leading to remedial filings were as follows:

Unfamiliarity with definition of "reporting insider"	Some reporting insiders were not aware that they had reporting obligations under NI 55-104.[6]
Unfamiliarity with definition of "significant shareholder" in NI 55-104	Some reporting insiders were not aware that when an individual holds more than 10% of the outstanding shares of an issuer through a holding company, that holding company is also a "significant shareholder" under NI 55-104, which is required to have its own insider profile and file its own insider reports.[7]
Failure to file reports for acquisitions under a NCIB	Some issuers failed to file insider reports for acquisitions of a security of its own issue under a NCIB in accordance with Part 7 of NI 55-104, which requires issuers to file an insider report disclosing each acquisition under a NCIB within 10 days of the end of the month in which the acquisition was completed.[8]
Failure to report expiration of securities	Many insiders failed to report expiration of certain issuer derivative securities such as options or warrants within the required 5 day period.[9]
Late reporting due to issuer delays	Some insiders failed to file insider reports on time because they did not receive certain key information from issuers on a timely basis. In some cases, this was due to the fact that issuers failed to file issuer event reports as required under NI 55-102 to alert insiders to changes affecting all holdings of a class of securities.[10]
Reliance on third parties	Some reporting insiders relied on third parties to make their filings and had genuinely believed that such filings had been made.

Notes:

6 See definition of "reporting insider" in NI 55-104 and Part 3 of NI 55-104 for primary insider reporting requirements.

7 See definition of "significant shareholder" in NI 55-104 which includes a person *or company* that has beneficial ownership of, or control or direction over, whether direct or indirect, securities of an issuer carrying more than 10% of the voting rights attached to all the issuer's outstanding voting securities. In general, there is no reporting exemption available for a holding company that is a significant shareholder and whose share holdings are only reported by the ultimate individual shareholder.

8 See Part 7 of NI 55-104 and item 4.5.1 of Staff Notice 55-316.

9 See section 3.3 of NI 55-104 which requires a reporting insider to file a report to disclose *any change* in the reporting insider's beneficial ownership of, or control or direction over, whether direct or indirect, securities of the reporting issuer.

10 See section 2.4 of NI 55-102 as well as Form 55-102F4 *Issuer Event Report* and Part 8 of NI 55-104.

Staff Recommendation:

As responsibility to file insider reports remains with the reporting insider regardless of whether they use a third party agent, reporting insiders should periodically review SEDI to make sure their reports are being filed correctly.

b) — Non-material deficiencies leading to correctional filings

- *In approximately 45% of issuers reviewed, at least one insider filed inaccurate insider reports on SEDI (with one or more non-material deficiencies (as described below)) which resulted in approximately 150 reporting insiders making correctional filings to address the non-material deficiencies.*

These reporting insiders were not subjected to late fees or other penalties.

Some of the non-material deficiencies resulting in correctional filings were as follows:

- inaccurate transaction codes;

- inaccurate transaction dates;

- inaccurate reporting with respect to type of ownership (direct, indirect or control or direction);

- not reporting the name of the registered holder; and

- use of incorrect security designations by issuers, precluding their insiders from correctly reporting their transactions (see discussion below under the heading "Use of incorrect security designations").

c) — Other common findings

In addition to the above, staff observed the following:

i. — Unfamiliarity with requirement to update insider profiles and issuer profile supplements on SEDI

Reporting insider profiles

Some reporting insiders were not aware that when they cease to be a reporting insider of a reporting issuer, their insider profile on SEDI must be amended to reflect this fact within 10 calendar days of the change.

- *Approximately 500 insiders were asked to update their profile on SEDI to disclose that they had ceased to be reporting insiders of reporting issuers.*

Some reporting insiders were also not aware that their contact information was out of date.

- *Approximately 300 insiders were required to update their profile on SEDI as their contact information was out of date.*

Staff Recommendation:

Reporting insiders should be proactive and periodically review their insider profiles on SEDI to determine whether they continue to be shown as reporting insiders of issuers and whether their contact information is current.

Issuer profile supplements

Some reporting issuers were not aware that they are required to file an amended issuer profile supplement on SEDI immediately if there is a change in the information disclosed in their issuer profile supplement.

- *Approximately 60% of issuers had out of date issuer profile supplements which required updating.*

Some of the common issues noted were as follows:

- the insider affairs contact was out of date; and
- security designations needed to be updated (see below).

Staff Recommendation:

Issuers should be proactive and periodically review their issuer profile supplement to see if any updates are required and remind their insiders to review their insider profiles for accuracy and completeness.

ii. — Use of incorrect security designations by issuers

In their issuer profile supplements, reporting issuers are required to designate all types of securities and related financial instruments that are held by insiders.

- *Security designations were required to be updated for approximately 40% of reporting issuers reviewed.*

Security designations needed to be updated for the following reasons:

- security designations were omitted;

- security designations were set up incorrectly; or

- security designations needed to be archived.

The majority of security designations that required updating were issuer derivative securities (e.g., stock options, rights, RSAs, DSAs and PSAs). Incorrect designation of issuer derivative securities as simple equity securities precluded insiders from properly reporting the characteristics of these securities (e.g., exercise price and vesting or expiration date) and transactions in these securities (e.g., the exercise or vesting of such securities).

Staff Recommendation:

Guidance on creating security designations can be found in Staff Notice 55-316. However, issuers should contact the OSC if they have further questions to ensure new securities designations are set up properly in SEDI.

iii. — Limited use of issuer grant reports by issuers

- *Only 10% of issuers filed one or more issuer grant reports since January 2014.*[5]

An issuer grant report is a report that may be voluntarily filed by a reporting issuer on SEDI which discloses the details of a grant of stock options or similar instruments to its insiders under a compensation arrangement which has already been described in a public document filed on SEDAR.

While there is no obligation for an issuer to file issuer grant reports, staff believe that increased use of issuer grant reports by issuers would be beneficial to all stakeholders as it would provide the market with timely information about the existence and material terms of a grant and provide insiders with relief from having to report the grant within the ordinary reporting time periods.[6]

Staff Recommendation:

To communicate information about a grant in a timely manner and to help avoid late fees being charged against its insiders, issuers should consider filing an issuer grant report within 5 days of a grant.

iv. — Lack of internal processes to reconcile insider reports on SEDI with issuers' CD records on SEDAR

As mentioned above, we observed that in many cases, information contained in SEDI filings did not reconcile to the related issuer's CD records available on SEDAR. Some issuers noted that the information contained in CD documents was incorrect as the issuer relied solely on the information communicated by insiders and did not compare such information to the insiders' SEDI filings.

- *Staff issued comments to approximately 20% of the reporting issuers reviewed requesting that they implement, on a going-forward basis, an internal process to reconcile insiders' reported holdings in CD documents to SEDI filings.*

Staff believe that such internal processes are an important element in the design and operation of issuers' internal control over financial reporting and disclosure controls and procedures.

Staff Recommendation:

Issuers should implement a process to annually verify the securities holdings communicated to them by insiders in order to avoid variances in the public records filed by the issuer on SEDAR versus the reports filed by insiders on SEDI.

Reporting insiders should be proactive and review information circulars annually and other CD records of the issuer on a regular basis to ensure their security holdings are properly reflected.

Improvement of Insider Trading Policies is Recommended

Most issuers had a written insider trading policy that was in accordance with the best practices set out in NP 51-201 and provided for "blackout periods" around regularly scheduled earnings announcements.

- *Approximately 85% of the issuers had written insider trading policies in place.*

However, as demonstrated in the chart below, certain policies reviewed by staff did not restrict derivative-based transactions or the grant of stock options or similar forms of stock-based compensation during blackout periods.

While these types of transactions are not specifically addressed in NP 51-201, staff believe that having a written insider trading policy which prohibits such transactions during blackout periods is essential to avoid public and regulatory scrutiny relating to the opportunistic timing of such actions taken on the basis of market prices which do not reflect material undisclosed information.

---

[5]While it is possible that other issuers did not have a reason to file issuer grant reports since January 2014, staff believe that this is highly unlikely given that many reporting issuers have compensation plans which contemplate granting of stock options or similar instruments.

[6]See section 6.2 of NI 55-104 for the terms of the insider reporting exemption for certain issuer grants.

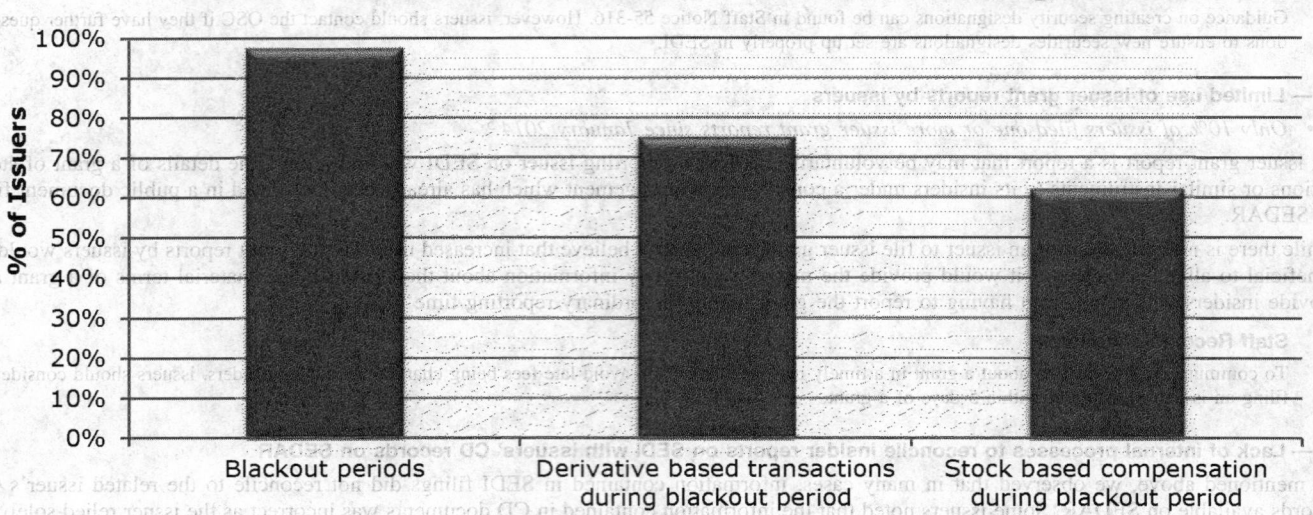

Areas Addressed in Issuers' Insider Trading Policies

Staff Recommendation:

Issuers should annually review their insider trading policies to ensure they align with current Canadian securities legislation.

Issuers should also adopt a written policy which, among other things, specifically prohibits derivative-based transactions, the grant of options and the setting of the exercise price during blackout periods. The written policy should also provide for a senior officer to approve and monitor the trading activity of all insiders, officers, and senior employees.

7. — Examples

For examples of common deficiencies noted by staff during this review, please see **Appendix A**.

8. — Conclusion

Our findings suggest that many reporting insiders need to improve the quality of their insider reporting for accuracy, completeness and timeliness. Staff strongly recommend that issuers and reporting insiders take note of the recommendations made in this notice and consider other processes that can be put in place to increase the rate of compliance with insider reporting obligations.

To assist issuers and their reporting insiders, we have included as **Appendix B** and **Appendix C**, checklists which highlight some of the key points that reporting insiders and issuers, respectively, should consider in complying with insider reporting requirements.

Staff remind issuers and reporting insiders of their responsibility to ensure that their filing obligations under NI 55-102 and NI 55-104 are satisfied. We also remind issuers and reporting insiders that regulatory action may be taken against issuers and reporting insiders who have not fulfilled their insider reporting requirements.

We will continue to monitor and review insider reporting as part of our normal course CD review program with an emphasis on continuing to educate issuers and reporting insiders on their obligations. We will also focus on identifying those reporting insiders who fail to file reports given the negative impact this non-compliance has on our insider reporting regime and market efficiency.

9. — Questions

If you have any questions, please feel free to contact any of the following individuals:

Inquiries and Contact Centre, Strategy and Operations Branch Tel: 416.593.8314 / 1.877.785.1555 Email: inquiries@osc.gov.on.ca	**Julie Erion, Supervisor, Insider Reporting, Corporate Finance Branch** Tel: 416.593.8154 Email: jerion@osc.gov.on.ca
Shannon O'Hearn, Manager, Corporate Finance Branch Tel: 416.595.8944 Email: sohearn@osc.gov.on.ca	**Katie DeBartolo, Accountant, Corporate Finance Branch** Tel: 416.593.2166 Email: kdebartolo@osc.gov.on.ca
Gina You, Legal Counsel, Corporate Finance Branch Tel: 416.595.8934 Email: gyou@osc.gov.on.ca	**Krstina Skocic, Legal Counsel, Corporate Finance Branch** Tel: 416.263.3769 Email: kskocic@osc.gov.on.ca

Appendix A

Examples

Refer to the following diagram for Examples 1 and 2.

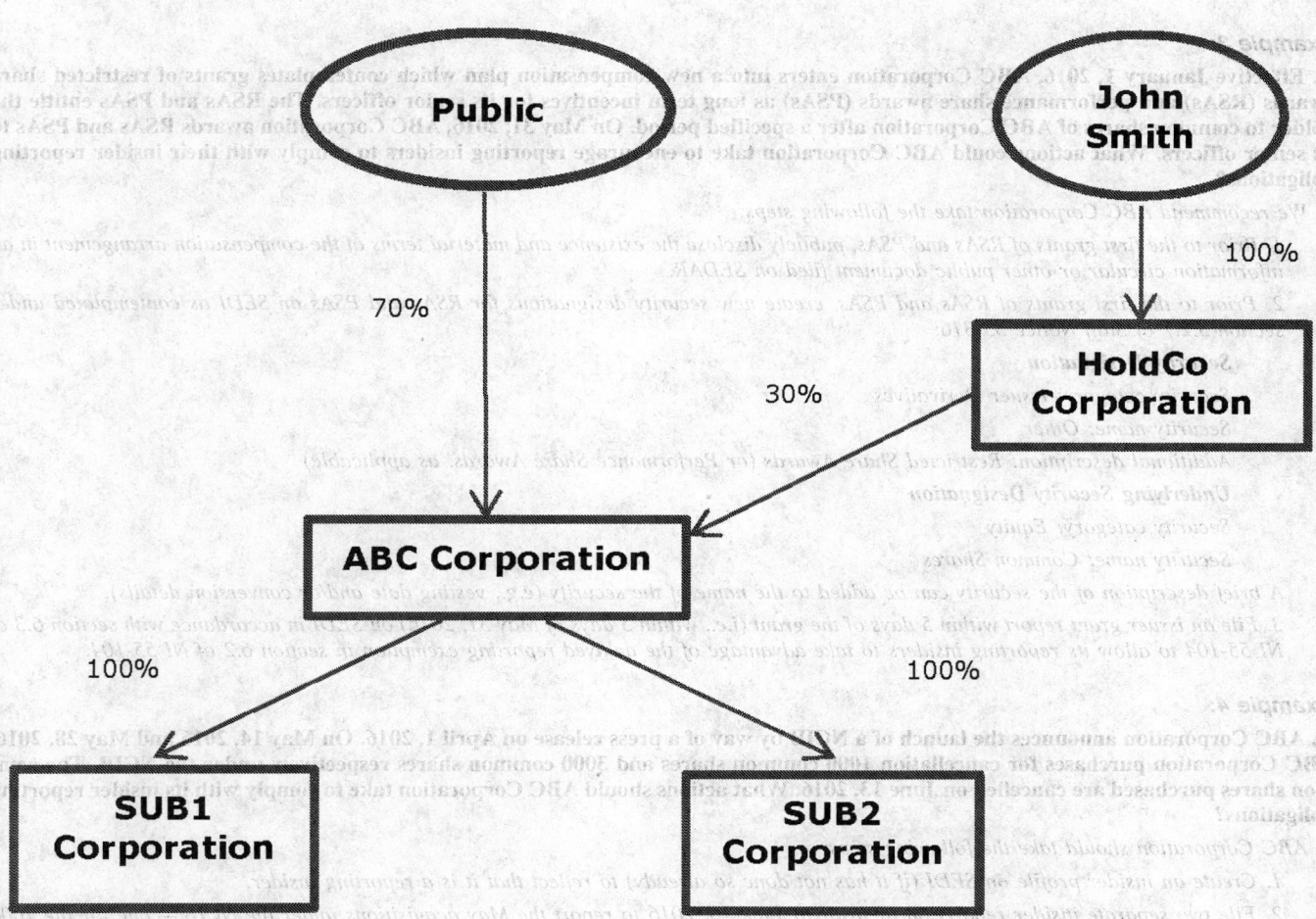

Example 1:

Q. ABC Corporation is a reporting issuer. It has two subsidiaries, SUB1 Corporation and SUB2 Corporation, each of which is wholly owned and considered a "major subsidiary" for purposes of NI 55-104. Each of the directors and senior officers of SUB1 Corporation and SUB2 Corporation holds common shares of ABC Corporation. Do these directors and senior officers need to file insider reports?

A. Yes, the directors and senior officers[7] of SUB1 Corporation and SUB 2 Corporation need to file insider reports in respect of their holdings in the common shares of ABC Corporation.

We note that senior officers and directors of major subsidiaries of an issuer are "reporting insiders" under NI 55-104. "Major subsidiary" is defined in NI 55-104 as a subsidiary of an issuer if the assets or revenue of the subsidiary are 30 percent or more of the consolidated assets or revenue of the issuer, as applicable.

Example 2:

Q. Holdco Corporation is a private holding company. Mr. John Smith owns all of the common shares of Holdco Corporation. Holdco Corporation owns 30% of the shares in ABC Corporation. Mr. John Smith has a SEDI insider profile and reports his indirect owner-

---

[7]"Senior officer" refers to persons acting as the CEO, CFO and COO of an issuer. See the definitions of CEO, CFO and COO in NI 55-104.

ship in ABC Corporation through Holdco Corporation. Is Holdco Corporation required to have its own insider profile and file its own insider reports in respect of the common shares it holds in ABC Corporation?

A. Yes, Holdco Corporation is required to have its own insider profile and file its own insider reports. The definition of "significant share-holder" means a person or company that has beneficial ownership of, or control or direction over, whether direct or indirect, securities of an issuer carrying more than 10 percent of the voting rights. As Holdco Corporation has control or direction over the securities that are held in its name representing 30% of the shares of ABC Corporation, and it does not otherwise qualify for a reporting exemption under NI 55-104, it should have its own filings on SEDI.

Example 3:

Q. Effective January 1, 2016, ABC Corporation enters into a new compensation plan which contemplates grants of restricted share awards (RSAs) and performance share awards (PSAs) as long term incentives for its senior officers. The RSAs and PSAs entitle the holder to common shares of ABC Corporation after a specified period. On May 31, 2016, ABC Corporation awards RSAs and PSAs to its senior officers. What actions could ABC Corporation take to encourage reporting insiders to comply with their insider reporting obligations?

A. We recommend ABC Corporation take the following steps:

1. Prior to the first grants of RSAs and PSAs, publicly disclose the existence and material terms of the compensation arrangement in an information circular or other public document filed on SEDAR.

2. Prior to the first grants of RSAs and PSAs, create new security designations for RSAs and PSAs on SEDI as contemplated under section 3.2.7 of Staff Notice 55-316:

> **Security Designation**
>
> *Security category: Issuer Derivatives*
>
> *Security name: Other*
>
> *Additional description: Restricted Share Awards (or Performance Share Awards, as applicable)*
>
> **Underlying Security Designation**
>
> *Security category: Equity*
>
> *Security name: Common Shares*
>
> *A brief description of the security can be added to the name of the security (e.g., vesting date and/or conversion details).*

3. File an issuer grant report within 5 days of the grant (i.e., within 5 days of May 31, 2016) on SEDI in accordance with section 6.3 of NI 55-104 to allow its reporting insiders to take advantage of the delayed reporting exemption in section 6.2 of NI 55-104.

Example 4:

Q. ABC Corporation announces the launch of a NCIB by way of a press release on April 1, 2016. On May 14, 2016 and May 28, 2016, ABC Corporation purchases for cancellation 1000 common shares and 3000 common shares respectively under the NCIB. The common shares purchased are cancelled on June 13, 2016. What actions should ABC Corporation take to comply with its insider reporting obligations?

A. ABC Corporation should take the following steps:

1. Create an insider profile on SEDI (if it has not done so already) to reflect that it is a reporting insider.

2. File two separate insider reports on or prior to June 10, 2016 to report the May acquisitions under the NCIB — one for the 1000 common shares purchased on May 14, 2016 and one for the 3000 common shares purchased on May 28, 2016.

3. File two separate insider reports on or prior to July 10, 2016 to report the cancellation of common shares purchased on May 14, 2016 (1000 common shares) and May 28, 2016 (3000 common shares), respectively.

For more information, see section 4.5.1 of Staff Notice 55-316.

Appendix B

User Guide for Reporting Insiders

This user guide is provided to assist reporting insiders with their insider reporting obligations. This guide is not meant to be exhaustive and we remind reporting insiders that responsibility for complying with the insider reporting requirements under Ontario securities laws rests with the reporting insiders themselves.

		Yes	No	N/A
Part A: Reporting Insider Profile on SEDI				
1	I have reviewed the definition of "reporting insider" under NI 55-104 and I am considered a reporting insider of the reporting issuer. *Note: You may need to seek advice about this item. You should also determine whether you qualify for an insider reporting exemption under NI 55-104 or otherwise under Ontario securities laws.*			
2	I hold securities of the reporting issuer.[1]			

		Yes	No	N/A
3	If "yes" to items 1 and 2, within 10 calendar days of becoming a reporting insider, I have registered as a SEDI user and filed my insider profile on SEDI identifying my relationship with the reporting issuer.			
4	I periodically review my SEDI insider profile and make updates to my profile where required.			
5	I am no longer a reporting insider of the reporting issuer and I have amended my SEDI insider profile within 10 calendar days of that change in status to indicate that I have ceased to be a reporting insider of the reporting issuer.			
Part B: Insider Reports on SEDI				
6	I have filed insider reports on SEDI that reflect all of my securities holdings and related transactions.			
7	I periodically review records of my securities holdings and compare those records to the filings I have made on SEDI for purposes of accuracy and completeness. *Note: This should include a review of:* — *balances in securities holdings* — *transaction dates* — *transaction codes* — *type of ownership (direct, indirect or control or direction)*			
8	I use a filing agent or other third party for my reporting insider filings on SEDI.			
9	If "yes" to item 8, I review my SEDI filings on a periodic basis to ensure all requested filings are accurate and complete.			
10	I hold issuer derivatives with expiration dates (e.g., stock options).			
11	If "yes" to item 10, I have reported the expiration of any issuer derivative securities on SEDI within 5 days of the expiration date.			
Part C: Holding Companies that are Significant Shareholders				
12	I hold more than 10% of the outstanding shares of the reporting issuer through a holding company that I control.			
13	If "yes" to item 12, I have reported on SEDI that I have control or direction over those shares through my holding company.			
14	If "yes" to item 13, my holding company has filed its own insider reports on SEDI for the shares that it directly owns.			
Part D: Grants of Stock Options and Other Forms of Compensation				
15	I have received stock options or other forms of compensation under the reporting issuer's compensation plans.			
16	If "yes" to item 15, I have checked the reporting issuer's SEDI profile to determine if the reporting issuer has filed an issuer grant report within 5 days of each grant. *Note: If an issuer grant report has been filed by the issuer within 5 days of the grant in accordance with Part 6 of NI 55-104, you have until March 31 of the next calendar year to report the grant, unless you transfer or dispose of the granted securities before such date (in which case the grant needs to be reported within 5 days of the transfer or disposition).*[2]			
17	If an issuer grant report has not been filed by the reporting issuer, I have reported each grant on SEDI within 5 days of the grant.			
Part E: Continuous Disclosure Filings of the Reporting Issuer				
18	I have reviewed the continuous disclosure filings of the reporting issuer (e.g., management information circulars) that include my securities holdings for accuracy and completeness and reported any discrepancies to the reporting issuer.			

Notes:

1   In this guide, "hold" or "holdings" refer to beneficial ownership of, or control or direction over, whether direct or indirect, securities of the reporting issuer.

2   There are certain exceptions for "specified dispositions". See Part 6 of NI 55-104.

Part 5: ONGOING REQUIREMENTS

Appendix C

User Guide for Reporting Issuers

This user guide is provided to assist reporting issuers with their insider reporting obligations as well as the reporting obligations of their reporting insiders. This guide is not meant to be exhaustive and we remind reporting issuers that responsibility for complying with the insider reporting requirements under Ontario securities laws rests with the issuers themselves (if applicable) and their reporting insiders.

		Yes	No	N/A
Part A: Issuer Profile Supplement on SEDI				
1	The reporting issuer periodically reviews the insider affairs contact information on its issuer supplement on SEDI and makes updates where required.			
2	The reporting issuer periodically reviews its security designations on its issuer supplement on SEDI to ensure that all securities have been designated and archived as appropriate. *Note: The reporting issuer should ensure that "issuer derivative securities" such as stock options, restricted share awards, deferred share awards and performance share awards have been categorized as issuer derivative securities.*			
Part B: Insider Reports on SEDI				
3	The reporting issuer engages in NCIBs.			
4	If "yes" to item 3, the issuer has created an insider profile on SEDI so that it can report acquisitions under a NCIB.			
5	If "yes" to item 3, the reporting issuer has reviewed its filings on SEDI to ensure that all transactions related to NCIBs have been reported on SEDI within 10 days of the end of the month in which the transaction was completed.			
6	The reporting issuer has recently announced an "issuer event" that affects all holdings of an entire class of its securities in the same manner. *Note: An "issuer event" includes:* *— stock dividend* *— stock split* *— consolidation* *— amalgamation* *— reorganization* *— merger* *— other similar event*			
7	If "yes" to item 6, the reporting issuer has filed an issuer event report on SEDI no later than one business day following the occurrence of the issuer event.			
Part C: Grants of Stock Options and Other Forms of Compensation				
8	The reporting issuer has compensation arrangements under which grants of stock options and similar instruments may be made to reporting insiders. *Note: The reporting issuer should consider filing an issuer grant report within 5 days of a grant to provide the market with timely information about the existence and material terms of a grant and allow reporting insiders to take advantage of the delayed reporting exemption in section 6.2 of NI 55-104.*			
9	If "yes" to item 8, the reporting issuer notifies its reporting insiders of such grants in a timely manner (by filing an issuer grant report or otherwise).			
Part D: Continuous Disclosure Filings of the Reporting Issuer				
10	The reporting issuer relies on information communicated by its reporting insiders to prepare its continuous disclosure records (e.g., management information circulars). *Note: To avoid discrepancies in public records, the reporting issuer should consider implementing a process to compare securities holdings disclosed by its reporting insiders on SEDI to the balances communicated to the reporting issuer.*			

OSC Rule 51-801 — Implementing National Instrument 51-102 Continuous Disclosure Obligations

Date: March 30, 2004, as amended May 16, 2005, December 29, 2006, December 31, 2007 and January 1, 2011

27 O.S.C.B. 3555, 28 O.S.C.B. 4559, 29 O.S.C.B. (Supp-2) 28, 30 O.S.C.B. 10510 and 33 O.S.C.B. (Supp. 5) 79

PART 1 — DEFINITIONS

1.1 Definitions — (1) In this Rule, "NI 51-102" means "National Instrument 51-102 *Continuous Disclosure Obligations*".

(2) Each term used in this Rule that is defined or interpreted in Part 1 of NI 51-102 has the meaning ascribed to it in that Part.

PART 2 — APPLICATION

2.1 Application — This Rule does not apply to investment funds.

PART 3 — INTERRELATIONSHIP WITH LEGISLATION

3.1 Annual financial statements — content — (1) The financial statements required under subsection 78(1) of the Act must include the statements and notes described in subsections 4.1(1) ad 4.1(3) of NI 51-102.

(2) Subsections 4.5(1), 4.8(4) and 4.8(6) and sections 4.2, 4.7, and 4.10 of NI 51-102 apply to financial statements and auditor's reports required under section 78 of the Act as if any reference to section 4.1 in sections 4.2, 4.5, 4.7, 4.8 and 4.10 of NI 51-102 is a reference to section 78 of the Act.

(3) This section applies for financial years beginning on or after January 1, 2004.

3.2 Interim financial statements — content — (1) The financial statements required under subsection 77(1) of the Act must include the statements and notes described in subsections 4.3(1), 4.3(2) and 4.3(2.1) of NI 51-102.

(2) Subsections 4.3(3), 4.3(4), 4.5(2), 4.8(4), 4.8(5), 4.8(7) and 4.8(8) and sections 4.4, 4.7 and 4.10 of NI 51-102 apply to financial statements required under subsection 77(1) of the Act as if any reference to section 4.3 in sections 4.4, 4.5, 4.7, 4.8 and 4.10 of NI 51-102 is a reference to subsection 77(1) of the Act.

(3) This section applies for interim periods in financial years beginning on or after January 1, 2004.

3.3 Filing annual financial statements — exemption — Section 78 of the Act does not apply to a reporting issuer that complies with, including in reliance on any applicable exemption or exclusion from, subsections 4.5(1), 4.7(1), 4.7(2), 4.8(4) and 4.8(6) and sections 4.1, 4.2 and 4.10 of NI 51-102 for financial years beginning on or after January 1, 2004.

3.4 Filing interim financial report — exemption — Subsection 77(1) of the Act does not apply to a reporting issuer that complies with, including in reliance on any applicable exemption or exclusion from, subsections 4.5(2), 4.7(1), 4.7(3), 4.7(4), 4.8(4), 4.8(5), 4.8(7) and 4.8(8) and sections 4.3, 4.4, and 4.10 of NI 51-102 for interim periods in financial years beginning on or after January 1, 2004.

3.5 Delivering financial statements — exemption — Section 79 of the Act does not apply to a reporting issuer that complies with, including in reliance on any applicable exemption or exclusion from, section 4.6 of NI 51-102 in the case of

    (a) annual financial statements for financial years beginning on or after January 1, 2004; and

    (b) interim financial reports for interim periods in financial years beginning on or after January 1, 2004.

3.6 Material change reports — form — Except as otherwise provided in National Instrument 71-101 *The Multijurisdictional Disclosure System* and in National Instrument 71-102 *Continuous Disclosure and other Exemptions Relating to Foreign Issuers*, every report required under subsection 75(2) of the Act must be a completed Form 51-102F3 except that the reference in Item 3 of Form 51-102F3 to section 7.1 of NI 51-102 shall be read as referring to subsection 75(1) of the Act and references in Items 6 and 7 of Form 51-102F3 to subsections 7.1(2), 7.1(5) or 7.1(7) of NI 51-102 shall be read as referring to subsections 75(3), 75(4) or 75(5), respectively, of the Act.

3.7 Issuance of material change news release — exemption — Subsection 75(1) of the Act does not apply to a reporting issuer that complies with, including in reliance on any applicable exemption or exclusion from, paragraph 7.1(1)(a) of NI 51-102.

3.8 Filing material change report — exemption — Subsection 75(2) of the Act does not apply to a reporting issuer that complies with, including in reliance on any applicable exemption or exclusion from, paragraph 7.1(1)(b) of NI 51-102.

3.9 Annual filing — exemption — Reporting issuers are exempt from subsection 81(2) of the Act.

3.10 Information circulars — form — Except as otherwise provided in National Instrument 71-101 *The Multijurisdictional Disclosure System* and in National Instrument 71-102 *Continuous Disclosure and Other Exemptions Relating to Foreign Issuers*, an information circular referred to in clause (a) or (b) of subsection 86(1) of the Act must be a completed Form 51-102F5, from and after June 1, 2004.

3.11 Filing information circular — exemption — Subsection 81(1) of the Act does not apply to a reporting issuer that complies with, including in reliance on any applicable exemption or exclusion from, the requirement in section 9.3 of NI 51-102 to file an information circular, from and after June 1, 2004.

3.12 Solicitation of proxies — exemption — Section 85 of the Act does not apply to a reporting issuer that complies with, including in reliance on any applicable exemption or exclusion from, subsection 9.1(1) of NI 51-102, from and after June 1, 2004.

3.13 Sending information circular — exemption — Section 86 of the Act does not apply to a person or company that complies with, including in reliance on any applicable exemption or exclusion from, subsection 9.1(2) of NI 51-102, from and after June 1, 2004.

PART 4 — REVOCATIONS AND AMENDMENTS OF RULES

4.1 Ontario Securities Commission Rule 51-501 AIF & MD&A (Rule 51-501) — (1) Rule 51-501 is amended by:

    (a) adding subsection 1.2(3):

        (3) This Rule does not apply to financial years beginning on or after January 1, 2004 nor to interim periods in financial years beginning on or after January 1, 2004.

    (b) in subsection 2.1(1) inserting "or Form 51-102F2" after "Form 44-101F1".

(2) [revoked]

4.2 Ontario Securities Commission Rule 52-501 Financial Statements (Rule 52-501) — (1) Rule 52-501 is amended by adding the following as new subsection 1.2(3):

(3) This Rule does not apply to:

a) annual financial statements for financial years of the issuer beginning on or after January 1, 2004;

b) interim financial statements for interim periods in financial years of the issuer beginning on or after January 1, 2004.

(2) Rule 52-501 is revoked effective May 19, 2005.

4.3 Ontario Securities Commission Rule 54-501 Prospectus Disclosure in Information Circulars (Rule 54-501) — Rule 54-501 is revoked effective June 1, 2004.

4.4 Ontario Securities Commission Rule 56-501 Restricted Shares (Rule 56-501): — (1) Rule 56-501 is amended by:

(a) deleting subsection 1.2(2);

(b) deleting section 2.1; and

(c) deleting the words "and an information circular concerning a proposed reorganization" in subsection 2.3(1).

(2) This section applies from and after May 19, 2005.

4.5 Form 41-501F1 Information Required in a Prospectus — Item 8.5 of Form 41-501F1 is amended by:

(a) in subsection(1), deleting the words "Form 44-101F2" and substituting the following:

(1) Form 51-102F1; or

(2) Form 51-102F1 or Form 44-102F2, if the financial statements relate to financial years beginning before January 1, 2004.

(b) deleting subsection (5) and substituting the following:

(5) Include MD&A for the interim financial statements of the issuer included in the prospectus, prepared in accordance with:

(1) Form 51-102F1; or

(2) Form 51-102F1 or Rule 51-501 *AIF and MD&A*, if the financial statements relate to an interim period in a financial year beginning on or after January 1, 2004.

PART 5 — EFFECTIVE DATE AND TRANSITION

5.1 Effective date — This Rule comes into force on March 30, 2004.

5.2 Transition — (1) Despite section 5.1, sections 3.1, 3.3 and paragraph 3.5(a) apply for financial years beginning on or after January 1, 2004.

(2) Despite section 5.1, sections 3.2, 3.4 and paragraph 3.5(b) apply for interim periods in financial years beginning on or after January 1, 2004.

(3) Despite section 5.1, sections 3.10, 3.11, 3.12 and 3.13 apply from and after June 1, 2004.

(4) Despite section 5.1, subsections 4.1(2) and 4.2(2) are effective on May 19, 2005.

(5) Despite section 5.1, section 4.3 is effective on June 1, 2004.

(6) Despite section 5.1, section 4.4 applies from and after May 19, 2005.

Final Rule: (2004) 27 O.S.C.B. 3555; Approval by OSC: (2003) 26 O.S.C.B. (Supp-3) 183 (December 19, 2003); Request for Comments: (2003) 26 O.S.C.B. 4577 and (2002) 25 O.S.C.B. 3701.

Amendment to Rule: (2005) 28 O.S.C.B. 4559; Approval by OSC: (2005) 28 O.S.C.B. 2232.

Amendment to Rule: Approval by OSC: (2006) 29 O.S.C.B. (Supp-2) 1; Request for Comments: (2005) 28 O.S.C.B. 9845.

Amendment to Rule: (2007) 30 O.S.C.B. 10510; Approval by OSC: (2007) 30 O.S.C.B. 8570.

Amendment to Rule: (2010) 33 O.S.C.B. (Supp. 5) 79; Approval by OSC: (2010) 33 O.S.C.B. (Supp. 3) 113; Request for Comments: (2009) 32 O.S.C.B. (Supp. 6) 1.

Companion Policy 51-801CP — To Ontario Securities Commission Rule 51-801 Implementing National Instrument 51-102 Continuous Disclosure Obligations

1.1 Introduction — The purpose of this Companion Policy is to provide information relating to the manner in which the Ontario Securities Commission (The Commission") interprets or applies certain provisions of Commission Rule 51-801 Implementing National Instrument 51-102 *Continuous Disclosure Obligations* (the "Implementing Rule") and National Instrument 51-102 *Continuous Disclosure Obligations* ("NI 51-102")

1.2 Interrelationship between NI 51-102 and the Securities Act Ontario (the "Act") — NI 51-102 is intended to provide a single source of harmonized continuous disclosure obligations for reporting issuers other than investment funds. As a result, NI 51-102 sometimes repeats (without any substantive change) certain requirements that are also dealt with in the Act under Part XVIII *Continuous Disclosure* and Part XIX *Proxies and Proxy Solicitation*. In addition NI 51-102, through the Implementing Rule, varies or adds to some of the requirements contained in Parts XVIII and XIX of the Act. The cumulative effect of NI 51-102 and the Implementing Rule is that NI 51-102 supersedes the requirements applicable to reporting issuers (other than investment funds) found in Parts XVIII and XIX (other than sections 76 and 87 of the Act, the subject matter of which are not dealt with in NI 51-102). Reporting Issuers can and should therefore refer to NI 51-102 in place of the requirements contained in Parts XVIII and XIX of the Act (other than sections 76 and 87).

Adoption by OSC: (2004) 27 O.S.C.B. 3559 and (2003) 26 O.S.C.B. (Supp-3) 183; Request for Comments: (2003) 26 O.S.C.B. 4577 and (2002) 25 O.S.C.B. 3701.

5.2 — Financial Disclosure

National Instrument 52-107 — Acceptable Accounting Principles and Auditing Standards

Date: March 30, 2004, as amended effective June 1, 2005, December 29, 2006, December 31, 2007, as replaced effective January 1, 2011, as amended effective May 14, 2013, January 11, 2015, May 5, 2015 and January 13, 2016

27 O.S.C.B. 3949, 28 O.S.C.B. 4976, 30 O.S.C.B. (Supp-1) 31, 30 O.S.C.B. 10505, 33 O.S.C.B. (Supp. 5) 1, 36 O.S.C.B. 4935, 37 O.S.C.B. (Supp. 5), 38 O.S.C.B. 4155 and 38 O.S.C.B. (Supp. 5) 28.

[This version of the Instrument reflects changes scheduled to come into force in Ontario on January 13, 2016, and in Alberta, New Brunswick, Nova Scotia, Québec and Saskatchewan on April 30, 2016.]

Part 5: ONGOING REQUIREMENTS

Table of Contents

PART 1 — DEFINITIONS AND INTERPRETATION

1.1 Definitions — In this Instrument:

"accounting principles" means a body of principles relating to accounting that are generally accepted in a jurisdiction of Canada or a foreign jurisdiction and includes, without limitation, IFRS, Canadian GAAP and U.S. GAAP;

"acquisition statements" means financial statements of an acquired business or a business to be acquired, or an operating statement for an oil and gas property that is an acquired business or a business to be acquired, that are

    (a) required to be filed under National Instrument 51-102 *Continuous Disclosure Obligations*,

    (b) included in a prospectus pursuant to Item 35 of Form 41-101F1 *Information Required in a Prospectus*,

    (c) required to be included in a prospectus under National Instrument 44-101 *Short Form Prospectus Distributions*, or

    (d) included in an offering memorandum required under National Instrument 45-106 *Prospectus Exemptions*;

"auditing standards" means a body of standards relating to auditing that are generally accepted in a jurisdiction of Canada or a foreign jurisdiction and includes, without limitation, Canadian GAAS, International Standards on Auditing, U.S. AICPA GAAS and U.S. PCAOB GAAS;

"business acquisition report" means a completed Form 51-102F4 *Business Acquisition Report*;

"convertible security" means a security of an issuer that is convertible into, or carries the right of the holder to acquire, or of the issuer to cause the acquisition of, a security of the same issuer;

"credit support issuer" means an issuer of securities for which a credit supporter has provided a guarantee or alternative credit support;

"credit supporter" means a person or company that provides a guarantee or alternative credit support for any of the payments to be made by an issuer of securities as stipulated in the terms of the securities or in an agreement governing rights of, or granting rights to, holders of the securities;

"designated foreign issuer" means a foreign issuer

    (a) that does not have a class of securities registered under section 12 of the 1934 Act and is not required to file reports under section 15(d) of the 1934 Act,

    (b) that is subject to foreign disclosure requirements in a designated foreign jurisdiction, and

    (c) for which the total number of equity securities beneficially owned by residents of Canada does not exceed 10%, on a fully-diluted basis, of the total number of equity securities of the issuer, calculated in accordance with sections 1.2 and 1.3;

"designated foreign jurisdiction" means Australia, France, Germany, Hong Kong, Italy, Japan, Mexico, the Netherlands, New Zealand, Singapore, South Africa, Spain, Sweden, Switzerland or the United Kingdom of Great Britain and Northern Ireland;

"exchangeable security" means a security of an issuer that is exchangeable for, or carries the right of the holder to acquire, or of the issuer to cause the acquisition of, a security of another issuer;

"exchange-traded security" means a security that is listed on a recognized exchange or is quoted on a recognized quotation and trade reporting system or is listed on an exchange or quoted on a quotation and trade reporting system that is recognized for the purposes of National Instrument 21-101 *Marketplace Operation* and National Instrument 23-101 *Trading Rules*;

"executive officer" means, for an issuer, an individual who is

    (a) a chair, vice-chair or president;

    (b) a vice-president in charge of a principal business unit, division or function including sales, finance or production; or

    (c) performing a policy-making function in respect of the issuer;

"financial statements" includes interim financial reports;

"foreign disclosure requirements" means the requirements to which a foreign issuer is subject concerning disclosure made to the public, to securityholders of the issuer or to a foreign regulatory authority

    (a) relating to the foreign issuer and the trading in its securities, and

    (b) that is made publicly available in the foreign jurisdiction under

        (i) the securities laws of the foreign jurisdiction in which the principal trading market of the foreign issuer is located, or

        (ii) the rules of the marketplace that is the principal trading market of the foreign issuer;

"foreign issuer" means an issuer that is incorporated or organized under the laws of a foreign jurisdiction, unless

    (a) outstanding voting securities of the issuer carrying more than 50% of the votes for the election of directors are beneficially owned by residents of Canada, and

    (b) any of the following apply:

        (i) the majority of the executive officers or directors of the issuer are residents of Canada;

        (ii) more than 50% of the consolidated assets of the issuer are located in Canada; or

(iii) the business of the issuer is administered principally in Canada;

"foreign registrant" means a registrant that is incorporated or organized under the laws of a foreign jurisdiction, unless

(a) outstanding voting securities of the registrant carrying more than 50% of the votes for the election of directors are beneficially owned by residents of Canada, and

(b) any of the following apply:

(i) the majority of the executive officers or directors of the registrant are residents of Canada;

(ii) more than 50% of the consolidated assets of the registrant are located in Canada; or

(iii) the business of the registrant is administered principally in Canada;

"foreign regulatory authority" means a securities commission, exchange or other securities market regulatory authority in a designated foreign jurisdiction;

"IAS 27" means International Accounting Standard 27 *Consolidated and Separate Financial Statements*, as amended from time to time;

"IAS 34" means International Accounting Standard 34 *Interim Financial Reporting*, as amended from time to time;

"inter-dealer bond broker" means a person or company that is approved by the Investment Industry Regulatory Organization of Canada under its Rule No. 36 *Inter-Dealer Bond Brokerage Systems*, as amended, and is subject to its Rule No. 36 and its Rule 2100 *Inter-Dealer Bond Brokerage Systems*, as amended from time to time;

"IPO venture issuer" has the same meaning as in section 1.1 of National Instrument 41-101 *General Prospectus Requirements*;

"issuer's GAAP" means the accounting principles used to prepare an issuer's financial statements, as permitted by this Instrument;

"marketplace" means

(a) an exchange,

(b) a quotation and trade reporting system,

(c) a person or company not included in paragraph (a) or (b) that

(i) constitutes, maintains or provides a market or facility for bringing together buyers and sellers of securities,

(ii) brings together the orders for securities of multiple buyers and sellers, and

(iii) uses established, non-discretionary methods under which the orders interact with each other, and the buyers and sellers entering the orders agree to the terms of a trade, or

(d) a dealer that executes a trade of an exchange-traded security outside of a marketplace,

but does not include an inter-dealer bond broker;

"multiple convertible security" means a security of an issuer that is convertible into, or exchangeable for, or carries the right of the holder to acquire, or of the issuer to cause the acquisition of, a convertible security, an exchangeable security or another multiple convertible security;

"predecessor statements" mean the financial statements referred to in paragraph 32.1(1)(a) of Form 41-101F1 *Information Required in a Prospectus*;

"primary business statements" mean the financial statements referred to in paragraph 32.1(1)(b) of Form 41-101F1 *Information Required in a Prospectus*;

"principal trading market" means the published market on which the largest trading volume in the equity securities of the issuer occurred during the issuer's most recently completed financial year that ended before the date the determination is being made;

"published market" means, for a class of securities, a marketplace on which the securities have traded that discloses, regularly in a publication of general and regular paid circulation or in a form that is broadly distributed by electronic means, the prices at which those securities have traded;

"recognized exchange" means

(a) in Ontario, an exchange recognized by the securities regulatory authority to carry on business as a stock exchange;

(b) in Québec, a person or company authorized by the securities regulatory authority to carry on business as an exchange; and

(c) in every other jurisdiction of Canada, an exchange recognized by the securities regulatory authority as an exchange, self-regulatory organization or self-regulatory body;

"recognized quotation and trade reporting system" means

(a) in every jurisdiction of Canada other than British Columbia, a quotation and trade reporting system recognized by the securities regulatory authority under securities legislation to carry on business as a quotation and trade reporting system, and

(b) in British Columbia, a quotation and trade reporting system recognized by the securities regulatory authority under securities legislation as a quotation and trade reporting system or as an exchange;

"SEC issuer" means an issuer that

(a) has a class of securities registered under section 12 of the 1934 Act or is required to file reports under section 15(d) of the 1934 Act, and

(b) is not registered or required to be registered as an investment company under the *Investment Company Act of 1940* of the United States of America, as amended from time to time;

"SEC foreign issuer" means a foreign issuer that is also an SEC issuer;

"underlying security" means a security issued or transferred, or to be issued or transferred, in accordance with the terms of a convertible security, an exchangeable security or a multiple convertible security;

"U.S. GAAP" means generally accepted accounting principles in the United States of America that the SEC has identified as having substantial authoritative support, as supplemented by Regulation S-X under the 1934 Act, as amended from time to time;

"U.S. AICPA GAAS" means auditing standards of the American Institute of Certified Public Accountants, as amended from time to time;

"U.S. PCAOB GAAS" means auditing standards of the Public Company Accounting Oversight Board (United States of America), as amended from time to time;

"venture issuer",

    (a) in the case of acquisition statements required by National Instrument 51-102 *Continuous Disclosure Obligations*, has the same meaning as in subsection 1.1(1) of that Instrument, and

    (b) in the case of acquisition statements referred to in paragraph (b), (c) or (d) of the definition of "acquisition statements", has the same meaning as in section 1.1 of National Instrument 41-101 *General Prospectus Requirements*.

1.2 Determination of Canadian Shareholders for Calculation of Designated Foreign Issuer and Foreign Issuer — (1) For the purposes of paragraph (c) of the definition of "designated foreign issuer" in section 1.1 and for the purposes of paragraphs 3.9(1)(c) and 4.9(c), a reference to equity securities beneficially owned by residents of Canada includes

    (a) any underlying securities that are equity securities of the foreign issuer, and

    (b) the equity securities of the foreign issuer represented by an American depositary receipt or an American depositary share issued by a depositary holding equity securities of the foreign issuer.

(2) For the purposes of paragraph (a) of the definition of "foreign issuer" in section 1.1, securities represented by American depositary receipts or American depositary shares issued by a depositary holding voting securities of the foreign issuer must be included as outstanding in determining both the number of votes attached to securities beneficially owned by residents of Canada and the number of votes attached to all of the issuer's outstanding voting securities.

1.3 Timing for Calculation of Designated Foreign Issuer, Foreign Issuer and Foreign Registrant — For the purposes of paragraph (c) of the definition of "designated foreign issuer" in section 1.1, paragraph (a) of the definition of "foreign issuer" in section 1.1, and paragraph (a) of the definition of "foreign registrant" in section 1.1, the calculation is made

    (a) if the issuer has not completed one financial year, on the earlier of

        (i) the date that is 90 days before the date of its prospectus, and

        (ii) the date that it became a reporting issuer; and

    (b) for all other issuers and for registrants, on the first day of the most recent financial year or interim period for which financial performance is presented in the financial statements or interim financial information filed or delivered or included in a prospectus.

1.4 Interpretation — (1) For the purposes of this Instrument, a reference to "prospectus" includes a preliminary prospectus, a prospectus, an amendment to a preliminary prospectus and an amendment to a prospectus.

(2) For the purposes of this Instrument, a reference to information being "included in" another document means information reproduced in the document or incorporated into the document by reference.

PART 2 — APPLICATION

2.1 Application — (1) This Instrument does not apply to investment funds that are subject to National Instrument 81-106 *Investment Fund Continuous Disclosure* in respect of their reporting requirements as investment funds.

(2) This Instrument applies to

    (a) all financial statements and interim financial information delivered by registrants to the securities regulatory authority or regulator under National Instrument 31-103 *Registration Requirements, Exemptions and Ongoing Registrant Obligations*,

    (b) all financial statements filed, or included in a document that is filed, by an issuer under National Instrument 51-102 *Continuous Disclosure Obligations* or National Instrument 71-102 *Continuous Disclosure and Other Exemptions Relating to Foreign Issuers*,

    (c) all financial statements included in

        (i) a prospectus, a take-over bid circular or any other document that is filed by or in connection with an issuer, or

        (ii) an offering memorandum required to be delivered by an issuer under National Instrument 45-106 *Prospectus Exemptions*,

    (d) any acquisition statements, predecessor statements, or primary business statements, that are an operating statement for an oil and gas property that is an acquired business or a business to be acquired, that is

        (i) filed by an issuer under National Instrument 51-102 *Continuous Disclosure Obligations*,

        (ii) included in a prospectus, take-over bid circular or any other document that is filed by or in connection with an issuer, or

        (iii) included in an offering memorandum required to be delivered by an issuer under National Instrument 45-106 *Prospectus Exemptions*,

    (e) any other financial statements filed, or included in a document that is filed, by a reporting issuer,

    (f) summary financial information for a credit supporter or credit support issuer that is

        (i) filed under National Instrument 51-102 *Continuous Disclosure Obligations*,

        (ii) included in a prospectus, take-over bid circular or any other document that is filed by or in connection with an issuer, or

        (iii) included in an offering memorandum required to be delivered by an issuer under National Instrument 45-106 *Prospectus Exemptions*,

    (g) summarized financial information of an acquired business or business to be acquired that is, or will be, an investment accounted for by the issuer using the equity method, that is

        (i) filed by an issuer under National Instrument 51-102 *Continuous Disclosure Obligations*,

        (ii) included in a prospectus, take-over bid circular or any other document that is filed by or in connection with an issuer, or

        (iii) included in an offering memorandum required to be delivered by an issuer under National Instrument 45-106 *Prospectus Exemptions*,

    (h) *pro forma* financial statements

        (i) filed, or included in a document that is filed, by an issuer under National Instrument 51-102 *Continuous Disclosure Obligations* or National Instrument 71-102 *Continuous Disclosure and Other Exemptions Relating to Foreign Issuers*,

        (ii) included in a prospectus, take-over bid circular or any other document that is filed by or in connection with an issuer, or

        (iii) otherwise filed, or included in a document that is filed, by a reporting issuer, and

(i) all financial statements

(i) filed by an issuer under subsection 2.9(17.4) of National Instrument 45-106 *Prospectus Exemptions*,

(ii) delivered by an issuer under subsection 2.9(17.5) of National Instrument 45-106 *Prospectus Exemptions*, or

(iii) made reasonably available by an issuer under subsection 2.9(17.6) of National Instrument 45-106 *Prospectus Exemptions*.

PART 3 — RULES APPLYING TO FINANCIAL YEARS BEGINNING ON OR AFTER JANUARY 1, 2011

3.1 Definitions and Application — (1) In this Part:

"publicly accountable enterprise" means a publicly accountable enterprise as defined in the Handbook;

"private enterprise" means a private enterprise as defined in the Handbook.

(2) This Part applies to financial statements, financial information, operating statements and *pro forma* financial statements for periods relating to financial years beginning on or after January 1, 2011.

3.2 Acceptable Accounting Principles — General Requirements — (1) Financial statements referred to in paragraphs 2.1(2)(b), (c), (e) and (i) other than acquisition statements, must

(a) be prepared in accordance with Canadian GAAP applicable to publicly accountable enterprises, and

(b) disclose

(i) in the case of annual financial statements, an unreserved statement of compliance with IFRS, and

(ii) in the case of an interim financial report, an unreserved statement of compliance with IAS 34.

(2) Despite subsection (1), in the case of an interim financial report that is not required under securities legislation to provide comparative interim financial information,

(a) the statement of financial position, statement of comprehensive income, statement of changes in equity, statement of cash flows and explanatory notes must be prepared in accordance with IAS 34 other than the requirement in IAS 34 to include comparative financial information; and

(b) the interim financial report must disclose that

(i) it does not comply with IAS 34 because it does not include comparative interim financial information, and

(ii) the statement of financial position, statement of comprehensive income, statement of changes in equity, statement of cash flows and explanatory notes have been prepared in accordance with IAS 34 other than the requirement in IAS 34 to include comparative financial information.

(3) Financial statements and interim financial information referred to in paragraph 2.1(2)(a) must

(a) be prepared in accordance with Canadian GAAP applicable to publicly accountable enterprises, except that any investments in subsidiaries, jointly controlled entities and associates must be accounted for as specified for separate financial statements in IAS 27, and

(b) in the case of annual financial statements,

(i) include the following statement:

These financial statements are prepared in accordance with the financial reporting framework specified in [*insert* "paragraph 3.2(3)(a)", "subsection 3.2(4)" *or* "section 3.15" *as applicable*] of National Instrument 52-107 *Acceptable Accounting Principles and Auditing Standards* for financial statements delivered by registrants.

and

(ii) describe the financial reporting framework used to prepare the financial statements.

(4) Despite paragraph (3)(a), financial statements and interim financial information referred to in paragraph 2.1(2)(a) for periods relating to a financial year beginning in 2011 may be prepared in accordance with Canadian GAAP applicable to publicly accountable enterprises, except that

(a) any investments in subsidiaries, jointly controlled entities and associates must be accounted for as specified for separate financial statements in IAS 27,

(b) comparative information relating to the preceding financial year must be excluded, and

(c) the first day of the financial year to which the financial statements or interim financial information relates must be used as the date of transition to the financial reporting framework.

(5) Financial statements must be prepared in accordance with the same accounting principles for all periods presented in the financial statements.

(6) Financial information referred to in paragraphs 2.1(2)(f) and (g) must

(a) present the line items for summary financial information or summarized financial information required by National Instrument 45-106 *Prospectus Exemptions* or National Instrument 51-102 *Continuous Disclosure Obligations*, as the case may be, and

(b) in the case of summarized financial information of an acquired business or business to be acquired that is, or will be, an investment accounted for by the issuer using the equity method,

(i) be prepared using accounting policies that

(A) are permitted by one of Canadian GAAP applicable to publicly accountable enterprises, IFRS, U.S. GAAP or Canadian GAAP applicable to private enterprises, and

(B) would apply to the information if the information were presented as part of a complete set of financial statements,

(ii) include the following statement:

This information is prepared in accordance with the financial reporting framework specified in subsection 3.2(6) of National Instrument 52-107 *Acceptable Accounting Principles and Auditing Standards* for summarized financial information of a business accounted for using the equity method.

and

(iii) describe the accounting policies used to prepare the information.

3.3 Acceptable Auditing Standards — General Requirements — (1) Financial statements, other than acquisition statements, that are required by securities legislation to be audited must

(a) be audited in accordance with Canadian GAAS and be accompanied by an auditor's report that

(i) expresses an unmodified opinion,

(ii) identifies all financial periods presented for which the auditor has issued an auditor's report,

(iii) is in the form specified by Canadian GAAS for an audit of financial statements prepared in accordance with a fair presentation framework, and

(iv) refers to IFRS as the applicable fair presentation framework if the financial statements are prepared in accordance with Canadian GAAP applicable to publicly accountable enterprises, and

(b) if the issuer or registrant has changed its auditor and one or more of the comparative periods presented in the financial statements were audited by a predecessor auditor, be accompanied by the predecessor auditor's reports on the comparative periods.

(2) Paragraph (1)(b) does not apply to financial statements referred to in paragraphs 2.1(2)(a) and (b) if the auditor's report described in paragraph (1)(a) refers to the predecessor auditor's reports on the comparative periods.

3.4 Acceptable Auditors — An auditor's report filed by an issuer or delivered by a registrant must be prepared and signed by a person or company that is authorized to sign an auditor's report under the laws of a jurisdiction of Canada or a foreign jurisdiction, and that meets the professional standards of that jurisdiction.

3.5 Presentation and Functional Currencies — (1) The presentation currency must be prominently displayed in financial statements.

(2) Financial statements must disclose the functional currency if it is different than the presentation currency.

3.6 Credit Supporters — (1) Unless subsection 3.2(1) applies, if a credit support issuer files, or includes in a prospectus, financial statements of a credit supporter, the credit supporter's financial statements must

(a) be prepared in accordance with the accounting principles and audited in accordance with the auditing standards that would apply under this Instrument if the credit supporter were to file financial statements referred to in paragraph 2.1(2)(b), and

(b) identify the accounting principles used to prepare the financial statements.

(2) If a credit support issuer files, or includes in a prospectus, summary financial information for the credit supporter or credit support issuer,

(a) the summary financial information must, in addition to satisfying other requirements in this Instrument

(i) prominently display the presentation currency, and

(ii) disclose the functional currency if it is different from the presentation currency, and

(b) the amounts presented in the summary financial information must be derived from financial statements of the credit supporter or credit support issuer that, if required by securities legislation to be audited, are audited in accordance with the auditing standards that would apply under this Instrument if the credit supporter or credit support issuer, as the case may be, were to file financial statements referred to in paragraph 2.1(2)(b).

3.7 Acceptable Accounting Principles for SEC Issuers — (1) Despite subsection 3.2(1), an SEC issuer's financial statements referred to in paragraphs 2.1(2)(b), (c), (e) and (i) and financial information referred to in paragraphs 2.1(2)(f) and (g) that are filed with or delivered to a securities regulatory authority or regulator, other than acquisition statements, may be prepared in accordance with U.S. GAAP.

(2) The notes to the financial statements referred to in subsection (1) must identify the accounting principles used to prepare the financial statements.

3.8 Acceptable Auditing Standards for SEC Issuers — (1) Despite subsection 3.3(1), an SEC issuer's financial statements referred to in paragraphs 2.1(2)(b), (c), (e) and (i) and financial information referred to in paragraphs 2.1(2)(f) and (g) that are filed with or delivered to a securities regulatory authority or regulator, other than acquisition statements, and that are required by securities legislation to be audited, may be audited in accordance with U.S. PCAOB GAAS if the financial statements are accompanied by

(a) an auditor's report prepared in accordance with U.S. PCAOB GAAS that

(i) expresses an unqualified opinion,

(ii) identifies all financial periods presented for which the auditor has issued an auditor's report, and

(iii) identifies the auditing standards used to conduct the audit and the accounting principles used to prepare the financial statements, and

(b) the predecessor auditor's reports on the comparative periods, if the issuer has changed its auditor and one or more of the comparative periods presented in the financial statements were audited by the predecessor auditor.

(2) Paragraph (1)(b) does not apply to financial statements referred to in paragraph 2.1(2)(b) if the auditor's report described in paragraph (1)(a) refers to the predecessor auditor's reports on the comparative periods.

3.9 Acceptable Accounting Principles for Foreign Issuers — (1) Despite subsection 3.2(1), a foreign issuer's financial statements referred to in paragraphs 2.1(2)(b), (c), (e) and (i) that are filed with or delivered to a securities regulatory authority or regulator, other than acquisition statements, may be prepared in accordance with

(a) IFRS,

(b) U.S. GAAP, if the issuer is an SEC foreign issuer,

(c) accounting principles that meet the disclosure requirements for foreign private issuers, as that term is defined for the purposes of the 1934 Act, if

(i) the issuer is an SEC foreign issuer,

(ii) on the last day of the most recently completed financial year the total number of equity securities of the issuer beneficially owned by residents of Canada does not exceed 10%, on a fully-diluted basis, of the total number of equity securities of the issuer, and

(iii) the financial statements include any reconciliation to U.S. GAAP required by the SEC, or

(d) accounting principles that meet the foreign disclosure requirements of the designated foreign jurisdiction to which the issuer is subject, if the issuer is a designated foreign issuer.

(2) The notes to the financial statements must identify the accounting principles used to prepare the financial statements.

3.10 Acceptable Auditing Standards for Foreign Issuers — (1) Despite subsection 3.3(1), a foreign issuer's financial statements referred to in paragraphs 2.1(2)(b), (c), (e) and (i) that are filed with or delivered to a securities regulatory authority or regulator, other than acquisition statements, that are required by securities legislation to be audited may be audited in accordance with

(a) International Standards on Auditing if the financial statements are accompanied by

(i) an auditor's report that

(A) expresses an unmodified opinion,

(B) identifies all financial periods presented for which the auditor has issued the auditor's report,

(C) identifies the auditing standards used to conduct the audit and the accounting principles used to prepare the financial statements, and

(D) is prepared in accordance with the same auditing standards used to conduct the audit, and

(ii) the predecessor auditor's reports on the comparative periods, if the issuer has changed its auditor and one or more of the comparative periods presented in the financial statements were audited by the predecessor auditor,

(b) U.S. PCAOB GAAS if the financial statements are accompanied by

(i) an auditor's report that

(A) expresses an unqualified opinion,

(B) identifies all financial periods presented for which the auditor has issued the auditor's report,

(C) identifies the auditing standards used to conduct the audit and the accounting principles used to prepare the financial statements, and

(D) is prepared in accordance with the same auditing standards used to conduct the audit, and

(ii) the predecessor auditor's reports on the comparative periods, if the issuer has changed its auditor and one or more of the comparative periods presented in the financial statements were audited by the predecessor auditor, or

(c) auditing standards that meet the foreign disclosure requirements of the designated foreign jurisdiction to which the issuer is subject if

(i) the issuer is a designated foreign issuer,

(ii) the financial statements are accompanied by an auditor's report prepared in accordance with the same auditing standards used to conduct the audit, and

(iii) the auditor's report identifies the auditing standards used to conduct the audit and the accounting principles used to prepare the financial statements.

(2) Subparagraph (1)(a)(ii) or (b)(ii) does not apply to financial statements referred to in paragraph 2.1(2)(b) if the auditor's report described in subparagraph (1)(a)(i) or (b)(i), as the case may be, refers to the predecessor auditor's reports on the comparative periods.

3.11 Acceptable Accounting Principles for Acquisition Statements — (1) Acquisition statements must be prepared in accordance with one of the following accounting principles:

(a) Canadian GAAP applicable to publicly accountable enterprises;

(b) IFRS;

(c) U.S. GAAP;

(d) accounting principles that meet the disclosure requirements for foreign private issuers, as that term is defined for the purposes of the 1934 Act, if

(i) the issuer or the acquired business or business to be acquired is an SEC foreign issuer,

(ii) on the last day of the most recently completed financial year the total number of equity securities of the SEC foreign issuer beneficially owned by residents of Canada does not exceed 10%, on a fully-diluted basis, of the total number of equity securities of the SEC foreign issuer, and

(iii) the financial statements include any reconciliation to U.S. GAAP required by the SEC;

(e) accounting principles that meet the foreign disclosure requirements of the designated foreign jurisdiction to which the issuer or the acquired business or business to be acquired is subject, if

(i) the issuer or business is a designated foreign issuer, and

(ii) in the case where the issuer's GAAP differs from the accounting principles used to prepare the acquisition statements, for the most recently completed financial year and interim period presented, the notes to the acquisition statements:

(A) describe the material differences between the issuer's GAAP and the accounting principles used to prepare the acquisition statements that relate to recognition, measurement and presentation, and

(B) quantify the effect of each difference referred to in clause (A) and include a tabular reconciliation between profit or loss reported in the acquisition statements and profit or loss computed in accordance with the issuer's GAAP;

(f) Canadian GAAP applicable to private enterprises if

(i) the acquisition statements consolidate any subsidiaries and account for significantly influenced investees and joint ventures using the equity method,

(ii) financial statements for the acquired business or business to be acquired were not previously prepared in accordance with one of the accounting principles specified in paragraphs (a) to (e) for the periods presented in the acquisition statements,

(iii) the acquisition statements are accompanied by a notice stating:

These financial statements are prepared in accordance with Canadian GAAP applicable to private enterprises, which are Canadian accounting standards for private enterprises in Part II of the Handbook.

The recognition, measurement and disclosure requirements of Canadian GAAP applicable to private enterprises differ from those of Canadian GAAP applicable to publicly accountable enterprises, which are International Financial Reporting Standards incorporated into the Handbook.

The *pro forma* financial statements included in the document include adjustments relating to the [*insert* "acquired business" *or* "business to be acquired" *as applicable*] and present *pro forma* information prepared using principles that are consistent with the accounting principles used by the issuer.

and

(iv) in the case of acquisition statements included in a document filed by an issuer that is not a venture issuer, and is not an IPO venture issuer, for all financial years and the most recently completed interim period presented, the notes to the acquisition statements

(A) describe the material differences between the issuer's GAAP and the accounting principles used to prepare the acquisition statements that relate to recognition, measurement and presentation,

(B) quantify the effect of each difference referred to in clause (A), and include a tabular reconciliation between profit or loss reported in the acquisition statements and profit or loss computed in accordance with the issuer's GAAP, and

(C) for each difference referred to in clause (A) that relates to measurement, disclose and discuss the material inputs or assumptions underlying the measurement of the relevant amount computed in accordance with the issuer's GAAP, consistent with the disclosure requirements of the issuer's GAAP.

(2) Acquisition statements must be prepared in accordance with the same accounting principles for all periods presented.

(3) Acquisition statements to which paragraph (1)(a) applies must disclose

(a) in the case of annual financial statements, an unreserved statement of compliance with IFRS, and

(b) in the case of interim financial reports, an unreserved statement of compliance with IAS 34.

(4) Unless paragraph (1)(a) applies, the notes to the acquisition statements must identify the accounting principles used to prepare the acquisition statements.

(5) Despite subsections (1) and (2), if acquisition statements are an operating statement for an oil and gas property that is an acquired business or business to be acquired

(a) the operating statement must include at least the following line items:

(i) gross sales;

(ii) royalties;

(iii) production costs;

(iv) operating income;

(b) the line items in the operating statement must be prepared using accounting policies that

(i) are permitted by one of Canadian GAAP applicable to publicly accountable enterprises, IFRS, U.S. GAAP or Canadian GAAP applicable to private enterprises, and

(ii) would apply to those line items if those line items were presented as part of a complete set of financial statements, and

(c) the operating statement must

(i) include the following statement:

This operating statement is prepared in accordance with the financial reporting framework specified in subsection 3.11(5) of National Instrument 52-107 *Acceptable Accounting Principles and Auditing Standards* for an operating statement.

and

(ii) describe the accounting policies used to prepare the operating statement.

3.12 Acceptable Auditing Standards for Acquisition Statements — (1) Acquisition statements that are required by securities legislation to be audited must be accompanied by an auditor's report and audited in accordance with one of the following auditing standards:

(a) Canadian GAAS;

(b) International Standards on Auditing;

(c) U.S. PCAOB GAAS;

(d) U.S. AICPA GAAS, if the acquired business or business to be acquired is not an SEC issuer;

(e) auditing standards that meet the foreign disclosure requirements of the designated foreign jurisdiction to which the issuer is subject, if the issuer is a designated foreign issuer.

(2) The auditor's report must,

(a) if paragraph (1)(a) or (b) applies, express an unmodified opinion,

(b) if paragraph (1)(c) or (d) applies, express an unqualified opinion,

(c) unless paragraph (1)(e) applies, identify all financial periods presented for which the auditor's report applies,

(d) identify the auditing standards used to conduct the audit,

(e) identify the accounting principles used or, if subsection 3.11(5) applies, the financial reporting framework used, to prepare the acquisition statements, unless the auditor's report accompanies acquisition statements prepared in accordance with Canadian GAAP applicable to publicly accountable enterprises and audited in accordance with Canadian GAAS, and

(f) if paragraph (1)(a) or (b) applies and subsection 3.11(5) does not,

(i) be in the form specified by the standards referred to in paragraph (1)(a) or (b), as applicable, for an audit of financial statements prepared in accordance with a fair presentation framework, and

(ii) refer to IFRS as the applicable fair presentation framework if the financial statements are prepared in accordance with Canadian GAAP applicable to publicly accountable enterprises.

(3) Despite paragraphs (2)(a) and (b), an auditor's report that accompanies acquisition statements may express a qualification of opinion relating to inventory if

(a) the issuer includes in the business acquisition report, prospectus or other document containing the acquisition statements, a statement of financial position for the acquired business or business to be acquired that is for a date that is subsequent to the date to which the qualification relates, and

(b) the statement of financial position referred to in paragraph (a) is accompanied by an auditor's report that does not express a qualification of opinion relating to closing inventory.

3.13 Financial Information for Acquisitions Accounted for by the Issuer Using the Equity Method — (1) If an issuer files, or includes in a prospectus, summarized financial information of an acquired business or business to be acquired that is, or will be, an investment accounted for by the issuer using the equity method, the financial information must

(a) meet the requirements in subsections 3.11(1), (2) and (4) if the term "acquisition statements" in those subsections is read as "summarized financial information", and

(b) disclose the presentation currency for the financial information, and disclose the functional currency if it is different than the presentation currency.

(2) If the financial information referred to in subsection (1) is required by securities legislation to be audited or derived from audited financial statements, the financial information must

(a) either

(i) meet the requirements in section 3.12 if the term "acquisition statements" in that section is read as "summarized financial information", or

(ii) be derived from financial statements that meet the requirements in section 3.12 if the term "acquisition statements" in that section is read as "financial statements from which is derived summarized financial information", and

(b) be audited, or derived from financial statements that are audited, by a person or company that is authorized to sign an auditor's report under the laws of a jurisdiction of Canada or a foreign jurisdiction, and that meets the professional standards of that jurisdiction.

3.14 Acceptable Accounting Policies for Pro Forma Financial Statements — (1) An issuer's *pro forma* financial statements must be prepared using accounting policies that

(a) are permitted by the issuer's GAAP, and

(b) would apply to the information presented in the *pro forma* financial statements if that information were included in the issuer's financial statements for the same period as that of the *pro forma* financial statements.

(2) Despite subsection (1), if an issuer's financial statements include, or are accompanied by, a reconciliation to U.S. GAAP, the issuer's *pro forma* financial statements for the same period as the issuer's financial statements may be prepared using accounting policies that

(a) are permitted by U.S. GAAP, and

(b) would apply to the information presented in the *pro forma* financial statements if that information were included in the reconciliation.

(3) Despite subsection (1), if the accounting principles used to prepare an issuer's most recent annual financial statements differ from the accounting principles used to prepare the issuer's interim financial report for a subsequent period, the issuer may prepare a *pro forma* income statement for the same period as that of its most recent annual financial statements using accounting policies that

(a) are permitted by the accounting principles that were used to prepare the issuer's interim financial report, and

(b) would apply to the information presented in the *pro forma* income statement if that information were included in the issuer's interim financial report.

3.15 Acceptable Accounting Principles for Foreign Registrants — Despite paragraph 3.2(3)(a), financial statements and interim financial information delivered by a foreign registrant may be prepared in accordance with

(a) IFRS, except that any investments in subsidiaries, jointly controlled entities and associates must be accounted for as specified for separate financial statements in IAS 27,

(b) U.S. GAAP, except that any investments in subsidiaries, jointly controlled entities and associates must be accounted for as specified for separate financial statements in IAS 27, or

(c) accounting principles that meet the disclosure requirements of a foreign regulatory authority to which the registrant is subject, if it is a foreign registrant incorporated or organized under the laws of that designated foreign jurisdiction.

3.16 Acceptable Auditing Standards for Foreign Registrants — (1) Despite subsection 3.3(1), financial statements referred to in paragraph 2.1(2)(a) that are delivered by a foreign registrant and required by securities legislation to be audited may be audited in accordance with

(a) International Standards on Auditing if the financial statements are accompanied by

(i) an auditor's report that

(A) expresses an unmodified opinion,

(B) identifies all financial periods presented for which the auditor has issued the auditor's report,

(C) identifies the auditing standards used to conduct the audit and the accounting principles used to prepare the financial statements, and

(D) is prepared in accordance with the same auditing standards used to conduct the audit, and

(ii) the predecessor auditor's reports on the comparative periods, if the foreign registrant has changed its auditor and one or more of the comparative periods presented in the financial statements were audited by the predecessor auditor,

(b) U.S. PCAOB GAAS or U.S. AICPA GAAS if the financial statements are accompanied by

(i) an auditor's report that

(A) expresses an unqualified opinion,

(B) identifies all financial periods presented for which the auditor has issued the auditor's report,

(C) identifies the auditing standards used to conduct the audit and the accounting principles used to prepare the financial statements, and

(D) is prepared in accordance with the same auditing standards used to conduct the audit, and

(ii) the predecessor auditor's reports on the comparative periods, if the foreign registrant has changed its auditor and one or more of the comparative periods presented in the financial statements were audited by the predecessor auditor, or

(c) auditing standards that meet the foreign disclosure requirements of the designated foreign jurisdiction to which the registrant is subject if

(i) it is a foreign registrant incorporated or organized under the laws of that designated foreign jurisdiction,

(ii) the financial statements are accompanied by an auditor's report prepared in accordance with the same auditing standards used to conduct the audit, and

(iii) the auditor's report identifies the accounting principles used to prepare the financial statements.

(2) Subparagraph (1)(a)(ii) or (b)(ii) does not apply if the auditor's report described in subparagraph (1)(a)(i) or (b)(i), as the case may be, refers to the predecessor auditor's reports on the comparative periods.

3.17 Acceptable Accounting Principles for Predecessor Statements or Primary Business Statements that are an Operating Statement — If predecessor statements or primary business statements are an operating statement for an oil and gas property,

(a) the operating statement must include at least the following line items:

(i) gross sales;

(ii) royalties;

(iii) production costs;

(iv) operating income;

(b) the line items in the operating statement must be prepared using accounting policies that

(i) are permitted by one of:

(A) Canadian GAAP applicable to publicly accountable enterprises;

(B) U.S. GAAP if the issuer is an SEC issuer or an SEC foreign issuer;

(C) IFRS if the issuer is a foreign issuer, and

(ii) would apply to those line items if those line items were presented as part of a complete set of financial statements, and

(c) the operating statement must

(i) include the following statement:

This operating statement is prepared in accordance with the financial reporting framework specified in section 3.17 of National Instrument 52-107 *Acceptable Accounting Principles and Auditing Standards* for an operating statement.

and

(ii) describe the accounting policies used to prepare the operating statement.

3.18 Acceptable Auditing Standards for Predecessor Statements or Primary Business Statements that are an Operating Statement — (1) If predecessor statements or primary business statements are an operating statement for an oil and gas property that are required by securities legislation to be audited, the operating statement must be accompanied by an auditor's report and audited in accordance with one of the following auditing standards:

(a) Canadian GAAS;

(b) U.S. PCAOB GAAS if the issuer is an SEC issuer or an SEC foreign issuer;

(c) International Standards on Auditing if the issuer is a foreign issuer.

(2) The auditor's report must,

(a) if paragraph 1(a) or (c) applies, express an unmodified opinion,

(b) if paragraph 1(b) applies, express an unqualified opinion,

(c) identify all financial periods presented for which the auditor's report applies,

(d) identify the auditing standards used to conduct the audit, and

(e) identify the financial reporting framework used to prepare the operating statement.

PART 4 — RULES APPLYING TO FINANCIAL YEARS BEGINNING BEFORE JANUARY 1, 2011

4.1 Definitions and Application — (1) In this Part:

"Canadian GAAP — Part V" means generally accepted accounting principles determined with reference to Part V of the Handbook applicable to public enterprises;

"public enterprise" means a public enterprise as defined in Part V of the Handbook.

(2) This Part applies to financial statements, financial information, operating statements and *pro forma* financial statements for periods relating to financial years beginning before January 1, 2011.

4.2 Acceptable Accounting Principles — General Requirements — (1) Financial statements, other than financial statements delivered by registrants and acquisition statements, must be prepared in accordance with Canadian GAAP — Part V.

(2) Financial statements and interim financial information delivered by a registrant to the securities regulatory authority, must be prepared in accordance with Canadian GAAP — Part V except that the financial statements and interim financial information must be prepared on a non-consolidated basis.

(3) Financial statements must be prepared in accordance with the same accounting principles for all periods presented in the financial statements.

(4) The notes to the financial statements must identify the accounting principles used to prepare the financial statements.

4.3 Acceptable Auditing Standards — General Requirements — Financial statements, other than acquisition statements, that are required by securities legislation to be audited must be audited in accordance with Canadian GAAS and be accompanied by an auditor's report that

    (a) expresses an unmodified opinion,

    (b) identifies all financial periods presented for which the auditor has issued an auditor's report,

    (c) refers to the predecessor auditor's reports on the comparative periods, if the issuer or registrant has changed its auditor and one or more of the comparative periods presented in the financial statements were audited by the predecessor auditor, and

    (d) identifies the accounting principles used to prepare the financial statements.

4.4 Acceptable Auditors — An auditor's report filed by an issuer or delivered by a registrant must be prepared and signed by a person or company that is authorized to sign an auditor's report under the laws of a jurisdiction of Canada or a foreign jurisdiction, and that meets the professional standards of that jurisdiction.

4.5 Measurement and Reporting Currencies — (1) The reporting currency must be disclosed on the face page of the financial statements or in the notes to the financial statements unless the financial statements are prepared in accordance with Canadian GAAP — Part V and the reporting currency is the Canadian dollar.

(2) The notes to the financial statements must disclose the measurement currency if it is different than the reporting currency.

4.6 Credit Supporters — (1) Unless subsection 4.2(1) applies, if a credit support issuer files, or includes in a prospectus, financial statements of a credit supporter, the credit supporter's financial statements must

    (a) be prepared in accordance with the accounting principles and audited in accordance with the auditing standards that apply under this Instrument if the credit supporter were to file financial statements referred to in paragraph 2.1(2)(b),

    (b) identify the accounting principles used to prepare the financial statements, and

    (c) disclose the reporting currency for the financial statements, and disclose the measurement currency if it is different than the reporting currency.

(2) If a credit support issuer files, or includes in a prospectus, summary financial information for the credit supporter or credit support issuer,

    (a) the summary financial information must

        (i) be prepared in accordance with the accounting principles that this Instrument requires to be used in preparing financial statements if the credit supporter or credit support issuer, as the case may be, were to file financial statements referred to in paragraph 2.1(2)(b),

        (ii) identify the accounting principles used to prepare the summary financial information, and

        (iii) disclose the reporting currency for the financial information, and disclose the measurement currency if it is different than the reporting currency, and

    (b) the amounts presented in the summary financial information must be derived from financial statements of the credit supporter or credit support issuer that, if required by securities legislation to be audited, are audited in accordance with the auditing standards that apply under this Instrument if the credit supporter or credit support issuer, as the case may be, were to file financial statements referred to in paragraph 2.1(2)(b).

4.7 Acceptable Accounting Principles for SEC Issuers — (1) Despite subsections 4.2(1) and (3), financial statements of an SEC issuer that are filed with or delivered to a securities regulatory authority or regulator, other than acquisition statements, may be prepared in accordance with U.S. GAAP provided that, if the SEC issuer previously filed or included in a prospectus financial statements prepared in accordance with Canadian GAAP — Part V, the SEC issuer complies with the following:

    (a) the notes to the first two sets of the issuer's annual financial statements after the change from Canadian GAAP — Part V to U.S. GAAP and the notes to the issuer's interim financial statements for interim periods during those two years

        (i) explain the material differences between Canadian GAAP — Part V and U.S. GAAP that relate to recognition, measurement and presentation,

        (ii) quantify the effect of material differences between Canadian GAAP — Part V and U.S. GAAP that relate to recognition, measurement and presentation, including a tabular reconciliation between net income reported in the financial statements and net income computed in accordance with Canadian GAAP — Part V, and

        (iii) provide disclosure consistent with disclosure requirements of Canadian GAAP — Part V to the extent not already reflected in the financial statements;

    (b) financial information for any comparative periods that were previously reported in accordance with Canadian GAAP — Part V are presented

        (i) as previously reported in accordance with Canadian GAAP — Part V,

        (ii) as restated and presented in accordance with U.S. GAAP, and

        (iii) supported by an accompanying note that

            (A) explains the material differences between Canadian GAAP — Part V and U.S. GAAP that relate to recognition, measurement and presentation, and

(B) quantifies the effect of material differences between Canadian GAAP — Part V and U.S. GAAP that relate to recognition, measurement and presentation, including a tabular reconciliation between net income as previously reported in the financial statements in accordance with Canadian GAAP — Part V and net income as restated and presented in accordance with U.S. GAAP, and

(c) if the SEC issuer has filed financial statements prepared in accordance with Canadian GAAP — Part V for one or more interim periods of the current year, those interim financial statements are restated in accordance with U.S. GAAP and comply with paragraphs (a) and (b).

(2) The comparative information specified in subparagraph (1)(b)(i) may be presented on the face of the balance sheet and statements of income and cash flow or in the note to the financial statements required by subparagraph (1)(b)(iii).

4.8 Acceptable Auditing Standards for SEC Issuers — Despite section 4.3, financial statements of an SEC issuer that are filed with or delivered to the securities regulatory authority or regulator, other than acquisition statements, and that are required by securities legislation to be audited, may be audited in accordance with U.S. PCAOB GAAS if the financial statements are accompanied by an auditor's report prepared in accordance with U.S. PCAOB GAAS that

(a) expresses an unqualified opinion,

(b) identifies all financial periods presented for which the auditor has issued an auditor's report,

(c) refers to the predecessor auditor's reports on the comparative periods, if the issuer has changed its auditor and one or more of the comparative periods presented in the financial statements were audited by the predecessor auditor, and

(d) identifies the accounting principles used to prepare the financial statements.

4.9 Acceptable Accounting Principles for Foreign Issuers — Despite subsection 4.2(1), financial statements of a foreign issuer that are filed with or delivered to a securities regulatory authority or regulator, other than acquisition statements, may be prepared in accordance with one of the following accounting principles:

(a) U.S. GAAP, if the issuer is an SEC foreign issuer;

(b) IFRS;

(c) accounting principles that meet the disclosure requirements for foreign private issuers, as that term is defined for the purposes of the 1934 Act, if

(i) the issuer is an SEC foreign issuer,

(ii) on the last day of the most recently completed financial year the total number of equity securities of the issuer beneficially owned by residents of Canada does not exceed 10%, on a fully-diluted basis, of the total number of equity securities of the issuer, and

(iii) the financial statements include any reconciliation to U.S. GAAP required by the SEC;

(d) accounting principles that meet the foreign disclosure requirements of the designated foreign jurisdiction to which the issuer is subject, if the issuer is a designated foreign issuer;

(e) accounting principles that cover substantially the same core subject matter as Canadian GAAP — Part V, including recognition and measurement principles and disclosure requirements, if the notes to the financial statements

(i) explain the material differences between Canadian GAAP — Part V and the accounting principles used that relate to recognition, measurement and presentation,

(ii) quantify the effect of material differences between Canadian GAAP — Part V and the accounting principles used that relate to recognition, measurement and presentation, including a tabular reconciliation between net income reported in the issuer's financial statements and net income computed in accordance with Canadian GAAP — Part V, and

(iii) provide disclosure consistent with Canadian GAAP — Part V requirements to the extent not already reflected in the financial statements.

4.10 Acceptable Auditing Standards for Foreign Issuers — Despite section 4.3, financial statements of a foreign issuer that are filed with or delivered to a securities regulatory authority or regulator, other than acquisition statements, that are required by securities legislation to be audited may, if the financial statements are accompanied by an auditor's report prepared in accordance with the same auditing standards used to conduct the audit and the auditor's report identifies the accounting principles used to prepare the financial statements, be audited in accordance with

(a) U.S. PCAOB GAAS, if the auditor's report

(i) expresses an unqualified opinion,

(ii) identifies all financial periods presented for which the auditor has issued an auditor's report, and

(iii) refers to the predecessor auditor's reports on the comparative periods, if the issuer has changed its auditor and one or more of the comparative periods presented in the financial statements were audited by the predecessor auditor,

(b) International Standards on Auditing, if the auditor's report is accompanied by a statement by the auditor that

(i) describes any material differences in the form and content of the auditor's report as compared to an auditor's report prepared in accordance with Canadian GAAS, and

(ii) indicates that an auditor's report prepared in accordance with Canadian GAAS would express an unmodified opinion, or

(c) auditing standards that meet the foreign disclosure requirements of the designated foreign jurisdiction to which the issuer is subject, if the issuer is a designated foreign issuer.

4.11 Acceptable Accounting Principles for Acquisition Statements — (1) Acquisition statements must be prepared in accordance with one of the following accounting principles:

(a) Canadian GAAP — Part V;

(b) U.S. GAAP;

(c) IFRS;

(d) accounting principles that meet the disclosure requirements for foreign private issuers, as that term is defined for the purposes of the 1934 Act, if

    (i) the issuer or the acquired business or business to be acquired is an SEC foreign issuer,

    (ii) on the last day of the most recently completed financial year the total number of equity securities of the SEC foreign issuer beneficially owned by residents of Canada does not exceed 10%, on a fully-diluted basis, of the total number of equity securities of the SEC foreign issuer, and

    (iii) the financial statements include any reconciliation to U.S. GAAP required by the SEC;

(e) accounting principles that meet the foreign disclosure requirements of the designated foreign jurisdiction to which the issuer or the acquired business or business to be acquired is subject, if the issuer or business is a designated foreign issuer;

(f) accounting principles that cover substantially the same core subject matter as Canadian GAAP — Part V, including recognition and measurement principles and disclosure requirements.

(2) Acquisition statements must be prepared in accordance with the same accounting principles for all periods presented.

(3) The notes to the acquisition statements must identify the accounting principles used to prepare the acquisition statements.

(4) If acquisition statements are prepared using accounting principles that are different from the issuer's GAAP, the acquisition statements for the most recently completed financial year and interim period that are required to be filed must be reconciled to the issuer's GAAP and the notes to the acquisition statements must

(a) explain the material differences between the issuer's GAAP and the accounting principles used to prepare the acquisition statements that relate to recognition, measurement, and presentation,

(b) quantify the effect of material differences between the issuer's GAAP and the accounting principles used to prepare the acquisition statements that relate to recognition, measurement and presentation, including a tabular reconciliation between net income reported in the acquisition statements and net income computed in accordance with the issuer's GAAP, and

(c) provide disclosure consistent with the issuer's GAAP to the extent not already reflected in the acquisition statements.

(5) Despite subsections (1) and (4), if the issuer is required to reconcile its financial statements to Canadian GAAP — Part V, the acquisition statements for the most recently completed financial year and interim period that are required to be filed must be

(a) prepared in accordance with Canadian GAAP — Part V, or

(b) reconciled to Canadian GAAP — Part V and the notes to the acquisition statements must

    (i) explain the material differences between Canadian GAAP — Part V and the accounting principles used to prepare the acquisition statements that relate to recognition, measurement, and presentation,

    (ii) quantify the effect of material differences between Canadian GAAP — Part V and the accounting principles used to prepare the acquisition statements that relate to recognition, measurement and presentation, including a tabular reconciliation between net income reported in the acquisition statements and net income computed in accordance with Canadian GAAP — Part V, and

    (iii) provide disclosure consistent with disclosure requirements of Canadian GAAP — Part V to the extent not already reflected in the acquisition statements.

4.12 Acceptable Auditing Standards for Acquisition Statements — (1) Acquisition statements that are required by securities legislation to be audited must be audited in accordance with one of the following auditing standards:

(a) Canadian GAAS;

(b) U.S. PCAOB GAAS;

(c) U.S. AICPA GAAS, if the acquired business or business to be acquired is not an SEC issuer.

(2) Despite subsection (1), acquisition statements filed by or included in a prospectus of a foreign issuer may be audited in accordance with

(a) International Standards on Auditing, if the auditor's report is accompanied by a statement by the auditor that

    (i) describes any material differences in the form and content of the auditor's report as compared to an auditor's report prepared in accordance with Canadian GAAS, and

    (ii) indicates that an auditor's report prepared in accordance with Canadian GAAS would express an unmodified opinion, or

(b) auditing standards that meet the foreign disclosure requirements of the designated foreign jurisdiction to which the issuer is subject, if the issuer is a designated foreign issuer.

(3) Acquisition statements must be accompanied by an auditor's report prepared in accordance with the same auditing standards used to conduct the audit and the auditor's report must identify the accounting principles used to prepare the acquisition statements.

(4) If acquisition statements are audited in accordance with paragraph (1)(a), the auditor's report must express an unmodified opinion.

(5) If acquisition statements are audited in accordance with paragraph (1)(b) or (c), the auditor's report must express an unqualified opinion.

(6) Despite paragraph (2)(a) and subsections (4) and (5) an auditor's report that accompanies acquisition statements may express a qualification of opinion relating to inventory if

(a) the issuer includes in the business acquisition report, prospectus or other document containing the acquisition statements, a balance sheet for the acquired business or business to be acquired that is for a date that is subsequent to the date to which the qualification relates, and

(b) the balance sheet referred to in paragraph (a) is accompanied by an auditor's report that does not express a qualification of opinion relating to closing inventory.

4.13 Financial Information for Acquisitions Accounted for by the Issuer Using the Equity Method — (1) If an issuer files, or includes in a prospectus, summarized financial information as to the assets, liabilities and results of operations of an acquired business or business to be acquired that is, or will be, an investment accounted for by the issuer using the equity method, the financial information must

(a) meet the requirements in section 4.11 if the term "acquisition statements" in that section is read as "summarized financial information", and

Part 5: ONGOING REQUIREMENTS

(b) disclose the reporting currency for the financial information, and disclose the measurement currency if it is different than the reporting currency.

(2) If the financial information referred to in subsection (1) is for any completed financial year, the financial information must

(a) either

(i) meet the requirements in section 4.12 if the term "acquisition statements" in that section is read as "summarized financial information", or

(ii) be derived from financial statements that meet the requirements in section 4.12 if the term "acquisition statements" in that section is read as "financial statements from which is derived summarized financial information", and

(b) be audited, or derived from financial statements that are audited, by a person or company that is authorized to sign an auditor's report under the laws of a jurisdiction of Canada or a foreign jurisdiction, and that meets the professional standards of that jurisdiction.

4.14 Acceptable Accounting Principles for *Pro Forma* Financial Statements — (1) *Pro forma* financial statements must be prepared in accordance with the issuer's GAAP.

(2) Despite subsection (1), if an issuer's financial statements have been reconciled to Canadian GAAP — Part V under subsection 4.7(1) or paragraph 4.9(e), the issuer's *pro forma* financial statements must be prepared in accordance with, or reconciled to, Canadian GAAP — Part V.

(3) Despite subsection (1), if an issuer's financial statements have been prepared in accordance with the accounting principles referred to in paragraph 4.9(c) and those financial statements are reconciled to U.S. GAAP, the *pro forma* financial statements may be prepared in accordance with, or reconciled to, U.S. GAAP.

4.15 Acceptable Accounting Principles for Foreign Registrants — (1) Despite subsection 4.2(2), and subject to subsection (2), financial statements delivered by a foreign registrant may be prepared in accordance with one of the following accounting principles:

(a) U.S. GAAP;

(b) IFRS;

(c) accounting principles that meet the disclosure requirements of a foreign regulatory authority to which the registrant is subject, if it is a foreign registrant incorporated or organized under the laws of that designated foreign jurisdiction;

(d) accounting principles that cover substantially the same core subject matter as Canadian GAAP — Part V, including recognition and measurement principles and disclosure requirements, if the notes to the financial statements, interim balance sheets, or interim income statements

(i) explain the material differences between Canadian GAAP — Part V and the accounting principles used that relate to recognition, measurement and presentation,

(ii) quantify the effect of material differences between Canadian GAAP — Part V and the accounting principles used that relate to recognition, measurement, and presentation, and

(iii) provide disclosure consistent with disclosure requirements of Canadian GAAP — Part V to the extent not already reflected in the financial statements, interim balance sheets or interim income statements.

(2) Financial statements, interim balance sheets, and interim income statements delivered by a foreign registrant prepared in accordance with accounting principles specified in paragraph (1)(a), (b) or (d) must be prepared on a non-consolidated basis.

4.16 Acceptable Auditing Standards for Foreign Registrants — Despite section 4.3, financial statements delivered by a foreign registrant that are required by securities legislation to be audited may, if the financial statements are accompanied by an auditor's report prepared in accordance with the same auditing standards used to conduct the audit and the auditor's report identifies the accounting principles used to prepare the financial statements, be audited in accordance with

(a) U.S. PCAOB GAAS or U.S. AICPA GAAS if the auditor's report expresses an unqualified opinion,

(b) International Standards on Auditing, if the auditor's report is accompanied by a statement by the auditor that

(i) describes any material differences in the form and content of the auditor's report as compared to an auditor's report prepared in accordance with Canadian GAAS, and

(ii) indicates that an auditor's report prepared in accordance with Canadian GAAS would express an unmodified opinion, or

(c) auditing standards that meet the foreign disclosure requirements of the designated foreign jurisdiction to which the registrant is subject, if it is a foreign registrant incorporated or organized under the laws of that designated foreign jurisdiction.

PART 5 — EXEMPTIONS

5.1 Exemptions — (1) The regulator or securities regulatory authority may grant an exemption from this Instrument, in whole or in part, subject to such conditions or restrictions as may be imposed in the exemption.

(2) Despite subsection (1), in Ontario, only the regulator may grant an exemption.

(3) Except in Ontario, an exemption referred to in subsection (1) is granted under the statute referred to in Appendix B of National Instrument 14-101 *Definitions* opposite the name of the local jurisdiction.

5.2 Certain Exemptions Evidenced by Receipt — (1) Subject to subsections (2) and (3), without limiting the manner in which an exemption may be evidenced, an exemption from this Instrument as it pertains to financial statements or auditor's reports included in a prospectus, may be evidenced by the issuance of a receipt for the prospectus or an amendment to the prospectus.

(2) A person or company must not rely on a receipt as evidence of an exemption unless the person or company

(a) sent to the regulator or securities regulatory authority, on or before the date the preliminary prospectus or the amendment to the preliminary prospectus or prospectus was filed, a letter or memorandum describing the matters relating to the exemption application, and indicating why consideration should be given to the granting of the exemption, or

(b) sent to the regulator or securities regulatory authority the letter or memorandum referred to in paragraph (a) after the date of the preliminary prospectus or the amendment to the preliminary prospectus or prospectus has been filed and receives a written acknowledgement from the securities regulatory authority or regulator that issuance of the receipt is evidence that the exemption is granted.

(3) A person or company must not rely on a receipt as evidence of an exemption if the regulator or securities regulatory authority has before, or concurrently with, the issuance of the receipt for the prospectus, sent notice to the person or company that the issuance of a receipt does not evidence the granting of the exemption.

(4) For the purpose of this section, a reference to a prospectus does not include a preliminary prospectus.

5.3 Financial Years ending between December 21 and 31, 2010 — Despite subsections 3.1(2) and 4.1(2), Part 3 may be applied by an issuer or registrant to all financial statements, financial information, operating statements and *pro forma* financial statements for periods relating to a financial year that begins before January 1, 2011 if the immediately preceding financial year ends no earlier than December 21, 2010.

5.4 Rate-Regulated Activities — (1) Despite subsections 3.1(2) and 4.1(2),

(a) Part 3 may be applied by a qualifying entity to all financial statements, financial information, operating statements and *pro forma* financial statements as if the expression "January 1, 2011" in subsection 3.1(2) were read as "January 1, 2012", and

(b) if the qualifying entity relies on paragraph (a) in respect of a period, Part 4 must be applied as if the expression "January 1, 2011" in subsection 4.1(2) were read as "January 1, 2012".

(2) For the purposes of subsection (1), a "qualifying entity" means a person or company that

(a) has activities subject to rate regulation, as defined in Part V of the Handbook, and

(b) is permitted under Canadian GAAP to apply Part V of the Handbook.

PART 6 — REPEAL, TRANSITION AND EFFECTIVE DATE

6.1 Repeal — National Instrument 52-107 *Acceptable Accounting Principles, Auditing Standards and Reporting Currency*, which came into force on March 30, 2004, is repealed.

6.2 Effective Date — This Instrument comes into force on January 1, 2011.

6.3 Existing Exemptions — A person or company that has obtained an exemption from National Instrument 52-107 *Acceptable Accounting Principles, Auditing Standards and Reporting Currency*, in whole or in part, is exempt from any substantially similar provision of this Instrument to the same extent and on the same conditions, if any, as contained in the exemption, unless the regulator or securities regulatory authority has revoked that exemption.

Final Rule: (2004) 27 O.S.C.B. 3949; Approval by OSC: (2004) 27 O.S.C.B. 755; Request for Comments: (2003) 26 O.S.C.B. 3735.

Amendment to Rule: (2005) 28 O.S.C.B. 4976; Approval by OSC: (2005) 28 O.S.C.B. (Supp-1) 53.

Amendment to Rule: (2007) 30 O.S.C.B. (Supp-1) 31; Approval by OSC: (2006) 29 O.S.C.B. (Supp-2) 1.

Amendment to Rule: (2007) 30 O.S.C.B. 10505; Approval by OSC: (2007) 30 O.S.C.B. 8570.

Revised Rule: (2010) 33 O.S.C.B. (Supp. 5) 1; Approval by OSC: (2010) 33 O.S.C.B. (Supp. 3) 1; Request for Comments: (2009) 32 O.S.C.B. 7581.

Amendment to Rule: (2013) 36 O.S.C.B. 4935 Approval by OSC: (2013) 36 O.S.C.B. (Supp. 2) 1; Request for Comments: (2011) 34 O.S.C.B. (Supp. 4) 1.

Policies and Orders: OPS 51-601; CSAN 52-320, 52-321, 52-324, 52-326; OSCN 41-703.

Companion Policy 52-107CP — To National Instrument 52-107 Acceptable Accounting Principles and Auditing Standards

PART 1 — INTRODUCTION AND DEFINITIONS

1.1 Introduction and Purpose — This Companion Policy provides information about how the securities regulatory authorities interpret or apply National Instrument 52-107 *Acceptable Accounting Principles and Auditing Standards* (the Instrument). The Instrument is linked closely with the application of other national instruments, including National Instrument 51-102 *Continuous Disclosure Obligations* (NI 51-102) and National Instrument 71-102 *Continuous Disclosure and Other Exemptions Relating to Foreign Issuers* (NI 71-102). These and other national instruments also contain a number of references to International Financial Reporting Standards (IFRS) and the requirements in the Handbook of the Canadian Institute of Chartered Accountants (the Handbook). Full definitions of IFRS and the Handbook are provided in National Instrument 14-101 *Definitions*.

The Instrument does not apply to investment funds. National Instrument 81-106 *Investment Fund Continuous Disclosure* applies to investment funds.

1.2 Multijurisdictional Disclosure System — National Instrument 71-101 *The Multijurisdictional Disclosure System* (NI 71-101) permits certain U.S. incorporated issuers to satisfy Canadian disclosure filing obligations, including financial statements, by using disclosure documents prepared in accordance with U.S. federal securities laws. The Instrument does not replace or alter NI 71-101. There are instances in which NI 71-101 and the Instrument offer similar relief to a reporting issuer. There are other instances in which the relief differs. If both NI 71-101 and the Instrument are available to a reporting issuer, the issuer should consider both instruments. It may choose to rely on the less onerous instrument in a given situation.

1.3 Calculation of Voting Securities Owned by Residents of Canada — The definition of "foreign issuer" is based upon the definition of foreign private issuer in Rule 405 of the 1933 Act and Rule 3b-4 of the 1934 Act. For the purposes of the definition of "foreign issuer", in determining the outstanding voting securities that are beneficially owned by residents of Canada, an issuer should

(a) use reasonable efforts to identify securities held by a broker, dealer, bank, trust company or nominee or any of them for the accounts of customers resident in Canada,

(b) count securities beneficially owned by residents of Canada as reported on reports of beneficial ownership, including insider reports and early warning reports, and

(c) assume that a customer is a resident of the jurisdiction or foreign jurisdiction in which the nominee has its principal place of business if, after reasonable inquiry, information regarding the jurisdiction or foreign jurisdiction of residence of the customer is unavailable.

This method of calculation differs from that in NI 71-101 which only requires a calculation based on the address of record. Some SEC foreign issuers may therefore qualify for exemptive relief under NI 71-101 but not under the Instrument.

1.4 Exemptions Evidenced by the Issuance of a Receipt — Section 5.2 of the Instrument states that an exemption from any of the requirements of the Instrument pertaining to financial statements or auditor's reports included in a prospectus may be evidenced by the issuance of a receipt for that prospectus. Issuers should not assume that the relief evidenced by the receipt will also apply to financial statements or auditors' reports filed in satisfaction of continuous disclosure obligations or included in any other filing.

1.5 Filed or Delivered — Financial statements that are filed in a jurisdiction will be made available for public inspection in that jurisdiction, subject to the provisions of securities legislation in the local jurisdiction regarding confidentiality of filed material. Material that is delivered to a regulator, but not filed, is not required under securities legislation to be made available for public inspection. However, the regulator may choose to make such material available for inspection by the public.

1.6 Other Legal Requirements — Issuers and auditors should refer to National Instrument 52-108 *Auditor Oversight* for requirements relating to auditor oversight by the Canadian Public Accountability Board. In addition, issuers and registrants are reminded that they and their auditors may be subject to requirements under the laws and professional standards of a jurisdiction that address matters similar to those addressed by the Instrument, and which may impose additional or more onerous requirements. For example, applicable corporate law may prescribe the accounting principles or auditing standards required for financial statements. Similarly, applicable federal, provincial or state law may impose licensing requirements on an auditor practising public accounting in certain jurisdictions.

1.7 Investment Funds — Section 2.1 of the Instrument provides that it does not apply to investment funds that are subject to NI 81-106 *Investment Fund Continuous Disclosure* (NI 81-106) in respect of their reporting requirements as investment funds. If an investment fund is also a registrant, it is subject to the requirements of this Instrument in relation to its reporting requirements as a registrant. Accordingly, if the same legal entity is both an investment fund that is subject to NI 81-106 and is also a registrant, it will be subject to both the requirements of this Instrument and NI 81-106.

PART 2 — APPLICATION — ACCOUNTING PRINCIPLES

2.1 Application of Part 3 — Part 3 of the Instrument generally applies to periods relating to financial years beginning on or after January 1, 2011. Part 3 refers to Canadian GAAP applicable to publicly accountable enterprises, which is IFRS incorporated into the Handbook, contained in Part I of the Handbook.

2.2 Application of Part 4 — Part 4 of the Instrument generally applies to periods relating to financial years beginning before January 1, 2011. Part 4 refers to Canadian GAAP-Part V, which is generally accepted accounting principles determined with reference to Part V of the Handbook applicable to public enterprises. These are the pre-changeover accounting standards for public companies. Part V of the Handbook has differing requirements for public enterprises and non-public enterprises. The following are some of the significant differences in Canadian GAAP applicable to public enterprises compared to those applicable to non-public enterprises:

(a) financial statements for public enterprises cannot be prepared using the differential reporting options as set out in Part V of the Handbook;

(b) transition provisions applicable to enterprises other than public enterprises are not available; and

(c) financial statements must include any additional disclosure requirements applicable to public enterprises.

2.3 IFRS in English and French — The Handbook provides IFRS in English and French. Both versions have equal status and effect under Canadian GAAP. Issuers, auditors, and other market participants may use either version to comply with the requirements in the Instrument.

2.4 Reference to accounting principles — Section 3.2 of the Instrument requires certain financial statements to be prepared in accordance with Canadian GAAP applicable to publicly accountable enterprises. This section includes requirements for an unreserved statement of compliance with IFRS in annual financial statements, and an unreserved statement of compliance with International Accounting Standard 34 *Interim Financial Reporting* in interim financial reports. These provisions distinguish between the basis of preparation and disclosure requirements.

There are two options for referring to accounting principles in the applicable financial statements and, in the case of annual financial statements, accompanying auditor's reports referred to in section 3.3 of the Instrument:

(a) refer only to IFRS in the notes to the financial statements and in the auditor's report, or

(b) refer to both IFRS and Canadian GAAP in the notes to the financial statements and in the auditor's report.

2.5 IFRS as adopted by the IASB — The definition of IFRS in National Instrument 14-101 *Definitions* refers to standards and interpretations adopted by the International Accounting Standards Board. The definition does not extend to national accounting standards that are modified or adapted from IFRS, sometimes referred to as a "jurisdictional" version of IFRS.

2.6 Presentation and functional currencies — If financial statements comply with requirements contained in IFRS in International Accounting Standard 1 *Presentation of Financial Statements* and International Accounting Standard 21 *The Effects of Changes in Foreign Exchange Rates* relating to the disclosure of presentation currency and functional currency, then they will comply with section 3.5 of the Instrument.

2.7 Registrants' financial statements and interim financial information — Subsections 3.2(3) and (4) and paragraphs 3.15(a) and (b) of the Instrument mandate accounting for any investments in subsidiaries, jointly controlled entities and associates as specified for separate financial statements in International Accounting Standard 27 *Consolidated and Separate Financial Statements* (IAS 27). Separate financial statements are sometimes referred to as non-consolidated financial statements. These requirements apply regardless of whether a registrant meets the criteria set out in IAS 27 for not presenting consolidated financial statements. Paragraph 3.2(3)(b) also requires a registrant's annual financial statements to describe the financial reporting framework used to prepare the financial statements. The description should refer to the requirement to account for any investments in subsidiaries, jointly controlled entities and associates as specified for separate financial statements in IAS 27, even if the registrant does not have these types of investments. In addition, if annual financial statements for a year beginning in 2011 are prepared using the financial reporting framework permitted by subsection 3.2(4), the description of the framework should explain the lack of comparatives and the date of transition, as specified in paragraphs 3.2(4)(b) and (c).

The financial reporting frameworks prescribed by subsections 3.2(3) and (4) are Canadian GAAP applicable to publicly accountable enterprises with specified differences. Although these frameworks differ in specified ways from IFRS, the exceptions and exemptions included as Appendices in IFRS 1 *First-time Adoption of International Financial Reporting Standards* (IFRS 1) would be relevant for determining an opening statement of financial position at the date of transition to the financial reporting framework prescribed in subsection 3.2(3) or (4).

Subparagraph 3.3(1)(a)(iii) requires an auditor's report in the form specified by Canadian GAAS for an audit of financial statements prepared in accordance with a fair presentation framework. The financial reporting frameworks prescribed by subsections 3.2(3) and (4) are fair presentation frameworks.

Subsection 3.2(4) of the Instrument allows a registrant to file financial statements and interim financial information for periods relating to a financial year beginning in 2011 that exclude comparative information relating to the preceding year and to use a date of transition to the financial reporting framework that is the first day of the financial year beginning in 2011. When such a registrant prepares the comparative information for financial statements and interim financial information for periods relating to a financial year beginning in 2012, the registrant should consider whether it must adjust the comparative information in order to comply with subsection 3.2(3). Adjustments may be necessary if a registrant changes one or more accounting policies for its year beginning in 2012 compared to its year beginning in 2011.

2.8 Use of different accounting principles — Subsection 3.2(5) of the Instrument requires financial statements to be prepared in accordance with the same accounting principles for all periods presented in the financial statements.

An issuer that is required to file, or include in a document that is filed, financial statements for three years can, except in the situation discussed in section 2.9 of this Companion Policy, choose to present two sets of financial statements. For example, if the earliest of the three financial years relates to a financial year beginning before January 1, 2010, the issuer should provide one set of financial statements that presents information for the most recent two years using the accounting principles in Part 3 of the Instrument and one set of financial statements that either:

(a) presents information for a third and fourth year using the accounting principles in Part 4, or

(b) presents information for a second and third year using the accounting principles in Part 4.

Note that under option (a), a fourth year not otherwise required would be included to satisfy the requirement in the issuer's GAAP for comparative financial statements. Under option (b), information for a second year would be presented in both sets of financial statements. This second year would be included in the most recent set of financial statements using accounting principles in Part 3 of the Instrument and also in the earliest set of financial statements using accounting principles in Part 4 of the Instrument.

If the accounting principles used for the earliest of the three financial years and the most recent two years differ, but both are acceptable in Part 3 of the Instrument, presentation of information for the earliest year would be similar to the example described above.

2.9 Date of transition to IFRS if financial statements include a transition year of less than nine months — Subsection 4.8(6) of NI 51-102 states that if a transition year is less than nine months in length, the reporting issuer must include comparative financial information for the transition year and old financial year in its financial statements for its new financial year. Similarly, subsection 32.2(4) in Form 41-101F1 states that if an issuer changed its financial year end during any of the financial years referred to in section 32.2 and the transition year is less than nine months, the transition year is deemed not to be a financial year for purposes of the requirement to provide financial statements for a specified number of financial years in section 32.2.

If an issuer's first set of annual financial statements with an unreserved statement of compliance with IFRS includes comparatives for both a transition year of less than nine months and the old financial year, the date of transition to IFRS should be the first day of the old financial year. Since subsection 3.2(5) of the Instrument requires financial statements to be prepared in accordance with the same accounting principles for all periods presented in the financial statements, a date of transition to IFRS using the first day of the transition year would not be appropriate.

2.10 Acceptable Accounting Principles — Readers are likely to assume that financial information disclosed in a news release is prepared on a basis consistent with the accounting principles used to prepare the issuer's most recently filed financial statements. To avoid misleading readers, an issuer should alert readers if financial information in a news release is prepared using accounting principles that differ from those used to prepare an issuer's most recently filed financial statements or includes non-GAAP financial measures discussed in CSA Staff Notice 52-306 *Non-GAAP Financial Measures*.

2.11 Financial statements for a reverse takeover or capital pool company acquisition — Subsection 8.1(2) of NI 51-102 states that Part 8 of that rule does not apply to a transaction that is a reverse takeover. Similarly, subsection 35.1(1) in Form 41-101F1 indicates that item 35 of that Form does not apply to a completed or proposed transaction that was or will be accounted for as a reverse takeover. Therefore, if a document includes financial statements for a reverse takeover acquirer, as defined in NI 51-102, for a period prior to completion of the reverse takeover, section 3.11 of the Instrument does not apply to the financial statements. Such financial statements must comply with section 3.2, 3.7, 3.9, 4.2, 4.7 or 4.9 of the Instrument as applicable.

Paragraph 32.1(b) of Form 41-101F1 indicates that financial statements of an issuer required under Item 32 of that Form include the financial statements of a business acquired or business proposed to be acquired by the issuer if a reasonable investor would regard the primary business of the issuer upon completion of the acquisition to be the acquired business or business proposed to be acquired. Consistent with this provision, if a capital pool company acquires or proposes to acquire a business, regardless of whether or not the transaction will be accounted for as a reverse takeover, financial statements for the acquired business or business proposed to be acquired must comply with section 3.2, 3.7, 3.9, 4.2, 4.7 or 4.9 of the Instrument as applicable.

2.12 Acquisition statements prepared using Canadian GAAP applicable to private enterprises — Paragraph 3.11(1)(f) of the Instrument permits acquisition statements to be prepared using Canadian GAAP applicable to private enterprises, which is Canadian accounting standards for private enterprises in Part II of the Handbook.

2.13 Conditions for acquisition statements prepared using Canadian GAAP applicable to private enterprises — Paragraph 3.11(1)(f) of the Instrument specifies certain conditions for the use of Canadian GAAP applicable to private enterprises. One of these conditions, in subparagraph 3.11(1)(f)(ii), is that financial statements for the business were not previously prepared in accordance with any of the accounting principles specified in paragraphs 3.11(1)(a) through (e) for the periods presented in the acquisition statements. Paragraph 3.11(1)(a) refers to Canadian GAAP applicable to publicly accountable enterprises, which is IFRS incorporated into the Handbook contained in Part I of the Handbook. The condition in subparagraph 3.11(1)(f)(ii) does not preclude Canadian GAAP — Part V, as defined in section 4.1 of the Instrument.

2.14 Acquisition statements prepared using Canadian GAAP applicable to private enterprises that include a reconciliation to the issuer's GAAP — If acquisition statements included in a document filed by an issuer that is not a venture issuer and not an IPO venture issuer are prepared using Canadian GAAP applicable to private enterprises, the reconciliation requirement in subparagraph 3.11(1)(f)(iv) applies.

For each difference presented in the quantified reconciliation that relates to measurement, clause 3.11(1)(f)(iv)(C) requires disclosure and discussion of the material inputs or assumptions underlying the measurement of the relevant amount computed in accordance with the issuer's GAAP, consistent

Part 5: ONGOING REQUIREMENTS

with the disclosure requirements of the issuer's GAAP. If the relevant amount was measured using a valuation technique, disclose the valuation technique, and disclose and discuss the inputs used. If changing one or more of the inputs to reasonably possible alternative assumptions would change the measurement significantly, a discussion of that fact and the effect of the changes on the measurement would facilitate readers' understanding of the measurement.

Clause 3.11(1)(f)(iv)(C) does not require disclosure and discussion of all the disclosure elements identified in the issuer's GAAP that relate to a difference presented in the reconciliation. As well, the clause does not require disclosure of information not required by the issuer's GAAP.

As an example of the disclosure required by clause 3.11(1)(f)(iv)(C), if the issuer's GAAP is IFRS and the relevant amount is share based payments measured using an option pricing model, disclose the option pricing model used and the inputs used in the model (i.e., weighted average share price, exercise price, expected volatility, option life, expected dividends, risk-free interest rate and any other inputs to the model). Also, discuss how expected volatility was determined and how any other features of the option grant (e.g., market condition) were incorporated into the measurement of the relevant amount.

2.15 Acquisition statements prepared using Canadian GAAP applicable to private enterprises that include a reconciliation to IFRS — If the reconciliation requirement in subparagraph 3.11(1)(f)(iv) applies, and the issuer's GAAP requires the annual financial statements to include an explicit and unreserved statement of compliance with IFRS, the reconciliation information in annual and interim acquisition statements must address material differences between Canadian GAAP applicable to private enterprises and IFRS that relate to recognition, measurement and presentation.

Consistent with IFRS requirements, for the purpose of preparing the reconciliation information required by subparagraph 3.11(1)(f)(iv), the date of transition to IFRS would be the first day of the earliest period for which comparative information is presented in the annual acquisition statements. For example, if annual acquisition statements present information for the most recently completed financial year and the comparative year, the date of transition to IFRS would be the first day of the comparative year.

Also consistent with IFRS, for the purpose of preparing the reconciliation, IFRS 1 would be applied to determine the opening IFRS statement of financial position at the date of transition to IFRS. The exceptions and exemptions included as Appendices in IFRS 1 would be relevant for determining the entity's statement of financial position at the date of transition to IFRS.

The opening IFRS statement of financial position is the starting point for identifying material differences from Canadian GAAP applicable to private enterprises. Although an opening IFRS statement of financial position must be prepared in order to prepare the information required by subparagraph 3.11(1)(f)(iv), that subparagraph does not require disclosure of the opening IFRS statement of financial position. Similarly, that subparagraph does not require disclosure of differences relating to equity as at the date of transition to IFRS.

As discussed in section 2.14 of this Companion Policy, clause 3.11(1)(f)(iv)(C) does not require disclosure and discussion of all the disclosure elements identified in the issuer's GAAP that relate to a difference presented in the reconciliation. Therefore, it would be inappropriate to include an explicit and unreserved statement of compliance with IFRS in acquisition statements that include reconciliation information for material differences between Canadian GAAP applicable to private enterprises and IFRS.

2.16 Acquisition statements prepared using Canadian GAAP applicable to private enterprises that do not include a reconciliation to the issuer's GAAP — If acquisition statements included in a document filed by a venture issuer or IPO venture issuer are prepared using Canadian GAAP applicable to private enterprises, the reconciliation requirements in subparagraph 3.11(1)(f)(iv) do not apply. However, subsection 3.14(1) requires *pro forma* financial statements to be prepared using accounting policies that are permitted by the issuer's GAAP and would apply to the information presented in the *pro forma* financial statements if that information were included in the issuer's financial statements for the same time. Companion Policy 51-102CP *Continuous Disclosure Obligations* provides further guidance on preparation of *pro forma* financial statements in this circumstance.

2.17 Acquisition statements, predecessor statements, or primary business statements that are an operating statement — In the case of acquisition statements that are an operating statement, subsection 3.11(5) requires the line items in the operating statement to be prepared in accordance with accounting policies that comply with the accounting policies permitted by one of Canadian GAAP applicable to publicly accountable enterprises, IFRS, U.S. GAAP, or Canadian GAAP applicable to private enterprises. In the case of predecessor statements or primary business statements that are an operating statement, section 3.17 requires the line items in the operating statement to be prepared in accordance with accounting policies that comply with the accounting policies permitted by one of: Canadian GAAP applicable to publicly accountable enterprises, U.S. GAAP if the issuer is an SEC issuer or SEC foreign issuer, or IFRS if the issuer is a foreign issuer. For the purpose of preparing an operating statement, the exceptions and exemptions included as Appendices in IFRS 1 would be relevant for determining the opening statement of financial position at the date of transition to IFRS.

2.18 Acquisition statements, predecessor statements, or primary business statements that are carve-out financial statements — Acquisition statements, predecessor statements or primary business statements may be based on information from the financial records of another entity whose operations included the acquired business, the business to be acquired, the predecessor entity or primary business. In some cases, there are no separate financial records for the business. Such financial statements, which are commonly referred to as carve-out financial statements, should generally include:

    (a) all assets and liabilities directly attributable to the business;

    (b) all revenue and expenses directly attributable to the business;

    (c) if there are expenses for the business that are common expenses shared with the other entity, a portion of those expenses allocated on a reasonable basis to the business;

    (d) income and capital taxes calculated as if the business had been a separate legal entity and had filed a separate tax return for the period presented; and

    (e) a description of the method of allocation for each significant line item presented in financial statements.

2.19 Preparation of pro forma financial statements when there is a change in accounting principles — Subsection 3.14(1) requires *pro forma* financial statements to be prepared using accounting policies that are permitted by the issuer's GAAP and would apply to the information presented in the *pro forma* financial statements if that information were included in the issuer's financial statement for the same period as that of the *pro forma* financial statements. If the accounting principles used to prepare an issuer's most recent annual financial statements differ from the accounting principles used to prepare the issuer's interim financial report for a subsequent period, subsection 3.14(3) provides an issuer the option of preparing its annual *pro forma* income statement using accounting policies that are permitted by the accounting principles used to prepare the interim financial report and would apply to the information presented in the *pro forma* income statement if that information were included in the interim financial report. In this case, the annual *pro forma* income statement should include adjustments to the amounts reported in the issuer's most recent statement of comprehensive income in order to restate the amounts on the basis of the accounting principles used to prepare the issuer's interim financial report. The *pro forma* income statement should present such adjustments separate from other adjustments relating to significant acquisitions.

If an issuer does not use the option provided by subsection 3.14(3), in order to avoid confusion, it would be appropriate to present the issuer's annual and interim *pro forma* financial statements as separate sets of *pro forma* financial statements.

2.20 Reconciliation requirements for an SEC issuer — If financial statements of an SEC issuer, other than acquisition statements, filed with or delivered to a securities regulatory authority or regulator are

    (a) for a financial year beginning before January 1, 2011,

    (b) prepared in accordance with U.S. GAAP, and

    (c) the SEC issuer previously filed or included in a prospectus financial statements prepared in accordance with Canadian GAAP — Part V,

then subsection 4.7(1) applies. Subsection 4.7(1) requires the notes of the first two sets of the SEC issuer's annual financial statements, and interim financial report during those first two years, to provide reconciling information between Canadian GAAP — Part V and U.S. GAAP that complies with subparagraphs 4.7(1)(a)(i) to (iii).

If an SEC issuer's second set of annual financial statements after a change in accounting principles is for a financial year beginning after January 1, 2011, the reconciliation requirements in subsection 4.7(1) no longer apply. Financial statements for a financial year beginning after January 1, 2011 are required to be prepared in accordance with Part 3 of the Instrument, which does not include any reconciliation requirements when an SEC issuer changes its accounting principles.

PART 3 — APPLICATION — AUDITING STANDARDS

3.1 Auditor's Expertise — The securities legislation in most jurisdictions prohibits a regulator or securities regulatory authority from issuing a receipt for a prospectus if it appears to the regulator or securities regulatory authority that a person or company who has prepared any part of the prospectus or is named as having prepared or certified a report used in connection with a prospectus is not acceptable.

3.2 Canadian Auditors for Canadian GAAP and GAAS Financial Statements — A Canadian auditor is a person or company that is authorized to sign an auditor's report by the laws, and that meets the professional standards, of a jurisdiction of Canada. We would normally expect issuers and registrants incorporated or organized under the laws of Canada or a jurisdiction of Canada, and any other issuer or registrant that is not a foreign issuer nor a foreign registrant, to engage a Canadian auditor to audit the issuer's or registrant's financial statements if those statements are prepared in accordance with Canadian GAAP applicable to publicly accountable enterprises and will be audited in accordance with Canadian GAAS unless a valid business reason exists to use a non-Canadian auditor. A valid business reason would include a situation where the principal operations of the company and the essential books and records required for the audit are located outside of Canada.

3.3 Auditor Oversight — In addition to the requirements in sections 3.4 and 4.4 of the Instrument, National Instrument 52-108 *Auditor Oversight* also contains certain requirements related to auditors and auditor reports.

3.4 Modification of opinion — Part 5 of the Instrument permits the regulator or securities regulatory authority to grant exemptive relief from the Instrument, including the requirement that an auditor's report express an unmodified opinion. A modification of opinion includes a qualification of opinion, an adverse opinion, and a disclaimer of opinion. However, staff will generally recommend that relief not be granted if the modification of opinion or other similar communication is:

    (a) due to a departure from accounting principles permitted by the Instrument, or

    (b) due to a limitation in the scope of the auditor's examination that

        (i) results in the auditor being unable to form an opinion on the financial statements as a whole,

        (ii) is imposed or could reasonably be eliminated by management, or

        (iii) could reasonably be expected to be recurring.

3.5 Identification of the financial reporting framework used to prepare an operating statement — Paragraphs 3.12(2)(e) and 3.18(2)(e) require an auditor's report to identify the financial reporting framework used to prepare an operating statement as addressed in subsections 3.11(5) and section 3.17. To comply with this requirement, the auditor's report may identify the applicable requirement in the Instrument, and refer the reader's attention to the note in the operating statement that describes the financial reporting framework.

Adoption by OSC: (2004) 27 O.S.C.B. 3962 and 755; Request for Comments: (2003) O.S.C.B. 3735.

Adoption of Revised Policy: (2010) 33 O.S.C.B. (Supp. 3) 1; Request for Comments: (2009) 32 O.S.C.B. 8469.

Adoption of Amendment by OSC: (2013) 36 O.S.C.B. 4937 and (Supp. 2) 1; Request for Comments: (2011) 34 O.S.C.B. (Supp. 4) 1.

National Instrument 52-108 — Auditor Oversight

Date: March 30, 2004, as amended effective July 4, 2008 and as repealed and replaced effective September 30, 2014

27 O.S.C.B. 3227, 31 O.S.C.B. 6575 and [37 O.S.C.B. 6753]

PART 1 — DEFINITIONS AND APPLICATION

1. Definitions — In this Instrument

"CPAB" means the Canadian Public Accountability Board/Conseil canadien sur la reddition de comptes, incorporated as a corporation without share capital under the *Canada Corporations Act* by Letters Patent dated April 15, 2003;

"CPAB rules" means the rules and bylaws of CPAB, as amended from time to time;

"participating audit firm" means a public accounting firm that has entered into a participation agreement and that has not had its participant status terminated or, if its participant status was terminated, the status has been reinstated by CPAB;

"participation agreement" means a written agreement between CPAB and a public accounting firm in connection with CPAB's program of practice inspections and the establishment of practice requirements;

"professional standards" means the standards, as amended from time to time, listed in section 300 of CPAB rules that are applicable to participating audit firms;

"public accounting firm" means a person or company engaged in the business of providing the services of a public accountant.

PART 2 — AUDITOR OVERSIGHT

2. **Public accounting firms** — A public accounting firm that prepares an auditor's report with respect to the financial statements of a reporting issuer must be, as of the date of the auditor's report

    (a) a participating audit firm,

    (b) in compliance with any remedial action referred to in subsection 5(1), and

    (c) in compliance with the notice requirements of subsections 5(1) and (2

3. **Notice to Reporting Issuer if Public Accounting Firm Not in Compliance** — (1) If a public accounting firm has been appointed to prepare an auditor's report with respect to the financial statements of a reporting issuer and, at any time before signing the auditor's report, the public accounting firm is not in compliance with the requirements of paragraphs 2(a), (b) or (c), the public accounting firm must deliver to the reporting issuer a notice in writing that it is not in compliance within 2 business days of first becoming aware of its non-compliance.

(2) A public accounting firm that previously delivered a notice to a reporting issuer under subsection(1) must not notify the reporting issuer that it is in compliance with paragraph 2(a), (b) or (c) unless the public accounting firm has been informed in writing by CPAB that the circumstances that gave rise to the notice no longer apply.

(3) A public accounting firm must deliver a copy of a notice required under this section to CPAB on the same day that the notice is delivered to the reporting issuer.

4. **Reporting Issuers** — A reporting issuer that files its financial statements accompanied by an auditor's report must have the auditor's report prepared by a public accounting firm that, as of the date of the auditor's report,

    (a) is a participating audit firm, and

    (b) has not delivered to the reporting issuer a notice under subsection 3(1) or, if it has delivered to the reporting issuer a notice under subsection 3(1), the public accounting firm has notified the reporting issuer that the circumstances that gave rise to the notice no longer apply.

PART 3 — NOTICE

5. **Notice of Remedial Action to the Regulator or the Securities Regulatory Authority** — (1) A participating audit firm appointed to prepare an auditor's report with respect to the financial statements of a reporting issuer must deliver a notice to the regulator or, in Quebec, the securities regulatory authority, if any of the following occurs:

    (a) CPAB notifies the participating audit firm in writing that it requires the participating audit firm to take one or more of the following remedial actions:

        (i) terminate an audit engagement;

        (ii) engage an independent monitor to observe and report to CPAB on the participating audit firm's compliance with professional standards;

        (iii) engage an external reviewer or supervisor to oversee the work of the participating audit firm;

        (iv) mit the type or number of new reporting issuer audit clients the participating audit firm may accept;

    (b) CPAB notifies the participating audit firm in writing that it must disclose to the regulator or, in Quebec, the securities regulatory authority, any remedial action not referred to in paragraph (a);

    (c) CPAB publicly discloses a remedial action with which the participating audit firm must comply.

(2) The notice required under subsection (1) must be in writing and must include all of the following:

    (a) how the participating audit firm failed to comply with professional standards;

    (b) the name of each reporting issuer whose audit file was referred to by CPAB in its communications with the participating audit firm as the basis, in whole or in part, for CPAB's conclusion that the participating audit firm failed to comply with professional standards;

    (c) each remedial action that CPAB imposed on the participating audit firm, as described by CPAB;

    (d) the time period within which the participating audit firm must comply with each remedial action, as described by CPAB.

(3) A participating audit firm must deliver the notice required under subsection (2) to the regulator or, in Quebec, the securities regulatory authority, no later than 2 business days after the date that CPAB notifies the participating audit firm that it must comply with any remedial action under paragraph (1)(a), (b) or (c).

(4) The participating audit firm must deliver a copy of a notice required under this section to CPAB on the same day that the notice is delivered to the regulator or, in Quebec, the securities regulatory authority.

6. **Additional Notice Relating to Defects in the System of Quality Control** — (1) If CPAB required a participating audit firm to comply with any remedial action relating to a defect in the participating audit firm's system of quality control, and CPAB notifies the participating audit firm in writing that it has failed to address the defect in its system of quality control to the satisfaction of CPAB within the time period required by CPAB, the participating audit firm must deliver a notice to all of the following:

    (a) for each reporting issuer for which the participating audit firm is appointed to prepare an auditor's report,

        (i) the audit committee, or

        (ii) if the reporting issuer does not have an audit committee, the person or company responsible for reviewing and approving the reporting issuer's financial statements before they are filed;

    (b) the regulator or, in Quebec, the securities regulatory authority.

(2) The notice required under subsection (1) must be in writing and must describe all of the following:

(a) the defect in the participating audit firm's system of quality control identified by CPAB;

(b) the remedial action imposed by CPAB, including the date the remedial action was imposed and the time period within which CPAB required the participating audit firm to address the defect in its system of quality control;

(c) why the participating audit firm failed to address the defect in its system of quality control within the time period required by CPAB.

(3) A participating audit firm must deliver the notice required under subsection (1) no later than 10 business days after the participating audit firm received notice from CPAB in writing that the participating audit firm failed to address the defect in its system of quality control within the time period required by CPAB.

(4) The participating audit firm must deliver a copy of a notice required under this section to CPAB on the same day the notice is delivered to the regulator or, in Quebec, the securities regulatory authority.

7. Notice Before New Appointment — (1) A participating audit firm that is seeking an appointment to prepare an auditor's report with respect to the financial statements for a financial year of a reporting issuer must deliver a notice to the reporting issuer's audit committee or, if the reporting issuer does not have an audit committee, the person or company responsible for reviewing and approving the reporting issuer's financial statements before they are filed, if

(a) the participating audit firm did not audit the financial statements of the reporting issuer for the immediately preceding financial year, and

(b) CPAB informed the participating audit firm within the preceding 12-month period that the participating audit firm failed to address a defect in its system of quality control to the satisfaction of CPAB.

(2) The notice required under subsection (1) must be in writing and include the information referred to in subsection 6(2).

PART 4 — EXEMPTION

8. Exemption — (1) The regulator or the securities regulatory authority may grant an exemption from this Instrument, in whole or in part, subject to such conditions and restrictions as may be imposed in the exemption.

(2) Despite subsection (1), in Ontario, only the regulator may grant such an exemption.

(3) Except in Ontario, an exemption referred to in subsection (1) is granted under the statute referred to in Appendix B of NI 14-101 opposite the name of the local jurisdiction.

4.1 Exemption — (1) The regulator or the securities regulatory authority may grant an exemption from this Instrument, in whole or in part, subject to such conditions or restrictions as may be imposed in the exemption.

(2) Despite subsection (1), in Ontario, only the regulator may grant such an exemption.

PART 5 — REPEAL AND EFFECTIVE DATE

9. Repeal — National Instrument 52-108 *Auditor Oversight* is repealed.

10. Effective Date — This Instrument comes into force on September 30, 2014.

Final Rule: (2004) 27 O.S.C.B. 3227; Approval by OSC: (2004) 27 O.S.C.B. 853; Request for Comments; (2003) 26 O.S.C.B. 4945.

Amendment to Rule: 31 O.S.C.B. 6575; Approval by OSC: 31 O.S.C.B. 4261; Request for Comments: 30 O.S.C.B. 8570.

Repealed and Replaced: Approval by OSC: (2014) 37 O.S.C.B. 6753; Request for Comments: (2013) 36 O.S.C.B. 10147

Companion Policy 52-108CP — Auditor Oversight

Introduction

CPAB is an independent oversight body for public accounting firms that audit financial statements of reporting issuers. The purpose of CPAB is to promote high quality external audits of reporting issuers. It is responsible for developing and implementing an oversight program that includes regular inspections of participating audit firms. CPAB's primary means of assessing the quality of audits is through the inspection of selected high-risk sections of audit files and elements of a participating audit firm's system of quality control.

The purpose of National Instrument 52-108 is to contribute to public confidence in the integrity of financial reporting by reporting issuers by requiring:

- a reporting issuer to engage an auditor that has entered into a participation agreement with CPAB in connection with CPAB's program of practice inspections and the establishment of practice requirements,

- a participating audit firm to be in compliance with specified remedial actions imposed by CPAB,

- a participating audit firm to deliver a notice to the regulator or, in Quebec, the securities regulatory authority, if CPAB imposes specified remedial actions, including the termination of an audit engagement or the engagement of an independent monitor to observe and report on compliance with professional standards, and

- a participating audit firm to deliver a notice to the reporting issuer's audit committee or the person or company responsible for reviewing and approving financial statements, of its reporting issuer clients if the firm failed to address a defect in the firm's system of quality control that was previously identified by CPAB.

The purpose of this Companion Policy is to state the view of the securities regulatory authorities on various matters related to the Instrument.

Section 1 — Definition of Participating Audit Firm

Many of the requirements in the Instrument are linked to the definition of participating audit firm in section 1. For example, section 5 of the Instrument imposes a notice requirement on a participating audit firm in a number of circumstances, including where CPAB requires the firm to terminate an audit engagement. CPAB may impose a remedial action on a participating audit firm that specifically pertains to one or more individuals involved in a professional capacity with the participating audit firm. If a remedial action imposed by CPAB on a participating audit firm specifically pertains to an individual acting in a professional capacity with the participating audit firm, this remedial action would be included in the content of a notice to the regulator or, in Quebec, the securities regulatory authority in accordance with paragraph 5(2)(c).

Section 1 — Definition of Professional Standards

The definition of professional standards refers to the standards listed in section 300 of CPAB rules, which are standards relating to auditing, ethics, independence and quality control.

Subsection 5(1) and Paragraph 6(1)(b) — Notice to the Regulator or the Securities Regulatory Authority

Both subsection 5(1) and paragraph 6(1)(b) of the Instrument require a participating audit firm to deliver a notice to the regulator or, in Quebec, the securities regulatory authority. "Regulator" and "securities regulatory authority" are defined in NI 14-101 — *Definitions*. Each participating audit firm that is subject to either of these provisions must deliver the notice to the regulator or, in Quebec, the securities regulatory authority, in each jurisdiction in which the firm is appointed by one or more reporting issuers to prepare an auditor's report with respect to their financial statements. The securities regulatory authorities will consider the notice requirement in each of these provisions of the Instrument to have been satisfied if the notice is sent to auditor.notice@acvm-csa.ca and identifies each jurisdiction that is to receive notice.

Subsection 5(1) — Remedial Action Imposed by CPAB

Subsection 5(1) of the Instrument requires a participating audit firm to deliver a notice to the regulator or, in Quebec, the securities regulatory authority, of certain remedial actions imposed by CPAB. CPAB may refer to an item in subsection 5(1) of the Instrument as a recommendation, a requirement, a restriction or a sanction, or CPAB may use a different term. A participating audit firm must deliver the notice under section 5 of the Instrument if the remedial action is described in that section, without regard to how CPAB refers to it. For example, a notice is required by subparagraph 5(1)(a)(i) of the Instrument if CPAB requires a participating audit firm to terminate an audit engagement regardless of whether CPAB refers to it as a recommendation, requirement, restriction, sanction or uses a different term.

Subparagraph 5(1)(a)(iii) — Engagement of an External Reviewer or Supervisor

Subparagraph 5(1)(a)(iii) of the Instrument requires a participating audit firm to deliver a notice to the regulator or, in Quebec, the securities regulatory authority, if CPAB requires a participating audit firm to engage an external reviewer or supervisor to oversee its work. One example of when a participating audit firm would notify the regulator is when CPAB requires the firm to engage an external engagement quality control reviewer to perform a technical review of one or more audits performed by the firm.

Subparagraph 5(1)(a)(iv) — Limitation on a Participating Audit Firm from Accepting New Reporting Issuer Audit Clients

Subparagraph 5(1)(a)(iv) of the Instrument requires a participating audit firm to deliver a notice to the regulator or, in Quebec, the securities regulatory authority, if CPAB limits the type or number of new reporting issuer audit clients the firm accepts. The securities regulatory authorities consider this type of limitation to include restrictions on accepting audit engagements of reporting issuers in a particular industry. For example, a participating firm that is limited for any period of time from auditing the financial statements of mining companies is subject to subparagraph 5(1)(a)(iv) in the Instrument even if the firm may continue to audit reporting issuers in other industries.

The securities regulatory authorities also consider the term "new reporting issuer audit client" to refer to any reporting issuer the financial statements of which were not audited by the participating audit firm for the reporting issuer's most recently completed financial year. For example, if a participating firm was asked to audit the financial statements of a reporting issuer for the first time in respect of its 2013 fiscal year, that issuer would be a new reporting issuer audit client of the firm. Similarly, if a participating audit firm had audited the reporting issuer's 2011 financial statements but did not audit the 2012 financial statements, the securities regulatory authorities would also consider the issuer to be a new reporting issuer audit client of the firm in respect of the 2013 financial statement audit.

Paragraph 5(1)(b) — Notice Required at Discretion of CPAB

Paragraph 5(1)(b) of the Instrument requires a participating audit firm to deliver a notice to the regulator or, in Quebec, the securities regulatory authority, at the discretion of CPAB. One example of when CPAB may require a participating audit firm to notify the regulator is when the firm failed to comply with a remedial action within the period CPAB required.

Subsection 5(2) — Contents of Notice

Subsection 5(2) of the Instrument sets out the content requirements for a notice delivered to the regulator or, in Quebec, the securities regulatory authority, by a participating audit firm.

Paragraph 5(2)(a) requires a participating audit firm to include a description of how the participating audit firm failed to comply with professional standards. The description included in the notice should be substantially similar to the description CPAB has provided the participating audit firm. There may be situations in which the description may need to be modified to remove reference to information protected by professional secrecy in Quebec.

Paragraph 5(2)(c) requires a participating audit firm to include a description of each remedial action that CPAB imposed on the firm, as described by CPAB. This includes, but is not limited to, remedial actions referred to in subsection 5(1). For example, if CPAB requires a participating audit firm to engage an independent monitor under subparagraph 5(1)(a)(ii) of the Instrument and also imposes additional remedial actions on the firm other than those referred to in subsection 5(1), the notice must include a complete description of such other remedial actions.

Adoption by OSC: (2014) 37 6753; Request for Comments: (2013) O.S.C.B. 10147

National Instrument 52-109 — Certification of Disclosure in Issuers' Annual and Interim Filings

Date: March 30, 2004, as amended effective June 6, 2005 and December 31, 2007; replaced effective December 15, 2008, as amended effective January 1, 2011 and November 17, 2015

27 O.S.C.B. 3230, 28 O.S.C.B. 4979, 30 O.S.C.B. 10506, 31 O.S.C.B. 10435, 33 O.S.C.B. (Supp. 5) 102 and 38 O.S.C.B. 7559

Form 52-109F1R Certification of refiled annual filings

Form 52-109F1 — AIF Certification of annual filings in connection with voluntarily filed AIF

Form 52-109F2 Certification of interim filings — full certificate

Form 52-109FV2 Certification of interim filings — venture issuer basic certificate

Form 52-109F2 — IPO/RTO Certification of interim filings following an initial public offering, reverse takeover or becoming a non-venture issuer

Form 52-109F2R Certification of refiled interim filings

PART 1 — DEFINITIONS AND APPLICATION

1.1 Definitions — In this Instrument,

"AIF" has the meaning ascribed to it in NI 51-102;

"accounting principles" has the meaning ascribed to it in NI 52-107;

"annual certificate" means the certificate required to be filed under Part 4 or section 6.1;

"annual filings" means an issuer's AIF, if any, its annual financial statements and its annual MD&A filed under securities legislation for a financial year, including, for greater certainty, all documents and information that are incorporated by reference in the AIF;

"annual financial statements" means the annual financial statements required to be filed under NI 51-102;

"certifying officer" means each chief executive officer and each chief financial officer of an issuer, or in the case of an issuer that does not have a chief executive officer or a chief financial officer, each individual performing similar functions to those of a chief executive officer or chief financial officer;

"DC&P" means disclosure controls and procedures;

"disclosure controls and procedures" means controls and other procedures of an issuer that are designed to provide reasonable assurance that information required to be disclosed by the issuer in its annual filings, interim filings or other reports filed or submitted by it under securities legislation is recorded, processed, summarized and reported within the time periods specified in the securities legislation and include controls and procedures designed to ensure that information required to be disclosed by an issuer in its annual filings, interim filings or other reports filed or submitted under securities legislation is accumulated and communicated to the issuer's management, including its certifying officers, as appropriate to allow timely decisions regarding required disclosure;

"financial period" means a financial year or an interim period;

"financial statements" has the meaning ascribed to it in section 1.1 of NI 51-102;

"ICFR" means internal control over financial reporting;

"internal control over financial reporting" means a process designed by, or under the supervision of, an issuer's certifying officers, and effected by the issuer's board of directors, management and other personnel, to provide reasonable assurance regarding the reliability of financial reporting and the preparation of financial statements for external purposes in accordance with the issuer's GAAP and includes those policies and procedures that:

(a) pertain to the maintenance of records that in reasonable detail accurately and fairly reflect the transactions and dispositions of the assets of the issuer;

(b) are designed to provide reasonable assurance that transactions are recorded as necessary to permit preparation of financial statements in accordance with the issuer's GAAP, and that receipts and expenditures of the issuer are being made only in accordance with authorizations of management and directors of the issuer; and

(c) are designed to provide reasonable assurance regarding prevention or timely detection of unauthorized acquisition, use or disposition of the issuer's assets that could have a material effect on the annual financial statements or interim financial reports;

"interim certificate" means the certificate required to be filed under Part 5 or section 6.2;

"interim filings" means an issuer's interim financial report and its interim MD&A filed under securities legislation for an interim period;

"interim financial report" means the interim financial report required to be filed under NI 51-102;

"interim period" has the meaning ascribed to it in NI 51-102;

"issuer's GAAP" has the meaning ascribed to it in NI 52-107;

"marketplace" has the meaning ascribed to it in National Instrument 21-101 *Marketplace Operation*;

"material weakness" means a deficiency, or a combination of deficiencies, in ICFR such that there is a reasonable possibility that a material misstatement of the reporting issuer's annual financial statements or interim financial report will not be prevented or detected on a timely basis;

"MD&A" has the meaning ascribed to it in NI 51-102;

"NI 51-102" means National Instrument 51-102 *Continuous Disclosure Obligations*;

"NI 52-107" means National Instrument 52-107 *Acceptable Accounting Principles and Auditing Standards*;

"non-venture issuer" means a reporting issuer that is not a venture issuer;

"proportionately consolidated entity" means an entity in which an issuer has an interest that is accounted for by combining, on a line-by-line basis, the issuer's *pro rata* share of each of the assets, liabilities, revenue and expenses of the entity with similar items in the issuer's financial statements;

"reverse takeover" has the meaning ascribed to it in NI 51-102;

"reverse takeover acquiree" has the meaning ascribed to it in NI 51-102;

"reverse takeover acquirer" has the meaning ascribed to it in NI 51-102;

"Sarbanes-Oxley Act" means the Sarbanes-Oxley Act of 2002 of the United States of America, Pub.L. 107-204, 116 Stat. 745 (2002), as amended from time to time;

"special purpose entity" has, in respect of an issuer, the meaning ascribed to that term in the issuer's GAAP;

"SOX 302 Rules" means U.S. federal securities laws implementing the annual report certification requirements in section 302(a) of the Sarbanes-Oxley Act;

"SOX 404 Rules" means U.S. federal securities laws implementing the internal control report requirements in sections 404(a) and (b) of the Sarbanes-Oxley Act;

"U.S. marketplace" has the meaning ascribed to it in NI 51-102; and

"venture issuer" means a reporting issuer that, as at the end of the period covered by the annual or interim filings, as the case may be, did not have any of its securities listed or quoted on any of the Toronto Stock Exchange, Aequitas NEO Exchange Inc., a U.S. marketplace, or a marketplace outside of Canada and the United States of America other than the Alternative Investment Market of the London Stock Exchange or the PLUS markets operated by PLUS Markets Group plc.

1.2 Application — (1) This Instrument applies to a reporting issuer other than an investment fund.

(2) This Instrument applies in respect of annual filings and interim filings for financial periods ending on or after December 15, 2008.

PART 2 — CERTIFICATION OBLIGATION

2.1 Certifying officers' certification obligation — Each certifying officer must certify the matters prescribed by the required form that must be filed under Part 4 or Part 5.

PART 3 — DC&P AND ICFR

3.1 Establishment and maintenance of DC&P and ICFR — A non-venture issuer must establish and maintain DC&P and ICFR.

3.2 MD&A disclosure of material weakness — Despite section 3.1, if a non-venture issuer determines that it has a material weakness which exists as at the end of the period covered by its annual or interim filings, as the case may be, it must disclose in its annual or interim MD&A for each material weakness

    (a) a description of the material weakness;

    (b) the impact of the material weakness on the issuer's financial reporting and its ICFR; and

    (c) the issuer's current plans, if any, or any actions already undertaken, for remediating the material weakness.

3.3 Limitations on scope of design — (1) Despite section 3.1, a non-venture issuer may limit its design of DC&P or ICFR to exclude controls, policies and procedures of

    (a) subject to subsection (3), a proportionately consolidated entity or a special purpose entity in which the issuer has an interest; or

    (b) subject to subsection (4), a business that the issuer acquired not more than 365 days before the end of the financial period to which the certificate relates.

(2) An issuer that limits its design of DC&P or ICFR under subsection (1) must disclose in its MD&A

    (a) the limitation; and

    (b) summary financial information about the proportionately consolidated entity, special purpose entity or business that the issuer acquired that has been proportionately consolidated or consolidated in the issuer's financial statements.

(3) An issuer must not limit its design of DC&P or ICFR under paragraph (1)(a) except where the certifying officers would not have a reasonable basis for making the representations in the annual or interim certificates because they do not have sufficient access to a proportionately consolidated entity or special purpose entity, as applicable, to design and evaluate controls, policies and procedures carried out by that entity.

(4) An issuer must not limit its design of DC&P or ICFR under paragraph (1)(b) except in the case of

    (a) an annual certificate relating to the financial year in which the issuer acquired the business; and

    (b) an interim certificate relating to the first, second or third interim period ending on or after the date the issuer acquired the business.

3.4 Use of a control framework for the design of ICFR — (1) A non-venture issuer must use a control framework to design the issuer's ICFR.

(2) If a venture issuer files a Form 52-109F1 or Form 52-109F2 for a financial period, the venture issuer must use a control framework to design the issuer's ICFR.

PART 4 — CERTIFICATION OF ANNUAL FILINGS

4.1 Requirement to file — (1) A reporting issuer must file a separate annual certificate in the wording prescribed by the required form

    (a) for each individual who, at the time of filing the annual certificate, is a certifying officer; and

    (b) signed by the certifying officer.

(2) A reporting issuer must file a certificate required under subsection (1) on the later of the dates on which it files the following:

    (a) its AIF if it is required to file an AIF under NI 51-102; or

    (b) its annual financial statements and annual MD&A.

(3) If a venture issuer voluntarily files an AIF for a financial year after it has filed its annual financial statements, annual MD&A and annual certificates for the financial year, the venture issuer must file on the same date that it files its AIF a separate annual certificate in the wording prescribed by the required form

    (a) for each individual who, at the time of filing the annual certificate, is a certifying officer; and

    (b) signed by the certifying officer.

(4) A reporting issuer must file a certificate required under subsection (1) or (3) separately from the documents to which the certificate relates.

4.2 Required form of annual certificate — (1) The required form of annual certificate under subsection 4.1(1) is

    (a) Form 52-109F1, in the case of an issuer that is a non-venture issuer; and

(b) Form 52-109FV1, in the case of an issuer that is a venture issuer.

(2) Despite subsection (1)(b), a venture issuer may file Form 52-109F1 in the wording prescribed by that Form instead of Form 52-109FV1 for a financial year.

(3) The required form of annual certificate under subsection 4.1(3) is Form 52-109F1 — AIF.

4.3 Alternative form of annual certificate for first financial period after initial public offering — Despite subsection 4.2(1), an issuer may file an annual certificate in Form 52-109F1 — IPO/RTO for the first financial year that ends after the issuer becomes a reporting issuer if

(a) the issuer becomes a reporting issuer by filing a prospectus; and

(b) the first financial period that ends after the issuer becomes a reporting issuer is a financial year.

4.4 Alternative form of annual certificate for first financial period after certain reverse takeovers — Despite subsection 4.2(1), an issuer may file an annual certificate in Form 52-109F1 — IPO/RTO for the first financial year that ends after the completion of a reverse takeover if

(a) the issuer is the reverse takeover acquiree in the reverse takeover;

(b) the reverse takeover acquirer was not a reporting issuer immediately before the reverse takeover; and

(c) the first financial period that ends after the completion of the reverse takeover is a financial year.

4.5 Alternative form of annual certificate for first financial period after becoming a non-venture issuer — Despite subsection 4.2(1), an issuer may file an annual certificate in Form 52-109F1 — IPO/RTO for the first financial year that ends after the issuer becomes a non-venture issuer if the first financial period that ends after the issuer becomes a non-venture issuer is a financial year.

4.6 Exception for new reporting issuers — Despite section 4.1, a reporting issuer does not have to file an annual certificate relating to

(a) the annual financial statements required under section 4.7 of NI 51-102 for financial years that ended before the issuer became a reporting issuer; or

(b) the annual financial statements for a reverse takeover acquirer required under section 4.10 of NI 51-102 for financial years that ended before the completion of the reverse takeover.

PART 5 — CERTIFICATION OF INTERIM FILINGS

5.1 Requirement to file — (1) A reporting issuer must file a separate interim certificate in the wording prescribed by the required form

(a) for each individual who, at the time of filing the interim certificate, is a certifying officer; and

(b) signed by the certifying officer.

(2) A reporting issuer must file a certificate required under subsection (1) on the same date that the issuer files its interim filings.

(3) A reporting issuer must file a certificate required under subsection (1) separately from the documents to which the certificate relates.

5.2 Required form of interim certificate — (1) The required form of interim certificate under subsection 5.1(1) is

(a) Form 52-109F2, in the case of an issuer that is a non-venture issuer; and

(b) Form 52-109FV2, in the case of an issuer that is a venture issuer.

(2) Despite subsection (1)(b), a venture issuer may file Form 52-109F2 in the wording prescribed by that Form instead of Form 52-109FV2 for an interim period.

5.3 Alternative form of interim certificate for first financial period after initial public offering — Despite subsection 5.2(1), an issuer may file an interim certificate in Form 52-109F2 — IPO/RTO for the first interim period that ends after the issuer becomes a reporting issuer if

(a) the issuer becomes a reporting issuer by filing a prospectus; and

(b) the first financial period that ends after the issuer becomes a reporting issuer is an interim period.

5.4 Alternative form of interim certificate for first financial period after certain reverse takeovers — Despite subsection 5.2(1), an issuer may file an interim certificate in Form 52-109F2 — IPO/RTO for the first interim period that ends after the completion of a reverse takeover if

(a) the issuer is the reverse takeover acquiree in the reverse takeover;

(b) the reverse takeover acquirer was not a reporting issuer immediately before the reverse takeover; and

(c) the first financial period that ends after the completion of the reverse takeover is an interim period.

5.5 Alternative form of interim certificate for first financial period after becoming a non-venture issuer — Despite subsection 5.2(1), an issuer may file an interim certificate in Form 52-109F2 — IPO/RTO for the first interim period that ends after the issuer becomes a non-venture issuer if the first financial period that ends after the issuer becomes a non-venture issuer is an interim period.

5.6 Exception for new reporting issuers — Despite section 5.1, a reporting issuer does not have to file an interim certificate relating to

(a) the interim financial reports required under section 4.7 of NI 51-102 for interim periods that ended before the issuer became a reporting issuer; or

(b) the interim financial reports for a reverse takeover acquirer required under section 4.10 of NI 51-102 for interim periods that ended before the completion of the reverse takeover.

PART 6 — REFILED FINANCIAL STATEMENTS, MD&A OR AIF

6.1 Refiled annual financial statements, annual MD&A or AIF — If an issuer refiles its annual financial statements, annual MD&A or AIF for a financial year, it must file separate annual certificates for that financial year in Form 52-109F1R on the date that it refiles the annual financial statements, annual MD&A or AIF, as the case may be.

6.2 Refiled interim financial report or interim MD&A — If an issuer refiles its interim financial report or interim MD&A for an interim period, it must file separate interim certificates for that interim period in Form 52-109F2R on the date that it refiles the interim financial report or interim MD&A, as the case may be.

PART 7 — GENERAL REQUIREMENTS FOR CERTIFICATES

7.1 Dating of certificates — A certifying officer must date a certificate filed under this Instrument the same date the certificate is filed.

7.2 French or English — (1) A certificate filed by an issuer under this Instrument must be in French or in English.

(2) In Québec, an issuer must comply with linguistic obligations and rights prescribed by Québec law.

PART 8 — EXEMPTIONS

8.1 Exemption from annual requirements for issuers that comply with U.S. laws — (1) Subject to subsection (2), Parts 2, 3, 4, 6 and 7 do not apply to an issuer for a financial year if

(a) the issuer is in compliance with the SOX 302 Rules and the issuer files signed certificates relating to its annual report under the 1934 Act separately, but concurrently, and as soon as practicable after they are filed with or furnished to the SEC; and

(b) the issuer is in compliance with the SOX 404 Rules, and the issuer files management's annual report on internal control over financial reporting and the attestation report on management's assessment of internal control over financial reporting included in the issuer's annual report under the 1934 Act for the financial year, if applicable, as soon as practicable after they are filed with or furnished to the SEC.

(2) Despite subsection (1), Parts 2, 3, 4, 6 and 7 apply to an issuer for a financial year if the issuer's annual financial statements, annual MD&A or AIF, that together comprise the issuer's annual filings, differ from the annual financial statements, annual MD&A or AIF filed with or furnished to the SEC, or included as exhibits to other documents filed with or furnished to the SEC, and certified in compliance with the SOX 302 Rules.

8.2 Exemption from interim requirements for issuers that comply with U.S. laws — (1) Subject to subsection (3), Parts 2, 3, 5, 6 and 7 do not apply to an issuer for an interim period if the issuer is in compliance with the SOX 302 Rules and the issuer files signed certificates relating to its quarterly report under the 1934 Act for the quarter separately, but concurrently, and as soon as practicable after they are filed with or furnished to the SEC.

(2) Subject to subsection (3), Parts 2, 3, 5, 6 and 7 do not apply to an issuer for an interim period if

(a) the issuer files with or furnishes to the SEC a report on Form 6-K containing the issuer's quarterly financial statements and MD&A ;

(b) the Form 6-K is accompanied by signed certificates that are filed with or furnished to the SEC in the same form required by the SOX 302 Rules; and

(c) the issuer files signed certificates relating to the quarterly report filed or furnished under cover of the Form 6-K as soon as practicable after they are filed with or furnished to the SEC.

(3) Despite subsections (1) and (2), Parts 2, 3, 5, 6 and 7 apply to an issuer for an interim period if the issuer's interim financial report or interim MD&A, that together comprise the issuer's interim filings, differ from the interim financial report or interim MD&A filed with or furnished to the SEC, or included as exhibits to other documents filed with or furnished to the SEC, and certified in compliance with the SOX 302 Rules.

8.3 Exemption for certain foreign issuers — This Instrument does not apply to an issuer if it qualifies under, and is in compliance with, sections 5.4 and 5.5 of National Instrument 71-102 *Continuous Disclosure and Other Exemptions Relating to Foreign Issuers*.

8.4 Exemption for certain exchangeable security issuers — This Instrument does not apply to an issuer if it qualifies under, and is in compliance with, subsection 13.3(2) of NI 51-102.

8.5 Exemption for certain credit support issuers — This Instrument does not apply to an issuer if it qualifies under, and is in compliance with, subsection 13.4(2) of NI 51-102.

8.6 General exemption — (1) The regulator or securities regulatory authority may grant an exemption from this Instrument, in whole or in part, subject to such conditions or restrictions as may be imposed in the exemption.

(2) Despite subsection (1), in Ontario only the regulator may grant such an exemption.

(3) Except in Ontario, an exemption referred to in subsection (1) is granted under the statute referred to in Appendix B of National Instrument 14-101 *Definitions* opposite the name of the local jurisdiction.

PART 9 — EFFECTIVE DATE AND REPEAL

9.1 Effective date — This Instrument comes into force on December 15, 2008.

9.2 Repeal — Multilateral Instrument 52-109 *Certification of Disclosure in Issuers' Annual and Interim Filings*, which came into force on

(a) March 30, 2004, in all jurisdictions other than British Columbia, New Brunswick and Québec,

(b) June 30, 2005, in Québec,

(c) July 28, 2005, in New Brunswick, and

(d) September 19, 2005 in British Columbia,

is repealed.

Final Rule: (2004) 27 O.S.C.B. 3230; Approval of OSC: (2004) 27 O.S.C.B. 877; Request for Comments: (2003) 26 O.S.C.B. 4980.

Amendment to Rule: (2005) 28 O.S.C.B. 4979; Approval of OSC: (2005) 28 O.S.C.B. 3089.

Amendment to Rule: 30 O.S.C.B. 10506; Approval by OSC: (2007) 30 O.S.C.B. 8570.

Replacement Rule: 31 O.S.C.B. 10435 Approval by OSC: 31 O.S.C.B. 7949; Request for Comments: 31 O.S.C.B. (Supp. 3) 1 (April 18, 2008), 30 O.S.C.B. 2877 and 28 O.S.C.B. 1318.

Amendment to Rule: (2010) 33 O.S.C.B. (Supp. 5) 102; Approval by OSC: (2010) 33 O.S.C.B. (Supp. 3) 191; Request for Comments: (2009) 32 O.S.C.B. (Supp. 6) 395.

Rules: NI 51-102, 71-102, 52-107.

Policies and Orders: CSAN 52-315, 52-325, 52-327, 51-332, 51-333; OSCN 51-706.

Form 52-109F1 — Certification of Annual Filings — Full Certificate

I, *<identify (i) the certifying officer, (ii) his or her position at the issuer, (iii) the name of the issuer and (iv) if the certifying officer's title is not "chief executive officer" or "chief financial officer", indicate in which of these capacities the certifying officer is providing the certificate>*, certify the following:

1. *Review:* I have reviewed the AIF, if any, annual financial statements and annual MD&A, including, for greater certainty, all documents and information that are incorporated by reference in the AIF (together, the "annual filings") of *<identify issuer>* (the "issuer") for the financial year ended *<state the relevant date>*.

2. *No misrepresentations:* Based on my knowledge, having exercised reasonable diligence, the annual filings do not contain any untrue statement of a material fact or omit to state a material fact required to be stated or that is necessary to make a statement not misleading in light of the circumstances under which it was made, for the period covered by the annual filings.

3. *Fair presentation:* Based on my knowledge, having exercised reasonable diligence, the annual financial statements together with the other financial information included in the annual filings fairly present in all material respects the financial condition, financial performance and cash flows of the issuer, as of the date of and for the periods presented in the annual filings.

4. *Responsibility:* The issuer's other certifying officer(s) and I are responsible for establishing and maintaining disclosure controls and procedures (DC&P) and internal control over financial reporting (ICFR), as those terms are defined in National Instrument 52-109 *Certification of Disclosure in Issuers' Annual and Interim Filings*, for the issuer.

5. *Design:* Subject to the limitations, if any, described in paragraphs 5.2 and 5.3, the issuer's other certifying officer(s) and I have, as at the financial year end

    (a) designed DC&P, or caused it to be designed under our supervision, to provide reasonable assurance that

        (i) material information relating to the issuer is made known to us by others, particularly during the period in which the annual filings are being prepared; and

        (ii) information required to be disclosed by the issuer in its annual filings, interim filings or other reports filed or submitted by it under securities legislation is recorded, processed, summarized and reported within the time periods specified in securities legislation; and

    (b) designed ICFR, or caused it to be designed under our supervision, to provide reasonable assurance regarding the reliability of financial reporting and the preparation of financial statements for external purposes in accordance with the issuer's GAAP.

5.1 *Control framework:* The control framework the issuer's other certifying officer(s) and I used to design the issuer's ICFR is *<insert the name of the control framework used>*.

<insert paragraph 5.2 or 5.3 if applicable. If paragraph 5.2 or 5.3 is not applicable, insert "5.2 N/A" or "5.3 N/A" as applicable. For paragraph 5.3, include (a)(i), (a)(ii) or (a)(iii) as applicable, and subparagraph (b).>

5.2 *ICFR — material weakness relating to design:* The issuer has disclosed in its annual MD&A for each material weakness relating to design existing at the financial year end

    (a) a description of the material weakness;

    (b) the impact of the material weakness on the issuer's financial reporting and its ICFR; and

    (c) the issuer's current plans, if any, or any actions already undertaken, for remediating the material weakness.

5.3 *Limitation on scope of design:* The issuer has disclosed in its annual MD&A

    (a) the fact that the issuer's other certifying officer(s) and I have limited the scope of our design of DC&P and ICFR to exclude controls, policies and procedures of

        (i) a proportionately consolidated entity in which the issuer has an interest;

        (ii) a special purpose entity in which the issuer has an interest; or

        (iii) a business that the issuer acquired not more than 365 days before the issuer's financial year end; and

    (b) summary financial information about the proportionately consolidated entity, special purpose entity or business that the issuer acquired that has been proportionately consolidated or consolidated in the issuer's financial statements.

<insert subparagraph 6(b)(ii) if applicable. If subparagraph 6(b)(ii) is not applicable, insert "(ii) N/A".>

6. *Evaluation:* The issuer's other certifying officer(s) and I have

    (a) evaluated, or caused to be evaluated under our supervision, the effectiveness of the issuer's DC&P at the financial year end and the issuer has disclosed in its annual MD&A our conclusions about the effectiveness of DC&P at the financial year end based on that evaluation; and

    (b) evaluated, or caused to be evaluated under our supervision, the effectiveness of the issuer's ICFR at the financial year end and the issuer has disclosed in its annual MD&A

        (i) our conclusions about the effectiveness of ICFR at the financial year end based on that evaluation; and

        (ii) for each material weakness relating to operation existing at the financial year end

              (A) a description of the material weakness;

              (B) the impact of the material weakness on the issuer's financial reporting and its ICFR; and

              (C) the issuer's current plans, if any, or any actions already undertaken, for remediating the material weakness.

7. *Reporting changes in ICFR:* The issuer has disclosed in its annual MD&A any change in the issuer's ICFR that occurred during the period beginning on *<insert the date immediately following the end of the period in respect of which the issuer made its most recent interim or annual filing, as applicable>* and ended on *<insert the last day of the financial year>* that has materially affected, or is reasonably likely to materially affect, the issuer's ICFR.

8. *Reporting to the issuer's auditors and board of directors or audit committee:* The issuer's other certifying officer(s) and I have disclosed, based on our most recent evaluation of ICFR, to the issuer's auditors, and the board of directors or the audit committee of the board of directors any fraud that involves management or other employees who have a significant role in the issuer's ICFR.

Date: *<insert date of filing>*

.... [Signature]

[Title]

    <If the certifying officer's title is not "chief executive officer" or "chief financial officer", indicate in which of these capacities the certifying officer is providing the certificate.>

Form 52-109FV1 — Certification of Annual Filings — Venture Issuer Basic Certificate

I, *<identify (i) the certifying officer, (ii) his or her position at the issuer, (iii) the name of the issuer and (iv) if the certifying officer's title is not "chief executive officer" or "chief financial officer", indicate in which of these capacities the certifying officer is providing the certificate>*, certify the following:

1. *Review:* I have reviewed the AIF, if any, annual financial statements and annual MD&A, including, for greater certainty, all documents and information that are incorporated by reference in the AIF (together, the "annual filings") of *<identify issuer>* (the "issuer") for the financial year ended *<state the relevant date>*.

2. *No misrepresentations:* Based on my knowledge, having exercised reasonable diligence, the annual filings do not contain any untrue statement of a material fact or omit to state a material fact required to be stated or that is necessary to make a statement not misleading in light of the circumstances under which it was made, for the period covered by the annual filings.

3. *Fair presentation:* Based on my knowledge, having exercised reasonable diligence, the annual financial statements together with the other financial information included in the annual filings fairly present in all material respects the financial condition, financial performance and cash flows of the issuer, as of the date of and for the periods presented in the annual filings.

Date: *<insert date of filing>*

.... [Signature]

[Title]

<If the certifying officer's title is not "chief executive officer" or "chief financial officer", indicate in which of these capacities the certifying officer is providing the certificate.>

Note to Reader

In contrast to the certificate required for non-venture issuers under National Instrument 52-109 *Certification of Disclosure in Issuers' Annual and Interim Filings* (NI 52-109), this Venture Issuer Basic Certificate does not include representations relating to the establishment and maintenance of disclosure controls and procedures (DC&P) and internal control over financial reporting (ICFR), as defined in NI 52-109. In particular, the certifying officers filing this certificate are not making any representations relating to the establishment and maintenance of

    i) controls and other procedures designed to provide reasonable assurance that information required to be disclosed by the issuer in its annual filings, interim filings or other reports filed or submitted under securities legislation is recorded, processed, summarized and reported within the time periods specified in securities legislation; and

    ii) a process to provide reasonable assurance regarding the reliability of financial reporting and the preparation of financial statements for external purposes in accordance with the issuer's GAAP.

The issuer's certifying officers are responsible for ensuring that processes are in place to provide them with sufficient knowledge to support the representations they are making in this certificate. Investors should be aware that inherent limitations on the ability of certifying officers of a venture issuer to design and implement on a cost effective basis DC&P and ICFR as defined in NI 52-109 may result in additional risks to the quality, reliability, transparency and timeliness of interim and annual filings and other reports provided under securities legislation.

Form 52-109F1–IPO/RTO — Certification of Annual Filings Following an Initial Public Offering, Reverse Takeover or Becoming a Non-Venture Issuer

I, *<identify (i) the certifying officer, (ii) his or her position at the issuer, (iii) the name of the issuer and (iv) if the certifying officer's title is not "chief executive officer" or "chief financial officer", indicate in which of these capacities the certifying officer is providing the certificate>*, certify the following:

1. *Review:* I have reviewed the AIF, if any, annual financial statements and annual MD&A, including, for greater certainty, all documents and information that are incorporated by reference in the AIF (together, the "annual filings") of *<identify issuer>* (the "issuer") for the financial year ended *<state the relevant date>*.

2. *No misrepresentations*: Based on my knowledge, having exercised reasonable diligence, the annual filings do not contain any untrue statement of a material fact or omit to state a material fact required to be stated or that is necessary to make a statement not misleading in light of the circumstances under which it was made, for the period covered by the annual filings.

3. *Fair presentation*: Based on my knowledge, having exercised reasonable diligence, the annual financial statements together with the other financial information included in the annual filings fairly present in all material respects the financial condition, financial performance and cash flows of the issuer, as of the date of and for the periods presented in the annual filings.

Date: *<insert date of filing>*

.... [Signature]

[Title]

<If the certifying officer's title is not "chief executive officer" or "chief financial officer", indicate in which of these capacities the certifying officer is providing the certificate.>

Note to Reader

In contrast to the usual certificate required for non-venture issuers under National Instrument 52-109 *Certification of Disclosure in Issuers' Annual and Interim Filings* (NI 52-109), namely, Form 52-109F1, this Form 52-109F1 — IPO/RTO does not include representations relating to the establishment and maintenance of disclosure controls and procedures (DC&P) and internal control over financial reporting (ICFR), as defined in NI 52-109. In particular, the certifying officers filing this certificate are not making any representations relating to the establishment and maintenance of

i) controls and other procedures designed to provide reasonable assurance that information required to be disclosed by the issuer in its annual filings, interim filings or other reports filed or submitted under securities legislation is recorded, processed, summarized and reported within the time periods specified in securities legislation; and

ii) a process to provide reasonable assurance regarding the reliability of financial reporting and the preparation of financial statements for external purposes in accordance with the issuer's GAAP.

The issuer's certifying officers are responsible for ensuring that processes are in place to provide them with sufficient knowledge to support the representations they are making in this certificate.

Investors should be aware that inherent limitations on the ability of certifying officers of an issuer to design and implement on a cost effective basis DC&P and ICFR as defined in NI 52-109 in the first financial period following

- completion of the issuer's initial public offering in the circumstances described in s. 4.3 of NI 52-109;

- completion of a reverse takeover in the circumstances described in s. 4.4 of NI 52-109; or

- the issuer becoming a non-venture issuer in the circumstances described in s. 4.5 of NI 52-109;

may result in additional risks to the quality, reliability, transparency and timeliness of interim and annual filings and other reports provided under securities legislation.

Form 52-109F1R — Certification of Refiled Annual Filings

This certificate is being filed on the same date that *<identify the issuer>* (the "issuer") has refiled *<identify the filing(s) that have been refiled>*.

I, *<identify (i) the certifying officer, (ii) his or her position at the issuer, (iii) the name of the issuer and (iv) if the certifying officer's title is not "chief executive officer" or "chief financial officer", indicate in which of these capacities the certifying officer is providing the certificate>*, certify the following:

1. *Review:* I have reviewed the AIF, if any, annual financial statements and annual MD&A, including, for greater certainty, all documents and information that are incorporated by reference in the AIF (together, the "annual filings") of the issuer for the financial year ended *<state the relevant date>*.

<Insert all paragraphs included in the annual certificates originally filed with the annual filings, other than paragraph 1. If the originally filed annual certificates were in Form 52-109FV1 or Form 52-109F1 — IPO/RTO, include the "note to reader" contained in Form 52-109FV1 or Form 52-109F1 — IPO/RTO, as the case may be, in this certificate.>

Date: *<insert date of filing>*

.... [Signature]

[Title]

<If the certifying officer's title is not "chief executive officer" or "chief financial officer", indicate in which of these capacities the certifying officer is providing the certificate.>

Form 52-109F1–AIF — Certification of Annual Filings in Connection with Voluntarily Filed AIF

This certificate is being filed on the same date that *<identify the issuer>* (the "issuer") has voluntarily filed an AIF.

I, *<identify (i) the certifying officer, (ii) his or her position at the issuer, (iii) the name of the issuer and (iv) if the certifying officer's title is not "chief executive officer" or "chief financial officer", indicate in which of these capacities the certifying officer is providing the certificate>*, certify the following:

1. *Review:* I have reviewed the AIF, annual financial statements and annual MD&A, including for greater certainty all documents and information that are incorporated by reference in the AIF (together, the "annual filings") of the issuer for the financial year ended *<state the relevant date>*.

<Insert all paragraphs included in the annual certificates originally filed with the annual filings, other than paragraph 1. If the originally filed annual certificates were in Form 52-109FV1 or Form 52-109F1 — IPO/RTO, include the "note to reader" contained in Form 52-109FV1 or Form 52-109F1 — IPO/RTO, as the case may be, in this certificate.>

Date: *<insert date of filing>*

.... [Signature]

[Title]

<If the certifying officer's title is not "chief executive officer" or "chief financial officer", indicate in which of these capacities the certifying officer is providing the certificate.>

Form 52-109F2 — Certification of Interim Filings — Full Certificate

I, *<identify (i) the certifying officer, (ii) his or her position at the issuer, (iii) the name of the issuer and (iv) if the certifying officer's title is not "chief executive officer" or "chief financial officer", indicate in which of these capacities the certifying officer is providing the certificate>*, certify the following:

1. *Review:* I have reviewed the interim financial report and interim MD&A (together, the "interim filings") of *<identify the issuer>* (the "issuer") for the interim period ended *<state the relevant date>*.

2. *No misrepresentations:* Based on my knowledge, having exercised reasonable diligence, the interim filings do not contain any untrue statement of a material fact or omit to state a material fact required to be stated or that is necessary to make a statement not misleading in light of the circumstances under which it was made, with respect to the period covered by the interim filings.

3. *Fair presentation:* Based on my knowledge, having exercised reasonable diligence, the interim financial report together with the other financial information included in the interim filings fairly present in all material respects the financial condition, financial performance and cash flows of the issuer, as of the date of and for the periods presented in the interim filings.

4. *Responsibility:* The issuer's other certifying officer(s) and I are responsible for establishing and maintaining disclosure controls and procedures (DC&P) and internal control over financial reporting (ICFR), as those terms are defined in National Instrument 52-109 *Certification of Disclosure in Issuers' Annual and Interim Filings*, for the issuer.

5. *Design:* Subject to the limitations, if any, described in paragraphs 5.2 and 5.3, the issuer's other certifying officer(s) and I have, as at the end of the period covered by the interim filings

    (a) designed DC&P, or caused it to be designed under our supervision, to provide reasonable assurance that

        (i) material information relating to the issuer is made known to us by others, particularly during the period in which the interim filings are being prepared; and

        (ii) information required to be disclosed by the issuer in its annual filings, interim filings or other reports filed or submitted by it under securities legislation is recorded, processed, summarized and reported within the time periods specified in securities legislation; and

    (b) designed ICFR, or caused it to be designed under our supervision, to provide reasonable assurance regarding the reliability of financial reporting and the preparation of financial statements for external purposes in accordance with the issuer's GAAP.

5.1 *Control framework:* The control framework the issuer's other certifying officer(s) and I used to design the issuer's ICFR is *<insert the name of the control framework used>*.

<insert paragraph 5.2 or 5.3 if applicable. If paragraph 5.2 or 5.3 is not applicable, insert "5.2 N/A" or "5.3 N/A" as applicable. For paragraph 5.3, include (a)(i), (a)(ii) or (a)(iii) as applicable, and subparagraph (b).>

5.2 *ICFR — material weakness relating to design:* The issuer has disclosed in its interim MD&A for each material weakness relating to design existing at the end of the interim period

    (a) a description of the material weakness;

    (b) the impact of the material weakness on the issuer's financial reporting and its ICFR; and

    (c) the issuer's current plans, if any, or any actions already undertaken, for remediating the material weakness.

5.3 *Limitation on scope of design:* The issuer has disclosed in its interim MD&A

    (a) the fact that the issuer's other certifying officer(s) and I have limited the scope of our design of DC&P and ICFR to exclude controls, policies and procedures of

        (i) a proportionately consolidated entity in which the issuer has an interest;

(ii) a special purpose entity in which the issuer has an interest; or

(iii) a business that the issuer acquired not more than 365 days before the last day of the period covered by the interim filings; and

(b) summary financial information about the proportionately consolidated entity, special purpose entity or business that the issuer acquired that has been proportionately consolidated or consolidated in the issuer's financial statements.

6. *Reporting changes in ICFR:* The issuer has disclosed in its interim MD&A any change in the issuer's ICFR that occurred during the period beginning on *<insert the date immediately following the end of the period in respect of which the issuer made its most recent interim or annual filing, as applicable>* and ended on *<insert the last day of the period covered by the interim filings>* that has materially affected, or is reasonably likely to materially affect, the issuer's ICFR.

Date: *<insert date of filing>*

.... [Signature]

[Title]

<If the certifying officer's title is not "chief executive officer" or "chief financial officer", indicate in which of these capacities the certifying officer is providing the certificate.>

Form 52-109FV2 — Certification of Interim Filings — Venture Issuer Basic Certificate

I, *<identify (i) the certifying officer, (ii) his or her position at the issuer, (iii) the name of the issuer and (iv) if the certifying officer's title is not "chief executive officer" or "chief financial officer", indicate in which of these capacities the certifying officer is providing the certificate>*, certify the following:

1. *Review:* I have reviewed the interim financial report and interim MD&A (together, the "interim filings") of *<identify the issuer>* (the "issuer") for the interim period ended *<state the relevant date>*.

2. *No misrepresentations:* Based on my knowledge, having exercised reasonable diligence, the interim filings do not contain any untrue statement of a material fact or omit to state a material fact required to be stated or that is necessary to make a statement not misleading in light of the circumstances under which it was made, with respect to the period covered by the interim filings.

3. *Fair presentation:* Based on my knowledge, having exercised reasonable diligence, the interim financial report together with the other financial information included in the interim filings fairly present in all material respects the financial condition, financial performance and cash flows of the issuer, as of the date of and for the periods presented in the interim filings.

Date: *<insert date of filing>*

.... [Signature]

[Title]

<If the certifying officer's title is not "chief executive officer" or "chief financial officer", indicate in which of these capacities the certifying officer is providing the certificate.>

Note to Reader

In contrast to the certificate required for non-venture issuers under National Instrument 52-109 *Certification of Disclosure in Issuers' Annual and Interim Filings* (NI 52-109), this Venture Issuer Basic Certificate does not include representations relating to the establishment and maintenance of disclosure controls and procedures (DC&P) and internal control over financial reporting (ICFR), as defined in NI 52-109. In particular, the certifying officers filing this certificate are not making any representations relating to the establishment and maintenance of

i) controls and other procedures designed to provide reasonable assurance that information required to be disclosed by the issuer in its annual filings, interim filings or other reports filed or submitted under securities legislation is recorded, processed, summarized and reported within the time periods specified in securities legislation; and

ii) a process to provide reasonable assurance regarding the reliability of financial reporting and the preparation of financial statements for external purposes in accordance with the issuer's GAAP.

The issuer's certifying officers are responsible for ensuring that processes are in place to provide them with sufficient knowledge to support the representations they are making in this certificate. Investors should be aware that inherent limitations on the ability of certifying officers of a venture issuer to design and implement on a cost effective basis DC&P and ICFR as defined in NI 52-109 may result in additional risks to the quality, reliability, transparency and timeliness of interim and annual filings and other reports provided under securities legislation.

Form 52-109F2–IPO/RTO — Certification of Interim Filings Following an Initial Public Offering, Reverse Takeover or Becoming a Non-Venture Issuer

I, *<identify (i) the certifying officer, (ii) his or her position at the issuer, (iii) the name of the issuer and (iv) if the certifying officer's title is not "chief executive officer" or "chief financial officer", indicate in which of these capacities the certifying officer is providing the certificate>*, certify the following:

1. *Review:* I have reviewed the interim financial report and interim MD&A (together, the "interim filings") of *<identify the issuer>* (the "issuer") for the interim period ended *<state the relevant date>*.

2. *No misrepresentations:* Based on my knowledge, having exercised reasonable diligence, the interim filings do not contain any untrue statement of a material fact or omit to state a material fact required to be stated or that is necessary to make a statement not misleading in light of the circumstances under which it was made, with respect to the period covered by the interim filings.

3. *Fair presentation:* Based on my knowledge, having exercised reasonable diligence, the interim financial report together with the other financial information included in the interim filings fairly present in all material respects the financial condition, financial performance and cash flows of the issuer, as of the date of and for the periods presented in the interim filings.

Date: *<insert date of filing>*

.... [Signature]

[Title]

<If the certifying officer's title is not "chief executive officer" or "chief financial officer", indicate in which of these capacities the certifying officer is providing the certificate.>

Note to Reader

In contrast to the usual certificate required for non-venture issuers under National Instrument 52-109 *Certification of Disclosure in Issuers' Annual and Interim Filings* (NI 52-109), namely, Form 52-109F2, this Form 52-109F2 — IPO/RTO does not include representations relating to the establishment and maintenance of disclosure controls and procedures (DC&P) and internal control over financial reporting (ICFR), as defined in NI 52-109. In particular, the certifying officers filing this certificate are not making any representations relating to the establishment and maintenance of

i) controls and other procedures designed to provide reasonable assurance that information required to be disclosed by the issuer in its annual filings, interim filings or other reports filed or submitted under securities legislation is recorded, processed, summarized and reported within the time periods specified in securities legislation; and

ii) a process to provide reasonable assurance regarding the reliability of financial reporting and the preparation of financial statements for external purposes in accordance with the issuer's GAAP.

The issuer's certifying officers are responsible for ensuring that processes are in place to provide them with sufficient knowledge to support the representations they are making in this certificate.

Investors should be aware that inherent limitations on the ability of certifying officers of an issuer to design and implement on a cost effective basis DC&P and ICFR as defined in NI 52-109 in the first financial period following

- completion of the issuer's initial public offering in the circumstances described in s. 5.3 of NI 52-109;
- completion of a reverse takeover in the circumstances described in s. 5.4 of NI 52-109; or
- the issuer becoming a non-venture issuer in the circumstances described in s. 5.5 of NI 52-109;

may result in additional risks to the quality, reliability, transparency and timeliness of interim and annual filings and other reports provided under securities legislation.

Form 52-109F2R — Certification of Refiled Interim Filings

This certificate is being filed on the same date that *<identify the issuer>* (the "issuer") has refiled *<identify the filing(s) that have been refiled>*.

I, *<identify (i) the certifying officer, (ii) his or her position at the issuer, (iii) the name of the issuer and (iv) if the certifying officer's title is not "chief executive officer" or "chief financial officer", indicate in which of these capacities the certifying officer is providing the certificate>*, certify the following:

1. *Review:* I have reviewed the interim financial report and interim MD&A (together, the "interim filings") of the issuer for the interim period ended *<state the relevant date>*.

<Insert all paragraphs included in the interim certificates originally filed with the interim filings, other than paragraph 1. If the originally filed interim certificates were in Form 52-109FV2 or Form 52-109F2 — IPO/RTO, include the "note to reader" contained in Form 52-109FV2 or Form 52-109F2 — IPO/RTO, as the case may be, in this certificate.>

Date: *<insert date of filing>*

.... [Signature]

[Title]

<If the certifying officer's title is not "chief executive officer" or "chief financial officer", indicate in which of these capacities the certifying officer is providing the certificate.>

Companion Policy 52-109CP — To National Instrument 52-109 Certification of Disclosure in Issuers' Annual and Interim Filings

PART 9 — MATERIAL WEAKNESS

    9.1 Identifying a deficiency in ICFR

    9.2 Assessing significance of deficiencies in ICFR

    9.3 Factors to consider when assessing significance of deficiencies in ICFR

    9.4 Indicators of a material weakness

    9.5 Conclusions on effectiveness if a material weakness exists

    9.6 Disclosure of a material weakness

    9.7 Disclosure of remediation plans and actions undertaken

PART 10 — WEAKNESS IN DC&P THAT IS SIGNIFICANT

    10.1 Conclusion on effectiveness of DC&P if a weakness exists that is significant

    10.2 Interim certification of DC&P design if a weakness exists that is significant

    10.3 Certification of DC&P if a material weakness in ICFR exists

PART 11 — REPORTING CHANGES IN ICFR

    11.1 Assessing the materiality of a change in ICFR

PART 12 — ROLE OF BOARD OF DIRECTORS AND AUDIT COMMITTEE

    12.1 Board of directors

    12.2 Audit committee

    12.3 Reporting fraud

PART 13 — CERTAIN LONG TERM INVESTMENTS

    13.1 Underlying entities

    13.2 Fair presentation

    13.3 Design and evaluation of DC&P and ICFR

PART 14 — BUSINESS ACQUISITIONS

    14.1 Access to acquired business

    14.2 Disclosure of scope limitation

PART 15 — VENTURE ISSUER BASIC CERTIFICATES

    15.1 Venture issuer basic certificates

    15.2 Note to reader included in venture issuer basic certificates

    15.3 Voluntary disclosure regarding DC&P and ICFR

PART 16 — CERTIFICATION REQUIREMENTS FOR A NEW REPORTING ISSUER AND AN ISSUER THAT BECOMES A NON-VENTURE ISSUER

    16.1 Certification requirements after becoming a non-venture issuer

PART 17 — EXEMPTIONS

    17.1 Issuers that comply with U.S. laws

PART 18 — LIABILITY FOR CERTIFICATES CONTAINING MISREPRESENTATIONS

    18.1 Liability for certificates containing misrepresentations

PART 19 — TRANSITION

    19.1 Representations regarding DC&P and ICFR following the transition periods

    19.2 Application of Amendments

PART 20 — CERTIFICATION OF REVISED OR RESTATED ANNUAL OR INTERIM FILINGS

    20.1 Certification of revised or restated annual or interim filings

    20.2 Disclosure considerations if an issuer revises or restates a continuous disclosure document

PART 1 — GENERAL

1.1 Introduction and purpose — National Instrument 52-109 *Certification of Disclosure in Issuers' Annual and Interim Filings* (the Instrument) sets out disclosure and filing requirements for all reporting issuers, other than investment funds. The objective of these requirements is to improve the quality, reliability and transparency of annual filings, interim filings and other materials that issuers file or submit under securities legislation.

This Companion Policy (the Policy) describes how the provincial and territorial securities regulatory authorities intend to interpret and apply the provisions of the Instrument.

1.2 Application to non-corporate entities — The Instrument applies to both corporate and non-corporate entities. Where the Instrument or the Policy refers to a particular corporate characteristic, such as the audit committee of the board of directors, the reference should be read to also include any equivalent characteristic of a non-corporate entity.

1.3 Application to venture issuers — Venture issuers should note that the guidance provided in Parts 5 through 14 of this Policy is intended for issuers filing Form 52-109F1 and Form 52-109F2. Under Parts 4 and 5 of the Instrument venture issuers are not required, but may elect, to use those Forms.

1.4 Definitions — For the purposes of the Policy, "DC&P" means disclosure controls and procedures (as defined in the Instrument) and "ICFR" means internal control over financial reporting (as defined in the Instrument).

1.5 Accounting terms — The Instrument uses accounting terms that are defined or used in Canadian GAAP applicable to publicly accountable enterprises. In certain cases, some of those terms are defined differently in securities legislation. In deciding which meaning applies, you should consider that National Instrument 14-101 *Definitions* provides that a term used in the Instrument and defined in the securities statute of a local jurisdiction has the meaning given to it in the statute unless: (a) the definition in that statute is restricted to a specific portion of the statute that does not govern continuous disclosure; or (b) the context otherwise requires.

1.6 Acceptable accounting principles other than Canadian GAAP applicable to publicly accountable enterprises — If an issuer is permitted under NI 52-107 to file financial statements in accordance with acceptable accounting principles other than Canadian GAAP applicable to publicly accountable enterprises, then the issuer may interpret any reference in the Instrument to a term or provision defined or used in Canadian GAAP applicable to publicly accountable enterprises as a reference to the corresponding term or provision in the other acceptable accounting principles.

1.7 Rate-regulated activities — If a qualifying entity is relying on the exemption in paragraph 5.4(1)(a) of NI 52-107, then the qualifying entity may interpret any reference in the Instrument to a term or provision defined or used in Canadian GAAP applicable to publicly accountable enterprises as a reference to the corresponding term or provision in Part V of the Handbook.

PART 2 — FORM OF CERTIFICATES

2.1 Prescribed wording — Parts 4 and 5 of the Instrument require the annual and interim certificates to be filed in the exact wording prescribed by the required form (including the form number and form title) without any amendment. Failure to do so will be a breach of the Instrument.

PART 3 — CERTIFYING OFFICERS

3.1 One individual acting as chief executive officer and chief financial officer — If only one individual is serving as the chief executive officer and chief financial officer of an issuer, or is performing functions similar to those performed by such officers, that individual may either:

(a) provide two certificates (one in the capacity of the chief executive officer and the other in the capacity of the chief financial officer); or

(b) provide one certificate in the capacity of both the chief executive officer and chief financial officer and file this certificate twice, once in the filing category for certificates of chief executive officers and once in the filing category for certificates of chief financial officers.

3.2 Individuals performing the functions of a chief executive officer or chief financial officer — (1) No chief executive officer or chief financial officer — If an issuer does not have a chief executive officer or chief financial officer, each individual who performs functions similar to those performed by a chief executive officer or chief financial officer must certify the annual filings and interim filings. If an issuer does not have a chief executive officer or chief financial officer, in order to comply with the Instrument the issuer will need to identify at least one individual who performs functions similar to those performed by a chief executive officer or chief financial officer, as applicable.

(2) Management resides at underlying business entity level or external management company — In the case of a reporting issuer where executive management resides at the underlying business entity level or in an external management company such as for an income trust (as described in National Policy 41-201 *Income Trusts and Other Indirect Offerings*), the chief executive officer and chief financial officer of the underlying business entity or the external management company should generally be identified as individuals performing functions for the reporting issuer similar to a chief executive officer and chief financial officer.

(3) Limited partnership — In the case of a limited partnership reporting issuer with no chief executive officer and chief financial officer, the chief executive officer and chief financial officer of its general partner should generally be identified as individuals performing functions for the limited partnership reporting issuer similar to a chief executive officer and chief financial officer.

3.3 "New" certifying officers — An individual who is the chief executive officer or chief financial officer at the time that an issuer files annual and interim certificates is the individual who must sign a certificate.

Certain forms included in the Instrument require each certifying officer to certify that he or she has designed, or caused to be designed under his or her supervision, the issuer's DC&P and ICFR. If an issuer's DC&P and ICFR have been designed prior to a certifying officer assuming office, the certifying officer would:

(a) review the design of the existing DC&P and ICFR after assuming office; and

(b) design any modifications to the existing DC&P and ICFR determined to be necessary following his or her review,

prior to certifying the design of the issuer's DC&P and ICFR.

PART 4 — FAIR PRESENTATION, FINANCIAL CONDITION AND RELIABILITY OF FINANCIAL REPORTING

4.1 Fair presentation of financial condition, financial performance and cash flows — (1) Fair presentation not limited to issuer's GAAP — The forms included in the Instrument require each certifying officer to certify that an issuer's financial statements (including prior period comparative financial information) and other financial information included in the annual or interim filings fairly present in all material respects the financial condition, financial performance and cash flows of the issuer, as of the date and for the periods presented.

This certification is not qualified by the phrase "in accordance with generally accepted accounting principles" which is typically included in audit reports accompanying annual financial statements. The forms specifically exclude this qualification to prevent certifying officers from relying entirely on compliance with the issuer's GAAP in this representation, particularly as the issuer's GAAP financial statements might not fully reflect the financial condition of the issuer. Certification is intended to provide assurance that the financial information disclosed in the annual filings or interim filings, viewed in its entirety, provides a materially accurate and complete picture that may be broader than financial reporting under the issuer's GAAP. As a result, certifying officers cannot limit the fair presentation representation by referring to the issuer's GAAP.

Although the concept of fair presentation as used in the annual and interim certificates is not limited to compliance with the issuer's GAAP, this does not permit an issuer to depart from the issuer's GAAP in preparing its financial statements. If a certifying officer believes that the issuer's financial statements do not fairly present the issuer's financial condition, the certifying officer should ensure that the issuer's MD&A includes any necessary additional disclosure.

(2) **Quantitative and qualitative factors** — The concept of fair presentation encompasses a number of quantitative and qualitative factors, including:

(a) selection of appropriate accounting policies;

(b) proper application of appropriate accounting policies;

(c) disclosure of financial information that is informative and reasonably reflects the underlying transactions; and

(d) additional disclosure necessary to provide investors with a materially accurate and complete picture of financial condition, financial performance and cash flows.

4.2 Financial condition — The Instrument does not formally define financial condition. However, the term "financial condition" in the annual certificates and interim certificates reflects the overall financial health of the issuer and includes the issuer's financial position (as shown on the statement of financial position) and other factors that may affect the issuer's liquidity, capital resources and solvency.

4.3 Reliability of financial reporting — The definition of ICFR refers to the reliability of financial reporting and the preparation of financial statements for external purposes in accordance with the issuer's GAAP. In order to have reliable financial reporting and financial statements to be prepared in accordance with the issuer's GAAP, the amounts and disclosures in the financial statements must not contain any material misstatement.

PART 5 — CONTROL FRAMEWORKS FOR ICFR

5.1 Requirement to use a control framework — Section 3.4 of the Instrument requires an issuer to use a control framework in order to design the issuer's ICFR. The framework used should be a suitable control framework that is established by a body or group that has followed due-process procedures, including the broad distribution of the framework for public comment.

Examples of suitable frameworks that an issuer could use to design ICFR are:

(a) the *Risk Management and Governance: Guidance on Control* (COCO Framework), formerly known as Guidance of the Criteria of Control Board, published by The Canadian Institute of Chartered Accountants;

(b) the *Internal Control — Integrated Framework* (COSO Framework) published by The Committee of Sponsoring Organizations of the Treadway Commission (COSO); and

(c) the *Guidance on Internal Control* (Turnbull Guidance) published by The Institute of Chartered Accountants in England and Wales.

A smaller issuer can also refer to *Internal Control over Financial Reporting — Guidance for Smaller Public Companies* published by COSO, which provides guidance to smaller public companies on the implementation of the COSO Framework.

In addition, *IT Control Objectives for Sarbanes-Oxley* published by the IT Governance Institute, might provide useful guidance for the design and evaluation of information technology controls that form part of an issuer's ICFR.

5.2 Scope of control frameworks — The control frameworks referred to in section 5.1 include in their definition of "internal control" three general categories: effectiveness and efficiency of operations, reliability of financial reporting and compliance with applicable laws and regulations. ICFR is a subset of internal controls relating to financial reporting. ICFR does not encompass the elements of these control frameworks that relate to effectiveness and efficiency of an issuer's operations or an issuer's compliance with applicable laws and regulations, except for compliance with the applicable laws and regulations directly related to the preparation of financial statements.

PART 6 — DESIGN OF DC&P AND ICFR

6.1 General — Most sections in this Part apply to the design of both DC&P (DC&P design) and ICFR (ICFR design); however, some sections provide specific guidance relating to DC&P design or ICFR design. The term "design" in this context generally includes both developing and implementing the controls, policies and procedures that comprise DC&P and ICFR. This Policy often refers to such controls, policies and procedures as the "components" of DC&P and ICFR.

A control, policy or procedure is implemented when it has been placed in operation. An evaluation of effectiveness does not need to be performed to assess whether the control, policy or procedure is operating as intended in order for it to be placed in operation.

6.2 Overlap between DC&P and ICFR — There is a substantial overlap between the definitions of DC&P and ICFR. However, some elements of DC&P are not subsumed within the definition of ICFR and some elements of ICFR are not subsumed within the definition of DC&P. For example, an issuer's DC&P should include those elements of ICFR that provide reasonable assurance that transactions are recorded as necessary to permit the preparation of financial statements in accordance with the issuer's GAAP. However, the issuer's DC&P might not include certain elements of ICFR, such as those pertaining to the safeguarding of assets.

6.3 Reasonable assurance — The definition of DC&P includes reference to reasonable assurance that information required to be disclosed by the issuer in its annual filings, interim filings or other reports filed or submitted by it under securities legislation is recorded, processed, summarized and reported within the time periods specified in securities legislation. The definition of ICFR includes the phrase "reasonable assurance regarding the reliability of financial reporting and the preparation of financial statements for external purposes in accordance with the issuer's GAAP". In this Part the term "reasonable assurance" refers to one or both of the above uses of this term.

Reasonable assurance is a high level of assurance, but does not represent absolute assurance. DC&P and ICFR cannot provide absolute assurance due to their inherent limitations. Each involves diligence and compliance and is subject to lapses in judgment and breakdowns resulting from human error. As a result of these limitations, DC&P and ICFR cannot prevent or detect all errors or intentional misstatements resulting from fraudulent activities.

The terms "reasonable", "reasonably" and "reasonableness" in the context of the Instrument do not imply a single conclusion or methodology, but encompass a range of potential conduct, conclusions or methodologies upon which certifying officers may base their decisions.

6.4 Judgment — The Instrument does not prescribe specific components of DC&P or ICFR or their degree of complexity. Certifying officers should design the components and complexity of DC&P and ICFR using their judgment, acting reasonably, giving consideration to various factors particular to an issuer, including its size, nature of business and complexity of operations.

6.5 Delegation permitted in certain cases — Section 3.1 of the Instrument requires a non-venture issuer to establish and maintain DC&P and ICFR. Employees or third parties, supervised by the certifying officers, may conduct the design of the issuer's DC&P and ICFR. Such employees should individually and collectively have the necessary knowledge, skills, information and authority to design the DC&P and ICFR for which they have been assigned responsibilities. Nevertheless, certifying officers of the issuer must retain overall responsibility for the design and resulting MD&A disclosure concerning the issuer's DC&P and ICFR.

6.6 Risk considerations for designing DC&P and ICFR — (1) *Approaches to consider for design* — The Instrument does not prescribe the approach certifying officers should use to design the issuer's DC&P or ICFR. However, we believe that a top-down, risk-based approach is an efficient and cost-effective approach that certifying officers should consider. This approach allows certifying officers to avoid unnecessary time and effort designing components of DC&P and ICFR that are not required to obtain reasonable assurance. Alternatively, certifying officers might use some other approach to design, depending on the issuer's size, nature of business and complexity of operations.

(2) *Top-down, risk-based approach* — Under a top-down, risk-based approach to designing DC&P and ICFR certifying officers first identify and assess risks faced by the issuer in order to determine the scope and necessary complexity of the issuer's DC&P or ICFR. A top-down, risk-based approach helps certifying officers to focus their resources on the areas of greatest risk and avoid expending unnecessary resources on areas with little or no risk.

Under a top-down, risk-based approach, certifying officers initially consider risks without considering any existing controls of the issuer. Using this approach to design DC&P, the certifying officers identify the risks that could, individually or in combination with others, reasonably result in a material misstatement in its annual filings, interim filings or other reports filed or submitted by it under securities legislation. Using this approach to design ICFR, the certifying officers identify those risks that could, individually or in combination with others, reasonably result in a material misstatement of the financial statements (financial reporting risks). A material misstatement includes misstatements due to error, fraud or omission in disclosure.

Identifying risks involves considering the size and nature of the issuer's business and the structure and complexity of business operations. If an issuer has multiple locations or business units, certifying officers initially identify the risks that could reasonably result in a material misstatement and then consider the significance of these risks at individual locations or business units. If the officers identify a risk that could reasonably result in a material misstatement, but the risk is either adequately addressed by controls, policies or procedures that operate centrally or is not present at an individual location or business unit, then certifying officers do not need to focus their resources at that location or business unit to address the risk.

For the design of DC&P, the certifying officers assess risks for various types and methods of disclosure. For the design of ICFR, identifying risks involves identifying significant accounts and disclosures and their relevant assertions. After identifying risks that could reasonably result in a material misstatement, the certifying officers then ensure that the DC&P and ICFR designs include controls, policies and procedures to address each of the identified risks.

(3) *Fraud risk* — When identifying risks, certifying officers should explicitly consider the vulnerability of the entity to fraudulent activity (e.g., fraudulent financial reporting and misappropriation of assets). Certifying officers should consider how incentives (e.g., compensation programs) and pressures (e.g., meeting analysts' expectations) might affect risks, and what areas of the business provide opportunity for an individual to commit fraud. For the purposes of this Instrument, fraud would generally include an intentional act by one or more individuals among management, other employees, those charged with governance or third parties, involving the use of deception to obtain an unjust or illegal advantage. Although fraud is a broad legal concept, for the purposes of this Instrument, the certifying officers should be concerned with fraud that could cause a material misstatement in the issuer's annual filings, interim filings or other reports filed or submitted under securities legislation.

(4) *Designing controls, policies and procedures* — If the certifying officers choose to use a top-down, risk-based approach, they design specific controls, policies and procedures that, in combination with an issuer's control environment, appropriately address the risks discussed in subsections (2) and (3).

If certifying officers choose to use an approach other than a top-down, risk-based approach, they should still consider whether the combination of the components of DC&P and ICFR that they have designed are a sufficient basis for the representations about reasonable assurance required in paragraph 5 of the certificates.

6.7 Control environment — (1) *Importance of control environment* — An issuer's control environment is the foundation upon which all other components of DC&P and ICFR are based and influences the tone of an organization. An effective control environment contributes to the reliability of all other controls, processes and procedures by creating an atmosphere where errors or fraud are either less likely to occur, or if they occur, more likely to be detected. An effective control environment also supports the flow of information within the issuer, thus promoting compliance with an issuer's disclosure policies.

An effective control environment alone will not provide reasonable assurance that any of the risks identified will be addressed and managed. An ineffective control environment, however, can undermine an issuer's controls, policies and procedures designed to address specific risks.

(2) *Elements of a control environment* — A key element of an issuer's control environment is the attitude towards controls demonstrated by the board of directors, audit committee and senior management through their direction and actions in the organization. An appropriate tone at the top can help to develop a culture of integrity and accountability at all levels of an organization which support other components of DC&P and ICFR. The tone at the top should be reinforced on an ongoing basis by those accountable for the organization's DC&P and ICFR.

In addition to an appropriate tone at the top, certifying officers should consider the following elements of an issuer's control environment:

    (a) *organizational structure of the issuer* — a structure which relies on established and documented lines of authority and responsibility may be appropriate for some issuers, whereas a structure which allows employees to communicate informally with each other at all levels may be more appropriate for some issuers;

    (b) *management's philosophy and operating style* — a philosophy and style that emphasises managing risks with appropriate diligence and demonstrates receptiveness to negative as well as positive information will foster a stronger control environment;

    (c) *integrity, ethics, and competence of personnel* — controls, policies and procedures are more likely to be effective if they are carried out by ethical, competent and adequately supervised employees;

    (d) *external influences that affect the issuer's operations and risk management practices* — these could include global business practices, regulatory supervision, insurance coverage and legislative requirements; and

    (e) *human resources policies and procedures* — an issuer's hiring, training, supervision, compensation, termination and evaluation practices can affect the quality of the issuer's workforce and its employees' attitudes towards controls.

(3) *Sources of information about the control environment* — The following documentation might provide useful information about an issuer's control environment:

    (a) written codes of conduct or ethics policies;

(b) procedure manuals, operating instructions, job descriptions and training materials;

(c) evidence that employees have confirmed their knowledge and understanding of items (a) and (b);

(d) organizational charts that identify approval structures and the flow of information; and

(e) written correspondence provided by an issuer's external auditor regarding the issuer's control environment.

6.8 Controls, policies and procedures to include in DC&P design — In order for DC&P to provide reasonable assurance that information required by securities legislation to be disclosed by an issuer is recorded, processed, summarized and reported within the required time periods, DC&P should generally include the following components:

(a) written communication to an issuer's employees and directors of the issuer's disclosure obligations, including the purpose of disclosure and DC&P and deadlines for specific filings and other disclosure;

(b) assignment of roles, responsibilities and authorizations relating to disclosure;

(c) guidance on how authorized individuals should assess and document the materiality of information or events for disclosure purposes; and

(d) a policy on how the issuer will receive, document, evaluate and respond to complaints or concerns received from internal or external sources regarding financial reporting or other disclosure issues.

An issuer might choose to include these components in a document called a disclosure policy. Part 6 of National Policy 51-201 *Disclosure Standards* encourages issuers to establish a written disclosure policy and discusses in more detail some of these components. For issuers that are subject to National Instrument 52-110 *Audit Committees* (NI 52-110), compliance with the instrument will also form part of the issuer's DC&P design.

6.9 Controls, policies and procedures to include in ICFR design — In order for ICFR to provide reasonable assurance regarding the reliability of financial reporting and the preparation of financial statements for external purposes in accordance with the issuer's GAAP, ICFR should generally include the following components:

(a) controls for initiating, authorizing, recording and processing transactions relating to significant accounts and disclosures;

(b) controls for initiating, authorizing, recording and processing non-routine transactions and journal entries, including those requiring judgments and estimates;

(c) procedures for selecting and applying appropriate accounting policies that are in accordance with the issuer's GAAP;

(d) controls to prevent and detect fraud;

(e) controls on which other controls are dependent, such as information technology general controls; and

(f) controls over the period-end financial reporting process, including controls over entering transaction totals in the general ledger, controls over initiating, authorizing, recording and processing journal entries in the general ledger and controls over recording recurring and non-recurring adjustments to the financial statements (e.g., consolidating adjustments and reclassifications).

6.10 Identifying significant accounts and disclosures and their relevant assertions — (1) **Significant accounts and disclosures and their relevant assertions** — As described in subsection 6.6(2) of the Policy, a top-down, risk-based approach to designing ICFR involves identifying significant accounts and disclosures and the relevant assertions that affect each significant account and disclosure. This method assists certifying officers in identifying the risks that could reasonably result in a material misstatement in the issuer's financial statements and not all possible risks the issuer faces.

(2) **Identifying significant accounts and disclosures** — A significant account could be an individual line item on the issuer's financial statements, or part of a line item. For example, an issuer might present "net revenue", which represents a combination of "gross revenue" and "returns", but might identify "gross revenue" as a significant account. By identifying part of a line item as a significant account, certifying officers might be able to focus on balances that are subject to specific risks that can be separately identified.

A significant disclosure relating to the design of ICFR could be any form of disclosure included in the issuer's financial statements, or notes to the financial statements, that is presented in accordance with the issuer's GAAP. The identification of significant disclosures for the design of ICFR does not extend to the preparation of the issuer's MD&A or other similar financial information presented in a continuous disclosure filing other than financial statements.

(3) **Considerations for identifying significant accounts and disclosures** — A minimum threshold expressed as a percentage or a dollar amount could provide a reasonable starting point for evaluating the significance of an account or disclosure. However, certifying officers should use their judgment, taking into account qualitative factors, to assess accounts or disclosures for significance above or below that threshold. The following factors will be relevant when determining whether an account or disclosure is significant:

(a) the size, nature and composition of the account or disclosure;

(b) the risk of overstatement or understatement of the account or disclosure;

(c) the susceptibility to misstatement due to errors or fraud;

(d) the volume of activity, complexity and homogeneity of the individual transactions processed through the account or reflected in the disclosure;

(e) the accounting and reporting complexities associated with the account or disclosure;

(f) the likelihood (or possibility) of conditions that will give rise to significant contingent liabilities in the account or disclosure;

(g) the existence of related party transactions; and

(h) the impact of the account on existing debt covenants.

(4) **Assertions** — Using a top-down, risk-based approach, the certifying officers identify those assertions for each significant account and disclosure that presents a risk that could reasonably result in a material misstatement in that significant account or disclosure. For each significant account and disclosure the following assertions could be relevant:

(a) **existence or occurrence** — whether assets or liabilities exist and whether transactions and events that have been recorded have occurred and pertain to the issuer;

(b) **completeness** — whether all assets, liabilities and transactions that should have been recorded have been recorded;

(c) **valuation or allocation** — whether assets, liabilities, equity, revenue and expenses have been included in the financial statements at appropriate amounts and any resulting valuation or allocation adjustments are appropriately recorded;

(d) **rights and obligations** — whether assets are legally owned by the issuer and liabilities are the obligations of the issuer; and

(e) **presentation and disclosure** — whether particular components of the financial statements are appropriately presented and described and disclosures are clearly expressed.

The certifying officers might consider assertions that differ from those listed above if the certifying officers determine that they have identified the pertinent risks in each significant account and disclosure that could reasonably result in a material misstatement.

(5) **Identifying relevant assertions for each significant account and disclosure** — To identify relevant assertions for each significant account and disclosure, the certifying officers determine the source of potential misstatements for each significant account or disclosure. When determining whether a particular assertion is relevant, the certifying officers would consider the nature of the assertion, the volume of transactions or data related to the assertion and the complexity of the underlying systems supporting the assertion. If an assertion does not present a risk that could reasonably result in a material misstatement in a significant account, it is likely not a relevant assertion.

For example, valuation might not be relevant to the cash account unless currency translation is involved; however, existence and completeness are always relevant. Similarly, valuation might not be relevant to the gross amount of the accounts receivable balance, but is relevant to the related allowance accounts.

(6) **Identifying controls, policies and procedures for relevant assertions** — Using a top-down, risk-based approach, the certifying officers design components of ICFR to address each relevant assertion. The certifying officers do not need to design all possible components of ICFR to address each relevant assertion, but should identify and design an appropriate combination of controls, policies and procedures to address all relevant assertions.

The certifying officers would consider the efficiency of evaluating an issuer's ICFR design when designing an appropriate combination of ICFR components. If more than one potential control, policy or procedure could address a relevant assertion, certifying officers could select the control, policy or procedure that would be easiest to evaluate (e.g., automated control vs. manual control). Similarly, if a control, policy or procedure can be designed to address more than one relevant assertion, then certifying officers could choose it rather than a control, policy or procedure that addresses only one relevant assertion. For example, the certifying officers would consider whether any entity-wide controls exist that adequately address more than one relevant assertion or improve the efficiency of evaluating operating effectiveness because such entity-wide controls negate the need to design and evaluate other components of ICFR at multiple locations or business units.

When designing a combination of controls, policies and procedures, the certifying officers should also consider how the components in subsection 6.7(2) of the Policy interact with each other. For example, the certifying officers should consider how information technology general controls interact with controls, policies and procedures over initiating, authorizing, recording, processing and reporting transactions.

6.11 **ICFR design challenges** — Key features of ICFR and related design challenges are described below.

(a) **Segregation of duties** — The term "segregation of duties" refers to one or more employees or procedures acting as a check and balance on the activities of another so that no one individual has control over all steps of processing a transaction or other activity. Assigning different people responsibility for authorizing transactions, recording transactions, reconciling information and maintaining custody of assets reduces the opportunity for any one employee to conceal errors or perpetrate fraud in the normal course of his or her duties. Segregating duties also increases the chance of discovering inadvertent errors early. If an issuer has few employees, a single employee may be authorized to initiate, approve and effect payment for transactions and it might be difficult to re-assign responsibilities to segregate those duties appropriately.

(b) **Board expertise** — An effective board objectively reviews management's judgments and is actively engaged in shaping and monitoring the issuer's control environment. An issuer might find it challenging to attract directors with the appropriate financial reporting expertise, objectivity, time, ability and experience.

(c) **Controls over management override** — An issuer might be dominated by a founder or other strong leader who exercises a great deal of discretion and provides personal direction to other employees. Although this type of individual can help an issuer meet its growth and other objectives, such concentration of knowledge and authority could allow the individual an opportunity to override established policies or procedures or otherwise reduce the likelihood of an effective control environment.

(d) **Qualified personnel** — Sufficient accounting and financial reporting expertise is necessary to ensure reliable financial reporting and the preparation of financial statements in accordance with the issuer's GAAP. Some issuers might be unable to obtain qualified accounting personnel or outsourced expert advice on a cost-effective basis. Even if an issuer obtains outsourced expert advice, the issuer might not have the internal expertise to understand or assess the quality of the outsourced advice. If an issuer consults on technically complex accounting matters, this consultation alone is not indicative of a deficiency relating to the design of ICFR.

An issuer's external auditor might perform certain services (e.g., income tax, valuation or internal audit services), where permitted by auditor independence rules, that provide skills which would otherwise be addressed by hiring qualified personnel or outsourcing expert advice from a party other than the external auditor. This type of arrangement should not be considered to be a component of the issuer's ICFR design.

If an issuer identifies one or more of these ICFR design challenges, additional involvement by the issuer's audit committee or board of directors could be a suitable compensating control or alternatively could mitigate risks that exist as a result of being unable to remediate a material weakness relating to the design challenge. The control framework the certifying officers use to design ICFR could include further information on these design challenges. See section 9.1 of the Policy for a discussion of compensating controls versus mitigating procedures.

6.12 **Corporate governance for internal controls** — The board of directors of an issuer is encouraged to consider adopting a written mandate to explicitly acknowledge responsibility for the stewardship of the issuer, including responsibility for internal control and management information systems.

6.13 **Maintaining design** — Following their initial development and implementation of DC&P and ICFR, and prior to certifying design each quarter, certifying officers should consider:

(a) whether the issuer faces any new risks and whether each design continues to provide a sufficient basis for the representations about reasonable assurance required in paragraph 5 of the certificates;

(b) the scope and quality of ongoing monitoring of DC&P and ICFR, including the extent, nature and frequency of reporting the results from the ongoing monitoring of DC&P and ICFR to the appropriate levels of management;

(c) the work of the issuer's internal audit function;

(d) communication, if any, with the issuer's external auditors; and

(e) the incidence of weaknesses in DC&P or material weaknesses in ICFR that have been identified at any time during the financial year.

6.14 Efficiency and effectiveness — In addition to the considerations set out in this Part that will assist certifying officers in appropriately designing DC&P and ICFR, other steps that certifying officers could take to enhance the efficiency and effectiveness of the designs are:

(a) embedding DC&P and ICFR in the issuer's business processes;

(b) implementing consistent policies and procedures and issuer-wide programs at all locations and business units;

(c) including processes to ensure that DC&P and ICFR are modified to adapt to any changes in business environment; and

(d) including procedures for reporting immediately to the appropriate levels of management any identified issues with DC&P and ICFR together with details of any action being undertaken or proposed to be undertaken to address such issues.

6.15 Documenting design — (1) **Extent and form of documentation for design** — The certifying officers should generally maintain documentary evidence sufficient to provide reasonable support for their certification of design of DC&P and ICFR. The extent of documentation supporting the certifying officers' design of DC&P and ICFR for each interim and annual certificate will vary depending on the certifying officers' assessment of risk, as discussed in section 6.6 of the Policy, as well as the size and complexity of the issuer's DC&P and ICFR. The documentation might take many forms (e.g., paper documents, electronic, or other media) and could be presented in a number of different ways (e.g., policy manuals, process models, flowcharts, job descriptions, documents, internal memoranda, forms, etc). Certifying officers should use their judgment, acting reasonably, to determine the extent and form of documentation.

(2) **Documentation of the control environment** — To provide reasonable support for the certifying officers' design of DC&P and ICFR, the certifying officers should generally document the key elements of an issuer's control environment, including those described in subsection 6.7(2) of the Policy.

(3) **Documentation for design of DC&P** — To provide reasonable support for the certifying officers' design of DC&P, the certifying officers should generally document:

(a) the processes and procedures that ensure information is brought to the attention of management, including the certifying officers, in a timely manner to enable them to determine if disclosure is required; and

(b) the items listed in section 6.8 of the Policy.

(4) **Documentation for design of ICFR** — To provide reasonable support for the certifying officers' design of ICFR, the certifying officers should generally document:

(a) the issuer's ongoing risk-assessment process and those risks which need to be addressed in order to conclude that the certifying officers have designed ICFR;

(b) how significant transactions, and significant classes of transactions, are initiated, authorized, recorded and processed;

(c) the flow of transactions to identify when and how material misstatements or omissions could occur due to error or fraud;

(d) a description of the controls over relevant assertions related to all significant accounts and disclosures in the financial statements;

(e) a description of the controls designed to prevent or detect fraud, including who performs the controls and, if applicable, how duties are segregated;

(f) a description of the controls over period-end financial reporting processes;

(g) a description of the controls over safeguarding of assets; and

(h) the certifying officers' conclusions on whether a material weakness relating to the design of ICFR exists at the end of the period.

PART 7 — EVALUATING OPERATING EFFECTIVENESS OF DC&P AND ICFR

7.1 General — Most sections in this Part apply to both an evaluation of the operating effectiveness of DC&P (DC&P evaluation) and an evaluation of the operating effectiveness of ICFR (ICFR evaluation); however, some sections apply specifically to an ICFR evaluation.

7.2 Scope of evaluation of operating effectiveness — The purpose of the DC&P and ICFR evaluations is to determine whether the issuer's DC&P and ICFR designs are operating as intended. To support a conclusion that DC&P or ICFR is effective, certifying officers should obtain sufficient appropriate evidence at the date of their assessment that the components of DC&P and ICFR that they designed, or caused to be designed, are operating as intended. Regardless of the approach the certifying officers use to design DC&P or ICFR, they could use a top-down, risk-based approach to evaluate DC&P or ICFR in order to limit the evaluation to those controls and procedures that are necessary to address the risks that might reasonably result in a material misstatement.

Form 52-109F1 requires disclosure of each material weakness relating to the operation of the issuer's ICFR. Therefore, the scope of the ICFR evaluation must be sufficient to identify any such material weaknesses.

7.3 Judgment — The Instrument does not prescribe how the certifying officers should conduct their DC&P and ICFR evaluations. Certifying officers should exercise their judgment, acting reasonably, and should apply their knowledge and experience in determining the nature and extent of the evaluation.

7.4 Knowledge and supervision — Form 52-109F1 requires the certifying officers to certify that they have evaluated, or supervised the evaluation of, the issuer's DC&P and ICFR. Employees or third parties, supervised by the certifying officers, may conduct the evaluation of the issuer's DC&P and ICFR. Such employees should individually and collectively have the necessary knowledge, skills, information and authority to evaluate the DC&P and ICFR for which they have been assigned responsibilities. Nevertheless, certifying officers must retain overall responsibility for the evaluation and resulting MD&A disclosure concerning the issuer's DC&P and ICFR.

Certifying officers should ensure that the evaluation is performed with the appropriate level of objectivity. Generally, the individuals who evaluate the operating effectiveness of specific controls or procedures should not be the same individuals who perform the specific controls or procedures. See section 7.10 of the Policy for guidance on self-assessments.

7.5 Use of external auditor or other third party — The certifying officers might decide to use a third party to assist with their DC&P or ICFR evaluations. In these circumstances, the certifying officers should assure themselves that the individuals performing the agreed-upon evaluation procedures have the appropriate knowledge and ability to complete the procedures. The certifying officers should be actively involved in determining the procedures to be performed, the findings to be communicated and the manner of communication.

If an issuer chooses to engage its external auditor to assist the certifying officers in the DC&P and ICFR evaluations, the certifying officers should determine the procedures to be performed, the findings to be communicated and the manner of communication. The certifying officers should not rely on ICFR-related procedures performed and findings reported by the issuer's external auditor solely as part of the financial statement audit. However, if the external auditor is separately engaged to perform specified ICFR-related procedures, the certifying officers might use the results of those procedures as part of their evaluation even if the auditor uses those results as part of the financial statement audit.

If the issuer refers, in a continuous disclosure document, to an audit report relating to the issuer's ICFR, prepared by its external auditor, then it would be appropriate for the issuer to file a copy of the internal control audit report with its financial statements.

7.6 Evaluation tools — Certifying officers can use a variety of tools to perform their DC&P and ICFR evaluations. These tools include:

> (a) certifying officers' daily interaction with the control systems;
>
> (b) walkthroughs;
>
> (c) interviews of individuals who are involved with the relevant controls;
>
> (d) observation of procedures and processes, including adherence to corporate policies;
>
> (e) reperformance; and
>
> (f) review of documentation that provides evidence that controls, policies or procedures have been performed.

Certifying officers should use a combination of tools for the DC&P and ICFR evaluations. Although inquiry and observation alone might provide an adequate basis for an evaluation of an individual control with a lower risk, they will not provide an adequate basis for the evaluation as a whole.

The nature, timing and extent of evaluation procedures necessary for certifying officers to obtain reasonable support for the effective operation of a component of DC&P or ICFR depends on the level of risk the component of DC&P or ICFR is designed to address. The level of risk for a component of DC&P or ICFR could change each year to reflect management's experience with a control's operation during the year and in prior evaluations.

7.7 Certifying officers' daily interaction — The certifying officers' daily interaction with their control systems provides them with opportunities to evaluate the operating effectiveness of the issuer's DC&P and ICFR during a financial year. This daily interaction could provide an adequate basis for the certifying officers' evaluation of DC&P or ICFR if the operation of controls, policies and procedures is centralized and involves a limited number of personnel. Reasonable support of such daily interaction would include memoranda, e-mails and instructions or directions from the certifying officers to other employees.

7.8 Walkthroughs — A walkthrough is a process of tracing a transaction from origination, through the issuer's information systems, to the issuer's financial reports. A walkthrough can assist certifying officers to confirm that:

> (a) they understand the components of ICFR, including those components relating to the prevention or detection of fraud;
>
> (b) they understand how transactions are processed;
>
> (c) they have identified all points in the process at which misstatements related to each relevant financial statement assertion could occur; and
>
> (d) the components of ICFR have been implemented.

7.9 Reperformance — (1) General — Reperformance is the independent execution of certain components of the issuer's DC&P or ICFR that were performed previously. Reperformance could include inspecting records whether internal (e.g., a purchase order prepared by the issuer's purchasing department) or external (e.g., a sales invoice prepared by a vendor), in paper form, electronic form or other media. The reliability of records varies depending on their nature, source and the effectiveness of controls over their production. An example of reperformance is inspecting whether the quantity and price information in a sales invoice agree with the quantity and price information in a purchase order, and confirming that an employee previously performed this procedure.

(2) Extent of reperformance — The extent of reperformance of a component of DC&P or ICFR is a matter of judgment for the certifying officers, acting reasonably. Components that are performed more frequently (e.g., controls for recording revenue) will generally require more testing than components that are performed less frequently (e.g., controls for monthly bank reconciliations). Components that are manually operated will likely require more rigorous testing than automated controls. Certifying officers could determine that they do not have to test every individual step comprising a control in order to conclude that the overall control is operating effectively.

(3) Reperformance for each evaluation — Certifying officers might find it appropriate to adjust the nature, extent and timing of reperformance for each evaluation. For example, in "year 1", certifying officers might test information technology controls extensively, while in "year 2", they could focus on monitoring controls that identify changes made to the information technology controls. Certifying officers should consider the specific risks the controls address when making these types of adjustments. It might also be appropriate to test controls at different interim periods, increase or reduce the number and types of tests performed or change the combination of procedures used in order to introduce unpredictability into the testing and respond to changes in circumstances.

7.10 Self-assessments — A self-assessment is a walk-through or reperformance of a control, or another procedure to analyze the operation of controls, performed by an individual who might or might not be involved in operating the control. A self-assessment could be done by personnel who operate the control or members of management who are not responsible for operating the control. The evidence of operating effectiveness from self-assessment activities depends on the personnel involved and how the activities are conducted.

A self-assessment performed by personnel who operate the control would normally be supplemented with direct testing by individuals who are independent from the operation of the control being tested and who have an equal or higher level of authority. In these situations, direct testing of controls would be needed to corroborate evidence from the self-assessment since the self-assessment alone would not have a reasonable level of objectivity.

In some situations a certifying officer might perform a self-assessment and the certifying officer is involved in operating the control. Even if no other members of management independent from the operation of the control with equal or higher level of authority can perform direct testing, the certifying officer's self-assessment alone would normally provide sufficient evidence since the certifying officer signs the annual certificate. In situations where there are two certifying officers and one is performing a self-assessment, it would be appropriate for the other certifying officer to perform direct testing of the control.

7.11 Timing of evaluation — Form 52-109F1 requires certifying officers to certify that they have evaluated the effectiveness of the issuer's DC&P and ICFR, as at the financial year end. Certifying officers might choose to schedule testing of some DC&P and ICFR components throughout the issuer's financial year. However, since the evaluation is at the financial year end, the certifying officers will have to perform sufficient procedures to evaluate the operation of the components at year end.

Since some year-end procedures occur subsequent to the year end (e.g., financial reporting close process), some testing of DC&P and ICFR components could also occur subsequent to year-end. The timing of evaluation activities will depend on the risk associated with the components being evaluated, the tools used to evaluate the components, and whether the components being evaluated are performed prior to, or subsequent to, year end.

7.12 Extent of examination for each annual evaluation — For each annual evaluation the certifying officers must evaluate those components of ICFR that, in combination, provide reasonable assurance regarding the reliability of financial reporting. For example, the certifying officers cannot decide to exclude components of ICFR for a particular process from the scope of their evaluation simply based on prior-year evaluation results. To have a reasonable basis for their assessment of the operating effectiveness of ICFR, the certifying officers must have sufficient evidence supporting operating effectiveness of all relevant components of ICFR as of the date of their assessment.

7.13 Documenting evaluations — (1) Extent of documentation for evaluation — The certifying officers should generally maintain documentary evidence sufficient to provide reasonable support for their certification of a DC&P and ICFR evaluation. The extent of documentation used to support the certifying officers' evaluations of DC&P and ICFR for each annual certificate will vary depending on the size and complexity of the issuer's DC&P and ICFR. The extent of documentation is a matter of judgment for the certifying officers, acting reasonably.

(2) Documentation for evaluations of DC&P and ICFR — To provide reasonable support for a DC&P or ICFR evaluation the certifying officers should generally document:

> (a) a description of the process the certifying officers used to evaluate DC&P or ICFR;
>
> (b) how the certifying officers determined the extent of testing of the components of DC&P or ICFR;
>
> (c) a description of, and results from applying, the evaluation tools discussed in sections 7.6 and 7.7 of the Policy or other evaluation tools; and
>
> (d) the certifying officers' conclusions about:
>
>> (i) the operating effectiveness of DC&P or ICFR, as applicable; and
>>
>> (ii) whether a material weakness relating to the operation of ICFR existed as at the end of the period.

PART 8 — USE OF A SERVICE ORGANIZATION OR SPECIALIST FOR AN ISSUER'S ICFR

8.1 Use of a service organization — An issuer might outsource a significant process to a service organization. Examples include payroll, production accounting for oil and gas companies, or other bookkeeping services. Based on their assessment of risks as discussed in subsection 6.6(2) of the Policy, the certifying officers might identify the need for controls, policies and procedures relating to an outsourced process. In considering the design and evaluation of such controls, policies and procedures, the officers should consider whether:

> (a) the service organization can provide a service auditor's report on the design and operation of controls placed in operation and tests of the operating effectiveness of controls at the service organization;
>
> (b) the certifying officers have access to the controls in place at the service organization to evaluate the design and effectiveness of such controls; or
>
> (c) the issuer has controls that might eliminate the need for the certifying officers to evaluate the design and effectiveness of the service organization's controls relating to the outsourced process.

8.2 Service auditor's reporting on controls at a service organization — If a service auditor's report on controls placed in operation and tests of the operating effectiveness of controls is available, the certifying officers should evaluate whether the report provides them sufficient evidence to assess the design and effectiveness of controls relating to the outsourced process. The following factors will be relevant in evaluating whether the report provides sufficient evidence:

> (a) the time period covered by the tests of controls and its relation to the as-of date of the certifying officers' assessment of the issuer's ICFR;
>
> (b) the scope of the examination and applications covered and the controls tested; and
>
> (c) the results of the tests of controls and the service auditor's opinion on the operating effectiveness of controls.

8.3 Elapsed time between date of a service auditor's report and date of certificate — If a significant period of time has elapsed between the time period covered by the tests of controls in a service auditor's report and the date of the certifying officer's assessment of ICFR, the certifying officers should consider whether the service organization's controls have changed subsequent to the period covered by the service auditor's report. The service organization might communicate certain changes such as changes in its personnel or changes in reports or other data that it provides. Changes might also be indicated by errors identified in the service organization's processing. If the certifying officers identify changes in the service organization's controls, they should evaluate the effect of these changes and consider the need for additional procedures. These might include obtaining further information from the service organization, performing procedures at the service organization, or requesting that a service auditor perform specified procedures.

8.4 Indicators of a material weakness relating to use of a service organization — There could be circumstances in which a service auditor's report is not available, the certifying officers do not have access to controls in place at the service organization and the certifying officers have not identified any compensating controls performed by the issuer. In these circumstances the inability to assess the service organization's controls, policies and procedures might represent a material weakness since the certifying officers might not have sufficient evidence to conclude whether the components of the issuer's ICFR at the service organization have been designed or are operating as intended.

8.5 Use of a specialist — A specialist is a person or firm possessing expertise in specific subject matter. A reporting issuer might arrange for a specialist to provide certain specialized expertise such as actuarial services, taxation services or valuation services. Based on their assessment of risks as discussed in subsection 6.6(2) of the Policy, the certifying officers might identify the need for the services provided by a specialist. The certifying officers should ensure the issuer has controls, policies or procedures in place relating to the source data and the reasonableness of the assumptions used to support the specialist's findings. The certifying officers should also consider whether the specialist has the necessary competence, expertise and integrity.

PART 9 — MATERIAL WEAKNESS

9.1 Identifying a deficiency in ICFR — (1) **Deficiency relating to the design of ICFR** — A deficiency relating to the design of ICFR exists when:

(a) necessary components of ICFR are missing from the design;

(b) an existing component of ICFR is designed so that, even if the component operates as designed, the financial reporting risks would not be addressed; or

(c) a component of ICFR has not been implemented and, as a result, the financial reporting risks have not been addressed.

Subsection 6.6(2) of the Policy provides guidance on financial reporting risks.

(2) **Deficiency relating to the operation of ICFR** — A deficiency relating to the operation of ICFR exists when a properly designed component of ICFR does not operate as intended. For example, if an issuer's ICFR design requires two individuals to sign a cheque in order to authorize a cash disbursement and the certifying officers conclude that this process is not being followed consistently, the control may be designed properly but is deficient in its operation.

(3) **Compensating controls versus mitigating procedures** — If the certifying officers identify a component of ICFR that does not operate as intended they should consider whether there is a compensating control that addresses the financial reporting risks that the deficient ICFR component failed to address. If the certifying officers are unable to identify a compensating control, then the issuer would have a deficiency relating to the operation of ICFR.

In the process of determining whether there is a compensating control, the certifying officers might identify mitigating procedures which help to reduce the financial reporting risks that the deficient ICFR component failed to address, but do not meet the threshold of being a compensating control because:

(a) the procedures only partially address the financial reporting risks or

(b) the procedures are not designed by, or under the supervision of, the issuer's certifying officers, and thus may not represent an internal control.

In these circumstances, since the financial reporting risks are not addressed with an appropriate compensating control, the issuer would continue to have a deficiency relating to the operation of ICFR and would have to assess the significance of the deficiency. The issuer may have one or more mitigating procedures that reduce the financial reporting risks that the deficient ICFR component failed to address and may consider disclosure of those procedures, as discussed in section 9.7 of the Policy. In disclosing these mitigating procedures in its MD&A, an issuer should not imply that the procedures eliminate the existence of a material weakness.

9.2 Assessing significance of deficiencies in ICFR — If a deficiency or combination of deficiencies in the design or operation of one or more components of ICFR is identified, certifying officers should assess the significance of the deficiency, or combination of deficiencies, to determine whether a material weakness exists. Their assessment should generally include both qualitative and quantitative analyses.

Certifying officers evaluate the severity of a deficiency, or combination of deficiencies, by considering whether (a) there is a reasonable possibility that the issuer's ICFR will fail to prevent or detect a material misstatement of a financial statement amount or disclosure; and (b) the magnitude of the potential misstatement resulting from the deficiency or deficiencies. The severity of a deficiency in ICFR does not depend on whether a misstatement has actually occurred but rather on whether there is a reasonable possibility that the issuer's ICFR will fail to prevent or detect a material misstatement on a timely basis.

9.3 Factors to consider when assessing significance of deficiencies in ICFR — (1) **Reasonable possibility of misstatement** — Factors that affect whether there is a reasonable possibility that a deficiency, or combination of deficiencies would result in ICFR not preventing or detecting in a timely manner a misstatement of a financial statement amount or disclosure, include, but are not limited to:

(a) the nature of the financial statement accounts, disclosures and assertions involved (e.g., related-party transactions involve greater risk);

(b) the susceptibility of the related asset or liability to loss or fraud (e.g., greater susceptibility increases risk);

(c) the subjectivity, complexity, or extent of judgment required to determine the amount involved (e.g., greater subjectivity, complexity, or judgment increases risk);

(d) the interaction or relationship of the control with other controls, including whether they are interdependent or address the same financial reporting risks;

(e) the interaction of the deficiencies (e.g., when evaluating a combination of two or more deficiencies, whether the deficiencies could affect the same financial statement amounts or disclosures); and

(f) the possible future consequences of the deficiency.

(2) **Magnitude of misstatement** — Various factors affect the magnitude of a misstatement that might result from a deficiency or deficiencies in ICFR. These factors include, but are not limited, to the following:

(a) the financial statement amounts or total of transactions relating to the deficiency; and

(b) the volume of activity in the account balance or class of transactions relating to the deficiency that has occurred in the current period or that is expected in future periods.

9.4 Indicators of a material weakness — It is a matter for the certifying officers' judgment whether the following situations indicate that a deficiency in ICFR exists and, if so, whether it represents a material weakness:

(a) identification of fraud, whether or not material, on the part of the certifying officers or other senior management who play a significant role in the issuer's financial reporting process;

(b) restatement of previously issued financial statements to reflect the correction of a material misstatement;

(c) identification by the issuer or its external auditor of a material misstatement in the financial statements in the current period in circumstances that indicate that the misstatement would not have been detected by the issuer's ICFR; and

(d) ineffective oversight of the issuer's external financial reporting and ICFR by the issuer's audit committee.

9.5 Conclusions on effectiveness if a material weakness exists — If the certifying officers identify a material weakness relating to the design or operation of ICFR existing as at the period-end date, the certifying officers could not conclude that the issuer's ICFR is effective. Certifying officers may not qualify their assessment by stating that the issuer's ICFR is effective subject to certain qualifications or exceptions unless the qualification pertains to one of the permitted scope limitations available in section 3.3 of the Instrument. As required by paragraph 6 in Form 52-109F1, the certifying officers must ensure the issuer has disclosed in the annual MD&A the certifying officers' conclusions about the effectiveness of ICFR at the financial year end.

9.6 Disclosure of a material weakness — **(1) Disclosure of a material weakness relating to the design of ICFR** — If the certifying officers become aware of a material weakness relating to the design of ICFR that existed at the end of the annual or interim period, the issuer's annual or interim MD&A must describe each material weakness relating to design, the impact of each material weakness on the issuer's financial reporting and its ICFR, and the issuer's current plans, if any, or any actions already undertaken, for remediating each material weakness as required by paragraph 5.2 of Form 52-109F1 and Form 52-109F2.

(2) Disclosure of a material weakness relating to the operation of ICFR — If the certifying officers become aware of a material weakness relating to the operation of ICFR that existed at the financial year end, the issuer's annual MD&A must describe each material weakness relating to operation, the impact of each material weakness on the issuer's financial reporting and its ICFR, and the issuer's current plans, if any, or any actions already undertaken, for remediating each material weakness as required by subparagraphs 6(b)(ii)(A), (B) and (C) of Form 52-109F1.

If a material weakness relating to the operation of ICFR continues to exist, the certifying officers should consider whether the deficiency initially relating to the operation of ICFR has become a material weakness relating to the design of ICFR that must be disclosed in the interim, as well as the annual MD&A under paragraph 5.2 of Form 52-109F1 and Form 52-109F2.

(3) Description of a material weakness — Disclosure pertaining to an identified material weakness should provide investors with an accurate and complete picture of the material weakness, including its effect on the issuer's ICFR. Issuers should consider providing disclosure in the annual or interim MD&A that allows investors to understand the cause of the material weakness and assess the potential impact on, and importance to, the financial statements of the identified material weakness. The disclosure will be more useful to investors if it distinguishes between those material weaknesses that may have a pervasive impact on ICFR from those material weaknesses that do not.

9.7 Disclosure of remediation plans and actions undertaken — If an issuer commits to a remediation plan to correct a material weakness relating to the design or operation of ICFR prior to filing a certificate, the annual or interim MD&A would describe the issuer's current plans, or any actions already undertaken, for remediating each material weakness.

Once an issuer has completed its remediation it would disclose information about the resulting change in the issuer's ICFR in its next annual or interim MD&A as required by paragraph 7 of Form 52-109F1 or paragraph 6 of Form 52-109F2.

If an issuer is unable to, or chooses not to, remediate a material weakness, but identifies mitigating procedures that reduce the impact of the material weakness on the issuer's ICFR, then disclosure about these mitigating procedures could provide investors with an accurate and complete picture of the material weakness, including its effect on the issuer's ICFR. If an issuer does not plan to remediate the material weakness, regardless of whether there are mitigating procedures, the issuer would continue to have a material weakness that the issuer must disclose in the annual or interim MD&A.

Part 10 — Weakness in DC&P that is Significant

10.1 Conclusions on effectiveness of DC&P if a weakness exists that is significant — If the certifying officers identify a weakness relating to the design or operation of DC&P that is significant existing as at the period-end date, the certifying officers could not conclude that the issuer's DC&P is effective. Certifying officers may not qualify their assessment by stating that the issuer's DC&P is effective subject to certain qualifications or exceptions unless the qualification pertains to one of the permitted scope limitations available in section 3.3 of the Instrument. A certifying officer could not conclude that the issuer's DC&P is effective if there is a deficiency, or combination of deficiencies, in DC&P such that there is a reasonable possibility that the issuer will not disclose material information required to be disclosed under securities legislation, within the time periods specified in securities legislation.

As required by paragraph 6(a) in Form 52-109F1, the certifying officers must ensure the issuer has disclosed in its annual MD&A the certifying officers' conclusions about the effectiveness of DC&P. The MD&A disclosure about the effectiveness of DC&P will be useful to investors if it discusses any identified weaknesses that are significant, whether the issuer has committed, or will commit, to a plan to remediate the identified weaknesses, and whether there are any mitigating procedures that reduce the risks that have not been addressed as a result of the identified weaknesses.

10.2 Interim certification of DC&P design if a weakness exists that is significant — If the certifying officers identify a weakness in the design of DC&P that is significant at the time of filing an interim certificate, to provide reasonable context for their certifications of the design of DC&P, it would be appropriate for the issuer to disclose in its interim MD&A the identified weakness and any other information necessary to provide an accurate and complete picture of the condition of the design of the issuer's DC&P.

10.3 Certification of DC&P if a material weakness in ICFR exists — As discussed in section 6.2 of the Policy, there is a substantial overlap between the definitions of DC&P and ICFR. If the certifying officers identify a material weakness in the issuer's ICFR, this will almost always represent a weakness that is significant in the issuer's DC&P.

Part 11 — Reporting Changes in ICFR

11.1 Assessing the materiality of a change in ICFR — Paragraph 7 of Form 52-109F1 and paragraph 6 of Form 52-109F2 require an issuer to disclose any change in the issuer's ICFR that has materially affected, or is reasonably likely to materially affect, the issuer's ICFR. A material change in ICFR might occur regardless of whether the change is being made to remediate a material weakness (e.g., a change from a manual payroll system to an automated payroll system). A change in an issuer's ICFR that was made to remediate a material weakness would generally be considered a material change in an issuer's ICFR.

Part 12 — Role of Board of Directors and Audit Committee

12.1 Board of directors — Form 52-109F1 requires the certifying officers to represent that the issuer has disclosed in its annual MD&A certain information about the certifying officers' evaluation of the effectiveness of DC&P. Form 52-109F1 also requires the certifying officers to represent that the issuer has disclosed in its annual MD&A certain information about the certifying officers' evaluation of the effectiveness of ICFR. Under National Instrument 51-102 *Continuous Disclosure Obligations* (NI 51-102), the board of directors must approve the issuer's annual MD&A, including the required disclosure concerning DC&P and ICFR, before it is filed. To provide reasonable support for the board of directors' approval of an issuer's MD&A disclosure concerning ICFR, including any material weaknesses, the board of directors should understand the basis upon which the certifying officers concluded that any particular deficiency or combination of deficiencies did or did not constitute a material weakness (see section 9.2 of the Policy).

12.2 Audit committee — NI 52-110 requires the audit committee to review an issuer's financial disclosure and to establish procedures for dealing with complaints and concerns about accounting or auditing matters. Issuers subject to NI 52-110 should consider its specific requirements in designing and evaluating their DC&P and ICFR.

12.3 Reporting fraud — Paragraph 8 of Form 52-109F1 requires certifying officers to disclose to the issuer's auditors, the board of directors or the audit committee of the board of directors any fraud that involves management or other employees who have a significant role in the issuer's ICFR. Subsection 6.6(3) of the Policy provides guidance on the term "fraud" for purposes of this Instrument.

Two types of intentional misstatements are (i) misstatements resulting from fraudulent financial reporting, which includes omissions of amounts or disclosures in financial statements to deceive financial statement users, and (ii) misstatements resulting from misappropriation of assets.

PART 13 — CERTAIN LONG TERM INVESTMENTS

13.1 Underlying entities — An issuer might have a variety of long term investments that affect how the certifying officers design and evaluate the effectiveness of the issuer's DC&P and ICFR. In particular, an issuer could have any of the following interests:

    (a) an interest in an entity that is a subsidiary which is consolidated in the issuer's financial statements;

    (b) an interest in an entity that is a special purpose entity (a SPE) which is consolidated in the issuer's financial statements;

    (c) an interest in an entity that is proportionately consolidated in the issuer's financial statements;

    (d) an interest in an entity that is accounted for using the equity method in the issuer's financial statements (an equity investment); or

    (e) an interest in an entity that is not accounted for by consolidation, proportionate consolidation or the equity method (a portfolio investment).

In this Part, the term entity is meant to capture a broad range of structures, including, but not limited to, corporations. The terms "consolidated", "subsidiary", "SPE", "proportionately consolidated", and "equity method" have the meaning ascribed to such terms under the issuer's GAAP. In this Part, the term "underlying entity" refers to one of the entities referred to in items (a) through (e) above.

13.2 Fair presentation — As discussed in section 4.1 of the Policy, the concept of fair presentation is not limited to compliance with the issuer's GAAP. If the certifying officers believe that an issuer's financial statements do not fairly present its financial condition insofar as it relates to an underlying entity, the certifying officers should cause the issuer to provide additional disclosure in its MD&A.

13.3 Design and evaluation of DC&P and ICFR — (1) **Access to underlying entity** — The nature of an issuer's interest in an underlying entity will affect the certifying officer's ability to design and evaluate the effectiveness of the controls, policies and procedures carried out by the underlying entity.

Subsidiary — In the case of an issuer with an interest in a subsidiary, as the issuer controls the subsidiary, certifying officers will have sufficient access to the subsidiary to design and evaluate the effectiveness of the controls, policies and procedures carried out by the underlying entity.

Proportionately consolidated entity or SPE — In the case of an issuer with an interest in a proportionately consolidated entity or a SPE, certifying officers might not always have sufficient access to the underlying entity to design and evaluate the effectiveness of the controls, policies and procedures carried out by the underlying entity.

Whether the certifying officers have sufficient access to a proportionately consolidated entity or a SPE to design and evaluate the effectiveness of the controls, policies and procedures carried out by the underlying entity is a question of fact. The sufficiency of their access could depend on, among other things:

    (a) the issuer's percentage ownership of the underlying entity;

    (b) whether the other underlying entity owners are reporting issuers;

    (c) the nature of the relationship between the issuer and the operator of the underlying entity if the issuer is not the operator;

    (d) the terms of the agreement(s) governing the underlying entity; and

    (e) the date of creation of the underlying entity.

Portfolio investment or equity investment — In the case of an issuer with a portfolio investment or an equity investment, certifying officers will generally not have sufficient access to the underlying entity to design and evaluate the effectiveness of the controls, policies and procedures carried out by the underlying entity.

(2) **Access to an underlying entity in certain indirect offering structures** — In the case of certain indirect offering structures, including certain income trust and limited partnership offering structures, the issuer could have:

    (a) a significant equity interest in the underlying entity but not legally control the underlying entity, since legal control is retained by a third party (typically the party involved in establishing the indirect offering structure) or

    (b) an equity interest in an underlying entity that represents a significant asset of the issuer and results in the issuer providing the issuer's equity holders with separate audited annual financial statements and interim financial reports prepared in accordance with the same accounting principles as the issuer's financial statements.

In these cases, we generally expect the trust indenture, limited partnership agreement or other constating documents to include appropriate terms ensuring the certifying officers will have sufficient access to the underlying entity to design and evaluate the effectiveness of the controls, policies and procedures carried out by the underlying entity.

(3) **Reasonable steps to design and evaluate** — Certifying officers should take all reasonable steps to design and evaluate the effectiveness of the controls, policies and procedures carried out by the underlying entity that provide the certifying officers with a basis for the representations in the annual and interim certificates. However, it is left to the discretion of the certifying officers, acting reasonably, to determine what constitutes "reasonable steps".

If the certifying officers have access to the underlying entity to design the controls, policies and procedures discussed in subsection (2) and they are not satisfied with those controls, policies and procedures, the certifying officers should consider whether there exists a material weakness or a weakness in DC&P that is significant.

(4) Disclosure of a scope limitation relating to a proportionately consolidated entity or SPE — A scope limitation exists if the certifying officers would not have a reasonable basis for making the representations in the annual or interim certificates because they do not have sufficient access to a proportionately consolidated entity or SPE, as applicable, to design and evaluate the controls, policies and procedures carried out by that underlying entity.

When determining whether a scope limitation exists, certifying officers must initially consider whether one, or a combination of more than one, proportionately consolidated entity or SPE includes risks that could reasonably result in a material misstatement in the issuer's annual filings, interim filings or other reports. The certifying officers would consider such risks when the certifying officers first identify the risks faced by the issuer in order to determine the scope and necessary complexity of the issuer's DC&P or ICFR, as discussed in subsection 6.6(2) of the Policy.

The certifying officers would disclose a scope limitation if one, or a combination of more than one, proportionately consolidated entity or SPE includes risks that could reasonably result in a material misstatement and the certifying officers do not have sufficient access to design and evaluate the controls, policies and procedures carried out by each underlying entity.

The certifying officers would not disclose a scope limitation if a proportionately consolidated entity or SPE, individually or in combination with another such entity, does not include risks that could reasonably result in a material misstatement.

The issuer must disclose in its MD&A a scope limitation and summary financial information about each underlying entity in accordance with section 3.3 of the Instrument. The summary financial information may be disclosed in aggregate or individually for each proportionately consolidated entity or SPE.

Meaningful summary financial information about an underlying entity, or combination of underlying entities, that is the subject of a scope limitation would include:

(a) revenue;

(b) profit or loss before discontinued operations;

(c) profit or loss for the period; and

unless (i) the accounting principles used to prepare the financial statements of the underlying entity permit the preparation of its statement of financial position without classifying assets and liabilities between current and non-current, and (ii) the MD&A includes alternative meaningful financial information about the underlying entity, or combination of underlying entities, which is more appropriate to the underlying entity's industry,

(d) current assets;

(e) non-current assets;

(f) current liabilities; and

(g) non-current liabilities.

Meaningful disclosure about an underlying entity that is the subject of a scope limitation would also include any contingent liabilities and commitments for the proportionately consolidated entity or SPE.

(5) Limited access to the underlying entity of a portfolio investment or equity investment — Although the certifying officers may not have sufficient access to design and evaluate controls, policies and procedures carried out by the underlying entity of a portfolio investment or equity investment, the issuer's DC&P and ICFR should address the issuer's controls over its disclosure of material information relating to:

(a) the carrying amount of the investment;

(b) any dividends the issuer receives from the investment;

(c) any impairment loss in the investment; and

(d) if applicable, the issuer's share of any profit or loss from the equity investment.

(6) Reliance on financial information of underlying entity — In most cases, certifying officers will have to rely on the financial information reported by a proportionately consolidated entity, SPE or the underlying entity of an equity investment. In order to certify an issuer's annual or interim filings that include information regarding the issuer's investment in these underlying entities, the certifying officers should perform the following minimum procedures:

(a) ensure that the issuer receives the underlying entity's financial information on a timely basis;

(b) review the underlying entity's financial information to determine whether it has been prepared in accordance with the issuer's GAAP; and

(c) review the underlying entity's accounting policies and evaluate whether they conform to the issuer's accounting policies.

PART 14 — BUSINESS ACQUISITIONS

14.1 Access to acquired business — In many circumstances it is difficult for certifying officers to design or evaluate controls, policies and procedures carried out by an acquired business shortly after acquiring the business. In order to address these situations, paragraph 3.3(1)(c) of the Instrument permits an issuer to limit the scope of its design of DC&P and ICFR for a business that the issuer acquired not more than 365 days before the end of the financial period to which the certificate relates. Generally this will result in an issuer limiting the scope of its design for a business acquisition for three interim certificates and one annual certificate.

14.2 Disclosure of scope limitation — When determining whether a scope limitation exists, certifying officers must initially consider whether an acquired business includes risks that could reasonably result in a material misstatement in the issuer's annual filings, interim filings or other reports. The certifying officers would consider such risks when the certifying officers first identify the risks faced by the issuer in order to determine the scope and necessary complexity of the issuer's DC&P or ICFR, as discussed in subsection 6.6(2) of the Policy. If the certifying officers limit the scope of their design of DC&P and ICFR for a recent business acquisition, this scope limitation and summary financial information about the business must be disclosed in the issuer's MD&A in accordance with section 3.3 of the Instrument and paragraph 5.3 in Form 52-109F1, or 52-109F2 as applicable. Meaningful summary financial information about the acquired business would include:

(a) revenue;

(b) profit or loss before discontinued operations;

(c) profit or loss for the period; and

unless (i) the accounting principles used to prepare the financial statements of the acquired business permit the preparation of its statement of financial position without classifying assets and liabilities between current and non-current, and (ii) the MD&A includes alternative meaningful financial information about the acquired business which is more appropriate to the acquired business' industry,

    (d) current assets;

    (e) non-current assets;

    (f) current liabilities; and

    (g) non-current liabilities.

Meaningful disclosure about the acquired business would also include the issuer's share of any contingent liabilities and commitments, which arise as a result of the acquisition. In the case of related businesses, as defined in NI 51-102, the issuer may present the summary financial information about the businesses on a combined basis.

PART 15 — VENTURE ISSUER BASIC CERTIFICATES

15.1 Venture issuer basic certificates — Many venture issuers have few employees and limited financial resources which make it difficult for them to address the challenges described in section 6.11 of the Policy. As a result, many venture issuers are unable to design DC&P and ICFR without (i) incurring significant additional costs, (ii) hiring additional employees, or (iii) restructuring the board of directors and audit committee. Since these inherent limitations exist for many venture issuers, the required forms of certificate for venture issuers are Forms 52-109FV1 and 52-109FV2. These forms do not include representations relating to the establishment and maintenance of DC&P and ICFR.

Although Forms 52-109FV1 and 52-109FV2 are the required forms for venture issuers, a venture issuer may elect to file Forms 52-109F1 or 52-109F2, which include representations regarding the establishment and maintenance of DC&P and ICFR.

Certifying officers of a non-venture issuer are not permitted to use Forms 52-109FV1 and 52-109FV2. Although a non-venture issuer may face similar challenges in designing its ICFR, such as those described in section 6.11 of the Policy, the issuer is still required to file Forms 52-109F1 and 52-109F2 and disclose in the MD&A a description of each material weakness existing at the end of the financial period.

15.2 Note to reader included in venture issuer basic certificates — Forms 52-109FV1 and 52-109FV2 include a note to reader that clarifies the responsibility of certifying officers and discloses that inherent limitations on the ability of certifying officers of a venture issuer to design and implement on a cost effective basis DC&P and ICFR may result in additional risks to the quality, reliability, transparency and timeliness of interim and annual filings and other reports provided under securities legislation.

15.3 Voluntary disclosure regarding DC&P and ICFR — If a venture issuer files Form 52-109FV1 or 52-109FV2, it is not required to discuss in its annual or interim MD&A the design or operating effectiveness of DC&P or ICFR. If a venture issuer files Form 52-109FV1 or 52-109FV2 and chooses to discuss in its annual or interim MD&A or other regulatory filings the design or operation of one or more components of its DC&P or ICFR, it should also consider disclosing in the same document that:

    (a) the venture issuer is not required to certify the design and evaluation of the issuer's DC&P and ICFR and has not completed such an evaluation; and

    (b) inherent limitations on the ability of the certifying officers to design and implement on a cost effective basis DC&P and ICFR for the issuer may result in additional risks to the quality, reliability, transparency and timeliness of interim and annual filings and other reports provided under securities legislation.

A selective discussion in a venture issuer's MD&A about one or more components of a venture issuer's DC&P or ICFR without these accompanying statements will not provide transparent disclosure of the state of the venture issuer's DC&P or ICFR.

PART 16 — CERTIFICATION REQUIREMENTS FOR A NEW REPORTING ISSUER AND AN ISSUER THAT BECOMES A NON-VENTURE ISSUER

16.1 Certification requirements after becoming a non-venture issuer — Sections 4.5 and 5.5 of the Instrument permit an issuer that becomes a non-venture issuer to file Forms 52-109F1 — IPO/RTO and 52-109F2 — IPO/RTO for the first certificate that the issuer is required to file under this Instrument, for a financial period that ends after the issuer becomes a non-venture issuer. If, subsequent to becoming a non-venture issuer, the issuer is required to file an annual or interim certificate for a period that ended while it was a venture issuer, the required form of certificate for that annual or interim filing is Form 52-109FV1 or 52-109FV2.

PART 17 — EXEMPTIONS

17.1 Issuers that comply with U.S. laws — Some Canadian issuers that comply with U.S. laws might choose to prepare two sets of financial statements and file financial statements in Canada with accounting principles that differ from those that are filed or furnished in the U.S. For example, an issuer may file U.S. GAAP financial statements in the U.S. and financial statements using another acceptable form of accounting principles in Canada. In order to ensure that the financial statements filed in Canada are certified (under either the Instrument or SOX 302 Rules), those issuers will not have recourse to the exemptions in sections 8.1 and 8.2 of the Instrument.

PART 18 — LIABILITY FOR CERTIFICATES CONTAINING MISREPRESENTATIONS

18.1 Liability for certificates containing misrepresentations — A certifying officer providing a certificate containing a misrepresentation potentially could be subject to quasi-criminal, administrative or civil proceedings under securities law.

A certifying officer providing a certificate containing a misrepresentation could also potentially be subject to private actions for damages either at common law or, in Québec, under civil law, or under the statutory civil liability regimes in certain jurisdictions.

PART 19 — TRANSITION

19.1 Representations regarding DC&P and ICFR following the transition periods — If an issuer files an annual certificate in Form 52-109F1 or an interim certificate in Form 52-109F2 that includes representations regarding DC&P or ICFR, these representations would not extend to the prior period comparative information included in the annual filings or interim filings if:

(a) the prior period comparative information was previously the subject of certificates that did not include these representations; or

(b) no certificate was required for the prior period.

19.2 Application of Amendments — The amendments to the Instrument and this Policy which came into effect on January 1, 2011 only apply to annual filings and interim filings for periods relating to financial years beginning on or after January 1, 2011.

PART 20 — CERTIFICATION OF REVISED OR RESTATED ANNUAL OR INTERIM FILINGS

20.1 Certification of revised or restated annual or interim filings — If an issuer files a revised or restated continuous disclosure document that was originally certified as part of its annual or interim filings, the certifying officers would need to file Form 52-109F1R or Form 52-109F2R. These certificates would be dated the same date the certificate is filed and filed on the same date as the revised or restated continuous disclosure document.

20.2 Disclosure considerations if an issuer revises or restates a continuous disclosure document — If an issuer determines that it needs to revise or restate previously issued financial statements, the issuer should consider whether its original disclosures regarding the design or operating effectiveness of ICFR are still appropriate and should modify or supplement its original disclosure to include any other material information that is necessary for such disclosures not to be misleading in light of the revision or restatement.

Similarly, if an issuer determines that it needs to revise or restate a previously issued continuous disclosure document, the issuer should consider whether its original disclosures regarding the design or operating effectiveness of DC&P are still appropriate and should modify or supplement its original disclosure to include any other material information that is necessary for such disclosures not to be misleading in light of the revision or restatement.

Adoption by OSC: (2004) 27 O.S.C.B. 3238 and 877; Request for Comments: (2003) 26 O.S.C.B. 4980.

Adoption of Amendment by OSC: (2005) 28 O.S.C.B. 3089.

Adoption of Replacement Policy: (2008) 31 O.S.C.B. 7949; Request for Comments: 31 O.S.C.B. (Supp. 3) 1 (April 18, 2008), 30 O.S.C.B. 2877 and 28 O.S.C.B. 1318.

Adoption of Amendment to Policy: (2010) 33 O.S.C.B. (Supp. 5) 104 and (Supp. 3) 191; Request for Comments: (2009) 32 O.S.C.B. (Supp. 6) 395.

National Instrument 52-110 — Audit Committees

Date: March 30, 2004, as amended effective June 30, 2005, December 31, 2007, March 17, 2008, July 4, 2008, January 1, 2011, June 30, 2015 and November 17, 2015

27 O.S.C.B. 3252, 28 O.S.C.B. 5387, 30 O.S.C.B. 10507, 31 O.S.C.B. 1009, 31 O.S.C.B. 6576, 33 O.S.C.B. (Supp. 5) 35, 38 O.S.C.B. 3430 and 38 O.S.C.B. 9332.

Table of Contents

PART 1 — DEFINITIONS AND APPLICATION

1.1 Definitions — In this Instrument,

"accounting principles" has the meaning ascribed to it in National Instrument 52-107 *Acceptable Accounting Principles and Auditing Standards*;

"AIF" has the meaning ascribed to it in NI 51-102;

"asset-backed security" has the meaning ascribed to it in NI 51-102;

"audit committee" means a committee (or an equivalent body) established by and among the board of directors of an issuer for the purpose of overseeing the accounting and financial reporting processes of the issuer and audits of the financial statements of the issuer, and, if no such committee exists, the entire board of directors of the issuer;

"audit services" means the professional services rendered by the issuer's external auditor for the audit and review of the issuer's financial statements or services that are normally provided by the external auditor in connection with statutory and regulatory filings or engagements;

"credit support issuer" has the meaning ascribed to it in section 13.4 of NI 51-102;

"designated foreign issuer" has the meaning ascribed to it in National Instrument 71-102 *Continuous Disclosure and Other Exemptions Relating to Foreign Issuers*;

"exchangeable security issuer" has the meaning ascribed to it in section 13.3 of NI 51-102;

"executive officer" of an entity means an individual who is:

    (a) a chair of the entity;

    (b) a vice-chair of the entity;

    (c) the president of the entity;

    (d) a vice-president of the entity in charge of a principal business unit, division or function including sales, finance or production;

    (e) an officer of the entity or any of its subsidiary entities who performs a policy-making function in respect of the entity; or

    (f) any other individual who performs a policy-making function in respect of the entity;

"foreign private issuer" means an issuer that is a foreign private issuer within the meaning of Rule 405 under the 1934 Act;

"immediate family member" means an individual's spouse, parent, child, sibling, mother or father-in-law, son or daughter-in-law, brother or sister-in-law, and anyone (other than an employee of either the individual or the individual's immediate family member) who shares the individual's home;

"marketplace" has the meaning ascribed to it in National Instrument 21-101 *Marketplace Operation*;

"MD&A" has the meaning ascribed to it in NI 51-102;

"NI 51-102" means National Instrument 51-102 *Continuous Disclosure Obligations*;

"non-audit services" means services other than audit services;

"SEC foreign issuer" has the meaning ascribed to it in National Instrument 71-102 *Continuous Disclosure and Other Exemptions Relating to Foreign Issuers*;

"U.S. marketplace" means an exchange registered as a 'national securities exchange' under section 6 of the 1934 Act, or the Nasdaq Stock Market;

"venture issuer" means an issuer that, at the end of its most recently completed financial year, does not have any of its securities listed or quoted on any of the Toronto Stock Exchange, Aequitas NEO Exchange Inc., a U.S. marketplace or a marketplace outside of Canada and the United States of America other than the Alternative Investment Market of the London Stock Exchange or the PLUS markets operated by PLUS Markets Group plc.

1.2 Application — This Instrument applies to all reporting issuers other than:

    (a) investment funds;

    (b) issuers of asset-backed securities;

    (c) designated foreign issuers;

    (d) SEC foreign issuers;

(e) issuers that are subsidiary entities, if

    (i) the subsidiary entity does not have equity securities (other than non-convertible, non-participating preferred securities) trading on a marketplace, and

    (ii) the parent of the subsidiary entity is

        (A) subject to the requirements of this Instrument, or

        (B) an issuer that (1) has securities listed or quoted on a U.S. marketplace, and (2) is in compliance with the requirements of that U.S. marketplace applicable to issuers, other than foreign private issuers, regarding the role and composition of audit committees;

(f) exchangeable security issuers, if the exchangeable security issuer qualifies for the relief contemplated by, and is in compliance with the requirements and conditions set out in, section 13.3 of NI 51-102; and

(g) credit support issuers, if the credit support issuer qualifies for the relief contemplated by, and is in compliance with the requirements and conditions set out in, section 13.4 of NI 51-102.

1.3 Meaning of Affiliated Entity, Subsidiary Entity and Control — (1) For the purposes of this Instrument, a person or company is considered to be an affiliated entity of another person or company if

(a) one of them controls or is controlled by the other or if both persons or companies are controlled by the same person or company, or

(b) the person is an individual who is

    (i) both a director and an employee of an affiliated entity, or

    (ii) an executive officer, general partner or managing member of an affiliated entity.

(2) For the purposes of this Instrument, a person or company is considered to be a subsidiary entity of another person or company if

(a) it is controlled by,

    (i) that other, or

    (ii) that other and one or more persons or companies each of which is controlled by that other, or

    (iii) two or more persons or companies, each of which is controlled by that other; or

(b) it is a subsidiary entity of a person or company that is the other's subsidiary entity.

(3) For the purpose of this Instrument, "control" means the direct or indirect power to direct or cause the direction of the management and policies of a person or company, whether through ownership of voting securities or otherwise.

(4) Despite subsection (1), an individual will not be considered to control an issuer for the purposes of this Instrument if the individual:

(a) owns, directly or indirectly, ten per cent or less of any class of voting securities of the issuer; and

(b) is not an executive officer of the issuer.

1.4 Meaning of Independence — (1) An audit committee member is independent if he or she has no direct or indirect material relationship with the issuer.

(2) For the purposes of subsection (1), a "material relationship" is a relationship which could, in the view of the issuer's board of directors, be reasonably expected to interfere with the exercise of a member's independent judgement.

(3) Despite subsection (2), the following individuals are considered to have a material relationship with an issuer:

(a) an individual who is, or has been within the last three years, an employee or executive officer of the issuer;

(b) an individual whose immediate family member is, or has been within the last three years, an executive officer of the issuer;

(c) an individual who:

    (i) is a partner of a firm that is the issuer's internal or external auditor,

    (ii) is an employee of that firm, or

    (iii) was within the last three years a partner or employee of that firm and personally worked on the issuer's audit within that time;

(d) an individual whose spouse, minor child or stepchild, or child or stepchild who shares a home with the individual:

    (i) is a partner of a firm that is the issuer's internal or external auditor,

    (ii) is an employee of that firm and participates in its audit, assurance or tax compliance (but not tax planning) practice, or

    (iii) was within the last three years a partner or employee of that firm and personally worked on the issuer's audit within that time;

(e) an individual who, or whose immediate family member, is or has been within the last three years, an executive officer of an entity if any of the issuer's current executive officers serves or served at that same time on the entity's compensation committee; and

(f) an individual who received, or whose immediate family member who is employed as an executive officer of the issuer received, more than $75,000 in direct compensation from the issuer during any 12 month period within the last three years.

(4) Despite subsection (3), an individual will not be considered to have a material relationship with the issuer solely because

(a) he or she had a relationship identified in subsection (3) if that relationship ended before March 30, 2004; or

(b) he or she had a relationship identified in subsection (3) by virtue of subsection (8) if that relationship ended before June 30, 2005.

(5) For the purposes of clauses (3)(c) and (3)(d), a partner does not include a fixed income partner whose interest in the firm that is the internal or external auditor is limited to the receipt of fixed amounts of compensation (including deferred compensation) for prior service with that firm if the compensation is not contingent in any way on continued service.

(6) For the purposes of clause (3)(f), direct compensation does not include:

(a) remuneration for acting as a member of the board of directors or of any board committee of the issuer, and

(b) the receipt of fixed amounts of compensation under a retirement plan (including deferred compensation) for prior service with the issuer if the compensation is not contingent in any way on continued service.

(7) Despite subsection (3), an individual will not be considered to have a material relationship with the issuer solely because the individual or his or her immediate family member

    (a) has previously acted as an interim chief executive officer of the issuer, or

    (b) acts, or has previously acted, as a chair or vice-chair of the board of directors or of any board committee of the issuer on a part-time basis.

(8) For the purpose of section 1.4, an issuer includes a subsidiary entity of the issuer and a parent of the issuer.

1.5 Additional Independence Requirements — (1) Despite any determination made under section 1.4, an individual who

    (a) accepts, directly or indirectly, any consulting, advisory or other compensatory fee from the issuer or any subsidiary entity of the issuer, other than as remuneration for acting in his or her capacity as a member of the board of directors or any board committee, or as a part-time chair or vice-chair of the board or any board committee; or

    (b) is an affiliated entity of the issuer or any of its subsidiary entities,

is considered to have a material relationship with the issuer.

(2) For the purposes of subsection (1), the indirect acceptance by an individual of any consulting, advisory or other compensatory fee includes acceptance of a fee by

    (a) an individual's spouse, minor child or stepchild, or a child or stepchild who shares the individual's home; or

    (b) an entity in which such individual is a partner, member, an officer such as a managing director occupying a comparable position or executive officer, or occupies a similar position (except limited partners, non-managing members and those occupying similar positions who, in each case, have no active role in providing services to the entity) and which provides accounting, consulting, legal, investment banking or financial advisory services to the issuer or any subsidiary entity of the issuer.

(3) For the purposes of subsection (1), compensatory fees do not include the receipt of fixed amounts of compensation under a retirement plan (including deferred compensation) for prior service with the issuer if the compensation is not contingent in any way on continued service.

1.6 Meaning of Financial Literacy — For the purposes of this Instrument, an individual is financially literate if he or she has the ability to read and understand a set of financial statements that present a breadth and level of complexity of accounting issues that are generally comparable to the breadth and complexity of the issues that can reasonably be expected to be raised by the issuer's financial statements.

PART 2 — AUDIT COMMITTEE RESPONSIBILITIES

2.1 Audit Committee — Every issuer must have an audit committee that complies with the requirements of the Instrument.

2.2 Relationship with External Auditors — Every issuer must require its external auditor to report directly to the audit committee.

2.3 Audit Committee Responsibilities — (1) An audit committee must have a written charter that sets out its mandate and responsibilities.

(2) An audit committee must recommend to the board of directors:

    (a) the external auditor to be nominated for the purpose of preparing or issuing an auditor's report or performing other audit, review or attest services for the issuer; and

    (b) the compensation of the external auditor.

(3) An audit committee must be directly responsible for overseeing the work of the external auditor engaged for the purpose of preparing or issuing an auditor's report or performing other audit, review or attest services for the issuer, including the resolution of disagreements between management and the external auditor regarding financial reporting.

(4) An audit committee must pre-approve all non-audit services to be provided to the issuer or its subsidiary entities by the issuer's external auditor.

(5) An audit committee must review the issuer's financial statements, MD&A and annual and interim profit or loss press releases before the issuer publicly discloses this information.

(6) An audit committee must be satisfied that adequate procedures are in place for the review of the issuer's public disclosure of financial information extracted or derived from the issuer's financial statements, other than the public disclosure referred to in subsection (5), and must periodically assess the adequacy of those procedures.

(7) An audit committee must establish procedures for:

    (a) the receipt, retention and treatment of complaints received by the issuer regarding accounting, internal accounting controls, or auditing matters; and

    (b) the confidential, anonymous submission by employees of the issuer of concerns regarding questionable accounting or auditing matters.

(8) An audit committee must review and approve the issuer's hiring policies regarding partners, employees and former partners and employees of the present and former external auditor of the issuer.

2.4 De Minimis Non-Audit Services — An audit committee satisfies the pre-approval requirement in subsection 2.3(4) if:

    (a) the aggregate amount of all the non-audit services that were not pre-approved is reasonably expected to constitute no more than five per cent of the total amount of fees paid by the issuer and its subsidiary entities to the issuer's external auditor during the fiscal year in which the services are provided;

    (b) the issuer or the subsidiary entity of the issuer, as the case may be, did not recognize the services as non-audit services at the time of the engagement; and

    (c) the services are promptly brought to the attention of the audit committee of the issuer and approved, prior to the completion of the audit, by the audit committee or by one or more of its members to whom authority to grant such approvals has been delegated by the audit committee.

2.5 Delegation of Pre-Approval Function — (1) An audit committee may delegate to one or more independent members the authority to pre-approve non-audit services in satisfaction of the requirement in subsection 2.3(4).

(2) The pre-approval of non-audit services by any member to whom authority has been delegated pursuant to subsection (1) must be presented to the audit committee at its first scheduled meeting following such pre-approval.

2.6 Pre-Approval Policies and Procedures — An audit committee satisfies the pre-approval requirement in subsection 2.3(4) if it adopts specific policies and procedures for the engagement of the non-audit services, if:

(a) the pre-approval policies and procedures are detailed as to the particular service;

(b) the audit committee is informed of each non-audit service; and

(c) the procedures do not include delegation of the audit committee's responsibilities to management.

PART 3 — COMPOSITION OF THE AUDIT COMMITTEE

3.1 Composition — (1) An audit committee must be composed of a minimum of three members.

(2) Every audit committee member must be a director of the issuer.

(3) Subject to sections 3.2, 3.3, 3.4, 3.5 and 3.6, every audit committee member must be independent.

(4) Subject to sections 3.5 and 3.8, every audit committee member must be financially literate.

3.2 Initial Public Offerings — (1) Subject to section 3.9, if an issuer has filed a prospectus to qualify the distribution of securities that constitutes its initial public offering, subsection 3.1(3) does not apply for a period of up to 90 days commencing on the date of the receipt for the prospectus, provided that one member of the audit committee is independent.

(2) Subject to section 3.9, if an issuer has filed a prospectus to qualify the distribution of securities that constitutes its initial public offering, subsection 3.1(3) does not apply for a period of up to one year commencing on the date of the receipt for the prospectus, provided that a majority of the audit committee members are independent.

3.3 Controlled Companies — (1) An audit committee member that sits on the board of directors of an affiliated entity is exempt from the requirement in subsection 3.1(3) if the member, except for being a director (or member of a board committee) of the issuer and the affiliated entity, is otherwise independent of the issuer and the affiliated entity.

(2) Subject to section 3.7, an audit committee member is exempt from the requirement in subsection 3.1(3) if:

(a) the member would be independent of the issuer but for the relationship described in paragraph 1.5(1)(b) or as a result of subsection 1.4(8);

(b) the member is not an executive officer, general partner or managing member of a person or company that

(i) is an affiliated entity of the issuer, and

(ii) has its securities trading on a marketplace;

(c) the member is not an immediate family member of an executive officer, general partner or managing member referred to in paragraph (b), above;

(d) the member does not act as the chair of the audit committee; and

(e) the board determines in its reasonable judgement that

(i) the member is able to exercise the impartial judgement necessary for the member to fulfill his or her responsibilities as an audit committee member, and

(ii) the appointment of the member is required by the best interests of the issuer and its shareholders.

3.4 Events Outside Control of Member — Subject to section 3.9, if an audit committee member ceases to be independent for reasons outside the member's reasonable control, the member is exempt from the requirement in subsection 3.1(3) for a period ending on the later of:

(a) the next annual meeting of the issuer, and

(b) the date that is six months from the occurrence of the event which caused the member to not be independent.

3.5 Death, Disability or Resignation of Member — Subject to section 3.9, if the death, disability or resignation of an audit committee member has resulted in a vacancy on the audit committee that the board of directors is required to fill, an audit committee member appointed to fill such vacancy is exempt from the requirements in subsections 3.1(3) and (4) for a period ending on the later of:

(a) the next annual meeting of the issuer, and

(b) the date that is six months from the day the vacancy was created.

3.6 Temporary Exemption for Limited and Exceptional Circumstances — Subject to section 3.7, an audit committee member is exempt from the requirement in subsection 3.1(3) if:

(a) the member is not an individual described in subsection 1.5(1);

(b) the member is not an employee or officer of the issuer, or an immediate family member of an employee or officer of the issuer;

(c) the board, under exceptional and limited circumstances, determines in its reasonable judgement that

(i) the member is able to exercise the impartial judgement necessary for the member to fulfill his or her responsibilities as an audit committee member, and

(ii) the appointment of the member is required by the best interests of the issuer and its shareholders;

(d) the member does not act as chair of the audit committee; and

(e) the member does not rely upon this exemption for a period of more than two years.

3.7 Majority Independent — The exemptions in subsection 3.3(2) and section 3.6 are not available to a member unless a majority of the audit committee members would be independent.

3.8 Acquisition of Financial Literacy — Subject to section 3.9, an audit committee member who is not financially literate may be appointed to the audit committee provided that the member becomes financially literate within a reasonable period of time following his or her appointment.

3.9 Restriction on Use of Certain Exemptions — The exemptions in sections 3.2, 3.4, 3.5 and 3.8 are not available to a member unless the issuer's board of directors has determined that the reliance on the exemption will not materially adversely affect the ability of the audit committee to act independently and to satisfy the other requirements of this Instrument.

PART 4 — AUTHORITY OF THE AUDIT COMMITTEE

4.1 Authority — An audit committee must have the authority

    (a) to engage independent counsel and other advisors as it determines necessary to carry out its duties,

    (b) to set and pay the compensation for any advisors employed by the audit committee, and

    (c) to communicate directly with the internal and external auditors.

PART 5 — REPORTING OBLIGATIONS

5.1 Required Disclosure — Every issuer must include in its AIF the disclosure required by Form 52-110F1.

5.2 Management Information Circular — If management of an issuer solicits proxies from the security holders of the issuer for the purpose of electing directors to the issuer's board of directors, the issuer must include in its management information circular a cross-reference to the sections in the issuer's AIF that contain the information required by section 5.1.

PART 6 — VENTURE ISSUERS

6.1 Venture Issuers — Venture issuers are exempt from the requirements of Parts 3 (*Composition of the Audit Committee*) and 5 (*Reporting Obligations*).

6.1.1 Composition of Audit Committee — (1) An audit committee of a venture issuer must be composed of a minimum of three members.

(2) Every member of an audit committee of a venture issuer must be a director of the issuer.

(3) Subject to subsections (4), (5) and (6), a majority of the members of an audit committee of a venture issuer must not be executive officers, employees or control persons of the venture issuer or of an affiliate of the venture issuer.

(4) If a circumstance arises that affects the business or operations of the venture issuer, and a reasonable person would conclude that the circumstance can be best addressed by a member of the audit committee becoming an executive officer or employee of the venture issuer, subsection (3) does not apply to the audit committee in respect of the member until the later of:

    (a) the next annual meeting of the venture issuer;

    (b) the date that is six months after the date on which the circumstance arose.

(5) If an audit committee member becomes a control person of the venture issuer or of an affiliate of the venture issuer for reasons outside the member's reasonable control, subsection (3) does not apply to the audit committee in respect of that member until the later of:

    (a) the next annual meeting of the venture issuer;

    (b) the date that is six months after the event which caused the member to become a control person.

(6) If a vacancy on the audit committee arises as a result of the death, incapacity or resignation of an audit committee member and the board of directors is required to fill the vacancy, subsection (3) does not apply to the audit committee, in respect of the member appointed to fill the vacancy, until the later of:

    (a) the next annual meeting of the venture issuer;

    (b) the date that is six months from the day the vacancy was created.

(7) This section applies to a venture issuer in respect of a financial year beginning on or after January 1, 2016.

6.2 Required Disclosure — (1) Subject to subsection (2), if management of a venture issuer solicits proxies from the security holders of the venture issuer for the purpose of electing directors to its board of directors, the venture issuer must include in its management information circular the disclosure required by Form 52-110F2.

(2) A venture issuer that is not required to send a management information circular to its security holders must provide the disclosure required by Form 52-110F2 in its AIF or annual MD&A.

PART 7 — U.S. LISTED ISSUERS

7.1 U.S. Listed Issuers — An issuer that has securities listed or quoted on a U.S. marketplace is exempt from the requirements of Parts 2 (*Audit Committee Responsibilities*), 3 (*Composition of the Audit Committee*), 4 (*Authority of the Audit Committee*), and 5 (*Reporting Obligations*), if:

    (a) the issuer is in compliance with the requirements of that U.S. marketplace applicable to issuers, other than foreign private issuers, regarding the role and composition of audit committees; and

    (b) if the issuer is incorporated, continued or otherwise organized in a jurisdiction in Canada, the issuer includes in its AIF the disclosure (if any) required by paragraph 7 of Form 52-110F1.

PART 8 — EXEMPTIONS

8.1 Exemptions — (1) The securities regulatory authority or regulator may grant an exemption from this rule, in whole or in part, subject to such conditions or restrictions as may be imposed in the exemption.

(2) Despite subsection (1), in Ontario, only the regulator may grant such an exemption.

PART 9 — EFFECTIVE DATE

9.1 Effective Date — (1) This Instrument comes into force on March 30, 2004.

(2) Despite subsection (1), this Instrument applies to an issuer commencing on the earlier of:

(a) the first annual meeting of the issuer after July 1, 2004, and

(b) July 1, 2005.

Final Rule: (2004) 27 O.S.C.B. 3252; Approval of OSC: (2004) 27 O.S.C.B. 792; Request for Comments: (2003) 26 O.S.C.B. 4996.

Amendment to Rule: (2005) 28 O.S.C.B. 5387; Approval of OSC: (2005) 28 O.S.C.B. 3644; Request for Comments: (2004) 28 O.S.C.B. 8825.

Amendment to Rule: 30 O.S.C.B. 10507; Approval by OSC: (2007) 30 O.S.C.B. 8570.

Amendment to Rule and Approval by OSC: 31 O.S.C.B. 1009.

Amendment to Rule: (2010) 33 O.S.C.B. (Supp. 5) 35; Approval by OSC: (2010) 33 O.S.C.B. (Supp. 3) 1.

Amendment to Rule: (2015) 38 O.S.C.B. 3430.

Policies and Orders: CSAN 52-309, 52-312, 52-318, 51-333.

Form 52-110F1 — Audit Committee Information Required in an AIF

1. — The Audit Committee's Charter

Disclose the text of the audit committee's charter.

2. — Composition of the Audit Committee

Disclose the name of each audit committee member and state whether or not the member is (i) independent and (ii) financially literate.

3. — Relevant Education and Experience

Describe the education and experience of each audit committee member that is relevant to the performance of his or her responsibilities as an audit committee member and, in particular, disclose any education or experience that would provide the member with:

(a) an understanding of the accounting principles used by the issuer to prepare its financial statements;

(b) the ability to assess the general application of such accounting principles in connection with the accounting for estimates, accruals and provisions;

(c) experience preparing, auditing, analyzing or evaluating financial statements that present a breadth and level of complexity of accounting issues that are generally comparable to the breadth and complexity of issues that can reasonably be expected to be raised by the issuer's financial statements, or experience actively supervising one or more individuals engaged in such activities; and

(d) an understanding of internal controls and procedures for financial reporting.

4. — Reliance on Certain Exemptions

If, at any time since the commencement of the issuer's most recently completed financial year, the issuer has relied on

(a) the exemption in section 2.4 (*De Minimis Non-audit Services*),

(b) the exemption in section 3.2 (*Initial Public Offerings*),

(c) the exemption in section 3.4 (*Events Outside Control of Member*),

(d) the exemption in section 3.5 (*Death, Disability or Resignation of Audit Committee Member*) or

(e) an exemption from this Instrument, in whole or in part, granted under Part 8 (*Exemptions*),

state that fact.

5. — Reliance on the Exemption in Subsection 3.3(2) or Section 3.6

If, at any time since the commencement of the issuer's most recently completed financial year, the issuer has relied upon the exemption in subsection 3.3(2) (*Controlled Companies*) or section 3.6 (*Temporary Exemption for Limited and Exceptional Circumstances*), state that fact and disclose

(a) the name of the member, and

(b) the rationale for appointing the member to the audit committee.

6. — Reliance on Section 3.8

If, at any time since the commencement of the issuer's most recently completed financial year, the issuer has relied upon section 3.8 (*Acquisition of Financial Literacy*), state that fact and disclose

(a) the name of the member,

(b) that the member is not financially literate, and

(c) the date by which the member expects to become financially literate.

7. — Audit Committee Oversight

If, at any time since the commencement of the issuer's most recently completed financial year, a recommendation of the audit committee to nominate or compensate an external auditor was not adopted by the board of directors, state that fact and explain why.

8. — Pre-Approval Policies and Procedures

If the audit committee has adopted specific policies and procedures for the engagement of non-audit services, describe those policies and procedures.

9. — External Auditor Service Fees (By Category)

(a) Disclose, under the caption "Audit Fees", the aggregate fees billed by the issuer's external auditor in each of the last two fiscal years for audit services.

(b) Disclose, under the caption "Audit-Related Fees", the aggregate fees billed in each of the last two fiscal years for assurance and related services by the issuer's external auditor that are reasonably related to the performance of the audit or review of the issuer's financial statements and are not reported under clause (a) above. Include a description of the nature of the services comprising the fees disclosed under this category.

(c) Disclose, under the caption "Tax Fees", the aggregate fees billed in each of the last two fiscal years for professional services rendered by the issuer's external auditor for tax compliance, tax advice, and tax planning. Include a description of the nature of the services comprising the fees disclosed under this category.

(d) Disclose, under the caption "All Other Fees", the aggregate fees billed in each of the last two fiscal years for products and services provided by the issuer's external auditor, other than the services reported under clauses (a), (b) and (c), above. Include a description of the nature of the services comprising the fees disclosed under this category.

Instruction

The fees required to be disclosed by this paragraph 9 relate only to services provided to the issuer or its subsidiary entities by the issuer's external auditor.

Form 52-110F2 — Disclosure by Venture Issuers

1. — The Audit Committee's Charter

Disclose the text of the audit committee's charter.

2. — Composition of the Audit Committee

Disclose the name of each audit committee member and state whether or not the member is (i) independent and (ii) financially literate.

3. — Relevant Education and Experience

Describe the education and experience of each audit committee member that is relevant to the performance of his or her responsibilities as an audit committee member and, in particular, disclose any education or experience that would provide the member with:

(a) an understanding of the accounting principles used by the issuer to prepare its financial statements;

(b) the ability to assess the general application of such accounting principles in connection with the accounting for estimates, accruals and provisions;

(c) experience preparing, auditing, analyzing or evaluating financial statements that present a breadth and level of complexity of accounting issues that are generally comparable to the breadth and complexity of issues that can reasonably be expected to be raised by the issuer's financial statements, or experience actively supervising one or more individuals engaged in such activities; and

(d) an understanding of internal controls and procedures for financial reporting.

4. — Audit Committee Oversight

If, at any time since the commencement of the issuer's most recently completed financial year, a recommendation of the audit committee to nominate or compensate an external auditor was not adopted by the board of directors, state that fact and explain why.

5. — Reliance on Certain Exemptions

If, at any time since the commencement of the issuer's most recently completed financial year, the issuer has relied on

(a) the exemption in section 2.4 *(De Minimis Non-audit Services)*, or

(b) the exemption in subsection 6.1.1(4) *(Circumstances Affecting the Business or Operations of the Venture Issuer)*,

(c) the exemption in subsection 6.1.1(5) *(Events Outside Control of Member)*,

(d) the exemption in subsection 6.1.1(6) *(Death, Incapacity or Resignation)*, or

(e) an exemption from this Instrument, in whole or in part, granted under Part 8 *(Exemption)*,

state that fact.

6. — Pre-Approval Policies and Procedures

If the audit committee has adopted specific policies and procedures for the engagement of non-audit services, describe those policies and procedures.

7. — External Auditor Service Fees (By Category)

(a) Disclose, under the caption "Audit Fees", the aggregate fees billed by the issuer's external auditor in each of the last two fiscal years for audit fees.

(b) Disclose, under the caption "Audit-Related Fees", the aggregate fees billed in each of the last two fiscal years for assurance and related services by the issuer's external auditor that are reasonably related to the performance of the audit or review of the issuer's financial statements and are not reported under clause (a) above. Include a description of the nature of the services comprising the fees disclosed under this category.

(c) Disclose, under the caption "Tax Fees", the aggregate fees billed in each of the last two fiscal years for professional services rendered by the issuer's external auditor for tax compliance, tax advice, and tax planning. Include a description of the nature of the services comprising the fees disclosed under this category.

(d) Disclose, under the caption "All Other Fees", the aggregate fees billed in each of the last two fiscal years for products and services provided by the issuer's external auditor, other than the services reported under clauses (a), (b) and (c), above. Include a description of the nature of the services comprising the fees disclosed under this category.

Instruction

The fees required to be disclosed by this paragraph 7 relate only to services provided to the issuer or its subsidiary entities by the issuer's external auditor.

8. — Exemption

Disclose that the issuer is relying upon the exemption in section 6.1 of the Instrument.

Companion Policy 52-110CP — To National Instrument 52-110 Audit Committees

PART 1 — GENERAL

1.1 Purpose — National Instrument 52-110 *Audit Committees* (the Instrument) is a rule in each of Québec, Alberta, Manitoba, Ontario, New Brunswick, Nova Scotia, Newfoundland and Labrador and British Columbia, a Commission regulation in Saskatchewan and Nunavut, a policy in Prince Edward Island and the Yukon Territory, and a code in the Northwest Territories. We, the securities regulatory authorities in each of the foregoing jurisdictions (the Jurisdictions), have implemented the Instrument to encourage reporting issuers to establish and maintain strong, effective and independent audit committees. We believe that such audit committees enhance the quality of financial disclosure made by reporting issuers, and ultimately foster increased investor confidence in Canada's capital markets.

This companion policy (the Policy) provides information regarding the interpretation and application of the Instrument.

1.2 Application to Non-Corporate Entities — The Instrument applies to both corporate and non-corporate entities. Where the Instrument or this Policy refers to a particular corporate characteristic, such as a board of directors, the reference should be read to also include any equivalent characteristic of a non-corporate entity. For example, in the case of a limited partnership, the directors of the general partner who are independent of the limited partnership (including the general partner) should form an audit committee which fulfils these responsibilities.

Income trust issuers should apply the Instrument in a manner which recognizes that certain functions of a corporate issuer, its board and its management may be performed by any or all of the trustees, the board or management of a subsidiary of the trust, or the board, management or employees of a management company. For this purpose, references to "the issuer" refer to both the trust and any underlying entities, including the operating entity.

If the structure of an issuer will not permit it to comply with the Instrument, the issuer should seek exemptive relief.

1.3 Management Companies — The definition of "executive officer" includes any individual who performs a policy-making function in respect of the entity in question. We consider this aspect of the definition to include an individual who, although not employed by the entity in question, nevertheless performs a policy-making function in respect of that entity, whether through another person or company or otherwise.

1.4 Audit Committee Procedures — The Instrument establishes requirements for the responsibilities, composition and authority of audit committees. Nothing in the Instrument is intended to restrict the ability of the board of directors or the audit committee to establish the committee's quorum or procedures, or to restrict the committee's ability to invite additional parties to attend audit committee meetings.

PART 2 — THE ROLE OF THE AUDIT COMMITTEE

2.1 The Role of the Audit Committee — An audit committee is a committee of a board of directors to which the board delegates its responsibility for oversight of the financial reporting process. Traditionally, the audit committee has performed a number of roles, including

helping directors meet their responsibilities,

providing better communication between directors and the external auditors,

enhancing the independence of the external auditor,

increasing the credibility and objectivity of financial reports, and

strengthening the role of the directors by facilitating in-depth discussions among directors, management and the external auditor.

The Instrument requires that the audit committee also be responsible for managing, on behalf of the shareholders, the relationship between the issuer and the external auditors. In particular, it provides that an audit committee must have responsibility for:

(a) overseeing the work of the external auditors engaged for the purpose of preparing or issuing an auditor's report or related work; and

(b) recommending to the board of directors the nomination and compensation of the external auditors.

Although under corporate law an issuer's external auditors are responsible to the shareholders, in practice, shareholders have often been too dispersed to effectively exercise meaningful oversight of the external auditors. As a result, management has typically assumed this oversight role. However, the

Part 5: ONGOING REQUIREMENTS

auditing process may be compromised if the external auditors view their main responsibility as serving management rather than the shareholders. By assigning these responsibilities to an independent audit committee, the Instrument ensures that the external audit will be conducted independently of the issuer's management.

2.2 Relationship between External Auditors and Shareholders — Subsection 2.3(3) of the Instrument provides that an audit committee must be directly responsible for overseeing the work of the external auditors engaged for the purpose of preparing or issuing an auditor's report or performing other audit, review or attest services for the issuer, including the resolution of disagreements between management and the external auditors regarding financial reporting. Notwithstanding this responsibility, the external auditors are retained by, and are ultimately accountable to, the shareholders. As a result, subsection 2.3(3) does not detract from the external auditors' right and responsibility to also provide their views directly to the shareholders if they disagree with an approach being taken by the audit committee.

2.3 Public Disclosure of Financial Information — Issuers are reminded that, in our view, the extraction of information from financial statements that have not previously been reviewed by the audit committee and the release of that information into the marketplace is inconsistent with the issuer's obligation to have its audit committee review the financial statements. See also National Policy 51-201 *Disclosure Standards*.

PART 3 — INDEPENDENCE

3.1 Meaning of Independence — The Instrument generally requires every member of an audit committee to be independent. Subsection 1.4(1) of the Instrument defines independence to mean the absence of any direct or indirect material relationship between the director and the issuer. In our view, this may include a commercial, charitable, industrial, banking, consulting, legal, accounting or familial relationship, or any other relationship that the board considers to be material. Although shareholding alone may not interfere with the exercise of a director's independent judgement, we believe that other relationships between an issuer and a shareholder may constitute material relationships with the issuer, and should be considered by the board when determining a director's independence. However, only those relationships which could, in the view of the issuer's board of directors, be reasonably expected to interfere with the exercise of a member's independent judgement should be considered material relationships within the meaning of section 1.4.

Subsection 1.4(3) and section 1.5 of the Instrument describe those individuals that we believe have a relationship with an issuer that would reasonably be expected to interfere with the exercise of the individual's independent judgement. Consequently, these individuals are not considered independent for the purposes of the Instrument and are therefore precluded from serving on the issuer's audit committee. Directors and their counsel should therefore consider the nature of the relationships outlined in subsection 1.4(3) and section 1.5 as guidance in applying the general independence requirement set out in subsection 1.4(1).

3.2 Derivation of Definition — In the United States, listed issuers must comply with the audit committee requirements contained in SEC rules as well as the director independence and audit committee requirements of the applicable securities exchange or market. The definition of independence included in the Instrument has therefore been derived from both the applicable SEC rules and the corporate governance rules issued by the New York Stock Exchange. The portion of the definition of independence that parallels the NYSE rules is found in section 1.4 of the Instrument. Section 1.5 of the Instrument contains additional rules regarding audit committee member independence that were derived from the applicable SEC rules. To be independent for the purposes of the Instrument, a director must satisfy the requirements in both sections 1.4 and 1.5.

3.3 Safe Harbour — Subsection 1.3(1) of the Instrument provides, in part, that a person or company is an affiliated entity of another entity if the person or company controls the other entity. Subsection 1.3(4), however, provides that an individual will not be considered to control an issuer if the individual:

    (a) owns, directly or indirectly, ten per cent or less of any class of voting equity securities of the issuer; and

    (b) is not an executive officer of the issuer.

Subsection 1.3(4) is intended only to identify those individuals who are not considered to control an issuer. The provision is not intended to suggest that an individual who owns more than ten percent of an issuer's voting equity securities automatically controls an issuer. Instead, an individual who owns more than ten percent of an issuer's voting equity securities should examine all relevant facts and circumstances to determine if he or she controls the issuer and is therefore an affiliated entity within the meaning of subsection 1.3(1).

3.4 Remuneration of Chair of Board, Etc. — Subsection 1.4(6) of the Instrument provides that, for the purpose of the prescribed relationship described in clause 1.4(3)(f), direct compensation does not include remuneration for acting as a member of the board of directors or of any board committee of the issuer. In our view, remuneration for acting as a member of the board also includes remuneration for acting as the chair of the board or of any committee of the board.

PART 4 — FINANCIAL LITERACY, FINANCIAL EDUCATION AND EXPERIENCE

4.1 Financial Literacy — For the purposes of the Instrument, an individual is financially literate if he or she has the ability to read and understand a set of financial statements that present a breadth and level of complexity of accounting issues that are generally comparable to the breadth and complexity of the issues that can reasonably be expected to be raised by the issuer's financial statements. In our view, it is not necessary for a member to have a comprehensive knowledge of GAAP and GAAS to be considered financially literate.

4.2 Disclosure of Relevant Education and Experience — (1) Item 3 of Forms 52-110F1 and 52-110F2 require an issuer to disclose any education or experience of an audit committee member that would provide the member with, among other things, an understanding of the accounting principles used by the issuer to prepare its financial statements. The level of understanding that is requisite is influenced by the complexity of the business being carried on. For example, if the issuer is a complex financial institution, a greater degree of education and experience is necessary than would be the case for an audit committee member of an issuer with a more simple business.

(2) Item 3 of Forms 52-110F1 and 52-110F2 also require an issuer to disclose any experience that the member has, among other things, actively supervising persons engaged in preparing, auditing, analyzing or evaluating certain types of financial statements. The phrase active supervision means more than the mere existence of a traditional hierarchical reporting relationship between supervisor and those being supervised. An individual engaged in active supervision participates in, and contributes to, the process of addressing (albeit at a supervisory level) the same general types of issues regarding preparation, auditing, analysis or evaluation of financial statements as those addressed by the individual or individuals being supervised. The supervisor should also have experience that has contributed to the general expertise necessary to prepare, audit, analyze or evaluate financial statements that is at least comparable to the general expertise of those being supervised. An executive officer should not be presumed to qualify. An executive officer with considerable operations involvement, but little financial or accounting involvement, likely would not be exercising the necessary active

PART 5 — NON-AUDIT SERVICES

5.1 Pre-Approval of Non-Audit Services — Section 2.6 of the Instrument allows an audit committee to satisfy, in certain circumstances, the pre-approval requirements in subsection 2.3(4) by adopting specific policies and procedures for the engagement of non-audit services. The following guidance should be noted in the development and application of such policies and procedures:

Monetary limits should not be the only basis for the pre-approval policies and procedures. The establishment of monetary limits will not, alone, constitute policies that are detailed as to the particular services to be provided and will not, alone, ensure that the audit committee will be informed about each service.

The use of broad, categorical approvals (*e.g.* tax compliance services) will not meet the requirement that the policies must be detailed as to the particular services to be provided.

The appropriate level of detail for the pre-approval policies will differ depending upon the facts and circumstances of the issuer. The pre-approval policies must be designed to ensure that the audit committee knows precisely what services it is being asked to pre-approve so that it can make a well-reasoned assessment of the impact of the service on the auditor's independence. Furthermore, because the Instrument requires that the policies cannot result in a delegation of the audit committee's responsibility to management, the pre-approval policies must be sufficiently detailed as to particular services so that a member of management will not be called upon to determine whether a proposed service fits within the policy.

PART 6 — DISCLOSURE OBLIGATIONS

6.1 Incorporation by Reference — National Instrument 51-102 permits disclosure required to be included in an issuer's AIF or information circular to be incorporated by reference, provided that the referenced document has already been filed with the applicable securities regulatory authorities.[1] Any disclosure required by the Instrument to be included in an issuer's AIF or management information circular may also incorporated by reference, provided that the procedures set out in National Instrument 51-102 are followed.

Adoption by OSC: (2004) 27 O.S.C.B. 3264 and 792; Reqest for Comments: (2003) 26 O.S.C.B. 4996.

Adoption of Amendment to Policy by OSC: (2005) 28 O.S.C.B. 5387 and 3644; Request for Comments: (2004) 27 O.S.C.B. 8859.

Adoption of Amendment to Policy by OSC: (2008) 31 O.S.C.B. 1009.

Adoption of Amendment to Policy by OSC: (2008) 31 O.S.C.B. 6576 and 4261.

CSA Staff Notice 52-306 (Revised) — Non-GAAP Financial Measures

Date: **January 14, 2016**

39 O.S.C.B. 229

I. — Purpose

The primary purpose of this notice is to provide guidance to an issuer that discloses non-GAAP financial measures. The guidance applies both to an issuer that uses International Financial Reporting Standards (IFRS) and to an issuer that uses accounting principles other than IFRS. Non-GAAP financial measures may mislead investors if they are not accompanied by the appropriate disclosure. Therefore, staff will monitor disclosure accompanying non-GAAP financial measures.

The notice also provides guidance on additional subtotals presented in the financial statements but disclosed before the financial statements are filed, and additional subtotals presented in the statement of cash flows for IFRS financial statements.

The guidance is intended to help ensure that the information disclosed does not mislead investors.

Staff cautions issuers that regulatory action may be taken if an issuer discloses information in a manner considered misleading and therefore potentially harmful to the public interest.

II. — Non-GAAP Financial Measures

For the purpose of this notice, a non-GAAP financial measure is a numerical measure of an issuer's historical or future financial performance, financial position or cash flow that is not specified, defined or determined under the issuer's GAAP (as that term is defined in National Instrument 52-107 *Acceptable Accounting Principles and Auditing Standards*) and is not presented in an issuer's financial statements. A non-GAAP financial measure excludes amounts that are included in, or includes amounts that are excluded from, the most directly comparable measure specified, defined or determined under the issuer's GAAP.

Some issuers disclose non-GAAP financial measures in press releases, management's discussion and analysis, prospectus filings, websites and marketing materials.

Many non-GAAP financial measures are derived from profit or loss determined under an issuer's GAAP and, by omission of selected items, present a more positive picture of financial performance. Terms used to identify non-GAAP financial measures may include "pro forma earnings", "cash earnings", "free cash flow", "distributable cash", "Adjusted EBITDA", "adjusted earnings", and "earnings before non-recurring items". Many of these terms lack standard meanings and different issuers may use the same term to refer to different calculations.

Staff is concerned that investors may be confused or even misled by non-GAAP financial measures. Staff is also concerned about the prominence of disclosure given to non-GAAP financial measures related to earnings compared to the prominence of earnings measures specified,

---

[1]See Part 1, paragraph (f) of Form 51-102F2 (*Annual Information Form*) and Part 1, paragraph (c) of Form 51-102F5 (*Information Circular*).

defined or determined under an issuer's GAAP. In staff's view, these concerns can be addressed by appropriate disclosure accompanying non-GAAP financial measures.

Some issuers disclose performance measures that are calculated without using financial measures (for example, number of units or number of subscribers). Some issuers disclose performance measures that are calculated using financial information presented in the financial statements (for example, sales per square foot, where the sales figure is extracted directly from the financial statements). In both of the preceding scenarios, such performance measures are not considered to be non-GAAP financial measures. However, if a non-GAAP financial measure is used to calculate a performance measure (such as an "adjusted earnings" financial measure used to calculate an "adjusted earnings per unit" measure), then that non-GAAP financial measure should be disclosed and Section III of this notice applies to that non-GAAP financial measure.

III. — Disclosure Accompanying Non-GAAP Financial Measures

Financial statements prepared in accordance with an issuer's GAAP provide investors with a clear basis for financial analysis and comparison among issuers. Staff recognizes that non-GAAP financial measures may provide investors with additional information to assist them in understanding critical components of an issuer's financial performance. However, an issuer should not present a non-GAAP financial measure in a way that confuses or obscures the most directly comparable measure specified, defined or determined under the issuer's GAAP presented in its financial statements.

Staff reminds issuers of their responsibility to ensure that information they provide to the public is not misleading. Staff also reminds certifying officers of their obligations under National Instrument 52-109 *Certification of Disclosure in Issuers' Annual and Interim Filings* to make certifications regarding misrepresentations, fair presentation, and disclosure controls and procedures. A non-GAAP financial measure may be misleading if it includes positive components of the most directly comparable measure specified, defined or determined under the issuer's GAAP presented in its financial statements but omits similar negative components.

In order to ensure that a non-GAAP financial measure does not mislead investors, an issuer should:

1. state explicitly that the non-GAAP financial measure does not have any standardized meaning under the issuer's GAAP and therefore may not be comparable to similar measures presented by other issuers;

2. name the non-GAAP financial measure in a way that distinguishes it from disclosure items specified, defined or determined under an issuer's GAAP and in a way that is not misleading. For example, in presenting EBITDA as a non-GAAP financial measure, it would be misleading to exclude amounts for items other than interest, taxes, depreciation and amortization;

3. explain why the non-GAAP financial measure provides useful information to investors and the additional purposes, if any, for which management uses the non-GAAP financial measure;

4. present with equal or greater prominence to that of the non-GAAP financial measure, the most directly comparable measure specified, defined or determined under the issuer's GAAP presented in its financial statements;

5. provide a clear quantitative reconciliation from the non-GAAP financial measure to the most directly comparable measure specified, defined or determined under the issuer's GAAP and presented in its financial statements, referencing to the reconciliation when the non-GAAP financial measure first appears in the document, or in the case of content on a website, in a manner that meets this objective (for example, by providing a link to the reconciliation);

6. ensure that the non-GAAP financial measure does not describe adjustments as non-recurring, infrequent or unusual, when a similar loss or gain is reasonably likely to occur within the next two years or occurred during the prior two years; and

7. present the non-GAAP financial measure on a consistent basis from period to period; however, where an issuer changes the composition of the non-GAAP financial measure, explain the reason for the change and restate any comparative period presented.

IV. — Disclosing Additional Subtotals before Filing Financial Statements

An issuer's GAAP may require the presentation of additional subtotals in the financial statements when such presentation is relevant to an understanding of the issuer's financial position or financial performance. An example of this requirement is found in paragraphs 55 and 85 of IAS 1 *Presentation of Financial Statements* (IAS 1). An issuer may choose to present these additional subtotals in a press release or some other location outside of an issuer's financial statements before filing on SEDAR its financial statements. In order to avoid any confusion about these additional subtotals, management should explain their composition. This may be accomplished by:

- including a copy of the statement that contains these additional subtotals (for example, the statement of profit or loss and other comprehensive income), or

- reconciling these additional subtotals to the most directly comparable line item specified or defined by IFRS that will be presented in financial statements (for example, profit or loss).

V. — Presentation of Additional Subtotals in the Statement of Cash Flows for IFRS Financial Statements

IAS 1 includes requirements that apply to additional subtotals presented in the statement of financial position and statement of profit or loss and other comprehensive income (see paragraphs 55A, 85A and 85B of IAS 1). The practices outlined in the paragraphs noted, will also help ensure that additional subtotals presented in the statement of cash flows do not mislead investors.

In addition, if an issuer chooses to present additional subtotals from the statement of cash flows in a press release or some other location outside of an issuer's financial statements before filing on SEDAR its financial statements, then in order to avoid any confusion about these additional subtotals, management should explain their composition (as discussed in Section IV of this notice).

VI. — Distributable Cash

National Policy 41-201 *Income Trusts and Other Indirect Offerings* provides additional guidance on measures of cash available for distribution.

VII. — Forward-Looking Information

The contents of this notice apply equally to disclosure of forward-looking non-GAAP financial measures.

VIII. — Revision and Republication

Staff updated this notice on November 9, 2010 to reflect the changeover to IFRS.

Staff updated this notice on February 17, 2012 to provide further guidance on accompanying disclosure for additional line items, headings or subtotals presented in financial statements and additional financial measures presented in notes to financial statements under IFRS.

Staff updated this notice on January 14, 2016 to reflect amendments to IAS 1 regarding additional subtotals presented in the financial statements.

IX. — Questions

Please refer your questions to any of the following individuals:

[Names not reproduced]

CSA Staff Notice 52-309 — Multilateral Instrument 52-110 Audit Committees Compliance Review

Date: May 6, 2005
28 O.S.C.B. 4172

Multilateral Instrument 52-110 *Audit Committees* (the Instrument) came into force on March 30, 2004 in every jurisdiction in Canada except British Columbia and Quebec. In Quebec, it will come into force once it is approved by the Minister of Finance. With limited exceptions, the Instrument applies to all reporting issuers.

Issuers subject to the Instrument are reminded that they must comply with the Instrument's requirements beginning on the earlier of

- the issuer's first annual meeting after July 1, 2004, and

- July 1, 2005.

Commencing shortly, staff from certain CSA jurisdictions will conduct a compliance review of a sample of issuers. This review will focus on each issuer's compliance with the Instrument's requirements regarding audit committee composition and responsibilities. Issuers that have been selected for this review will be contacted by CSA staff.

We will publish the results and outcomes of this review upon its completion.

CSA Staff Notice 52-312 — Audit Committee Compliance Review

Date: January 13, 2006
29 O.S.C.B. 259

As announced on May 6, 2005, staff of the securities regulatory authorities in Alberta, Saskatchewan, Manitoba, Ontario and Québec conducted a review of compliance with the provisions of Multilateral Instrument 52-110 *Audit Committees* (the Instrument). This notice outlines the results of our review.

The Instrument

The Instrument came into force on March 30, 2004 in every jurisdiction in Canada except British Columbia and Québec. In Québec, it came into force on June 30, 2005. With limited exceptions, the Instrument applies to all reporting issuers. Issuers subject to the Instrument were required to comply with its requirements beginning on the earlier of: (i) the issuer's first annual meeting after July 1, 2004, and (ii) July 1, 2005.

The Instrument prescribes four broad sets of requirements:

- an issuer must have an audit committee that complies with the Instrument;

- all members of the audit committee must be independent and financially literate (venture issuers are exempt from these requirements);

- an audit committee must have a written charter that includes prescribed responsibilities; and

- an issuer must include certain disclosure in its AIF, management information circular or MD&A.

The Review Program

A sample of 95 issuers was selected from across the country. The selection criteria included the issuer's head office location, its industry sector, and its listing status. The sample included 40 issuers listed on the TSX on an exempt basis (exempt TSX issuers); 23 issuers listed on the TSX on a non-exempt basis (non-exempt TSX issuers)[1]; and 30 issuers listed on the TSX Venture Exchange and 2 other issuers which did not have securities listed or quoted on any of these markets (collectively, venture issuers).

The review focused on each issuer's compliance with the Instrument's requirements regarding audit committee composition and responsibilities. Each issuer was requested to provide us with a copy of its audit committee charter together with the following information:

- for each member of the audit committee, all direct or indirect relationships that the member had with the issuer and the basis upon which the member was determined to be independent or non-independent;

- for each member of the audit committee, the basis upon which the member was determined to be financially literate; and

- any exemptions that were being relied upon in connection with audit committee member independence or financial literacy.

Results

The statistical results of the compliance review are included in Appendix A.

All section references are to the Instrument as it read prior to amendments that came into force on June 30, 2005.

Audit Committee Responsibilities

Overall, 64% of the audit committee charters reviewed set out all of the responsibilities prescribed by the Instrument. This included 68% of exempt TSX issuers, 57% of non-exempt TSX issuers, and 66% of venture issuers. In our view, a 64% overall compliance level is inadequate. It appears that many issuers were either unaware of the provisions of the Instrument or were at least unaware of its transition provisions.

While the non-compliance was broadly dispersed across all responsibilities, the responsibilities that were most commonly excluded from non-compliant charters were the responsibility to establish procedures for the handling of complaints and employee concerns regarding accounting or auditing matters (s. 2.3(7)) (17 instances of non-compliance) and the responsibility to review and approve the issuer's hiring policies for partners and employees of the issuer's current and former auditors (s. 2.3(8)) (20 instances of non-compliance).

Three other responsibilities were commonly excluded from the audit committee charters of non-exempt TSX issuers. The charters of 5 issuers did not include the requirement to directly oversee the work of the external auditor (s. 2.3(3)); the charters of 6 issuers did not include the requirement to review the issuer's financial statements, MD&A and annual and interim earnings press releases prior to their release (s. 2.3(5)); and the charters of 6 issuers did not include the requirement that the audit committee satisfy itself as to the adequacy of review procedures for other financial information (s. 2.3(6)). Additionally, 4 venture issuers did not have an audit committee charter.

In several instances, issuers asserted that their audit committee charter complied with the Instrument because certain responsibilities not specifically enumerated were implied by the language in the audit committee's charter. In other instances, the audit committee was provided with discretion in its charter as to whether or not to assume certain of the responsibilities outlined therein.

In our view, neither position is justifiable. In order to satisfy the provisions of the Instrument, the prescribed responsibilities must be directly and clearly set out in the audit committee's charter. Further, the audit committee must not be provided with discretion as to whether or not to assume certain of the responsibilities.

Where we identified non-compliance during the course of a review, the audit committee charter was generally amended prior to the completion of the review. In several instances, however, an undertaking was filed by the issuer to amend the charter within a specified period of time prior to the date of the issuer's next annual meeting.

Audit Committee Member Independence

92% of TSX issuers had audit committees comprised solely of independent directors.

All 5 TSX issuers that did not have fully independent audit committees had only one member who was not independent. The basis for the determination of non-independence in each instance was that the individual received, directly or indirectly, a consulting, advisory or compensatory fee from the issuer which is a deemed material relationship under s. 1.4(3)(f)(i). In this regard, there appeared to be confusion as to the interpretation and application of s. 1.4(7)(b). That section deems an individual to be in receipt of indirect compensation if they are a partner of a law, accounting or consulting firm that receives fees from the issuer.

In 3 instances of non-compliance by TSX issuers, the individual was the issuer's counsel or was a partner in a law firm that received fees from the issuer. The individual in one instance provided accounting services to the issuer. In the remaining instance, the individual's consulting firm received fees from the issuer. In one of these instances, the issuer responded that its board had determined that a director contravened s. 1.4(3)(f)(i) but was nonetheless independent. It should be noted that s. 1.4(3) does not provide a board with this discretion.

In 4 instances where we determined that a member of the audit committee of a TSX issuer was not independent, the member was replaced by an independent director prior to the completion of the review. In one instance, however, an undertaking was filed by the issuer to replace the member within a specified period of time prior to the date of the issuer's next annual meeting.

Interestingly, notwithstanding that venture issuers are not required to comply with the audit committee independence requirements of the Instrument on the basis of the exemption included in Part 6, 31% of venture issuers had audit committees comprised solely of independent directors.

---

[1] An exempt issuer is an issuer that is at a more advanced development stage based on factors such as higher levels of profitability, cash flow, net tangible assets and market capitalization as outlined in the TSX original listing requirements for exempt issuers. As a result, exempt issuers are entitled to reduced filing requirements in some circumstances. Non-exempt issuers are subject to additional TSX oversight, as provided in Part 5 of the TSX Company Manual, for any proposed material change in their business or affairs.

Of the 22 venture issuers that did not have fully independent audit committees, 13 had one member who was not independent while 9 had two members who were not independent.

In 18 instances where a member of the audit committee of a venture issuer was determined not to be independent, the member was an employee or executive officer of the issuer which is a deemed material relationship under s. 1.4(3)(a). In 15 of those instances, the individual was the CEO of the issuer. In one instance, a member was determined not to be independent as the individual was an immediate family member of an executive officer which is a deemed material relationship under s. 1.4(3)(b). The basis for the determination of non-independence in 9 instances was that the individual received, directly or indirectly, a consulting, advisory or compensatory fee which is a deemed material relationship under s. 1.4(3)(f)(i). In 3 of these instances, the individual was the issuer's counsel or was a partner in a law firm that received fees from the issuer; in one instance, the individual was a partner of an accounting firm that received fees from the issuer; and in 5 instances, the individual received fees from the issuer for providing consulting or investment banking services.

Audit Committee Member Financial Literacy

We did not find any instances where an issuer determined that an audit committee member was not financially literate. This finding is particularly noteworthy for venture issuers as they are not required to comply with the audit committee financial literacy requirements of the Instrument on the basis of the exemption included in Part 6.

We note that, in several instances, the assertion by an issuer of the financial literacy of an audit committee member was the subject of further scrutiny in our review. In several instances it appears that, although an audit committee member was ultimately determined to be financially literate, the matter had not been carefully considered by the issuer prior to our enquiry. The financial literacy of each director should be carefully assessed prior to that individual's appointment to the audit committee. The assessment should generally be supportable on the basis of the individual's relevant education and/or experience.

Future Reviews

In our view, the level of compliance by issuers with the provisions of the Instrument was unacceptable. We were particularly concerned to learn that even the largest issuers, exempt TSX issuers, were not fully compliant.

We expect issuers to fully comply with the Instrument.

We intend to conduct additional reviews of compliance by issuers with the Instrument in the near future. We will actively follow up on deficiencies identified in those reviews and will pursue appropriate remedies where we deem it appropriate.

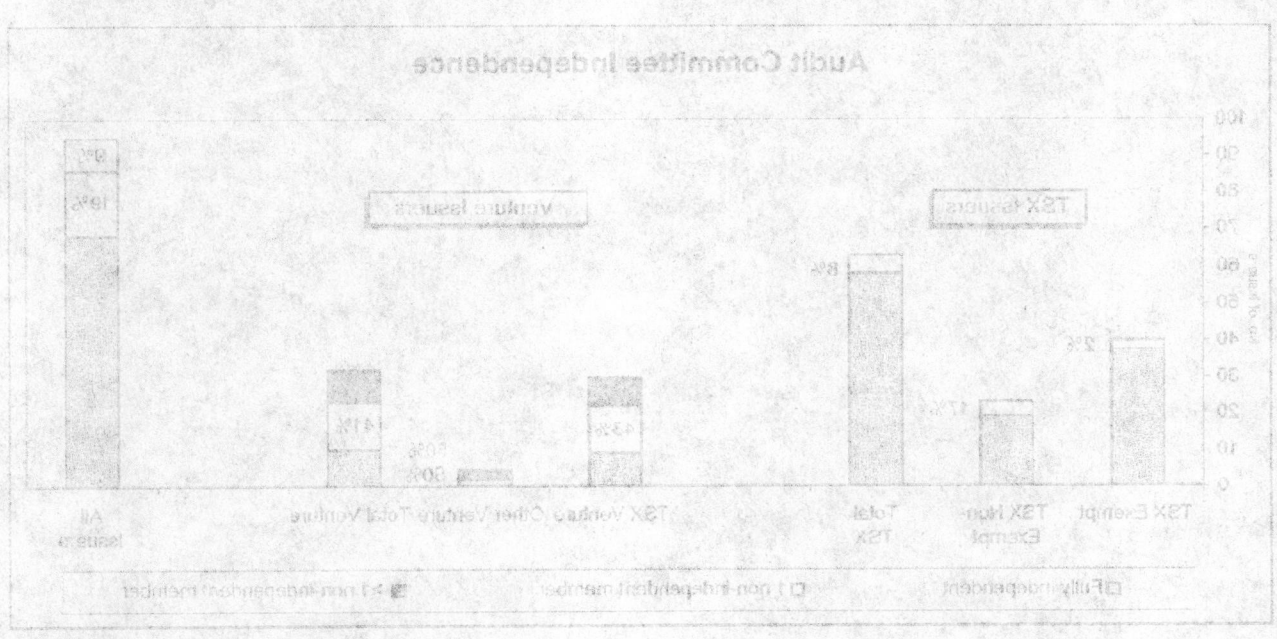

Appendix A — Audit Committee Compliance Review Summary of Compliance

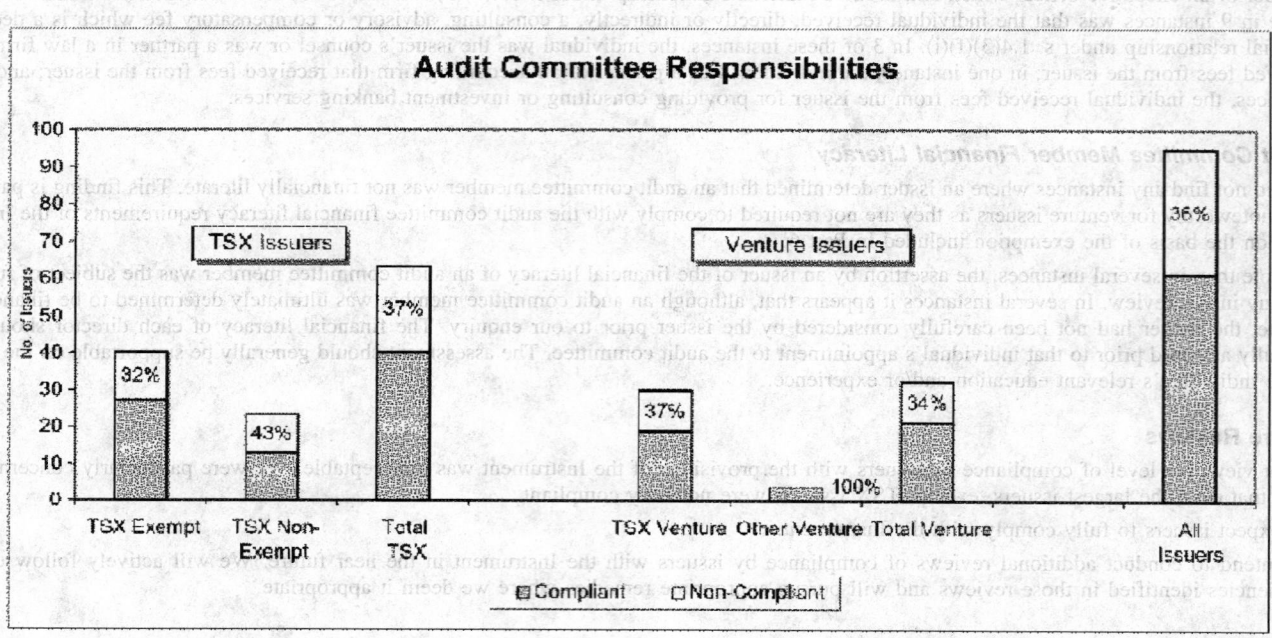

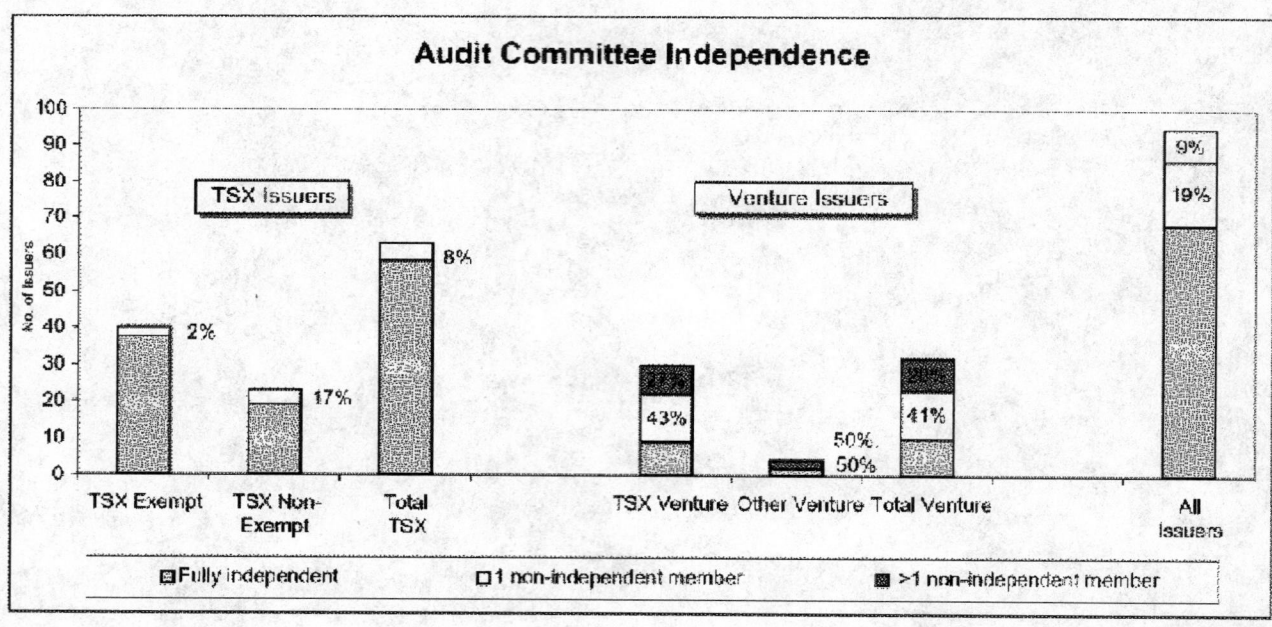

Policies and Orders: CSAN 52-318.

CSA Staff Notice 52-315 — Certification Compliance Review

Date: September 22, 2006, as amended effective December 15, 2008

29 O.S.C.B. 7556 and 31 O.S.C.B. 11971

Note: This Notice concerns an historical compliance review and contains staff guidance and references to requirements under Multilateral Instrument 52-109 (MI 52-109). MI 52-109 was repealed and replaced by National Instrument 52-109 Certification of Issuers' Annual and Interim Filings effective December 15, 2008. Issuers and certifying officers are advised to refer to National instrument 52-109 Certification of Issuers' Annual and Interim Filings and related documents for information regarding current certification requirements.

Purpose of notice

Staff of the securities regulatory authorities in British Columbia, Alberta, Manitoba, Ontario and Quebec conducted a review of compliance with the provisions of Multilateral Instrument 52-109 *Certification of Disclosure in Issuers' Annual and Interim Filings* (the Certification Instrument).

This notice outlines the results of our review and provides guidance to issuers and certifying officers in complying with the certification requirements.

Certification Instrument

The Certification Instrument came into force in all CSA jurisdictions, except British Columbia and Quebec, on March 30, 2004. The Certification Instrument came into force in Quebec on June 30, 2005 and in British Columbia on September 19, 2005.

With limited exceptions, the Certification Instrument applies to all reporting issuers other than investment funds.[1]

Under the Certification Instrument, issuers are required to file certificates for financial years and interim periods beginning on or after January 1, 2004.[2] Issuers must file a separate certificate for each person who, at the time of filing the certificate, is a chief executive officer or a chief financial officer, or in the case of an issuer that does not have a chief executive officer or chief financial officer, performs similar functions to a chief executive officer or chief financial officer (each a certifying officer).[3]

The form of annual certificate is Form 52-109F1 (the full annual certificate). However, the Certification Instrument permits issuers to file:

- annual certificates in Form 52-109FT1 (the bare annual certificate) for financial years ending on or before March 30, 2005; and

- annual certificates in Form 52-109F1 with the certifications regarding internal control over financial reporting deleted (the modified annual certificate) for financial years ending on or before June 29, 2006.[4]

The form of interim certificate is Form 52-109F2. However, during certain transition periods, the Certification Instrument permits issuers to file interim certificates in Form 52-109FT2 or Form 52-109F2 with the certifications regarding internal control over financial reporting deleted.[5]

Review program

We selected a sample of 286 issuers from across the country. This sample included:

- 229 issuers (together the TSX Issuers) listed on the Toronto Stock Exchange (the TSX);

- 52 issuers (together the Venture Issuers) listed on the TSX Venture Exchange; and

- 5 issuers (together the CNQ Issuers) listed on the Canadian Trading and Quotation System Inc.

We reviewed the annual certificates of the issuers in our sample for the most recently completed financial year. Our review focused on the following two aspects of compliance with the Certification Instrument:

- whether the issuer filed the correct form of certificate, which in all cases was either the modified annual certificate or the full annual certificate;[6] and

- whether the issuer's annual MD&A contained disclosure regarding the certifying officers' conclusions about the effectiveness of disclosure controls and procedures, as represented in the modified annual certificate and the full annual certificate.[7]

Results of the review

The results of the review are summarized below:

---

[1]See section 1.2 and Part 4 of the Certification Instrument.

[2]See sections 2.1, 3.1 and 5.2 of the Certification Instrument.

[3]See sections 2.1 and 3.1 of the Certification Instrument.

[4]See sections 2.1 and 5.2 of the Certification Instrument.

[5]See sections 3.1 and 5.2 of the Certification Instrument.

[6]See sections 2.1 and 5.2 of the Certification Instrument.

[7]See paragraph 4(c) of the full annual certificate and the modified annual certificate.

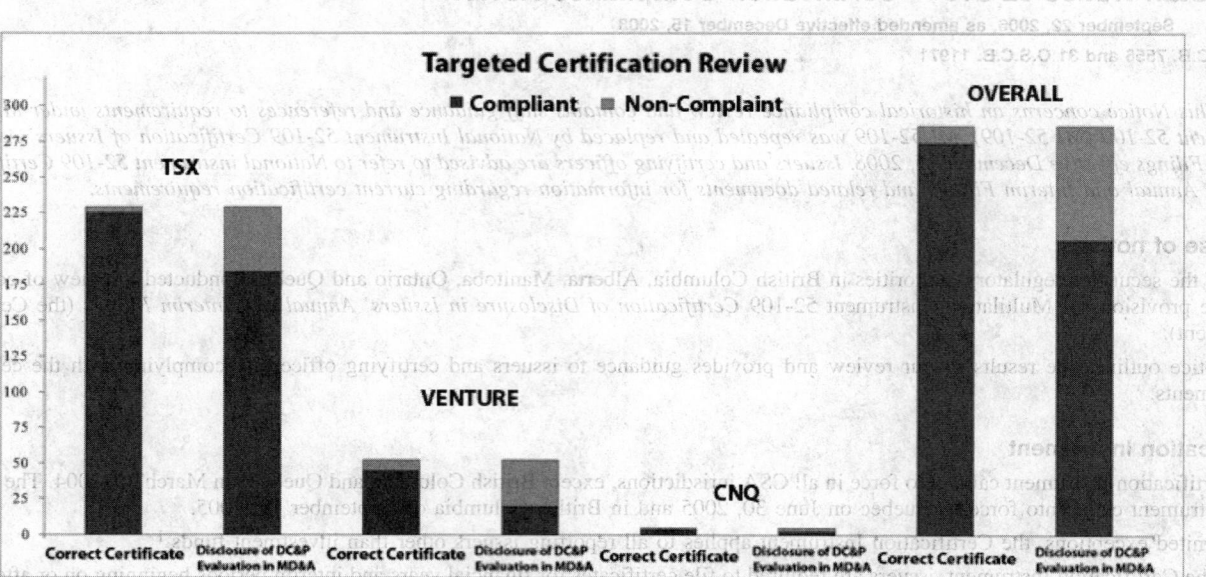

Overall, 96% of issuers in our sample filed the correct form of certificate. However, 4% of issuers filed bare annual certificates when modified annual certificates or full annual certificates were required. Most of the issuers that filed the incorrect form of certificate were either Venture Issuers, of which 87% filed the correct form of certificate, or CNQ Issuers, of which 80% filed the correct form of certificate. In contrast, 98% of the TSX Issuers filed the correct form of certificate.

Overall, 72% of issuers in our sample included disclosure in their annual MD&A regarding the certifying officers' conclusions about the effectiveness of disclosure controls and procedures. This included 80% of the TSX Issuers, 38% of the Venture Issuers and 40% of the CNQ Issuers. Approximately 28% of issuers in our sample, however, failed to include this disclosure in their annual MD&A. This widespread non-compliance with such a clear and basic requirement shows that many issuers are not paying adequate attention to their disclosure obligations. We are particularly concerned by the failure to include the disclosure regarding disclosure controls and procedures in the annual MD&A given that, in most cases, the certifying officers specifically represented in their certificates that they had caused the issuer to include this disclosure in the annual MD&A.

Our response to review results

Although most of the issuers in our sample appeared to comply with the certification requirements, there was a significant percentage of issuers that did not comply. This shows that many issuers need to pay greater attention to their obligations under the Certification Instrument.

We will actively follow up on the deficiencies identified during our review and will take action where we decide it is appropriate.

We will conduct additional reviews of compliance by issuers with the Certification Instrument as part of our ongoing continuous disclosure review program. Issuers and certifying officers should review their certificates and annual MD&A, both those that have been filed and those that are to be filed, to ensure that they comply with the requirements of the Certification Instrument.

Reminders for issuers and certifying officers

Issuers and certifying officers should note the following:

- *Correct form of certificates:* Issuers and certifying officers may refer to CSA Staff Notice 52-311 *Regarding the Required Forms of Certificates under Multilateral Instrument 52-109 Certification of Disclosure in Issuers' Annual and Interim Filings* dated December 16, 2005 for guidance on the correct forms of certificates. The notice is on various CSA websites, including the Ontario Securities Commission's website at the following link: http://www.osc.gov.on.ca/Regulation/Rulemaking/Current/Part5/csa_20051216_52-311_not-reg-req-forms.jsp

  The transition period in section 5.2 of the Certification Instrument for annual certificates is now over. Issuers and certifying officers should note that the required form of certificate for financial years ending on or after June 30, 2006 is the full annual certificate, which includes the certifications regarding internal control over financial reporting.

- *Date of certificates:* Certifying officers must certify that they have reviewed their issuer's financial statements, MD&A and AIF, if applicable (each a CD document).[8] As a result, certificates should not be dated earlier than the date of those CD documents. Certificates should be dated the date that they are filed.

---

[8]See paragraph 2 of the full annual certificate and the modified annual certificate

- *AIFs voluntarily filed by venture issuers:* If a venture issuer voluntarily files an AIF for a financial year after the issuer has filed its annual financial statements, annual MD&A and annual certificates for that financial year, it must file new annual certificates for that financial year separately but concurrently with the filing of its AIF.[9]

- *Disclosure in the issuer's annual MD&A:* Instruction to Item 1.15 of Form 51-102F1 *Management's Discussion & Analysis* states that "Your company may also be required to provide additional disclosure in its MD&A as set out in Form 52-109F1 *Certification of Annual Filings* and Form 52-109F2 *Certification of Interim Filings*". In the modified annual certificate, certifying officers are required to certify that they have evaluated the effectiveness of the issuer's disclosure controls and procedures as of the end of the period covered by the annual filings and *have caused the issuer to disclose in the annual MD&A* their conclusions about the effectiveness of the disclosure controls and procedures as of the end of the period covered by the annual filings based on such evaluation. Issuers and certifying officers should ensure that their conclusions about the effectiveness of disclosure controls and procedures are *in fact* disclosed in the annual MD&A.

- *Refiled continuous disclosure documents:* An issuer may refile a CD document for a financial period. If the original CD document was required to be certified, then the revised CD document should be certified under the same form of certificate that was required to be filed for the original CD document. As a result, the issuer must file new certificates for that financial period separately but concurrently with the filing of the revised CD document.[10]

CSA Staff Notice 52-318 — Audit Committee Follow-up Compliance Review

Date: June 29, 2007

30 O.S.C.B. 5823

Part 5: ONGOING REQUIREMENTS

As announced in CSA Staff Notice 52-312 that was published on January 13, 2006, staff of the securities regulatory authorities in Alberta, Saskatchewan, Manitoba, Ontario and Québec (the participating jurisdictions) conducted a follow-up review of compliance with the provisions of Multilateral Instrument 52-110 *Audit Committees* (the Instrument). The follow-up review was necessitated by the inadequate level of compliance with the Instrument that was communicated in CSA Staff Notice 52-312. This notice outlines the results of our follow-up review.

The Instrument

The Instrument came into force on March 30, 2004 in every jurisdiction in Canada except British Columbia and Québec. In Québec, it came into force on June 30, 2005. The Instrument applies to all reporting issuers with limited exceptions.

The Instrument prescribes three broad sets of requirements:

- all members of the audit committee must be independent and financially literate (venture issuers, as that term is defined in the Instrument, are exempt from these requirements);

- an audit committee must have all of the responsibilities prescribed by the Instrument which should be set out in its charter; and

- a reporting issuer must include certain disclosure in its AIF, management information circular or MD&A.

The Review Program

We selected a sample of 25 issuers for review where a participating jurisdiction was the issuer's principal regulator. Our selection criteria included the size of the issuer's market capitalization, its industry sector, and its listing status. Our sample included 15 TSX listed issuers (TSX issuers) and 10 venture issuers.

Our review focused on each issuer's compliance with the Instrument's requirements related to audit committee composition and responsibilities. In conducting our review, we examined:

- the responsibilities of the audit committee;

- all direct or indirect relationships that each audit committee member had with the issuer;

- the basis upon which each audit committee member was determined to be independent or non-independent;

- the relevant education and experience of each audit committee member;

- the basis upon which each audit committee member was determined to be financially literate; and

- any exemptions that the issuer relied on in connection with the independence or financial literacy of an audit committee member.

Results

Audit Committee Responsibilities

Overall, the audit committees of 18 issuers (72% of issuers reviewed) had all of the responsibilities prescribed by the Instrument. This included 10 TSX issuers (67% of TSX issuers reviewed) and 8 venture issuers (80% of venture issuers reviewed).

---

[9]See section 2.2 of the Certification Instrument.

[10]See section 2.2 of the Certification Instrument.

Our review identified several instances where an issuer's audit committee was not assigned one or more of the responsibilities prescribed by the Instrument. The non-compliance related to a range of different responsibilities as set out below:

Responsibility	Section Number in Instrument	Number of Instances of Non-Compliance
Oversee work of external auditor	s. 2.3(3)	6
Review and approve issuer's hiring policies for partners and employees of issuer's current and former external auditors	s. 2.3(8)	4
Pre-approve non-audit services to be provided by external auditor	s. 2.3(4)	3
Establish procedures for handling complaints and employee concerns regarding accounting or auditing matters	s. 2.3(7)	3
Review issuer's financial statements, MD&A and annual and interim earnings press releases prior to their release	s. 2.3(5)	2
Recommend to board the external auditor to be nominated and their compensation	s. 2.3(2)	1

For each of the seven issuers where we identified instances of non-compliance, we accepted an undertaking from the issuer to address the deficiencies within a specified period of time prior to its next annual meeting.

Audit Committee Member Independence

All of the TSX issuers reviewed had audit committees comprised solely of independent directors.

While venture issuers are not required to comply with the audit committee independence requirements of the Instrument on the basis of the exemption included in Part 6, six venture issuers (60% of venture issuers reviewed) had audit committees comprised solely of independent directors.

Each of the four venture issuers that did not have fully independent audit committees had one member who was not independent. In each instance, the member was an employee or executive officer of the issuer which is a deemed material relationship under s. 1.4(3)(a). In two of those instances the individual was the issuer's president and CEO, in one instance the individual was the issuer's CFO, and in one instance the individual was an employee of the issuer.

Audit Committee Member Financial Literacy

We did not find any instances where an issuer determined that an audit committee member was not financially literate. This finding is particularly noteworthy for venture issuers as they are not required to comply with the audit committee financial literacy requirements of the Instrument on the basis of the exemption included in Part 6.

In a few instances, however, the assertion by an issuer of the financial literacy of an audit committee member was the subject of further scrutiny in our review. In these instances, we found that, although an audit committee member was ultimately determined to be financially literate, the matter had not been carefully considered by the issuer prior to our enquiry.

Issuers are reminded that the financial literacy of each director should be carefully assessed prior to that individual's appointment to the audit committee. The assessment should generally be supportable on the basis of the individual's relevant education and/or experience.

Future Reviews

All of the TSX issuers reviewed complied with the Instrument's audit committee composition requirements. However, we are concerned about the number of instances identified in our review where the audit committees of both TSX issuers and venture issuers were not assigned all of the responsibilities prescribed by the Instrument. We therefore intend to review issuers' compliance with the Instrument selectively as part of our ongoing continuous disclosure review program.

CSA Staff Notice 52-320 — Disclosure of Expected Changes in Accounting Policies Relating to Changeover to International Financial Reporting Standards

Date: May 9, 2008

31 O.S.C.B. 4744

Purpose

This notice provides guidance to an issuer on disclosure of expected changes in accounting policies relating to an issuer's changeover to International Financial Reporting Standards (IFRS) as the basis for preparing its financial statements. This guidance applies to disclosure relating to each financial reporting period in the three years before the first year for which an issuer prepares its financial statements in accordance with IFRS.

Background

The Canadian Accounting Standards Board recently confirmed January 1, 2011 as the date IFRS will replace current Canadian standards and interpretations as Canadian generally accepted accounting principles (Canadian GAAP) for publicly accountable enterprises (which include investment funds and other reporting issuers). As discussed in CSA Concept Paper 52-402 *Possible changes to securities rules relating to International Financial Reporting Standards*, the Canadian Securities Administrators (the CSA) is considering allowing domestic issuers to adopt IFRS at an earlier date.

Changing from current Canadian GAAP to IFRS will be a significant undertaking that may materially affect an issuer's reported financial position and results of operations. It may also affect certain business functions. Investors and other market participants will need timely and meaningful information about these matters during the reporting periods leading up to an issuer's changeover to IFRS.

Disclosure of changeover to IFRS by issuers other than investment funds

Form 51-102F1 *Management's Discussion & Analysis* (the MD&A form or 51-102F1) requires an issuer to discuss and analyze any changes in the issuer's accounting policies that the issuer has adopted or expects to adopt subsequent to the end of its most recently completed financial year, including changes due to a new accounting standard that the issuer does not have to adopt until a future date. Changes in an issuer's accounting policies that an issuer expects to make on changeover to IFRS are changes due to new accounting standards and therefore fall within the scope of section 1.13(a) of the MD&A form. That section specifies that the discussion and analysis should include:

- a description of the new accounting standard,

- disclosure of methods of adoption permitted and the method the issuer expects to use,

- discussion of expected effects on the issuer's financial statements, and

- potential effects on the issuer's business.

The MD&A form requirements apply to annual and interim MD&A filed by a reporting issuer in compliance with National Instrument 51-102 *Continuous Disclosure Obligations* as well as MD&A in the form of 51-102F1 that is included in a prospectus filed in compliance with Form 41-101F1 *Information Required in a Prospectus*.

CSA staff recognize that an issuer will likely be able to provide only limited information on the topics specified in section 1.13(a) in its MD&A three and two years before the first day of an issuer's financial year for which financial statements are prepared in accordance with IFRS (issuer's changeover date). An issuer will generally be able to provide more detailed information about the expected effects of IFRS on its specific circumstances in its MD&A for interim and annual periods of the year before the issuer's changeover date. As an issuer moves closer to its changeover date, the issuer should consider how it might make available meaningful quantified information to allow investors to understand the impact of IFRS on the issuer's financial statements. The following sections describe this incremental approach to disclosure for the reporting periods prior to adoption of IFRS.

This guidance applies to an issuer whose changeover date is on or after January 1, 2011. It also applies to an issuer that adopts IFRS earlier if permitted by the CSA, to the extent that the periods referred to in the guidance have not already passed.

While this notice focuses on disclosure in MD&A, we encourage an issuer to consider whether additional disclosure beyond MD&A might contribute to informing investors about how the issuer expects it will be affected by changeover to IFRS. An issuer should also consider whether requirements in securities legislation other than section 1.13 of the MD&A form might also require the issuer to disclose specific information about the broader implications of its changeover to IFRS.

Interim and annual MD&A three years before changeover to IFRS

(e.g., the interim and annual periods of the financial year ending December 31, 2008 in the case of an issuer that will change to IFRS for its financial year beginning January 1, 2011)

If at the time of preparing its MD&A for the interim periods of the financial year beginning three years before the issuer's changeover date, an issuer has developed an IFRS changeover plan, the issuer should discuss in the interim MD&A the key elements and timing of its plan. No later than in its annual MD&A for the year beginning three years before an issuer's changeover date, the issuer should discuss the status of the key elements and timing of its changeover plan. Key elements of an issuer's plan may address the impact of IFRS on:

- accounting policies, including choices among policies permitted under IFRS, and implementation decisions such as whether certain changes will be applied on a retrospective or a prospective basis,

- information technology and data systems,

- internal control over financial reporting,

- disclosure controls and procedures, including investor relations and external communications plans,

- financial reporting expertise, including training requirements, and

- business activities, such as foreign currency and hedging activities, as well as matters that may be influenced by GAAP measures such as debt covenants, capital requirements and compensation arrangements.

If at the time of preparing its MD&A for the interim and annual periods in the financial year beginning three years before an issuer's changeover date, an issuer is well advanced in its IFRS changeover project, then the issuer should discuss the impact of IFRS changeover on its financial reporting.

Interim MD&A two years before changeover to IFRS

(e.g., the interim periods of the financial year ending December 31, 2009 in the case of an issuer that will change to IFRS for its financial year beginning January 1, 2011)

An issuer should provide an update of progress on its IFRS changeover plan and any changes in its plan, in the issuer's MD&A for interim periods of the financial year beginning two years before the issuer's changeover date.

Part 5: ONGOING REQUIREMENTS

Annual MD&A two years before changeover to IFRS

(e.g., the financial year ending December 31, 2009 in the case of an issuer that will change to IFRS for its financial year beginning January 1, 2011)

To comply with section 1.13 of the MD&A form, an issuer should discuss in its MD&A for the financial year beginning two years before an issuer's changeover date, the issuer's preparations for changeover to IFRS. Relevant details include those discussed in the preceding two sections. In addition, an issuer should describe the major identified differences between the issuer's current accounting policies and those the issuer is required or expects to apply in preparing IFRS financial statements. Such differences include any difference due to an expected change in accounting policy even though the issuer's existing policy under Canadian GAAP is permissible under IFRS. While such information may be narrative only at this stage, it should enable an investor to understand the key elements of the issuer's financial statements that will be affected by the changeover to IFRS. In identifying the accounting policies that an issuer is required or expects to apply under IFRS, an issuer should consider IFRS as they exist at the date the issuer prepares its MD&A. When an issuer believes it is also appropriate to consider the potential impact of projects that the International Accounting Standards Board currently has in process in identifying the accounting policies the issuer expects to apply on initial adoption of IFRS, the issuer should disclose any assumptions made about future changes to IFRS.

Annual and Interim MD&A for the year before changeover to IFRS

(e.g., the interim and annual periods of the financial year ending December 31, 2010 in the case of an issuer that will change to IFRS for its financial year beginning January 1, 2011)

To comply with section 1.13 of the MD&A form, an issuer should provide an updated discussion of the issuer's preparations for changeover to IFRS in its annual and interim MD&A for the financial year beginning one year before an issuer's changeover date. Relevant details include those discussed in the preceding sections. By this time, an issuer will generally be able to discuss in more detail the key decisions and changes the issuer has made, or will have to make, relating to the changeover to IFRS. The issuer's discussion of changes relating to accounting policies should include decisions about accounting policy choices available under IFRS 1 *First-time Adoption of International Financial Reporting Standards* and other individual IFRS standards that are relevant to the issuer.

IFRS 1 requires disclosure of comparative and reconciliation information in the interim and annual financial statements of the year beginning on an issuer's changeover date. To comply with this requirement, an issuer will need to prepare quantified information about the impact of IFRS on each line item presented in the financial statements for the interim and annual periods of the year preceding changeover (e.g., for the year ending December 31, 2010 in the case of an issuer that will change to IFRS for the financial year beginning January 1, 2011). If an issuer has quantified information about the impact of IFRS on the key line items in the issuer's financial statements available when it prepares its interim and annual MD&A for the financial year beginning one year before an issuer's changeover date, an issuer should include this information in its MD&A.

Disclosure of changeover to IFRS by investment funds

An investment fund that is a reporting issuer is required under item 2.4 of Form 81-106F1 *Contents of Annual and Interim Management Report of Fund Performance* (MRFP) to discuss developments affecting the investment fund. As well, section 2.1(2) of Companion Policy 81-106 *Investment Fund Continuous Disclosure* discusses disclosure in an investment fund's financial statements and indicates that an investment fund should include information necessary to ensure disclosure of all material information concerning the financial position and results of the investment fund. An investment fund should discuss the changeover to IFRS for each fund or fund family in either the MRFP or the notes to the financial statements.

In the annual and interim filings three, two and one year(s) before changeover, as appropriate, an investment fund should disclose relevant information about its changeover to IFRS, including:

- the key elements and timing of its changeover plan,

- impact on business arrangements,

- impact, if any, on net asset value per unit,

- accounting policy and implementation decisions the fund will have to make,

- major differences the fund has identified between its current accounting policies and those it expects to apply under IFRS, and

- progress made on the fund's changeover plan.

In the year before changeover, disclosure should include quantitative impact of the changeover to IFRS. Consistent with Instructions for the MRFP, disclosure should be clear and concise, focusing on specific material information, risks and uncertainties to enable readers to better assess the impact on the investment fund.

Policies and Orders: CSAN 52-321, 52-324, 52-326; OSCN 52-718.

CSA Staff Notice 52-321 — Early Adoption of International Financial Reporting Standards, Use of US GAAP and Reference to IFRS-IASB

Date: **June 27, 2008**

31 O.S.C.B. 6453

Purpose

This notice updates the market on CSA staff's views on the issues addressed in CSA Concept Paper 52-402 *Possible changes to securities rules relating to International Financial Reporting Standards* (the concept paper), published on February 13, 2008, namely:

- use of International Financial Reporting Standards (IFRS) by a domestic issuer[1] before January 1, 2011,

- use of US generally accepted accounting principles (US GAAP) by a domestic issuer that is an SEC issuer, and

- reference to IFRS as issued by the International Accounting Standards Board (IFRS-IASB) instead of Canadian generally accepted accounting principles (Canadian GAAP).

Background

We have reviewed the 42 comment letters and other feedback received in response to the concept paper. Based on that input, staff have further developed their views on the three issues addressed in the paper.

Early adoption of IFRS

Staff recognize that some issuers might want to prepare their financial statements in accordance with IFRS for periods beginning prior to January 1, 2011, the mandatory date for changeover to IFRS for Canadian publicly accountable enterprises[2]. Staff are prepared to recommend exemptive relief on a case by case basis to permit a domestic issuer to prepare its financial statements in accordance with IFRS-IASB for financial periods beginning before January 1, 2011.

We expect an issuer contemplating the possibility of adopting IFRS before 2011 would carefully assess the readiness of its staff, board of directors, audit committee, auditors, investors and other market participants to deal with the change. An issuer should also consider the implications of adopting IFRS before 2011 on its obligations under securities legislation including those relating to CEO and CFO certifications, business acquisition reports, offering documents, and previously released material forward-looking information.

A domestic issuer may have previously filed financial statements prepared in accordance with Canadian GAAP or US GAAP for interim periods in the first year that the issuer proposes to adopt IFRS. In such cases, staff will recommend as a condition of the exemptive relief that the issuer file revised interim financial statements prepared in accordance with IFRS-IASB, revised interim management discussion and analysis, and new interim certificates.

Domestic issuers' use of US GAAP

Staff propose retaining the existing option in NI 52-107 for a domestic issuer that is also an SEC issuer to use US GAAP.

Reference to IFRS-IASB instead of Canadian GAAP

Staff have concluded that it is preferable for securities rules to require a domestic issuer to prepare its financial statements in accordance with IFRS-IASB after the mandatory changeover date, rather than Canadian GAAP, and require an audit report on such annual financial statements to refer to IFRS-IASB. However, we continue to consider issues relating to the availability of an appropriate French translation of IFRS and reference to both IFRS-IASB and Canadian GAAP.

Policies and Orders: CSAN 52-320, 52-324.

CSA Staff Notice 52-323 — Coming into Force of National Instrument 52-109 *Certification of Disclosure in Issuers' Annual and Interim Filings* and Consequential Policy Amendments

Date: November 28, 2008

31 O.S.C.B. 11350

[Not reproduced]

CSA Staff Notice 52-324 — Issues relating to changeover to International Financial Reporting Standards

Date: May 21, 2009

Citation: 32 O.S.C.B. 4157

---

[1] The term "domestic issuer" in this notice refers to a reporting issuer that is not a "foreign issuer" as defined in NI 52-107. Most domestic issuers are incorporated or organized in a Canadian jurisdiction. Depending on its circumstances, an issuer incorporated or organized in a foreign jurisdiction may not meet the definition of "foreign issuer" and would therefore be considered a "domestic issuer."

[2] Following a period of public consultation, the Canadian Accounting Standards Board (AcSB) has adopted a strategic plan to move financial reporting for Canadian publicly accountable enterprises to IFRS as issued by the IASB. The AcSB recently confirmed January 1, 2011 as the changeover date; publicly accountable enterprises will be required to prepare their financial statements in accordance with IFRS for interim and annual financial statements relating to fiscal years beginning on or after January 1, 2011.

Purpose

The Canadian Accounting Standards Board (AcSB) has confirmed that Canadian generally accepted accounting principles (Canadian GAAP) for publicly accountable enterprises will be replaced by International Financial Reporting Standards (IFRS) for fiscal years beginning on or after January 1, 2011.

This notice is an update on issues related to the changeover to IFRS in Canada, including:

- use of IFRS by a domestic issuer[1] for periods beginning prior to January 1, 2011,

- requirements for interim financial statements in the year of IFRS adoption, and

- reference to IFRS and Canadian GAAP.

Exemptive relief for early adoption of IFRS

Domestic issuers may apply for exemptive relief to prepare their financial statements in accordance with IFRS as issued by the International Accounting Standards Board (IASB) for financial periods beginning before January 1, 2011.

As outlined in our June 2008 notice,[2] staff of the Canadian Securities Administrators (CSA staff or we) are prepared to recommend exemptive relief on a case-by-case basis. If a domestic issuer previously filed financial statements for interim periods in the first year that the issuer proposed to adopt IFRS, we will recommend as a condition of the exemptive relief that the issuer file revised interim financial statements prepared in accordance with IFRS, revised interim management discussion and analysis, and new interim certificates. Several exemption orders for early adoption of IFRS have been issued with this condition.

On March 12, 2009,[3] the AcSB published "Adopting IFRSs in Canada, II", which provides further details of the AcSB's strategy to incorporate IFRS into the CICA Handbook — Accounting (Handbook) as Canadian GAAP. In its proposal, the AcSB has stated that it expects to incorporate IFRS into the Handbook in the second half of 2009.

In its proposal, the AcSB states that IFRS as incorporated into the Handbook are effective for publicly accountable enterprises for interim and annual financial statements relating to financial years beginning on or after January 1, 2011 (the mandatory effective date). The proposal also indicates that an entity may choose to adopt IFRS as incorporated into the Handbook before the mandatory effective date but that an entity choosing this option does not have to apply the standards to interim financial statements in the year of adoption, unless required to do so by another authoritative body.

Securities legislation refers to Canadian GAAP as applicable to public enterprises. It defines Canadian GAAP as generally accepted accounting principles determined with reference to the Handbook. Once the AcSB incorporates IFRS into the Handbook, the Handbook will contain two versions of Canadian GAAP for publicly accountable enterprises:

- IFRS (proposed "Part I" of the Handbook), and

- the standards constituting Canadian GAAP before the mandatory effective date (proposed "Part IV" of the Handbook).

Prior to the mandatory effective date, CSA staff consider the standards in proposed Part IV of the Handbook to be Canadian GAAP as applicable to public enterprises for securities legislation purposes. Therefore, a domestic issuer that wants to use IFRS for periods beginning prior to January 1, 2011 must apply for exemptive relief from the requirement to prepare its financial statements in accordance with Canadian GAAP as applicable to public enterprises. We will use the same approach to these applications as discussed above.

Issuers that are considering early adoption of IFRS should carefully assess the readiness of their staff, board of directors, audit committee, auditors, investors and other market participants to deal with the change. Issuers should also consider how early adoption would affect their obligations under securities legislation, including those relating to certifications, business acquisition reports, offering documents, and previously released material forward-looking information.

Interim financial statements in the year of IFRS adoption

We propose to require an issuer to disclose compliance with International Accounting Standard 34 *Interim Financial Reporting*[4] in its interim financial statements. The first time a domestic issuer would have to comply with this requirement would be in its first interim financial statements in its financial year beginning on or after January 1, 2011.

We also propose to require a domestic issuer to include a balance sheet that complies with IFRS as at the issuer's "transition date" in its first interim financial statements in the first financial year that the issuer adopts IFRS. An issuer's transition date is the beginning of the earliest comparative period presented in the financial statements. For example, an issuer with a calendar year end will have a transition date of January 1, 2010.

We think that the transition date balance sheet will assist users of an issuer's interim financial statements in understanding the impact of changeover to IFRS. The transition date balance sheet would be subject to the existing requirements in securities legislation relating to auditor

---

[1]The term "domestic issuer" in this notice refers to a reporting issuer that is not a "foreign issuer" as defined in NI 52-107. Most domestic issuers are incorporated or organized in a Canadian jurisdiction. Depending on its circumstances, an issuer incorporated or organized in a foreign jurisdiction may not meet the definition of "foreign issuer" and would therefore be considered a "domestic issuer."

[2]See CSA Staff Notice 52-321 *Early adoption of International Financial Reporting Standards, use of US GAAP and reference to IFRS-IASB* published June 27, 2008 and CSA Concept Paper 52-402 *Possible changes to securities rules relating to International Financial Reporting Standards* published February 13, 2008

[3]The AcSB's publication "Adopting IFRSs in Canada, II" is available on the AcSB's website at http://www.acsbcanada.org

[4]This standard within IFRS prescribes the contents of, and principles for recognition and measurement for, interim financial reports.

review of interim financial statements. For example, if an auditor has not performed a review of interim financial statements required to be filed under National Instrument 51-102 *Continuous Disclosure Obligations*, the statements must be accompanied by a notice indicating that fact. A transition date balance sheet presented in an issuer's annual financial statements would be subject to the external audit required for those statements.

We propose similar requirements for interim financial statements of investment funds subject to National Instrument 81-106 *Investment Fund Continuous Disclosure*.

Reference to IFRS and Canadian GAAP

In our June 2008 notice, we stated that we prefer reference to IFRS as issued by the IASB, rather than Canadian GAAP, in both financial statements and audit reports for domestic issuers. We also indicated we would continue to consider issues relating to the availability of an appropriate French translation of IFRS and reference to both IFRS and Canadian GAAP.

We have continued to discuss these issues with AcSB staff, Canadian Auditing and Assurance Standards Board staff, Canadian Public Accountability Board staff, reporting issuers, auditors, other Canadian and foreign regulators, and other stakeholders.

Based on input from stakeholders and the AcSB's proposal, we propose to allow two options for referring to accounting principles in a domestic issuer's financial statements and accompanying auditor's reports:

- refer only to IFRS in the notes to the financial statements and in the auditor's report, or

- refer to both IFRS and Canadian GAAP in the notes to the financial statements and in the auditor's report.

To implement these two options, we propose to distinguish between the basis of preparation and disclosure requirements. We propose the following requirements for domestic issuers for annual and interim financial statements relating to financial years beginning on or after January 1, 2011:

- issuers must prepare their annual and interim financial statements in accordance with Canadian GAAP for publicly accountable enterprises,

- issuers must make an explicit and unreserved statement of compliance with IFRS[5] in the notes to their annual financial statements, and disclose compliance with International Accounting Standard 34 *Interim Financial Reporting* in their interim financial statements, and

- auditor's reports accompanying an issuer's financial statements must refer to IFRS and be in the form specified by Canadian generally accepted auditing standards for financial statements prepared in accordance with a fair presentation framework.[6]

The AcSB's proposal states that the Handbook provides IFRS in English and French. Therefore, preparers and auditors will be able to use either version to comply with the proposed requirement to prepare financial statements in accordance with Canadian GAAP for publicly accountable enterprises. The proposed requirements ensure reference to IFRS and address the continuing need for some entities to refer to Canadian GAAP to satisfy existing contractual obligations, other federal, provincial and territorial laws, regulatory rules and other statutory or regulatory requirements.

We propose a similar approach for reference to accounting principles by investment funds subject to National Instrument 81-106 *Investment Fund Continuous Disclosure*.

Relief from using the same accounting principles for all periods

We propose to provide relief from the existing requirement in securities legislation for financial statements to be prepared in accordance with the same accounting principles for all periods presented in the financial statements.[7]

If the periods for the financial information straddle a domestic issuer's adoption of IFRS, the proposed relief would allow the domestic issuer to present financial information in certain offering and continuous disclosure documents in accordance with Canadian GAAP alongside financial information prepared in accordance with IFRS.

Meeting filing deadlines

We are aware of the challenges domestic issuers will face to meet the filing deadline for their first interim financial statements beginning on or after January 1, 2011. We are exploring ways to assist issuers with these challenges, including extending the filing deadline for a domestic issuer's first interim filings for a period beginning on or after January 1, 2011.

Next steps

We expect to publish for comment details of our proposals discussed in this notice later this year.

Policies and Orders: CSAN 52-320, 52-321; OSCN 52-718.

---

[5]We propose to define IFRS in securities legislation as IFRS as issued by the IASB.

[6]The term "fair presentation framework" is described in proposed Canadian Auditing Standard 700 — "Forming an Opinion and Reporting on Financial Statements."

[7]See section 3.1 of National Instrument 52-107 *Acceptable Accounting Principles, Auditing Standards and Reporting Currency*.

CSA Staff Notice 52-325 — Certification Compliance Review

Date: **September 11, 2009**

32 O.S.C.B. 7086

Purpose

This notice outlines the results of a recent review conducted by staff of the Canadian Securities Administrators (staff or we) of compliance with the provisions of National Instrument 52-109 *Certification of Disclosure in Issuers' Annual and Interim Filings* (Certification Instrument or NI 52-109).

NI 52-109 came into force on December 15, 2008, at which time Multilateral Instrument 52-109 *Certification of Disclosure in Issuers' Annual and Interim Filings* (MI 52-109) was repealed. The purpose of the Certification Instrument is to improve the quality and reliability of reporting issuers' annual and interim disclosure. We believe that this, in turn, will help to maintain and enhance investors confidence in the integrity of our capital markets. See Appendix A of this notice for a summary of the most significant changes from MI 52-109 to NI 52-109.

Executive Summary

Of the total reporting issuers reviewed, 38% appeared to substantively comply with the requirements of NI 52-109 such that no action was required. However, of the remaining 62% of issuers reviewed, we identified some level of non-compliance with the provisions of the Certification Instrument. For 30% of reporting issuers reviewed, the filings were so deficient that the issuers were required to refile their annual MD&A and/or certificates. For 32% of the issuers reviewed, we required the issuers to make prospective changes in future filings. Staff expects that issuers' compliance with NI 52-109 will improve as issuers become more familiar with the requirements. Meanwhile, we will continue to monitor compliance with these requirements closely.

Review program

We selected a sample of 198 non-venture issuers and 53 venture issuers with a December 31, 2008 year-end.

Our review focused on the following questions:

- Did the certifying officers and issuer use the correct form of certificate for their circumstance?
- Did the issuer's annual management discussion and analysis (MD&A) include disclosure that corresponds to the representations contained in the certificates?
- Was the MD&A disclosure consistent with the guidance in the Companion Policy to NI 52-109 (52-109CP)?
- Were the annual certificates dated and filed on the correct date?
- If the issuer refiled its annual financial statements, annual MD&A or Annual Information Form (AIF), did the issuer also file Form 52-109F1R — *Certification of refiled annual filings* (Form 52-109F1R)?
- Were the annual certificates filed in the exact wording prescribed by the required form without any amendments?

Results of the review

The table below summarizes the results of the review. In some cases, issuers did not comply with more than one provision of the Certification Instrument.

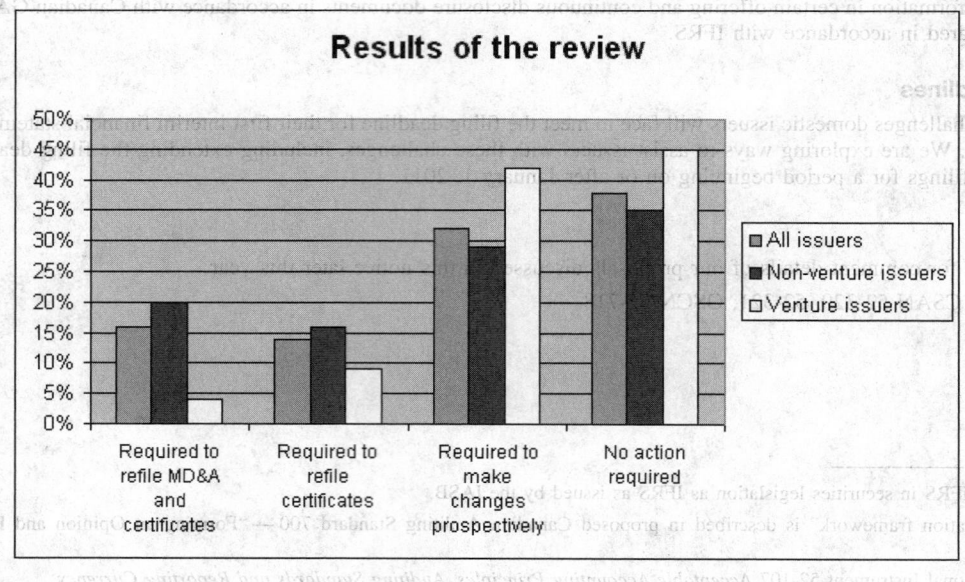

We characterized the level of non-compliance into three categories (refiling of MD&A and certificates, refiling of certificates and prospective changes) based upon the nature and severity of the deficiencies identified.

For 30% of reporting issuers reviewed, the filings were so deficient that the issuers were required to refile their annual MD&A and/or certificates. This was the situation for 36% of non-venture issuers and 13% of venture issuers reviewed. The majority of the refilings related to:

- conclusions about the effectiveness of disclosure controls and procedures (DC&P) and internal control over financial reporting (ICFR) in the annual MD&A, and

- significant amendments to the wording prescribed by the certificates.

Prospective changes were required for 32% of reporting issuers reviewed to correct some aspect of their compliance with the Certification Instrument provisions going forward. A significant number of these commitments related to:

- amendments to the wording prescribed by the certificate, and

- the use of incorrect dates.

The results of the review are described in greater detail below. We encourage certifying officers and issuers to use this notice and to thoroughly review the Certification Instrument and 52-109CP in order to fully comply with the certification requirements.

A — Refiling of MD&A and certificates

As a result of our review, we recommended that 20% of non-venture issuers and 4% of venture issuers reviewed refile their MD&A and certificates due to the following deficiencies.

Issuers did not fully disclose their conclusions about the effectiveness of DC&P and ICFR in their MD&A

In accordance with the representations in subparagraphs 6(a) and (b)(i) of Form 52-109F1 — *Certification of annual filings full certificate* (Form 52-109F1), the annual MD&A must disclose the certifying officers' conclusions about the effectiveness of the issuer's DC&P and ICFR.

Eleven percent of non-venture issuers did not disclose in their annual MD&A the certifying officers' conclusions about the effectiveness of DC&P or the ICFR. Four percent of venture issuers reviewed, that elected to file Form 52-109F1, also did not disclose these conclusions. This includes issuers that did not disclose conclusions about the effectiveness of both the design and operation of DC&P or ICFR. Guidance on evaluating operating effectiveness of DC&P and ICFR can be found in Part 7 of 52-109CP.

Issuers qualified their conclusions about the effectiveness of DC&P and/or ICFR

As discussed in Parts 9.5 and 10.1 of 52-109CP, certifying officers may not qualify their assessment by stating that the issuer's DC&P and ICFR are effective, subject to certain qualifications or exceptions, unless the qualification pertains to one of the scope limitations explicitly permitted by section 3.3 of the Certification Instrument.

Eleven percent of non-venture issuers reviewed qualified their conclusions about the effectiveness of DC&P and ICFR. While some of these issuers concluded that DC&P and ICFR were effective, they also disclosed a "weakness", "design challenge" or "deficiency," (collectively, a limitation), such as lack of segregation of duties or a lack of knowledgeable accounting staff in technically complex areas. This type of disclosure is potentially confusing to readers of the annual MD&A because it is difficult to discern if such a description constitutes a material weakness relating to ICFR or a weakness in DC&P that is significant.

If issuers elect to discuss a limitation in their annual MD&A that is not a material weakness relating to their ICFR or a weakness in DC&P that is significant, the discussion should avoid any ambiguity about the nature of the limitation. The MD&A should clearly disclose if the limitation constitutes a material weakness relating to ICFR or a weakness in DC&P that is significant. Guidance on assessing the significance of deficiencies in ICFR can be found in Part 9 of 52-109CP.

Some issuers concluded that DC&P and ICFR were effective because they had procedures for addressing the limitation. In some cases, an issuer's discussion did not clarify if a material weakness relating to ICFR or a weakness in DC&P that is significant existed after implementing the procedures. A reader could infer that although there was a material weakness relating to ICFR or a weakness in DC&P that was significant, it was fully addressed at the reporting date due to the implementation of the procedures. If the control deficiencies were fully addressed, the limitation would not exist at the financial reporting date.

Several issuers confused the concepts of "mitigating procedures" and "compensating controls". As discussed in subsection 9.1(3) of 52-109CP, a mitigating procedure may help to reduce, but does not eliminate, the financial reporting risk that the deficient ICFR component failed to address. Certifying officers and issuers should not imply that a mitigating procedure eliminates a material weakness and should not conclude that ICFR and DC&P are effective. In contrast to a mitigating procedure, a compensating control fully addresses a material weakness and allows certifying officers to conclude that ICFR and DC&P are effective. In the case of a compensating control, the material weakness relating to ICFR or the weakness in DC&P that is significant is fully addressed and there is no associated reporting obligation.

As discussed in section 6.11 of 52-109CP, the lack of segregation of duties is a significant ICFR challenge. An issuer may address this challenge through additional involvement by its audit committee or board of directors. This involvement could represent either a mitigating procedure or a compensating control, depending on the nature of procedures performed by the directors, the volume of transactions and the complexity of the business. Staff believes that the threshold is high for the additional involvement of the audit committee or board of directors to constitute a compensating control, rather than a mitigating procedure. If the issuer has implemented only a mitigating procedure, it should identify the lack of segregation of duties as a material weakness and conclude that ICFR is not effective. Further, section 10.3 of 52-109CP states that if the certifying officers identify a material weakness in the issuer's ICFR, this will almost always represent a weakness that is significant in the issuer's DC&P.

Issuers limited the scope of design of DC&P and ICFR

In accordance with section 3.3(2) of NI 52-109, an issuer that limits its scope of DC&P or ICFR design to exclude controls, policies and procedures of a proportionately consolidated entity, a variable interest entity or a business acquired not more than 365 days before the end of the financial period to which the certificates relate must disclose in its MD&A the limitation and provide summary financial information about these entities. Guidance on meaningful summary financial information is included in section 13.3 and section 14.2 of 52-109CP.

Two percent of the non-venture issuers reviewed, that relied on a scope limitation, failed to disclose in their MD&A summary financial information. In addition, one non-venture issuer did not disclose in its MD&A the fact that it had limited the scope of its design of DC&P and ICFR.

B — Refiling of certificates

Staff recommended that 16% of non-venture issuers and 9% of venture issuers reviewed refile their certificates due to the following deficiencies.

Significant amendments to the wording of the form

In accordance with sections 4.1 and 5.1 of NI 52-109, issuers are required to file the annual and interim certificates in the exact wording prescribed by the required form. This includes the form number and the form title.

Six percent of non-venture issuers reviewed made significant amendments to the wording prescribed by the required form.

The most common amendments were:

- omitting paragraphs;

- removing paragraph 5.2 on ICFR material weakness relating to design, paragraph 5.3 on limitation of scope of design and subparagraph 6(b)(ii) on ICFR material weakness relating to operation when they did not apply;

- reporting changes in ICFR for a shorter period than the issuer's interim period by inserting the incorrect date in paragraph 7, and

- adding text.

No material weakness or scope limitation

In accordance with the instruction included in the required form, the certifying officers and the issuer must insert paragraph 5.2, subparagraph 6(b)(ii) and paragraph 5.3 in the certificates only if they are applicable. If they are not applicable, they must insert "N/A".

Eleven percent of non-venture issuers reviewed:

- incorrectly referred, by the inclusion of paragraph 5.2 and/or subparagraph 6(b)(ii) in their certificates, to the existence of a material weakness relating to ICFR when one did not exist, or

- incorrectly referred, by the inclusion of paragraph 5.3 in their certificates, to a limitation in the scope of the design of DC&P and ICFR when no scope limitation was required.

Refiled financial statements, MD&A or AIF

In accordance with Part 6 of NI 51-109, if an issuer refiles its financial statements, MD&A or AIF, it must file separate certificates for the period in Form 52-109F1R for refiled annual filings or Form 52-109F2R — *Certification of refiled interim filings* for refiled interim filings.

Two percent of non-venture issuers reviewed did not refile certificates when they filed amended financial statements or MD&A.

AIF filed subsequently

In accordance with subsection 4.1(2) of NI 52-109, a reporting issuer must file its certificates on the later of the dates on which it files its AIF (if it is required to file an AIF), or files its annual financial statements and annual MD&A. A non-venture issuer that chooses to file annual certificates at the date of the filing of its annual financial statements and annual MD&A must refile the annual certificates if the AIF is subsequently filed.

In addition, if a venture issuer voluntarily files an AIF for a financial year after it has filed its annual financial statements, annual MD&A and annual certificates for the financial year, the venture issuer must file separate annual certificates on the same date that it files its AIF (Form 52-109F1-AIF — *Certification of Annual Filings in Connection with Voluntarily Filed AIF*). This is in accordance with subsection 4.1(3) of NI 52-109.

Two percent of non-venture issuers reviewed and 4% of venture issuers reviewed did not refile certificates when they filed an AIF subsequent to filing their financial statements and MD&A.

Note to reader

The note to reader is an integral part of the Form 52-109FV1 — *Certification of annual filings — venture issuer basic certificate* (Form 52-109FV1). It clarifies the responsibility of certifying officers and discloses that inherent limitations on the ability of certifying officers of a venture issuer to design and implement on a cost-effective basis DC&P and ICFR may result in additional risks to the quality, reliability, transparency and timeliness of interim and annual filings and other reports provided under securities legislation.

Five percent of venture issuers reviewed did not include the "Note to reader" in their Form 52-109FV1.

C — Prospective changes to the certificates and/or the MD&A

Twenty-nine percent of non-venture issuers and 42% of venture issuers were required to make prospective changes in the following areas.

- *Amendments to wording on forms.* Certifying officers and issuers were advised not to make any amendment to the wording prescribed by the required form even if they considered those amendments to be minor. In most of these instances, certifying officers and issuers did not include the paragraph titles, the title of the form or the form number. Some certifying officers of non-venture issuers removed "if any" after "AIF" from paragraph 1 of the annual certificates and some venture issuers removed the reference to "the AIF" in the same paragraph. None of these alterations are permitted.

- *Date in paragraph 7 of the certificates.* When certifying officers certify that the issuer disclosed in its annual MD&A any change in the issuer's ICFR that occurred during the period, they must insert the date immediately following the end of the period in respect of which the issuer made its most recent interim or annual filing, as applicable. This date would generally be October 1, 2008 for issuers with December 31, 2008 year-end. We note that many certifying officers inserted January 1, 2008.

- *Certificate date.* Some certifying officers did not date the certificates the same date that the certificates were filed. In accordance with section 7.1 of NI 52-109, a certifying officer must date a certificate filed under NI 52-109 the same date the certificate is filed.

- *Filing date of certificates.* Some issuers did not file the certificates concurrently with the filing of their AIF or financial statements and MD&A, whichever is later. Certifying officers and issuers were advised that in accordance with subsections 4.1(2) and 5.1(2) of NI 52-109, they are required to file their certificates on the later of the dates on which they file their AIF (if they are required to file an AIF) or their annual financial statements and annual MD&A. Interim certificates must be filed on the same date the interim financial statements and interim MD&A are filed.

- *Venture issuer disclosure.* Some venture issuers discussed DC&P or ICFR in the MD&A but did not include cautionary language. In accordance with section 15.3 of 52-109CP, if a venture issuer and its certifying officers file Form 52-109FV1 or Form 52-109FV2 — *Certification off interim filings — venture issuer basic certificate* and chooses to discuss the design or operation of one or more components of their ICFR and DC&P in the MD&A or other regulatory filings, they should consider disclosing in the same document that:

  (a) the venture issuer is not required to certify the design and evaluation of its DC&P and ICFR and has not completed such an evaluation, and

  (b) inherent limitations on the ability of the certifying officers to design and implement on a cost-effective basis DC&P and ICFR for the issuer may result in additional risks to the quality, reliability, transparency and timeliness of interim and annual filings and other reports provided under securities legislation.

D — No action required

No action was taken with 35% of non-venture issuers and 45% of venture issuers reviewed. In these cases, the issuer either fully complied with the Certification Instrument, or the level of non-compliance was insignificant.

Next steps

We will continue to review compliance with the Certification Instrument as part of our ongoing compliance reviews and our continuous disclosure review program. We will take action when deficiencies are identified.

Appendix A — Certification Instrument

On December 15, 2008, the Certification Instrument came into force and MI 52-109 was repealed. The most significant changes introduced by NI 52-109 are set out below.

Non-venture issuers

Full Annual Certificate

A representation has been added to this certificate to the effect that the certifying officers have evaluated, or have caused to be evaluated under their supervision, the effectiveness of the issuer's ICFR at the financial year-end and that the issuer has disclosed in its annual MD&A the certifying officers' conclusions about the effectiveness of ICFR at the financial year-end based on their evaluation.

Design of DC&P and ICFR

Non-venture issuers:

- are required to use a control framework in the design of ICFR

- may limit the scope of their design of DC&P and ICFR to exclude controls, policies and procedures of a proportionately consolidated entity or variable interest entity in which the issuer has an interest or a business that the issuer acquired not more than 365 days before the end of the financial period to which the certificate relates

- must disclose in their MD&A any scope limitation in the design of DC&P and ICFR and provide summary financial information about the proportionately consolidated entity, variable interest entity or acquired business that has been proportionately consolidated or consolidated in the issuer's financial statements

Material weakness in design or operation of ICFR

If the certifying officers of a non-venture issuer determine that a material weakness relating to either the design or operation of ICFR exists at the end of the period covered by the annual or interim filings, the issuer must disclose the following in its annual or interim MD&A:

- a description of each material weakness

- the impact of the material weakness on the issuer's financial reporting and its ICFR, and

- any plans or any actions undertaken for remediating the material weakness

Venture issuers

Venture Issuer Basic Certificate

There is a new form of certificate for venture issuers. It does not include representations relating to the establishment and maintenance of DC&P and ICFR.

CSA Staff Notice 52-326 — IFRS Transition Disclosure Review

Date: **July 23, 2010**

33 O.S.C.B. 6642

Introduction

Canadian Securities Administrators (CSA) staff conducted a review to assess the extent and quality of International Financial Reporting Standards (IFRS) transition disclosure made by issuers in 2009 annual Management's Discussion & Analysis (MD&A). We compared the IFRS transition disclosure of 196 calendar year-end issuers to the disclosure guidance provided in CSA Staff Notice 52-320 *Disclosure of Expected Changes in Accounting Policies Relating to Changeover to International Financial Reporting Standards* (SN 52-320). SN 52-320 provides guidance on the requirement in Form 51-102F1 *Management's Discussion & Analysis* (Form 51-102F1) for an issuer's disclosure of expected changes in accounting policies related to IFRS changeover for the three year period prior to financial years beginning on or after January 1, 2011 (the changeover date).

We expected issuers to have provided in their 2009 annual MD&A a progress update on their IFRS changeover plans. In addition, issuers should have described the major identified differences between their current accounting policies and those they will be required to apply, or expect to apply, in preparing their IFRS financial statements.

Based on these expectations, our review focused on the disclosure of an issuer's IFRS changeover plan and the related discussion of the accounting policy effects of IFRS on the issuer's financial reporting. Overall, we found improvement in the amount and quality of IFRS transition disclosure provided by issuers. Issuers recognized the importance of this disclosure to their stakeholders and demonstrated a willingness to provide disclosure consistent with the guidance in SN 52-320. However, we identified areas where disclosure could be improved and consequently we asked, when appropriate, that these issuers confirm future MD&A filings would contain enhanced IFRS transition disclosure.

This notice summarizes the results of our review and provides additional guidance for issuers preparing their MD&A. We did not assess an issuer's preparedness for IFRS transition. That assessment is best done by an issuer's management, board of directors and external advisors. Issuers and their directors and advisors, should take this notice into account when assessing the extent to which future MD&A disclosure meets the requirements of securities legislation and their investors' need for meaningful IFRS disclosure.

It is critical that issuers communicate the potential impact of the IFRS changeover. Investors need to be properly informed during the IFRS transition on whether reported changes in financial performance relate to the adoption of different accounting standards or relate to a change in the issuer's business. Changes in accounting policies necessitated by transition to IFRS may result in greater volatility in reported results depending upon the issuer's industry and its entity-specific circumstances.

As discussed in SN 52-320, issuers should provide detailed information about the impacts of adopting IFRS in their 2010 interim and annual filings. Staff will continue to review IFRS transition disclosure provided by issuers as part of our continuous disclosure review program.

Investor Impact

The changeover from Canadian GAAP to IFRS could have a material impact on an issuer's business functions and reported financial results. Disclosure is important to assist investors in assessing an issuer's readiness to transition to IFRS and the related impact that the adoption of IFRS may have on the entity.

The disclosure expectations outlined in SN 52-320 for 2009 annual MD&A directs issuers to provide investors with the following information:

- A status update on their IFRS changeover plan, including a detailed discussion of each of the key elements of the plan;

- A discussion of the significant differences between the issuer's current accounting policies and those the issuer is required or expects to apply in preparing IFRS financial statements;

- A description of the impact that the above noted differences may have on the issuer's reported financial statements and results; and

- Whether the transition to IFRS has, or will, result in a change to the issuer's business functions and activities.

Issuers that provide sufficient information about their conversion process and its effects prior to the changeover date will reduce the level of investor uncertainty about IFRS readiness and inform readers about the potential for volatility in future reported results. This disclosure should lead to a more stable and less disruptive transition to IFRS, which will be beneficial to both issuers and their investors.

Summary of Findings

Overall, we found an improvement in the amount and quality of IFRS transition disclosure provided by issuers in their 2009 annual MD&A compared to the prior year. Such improvement should be expected since we are closer to the changeover date and issuers generally are farther along in implementing their changeover plans and assessing the impact of accounting policy differences. A summary of our findings follows:

- 95% of issuers reviewed disclosed their IFRS changeover plan, which is a significant improvement over the prior year. We did, however, note some areas where investors would benefit from more information. In particular, issuers should have provided an in-depth discussion of all key elements which were assessed as part of their changeover plan.

- 60% of issuers described milestones and anticipated timelines associated with each of the key elements of their IFRS changeover plan. All issuers should continue to focus on enhancing disclosure in this area so that investors can readily assess whether the project is progressing in accordance with the IFRS changeover plan.

- 82% of issuers identified significant accounting policy differences between Canadian GAAP and IFRS. However, issuers could improve their discussion of accounting differences to enhance investors' understanding of the impact of adopting IFRS on the issuer. Specifically, disclosure should have linked accounting differences to various financial statement categories in the balance sheet or the income statement. Such disclosure would have provided a basis for discussing the quantified effects of IFRS conversion in future MD&A filings.

- 80% of issuers provided an update of IFRS transition information from disclosure made in 2008 annual MD&A and 2009 interim MD&A. This improvement over the prior year suggests that investors are generally being provided with information that is timely, reflecting an issuer's IFRS transition efforts.

Findings

This section discusses the results of our review in detail.

IFRS Changeover Plan

No Disclosure of a Changeover Plan

SN 52-320 states that if an issuer has developed an IFRS changeover plan, this plan should be disclosed in its MD&A. The vast majority of issuers reviewed, 95%, disclosed a changeover plan. This is a significant improvement over the prior year. For those issuers that did not provide IFRS disclosure, a reader was unable to assess whether the issuer is taking the appropriate steps to manage its transition to IFRS. If an issuer does not have a changeover plan, we generally believe this to be material information that should have been disclosed in its MD&A.

Given the short time remaining before the changeover date, we are concerned that issuers without a plan may be at greater risk of not meeting their future filing obligations. We asked issuers without a changeover plan to provide us with their assessment of how they intend to meet future reporting obligations in the absence of a comprehensive plan. Management and audit committees need to carefully consider this issue and the impact on their investors if they have not planned for IFRS transition.

If issuers continue filing financial statements using Canadian GAAP after the changeover date, the issuer's principal regulator may issue a cease trade order that will prohibit trading in securities of the issuer in accordance with the guidance in National Policy 12-203 *Cease Trade Orders for Continuous Disclosure Defaults*. Furthermore, if an issuer determines that it will not be able to prepare IFRS financial statements by the required deadlines after the changeover date, this will often be a material change that the issuer should immediately communicate to the securities marketplace by way of a news release and material change report in accordance with Part 7 of NI 51-102 *Continuous Disclosure Obligations*.

Disclosure of a Changeover Plan

As outlined in SN 52-320, discussion in the 2009 annual MD&A should have provided an update to an issuer's previously disclosed IFRS changeover plan. This includes an update on the key elements specific to the issuer's changeover plan that address the impact of IFRS and may include accounting policies, internal control over financial reporting (ICFR), disclosure controls and procedures (DC&P), financial reporting expertise, business activities, information technology systems (IT) or other elements. For the 95% of issuers that included IFRS transition disclosure in their 2009 MD&A, the chart below shows the extent to which each of the potential key elements outlined in SN 52-320 were specifically addressed.

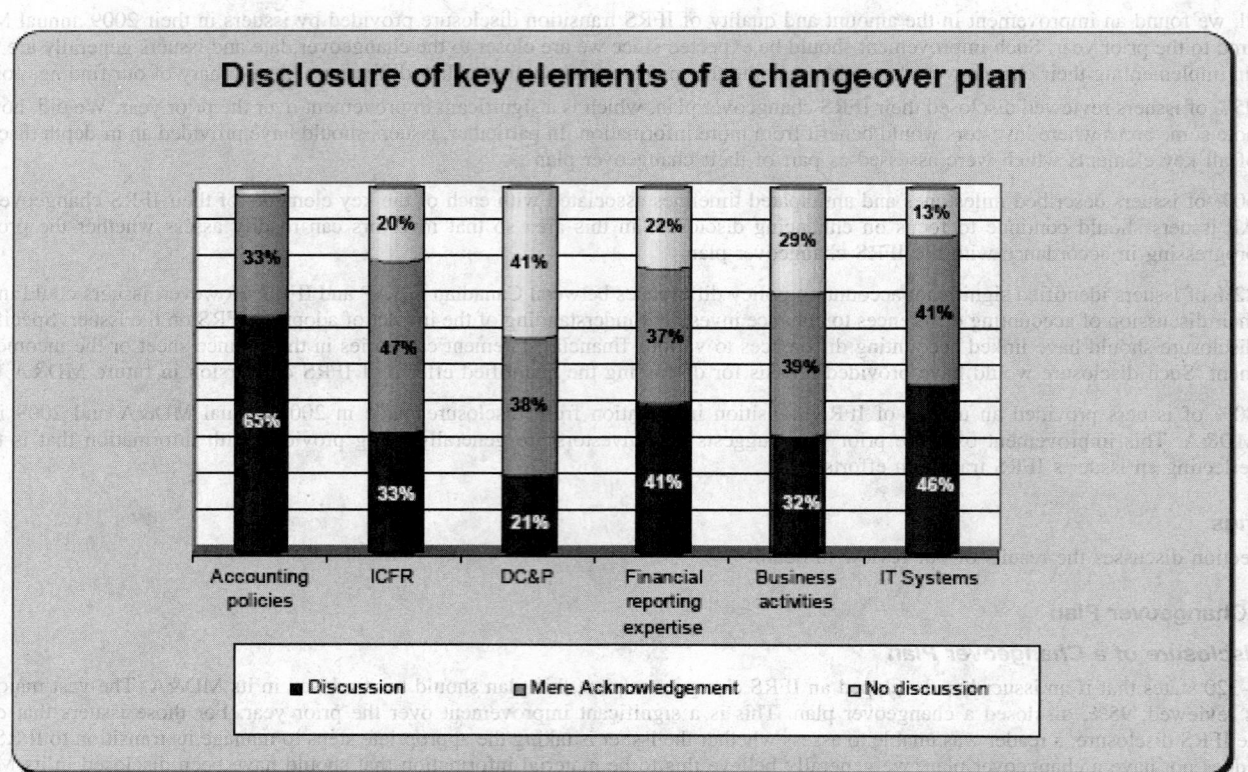

Generally, we noted improvement in the extent to which issuers discussed each of these key elements in their 2009 annual MD&A over the prior year. Many issuers provided entity-specific and comprehensive information that would be useful to investors. We did, however, note some areas where investors would benefit from more information. Specifically, we found that many issuers provided an in-depth discussion of certain key elements of their changeover plan, most commonly accounting policies and IT systems, while other key elements that were considered as part of their plan were not discussed.

In response to our comment letters, some issuers explained that they had assessed a specific element as part of their IFRS changeover plan and had determined there was no impact as a result of the changeover to IFRS. Rather than disclose the results of this assessment, issuers only discussed the elements that would likely be impacted by IFRS. A comprehensive discussion of the assessment, and related conclusion, for all key elements included in their changeover plan would have enhanced a reader's understanding of the IFRS impacts on the issuer and reduced the potential for investor uncertainty. As a result, we asked these issuers to discuss the complete results of this assessment in their next MD&A filing.

For each key element of an IFRS changeover plan discussed in MD&A, issuers should have described the significant milestones and anticipated timelines. This provides a reader with the information necessary to assess an issuer's readiness to meet the changeover to IFRS.

Our review found 60% of issuers described the significant milestones and anticipated timelines associated with each of the plan's key elements. While this represents an improvement over the prior year, issuers still need to focus on enhancing their disclosure in this area. We also noted that some issuers did not discuss conclusions reached as these milestones were completed. It is important that issuers discuss the outcomes and implications associated with the completion of key milestones so that investors can readily assess whether the project is progressing in accordance with the changeover plan.

Identified Differences between Canadian GAAP and IFRS

As outlined in SN 52-320, issuers should have described the major identified differences between the issuer's current accounting policies and those the issuer is required to apply, or expects to apply, in preparing IFRS financial statements. Such differences should have included any difference due to an expected change in accounting policy even though the issuer's existing policy under Canadian GAAP is permissible under IFRS. The discussion should have been comprehensive enough for an investor to understand the impact of these policy changes on the issuer's financial statements.

Of the issuers reviewed, 82% identified differences between the accounting policies currently applied under Canadian GAAP and those policies required, or expected, to be applied under IFRS. However, we noted improvements could be made. For example, rather than simply listing the accounting standards to be adopted upon transition, and providing a limited description of accounting policy differences between Canadian GAAP and IFRS, an issuer should have explained the full implications of these differences on the issuer's expected reporting under IFRS. The discussion should have focused on only the policy differences that would likely be material to the issuer. While we expected this information to likely only be narrative for 2009, enhanced entity-specific disclosure would have provided an investor with information about the potential impact of identified IFRS accounting policy differences on an issuer's future balance sheet, income statement and key performance metrics.

Our review identified two types of accounting differences — differences that are common across various industries and differences that are industry-specific. We discuss each of these differences in more detail below and provide examples of entity-specific disclosures that may assist issuers in preparing their MD&A. These examples form only one part of a complete IFRS transition discussion and are for illustrative purposes only. Accordingly, they may not be sufficient or appropriate for any particular issuer depending on its circumstances and the needs of its investors. Responsibility for making sufficient and appropriate disclosure and complying with applicable securities legislation remains with issuers.

Common accounting policy differences

We reviewed issuers from various industries, including biotechnology, financial services, insurance, manufacturing, mining, real estate, oil and gas, retail, services and technology and found many accounting policy differences that were common to each of these industries. For differences that are common across industries and entities, it is imperative the issuer discuss the potential entity-specific impact of these differences on its financial reporting to increase an investor's understanding of the full implications of the IFRS transition. Some of the common accounting differences disclosed by issuers included impairment of assets, revenue recognition and property, plant and equipment. An example of entity-specific disclosure for each of these accounting differences is provided below.

Impairment of assets

Under IFRS, the methods for recognizing and measuring impairment losses vary from existing Canadian GAAP. Issuers commonly identified that IFRS only requires a one-step impairment process, which may increase the amount of recognized impairment losses. In addition, unlike existing Canadian GAAP, IFRS generally permits the reversal of impairment losses if there is a change in the estimate used to determine the asset's recoverable amount.

We found an issuer's disclosure was limited to identifying these IFRS differences. More meaningful information to investors would have identified and explained that such differences in the measurement and recognition of impairment losses and reversals could lead to increased income statement volatility under IFRS. We have provided below an entity-specific example of accounting policy disclosure related to the method of calculating impairment losses under IFRS.

Entity-Specific Impairment of Assets Disclosure: Canadian GAAP generally uses a two-step approach to impairment testing: first comparing asset carrying values with undiscounted future cash flows to determine whether impairment exists, and then measuring impairment by comparing asset carrying values to their fair value (which is calculated using discounted cash flows). IAS 36 *Impairment of Assets* (IAS 36) uses a one-step approach for testing and measuring impairment, with asset carrying values compared directly with the higher of fair value less costs to sell and value in use (which uses discounted cash flows). This may potentially result in write-downs where the carrying value of assets were previously supported under Canadian GAAP on an undiscounted cash flow basis, but could not be supported on a discounted cash flow basis. This difference could lead to income statement and earnings volatility in future periods. The Company assessed the carrying value of its assets in accordance with IAS 36 and found that no impairment losses were required to be recognized as at the date of transition, January 1, 2010.

Canadian GAAP generally uses a two-step approach to impairment testing: first comparing asset carrying values with undiscounted future cash flows to determine whether impairment exists, and then measuring impairment by comparing asset carrying values to their fair value (which is calculated using discounted cash flows). IAS 36 *Impairment of Assets* (IAS 36) uses a one-step approach for testing and measuring impairment, with asset carrying values compared directly with the higher of fair value less costs to sell and value in use (which uses discounted cash flows). This may potentially result in write-downs where the carrying value of assets were previously supported under Canadian GAAP on an undiscounted cash flow basis, but could not be supported on a discounted cash flow basis. This difference could lead to income statement and earnings volatility in future periods. The Company assessed the carrying value of its assets in accordance with IAS 36 and found that no impairment losses were required to be recognized as at the date of transition, January 1, 2010.

Revenue recognition

Revenue is often the single largest item reported in an issuer's financial statements. In addition to the direct impact that it has on an issuer's bottom line, investors also place great importance on revenue when making investment decisions. Our review found issuers were generally silent on revenue recognition accounting differences. We would have expected issuers to focus on the IFRS accounting standards governing revenue recognition, including the absence of detailed standards in IFRS compared to Canadian GAAP.

Disclosure addressing the potential timing differences in revenue recognition would have provided important information to readers of the issuer's financial statements. Absent this disclosure, an investor may have difficulty interpreting a change in accounting policy versus a change in an issuer's revenue generating activities during the year of IFRS adoption. We have provided below an example of disclosure related to revenue recognition accounting policy differences specific to an entity.

Entity-Specific Revenue Recognition Disclosure:

In reviewing IAS 18 *Revenue*, we have determined that certain changes will be made in the manner in which we recognize revenue in arrangements that have multiple deliverables. In accordance with Canadian GAAP, we recognize revenue for all delivered elements in an arrangement when there is objective and reliable evidence of fair value for the undelivered elements (commonly referred to as the residual method). Under the residual method, the amount of consideration allocated to the delivered elements equals the total arrangement consideration less the fair value of the undelivered item. However, in accordance with IFRS, revenue is allocated and recognized for each separately identifiable component in a multiple deliverable arrangement. The residual method is not permitted. As a result, for certain arrangements, the amount and timing of revenue recorded for each identifiable components may differ under IFRS.

Property, plant and equipment (PP&E)

IAS 16 *Property, plant and equipment* requires separate accounting for the different components of an asset when the associated depreciation methods or rates are different. While existing Canadian GAAP also refers to componentization of PP&E, the requirements in IFRS on this issue are more explicit. IFRS also permits PP&E to be revalued to fair value at the end of each reporting period.

We found issuers generally discussed both of these differences. However, to have provided meaningful information to investors, issuers should have disclosed the effects of asset componentization on the balance sheet and depreciation expense in net income. For those issuers identifying the revaluation option as a possible alternative, disclosure would have provided the impact of the revaluation surplus amount on equity. An example of entity-specific disclosure on the effects of componentization of PP&E is provided below.

Entity-Specific Property, Plant and Equipment Disclosure:

The Company expects the carrying value of certain property, plant and equipment may decrease upon conversion to IFRS compared to the carrying value under Canadian GAAP. The decrease may result from increased depreciation expense due to asset componentization and the requirement to depreciate property, plant and equipment when the assets are available for use, rather than when the assets are put into use. Asset componentization, which may result in increased depreciation expense, involves breaking down an asset by identifying significant individual components and separately depreciating those individual components over their useful lives.

Industry specific accounting policy differences

While performing our review we also noted various industry issues. We have highlighted below some of the industry-specific issues identified in our review.

Mining

The most common accounting standard identified by issuers in the mining sector was IFRS 6 *Exploration for and Evaluation of Mineral Resources* (IFRS 6). IFRS 6 allows issuers to follow an approach similar to Canadian GAAP, and therefore, exploration and evaluation (E&E) expenditures can be either expensed or capitalized. Our review found that half of the mining issuers reviewed discussed this standard in enough detail for an investor to understand the policy choices available to the issuer under IFRS.

While we found many issuers plan to continue to apply their current accounting policy for E&E expenditure post-IFRS transition, not all issuers discussed the accounting policy they expect to adopt for these costs. Given that IFRS permits the alternative of expensing or capitalizing E&E expenditures, issuers should have had discussed their accounting policy choice, including any possible changes that this choice would likely have on its balance sheet and income statement. Alternatively, an issuer should have disclosed that it is still considering its accounting policy decision. Below is an example of entity-specific disclosure related to IFRS 6 accounting differences.

Entity-Specific Mining Disclosure:

IFRS 6, *Exploration for and Evaluation of Mineral Resources* (IFRS 6), applies to expenditures incurred on properties in the exploration and evaluation (E&E) phase. The E&E phase begins when an entity obtains the legal rights to explore a specific area and ends when the technical feasibility and commercial viability of extracting a mineral resource are demonstrable. IFRS 6 requires entities to select and consistently apply an accounting policy specifying which E&E expenditures are capitalized and which are expensed. Our project team is developing a policy that includes defining the E&E phase and accounting for E&E expenditures.

The Company expects to establish an accounting policy to expense, as incurred, all costs relating to E&E until such time as it is determined that a property has economically recoverable reserves. On adoption of IFRS, the carrying value of the unproven properties will be reduced to zero (at the transition date), with a corresponding adjustment to accumulated deficit. All subsequent E&E expenditure will be expensed as incurred until such time as it has been determined that a property has economically recoverable reserves.

Oil & Gas

Most oil and gas issuers currently apply full cost accounting under Canadian GAAP. Full cost accounting allows an issuer to capitalize costs incurred to locate, acquire and develop reserves for multiple projects in a cost centre which may be a large geographical area. IFRS 6 limits this type of accounting to exploration and evaluation activities only. Costs incurred for all other activities must be accounted for on a successful efforts or comparable basis. Many issuers currently applying full cost accounting disclosed that they will have to revise their accounting policy for the recognition of these costs and assess the appropriateness of their current depletion policies. Issuers should also have described the potential impact on the key balance sheet and income statement areas that are expected to be affected as a result.

Some issuers also discussed the IFRS 1 *First-time Adoption of International Financial Reporting Standards* (IFRS 1) exemptions that were applicable. An entity that currently uses full cost accounting can elect to measure E&E assets at the amount determined under Canadian GAAP and to measure oil and natural gas assets in the development or production phases by allocating the amount determined under the Canadian GAAP to the underlying assets pro rata using reserve volumes or reserve values as of the date of adoption. This is a significant exemption that many oil and gas issuers expect to adopt, therefore, disclosure of this fact was expected. An example of an oil and gas issuer's PP&E disclosure is provided below.

Entity-Specific Oil and Gas Disclosure for PP&E:

Under Canadian GAAP, the Company follows the CICA's guidance on full cost accounting, while IFRS has no equivalent guideline. Under GAAP, the Company accounts for its petroleum and natural gas properties whereby all costs directly associated with the exploration and development of natural gas reserves are capitalized. Upon transition to IFRS, the Company will be required to adopt new accounting policies to account for certain of these expenditures.

According to IFRS 6, *Exploration for and Evaluation of Mineral Resources* (IFRS 6), pre-exploration costs must be expensed in the period incurred. Currently, the Company capitalizes and depletes pre-exploration costs; however, these costs have been insignificant for the Company in the past, therefore, this difference is not expected to be material.

IFRS 6 defines exploration and evaluation (E&E) expenditures under IFRS and states that, upon transition, the Company will need to reclassify all E&E expenditures that are currently included in PP&E on the balance sheet as E&E assets. Under IFRS, the Company will have the option to initially capitalize these costs as E&E assets on the balance sheet or expense them in the period incurred. The Company has not concluded at this time the preferred accounting policy for E&E assets.

Under IFRS, the Company will continue to capitalize development and production costs in PP&E on the balance sheet. However, the depletion basis for these costs will likely change from a country cost centre to a smaller unit of measure. The Company has not finalized the inputs to be utilized in the unit-of-production depletion calculation. Under GAAP, the Company calculates depletion expense using the unit-of-production method based on estimated proved natural gas reserves. The Company can comply with IFRS by using a reserve base of either proved reserves or proved plus probable reserves. The Company has concluded at this time that it will continue to use proved reserves as the basis, therefore this difference is not anticipated to be material.

Real estate

The real estate industry faces potential significant changes in financial reporting with the adoption of IFRS. IAS 40 *Investment Property* (IAS 40) gives issuers the option to record investment property at fair value on the balance sheet with the gains and losses recorded through income in each reporting period. Alternatively, an issuer can elect to continue measuring investment property using the historical cost model as currently required under Canadian GAAP; however, IFRS requires the fair value of the investment property to be disclosed in the financial statement notes.

We noted many issuers expect to use the fair value method to account for their investment properties. Given this is a significant difference from existing Canadian GAAP and will likely lead to greater volatility in reported results, issuers should have described the potential impact to the balance sheet and income statement resulting from this accounting policy choice. An example of entity-specific IAS 40 disclosure is provided below.

Entity-Specific Real Estate Disclosure:

IFRS defines investment property as property held by the owner to earn rental income, capital appreciation or both. Assets classified as income producing properties on the balance sheet of the Company qualify as investment property under IFRS.

Under IFRS, the Company has a choice of measuring investment property using the historical cost model or the fair value model. The cost model is generally consistent with Canadian GAAP and would require that the fair value be disclosed in the notes to the financial statements. Under the fair value model, investment property is measured at fair value, and changes in fair value are recorded through income each reporting period. Under the fair value model there are no charges for depreciation like under the cost model.

The Company expects to use the fair value model when preparing its IFRS financial statements. The Company has substantially completed the design of the investment property valuation process and has commenced implementation. The magnitude of the impact to the Company's balance sheet cannot be quantified at this time but is expected to be significant.

Quarterly Updates

SN 52-320 sets out an incremental approach to disclosure of the impact of IFRS changeover leading up to 2011. Issuers should provide more detailed disclosure in each successive reporting period as the changeover date approaches. Alternatively, disclosure should confirm that no progress has been made during the quarter.

Our review found that 80% of issuers provided an update on the status of their IFRS changeover plan when comparing disclosure in 2009 annual MD&A to 2009 Q3 interim MD&A. This represents an improvement over the quarterly progress updates provided by issuers in 2008. We expect updates in each reporting period in 2010.

Future Action

We expect incremental disclosure will become more robust and complete as transition approaches. It is critical for investors that issuers provide timely transition disclosure. Issuers with calendar year-ends only have the remaining reporting periods in 2010 to communicate the potential impact of IFRS transition. Since IFRS will be implemented in the first quarter of 2011 for calendar year-end issuers, we expect issuers to provide, through interim and annual 2010 MD&A disclosure, more detailed disclosure of their changeover plan and information about key decisions on policy choices under IFRS 1 and other standards to the extent these choices were not disclosed in 2009 MD&A.

As required by Form 51-102F1, disclosure of expected changes in accounting policies should include a discussion of the expected effect on the issuer's financial statements or a statement that the issuer cannot reasonably estimate the effect. During late 2009 and the first half of 2010, many companies started preparing quantitative information for the opening IFRS statement of financial position. As the process for preparing this information continues, more quantitative information will become available during 2010, and we believe it is important for investors to start to understand the quantitative impacts that they will begin to see in 2011. Given this, issuers should consider when they can communicate quantified information in their 2010 interim and annual MD&A prior to final approval of IFRS balances. For example, in communicating the expected effects of IFRS changeover on significant financial statement items, issuers may want to consider indicating, directionally, how significant asset and liability balances may change as a result of accounting policy decisions, or providing estimates of balances relating to the transition date balance sheet.

We will continue to review IFRS transition disclosure as part of our overall continuous disclosure review program. Issuers should anticipate staff requests for re-filings of MD&A in the future if an issuer has not met its disclosure obligations.

CSA Staff Notice 52-327 — Certification Compliance Update

Date: October 15, 2010

33 O.S.C.B. 9427

Introduction

The Canadian Securities Administrators (CSA) staff (staff or we) conducted a review of the 2009 annual Management's Discussion & Analysis (MD&A) and the annual certificates[1] for a sample of 195 reporting issuers, composed of 145 non-venture and 50 venture issuers[2], to assess compliance with the provisions of National Instrument 52-109 *Certification of Disclosure in Issuers' Annual and Interim Filings* (Certification Instrument or NI 52-109). In 2009, we conducted a review of the 2008 annual MD&A and certificates to assess compliance with the Certification Instrument. The results of last year's review are summarized in CSA Staff Notice 52-325 *Certification Compliance Review* (CSA Staff Notice 52-325), published on September 11, 2009. A follow-up review was conducted this year to evaluate the level of improvement in reporting issuers' compliance with the Certification Instrument with respect to their 2009 annual filings and to raise awareness and educate issuers on their certification disclosure obligations.

This year's review focused on the following aspects:

- Compliance of NI 52-109 related MD&A disclosure;

- Compliance of NI 52-109 certificates;

- Further review of issuers identified in last year's review that did not fully comply;

- Certificates and related MD&A disclosure of issuers that restated and re-filed 2009 interim or annual financial statements to correct accounting errors; and

- MD&A disclosure relating to the impact of International Financial Reporting Standards (IFRS) on internal control over financial reporting (ICFR) and disclosure controls and procedures (DC&P).

This notice summarizes the results of the review and provides issuers with further guidance.[3]

Overall, the results of this year's review indicate moderate improvement in the level of issuers' compliance with NI 52-109 as compared to the results of last year's review. In view of the high number of refilings resulting from this year's review, we think that issuers can further improve form compliance and related MD&A disclosure in future filings. We recommend that issuers and their certifying officers review the requirements outlined in the Certification Instrument and review its Companion Policy NI 52-109CP (52-109CP). Issuers and their certifying officers should also refer to the guidance in this staff notice and in CSA Staff Notice 52-325.

Investor Impact

As noted in section 1.1 of 52-109CP, the objective of the Certification Instrument is to improve the quality, reliability and transparency of reporting issuers' annual filings, interim filings and other materials that issuers file or submit under securities legislation. We think this improvement in turn helps maintain and enhance investors' confidence in the integrity of our capital markets. In order to provide investors with a better understanding of the non-venture issuers' ICFR and DC&P, non-venture issuers should fully and clearly disclose in their MD&A:

- Their certifying officers' conclusions about the effectiveness of the issuers' ICFR and DC&P;

- Any material weakness in ICFR and any weakness that is significant in DC&P; and

- Any material change in ICFR.

Summary of Findings

The table below summarizes the results of this year's review compared to the results of last year's review.

---

[1] A "certificate" or "form" is any of the forms associated with NI 52-109.

[2] All but one of the venture issuers in our sample filed basic certificates.

[3] Venture issuers that choose to file full certificates should consider all comments and guidance of this staff notice addressed to non-venture issuers.

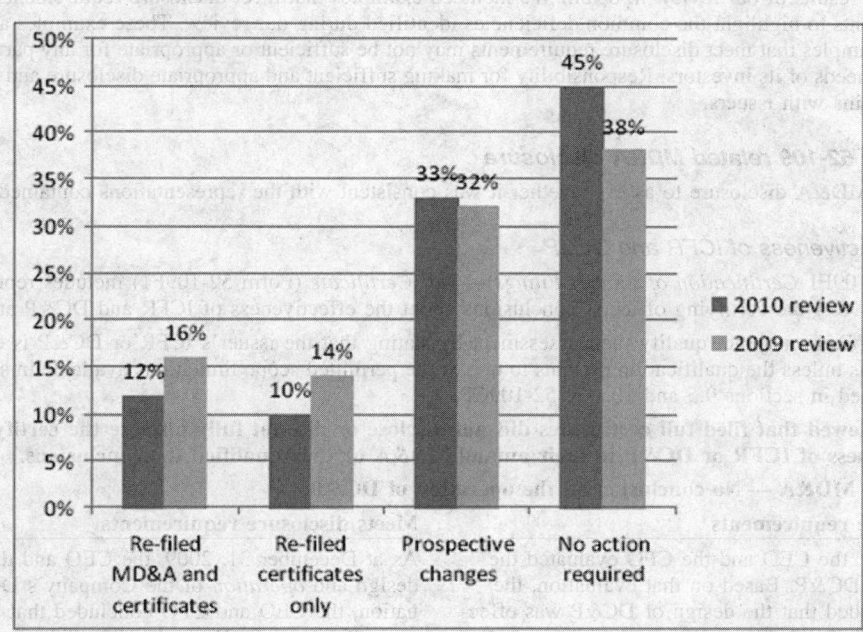

As illustrated above, the percentage of issuers that were requested to re-file their MD&A and certificates declined as we saw a decrease in the severity of the deficiencies. We also observed some improvement in the percentage of issuers for which no action was taken because the issuer fully or substantively complied with the Certification Instrument. A summary of our findings is set out below.

A — Compliance of NI 52-109 related MD&A disclosure

We reviewed the annual MD&A disclosure to assess whether it was consistent with the representations contained in the annual certificates. As a result of our review, 12% of issuers were asked to re-file their 2009 annual MD&A and certificates. In instances where issuers did not disclose the certifying officers' conclusions about the effectiveness of ICFR or DC&P or when the disclosure was unclear or incomplete, we asked issuers to re-file their 2009 annual MD&A and certificates.

B — Compliance of NI 52-109 certificates

We reviewed the annual certificates to determine if they were filed in the exact wording prescribed by the required form, if the certificates were filed on the proper date and to assess whether the representations included in the certificates were consistent with the disclosure in the related annual MD&A. As a result of our review, 10% of issuers were asked to re-file their 2009 annual certificates because of material amendments to the wording of the certificates and certificate content that was inconsistent with related MD&A disclosure.

C — Further review of issuers identified in last year's review that did not fully comply

Our review sample of 195 reporting issuers included 45 issuers (33 non-venture issuers and 12 venture issuers) identified in last year's review as not fully compliant. We asked two issuers to re-file their 2009 annual MD&A or certificates for the same reasons that they were asked to re-file in last year's review.

D — Certificates and related MD&A disclosure of issuers that restated and re-filed 2009 interim or annual financial statements to correct accounting errors

We selected a sample of eight non-venture issuers that restated and re-filed their 2009 interim or annual financial statements to correct accounting errors. Based on our discussion with the issuers, we concluded that issuers did not always consider if the misstatement in the financial statements related to a material weakness in the issuer's ICFR. As a result, we found deficiencies in the disclosure of material weaknesses, in the conclusions about the effectiveness of ICFR and DC&P and in the disclosure of material changes to ICFR that were made to remediate a material weakness.

E — MD&A disclosure relating to the impact of IFRS on ICFR and DC&P

We reviewed the MD&A disclosure relating to the ICFR and DC&P components of the IFRS transition plan of the non-venture issuers in our sample and noted the majority of these issuers provided generic disclosure or did not discuss the impact of the transition to IFRS on ICFR and DC&P. We reminded the issuers, in advance of their first IFRS financial statement filings, of the requirement to disclose any material change in ICFR that may occur due to the transition to IFRS and the ongoing preparation of financial statements in accordance with IFRS.

Findings

This section discusses the results of our review in detail. We included examples that meet disclosure requirements and examples that do not meet disclosure requirements to highlight the common deficiencies identified during our review. These examples are for illustrative purposes only. Accordingly, the examples that meet disclosure requirements may not be sufficient or appropriate for any particular issuer depending on its circumstances and the needs of its investors. Responsibility for making sufficient and appropriate disclosure and complying with applicable securities legislation remains with issuers.

A — Compliance of NI 52-109 related MD&A disclosure

We reviewed the annual MD&A disclosure to assess whether it was consistent with the representations contained in the annual certificates.

Conclusions on the effectiveness of ICFR and DC&P

Paragraph 6 of Form 52-109F1 *Certification of Annual Filings — Full Certificate* (Form 52-109F1) includes representations that the issuer disclosed in its annual MD&A the certifying officers' conclusions about the effectiveness of ICFR and DC&P at the financial year end.

Additionally, certifying officers may not qualify their assessment by stating that the issuer's ICFR or DC&P is effective subject to certain qualifications or exceptions unless the qualification pertains to one of the permitted scope limitations available in section 3.3 of the Certification Instrument as discussed in sections 9.5 and 10.1 of 52-109CP.

- **26% of issuers reviewed that filed full certificates did not disclose or did not fully disclose the certifying officers' conclusions about the effectiveness of ICFR or DC&P in their annual MD&A or they qualified the conclusions.**

Example 1 — Extract of MD&A — No conclusion on the operation of DC&P:

Does not meet disclosure requirements	Meets disclosure requirements
As at December 31, 2009, the CEO and the CFO evaluated the design of the Company's DC&P. Based on that evaluation, the CEO and the CFO concluded that the design of DC&P was effective as at December 31, 2009.	As at December 31, 2009, the CEO and the CFO evaluated the design and *operation* of the Company's DC&P. Based on that evaluation, the CEO and CFO concluded that the Company's *DC&P was effective* as at December 31, 2009.

In Example 1, the issuer has disclosed the certifying officers' conclusion on the design of DC&P but not its operation. Since the issuer's DC&P may be designed effectively but may not operate as intended, it is important for issuers to disclose the certifying officers' conclusion about both the design and operation of ICFR and DC&P. To cover the entirety of ICFR and DC&P, certifying officers may simply conclude on the effectiveness of ICFR and DC&P without referring to the design and operation separately.

Example 2 — Extract of MD&A — Incomplete conclusion about the effectiveness of ICFR:

Does not meet disclosure requirements	Meets disclosure requirements
Based on the evaluation of the design and operating effectiveness of the company's ICFR, the CEO and the CFO concluded that the company's ICFR was effective to provide reasonable assurance regarding the reliability of financial reporting as at December 31, 2009.	Based on the evaluation of the design and operating effectiveness of the company's ICFR, the CEO and the CFO concluded that the company's ICFR was *effective* as at December 31, 2009.

In Example 2, the conclusion does not contain the exact definition of ICFR, as noted in the Certification Instrument. Issuers are not required to include the definition of ICFR or DC&P in their conclusion of the effectiveness. However, if issuers and their certifying officers choose to include the definition of ICFR and DC&P in their MD&A, the definitions should be replicated in their entirety and verbatim to avoid concluding on only a portion of ICFR or DC&P.

While the Certification Instrument does not specifically prescribe the language used to conclude on the effectiveness of the issuer's DC&P and ICFR, explicit disclosure as to whether the issuer's ICFR and DC&P are "effective" or "ineffective" at the financial year end improves transparency and avoids ambiguity.

Example 3 — Extract of MD&A — Qualification of the conclusion regarding the effectiveness of ICFR:

Does not meet disclosure requirements	Meets disclosure requirements — If the "disclosable weakness" is not a material weakness:
The CEO and the CFO have determined that as at December 31, 2009, the Company's ICFR was effective except for a disclosable weakness with respect to segregation of duties.	Based on an evaluation of the Company's ICFR as at December 31, 2009, the CEO and CFO concluded that the Company's ICFR was *effective*.
	Meets disclosure requirements — If the "disclosable weakness" is a material weakness
	Based on an evaluation of the Company's DC&P and ICFR as at December 31, 2009, the CEO and CFO concluded that the company's ICFR was *ineffective*.

In Example 3, the certifying officers qualified their assessment by stating that the issuer's ICFR was effective subject to a qualification. Furthermore, the disclosure is confusing since "disclosable weakness" is not a defined term under NI 52-109.

There is no requirement to discuss a "weakness", "design challenge" or "deficiency" in ICFR or DC&P if it is not significant enough to constitute a material weakness in ICFR or a weakness in DC&P that is significant. If an issuer elects to discuss such "weakness", "design challenge" or "deficiency" in its annual MD&A, to improve transparency and avoid ambiguity, the disclosure should clearly indicate that these items do not constitute a material weakness or a weakness in DC&P that is significant. Guidance on assessing the significance of deficiencies in ICFR and DC&P can be found in Part 9 and Part 10 of 52-109CP, respectively.

In instances where issuers did not disclose the certifying officers' conclusions about the effectiveness of ICFR or DC&P or when the disclosure was unclear or incomplete, we asked issuers to re-file their 2009 annual MD&A and certificates.

Material weakness

As discussed in sections 9.5 and 10.1 of 52-109CP, the certifying officers cannot conclude that the issuer's ICFR or DC&P is effective if they identify a material weakness or a weakness in DC&P that is significant, as in Example 4 below. Additionally, section 10.3 of 52-109CP notes that the existence of a material weakness in the issuer's ICFR will almost always represent a weakness that is significant in the issuer's DC&P given the substantial overlap between the definitions of DC&P and ICFR.

- **3% of issuers reviewed that filed full certificates disclosed that their certifying officers concluded that ICFR was "effective" despite the disclosure of a material weakness in the annual MD&A.**

Example 4 — Extract of MD&A — Conclusion that ICFR was effective when a material weakness exists:

Does not meet disclosure requirements	Meets disclosure requirements
As at December 31, 2009, the CEO and the CFO evaluated and concluded that the Company's ICFR and DC&P were effective as at December 31, 2009.	As at December 31, 2009, the CEO and the CFO evaluated and concluded that the Company's ICFR and DC&P were *ineffective* as at December 31, 2009.
During their evaluation of ICFR, the CEO and the CFO noted a material weakness. The Company's accounting staff has limited knowledge of Canadian GAAP. As such, there is a reasonable possibility that the issuer's ICFR will fail to prevent or detect a material misstatement in the financial statements on a timely basis. To improve the accounting staff's knowledge, the Company will seek external consultants to train accounting staff.	During their evaluation of ICFR, the CEO and the CFO noted a material weakness. The Company's accounting staff has limited knowledge of Canadian GAAP. As such, there is a reasonable possibility that the issuer's ICFR will fail to prevent or detect a material misstatement in the financial statements on a timely basis. To improve the accounting staff's knowledge, the Company will seek external consultants to train accounting staff.

In Example 4, despite the existence of a remediation plan, the certifying officers could not conclude that the issuer' ICFR and DC&P were effective because the material weakness existed at year end.

Voluntary disclosure about DC&P and ICFR by venture issuers

If a venture issuer files Form 52-109FV1 *Certification of Annual Filings — Venture Issuer Basic Certificates* (Form 52-109FV1) or Form 52-109FV2 *Certification of Interim Filings — Venture Issuer Basic Certificates* (Form 52-109FV2), it is not required to discuss in the MD&A the design or operating effectiveness of DC&P and ICFR. If an issuer chooses to discuss the design or operation of one or more components of its DC&P and ICFR, section 15.3 of 52-109CP recommends disclosure to accompany the issuer's discussion about DC&P or ICFR.

- **35% of venture issuers that filed basic certificates voluntarily discussed DC&P or ICFR in their annual MD&A but did not include cautionary language.**

The "Note to Reader" included in Form 52-109FV1 and Form 52-109FV2 states that the certifying officers have not made any representations relating to the establishment and maintenance of DC&P and ICFR. By including a discussion of DC&P and ICFR in the MD&A without the language noted in section 15.3 of 52-109CP, the "Note to Reader" conflicts with the disclosure included in the MD&A.

If the certifying officers of a venture issuer choose to establish and maintain the issuer's DC&P and ICFR and evaluate their operating effectiveness, as required for non-venture issuers, and wish to provide disclosure to that effect in the MD&A, the venture issuer may consider filing full certificates in Form 52-109F1 and Form 52-109F2 *Certification of Interim Filings — Full Certificate*.

B — Compliance of NI 52-109 certificates

We reviewed the issuers' annual certificates to determine if they were filed in the exact wording prescribed by the required form, if the certificates were filed on the proper date and to assess whether the representations included in the certificates were consistent with the disclosure in the related annual MD&A.

Amendments to the form

Subsections 4.1(1) and 5.1(1) of NI 52-109 require issuers to file annual and interim certificates in the wording prescribed by the required form.

- **23% of issuers reviewed amended the wording prescribed by the form.**

Some issuers omitted or modified the sequence of paragraphs and removed or added text. For example, some issuers inappropriately deleted paragraphs 5.2 and 5.3 and subparagraph 6(b)(ii) of Form 52-109F1 or did not insert "N/A" when they were not applicable. Those paragraphs relate to material weaknesses and scope limitations. If they do not apply to the issuer, the paragraph number must be included in the certificates to maintain the sequence of the paragraphs and certifying officers must insert "N/A" after the paragraph number.

In instances where issuers deleted paragraphs 5.2 and 5.3 and subparagraph 6(b)(ii) of Form 52-109F1, did not insert "N/A" when they were not applicable or made major amendments to the certificates, we asked issuers to re-file their 2009 annual certificates.

Other deficiencies identified

The following is a non-exhaustive list of other deficiencies identified in our review of certificates:

- The certifying officers did not date the certificates the same date the certificates were filed; (Section 7.1 of NI 52-109);

- Certificates were not filed concurrently with the filing of an AIF, when the AIF was filed after the financial statements and MD&A; (Subsection 4.1(2) of NI 52-109); and

- The date in paragraph 7 of the Form 52-109F1 certificate was not the date immediately following the end of the period covered by the issuer's most recent interim filing. An issuer with a December 31, 2009 year end should have indicated October 1, 2009 in paragraph 7 because this was the date immediately following the end of its September 30, 2009 interim period filing.

C — Further review of issuers identified in last year's review that did not fully comply

We conducted a further review of a sample of 45 reporting issuers (33 non-venture issuers and 12 venture issuers) that were identified in last year's review as not fully compliant with NI 52-109 requirements. The purpose of this review was to determine whether these issuers appropriately addressed the deficiencies that we raised in last year's review in respect of this year's filings. As a result of our review, we asked two of the issuers in our sample to re-file their 2009 annual MD&A or certificates for the same reasons they were asked to re-file in last year' review. Many of the issues identified in this part of our review resulted from new deficiencies and were not a continuation of deficiencies identified in last year's review.

At the end of every reporting period, we encourage issuers to review the Certification Instrument and any past correspondence with CSA staff to ensure that their filings fully comply with the current requirements. Issuers should anticipate staff requests for refiling of certificates or related MD&A in the future if an issuer has not met its certification obligations. As well, staff may consider other regulatory action as circumstances warrant.

D — Certificates and related MD&A disclosure of issuers that restated and re-filed 2009 interim or annual financial statements to correct accounting errors

We selected a sample of eight non-venture issuers that restated and re-filed their 2009 interim or annual financial statements to correct accounting errors. Section 9.4 of 52-109CP mentions that the restatement of previously issued financial statements to reflect the correction of a material misstatement may suggest the existence of a material weakness in ICFR. Based on our discussions with the issuers, we concluded that issuers did not always consider if the misstatement in the financial statements was related to a material weakness in the issuer's ICFR. As a result, we found deficiencies in the disclosure of material weaknesses, in the conclusions of the effectiveness of ICFR and DC&P and in the disclosure of material changes to ICFR when a material weakness was remediated.

MD&A disclosure of material weakness

Timely disclosure of any material weakness, whether it is related to design or operation, allows investors to understand and assess the potential impact on the financial statements. We remind issuers that if the certifying officers become aware of a material weakness, the MD&A for the applicable period must include the disclosure required under paragraph 3.2 of NI 52-109 (the Material Weakness Disclosure).

Until the issuer remediates the material weakness, it will continue to exist. Therefore, the issuer must provide the Material Weakness Disclosure in the reporting period in which it is discovered and in all subsequent reporting periods until the material weakness is remediated.

- **50% of issuers did not disclose a material weakness in their interim or annual MD&A.**

In our review, we noted that some issuers did not disclose the material weakness relating to the design or operation of ICFR. In Example 5 below, the issuer had a material weakness existing as at September 30, 2009 that was not remediated until June 2010.

MD&A disclosure of remediation plan

The representation of paragraph 7 in Form 52-109F1 and paragraph 6 of Form 52-109F2 requires issuers to disclose in their MD&A any change in ICFR that occurred during the period that has materially affected, or is reasonably likely to materially affect, the issuer's ICFR.

- **50% of issuers did not disclose the change in their ICFR that was made to address the material weakness.**

As discussed in section 11.1 of 52-109CP, a change in an issuer's ICFR that was made to remediate a material weakness would generally be considered a material change in an issuer's ICFR. Although some issuers in our sample represented that they had remediated the material weakness, these issuers did not always disclose the change in their ICFR that was made to address the material weakness. It is critical for issuers to disclose such changes in a timely manner so that investors can better understand how the issuer has addressed its financial reporting risks that the deficient ICFR component previously failed to address.

Annual conclusions on effectiveness if a material weakness in ICFR or a weakness in DC&P that is significant exists as at the financial year end

As noted in sections 9.5 and 10.1 of 52-109CP, the certifying officers could not conclude that the issuer's ICFR and DC&P are "effective" if the certifying officers identify a material weakness relating to the design or operation of ICFR or a weakness relating to the design or operation of DC&P that is significant. In addition, as noted in section 10.3 of 52-109CP, the existence of a material weakness in the issuer's ICFR will almost always represent a weakness that is significant in the issuer's DC&P given the substantial overlap between the definitions of DC&P and ICFR.

- **37% of issuers did not remediate the material weakness by the end of the year but concluded that their DC&P and ICFR were "effective" in their annual MD&A.**

In Example 5 below, the issuer re-filed its September 30, 2009 interim financial statements on April 15, 2010. Given that the material weakness that related to the restatement of the previously filed financial statements was identified subsequent to the financial year end, this suggests that the issuer's ICFR had a material weakness existing at the December 31, 2009 year end. As such, the non-venture issuer in Example 5 amended and re-filed its 2009 annual MD&A to disclose that the certifying officers concluded that the issuer's ICFR was "ineffective" at the financial year end. The amended MD&A also provides the Material Weakness Disclosure as defined above.

Example 5 — Non-venture issuer re-files 2009 interim financial statements to correct a material misstatement:

Facts — December 31 year end:

— Filed September 30, 2009 interim financial statements and MD&A on November 14, 2009.

— Filed December 31, 2009 annual financial statement and MD&A on March 15, 2010.

— Amended and restated the September 30, 2009 interim financial statements and MD&A on April 15, 2010.

Certification Requirements:

— *On November 14, 2009, the issuer filed interim certificates (Form 52-109F2).*

— *On March 15, 2010, the issuer filed annual certificates (Form 52-109F1).*

— *On April 15, 2010 the issuer:*

1)   *Disclosed a material weakness relating to design in the September 30, 2009 amended and re-filed interim MD&A.*

2)   *Filed Form 52-109F2R Certification of re-filed interim filings (Form 52-109F2R)in conjunction with the refiling of the September 30, 2009 financial statements and corresponding MD&A.*

3)   *Amended and re-filed the 2009 annual MD&A to disclose as at December 31, 2009:*
     — *the material weakness relating to design and operation of ICFR [and likely a weakness that is significant in DC&P]; and*
     — *Conclusions that ICFR [and likely DC&P] is "ineffective".*

4)   *Filed Form 52-109F1R Certification of re-filed annual filings (Form 52-109F1R)in conjunction with the re-filed annual MD&A.*

— *On August 14, 2010 the issuer:*

— The material weakness related to the refiling was remediated on June 30, 2010.

1)   *Filed interim certificates (Form 52-109F2)*

— Filed June 30, 2010 interim financial statements and MD&A on August 14, 2010.

2)   *Disclosed in the June 30, 2010 MD&A the changes made to ICFR during the period.*

Other considerations

Venture issuers that re-file financial statements to correct an accounting error should be cautious if they voluntarily discuss the design or operation of DC&P or ICFR in their re-filed MD&A. We would expect these issuers to disclose that DC&P or ICFR are ineffective for the same reasons as noted above.

E — MD&A disclosure relating to the impact of IFRS on ICFR and DC&P

The transition to IFRS from Canadian GAAP may have a material impact on issuers' ICFR and DC&P due to changes in both accounting policies and in financial reporting disclosure requirements. In this year's review, staff assessed the quality of issuers' IFRS transition disclosure relating to ICFR and DC&P. As specified in CSA Staff Notice 52-320 *Disclosure of Expected Changes in Accounting Policies Relating to Changeover to International Financial Reporting Standards* (CSA Staff Notice 52-320), investors need meaningful information about the transition to IFRS.

CSA Staff Notice 52-320 provides guidance on the requirement in Form 51-102F1 *Management's Discussion & Analysis* for an issuer's disclosure of expected changes in accounting policies related to the IFRS transition for the three years before the changeover to IFRS. CSA Staff Notice 52-320 indicates that an issuer's IFRS changeover plan may address the impact of IFRS on ICFR and DC&P if it is a key element of the IFRS transition plan. Key elements should be discussed in the issuer's MD&A.

Part 5: ONGOING REQUIREMENTS

We reviewed MD&A disclosure relating to the IFRS transition of all non-venture issuers in our sample. A total of 79% of non-venture issuers reviewed identified in their MD&A accounting policy differences, including choices among policies permitted under IFRS. For those issuers we noted the following:

- 46% did not discuss the impact of the IFRS transition on their DC&P and ICFR in their MD&A;

- 37% provided generic disclosure of the impact of the IFRS transition on their DC&P and ICFR; and

- 17% provided entity-specific disclosure of the impact of the IFRS transition on their DC&P and ICFR.

Considerations for assessing ICFR and DC&P

Part 6 of 52-109CP directs issuers to identify the risks that could reasonably result in a material misstatement in the financial information. To address these risks appropriately, an issuer may need to establish specific ICFR and DC&P or modify existing ICFR and DC&P in order to prepare its financial statements in accordance with IFRS. We suggest issuers assess whether they have appropriate controls over the transition process and the preparation of IFRS compliant financial information.

We encourage issuers to review the adequacy of their ICFR to ensure the information on how the transition from Canadian GAAP to IFRS affected their reported financial position, financial performance and cash flows is reliable.

Disclosure requirements

NI 52-109 requires non-venture issuers to establish and maintain ICFR and DC&P. Paragraph 7 of Form 52-109F1 and paragraph 6 of Form 52-109F2 require certifying officers to certify that the issuer disclosed in its MD&A any change in the issuer's ICFR that occurred during the period that has materially affected, or is reasonably likely to materially affect, the issuer's ICFR. Therefore, any change in the issuer's ICFR relating to IFRS that will materially affect, or is reasonably likely to materially affect, the issuer's ICFR must be disclosed in the period in which the change first impacts the reliability of financial reporting and the preparation of financial statements for external purposes in accordance with the issuer's GAAP.

Future Action

While we found moderate levels of improvement in compliance with NI 52-109 since last year's review, further focus on the Certification Instrument by issuers and their certifying officers will help compliance. Compliance with NI 52-109 will enhance investors' confidence in the quality, reliability and transparency of the annual filings, interim filings and other materials that issuers file or submit under securities legislation.

We will continue to review issuers' compliance with the Certification Instrument as part of our overall continuous disclosure review program and we will take action when deficiencies are identified.

CSA Staff Notice 52-328 — Disclosures About Accounting Policies in the Year of Changeover to International Financial Reporting Standards

Date: April 15, 2011

34 O.S.C.B. 4364

Purpose

This notice responds to specific questions CSA staff have received on disclosure about accounting policies in an issuer's interim and annual Management's Discussion and Analysis (MD&A) in the year of changeover to International Financial Reporting Standards (IFRS).

Background

For many issuers, the adoption of IFRS will result in one or more significant changes in an issuer's accounting policies.

CSA Staff Notice 52-320 *Disclosure of Expected Changes in Accounting Policies Relating to Changeover to International Financial Reporting Standards* (SN 52-320), issued in 2008, provides guidance to an issuer on disclosure of expected changes in accounting policies relating to an issuer's changeover to IFRS. It discusses Item 1.13(a) of Form 51-102F1 *Management's Discussion and Analysis* (51-102F1) and disclosure about expected changes in an issuer's accounting policies. While SN 52-320 addresses disclosure in MD&A for periods prior to changeover to IFRS, this notice addresses disclosure in the year of changeover.

MD&A disclosure about accounting policies in the year of changeover to IFRS

Item 1.13(b) of 51-102F1 addresses MD&A disclosures about accounting policies initially adopted during the most recently completed financial year. The instruction to Item 1.13 indicates that MD&A does not need to include the discussion under Item 1.13(b) for the initial adoption of accounting policies resulting from the adoption of new accounting standards. We have received questions about how the instruction relates to IFRS changeover.

Item 1.13(b) does not apply to accounting policies initially adopted as a result of changeover to IFRS. However, in its year of adopting IFRS, if an issuer voluntarily changes an accounting policy subsequent to filing its first interim financial report (other than due to the early adoption of a new or revised IFRS standard), Item 1.13(b) applies to the change in accounting policy. In this case, an issuer should provide the disclosure specified in Item 1.13(b) to the extent it is not provided in the financial statements.

An issuer's interim financial reports and annual financial statements in its year of changeover to IFRS will include information about the transition to IFRS and the issuer's accounting policies. In the accompanying MD&A, management has the opportunity to supplement this information by highlighting significant entity-specific features of the issuer's transition to IFRS. Although Item 1.13(b) does not apply to accounting policies initially adopted on changeover to IFRS, management may conclude that investors would benefit from further information.

For example, management may discuss an issuer's choices among alternative acceptable accounting policies under IFRS, including the reasons for a particular choice. MD&A disclosure should not simply replicate disclosure in the financial statements but instead should complement the information provided in the financial statements.

Interim MD&A updates an issuer's annual MD&A. As discussed in SN 52-320, an issuer may have provided comprehensive information about accounting policy choices in its annual MD&A prior to changeover to IFRS. MD&A disclosures about IFRS transition in the year of IFRS adoption need not repeat information included in the annual MD&A. However, an issuer should consider discussing significant differences between MD&A disclosure made prior to the changeover to IFRS and information reported in the current period about accounting policy choices.

To avoid confusion, issuers should consider presenting information pertaining to an issuer's transition to IFRS and its accounting policies:

- in one section of the MD&A, and

- separately from the discussion of financial performance and financial condition.

In an issuer's year of changeover to IFRS, investors will need information about the issuer's accounting policies. Management should consider how the combination of the information in the financial statements and the MD&A responds to investors' needs.

OSC Rule 52-501 — Financial Statements

Date: December 15, 2000 and March 30, 2004 (by Rule 51-801)
23 O.S.C.B. 8372

[revoked by Rule 51-801]

Companion Policy 52-501CP — To OSC Rule 52-501 Financial Statements

[revoked]

OSC Staff Notice 52-701 — Initial Report on Staff's Review of Revenue Recognition, Continuous Disclosure Team and Corporate Finance Branch, February 2001

Date: March 9, 2001
24 O.S.C.B. 1483

1. — Purpose

The purpose of this notice is to report the preliminary findings and comments of staff of the Continuous Disclosure Team of the Corporate Finance Branch (the "staff") arising from staff's review of the practices of a sample of Canadian reporting issuers in recognizing, measuring, presenting and disclosing revenue (the "review").

2. — Scope of Review

The review commenced in August 2000 with the objective of identifying whether the accounting practices of Canadian issuers in recognizing, measuring, presenting and disclosing revenue reflect an appropriate application of the standards set out in the Handbook of The Canadian Institute of Chartered Accountants (the "CICA HB").

In a letter sent to a sample of 75 reporting issuers, staff asked for a detailed explanation of how the issuers apply revenue recognition policies in their financial statements. Staff also asked the issuers to provide the following information:

   for revenue recognition on the sale of goods, an explanation of how the issuers deal with retained risks or obligations; including customer right of return, obligations under maintenance contracts and obligations to provide complimentary upgrades;

   a description of how revenue is accrued for service contracts;

   whether any portion of the issuer's reported revenue represents the "gross" amount of sales transactions in which the issuer acts essentially as an agent or broker rather than as principal and for which it is compensated on a commission or fee basis; and

   whether, and if so how, the issuer compared its revenue recognition accounting practices with those applied generally within the industry in which it operates or by specific issuers within that industry.

Staff's choice of revenue recognition as the subject for its earnings management review was influenced by numerous factors. Clearly, revenue is a highly significant element of financial reporting because of its direct effect on reported earnings. In addition, some users of financial statements are placing increased emphasis on revenue growth as a key indicator of value and performance, particularly for companies in the technology sector.

Canadian accounting standards set out the principles governing recognition of revenue of all types but provide relatively little detailed and specific guidance on how those principles should be applied in specific circumstances. In a business environment in which revenue-generating transactions may involve complex combinations of customized technology and services, as well as new forms of product delivery and distribution channels, questions arise as to whether revenue recognition practices reflect a rigorous application of the relevant standards.

Staff's objectives for the review are to ensure that the standards are being applied appropriately and to identify any areas in which more specific guidance may be required, for example, in the form of new standards, or interpretations issued by the Emerging Issues Committee ("EIC") of The Canadian Institute of Chartered Accountants.

The issuers chosen for review were primarily in the technology and related industries. Of the sample chosen:

- 38% were software providers;
- 25% were service providers (technology, internet, data processing and e-commerce);
- 24% sold hardware products (which could include software as a component); and
- 13% of the issuers were in some other industry.

91% of the issuers were listed on the Toronto Stock Exchange. 27% of the issuers were listed or quoted on an exchange or market in the United States ("US") and therefore reconciled their financial results to accounting principles generally accepted in the United States ("US GAAP").

3. — Summary of Findings and Comments

5% of the issuers provided sufficient information in response to staff's questions and did not generate any follow-up questions.

35% of the responses generated follow-up questions or comments on disclosure issues only. These are discussed further in Part 4 of this notice.

60% of the responses generated follow-up questions on recognition, measurement or presentation issues. These are discussed further in Part 5 of this notice.

The initial results of the review suggest a need for significant improvement in the nature and extent of disclosure in both the financial statements and Management's Discussion and Analysis ("MD&A"). Staff have also identified certain situations in which they are continuing to investigate whether particular revenue recognition, measurement and presentation practices reflect an appropriate application of the relevant standards.

As a result of the review, a number of issuers will be required to provide significantly more detailed disclosure in their financial statement notes or MD&A. Staff recommend that issuers review the quality of their disclosures with a view to implementing immediate improvements, taking into account the commentary and guidance provided in Part 4 of this notice. Where an issuer has not previously disclosed its accounting policies or other significant information regarding revenue, it should consider providing that information in a press release pending the release of the issuer's next financial statements.

Other issuers may be required, following further investigation and discussion, to revise their accounting policies or to restate previously issued financial statements to address the recognition and measurement issues raised in this report. Staff continues to correspond with issuers on many of the specific issues identified in this notice, and will issue a final report following the resolution of all matters. Where issues have been identified for follow up and an issuer files a prospectus, staff will require the issuer to address and resolve these matters prior to a final receipt being issued. The major issues identified to date are summarized in Part 5 of this notice. The issues are typical of matters that will be questioned by staff on an ongoing basis as part of the continuous disclosure review program described in Staff Notice 51-703, *Implementation of Reporting Issuer Continuous Disclosure Review Program* and in the context of offering document reviews.

Staff recommend that Boards and Audit Committees evaluate and regularly reassess whether:

- management has established and is following a set of revenue recognition policies that is sufficiently comprehensive to provide sound practices across the issuer's full range of activities; and
- management has sufficient controls in place to monitor, report and respond to the key factors and functions that affect revenue recognition. Such controls would include, for instance, controls to ensure the appropriate coordination between the issuer's sales and accounting departments on major contractual items that impact the amount of revenue recognized and the timing of recognition.

Staff remind issuers that more detailed accounting literature exists in the US and elsewhere, providing a valuable point of reference in considering accounting treatments under Canadian GAAP. Specifically, in the Spring 2000 issue of *OSC Perspectives*, staff made the following statement:

> (The) fundamental accounting concepts pertaining to revenue recognition are similar under both US and Canadian GAAP. Accordingly, Canadian issuers and their auditors should consider carefully the basis in Canadian authoritative literature for all revenue recognition policies that differ from the interpretations set out in SEC Staff Accounting Bulletin ("SAB") No. 101. Where a policy adopted under Canadian GAAP differs from the requirements of SAB No. 101, and the difference cannot be justified with specific reference to underlying authoritative literature, or to clearly established practice that is consistent with fundamental accounting concepts, staff will be likely to take the view that the policy is not in accordance with Canadian GAAP.

Staff believe that analyses built on the criteria outlined in SAB 101 will generally be consistent with the requirements of Canadian GAAP as set out in CICA HB 3400, *Revenue*. As discussed in more detail below, the initial results of this review suggest that in many cases issuers have not looked to all appropriate sources of accounting literature when applying Canadian GAAP.

4. — Significant Disclosure Issues

4.1 — Revenue Recognition Policies

Staff identified some issuers that provided no disclosure of revenue recognition policies in the notes to the financial statements. CICA HB 1505, *Disclosure of Accounting Policies*, requires "a clear and concise description of the significant accounting policies of an enterprise". Staff believe that the degree of judgement involved in determining the appropriate application of revenue recognition principles for the specific circumstances of a particular business is such that revenue recognition policies should always be viewed as significant and therefore disclosed.

When revenue recognition policies were disclosed, they were often limited to vague or boilerplate language that provided little information relevant to the issuer's specific circumstances. For example, the disclosure stated merely that revenue is recognized when earned. It is staff's view that such disclosure provides no useful information and does not meet the requirements of CICA 1505.

For the sale of goods, the disclosure often stated only that revenue is recognized when goods are shipped. Staff view such disclosure as insufficiently specific in cases where the issuer does not always sell its product directly to end users. For issuers that use distribution channels such as resellers, distributors, e-tailers or retailers, a reader of the financial statements would not be able to determine whether revenue was recognized on shipment to the distributor or only on shipment to the end-user.

Through its review of some issuer response letters, staff established that sales to distribution channels were recognized based on more extensive criteria than merely shipment. In such cases, staff questioned the accuracy of the disclosed policy. For example, one issuer's response stated that criteria for revenue recognition included agreement in writing by the customer to all terms and conditions, delivery to and acceptance by the customer, and assessment of collection of the sales proceeds as probable. The disclosed policy stated only that such revenues were "recognized when shipped." Staff emphasize that a full discussion of the key criteria assessed in recognizing revenue is necessary for a user to obtain an adequate understanding of the accounting policy applied.

Staff noted that the policies disclosed by issuers commonly failed to address separately major categories of goods or services provided by the issuer. In some cases, the policies had not been updated for recent shifts in the issuer's products and services. In other cases, the policies disclosed were not consistent with the description of revenue recognition policies submitted in response to the review letter. Issuers should regularly assess their disclosed policies to ensure that they provide a complete and current description of all significant elements of their revenue recognition practices.

4.2 — Issuers Reporting in the US

Some issuers prepared and distributed financial statements under both US GAAP and Canadian GAAP. In these cases, staff found that the disclosure of revenue recognition practices provided for US GAAP purposes was generally more detailed than that presented in the Canadian GAAP financial statements. Staff expect a consistent level of disclosure of revenue recognition policies in both sets of statements.

In some cases, issuers that prepared their results solely in accordance with Canadian GAAP nevertheless indicated in their responses to staff's letter that the accounting principles applied were consistent with certain US pronouncements. Staff believe such information provides a useful insight into the basis of preparation of the financial statements and its disclosure is therefore encouraged. Other Canadian issuers reconciled their financial results to US GAAP without reporting any differences relating to recognition of revenue, but did not address in the financial statements or in their responses to staff which US pronouncements were applied.

Staff remind issuers that, when financial statements contain a reconciliation to US GAAP, staff may as part of the continuous disclosure review and offering document review programs consider whether the reconciling items are indicative of a potential misapplication of Canadian accounting standards.

4.3 — Software Revenue Recognition

Many Canadian software vendors stated in their responses that they follow US accounting pronouncements, particularly SOP 97-2, *Software Revenue Recognition*, for Canadian accounting purposes. In some cases, staff asked for additional information on certain key aspects of how these pronouncements were applied. These included questions regarding:

- the terms of multiple element arrangements;
- the determination of vendor-specific objective evidence as a basis for allocating revenue to each element;
- how it was determined that fees are fixed and determinable given the existence of extended payment terms; and
- how it was determined that delivery had occurred when goods were sold to resellers.

Staff believe that information on these matters is important to an adequate understanding of the revenue recognition policy followed by an issuer and should be addressed in the notes to the financial statements.

4.4 — Segmented Information

In many cases, the responses provided by issuers contained a description of how the issuers are organized for internal reporting and decision-making purposes. Staff's review of this information sometimes raised concerns that the issuers might not be providing segment information in accordance with CICA HB 1701, *Segment Disclosures*. CICA HB 1701 requires that segment information be provided based on the way that management organizes the enterprise for its own internal monitoring and decision-making purposes. Staff note that the recent release of EIC No. 115, *Segment disclosure — Application of the aggregation criteria in CICA HB 1701*, provides further guidance on the circumstances in which operating segments may be aggregated for external reporting purposes.

Even where the segment information itself appeared to be provided appropriately, many issuers failed to comply with the requirements of CICA HB 1701.39 that revenue from external customers should be disclosed for each product and service or each group of similar products and services, unless it is impracticable to do so, in which case that fact is required to be disclosed.

4.5 — Economic Dependence

Staff identified several situations in which particular customers, distributors or suppliers appeared to generate or provide a significant volume of the issuer's business. In such circumstances, staff remind issuers of the disclosure requirements of CICA HB 1701.42 and 1701.43, regarding information about major customers, and CICA HB 3841, *Economic Dependence*.

Staff encourage issuers, when disclosing such relationships, to provide the desirable disclosures set out in CICA HB 3841.06 and 3841.07, including the amount of the transactions and an explanation of whether the volume is normal for the issuer and the industry in which it

Part 5: ONGOING REQUIREMENTS

operates. Such disclosures appear particularly useful when the stage of development of an issuer's business is such that it has only a small number of customers, distributors or major suppliers.

4.6 — *Management's Discussion and Analysis*

Management's Discussion and Analysis ("MD&A") as required by OSC Rule 51-501, *AIF & MD&A*, effective January 1, 2001 (as prescribed in forms 44-101F1 and 44-101F2 contained in National Instrument 44-101, *Short Form Prospectus Distributions*) requires a discussion, analysis and comparison of an issuer's financial condition, cash flows and results of operations.

In particular, form 44-101F2, Item 4(3) requires "a discussion of the extent to which any changes in net sales or revenues are attributable to changes in selling prices, to changes in the volume or quantity of goods or services being sold, or the introduction of new products or services" (this requirement was previously contained in OSC Policy 5.10).

It is staff's view that such discussion increases in usefulness when it specifically identifies, analyses and to the extent possible quantifies the significant underlying factors contributing to changes in selling price or in volumes or quantity of goods or services sold. The discussion should provide a full and balanced historical perspective, addressing both the absolute amount of revenue for the year and the change from previous years. In providing this perspective, issuers may find it necessary to address a period longer than two years.

The discussion should also provide a forward-looking assessment of the likely ongoing impact of the significant factors that contributed to changes in selling price or in volumes or quantity of goods or services sold. Staff's review identified many issuers that merely listed various factors underlying the change in revenue without providing any meaningful discussion or sensitivity analysis.

Other common deficiencies noted by staff in reviewing the MD&A of the sample issuers included an absence of discussion or analysis of the following areas:

- changes in revenue by operational or geographic segment;
- the impact of new products or services on reported revenues;
- the issuer's relationships with customers or suppliers representing a significant volume of business; and
- the significance of related parties to the issuer's operations.

Factors that might be identified, analysed and explained include, but are not limited to:

- changes in customer buying patterns due to new technologies, changes in demographics, or other factors;
- changes in selling practices, such as new distribution arrangements or a reorganization of a direct sales force;
- changes in competition, including an assessment of the issuer's resources, strengths and weaknesses relative to those of its competitors;
- the impact of exchange rates on foreign revenues;
- changes in pricing of inputs, constraints on supply, order backlog, or other input-related matters affecting sales volume;
- changes in production capacity due to plant closures, work stoppages or other matters;
- changes in the volume of discounts granted to customers, volumes of returns and allowances, excise and other taxes or other amounts reflected on a net basis against revenues;
- changes in the terms and conditions of service contracts;
- the impact of new products or services, or discontinuances of specific products or services or operations; and
- industry-wide changes, including matters that did not impact on the issuer if such impact might reasonably have been expected to occur.

Staff plan to increase their focus on the quality of MD&A disclosure, including carrying out a future targeted review in the context of continuous disclosure.

4.7 — *Interim Financial Statements*

Staff noted that the interim financial statements of issuers that had changed or expanded their revenue recognition accounting policies during a specific quarter due to a change in their business seldom provided information about the revised accounting policies as required by CICA HB 1750.06(d)(i) (or, for interim periods in fiscal years beginning on or after January 1, 2001, by CICA HB 1751.14(b)). In addition, staff noted that few issuers included the segmented disclosure required by CICA HB 1750.06(e) (or, for interim periods in fiscal years beginning on or after January 1, 2001, by CICA HB 1751.14(e)) *Interim Financial Reporting to Shareholders*.

Staff also noted that notes were often not included in the interim financial statements filed by the issuers. Staff remind issuers that for interim periods in fiscal years beginning on or after January 1, 2001, the disclosure requirements for interim financial statements outlined in CICA HB 1751.13 — 1751.15, *Interim Financial Statements,* and OSC Rule 51-501, *AIF & MD&A,* are effective for public enterprises. To comply with these new requirements, issuers will need to provide notes to their interim financial statements.

5. — Significant Accounting Issues

The issues are categorized here with reference to the accounting recommendations set out in the CICA HB.

5.1. — Transfer of significant risks and rewards of ownership

Revenue should be recognized only when performance of the transaction has been achieved and ultimate collection of the consideration is reasonably assured. CICA HB 3400.07(a) contains the following necessary condition that must be fulfilled if performance is to be regarded as achieved:

> the seller of the goods has transferred to the buyer the significant risks and rewards of ownership, in that all significant acts have been completed and the seller retains no continuing managerial involvement in, or effective control of, the goods transferred to a degree usually associated with ownership

The following issues raise concerns regarding the appropriate application of this condition:

5.1 (1) — Completion of all Significant Acts

In some cases, revenue was recognized even though all activities had not been completed. For example, one issuer recognized revenue when items were shipped, even though these items were subject to a subsequent installation process to be carried out by the issuer. In other cases, revenue from software products which were not standard and required extensive customization specific to each customer was recognized upon shipment.

There may be limited circumstances in which the additional time and risk associated with an installation process is so minimal as to be insignificant. However, when installation and testing of the product at the customer's business site are more than non-substantive, staff believe they should be regarded as significant acts, the completion of which are a necessary condition for the recognition of revenue. Staff note that International Accounting Standard IAS 18, *Revenue*, cites an example of a situation in which the installation process is insignificant, a factory tested television receiver which only requires unpacking and connection of power and antennae. Questions as to whether all significant acts have been completed also arise when issuers have continuing obligations to provide free upgrades.

5.1 (2) — Delivery and Customer Acceptance

Canadian accounting standards require all significant risks and rewards of ownership to be transferred to the buyer before revenue is recognized. Many issuers follow a policy of recognizing revenue when goods are shipped. In some cases, staff question whether a sufficiently detailed assessment has been made of whether the significant risks and rewards of ownership are in fact transferred at the point of shipment.

Staff note that even when goods have been shipped to the customer, if contractual customer acceptance provisions exist, and there remains some uncertainty regarding the customer's acceptance of the products, it will often be unlikely that the significant risks and rewards of ownership could be concluded to have been transferred.

5.1 (3) — "Bill and Hold" Sales

In some cases, issuers recognized revenue before possession of the goods had been transferred to the customer. Staff questioned in such cases whether all significant risks and rewards of ownership had been transferred and all significant acts completed. In such circumstances, staff will use the following factors as a reference point in assessing whether the risks and rewards of ownership of the goods have passed to the buyer:

- whether the customer has made a fixed commitment to purchase the goods (preferably evidenced in written documentation);
- whether the buyer, rather than the seller, requested that the transaction be on a bill and hold basis, and whether the buyer had a substantial business purpose for ordering the goods on such a basis;
- whether there is a fixed schedule for delivery of the goods that is reasonable and consistent with the buyer's business purpose;
- whether the seller retains any specific performance obligations such that the earning process is not complete;
- whether the ordered goods are segregated from the seller's inventory or are subject to being used to fill other orders; and
- whether the product is complete and ready for shipment.

5.1 (4) — Contracts with multiple elements

In some cases, staff noted customer contracts or agreements that had more than one deliverable product or service, each of which was accounted for as a different revenue stream. For example, some contracts for the sale of software also included obligations to provide maintenance, training services or free upgrades. Staff asked issuers to discuss and explain how the revenue allocated to each deliverable was determined. Where the basis of such allocations cannot be supported, staff will question how an issuer concludes that all significant acts pertaining to a particular revenue stream have been completed.

5.1 (5) — Issues involving legal title

CICA HB 3400.11 states that, in most cases, revenue is recognized on the passing of possession of goods which, in the case of retail sales, is usually coincident with the passing of legal title. However, it also notes that the passing of legal title may occur at a different time from the passing of possession or of the risks and rewards of ownership. In many cases, staff's review suggested that issuers had not made a detailed assessment of title issues for their various products and how this might impact on their accounting practices.

Traditionally, revenue was considered earned at the point of sale, either when a product was delivered to the customer's delivery site (FOB destination) or when a product was shipped to the customer (FOB shipping point). This practice was based on a traditional business making standardized products with few, if any, obligations to the customer after the sale. A more transaction-specific approach appears to be appropriate when products are more complex and less homogenous, undergo significant customization or involve a greater ongoing collaboration between the seller and the customer. However, as noted previously, such a transaction-specific approach requires adequate controls and established revenue recognition policies that are sufficiently comprehensive to provide sound practices across the issuer's full range of activities.

Part 5: ONGOING REQUIREMENTS

5.2 — Measurement of consideration and assessment of returns

CICA HB 3400.07(b) contains the following further condition that must be fulfilled if performance is to be regarded as achieved:

reasonable assurance exists regarding the measurement of the consideration that will be derived from the sale of goods, and the extent to which goods may be returned

The following issues raise concerns regarding the appropriate application of this condition:

5.2 (1) — Right of Return

Staff identified issuers that recognized revenue at the time of product shipment despite being exposed to potentially significant returns which, historically, have large fluctuations. In staff's view, a history of large fluctuations in actual returns raises concerns with regard to the issuer's ability to make reliable estimates of returns and may suggest that the amount of revenue is not measurable with sufficient reliability to be recognized.

CICA HB 3400.18(b) indicates that when the market for a returnable good is untested and when an issuer is subject to significant and unpredictable returns, revenue would not be recognized. When the volume of returns is large relative to the total revenue recognized, staff may also question how the issuer assesses the predictability of returns. Such cases may also call into question whether the significant risks and rewards of ownership have been transferred at the time revenue is recognized.

Issuers should ensure that they have adequate systems in place to support the assumption that returns can be reasonably estimated. Staff note it is particularly difficult to establish a sound basis for predicting the extent of returns in businesses that are characterized by rapid and unpredictable technological change.

CICA HB 3400.18(a) also states that when consideration is not determinable within reasonable limits, for example when payment relating to goods sold depends on the resale of goods by the buyer, revenue would not be recognized. In certain circumstances where an issuer sells its products through resellers rather than directly to end users, staff may question the issuer regarding the terms of its agreements with the resellers, the history of returns or any adjustments that have occurred as a result of these agreements.

5.2 (2) — Price protection arrangements

Staff noted cases where revenue was recognized even though the issuer continued to offer price protection with regard to the products in question. Under these arrangements, when an issuer reduces its published price list for products, it provides credit to customers (resellers) for products held in their inventories. It appears to staff that the existence of price protection and inventory credit arrangements raise significant concerns as to whether the issuer has reasonable assurance with respect to the measurement of the consideration that will be derived from the sale of the goods. Further, arrangements that leave the seller exposed to price risk with respect to the products sold may raise questions as to whether the significant risks and rewards of ownership have been substantially transferred to the customer. Such concerns are magnified when the price protection arrangements coexist with right of return provisions or other contractual provisions that might also result in an adjustment to revenue.

5.2 (3) — Valuing of Consideration

Staff identified an issuer that receives equity interests in customers as compensation for providing professional services. However, due to uncertainty in the value of the equity interests, the issuer disclosed that no amount had been attributed to those equity interests. Staff questioned this accounting, noting that CICA HB 3830.05, *Non-Monetary Transactions*, requires that such non-monetary exchanges be recorded at the fair value of the asset or service given up or, if more clearly determinable, the fair value of the asset or service received. Where uncertainties exist regarding the computation of fair value, those uncertainties may, if material, be dealt with by disclosure under CICA HB 1508, *Measurement Uncertainty*.

Staff noted some issuers that issued warrants or equity instruments to arm's length customers as part of a revenue-generating transaction. Staff take the view that where such instruments are issued to a customer in combination with a sale, then the consideration received would be allocated between the goods or services provided and the warrants or equity issued based on their fair value. In such cases, the issuance of the warrants or equity instruments effectively returns to the customer a portion of the contracted or stated amount of revenue.

5.3 — Rendering of Services and Long-Term Contracts

CICA HB 3400.08 states that for the rendering of services and long-term contracts, performance should be determined using either the percentage of completion method or the completed contract method, whichever relates the revenue to the work accomplished. The following issue raises concerns regarding the appropriate application of this principle:

5.3 (1) — Up-front fees

Staff noted certain arrangements where up-front fees are received at the inception of a licensing or similar agreement and are accounted for as earned as the products are delivered or services are performed over the term of the arrangement. Staff questioned cases in which these fees appeared to be amortized over a period shorter than that of the term of the arrangement. Staff also questioned cases where such up-front fees were recognized in income immediately by the issuer because they were considered to be non-refundable and not dependent on any subsequent activity to be fully earned. Staff also questioned such treatment where it appeared that the fees were potentially refundable. For example, staff questioned a situation in which an up-front fee, recognized in revenue, appeared to be received in consideration of entering into an exclusive nine-month negotiating period, and would have been refundable if the terms of that agreement were breached.

5.4 — Other issues identified

5.4 (1) — "Gross vs. Net" Presentation

Staff noted an internet retailer which places a purchase order with a supplier for a product only after a customer of the issuer has placed a sales order; the supplier then ships the product directly to the customer. The issuer acquires title to the product and retains such title during shipment. However, in some respects the issuer's assumption of the risks of ownership of the product is relatively minimal; for instance, it never has any of the risks associated with bringing goods into inventory. When an issuer's interest in a transaction is such that it is not exposed to the significant risks and rewards of ownership of the items that are the subject of the transaction, this may be indicative of an agency type of relationship. In such cases, even where the issuer does not legally act as agent or broker, revenue reported by the issuer should be limited to the amount of the commission earned.

"Gross vs net" issues have recently been considered by the Emerging Issues Task Force in the US. Canadian issuers may find the US guidance helpful. Staff believe that detailed guidance on these issues is required in Canada.

5.4 (2) — Evidence Of Arrangement

CICA HB 3400.11 states that "assessing when the risks and rewards of ownership are transferred to the buyer with sufficient certainty requires an examination of the circumstances of the transaction." In staff's view, to achieve sufficient certainty it is usually necessary to have persuasive evidence regarding the existence and major terms of the transaction. The nature of this evidence would depend largely on the issuer's business, customers, organization, practices and processes and could take many forms including a final written agreement that is executed and properly authorized by the customer, binding purchase orders from third parties or on-line authorizations that are binding and include terms of sale.

Very few issuers provided contracts or other supporting documentation as part of their response to staff's letter. Staff expect to request such support as part of its continuing correspondence with certain issuers.

6. — Conclusion

In many cases, staff continue to correspond with issuers to obtain additional information and resolve the issues identified as a result of the review. A final report will be issued following the resolution of all issues. As mentioned, these issues are typical of matters that will be questioned by staff on an ongoing basis as part of the continuous disclosure review program described in Staff Notice 51-703 and in the context of offering document reviews. Staff encourage issuers to discuss questions and issues with staff on a pre-filing basis.

On completion of this review, staff are planning a targeted review of interim financial statements which will commence in April 2001. These reviews are part of staff's increasing shift towards the review of more continuous disclosure documents. In addition to targeted reviews, staff carry out a range of other reviews as described in OSC Staff Notice 51-703.

Policies and Orders: OSCN 51-708.

OSC Notice 52-703 — Pre-Filing Consultation on Innovative or Unusual Financial Reporting

Date: October 2, 1987

10 O.S.C.B. 5687 , Assigned number: (2001) 24 O.S.C.B. 2405

With the increasing importance and complexity of financial reporting requirements, Commission staff have recently augmented procedures designed to improve the quality and clarity of financial disclosure and compliance with generally accepted accounting and auditing standards. New initiatives include a program to review, on a sample basis, renewal Annual Information Forms and annual financial statements. Staff continue to review all financial disclosures contained in prospectuses.

These procedures are increasingly focussed on substantive issues such as the appropriateness of accounting policies and of particular financial statement presentation. Issuers should not assume that staff will not question an item simply because the issuer and its auditors are satisfied with it. To the contrary, as the recent legislative report involving the Argosy matter indicates, staff have an obligation to look behind the opinions of professional advisers. Unusual or innovative accounting treatments or presentations may be challenged.

Accordingly, staff encourage issuers and their advisers to consult with them on difficult or unusual financial reporting issues as far in advance of filing as possible. Such meetings avoid both the delay which results from the identification of issues late in the process and the risk of Commission intervention. Issuers should submit background information, an analysis of all the relevant issues and a proposed course of action. Staff will endeavour to respond expeditiously to reasonable inquiries and may, in appropriate circumstances, pre-clear issues on a confidential basis. Failure to pre-clear difficult issuers runs the risk that staff will not be able to resolve a matter quickly, which may delay the issuance of a receipt for a prospectus or lead to a cease trade order for failure to file material which complies with the Commission's requirements.

OSC Staff Notice 52-718 — IFRS Transition Disclosure Review

Date: February 5, 2010

33 O.S.C.B. 1161

Introduction

Recently staff of the Ontario Securities Commission conducted a review to assess the extent and quality of International Financial Reporting Standards (IFRS) transition disclosures made by issuers in light of the disclosure guidance provided in CSA Staff Notice 52-320 *Disclosure of Expected Changes in Accounting Policies Relating to Changeover to International Financial Reporting Standards* (SN 52-320).

Part 5: ONGOING REQUIREMENTS

SN 52-320 provides guidance on the requirement in Form 51-102F1 *Management's Discussion & Analysis* (MD&A) for an issuer's disclosure of the expected changes in accounting policies related to IFRS changeover for the three-year period prior to financial years beginning on or after January 1, 2011 (the changeover date). This disclosure is important to assist investors in assessing the readiness of an issuer's transition to IFRS and the impact the adoption of IFRS may have on the issuer.

Our review focused on reporting issuers' IFRS transition disclosure provided in 2008 annual and 2009 interim MD&A. We used a risk-based approach to select issuers, supplemented by a random selection of issuers across various industries. Generally, the criteria used in our selection process was designed to identify issuers whose disclosure was likely to be materially improved relative to the guidance set out in SN 52-320.

In 2008 MD&A, we expected issuers to have discussed the status of the key elements and timing of their IFRS changeover plan. As explained in SN 52-320, developing and implementing an IFRS conversion plan is not just an accounting exercise, since IFRS adoption will affect a wide variety of an issuer's business activities. SN 52-320 directs issuers to consider how the transition to IFRS will affect all business functions that rely on financial information and to communicate this to investors. We also expected issuers to have provided a status update in their 2009 interim MD&A against previously disclosed timelines so that readers of the MD&A could have assessed an issuer's transition progress.

Of the 106 reporting issuers reviewed, 60% discussed an IFRS changeover plan, while the remaining 40% did not provide any IFRS transition disclosure. Overall, our findings suggest that reporting issuers are not adequately discussing, in MD&A, the key elements of their IFRS changeover plan or their progress towards achieving this plan. We did not request, however, that issuers re-file MD&A to improve the quality of historical IFRS transition disclosure because the focus of this particular review was to raise awareness about the IFRS changeover and to educate issuers on our disclosure expectations related to transition. Issuers were asked to confirm that future MD&A filings would address the disclosure concerns identified by staff and contain enhanced disclosure of their IFRS transition plan, along with related progress updates. We will follow up on those commitments in our subsequent reviews.

The purpose of this notice is to summarize the results of our review and to provide additional guidance for issuers in filing future MD&A. Our findings do not reflect an assessment of any issuer's preparedness for IFRS transition as this assessment is best done by an issuer's management, board of directors and external advisors. Issuers and their management, directors and advisors, should take into account the issuer's level of IFRS preparedness when assessing the extent to which future MD&A disclosures meet the requirements of securities law and their investors' need for meaningful IFRS disclosure.

It is critical that investors are properly informed during the IFRS transition on whether reported changes in financial performance relate to the adoption of different accounting standards or relate to a change in the issuer's business. Issuers that provide sufficient information about their conversion process and its effects prior to the changeover will reduce the level of investor uncertainty. Ultimately, this should lead to a more stable and less disruptive transition to IFRS, which will be beneficial to both issuers and their investors.

As discussed in SN 52-320 issuers will need to provide more detailed information about the expected effects of IFRS as the changeover date approaches. Accordingly, we will conduct future targeted reviews of issuers' IFRS transition disclosures. While the focus of our current review was education and awareness, we caution issuers that we may request re-filings of MD&A in the future if disclosure obligations are not met.

Summary of Findings

Overall, we found that issuers are not adequately disclosing information related to their IFRS transition efforts. A summary of our findings is as follows:

- 40% of issuers received a letter from staff questioning whether a changeover plan was in place as it was not evident from reading their MD&A disclosure. Given the short time remaining before the changeover date this raises concerns that issuers may not be able to comply with future filing obligations.

- Of the 60% of issuers that discussed an IFRS changeover plan in their 2008 annual MD&A, approximately half simply provided a generic description of the plan without any direct application to their own circumstances. The most valuable information for investors is IFRS transition disclosure that is specific to the issuer.

- 80% of issuers that discussed an IFRS changeover plan failed to describe significant milestones and anticipated timelines associated with each of the key elements of the plan. It is important that issuers discuss the timing associated with key elements so that investors can readily assess whether the project is progressing in accordance with the changeover plan.

- 48% of issuers that discussed IFRS transition in 2008 annual MD&A failed to provide quarterly updates in 2009 interim MD&A on the progress related to their changeover plan. Investors need progress updates to assist them in assessing the likelihood that the issuer will be able to complete its IFRS conversion on time.

Findings

This section discusses the results of our review in detail.

No Disclosure of a Changeover Plan

While many of the issuers reviewed identified that they already had or were going to have a changeover plan in place, 40% of issuers did not discuss an IFRS changeover plan at all in their MD&A. In our view, the fact that an issuer has not provided any disclosure about an IFRS changeover plan implies that the issuer has not begun to prepare for the IFRS transition or does not believe it is necessary to do so. If an issuer does not have a changeover plan, we generally believe this to be material information that should be disclosed in MD&A.

In response to our comment letters, many of these issuers explained that the reason for the absence of an IFRS changeover plan was due to such factors as the lack of complexity of business operations or resource constraints. These reasons should have been disclosed in the MD&A so that investors could have assessed the potential impact that the absence of a transition plan may have on the issuer.

Given the short time remaining before the changeover date, we are concerned that issuers without a plan may be at greater risk of not meeting their future filing obligations. We asked issuers without a changeover plan to provide us with their assessment of how they intend to meet future reporting obligations in the absence of a comprehensive plan. Management and audit committees need to carefully consider this issue and the impact on their investors if they are unable or unwilling to plan for the IFRS transition. We will continue to monitor these issuers during the period leading up to the changeover date.

Disclosure of an IFRS Changeover Plan

For the 60% of issuers that discussed an IFRS changeover plan, approximately half simply provided generic or boilerplate disclosure of the transition. We assessed disclosure as boilerplate when it reflected the following two characteristics:

- The disclosure consisted of a brief description and timeline for Canada's transition to IFRS, accompanied by a statement that the impact on the issuer's financial statements could not be determined at this time; and

- The disclosure lacked entity-specific information that would have allowed a reader to assess the current status of an issuer's conversion efforts.

Example of Boilerplate Disclosure:

Accounting standards in Canada are to converge with International Financial Reporting Standards (IFRS). The Company is required to begin reporting under IFRS by the first quarter of 2011 with comparative data also reported under IFRS. The Company is assessing the impact on accounting policies, data systems, internal controls over financial reporting, and business activities, such as financing and compensation arrangements during the period leading up to the transition date.

This type of disclosure does not allow an investor to even begin to assess the readiness of an issuer to transition to IFRS and the possible impact that IFRS adoption may have on the issuer. To have provided meaningful information to investors and market participants, reporting issuers should have discussed in reasonable detail the key elements of their IFRS changeover plan, including the applicability of each element to the issuer's specific circumstances. In addition, issuers should have described the significant milestones and anticipated timelines for each of the elements in the plan.

Key Elements of an IFRS Changeover Plan

As outlined in SN 52-320, key elements of a plan may address the impact of IFRS on accounting policies, internal control over financial reporting (ICFR), disclosure controls and procedures (DC&P), financial reporting expertise, business activities and IT systems.

For the 60% of issuers that included IFRS transition disclosure in their MD&A, the chart below shows the extent to which each of the key elements of an IFRS changeover plan, as described in SN 52-320, was specifically addressed. While many of the issuers with a plan acknowledged some key elements, most did not provide a comprehensive discussion of the impact that IFRS would have on each element affecting the entity.

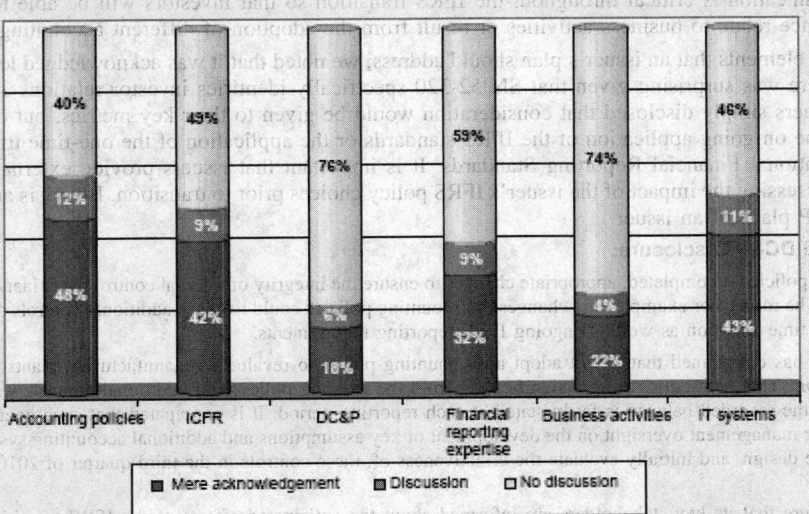

Disclosure of key elements of a changeover plan

We discuss each of these key elements in more detail below and provide examples of entity-specific disclosures that may assist issuers in filing future MD&A. These examples form only one part of a complete IFRS transition plan and are for illustrative purposes only. Accordingly, they may not be sufficient for any particular issuer given its complexity and the needs of its investors.

Accounting policies

An IFRS changeover plan should address the impact of IFRS on an issuer's accounting policies, including choices among policies permitted under IFRS and implementation decisions such as whether changes will be applied on a retrospective or prospective basis. For those issuers that disclosed an IFRS changeover plan, more than half identified that IFRS would affect their accounting policies. This is not surprising since the accounting policy choices available under IFRS will likely result in differences in recognition, measurement and disclosure in an issuer's financial statements upon conversion. Changes in accounting policies may significantly impact other elements of a changeover plan, such as information technology and data systems.

Most issuers identifying this element simply acknowledged that differences between Canadian GAAP and IFRS were being considered but did not provide any further discussion on accounting policies that were of specific interest to the issuer or its industry. Enhanced, entity-specific disclosure would have provided information about the identified accounting policy differences and the potential impact on an issuer's future balance sheet, income statement and key performance metrics. Below is an example of this type of entity-specific accounting policy disclosure for a real estate company.

Entity-Specific Accounting Policy Disclosure:

The following paragraph describes the expected impact of a significant difference between Canadian GAAP and IFRS for the Company's investment properties. Under International Accounting Standard 40 *Investment Property* (IAS 40), investment property includes land and buildings held primarily to earn rental income or for capital appreciation or both, rather than for use in the production or supply of goods or for sale in the ordinary course of business. While under both IFRS and Canadian GAAP investment property is initially measured at cost, IFRS will allow investment property to subsequently be measured using the fair value model. The Company will use the fair value model when preparing its IFRS financial statements and expects the fair value of its investment properties to be greater than the properties' previous carrying value under Canadian GAAP. The Company will determine the fair value of each investment property based upon net rental income from current leases combined with projected net rental income from future leases that best reflect market conditions at the reporting date.

Internal control over financial reporting

Internal control over financial reporting (ICFR) is another key element of an issuer's changeover plan given that the conversion from Canadian GAAP to IFRS will require the implementation of a new set of accounting standards. Depending on the nature and complexity of the issuer's business, the financial reporting effects of this conversion may be significant. Issuers will therefore need to ensure that their ICFR is sufficiently robust to address the changes resulting from IFRS transition. ICFR will need to address the initial reporting of IFRS financial statements, including related note disclosures, as well as on-going financial reporting. As well, a non-venture issuer's periodic MD&A must also disclose any material changes made to these internal controls.

We noted that many issuers acknowledged that ICFR would be assessed once accounting policy choices have been finalized. Those issuers that discussed ICFR in more detail also described the activities required to ensure that proper controls would be designed to support the initial reporting under IFRS, including appropriate management oversight. Some issuers provided a discussion of their plan to test controls throughout 2010 to facilitate certification in 2011. An example of entity-specific ICFR disclosure is included in the related section below.

Disclosure controls and procedures

An issuer's changeover plan should also consider the impact of IFRS on disclosure controls and procedures (DC&P). As discussed in National Instrument 52-109 *Certification of Disclosure in Issuers' Annual and Interim Filings*, DC&P should provide reasonable assurance that the information required by securities legislation to be disclosed by an issuer, including interim and annual financial statements and MD&A, is recorded, processed, summarized and reported within required deadlines. It is particularly important for issuers as they progress through their IFRS changeover plan that DC&P be updated to ensure that accurate information about the conversion process is communicated in MD&A in a timely manner. This communication is critical throughout the IFRS transition so that investors will be able to identify whether reported changes in financial performance relate to business activities or result from the adoption of different accounting standards.

While DC&P is one of the key elements that an issuer's plan should address, we noted that it was acknowledged less frequently than any other element. This lack of disclosure was surprising given that SN 52-320 specifically identifies investor relations and external communication plans within DC&P. Most issuers simply disclosed that consideration would be given to their key metrics, but did not discuss whether this consideration would include the on-going application of the IFRS standards or the application of the one-time transitioning standard IFRS 1 *First-time Adoption of International Financial Reporting Standards*. It is important that issuers provide external stakeholders with enough information to assist them in assessing the impact of the issuer's IFRS policy choices prior to transition. Below is an example of disclosure that addresses the ICFR and DC&P plans of an issuer.

Entity-Specific ICFR and DC&P Disclosure:

As the review of accounting policies is completed, appropriate changes to ensure the integrity of internal control over financial reporting and disclosure controls and procedures will be made. For example, any changes in accounting policies could result in additional controls or procedures being required to address reporting of first time adoption as well as ongoing IFRS reporting requirements.

At this point, the Company has determined that it will adopt an accounting policy to revalue its manufacturing plants in accordance with IAS 16 *Property, Plant & Equipment*. This new policy differs significantly from the existing policy, and additional controls will need to be designed and implemented to ensure that the recorded balance is fairly stated at each reporting period. It is anticipated that such controls will include the use of independent valuators, senior management oversight on the development of key assumptions and additional accounting system changes. The certifying officers plan to complete the design, and initially evaluate the effectiveness of, these controls in the third quarter of 2010 to prepare for certification under IFRS in 2011.

The Company will also ensure that its key stakeholders are informed about the anticipated effects of the IFRS transition. In the current year, the Company provided IFRS information as part of its investor day presentations to highlight such anticipated effects on the Company.

Financial reporting expertise

One of the most critical elements of an IFRS conversion plan is technical training for an issuer's board, management and employees. An issuer's management and its employees need the technical knowledge to lead the IFRS conversion and implement the accounting policy changes throughout the organization. Similarly, board and/or audit committee members will need to be sufficiently knowledgeable about IFRS in order to evaluate management's selection of accounting policy choices permitted under IFRS and to consider the impact of IFRS conversion on the various aspects of the issuer's operations.

Our review found most issuers simply acknowledged that the financial reporting management team would obtain the appropriate training to prepare IFRS compliant financial statements. Some issuers, however, provided disclosure about the involvement of their board of directors and audit committees and the deployment of internal and external resources to prepare for the IFRS transition. A limited number of issuers also disclosed they do not have sufficient resources in-house and would be relying on external advisers to assist with the transition. This type of entity-specific disclosure allows investors to understand the extent of resources the issuer is dedicating to the conversion process and the level of involvement of the audit committee or board of directors of the issuer. An example of disclosure around planning for an entity's IFRS reporting expertise is provided below.

Entity-Specific Financial Reporting Expertise Disclosure:

The Company has identified resource requirements to establish appropriate IFRS financial reporting expertise at all levels of the business. Training of key finance and operational staff is to be delivered starting in the second quarter of 2009. Educational information regarding IFRS implications will be issued to external constituents, such as rating agencies, during the third quarter of 2010.

The Company also held an IFRS information session with members of the Board of Directors (including Audit Committee members). During this session, management and external consultants provided the Board with a review of the timeline for implementation, the implications of IFRS standards to the business and an overview of the impact to the financial statements (as experienced in Europe by comparable companies).

As a result of the information session, the Audit Committee members will review the Audit Committee Charter and make the necessary changes to reflect the requirements for IFRS financial expertise. The Audit Committee will continue to receive quarterly presentations and project status updates from management.

Business activities

Issuers will also need to plan for the impact of IFRS on their business activities. This is a wide ranging element and may include foreign currency, hedging activities, debt covenants, compensation arrangements and risk management practices. It is important to note that any activity that relies on financial information will need to be considered in the context of the broader consequences of IFRS conversion.

Most issuers that acknowledged this element identified debt covenants and executive compensation as arrangements that would be considered. Many issuers also discussed the need to review contracts for IFRS impact as part of the changeover plan but very few provided entity-specific information that would be useful to investors. Where entity-specific information was provided, one issuer identified certain material contracts and explained, in detail, the process required to amend the contracts before the changeover date. This disclosure enabled users to understand the IFRS impact of the contracts on the issuer's operations and how the matter was being addressed in advance of the transition. Below is an example of disclosure related to the impact of IFRS on an issuer's business activities.

Entity-Specific Business Activities Disclosure:

The Company is required to meet its financial covenants included in the Declaration of Trust and the debenture agreement. Within each of the previously mentioned documents, the Company's debt cannot exceed 65% of gross book value (GBV). As discussed above, an accounting policy choice exists which would allow the Company to record its investment properties at fair value resulting in the Company's debt being significantly less than 65% of GBV, which provides less protection to stakeholders. As a result of this expected change, the debenture agreement has already been revised to state that the indebtedness percentage will decrease to 55% from the current 65% when the Company elects to report the fair value of its investment properties in accordance with IFRS. This change ensures that the financial covenant is still addressing the concerns of the stakeholders and similar revisions are expected in the other documents.

IT systems

Another key element issuers should consider in transition planning is the impact of IFRS on IT systems (IT). Any changes made to accounting policies for the recognition, measurement and disclosure requirements of IFRS may necessitate system changes to accurately support these new requirements. These changes will generally need to be made prior to the changeover date to ensure the issuer's systems can generate the comparative 2010 IFRS data required for its first interim IFRS filing in 2011. While system changes for IFRS will likely impact the general ledger, an issuer's changeover plan may also consider any implications for other applications such as, treasury, payroll and risk management systems.

Most of the issuers that addressed IT acknowledged systems changes would be needed the year before the changeover date to capture the comparative data required for their first IFRS financial statements. Issuers that discussed IT in more detail provided further, entity-specific information requirements that would arise from the adoption of IFRS. As described below for example, some issuers with investment properties disclosed that system changes would be needed to track additional fair value information for their properties. This type of disclosure allows investors to assess the extent to which an issuer's systems will be impacted by transition.

Entity-Specific Information Technology and Data Systems Disclosure:

A significant IT initiative is underway in anticipation of the implementation of IFRS standards on January 1, 2011. The initiative relates to the development of a fixed asset module that will be used to track all assets within the organization. This system will allow the Company to track all assets as required under current Canadian GAAP (requirement from now until January 1, 2011), under IFRS (required as at January 1, 2011) and for the compilation of a comparative year of financial information beginning January 1, 2010. In addition to tracking the cost basis of all the Company's real estate assets, it will track the fair value of each the Company's properties as required under IAS 40.

Milestones and Timelines

For each key element of an IFRS changeover plan discussed in MD&A, issuers should describe the significant milestones and anticipated timelines. This provides users of the financial statements with the information necessary to assess an issuer's readiness to meet the changeover to IFRS.

Our review found that only 20% of the issuers that discussed an IFRS changeover plan also described the significant milestones and anticipated timelines for each of the key elements comprising the plan. It is important that issuers discuss the timing associated with key elements so that investors can readily assess whether the project is progressing in accordance with the changeover plan.

Quarterly Updates

SN 52-320 sets out an incremental approach to disclosure of the impact of IFRS changeover leading up to 2011. Issuers should provide quarterly MD&A updates on the status of their changeover plan, along with an assessment of their progress in relation to expected milestone completion dates. Alternatively, disclosure should confirm that no progress has been made during the quarter.

We found only approximately half of the issuers that discussed IFRS transition in 2008 annual MD&A provided quarterly updates in 2009 interim MD&A on the progress related to their changeover plan. In our view, if an issuer does not provide updated information on the status of its IFRS transition in interim MD&A, this suggests the issuer has not made any progress in relation to its changeover plan. It is important for investors that an issuer communicate its progress towards IFRS conversion in a timely manner.

Future Action

As described in SN 52-320, we expect issuers to provide more detailed information about the expected effects of IFRS as we move closer to the changeover date. Specifically, an issuer's 2009 annual MD&A disclosures should provide a progress update on their conversion plan, along with a description of the major identified accounting differences between the issuer's current accounting policies and those the issuer expects to apply when preparing its IFRS financial statements. In 2010, we expect issuers to provide significant details of their changeover plan and information about key decisions on policy choices under IFRS 1 *First-time Adoption of International Financial Reporting Standards*. As well, if an issuer has quantified information about the impact of IFRS on key financial statement line items when it prepares MD&A in 2010, the issuer should include this information in its MD&A.

We will conduct reviews of selected 2009 and 2010 annual and interim MD&A filings. We will also follow up on the commitments made by issuers during this review to improve future MD&A disclosure. While the focus of our current review was to increase issuer awareness and prospectively improve IFRS disclosures, issuers should anticipate staff requests for re-filings of MD&A in the future if an issuer has not met its disclosure obligations. As well, staff may consider other regulatory action as circumstances warrant.

OSC Staff Notice 52-719 — Going Concern Disclosure Review

Date: December 17, 2010

33 O.S.C.B. 11656

Introduction

Staff of the Ontario Securities Commission conducted a review to assess the timeliness and adequacy of disclosures in financial statements and management's discussion and analysis related to the going concern assumption. The purpose of this Notice is to summarize our findings and to provide guidance to issuers on going concern disclosures to assist them in improving the disclosures and in providing robust information to investors. Smaller issuers and start-up operations often face more going concern uncertainties, and may therefore find this Notice of particular interest.

The going concern assumption is a fundamental principle in the preparation of financial statements. Under the going concern assumption it is presumed that an issuer will continue in operation and that there will be no need to liquidate or cease operating. Going concern disclosures are important to investors as they provide warnings about significant risks that the issuer is facing and may help investors avoid or minimize negative consequences when making investment decisions. It is important that the assessment issuers make with respect to the going concern assumption is rigorous and that the corresponding disclosure provides a balanced and transparent view of material uncertainties that may cast significant doubt on the issuer's ability to continue as a going concern.

> **Importance of going concern disclosure to investors**
>
> Going concern disclosures are important to investors as they provide warnings about significant risks that the issuer is facing and may help investors avoid or minimize negative consequences when making investment decisions. Each of an issuer's management, audit committee and auditors has a part to play in ensuring that investors are provided with timely and accurate information related to going concern risks.

Canadian Generally Accepted Accounting Principles (CGAAP) require management to assess the issuer's ability to continue as a going concern. If management's assessment identifies material uncertainties related to events or conditions that may cast significant doubt upon the entity's ability to continue as a going concern (for ease of reference, we will refer to these uncertainties in this Notice as a going concern risk), the financial statements should disclose such risk. Disclosure in the management's discussion and analysis (MD&A) should complement and expand upon the financial statement disclosure to provide a complete discussion of the uncertainties and the effect that they have on the issuers' operations, liquidity and capital.

Overall, we found that there is need for improvement in both the timeliness and robustness of the going concern disclosures, particularly in the MD&A. As a result of our review, certain issuers were required to make prospective improvements in their disclosure, and in some cases were required to file material change reports. Disclosure of going concern risks will continue to be an area of focus in our continuous disclosure and prospectus reviews, and issuers should be aware that we will require refilings of documents where appropriate.

Management's responsibility	**Audit committee's responsibility**
The assessment of an issuer's ability to continue as a going concern is the responsibility of its management. Management should satisfy themselves that it is reasonable for them to conclude that it is appropriate to prepare the financial statements on a going concern basis. If a material going concern risk exists, management should ensure that adequate disclosures are included in the issuer's continuous disclosure filings so that these filings fairly present the issuers financial condition, results of operations and cash flows.	The audit committee of an issuer must review the issuer's financial statements, MD&A and earnings press releases before the information is publicly disclosed. An audit committee should ensure that management has made an appropriate assessment of the issuer's ability to continue as a going concern and has made the necessary disclosures in its continuous disclosure filings. An audit committee must also be satisfied that adequate procedures are in place for the review of the issuer's other financial information disclosure.

Findings

We reviewed a total of 105 issuers. These issuers comprised the following three main groups:

1. issuers with indications of financial difficulty that had no going concern disclosure (28);
2. issuers with indications of financial difficulty that had some going concern disclosure (48); and
3. issuers that had recently ceased operations (29).

1. — Issuers with indications of financial difficulty that had no going concern disclosure

For the group of 28 issuers that had indicators suggesting financial difficulty where no going concern risk was disclosed, our review focused on the appropriateness of management's assessment to determine if a going concern risk should have been disclosed. Overall we were satisfied with management's assessment. The issuers reviewed provided sufficient evidence supporting management's belief that there were no material uncertainties creating a going concern risk. Generally, management's assessment of the issuer's ability to continue as a going concern included consideration of unusual or one-time charges, forecasts, and improvements in operations or changes in circumstances. A follow up review of these issuers found that all continue to operate, with only one issuer now disclosing a going concern risk in its financial statements.

Evidence supporting management's assessment
If events or conditions have been identified that may cast significant doubt on the entity's ability to continue as a going concern (such as the incidence of serious financial difficulty), sufficient appropriate evidence is required to demonstrate that a material uncertainty does not exist so that additional disclosures are not required. The following are two examples of situations where additional going concern disclosure was not required.
Examples:
Non-recurring charges
An issuer incurred a significant net loss in its most recent financial year. The issuer cited an unusual event — foreign currency restrictions in one of the primary markets in which the issuer operates — as the primary cause of the loss. The government restrictions had since been lifted and were not expected to recur in the foreseeable future. Absent such restrictions, the issuer was expected to return to profitability. This supported management's assessment that disclosure of a going concern risk was not necessary.
Amended financing arrangements and improvement in operations
An issuer had a significant working capital deficiency as a result of a violation of certain debt covenants. Subsequent to the year end, the issuer entered into an amended financing agreement with amended terms such that the risk of covenant violation was substantially reduced. In addition, the issuer obtained a new customer contract, and a revised forecast incorporating this new contract showed significant improvement in the issuer's results. This supported management's assessment that disclosure of a going concern risk was not necessary.

2. — Issuers with going concern disclosure

For the group of 48 issuers with indications of financial difficulty where there was some going concern disclosure, we focused our review on assessing the quality and sufficiency of the going concern disclosure in both the financial statements and MD&A.

Financial statement going concern disclosure

CGAAP requires financial statements to disclose the material uncertainties related to events or conditions identified by management's assessment that may cast significant doubt upon an issuer's ability to continue as a going concern. In assessing whether the going concern assumption is appropriate, management should take into account all available information about the future, which is at least, but is not limited to, twelve months from the balance sheet date[1]

Part 5: ONGOING REQUIREMENTS

---

[1]See CICA Handbook Section 1400 *General Standards of Financial Statement Presentation*, paragraphs 1400.08A and 1400.08B.

Auditors' responsibility

We remind auditors of their responsibilities under Canadian generally accepted auditing standards to obtain sufficient appropriate audit evidence about the appropriateness of management's use of the going concern assumption in the preparation and presentation of the financial statements and to conclude whether there is a material uncertainty about the entity's ability to continue as a going concern. We also remind auditors that if a material uncertainty exists, they are responsible for determining whether the financial statements adequately disclose and describe the going concern risk, and, therefore, that the issuer may be unable to realize its assets and discharge its liabilities in the normal course of business. Beginning for audits of financial statements for periods ending on or after December 14, 2010, an auditor's report is required to include a paragraph that highlights the existence of the material going concern risk even when adequate disclosure is made in the financial statements.

Overall, we found that issuers disclosed material uncertainties in the notes to their financial statements. However, 41% did not explicitly state that the disclosed uncertainties may cast significant doubt upon the entity's ability to continue as a going concern. This omission is significant because, absent such linking disclosure, the going concern risk is not highlighted for readers to assess the likelihood and impact of the uncertainties disclosed on the issuers' financial condition. During our review, we often found it difficult, based on the entity's public disclosures alone, to differentiate uncertainties that cast significant doubt on an entity's ability to continue as a going concern from uncertainties that do not cast such doubt, and had to request additional information from the issuer for clarification. Investors do not have the ability to request this additional information and rely on the public disclosure record to make investment decisions. That is why clear robust disclosure is important. In order for the going concern disclosures to be useful to investors, the going concern disclosures should explicitly identify that the disclosed uncertainties may cast significant doubt upon the entity's ability to continue as a going concern.

> **Impact of transition to IFRS**
>
> The disclosure requirements for going concern under CGAAP are fully converged with the requirements in paragraph 25 of International Accounting Standards 1 *Presentation of Financial Statements* (IAS 1). The IFRS Interpretations Committee (the Committee) recently considered the need for further guidance on the going concern disclosure requirements in IAS 1. While the Committee decided not to add the issue to its agenda as they believe IAS 1 provides sufficient guidance, the Committee indicated that for the going concern disclosure required by IAS 1 to be useful, **that disclosure must also identify that the uncertainties may cast significant doubt upon the entity's ability to continue as a going concern**.

Below is an example of a financial statement disclosure that does not explicitly link the disclosed uncertainties to the fact that they may cast significant doubt upon the entity's ability to continue as a going concern:

> *At year-end the Company had cash of $1,000,000 and a working capital deficiency of $2,000,000. The Company's ability to continue operations and fund its expenditures is dependent on management's ability to secure additional financing. Management is actively pursuing such additional sources of financing, and while it has been successful in doing so in the past, there can be no assurance it will be able to do so in the future.*

The example below provides the link between the uncertainties and going concern that would be meaningful to investors:

> *The financial statements were prepared on a going concern basis. The going concern basis assumes that the Company will continue in operation for the foreseeable future and will be able to realize its assets and discharge its liabilities and commitments in the normal course of business.*
>
> *The Company has incurred significant operating losses and negative cash flows from operations in recent years, and has a working capital deficiency. Whether and when the Company can attain profitability and positive cash flows is uncertain. These uncertainties cast significant doubt upon the Company's ability to continue as a going concern.*
>
> *The Company will need to raise capital in order to fund its operations. This need may be adversely impacted by: a lack of normally available financing, the ongoing lawsuit, an accelerating loss of customers, and falling sales per customer. To address its financing requirements, the Company will seek financing through joint venture agreements, debt and equity financings, asset sales, and rights offerings to existing shareholders. The outcome of these matters cannot be predicted at this time.*

MD&A going concern disclosure

MD&A should clearly communicate, through the eyes of management, an issuer's financial condition and future prospects. Various disclosure requirements for MD&A are applicable to an issuer with a going concern risk[2].

Generally, we found that issuers' discussion in MD&A related to their going concern risk needed improvement. 17% of the MD&A reviewed contained no discussion of going concern risk, and 61% of the going concern disclosures that were included were generic or incomplete.

---

[2]See Form 51-102F1 — *MD&A*, Part 1(a), sections 1.2, 1.4(g), 1.6, and 1.7.

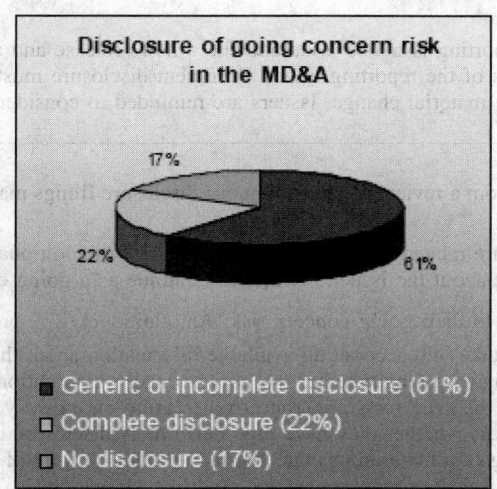

Disclosure of going concern risk
in the MD&A

17%

22%

61%

■ Generic or incomplete disclosure (61%)
□ Complete disclosure (22%)
□ No disclosure (17%)

Most commonly, we noted deficiencies in the following areas of disclosure:

- the risks and uncertainties resulting from the doubt that an issuer would be able to continue as a going concern;

- the impact of the going concern risk on the issuer's financial condition; and

- the impact of the going concern risk on the issuer's liquidity requirements, including mitigating factors and plans.

A complete MD&A discussion of going concern risk should address:

- the financial position (as shown on the balance sheet) and other factors that may affect the issuer's liquidity, capital resources and solvency;

- trends or expected fluctuations in liquidity, taking into account demands, commitments, events or uncertainties;

- risks or uncertainties that management reasonably believes will materially affect the issuer's future performance, including the possibility of discontinuance of operations;

- mitigating factors, and management's evaluation of the impact of such factors on the issuer's going concern risk; and

- management's plans to mitigate the events and uncertainties, and management's evaluation of the effectiveness and likelihood of successful implementation of these plans.

Below is an example of an incomplete MD&A disclosure.

> *The Company is focusing on developing its technology and building its business. The Company has started to generate sales but has incurred significant losses to date. The Company's ability to continue is dependent on its ability to obtain sufficient funding to sustain operations, promote its products and achieve profitable operations.*

Below is an example of a more robust MD&A discussion that addresses an issuer's going concern risk.

> *The Company has financed its operations through debt and equity issuances. During the period, sales funded 60% of operating costs (40% in the prior period).*
>
> *The Company has a working capital deficiency of $9,000,000 and an accumulated deficit of $40,000,000. After adjusting working capital for the current related party debt of $10,000,000, the Company expects it will have sufficient liquidity to finance its operations for no more than twelve months. The working capital deficiency limits the Company's ability to fund capital expenditures and operations. The Company is in breach of the minimum working capital and earnings covenants of its credit agreement, which resulted in the lender having the right to demand full repayment.*
>
> *As a result there is significant doubt about the Company's ability to continue as a going concern. The continuation of the Company as a going concern is dependent on completing a short-term financing to make a $1,000,000 payment to the Company's lender, raising sufficient working capital to maintain operations, reducing operating expenses, and increasing revenues. Subsequent to the year end, the Company has engaged a financial advisor to assist in seeking short-term financing to maintain operations and to work towards a long-term financial restructuring. The Company has also initiated an internal restructuring to sell redundant assets and reduce operating expenses. These plans are expected to be completed within nine months, and are expected to generate sufficient liquidity to finance operations until the launch of the Company's New Product. While management believes that the likelihood of completing these plans is high given the economic recovery and the rebound of the industry, a new financing has not yet been completed and there is no assurance that it will be. Without this financing the Company may be forced to cease operations.*

3. — Issuers that had recently ceased operations

For the 29 issuers that had ceased operations (i.e., filed for bankruptcy, entered receivership, became dormant) we reviewed the disclosure filed before they ceased operations to assess whether the financial statements and MD&A adequately disclosed their going concern risk. A significant number of these issuers did not draw attention to their going concern risk in the disclosure leading up to their ceasing operations. In some cases, the disclosure was boilerplate and did not clearly communicate the severity of the risk; in others, the disclosure was absent.

Timely disclosure of material change

Securities legislation generally requires a reporting issuer to issue and file a news release and a material change report on a timely basis where a material change occurs in the affairs of the reporting issuer. Sufficient disclosure must be provided to enable a reader to appreciate the significance and impact of the material change. Issuers are reminded to consider whether the occurrence of a going concern risk constitutes a material change.

The following is a summary of the findings from a review of the continuous disclosure filings made by these issuers in the period immediately before they ceased operations:

- 28% had no financial statement disclosure related to their going concern risk. An additional 20% had incomplete disclosure and did not explain that there was significant doubt about the issuer's ability to continue as a going concern.

- 21% had no MD&A discussion related to their going concern risk. An additional 52% provided incomplete or generic disclosure.

Given that CGAAP requires management to take into account all available information about the future, which is at least, but not limited to, twelve months from the balance sheet date, in assessing whether the going concern assumption is appropriate, it is important for issuers to consider all available information and assess the need for going concern disclosure on a timely basis. In addition to the financial statements and MD&A requirements, issuers should assess whether they have met their timely disclosure obligation under securities law, including the disclosure of a material fact and the reporting of a material change. We may require refiling of documents or may take additional actions in situations where issuers have not met their disclosure requirements or reporting obligations.

Going Concerns and Prospectus Offerings: Additional Concerns

Further attention to an issuer's going concern risk is necessary when the issuer undertakes to distribute securities under a prospectus.

Subsection 61(2)(c) of the *Securities Act* (Ontario) prohibits the Director from issuing a receipt for a prospectus if it appears that the proceeds from the prospectus offering, along with the issuer's other resources, will be insufficient to accomplish the purpose of the issue stated in its prospectus. A principal purpose of this provision is to protect the integrity of the capital markets, which would be harmed if an issuer ceased operations on account of insufficient funds shortly after completing a public securities offering.

The proceeds raised under a prospectus may be insufficient if they are raised:

- for a specific purpose but do not address the issuer's short-term liquidity requirements,

- through a best efforts offering without a minimum subscription, or a minimum subscription that does not appear to be sufficient to satisfy the issuer's short-term liquidity requirements, or

- through a shelf prospectus offering that can be drawn down in small increments that may not be sufficient to satisfy the issuer's short-term liquidity requirements.

A prospectus should clearly disclose an issuer's going concern risk to allow its readers to make an informed investment decision. The Director may not issue a receipt for a prospectus if it appears that the prospectus inadequately discloses an issuer's going concern risk. Additional requirements aimed at the disclosure of going concern risk may be found in both NI 41-101 *General Prospectus Requirements* and NI 44-101 *Short Form Prospectus Distributions*.

Section 21.1 of Form 41-101F1 *Information Required in a Prospectus* and section 17.1 of 44-101F1 *Short Form Prospectus* require disclosure of risk factors relating to an issuer and its business, such as cash flow and liquidity problems. The accompanying instructions require the risks to be disclosed in order of seriousness. An issuer with a going concern risk should disclose this risk in the prospectus. This disclosure should explain the uncertainties that may create a going concern risk and how the issuer is addressing it.

Material fact disclosure requirements

In addition to considering whether the occurrence of a going concern risk constitutes a material change, reporting issuers are reminded to also consider whether the presence of a going concern risk constitutes a material fact. If this is the case, to the extent that the issuer wishes to make a prospectus offering prior to general disclosure of this information, the issuer will be required to disclose the information in the prospectus in order to be able to certify that the prospectus contains full, true and plain disclosure of all material facts. Issuers should also note that persons in a "special relationship" with the reporting issuer with knowledge of a material fact will generally be prohibited from trading in securities of the issuer prior to disclosure of this information.

In many circumstances an issuer with a going concern risk should also include the disclosure required by section 8.7 of Form 41-101F1 for junior issuers. This section requires disclosure of:

- the period of time the proceeds raised under the prospectus are expected to fund operations,

- the estimated total operating costs necessary for the issuer to achieve its stated business objectives during that period of time, and

- the estimated amount of other material capital expenditures during that period of time.

Similarly, section 4.3 of Companion Policy 41-101CP and section 4.4 of Companion Policy 44-101CP explain that an issuer with negative operating cash flow in its most recently completed financial year for which financial statements have been included in the prospectus should:

- prominently disclose that fact in the use of proceeds section of the prospectus,

- disclose whether, and if so, to what extent, it will use the proceeds of the distribution to fund any anticipated negative operating cash flow in future periods, and

- disclose negative operating cash flow as a risk factor.

Below is an example of a Use or Proceeds disclosure that adequately addresses the two above disclosure requirements.

USE OF PROCEEDS

At period end, the Company had negative operating cash flow of $1,500,000 and a working capital deficit of $1,000,000. The net proceeds of the Offering will be used by the Company as follows:

Proceeds of the Offering

Working capital (future negative operating cash flows)	$2,000,000
Product development	1,000,000
General corporate purposes	200,000
Total	$3,200,000

The Company will use the proceeds to:

(i) ensure adequate working capital to fund operations for the next 9 months; and

(ii) complete the development phase of its product over the next 6 months.

If the product is successfully developed, the Company expects it will require an additional $2,000,000 to acquire regulatory approvals and implement a marketing plan.

Future Action

Our reviews identified areas where going concern disclosures need improvement. While the economic environment for issuers has begun to improve, many issuers still face a going concern risk and will need to provide clear disclosure about this risk. We will continue to focus on going concern risk disclosure as part of our continuous disclosure and prospectus reviews, and require issuers to enhance their disclosure prospectively or to refile their continuous disclosure documents, depending on the severity of the deficiency.

OSC Staff Notice 52-720 — Office of the Chief Accountant — Financial Reporting Bulletin — February 2012

Date: February 24, 2012

35 O.S.C.B. 1876

Table of Contents

Introduction

During the course of 2011, most publicly accountable enterprises transitioned from previous Canadian accounting standards to International Financial Reporting Standards (IFRS). The Office of the Chief Accountant (OCA) of the Ontario Securities Commission is publishing this bulletin to highlight selected financial reporting areas of interest that we have observed from ourexperiences with IFRS during 2011, and to identify topics that we are interested in examining more closely during 2012. The objective of this bulletin is to provide information to market participants that may be useful in preparing financial reports during 2012.

Business Combinations — IFRS 3

During the course of 2011, Staff in the OCA (we or Staff) have been interested in looking more closely at the application of accounting standards that contain different recognition, measurement and disclosure requirements under IFRS compared to pre-changeover Canadian generally accepted accounting principles (GAAP). IFRS financial reporting requirements for business combinations as prescribed by IFRS 3 *Business Combinations* (IFRS 3) may be similar to prechangeover Canadian GAAP in some respects, however, there are differences between the two reporting standards — the significance of the differences will vary from one issuer to the next depending on the facts and circumstances. As such, Staff undertook an examination of selected Canadian interim financial reports filed in 2011 to determine the level of compliance with certain features of these standards that are "new" to our capital markets. Our objective was primarily to assess whether issuers complied with IFRS 3 requirements during this important year of IFRS implementation.

Findings

Overall, issuers complied with the IFRS 3 recognition, measurement and disclosure requirements that were similar to those required under pre-changeover Canadian GAAP. However, Staff noted the following recognition and measurement issues that had not been fully reflected in financial statements in all instances:

- *Step acquisitions* — requirement to remeasure previously-held interests at fair value at the date of acquisition, and recognize the resulting gain/loss;

- *Method of acquisition accounting* — requirement to recognize identifiable assets acquired and liabilities assumed at full fair value (with limited exceptions) even when the acquirer's interest in the acquiree is less than 100%;

- *Transactions outside of the business combination* — requirement to identify, measure and appropriately disclose how certain transactions such as "payouts to employees of acquiree" or extension of an existing contract with the acquiree were accounted for separately from the acquisition of assets and assumption of liabilities in the business combination.

In addition, the following deficiencies were noted in areas of **new disclosure requirements** such as:

- Qualitative description of what makes up goodwill

- Revenue and profit or loss of the acquiree since the acquisition date

- Pro-forma revenue and profit or loss for the combined entity

- Reason for the business combination

- Gross contractual amounts of acquired receivable and an estimate of the contractual cash flows not expected to be collected

The significant accounting policy note (related to business combination) that was included in the interim financial reports provided limited information in some instances, and some issuers did not appear to have updated their accounting policy note to be in accordance with IFRS 3.

Our examination of IFRS 3 compliance included a sample of interim financial reports that were subject to auditor review as well as those that did not have auditor involvement. In general, we noted that interim financial reports that were subject to auditor review had fewer deficiencies than those without auditor involvement.

- Preparers need to provide important *new* disclosure for business combinations — **more extensive** under IFRS than previous Canadian GAAP
- Do investors understand *what* has been acquired, *how* it was acquired and *why*?

Common Control Business Combination Transactions

Business combinations under common control are combinations whereby businesses are ultimately controlled by the same party or parties both before and after the business combination transaction. Accounting for business combinations under common control is a complex area because of the wide array of such transactions that occur in practice.

IFRS currently does not provide guidance on accounting for common control transactions, and as a result, financial statement preparers look to IAS 8 *Accounting Policies, Changes in Estimates, and Errors* to determine an accounting policy that is appropriate for its specific circumstances. In Canada and in other jurisdictions, we have noted the following financial reporting approaches for the "acquired" business that is, in essence, a transfer between entities under common control:

    (i) Book value (carry-over basis) accounting of the assets and liabilities acquired for current and comparative years — the financial statements of both entities are combined together at book value for the current and comparative years to account for the entities as though they had always been combined together as one entity,

    (ii) Book value (carry-over basis) accounting of the assets and liabilities acquired from the date of acquisition — the financial statements of both entities are combined together at book value only from the date of acquisition without restatement of comparative years; or

    (iii) Purchase accounting analogous to IFRS 3 on the basis that the acquirer is a separate entity in its own right.

Consider:
- Is **complete** information about the acquiree being provided?
  - **with comparative information**?
  - **without gaps** in periods in the current year?
- Is the selected accounting policy resulting in **useful information** to an investor?

Staff have encountered instances where the accounting approach outlined in (ii) and (iii) above can result in the omission of important financial information about the acquiree. Such information includes current period pre-acquisition information, as well as comparative period information. Staff are of the view that it is important for investors to have financial information about the acquiree that relates to periods both **before and after** the common control transaction, **without gaps** in the periods being presented. In many of these transactions, there has often been no substantive change regarding the ultimate ownership structure or ongoing operations of the acquiree, and therefore it is important that investors are provided with the current period preacquisition as well as comparative financial information for making an investment decision.

Accounting for a common control business combination transaction only from the date of acquisition forward can also result in the omission of information that may otherwise not have been available to the users of the financial statements, for example, when the business combination takes place at a time between reporting periods. To illustrate, a business combination under common control takes place on December 1, 2011. The most recent financial statements of both the acquirer and the acquiree are available for the quarter ended September 30, 2011. If the acquirer accounts for the transaction from the acquisition date forward, the operating results of the acquiree for the period from October 1 to November 30, 2011 may not otherwise be available to the investor group. **Staff are concerned that the absence of such information may not result in complete financial information that is important for the investment decision-making needs of users**.

In summary, common control business combination transactions can take various forms, and facts and circumstances will inevitably be different in each situation. When determining an accounting approach for such transactions, issuers and their advisors should carefully consider whether the resulting publicly available financial reporting and disclosure will provide investors with information about the acquiree that is complete with comparative period information and without gaps in the periods being presented. We would encourage issuers and their advisors to consult with us regarding proposed accounting treatments for these types of complex common control business combination transactions in advance of filing financial statements. Please refer to the OCA consultations procedures discussed at the end of this bulletin.

Impairment

There are significant differences between the requirements of IAS 36 *Impairment of Assets* (IAS 36) and pre-changeover Canadian GAAP with respect to the recognition and measurement of impairment. The application of these requirements that are new to Canada are of a particular interest to Staff given the current local and global economic environment. Key areas of interest are as follows:

- disclosures for each material impairment loss or reversal including the following:

  - events and circumstances that led to the recognition or reversal of the impairment loss;

  - a description of the cash generating unit (CGU);

  - whether the recoverable amount is fair value less costs to sell or value in use;

  - if recoverable amount is fair value less costs to sell, the basis used to determine fair value less costs to sell;

  - if recoverable amount is value in use, the discount rate(s) used in the estimate;

- disclosures required for estimates used to measure recoverable amounts of CGUs containing significant goodwill or intangible assets with indefinite useful lives, irrespective of whether there has been an impairment or not:

  If recoverable amount is based on **value in use**:

  - description of key assumptions that management has based its cash flow projections on;

  - description of management's approach to making these determinations;

  - the period over which management has projected cash flows, and the growth rates used

  If recoverable amount is based on **fair value less costs to sell**:

  - the methodology used to determine fair value less costs to sell;

  - If fair value less costs to sell is not determined using an observable market price for the CGU(s), a description of the key assumptions and management's approach;

  - If fair value less costs to sell is determined using discounted cash flow projections, disclosures about the period over which management has projected cash flows, and growth rates;

IAS 36 is a complex standard that involves numerous judgements and estimation uncertainties. As a result, IAS 36 disclosure requirements are aimed at providing users with useful information for evaluating the reliability of the impairment tests. IAS 36 requires these disclosures to be provided appropriately, when applicable, in the annual financial statements.

Consider:
- Are financial statement disclosures providing the necessary information to allow investors to **easily understand** how 'recoverable amount' was determined?

Indicators of impairment

Similar to 2011, 2012 continues to be a year of global economic uncertainty and issuers may experience the impact of these events in their global operations as well as through direct and indirect international debt and equity holdings. As the European sovereign debt crisis continues to impact the global economy, issuers should remain alert of the impacts of the crisis locally. Although sovereign debt concerns may not be significant for Canadian issuers who do not hold debt instruments of affected countries, there may be considerations for reporting issuers who hold debt or equity investments in entities that operate in or are impacted by a jurisdiction experiencing sovereign debt issues. Guarantees of third party investments in entities operating in or who hold debt instruments of affected Eurozone countries may also create increased exposures to a Canadian guarantor.

Part 5: ONGOING REQUIREMENTS

Consider:
- Indicators of impairment as a result of the current economic environment?
- Indirect impact of European sovereign debt crisis on investments held in affected entities?

Staff remind issuers to carefully assess whether the impact of these exposures:

- are indicators that the recoverable value of an asset/CGU may be lower than its carrying value, and
- are appropriately reflected in the valuation of investments in affected debt or equity instruments accounted for in accordance with IAS 39 *Financial Instruments*.

When applying IAS 36, various sources of information are required to be considered in assessing whether an indicator of impairment exists. In the current economic climate, the market capitalization of some reporting issuers may be less than the carrying amount of the issuer's net asset. In this situation, **investors will benefit from disclosure that explains the shortfall and why the carrying value of the net assets is supported**.

This area of impairment, as well as other indicators identified in IAS 36, will be examined more closely by Staff as we review this area of IFRS during 2012.

Discounted cash flow calculations

In the past, Staff have encountered filings where issuers have been overly optimistic in establishing assumptions used to determine the fair value of their reporting units (under pre-changeover Canadian GAAP). Problems include incomplete or unrealistic cash flow forecasts that reflect excessive growth rates, unproven sales trends, or insufficient consideration for working capital or capital expenditure requirements going forward.

Staff have also encountered filings where the discount rate incorporated in discounted cash flow calculations did not appropriately reflect current market assessments of the time value of money and the risks specific to the asset.

This will continue to be an area of interest for Staff in 2012 given the current economic environment and the areas of judgement and/or estimates when assessing impairment. It is the responsibility of issuers to ensure they are not **unduly inflating fair value determinations** by incorporating overly optimistic assumptions in discounted cash flows calculations.

Consider:
- Are cash flow projections based on **reasonable and supportable** assumptions?
- Do discount rates reflect current market assessments and specific risk of the asset or CGU?

Critical Judgements and Sources of Estimation Uncertainty

Critical Judgements

IAS 1 *Presentation of Financial Statements* (IAS 1) paragraph 122 requires the disclosure of judgements, apart from those involving estimations, that management has made in the process of applying the entity's accounting policies and that have the **most significant effect** on the amounts recognized in the financial statements. IAS 1.BC77 notes that the disclosure of **the most important of these judgements** enable users of financial statements to better understand how the accounting policies are applied and to make comparisons between issuers regarding the basis on which management make these judgements. Disclosures of judgements that are immaterial may obscure those that are most important, and may make it difficult for an investor to understand the most important features of the critical judgements disclosures.

Consider:
- Do the disclosures focus on the **most significant** judgements?
- Are disclosures of insignificant (**immaterial**) judgements "cluttering up" the financial statements?

Pre-changeover Canadian GAAP did not have a similar requirement, and therefore this disclosure is likely new to reporting issuers. In our examination of practices of disclosure in this area for interim financial reports, we noted that such disclosures were either **omitted** from the financial statements or were **lacking in substance (boilerplate)**. The purpose of such disclosures is to enable users of financial statements to better understand how the accounting policies are applied and to make comparisons between issuers regarding the basis on which management make these judgements. Some examples of areas of material judgement may include:

- going concern risk assessment;
  - refer to further discussion in the section *Going Concern*
- determination of CGUs;
  - significant judgement may be involved in determining the *smallest* group of assets that generates independent cash *inflows*
- determination of functional currency;
  - significant judgement may be involved where primary and secondary indicators are mixed, and management's judgement should be appropriately disclosed

It is also important to note that IAS 1.132 requires the disclosures of judgements made by management in the process of applying the issuer's accounting policies *separately* from the disclosures of judgements involving estimation uncertainty (see below).

Sources of estimation uncertainty

IAS 1.125 requires an issuer to disclose information about the assumptions made about the future and other major sources of estimation uncertainty at the end of the reporting period, that have a significant risk of resulting in a material adjustment to the carrying amounts of assets and liabilities within the next financial year. In respect of those assets and liabilities, notes to the financial statements shall include details of their nature and their carrying amount as at the end of the reporting period.

Similar to the disclosure of judgements, Staff noted that disclosures in this area either **lacked substance** (boilerplate) **or included every source of estimation uncertainty**. Staff remind issuers that the disclosure requirements here are for estimates that require **management's** *most difficult, subjective or complex* **judgements**. The basis of conclusion also stresses that few items are disclosed here [IAS 1.BC81].

Consider:
- Do the estimates require management's **most difficult, subjective or complex** judgements?
- Separate disclosures of estimation uncertainty apart from judgements is helpful to an investor's understanding of both of these requirements.

Examples

Below are examples of estimation uncertainty disclosures that did not meet Staff's expectation, followed by an example of improved disclosure:

1. — Disclosure that did not meet Staff's expectation

Problems

- **lacks substance (boilerplate)**

- **does not separate critical judgements from sources of estimation uncertainty**

The preparation of financial statements in conformity with IFRS requires management to make estimates and assumptions that affect the application of accounting policies and the reported amounts of assets, liabilities, income and expenses. Estimates and judgements are reviewed on a continuous basis and are based on a management's historical experience, knowledge of current conditions and other factors believed to be reasonable under the circumstances.

Material estimates and assumptions are made with respect to establishing the following: depreciation and amortization periods; goodwill and indefinite life intangible assets; the valuation of inventories; allowance for doubtful accounts; impairment of financial assets; customer rebates; current and deferred income taxes; impairment of non-financial assets (if any); fair value and level of financial instruments; and the remeasurement of employee future benefits. Actual results could differ from those estimates under different assumptions and conditions.

2. — Improved disclosure

Improvements

- **entity specific**

- **separation of critical judgements from sources of estimation uncertainty** *The preparation of financial statements in conformity with IFRS requires management to make estimates and assumptions that affect the application of accounting policies and the reported amounts of assets, liabilities, income and expenses. Actual results may differ from these estimates.*

Estimates and underlying assumptions are reviewed on an ongoing basis. Revisions to accounting estimates are recognized in the period in which the estimates are revised and in any future periods affected.

Critical judgements in applying accounting policies:

The following are critical judgements that management has made in the process of applying accounting policies and that have the most significant effect on the amounts recognized in the consolidated financial statement:

Determination of a Cash Generating Unit (CGU) (an excerpt):

The Company's production facility in London produces the specialized chip that is then transferred to the production facility in Waterloo for use in the final product sold by the Company. The transfer price is determined internally which includes a level of margin for the London production facility.

Currently, there is no active market for specialized chip and the cash inflows of the London production facility is dependant on the demand for the final product. As such, management has concluded that the London production facility does not generate cash flows that are largely independent of the cash flows of assets of the Waterloo production facility. The two facilities are managed together and hence, management has treated the two facilities as a single CGU.

Key sources of estimation uncertainty:

The following are key assumptions concerning the future and other key sources of estimation uncertainty that have a significant risk of resulting in a material adjustment to the carrying amount of assets and liabilities within the next financial year:

Decommissioning liabilities (an excerpt):

As part of the long-term lease agreement on the production facility with ABC Company, the Company has recognized a provision for decommissioning obligations associated with the production facility. In determining the fair value of the provision, assumptions and estimates are made in relation to discount rates, the expected cost to dismantle and restore the facility to its original condition and the expected timing of those costs. The carrying amount of the provision at December 31, 2011 is $1,850,000 (2010: $1,600,000).

Part 5: ONGOING REQUIREMENTS

If the estimated pre-tax discount rate used in the calculation had been 10% higher than management's estimate, the carrying amount of the provision would have been $75,000 lower.

Going Concern

Many issuers continue to face ongoing challenges as a result of economic conditions and uncertainties stemming from the impact of international events such as the European sovereign debt situation. National growth rates (actual and expected) continue to be low in most countries.

As volatile market conditions continue into 2012, Staff remain focused on reviewing financial statements for compliance with financial reporting standards related to the assessment and disclosure of going concern risks. This has been an area of focus in prior years, and further detailed information can be found in OSC Staff Notice 52-719 *Going Concern Disclosure Review* (SN 52-719). Although the notice refers to prechangeover Canadian GAAP, it is still applicable for issuers reporting under IFRS as the disclosure requirements for going concern under prechangeover Canadian GAAP were fully converged with IFRS.

Going concern disclosures are important to investors as they provide warnings about significant risks that the issuer is facing and are of critical importance to assist investors when making investment decisions. Therefore, it is important that the assessment issuers make with respect to the going concern assumption is rigorous and that the corresponding disclosure provides a balanced and transparent view of material uncertainties related to events or conditions that may cast significant doubt on the issuer's ability to continue as a going concern.

Staff remind issuers that it is important to differentiate uncertainties that cast significant doubt on an entity's ability to continue as a going concern from uncertainties that do not cast such doubt. This may not be easily determinable if the disclosures provided are "boilerplate" and lack specificity. Therefore, it is important that the going concern disclosures explicitly identify that the disclosed *material uncertainties may cast significant doubt* upon the entity's ability to continue as a going concern. The IFRS Interpretations Committee (IFRIC) had considered the need for further guidance on the going concern disclosure requirements in IFRS. While IFRIC decided not to add the issue to its agenda, IFRIC indicated that for the going concern disclosure required by IFRS to be useful, that disclosure **must also identify that the uncertainties may cast significant doubt upon the entity's ability to continue as a going concern**. Staff will continue to monitor going concern disclosures and will look for and expect the explicit use of the words "material uncertainty...casts significant doubt" in disclosures relating to going concern.

In these circumstances, an "emphasis of matter" paragraph is also required to be included in an auditor's report accompanying the annual financial statements. This paragraph should highlight the existence of the material uncertainties which may cast significant doubt upon the entity's ability to continue as a going concern even when adequate disclosure is made in the financial statements. The emphasis of matter paragraph also draws users' attention to the note in the financial statements that discloses the matters. Staff will continue to look for and expect such emphasis of matter paragraph in the auditor's report when appropriate.

Consider:
- Can a reader identify going concern disclosures **apart** from those that are associated with other uncertainties / estimation uncertainty?
- Are the words "**material uncertainty . . . casts significant doubt**" explicitly used in the disclosure?
- Does the auditor's report include an "**emphasis of matter**" paragraph highlighting the existence of the going concern risk?

Each of an issuer's management, audit committee and auditors has an important part to play to ensure that investors are provided with timely and accurate information related to going concern risks. Staff remind issuers that this will continue to be an area of focus as part of ongoing financial statement reviews.

Please refer to SN 52-719 for further information and examples on going concern risks disclosures.

Non-GAAP Financial Measures and Additional Gaap Measures

Staff of the Canadian Securities Administrators (CSA) have recently published revised CSA Staff Notice 52-306 *Non-GAAP Financial Measures and Additional GAAP Measures* (SN 52-306). This notice has been revised to provide additional information on Staff's expectations for disclosure of additional GAAP measures presented under IFRS.

The notice describes practices that help issuers and certifying officers address their obligations to ensure that the information they provide to the public is not misleading. The practices contain examples of subtotals that should not be presented in the statement of comprehensive income. These examples include subtotals without labels, "income before the undernoted items", adjusted EBITDA and adjusted EBIT. Staff also remind issuers who include "operating earnings" or similar subtotals to include all items of an operating nature within the subtotal.

The use of additional GAAP measures will continue to be an area of focus as part of ongoing reviews of financial statements.

Areas of Interest for 2012

We will continue to examine the implementation of IFRS standards that are "new" to the Canadian capital markets, some of which are identified in the table below. The financial reporting areas of focus cited in this bulletin are not an exhaustive list of all areas that will be explored by OSC staff during the course of financial statement reviews in 2012, and application of specific IFRS standards depends on the facts and circumstances of each issuer. Successful compliance with IFRS in all material respects is important in order to provide relevant information for investors to make informed investment decisions.

Areas of Interest for further examination during 2012

Business combinations   **Additional GAAP Measures**

Critical judgements   **Impairment**   • See above discussion in this bulletin

Provisions

- Threshold for recognition (*probable*) lower under IFRS than under pre-changeover Canadian GAAP (*more likely than not*)

- Disclosure of whether the discount rate is credit risk adjusted or not

- Provisions for loss-making executory contracts

- Disclosure of the **nature and amount of changes in estimates** when an estimate previously reported in an interim period is significantly changed during the final interim period.

Fair value measurement

- Consideration of the **impact of the current economic conditions** on the risk adjustments (if any) and discount rates

- Reasonable and supportable assumptions, and a **rigorous process** applied to determining fair value calculations

Debt classification

- Long-term classification when an issuer has an *"unconditional right"* to defer settlement of the liability for at least twelve months after the end of the reporting period [IAS 1.69(d)]

- Refinancing / rollover arrangements in place at the financial statement date **with the same party** in order to achieve long-term classification

Statement of comprehensive income — presentation

- Additional supplementary disclosure 'by nature' when functional approach is utilized

- Use of additional subtotals in the statement of comprehensive income (i.e. additional GAAP measures)

Questions

As part of its on-going efforts to promote high-quality financial reporting, the OCA has established an external consultation process for consultations on unusual or complex technical accounting issues and financial statement disclosures. *Click here [Editor's note: http://www. osc.gov.on.ca/en/Companies_oca_20111130_rfc-with-oca.htm]* for the *Guidelines for Requests for Consultations with the Office of the Chief Accountant*. Note that this protocol does not replace and is not a substitute for the existing process for pre-filings and applications made under National Instrument 11-203 — *Process for Exemptive Relief Applications in Multiple Jurisdictions*.

OSC Staff Notice 52-721 — Office of the Chief Accountant Financial Reporting Bulletin

Issue: September 19, 2013

Citation: 36 O.S.C.B. 9116

Table of Contents

1. — Introduction
2. — Executive summary
3. — Asset Impairment
4. — Segment Reporting
5. — Questions

1. — Introduction

The Office of the Chief Accountant (OCA) of the Ontario Securities Commission is publishing this bulletin to highlight observations about asset impairment and segment disclosures in reporting issuer financial statements prepared in accordance with International Financial Reporting Standards (IFRS). The objective of this bulletin is to provide useful information to market participants that may assist in preparing future financial reports.

2. — Executive summary

International Accounting Standard 36 *Impairment of Assets* (IAS 36) and International Financial Reporting Standard 8 *Operating Segments* (IFRS 8) require comprehensive disclosures that are designed to provide users of financial statements with useful information. This includes insights about important areas such as the valuation of assets, how assets are being used within an organization, and how management has exercised its judgement in making the determinations that result in the information provided in the financial statements. Staff in the OCA (we or Staff) have recently been focussing on disclosures provided by reporting issuers in the area of asset impairment and segment reporting in order to assess the overall quality of disclosures and identify areas of concern in the application of the two standards.

Our observations in the area of asset impairment disclosures identified the following areas that could be improved to provide investors with useful and meaningful disclosure:

- description of the issuer s cash generating units (CGUs);
- explanations of the events and circumstances that contributed to the impairment loss; and
- explanations of the basis of key assumptions and the valuation approach used to determine the recoverable amount

Our observations in the area of *segment reporting* identified the following areas where we believe reporting issuers should pay particular attention when applying IFRS 8:

- identification of the Chief Operating Decision Maker (CODM);
- identification of operating segments;
- aggregation of operating segments to form reportable segments;
- change in reportable segments; and
- entity-wide disclosures

Our observations have been derived from OCA and Corporate Finance involvement in the review of selected annual IFRS financial statements and interim financial reports through various reporting periods in 2011 and 2012.

3. — Asset Impairment

Given the challenging economic environment that has been present for several years in Canada and throughout various regions of the world, Staff have been interested in how reporting issuers have been complying with the disclosure requirements of IAS 36 with the objective of assessing the overall quality of disclosure and to identify areas where disclosure could be enhanced. In addition, the application of IAS 36 is an area of interest to Staff given that it contains different recognition, measurement and disclosure requirements compared to pre-changeover Canadian generally accepted accounting principles (GAAP) that was in effect prior to 2011.

A. — Determination of cash-generating units (CGUs)

Determination of a CGU and the allocation of goodwill to each CGU is an important initial step in performing annual and periodic goodwill impairment testing. IAS 36 defines a CGU to be the smallest identifiable group of assets that generates cash inflows that are largely independent of the cash inflows from other assets or group of assets. IAS 36 paragraph 130(d) requires specific disclosures about CGUs when an impairment loss is recognized. We note the following observations pertaining to CGU disclosure:

- In many instances, reporting issuers who recognized an impairment loss did not provide a description of the CGU (such as whether it is a product line, a plant, a business operation, a geographical area, or a reportable segment). Without this required information, financial statement users will not have sufficient context regarding the impact of the impairment on the overall activities and operations of the entity.
- In circumstances where an entity changed how it had aggregated its assets into CGUs from the prior year, reporting issuers often failed to provide disclosures to identify the change in the aggregation and the reason for the change. Since a change in the grouping of assets for a CGU from year to year may affect impairment testing results, a description and reason for the current and former aggregation approach is important since it provides financial statement users with insight as to why management is making this change.

3A.1 — EXAMPLE — description of CGUs that did not meet Staff's expectation Problems:

- *lacks substance (boilerplate)*
- *vague disclosures to describe the CGUs*

For the purposes of assessing impairment, Issuer ABC s assets are grouped and tested at the cash generating unit (CGU) level. ABC's CGUs are the smallest identifiable group of assets that generates cash inflows that are largely independent of the cash inflows from other assets or groups of assets.

3A.2 — EXAMPLE — improved CGU disclosure

Improvements:

- *greater specificity about the CGUs*
- *informs users of the level tested for impairment*

For the purposes of assessing impairment, Issuer XYZ's assets are grouped and tested at the cash generating unit level. Issuer XYZ owns 20 retail stores in various cities in Ontario, with no more than one store residing in each city.

Each store is managed at the corporate level, with internal reporting organized to measure performance of each retail store. Management has determined that its cash generating units are identifiable at the individual retail store level since the assets devoted to and cash inflows generated by each store are separately identifiable and independent of each other.

B. — Indicators of impairment

An asset is impaired when its carrying amount exceeds its recoverable amount. An entity is required to assess at the end of each reporting period whether there is any indication that an asset is impaired, and if any such indication is present, an entity is required to estimate the recoverable amount of the asset. If an entity determines that there is an impairment loss to be recognized, or reversed, during the period, IAS 36 paragraph 130(a) requires an entity to disclose the events and circumstances that led to the recognition or reversal of the impairment loss.

We noted that in many instances reporting issuers provided only general disclosure about the events and circumstances that led to a material impairment loss. The disclosures were broad, vague and did not explain the entity-specific factors of the main events and circumstances that resulted in the impairment.

3B.1 — EXAMPLE — disclosure of events and circumstances which led to an impairement loss — that did not meet Staff's expectation

Problems:

- *lacks substance (boilerplate)*
- *not entity-specific*

During the period, ABC company recorded an impairment charge in CGU X due to weaker than expected performance.

3B.2 — EXAMPLE — improved disclosure of events and circumstances which led to an impairement loss

Improvements:

- *greater specificity about the indicators of and reasons for impairment*

Issuer XYZ considers both qualitative and quantitative factors when determining whether an asset may be impaired. In the fourth quarter management noted indications that CGU X may be impaired in light of the following conditions:

- *The technology underlying CGU X's products has recently been challenged by newer products that offer additional functionality that the CGU X product is not able to support. In order to remain competitive in the marketplace CGUX has reduced CGU X's product prices.*
- *The primary customers for CGU X's products have informed Issuer XYZ that future orders will be lower than originally anticipated in light of the recent functionality limitations noted above.*
- *CGU Y recently introduced a new product that has received a strong response in the marketplace, which unexpectedly resulted in customers who were anticipated to purchase CGU X's products to instead early adopt CGU Y's new product sooner than anticipated.*

A plan to discontinue or restructure the operation to which the asset, CGU or group of CGUs belong

Significant changes with an adverse effect on the entity that have taken place, *or are expected to take place* in the near future, are an important source of internal information that is identified in paragraph 12(f) of IAS 36. A significant change, specifically, includes a plan to discontinue or restructure the operation that the asset belongs to. Staff have observed instances where the statement of comprehensive income would identify a loss from discontinued operations that includes asset disposals, yet there were no impairment losses recorded in prior periods when the reporting issuer had originally identified the asset as held for sale. We remind management that a *plan by management to dispose of an asset*, or discontinue or restructure a CGU is an indicator of impairment, and that the asset should be assessed when the decision to dispose, discontinue, or restructure is made.

Market capitalization lower than net book value

In the current economic climate, reporting issuers' market capitalization may be less than the carrying amount of the issuer's net assets. We remind reporting issuers that IAS 36, paragraph 12 (d) specifically states that when an entity's carrying amount of the net assets is more than its market capitalization, this is an external source of information which may indicate impairment that must be carefully considered by management. Although this factor alone may not lead to a determination that an asset is impaired, management should understand what factors may have contributed to the decline in market capitalization in order to assess whether there are additional indications of impairment that may be present.

Consider and assess:

- *Are there identifiable factors that contributed to the decline in market capitalization?*
- *How do these factors affect the cash inflows of your product line, business line etc., in the current period and in future periods?*

C. — Allocating goodwill to CGUs and timing of impairment

For the purpose of impairment testing, IAS 36 requires that goodwill be allocated to the company's CGUs, or groups of CGUs that are expected to benefit from the synergies. IAS 36 states that each CGU or group of CGUs to which the goodwill is allocated should represent the *lowest level* within the entity at which the goodwill is monitored for internal management purposes, and not be larger than an operating segment (as defined in IFRS 8).

During the course of our work, we observed reporting issuers disclosing that they monitored goodwill at the operating segment level. We recognize that this represents the highest level at which goodwill is allowed to be tested for impairment, however in some instances we questioned whether the *operating segment level* is in fact, the lowest level where other disclosures within the financial statements as well as other public documents (e.g., management's discussion and analysis) indicated that management monitored its operations, including its goodwill, at a lower level than an operating segment.

D. — Measuring the recoverable amount

The recoverable amount of a CGU is determined to be the higher of its fair value less cost to sell (FVLCS) or value in use (VIU). Measuring the recoverable amount (whether it is FVLCS or VIU) is a critical step in the impairment analysis as it determines whether an impairment charge should be recognized in the financial statements. This step often involves significant judgement on the part of management to develop assumptions and estimates in determining its recoverable amount.

During the course of our work, we observed that, certain reporting issuers failed to comply with the disclosure requirements in IAS 36 in identifying whether FVLCS or VIU was determined to be the recoverable amount. Without this disclosure, investors are not able to fully understand and evaluate the reporting issuer's approach to determining the recoverable amount.

Disclosure of estimates and key assumptions

IAS 36 requires an entity to disclose information about the key assumptions used to determine the recoverable amount when it is based on VIU or FVLCS using a valuation technique (e.g., discount cash flow method). During the course of our work, we observed that the disclosure required for key assumptions was not always provided, such as management's approach for determining the discount rate or growth rate used for discounted cash flow calculations.

3D.1 — EXAMPLE — disclosure of the basis for management's key assumptions in determining FVLCS — that did not meet Staff's expectation

Problems:

- *. valuation approach was not explained*
- *no explanations for the basis of the key assumptions used*

Issuer ABC recorded a goodwill impairment loss of $2 million. The recoverable amount of this CGU was based on the estimated fair value less cost to sell based on estimated cash flows over a 5 year period and a discount rate of 11%.

3D.2 — EXAMPLE — improved disclsoure of the basis for management's key assumptions in determining FVLCS

Improvements:

- *enhanced explanations about the key assumptions used*

Issuer XYZ recorded a goodwill impairment loss of $2 million. The recoverable amount was based on FVLCS using discounted cash flow projections. The significant assumptions applied in goodwill impairment test are described below.

Cash Flows

Estimated cash flows are based on budgeted earnings before interest, taxes, depreciation and amortization (EBITDA) for the next three years. The forecast is extended for an additional two years based on an analysis of industry reports, historical and forecast volume changes, growth rates, and inflation rates.

Discount rate

The weighted average cost of capital (WACC) was determined to be in the range of 10% to 14% and is based on market capital structure of debt, risk-free rate, equity risk premium, beta adjustment to the equity risk premium based on a review of betas of comparable publicly traded companies, an unsystematic risk premium, and after-tax cost of debt based on corporate bond yields.

Terminal value growth rate

Five years of cash flows have been included in the discounted cash flow models. Maintainable debtfree net cash flow beyond the forecast period is estimated to approximate the 20X7 cash flows increased by a terminal growth rate in the range of 1% to 3% and is based on the industry's expected growth rates, forecast inflation rates, and management s experiences.

Sensitivity analysis

IAS 36 paragraph 134(f) states that, if a reasonably possible change in a key assumption on which management has based its determination of the CGUs' (group of CGUs') recoverable amount would cause the CGUs' (group of CGUs') carrying amount to exceed its recoverable amount, management should provide users of the financial statements with information on how much the key assumption must change in order for the recoverable amount to be equal to the carrying amount.

We observed that such analysis was often not provided. During this uncertain and volatile economic climate, we expect that changes in key assumptions are likely to occur more frequently than in stable conditions. We remind reporting issuers of the importance of critically analyzing the sensitivity of their key assumptions and providing material disclosures in their financial reports. *This information is especially important in a situation where key assumptions result in a recoverable amount that exceeds, but is very close to, the carrying amount of a CGU.*

4. — Segment Reporting

Segment disclosures required by IFRS 8 assist investors in analyzing reporting issuers that are involved in diverse businesses. Financial information about business segments can be as important as information about the reporting issuer as a whole. Investors and analysts have emphasized the importance of transparent disclosure about operating segments because it gives a view of the business as it is seen through the eyes of management.

A. — Identification of the chief operating decision maker (CODM)

The disclosure required by IFRS 8 is primarily driven by the determination of what information is used internally by the CODM. IFRS 8 identifies the CODM as the function that reviews the operating results of segments regularly to assess its performance and make decisions about allocation of resources. IFRS 8 further explains that the term CODM identifies a function, and not necessarily a manager with a specific title. Identification of such function may require an entity to exercise judgement in making such a determination.

While IFRS 8 does not require entities to identify the CODM in their disclosure, we observed that reporting issuers frequently provide this disclosure and most often identify the CODM as the CEO of the entity. However, we also noted that some other reporting issuers identified the CODM to be the entire Board of Directors or the executive team.

When determining the CODM, reporting issuers should consider whether the management level identified is appropriate for the organization and whether the disclosure is appropriately reflecting how operating decisions are made. IFRS 8 paragraph 5(b) defines an operating segment to be a component of an entity at the level at which the relevant operating decisions are made, rather than the overall strategic decisions.

Identification of the CODM at a level that is too high within the organization (i.e. at the 'strategic level' vs. the 'operating level') could result in too low of a number of segments being identified, and inadequate information provided to investors about the various business operations.

Consider and assess:

- *Is the CODM identified at an appropriate 'operating' level within the organization?*
- *Are investors receiving an adequate level of information about the various business operations of the entity?*

B. — Identification of operating segments

Correct identification of operating segments is also critical in ensuring appropriate segment disclosures are provided. IFRS 8 paragraph 5 defines operating segments as a component of an entity that:

- *engages in business activities from which it may earn revenues and incur expenses,*
- *whose operating results are regularly reviewed by the entity's CODM to make decisions about resources to be allocated to the segment and assess its performance, and*
- *for which discrete financial information is available.*

In assessing whether reporting issuers correctly identified operating segments, we considered financial statement disclosures as well as information presented in other continuous disclosure documents that might provide useful insights in the various segments of an issuer. These documents included a reporting issuer's management discussion and analysis (MD&A), press releases, annual information form, investor presentation materials and other information presented on company websites. In some cases, we noted that discrete financial information was available that appeared to be reviewed by the CODM, which suggests that an operating segment exists. In the absence of segment disclosures in such circumstances, Staff questioned whether the requirements of IFRS 8 had been complied with.

Consistency of segment disclosure

The financial information presented outside of the financial statements in some instances included quantitative information that was useful and appropriate. However, in some instances Staff observed that information in these other documents related to components of the business that were not consistent with the number of segments identified (and the resulting segment disclosure) in the financial statements, which raised questions relating to the inconsistencies. In Staff's view, when this type of information is provided outside of the financial statements that is not consistent with segment disclosures within the financial statements, investors would benefit from an explanation of the reason for the inconsistencies.

Consider:

- *Has the entity provided appropriate segment information throughout the various filings of financial information?*
- *Is the information consistent with the financial statements? If not, is there sufficient explanation provided to investors?*

4B.1 — EXAMPLE — inconsistent segment disclosure

Concerns:

- *consistent presentation between financial statement note disclosure and the MD&A disclosure*

Financial statement note disclosure:

> *Segmented information*
>
> *The Company has one reportable segment, MMM. Through its MMM segment, the Company enters into a variety of business in the media industry. It derives its revenues from advertising, marketing, circulation, distribution, printing and other. Segment profit or loss has been defined as operating profit which corresponds to operating profit as presented in the consolidated statement of income.*

MD&A disclosure:

> *Business activities*
>
> *The Company s primary business activities include the publication of hard copy subscription materials as well as online media. ABC Group (ABC) operations includes hard copy publications operating under the name AAA, BBB and CCC. XYZ Group (XYZ) operations comprise of the online media business including commercial and non-commercial.*

Operating Results

> *The following table sets out operating earnings for the years ended December 31, 20X2 and 20X1.*

In M's	20X2			20X1		
	ABC	XYZ	Total	ABC	XYZ	Total
Operating revenue	53.4	46.6	100	53.3	46.7	100

Single operating segment

Regardless of the different business activities and different economic characteristics of businesses, some reporting issuers' note disclosure indicated that they operated in only one segment since they were not earning any revenues in their various businesses. IFRS 8 paragraph 5 states that an operating segment can be one which engages in business activities for which it has yet to begin to earn revenues. For example, start-up operations may be considered operating segments before earning revenues. As such, it is not adequate to solely rely on the fact that the entity has yet to begin its generation of revenues to conclude that the entity operates in a single operating segment.

4B.2 — EXAMPLES — insufficient disclosures about segment determination

Example 1
   Concern:

   • *segment determination based solely on the absence of revenue generation*

   The Company has not begun earning revenues. Accordingly, no segment information has been provided in these consolidated financial statements.

Example 2
   Concern:

   • *vague disclosure of management s assessment of operating segments and how the management has determined it operates in one reportable segment.*

   The Company reports its continuing operations in one reportable segment, 'marketing', based on the business activity of the Company and its subsidiaries. The Company provides various online and hardcopy advertising publications and online marketing services to various types of customers in the many different industries locally and internationally. Revenues are derived mainly from sales of online advertisements and other services.

4B.3 — EXAMPLES — improved disclosure on identification of operating segments

Significant Accounting Policies

The Company's operating segments, before aggregation, have been identified as the Company's individual operating and development stage mines. Each operating and development mine is reviewed by the CODM in reviewing their profitability so that the information can be used to ensure adequate resources are allocated to that part of the Company's operations.

In Staffs view, the significant accounting policy disclosure in the above example provides entity specific and improved disclosures regarding the application of IFRS 8 criteria in the identification of operating segments, compared to the examples in 4B.2 above.

Multiple operating segments based on geographic locations

Depending on how the CODM reviews the operations, operating segments may be based on geographical area. Staff have observed instances where reporting issuers that identified operating segments by geographical area have provided only the entity-wide disclosures set out in paragraphs 31 to 34 and omit the disclosure requirements in paragraphs 20 to 30. Regardless of whether an operating segment is defined by the nature of products or services or the geographical area, reporting issuers must provide complete information of all material disclosures required by IFRS 8.

C. — Aggregation of operating segments to form reportable segments

IFRS 8 permits reporting issuers to aggregate operating segments when certain qualitative criteria are met, as well as certain quantitative thresholds.

Currently, IFRS 8 does not require detailed disclosure on aggregation of operating segments. However, paragraph 22(a) requires the disclosure of factors used to identify the entity's reportable segments, including the basis of organization and whether segments have been aggregated.*

Staff found that many reporting issuers provided sufficient disclosure to comply with paragraph 22(a) of IFRS 8. However, the following are the common areas of deficiency that we noted from our work:

   • Lack of explicit disclosure as to whether aggregation was used to identify reportable segments.

   • For some entities where it was apparent that aggregation was applied, it was unclear to Staff as to how the specific aggregation criteria in IFRS 8 were met after considering other information presented in an entity's MD&A or other notes to the financial statements. In certain cases, this led Staff to question whether the aggregation applied was appropriate.

   • Information presented in other documents, including MD&A, press releases and investor presentations, where the disclosure of quantitative data indicated that the quantitative thresholds for segment disclosure were exceeded.

Consider:

   • Has the entity provided sufficient information such that the investor would be able to determine what segments have been aggregated, if any?

Presentation of "all other segments"

Staff observed instances where relatively smaller segments had been aggregated with certain reportable segments. Staff note that IFRS 8 paragraph 16 requires operating segments which are not reportable to be combined and disclosed in an all other segments category rather than aggregating with an identifiable reportable segment.

4C.1 — EXAMPLE — entity-specific disclosure on aggregation of operating segments

Note X: Operating Segments

   The Company's reportable segments are components of the Company's operating segments after aggregation and consist of the geographical regions in which the Company operates. The Company's chief operating decision maker reviews the financial and operational performance of the Company on a mine by mine basis which share similar economic, operational and regulatory characteristics. Management uses the information presented for each mine in setting the budget and dedicate other resources to the individual mine.

---

*The Annual Improvements to IFRS cycle 20102012 included an amendment to IFRS 8 proposing additional disclosure regarding what aggregation criteria was applied in determining reportable segments. In their February 2013 meeting, the International Accounting Standards Board tentatively decided to amend the Standard as proposed.

The Company has three reportable segments, as follow (where each mine has been identified as an operating segment):

- *Brazil: Mine 1, Mine 2, and Mine 3*
- *Columbia: Mine 5 and Mine 6 .*
- *Canada: Mine 4 — development stage.*

'Other' consists of the Company s business activities of exploration properties which are not operating segments on their own.

D. — Change in reportable segments

IFRS 8 paragraph 29 requires an entity to reflect any changes in reportable segments in the comparative financial statements by restating the segment data for a prior period to be consistent with that of the current period unless the information is not available and the cost to develop it would be excessive. Staff observed instances of reporting issuers that had not restated prior period data to reflect a change in reportable segments and did not provide the additional disclosure required by IFRS 8 paragraph 30. Restated financial statement information is important as it allows investors to compare year over year trends in the reportable segments.

Consider:

- Are the segment disclosures providing sufficient information to allow investors to *easily understand* how the segments have changed?

E. — Entity-wide disclosure

Regardless of whether an entity has single or multiple reportable segments, IFRS 8 paragraphs 31 to 34 require entity-wide disclosures, where applicable unless the information is not available and the cost to develop it would be excessive. These include information relating to products and services of the entity, geographic areas of operations, as well as major customers.

Products and services

Staff observed this to be an area of deficiency where information was not always provided, or was unclear. Information on products and services provides valuable information as it assists users of financial statements in the assessment of both past performance and future prospects for growth of the entity.

Geographic information

IFRS 8 requires disclosures of the revenues and non-current assets attributed to individual countries if they are material. Staff observed instances of reporting issuers not providing this disclosure when it appeared, from an examination of other disclosure documents, that these amounts were material. We remind reporting issuers that when determining whether information about individual countries is material, management should consider whether the information would influence the economic decisions of users. For example, requests by analysts and users for this type of information would be a strong indicator of the material nature of this information.

In addition, Staff observed instances of reporting issuers not providing the required disclosure of the *basis for attributing revenues* from external customers to individual countries. Information about the extent of operations in foreign countries can be useful information to investors as it allows them to understand the extent of foreign operations and the exposure to foreign economies, and how this is changing year over year.

4E.1 — EXAMPLE — geographic disclosure that did not meet Staff's expectation

Concerns:

- significant portion of revenue attributed to "Other" category, which should be further expanded to identify all material individual countries, if applicable.
- basis for attribution of revenues to the individual countries is not provided

% of total revenue	December 31, 20X2	December 31, 20X1
Canada	6	5
United States	20	40
Australia	10	10
Other	64	45
Total	100	100

4E.2 — EXAMPLE — improved geographic disclosure

Informative Disclosure:

- *Provides clear and detailed revenue information for individual countries for which the amounts are considered to be material*

% of total revenue	December 31, 20X2	December 31, 20X1
Canada	6	5
United States	21	40
Australia	10	10
China	26	24
Japan	15	9
Germany	13	10

% of total revenue	December 31, 20X2	December 31, 20X1
Other	9	2
Total	*100*	*100*

The revenue has been attributed to the individual countries based on the location of the customer. In the above table, "Other" represents revenues attributed to countries to which the attributable revenues are less than 10% of total consolidated revenues.

Major Customers

IFRS 8 paragraph 34 requires an entity to provide information about the extent of its reliance on its major customers by providing specific disclosure relating to the amount of revenues attributed to its major customers. This includes separate disclosure of revenues from each customer and the identity of the segment or segments reporting the revenues.

Staff found that for those reporting issuers that disclosed major customers, many only presented aggregated revenue information, as shown in the example below.

4E.3 — EXAMPLE — major customer disclosure that did not meet Staff's expectation

Approximately 70% of the Company's consolidated revenues are generated from sales made to three customers.

4E.4 — EXAMPLE — improved major customer disclosure

During the year ended December 31, 20X2, the Company earned significant sales revenue from two customers in the amount of $633 (20X1 — $650) and $563 (20X1 — $642). The two customers were located in Brazil and Colombia, with each having their entire revenue reported in the Brazil and Colombia reportable segments, respectively.

Competitive harm

We have encountered instances where the segment disclosure omitted the entitywide information required by IFRS 8. The absence of this information was due to concerns related to a potential competitive harm; however, we note that IFRS 8 does not exempt issuers from providing these important disclosures for reasons of competitive harm. We note the Board's explicit consideration of this point in IFRS 8 BC paragraph 44, "Lack of a competitive harm exemption".

> BC44 The Board concluded that a 'competitive harm' exemption would be inappropriate because it would provide a means for broad non-compliance with the IFRS. The Board noted that entities would be unlikely to suffer competitive harm from the required disclosures since most competitors have sources of detailed information about an entity other than its financial statements.

This information is important in meeting the overall objective of IFRS 8 to provide insights as to the different types of business activities that an entity engages in and the different economic environments in which it operates, as well as to provide some comparability amongst entities.

5. — Questions

[Omitted]

OSC Staff Notice 52-722 — Report on Staff's Review of Non-GAAP Financial Measures and Additional GAAP Measures

Date: December 12, 2013

36 O.S.C.B. 11773

[Not reproduced.]

5.3 — Timely Disclosure

OSC Staff Notice 53-701 — Staff Report on Corporate Disclosure Survey

Date: July 28, 2000

23 O.S.C.B. 5098

On December 22, 1999 the Ontario Securities Commission (the "Commission") released the preliminary results of the corporate disclosure survey that Staff in the Continuous Disclosure Team had conducted as part of its initiative to examine the issue of "selective disclosure". Staff has completed its analysis of the survey and the Commission is publishing this Staff Report detailing the final survey results.

What is Selective Disclosure?

Selective disclosure occurs when corporate officers disclose material corporate information to select groups or individuals such as analysts or institutional investors that has not been disclosed to the public. In Canada, attention was focused on selective disclosure in 1995 when The Toronto Stock Exchange Committee on Corporate Disclosure (the "Allen Committee") released its Interim Report. In the report the Allen Committee acknowledged the importance of meetings with analysts in "fostering open and thorough continuous disclosure practices". The Allen Committee recognized that "benefits may flow to the markets from the legitimate efforts of securities analysts who use their professional expertise to process detailed data and information into commentary that investors find useful and can digest relatively quickly and improve the flow of corporate information into the marketplace". Nevertheless the Allen Committee remained concerned that private meetings with analysts and professional investors had resulted in "selective disclosure of information that should have been disclosed on a general basis". "Quite apart from any questions of compliance with securities laws", the Allen Committee noted that this causes "unfairness in the marketplace".[1]

These concerns about selective disclosure are widely shared, as reflected in stock exchange listing standards and in "best practices" guidelines of investor relations groups. The Toronto Stock Exchange's (the "TSE") Policy Statement on Timely Disclosure requires listed companies to disclose material information immediately upon the information becoming known to management of the company or upon it becoming apparent that the information is material. The TSE notes that "immediate release of information is necessary to ensure that it is promptly available to all investors and to reduce the risk of persons with access to the information acting upon undisclosed information". The Canadian Investor Relations Institute (CIRI) guidance in this area goes one step further and discourages companies from disclosing "more detailed, non-material information" to analysts and institutional investors in circumstances where a company would be unwilling to provide the same level of information to individual investors upon request.[2]

Staff has become increasingly concerned about the growing reports in the financial press of "selective disclosure" and the potential impact of this practice on market integrity. Selective disclosure can create opportunities for insider trading and also undermines retail investors' confidence in the market as a level playing field by creating a perception that analysts and institutional investors have access to information that is not available to other investors. In Staff's view, the best solution to these negative perceptions is for companies to adopt best practices in the area of disclosure and communications with analysts, the media and investors. Chairman David Brown recently made the following comments in a public address:

> In today's market atmosphere, with so much riding on share price, it's understandable that companies would want to keep analysts and institutional investors well informed. But when information is shared selectively, the result may be unfair trading opportunities. Retail investors have a right to trade on a level playing field. That means they must have the opportunity to share in all relevant information, along with institutional investors and market analysts. Retail investors suffer, however, when companies announce major events or disclose new or more detailed information about their affairs in one-on-one meetings or closed conference calls with institutions and analysts. With recent improvements in technology, no one need be left out. More and more companies are giving retail investors access to analyst meetings, through the Internet and 1-800 numbers. We applaud these efforts.

The Survey

As a first step in addressing the issue of selective disclosure Staff conducted a survey of disclosure practices of public companies (the "Survey"). Four hundred public companies were randomly selected across all industries to participate in the Survey. The Survey was sent to reporting issuers in October 1999 and 170 responses were received, a 43% response rate. Companies that did not receive a copy of the survey and wished to provide input were encouraged to do so by completing the survey on the Commission website.

The Survey explored several areas including: (i) company policies surrounding meetings and discussions with analysts and other groups; (ii) company responses to requests for information that is not available on the public record; (iii) company procedures if material non-public information is inadvertently disclosed to select groups; and (iv) the existence of company disclosure policies that address these and related issues.

The Survey was not intended to identify companies that may be selectively disclosing information. Rather the objective of the Survey was to seek input from reporting issuers on current practices and identify areas where additional guidance from the Commission would be appropriate.

Results of the Survey

In general, the results of the Survey indicate that the extent and nature of corporate disclosure policies and practices of issuers is not sufficient to reduce the potential for selective disclosure. For example:

- 71% of the respondents do not have written corporate disclosure policies;

- 81% of the respondents reported that they have one-on-one meetings with analysts;

- 98% of the respondents reported that they typically comment in some form on draft analyst reports; and

- 27% of the respondents indicated that they express a level of comfort on earnings projections.

Avoiding Selective Disclosure

The following, in Staff's view, are some good disclosure practices that emerged from the Survey:

1. — Have a Written Disclosure Policy

Survey Result: 29% of respondents have a written disclosure policy.

A written disclosure policy can assist a company in meeting its regulatory disclosure obligations as it provides a framework for disclosure and raises the level of awareness and understanding of regulatory requirements. Disclosure policies should also be broadly communicated throughout the organization and monitored for compliance in order for them to be effective.

There are also practical benefits for a company in having one of its senior officers take overall responsibility for ensuring compliance with regulatory requirements on continuous disclosure; and overseeing and coordinating disclosure of information to market participants.

---

[1] These concerns were reiterated by the Allen Committee in 1997 when it released its Final Report. The Allen Committee also made a number of recommendations designed to equalize access to information among investors including group analyst meetings with retail investor access; wide availability of data books and additional information; and electronic access to corporate information.

[2] Canadian Investor Relations Institute, *Standards and Guidance for Disclosure*. First Edition (February 1998) at page 8.

2. — Limit the Number of Authorized Spokespersons

Survey Result: 69% of respondents indicated that all communications are handled through three or less key officers.

Companies can designate a limited number of persons, usually not more than two or three in charge of investors relations, as the only representatives of the company authorized to communicate with analysts. Other employees can then be instructed to refer all requests for information to those authorized to speak on the company's behalf. Such a policy helps to ensure that all communications to analysts are made by persons who are fully informed about the company and its disclosure policies and the risks applicable to analyst communications. This practice also reduces the risk of (i) different company representatives making inconsistent statements; and (ii) company representatives making inconsistent statements from the information contained in the company's regulatory filings.

3. — Open Up Access to Conference Calls

Survey Result: 19% of respondents invite retail investors to the quarterly conference call

Many companies hold conference calls with analysts shortly following the public disclosure of quarterly financial results. Some companies adopt a complete "open door" policy with respect to who is permitted to participate in conference calls by publicly disclosing the date, time and dial-in number for their conference calls (such as by including it in their press releases or posting it on their web site) or simulcasting the conference call over the internet, thus allowing access to everyone. As a matter of good practice, company officers who will be making presentations during a conference call prepare a script in advance of their remarks, which is reviewed internally for accuracy and also reviewed by counsel. Scripting a call can help to identify any "material changes" and "material facts" that ought to be publicly disclosed prior to the call and reduces the risk of inappropriate statements being made.

As a matter of law, conference calls should not divulge any "material facts" about the company which have not already been generally disclosed. In this context, companies and their spokespersons should be aware that there may be dangers in disclosing even seemingly innocuous information to a select group without first releasing it publically. Staff encourage companies to maintain an "open door" policy with respect to who is permitted to listen in on conference calls, although companies may legitimately want to restrict who can actively participate in such calls.

4. — Dissemination of Information

Survey Result: 18% of respondents broadcast their quarterly conference calls via Internet or by other means.

Advances in technology are being utilized by some issuers to provide wide dissemination of information and at a relatively low cost. Posting information on the company's web site is an effective and efficient way of disseminating information to the marketplace as well as investors simultaneously.

In this context, it should be noted that on March 25, 1999, the TSE released guidelines for electronic communications by listed companies.[3] The accompanying press release stated that the guidelines reflect the "growing importance of the internet as a preferred medium of communication", with more than 70 per cent of TSE listed companies using the internet for some aspects of their communication, marketing or promotion. The guidelines aim to encourage the use of electronic media while ensuring that information disclosed in this way complies with regulatory requirements. The TSE recommends that "companies develop policies for disseminating information by electronic means as part of their corporate disclosure policies". In this regard, the TSE's guidelines include a recommendation that companies make available to all investors through their web sites all supplemental information provided at briefings to analysts and institutional investors, such as fact sheets, slides and transcripts of speeches.

Next Steps

The Commission will publish a policy statement which will address best disclosure practices for issuers with regard to (i) providing investors with fair access to information and; (ii) avoiding selective disclosure in their dealings with analysts and institutional investors. The policy will suggest practical steps that reporting issuers can take to ensure that they meet the letter and spirit of Ontario's regulatory requirements. The Commission's goal in proposing the policy is to encourage companies to aim for best practice in their disclosure regime, not just minimum level of compliance with the law.

In the interim, Staff reminds market participants that the *Securities Act* (the "Act") has existing provisions that prohibit the selective disclosure of "material changes" and "material facts". The Act provides that "no reporting issuer and no person or company in a special relationship with a reporting issuer shall inform, other than in the necessary course of business, another person or company of a material fact or material change with respect to the reporting issuer before the material fact or material change has been generally disclosed". In addition, the Act requires that, where a material change occurs in the affairs of a reporting issuer, it shall issue and file a news release disclosing the nature and substance of the change.

Finally, it should be noted that The Toronto Stock Exchange, the Vancouver Stock Exchange, the Alberta Stock Exchange and the Investment Dealers Association recently established the Securities Industry Committee on Analyst Standards (the "Committee"). The Committee's mandate is "to review the practices and activities of securities research analysts employed by dealers in Canada and the standards of conduct and supervision of the analysts; and to report and make recommendation on securities industry standards governing the conduct and supervision of analysts as considered appropriate to preserve the integrity of the capital markets".[4] The Committee plans to produce a preliminary report, covering its findings and recommendations. A final report will be tabled following a comment period on the preliminary report. The Commission is awaiting the release of these reports and will evaluate at that time whether further Commission action in this area is desirable.

---

[3]The guidelines are available on the TSE's Web site, tse.com, and are located under "Market Regulation" among the "TSE/SRO Position Papers/Reports".

[4]Investment Dealers Association of Canada — Bulletin #2632 (September 29, 1999).

Policies and Orders: OSCN 51-706.

5.4 — Proxy Solicitation

National Instrument 54-101 — Communication with Beneficial Owners of Securities of a Reporting Issuer

Date: June 14, 2002, as amended effective February 9, 2005, January 1, 2011 and February 11, 2013

25 O.S.C.B. 3361, 28 O.S.C.B. 3991, 33 O.S.C.B. (Supp. 5) 35 and 35 O.S.C.B. 10709

Table of Contents

PART 1 — DEFINITIONS AND INTERPRETATION

1.1 Definitions — In this Instrument

"affairs" means the relationship among a reporting issuer, its affiliates, and their securityholders, partners, directors and officers, other than the business carried on by the reporting issuer;

"annual report" means an annual report of a reporting issuer that includes the audited annual financial statements of the reporting issuer, and any other document required by Canadian securities legislation to be included in or sent with an annual report;

"beneficial owner" means, for a security held by an intermediary in an account, the person or company that is identified as providing the instructions contained in a client response form or, if no instructions are provided, the person or company that has the authority to provide those instructions;

"beneficial ownership determination date" means, for a meeting,

    (a) the record date for voting, or

    (b) in the absence of a record date for voting, the record date for notice;

"business day" means a day other than a Saturday, Sunday or statutory holiday in the local jurisdiction;

"CDS" means the Canadian Depository for Securities Limited and any successor to its depository business;

"client" means a person or company on whose behalf an intermediary directly holds a security;

"client response form" means the form of response set out in Form 54-101F1;

"corporate law" means, for a reporting issuer, any legislation, constating instrument or agreement that governs the affairs of the reporting issuer;

"day" means a calendar day unless express reference is made to a business day;

"depository" means CDS and any other person or company recognized as a depository by the securities regulatory authority for the purpose of this Instrument;

"explanation to clients" means an explanation to clients set out in the form of Form 54-101F1;

"FINS" means Financial Institution Numbering System;

"intermediary" means, for a security, a person or company that, in connection with its business, holds the security on behalf of another person or company, and that is not

(a) a person or company that holds the security only as a custodian, and is not the registered securityholder of the security nor holding the security as a participant in a depository,

(b) a depository, or

(c) a beneficial owner of the security;

"intermediary master list" means a list of intermediaries that a depository maintains under section 5.1;

"intermediary search request" means the request referred to in section 2.3;

"meeting" means a meeting of securityholders of a reporting issuer;

"NOBO" means a non-objecting beneficial owner;

"NOBO list" means a non-objecting beneficial owner list;

"nominee" means a person or company that acts as a passive title-holder to hold securities and does not carry on business in its own right;

"non-objecting beneficial owner" means a beneficial owner of securities that

(a) has provided instructions to an intermediary holding the securities in an account on behalf of the beneficial owner that the beneficial owner does not object, for that account, to the intermediary disclosing ownership information about the beneficial owner under this Instrument, or

(b) is a non-objecting beneficial owner under subparagraph (i) or (ii) of paragraph 3.3(b);

"non-objecting beneficial owner list" means, for an intermediary, a list that includes ownership information concerning NOBOs on whose behalf the intermediary, or another intermediary holding directly or indirectly through the intermediary, holds securities and information regarding instructions from those NOBOs concerning receipt of securityholder materials and

(a) if prepared in non-electronic form, is in a clear and readable format and contains the information referred to in paragraph (b), or

(b) if prepared in electronic form, is prepared in the form of, and contains the information prescribed in, Form 54-101F5;

"notice-and-access" means

(a) in respect of registered holders of voting securities of a reporting issuer, the delivery procedures referred to in section 9.1.1 of National Instrument 51-102 *Continuous Disclosure Obligations*, or

(b) in respect of beneficial owners of securities of a reporting issuer, the delivery procedures referred to in section 2.7.1;

"notification of meeting and record dates" means the notification referred to in section 2.2;

"NP41" means National Policy Statement No. 41;

"objecting beneficial owner" means a beneficial owner of securities that

(a) has provided instructions to an intermediary holding the securities in an account on behalf of the beneficial owner that the beneficial owner objects, for that account, to the intermediary disclosing ownership information about the beneficial owner under this Instrument, or

(b) is an objecting beneficial owner under subparagraph (iii) of paragraph 3.3(b);

"OBO" means an objecting beneficial owner;

"omnibus proxy" means, for a meeting,

(a) for a depository, a proxy in the form of Form 54-101F3, and

(b) for an intermediary, a proxy in the form of Form 54-101F4;

"ownership information" means, for a beneficial owner of securities that holds the securities through an intermediary in an account of the intermediary, the beneficial owner's name, address, holdings of the securities in the account, preferred language of communication, if known, the electronic mail address of the beneficial owner, and whether the beneficial owner has given to the intermediary a currently valid consent to the electronic delivery of documents from the intermediary;

"participant in a depository" means a person or company for whom a depository maintains an account in which entries may be made to effect a transfer or pledge of a security;

"preferred language of communication" means either the English language or the French language;

"proximate intermediary" means, for a security,

(a) a participant in a depository holding the security, or

(b) an intermediary that is the registered holder of the security;

"proxy-related materials" means securityholder material relating to a meeting that the reporting issuer is required under corporate law or securities legislation to send to the registered holders or beneficial owners of the securities;

"record date for notice" means, for a meeting, the date established in accordance with corporate law for the determination of the registered holders of securities that are entitled to receive notice of the meeting;

"record date for voting" means, for a meeting, the date, if any, established in accordance with corporate law for the determination of the registered holders of securities that are entitled to vote at the meeting;

"registered holder" means, for a security, the person or company shown as the holder of the security on the books or records of the reporting issuer;

"request for beneficial ownership information" means, for a security, a request for beneficial ownership information in the form of Form 54-101F2 sent by a reporting issuer to a proximate intermediary holding the security;

"SEC issuer" means an issuer that

(a) has a class of securities registered under section 12 of the 1934 Act or is required to file reports under section 15(d) of the 1934 Act, and

(b) is not registered or required to be registered as an investment company under the *Investment Company Act of 1940* of the United States of America, as amended;

"security" means a security of a reporting issuer;

"securityholder" means, for a security, the registered holder of the security, the beneficial owner of the security, or both, depending upon the context;

"securityholder materials" means, for a reporting issuer, materials that are sent to registered holders or beneficial owners of securities of the reporting issuer;

"send" means to deliver, send or forward or arrange to deliver, send or forward in any manner, including by prepaid mail, courier or by electronic means; and

"special resolution" for a meeting,

    (a) has the same meaning given to the term "special resolution" under corporate law, or

    (b) if no such term exists under corporate law, means a resolution that is required to be passed by at least two-thirds of the votes cast;

"special meeting" means a meeting at which a special resolution is being submitted to the securityholders of a reporting issuer;

"stratification", in relation to a reporting issuer using notice-and-access, means procedures whereby a paper copy of the information circular and, if applicable, the documents in paragraph 2.7.1(2)(b), are included with either or both of the following:

    (a) the documents required to be sent to registered holders under subsection 9.1(1) of National Instrument 51-102 *Continuous Disclosure Obligations*;

    (b) the documents required to be sent to beneficial owners under subsection 2.7.1(1);

"transfer agent" means a person or company that carries on the business of a transfer agent.

1.2 Holding of security by intermediary — In this Instrument, an intermediary is considered to hold a security if the security is held

    (a) by the intermediary directly; or

    (b) by the intermediary indirectly through another person or company on behalf of the intermediary.

1.3 Use of required forms — (1) A person or company required to send or use a required form or document under a provision of this Instrument may substitute for that form or document another form or document, or combine the required form or document with another form or document, if the substituted or combined form or document requests or includes the same information contemplated by the form or document that is otherwise required.

(2) Subsection (1) does not apply to a NOBO list in the form of Form 54-101F5 unless both the party requesting and the party providing the NOBO list agree to an alternative form.

1.4 Fees — A fee payable under this Instrument shall be, unless prescribed by the regulator or securities regulatory authority, a reasonable amount.

PART 2 — REPORTING ISSUERS

2.1 Establishment of meeting and record dates — A reporting issuer that is required to give notice of a meeting to the registered holders of any of its securities shall fix

    (a) a date for the meeting;

    (b) a record date for notice of the meeting, which shall be no fewer than 30 and no more than 60 days before the meeting date; and

    (c) if required or permitted by corporate law, a record date for voting at the meeting.

2.2 Notification of meeting and record dates — (1) Subject to section 2.20, at least 25 days before the record date for notice of a meeting, the reporting issuer shall send a notification of meeting and record dates [to]

    (a) all depositories;

    (b) the securities regulatory authority; and

    (c) each exchange in Canada on which securities of the reporting issuer are listed.

(2) The notification of meeting and record dates referred to in subsection (1) shall specify

    (a) the name of the reporting issuer;

    (b) the date fixed for the meeting;

    (c) the record date for notice;

    (d) the record date for voting, if any;

    (e) the beneficial ownership determination date;

    (f) the classes or series of securities that entitle the holder to receive notice of the meeting;

    (g) the classes or series of securities that entitle the holder to vote at the meeting;

    (h) whether the meeting is a special meeting;

    (i) whether the reporting issuer is sending proxy-related materials to registered holders or beneficial owners using notice-and-access and, if stratification will be used, the types of registered holders or beneficial owners who will receive paper copies of the information circular or other proxy-related materials;

    (j) whether the reporting issuer is sending the proxy-related materials directly to NOBOs; and

    (k) whether the reporting issuer intends to pay for a proximate intermediary to send the proxy-related materials to OBOs.

2.3 Intermediary search request — Request to depository — (1) At the same time as a reporting issuer sends a notification of meeting and record dates for a meeting to a depository, the reporting issuer shall request the depository to send to the reporting issuer

    (a) subject to section 2.4, a report that specifies the number of securities of the reporting issuer of each class or series that entitle the holder to receive notice of the meeting or to vote at the meeting that are currently registered in the name of the depository, the identity of any other person or company that holds securities of the reporting issuer of the series or class specified in the request on behalf of the depository and the number of those securities held by that other person or company;

    (b) subject to section 2.4, a list of all intermediaries and their nominees shown on the intermediary master list;

(c) subject to section 2.4, a list setting out the names, addresses, telephone numbers, fax numbers, any electronic mail addresses and the respective holdings of participants in the depository of each class or series of securities that entitle the holder to receive notice of the meeting or to vote at the meeting; and

(d) the omnibus proxy required to be sent under subsection 5.4(1).

(2) In addition to the request referred to in subsection (1), a reporting issuer may request, at any time, a depository to send any or all of the information referred to in subsection (1), other than paragraph (1)(d), for any class or series of securities of the reporting issuer, and as of a date, specified in the request.

2.4 No intermediary search request if reporting issuer has electronic access — A reporting issuer shall not request from the depository information referred to in paragraph 2.3(1)(a), 2.3(1)(b) or 2.3(1)(c) if the information is included on a file maintained by the depository in electronic format and the reporting issuer has access to the file.

2.5 Request for beneficial ownership information — (1) Subject to section 2.20, at least 20 days before the record date for notice of a meeting, the reporting issuer, using information, including the intermediary master lists, provided by depositories under section 5.3 or referred to in section 2.4, shall complete Part 1 of a request for beneficial ownership information and send it to each proximate intermediary that is

(a) identified by a depository as a participant in the depository holding securities that entitle the holder to receive notice of the meeting or to vote at the meeting; or

(b) listed as an intermediary on the intermediary master list provided by a depository where the intermediary, or a nominee of the intermediary that is identified on the intermediary master list, is a registered holder of securities that entitle the holder to receive notice of the meeting or to vote at the meeting.

(2) In addition to making the request referred to in subsection (1) in connection with a meeting, a reporting issuer, using information, including the intermediary master lists, provided by depositories under section 5.3 or referred to in section 2.4, may make, for any class or series of securities of the reporting issuer, at any time, a request for beneficial ownership information by completing Part 1 of a request for beneficial ownership information and sending it to any proximate intermediary that is

(a) identified by a depository as a participant in the depository holding the securities; or

(b) listed as an intermediary on the intermediary master list provided by a depository where the intermediary, or a nominee of the intermediary that is identified on the intermediary master list, is a registered holder of the securities.

(3) A reporting issuer that makes a request for beneficial ownership information under either subsection (1) or subsection (2) that includes a request for NOBO lists shall provide a written undertaking to the proximate intermediary in the form of Form 54-101F9.

(4) A reporting issuer that requests beneficial ownership information under this section must do so through a transfer agent.

(5) Despite subsection (4), a reporting issuer may request beneficial ownership information without using a transfer agent for the sole purpose of obtaining a NOBO list if the reporting issuer has provided an undertaking using Form 54-101F9.

2.6 No depositories or intermediaries are registered holders — A reporting issuer is not subject to section 2.3 or 2.5 if, on the 25th day before the record date for notice of the meeting,

(a) none of the registered holders of its securities is a depository, a nominee of a depository, or a person or company listed as an intermediary or the nominee of an intermediary on the intermediary master list of any depository; or

(b) all of the information contemplated in Part 2 of the request for beneficial ownership information is known to the reporting issuer.

2.7 Sending proxy-related materials to beneficial owners — A reporting issuer that is required by Canadian securities legislation to send proxy-related materials to the registered holders of any class or series of its securities shall, subject to section 2.10 and subsection 2.12(3) send the proxy-related materials to beneficial owners of the securities, by either sending

(a) directly to NOBOs, and indirectly under section 2.12 to OBOs; or

(b) indirectly under section 2.12 to beneficial owners.

2.7.1 Notice-and-Access — (1) A reporting issuer that is not an investment fund may use notice-and-access to send proxy-related materials relating to a meeting to a beneficial owner of its securities if all of the following apply:

(a) the beneficial owner is sent a notice that contains the following information and no other information:

    (i) the date, time and location of the meeting for which the proxy-related materials are being sent;

    (ii) a description of each matter or group of related matters identified in the form of proxy to be voted on, unless that information is already included in a Form 54-101F6 or Form 54-101F7 as applicable, that is being sent to the beneficial owner under paragraph (b);

    (iii) the website addresses for SEDAR and the non-SEDAR website where the proxy-related materials are posted;

    (iv) a reminder to review the information circular before voting;

    (v) an explanation of how to obtain a paper copy of the information circular and, if applicable, the documents in paragraph (2)(b) from the reporting issuer;

    (vi) a plain-language explanation of notice-and-access that includes the following information:

        (A) if the reporting issuer is using stratification, a list of the types of registered holders or beneficial owners who will receive paper copies of the information circular, and if applicable, the documents in paragraph (2)(b);

        (B) the estimated date and time by which a request for a paper copy of the information circular and, if applicable, the documents in paragraph (2)(b), is to be received in order for the requester to receive the paper copy in advance of any deadline for the submission of voting instructions and the date of the meeting;

        (C) an explanation of how the beneficial owner is to return voting instructions, including any deadline for return of those instructions;

        (D) the sections of the information circular where disclosure regarding each matter or group of related matters identified in the notice can be found;

    (E) a toll-free telephone number the beneficial owner can call to get information about notice-and-access;

(b) using the procedures referred to in section 2.9 or 2.12, as applicable, the beneficial owner is sent, by prepaid mail, courier or the equivalent, the notice required by paragraph (a) and a Form 54-101F6 or Form 54-101F7, as applicable;

(c) the reporting issuer files on SEDAR the notification of meeting and record dates on the same date that it sends the notification under subsection 2.2(1);

(d) public electronic access to the information circular and the notice in paragraph (a) is provided on or before the date that the reporting issuer sends the notice in paragraph (a) to beneficial owners, in the following manner:

    (i) the documents are filed on SEDAR;

    (ii) the documents are posted until the date that is one year from the date that the documents are posted, on a website other than the website for SEDAR;

(e) a toll-free telephone number is provided for use by the beneficial owner to request a paper copy of the information circular and, if applicable, the documents in paragraph (2)(b), at any time from the date that the reporting issuer sends the notice in paragraph (a) to the beneficial owner up to and including the date of the meeting, including any adjournment;

(f) if a request for a paper copy of the information circular and, if applicable, the documents in paragraph (2)(b), is received at the toll-free telephone number provided under paragraph (e) or by any other means, a paper copy of any such document requested is sent free of charge by the reporting issuer to the requester at the address specified in the request in the following manner:

    (i) in the case of a request received prior to the date of the meeting, within 3 business days after receiving the request, by first class mail, courier or the equivalent;

    (ii) in the case of a request received on or after the date of the meeting, and within one year of the information circular being filed, within 10 calendar days after receiving the request, by prepaid mail, courier or the equivalent.

(2) Unless an information circular is included with the proxy-related materials, a reporting issuer that sends proxy-related materials to a beneficial owner of its securities using notice-and-access must not include with the proxy-related materials any information or document that relates to the particulars of any matter to be submitted to the meeting, except for the following:

(a) the information required to be included in the notice under paragraph (1)(a);

(b) financial statements of the reporting issuer to be approved at the meeting, and MD&A related to those financial statements, which may be part of an annual report.

2.7.2 Notice in advance of first use of notice-and-access — Despite paragraph 2.7.1(1)(c) and subsection 2.20(a.1), the first time that a reporting issuer uses notice-and-access to send proxy-related materials to a beneficial owner of its securities, the reporting issuer must file on SEDAR the notification of meeting and record dates at least 25 days before the record date for notice.

2.7.3 Restrictions on information gathering — (1) A reporting issuer that receives a request for a paper copy of the information circular or other documents referred to in paragraph 2.7.1(1)(e) using the toll-free telephone number or by any other means must not do any of the following:

(a) ask for any information about the requester, other than the name and address to which the information circular and, if applicable, the documents in paragraph 2.7.1(2)(b), are to be sent;

(b) disclose or use the name or address of the requester for any purpose other than sending the information circular and, if applicable, the documents in paragraph 2.7.1(2)(b).

(2) A reporting issuer that posts proxy-related materials pursuant to subparagraph 2.7.1(1)(d)(ii) must not collect information that can be used to identify a person or company who has accessed the website address where the proxy-related materials are posted.

2.7.4 Posting materials on non-SEDAR website — (1) A reporting issuer that posts proxy-related materials in the manner referred to in subparagraph 2.7.1(1)(d)(ii) must also post on the website the following documents:

(a) any disclosure material regarding the meeting that the reporting issuer has sent to registered holders or beneficial owners of its securities;

(b) any written communications the reporting issuer has made available to the public regarding each matter or group of matters to be voted on at the meeting, whether or not they were sent to registered holders or beneficial owners of its securities.

(2) Proxy-related materials that are posted under subparagraph 2.7.1(1)(d)(ii) must be posted in a manner and be in a format that permit an individual with a reasonable level of computer skill and knowledge to do all of the following easily:

(a) access, read and search the documents on the website;

(b) download and print the documents.

2.7.5 Consent to other delivery methods — For greater certainty, section 2.7.1 does not

(a) prevent a beneficial owner from consenting to a reporting issuer, an intermediary or another person or company's use of other delivery methods to send proxy-related materials,

(b) terminate or modify a consent that a beneficial owner of voting securities previously gave to a reporting issuer, an intermediary or another person or company regarding the use of other delivery methods to send proxy-related materials, or

(c) prevent a reporting issuer, an intermediary or another person or company from sending proxy-related materials using a delivery method to which a beneficial owner has consented prior to February 11, 2013.

2.7.6 Instructions to receive paper copies — (1) Despite section 2.7.1, an intermediary may obtain standing instructions from a beneficial owner that is a client of the intermediary that a paper copy of the information circular and, if applicable, the documents in paragraph 2.7.1(2)(b), be sent to the beneficial owner in all cases when a reporting issuer uses notice-and-access.

(2) If an intermediary has obtained standing instructions from a beneficial owner under subsection (1), the intermediary must do all of the following:

(a) if the reporting issuer is sending proxy-related materials directly under section 2.9, indicate in the NOBO list provided to the reporting issuer those NOBOs who have provided standing instructions under subsection (1) as at the date the NOBO list is generated;

(b) if the intermediary is sending proxy-related materials to a beneficial owner on behalf of a reporting issuer using notice-and-access, request appropriate quantities of paper copies of the information circular and, if applicable, the documents in paragraph 2.7.1(2)(b), from the reporting issuer for forwarding to beneficial owners who have provided standing instructions to be sent paper copies;

(c) include with the proxy-related materials a description, or otherwise inform the beneficial owner of, the means by which the beneficial owner may revoke the beneficial owner's standing instructions.

2.7.7 Application to non-management solicitations — (1) A person or company other than management of a reporting issuer that is required by law to send materials to registered holders or beneficial owners of securities in connection with a meeting may use notice-and-access to send the materials.

(2) Section 2.7.1, other than paragraph (1)(c), and sections 2.7.3, 2.7.4 and 2.7.5 apply to a person or company in subsection (1) as if the person or company were a reporting issuer.

(3) Paragraph 2.7.1(1)(c) and section 2.7.8 apply to a person or company referred to in subsection (1) only if the person or company has requisitioned a meeting.

2.7.8 Record date for notice — Despite subsection 2.1(b), a reporting issuer that uses notice-and-access must set a record date for notice that is no fewer than 40 days before the date of the meeting.

2.8 Other securityholder materials — A reporting issuer may, but is not required to, send securityholder materials other than proxy-related materials to beneficial owners of its securities, by either sending

(a) directly to NOBOs, and indirectly under section 2.12 to OBOs; or

(b) indirectly under section 2.12 to beneficial owners.

2.9 Direct sending of proxy-related materials to NOBOs by a reporting issuer — (1) A reporting issuer that has stated in its request for beneficial ownership information sent in connection with a meeting, that it will send proxy-related materials to, and seek voting instructions from, NOBOs must send at its own expense the proxy-related materials for the meeting directly to the NOBOs on the NOBO lists received in response to the request.

(2) A reporting issuer that sends by prepaid mail, courier or the equivalent, paper copies of proxy-related materials directly to a NOBO must send the proxy-related materials at least 21 days before the date of the meeting.

(3) A reporting issuer that sends proxy-related materials directly to a NOBO using notice-and-access must send the notice required by paragraph 2.7.1(1)(a) and, if applicable, any paper copies of information circulars and documents in paragraph 2.7.1(2)(b), at least 30 days before the date of the meeting.

2.10 Sending securityholder materials against instructions — Except as required by securities legislation, and despite subsection 2.9(1), no reporting issuer that uses a NOBO list to send securityholder materials directly to NOBOs on the NOBO list shall send the securityholder materials to NOBOs that are identified on the NOBO list as having declined to receive those materials unless the reporting issuer has specified in the request for beneficial ownership information sent under section 2.5 in connection with the sending of materials that the securityholder materials will be sent to all beneficial owners of securities.

2.11 Disclose how information obtained — (1) A reporting issuer that uses a NOBO list to send securityholder materials directly to NOBOs on the NOBO list shall include in the materials the following statement:

These securityholder materials are being sent to both registered and non-registered owners of the securities. If you are a non-registered owner, and the issuer or its agent has sent these materials directly to you, your name and address and information about your holdings of securities, have been obtained in accordance with applicable securities regulatory requirements from the intermediary holding on your behalf.

(2) A reporting issuer that uses a NOBO list to send proxy-related materials that solicit votes or voting instructions directly to a NOBO on the NOBO list shall include, after the text required by subsection (1), the following statement:

By choosing to send these materials to you directly, the issuer (and not the intermediary holding on your behalf) has assumed responsibility for (i) delivering these materials to you, and (ii) executing your proper voting instructions. Please return your voting instructions as specified in the request for voting instructions.

2.12 Indirect sending of securityholder materials by a reporting issuer — (1) A reporting issuer sending securityholder materials indirectly to beneficial owners must send to each proximate intermediary that responded to the applicable request for beneficial ownership information the number of sets of those materials specified by that proximate intermediary for sending to beneficial owners.

(2) A reporting issuer that sends proxy-related materials indirectly to a beneficial owner by having the proximate intermediary send the proxy-related materials by prepaid mail must send the proxy-related materials to the proximate intermediary

(a) at least 3 business days before the 21st day before the date of the meeting, in the case of proxy-related materials that are to be sent on by the proximate intermediary by first class mail, courier or the equivalent, or

(b) at least 4 business days before the 21st day before the date of the meeting, in the case of proxy-related materials that are to be sent using any other type of prepaid mail.

(3) A reporting issuer that sends proxy-related materials indirectly to a beneficial owner using notice-and-access must send the notice required by paragraph 2.7.1(1)(a) and, if applicable, any paper copies of information circulars and documents in paragraph 2.7.1(2)(b), to the proximate intermediary

(a) at least 3 business days before the 30th day before the date of the meeting, in the case of proxy-related materials that are to be sent on by the proximate intermediary by first class mail, courier or the equivalent, or

(b) at least 4 business days before the 30th day before the date of the meeting, in the case of proxy-related materials that are to be sent using any other type of prepaid mail.

(4) A reporting issuer that sends securityholder materials that are not proxy-related materials indirectly to beneficial owners must send the securityholder materials to the intermediary on the date specified in the request for beneficial ownership information.

(5) Despite section 2.9, a reporting issuer must not send securityholder materials directly to a NOBO if a proximate intermediary in a foreign jurisdiction holds securities on behalf of the NOBO and one or both of the following applies:

(a) the law of the foreign jurisdiction does not permit the reporting issuer to send securityholder materials directly to NOBOs;

(b) the proximate intermediary has stated in a response to a request for beneficial ownership information that the law in the foreign jurisdiction requires the proximate intermediary to deliver securityholder materials to beneficial owners.

2.13 Fee for search — A reporting issuer shall pay a fee to a proximate intermediary for furnishing the information requested in a request for beneficial ownership information made by the reporting issuer.

2.14 Fee for sending materials indirectly — (1) A reporting issuer that sends securityholder materials indirectly to NOBOs through a proximate intermediary shall pay to the proximate intermediary, upon receipt by the reporting issuer of a certificate of sending to NOBOs in accordance with the instructions specified by the reporting issuer in the request for beneficial ownership information

(a) a fee for sending the securityholder materials to the NOBOs;

(b) the actual cost of any postage incurred by the proximate intermediary in sending the securityholder materials to the NOBOs in accordance with any mailing instructions specified by the reporting issuer in the request for beneficial ownership information; and

(c) if the securityholder materials were sent by mail other than first class mail in accordance with the mailing instructions specified by the reporting issuer in the request for beneficial ownership information, the reasonable additional handling costs associated with the preparation by the proximate intermediary of the securityholder materials for mailing to NOBOs.

(2) A reporting issuer that sends securityholder materials, indirectly through a proximate intermediary, to OBOs that have declined in accordance with this Instrument to receive those materials, shall pay to the proximate intermediary, upon receipt by the reporting issuer of a certificate of sending to OBOs in accordance with the instructions specified by the reporting issuer in the request for beneficial information

(a) a fee for sending the securityholder materials to the OBOs;

(b) the actual cost of any postage incurred by the proximate intermediary in sending the securityholder materials to the OBOs in accordance with any mailing instructions specified by the reporting issuer in the request for beneficial ownership information; and

(c) if the securityholder materials were sent by mail other than first class mail in accordance with the mailing instructions specified by the reporting issuer in the request for beneficial information, the reasonable additional handling costs associated with the preparation by the proximate intermediary of the securityholder materials for mailing to OBOs.

2.15 Adjournment or change in meeting — A reporting issuer that sends a notice of adjournment or other change for a meeting to registered holders of its securities shall concurrently send the notice, including any change in the beneficial ownership determination date,

(a) to each of the persons or companies referred to in subsection 2.2(1);

(b) to each proximate intermediary to which the reporting issuer sent a request for beneficial ownership information for the meeting under subsection 2.5(1);

(c) directly, in accordance with section 2.9, other than the timing requirement of that section, to each of the NOBOs to which it previously directly sent proxy-related materials for the meeting under section 2.9; and

(d) indirectly, in accordance with section 2.12, other than the timing requirement of that section, to each of the NOBOs and OBOs to which it previously indirectly sent proxy-related materials for the meeting under section 2.12.

2.16 Explanation of voting rights — (1) If a reporting issuer sends proxy-related materials for a meeting to a beneficial owner of its securities, the materials must explain, in plain language, how the beneficial owner can exercise voting rights attached to the securities, including an explanation of how to attend and vote the securities directly at the meeting.

(2) Management of a reporting issuer must provide the following disclosure in the information circular:

(a) whether the reporting issuer is sending proxy-related materials to registered holders or beneficial owners using notice-and-access, and if stratification will be used, the types of registered holders or beneficial owners who will receive paper copies of the information circular and, if applicable, the documents in paragraph 2.7.1(2)(b);

(b) whether the reporting issuer is sending proxy-related materials directly to NOBOs;

(c) whether the reporting issuer intends to pay for an intermediary to deliver to OBOs the proxy-related materials and Form 54-101F7, and if the reporting issuer does not intend to pay for such delivery, a statement that OBOs will not receive the materials unless their intermediary assumes the costs of delivery.

2.17 Voting instruction form (Form 54-101F6) — A reporting issuer that sends proxy-related materials directly to a NOBO that solicit votes or voting instructions from securityholders must include with the proxy-related materials a Form 54-101F6.

2.18 Appointing beneficial owner as proxy holder — (1) A reporting issuer whose management holds a proxy in respect of securities beneficially owned by a NOBO must arrange, without expense to the NOBO, to appoint the NOBO or a nominee of the NOBO as a proxy holder in respect of those securities if the NOBO has instructed the reporting issuer to do so using either of the following methods:

(a) the NOBO filled in and submitted the Form 54-101F6 previously sent to the NOBO by the reporting issuer;

(b) the NOBO submitted any other document in writing that requests that the NOBO or a nominee of the NOBO be appointed as a proxyholder.

(2) If management appoints a NOBO or a nominee of the NOBO as a proxy holder under subsection (1), the NOBO or nominee of the NOBO, as applicable, must be given authority to attend, vote and otherwise act for and on behalf of management of the reporting issuer in respect of all matters that may come before the applicable meeting and at any adjournment or continuance, unless corporate law prohibits the giving of that authority.

(3) A reporting issuer who appoints a NOBO as a proxy holder pursuant to subsection (1) must deposit the proxy within any time specified for the deposit in the information circular if the reporting issuer obtains the instructions under subsection (1) at least one business day before the termination of that time.

(4) If corporate law requires an intermediary or depository to appoint the NOBO or nominee of the NOBO as a proxy holder in respect of securities beneficially owned by the NOBO in accordance with any written voting instructions received from the NOBO, and the intermediary has received the written voting instructions, the reporting issuer must provide, upon request by the intermediary, confirmation of both of the following:

 (a) management of the reporting issuer will comply with subsections 2.18(1) and (2);

 (b) management of the reporting issuer is acting on behalf of the intermediary or depository to the extent it appoints the NOBO or nominee of the NOBO as proxy holder in respect of the securities of the reporting issuer beneficially owned by the NOBO.

(5) A confirmation provided under subsection (4) must identify the specific meeting to which the confirmation applies, but is not required to specify each proxy appointment that management of the reporting issuer has made.

2.19 Tabulation and execution of voting instructions — A reporting issuer shall

 (a) tabulate the voting instructions received from NOBOs in response to a request for voting instructions referred to in section 2.17; and

 (b) through the actions of management of the reporting issuer, execute the voting instructions as instructed by the NOBOs, to the extent that the management of the reporting issuer holds the corresponding proxy.

2.20 Abridging time — A reporting issuer may abridge the time prescribed in subsections 2.1(b), 2.2(1) or 2.5(1) if the reporting issuer

 (a) arranges to have proxy-related materials for the meeting sent in compliance with the applicable timing requirements in sections 2.9 and 2.12;

 (a.1) if the reporting issuer uses notice-and-access, fixes the record date for notice to be at least 40 days before the date of the meeting and sends the notification of meeting and record dates under section 2.2 at least 3 business days before the record date for notice;

 (b) arranges to have carried out all of the requirements of this Instrument in addition to those described in subparagraph (a); and

 (c) files at the time it files the proxy-related materials, a certificate of one of its officers reporting that it made the arrangements described in paragraphs (a) and (b) and that the reporting issuer is relying upon this section.

PART 3 — INTERMEDIARIES' OBLIGATIONS CONCERNING THE OBTAINING OF BENEFICIAL OWNER INSTRUCTIONS

3.1 Intermediary information to depository — (1) Before a person or company acts as an intermediary, the person or company shall send the following information to each depository:

 (a) the intermediary's name and address;

 (b) the name and address of each nominee of the intermediary in whose name the intermediary holds securities on behalf of beneficial owners; and

 (c) the name, address, telephone number, fax number and any electronic mail address of a representative of the intermediary.

(2) A person or company that is an intermediary on the date of the coming into force of this Instrument shall, on that date, send to each depository the information referred to in subsection (1), unless it has already done so.

(3) An intermediary shall send notice to each depository of a change in the information contained in a notice given under this section within five business days after the change.

3.2 Instructions from new clients — Subject to section 3.4, an intermediary that opens an account for a client shall,

 (a) as part of its procedures to open the account, send to the client an explanation to clients and a client response form; and

 (b) before the intermediary holds securities on behalf of the client in the account

  (i) obtain instructions from the client on the matters to which the client response form pertains;

  (ii) obtain the electronic mail address of the client, if available; and

  (iii) if applicable, enquire whether the client wishes to consent and, if so, obtain the consent of the client, to electronic delivery of documents by the intermediary to the client.

3.3 Transitional — Instructions from existing clients — An intermediary that holds securities on behalf of a client in an account that was opened before the coming into force of this Instrument

 (a) may seek new instructions from its client in relation to the matters to which the client response form pertains; and

 (b) in the absence of new instructions from the client, shall rely on the instructions previously given or deemed to have been given by the client under NP41 in respect of that account, on the following basis:

  (i) If the client chose to permit the intermediary to disclose the client's name and security holdings to the issuer of the security or other sender of material, the client is a NOBO under this Instrument.

  (ii) If the client was deemed to have permitted the intermediary to disclose the client's name and security holdings to the issuer of the security or other sender of material, the intermediary may choose to treat the client as a NOBO under this Instrument.

  (iii) If the client chose not to permit the intermediary to disclose the client's name and security holdings to the issuer of the security or other sender of material, the client is an OBO under this Instrument.

  (iv) If the client chose not to receive material relating to annual or special meetings of securityholders or audited financial statements, the client is considered to have declined under this Instrument to receive:

   (A) proxy-related materials that are sent in connection with a securityholder meeting;

   (B) financial statements and annual reports that are not part of proxy-related materials; and

   (C) materials sent to securityholders that are not required by corporate or securities law to be sent to registered securityholders.

  (v) If the intermediary was permitted not to provide material relating to annual meetings of securityholders or audited financial statements, the client is considered to have declined under this Instrument to receive:

   (A) proxy-related materials that are sent in connection with a securityholder meeting that is not a special meeting;

Part 5: ONGOING REQUIREMENTS

(B) financial statements and annual reports that are not part of proxy-related materials; and

(C) materials sent to securityholders that are not required by corporate or securities law to be sent to registered securityholders;

(vi) If the client chose to receive material relating to annual or special meetings of securityholders and audited financial statements, the client is considered to have chosen under this Instrument to receive all securityholder materials sent to beneficial owners of securities.

(vii) The client is considered to have chosen under this Instrument as the client's preferred language of communication the language that has been customarily used by the intermediary to communicate with the client.

3.4 Amending client instructions — A client may at any time change the instructions it has given or is deemed to have given in connection with any of the choices provided for in the client response form by advising the intermediary that holds securities on the client's behalf of the change.

3.5 Application of instructions to accounts — The instructions given to an intermediary by a beneficial owner under this Part apply in respect of all securities held by the beneficial owner in the account of the intermediary identified in the client response form.

PART 4 — INTERMEDIARIES' OTHER OBLIGATIONS

4.1 Request for beneficial ownership information — Response — (1) A proximate intermediary that receives a request for beneficial ownership information from a reporting issuer, that pertains to a meeting, shall send to the reporting issuer, through the transfer agent, or in the case of a NOBO list, a person or company described in subsection 2.5(5) that sent the request

(a) within three business days of receiving the request, the information referred to in Part 2 of the request for beneficial ownership information other than Item 7;

(b) if the request contains a request for a NOBO list, within three business days after the beneficial ownership determination date for the meeting specified in the request, the NOBO list and other information required in accordance with Item 7 of Part 2 of the request for beneficial ownership information as at the beneficial ownership determination date of the meeting; and

(c) within three business days after the beneficial ownership determination date for the meeting specified in the request, if the request stated that the reporting issuer will send proxy-related materials to, and seek voting instructions from, NOBOs, a form of omnibus proxy that appoints management of the reporting issuer as the proximate intermediary's proxy holder for the securities held, as of the beneficial ownership determination date, on behalf of each NOBO identified on the NOBO list, in respect of which the proximate intermediary is either the registered holder or proxy holder.

(2) A proximate intermediary that receives a request for beneficial ownership information from a reporting issuer that pertains to the sending of securityholder materials other than in connection with a meeting shall, within three business days of receiving the request, send to the reporting issuer, through the transfer agent of the reporting issuer that sent the request, the NOBO lists if applicable and the other information referred to in Part 2 of the request for beneficial ownership information.

(3) A proximate intermediary that receives a request for beneficial ownership information from a reporting issuer that contains a request for a NOBO list but does not pertain to a meeting or the sending of securityholder materials shall, within three business days of receiving the request, send to the reporting issuer, through the transfer agent of the reporting issuer that sent the request, the NOBO lists if applicable and the other information referred to in Part 2 of the request for beneficial ownership information.

(4) The response of a proximate intermediary to a reporting issuer given under this section shall be a consolidated response relating to all beneficial owners of each class and series of securities, specified in the request for beneficial ownership information, that hold, directly or indirectly, through the proximate intermediary.

(5) An intermediary holding securities, directly or indirectly, through a proximate intermediary, shall take all necessary steps to ensure that the proximate intermediary is provided with the information required to enable it to satisfy its obligations under this section within the times required by this section.

(6) An intermediary is not required under this Instrument to provide ownership information concerning an OBO to any person or company.

4.2 Sending of securityholder materials to beneficial owners by intermediaries — (1) Subject to sections 4.3 and 4.7, a proximate intermediary that receives securityholder materials from a reporting issuer for sending to beneficial owners shall send

(a) one set of the materials to each OBO of the relevant securities that is a client of the proximate intermediary;

(b) one set of the materials to each NOBO of the relevant securities if the reporting issuer stated in the applicable request for beneficial ownership information, or otherwise advised the proximate intermediary, that the reporting issuer will send the materials to NOBOs indirectly through intermediaries; and

(c) appropriate quantities of materials to all intermediaries holding securities of the relevant class or series that are clients of the proximate intermediary, for sending by them under subsection (3).

(2) A proximate intermediary shall comply with subsection (1)

(a) within four business days after receipt in the case of securityholder materials to be sent by prepaid mail other than first class mail; and

(b) within three business days after receipt in the case of securityholder materials to be sent by any other means.

(3) An intermediary that receives securityholder materials from another intermediary under this section shall send, within one business day of receipt

(a) one set of the materials to each OBO that is a client of the intermediary; and

(b) appropriate quantities of the materials to all intermediaries holding securities of the relevant class or series that are clients of the intermediary for sending by them under this subsection.

(4) The persons or companies to whom securityholder materials are sent under this section shall be determined

(a) as at the beneficial ownership determination date, in the case of proxy-related materials; and

(b) as at the date specified in the relevant request for beneficial ownership information, in the case of securityholder materials not sent in connection with a meeting.

(5) An intermediary may satisfy its obligation to send securityholder materials to another intermediary under this section by sending the securityholder materials to a person or company designated by the other intermediary.

4.3 Sending securityholder materials against instructions — An intermediary that receives securityholder materials that are to be sent to a beneficial owner of securities shall not send the securityholder materials to the beneficial owner if the beneficial owner has declined in accordance with this Instrument to receive those materials unless the reporting issuer has specified in the request for beneficial ownership information sent under section 2.5 in connection with the sending of the securityholder materials that the securityholder materials shall be sent to all beneficial owners of securities.

4.4 Voting instruction form (Form 54-101F7) — An intermediary that forwards proxy-related materials to a beneficial owner that solicit votes or voting instructions from securityholders must include with the proxy-related materials a Form 54-101F7.

4.5 Appointing beneficial owner as proxy holder — (1) An intermediary who is the registered holder of, or holds a proxy in respect of, securities owned by a beneficial owner must arrange, without expense to the beneficial owner, to appoint the beneficial owner or a nominee of the beneficial owner as a proxy holder in respect of those securities if the beneficial owner has instructed the intermediary to do so using either of the following methods:

    (a) the beneficial owner filled in and submitted the Form 54-101F7 previously sent to the beneficial owner by the intermediary;

    (b) the beneficial owner submitted any other document in writing that requests that the beneficial owner or a nominee of the beneficial owner be appointed as a proxy holder.

(2) If an intermediary appoints a beneficial owner or a nominee of the beneficial owner as a proxy holder under subsection (1), the beneficial owner or nominee of the beneficial owner, as applicable, must be given authority to attend, vote and otherwise act for and on behalf of the intermediary in respect of all matters that may come before the applicable meeting and at any adjournment or continuance, unless corporate law does not permit the giving of that authority.

(3) An intermediary who appoints a beneficial owner as proxy holder pursuant to subsection (1) must deposit the proxy within any time specified for deposit in the information circular if the intermediary obtains the instructions under subsection (1) at least one business day before the termination of that time.

4.6 Tabulation and execution of voting instructions — An intermediary shall

    (a) tabulate voting instructions received from beneficial owners of securities in response to a request for voting instructions sent by the intermediary under section 4.4; and

    (b) for each beneficial owner, execute the voting instructions received from the beneficial owner to the extent that the intermediary holds a proxy directly given by the registered holder, or indirectly given by the registered holder through one or more other proxy holders, in respect of the securities held by the intermediary for the beneficial owner.

4.7 Securities legislation — Despite any other provision of this Part, nothing in this Part requires a person or company to send securityholder materials to a beneficial owner if securities legislation specifically permits the person or company to decline to send those materials to the beneficial owner.

4.8 Fees from Persons or Companies other than Reporting Issuers — A proximate intermediary that receives securityholder materials from a person or company that is not a reporting issuer for sending to beneficial owners is not required to send the securityholder materials to any beneficial owners or intermediaries that are clients of the proximate intermediary unless the proximate intermediary receives reasonable assurance of payment for the delivery of the securityholder materials.

PART 5 — DEPOSITORIES

5.1 Intermediary master list — A depository shall maintain a current list of intermediaries containing the information received by the depository from intermediaries under section 3.1 and shall send a copy of that list to any new depository recognized under this Instrument.

5.2 Index of meeting and record dates — (1) A depository shall maintain an index of pending meetings containing the information that it receives from reporting issuers under section 2.2.

(2) A depository shall arrange for the timely publication of the information it receives from a reporting issuer under section 2.2 in the national financial press and may charge the reporting issuer a publication fee in a reasonable amount for the publication.

5.3 Depository response to intermediary search request by reporting issuer — Within two business days of its receipt of an intermediary search request from a reporting issuer, a depository shall send to the reporting issuer a report, containing information that is as current as possible, that

    (a) specifies the number of securities of the reporting issuer of the series or class specified in the request that are registered in the name of the depository, the identity of any other person or company that holds on behalf of the depository securities of the reporting issuer of the series or class specified in the request and the number of such securities held by that other person or company;

    (b) specifies the names, addresses, telephone numbers, fax numbers, any electronic mail addresses and respective holdings of participants in the depository of securities of the series or class specified in the request, on whose behalf the depository holds the securities; and

    (c) contains a copy of the intermediary master list.

5.4 Depository to send participant omnibus proxy to reporting issuer — (1) Within two business days after the beneficial ownership determination date specified in the notification of meeting and record dates referred to in section 2.2, the depository shall send to the reporting issuer an omnibus proxy, appointing each participant, on whose behalf, and to the extent that, the depository holds, as of the beneficial ownership determination date, securities that entitle the holder to vote at the meeting, as the depository's proxy holder in respect of the securities held by the depository on behalf of the participant.

(2) The depository shall send to each of the participants named in an omnibus proxy referred to in subsection (1), at the same time as the depository sends the omnibus proxy to the reporting issuer, confirmation of the proxy given by the depository.

(3) If corporate law requires a depository to appoint a beneficial owner or nominee of the beneficial owner as a proxy holder in respect of securities beneficially owned by the beneficial owner in accordance with any written voting instructions received from the beneficial owner, and the depository has received the written voting instructions, any participant described in subsection (1) must provide, upon request by the depository, confirmation of all of the following:

    (a) the participant will comply with subsections 4.5(1) and (2);

    (b) the participant is acting on behalf of the depository to the extent it appoints a beneficial owner or nominee of a beneficial owner as proxy holder in respect of the securities of the reporting issuer beneficially owned by the beneficial owner;

(c) if the participant is required to execute an omnibus proxy under section 4.1, that the participant will take reasonable steps to request the confirmation set out in subsection 2.18(4).

(4) A confirmation provided under subsection (3) must identify the specific securityholder meeting to which the confirmation applies, but is not required to specify each proxy appointment that the participant has made.

PART 6 — OTHER PERSONS OR COMPANIES

6.1 Requests for NOBO Lists from a reporting issuer — (1) A person or company may request from a reporting issuer the most recently prepared NOBO list, for any proximate intermediary holding securities of the reporting issuer, that is in the reporting issuer's possession.

(2) A request for a NOBO list under this section shall be accompanied by an undertaking in the form of Form 54-101F9 of the person or company making the request.

(3) The person or company making a request under subsection (1) shall pay a fee to the reporting issuer for preparing the NOBO list for sending under this section.

(4) A reporting issuer shall send any NOBO list requested under this section, within ten days of receipt of both the request and the fee for preparing the list for sending under this section.

(5) A reporting issuer shall delete from any NOBO list sent under this section any reference to FINS numbers referred to in any form and any other information that would identify the intermediary through which a NOBO holds securities.

6.2 Other rights and obligations of persons and companies other than reporting issuers — (1) A person or company may take any action permitted under this Instrument to be taken by a reporting issuer and, in so doing, has all the rights, and is subject to all of the obligations, of a reporting issuer in connection with that action, unless this Instrument specifies a different right or obligation.

(2) In connection with actions taken under subsection (1) by a person or company other than the reporting issuer, references in this Instrument to a "reporting issuer" shall be read as references to that person or company and all other persons and companies will have the same obligations under this Instrument to that person or company as they would have if the person or company were the reporting issuer.

(3) Subsections (1) and (2) do not apply to sections 2.1, 2.2, subsections 2.3(1) and 2.5(1), paragraphs 2.12(1)(a) and (b), sections 2.14 and 2.18, paragraph 4.1(1)(c), section 5.4.

(4) A person or company other than the reporting issuer to which the request relates that makes an intermediary search request under subsection 2.3(2) or a request for beneficial ownership information under subsection 2.5(2) shall concurrently send a copy of that request to the reporting issuer of the securities to which the request relates.

(5) A person or company other than the reporting issuer to which the request relates that makes an intermediary search request under subsection 2.3(2) or a request for beneficial ownership information under subsection 2.5(2) shall provide an undertaking in the form of Form 54-101F9.

(6) A person or company, other than the reporting issuer to which the request relates, that sends materials indirectly to beneficial owners must comply with the following:

(a) the person or company must pay to the proximate intermediary a fee for sending the securityholder materials to the beneficial owners;

(b) the person or company must provide an undertaking to the proximate intermediary in the form of Form 54-101F10.

PART 7 — USE OF NOBO LIST AND INDIRECT SENDING OF MATERIALS

7.1 Use of NOBO list — (1) A reporting issuer may use a NOBO list, or a report prepared under section 5.3 relating to the reporting issuer and obtained under this Instrument, in connection with any matter relating to the affairs of the reporting issuer.

(2) A person or company that is not the reporting issuer must not use a NOBO list, or a report prepared under section 5.3 relating to the reporting issuer and obtained under this Instrument, in any manner other than any of the following:

(a) for sending securityholder materials directly to NOBOs in accordance with this Instrument;

(b) in respect of an effort to influence the voting of securityholders of the reporting issuer;

(c) in respect of an offer to acquire securities of the reporting issuer.

7.2 Sending of Materials — (1) A reporting issuer may send securityholder materials indirectly to beneficial owners of securities of the reporting issuer using the procedures in section 2.12, or directly to NOBOs of the reporting issuer using a NOBO list, in connection with any matter relating to the affairs of the reporting issuer.

(2) A person or company that is not the reporting issuer may send securityholder materials indirectly to beneficial owners of securities of the reporting issuer using the procedures in section 2.12, or directly to NOBOs of the reporting issuer using a NOBO list, only in connection with one or both of the following:

(a) an effort to influence the voting of securityholders of the reporting issuer;

(b) an offer to acquire securities of the reporting issuer.

PART 8 — MISCELLANEOUS

8.1 Default of party in communication chain — If a person or company fails to send information or materials in accordance with the requirements of this Instrument, the person or company whose required response or action under this Instrument is dependent upon receiving the information or materials shall use reasonable efforts to obtain the information or materials from the other person or company, and in so doing is exempt from the timing provisions of this Instrument in connection with the response or action to the extent that the delay arose from the failure of the other person or company.

8.2 Right to proxy — Nothing in this Instrument shall be interpreted to restrict in any way

(a) a beneficial owner's right to demand and to receive from an intermediary holding securities on behalf of the beneficial owner a proxy enabling the beneficial owner to vote the securities; or

(b) the right of a depository or intermediary to vary an omnibus proxy in respect of securities to properly reflect a change in the registered or beneficial ownership of the securities.

PART 9 — EXCEPTIONS AND EXEMPTIONS

9.1 Audited annual financial statements or annual report — The time periods applicable to sending of proxy-related materials prescribed in this Instrument do not apply to the sending of proxy-related materials that are annual financial statements or an annual report if the statements or report are sent directly or indirectly in accordance with the Instrument to beneficial owners of the securities within the time limitations established in applicable corporate law and securities legislation for the sending of the statements or report to registered holders of the securities.

9.1.1 Compliance with SEC Notice-and-Access Rules — (1) Despite section 2.7, a reporting issuer that is an SEC issuer can send proxy-related materials to beneficial owners using a delivery method permitted under U.S. federal securities law, if all of the following apply:

(a) the SEC issuer is subject to, and complies with Rule 14a-16 under the 1934 Act;

(b) the SEC issuer has arranged with each intermediary through whom the beneficial owner holds its interest in the reporting issuer's securities to have each intermediary send the proxy-related materials to the beneficial owner by implementing the procedures under Rule 14b-1 or Rule 14b-2 of the 1934 Act that relate to the procedures in Rule 14a-16 under the 1934 Act;

(c) residents of Canada do not own, directly or indirectly, outstanding voting securities of the issuer carrying more than 50% of the votes for the election of directors, and none of the following apply:

(i) the majority of the executive officers or directors of the issuer are residents of Canada;

(ii) more than 50% of the consolidated assets of the issuer are located in Canada;

(iii) the business of the issuer is administered principally in Canada.

(2) Part 4 does not apply to an intermediary with whom a reporting issuer has made arrangements under paragraph (1)(b) if the intermediary implements the procedures under Rule 14b-1 or Rule 14b-2 of the 1934 Act that relate to the procedures in Rule 14a-16 under the 1934 Act.

9.2 Exemptions — (1) The regulator or the securities regulatory authority may grant an exemption from this Instrument, in whole or in part, subject to such conditions or restrictions as may be imposed in the exemption.

(2) Despite subsection (1), in Ontario only the regulator may grant such an exemption.

PART 10 — EFFECTIVE DATES AND TRANSITION

10.1 Effective date of instrument — This Instrument comes into force on July 1, 2002.

10.2 Transition — A reporting issuer that has filed a notice of a meeting and record date with the securities regulatory authority in accordance with the provisions of NP41 before the coming into force of this Instrument is, with respect to that meeting, exempt from the provisions of this Instrument if the reporting issuer complies with the provisions of NP41.

10.3 Sending of proxy-related materials — Despite section 2.7, a reporting issuer sending proxy-related materials to beneficial owners of securities under section 2.7 for a meeting to be held before September 1, 2004 shall send those materials only indirectly to the beneficial owners under section 2.12.

10.4 NOBO lists — No person or company shall be obliged to furnish a NOBO list under this Instrument before September 1, 2002.

Final Rule: (2002) 25 O.S.C.B. 3361; Approved by OSC: (2002) 25 O.S.C.B. 1863; Request for Comments: (2000) 23 O.S.C.B. 5937, (1998) 21 O.S.C.B. 4491 and (1998) 21 O.S.C.B. 1388. Replaced in part NPS 41.

Amendment to Rule: (2005) 28 O.S.C.B. 3991; Approval by OSC: (2004) 27 O.S.C.B. 9463; Request for Comments: (2003) 26 O.S.C.B. 6759.

Amendment to Rule: (2010) 33 O.S.C.B. (Supp. 5) 35; Approval by OSC: (2010) 33 O.S.C.B. (Supp. 3) 1.

Amendment to Rule: Approval by OSC: (2012) 35 O.S.C.B. 10709; Request for Comments: (2011) 34 O.S.C.B. 6769 and (2010) 33 O.S.C.B. 3109.

Policies and Orders: CSAN 54-301.

Form 54-101F1 — Explanation to Clients and Client Response Form

Note: Terms used in this Form have the meanings given to them in National Instrument 54-101.

The use of this Form is referenced in sections 1.1, 3.2, 3.3, 3.4 and 3.5 of National Instrument 54-101.

Explanation to Clients

[Letterhead of Intermediary]

Based on your instructions, the securities in your account with us are not registered in your name but in our name or the name of another person or company holding your securities on our behalf. The issuers of the securities in your account may not know the identity of the beneficial owner of these securities.

We are required under securities law to obtain your instructions concerning various matters relating to your holding of securities in your account.

Disclosure of Beneficial Ownership Information

Securities law permits reporting issuers and other persons and companies to send materials related to the affairs of the reporting issuer directly to beneficial owners of the reporting issuer's securities if the beneficial owner does not object to having information about it disclosed to the reporting issuer or other persons and companies. Part 1 of the client response form allows you to tell us if you *OBJECT* to the disclosure by us to the reporting issuer or other persons or companies of your beneficial ownership information, consisting of your name, address, electronic mail address, securities holdings and preferred language of communication. Securities legislation restricts the use of your beneficial ownership information to matters relating to the affairs of the reporting issuer.

If you *DO NOT OBJECT* to the disclosure of your beneficial ownership information, please mark the first box on Part 1 of the form. In those circumstances, you will not be charged with any costs associated with sending securityholder materials to you.

If you *OBJECT* to the disclosure of your beneficial ownership information by us, please mark the second box in Part 1 of the form. If you do this, all materials to be delivered to you as a beneficial owner of securities will be delivered by us. *[Instruction: Disclose particulars of any fees or charges that the intermediary may require an objecting beneficial owner to pay in connection with the sending of securityholder materials.]*

Receiving Securityholder Materials

For securities that you hold through your account, you have the right to receive proxy-related materials sent by reporting issuers to registered holders of their securities in connection with meetings of such securityholders. Among other things, this permits you to receive the necessary information to allow you to have your securities voted in accordance with your instructions at a securityholder meeting. *[Optional: Revise this paragraph, if appropriate, to state that objecting beneficial owners will not receive materials unless they or the relevant issuers bear the costs.]*

In addition, reporting issuers may choose to send other securityholder materials to beneficial owners, although they are not obliged to do so.

Securities law permits you to decline to receive securityholder materials. The three types of materials that you may decline to receive are:

    (a) proxy-related materials, including annual reports and financial statements, that are sent in connection with a securityholder meeting;

    (b) annual reports and financial statements that are not part of proxy-related materials; and

    (c) materials that a reporting issuer or other person or company sends to securityholders that are not required by corporate or securities law to be sent to registered holders.

Part 2 of the client response form allows you to receive all materials sent to beneficial owners of securities or to decline to receive the three types of materials referred to above.

If you want to receive *ALL* materials that are sent to beneficial owners of securities, please mark the first box on Part 2 of the enclosed client response form. If you want to *DECLINE* to receive the three types of materials referred to above, please mark the second box in Part 2 of the form.

(Note: Even if you decline to receive the three types of materials referred to above, a reporting issuer or other person or company is entitled to deliver these materials to you, provided that the reporting issuer or other person or company pays all costs associated with the sending of these materials. These materials would be delivered to you through your intermediary if you have objected to the disclosure of your beneficial ownership information to reporting issuers.)

Preferred Language of Communication

Part 3 of the client response form allows you to tell us your preferred language of communication (English or French). You will receive materials in your preferred language of communication if the materials are available in that language.

Electronic Delivery of Documents

Securities law permits us to deliver some documents by electronic means if the consent of the recipient to the means of delivery has been obtained. Please provide your electronic mail address if you have one. *[Instruction: If applicable, either state (1) if the client wishes to receive documents by electronic delivery from the intermediary, the client should complete, sign and return the enclosed consent form with the client response form or (2) inform the client that electronic delivery of documents by the intermediary may be available upon his or her consent, and provide information as to how the client may provide that consent.]*

Contact

If you have any questions or want to change your instructions in the future, please contact [name] at [phone number] or [address, fax number, electronic mail address and/or website].

Client Response Form

TO: [NAME OF INTERMEDIARY]

Account Number(s) ....

I have read and understand the explanation to clients that you have provided me in connection with this form and the choices indicated by me apply to all of the securities held in the above account(s).

Part 1 — Disclosure of Beneficial Ownership Information

Please mark the corresponding box to show whether you DO NOT OBJECT or OBJECT to us disclosing your name, address, electronic mail address, securities holdings and preferred language of communication (English or French) to issuers of securities you hold with us and to other persons or companies in accordance with securities law. [Optional: For clients that OBJECT, disclose particulars of any fees or charges that the intermediary may require the client to pay in connection with the sending of securityholder materials.] [Note: The client response form may contain a place where an objecting beneficial owner can indicate its agreement to pay costs of delivery of securityholder materials that are not borne or required to be borne by another person or company.]

❏ *I DO NOT OBJECT to you disclosing the information described above.*

❏ *I OBJECT to you disclosing the information described above.*

Part 2 — Receiving Securityholder Materials

Please mark the corresponding box to show what materials you want to receive. Securityholder materials sent to beneficial owners of securities consist of the following materials: (a) proxy-related materials for annual and special meetings; (b) annual reports and financial statements that are not part of proxy-related materials; and (c) materials sent to securityholders that are not required by corporate or securities law to be sent.

❏ *I WANT to receive ALL securityholder materials sent to beneficial owners of securities.*

❏ *I DECLINE to receive ALL securityholder materials sent to beneficial owners of securities. (Even if I decline to receive these types of materials, I understand that a reporting issuer or other person or company is entitled to send these materials to me at its expense.)*

❏ *I WANT to receive ONLY proxy-related materials that are sent in connection with a special meeting.*

(Important note: These instructions do not apply to any specific request you give or may have given to a reporting issuer concerning the sending of interim financial reports of the reporting issuer. In addition, in some circumstances, the instructions you give in this client response form will not apply to annual reports or financial statements of an investment fund that are *not* part of proxy-related materials. An investment fund is also entitled to obtain specific instructions from you on whether you wish to receive its annual report or financial statements, and where you provide specific instructions, the instructions in this form with respect to financial statements will not apply.)

Part 3 — Preferred Language of Communication

Please mark the corresponding box to show your preferred language of communication.

❏ *ENGLISH*

❏ *FRENCH*

I understand that the materials I receive will be in my preferred language of communication if the materials are available in that language.

Form 54-101F2 — Request for Beneficial Ownership Information

Note: Terms used in this Form have the meanings given to them in National Instrument 54-101.

The use of this Form is referenced in sections 1.1, 2.5, 2.6, 2.9, 2.10, 2.12, 2.13, 2.14 and 4.1, 4.2, 4.3 and 6.2 of National Instrument 54-101.

References in this Form should be amended as appropriate to refer to any person or company using this Form in accordance with section 6.2 of National Instrument 54-101.

Part 1 — Reporting Issuer Information

Item 1 — Name and address of the reporting issuer.

State the name and address of the reporting issuer in English and, if applicable, French.

Item 2 — Contact person(s)

State the name, address, telephone number, facsimile number and email address of the contact person(s) of the reporting issuer, and of the reporting issuer's agent, if applicable, with whom the intermediary should deal. If different from the foregoing, also state the name, address, telephone number, facsimile number and email address of the contact person(s) of the reporting issuer responsible for dealing with invoices.

Item 3 — Name and ISIN[1] number of each class or series of securities to be searched

State the name and ISIN number of each class or series of securities of the reporting issuer for which information is requested.

Item 4 — Purpose of the request for beneficial ownership information

State whether the request is being made

(a) in connection with neither a meeting nor the sending of securityholder materials;

(b) for the purpose of obtaining a NOBO list, and in connection with sending securityholder materials, but not in connection with a meeting;

(c) for the purpose of obtaining a NOBO list, and in connection with a meeting;

(d) in connection with sending securityholder materials, not in connection with a meeting, and without a NOBO list being requested; or

(e) in connection with a meeting, without a NOBO list being requested.

---

[1]"ISIN" means International Stock Identification Number.

Item 5 — Information to be Included or Requested if Item 4(a) is Applicable

5.1 If a NOBO list is desired, request a NOBO list without FINS number information.

5.2 If desired, request information on the number of OBOs and NOBOs of the reporting issuer, indicating the number of each that have declined to accept materials to the extent applicable and the number of OBOs and NOBOs who have consented to electronic delivery of documents.

5.3 Specify the date as of which the NOBO list or the information referred to in item 5.2 is to be prepared.

5.4 If a NOBO list is requested, confirm that an undertaking of the reporting issuer in the form of Form 54-101F9 is enclosed or is being concurrently provided with the request for beneficial ownership information.

Item 6 — Information to be Included or Requested if Item 4(b) is Applicable

6.1 Request a NOBO list without FINS number information.

6.2 Provide an itemized list of the securityholder materials to be sent.

6.3 Indicate whether the securityholder materials are available in English or French only or in both English and French.

6.4 State whether the reporting issuer will send the materials directly to NOBOs or whether the reporting issuer will send the materials to the proximate intermediary for sending to NOBOs.

6.5 State the date as of which information provided in response to the request, including the NOBO lists, is to be provided.

6.6 State the date when the reporting issuer anticipates that proximate intermediaries will receive the materials referred to in item 6.2.

6.7 State whether the materials are to be sent by first class mail to the beneficial owners of securities and if not, state what method is to be used to send the materials, bearing in mind the different timing requirements in section 2.12 of the National Instrument. State whether the reporting issuer would like materials to be sent electronically when consent has been obtained from the beneficial owner of securities. *[If materials are to be sent electronically, the sender should bear in mind the principles of National Policy 11-201 Electronic Delivery of Documents.]*

6.8 Confirm that an undertaking of the reporting issuer in the form of Form 54-101F9 is enclosed or is being concurrently provided with the request for beneficial ownership information.

6.9 State if securityholder materials are to be sent to (a) all beneficial owners of securities (including beneficial owners that have declined to receive them), (b) only those beneficial owners who have requested to receive all securityholder materials, or (c) only those beneficial owners who have requested to receive all securityholder materials or special meeting materials.

Item 7 — Information to be Included or Requested if Item 4(c) is Applicable

7.1 Request a NOBO list. If the reporting issuer will send proxy-related materials directly to NOBOs and seek voting instructions from NOBOs, specify that the NOBO list will include FINS number information. Otherwise, specify that the NOBO list will exclude FINS number information.

7.2 Provide an itemized list of the proxy-related materials to be sent.

7.3 Indicate whether the proxy-related materials are available in English or French only or in both English and French.

7.4 State whether the reporting issuer will send the materials directly to NOBOs or whether the reporting issuer will send the materials to the proximate intermediary for sending to NOBOs. If the reporting issuer will send materials directly to NOBOs, state whether the reporting issuer will be seeking voting instructions from NOBOs in connection with the meeting.

7.5 State:

    (a) the type of meeting (annual, special or annual and special);

    (b) the beneficial ownership determination date of the meeting;

    (c) the date, time and place of meeting; and

    (d) the cut-off date and time for proxy receipt, if applicable.

7.6 State the name and ISIN number of each class or series of securities that carry the right to receive notice of the meeting or the right to vote at the meeting.

7.7 State that the information to be provided in response to the request, including the NOBO list, is to be provided as at the beneficial ownership determination date of the meeting.

7.8 State the date when the reporting issuer anticipates that proximate intermediaries will receive the materials referred to in item 7.2.

7.9 State whether the materials are to be sent by first class mail to the beneficial owners of securities and if not, state what method is to be used to send the materials, bearing in mind the different timing requirements in section 2.12 of the National Instrument. State whether the reporting issuer would like materials to be sent electronically when consent has been obtained from the beneficial owner of securities. *[If materials are to be sent electronically, the sender should bear in mind the principles of National Policy 11-201 Electronic Delivery of Documents.]*

7.10 Confirm that an undertaking of the reporting issuer in the form of Form 54-101F9 is enclosed or is being concurrently provided with the request for beneficial ownership information.

7.11 State if securityholder materials are to be sent to (a) all beneficial owners of securities (including beneficial owners that have declined to receive them), (b) only those beneficial owners who have requested to receive all securityholder materials, or (c) only those beneficial owners who have requested to receive all securityholder materials or special meeting materials.

7.12 State whether the reporting issuer is using notice-and-access, and any stratification criteria to be used. *[Before completing this item, the reporting issuer should discuss with the intermediary what stratification criteria the intermediary is able to apply.];*

Item 8 — Information to be Included or Requested if Item 4(d) is Applicable

8.1 Provide an itemized list of the securityholder materials to be sent.

8.2 Indicate whether the securityholder materials are available in English or French only or in both English and French.

8.3 State the date as at which information provided in response to the request is to be provided.

8.4 State the date when the reporting issuer anticipates that proximate intermediaries will receive the materials referred to in item 8.1.

8.5 State whether the materials are to be sent by first class mail to the beneficial owners of securities, and, if not, state what method is to be used to send the materials, bearing in mind the different timing requirements in section 2.12 of the National Instrument. State whether the reporting issuer would like materials to be sent electronically when consent has been obtained from the beneficial owner of securities. *[If materials are to be sent electronically, the sender should bear in mind the principles of National Policy 11-201 Electronic Delivery of Documents.]*

8.6 State if securityholder materials are to be sent to (a) all beneficial owners of securities (including beneficial owners that have declined to receive them), (b) only those beneficial owners who have requested to receive all securityholder materials, or (c) only those beneficial owners who have requested to receive all securityholder materials or special meeting materials.

Item 9 — Information to be Included or Requested if Item 4(e) is Applicable

9.1 Provide an itemized list of the proxy-related materials to be sent.

9.2 Indicate whether the proxy-related materials are available in English or French only or in both English and French.

9.3 State:

(a) the type of meeting (annual, special or annual and special);

(b) the beneficial ownership determination date of the meeting;

(c) the date, time and place of meeting; and

(d) the cut-off date and time for proxy receipt, if applicable.

9.4 State the name and ISIN number of each class or series of securities that carry the right to receive notice of the meeting or the right to vote at the meeting.

9.5 State that the information to be provided in response to the request is to be provided as at the beneficial ownership determination date of the meeting.

9.6 State the date when the reporting issuer anticipates that proximate intermediaries will receive the materials referred to in item 9.1.

9.7 State whether the materials are to be sent by first class mail to the beneficial owners of securities and, if not, state what method is to be used to send the materials, bearing in mind the different timing requirements in section 2.12 of the National Instrument. State whether the reporting issuer would like materials to be sent electronically when consent has been obtained from the beneficial owner of securities. *[If materials are to be sent electronically, the sender should bear in mind the principles of National Policy 11-201 Electronic Delivery of Documents.]*

9.8 State if securityholder materials are to be sent to (a) all beneficial owners of securities (including beneficial owners that have declined to receive them), (b) only those beneficial owners who have requested to receive all securityholder materials, or (c) only those beneficial owners who have requested to receive all securityholder materials or special meeting materials.

9.9 State whether the reporting issuer is using notice-and-access, and any stratification criteria to be used. *[Before completing this item, the reporting issuer should discuss with the intermediary what stratification criteria the intermediary is able to apply.]*

Item 10 — Payment of Costs of Sending to OBOs

10.1 State whether the reporting issuer will pay the costs associated with the delivery of the securityholder materials to OBOs by intermediaries.

Part 2 — Proximate Intermediary Response

Item 1 — Name and address of proximate intermediary

State the name and address of the proximate intermediary.

Item 2 — Contact person

State the name, telephone number, fax number and any electronic mail address and website of the contact person(s) of the proximate intermediary, or of the proximate intermediary's agent, if applicable, with whom the reporting issuer should deal.

Item 3 — Consolidation of replies

3.1 If applicable, provide a list of

(a) all nominees and depositories who hold securities on behalf of the proximate intermediary; and

(b) all nominees, depositories and other intermediaries for whom the proximate intermediary, directly or indirectly, holds securities.

3.2 Provide a list showing the number and class of securities held by each of the persons or companies referred to in Item 3.1.

3.3 Confirm that the information provided in the response includes securities held through those nominees, depositories and intermediaries holding, directly or indirectly, through the proximate intermediary.

Item 4 — Address for receipt of materials

If the request for beneficial ownership information was made either in connection with sending securityholder materials apart from a meeting, or in connection with a meeting, provide, if different from the information provided under Item 2, the name and municipal address to which the materials are to be sent for forwarding by the intermediary to beneficial owners or other intermediaries.

Also provide the name, telephone number, fax number and any electronic mail address and website of the contact person at that address if different from the information provided under item 2.

Item 5 — Number of sets of materials required for forwarding by proximate intermediary to beneficial owners

5.1 Unless the request for beneficial ownership information was made only to obtain NOBO lists, state the number, including the number required in each case in English and French, of materials specified in Part 1 of this form required for forwarding by the proximate intermediary to beneficial owners. If the proximate intermediary is in a foreign jurisdiction and the law in that jurisdiction requires the proximate intermediary to send securityholder materials to beneficial owners including NOBOs, this fact may be stated and the number of sets of materials specified may include the number required for such NOBOs.

5.2 If the reporting issuer has specified that it will send documents electronically, state the

    (a) aggregate number of beneficial owners that hold securities, directly or indirectly, through the proximate intermediary; and

    (b) the aggregate number of the beneficial owners referred to in paragraph (a) that have consented to electronic delivery of the documents by the intermediary through whom they hold the relevant securities.

5.3 State the number of OBOs with addresses, as shown in the records of the intermediary through which the OBO holds securities, in each jurisdiction.

Item 6 — Preliminary Search Information

If the request for beneficial ownership information was made to receive information under item 5.2 of the request, provide information on the number of OBOs and NOBOs of the reporting issuer, indicating the number of each that have declined to receive materials in accordance with the Instrument.

Item 7 — NOBO Lists

If a NOBO list was requested and if the proximate intermediary is able to provide the list in electronic form in the form of Form 54-101F5, confirm that the proximate intermediary shall send it electronically in that form. If a NOBO list was requested and if the proximate intermediary is unable to provide the list electronically in the form of Form 54-101F5, enclose the list with the response. Unless the request for beneficial ownership information stated that the request was being made for the purpose of obtaining NOBO lists and in connection with a meeting where the reporting issuer would be sending materials to NOBOs and seeking voting instructions from NOBOs, exclude from the NOBO list the FINS number information.

Item 8 — Confirmation of the search

Confirm the completeness and accuracy of the foregoing information.

Item 9 — Warning

If NOBO lists were requested, the response shall contain the following statement:

    WARNING: IT IS AN OFFENCE TO USE A NOBO LIST FOR PURPOSES OTHER THAN IN CONNECTION WITH:

        a. sending securityholder materials to NOBOs in accordance with National Instrument 54-101;

        b. an effort to influence the voting of securityholders of the reporting issuer;

        c. an offer to acquire securities of the reporting issuer; or

        d. any other matter relating to the affairs of the reporting issuer.

Item 10 — Non-Delivery to OBOs

10.1 State whether the proximate intermediary or any other intermediaries on whose behalf the proximate intermediary holds securities are entitled to decline to send, and will not send, securityholder materials to an OBO unless the OBO, or the relevant issuer, pays the costs of sending. *[This provision is not necessary if a reporting issuer has indicated in Form 54-102F2 that it will pay the costs of the intermediaries sending materials to OBOs.]*

10.2 Estimate the number of OBOs and their aggregate approximate holdings in securities of the reporting issuer that hold through the intermediaries referred to in item 10.1.

Form 54-101F3 — Omnibus Proxy (Depositories)

Note: Terms used in this Form have the meanings given to them in National Instrument 54-101.

The use of this Form is referenced in sections 1.1, 2.3, 5.4 and 8.2 of National Instrument 54-101.

[Letterhead of Depository]

Omnibus Proxy

Subject to the paragraph that follows, [the undersigned], being a registered holder or proxy holder in respect of securities of the reporting issuer specified below, as at the beneficial ownership determination date, hereby appoints each of the persons or companies identified in the attached schedule, in respect of the corresponding securities referred to below, with power of substitution in each, to attend, vote and otherwise act for and on behalf of [the undersigned] to the extent of the number of securities specified, in respect of all matters that may come before the meeting of securityholders described below, and at any adjournment or continuance thereof.

The appointees shall not vote, or give a proxy requiring or authorizing another person or company to vote, the securities represented by this omnibus proxy except in accordance with voting instructions received from the beneficial owners whose securities are represented by this omnibus proxy or in accordance with other legal authority to vote the securities.

This instrument supersedes and revokes any prior appointment of proxy made by [the undersigned] with respect to the voting of the securities specified below at such meeting, or at any adjournment thereof.

Reporting issuer: ....

Class/Series of Security: ....

ISIN Number: ....

Number of Securities: ....

Date of Meeting: ....

Beneficial Ownership Determination Date: ....

[Include date and signature]

Schedule To Form 54-101F3

[Letterhead of Depository]

Schedule to Omnibus Proxy

Participant Security Positions

Reporting issuer: ....

ISIN Number: ....

Effective Date/Beneficial Ownership Determination Date: ....

Participant	Total Number of Securities of the relevant class or series
[Name/address of participant]	[position held by participant]
[Name/address of participant]	[position held by participant]
[Name/address of participant]	[position held by participant]
Total Number of Securities held by Participants for the relevant class or series	[Total]

Form 54-101F4 — Omnibus Proxy (Proximate Intermediaries)

Note: Terms used in this Form have the meanings given to them in National Instrument 54-101.

The use of this Form is referenced in sections 1.1, 4.1 and 8.2 of National Instrument 54-101.

[Letterhead of Proximate Intermediary]

Omnibus Proxy

Subject to the paragraph that follows, [the undersigned], being a registered holder or proxy holder in respect of securities of the reporting issuer specified below, as at the beneficial ownership determination date, hereby appoints [*insert names from reporting issuer's management proxy*], with power of substitution, to attend, vote and otherwise act for and on behalf of [the undersigned] to the extent of the number of securities specified, in respect of all matters that may come before the meeting of securityholders described below, and at any adjournment or continuance.

The appointees shall not vote, or give a proxy requiring or authorizing another person or company to vote, the securities represented by this omnibus proxy except in accordance with voting instructions received from the beneficial owners whose securities are represented by this omnibus proxy or in accordance with other legal authority to vote the securities.

This instrument supersedes and revokes any prior appointment of proxy made by [the undersigned] with respect to the voting of the securities specified below at such meeting, or at any adjournment thereof.

Reporting issuer: ....

Class/Series of Security: ....

ISIN Number: ....

Number of Securities: ....

Name of Registered Holder of Securities[1]: ....

Date of Meeting: ....

Beneficial Ownership Determination Date: ....

[Include date and signature]

Form 54-101F5 — Electronic Format for NOBO List

HEADER RECORD DESCRIPTION	TYPE	LENGTH	POSITION	COMMENTS
RECORD TYPE	A	1	1	Header record = A
FINS NUMBER	A	4	2–5	Prefix T, M, V or C
ISIN	A	12	6–17	
FILLER	X	3	18–20	Blank
SECURITY DESC.	A	32	21–52	Security Description
RECORD DATE	N	8	53–60	Format YYYYMMDD
CREATION DATE	N	8	61–68	Format YYYYMMDD
FILLER	X	250	69–318	Blank

DETAIL RECORD DESCRIPTION	TYPE	LENGTH	POSITION	COMMENTS
RECORD TYPE	A	1	1	Detail Record = B
FINS NUMBER	A	4	2–5	Same as in Header record
ISIN	A	12	6–17	
FILLER	X	3	18–20	Blank
FILLER	X	20	21–40	Blank
NAME	A	32	41–72	Holder Name
ADDRESS	A	32 × 6	73–264	Occurs 6 times
FILLER	X	32	265–296	Blank
POSTAL CODE	A	9	297–305	
POSTAL REGION	A	1	306	C=Canada; U=USA; F=Foreign; (other than USA); H=Hand Deliver
NOTICE AND ACCESS	A	1	307	Y=Full Package; N=Notice Only
FILLER	X	1	308	Blank
E-MAIL ADDRESS	A	32	309–340	
LANGUAGE CODE	A	1	341	E=English; F=French
NUMBER OF SHARES	N	9	342–350	Shareholder Position
RECEIVE ALL MATERIAL	A	1	351	A — ALL Material, S — Material for SPECIAL Meetings only, D — DECLINE to receive Materials
AGREE TO ELECTRONIC DELIVERY BY INTERMEDIARY	A	1	352	Y/N

TRAILER RECORD DESCRIPTION	TYPE	LENGTH	POSITION	COMMENTS
RECORD TYPE	A	1	1	Trailer record = C
FINS NUMBER	A	4	2–5	Same as in Header Record

---

[1]*[Instruction: Specify if securities are held through more than one registered holder, and specify the number of securities held through each registered holder.]*

ISIN	A	12	6–17	
FILLER	X	3	18–20	
TOTAL SHAREHOLDERS	N	7	21–27	Number of "B" type records
TOTAL SHARES	N	11	27–38	Total Shares on "B" type records
FILLER	X	280	39–318	Blank

Form 54-101F6 — Request for Voting Instructions Made by Reporting Issuer

Note: Terms used in this Form have the meanings given to them in National Instrument 54-101.

The use of this Form is referenced in sections 1.1, 2.11, 2.17 and 2.19 of National Instrument 54-101.

References in this Form should be amended as appropriate to refer to the person or company using this Form, in accordance with section 6.2 of National Instrument 54-101.

[Letterhead of Reporting issuer]

Request for Voting Instructions

To our securityholders:

We are sending to you the enclosed proxy-related materials that relate to a meeting of the holders of the series or class of securities that are held on your behalf by the intermediary identified below. Unless you attend the meeting and vote in person, your securities can be voted only by management, as proxy holder of the registered holder, in accordance with your instructions.

[Include instructions for appointing alternative proxy.]

We are prohibited from voting these securities on any of the matters to be acted upon at the meeting without your specific voting instructions. In order for these securities to be voted at the meeting, it will be necessary for us to have your specific voting instructions. Please complete and return the information requested in this form to provide your voting instructions to us promptly.

[Specify how and to whom the voting instructions may be returned.]

If you want to attend the meeting and vote in person, write your name in the place provided for that purpose in this form. You can also write the name of someone else whom you wish to attend the meeting and vote on your behalf. Unless prohibited by law, the person whose name is written in the space provided will have full authority to present matters to the meeting and vote on all matters that are presented at the meeting, even if those matters are not set out in this form or the information circular. Consult a legal advisor if you wish to modify the authority of that person in any way. If you require help, contact *[insert name]*.

[Insert proximate intermediary name, code or identifier; name, address and respective holdings of securities of the relevant series or class held for the NOBO.]

[Insert description of proposals to be voted upon, other instructions or explanations, etc.]

By providing voting instructions as requested, you are acknowledging that you are the beneficial owner of, and are entitled to instruct us with respect to the voting of, these securities.

(If these voting instructions are given on behalf of a body corporate set out the full legal name of the body corporate, the name and position of the person giving voting instructions on behalf of the body corporate and the address for service of the body corporate.)

Form 54-101F7 — Request for Voting Instructions Made by Intermediary

Note: Terms used in this Form have the meanings given to them in National Instrument 54-101.

The use of this Form is referenced in sections 1.1, 4.4 and 4.6 of National Instrument 54-101.

References in this Form should be amended as appropriate to refer to the person or company using this Form, in accordance with section 6.2 of National Instrument 54-101.

[Letterhead of Intermediary]

Request for Voting Instructions

To our clients:

We are sending to you the enclosed proxy-related materials that relate to a meeting of the holders of securities of the series or class held by us in your account but not registered in your name. Unless you attend the meeting and vote in person, your securities can be voted only by us, as registered holder or proxy holder of the registered holder, in accordance with your written instructions.

[Include instructions for appointing alternative proxy.]

We are prohibited from voting these securities on any of the matters to be acted upon at the meeting without your specific voting instructions. In order for these securities to be voted at the meeting, it will be necessary for us to have your specific voting instructions. Please complete and return the information requested in this form to provide your voting instructions to us promptly.

[Specify how and to whom the voting instructions may be returned.]

If you want to attend the meeting and vote in person, write your name in the place provided for that purpose in this form. You can also write the name of someone else whom you wish to attend the meeting and vote on your behalf. Unless prohibited by law, the person whose name is written in the space provided will have full authority to present matters to the meeting and vote on all matters that are presented at the meeting, even if those matters are not set out in this form or the information circular. Consult a legal advisor if you wish to modify the authority of that person in any way. If you require help, contact *[insert name]*.

[Insert intermediary name, code or identifier; name, address and respective holdings of securities of the relevant series or class held for the beneficial owner.]

[Insert description of proposals to be voted upon, other instructions or explanations, etc.]

By providing voting instructions as requested, you are acknowledging that you are the beneficial owner of, and are entitled to instruct us with respect to the voting of, these securities.

(If these voting instructions are given on behalf of a body corporate set out the full legal name of the body corporate, the name and position of the person giving voting instructions on behalf of the body corporate and the address for service of the body corporate.)

Form 54-101F8 — [repealed]

Form 54-101F9 — Undertaking

Note: Terms used in this Form have the meanings given to them in National Instrument 54-101.

The use of this Form is referenced in sections 2.5, 6.1 and 6.2 of National Instrument 54-101.

I, ...

(Full Residence Address) ....

(If this undertaking is made on behalf of a body corporate, set out the full legal name of the body corporate, position of person signing and address for service of the body corporate).

SOLEMNLY DECLARE AND UNDERTAKE THAT:

1. I require a list in the required format of the non-objecting beneficial owners of securities of *[insert name of the reporting issuer]* on whose behalf intermediaries hold securities (a NOBO list), as shown on the records of the intermediaries.

<Option #1: *use this alternative if the reporting issuer is providing the undertaking>*

2. I undertake that the information set out on the NOBO list will be used only in connection with matters relating to the affairs of the reporting issuer.

<Option #2: *use this alternative if a person or company other than the reporting issuer is providing the undertaking>*

2. I undertake that the information set out on the NOBO list will be used only for one or more of the following purposes:

(a) sending securityholder materials directly to NOBOs in accordance with National Instrument 54-101;

(b) an effort to influence the voting of securityholders of the reporting issuer;

(c) an offer to acquire securities of the reporting issuer.

3. I undertake that, except as permitted under National Instrument 54-101, the NOBO list will not be used to send securityholder materials to those NOBOs that are identified on the NOBO list as having chosen not to receive the materials, and that the materials sent shall include the following statement:

These securityholder materials are being sent to both registered and non-registered owners of the securities. If you are a non-registered owner, and the issuer or its agent has sent these materials directly to you, your name and address and information about your holdings of securities, have been obtained in accordance with applicable securities regulatory requirements from the intermediary holding on your behalf.

4. I am aware that it is a contravention of the law to use a NOBO list for purposes other than in connection with one or more of the following:

(a) sending securityholder materials directly to NOBOs in accordance with National Instrument 54-101;

(b) an effort to influence the voting of securityholders of the reporting issuer;

(c) an offer to acquire securities of the reporting issuer.

5. I declare that I (or the person or company I am using to make this request) has the technological capacity to receive the NOBO list.

.... Signature

.... Name of person signing

.... Date

Form 54-101F10 — Undertaking

Note: Terms used in this Form have the meaning given to them in National Instrument 54-101.

The use of this Form is referenced in section 6.2 of National Instrument 54-101.

I, ..., (Full Residence Address) .... *(If this undertaking is made on behalf of a person or company other than an individual, set out the full legal name of that person or company, position of the individual signing on behalf of that person or company and address for service.)* SOLEMNLY DECLARE AND UNDERTAKE THAT:

1. I wish to send materials to beneficial owners of securities of [*insert name of the reporting issuer*] on whose behalf intermediaries hold securities, using the indirect sending procedures provided in National Instrument 54-101 (the "NI 54-101 Procedures").

2. I undertake that I am using the NI 54-101 Procedures to send materials to beneficial owners only for the purpose of one or both of the following:

(a) an effort to influence the voting of securityholders of the reporting issuer;

(b) an offer to acquire securities of the reporting issuer.

3. I am aware that it is a contravention of t\he law to send materials using the NI 54-101 Procedures for purposes other than in connection with one or both of the following:

(a) an effort to influence the voting of securityholders of the reporting issuer;

(b) an offer to acquire securities of the reporting issuer.

.... Signature

.... Name of person signing

.... Date

Companion Policy 54-101CP — Communication with Beneficial Owners of Securities of a Reporting Issuer

Table of Contents

PART 1 — BACKGROUND

1.1 History — (1) Obligations imposed on reporting issuers under corporate law and securities legislation to communicate with securityholders are typically cast as obligations in respect of registered holders and not in respect of beneficial owners. For purposes of market efficiency, securities are increasingly not registered in the names of the beneficial owners but rather in the names of depositories, or their nominees, who hold on behalf of intermediaries, such as dealers, trust companies or banks, who, in turn, hold on behalf of the beneficial owners. Securities may also be registered directly in the names of intermediaries who hold on behalf of the beneficial owners.

(2) Corporate law and securities legislation require reporting issuers to send to their registered holders information and materials that enable such holders to exercise their right to vote. To address concerns that beneficial owners who hold their securities through intermediaries or their nominees may not receive the information and materials, in 1987, the CSA approved National Policy Statement No. 41 ("NP41"), which has since been replaced by National Instrument 54-101 (the "Instrument").

(3) The purpose of this Policy is to state the views of the Canadian securities regulatory authorities on various matters relating to the Instrument in order to provide guidance and interpretation to market participants in the practical application of the Instrument.

1.2 Fundamental principles — The following fundamental principles have guided the preparation of the Instrument:

(a) all securityholders of a reporting issuer, whether registered holders or beneficial owners, should have the opportunity to be treated alike as far as is practicable;

(b) efficiency should be encouraged; and

(c) the obligations of each party in the securityholder communication process should be equitable and clearly defined.

PART 2 — GENERAL

2.1 Application of instrument — (1) The securityholder communication procedures in the Instrument are relevant to all securityholder materials sent by a reporting issuer to beneficial owners of its securities under Canadian securities legislation. Securityholder materials include, but are not limited to, proxy-related materials. Securityholder materials include:

(a) materials required by securities legislation or applicable corporate law to be sent to registered holders or beneficial owners of a reporting issuer's securities, such as interim financial reports or annual financial statements;

(b) materials required by securities legislation or applicable corporate law to be sent only to registered holders of a reporting issuer's securities, such as issuer bid and directors circulars and dissident proxy-related materials;

(c) materials sent to registered holders or beneficial owners of a reporting issuer's securities absent any legal requirement to do so.

(2) As provided in section 2.7 of the Instrument, compliance with the procedures set out in the Instrument is mandatory for reporting issuers when sending proxy-related materials to beneficial owners, and, under section 2.8 of the Instrument, is optional for the sending of other materials. Once a reporting issuer, or another person or company pursuant to Part 6 of the Instrument, chooses to use the communications procedures specified in the Instrument for a reporting issuer, depositories, intermediaries and other persons or companies must comply with their corresponding obligations under the Instrument.

2.2 Application to foreign securityholders and U.S. issuers — (1) As provided in subsection 2.12(5) of the Instrument, a reporting issuer that is precluded from sending securityholder materials directly to NOBOs because of conflicting legal requirements in the United States or elsewhere outside of Canada shall send the materials indirectly, i.e., by forwarding the materials to NOBOs through proximate intermediaries for those securities. Subsection 2.12(3) does not require a reporting issuer to send proxy-related materials to all beneficial owners outside Canada. A reporting issuer need only send proxy-related materials to beneficial owners who hold through proximate intermediaries that are either participants in a recognized depository, or intermediaries on the depository's intermediary master list.

(2) National Instrument 71-101 *The Multijurisdictional Disclosure System* provides, in Part 18, that a "U.S. issuer", as defined in that Instrument, is considered to satisfy the requirements of National Instrument 54-101, other than in respect of fees, if the issuer complies with the requirements of Rule 14a-13 under the 1934 Act for any Canadian clearing agency and any intermediary whose last address as shown on the books of the issuer is in the local jurisdiction. Those requirements are designed to achieve the same purpose as the requirements of the Instrument.

(3) A Canadian reporting issuer may be exempt from complying with U.S. requirements under a reciprocal provision in the U.S. Multijurisdictional Disclosure regime.

2.3 [deleted]

2.4 "Client" and "Intermediary" to be distinguished from "Beneficial Owner" — (1) Section 1.1 of the Instrument distinguishes between "client" and "beneficial owner". The two definitions recognize that, for many reporting issuers, there may be layers of intermediaries between the registered holder of a security and the ultimate beneficial owner. For example, a dealer could hold a security on behalf of another dealer that in turn holds the security for the beneficial owner.

(2) For the purposes of the Instrument, if an intermediary that holds securities has discretionary voting authority over the securities, it will be the beneficial owner of those securities for purposes of providing instructions in a client response form, and would not also be an "intermediary" with respect to those securities.

(3) The term "client" refers to the person or company for whom an intermediary directly holds securities, regardless of whether the client is a beneficial owner. For example, if a dealer holds securities on behalf of a bank that in turn holds the securities on behalf of the beneficial owner, the bank is a client of the dealer, and the beneficial owner is a client of the bank. The beneficial owner is not a client of the dealer. Section 1.2 of the Instrument recognizes that, under the Instrument, an intermediary may "hold" securities for a client, even if another person or company is shown on the books or records of the reporting issuer or the records of another intermediary or depository as the holder of the securities.

2.5 Definition of "Corporate Law" — Section 1.1 of the Instrument defines "corporate law" as any legislation, constating instrument or agreement that governs the affairs of a reporting issuer. The term "corporate law" therefore encompasses Canadian and foreign laws, a declaration or deed of trust in the case of a trust, and the partnership agreement in the case of a partnership.

2.6 Fees — Section 1.4 provides that fees payable under the Instrument, unless prescribed by the regulator or securities regulatory authority, shall be a reasonable amount. Section 2.13 provides that a reporting issuer shall pay a fee to a proximate intermediary for furnishing the information requested in a request for beneficial ownership information (which would be used by reporting issuer to request a NOBO list) made by the reporting issuer. Paragraph 2.14(1)(a) provides that a reporting issuer that sends securityholder materials indirectly to NOBOs through a proximate intermediary shall pay to the proximate intermediary, upon receipt by the reporting issuer of a certificate of sending to NOBOs in accordance with the instructions specified by the reporting issuer and the request for beneficial ownership information, a fee for sending the securityholder materials to the NOBOs. In determining what is a reasonable amount the Canadian securities regulatory authorities expect that market participants will be guided by fees previously prescribed by Canadian securities regulatory authorities and by the fees payable for comparable services in other jurisdictions such as the United States, as well as by technological developments. In the case of fees for sending securityholder materials to NOBOs, referred to in paragraph 2.14(1)(a), the CSA would regard as currently reasonable an amount not exceeding $1 (being the amount previously specified in NP41).

2.7 Agent — A depository, intermediary, reporting issuer or any other person or company subject to obligations under the Instrument's securityholder communication procedures may use a service provider as its agent to fulfil its obligations. A person or company that uses an agent remains fully responsible for fulfilling its obligations under the Instrument, and for the conduct of the agent in this regard. In particular, section 11.1 of National Instrument 31-103 *Registration Requirements, Exemptions and Ongoing Registrant Obligations* ("NI 31-103") requires any person or company that is a registered firm under NI 31-103 to establish, maintain and apply policies and procedures that establish a system of controls and supervision sufficient to provide reasonable assurance that the firm and each individual acting on its behalf complies with securities legislation.

A person or company is permitted to fulfil its obligations relating to another party through an agent of that other party. For example, under section 2.12 of the Instrument, a reporting issuer fulfills its obligation to send securityholder materials to a proximate intermediary if the proximate intermediary designates an agent to whom the reporting issuer will provide the materials, and the reporting issuer sends the materials to such agent. If an intermediary has designated an agent in the foregoing circumstances, we expect reporting issuers to send materials to that designated agent unless a reporting issuer previously has made alternate arrangements agreeable to that intermediary well in advance of the reporting issuer's meeting. We expect that any such alternate arrangements would be at least as efficient and user-friendly as established industry practices.

PART 3 — REPORTING ISSUERS

3.1 Timing for notice of meeting and record dates and intermediary searches — (1) Section 2.2 of the Instrument requires that, 25 days before the record date for notice of a meeting, a reporting issuer send to the entities named in that section a notification of meeting and record dates that includes certain basic information about the meeting. Section 2.5 of the Instrument requires that 20 days before the record date for notice, a reporting issuer send a request for beneficial ownership information to proximate intermediaries. Section 2.20 allows these timing requirements to be abridged so long as the reporting issuer arranges to have the proxy-related materials for the meeting sent in compliance with the applicable timing requirements in sections 2.9 and 2.12, and upon filing of an officer's certificate containing the information specified in section 2.20. Where the reporting issuer uses notice-and-access, the reporting issuer also must fix the record date for notice to be at least 40 days before the date of the meeting, and send the notification of meeting and record dates at least 25 days before the meeting.

(2) The time frames stipulated by sections 2.9 and 2.12 of the Instrument are minimum requirements. For a meeting that will deal with contentious matters, the CSA expect that good corporate practice will often require that materials be sent earlier than the minimum required dates to ensure that securityholders have a full opportunity to understand and react to the matters raised.

(3) It remains the reporting issuer's responsibility when planning a meeting timetable to factor in all timing considerations, including deadlines external to the Instrument. For example, reporting issuers that have obligations under corporate law to advertise in advance of a record date for notice, or satisfy other publication obligations, would need to comply with those obligations. Reporting issuers that intend to satisfy their advance publication obligation by relying upon publication by CDS of meeting and record dates under subsection 5.2(2) of the Instrument would need to factor in the timing of publication by CDS and the advance notice required by CDS, as described in section 3.4 of this Policy, in order to permit inclusion of meeting and record date information in the publication. Reporting issuers will also need to factor in the time needed to produce and assemble the relevant securityholder materials after quantities have been determined.

(4) Proximate intermediaries are required under section 4.1 of the Instrument to furnish the information requested in a request for beneficial ownership information, in certain circumstances, within three business days of receipt. It should be noted that this timing refers to receipt of the request by the proximate intermediary, which may not be the same date as the request was sent by the reporting issuer. The time necessary for a request for beneficial ownership information to be received by a proximate intermediary should be factored into a reporting issuer's planning.

3.2 Adjournment or change in meeting — (1) Under section 2.15, a reporting issuer that sends a notice of adjournment or other change for a meeting to registered holders of its securities shall concurrently send the notice, including any change in the beneficial ownership determination date, to the persons and companies listed in section 2.15. Issuers are reminded of a number of other potential implications associated with an adjournment or other change, including those set out below.

(2) If additional proxy-related materials are sent in connection with the meeting after proxy-related materials have previously been sent, a new intermediary search may be required if the beneficial ownership determination date for the meeting is changed.

(3) New intermediary searches may have to be conducted if the nature of the business to be transacted at the meeting is materially changed. If the nature of the business is changed to add business that results in the meeting becoming a special meeting, it may be necessary to conduct new intermedi-

ary searches in order to ensure that beneficial owners that had elected to receive only proxy-related materials that are sent in connection with a special meeting receive proxy-related materials for the meeting.

(4) If an adjournment or other change to the business of the meeting requires that new proxy-related materials be sent to securityholders, the meeting date or the date of the adjourned meeting may have to be delayed to satisfy the time periods specified in the Instrument, unless an exemption from the time periods of the Instrument is obtained. If the change in the business of the meeting is significant, such as a change from only routine business to special business, Canadian securities regulatory authorities will not generally grant exemptions from timing requirements for sending proxy-related materials in the absence of exceptional circumstances.

3.3 Request for beneficial ownership information — (1) A request for beneficial ownership information made under subsection 2.5(2) of the National Instrument may be for any class or series of securities and is not restricted to only those securities carrying the right to receive notice of, or to vote at, a meeting, as is the case with a request under subsection 2.5(1). A request under subsection 2.5(2) need not necessarily be addressed to all proximate intermediaries holding the class or series of securities.

(2) If it is able to do so, a proximate intermediary is required to respond to a request for a NOBO list by providing the NOBO list in electronic format. Subsection 2.5(4) provides that a request for beneficial ownership information must be made through a transfer agent. However, where only a NOBO list is being requested, the request may be made by the reporting issuer (or another person or company retained by the reporting issuer), provided the requester has provided the necessary undertaking in Form 54-101F10.

3.4 Depository's index of meetings — CDS advises that the index referred to in section 5.2 of the Instrument is currently published in the Monday edition of *The Globe and Mail Report on Business* and in the Tuesday edition of *La Presse*. CDS advises that notices of meetings received by CDS by noon on Wednesday are usually published in *The Globe and Mail* on the following Monday and in *La Presse* on the following Tuesday. A reporting issuer should contact CDS for current forms and fee schedules of CDS.

3.4.1 Explanation of Voting Rights — (1) Subsection 2.16(1) of the Instrument requires a reporting issuer's proxy-related materials to contain a plain language explanation of how the beneficial owner can exercise the voting rights attached to the securities.

(2) Subsection 2.16(2) of the Instrument requires management of a reporting issuer to provide in the information circular disclosure about the following:

(a) whether the reporting issuer is sending proxy-related materials to registered holders or beneficial owners using notice-and-access, and if stratification will be used, the types of registered holders or beneficial owners who will receive paper copies of the information circular;

(b) whether the reporting issuer is sending proxy-related materials directly to NOBOs;

(c) whether the reporting issuer intends to pay for delivery to OBOs. If the reporting issuer does not intend to pay for such delivery, the information circular must disclose this fact and state that an OBO will not receive the materials unless the OBO's intermediary assumes the costs of delivery.

This disclosure is intended to explain to beneficial owners why they may receive different proxy-related materials than other beneficial owners and why they may not receive proxy-related materials even if they have requested them. Item 4.3 of Form 51-102F5 Information Circular also requires this disclosure.

We also encourage reporting issuers to disclose whether they are sending proxy-related materials to beneficial owners who have declined to receive them and explain their decision.

(3) If a reporting issuer has chosen not to pay for proximate intermediaries to deliver proxy-related materials and Form 54-101F7 to OBOs, section 2.12 still requires that it send to a proximate intermediary the number of sets of proxy-related materials that the proximate intermediary requested for forwarding to OBOs.

3.5 NOBO Voting instructions — (1) Voting instructions that the reporting issuer requests directly from NOBOs will be returned directly to the reporting issuer. Management of the reporting issuer will then vote the securities beneficially owned by NOBOs according to the instructions received from the NOBOs to the extent that management has the corresponding proxy. The proximate intermediary that provides the NOBO list under subsection 4.1(1) of the Instrument gives management that proxy.

We expect reporting issuers that choose to solicit voting instructions directly from NOBOs to have appropriate procedures for NOBO voting, which includes doing the following in a timely manner:

(a) responding to inquiries from NOBOs or intermediaries with NOBO clients about the voting process;

(b) appointing a NOBO or nominee of the NOBO as a proxyholder in respect of securities beneficially owned by the NOBO;

(c) generating a new Form 54-101F6 if a NOBO requests one. For example, a NOBO may have misplaced a Form 54-101F6 that he or she had received; or may now wish to provide voting instructions although he or she had previously indicated on his or her client response form that he or she did not wish to receive proxy-related materials.

We expect reporting issuers and intermediaries to work together to address any issues arising from the NOBO voting process.

3.6 Appointing NOBO as Proxy Holder — Section 2.18 of the Instrument requires reporting issuers who request voting instructions from NOBOs to:

• arrange to appoint the NOBO as proxy holder, if he or she so instructs, at no expense to the NOBO; and

• deposit the proxy within any time specified in the information circular for the deposit of proxies (a "proxy cut-off") if the reporting issuer obtains the instructions at least one business day before the proxy cut-off. We expect reporting issuers to make best efforts to deposit the proxy even if the instructions are obtained less than one business day before the proxy cut-off.

However, subject to these basic obligations, reporting issuers have flexibility as to the specific mechanism used to appoint the beneficial owner as proxy holder.

PART 4 — INTERMEDIARIES

4.1 Client response form — By completing a client response form as provided in Part 3 of the Instrument, a beneficial owner gives notice of its choices concerning the receipt of materials and the disclosure of ownership information concerning it. Pursuant to section 3.4 of the Instrument, a beneficial owner may, by notice to the intermediary through which it holds, change any prior instructions given in a client response form. Proximate intermediaries should alert their clients to the costs and other consequences of the options in the client response form. Section 4.6 of National Instrument 51-102 *Continuous Disclosure Obligations* requires reporting issuers to send annually a request form to the registered holders and beneficial holders of its securities that the holders may use to request a copy of the reporting issuer's financial statements and MD&A. Failing to return the request form or otherwise specifically request a copy of the financial statements or MD&A from the reporting issuer will override the beneficial owner's standing instructions under this Instrument in respect of the financial statements.

4.2 Separate accounts — A client that wishes to make different choices concerning receipt of securityholder materials or disclosure of ownership information with respect to some of the securities beneficially owned by it should hold those securities in separate accounts.

4.3 Reconciliation of positions — (1) The records of an intermediary must show which of its clients are NOBOs, OBOs or other intermediaries, and specify the holdings of each of those clients.

(2) In order that the Instrument work properly, it is important that the records of an intermediary be accurate. Its records must reconcile accurately with the records of the person or company through whom the intermediary itself holds the securities, which could either be another intermediary or a depository, or the security register of the relevant issuer, if the intermediary is a registered securityholder. This reconciliation must include securities held both directly and through nominees.

(3) A proximate intermediary should provide accurate responses to requests for beneficial ownership information. Information about the holdings of NOBOs, when added to the holdings of OBOs, the holdings of other intermediaries holding through the proximate intermediary and the holdings that the proximate intermediary holds as principal, must not exceed the total security holdings of the proximate intermediary, including its nominees, as shown on the register of the issuer or in the records of the depository.

(4) It is important as well that the total number of votes cast at a meeting by an intermediary or persons or companies holding through an intermediary not exceed the number of votes for which the intermediary itself is a proxyholder.

4.4 Identification of intermediary — (1) A NOBO list with FINS numbers will only be provided where the list is sought by a reporting issuer in conjunction with a meeting of its securityholders in circumstances in which the issuer is sending proxy-related materials under paragraph 4.1(1)(c) of the Instrument. The FINS number should not be required in circumstances where it is not necessary to reconcile voting instructions and/or proxies.

(2) Identification of the intermediary and the holdings specified in the corresponding NOBO list on requests for voting instructions as required in Form 54-101F6 is necessary for the reporting issuer to be able to reconcile voting instructions received from a NOBO to the corresponding position registered in the name of the intermediary or its nominee or in respect of which the intermediary holds a proxy. In addition, should a NOBO wish to change its voting instructions, before or at a meeting of securityholders, knowledge of the corresponding intermediary and the NOBO's holdings is necessary.

4.5 Changes to intermediary master list — It is the obligation of intermediaries under section 3.1 of the Instrument to notify each depository of any changes in the information required to be provided under that section within five business days after the change. The five business days is a maximum requirement and it is expected that intermediaries will provide notice of such changes as soon as possible and, if possible in advance, in order that their clients not be prejudiced.

4.6 Incomplete or late deliveries — If sets of securityholder materials of a reporting issuer are incomplete or received after the prescribed time limits, the intermediary should advise the reporting issuer and request instructions.

4.7 Other obligations of intermediaries — The Instrument addresses the obligations of intermediaries in connection with the forwarding of securityholder materials. It is noted that intermediaries will have other obligations to the beneficial owners holding through them that arise from the nature of the relationship between the intermediary and the beneficial owners. These obligations will likely include advising the beneficial owners of the commencement of take-over bids, issuer bids, rights offerings and other events, and advising as to how the beneficial owners can obtain the relevant materials.

4.8 Instructions from Existing Clients — A client deemed to be a NOBO under NP41 can continue to be treated as a NOBO under paragraph 3.3(b)(ii) of this Instrument. However, intermediaries are responsible for ensuring that they comply with their obligations under privacy legislation with respect to their clients' personal information. Intermediaries may find that, notwithstanding paragraph 3.3(b)(ii), privacy legislation requires that they take measures to obtain their clients' consent before they disclose their clients' names and security holdings to a reporting issuer or other sender of material.

4.9 Appointing Beneficial Owner as Proxy Holder — Section 4.5 of the Instrument requires intermediaries to:

- arrange to appoint the beneficial owner as proxy holder, if he or she so instructs, at no expense to the beneficial owner; and
- deposit the proxy within any proxy cut-off if the intermediary obtains the instructions at least one business day before the proxy cut-off. We encourage intermediaries to make best efforts to deposit the proxy even if the instructions are obtained less than one business day before the proxy cut-off.

However, subject to these basic obligations, intermediaries have flexibility as to the specific method used to appoint the beneficial owner as proxy holder. One method in current use and permitted under section 4.5 of the Instrument is the "appointee system". Under the appointee system, a beneficial owner who wishes to be appointed as proxy holder for the intermediary in respect of securities that he or she beneficially owns can print his or her name or the name of his or her appointee in a space provided on the voting instruction form. The name of the beneficial owner or her appointee is then recorded on a cumulative proxy, which is provided to the proxy tabulator or meeting scrutineer. When the beneficial owner or his or her appointee arrives at the meeting, the scrutineer has all the necessary proxies and information at hand to enable the beneficial owner or other appointees to vote at the meeting.

PART 5 — MEANS OF SENDING

5.1 General — The following tables illustrate the options available for sending proxy-related materials to beneficial owners.

Table A: Direct Sending to NOBOs

Delivery Method	Documents Sent	Beneficial Owner Prior Consent Required?
Prepaid mail, courier or the equivalent	Reporting issuer sends paper copies of proxy-related materials, including notice of meeting, management information circular, Form 54-101F6 and, if applicable, annual financial statements and related MD&A, which may be part of an annual report.	No.
Notice-and-access	Reporting issuer files management information circular and notice on SEDAR and posts on non-SEDAR website. Reporting issuer sends notice and Form 54-101F6. Reporting issuer is responsible for providing on request paper copy of information circular and, if applicable, the annual financial statements and related MD&A. Reporting issuer may send some NOBOs paper copies of the information circular and, if applicable, the annual financial statements and related MD&A, pursuant to stratification and/or previously obtained or standing instructions.	No, if notice package is sent using prepaid mail, courier or the equivalent. Yes, if notice package is being sent by other method, i.e., electronically.
Other delivery method	Reporting issuer sends proxy-related materials and Form 54-101F6 using delivery method that is not (i) prepaid mail, courier or the equivalent, or (ii) notice-and-access, e.g., an e-mail with embedded links.	Yes.

Table B: Indirect Sending to Beneficial Owners

Delivery Method	Documents Sent	Beneficial Owner Prior Consent Required?
Prepaid mail, courier or the equivalent	Reporting issuer sends paper copies of proxy-related materials, including notice of meeting, management information circular and, if applicable, annual financial statements and related MD&A, which may be part of an annual report. Proximate intermediary (or in some cases, intermediary) will add to that package a paper copy of Form 54-101F7.	No.
Notice-and-access	Reporting issuer files management information circular and notice on SEDAR and posts on non-SEDAR website. Reporting issuer sends requested number of copies of notice to proximate intermediaries (and in some cases, intermediaries) for sending to beneficial owners. Reporting issuer also sends appropriate numbers of paper copies of the information circular and, if applicable, annual financial statements and related MD&A, for proximate intermediaries (in some cases, intermediaries) to send pursuant to stratification and/or previously obtained or standing instructions. Proximate intermediary (or in some cases, intermediary) will add to that package a paper copy of Form 54-101F7.	No, if notice package is sent using prepaid mail, courier or the equivalent. Yes, if notice package is being sent by other method, i.e., electronically.
Other delivery method	Proximate intermediary (or in some cases, intermediary) sends proxy-related materials and Form 54-101F7 using delivery method that is not (i) prepaid mail, courier or the equivalent, or (ii) notice-and-access, e.g., email with embedded links.	Yes.

5.2 Securityholder Materials Sent to Intermediaries — Reporting issuers and other persons or companies should make arrangements with proximate intermediaries to send securityholder materials to beneficial owners in a timely manner. A proximate intermediary should not request sets of securityholder materials for NOBOs if the reporting issuer will be sending the materials directly to those NOBOs.

5.3 Prepaid Mail, Courier or the Equivalent — Paper copies of proxy-related materials must be sent using prepaid mail, courier or an equivalent delivery method. We consider "first class mail" to be the equivalent of Canada Post Lettermail. An equivalent delivery method is any delivery method where the beneficial owner receives paper copies in a similar time frame as prepaid mail or courier. For example, a reporting issuer that sponsors an employee share purchase plan could arrange for the proximate intermediary to deliver proxy-related materials to beneficial owner employees through the reporting issuer's internal mail system.

5.4 Notice-and-Access — (1) The Instrument permits a reporting issuer to use notice-and-access to send proxy-related materials to beneficial owners. Notice-and-access cannot be used for sending proxy-related materials relating to meetings of investment fund reporting issuers. However, it can be used for all other types of meetings.

When using notice-and-access for the first time, a reporting issuer must file on SEDAR the notification of meeting and record dates at least 25 days before the record date for notice, i.e., the abridgment provisions in section 2.20 do not apply. We also encourage issuers to consider what additional methods of advance notice are appropriate. For example, an issuer could consider a special purpose mailing to its retail beneficial owners in advance of the first meeting for which notice-and-access is used.

We expect reporting issuers to evaluate the potential impact of using notice-and-access on beneficial owners of their voting securities when deciding whether to use notice-and-access. Factors that reporting issuers should take into account include:

- the nature of the meeting business (including whether it is expected to be contentious); and
- whether notice-and-access resulted in material declines in beneficial owner voting rates in prior meetings where notice-and-access was used.

(2) Notice-and-access can be used by reporting issuers to send proxy-related materials directly to NOBOs under section 2.9 of the Instrument or indirectly under section 2.12 of the Instrument.

Direct sending to NOBOs: — The reporting issuer must send at least 30 days before the meeting the notice required by paragraph 2.7.1(1)(a) and Form 54-101F6 (subsection 2.9(3) of the Instrument). The reporting issuer also must at the same time send any paper copies of the information circular and, if applicable, annual financial statements and annual MD&A required to comply with previously obtained or standing instructions.

Indirect sending to beneficial owners: — The reporting issuer must send within the relevant timelines set out in subsection 2.12(3) the notice required by paragraph 2.7.1(1)(a). The reporting issuer also must at the same time send any paper copies of the information circular and, if applicable, annual financial statements and annual MD&A required to comply with previously obtained or standing instructions. The proximate intermediary (or in some cases, the intermediary) must prepare a Form 54-101F7 and forward it with the foregoing documents (section 4.4 of the Instrument). The notice can be combined with Form 54-101F7 in a single document.

(3) With respect to matters to be voted on at the meeting, the notice must only contain a description of each matter or group of related matters identified in the form of proxy, unless the information is already included in an applicable voting instruction form. We expect that reporting issuers will state each matter or group of related matters in the proxy (or voting instruction form) in a reasonably clear and user-friendly manner. For example, it would be inappropriate to identify the matter to be voted on solely by referring to disclosure contained in the information circular as follows: "To vote For or Against the resolution in Schedule A of management's information circular".

The notice must contain a plain-language explanation of notice-and-access. The explanation also can address other aspects of the proxy voting process. However, there should not be any substantive discussion of the matters to be considered at the meeting.

(4) Paragraph 2.7.1(1)(b) of the Instrument requires the beneficial owner to be sent as part of the notice package the appropriate voting instruction form, i.e., a Form 54-101F6 where the reporting issuer is sending proxy-related materials directly and soliciting voting instructions from NOBOs, and a Form 54-101F7 where an intermediary is doing so.

(5) Paragraph 2.7.1(1)(c) of the Instrument requires the reporting issuer to file on SEDAR the notification of meeting and record dates required by subsection 2.2(1) on the same date that it sends the notification under subsection 2.2(1). This provision is subject to section 2.7.2, which specifies that the first time that a reporting issuer uses notice-and-access, the reporting issuer must file on SEDAR the notification of meeting and record dates at least 25 days before the record date for notice.

(6) Paragraph 2.7.1(1)(d) of the Instrument requires the notice and the information circular to be filed on SEDAR and posted on a website other than SEDAR. The non-SEDAR website can be the reporting issuer's website or the website of a service provider.

(7) Paragraph 2.7.1(1)(e) of the Instrument requires the reporting issuer to establish a toll-free telephone number for the beneficial owner to request a paper copy of the information circular. A reporting issuer may choose to, but is not required to, provide additional methods for requesting a paper copy of the information circular. If a reporting issuer does so, it must still comply with the fulfillment timelines in paragraph 2.7.1(1)(f) of the Instrument and the restrictions on use of information obtained in connection with the request.

(8) Section 2.7.3 of the Instrument is intended to restrict intentional information gathering about beneficial owners by reporting issuers who receive requests for paper copies of information circulars or via the website other than SEDAR.

(9) Section 2.7.4 of the Instrument is intended to allow beneficial owners to access the posted proxy-related materials in a user-friendly manner. For example, requiring the beneficial owner to navigate through several web pages to access the proxy-related materials would not be user-friendly. Providing the beneficial owner with the specific URL where the documents are posted would be more user-friendly. We encourage reporting issuers and their service providers to develop best practices in this regard.

(10) Where a reporting issuer uses notice-and-access, it generally must send the same basic notice package to all beneficial owners. However, the following are exceptions to this general principle:

- Section 2.7.5 of the Instrument provides that where a reporting issuer uses notice-and-access, a beneficial owner still can be sent proxy-related materials using an alternate method to which the beneficial owner has previously consented. For example, service providers acting on behalf of reporting issuers or intermediaries may have previously obtained (and continue to obtain) consents from beneficial owners for proxy-related materials to be sent by email. This delivery method would still be available.

- Section 2.7.6 of the Instrument permits an intermediary to obtain standing instructions from a beneficial owner client to be sent a paper copy of the information circular and if applicable, annual financial statements and annual MD&A in all cases where a reporting issuer uses notice-and-access. Where such standing instructions have been obtained, the notice package for the beneficial owner will contain a paper copy of the relevant documents.

- Subsection 4.6 of National Instrument 51-102 *Continuous Disclosure Obligations* ("NI 51-102") establishes an annual request form mechanism for registered holders and beneficial owners to request copies of a reporting issuer's annual financial statements and annual MD&A for the following year. A request for annual financial statements and annual MD&A can also contain a request that the notice package for the registered holder or beneficial owner contain a paper copy of the information circular.

- Notice-and-access also can be used to send annual financial statements and annual MD&A pursuant to subsection 4.6(5) of NI 51-102. Notice-and-access is consistent with the principles for electronic delivery set out in National Policy 11-201 *Electronic Delivery of Documents* ("NP 11-201").

(11) The addition of a paper information circular to the notice package sent to some beneficial owners is referred to as "stratification", and is a term defined in section 1.1 of the Instrument.

We do not mandate the use of stratification, except if it is necessary to comply with standing instructions or other requests for paper copies of information circulars that reporting issuers or intermediaries have chosen to obtain from registered holders or beneficial owners. We expect that any additional stratification criteria will develop and evolve through market demand and practice. However, we expect that a reporting issuer that uses stratification for purposes other than complying with beneficial owner instructions does so in order to enhance effective communication, and not to disenfranchise beneficial owners. We require reporting issuers to disclose whether they are using stratification, and what criteria they are applying to determine which types of beneficial owners will receive a copy of the information circular.

One example of how stratification could enhance communication is where a reporting issuer wishes to send proxy-related materials to all its beneficial owners, including those who have declined to receive materials ("declining beneficial owners"). These declining beneficial owners could be sent a notice package only, while the reporting issuer would send other beneficial owners who wished to receive all materials the notice package and the information circular. All beneficial owners thus would receive the documentation necessary to vote, but those declining to receive materials would not receive a paper copy of the information circular unless they requested it.

5.5 Consent to Electronic Delivery — NP 11-201 discusses the sending of materials by electronic means. The guidelines set out in NP 11-201, particularly the suggestion that consent be obtained to an electronic transmission of a document, are applicable to documents sent under the Instrument.

5.6 Multiple Deliveries to One Person or Company — A single investor may hold securities of the same class in two or more accounts with the same address. Delivering a single set of securityholder materials to that person or company would satisfy the delivery requirements under the Instrument. We encourage this practice as a way to help reduce the costs of securityholder communications.

PART 6 — USE OF NOBO LIST

6.1 Permitted Uses — (1) A person or company that is not a reporting issuer may only use the NOBO list and the procedures in sections 2.9 or 2.12 of the Instrument in connection with an effort to influence voting or an offer to acquire securities of a reporting issuer. In our view, a person or company may obtain the NOBO list if the person or company, acting reasonably and in good faith, intends to use the NOBO list to determine whether to begin an effort to influence securityholder voting or an offer to acquire securities of the reporting issuer.

(2) Using a NOBO list contrary to Part 7 of the Instrument will constitute a breach of the Instrument and securities legislation. Penalty provisions of securities legislation may be applied.

PART 7 — EXEMPTIONS

7.1 Materials Sent in Less Than the Required Number of Days Before Meeting — In general, exemptive relief to shorten the relevant periods in sections 2.9 and 2.12 of the Instrument will not be granted, except in extraordinary circumstances.

7.2 Delay of audited annual financial statements or annual report — Section 9.1 of the Instrument recognizes that corporate law or securities legislation may permit a reporting issuer to send its audited annual financial statements or annual report to registered holders of its securities later than other proxy-related materials. The Instrument provides that the time periods applicable to sending proxy-related materials prescribed in the Instrument do not apply to the sending of proxy-related materials that are annual financial statements or an annual report if the statements or report are sent by the reporting issuer to beneficial owners of the securities within the time limitations established in applicable corporate law and securities legislation for the sending of the statements or report to registered holders of the securities. Reporting issuers are nonetheless encouraged to send their audited annual financial statements or annual report at the same time as other proxy-related materials.

7.3 Additional Costs for Expedited Processing — Where reporting issuers wish to have intermediaries comply with the procedures in the Instrument within shorter time limits than provided in the Instrument, they should provide for recovery by the intermediary of reasonable costs incurred in expedited processing of securityholder materials in order to ensure forwarding of the materials to beneficial owners. Examples of such costs include courier, long distance telephone and overtime costs.

7.4 Applications — Major exemptions from the requirements of the Instrument will likely be granted infrequently. We encourage applicants to discuss requests for exemptive relief on a pre-file basis with the relevant Canadian securities regulatory authorities.

PART 8 — APPENDIX A

8.1 Appendix A — This Companion Policy contains, as Appendix A, a flow chart outlining the processes prescribed by the Instrument for the sending of proxy-related materials by prepaid mail.

Appendix A — Proxy Solicitation under NI 54-101

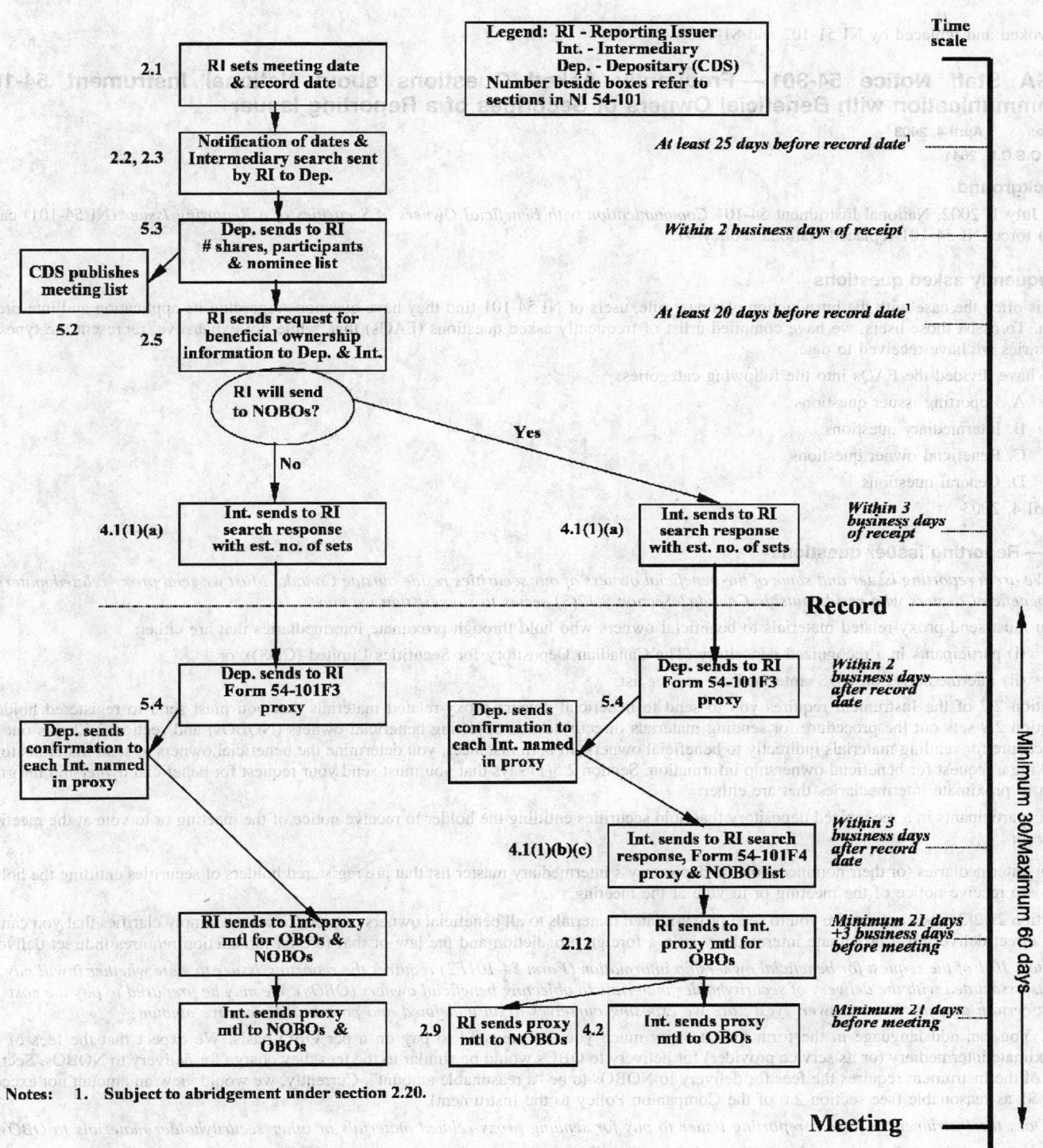

Legend: RI - Reporting Issuer
Int. - Intermediary
Dep. - Depositary (CDS)
Number beside boxes refer to sections in NI 54-101

Time scale

Section	Box	Timing
2.1	RI sets meeting date & record date	
2.2, 2.3	Notification of dates & Intermediary search sent by RI to Dep.	*At least 25 days before record date[1]*
5.3	Dep. sends to RI # shares, participants & nominee list	*Within 2 business days of receipt*
5.2	CDS publishes meeting list	
2.5	RI sends request for beneficial ownership information to Dep. & Int.	*At least 20 days before record date[1]*

RI will send to NOBOs?

No → Yes

4.1(1)(a) — Int. sends to RI search response with est. no. of sets

4.1(1)(a) — Int. sends to RI search response with est. no. of sets

Within 3 business days of receipt

Record

5.4 — Dep. sends to RI Form 54-101F3 proxy

5.4 — Dep. sends to RI Form 54-101F3 proxy

Within 2 business days after record date

Dep. sends confirmation to each Int. named in proxy

Dep. sends confirmation to each Int. named in proxy

4.1(1)(b)(c) — Int. sends to RI search response, Form 54-101F4 proxy & NOBO list

Within 3 business days after record date

RI sends to Int. proxy mtl for OBOs & NOBOs

2.12 — RI sends to Int. proxy mtl for OBOs

Minimum 21 days +3 business days before meeting

Int. sends proxy mtl to NOBOs & OBOs

2.9 — RI sends proxy mtl to NOBOs

4.2 — Int. sends proxy mtl to OBOs

Minimum 21 days before meeting

Minimum 30/Maximum 60 days

Meeting

Notes: 1. Subject to abridgement under section 2.20.

Adoption by OSC: (2002) 25 O.S.C.B. 3361 and 1863. Request for Comments: (2000) 23 O.S.C.B. 5937, (1998) 21 O.S.C.B. 4491 and (1998) 21 O.S.C.B. 1388.

Adoption of Amendment by OSC: (2005) 28 O.S.C.B. 3995 and (2004) 27 O.S.C.B. 9463.

Adoption of Amendment by OSC: (2012) 35 O.S.C.B. 10709; Request for Comments: (2011) 34 O.S.C.B. 6769 and (2010) 33 O.S.C.B. 3109.

National Instrument 54-102 — Interim Financial Statement & Report Exemption

Date: June 14, 2002

25 O.S.C.B. 3403

[revoked and replaced by NI 51-102 and 81-106]

CSA Staff Notice 54-301 — Frequently Asked Questions about National Instrument 54-101 Communication with Beneficial Owners of Securities of a Reporting Issuer

Date: April 4, 2003

26 O.S.C.B. 2641

Background

On July 1, 2002, National Instrument 54-101 *Communication with Beneficial Owners of Securities of a Reporting Issuer* (NI 54-101) came into force. NI 54-101 replaced National Policy 41.

Frequently asked questions

As is often the case with the introduction of a new rule, users of NI 54-101 find they have questions regarding its application and interpretation. To assist those users, we have compiled a list of frequently asked questions (FAQs) that, while not exhaustive, represent the types of inquiries we have received to date.

We have divided the FAQs into the following categories:

A. Reporting issuer questions

B. Intermediary questions

C. Beneficial owner questions

D. General questions

April 4, 2003

A. — Reporting issuer questions

1. *We are a reporting issuer and some of the beneficial owners of our securities reside outside Canada. Must we send proxy-related materials to beneficial owners who reside outside Canada? Section 2.12(3) seems to suggest that we must.*

You must send proxy-related materials to beneficial owners who hold through proximate intermediaries that are either:

(i) participants in a recognized depository (The Canadian Depository for Securities Limited (CDS)), or

(ii) intermediaries on CDS' intermediary master list.

Section 2.7 of the Instrument requires you to send to beneficial owners proxy-related materials that you must send to registered holders. Section 2.9 sets out the procedure for sending materials directly to non-objecting beneficial owners (NOBOs) and section 2.12 sets out the procedure for sending materials indirectly to beneficial owners. In both instances, you determine the beneficial owners to send materials to by making a request for beneficial ownership information. Section 2.5(1) says that you must send your request for beneficial ownership information to proximate intermediaries that are either:

- participants in a recognized depository that hold securities entitling the holder to receive notice of the meeting or to vote at the meeting, or

- intermediaries (or their nominees) on the depository's intermediary master list that are registered holders of securities entitling the holder to receive notice of the meeting or to vote at the meeting.

Section 2.12(3) does not require you to send proxy-related materials to all beneficial owners outside Canada. It simply clarifies that you cannot use direct delivery if a proximate intermediary is in a foreign jurisdiction and the law of that foreign jurisdiction requires indirect delivery.

2. *Item 10.1 of the request for beneficial ownership information (Form 54-101F2) requires the reporting issuer to state whether it will pay the costs associated with the delivery of securityholder materials to objecting beneficial owners (OBOs). We may be prepared to pay the costs up to a certain amount. If we answer "yes", are we exposing ourselves to an undefined and potentially excessive amount?*

No. You can add language in the form to state how much you are prepared to pay on a per OBO basis. We expect that the fees of the proximate intermediary (or its service provider) for delivery to OBOs would be similar to the fees they charge for delivery to NOBOs. Section 1.4 of the Instrument requires the fees for delivery to NOBOs to be "a reasonable amount". Currently, we would view an amount not exceeding $1 as reasonable (see section 2.6 of the Companion Policy to the Instrument).

3. *Does the Instrument require a reporting issuer to pay for sending proxy-related materials or other securityholder materials to OBOs?*

No. You are only required to pay the proximate intermediary for sending securityholder materials (including proxy-related materials) to OBOs if the OBO has declined to receive those materials under section 2.14. However, if you decline to pay in other circumstances, there are three possible consequences:

(i) the intermediary pays (see Part B question 9 of these FAQs);

   (ii) the OBO pays; or

   (iii) neither the intermediary nor the OBO pays and the intermediary does not send the materials. If OBOs do not receive proxy-related materials, they may not be in a position to provide voting instructions for the meeting.

4. What is "routine" business?

"Routine business" is defined in the Instrument. Any matters that fall outside those listed in the definition are not "routine business". The definition is:

   "routine business" means, for a meeting,

      (a) consideration of the minutes of an earlier meeting,

      (b) consideration of the financial statements of the reporting issuer or an auditor's report on the financial statements of the reporting issuer,

      (c) election of directors of the reporting issuer,

      (d) setting or changing of the number of directors to be elected within a range permitted by corporate law, if no change to the constating documents of the reporting issuer is required in connection with that action, or

      (e) reappointment of an incumbent auditor of the reporting issuer.

5. Mutual funds (or their managers) have historically sent meeting materials directly to unitholders under NP 41. Does section 10.3 prevent mutual funds from continuing to send materials directly to their unitholders who hold through mutual fund dealers or investment dealers?

Despite section 10.3, a mutual fund can continue, as a person or company designated by the intermediary under section 2.12(2), to send unitholder meeting materials directly to unitholders who hold through mutual fund dealers or investment dealers.

B. — Intermediary questions

1. Under section 3.2 and the Explanation to Clients (Form 54-101F1), must we ask clients whether they will consent to electronic delivery even if we (or our service provider) do not offer electronic delivery?

No. The consent provisions only apply if you (or your service provider) intend to provide electronic delivery of securityholder materials to clients. You should still obtain the client's electronic mail address, if available, as it forms part of the ownership information defined in the Instrument and may be of interest to reporting issuers (see section 5.4(4) of the Companion Policy). There are electronic delivery technologies available and we encourage intermediaries to take advantage of them to increase efficiency and cost-effectiveness.

2. The "Electronic Delivery of Documents" section in the Explanation to Clients and Client Response Form (Form 54-101F1) refers to an "enclosed consent form". There is no "enclosed consent form".

We have not provided a consent form in the Instrument because proximate intermediaries can prepare appropriate consents themselves. We expect proximate intermediaries to follow the guidelines for meaningful consent set out in National Policy 11-201.

3. In the Explanation to Clients and Client Response Form (Form 54-101F1), the boxes for checking OBO and NOBO status are the wrong way round.

The English version of Form 54-101F1 is incorrect. The French version is correct. We will amend the Form as soon as possible. In the meantime, you should ensure that the forms you use show the boxes correctly.

4. As part of our account opening procedures, we have already asked clients for their preferred language of communication. Can we rely on our previous instructions or must we ask them again?

You may rely on previously obtained instructions on preferred language if the instructions cover the issues set out in the Explanation to Clients and Client Response Form (Form 54-101F1).

5. Under section 3.2, must we have a completed client response form before we can hold securities on behalf of our client?

No. Section 3.2(b)(i) requires you to have obtained instructions from the client on the matters in the client response form before you can hold securities on behalf of the client. The Instrument does not say you must obtain a completed client response form. You must satisfy yourself that you have got instructions on the matters in the client response form. You must also bear in mind your responsibilities under any relevant IDA requirements.

6. If we have the client's consent to deliver securityholder materials electronically, must the reporting issuer also get consent for us to send the materials electronically?

No. Under section 4.2, if a reporting issuer gives materials to an intermediary for sending indirectly to beneficial owners, the obligation to send them is on the intermediary, not the reporting issuer. If the intermediary sends the materials electronically, it is the intermediary that must have the client's consent.

If a reporting issuer sends materials directly to beneficial owners under section 2.8 or 2.9, the reporting issuer must have the client's consent to electronic delivery.

If an intermediary seeks the consent of a beneficial owner to electronic delivery *by the reporting issuer*, both the intermediary and the reporting issuer must ensure that the consent is consistent with the guidelines in NP 11-201.

7. In the Explanation to Clients and Client Response Form (Form 54-101F1), under Disclosure of Beneficial Ownership Information, there is an instruction to disclose particulars of fees or charges that the intermediary may ask an OBO to pay. As the fees or charges will differ depending on the reporting issuer, the bulkiness of the materials, whether it is insured mail or regular mail, etc., what exact particulars must we provide?

You need not set out detailed fee information. The instruction and the optional disclosure in the client response form clarify that, if you intend to recover the costs of delivery to OBOs where the reporting issuer does not pay, you must explain how you intend to recover the costs from the OBO. The specific mechanism by which you recoup your costs from the OBO is a business decision.

8. Must mutual fund dealers send their details to the depository under section 3.1 and must they send their clients the Explanation to Clients and Client Response Form (Form 54-101F1)?

The answer depends on whether the mutual fund dealer is an intermediary as defined in the Instrument. If the mutual fund dealer does not hold shares or units of a mutual fund on behalf of its clients, then it would not be an intermediary for the purposes of section 3.1. If it does hold shares or units of mutual funds on behalf of clients, it is an intermediary and must comply with sections 3.1 and 3.2. Mutual fund dealers that are intermediaries need only send Form 54-101F1 to those clients on whose behalf they actually hold securities.

9. Under the Instrument, can intermediaries charge OBOs for sending them proxy-related materials provided by a reporting issuer?

The Instrument does not prohibit intermediaries from charging OBOs for sending proxy-related or other securityholder materials. Provincial securities legislation may regulate whether intermediaries can charge and whether they must send proxy-related materials if neither the reporting issuer nor the OBO has agreed to pay the costs of sending. You should confirm the position under the appropriate securities legislation.

For example, in Ontario (section 49(2) of the *Securities Act*), the registrant or custodian is not required to send proxy-related materials to a beneficial securityholder if neither the reporting issuer nor the beneficial owner has agreed to pay the reasonable costs of sending. In Alberta (section 104(2) of the *Securities Act*), the registrant or custodian must send proxy-related materials if the beneficial securityholder has agreed to pay the reasonable costs. In British Columbia (section 182 of the *Securities Rules*), the registrant or custodian is not required to send materials if the beneficial owner has not declined to receive the materials and has not agreed to pay the reasonable costs. In Québec (section 165 of the *Securities Act*), a dealer or any other person holding the securities of a reporting issuer on behalf of clients must forward all securityholder materials to the owner at the expense of a person designated by regulation. The regulation does not designate any person.

In contrast, in Manitoba (section 79(1) of the *Securities Act*), shares of a company registered in the name of a registrant or its nominee and not beneficially owned by the registrant cannot be voted at any shareholders meeting unless the registrant sends the proxy-related materials to the beneficial owner at no expense to the beneficial owner.

We expect that fees for sending securityholder materials to OBOs would be similar to those for sending to NOBOs. Section 1.4 of the Instrument requires the fees for delivery to NOBOs to be "a reasonable amount". Currently, we would view an amount not exceeding $1 as reasonable (see section 2.6 of the Companion Policy to the Instrument).

10. Why is there a reference, in the indirect delivery flow of the flowchart, to the intermediary sending the reporting issuer a search response and omnibus proxy (Form 54-101F4)?

The reference is incorrect. We will amend the flowchart as soon as possible. We remind you to refer to the Instrument to determine your obligations.

11. Managers of discretionary managed accounts have authority in the management agreement to vote the securities on behalf of the underlying beneficial owner. These managers fall within the definition of "intermediary". As they do not hold a general power of attorney, it is arguable that they do not have authority to provide the instructions in the Explanation to Clients and Client Response Form (Form 54-101F1). Must they obtain authority from the underlying beneficial owner to provide the instructions in the Form?

No. For the purposes of the Instrument, we take the view that the manager can provide the instructions in the Form without seeking additional authority from the underlying beneficial owner.

C. — Beneficial owner questions

1. Under National Policy 41, non-registered owners could revoke their voting instructions. Can beneficial owners revoke their voting instructions under the Instrument?

Yes. We take the view that a written revocation of voting instructions constitutes new voting instructions. Reporting issuers and intermediaries must use their best efforts to comply with the most current voting instructions. Under the omnibus proxies, they are not allowed to vote except in accordance with the voting instructions received from beneficial owners. Securities legislation also requires intermediaries who are registrants to vote or give a proxy in accordance with written voting instructions received from beneficial owners.

2. Can a beneficial owner decline to receive proxy-related materials relating to meetings involving non-routine business?

No. The client response form permits beneficial owners to decline proxy-related materials only for meetings involving "routine business" as defined in the Instrument.

3. Can beneficial owners of a debenture issued under a trust indenture get proxy-related materials for meetings where registered holders are entitled to vote?

The answer depends on the securities legislation of the relevant jurisdiction. A reporting issuer must, under section 2.7, send proxy-related materials to beneficial owners if, under Canadian securities legislation (defined in National Instrument 14-101), it must send those materials to registered holders. For example, section 83.1 of the Securities Act in Québec would result in proxy-related materials having to be sent to beneficial owners of a debenture issued under a trust indenture if the registered holders of the debenture have the right to vote at a meeting

4. I am a beneficial owner of securities and I have asked my broker to forward all meeting materials to me. Can I vote or ask someone to vote on my behalf at meetings of the reporting issuer of my securities?

Yes. When you receive the request for voting instructions, you can ask your broker (the intermediary) in writing for a legal proxy. The legal proxy grants you the right to vote the securities that you beneficially own. If you wish to nominate someone to vote on your behalf, you can ask your broker to modify the legal proxy to grant your nominee the right to vote.

D. — General questions

1. Can a person or company that is not the relevant reporting issuer obtain a NOBO list?

Yes. There are two ways that a third party can obtain the NOBO list:

(i) Under section 6.1, a third party can ask a reporting issuer for its most recent NOBO list for any proximate intermediary.

(ii) Under section 6.2(1), a third party can use the same process for requesting beneficial ownership information from a proximate intermediary that a reporting issuer uses under section 2.5(2) of the Instrument. The third party has the same rights and obligations under the Instrument as a reporting issuer that requests beneficial ownership information, except for:

- fixing a meeting and record date (section 2.1)

- sending a notice of meeting and record dates (section 2.2)

- requesting depository information (section 2.3(1))

- sending a request for beneficial ownership information 20 days before the record date (section 2.5(1))

- sending a legal proxy (section 2.18)

- receiving an omnibus proxy (section 4.1(1)(c))

- receiving a participant omnibus proxy (section 5.4)

The third party must also send a copy of the request for beneficial ownership information concurrently to the reporting issuer and must provide an undertaking (Form 54-101F9) to the proximate intermediary.

2. *Section 6.2(3) provides that certain subsections of Parts 2, 4 and 5 do not apply to third parties requesting beneficial ownership information. The exclusions do not include references to section 2.9 and 2.12. Is a dissident shareholder that sends materials to beneficial owners about a meeting subject to the same timing requirements under section 2.9 and 2.12 as a reporting issuer?*

No. Dissident shareholder materials are not "proxy related materials" as defined in the Instrument. Sections 2.9 and 2.12 only apply to proxy-related materials.

3. *Is the ISIN the same as the CUSIP and, if not, what is the difference?*

The ISIN (International Securities Identification Number) is the number issued to a security under the international standard ISO 6166. The National Numbering Agency of the country in which the security is domiciled issues the number. The CUSIP is the number used for Canadian and U.S. securities. The CUSIP number follows the ISO 6166 guidelines for ISINs, except that it does not contain the country code (the first two characters of the ISIN).

OSC Rule 54-302 — Update on CSA Consultation Paper 54-401 Review of the Proxy Voting Infrastructure

Date: October 31, 2013

36 O.S.C.B. 10598

[Not reproduced]

CSA Multilateral Staff Notice 54-304 — Final Report on Review of the Proxy Voting Infrastructure and Request for Comments on Proposed Meeting Vote Reconciliation Protocols

Date: March 31, 2016

39 OSCB 2915

[Not reproduced]

OSC Rule 54-303 — Progress Report on Review of the Proxy Voting Infrastructure

Date: January 29, 2015

38 O.S.C.B. 772

[Not reproduced]

OSC Rule 54-501 — Prospectus Disclosure

Date: December 22, 2000

23 O.S.C.B. 8519

[Revoked effective June 1, 2004 by Rule 51-801]

OSC Staff Notice 54-701 — Regulatory Developments Regarding Shareholder Democracy Issues

Date: January 14, 2011

34 O.S.C.B. 404

The Ontario Securities Commission's 2010-2011 Statement of Priorities included a commitment to review protections for shareholders' rights and corporate governance. In addition, the Standing Committee on Government Agencies (SCOGA) March 2010 report on the Ontario Securities Commission (the OSC) recommended that the province of Ontario institute a formal review of democracy in corporate governance in Ontario. The OSC's submissions to SCOGA noted that the OSC was in the process of a significant review of shareholder democracy.

This Notice provides an update from OSC staff on the current status of our work in the area of shareholder democracy issues. We have identified the following issues as requiring additional review at this time and, potentially, the development of regulatory proposals for reporting issuers:

- slate voting and majority voting for uncontested director elections,

- shareholder advisory votes on executive compensation, and

- the effectiveness of the proxy voting system.

We may identify additional issues as a result of our continued review and developments in the capital markets.

Slate voting and majority voting for uncontested director elections

Slate voting refers to a voting practice by which shareholders are able only to vote in respect of the entire slate of director nominees presented by management. Slate voting is in contrast to individual director voting, where shareholders are able to vote in respect of individual director nominees. Ontario securities legislation does not currently prohibit or restrict slate voting at shareholder meetings, through proxy requirements or otherwise. The dominant voting standard in Ontario is plurality voting, which permits directors to be elected without receiving a majority of votes in their favour.

We are assessing whether reforms to securities law are appropriate to facilitate individual director voting and majority voting for director elections of reporting issuers.

Mandated shareholder advisory votes on executive compensation

The issue of whether shareholders should have a separate advisory vote on executive compensation and "golden parachute" payments (Say-on-Pay) has recently been receiving increased attention from various stakeholders.

Legislation in the United Kingdom, Australia and some European countries already requires public companies to give shareholders a Say-on-Pay, and the United States is expected to impose a similar obligation. In particular, the Dodd-Frank Act requires every public company in the United States to include in the proxy for its first shareholder meeting held on or after January 21, 2011 an advisory Say-on-Pay vote on executive compensation, as well as a separate vote to determine whether subsequent Say-on-Pay votes will be held annually, or at intervals of two or three years. The Dodd-Frank Act also requires any public company seeking shareholder approval of a merger or acquisition at a meeting held on or after January 21, 2011 to include in its proxy an advisory vote on certain "golden parachute" payments to its executive officers in accordance with SEC regulations. On October 18, 2010, the SEC proposed rules to implement the various Say-on-Pay votes required by the *Dodd-Frank Act*.

While a number of large public companies are voluntarily giving their shareholders a Say-on-Pay, there is no current initiative to implement a mandatory Say-on-Pay regime for all reporting issuers.

Over the past few years, securities regulators have focused on improving executive compensation disclosure to provide shareholders with meaningful information to exercise their voting rights. However, we have also been monitoring international developments in respect of Say-on-Pay and are considering whether securities regulators should consider introducing mandatory Say-on-Pay.

Effectiveness of proxy voting system

We recognize the need for an effective proxy voting system that allows shareholders to make informed voting decisions and ensures that their votes are counted at shareholder meetings. In addition to the issues being considered by the Canadian Securities Administrators (CSA) in relation to its proposed amendments to National Instrument 54-101 *Communications with Beneficial Owners of Securities of a Reporting Issuer*, OSC staff are generally reviewing the proxy voting system to determine whether there is a need for additional reforms and to what extent securities law should address these matters.

Next steps

We intend to coordinate our review and the development of regulatory proposals relating to this review with other members of the CSA.

We also anticipate additional consultations with interested stakeholders on the appropriate scope of any regulatory proposals, their impact on investor protection and the implications for the role of the board of directors.

At this time, we would be pleased to receive any comments on whether it is desirable that staff develop proposals in these areas and the appropriate scope of such proposals. Please send your comments to the address below by **March 31, 2011.** If you are sending your comments by email, you should also send an electronic file containing the submissions (in Windows format, Microsoft Word).

OSC Staff Notice 54-702 — Corporate Finance Guidance — Notice-and-access: Interaction with National Policy 11-201 Electronic Delivery of Documents and the Ontario *Business Corporations Act*

Date: **February 28, 2013**

36 O.S.C.B. 1975

The purpose of this staff notice is to provide staff guidance to reporting issuers, intermediaries and others involved in the sending of proxy-related materials to registered holders and beneficial owners of an issuer's securities (collectively, **shareholders**) on:

- the interaction of notice-and-access with National Policy 11-201 *Electronic Delivery of Documents* (**NP 11-201**); and

- whether reporting issuers incorporated under the *Ontario Business Corporations Act* (**OBCA**) can use notice-and-access.

This notice represents the views of Commission staff which do not have the force of law. These views are also not legal advice and should not be relied on as such.

Introduction to notice-and-access and interaction with NP 11-201

1. — What is notice-and-access?

Notice-and-access is a method for reporting issuers to send proxy-related materials to shareholders that is set out in National Instrument 51-102 *Continuous Disclosure Obligations* (**NI 51-102**) and National Instrument 54-101 *Communication with Beneficial Owners of a Reporting Issuer* (**NI 54-101**). Amendments to NI 51-102 and NI 54-101 adopting notice-and-access came into force on February 11, 2013. In particular, notice-and-access can be used to deliver proxy-related materials for meetings that take place on or after March 1, 2013.

Under notice-and-access, a reporting issuer can send proxy-related materials to a shareholder by:

- posting the relevant management information circular and other proxy-related materials on a website that is not SEDAR;

- sending (by prepaid mail, courier or the equivalent, or any other agreed-upon method) a notice package consisting of:

  - a notice informing shareholders that the proxy-related materials have been posted, and an explanation of how to access the materials; and

  - the relevant voting document (a form of proxy or voting instruction form); and

- providing a toll-free telephone number for the shareholder to request a paper copy of the information circular (and if applicable, other proxy-related materials) at no charge.

Notice-and-access therefore incorporates the use of documents in electronic form that are posted on a website as a method of satisfying the obligation to send proxy-related materials. A reporting issuer generally will send shareholders a paper copy of the notice of meeting and the form of proxy. However, it will not send a paper copy of the management information circular. Instead, the circular is sent through a combination of (i) the issuer posting the information circular on a website, and (ii) the shareholder being notified of its availability and how to access the electronic document. The shareholder is also notified that the shareholder can call the toll-free number provided by the issuer to request that a paper copy of the information circular be sent to him or her free of charge. Upon receiving the request, the reporting issuer must send the information circular by first class mail, courier or the equivalent, within specified timeframes.

2. — How does notice-and-access interact with NP 11-201?

NP 11-201 sets out the Commission's views on how the delivery requirements of Ontario securities legislation can be satisfied through electronic delivery — see in particular section 2.1(1) of NP 11-201.[1] The Commission has stated, in connection with delivering proxy-related materials and annual financial statements and MD&A under section 4.6(5) of NI 51-102, that notice-and-access is consistent with the principles for electronic delivery set out in NP 11-201. The Commission also has provided guidance on interpreting the provisions of NI 51-102 and NI 54-101 relating to notice-and-access in the Companion Policies to those instruments.

Notice-and-access is not the only means by which a reporting issuer can satisfy its obligations to send proxy-related materials using electronic delivery or electronic documents. While there is no specific requirement under securities legislation to obtain the consent of an intended recipient prior to using electronic delivery, the Commission has stated that prior consent should be obtained when issuers deliver proxy-related materials using methods other than (i) notice-and-access; or (ii) prepaid mail, courier or the equivalent.[2] The process of obtaining express consent, and then delivering the document in accordance with that consent, can enable the issuer to achieve some of the basic components of electronic delivery under NP 11-201.[3]

Notice-and-access and reporting issuers incorporated under the OBCA

We do not think that it is necessary for reporting issuers incorporated under the OBCA to obtain exemptive relief from the Commission under section 113 of the OBCA in order to use notice-and-access. In our view, and as explained in more detail below, the OBCA does not prevent a reporting issuer from sending proxy-related materials using notice-and-access in compliance with NI 51-102 and NI 54-101.

The OBCA does not contain any provisions regarding the sending of proxy-related materials to beneficial owners. The OBCA does, however, contain provisions regarding the sending of proxy-related materials to registered shareholders.[4] The OBCA also requires that an OBCA corporation send a copy of the annual financial statements and auditor's report to all registered shareholders who have informed the corporation that they wish to receive a copy of those documents.[5]

---

[1] See section 3.5 of the Companion Policy to NI 51-102 (51-102CP) and section 5.4(10) of the Companion Policy to NI 54-101 (54-101CP).

[2] See section 5.1 of 54-101CP.

[3] See section 2.2 of NP 11-201. The Commission also has noted in section 5.5 of 54-101CP that where documents are sent electronically under NI 54-101, it may still be appropriate to obtain consent in order to achieve the basic components of electronic delivery set out in section 2.1 of NP 11-201.

[4] See sections 96 (notice of meeting), 111 (form of proxy) and 112 (circular) of the OBCA.

[5] See section 154(3) of the OBCA.

The definition of the term "send" in the OBCA is inclusive, and includes to "deliver" and "mail." It does not prohibit the use of electronic delivery or electronic documents, including the procedures contemplated by notice-and-access. Nor does the OBCA impose an obligation that a reporting issuer obtain consent in order for a reporting issuer to use electronic delivery methods to send proxy-related materials. The OBCA also provides that a document or notice "may" be sent by:

- prepaid mail;
- personal delivery; or
- electronic means in accordance with the *Electronic Commerce Act, 2000* (the **ECA**).[6]

We note that the ECA states that a recipient cannot be required to use or accept a document in electronic form without his or her consent. Our view is that under notice-and-access, a shareholder is not required to use or accept the electronic form of information circular (or any other relevant proxy-related materials) since shareholders have the option of requesting a paper copy at no charge to the shareholder. The ECA also states that electronic information or an electronic document is not provided if the information or document is merely posted on a website. Under notice-and-access, issuers must do more than merely post their proxy-related materials on a website. In particular, issuers must mail the notice package to shareholders in advance of a meeting, which will inform them of, among other things, the website posting of the proxy-related materials.[7]

5.5 — Insider Reporting

National Instrument 55-101 — Insider Reporting Exemptions

[Repealed upon the coming into force of NI 55-104]

Revised Rule: (2005) 28 O.S.C.B. 3981; Approval by OSC: (2005) 28 O.S.C.B. 1597; Request for Comments: (2004) 27 O.S.C.B. 4681.

Amendment to Revised Rule: (2007) 30 O.S.C.B. 7711: Approval by OSC: (2007) 30 O.S.C.B. 5263; Request for Comments: (2006) 29 O.S.C.B. 2441.

Final Rule: 24 O.S.C.B. 3025 (May 11, 2001); Approval by OSC: 24 O.S.C.B. 1283 (February 23, 2001); Request for Comments: 23 O.S.C.B. 4212 (June 16, 2000) and 22 O.S.C.B. 5161 (August 20, 1999).

Amendment to Revised Rule: (2007) 30 O.S.C.B. 7711; Approval by OSC: (2007) 30 O.S.C.B. 5263; Request for Comments: (2006) 29 O.S.C.B. 8441.

Companion Policy 55-101CP — To National Instrument 55-101 Insider Reporting Exemptions

[Repealed upon the coming into force of NI 55-104]

Adoption of Amendments: (2007) 30 O.S.C.B. 7717 and 5263; Request for Comments: (2006) 29 O.S.C.B. 8441.

Adoption of Revised Companion Policy by OSC: (2005) 28 O.S.C.B. 3986 and 1597; Request for Comments: (2004) 27 O.S.C.B. 4681.

Adoption by OSC: 24 O.S.C.B. 3025 (May 11, 2001) and 24 O.S.C.B. 1283 (February 23, 2001); Request for Comments: 23 O.S.C.B. 4212 (June 16, 2000) and 22 O.S.C.B. 5161 (August 20, 1999).

National Instrument 55-102 — System for Electronic Disclosure by Insiders (SEDI)

Date: **October 19, 2001, as amended effective April 29, 2003, June 13, 2008, May 6, 2011 and October 12, 2013**

24 O.S.C.B. 6325, 26 O.S.C.B. 3163, 31 O.S.C.B. 6571, 34 O.S.C.B. 5171 and 36 O.S.C.B. 9609

PART 1 — DEFINITIONS AND INTERPRETATION

1.1 Definitions — In this Instrument

"access key" means an alpha-numeric code issued by SEDI or the SEDI operator in respect of an insider that files an insider profile in SEDI format or in respect of a SEDI issuer that files an issuer profile supplement in SEDI format;

"class" includes a series of a class;

"filing agent" means a person or company that is authorized by a SEDI filer to make a SEDI filing on behalf of the SEDI filer;

"insider profile" means the information that is required under Form 55-102F1;

"insider report" means a report required to be filed under the insider reporting requirement;

"issuer event" means a stock dividend, stock split, consolidation, amalgamation, reorganization, merger or other similar event that affects all holdings of a class of securities of an issuer in the same manner, on a per share basis;

"issuer event report" means the information that is required under Form 55-102F4;

---

[6]The Commission previously has reviewed the legal framework for electronic delivery under the ECA, and has stated that the components of electronic delivery in NP 11-201 are compatible with the legal framework for electronic delivery under the ECA. See section 2.1(2) of NP 11-201.

[7]See also section 4.1(3) of NP 11-201, which states that merely making proxy documents available for access on a website will not constitute delivery of these documents in accordance with the four components of effective delivery set out in NP 11-201.

"issuer profile supplement" means the information that is required under Form 55-102F3;

"paper format" means information printed on paper;

"SEDI" means the online computer system providing for the transmission, receipt, review and dissemination of insider reports and related information filed electronically, which is known as the System for Electronic Disclosure by Insiders;

"SEDI filer" means a person or company that is required to make a SEDI filing in accordance with this Instrument;

"SEDI filing" means information that is filed under securities legislation or securities directions in SEDI format, or the act of filing information under securities legislation or securities directions in SEDI format, as the context indicates;

"SEDI format" means information entered electronically in SEDI using the SEDI software application located at the SEDI web site;

"SEDI issuer" means a reporting issuer, other than a mutual fund, that is required to comply with National Instrument 13-101 *System for Electronic Document Analysis and Retrieval (SEDAR)*, including a foreign issuer referred to under paragraph 2 of subsection 2.1(1) of that Instrument;

"SEDI operator" means the Alberta Securities Commission or a successor appointed by the securities regulatory authority to operate SEDI;

"SEDI software application" means the software on the SEDI web site that provides SEDI users with the functionality to make SEDI filings;

"SEDI user" means an individual who has registered in accordance with subsection 2.5(2);

"SEDI web site" means the web site maintained by the SEDI operator for the filing of information in SEDI format;

"transfer report" means

> (a) in Alberta, Saskatchewan, Ontario, New Brunswick, Northwest Territories, Nova Scotia, Prince Edward Island, Newfoundland, Nunavut or Yukon, a report required to be filed by an insider of a reporting issuer under securities legislation if the insider transfers securities of the reporting issuer into the name of an agent, nominee or custodian; or

> (b) in Quebec, a report required to be filed by an insider of a reporting issuer under securities legislation if the insider registers or causes to be registered any security of the reporting issuer in the name of a third person;

"user registration form" means the information that is required under Form 55-102F5.

PART 2 — SEDI FILING REQUIREMENTS

2.1 Filing of Insider Profile — (1) An insider of a SEDI issuer shall file an insider profile or an amended insider profile in SEDI format before the insider files an insider report in SEDI format in respect of that SEDI issuer.

(2) An insider profile shall contain the information required under Form 55-102F1.

(3) An insider that has filed an insider profile under subsection (1) shall file an amended insider profile in SEDI format containing the information required under Form 55-102F1

> (a) if there is a change in the insider's name or the insider's relationship to any SEDI issuer disclosed in the insider's most recently filed insider profile, or if the insider ceases to be an insider of any such SEDI issuer, within 10 days after the occurrence of the event, or

> (b) if there has been any other change in the information disclosed in the insider's most recently filed insider profile, at the time that the insider next files an amended insider profile or an insider report in SEDI format.

(4) An insider that is required to file an insider profile in SEDI format shall not file more than one insider profile.

2.2 Filing of Insider Reports in SEDI Format — (1) An insider of a SEDI issuer that is required by securities legislation to file an insider report in that capacity shall file the insider report in SEDI format through a SEDI user.

(2) For greater certainty, a SEDI user under subsection (1) includes the insider if that insider becomes registered as a SEDI user on or before the time that the insider report is due to be filed.

(3) An insider report that is filed in SEDI format shall contain the information required under Form 55-102F2.

2.3 Filing of Issuer Profile Supplement — (1) A SEDI issuer shall file an issuer profile supplement in SEDI format within three business days after the date that it becomes a SEDI issuer.

(2) An issuer profile supplement that is required to be filed under subsection (1) shall contain the information required under Form 55-102F3.

(3) A SEDI issuer shall file an amended issuer profile supplement in SEDI format immediately if

> (a) the SEDI issuer issues any security or class of securities to any insider of the SEDI issuer, unless that issuance has already been disclosed in its issuer profile supplement;

> (b) there is any change in the designation of any security or class of securities of the SEDI issuer disclosed or required to be disclosed in its issuer profile supplement;

> (c) any security or class of securities of the SEDI issuer disclosed or required to be disclosed in its issuer profile supplement has ceased to be outstanding and is not subject to issuance at a future date; or

> (d) there is any other change in the information disclosed or required to be disclosed in its issuer profile supplement.

2.4 Filing of Issuer Event Report — (1) A SEDI issuer shall file an issuer event report in SEDI format no later than one business day following the occurrence of an issuer event.

(2) An issuer event report that is required to be filed under subsection (1) shall contain the information required under Form 55-102F4.

2.5 SEDI Users — (1) An individual who is a SEDI filer, a filing agent, or an authorized representative of a SEDI filer or filing agent, may use SEDI for the purpose of making SEDI filings.

(2) Before using SEDI to make SEDI filings, an individual referred to in subsection (1) shall register as a SEDI user by

> (a) completing and submitting a user registration form in SEDI format; and

> (b) delivering a copy of the completed user registration form in paper format to the SEDI operator for verification by the SEDI operator.

(3) A user registration form under subsection (2) shall contain the information required under Form 55-102F5 and the paper format copy of the user registration form under paragraph (2)(b) shall contain the manual or facsimile signature of the individual being registered.

(4) The paper format copy of the user registration form referred to in paragraph (2)(b) shall be delivered to the SEDI operator by prepaid mail, personal delivery or facsimile at the address or facsimile number indicated on the printed copy of Form 55-102F5, as applicable.

PART 3 — FILING OF REPORTS IN PAPER FORMAT

3.1 Filing of Insider Reports in Paper Format — (1) An insider report that is not required to be filed in SEDI format under this Instrument shall be filed in paper format.

(2) An insider report that is required to be filed in paper format shall be prepared in accordance with Form 55-102F6, subject to any provision of securities legislation that permits the use of an alternative form of report in the particular circumstances.

(3) An insider report that is prepared in accordance with Form 55-102F6 shall be manually signed and shall be filed either

(a) by prepaid mail or personal delivery to the address of the securities regulatory authority set forth on Form 55-102F6; or

(b) by facsimile to the facsimile number of the securities regulatory authority set forth on Form 55-102F6.

3.2 Filing of Transfer Reports in Paper Format — (1) In Alberta, Saskatchewan, Ontario, New Brunswick, Northwest Territories, Quebec, Nova Scotia, Prince Edward Island, Newfoundland, Nunavut or Yukon, a transfer report shall be filed in paper format and shall be prepared in accordance with Form 55-102F6.

(2) A transfer report that is prepared in accordance with Form 55-102F6 shall be manually signed and shall be filed either

(a) by prepaid mail or personal delivery to the address of the securities regulatory authority set forth on Form 55-102F6; or

(b) by facsimile to the facsimile number of the securities regulatory authority set forth on Form 55-102F6.

PART 4 — SEDI FILING EXEMPTION

4.1 Temporary Hardship Exemption — (1) If unanticipated technical difficulties or failure by a SEDI issuer to file its issuer profile supplement prevent the timely submission of an insider report in SEDI format, a SEDI filer shall file the insider report in paper format as soon as practicable and in any event no later than two business days after the day on which the insider report was required to be filed.

(2) An insider report filed in paper format under subsection (1) shall be prepared in accordance with Form 55-102F6 and shall include the following legend in capital letters at the top of the front page:

IN ACCORDANCE WITH SECTION 4.1 OF NATIONAL INSTRUMENT 55-102 SYSTEM FOR ELECTRONIC DISCLOSURE BY INSIDERS (SEDI), THIS INSIDER REPORT IS BEING FILED IN PAPER FORMAT UNDER A TEMPORARY HARDSHIP EXEMPTION.

(3) The requirements of securities legislation relating to paper format filings of insider reports apply to a filing under subsection (1) except that signatures to the paper format document may be in typed form rather than manual format and an agent may sign the paper format document on behalf of an insider who is an individual without filing a completed power of attorney.

(4) If an insider report is filed in paper format in the manner and within the time prescribed in this section, the date by which the information is required to be filed under securities legislation is extended to the date on which the filing is made in paper format.

(5) If a SEDI filer makes a paper format filing under this section, the SEDI filer shall file the insider report in SEDI format as soon as practicable after the unanticipated technical difficulties have been resolved or the insider has become aware that the SEDI issuer has filed its issuer profile supplement, whichever is applicable.

(6) Despite subsection 2.1(3) and sections 2.3 and 2.4, if unanticipated technical difficulties prevent a SEDI filer from filing an issuer profile supplement, an amended issuer profile supplement, an issuer event report or an amended insider profile within the specified time, the SEDI filer shall file such document as soon as practicable after the unanticipated technical difficulties have been resolved.

PART 5 — PREPARATION AND TRANSMISSION OF SEDI FILINGS

5.1 Manner of Effecting SEDI Filings — A SEDI filing shall be prepared and transmitted using the SEDI software application located at the SEDI web site.

5.2 Access Key — After an issuer profile supplement or an insider profile has been filed by or for a SEDI filer, all information filed in SEDI format by or for the SEDI filer shall be authenticated using the SEDI filer's access key.

5.3 Format of Information and Number of Copies — A requirement in securities legislation relating to the format in which a report or other information to be filed must be printed or specifying the number of copies of a report or other information that must be filed does not apply to a SEDI filing made in accordance with this Instrument.

PART 6 — EXEMPTION

6.1 Exemption — (1) The regulator or the securities regulatory authority may grant an exemption from this Instrument, in whole or in part, subject to such conditions or restrictions as may be imposed in the exemption.

(2) Despite subsection (1), in Ontario only the regulator may grant such an exemption.

PART 7 — TRANSITION TO ELECTRONIC FILING

7.1 SEDI Issuers — An issuer that is a SEDI issuer on October 29, 2001 shall file an issuer profile supplement in SEDI format within five business days after that date.

7.2 Transactions Before Effective Date — If, at any time on or after November 13, 2001, an insider of a SEDI issuer is filing an insider report, including an amended insider report, in respect of a relationship to, or a transaction in securities of, the SEDI issuer which arose or occurred prior to that date, the insider shall file the insider report in SEDI format.

PART 8 — EFFECTIVE DATE

8.1 Effective Date — (1) Except for sections 2.1, 2.2, 2.4, 3.1 and 3.2, this Instrument comes into force on October 29, 2001.

(2) Sections 2.1, 2.2, 2.4, 3.1 and 3.2 come into force on November 13, 2001.

PART 9 — FILING OF ISSUER PROFILE SUPPLEMENT

9.1 Filing of Issuer Profile Supplement — (1) A SEDI issuer that filed an issuer profile supplement in SEDI format on or before January 31, 2002 shall file a new and current issuer profile supplement in SEDI format not later than the date specified by the regulator under subsection (2).

(2) For the purposes of subsection (1), the regulator may specify a period and that period must

    (a) begin no earlier than the date that the notice is published under subsection (3), and

    (b) be at least 18 days in length.

(3) After specifying a period under subsection (2), the regulator shall

    (a) publish a notice specifying the date the period ends and the filing requirement under subsection (1), and

    (b) issue a press release summarizing the notice given under paragraph (a).

Final Rule: 24 O.S.C.B. 6325; Approval by OSC: 24 O.S.C.B. 4414; Request for Comments: 23 O.S.C.B. 4427; Replaced Rule 55-501.

Amendment to Rule: 26 O.S.C.B. 3163; Approval by OSC: 26 O.S.C.B. 1637.

Amendment to Rule: 31 O.S.C.B. 6571; Approval by OSC: 31 O.S.C.B. 3565; Request for Comments: 30 O.S.C.B. 10093.

Amendment to Rule: CSAN 11-314.

Amendment to Rule: (2013) 36 O.S.C.B. 9601; Approval by OSC: (2013) O.S.C.B. 8569 (corrections) and 7217; Request for Comments: (2013) 36 O.S.C.B. 1081.

Rules: NI 55-103.

Policies and Orders: CSAN 55-312, 55-315, 55-316, NPS 55-102CP.

Form 55-102F1 — Insider Profile

An insider profile filed in SEDI format shall contain the information prescribed below. The information shall be entered using the online version of this form accessible by SEDI users at the SEDI web site (www.sedi.ca). All references to web pages, fields and lists relate to the online version of the form.

If the insider is an individual, start entering information on the web page titled "Create insider profile (Form 55-102F1) — Enter individual information". If the individual insider has submitted a SEDI user registration form, select "Copy your user registration information" to avoid re-entering the insider's personal information. If the insider is not an individual, select "Enter company information" and start entering information on the web page titled "Create insider profile (Form 55-102F1) — Enter company information".

1. — Insider's full legal name

Provide the full legal name of the insider. Use upper and lower case letters as applicable. Do not use initials, nicknames or abbreviations. If the insider is an individual, complete the "Insider family name" and the "Insider given names" fields. If the insider is not an individual, provide the full legal name of the insider in the "Insider company name" field.

2. — Name of insider representative (if applicable)

If the insider is not an individual, provide the full legal name of an individual representative of the insider using the "Family name" and "Given names" fields. Use upper and lower case letters as applicable. Do not use initials, nicknames or abbreviations.

3. — Insider's address

If the insider is an individual, provide the insider's principal residential address. Otherwise, provide the business address where the insider's representative (provided in item 2 above) is employed. In either case, select or provide the country and provide the address (street name and number, etc.), the municipality (city, town, etc.), province, territory or state and postal or zip code, as applicable. A post office box or similar mailing address is not acceptable.

4. — Insider's telephone number

Provide a daytime telephone number for the insider (if the insider is an individual) or for the insider's representative (if the insider is not an individual).

5. — Insider's fax number (if applicable)

If available, provide a fax number for the insider (if the insider is an individual) or for the insider's representative (if the insider is not an individual).

6. — Insider's e-mail address (if applicable)

If available, provide an e-mail address for the insider (if the insider is an individual) or for the insider's representative (if the insider is not an individual).

7. — Correspondence in English or French

If the insider is an individual resident in Quebec, the insider may choose to receive any correspondence from the Quebec securities regulatory authority in English. If no choice is made, any correspondence from the Quebec securities regulatory authority shall be in French. If the insider is a person or company other than an individual and is resident in Quebec, any correspondence from the Quebec securities regulatory authority shall be in French.

If the insider is resident in Manitoba or Ontario, the insider may choose to receive any correspondence from the local securities regulatory authority in French. If no choice is made, any correspondence from the local securities regulatory authority shall be in English.

If the insider is resident in New Brunswick, the insider may choose to receive any correspondence from the New Brunswick securities regulatory authority in French or English.

8. — Confidential question and answer

Provide a "confidential question" and an answer to the confidential question for use in verifying the identity of the insider or the insider's representative if a request is being made to the SEDI operator for a new insider access key. Keep a record of the confidential question and answer in a secure location.

9. — Add name(s) of reporting issuer(s)

Add the name of each reporting issuer in respect of which the insider is required to file an insider report in SEDI format. Search for and select each reporting issuer to be added from a database of all SEDI issuers provided for this purpose. Use the reporting issuer's SEDAR number or its legal name (in English or French) to conduct your search. Make sure you select the correct reporting issuer before you proceed further. If you are unable to find the reporting issuer that you are searching for, contact the reporting issuer or the SEDI operator for assistance. Note that the reporting issuer will not appear in your search results unless the reporting issuer has created an issuer profile in SEDAR and filed an issuer profile supplement in SEDI.

If the insider has ceased to be an insider of a reporting issuer added previously to the insider profile, see item 12 below.

10. — Insider's relationship to reporting issuer

For each reporting issuer added under item 9 above, disclose all of the insider's relationships to that reporting issuer by selecting from the list of relationship types provided.

11. — Date the insider became an insider or date of opening balance

For each reporting issuer added under item 9 above, if the insider has not filed an insider report in respect of the reporting issuer since becoming an insider, provide the date on which the insider became an insider of the reporting issuer. Otherwise, provide an opening balance date. This opening balance date will be used as the date for all opening balances of securities of this reporting issuer. The opening balance date should be a date prior to the date of any transactions that will be reported for this reporting issuer in SEDI.

12. — Date the insider ceased to be an insider

If the insider has ceased to be an insider of a reporting issuer added previously to the insider profile, amend the insider profile by providing the date on which the insider ceased to be an insider of the reporting issuer in the fields provided for this purpose on the web page titled "Amend insider profile — Amend issuer information."

Optional Information

An insider profile filed in SEDI format may, at the option of the insider, contain the following additional information:

13. — Additional contact information

For each reporting issuer added to the insider profile, the insider may provide another address at which the insider prefers to be contacted (such as a business address) or may provide contact information for another individual who is to be contacted by the securities regulatory authority instead of the insider. To provide additional contact information, check the applicable box under "Optional information" on the web page titled "Create insider profile — Enter information about the insider's relationship to the issuer".

14. — Add name(s) of registered holder(s) of securities

If the insider is required to file an insider report in respect of securities owned indirectly or over which control or direction is exercised, the insider must provide the name of the registered holder of the securities at the time the insider report is filed. To assist the insider in complying with this requirement, for each reporting issuer added to the insider's profile the insider may add the name(s) of the registered holder(s) of securities of the reporting issuer that the insider is required to provide in an insider report.

To add the name(s) of the registered holder(s) for the reporting issuer, check the applicable box under "Optional information" on the web page titled "Create insider profile — Enter information about the insider's relationship to the issuer". Any name added to the insider's profile in this manner may be selected when an insider report is prepared in SEDI format and registered holder information is required. The full legal name of the registered holder must be provided in each case.

Securities beneficially owned directly but held through a nominee such as a broker or book-based depository are considered direct holdings.

Amending Insider Profile To Add a Reporting Issuer

If an insider that has previously filed an insider profile is required to file an insider report in SEDI format in respect of a reporting issuer that is not already disclosed in the insider profile, amend the insider profile to add the name of the reporting issuer, to disclose all of the insider's relationships to the reporting issuer and to provide the date the insider became an insider or the date of the previous paper filing, as applicable. Provide the information required in items 9, 10 and 11 above.

Certification

Prior to submitting an insider profile, the insider or the insider's agent must certify that the information is true and complete in every respect by selecting "Certify" on the web page titled "Create insider profile — Certify and file insider profile" and following the instructions provided for this purpose. In the case of an agent, the certification is based on the agent's best knowledge, information and belief but the insider is still responsible for ensuring that the information filed by the agent is true and complete. It is an offence to submit information that, in a material respect and at the time and in the light of the circumstances in which it is submitted, is misleading or untrue.

Notice — Collection and Use of Personal Information

The personal information required under this form is collected on behalf of and used by the securities regulatory authorities set out below for purposes of the administration and enforcement of certain provisions of the securities legislation in British Columbia, Alberta, Saskatchewan, Manitoba, Ontario, Northwest Territories, Quebec, New Brunswick, Nova Scotia, Prince Edward Island, Newfoundland and Yukon. Some of the required information will be made public pursuant to the securities legislation in each of the jurisdictions indicated above. Other required information will remain confidential and will not be disclosed to any person or company except to any of the securities regulatory authorities or their authorized representatives. If you have any questions about the collection and use of this information, you may contact the securities regulatory authority in any jurisdiction(s) in which the required information is filed, at the address(es) or telephone number(s) set out below. In Quebec, questions may also be addressed to the Commission d'accès à l'information du Québec (1-888-528-7741, web site: www.cai.gouv.qc.ca).

Alberta Securities Commission
Suite 600, 250-5th Street SW
Calgary, AB T2P 0R4
Attention: Information Officer
Telephone: (403) 297-6454

The Manitoba Securities Commission
500-400 St. Mary Avenue
Winnipeg, MB R3C 4K5
Attention: Director, Legal
Telephone: (204) 945-4508

Nova Scotia Securities Commission
Suite 400, 5251 Duke Street
Halifax, NS B3J 1P3
Attention: FOI Officer
Telephone: (902) 424-7768

Autorité des marchés financiers
Stock Exchange Tower
P.O. Box 246, 22nd Floor
800 Victoria Square
Montréal, PQ H4Z 1G3
Attention: Responsable de l'accès à l'information
Telephone: (514) 940-2150 or (800) 361-5072 (in Quebec)

British Columbia Securities Commission
P.O. Box 10142, Pacific Centre
701 West Georgia Street
Vancouver, BC V7Y 1L2
Attention: Supervisor, Insider Reporting
Telephone: (604) 899-6500 or (800) 373-6393 (in BC)

Securities Commission of Newfoundland
P.O. Box 8700
2nd Floor, West Block
Confederation Building
St. John's, NFLD A1B 4J6
Attention: Director of Securities
Telephone: (709) 729-4189

Ontario Securities Commission
Suite 1903, Box 55
20 Queen Street West
Toronto, ON M5H 3S8
Attention: FOI Coordinator
Telephone: (416) 593-8314

Saskatchewan Financial Services Commission, Securities Division
6th Floor, 1919 Saskatchewan Drive
Regina, SK S4P 3V7
Attention: Director
Telephone: (306) 787-5645

New Brunswick Securities Commission
85 Charlotte Street, Suite 300
Saint John, NB E2L 2J2
Attention: Corporate Finance Officer
Telephone: (506) 658-3060 or (866) 933-2222 (in New Brunswick)

Superintendent of Securities
Department of Justice
Government of the Northwest Territories
1st Floor, Stuart M. Hogson Building
5009-49th Street
P.O. Box 1320
Yellowknife, Northwest Territories, X1A 2L9
Attention: Deputy Superintendent of Securities
Tel:(867) 920-3318

Government of Nunavut
Legal Registries Division
P.O. Box 100, Station 570
1st Floor, Brown Building
Iqualuit, Nunavut, X0A 0H0
Contact person: Superintendent of Securities
Tel: (867) 975-6590
Fax: (867) 975-6595
Email: legal.registries@gov.nu.ca

Superintendent of Securities
Government of Prince Edward Island
4th Floor, Shaw Building
95 Rochford Street
P.O. Box 2000

Charlottetown PE C1A 7N8
Tel: (902) 368-4550

Office of the Yukon Superintendent of Securities
Government of Yukon
Department of Community Services
307 Black Street, 1st Floor
PO Box 2703 (C-6)
Whitehorse, Yukon Y1A 2C6
Telephone: 867-667-5466
Facsimile: 867-393-6251
http://www.community.gov.yk.ca/corp/securities_about.html

Form 55-102F2 — Insider Report

An insider report filed in SEDI format shall contain the information prescribed below. The information shall be entered using the online version of this form accessible by SEDI users at the SEDI web site (www.sedi.ca). All references to web pages, fields and lists relate to the online version of the form.

If a position or transaction being reported by the insider involves an option, warrant, right or other derivative, the information prescribed by items 18 to 25 below must be included in the insider report, if applicable.

For each reporting issuer in respect of which one or more positions or transactions are being reported by an insider, start by navigating to the web page titled "File insider report (Form 55-102 F2) — Select issuer" and then provide the information required in the circumstances.

1. — Name of reporting issuer

Provide the name of the reporting issuer for the securities that are the subject of the insider report by selecting the reporting issuer's name from the list of one or more reporting issuer names added previously to the insider's profile. If the name of the applicable reporting issuer does not appear in the list, the insider's profile must be amended to add the name of the applicable reporting issuer before the insider report can be completed. A separate insider report must be completed for each reporting issuer in respect of which the insider has a reporting obligation.

2. — Amended insider report

If the insider is amending information contained in an insider report filed previously in SEDI format, the amended insider report shall contain all of the information required to be disclosed in the previous insider report in its amended form.

If the insider is amending information contained in an insider report filed previously in paper format, select "Amend paper filing" on the "Amend insider transaction" web page and complete a new insider report in SEDI format containing all of the information required to be disclosed in the previous paper filing in its amended form. In the "General remarks" field on the "File insider report — Enter transaction information" web page, provide the date on which the previous paper filing was made.

3. — Review issuer information

Review the information contained in the insider profile with respect to the selected reporting issuer to ensure that the information is correct. To do this, click on "Insider profile" in the top bar and the "Introduction to insider profile activities (Form 55-102F1)" screen will appear.

You must review the information in the insider profile with respect to the selected reporting issuer and, if the information is not correct, you must amend it by filing an amended insider profile. To do this, click on "Amend insider profile" in the bar on the left side and make the necessary corrections.

4. — Review new issuer event reports

If the reporting issuer has filed an issuer event report that has not previously been viewed or that has been previously flagged for further viewing, you must review the issuer event report.

To do this you must do the following: i) After you have selected an issuer and before selecting the "File insider report" feature, on the screen entitled "File insider report (Form 55-102F2) — Select issuer", click on the feature entitled "View issuer event reports" and the "Listing of issuer event reports" screen appears. ii) Next, click on the radio button for the report you wish to see and then select "View Report" and the "View issuer report information" screen appears with the text of the issuer event report.

If the insider's holdings of securities of the reporting issuer have been affected by an issuer event, the change in holdings must be reported.

5. — Security designation

For each position or transaction being reported, provide the security designation for the applicable security or class of securities. For this purpose, select the applicable security designation from the list shown for the reporting issuer's outstanding securities.

If the applicable security designation does not appear in the list, check the "archived security designation" list containing designations of securities of the reporting issuer that are no longer outstanding and that may no longer be issued. Alternatively, check the "Insider defined security" list that will contain one or more security designations for the reporting issuer if any have been defined previously by or for the insider. In either case, if the applicable securities designation appears in the list, select it.

If the applicable security designation does not appear in any of the lists described above, the insider must define the applicable security designation. For this purpose, select the appropriate "Security category" by choosing "Debt", "Equity", "Issuer Derivative" or "Third Party Derivative" from the list provided. For purposes of the insider reporting requirement, "issuer derivative" means a derivative issued by the reporting issuer to which the insider reporting requirement relates and "third party derivative" means a derivative issued by a person or company other than the reporting issuer to which the insider reporting requirement relates. The security category selected will determine the nature of the information that is required to be reported in relation to positions or transactions involving the applicable security designation.

Next, create the "insider defined" security designation by selecting the most appropriate "Security name" from the list provided and, if applicable, use the "Additional description" field to enter any additional words used to describe the specific security or class of securities. For example, to provide the security designation of "Class A Preferred Shares, Series 1", select "Preferred Shares" from the "Security name" list and then type "Class A, Series 1" in the "Additional description" field.

Important Note: If the security or class of securities being designated is a security that has been issued by the reporting issuer, it is important to try to avoid creating an "insider defined" security designation. If a security designation has not been created by the reporting issuer in respect of a security or class of securities issued by the reporting issuer, contact the reporting issuer to request that the security designation be added to the list of security designations for the reporting issuer's outstanding securities in its issuer profile supplement. However, you must create an "insider defined" security designation if this becomes necessary to ensure that the insider report is filed on a timely basis.

Derivatives: If the security or class of securities being designated is an issuer derivative or a third party derivative, provide the security designation for the derivative and the security designation for the underlying security. See item 18 below. In addition, if the security or class of securities being designated is a third party derivative, the insider will have to provide the applicable security designation in all cases.

6. — Ownership type

Indicate whether the securities in respect of which a position or transaction is being reported are (1) beneficially owned directly, (2) beneficially owned indirectly or (3) controlled or directed. Securities beneficially owned directly but held through a nominee such as a broker or book-based depository are considered direct holdings.

7. — Identity of registered holder of securities where ownership is indirect or where control or direction is exercised

If beneficial ownership of the securities is indirect or if control or direction is exercised over the securities, provide the name of the registered holder of the securities. If the name of the registered holder has been previously added to the insider's profile in respect of the reporting issuer, select the name of the registered holder from the list shown. Otherwise, enter the full legal name of the registered holder in the field provided.

8. — Opening balance of securities held (initial SEDI report only)

If the insider is filing an initial report in respect of securities held on becoming an insider or is reporting a change in a security or class of securities previously reported only in paper format, for each security or class of securities held directly or by a particular registered holder, disclose the initial number or amount of securities so held in the field provided for this purpose on the web page titled "File insider report — Opening balance on initial SEDI report (Non-Derivatives)", or the corresponding web page for derivatives, as applicable. For debt securities, provide the aggregate nominal value of the securities held.

If an opening balance of securities held is required to be disclosed, the information with respect to the "Opening/initial balance date" and "nature of transaction" required under items 9 and 10 below will be generated by the SEDI software application. The "Opening/initial balance date" will be the date the insider became an insider or the date the insider entered for all opening balances for securities of this issuer.

If the insider has previously filed a report in SEDI disclosing the balance of the security or class of securities held directly or by a particular registered holder, the opening balance of the security or class of securities so held is generated by the SEDI software application based on all previous reports filed in respect of the particular holding.

If an initial SEDI report involves the holding of a derivative, see item 19 below.

9. — Date of transaction

Provide the date of each transaction being reported using the fields provided for this purpose. Provide the "trade date" not the "settlement date".

10. — Nature of transaction

Indicate the nature of each transaction being reported by selecting the most appropriate transaction type from the list provided for this purpose.

11. — Number or value of securities acquired

Disclose the number or value of securities acquired for each transaction involving an acquisition of securities. For debt securities, provide the aggregate nominal value. If the transaction involved the acquisition of an option, warrant, right or other derivative, see items 21 and 22 below.

12. — Number or value of securities disposed of

Disclose the number or value of securities disposed of for each transaction involving a disposition of securities. For debt securities, provide the aggregate nominal value. If the transaction involved the disposition of an option, warrant, right or other derivative, see items 21 and 22 below.

13. — Unit price or exercise price

Disclose the price per security paid or received by the insider for each transaction being reported, if applicable. Do not reduce the price being reported to reflect the amount of any commission paid. If the insider acquired or disposed of a security upon the exercise of an option, warrant, right or other derivative, report the exercise price per security. If the insider acquired or disposed of an option, warrant, right or other derivative, see item 23 below.

If the transaction involved consideration other than cash, provide the approximate fair value of the consideration in Canadian dollars and describe the consideration in the "General remarks" field. If no consideration was paid or received by the insider, check "Not applicable".

14. — Currency

If the price paid or received in any transaction was in a currency other than Canadian dollars, provide the amount in that other currency and select the other currency from the list provided for this purpose.

15. — Closing balance of securities held

After each new transaction being reported in respect of a security or class of securities held directly or through a particular registered holder has been entered, a new balance of the security or class of securities held directly or by the particular registered holder will be generated automatically by SEDI prior to filing. If the insider believes that the closing balance reported by SEDI is not correct, the closing balance calculated by the insider must be reported in the field provided for this purpose. The insider shall make all reasonable efforts to reconcile the balance calculated by SEDI with the balance believed by the insider to be correct. An incorrect balance may have resulted from an error in a previous insider report or from a failure to report a previous transaction.

16. — General remarks

Provide additional information if necessary to provide an accurate description of each position and/or transaction in securities being reported. Information provided in this field will be accessible by the public.

17. — Private remarks to securities regulatory authority

Using the field provided, the insider may disclose additional information with respect to the position or transaction being reported to staff of the securities regulatory authority. Information provided in this field will not be accessible by the public.

Holdings or Transactions Involving Derivatives

If a holding or transaction being reported by the insider involves an issuer derivative or a third party derivative, the additional information prescribed below shall be disclosed, if applicable. For this purpose, "issuer derivative" means a derivative issued by the reporting issuer to which the insider reporting requirement relates, and "third party derivative" means a derivative issued by a person or company other than the reporting issuer to which the insider reporting requirement relates.

18. — Security designation of derivative and underlying security

Provide the security designation for the derivative in the manner described under item 5 above. Next, select the appropriate security category for the underlying security from the list provided and then provide the security designation for the underlying security in a similar manner to that described under item 5 above. If the security or class of securities being designated is a third party derivative, the insider will have to define the applicable security designation in all cases. If the derivative security has been defined by the insider, the underlying security must also be defined by the insider.

19. — Opening balance of derivative securities or contracts held (initial SEDI report only)

If the insider is filing an initial report disclosing an option, warrant, right or other derivative held on becoming an insider or is reporting a change in such a derivative not previously reported in SEDI format, for each such derivative position so held directly or by a particular registered holder, disclose the initial number of derivative securities or contracts held in the field provided for this purpose.

20. — Opening balance of equivalent number of underlying securities (initial SEDI report only)

If the insider is filing an initial report of an option, warrant, right or other derivative held on becoming an insider or is reporting a change in any such derivative not previously reported in SEDI format, for each such derivative position held directly or by a particular registered holder, disclose the actual or notional number or amount of underlying securities that may be acquired or disposed of upon exercise or settlement of such derivative. If the underlying securities are debt securities, provide the aggregate nominal value of the actual or notional amount of underlying debt securities that may be acquired or disposed of upon exercise or settlement of such derivative.

21. — Number of derivative securities or contracts acquired or disposed of

Disclose the number of derivative securities or contracts acquired for each transaction involving an acquisition of a derivative or the number of derivative securities or contracts disposed of for each transaction involving a disposition of a derivative.

22. — Equivalent number of underlying securities acquired or disposed of

For each transaction involving an acquisition or disposition of a derivative, disclose the actual or notional number or amount of underlying securities that may be acquired or disposed of upon exercise or settlement of the derivative. If the underlying securities are debt securities, provide the aggregate nominal value of the equivalent amount of underlying debt securities that may be acquired or disposed of upon exercise or settlement of the derivative.

23. — Unit price of derivative

Disclose the premium or other amount paid or received by the insider in connection with the acquisition or disposition of the derivative (per contract if applicable). If the premium or other amount paid or received was in a currency other than Canadian dollars, provide the amount in that other currency and select the other currency from the list provided for this purpose.

24. — Conversion or exercise price of derivative

Provide the conversion or exercise price of the derivative by entering the amount in the field provided for this purpose (per underlying security if applicable). If the conversion or exercise price is in a currency other than Canadian dollars, select the relevant currency from the list provided for this purpose. If the conversion or exercise price of the derivative will adjust on one or more specified dates, provide the details of the adjustment terms in the "General remarks" field.

25. — Date of expiry or maturity of derivative

If the derivative expires or matures on a given date, specify the date of expiry or maturity using the fields provided for this purpose.

Certification

Prior to filing an insider report, the insider or the insider's agent must certify that the information is true and complete in every respect. In the case of an agent, the certification is based on the agent's best knowledge, information and belief but the insider is still responsible for ensuring that the information filed by the agent is true and complete. It is an offence to submit information that, in a material respect and at the time and in the light of the circumstances in which it is submitted, is misleading or untrue.

Notice — Collection and Use of Personal Information

The personal information required under this form is collected on behalf of and used by the securities regulatory authorities set out below for purposes of the administration and enforcement of certain provisions of the securities legislation in British Columbia, Alberta, Saskatchewan, Manitoba, Ontario, Northwest Territories, Quebec, New Brunswick, Nova Scotia, Prince Edward Island, Newfoundland and Yukon. Some of the required information will be made public pursuant to the securities legislation in each of the jurisdictions indicated above. Other required information will remain confidential and will not be disclosed to any person or company except to any of the securities regulatory authorities or their authorized representatives. If you have any questions about the collection and use of this information, you may contact the securities regulatory authority in any jurisdiction(s) in which the required information is filed, at the address(es) or telephone number(s) set out below. In Quebec, questions may also be addressed to the Commission d'accès à l'information du Québec (1-888-528-7741, web site: www.cai.gouv.qc.ca).

Alberta Securities Commission

Suite 600, 250-5th Street SW

Calgary, AB T2P 0R4

Attention: Information Officer

Telephone: (403) 297-6454

The Manitoba Securities Commission

500-400 St. Mary Avenue

Winnipeg, MB R3C 4K5

Attention: Director, Legal

Telephone: (204) 945-4508

Nova Scotia Securities Commission

Suite 400, 5251 Duke Street

Halifax, NS B3J 1P3

Attention: FOI Officer

Telephone: (902) 424-7768

Autorité des marchés financiers

Stock Exchange Tower

P.O. Box 246, 22nd Floor

800 Victoria Square

Montréal, PQ H4Z 1G3

Attention: Responsable de l'accès à l'information

Telephone: (514) 940-2150 or (800) 361-5072 (in Quebec)

British Columbia Securities Commission
P.O. Box 10142, Pacific Centre
701 West Georgia Street
Vancouver, BC V7Y 1L2
Attention: Supervisor, Insider Reporting
Telephone: (604) 899-6500 or (800) 373-6393 (in BC)

Securities Commission of Newfoundland
P.O. Box 8700
2nd Floor, West Block
Confederation Building
St. John's, NFLD A1B 4J6
Attention: Director of Securities
Telephone: (709) 729-4189

Ontario Securities Commission
Suite 1903, Box 55
20 Queen Street West
Toronto, ON M5H 3S8
Attention: FOI Coordinator
Telephone: (416) 593-8314

Saskatchewan Financial Services Commission, Securities Division
6th Floor, 1919 Saskatchewan Drive
Regina, SK S4P 3V7
Attention: Director
Telephone: (306) 787-5645

New Brunswick Securities Commission
85 Charlotte Street, Suite 300
Saint John, NB E2L 2J2
Attention: Corporate Finance Officer
Telephone: (506) 658-3060 or (866) 933-2222 (in New Brunswick)

Superintendent of Securities
Department of Justice
Government of the Northwest Territories
1st Floor, Stuart M. Hogson Building
5009-49th Street
P.O. Box 1320
Yellowknife, Northwest Territories, X1A 2L9
Attention: Deputy Superintendent of Securities
Tel:(867) 920-3318

Government of Nunavut
Legal Registries Division
P.O. Box 100, Station 570
1st Floor, Brown Building
Iqaluit, Nunavut, X0A 0H0
Contact person: Superintendent of Securities
Tel: (867) 975-6590

Fax: (867) 975-6595

Email: legal.registries@gov.nu.ca

Superintendent of Securities

Government of Prince Edward Island

4th Floor, Shaw Building

95 Rochford Street

P.O. Box 2000

Charlottetown PE C1A 7N8

Tel: (902) 368-4550

Office of the Yukon Superintendent of Securities

Government of Yukon

Department of Community Services

307 Black Street, 1st Floor

PO Box 2703 (C-6)
Whitehorse, Yukon Y1A 2C6
Telephone: 867-667-5466
Facsimile: 867-393-6251
http://www.community.gov.yk.ca/corp/securities_about.html

Form 55-102F3 — Issuer Profile Supplement

An issuer profile supplement filed in SEDI format shall contain the information prescribed below. The information shall be entered using the online version of this form accessible by SEDI users at the SEDI web site (www.sedi.ca). All references to web pages, fields and lists relate to the online version of the form.

1. — Name of reporting issuer

Provide the name of the reporting issuer for which the issuer profile supplement is being created by searching for the reporting issuer using the reporting issuer's SEDAR number or the reporting issuer's legal name (in English or French). If the reporting issuer's name does not appear in the search results, an issuer profile must be created for the reporting issuer in SEDAR before proceeding further with any SEDI filings. See National Instrument 13-101 *System for Electronic Document Analysis and Retrieval (SEDAR)*.

2. — Name of insider affairs contact

Provide the full legal name of an individual who will act as "insider affairs contact" for the reporting issuer. Use the "Family name" and "Given names" fields for this purpose. Use upper and lower case letters as applicable. Do not use initials, nicknames or abbreviations. SEDI will automatically deliver an e-mail message to the e-mail address provided for the insider affairs contact each time an insider profile or an amended insider profile is filed by or on behalf of a person or company disclosing an insider relationship with the reporting issuer. This is intended to assist the reporting issuer in identifying any incorrect or inappropriate SEDI filings made in respect of the reporting issuer. Insider affairs contact information is not accessible by the public.

3. — Address of insider affairs contact

Provide a business address for the insider affairs contact. Indicate the country and provide the address (street name and number, etc.), the municipality (city, town, etc.), province, territory or state and postal or zip code, as applicable. A post office box or similar mailing address is not acceptable.

4. — Telephone number and e-mail address of insider affairs contact

Provide a business telephone number and a business e-mail address for the insider affairs contact.

5. — Fax number of insider affairs contact (if applicable)

If available, provide a business fax number for the insider affairs contact.

6. — Confidential question and answer

Provide a "confidential question" and an answer to the confidential question for use in identifying the issuer's representative if a request is being made to the SEDI operator for a new issuer access key. Keep a record of the confidential question and answer in a secure location.

7. — Security designations

Provide the security designation for each outstanding security and each class of outstanding securities of the reporting issuer that is held by an insider of the reporting issuer who has direct or indirect beneficial ownership of, or control or direction over, that security or class of security.

For each security or class of securities, select the appropriate "Security category" by choosing "Debt", "Equity" or "Issuer Derivative" from the list provided. Then provide a designation of the security or class of securities using the fields provided for this purpose, as follows. First, select the "Security name" from the list of generic security names provided. Second, if applicable, enter any additional words used to describe the specific security or class of securities. For example, to provide the designation of "Class A Preferred Shares, Series 1", select "Preferred Shares" from the "Security name" field and then type "Class A, Series 1" in the "Additional description" field.

If the security whose designation is being added is an issuer derivative, provide the designation of the underlying security or class of underlying securities in addition to the designation of the issuer derivative itself. First, select the applicable securities category for the underlying security and then provide the designation for the underlying security using the "Security name" and "Additional description" fields in the same manner as described above.

8. — Amending a security designation

If there is any change in the security designation disclosed previously for a security or class of securities of the reporting issuer that is outstanding or that may be issued in the future, use the "Amend security designation" function to amend the applicable security designation in the issuer profile supplement. Select the applicable security designation to be amended and a web page with pre-populated fields containing the existing security designation information will be displayed for purposes of making the necessary amendment(s).

Note that a security designation should only be amended for corrections or for changes that do not result in the security or class of securities ceasing to exist. If a security or class of securities ceases to exist and is replaced by another security or class of securities, the "old" security must be archived in the manner described under item 9 below and a security designation must be added for the "new" security in the manner described under item 7 above.

If the security or class of securities affected by the change is an underlying security for an issuer derivative, use the "Amend security designation" function to amend the security designation of the underlying security as well.

9. — Archiving a security designation

If any security or class of securities designated previously by the reporting issuer has ceased to be outstanding and the security or class of securities may no longer be issued, use the "Archive security designation" function to remove the relevant security designation from the reporting issuer's list of "outstanding securities" and place it in the reporting issuer's list of "archived securities". Archived security designations may not be reactivated if the applicable security or class of securities is re-issued or becomes subject to the issuance. In such circumstances, a new security designation must be added to the issuer profile supplement in the manner described under item 7 above.

Notice — Collection and Use of Personal Information

The personal information required under this form is collected on behalf of and used by the securities regulatory authorities set out below for purposes of the administration and enforcement of certain provisions of the securities legislation in British Columbia, Alberta, Saskatchewan, Manitoba, Ontario, Northwest Territories, Quebec, New Brunswick, Nova Scotia, Prince Edward Island, Newfoundland and Yukon. Some of the required information will be made public pursuant to the securities legislation in each of the jurisdictions indicated above. Other required information will remain confidential and will not be disclosed to any person or company except to any of the securities regulatory authorities or their authorized representatives. If you have any questions about the collection and use of this information, you may contact the securities regulatory authority in any jurisdiction(s) in which the required information is filed, at the address(es) or telephone number(s) set out below. In Quebec, questions may also be addressed to the Commission d'accès à l'information du Québec (1-888-528-7741, web site: www.cai.gouv.qc.ca).

Alberta Securities Commission
Suite 600, 250-5th Street SW
Calgary, AB T2P 0R4
Attention: Information Officer
Telephone: (403) 297-6454

The Manitoba Securities Commission
500-400 St. Mary Avenue
Winnipeg, MB R3C 4K5
Attention: Director, Legal
Telephone: (204) 945-4508

Nova Scotia Securities Commission
Suite 400, 5251 Duke Street
Halifax, NS B3J 1P3
Attention: FOI Officer
Telephone: (902) 424-7768

Autorité des marchés financiers

Stock Exchange Tower
P.O. Box 246, 22nd Floor
800 Victoria Square
Montréal, PQ H4Z 1G3
Attention: Responsable de l'accès à l'information
Telephone: (514) 940-2150 or (800) 361-5072 (in Quebec)

British Columbia Securities Commission
P.O. Box 10142, Pacific Centre
701 West Georgia Street
Vancouver, BC V7Y 1L2
Attention: Supervisor, Insider Reporting
Telephone: (604) 899-6500 or (800) 373-6393 (in BC)

Securities Commission of Newfoundland
P.O. Box 8700
2nd Floor, West Block
Confederation Building
St. John's, NFLD A1B 4J6
Attention: Director of Securities
Telephone: (709) 729-4189

Ontario Securities Commission
Suite 1903, Box 55
20 Queen Street West
Toronto, Ontario
M5H 3S8
Attention: FOI Coordinator
Telephone: (416) 593-8314

Saskatchewan Financial Services Commission, Securities Division
6th Floor, 1919 Saskatchewan Drive
Regina, SK S4P 3V7
Attention: Director
Telephone: (306) 787-5645

New Brunswick Securities Commission
85 Charlotte Street, Suite 300
Saint John, NB E2L 2J2
Attention: Corporate Finance Officer
Telephone: (506) 658-3060 or (866) 933-2222 (in New Brunswick)

Superintendent of Securities
Department of Justice
Government of the Northwest Territories
1st Floor, Stuart M. Hogson Building
5009-49th Street
P.O. Box 1320
Yellowknife, Northwest Territories, X1A 2L9
Attention: Deputy Superintendent of Securities
Tel:(867) 920-3318

Government of Nunavut

Legal Registries Division

P.O. Box 100, Station 570

1st Floor, Brown Building

Iqaluit, Nunavut, X0A 0H0

Contact person: Superintendent of Securities

Tel: (867) 975-6590

Fax: (867) 975-6595

Email: legal.registries@gov.nu.ca

Superintendent of Securities

Government of Prince Edward Island

4th Floor, Shaw Building

95 Rochford Street

P.O. Box 2000

Charlottetown PE C1A 7N8

Tel: (902) 368-4550

Office of the Yukon Superintendent of Securities

Government of Yukon

Department of Community Services

307 Black Street, 1st Floor

PO Box 2703 (C-6)

Whitehorse, Yukon Y1A 2C6

Telephone: 867-667-5466

Facsimile: 867-393-6251

http://www.community.gov.yk.ca/corp/securities_about.html

Part 5: ONGOING
REQUIREMENTS

Form 55-102F4 — Issuer Event Report

An issuer event report in SEDI format shall contain the information prescribed below. The information shall be entered using the online version of this form accessible by SEDI users at the SEDI web site (www.sedi.ca). All references to web pages, fields and lists relate to the online version of the form.

1. — Issuer event type

Starting at the web page titled "File issuer event report — Form 55-102F4", select the "Issuer event type" that appropriately describes the issuer event from the list of transactions and other events provided for this purpose. If an appropriate issuer event type is not provided in the list, select "Other Issuer Event" and enter an appropriate generic term for the type of issuer event being reported in the "Other issuer event type" field provided for this purpose.

2. — Effective date of issuer event

Disclose the effective date of the issuer event using the fields provided for this purpose.

3. — Issuer event title

Provide a descriptive title for the issuer event that will distinguish the issuer event from other issuer events of the same type. For example, in the case of a merger, refer to another merging issuer, or in the case of a stock split, indicate the approximate date.

4. — Issuer event details

Describe the issuer event in plain language. Provide the security designation of each security or class of securities of the issuer affected by the issuer event and explain the adjustment or other change in holdings that affected insiders of the issuer would be required to report as a result of the issuer event. If applicable, provide the ratio by which each security or class of securities affected has been or will be adjusted by the issuer event.

If the required adjustment(s) will result in a fractional number of securities when applied to the number of securities held by affected insiders, indicate whether the number of securities held by the insider shall be rounded up or down.

If the issuer event involved the creation of a new security or class of securities or the formation of a new reporting issuer, disclose this information. If applicable, amend the issuer profile supplement for the reporting issuer.

Optional Information

An issuer event report filed in SEDI format may, at the option of the reporting issuer, contain the following additional information:

5. — Private remarks to securities regulatory authority

Using the field provided, the issuer may disclose additional information concerning the issuer event to staff of the securities regulatory authority. Information provided in this field will not be accessible by the public.

Form 55-102F5 — SEDI User Registration Form

An individual who intends to use SEDI to file information with the securities regulatory authority is required to complete and submit a user registration form in SEDI format containing the information prescribed below. The information must be entered using the online version of this form accessible at the SEDI web site (www.sedi.ca). To access the online user registration form, select "Register as a SEDI user" on the navigation bar at the top of the web page titled "Welcome to SEDI".

1. — Full legal name of SEDI user

Provide your family name and your given names. Use upper and lower case letters as applicable. Do not use initials, nicknames or abbreviations.

2. — Name of employer and position of SEDI user

If you are acting on behalf of an employer, provide the full legal name of your employer and your position with that employer.

3. — Address of SEDI user

If you are an insider, provide your principal residential address. Otherwise, provide the business address where you are employed. A post office box or other mailing address is not sufficient.

4. — SEDI user's telephone number

Provide your daytime telephone number.

5. — SEDI user's fax number

If available, provide your fax number.

6. — SEDI user's e-mail address

If available, provide your e-mail address.

7. — Check the appropriate box for SEDI user classification

Indicate whether you expect to access SEDI as an insider, an agent and/or an issuer's representative by checking the appropriate box or boxes. The type of user classification will determine the amount of functionality you will have in the SEDI application software.

8. — Confidential question and answer

Provide a "confidential question" and an answer to the confidential question for use in verifying your identity if a request in your name is being made to the SEDI operator for a new password.

Certification

Prior to submitting the completed online user registration form, you must certify that the information is true in all material respects and you must agree to update the information submitted as soon as practicable following any material change in the information.

Delivery of Signed Copy to SEDI Operator

Before you may make a valid SEDI filing, you must deliver a manually signed paper copy of the completed user registration form to the SEDI operator for verification purposes. To satisfy this requirement, you may print a copy of the online user registration form once you have certified and submitted it. You must deliver a manually signed and dated copy of the completed user registration form via prepaid mail, personal delivery or facsimile to the SEDI operator at the following address or fax number, as applicable:

CSA Service Desk

Attn: SEDI Operator

12 Millennium Blvd, Suite 210

Moncton, NB E1C 0M3

or at such other address(es) or fax number(s) as may be provided on the SEDI web site (www.sedi.ca).

Questions

Questions may be directed to the SEDI operator at 1-800-219-5381 or such other number as may be provided on the SEDI web site.

Notice — Collection and Use of Personal Information

The personal information that you provide on this form is used to facilitate your access to and use of the SEDI system and is not used for any other purpose. The signed copy of the completed form that you deliver to the SEDI operator is retained by the SEDI operator as evidence of your registration as a SEDI user. The information you provide on this form will not be disclosed to any third party except any of the securities regulatory authorities or their authorized representatives for purposes of the administration or enforcement of securities legislation in the applicable jurisdictions. For information about the use of the information collected on this form or if you would like to obtain access to the information you have submitted, contact the SEDI operator at the address or telephone number provided above. In Quebec, questions may also be addressed to the Commission d'accès à l'information du Québec (1-888-528-7741, web site: www.cai.gouv.qc.ca).

SEDI User Registration Form

Note: Before an individual registering as a SEDI user may make a valid SEDI filing, the registering individual must deliver a manually signed paper copy of the completed user registration form to the SEDI operator for verification purposes. The registering individual may print a copy of the online version using the "Print" function provided for this purpose in SEDI. The signed paper copy must be delivered by prepaid mail, personal delivery or facsimile to:

> CSA Service Desk
> Attn: SEDI Operator
> 12 Millennium Blvd, Suite 210
> Moncton, NB E1C 0M3

Section 1 — SEDI User Information

Family name:

Given names (in full):

Employer name and position (if applicable):

Address (street name and number, etc.):

Municipality (city, town, etc.):

Province, territory or state:

Country:

Postal code or zip code:

Telephone number: ( )

Fax number (if available): ( )

E-mail address (if available):

Section 2 — SEDI User Classification

Check the appropriate box or boxes:

> ❑ Insider ❑ Issuer representative
> ❑ Agent

Section 3 — Certification of SEDI User

I certify that the foregoing information is true in all material respects. I agree to update the information submitted on this form in SEDI as soon as practicable following any material change in the information. I agree that an executed copy of Form 55-102F5, if delivered to the SEDI operator by facsimile, shall have the same effect as an originally executed copy delivered to the SEDI operator.

Signature of SEDI user: Date:

Part 5: ONGOING REQUIREMENTS

55-102F6 — Insider Report

FORM 55-102F6

INSIDER REPORT

(See instructions on the back of this report)

Notice – Collection and Use of Personal Information: The personal information required under this form is collected on behalf of and used by the securities regulatory authorities set out below for purposes of the administration and enforcement of certain provisions of the securities legislation in British Columbia, Alberta, Saskatchewan, Manitoba, Ontario, Northwest Territories, Quebec, New Brunswick, Nova Scotia, Prince Edward Island, Newfoundland and Yukon. Some of the required information will be made public pursuant to the securities legislation in each of the jurisdictions indicated above. Other required information will remain confidential and will not be disclosed to any person or company except to any of the securities regulatory authorities or their authorized representatives. If you have any questions about the collection and use of this information, you may contact the securities regulatory authority in any jurisdiction(s) in which the required information is filed, at the address(es) or telephone number(s) set out on the back of this report.

BOX 1. NAME OF THE REPORTING ISSUER (BLOCK LETTERS)

BOX 2. INSIDER DATA

RELATIONSHIP(S) TO REPORTING ISSUER

CHANGE IN RELATIONSHIP FROM LAST REPORT   ☐ YES   ☐ NO

DATE OF LAST REPORT FILED OR IF INITIAL REPORT, DATE ON WHICH YOU BECAME AN INSIDER

DD   MM   YY

DD   MM   YY

BOX 3. NAME, ADDRESS AND TELEPHONE NUMBER OF THE INSIDER (BLOCK LETTERS)

FAMILY NAME OR CORPORATE NAME

GIVEN NAMES

NO.   STREET   APT

CITY   PROV   POSTAL CODE

BUSINESS TELEPHONE NUMBER   EXT

BUSINESS FAX NUMBER

CHANGE IN NAME, ADDRESS OR TELEPHONE NUMBER FROM LAST REPORT   ☐ YES   ☐ NO

BOX 4. JURISDICTION(S) WHERE THE ISSUER IS A REPORTING ISSUER OR THE EQUIVALENT

☐ ALBERTA   ☐ PRINCE EDWARD ISLAND
☐ BRITISH COLUMBIA   ☐ NORTHWEST TERRITORIES
☐ MANITOBA   ☐ ONTARIO
☐ NEW BRUNSWICK   ☐ QUÉBEC
☐ NEWFOUNDLAND   ☐ SASKATCHEWAN
☐ NOVA SCOTIA   ☐ YUKON

BOX 5. INSIDER HOLDINGS AND CHANGES (IF INITIAL REPORT, COMPLETE SECTIONS A AND D ONLY. SEE ALSO INSTRUCTIONS TO BOX 6)

TRANSACTIONS

A	B			C	D	E	F
DESIGNATION OF CLASS OF SECURITIES	BALANCE OF CLASS OF SECURITIES ON LAST REPORT	DATE		NATURE	NUMBER/VALUE ACQUIRED	NUMBER/VALUE DISPOSED OF	PRESENT BALANCE OF CLASS OF SECURITIES HELD
		DD MM YY				UNIT PRICE / EXERCISE PRICE $ US	DIRECT / INDIRECT OWNERSHIP / CONTROL OR DIRECTION	IDENTIFY THE REGISTERED HOLDER WHERE OWNERSHIP IS INDIRECT OR WHERE CONTROL OR DIRECTION IS EXERCISED

BOX 6. REMARKS

BOX 7. SIGNATURE

The undersigned certifies that the information given in this report is true and complete in every respect. It is an offence to submit information that, in a material respect and at the time and in the light of the circumstances in which it is submitted, is misleading or untrue.

NAME (BLOCK LETTERS)

SIGNATURE

DATE OF THIS REPORT   DD   MM   YY

ATTACHMENT   ☐ YES   ☐ NO

This form is used as a uniform report for the insider reporting requirements under all provincial securities Acts. The terminology used is generic to accommodate the various Acts.

CORRESPONDENCE   ☐ ENGLISH   ☐ FRENCH

KEEP A COPY FOR YOUR FILE

ASC 55-102F6 Rev. 2011/06/01 — VERSION FRANÇAISE DISPONIBLE SUR DEMANDE

INSTRUCTIONS

Insider Reports in English and French are available from Manitoba, Ontario, Québec and New Brunswick. If you are a corporate insider in the province of Québec, you will receive correspondence in French. Individuals in the province of Québec will receive, upon request, correspondence in French.

Where an insider of a reporting issuer does not own or have control or direction over securities of the reporting issuer, or where an insider's ownership or direction or control over securities of the reporting issuer remains unchanged from the last report filed, a report is not required. Insider reports are not required to be filed in, Nunavut.

If you have any questions about the form you should be using to file your report, see National Instrument 55-102 *System for Electronic Disclosure by Insiders (SEDI)*.

BOX 1   Name of reporting issuer
Provide the full legal name of the reporting issuer. Use a separate report for each reporting issuer.

BOX 2   Insider data
Indicate all of your relationship(s) to the reporting issuer using the following codes:

Reporting issuer that has acquired securities issued by itself	1
Subsidiary of the reporting issuer	2
Security holder who beneficially owns or who exercises control or direction over more than 10% of the securities of the reporting issuer (Québec Securities Act – 10% of a class of shares) to which are attached voting rights or an unlimited right to a share of the profits and to its assets in case of winding up	3
Director of a reporting issuer	4
Senior officer of a reporting issuer	5
Director or senior officer of a security holder referred to in 3	6
Director or senior officer of an insider or subsidiary of the reporting issuer, other than in 4, 5 and 6	7
Deemed insider – 6 months before becoming an insider	8

If you have filed a report before, indicate whether your relationship to the reporting issuer has changed.

Specify the date of the last report you filed, and if it is an initial report, the date on which you became an insider.

BOX 3   Name, address and telephone number of the insider
Provide your name, address and business telephone number.

BOX 4   Jurisdiction
Indicate each jurisdiction where the issuer is a reporting issuer or the equivalent.

BOX 5   Insider holdings and changes
Show direct and indirect holdings separately, both in the initial report and where a transaction is reported. Indicate only one transaction per line.

For an initial report complete only:
A designation of class of securities held
D present balance of class of securities held
E nature of ownership (see List of Codes)
F identification of the registered holder where ownership is not direct

If you acquired or disposed of securities while an insider, complete sections **A** to **F**:
A Indicate a designation of the securities traded that is sufficient to identify the class, including yield, series, maturity.
B Indicate the number of securities, or for debt securities, the aggregate nominal value, of the class held, directly and indirectly, before the transaction that is being reported.
C Indicate for each transaction:
- the date of the transaction (not the settlement date)
- the nature of the transaction (see List of Codes)
- the number of securities acquired or disposed of, or for debt securities, the aggregate nominal value
- the unit price paid or received on the day of the transaction, excluding the commission
- if the report is in American dollars, check the space under "$ US"

List of Codes

BOX 5 C   Nature of transaction

General

Acquisition or disposition in the public market	10
Acquisition or disposition carried out privately	11
Acquisition or disposition under a prospectus	15
Acquisition or disposition under a prospectus exemption	16
Acquisition or disposition pursuant to a take-over bid, merger or acquisition	22
Acquisition or disposition under a purchase/ownership plan	30
Stock dividend	35
Conversion or exchange	36
Stock split or consolidation	37
Redemption/retraction/cancellation/repurchase	38
Short sale	40
Compensation for property	45
Compensation for services	46
Acquisition or disposition by gift	47
Acquisition by inheritance or disposition by bequest	48

Issuer Derivatives

Grant of options	50
Exercise of options	51
Expiration of options	52
Grant of warrants	53
Exercise of warrants	54
Expiration of warrants	55
Grant of rights	56
Exercise of rights	57
Expiration of rights	58
Exercise for cash	59

Third Party Derivatives

Acquisition or disposition (writing) of third party derivative	70
Exercise of third party derivative	71
Other settlement of third party derivative	72
Expiration of third party derivative	73

Miscellaneous

Change in nature of ownership	90
Other	97
Correction of information	99

D Indicate the number of securities, or for debt securities, the aggregate nominal value, of the class held, directly and indirectly, after the transaction is being reported.

E Indicate the nature of ownership, control or direction of the class of securities held using the following codes:

Direct ownership	1
Indirect ownership (identify the registered holder)	2
Control or direction (identify the registered holder)	3

F For securities that are indirectly held, or over which control or direction is exercised, identify the registered holder.

BOX 6   Remarks
Add any explanation necessary to make the report clearly understandable.

If space provided for any item is insufficient, additional sheets may be used. Additional sheets must refer to the appropriate Box and must be properly identified and signed.

Office staff are not permitted to alter a report.

BOX 7   Signature and filing
Sign and date the report.

File one copy of each of the report in each jurisdiction in which the issuer is reporting within the time limits prescribed by the applicable laws of that jurisdiction.

Manually sign the report.

Legibly print or type the name of each individual signing the report.

If the report is filed on behalf of a company, partnership, trust or other entity, legibly print or type the name of that entity after the signature.

If the report is signed on behalf of an individual by an agent, there shall be filed with each jurisdiction in which the report is filed a duly completed power of attorney.

If the report is filed by facsimile in accordance with National instrument 55-102 *System for Electronic Disclosure by Insiders (SEDI)*, the report should be sent to the applicable securities regulatory authority at the fax number set out below.

Alberta Securities Commission
Suite 600, 250 – 5th Street SW
Calgary, AB, T2P 0R4
Attention: Information Officer *
Telephone: (403) 297-6454
Telephone: (403) 297-6156

British Columbia Securities Commission
PO Box 10142, Pacific Centre
701 West Georgia Street
Vancouver, BC, V7Y 1L2
Attention: Supervisor, Insider Reporting *
Telephone: (604) 899-6500 or
(800) 373-6393 (in BC)
Facsimile: (604) 899-6550

The Manitoba Securities Commission
500 – 400 St. Mary Avenue
Winnipeg, MB, R3C 4K5
Attention: Continuous Disclosure *
Telephone: (204) 945-2548
Facsimile: (204) 945-0330

Securities Commission of Newfoundland
P.O. Box 8700, 2nd Floor West Block
Confederation Building
St. John's, NFLD, A1B 4J6
Attention: Director of Securities *
Telephone: (709) 729-4189
Facsimile: (709) 729-6187

Superintendent of Securities
Department of Justice
Government of the Northwest Territories
1st Floor, Stuart M. Hodgson Building
5009-49th Street
P.O. Box 1320
Yellowknife, Northwest Territories, X1A 2L9
Attention: Deputy Superintendent of Securities
Tel: (867) 920-3318
Facsimile: (867) 873-0243

Nova Scotia Securities Commission
Suite 400, 5251 Duke Street
Halifax, Nova Scotia B3J 1P3
Attention: FOI Officer *
Telephone: (902) 424-7768
Facsimile: (902) 424-4625

Government of Nunavut
Legal Registries Division
P.O. Box 100, Station 570
1st Floor, Brown Building
Iqaluit, Nunavut, X0A 0H0
Contact person: Superintendent of Securities
Tel: (867) 975-6590
Fax: (867) 975-6595
Email: legal.registries@gov.nu.ca

Ontario Securities Commission
Suite 1903, Box 55, 20 Queen Street West
Toronto, ON, M5H 3S8
Attention: FOI Coordinator *
Telephone: (416) 593-8314
Facsimile: (416) 593-3666

Office of the Yukon Superintendent of Securities
Government of Yukon Department of Community Services
307 Black Street, 1st Floor
PO Box 2703 (C-6)
Whitehorse, Yukon Y1A 2C6
Telephone: (867)667-5466
Facsimile: (867)393-6251

Autorité des marchés financiers**
Stock Exchange Tower
P.O. Box 246, 22nd Floor
800 Victoria Square
Montreal, PQ, H4Z 1G3
Attention: Responsable de l'accès à l'information
Telephone: (514) 940-2150 or
(800) 361-5072 (in Québec)
Facsimile: (514) 873-3120

Saskatchewan Financial Services Commission
Securities Division
6th Floor, 1919 Saskatchewan Drive
Regina, SK, S4P 3V7
Attention: Director *
Telephone: (306) 787-5645
Facsimile: (306) 787-5899

New Brunswick Securities Commission
85 Charlotte Street, Suite 300
Saint John, NB, E2L 2J2
Attention: Corporate Finance Officer
Telephone: (506) 658-3060 or
(866) 933-2222 (in New Brunswick)

Superintendent of Securities
Government of Prince Edward Island
4th Floor, Shaw Building
95 Rochford Street
P.O. Box 2000
Charlottetown PE C1A 7N8
Tel: (902) 368-4550

*   For questions about the collection and use of personal information

** In Québec questions about the collection and use of personal information may also be addressed to the Commission d'accès à l'information du Québec (1-888-528-7741)

ASC 55-102F6 Rev. 2011/ 05 /01

Note: [01 May 2011] *– The above is a consolidation of 55-102F6. It incorporates the amendments to this document that came into effect on May 6, 2003, June 13, 2008, May 1, 2011, local amendments in Nova Scotia and Yukon as described in CSA Notice 11-320, and local amendments made by Yukon Rule 11-802 and 11-803, PEI Rule 55-802, Nunavut Rule 11-801, NWT Rule 11-801 and Nova Scotia Rule 11-506. This consolidation is provided for your convenience and should not be relied on as authoritative.*

Companion Policy 55-102CP — To National Instrument 55-102 System for Electronic Disclosure by Insiders (SEDI)

PART 1 — PUBLIC AVAILABILITY OF SEDI INFORMATION

1.1 The securities legislation of several provinces requires, in effect, that information filed with the securities regulatory authority or, where applicable, the regulator under such securities legislation, be made available for public inspection during normal business hours except for information that the securities regulatory authority or, where applicable, the regulator,

(a) believes to be personal or other information of such a nature that the desirability of avoiding disclosure thereof in the interest of any affected individual outweighs the desirability of adhering to the principle that information filed with the securities regulatory authority or the regulator, as applicable, be available to the public for inspection, or

(b) in Alberta, considers that it would not be prejudicial to the public interest to hold the information in confidence, or

(c) in Quebec, considers that access to the information could be prejudicial for the affected persons.

Based on the above mentioned provisions of the securities legislation, the securities regulatory authority or the regulator, as applicable, has determined that the information listed in Schedule A to this Companion Policy discloses personal or other information or such a nature that the desirability of avoiding disclosure of this personal or other information in the interests of the affected persons outweighs the desirability of making the information available to the public for inspection. In addition, in Alberta, the securities regulatory authority and the regulator consider that it would not be prejudicial to the public interest to hold the information listed in Schedule A to this Companion Policy in confidence and in Quebec, the security regulatory authority considers that access to the information by the public in general could be prejudicial for the affected persons. Accordingly, the information listed in Schedule A to this Companion Policy will not be made publicly available.

1.2 The securities regulatory authority or the regulator, as applicable, has further determined that, in the case of information filed in SEDI format other than information listed in Schedule A to this Companion Policy, the requirement that this information be made available for public inspection will be satisfied by making the information available on the SEDI web site.

PART 2 — PRODUCTION OF SEDI FILINGS

2.1 The securities legislation of several provinces contains a requirement to produce or make available an original or certified copy of information filed under the securities legislation. The securities regulatory authority or the regulator, as applicable, considers that it may satisfy such a requirement in the case of information filed in SEDI format by providing a printed copy or other output of the information in readable form that contains or is accompanied by a certification by the regulator that the printed copy or output is a copy of the information filed in SEDI format.

PART 3 — JURISDICTION OF FILING

3.1 The SEDI software application located at the SEDI web site does not provide a SEDI user with the functionality to select the jurisdiction(s) in which a SEDI filing is being submitted for filing. However, the securities regulatory authority takes the view that the submission of information in SEDI format in accordance with the National Instrument constitutes the filing of that information under securities legislation if the information is required to be filed under the securities legislation.

PART 4 — DATE OF FILING AND USER REGISTRATION

4.1 The securities regulatory authority takes the view that information filed in SEDI format is, for purposes of securities legislation, filed on the day that the transmission of the information to the SEDI server is completed. Once SEDI receives that information, the system will allow the SEDI user to print a copy of the filed information showing the date and time SEDI received it.

4.2 Subsection 2.5(1) of the National Instrument permits an individual who is a SEDI filer, a filing agent, or an authorized representative of a SEDI filer or filing agent to use SEDI to make SEDI filings. Subsection 2.5(2) of the National Instrument requires such an individual to register before using SEDI to make a SEDI filing. To do so, the individual must complete, and submit, an online user registration form, and must deliver a signed paper copy of the completed user registration form to the SEDI operator, for verification. Until an individual has completed registration as a SEDI user in accordance with subsection 2.5(2) of the National Instrument, the individual cannot use SEDI to make filings.

The SEDI operator will promptly process the signed paper copies of the registration form that it receives for verification. If there is a problem with the verification process, the SEDI operator or the securities regulatory authority, depending on the problem, will work with the registering individual to try to resolve it.

PART 5 — OFFICIAL COPY OF SEDI FILINGS

5.1 For purposes of securities legislation, securities directions or any other related purpose, the securities regulatory authority takes the view that the official record of any information filed in SEDI format by a SEDI filer is the electronic information stored in SEDI.

PART 6 — COLLECTION, USE AND DISCLOSURE OF PERSONAL INFORMATION

6.1 The *Personal Information Protection and Electronic Documents Act* (Canada) (the "Federal Privacy Act") requires an organization that is collecting, using or disclosing personal information to obtain the individual's consent in most circumstances. While certain information filed in SEDI is personal information within the meaning of the Federal Privacy Act, the Act provides an exemption from the consent requirement in respect of personal information that is, by law, collected and placed in a public registry if the collection, use and disclosure relates directly to the purposes for which the personal information appears in the public registry. This exemption is based on the recognition that often there are legitimate primary purposes for which the personal information is collected, used or disclosed and, therefore, as long as the information is collected, used or disclosed for the primary purposes, no consent is required.

In Quebec, the *Act Respecting Access to Documents Held by Public Bodies and the Protection of Personal Information*, R.S.Q. c. A-2.1 (the "Public Sector Act") and the *Act Respecting the Protection of Personal Information in the Private Sector*, R.S.Q. c. P-39.1 (the "Private Sector Act") are both applicable to information filed in SEDI. Under the Public Sector Act, personal information which, by law, is public is not considered to be nominative (or personal) and, therefore, is not confidential. The Private Sector Act, which applies to persons engaged in carrying on an enterprise (excluding a public body within the meaning of the Public Sector Act and any person that holds information on behalf of the public body), requires an individual's consent to the use or disclosure of personal information concerning the individual in most circumstances. Further, this consent must be manifest, free and enlightened, and must be given for specific purposes. However, Bill 122, which will amend the Private Sector Act and which was introduced in the Quebec legislature on May 11, 2000, will harmonize the Private Sector Act with the Public Sector Act. Bill 122 provides that personal information which, by law, is public is not confidential. Consequently, if the Quebec legislature adopts Bill 122, the use and communication of publicly available information filed in SEDI will not be subject to the consent requirement in the Private Sector Act.

6.2 For purposes of determining the scope of the exemption from the consent requirement in the Federal Privacy Act discussed in section 6.1, the securities regulatory authority takes the view that the primary purposes for the collection, use and disclosure of personal information relating to insiders of reporting issuers and their security holdings in these issuers include the following:

(a) protecting the investing public against unfair, improper or fraudulent use of material undisclosed information relating to publicly traded issuers;

(b) enhancing the ability of investors to make well-informed investment decisions;

(c) promoting efficiency in the capital markets;

(d) promoting fair, honest and responsible market practices by market participants; and

(e) promoting confidence in the transparent operation of the capital markets in Canada.

Schedule A — To Companion Policy 55-102CP System for Electronic Disclosure by Insiders (SEDI)

Form 55-102F1 — Insider Profile

The following information filed in Form 55-102F1 Insider Profile will not be made available for public inspection:

1. Name of insider representative (if applicable) (item 2)

2. Insider's address including postal code but excluding municipality (city, town, etc.), province, territory, state and/or country (item 3)

3. Insider's telephone number (item 4)

4. Insider's fax number (if applicable) (item 5)

5. Insider's e-mail address (if applicable) (item 6)

6. Correspondence in English or French (item 7)

7. Confidential question and answer (item 8)

8. Additional contact information (item 13)

Form 55-102F2 — Insider Report

The following information filed in Form 55-102F2 Insider Report will not be made available for public inspection:

1. Private remarks to securities regulatory authority (item 17)

Form 55-102F3 — Issuer Profile Supplement

The following information filed in Form 55-102F3 Issuer Profile Supplement will not be made available for public inspection:

1. Name of insider affairs contact (item 2)

2. Address of insider affairs contact (item 3)

3. Telephone number and e-mail address of insider affairs contact (item 4)

4. Fax number of insider affairs contact (if applicable) (item 5)

5. Confidential question and answer (item 6)

Form 55-102F4 — Issuer Event Report

The following information filed in Form 55-102F4 Issuer Event Report will not be made available for public inspection:

1. Private remarks to securities regulatory authority (item 6)

Form 55-102F5 — SEDI User Registration Form

None of the information submitted in Form 55-102F5 SEDI User Registration Form will be made available for public inspection.

Form 55-102F6 — Insider Report

The following information filed in Form 55-102F6 Insider Report will not be made available for public inspection:

1. Insider's address including postal code but excluding municipality (city, town, etc.), province, territory, state and/or country (Box 3)

2. Insider's telephone number (Box 3)

3. Insider's fax number (Box 3)

4. Correspondence in English or French

Adoption by OSC: 24 O.S.C.B. 6325 (October 19, 2001) and 24 O.S.C.B. 4414 (July 20, 2001); Request for Comments: 23 O.S.C.B. 4427 (June 16, 2000).

Adoption of amendments to Policy: 26 O.S.C.B. 1637 (February 21, 2003) and 28 O.S.C.B. 6231 (August 20, 2005).

Policies and Orders: CSAN 55-305.

Multilateral Instrument 55-103 — Insider Reporting for Certain Derivative Transactions (Equity Monetization)

[Revoked upon the coming into force of NI 55-104]

Final Rule: (2004) 27 O.S.C.B. 2361; Approval by OSC: (2003) 26 O.S.C.B. 7699; Request for Comments: (2003) 26 O.S.C.B. 1805.

Companion Policy 55-103CP — To Multilateral Instrument 55-103 Insider Reporting for Certain Derivative Transactions (Equity Monetization)

[Revoked upon the coming into force of NI 55-104]

Adoption by OSC: (2004) 27 O.S.C.B. 2365 and (2003) 26 O.S.C.B. 7699; Request for Comments: (2003) 26 O.S.C.B. 1805.

National Instrument 55-104 — Insider Reporting Requirements and Exemptions

Date: **January 22, 2010**
33 O.S.C.B. 3673

PART 1 — DEFINITIONS AND INTERPRETATION

1.1 Definitions and interpretation — (1) In this Instrument

"acceptable summary form" means, in relation to the alternative form of insider report described in sections 5.4 and 6.4, an insider report that discloses as a single transaction, with December 31 of the relevant year as the date of the transaction, using an average unit price of the securities,

(a) the total number of securities of the same type acquired under an automatic securities purchase plan or compensation arrangement, or under all such plans or arrangements, for the calendar year; and

(b) the total number of securities of the same type disposed of under all specified dispositions of securities under an automatic securities purchase plan or compensation arrangement, or under all such plans or arrangements, for the calendar year;

"automatic securities purchase plan" means a dividend or interest reinvestment plan, a stock dividend plan, or any other plan established by an issuer or by a subsidiary of an issuer to facilitate the acquisition of securities of the issuer if the timing of acquisitions of securities, the number of securities which may be acquired under the plan by a director or officer of the issuer or of the subsidiary of the issuer, and the price payable for the securities are established in advance by written formula or criteria set out in a plan document and not subject to a subsequent exercise of discretion;

"cash payment option" means a provision in a dividend or interest reinvestment plan under which a participant is permitted to make cash payments to purchase from the issuer, or from an administrator of the plan, securities of the issuer's own issue;

"CEO" means a chief executive officer and any other individual who acts as chief executive officer for an issuer or acts in a similar capacity for the issuer;

"CFO" means a chief financial officer and any other individual who acts as chief financial officer for an issuer or acts in a similar capacity for the issuer;

"compensation arrangement" includes, but is not limited to, an arrangement, whether or not set out in any formal document and whether or not applicable to only one individual, under which cash, securities or related financial instruments, including, for greater certainty, options, stock appreciation rights, phantom shares, restricted shares or restricted share units, deferred share units, performance units or performance shares, stock, stock dividends, warrants, convertible securities, or similar instruments, may be received or purchased as compensation for services rendered, or otherwise in connection with holding an office or employment with a reporting issuer or a subsidiary of a reporting issuer;

"convertible security" means a security of an issuer that is convertible into, or carries the right of the holder to purchase or otherwise acquire, or of the issuer to cause the purchase or acquisition of, a security of the same issuer;

"COO" means a chief operating officer and any other individual who acts as chief operating officer for an issuer or acts in a similar capacity for the issuer;

"credit derivative" means a derivative in respect of which the underlying security, interest, benchmark or formula is, or is related to or derived from, in whole or in part, a debt or other financial obligation of an issuer;

"derivative"

(a) means, other than in New Brunswick, the Northwest Territories, Nunavut, Ontario, Prince Edward Island, Québec and the Yukon Territory, an instrument, agreement, security or exchange contract, the market price, value or payment obligations of which is derived from, referenced to, or based on an underlying security, interest, benchmark or formula;

(b) in New Brunswick, the Northwest Territories, Nunavut, Ontario, Prince Edward Island and the Yukon Territory, has the same meaning as in securities legislation; and

(c) in Québec, has the same meaning as in *The Derivatives Act*;

"dividend or interest reinvestment plan" means an arrangement under which a holder of securities of an issuer is permitted to direct that the dividends, interest or distributions paid on the securities be applied to the purchase, from the issuer or an administrator of the issuer, of securities of the issuer's own issue;

"economic exposure" in relation to an issuer

(a) means, other than in Ontario, the extent to which the economic or financial interests of a person or company are aligned with the trading price of securities of the issuer or the economic or financial interests of the issuer;

(b) in Ontario, has the same meaning as in securities legislation;

"economic interest" in a security or an exchange contract

(a) means, other than in British Columbia, New Brunswick, the Northwest Territories, Nunavut, Ontario, Prince Edward Island, Québec, Saskatchewan and the Yukon Territory,

(i) a right to receive or the opportunity to participate in a reward, benefit or return from a security or an exchange contract, or

(ii) exposure to a risk of a financial loss in respect of a security or an exchange contract;

(b) in British Columbia, New Brunswick, the Northwest Territories, Nunavut, Ontario, Prince Edward Island, Québec, Saskatchewan and the Yukon Territory, has the same meaning as in securities legislation;

"exchange contract"

(a) means, other than in Alberta, British Columbia, New Brunswick and Saskatchewan, a futures contract or an option that meets both of the following requirements:

(i) its performance is guaranteed by a clearing agency; and

(ii) it is traded on an exchange pursuant to standardized terms and conditions set out in that exchange's by-laws, rules or regulatory instruments, at a price agreed on when the futures contract or option is entered into on the exchange;

(b) in Alberta, British Columbia, New Brunswick and Saskatchewan, has the same meaning as in securities legislation;

"exchangeable security" means a security of an issuer that is exchangeable for, or carries the right of the holder to purchase or otherwise acquire, or of the issuer to cause the purchase or acquisition of, a security of another issuer;

"income trust" means a trust or an entity, including corporate and non-corporate entities, the securities of which entitle the holder to net cash flows generated by an underlying business or income-producing properties owned through the trust or by the entity;

"insider report" means a report to be filed by an insider under securities legislation;

"insider reporting requirement" means

(a) a requirement to file insider reports under Parts 3 and 4;

(b) a requirement to file insider reports under any provisions of Canadian securities legislation substantially similar to Parts 3 and 4; and

(c) a requirement to file an insider profile under NI 55-102;

"investment issuer" means, in relation to an issuer, another issuer in respect of which the issuer is an insider;

"issuer event" means a stock dividend, stock split, consolidation, amalgamation, reorganization, merger or other similar event that affects all holdings of a class of securities of an issuer in the same manner, on a per share basis;

"lump-sum provision" means a provision of an automatic securities purchase plan that allows a director or officer to acquire securities in consideration of an additional lump-sum payment, and includes a cash payment option;

"major subsidiary" means a subsidiary of an issuer if

(a) the assets of the subsidiary, as included in the issuer's most recent annual audited or interim balance sheet, or, for a period relating to a financial year beginning on or after January 1, 2011, a statement of financial position, are 30 per cent or more of the consolidated assets of the issuer reported on that balance sheet or statement of financial position, as the case may be, or

(b) the revenue of the subsidiary, as included in the issuer's most recent annual audited or interim income statement, or, for a period relating to a financial year beginning on or after January 1, 2011, a statement of comprehensive income, is 30 per cent or more of the consolidated revenue of the issuer reported on that statement;

"management company" means a person or company established or contracted to provide significant management or administrative services to an issuer or a subsidiary of the issuer;

"NI 55-102" means National Instrument 55-102 *System for Electronic Disclosure by Insiders (SEDI)*;

"normal course issuer bid" means

(a) an issuer bid that is made in reliance on the exemption, contained in securities legislation from requirements relating to issuer bids, that is available if the number of securities acquired by the issuer within a period of twelve months does not exceed 5 per cent of the securities of that class issued and outstanding at the commencement of the period, or

(b) a normal course issuer bid as defined in the rules or policies of the Toronto Stock Exchange, the TSX Venture Exchange or an exchange that is a recognized exchange, as defined in National Instrument 21-101*Marketplace Operation*, and that is conducted in accordance with the rules or policies of that exchange;

"operating entity" means a person or company with an underlying business or with assets owned in whole or in part by an income trust for the purposes of generating cash flow;

"principal operating entity" means an operating entity that is a major subsidiary of an income trust;

"related financial instrument"

(a) means, other than in British Columbia, New Brunswick, the Northwest Territories, Nunavut, Ontario, Prince Edward Island, Québec, Saskatchewan and the Yukon Territory,

(i) an instrument, agreement, security or exchange contract the value, market price or payment obligations of which are derived from, referenced to or based on the value, market price or payment obligations of a security, or,

(ii) any other instrument, agreement, or understanding that affects, directly or indirectly, a person or company's economic interest in a security or an exchange contract;

(b) in British Columbia, New Brunswick, the Northwest Territories, Nunavut, Ontario, Prince Edward Island, Québec, Saskatchewan and the Yukon Territory, has the same meaning as in securities legislation;

"reporting insider" means an insider of a reporting issuer if the insider is

(a) the CEO, CFO or COO of the reporting issuer, of a significant shareholder of the reporting issuer or of a major subsidiary of the reporting issuer;

(b) a director of the reporting issuer, of a significant shareholder of the reporting issuer or of a major subsidiary of the reporting issuer;

(c) a person or company responsible for a principal business unit, division or function of the reporting issuer;

(d) a significant shareholder of the reporting issuer;

(e) a significant shareholder based on post-conversion beneficial ownership of the reporting issuer's securities and the CEO, CFO, COO and every director of the significant shareholder based on post-conversion beneficial ownership;

(f) a management company that provides significant management or administrative services to the reporting issuer or a major subsidiary of the reporting issuer, every director of the management company, every CEO, CFO and COO of the management company, and every significant shareholder of the management company;

(g) an individual performing functions similar to the functions performed by any of the insiders described in paragraphs (a) to (f);

(h) the reporting issuer itself, if it has purchased, redeemed or otherwise acquired a security of its own issue, for so long as it continues to hold that security; or

(i) any other insider that

(i) in the ordinary course receives or has access to information as to material facts or material changes concerning the reporting issuer before the material facts or material changes are generally disclosed; and

(ii) directly or indirectly exercises, or has the ability to exercise, significant power or influence over the business, operations, capital or development of the reporting issuer;

"significant shareholder" means a person or company that has beneficial ownership of, or control or direction over, whether direct or indirect, or a combination of beneficial ownership of, and control or direction over, whether direct or indirect, securities of an issuer carrying more than 10 per cent of the voting rights attached to all the issuer's outstanding voting securities, excluding, for the purpose of the calculation of the percentage held, any securities held by the person or company as underwriter in the course of a distribution;

"stock dividend plan" means an arrangement under which securities of an issuer are issued by the issuer to holders of securities of the issuer as a stock dividend or other distribution out of earnings, retained earnings or capital; and

"underlying security" means a security issued or transferred, or to be issued or transferred, in accordance with the terms of a convertible security, an exchangeable security or a multiple convertible security.

(2) **Affiliate** — In this Instrument, an issuer is an affiliate of another issuer if

(a) one of them is the subsidiary of the other, or

(b) each of them is controlled by the same person or company.

(3) **Control** — In this Instrument, a person or company (first person or company) is considered to control another person or company (second person or company) if

(a) the first person or company beneficially owns or has control or direction over, whether direct or indirect, securities of the second person or company carrying votes which, if exercised, would entitle the first person or company to elect a majority of the directors of the second person or company, unless that first person or company holds the voting securities only to secure an obligation,

(b) the second person or company is a partnership, other than a limited partnership, and the first person or company holds more than 50 per cent of the interests of the partnership, or

(c) the second person or company is a limited partnership and the general partner of the limited partnership is the first person or company.

(4) **Post-conversion beneficial ownership** — In this Instrument, a person or company is considered to have, as of a given date, post-conversion beneficial ownership of a security, including an unissued security, if the person or company is the beneficial owner of a security convertible into the security within 60 days following that date or has a right or obligation permitting or requiring the person or company, whether or not on conditions, to acquire beneficial ownership of the security within 60 days, by a single transaction or a series of linked transactions.

(5) **Significant shareholder based on post-conversion beneficial ownership** — In this Instrument, a person or company is a significant shareholder based on post-conversion beneficial ownership if the person or company is not a significant shareholder but the person or company has beneficial ownership of, post-conversion beneficial ownership of, control or direction over, whether direct or indirect, or any combination of beneficial ownership of, post-conversion beneficial ownership of, or control or direction over, whether direct or indirect, securities of an issuer carrying more than 10 per cent of the voting rights attached to all the issuer's outstanding voting securities, calculated in accordance with subsections (6) and (7).

(6) For the purposes of the calculation in subsection (5), an issuer's outstanding voting securities include securities in respect of which a person or company has post-conversion beneficial ownership.

(7) For the purposes of the calculation in subsections (4) and (5), a person or company may exclude any securities held by the person or company as underwriter in the course of a distribution.

1.2 **Persons and companies designated or determined to be insiders for the purposes of this Instrument** — (1) The following persons and companies are designated or determined to be insiders of an issuer:

(a) a significant shareholder of the issuer based on post-conversion beneficial ownership of the issuer's securities;

(b) a management company that provides significant management or administrative services to the issuer or a major subsidiary of the issuer, and every director, officer and significant shareholder of the management company; and

(c) if the issuer is an income trust, every director, officer and significant shareholder of a principal operating entity of the issuer.

(2) **Issuer as insider of reporting issuer** — If an issuer (the first issuer) becomes an insider of a reporting issuer (the second issuer), the CEO, CFO, COO and every director of the first issuer are designated or determined to be an insider of the second issuer and must file insider reports in accordance with section 3.5 in respect of transactions relating to the second issuer that occurred in the previous six months or for such shorter period that the individual was a CEO, CFO, COO or director of the first issuer.

(3) **Reporting issuer as insider of other issuer** — If a reporting issuer (the first issuer) becomes an insider of another issuer (the second issuer), the CEO, CFO, COO and every director of the second issuer is designated or determined to be an insider of the first issuer and must file insider reports in accordance with section 3.5 in respect of transactions relating to the first issuer that occurred in the previous six months or for such shorter period that the individual was a CEO, CFO, COO or director of the second issuer.

1.3 Reliance on Reported Outstanding Shares — (1) In determining the securityholding percentage of a person or company in a class of securities for the purposes of the definition "significant shareholder" and in determining if the person or company is a significant shareholder based on post-conversion beneficial ownership, the person or company may rely upon information most recently filed by the issuer of the securities in a material change report or under section 5.4 of National Instrument 51-102 *Continuous Disclosure Obligations*, whichever contains the most recent relevant information.

(2) Subsection (1) does not apply if the person or company has knowledge both

> (a) that the information filed is inaccurate or has changed; and

> (b) of the correct information.

PART 2 — APPLICATION

2.1 Insider reporting requirements (insiders of Ontario reporting issuers) — In Ontario, the insider reporting requirements in sections 3.2 and 3.3 do not apply to an insider of a reporting issuer under the *Securities Act* (Ontario).

Note: *In Ontario, requirements similar to the insider reporting requirements in sections 3.2 and 3.3 of this Instrument are contained in section 107 of the* Securities Act *(Ontario).*

2.2 Reporting deadline — In Ontario, for the purposes of subsection 107(2) of the *Securities Act* (Ontario), in the case of a transaction occurring after October 31, 2010, the prescribed period is within five days of any change in the beneficial ownership of, or control or direction over, whether direct or indirect, securities of the reporting issuer or any interest in, or right or obligation associated with, a related financial instrument.

PART 3 — PRIMARY INSIDER REPORTING REQUIREMENT

3.1 Reporting requirement — An insider must file insider reports under this Part and Part 4 in respect of a reporting issuer if the insider is a reporting insider of the reporting issuer.

3.2 Initial report — A reporting insider must file an insider report in respect of a reporting issuer, within 10 days of becoming a reporting insider, disclosing the reporting insider's

> (a) beneficial ownership of, or control or direction over, whether direct or indirect, securities of the reporting issuer, and

> (b) interest in, or right or obligation associated with, a related financial instrument involving a security of the reporting issuer.

3.3 Subsequent report — A reporting insider must within five days of any of the following changes file an insider report in respect of a reporting issuer disclosing a change in the reporting insider's

> (a) beneficial ownership of, or control or direction over, whether direct or indirect, securities of the reporting issuer, or

> (b) interest in, or right or obligation associated with, a related financial instrument involving a security of the reporting issuer.

3.4 Reporting requirements in connection with convertible or exchangeable securities — For greater certainty, a reporting insider who exercises an option, warrant or other convertible or exchangeable security must file, within five days of the exercise, separate insider reports in accordance with section 3.3 disclosing the resulting change in the reporting insider's beneficial ownership of, or control or direction over, whether direct or indirect, each of

> (a) the option, warrant or other convertible or exchangeable security, and

> (b) the common shares or other underlying securities.

3.5 Report by certain designated insiders for certain historical transactions — A CEO, CFO, COO or director of an issuer (the first issuer) who is designated or determined to be an insider of another issuer (the second issuer) under subsection 1.2(2) or 1.2(3) must file, within 10 days of being designated or determined to be an insider of the second issuer, the insider reports that a reporting insider of the second issuer would have been required to file under Part 3 and Part 4 for all transactions involving securities of the second issuer or related financial instruments involving securities of the second issuer, that occurred in the previous six months or for such shorter period that the individual was a CEO, CFO, COO or director of the first issuer.

PART 4 — SUPPLEMENTAL INSIDER REPORTING REQUIREMENT

4.1 Other agreements, arrangements or understandings — (1) If a reporting insider of a reporting issuer enters into, materially amends, or terminates an agreement, arrangement or understanding described in subsection (2), the reporting insider must, within five days of this event, file an insider report in respect of the reporting issuer in accordance with section 4.3.

(2) An agreement, arrangement or understanding must be reported under subsection (1) in an insider report in respect of a reporting issuer if

> (a) the agreement, arrangement or understanding has the effect of altering, directly or indirectly, the reporting insider's economic exposure to the reporting issuer;

> (b) the agreement, arrangement or understanding involves, directly or indirectly, a security of the reporting issuer or a related financial instrument involving a security of the reporting issuer; and

> (c) the reporting insider is not otherwise required to file an insider report in respect of this event under Part 3 or any corresponding provision of Canadian securities legislation.

4.2 Report of prior agreements, arrangements or understandings — A reporting insider must, within 10 days of becoming a reporting insider of a reporting issuer, file an insider report in accordance with section 4.3 in respect of the reporting issuer if

> (a) the reporting insider, prior to the date the reporting insider most recently became a reporting insider, entered into an agreement, arrangement or understanding in respect of which the reporting insider would have been required to file an insider report under section 4.1 if the agreement, arrangement or understanding had been entered into on or after the date the reporting insider most recently became a reporting insider, and

> (b) the agreement, arrangement or understanding remains in effect on or after the date the reporting insider most recently became a reporting insider.

4.3 Contents of report — An insider report required to be filed under section 4.1 or 4.2 must disclose the existence and material terms of the agreement, arrangement or understanding.

PART 5 — EXEMPTION FOR AUTOMATIC SECURITIES PURCHASE PLANS

5.1 Interpretation — (1) In this Part, a reference to a director or officer means a director or officer who is

    (a) a director or officer of a reporting issuer and a reporting insider of the reporting issuer, or

    (b) a director or officer of a subsidiary of a reporting issuer and a reporting insider of the reporting issuer.

(2) In this Part, a reference to a security of a reporting issuer includes a related financial instrument involving a security of the reporting issuer.

(3) In this Part, a disposition or transfer of securities acquired under an automatic securities purchase plan is a specified disposition of securities if

    (a) the disposition or transfer is incidental to the operation of the automatic securities purchase plan and does not involve a discrete investment decision by the director or officer; or

    (b) the disposition or transfer is made to satisfy a tax withholding obligation arising from the distribution of securities under the automatic securities purchase plan and either

        (i) the director or officer has elected that the tax withholding obligation will be satisfied through a disposition of securities, has communicated this election to the reporting issuer or the plan administrator at least 30 days before the disposition and this election is irrevocable as of the 30th day before the disposition; or

        (ii) the director or officer has not communicated an election to the reporting issuer or the plan administrator and, in accordance with the terms of the plan, the reporting issuer or the plan administrator is required to sell securities automatically to satisfy the tax withholding obligation.

5.2 Reporting exemption — (1) The insider reporting requirement does not apply to a director or officer for an acquisition or disposition of securities described in subsection (2) if the director or officer complies with the alternative reporting requirement in section 5.4.

(2) The exemption in subsection (1) applies to

    (a) an acquisition of securities of the reporting issuer under an automatic securities purchase plan, other than an acquisition of securities under a lump-sum provision of the plan; or

    (b) a specified disposition of securities of the reporting issuer under an automatic securities purchase plan.

5.3 Acquisition of options or similar securities — The exemption in section 5.2 does not apply to an acquisition of options or similar securities granted to a director or officer.

5.4 Alternative reporting requirement — (1) A director or officer is exempt under section 5.2 from the insider reporting requirement if the insider files an insider report within the time period described in subsection (2) disclosing, on a transaction-by-transaction basis or in acceptable summary form, each acquisition and each specified disposition of a security under an automatic securities purchase plan that has not previously been disclosed by or on behalf of the director or officer.

(2) The deadline for filing the insider report under subsection (1) is,

    (a) in the case of any securities acquired under the automatic securities purchase plan that have been disposed of or transferred, other than securities that have been disposed of or transferred as part of a specified disposition of securities, within five days of the disposition or transfer; and

    (b) in the case of any securities acquired under the automatic securities purchase plan during a calendar year that have not been disposed of or transferred, and any securities that have been disposed of or transferred as part of a specified disposition of securities, on or before March 31 of the next calendar year.

(3) Subsection (1) does not apply to a director or officer if, at the time the insider report described in subsection (1) is due,

    (a) the director or officer is not a reporting insider; or

    (b) the director or officer is exempt from the insider reporting requirement.

PART 6 — EXEMPTION FOR CERTAIN ISSUER GRANTS

6.1 Interpretation — (1) In this Part, a reference to a director or officer means a director or officer who is

    (a) a director or officer of a reporting issuer and a reporting insider of the reporting issuer, or

    (b) a director or officer of a subsidiary of a reporting issuer and a reporting insider of the reporting issuer.

(2) In this Part, a reference to a security of a reporting issuer includes a related financial instrument involving a security of the reporting issuer.

(3) In this Part, a disposition or transfer of a security acquired under a compensation arrangement is a specified disposition of a security if

    (a) the disposition or transfer is incidental to the operation of the compensation arrangement and does not involve a discrete investment decision by the director or officer; or

    (b) the disposition or transfer is made to satisfy a tax withholding obligation arising from the distribution of a security under the compensation arrangement and either

        (i) the director or officer has elected that the tax withholding obligation will be satisfied through a disposition of securities, has communicated this election to the reporting issuer or the administrator of the compensation arrangement at least 30 days before the disposition and this election is irrevocable as of the 30th day before the disposition; or

        (ii) the director or officer has not communicated an election to the reporting issuer or the administrator of the compensation arrangement and, in accordance with the terms of the arrangement, the reporting issuer or the administrator is required to sell securities automatically to satisfy the tax withholding obligation.

6.2 **Reporting exemption** — The insider reporting requirement does not apply to a director or officer for the acquisition of a security of the reporting issuer, or a specified disposition of a security of the reporting issuer, under a compensation arrangement established by the reporting issuer or by a subsidiary of the reporting issuer, if

(a) the reporting issuer has previously disclosed the existence and material terms of the compensation arrangement in an information circular or other public document filed on SEDAR;

(b) in the case of an acquisition of securities, the reporting issuer has previously filed in respect of the acquisition an issuer grant report on SEDI in accordance with section 6.3; and

(c) the director or officer complies with the alternative reporting requirement in section 6.4.

6.3 **Issuer grant report** — An issuer grant report filed under this Part in respect of a compensation arrangement must include

(a) the date the option or other security was issued or granted;

(b) the number of options or other securities issued or granted to each director or officer;

(c) the price at which the option or other security was issued or granted and the exercise price;

(d) the number and type of securities issuable on the exercise of the option or other security; and

(e) any other material terms that have not been previously disclosed or filed in a public filing on SEDAR.

6.4 **Alternative reporting requirement** — (1) A director or officer is exempt under section 6.2 from the insider reporting requirement if the insider files an insider report within the time period described in subsection (2) disclosing, on a transaction-by-transaction basis or in acceptable summary form, each acquisition and each specified disposition of a security under a compensation arrangement that has not previously been disclosed by or on behalf of the director or officer.

(2) The deadline for filing the insider report under subsection (1) is

(a) in the case of any security acquired under the compensation arrangement that has been disposed of or transferred, other than a security that has been disposed of or transferred as part of a specified disposition of a security, within five days of the disposition or transfer; and

(b) in the case of any security acquired under the compensation arrangement during a calendar year that has not been disposed of or transferred, and any security that has been disposed of or transferred as part of a specified disposition of a security, on or before March 31 of the next calendar year.

(3) Subsection (1) does not apply to a director or officer if, at the time the insider report described in subsection (1) is due,

(a) the director or officer is not a reporting insider; or

(b) the director or officer is exempt from the insider reporting requirement.

PART 7 — EXEMPTIONS FOR NORMAL COURSE ISSUER BIDS AND PUBLICLY DISCLOSED TRANSACTIONS

7.1 **Reporting exemption for normal course issuer bids** — The insider reporting requirement does not apply to an issuer for an acquisition of a security of its own issue by the issuer under a normal course issuer bid if the issuer complies with the alternative reporting requirement in section 7.2.

7.2 **Reporting requirement** — An issuer who relies on the exemption in section 7.1 must file an insider report disclosing each acquisition of securities by it under a normal course issuer bid within 10 days of the end of the month in which the acquisition occurred.

7.3 **General exemption for other transactions that have been otherwise disclosed** — The insider reporting requirement does not apply to an issuer in connection with a transaction, other than a normal course issuer bid, involving a security of its own issue if the existence and material terms of the transaction have been generally disclosed in a public filing on SEDAR.

PART 8 — EXEMPTION FOR CERTAIN ISSUER EVENTS

8.1 **Reporting exemption** — The insider reporting requirement in respect of a reporting issuer does not apply to a reporting insider whose beneficial ownership of, or control or direction over, whether direct or indirect, a security of the reporting issuer changes as a result of an issuer event of the reporting issuer.

8.2 **Reporting requirement** — A reporting insider who relies on the exemption in section 8.1 in respect of a reporting issuer must file an insider report, disclosing all changes in beneficial ownership of, or control or direction over, whether direct or indirect, a security of the reporting issuer as a result of an issuer event if those changes have not previously been reported by or on behalf of the insider, within the time required by securities legislation for the insider to report any other subsequent change in beneficial ownership of, or control or direction over, whether direct or indirect, a security of the reporting issuer.

PART 9 — GENERAL EXEMPTIONS

9.1 **Reporting exemption (mutual funds)** — The insider reporting requirement does not apply to an insider of an issuer that is a mutual fund.

9.2 **Reporting exemption (non-reporting insiders)** — The insider reporting requirement does not apply to an insider of an issuer if the insider is not a reporting insider of that issuer.

9.3 **Reporting exemption (certain insiders of investment issuers)** — The insider reporting requirement does not apply to a director or officer of a significant shareholder, or a director or officer of a subsidiary of a significant shareholder, in respect of securities of an investment issuer or a related financial instrument involving a security of the investment issuer if the director or officer

(a) does not in the ordinary course receive or have access to information as to material facts or material changes concerning the investment issuer before the material facts or material changes are generally disclosed; and

(b) is not a reporting insider of the investment issuer in any capacity other than as a director or officer of the significant shareholder or a subsidiary of the significant shareholder.

9.4 Reporting exemption (nil report) — The insider reporting requirement does not apply to a reporting insider if the reporting insider

(a) does not have any beneficial ownership of, or control or direction over, whether direct or indirect, a security of the issuer;

(b) does not have any interest in, or right or obligation associated with, a related financial instrument involving a security of the issuer;

(c) has not entered into any agreement, arrangement or understanding as described in section 4.1; and

(d) is not a significant shareholder based on post-conversion beneficial ownership.

9.5 Reporting exemption (corporate group) — The insider reporting requirement does not apply to a reporting insider if

(a) the reporting insider is a subsidiary or other affiliate of another reporting insider (the affiliated reporting insider); and

(b) the affiliated reporting insider has filed an insider report in respect of the reporting issuer that discloses substantially the same information as would be contained in an insider report filed by the reporting insider, including details of the reporting insider's

(i) beneficial ownership of, or control or direction over, whether direct or indirect, securities of the reporting issuer; and

(ii) interest in, or right or obligation associated with, any related financial instrument involving a security of the reporting issuer.

9.6 Reporting exemption (executor and co-executor) — The insider reporting requirement does not apply to a reporting insider for a security of an issuer beneficially owned or controlled, directly or indirectly, by an estate if

(a) the reporting insider is an executor, administrator or other person or company who is a representative of the estate (referred to in this section as an executor of the estate), or a director or officer of an executor of the estate;

(b) the reporting insider is subject to the insider reporting requirement solely because of the reporting insider being an executor or a director or officer of an executor of the estate; and

(c) another executor or director or officer of an executor of the estate has filed an insider report that discloses substantially the same information as would be contained in an insider report filed by the reporting insider for securities of an issuer beneficially owned or controlled, directly or indirectly, by the estate.

9.7 Exempt persons and transactions — The insider reporting requirement does not apply to

(a) an agreement, arrangement or understanding which does not involve, directly or indirectly,

(i) a security of the reporting issuer;

(ii) a related financial instrument involving a security of the reporting issuer; or

(iii) any other derivative in respect of which the underlying security, interest, benchmark or formula is or includes as a material component a security of the reporting issuer or a related financial instrument involving a security of the reporting issuer;

(b) a transfer, pledge or encumbrance of a security by a reporting insider for the purpose of giving collateral for a debt made in good faith so long as there is no limitation on the recourse available against the insider for any amount payable under such debt;

(c) the receipt by a reporting insider of a transfer, pledge or encumbrance of a security of an issuer if the security is transferred, pledged or encumbered as collateral for a debt under a written agreement and in the ordinary course of business of the insider;

(d) a reporting insider, other than a reporting insider that is an individual, that enters into, materially amends or terminates an agreement, arrangement or understanding which is in the nature of a credit derivative;

(e) a reporting insider who did not know and, in the exercise of reasonable diligence, could not have known of the alteration to economic exposure described in section 4.1;

(f) the acquisition or disposition of a security, or an interest in a security, of an investment fund, provided that securities of the reporting issuer do not form a material component of the investment fund's market value; or

(g) the acquisition or disposition of a security, or an interest in a security, of an issuer that holds directly or indirectly securities of the reporting issuer, if

(i) the reporting insider is not a control person of the issuer; and

(ii) the reporting insider does not have or share investment control over the securities of the reporting issuer.

Part 10 — Discretionary Exemptions

10.1 Exemptions from this Instrument — (1) The regulator or securities regulatory authority may grant an exemption from this Instrument, in whole or in part, subject to such conditions or restrictions as may be imposed in the exemption.

(2) Despite subsection (1), in Ontario only the regulator may grant such an exemption.

(3) Except in Ontario, an exemption referred to in subsection (1) is granted under the statute referred to in Appendix B of National Instrument 14-101 *Definitions* opposite the name of the local jurisdiction.

Part 11 — Effective Date and Transition

11.1 Effective Date — This Instrument comes into force on April 30, 2010.

(1) Except in Ontario, this Instrument comes into force on April 30, 2010.

(2) In Ontario, this Instrument comes into force on the later of the following:

(a) April 30, 2010; and

(b) the day on which subsection 1(8) and sections 9 and 10 of Schedule Z.5 to Bill 151, Budget Measures Act, 2006 (No. 2) are proclaimed in force.

11.2 Transition — (1) Despite sections 3.3 and 3.4, a reporting insider may file an insider report required by either of those sections within 10 days of a change described in those sections if the change relates to a transaction that occurred on or before October 31, 2010.

(2) Despite section 4.1, a reporting insider may file an insider report required under that section within 10 days of an event described in that section if the event relates to a transaction that occurred on or before October 31, 2010.

(3) Despite paragraph 5.4(2)(a), a reporting insider may file an insider report required under that paragraph within 10 days of a disposition or transfer described in that paragraph if the disposition or transfer occurred on or before October 31, 2010.

(4) Despite paragraph 6.4(2)(a), a reporting insider may file an insider report required under that paragraph within 10 days of a disposition or transfer described in that paragraph if the disposition or transfer occurred on or before October 31, 2010.

Final Rule: (2010) 33 O.S.C.B. 3673; Approval by OSC: (2010) 33 O.S.C.B. 689; Request for Comments: (2008) 31 O.S.C.B. 12117.

Rules: NI 55-102.

Policies and Orders: CSAN 55-312, 55-315, 55-316.

Companion Policy 55-104CP — Insider Reporting Requirements and Exemptions

PART 1 — INTRODUCTION AND DEFINITIONS

1.1 Introduction and Purpose — (1) National Instrument 55-104 *Insider Reporting Requirements and Exemptions* (the Instrument) sets out the principal insider reporting requirements and exemptions for insiders of reporting issuers.[1]

(2) The purpose of this Policy is to help you understand how the Canadian Securities Administrators (the CSA or we) interpret or apply certain provisions of the Instrument.

1.2 Background to the Instrument — (1) The Instrument consolidates the principal insider reporting requirements and most exemptions in one location. This will make it easier for issuers and insiders to locate and understand their obligations and will help promote timely and effective compliance.

(2) The focus of the Instrument is on the substantive legal insider reporting requirements rather than the procedural requirements relating to the filing of insider reports. Issuers and insiders should review National Instrument 55-102 *System for Electronic Disclosure by Insiders (SEDI)* (NI 55-102) in order to determine their obligations for the filing of insider reports.

(3) Although the Instrument sets out the principal insider reporting requirements and exemptions for issuers and insiders in Canada, a number of other CSA instruments also contain exemptions from the insider reporting requirements, including

(a) National Instrument 51-102 *Continuous Disclosure Obligations* (NI 51-102);

(b) National Instrument 62-103 *The Early Warning System and Related Take-Over Bid and Insider Reporting Issues* (NI 62-103);

(c) National Instrument 71-101 *The Multijurisdictional Disclosure System* (NI 71-101); and

(d) National Instrument 71-102 *Continuous Disclosure and Other Exemptions Relating to Foreign Issuers* (NI 71-102).

We have not included the insider reporting exemptions from these instruments in the Instrument because we think these exemptions are better situated within the context of these other instruments. Issuers and insiders therefore may wish to review these instruments in determining whether any additional exemptions from the insider reporting requirements are available.

1.3 Policy Rationale for Insider Reporting in Canada — (1) The insider reporting requirements serve a number of functions. These include deterring improper insider trading based on material undisclosed information and increasing market efficiency by providing investors with information concerning the trading activities of insiders of an issuer, and, by inference, the insiders' views of their issuer's prospects.

(2) Insider reporting also helps prevent illegal or otherwise improper activities involving stock options and similar equity-based instruments, including stock option backdating, option repricing, and the opportunistic timing of option grants (spring-loading or bullet-dodging). This is because the requirement for timely disclosure of option grants and public scrutiny of such disclosure will generally limit opportunities for issuers and insiders to engage in improper dating practices.

(3) Insiders should interpret the insider reporting requirements in the Instrument with these policy rationales in mind and comply with the requirements in a manner that gives priority to substance over form.

1.4 Definitions used in the Instrument — (1) **General** — The Instrument provides definitions of many terms that are defined in the securities legislation of some local jurisdictions but not others. A term used in the Instrument and defined in the securities statute of a local jurisdiction has the meaning given to it in the local securities statute unless: (a) the definition in that statute is restricted to a specific portion of the statute that does not govern insider reporting; or (b) the context otherwise requires.

This means that, in the jurisdictions specifically excluded from the definition, the definition in the local securities statute applies. However, in the jurisdictions not specifically excluded from the definition, the definition in the Instrument applies.

The provincial and territorial regulatory authorities consider the meanings given to these terms in securities legislation to be substantially similar to the definitions set out in the Instrument.

(2) **Directors and Officers** — Where the Instrument uses the term "directors" or "officers", insiders of an issuer that is not a corporation must refer to the definitions in securities legislation of "director" and "officer". The definitions of "director" and "officer" typically include persons acting in capacities similar to those of a director or an officer of a company or individuals who perform similar functions. Corporate and non-corporate issuers and their insiders must determine, in light of the particular circumstances, which individuals or persons are acting in such capacities for the purposes of complying with the Instrument.

Similarly, the terms "CEO", "CFO" and "COO" include the individuals that have the responsibilities normally associated with these positions or act in a similar capacity. This determination is to be made irrespective of an individual's corporate title or whether that individual is employed directly or acts pursuant to an agreement or understanding.

---

[1]In Ontario, the principal insider reporting requirements are set out in Part XXI of the *Securities Act* (Ontario) (the Ontario Act). See Part 2 of this Policy.

(3) **Economic Interest** — The term "economic interest" in a security is a core component of the definition of "related financial instrument" which is part of the primary insider reporting requirement in Part 3 of the Instrument. We intend the term to have broad application and to refer to the economic attributes ordinarily associated in common law with beneficial ownership of a security, including

- the potential for gain in the nature of interest, dividends or other forms of distributions or reinvestments of income on the security;

- the potential for gain in the nature of a capital gain realized on a disposition of the security, to the extent that the proceeds of disposition exceed the tax cost (that is, gains associated with an appreciation in the security's value); and

- the potential for loss in the nature of a capital loss on a disposition of the security, to the extent that the proceeds of disposition are less than the tax cost (that is, losses associated with a fall in the security's value).

For example, a reporting insider who owns securities of his or her reporting issuer could reduce or eliminate the risk associated with a fall in the value of the securities while retaining ownership of the securities by entering into a derivative transaction such as an equity swap. The equity swap would represent a "related financial instrument" since, among other things, the agreement would affect the reporting insider's economic interest in a security of the reporting issuer.

(4) **Economic Exposure** — The term "economic exposure" is used in Part 4 of the Instrument and is part of the supplemental insider reporting requirement. The term generally refers to the link between a person's economic or financial interests and the economic or financial interests of the reporting issuer of which the person is an insider.

For example, an insider with a substantial proportion of his or her personal wealth invested in securities of his or her reporting issuer will be highly exposed to changes in the fortunes of the reporting issuer. By contrast, an insider who does not hold securities of a reporting issuer (and does not participate in a compensation arrangement involving securities of the reporting issuer) will generally be exposed only to the extent of their salary and any other compensation arrangements provided by the issuer that do not involve securities of the reporting issuer.

All other things being equal, if an insider changes his or her ownership interest in a reporting issuer (either directly, through a purchase or sale of securities of the reporting issuer, or indirectly, through a derivative transaction involving securities of the reporting issuer), the insider will generally be changing his or her economic exposure to the reporting issuer. Similarly, if an insider enters into a hedging transaction that has the effect of reducing the sensitivity of the insider to changes in the reporting issuer's share price or performance, the insider will generally be changing his or her economic exposure to the reporting issuer.

(5) **Major Subsidiary** — The definition of "major subsidiary" is a key element of the definition of "reporting insider". The determination of whether a subsidiary is a major subsidiary will generally require a backward-looking determination based on the issuer's most recent financial statements.

If an issuer acquires a subsidiary or undertakes a reorganization, with the result that a subsidiary will come within the definition of major subsidiary once the issuer next files its financial statements, the subsidiary will not be a major subsidiary until such filing, and directors and the CEO, CFO and COO of the subsidiary will not be reporting insiders until such filing.

Although not required to do so, insiders may choose to file insider reports upon completion of the acquisition or reorganization rather than wait for the issuer to file its next set of financial statements. Similarly, if a subsidiary ceases to be a major subsidiary because of an acquisition or other reorganization by the parent issuer, but the subsidiary continues to be a major subsidiary based on information contained within the issuer's most recently filed financial statements, the issuer or reporting insiders may wish to consider applying for an exemption from the insider reporting requirement as the reporting obligation will continue until the issuer next files its financials statements.

(6) **Related Financial Instrument** — Historically, there has been some uncertainty as to whether, as a matter of law, certain derivative instruments involving securities are themselves securities. This uncertainty has resulted in questions as to whether a reporting obligation existed or how insiders should report a derivative instrument. The Instrument resolves this uncertainty by including derivative instruments in the definition of "related financial instrument". Under the Instrument, it is not necessary to determine whether a particular derivative instrument is a security or a related financial instrument since the insider reporting requirement in Part 3 of the Instrument applies to both securities and related financial instruments.

To the extent the following derivative instruments do not, as a matter of law, constitute securities, they will generally be related financial instruments:

- a forward contract, futures contract, stock purchase contract or similar contract involving securities of the insider's reporting issuer;

- options issued by an issuer other than the insider's reporting issuer;

- stock-based compensation instruments, including phantom stock units, deferred share units (DSUs), restricted share awards (RSAs), performance share units (PSUs), stock appreciation rights (SARs) and similar instruments;

- a debt instrument or evidence of deposit issued by a bank or other financial institution for which part or all of the amount payable is determined by reference to the price, value or level of a security of the insider's reporting issuer (a linked note); and

- most other agreements, arrangements or understandings that were previously subject to an insider reporting requirement under former Multilateral Instrument 55-103 *Insider Reporting for Certain Derivative Transactions (Equity Monetization)* (MI 55-103).

(7) **Reporting insider** — We developed the term "reporting insider" specifically for the purposes of the insider reporting requirements and exemptions in the Instrument. It allows us to focus the insider reporting requirement on a core group of persons and companies who in some cases are not "insiders" as defined in securities legislation. There are additional obligations and prohibitions on "insiders" as defined in our Acts, such as the important prohibition on illegal insider trading. The concept of reporting insider is discussed in section 3.1 of this Policy.

1.5 References to the term "day" in the Instrument — References in the Instrument to the term "day" mean calendar day (as opposed to business day). This is consistent with how we use this term elsewhere in securities legislation and the statutory interpretation of the term "day" in each of the CSA jurisdictions.

1.6 Persons and companies designated or determined to be insiders — Section 1.2 of the Instrument designates or determines certain persons and companies to be insiders of a reporting issuer. The Instrument uses the terms "designate" and "determine" since these are the terms used in securities legislation in different jurisdictions. The designation or determination is for the purposes of the insider reporting requirements in the Instrument only. However, in many cases, persons and companies designated or determined to be insiders will also be insiders in another capacity. For example, section 1.2 designates or determines officers and directors of a management company that provides significant management or administrative services to a reporting issuer to be insiders of that reporting issuer. These individuals may also be officers and directors of the reporting issuer under the extended definitions of "officer" and "director" which typically include persons acting in capacities similar to those of a director or an officer or individuals who perform similar functions. The purpose of designating or determining these individuals to be insiders is to clarify these individuals' insider reporting obligations and to avoid uncertainty.

PART 2 — APPLICATION

2.1 Application in Ontario — In Ontario, the insider reporting requirements are set out in Part XXI of the Ontario Act. For this reason, sections 3.2 and 3.3 of the Instrument do not apply in Ontario. However, the insider reporting requirements set out in the Instrument and in Part XXI of the Ontario Act are substantially harmonized. Accordingly, in this Policy, we omit separate references to the requirements of the Ontario Act except where it is necessary to highlight a difference between the requirements of the Instrument and the Ontario Act.

PART 3 — PRIMARY INSIDER REPORTING REQUIREMENT

3.1 Concept of reporting insider — (1) General — Subsection 1.1(1) of the Instrument contains the definition of "reporting insider". The definition represents a principles-based approach to determining which insiders should file insider reports and enumerates a list of insiders whom we think generally satisfy both of the following criteria:

(i) the insider in the ordinary course receives or has access to information as to material facts or material changes concerning the reporting issuer before the material facts or material changes are generally disclosed; and

(ii) the insider directly or indirectly, exercises, or has the ability to exercise, significant power or influence over the business, operations, capital or development of the reporting issuer.

In addition to enumerating a list of insiders, the definition also includes, in paragraph (i), a "basket" provision that explicitly states these two criteria. The basket provision articulates the fundamental principle that an insider who satisfies the criteria of routine access to material undisclosed information concerning a reporting issuer and significant influence over the reporting issuer should file insider reports.

(2) Interpreting the basket criteria — The CSA consider that insiders who come within the enumerated list of positions in the definition of reporting insider will generally satisfy the criteria of routine access to material undisclosed information and significant influence over the reporting issuer. We recognize that this may not always be the case for certain positions in the definition and have therefore included an exemption in section 9.3 of the Instrument for directors and officers of significant shareholders based on lack of routine access to material undisclosed information.

If an insider does not fall within any of the enumerated positions, the insider should consider whether the insider has access to material undisclosed information and has influence over the reporting issuer that is reasonably commensurate with that of one or more of the enumerated positions. If the insider satisfies both of these criteria, the insider will fall within the basket provision of the reporting insider definition.

(3) Meaning of significant power or influence — In determining whether an insider satisfies the significant influence criterion, the insider should consider whether the insider exercises, or has the ability to exercise, significant influence over the business, operations, capital or development of the issuer that is reasonably comparable to that exercised by one or more of the enumerated positions in the definition.

Certain positions or relationships with the issuer may give rise to reporting insider status in the case of certain issuers but not others, depending on the importance of the position or relationship to the business, operations, capital or development of the particular issuer. Similarly, the importance of a position or relationship to an issuer may change over time. For example, the directors and the CEO, CFO and COO of a 20 per cent subsidiary (i.e. not a "major subsidiary", as defined in the Instrument) who are not reporting insiders for any other reason may be reporting insiders prior to and during a significant business acquisition or reorganization, or a market moving announcement.

(4) Exercise of reasonable judgment — The determination of whether an insider is a reporting insider based on the criteria in the basket provision will generally be a question of reasonable judgment. The CSA expect insiders to make reasonable determinations after careful consideration of all relevant facts but recognize that a reasonable determination may not always be a correct determination. The CSA recommend that insiders consult with their issuers when making this determination since confirming that the insider's conclusion is consistent with the issuer's view may help establish that a determination was reasonable. Insiders may also wish to seek professional advice or consider the reporting status of individuals in similar positions with the issuer or other similarly situated issuers.

3.2 Meaning of beneficial ownership — (1) General — The term "beneficial ownership" is not defined in securities legislation. Accordingly, beneficial ownership must be determined in accordance with the ordinary principles of property and trust law of a local jurisdiction. In Québec, due to the fact that the concept of beneficial ownership does not exist in civil law, the meaning of beneficial ownership has the meaning ascribed to it in section 1.4 of Regulation 14-501Q. The concept of beneficial ownership in Québec legislation is often used in conjunction with the concept of control and direction, which allows for a similar interpretation of the concept of common law beneficial ownership in most jurisdictions.

(2) Deemed beneficial ownership — Although securities legislation does not define beneficial ownership, securities legislation in certain jurisdictions may deem a person to beneficially own securities in certain circumstances. For example, in some jurisdictions, a person is deemed to beneficially own securities that are beneficially owned by a company controlled by that person or by an affiliate of such company.

(3) Post-conversion beneficial ownership — Under the Instrument, a person has "post-conversion beneficial ownership" of a security, including an unissued security, if the person is the beneficial owner of a security convertible into the security within 60 days. For example, a person who owns special warrants convertible at any time and without payment of additional consideration into common shares will be considered to have post-conversion beneficial ownership of the underlying common shares. Under the Instrument, a person who has post-conversion beneficial ownership of securities may in certain circumstances be designated or determined to be an insider and may be a reporting insider. For example, if a person owns 9.9% of an issuer's common shares and then acquires special warrants convertible into an additional 5% of the issuer's common shares, the person will be designated or determined to be an insider under section 1.2 of the Instrument and will be a reporting insider under subsection 1.1(1) of the Instrument.

The concept of post-conversion beneficial ownership of the underlying securities into which securities are convertible within 60 days is consistent with similar provisions for determining beneficial ownership of securities for the purposes of the early warning requirements in section 1.8 of National Instrument 62-104 *Take-Over Bids and Issuer Bids*.

(4) Beneficial ownership of securities held in a trust — Under common law trust law, legal ownership is commonly distinguished from beneficial ownership. A trustee is generally considered to be the legal owner of the trust property; a beneficiary, the beneficial owner. Under the Québec civil law, a trust is governed by the Québec Civil Code.

A reporting insider who has a beneficial interest in securities held in a trust may have or share beneficial ownership of the securities for insider reporting purposes, depending on the particular facts of the arrangement and upon the governing law of the trust, whether common law or civil law. We will generally consider a person to have or share beneficial ownership of securities held in a trust if the person has or shares

(a) a beneficial interest in the securities held in the trust and has or shares voting or investment power over the securities held in the trust; or

(b) legal ownership of the securities held in the trust and has or shares voting or investment power over the securities held in the trust.

(5) Disclaimers of beneficial ownership — The CSA generally will not regard a purported disclaimer of a beneficial interest in, or beneficial ownership of, securities as being effective for the purposes of determining beneficial ownership under securities legislation unless such disclaimer is irrevocable and has been generally disclosed to the public.

(6) When ownership passes — Securities legislation of certain local jurisdictions provides that ownership is deemed to pass at the time an offer to sell is accepted by the purchaser or the purchaser's agent or an offer to buy is accepted by the vendor or the vendor's agent. The CSA is of the view that, for the purposes of the insider reporting requirement beneficial ownership passes at the same time.

3.3 Meaning of control or direction — (1) The term "control or direction" is not defined in Canadian securities legislation except in Québec, where the *Securities Act* (Québec), in sections 90, 91 and 92, defines the concept of control and deems situations where a person has control over securities. For purposes of the Instrument, a person will generally have control or direction over securities if the person, directly or indirectly, through any contract, arrangement, understanding or relationship or otherwise has or shares

    (a) voting power, which includes the power to vote, or to direct the voting of, such securities and/or

    (b) investment power, which includes the power to acquire or dispose, or to direct the acquisition or disposition of such securities.

(2) A reporting insider may have or share control or direction over securities through a power of attorney, a grant of limited trading authority, or a management agreement. This would also include a situation where a reporting insider acts as a trustee for an estate (or in Québec as a liquidator) or other trust in which securities of the reporting insider's issuer are included within the assets of the trust. This may also be the case if a spouse (or any other person related to the reporting insider) owns the securities or acts as trustee, but the reporting insider has or shares control or direction over the securities held in trust. In addition, this may be the case where the reporting insider is an officer or director of another issuer that owns securities of the reporting insider's issuer and the reporting insider is able to influence the investment or voting decisions of the issuer.

PART 4 — SUPPLEMENTAL INSIDER REPORTING REQUIREMENT

4.1 Supplemental insider reporting requirement — (1) Part 4 of the Instrument contains the supplemental insider reporting requirement. The supplemental insider reporting requirement is consistent with the predecessor insider reporting requirement for derivatives that previously existed in some jurisdictions under former MI 55-103. However, because Part 3 of the Instrument requires insiders, as part of the primary insider reporting requirement, to file insider reports about transactions involving "related financial instruments", most transactions that were previously subject to a reporting requirement under former MI 55-103 will be subject to the primary insider reporting requirement under Part 3 of the Instrument.

(2) If a reporting insider enters into an equity monetization transaction or other derivative-based transaction that falls outside of the primary insider reporting requirement in Part 3 of the Instrument, the reporting insider must report the transaction under Part 4. For example, certain types of monetization transactions may be found to alter an insider's "economic exposure" to the insider's issuer but not alter the insider's "economic interest in a security". If a reporting insider enters into, materially amends or terminates this type of transaction, the insider must report the transaction under Part 4.

4.2 Insider reporting of equity monetization transactions — (1) What are equity monetization transactions? — There are a variety of sophisticated derivative-based strategies that permit investors to dispose of, in economic terms, an equity position in a public company without attracting certain tax and non-tax consequences associated with a conventional disposition of such position. These strategies, which are sometimes referred to as "equity monetization" strategies, allow an investor to receive a cash amount similar to proceeds of disposition, and transfer part or all of the economic risk and/or return associated with securities of an issuer, without actually transferring ownership of or control over such securities. (The term "monetization" generally refers to the conversion of an asset (such as securities) into cash.)

(2) What are the concerns with equity monetization transactions? — Where a reporting insider enters into a monetization transaction, and does not disclose the existence or material terms of that transaction, there is potential for harm to investors and the integrity of the insider reporting regime because

- an insider in possession of material undisclosed information, although prohibited from trading in securities of the issuer, may be able to profit improperly from such information by entering into derivative-based transactions that mimic trades in securities of the reporting issuer;

- market efficiency will be impaired since the market is deprived of important information relating to the market activities of the insider; and

- since the insider's publicly reported holdings no longer reflect the insider's true economic position in the issuer, the public reporting of such holdings (e.g., in an insider report or a proxy circular) may in fact materially mislead investors.

If a reporting insider enters into a transaction which satisfies one or more of the policy rationales for insider reporting, but for technical reasons it may be argued that the transaction falls outside of the primary insider reporting requirement in Part 3 of the Instrument, the insider will be required to file an insider report under Part 4 unless an exemption is available. In this way, the market can make its own determination as to the significance, if any, of the transaction in question.

PART 5 — AUTOMATIC SECURITIES PURCHASE PLANS

5.1 Automatic Securities Purchase Plans — (1) Section 5.1 of the Instrument contains an interpretation provision that applies to Part 5. Because of this provision, directors and officers of a reporting issuer and of a major subsidiary of a reporting issuer can use the exemption in this Part for both acquisitions and specified dispositions of securities and related financial instruments under an automatic securities purchase plan (ASPP).

(2) The exemption does not apply to securities acquired under a cash payment option of a dividend or interest reinvestment plan or a lump-sum provision of a share purchase plan.

(3) The exemption does not apply to an "automatic securities disposition plan" (sometimes referred to as a "pre-arranged structured sales plan") (an ASDP) established between a reporting insider and a broker, since an ASDP is designed to facilitate dispositions not acquisitions. However, if a reporting insider can demonstrate that an ASDP is genuinely an automatic plan and that the insider cannot make discrete investment decisions through the plan, we may consider granting exemptive relief on an application basis to permit the insider to file reports on an annual basis.

(4) The exemption is not available for a grant of options or similar securities to reporting insiders, since, in many cases, the reporting insider will be able to make an investment decision in respect of the grant. If an insider is an executive officer or a director of the reporting issuer or a major subsidiary, the insider may be participating in the decision to grant the options or other securities. Even if the insider does not participate in the decision, we think information about options or similar securities granted to this group of insiders is important to the market and the insider should disclose this information in a timely manner.

5.2 Specified Dispositions of Securities — (1) Paragraph 5.1(3)(a) of the Instrument provides that a disposition or transfer of securities is a specified disposition if, among other things, it does not involve a "discrete investment decision" by the director or officer. The term "discrete investment decision" generally refers to the exercise of discretion involved in a specific decision to purchase, hold or sell a security. The purchase of a security as a result of the application of a pre-determined, mechanical formula does not generally represent a discrete investment decision (other than the initial decision to enter into the plan). For example, for an individual who holds stock options in a reporting issuer, the decision to exercise the stock options will generally represent a discrete investment decision. If the individual is a reporting insider, we think the individual should report this information in a timely fashion, since this decision may convey information that other market participants may consider relevant to their own investing decisions.

(2) The definition of "specified disposition of securities" contemplates, among other things, a disposition made to satisfy a tax withholding obligation arising from the acquisition of securities under an ASPP in certain circumstances. Under some types of ASPPs, an issuer or plan administrator may sell, on behalf of a plan participant, a portion of the securities that would otherwise be distributed to the plan participant in order to satisfy a tax withholding obligation. In such plans, the participant typically may elect either to provide the issuer or the plan administrator with a cheque to cover this liability or to direct the issuer or plan administrator to sell a sufficient number of the securities that would otherwise be distributed to cover this liability. In many cases, for reasons of convenience, a plan participant will simply direct the issuer or the plan administrator to sell a portion of the securities.

Although we think that the election as to how a tax withholding obligation will be funded contains an element of a discrete investment decision, we are satisfied that, where the election occurs sufficiently in advance of the actual disposition of securities, it is acceptable for a report of a disposition made to satisfy a tax withholding obligation to be made on an annual basis. Accordingly, a disposition made to satisfy a tax withholding obligation will be a specified disposition of securities if it meets the criteria contained in paragraph 5.1(3)(b) of the Instrument.

5.3 Alternative Reporting Requirements — If securities acquired under an ASPP are disposed of or transferred, other than through a specified disposition of securities, and the insider has not previously disclosed the acquisition of these securities, the insider report should disclose, for each acquisition of securities which the insider is now disposing of or transferring, information about the date of acquisition of the securities, the number of securities acquired and the acquisition price of such securities. The report should also disclose, for each disposition or transfer, information about each disposition or transfer of securities.

5.4 Exemption from the Alternative Reporting Requirement — The rationale underlying the alternative reporting requirement is the need for reporting insiders to periodically update their publicly disclosed holdings to ensure that their publicly disclosed holdings convey an accurate picture of their holdings. If an individual has ceased to be subject to the insider reporting requirements at the time the alternative report becomes due, the market generally would not benefit from the information in the alternative report. Accordingly, we provided an exemption in subsection 5.4(3) of the Instrument in these circumstances.

5.5 Design and Administration of Plans — (1) Part 5 of the Instrument provides a limited exemption from the insider reporting requirement only in circumstances in which an insider, by virtue of participation in an ASPP, is not making discrete investment decisions for acquisitions under such plan. Accordingly, if it is intended that insiders of an issuer rely on this exemption for a particular plan of an issuer, the issuer should design and administer the plan in a manner that is consistent with this limitation.

(2) To fit within the definition of an ASPP, the plan must set out a written formula or criteria for establishing the timing of the acquisitions, the number of securities that the insider can acquire and the price payable. If a plan participant is able to exercise discretion in relation to these matters either in the capacity of a recipient of the securities or through participating in the decision-making process of the issuer making the grant, he or she may be able to make a discrete investment decision in respect of the grant or acquisition. We think a reporting insider in these circumstances should disclose information about the grant within the normal timeframe and not on a deferred basis.

PART 6 — ISSUER GRANT REPORTS

6.1 Overview — (1) Section 6.1 of the Instrument contains an interpretation provision that applies to Part 6. Because of this provision, directors and officers of a reporting issuer or a major subsidiary of a reporting issuer who are reporting insiders of the reporting issuer can use the exemption in this Part for grants of securities and related financial instruments.

(2) A reporting insider who intends to rely on the exemption in Part 6 for a grant of stock options or similar securities must first confirm that the issuer has made the public disclosure required by section 6.3 of the Instrument. If the issuer has not made the required disclosure within the required time, the reporting insider must report the grant within the required time and in accordance with the normal reporting requirements under Part 3 of the Instrument.

6.2 Policy rationale for the issuer grant report exemption — (1) The issuer grant report exemption reduces the regulatory burden on insiders that is associated with insider reporting of stock options and similar instruments since it allows an issuer to make a single filing on SEDI. This filing provides the market with timely information about the existence and material terms of the grant, making it unnecessary for each of the affected reporting insiders to file an insider report about the grant within the ordinary time periods.

(2) The concept of an issuer grant report is generally similar to the concept of an issuer event report in that the decision to make the grant originates with the issuer. Accordingly, at the time of the grant, the issuer will generally be in a better position than the reporting insiders who are the recipients of the grant to communicate information about the grant to the market in a timely manner.

(3) There is no obligation for an issuer to file an issuer grant report for a grant of stock options or similar instruments. An issuer may choose to do so to assist its reporting insiders with their reporting obligations and to communicate material information about its compensation practices to the market in a timely manner.

(4) If an issuer chooses not to file an issuer grant report, the issuer should take all reasonable steps to notify reporting insiders of their grants in a timely manner to allow reporting insiders to comply with their reporting obligations.

(5) The concept of an issuer grant report is different from the issuer event report that an issuer is required to make under Part 2 of NI 55-102 in that an issuer is not required to file an issuer grant report.

6.3 Format of an issuer grant report — There is no required format for an issuer grant report. However, an issuer grant report must include the information required by section 6.3 of the Instrument.

PART 7 — EXEMPTIONS FOR NORMAL COURSE ISSUER BIDS AND PUBLICLY DISCLOSED TRANSACTIONS

7.1 Introduction — Under securities legislation, a reporting issuer may become an insider of itself in certain circumstances and therefore subject to an insider reporting requirement in relation to transactions involving its own securities. Under the definition of "insider" in securities legislation, a reporting issuer becomes an insider of itself if it "has purchased, redeemed or otherwise acquired a security of its own issue, for so long as it continues to hold that security". In certain jurisdictions, a reporting issuer may also become an insider of itself if it acquires and holds securities of its own issue through an affiliate, because in certain jurisdictions a person is deemed to beneficially own securities beneficially owned by affiliates. Where a reporting issuer is an insider of itself, the reporting issuer will also be a reporting insider under the Instrument.

7.2 General exemption for transactions that have been generally disclosed — Section 7.3 of the Instrument provides that the insider reporting requirement does not apply to an issuer in connection with a transaction, other than a normal course issuer bid, involving securities of its own issue if the existence and material terms of the transaction have been generally disclosed in a public filing made on SEDAR. Because of this exemption and the exemption for normal course issuer bids in section 7.1, a reporting issuer that is an insider of itself will not generally need to file insider reports under Part 3 or Part 4 provided the issuer complies with the alternative reporting requirement in section 7.2 of the Instrument.

PART 8 — EXEMPTION FOR CERTAIN ISSUER EVENTS

8.1 [Intentionally left blank]

PART 9 — EXEMPTIONS

9.1 Scope of exemptions — The exemptions under the Instrument are only exemptions from the insider reporting requirements contained in the Instrument and are not exemptions or defences from the provisions in Canadian securities legislation imposing liability for improper insider trading.

9.2 Reporting Exemption — The definition of "reporting insider" includes certain enumerated persons or companies that generally satisfy the criteria contained in subsection (i) of the definition of reporting insider, namely, routine access to material undisclosed information and significant power or influence over the reporting issuer. Although there is no general exemption for the enumerated persons or companies based on lack of routine access to material undisclosed information or lack of power or influence, we will consider applications for exemptive relief where the issuer or reporting insider can demonstrate that the reporting insider does not satisfy these criteria. This might include, for example, a situation where a foreign subsidiary may appoint a locally resident individual as a director to meet residency requirements under applicable corporate legislation, but remove the individual's powers and liabilities through a unanimous shareholder declaration.

9.3 Reporting Exemption (certain directors and officers of insider issuers) — The reference to "material facts or material changes concerning the investment issuer" in section 9.3 of the Instrument is intended to include information that originates at the insider issuer level but which concerns or is otherwise relevant to the investment issuer. For example, in the case of an issuer that has a subsidiary investment issuer, a decision at the parent issuer level that the subsidiary investment issuer will commence or discontinue a line of business would generally represent a "material fact or material change concerning the investment issuer". Similarly, a decision at the parent issuer level that the parent issuer will seek to sell its holding in the subsidiary investment issuer would also generally represent a "material fact or material change concerning the investment issuer." Accordingly, a director or officer of the parent issuer who routinely had access to such information concerning the investment issuer would not be entitled to rely on the exemption for trades in securities of the investment issuer.

9.4 Exemption for a pledge where there is no limitation on recourse — The exemption in paragraph 9.7(b) of the Instrument is limited to pledges of securities in which there is no limitation on recourse since a limitation on recourse may effectively allow the borrower to "put" the securities to the lender to satisfy the debt. The limitation on recourse may effectively represent a transfer of the risk that the securities may fall in value from the insider to the lender. In these circumstances, the transaction should be transparent to the market.

A loan secured by a pledge of securities may contain a term limiting recourse against the borrower to the pledged securities (a legal limitation on recourse). Similarly, a loan secured by a pledge of securities may be structured as a limited recourse loan if the loan is made to a limited liability entity (such as a holding corporation) owned or controlled by the insider (a structural limitation on recourse). If there is a limitation on recourse as against the insider either legally or structurally, the exemption would not be available.

9.5. Exemption for certain investment funds — The exemption in paragraph 9.7(f) of the Instrument is limited to situations where securities of the reporting issuer do not form a material component of the investment fund's market value. In determining materiality, similar considerations to those involved in the concepts of material fact and material change would apply.

PART 10 — CONTRAVENTION OF INSIDER REPORTING REQUIREMENTS

10.1 Contravention of insider reporting requirements — (1) It is an offence to fail to file an insider report in accordance with the filing deadlines prescribed by the Instrument or to submit information in an insider report that, in a material respect and at the time and in the light of the circumstances in which it is submitted, is misleading or untrue.

(2) A failure to file an insider report in a timely manner or the filing of an insider report that contains information that is materially misleading may result in one or more of the following

- the imposition of a late filing fee;

- the reporting insider being identified as a late filer on a public database of late filers maintained by certain securities regulators;

- the issuance of a cease trade order that prohibits the reporting insider from directly or indirectly trading in or acquiring securities or related financial instruments of the applicable reporting issuer or any reporting issuer until the failure to file is corrected or a specified period of time has elapsed; or

- in appropriate circumstances, enforcement proceedings.

(3) Members of the CSA may also consider information relating to wilful or repeated non-compliance by directors and executive officers of a reporting issuer with their insider reporting obligations in the context of a prospectus review or continuous disclosure review, since this may raise questions relating to the integrity of the insiders and the adequacy of the issuer's policies and procedures relating to insider reporting and insider trading.

PART 11 — INSIDER TRADING

11.1 Non-reporting insiders — Insiders who are not reporting insiders are still subject to the provisions in Canadian securities legislation prohibiting improper insider trading.

11.2 Written disclosure policies — National Policy 51-201 *Disclosure Standards* outlines detailed best practices for issuers for disclosure and information containment and provides interpretive guidance of insider trading laws. We recommend that issuers adopt written disclosure policies to assist directors, officers, employees and other representatives in discharging timely disclosure obligations. Written disclosure policies also should provide guidance on how to maintain the confidentiality of corporate information and to prevent improper trading based on inside information. Adopting the CSA best practices may assist issuers to ensure that they take all reasonable steps to contain inside information.

11.3 Insider Lists — Reporting issuers may also wish to consider preparing and periodically updating a list of the persons working for them or their affiliates who have access to material facts or material changes concerning the reporting issuer before those facts or changes are generally disclosed. This type of list may allow reporting issuers to control the flow of undisclosed information. The CSA may request additional information from time to time, including asking the reporting issuer to prepare and provide a list of insiders and reporting insiders, in the context of an insider reporting review.

Adoption by OSC: (2010) 33 O.S.C.B. 689; Request for Comments: (2009) 32 O.S.C.B. 12117.

Amendment to Policy: (2016) 39 O.S.C.B. (Supp. 1) 55

CSA Staff Notice 55-312 — Insider Reporting Guidelines for Certain Derivative Transactions (Equity Monetization) (Revised)

Date: February 27, 2004 as revised June 11, 2010

27 O.S.C.B. 2309 and 33 O.S.C.B. 5205

Purpose

The purpose of this notice is to provide guidance to reporting insiders[1] in relation to the reporting of certain derivative-based transactions, including transactions that are commonly referred to as "equity monetization" transactions.

The staff of the Canadian Securities Administrators have prepared this notice to assist reporting insiders who have entered into such transactions and to promote consistency in filings. The notice contains a number of examples of arrangements and transactions involving derivatives together with examples of how to report these arrangements and transactions. The instructions contained in this notice are guidelines only, and do not necessarily represent the only way that such arrangements and transactions may be reported.

If you have questions or comments with respect to the contents of this notice, please feel free to contact a member of staff. Contact information is included at the end of this notice. This notice is dated June 11, 2010. We may from time to time reissue this notice to reflect frequently asked questions or concerns.

Background

1. — What are equity monetization transactions?

Equity monetization transactions are derivative-based transactions that allow an investor to receive a cash amount similar to proceeds of disposition, and to transfer part or all of the economic risk and/or return associated with securities of an issuer, without actually transferring ownership of or control over such securities. (The term "monetization" generally refers to the conversion of an asset (such as securities) into cash.)

You can find more information about how to file insider reports, including insider reports about equity monetization transactions and other derivative-based transactions, in the following materials:

- National Instrument 55-102 *System for Electronic Disclosure By Insiders (SEDI)* (NI 55-102)

- Companion Policy 55-102CP *System for Electronic Disclosure By Insiders (SEDI)* (55-102CP)

- National Instrument 55-104 *Insider Reporting Requirements and Exemptions* (NI 55-104)

- Companion Policy 55-104CP *Insider Reporting Requirements and Exemptions* (55-104CP)

- CSA Staff Notice 55-315 *Frequently Asked Questions about National Instrument 55-104 Insider Reporting Requirements and Exemptions*

- CSA Staff Notice 55-316 *Questions and Answers on Insider Reporting and the System for Electronic Disclosure by Insiders (SEDI)* (SN 55-316)

- SEDI online help relating to Third-Party Derivatives (available by clicking "help" at any time once you are in the SEDI website (www.sedi.ca)).

---

[1]Prior to April 30, 2010, Canadian securities legislation generally required all persons and companies who are "insiders" (as defined in securities legislation) to file insider reports unless they had an exemption from the insider reporting requirement. On April 30, 2010, the Canadian Securities Administrators introduced a new insider reporting regime established by NI 55-104. Under NI 55-104, the insider reporting requirement is generally limited to "reporting insiders" (as defined in NI 55-104) and certain persons who may be designated insiders for certain historical transactions (see s. 3.5 of NI 55-104). For convenience, this notice will refer to insiders subject to a reporting requirement as "reporting insiders".

These materials are available at the websites of the securities regulatory authorities indicated below:

- www.bcsc.bc.ca
- www.albertasecurities.com
- www.sfsc.gov.sk.ca
- www.msc.gov.mb.ca
- www.osc.gov.on.ca
- www.lautorite.qc.ca
- www.nbsc-cvmnb.ca

2. — How are these transactions reported in SEDI?

We have set out below a number of examples of arrangements and transactions involving derivatives together with examples of how to report these arrangements and transactions in SEDI.

The first example is considered in detail. The subsequent examples generally refer the reader back to the step-by-step approach taken in the first example, highlighting necessary changes.

The examples discussed in this notice have necessarily been simplified and are for illustrative purposes only. The examples assume the following set of facts:

ABC Inc. is a reporting issuer. John is a director of ABC Inc. and is therefore a reporting insider (as defined in NI 55-104) of ABC Inc. On March 1, 2010, John acquired 10 shares of ABC Inc. at a fair market value (FMV) price of $10 per share. On March 1, 2011, shares of ABC Inc. have a FMV of $100 per share. John does not wish to sell the shares, but is concerned that the shares might fall in value, and wishes to protect at least $80 of the gain (that is, to "lock in" the share price at at least $90).

The examples also assume that the following necessary preliminary steps have been taken:

- ABC Inc. has completed an issuer profile supplement;
- John has a valid SEDI user ID and password;
- John has created his insider profile in SEDI and has his insider access key; and
- John has previously added ABC Inc. to his insider profile.

For additional information about filing an insider report under SEDI, please refer to 55-102CP, SN 55-316 and the SEDI online help available on the SEDI website (www.sedi.ca).

Example 1

On March 1, 2011, John enters into a **forward contract** with InvestBank under which John agrees to sell, and InvestBank agrees to purchase, 10 shares of ABC Inc. at a price of $109.50 per share.[2] The sale will take place on March 1, 2016. The parties may settle their obligations under the forward contract on a cash settlement basis or by physical delivery of 10 ABC Inc. shares. This contract may be settled at an earlier date, subject to an adjustment to the settlement price. InvestBank hedges its risk under the forward contract through a hedging strategy involving short sales into the secondary market.

Insider Reporting Requirement: John is required to file an insider report within five (calendar) days of March 1, 2011. (See Part 3 of NI 55-104.) For an example of how this transaction would be reported, see below. Unless InvestBank is also a reporting insider of ABC Inc., InvestBank is not required to file an insider report.

Instructions for Example 1

Note: John has accessed the SEDI website at www.sedi.ca, selected "English" as his language of preference, selected "login" at the "Welcome to SEDI" screen, and has logged in by entering his SEDI user ID and his password. John will now see the following screen: "Insider home page".

1. Enter your **insider access key** and click **Next.**

SCREEN: Insider activities

2. Click **Insider report** (at the top of the screen).

SCREEN: Introduction to insider report activities (Form 55-102F2)

3. Click **File insider report** (on the navigation bar at the left of the screen)

SCREEN: File insider report (Form 55-102F2) — Select issuer

4. Select and highlight "ABC Inc." in the list of issuers from the insider profile.

---

[2]In this example, $90 is assumed to represent the present value of $109.50 on March 1, 2016. Assuming an annual compounding of 4%, John and InvestBank are in the same position (absent any consideration of taxes) whether they proceed by way of a sale today at $90 or a sale five years from today at $109.50. In the case of a sale today, John receives $90, which he may then invest at 4%. Assuming an annual compounding return of 4%, at the end of five years, John will have received cash in the amount of $109.50. In the case of the forward sale at the end of five years, John will have received cash in the amount of $109.50.

5. Click **File insider report**.

SCREEN: File insider report — Select security designation

6. Click on **Add insider-defined security** (at the bottom of the screen).

Note: Since the forward contract is not a class of security defined by the issuer in its issuer profile supplement, it will be necessary for John to create a new insider-defined security designation for the forward contract.

Note: In SEDI, third-party derivative arrangements are considered to be "securities". Such arrangements may or may not be considered "securities" under securities law generally, depending upon the facts and circumstances of the arrangement in question. To the extent derivative instruments do not, as a matter of law, constitute securities, they will generally be related financial instruments. See commentary in subsection 1.4(6) of 55-104CP. For insider reporting purposes, it is not necessary to determine whether a derivative instrument is a security or a related financial instrument since both are subject to insider reporting requirements under Part 3 of NI 55-104.

SCREEN: Pop-up warning

Note: At this point, a warning pop-up box should appear: "Warning: You are about to specify an insider-defined security. You must ensure that the security is not already listed."

7. Click **OK.**

SCREEN: File insider report — Add insider-defined security designation

8. Use the drop-down menu under the heading **Security category**, select and highlight **Third Party Derivatives**.

9. Under the heading **Security designation**, in the drop-down menu under the subheading **Security name**, select and highlight **Forward Sale**.

10. Then, for the **Additional description**, briefly describe. For example, "10 common shares — settlement date March 2016".

Note: This adds the security designation "Forward sale (10 common shares — settlement date March 2016)" to your list of insider-defined securities.

*Note: Not all of this text will currently be visible in the **Additional description** box. (The box will only show a limited number of characters at any one time.) However, the full text in this example will be accepted, and will be visible at later stages of the filing process.*

11. Under the heading **Underlying security designation**, in the drop-down menu under the subheading **Security category**, select and highlight **Equity**.

12. Then, in the drop-down menu under the subheading **Security name**, select and highlight **Common Shares**.

Note: In the context of a forward sale, the underlying security is the security that is the subject of the forward sale.

13. Click **Next**.

SCREEN: File insider report — Select ownership type

14. In the drop-down menu **Ownership type**, select and highlight **Direct Ownership** and click **Next.**

SCREEN: File insider report — opening balance on initial SEDI report

*Note: SEDI requires an opening balance for each type of security. This has to be entered before a report can be filed about a transaction in the security. If the reporting insider has never filed a report about this specific type of security, the reporting insider must enter **0** (zero) as the opening balance. If John has previously entered into another forward contract that has different terms (e.g., a different settlement date or price) from the present forward contract, the present contract would be considered a separate type of security.*

15. In the field **Opening balance of securities or contracts held**, enter **0**.

16. In the field **Opening balance of equivalent number or value of underlying securities**, enter **0.**

*Note: This screen contains additional fields: **General remarks** and **Private remarks to securities regulatory authorities**. In this example, it is not necessary to include any information here.*

17. Click **Next** (at the bottom of the screen).

SCREEN: File insider report — Final review

18. Click **Certify**.

SCREEN: Certification

19. Click **OK** to Accept.

SCREEN: File insider report — Completed

Note: John has now filed his opening balance for the security designated "Forward sale (10 common shares — settlement date March 2016)". It is now necessary to file a report about the transaction involving this security entered into on March 1, 2011.

20. At the prompt *"File another transaction?"* click **Yes**.

SCREEN: File insider report — Select a transaction option

Note: Make sure "Same security & holder" is selected.

SCREEN: File insider report — Enter transaction information

21. In the **Date of transaction** field, select **March 1, 2011**.

Note: Since John entered into the forward contract on March 1, 2011, enter this date. Do not enter the date of the anticipated settlement (i.e., March 1, 2016) here.

22. In the drop-down menu **Nature of transaction**, select and highlight the appropriate code. Since John has acquired rights and obligations under a derivative contract, select "70 — Acquisition or disposition (writing) of third party derivative".

Note: For information about "nature of transaction" codes, see the online help function on SEDI.

23. Enter a number in the **Number or value of securities or contracts acquired** field. Enter **1** here.

*Note: Since John has acquired rights and obligations under a derivative contract, enter **1** after the field **Number or value of securities or contracts acquired**. Leave the **Number or value of securities or contracts disposed of** field blank.*

Note: Since John has specified a derivative as the security, there are additional fields in which to enter the equivalent number or value of the underlying securities to which the derivative relates.

24. Enter a number in the **Equivalent number or value of underlying securities disposed of** field. Enter **10** here.

25. Next to the field **Unit price or exercise price**, click the **Not Applicable** box.

26. In the field **Conversion or exercise price**, enter **109.50**.

*Note: Since John has not paid any consideration (in this example) for the forward contract, he would click the **Not Applicable** box next to the field **Unit price or exercise price**. Since the forward contract obliges John to sell 10 ABC Inc. shares at $109.50 per share on March 1, 2016, John would enter **109.50** in the field **Conversion or exercise price**.*

27. In the **Date of expiry or maturity** field, select **March 1, 2016**.

Note: Since the anticipated date of settlement is March 1, 2016, this will be the date of expiry or maturity.

28. Enter the following information in the **General remarks** field:

> Forward contract to sell 10 shares at $109.50 per share on March 1, 2016. Contract may be settled by cash or by delivery of 10 shares. Contract may be settled at earlier date, subject to price adjustment.

*Note: If it is not possible to adequately describe a transaction or to include all of the material terms of a transaction in the space provided, consider making reference to a public document (e.g., a news release issued by the issuer) that further describes the transaction. Alternatively, this information may be included in a schedule that may be filed in paper format by facsimile in accordance with the provisions of Part 3 of NI 55-102. Fax the schedule to the facsimile number of the securities commission set out on Form 55-102F6. We recommend that you make reference to this filing by facsimile in the **General remarks** field on SEDI. Staff will make this schedule available to the public on request.*

29. Enter additional information, as necessary, in the **Private remarks to securities regulatory authorities** field.

Note: This is an optional field. These remarks will only be accessible by securities regulatory authorities. Leave this field blank if no remarks are necessary.

SUMMARY — The information should appear as follows:

File insider report - Enter transaction information

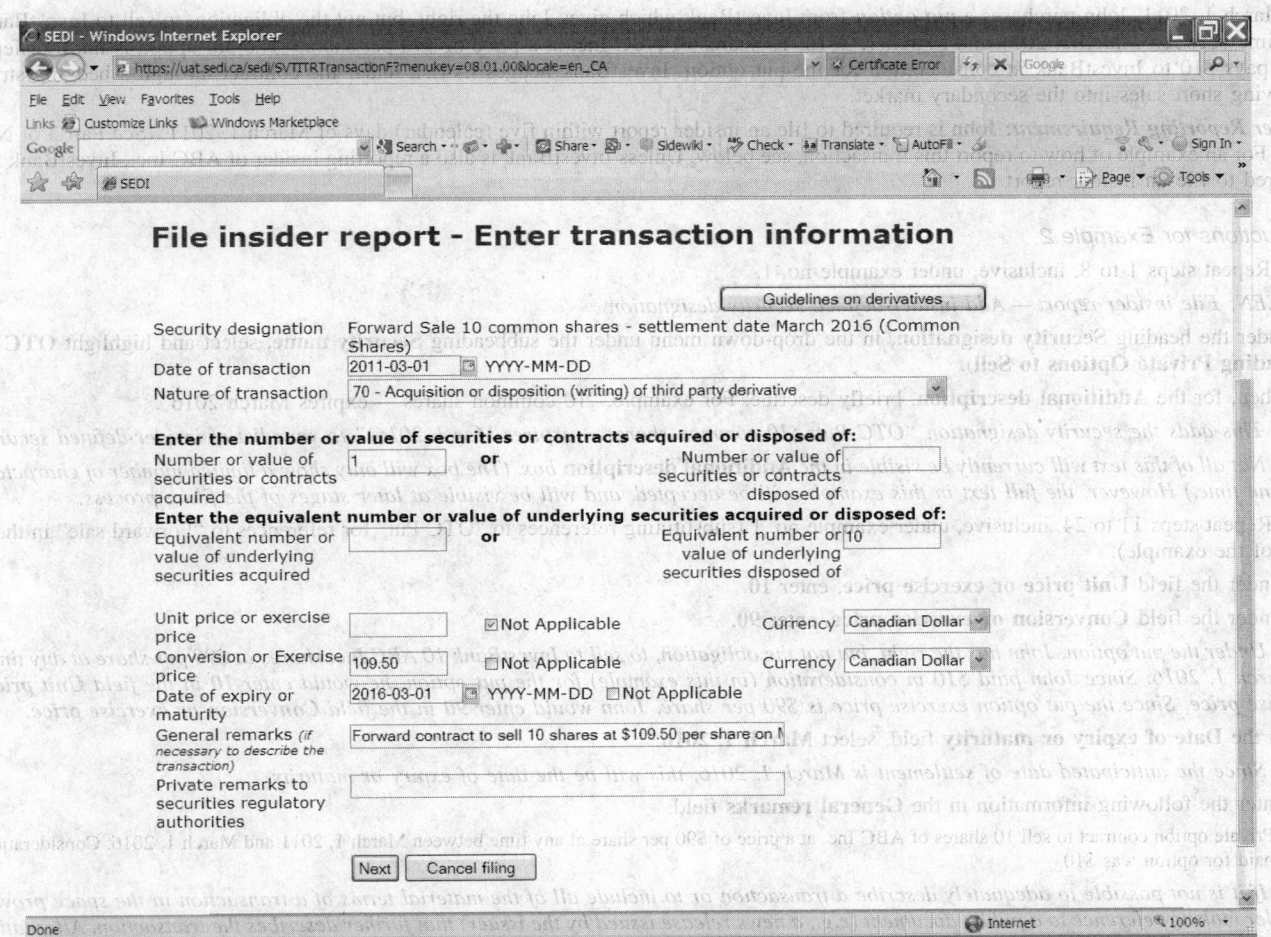

30. Click **Next**.

SCREEN: File insider report — Final review

31. Ensure that the details of your report are complete and accurate.

32. Click **Certify** (at the bottom of the screen).

SCREEN: Certification Pop-Up

33. Review the certification information carefully.

34. Click **OK** to accept.

SCREEN: File insider report — Completed

35. At the prompt "*File another transaction?*" click **No**.

36. Logout

John has now completed the filing of his insider report relating to the forward contract. This report will normally be publicly available on SEDI within five minutes of filing.

Note: Generally, where a reporting insider files an insider report in respect of a third-party derivative such as a forward contract, the reporting insider will be required to file a second report at the time the derivative is settled, matures or otherwise closed out. For example, John in this example will be required to file an insider report within five days of March 1, 2016 (assuming that the contract settles on that date and that John is still a reporting insider on that date). The report will show i) a disposition of the forward contract, and ii) a disposition of the underlying common shares.

Example 2

On March 1, 2011, John purchases a ***put option*** from InvestBank which gives John the right, but not the obligation, to sell to InvestBank, at any time between March 1, 2011 and March 1, 2016, 10 shares of ABC Inc. at a price of $90 per share.[3] The put option is not transferable. John pays $10 to InvestBank in consideration for the put option. InvestBank hedges its risk under the contract through a hedging strategy involving short sales into the secondary market.

Insider Reporting Requirement: John is required to file an insider report within five (calendar) days of March 1, 2011. (See Part 3 of NI 55-104.) For an example of how to report this transaction, see below. Unless InvestBank is also a reporting insider of ABC Inc., InvestBank is not required to file an insider report.

Instructions for Example 2

- Repeat steps 1 to 8, inclusive, under example no. 1.

SCREEN: File insider report — Add insider-defined security designation

9. Under the heading **Security designation**, in the drop-down menu under the subheading **Security name**, select and highlight **OTC Puts (including Private Options to Sell)**.

10. Then, for the **Additional description**, briefly describe. For example, "10 common shares — expires March 2016".

Note: This adds the security designation "OTC Puts (10 common shares — expires March 2016)" to your list of insider-defined securities.

*Note: Not all of this text will currently be visible in the **Additional description** box. (The box will only show a limited number of characters at any one time.) However, the full text in this example will be accepted, and will be visible at later stages of the filing process.*

- Repeat steps 11 to 24, inclusive, under example no. 1 (substituting references to "OTC Put" for references to "Forward sale" in the text of the example).

25. Under the field **Unit price or exercise price**, enter **10**.

26. Under the field **Conversion or exercise price**, enter **90**.

*Note: Under the put option, John has the right, but not the obligation, to sell to InvestBank 10 ABC Inc. shares at $90 per share at any time up to March 1, 2016. Since John paid $10 in consideration (in this example) for the put option, he would enter **10** in the field **Unit price or exercise price**. Since the put option exercise price is $90 per share, John would enter **90** in the field **Conversion or exercise price**.*

27. In the **Date of expiry or maturity** field, select **March 1, 2016**.

Note: Since the anticipated date of settlement is March 1, 2016, this will be the date of expiry or maturity.

28. Enter the following information in the **General remarks** field:

> Private option contract to sell 10 shares of ABC Inc. at a price of $90 per share at any time between March 1, 2011 and March 1, 2016. Consideration paid for option was $10.

*Note: If it is not possible to adequately describe a transaction or to include all of the material terms of a transaction in the space provided, consider making reference to a public document (e.g., a news release issued by the issuer) that further describes the transaction. Alternatively, this information may be included in a schedule that may be filed in paper format by facsimile in accordance with the provisions of Part 3 of NI 55-102. Fax the schedule to the facsimile number of the securities commission set out on Form 55-102F6. We recommend that you refer to this filing by facsimile in the **General remarks** field on SEDI. Staff will make this schedule available to the public on request.*

- Repeat steps 29 to 36, inclusive, under example no. 1, with necessary changes (i.e., substituting references to "OTC Puts" for references to "forward sale" in the text of the example).

Example 3

On March 1, 2011, John purchases a ***put option*** from InvestBank and simultaneously sells a ***call option*** to InvestBank. (The combination of a put option and call option is sometimes referred to as a ***collar***.) The put option gives John the right, but not the obligation, to sell to InvestBank, at any time between March 1, 2011 and March 1, 2016, 10 shares of ABC Inc. at a price of $90 per share. The call option gives InvestBank the right, but not the obligation, to require John to sell to InvestBank at any time between March 1, 2011 and March 1, 2016, 10 shares of ABC Inc. at $115 per share.

The options are not transferable. John finances the purchase of the put option by the simultaneous sale of the call option. InvestBank hedges its risk under the contract through a hedging strategy involving short sales into the secondary market.

Insider Reporting Requirement: John is required to file an insider report within five (calendar) days of March 1, 2011. (See Part 3 of NI 55-104.) For an example of how to report this transaction, see below. Unless InvestBank is also a reporting insider of ABC Inc., InvestBank is not required to file an insider report.

Instructions for Example 3

In the above example, a separate report will be filed for the **put option** component and the **call option** component.

---

[3]This example and the subsequent examples assume a fixed exercise price of $90 per share for the sake of simplicity. If the exercise price is based upon a formula, a note to this effect can be included in the **General remarks** field.

Instructions for filing a report in respect of the **put option** component are contained in example 2. Under the **General remarks** field (step 28), a reference to the call option can be made as follows:

> Private option contract to sell 10 shares of ABC Inc. at a price of $90 per share at any time between March 1, 2011 and March 1, 2016. Acquisition of put option financed by simultaneous sale of call option (see separate report).

The following instructions relate to the **call option** component.

- Repeat steps 1 to 8, inclusive, under example no. 1.

SCREEN: File insider report — Add security designation

9. Under the heading **Security designation**, in the drop-down menu under the subheading **Security name**, select and highlight **OTC Calls (including Private Options to Purchase)**.

10. Then, for the **Additional description**, briefly describe. For example, "10 common shares — expires March 2016".

Note: This adds the security designation "OTC Calls (10 common shares — expires March 2016)" to your list of insider-defined securities.

*Note: Not all of this text will currently be visible in the **Additional description** box. (The box will only show a limited number of characters at any one time.) However, the full text in this example will be accepted, and will be visible at later stages of the filing process.*

- Repeat steps 11 to 22, inclusive, under example no. 1 (substituting references to "OTC Calls" for references to "Forward sale" in the text of the example (step 11)).

23. Enter a number in the **Number or value of securities or contracts disposed of** field. Enter **1** here.

*Note: Since John has entered into a new contract that requires John to sell, if and when called upon, 10 shares of ABC Inc. at a price of $115 per share at any time between March 1, 2011 and March 1, 2016, enter a **1** after the field **Number or value of securities or contracts disposed of**. Since John has sold a call option (i.e., written an option to purchase shares of ABC Inc.), John is considered to have "disposed" of an OTC Call contract for the purposes of this field. Leave the field **Number or value of securities or contracts acquired** blank.*

Note: Since John has specified a derivative as the security, there are additional fields in which to enter the equivalent number or value of the underlying securities to which the derivative relates.

24. Enter a number in the **Equivalent number or value of underlying securities disposed of** field. Enter **10** here.

25. Next to the field **Unit price or exercise price**, click the **Not Applicable** box.

*Note: In example no. 2, John paid $10 as a premium for the acquisition of the put option. Accordingly, in example no. 2, John would enter **10** in the field **Unit price or exercise price**. In the present example, the consideration for the put option component of the collar is the sale of the related call option. Accordingly, John will click the **Not Applicable** box next to the field **Unit price or exercise price**, and make reference to the related put option in the **General remarks** field.*

26. Under the field **Conversion or exercise price**, enter **115**.

*Note: Since the call option exercise price is $115 per share, John would enter **115** in the field **Conversion or exercise price**.*

27. In the **Date of expiry or maturity** field, enter **March 1, 2016**.

Note: Since the anticipated date of settlement is March 1, 2016, this will be the date of expiry or maturity.

28. Enter the following information in the **General remarks** field:

> Private option contract requiring John to sell 10 ABC Inc. shares at $115 per share at any time between March 1, 2011 and March 1, 2016. Proceeds from sale of call option used to finance acquisition of put option (see separate report).

*Note: If it is not possible to adequately describe a transaction or to include all of the material terms of a transaction in the space provided, consider making reference to a public document (e.g., a news release issued by the issuer) that further describes the transaction. Alternatively, this information may be included in a schedule that may be filed in paper format by facsimile in accordance with the provisions of Part 3 of NI 55-102. Fax the schedule to the facsimile number of the securities commission set out on Form 55-102F6. We recommend that you refer to this filing by facsimile in the **General remarks** field on SEDI. Staff will make this schedule available to the public on request.*

- Repeat steps 29 to 36, inclusive, under example no. 1, with necessary changes.

Example 4

On March 1, 2011, John enters into a secured loan arrangement with InvestBank under which John agrees to borrow, and InvestBank agrees to lend, an amount equal to 90% of the FMV of the ABC Inc. shares, or $900. The loan bears interest at 6 per cent per annum. The loan has a term of approximately five years, and matures on March 1, 2016. As security for the loan, John pledges the 10 ABC Inc. shares. Recourse under the loan is limited to the pledged securities (or identical collateral substituted therefor). (In other words, John may settle his obligations under the loan on a cash settlement basis or by physical delivery of 10 ABC Inc. shares.) InvestBank hedges its risk under the contract through a hedging strategy involving short sales into the secondary market.

Insider Reporting Requirement: John is required to file an insider report within five (calendar) days of March 1, 2011. (See Part 3 of NI 55-104.) For an example of how to report this transaction, see below. Unless InvestBank is also a reporting insider of ABC Inc., InvestBank is not required to file an insider report.

Instructions for Example 4

In the above example, the term of the loan agreement limiting recourse to the collateral (or to identical collateral delivered in substitution for the original collateral) effectively operates as a "put" option. John can repay the principal amount of $900 at the term of the loan. Alternatively, John can satisfy his obligation under the loan agreement to repay the principal amount of $900 by releasing his interest in the collateral (or by delivering another 10 ABC Inc. shares in substitution for the pledged shares), regardless of their value at the term of the loan.

John can report this transaction in a number of ways. One approach would be to report this transaction as an acquisition of an OTC Put Option. (See example no. 2 for instructions as to how this may be reported.)

Another approach would be to define the secured loan agreement as an insider-defined derivative, as follows.

- Repeat steps 1 to 8, inclusive, under example no. 1.

SCREEN: File insider report — Add insider-defined security designation

9. Under the heading **Security designation**, in the drop-down menu under the subheading **Security name**, select and highlight **Other**.

10. Then, for the **Additional description**, briefly describe. For example, "Loan secured by pledge (limited recourse) matures March 2016".

Note: This adds the security designation "Loan secured by pledge (limited recourse) matures March 2016" to your list of insider-defined securities.

- Repeat steps 11 to 24, inclusive, under example no. 1, with necessary changes.

25. Under the field **Unit price or exercise price**, enter **0**.

26. Under the field **Conversion or exercise price**, enter **900**.

*Note: Under the loan agreement, John can repay the principal amount of $900 at the term of the loan. Alternatively, John can satisfy his obligation under the loan agreement to repay the principal amount of $900 by releasing his interest in the collateral (or by delivering another 10 ABC Inc. shares in substitution for the pledged shares), regardless of their value at the term of the loan. Effectively, John has an option to put 10 shares to InvestBank at a notional price of $900 (or $90 per share). Since the put option exercise price is $900, John would enter **900** in the field **Conversion or exercise price**.*

27. In the **Date of expiry or maturity** field, select **March 1, 2016**.

Note: Since the anticipated date of settlement is March 1, 2016, this will be the date of expiry or maturity.

28. Enter the following information in the **General remarks** field:

> Pledge of shares as collateral for loan (principal amount $900; interest at 6 per cent per annum). Loan may be repaid in cash or settled by delivery of 10 shares.

*Note: If it is not possible to adequately describe a transaction or to include all of the material terms of a transaction in the space provided, consider making reference to a public document (e.g., a news release issued by the issuer) that further describes the transaction. Alternatively, this information may be included in a schedule that may be filed in paper format by facsimile in accordance with the provisions of Part 3 of NI 55-102. Fax the schedule to the facsimile number of the securities commission set out on Form 55-102F6. We recommend that you refer to this filing by facsimile in the **General remarks** field on SEDI. Staff will make this schedule available to the public on request.*

SUMMARY — The information should appear as follows:

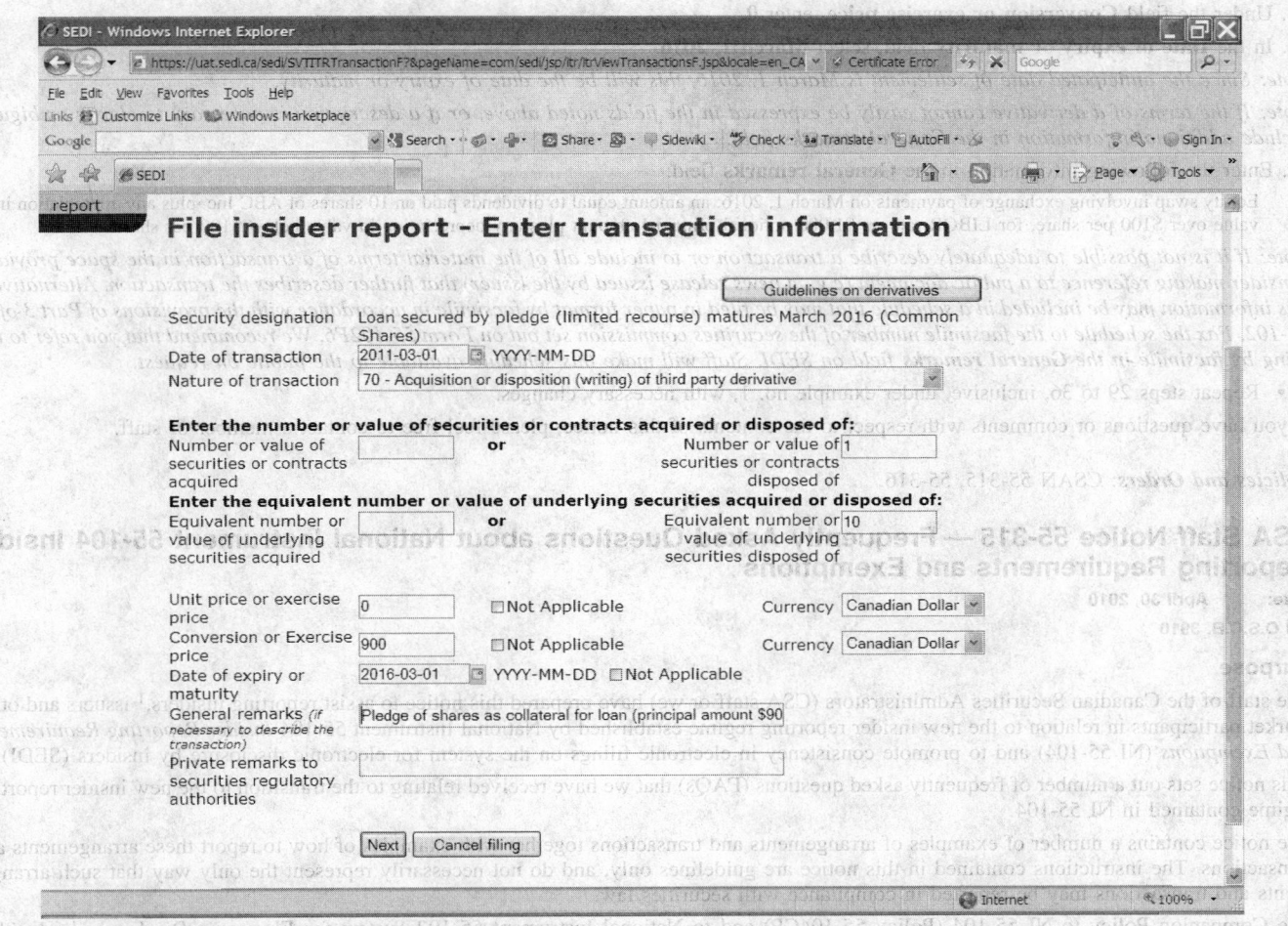

- Repeat steps 29 to 36, inclusive, under example no. 1, with necessary changes.

Example 5

On March 1, 2011, John enters into a swap agreement with InvestBank whereby he agrees to pay InvestBank, on March 1, 2016, an amount equal to dividends paid on the 10 shares of ABC Inc. plus any appreciation in value over $100 per share. In return, InvestBank agrees to pay John the London interbank offered rate (LIBOR) on a notional principal amount of $1,000 (i.e., the FMV of the 10 ABC Inc. shares) plus any depreciation in the value of the shares below $100 per share. InvestBank hedges its risk under the contract through a hedging strategy involving short sales into the secondary market.

Insider Reporting Requirement: John is required to file an insider report within five (calendar) days of March 1, 2011. (See Part 3 of NI 55-104.) For an example of how to report this transaction, see below. Unless InvestBank is also a reporting insider of ABC Inc., InvestBank is not required to file an insider report.

Instructions for Example 5

- Repeat steps 1 to 8, inclusive, under example no. 1.

SCREEN: File insider report — Add insider-defined security designation

9. Under the heading **Security designation**, in the drop-down menu under the subheading **Security name**, select and highlight **Equity Swap — Short Position**.

10. Then, for the **Additional description**, briefly describe. For example, "10 common shares — expires March 2016".

Note: John is considered to have the short position on the equity swap since John has swapped the cash flows associated with ownership (i.e., a long position) for cash flows generated by another instrument, a notional investment of $1,000 at the LIBOR rate.

Note: This adds the security designation "Equity Swap — Short Position (10 common shares — expires March 2016)" to your list of insider-defined securities.

*Note: Not all of this text will currently be visible in the **Additional description** box. (The box will only show a limited number of characters at any one time.) However, the full text in this example will be accepted, and will be visible at later stages of the filing process.*

- Repeat steps 11 to 24, inclusive, under example no. 1, with necessary changes.

25. Under the field **Unit price or exercise price**, enter **0**.

26. Under the field **Conversion or exercise price**, enter **0**.

27. In the **Date of expiry or maturity** field, select **March 1, 2016**.

Note: Since the anticipated date of settlement is March 1, 2016, this will be the date of expiry or maturity.

*Note: If the terms of a derivative cannot easily be expressed in the fields noted above, or if a description is necessary to clarify ambiguity, include additional information in the **General remarks** field.*

28. Enter the following information in the **General remarks** field:

> Equity swap involving exchange of payments on March 1, 2016: an amount equal to dividends paid on 10 shares of ABC Inc. plus any appreciation in value over $100 per share, for LIBOR rate on $1,000 notional principal amount plus any depreciation in value below $100 per share.

*Note: If it is not possible to adequately describe a transaction or to include all of the material terms of a transaction in the space provided, consider making reference to a public document (e.g., a news release issued by the issuer) that further describes the transaction. Alternatively, this information may be included in a schedule that may be filed in paper format by facsimile in accordance with the provisions of Part 3 of NI 55-102. Fax the schedule to the facsimile number of the securities commission set out on Form 55-102F6. We recommend that you refer to this filing by facsimile in the **General remarks** field on SEDI. Staff will make this schedule available to the public on request.*

- Repeat steps 29 to 36, inclusive, under example no. 1, with necessary changes.

If you have questions or comments with respect to the contents of this notice, please feel free to contact a member of staff.

Policies and Orders: CSAN 55-315, 55-316.

CSA Staff Notice 55-315 — Frequently Asked Questions about National Instrument 55-104 Insider Reporting Requirements and Exemptions

Date: April 30, 2010

33 O.S.C.B. 3910

Purpose

The staff of the Canadian Securities Administrators (CSA staff or we) have prepared this notice to assist reporting insiders,[1] issuers and other market participants in relation to the new insider reporting regime established by National Instrument 55-104 *Insider Reporting Requirements and Exemptions* (NI 55-104) and to promote consistency in electronic filings on the system for electronic disclosure by insiders (SEDI).

This notice sets out a number of frequently asked questions (FAQs) that we have received relating to the transition to the new insider reporting regime contained in NI 55-104.

The notice contains a number of examples of arrangements and transactions together with examples of how to report these arrangements and transactions. The instructions contained in this notice are guidelines only, and do not necessarily represent the only way that such arrangements and transactions may be reported in compliance with securities law.

The Companion Policy to NI 55-104 (Policy 55-104CP) and to National Instrument 55-102 *System for Electronic Disclosure by Insiders (SEDI)* (NI 55-102) also contain explanation and guidance on the insider reporting requirements.

CSA Staff will also shortly publish the following general guidance:

- CSA Staff 55-312 *Insider Reporting Guidelines for Certain Derivative Transactions (Equity Monetization) (REVISED)*

- CSA Staff Notice 55-316 *Questions and Answers on Insider Reporting and the System for Electronic Disclosure by Insiders (SEDI)* which will replace CSA Staff Notice 55-308 *Questions on Insider Reporting* and CSA Staff Notice 55-310 *Questions and Answers on the System for Electronic Disclosure by Insiders (SEDI)*.

If you have questions or comments with respect to the contents of this notice, please contact a member of staff. Contact information is included at the end of this notice. This notice is dated April 28, 2010. We may from time to time reissue this notice to reflect additional frequently asked questions or concerns.

1. — *Do existing insiders have to file a new initial report within 10 days of April 30, 2010?*

Background

1. ABC Inc. (the Issuer) is a reporting issuer in all provinces and territories.

2. On January 1, 2009, I became the CEO of the Issuer. I am therefore an "insider" of the Issuer under Canadian securities legislation. I have filed all required insider reports since becoming CEO.

3. On April 30, 2010, NI 55-104 came into force.

---

[1]Prior to April 30, 2010, Canadian securities legislation generally required all persons and companies who are "insiders" (as defined in securities legislation) to file insider reports unless they had an exemption from the insider reporting requirement. On April 30, 2010, the Canadian Securities Administrators introduced a new insider reporting regime established by NI 55-104. Under NI 55-104, the insider reporting requirement is generally limited to "reporting insiders" (as defined in NI 55-104) and certain persons who may be designated insiders for certain historical transactions (see s. 3.5 of NI 55-104). For convenience, this notice will refer to insiders subject to a reporting requirement as "reporting insiders".

4. NI 55-104 contains a new definition of "reporting insider". The definition of "reporting insider" includes a CEO of a reporting issuer. I am therefore a "reporting insider" for this Issuer under NI 55-104.

5. Section 3.2 of NI 55-104 states that a reporting insider must file an insider report in respect of a reporting issuer, "within 10 days of becoming a reporting insider", disclosing certain prescribed information.

Question

1. Do I have to file a new initial report under section 3.2 within 10 days of April 30, 2010? (In other words, have I "become" a reporting insider as a result of NI 55-104 coming into force?) I do not otherwise have any transactions involving securities or related financial instruments to report.

Response

1. No, you do not have to file a new initial report. The term "reporting insider" is simply intended to refer to a defined class of insiders who have reporting obligations. A person is determined to be an insider by operation of the statutory definition of "insider". A person is a reporting insider for the purposes of the insider reporting requirements in NI 55-104 if the person has a position or function, such as CEO or director, or has a particular type of relationship to a reporting issuer, described in the definition of "reporting insider". We do not consider you to have "become" a reporting insider simply through the introduction of this term in NI 55-104.

2. — Do insiders who previously filed reports but who are not reporting insiders under NI 55-104 have to file anything to show their change in reporting status?

Background

1. ABC Inc. (the Issuer) is a reporting issuer in all provinces and territories.

2. I am the CEO of a subsidiary of the Issuer (SubCo). Prior to April 30, 2010, I was required to file insider reports because SubCo was a "major subsidiary" of the Issuer as that term was defined in former National Instrument 55-101 *Insider Reporting Exemptions* (NI 55-101).

3. On April 30, 2010, NI 55-104 came into force. The definition of "major subsidiary" in NI 55-104 has been amended from the definition in NI 55-101 in that the assets and revenue thresholds have been increased from 20% to 30%.

4. SubCo is not a "major subsidiary" of the Issuer as defined in NI 55-104. I am not an insider of the Issuer in any capacity other than as CEO of SubCo. I am therefore not a "reporting insider" for this Issuer under NI 55-104.

Question

1. Do I need to amend my SEDI profile, or otherwise do anything, to disclose the fact that I am not a reporting insider under NI 55-104?

Response

1. No. There is no requirement to file an amended insider profile on SEDI for an insider who has ceased to have reporting obligations because the insider is not a reporting insider under NI 55-104.

2. However, we recommend that an insider who has previously filed insider reports, but as of April 30, 2010 is no longer required to file insider reports because they are not a "reporting insider" under NI 55-104, add a comment on SEDI in the "Remarks" field regarding their change of status. This can be done on either their next transaction to be filed on SEDI or by amending their last transaction already filed on SEDI. A member of the public viewing the insider reports on SEDI will then know why the insider ceased reporting.

Note: section 4.3.1.19 of CSA Staff Notice 55-310 included similar guidance for insiders who previously filed insider reports and then proposed to rely on an exemption from insider reporting in Part 2 or Part 3 of NI 55-101.

3. — Can a reporting insider rely on the exemption in Part 5 of NI 55-104 (exemption for automatic securities purchase plans) for a grant of related financial instruments under a compensation arrangement?

Response

1. No. See section 5.3 of NI 55-104 which states that the exemption in section 5.2 does not apply to an acquisition of options or similar securities granted to a director or officer. Subsection 5.1(2) states that, in Part 5, a reference to a security of a reporting issuer includes a related financial instrument involving a security of the reporting issuer. See section 5.1 of Policy 55-104CP for related commentary.

A reporting insider can rely on the exemption in Part 6 of NI 55-104 (exemption for certain issuer grants) for a grant of related financial instruments under a compensation arrangement if the issuer files an issuer grant report in accordance with Part 6.

Despite the above, if a compensation arrangement provides for the automatic issuance of related financial instruments as dividend equivalents, staff would accept that aspect of the compensation arrangement as coming within the definition of "automatic securities purchase plan" for the purposes of Part 5 of NI 55-104. We would not consider an issuance in these circumstances to be a grant for the purposes of section 5.3 of NI 55-104.

4. — How do I report a grant of related financial instruments made prior to April 30, 2010?

Background

1. ABC Inc. (the Issuer) is a reporting issuer in all provinces and territories.

2. I am the CEO of the Issuer and therefore a "reporting insider" for this Issuer under NI 55-104. I did not hold any deferred share units (DSUs) when I became an insider of the Issuer.

3. On March 15, 2010, I received a grant of 100 DSUs.

4. The redemption value of a DSU is equal to the market value of a common share of the Issuer at the time of redemption, in accordance with the DSU Plan. The DSUs are cash-settled and do not provide for or permit settlement in securities of the Issuer. The DSUs do not entitle the holder to voting or other shareholder rights. The DSUs cannot be redeemed for cash until the holder has ceased to be a director, officer or employee of the Issuer.

5. At the time of the grant, I confirmed that the DSUs do not, as a matter of law, constitute securities and are therefore not subject to the ordinary insider reporting requirements applicable to securities. I also confirmed that the Issuer has disclosed the existence and material terms of the DSU Plan in its circular and that I was therefore eligible for the reporting exemption in s. 2.2(b) of Multilateral Instrument 55-103 *Insider Reporting for Certain Derivative Transactions (Equity Monetization)* (MI 55-103) and, in British Columbia, Part 3 of BCI 55-506 *Exemption from insider reporting requirements for certain derivative transactions* (BCI 55-506).

6. Accordingly, I did not file an insider report to report the grant of 100 DSUs on March 15, 2010.

7. On April 30, 2010, NI 55-104 came into force.

8. On May 15, 2010, I received a further grant of 100 DSUs.

9. The Issuer has not filed an issuer grant report about this grant.

Questions

1. Do I need to file a report about the March grant of DSUs? If yes, when do I need to file it by? (For example, do I need to file it within 10 days of April 30, 2010?)

2. Do I need to file a report about the May grant of DSUs? If yes, when do I need to file it by?

3. If I need to file a report about the May grant, do I show a balance of 100 or 200 DSUs?

Responses

1. Assuming the DSUs are not securities, and the March grant was properly covered by the exemptions in MI 55-103 and BCI 55-506, you do not need to file an insider report about the March grant. Accordingly, there is no requirement to file a report about the March grant within 10 days of April 30, 2010. However, the next time there is a change in your holdings of DSUs (i.e., the May 15 grant), before you can report this change, you will first need to take a step to reflect the March grant in your holdings. We have set out below two methods for doing this. Either method is acceptable so long as you explain in the General Remarks section which method you are using.

2. Assuming the DSUs are not securities, they would likely be considered "related financial instruments" under NI 55-104. Accordingly, you are required to file an insider report about the May grant within 10 days of the grant, or by May 25, 2010.

Note: If the issuer files an issuer grant report about this grant on or before May 25, 2010, the deadline for the insider report is March 31, 2011. When filing this report, use nature of transaction code 56 — grant of rights. See Part 6 of NI 55-104 for more information.

Note: SEDI does not use the term "related financial instrument". For the purposes of filing on SEDI, the term "security" applies to both securities and related financial instruments.

3. Before you can file a report about the May 15 grant of 100 DSUs, you will need to reflect the March 15 grant in your holdings. There are two methods for doing this. These are described below.

In order to file an insider report about a grant of securities or related financial instruments, it is first necessary

    a. to confirm that the Issuer has created a security designation for this type of instrument, and

    b. record an Opening Balance on Initial Report for the DSUs.

If the Issuer has not created a security designation for DSUs, you should contact the Issuer and request the Issuer to add the security designation to its issuer profile supplement. If the Issuer is unable to comply in a timely manner, you should contact the securities regulatory authority that is the principal regulator for the Issuer (generally, the securities regulatory authority in the jurisdiction where the Issuer's head office is located).

Method 1 — filing an opening balance that shows the March grant

4. Under this method, you can reflect the March grant in your opening balance. (If there are other prior grants of the same type of DSU, aggregate all such grants.)

5. When you record an Opening Balance for the DSUs, you should include a remark in the General Remarks section to explain that you are using method 1. Failure to do this may result in the filing being misleading. For example,

> "Opening balance for DSUs reflects grant of 100 DSUs on March 15, 2010. At the time of the grant, the grant was exempt from reporting requirements under Part 2 of MI 55-103 and Part 3 of BCI 55-506".

Note: Ordinarily, the Opening Balance is intended to reflect the insider's holdings as of the date the insider became an insider. In this case, if the individual first became an insider on January 1, 2009, but did not receive any DSUs until the March 15, 2010 grant, then the record will be potentially misleading unless the insider also includes a comment in the general remarks section to explain that opening balance for DSUs reflects the grant of 100 DSUs on March 15, 2010.

6. When filing the insider report about the May 15, 2010 grant of DSUs, report the number of DSUs awarded and the equivalent number of underlying common shares. Use nature of transaction code 56 — grant of rights.

For more information, please refer to the section "Insider Report for Deferred Share Units (DSU) or Restricted Share Awards" in the online SEDI help.

Method 2 — notional adjusting transaction

7. Under this method, you would first file an opening balance of "0" for the DSUs.

8. Then, prior to filing an insider report to reflect the May 15 grant of 100 DSUs, you would file a report to show a *notional* acquisition of the 100 DSUs that were granted on March 15, 2010. (If there are other prior grants of the same type of DSU, aggregate all such grants.)

9. If this method is used, you should use the *date of filing* as the date of the notional acquisition, and not the actual date of acquisition (i.e., March 15, 2010) for the transaction date.

Note: If you use the actual date of acquisition, or March 15, 2010, this may generate a late filing invoice. If this occurs, contact CSA staff in the jurisdiction which acts as principal regulator for the Issuer for assistance.

10. When you file the report about the notional acquisition, you should include a remark in the General Remarks section to explain that you are using method 2. Failure to do this may result in the filing being misleading. For example,

> "Notional transaction to reflect grant of 100 DSUs on March 15, 2010. At the time of the grant, the grant was exempt from reporting requirements under Part 2 of MI 55-103 and Part 3 of BCI 55-506".

Note: If you do not include an explanation in the general remarks section, this may suggest there was an actual acquisition of 100 DSUs on the date of filing (in addition to the grant of 100 DSUs granted on May 15, 2010). This may result in the public record being misleading. In addition, if the DSU exercise price is based on the share price on the actual date of grant (i.e., March 15, 2010), but the filing date is used as the transaction date without explanation in the general remarks section, this may suggest that DSUs have not been granted in accordance with the DSU plan.

5. — How do I report additional DSUs received as dividends?

Background

1. Same facts as in preceding FAQ.

2. The Issuer has a dividend reinvestment plan (the DRIP) that provides that a holder of common shares may choose to receive additional common shares in lieu of cash dividends.

3. On June 30, 2010, the Issuer declared a dividend on its common shares. Under the Issuer's DRIP, a holder of common shares would receive one additional common share for each 10 common shares held.

4. Similarly, under the DSU Plan, additional DSUs are received as dividend equivalents. A participant in the DSU Plan cannot exercise any discretion in terms of the receipt of additional DSUs as dividend equivalents (i.e., the participant cannot choose between receiving DSUs or cash).

5. Accordingly, on June 30, 2010, I received an additional 20 DSUs as a dividend on the 200 DSUs I currently hold.

Question

1. Do I need to file an insider report about the additional 20 DSUs received on June 30, 2010 within 10 days of the acquisition?

Response

1. If the issuer files an issuer grant report about a grant of DSUs after April 30, 2010, and the issuer grant report discloses, in addition to all other required information, the fact that each time the issuer issues common shares as dividends on its common shares, holders of DSUs will automatically receive corresponding DSUs as dividends, staff will accept that the exemption in section 6.2 of NI 55-104 is available for the issuance of the additional DSUs as dividend equivalents.

2. In this case, the information required by section 6.3 will be readily determinable based on the issuer grant report and public disclosure by the issuer about the declaration of a dividend. You would need to file an alternative report by March 31, 2011 showing all DSUs received as dividend equivalents.

3. Alternatively, so long as the reporting insider cannot exercise any discretion in terms of the issuance of additional DSUs as dividend equivalents under the DSU Plan, staff would accept that aspect of the DSU Plan as coming within the definition of "automatic securities purchase plan" for the purposes of Part 5 of NI 55-104. (Note that we would not accept that the DSU Plan generally constitutes an automatic plan for the purposes of the *initial grant* of DSUs under the Plan. This is because timely disclosure of grants of securities and similar instruments, whether through the insider reporting system or through the issuer filing an issuer grant report, can provide important information to investors and allows investors to monitor whether insiders may be causing issuers to engage in improper or unauthorized dating practices including backdating, spring-loading and bullet-dodging. See section 5.1 of Policy 55-104CP.)

4. Accordingly, you can rely on the exemption in Part 5 of NI 55-104 for acquisitions of securities and related financial instruments under an automatic plan. You would need to file an alternative report by March 31, 2011 showing all DSUs received as dividend equivalents.

6. — What information do I need to include in an issuer grant report?

Response

1. The issuer grant report must contain the information required by section 6.3 of NI 55-104.

2. An example of a report would be as follows:

On November 1, 2010, ABC Inc. granted a total of 1,000,000 incentive stock options to directors, officers, employees and consultants of ABC Inc. Details of options granted to reporting insiders are:

Name	Number of Options
[Insert name of recipient]	10,000
[Insert name of recipient]	10,000
[Insert name of recipient]	10,000
[Insert name of recipient]	10,000
[Insert name of recipient]	10,000
[Insert name of recipient]	10,000
[Insert name of recipient]	10,000
[Insert name of recipient]	10,000
TOTAL	80,000

These stock options have an exercise price of $2.00 and expire on October 31, 2015.

The options were granted under the stock option plan described in the ABC Inc. Information Circular dated June 30, 2010.

3. The issuer grant report function on SEDI is subject to the following restrictions:

Title box character limit: 120

Text box character limit: 4,000

Private remarks to regulators box character limit: 256

Note: If it is not possible to adequately describe a transaction or to include all of the material terms of a transaction in the space provided, consider making reference to a public document (e.g., a news release issued by the issuer) that further describes the transaction. Alternatively, this information may be included in a schedule that may be filed in paper format by facsimile in accordance with the provisions of Part 3 of NI 55-102. Fax the schedule to the facsimile number of the securities regulatory authority set out on Form 55-102F6. We recommend that you make reference to this filing by facsimile in the general remarks field on SEDI. Staff will make this schedule available to the public on request.

7. — If an issuer files an issuer grant report within the normal filing period (i.e., 10-days in the case of grants prior to November 1, 2010, five days in the case of grants on or after November 1, 2010), but an insider then files an insider report about the grant after the normal filing deadline has expired, will there be a late fee for that filing?

Response

Late fees will be levied based on the information we receive from issuers and reporting insiders. In the example above, if the insider filed an insider report about a grant outside the normal filing period, and we levied a late fee based on this filing, and the insider then advised us that the issuer *had* in fact filed an issuer grant report within the filing period, staff would likely recommend a waiver of the late fee because the insider had an exemption available.

Policies and Orders: 55-312, 55-316.

CSA Staff Notice 55-316 — Questions and Answers on Insider Reporting and the System for Electronic Disclosure by Insiders (SEDI)

Date: **June 11, 2010**

33 O.S.C.B. 5217

Table of Contents
INTRODUCTION
SOME DEFINED TERMS
1. GENERAL

1.12 Where can I get information about how to use SEDI?

1.13 Will the information I enter on SEDI be publicly available?

1.14 What are some of the technical features I should keep in mind when using SEDI?

2. REGISTRATION

2.1 General

2.1.1 Do I need to register to use SEDI?

2.1.2 When do I need to register as a SEDI user?

2.1.3 What information do I need to provide to register as a SEDI user?

2.1.4 In what category should I register on SEDI?

2.1.5 When should I register as an insider?

2.1.6 When should I register as an issuer representative?

2.1.7 When should I register as an agent?

2.1.8 How do I register on SEDI?

2.1.9 What is the confidential question and answer I need to give?

2.1.10 Once I enter all the information on the registration form (Form 55 102F5), how do I have it validated?

2.1.11 How long will it take for the SEDI operator to validate my registration?

2.1.12 Can I file information on SEDI before my registration is validated?

2.1.13 How do I find out if my account has been validated?

2.1.14 What if my information changes after I have submitted the form?

2.1.15 Can I still submit my SEDI user registration without entering a postal/zip code because I reside outside North America?

2.2 Agents

2.2.1 Can an issuer or a reporting insider have several agents?

2.2.2 Can a law firm register as an agent?

2.2.3 Can law clerks register as agents?

2.2.4 Can I register as an insider, an issuer representative and an agent?

2.2.5 Do insiders who will only file through an agent need to register on SEDI?

2.2.6 Do issuers who will only file through an agent need an issuer representative?

2.2.7 As an agent, how do I access each of my client's filings?

2.2.8 Do I, as the agent for a reporting insider, have to file a power of attorney for insider reports filed on SEDI?

2.2.9 Can I, as an agent, register someone else as a SEDI user?

2.3 Passwords

2.3.1 How many passwords and access keys will I have as an agent?

2.3.2 What do I do if I cannot remember my password?

2.3.3 When will I be issued my password and ID, as opposed to my access key? How are they different?

3. ISSUER INFORMATION

3.1 General

3.1.1 Which issuers must use SEDI?

3.1.2 Do I have to file a report if I am a reporting insider of (a) an income trust, (b) a labour sponsored investment fund corporations (LSIFs) or a labour sponsored venture capital fund corporation (LSVCF), (c) a mutual fund or (d) a limited partnership?

3.1.3 If the reporting insiders of a SEDI issuer are exempt from insider reporting requirements, does the SEDI issuer have to file issuer information on SEDI?

3.1.4 Why do I need to file on SEDI as an issuer?

3.1.5 Who can file for an issuer?

3.1.6 Can an issuer have several issuer representatives?

3.1.7 What do I need to file on SEDI?

3.1.8 How do I file issuer information on SEDI?

3.1.9 Do issuers pay fees to file on SEDI? What are they, how are they paid and when?

3.1.10 What do I do if cannot access SEDI to file issuer information?

3.2 Issuer Profile Supplement

3.2.1 What is an issuer profile supplement?

3.2.2 When do I need to file an issuer profile supplement?

3.2.3 What if I do not file an issuer profile supplement on SEDI?

3.2.4 How do I designate the issuer's outstanding securities and related financial instruments?

3.2.5 What securities can I designate under the 'Equity' category?

3.2.6 What securities can I designate under the 'Debt' category?

3.2.7 How do I designate the following types of securities?

3.2.8 Do I need to file an issuer profile supplement if the issuer is only offering limited partnership units?

3.2.9 Are shares and options the same thing?

3.2.10 What derivatives can I select as a category of securities?

3.2.11 What if a class of securities on the drop-down list box of security designations is no longer issued or outstanding?

3.2.12 What if I entered the wrong type of security or related financial instrument? Can I remove it?

3.2.13 Who is an insider affairs contact?

3.2.14 Why do I need to give insider affairs contact information?

3.2.15 How does a SEDI issuer change its information on SEDI?

3.2.16 Do I designate in the issuer profile supplement all types of issued securities and related financial instruments, not just the ones issued currently to the insiders?

3.2.17 If I issue common shares through both an employee share ownership plan (ESOP) and a dividend reinvestment plan (DRIP), do I have to create two separate security designations for common shares of the ESOP and common shares of the DRIP?

3.3 Issuer Event Report

3.3.1 What is an issuer event?

3.3.2 What is an issuer event report?

3.3.3 Who must file an issuer event report?

3.3.4 When do I need to file an issuer event report?

3.3.5 What information do I need to file?

3.3.6 Why do I need to file this report?

3.3.7 What if I do not file this report?

3.3.8 Do I file one report or several reports if a number of transactions comprise the issuer event?

3.3.9 What information do I need to provide in the 'Issuer report details' field?

3.3.10 What if there is not enough space in the 'Issuer report details' field to adequately describe the event?

3.3.11 Can I provide some information just to the securities regulators that is not viewable by the public?

3.3.12 When do I file an issuer event report versus a material change report?

3.3.13 What is the "Effective date" on an issuer event report form?

3.4 Issuer Grant Report

3.4.1 What is an issuer grant report?

3.4.2 Who files an issuer grant report?

3.4.3 When do I file an issuer grant report?

3.4.4 What information do I need to provide in an issuer grant report?

3.4.5 Where do I file an issuer grant report?

3.4.6 If an issuer files an issuer grant report, when do the reporting insiders need to file insider reports about the grant?

3.4.7 What happens if I do not file an issuer grant report?

4. INSIDER INFORMATION

4.1 General

4.1.1 Do I have to use SEDI to file my insider reports?

4.1.2 Do I have to file my reports myself?

4.1.3 What do I need to file on SEDI?

4.1.4 When do I need to file my insider reports on SEDI?

4.1.5 Do I need to do anything on SEDI before using SEDI to report my transactions?

4.1.6 Can I make a filing after I have completed the online registration form on SEDI but before my registration has been validated?

4.1.7 What if I need to file my insider profile or insider reports and SEDI is unavailable?

4.1.8 Am I a reporting insider?

4.1.9 Do I have to file reports if I am a reporting insider?

4.1.10 Do I need to report for a period before I was a director, CEO, CFO or COO of the relevant reporting issuer?

4.1.11 As a reporting insider, do I need to report securities and related financial instruments that my spouse owns or controls?

4.1.12 What if I already have an insider profile and need to add new reportable securities or related financial instruments?

4.1.13 What if I am no longer required under securities legislation to file insider reports in relation to a particular company?

4.2 Insider Profile

4.2.1 What is an insider profile?

4.2.2 When do I file an insider profile?

4.2.3 What information do I need to include in my insider profile?

4.2.4 What do I need to do if I am a reporting insider of several companies?

4.2.5 What if the information in my insider profile changes?

4.2.6 What if I cannot find a SEDI issuer in the database that I need to add to my insider profile?

4.2.7 Do I need to add the name of the broker or depository as the registered holder of the securities if I own the securities directly?

4.2.8 When do I need to add registered holders and in what circumstances?

4.2.9 If I am no longer an insider, what do I have to do on SEDI?

4.2.10 If I cease to be a reporting insider, but am still an insider, how do I update my insider profile to reflect the change?

4.2.11 What is the additional contact information that I can provide on my insider profile?

4.2.12 What date do I report: an opening balance date or the date I became an insider?

4.2.13 What if I have filed a duplicate insider profile by mistake?

4.3 Insider Report

4.3.1 General

4.3.2 When do I file my insider report on SEDI?

4.3.3 Do I need to file a separate report on SEDI for each province and territory where I have insider reporting obligations?

4.3.4 What type of report do I file when I first become a reporting insider of a SEDI issuer and own securities or related financial instruments of that issuer?

4.3.5 What type of report do I file after I have made my initial SEDI report?

4.3.6 How do I know if my insider report is successfully filed on SEDI?

4.3.7 When do I file insider reports in paper format?

4.3.8 How do I check if my filing was completed?

4.3.9 As an agent can I make a bulk filing for a number of reporting insiders?

4.3.10 Do I need to file on SEDI insider reports required under federal legislation, such as the Canada Business Corporations Act?

4.3.11 What do I file if I am an insider of a U.S. issuer that is a registrant with the SEC and I file insider reports with the SEC?

4.3.12 What do I file if I am an insider of a Designated Foreign Issuer under NI 71-102?

4.3.13 What is the significance of the codes used on SEDI?

4.3.14 I want to report a transaction but SEDI keeps asking me for an opening balance for my securities. What do I do?

4.3.15 When reporting values and amounts, can I enter commas, decimals or fractions?

4.3.16 How do I add more information about the transaction I am reporting?

4.3.17 What if I have to change information that I already filed in a report on SEDI?

4.3.18 Do I have to report all my holdings of securities and related financial instruments of the SEDI issuer or just the securities and related financial instruments in respect of which my ownership or control has changed?

4.3.19 What do I do if I have been previously filing insider reports but am no longer required to?

4.3.20 Do I also need to file an insider report if I file an early warning report (EWR) or an alternative monthly report (AMR) for a particular transaction?

4.3.21 Do I need to file a report when I become a reporting insider if I do not own or control any securities or related financial instruments of the issuer?

4.4 Reporting for Related Financial Instruments

4.4.1 What is a related financial instrument?

4.4.2 What related financial instruments do I need to report on SEDI?

4.4.3 What is an underlying security and how do I report it?

4.5 Reporting Transactions

4.5.1 How does an issuer that is an insider report transactions under a normal course issuer bid?

4.5.2 How do I report acquisitions under an automatic securities purchase plan (including employee share ownership plans (ESOP) and dividend reinvestment plans (DRIP))?

4.5.3 If I acquire securities through an employee share ownership plan (ESOP) or a dividend reinvestment plan (DRIP), do I hold these securities directly or indirectly (do I indicate the "registered owner" on my report)?

4.5.4 How do I report holdings of securities under an RRSP?

4.5.5 How do I report share-based compensation (other than options) such as deferred share units (DSUs), restricted share awards (RSAs), and stock appreciation rights (SARs)?

4.5.6 How do I report a grant of related financial instruments which predates April 30, 2010?

4.5.7 When do I report changes to my holdings as a result of share consolidations/splits?

4.5.8 For what issuer events do I need to report changes in my securities holdings?

4.5.9 How do I report the change in my holdings resulting from an issuer event?

4.5.10 What are equity monetization transactions?

4.5.11 Do I have to file insider reports for securities that I have monetized?

4.5.12 How do I report an exercise of options?

4.5.13 What are the most common filing errors on insider reports?

5. PUBLIC ACCESS

5.1 Can I search for information filed on SEDI?

5.2 What reports can I view on SEDI?

5.3 Do I need to be registered on SEDI to view these reports?

5.4 What weekly summaries can I view?

5.5 Does the weekly summary include reports only from one province or reports from all provinces and territories?

5.6 Does SEDI list the number of issued and outstanding securities for each issuer?

5.7 Can I subscribe to receive information on filings by certain insiders, or by insiders of particular companies or other information filed on SEDI?

5.8 Where can I look at insider reports filed in paper format?

Appendix A

Securities Regulatory Authorities and SEDI Contact and Website Information

Introduction

Under Canadian securities legislation, certain insiders (referred to as "reporting insiders") of reporting issuers, other than mutual funds, are required to file insider reports about their transactions in securities and related financial instruments of their public companies using an internet-based reporting system called SEDI.

SEDI, or the System for Electronic Disclosure by Insiders, is the electronic insider reporting system for reporting insiders to file their insider reports. Reporting issuers also use SEDI to file certain required information that is necessary for their reporting insiders to comply with the insider reporting requirements. The SEDI website is located at www.sedi.ca.

SEDI is also available to members of the public to search for and view public information about the trading activities of reporting insiders free of charge.

The SEDI electronic reporting requirements for issuers and reporting insiders (referred to as SEDI users) are found in National Instrument 55-102 *System for Electronic Disclosure by Insiders (SEDI)*. Companion Policy 55-102CP contains commentary and guidance on the electronic reporting requirements in NI 55-102.

The substantive insider reporting requirements and specific insider reporting obligations are found in National Instrument 55-104 *Insider Reporting Requirements and Exemptions*. Companion Policy 55-104CP contains commentary and guidance on the insider reporting requirements in NI 55-104.

The Canadian Securities Administrators (CSA) have prepared the questions and answers in this Staff Notice (the QAs) to help SEDI users file information on SEDI. Accordingly, the QAs focus on the *filing* requirements under NI 55-102. They are intended for general application and should not be relied upon as legal advice. Information about the substantive legal insider reporting requirements is in NI 55-104 and its Companion Policy 55-104CP.

This notice replaces CSA Staff Notice 55-308 *Questions on Insider Reporting* and CSA Staff Notice 55-310 *Questions and Answers on the System for Electronic Disclosure by Insiders (SEDI)*, which have been or will be withdrawn in the various CSA jurisdictions.

In cases of doubt, SEDI users should obtain appropriate legal advice to determine their obligations under securities legislation.

How are the QAs organized?

The QAs are divided into different sections based on the logical or technical steps in the filing process on SEDI and the type of SEDI filer — insider or issuer. There is also a section on public access to filings and profile information on SEDI.

Please refer to Appendix A for information on how to contact the various securities regulatory authorities and the SEDI operator. Appendix A includes the website addresses of the securities regulatory authorities that publish information on SEDI and the website address of the CSA.

You can also refer to the factsheets and online help feature on the SEDI website (www.sedi.ca).

Some Defined Terms

To help you understand some of the frequently used defined terms referred to in the QAs, here is a list of these terms, along with their meanings.

CSA means the Canadian Securities Administrators

NI 55-102 means National Instrument 55-102 *System for Electronic Disclosure by Insiders (SEDI)*

NI 55-104 means National Instrument 55-104 *Insider Reporting Requirements and Exemptions*

NI 62-103 means National Instrument 62-103 *The Early Warning System and Related Take-over Bid and Insider Reporting Issues*

related financial instrument[1] generally refers to

(i) a derivative, the value, market price or payment obligations of which are derived from, referenced to or based on the value, market price or payment obligations of a security, or

(ii) any other instrument, agreement, or understanding that affects, directly or indirectly, a person or company's economic interest in a security

Important note: SEDI does not use the term "related financial instrument". Instead, for the purposes of SEDI, all instruments — whether securities or related financial instruments — are considered securities.

reporting insider[2] means an insider of a reporting issuer if the insider is

(a) the CEO, CFO or COO of the reporting issuer, of a significant shareholder of the reporting issuer or of a major subsidiary of the reporting issuer;

(b) a director of the reporting issuer, of a significant shareholder of the reporting issuer or of a major subsidiary of the reporting issuer;

(c) a person or company responsible for a principal business unit, division or function of the reporting issuer;

(d) a significant shareholder of the reporting issuer;

(e) a significant shareholder based on post-conversion beneficial ownership of the reporting issuer's securities and the CEO, CFO, COO and every director of the significant shareholder based on post-conversion beneficial ownership;

(f) a management company that provides significant management or administrative services to the reporting issuer or a major subsidiary of the reporting issuer, every director of the management company, every CEO, CFO and COO of the management company, and every significant shareholder of the management company;

(g) an individual performing functions similar to the functions performed by any of the insiders described in paragraphs (a) to (f);

(h) the reporting issuer itself, if it has purchased, redeemed or otherwise acquired a security of its own issue, for so long as it continues to hold that security; or

(i) any other insider that

(i) in the ordinary course receives or has access to information as to material facts or material changes concerning the reporting issuer before the material facts or material changes are generally disclosed; and

(ii) directly or indirectly, exercises, or has the ability to exercise, significant power or influence over the business, operations, capital or development of the reporting issuer

reporting issuer[3] means, generally, a company or other entity that has certain public reporting and other obligations under securities legislation because its securities are publicly traded in the relevant province or territory (please see the definition of 'reporting issuer' under securities legislation)

SEC means the United States Securities and Exchange Commission

SEDAR means the System for Electronic Document Analysis and Retrieval

SEDI means the System for Electronic Disclosure by Insiders

SEDI issuer[4] means a reporting issuer, other than a mutual fund, that is required to comply with National Instrument 13-101 *System for Electronic Document Analysis and Retrieval (SEDAR)*

1. — General

Initial steps

SEDI issuers and their reporting insiders must take certain initial steps before they will be able to file information on SEDI.

SEDI Issuers: As a SEDI issuer (or agent of a SEDI issuer), you need to

- ensure your existing SEDAR profile is accurate and complete

- register on SEDI

---

[1]The term "related financial instrument' is defined in securities legislation. The concept of "related financial instrument" is generally intended to refer to derivatives of securities. Commentary and guidance on this term can be found in Companion Policy 55-104CP.

[2]As defined in NI 55-104.

[3]The term "reporting issuer" is defined in securities legislation.

[4]As defined in NI 55-102

- file an issuer profile supplement including information about your outstanding securities and related financial instruments that may be held by your reporting insiders

Reporting Insiders: As a reporting insider (or agent of a reporting insider) of a SEDI issuer, or any other person required under securities legislation to file insider reports in relation to a SEDI issuer, you need to

- register on SEDI

- file an insider profile

- file an initial insider report within **10 days** of becoming a reporting insider disclosing the reporting insider's

(a) beneficial ownership of, or control or direction over, whether direct or indirect, securities of the reporting issuer, and

(b) interest in, or right or obligation associated with, a related financial instrument involving a security of the reporting issuer.

For more information on registering on SEDI, please see section 2.1 General under Part 2 Registration.

Ongoing requirements

After the initial SEDI registration, profile and initial report are filed, SEDI issuers and their reporting insiders have ongoing obligations and must take certain steps on a continuous basis.

SEDI Issuers: As a SEDI issuer (or agent of a SEDI issuer), your ongoing obligation is to

- file issuer event reports (to report stock dividends, stock splits, etc.)

- amend your profile supplement if there is any change in the information disclosed.

SEDI issuers may also choose to file issuer grant reports to report grants of securities and related financial instruments to reporting insiders. For more information on issuer grant reports, see section 3.4 Issuer Grant Report.

Reporting Insiders: As a reporting insider (or agent of a reporting insider) of a SEDI issuer, or any other person required under securities legislation to file insider reports in relation to a SEDI issuer, your ongoing obligation is:

- within **five**[5] **calendar days** of any of the following changes, to file an insider report disclosing a change in the reporting insider's

(a) beneficial ownership of, or control or direction over, whether direct or indirect, securities of the reporting issuer, or

(b) interest in, or right or obligation associated with, a related financial instrument involving a security of the reporting issuer.

- Amend your insider profile if there is any change in the information disclosed.

1.1 — Who uses SEDI?

The following persons and companies use SEDI:

- SEDI issuers to file their issuer profile supplement and issuer reports

- Reporting insiders of SEDI issuers to file their insider profile and insider reports

- Any other person required under securities legislation to file insider reports in respect of a SEDI issuer.

SEDI issuers and their reporting insiders (or agents on their behalf) use SEDI to file insider and issuer information as well as to file reports disclosing the insider's beneficial ownership of, or control or direction over, whether direct or indirect, securities and related financial instruments of that company, and any changes in that ownership and certain other issuer events.

The public has free access to public information contained on the SEDI website (www.sedi.ca) and can search for and view insider and issuer information filed on SEDI.

1.2 — What computer systems requirements do I need to use SEDI?

Generally, you can use SEDI if you can access the Internet from your computer. Recommended system requirements are on the SEDI website (www.sedi.ca).

1.3 — Who do I call for help with SEDI?

Depending on the type of help you need, call your securities regulatory authority or the SEDI Technical Service Desk.

For example, if you have filing or compliance-related questions regarding SEDI or NI 55-102, such as

- how to use SEDI to report your insider transactions

- what information you need to enter on SEDI

- who must register to use SEDI

- when must you report transactions

contact your securities regulatory authority (see Appendix A).

---

[5]Prior to November 1, 2010, within 10 calendar days.

Or, if you are having technical problems using SEDI, such as

- seeing error messages on the screen

- forgetting your password and/or access key

- needing your access key or password reset

- having printing problems

contact the SEDI Technical Service Desk toll-free at 1-800-219-5381 for assistance in English or French.

If you have questions relating to the substantive legal insider reporting requirements in NI 55-104 you should seek legal advice.

1.4 — Do I need to pay to use SEDI?

SEDI issuers have to pay an annual service charge related to SEDI. (See question 3.1.9 for more detailed information on fees payable by SEDI issuers.) There are no service charges payable either by insiders for filing on SEDI or by the public for accessing information filed on the SEDI website (www.sedi.ca).

1.5 — How do I access SEDI?

Go to the SEDI website at www.sedi.ca. On the introductory page of the website, select the language in which you wish to use the site, either French or English. A 'Welcome to SEDI' page will then appear. If you want to search for information filed on SEDI, click on the 'Access public filings' link.

If you need to file information for the first time, you must register as a SEDI user by clicking on *'Register as a SEDI user'*. For more information on registering, please see section 2.1 General under Part 2 Registration.

1.6 — Where must I file my insider report?

Insider reports must be filed on the SEDI website (www.sedi.ca).

1.7 — When can I use SEDI?

You can use SEDI 24 hours a day, seven days a week to make filings once your SEDI user account has been activated, subject to service interruptions for system maintenance.

1.8 — What if I file my report late, it is inaccurate, or I do not file it at all?

Reporting insiders and all other persons required under securities legislation to file insider reports in respect of a SEDI issuer are responsible for the filing of complete, accurate and timely insider reports. This is the case whether or not an insider is reporting the information directly or through an agent, or in the case of an issuer that is a reporting insider, through an issuer representative.

The information provided by insiders is published as filed on the SEDI website (www.sedi.ca).

Under securities legislation, it is an offence to fail to file an insider report in accordance with the requirements and filing deadlines prescribed by NI 55-104 or to submit information in an insider report that, in a material respect and at the time and in the light of the circumstance in which it is submitted, is misleading or untrue. Failure to file an insider report in a timely manner or the filing of an insider report that contains information that is materially misleading may result in one or more of the following:

- in some jurisdictions, a late filing fee;

- the reporting insider being identified as a late filer on a public database of late filers maintained by certain securities regulators;

- the issuance of a cease trade order that prohibits the reporting insider from directly or indirectly trading in or acquiring securities or related financial instruments of the applicable reporting issuer or any reporting issuer until the failure to file is corrected or a specific period of time has elapsed; or

- in appropriate circumstances, enforcement proceedings.

Securities regulators may also consider information relating to wilful, or repeated, non-compliance by directors and executive officers of a reporting issuer with their insider reporting obligations in the context of a prospectus review or continuous disclosure review. This is because this information may raise questions relating to the integrity of the insiders and the adequacy of the issuer's policies and procedures relating to insider reporting and insider trading.

For details on late filing fees, and other consequences for late filing, please refer to the factsheet on Late Filing available from the SEDI online help or on the website of the securities regulatory authorities that publish information on SEDI. Also, see Part 10 of Companion Policy 55-104CP.

1.9 — What if I am required to file an insider report and SEDI is not available?

If you experience unanticipated technical difficulties that make SEDI unavailable, you can meet your obligations to file your insider report by filing your report in paper format with the relevant securities regulatory authority no later than two days after your report is due. As soon as practicable after the technical difficulties have been resolved, you must re-file your report on SEDI.

Prepare your report using Form 55-102F6 and write the words "IN ACCORDANCE WITH SECTION 4.1 OF NATIONAL INSTRUMENT 55-102 SYSTEM FOR ELECTRONIC DISCLOSURE BY INSIDERS, THIS INSIDER REPORT IS BEING FILED IN PAPER FORMAT UNDER A TEMPORARY HARDSHIP EXEMPTION." in capital letters at the top of the front page.

For more information on the temporary hardship exemption, please refer to Part 4 of NI 55-102 which sets out the temporary hardship exemption.

1.10 — Where can I find the legal requirements for SEDI?

You can find the legal requirements for SEDI, including the requirement to create an Insider Profile and file insider reports on the SEDI website (www.sedi.ca), in NI 55-102 and related materials.

You can find both the legal requirements and exemptions for reporting by insiders in NI 55-104. In Ontario, the principal insider reporting requirements are in Part XXI of the *Securities Act* (Ontario), but are substantially harmonized with the insider reporting requirements set out in NI 55-104. See Appendix A for a list of the securities regulatory authorities with their contact information and website addresses.

1.11 — When should I seek legal advice?

The consequences of non-compliance can be serious. If you are uncertain about your legal obligations, you should seek advice from legal counsel that practises securities law.

1.12 — Where can I get information about how to use SEDI?

You can get information from the SEDI website itself at www.sedi.ca. It has an online help function which contains a list of frequently asked questions (FAQs), factsheets containing helpful hints, detailed guidance and additional information.

You can also get additional information on SEDI through the

- Securities regulatory authorities' websites and contact numbers (see Appendix A), or
- SEDI Technical Service Desk — 1-800-219-5381 (Toll Free) for technical assistance.

Please see question 1.3 for when to contact the SEDI operator and for when to contact a securities regulatory authority.

1.13 — Will the information I enter on SEDI be publicly available?

Yes. Insider reports filed on SEDI with the securities regulatory authorities are publicly available. However, the reporting insider's personal information given on the form and some remarks are confidential.

1.14 — What are some of the technical features I should keep in mind when using SEDI?

Browser Back Button — Try not to use your browser 'Back' button to navigate on SEDI. Where it affects system operability, SEDI will disable the use of your browser's 'Back' button. In these instances, clicking the browser 'Back' button will not return you to a prior screen — you will remain on the current screen. Alternatively, SEDI will bring you to a screen indicating that you have performed an unauthorized sequence of actions. You can try to exit from this screen by clicking any of the primary or secondary navigation buttons available on the screen (i.e., insider report, insider profile, file insider report, amend or delete insider report, etc.). Depending on the navigation button selected, SEDI will take you out of the "unauthorized sequence of actions" screen to the applicable SEDI screen.

- **Browser Stop Button** — If for any reason you click the browser 'Stop' button, you must click the browser 'Refresh' button in order to proceed.

- **Cancel Button** — The 'Cancel' button will delete all information previously entered and will cancel the current option. For example, if you selected 'Create insider profile' and decide in mid-process that you prefer another option, you would click the 'Cancel' button. SEDI would display the previous option you had selected.

- **Certify Button** — The 'Certify' button is used to confirm that the information filed electronically is true and complete in every respect. In the case of a filing agent, the certification is based on the agent's best knowledge, information and belief.

- **Language** — The SEDI site is fully bilingual (French and English). You can change to the other language within the site by returning to the '*Welcome*' page and clicking the appropriate language button available from the main navigation bar (top right portion of the screen).

- **Next Button** — The 'Next' button appears when SEDI prompts you to proceed to the next screen.

- **No Draft Capability** — SEDI has no draft capability. Make sure you have all the necessary information with you before you begin to file. For security reasons, if you stop entering information on SEDI for more than 20 minutes you will lose all the information you just entered. If you close the browser without properly logging-out, you will be temporarily locked out of SEDI for 30 minutes. You will have to log in and enter the information again.

- **'Not Applicable' Checkbox** — All SEDI fields are mandatory, except for certain search criterion fields in the public reports. If the fields do not apply in your case, place a check mark in the 'Not Applicable' checkbox.

- **Printer Friendly Version Button** — Use the 'Printer friendly version' button to display a separate browser window with pre-formatted data that was previously entered. SEDI will trigger a print window offering you print options.

2. — *Registration*

Before filing any information on SEDI, a reporting insider, issuer representative or agent must register as a user on SEDI. To do so, you need to

- *go to the SEDI website (www.sedi.ca) and click on 'Register as a SEDI User'*

- *follow the screen instructions and complete Form 55-102F5 — Register as a SEDI user*
- *print the completed form that is dated and time stamped, and sign it in the space provided*
- *fax or send it to the SEDI operator at the address provided on Form 55-102F5 (fax: 1-866-729-8011 within North America or 416-365-9194 outside of North America)*

The SEDI operator will then process your registration and activate your SEDI user account.

In order to make filings, you must complete this registration process and have your SEDI user account activated.

2.1 — General

2.1.1 — Do I need to register to use SEDI?

You need to register on SEDI as a SEDI user only if you need to file something on SEDI. You do not need to register if you simply want to search for information on the SEDI website.

You must be an individual to register on SEDI as a SEDI user. An issuer that has information to file either as a reporting insider or as an issuer must do so through an individual who is registered as the issuer's representative or agent.

2.1.2 — When do I need to register as a SEDI user?

You need to register as a SEDI user in order to file information on SEDI.

An individual who is a reporting insider must either register as a SEDI user or have an agent who is a registered SEDI user before an insider profile or initial insider report can be filed on SEDI.

An issuer that has information to file either as a reporting insider or an issuer must do so through an individual who is registered as the issuer's representative or agent.

2.1.3 — What information do I need to provide to register as a SEDI user?

You need to provide the following information:

- your name
- name of your employer and your position (if you are registering as an agent)
- your address (your principal residence if you are a reporting insider or your business address if you are an agent or issuer representative)
- your daytime telephone number
- your fax number if available
- your e-mail address if available
- the capacity in which you will be using the system, i.e., as a reporting insider, as an agent for reporting insider(s) and/or issuer(s), or as an issuer representative. (You can select more than one SEDI user classification by holding the "CTRL" key.)
- confidential question and answer (see question 2.1.9)

Note: You should register as a SEDI user only once, even though you may be an agent for many reporting insiders.

2.1.4 — In what category should I register on SEDI?

There are different categories of SEDI user depending on whether you are using SEDI as a reporting insider, as an issuer representative, or as an agent.

Each category of SEDI user has access to different functions on SEDI. Depending on the category chosen, you will be able to log on to the relevant SEDI user home page and access the various functions available. Please see questions 2.1.5 to 2.1.7.

2.1.5 — When should I register as an insider?

If you are a reporting insider, you should register as an insider if you will be filing an insider profile and insider reports only for yourself and no one else.

If you are filing insider profiles and insider reports for one or more reporting insiders (other than yourself), or information for several issuers you should register as an agent (see question 2.1.7), and not as an insider.

2.1.6 — When should I register as an issuer representative?

You should register as an issuer representative if you will only be filing an issuer profile supplement for one issuer and any subsequent issuer reports for that one issuer. If you are filing for more than one issuer, you should register as an agent (see question 2.1.7), not as an issuer representative.

2.1.7 — When should I register as an agent?

You should register as an agent when you will be filing:

- insider information for one or several reporting insiders other than yourself

- issuer information for more than one issuer

- insider and issuer information for yourself, several reporting insiders and an issuer.

Please see section 2.2 Agents.

2.1.8 — How do I register on SEDI?

Go to the SEDI website (www.sedi.ca). After you have selected the appropriate language, click on 'Register as a SEDI user', and follow the instructions to enter the required information. When you are finished, click 'Next' (See the following question for the next steps.)

2.1.9 — What is the confidential question and answer I need to give?

If you forget your password, the SEDI operator will ask you this question to verify that you are who you say you are. You should provide a question for which only you would know the answer. For example, "What is your favourite movie?", rather than "Which country won the most gold medals at the 2010 Winter Olympics?" You must also provide an answer to the question.

2.1.10 — Once I enter all the information on the registration form (Form 55-102F5), how do I have it validated?

- After entering all the information, including your confidential question and answer, you click 'Next'.

- SEDI will then display the *Register as a SEDI user — Accept terms of use — SEDI user* page.

- Read the *Terms of Use — SEDI user* and the *Collection and use of personal information* notice and click 'Accept'.

- SEDI will then display the *Register as a SEDI user — Certify and submit registration information — Form 55-102F5* page. Click 'Certify'. SEDI will then display the *Certification* page. Click 'OK'.

- SEDI will then display the *Register as a SEDI user — Conditional registration completed* page, which will list your SEDI user ID and password. While on this screen, you can either write your SEDI user ID and password down or click on the 'Print' button on your browser bar at the top of the page to get a screen print with your SEDI user ID and password. (Note that passwords are case-sensitive. It is recommended that you keep them in a confidential secure place.) You will need them to log on to SEDI in the future.

- To complete your SEDI registration, click 'Printer friendly version' to get a copy of your registration form. You will not get your password on this printout.

- Sign your registration form and then either fax, deliver or courier it to the SEDI operator using the appropriate address or fax number listed on the form. The SEDI operator will then validate it.

2.1.11 — How long will it take for the SEDI operator to validate my registration?

The SEDI operator anticipates a turnaround time of 24 hours on business days, assuming your form is properly completed and signed. However, you are encouraged to register well before you need to file an insider report or an issuer profile supplement or issuer report.

2.1.12 — Can I file information on SEDI before my registration is validated?

No. You cannot make filings while your registration form is being validated. Once your registration as a SEDI user (whether as an insider, issuer representative or agent) is validated, you will be able to make valid filings that will be made public on the SEDI website (www.sedi.ca).

2.1.13 — How do I find out if my account has been validated?

When your account has been activated, you will be taken to the proper homepage for your SEDI user type (e.g., insider, agent or issuer representative), and be granted access to the functions associated with your SEDI user type. A SEDI user can also log on to SEDI, and click 'Your user information' and verify the Registration status field on the *View your user information* page. If your SEDI user account has been validated, your registration status should display the word 'Activated'.

If your account has not been validated, when you log on to SEDI you will be taken to a homepage that advises you to complete the registration process and will only allow you to access your SEDI user information.

2.1.14 — What if my information changes after I have submitted the form?

You can make changes electronically to your SEDI registration form by amending, certifying and submitting the changes to the form online on SEDI. See the SEDI online help available on the SEDI website for instructions. However, we also recommend that you then print the form and fax it to the SEDI operator (fax: 1-866-729-8011).

When registering as a SEDI user, you may elect to receive an e-mail notification of your account activation. If you would like an e-mail notification to be sent when your account is activated, then you must enter an e-mail address in your user registration (Form 55-102F5). If you choose not to enter an e-mail address, then no notification will be sent that your account has been activated (see question 2.1.3)

2.1.15 — Can I still submit my SEDI user registration without entering a postal/zip code because I reside outside North America?

Yes. You do not need to enter a postal code or zip code if you live outside North America. Complete the field by entering 'not applicable'.

2.2 — Agents

2.2.1 — Can an issuer or a reporting insider have several agents?

Yes. For example, if an individual is a reporting insider of several SEDI issuers, and each of these issuers has arrangements to file insider reports on behalf of that individual, then it is possible that this individual will have a different agent for each issuer.

2.2.2 — Can a law firm register as an agent?

No. Only individuals can register as agents.

2.2.3 — Can law clerks register as agents?

Yes, any individual can register as an agent. Therefore, any number of law clerks at a particular law firm can register. Each SEDI user should register individually so that he or she has his or her own SEDI user ID and password.

2.2.4 — Can I register as an insider, an issuer representative and an agent?

Generally, yes. However, you must select the category that best suits your activity. For example, if you are a reporting insider and you will only be filing insider reports for yourself, you should register as an "insider".

If you fulfill multiple roles, you must register as an agent. For example, you would register as an agent if you will be filing:

- insider information for one or more reporting insiders other than yourself
- issuer information for more than one issuer
- insider and issuer information for yourself, several insiders and an issuer

Please see questions 2.1.4 to 2.1.7.

2.2.5 — Do insiders who will only file through an agent need to register on SEDI?

No.

2.2.6 — Do issuers who will only file through an agent need an issuer representative?

No.

2.2.7 — As an agent, how do I access each of my client's filings?

You will need to have each client's access key.

An access key is a unique case-sensitive alpha-numeric code issued by SEDI or the SEDI operator to an insider or SEDI issuer that has filed an insider profile or issuer profile supplement on SEDI. If you set up a client's insider profile or issuer profile supplement, SEDI will give you their access key. If someone else sets up the client's profile information, you will need to request the access key from your client.

2.2.8 — Do I, as the agent for a reporting insider, have to file a power of attorney for insider reports filed on SEDI?

No. However, if you, as an agent, are filing an insider report in paper format in certain circumstances (see question 4.3.7), you still need to file with the relevant securities regulatory authority a power of attorney. However, an agent does not need to file a power of attorney for an insider report of an individual that is filed in paper format under the temporary hardship exemption.

2.2.9 — Can I, as an agent, register someone else as a SEDI user?

No. You, as an agent, cannot register someone else as a SEDI user. The paper format copy of the SEDI user registration form that is sent to the SEDI operator for validation purposes must contain the manual or facsimile signature of the individual being registered.

2.3 — Passwords

2.3.1 — How many passwords and access keys will I have as an agent?

You will have one password as an agent. You will be issued a SEDI user ID and a password for yourself that you will need to log on to SEDI. In addition, if you are filing for a reporting insider, you will be given an insider number and a distinct access key for each insider whose insider profile you create. If you are filing for an issuer, you will be given a distinct access key for each issuer whose issuer profile supplement you create.

2.3.2 — What do I do if I cannot remember my password?

Call the SEDI Technical Service Desk at 1-800-219-5381. You will be asked a number of questions, including the confidential question you provided when you registered. If your answer is correct, a SEDI operator will give you a single use password. You will need to use this single use password the next time you log on to SEDI. After logging on, SEDI will require you to generate your own permanent password.

2.3.3 — When will I be issued my password and ID, as opposed to my access key? How are they different?

You will be issued a password and a SEDI user ID after you complete, certify and submit your SEDI user registration on the system. The password is tied to the SEDI user ID and allows you, as that SEDI user, to log on to SEDI.

Each time you create an insider profile or an issuer profile supplement, SEDI will display an insider number (if you are an insider) and an access key online to you as creator of the profile. In addition, SEDI will also send an e-mail (if an e-mail address is provided) or letter containing the access key to the insider or issuer representative or agent.

An access key is a case-sensitive alpha-numeric code that is connected either to an insider or issuer profile supplement and issued once an insider profile or issuer profile supplement is created. It allows you, as an agent, insider, or issuer representative, to make a filing once the insider profile or issuer profile supplement is created. The system gives one access key per profile. Call the SEDI Technical Service Desk at 1-800-219-5381 if you forget your password or your access key.

3. — Issuer Information

SEDI issuers need to file certain information on SEDI. SEDI issuers must create their issuer profile supplement before insiders can file their insider reports.

As a SEDI issuer, you need to

  • *ensure your SEDAR profile is accurate and up to date*

  • *register on SEDI through a registered issuer representative or agent (see Part 2 Registration)*

  • *file your issuer profile supplement (including a list of your issued and outstanding securities and related financial instruments) on SEDI through a registered issuer representative or agent*

And then, on a continuous basis:

  • *file any change in the information disclosed*

  • *file on SEDI an issuer report when required*

3.1 — General

3.1.1 — Which issuers must use SEDI?

All reporting issuers, except mutual funds, that file disclosure documents on SEDAR must file information on SEDI unless exempted. These issuers are referred to as SEDI issuers.

3.1.2 — Do I have to file a report if I am a reporting insider of (a) an income trust, (b) a labour sponsored investment fund corporations (LSIFs) or a labour sponsored venture capital fund corporation (LSVCF), (c) a mutual fund or (d) a limited partnership?

(a) an income trust?

Yes

(b) a labour-sponsored investment fund (LSIF) or labour-sponsored venture capital fund corporation (LSVCF)?

The answer depends on the province(s) where the LSIF or LSVCF is a reporting issuer (or equivalent). In certain jurisdictions, such as Alberta, LSIFs and their insiders do not have to file on SEDI because LSIFs are considered mutual funds. In other jurisdictions, such as Ontario and Manitoba, LSIFs and their reporting insiders must file on SEDI because LSIFs are not considered to be mutual funds for insider reporting purposes.

(c) a mutual fund?

No. The insider reporting requirement does not apply to an insider of an issuer that is a mutual fund (see section 9.1 of NI 55-104).

(d) a limited partnership?

Yes. You need to file insider reports if you are a reporting insider of a limited partnership that is a reporting issuer and hold securities or related financial instruments of that limited partnership.

3.1.3 — If the reporting insiders of a SEDI issuer are exempt from insider reporting requirements, does the SEDI issuer have to file issuer information on SEDI?

Generally, the SEDI issuer will still be required to file information on SEDI.

3.1.4 — Why do I need to file on SEDI as an issuer?

As a SEDI issuer, you are required to file certain information on SEDI. You need to file this information so that your insiders who are required by securities legislation to report can meet their legal obligation to file insider reports on SEDI. This information also helps your insiders to file accurate insider reports.

3.1.5 — Who can file for an issuer?

An agent or issuer representative registered as a SEDI user can file information on SEDI for an issuer.

3.1.6 — Can an issuer have several issuer representatives?

Yes, but each issuer can only have one insider affairs contact.

3.1.7 — What do I need to file on SEDI?

As a SEDI issuer, you need to file, through a registered issuer representative or agent:

  • an issuer profile supplement (see 'Issuer Profile Supplement' section)

  • issuer event reports if an issuer event has occurred (see 'Issuer Event Report' section)

• any change in the information disclosed.

The issuer profile supplement contains information about the issuer, including the designations of its outstanding securities and related financial instruments that its insiders hold, and contact information for the person responsible for insider affairs. The legal form is Form 55-102F3.

The issuer event report contains information about an issuer event. An issuer event is a stock dividend, stock split, consolidation, amalgamation, reorganization, merger or other similar event that affects all holdings of a class of the issuer's securities in the same manner. The legal form is Form 55-102F4.

An issuer may choose to file issuer grant reports. Issuer grant reports disclose specific information relating to the grant or issue of an issuer's securities and related financial instruments made to insiders of the issuer pursuant to compensation arrangements.

3.1.8 — How do I file issuer information on SEDI?

You must be a registered SEDI user and have an active SEDI user account (see Part 2 Registration). Once registered and validated, log onto the system. At your home page, select 'Create issuer profile supplement' in order to create the issuer profile supplement for the issuer. Simply follow the on-screen instructions to complete the process. Once this process is completed, you will obtain the issuer access key.

To file an issuer event report you must log on to SEDI and enter the issuer access key for that issuer. From the *Issuer activities* page, click 'Issuer event report' and follow the on-screen instructions to complete the process.

To file an issuer grant report when an issuer grants or issues securities or related financial instruments pursuant to a compensation arrangement, you must log on to SEDI and enter the issuer access key for that issuer. From the *Issuer activities* page, click 'Issuer grant report' and follow the on-screen instructions to complete the process.

3.1.9 — Do issuers pay fees to file on SEDI? What are they, how are they paid and when?

SEDI issuers pay fees through the SEDAR system as SEDAR annual filing service charges related to SEDI. The fees are implemented by the SEDAR operator in SEDAR in code updates. The annual filing service charges effective as of January 1, 2005 are set out in CSA Staff Notice 13-314 *2005 Changes to SEDAR Annual Filing Service Charges.*

Insiders and the public are not charged any fees to use the system.

3.1.10 — What do I do if I cannot access SEDI to file issuer information?

If SEDI is unavailable due to technical difficulties for more than a short period, the CSA would consider, depending on the jurisdiction and the circumstances, providing blanket relief from the filing requirements, or otherwise varying the time periods for filing during the period of service interruption.

If unanticipated technical difficulties prevent a SEDI issuer from filing issuer information on SEDI, then that issuer must file that information as soon as practicable after these difficulties have been resolved.

3.2 — Issuer Profile Supplement

3.2.1 — What is an issuer profile supplement?

The issuer profile supplement provides certain information about the issuer, particularly relating to its outstanding securities and related financial instruments that may be held by insiders, that is additional to the information the issuer files on SEDAR. The issuer profile supplement must contain the information required under Form 55-102F3.

As a SEDI issuer, you need to designate on your issuer profile supplement all types of securities and related financial instruments that may be held by your insiders. However, we recommend that you designate all your issued and outstanding securities and related financial instruments.

3.2.2 — When do I need to file an issuer profile supplement?

You need to file an issuer profile supplement within three business days after the issuer becomes a SEDI issuer.

3.2.3 — What if I do not file an issuer profile supplement on SEDI?

If you do not file an issuer profile supplement, you will be in breach of securities legislation. The securities regulatory authorities can take certain actions against issuers not complying with the law, including placing the issuer on a public default list.

Also, by not filing your issuer profile supplement, your insiders will not be able to file their reports on SEDI. You will cause unnecessary inconvenience to them. Your insiders will have to file paper reports relying on the temporary hardship exemption. After you do complete your issuer profile supplement, your insiders will have to file on SEDI every report previously filed in paper format under the temporary hardship exemption.

3.2.4 — How do I designate the issuer's outstanding securities and related financial instruments?

Important note: SEDI does not use the term "related financial instrument". Instead, for the purposes of SEDI, all instruments — whether securities or related financial instruments — are considered securities.

To create a security designation for an outstanding security or related financial instrument, you need to do the following for each:

• select the security category (Debt, Equity or Issuer derivative)

• select the security name (from a drop down list)

• if you need to, you can type in a brief description of a particular security so there is no confusion with a security that may be similar

- if you selected 'Issuer derivative' in the first step, you need to select the underlying security. To do this,
  - select the securities category of the underlying security (Debt, Equity or Issuer derivative)
  - select the underlying security name
  - if applicable, enter any additional words to describe the specific underlying security

A list of the security names under each security category on SEDI is set out in Appendix 1 of the SEDI User Guide available on the SEDI website (www.sedi.ca).

See question 3.2.7 for examples on how to designate specific securities.

3.2.5 — What securities can I designate under the 'Equity' category?

You can designate, for example, common shares, preferred shares, non-voting shares and multiple voting shares under the 'Equity' category.

3.2.6 — What securities can I designate under the 'Debt' category?

You can designate, for example, bonds, debentures, convertible debentures and notes under the 'Debt' category.

3.2.7 — How do I designate the following types of securities?

1.	Asset-backed securities	a)	Select	'Equity' or 'Debt' category
		b)	Select	'Other' as security name
		c)	Describe	type 'Asset-backed Securities' in the additional description field
2.	Options• (exercisable into common shares under plan)			
	for the options	a)	Select	'Issuer derivative' category
		b)	Select	'Options' as security name
		c)	Describe	(if needed, add description)
	for the underlying security (common shares)	d)	Select	'Equity' category
		e)	Select	'Common shares' as security name
		f)	Describe	(if needed, add description)
3.	Convertible debentures	a)	Select	'Debt' category
		b)	Select	'Convertible debentures' as security name
		c)	Describe	(if needed, add description)

Notes:

- See also the questions and answers under section 4.4. Reporting for Related Financial Instruments for an explanation of "issuer derivatives" and "underlying security".

Suggestion: Together, the security name and description will appear as one of the designated securities on this issuer's list of securities. Its insiders will see and select from this list in order to report transactions and holdings in securities or related financial instruments of that issuer. Make sure to enter any additional words used to describe the specific security or class of security that will distinguish this security or class of security from another that will allow your reporting insiders to choose the appropriate security or related financial instrument. SEDI will compute the total balances of securities and related financial instruments that have the same designation, ownership type and registered holder name combination.

3.2.8 — Do I need to file an issuer profile supplement if the issuer is only offering limited partnership units?

Yes.

3.2.9 — Are shares and options the same thing?

No. An option is the *right* to buy or sell a specific security, such as a common share, at a predetermined price within a specified time. A share is a security that represents a residual ownership interest in a company and generally carries voting privileges.

The two are often linked. For example, in the case of an option to acquire shares in a reporting issuer, you must file separate insider reports for each of the following if they occur while you are reporting insider:

- the acquisition (i.e., grant) of an option;
- the exercise of an option;
- the acquisition of the underlying shares;
- any subsequent sale or transfer of the shares.

3.2.10 — What derivatives can I select as a category of securities?

A derivative is generally an instrument that derives its value, directly or indirectly, from an underlying interest, such as a security.

For SEDI, derivatives that are subject to insider reporting requirements may be classified as either "issuer derivatives" or "third party derivatives". Issuer derivatives are derivatives such as options, warrants and rights issued by a company or other entity directly to its insiders. Share-based compensation instruments, including phantom stock units, deferred share units (DSUs), restricted share awards (RSAs), performance share units (PSUs), stock appreciation rights (SARs) and similar instruments are also generally issuer derivatives.

You can select 'Issuer derivative' as a category of security if you, as the issuer, have issued the derivatives. You would then select the appropriate name of the security: 'options', 'rights', 'warrants' or 'other'. If necessary, you could also add a brief description to the name of the security.

A SEDI issuer cannot designate a third party derivative. Third party derivatives are designated by the insider when the insider files an insider report for those derivatives. Futures, forwards and exchange-traded call or put options are examples of third party derivatives.

For further guidance on how derivatives are reported, please refer to CSA Staff Notice 55-312 *Insider Reporting Guidelines for Certain Derivative Transactions (Equity Monetization)* (REVISED).

3.2.11 — What if a class of securities on the drop-down list box of security designations is no longer issued or outstanding?

You should amend your issuer profile supplement and indicate that this security is now to be listed as an 'Archived security'. Insiders will still be able to report transactions in these securities, using the 'Archived security' list.

3.2.12 — What if I entered the wrong type of security or related financial instrument? Can I remove it?

No. You must contact your securities regulatory authority (see Appendix A) and request that the SEDI operator remove that security from your list of designated securities and related financial instruments. The SEDI operator can only remove the security or related financial instrument after receiving written authorization from the issuer's representative to remove it.

3.2.13 — Who is an insider affairs contact?

An insider affairs contact is the contact person for an issuer whom any of the securities regulatory authorities will contact regarding the issuer and the issuer profile supplement, if there is an issue that a securities regulatory authority needs to discuss with that issuer. You need to include this individual's full name, business address, business telephone number and business e-mail address on the issuer profile supplement.

3.2.14 — Why do I need to give insider affairs contact information?

When an insider creates an insider profile and therefore specifies that insider's relationship with at least one SEDI issuer, SEDI will send an e-mail notification to the insider affairs contact for that issuer. If at any point the issuer has any concerns about the individual identified as the insider, the issuer should contact their local securities regulatory authority.

3.2.15 — How does a SEDI issuer change its information on SEDI?

Your issuer information on SEDI is composed of the information you filed on SEDAR (SEDAR profile) and the information you filed on SEDI under the issuer profile supplement. Your SEDAR profile information is automatically transferred over to SEDI.

Your issuer profile supplement includes your

- issuer name
- insider affairs contact information
- security designations
- confidential question and answer.

You amend SEDI information, such as your insider affairs contact information and security designations, on SEDI as an amended issuer profile supplement. You need to amend SEDAR information, such as your head office or mailing address, on SEDAR.

If you need to change information filed on SEDI, log on, go to the *Issuer Profile Supplement* page, and follow the on-screen instructions. If you need to change the information that comes from SEDAR, you need to contact your SEDAR filing agent and have the agent amend this information.

3.2.16 — Do I designate in the issuer profile supplement all types of issued securities and related financial instruments, not just the ones issued currently to insiders?

We recommend that you designate all your issued and outstanding securities and related financial instruments.

Remember: SEDI does not use the term "related financial instrument". Instead, for the purposes of SEDI, all instruments — whether securities or related financial instruments — are considered securities.

3.2.17 — If I issue common shares through both an employee share ownership plan (ESOP) and a dividend reinvestment plan (DRIP), do I have to create two separate security designations for common shares of the ESOP and common shares of the DRIP?

No. Issuers should not create separate security designations for common shares acquired through different plans.

3.3 — Issuer Event Report

3.3.1 — What is an issuer event?

An issuer event is a stock dividend, stock split, consolidation, amalgamation, reorganization, merger or other similar event that affects the entire class of securities of a SEDI issuer in the same manner. A cash dividend, for example, would not be an issuer event reportable on SEDI.

3.3.2 — What is an issuer event report?

It is a report filed by a SEDI issuer on SEDI. This report provides notice to insiders and members of the public that an issuer event has occurred. It helps insiders to report more accurately any changes in their securities or related financial instrument holdings that may result from the issuer event. The information that you need to complete this report is set out in Form 55-102F4.

3.3.3 — Who must file an issuer event report?

A SEDI issuer whose securities or related financial instruments are affected by an issuer event must file an issuer event report.

3.3.4 — When do I need to file an issuer event report?

You need to file an issuer event report no later than one business day following the occurrence of an issuer event. For example, for a stock split, you report the event within one business day after the issuer issues the securities resulting from the stock split. As a preferred practice, you should report the event following the close of markets on the day of the event or before the opening of the markets on the day after the event occurred. See question 3.3.12.

3.3.5 — What information do I need to file?

The information is set out in Form 55-102F4. This information includes the:

- issuer event type (e.g., stock dividend, stock split, reorganization)

- date the issuer event occurred

- brief description of the issuer event (e.g., 3 for 1 Stock Split — Class A and Class B Shares)

- summary of the issuer report details.

The online help guide (available on the SEDI website by clicking 'Help') gives additional instructions on how to complete the report and provides examples.

3.3.6 — Why do I need to file this report?

The report notifies your insiders that an issuer event has occurred that may affect their holdings. It helps them to report accurately changes in their holdings in the securities or related financial instruments affected by the event. Whenever you file an issuer event report, an alert will appear on the screen the next time an affected insider logs on to SEDI. The alert notifies the insider an issuer event report was filed and identifies the particulars of that event.

3.3.7 — What if I do not file this report?

You are in breach of your obligations under securities legislation as a SEDI issuer. In addition, your insiders may not be able to file accurate reports reflecting changes in their securities or related financial instrument holdings arising as a result of the issuer event.

3.3.8 — Do I file one report or several reports if a number of transactions comprise the issuer event?

One report can be used to report several 'sub-events' in connection with the same event, all happening on the same day. However, you should fully describe all pertinent 'sub-events' in the issuer event title and issuer report details fields.

For example, an issuer event can be an amalgamation that is composed of a share exchange and also a consolidation (of the resulting company's) share capital. You would report the event as follows:

- Issuer event: Amalgamation, merger or reorganization

- Issuer event title: Amalgamation of ABC Ltd. and DEF Corp. into XYZ Ltd. and consolidation of DEF Corp. shares

- Issuer report details: describe the relevant information for both the amalgamation and consolidation aspects of the event and the impact on insider holdings.

3.3.9 — What information do I need to provide in the 'Issuer report details' field?

You need to include a description of the issuer event by providing the following information:

- a description of the affected securities and related financial instruments along with their respective numbers or amounts, as disclosed in the issuer profile supplement, for that issuer

- the name of the resulting issuer, if applicable

- designation of all resulting securities and related financial instruments along with their respective numbers or amounts, if applicable

- the exchange or conversion rates, if applicable

- a description of the resulting securities and related financial instruments as created in the issuer profile supplement in SEDI, if applicable

- the number of resulting securities and related financial instruments rounded up or down to the nearest share.

Include a description of the issuer event in either English or French, or both where appropriate.

3.3.10 — What if there is not enough space in the 'Issuer report details' field to adequately describe the event?

You should provide a summary of the event. However, to the extent that you need more space, consider cross-referencing a public document that adequately discloses the necessary information about the event.

3.3.11 — Can I provide some information just to the securities regulators that is not viewable by the public?

Yes, you can provide additional information concerning the issuer event to staff of the securities regulatory authorities in the 'Private remarks to securities regulatory authority' field. The public, including the issuer's insiders, will not have access to this information.

3.3.12 — When do I file an issuer event report versus a material change report?

You need to file an issuer event report when an event affects the entire class of securities or related financial instruments in the same manner. This may also be a material change.[6] If so, you will also need to file a material change report. However, not all material changes are issuer events. For example, while a company buy-back of shares might be considered a material change, it would not be an issuer event. Please see question 4.5.1 for how to report transactions under a normal course issuer bid.

3.3.13 — What is the "Effective date" on an issuer event report form?

The "Effective date" is the date on which the change to the number of securities and related financial instruments happens as a result of the issuer event. It is the date of the occurrence of the event.

3.4 — Issuer Grant Report

3.4.1 — What is an issuer grant report?

An issuer grant report is a report filed by an issuer on SEDI that publicly discloses the details of compensation arrangements under which grants of stock options or similar instruments are made to reporting insiders. While there is no obligation for an issuer to file an issuer grant report, it may choose to do so to assist its reporting insiders with their reporting obligations, provide them with the benefits of an exemption and communicate material information about its compensation practices to the market in a timely manner.

The issuer grant report exemption reduces the regulatory burden on reporting insiders that is associated with insider reporting of stock options and similar instruments since it allows an issuer to make a single filing on SEDI. This filing provides the market with timely information about the existence and material terms of the grant, and makes it unnecessary for each of the affected reporting insiders to file an insider report about the grant within the ordinary reporting time periods.

It contains the information listed in question 3.4.4.

3.4.2 — Who files an issuer grant report?

A SEDI issuer that *chooses* to report details of a grant or an issue of interests in its securities and related financial instruments to insiders pursuant to a compensation arrangement.

3.4.3 — When do I file an issuer grant report?

The deadline for an issuer to file an issuer grant report is effectively within five days[7] of a grant or award. This is because the exemption in Part 6 of NI 55-104 for reporting insiders is available only when an issuer grant report is filed within the time prescribed for filing insider reports.

Reporting insiders will be in breach of their *individual* insider reporting obligations if the issuer has not filed the report within five days of the grant, and the reporting insiders have not filed their insider reports. We therefore recommend that the issuer file the issuer grant report as soon as reasonably practicable following the grant, award or issue of securities or related financial instruments to reporting insiders.

3.4.4 — What information do I need to provide in an issuer grant report?

The issuer grant report discloses the details of a compensation arrangement and must include

- the date the option or other security or related financial instrument was issued or granted;

- the number of options or other securities or related financial instruments issued or granted to each director or officer;

- the price at which the option or other security or related financial instrument was issued or granted and the exercise price;

- the number and type of securities or related financial instruments issuable on the exercise of the option or other security or instrument; and

- any other material terms that have not been previously disclosed or filed in a public filing on SEDAR.

3.4.5 — Where do I file an issuer grant report?

---

[6]As defined in securities legislation.

[7]Prior to November 1, 2010, within 10 calendar days.

Issuer grant reports are filed on SEDI.

3.4.6 — If an issuer files an issuer grant report, when do the reporting insiders need to file insider reports about the grant?

If an issuer files an issuer grant report within five days[8] of a grant, award or issue of securities or related financial instruments, the reporting insiders named in the issuer grant report can report the grant on a deferred basis. Instead of reporting the grant within the usual five day reporting timeframe, the reporting insiders have until March 31 of the next calendar year to report the grant or award.

If, subsequent to the grant and prior to **March 31** of the next calendar year, the reporting insider disposes of or transfers the securities or related financial instruments identified in the issuer grant report (other than as part of a specified disposition), the reporting insider must file an insider report within five days of the disposition or transfer.

3.4.7 — What happens if I do not file an issuer grant report?

There is no requirement to file issuer grant reports. If an issuer chooses not to file an issuer grant report, the issuer should notify reporting insiders of a grant, award or issue of securities and related financial instruments in a timely manner so that those insiders can meet their individual reporting obligations within the period prescribed for filing insider reports.

4. — Insider Information

Reporting insiders of SEDI issuers, and any other person required under securities legislation to file insider reports, must file insider reports in electronic format using SEDI. To file your insider reports on SEDI, you need to:

- *register as a SEDI user (or use a registered SEDI user as your agent) (see Part 2 Registration)*
- *file your insider profile (see section 4.2 Insider Profile)*
- *file your insider reports when they are due (see section 4.3 Insider Report)*

4.1 — General

4.1.1 — Do I have to use SEDI to file my insider reports?

If you are a reporting insider of a SEDI issuer, you need to file insider reports using SEDI unless you are exempt under NI 55-104 or NI 62-103 or have been otherwise exempted by a securities regulatory authority. In certain cases, you may file insider reports in paper format rather than on SEDI. Please see question 4.3.7 below for a list of exceptional situations where you may file your report in paper format.

4.1.2 — Do I have to file my reports myself?

No. You can have an agent that is registered as a SEDI user file the reports for you. (See Part 2 Registration)

4.1.3 — What do I need to file on SEDI?

As an insider required by securities legislation to file insider reports, you (or your agent) must file on SEDI your insider profile (see section 4.2 Insider Profile) and your insider reports (see section 4.3 Insider Report).

4.1.4 — When do I need to file my insider reports on SEDI?

You need to file your insider reports on SEDI as follows:

- if you beneficially own (or have, or share, direct or indirect control or direction over) securities or related financial instruments of a SEDI issuer, within 10 calendar days of first becoming an insider required by securities legislation to file insider reports,
- if you are already a reporting insider of a SEDI issuer, within five calendar days[9] of:
  - the date of any change in your ownership of, or control or direction over, securities of the SEDI issuer; and
  - the date of any change in your interest in, or right or obligation associated with, a related financial instrument involving a security of the SEDI issuer.

SEDI issuers are reporting issuers, other than mutual funds, that file disclosure documents on SEDAR. You can check the SEDAR website, www.sedar.com, to find out whether your company files disclosure documents on SEDAR.

4.1.5 — Do I need to do anything on SEDI before using SEDI to report my transactions?

To use SEDI to file your own insider reports, you first need to register as a SEDI user. To register, complete the SEDI User Registration Form (Form 55-102F5), sign a printed copy and send it to the SEDI operator. The SEDI operator will review your registration request and, once validated, will activate a SEDI user account for you on SEDI. You cannot file insider reports until the registration process is completed. Please refer to Part 2 Registration.

You do not need to register or file insider reports on SEDI yourself. You can use an agent to file for you. The agent must be an individual who is already registered as a SEDI user.

---

[8]Prior to November 1, 2010, within 10 calendar days.

[9]Prior to November 1, 2010, within 10 calendar days.

4.1.6 — Can I make a filing after I have completed the online registration form on SEDI but before my registration has been validated?

No, you cannot file your insider profile or your insider report until your registration is validated. Once the registration process is complete, you will be able to make filings that will be made publicly accessible.

4.1.7 — What if I need to file my insider profile or insider reports and SEDI is unavailable?

Please see question 1.9.

4.1.8 — Am I a reporting insider?

See the definition of reporting insider in the Defined Terms section of this notice or seek legal advice.

4.1.9 — Do I have to file reports if I am a reporting insider?

Yes. You need to report your holdings of securities and related financial instruments of the SEDI issuer of which you are a reporting insider, and any changes in these holdings unless you are within an exemption in NI 55-104 or NI 62-103 or have been otherwise exempted by a securities regulatory authority.

4.1.10 — Do I need to report for a period before I was a director, CEO, CFO or COO of the relevant reporting issuer?

Yes. In certain situations, the "look-back" rules in subsections 1.2(2) and 1.2(3) and section 3.5 of NI 55-104 may require you to file an insider report on SEDI in relation to certain historical transactions.

Issuer as insider of reporting issuer — If an issuer (the first issuer) becomes an insider of a reporting issuer (the second issuer), the CEO, CFO, COO and every director of the first issuer must file insider reports in respect of transactions relating to securities and related financial instruments of the second issuer that occurred in the previous six months or for such shorter period that the individual was a CEO, CFO, COO or director of the first issuer.

Reporting issuer as insider of other issuer — If a reporting issuer (the first issuer) becomes an insider of another issuer (the second issuer), the CEO, CFO, COO and every director of the second issuer must file insider reports in respect of transactions relating to securities and related financial instruments of the first issuer that occurred in the previous six months or for such shorter period that the individual was a CEO, CFO, COO or director of the second issuer.

Example — If a reporting issuer (A Co) owns 5% of the common shares of another reporting issuer (B Co), and then acquires, on June 30, 2011, an additional 25% of B Co's common shares through an exempt take-over bid, A Co will have become an "insider" (as defined in securities legislation) of B Co on June 30, 2011 because A Co has become a "significant shareholder" (as defined in NI 55-104) of B Co as of that date.

As a result of the special designation/determination provisions in subsections 1.2(2) and (3) of NI 55-104, the CEO, CFO, COO and every director of A Co are designated or determined to be insiders of B Co and the CEO, CFO, COO and every director of B Co are designated or determined to be insiders of A Co. (Section 1.2 of NI 55-104 uses the terms "designated" and "determined" to reflect the different terms used in securities legislation across Canada. They mean the same thing.)

Note that the CEO, CFO, COO and every director of A Co will also be insiders and reporting insiders of B Co under the ordinary definition of "insider" and "reporting insider". However, the CEO, CFO, COO and every director of B Co would not normally be insiders and reporting insiders of A Co (unless they were insiders and reporting insiders in another capacity) since B Co would not be a "subsidiary" of A Co.

There are special reporting rules that apply to the period that precedes a take-over bid or similar acquisition. The purpose of these provisions is to address concerns over directors and officers of a company proposing to acquire a significant interest in another company by unlawfully "frontrunning" the acquisition through personal purchases of shares of the second company.

Section 3.5 of NI 55-104 requires the CEO, CFO, COO and every director of A Co to file insider reports in respect of transactions relating to securities and related financial instruments of B Co that occurred in the previous six months or for such shorter period that the individual was a CEO, CFO, COO or director of A Co. Similarly, the CEO, CFO, COO and every director of B Co must file insider reports in respect of transactions relating to securities and related financial instruments of A Co that occurred in the previous six months or for such shorter period that the individual was a CEO, CFO, COO or director of B Co. When filing these transactions, we recommend that you select relationship code 8 on your insider profile.

4.1.11 — As a reporting insider, do I need to report securities and related financial instruments that my spouse owns or controls?

As a reporting insider of a SEDI issuer, you need to report any securities and any related financial instruments of that SEDI issuer that your spouse (or any other person) owns if you *have* or *share* control or direction, whether direct or indirect, over those securities or related financial instruments.

A person will generally have or share control or direction over securities if the person directly or indirectly through any contract, arrangement, understanding or relationship or otherwise has or shares

- voting power, which includes the power to vote, or to direct the voting of, such securities and/or

- investment power, which includes the power to acquire or dispose, or to direct the acquisition or disposition of such securities.

4.1.12 — What if I already have an insider profile and need to add new reportable securities or related financial instruments?

We recommend that you file an opening balance for the new reportable security or related financial instrument and add a note in the general remarks field to explain that the balance reflects what you held on a specific date (e.g. April 30, 2010, the date NI 55-104 came into effect) rather than what you held on the date you became an insider.

4.1.13 — What if I am no longer required under securities legislation to file insider reports in relation to a particular company?

You can cease filing insider reports on SEDI, provided you have reported all transactions that took place when you were required to file insider reports. Also, see question 4.2.10.

4.2 — Insider Profile

4.2.1 — What is an insider profile?

An insider profile contains information identifying you as the insider, and your relationship with one or more SEDI issuers. The information required is set out in Form 55-102F1. You must not file more than one insider profile.

4.2.2 — When do I file an insider profile?

You need to file your insider profile and opening balance reports **within 10 calendar days of becoming a reporting insider** if you beneficially own, or have or share direct or indirect control or direction over, securities or related financial instruments of the issuer of which you are a reporting insider.

Note that if you enter into a reportable transaction within 10 calendar days of becoming a reporting insider, this may have the effect of accelerating your requirement to file an insider profile and opening balance report, since you need to take these steps before you can file a report about the reportable transaction. See example below.

If you are a reporting insider or otherwise required by securities legislation to file insider reports in respect of a SEDI issuer, but do not own or control securities or related financial instruments relating to that SEDI issuer, you do not need to file an insider profile until an insider report is required. However, if you wait until you are required to file an insider report, you must file your insider profile at the same time.

Alternatively, you can set up and file your insider profile with a zero opening balance report (for each security, ownership type and registered holder combination) after you or your agent are registered as a SEDI user, but before any of your insider reports are due.

Example: New Reporting Insider
Question

1. On November 1, 2010, I became a director of ABC Inc. and therefore a "reporting insider" for this issuer under NI 55-104.

2. I understand that, in accordance with section 3.2 of NI 55-104, I am required to file my initial report within 10 calendar days of becoming a reporting insider. Accordingly, my initial report would appear to be due on November 10, 2010.

3. On November 3, 2010, I purchased 100 common shares of ABC Inc. in a market transaction.

4. According to section 3.3 of NI 55-104, I am required to file an insider report within five calendar days of any change in my ownership or control of securities or interests in or rights or obligations associated with a related financial instrument. Accordingly, my insider report for this transaction would appear to be due on November 8, 2010.

5. What is my deadline for the initial report? What is my deadline for reporting the purchase of 100 shares?

Response

1. The deadline for filing the initial report would ordinarily be November 10, 2010. However, as a result of the purchase of 100 shares on November 3, 2010, the deadline for filing the initial report has effectively been accelerated to November 8, 2010. This is because, in order to be able to file an insider report about the purchase of 100 shares by the required due date of November 8, 2010, it will first be necessary to file the initial report.

2. The deadline for filing the report about the purchase of 100 shares is, in this example, November 8, 2010.

4.2.3 — What information do I need to include in my insider profile?

You need to include:

- full legal name (if an individual insider)

- company name (if not an individual insider)

- full legal name of individual representative of insider (if insider is not an individual)

- residential address (business address for insider's representative, if insider is not an individual)

- street name and number

- municipality (city or town)

- province, territory or state

- postal code or zip code (if in North America)

- country of residence

- daytime telephone number

- fax number (if applicable)

- e-mail address (Note: if you would like to receive notifications of access key changes or other updates via e-mail, you will need to provide an e-mail address)

- confidential question and answer (see next paragraph)

- Issuer number or name of SEDI issuer

- the date you became an insider of the SEDI issuer (if you have not already filed an insider report for the issuer) or the opening balance date (if you have previously filed an insider report for this issuer) (see next paragraph)

- relationship with SEDI issuer

- registered holders (if applicable)

- date you ceased to be an insider (when applicable)

For the confidential question and answer, you should provide a question for which only you would know the answer. For example, "What is your favourite movie?" rather than "Which country won the most gold medals at the 2010 Winter Olympics?" You must provide an answer to this question. If you forget your password, the SEDI operator will ask you this question to verify that you are who you say you are.

The opening balance date is used for all opening balances for this issuer and should be a date prior to the date of any transactions that you are required to report on SEDI in connection with a SEDI issuer.

4.2.4 — What do I need to do if I am a reporting insider of several companies?

You need to file a separate insider report for each company that is a reporting issuer and in which you own or have interests in securities or related financial instruments. You need to file one insider profile and indicate the names of all the companies of which you are a reporting insider. If you use an agent to file for you, we recommend that you only use one. However, if you choose to have different people file insider reports for you for these different companies, you must make sure that only one insider profile is created for you. You may wish to have one agent set up the profile for you, and then share your access key with all of your other filing agents.

4.2.5 — What if the information in my insider profile changes?

You need to amend your profile on SEDI. You must do this within 10 days if you change your name or your relationship to a SEDI issuer, or if you cease to be a reporting insider of a SEDI issuer. For other changes, you can amend your profile the next time you have to file an insider report.

4.2.6 — What if I cannot find a SEDI issuer in the database that I need to add to my insider profile?

You should contact the issuer to ask whether the issuer has filed its issuer profile supplement on SEDI. If the issuer has not yet done so, it may be in default of its reporting requirements and you will be unable to file an insider report on SEDI for any securities and related financial instruments of that issuer. Encourage the issuer to file its issuer profile supplement so that you can file your insider profile. You may also contact your local securities regulatory authority as soon as possible to advise them of this.

If your report is due and you cannot file your insider report on SEDI because the issuer has not filed its issuer profile supplement, you can file your report in paper form (Form 55-102F6) under the temporary hardship exemption. However, when you become aware that the issuer has filed its issuer profile supplement, you will have to re-file your insider report on SEDI. See NI 55-102, section 4.1. See questions 1.9 and 4.3.7 (temporary hardship exemption).

4.2.7 — Do I need to add the name of the broker or depository as the registered holder of the securities if I own the securities directly?

No. For insider reporting, the term "registered holder" means the entity through which you beneficially own or control securities such as an RRSP, holding company, family trust, or the person or company that owns the securities over which you have control or direction. Securities owned directly but held through a nominee such as a broker or book-based depository, are considered direct holdings. See Form 55-102F1, item 14, and Form 55-102F2, item 6.

4.2.8 — When do I need to add registered holders and in what circumstances?

Whenever you create an insider profile and file an insider report, SEDI will prompt you to indicate how you (or your insider, if you are an agent, filing for an insider) hold the securities.

You can hold your securities in the following three ways:

(1) You can hold them *directly*. For example, you can hold the securities in an account with your broker, but the account is in your name.

(2) You can hold them *indirectly*. For example, you beneficially own common shares in X Co. but the registered owner is another entity such as a holding company, an RRSP, or a family trust.

(3) You can have *control or direction* over them. You have control or direction over the securities if you, directly or indirectly, through any contract, arrangement, understanding or relationship or otherwise have or share

- voting power, or

- investment power.

This would include having control or direction over the securities through a power of attorney, a grant of limited trading authority, or management agreement. For example, you set up a trust for your children in which X Co. securities are held. Because of your relation-

Part 5: ONGOING REQUIREMENTS

ship with your children, you need to report your children's holdings, because you could direct your children to purchase or sell those securities. This may also be the case if your spouse owns the securities, but you have control or direction over those securities.

If you choose either 'Indirect' or 'Control or Direction', SEDI will prompt you to add the name of a registered holder. The registered holder is the entity through which you beneficially own the securities, such as an RRSP, holding company, family trust, or the person or company that owns the securities over which you have control or direction.

4.2.9 — If I am no longer an insider, what do I have to do on SEDI?

You have to amend your insider profile using the "add or amend issuer information" button, to indicate in the "Date the insider ceased being an insider of this issuer" field that you have ceased to be an insider of that issuer. (See item 12 of Form 55-102F1).

4.2.10 — If I cease to be a reporting insider, but am still an insider, how do I update my insider profile to reflect the change?

Once you have ceased to be a reporting insider you are no longer required to report your insider transactions on SEDI. There are no requirements to update your insider profile to reflect the change. However, we recommend that you add a public remark to your last filed transaction advising that you are no longer required to report and will cease reporting your transactions on SEDI effective the date of the change in your status.

4.2.11 — What is the additional contact information that I can provide on my insider profile?

If you wish, you can add the name and contact information of a person that the securities regulatory authorities or the SEDI operator could contact, instead of you, regarding your filings for a particular SEDI issuer. This person should be an individual who has your permission and authority to speak on your behalf regarding your insider reports and filings on SEDI. Alternatively, you could also put additional contact information for yourself if you do not wish to be contacted at your residential address. None of this additional contact information is released to the public. If you wish to provide this optional information, you need to enter the information for each particular issuer for which you are an insider.

4.2.12 — What date do I report: an opening balance date or the date I became a reporting insider?

If you *have not* previously filed an insider report for the issuer, enter the date on which you became an insider of this issuer.

If you *have* previously filed an insider report for this issuer, enter the opening balance date. This date will be used for all opening balances for this issuer and should be prior to the date of any transactions required to be reported for this issuer on SEDI.

4.2.13 — What if I have filed a duplicate insider profile by mistake?

Each insider should only have one insider profile on SEDI. However, if you inadvertently filed more than one, please advise your securities regulatory authority in writing (see Appendix A) who will then take the necessary steps to have the SEDI operator remove the duplicate profiles from SEDI.

4.3 — Insider Report

4.3.1 — General

4.3.2 — When do I file my insider report on SEDI?

If you already own or control, directly or indirectly, securities or related financial instruments relating to a SEDI issuer, you need to file your insider profile and opening balance reports within 10 calendar days of becoming a reporting insider. You need to file a report of any changes to your holdings within five calendar days[10] of the change.

Note that if you enter into a reportable transaction within 10 calendar days of becoming a reporting insider, this may have the effect of accelerating your requirement to file an insider profile and opening balance report, since you need to take these steps before you can file a report about the reportable transaction. See the example in question 4.2.2.

Certain exemptions may allow you to report changes in your holdings later, for example, changes resulting from an automatic share purchase plan. See question 4.5.2.

4.3.3 — Do I need to file a separate report on SEDI for each province and territory where I have insider reporting obligations?

SEDI is the electronic filing system for insider reporting. You need to file an insider report in all provinces and territories in which the company (or other entity) of which you are a reporting insider is a reporting issuer.

Filing an insider report on SEDI satisfies the insider reporting requirements in all provinces and territories in which you have insider reporting obligations relating to that reporting issuer.

4.3.4 — What type of report do I file when I first become a reporting insider of a SEDI issuer and own securities or related financial instruments of that issuer?

You need to file an initial opening balance report within 10 calendar days of the date you first become a reporting insider of a reporting issuer *if you have reportable securities or related financial instruments on that date*. In your report, you must disclose your beneficial ownership of,

---

[10]Prior to November 1, 2010, within 10 calendar days.

or control or direction over (whether direct or indirect), securities and interests in or rights or obligations associated with related financial instruments of that issuer.

You will initially need to file (create) an insider profile in the system before you can file this opening balance report. Once your insider profile is filed, you can then file your opening balance report, disclosing all your current holdings in the securities and related financial instruments of the SEDI issuer. For each particular type of security and related financial instrument, the system will ask you to input an opening balance.

If you do not have any interests in any securities or related financial instruments of the reporting issuer when you first become a reporting insider, you do not need to file an insider profile or an initial opening balance. You may choose to set up an insider profile and file a zero balance opening balance report. If you choose to file a zero opening balance report, all subsequent reports, including your first insider report of a transaction in the securities or related financial instruments of the issuer must be filed within five calendar days[11].

Otherwise, the first insider report you will file will be when you have your first transaction in securities or related financial instruments of the reporting issuer. At this time you will need to set up an insider profile (if you have not already done so) and file the initial report within five calendar days after you made this first transaction. All subsequent reports must also be filed within five calendar days.

Note that if you enter into a reportable transaction within 10 calendar days of becoming a reporting insider, this may have the effect of accelerating your requirement to file an insider profile and opening balance report, since you need to take these steps before you can file a report about the reportable transaction. See the example in question 4.2.2.

4.3.5 — What type of report do I file after I have made my initial SEDI report?

After you have made your initial SEDI report, you need to file an insider report within five calendar days[12] of the date on which any change in your holdings of the reporting issuer occurs.

You need to file an insider report on SEDI, disclosing your transactions in those securities that have resulted in a change in your beneficial ownership of, or control or direction over, them. You do not need to report closing balances if the balances did not change and you have already reported them. SEDI calculates and maintains a record of all these holdings as reported previously.

4.3.6 — How do I know if my insider report is successfully filed on SEDI?

SEDI will automatically record the date and time (in the Eastern Time Zone) that your insider report is filed on SEDI. To print the insider report you have filed and certified with the date and time of filing, click the "Printer friendly version" button from the File insider report — Completed screen. You can also verify that your insider report has been filed by logging off and then accessing the public reports. You will need to wait about five minutes for the system to update the information you have just filed before your transactions will appear on the public reports.

4.3.7 — When do I file insider reports in paper format?

You (or an agent on your behalf) need to file insider reports electronically on SEDI, unless you are exempt from insider reporting requirements under provincial securities legislation or an order of the relevant securities regulatory authority. In certain circumstances, however, you may need to file insider reports in paper format rather than on SEDI. These would include:

(1) **Reporting insider of a non-SEDI issuer** — You are a reporting insider of a non-SEDI issuer (i.e., a foreign reporting issuer who has not elected to file disclosure documents on SEDAR) that is required by securities legislation to report insider transactions and you are not otherwise exempt from the insider reporting requirements;

(2) **Report by Registered Holder** — You are a registered holder of voting securities of an issuer and you know the beneficial owner (or in Quebec the person who has control or direction over such securities) is a reporting insider that is required by securities legislation to report insider transactions but this insider has not filed a report of the ownership or control (except where there was a transfer for giving collateral for a genuine debt);

(3) **General Exemption** — You are granted a discretionary exemption from filing insider reports on SEDI by the relevant securities regulators, upon application under NI 55-102, Part 6. Depending on the circumstances, one of the conditions to that exemption may be that you file insider reports in paper format;

(4) **Unanticipated Technical Difficulties (Temporary)** — You are having unanticipated technical difficulties, i.e., SEDI is unavailable due to technical problems with SEDI, when trying to file your insider report in electronic format;

(5) **No Issuer Profile Supplement (Temporary)** — You are the insider of a SEDI issuer that has not yet filed its issuer profile supplement and your insider report is due.

Note that (4) and (5) are only temporary exemptions from filing on SEDI. They are available to insiders. (However, for issuers, please see the exemption in the answer to question 3.1.10.) You need to file the report in paper format using Form 55-102F6. See question 1.9 for further details.

You must file this report within two business days of when the report was due to be filed on SEDI. Once you have resolved the technical difficulties or you become aware that the issuer has filed its issuer profile supplement, as applicable, you must re-file your insider report on SEDI. You should therefore only use the exemptions in (4) and (5) when the circumstances allowing you to use the exemption arise and your report is due. See Part 4 of NI 55-102.

You can find Form 55-102F6 in the additional information section of the SEDI online help.

---

[11]Prior to November 1, 2010, within 10 calendar days.

[12]Prior to November 1, 2010, within 10 calendar days.

4.3.8 — How do I check if my filing was completed?

Your report will be filed only if you completed the process and certified your filing. To check, log off the system and wait at least five minutes. After waiting, go to the SEDI website and click on "Access public filings" to now view your report as a public record.

4.3.9 — As an agent can I make a bulk filing for a number of reporting insiders?

No.

4.3.10 — Do I need to file on SEDI insider reports required under federal legislation, such as the *Canada Business Corporations Act*?

SEDI only supports filing under provincial securities legislation. However, there are no insider reporting requirements currently under the *Canada Business Corporations Act, Bank Act, Cooperative Credit Associations Act, Insurance Companies Act* or *Trust and Loan Companies Act*.

4.3.11 — What do I file if I am an insider of a U.S. issuer that is a registrant with the SEC and I file insider reports with the SEC?

Generally, you need to file your reports on SEDI if that issuer files disclosure documents on SEDAR.

However, you do not need to file insider reports if:

- the issuer is a "U.S. issuer" under National Instrument 71-101, *The Multijurisdictional Disclosure System* that has securities registered under the United States Securities Exchange Act of 1934, or

- the issuer is a "SEC foreign issuer" under National Instrument 71-102, *Continuous Disclosure and Other Exemptions Relating to Foreign Issuers* (NI 71-102)

and you comply with the U.S. federal securities law regarding insider reporting and you file the required reports with the SEC.

4.3.12 — What do I file if I am an insider of a Designated Foreign Issuer under NI 71-102?

Generally, the insider reporting requirement does not apply to an insider of a Designated Foreign Issuer provided you comply with the disclosure requirements related to insider reporting in the jurisdiction where the foreign issuer is regulated. See Part 5 of NI 71-102.

4.3.13 — What is the significance of the codes used on SEDI?

It is important to use the correct codes to avoid any uncertainty as to the nature of your transaction and to avoid misleading the marketplace. You use codes to describe:

- the type of the transaction you are reporting (nature of transaction),

- the type of ownership or other interest you have of the securities, and

- your relationship with the issuer

For a current list, see the instruction page of Form 55-102F6 (available on SEDI though the on-line help and the securities regulatory authorities' websites — see Appendix A).

4.3.14 — I want to report a transaction but SEDI keeps asking me for an opening balance for my securities. What do I do?

When you file your first insider report for a particular security (and registered holder, if applicable), the system will always ask for the opening balance before you can file actual transaction details. This is required in order to enable SEDI to automatically calculate your holdings of that security as of the date of your transaction.

You should enter the total number for the type of security you held as of your opening balance date. (You will have entered this date on your insider profile and it will appear on the opening balance screen as 'Date of transaction'). If you did not hold that type of security as of the date of your last opening balance, you should enter '0' as your opening balance.

4.3.15 — When reporting values and amounts, can I enter commas, decimals or fractions?

You can use decimals and fractions in the unit price or exercise price and conversion or exercise price fields on SEDI. When a decimal is used for amounts in cents (with no dollars), please also enter the '0' before the decimal, i.e., '0.11' for eleven cents. Please round up or down fractional amounts for securities. SEDI allows the use of a comma in the General or Private remarks fields only.

4.3.16 — How do I add more information about the transaction I am reporting?

You can add additional information in the 'Remarks' field. If you do not want the additional information to be public, use the 'Private remarks to securities regulatory authority'. To the extent that more space is needed, you may wish to consider cross-referencing a document already publicly disclosed that has this information, such as a press release or a material change report.

4.3.17 — What if I have to change information that I already filed in a report on SEDI?

You can change this information by filing on SEDI an amended insider report.

4.3.18 — Do I have to report all my holdings of securities and related financial instruments of the SEDI issuer or just the securities and related financial instruments in respect of which my ownership or control has changed?

The first time you file on SEDI, you must report all of your holdings of securities and related financial instruments of the SEDI issuer. Subsequently, you only need to report changes in interests in, or new interests in securities and related financial instruments, or changes in control or direction over, securities and related financial instruments of the SEDI issuer.

4.3.19 — What do I do if I have been previously filing insider reports but am no longer required to?

You should add a comment in the "Remarks" field explaining that you are no longer a reporting insider or are exempt. You can do this either on your next transaction to be filed on SEDI or by amending your last report already filed on SEDI. A member of the public viewing your insider reports on SEDI will then know why you have ceased reporting.

4.3.20 — Do I also need to file an insider report if I file an early warning report (EWR) or an alternative monthly report (AMR) for a particular transaction?

You may not need to file an insider report when you file an EWR or AMR if you can use the exemption provided in Part 9 of NI 62-103. The EWRs and AMRs are filed on SEDAR.

4.3.21 — Do I need to file a report when I become a reporting insider if I do not own or control any securities or related financial instruments of the issuer?

Generally no. Please see the exemption in section 9.4 of NI 55-104.

4.4 — Reporting for Related Financial Instruments

4.4.1 — What is a related financial instrument?

A related financial instrument is an instrument, agreement, security or, in some jurisdictions an exchange contract, that has a value based on, derived from, or otherwise referenced to the value, market price or payment obligations of a security. The term also includes any other type of instrument, agreement or understanding that affects, whether directly or indirectly, a person or company's economic interest in a security or exchange contract.

For further explanation of related financial instruments and economic interest, see Part 1 of Companion Policy 55-104CP.

Important note: SEDI does not use the term "related financial instrument". Instead, for the purposes of SEDI, all instruments — whether securities or related financial instruments — are considered securities. For the purposes of SEDI, the category of "security" includes two subcategories relating to derivatives:

- "Issuer derivatives" are derivatives issued by the issuer. Issuer derivatives include options, warrants, rights and special warrants issued by an issuer. Share-based compensation instruments, including phantom stock units, deferred share units (DSUs), restricted share awards (RSAs), performance share units (PSUs), stock appreciation rights (SARs) and similar instruments are also generally issuer derivatives. The issuer designates these derivatives in its issuer profile supplement.

- "Third party derivatives" are derivatives offered by someone other than the issuer. The price, value or payment obligations of third party derivatives are based on an underlying interest (such as common shares) issued by the issuer as the underlying security. Third party derivatives include exchange-traded options or over-the-counter (OTC) options.

Please refer to the derivatives section in the online help on SEDI for additional information about derivatives reporting.

4.4.2 — What related financial instruments do I need to report on SEDI?

You need to report all of your interests in, or rights or obligations associated with, related financial instruments in accordance with the requirements of securities legislation.

For guidance on reporting related financial instruments and economic interest, see Part 1 of Companion Policy 55-104CP.

4.4.3 — What is an underlying security and how do I report it?

An underlying security is a security you would acquire or dispose of if you exercised the rights you acquired when you purchased a different security. For example, if you have options that are exercisable into common shares, the common shares are the "underlying securities". On SEDI, you must report both the initial securities you acquired and their underlying securities and related financial instruments.

Example: You were granted options under your company's stock option plan. The options are convertible into common shares on a 1:1 basis when you exercise your options.

You must report the grant as follows:

- Report the number of options granted as an acquisition. Use nature of transaction code 50 to report the acquisition. Report the equivalent number of underlying securities acquired. Enter the date of the transaction, the grant price, etc. and then go through the steps required to certify and file your report.

If you exercise the options, you must report the exercise as follows:

- Report the number of options being exercised as a disposition. Use nature of transaction code 51 to report the disposition. Enter the date of the transaction, the exercise price, etc. and then go through the steps required to certify and file your report.

- Show an acquisition of the underlying security (e.g., common shares) equal to the appropriate number of options exercised. Use nature of transaction code 51 to report the acquisition of the common shares.

- If you subsequently sell the common shares, you must file a separate report for the sale.

4.5 — Reporting Transactions

4.5.1 — How does an issuer that is an insider report transactions under a normal course issuer bid?

Under NI 55-104 an issuer can report acquisitions in connection with normal course issuer bids (as defined in NI 55-104) within 10 days of the end of the month in which the acquisitions occurred, as opposed to within five calendar days[13] of the transaction. NI 55-104 requires you to report each acquisition.

We recommend that you report transactions under a normal course issuer bid within 10 calendar days of the end of the month, in the following manner.

Step 1:

Report *each acquisition* of securities that took place under the normal course issuer bid as a separate transaction, with the appropriate nature of transaction code 38 — Redemption/ retraction/cancellation/repurchase.

Step 2:

Report *each cancellation* of securities acquired under the normal course issuer bid as a separate transaction using the relevant nature of transaction code 38 — Redemption/retraction/cancellation/repurchase.

4.5.2 — How do I report acquisitions under an automatic securities purchase plan (including employee share ownership plans (ESOP) and dividend reinvestment plans (DRIP))?

Any securities acquired under an automatic securities purchase plan during a calendar year that have not been disposed of or transferred, and any securities that have been disposed of or transferred as part of a specified disposition of securities, must be reported on or before March 31 of the next calendar year. You should report acquisitions under your automatic share purchase plan using the nature of transaction code 30 for each transaction.

Any securities acquired under an automatic securities purchase that are subsequently disposed of or transferred, other than as part of a specified disposition of those securities, must be reported within five days[14] of the disposition or transfer.

For further guidance on reporting securities acquired, disposed of or transferred under an automatic securities purchase plan, see question 4.5.3 below, and refer to Part 5 of Companion Policy 55-104CP. See also Part 6 of NI 55-104 for reporting exemptions for issuer grants.

4.5.3 — If I acquire securities through an employee share ownership plan (ESOP) or a dividend reinvestment plan (DRIP), do I hold these securities directly or indirectly (do I indicate the "registered owner" on my report)?

Whether or not you should indicate the ESOP or DRIP as the "registered owner" depends on whether the ESOP or DRIP is the "beneficial owner" of, or has control over, the securities. The answer may be different depending on the terms of the particular plan. If you have the right to vote or sell securities held in a plan, you would normally be considered to hold these securities directly. You should speak to your employer to find out whether the ESOP or DRIP is the registered owner, or whether you hold these securities directly.

4.5.4 — How do I report holdings of securities under an RRSP?

You should report that you hold these securities *indirectly* and indicate that the "registered holder" is the RRSP.

4.5.5 — How do I report share-based compensation (other than options) such as deferred share units (DSUs), restricted share awards (RSAs), and stock appreciation rights (SARs)?

One of the most common forms of share-based compensation is granting options that, upon exercise, are converted into the issuer's common shares. However, there are other types of share-based compensation. For example, restricted share awards (RSAs) and deferred share units (DSUs) entitle recipients to an award of the issuer's common shares after a specified period or cash payments based on the value or growth in value of the issuer's common shares over a specified period. In contrast, stock appreciation rights (SARs) typically only entitle employees to cash payments based on the value or growth in value of the issuer's common shares over a specified period.

Historically, there has been some uncertainty as to whether, as a matter of law, certain derivative instruments involving securities are themselves securities. Under NI 55-104, it is not necessary to determine whether a particular derivative instrument is a security or a related financial instrument since the insider reporting requirement in Part 3 of NI 55-104 applies to both securities and related financial instruments. To the extent DSUs, RSAs and SARs do not, as a matter of law, constitute securities, they will generally be related financial instruments.

- *RSAs and DSUs*

Step 1 — Grant of RSAs or DSUs:

Report the number of RSAs or DSUs awarded and report the equivalent amount of underlying common shares using nature of transaction code 56 — Grant of rights. On SEDI, report the underlying common shares in the "Equivalent number of underlying securities" box. In SEDI, issuers should have created a security designation for the RSAs or DSUs in the issuer profile supplement, and selected the "Issuer derivative" category.

---

[13]Prior to November 1, 2010, within 10 calendar days.

[14]Prior to November 1, 2010, within 10 calendar days.

Step 2 — *Vesting and distribution of underlying common shares or cash:*

When the RSAs or DSUs vest and are settled in underlying common shares, report an acquisition of the relevant number of underlying common shares as one transaction using nature of transaction code 57 — Exercise of rights. You will also need to report a disposition of the corresponding number of the RSAs or DSUs, using nature of transaction code 57, as another transaction.

When the RSAs or DSUs vest and are settled by a cash payment, report a disposition of the relevant number of the RSAs or DSUs using nature of transaction code 59 — Exercise for cash.

- *SARs*

Step 1 — *Grant of SARs*

Report the number of SARs awarded, and the exercise price, and report the equivalent amount of underlying common shares using nature of transaction code 56 — Grant of rights. Issuers should have created a security designation for the SARs in the issuer profile supplement, and selected the "Issuer derivative" category.

Step 2 — *Vesting and distribution of cash*

Report a disposition of the relevant number of SARs using nature of transaction code 59 — Exercise for cash.

4.5.6 — How do I report a grant of related financial instruments which predates April 30, 2010?

See CSA Staff Notice 55-315 *Frequently Asked Questions about National Instrument 55-104 Insider Reporting Requirements and Exemptions.*

4.5.7 — When do I report changes to my holdings as a result of share consolidations/splits?

You, the reporting insider, need to report these changes in your holdings resulting from an issuer event the next time you need to file an insider report. See Part 8 of NI 55-104.

4.5.8 — For what issuer events do I need to report changes in my securities holdings?

You need to report changes in your holdings in securities of a reporting issuer resulting from such events as a stock dividend, stock split, consolidation, amalgamation, reorganization or other similar event that affects all holdings of a class of securities of an issuer in the same manner, on a per share basis.

4.5.9 — How do I report the change in my holdings resulting from an issuer event?

Example: a 4-for-1 consolidation of 100 common shares

If you held 100 common shares that were consolidated on a 4:1 basis (so that you now hold 25 common shares), you report the change as follows. Calculate the new number of common shares you hold after the consolidation — in this case, 25 common shares. Subtract your new holdings from what you held before the stock consolidation; in this case, 100 — 25, and then report the difference — i.e. 75 common shares, using nature of transaction code 37 — Stock split or consolidation.

Example: a 4-for-1 split of 100 common shares

If you held 100 common shares that were split on a 4:1 basis (so that you now hold 400 common shares), you report the change as follows. Calculate the new number of common shares you hold after the split — in this case, 400 common shares. Subtract from this number the number of common shares you held before the split: 400 — 100, and report the difference — i.e. 300 common shares as an acquisition using nature of transaction code 37.

4.5.10 — What are equity monetization transactions?

Equity monetization transactions are transactions that allow an investor to receive a cash amount similar to proceeds of disposition, and to transfer all or part of the economic risk and/or return associated with securities of an issuer, without actually transferring the legal and beneficial ownership of such securities.

The term "monetization" generally refers to the conversion of an asset (such as securities) into cash.

For additional guidance on how to report these types of transactions, please refer to CSA Staff Notice 55-312 *Insider Reporting Guidelines for Certain Derivative Transactions (Equity Monetization)* (REVISED).

See Part 4 of NI 55-104 for the supplemental insider reporting requirements for equity monetization transactions and Part 4 of Companion Policy 55-104CP.

4.5.11 — Do I have to file insider reports for securities that I have monetized?

Yes.

4.5.12 — How do I report an exercise of options?

There are the following two steps to report the exercise of an option:

Step 1 — Report the number of options being exercised as a disposition. Use nature of transaction code 51 to show the disposition. If you are not sure of the number of underlying shares, you can ask the insider affairs contact person found in the issuer profile supplement of the company. Enter the date of the transaction, the exercise price, etc. and then go through the steps required to certify and file your report.

Step 2 — Show an acquisition of the underlying security (e.g., common shares) equal to the appropriate number of options exercised. Use nature of transaction code 51 to report the acquisition of the common shares.

4.5.13 — What are the most common filing errors on insider reports?

Here is a list of the most common filing errors made on insider reports. We strongly suggest that you check your proposed filing for these types of errors in order to lessen the likelihood that a securities regulatory authority will consider your report incorrect and contact you.

- Problems with reporting your type of ownership — Not reporting by type of holding (direct ownership, indirect ownership, or control or direction)

- Reporting escrowed shares as a separate class of securities

- Not reporting the name of the registered holder (for indirect or control/direction holdings)

- Not showing both sides of the transaction, if applicable (e.g., exercise of options — disposition of options/acquisition of common shares). See question 4.5.12.

5. — Public Access

Any member of the public can view information filed on SEDI by clicking 'Access public filings' on the Welcome to SEDI page on the SEDI website (www.sedi.ca). The information is available in either French or English. Four reports (described below), including the weekly summary report of insider transactions, are available to you to use in accordance with the Terms of Use — Public. You can download the reports to your computer (PDF format only) and you can print them.

5.1 — Can I search for information filed on SEDI?

Yes. SEDI provides extensive search capabilities for public users. You can either download a weekly report, capturing all insider reports filed for a Friday through Thursday period, or search the database using an extensive set of parameters such as insider's name, issuer, date ranges or types of securities.

5.2 — What reports can I view on SEDI?

You can view the following reports:

- Weekly summary — provides a summary of all insider reports filed after Thursday at 4 p.m. Eastern Time and before Thursday at 4 p.m. of the following week (for each of the three preceding weeks only)

- Insider transaction detail — provides a summary of all individual transactions filed by insiders, based on the search criteria used

- Insider information by issuer — provides a list of all registered insiders by each SEDI issuer, based on the search criteria used

- Issuer event history — provides a list of all issuer events reported by an issuer.

Except for the Weekly summary report which displays only in PDF format, the above reports are displayed online in HTML format and can also be downloaded in PDF format. You can view these reports in a Web browser.

5.3 — Do I need to be registered on SEDI to view these reports?

No. To view these reports go to the SEDI website (www.sedi.ca) and, on the *Welcome to SEDI* page, click 'Access public filings'.

5.4 — What weekly summaries can I view?

You can view one of three weekly summary reports (1 or 2 or 3 weeks back only) by clicking on the week requested. For insider reports older than three weeks, you need to do a specific search using the insider transaction detail report.

5.5 — Does the weekly summary include reports only from one province or reports from all provinces and territories?

The weekly summary reports includes consolidated reports from all provinces and territories. However, you can search the database for an insider transaction detail report using certain parameters so that such reports include specific provinces or territories, for example, only Ontario reports. For certain provinces you can go to the website of the securities regulatory authority to obtain the weekly summary of reports filed in that province.

5.6 — Does SEDI list the number of issued and outstanding securities for each issuer?

No, that information is not available on SEDI. This information will generally be available on SEDAR in the issuer's most recent information circular and other continuous disclosure filings. You can generally rely on an issuer's disclosure of its outstanding securities to determine if you are a "significant shareholder" and therefore a "reporting insider", unless you know the issuer's disclosed information is not correct. See section 1.3 of NI 55-104 (Reliance on Reported Outstanding Shares).

5.7 — Can I subscribe to receive information on filings by certain insiders, or by insiders of particular companies or other information filed on SEDI?

These services are not part of SEDI. However, bulk and/or real-time SEDI data feeds may be available for resale. Please contact the SEDI operator.

5.8 — Where can I look at insider reports filed in paper format?

You can look at these reports at the offices of the relevant securities regulatory authority during business hours or, to see a summary of insider transactions, on their respective websites.

Appendix A — Securities Regulatory Authorities and SEDI Contact and Website Information

Canadian Securities Administrators (CSA)

website: www.securities-administrators.ca

Securities Regulatory Authorities

Alberta Securities Commission

4th Floor, 300-5th Avenue S.W.

Calgary, AB, Canada

T2P 3C4

Attention: Compliance Officer, Corporate Finance

Telephone: 403-297-2489

Facsimile: 403-297-6156

E-mail: Inquiry@asc.ca

Website: www.albertasecurities.com

Autorité des marchés financiers

800, square Victoria, 22e étage

C.P. 246, tour de la Bourse

Montréal, Québec

H4Z 1G3

Attention: Information Center

Telephone: 514-395-0337 or 877-525-0337

Facsimile: 514-873-3090

For insider reports:

    Telephone: 514-395-0337 ext. 4200

    Facsimile: 514-873-3120

    E-mail: inities@lautorite.qc.ca

    Website: http://www.lautorite.qc.ca

British Columbia Securities Commission

P.O. Box 10142 Pacific Centre

701 West Georgia Street

Vancouver, BC Canada

V7Y 1L2

Attention: Insider Reporting

Telephone: 604-899-6500 or 800-373-6393 (in BC)

Facsimile: 604-899-6506 (for correspondence)

E-mail: inquiries@bcsc.bc.ca

Website: www.bcsc.bc.ca

Manitoba Securities Commission

500-400 St. Mary Avenue

Winnipeg, MB, Canada

R3K 4K5

Attention: Insider Reporting

Telephone: 204-945-2548 or 800-655-5244 (Manitoba only)

Email: securities@gov.mb.ca

Facsimile: 204-945-0330

Website: www.msc.gov.mb.ca

New Brunswick Securities Commission

85 Charlotte Street, Suite 300

Saint John, NB, Canada

E2L 2J2

Telephone: 506-658-3060

Facsimile: 506-658-3059

E-mail: information@nbsc-cvmnb.ca

Website: www.nbsc-cvmnb.ca

Nova Scotia Securities Commission

2nd Floor, Joseph Howe Building

1690 Hollis Street

P.O. Box 458

Halifax, NS, Canada

B3J 3J9

Attention: Corporate Finance

Telephone: 902-424-7768

Facsimile: 902-424-4625

Website: http://www.gov.ns.ca/nssc

Ontario Securities Commission

Suite 1903, Box 55

20 Queen Street West

Toronto, ON, Canada

M5H 3S8

Attention: Review Officer, Insider Reporting

Telephone:

    416-593-8314

    1-877-785-1555 (toll free)

Facsimile for filing insider reports: 416-593-3666

E-mail: inquiries@osc.gov.on.ca

Website: www.osc.gov.on.ca

Saskatchewan Financial Services Commission

Securities Division

6th Floor, 1919 Saskatchewan Dr.

Regina, SK, Canada

S4P 3V7

Attention: Deputy Director, Corporate Finance

Telephone: 306-787-5867

Facsimile: 306-787-5899

Website: http://www.sfsc.gov.sk.ca

Securities Commission of Newfoundland and Labrador

Financial Services Regulation Division

Department of Government Services

P.O. Box 8700

2nd Floor, West Block

Confederation Building

St. John's NL

Canada

A1B 4J6

Telephone: 709-729-4189

Facsimile: 709-729-6187

Website: http://www.gs.gov.nl.ca/insurance/index.html

SEDI Technical Service Desk

Telephone: 1-800-219-5381

Facsimile: 1-866-729-8011

Policies and Orders: CSAN 55-312, 55-315.

OSC Rule 55-501 — Insider Report
Date: February 9, 1996
Amended: February 13, 1998
 19 O.S.C.B. 821

[Replaced by NI 55-102]

OSC Rule 55-502 — Facsimile Filing or Delivery of Section 109 Reports
Date: May 8, 1998
 21 O.S.C.B. 2925

1.1 Facsimile Signatures — A report required or permitted to be filed or delivered under section 109 of the Act may contain the facsimile signature of the person or company signing the report.

1.2 Facsimile Filings and Delivery — A person or company may deliver or file a report under section 109 of the Act by sending the report to the Commission by way of facsimile at the number specified by the Commission.

1.3 Filing or Delivery For Purposes of the Act — The sending of a report to the Commission by way of facsimile under section 1.2 constitutes

(1) if the report is required or permitted to be filed under the Act, the filing of that report under the Act; and

(2) if the report is required or permitted to be delivered under the Act, the delivery of that report.

1.4 Date of Filing — A report sent by facsimile under section 1.2 is considered to be filed or delivered on the day that the facsimile transmission of the report is completed.

Final Rule: (1998) 21 O.S.C.B. 2925; Approval by OSC: (1998) 21 O.S.C.B. 2326; Reqeust for Comments: (1997) 20 O.S.C.B. 378.

Amendment to Rule: (2001) 24 O.S.C.B. 4418.

OSC Staff Notice 55-701 — Automatic Securities Disposition Plans and Automatic Securities Purchase Plans
Date: June 2, 2006
 29 O.S.C.B. 4513

Purpose

Staff of the Ontario Securities Commission (staff or we) have recently received a number of questions on behalf of insiders who wish to establish an "automatic securities disposition plan" (sometimes referred to as a "pre-arranged structured sales plan") (an ASDP) with their broker.

We have compiled a list of the most frequently asked questions (the FAQs) and have set out our responses to such questions below.

This notice represents staff's views on the interpretation of certain requirements of Ontario securities law that apply to ASDPs. Although the focus of this notice is on ASDPs, we would generally consider the views set out below as also being applicable to "automatic securities purchase plans" (ASPPs) as described in National Instrument 55-101 *Insider Reporting Exemptions* (NI 55-101). Accordingly, unless otherwise indicated, a reference in this notice to a "plan" should be read as referring to both an ASDP and an ASPP.

This notice is intended to be a temporary notice pending the development by staff of the Canadian Securities Administrators (the CSA) of a CSA Staff Notice in relation to ASDPs and similar plans generally. We expect that the proposed CSA Staff Notice will also address additional questions, such as the application of certain requirements of Canadian securities legislation to insiders who wish to establish a managed account where full discretionary authority over the securities in the account rests with the manager of the account. Questions relating to managed accounts are beyond the scope of this notice.

In the meantime, we would remind issuers, insiders and other market participants that there may be differences in the securities law requirements of the other CSA jurisdictions that apply to automatic securities plans, and that the specific requirements of the other jurisdictions' securities legislation should be reviewed prior to establishing an ASDP or ASPP.

Background

We have recently received a number of enquiries on behalf of insiders who wish to establish an ASDP with their broker.

These types of plans typically involve an insider instructing a broker to sell securities from the insider's holdings in accordance with a pre-arranged set of instructions. The plans typically contemplate that the broker will continue to sell the securities regardless of whether a "blackout period" established by the issuer may be in effect and regardless of whether the insider may be in possession of material undisclosed information about the issuer at the time of the sale.

The most common questions that we have received in relation to ASDPs are as follows:

- If an insider sells securities of a reporting issuer under an ASDP at a time when the insider has knowledge of material undisclosed information about the issuer, can the insider rely on the exemption contained in subsection 175(2)(b) of the regulations? In other words, is an ASDP an "other similar automatic plan" for the purposes of the exemption in s. 175(2)(b), with the result that the insider is exempt from the prohibition in subsection 76(1) of the Act and liability under section 134 of the Act?

- Is there a disclosure obligation at the time the insider enters into the ASDP?

- Does the insider have to file an insider report each time there is a disposition under an ASDP? Or can the insider rely on the insider reporting exemption for "automatic securities purchase plans" (ASPPs) in NI 55-101 which allows an insider to file a report on an annual basis rather than a transaction-by-transaction basis?

We have responded to these questions as follows.

1. — Is the exemption in s. 175(2)(b) of the regulations available?

Although the exemption in s. 175(2)(b) refers to plans that are typically established by the issuer, staff take the view that this is not a necessary element under Ontario securities law, and an "other similar automatic plan" can include a plan established by an insider and the insider's broker, provided that the plan is "automatic", as discussed below, and the other conditions to the exemption are satisfied. (It should be noted, however, that securities legislation in other jurisdictions may limit this exemption to plans established by the issuer.)

We accept that a plan is "automatic" where the insider is able to demonstrate that the insider no longer has the ability to make decisions relating to trading in the securities in the plan and cannot make "discrete investment decisions" through the plan. (For more information on the concept of "discrete investment decisions", please see, for example, sections 5.2 and 5.5 of the Companion Policy to NI 55-101.)

Accordingly, we will generally accept that a plan is an "automatic" plan for the purposes of s. 175(2)(b) of the regulations if it meets the following conditions:

a) At the time of entry into the plan, the insider is not in possession of any material undisclosed information in relation to the issuer.

b) At the time of entry into the plan, in the case of plans that have not been established by the issuer, the insider provides the broker with a certificate from the issuer confirming that the issuer is aware of the plan and certifying that, to the best of its knowledge, the insider is not in possession of material undisclosed information about the issuer.

c) The trading parameters and other instructions are set out in a written plan document at the time of the establishment of the plan.

d) The plan contains meaningful restrictions on the ability of the insider to vary, suspend or terminate the plan that have the effect of ensuring that the insider cannot profit from material undisclosed information through a decision to vary, suspend or terminate the plan.

e) The plan provides that the broker is not permitted to consult with the insider regarding any sales under the plan and that the insider cannot disclose to the broker any information concerning the issuer that might influence the execution of the plan.

f) The plan to purchase or sell securities was given or entered into in good faith and not as part of a plan or scheme to evade the insider trading prohibitions.

Where an insider's ability to vary, suspend or terminate the plan is not meaningfully restricted, we would likely question whether the plan may genuinely be regarded as an "automatic" plan for the purposes of s. 175(2)(b) of the regulations. This is because the insider retains discretionary authority over the securities in the plan and may be in a position to profit from material undisclosed information by varying, suspending or terminating the plan. For example, if an insider of an issuer establishes an ASDP and then comes into possession of material undisclosed information that is favourable to the issuer, the insider may profit from that information by terminating the plan. Similarly, if the insider comes into possession of material undisclosed information that is adverse to the issuer, the insider could vary the instructions to accelerate the dispositions. In both cases, we would likely take the view that the insider was making discrete investment decisions through the plan.

Where a plan contains meaningful restrictions on the ability to vary, suspend or terminate the plan, we will generally accept that the plan is an "automatic" plan for the purposes of s. 175(2)(b). We have previously advised insiders and their advisers that a simple requirement that the insider represent to the broker that the insider is not in possession of material undisclosed information at the time of the variation, suspension or termination would likely not be sufficient. Meaningful restrictions could include, for example, a requirement that the insider notify the issuer and the public (via a SEDI filing) of a change in instructions which filing would include a representation that the insider is not in possession of any material undisclosed information.

2. — Is there a disclosure obligation at the time the insider enters into the ASDP?

Staff take the view that this will depend on the particular circumstances of the plan. In making this determination, the following questions should be considered:

- Where the plan is established by the issuer, the issuer should consider whether establishing the plan constitutes a "material change", thereby triggering a news release and a material change report.

- Similarly, the issuer and the insider should consider whether the establishment of the plan constitutes a "material fact", with the result that no person with knowledge of the material fact can trade so long as it has not been generally disclosed. In discussions with staff, insiders and their advisers have in some cases expressed the concern that public disclosure of the plan at the time the plan is established may have a negative impact on share price as it will indicate that a large block of securities may shortly come onto the market. We note that this concern would appear to suggest that the establishment of the plan constitutes a material change and/or a material fact.

- The insider should consider whether entering into the arrangement involves a change in "direct or indirect ... control or direction" over the insider's securities. If yes, then an insider report is required at the time the arrangement is entered into by virtue of s. 107(2) of the *Securities Act* (Ontario).

- The insider should consider whether entering into the arrangement involves a change in the insider's "economic interest" in a security of the reporting issuer, or the insider's "economic exposure to the reporting issuer". If yes, then entering into the arrangement will trigger a disclosure requirement under MI 55-103 *Insider Reporting for Certain Derivative Transactions (Equity Monetization)*, unless an exemption in that instrument is available.

Where the issuer and insider conclude that there is no legal requirement to disclose the existence of the plan at the time the plan is established, it may nevertheless be advisable to disclose the existence of the plan on a voluntary basis. Disclosure about the plan may eliminate questions about apparent trading activity by insiders during blackout periods and periods when the insiders may have access to material undisclosed information.

3. — Does the insider have to file an insider report each time there is a disposition under an ASDP?

Generally the insider (or the broker on behalf of the insider) will be required to file insider reports each time there is a disposition under an ASDP. We recommend that the insider include a statement in the general remarks section that the sale is pursuant to an ASDP.

NI 55-101 allows for reporting on an annual basis for certain acquisitions of securities under an ASPP. As a result of recent amendments to NI 55-101, effective April 30, 2005, insiders can now report certain "specified dispositions" in connection with an ASPP on an annual basis. An ASDP is not an ASPP since it is designed to facilitate dispositions not acquisitions. However, if an insider wishes to make an application for exemptive relief, and is able to demonstrate that the plan is genuinely an automatic plan and the insider cannot make discrete investment decisions through the plan, staff may be prepared to recommend exemptive relief to allow the insider to file reports on an annual basis.

5.6 — Restricted Shares

OSC Rule 56-501 — Restricted Shares

Date: October 29, 1999, as amended effective March 30, 2004 (by Rule 51-801), March 17, 2008 and November 17, 2015

22 O.S.C.B. 6804, 31 O.S.C.B. (Supp. 2) 261 and 38 O.S.C.B. 9338

Part 5: ONGOING REQUIREMENTS

Table of Contents

PART 1 — DEFINITIONS AND APPLICATION

1.1 Definitions — In this Rule

"CDN issuer" means an issuer, other than a reporting issuer, any of the equity shares of which are quoted on the CDN system, if the shares are not listed or quoted on any other published market;

"CDN system" means the trade reporting and quotation system for over-the-counter trading operated by The Canadian Dealing Network Inc.;

"class" includes a series of a class;

"common shares" means equity shares to which are attached voting rights exercisable in all circumstances, irrespective of the number or percentage of shares owned, that are not less, on a per share basis, than the voting rights attaching to any other shares of an outstanding class of shares of the issuer, unless the Director makes a determination under section 4.1 that the shares are restricted shares;

"control person" means, with respect to an issuer, any person, company or combination of persons or companies holding a sufficient number of any securities of that issuer to affect materially the control of that issuer, and any holding of any person, company or combination of persons or companies holding more than 20 per cent of the voting rights attached to all of the outstanding voting securities of an issuer shall, in the absence of evidence to the contrary, be deemed to affect materially the control of that issuer;

"equity shares" means shares of an issuer that carry a residual right to participate in the earnings of the issuer and, upon the liquidation or winding up of the issuer, in its assets;

"minority approval" means approval of a proposed reorganization or stock distribution given at a meeting of shareholders of an issuer called to consider the reorganization or stock distribution by a majority of the votes cast by holders of voting shares and, if required by corporate law governing the issuer, by a majority of the votes cast by holders of a class of shares voting separately as a class other than, in both cases, the votes attaching at the time to securities held directly or indirectly by affiliates of the issuer and securities held directly or indirectly by control persons of the issuer;

"non-voting shares" means restricted shares that do not carry the right to vote generally, except for a right to vote that is mandated in special circumstances by law;

"preference shares" means shares to which are attached a preference or right over the shares of any class of equity shares of the issuer, but does not include equity shares;

"reorganization" means

(a) the creation of a class of shares that are restricted shares, either directly or through the creation of a class of subject securities, including by way of

(i) an amendment to an issuer's constating documents,

(ii) a resolution of the board of directors of an issuer setting the terms of a series of shares of the issuer, or

(iii) a restructuring, recapitalization, reclassification, arrangement, amalgamation or merger, or

(b) if the issuer has one or more classes of restricted shares outstanding, an amendment to an issuer's constating documents to increase

(i) the per share voting rights attached to an issuer's common shares without at the same time making a proportionate increase in the per share voting rights attached to an existing class of restricted shares of the issuer, or

(ii) the number of common shares authorized;

"restricted share term" means each of "non-voting shares", "subordinate voting shares", "restricted voting shares" and every other term designated by the Director under subsection 4.1(2);

"restricted shares" means

(a) equity shares that are not common shares, and

(b) equity shares determined to be restricted shares under subsection 4.1(1);

"restricted voting shares" means restricted shares that carry a right to vote subject to a restriction on the number or percentage of shares that may be voted by a person, a company or any combination of persons and companies, except to the extent the restriction or limit is permitted or prescribed by statute and is applicable only to persons or companies that are not citizens or residents of Canada or that are otherwise considered as a result of any law applicable to the issuer to be non-Canadians;

"stock distribution" means a distribution of restricted shares or subject securities, or securities that are directly or indirectly convertible into or exercisable or exchangeable for restricted shares or subject securities, whether in conjunction with a reorganization or otherwise, other than

(a) a distribution of previously unissued restricted shares by way of stock dividend in the ordinary course to shareholders instead of a cash dividend if at the time of distribution there is a published market for the restricted shares, or

(b) a stock split that takes the form of a distribution of previously unissued restricted shares by way of stock dividend to holders of the same class of restricted shares if at the time of distribution there is a published market for the restricted shares and the distribution is part of a concurrent distribution by way of stock dividend to holders of all equity shares under which all outstanding equity shares of the issuer are increased in the same proportion;

"subject securities" means shares that have the effect, or would have the effect if and when issued, of changing a class of outstanding equity shares into restricted shares;

"subordinate voting shares" means restricted shares that carry a right to vote, if there are shares of another class of shares outstanding that carry a greater right to vote on a per share basis; and

"U.S. issuer" has the meaning set out in National Instrument 71-101 Multijurisdictional Disclosure System.

1.2 Application — (1) This Rule does not apply to

(a) shares of mutual funds;

(b) shares that carry a right to vote subject to a restriction on the number or percentage of shares that may be voted or owned by persons or companies that are not citizens or residents of Canada or that are otherwise considered as a result of any law applicable to the issuer to be non-Canadians, but only to the extent of the restriction; or

(c) shares that are subject to a restriction, imposed by any law governing the issuer, on the level of ownership of the shares by a person, company or combination of persons or companies, but only to the extent of the restriction.

(2) [deleted]

(3) Sections 2.3 and 3.2 do not apply to an issuer distributing securities in accordance with National Instrument 71-101 Multijurisdictional Disclosure System.

(4) Section 2.3 does not apply to an issuer if as of a date not more than seven days before the date that the issuer finalizes the final offering document or information circular being used in connection with the stock distribution or reorganization, the issuer expects that the number of shares of each class of equity shares of the issuer held by registered holders whose last address as shown on the books of the issuer is in Ontario or beneficially owned by persons or companies in Ontario will be less than two percent of the outstanding shares of the class after giving effect to the proposed stock distribution or reorganization.

(5) Section 3.2 does not apply to an issuer if,

(a) as of a date not more than seven days before the date that the issuer finalizes the final offering document or information circular; or

(b) as of a date not more than seven days before completion of the stock distribution if there is no offering document or information circular;

the issuer expects that the number of shares of each class of equity shares of the issuer held by registered holders whose last address as shown on the books of the issuer is in Ontario or beneficially owned by persons or companies in Ontario will be less than two percent of the outstanding shares of the class after giving effect to the proposed stock distribution.

PART 2 — DISCLOSURE REQUIREMENTS

2.1 [deleted]

2.2 Dealer and Adviser Documentation — (1) If restricted shares and the appropriate restricted share term, or a code reference to restricted shares or the appropriate restricted share term, are included in a trading record published by the TSX Venture Exchange, the Canadian Securities Exchange or Aequitas NEO Exchange Inc., the appropriate restricted share term shall be included in

(a) any confirmation sent in accordance with section 36 of the Act in respect of transactions in restricted shares;

(b) any statement of transactions or security positions sent by a registered dealer to a customer that refers to restricted shares; and

(c) all recommendations, selling documents and other literature prepared by or on behalf of a registered dealer or adviser and published by a registered dealer or adviser or sent by a registered dealer or adviser to a customer or potential customer that refer to restricted shares.

(2) Despite subsection (1), a registered dealer or adviser may use an abbreviation for the restricted share term in confirmations and statements of transactions or security positions if an explanation of the abbreviation is given in the document.

2.3 Minimum Disclosure in Offering Documents — (1) A rights offering circular or offering memorandum for a stock distribution,

(a) prepared for a reporting issuer or a CDN issuer;

(b) prepared for an issuer that will, upon or in connection with the filing of the document, become a reporting issuer; or

(c) that refers to an issuer intending to become a CDN issuer concurrently with or following completion of the stock distribution or reorganization

shall comply with the following requirements:

1. Each class of securities that is or may become restricted shares shall be referred to using a term or a defined term that includes the appropriate restricted share term.

2. No shares may be referred to by a term or a defined term that includes "common", or "preference" or "preferred", unless the shares are common shares or preference shares, respectively.

3. The description on the front page of the document, if any, showing the number and class or classes of restricted shares being distributed shall include the appropriate restricted share term in the same type face and type size as the rest of the description.

4. A detailed description shall be included, and a summary, if a summary is mandated by Ontario securities law or is otherwise included, shall be cross-referenced to the detailed description, describing

(i) the voting rights attached to the restricted shares that are the subject of the stock distribution or reorganization or that will result from the stock distribution or reorganization either directly or following a conversion, exchange or exercise, and the voting rights, if any, attached to the shares of any other class of shares of the issuer that are the same or greater on a per share basis than those attached to the restricted shares that are the subject of the stock distribution or reorganization or that will result from the stock distribution or reorganization either directly or following a conversion, exchange or exercise;

(ii) any significant provisions under applicable corporate and securities law that do not apply to the holders of the restricted shares that are the subject of the stock distribution or reorganization or that will result from the stock distribution or reorganization either directly or following a conversion, exchange or exercise, but do apply to the holders of another class of equity shares, and the extent of any rights provided in the constating documents or otherwise for the protection of holders of the restricted shares; and

(iii) any rights under applicable corporate law, in the constating documents or otherwise, of holders of restricted shares that are the subject of the stock distribution or reorganization or that will result from the stock distribution or reorganization either directly or following a conversion, exchange or exercise, to attend, in person or by proxy, meetings of holders of equity shares of the issuer and to speak at the meetings to the same extent that holders of equity shares are entitled.

5. If holders of restricted shares do not have all of the rights referred to in paragraphs 4(i), (ii) and (iii), the detailed description and summary referred to in paragraph 4 shall include, in bold-face type, a statement of the rights the holders do not have.

6. Restricted shares shall be separately identified on any balance sheet contained in any financial statements unless there is only a one-line reference in the balance sheet to "capital", "shareholders' capital", "share capital", "equity capital" or a like term.

(2) Despite paragraph 2 of subsection (1), a document referred to in subsection (1) may, in one place only in the document, describe the restricted shares by the term used in the constating documents of the issuer, to the extent it differs from the appropriate restricted share term, if the description is not on the front page of the document and is in the same type face and type size as that used generally in the document.

PART 3 — WITHDRAWAL OF PROSPECTUS EXEMPTIONS

3.1 [Repealed]

3.2 Prospectus Exemptions Not Available — (1) The prospectus exemptions under Ontario securities law are not available for a stock distribution of securities of

(a) a reporting issuer or CDN issuer;

(b) an issuer if the issuer will become a reporting issuer as a result of the stock distribution; or

(c) an issuer if it is represented in any offering documentation used in connection with the stock distribution that the issuer intends to become a CDN issuer concurrently with or following completion of the stock distribution;

unless

(d) either

(i) the stock distribution received minority approval, or

(ii) all of the conditions set out in subsection (2) are satisfied, and

(e) the information circular in connection with the shareholders' meeting held to obtain minority approval for the stock distribution or each reorganization carried out by the issuer related to the restricted shares that are the subject of the stock distribution,

(i) included, if known after reasonable inquiry,

(A) the name of each affiliate of the issuer that is or was a beneficial owner of securities of the issuer and the number of securities beneficially owned, directly or indirectly, by the affiliate as of the date of the information circular;

           (B) the name of each control person and the number of securities beneficially owned, directly or indirectly, by the control person as of the date of the information circular; and

           (C) a statement of the number of votes attaching to the securities that are or were not to be counted for the purpose of the approval, and

        (ii) if mailed after the coming into force of this Rule, described the purpose and business reasons for the use of the restricted shares or subject securities.

(2) The conditions are as follows:

       1. Each reorganization carried out by the issuer related to the restricted shares that are the subject of the stock distribution received minority approval.

       2. At the time of each reorganization referred to in paragraph 1, the issuer was either a reporting issuer in any jurisdiction or a CDN issuer.

       3. If any proposed uses for the restricted shares were described in the information circular sent to shareholders in connection with the shareholders' meeting held to approve a reorganization referred to in paragraph 1, the reason for the stock distribution is not inconsistent with those uses.

(3) Subsection (1) does not apply to a stock distribution if

      (a) the reorganization took place before December 21, 1984, or

      (b) the stock distribution is

          (i) of securities of an issuer that was a private company immediately before the completion of the stock distribution; or

          (ii) a subsequent distribution by an issuer described in clause (i) of securities of the same class that were the subject of the stock distribution described in clause (i).

PART 4 — DETERMINATIONS AND EXEMPTIONS

4.1 Determination of Status — (1) The Director may determine that equity shares of an issuer are restricted shares for purposes of this Rule, if one of the following factors is present:

       1. There is another class of shares that, in view of the consideration and time at which the shares were or are being issued, carries a disproportionate vote per share relative to the equity shares.

       2. The conditions of the equity shares, the conditions of other classes of shares or the issuer's constating documents have provisions that tend to nullify or significantly restrict the voting rights or voting interests of the equity shares.

       3. There is another class of equity shares, the shares of which are entitled to participate in earnings or assets to a substantially lesser extent, on a per share basis, than the extent to which the first class of equity shares is entitled to participate.

(2) If the Director determines that equity shares are restricted shares, the Director may also determine the appropriate restricted share term to be used to designate the shares, taking into account the voting attributes attached to the shares and the term that will best describe the attributes.

4.2 Exemption — The Director may grant an exemption to this Rule, in whole or in part, subject to such conditions or restrictions as may be imposed in the exemption.

Final Rule: (1999) 22 O.S.C.B. 6803, corrected (1999) 22 O.S.C.B. 7091; Approval by OSC: (1999) 22 O.S.C.B. 5005; Request for Comments: (1999) 22 O.S.C.B. 3123 and (1995) 18 O.S.C.B. 4903. A version of this Rule was approved by the OSC, (1997) 20 O.S.C.B. 1863, but returned by the Minister for further consideration, (1997) 20 O.S.C.B. 3592; Replaced ON LPS 1.3.

Rules: Rule 51-801; NI 51-102, Part 10.

5.7 — Cease Trade Orders

See also OPS 1.4.

OSC Policy 57-602 — Cease Trading Orders — Applications for Partial Revocation to Permit a Securityholder to Establish a Tax Loss

Date: **February 27, 1998**
21 O.S.C.B. 1379

[Revoked upon the coming into force of NPS 12-202; (2007) 30 O.S.C.B. 6742.]

Adoption by OSC: (1998) 21 O.S.C.B. 1379; Request for Comments: (1997) 20 O.S.C.B. 3365. Replaced ON LPS 2.9.

OSC Policy 57-603 — Defaults by Reporting Issuers in Complying with Financial Statement Filing Requirements

Date: **April 27, 2001**
24 O.S.C.B. 2705

[Replaced by NPS 12-203; (2008) 31 O.S.C.B. 8375.]

Adoption by OSC: 24 O.S.C.B. 2700 (April 27, 2001); Request for Comments: 23 O.S.C.B. 2368 (March 31, 2000).

5.8 — Corporate Governance

National Instrument 58-101 — Disclosure of Corporate Governance Practices

Date: June 30, 2005, as amended effective December 31, 2007, March 17, 2008, October 31, 2011, December 31, 2014 and November 17, 2015.

28 O.S.C.B. 5377, 30 O.S.C.B. 10508, 31 O.S.C.B. 1009, 34 O.S.C.B. 11499, 37 O.S.C.B. 9370 and 38 O.S.C.B. 7561

PART 1 — DEFINITIONS AND APPLICATION

1.1 Definitions — In this Instrument,

"AIF" has the same meaning as in NI 51-102;

"asset-backed security" has the same meaning as in NI 51-102;

"CEO" means a chief executive officer;

"code" means a code of business conduct and ethics;

"executive officer" has the same meaning as in NI 51-102;

"major subsidiary" has the same meaning as in National Instrument 55-104 *Insider Reporting Requirements and Exemptions*;

"marketplace" has the same meaning as in National Instrument 21-101 *Marketplace Operation*;

"MD&A" has the same meaning as in NI 51-102;

"NI 51-102" means National Instrument 51-102 *Continuous Disclosure Obligations*;

"NI 52-110" means National Instrument 52-110 *Audit Committees*;

"SEDAR" has the same meaning as in National Instrument 13-101 *System for Electronic Document Analysis and Retrieval (SEDAR)*;

"significant security holder" means, in relation to an issuer, a security holder that

(a) owns or controls 10% or more of any class of the issuer's voting securities, or

(b) is able to affect materially the control of the issuer, whether alone or by acting in concert with others;

"subsidiary entity" has the meaning set out in NI 52-110;

"U.S. marketplace" means an exchange registered as of the effective date of this Instrument as a 'national securities exchange' under section 6 of the 1934 Act, or the Nasdaq Stock Market; and

"venture issuer" means a reporting issuer that, at the end of its most recently completed financial year, does not have any of its securities listed or quoted on any of the Toronto Stock Exchange, Aequitas NEO Exchange Inc., a U.S. marketplace, or a marketplace outside of Canada and the United States of America other than the Alternative Investment Market of the London Stock Exchange or the PLUS markets operated by PLUS Markets Group plc.

1.2 Meaning of Independence — For the purposes of this Instrument, a director is independent if he or she would be independent within the meaning of section 1.4 of NI 52-110.

1.3 Application — This Instrument applies to a reporting issuer other than:

(a) an investment fund or issuer of asset-backed securities, as defined in NI 51-102;

(b) a designated foreign issuer or SEC foreign issuer, as defined in National Instrument 71-102 *Continuous Disclosure and Other Exemptions Relating to Foreign Issuers*;

(c) an exchangeable security issuer or credit support issuer that is exempt under sections 13.3 and 13.4 of NI 51-102, as applicable; and

(d) an issuer that is a subsidiary entity, if

(i) the issuer does not have equity securities, other than non-convertible, non-participating preferred securities, trading on a marketplace, and

(ii) the person or company that owns the issuer is

(A) subject to the requirements of this Instrument, or

(B) an issuer that has securities listed or quoted on a U.S. marketplace, and is in compliance with the corporate governance disclosure requirements of that U.S. marketplace.

PART 2 — DISCLOSURE AND FILING REQUIREMENTS

2.1 Required Disclosure — (1) If management of an issuer, other than a venture issuer, solicits a proxy from a security holder of the issuer for the purpose of electing directors to the issuer's board of directors, the issuer must include in its management information circular the disclosure required by Form 58-101F1.

(2) An issuer, other than a venture issuer, that does not send a management information circular to its security holders must provide the disclosure required by Form 58-101F1 in its AIF.

2.2 Venture Issuers — (1) If management of a venture issuer solicits a proxy from a security holder of the venture issuer for the purpose of electing directors to the issuer's board of directors, the venture issuer must include in its management information circular the disclosure required by Form 58-101F2.

(2) A venture issuer that does not send a management information circular to its security holders must provide the disclosure required by Form 58-101F2 in its AIF or annual MD&A.

2.3 Filing of Code — If an issuer has adopted or amended a written code, the issuer must file a copy of the code or amendment on SEDAR no later than the date on which the issuer's next financial statements must be filed, unless a copy of the code or amendment has been previously filed.

PART 3 — EXEMPTIONS AND EFFECTIVE DATE

3.1 Exemptions — (1) The securities regulatory authority or regulator may grant an exemption from this rule, in whole or in part, subject to any conditions or restrictions imposed in the exemption.

(2) Despite subsection (1), in Ontario, only the regulator may grant an exemption.

3.2 Effective Date — (1) This Instrument comes into force on June 30, 2005.

(2) Despite subsection (1), sections 2.1 and 2.2 only apply to management information circulars, AIFs and annual MD&A, as the case may be, which are filed following an issuer's financial year ending on or after June 30, 2005.

Final Rule: (2005) 28 O.S.C.B. 5377; Approval by OSC: (2005) 28 O.S.C.B. 3615; Request for Comments: (2004) 27 O.S.C.B. 8825 and 961.

Amendment to Rule: (2007) 30 O.S.C.B. 10508; Approval by OSC: (2007) 30 O.S.C.B. 8570.

Amendment to Rule and Approval by OSC: (2008) 31 O.S.C.B. 1009.

Amendment to Rule: (2011) 34 O.S.C.B. 11499; Approval by OSC: (2011) 34 O.S.C.B. 8047; Request for Comments: (2010) 33 O.S.C.B. 10723.

Related provisions: OSA Part XX1.I.

Policies and Orders: NP 58-201; CSAN 58-303, 58-304, 58-305, 58-306; OSCN 51-706, 51-717.

Form 58-101F1 — Corporate Governance Disclosure

[Editor's note: Included in the amendments to NI 58-101 Disclosure of Corporate Governance Practices, effective December 31, 2014 (the "2014 Amendments"), is a transition provision which states that the 2014 Amendments only apply to management information circulars and AIFs , as the case may be, which are filed following an issuer's financial year ending on or after December 31, 2014.]

1. Board of Directors —

    (a) Disclose the identity of directors who are independent.

    (b) Disclose the identity of directors who are not independent, and describe the basis for that determination.

    (c) Disclose whether or not a majority of directors are independent. If a majority of directors are not independent, describe what the board of directors (the *board*) does to facilitate its exercise of independent judgement in carrying out its responsibilities.

    (d) If a director is presently a director of any other issuer that is a reporting issuer (or the equivalent) in a jurisdiction or a foreign jurisdiction, identify both the director and the other issuer.

    (e) Disclose whether or not the independent directors hold regularly scheduled meetings at which non-independent directors and members of management are not in attendance. If the independent directors hold such meetings, disclose the number of meetings held since the beginning of the issuer's most recently completed financial year. If the independent directors do not hold such meetings, describe what the board does to facilitate open and candid discussion among its independent directors.

    (f) Disclose whether or not the chair of the board is an independent director. If the board has a chair or lead director who is an independent director, disclose the identity of the independent chair or lead director, and describe his or her role and responsibilities. If the board has neither a chair that is independent nor a lead director that is independent, describe what the board does to provide leadership for its independent directors.

    (g) Disclose the attendance record of each director for all board meetings held since the beginning of the issuer's most recently completed financial year.

2. Board Mandate — Disclose the text of the board's written mandate. If the board does not have a written mandate, describe how the board delineates its role and responsibilities.

3. Position Descriptions —

    (a) Disclose whether or not the board has developed written position descriptions for the chair and the chair of each board committee. If the board has not developed written position descriptions for the chair and/or the chair of each board committee, briefly describe how the board delineates the role and responsibilities of each such position.

    (b) Disclose whether or not the board and CEO have developed a written position description for the CEO. If the board and CEO have not developed such a position description, briefly describe how the board delineates the role and responsibilities of the CEO.

4. Orientation and Continuing Education —

    (a) Briefly describe what measures the board takes to orient new directors regarding

        (i) the role of the board, its committees and its directors, and

        (ii) the nature and operation of the issuer's business.

    (b) Briefly describe what measures, if any, the board takes to provide continuing education for its directors. If the board does not provide continuing education, describe how the board ensures that its directors maintain the skill and knowledge necessary to meet their obligations as directors.

5. Ethical Business Conduct —

    (a) Disclose whether or not the board has adopted a written code for the directors, officers and employees. If the board has adopted a written code:

        (i) disclose how a person or company may obtain a copy of the code;

(ii) describe how the board monitors compliance with its code, or if the board does not monitor compliance, explain whether and how the board satisfies itself regarding compliance with its code; and

(iii) provide a cross-reference to any material change report filed since the beginning of the issuer's most recently completed financial year that pertains to any conduct of a director or executive officer that constitutes a departure from the code.

(b) Describe any steps the board takes to ensure directors exercise independent judgement in considering transactions and agreements in respect of which a director or executive officer has a material interest.

(c) Describe any other steps the board takes to encourage and promote a culture of ethical business conduct.

6. Nomination of Directors —

(a) Describe the process by which the board identifies new candidates for board nomination.

(b) Disclose whether or not the board has a nominating committee composed entirely of independent directors. If the board does not have a nominating committee composed entirely of independent directors, describe what steps the board takes to encourage an objective nomination process.

(c) If the board has a nominating committee, describe the responsibilities, powers and operation of the nominating committee.

7. Compensation —

(a) Describe the process by which the board determines the compensation for the issuer's directors and officers.

(b) Disclose whether or not the board has a compensation committee composed entirely of independent directors. If the board does not have a compensation committee composed entirely of independent directors, describe what steps the board takes to ensure an objective process for determining such compensation.

(c) If the board has a compensation committee, describe the responsibilities, powers and operation of the compensation committee.

8. Other Board Committees — If the board has standing committees other than the audit, compensation and nominating committees, identify the committees and describe their function.

9. Assessments — Disclose whether or not the board, its committees and individual directors are regularly assessed with respect to their effectiveness and contribution. If assessments are regularly conducted, describe the process used for the assessments. If assessments are not regularly conducted, describe how the board satisfies itself that the board, its committees, and its individual directors are performing effectively.

10. Director Term Limits and Other Mechanisms of Board Renewal — (Manitoba, New Brunswick, Newfoundland and Labrador, Northwest Territories, Nova Scotia, Nunavut, Ontario, Québec and Saskatchewan only) — Disclose whether or not the issuer has adopted term limits for the directors on its board or other mechanisms of board renewal and, if so, include a description of those director term limits or other mechanisms of board renewal. If the issuer has not adopted director term limits or other mechanisms of board renewal, disclose why it has not done so.

11. Policies Regarding the Representation of Women on the Board — (Manitoba, New Brunswick, Newfoundland and Labrador, Northwest Territories, Nova Scotia, Nunavut, Ontario, Québec and Saskatchewan only) —

(a) Disclose whether the issuer has adopted a written policy relating to the identification and nomination of women directors. If the issuer has not adopted such a policy, disclose why it has not done so.

(b) If an issuer has adopted a policy referred to in (a), disclose the following in respect of the policy:

(i) a short summary of its objectives and key provisions,

(ii) the measures taken to ensure that the policy has been effectively implemented,

(iii) annual and cumulative progress by the issuer in achieving the objectives of the policy, and

(iv) whether and, if so, how the board or its nominating committee measures the effectiveness of the policy.

12. Consideration of the Representation of Women in the Director Identification and Selection Process — (Manitoba, New Brunswick, Newfoundland and Labrador, Northwest Territories, Nova Scotia, Nunavut, Ontario, Québec and Saskatchewan only) — Disclose whether and, if so, how the board or nominating committee considers the level of representation of women on the board in identifying and nominating candidates for election or re-election to the board. If the issuer does not consider the level of representation of women on the board in identifying and nominating candidates for election or re-election to the board, disclose the issuer's reasons for not doing so.

13. Consideration Given to the Representation of Women in Executive Officer Appointments — (Manitoba, New Brunswick, Newfoundland and Labrador, Northwest Territories, Nova Scotia, Nunavut, Ontario, Québec and Saskatchewan only) — Disclose whether and, if so, how the issuer considers the level of representation of women in executive officer positions when making executive officer appointments. If the issuer does not consider the level of representation of women in executive officer positions when making executive officer appointments, disclose the issuer's reasons for not doing so.

14. Issuer's Targets Regarding the Representation of Women on the Board and in Executive Officer Positions — (Manitoba, New Brunswick, Newfoundland and Labrador, Northwest Territories, Nova Scotia, Nunavut, Ontario, Québec and Saskatchewan only) —

(a) For purposes of this Item, a "target" means a number or percentage, or a range of numbers or percentages, adopted by the issuer of women on the issuer's board or in executive officer positions of the issuer by a specific date.

(b) Disclose whether the issuer has adopted a target regarding women on the issuer's board. If the issuer has not adopted a target, disclose why it has not done so.

(c) Disclose whether the issuer has adopted a target regarding women in executive officer positions of the issuer. If the issuer has not adopted a target, disclose why it has not done so.

(d) If the issuer has adopted a target referred to in either (b) or (c), disclose:

    (i) the target, and

    (ii) the annual and cumulative progress of the issuer in achieving the target.

15. Number of Women on the Board and in Executive Officer Positions (Manitoba, New Brunswick, Newfoundland and Labrador, Northwest Territories, Nova Scotia, Nunavut, Ontario, Québec and Saskatchewan only) —

    (a) Disclose the number and proportion (in percentage terms) of directors on the issuer's board who are women.

    (b) Disclose the number and proportion (in percentage terms) of executive officers of the issuer, including all major subsidiaries of the issuer, who are women.

INSTRUCTION:

(1) This Form applies to both corporate and non-corporate entities. Reference to a particular corporate characteristic, such as a board, includes any equivalent characteristic of a non-corporate entity.

Income trust issuers must provide disclosure in a manner which recognizes that certain functions of a corporate issuer, its board and its management may be performed by any or all of the trustees, the board or management of a subsidiary of the trust, or the board, management or employees of a management company. In the case of an income trust, references to "the issuer" refer to both the trust and any underlying entities, including the operating entity.

(2) If the disclosure required by Item 1 is included in a management information circular distributed to security holders of the issuer for the purpose of electing directors to the issuer's board of directors, provide disclosure regarding the existing directors and any proposed directors.

(3) Disclosure regarding board committees made under Item 8 of this Form may include the existence and summary content of any committee charter.

(3.1) Issuers may incorporate disclosure regarding compensation made under Item 7 of this Form by reference to the information required to be included in Form 51-102F6 Statement of Executive Compensation. Clearly identify the information that is incorporated by reference into this Form.

(4) An issuer may disclose any additional information that is relevant in order to understand the context of the information disclosed by the issuer under Item 15(a) or (b) of this Form.

(5) An issuer may incorporate information required to be disclosed under Items 10 to 15 by reference to another document. The issuer must clearly identify the reference document or any excerpt of it that the issuer incorporates into the disclosure provided under Items 10 to 15. Unless the issuer has already filed the reference document or excerpt under its SEDAR profile, the issuer must file it at the same time as it files the document containing the disclosure required under this Form.

Form 58-101F2 — Corporate Governance Disclosure (Venture Issuers)

1. Board of Directors — Disclose how the board of directors (the board) facilitates its exercise of independent supervision over management, including

    (i) the identity of directors that are independent, and

    (ii) the identity of directors who are not independent, and the basis for that determination.

2. Directorships — If a director is presently a director of any other issuer that is a reporting issuer (or the equivalent) in a jurisdiction or a foreign jurisdiction, identify both the director and the other issuer.

3. Orientation and Continuing Education — Describe what steps, if any, the board takes to orient new board members, and describe any measures the board takes to provide continuing education for directors.

4. Ethical Business Conduct — Describe what steps, if any, the board takes to encourage and promote a culture of ethical business conduct.

5. Nomination of Directors — Disclose what steps, if any, are taken to identify new candidates for board nomination, including:

    (i) who identifies new candidates, and

    (ii) the process of identifying new candidates.

6. Compensation — Disclose what steps, if any, are taken to determine compensation for the directors and CEO, including:

    (i) who determines compensation, and

    (ii) the process of determining compensation.

7. Other Board Committees — If the board has standing committees other than the audit, compensation and nominating committees, identify the committees and describe their function.

8. Assessments — Disclose what steps, if any, that the board takes to satisfy itself that the board, its committees, and its individual directors are performing effectively.

INSTRUCTION:

(1) This form applies to both corporate and non-corporate entities. Reference to a particular corporate characteristic, such as a board, includes any equivalent characteristic of a non-corporate entity.

Income trust issuers must provide disclosure in a manner which recognizes that certain functions of a corporate issuer, its board and its management may be performed by any or all of the trustees, the board or management of a subsidiary of the trust, or the board, management or employees of a management company. In the case of an income trust, references to "the issuer" refer to both the trust and any underlying entities, including the operating entity.

(2) If the disclosure required by Items 1 and 2 is included in a management information circular distributed to security holders of the issuer for the purpose of electing directors to the issuer's board of directors, provide disclosure regarding the existing directors and any proposed directors.

(3) Disclosure regarding board committees made under Item 7 of this Form may include the existence and summary content of any committee charter.

(3.1) Issuers may incorporate disclosure regarding compensation made under Item 6 of this Form by reference to the information required to be included in Form 51-102F6 Statement of Executive Compensation. Clearly identify the information that is incorporated by reference into this Form.

National Policy 58-201 — Corporate Governance Guidelines

Date: **June 30, 2005**
28 O.S.C.B. 5383

PART 1 — PURPOSE AND APPLICATION

1.1 Purpose of this Policy — This Policy provides guidance on corporate governance practices which have been formulated to:

- achieve a balance between providing protection to investors and fostering fair and efficient capital markets and confidence in capital markets;

- be sensitive to the realities of the greater numbers of small companies and controlled companies in the Canadian corporate landscape;

- take into account the impact of corporate governance developments in the U.S. and around the world; and

- recognize that corporate governance is evolving.

The guidelines in this Policy are not intended to be prescriptive. We encourage issuers to consider the guidelines in developing their own corporate governance practices.

We do, however, understand that some parties have concerns about how this Policy and National Instrument 58-101 *Disclosure of Corporate Practices* affect controlled companies. Accordingly, we intend, over the next year, to carefully consider these concerns in the context of a study to examine the governance of controlled companies. We will consult market participants in conducting the study. After completing the study, we will consider whether to change how this Policy and National Instrument 58-101 treat controlled companies.

1.2 Application — This Policy applies to all reporting issuers, other than investment funds. Consequently, it applies to both corporate and non-corporate entities. Reference to a particular corporate characteristic, such as a board of directors (the board), includes any equivalent characteristic of a non-corporate entity. For example, in the case of a limited partnership, we recommend that a majority of the directors of the general partner should be independent of the limited partnership (including the general partner).

Income trust issuers should, in applying these guidelines, recognize that certain functions of a corporate issuer, its board and its management may be performed by any or all of the trustees, the board or management of a subsidiary of the trust, or the board, management or employees of a management company. For this purpose, references to "the issuer" refer to both the trust and any underlying entities, including the operating entity.

PART 2 — MEANING OF INDEPENDENCE

2.1 Meaning of Independence — For the purposes of this Policy, a director is independent if he or she would be independent for the purposes of National Instrument 58-101 *Disclosure of Corporate Governance Practices.*

PART 3 — CORPORATE GOVERNANCE GUIDELINES

Composition of the Board

3.1 The board should have a majority of independent directors.

3.2 The chair of the board should be an independent director. Where this is not appropriate, an independent director should be appointed to act as "lead director". However, either an independent chair or an independent lead director should act as the effective leader of the board and ensure that the board's agenda will enable it to successfully carry out its duties.

Meetings of Independent Directors

3.3 The independent directors should hold regularly scheduled meetings at which non-independent directors and members of management are not in attendance.

Board Mandate

3.4 The board should adopt a written mandate in which it explicitly acknowledges responsibility for the stewardship of the issuer, including responsibility for:

(a) to the extent feasible, satisfying itself as to the integrity of the chief executive officer (the CEO) and other executive officers and that the CEO and other executive officers create a culture of integrity throughout the organization;

(b) adopting a strategic planning process and approving, on at least an annual basis, a strategic plan which takes into account, among other things, the opportunities and risks of the business;

(c) the identification of the principal risks of the issuer's business, and ensuring the implementation of appropriate systems to manage these risks;

(d) succession planning (including appointing, training and monitoring senior management);

(e) adopting a communication policy for the issuer;

(f) the issuer's internal control and management information systems; and

(g) developing the issuer's approach to corporate governance, including developing a set of corporate governance principles and guidelines that are specifically applicable to the issuer.[1]

The written mandate of the board should also set out:

(i) measures for receiving feedback from stakeholders (*e.g.*, the board may wish to establish a process to permit stakeholders to directly contact the independent directors), and

(ii) expectations and responsibilities of directors, including basic duties and responsibilities with respect to attendance at board meetings and advance review of meeting materials.

In developing an effective communication policy for the issuer, issuers should refer to the guidance set out in National Policy 51-201 *Disclosure Standards*.

For purposes of this Policy, "executive officer" has the same meaning as in National Instrument 51-102 *Continuous Disclosure Obligations*.

Position Descriptions

3.5 The board should develop clear position descriptions for the chair of the board and the chair of each board committee. In addition, the board, together with the CEO, should develop a clear position description for the CEO, which includes delineating management's responsibilities. The board should also develop or approve the corporate goals and objectives that the CEO is responsible for meeting.

Orientation and Continuing Education

3.6 The board should ensure that all new directors receive a comprehensive orientation. All new directors should fully understand the role of the board and its committees, as well as the contribution individual directors are expected to make (including, in particular, the commitment of time and resources that the issuer expects from its directors). All new directors should also understand the nature and operation of the issuer's business.

3.7 The board should provide continuing education opportunities for all directors, so that individuals may maintain or enhance their skills and abilities as directors, as well as to ensure their knowledge and understanding of the issuer's business remains current.

Code of Business Conduct and Ethics

3.8 The board should adopt a written code of business conduct and ethics (a code). The code should be applicable to directors, officers and employees of the issuer. The code should constitute written standards that are reasonably designed to promote integrity and to deter wrongdoing. In particular, it should address the following issues:

(a) conflicts of interest, including transactions and agreements in respect of which a director or executive officer has a material interest;

(b) protection and proper use of corporate assets and opportunities;

(c) confidentiality of corporate information;

(d) fair dealing with the issuer's security holders, customers, suppliers, competitors and employees;

(e) compliance with laws, rules and regulations; and

(f) reporting of any illegal or unethical behaviour.

3.9 The board should be responsible for monitoring compliance with the code. Any waivers from the code that are granted for the benefit of the issuer's directors or executive officers should be granted by the board (or a board committee) only.

Although issuers must exercise their own judgement in making materiality determinations, the Canadian securities regulatory authorities consider that conduct by a director or executive officer which constitutes a material departure from the code will likely constitute a "material change" within the meaning of National Instrument 51-102 *Continuous Disclosure Obligations*. National Instrument 51-102 requires every material change report to include a full description of the material change. Where a material departure from the code constitutes a material change to the issuer, we expect that the material change report will disclose, among other things:

- the date of the departure(s),

- the party(ies) involved in the departure(s),

- the reason why the board has or has not sanctioned the departure(s), and

- any measures the board has taken to address or remedy the departure(s).

Nomination of Directors

3.10 The board should appoint a nominating committee composed entirely of independent directors.

3.11 The nominating committee should have a written charter that clearly establishes the committee's purpose, responsibilities, member qualifications, member appointment and removal, structure and operations (including any authority to delegate to individual members and subcommittees), and manner of reporting to the board. In addition, the nominating committee should be given authority to engage and compensate any outside advisor that it determines to be necessary to permit it to carry out its duties. If an issuer is legally required by contract or otherwise to provide third parties with the right to nominate directors, the selection and nomination of those directors need not involve the approval of an independent nominating committee.

---

[1]Issuers may consider appointing a corporate governance committee to consider these issues. A corporate governance committee should have a majority of independent directors, with the remaining members being "non-management" directors.

3.12 Prior to nominating or appointing individuals as directors, the board should adopt a process involving the following steps:

(A) Consider what competencies and skills the board, as a whole, should possess. In doing so, the board should recognize that the particular competencies and skills required for one issuer may not be the same as those required for another.

(B) Assess what competencies and skills each existing director possesses. It is unlikely that any one director will have all the competencies and skills required by the board. Instead, the board should be considered as a group, with each individual making his or her own contribution. Attention should also be paid to the personality and other qualities of each director, as these may ultimately determine the boardroom dynamic.

The board should also consider the appropriate size of the board, with a view to facilitating effective decision-making.

In carrying out each of these functions, the board should consider the advice and input of the nominating committee.

3.13 The nominating committee should be responsible for identifying individuals qualified to become new board members and recommending to the board the new director nominees for the next annual meeting of shareholders.

3.14 In making its recommendations, the nominating committee should consider:

(a) the competencies and skills that the board considers to be necessary for the board, as a whole, to possess;

(b) the competencies and skills that the board considers each existing director to possess; and

(c) the competencies and skills each new nominee will bring to the boardroom.

The nominating committee should also consider whether or not each new nominee can devote sufficient time and resources to his or her duties as a board member.

Compensation

3.15 The board should appoint a compensation committee composed entirely of independent directors.

3.16 The compensation committee should have a written charter that establishes the committee's purpose, responsibilities, member qualifications, member appointment and removal, structure and operations (including any authority to delegate to individual members or subcommittees), and the manner of reporting to the board. In addition, the compensation committee should be given authority to engage and compensate any outside advisor that it determines to be necessary to permit it to carry out its duties.

3.17 The compensation committee should be responsible for:

(a) reviewing and approving corporate goals and objectives relevant to CEO compensation, evaluating the CEO's performance in light of those corporate goals and objectives, and determining (or making recommendations to the board with respect to) the CEO's compensation level based on this evaluation;

(b) making recommendations to the board with respect to non-CEO officer and director compensation, incentive-compensation plans and equity-based plans; and

(c) reviewing executive compensation disclosure before the issuer publicly discloses this information.

Regular Board Assessments

3.18 The board, its committees and each individual director should be regularly assessed regarding his, her or its effectiveness and contribution. An assessment should consider

(a) in the case of the board or a board committee, its mandate or charter, and

(b) in the case of an individual director, the applicable position description(s), as well as the competencies and skills each individual director is expected to bring to the board.

Adoption by OSC: (2005) 28 O.S.C.B. 5383 and 3615; Request for Comments: (2004) 27 O.S.C.B. 8825 and 961.

Policies and Orders: CSAN 51-320, 51-333, 58-303, 58-305, 58-306.

CSA Staff Notice 58-303 — Corporate Governance Disclosure Compliance Review

Date: June 29, 2007
30 O.S.C.B. 5818

Staff of the securities regulatory authorities in British Columbia, Alberta, Saskatchewan, Manitoba, Ontario, Québec and New Brunswick (the participating jurisdictions) conducted a review of compliance with the requirements of National Instrument 58-101 *Disclosure of Corporate Governance Practices* (the Instrument). The Instrument came into force on June 30, 2005 in conjunction with National Policy 58-201 *Corporate Governance Guidelines* (the Policy).

The Instrument

The Instrument applies to all reporting issuers with limited exceptions. Part 2 of the Instrument requires a reporting issuer to disclose its corporate governance practices and file any written code it has adopted. TSX-listed issuers must comply with the disclosure requirements in Form 58-101F1 *Corporate Governance Disclosure*. Because smaller issuers may have less formal procedures in place to ensure effective corporate governance, the Instrument's disclosure requirements for venture issuers (as defined) are less extensive than those applicable to TSX issuers. These requirements for venture issuers are set out in Form 58-101F2 *Corporate Governance Disclosure* (Venture Issuers).

The Policy

The Policy provides guidance on corporate governance practices for all reporting issuers, other than investment funds. The guidelines, which are included in Part 3 of the Policy, are not intended to be prescriptive. We provide them to assist issuers in developing their own corporate governance practices.

The Review Program

We selected a sample of 100 reporting issuers for review. Our selection criteria included the size of the issuer's market capitalization, its industry sector, and its listing status to achieve a broad cross-section of all reporting issuers. Our sample included 65 TSX issuers and 35 venture issuers. We reviewed each issuer's corporate governance disclosure to determine whether it complied with the Instrument's requirements. We also reviewed the substance of the disclosure to assess whether the quality was sufficient to provide a clear and complete account of its governance practices, while taking account of the realities faced by a diversity of issuers in a changing corporate governance landscape. In our view, disclosure that is not of sufficient quality does not meet the requirements of the Instrument.

Results

TSX Issuers

Form 58-101F1 requires a TSX issuer to disclose its governance practices. The table below sets out the average response rate for the required disclosure in each category. The response rates do not necessarily reflect the quality of the disclosure. We comment on the quality of disclosure in the discussion that follows the table.

Category	Item Number of Form 58-101F1	Response Rate
Board Independence	1	94%
Board Mandate	2	77%
Position Descriptions	3	70%
Orientation & Continuing Education	4	85%
Ethical Business Conduct	5	86%
Nomination of Directors	6	82%
Compensation	7	80%
Assessments	9	85%

To assist issuers to make disclosure that meets the requirements of the Instrument, we provide some examples of deficient disclosure in each category of disclosure required in Form 58-101F1:

- *Board Independence — Leadership for Independent Directors*

  Item 1(f) requires a TSX issuer to disclose what the board does to provide leadership for its independent directors if it has neither a chair nor a lead director that is independent.

  One issuer disclosed that leadership is provided through contact with the independent directors, but failed to disclose how or when such contact is established, nor the forum for the contact. It was therefore unclear from the disclosure what the measure was or how the measure provided leadership for the independent directors.

- *Board Mandate*

  Item 2 requires a TSX issuer to disclose the text of the board's written mandate or, if it does not have a written mandate, to describe how the board delineates its roles and responsibilities.

  Several issuers disclosed summarized information that was insufficient for a reader to fully understand the board's responsibilities. In addition, several issuers disclosed a cross-reference to their website for the text of the mandate. Any information required to be included in a management information circular may be incorporated by reference, but the document from which it is incorporated must be filed on SEDAR.[1]

- *Position Descriptions*

  Item 3(a) requires a TSX issuer to disclose whether or not the board has developed written position descriptions for the chair and the chair of each board committee. Item 3(b) requires a TSX issuer to disclose whether or not the board and CEO have developed a written position description for the CEO. In both instances, a TSX issuer is required to disclose how the board delineates the role and responsibilities of the individual if a written position description has not been developed.

  Where there was not a position description for one or more of these parties, the disclosure as to how the board delineates their respective roles and responsibilities was often vague and uninformative. In some instances, it was not obvious how the measures the board adopted facilitated the delineation. For example, one issuer merely disclosed that it relied on a "mutual understanding" without further explanation. In connection with the CEO's position description, it was sometimes unclear whether both the board and the CEO had been involved in the development of the position description.

- *Orientation and Education of Directors*

  Item 4 requires a TSX issuer to disclose what measures the board takes to orient new directors regarding their role and the nature and operations of the issuer's business, and to provide continuing education for all directors.

  Several issuers disclosed that they provide a package of materials to the directors to address these responsibilities. Without knowing the general nature and content of the materials, a reader could neither discern the range of matters the materials addressed nor assess their adequacy.

---

[1]Part 1(c) of Form 51-102F5 — *Information Circular.*

- *Ethical Business Conduct — Monitoring Compliance with Code of Conduct*

  Item 5(a) (ii) requires a TSX issuer to describe how the board monitors compliance with its code, or if the board does not monitor compliance, explain whether and how the board satisfies itself regarding compliance with its code.

  One issuer disclosed that its board delegated this responsibility to its governance committee. However, the disclosure did not indicate how the governance committee fulfilled this responsibility. Another issuer disclosed that it addressed this responsibility through interviews or discussions, without further explanation. It was unclear from these brief accounts how either measure enabled the board to monitor or otherwise satisfy itself regarding compliance with its code.

- *Nomination of Directors*

  Item 6 requires a TSX issuer to describe the process by which the board identifies new candidates for board nomination, and to describe what steps the board takes to encourage an objective nomination process if it does not have a nominating committee composed entirely of independent directors.

  In several instances, the disclosure was vague and uninformative with issuers merely disclosing that the board fills vacancies with required skill sets. In other instances, the disclosure included descriptions of the required skill sets, but not the process by which the board identifies new candidates.

- *Compensation*

  Item 7 requires a TSX issuer to describe the process by which the board determines the compensation for the issuer's directors and officers, and to describe what steps the board takes to ensure an objective process for determining such compensation if it does not have a compensation committee composed entirely of independent directors.

  The disclosure in this area was often vague and uninformative. For directors, several issuers disclosed the amount of their compensation but not the process by which it is determined. Where issuers did not have a fully independent compensation committee, there was often either no disclosure or only a very general description of how the board determines compensation that did not focus on the objectivity of the compensation setting process.

- *Assessments*

  Item 9 requires a TSX issuer to disclose whether or not the board, its committees and individual directors are regularly assessed with respect to their effectiveness and contribution. If assessments are regularly conducted, the issuer is required to describe the process used for the assessments. If assessments are not regularly conducted, the issuer is required to describe how the board satisfies itself that these parties are performing effectively.

  Where issuers included disclosure of this nature, it was often vague and uninformative. In some instances, it was not obvious how the measures adopted enabled the board to satisfy itself that the board, its committees, and individual directors are performing effectively. For example, several issuers disclosed that the performance of officers and directors is informally touched on in board meetings. Another issuer disclosed that the board informally supervises its officers and directors, without further elaboration.

TSX Issuer Outcomes

As a result of our review, we required 27 TSX issuers to address the deficiencies identified in our review in their next management information circular or annual information form, as applicable.

Venture Issuers

The disclosure requirements for venture issuers included in Form 58-101F2 are less extensive than those applicable to TSX issuers. However, the requirements generally cover the same categories as those for TSX issuers, with the exception of the board mandate and position descriptions. There were significant deficiencies in the quality of the disclosure that was filed. Eight issuers, representing 23% of the 35 venture issuers reviewed, did not provide any corporate governance disclosure.

Similar to the disclosure for TSX issuers, there were instances where the nature of a practice was not adequately described, where it was unclear how a practice achieved its purpose, or both. This was particularly evident in the following three areas:

- *Board Supervision over Management*

  Item 1 requires a venture issuer to disclose how the board facilitates its exercise of independent supervision over management, including (i) the identity of directors that are independent, and (ii) the identity of directors who are not independent, and the basis for that determination.

  Several issuers did not provide disclosure with a sufficiently comprehensive description for a reader to understand how the board facilitates its exercise of independent supervision over management.

- *Nomination of Directors*

  Item 5 requires a venture issuer to disclose what steps, if any, are taken to identify new candidates for board nomination, including who identifies new candidates and the process for identifying new candidates.

  Several issuers merely disclosed that the board fills vacancies with required skill sets, without further elaboration. Those issuers did not discuss how the board determines the competencies and skills it should possess or how it identifies potential candidates to address its needs.

- *Assessments*

  Item 8 requires a venture issuer to disclose what steps, if any, the board takes to satisfy itself that the board, its committees, and its individual directors are performing effectively.

  One issuer disclosed that the board conducts assessments without identifying who is assessed or how assessments are performed.

Venture Issuer Outcomes

As a result of our review, we required two venture issuers that did not provide any corporate governance disclosure to restate and refile their management information circulars. In addition, we required the other six venture issuers that did not provide any corporate governance disclosure to include the relevant disclosure in their imminent management information circular filing. We also required three other venture issuers to address significant deficiencies identified in our review in their next management information circular, annual information form, or annual management discussion and analysis, as applicable.

Future Reviews

Reporting issuers must provide corporate governance disclosure that addresses the requirements of the Instrument by providing meaningful information to capital market participants.

We are concerned about those issuers that did not comply with all of the Instrument's disclosure requirements. We are equally concerned about the qualitative deficiencies in the disclosure that was provided by both TSX and venture issuers, in particular, the extent to which issuers failed to provide clear or complete accounts of their governance practices in their disclosures. To comply with the requirements of the Instrument, issuers must provide meaningful, informative disclosure of their corporate governance practices. Avoiding the use of boiler-plate language would help issuers to provide investors with more specific information about their corporate governance practices.

We intend to selectively review issuers' compliance with the Instrument as part of our ongoing continuous disclosure review program and will take appropriate regulatory action for non-compliance.

Policies and Orders: OSCN 51-717, 58-306.

CSA Staff Notice 58-305 — Status Report on the Proposed Changes to the Corporate Governance Regime

Date:　　　November 13, 2009

32 O.S.C.B. 9347

On December 19, 2008, the Canadian Securities Administrators (CSA) published for comment proposed changes to the corporate governance regime entitled "Proposed Repeal and Replacement of National Policy 58-201 *Corporate Governance Guidelines*, National Instrument 58-101 *Disclosure of Corporate Governance Practices*, and National Instrument 52-110 *Audit Committees* and Companion Policy 52-110CP *Audit Committees*" (the **Proposal**).

We received numerous comments about the timing of the Proposal. A majority of commenters expressed the view that now is not an appropriate time to introduce significant changes to the corporate governance regime in Canada. Commenters pointed out that issuers are currently focused on business sustainability issues in a challenging economic climate, and on the transition to International Financial Reporting Standards. We also received significant comments on a wide range of other matters related to the Proposal.

Based on the comments we received, the CSA does not intend to implement the Proposal as originally published. We have concluded that now is not an appropriate time to recommend significant changes to the corporate governance regime.

We are reconsidering whether to recommend any changes to the corporate governance regime. We will publish any proposed changes for comment. They would not be effective until the 2011 proxy season at the earliest. The CSA will provide sufficient advance notice for issuers to adapt their corporate governance practices to fully comply with any revised regime.

CSA Staff Notice 58-306 — 2010 Corporate Governance Disclosure Compliance Review

Date:　　　December 2, 2010

33 O.S.C.B. 11134

Contents

1. Introduction

        C. Orientation and continuing education
        D. Ethical business conduct
        E. Nomination of directors
        F. Assessments
    3.2 Requirements for venture issuers
        A. Board of directors
        B. Other board committees
    3.3 Executive Compensation
    3.4 Risk management
4. **Conclusion and questions**

1. — Introduction

The purpose of this notice is to:

- summarize the results of a corporate governance disclosure compliance review, and

- provide guidance on compliance with the existing corporate governance disclosure requirements in the areas of concern identified during the review.

Compliance review

Staff of the securities regulatory authorities in Ontario, British Columbia, Manitoba and Québec (the Participating Jurisdictions or we) conducted a review (the 2010 review) of compliance with the requirements of National Instrument 58-101 *Disclosure of Corporate Governance Practices* (the Corporate Governance Instrument). We reviewed the corporate governance disclosure of 72 reporting issuers (other than investment funds) in the Participating Jurisdictions. The review was intended to build on the results of the 2007 CSA compliance review, outlined in CSA Staff Notice 58-303 *Corporate Governance Disclosure Compliance Review* (the 2007 review).

Guidance

This notice sets out guidance to reporting issuers, other than investment funds (referred to in this notice as issuers) on the existing continuous disclosure (CD) requirements under securities legislation relating to corporate governance matters. It is intended to clarify existing disclosure requirements relating to corporate governance matters and does not create any new legal requirements or modify existing ones. It is also intended to assist issuers in (1) determining what information about corporate governance matters needs to be disclosed, and (2) enhancing or supplementing their disclosure regarding corporate governance matters. Issuers should consider this guidance when preparing their corporate governance disclosure in their next management information circular or other filing.

Summary of results and future action

Over half of the issuers reviewed were required to make prospective enhancements to their corporate governance disclosure. We view the level of non-compliance with the disclosure requirements of the Corporate Governance Instrument to be unacceptable. Although significant efforts have been made to comply with the corporate governance disclosure requirements, issuers need to further improve their disclosure. We will continue to review corporate governance disclosure as part of our overall CD review program. Issuers should anticipate staff requests for additional disclosure, re-filings or other staff action, where appropriate, if an issuer has not fully met its corporate governance disclosure obligations.

1.1 — *Corporate governance regime*

The Corporate Governance Instrument came into force on June 30, 2005 in conjunction with National Policy 58-201 *Corporate Governance Guidelines* (the Corporate Governance Policy).

Corporate Governance Policy

The Corporate Governance Policy applies to all issuers. Part 3 sets out guidelines for corporate governance practices. The guidelines are not intended to be prescriptive. Issuers are encouraged to consider the guidelines in developing their own corporate governance practices.

Corporate Governance Instrument

The Corporate Governance Instrument applies to all issuers with limited exceptions. It requires, among other things, that issuers disclose their corporate governance practices in their management information circulars (or in their annual information forms (AIF) or management's discussion and analysis (MD&A), as applicable).

There are two sets of disclosure requirements:

- **TSX-listed issuers.**[1] TSX-listed issuers must comply with the disclosure requirements in Form 58-101F1 *Corporate Governance Disclosure* (Form 58-101F1). Under Form 58-101F1, they must provide disclosure about their corporate governance practices with reference to the guidelines set out in the Corporate Governance Policy.

- **Venture issuers.** The Corporate Governance Instrument's disclosure requirements for venture issuers are less extensive than those applicable to TSX-listed issuers. The requirements for venture issuers are set out in Form 58-101F2 *Corporate Governance Disclosure (Venture Issuers)* (Form 58-101F2). They must provide disclosure regarding their practices in the areas addressed by the guidelines set out in the Corporate Governance Policy, but they are not required to compare their practices against the guidelines.

1.2 — Importance of corporate governance information to investors and the market

A strong corporate governance disclosure regime is a key feature of market-based monitoring of corporate conduct and is central to the ability of shareholders to exercise their voting rights effectively. Disclosure can be a powerful tool for protecting investors. Shareholders and potential investors require access to regular, reliable and comparable information in sufficient detail for them to assess the stewardship of the board and management and make informed decisions about the valuation, ownership and voting of shares. Insufficient or unclear information may hamper the ability of markets to function, may increase the cost of capital and may result in a poor allocation of resources.

2. — Review Results

2.1 — Review program

We selected a sample of 72 issuers for review. Our selection criteria included the size of the issuer's market capitalization, its industry sector and its listing status to achieve a broad cross-section of all issuers. Our sample included 46 TSX-listed issuers and 26 venture issuers. In the 2007 review, a sample of 100 issuers was selected, including 65 TSX-listed issuers and 35 venture issuers.

We reviewed each issuer's corporate governance disclosure in its most recently filed management information circular to determine whether it complied with the requirements in the Corporate Governance Instrument. In our view, disclosure that does not sufficiently describe the corporate governance practices of an issuer or that is boilerplate does not meet those requirements.

2.2 — Summary of results

We found an unacceptable level of compliance with the Corporate Governance Instrument. In 2010, 55% of the total number of issuers reviewed were required to make prospective enhancements to their corporate governance disclosure, compared to 36% in the 2007 review. However, no issuers reviewed in 2010 were required to restate and refile their corporate governance disclosure. In contrast, two issuers in the 2007 review did not provide any corporate governance disclosure and were required to restate and refile their management information circulars. A summary of our review outcomes is set out below:

TSX-listed issuers			Venture issuers		
	2010 review	**2007 review**		**2010 review**	**2007 review**
Prospective enhancements	63%	42%	**Prospective enhancements**	42%	26%
Restatements	0%	0%	**Restatements**	0%	6%

The results of the review identified significant and frequent disclosure deficiencies in each of the following areas:

- board of directors
- position descriptions
- orientation and continuing education
- ethical business conduct
- nomination of directors, and
- assessments.

Guidance on the disclosure requirements relating to these areas is set out in Part 3 of this notice. Given that a higher percentage of the issuers reviewed in the 2010 review compared to the 2007 review were required to make prospective enhancements to their corporate governance disclosure, this notice is meant to be an educational tool for issuers when preparing their corporate governance disclosure. As noted above, we will continue to monitor corporate governance disclosure as a part of our overall CD review program.

3. — Guidance for Corporate Governance Disclosure in Areas of Concern

To further assist issuers in complying with the disclosure requirements in the Corporate Governance Instrument, we have set out guidance and examples of disclosure below in the areas where we noted deficiencies during our review.

---

[1]References to TSX-listed Issuers in this notice include references to all reporting issuers that are not venture issuers (as defined in National Instrument 51-102 *Continuous Disclosure Obligations*).

Examples of entity-specific disclosure

The examples have been included for illustration purposes only, and should not be viewed as applicable to all issuers, or comprehensive in all cases. Issuers are reminded that their CD documents filed with the securities regulatory authorities must comply with all applicable disclosure requirements. While particular corporate governance practices are identified in the examples, we are not suggesting that all issuers adopt those practices. We recognize that there is no single model of good corporate governance and that the practices that are most appropriate will vary among issuers. Nonetheless, the practices adopted by issuers need to be clearly articulated and disclosed so that investors can make their own assessments.

3.1 — Requirements for TSX-listed issuers

A. — Board of directors

Identity of non-independent directors and basis for determination

Disclosure requirement

Item 1(b) of Form 58-101F1 requires an issuer to disclose the identity of directors who are not independent (as defined in National Instrument 52-110 *Audit Committees*), and describe the basis for that determination.

Findings of review

The majority of issuers reviewed disclosed the identity of non-independent directors. However, many issuers did not disclose the basis for that determination. While for many issuers it was obvious that those directors were not independent because of their position with the issuer, the issuer did not explicitly note the executive relationship. For other issuers, no disclosure was included to facilitate a reader's understanding of why the director was considered to be non-independent.

Commentary

An issuer must explain why directors are identified as non-independent. It is not sufficient to include vague and general statements regarding the non-independence of directors, such as "when deciding whether a particular director is or is not an independent director, the board will examine the factual circumstances of each director and consider them in the context of many factors".

Where a director has been identified as non-independent, the issuer must disclose, at a minimum:

- the fact that the non-independent director has a direct or indirect material relationship with the issuer, or a subsidiary entity or parent of the issuer, which could, in the view of the board of directors, be reasonably expected to interfere with the exercise of his or her independent judgement

- how it determined whether a director has such a material relationship, and

- the nature of the material relationship in sufficient detail for investors to understand it.

Below is an example of entity-specific disclosure that elaborates on the basis for determining if a director is independent.

Example of entity-specific disclosure

A director is considered independent only where the board determines that the director has no direct or indirect material relationship with the company or its subsidiaries (together referred to as the company). A "material relationship" is defined in National Instrument 52-110 *Audit Committees* to mean any relationship, which could, in the view of the board, be reasonably expected to interfere with the exercise of a director's independent judgement.

On an annual basis, the board of directors, in consultation with the x committee, reviews each relationship that a director has with the company in order to determine whether the director is or remains independent.

Based on reference to these requirements and a review of the applicable factual circumstances against these standards, the board, in consultation with the x committee, has determined that the majority of its directors are independent. The following table identifies which directors are not independent and the basis for that determination.

Director	Independence status	Basis for determination of non-independence
Director A	Independent	Not applicable — no material relationship
Director B	Not independent	Director B is considered to have a material relationship with the company by virtue of her executive officer position with the company since 20XX.
Director C	Independent	Not applicable — no material relationship
Director D	Independent	Not applicable — no material relationship
Director E	Not independent	Director E is considered to have a material relationship with the company as a result of being the relationship partner of the company's primary external legal counsel.
Director F	Not independent	Director F is considered to have a material relationship with the company's subsidiary, subsidiary x, because Director F is the CEO of supplier Y, and subsidiary x is the most significant customer of supplier Y's products.
Director G	Independent	Not applicable — no material relationship

Meetings of independent directors

Disclosure requirement

Item 1(e) of Form 58-101F1 requires, among other things, an issuer to disclose whether or not the independent directors hold regularly scheduled meetings at which non-independent directors and members of management are not in attendance. If the independent directors hold such meetings, the issuer must disclose the number of meetings held since the beginning of the issuer's most recently completed financial year. If the independent directors do not hold such meetings, the issuer must describe what the board does to facilitate open and candid discussion among its independent directors.

Findings of review

A significant portion of the issuers reviewed met part of the disclosure requirement in Item 1(e).

- **Held meetings with only independent directors.** The majority of issuers disclosed that they held meetings of the independent directors, but they did not disclose how many meetings were held or if such meetings were held regularly.

- **Did not hold meetings with only independent directors.** Other issuers disclosed that they did not hold regularly scheduled meetings at which non-independent directors and members of management are not in attendance, but failed to explain how the board facilitates open and candid discussion among the independent directors. Some issuers included a general statement on why they did not hold regularly scheduled meetings of their independent directors. For example, they may have disclosed that they believed there is active discussion among the independent directors outside of formal meetings or that appropriate structures and procedures are in place to ensure that the board can function independently of the management, but did not elaborate on the basis for that belief or describe what the appropriate structures and procedures are. In particular, they did not specifically explain what the board does to facilitate open and candid discussion among its independent directors, as required by Form 58-101F1.

Commentary

It is important for investors to understand whether an issuer facilitates open and candid discussions among its independent directors, either through holding regular meetings with only the independent directors in attendance or through other practices.

Below are examples of questions an issuer should consider when drafting this disclosure.

- Do the independent directors of the board have a forum in which to address issues or concerns?

- At each board meeting, is a portion of the meeting reserved for independent directors where the non-independent directors and members of management are not in attendance?

- At each committee meeting, is a portion of the meeting reserved for independent directors where the non-independent directors and members of management are not in attendance?

- If a portion of the board and committee meetings is not reserved for independent directors where the non-independent directors and members of management are not in attendance, do the independent directors have the opportunity to meet regularly and discuss matters of interest, independently of any managerial influence?

- If the issuer has no formal structures in place to ensure that the independent directors can meet without the non-independent directors and management:

    - what does the issuer do to ensure open and candid discussions?
    - does the issuer put procedures in place to have ad hoc in-camera meetings?
    - does the issuer have in-camera meetings on a regular basis or on an as needed basis?
    - what does the issuer consider when deciding if an in-camera meeting is needed?
    - are in-camera meetings held at the beginning or end of the meeting and why does the board consider this approach to be effective?

- does the board ask one or more members of management or non-independent directors to withdraw during certain discussions, if the circumstances require it?

Below are examples of entity-specific disclosure elaborating on how a board facilitates open and candid discussion among its independent directors.

Example 1 – Entity-specific disclosure where regular meetings with only independent directors

The board regularly meets independently of management and non-independent directors at the request of any independent director, or may excuse members of management and non-independent directors from all or a portion of any meeting where a potential conflict of interest arises or where otherwise appropriate. The board is also scheduled to meet without management and non-independent directors before or after each board meeting. In addition, after each board meeting held to consider interim and annual financial statements, the board meets without management and non-independent directors. In 20XX, the board met without management and non-independent directors at each board meeting, being seven separate occasions, including the four regularly scheduled quarterly meetings.

Example 2 – Entity-specific disclosure where no regular meetings with only independent directors

The independent directors do not have regularly scheduled meetings. However, they have the opportunity to hold ad hoc meetings that are not attended by the non-independent directors and members of management and they avail themselves of this opportunity, at their entire discretion, whenever they deem necessary. Among other things, during meetings of the x committee, non-independent directors, executive officers who are not members of the board and other guests attending these meetings are asked to withdraw from these meetings for a certain period in order to allow the independent directors to discuss issues freely among themselves. In 20XX, no such meetings were held. In 20XX and to date, x such meetings were held.

Independent chair and independent lead director

Disclosure requirement

Item 1(f) of Form 58-101F1 requires an issuer to describe what the board does to provide leadership for its independent directors if it has neither a chair nor a lead director that is independent.

Findings of review

Our review found that some of the issuers reviewed did not meet this disclosure requirement. In many cases, the chair was identified as a non-independent chair, but there was no disclosure on whether the board had an independent lead director. In other cases, the non-independent chair or non-independent lead director was identified, but it was unclear as to what steps the board took to provide leadership for its independent directors.

We also found that some issuers simply stated that their current independence structure was an appropriate leadership structure for the issuer and that they would periodically evaluate whether such structure continued to be in the best interests of the issuer and its shareholders.

Commentary

An issuer must clearly disclose whether the chair or lead director is independent.

Where the chair or the lead director is not independent, the issuer must disclose what specific steps the board takes to provide leadership to its independent directors. Below are examples of questions an issuer should consider when drafting this disclosure.

- Has an independent director been tasked with the function of identifying whether the board's mandate is being effectively carried out by the board and its committees?
- How does the board create a balance of authority and provide for objective leadership?
- How does the issuer ensure that the responsibilities of the board are understood by both the board and management and that the boundaries between board and management responsibilities are understood and respected?
- Does the board provide all directors, including its non-independent directors, with unfettered access to information regarding the issuer's activities?
- How does the board ensure that the views of its independent directors are heard?
- Do the independent directors have the ability to engage outside advisors?

If a board does not take any steps to provide leadership for its independent directors, it should disclose that fact and explain its rationale for that decision.

Below are examples of entity-specific disclosure on what a board with an independent chair, and an independent lead director, does to provide leadership for its independent directors.

Example 1 – Entity-specific disclosure for board with independent chair

In addition to chairing all board meetings and setting the board's agenda, the chair's role is to facilitate and chair discussions among the company's independent directors, and to facilitate communication between the independent directors and the company's management. The chair is also charged with the responsibility of leading the board and organizing it to function in partnership with, but independently of, management of the company in order to facilitate the achievement of the goals of the company. The chair reviews any comments or requests made by an independent director and oversees the process by which unfettered information to independent directors is made available regarding the company's activities.

Example 2 – Entity-specific disclosure for board with independent lead director

The responsibilities of the lead independent director are, among other things, to ensure that the board is able to function independently of management, set board agendas, oversee the quality of the information sent to directors and review any comments or requests made by an independent director. The independent lead director also chairs periodic meetings of the independent directors without management and non-independent directors and reports to the board on their deliberations, as required. In addition, the independent lead director is charged with the responsibility of assisting the independent directors with fulfilling their governance responsibilities and to oversee the governance obligations of the board and its committees generally. The lead director is elected annually by a vote of the directors who qualify as independent directors.

B. — Position descriptions

Disclosure requirement

Item 3 of Form 58-101F1 requires an issuer to disclose whether or not:

- the board has developed written position descriptions for the chair and the chair of each board committee, and

- the board and CEO have developed a written position description for the CEO.

If written position descriptions have not been developed, the issuer must briefly describe how the board delineates the roles and responsibilities of each such position.

Findings of review

While some of the issuers reviewed included this disclosure, we found that improvements could be made and that a significant number of issuers did not fully meet this disclosure requirement.

Many issuers did not disclose whether they developed written position descriptions, nor did they disclose what the board does to delineate the roles and responsibilities of the specified individuals.

Other issuers disclosed that they had not developed written position descriptions, but they did not adequately explain how the board delineates the role and responsibilities of the specified individuals. In some instances, issuers disclosed that they had adopted written position descriptions for only some of the specified individuals, but failed to describe how the board delineates roles and responsibilities for the other specified individuals.

Some issuers simply made positive statements that they had created position descriptions as required by the Corporate Governance Instrument and that all position descriptions are reviewed and approved on an annual basis.

Commentary

It is important for an issuer to clearly disclose whether or not it has developed written position descriptions for each of the chair, the chair of each board committee and the CEO.

If an issuer has developed written position descriptions, it is not required to include the text of those position descriptions in its disclosure. However, it may be helpful to provide investors trying to understand the issuer's corporate governance structure with a cross-reference or a link to a website where those written position descriptions can be found.

Where an issuer has not developed written position descriptions, it should include a brief summary of the roles and responsibilities of each of the chair, the chair of each board committee and the CEO. It is not sufficient to disclose that the issuer relies on a mutual understanding of these roles and responsibilities.

Below are two examples of entity-specific disclosure regarding the position description for the chair. In the first example, a written position description has been developed, and in the second example, the issuer is relying on less formal means for delineating roles and responsibilities.

Example 1 – Entity-specific disclosure where written position description for chair developed

The board mandate includes a position description of the chair, which sets out his or her duties and responsibilities. A copy of the position description, together with the rest of the board mandate, can be found at: www.x.ca. This position description is reviewed by the x committee on an annual basis.

Example 2 – Entity-specific disclosure where position description for chair not developed

The board does not believe that it is necessary to develop a formal written position description for the chair of the board, given the size of the company and the fact that the board has not changed in the last x years.

The chair is responsible for the management, development and effective performance of the board, and for providing leadership to the directors in carrying out their collective responsibilities to supervise the management of the business and affairs of the company. The chair is also charged with the responsibility of leading the board and organizing it to function in partnership with, but independently of, management of the company in order to facilitate the achievement of the goals of the company, including sustainable growth and maximizing shareholder value. In particular, the chair

- sets all board meeting agendas with the CEO, and leads all board discussions
- facilitates and chairs discussions among the company's independent directors, facilitates communication between the independent directors and the company's management, and is responsible for discussing any performance issues of any director, and
- if and when necessary, acts as a spokesperson on behalf of the board in dealing with the press and members of the public.

C. — Orientation and continuing education

Orientation of new directors

Disclosure requirement

Item 4(a) of Form 58-101F1 requires an issuer to briefly describe what measures the board takes to orient new directors regarding:

- the role of the board, its committees and its directors, and
- the nature and operation of the issuer's business.

Findings of review

We found that the majority of issuers' disclosure was limited to identifying that an orientation and training program exists, but did not describe what comprises such orientation and training. In other cases, issuers simply disclosed that they did not provide a formal orientation or education program for board members because they did not believe those programs were appropriate given the size of the issuer, its geographic concentration and board member expertise.

Commentary

To satisfy this disclosure requirement, an issuer must disclose the measures that the board takes to orient new directors, regardless of whether the issuer has a formal orientation program for new directors. It is not sufficient to merely state that the board has or does not have an orientation and training program. Understanding how a board orients its new members contributes to investors' understanding of how a board effectively functions.

Below are examples of questions that an issuer should consider when drafting this disclosure.

- Do new directors meet with the chair, other directors and CEO? If so, when do they meet?

- Are new directors given the opportunity to ask questions about the role of the board, its committees and its directors, and about the nature of the issuer and its operations?

- Are new directors provided with briefings and copies of the issuer's key documents, including a code of business conduct and ethics, insider trading and continuous disclosure policies, and board and committee mandates and charters?

- Do new directors receive an orientation session in order to familiarize themselves with the issuer, its business, industry, senior management team and the contribution individual directors are expected to make?

- Are new directors informed of the legal duties and obligations required of a director of a publicly-held entity?

- Are new directors provided with up-to-date information on the issuer's corporate organization, operations and strategy, its current year business plan and financial information?

- Does the issuer offer on-site visits to its corporate headquarters and main facilities?

- Has the board assigned a standing committee to be responsible for carrying out its orientation function?

Below is an example of entity-specific disclosure on the measures a board takes to orient new directors regarding (i) the role of the board, its committees and directors, and (ii) the nature and operation of the issuer's business.

Example of entity-specific disclosure

All new directors receive a comprehensive orientation on their election or appointment to the board. The orientation includes:
- a detailed briefing with the chair of the board
- a detailed briefing with the chair of each of the Audit Committee, x committee and x committee
- a detailed briefing with the independent directors
- a detailed briefing on the role of the director in the company and other matters by the company's general counsel and external legal counsel
- a detailed briefing on the legal duties and obligations required of a director of a publicly-held company
- a detailed briefing on the company and its business by the CEO, CFO and other members of senior management, including a discussion of the company's key products and operations, and
- a tour of the company's head office and main facility.

The orientation program is reviewed regularly by either the board or the x committee in connection with new appointments.

Below is an example of entity-specific disclosure where an issuer has no formal orientation program in place for its new directors.

Example of entity-specific disclosure

Given that the board of directors of the company has not changed in the last x years, the board has not been required to take any measures to orient new directors. If and when a new director is appointed to the board, the board will consider what orientation measures are appropriate at such time.

Continuing education

Disclosure requirement

Item 4(b) of Form 58-101F1 requires an issuer to briefly describe what measures, if any, the board takes to provide continuing education for its directors, and if it does not provide continuing education, how it ensures that its directors maintain the skill and knowledge necessary to meet their obligations as directors.

Findings of review

We observed a range of disclosure from the issuers reviewed. Some issuers disclosed that directors attend presentations and information sessions concerning board responsibilities, as well as education on current trends in governance that is available to the directors through their membership in various governance-related organizations. Other issuers explained that board members are encouraged to attend conferences, seminars or courses at the issuer's expense. However, many issuers included blanket statements that the board would ascertain and make continuing education available to its directors when required, but did not elaborate on how it determines when continuing education is needed or the nature of such continuing education.

Commentary

To satisfy this requirement, an issuer must provide meaningful disclosure on how it encourages its directors to maintain the skill and knowledge necessary to meet their obligations as directors. It is not sufficient to merely state that continuing education will be available when needed. Understanding how a board ensures that its directors maintain their skills and knowledge contributes to investors' understanding of how a board effectively functions.

Below are examples of questions that an issuer should consider when preparing this disclosure.

- What continuing education opportunities are provided to directors to increase their knowledge and understanding of the issuer and its business?

- Are the directors regularly briefed on strategic issues? Do these briefings include assessments of the issuer's competitive environment, the issuer's performance relative to its peers, and any other developments that could materially affect the issuer's business?

- What steps does the issuer take to keep directors informed about their fiduciary duties and trends in corporate governance?

- What steps does the issuer take to keep directors informed about significant regulatory developments that affect the issuer?

- Who is responsible for planning training activities for the directors?

- Do directors participate in the issuer's continuing education program or opportunities?

Below is an example of entity-specific disclosure of the measures a board takes to provide continuing education for its directors.

Example of entity-specific disclosure

The company has a continuing education program for its directors, for which the x committee is responsible. The program was developed to help directors maintain or enhance their skills and abilities, and update their knowledge and understanding of the company and its industry. The key components of the program include:

- **Regular briefings.** Directors are briefed regularly (and at least on a quarterly basis) on strategic issues affecting the company, and these briefings include reviews of the competitive environment, the company's performance relative to its peers, and any other developments that could materially affect the company's business such as the enactment of Act x, which is expected to have a significant impact on the company's operations in the Province of x. The briefings are conducted by the CEO, CFO and other members of the executive management team, as well as external advisors to the company.

- **Internal educational seminars.** The x committee also plans training activities to be held at certain board meetings, in addition to regular education sessions and presentations made to the board. For example, recent presentations have been made to the board relating to proposed new regulations, trends in corporate governance and certain specific business units. In 20xx, x seminars were held.

- **Conferences and other industry events.** Directors also participate in external education seminars at the company's expense that are relevant to their role on the board. As part of the company's continuing education program, the company provides directors with a list of the principal education activities that are aimed at the company's industry and the role of a director of a public company. In 20xx, the directors attended x conferences in relation to the company's business and industry.

D. — Ethical business conduct

Disclosure requirement

Item 5 of Form 58-101F1 requires, among other things, an issuer to disclose whether or not the board has adopted a written code of business conduct and ethics (a code) for directors, officers and employees. If so, the issuer must, among other things,

- disclose how a person or company may obtain a copy of the code, and

- describe how the board monitors compliance with its code, or if the board does not monitor compliance, explain whether and how the board satisfies itself regarding compliance with its code.

Findings of review

Generally, our review revealed that many issuers disclosed that they adopted a code, but did not provide any of the other required information contained in Item 5. Particularly, we identified disclosure gaps when addressing how an issuer monitors compliance with its code. A significant portion of issuers included a positive statement in their disclosure that the board and/or a designated standing committee of the board monitors compliance, but did not provide a description or explanation of that process. Some issuers disclosed that they "take the necessary steps to ensure that all those covered by the relevant policies comply with such policies", but failed to include a description of those "necessary steps". Other issuers simply stated that when situations of non-compliance become known to management, appropriate disciplinary actions are taken.

Commentary

Blanket statements that a board monitors compliance with its code are not sufficient to satisfy this disclosure requirement. It is important for investors to understand what procedures the issuer has implemented or what actions it has undertaken to monitor compliance with the code.

Below are examples of questions that an issuer should consider when preparing this disclosure.

- Has the board delegated oversight of compliance with the code to one of its standing committees?

- Does the board or a designated standing committee annually or quarterly review with management compliance with the code and any issues arising from non-compliance?

- How does the board or a designated standing committee become aware of non-compliance with the code?

- Does the issuer require its directors, officers and employees to complete an acknowledgement (on an annual, semi-annual or other basis) whereby they confirm they have read the code and agree to follow its terms and fully comply? If not, is there a process whereby members of management and employees confirm they have read and understand the code?

- Has the issuer appointed a compliance officer? If so, what are the compliance officer's roles and responsibilities? Does the compliance officer report regularly to the board (or its designated standing committee) on compliance with the code?

- Does the issuer have a process in place whereby directors or officers disclose transactions or holdings that may be, or appear to be, in conflict with the code?

- Does the issuer have a whistleblower program or other compliance program available to employees that allows for anonymous reports to be made?

- Has the issuer designated a person with whom employees can discuss any issues regarding the code?

An issuer may include a description of its process to monitor compliance with the code in the code itself. In order to meet this disclosure requirement, the issuer must either describe the process in its corporate governance disclosure, or incorporate that description by reference. Providing investors with a cross-reference or a link to a website where the code can be found may also be useful.

Below is an example of entity-specific disclosure of the measures a board takes to monitor compliance with its code.

Example of entity-specific disclosure

The board reviews its code of conduct on an annual basis and has delegated compliance oversight to the x committee. The company monitors compliance with its code as follows:

- **External Reporting System**. The company uses a confidential and anonymous reporting system that allows officers and employees to report suspected illegal, unethical or improper conduct in violation of the code through the Internet, a toll-free telephone number and/or by mail. The reporting system is run by an independent third party and generates reports for management. Management reviews the reports on a [quarterly/monthly/other basis] and investigates any alleged breaches of the code. The chairs of the x committee and Audit Committee also have access to all reports filed through the reporting system.

- **Internal Reporting System**. Complaints can also be made internally to the following members of the executive management team: x, x and x.

Management prepares reports for the x committee, noting any alleged violations of the code on a [quarterly/monthly/other basis]. The x committee updates the board on a [quarterly/monthly/other basis] about compliance with the code, and reports any alleged violations to the board as necessary. The Audit Committee is also notified of any alleged violations of the code relating to accounting, internal controls or auditing matters. The x committee, in consultation with the board, reviews the process for administering the code every year.

The board believes that providing a procedure for employees and officers to raise concerns about ethical conduct on an anonymous and confidential basis fosters a culture of ethical conduct within the company. The company requires that directors, officers and employees annually certify they have complied with the code. To date, the company has not been required to file a material change report relating to a departure from the code.

E. — Nomination of directors

Disclosure requirement

Item 6 of Form 58-101F1 requires, among other things, an issuer to describe the process by which the board identifies new candidates for board nomination.

Findings of review

Generally, this was an area where staff identified significant disclosure deficiencies. Many issuers included positive statements in their corporate governance disclosure acknowledging that they had a process in place for identifying candidates, but failed to describe the process itself. Similarly, many issuers disclosed who is responsible for identifying new candidates, but did not describe the process undertaken by such person or committee identified. Other issuers disclosed that the process for identifying new candidates for board nomination was outlined in the nominating committee's charter, but did not include the text of the charter in its disclosure.

Commentary

It is not sufficient to merely state that the board has a process in place for identifying new candidates. To comply with this requirement, the issuer must describe that process, regardless of whether that process has been formalized. A description of that process provides meaningful information to investors.

Below are examples of questions that an issuer should consider when preparing this disclosure.

- Who leads the candidate selection process and what is such person/committee's mandate in this respect?

- Does the board or the person/committee responsible for the nomination process identify any gaps in the board's composition or expertise before it seeks candidates to fill those gaps?

- Does the board have a formal policy on the recruitment of new candidates to the board?

- Does the board or the person/committee responsible for the nomination process invite suggestions for potential candidates from other directors, management, shareholders, external sources or does it consider self-nominated candidates?

- What is the role, if any, of the CEO in the nomination process?

- Does the board or the person/committee responsible for the nomination process take into account the appropriate size of the board, with a view to facilitating effective decision making?

- Does the board or the person/committee responsible for the nomination process establish criteria in respect of the competencies, skills and characteristics, and expertise that each candidate for appointment or election to the board would bring to the board?

- Does the board consider diversity of experience, background and views when considering a candidate for appointment or election to the board?

- Does the board or the person/committee responsible for the nomination process consider the following criteria when considering a candidate for appointment or election to the board:

  - a proven track record of substantial achievement

  - specific industry or geographic experience

  - the ability of the candidate to bring an objective appraisal of management's plans

  - potential conflicts that could arise

  - personal characteristics and other considerations,

  - the integrity of the candidate, and

  - the ability of the candidate to devote sufficient time and resources to his or her duties as a board member?

If an issuer does not have a process for identifying new candidates, it should explain why. For example, an issuer may not have a process for identifying new candidates as changes are made to the board very infrequently.

Below is an example of entity-specific disclosure of the measures a board takes to identify new candidates for board nomination.

Example of entity-specific disclosure

The x committee, which is comprised entirely of independent directors, is responsible for participating in the recruitment and recommendation of new candidates for appointment or election to the board. When considering a potential candidate, the x committee considers the qualities and skills that the board, as a whole, should have and assesses the competencies and skills of the current members of the board. Based on the talent already represented on the board, the x committee then identifies the specific skills, personal qualities or experiences that a candidate should possess in light of the opportunities and risks facing the company. Potential candidates are screened to ensure that they possess the requisite qualities, including integrity, business judgment and experience, business or professional expertise, independence from management, international experience, financial literacy, excellent communications skills and the ability to work well with the board and company. The x committee considers the existing commitments of a potential candidate to ensure that such candidate will be able to fulfill his or her obligations as a board member.

The x committee maintains a list of potential director candidates for its future consideration and may engage outside advisors to assist in identifying potential candidates. The x committee also considers recommendations for director nominees submitted by the company's shareholders.

F. — Assessments

Disclosure Requirement

Item 9 of Form 58-101F1 requires an issuer to describe the process used for assessments, if the board, its committees and individual directors are regularly assessed with respect to their effectiveness and contribution. If assessments are not regularly conducted, the issuer is required to describe how the board satisfies itself that the board, its committees, and its individual directors are performing effectively.

Findings of review

A significant portion of the issuers reviewed did not fully satisfy this requirement.

- **Regular assessments conducted.** A significant portion of the issuers reviewed did not describe the process used for assessments. Many issuers disclosed that they conduct regular assessments and other issuers included disclosure on the importance of completing assessments, but they did not in either case describe the process used for the assessments. In addition, we often noticed that issuers did not disclose how "regularly" these assessments are conducted.

- **Regular assessments not conducted.** Other issuers reviewed indicated that they did not have a formal assessment procedure in place because the board believes that such assessments are generally more appropriate for issuers of significantly larger size and complexity and which may have significantly larger boards of directors. However, they did not describe how the board satisfies itself that the board, its committees, and its individual directors are performing effectively.

Commentary

It is not sufficient to merely state whether or not the board conducts regular assessments. To satisfy this requirement, the issuer must either describe the process used for any assessments or describe how the board satisfies itself that the board, its committees, and its individual directors are performing effectively. Understanding how a board manages its performance is important for investors.

Below are examples of questions that an issuer should consider when preparing this disclosure.

Assessments

- Are assessments conducted annually, semi-annually or at different intervals?

- Are assessments undertaken through the use of questionnaires and/or confidential interviews, or by third parties hired for this purpose?

- Who is responsible for conducting the assessments?

- If a questionnaire is the method used for the assessment:

  - Is it reviewed and approved by the board or a board committee in advance of its use?

  - Is it submitted on a confidential basis?

  - Does it facilitate a written evaluation of the performance and effectiveness of the board and each board committee?

  - Does it incorporate peer assessments and self-assessments on the part of individual board members?

  - Does it cover such matters, among other things, as the operation of the board and its committees, the adequacy and timeliness of the information provided to directors, agenda planning for board meetings and contributions of board and committee members?

  - Are the findings analyzed and presented to the board for further consideration?

- Upon review of the results of the assessment, do the board and members of each board committee consider whether any changes to the composition, structure or charter of the board or committee are appropriate?

Other measures

- Are board members free to discuss the performance of a fellow director with the chair of the board or with an appropriate board committee?

- Is there a dialogue between the chair or lead director and each individual director regarding his or her performance and continuance on the board?

- Is there a review of individual directors' performance when they are standing for re-election? If so, who conducts the review?

Below are examples of entity-specific disclosure of formal and informal processes used for assessments.

Example 1 – Entity-specific disclosure for formal assessment process

The board of directors conducts an annual evaluation of the performance and effectiveness of the board in light of its charter. The results of the evaluation are analysed and reviewed by members of the x committee and the board, who consider whether any changes to the board's processes, composition or committee structure are appropriate. Additionally, senior management is advised of any suggestions made by directors for enhancement of processes to support the work of the board.

Assessment of individual board members involves directors participating in an annual written peer review to assess individual directors on the board and attributes that contribute to an effective board. This consists of both an evaluation of each directors' peers and a self-evaluation which are based on questionnaires approved by the board. The written peer evaluation process is complemented with one-on-one meetings between the chair of the board and each director. In addition, each board committee annually evaluates its effectiveness in carrying out the duties specified in its charter. The results are reviewed by the members of each committee who consider whether any changes to its structure or charter may be appropriate.

Example 1 – Entity-specific disclosure for informal assessment process

The board, its committees and individual directors are not regularly assessed with respect to their effectiveness and contribution, as the board believes that such assessments are generally more appropriate for corporations of significantly larger size and complexity than the company and which may have significantly larger boards of directors. However, the chair of the board meets annually with each director individually which facilitates a discussion of his or her contribution and that of other directors. When needed, time is set aside at a meeting of the board for a discussion regarding the effectiveness of the board and its committees. If appropriate, the board then considers procedural or substantive changes to increase the effectiveness of the board and its committees. On an informal basis, the chair is also responsible for reporting to the board on areas where improvements can be made. Any agreed upon improvements required to be made are implemented and overseen by the x committee. A more formal assessment process will be instituted as, if, and when the board considers it to be necessary.

3.2 — Requirements for venture issuers

A. — Board of directors

Disclosure requirement

Item 1 of Form 58-101F2 requires a venture issuer to disclose how its board of directors facilitates its exercise of independent supervision over management, including,

- the identity of directors who are independent, and

- those who are not independent, and the basis for that determination.

Findings of review

While the majority of issuers disclosed the identity of independent and non-independent directors, many issuers did not disclose how the board facilitates its exercise of independent supervision over management.

Commentary

More meaningful disclosure to investors would have identified and explained what the board does to facilitate its exercise of independent supervision over management. In particular, issuers should describe what processes are in place to safeguard the independent supervisory role of the board in relation to management.

Below are examples of questions that an issuer should consider when preparing this disclosure.

- Does the board operate in an independent manner, generally, from management?

- Does the board meet regularly without the presence of management to ensure the independence of the board from management?

- Is the independence of the board enabled through the separation of the positions of chair and CEO?

- Does the board hold periodic meetings to approve various matters and discuss the business and operations of the issuer in the absence of management?

- Does the board have free access to the issuer's external auditor, legal counsel and to any of the issuer's officers?

- If the chair is not independent, is there an independent lead director?

B. — Other board committees
Disclosure requirement

Item 7 of Form 58-101F2 requires a venture issuer to disclose if the board has standing committees other than the audit, compensation and nominating committees and if so, to identify the committees and describe their function.

Findings of review

Many of the issuers reviewed disclosed that they did not have other standing committees. However, some issuers noted that they did have standing committees and identified such committees (i.e. industry specific committees), but did not describe their function.

Commentary

It is helpful for investors to understand what functions standing committees of the board have in regards to the overall functioning of the issuer.

Below are examples of questions that an issuer should consider when preparing this disclosure.

- Why was the standing committee formed?

- What are the standing committee's responsibilities?

- What functions is the standing committee tasked to perform?

3.3 — Executive compensation

In light of the proposed amendments to Form 51-102F6 *Statement of Executive Compensation* of National Instrument 51-102 *Continuous Disclosure Obligations* published for comment on November 19, 2010 (the Proposed Executive Compensation Amendments), we will not provide commentary on the corporate governance disclosure requirements relating to compensation. Please refer to the Proposed Executive Compensation Amendments for further information on changes that may impact your corporate governance disclosure regarding compensation made in regards to Item 7 of Form 58-101F1 for TSX-listed issuers and Item 6 of Form 58-101F2 for venture issuers.

3.4 — Risk management

Understanding how the board manages risk is very important for investors. Intensified concerns about risk management, auditing and fraud detection, and corporate governance have sensitized boards and management to adopt a more active role in the oversight of business strategy and operations. Boards and other market participants are receiving increased scrutiny regarding their risk management practices.

Disclosure requirements

There are two sets of disclosure requirements relating to risk management:

1. Board mandate. Item 2 of Form 58-101F1 requires TSX-listed issuers to disclose the text of the board's written mandate, or if the board does not have a written mandate, to describe how the board delineates its role and responsibilities. Section 3.4 of the Corporate Governance Policy states that the board should adopt a written mandate in which it explicitly acknowledges responsibility for, among other things:

- adopting a strategic planning process and approving, on at least an annual basis, a strategic plan which takes into account, among other things, the opportunities and risks of the business, and

- identifying the principal risks of the issuer's business and ensuring the implementation of appropriate systems to manage those risks.

2. Board committees. There are two relevant disclosure requirements relating to board standing committees and audit committees:

- Item 8 of Form 58-101F1 requires TSX-listed issuers to disclose if their boards have standing committees other than the audit, compensation and nominating committees, and if so, to identify the committees and describe their function. The mandate of those committees may include responsibility for risk management.

- Item 1 of Form 52-110F1 *Audit Committee Information Required in an AIF* and Form 52-110F2 *Disclosure by Venture Issuers* requires issuers to disclose the text of the audit committee's charter in the AIF. The audit committee may have responsibility for risk management.

Findings of review

A significant portion of the issuers reviewed included disclosure in the board's mandate relating to how the issuer manages risk and explained that risk management was a part of the board's oversight function. Similarly, many issuers disclosed that the board's mandate includes responsibility for a strategic plan taking into account the risks of the business. However, many of the issuers reviewed did not disclose whether the board's standing committees addressed risk management. For some issuers, the disclosure indicated that the audit committee was charged with this responsibility or that the board oversees the process by which the issuer assesses and manages risk.

Commentary

Material risks are required to be disclosed in regulatory filings such as an AIF or a prospectus. The way in which an issuer manages those risks may vary between industries and even between issuers within an industry according to their particular circumstances. It is important for investors to understand how issuers manage those risks. Disclosure regarding oversight and management of risks should indicate:

- the board's responsibility for oversight and management of risks, and

- any board and management-level committee to which responsibility for oversight and management of risks has been delegated.

The disclosure should provide insight into:

- the development and periodic review of the issuer's risk profile

- the integration of risk oversight and management into the issuer's strategic plan

- the identification of significant elements of risk management, including policies and procedures to manage risk, and

- the board's assessment of the effectiveness of risk management policies and procedures, where applicable.

In light of ongoing international developments regarding the disclosure of risk management practices, this is an area that we will continue to monitor.

4. — Conclusion and Questions

Issuers should consider the Corporate Governance Instrument, Corporate Governance Policy and the guidance in this notice when preparing their corporate governance disclosure to ensure that it complies with securities legislation and provides investors with meaningful information for making investment decisions. It is important for investors to understand what corporate governance practices an issuer has adopted and why.

CSA Multilateral Staff Notice 58-307 — Staff Review of Women on Boards and in Executive Officer Positions — Compliance with NI 58-101 Disclosure of Corporate

Date: October 1, 2015

38 O.S.C.B. 8435

[Not reproduced]

OSC Staff Notice 58-701 — Extension of Consultation Period — OSC Staff Consultation Paper 58-401 — *Disclosure Requirements Regarding Women on Boards and In Senior Management*

Date: September 20, 2013

36 O.S.C.B. 9288

[Not reproduced]

PART VI — TAKE-OVER BIDS AND SPECIAL TRANSACTIONS

6.1 — Special Transactions

Multilateral Instrument 61-101 — Protection of Minority Security Holders in Special Transactions

Date: February 1, 2008, amended November 17, 2015, December 8, 2015 and May 9, 2016.
31 O.S.C.B. 1321, 38 O.S.C.B. 7562, 38 O.S.C.B. 8332 and 39 O.S.C.B. 4281.

[Editor's note: MI 61-101 has been adopted in Ontario and Quebec.]

PART 1 — DEFINITIONS AND INTERPRETATION

1.1 Definitions — In this Instrument

"affected security" means

(a) for a business combination of an issuer, an equity security of the issuer in which the interest of a security holder would be terminated as a consequence of the transaction, and

(b) for a related party transaction of an issuer, an equity security of the issuer;

"affiliated entity": a person is considered to be an affiliated entity of another person if one is the subsidiary entity of the other or if both are subsidiary entities of the same person,

"arm's length" has the meaning ascribed to that term in section 251 of the *Income Tax Act* (Canada), or any successor to that legislation, and, in addition to that meaning, a person is deemed not to deal at arm's length with a related party of that person;

"associated entity", when used to indicate a relationship with a person, means

(a) an issuer of which the person beneficially owns or controls, directly or indirectly, voting securities entitling the person to more than 10% of the voting rights attached to outstanding securities of the issuer,

(b) any partner of the person,

(c) any trust or estate in which the person has a substantial beneficial interest or in respect of which a person serves as trustee or in a similar capacity,

(d) a relative of that person, including

(i) the spouse, or

(ii) a relative of the person's spouse

if the relative has the same home as that person;

"beneficially owns" includes direct or indirect beneficial ownership of a security holder;

"bid" means a take-over bid or an issuer bid to which Part 2 of National Instrument 62-104 *Take-Over Bids and Issuer Bids* applies;

"bona fide lender" means a person that

(a) is an issuer insider of an issuer solely through the holding of, or the exercise of control or direction over, securities used as collateral for a debt under a written agreement entered into by the person as a lender, assignee, transferee or participant,

(b) is not yet legally entitled to dispose of the securities for the purpose of applying proceeds of realization in repayment of the secured debt, and

(c) was not a related party of the issuer at the time the agreement referred to in paragraph (a) was entered into;

"business combination" means, for an issuer, an amalgamation, arrangement, consolidation, amendment to the terms of a class of equity securities or any other transaction of the issuer, as a consequence of which the interest of a holder of an equity security of the issuer may be terminated without the holder's consent, regardless of whether the equity security is replaced with another security, but does not include

(a) an acquisition of an equity security of the issuer under a statutory right of compulsory acquisition or, if the issuer is not a corporation, under provisions substantially equivalent to those comprising section 206 of the CBCA,

(b) a consolidation of securities that does not have the effect of terminating the interests of holders of equity securities of the issuer in those securities without their consent, through the elimination of post-consolidated fractional interests or otherwise, except to an extent that is nominal in the circumstances,

(c) a termination of a holder's interest in a security, under the terms attached to the security, for the purpose of enforcing an ownership or voting constraint that is necessary to enable the issuer to comply with legislation, lawfully engage in a particular activity or have a specified level of Canadian ownership,

(d) a downstream transaction for the issuer, or

(e) a transaction in which no person that is a related party of the issuer at the time the transaction is agreed to

(i) would, as a consequence of the transaction, directly or indirectly acquire the issuer or the business of the issuer, or combine with the issuer, through an amalgamation, arrangement or otherwise, whether alone or with joint actors,

(ii) is a party to any connected transaction to the transaction, or

(iii) is entitled to receive, directly or indirectly, as a consequence of the transaction

(A) consideration per equity security that is not identical in amount and form to the entitlement of the general body of holders in Canada of securities of the same class,

(B) a collateral benefit, or

(C) consideration for securities of a class of equity securities of the issuer if the issuer has more than one outstanding class of equity securities, unless that consideration is not greater than the entitlement of the general body of holders in Canada of every other class of equity securities of the issuer in relation to the voting and financial participating interests in the issuer represented by the respective securities;

"CBCA" means the *Canada Business Corporations Act*, R.S.C. 1985, c. C-44;

"class" includes a series of a class;

"collateral benefit", for a transaction of an issuer or for a bid for securities of an issuer, means any benefit that a related party of the issuer is entitled to receive, directly or indirectly, as a consequence of the transaction or bid, including, without limitation, an increase in salary, a lump sum payment, a payment for surrendering securities, or other enhancement in benefits related to past or future services as an employee, director or consultant of the issuer or of another person, regardless of the existence of any offsetting costs to the related party or whether the benefit is provided, or agreed to, by the issuer, another party to the transaction or the offeror in the bid, but does not include

(a) a payment or distribution per equity security that is identical in amount and form to the entitlement of the general body of holders in Canada of securities of the same class,

(b) an enhancement of employee benefits resulting from participation by the related party in a group plan, other than an incentive plan, for employees of a successor to the business of the issuer, if the benefits provided by the group plan are generally provided to employees of the successor to the business of the issuer who hold positions of a similar nature to the position held by the related party, or

(c) a benefit, not described in paragraph (b), that is received solely in connection with the related party's services as an employee, director or consultant of the issuer, of an affiliated entity of the issuer or of a successor to the business of the issuer, if

(i) the benefit is not conferred for the purpose, in whole or in part, of increasing the value of the consideration paid to the related party for securities relinquished under the transaction or bid,

(ii) the conferring of the benefit is not, by its terms, conditional on the related party supporting the transaction or bid in any manner,

(iii) full particulars of the benefit are disclosed in the disclosure document for the transaction, or in the directors' circular in the case of a take-over bid, and

(iv)   (A) at the time the transaction is agreed to or the bid is publicly announced, the related party and its associated entities beneficially own or exercise control or direction over less than one per cent of the outstanding securities of each class of equity securities of the issuer, or

(B) if the transaction is a business combination for the issuer or a bid for securities of the issuer,

(I) the related party discloses to an independent committee of the issuer the amount of consideration that the related party expects it will be beneficially entitled to receive, under the terms of the transaction or bid, in exchange for the equity securities beneficially owned by the related party,

(II) the independent committee, acting in good faith, determines that the value of the benefit, net of any offsetting costs to the related party, is less than five per cent of the value referred to in subclause (I), and

(III) the independent committee's determination is disclosed in the disclosure document for the transaction, or in the directors' circular in the case of a take-over bid;

"connected transactions" means two or more transactions that have at least one party in common, directly or indirectly, other than transactions related solely to services as an employee, director or consultant, and

(a) are negotiated or completed at approximately the same time, or

(b) the completion of at least one of the transactions is conditional on the completion of each of the other transactions;

"consultant" means, for an issuer, a person, other than an employee or senior officer of the issuer or of an affiliated entity of the issuer, that

(a) is engaged to provide services to the issuer or an affiliated entity of the issuer, other than services provided in relation to a distribution,

(b) provides the services under a written contract with the issuer or an affiliated entity of the issuer, and

(c) spends or will spend a significant amount of time and attention of the affairs and business of the issuer or an affiliated entity or the issuer

and includes, for an individual consultant a corporation of which the individual consultant is an employee or shareholder, and a partnership of which the individual consultant is an employee or partner;

"convertible" means convertible into, exchangeable for, or carrying the right or obligation to purchase or otherwise acquire or cause the purchase or acquisition of, another security;

"director", for an issuer that is a limited partnership, includes a director of the general partner of the issuer, except for the purposes of the interpretation of "control";

"disclosure document" means

(a) for a take-over bid including an insider bid, a take-over bid circular sent to holders of offeree securities,

(b) for an issuer bid, an issuer bid circular sent to holders of offeree securities, and

(c) for a business combination or a related party transaction,

(i) an information circular sent to holders of affected securities,

(ii) if no information circular is required, another document sent to holders of affected securities in connection with a meeting of holders of affected securities, or

(iii) if no information circular or other document referred to in subparagraph (ii) is required, a material change report filed for the transaction;

"downstream transaction" means, for an issuer, a transaction between the issuer and a related party of the issuer if, at the time the transaction is agreed to

(a) the issuer is a control person of the related party, and

(b) to the knowledge of the issuer after reasonable inquiry, no related party of the issuer, other than a wholly-owned subsidiary entity of the issuer, beneficially owns or exercises control or direction over, other than through its interest in the issuer, more than five per cent of any class of voting or equity securities of the related party that is a party to the transaction;

"equity security" means a security of an issuer that carries a residual right to participate in the earnings of the issuer and, on liquidation or winding up of the issuer, in its assets;

"fair market value" means, except as provided in paragraph 6.4(2)(d), the monetary consideration that, in an open and unrestricted market, a prudent and informed buyer would pay to a prudent and informed seller, each acting at arm's length with the other and under no compulsion to act;

"formal valuation" means a valuation prepared in accordance with Part 6;

"freely tradeable" means, for securities, that

(a) the securities are transferable,

(b) the securities are not subject to any escrow requirements,

(c) the securities do not form part of the holdings of any control person,

(d) the securities are not subject to any cease trade order imposed by a securities regulatory authority,

(e) all hold periods imposed by securities legislation before the securities can be traded without a prospectus or in reliance on a prospectus exemption have expired, and

(f) any period of time imposed by securities legislation for which the issuer has to have been a reporting issuer in a jurisdiction before the securities can be traded without a prospectus or in reliance on a prospectus exemption has passed;

"incentive plan" means a group plan that provides for stock options or other equity incentives, profit sharing, bonuses, or other performance-based payments;

"independent committee" means, for an issuer, a committee consisting exclusively of one or more independent directors of the issuer;

"independent director" means, for an issuer in respect of a transaction or bid, a director who is independent as determined in section 7.1;

"independent valuator" means, for a transaction or bid, a valuator that is independent of all interested parties in the transaction, as determined in section 6.1;

"insider bid" means a take-over bid made by

(a) an issuer insider of the offeree issuer,

(b) an associated or affiliated entity of an issuer insider of the offeree issuer,

(c) an associated or affiliated entity of the offeree issuer,

(d) a person described in paragraph (a), (b) or (c) at any time within 12 months preceding the commencement of the bid, or

(e) a joint actor with a person referred to in paragraph (a), (b), (c) or (d);

"interested party" means

(a) for a take-over bid including an insider bid, the offeror or a joint actor with the offeror,

(b) for an issuer bid

(i) the issuer, and

(ii) any control person of the issuer, or any person that would reasonably be expected to be a control person of the issuer upon successful completion of the issuer bid,

(c) for a business combination, a related party of the issuer at the time the transaction is agreed to, if the related party

(i) would, as a consequence of the transaction, directly or indirectly acquire the issuer or the business of the issuer, or combine with the issuer, through an amalgamation, arrangement or otherwise, whether alone or with joint actors,

(ii) is a party to any connected transaction to the business combination, or

(iii) is entitled to receive, directly or indirectly, as a consequence of the transaction

(A) consideration per affected security that is not identical in amount and form to the entitlement of the general body of holders in Canada of securities of the same class,

(B) a collateral benefit, or

(C) consideration for securities of a class of equity securities of the issuer if the issuer has more than one outstanding class of equity securities, unless that consideration is not greater than the entitlement of the general body of holders in Canada of every other class of equity securities of the issuer in relation to the voting and financial participating interests in the issuer represented by the respective securities, and

(d) for a related party transaction, a related party of the issuer at the time the transaction is agreed to, if the related party

(i) is a party to the transaction, unless it is a party only in its capacity as a holder of affected securities and is treated identically to the general body of holders in Canada of securities of the same class on a per security basis, or

(ii) is entitled to receive, directly or indirectly, as a consequence of the transaction

(A) a collateral benefit, or

(B) a payment or distribution made to one or more holders of a class of equity securities of the issuer if the issuer has more than one outstanding class of equity securities, unless the amount of that payment or distribution is not greater than the entitlement of the general body of holders in Canada of every other class of equity securities of the issuer in relation to the voting and financial participating interests in the issuer represented by the respective securities;

"issuer bid" has the meaning ascribed to that term in section 1.1 of National Instrument 62-104 *Take-Over Bids and Issuer Bids*;

"issuer insider" means, for an issuer

(a) a director or senior officer of the issuer,

(b) a director or senior officer of a person that is itself an issuer insider or subsidiary entity of the issuer, or

(c) a person that has

(i) beneficial ownership of, or control or direction over, directly or indirectly, or

(ii) a combination of beneficial ownership of, and control or direction over, directly or indirectly,

securities of the issuer carrying more than 10% of the voting rights attached to all the issuer's outstanding voting securities;

"joint actors", when used to describe the relationship among two or more persons, means persons "acting jointly or in concert" as determined in accordance with section 1.9 of National Instrument 62-104 *Take-Over Bids and Issuer Bids*, with necessary modifications where the term is used in the context of a transaction that is not a take-over bid or issuer bid, but a security holder is not considered to be a joint actor with an offeror making a bid, or with a person involved in a business combination or related party transaction, solely because there is an agreement, commitment or understanding that the security holder will tender to the bid or vote in favour of the transaction;

"liquid market" means a market that meets the criteria specified in section 1.2;

"market capitalization" of an issuer means, for a transaction, the aggregate market price of all outstanding securities of all classes of equity securities of the issuer, the market price of the outstanding securities of a class being

(a) in the case of equity securities of a class for which there is a published market, the product of

(i) the number of securities of the class outstanding as of the close of business on the last business day of the calendar month preceding the calendar month in which the transaction is agreed to or, if no securities of the class were outstanding on that day, on the first business day after that day that securities of the class became outstanding, so long as that day precedes the date the transaction is agreed to, and

(ii) the market price of the securities at the time referred to in subparagraph (i), on the published market on which the class of securities is principally traded, as determined in accordance with subsections 1.11(1), (2) and (3) of National Instrument 62-104 *Take-Over Bids and Issuer Bids*,

(b) in the case of equity securities of a class for which there is no published market but that are currently convertible into a class of equity securities for which there is a published market, the product of

(i) the number of equity securities into which the convertible securities were convertible as of the close of business on the last business day of the calendar month preceding the calendar month in which the transaction is agreed to or, if no convertible securities were outstanding or convertible on that day, on the first business day after that day that the convertible securities became outstanding or convertible, so long as that day precedes the date the transaction is agreed to, and

(ii) the market price of the securities into which the convertible securities were convertible, at the time referred to in subparagraph (i), on the published market on which the class of securities is principally traded, as determined in accordance with subsections 1.11(1), (2) and (3) of National Instrument 62-104 *Take-Over Bids and Issuer Bids*, and

(c) in the case of equity securities of a class not referred to in paragraph (a) or (b), the amount determined by the issuer's board of directors in good faith to represent the fair market value of the outstanding securities of that class;

"minority approval" means, for a business combination or related party transaction of an issuer, approval of the proposed transaction by a majority of the votes as specified in Part 8, cast by holders of each class of affected securities at a meeting of security holders of that class called to consider the transaction;

"offeree issuer" has the meaning ascribed to that term in section 1.1 of National Instrument 62-104 *Take-Over Bids and Issuer Bids*;

"offeree security" means a security that is subject to a take-over bid or issuer bid;

"offeror" has the meaning ascribed to that term in section 1.1 of National Instrument 62-104 *Take-Over Bids and Issuer Bids*;

"person" in Ontario, includes

(a) an individual,

(b) a corporation,

(c) a partnership, trust, fund and an association, syndicate, organization or other organized group of persons, whether incorporated or not, and

(d) an individual or other person in that person's capacity as a trustee, executor, administrator or personal or other legal representative;

"prior valuation" means a valuation or appraisal of an issuer or its securities or material assets, whether or not prepared by an independent valuator, that, if disclosed, would reasonably be expected to affect the decision of a security holder to vote for or against a transaction, or to retain or dispose of affected securities or offeree securities, other than

(a) a report of a valuation or appraisal prepared by a person other than the issuer, if

(i) the report was not solicited by the issuer, and

(ii) the person preparing the report did so without knowledge of any material information concerning the issuer, its securities or any of its material assets, that had not been generally disclosed at the time the report was prepared,

(b) an internal valuation or appraisal prepared for the issuer in the ordinary course of business that has not been made available to, and has been prepared without the participation of

(i) the board of directors of the issuer, or

(ii) any director or senior officer of an interested party, except a senior officer of the issuer in the case of an issuer bid,

(c) a report of a market analyst or financial analyst that

(i) has been prepared by or for and at the expense of a person other than the issuer, an interested party, or an associated or affiliated entity of the issuer or an interested party, and

(ii) is either generally available to clients of the analyst or of the analyst's employer or of an associated or affiliated entity of the analyst's employer or, if not, is not based, so far as the person required to disclose a prior valuation is aware, on any material information concerning the issuer, its securities or any of its material assets, that had not been generally disclosed at the time the report was prepared,

(d) a valuation or appraisal prepared by a person or a person retained by that person, for the purpose of assisting the person in determining the price at which to propose a transaction that resulted in the person becoming an issuer insider, if the valuation or appraisal is not made available to any of the independent directors of the issuer, or

(e) a valuation or appraisal prepared by an interested party or a person retained by the interested party, for the purpose of assisting the interested party in determining the price at which to propose a transaction that, if pursued, would be an insider bid, business combination or related party transaction, if the valuation or appraisal is not made available to any of the independent directors of the issuer;

"published market" means, with respect to any class of securities, a market in Canada or outside of Canada on which the securities are traded, if the prices at which they have been traded on that market are regularly

(a) disseminated electronically, or

(b) published in a newspaper or business or financial publication of general and regular paid circulation;

"related party" of an entity means a person, other than a person that is solely a bona fide lender, that, at the relevant time and after reasonable inquiry, is known by the entity or a director or senior officer of the entity to be

(a) a control person of the entity,

(b) a person of which a person referred to in paragraph (a) is a control person,

(c) a person of which the entity is a control person,

(d) a person that has

(i) beneficial ownership of, or control or direction over, directly or indirectly, or

(ii) a combination of beneficial ownership of, and control or direction over, directly or indirectly,

securities of the entity carrying more than 10% of the voting rights attached to all the entity's outstanding voting securities;

(e) a director or senior officer of

(i) the entity, or

(ii) a person described in any other paragraph of this definition,

(f) a person that manages or directs, to any substantial degree, the affairs or operations of the entity under an agreement, arrangement or understanding between the person and the entity, including the general partner of an entity that is a limited partnership, but excluding a person acting under bankruptcy or insolvency law,

(g) a person of which persons described in any paragraph of this definition beneficially own, in the aggregate, more than 50 per cent of the securities of any outstanding class of equity securities, or

(h) an affiliated entity of any person described in any other paragraph of this definition;

"related party transaction" means, for an issuer, a transaction between the issuer and a person that is a related party of the issuer at the time the transaction is agreed to, whether or not there are also other parties to the transaction, as a consequence of which, either through the transaction itself or together with connected transactions, the issuer directly or indirectly

(a) purchases or acquires an asset from the related party for valuable consideration,

(b) purchases or acquires, as a joint actor with the related party, an asset from a third party if the proportion of the asset acquired by the issuer is less than the proportion of the consideration paid by the issuer,

(c) sells, transfers or disposes of an asset to the related party,

(d) sells, transfers or disposes of, as a joint actor with the related party, an asset to a third party if the proportion of the consideration received by the issuer is less than the proportion of the asset sold, transferred or disposed of by the issuer,

(e) leases property to or from the related party,

(f) acquires the related party, or combines with the related party, through an amalgamation, arrangement or otherwise, whether alone or with joint actors,

(g) issues a security to the related party or subscribes for a security of the related party,

(h) amends the terms of a security of the issuer if the security is beneficially owned, or is one over which control or direction is exercised, by the related party, or agrees to the amendment of the terms of a security of the related party if the security is beneficially owned by the issuer or is one over which the issuer exercises control or direction,

(i) assumes or otherwise becomes subject to a liability of the related party,

(j) borrows money from or lends money to the related party, or enters into a credit facility with the related party,

(k) releases, cancels or forgives a debt or liability owed by the related party,

(l) materially amends the terms of an outstanding debt or liability owed by or to the related party, or the terms of an outstanding credit facility with the related party, or

(m) provides a guarantee or collateral security for a debt or liability of the related party, or materially amends the terms of the guarantee or security;

"senior officer" means the chair or a vice-chair of the board of directors, a president, a vice-president, the secretary, the treasurer or the general manager of an issuer or any other individual who performs functions for an issuer similar to those normally performed by an individual occupying any such office, and for an issuer that is a limited partnership, includes a senior officer of the general partner of the issuer;

"subsidiary entity" means a person that is controlled directly or indirectly by another person and includes a subsidiary of that subsidiary;

"take-over bid" has the meaning ascribed to that term in section 1.1 of National Instrument 62-104 *Take-Over Bids and Issuer Bids*; and

"wholly-owned subsidiary entity": a person is considered to be a wholly-owned subsidiary entity of an issuer if the issuer owns, directly or indirectly, all the voting and equity securities and securities convertible into voting and equity securities of the person.

1.2 Liquid Market — (1) For the purposes of this Instrument, a liquid market in a class of securities of an issuer in respect of a transaction exists at a particular time only if

    (a) there is a published market for the class of securities,

        (i) during the period of 12 months before the date the transaction is agreed to in the case of a business combination, or 12 months before the date the transaction is publicly announced in the case of an insider bid or issuer bid,

            (A) the number of outstanding securities of the class was at all times at least 5,000,000, excluding securities beneficially owned, or over which control or direction was exercised, by related parties and securities that were not freely tradeable,

            (B) the aggregate trading volume of the class of securities on the published market on which the class was principally traded was at least 1,000,000 securities,

            (C) there were at least 1,000 trades in securities of the class on the published market on which the class was principally traded, and

            (D) the aggregate value of the trades in securities of the class on the published market on which the class was principally traded was at least $15,000,000, and

        (ii) the market value of the class of securities on the published market on which the class was principally traded, as determined in accordance with subsection (2), was at least $75,000,000 for the calendar month preceding the calendar month

            (A) in which the transaction is agreed to, in the case of a business combination, or

            (B) in which the transaction is publicly announced, in the case of an insider bid or issuer bid, or

    (b) if the test set out in paragraph (a) is not met and there is a published market for the class of securities,

        (i) a person that is qualified and independent of all interested parties to the transaction, as determined on the same basis applicable to a valuator preparing a formal valuation under section 6.1, provides an opinion to the issuer that there is a liquid market in the class at the date the transaction is agreed to in the case of a business combination, or at the date the transaction is publicly announced in the case of an insider bid or issuer bid,

        (ii) the opinion is included in the disclosure document for the transaction, and

        (iii) the disclosure document for the transaction includes the same disclosure regarding the person providing the opinion as is required for a valuator under section 6.2.

(2) For the purpose of determining whether an issuer satisfies the market value requirement of subparagraph (1)(a)(ii), the market value of a class of securities for a calendar month is calculated by multiplying

    (a) the number of securities of the class outstanding as of the close of business on the last business day of the calendar month, excluding securities beneficially owned, or over which control or direction was exercised, by related parties of the issuer and securities that were not freely tradeable, by

    (b) the arithmetic average of the closing prices of the securities of that class on the published market on which that class was principally traded for each of the trading days during the calendar month, if the published market provides a closing price for the securities, or

    (c) the arithmetic average of the simple averages of the highest and lowest prices of the securities of that class on the published market on which that class was principally traded for each of the trading days for which the securities traded during the calendar month, if the published market does not provide a closing price, but provides only the highest and lowest prices of securities traded on a particular day.

1.3 Transactions by Wholly-Owned Subsidiary Entity — For the purposes of this Instrument, a transaction of a wholly-owned subsidiary entity of an issuer is deemed to be also a transaction of the issuer, and, for greater certainty, a bid made by a wholly-owned subsidiary entity of an issuer for securities of the issuer is deemed to be also an issuer bid made by the issuer.

1.4 Transactions by Underlying Operating Entity of Income Trust — For the purposes of this Instrument, a transaction of an underlying operating entity of an income trust within the meaning of National Policy 41-201 *Income Trusts and Other Indirect Offerings* is deemed to be a transaction of the income trust, and a related party of the underlying operating entity is deemed to be a related party of the income trust.

1.5 Redeemable Securities as Consideration in Business Combination — For the purposes of this Instrument if all or part of the consideration that holders of affected securities receive in a business combination consists of securities that are redeemed for cash within seven days of their issuance, the cash proceeds of the redemption, rather than the redeemed securities, are deemed to be consideration that the holders of the affected securities receive in the business combination.

1.6 Beneficial Ownership — (1) Despite any other provision in securities legislation, for the purposes of this Instrument,

    (a) a person is deemed to own beneficially securities beneficially owned by a person it controls or by an affiliated entity of the controlled person if the affiliated entity is a subsidiary entity of the controlled person,

    (b) a person is deemed to own beneficially securities beneficially owned by its affiliated entity if the affiliated entity is a subsidiary entity of the person,

(2) For the purposes of the definitions of collateral benefit, control person, downstream transaction and related party, in determining beneficial ownership, the provisions of section 1.8 of National Instrument 62-104 *Take-Over Bids and Issuer Bids* apply.

(3) In Québec, for the purposes of this Instrument, a person that beneficially owns securities means a person that owns the securities or that holds securities registered under the name of an intermediary acting as nominee, including a trustee or agent.

1.7 Control — For the purposes of the definition of "subsidiary entity", a person controls a second person if

    (a) the person, directly or indirectly, beneficially owns or exercises control or direction over securities of the second person carrying votes which, if exercised, would entitle the person to elect a majority of the directors of the second person, unless the person beneficially owns or exercises control or direction over voting securities only to secure an obligation,

    (b) the second person is a partnership, the person beneficially owns or exercises control or direction over more than 50 per cent of the interests in the partnership, or

    (c) the second person is a limited partnership, the person is the general partner of the limited partnership or the control person of the general partner.

1.8 **Entity** — For the purposes of the definition of "related party", an entity has the meaning ascribed to the term "person" in section 1.1, other than an individual.

PART 2 — INSIDER BIDS

2.1 **Application** — (1) This Part applies to a bid that is an insider bid.

(2) This Part does not apply to an insider bid in respect of which the offeror complies with National Instrument 71-101 *The Multijurisdictional Disclosure System*, unless persons whose last address as shown on the books of the offeree issuer is in Canada, as determined in accordance with subsections 12.1(2) to (4) of that instrument, hold 20 per cent or more of the class of securities that is the subject of the bid.

2.2 **Disclosure** — (1) The offeror shall disclose in the disclosure document for an insider bid

(a) the background to the insider bid,

(b) in accordance with section 6.8, every prior valuation in respect of the offeree issuer that has been made in the 24 months before the date of the insider bid, and the existence of which is known, after reasonable inquiry, to the offeror or any director or senior officer of the offeror,

(c) the formal valuation exemption, if any, on which the offeror is relying under section 2.4 and the facts supporting that reliance, and

(d) the disclosure required by Form 62-104F2 *Issuer Bid Circular* of National Instrument 62-104 *Take-Over Bids and Issuer Bids*, to the extent applicable and with necessary modifications.

(2) The board of directors of the offeree issuer shall include in the directors' circular for an insider bid

(a) disclosure, in accordance with section 6.8, of every prior valuation in respect of the offeree issuer not disclosed in the disclosure document for the insider bid

(i) that has been made in the 24 months before the date of the insider bid, and

(ii) the existence of which is known, after reasonable inquiry, to the offeree issuer or to any director or senior officer of the offeree issuer,

(b) a description of the background to the insider bid to the extent the background has not been disclosed in the disclosure document for the insider bid,

(c) disclosure of any bona fide prior offer that relates to the offeree securities or is otherwise relevant to the insider bid, which offer was received by the issuer during the 24 months before the insider bid was publicly announced, and a description of the offer and the background to the offer, and

(d) a discussion of the review and approval process adopted by the board of directors and the special committee, if any, of the offeree issuer for the insider bid, including a discussion of any materially contrary view or abstention by a director and any material disagreement between the board and the special committee.

2.3 **Formal Valuation** — (1) The offeror in an insider bid shall

(a) obtain, at its own expense, a formal valuation,

(b) provide the disclosure required by section 6.2,

(c) include, in accordance with section 6.5, a summary of the formal valuation in the disclosure document for the insider bid, unless the formal valuation is included in its entirety in the disclosure document, and

(d) comply with the other provisions of Part 6 applicable to it relating to formal valuations.

(2) An independent committee of the offeree issuer shall, and the offeror shall enable the independent committee to

(a) determine who the valuator will be,

(b) supervise the preparation of the formal valuation, and

(c) use its best efforts to ensure that the formal valuation is completed and provided to the offeror in a timely manner.

2.4 **Exemptions from Formal Valuation Requirement** — (1) Section 2.3 does not apply to an offeror in connection with an insider bid in any of the following circumstances:

(a) **Lack of Knowledge and Representation** — neither the offeror nor any joint actor with the offeror has, or has had within the preceding 12 months, any board or management representation in respect of the offeree issuer, or has knowledge of any material information concerning the offeree issuer or its securities that has not been generally disclosed,

(b) **Previous Arm's Length Negotiations** — all of the following conditions are satisfied:

(i) the consideration per security under the insider bid is at least equal in value to and is in the same form as the highest consideration agreed to with one or more selling security holders of the offeree issuer in arm's length negotiations in connection with

(A) the making of the insider bid,

(B) one or more other transactions agreed to within 12 months before the date of the first public announcement of the insider bid, or

(C) a combination of transactions referred to in clauses (A) and (B),

(ii) at least one of the selling security holders party to an agreement referred to in clause (i)(A) or (B) beneficially owns or exercises control or direction over, or beneficially owned or exercised control or direction over, and agreed to sell

(A) at least five per cent of the outstanding securities of the class of offeree securities, as determined in accordance with subsection (2), if the person that entered into the agreement with the selling security holder beneficially owned 80 per cent or more of the outstanding securities of the class of offeree securities, as determined in accordance with subsection (2), or

(B) at least 10 per cent of the outstanding securities of the class of offeree securities, as determined in accordance with subsection (2), if the person that entered into the agreement with the selling security holder beneficially owned less than 80 per cent of the outstanding securities of the class of offeree securities, as determined in accordance with subsection (2),

(iii) one or more of the selling security holders party to any of the transactions referred to in subparagraph (i) beneficially own or exercise control or direction over, or beneficially owned or exercised control or direction over, and agreed to sell, in the aggregate, at least 20 per cent of the outstanding securities of the class of offeree securities, as determined in accordance with subsection (3), beneficially owned, or over which control or direction was exercised, by persons other than the person, and joint actors with the person, that entered into the agreements with the selling security holders,

(iv) the offeror reasonably believes, after reasonable inquiry, that at the time of each of the agreements referred to in subparagraph (i)

(A) each selling security holder party to the agreement had full knowledge and access to information concerning the offeree issuer and its securities, and

(B) any factors peculiar to a selling security holder party to the agreement, including non-financial factors, that were considered relevant by that selling security holder in assessing the consideration did not have the effect of reducing the price that would otherwise have been considered acceptable by that selling security holder,

(v) at the time of each of the agreements referred to in subparagraph (i), the offeror did not know of any material information in respect of the offeree issuer or the offeree securities that

(A) had not been generally disclosed, and

(B) if generally disclosed, could have reasonably been expected to increase the agreed consideration,

(vi) if any of the agreements referred to in subparagraph (i) was entered into with a selling security holder by a person other than the offeror, the offeror reasonably believes, after reasonable inquiry, that at the time of that agreement, the person did not know of any material information in respect of the offeree issuer or the offeree securities that

(A) had not been generally disclosed, and

(B) if disclosed, could have reasonably been expected to increase the agreed consideration,

(vii) the offeror does not know, after reasonable inquiry, of any material information in respect of the offeree issuer or the offeree securities since the time of each of the agreements referred to in subparagraph (i) that has not been generally disclosed and could reasonably be expected to increase the value of the offeree securities;

(c) **Auction** — all of the following conditions are satisfied:

(i) the insider bid is publicly announced or made while

(A) one or more bids for securities of the same class that is the subject of the insider bid have been made and are outstanding, or

(B) one or more proposed transactions are outstanding that

(I) are business combinations in respect of securities of the same class that is the subject of the insider bid and ascribe a per security value to those securities, or

(II) would be business combinations in respect of securities of the same class that is the subject of the insider bid, except that they come within the exception in paragraph (e) of the definition of business combination and ascribe a per security value to those securities,

(ii) at the time the insider bid is made, the offeree issuer has provided equal access to the offeree issuer, and to information concerning the offeree issuer and its securities, to the offeror in the insider bid, all offerors in the other bids, and all parties to the proposed transactions described in clause (i)(B),

(iii) the offeror, in the disclosure document for the insider bid,

(A) includes all material information concerning the offeree issuer and its securities that is known to the offeror after reasonable inquiry but has not been generally disclosed, together with a description of the nature of the offeror's access to the issuer, and

(B) states that the offeror does not know, after reasonable inquiry, of any material information concerning the offeree issuer and its securities other than information that has been disclosed under clause (A) or that has otherwise been generally disclosed.

(2) For the purposes of subparagraph (b)(ii) of subsection (1), the number of outstanding securities of the class of offeree securities

(a) is calculated at the time of the agreement referred to in clause (b)(i)(A) or (B) of subsection (1), if the offeror knows the number of securities of the class outstanding at that time, or

(b) if paragraph (a) does not apply, is determined based on the information most recently provided by the offeree issuer in a material change report, or section 5.4 of National Instrument 51-102 Continuous Disclosure Obligations, immediately preceding the date of the agreement referred to in clause (b)(i)(A) or (B) of subsection (1).

(3) For the purposes of subparagraph (b)(iii) of subsection (1), the number of outstanding securities of the class of offeree securities

(a) is calculated at the time of the last of the agreements referred to in subparagraph (b)(i) of subsection (1), if the offeror knows the number of securities of the class outstanding at that time, or

(b) if paragraph (a) does not apply, is determined based on the information most recently provided by the offeree issuer in a material change report, or section 5.4 of National Instrument 51-102 *Continuous Disclosure Obligations*, immediately preceding the date of the last of the agreements referred to in subparagraph (b)(i) of subsection (1).

PART 3 — ISSUER BIDS

3.1 **Application** — (1) This Part applies to a bid that is an issuer bid.

(2) This Part does not apply to an issuer bid that complies with National Instrument 71-101 *The Multijurisdictional Disclosure System*, unless persons whose last address as shown on the books of the issuer is in Canada, as determined in accordance with subsections 12.1(2) to (4) of that instrument, hold 20 per cent or more of the class of securities that is the subject of the bid.

3.2 **Disclosure** — The issuer shall include in the disclosure document for an issuer bid

(a) a description of the background to the issuer bid,

(b) disclosure, in accordance with section 6.8, of every prior valuation in respect of the issuer

(i) that has been made in the 24 months before the date of the issuer bid, and

(ii) the existence of which is known, after reasonable inquiry, to the issuer or to any director or senior officer of the issuer,

(c) disclosure of any bona fide prior offer that relates to the offeree securities or is otherwise relevant to the issuer bid, which offer was received by the issuer during the 24 months before the issuer bid was publicly announced, and a description of the offer and the background to the offer,

(d) a discussion of the review and approval process adopted by the board of directors and the special committee, if any, of the issuer for the issuer bid, including a discussion of any materially contrary view or abstention by a director and any material disagreement between the board and the special committee,

(e) a statement of the intention, if known to the issuer after reasonable inquiry, of every interested party to accept or not to accept the issuer bid,

(f) a description of the effect that the issuer anticipates the issuer bid, if successful, will have on the direct or indirect voting interest in the issuer of every interested party, and

(g) disclosure of the formal valuation exemption, if any, on which the issuer is relying under section 3.4 and the facts supporting that reliance.

3.3 Formal Valuation — (1) An issuer that makes an issuer bid shall

(a) obtain a formal valuation,

(b) provide the disclosure required by section 6.2,

(c) include, in accordance with section 6.5, a summary of the formal valuation in the disclosure document for the issuer bid, unless the formal valuation is included in its entirety in the disclosure document,

(d) if there is an interested party other than the issuer, state in the disclosure document who will pay or has paid for the valuation, and

(e) comply with the other provisions of Part 6 applicable to it relating to formal valuations.

(2) The board of directors of the issuer or an independent committee of the board shall

(a) determine who the valuator will be, and

(b) supervise the preparation of the formal valuation.

3.4 Exemptions from Formal Valuation Requirement — Section 3.3 does not apply to an issuer in connection with an issuer bid in any of the following circumstances:

(a) Bid for Non-Convertible Securities — the issuer bid is for securities that are not equity securities and that are not, directly or indirectly, convertible into equity securities,

(b) Liquid Market — the issuer bid is made for securities for which

(i) a liquid market exists,

(ii) it is reasonable to conclude that, following the completion of the bid, there will be a market for holders of the securities who do not tender to the bid that is not materially less liquid than the market that existed at the time of the making of the bid, and

(iii) if an opinion referred to in paragraph (b) of subsection 1.2(1) is provided, the person providing the opinion reaches the conclusion described in subparagraph (b)(ii) of this section 3.4 and so states in its opinion.

PART 4 — BUSINESS COMBINATIONS

4.1 Application — This Part does not apply to an issuer carrying out a business combination if

(a) the issuer is not a reporting issuer,

(b) the issuer is a mutual fund, or

(c) (i) at the time the business combination is agreed to, securities held by beneficial owners in the local jurisdiction constitute less than two per cent of the outstanding securities of each class of affected securities of the issuer, and

(ii) all documents concerning the transaction that are sent generally to other holders of affected securities of the issuer are concurrently sent to all holders of the securities in the local jurisdiction.

4.2 Meeting and Information Circular — (1) Without limiting the application of any other legal requirements that apply to meetings of security holders and information circulars, this section applies only to a business combination for which section 4.5 requires the issuer to obtain minority approval.

(2) An issuer proposing to carry out a business combination shall call a meeting of holders of affected securities and send an information circular to those holders.

(3) The issuer shall include in the information circular

(a) the disclosure required by Form 62-104F2 *Issuer Bid Circular* of National Instrument 62-104 *Take-Over Bids and Issuer Bids*, to the extent applicable and with necessary modifications,

(b) a description of the background to the business combination,

(c) disclosure in accordance with section 6.8 of every prior valuation in respect of the issuer

(i) that has been made in the 24 months before the date of the information circular, and

(ii) the existence of which is known, after reasonable inquiry, to the issuer or to any director or senior officer of the issuer,

(d) disclosure of any bona fide prior offer that relates to the subject matter of or is otherwise relevant to the transaction, which offer was received by the issuer during the 24 months before the business combination was agreed to, and a description of the offer and the background to the offer,

(e) a discussion of the review and approval process adopted by the board of directors and the special committee, if any, of the issuer for the transaction, including a discussion of any materially contrary view or abstention by a director and any material disagreement between the board and the special committee,

(f) disclosure of the formal valuation exemption, if any, on which the issuer is relying under section 4.4 and the facts supporting that reliance,

(g) disclosure of the number of votes attached to the securities that, to the knowledge of the issuer after reasonable inquiry, will be excluded in determining whether minority approval for the business combination is obtained, and

(h) the identity of the holders of securities specified in paragraph (g) together with their individual holdings.

(4) If, after sending the information circular and before the meeting, a change occurs that, if disclosed, would reasonably be expected to affect the decision of a holder of affected securities to vote for or against the business combination or to retain or dispose of affected securities, the issuer shall promptly disseminate disclosure of the change

    (a) in a manner that the issuer reasonably determines will inform beneficial owners of affected securities of the change, and

    (b) sufficiently in advance of the meeting that the beneficial owners of affected securities will be able to assess the impact of the change.

(5) If subsection (4) applies, the issuer shall file a copy of the disseminated information contemporaneously with its dissemination.

4.3 Formal Valuation — (1) An issuer shall obtain a formal valuation for a business combination if

    (a) an interested party would, as a consequence of the transaction, directly or indirectly acquire the issuer or the business of the issuer, or combine with the issuer, through an amalgamation, arrangement or otherwise, whether alone or with joint actors, or

    (b) an interested party is a party to any connected transaction to the business combination, if the connected transaction is a related party transaction for which the issuer is required to obtain a formal valuation under section 5.4.

(2) If a formal valuation is required under subsection (1), the issuer shall

    (a) provide the disclosure required by section 6.2,

    (b) include, in accordance with section 6.5, a summary of the formal valuation in the disclosure document for the business combination, unless the formal valuation is included in its entirety in the disclosure document,

    (c) state in the disclosure document for the business combination who will pay or has paid for the valuation, and

    (d) comply with the other provisions of Part 6 applicable to it relating to formal valuations.

(3) The board of directors of the issuer or an independent committee of the board shall

    (a) determine who the valuator will be, and

    (b) supervise the preparation of the formal valuation.

4.4 Exemptions from Formal Valuation Requirement — (1) Section 4.3 does not apply to an issuer carrying out a business combination in any of the following circumstances:

    (a) **Issuer Not Listed on Specified Markets** — no securities of the issuer are listed or quoted on the Toronto Stock Exchange, Aequitas NEO Exchange Inc., the New York Stock Exchange, the American Stock Exchange, the NASDAQ Stock Market, or a stock exchange outside of Canada and the United States other than the Alternative Investment Market of the London Stock Exchange or the PLUS markets operated by PLUS Markets Group plc,

    (b) **Previous Arm's Length Negotiations** — all of the following conditions are satisfied:

        (i) the consideration per affected security under the business combination is at least equal in value to and is in the same form as the highest consideration agreed to with one or more selling security holders of the issuer in arm's length negotiations in connection with

            (A) the business combination,

            (B) one or more other transactions agreed to within 12 months before the date of the first public announcement of the business combination, or

            (C) a combination of transactions referred to in clauses (A) and (B),

        (ii) at least one of the selling security holders party to an agreement referred to in clause (i)(A) or (B) beneficially owns or exercises control or direction over, or beneficially owned or exercised control or direction over, and agreed to sell

            (A) at least five per cent of the outstanding securities of the class of affected securities, as determined in accordance with subsection (2), if the person that entered into the agreement with the selling security holder beneficially owned 80 per cent or more of the outstanding securities of the class of affected securities, as determined in accordance with subsection (2), or

            (B) at least 10 per cent of the outstanding securities of the class of affected securities, as determined in accordance with subsection (2), if the person that entered into the agreement with the selling security holder beneficially owned less than 80 per cent of the outstanding securities of the class of affected securities, as determined in accordance with subsection (2),

        (iii) one or more of the selling security holders party to any of the transactions referred to in subparagraph (i) beneficially owns or exercises control or direction over, or beneficially owned or exercised control or direction over, and agreed to sell, in the aggregate, at least 20 per cent of the outstanding securities of the class of affected securities, as determined in accordance with subsection (3), beneficially owned or over which control or direction was exercised by persons other than the person, and joint actors with the person, that entered into the agreements with the selling security holders,

        (iv) the person proposing to carry out the business combination with the issuer reasonably believes, after reasonable inquiry, that at the time of each of the agreements referred to in subparagraph (i)

            (A) each selling security holder party to the agreement had full knowledge of and access to information concerning the issuer and its securities, and

            (B) any factors peculiar to a selling security holder party to the agreement, including non-financial factors, that were considered relevant by the selling security holder in assessing the consideration did not have the effect of reducing the price that would otherwise have been considered acceptable by that selling security holder,

        (v) at the time of each of the agreements referred to in subparagraph (i), the person proposing to carry out the business combination with the issuer did not know of any material information in respect of the issuer or the affected securities that

            (A) had not been generally disclosed, and

            (B) if disclosed, could have reasonably been expected to increase the agreed consideration,

        (vi) any of the agreements referred to in subparagraph (i) was entered into with a selling security holder by a person other than the person proposing to carry out the business combination with the issuer, the person proposing to carry out the business combination with the issuer reasonably believes, after reasonable inquiry, that at the time of that agreement, the person entering into the agreement with the selling security holder did not know of any material information in respect of the issuer or the affected securities that

    (A) had not been generally disclosed, and

    (B) if disclosed, could have reasonably been expected to increase the agreed consideration,

(vii) the person proposing to carry out the business combination with the issuer does not know, after reasonable inquiry, of any material information in respect of the issuer or the affected securities since the time of each of the agreements referred to in subparagraph (i) that has not been generally disclosed and could reasonably be expected to increase the value of the affected securities,

(c) **Auction** — all of the following conditions are satisfied:

(i) the business combination is publicly announced while

    (A) one or more proposed transactions are outstanding that

        (I) are business combinations in respect of the affected securities, and ascribe a per security value to those securities, or

        (II) would be business combinations in respect of the affected securities, except that they come within the exception in paragraph (e) of the definition of business combination, and ascribe a per security value to those securities,

    (B) one or more bids for the affected securities have been made and are outstanding,

(ii) at the time the disclosure document for the business combination is sent to the holders of affected securities, the issuer has provided equal access to the issuer, and to information concerning the issuer and its securities, to the person proposing to carry out the business combination with the issuer, all parties to the proposed transactions described in clause (i)(A), and all offerors in the bids,

(d) **Second Step Business Combination** — all of the following conditions are satisfied:

(i) the business combination is being effected by an offeror that made a bid, or an affiliated entity of that offeror, and is in respect of the securities of the same class for which the bid was made and that were not acquired in the bid,

(ii) the business combination is completed no later than 120 days after the date of expiry of the bid,

(iii) the consideration per security that the security holders would be entitled to receive in the business combination is at least equal in value to and is in the same form as the consideration that the tendering security holders were entitled to receive in the bid,

(iv) the disclosure document for the bid

    (A) disclosed that if the offeror acquired securities under the bid, the offeror intended to acquire the remainder of the securities under a statutory right of acquisition or under a business combination that would satisfy the conditions in subparagraphs (ii) and (iii),

    (B) described the expected tax consequences of both the bid and the business combination if, at the time the bid was made, the tax consequences arising from the business combination

        (I) were reasonably foreseeable to the offeror, and

        (II) were reasonably expected to be different from the tax consequences of tendering to the bid, and

    (C) disclosed that the tax consequences of the bid and the business combination may be different if, at the time the bid was made, the offeror could not reasonably foresee the tax consequences arising from the business combination,

(e) **Non-redeemable Investment Fund** — the issuer is a non-redeemable investment fund that

(i) at least once each quarter calculates and publicly disseminates the net asset value of its securities, and

(ii) at the time of publicly announcing the business combination, publicly disseminates the net asset value of its securities as of the business day before the announcement,

(f) **Amalgamation or Equivalent Transaction with No Adverse Effect on Issuer or Minority** — the transaction is a statutory amalgamation, or substantially equivalent transaction, resulting in the combination of the issuer or a wholly-owned subsidiary entity of the issuer with an interested party, that is undertaken in whole or in part for the benefit of another related party, if all of the following conditions are satisfied:

(i) the transaction does not and will not have any adverse tax or other consequences to the issuer, the person resulting from the combination, or beneficial owners of affected securities generally,

(ii) no material actual or contingent liability of the interested party with which the issuer or a wholly-owned subsidiary entity of the issuer is combining will be assumed by the issuer, the wholly-owned subsidiary entity of the issuer or the person resulting from the combination,

(iii) the related party benefiting from the transaction agrees to indemnify the issuer against any liabilities of the interested party with which the issuer, or a wholly-owned subsidiary entity of the issuer, is combining,

(iv) after the transaction, the nature and extent of the voting and financial participating interests of holders of affected securities in the person resulting from the combination will be the same as, and the value of their financial participating interests will not be less than, that of their interests in the issuer before the transaction,

(v) the related party benefiting from the transaction pays for all of the costs and expenses resulting from the transaction.

(2) For the purposes of subparagraph (b)(ii) of subsection (1), the number of outstanding securities of the class of affected securities

(a) is calculated at the time of the agreement referred to in clause (b)(i)(A) or (B) of subsection (1), if the person proposing to carry out the business combination with the issuer knows the number of securities of the class outstanding at that time; or

(b) if paragraph (a) does not apply, is determined based on the information most recently provided by the issuer in a material change report, or section 5.4 of NI 51-102 *Continuous Disclosure Obligations*, immediately preceding the date of the agreement referred to in clause (b)(i)(A) or (B) of subsection (1).

(3) For the purposes of subparagraph (b)(iii) of subsection (1), the number of outstanding securities of the class of affected securities

(a) is calculated at the time of the last of the agreements referred to in subparagraph (b)(i) of subsection (1), if the person proposing to carry out the business combination with the issuer knows the number of securities of the class outstanding at that time; or

(b) if paragraph (a) does not apply, is determined based on the information most recently provided by the issuer in a material change report, or section 5.4 of National Instrument 51-102 Continuous Disclosure Obligations, immediately preceding the date of the last of the agreements referred to in subparagraph (b)(i) of subsection (1).

4.5 Minority Approval — An issuer shall not carry out a business combination unless the issuer has obtained minority approval for the business combination under Part 8.

4.6 Exemptions from Minority Approval Requirement — (1) Section 4.5 does not apply to an issuer carrying out a business combination in any of the following circumstances if the exemption relied on, any formal valuation exemption relied on, and the facts supporting reliance on those exemptions are disclosed in the disclosure document for the business combination:

(a) **90 Per Cent Exemption** — subject to subsection (2), one or more persons that are interested parties within the meaning of subparagraph (c)(i) of the definition of interested party beneficially own, in the aggregate, 90 per cent or more of the outstanding securities of a class of affected securities at the time that the business combination is agreed to, and either

(i) an appraisal remedy is available to holders of the class of affected securities under the statute under which the issuer is organized or is governed as to corporate law matters, or

(ii) if an appraisal remedy referred to in subparagraph (i) is not available, holders of the class of affected securities are given an enforceable right that is substantially equivalent to the appraisal remedy provided for in section 190 of the CBCA and that is described in the disclosure document for the business combination;

(b) **Other Transactions Exempt from Formal Valuation** — the circumstances described in paragraph (f) of subsection 4.4(1).

(2) If there are two or more classes of affected securities, paragraph (a) of subsection (1) applies only to a class of which the applicable interested parties beneficially own, in the aggregate, 90 per cent or more of the outstanding securities.

4.7 Conditions for Relief from Business Corporations Act Requirements — In Ontario, an issuer that is governed by the *Business Corporations Act* ("OBCA") and proposes to carry out a "going private transaction", as defined in subsection 190(1) of the OBCA, is exempt from subsections (2), (3) and (4) of section 190 of the OBCA, and is not required to make an application for exemption from those subsections under subsection 190(6) of the OBCA, if

(a) the transaction is not a business combination,

(b) Part 4 does not apply to the transaction by reason of section 4.1, or

(c) the transaction is carried out in compliance with Part 4, and, for this purpose, compliance includes reliance on any applicable exemption from a requirement of Part 4, including a discretionary exemption granted under section 9.1.

PART 5 — RELATED PARTY TRANSACTIONS

5.1 Application — This Part does not apply to an issuer carrying out a related party transaction if

(a) the issuer is not a reporting issuer,

(b) the issuer is a mutual fund,

(c)   (i) at the time the transaction is agreed to, securities held by beneficial owners in the local jurisdiction constitute less than two per cent of the outstanding securities of each class of affected securities of the issuer, and

(ii) all documents concerning the transaction that are sent generally to other holders of affected securities of the issuer are concurrently sent to all holders of the securities in the local jurisdiction,

(d) the parties to the transaction consist solely of

(i) an issuer and one or more of its wholly-owned subsidiary entities, or

(ii) wholly-owned subsidiary entities of the same issuer,

(e) the transaction is a business combination for the issuer,

(f) the transaction would be a business combination for the issuer except that it comes within an exception in any of paragraphs (a) to (e) of the definition of business combination,

(g) the transaction is a downstream transaction for the issuer,

(h) the issuer is obligated to and carries out the transaction substantially under the terms

(i) that were agreed to, and generally disclosed, before December 15, 2000 in Québec and before May 1, 2000 in Ontario,

(ii) that were agreed to, and generally disclosed, before the issuer became a reporting issuer, or

(iii) of a previous transaction the terms of which were generally disclosed, including an issuance of a convertible security, if the previous transaction was carried out in compliance with this Instrument, including in reliance on any applicable exemption or exclusion, or was not subject to this Instrument,

(i) the transaction is a distribution

(i) of securities of the issuer and is a related party transaction for the issuer solely because the interested party is an underwriter of the distribution, and

(ii) carried out in compliance with, including in reliance on any applicable exemption from, National Instrument 33-105 *Underwriting Conflicts*;

(j) the issuer is subject to the requirements of Part IX of the *Loan and Trust Corporations Act* (Ontario), the *Act respecting Trust Companies and Savings Companies* (Quebec), Part XI of the *Bank Act* (Canada), Part XI of the *Insurance Companies Act* (Canada), or Part XI of the *Trust and Loan Companies Act* (Canada), or any successor to that legislation, and the issuer complies with those requirements, or

(k) the transaction is a rights offering, dividend distribution, or any other transaction in which the general body of holders in Canada of affected securities of the same class are treated identically on a per security basis, if

(i) the transaction has no interested party within the meaning of paragraph (d) of the definition of interested party, or

(ii) the transaction is a rights offering, there is an interested party only because a related party of the issuer provides a stand-by commitment for the rights offering, and the stand-by commitment complies with National Instrument 45-106 *Prospectus Exemptions*.

5.2 Material Change Report — (1) An issuer shall include in a material change report, if any, required to be filed under securities legislation for a related party transaction

(a) a description of the transaction and its material terms,

(b) the purpose and business reasons for the transaction,

(c) the anticipated effect of the transaction on the issuer's business and affairs,

(d) a description of

(i) the interest in the transaction of every interested party and of the related parties and associated entities of the interested parties, and

(ii) the anticipated effect of the transaction on the percentage of securities of the issuer, or of an affiliated entity of the issuer, beneficially owned or controlled by each person referred to in subparagraph (i) for which there would be a material change in that percentage,

(e) unless this information will be included in another disclosure document for the transaction, a discussion of the review and approval process adopted by the board of directors and the special committee, if any, of the issuer for the transaction, including a discussion of any materially contrary view or abstention by a director and any material disagreement between the board and the special committee,

(f) a summary, in accordance with section 6.5, of the formal valuation, if any, obtained for the transaction, unless the formal valuation is included in its entirety in the material change report or will be included in its entirety in another disclosure document for the transaction,

(g) disclosure, in accordance with section 6.8, of every prior valuation in respect of the issuer that relates to the subject matter of or is otherwise relevant to the transaction

(i) that has been made in the 24 months before the date of the material change report, and

(ii) the existence of which is known, after reasonable inquiry, to the issuer or to any director or senior officer of the issuer,

(h) the general nature and material terms of any agreement entered into by the issuer, or a related party of the issuer, with an interested party or a joint actor with an interested party, in connection with the transaction, and

(i) disclosure of the formal valuation and minority approval exemptions, if any, on which the issuer is relying under sections 5.5 and 5.7, respectively, and the facts supporting reliance on the exemptions.

(2) If the issuer files a material change report less than 21 days before the expected date of the closing of the transaction, the issuer shall explain in the news release required to be issued under National Instrument 51-102 *Continuous Disclosure Obligations* and in the material change report why the shorter period is reasonable or necessary in the circumstances.

(3) Despite paragraphs (1)(f) and 5.4(2)(a), if the issuer is required to include a summary of the formal valuation in the material change report and the formal valuation is not available at the time the issuer files the material change report, the issuer shall file a supplementary material change report containing the disclosure required by paragraph (1)(f) as soon as the formal valuation is available.

(4) The issuer shall send a copy of any material change report prepared by it in respect of the transaction to any security holder of the issuer upon request and without charge.

5.3 Meeting and Information Circular — (1) Without limiting the application of any other legal requirements that apply to meetings of security holders and information circulars, this section applies only to a related party transaction for which section 5.6 requires the issuer to obtain minority approval.

(2) An issuer proposing to carry out a related party transaction to which this section applies shall call a meeting of holders of affected securities and send an information circular to those holders.

(3) The issuer shall include in the information circular

(a) the disclosure required by Form 62-104F2 *Issuer Bid Circular* of National Instrument 62-104 *Take-Over Bids and Issuer Bids*, to the extent applicable and with necessary modifications,

(b) a description of the background to the transaction,

(c) disclosure, in accordance with section 6.8, of every prior valuation in respect of the issuer that relates to the subject matter of or is otherwise relevant to the transaction

(i) that has been made in the 24 months before the date of the information circular, and

(ii) the existence of which is known, after reasonable inquiry, to the issuer or to any director or senior officer of the issuer,

(d) disclosure of any bona fide prior offer that relates to the subject matter of or is otherwise relevant to the transaction, which offer was received by the issuer during the 24 months before the transaction was agreed to, and a description of the offer and the background to the offer,

(e) a discussion of the review and approval process adopted by the board of directors and the special committee, if any, of the issuer for the transaction, including a discussion of any materially contrary view or abstention by a director and any material disagreement between the board and the special committee,

(f) disclosure of the formal valuation exemption, if any, on which the issuer is relying under section 5.5 and the facts supporting that reliance,

(g) disclosure of the number of votes attached to the securities that, to the knowledge of the issuer after reasonable inquiry, will be excluded in determining whether minority approval for the related party transaction is obtained, and

(h) the identity of the holders of securities specified in paragraph (g) together with their individual holdings.

(4) If, after sending the information circular and before the meeting, a change occurs that, if disclosed, would reasonably be expected to affect the decision of a holder of affected securities to vote for or against the related party transaction or to retain or dispose of affected securities, the issuer shall promptly disseminate disclosure of the change

(a) in a manner that the issuer reasonably determines will inform beneficial owners of affected securities of the change, and

(b) sufficiently in advance of the meeting that the beneficial owners of affected securities will be able to assess the impact of the change.

(5) If subsection (4) applies, the issuer shall file a copy of the disseminated information contemporaneously with its dissemination.

5.4 Formal Valuation — (1) An issuer shall obtain a formal valuation for a related party transaction described in any of paragraphs (a) to (g) of the definition of related party transaction.

(2) If a formal valuation is required under subsection (1), the issuer shall

    (a) include, in accordance with section 6.5, a summary of the formal valuation in the disclosure document for the related party transaction, unless the formal valuation is included in its entirety in the disclosure document,

    (b) state in the disclosure document who will pay or has paid for the valuation, and

    (c) comply with the other provisions of Part 6 applicable to it relating to formal valuations.

(3) The board of directors of the issuer or an independent committee of the board shall

    (a) determine who the valuator will be, and

    (b) supervise the preparation of the formal valuation.

5.5 Exemptions from Formal Valuation Requirement — Section 5.4 does not apply to an issuer carrying out a related party transaction in any of the following circumstances:

    (a) **Fair Market Value Not More Than 25% of Market Capitalization** — at the time the transaction is agreed to, neither the fair market value of the subject matter of, nor the fair market value of the consideration for, the transaction, insofar as it involves interested parties, exceeds 25 per cent of the issuer's market capitalization, and for this purpose

        (i) if either of the fair market values is not readily determinable, any determination as to whether that fair market value exceeds the threshold for this exemption shall be made by the issuer's board of directors acting in good faith,

        (ii) if the transaction is one in which the issuer or a wholly-owned subsidiary entity of the issuer combines with a related party, through an amalgamation, arrangement or otherwise, the subject matter of the transaction shall be deemed to be the securities of the related party held, at the time the transaction is agreed to, by persons other than the issuer or a wholly-owned subsidiary entity of the issuer, and the consideration for the transaction shall be deemed to be the consideration received by those persons,

        (iii) if the transaction is one of two or more connected transactions that are related party transactions and would, without the exemption in this paragraph (a), require formal valuations under this Instrument, the fair market values for all of those transactions shall be aggregated in determining whether the tests for this exemption are met, and

        (iv) if the assets involved in the transaction (the "initial transaction") include warrants, options or other instruments providing for the possible future purchase of securities or other assets (the "future transaction"), the calculation of the fair market value for the initial transaction shall include the fair market value, as of the time the initial transaction is agreed to, of the maximum number of securities or other consideration that the issuer may be required to issue or pay in the future transaction,

    (b) **Issuer Not Listed on Specified Markets** — no securities of the issuer are listed or quoted on the Toronto Stock Exchange, Aequitas NEO Exchange Inc., the New York Stock Exchange, the American Stock Exchange, the NASDAQ Stock Market, or a stock exchange outside of Canada and the United States other than the Alternative Investment Market of the London Stock Exchange or the PLUS markets operated by PLUS Markets Group plc,

    (c) **Distribution of Securities for Cash** — the transaction is a distribution of securities of the issuer to a related party for cash consideration, if

        (i) neither the issuer nor, to the knowledge of the issuer after reasonable inquiry, the related party has knowledge of any material information concerning the issuer or its securities that has not been generally disclosed, and the disclosure document for the transaction includes a statement to that effect, and

        (ii) the disclosure document for the transaction includes a description of the effect of the distribution on the direct or indirect voting interest of the related party,

    (d) **Certain Transactions in the Ordinary Course of Business** — the transaction is

        (i) a purchase or sale, in the ordinary course of business of the issuer, of inventory consisting of personal or movable property under an agreement that has been approved by the board of directors of the issuer and the existence of which has been generally disclosed, or

        (ii) a lease of real or immovable property or personal or movable property under an agreement on reasonable commercial terms that, considered as a whole, are not less advantageous to the issuer than if the lease was with a person dealing at arm's length with the issuer and the existence of which has been generally disclosed,

    (e) **Transaction Supported by Arm's Length Control Person** — the interested party beneficially owns, or exercises control or direction over, voting securities of the issuer that carry fewer voting rights than the voting securities beneficially owned, or over which control or direction is exercised, by another security holder of the issuer who is a control person of the issuer and who, in the circumstances of the transaction

        (i) is not also an interested party,

        (ii) is at arm's length to the interested party, and

        (iii) supports the transaction,

    (f) **Bankruptcy, Insolvency, Court Order** —

        (i) the transaction is subject to court approval, or a court orders that the transaction be effected, under

            (A) bankruptcy or insolvency law, or

            (B) section 191 of the CBCA, any successor to that section, or equivalent legislation of a jurisdiction,

        (ii) the court is advised of the requirements of this Instrument regarding formal valuations for related party transactions, and of the provisions of this paragraph (f), and

        (iii) the court does not require compliance with section 5.4,

    (g) **Financial Hardship** —

        (i) the issuer is insolvent or in serious financial difficulty,

        (ii) the transaction is designed to improve the financial position of the issuer,

        (iii) paragraph (f) is not applicable,

        (iv) the issuer has one or more independent directors in respect of the transaction, and

(v) the issuer's board of directors, acting in good faith, determines, and at least two-thirds of the issuer's independent directors, acting in good faith, determine that

(A) subparagraphs (i) and (ii) apply, and

(B) the terms of the transaction are reasonable in the circumstances of the issuer,

(h) Asset Resale —

(i) the subject matter of the related party transaction was acquired by the issuer or an interested party, as the case may be, in a prior arm's length transaction that was agreed to not more than 12 months before the date that the related party transaction is agreed to, and a qualified, independent valuator provides a written opinion that, after making such adjustments, if any, as the valuator considers appropriate in the exercise of the valuator's professional judgment

(A) the value of the consideration payable by the issuer for the subject matter of the related party transaction is not more than the value of the consideration paid by the interested party in the prior arm's length transaction, or

(B) the value of the consideration to be received by the issuer for the subject matter of the related party transaction is not less than the value of the consideration paid by the issuer in the prior arm's length transaction, and

(ii) the disclosure document for the related party transaction includes the same disclosure regarding the valuator as is required in the case of a formal valuation under section 6.2,

(i) Non-redeemable Investment Fund — the issuer is a non-redeemable investment fund that

(i) at least once each quarter calculates and publicly disseminates the net asset value of its securities, and

(ii) at the time of publicly announcing the related party transaction, publicly disseminates the net asset value of its securities as of the business day before the announcement,

(j) Amalgamation or Equivalent Transaction with No Adverse Effect on Issuer or Minority — the transaction is a statutory amalgamation, or substantially equivalent transaction, resulting in the combination of the issuer or a wholly-owned subsidiary entity of the issuer with an interested party, that is undertaken in whole or in part for the benefit of another related party, if all of the following conditions are satisfied:

(i) the transaction does not and will not have any adverse tax or other consequences to the issuer, the person resulting from the combination, or beneficial owners of affected securities generally,

(ii) no material actual or contingent liability of the interested party with which the issuer or a wholly-owned subsidiary entity of the issuer is combining will be assumed by the issuer, the wholly-owned subsidiary entity of the issuer or the person resulting from the combination,

(iii) the related party benefiting from the transaction agrees to indemnify the issuer against any liabilities of the interested party with which the issuer, or a wholly-owned subsidiary entity of the issuer, is combining,

(iv) after the transaction, the nature and extent of the voting and financial participating interests of holders of affected securities in the person resulting from the combination will be the same as, and the value of their financial participating interests will not be less than, that of their interests in the issuer before the transaction,

(v) the related party benefiting from the transaction pays for all of the costs and expenses resulting from the transaction.

5.6 Minority Approval — An issuer shall not carry out a related party transaction unless the issuer has obtained minority approval for the transaction under Part 8.

5.7 Exemptions from Minority Approval Requirement — (1) Subject to subsections (2), (3), (4) and (5), section 5.6 does not apply to an issuer carrying out a related party transaction in any of the following circumstances if the exemption relied on, any formal valuation exemption relied on, and the facts supporting reliance on those exemptions are disclosed in the disclosure document, if any, for the transaction:

(a) Fair Market Value Not More Than 25 Per Cent of Market Capitalization — the circumstances described in paragraph (a) of section 5.5,

(b) Fair Market Value Not More Than $2,500,000 — Distribution of Securities for Cash — the circumstances described in paragraph (c) of section 5.5, if

(i) no securities of the issuer are listed or quoted on the Toronto Stock Exchange, Aequitas NEO Exchange Inc., the New York Stock Exchange, the American Stock Exchange, the NASDAQ Stock Market, or a stock exchange outside of Canada and the United States other than the Alternative Investment Market of the London Stock Exchange or the PLUS markets operated by PLUS Markets Group plc,

(ii) at the time the transaction is agreed to, neither the fair market value of the securities to be distributed in the transaction nor the consideration to be received for those securities, insofar as the transaction involves interested parties, exceeds $2,500,000,

(iii) the issuer has one or more independent directors in respect of the transaction who are not employees of the issuer, and

(iv) at least two-thirds of the directors described in subparagraph (iii) approve the transaction,

(c) Other Transactions Exempt from Formal Valuation — the circumstances described in paragraphs (d), (e) and (j) of section 5.5,

(d) Bankruptcy, Insolvency, Court Order — the circumstances described in subparagraph (f)(i) of section 5.5, if the court is advised of the requirements of this Instrument regarding minority approval for related party transactions, and of the provisions of this paragraph, and the court does not require compliance with section 5.6,

(e) Financial Hardship — the circumstances described in paragraph (g) of section 5.5, if there is no other requirement, corporate or otherwise, to hold a meeting to obtain any approval of the holders of any class of affected securities,

(f) Loan to Issuer, No Equity or Voting Component —

(i) the transaction is a loan, or the creation of a credit facility, that is obtained by the issuer from a related party on reasonable commercial terms that are not less advantageous to the issuer than if the loan or credit facility were obtained from a person dealing at arm's length with the issuer, and the loan, or each advance under the credit facility, as the case may be, is not

(A) convertible, directly or indirectly, into equity or voting securities of the issuer or a subsidiary entity of the issuer, or otherwise participating in nature, or

(B) repayable as to principal or interest, directly or indirectly, in equity or voting securities of the issuer or a subsidiary entity of the issuer,

(ii) and for this purpose, any amendment to the terms of a loan or credit facility is deemed to create a new loan or credit facility,

(g) **90 Per Cent Exemption** — one or more persons that are interested parties within the meaning of subparagraph (d)(i) of the definition of interested party beneficially own, in the aggregate, 90 per cent or more of the outstanding securities of a class of affected securities at the time the transaction is agreed to, and either

(i) an appraisal remedy is available to holders of the class of affected securities under the statute under which the issuer is organized or is governed as to corporate law matters, or

(ii) if an appraisal remedy referred to in subparagraph (i) is not available, holders of the class of affected securities are given an enforceable right that is substantially equivalent to the appraisal remedy provided for in section 190 of the CBCA and that is described in an information circular or other document sent to holders of that class of affected securities in connection with a meeting to approve the related party transaction, or, if there is no such meeting, in another document that is sent to those security holders not later than the time by which an information circular or other document would have been required to be sent to them if there had been a meeting.

(2) Despite subparagraph (a)(iii) of section 5.5, if the transaction is one of two or more connected transactions that are related party transactions and would, without the exemptions in paragraphs (a) and (b) of subsection (1), require minority approval under this Instrument, the fair market values for all of those transactions shall be aggregated in determining whether the tests for those exemptions are met.

(3) If the transaction is a material amendment to the terms of a security, or of a loan or credit facility to which the exemption in paragraph (f) of subsection (1) does not apply, the fair market value tests for the exemptions in paragraphs (a) and (b) of subsection (1) shall be applied to the whole transaction as amended, insofar as it involves interested parties, rather than just to the amendment, and, for this purpose, any addition of, or amendment to, a term involving a right to convert into or otherwise acquire equity or voting securities is deemed to be a material amendment.

(4) Subparagraphs (a)(i), (iii) and (iv) of section 5.5 apply to paragraph (b) of subsection 5.7(1) with appropriate modifications.

(5) If there are two or more classes of affected securities, paragraph (g) of subsection (1) applies only to a class of which the applicable interested parties beneficially own, in the aggregate, 90 per cent or more of the outstanding securities.

PART 6 — FORMAL VALUATIONS AND PRIOR VALUATIONS

6.1 Independence and Qualifications of Valuator — (1) Every formal valuation required by this Instrument for a transaction shall be prepared by a valuator that is independent of all interested parties in the transaction and that has appropriate qualifications.

(2) It is a question of fact as to whether a valuator is independent of an interested party or has appropriate qualifications.

(3) A valuator is not independent of an interested party in connection with a transaction if

(a) the valuator is an associated or affiliated entity or issuer insider of the interested party,

(b) except in the circumstances described in paragraph (e), the valuator acts as an adviser to the interested party in respect of the transaction, but for this purpose, a valuator that is retained by an issuer to prepare a formal valuation for an issuer bid is not, for that reason alone, considered to be an adviser to the interested party in respect of the transaction,

(c) the compensation of the valuator depends in whole or in part on an agreement, arrangement or understanding that gives the valuator a financial incentive in respect of the conclusion reached in the formal valuation or the outcome of the transaction,

(d) the valuator is

(i) a manager or co-manager of a soliciting dealer group for the transaction, or

(ii) a member of a soliciting dealer group for the transaction, if the valuator, in its capacity as a soliciting dealer, performs services beyond the customary soliciting dealer's function or receives more than the per security or per security holder fees payable to other members of the group,

(e) the valuator is the external auditor of the issuer or of an interested party, unless the valuator will not be the external auditor of the issuer or of an interested party upon completion of the transaction and that fact is publicly disclosed at the time of or prior to the public disclosure of the results of the valuation, or

(f) the valuator has a material financial interest in the completion of the transaction,

and for the purposes of this subsection, references to the valuator include any affiliated entity of the valuator.

(4) A valuator that is paid by one or more interested parties in a transaction, or paid jointly by the issuer and one or more interested parties in a transaction, to prepare a formal valuation for the transaction is not, by virtue of that fact alone, not independent.

6.2 Disclosure Regarding Valuator — An issuer or offeror required to obtain a formal valuation for a transaction shall include in the disclosure document for the transaction

(a) a statement that the valuator has been determined to be qualified and independent,

(b) a description of any past, present or anticipated relationship between the valuator and the issuer or an interested party that may be relevant to a perception of lack of independence,

(c) a description of the compensation paid or to be paid to the valuator,

(d) a description of any other factors relevant to a perceived lack of independence of the valuator,

(e) the basis for determining that the valuator is qualified, and

(f) the basis for determining that the valuator is independent, despite any perceived lack of independence, having regard to the amount of the compensation and any factors referred to in paragraphs (b) and (d).

6.3 Subject Matter of Formal Valuation — (1) An issuer or offeror required to obtain a formal valuation shall provide the valuation in respect of

(a) the offeree securities, in the case of an insider bid or issuer bid,

(b) the affected securities, in the case of a business combination,

(c) any non-cash consideration being offered to, or to be received by, the holders of securities referred to in paragraph (a) or (b), and

(d) the non-cash assets involved in a related party transaction.

(2) A formal valuation of non-cash consideration or assets referred to in paragraph (1)(c) or (d) is not required if

(a) the non-cash consideration or assets are securities of a reporting issuer or are securities of a class for which there is a published market,

(b) the person that would otherwise be required to obtain the formal valuation of those securities states in the disclosure document for the transaction that the person has no knowledge of any material information concerning the issuer of the securities, or concerning the securities, that has not been generally disclosed,

(c) in the case of an insider bid, issuer bid or business combination

(i) a liquid market in the class of securities exists,

(ii) the securities constitute 25 per cent or less of the number of securities of the class that are outstanding immediately before the transaction,

(iii) the securities are freely tradeable at the time the transaction is completed, and

(iv) the valuator is of the opinion that a valuation of the securities is not required, and

(d) in the case of a related party transaction for the issuer of the securities, the conditions in subparagraphs (c)(i) and (ii) of section 5.5 are satisfied, regardless of the form of the consideration for the securities.

6.4 Preparation of Formal Valuation — (1) A formal valuation shall contain the valuator's opinion as to a value or range of values representing the fair market value of the subject matter of the valuation.

(2) A person preparing a formal valuation under this Instrument shall

(a) prepare the formal valuation in a diligent and professional manner,

(b) prepare the formal valuation as of an effective date that is not more than 120 days before the earlier of

(i) the date that the disclosure document for the transaction is first sent to security holders, if applicable, and

(ii) the date that the disclosure document is filed,

(c) make appropriate adjustments in the formal valuation for material intervening events of which it is aware between the effective date of the valuation and the earlier of the dates referred to in subparagraphs (i) and (ii) of paragraph (b),

(d) in determining the fair market value of offeree securities or affected securities, not include in the formal valuation a downward adjustment to reflect the liquidity of the securities, the effect of the transaction on the securities or the fact that the securities do not form part of a controlling interest, and

(e) provide sufficient disclosure in the formal valuation to allow the readers to understand the principal judgments and principal underlying reasoning of the valuator so as to form a reasoned judgment of the valuation opinion or conclusion.

6.5 Summary of Formal Valuation — (1) An issuer or offeror required to provide a summary of a formal valuation shall ensure that the summary provides sufficient detail to allow the readers to understand the principal judgments and principal underlying reasoning of the valuator so as to form a reasoned judgment of the valuation opinion or conclusion.

(2) In addition to the disclosure referred to in subsection (1), if an issuer or offeror is required to provide a summary of a formal valuation, the issuer or offeror shall ensure that the summary

(a) discloses

(i) the effective date of the valuation, and

(ii) any distinctive material benefit that might accrue to an interested party as a consequence of the transaction, including the earlier use of available tax losses, lower income taxes, reduced costs or increased revenues,

(b) if the formal valuation differs materially from a prior valuation, explains the differences between the two valuations or, if it is not practicable to do so, the reasons why it is not practicable to do so,

(c) indicates an address where a copy of the formal valuation is available for inspection, and

(d) states that a copy of the formal valuation will be sent to any security holder upon request and without charge or, if the issuer or offeror providing the summary so chooses, for a nominal charge sufficient to cover printing and postage.

6.6 Filing of Formal Valuation — (1) An issuer or offeror required to obtain a formal valuation in respect of a transaction shall file a copy of the formal valuation

(a) concurrently with the sending of the disclosure document for the transaction to security holders, or

(b) concurrently with the filing of a material change report for a related party transaction for which no disclosure document is sent to security holders, or if the formal valuation is not available at the time of filing the material change report, as soon as the formal valuation is available.

(2) If the formal valuation is included in its entirety in the disclosure document, an issuer or offeror satisfies the requirement in subsection (1) by filing the disclosure document.

6.7 Valuator's Consent — An issuer or offeror required to obtain a formal valuation shall

(a) obtain the valuator's consent to the filing of the formal valuation and to the inclusion of the formal valuation or its summary in the disclosure document for the transaction for which the formal valuation was obtained, and

(b) include in the disclosure document a statement, signed by the valuator, substantially as follows:

We refer to the formal valuation dated •, which we prepared for (indicate name of the person) for (briefly describe the transaction for which the formal valuation was prepared). We consent to the filing of the formal valuation with the securities regulatory authority and the inclusion of [a summary of the formal valuation/the formal valuation] in this document.

6.8 Disclosure of Prior Valuation — (1) A person required to disclose a prior valuation shall, in the document in which the prior valuation is required to be disclosed

(a) disclose sufficient detail to allow the readers to understand the prior valuation and its relevance to the present transaction,

(b) indicate an address where a copy of the prior valuation is available for inspection, and

(c) state that a copy of the prior valuation will be sent to any security holder upon request and without charge or, if the issuer or offeror providing the summary so chooses, for a nominal charge sufficient to cover printing and postage.

(2) If there are no prior valuations, the existence of which is known after reasonable inquiry, the person that would be required to disclose prior valuations, if any existed, shall include a statement to that effect in the document.

(3) Despite anything to the contrary in this Instrument, disclosure of the contents of a prior valuation is not required in a document if

    (a) the contents are not known to the person required to disclose the prior valuation,

    (b) the prior valuation is not reasonably obtainable by the person required to disclose it, irrespective of any obligations of confidentiality, and

    (c) the document contains statements regarding the prior valuation substantially to the effect of paragraphs (a) and (b).

6.9 Filing of Prior Valuation — A person required to disclose a prior valuation shall file a copy of the prior valuation concurrently with the filing of the first document in which that disclosure is required.

6.10 Consent of Prior Valuator Not Required — Despite sections 2.15 and 2.21 of National Instrument 62-104 *Take-Over Bids and Issuer*, a person required to disclose a prior valuation under this Instrument is not required to obtain or file the valuator's consent to the filing or disclosure of the prior valuation.

PART 7 — INDEPENDENT DIRECTORS

7.1 Independent Directors — (1) For the purposes of this Instrument, it is a question of fact as to whether a director of an issuer is independent.

(2) A director of an issuer is not independent in connection with a transaction if the director

    (a) is an interested party in the transaction,

    (b) is currently, or has been at any time during the 12 months before the date the transaction is agreed to, an employee, associated entity or issuer insider of an interested party, or of an affiliated entity of an interested party, other than solely in his or her capacity as a director of the issuer,

    (c) is currently, or has been at any time during the 12 months before the date the transaction is agreed to, an adviser to an interested party in connection with the transaction, or an employee, associated entity or issuer insider of an adviser to an interested party in connection with the transaction, or of an affiliated entity of such an adviser, other than solely in his or her capacity as a director of the issuer,

    (d) has a material financial interest in an interested party or an affiliated entity of an interested party, or

    (e) would reasonably be expected to receive a benefit as a consequence of the transaction that is not also available on a pro rata basis to the general body of holders in Canada of offeree securities or affected securities, including, without limitation, the opportunity to obtain a financial interest in an interested party, an affiliated entity of an interested party, the issuer or a successor to the business of the issuer.

(3) A member of an independent committee for a transaction to which this Instrument applies shall not receive any payment or other benefit from an issuer, an interested party or a successor to any of them that is contingent upon the completion of the transaction.

(4) For the purposes of this section, in the case of an issuer bid, a director of the issuer is not, by that fact alone, not independent of the issuer.

PART 8 — MINORITY APPROVAL

8.1 General — (1) If minority approval is required for a business combination or related party transaction, it shall be obtained from the holders of every class of affected securities of the issuer, in each case voting separately as a class.

(2) In determining minority approval for a business combination or related party transaction, an issuer shall exclude the votes attached to affected securities that, to the knowledge of the issuer or any interested party or their respective directors or senior officers, after reasonable inquiry, are beneficially owned or over which control or direction is exercised by

    (a) the issuer,

    (b) an interested party,

    (c) a related party of an interested party, unless the related party meets that description solely in its capacity as a director or senior officer of one or more persons that are neither interested parties nor issuer insiders of the issuer, or

    (d) a joint actor with a person referred to in paragraph (b) or (c) in respect of the transaction.

8.2 Second Step Business Combination — Despite subsection 8.1(2), the votes attached to securities acquired under a bid may be included as votes in favour of a subsequent business combination in determining whether minority approval has been obtained if

    (a) the security holder that tendered the securities to the bid was not a joint actor with the offeror in respect of the bid,

    (b) the security holder that tendered the securities to the bid was not

        (i) a direct or indirect party to any connected transaction to the bid, or

        (ii) entitled to receive, directly or indirectly, in connection with the bid

            (A) consideration per offeree security that was not identical in amount and form to the entitlement of the general body of holders in Canada of securities of the same class,

            (B) a collateral benefit, or

            (C) consideration for securities of a class of equity securities of the issuer if the issuer had more than one outstanding class of equity securities, unless that consideration was not greater than the entitlement of the general body of holders in Canada of every other class of equity securities of the issuer in relation to the voting and financial participating interests in the issuer represented by the respective securities,

    (c) the business combination is being effected by the offeror that made the bid, or an affiliated entity of that offeror, and is in respect of the securities of the same class for which the bid was made and that were not acquired in the bid,

    (d) the business combination is completed no later than 120 days after the date of expiry of the bid,

    (e) the consideration per security that the holders of affected securities would be entitled to receive in the business combination is at least equal in value to and is in the same form as the consideration that the tendering security holders were entitled to receive in the bid, and

(f) the disclosure document for the bid

(i) disclosed that if the offeror acquired securities under the bid, the offeror intended to acquire the remainder of the securities under a statutory right of acquisition or under a business combination that would satisfy the conditions in paragraphs (d) and (e),

(ii) contained a summary of a formal valuation of the securities in accordance with the applicable provisions of Part 6, or contained the valuation in its entirety, if the offeror in the bid was subject to and not exempt from the requirement to obtain a formal valuation,

(iii) stated that the business combination would be subject to minority approval,

(iv) disclosed the number of votes attached to the securities that, to the knowledge of the issuer after reasonable inquiry, would be required to be excluded in determining whether minority approval for the business combination had been obtained,

(v) identified the holders of securities specified in subparagraph (iv) and set out their individual holdings,

(vi) identified each class of securities the holders of which would be entitled to vote separately as a class on the business combination,

(vii) described the expected tax consequences of both the bid and the business combination if, at the time the bid was made, the tax consequences arising from the business combination

(A) were reasonably foreseeable to the offeror, and

(B) were reasonably expected to be different from the tax consequences of tendering to the bid, and

(viii) disclosed that the tax consequences of the bid and the business combination may be different if, at the time the bid was made, the offeror could not reasonably foresee the tax consequences arising from the business combination.

PART 9 — EXEMPTION

9.1 Exemption — (1) In Québec, the securities regulatory authority may grant an exemption to this Instrument, in whole or in part, subject to those conditions or restrictions as may be imposed in the exemption. This exemption is granted under section 263 of the *Securities Act* (R.S.Q., C. V-1).

(2) In Ontario, the regulator may grant an exemption to this Instrument, in whole or in part, subject to those conditions or restrictions as may be imposed in the exemption.

PART 10 — EFFECTIVE DATE

10.1 Effective Date — This Instrument comes into force February 1, 2008.

Final Rule: (2008) 31 O.S.C.B. 1321; Approval by OSC: (2007) 30 O.S.C.B. (Supp. 6) 45; Request for Comments: (2006) 29 O.S.C.B. 6801.

Amendments to Rule: (2016) 39 O.S.C.B. 4281

Rules: Rule 61-801, 71-802.

Companion Policy 61-101CP — To Multilateral Instrument 61-101 Protection of Minority Security Holders in Special Transactions

PART 6 ROLE OF DIRECTORS

    6.1 Role of Directors

PART 1 — GENERAL

1.1 General — The Autorité des marchés financiers and the Ontario Securities Commission (or "we") regard it as essential, in connection with the disclosure, valuation, review and approval processes followed for insider bids, issuer bids, business combinations and related party transactions, that all security holders be treated in a manner that is fair and that is perceived to be fair. We are of the view that issuers and others who benefit from access to the capital markets assume an obligation to treat security holders fairly, and that the fulfillment of this obligation is essential to the protection of the public interest in maintaining capital markets that operate efficiently, fairly and with integrity.

We do not consider that the types of transactions covered by this Instrument are inherently unfair. We recognize, however, that these transactions are capable of being abusive or unfair, and have made the Instrument to address this.

This Policy expresses our views on certain matters related to the Instrument.

PART 2 — INTERPRETATION

2.1 Equal Treatment of Security Holders — (1) *Security Holder Choice* — The definitions of business combination, collateral benefit and interested party, as well as other provisions in the Instrument, include the concept of identical treatment of security holders in a transaction. For the purposes of the Instrument, if security holders have an identical opportunity under a transaction, then they are considered to be treated identically. For example, if under the terms of a business combination, each security holder has the choice of receiving, for each affected security, either $10 in cash or one common share of ABC Co., we regard the security holders as having identical entitlements in amount and form, and as receiving identical treatment, even though they may not all make the same choice. This interpretation also applies where the Instrument refers to consideration that is "at least equal in value" and "in the same form", such as in the provisions on second step business combinations.

(2) *Multiple Classes of Equity Securities* — The definitions of business combination and interested party, and the provisions on second step business combinations in section 8.2 of the Instrument, refer to circumstances where an issuer carrying out a business combination or related party transaction has more than one class of equity securities. The Instrument's treatment of these transactions depends on whether the entitlements of the holders of one class under the transaction are greater than those of the holders of the other classes in relation to the voting and financial participating interests in the issuer represented by the respective securities.

For example: An issuer has outstanding subordinate voting shares carrying one vote per share, and multiple voting shares carrying ten votes per share, with the shares of the two classes otherwise carrying identical rights. Under the terms of a business combination, holders of the subordinate voting shares will receive $10 per share. For the multiple voting shareholders to be regarded as not being entitled to greater consideration than the subordinate voting shareholders under the Instrument, the multiple voting shareholders must receive no more than $10 per share. As a second example: An issuer has the same share structure as the issuer in the first example. Under the terms of a business combination, subordinate voting shareholders will receive, for each subordinate voting Share, $10 and one subordinate voting share of a successor issuer, carrying one vote per share. For the multiple voting shareholders to be regarded as not being entitled to greater consideration than the subordinate voting shareholders under the Instrument, the multiple voting shareholders must receive, for each multiple voting share, no more than $10 and one multiple voting share of the successor issuer, carrying no more than ten votes per share and otherwise carrying no greater rights than those of the subordinate voting shares of the successor issuer.

(3) *Related Party Holding Securities of Other Party to Transaction* — The Instrument sets out specific criteria for determining related party and interested party status. Without limiting the application of those criteria, a related party of an issuer is not considered to be treated differently from other security holders of the issuer in a transaction, or to receive a collateral benefit, solely by reason of being a security holder of another party to the transaction. For example, if ABC Co. proposes to amalgamate with XYZ Co., the fact that a director of ABC Co., who is not a control person of ABC Co., owns common shares of XYZ Co. (but less than 50 per cent) will not, in and of itself, cause the amalgamation to be considered a business combination for ABC Co. under the Instrument.

(4) *Consolidation of Securities* — One of the methods that may be used to effect a business combination is a consolidation of an issuer's securities at a ratio that eliminates the entire holdings of most holders of affected securities, through the elimination of post-consolidated fractional interests. Where this or a similar method is used, the security holders whose entire holdings are not eliminated are not considered to be treated identically to the general body of security holders under the Instrument.

(5) *Principle of Equal Treatment in Business Combinations* — The Instrument contemplates that a related party of an issuer might not be treated identically to all other security holders in the context of a business combination in which a person other than that related party acquires the issuer. There are provisions in the Instrument, including the minority approval requirement, that are intended to address this circumstance. Despite these provisions, we are of the view that, as a general principle, security holders should be treated equally in the context of a business combination, and that differential treatment is only justified if its benefits to the general body of security holders outweigh the principle of equal treatment. While we will generally rely on an issuer's review and approval process, in combination with the provisions of the Instrument, to achieve fairness for security holders, we may intervene if it appears that differential treatment is not reasonably justified. Giving a security holder preferential treatment in order to obtain that holder's support of the transaction will not normally be considered justifiable.

2.2 Equity Participation by a Related Party — If a related party of an issuer is provided with the opportunity to maintain or acquire an equity interest in the issuer, or in a successor to the business of the issuer, upon completion of a bid or business combination, the following provisions of the Instrument may be relevant.

If the equity interest will be derived solely through securities-based compensation for services as an employee, director or consultant, the provisions of the Instrument regarding collateral benefits may be applicable. In other cases, the acquisition of the equity interest or opportunity to maintain an equity interest may be a connected transaction. In either of these instances, votes attaching to the securities owned by the related party may be excluded from the minority vote required for a business combination, including a second step business combination following a bid. We are of the view that the employee compensation exemptions to the collateral benefit and connected transaction definitions do not generally apply to an issuance of securities in the issuer or a successor issuer upon completion of the transaction.

Without limiting the application of the definition of joint actor, we may consider a related party to be a joint actor with the offeror in a bid, or with the acquirer in a business combination, if the related party becomes a control person of the issuer or a successor issuer upon completion of the transaction or if the related party, whether alone or with joint actors, beneficially owns securities with more than 20 per cent of the voting rights. We may also consider a related party's continuing equity interest in the issuer or a successor issuer upon completion of the transaction in making an assessment of joint actor status generally. A joint actor characterization could cause a bid to be regarded as an insider bid, or an otherwise arm's length transaction to be a regarded as a business combination, that requires preparation of a formal valuation.

2.3 Direct or Indirect Parties to a Transaction — (1) The Instrument makes references to direct and indirect parties to a transaction in the definition of connected transactions and in subparagraph 8.2(b)(i) regarding minority approval for a second step business combination. For the purposes of the Instrument, a person is considered to be an indirect party if, for example, a direct party to the transaction is a subsidiary entity, nominee or agent of the person. A person is not an indirect party merely because it negotiates or approves the transaction on behalf of a party, holds securities of a party or agrees to support the transaction in the capacity of a security holder of a party.

(2) For the purposes of the Instrument, we do not consider a person to be a direct or indirect party to a business combination solely because the person receives pro rata consideration in its capacity as a security holder of the issuer carrying out the business combination.

2.4 Amalgamations — Under the Instrument, an amalgamation may be a business combination, related party transaction or neither, depending on the circumstances. For example, an amalgamation is a business combination for an issuer if, as a consequence of the amalgamation, holders of equity securities of the issuer become security holders of the amalgamated entity, unless an exception in one of the lettered paragraphs in the definition of business combination applies. An amalgamation is a related party transaction for an issuer rather than a business combination if, for example, a wholly-owned subsidiary entity of the issuer amalgamates with a related party of the issuer, leaving the equity securities of the issuer unaffected.

2.5 Transactions Involving More than One Reporting Issuer — The characterization of a transaction or the availability of a valuation or minority approval exemption under the Instrument must be considered individually for each reporting issuer involved in the transaction. For example, an amalgamation may be a downstream transaction for one party and a business combination for the other, in which case the latter party is the only party to whom the requirements of the Instrument may apply.

2.6 Previous Arm's Length Negotiations Exemption — (1) For the purposes of the formal valuation exemptions based on previous arm's length negotiations in paragraph (b) of subsection 2.4(1) and paragraph (b) of subsection 4.4(1) of the Instrument for insider bids and business combinations, respectively, the arm's length relationship must be between the selling security holder and all persons or companies that negotiated with the selling security holder.

(2) We note that the previous arm's length negotiations exemption is based on the view that those negotiations can be a substitute for a valuation. An important requirement for the exemption to be available is that the offeror or proponent of the business combination, as the case may be, engages in "reasonable inquiries" to determine whether various circumstances exist. In our view, if this requirement cannot be satisfied through receipt of representations of the parties directly involved or some other suitable method, the offeror or proponent of the transaction is not entitled to rely on this exemption.

2.7 Connected Transactions — (1) "Connected transactions" is a defined term in the Instrument, and reference is made to connected transactions in a number of parts of the Instrument. For example, subparagraph (a)(iii) of section 5.5 of the Instrument requires connected transactions to be aggregated, in certain circumstances, for the purpose of determining the availability of the formal valuation exemption for a related party transaction that is not larger than 25 per cent of the issuer's market capitalization. In other circumstances, it is possible for an issuer to rely on an exemption for each of two or more connected transactions. However, we may intervene if we believe that a transaction is being carried out in stages or otherwise divided up for the purpose of avoiding the application of a provision of the Instrument.

(2) One method of acquiring all the securities of an issuer is through a plan of arrangement or similar process comprised of a series of two or more interrelated steps. The series of steps is the "transaction" for the purposes of the definition of business combination. However, a related party transaction that is carried out in conjunction with a business combination, and that is not simply one of the procedural steps in implementing the acquisition of the affected securities in the business combination, is subject to the Instrument's requirements for related party transactions. This applies where, for example, a related party buys some of the issuer's assets that the acquirer in the business combination does not want.

(3) An agreement, commitment or understanding that a security holder will tender to a bid or vote in favour of a transaction is not, in and of itself, a connected transaction to the bid or to the transaction for purposes of the Instrument.

2.8 Time of Agreement — A number of provisions in the Instrument refer to the time a business combination or related party transaction is agreed to. This should be interpreted as the time the issuer first makes a legally binding commitment to proceed with the transaction, subject to any conditions such as security holder approval. Where the issuer does not technically negotiate the transaction with another party, such as in the case of a share consolidation, the time the transaction is agreed to should be interpreted as the time at which the issuer's board of directors determines to proceed with the transaction, subject to any conditions.

2.9 "Acquire the Issuer" — In some definitions and elsewhere in the Instrument, reference is made to a transaction in which a related party would "directly or indirectly acquire the issuer . . . through an amalgamation, arrangement or otherwise, whether alone or with joint actors". This refers to the acquisition of all of the issuer, not merely the acquisition of a control position. For example, a related party "acquires" an issuer when it acquires all of the securities of the issuer that it does not already own, even if that related party held a control position in the issuer prior to the transaction.

PART 3 — MINORITY APPROVAL

3.1 Meeting Requirement — The definition of minority approval and subsections 4.2(2) and 5.3(2) of the Instrument provide that minority approval, if required, must be obtained at a meeting of holders of affected securities. The issuer may be able to demonstrate that holders of a majority of the securities that would be eligible to be voted at a meeting would vote in favour of the transaction under consideration. In this circumstance, the regulator or the securities regulatory authority will consider granting an exemption under section 9.1 of the Instrument from the requirement to hold a meeting, conditional on security holders being provided with disclosure similar to that which would be available to them if a meeting were held.

3.2 Second Step Business Combination Following an Unsolicited Take-over Bid — Section 8.2 of the Instrument allows the votes attached to securities acquired under a bid to be included as votes in favour of a subsequent business combination in determining whether minority approval has been obtained if certain conditions are met. One of the conditions is that the security holder that tendered the securities in the bid not receive an advantage in connection with the bid, such as a collateral benefit, that was not available to other security holders. There may be circumstances where this condition could cause difficulty for an offeror who wishes to acquire all of an issuer through a business combination following a bid that was unsolicited by the issuer. For example, in order to establish that a benefit received by a tendering security holder is not a collateral benefit under the Instrument, the offeror may need the cooperation of an independent committee of the offeree issuer during the bid. This cooperation may not be forthcoming if the bid is unfriendly. In this type of circumstance, the fact that the bid was unsolicited would normally be a factor the regulator or the securities regulatory authority would take into account in considering whether exemptive relief should be granted to allow the securities to be voted.

Part 6: TAKE-OVER BIDS

3.3 Special Circumstances — As the purpose of the Instrument is to ensure fair treatment of minority security holders, abusive minority tactics in a situation involving a minimal minority position may cause the regulator or the securities regulatory authority to grant an exemption from the requirement to obtain minority approval. Where an issuer has more than one class of equity securities, exemptive relief may also be appropriate if the Instrument's requirement of separate minority approval for each class could result in unfairness to security holders who are not interested parties, or if the policy objectives of the Instrument would be accomplished by the exclusion of an interested party's votes in one or more, but not all, of the separate class votes.

PART 4 — DISCLOSURE

4.1 Insider Bids — Disclosure — For an insider bid, in addition to the disclosure required by Form 62-104F1 *Take-Over Bid Circular* of National Instrument 62-104 *Take-Over Bids and Issuer Bids*, subsection 2.2(1)(d) of the Instrument requires the disclosure required by Form 62-104F2 *Issuer Bid Circular* of National Instrument 62-104 *Take-Over Bids and Issuer Bids*, appropriately modified. In our view, Form 62-104F2 disclosure would generally include disclosure for the following items, with necessary modifications, in the context of an insider bid:

1. Item 9 — Purpose of the bid
2. Item 13 — Acceptance of issuer bid
3. Item 14 — Benefits from the bid
4. Item 16 — Other benefits
5. Item 17 — Arrangements between issuer and security holders
6. Item 18 — Previous purchases and sales
7. Item 20 — Valuation
8. Item 23 — Previous distribution
9. Item 24 — Dividend policy
10. Item 25 — Tax consequences
11. Item 26 — Expenses of bid

4.2 Business Combinations and Related Party Transactions — Disclosure — Paragraphs 4.2(3)(a) and 5.3(3)(a) of the Instrument require in the information circulars for a business combination and a related party transaction, respectively, the disclosure required by Form 62-104F2 to the extent applicable and with necessary modifications. In our view, Form 62-104F2 disclosure would generally include disclosure for the following items, with necessary modifications, in the context of those transactions:

1. Item 4 — Consideration
2. Item 9 — Purpose of the bid
3. Item 10 — Trading in securities to be acquired
4. Item 11 — Ownership of securities of issuer
5. Item 12 — Commitments to acquire securities of issuer
6. Item 13 — Acceptance of issuer bid
7. Item 14 — Benefits from the bid
8. Item 15 — Material changes in the affairs of issuer
9. Item 16 — Other benefits
10. Item 17 — Arrangements between issuer and security holders
11. Item 18 — Previous purchases and sales
12. Item 19 — Financial statements
13. Item 20 — Valuation
14. Item 21 — Securities of issuer to be exchanged for others
15. Item 22 — Approval of issuer bid circular
16. Item 23 — Previous distribution
17. Item 24 — Dividend policy
18. Item 25 — Tax consequences
19. Item 26 — Expenses of bid
20. Item 29 — Other material information
21. Item 30 — Solicitations

PART 5 — FORMAL VALUATIONS

5.1 General — (1) The Instrument requires formal valuations in a number of circumstances. We are of the view that a conclusory statement of opinion as to the value or range of values of the subject matter of a valuation does not by itself fulfil this requirement.

(2) The disclosure standards for formal valuations in By-laws 29.14 to 29.23 of the Investment Dealers Association of Canada and Appendix A to Standard No. 110 of the Canadian Institute of Chartered Business Valuators each generally represent a reasonable approach to meeting the applicable legal requirements. Specific disclosure standards, however, cannot be construed as a substitute for the professional judgment and responsibility of the valuator and, on occasion, additional disclosure may be necessary.

(3) An issuer that is required to obtain a formal valuation, or the offeree issuer in the case of an insider bid, should work in cooperation with the valuator to ensure that the requirements of the Instrument are satisfied. At the valuator's request, the issuer should promptly furnish the valuator with access to the issuer's management and advisers, and to all material information in the issuer's possession relevant to the formal valuation. The valuator

is expected to use that access to perform a comprehensive review and analysis of information on which the formal valuation is based. The valuator should form its own independent views of the reasonableness of this information, including any forecasts, projections or other measurements of the expected future performance of the enterprise, and of any of the assumptions on which it is based, and adjust the information accordingly.

(4) The disclosure in the valuation of the scope of review should include a description of any limitation on the scope of the review and the implications of the limitation on the valuator's conclusion. Scope limitations should not be imposed by the issuer, an interested party or the valuator, but should be limited to those beyond their control that arise solely as a result of unusual circumstances. In addition, it is inappropriate for any interested party to exercise or attempt to exercise any influence over a valuator.

(5) Subsection 2.3(2) of the Instrument provides that in the context of an insider bid, an independent committee of the offeree issuer shall, and the offeror shall enable the independent committee to, determine who the valuator will be and supervise the preparation of the formal valuation. Although the subsection also requires the independent committee to use its best efforts to ensure that the valuation is completed and provided to the offeror in a timely manner, we are aware that an independent committee could attempt to use the subsection to delay or impede an insider bid viewed by the committee as unfriendly. In a situation where an offeror is of the view that an independent committee is not acting in a timely manner in having the formal valuation prepared, the offeror may seek relief under section 9.1 of the Instrument from the requirement that the offeror obtain a valuation.

(6) Similarly, in circumstances where an independent committee is of the view that a bid that has been announced will not actually be made or that the bid is not being made in good faith, the independent committee may apply for relief from the requirements of subsection 2.3(2) of the Instrument.

(7) Requirements in securities legislation relating to forward-looking information do not apply to a formal valuation for which financial forecasts and projections are relied on and disclosed.

5.2 **Independent Valuators** — While, except in certain prescribed situations, the Instrument provides that it is a question of fact as to whether a valuator (which for the purposes of this section includes a person providing a liquidity opinion) is independent, situations have been identified in the past that raise serious concerns for us. These situations, which are set out below, must be assessed for materiality by the board or committee responsible for choosing the valuator, and disclosed in the disclosure document for the transaction. In determining the independence of the valuator from an interested party, relevant factors may include whether

(a) the valuator or an affiliated entity of the valuator has a material financial interest in future business under an agreement, commitment or understanding involving the issuer, the interested party or an associated or affiliated entity of the issuer or interested party;

(b) during the 24 months before the valuator was first contacted for the purpose of the formal valuation or opinion, the valuator or an affiliated entity of the valuator

(i) had a material involvement in an evaluation, appraisal or review of the financial condition of the interested party, or an associated or affiliated entity of the interested party, other than the issuer,

(ii) had a material involvement in an evaluation, appraisal or review of the financial condition of the issuer, or an associated or affiliated entity of the issuer, if the evaluation, appraisal or review was carried out at the direction or request of the interested party or paid for by the interested party, other than the issuer in the case of an issuer bid,

(iii) acted as a lead or co-lead underwriter of a distribution of securities by the interested party, or acted as a lead or co-lead underwriter of a distribution of securities by the issuer if the retention of the underwriter was carried out at the direction or request of the interested party or paid for by the interested party, other than the issuer in the case of an issuer bid,

(iv) had a material financial interest in a transaction involving the interested party, other than the issuer in the case of an issuer bid, or

(v) had a material financial interest in a transaction involving the issuer other than by virtue of performing the services referred to in subparagraph (b)(ii) or (b)(iii), or

(c) the valuator or an affiliated entity of the valuator is

(i) a lead or co-lead lender or manager of a lending syndicate in respect of the transaction in question, or

(ii) a lender of a material amount of indebtedness in a situation where the interested party or the issuer is in financial difficulty, and the transaction would reasonably be expected to have the effect of materially enhancing the lender's position.

PART 6 — ROLE OF DIRECTORS

6.1 **Role of Directors** — (1) Paragraphs 2.2(2)(d), 3.2(d), 4.2(3)(e), 5.2(1)(e) and 5.3(3)(e) of the Instrument require that the disclosure for the applicable transaction include a discussion of the review and approval process adopted by the board of directors and the special committee, if any, of the issuer, including any materially contrary view or abstention by a director and any material disagreement between the board and the special committee.

(2) An issuer involved in any of the types of transactions regulated by the Instrument should provide sufficient information to security holders to enable them to make an informed decision. Accordingly, the directors should disclose their reasonable beliefs as to the desirability or fairness of the proposed transaction and make useful recommendations regarding the transaction. A statement that the directors are unable to make or are not making a recommendation regarding the transaction, without detailed reasons, generally would be viewed as insufficient disclosure.

(3) In reaching a conclusion as to the fairness of a transaction, the directors should disclose in reasonable detail the material factors on which their beliefs regarding the transaction are based. Their disclosure should discuss fully the background of deliberations by the directors and any special committee, and any analysis of expert opinions obtained.

(4) The factors that are important in determining the fairness of a transaction to security holders and the weight to be given to those factors in a particular context will vary with the circumstances. Normally, the factors considered should include whether the transaction is subject to minority approval, whether the transaction has been reviewed and approved by a special committee and, if there has been a formal valuation, whether the consideration offered is fair in relation to the valuation conclusion arrived at through the application of the valuation methods considered relevant for the subject matter of the formal valuation. A statement that the directors have no reasonable belief as to the desirability or fairness of the transaction or that the transaction is fair in relation to values arrived at through the application of valuation methods considered relevant, without more, generally would be viewed as insufficient disclosure.

(5) The directors of an issuer involved in a transaction regulated by the Instrument are generally in the best position to assess the formal valuation to be provided to security holders. Accordingly, we are of the view that, in discharging their duty to security holders, the directors should consider the formal valuation and all prior valuations disclosed and discuss them fully in the applicable disclosure document.

(6) To safeguard against the potential for an unfair advantage for an interested party as a result of that party's conflict of interest or informational or other advantage in connection with the proposed transaction, it is good practice for negotiations for a transaction involving an interested party to be carried out by or reviewed and reported upon by a special committee of disinterested directors. Following this practice normally would assist in addressing our interest in maintaining capital markets that operate efficiently, fairly and with integrity. While the Instrument only mandates an independent committee in limited circumstances, we are of the view that it generally would be appropriate for issuers involved in a material transaction to which the Instrument applies to constitute an independent committee of the board of directors for the transaction. Where a formal valuation is involved, we also would encourage an independent committee to select the valuator, supervise the preparation of the valuation and review the disclosure regarding the valuation.

(7) A special committee should, in our view, include only directors who are independent from the interested party. While a special committee may invite non-independent board members and other persons possessing specialized knowledge to meet with, provide information to, and carry out instructions from, the committee, in our view non-independent persons should not be present at or participate in the decision-making deliberations of the special committee.

(8) We recognize that directors who serve on a special committee or independent committee must be adequately compensated for their time and effort. However, members of the committee should ensure that compensation for serving on the committee will not compromise their independence. Subsection 7.1(3) of the Instrument prohibits members of an independent committee reviewing a transaction from receiving any payment that is contingent on completion of the transaction. We are of the view that the compensation of committee members should ideally be set when the committee is created and be based on fixed sum payments or the work involved.

Adoption by OSC: (2008) 31 O.S.C.B. 1358 and (2007) 30 O.S.C.B. (Supp 6) 45; Request for Comments: (2006) 29 O.S.C.B. 6801.

Amendments to Policy: (2016), 39 O.S.C.B. 4283.

CSA Staff Notice 61-301 — Staff Guidance on the Practice of "Mini-Tenders"

Date: December 10, 1999
22 O.S.C.B. 7797

On September 28, 1999, the Canadian Securities Administrators (the "CSA") released an Investor Alert entitled "Mini-Tender Offers — Watch Out for Mini-Tender Offers Below Market Price". This Investor Alert announced that the staff of each of the CSA ("Staff") was examining the phenomenon of mini-tenders to assess the appropriate regulatory response to this practice. Staff has discussed this issue with various market participants, including the Investment Dealers Association, The Toronto Stock Exchange, The Canadian Depository for Securities Limited, custodians of securities, issuers who have been targeted by mini-tenders and a Canadian firm currently engaged in the practice of making mini-tenders. The following sets out Staff's current views on mini-tenders.

What is a Mini-Tender?

A mini-tender is a widely-disseminated offer to purchase shares of a public company at a price below the current market price. A mini-tender is different from a take-over bid in Canada because a mini-tender offeror usually offers to acquire only a small percentage of the outstanding shares of a public company and in any event significantly less than 20% of the outstanding shares of a public company.

Numerous mini-tenders have taken place in the United States and Staff is aware of at least fourteen mini-tenders that have been made for Canadian companies.

Generally, mini-tenders offer consideration that is anywhere from 3–35% below the current market price of the shares sought. This discount invites the question of why securityholders would tender their securities to a mini-tender when they could sell them in the market for a greater price.

Based upon the inquiries of Staff, the only circumstance in which investors might benefit from tendering their securities to a mini-tender is in the circumstances where an individual investor holds less than a "board lot" of securities, (a "board lot" means 100 shares having a market value of $1.00 per share or greater; 500 shares having a market value of less than $1.00 and not less than $0.10 per share; or 1,000 shares having a market value of less than $0.10 per share). Generally, no commissions are payable in connection with the tender of securities to a mini-tender. Therefore, proponents of mini-tenders point out that in some circumstances the holder of less than a board lot of securities could tender to a mini-tender to avoid minimum brokerage commissions that make the sale of his or her securities relatively costly.

Whether or not tendering to a mini-tender might be attractive in these very limited circumstances, Staff would like to stress that investors should carefully examine a mini-tender to determine whether it is in their interests to tender to it. Investors are urged to consult their financial advisers in this regard.

Communication of Mini-Tenders Not Required

Currently, mini-tender offerors use the information systems put in place by market intermediaries to communicate their mini-tenders to the securityholders of target issuers. In this regard, Staff wishes to express its view that there is currently no specific requirement under Canadian securities legislation or policies that notice of a mini-tender must be delivered to registered holders of the securities subject to the mini-tender. A mini-tender is not a "take-over bid" as defined in Canadian securities legislation. Therefore, intermediaries are not obliged under Part IX of National Policy 41 to advise their clients who are non-registered holders of securities, of the commencement of a mini-tender.

Furthermore, Staff wishes to express its view that registrants are not obliged under securities laws to pass on mini-tenders to their clients. If registrants choose or are otherwise obliged to pass on information concerning a mini-tender to their clients, they should ensure that all relevant information concerning the mini-tender and the market for the affected security is given to their clients, including the warning referred to in item 2 below.

Staff Concerns

Staff has serious concerns that an investor might tender to a mini-tender based upon a misunderstanding of the mini-tender or the current market price of the security subject to the mini-tender. Mini-tenders bear a close resemblance to formal take-over bids, which are historically equated with an offering price that includes a premium to the current price. In Staff's opinion, causing investors to tender to a mini-tender based upon such a misunderstanding can be abusive of the capital markets and contrary to applicable anti-fraud provisions of certain securities legislation.

As a result, Staff suggests that a minimum level of disclosure be provided by the mini-tender offeror to holders of the securities subject to a mini-tender. By including this minimum disclosure with the information contained in a mini-tender, the risk that a securityholder would be tendering to a mini-tender through inadvertence or misunderstanding should be reduced or eliminated.

Suggested Disclosure in Mini-Tenders

Staff's view is that in order to avoid confusion and misunderstanding, a mini-tender offeror should ensure that the information that accompanies any widely-disseminated offer to purchase securities at a price below that security's current market price should prominently include the following information:

1. the principal market or markets for the securities of the issuer of the target securities sought to be acquired pursuant to the offer, the date of the offer and the market price of the securities immediately before the earlier of the public announcement of the offer or the date of the offer, as the case may be;

2. a warning that the offering price is below the current market price of those securities;

3. a statement that any person considering tendering to the offer should consult his or her financial adviser;

4. a description of the withdrawal rights of the securityholders under the offer and details of the withdrawal procedure; if no such withdrawal rights exist, a clear statement should be included to that effect;

5. if applicable, a statement that the offeror could revoke its offer at any time; and

6. a clear calculation of the final price to be paid for the target securities.

Staff also suggests that mini-tender offerors provide a copy of their mini-tenders directly to the issuer of the securities subject to the mini-tender.

Depositories, participants and intermediaries who summarize and forward notice of mini-tenders (notwithstanding that there is currently no specific requirement to do so under Canadian securities legislation or policies, as discussed above) should ensure that their summaries prominently include the warning referred to in item 2 above. The summary should also state that any person considering tendering to the offer should first consult his or her financial adviser.

Staff will continue to monitor mini-tenders and in the event that a mini-tender is conducted in a manner or in circumstances which are prejudicial to the public interest, Staff will recommend to CSA members that appropriate action be taken which could include seeking a cease-trade order in respect of the mini-tender or the person or company making the mini-tender.

OSC Rule 61-501 — Insider Bids, Issuer Bids, Business Combination and Related Party Transactions

Date: May 1, 2000 amended effective March 1, 2002 and replaced effective June 29, 2004

23 O.S.C.B. 971; 25 O.S.C.B. 943; 27 O.S.C.B. 5975

[Revoked by Rule 61-801; replaced by MI 61-101.]

Final Rule: (2000) 23 O.S.C.B. 2719; Approval by OSC: (2000) 23 O.S.C.B. 965; Request for Comments: (1999) 22 O.S.C.B. 7835; (1999) 22 O.S.C.B. 493 and (1996) 19 O.S.C.B. 2981. Replaced OPS 9.1 and two rules. The rules were originally blanket rulings which were deemed to be rules under section 143.1(1) of the Act and remade into rules. They were *In the Matter of Going Private Transactions* (1993) 16 O.S.C.B. 3428 and *In the Matter of Insider Bids, Issuer Bids and Take-Over Bids in Anticipation of Going Private Transactions* (1993) 16 O.S.C.B. 3429, remade into rules (1997) 20 O.S.C.B. 1219, amended (1998) 21 O.S.C.B. 3361, (1999) 22 O.S.C.B. 148 and (2000) 23 O.S.C.B. 285. ON LPS 9.1 was former Policy 3-37; First published (1977) O.S.C.B. 253; amended (1977) O.S.C.B. 268; notices (1977) O.S.C.B. 273, (1978) O.S.C.B. 60; exemptions (1978) O.S.C.B. 114; amended (1978) O.S.C.B. 224; interpretation statement (1978) O.S.C.B. 323; draft amendment (1981) 1 O.S.C.B. 7E; addendum to draft (1981) 1 O.S.C.B. 24E; published as 9.1 (1982) 4 O.S.C.B. 538E; draft (1990) 13 O.S.C.B. 2021; replaced (1991) 14 O.S.C.B. 3345; amended (1992) 15 O.S.C.B. 2921.

Amendment to Rule: (2002) 25 O.S.C.B. 943; Approval by OSC: (2001) 24 O.S.C.B. 7308; Request for Comments: (2001) 24 O.S.C.B. 5179.

Amendment to Rule: (2004) 27 O.S.C.B. 5975; Approval by OSC: (2004) 27 O.S.C.B. 4483; Request for Comments: (2004) 27 O.S.C.B. 550 and (2003) 26 O.S.C.B. 1822.

Companion Policy 61-501CP — To Ontario Securities Commission Rule 61-501 Insider Bids, Issuer Bids, Going Private Transactions and Related Party Transactions

[Revoked: (2008) 31 O.S.C.B. 1230]

Adoption by OSC: (2000) 23 O.S.C.B. 2719 and (2000) 23 O.S.C.B. 965; Request for Comments: (1999) 22 O.S.C.B. 7835, (1999) 22 O.S.C.B. 493 and (1996) 19 O.S.C.B. 2981.

Adoption of replacement Policy: (2004) 27 O.S.C.B. 6011 and (2004) 27 O.S.C.B. 4483; Request for Comments (2004) 27 O.S.C.B. 550 and (2003) 26 O.S.C.B. 1822.

OSC Rule 61-801 — Implementing Multilateral Instrument 61-101 Protection of Minority Security Holders in Special Transactions

Date: **February 1, 2008**

31 O.S.C.B. 1365

1.1 Rule 61-501 — Rule 61-501 *Insider Bids, Issuer Bids, Business Combinations and Related Party Transactions* is revoked.

1.2 Rule 71-802 — Section 2.4 of Rule 71-802 *Implementing National Instrument 71-102 Continuous Disclosure and Other Exemptions Relating to Foreign Issuers* is amended by:

(i) replacing the title "Going Private Transactions and Related Party Transactions" with the title "Business Combinations and Related Party Transactions", and

(ii) replacing the words "Rule 61-501 *Insider Bids, Issuer Bids, Going Private Transactions and Related Party Transactions*" with "MI 61-101 *Protection of Minority Security Holders in Special Transactions*".

1.3 Effective Date — This rule comes into force on February 1, 2008.

Final Rule: (2008) 31 O.S.C.B. 1325; Approval by OSC: (2007) 30 O.S.C.B. (Supp 6) 45; Request for Comments: (2006) 29 O.S.C.B. 6801.

6.2 — Take-Over Bids

National Instrument 62-101 — Control Block Distribution Issues

[Repealed]

Final Rule: (2000) 23 O.S.C.B. 1368; Approval by OSC: (1999) 22 O.S.C.B. 8111; Request for Comments: (1998) 21 O.S.C.B. 5637 and (1995) 18 O.S.C.B. 4887.

Amendments to Rule: (2004) 27 O.S.C.B. 3602; Approval of OSC: (2003) 26 O.S.C.B. 8217; Request for Comments: (2003) 26 O.S.C.B. 991.

Repeal: (2005) 28 O.S.C.B. (Supp-4) 117; Approval by OSC: (2005) 28 O.S.C.B. (Supp-3) 83; Request for Comments: (2004) 27 O.S.C.B. 1.

National Instrument 62-102 — Disclosure of Outstanding Share Data

Date: **February 25, 2000, as amended effective March 30, 2004**

23 O.S.C.B. 1370 and 26 O.S.C.B. (Supp-3) 59 (December 19, 2003)

[Revoked]

National Instrument 62-103 — The Early Warning System and Related Take-Over Bid and Insider Reporting Issues

Date: **February 25, 2000, as amended effective March 30, 2004, September 14, 2005, December 31, 2007 (by Rule 62-504), April 30, 2010, May 6, 2011, September 22, 2014, May 5, 2015 and February 25, 2016**

23 O.S.C.B. 1372, 26 O.S.C.B. (Supp-3) 60 (December 19, 2003), 28 O.S.C.B. (Supp-4) 120 (September 9, 2005), 33 O.S.C.B. 3700, 34 O.S.C.B. 5171, 37 O.S.C.B. (Supp. 4), 38 O.S.C.B. (Supp. 1) 165 and 39 O.S.C.B. 1779

PART 1 — DEFINITIONS AND INTERPRETATION

1.1 **Definitions** — (1) In this Instrument

"acquiror" has the meaning ascribed to that term in Part 5 of NI 62-104;

"acquiror's securities" has the meaning ascribed to that term in Part 5 of NI 62-104;

"acquisition announcement provisions" means the requirement in securities legislation for an offeror to issue a news release if, during a formal bid for voting or equity securities of a reporting issuer by an entity other than the acquiror, the acquiror acquires ownership of, or control over, securities of the class subject to the bid that, together with the acquiror's securities of the class, constitute an amount equal to or greater than the amount specified in securities legislation;

"acting jointly or in concert" has the meaning ascribed to that phrase in securities legislation, and, when used in connection with an entity, has the meaning ascribed in securities legislation as if the term "entity" replaced the term "person or company" or similar term;

"applicable definitions" means

(a) the definitions of "take-over bid" and "offeror's securities" in the take-over provisions, and

(b) the control block distribution definition;

"applicable provisions" means

(a) the early warning requirements,

(b) Part 4,

(c) the moratorium provisions,

(d) the insider reporting requirement, and

(e) the acquisition announcement provisions;

"associate" has the meaning ascribed to that term in section 1.1 of NI 62-104;

"business unit" means a legal entity or part of a legal entity, or a combination of legal entities or parts of legal entities, that engage in a distinct business or investment activity separately from other businesses and investment activities of the relevant entities;

"class" means, in relation to a security, a class or series of a class of the security;

"control" means, for a security

(a) when used in connection with the insider reporting requirements, the take-over bid requirements and related definitions and the early warning requirements, the power to exercise control or direction over the security, or similar term or expression used in securities legislation; and

(b) when used in connection with the control block distribution definition, holding the security, or similar term or expression used in securities legislation;

"control block distribution definition" means the provisions of securities legislation listed in Appendix A;

"early warning requirements" means the requirements set out in section 5.2 of NI 62-104;

"economic exposure" has the meaning ascribed to that term in NI 55-104;

"effective control" means, for a reporting issuer, the control in fact of the reporting issuer by an entity through the ownership of, or control over, voting securities of the reporting issuer, other than securities held by way of security only;

"eligible institutional investor" means

(a) a financial institution,

(b) a pension fund that is regulated by either the Office of the Superintendent of Financial Institutions (Canada), a pension commission of a jurisdiction, or a similar regulatory authority,

(c) a mutual fund that is not a reporting issuer,

(d) an investment manager in relation to securities over which it exercises discretion to vote, acquire or dispose without the express consent of the beneficial owner, subject to applicable legal requirements, general investment policies, guidelines, objectives or restrictions, or

(e) an entity referred to in clauses (D) or (F) of Rule 13d- 1(b)(1)(ii) under the 1934 Act;

"entity" means a person or company or a business unit;

"equity security" has the meaning ascribed to that term in securities legislation;

"financial institution" means

(a) a Canadian financial institution,

(b) an entity that is engaged in financial services activities and that is supervised and regulated under the banking, insurance, trust or similar laws of, and incorporated in, the United States of America or Japan, or

(c) a credit institution, within the meaning of European Union Directive 77/780/EEC, whose home member state for purposes of that European Union Directive is France, Germany, Italy or the United Kingdom of Great Britain and Northern Ireland;

"formal bid" means a take-over bid or issuer bid made in accordance with Part 2 of NI 62-104;

"investment manager" means an entity that

(a) either

(i) is registered or licensed to provide investment counselling, portfolio management or similar advisory services in respect of securities, or is exempt from the requirement to be so registered or licensed, under the securities laws of a jurisdiction or of Japan or under the Investment Advisers Act of 1940 of the United States of America, as amended, or

(ii) is subject to European Union Directive 93/22 on investment services in the securities field, and provides the portfolio management services referred to in Section A(3) of the Annex to that Directive, and whose home member state is France, Germany, Italy or the United Kingdom of Great Britain and Northern Ireland, and

(b) provides the services referred to in paragraph (a) for valuable consideration under a contractual arrangement;

"joint actor" means, in relation to an entity and a security, another entity acting jointly or in concert with the entity in connection with the ownership of, or control over, the security;

"moratorium provisions" means the provisions set out in subsection 5.3(1) of NI 62-104;

"news release" includes a press release;

"NI 55-104" means National Instrument 55-104 *Insider Reporting Requirements and Exemptions*;

"NI 62-104" means National Instrument 62-104 *Take-Over Bids and Issuer Bids*;

"ownership" means, in relation to a security, the beneficial ownership of the security, and "owns", "owned" and similar words have corresponding meanings;

"pledgee" includes a holder of any type of security interest;

"portfolio adviser" means an entity that provides investment advice or portfolio management services to, or for, an investment fund;

"private mutual fund" means

(a) a private investment club referred to in section 2.20 of National Instrument 45-106 *Prospectus Exemptions*, or

(b) a private investment fund referred to in section 2.21 of National Instrument 45-106 *Prospectus Exemptions*;

"related financial instrument" has the meaning ascribed to that term in NI 55-104;

"securities lending arrangement" has the meaning ascribed to that term in Part 5 of NI 62-104;

"securityholding percentage" means, in relation to an entity and a class of securities, the percentage of the outstanding securities of the class owned, together with the percentage controlled by the entity, determined in accordance with the provisions of applicable securities legislation listed in Appendix D and after application of any aggregation relief available under Part 5 that is relied on by the entity;

"significant change in a related financial instrument position" means, in relation to an entity and a related financial instrument that involves, directly or indirectly, a security of a reporting issuer, any change in the entity's interest in, or rights or obligations associated with, the related financial instrument if the change has a similar economic effect to an increase or decrease in the entity's securityholding percentage in a class of voting or equity securities of the reporting issuer by 2.5 percent or more;

"take-over provisions" means the provisions in securities legislation that regulate take-over bids and issuer bids; and

"underwriting period" means, for an entity acting as an underwriter of securities, the period commencing from the date of execution of an underwriting agreement or commitment until

(a) for securities acquired by the entity upon the exercise of an over-allotment option, four business days after the acquisition of those securities, and

(b) for all other securities, the earlier of

(i) the expiration of 40 days after the date of the closing of the purchase of the securities, and

(ii) the date of the completion of the distribution by the underwriter of the securities.

1.2 Deemed Effective Control — For the purposes of the definition of "effective control", an entity that, either alone or together with one or more joint actors, owns or controls voting securities carrying more than 30 percent of the votes attached to all of the outstanding voting securities of a reporting issuer shall, in the absence of evidence to the contrary, be deemed to possess effective control over the reporting issuer.

PART 2 — GENERAL RELIANCE AND REPORTING PROVISIONS

2.1 Reliance on Reported Outstanding Shares — (1) Subject to subsection (2), in determining its securityholding percentage in a class of securities for the purposes of the early warning requirements or Part 4, an entity may rely upon information most recently provided by the issuer of the securities in a material change report or under section 5.4 of National Instrument 51-102 *Continuous Disclosure Obligations*, whichever contains the most recent relevant information.

(2) Subsection (1) does not apply if the entity has knowledge both

(a) that the information filed is inaccurate or has changed; and

(b) of the correct information.

2.2 Copies of News Release and Report — An entity that files a news release and report under the early warning requirements, or a report under Part 4, in relation to a reporting issuer shall immediately send a copy of each filing to the reporting issuer.

2.3 No Duplication of News Releases or Reports — (1) An entity that is required to issue a news release under both the early warning requirements and the acquisition announcement provisions is exempt from the requirement to issue the news release contained in the provision requiring the later release if

(a) the news release is filed under the provision with the earlier reporting requirement; and

(b) the facts required to be contained in the two news releases are identical.

(2) An entity that is required to file a report under the acquisition announcement provisions and either the early warning requirements or Part 4 is exempt from the requirement to file the report under the provision requiring the later report if

(a) the report is filed under the provision requiring the earlier report; and

(b) the facts required to be contained in the two reports are identical.

PART 3 — EARLY WARNING REQUIREMENTS

3.1 Contents of News Releases and Reports — (1) A news release and report required under the early warning requirements shall contain the information required by Form 62-103F1 *Required Disclosure under the Early Warning Requirements*.

(2) Despite subsection (1), a news release required under the early warning requirements may omit the information otherwise required by Items 2.3, 3.3, 3.5 through 3.8, 4.2, 4.3, 6 and 9, and Item 7 to the extent that the information relates to those sections and items, of Form 62-103F1 *Required Disclosure under the Early Warning Requirements*, if

(a) the omitted information is included in the corresponding report required by the early warning requirements, and

(b) the news release indicates the name and telephone number of an individual to contact to obtain a copy of the report.

(3) The acquiror shall send a copy of the report referred to in paragraph (2)(a) promptly to any entity requesting it.

3.2 Filing Relief for Joint Actors — The early warning requirements and the acquisition announcement provisions do not apply to a joint actor of an acquiror in connection with the obligation to make a specific filing of a news release or report if

(a) the acquiror files a news release or report at the time that the joint actor would be required to file; and

(b) the news release or report filed discloses the information concerning the joint actor required by securities legislation.

3.3 Exemption from Early Warning Requirements for Mutual Fund Securities — The early warning requirements do not apply in connection with the ownership or control of securities issued by a mutual fund to which National Instrument 81-102 *Investment Funds* applies.

PART 4 — ALTERNATIVE MONTHLY REPORTING SYSTEM

4.1 Exemption from the Early Warning Requirements — The early warning requirements do not apply to an eligible institutional investor for a reporting issuer if the eligible institutional investor

(a) is not disqualified by section 4.2 from filing reports under this Part for the reporting issuer; and

(b) either

(i) intends to file reports under this Part for the reporting issuer, if no reports are yet required to be filed; or

(ii) is not in arrears of filing reports under this Part for the reporting issuer, if a report has been required by this Part to be filed.

Part 6: TAKE-OVER BIDS

4.2 Disqualification — (1) An eligible institutional investor shall not file reports under this Part for a reporting issuer if the eligible institutional investor, or a joint actor,

(a) makes or intends to make a formal bid for securities of the reporting issuer;

(b) proposes or intends to propose a reorganization, amalgamation, merger, arrangement or similar business combination with a reporting issuer that if completed would reasonably be expected to result in the eligible institutional investor, either alone or together with any joint actors, possessing effective control over the reporting issuer or a successor to all or a part of the business of the reporting issuer; or

(c) solicits proxies from securityholders of the reporting issuer in any of the following circumstances:

(i) in support of the election of one or more persons as directors of the reporting issuer other than the persons proposed to be nominated by management of the reporting issuer;

(ii) in support for a reorganization, amalgamation, merger, arrangement or other similar corporate action involving the securities of the reporting issuer if that action is not supported by management of the reporting issuer;

(iii) in opposition to a reorganization, amalgamation, merger, arrangement or other similar corporate action involving the securities of the reporting issuer if that action is proposed by management of the reporting issuer.

(2) For the purposes of this section, "solicit" has the meaning ascribed to that term in National Instrument 51-102 *Continuous Disclosure Obligations.*.

4.3 Reporting and Filing Requirements — (1) If an eligible institutional investor is relying on the exemption in section 4.1 for a reporting issuer and becomes disqualified under section 4.2 from filing, or no longer intends to file, reports under this Part for the reporting issuer, the eligible institutional investor shall

(a) immediately issue and file a news release; and

(b) within two business days after filing the news release, file a report.

(2) The news release and report required by subsection (1) shall contain the information required by Form 62-103F2 *Required Disclosure by an Eligible Institutional Investor under Section 4.3.*

(3) An eligible institutional investor that is required to file a report under subsection (1) for a reporting issuer is not exempt from the early warning requirements for that reporting issuer as of the date on which the news release required by subsection (1) is required to be filed.

(4) An eligible institutional investor that files reports under this Part for a reporting issuer and that controls securities of the reporting issuer that are owned by another entity shall

(a) on request by the entity, promptly advise the entity of the number of securities held on its behalf; and

(b) if the eligible institutional investor has reason to believe that the securityholding percentage of the entity in a class of voting or equity securities of the reporting issuer equals 10 percent or more, promptly advise the entity of the number of securities held on its behalf.

4.4 Restrictions on Acquisitions — An eligible institutional investor that has become disqualified under section 4.2 from filing reports under this Part for a reporting issuer, if the securityholding percentage of the eligible institutional investor in a class of voting or equity securities of the reporting issuer is 10 percent or more, shall not acquire ownership of, or control over, any additional securities of the reporting issuer for the period

(a) starting at the time that the news release referred to in paragraph 4.3(1)(a) is required to be filed; and

(b) ending 10 days after the news release is filed.

4.5 Filing Obligations under this Part — In order to rely on the exemption provided by section 4.1, an eligible institutional investor shall file a report

(a) within 10 days after the end of the month in which the eligible institutional investor elected to begin to file reports for the reporting issuer under this Part, if the securityholding percentage of the eligible institutional investor in a class of voting or equity securities of the reporting issuer at the end of the month is 10 percent or more;

(b) within 10 days after the end of the month in which the securityholding percentage of the eligible institutional investor in a class of voting or equity securities of the reporting issuer, as at the end of the month, increased to 10 percent or more;

(c) within 10 days after the end of the month in which the securityholding percentage of the eligible institutional investor in a class of voting or equity securities of the reporting issuer, as at the end of the month, increased or decreased past thresholds that are products of whole numbers multiplied by 2.5 percent of the outstanding securities of the class and that are in excess of 10 percent of the outstanding securities of the class; and

(d) within 10 days after the end of the month in which the securityholding percentage of the eligible institutional investor in a class of voting or equity securities of the reporting issuer, as at the end of the month, decreased to less than 10 percent.

4.6 Change Reports — In addition to the filing requirements of section 4.5, an eligible institutional investor shall file a report within 10 days after the end of the month in which there has been a change in a material fact contained in the report of the eligible institutional investor most recently filed under this Part.

4.7 Contents of Reports — (1) A report filed under this Part shall contain the information required by Form 62-103F3 *Required Disclosure by an Eligible Institutional Investor under Part 4.*

(2) Despite subsection (1), a report filed under paragraph 4.5(d) may be limited to

(a) the name and address of the eligible institutional investor;

(b) the name of the reporting issuer and the designation and number or principal amount of voting or equity securities of the reporting issuer in respect of which the report is being filed and the securityholding percentage of the eligible institutional investor in the class of securities; and

(c) a statement that the eligible institutional investor is eligible to file reports under this Part.

4.8 Exemptions — The requirement to file a report under this Part does not apply to a joint actor with an eligible institutional investor in connection with a specific filing if

(a) the eligible institutional investor files a report under this Part at the time that the joint actor is required to file; and

(b) the report discloses the information concerning the joint actor required by this Instrument.

PART 5 — AGGREGATION RELIEF

5.1 Separate Business Units — An eligible institutional investor, or an affiliate or associate of an eligible institutional investor, that conducts business or investment activities through business units may, for the purposes of the applicable provisions and securities legislation related to the applicable definitions, treat securities that are owned or controlled through a business unit, or securities into which those securities are convertible, exerciseable or exchangeable, separately from securities owned or controlled through any other of its business units if

(a) decisions on each of the acquisition, disposition, holding or voting of the securities owned or controlled by a business unit are made in all circumstances by that business unit;

(b) the business unit is not a joint actor with any other business unit with respect to the securities, determined without regard to the provision of securities legislation that deem an affiliate, and presume an associate, to be acting jointly or in concert with the acquiror;

(c) no entity that makes, advises on, participates in the formulation of, or exercises influence over, decisions on the acquisition, disposition, holding or voting of securities owned or controlled by or on behalf of a business unit also makes, advises on, participates in the formulation of or exercises influence over, decisions on the acquisition, disposition, holding or voting of securities owned or controlled by or on behalf of any other business unit, except for the purposes of

    (i) preparing research reports,

    (ii) monitoring or ensuring compliance with regulatory requirements, or

    (iii) setting, monitoring or ensuring compliance with general investment policies, guidelines, objectives or restrictions;

(d) the eligible institutional investor or affiliate or associate has reasonable grounds for believing that each business unit complies with the applicable provisions and securities legislation related to the applicable definitions in connection with the securities owned or controlled by the business unit;

(e) the eligible institutional investor or affiliate or associate has taken reasonable steps to ensure that each business unit complies with the requirements of this Part; and

(f) the eligible institutional investor or affiliate or associate complies with section 5.3.

5.2 Securities Held by an Investment Fund — An eligible institutional investor, or an affiliate or associate of an eligible institutional investor, may, for the purposes of the applicable provisions and securities legislation related to the applicable definitions, treat securities owned or controlled by an investment fund over which the eligible institutional investor, affiliate or associate exercises or shares control, or securities into which those securities are convertible, exerciseable or exchangeable, separately from other securities owned or controlled by the eligible institutional investor or affiliate or associate if

(a) the investment fund is not a private mutual fund;

(b) a portfolio adviser manages the investment fund on behalf of the eligible institutional investor under a written agreement;

(c) the portfolio adviser has been identified as managing the investment fund in a document provided to an investor;

(d) none of the eligible institutional investor, its affiliates or associates, or a director, officer, partner, employee or agent of the eligible institutional investor or its affiliates or associates, makes, advises on, participates in the formulation of, or exercises influence over, decisions made by the portfolio adviser on the acquisition, disposition, holding or voting of securities, except for the purposes of

    (i) preparing research reports,

    (ii) monitoring or ensuring compliance with regulatory requirements, or

    (iii) setting, monitoring or ensuring compliance with general investment policies, guidelines, objectives or restrictions;

(e) the eligible institutional investor or affiliate or associate has reasonable grounds for believing that the portfolio adviser complies with the applicable provisions and securities legislation related to the applicable definitions in connection with securities owned or controlled by the investment fund;

(f) the portfolio adviser neither controls nor is controlled by the eligible institutional investor or an affiliate or associate of the eligible institutional investor; and

(g) the eligible institutional investor or affiliate or associate complies with section 5.3.

5.3 Reporting and Record Keeping — (1) In addition to the requirements of sections 5.1 and 5.2, in order to rely on section 5.1 or 5.2, an eligible institutional investor or an affiliate or associate shall indicate in any document released or filed under the applicable provisions or securities legislation related to the applicable definitions

(a) its reliance on either section 5.1 or 5.2;

(b) the identity of the business units or investment funds for which ownership and control of the securities has been disclosed; and

(c) the fact that securities owned or controlled by other business units or investment funds have not been, or may not have been, disclosed.

(2) An eligible institutional investor or affiliate or associate shall maintain records of the details concerning

(a) business units of the entity that are treated separately, by reason of section 5.1, for the purposes of compliance with the applicable provisions and securities legislation related to the applicable definitions; and

(b) investment funds whose ownership of, or control over, securities are treated separately, by reason of section 5.2, for the purposes of compliance with the applicable provisions and securities legislation related to the applicable definitions.

5.4 No Requirement to Satisfy Insider Reporting Requirement — If an eligible institutional investor, or an affiliate or associate of an eligible institutional investor, is relying on this Part so that it is not subject to the insider reporting requirement for a reporting issuer, then every director or senior officer of the eligible institutional investor, or of the affiliate or associate of an eligible institutional investor, who is an insider of the reporting issuer solely as a result of being a director or senior officer of the eligible institutional investor, or the affiliate or associate of an eligible institutional investor, is not subject to the insider reporting requirement for the reporting issuer.

Part 6: TAKE-OVER BIDS

PART 6 — ISSUER ACTIONS

6.1 Issuer Actions — (1) An entity is exempt from the early warning requirements and the obligation to report under Part 4 in connection with an increase in the securityholding percentage of the entity in a class of securities of a reporting issuer that arises without any action being taken by the entity and solely from a reduction in outstanding securities that occurs as a result of redemptions, retractions or other repurchases by the reporting issuer, that affect or are offered to all securityholders of the relevant class.

(2) An entity is exempt from the early warning requirements and the obligation to report under Part 4 in connection with a decrease in the securityholding percentage of the entity in a class of securities of a reporting issuer that arises without any action being taken by the entity and solely from an increase in outstanding securities that occurs as a result of treasury issuances of securities by the reporting issuer.

(3) An entity may rely upon an exemption provided by this section in connection with a class of securities only until the entity undertakes any transaction that changes the securityholding percentage of the entity in that class of securities.

(4) An entity that undertakes a transaction described in subsection (3) shall comply with the early warning requirements or Part 4 in connection with the class of securities referred to in that subsection in a manner that reflects the changes in the securityholding percentage of the entity in that class of securities since the last news release or report made or filed under the early warning requirements or Part 4.

PART 7 — UNDERWRITING EXEMPTION

7.1 Underwriting Exemption — An entity is exempt from the early warning requirements and the obligation to report under Part 4 in respect of securities owned by the entity in its capacity as underwriter or securities into which those securities are convertible, or exerciseable or exchangeable, during the underwriting period, if

(a) the entity is engaged in the business of an underwriter of securities; and

(b) the entity or the issuer of the securities has issued and filed a news release that

(i) announces the proposed underwriting, and

(ii) identifies the reporting issuer and the designation and number or principal amount of the securities underwritten.

PART 8 — RELIEF FOR PLEDGEES

8.1 Relief for Pledgees — (1) For securities that are controlled by a person or company as a pledgee, and any securities into which those securities are convertible, exercisable or exchangeable, in either case that are pledged, mortgaged or otherwise encumbered as collateral for a debt under a written pledge agreement and in the ordinary course of the business of the person or company, the person or company is exempt from the applicable provisions, and those securities are not required to be taken into account for the purposes of securities legislation related to the applicable definitions.

(2) Subsection (1) does not apply at any time that the person or company is legally entitled to dispose of the securities as pledgee for the purpose of applying proceeds of realization in repayment of the secured debt.

8.2 Further Relief for de minimis Pledgees — Despite subsection 8.1(2), for securities that are controlled by a person or company as a pledgee, and any securities into which those securities are convertible, exercisable or exchangeable, in either case that are or were pledged, mortgaged or otherwise encumbered as collateral for a debt, under a written pledge agreement and in the ordinary course of the business of the person or company, the person or company is exempt from the applicable provisions, and those securities are not required to be taken into account for the purposes of securities legislation related to the applicable definitions, even if the person or company is legally entitled to dispose of the securities as pledgee for the purpose of applying proceeds of realization in repayment of the secured debt, if

(a) the principal amount of the debt, together with the principal amount of all other debts of or guaranteed by the same borrower to the person or company, does not exceed $2,000,000; and

(b) the pledged securities, and securities into which the pledged securities are convertible, exercisable or exchangeable, constitute less than 10 percent of a class of voting or equity securities.

8.3 Corresponding Insider Reporting Relief — If a person or company is exempt under section 8.1 or 8.2 from the insider reporting requirement for those securities of a reporting issuer that it controls as pledgee, every director or senior officer of the person or company who is an insider of the reporting issuer solely as a result of being a director or senior officer of the person or company that is an insider of the reporting issuer is exempt from the insider reporting requirement for those securities.

PART 9 — INSIDER REPORTING EXEMPTION

9.1 Insider Reporting Exemption — (1) Subject to subsections (3.1) and (4), an eligible institutional investor is exempt from the insider reporting requirement for a reporting issuer if

(a) the eligible institutional investor has filed the report required under the early warning requirements or Part 4 for the reporting issuer in connection with the current securityholding percentage of the eligible institutional investor in the classes of voting and equity securities of the reporting issuer;

(a.1) the report referred to in paragraph (a) discloses, in addition to any other required disclosure,

(i) the eligible institutional investor's interest in any related financial instrument involving a security of the reporting issuer that is not otherwise reflected in the current securityholding percentage of the eligible institutional investor; and

(ii) the material terms of the related financial instrument;

(b) the eligible institutional investor is not disqualified under section 4.2 from filing reports under Part 4;

(c) the eligible institutional investor does not have knowledge of any material fact or material change with respect to the reporting issuer that has not been generally disclosed;

(d) the eligible institutional investor does not receive in the ordinary course of its business and investment activities knowledge of any material fact or material change with respect to the reporting issuer that has not been generally disclosed;

(e) there are no directors or officers of the reporting issuer who were, or could reasonably be seen to have been, selected, nominated or designated by the eligible institutional investor or any joint actor; and

(f) the eligible institutional investor, either alone or together with any joint actors, does not possess effective control of the reporting issuer.

(2) An eligible institutional investor relying on the exemption in subsection (1) shall maintain records that include the information that, absent this section, would have been required to be included in a report filed under the insider reporting requirement.

(3) [Repealed]

(3.1) Despite subsection (1), an eligible institutional investor that is filing reports under the early warning requirements or Part 4 for a reporting issuer may rely upon the exemption contained in subsection (1) only if the eligible institutional investor treats a significant change in a related financial instrument position as a change in a material fact for the purposes of securities legislation pertaining to the early warning requirements or section 4.6 of this Instrument.

(4) Despite subsection (1), an eligible institutional investor that is an insider of a reporting issuer may not rely upon the exemption contained in subsection (1) if

(a) the eligible institutional investor, either alone or with a joint actor or joint actors, purchased in the previous month, directly or indirectly, 50 percent or more of all of the securities of a class that were reported sold on stock exchanges, over-the-counter markets or both in the previous month; or

(b) the eligible institutional investor, either alone or with a joint actor or joint actors, sold in the previous month, directly or indirectly, 50 percent or more of all of the securities of a class that were reported sold on stock exchanges, over-the-counter markets or both in the previous month.

(5) If an eligible institutional investor is exempt under subsection (1) from the insider reporting requirement for a reporting issuer, every director or senior officer of the eligible institutional investor who is an insider of the reporting issuer solely as a result of being director or senior officer of the eligible institutional investor is exempt from the insider reporting requirement for the reporting issuer.

PART 10 — MORATORIUM RELIEF

10.1 Moratorium Relief — (1) An entity is exempt from the moratorium provisions in respect of the acquisition of, or offers to acquire, securities, if those acquisitions or offers are made by an investment manager acting on behalf of the entity without the direction or prior knowledge of the entity.

(2) Subsection (1) does not apply to an investment manager acting as principal.

(3) An entity is exempt from the moratorium provisions in respect of any acquisitions of, or offers to acquire, securities made solely in its capacity as an approved specialist, or market maker, recognized by a stock exchange or an over-the-counter market that represents a published market for the securities.

(4) An eligible institutional investor is exempt from the moratorium provisions in respect of securities of a reporting issuer at any time in which

(a) the eligible institutional investor is using the exemption in section 4.1 in connection with filings relating to securities of that reporting issuer; or

(b) the eligible institutional investor is subject to the restrictions contained in section 4.4.

PART 11 — EXEMPTIONS

11.1 Exemptions — (1) The regulator or the securities regulatory authority may grant an exemption to this Instrument, in whole or in part, subject to such conditions or restrictions as may be imposed in the exemption.

(2) Despite subsection (1), in Ontario only the regulator may grant such an exemption.

PART 12 — EFFECTIVE DATE

12.1 Effective Date — This Instrument comes into force on March 15, 2000.

APPENDIX A — CONTROL BLOCK DISTRIBUTIONS DEFINITION

JURISDICTION	SECURITIES LEGISLATION REFERENCE
ALBERTA	Clause 1(p)(iii) of the *Securities Act* (Alberta)
BRITISH COLUMBIA	Paragraph (c) of the definition of "distribution" contained in subsection 1(1) of the *Securities Act* (British Columbia)
MANITOBA	Paragraph 1(b) of the definition of "primary distribution to the public" contained in subsection 1(1) of the *Securities Act* (Manitoba)
NEW BRUNSWICK	Paragraph (c) of the definition of "distribution" contained in section 1(1) of the *Securities Act* (New Brunswick)
NEWFOUNDLAND	Clause 2(1)(l)(iii) of the *Securities Act* (Newfoundland)
NORTHWEST TERRITORIES	Paragraph (c) of the definition of "distribution" contained in subsection 1(1) of the *Securities Act* (Northwest Territories),
NOVA SCOTIA	Clause 2(1)(l)(iii) of the *Securities Act* (Nova Scotia)
NUNAVUT	Paragraph (c) of the definition of "distribution" contained in subsection 1(1) of the *Securities Act* (Nunavut)
ONTARIO	Paragraph (c) of the definition of "distribution" contained in subsection 1(1) of the *Securities Act* (Ontario)
QUÉBEC	Subparagraph 9 of the definition of "distribution" contained in section 5 of the *Securities Act* (Québec)
PRINCE EDWARD ISLAND	Subclause (iii) of the definition of "distribution" contained in clause 1(k) of the *Securities Act* (Prince Edward Island)
SASKATCHEWAN	Subclause 2(1)(r)(iii) of *The Securities Act, 1988* (Saskatchewan)
YUKON TERRITORY	Paragraph (c) of the definition of "distribution" contained in subsection 1(1) of the *Securities Act* (Yukon Territory).

Appendix B — [Repealed]

Appendix C — [Repealed]

Appendix D — Beneficial Ownership

JURISDICTION	SECURITIES LEGISLATION REFERENCE
ALBERTA	Sections 5 and 6 of the *Securities Act* (Alberta) and sections 1.8 and 1.9 of NI 62-104
BRITISH COLUMBIA	Subsections 1(4) of the *Securities Act* (British Columbia) and sections 1.8 and 1.9 of NI 62-104
MANITOBA	Subsections 1(6) and 1(7) of the *Securities Act* (Manitoba) and sections 1.8 and 1.9 of NI 104
NEW BRUNSWICK	Subsections 1(5) and 1(6) of the *Securities Act* (New Brunswick) and sections 1.8 and 1.9 of NI 62-104
NEWFOUNDLAND AND LABRADOR	Subsections 2(5) and 2(6) of the *Securities Act* (Newfoundland and Labrador) and sections 1.8 and 1.9 of NI 62-104
NORTHWEST TERRITORIES	Section 11 of the *Securities Act* (Northwest Territories) and sections 1.8 and 1.9 of NI 62-104
NOVA SCOTIA	Subsections 2(5) and 2(6) of the *Securities Act* (Nova Scotia) and sections 1.8 and 1.9 of NI 62-104
NUNAVUT	Sections 1.8 and 1.9 of NI 62-104
ONTARIO	Subsections 1(5) and 1(6) of the *Securities Act* (Ontario) and sections 1.8 and 1.9 of NI 62-104
PRINCE EDWARD ISLAND	Section 11 of the *Securities Act* (Prince Edward Island) and sections 1.8 and 1.9 of NI 62-104
QUEBEC	Sections 1.8 and 1.9 of NI 62-104
SASKATCHEWAN	Subsections 2(5) and 2(6) of *The Securities Act, 1988* (Saskatchewan) and sections 1.8 and 1.9 of NI 62-104
YUKON TERRITORY	Section 11 of the *Securities Act* (Yukon Territory) and sections 1.8 and 1.9 of NI 62-104

Form 62-103F1 — Required Disclosure under the Early Warning Requirements

State if the report is filed to amend information disclosed in an earlier report. Indicate the date of the report that is being amended.

Item 1 — Security and Reporting Issuer

1.1 State the designation of securities to which this report relates and the name and address of the head office of the issuer of the securities.

1.2 State the name of the market in which the transaction or other occurrence that triggered the requirement to file this report took place.

Item 2 — Identity of the Acquiror

2.1 State the name and address of the acquiror.

2.2 State the date of the transaction or other occurrence that triggered the requirement to file this report and briefly describe the transaction or other occurrence.

2.3 State the names of any joint actors.

INSTRUCTION

If the acquiror is a corporation, general partnership, limited partnership, syndicate or other group of persons, provide its name, the address of its head office, its jurisdiction of incorporation or organization, and its principal business.

Item 3 — Interest in Securities of the Reporting Issuer

3.1 State the designation and number or principal amount of securities acquired or disposed of that triggered the requirement to file the report and the change in the acquiror's securityholding percentage in the class of securities.

3.2 State whether the acquiror acquired or disposed ownership of, or acquired or ceased to have control over, the securities that triggered the requirement to file the report.

3.3 If the transaction involved a securities lending arrangement, state that fact.

3.4 State the designation and number or principal amount of securities and the acquiror's securityholding percentage in the class of securities, immediately before and after the transaction or other occurrence that triggered the requirement to file this report.

3.5 State the designation and number or principal amount of securities and the acquiror's securityholding percentage in the class of securities referred to in Item 3.4 over which

(a) the acquiror, either alone or together with any joint actors, has ownership and control,

(b) the acquiror, either alone or together with any joint actors, has ownership but control is held by persons or companies other than the acquiror or any joint actor, and

(c) the acquiror, either alone or together with any joint actors, has exclusive or shared control but does not have ownership.

3.6 If the acquiror or any of its joint actors has an interest in, or right or obligation associated with, a related financial instrument involving a security of the class of securities in respect of which disclosure is required under this item, describe the material terms of the related financial instrument and its impact on the acquiror's securityholdings.

3.7 If the acquiror or any of its joint actors is a party to a securities lending arrangement involving a security of the class of securities in respect of which disclosure is required under this item, describe the material terms of the arrangement including the duration of the arrangement, the number or principal amount of securities involved and any right to recall the securities or identical securities that have been transferred or lent under the arrangement.

State if the securities lending arrangement is subject to the exception provided in section 5.7 of NI 62-104.

3.8 If the acquiror or any of its joint actors is a party to an agreement, arrangement or understanding that has the effect of altering, directly or indirectly, the acquiror's economic exposure to the security of the class of securities to which this report relates, describe the material terms of the agreement, arrangement or understanding.

INSTRUCTIONS

(i) "Related financial instrument" has the meaning ascribed to that term in NI 55-104. Item 3.6 encompasses disclosure of agreements, arrangements or understandings where the economic interest related to a security beneficially owned or controlled has been altered.

(ii) For the purposes of Items 3.6, 3.7 and 3.8, a material term of an agreement, arrangement or understanding does not include the identity of the counterparty or proprietary or commercially sensitive information.

(iii) For the purposes of Item 3.8, any agreements, arrangements or understandings that have been disclosed under other items in this Form do not have to be disclosed under this item.

Item 4 — Consideration Paid

4.1 State the value, in Canadian dollars, of any consideration paid or received per security and in total.

4.2 In the case of a transaction or other occurrence that did not take place on a stock exchange or other market that represents a published market for the securities, including an issuance from treasury, disclose the nature and value, in Canadian dollars, of the consideration paid or received by the acquiror.

4.3 If the securities were acquired or disposed of other than by purchase or sale, describe the method of acquisition or disposition.

Item 5 — Purpose of the Transaction

State the purpose or purposes of the acquiror and any joint actors for the acquisition or disposition of securities of the reporting issuer. Describe any plans or future intentions which the acquiror and any joint actors may have which relate to or would result in any of the following:

(a) the acquisition of additional securities of the reporting issuer, or the disposition of securities of the reporting issuer;

(b) a corporate transaction, such as a merger, reorganization or liquidation, involving the reporting issuer or any of its subsidiaries;

(c) a sale or transfer of a material amount of the assets of the reporting issuer or any of its subsidiaries;

(d) a change in the board of directors or management of the reporting issuer, including any plans or intentions to change the number or term of directors or to fill any existing vacancy on the board;

(e) a material change in the present capitalization or dividend policy of the reporting issuer;

(f) a material change in the reporting issuer's business or corporate structure;

(g) a change in the reporting issuer's charter, bylaws or similar instruments or another action which might impede the acquisition of control of the reporting issuer by any person or company;

(h) a class of securities of the reporting issuer being delisted from, or ceasing to be authorized to be quoted on, a marketplace;

(i) the issuer ceasing to be a reporting issuer in any jurisdiction of Canada;

(j) a solicitation of proxies from securityholders;

(k) an action similar to any of those enumerated above.

Item 6 — Agreements, Arrangements, Commitments or Understandings With Respect to Securities of the Reporting Issuer

Describe the material terms of any agreements, arrangements, commitments or understandings between the acquiror and a joint actor and among those persons and any person with respect to securities of the class of securities to which this report relates, including but not limited to the transfer or the voting of any of the securities, finder's fees, joint ventures, loan or option arrangements, guarantees of profits, division of profits or loss, or the giving or withholding of proxies. Include such information for any of the securities that are pledged or otherwise subject to a contingency, the occurrence of which would give another person voting power or investment power over such securities, except that disclosure of standard default and similar provisions contained in loan agreements need not be included.

INSTRUCTIONS

(i) Agreements, arrangements or understandings that are described under Item 3 do not have to be disclosed under this item.

(ii) For the purposes of Item 6, the description of any agreements, arrangements, commitments or understandings does not include naming the persons with whom those agreements, arrangements, commitments or understandings have been entered into, or proprietary or commercially sensitive information.

Item 7 — Change in material fact

If applicable, describe any change in a material fact set out in a previous report filed by the acquiror under the early warning requirements or Part 4 in respect of the reporting issuer's securities.

Item 8 — Exemption

If the acquiror relies on an exemption from requirements in securities legislation applicable to formal bids for the transaction, state the exemption being relied on and describe the facts supporting that reliance.

Item 9 — Certification

The acquiror must certify that the information is true and complete in every respect. In the case of an agent, the certification is based on the agent's best knowledge, information and belief but the acquiror is still responsible for ensuring that the information filed by the agent is true and complete.

This report must be signed by each person on whose behalf the report is filed or his authorized representative.

It is an offence to submit information that, in a material respect and at the time and in the light of the circumstances in which it is submitted, is misleading or untrue.

Certificate

The certificate must state the following:

I, as the acquiror, certify, or I, as the agent filing the report on behalf of an acquiror, certify to the best of my knowledge, information and belief, that the statements made in this report are true and complete in every respect.

.... Date

.... Signature

.... Name/Title.

Form 62-103F2 — Required Disclosure by an Eligible Institutional Investor under Section 4.3

State if the report is filed to amend information disclosed in an earlier report. Indicate the date of the report that is being amended.

Item 1 — Security and Reporting Issuer

1.1 State the designation of securities to which this report relates and the name and address of the head office of the issuer of the securities.

1.2 State the name of the market in which the transaction or other occurrence that triggered the requirement to file this report took place.

Item 2 — Identity of the Eligible Institutional Investor

2.1 State the name and address of the eligible institutional investor.

2.2 State the date of the transaction or other occurrence that triggered the requirement to file this report and briefly describe the transaction or other occurrence.

2.3 State that the eligible institutional investor is ceasing to file reports under Part 4 for the reporting issuer.

2.4 Disclose the reasons for doing so.

2.5 State the names of any joint actors.

Item 3 — Interest in Securities of the Reporting Issuer

3.1 State the designation and number or principal amount of securities and the eligible institutional investor's securityholding percentage in the class of securities immediately before and after the transaction or other occurrence that triggered the requirement to file this report.

3.2 State whether the acquiror acquired or disposed ownership of, or acquired or ceased to have control over, the securities that triggered the requirement to file the report.

3.3 If the transaction involved a securities lending arrangement, state that fact.

3.4 State the designation and number or principal amount of securities and the eligible institutional investor's securityholding percentage in the class of securities, immediately before and after the transaction or other occurrence that triggered the requirement to file this report and over which

(a) the eligible institutional investor, either alone or together with any joint actors, has ownership and control,

(b) the eligible institutional investor, either alone or together with any joint actors, has ownership but control is held by persons or companies other than the eligible institutional investor or any joint actor, and

(c) the eligible institutional investor, either alone or together with any joint actors, has exclusive or shared control but does not have ownership.

3.5 If the eligible institutional investor or any of its joint actors has an interest in, or right or obligation associated with, a related financial instrument involving a security of the class of securities in respect of which disclosure is required under this item, describe the material terms of the related financial instrument and its impact on the eligible institutional investor's securityholdings.

3.6 If the eligible institutional investor or any of its joint actors is a party to a securities lending arrangement involving a security of the class of securities in respect of which disclosure is required under this item, describe the material terms of the arrangement including the duration of the arrangement, the number or principal amount of securities involved and any right to recall the securities or identical securities that have been transferred or lent under the arrangement.

State if the securities lending arrangement is subject to the exception provided in section 5.7 of NI 62-104.

3.7 If the eligible institutional investor or any of its joint actors is a party to an agreement, arrangement or understanding that has the effect of altering, directly or indirectly, the eligible institutional investor's economic exposure to the security of the class of securities to which this report relates, describe the material terms of the agreement, arrangement or understanding.

INSTRUCTIONS

(i) "Related financial instrument" has the meaning ascribed to that term in NI 55-104. Item 3.5 encompasses disclosure of agreements, arrangements or understandings where the economic interest related to a security beneficially owned or controlled has been altered.

(ii) For the purposes of Items 3.5, 3.6 and 3.7, a material term of an agreement, arrangement or understanding does not include the identity of the counterparty or proprietary or commercially sensitive information.

(iii) For the purposes of Item 3.7, any agreements, arrangements or understandings that have been disclosed under other items in this Form do not have to be disclosed under this item.

Item 4 — Consideration Paid

4.1 State the value, in Canadian dollars, of any consideration paid or received per security and in total.

4.2 In the case of a transaction or other occurrence that did not take place on a stock exchange or other market that represents a published market for the securities, including an issuance from treasury, disclose the nature and value, in Canadian dollars, of the consideration paid or received by the eligible institutional investor.

4.3 If the securities were acquired or disposed of other than by purchase or sale, describe the method of acquisition or disposition.

Item 5 — Purpose of the Transaction

State the purpose or purposes of the eligible institutional investor and any joint actors for the acquisition or disposition of securities of the reporting issuer. Describe any plans or future intentions which the eligible institutional investor and any joint actors may have which relate to or would result in any of the following:

(a) the acquisition of additional securities of the reporting issuer, or the disposition of securities of the reporting issuer;

(b) a corporate transaction, such as a merger, reorganization or liquidation, involving the reporting issuer or any of its subsidiaries;

(c) a sale or transfer of a material amount of the assets of the reporting issuer or any of its subsidiaries;

(d) a change in the board of directors or management of the reporting issuer, including any plans or intentions to change the number or term of directors or to fill any existing vacancy on the board;

(e) a material change in the present capitalization or dividend policy of the reporting issuer;

(f) a material change in the reporting issuer's business or corporate structure;

(g) a change in the reporting issuer's charter, bylaws or similar instruments or another action which might impede the acquisition of control of the reporting issuer by any person;

(h) a class of securities of the reporting issuer being delisted from, or ceasing to be authorized to be quoted on, a marketplace;

(i) the issuer ceasing to be a reporting issuer in any jurisdiction of Canada;

(j) a solicitation of proxies from securityholders;

(k) an action similar to any of those enumerated above.

Item 6 — Agreements, Arrangements, Commitments or Understandings With Respect to Securities of the Reporting Issuer

Describe the material terms of any agreements, arrangements, commitments or understandings between the eligible institutional investor and a joint actor and among those persons and any person with respect to any securities of the reporting issuer, including but not limited to the transfer or the voting of any of the securities, finder's fees, joint ventures, loan or option arrangements, guarantees of profits, division of profits or loss, or the giving or withholding of proxies. Include such information for any of the securities that are pledged or otherwise subject to a contingency, the occurrence of which would give another person voting power or investment power over such securities, except that disclosure of standard default and similar provisions contained in loan agreements need not be included.

> *INSTRUCTIONS*
>
> *(i) Agreements, arrangements or understandings that are described under Item 3 do not have to be disclosed under this item.*
>
> *(ii) For the purposes of Item 6, the description of any agreements, arrangements, commitments or understandings does not include naming the persons with whom those agreements, arrangements, commitments or understandings have been entered into, or proprietary or commercially sensitive information.*

Item 7 — Change in material fact

If applicable, describe any change in a material fact set out in a previous report filed by the eligible institutional investor under the early warning requirements or Part 4 in respect of the reporting issuer's securities.

Item 8 — Exemption

If the eligible institutional investor relies on an exemption from the requirement in securities legislation applicable to formal bids for the transaction, state the exemption being relied on and describe the facts supporting that reliance.

Item 9 — Certification

The eligible institutional investor must certify that the information is true and complete in every respect. In the case of an agent, the certification is based on the agent's best knowledge, information and belief but the eligible institutional investor is still responsible for ensuring that the information filed by the agent is true and complete.

This report must be signed by each person on whose behalf the report is filed or his authorized representative.

It is an offence to submit information that, in a material respect and at the time and in the light of the circumstances in which it is submitted, is misleading or untrue.

Certificate

The certificate must state the following:

I, as the eligible institutional investor, certify, or I, as the agent filing the report on behalf of the eligible institutional investor, certify to the best of my knowledge, information and belief, that the statements made in this report are true and complete in every respect.

.... Date

.... Signature

.... Name/Title.

Form 62-103F3 — Required Disclosure by an Eligible Institutional Investor under Part 4

State if the report is filed to amend information disclosed in an earlier report. Indicate the date of the report that is being amended.

Item 1 — Security and Reporting Issuer

1.1 State the designation of securities to which this report relates and the name and address of the head office of the issuer of the securities.

1.2 State the name of the market in which the transaction or other occurrence that triggered the requirement to file this report took place.

Item 2 — Identity of the Eligible Institutional Investor

2.1 State the name and address of the eligible institutional investor.

2.2 State the date of the transaction or other occurrence that triggered the requirement to file this report and briefly describe the transaction or other occurrence.

2.3 State the name of any joint actors.

2.4 State that the eligible institutional investor is eligible to file reports under Part 4 in respect of the reporting issuer.

Item 3 — Interest in Securities of the Reporting Issuer

3.1 State the designation and the net increase or decrease in the number or principal amount of securities, and in the eligible institutional investor's securityholding percentage in the class of securities, since the last report filed by the eligible institutional investor under Part 4 or the early warning requirements.

3.2 State the designation and number or principal amount of securities and the eligible institutional investor's securityholding percentage in the class of securities at the end of the month for which the report is made.

3.3 If the transaction involved a securities lending arrangement, state that fact.

3.4 State the designation and number or principal amount of securities and the percentage of outstanding securities of the class of securities to which this report relates and over which

(a) the eligible institutional investor, either alone or together with any joint actors, has ownership and control,

(b) the eligible institutional investor, either alone or together with any joint actors, has ownership but control is held by persons or companies other than the eligible institutional investor or any joint actor, and

(c) the eligible institutional investor, either alone or together with any joint actors, has exclusive or shared control but does not have ownership.

3.5 If the eligible institutional investor or any of its joint actors has an interest in, or right or obligation associated with, a related financial instrument involving a security of the class of securities in respect of which disclosure is required under this item, describe the material terms of the related financial instrument and its impact on the eligible institutional investor's securityholdings.

3.6 If the eligible institutional investor or any of its joint actors is a party to a securities lending arrangement involving a security of the class of securities in respect of which disclosure is required under this item, describe the material terms of the arrangement including the duration of the arrangement, the number or principal amount of securities involved and any right to recall the securities or identical securities that have been transferred or lent under the arrangement.

State if the securities lending arrangement is subject to the exception provided in section 5.7 of NI 62-104.

3.7 If the eligible institutional investor or any of its joint actors is a party to an agreement, arrangement or understanding that has the effect of altering, directly or indirectly, the eligible institutional investor's economic exposure to the security of the class of securities to which this report relates, describe the material terms of the agreement, arrangement or understanding.

INSTRUCTIONS

(i) *"Related financial instrument" has the meaning ascribed to that term in NI 55-104. Item 3.5 encompasses disclosure of agreements, arrangements or understandings where the economic interest related to a security beneficially owned or controlled has been altered.*

(ii) *An eligible institutional investor may omit the securityholding percentage from a report if the change in percentage is less than 1% of the class.*

(iii) *For the purposes of Item 3.5, 3.6 and 3.7, a material term of an agreement, arrangement or understanding does not include the identity of the counterparty or proprietary or commercially sensitive information.*

(iv) *For the purposes of Item 3.7, any agreements, arrangements or understandings that have been disclosed under other items in this Form do not have to be disclosed under this item.*

Item 4 — Purpose of the Transaction

State the purpose or purposes of the eligible institutional investor and any joint actors for the acquisition or disposition of securities of the reporting issuer. Describe any plans or future intentions which the eligible institutional investor and any joint actors may have which relate to or would result in any of the following:

(a) the acquisition of additional securities of the reporting issuer, or the disposition of securities of the issuer;

(b) a sale or transfer of a material amount of the assets of the reporting issuer or any of its subsidiaries;

(c) a change in the board of directors or management of the reporting issuer, including any plans or intentions to change the number or term of directors or to fill any existing vacancy on the board;

(d) a material change in the present capitalization or dividend policy of the reporting issuer;

(e) a material change in the reporting issuer's business or corporate structure;

(f) a change in the reporting issuer's charter, bylaws or similar instruments or another action which might impede the acquisition of control of the reporting issuer by any person;

(g) a class of securities of the reporting issuer being delisted from, or ceasing to be authorized to be quoted on, a marketplace;

(h) the issuer ceasing to be a reporting issuer in any jurisdiction of Canada;

(i) a solicitation of proxies from securityholders;

(j) an action similar to any of those enumerated above.

Item 5 — Agreements, Arrangements, Commitments or Understandings With Respect to Securities of the Reporting Issuer

Describe the material terms of any agreements, arrangements, commitments or understandings between the eligible institutional investor and a joint actor and among those persons and any person with respect to securities of the class of securities to which this report relates, including but not limited to the transfer or the voting of any of the securities, finder's fees, joint ventures, loan or option arrangements, puts or calls, guarantees of profits, division of profits or loss, or the giving or withholding of proxies. Include such information for any of the securities that are pledged or otherwise subject to a contingency, the occurrence of which would give another person voting power or investment power over such securities except that disclosure of standard default and similar provisions contained in loan agreements need not be included.

INSTRUCTIONS

> *(i) Agreements, arrangements or understandings that are described under Item 3 do not have to be disclosed under this item.*

> *(ii) For the purposes of Item 5, the description of any agreements, arrangements, commitments or understandings does not include naming the persons with whom those agreements, arrangements, commitments or understandings have been entered into, or proprietary or commercially sensitive information.*

Item 6 — Change in Material Fact

If applicable, describe any change in a material fact set out in a previous report filed by the eligible institutional investor under the early warning requirements or Part 4 in respect of the reporting issuer's securities.

Item 7 — Certification

The eligible institutional investor must certify that the information is true and complete in every respect. In the case of an agent, the certification is based on the agent's best knowledge, information and belief but the eligible institutional investor is still responsible for ensuring that the information filed by the agent is true and complete.

This report must be signed by each person on whose behalf the report is filed or his authorized representative.

It is an offence to submit information that, in a material respect and at the time and in the light of the circumstances in which it is submitted, is misleading or untrue.

Certificate

The certificate must state the following:

> I, as the eligible institutional investor, certify, or I, as the agent filing the report on behalf of the eligible institutional investor, certify to the best of my knowledge, information and belief, that the statements made in this report are true and complete in every respect.

.... Date

.... Signature

.... Name/Title.

National Instrument 62-104 — Take-Over Bids and Issuer Bids

Date: **February 25, 2016**

39 OSCB (Supp-1) 63

PART 1: — DEFINITIONS AND INTERPRETATION

1.1 Definitions — In this Instrument,

"Act" means, in the jurisdiction, the statute referred to in Appendix B to National Instrument 14-101 *Definitions*;

"alternative transaction" means, for an issuer:

(a) an amalgamation, merger, arrangement, consolidation, or any other transaction of the issuer, or an amendment to the terms of a class of equity securities of the issuer, as a consequence of which the interest of a holder of an equity security of the issuer may be terminated without the holder's consent, regardless of whether the equity security is replaced with another security, but does not include

(i) a consolidation of securities that does not have the effect of terminating the interests of holders of equity securities of the issuer in those securities without their consent, except to an extent that is nominal in the circumstances,

(ii) a circumstance in which the issuer may terminate a holder's interest in a security, under the terms attached to the security, for the purpose of enforcing an ownership or voting constraint that is necessary to enable the issuer to comply with legislation, lawfully engage in a particular activity or have a specified level of Canadian ownership, or

(iii) a transaction solely between or among the issuer and one or more subsidiaries of the issuer,

(b) a sale, lease or exchange of all or substantially all the property of the issuer if the sale, lease or exchange is not in the ordinary course of business of the issuer, but does not include a sale, lease or exchange solely between or among the issuer and one or more subsidiaries of the issuer;

"associate", when used to indicate a relationship with a person, means

(a) an issuer of which the person beneficially owns or controls, directly or indirectly, voting securities entitling the person to more than 10% of the voting rights attached to outstanding securities of the issuer,

(b) any partner of the person,

(c) any trust or estate in which the person has a substantial beneficial interest or in respect of which a person serves as trustee or in a similar capacity, or

(d) a relative of that person, if the relative has the same home as that person, including

(i) the spouse or, in Alberta, adult interdependent partner of that person, or

(ii) a relative of the person's spouse or, in Alberta, adult interdependent partner;

"bid circular" means a bid circular prepared in accordance with section 2.10;

"business day" means a day other than a Saturday, a Sunday or a day that is a statutory holiday in the jurisdiction;

"class of securities" includes a series of a class of securities;

"consultant" has the same meaning as in National Instrument 45-106 *Prospectus Exemptions*;

"deposit period news release" means a news release issued by an offeree issuer in respect of a proposed or commenced take-over bid for the securities of the offeree issuer and stating an initial deposit period for the bid of not more than 105 days and not less than 35 days, expressed as a number of days from the date of the bid;

"equity security" means a security of an issuer that carries a residual right to participate in the earnings of the issuer and, on liquidation or winding up of the issuer, in its assets;

"initial deposit period" means the period, including any extension, during which securities may be deposited under a take-over bid but does not include

(a) a mandatory 10-day extension period, or

(b) any extension to the period during which securities may be deposited if the extension is made after a mandatory 10-day extension period;

"issuer bid" means an offer to acquire or redeem securities of an issuer made by the issuer to one or more persons, any of whom is in the local jurisdiction or whose last address as shown on the books of the offeree issuer is in the local jurisdiction, and also includes an acquisition or redemption of securities of the issuer by the issuer from those persons, but does not include an offer to acquire or redeem, or an acquisition or redemption if

(a) no valuable consideration is offered or paid by the issuer for the securities,

(b) the offer to acquire or redeem, or the acquisition or redemption is a step in an amalgamation, merger, reorganization or arrangement that requires approval in a vote of security holders, or

(c) the securities are debt securities that are not convertible into securities other than debt securities;

"mandatory 10-day extension period" means the period referred to in paragraph 2.31.1(a);

"offer to acquire" means

(a) an offer to purchase, or a solicitation of an offer to sell, securities,

(b) an acceptance of an offer to sell securities, whether or not the offer has been solicited, or

(c) any combination of the above;

"offeree issuer" means an issuer whose securities are the subject of a take-over bid, an issuer bid or an offer to acquire;

"offeror" means, except in Division 1 of Part 2 of this Instrument, a person that makes a take-over bid, an issuer bid or an offer to acquire;

"offeror's securities" means securities of an offeree issuer beneficially owned, or over which control or direction is exercised, on the date of an offer to acquire, by an offeror or any person acting jointly or in concert with the offeror;

"partial take-over bid" means a take-over bid for less than all of the outstanding securities of the class of securities subject to the bid;

"person" includes

(a) an individual,

(b) a corporation,

(c) a partnership, trust, fund and an association, syndicate, organization or other organized group of persons, whether incorporated or not, and

(d) an individual or other person in that person's capacity as a trustee, executor, administrator or personal or other legal representative;

"published market" means, with respect to any class of securities, a market in Canada or outside of Canada on which the securities are traded, if the prices at which they have been traded on that market are regularly

(a) disseminated electronically, or

(b) published in a newspaper or business or financial publication of general and regular paid circulation;

"standard trading unit" means

(a) 1,000 units of a security with a market price of less than $0.10 per unit,

(b) 500 units of a security with a market price of $0.10 or more per unit and less than $1.00 per unit, and

(c) 100 units of a security with a market price of $1.00 or more per unit;

"subsidiary" means an issuer that is controlled directly or indirectly by another issuer and includes a subsidiary of that subsidiary;

"take-over bid" means an offer to acquire outstanding voting securities or equity securities of a class made to one or more persons, any of whom is in the local jurisdiction or whose last address as shown on the books of the offeree issuer is in the local jurisdiction, where the securities subject to the offer to acquire, together with the offeror's securities, constitute in the aggregate 20% or more of the outstanding securities of that class of securities at the date of the offer to acquire but does not include an offer to acquire if the offer to acquire is a step in an amalgamation, merger, reorganization or arrangement that requires approval in a vote of security holders.

1.2 Definitions for purposes of the Act — (1) Except in Saskatchewan, in the Act,

(a) "offer to acquire" has the same meaning as in this Instrument, and

(b) "offeror" has the same meaning as in section 1.1 of this Instrument.

(2) In the definition of "issuer bid" in the Act, the prescribed class of issuer bids is that set out in the definition of **"issuer bid"** in this Instrument.

(3) In the definition of "take-over bid" in the Act, the prescribed class of take-over bids is that set out in the definition of **"take-over bid"** in this Instrument.

1.3 Affiliate — In this Instrument, an issuer is an affiliate of another issuer if

(a) one of them is the subsidiary of the other, or

(b) each of them is controlled by the same person.

1.4 Control — In this Instrument, a person controls a second person if

(a) the first person, directly or indirectly, beneficially owns or exercises control or direction over securities of the second person carrying votes which, if exercised, would entitle the first person to elect a majority of the directors of the second person, unless the first person holds the voting securities only to secure an obligation,

(b) the second person is a partnership, other than a limited partnership, and the first person holds more than 50% of the interests of the partnership, or

(c) the second person is a limited partnership and the general partner of the limited partnership is the first person.

1.5 Computation of time — In this Instrument, a period of days is to be computed as beginning on the day following the event that began the period and ending at 11:59 p.m. on the last day of the period if that day is a business day or at 11:59 p.m. on the next business day if the last day of the period does not fall on a business day.

1.6 Expiry of bid — A take-over bid or an issuer bid expires at the later of

(a) the end of the period, including any extension, during which securities may be deposited under the bid, and

(b) the time at which the offeror becomes obligated by the terms of the bid to take up or reject securities deposited under the bid.

1.7 Convertible securities — In this Instrument,

(a) a security is deemed to be convertible into a security of another class if, whether or not on conditions, it is or may be convertible into or exchangeable for, or if it carries the right or obligation to acquire, a security of the other class, whether of the same or another issuer, and

(b) a security that is convertible into a security of another class is deemed to be convertible into a security or securities of each class into which the second-mentioned security may be converted, either directly or through securities of one or more other classes of securities that are themselves convertible.

1.8 Deemed beneficial ownership — (1) In this Instrument, in determining the beneficial ownership of securities of an offeror, of an acquiror or of any person acting jointly or in concert with the offeror or the acquiror, at any given date, the offeror, the acquiror or the person is deemed to have acquired and to be the beneficial owner of a security, including an unissued security, if the offeror, the acquiror or the person

(a) is the beneficial owner of a security convertible into the security within 60 days following that date, or

(b) has a right or obligation permitting or requiring the offeror, the acquiror or the person, whether or not on conditions, to acquire beneficial ownership of the security within 60 days by a single transaction or a series of linked transactions.

(2) The number of outstanding securities of a class in respect of an offer to acquire includes securities that are beneficially owned as determined in accordance with subsection (1).

(3) If 2 or more offerors acting jointly or in concert make one or more offers to acquire securities of a class, the securities subject to the offer or offers to acquire are deemed to be securities subject to the offer to acquire of each offeror for the purpose of determining whether an offeror is making a take-over bid.

(4) In this section, an offeror is not a beneficial owner of securities solely because there is an agreement, commitment or understanding that a security holder will tender the securities under a take-over bid or an issuer bid, made by the offeror, that is not exempt from Part 2.

(5) In Québec, for the purposes of this Instrument, a person that beneficially owns securities means a person that owns the securities or that holds securities registered under the name of an intermediary acting as nominee, including a trustee or agent.

1.9 Acting jointly or in concert — (1) In this Instrument, it is a question of fact as to whether a person is acting jointly or in concert with an offeror or an acquiror and, without limiting the generality of the foregoing,

(a) the following are deemed to be acting jointly or in concert with an offeror or an acquiror:

(i) a person that, as a result of any agreement, commitment or understanding with the offeror, the acquiror or with any other person acting jointly or in concert with the offeror or the acquiror, acquires or offers to acquire securities of the same class as those subject to the offer to acquire;

(ii) an affiliate of the offeror or the acquiror;

(b) the following are presumed to be acting jointly or in concert with an offeror or an acquiror:

(i) a person that, as a result of any agreement, commitment or understanding with the offeror, the acquiror or with any other person acting jointly or in concert with the offeror or the acquiror, intends to exercise jointly or in concert with the offeror, the acquiror or with any person acting jointly or in concert with the offeror or the acquiror any voting rights attaching to any securities of the offeree issuer;

(ii) an associate of the offeror or the acquiror.

(2) Subsection (1) does not apply to a registered dealer acting solely in an agency capacity for the offeror in connection with a bid and not executing principal transactions in the class of securities subject to the offer to acquire or performing services beyond the customary functions of a registered dealer.

(3) For the purposes of this section, a person is not acting jointly or in concert with an offeror solely because there is an agreement, commitment or understanding that the person will tender securities under a take-over bid or an issuer bid, made by the offeror, that is not exempt from Part 2.

1.10 Application to direct and indirect offers — In this Instrument, a reference to an offer to acquire or to the acquisition or ownership of securities or to control or direction over securities includes a direct or indirect offer to acquire or the direct or indirect acquisition or ownership of securities, or the direct or indirect control or direction over securities, as the case may be.

1.11 Determination of market price — (1) In this Instrument,

(a) the market price of a class of securities for which there is a published market, at any date, is an amount equal to the simple average of the closing price of securities of that class for each of the business days on which there was a closing price in the 20 business days preceding that date,

(b) if a published market does not provide a closing price, but provides only the highest and lowest prices of securities traded on a particular day, the market price of the securities, at any date, is an amount equal to the average of the simple averages of the highest and lowest prices for each of the business days on which there were highest and lowest prices in the 20 business days preceding that date, and

(c) if there has been trading of securities in a published market for fewer than 10 of the 20 business days preceding the date as of which the market price of the securities is being determined, the market price is the average of the following prices established for each day of the 20 business days preceding that date:

> (i) the average of the closing bid and ask prices for each day on which there was no trading; and

> (ii) either the closing price of securities of the class for each day that there has been trading, if the published market provides a closing price, or the average of the highest and lowest prices of securities of that class for each day that there has been trading, if the published market provides only the highest and lowest prices of securities traded on a particular day.

(2) If there is more than one published market for a security, the market price in paragraphs (1)(a), (b) and (c) must be determined as follows:

> (a) if only one of the published markets is in Canada, the market price must be determined solely by reference to that market;

> (b) if there is more than one published market in Canada, the market price must be determined solely by reference to the published market in Canada on which the greatest volume of trading in the particular class of securities occurred during the 20 business days preceding the date as of which the market price is being determined;

> (c) if there is no published market in Canada, the market price must be determined solely by reference to the published market on which the greatest volume of trading in the particular class of securities occurred during the 20 business days preceding the date as of which the market price is being determined.

(3) Despite subsections (1) and (2) for the purposes of section 4.1 and subsection 4.8(3), if an offeror acquires securities on a published market, the market price for those securities is the price of the last standard trading unit of securities of that class purchased, before the acquisition by the offeror, by a person who was not acting jointly or in concert with the offeror.

PART 2: — BIDS

DIVISION 1: — RESTRICTIONS ON ACQUISITIONS OR SALES

2.1 Definition of "offeror" — In this Division, "offeror" means

> (a) a person making a take-over bid or an issuer bid that is not exempt from Part 2,

> (b) a person acting jointly or in concert with a person referred to in paragraph (a),

> (c) a control person of a person referred to in paragraph (a), or

> (d) a person acting jointly or in concert with a control person referred to in paragraph (c).

2.2 Restrictions on acquisitions during take-over bid — (1) An offeror must not offer to acquire, or make or enter into an agreement, commitment or understanding to acquire beneficial ownership of any securities of the class that are subject to a take-over bid or securities convertible into securities of that class otherwise than under the bid on and from the day of the announcement of the offeror's intention to make the bid until the expiry of the bid.

(2) Subsection (1) does not apply to an agreement between a security holder and the offeror to the effect that the security holder will, in accordance with the terms and conditions of a take-over bid that is not exempt from Part 2, deposit the security holder's securities under the bid.

(3) Despite subsection (1), an offeror may purchase securities of the class that are subject to a take-over bid and securities convertible into securities of that class beginning on the 3rd business day following the date of the bid until the expiry of the bid if all of the following conditions are satisfied:

> (a) the intention of the offeror,

> > (i) on the date of the bid, is to make purchases and that intention is stated in the bid circular, or

> > (ii) to make purchases changes after the date of the bid and that intention is stated in a news release issued and filed at least one business day prior to making such purchases;

> (b) the number of securities beneficially acquired under this subsection does not exceed 5% of the outstanding securities of that class as at the date of the bid;

> (c) the purchases are made in the normal course on a published market;

> (d) the offeror issues and files a news release immediately after the close of business of the published market on each day on which securities have been purchased under this subsection disclosing the following information:

> > (i) the name of the purchaser;

> > (ii) if the purchaser is a person referred to in paragraph 2.1(b), (c) or (d), the relationship of the purchaser and the offeror;

> > (iii) the number of securities purchased on the day for which the news release is required;

> > (iv) the highest price paid for the securities on the day for which the news release is required;

> > (v) the aggregate number of securities purchased on the published market during the currency of the bid;

> > (vi) the average price paid for the securities that were purchased on the published market during the currency of the bid; and

> > (vii) the total number of securities owned by the purchaser after giving effect to the purchases that are the subject of the news release;

> (e) no broker acting for the offeror performs services beyond the customary broker's functions in regard to the purchases;

> (f) no broker acting for the offeror receives more than the usual fees or commissions in regard to the purchases than are charged for comparable services performed by the broker in the normal course;

> (g) the offeror or any person acting for the offeror does not solicit or arrange for the solicitation of offers to sell securities of the class subject to the bid, except for the solicitation by the offeror or members of the soliciting dealer group under the bid;

> (h) the seller or any person acting for the seller does not, to the knowledge of the offeror, solicit or arrange for the solicitation of offers to buy securities of the class subject to the bid.

(4) For the purposes of paragraph 2.2(3)(b), the acquisition of beneficial ownership of securities that are convertible into securities of the class that is subject to the bid shall be deemed to be an acquisition of the securities as converted.

2.3 Restrictions on acquisitions during issuer bid — (1) An offeror must not offer to acquire, or make or enter into an agreement, commitment or understanding to acquire, beneficial ownership of any securities of the class that are subject to an issuer bid, or securities that are convertible into securities of that class, otherwise than under the bid on and from the day of the announcement of the offeror's intention to make the bid until the expiry of the bid.

(2) Subsection (1) does not prevent the offeror from purchasing, redeeming or otherwise acquiring any securities of the class subject to the bid in reliance on an exemption under paragraph 4.6(a), (b) or (c).

2.4 Restrictions on acquisitions before take-over bid — (1) If, within the period of 90 days immediately preceding a take-over bid, an offeror acquired beneficial ownership of securities of the class subject to the bid in a transaction not generally available on identical terms to holders of that class of securities,

(a) the offeror must offer

(i) consideration for securities deposited under the bid at least equal to and in the same form as the highest consideration that was paid on a per security basis under any such prior transaction, or

(ii) at least the cash equivalent of that consideration, and

(b) the offeror must offer to acquire under the bid that percentage of the securities of the class subject to the bid that is at least equal to the highest percentage that the number of securities acquired from a seller in any such prior transaction was of the total number of securities of that class beneficially owned by that seller at the time of that prior transaction.

(2) Subsection (1) does not apply to a transaction that occurred within 90 days preceding the bid if either of the following conditions are satisfied:

(a) the transaction is a trade in a security of the issuer that had not been previously issued;

(b) the transaction is a trade by or on behalf of the issuer in a previously issued security of that issuer that had been redeemed or purchased by, or donated to, that issuer.

2.5 Restrictions on acquisitions after bid — During the period beginning with the expiry of a take-over bid or an issuer bid and ending at the end of the 20ᵗʰ business day after that, whether or not any securities are taken up under the bid, an offeror must not acquire or offer to acquire beneficial ownership of securities of the class that was subject to the bid except by way of a transaction that is generally available to holders of that class of securities on identical terms.

2.6 Exception — Subsection 2.4(1) and section 2.5 do not apply to purchases made by an offeror in the normal course on a published market if all of the following conditions are satisfied:

(a) no broker acting for the offeror performs services beyond the customary broker's functions in regard to the purchases;

(b) no broker acting for the offeror receives more than the usual fees or commissions in regard to the purchases than are charged for comparable services performed by the broker in the normal course;

(c) the offeror or any person acting for the offeror does not solicit or arrange for the solicitation of offers to sell securities of the class subject to the bid, except for the solicitation by the offeror or members of the soliciting dealer group under the bid;

(d) the seller or any person acting for the seller does not, to the knowledge of the offeror, solicit or arrange for the solicitation of offers to buy securities of the class subject to the bid.

2.7 Restrictions on sales during bid — (1) An offeror, except under a take-over bid or an issuer bid, must not sell, or make or enter into an agreement, commitment or understanding to sell, any securities of the class subject to the bid, or securities that are convertible into securities of that class, beginning on the day of the announcement of the offeror's intention to make the bid until the expiry of the bid.

(2) Despite subsection (1), an offeror may, before the expiry of a bid, make or enter into an agreement, commitment or understanding to sell securities that may be taken up by the offeror under the bid, after the expiry of the bid, if the intention to sell is disclosed in the bid circular.

(3) Subsection (1) does not apply to an offeror under an issuer bid in respect of the issue of securities under a dividend plan, dividend reinvestment plan, employee purchase plan or another similar plan.

DIVISION 2: — MAKING A BID

2.8 Duty to make bid to all security holders — An offeror must make a take-over bid or an issuer bid to all holders of the class of securities subject to the bid who are in the local jurisdiction by sending the bid to

(a) each holder of that class of securities whose last address as shown on the books of the offeree issuer is in the local jurisdiction, and

(b) each holder of securities that, before the expiry of the deposit period referred to in the bid, are convertible into securities of that class, whose last address as shown on the books of the offeree issuer is in the local jurisdiction.

2.9 Commencement of bid — (1) An offeror must commence a take-over bid by

(a) publishing an advertisement containing a brief summary of the take-over bid in at least one major daily newspaper of general and regular paid circulation in the local jurisdiction in English, and in Québec in French or in French and English, or

(b) sending the bid to security holders described in section 2.8.

(2) An offeror must commence an issuer bid by sending the bid to security holders described in section 2.8.

2.10 Offeror's circular — (1) An offeror making a take-over bid or an issuer bid must prepare and send, either as part of the bid or together with the bid, a take-over bid circular or an issuer bid circular, as the case may be, in the following form:

(a) Form 62-104F1 Take-Over Bid Circular, for a take-over bid; or

(b) Form 62-104F2 Issuer Bid Circular, for an issuer bid.

(2) An offeror commencing a take-over bid under paragraph 2.9(1)(a) must,

(a) on or before the date of first publication of the advertisement,

(i) deliver the bid and the bid circular to the offeree issuer's principal office,

(ii) file the bid, the bid circular and the advertisement,

(iii) request from the offeree issuer a list of security holders described in section 2.8, and

(b) not later than 2 business days after receipt of the list of security holders referred to in subparagraph (a)(iii), send the bid and the bid circular to those security holders.

(3) An offeror commencing a take-over bid under paragraph 2.9(1)(b) must file the bid and the bid circular and deliver them to the offeree issuer's principal office on the day the bid is sent, or as soon as practicable after that.

(4) An offeror making an issuer bid must file the bid and the bid circular on the day the bid is sent, or as soon as practicable after that.

2.11 Change in information — (1) If, before the expiry of a take-over bid or an issuer bid or after the expiry of a bid but before the expiry of all rights to withdraw the securities deposited under the bid, a change has occurred in the information contained in the bid circular or any notice of change or notice of variation that would reasonably be expected to affect the decision of the security holders of the offeree issuer to accept or reject the bid, the offeror must promptly

(a) issue and file a news release, and

(b) send a notice of the change to every person to whom the bid was required to be sent and whose securities were not taken up before the date of the change.

(1.1) Despite paragraph (1)(b), an offeror is not required to send a notice of change to a security holder if, under paragraph 2.30(2)(a.1), the security holder is restricted from withdrawing securities that have been deposited under the bid.

(2) Subsection (1) does not apply to a change that is not within the control of the offeror or of an affiliate of the offeror unless it is a change in a material fact relating to the securities being offered in exchange for securities of the offeree issuer.

(3) In this section, a variation in the terms of a bid does not constitute a change in information.

(4) A notice of change must be in the form of Form 62-104F5 Notice of Change or Notice of Variation.

(5) If, under subsection (1), an offeror is required to send a notice of change before the expiry of the initial deposit period

(a) the initial deposit period for the offeror's take-over bid must not expire before 10 days after the date of the notice of change, and

(b) the offeror must not take up securities deposited under the bid before 10 days after the date of the notice of change.

2.12 Variation of terms — (1) If there is a variation in the terms of a take-over bid or an issuer bid, including any reduction of the period during which securities may be deposited under the bid pursuant to section 2.28.2 or section 2.28.3, or any extension of the period during which securities may be deposited under the bid, and whether or not that variation results from the exercise of any right contained in the bid, the offeror must promptly

(a) issue and file a news release, and

(b) send a notice of variation to every person to whom the bid was required to be sent under section 2.8 and whose securities were not taken up before the date of the variation.

(1.1) Despite paragraph (1)(b), an offeror is not required to send a notice of variation to a security holder if, under paragraph 2.30(2)(a.1), the security holder is restricted from withdrawing securities that have been deposited under the bid.

(2) A notice of variation must be in the form of Form 62-104F5 Notice of Change or Notice of Variation.

(3) If there is a variation in the terms of a take-over bid or an issuer bid, the period during which securities may be deposited under the bid must not expire before 10 days after the date of the notice of variation.

(3.1) If, under subsection (1), an offeror is required to send a notice of variation before the expiry of the initial deposit period

(a) the initial deposit period for the offeror's take-over bid must not expire before 10 days after the date of the notice of variation, and

(b) the offeror must not take up securities deposited under the bid before 10 days after the date of the notice of variation.

(4) Subsections (1), (3) and (3.1) do not apply to a variation in the terms of a bid consisting solely of the waiver of a condition in the bid and any extension of the bid, other than an extension in respect of the mandatory 10-day extension period, resulting from the waiver where the consideration offered for the securities consists solely of cash, but in that case the offeror must promptly issue and file a news release announcing the waiver.

(5) An offeror must not make a variation in the terms of an issuer bid, other than a variation that is the waiver by the offeror of a condition that is specifically stated in the bid as being waivable at the sole option of the offeror, after the expiry of the period, including any extension of the period, during which the securities may be deposited under the bid.

(6) An offeror must not make a variation in the terms of a take-over bid, other than a variation to extend the time during which securities may be deposited under the bid or a variation to increase the consideration offered for the securities subject to the bid, after the offeror becomes obligated to take up securities deposited under the bid in accordance with section 2.32.1.

2.13 Filing and sending notice of change or notice of variation — A notice of change or notice of variation in respect of a take-over bid or an issuer bid must be filed and, in the case of a take-over bid, delivered to the offeree issuer's principal office, on the day the notice of change or notice of variation is sent to security holders of the offeree issuer, or as soon as practicable after that.

2.14 Change or variation in advertised take-over bid — (1) If a change or variation occurs to a take-over bid that was commenced by means of an advertisement, and if the offeror has complied with paragraph 2.10(2)(a) but has not yet sent the bid and the bid circular under paragraph 2.10(2)(b), the offeror must

(a) publish an advertisement that contains a brief summary of the change or variation in at least one major daily newspaper of general and regular paid circulation in the local jurisdiction in English, and in Québec in French or in French and English,

(b) concurrently with the date of first publication of the advertisement,

(i) file the advertisement, and

(ii) file and deliver a notice of change or notice of variation to the offeree issuer's principal office, and

(c) subsequently send the bid, the bid circular and the notice of change or notice of variation to the security holders of the offeree issuer before the expiration of the period set out in paragraph 2.10(2)(b).

(2) If an offeror satisfies the requirements of subsection (1), the notice of change or notice of variation is not required to be filed and delivered under section 2.13.

2.15 Consent of expert — bid circular — (1) In this section and section 2.21, an expert includes a notary in Québec, solicitor, auditor, accountant, engineer, geologist or appraiser or any other person whose profession or business gives authority to a report, valuation, statement or opinion made by that person.

(2) If a report, valuation, statement or opinion of an expert is included in or accompanies a bid circular or any notice of change or notice of variation to the circular, the written consent of the expert to the use of the report, valuation, statement or opinion must be filed concurrently with the bid circular, notice of change or notice of variation.

2.16 Delivery and date of bid documents — (1) A take-over bid, an issuer bid, a bid circular and every notice of change or notice of variation must be

(a) mailed by pre-paid mail to the intended recipient, or

(b) delivered to the intended recipient by personal delivery, courier or other manner acceptable to the regulator or securities regulatory authority.

(2) Except for a take-over bid commenced by means of an advertisement in accordance with paragraph 2.9(1)(a), a bid, bid circular, notice of change or notice of variation sent in accordance with this section is deemed to be dated as of the date it was sent to all or substantially all of the persons entitled to receive it.

(3) If a take-over bid is commenced by means of an advertisement in accordance with paragraph 2.9(1)(a), a bid, bid circular, notice of change or notice of variation is deemed to have been dated as of the date of first publication of the relevant advertisement.

DIVISION 3: — OFFEREE ISSUER'S OBLIGATIONS

2.17 Duty to prepare and send directors' circular — (1) If a take-over bid has been made, the board of directors of the offeree issuer must prepare and send, not later than 15 days after the date of the bid, a directors' circular to every person to whom the bid was required to be sent under section 2.8.

(2) The board of directors of the offeree issuer must evaluate the terms of the take-over bid and, in the directors' circular,

(a) must recommend to security holders that they accept or reject the bid and state the reasons for the recommendation,

(b) must advise security holders that the board is unable to make, or is not making, a recommendation and state the reasons for being unable to make a recommendation or for not making a recommendation, or

(c) must advise security holders that the board is considering whether to make a recommendation to accept or reject the bid, must state the reasons for not making a recommendation in the directors' circular and may advise security holders that they should not deposit their securities under the bid until they receive further communication from the board of directors in accordance with paragraph (a) or (b).

(3) If paragraph (2)(c) applies, the board of directors must communicate to security holders a recommendation to accept or reject the bid or the decision that it is unable to make, or is not making, a recommendation, together with the reasons for the recommendation or decision, at least 7 days before the scheduled expiry of the initial deposit period.

(4) A directors' circular must be in the form of Form 62-104F3 Directors' Circular.

2.18 Notice of change — (1) If, before the expiry of a take-over bid or after the expiry of a take-over bid but before the expiry of all rights to withdraw the securities deposited under the bid, a change has occurred in the information contained in a directors' circular or in any notice of change to the directors' circular that would reasonably be expected to affect the decision of the security holders to accept or reject the bid, the board of directors of the offeree issuer must promptly issue and file a news release relating to the change and send a notice of the change to every person to whom the take-over bid was required to be sent disclosing the nature and substance of the change.

(2) A notice of change must be in the form of Form 62-104F5 Notice of Change or Notice of Variation.

2.19 Filing directors' circular or notice of change — The board of directors of the offeree issuer must concurrently file the directors' circular or a notice of change in relation to it and deliver it to the principal office of the offeror not later than the date on which it is sent to the security holders of the offeree issuer, or as soon as practicable after that date.

2.20 Individual director's or officer's circular — (1) An individual director or officer may recommend acceptance or rejection of a take-over bid if the director or officer sends with the recommendation a separate director's or officer's circular to every person to whom the take-over bid was required to be sent under section 2.8.

(2) If, before the expiry of a take-over bid or after the expiry of a take-over bid but before the expiry of all rights to withdraw the securities deposited under the bid, a change has occurred in the information contained in a director's or officer's circular or any notice of change in relation to it that would reasonably be expected to affect the decision of the security holders to accept or reject the bid, other than a change that is not within the control of the director or officer, as the case may be, that director or officer must promptly send a notice of change to every person to whom the take-over bid was required to be sent under section 2.8.

(3) A director's or officer's circular must be in the form of Form 62-104F4 Director's or Officer's Circular.

(4) A director's or officer's obligation to send a circular under subsection (1) or to send a notice of change under subsection (2) may be satisfied by sending the circular or the notice of change, as the case may be, to the board of directors of the offeree issuer.

(5) If a director or officer sends to the board of directors of the offeree issuer a circular under subsection (1) or a notice of change under subsection (2), the board, at the offeree issuer's expense, must promptly send a copy of the circular or notice to every person to whom the take-over bid was required to be sent under section 2.8.

(6) The board of directors of the offeree issuer or the individual director or officer, as the case may be, must concurrently file the director's or officer's circular or a notice of change in relation to it and send it to the principal office of the offeror not later than the date on which it is sent to the security holders of the offeree issuer, or as soon as practicable after that.

(7) A notice of change in relation to a director's or officer's circular must be in the form of Form 62-104F5 Notice of Change or Notice of Variation.

2.21 Consent of expert — directors' circular/individual director's or officer's circular — If a report, valuation, statement or opinion of an expert is included in or accompanies a directors' circular, an individual director's or officer's circular or any notice of change to either circular, the written consent of the expert to the use of the report, valuation, statement or opinion must be filed concurrently with the circular or notice.

2.22 Delivery and date of offeree issuer's documents — (1) A directors' circular, an individual director's or officer's circular and every notice of change must be

    (a) mailed by pre-paid mail to the intended recipient, or

    (b) delivered to the intended recipient by personal delivery, courier or other manner acceptable to the regulator or securities regulatory authority.

(2) Any circular or notice sent in accordance with this section is deemed to be dated as of the date it was sent to all or substantially all of the persons entitled to receive it.

DIVISION 4: — OFFEROR'S OBLIGATIONS

2.23 Consideration — (1) If a take-over bid or an issuer bid is made, all holders of the same class of securities must be offered identical consideration.

(2) Subsection (1) does not prohibit an offeror from offering an identical choice of consideration to all holders of the same class of securities.

(3) If a variation in the terms of a take-over bid or an issuer bid before the expiry of the bid increases the value of the consideration offered for the securities subject to the bid, the offeror must pay that increased consideration to each person whose securities are taken up under the bid, whether or not the securities were taken up by the offeror before the variation of the bid.

2.24 Prohibition against collateral agreements — If a person makes or intends to make a take-over bid or an issuer bid, the person or any person acting jointly or in concert with that person must not enter into any collateral agreement, commitment or understanding that has the effect, directly or indirectly, of providing a security holder of the offeree issuer with consideration of greater value than that offered to the other security holders of the same class of securities.

2.25 Collateral agreements — exception — (1) Section 2.24 does not apply to an employment compensation arrangement, severance arrangement or other employment benefit arrangement that provides

    (a) an enhancement of employee benefits resulting from participation by the security holder of the offeree issuer in a group plan, other than an incentive plan, for employees of a successor to the business of the offeree issuer, if the benefits provided by the group plan are generally provided to employees of the successor to the business of the offeree issuer who hold positions of a similar nature to the position held by the security holder, or

    (b) a benefit not described in paragraph (a) that is received solely in connection with the security holder's services as an employee, director or consultant of the offeree issuer, of an affiliated entity of the offeree issuer, or of a successor to the business of the offeree issuer, if

        (i) at the time the bid is publicly announced, the security holder and its associates beneficially own or exercise control or direction over less than 1% of the outstanding securities of each class of securities of the offeree issuer subject to the bid, or

        (ii) an independent committee of directors of the offeree issuer, acting in good faith, has determined that

            (A) the value of the benefit, net of any offsetting costs to the security holder, is less than 5% of the amount referred to in paragraph 3(a), or

            (B) the security holder is providing at least equivalent value in exchange for the benefit.

(2) In order to rely on an exception under paragraph (1)(b) the following conditions must be satisfied:

    (a) the benefit is not conferred for the purpose, in whole or in part, of increasing the amount of the consideration paid to the security holder for securities deposited under the bid or providing an incentive to deposit under the bid;

    (b) the conferring of the benefit is not, by its terms, conditional on the security holder supporting the bid in any manner; and

    (c) full particulars of the benefit are disclosed in the issuer bid circular or, in the case of a take-over bid, in the take-over bid circular or directors' circular.

(3) In order to rely on an exception under subparagraph 1(b)(ii) the following conditions must be satisfied:

    (a) the security holder receiving the benefit has disclosed to the independent committee the amount of consideration that the security holder expects it will be beneficially entitled to receive under the terms of the bid in exchange for the securities beneficially owned by the security holder; and

    (b) the determination of the independent committee under subparagraph 1(b)(ii) is disclosed in the issuer bid circular or, in the case of a take-over bid, in the take-over bid circular or directors' circular.

(4) In this section, in determining the beneficial ownership of securities of a holder at a given date, any security or right or obligation permitting or requiring the security holder or any person acting jointly or in concert with the security holder, whether or not on conditions, to acquire a security, including an unissued security, of a particular class within 60 days by a single transaction or a series of linked transactions is deemed to be a security of a particular class.

2.26 Proportionate take up and payment — issuer bids — (1) If an issuer bid is made for less than all of the class of securities subject to the bid and a greater number of securities is deposited under the bid than the offeror is bound or willing to acquire under the bid, the offeror must take up and pay for the securities proportionately, disregarding fractions, according to the number of securities deposited by each security holder.

(2) Subsection (1) does not prohibit an offeror from acquiring securities under the terms of an issuer bid that, if not acquired, would constitute less than a standard trading unit for the security holder.

(3) Subsection (1) does not apply to securities deposited under the terms of an issuer bid by security holders who

    (a) are entitled to elect a minimum price per security, within a range of prices, at which they are willing to sell their securities under the bid, and

    (b) elect a minimum price which is higher than the price that the offeror pays for securities under the bid.

2.26.1 Proportionate take up and payment — take-over bids — (1) If a greater number of securities is deposited under a partial take-over bid than the offeror is bound or willing to acquire under the bid, the offeror must take up and pay for the securities proportionately, disregarding fractions, according to the number of securities deposited by each security holder.

(2) For the purposes of subsection (1), any securities acquired in a pre-bid transaction to which subsection 2.4(1) applies are deemed to have been deposited under the take-over bid by the person who was the seller in the pre-bid transaction.

2.27 Financing arrangements — (1) If a take-over bid or an issuer bid provides that the consideration for the securities deposited under the bid is to be paid in cash or partly in cash, the offeror must make adequate arrangements before the bid to ensure that the required funds are available to make full payment for the securities that the offeror has offered to acquire.

(2) The financing arrangements required to be made under subsection (1) may be subject to conditions if, at the time the take-over bid or the issuer bid is commenced, the offeror reasonably believes the possibility to be remote that, if the conditions of the bid are satisfied or waived, the offeror will be unable to pay for the securities deposited under the bid due to a financing condition not being satisfied.

DIVISION 5: — BID MECHANICS

2.28 Minimum deposit period — issuer bids — An offeror must allow securities to be deposited under an issuer bid for a minimum deposit period of at least 35 days from the date of the bid.

2.28.1 Minimum deposit period — take-over bids — An offeror must allow securities to be deposited under a take-over bid for an initial deposit period of at least 105 days from the date of the bid.

2.28.2 Shortened deposit period — deposit period news release — (1) Despite section 2.28.1, if at or after the time an offeror announces a take-over bid, the offeree issuer issues a deposit period news release in respect of the offeror's take-over bid, the offeror must allow securities to be deposited under its take-over bid for an initial deposit period of at least the number of days from the date of the bid as stated in the deposit period news release.

(2) Despite section 2.28.1, an offeror, other than an offeror under subsection (1), must allow securities to be deposited under its take-over bid for an initial deposit period of at least the number of days from the date of the bid as stated in the deposit period news release if either of the following applies:

> (a) the offeror commenced the take-over bid in respect of securities of the offeree issuer before the issuance of the deposit period news release referred to in subsection (1) and the bid has yet to expire;

> (b) the offeror, after the issuance of the deposit period news release referred to in subsection (1), commences a take-over bid in respect of securities of the offeree issuer and the bid is commenced before one of the following:

>> (i) the date of expiry of the take-over bid referred to in subsection (1),

>> (ii) the date of expiry of another take-over bid referred to in paragraph (a).

(3) For the purposes of subsections (1) and (2), an offeror must not allow securities to be deposited under its take-over bid for an initial deposit period of less than 35 days from the date of the bid.

2.28.3 Shortened deposit period — alternative transaction — Despite section 2.28.1, if an issuer issues a news release announcing that it intends to effect an alternative transaction, whether pursuant to an agreement or otherwise, an offeror must allow securities to be deposited under its take-over bid for an initial deposit period of at least 35 days from the date of the bid if either of the following applies:

> (a) the offeror commenced the take-over bid in respect of securities of the offeree issuer before the issuance of the news release and the bid has yet to expire;

> (b) the offeror, after the issuance of the news release, commences a take-over bid in respect of securities of the offeree issuer and the bid is commenced before one of the following:

>> (i) the date of completion or abandonment of the alternative transaction,

>> (ii) the date of expiry of another take-over bid referred to in paragraph (a).

2.29 Restriction on take up — issuer bids — An offeror must not take up securities deposited under an issuer bid until the expiration of 35 days from the date of the bid.

2.29.1 Restriction on take up — take-over bids — An offeror must not take up securities deposited under a take-over bid unless all of the following apply:

> (a) a period of 105 days, or the number of days determined in accordance with section 2.28.2 or section 2.28.3, has elapsed from the date of the bid;

> (b) all the terms and conditions of the bid have been complied with or waived;

> (c) more than 50% of the outstanding securities of the class that are subject to the bid, excluding securities beneficially owned, or over which control or direction is exercised, by the offeror or by any person acting jointly or in concert with the offeror, have been deposited under the bid and not withdrawn.

2.30 Withdrawal of securities — (1) A security holder may withdraw securities deposited under a take-over bid or an issuer bid

> (a) at any time before the securities have been taken up by the offeror,

> (b) at any time before the expiration of 10 days from the date of a notice of change under section 2.11 or a notice of variation under section 2.12, or

> (c) if the securities have not been paid for by the offeror within 3 business days after the securities have been taken up.

(1.1) Despite paragraph (1)(a), if an offeror that has made a partial take-over bid becomes obligated to take up securities under subsection 2.32.1(1), a security holder must not withdraw securities deposited before the expiry of the initial deposit period and not taken up by the offeror in reliance on subsection 2.32.1(6) during the period

> (a) commencing at the time the offeror became obligated to take up securities under subsection 2.32.1(1), and

> (b) ending at the time the offeror becomes obligated under either subsection 2.32.1(7) or (8) to take up securities not taken up by the offeror in reliance on subsection 2.32.1(6).

(2) Despite paragraph (1)(b), a security holder must not withdraw securities deposited if

> (a) the securities have been taken up by the offeror before the date of the notice of change or notice of variation,

(a.1) in the case of a partial take-over bid, the securities were deposited before the expiry of the initial deposit period and not taken up by the offeror in reliance on subsection 2.32.1(6) and the date of the notice of change or notice of variation is after the date that the offeror became obligated to take up securities under subsection 2.32.1(1), or

(b) any of the following apply:

(i) there is a variation in the terms of a take-over bid or issuer bid consisting solely of an increase in consideration offered for the securities and an extension of the time for deposit to not later than 10 days after the date of the notice of variation;

(ii) there is a variation in the terms of a take-over bid or issuer bid consisting solely of the waiver of one or more of the conditions of the bid where the consideration offered for the securities subject to the take-over bid or the issuer bid consists solely of cash;

(iii) in the case of a take-over bid, there is a variation in the terms after the expiry of the initial deposit period consisting of either an increase in the consideration offered for the securities subject to the bid or an extension of the time for deposit to not later than 10 days from the date of the notice of variation.

(3) The withdrawal of any securities under subsection (1) is made by sending a written notice to the depository designated in the bid circular and becomes effective on its receipt by the depository.

(4) If notice is given in accordance with subsection (3), the offeror must promptly return the securities to the security holder.

2.31 Effect of market purchases — If an offeror purchases securities under subsection 2.2(3), the purchased securities must not be counted in determining whether the minimum tender requirement in paragraph 2.29.1(c) is satisfied and the purchase does not reduce the number of securities the offeror is bound to take up under the take-over bid.

2.31.1 Mandatory 10-day extension period — take-over bids — If, at the expiry of the initial deposit period, an offeror is obligated to take up securities deposited under a take-over bid pursuant to subsection 2.32.1(1), the offeror must

(a) extend the period during which securities may be deposited under the bid for a period of at least 10 days, and

(b) promptly issue and file a news release disclosing the following:

(i) that the minimum tender requirement specified in paragraph 2.29.1(c) has been satisfied,

(ii) the number of securities deposited and not withdrawn as at the expiry of the initial deposit period,

(iii) that the period during which securities may be deposited under the bid has been extended for the mandatory 10-day extension period, and

(iv) in the case of a take-over bid that

(A) is not a partial take-over bid, that the offeror will immediately take up the deposited securities and pay for securities taken up as soon as possible, and in any event not later than 3 business days after the securities are taken up, or

(B) is a partial take-over bid, that the offeror will take up and pay for the deposited securities proportionately in accordance with applicable securities legislation and in any event will take up the deposited securities not later than one business day after the expiry of the mandatory 10-day extension period and pay for securities taken up as soon as possible and in any event not later than 3 business days after the securities are taken up.

2.31.2 Time limit on extension — partial take-over bids — In the case of a partial take-over bid,

(a) the mandatory 10-day extension period must not exceed 10 days, and

(b) the bid must not be extended after the expiry of the mandatory 10-day extension period.

2.32 Obligation to take up and pay for deposited securities — issuer bids — (1) If all the terms and conditions of an issuer bid have been complied with or waived, the offeror must take up and pay for securities deposited under the bid not later than 10 days after the expiry of the bid or at the time required by subsection (2) or (3), whichever is earliest.

(2) An offeror must pay for any securities taken up under an issuer bid as soon as possible, and in any event not later than 3 business days after securities deposited under the bid are taken up.

(3) Securities deposited under an issuer bid subsequent to the date on which the offeror first takes up securities deposited under the bid must be taken up and paid for by the offeror not later than 10 days after the deposit of securities.

(4) An offeror must not extend its issuer bid if all the terms and conditions of the bid have been complied with or waived, unless the offeror first takes up all securities deposited under the bid and not withdrawn.

(5) Despite subsections (3) and (4), if an issuer bid is made for less than all of the class of securities subject to the bid, an offeror is required to take up, by the times specified in those subsections, only the maximum number of securities that the offeror can take up without contravening section 2.23 or section 2.26 at the expiry of the bid.

(6) Despite subsection (4), if the offeror waives any terms or conditions of an issuer bid and extends the bid in circumstances where the rights of withdrawal conferred by paragraph 2.30(1)(b) are applicable, the bid must be extended without the offeror first taking up the securities which are subject to the rights of withdrawal.

2.32.1 Obligation to take up and pay for deposited securities — take-over bids — (1) An offeror must immediately take up securities deposited under a take-over bid if, at the expiry of the initial deposit period, all of the following apply:

(a) the deposit period referred to in section 2.28.1, section 2.28.2 or section 2.28.3, as applicable, has elapsed;

(b) all the terms and conditions of the bid have been complied with or waived;

(c) the requirement in paragraph 2.29.1(c) is satisfied.

(2) An offeror must pay for any securities taken up under a take-over bid as soon as possible, and in any event not later than 3 business days after the securities deposited under the bid are taken up.

(3) In the case of a take-over bid that is not a partial take-over bid, securities deposited under the bid during the mandatory 10-day extension period, or an extension period made after the mandatory 10-day extension period, must be taken up and paid for by the offeror not later than 10 days after the deposit of securities.

(4) In the case of a take-over bid that is not a partial take-over bid, an offeror must not extend its bid beyond the expiry of the mandatory 10-day extension period unless the offeror first takes up all securities deposited under the bid and not withdrawn.

(5) Despite subsection (4), if the offeror extends the bid in circumstances where the rights of withdrawal conferred by paragraph 2.30(1)(b) are applicable, the offeror must extend the bid without the offeror first taking up the securities which are subject to the rights of withdrawal.

(6) Despite subsection (1), an offeror that has made a partial take-over bid is required to take up, by the time specified in that subsection, only the maximum number of securities that the offeror can take up without contravening section 2.23 or section 2.26.1 at the expiry of the bid.

(7) In the case of a partial take-over bid, securities deposited before the expiry of the initial deposit period and not taken up by the offeror in reliance on subsection (6), and securities deposited during the mandatory 10-day extension period, must be taken up by the offeror, in the manner required under section 2.26.1, not later than one business day after the expiry of the mandatory 10-day extension period.

(8) Despite subsection (7), if at the expiry of the mandatory 10-day extension period rights of withdrawal conferred by paragraph 2.30(1)(b) are applicable, securities deposited before the expiry of the initial deposit period and not taken up by the offeror in reliance on subsection (6), and securities deposited during the mandatory 10-day extension period, must be taken up by the offeror, in the manner required under section 2.26.1, not later than one business day after the expiry of the withdrawal period conferred by paragraph 2.30(1)(b).

2.33 Return of deposited securities — If, following the expiry of a take-over bid or an issuer bid, an offeror knows that it will not take up securities deposited under the bid, the offeror must promptly issue and file a news release to that effect and return the securities to the security holders.

2.34 News release on expiry of bid — If all the terms and conditions of a take-over bid or an issuer bid have been complied with or waived, the offeror must issue and file a news release to that effect promptly after the expiry of the bid, and the news release must disclose

(a) the approximate number of securities deposited, and

(b) the approximate number that will be taken up.

PART 3: — GENERAL

3.1 Language of bid documents — (1) A person must file a document required under this Instrument in French or English.

(2) In Québec, a take-over bid circular, issuer bid circular, directors' circular, director's or officer's circular, notice of change or notice of variation required under Part 2 must be in French or in French and English.

(3) Subsection (1) does not apply to an exempt take-over bid made under section 4.4, or an exempt issuer bid made under section 4.10.

(4) Despite subsection (1), if a person files a document only in French or English, but delivers to a security holder a version of the document in the other language, the person must file that other version not later than when it is first delivered to the security holder.

3.2 Filing of documents — (1) An offeror making a take-over bid under Part 2 must file copies of the following documents, and any amendments to those documents:

(a) any agreement between the offeror and a security holder of the offeree issuer relating to the take-over bid, including any agreement to the effect that the security holder will deposit its securities to the take-over bid made by the offeror;

(b) any agreement between the offeror and directors or officers of an offeree issuer relating to the take-over bid;

(c) any agreement between the offeror and an offeree issuer relating to the take-over bid;

(d) any other agreement of which the offeror is aware that could affect control of the offeree issuer, including any agreement with change of control provisions, any security holder agreement or any voting trust agreement, that the offeror has access to and can reasonably be regarded as material to a security holder in deciding whether to deposit securities under the bid.

(2) An offeree issuer whose securities are the subject of a take-over bid under Part 2 must file copies of any agreement of which the offeree issuer is aware that could affect control of the offeree issuer, including an agreement with change of control provisions, a security holder agreement or a voting trust agreement, that the offeree issuer has access to and can reasonably be regarded as material to a security holder in deciding whether to deposit securities under the bid.

(3) The documents required to be filed

(a) under subsection (1) must be filed on the day the take-over bid circular is filed under section 2.10, and

(b) under subsection (2) must be filed on the day that the directors' circular is filed under section 2.19.

(4) If an agreement required to be filed under subsection (1) or (2) is entered into after a take-over bid circular referred to in subsection (1) or the directors' circular referred to in subsection (2) is filed, the agreement must be filed promptly but not later than 2 business days from the date that the agreement was entered into.

(5) If a document required to be filed under subsection (1) or (2) has already been filed in electronic format under National Instrument 13-101 *System for Electronic Document Analysis and Retrieval* (SEDAR), the requirement to file the document may be satisfied by filing a letter describing the document and stating the filing date and project number.

(6) A document dated before March 30, 2004 that is required to be filed under subsection (1) or (2) may be filed in paper format if it does not exist in an acceptable electronic format under National Instrument 13-101 *System for Electronic Document Analysis and Retrieval* (SEDAR).

(7) A provision in a document required to be filed under subsection (1) or (2) may be omitted or marked so as to be unreadable if

(a) the filer has reasonable grounds to believe that disclosure of the provision would be seriously prejudicial to the interests of the filer or would violate confidentiality provisions,

(b) the provision does not contain information relating to the filer or its securities that would be necessary to understand the document, and

(c) in the copy of the document filed by the filer, the filer includes a brief description of the information that has been omitted or marked so as to be unreadable immediately after the provision that has been omitted or marked.

3.3 Certification of bid circulars — (1) A bid circular or a notice of change or notice of variation in respect of the bid circular required under this Instrument must contain a certificate of the offeror in the required form signed

    (a) if the offeror is a person other than an individual, by each of the following:

        (i) the chief executive officer or, in the case of a person that does not have a chief executive officer, the individual who performs similar functions to a chief executive officer,

        (ii) the chief financial officer or, in the case of a person that does not have a chief financial officer, the individual who performs similar functions to a chief financial officer, and

        (iii) 2 directors, other than the chief executive officer and the chief financial officer, who are duly authorized by the board of directors of that person to sign on behalf of the board of directors, or

    (b) if the offeror is an individual, by the individual.

(2) For the purposes of subsection (1)(a), if the offeror has fewer than 4 directors and officers, the certificate must be signed by all of the directors and officers.

(3) A directors' circular or a notice of change in respect of a directors' circular required under this Instrument must contain a certificate of the board of directors of the offeree issuer in the required form signed by 2 directors who are duly authorized by the board of directors of that person to sign on behalf of the board of directors.

(4) Every person that files and sends an individual director's or officer's circular or a notice of change in respect of an individual director's or officer's circular under this Instrument must ensure that the circular or notice contains a certificate in the required form and signed by or on behalf of the director or officer sending the circular or notice.

(5) If the regulator or securities regulatory authority is satisfied that either or both of the chief executive officer or chief financial officer cannot sign a certificate required under this Instrument, the regulator or securities regulatory authority may accept a certificate signed by another officer or director.

3.4 Obligation to provide security holder list — (1) If a person makes or proposes to make a take-over bid under Part 2 for a class of securities of an issuer that is not otherwise required by law to provide a list of its security holders to the person, the issuer must provide a list of holders of that class of securities, and any known holder of an option or right to acquire securities of that class, to enable the person to carry out the bid in compliance with this Instrument.

(2) For the purposes of subsection (1), section 21 of the *Canada Business Corporations Act* applies with necessary modifications to the person making or proposing to make the take-over bid and to the issuer, except that the affidavit that accompanies the request for the list of security holders must state that the list will not be used except in connection with a bid made under Part 2 for securities of the issuer.

Part 4: — Exemptions

Division 1: — Exempt Take-Over Bids

4.1 Normal course purchase exemption — A take-over bid is exempt from Part 2 if all of the following conditions are satisfied:

    (a) the bid is for not more than 5% of the outstanding securities of a class of securities of the offeree issuer;

    (b) the aggregate number of securities acquired in reliance on this exemption by the offeror and any person acting jointly or in concert with the offeror within any period of 12 months, when aggregated with acquisitions otherwise made by the offeror and any person acting jointly or in concert with the offeror within the same 12-month period, other than under a bid that is subject to Part 2, does not exceed 5% of the securities of that class outstanding at the beginning of the 12-month period;

    (c) there is a published market for the class of securities that are the subject of the bid;

    (d) the value of the consideration paid for any of the securities acquired is not in excess of the market price at the date of acquisition, as determined in accordance with section 1.11, plus reasonable brokerage fees or commissions actually paid.

4.2 Private agreement exemption — (1) A take-over bid is exempt from Part 2 if all of the following conditions are satisfied:

    (a) purchases are made from not more than 5 persons in the aggregate, including persons located outside the local jurisdiction;

    (b) the bid is not made generally to security holders of the class of securities that is the subject of the bid, so long as there are more than 5 security holders of the class;

    (c) if there is a published market for the securities acquired, the value of the consideration paid for any of the securities, including brokerage fees or commissions, is not greater than 115% of the market price of the securities at the date of the bid as determined in accordance with section 1.11;

    (d) if there is no published market for the securities acquired, there is a reasonable basis for determining that the value of the consideration paid for any of the securities is not greater than 115% of the value of the securities.

(2) In subsection (1), if an offeror makes an offer to acquire securities from a person and the offeror knows or ought to know after reasonable enquiry that

    (a) the person acquired the securities in order that the offeror might make use of the exemption under subsection (1), then each person from whom those securities were acquired must be included in the determination of the number of persons to whom an offer to acquire has been made, or

    (b) the person from whom the acquisition is being made is acting as a nominee, agent, trustee, executor, administrator or other legal representative for one or more other persons having a direct beneficial interest in those securities, then each of those other persons must be included in the determination of the number of persons to whom an offer to acquire has been made.

(3) Despite paragraph (2)(b), a trust or estate is to be considered a single security holder in the determination of the number of persons to whom an offer to acquire has been made if

    (a) an inter vivos trust has been established by a single settlor, or

    (b) an estate has not vested in all persons who are beneficially entitled to it.

4.3 Non-reporting issuer exemption — A take-over bid is exempt from Part 2 if all of the following conditions are satisfied:

(a) the offeree issuer is not a reporting issuer;

(b) there is no published market for the securities that are the subject of the bid;

(c) the number of security holders of that class of securities at the commencement of the bid is not more than 50, exclusive of holders who

(i) are in the employment of the offeree issuer or an affiliate of the offeree issuer, or

(ii) were formerly in the employment of the offeree issuer or in the employment of an entity that was an affiliate of the offeree issuer at the time of that employment, and who while in that employment were, and have continued after that employment to be, security holders of the offeree issuer.

4.4 Foreign take-over bid exemption — A take-over bid is exempt from Part 2 if all of the following conditions are satisfied:

(a) security holders whose last address as shown on the books of the offeree issuer is in Canada hold less than 10% of the outstanding securities of the class subject to the bid at the commencement of the bid;

(b) the offeror reasonably believes that security holders in Canada beneficially own less than 10% of the outstanding securities of the class subject to the bid at the commencement of the bid;

(c) the published market on which the greatest volume of trading in securities of that class occurred during the 12 months immediately preceding the commencement of the bid was not in Canada;

(d) security holders in the local jurisdiction are entitled to participate in the bid on terms at least as favourable as the terms that apply to the general body of security holders of the same class;

(e) at the same time as material relating to the bid is sent by or on behalf of the offeror to security holders of the class that is subject to the bid, the material is filed and sent to security holders whose last address as shown on the books of the offeree issuer is in the local jurisdiction;

(f) if the bid materials referred to in paragraph (e) are not in English, a brief summary of the key terms of the bid prepared in English, and in Québec in French or French and English, is filed and sent to security holders whose last address as shown on the books of the offeree issuer is in the local jurisdiction at the same time as the bid materials are filed and sent;

(g) if no material relating to the bid is sent by or on behalf of the offeror to security holders of the class that is subject to the bid but a notice or advertisement of the bid is published by or on behalf of the offeror in the jurisdiction where the offeree issuer is incorporated or organized, an advertisement of the bid specifying where and how security holders may obtain a copy of, or access to, the bid documents is filed and published in English, and in Québec in French or French and English, in at least one major daily newspaper of general and regular paid circulation in the local jurisdiction.

4.5 De minimis exemption — A take-over bid is exempt from Part 2 if all of the following conditions are satisfied:

(a) the number of beneficial owners of securities of the class subject to the bid in the local jurisdiction is fewer than 50;

(b) the securities held by the beneficial owners referred to in paragraph (a) constitute, in aggregate, less than 2% of the outstanding securities of that class;

(c) security holders in the local jurisdiction are entitled to participate in the bid on terms at least as favourable as the terms that apply to the general body of security holders of the same class;

(d) at the same time as material relating to the bid is sent by or on behalf of the offeror to security holders of the class that is subject to the bid, the material is filed and sent to security holders whose last address as shown on the books of the offeree issuer is in the local jurisdiction.

DIVISION 2: — EXEMPT ISSUER BIDS

4.6 Issuer acquisition or redemption exemption — An issuer bid for a class of securities is exempt from Part 2 if any of the following conditions are satisfied:

(a) the securities are purchased, redeemed or otherwise acquired in accordance with the terms and conditions attaching to the class of securities that permit the purchase, redemption or acquisition of the securities by the issuer without the prior agreement of the owners of the securities, or the securities are acquired to meet sinking fund or purchase fund requirements;

(b) the purchase, redemption or other acquisition is required by the terms and conditions attaching to the class of securities or by the statute under which the issuer was incorporated, organized or continued;

(c) the terms and conditions attaching to the class of securities contain a right of the owner to require the issuer of the securities to redeem, repurchase, or otherwise acquire the securities, and the securities are acquired under the exercise of the right.

4.7 Employee, executive officer, director and consultant exemption — An issuer bid is exempt from Part 2 if the securities are acquired from a current or former employee, executive officer, director or consultant of the issuer or of an affiliate of the issuer and, if there is a published market in respect of the securities,

(a) the value of the consideration paid for any of the securities acquired is not greater than the market price of the securities at the date of the acquisition, determined in accordance with section 1.11, and

(b) the aggregate number of securities or, in the case of convertible debt securities, the aggregate principal amount of securities acquired by the issuer within any period of 12 months in reliance on the exemption provided by this paragraph does not exceed 5% of the securities of that class outstanding at the beginning of the 12-month period.

4.8 Normal course issuer bid exemptions — (1) In this section, "designated exchange" means the Toronto Stock Exchange, the TSX Venture Exchange or other exchange recognized or designated by the securities regulatory authorities for the purpose of this Instrument.

(2) An issuer bid that is made in the normal course through the facilities of a designated exchange is exempt from Part 2 if the bid is made in accordance with the bylaws, rules, regulations and policies of that exchange.

(3) An issuer bid that is made in the normal course on a published market, other than a designated exchange, is exempt from Part 2 if all of the following conditions are satisfied:

(a) the bid is for not more than 5% of the outstanding securities of a class of securities of the issuer;

(b) the aggregate number of securities or, in the case of convertible debt securities, the aggregate principal amount of securities acquired in reliance on this exemption by the issuer and any person acting jointly or in concert with the issuer within any 12-month period does not exceed 5% of the securities of that class outstanding at the beginning of the 12-month period;

(c) the value of the consideration paid for any of the securities acquired is not in excess of the market price at the date of acquisition as determined in accordance with section 1.11, plus reasonable brokerage fees or commissions actually paid.

(4) An issuer making a bid under subsection (2) must promptly file any news release required to be issued by the designated exchange.

(5) An issuer making a bid under subsection (3) must issue and file, at least 5 days before the commencement of the bid, a news release containing the following information:

(a) the class and number of securities or principal amount of debt securities sought;

(b) the dates, if known, on which the issuer bid will commence and expire;

(c) the value, in Canadian dollars, of the consideration offered per security;

(d) the manner in which the securities will be acquired; and

(e) the reasons for the issuer bid.

4.9 Non-reporting issuer exemption — An issuer bid is exempt from Part 2 if all of the following conditions are satisfied:

(a) the issuer is not a reporting issuer;

(b) there is no published market for the securities that are the subject of the bid;

(c) the number of security holders of that class of securities at the commencement of the bid is not more than 50, exclusive of holders who

(i) are in the employment of the issuer or an affiliate of the issuer, or

(ii) were formerly in the employment of the issuer or in the employment of an entity that was an affiliate of the issuer at the time of that employment, and who while in that employment were, and have continued after the employment to be, security holders of the issuer.

4.10 Foreign issuer bid exemption — An issuer bid is exempt from Part 2 if all of the following conditions are satisfied:

(a) security holders whose last address as shown on the books of the offeree issuer is in Canada hold less than 10% of the outstanding securities of the class subject to the bid at the commencement of the bid;

(b) the offeror reasonably believes that security holders in Canada beneficially own less than 10% of the outstanding securities of the class subject to the bid at the commencement of the bid;

(c) the published market on which the greatest volume of trading in securities of that class occurred during the 12 months immediately preceding the commencement of the bid was not in Canada;

(d) security holders in the local jurisdiction are entitled to participate in the bid on terms at least as favourable as the terms that apply to the general body of security holders of the same class;

(e) at the same time as material relating to the bid is sent by or on behalf of the offeror to security holders of the class that is subject to the bid, the material is filed and sent to security holders whose last address as shown on the books of the offeree issuer is in the local jurisdiction;

(f) if the bid materials referred to in paragraph (e) are not in English, a brief summary of the key terms of the bid prepared in English, and in Québec in French or French and English, is filed and sent to security holders whose last address as shown on the books of the offeree issuer is in the local jurisdiction at the same time as the bid materials are filed and sent;

(g) if no material relating to the bid is sent by or on behalf of the offeror to security holders of the class that is subject to the bid but a notice or advertisement of the bid is published by or on behalf of the offeror in the jurisdiction where the offeree issuer is incorporated or organized, an advertisement of the bid specifying where and how security holders may obtain a copy of, or access to, the bid documents is filed and published in English, and in Québec in French or French and English, in at least one major daily newspaper of general and regular paid circulation in the local jurisdiction.

4.11 De minimis exemption — An issuer bid is exempt from the requirements of Part 2 if all of the following conditions are satisfied:

(a) the number of beneficial owners of the class of securities subject to the bid in the local jurisdiction is fewer than 50;

(b) the securities held by the beneficial owners referred to in paragraph (a) constitute, in aggregate, less than 2% of the outstanding securities of that class;

(c) security holders in the local jurisdiction are entitled to participate in the bid on terms at least as favourable as the terms that apply to the general body of security holders of the same class;

(d) at the same time as material relating to the bid is sent by or on behalf of the offeror to security holders of the class that is subject to the bid, the material is filed and sent to security holders whose last address as shown on the books of the offeree issuer is in the local jurisdiction.

PART 5: — REPORTS AND ANNOUNCEMENTS OF ACQUISITIONS

5.1 Definitions and Interpretation — (1) In this Part,

"acquiror" means a person who acquires a security, other than by way of a take-over bid or an issuer bid made in compliance with Part 2;

"acquiror's securities" means securities of an issuer beneficially owned, or over which control or direction is exercised, on the date of the acquisition or disposition, by an acquiror or any person acting jointly or in concert with the acquiror;

"specified securities lending arrangement" means a securities lending arrangement if all of the following apply:

(a) the material terms of the securities lending arrangement are set out in a written agreement;

(b) the securities lending arrangement requires the borrower to pay to the lender amounts equal to all dividends or interest payments, if any, paid on the security that would have been received by the lender if the lender had held the security throughout the period beginning at the date of the transfer or loan and ending at the time the security or an identical security is transferred or returned to the lender;

(c) the lender has established policies and procedures that require the lender to maintain a record of all securities that it has transferred or lent under securities lending arrangements;

(d) the written agreement referred to in paragraph (a) provides for any of the following:

(i) the lender has an unrestricted right to recall all securities that it has transferred or lent under the securities lending arrangement, or an equal number of identical securities, before the record date for voting at any meeting of securityholders at which the securities may be voted;

(ii) the lender requires the borrower to vote the securities transferred or lent in accordance with the lender's instructions;

"securities lending arrangement" means an arrangement between a lender and a borrower with respect to which both of the following apply:

(a) the lender transfers or lends a security to the borrower;

(b) at the time that the security is lent or transferred, the lender and the borrower reasonably expect that the borrower will, at a later date, transfer or return to the lender the security or an identical security.

(2) For the purposes of this Part, if an acquiror and one or more persons acting jointly or in concert with the acquiror acquire or dispose of securities, the securities are deemed to be acquired or disposed of, as applicable, by the acquiror.

5.2 Early warning — (1) An acquiror who acquires beneficial ownership of, or control or direction over, voting or equity securities of any class of a reporting issuer, or securities convertible into voting or equity securities of any class of a reporting issuer, that, together with the acquiror's securities of that class, constitute 10% or more of the outstanding securities of that class, must

(a) promptly, and, in any event, no later than the opening of trading on the business day following the acquisition, issue and file a news release containing the information required by section 3.1 of National Instrument 62-103 *The Early Warning System and Related Take-Over Bid and Insider Reporting Issues*, and

(b) promptly, and, in any event, no later than 2 business days from the date of the acquisition, file a report containing the information required by section 3.1 of National Instrument 62-103 *The Early Warning System and Related Take-Over Bid and Insider Reporting Issues*.

(2) An acquiror who is required to make disclosure under subsection (1) must make further disclosure, in accordance with subsection (1), each time any of the following events occur:

(a) the acquiror or any person acting jointly or in concert with the acquiror, acquires or disposes beneficial ownership of, or acquires or ceases to have control or direction over, either of the following:

(i) securities in an amount equal to 2% or more of the outstanding securities of the class of securities that was the subject of the most recent report required to be filed by the acquiror under subsection (1) or under this subsection;

(ii) securities convertible into 2% or more of the outstanding securities referred to in subparagraph (i);

(b) there is a change in a material fact contained in the most recent report required to be filed under paragraph (1)(b) or under paragraph (a) of this subsection.

(3) An acquiror must issue and file a news release and file a report in accordance with subsection (1) if beneficial ownership of, or control or direction over, the outstanding securities of the class of securities that was the subject of the most recent report required to be filed by the acquiror under this section decreases to less than 10%.

(4) If an acquiror issues and files a news release and files a report under subsection (3), the requirements under subsection (2) do not apply unless subsection (1) applies in respect of a subsequent acquisition of beneficial ownership of, or control or direction over, voting or equity securities of any class of a reporting issuer, or securities convertible into voting or equity securities of any class of a reporting issuer, that, together with the acquiror's securities of that class, constitute 10% or more of the outstanding securities of that class.

5.3 Moratorium provisions — (1) During the period beginning on the occurrence of an event in respect of which a report is required to be filed under section 5.2 and ending on the expiry of the first business day following the date that the report is filed, an acquiror, or any person acting jointly or in concert with the acquiror, must not acquire or offer to acquire beneficial ownership of, or control or direction over, any securities of the class in respect of which the report is required to be filed or any securities convertible into securities of that class.

(2) Subsection (1) does not apply to an acquiror that has beneficial ownership of, or control or direction over, securities that, together with the acquiror's securities of that class, constitute 20% or more of the outstanding securities of that class.

5.4 Acquisitions during bid — (1) If, after a take-over bid or an issuer bid has been made under Part 2 for voting or equity securities of a reporting issuer and before the expiry of the bid, an acquiror acquires beneficial ownership of, or control or direction over, securities of the class subject to the bid which, when added to the acquiror's securities of that class, constitute 5% or more of the outstanding securities of that class, the acquiror must, before the opening of trading on the next business day, issue and file a news release containing the information required by subsection (3).

(2) An acquiror must issue and file an additional news release in accordance with subsection (3) before the opening of trading on the next business day each time the acquiror, or any person acting jointly or in concert with the acquiror, acquires beneficial ownership of, or control or direction over, in aggregate, an additional 2% or more of the outstanding securities of the class of securities that was the subject of the most recent news release required to be filed by the acquiror under this section.

(3) A news release or further news release required under subsection (1) or (2) must set out

(a) the name of the acquiror,

(b) the number of securities of the offeree issuer that were beneficially acquired, or over which control or direction was acquired, in the transaction that gave rise to the requirement under subsection (1) or (2) to issue the news release,

(c) the number of securities and the percentage of outstanding securities of the offeree issuer that the acquiror and all persons acting jointly or in concert with the acquiror, have beneficial ownership of, or control or direction over, immediately after the acquisition described in paragraph (b),

(d) the number of securities of the offeree issuer that were beneficially acquired, or over which control or direction was acquired, by the acquiror and all persons acting jointly or in concert with the acquiror, since the commencement of the bid,

(e) the name of the market in which the acquisition described in paragraph (b) took place, and

(f) the purpose of the acquiror and all persons acting jointly or in concert with the acquiror in making the acquisition described in paragraph (b), including any intention of the acquiror and all persons acting jointly or in concert with the acquiror to increase the beneficial ownership of, or control or direction over, any of the securities of the offeree issuer.

5.5 Duplicate news release not required — If the facts in respect of which a news release is required to be filed under sections 5.2 and 5.4 are identical, a news release is required only under the provision requiring the earlier news release.

5.6 Copies of news release and report — An acquiror that files a news release or report under section 5.2 or 5.4 must promptly send a copy of each filing to the reporting issuer.

5.7 Exception — Sections 5.2, 5.3 and 5.4 do not apply to either of the following:

(a) an acquiror that is a lender in respect of securities transferred or lent pursuant to a specified securities lending arrangement;

(b) an acquiror that is a borrower in respect of securities or identical securities borrowed, disposed of or acquired in connection with a securities lending arrangement if all of the following apply:

(i) the borrowed securities are disposed of by the borrower no later than 3 business days from the date of the transfer or loan;

(ii) the borrower will at a later date acquire the securities or identical securities and transfer or return those securities to the lender;

(iii) the borrower does not intend to vote and does not vote the securities or identical securities during the period beginning on the date of the transfer or loan and ending at the time the securities or identical securities are transferred or returned to the lender.

PART 6: — EXEMPTIONS

6.1 Exemption — general — (1) The regulator or the securities regulatory authority may grant an exemption from the provisions of this Instrument, in whole or in part, subject to such conditions or restrictions as may be imposed in the exemption.

(2) Despite subsection (1), in Ontario, only the regulator may grant such an exemption.

(3) Except in Alberta and Ontario, an exemption referred to in subsection (1) is granted under the statute referred to in Appendix B of National Instrument 14-101 *Definitions* opposite the name of the local jurisdiction.

6.2 Exemption — collateral benefit — (1) The regulator or the securities regulatory authority may decide for the purposes of section 2.24 that an agreement, commitment or understanding with a selling security holder is made for reasons other than to increase the value of the consideration paid to a selling security holder for the securities of the selling security holder and that the agreement, commitment or understanding may be entered into despite that section.

(2) Despite subsection (1), in Ontario, only the regulator may make such a decision.

PART 7: — TRANSITION AND COMING INTO FORCE

7.1 Transition — The take-over bid or issuer bid provisions in securities legislation that were in force immediately before May 9, 2016, continue to apply in respect of

(a) every take-over bid and issuer bid commenced before May 9, 2016,

(b) any take-over bid in respect of the securities of an offeree issuer subject to a take-over bid referred to in paragraph (a) commenced on or subsequent to May 9, 2016 and prior to the date of the expiry of a take-over bid referred to in paragraph (a), and

(c) any take-over bid in respect of the securities of an issuer that issued a news release before May 9, 2016 announcing that it intends to effect an alternative transaction, whether pursuant to an agreement or otherwise, commenced on or subsequent to May 9, 2016 and prior to the date of completion or abandonment of the alternative transaction.

7.2 Coming into force — (1) Except in Ontario, this Instrument comes into force on February 1, 2008.

(2) In Ontario, this Instrument comes into force on the later of the following:

(a) May 9, 2016;

(b) the day on which sections 1, 2 and 3, subsections 4(2) and (3), and sections 5, 7, 8 and 10 of Schedule 18 of the *Budget Measures Act, 2015* (Ontario) are proclaimed into force.

Form 62-104F1 — Take-Over Bid Circular

Part 1 — General Provisions

(a) — Defined terms

If a term is used but not defined in this Form, refer to Part 1 of National Instrument 62-104 *Take-Over Bids and Issuer Bids* (the Instrument) and to National Instrument 14-101 *Definitions*.

(b) — Incorporating information by reference

If you are qualified to file a short form prospectus under sections 2.2 to 2.7 of National Instrument 44-101 *Short Form Prospectus Distributions*, or by reason of an exemption granted by a securities regulatory authority, you may incorporate information required under item 19 to be included in your take-over bid circular by reference to another document. Clearly identify the referenced document or any excerpt of it that you incorporate into your take-over bid circular. Unless you have already filed the referenced document, you must file it with your take-over bid circular. You must also disclose that the document is on SEDAR at www.sedar.com and that, on request, you will promptly provide a copy of the document free of charge to a security holder of the offeree issuer.

(c) — Plain language

Write the take-over bid circular so that readers are able to understand it and make informed investment decisions. Offerors should apply plain language principles when they prepare a take-over bid circular including:

- using short sentences;

- using definite everyday language;

- using the active voice;

- avoiding superfluous words;

- organizing the document into clear, concise sections, paragraphs and sentences;
- avoiding jargon;
- using personal pronouns to speak directly to the reader;
- avoiding reliance on glossaries and defined terms unless it facilitates understanding of the disclosure;
- avoiding vague boilerplate wording;
- avoiding abstract terms by using more concrete terms or examples;
- avoiding multiple negatives;
- using technical terms only when necessary and explaining those terms;
- using charts, tables and examples where it makes disclosure easier to understand.

If you use technical terms, explain them in a clear and concise manner.

(d) — Numbering and headings

The numbering, headings and ordering of items included in this Form are guidelines only. You do not need to include the heading or numbering or follow the order of items in this Form. You do not need to refer to inapplicable items and, unless otherwise required in this Form, you may omit negative answers to items. Disclosure provided in response to any item need not be repeated elsewhere in the circular.

Part 2 — Contents of Take-Over Bid Circular

Item 1. — Name and description of offeror

State the corporate name of the offeror or, if the offeror is an unincorporated entity, the full name under which it exists and carries on business, and give a brief description of its activities.

Item 2. — Name of offeree issuer

State the corporate name of the offeree issuer or, if the offeree issuer is an unincorporated entity, the full name under which it exists and carries on business.

Item 3. — Securities subject to the bid

State the class and number of securities that are the subject of the take-over bid and a description of the rights of the holders of any other class of securities that have a right to participate in the offer.

Item 4. — Time period

State the dates on which the take-over bid will commence and expire.

Item 5. — Consideration

State the consideration to be offered. If the consideration includes securities, state the particulars of the designation, rights, privileges, restrictions and conditions attaching to those securities.

Item 6. — Ownership of securities of offeree issuer

State the number, designation and percentage of the outstanding securities of any class of securities of the offeree issuer beneficially owned or over which control or direction is exercised

    (a) by the offeror,

    (b) by each director and officer of the offeror, and

    (c) if known after reasonable enquiry, by

        (i) each associate or affiliate of an insider of the offeror,

        (ii) an insider of the offeror, other than a director or officer of the offeror, and

        (iii) any person acting jointly or in concert with the offeror.

In each case where no securities are owned, directed or controlled, state this fact.

Item 7. — Trading in securities of offeree issuer

State, if known after reasonable enquiry, the following information about any securities of the offeree issuer purchased or sold by the persons referred to in item 6 during the 6-month period preceding the date of the take-over bid:

    (a) the description of the security;

    (b) the number of securities purchased or sold;

    (c) the purchase or sale price of the security;

    (d) the date of the transaction.

If no such securities were purchased or sold, state this fact.

Item 8. — Commitments to acquire securities of offeree issuer

Disclose all agreements, commitments or understandings made by the offeror, and, if known after reasonable enquiry, by the persons referred to in item 6 to acquire securities of the offeree issuer, and the terms and conditions of those agreements, commitments or understandings.

Item 9. — Terms and conditions of the bid

State the terms of the take-over bid. If the obligation of the offeror to take up and pay for securities under the take-over bid is conditional, state the particulars of each condition.

Item 9.1. — Minimum Tender Requirement and Mandatory Extension Period

State the following in italics and boldface type at the top of the cover page of the take-over bid circular:

No securities tendered to this bid will be taken up until (a) more than 50% of the outstanding securities of the class sought (excluding those securities beneficially owned, or over which control or direction is exercised by the offeror or any person acting jointly or in concert with the offeror) have been tendered to the bid, (b) the minimum deposit period required under applicable securities laws has elapsed, and (c) any and all other conditions of the bid have been complied with or waived, as applicable. If these criteria are met, the offeror will take up securities deposited under the bid in accordance with applicable securities laws and extend its bid for an additional minimum period of 10 days to allow for further deposits of securities.

Item 10. — Payment for deposited securities

State the particulars of the method and time of payment of the consideration.

Item 11. — Right to withdraw deposited securities

Describe the withdrawal rights of the security holders of the offeree issuer under the take-over bid. State that the withdrawal is made by sending a written notice to the designated depository and becomes effective on its receipt by the depository.

Item 12. — Source of funds

State the source of any funds to be used for payment of deposited securities. If the funds are to be borrowed, state

    (a) the name of the lender,

    (b) the terms and financing conditions of the loan,

    (c) the circumstances under which the loan must be repaid, and

    (d) the proposed method of repayment.

Item 13. — Trading in securities to be acquired

Provide a summary showing

    (a) the name of each principal market on which the securities sought are traded,

    (b) any change in a principal market that is planned following the take-over bid, including but not limited to listing or de-listing on an exchange,

    (c) where reasonably ascertainable, in reasonable detail, the volume of trading and price range of the class of the securities in the 6-month period preceding the date of the take-over bid, or, in the case of debt securities, the prices quoted on each principal market, and

    (d) the date that the take-over bid to which the circular relates was announced to the public and the market price of the securities immediately before that announcement.

Item 14. — Arrangements between the offeror and the directors and officers of offeree issuer

Disclose the particulars of any agreement, commitment or understanding made or proposed to be made between the offeror and any of the directors or officers of the offeree issuer, including particulars of any payment or other benefit proposed to be made or given by way of compensation for loss of office or their remaining in or retiring from office if the take-over bid is successful.

Item 15. — Arrangements between the offeror and security holders of offeree issuer

(1) Disclose the particulars of any agreement, commitment or understanding made or proposed to be made between the offeror and a security holder of the offeree issuer relating to the bid, including a description of its purpose, its date, the identity of the parties, and its terms and conditions. Disclosure with respect to each agreement, commitment or understanding, other than an agreement that a security holder will tender securities to a take-over bid made by the offeror, must include

    (a) a detailed explanation as to how the offeror determined entering into it was not prohibited by section 2.24 of the Instrument, or

    (b) disclosure of the exception to, or exemption from, the prohibition against collateral agreements relied on by the offeror and the facts supporting that reliance.

(2) If the offeror is relying on an exception to the prohibition against collateral agreements under subparagraph 2.25(1)(b)(ii) of the Instrument, and if the information is available to the offeror, disclose the review process undertaken by the independent committee of directors of the issuer and the basis on which the independent committee made its determination under clause 2.25(1)(b)(ii)(A) or (B) of the Instrument.

Item 16. — Arrangements with or relating to the offeree issuer

Disclose the particulars of any agreement, commitment or understanding made between the offeror and the offeree issuer relating to the take-over bid and any other agreement, commitment or understanding of which the offeror is aware that could affect control of the offeree issuer, including an agreement with change of control provisions, a security holder agreement or a voting trust agreement that the offeror has access to and that can reasonably be regarded as material to a security holder in deciding whether to deposit securities under the bid.

Item 17. — Purpose of the bid

State the purpose of the take-over bid. Disclose the particulars of any plans or proposals for

    (a) subsequent transactions involving the offeree issuer such as a going private transaction, or

    (b) material changes in the affairs of the offeree issuer, including, for example, any proposal to liquidate the offeree issuer, to sell, lease or exchange all or a substantial part of its assets, to amalgamate it with any other business organization or to make any material changes in its business, corporate structure (debt or equity), management or personnel.

Item 18. — Valuation

If the take-over bid is an insider bid, as defined in applicable securities legislation, include the disclosure regarding valuations required by securities legislation.

Item 19. — Securities of an offeror or other issuer to be exchanged for securities of offeree issuer

(1) If a take-over bid provides that the consideration for the securities of the offeree issuer is to be, in whole or in part, securities of the offeror or other issuer, include the financial statements and other information required in a prospectus of the issuer whose securities are being offered in exchange for the securities of the offeree issuer.

(2) For the purposes of subsection (1), provide the pro forma financial statements that would be required in a prospectus assuming that

 (a) the likelihood of the offeror completing the acquisition of securities of the offeree issuer is high, and

 (b) the acquisition is a significant acquisition for the offeror.

(3) Despite subsection (1), the financial statements of the offeree issuer are not required to be included in the circular.

Item 20. — Right of appraisal and acquisition

State any rights of appraisal the security holders of the offeree issuer have under the laws or constating document governing, or contracts binding, the offeree issuer and state whether or not the offeror intends to exercise any right of acquisition the offeror may have.

Item 21. — Market purchases of securities

State whether or not the offeror intends to purchase in the market securities that are the subject of the take-over bid.

Item 22. — Approval of take-over bid circular

If the take-over bid is made by or on behalf of an offeror that has directors, state that the take-over bid circular has been approved and its sending has been authorized by the directors.

Item 23. — Other material facts

Describe

 (a) any material facts concerning the securities of the offeree issuer, and

 (b) any other matter not disclosed in the take-over bid circular that has not previously been generally disclosed, is known to the offeror, and that would reasonably be expected to affect the decision of the security holders of the offeree issuer to accept or reject the offer.

Item 24. — Solicitations

Disclose any person retained by or on behalf of the offeror to make solicitations in respect of the take-over bid and the particulars of the compensation arrangements.

Item 25. — Statement of rights

Include the following statement of rights provided under the securities legislation of the jurisdictions relating to this circular:

 Securities legislation in the provinces and territories of Canada provides security holders of the offeree issuer with, in addition to any other rights they may have at law, one or more rights of rescission, price revision or to damages, if there is a misrepresentation in a circular or notice that is required to be delivered to those security holders. However, such rights must be exercised within prescribed time limits. Security holders should refer to the applicable provisions of the securities legislation of their province or territory for particulars of those rights or consult a lawyer.

Item 26. — Certificate

A take-over bid circular certificate form must state:

 The foregoing contains no untrue statement of a material fact and does not omit to state a material fact that is required to be stated or that is necessary to make a statement not misleading in the light of the circumstances in which it was made.

Item 27. — Date of take-over bid circular

Specify the date of the take-over bid circular.

Form 62-104F2 — Issuer Bid Circular

Part 1 — General Provisions

(a) — Defined terms

If a term is used but not defined in this Form, refer to Part 1 of National Instrument 62-104 *Take-Over Bids and Issuer Bids* (the Instrument) and to National Instrument 14-101 *Definitions*.

(b) — Incorporating information by reference

If you are qualified to file a short form prospectus under sections 2.2 to 2.7 of National Instrument 44-101 *Short Form Prospectus Distributions*, or by reason of an exemption granted by a securities regulatory authority, you may incorporate information required under item 21 to be included in your issuer bid circular by reference to another document. Clearly identify the referenced document or any excerpt of it that you incorporate into your issuer bid circular. Unless you have already filed the referenced document, you must file it with your issuer bid circular. You must also disclose that the document is on SEDAR at www.sedar.com and that, on request, you will promptly provide a copy of the document free of charge to a security holder of the issuer.

(c) — Plain language

Write the issuer bid circular so that readers are able to understand it and make informed investment decisions. Issuers should apply plain language principles when they prepare an issuer bid circular including:

* using short sentences;

* using definite everyday language;

* using the active voice;

* avoiding superfluous words;

- organizing the document into clear, concise sections, paragraphs and sentences;
- avoiding jargon;
- using personal pronouns to speak directly to the reader;
- avoiding reliance on glossaries and defined terms unless it facilitates understanding of the disclosure;
- avoiding vague boilerplate wording;
- avoiding abstract terms by using more concrete terms or examples;
- avoiding multiple negatives;
- using technical terms only when necessary and explaining those terms;
- using charts, tables and examples where it makes disclosure easier to understand.

If you use technical terms, explain them in a clear and concise manner.

(d) — Numbering and headings

The numbering, headings and ordering of items included in this Form are guidelines only. You do not need to include the heading or numbering or follow the order of items in this Form. You do not need to refer to inapplicable items and, unless otherwise required in this Form, you may omit negative answers to items. Disclosure provided in response to any item need not be repeated elsewhere in the circular.

Part 2 — Contents of Issuer Bid Circular

Item 1. — Name of issuer

State the corporate name of the issuer or, if the issuer is an unincorporated entity, the full name under which it exists and carries on business.

Item 2. — Securities subject to the bid

State the class and number of securities that are the subject of the issuer bid and a description of the rights of the holders of any other class of securities that have a right to participate in the offer. Where the number of securities sought under the bid is subject to additional purchases by the issuer for the purpose of preventing security holders from being left with less than a standard trading unit, disclose this fact.

Where the issuer intends to rely on the exception from the proportionate take up and payment requirements found in subsection 2.26(3) of the Instrument relating to "dutch auctions", the issuer is not required to disclose the number of securities that are the subject of the issuer bid if the issuer discloses a maximum amount the issuer intends to spend making purchases pursuant to the bid.

Item 3. — Time period

State the dates on which the issuer bid will commence and expire.

Item 4. — Consideration

State the consideration to be offered. If the consideration includes securities, state the particulars of the designation, rights, privileges, restrictions and conditions attaching to those securities.

Item 5. — Payment for deposited securities

State the particulars of the method and time of payment of the consideration.

Item 6. — Right to withdraw deposited securities

Describe the right to withdraw securities deposited under the issuer bid. State that the withdrawal is made by sending a written notice to the designated depository and becomes effective on its receipt by the depository.

Item 7. — Source of funds

State the source of any funds to be used for payment of deposited securities. If the funds are to be borrowed, state

    (a) the name of the lender,

    (b) the terms and financing conditions of the loan,

    (c) the circumstances under which the loan must be repaid, and

    (d) the proposed method of repayment.

Item 8. — Participation

If the issuer bid is for less than all of the outstanding securities of that class, state that if a greater number or principal amount of the securities are deposited than the issuer is bound or willing to take up and pay for, the issuer will take up as nearly as may be proportionately, disregarding fractions, according to the number or principal amount of the securities deposited. To the extent that this is not the case, as permitted by securities legislation, the response to this item should be modified accordingly.

If an issuer intends to rely on one or both of the exceptions from the proportionate take up and payment requirements found in subsections 2.26(2) and (3) of the Instrument relating to standard trading units and "dutch auctions", describe the mechanism under which securities would be deposited and taken up without proration.

Item 9. — Purpose of the bid

State the purpose for the issuer bid, and if it is anticipated that the issuer bid will be followed by a going private transaction or other transaction such as a business combination, describe the proposed transaction.

Item 10. — Trading in securities to be acquired

Provide a summary showing

(a) the name of each principal market on which the securities sought are traded,

(b) any change in a principal market that is planned following the issuer bid,

(c) where reasonably ascertainable, in reasonable detail, the volume of trading and price range of the class of the securities in the 6-month period preceding the date of the issuer bid, or, in the case of debt securities, the prices quoted on each principal market, and

(d) the date that the issuer bid to which the circular relates was announced to the public and the market price of the securities of the issuer immediately before that announcement.

Item 11. — Ownership of securities of issuer

State the number, designation and the percentage of the outstanding securities of any class of securities of the issuer beneficially owned or over which control or direction is exercised

(a) by each director and officer of the issuer, and

(b) if known after reasonable enquiry, by

(i) each associate or affiliate of an insider of the issuer,

(ii) each associate or affiliate of the issuer,

(iii) an insider of the issuer, other than a director or officer of the issuer, and

(iv) each person acting jointly or in concert with the issuer.

In each case where no securities are owned, directed or controlled, state this fact.

Item 12. — Commitments to acquire securities of issuer

Disclose all agreements, commitments or understandings made by the issuer and, if known after reasonable enquiry, by the persons referred to in item 11, to acquire securities of the issuer, and the terms and conditions of those agreements, commitments or understandings.

Item 13. — Acceptance of issuer bid

If known after reasonable enquiry, state the name of every person named in item 11 who has accepted or intends to accept the issuer bid and the number of securities in respect of which the person has accepted or intends to accept the issuer bid.

Item 14. — Benefits from the bid

State the direct or indirect benefits to any of the persons named in item 11 of accepting or refusing the issuer bid.

Item 15. — Material changes in the affairs of issuer

Disclose the particulars of any plans or proposals for material changes in the affairs of the issuer, including, for example, any contract or agreement under negotiation, any proposal to liquidate the issuer, to sell, lease or exchange all or a substantial part of its assets, to amalgamate it or to make any material changes in its business, corporate structure (debt or equity), management or personnel.

Item 16. — Other benefits

If any material changes or subsequent transactions are contemplated, as described in item 9 or 15, state any specific benefit, direct or indirect, as a result of such changes or transactions to any of the persons named in item 11.

Item 17. — Arrangements between the issuer and security holders

(1) Disclose the particulars of any agreement, commitment or understanding made or proposed to be made between the issuer and a security holder of the issuer relating to the bid, including a description of its purpose, its date, the identity of the parties, and its terms and conditions. Disclosure with respect to each agreement, commitment or understanding, other than an agreement that a security holder will tender securities to an issuer bid, must include

(a) a detailed explanation as to how the issuer determined entering into it was not prohibited by section 2.24 of the Instrument, or

(b) disclosure of the exception to, or exemption from, the prohibition against collateral agreements relied on by the issuer and the facts supporting that reliance.

(2) If the issuer is relying on an exception to the prohibition against collateral agreements under subparagraph 2.25(1)(b)(ii) of the Instrument, and if the information is available to the issuer, disclose the review process undertaken by the independent committee of directors of the issuer and the basis on which the independent committee made its determination under clause 2.25(1)(b)(ii)(A) or (B) of the Instrument.

Item 18. — Previous purchases and sales

State the following information about any securities of the issuer purchased or sold by the issuer during the twelve months preceding the date of the issuer bid, excluding securities purchased or sold pursuant to the exercise of employee stock options, warrants and conversion rights:

(a) the description of the security,

(b) the number of securities purchased or sold,

(c) the purchase or sale price of the security, and

(d) the date and purpose of each transaction.

If no securities were purchased or sold, state this fact.

Item 19. — Financial statements

If the most recently available interim financial report is not included, include a statement that the most recent interim financial report will be sent without charge to any security holder requesting them.

Item 20. — Valuation

If a valuation is required by applicable securities legislation, include the disclosure regarding valuations required by securities legislation.

Item 21. — Securities of issuer to be exchanged for others

If an issuer bid provides that the consideration for the securities of the issuer is to be, in whole or in part, different securities of the issuer, include the financial and other information prescribed for a prospectus of the issuer.

Item 22. — Approval of issuer bid circular

State that the issuer bid circular has been approved by the issuer's directors, disclosing the name of any individual director of the issuer who has informed the directors in writing of their opposition to the issuer bid and that the delivery of the issuer bid circular to the security holders of the issuer has been authorized by the issuer's directors.

If the issuer bid is part of a transaction or to be followed by a transaction required to be approved by minority security holders, state the nature of the approval required.

Item 23. — Previous distribution

If the securities of the class subject to the issuer bid were distributed during the 5 years preceding the issuer bid, state the distribution price per share and the aggregate proceeds received by the issuer or selling security holder.

Item 24. — Dividend policy

State the frequency and amount of dividends with respect to shares of the issuer during the 2 years preceding the date of the issuer bid, any restrictions on the issuer's ability to pay dividends and any plan or intention to declare a dividend or to alter the dividend policy of the issuer.

Item 25. — Tax consequences

Provide a general description of the income tax consequences in Canada of the issuer bid to the issuer and to the security holders of any class affected.

Item 26. — Expenses of bid

Provide a statement of the expenses incurred or to be incurred in connection with the issuer bid.

Item 27. — Right of appraisal and acquisition

State any rights of appraisal the security holders of the issuer have under the laws or constating documents governing, or contracts binding, the issuer and state whether or not the issuer intends to exercise any right of acquisition the issuer may have.

Item 28. — Statement of rights

Include the following statement of rights provided under the securities legislation of the jurisdictions relating to this circular:

> *Securities legislation in the provinces and territories of Canada provides security holders of the offeree issuer with, in addition to any other rights they may have at law, one or more rights of rescission, price revision or to damages, if there is a misrepresentation in a circular or notice that is required to be delivered to those security holders. However, such rights must be exercised within prescribed time limits. Security holders should refer to the applicable provisions of the securities legislation of their province or territory for particulars of those rights or consult a lawyer.*

Item 29. — Other material facts

Describe

(a) any material facts concerning the securities of the issuer, and

(b) any other matter not disclosed in the issuer bid circular that has not previously been generally disclosed, is known to the issuer, and that would reasonably be expected to affect the decision of the security holders of the issuer to accept or reject the offer.

Item 30. — Solicitations

Disclose any person retained by or on behalf of the issuer to make solicitations in respect of the issuer bid and the particulars of the compensation arrangements.

Item 31. — Certificate

An issuer bid circular certificate form must state:

> *The foregoing contains no untrue statement of a material fact and does not omit to state a material fact that is required to be stated or that is necessary to make a statement not misleading in the light of the circumstances in which it was made.*

Item 32. — Date of issuer bid circular

Specify the date of the issuer bid circular.

Form 62-104F3 — Directors' Circular

Part 1 — General Provisions

(a) — Defined terms

If a term is used but not defined in this Form, refer to Part 1 of National Instrument 62-104 *Take-Over Bids and Issuer Bids* (the Instrument) and to National Instrument 14-101 *Definitions*.

(b) — Plain language

Write the directors' circular so that readers are able to understand it and make informed investment decisions. Directors should apply plain language principles when they prepare a directors' circular including:

- using short sentences;
- using definite everyday language;

- using the active voice;

- avoiding superfluous words;

- organizing the document into clear, concise sections, paragraphs and sentences;

- avoiding jargon;

- using personal pronouns to speak directly to the reader;

- avoiding reliance on glossaries and defined terms unless it facilitates understanding of the disclosure;

- avoiding vague boilerplate wording;

- avoiding abstract terms by using more concrete terms or examples;

- avoiding multiple negatives;

- using technical terms only when necessary and explaining those terms;

- using charts, tables and examples where it makes disclosure easier to understand.

If you use technical terms, explain them in a clear and concise manner.

(c) — Numbering and headings

The numbering, headings and ordering of items included in this Form are guidelines only. You do not need to include the heading or numbering or follow the order of items in this Form. You do not need to refer to inapplicable items and, unless otherwise required in this Form, you may omit negative answers to items. Disclosure provided in response to any item need not be repeated elsewhere in the circular.

Part 2 — Contents of Directors' Circular

Item 1. — Name of offeror

State the corporate name of the offeror or, if the offeror is an unincorporated entity, the full name under which it exists and carries on business.

Item 2. — Name of offeree issuer

State the corporate name of the offeree issuer or, if the offeree issuer is an unincorporated entity, the full name under which it exists and carries on business.

Item 3. — Names of directors of the offeree issuer

State the name of each director of the offeree issuer.

Item 4. — Ownership of securities of offeree issuer

State the number, designation and the percentage of the outstanding securities of any class of securities of the offeree issuer beneficially owned or over which control or direction is exercised

    (a) by each director and officer of the offeree issuer, and

    (b) if known after reasonable enquiry, by

        (i) each associate or affiliate of an insider of the offeree issuer,

        (ii) each associate or affiliate of the offeree issuer,

        (iii) an insider of the offeree issuer, other than a director or officer of the offeree issuer, and

        (iv) each person acting jointly or in concert with the offeree issuer.

In each case where no securities are owned, directed or controlled, state this fact.

Item 5. — Acceptance of take-over bid

If known after reasonable enquiry, state the name of every person named in item 4 who has accepted or intends to accept the offer and the number of securities in respect of which such person has accepted or intends to accept the offer.

Item 6. — Ownership of securities of offeror

If a take-over bid is made by or on behalf of an offeror that is an issuer, state the number, designation and percentage of the outstanding securities of any class of securities of the offeror beneficially owned or over which control or direction is exercised

    (a) by the offeree issuer,

    (b) by each director and officer of the offeree issuer, and

    (c) if known after reasonable enquiry, by

        (i) each associate or affiliate of an insider of the offeree issuer,

        (ii) each affiliate or associate of the offeree issuer, and

        (iii) an insider of the offeree issuer, other than a director or officer of the offeree issuer, and

        (iv) each person acting jointly or in concert with the offeree issuer.

In each case where no securities are so owned, directed or controlled, state this fact.

Item 7. — Relationship between the offeror and the directors and officers of the offeree issuer

Disclose the particulars of any agreement, commitment or understanding made or proposed to be made between the offeror and any of the directors or officers of the offeree issuer, including particulars of any payment or other benefit proposed to be made or given by way of compensation for loss of office or their remaining in or retiring from office if the take-over bid is successful. State also whether any directors or officers of the offeree issuer are also directors or officers of the offeror or any subsidiary of the offeror and identify those persons.

Item 8. — Arrangements between offeree issuer and officers and directors

Disclose the particulars of any agreement, commitment or understanding made or proposed to be made between the offeree issuer and any of the directors or officers of the offeree issuer, including particulars of any payment or other benefit proposed to be made or given by way of compensation for loss of office or their remaining in or retiring from office if the take-over bid is successful.

Item 9. — Arrangements between the offeror and security holders of offeree issuer

(1) If not already disclosed in the take-over bid circular, disclose the particulars of any agreement, commitment or understanding made or proposed to be made between the offeror and a security holder of the offeree issuer relating to the bid, including a description of its purpose, its date, the identity of the parties, and its terms and conditions. Disclosure with respect to each agreement, commitment or understanding, other than an agreement that a security holder will tender securities to a take-over bid made by the offeror, must include

    (a) a detailed explanation as to how the offeror determined entering into it was not prohibited by section 2.24 of the Instrument, or

    (b) disclosure of the exception to, or exemption from, the prohibition against collateral agreements relied on by the offeror and the facts supporting that reliance.

(2) If the offeror is relying on an exception to the prohibition against collateral agreements under subparagraph 2.25(1)(b)(ii) of the Instrument, and if not already disclosed in the take-over bid circular, disclose the review process undertaken by the independent committee of directors of the issuer and the basis on which the independent committee made its determination under clause 2.25(1)(b)(ii)(A) or (B) of the Instrument.

Item 10. — Interests of directors and officers of the offeree issuer in material transactions with offeror

State whether any director or officer of the offeree issuer and their associates and, if known to the directors or officers after reasonable enquiry, whether any person who owns more than 10% of any class of equity securities of the offeree issuer for the time being outstanding has any interest in any material transaction to which the offeror is a party, and if so, state particulars of the nature and extent of such interest.

Item 11. — Trading by directors, officers and other insiders

(1) State the number of securities of the offeree issuer traded, the purchase or sale price and the date of each transaction during the 6-month period preceding the date of the directors' circular by the offeree issuer and each director, officer or other insider of the offeree issuer, and, if known after reasonable enquiry, by

    (a) each associate or affiliate of an insider of the offeree issuer,

    (b) each affiliate or associate of the offeree issuer, and

    (c) each person acting jointly or in concert with the offeree issuer.

(2) Disclose the number and price of securities of the offeree issuer of the class of securities subject to the bid or convertible into securities of that class that have been issued to the directors, officers and other insiders of the offeree issuer during the 2-year period preceding the date of the circular.

Item 12. — Additional information

If any information required to be disclosed by the take-over bid circular prepared by the offeror has been presented incorrectly or is misleading, supply any additional information which will make the information in the circular correct or not misleading.

Item 13. — Material changes in the affairs of offeree issuer

State the particulars of any information known to any of the directors or officers of the offeree issuer that indicates any material change in the affairs of the offeree issuer since the date of the last published interim financial report or annual financial statements of the offeree issuer.

Item 14. — Other material information

State the particulars of any other information known to the directors but not already disclosed in the directors' circular that would reasonably be expected to affect the decision of the security holders of the offeree issuer to accept or reject the offer.

Item 15. — Recommending acceptance or rejection of the bid

Include either a recommendation to accept or reject the take-over bid and the reasons for such recommendation or a statement that the directors are unable to make or are not making a recommendation. If no recommendation is made, state the reasons for not making a recommendation. If the directors of an offeree issuer are considering recommending acceptance or rejection of a take-over bid after the sending of the directors' circular, state that fact.

Item 16. — Response of offeree issuer

Describe any transaction, directors' resolution, agreement in principle or signed contract of the offeree issuer in response to the bid. Disclose whether there are any negotiations underway in response to the bid, which relate to or would result in

    (a) an extraordinary transaction such as a merger or reorganization involving the offeree issuer or a subsidiary,

    (b) the purchase, sale or transfer of a material amount of assets by the offeree issuer or a subsidiary,

    (c) a competing take-over bid,

    (d) a bid by the offeree issuer for its own securities or for those of another issuer, or

    (e) any material change in the present capitalization or dividend policy of the offeree issuer.

If there is an agreement in principle, give full particulars.

Item 17. — Approval of directors' circular

State that the directors' circular has been approved and its sending has been authorized by the directors of the offeree issuer.

Item 18. — Statement of rights

Include the following statement of rights provided under the securities legislation of the jurisdictions relating to this circular:

Securities legislation in the provinces and territories of Canada provides security holders of the offeree issuer with, in addition to any other rights they may have at law, one or more rights of rescission, price revision or to damages, if there is a misrepresentation in a circular or notice that is required to be delivered to those security holders. However, such rights must be exercised within prescribed time limits. Security holders should refer to the applicable provisions of the securities legislation of their province or territory for particulars of those rights or consult a lawyer.

Item 19. — Certificate

A directors' circular certificate form must state:

The foregoing contains no untrue statement of a material fact and does not omit to state a material fact that is required to be stated or that is necessary to make a statement not misleading in the light of the circumstances in which it was made.

Item 20. — Date of directors' circular

Specify the date of the directors' circular.

Form 62-104F4 — Director's or Officer's Circular

Part 1 — General Provisions

(a) — Defined terms

If a term is used but not defined in this Form, refer to Part 1 of National Instrument 62-104 *Take-Over Bids and Issuer Bids* (the Instrument) and to National Instrument 14-101 *Definitions*.

(b) — Plain language

Write the director's or officer's circular so that readers are able to understand it and make informed investment decisions. Directors and officers should apply plain language principles when they prepare a director's or officer's circular including:

*   using short sentences;
*   using definite everyday language;
*   using the active voice;
*   avoiding superfluous words;
*   organizing the document into clear, concise sections, paragraphs and sentences;
*   avoiding jargon;
*   using personal pronouns to speak directly to the reader;
*   avoiding reliance on glossaries and defined terms unless it facilitates understanding of the disclosure;
*   avoiding vague boilerplate wording;
*   avoiding abstract terms by using more concrete terms or examples;
*   avoiding multiple negatives;
*   using technical terms only when necessary and explaining those terms;
*   using charts, tables and examples where it makes disclosure easier to understand.

If you use technical terms, explain them in a clear and concise manner.

(c) — Numbering and headings

The numbering, headings and ordering of items included in this Form are guidelines only. You do not need to include the heading or numbering or follow the order of items in this Form. You do not need to refer to inapplicable items and, unless otherwise required in this Form, you may omit negative answers to items. Disclosure provided in response to any item need not be repeated elsewhere in the circular.

Part 2 — Contents of Director's or Officer's Circular

Item 1. — Name of offeror

State the corporate name of the offeror or, if the offeror is an unincorporated entity, the full name under which it exists and carries on business.

Item 2. — Name of offeree issuer

State the corporate name of the offeree issuer or, if the offeree issuer is an unincorporated entity, the full name under which it exists and carries on business.

Item 3. — Name of director or officer of offeree issuer

State the name of each director or officer delivering the circular.

Item 4. — Ownership of securities of offeree issuer

State the number, designation and percentage of the outstanding securities of any class of securities of the offeree issuer beneficially owned or over which control or direction is exercised

(a) by the director or officer, and

(b) if known after reasonable enquiry, by the associates of the director or officer.

In each case where no securities are so owned, directed or controlled, state this fact.

Item 5. — Acceptance of bid

State whether the director or officer of the offeree issuer and, if known after reasonable enquiry whether any associate of such director or officer, has accepted or intends to accept the offer and state the number of securities in respect of which the director or officer, or any associate, has accepted or intends to accept the offer.

Item 6. — Ownership of securities of offeror

If a take-over bid is made by or on behalf of an issuer, state the number, designation and percentage of the outstanding securities of any class of securities of the offeror beneficially owned or over which control or direction is exercised

> (a) by the director or officer, or

> (b) if known after reasonable enquiry, by the associates of the director or officer.

In each case where no securities are so owned, directed or controlled, state this fact.

Item 7. — Arrangements between offeror and director or officer

Disclose the particulars of any agreement, commitment or understanding made or proposed to be made between the offeror and the director or officer, including particulars of any payment or other benefit proposed to be made or given by way of compensation for loss of office or the director or officer remaining in or retiring from office if the take-over bid is successful. State whether the director or officer is also a director or officer of the offeror or any subsidiary of the offeror.

Item 8. — Arrangements between offeree issuer and director or officer

Disclose the particulars of any agreement, commitment or understanding made or proposed to be made between the offeree issuer and the director or officer, including particulars of any payment or other benefit proposed to be made or given by way of compensation for loss of office or his or her remaining in or retiring from office if the take-over bid is successful.

Item 9. — Interests of director or officer in material transactions with offeror

State whether the director or officer or the associates of the director or officer have any interest in any material transaction to which the offeror is a party, and if so, state the particulars of the nature and extent of such interest.

Item 10. — Additional information

If any information required to be disclosed by the take-over bid circular prepared by the offeror or the directors' circular prepared by the directors has been presented incorrectly or is misleading, supply any additional information within the knowledge of the director or officer which would make the information in the take-over bid circular or directors' circular correct or not misleading.

Item 11. — Material changes in the affairs of offeree issuer

State the particulars of any information known to the director or officer that indicates any material change in the affairs of the offeree issuer since the date of the last published interim financial report or annual financial statements of the offeree issuer and not generally disclosed or in the opinion of the director or officer not adequately disclosed in the take-over bid circular or directors' circular.

Item 12. — Other material information

State the particulars of any other information known to the director or officer but not already disclosed in the director's or officer's circular that would reasonably be expected to affect the decision of the security holders of the offeree issuer to accept or reject the offer.

Item 13. — Recommendation

State the recommendation of the director or officer and the reasons for the recommendation.

Item 14. — Statement of rights

Include the following statement of rights provided under the securities legislation of the jurisdictions relating to this circular:

> *Securities legislation of the provinces and territories of Canada provides security holders of the offeree issuer with, in addition to any other rights they may have at law, one or more rights of rescission, price revision or to damages if there is a misrepresentation in a circular or notice that is required to be delivered to those security holders. However, such rights must be exercised within prescribed time limits. Security holders should refer to the applicable provisions of the securities legislation of their province or territory for particulars of those rights or consult a lawyer.*

Item 15. — Certificate

Include a certificate in the following form signed by or on behalf of each director or officer delivering the circular:

> *The foregoing contains no untrue statement of a material fact and does not omit to state a material fact that is required to be stated or that is necessary to make a statement not misleading in the light of the circumstances in which it was made.*

Item 16. — Date of director's or officer's circular

Specify the date of the director's or officer's circular.

Form 62-104F5 — Notice of Change or Notice of Variation

Part 1 — General Provisions

(a) — Defined terms

If a term is used but not defined in this Form, refer to Part 1 of National Instrument 62-104 *Take-Over Bids and Issuer Bids* (the Instrument) and to National Instrument 14-101 *Definitions*.

(b) — Plain language

Write the notice of change or notice of variation so that readers are able to understand it and make informed investment decisions. Plain language principles should be applied when preparing a notice of change or notice of variation including:

- using short sentences;

- using definite everyday language;

- using the active voice;

- avoiding superfluous words;

- organizing the document into clear, concise sections, paragraphs and sentences;

- avoiding jargon;

- using personal pronouns to speak directly to the reader;

- avoiding reliance on glossaries and defined terms unless it facilitates understanding of the disclosure;

- avoiding vague boilerplate wording;

- avoiding abstract terms by using more concrete terms or examples;

- avoiding multiple negatives;

- using technical terms only when necessary and explaining those terms;

- using charts, tables and examples where it makes disclosure easier to understand.

If you use technical terms, explain them in a clear and concise manner.

(c) — Numbering and headings

The numbering, headings and ordering of items included in this Form are guidelines only. You do not need to include the heading or numbering or follow the order of items in this Form. You do not need to refer to inapplicable items and, unless otherwise required in this Form, you may omit negative answers to items. Disclosure provided in response to any item need not be repeated elsewhere in the circular.

Part 2 — Contents of Notice of Change or Notice of Variation

Item 1. — Name of offeror

State the corporate name of the offeror or, if the offeror is an unincorporated entity, the full name under which it exists and carries on business.

Item 2. — Name of offeree issuer (if applicable)

State the corporate name of the offeree issuer or, if the offeree issuer is an unincorporated entity, the full name under which it exists and carries on business.

Item 3. — Particulars of notice of change or notice of variation

(1) A notice of change required under section 2.11 of the Instrument must contain

    (a) a description of the change in the information contained in

        (i) the take-over bid circular or issuer bid circular, and

        (ii) any notice of change previously delivered under section 2.11,

    (b) the date of the change,

    (c) the date up to which securities may be deposited,

    (d) the date by which securities deposited must be taken up by the offeror, and

    (e) a description of the rights of withdrawal that are available to security holders.

(2) A notice of variation required under section 2.12 of the Instrument must contain

    (a) a description of the variation in the terms of the take-over bid or issuer bid,

    (a.1) if one of the terms referred to in paragraph (a) is the mandatory 10-day extension period required pursuant to paragraph 2.31.1(a) of the Instrument, the number of securities deposited under the take-over bid and not withdrawn as at the date of the variation,

    (b) the date of the variation,

    (c) the date up to which securities may be deposited,

    (d) the date by which securities deposited must be taken up by the offeror,

    (e) if the date referred to in paragraph (d) is not known, a description of the legal requirements regarding the timing of take up of securities deposited under the bid,

    (f) a description of when payment will be made for deposited securities in relation to the time in which they are taken up by the offeror, and

    (g) a description of the rights of withdrawal that are available to security holders.

(3) A notice of change required under section 2.18 or subsection 2.20(2) of the Instrument must contain, as applicable, a description of the change in the information contained in

    (a) the directors' circular,

    (b) any notice of change previously delivered under section 2.18,

    (c) the director's or officer's circular, or 3

    (d) any notice of change previously delivered under subsection 2.20(2).

Item 4. — Statement of rights

Include the following statement of rights provided under the securities legislation of the jurisdictions relating to this notice:

Securities legislation of the provinces and territories of Canada provides security holders of the offeree issuer with, in addition to any other rights they may have at law, one or more rights of rescission, price revision or to damages if there is a misrepresentation in a circular or notice that is required to be delivered to those security holders. However, such rights must be exercised within prescribed time limits. Security holders should refer to the applicable provisions of the securities legislation of their province or territory for particulars of those rights or consult a lawyer.

Item 5. — Certificate

Include the signed certificate required in the bid circular, directors' circular or director's or officer's circular, amended to refer to the initial circular and to all subsequent notices of change or notices of variation.

Item 6. — Date of notice of change or notice of variation

Specify the date of the notice of change or notice of variation.

National Policy 62-201 — Bids Made Only in Certain Jurisdictions

Date: July 4, 1997
20 O.S.C.B. 3523

[Revoked: (2008) 31 O.S.C.B. 1229]

Adoption by OSC: (1997) 20 O.S.C.B. 3523; Request for Comments: (1996) 19 O.S.C.B. 6661. Replaced National Policy 37.

National Policy 62-202 — Take-Over Bids — Defensive Tactics

Date: July 4, 1997
20 O.S.C.B. 3525

PART 1 — DEFENSIVE TACTICS

1.1 Defensive Tactics — (1) The Canadian securities regulatory authorities recognize that take-over bids play an important role in the economy by acting as a discipline on corporate management and as a means of reallocating economic resources to their best uses. In considering the merits of a take-over bid, there is a possibility that the interests of management of the target company will differ from those of its shareholders. Management of a target company may take one or more of the following actions in response to a bid that it opposes:

    1. Attempt to persuade shareholders to reject the bid.

    2. Take action to maximize the return to shareholders including soliciting a higher bid from a third party.

    3. Take other defensive measures to defeat the bid.

(2) The primary objective of the take-over bid provisions of Canadian securities legislation is the protection of the bona fide interests of the shareholders of the target company. A secondary objective is to provide a regulatory framework within which take-over bids may proceed in an open and even-handed environment. The take-over bid provisions should favour neither the offeror nor the management of the target company, and should leave the shareholders of the target company free to make a fully informed decision. The Canadian securities regulatory authorities are concerned that certain defensive measures taken by management of a target company may have the effect of denying to shareholders the ability to make such a decision and of frustrating an open take-over bid process.

(3) The Canadian securities regulatory authorities have determined that it is inappropriate to specify a code of conduct for directors of a target company, in addition to the fiduciary standard required by corporate law. Any fixed code of conduct runs the risk of containing provisions that might be insufficient in some cases and excessive in others. However, the Canadian securities regulatory authorities wish to advise participants in the capital markets that they are prepared to examine target company tactics in specific cases to determine whether they are abusive of shareholder rights. Prior shareholder approval of corporate action would, in appropriate cases, allay such concerns.

(4) Without limiting the foregoing, defensive tactics that may come under scrutiny if undertaken during the course of a bid, or immediately before a bid, if the board of directors has reason to believe that a bid might be imminent, include

    (a) the issuance, or the granting of an option on, or the purchase of, securities representing a significant percentage of the outstanding securities of the target company,

    (b) the sale or acquisition, or granting of an option on, or agreeing to sell or acquire, assets of a material amount, and

    (c) entering into a contract other than in the normal course of business or taking corporate action other than in the normal course of business.

(5) The Canadian securities regulatory authorities consider that unrestricted auctions produce the most desirable results in take-over bids and they are reluctant to intervene in contested bids. However, they will take appropriate action if they become aware of defensive tactics that will likely result in shareholders being deprived of the ability to respond to a take-over bid or to a competing bid.

(6) The Canadian securities regulatory authorities appreciate that defensive tactics, including those that may consist of some of the actions listed in subsection (4), may be taken by a board of directors of a target company in a genuine attempt to obtain a better bid. Tactics that are likely to deny or limit severely the ability of the shareholders to respond to a take-over bid or a competing bid may result in action by the Canadian securities regulatory authorities.

(7) As a general rule, the Canadian securities regulatory authorities will not advise parties as to the propriety of proposed action in a particular case except in the context of a meeting or proceeding of which interested parties have been given notice.

PART 2 — EFFECTIVE DATE

2.1 Effective Date — This National Policy comes into force on August 4, 1997.

Adoption by OSC: (1997) 20 O.S.C.B. 3525; Request for Comments: (1996) 19 O.S.C.B. 6495. Replaced National Policy 38.

National Policy 62-203 — Take-Over Bids and Issuer Bids

Date: February 1, 2008 and May 9, 2016
31 O.S.C.B. 1319 and 39 O.S.C.B. 1778

PART 1 — INTRODUCTION AND PURPOSE

1.1 Introduction — National Instrument 62-104 *Take-Over Bids and Issuer Bids* (the Instrument) governs take-over bids and issuer bids in all jurisdictions of Canada. This Policy and the Instrument are together referred to as the "Bid Regime". This Policy outlines how the provincial and territorial securities regulatory authorities interpret or apply certain provisions of the Bid Regime and provides guidance on the conduct of parties involved in a bid.

PART 2 — BID REGIME FOR TAKE-OVER BIDS AND ISSUER BIDS IN CANADA

2.1 General — The Bid Regime is designed to establish a clear and predictable framework for the conduct of bids in a manner that achieves three primary objectives:

- equal treatment of offeree issuer security holders,
- provision of adequate information to offeree issuer security holders, and
- an open and even-handed bid process.

2.2 Identifying the offeror — More than one person may constitute an offeror under a take-over bid. This can arise if an offer is made indirectly, because the terms "offer to acquire" and "take-over bid" in section 1.1 of the Instrument apply to both direct and indirect offers to acquire securities.

For example, a party (the primary party) that uses an acquisition entity, subsidiary or other affiliate (the named offeror) to make a take-over bid, may itself be making an indirect bid. In that case, the named offeror and the primary party may be joint offerors. As joint offerors, both would be subject to the requirements of the Bid Regime, including the requirements to certify and deliver the bid circular.

If a take-over bid is made by a wholly-owned entity, we regard the entity's parent to be a joint offeror. If the named offeror is not a wholly-owned entity, assessment of whether the primary party is a joint offeror would depend on its role, taking into account, among other factors, the answers to the following questions:

- Did the primary party play a significant role in initiating, structuring and negotiating the bid?
- Does the primary party control any of the terms of the offer?
- Is the primary party financing the bid, guaranteeing the financing, or integral to obtaining the financing?
- Does the primary party directly or indirectly control the named offeror?
- Did the primary party form, or cause to be formed, the named offeror?
- Are the primary party's securities being offered as consideration under the bid?
- Will the primary party beneficially own the assets or securities of the target after completion of the bid?

We think a "yes" answer to any of these questions could mean that the primary party is making an indirect offer and is a joint offeror under the bid.

2.3 Bids made only in certain jurisdictions — The failure to make a bid to security holders of an offeree issuer in one or more jurisdictions if the bid is made to security holders in other jurisdictions is not consistent with the existing framework of securities regulation in Canada, which aims to ensure that all security holders of the offeree issuer in Canada are treated equally. If the bid is not made in all jurisdictions, securities regulatory authorities in the jurisdictions in which the bid is made may issue cease trade orders in respect of the bid.

2.4 Varying terms — If an offeror varies the terms of its bid after the bid has been commenced, the variation may have the effect of making the bid less favourable to offeree security holders in circumstances where the offeror

(a) lowers the consideration offered under the bid,

(b) changes the form of consideration offered under the bid, other than to add to the consideration already offered under the bid,

(c) lowers the proportion of outstanding securities for which the bid is made, or

(d) adds new conditions.

Depending on the circumstances, these variations may be so fundamental to the bid that we may exercise our public interest mandate to ensure that offeree security holders are not prejudiced by the variations. We may intervene to cease trade the bid, require that the deposit period be extended for a period longer than mandated under the Bid Regime or require that an offeror commence a new bid with the varied conditions.

2.5 Interpretation of prohibition against collateral agreements — An offeror or anyone acting jointly or in concert with an offeror is prohibited from entering into a collateral agreement, understanding or commitment that has the effect of providing a security holder of the offeree issuer with consideration of greater value than that offered to other security holders of the same class. This prohibition applies to a direct or indirect benefit being provided to a security holder and includes participation by the holder in another transaction with the offeror that has the effect of providing consideration of greater value to the holder than that offered to other security holders of the same class.

2.6 Independent committees for the collateral agreement exceptions — The Bid Regime excludes employment-related arrangements from the scope of the collateral agreement prohibition if, among other conditions, an independent committee of the offeree issuer has determined that the value of the benefit received by a security holder is less than 5% of the total consideration to be received by the holder under the bid or that a security holder is providing at least equivalent value in exchange for the benefit. For the purposes of these exceptions, we consider a director to be independent if the director is disinterested in the bid or any related transactions. Although this is a factual determination based on the particular circumstances of the bid, we think that the definitions of independent director and independent committee in Multilateral Instrument 61-101 *Protection of Minority Security Holders in Special Transactions* provide relevant guidance on determining director independence.

2.7 Equivalent value exception — In determining that a security holder is providing at least equivalent value in exchange for a benefit under clause 2.25(1)(b)(ii)(B) of the Instrument, an independent committee should consider, among other things, whether the employment compensation arrangement, severance arrangement or other employment benefit arrangement is on terms consistent with arrangements made with individuals holding comparable positions (i) with the offeror and (ii) in the industry generally. Where an independent committee does not have the expertise or resources to ascertain whether an arrangement is on terms consistent with industry standards, we recommend the committee retain an appropriately qualified independent expert to advise it concerning industry standards.

2.8 Redacting or omitting filed information — The Bid Regime requires the offeror and offeree issuer to file prescribed documents relating to control of the offeree issuer and to the bid. The filer is permitted, under certain conditions, to omit or mark provisions of a filed document so as to make the provisions unreadable. However, we do not think it appropriate for a filer to omit or redact an entire document on the basis that the information in the document is subject to confidentiality.

2.9 Section 1.2 of the Instrument — Saskatchewan is not included in subsection 1.2(1) of the Instrument because the definitions of "offer to acquire" and "offeror" are in the regulations to *The Securities Act, 1988* (Saskatchewan). The definitions are the same.

2.10 Take-over bid deposit period — The Bid Regime requires all non-exempt take-over bids to remain open for a minimum deposit period of 105 days (section 2.28.1 of the Instrument), except in the following circumstances:

    (a) the offeree issuer states in a news release a shorter deposit period for a bid of not less than 35 days (section 2.28.2 of the Instrument); or

    (b) the issuer issues a news release that it intends to effect a specified alternative transaction (section 2.28.3 of the Instrument).

Where a shorter minimum deposit period applies, an offeror that has not yet commenced its take-over bid can avail itself of the shorter minimum deposit period by establishing an expiry date for the initial deposit period based on the number of days specified for the bid referred to in the deposit period news release. In the case of an alternative transaction, section 2.28.3 of the Instrument permits an offeror to establish a minimum initial deposit period of at least 35 days. This provision applies regardless of the length of time that may be required to complete the alternative transaction.

If an offeror has already commenced a take-over bid when a deposit period news release is issued or an alternative transaction is announced, sections 2.28.2 and 2.28.3 of the Instrument do not require the offeror to shorten the deposit period for its bid, nor do they apply to automatically shorten the initial deposit period of its bid. To avail itself of the permitted shorter initial deposit period, the offeror must vary its take-over bid in accordance with section 2.12 of the Instrument to reflect the earlier expiry date for the bid. As a consequence, the offeror must allow securities to be deposited under its bid for at least 10 days after the notice of variation even if the offeror's take-over bid would otherwise have already satisfied the shorter minimum deposit period.

2.11 Deposit period news release — A "deposit period news release" is defined, in part, as a news release issued by an offeree issuer in respect of a "proposed or commenced" take-over bid. A take-over bid is "proposed" if a person publicly announces that it intends to make a take-over bid for the securities of an offeree issuer. An anticipated but unannounced take-over bid or possible future take-over bid would not constitute a "proposed" take-over bid within the meaning of this definition.

A deposit period news release will state an initial deposit period for a take-over bid of not more than 105 days and not less than 35 days. A deposit period news release must describe the minimum deposit period by referring to a number of days from the date of the bid and not to specific calendar dates in order to facilitate the generic application of the shorter minimum deposit period to multiple take-over bids.

2.12 Multiple deposit period news releases — The Bid Regime does not restrict an offeree issuer from issuing multiple deposit period news releases in respect of a take-over bid or contemporaneous bids. While likely rare, we anticipate that there may be circumstances where an offeree issuer determines to further shorten a previously stated minimum initial deposit period for a take-over bid or determines to state a shorter initial minimum deposit period for a take-over bid after it had previously stated an initial minimum deposit period for another take-over bid. In the event that an offeree issuer issues multiple deposit period news releases, the provisions in section 2.28.2 of the Instrument should be interpreted such that the shortest initial minimum deposit period stated in a deposit period news release applies to all take-over bids that are subject to section 2.28.2 of the Instrument.

2.13 Alternative transaction — The Bid Regime includes a definition for an "alternative transaction" that is based, with certain modifications, principally on the definition of "business combination" in Multilateral Instrument 61-101 *Protection of Minority Security Holders in Special Transactions*. This definition is intended to encompass transactions agreed to or initiated by the issuer that could result in the acquisition of the issuer or the business of the issuer as an alternative to doing so by means of a take-over bid.

2.14 Alternative transaction — time of agreement — Section 2.28.3 of the Instrument provides that, in certain circumstances, the initial deposit period for a bid must be at least 35 days from the date of the bid if an issuer issues a news release announcing that it "intends to effect an alternative transaction, whether pursuant to an agreement or otherwise". An agreement to enter into an alternative transaction should be interpreted as having occurred when the issuer first makes a legally binding commitment to proceed with the alternative transaction, subject to conditions such as security holder approval.

Where an issuer does not technically negotiate an alternative transaction with another party, such as in the case of a share consolidation, a determination to effect the alternative transaction should be interpreted as having occurred when the issuer's board of directors decides to proceed with the alternative transaction, subject to conditions.

2.15 Alternative transaction — reliance on issuer news release — Section 2.28.3 of the Instrument provides for the reduction of the minimum initial deposit period for a take-over bid to 35 days if an issuer issues a news release announcing that it intends to effect an alternative transaction. Section 2.28.3 applies in respect of an offeror's take-over bid, such that an offeror should reasonably determine whether an issuer's announced transaction is an "alternative transaction" before either, as the case may be, reducing the initial deposit period of its outstanding take-over bid to not less than 35 days or commencing a take-over bid for the issuer with an initial deposit period of not less than 35 days.

2.16 Change in information or variation of terms — Subsections 2.11(5) and 2.12(3.1) of the Instrument provide that the initial deposit period for a take-over bid must not expire before 10 days after the date of a notice of change or notice of variation, respectively. If an offeror is required to send a notice of change or a notice of variation in circumstances where the initial deposit period would expire less than 10 days from the date of the notice then the offeror would be obliged to further extend the initial deposit period to ensure that at least 10 days have elapsed before the expiry of the initial deposit period.

2.17 Partial take-over bids — The Bid Regime includes specific requirements for partial take-over bids, including that an offeror is required to take up securities deposited on a proportionate or *pro rata* basis where a greater number of securities is deposited under the bid than the offeror is bound or willing to acquire. The Bid Regime exempts an offeror making a partial take-over bid from the general obligation to immediately take up all deposited securities if, at the expiry of the initial deposit period, the specified bid conditions in subsection 2.32.1(1) of the Instrument are satisfied. Instead, subsection 2.32.1(6) of the Instrument provides that the offeror is required to take up at the expiry of the initial deposit period only the maximum number of securities that it can without contravening the *pro rata* requirement. An offeror would therefore make the determination of the maximum number of securities it can take up assuming that all other securities subject to the bid will be deposited during the mandatory 10-day extension period.

Subsection 2.32.1(7) of the Instrument further requires that an offeror making a partial take-over bid must take up any securities deposited during the initial deposit period and not already taken up by it in reliance on subsection s. 2.32.1(6), and securities deposited during the mandatory 10-day extension period, on a *pro rata* basis and not later than one business day after expiry of the mandatory 10-day extension period. This *pro rata* determination would take into account the fact that a portion of the securities deposited in the initial deposit period has already been taken up by the offeror.

The following are illustrative examples of how the proportionate take-up provisions in the Bid Regime would apply to partial take-over bids in different circumstances.

Partial take-over bid scenario	Offeree shares deposited as at expiry of initial deposit period (all other conditions satisfied)	Maximum number of offeree shares taken up pro rata by offeror at expiry of initial deposit period	Additional offeree shares deposited during mandatory 10-day extension period	Total offeree shares taken up at expiry of mandatory 10-day extension period
Bid for 3,000 offeree shares (30% of 10,000 issued and outstanding offeree shares) Offeror does not own offeree shares at commencement of bid and does not acquire offeree shares during the bid.	6,000 (60% of the 10,000 offeree shares subject to the bid) (minimum 50% tender is required to meet minimum tender requirement in s. 2.29.1(c))	1,800 (60% of 3,000 offeree shares bid for, or 30% of 6,000 shares deposited) Offeror cannot take-up more than 60% of the 3,000 shares it bid for (30% of deposited shares) to allow for possibility of additional deposit of all 4,000 (40%) remaining shares subject to the bid during mandatory 10-day extension period.	2,000 (20% of the 10,000 offeree shares subject to the bid)	3,000 (30% of 10,000 issued and outstanding offeree shares) *Summary* A total of 8,000 (80%) of the offeree shares subject to the bid deposited as at expiry of the mandatory 10-day extension period (6,000 as at expiry of initial deposit period plus 2,000 deposited during mandatory 10-day extension period). Proration factor: 3,000 / 8,000 (number of shares sought / number of shares tendered) = approx. 0.375. The offeror will take up and pay for 37.5% of shares deposited by each shareholder, taking into account any shares already taken up at expiry of initial deposit period.
Bid for 3,000 offeree shares (30% of 10,000 issued and outstanding offeree shares) in addition to shares held by offeror Offeror owns 1,000 (10%) of offeree shares at commencement of bid and does not acquire offeree shares during the bid.	6,000 (66⅔% of the 9,000 offeree shares subject to the bid) (minimum 50% tender of the 9,000 offeree shares not held by offeror (or 4,500 shares) is required to meet minimum tender requirement in s. 2.29.1(c))	2,000 (66⅔% of 3,000 offeree shares bid for, or 33⅓% of 6,000 shares deposited) Offeror cannot take-up more than 66⅔% of the 3,000 offeree shares it bid for to allow for possibility of additional deposit of all 3,000 (33⅓%) remaining shares subject to the bid during mandatory 10-day extension period.	2,000 (approx. 22% of the 9,000 offeree shares subject to the bid)	3,000 (30% of 10,000 issued and outstanding offeree shares) *Summary* A total of 8,000 (80%) of offeree shares subject to the bid deposited as at expiry of the mandatory 10-day extension period (6,000 as at expiry of initial deposit period plus 2,000 deposited during mandatory 10-day extension period). Pro ration factor: 3,000 / 8,000 (number of shares sought / number of shares deposited) = approx. 0.375. The offeror will take up and pay for 37.5% of shares deposited by each shareholder, taking into account any shares already taken up at expiry of initial deposit period.

PART 3 — TAKE-OVER BID AND EARLY WARNING REQUIREMENTS

3.1 Equity swap or similar derivative arrangement — An investor that is a party to an equity swap or similar derivative arrangement may under certain circumstances have deemed beneficial ownership, or control or direction, over the referenced voting or equity securities. This could occur where the investor has the ability, formally or informally, to obtain the voting or equity securities or to direct the voting of voting securities held by any counterparties to the transaction. This determination would be relevant for compliance with the early warning and take-over bid requirements under the Instrument.

3.2 Securities lending arrangements — Securities lending describes the market practice whereby securities are temporarily transferred from one party (the lender) to another party (the borrower) in return for a fee. As part of the lending arrangement, the borrower is obliged to redeliver to the lender the securities or identical securities to those that were transferred or lent, either on demand or at the end of the loan term.

Securities lending arrangements transfer title of securities from the lender to the borrower for the duration of the loan. During this period, the borrower has full ownership rights and may re-sell the securities as well as vote them. Securities lending arrangements between the lender and the borrower generally provide for payment to the lender of any economic benefits (for example, dividends) accruing to the securities while "on loan". Therefore, securities lending separates the economic interest in the securities which remains with the lender from the ownership and voting rights which are transferred to the borrower. If the lender wants to vote the loaned securities it must, in accordance with the terms of the securities lending arrangement, either recall the securities or identical securities from the borrower or otherwise direct the voting of the loaned securities.

Since securities lending arrangements involve a disposition and acquisition of securities, lenders and borrowers should consider securities lent (disposed) and borrowed (acquired) under securities lending arrangements in determining whether an early warning reporting obligation has been triggered.

Paragraph 5.7(a) of the Instrument provides an exception for the lender of securities under a securities lending arrangement from the early warning requirements if the securities are transferred or lent pursuant to a securities lending arrangement that meets the criteria of a specified securities lending arrangement. If the securities lending arrangement is not a specified securities lending arrangement, then the early warning reporting requirements for dispositions of securities will apply to the disposition of securities by the lender under the securities lending arrangement.

Paragraph 5.7(b) of the Instrument provides an exception for the borrower of securities under a securities lending arrangement from the early warning requirements if the securities or identical securities are borrowed, disposed of or acquired in connection with a borrower's short sale if certain conditions are met. Short selling is a trading strategy where the borrower uses securities borrowed under a securities lending arrangement to settle a sale (disposition) of the securities to another party with the objective of later repurchasing (acquiring) identical securities at a lower price on the market to return the securities to the lender. If all the conditions of paragraph 5.7(b) are not satisfied, then the early warning reporting requirements will apply to the borrower in respect of securities borrowed under the securities lending arrangement and the disposition of and acquisition of the securities or identical securities in the market in connection with the securities lending arrangement.

Adoption by OSC: (2008) 31 O.S.C.B. 1319, (2007) 30 O.S.C.B. (Supp 6) 39, (2016) 39 O.S.C.B. 1776 and (2016) 39 O.S.C.B. (Supp. 1) 46; Request for Comments: (2006) 29 O.S.C.B. 3553 and (2013) 36 O.S.C.B. 2675.

CSA Staff Notice 62-305 — Varying the Terms of Take-Over Bids

Date: **December 18, 2009**

32 O.S.C.B. 10449

As used in this notice, the term "Bid Regime" has the meaning ascribed to it in National Policy 62-203 *Take-Over Bids and Issuer Bids*.

The Bid Regime is designed to protect the *bona fide* interests of offeree security holders while establishing a transparent, even-handed and predictable framework for the conduct of formal bids. An important underpinning of the Bid Regime is that offerors make offers that they are prepared to honour. Upon commencement of a formal take-over bid, the market price of the securities of the offeree issuer may be affected. This creates a legitimate expectation among security holders, other potential offerors, the offeree issuer and other market participants that the bid will be completed at the specified price provided that the conditions of the bid are satisfied.

This notice sets out the view of the staff of the Canadian Securities Administrators (CSA staff) regarding the ability of an offeror in a formal take-over bid to vary the terms of a bid in a manner that makes the bid less favourable to offeree security holders (a "negative variation"). Variations of this nature may include cases where the offeror:

     (a) lowers the consideration offered under the bid,

     (b) changes the form of consideration offered, other than to add to the consideration already offered,

     (c) lowers the proportion of outstanding securities subject to the bid, or

     (d) adds new conditions.

CSA staff are concerned that some market participants have expressed the view that an offeror is entitled, at its discretion and at any time, to withdraw a bid or to vary a bid by reducing the offer price or otherwise making the bid less favourable to offeree security holders.

Does an offeror have the right to reduce its offer price or add new offer conditions for any reason, and at any time, prior to expiry of the bid?

The Bid Regime provides that the bid shall remain open for acceptance for at least 35 days and that securities are to be taken up and paid for under the bid, at the bid price, if the conditions of the bid have been satisfied or waived. The Bid Regime requires that an offeror have the funds in place to pay the consideration offered.

Accordingly, in the view of CSA staff, the Bid Regime does not contemplate the unilateral "withdrawal" of a formal take-over bid, or if all terms and conditions of a bid have been satisfied or waived, the offeror varying the offer price downwards or introducing new conditions.

CSA staff have noted that offer documents and bid circulars occasionally contain language to the effect that the offeror may vary the bid at any time in its sole discretion, including by reducing the consideration offered. CSA staff are of the view that such language may be inconsistent with the requirements of the Bid Regime.

Does an offeror have the right to reduce its offer price or add new conditions where all of the conditions of the offer have not yet been satisfied, or in response to the failure of a condition?

Where the terms and conditions of an offer have not been satisfied, an offeror is entitled to allow its bid to expire and not take up and pay for securities deposited under the bid. The offeror is then entitled to make a new offer on different terms. Where the terms and conditions of an offer have not been satisfied by the expiry of the bid or clearly will not be satisfied during the offer period, staff will not object to an offeror varying its bid by adding new conditions or reducing the consideration offered, provided such variation is not prejudicial to security holders.

National Policy 62-203 *Take-Over Bids and Issuer Bids* provides that negative variations are subject to review to ensure such variations are not prejudicial to security holders. In determining whether to challenge a negative variation, CSA staff will consider whether such a variation: (a) is in response to the failure of a *bona fide* condition of the offer; (b) is effected as an alternative to allowing the bid to expire unsuccessfully; (c) provides sufficient procedural protections to offeree security holders and other market participants affected by the variation; and (d) would not be abusive to offeree security holders.

In reviewing such a variation, CSA staff may request submissions and confirmation from the offeror as to the circumstances justifying the position that a *bona fide* condition of the offer has not been or will not be satisfied. This includes whether the offeror has informed the market in a timely manner as to such failure of a condition and the events giving rise to the failure, and the reasonableness of the procedural protections being put in place for the benefit of the offeree security holders and other affected market participants. The notice of variation to be filed by the offeror should disclose this information.

Where the onus is being placed on security holders to take active steps to withdraw securities tendered to an offer following a variation of that offer, there is a risk that some security holders may not become aware of the variation and would not have tendered on the varied terms. An offeror should consider and address this risk in deciding whether to vary a bid rather than to commence a new bid and in implementing the procedural protections to be provided to offeree security holders in the event it elects to proceed with a negative variation. The procedural protections, including period of extension, should also provide the offeree board of directors with sufficient time to assess the revised offer and communicate its views to its security holders. The time period must also provide sufficient time for other potential offerors to evaluate the revised offer and determine whether to participate in an auction for the offeree issuer.

In CSA staff's view, the offeror's conditions to a formal take-over bid should be *bona fide*, and should be interpreted in good faith and on a reasonable basis. If they are not, staff may take the position that reliance on a condition undermines the statutory requirement that shares be taken up under an offer where the terms and conditions have been satisfied. Where the failure of a condition is being relied upon to vary a bid or where a condition is expressed such that the offeror has sole judgment or discretion as to whether the condition has been satisfied, staff may intervene where necessary to ensure that such judgment or discretion is exercised in a reasonable manner. This is irrespective of whether it is stated in the bid circular that the offeror has sole discretion as to whether conditions are satisfied. In CSA staff's view, an offeror reserving "sole discretion" with respect to a condition should act honestly, in good faith and on reasonable grounds such that the exercise of such discretion is not capricious or arbitrary.

A negative variation should not be used to avoid the obligation on the offeror to have funds available to pay the consideration offered under a bid. For example, it would be a contravention of the Bid Regime to commence a bid at a specific price, but arrange financing at a lower price with the intention that the bid price will ultimately be reduced. In examining negative variations, staff may request documentation evidencing that funds were available to pay the initially offered consideration at the time the offer was made.

CSA Staff Notice 62-306 — Update on Proposed National Instrument 62-105 Security Holder Rights Plans and AMF Consultation Paper An Alternative Approach to Securities Regulators' Intervention in Defensive Tactics

Date: September 11, 2014
Citation: 37 O.S.C.B. 8299

Introduction

On March 14, 2013, the Canadian Securities Administrators (the **CSA** or **we**) published for comment proposed National Instrument 62-105 *Security Holder Rights Plans* and proposed Companion Policy 62-105CP *Security Holder Rights Plans* (together, the **CSA Proposal**). The Autorité des marchés financiers (the **AMF**), while participating in the publication for comment of the CSA Proposal, concurrently published a consultation paper entitled *An Alternative Approach to Securities Regulators' Intervention in Defensive Tactics* (the **AMF Proposal**). This notice provides an update on the CSA's consideration of these two defensive tactics policy proposals and our proposed regulatory approach going forward.

The CSA Proposal and the AMF Proposal sought to address, in different ways, concerns raised with the CSA's current approach to reviewing defensive tactics adopted by boards of directors of target issuers in response to, or in anticipation of, unsolicited or "hostile" take-over bids.

Canadian securities regulators currently review defensive tactics under their respective public interest jurisdictions in light of the guidance in National Policy 62-202 *Defensive Tactics* (the **Defensive Tactics Policy**). We developed the CSA Proposal, and the AMF developed the AMF Proposal, with a view to revising the application of the Defensive Tactics Policy by securities regulators in response to developments subsequent to the implementation of the Defensive Tactics Policy.

New Harmonized Bid Amendments Proposal

In light of the comments received and following further reflection and analysis, the CSA have determined not to proceed with the CSA Proposal and the AMF has determined not to proceed with the AMF Proposal. Instead, the CSA intend to publish for comment, subject to necessary approvals, a new harmonized regulatory proposal based on amendments to the take-over bid regime contained in Multilateral Instrument 62-104 *Take-Over Bids and Issuer Bids* (for jurisdictions other than Ontario) and Part XX of the *Securities Act* (Ontario) and Ontario Securities Commission Rule 62-504 *Take-Over Bids and Issuer Bids* (for Ontario) (collectively, the **Proposed Bid Amendments**).

The Proposed Bid Amendments will address key issues identified in the CSA Proposal and the AMF Proposal, as further informed by the comments received in respect of those proposals. In general, the Proposed Bid Amendments will aim to facilitate the ability of shareholders to make voluntary, informed and co-ordinated tender decisions and provide target boards with additional time to respond to hostile bids, each with the objective of rebalancing the current dynamics between hostile bidders and target boards.

Specifically, the Proposed Bid Amendments would require that all non-exempt take-over bids:

(1) be subject to a mandatory tender condition that a minimum of more than 50% of all outstanding target securities owned or held by persons other than the bidder and its joint actors be tendered and not withdrawn before the bidder can take up any securities under the bid;

(2) be extended by the bidder for an additional 10 days after the bidder achieves the mandatory minimum tender condition and the bidder announces its intention to immediately take up and pay for the securities deposited under the bid; and

(3) remain open for a minimum of 120 days, subject to the ability of the target board to waive, in a non-discriminatory manner when there are multiple bids, the minimum period to a period of no less than 35 days.

At this time, the CSA are not contemplating any changes to the current take-over bid exemptions or the Defensive Tactics Policy.

Subject to necessary approvals, we will publish for comment the complete details of the Proposed Bid Amendments and their application.

Overview of 2013 CSA Proposal and AMF Proposal

CSA Proposal

The purpose of the CSA Proposal was to create a framework for the regulation of security holder rights plans (**Rights Plans**) adopted by boards of directors of target issuers in response to, or in anticipation of, hostile bids. Rights Plans are the most common form of defensive measure adopted by target boards and, under the CSA's current approach, are typically cease traded by securities regulators within 45 to 55 days after the commencement of the hostile bid.

The CSA Proposal would have allowed a target board to maintain a Rights Plan in the face of a hostile bid if a majority of the equity or voting securities of the target issuer (excluding the securities of the hostile bidder and its joint actors) were voted in favour of the Rights Plan either in the face of the hostile bid or at the issuer's previous annual meeting. The CSA Proposal contemplated that securities regulators would generally not intervene to cease trade Rights Plans adopted under the CSA Proposal when security holders had approved the Rights Plan within 90 days from its adoption by the board or the commencement of the hostile bid.

We intended the CSA Proposal to address concerns about the utility of a Rights Plan to the target issuer in response to a hostile bid, while ensuring that a majority of the holders of equity or voting securities of the target issuer supported the application of the Rights Plan as proposed by the target board. The CSA Proposal would have potentially provided additional time for a target board to exercise its discretion in responding to a hostile bid, allowed target issuer security holders to, effectively, make a collective decision about a hostile bid by endorsing a Rights Plan and enhanced harmonization in the review of Rights Plans among the CSA.

AMF Proposal

While the CSA Proposal only addressed the use of Rights Plans by target boards, the AMF Proposal raised more fundamental issues regarding the regulation of defensive measures in Canada, including the role of boards of directors when faced with unsolicited take-over bids and the structural imbalance between bidders and target boards, and sought comments on the specific changes to the take-over bid regime set out in the AMF Proposal.

The AMF Proposal identified three main concerns with the current take-over bid regime and application of the Defensive Tactics Policy:

(1) the take-over bid regime has become too "bidder friendly" and is inconsistent with its stated goal of neutrality as between bidders and target boards and their management;

(2) the Defensive Tactics Policy is being applied to inappropriately limit the target board's ability to exercise its fiduciary duty, including to maximize security holder value in the long term; and

(3) the take-over bid regime is structurally coercive to target security holders as it does not permit them to make a collective decision about the transaction.

The AMF Proposal proposed two changes to address these concerns. First, it suggested replacing the Defensive Tactics Policy with a new policy that would recognize the fiduciary duty of the target board to the issuer when responding to a hostile bid. The new policy would limit the intervention of securities regulators to circumstances where security holders are deprived from considering a *bona fide* offer because the target board failed to take measures to address its conflicts of interest and risk of entrenchment.

Second, the AMF Proposal contemplated that the take-over bid regime be amended to require a minimum tender condition of more than 50% of all outstanding target securities owned or held by persons other than the bidder and its joint actors, along with a mandatory 10 day extension of the bid following the announcement that the minimum tender condition has been met to give the remaining security holders the opportunity to tender to the bid.

Public Comments on the CSA Proposal and the AMF Proposal

The comment period on the CSA Proposal and the AMF Proposal ended on July 12, 2013. We received approximately 70 comment letters from various market participants, including issuers, institutional investors, industry associations and law firms that reflected a broad diversity of opinions on the CSA Proposal and the AMF Proposal. Many commenters provided helpful substantive submissions, information and alternative considerations. We have reviewed the comments and wish to thank all of the commenters for their contributions.

We intend to provide a general summary of comments received in respect of the CSA Proposal and AMF Proposal when, subject to necessary approvals, we publish the Proposed Bid Amendments for comment.

Next Steps

We are in the process of developing the Proposed Bid Amendments and, subject to necessary approvals, intend to publish them for comment in the first quarter of 2015.

Questions

Please refer your questions to any of the following:

[Omitted.]

CSA Staff Notice 62-307 — Update on Proposed Amendments to Multilateral Instrument 62-104 Take-Over Bids and Issuer Bids, National Instrument 62-103 Early Warning System and Related Take-Over Bid and Insider Reporting Issues and National Policy 62-203 Take-Over Bids and Issuer Bids

Date: October 10, 2014

37 O.S.C.B. 9367

Introduction

On March 13, 2013, the Canadian Securities Administrators (the **CSA** or **we**) published for comment draft amendments and changes to:

- Multilateral Instrument 62-104 *Take-Over Bids and Issuer Bids* (MI 62-104),
- National Instrument 62-103 Early Warning System and Related Take-Over Bid and Insider Reporting Issues (NI 62-103), and
- National Policy 62-203 *Take-Over Bids and Issuer Bids* (NP 62-203) (collectively, the **Draft Amendments**).

The purpose of the publication was to address concerns about the level of transparency of significant holdings of issuers' securities under the early warning reporting system: in particular, the reporting threshold of 10%, and the adequacy of disclosure in early warning reports filed in Canada.

This notice provides an update to market participants on the status of the Draft Amendments.

Background

The Draft Amendments proposed a lower early warning reporting threshold of 5%, requiring disclosure of decreases in ownership of 2% or more of securities and enhancing the content of the disclosure in the early warning news releases and reports. We also proposed changes so that certain hidden ownership and empty voting arrangements would be disclosed and we proposed that eligible institutional investors that solicit proxies on matters relating to the election of directors or corporate actions involving an issuer's securities be unable to use the alternative monthly reporting system.

Summary of Comments

The comment period on the Draft Amendments ended on July 12, 2013. We received over 70 comment letters from various market participants that reflected a broad range of opinions. We wish to thank all of the commenters for their contributions.

We have reviewed and discussed the comments received. Many commenters provided helpful substantive submissions, information and perspectives on the Draft Amendments. We note that the commenters generally agreed with the enhanced transparency objective of the Draft Amendments. However, a majority of commenters raised various concerns about potential unintended consequences of certain Draft Amendments.

The comment process has assisted the CSA in re-considering certain elements of the Draft Amendments. Some of the views expressed and considered were the:

- unique features of the Canadian market, compared to the United States and other markets, including the large number of smaller issuers and the limited liquidity of these smaller issuers and of our market;
- potential detrimental or inadvertent impact of certain Draft Amendments, such as hindering an investor's ability to rapidly accumulate or reduce a large position and the signalling of investment strategies to the market;
- complexity and difficulty of applying a new early warning reporting trigger in respect of "equity equivalent derivatives";
- significant administrative and compliance burden associated with implementing additional reporting obligations; and
- potential benefits of the enhanced disclosure being outweighed by the potential negative impact of implementing certain Draft Amendments.

We intend to provide a summary of comments received in respect of the Draft Amendments in our next publication.

Final Amendments

In light of the comments received and following further reflection and analysis, the CSA have re-considered the proposals and have determined not to proceed with certain of the Draft Amendments. Instead, the CSA intend to proceed to publish final amendments to MI 62-104 and NI 62-103 as well as guidance in NP 62-203 (collectively, the Final Amendments) that will address certain key issues identified in the

Draft Amendments. In Ontario, we anticipate that amendments to the *Securities Act* (Ontario) and Ontario Securities Commission Rule *Take-Over Bids and Issuer Bids* will be proposed in order to allow the substance of the Final Amendments to apply fully.

The CSA have concluded that it is not appropriate at this time to proceed with:

- the proposal to reduce the reporting threshold from 10% to 5%; and
- the proposal to include "equity equivalent derivatives" for the purposes of determining the threshold for early warning reporting disclosure.

Nonetheless, subject to necessary approvals, we are proceeding with the following Final Amendments. These amendments will enhance transparency by:

- requiring disclosure of 2% decreases in ownership;
- requiring disclosure when a shareholder's ownership interest falls below the reporting threshold;
- making the alternative monthly reporting system unavailable to eligible institutional investors as described in the Draft Amendments, with additional clarification on the circumstances when they would be precluded;
- exempting lenders from disclosure requirements if they lend shares pursuant to a specified securities lending arrangement;
- exempting borrowers, in certain circumstances, from disclosure requirements if they borrow shares under a securities lending arrangement;
- providing guidance clarifying the current application of early warning reporting requirements to certain derivatives and requiring disclosure of derivatives in the early warning report;
- enhancing and improving the disclosure requirements in the early warning report; and
- clarifying the timeframe to file the early warning report and news release.

The CSA believe that the intended Final Amendments, while not as extensive as the Draft Amendments, will enhance the quality and integrity of the early warning reporting regime in a manner that is appropriate for the Canadian public capital markets

Next Steps

We are in the process of completing the Final Amendments and, subject to necessary approvals, intend to publish them in the second quarter of 2015.

Questions

[Omitted.]

OSC Rule 62-501 — Prohibited Stock Market Purchases of the Offeree's Securities by the Offeror During a Take-Over Bid

Date: **August 9, 2002**

25 O.S.C.B. 5356

[Revoked by s. 9.1 of Rule 62-504]

Final Rule: (2002) 25 O.S.C.B. 5356; Approval of OSC: (2002) 25. O.S.C.B. 3099; Request for Comments: (2001) 24 O.S.C.B. 7564.

OSC Rule 62-503 — Financing of Take-Over Bids and Issuer Bids

Date: **December 16, 2005**

28 O.S.C.B. 10149

[Revoked by s. 9.2 of Rule 62-504]

Final Rule: 28 O.S.C.B. 10149; Approval by OSC: 28 O.S.C.B. 8677; Request for Comments: 28 O.S.C.B. 5689.

OSC Rule 62-504 — Take-Over Bids and Issuer Bids

[Revoked effective May 9, 2016 upon the coming into force of NI 62-104, (2016) 39 O.S.C.B. 113]

OSC Policy 62-601 — Securities Exchange Take-Over Bids — Trades in the Offeror's Securities

[Revoked upon the coming into force of Rule 48-501]

OSC Policy 62-602 — Business and Asset Combinations

1. The Ontario Securities Commission is of the view that it is important, in order to maintain confidence in the integrity of the capital market, that adequate disclosure be made of complex and multi-step transactions. Such disclosure should provide a global view of the transactions and a more detailed analysis of the effect of the transaction on the security holders of each of the issuers involved in the

transaction. Disclosure can be made in a variety of ways including press releases and informal communications as well as in the types of disclosure documents required under the *Securities Act* (Ontario) or the applicable corporate statutes.

2. Certain complex business combinations are structured in such a manner that security holder approval is not required by the applicable statutes although the effect of the reorganization or combination is akin to that of an amalgamation where security holder approval would clearly be required. Issuers should give serious consideration to providing security holders with an opportunity to approve the corporate restructuring contemplated in such circumstances.

3. Issuers proposing to proceed with complex business and asset combination transactions may wish to discuss them with the Director of the Commission in order to review the proposed level of disclosure and to discuss whether security holder approval or a certain level of security holder approval would be appropriate in these circumstances. The Commission is prepared to review the Director's views with the interested parties.

(Renumbered as 62-602: (2001) 24 O.S.C.B. 2404; previously OSC Policy 7.4: (1982) 4 O.S.C.B. 535E; Former Policy 3-37: First published (1977) O.S.C.B. 253; amended (1977) O.S.C.B. 268; notices (1977) O.S.C.B. 273, (1978) O.S.C.B. 60; exceptions (1978) O.S.C.B. 114; amended (1978) O.S.C.B. 224; interpretation statement (1978) O.S.C.B. 323; draft amendment (1981) 1 O.S.C.B. 7E; addendum to draft (1981) 1 O.S.C.B. 24E.)

OSC Notice 62-701 — Staff Investigation in Respect of Loan by Stelco Inc. to Controlling Shareholder of Clarus Corporation

Date: May 3, 1991

14 O.S.C.B. 1807, Assigned number and amended (2001) 24 O.S.C.B. 2405

Commission staff has completed a review of the facts relating to the loan by Stelco Inc. ("Stelco") of approximately $16.5 million on August 18, 1989 to Canadian Investors Corp. and certain other private companies (collectively, the "Borrowers") controlled, directly or indirectly, by Michael Cochrane and members of his family. The loan was secured by a pledge of assets which included certain shares in the capital of Clarus Corporation ("Clarus") constituting a 66% voting interest in Clarus.

Following a demand by Stelco for repayment of the loan, Stelco announced by press release on March 26, 1990 that it had taken possession on that date of the Clarus shares which had been pledged as collateral for the loan. The allegation has been made to the Commission that the loan and the realization of the security constitute an illegal take-over bid for shares of Clarus in contravention of the Securities Act (Ontario) (the "Act").

Commission staff is of the view that a transaction structured as a loan secured by a pledge of securities, which transaction may result in the acquisition by the lender of outstanding voting or equity securities which, together with securities beneficially owned or over which control or direction is exercised, on the date of the loan, by the lender or any person or company acting jointly or in concert with the lender, constitute in the aggregate 20% or more of the outstanding securities of that class of securities at the date of the loan, may in appropriate circumstances properly be viewed as an "offer to acquire" the pledged securities, which transaction is subject to Part XX of the Act. Commission staff is of the view that the proper characterisation of such a transaction turns on whether the loan was bona fide at the time it was made or whether it was an indirect means of accomplishing a take-over bid not otherwise permitted by the Act.

In making an assessment of the characterisation of such a transaction, Commission staff considers relevant whether the loan was made in the ordinary course of business of the lender, on ordinary business terms and with a reasonable expectation of repayment in full.

Following an extensive investigation, Commission staff concluded that at the time the loan was made by Stelco on August 18, 1989 it was a bona fide loan transaction and consequently should not be characterized as a take-over bid by Stelco in respect of the Clarus shares pledged as collateral for the loan. Accordingly, staff has determined that it will not recommend proceedings against Stelco before the Commission in respect of this matter.

In reaching this conclusion, staff considered relevant the following facts:

- the loan was for the purposes of refinancing an existing bona fide loan, with all proceeds going to the previous lender, and not for the purposes of financing a share acquisition;

- based on representations made by the Borrowers to Stelco at the time of the loan, Stelco was of the view that the loan was reasonably secured by the security package indirectly assigned to it by Unicorp Canada Corporation, the previous lender to the Borrowers and a sophisticated merchant banker;

- based on the representations made by the Borrowers to Stelco at the time of the loan, Stelco had a reasonable expectation that the loan would be repaid in full;

- the loan was a full recourse loan;

- Stelco had on two previous occasions extended financial assistance to Continuous Colour Coat Limited, a subsidiary of Clarus and a significant Stelco customer; and

- Stelco had extended financial assistance of similar magnitude and on substantially similar terms to other significant customers in the past in order to ensure the continuity of supply relationships with these customers, such that these lending arrangements could be considered to be in the ordinary course of business for Stelco.

This conclusion by staff does not constitute an assessment of the appropriateness of other conduct of Clarus, the Borrowers or Stelco in respect of this matter. In particular, this conclusion does not constitute a determination of whether or not Clarus, the Borrowers or Stelco at all times complied fully with applicable disclosure requirements or fiduciary duties under securities, corporate or other laws. These matters, to the extent within the jurisdiction of the Commission, remain under review by the Commission's Enforcement Branch.

PART VII — SECURITIES TRANSACTIONS OUTSIDE THE JURISDICTIONS

7.1 — International Issuers

National Instrument 71-101 — The Multijurisdictional Disclosure System

Date: November 1, 1998
21 O.S.C.B. 6919

PART 1 — DEFINITIONS

1.1 Definitions — In this Instrument

"acting jointly or in concert" has the same interpretation as in securities legislation;

"affiliated party", for an issuer, means a person or company that directly, or indirectly through one or more intermediaries, controls or is controlled by, or is under common control with, the issuer;

"bid" means a take-over bid or an issuer bid;

"bid circular" means a take-over bid circular or an issuer bid circular as those terms are used in securities legislation;

"business combination" means a statutory merger or consolidation or similar plan or acquisition requiring the vote or consent of securityholders of a person or company, in which securities of the person or company or another person or company held by the securityholders will become or be exchanged for securities of any other person or company;

"commodity pool issuer" means an issuer formed and operated for the purpose of investing in commodity futures contracts, commodity futures, related products, or a combination of them;

"connected issuer" has the meaning ascribed to the term "connected issuer" or "connected party" in securities legislation;

"control", with respect to an issuer, means the possession, direct or indirect, of the power to direct or cause the direction of the management and policies of the issuer, whether through the ownership of voting securities, by contract or otherwise, and "under common control with" has a corresponding meaning;

"convertible", for debt or preferred shares, means that the rights and attributes attaching to the securities include a right or option to purchase, convert into, exchange for or otherwise acquire a security of the issuer or of another issuer that is

(a) an equity share,

(b) a debt or a preferred share not having an investment grade rating in the case of a debt or a preferred share having an investment grade rating, or

(c) another security that itself has a right or option to purchase, convert into, exchange for or otherwise acquire a security of the issuer or another issuer that is an equity share, or a debt or a preferred share not having an investment grade rating in the case of a debt or a preferred share having an investment grade rating;

"convert" has a corresponding meaning to the term "convertible";

"dealer registration requirement" means the requirement in securities legislation that prohibits a person or company from trading in a security unless the person or company is registered in the appropriate category of registration under securities legislation;

"equity shares" means common shares, non-voting equity shares and subordinate or restricted voting equity shares, but excludes preferred shares;

"expertised statement" means part of a disclosure document required to be filed for a distribution or bid made under this Instrument, a document that is incorporated by reference in the disclosure document, or a report used in or in connection with the disclosure document or any document incorporated by reference in the disclosure document, that in each case is purported to be made on the authority of an expert;

"foreign issuer" means an issuer that is not incorporated or organized under the laws of Canada or a jurisdiction, unless

(a) voting securities carrying more than 50 percent of the votes for the election of directors are held by persons or companies whose last address as shown on the books of the issuer is in Canada, and

(b) any one or more of

(i) the majority of the senior officers or directors of the issuer are citizens or residents of Canada,

(ii) more than 50 percent of the assets of the issuer are located in Canada, or

(iii) the business of the issuer is administered principally in Canada;

"independent underwriter" means a person or company that underwrites securities distributed by MJDS prospectus that is not the issuer and in respect of which

(a) if the person or company is a registrant, the issuer is not a connected issuer or related issuer, or

(b) if the person or company is not a registrant, would not be a connected issuer or related issuer if the person or company was a registrant;

"insider bid" has the meaning ascribed to that term in securities legislation;

"insider reporting requirement" means the requirement in securities legislation for an insider of a reporting issuer to file reports disclosing the insider's direct or indirect beneficial ownership of, or control or direction over, securities of the issuer;

"intermediary", for purposes of section 18.1, means a registered dealer or adviser, a bank or trust company, a participant in a clearing agency, a trustee or administrator of a self-administered retirement savings plan, retirement income fund, education savings plan, or other similar self-administered savings or investment plan registered under the ITA, or a nominee of any of those persons, that holds a security on behalf of another person or company that is not the registered holder of the security, unless excluded from the definition of "intermediary" by National Policy Statement No. 41 or any successor instrument to that national policy statement;

"investment grade rating" means a provisional rating by a rating organization in one of its generic rating categories that signifies investment grade;

"issuer tender offer statement" means an issuer tender offer statement on Schedule 13E-4 under Section 13(e)(1) of the 1934 Act;

"issuer bid" has the meaning ascribed to that term in securities legislation;

"majority-owned subsidiary" means a person or company of which voting securities carrying more than 50 percent of the votes for the election of directors are held by any one or more of

(a) another person or company, and

(b) the other majority-owned subsidiaries of that other person or company;

"method 1" means the first of the two alternative methods of providing prospectus certificates for rule 415 offerings made under this Instrument set forth in Appendix A;

"method 2" means the second of the two alternative methods of providing prospectus certificates for rule 415 offerings made under this Instrument set forth in Appendix B;

"MJDS" means the multijurisdictional disclosure system established by this Instrument;

"MJDS directors' circular" means, for a take-over bid for a class of securities of a U.S. issuer made under this Instrument, a tender offer solicitation/recommendation statement, amendments to that statement and all other information and materials required or permitted to be disseminated to holders of the securities by the offeree issuer or its board of directors for a tender offer made for the securities under U.S. federal securities law, that in each case complies with the form and content requirements of subsection 12.4(2);

"MJDS director's or officer's circular" means, for a take-over bid for a class of securities of a U.S. issuer made under this Instrument, a tender offer solicitation/recommendation statement, amendments to that statement and all other information and materials required or permitted to be disseminated to holders of the securities by an individual director or officer for a tender offer made for the securities under U.S. federal securities law, that in each case complies with the form and content requirements of subsection 12.4(2);

"MJDS issuer bid circular" means, for an issuer bid for a class of securities of a U.S. issuer made under this Instrument, an issuer tender offer statement, amendments to that statement and all other information and materials required to be disseminated to holders of the securities by the issuer for an issuer tender offer made for the securities under U.S. federal securities law, that in each case complies with the form and content requirements of subsection 12.4(1);

"MJDS prospectus" means, for a distribution of securities under this Instrument other than under section 12.3, a U.S. prospectus that contains the additional information, legends and certificates required by, and otherwise complies with the disclosure requirements of, this Instrument;

"MJDS take-over bid circular" means, for a take-over bid for a class of securities of a U.S. issuer made under this Instrument, a tender offer statement, amendments to that statement and all other information and materials required to be disseminated to holders of the securities by the offeror for a tender offer made for the securities under U.S. federal securities law, that in each case complies with the form and content requirements of subsection 12.4(1);

"MTN program" means a continuous rule 415 offering of debt in which the specific variable terms of the individual securities and the offering of the securities are determined at the time of sale;

"Nasdaq" means the Nasdaq Stock Market;

"NNM" means the Nasdaq National Market;

"non-convertible" means securities that are not convertible;

"offeree issuer" has the meaning ascribed to that term in securities legislation;

"offeror" has the meaning ascribed to that term in securities legislation;

"parent", for a majority-owned subsidiary, means a person or company that, alone or together with any one or more of the person or company's other majority-owned subsidiaries, holds voting securities of the majority-owned subsidiary carrying more than 50 percent of the votes for the election of directors;

"preliminary MJDS prospectus" means, for a distribution of securities under this Instrument other than under section 12.3, a preliminary form of MJDS prospectus;

"principal jurisdiction" means the jurisdiction specified in accordance with section 5.1;

"principal market", for a class of securities, means the single securities market with the largest aggregate trading volume for the class of securities in the preceding 12 calendar month period;

"prospectus requirement" means the prohibition in securities legislation from a person or company distributing a security unless a preliminary prospectus and prospectus for the distribution have been filed and receipts obtained for them;

"public float", for a class of securities, means

    (a) the aggregate market value of the securities held by persons or companies that are not affiliated parties of the issuer of the securities, calculated by using the price at which the securities were last sold in the principal market for the securities on the date specified in the applicable provision of this Instrument, or the average of the bid and asked prices of the securities in the principal market on that date if there were no sales on that date,

    (b) if there is no market for the class of securities, the book value of the securities held by persons or companies that are not affiliated parties of the issuer of the securities computed on that date, and

    (c) if the issuer of the class of securities is in bankruptcy or receivership or has an accumulated capital deficit, one-third of the principal amount, par value or stated value of the securities held by persons or companies that are not affiliated parties of the issuer of the securities computed on that date;

"rating organization" means each of CBRS Inc., Dominion Bond Rating Service Limited, Moody's Investors Service, Inc., Standard & Poor's Corporation and any entity recognized by the SEC as a nationally recognized statistical rating organization as that term is used in Rule 15c3-1(c)(2)(vi)(F) under the 1934 Act;

"related issuer" has the meaning ascribed to the term "related issuer" or "related party" in securities legislation;

"rule 415 offering" means a distribution under Rule 415 under the 1933 Act that is made under this Instrument;

"rule 415 prospectus supplement" means a form of prospectus supplement prepared for a rule 415 offering;

"rule 430A offering" means a distribution under Rule 430A under the 1933 Act that is made under this Instrument;

"rule 430A pricing prospectus" means a MJDS prospectus prepared for a rule 430A offering that contains the information omitted from the U.S. prospectus included as part of the registration statement at the time of effectiveness of the registration statement, as permitted by Rule 430A under the 1933 Act;

"securities exchange bid" means a bid in which the consideration for the securities of the offeree issuer consists, in whole or in part, of securities of an offeror or other issuer;

"specified predecessor" means, for a successor issuer continuing after a business combination, a predecessor to the successor issuer whose assets and gross revenues in aggregate would contribute less than 20 percent of the total assets and gross revenues from continuing operations of the successor issuer, based on a *pro forma* combination of each predecessor's financial position and results of operations for its most recently completed financial year ended before the business combination for which financial statements have been filed;

"successor issuer" means an issuer subsisting as an issuer after a business combination;

"take-over bid" has the meaning ascribed to that term in securities legislation;

"tender offer solicitation/recommendation statement" means a statement made under rule 14d-9 or 14e-2 under the 1934 Act;

"tender offer statement" means a tender offer statement on Schedule 14D-1 under section 14(d) of the 1934 Act;

"U.S. federal securities law" means the federal statutes of the United States of America concerning the regulation of securities markets and trading in securities and the regulations, rules, forms and schedules under those statutes;

"U.S. issuer" means a foreign issuer that is incorporated or organized under the laws of the United States of America or any state or territory of the United States of America or the District of Columbia;

"U.S. prospectus" means a prospectus that has been prepared in accordance with the disclosure and other requirements of U.S. federal securities law for an offering of securities registered under the 1933 Act, or if the offering is not being made contemporaneously in the U.S., as if the offering is being made on a registered basis in the United States of America;

"voting securities" means securities the holders of which have a present entitlement to vote for the election of directors;

"1934 Act filings" means all filings required to be made with the SEC under sections 13, 14 and 15(d) of the 1934 Act; and

"1940 Act" means the *Investment Company Act of 1940* of the United States of America.

PART 2 — GENERAL

2.1 Timing of Filing — Unless otherwise provided in this Instrument, documents that must be filed under this Instrument that are also filed with the SEC shall be filed as nearly as practicable contemporaneously with the filing with the SEC.

2.2 Successor Issuers — A successor issuer satisfies the eligibility criteria set forth in subparagraphs 3.1(a)(iii), 3.1(b)(ii) and (iii) and paragraphs 12.3(1)(c) and 13.1(1)(c) if

    (a) since the business combination the successor issuer has made all 1934 Act filings and, if applicable, has had a class of its securities listed on the New York Stock Exchange or the American Stock Exchange or quoted on NNM;

    (b) the successor issuer is in compliance with the obligations arising from the listing or quotation referred to in paragraph (a), if applicable; and

    (c) the filing, listing or quotation requirement to be satisfied for a period of 12 or 36 months is satisfied for each predecessor, other than a specified predecessor.

2.3 Successor Issuer Interpretation — In determining if the filing, listing or quotation requirement in paragraph 2.2(c) is satisfied for a period of 12 or 36 months for each predecessor, the period during which the successor issuer satisfied the requirement shall be added to the immediately preceding period during which the predecessor satisfied the requirement.

PART 3 — MJDS PROSPECTUS DISTRIBUTIONS OF SECURITIES OF U.S. ISSUERS

3.1 General Eligibility Criteria — Subject to section 3.3, this Instrument may be used to distribute

    (a) debt that has an investment grade rating or preferred shares that have an investment grade rating, in each case at the time the preliminary MJDS prospectus is filed in the principal jurisdiction, or rights that, upon issuance, are immediately exercisable for any of these securities, if

        (i) the issuer is a U.S. issuer,

(ii) the issuer

    (A) has a class of securities registered under section 12(b) or 12(g) of the 1934 Act, or

    (B) is required to file reports under section 15(d) of the 1934 Act,

(iii) the issuer has filed with the SEC all 1934 Act filings for a period of 12 calendar months immediately before the filing of the preliminary MJDS prospectus in the principal jurisdiction,

(iv) the issuer is not registered or required to be registered as an investment company under the 1940 Act,

(v) the issuer is not a commodity pool issuer, and

(vi) the securities being offered or issuable upon the exercise of the rights either,

    (A) are non-convertible, or

    (B) if convertible, may not be converted for at least one year after issuance, and the equity shares of the issuer of the securities into which the offered securities are convertible have a public float of not less than U.S. \$75,000,000, determined as of a date within 60 days before the filing of the preliminary MJDS prospectus in the principal jurisdiction;

(b) rights to purchase additional securities of its own issue issued by a U.S. issuer to its existing securityholders and the securities issued upon the exercise of the rights, if

(i) the issuer meets the eligibility criteria specified in subparagraphs (a)(ii), (iv) and (v),

(ii) the issuer has filed with the SEC all 1934 Act filings for a period of 36 calendar months immediately before the filing of the preliminary MJDS prospectus in the principal jurisdiction,

(iii) the issuer has had a class of its securities listed on the New York Stock Exchange or the American Stock Exchange or quoted on the NNM for a period of at least 12 calendar months immediately before the filing of the preliminary MJDS prospectus in the principal jurisdiction and is in compliance with the obligations arising from the listing or quotation,

(iv) the rights are exercisable immediately upon issuance,

(v) subject to subparagraph (vi), the rights issued to residents of Canada have the same terms and conditions as the rights issued to residents of the United States of America, and

(vi) beneficial ownership of rights issued to a resident of Canada are not transferable to a resident of Canada, other than residents to whom rights of the same issue were granted, provided that,

    (A) the securities issuable upon exercise of the rights may be so transferable, and

    (B) this limitation does not restrict the transfer of rights on a securities exchange or inter-dealer quotation system outside of Canada; or

(c) any securities of a U.S. issuer if

(i) the issuer meets the eligibility criteria specified in subparagraphs (a)(ii) to (v), and

(ii) the equity shares of the issuer have a public float of not less than U.S. \$75,000,000, determined as of a date within 60 days before the filing of the preliminary MJDS prospectus in the principal jurisdiction.

3.2 Alternative Eligibility Criteria for Certain Guaranteed Issues — Subject to section 3.3, this Instrument may also be used to distribute securities of an issuer, if

(a) the securities distributed are

(i) non-convertible debt having an investment grade rating, or non-convertible preferred shares having an investment grade rating, of a majority-owned subsidiary whose parent meets the eligibility criteria set forth in subparagraphs 3.1(a)(i) through (v),

(ii) convertible debt having an investment grade rating, or convertible preferred shares having an investment grade rating, of a majority-owned subsidiary that may not be converted for at least one year after issuance and are convertible only into securities of a parent that meets the eligibility requirements set forth in subparagraphs 3.1(a)(i) through (v) and sub-subparagraph 3.1(a)(vi)(B),

(iii) non-convertible debt, or non-convertible preferred shares, of a majority-owned subsidiary whose parent meets the eligibility requirements set forth in paragraph 3.1(c), or

(iv) convertible debt, or convertible preferred shares, of a majority-owned subsidiary that are convertible only into securities of a parent that meets the eligibility requirements set forth in paragraph 3.1(c);

(b) the issuer meets the eligibility criteria set forth in subparagraphs 3.1(a)(i), (iv) and (v); and

(c) the parent fully and unconditionally guarantees payment in respect of the securities being distributed, as to principal and interest if the securities are debt, and as to liquidation preference, redemption and dividends if the securities are preferred shares.

3.3 Limitation on Distribution of Derivative Securities — (1) No person or company shall file a prospectus for the distribution of derivative securities under this Instrument.

(2) Despite subsection (1), warrants, options, rights or convertible securities may be distributed under this Instrument if the issuer of the underlying securities to which the warrants, options, rights or convertible securities relate is eligible under this Instrument to distribute the underlying securities.

3.4 Preliminary MJDS Prospectus and MJDS Prospectus — (1) A U.S. issuer shall file a preliminary MJDS prospectus and a MJDS prospectus for a distribution of securities under this Instrument other than under section 12.3.

(2) A preliminary MJDS prospectus, an amendment to a preliminary MJDS prospectus, a MJDS prospectus and an amendment to a MJDS prospectus is a preliminary prospectus, an amendment to a preliminary prospectus, a prospectus and an amendment to a prospectus, respectively, for the purposes of securities legislation.

Part 7: TRANSACTIONS OUTSIDE JURISDICTIONS

PART 4 — FORM AND CONTENT OF MJDS PROSPECTUS

4.1 Distributions in Canada and the U.S. — Subject to section 4.2, an issuer of securities distributed under this Instrument shall file the registration statement and amendments to the registration statement filed for the offering with the SEC, together with the related preliminary MJDS prospectus and MJDS prospectus and amendments and supplements to the preliminary MJDS prospectus and MJDS prospectus.

4.2 Distributions only in Canada — If a distribution is being made only in Canada, the issuer does not need to file a registration statement and amendments to the registration statement, or other information required in a registration statement but not required in the U.S. prospectus.

4.3 Additional Legends and Disclosure — (1) The following statements shall be printed

    (a) in red ink on the outside front cover page, or on a sticker on that page, of each preliminary MJDS prospectus used for a distribution under this Instrument

        This preliminary MJDS prospectus relating to the securities described in it has been filed in [each of/certain of] the [provinces/provinces and territories] of Canada but has not yet become final for the purpose of a distribution. Information contained in this preliminary MJDS prospectus may not be complete and may have to be amended. The securities may not be distributed until a receipt is obtained for the MJDS prospectus.;

    (b) on the outside or inside front cover page, or on a sticker on that page, of each preliminary MJDS prospectus and MJDS prospectus

        (i) "This offering is being made by a U.S. issuer using disclosure documents prepared in accordance with U.S. securities laws. Purchasers should be aware that these requirements may differ from those of [insert the names of the provinces and territories where qualified]. The financial statements included or incorporated by reference in this prospectus have not been prepared in accordance with Canadian generally accepted accounting principles and may not be comparable to financial statements of Canadian issuers."

        (ii) "[All of] [Certain of] the directors and officers of the issuer and [all of] [certain of] the experts named in this prospectus reside outside of Canada. [[Substantially] [A]ll of the assets of these persons and of the issuer may be located outside Canada.] The issuer has appointed [name and address of agent for service] as its agent for service of process in Canada, but it may not be possible for investors to effect service of process within Canada upon the directors, officers and experts referred to above. It may also not be possible to enforce against the issuer, its directors and officers and [certain of] the experts named in this prospectus judgments obtained in Canadian courts predicated upon the civil liability provisions of applicable securities laws in Canada."

        (iii) "This prospectus constitutes a public offering of these securities only in those jurisdictions where they may be lawfully offered for sale and in those jurisdictions only by persons permitted to sell such securities. No securities commission or similar authority in Canada or the United States of America has in any way passed upon the merits of the securities offered by this prospectus and any representation to the contrary is an offence."; and

    (c) in each preliminary MJDS prospectus and MJDS prospectus

        Securities legislation in [certain of the provinces [and territories] of Canada] [the Province of... [insert name of local jurisdiction, if applicable]] provides purchasers with the right to withdraw from an agreement to purchase securities within two business days after receipt or deemed receipt of a prospectus and any amendment. [In several of the provinces [and territories], the] securities legislation further provides a purchaser with remedies for rescission [or [, in some jurisdictions,] damages] if the prospectus and any amendment contains a misrepresentation or is not delivered to the purchaser, provided that such remedies for rescission [or damages] are exercised by the purchaser within the time limit prescribed by the securities legislation of the purchaser's province [or territory]. The purchaser should refer to the applicable provisions of the securities legislation of the purchaser's province [or territory] for particulars of these rights or consult with a legal adviser. Rights and remedies also may be available to purchasers under U.S. law; purchasers may wish to consult with a U.S. legal adviser for particulars of these rights.

(2) A preliminary MJDS prospectus, MJDS prospectus or amendment or supplement to a preliminary MJDS prospectus or MJDS prospectus need not contain any disclosure relevant solely to U.S. offerees or purchasers, including

    (a) any "red herring" legend required by U.S. federal securities law;

    (b) except as provided in paragraph (1)(b)(iii), any legend regarding approval or disapproval by the SEC;

    (c) any discussion of U.S. tax considerations other than those material to Canadian purchasers; and

    (d) the names of U.S. underwriters not acting as underwriters in Canada or a description of the U.S. plan of distribution, except to the extent necessary to describe facts material to the Canadian distribution.

4.4 Incorporation by Reference — Except as otherwise provided in this Instrument, documents incorporated or deemed to be incorporated by reference into a U.S. prospectus under U.S. federal securities law shall be, and are deemed to be, incorporated by reference into a preliminary MJDS prospectus or MJDS prospectus.

4.5 Statements Modified or Superseded — (1) A statement in a document incorporated or deemed to be incorporated by reference into a MJDS prospectus shall be deemed to be modified or superseded, for the purposes of the MJDS prospectus, to the extent that a statement in the MJDS prospectus or in any other subsequently filed document that also is or is deemed to be incorporated by reference into the MJDS prospectus modifies or supersedes the statement.

(2) The modifying or superseding statement need not state that it has modified or superseded a prior statement or include any other information in the document that it modifies or supersedes.

(3) The making of a modifying or superseding statement shall not be deemed an admission for any purpose that the modified or superseded statement, when made, constituted a misrepresentation, an untrue statement of material fact or an omission to state a material fact that is required to be stated or that is necessary to make a statement not misleading in light of the circumstances in which it was made.

(4) A statement so modified or superseded shall not be deemed in its unmodified or superseded form to constitute part of the MJDS prospectus.

(5) If documents are incorporated by reference into a preliminary MJDS prospectus or MJDS prospectus, the section in the preliminary MJDS prospectus or MJDS prospectus that provides information about incorporation by reference shall include a statement that information has been incorporated by reference from documents filed with the Canadian securities regulatory authority in each jurisdiction in which the distribution is being made and shall state the name, address and telephone number of an officer of the issuer from whom copies of the documents may be obtained on request without charge.

4.6 Reconciliation of Financial Statements — (1) A preliminary MJDS prospectus and a MJDS prospectus used to distribute securities eligible under paragraph 3.1(c) shall include a reconciliation of the financial statements required to be included or incorporated by reference in the preliminary MJDS prospectus and MJDS prospectus to Canadian GAAP in the notes to the financial statements or as a supplement included or incorporated by reference in the preliminary MJDS prospectus and MJDS prospectus.

(2) A reconciliation required to be included in the financial statements under subsection (1) shall explain and quantify as a separate reconciling item any significant differences between the principles applied in the financial statements, including note disclosure, and Canadian GAAP and, in the case of the reconciliation of the annual financial statements, shall be covered by an auditor's report.

4.7 General Certification Requirements — Except as provided in sections 4.8 to 4.10, each preliminary MJDS prospectus and MJDS prospectus used for a distribution under this Part shall contain

    (a) a certificate in the following form, signed by the chief executive officer, the chief financial officer, and, on behalf of the board of directors of the issuer, any two directors of the issuer, other than the chief executive officer and the chief financial officer, any person or company who is a promoter of the issuer and each person or company who is a guarantor of the securities distributed under the MJDS prospectus

        The foregoing [insert, if applicable, — "together with the documents incorporated in this prospectus by reference,"] constitutes full, true and plain disclosure of all material facts relating to the securities offered by this prospectus as required by [insert applicable references] [insert if offering made in Quebec — "and does not contain any misrepresentation likely to affect the value or the market price of the securities to be distributed"]; and

    (b) if there is an underwriter, a certificate in the following form, signed by each underwriter who is in a contractual relationship with the issuer or selling securityholder for the securities distributed under the MJDS prospectus

        To the best of our knowledge, information and belief, the foregoing [insert, if applicable, — ", together with the documents incorporated in this prospectus by reference,"] constitutes full, true and plain disclosure of all material facts relating to the securities offered by this prospectus as required by [insert applicable references] [insert if offering made in Quebec — "and does not contain any misrepresentation likely to affect the value or the market price of the securities to be distributed."].

4.8 Certificate Requirement for Rule 415 Offerings — A preliminary MJDS prospectus, an amendment to a preliminary MJDS prospectus, a MJDS prospectus and an amendment to a MJDS prospectus filed for a rule 415 offering under this Part shall contain certificates prepared in accordance with method 1 or method 2.

4.9 Certificate Requirement for Rule 430A Offerings — For a rule 430A offering,

    (a) a preliminary MJDS prospectus, amendment to a preliminary MJDS prospectus and a MJDS prospectus,

    (b) an amended MJDS prospectus filed to commence a new period for filing a rule 430A pricing prospectus, and

    (c) an amendment to a MJDS prospectus filed for a rule 430A offering before the information omitted from the MJDS prospectus has been filed in either a rule 430A pricing prospectus or an amendment shall contain

        (i) a certificate in the following form, signed by the chief executive officer, the chief financial officer, and, on behalf of the board of directors of the issuer, any two directors of the issuer, other than the chief executive officer and chief financial officer, any person or company who is a promoter of the issuer and each person or company who is a guarantor of the securities to be distributed under the MJDS prospectus

            The foregoing, together with the documents incorporated in this prospectus by reference as of the date of the prospectus providing the information permitted to be omitted from this prospectus, will constitute full, true and plain disclosure of all material facts relating to the securities offered by this prospectus as required by [insert applicable references] [insert if offering made in Quebec — "and will not contain any misrepresentation likely to affect the value or the market price of the securities to be distributed."]; and

        (ii) if there is an underwriter, a certificate in the following form, signed by each underwriter who is in a contractual relationship with the issuer or selling securityholder for the securities distributed under the MJDS prospectus

            To the best of our knowledge, information and belief, the foregoing, together with the documents incorporated in this prospectus by reference, as of the date of the prospectus providing the information permitted to be omitted from this prospectus, will constitute full, true and plain disclosure of all material facts relating to the securities offered by this prospectus as required by [insert applicable references] [insert if offering made in Quebec — "and will not contain any misrepresentation likely to affect the value or the market price of the securities to be distributed".].

4.10 Certificates for Rule 430A Pricing Prospectus — A rule 430A pricing prospectus shall contain in place of the certificates referred to in section 4.9

    (a) a certificate in the following form, signed by the chief executive officer, the chief financial officer, and, on behalf of the board of directors of the issuer, any two directors of the issuer, other than the chief executive officer and chief financial officer, any person or company who is a promoter of the issuer and each person or company who is a guarantor of the securities distributed under the MJDS prospectus

        The foregoing [insert, if applicable — ", together with the documents incorporated in this prospectus by reference,"] constitutes full, true and plain disclosure of all material facts relating to the securities offered by this prospectus as required by [insert applicable references] [insert if offering made in Quebec — "and does not contain any misrepresentation likely to affect the value or the market price of the securities to be distributed."]; and

    (b) if there is an underwriter, a certificate in the following form, signed by each underwriter who is in a contractual relationship with the issuer or selling securityholder for securities distributed under the MJDS prospectus

        To the best of our knowledge, information and belief, the foregoing [insert, if applicable — ", together with the documents incorporated in this prospectus by reference,"] constitutes full, true and plain disclosure of all material facts relating to the securities offered by this prospectus as required by [insert applicable references] [insert if offering also made in Quebec — "and does not contain any misrepresentation likely to affect the value or the market price of the securities to be distributed."].

4.11 Signing of Certificates by Agent — Certificates contained in a preliminary MJDS prospectus, MJDS prospectus, amendment to a preliminary MJDS prospectus or MJDS prospectus, rule 415 prospectus supplement or rule 430A pricing prospectus shall be signed in accordance with securities legislation provided that any or all of the persons or companies required to sign a certificate may sign the certificate for a distribution made under this Instrument by an agent duly authorized in writing.

PART 5 — FILING PROCEDURES

5.1 Specification of Principal Jurisdiction — At the time of filing a preliminary MJDS prospectus, the issuer shall send written notice to the securities regulatory authority and, unless the distribution is being made in Canada only, to the SEC, stating that the distribution is being made under the MJDS and specifying the principal jurisdiction.

5.2 Alternate Principal Jurisdiction — If the securities regulatory authority in the jurisdiction specified in the notice sent under section 5.1 advises the issuer that it is not prepared to act as principal jurisdiction, the issuer shall specify another jurisdiction that is prepared to act as principal jurisdiction and notify the security regulatory authority in each jurisdiction in which the preliminary MJDS prospectus was filed and the SEC.

5.3 SEC Review — If the SEC notifies an issuer that a filing made under the MJDS has been selected for review, the issuer shall notify the securities regulatory authority in the principal jurisdiction.

PART 6 — FILING DOCUMENTS

6.1 Principal Jurisdiction — The issuer shall file in the principal jurisdiction

    (a) the preliminary MJDS prospectus, the MJDS prospectus, each amendment and supplement to the preliminary MJDS prospectus and MJDS prospectus, the rule 430A pricing prospectus and each rule 415 prospectus supplement used in Canada,

    (b) all documents incorporated or deemed to be incorporated by reference in the MJDS prospectus, and

    (c) all other documents required by this Instrument.

6.2 Canada-U.S. Offering — If the distribution is being made in Canada and the United States of America, the issuer shall also file in the principal jurisdiction one unsigned copy of the registration statement and all amendments and exhibits to the registration statement in addition to the documents specified in section 6.1.

6.3 Non-Principal Jurisdictions — In the jurisdictions other than the principal jurisdiction, the issuer shall file

    (a) the preliminary MJDS prospectus, the MJDS prospectus, each amendment and supplement to the preliminary MJDS prospectus and MJDS prospectus, the rule 430A pricing prospectus and, subject to section 7.6, each rule 415 prospectus supplement used in Canada,

    (b) all documents incorporated or deemed to be incorporated by reference in the MJDS prospectus, and

    (c) all other documents required by this Instrument.

6.4 Certificate Regarding Eligibility Criteria — At the time of filing a preliminary MJDS prospectus, an issuer shall file a certificate, signed on its behalf by a senior officer of the issuer, confirming that the issuer satisfies the applicable eligibility criteria.

6.5 Consents — (1) The issuer shall file the written consent of an attorney, auditor, accountant, engineer, appraiser or any other person or company named as having prepared or certified any expertised statement as follows:

    (a) if the expertised statement is in the preliminary MJDS prospectus, an amendment to the preliminary MJDS prospectus, the MJDS prospectus or a document incorporated by reference into the MJDS prospectus that was filed before the filing of the MJDS prospectus, the consent shall be filed at the time of filing the MJDS prospectus; and

    (b) if the expertised statement is in an amendment to the MJDS prospectus, a rule 415 prospectus supplement, a rule 430A pricing prospectus, or a document incorporated by reference into a MJDS prospectus that was filed after the filing of the MJDS prospectus, the consent shall be filed at the time of filing the amendment, the rule 415 prospectus supplement, the rule 430A pricing prospectus or the document.

(2) Despite subsection (1), the filing requirements in paragraphs (1)(a) and (b) do not apply to the consent of a rating organization that issues a rating or provisional rating that is used in or in connection with a preliminary MJDS prospectus, an amendment to a preliminary MJDS prospectus, a MJDS prospectus, an amendment to a MJDS prospectus, a rule 415 prospectus supplement or a rule 430A pricing prospectus.

6.6 Further Consents — If a change to the MJDS prospectus is material to the consent filed under subsection 6.5(1), the issuer shall file a further consent contemporaneously with the filing of the change to the MJDS prospectus.

6.7 Form of Consent — The consent referred to in sections 6.5 and 6.6 shall be prepared in accordance with securities legislation.

6.8 Reports on Property — An issuer satisfies the requirement of securities legislation to file a report on the property of a natural resource company if it files a report prepared in accordance with U.S. federal securities law if a report is required to be filed with the SEC.

6.9 Appointment of Agent for Service — At the time of filing of the MJDS prospectus, the issuer shall file a duly executed submission to jurisdiction and appointment of agent for service of process in the required form.

6.10 Powers of Attorney — If a person or company signs a certificate by an agent under section 4.11, the issuer shall file a duly executed copy of the document authorizing the agent to sign the certificate not later than the time of filing the document in which the certificate is included.

6.11 Notification of Effectiveness — If the securities distributed under this Instrument are also offered or sold in the United States of America, the issuer whose securities are being distributed under this Instrument shall notify in writing the principal jurisdiction once the related registration statement filed with the SEC has become effective.

6.12 Exhibits to Registration Statement — An issuer shall file any exhibits to a registration statement requested by the securities regulatory authority in a non-principal jurisdiction.

6.13 Rule 415 Offerings — A commercial copy of each MJDS prospectus and rule 415 prospectus supplement need not be refiled if it is used, without change, in distributions of additional tranches of securities.

6.14 French Language Documentation Not Required — A preliminary MJDS prospectus and a MJDS prospectus in the French language need not be filed in Quebec for an offering of rights eligible to be made under paragraph 3.1(b), unless

(a) the issuer is a reporting issuer in Quebec other than solely as a result of one or more rights offerings made under paragraph 3.1(b); or

(b) 20 percent or more of the class of securities in respect of which the rights are issued is held by persons or companies whose last address as shown on the books of the issuer is in Canada.

PART 7 — AMENDMENT AND SUPPLEMENT PROCEDURES

7.1 Form of Amendment or Supplement — (1) An issuer shall amend or supplement disclosure documents filed under this Instrument in accordance with U.S. federal securities law.

(2) The amending or supplementing document shall contain the legends and certificates required by this Instrument.

7.2 Modification or Amendment — (1) If a registration statement is amended in a manner that modifies the related U.S. prospectus, an issuer shall file the documents containing the modification.

(2) If the receipt for the MJDS prospectus has not been issued and the filing has been made as a result of the occurrence of an adverse material change since the filing of the preliminary MJDS prospectus or an amendment to the preliminary MJDS prospectus, an issuer shall file the documents as an amendment to the preliminary MJDS prospectus.

7.3 Post-Effective Amendment — If a modification is made to a U.S. prospectus by filing with the SEC a post-effective amendment to the registration statement, an issuer shall file an amendment to the MJDS prospectus.

7.4 Amendment to Additional Disclosure — An issuer shall file an amendment in the event of an adverse material change in the additional disclosure contained only in the preliminary MJDS prospectus or a material change in the additional disclosure contained only in the MJDS prospectus.

7.5 Filing of Rule 415 Prospectus Supplement — (1) An issuer shall file a rule 415 prospectus supplement.

(2) A rule 415 prospectus supplement filed under subsection (1) shall be deemed to be incorporated into the MJDS prospectus as of the date of filing with the SEC, but only for the purpose of the distribution of the securities covered by the supplement.

7.6 Rule 415 Prospectus Supplement Not Filed — Despite sections 6.3 and 7.5, an issuer is not required to file a rule 415 prospectus supplement in the local jurisdiction unless it is the principal jurisdiction, if

(a) the rule 415 prospectus supplement is used to describe the terms of a tranche of securities distributed under the MJDS prospectus, or is a preliminary form of the rule 415 prospectus supplement for use in marketing, and the securities covered by the supplement will not be distributed in the local jurisdiction; or

(b) the rule 415 prospectus supplement is used to establish an MTN program or other continuous offering program or to update disclosure for the program, and securities will not be distributed under the program in the local jurisdiction.

7.7 Filing of Rule 430A Pricing Prospectus — An issuer shall file a rule 430A pricing prospectus.

7.8 Incorporation by Reference of Pricing Information — The information contained in a rule 430A pricing prospectus that was omitted from the U.S. prospectus in accordance with Rule 430A under the 1933 Act and any other additional information that the issuer has elected to include in the rule 430A pricing prospectus in accordance with U.S. federal securities law shall be deemed to be incorporated by reference into the MJDS prospectus as of the date of the rule 430A pricing prospectus.

7.9 Filing of Revised U.S. Prospectus or Prospectus Supplement — (1) If an issuer files with the SEC a revised U.S. prospectus, other than as an amendment to the related registration statement under rule 424(b) or another rule under the 1933 Act, or a prospectus supplement, to modify a U.S. prospectus, other than a U.S. prospectus for a rule 415 offering or a rule 430A offering, the issuer shall file the revised U.S. prospectus or prospectus supplement.

(2) The revised U.S. prospectus or prospectus supplement shall be deemed to be incorporated into the MJDS prospectus as of the date of the revised U.S. prospectus or prospectus supplement.

PART 8 — DISSEMINATION REQUIREMENTS

8.1 General — Subject to section 8.3, a preliminary MJDS prospectus, a MJDS prospectus and amendments and supplements to either shall be sent to offerees and purchasers in accordance with prospectus delivery requirements of securities legislation.

8.2 Prospectus Supplements — All prospectus supplements applicable to the securities being distributed shall be attached to, or included with, the MJDS prospectus that is sent to offerees and purchasers of the securities.

8.3 Rule 430A Pricing Prospectus — Instead of the related MJDS prospectus, a rule 430A pricing prospectus shall be sent to offerees and purchasers in accordance with prospectus delivery requirements of securities legislation.

8.4 Documents Incorporated by Reference — Documents that are incorporated or deemed to be incorporated by reference into a preliminary MJDS prospectus or a MJDS prospectus, other than rule 415 prospectus supplements and rule 430A pricing prospectuses, shall be sent to offerees or purchasers if the documents are required to be sent to offerees or purchasers under U.S. federal securities law.

8.5 Provision of Documents Incorporated by Reference — Documents incorporated by reference or deemed to be incorporated by reference shall be provided by the issuer to any person or company upon request without charge.

PART 9 — REGISTRATION REQUIREMENTS

9.1 Rights offerings — The dealer registration requirement does not apply to a trade made by a U.S. issuer in accordance with this Instrument of a right to purchase additional securities of its own issue issued by a U.S. issuer to its existing securityholders and of the securities issued upon the exercise of the right.

PART 10 — CONFLICTS OF INTEREST

10.1 Distributions of a Registrant, Connected Issuer or a Related Issuer — The provisions of securities legislation that regulate conflicts of interest in connection with a distribution of securities of a registrant, a connected issuer of a registrant or a related issuer of a registrant that require specified disclosure in a preliminary prospectus or prospectus do not apply to a distribution under this Instrument.

PART 11 — GENERAL

11.1 Representations as to Listing — The prohibitions in securities legislation regarding representations as to the listing, posting for trading or quotation of securities or to an application having been made or to be made for the listing, posting for trading or quotation of securities do not apply to distributions made under this Instrument.

11.2 Solicitations of Expressions of Interest — The prospectus requirement does not apply to solicitations of expressions of interest for the purchase of securities before the filing of a preliminary MJDS prospectus if

(a) the issuer or selling securityholder has entered into an enforceable agreement with an underwriter who has, or underwriters who have, agreed to purchase the securities;

(b) the agreement referred to in paragraph (a) has fixed the terms of the distribution and requires that the issuer file a preliminary MJDS prospectus for the securities and obtain a receipt for the preliminary MJDS prospectus from

(i) the regulator in at least one jurisdiction dated not more than two business days after the date that the agreement is entered into, and

(ii) the Canadian securities regulatory authorities in any other jurisdictions in which the distribution is to be made dated not more than three business days after the date that the agreement is entered into;

(c) immediately upon entering into the agreement the issuer issues and files a news release announcing the agreement;

(d) upon issuance of the receipt for the preliminary MJDS prospectus, a preliminary MJDS prospectus is sent to the person or company who has expressed an interest in acquiring the securities; and

(e) except as provided in paragraph (a), no agreement of purchase and sale for the securities is entered into until the MJDS prospectus has been filed and a receipt obtained.

11.3 Other Prospectus Requirements — National Instrument 41-101 Prospectus Disclosure Requirements, National Instrument 43-101 Standards of Disclosure for Mineral Exploration and Development and Mining Properties, National Instrument 43-102 Guide for Engineers and Geologists Submitting Oil and Gas Reports and National Instrument 45-101 Rights Offerings do not apply to a distribution of securities under this Instrument.

PART 12 — BIDS FOR SECURITIES OF U.S. ISSUERS

12.1 General Eligibility Criteria — (1) A bid may be made under this Instrument if

(a) the offeree issuer is a U.S. issuer;

(b) the offeree issuer is not registered or required to be registered as an investment company under the 1940 Act;

(c) the offeree issuer is not a commodity pool issuer,

(d) the bid is subject to section 14(d) of the 1934 Act in the case of a take-over bid, or section 13(e) of the 1934 Act in the case of an issuer bid, and is not exempt from the 1934 Act;

(e) the bid is made to all holders of the class of securities in Canada and the United States of America;

(f) the bid is made to residents of Canada on the same terms and conditions as it is made to residents of the United States of America; and

(g) less than 40 percent of each class of securities that is the subject of the bid is held by persons or companies whose last address as shown on the books of the issuer is in Canada.

(2) Subject to subsection (3), the calculation under paragraph (1)(g) shall be made as of the end of the offeree issuer's last quarter before the date of filing the tender offer statement or issuer tender offer statement with the SEC or, if the quarter terminated within 60 days of the filing date, as of the end of the offeree issuer's preceding quarter.

(3) If another bid for securities of the same class of the offeree issuer is in progress at the date of the filing, the calculation for the subsequent bid shall be made as of the same date as for the first bid already in progress.

(4) If a take-over bid is made without the prior knowledge of the directors of the offeree issuer who are not insiders of the offeror or acting jointly or in concert with the offeror, or upon informing the directors of the proposed bid the offeror has a reasonable basis for concluding that the bid is being regarded as a hostile bid by a majority of the directors, and in either case the offeror lacks access to the relevant list of securityholders of the offeree issuer, it will be conclusively presumed that paragraph (1)(g) is satisfied and paragraph (a) in the definition of "foreign issuer" is not satisfied, unless

(a) the aggregate published trading volume of the class on The Toronto Stock Exchange, The Montreal Exchange, the Vancouver Stock Exchange, the Alberta Stock Exchange and the Canadian Dealing Network Inc. exceeded the aggregate published trading volume of the class on national securities exchanges in the United States of America and Nasdaq for the 12 calendar month period before commencement of the bid or, if another bid for securities of the same class is in progress, the 12 calendar month period before commencement of the first bid already in progress;

(b) disclosure that paragraph (1)(g) was not satisfied or paragraph (a) of the definition of "foreign issuer" was satisfied had been made by the issuer in its Form 10-K most recently filed with the SEC under the 1934 Act; or

(c) the offeror has actual knowledge that paragraph (1)(g) is not satisfied or paragraph (a) of the definition of foreign issuer is satisfied.

12.2 MJDS Take-Over Bid Circular and MJDS Issuer Bid Circular — (1) An offeror that makes a take-over bid or issuer bid under this Part shall file a MJDS take-over bid circular or MJDS issuer bid circular, respectively.

(2) A MJDS take-over bid circular, MJDS issuer bid circular, MJDS directors' circular, MJDS director's or officer's circular, a change to any of these documents or a variation to a MJDS take-over bid circular or a MJDS issuer bid circular, is a take-over bid circular, issuer bid circular, directors' circular, individual director's or officer's circular, a notice of change and a notice of variation, respectively, for purposes of securities legislation.

12.3 Securities Exchange Bids — (1) A securities exchange bid may be made under this Instrument if

(a) the eligibility criteria set out in section 12.1 are satisfied;

(b) the offeror or, if the securities being offered are of another issuer, the other issuer, meets the eligibility criteria set out in subparagraphs 3.1(a)(i), (ii), (iv) and (v) and has filed with the SEC all 1934 Act filings for a period of 36 calendar months immediately before the filing of the registration statement with the SEC;

(c) the offeror or, if the securities being offered are of another issuer, the other issuer, has had a class of its securities listed on the New York Stock Exchange or the American Stock Exchange or quoted on the NNM for a period of at least 12 calendar months immediately before the filing of the registration statement with the SEC and is in compliance with the obligations arising from the listing or quotation; and

(d) one of the following is satisfied:

(i) the equity shares of the offeror or, if the securities being offered are of another issuer, the other issuer, have a public float of not less than U.S. $75,000,000, determined as of a date within 60 days before the filing of the registration statement with the SEC;

(ii) the securities being offered are non-convertible debt having an investment grade rating or non-convertible preferred shares having an investment grade rating; or

(iii) the bid is an issuer bid made under this Instrument with securities of the issuer being offered as consideration.

(2) The dealer registration requirement does not apply to the trade of securities of an offeror or another issuer in a securities exchange issuer bid if the eligibility criteria in subsection (1) are met.

(3) The prospectus requirement does not apply to the distribution of securities of an offeror or another issuer in a securities exchange issuer bid if the eligibility criteria in subsection (1) are met and the offeror complies with the requirements of U.S. federal securities law applicable as a result of the consideration for the securities of the offeree issuer being at least in part securities of the offeror or other issuer.

12.4 Compliance with U.S. tender offer requirements — (1) If an offeror makes a bid under this Part, the offeror shall comply with the requirements of

(a) sections 14(d) and 14(e) of the 1934 Act and Regulations 14D and 14E under the 1934 Act for a take-over bid made under this Instrument; and

(b) sections 13(e) and 14(e) of the 1934 Act and Regulations 13E and 14E under the 1934 Act for an issuer bid made under this Instrument.

(2) If the directors or an individual director or officer of an offeree issuer elects to comply with this Part instead of securities legislation otherwise applicable in preparation of a directors' circular or individual director's or officer's circular for a take-over bid made under this Part, each person so electing shall comply with sections 14(d) and 14(e) of the 1934 Act and Regulations 14D and 14E under the 1934 Act.

12.5 Form and Content of Bid Documents — (1) A MJDS take-over bid circular or a MJDS issuer bid circular shall contain the additional information, legends and certificates required by this section.

(2) The U.S. prospectus forming part of the registration statement filed with the SEC for a securities exchange bid shall be included in, or incorporated by reference into, the MJDS take-over bid circular or MJDS issuer bid circular.

(3) If an offeror makes a take-over bid under this Part and the directors or an individual director or officer elects to comply with this Part, instead of the securities legislation otherwise applicable, the directors shall prepare a MJDS directors' circular and an individual director or officer may prepare a MJDS director's or officer's circular, in each case, that contains the additional information, legends and certificates required by this section.

(4) The following statements shall be printed on the outside front cover page, or on a sticker on that page, of a MJDS take-over bid circular or MJDS issuer bid circular

(a) "This bid is made in Canada [for applicable securities exchange bids — "by a U.S. issuer"] for securities of a U.S. issuer in accordance with U.S. federal securities laws. Securityholders should be aware that the U.S. requirements applicable to the bid may differ from those of [insert the names of the provinces and territories where bid is made]. [For securities exchange bids, also insert the following — "The financial statements included or incorporated by reference in this bid circular have not been prepared in accordance with Canadian generally accepted accounting principles and thus may not be comparable to financial statements of Canadian issuers."]

(b) "[All of] [Certain of] the directors and officers of the offeror and [all of] [certain of] the experts named in this bid circular reside outside of Canada. [[Substantially] all of the assets of these persons and of the offeror may be located outside of Canada.] The offeror has appointed [name and address of agent for service] as its agent for service of process in Canada, but it may not be possible for securityholders to effect service of process within Canada upon the directors, officers and experts referred to above. It may also not be possible to enforce against the offeror, its directors and officers and [certain of] the experts named in this bid circular judgments obtained in Canadian courts predicated upon the civil liability provisions of applicable securities laws in Canada."

(5) The legend contained in paragraph 4(b) is not required if the offeror is incorporated or organized under the laws of Canada or a jurisdiction.

(6) An offeror shall include the following statement in a MJDS take-over bid circular or MJDS issuer bid circular

Securities legislation in certain of the provinces [and territories] of Canada provides securityholders of the offeree issuer with, in addition to any other rights they may have at law, remedies for rescission [or [, in some jurisdictions,] damages if a circular or notice that is required to be delivered to such securityholders contains a misrepresentation or is not delivered to the securityholder, provided that such remedies for rescission [or damages] are exercised by the securityholder within the time limit prescribed by the securities legislation of the securityholder's province or territory. The securityholder should refer to the applicable provisions of the securities legislation of the securityholder's province [or territory] for particulars of these rights or consult with a legal adviser. Rights and remedies also may be available to securityholders under U.S. law; securityholders may wish to consult with a U.S. legal adviser for particulars of these rights.

(7) A MJDS take-over bid circular, MJDS issuer bid circular, MJDS directors' circular or MJDS director's or officer's circular need not contain disclosure relevant only to U.S. securityholders.

12.6 Incorporation by Reference — Except as otherwise provided in this Instrument, documents incorporated or deemed to be incorporated by reference into a tender offer statement, issuer tender offer statement or tender offer solicitation/recommendation statement under U.S. federal securities law shall be, and are deemed to be, incorporated by reference into a MJDS take-over bid circular, MJDS issuer bid circular, MJDS directors' circular or MJDS director's or officer's circular.

12.7 Statements Modified or Superseded — (1) A statement in a document incorporated or deemed to be incorporated by reference into a MJDS take-over bid circular, a MJDS issuer bid circular, a MJDS director's circular or a MJDS director's or officer's circular shall be deemed to be modified or superseded, for the purposes of the applicable circular, to the extent that a statement in the MJDS take-over bid circular, the MJDS issuer bid circular, the MJDS director's circular or the MJDS director's or officer's circular, or in any other subsequently filed document that also is or is deemed to be incorporated by reference into the applicable circular modifies or supersedes the statement.

(2) The modifying or superseding statement need not state that it has modified or superseded a prior statement or include any other information in the document that it modifies or supersedes.

(3) The making of a modifying or superseding statement shall not be deemed an admission for any purpose that the modified or superseded statement, when made, constituted a misrepresentation, an untrue statement of a material fact or an omission to state a material fact that is required to be stated or that is necessary to make a statement not misleading in light of the circumstances in which it was made.

(4) A statement so modified or superseded shall not be deemed in its unmodified or superseded form to constitute part of the MJDS take-over bid, the MJDS issuer bid circular, the MJDS directors' circular or the MJDS director's or officer's circular.

(5) If documents are incorporated by reference into a MJDS take-over bid circular, a MJDS issuer bid circular, a MJDS directors' circular or a MJDS director's or officer's circular, the section that provides information about incorporation by reference shall include a statement that information has been incorporated by reference from documents filed with securities regulatory authorities in each jurisdiction in Canada in which the documents have been filed and shall state the name, address and telephone number of a person in Canada or the United States of America from whom copies of the documents may be obtained on request without charge.

12.8 Reconciliation of Financial Statements — A MJDS take-over bid circular or a MJDS issuer bid circular for a securities exchange bid that satisfies the eligibility criteria of subsection 12.3(1) is not subject to the requirement of securities legislation to reconcile to Canadian GAAP the financial statements included in, or incorporated by reference into, the bid circular.

12.9 Certificates — (1) A MJDS take-over bid circular shall contain a certificate in the following form signed by the chief executive officer and the chief financial officer of the offeror and, on behalf of the board of directors, by any two directors of the offeror other than the chief executive officer and chief financial officer, and each person or company that is a promoter of the offeror or a guarantor of the securities being offered in a securities exchange bid:

> The foregoing [, together with documents incorporated by reference,] contains no untrue statement of a material fact and does not omit to state a material fact that is required to be stated or that is necessary to make a statement not misleading in the light of the circumstances in which it was made.

(2) A MJDS issuer bid circular shall contain a certificate in the form set out in subsection (1) signed by the chief executive officer and the chief financial officer of the issuer and, on behalf of the board of directors, by any two directors of the issuer other than the chief executive officer and chief financial officer, and each person or company that is a promoter of the issuer or a guarantor of the securities being offered in a securities exchange bid.

(3) A MJDS directors' circular shall contain a certificate in the form set out in subsection (1) signed on behalf of the board of directors by any two directors of the issuer.

(4) A MJDS director's or officer's circular shall contain a certificate in the form set out in subsection (1) signed by each director or officer sending the circular.

(5) The certificate for notices of variation and notices of change shall be in the form set out in subsection (1), amended to refer to the initial MJDS take-over bid circular or MJDS issuer bid circular and all notices of variation or change to the MJDS take-over bid circular or MJDS issuer bid circular.

(6) Any or all of the persons required to sign a certificate under subsections (1), (2), (3), (4) or (5) may sign by an agent duly authorized in writing.

12.10 Bid Circular Filing Procedures — (1) If an offeror makes a bid under this Instrument, the offeror shall file

    (a) the tender offer statement or issuer tender offer statement and all exhibits and amendments to the tender offer statement or issuer tender offer statement,

    (b) the MJDS take-over bid circular or MJDS issuer bid circular,

    (c) a certificate of the offeror, signed on its behalf by a senior officer, confirming that the eligibility criteria set forth in subsection 12.1(1) and, if applicable, section 12.3 are satisfied and that the circular has been prepared in accordance with U.S. federal securities law,

    (d) the written consent of an attorney, auditor, accountant, engineer, appraiser or any other person or company who is named as having prepared or certified any expertised statement in any document filed under this section or section 12.14,

    (e) a submission to jurisdiction and appointment of agent for service of process duly executed by the offeror in section 2 of the required form, and

    (f) if a person or company signs a certificate by an agent under subsection 12.9(6), a duly executed copy of the document authorizing the agent to sign the certificate.

(2) Despite subsection (1), the filing requirement in paragraph (1)(d) does not apply to the consent of a rating organization that issues a rating or provisional rating that is used in or in connection with a MJDS take-over bid circular or MJDS issuer bid circular.

12.11 Notification to Offeree Issuer — An offeror filing a MJDS take-over bid circular shall so notify the offeree issuer at its principal office not later than the business day following the day the MJDS take-over bid circular is filed.

12.12 French Language Documentation Not Required — A MJDS take-over bid circular or MJDS issuer bid circular in the French language is not required to be filed in Quebec unless

    (a) the offeree issuer is a reporting issuer in Quebec; or

    (b) 20 percent or more of the class of securities that is the subject of the bid is held by persons or companies whose last address as shown on the books of the issuer is in Canada.

12.13 MJDS Directors' Circulars and MJDS Director's or Officer's Circulars — If an offeror makes a take-over bid under this Part, and the directors or an individual director or officer of the offeree issuer elects to comply with this Instrument in preparation of a directors' circular or individual director's or officer's circular instead of securities legislation otherwise applicable, the directors or an individual director or officer who so elects shall file

(a) the tender offer solicitation/recommendation statement and all exhibits or amendments to that statement,

(b) the MJDS directors' circular or MJDS director's or officer's circular,

(c) a statement by the directors or an individual director or officer that the circular has been prepared in accordance with U.S. federal securities law,

(d) the written consent of an attorney, auditor, accountant, engineer, appraiser or any other person or company who is named as having prepared or certified an expertised statement contained in the MJDS directors' circular or MJDS director's or officer's circular, and

(e) if a person signs a certificate by an agent under subsection 12.9(3), a duly executed copy of the document authorizing the agent to sign the certificate.

12.14 Securities Exchange Bids — In the case of a securities exchange bid made under section 12.3 for which a registration statement is filed with the SEC, the offeror shall file contemporaneously with the filing of the bid circular the registration statement and all exhibits and amendments to the registration statement, together with all documents incorporated by reference into the registration statement.

12.15 Notice of Variation and Notice of Change — (1) Documents filed under this Part shall be changed or varied in accordance with U.S. federal securities law as additional tender offer materials, but the additional tender offer materials shall contain the legends and certificates required by this Part.

(2) An offeror shall file additional tender offer materials that vary the terms of the bid as a notice of variation and identify the materials as such.

(3) An offeror shall file additional tender offer materials that change the information in the tender offer materials or previous additional tender offer materials, other than information about a variation in the terms of the bid, as a notice of change and identify the materials as such.

(4) Additional tender offer materials required to be filed as a notice of variation and a notice of change shall be filed as both a notice of variation and a notice of change and identified as such.

(5) The directors or an individual director or officer of an offeror issuer shall file additional materials prepared by the directors or an individual director or officer as a notice of change.

(6) If a person or company signs a certificate by an agent under subsection 12.9(6), an offeror shall file a duly executed copy of a document authorizing an agent to sign a certificate.

(7) If a change to a MJDS take-over bid circular or MJDS issuer bid circular is material to the consent filed under paragraph 12.10(1)(d), an offeror shall file a further consent contemporaneously with the filing of the change to the MJDS take-over bid circular or MJDS issuer bid circular.

(8) If a change to a MJDS directors' circular or MJDS director's or officer's circular is material to the consent filed under paragraph 12.13(d), the directors in the case of a MJDS directors' circular or the director or officer sending the circular in the case of a MJDS director's or officer's circular shall file a further consent contemporaneously with the filing of the change to a MJDS directors' circular or MJDS director's or officer's circular.

12.16 Dissemination Requirements — (1) An offeror shall send a MJDS take-over bid circular, MJDS issuer bid circular, a notice of change and a notice of variation to each securityholder whose last address as shown on the books of the offeree issuer is in the local jurisdiction.

(2) Despite subsection (1), a notice of change or a notice of variation shall be sent only to those securityholders whose securities were not taken up at the date of the occurrence of the change or variation.

(3) An offeree issuer shall send a MJDS directors' circular, MJDS director's or officer's circular and a notice of change to the MJDS directors' circular or MJDS director's or officer's circular to every person or company to whom a MJDS take-over bid circular is required to be sent under subsections (1) and (2).

(4) Documents referred to in subsections (1) and (3) that are sent or given to securityholders resident in the United States of America shall be sent by the offeror or offeree issuer as appropriate to each securityholder whose last address as shown on the books of the offeree issuer is in the local jurisdiction as soon as practicable following the time they are sent or given to securityholders resident in the United States of America.

(5) Documents referred to in subsections (1) and (3) that are published by long form or summary publication in the United States of America shall be sent by the offeror or offeree issuer as appropriate to each securityholder whose last address as shown on the books of the offeree issuer is in the local jurisdiction as soon as practicable following publication.

(6) Documents that are incorporated or deemed to be incorporated by reference into documents filed under this Part shall be sent to each securityholder whose last address as shown on the books of the offeree issuer is in the local jurisdiction if those documents are required to be sent to securityholders under U.S. federal securities law.

(7) Documents incorporated or deemed to be incorporated by reference shall be provided to any person or company upon request without charge by the person or company that filed the documents into which the documents are incorporated or deemed to be incorporated by reference.

PART 13 — BUSINESS COMBINATIONS

13.1 Eligibility Criteria — (1) This Part may be used for the distribution of securities of a successor issuer in connection with a business combination if

(a) each person or company participating in the business combination meets the eligibility criteria specified in subparagraphs 3.1(a)(i), (iv) and (v) and, other than participating persons or companies that are specified predecessors, subparagraphs 3.1(a)(ii) and 3.1(b)(ii);

(b) the equity shares of each person or company participating in the business combination, other than a specified predecessor, have a public float of not less than U.S. $75,000,000, determined as of a date within 60 days before the filing of the preliminary MJDS prospectus with the principal jurisdiction;

(c) each person or company participating in the business combination, other than a specified predecessor, has had a class of its securities listed on the New York Stock Exchange or the American Stock Exchange or quoted on the NNM for a period of at least 12 calendar months immediately preceding the filing of the preliminary MJDS prospectus in the principal jurisdiction and is in compliance with the obligations arising from the listing or quotation;

(d) the issue or exchange of securities in the business combination is made to residents of Canada on the same basis, terms and conditions as it is made to residents of the United States of America; and

(e) less than 40 percent of the class of securities to be distributed in the business combination by the successor issuer will be distributed to persons or companies whose last address as shown on the books of the participating person or company is in Canada.

(2) The requirement in paragraph (1)(b) may be satisfied for a participating person or company whose securities were the subject of a bid made under or eligible to have been made under this Instrument that terminated within the preceding 12 months if the requirement would have been satisfied immediately before commencement of the bid.

(3) The calculation in paragraph 1(e) shall be made

    (a) for each participating person or company as of the end of the participating person's or company's last quarter before the date of filing of the preliminary MJDS prospectus in the principal jurisdiction or, if that quarter terminated within 60 days of the filing date, as of the end of the participating person's or company's preceding quarter; and

    (b) on the basis that all persons or companies that have an option in respect of the consideration to be received under the business combination elect the option that would result in the issuance of the greatest number of securities.

13.2 Form and Content of Disclosure Documents and Procedures — (1) If the eligibility criteria set forth in section 13.1 are satisfied, securities may be distributed under this Part in connection with a business combination by complying with the requirements set out in Part 4, other than section 4.6, Parts 5 through 9 and Part 11.

(2) If securities are being distributed under this Part in connection with a business combination, the disclosure documents prepared for the business combination shall be filed as a MJDS prospectus and, if proxies will be solicited from holders of voting securities of the issuer and the issuer is a reporting issuer in the local jurisdiction, as an information circular.

PART 14 — MATERIAL CHANGE REPORTING

14.1 News Release — A U.S. issuer that has a class of securities listed on the New York Stock Exchange or the American Stock Exchange or quoted on Nasdaq satisfies the requirement of securities legislation to issue and file a news release upon the occurrence of a material change in its affairs by

    (a) complying with the requirements of the exchange on which its securities are listed or Nasdaq, as applicable, for making public disclosure of material information on a timely basis; and

    (b) immediately issuing in Canada and filing each news release disclosed by it for the purpose of complying with the requirements referred to in paragraph (a).

14.2 Material Change Reports — A U.S. issuer that has a class of securities registered under section 12 of the 1934 Act or is required to file reports under section 15(d) of the 1934 Act satisfies the requirement of securities legislation to file a material change report upon the occurrence of a material change in its affairs by

    (a) complying with the requirements of U.S. federal securities law relating to current reports; and

    (b) filing the current report filed with the SEC.

PART 15 — FINANCIAL STATEMENTS, ANNUAL INFORMATION FORMS AND MANAGEMENT'S DISCUSSION AND ANALYSIS OF FINANCIAL CONDITION AND RESULTS OF OPERATIONS

15.1 Financial Statements — A U.S. issuer that has a class of securities registered under section 12 of the 1934 Act or is required to file reports under section 15(d) of the 1934 Act satisfies the requirements of securities legislation relating to the preparation, certification, filing and sending of interim financial statements, and annual financial statements and auditor's reports thereon by

    (a) complying with the requirements of U.S. federal securities law relating to quarterly reports and annual reports;

    (b) filing the quarterly reports and annual reports filed with the SEC; and

    (c) either

        (i) sending each financial statement included in the report required to be filed under paragraph (b) to each securityholder whose last address as shown on the books of the reporting issuer is in the local jurisdiction in the manner and at the time required by U.S. federal securities law if

            (A) the issuer is a reporting issuer solely as a result of a distribution or securities exchange bid made under this Instrument;

            (B) the issuer meets the eligibility requirements in paragraph 3.1(c); or

            (C) the issuer meets the eligibility requirements in subparagraphs 3.1(a)(i) to (v) and the issuer is a reporting issuer solely as the result of the distribution of securities that had an investment grade rating and met the eligibility requirements of subparagraph 3.1(a)(vi) at the time of distribution; or

        (ii) sending each financial statement included in the report required to be filed under paragraph (b) to each securityholder whose last address as shown on the books of the issuer is in the local jurisdiction in the manner and at the time required by securities legislation other than this Instrument.

15.2 Annual Reports, Annual Information Forms and Management's Discussion and Analysis — A U.S. issuer that has a class of securities registered under section 12 of the 1934 Act or that is required to file reports under section 15(d) of the 1934 Act satisfies the requirements of securities legislation to file annual reports, annual information forms and management's discussion and analysis of financial condition and results of operations by

    (a) complying with the requirements of U.S. federal securities law relating to annual reports, quarterly reports and management's discussion and analysis;

    (b) filing the annual report and quarterly report filed with the SEC; and

    (c) sending the annual report to each securityholder whose last address as shown on the books of the reporting issuer is in the local jurisdiction in the manner and at the time required by U.S. federal securities law.

PART 16 — PROXIES AND PROXY SOLICITATION

16.1 Proxy Solicitation by a U.S. Issuer — A U.S. issuer that has a class of securities registered under section 12 of the 1934 Act satisfies the requirements of securities legislation relating to information circulars, proxies and proxy solicitation by

(a) complying with the requirements of U.S. federal securities law relating to proxy statements, proxies and proxy solicitation;

(c) filing all material relating to the meeting that is filed with the SEC; and

(d) sending each document filed under paragraph (b) to each securityholder whose last address as shown on the books of the reporting issuer is in the local jurisdiction in the manner and at the time required by U.S. federal securities law.

16.2 Proxy Solicitation by Another Person or Company — A person or company other than the issuer satisfies the requirements of securities legislation relating to proxies and proxy solicitation with respect to a U.S. issuer that has a class of securities registered under section 12 of the 1934 Act by fulfilling the requirements of paragraphs 16.1(a), (b) and (c).

16.3 Determination of Eligibility — If a proxy solicitation is made under section 16.2 and the person or company soliciting proxies lacks access to the relevant list of securityholders of the issuer, it will be conclusively presumed that paragraph (a) of the definition of foreign issuer is not satisfied, unless

(a) the aggregate published trading volume of the class on The Toronto Stock Exchange, The Montreal Exchange, the Vancouver Stock Exchange, the Alberta Stock Exchange and the Canadian Dealing Network Inc. exceeded the aggregate published trading volume of the class on national securities exchanges in the United States of America and Nasdaq for the 12 calendar month period before commencement of the proxy solicitation or, if another proxy solicitation for securities of the same class is in progress, the 12 calendar month period before commencement of the first proxy solicitation already in progress;

(b) disclosure that paragraph (a) of the definition of foreign issuer was satisfied had been made by the issuer in its Form 10-K most recently filed with the SEC under the 1934 Act; or

(c) the person or company soliciting proxies has actual knowledge that paragraph (a) of the definition of foreign issuer is satisfied.

PART 17 — INSIDER REPORTING

17.1 Insider Reporting — The insider report filing requirement does not apply to an insider of a U.S. issuer that has a class of securities registered under section 12 of the 1934 Act if the insider

(a) complies with the requirements of U.S. federal securities law regarding insider reporting; and

(b) files with the SEC any insider report required to be filed with the SEC under section 16(a) of the 1934 Act and the rules and regulations under the 1934 Act.

PART 18 — COMMUNICATION WITH BENEFICIAL OWNERS OF SECURITIES OF A REPORTING ISSUER

18.1 Communication with Beneficial Owners of Securities of a Reporting Issuer — A U.S. issuer satisfies the requirements of securities legislation relating to communications with, delivery of materials to and conferring voting rights upon non-registered holders of its securities who hold their interests in the securities through one or more intermediaries by

(a) complying with the requirements of Rule 14a-13 under the 1934 Act for any Canadian clearing agency and any intermediary whose last address as shown on the books of the issuer is in the local jurisdiction; and

(b) complying with the requirements of National Policy Statement No. 41 or any successor instrument to that national policy statement with respect to fees payable to intermediaries, for any Canadian clearing agency and any intermediary whose last address as shown on the books of the issuer is in the local jurisdiction.

PART 19 — TRUST INDENTURE REQUIREMENTS

19.1 Trust Indenture Requirements — The requirements of the legislation of the local jurisdiction applicable to trust indentures, for debt outstanding or guaranteed under the indenture, including a requirement that a person or company appointed as a trustee under a trust indenture be resident or authorized to do business in the local jurisdiction, do not apply to distributions made under this Instrument, if

(a) the trust indenture under which the obligations are issued or guaranteed is subject to and complies with the *Trust Indenture Act of 1939* of the United States of America; and

(b) at least one person or company appointed as trustee under the trust indenture

(i) is resident in the local jurisdiction,

(ii) is authorized to do business in the local jurisdiction, or

(iii) has filed a duly executed submission to jurisdiction and appointment of agent for service of process in section 3 of the required form.

PART 20 — FINANCIAL DISCLOSURE

20.1 Financial Disclosure — National Instruments 52-101 Future-Oriented Financial Information [NPS 48], 52-102 Use of Currencies [NPS 14], 52-103 Change of Auditor [s. 4.11 of NI 51-102], 52-104 Basis of Accounting, Auditing and Reporting [NI 52-107] and 52-105 Change in the Ending Date of a Financial Year [s. 4.8 of NI 51-102] do not apply to a U.S. issuer distributing securities or making a bid or filings in accordance with this Instrument.

PART 21 — EXEMPTIONS

21.1 Exemption — (1) The regulator or the securities regulatory authority may grant an exemption to this Instrument, in whole or in part, subject to such conditions or restrictions as may be imposed in the exemption.

(2) Despite subsection (1), in Ontario, only the regulator may grant such an exemption.

(3) Despite subsection (1), in Alberta, only the regulator may grant such an exemption.

(4) An application made to the securities regulatory authority or regulator for an exemption from this Instrument shall include a letter or memorandum describing the matters relating to the exemption, and indicating why consideration should be given to the granting of the exemption.

21.2 Evidence of Exemption — Without limiting the manner in which an exemption under section 21.1 may be evidenced, the issuance by the regulator of a receipt for a MJDS prospectus or an amendment to a MJDS prospectus is evidence of the granting of the exemption if

(a) the person or company that sought the exemption sent to the regulator the letter or memorandum referred to in subsection 21.1(4)

(i) on or before the date of filing of the preliminary MJDS prospectus, or

(ii) after the date of filing of the preliminary MJDS prospectus and received a written acknowledgement from the regulator that the exemption may be evidenced by the issuance of a receipt for the MJDS prospectus or an amendment to the MJDS prospectus; and

(b) the regulator has not sent notice of refusal to grant the exemption to the person or company that sought the exemption before, or concurrent with, the issue of the receipt for the MJDS prospectus.

PART 22 — EFFECTIVE DATE

22.1 Effective Date — This Instrument comes into force on November 1, 1998.

APPENDIX A — METHOD 1 FOR PROSPECTUS CERTIFICATES FOR RULE 415 OFFERINGS

Method 1 — Forward Looking Certificates to be Included in a MJDS Prospectus for a Rule 415 Offering or Supplement Establishing an MTN Program or Other Continuous Distribution

Part 1 — MJDS Prospectus for a Rule 415 Offering

1.1 Certificate of Issuer and Promoter — If a MJDS prospectus for a rule 415 offering establishes an MTN program or other continuous distribution, or if method 2 has not been elected by an issuer, the preliminary MJDS prospectus and the MJDS prospectus for a rule 415 offering shall contain a certificate in the following form signed by

(a) the chief executive officer and the chief financial officer of the issuer;

(b) on behalf of the board of directors of the issuer, any two directors of the issuer, other than the chief executive officer or chief financial officer, duly authorized to sign; and

(c) any person or company who is a promoter of the issuer:

This MJDS prospectus, together with the documents incorporated in this prospectus by reference, will, as of the date of each supplement to this prospectus, constitute full, true and plain disclosure of all material facts relating to the securities offered by this MJDS prospectus and the supplement as required by [insert name of each jurisdiction in which qualified] [insert if distribution made in Quebec — "and will not contain any misrepresentation likely to affect the value or the market price of the securities to be distributed"]..

1.2 Underwriters' Certificates — A preliminary MJDS prospectus and a MJDS prospectus for a rule 415 offering shall contain an underwriter's certificate in the following form signed by each underwriter who, at the time of filing, is, or it is known will be, in a contractual relationship with the issuer or selling securityholder for the securities to be distributed under the MJDS prospectus, if

(a) the MJDS prospectus establishes an MTN program or other continuous distribution; or

(b) method 2 has not been elected by the underwriter:

To the best of our knowledge, information and belief, this short form prospectus, together with the documents incorporated in this prospectus by reference will, as of the date of each supplement to this prospectus, constitute full, true and plain disclosure of all material facts relating to the securities offered under this prospectus and the supplement as required by [insert name of each jurisdiction in which qualified] [insert if distribution made in Quebec — "and will not contain any misrepresentation likely to affect the value or the market price of the securities to be distributed"].

1.3 Guarantor's Certificate — A preliminary MJDS prospectus and a MJDS prospectus for a rule 415 offering shall contain a certificate in the form described in section 1.1 signed by a guarantor of the securities to be distributed under the MJDS prospectus, if

(a) this Instrument requires a prospectus certificate of the guarantor; and

(b) either

(i) the MJDS prospectus establishes an MTN program or other continuous distribution, or

(ii) method 2 has not been elected by the guarantor.

1.4 Amendments — (1) An amendment to a MJDS prospectus for a rule 415 offering or an amended and restated MJDS prospectus shall, subject to subsection (2), contain

(a) the certificates required under section 1.1 to be included in a MJDS prospectus, if the MJDS prospectus contains an issuer's certificate in the form described in section 1.1;

(b) the certificates required under section 1.2 to be included in a MJDS prospectus, if the MJDS prospectus contains an underwriter's certificate in the form described in section 1.2; and

(c) the certificate required under section 1.3 to be included in a MJDS prospectus, if the MJDS prospectus contains a guarantor's certificate in the form described in section 1.3.

(2) In each certificate required under subsection (1), the reference to "this MJDS prospectus" shall be omitted and replaced by

(a) in the case of an amendment to a MJDS prospectus, "the MJDS prospectus dated [insert date] as amended by this amendment"; and

(b) in the case of an amended and restated MJDS prospectus, "this amended and restated MJDS prospectus".

Part 2 — MJDS Prospectus Supplements establishing a MTN Program

2.1 Certificate of Issuer and Promoter — If an issuer's certificate in the form described in section 1.1 was not included in the corresponding MJDS prospectus, a MJDS prospectus supplement that establishes a MTN program or other continuous distribution shall contain a certificate in the following form signed by

(a) the chief executive officer and the chief financial officer of the issuer;

(b) on behalf of the board of directors of the issuer, any two directors of the issuer, other than the chief executive officer or chief financial officer, duly authorized to sign; and

(c) any person or company who is a promoter of the issuer:

The MJDS prospectus together with the documents incorporated in the prospectus, as supplemented by the foregoing, will, as of the date of each supplement to the MJDS prospectus, constitute full, true and plain disclosure of all material facts relating to the securities offered under the MJDS prospectus and by the supplement as required by [insert name of each jurisdiction in which qualified] [insert if distribution made in Quebec — "and will not contain any misrepresentation likely to affect the value or the market price of the securities to be distributed."].

2.2 Underwriters' Certificates — A MJDS prospectus supplement that establishes an MTN program or other continuous distribution shall contain a certificate in the following form signed by each underwriter who

(a) is in a contractual relationship with the issuer or selling securityholder for the securities being distributed under the MJDS prospectus supplement; and

(b) did not sign and include in the corresponding MJDS prospectus a certificate in the form described in section 1.2:

To the best of our knowledge, information and belief, the MJDS prospectus together with the documents incorporated in the prospectus, as supplemented by the foregoing, will, as of the date of each supplement to the MJDS prospectus, constitute full, true and plain disclosure of all material facts relating to the securities offered under the MJDS prospectus and by the supplement as required by [insert name of jurisdiction in which qualified] [insert if distribution made in Quebec — "and will not contain any misrepresentation likely to affect the value or the market price of the securities to be distributed."].

2.3 Guarantor's Certificate — A MJDS prospectus supplement that establishes an MTN program or other continuous distribution shall contain a certificate in the form described in section 2.1 signed by a guarantor of the securities being distributed under the MJDS prospectus supplement, if

(a) this Instrument requires a prospectus certificate of the guarantor; and

(b) a prospectus certificate of the guarantor in the form described in section 1.3 was not included in the corresponding MJDS prospectus.

2.4 Amendments — (1) An amendment to a MJDS prospectus supplement or an amended and restated MJDS prospectus supplement that establishes an MTN program or other continuous distribution shall, subject to subsection (2), contain

(a) the certificates required under section 2.1 to be included in a MJDS prospectus supplement, if the MJDS prospectus supplement contains an issuer's certificate in the form described in section 2.1;

(b) the certificates required under section 2.2 to be included in a MJDS prospectus supplement, if the MJDS prospectus supplement contains an underwriter's certificate in the form described in section 2.2; and

(c) the certificate required under section 2.3 to be included in a MJDS prospectus supplement, if the MJDS prospectus supplement contains a guarantor's certificate in the form described in section 2.3.

(2) In each certificate required under subsection (1), the reference to "this MJDS prospectus supplement" shall be omitted and replaced by

(a) in the case of an amendment to a MJDS prospectus supplement, "the MJDS prospectus supplement dated [insert date] as amended by this amendment"; and

(b) in the case of an amended and restated MJDS prospectus supplement, "this amended and restated MJDS prospectus supplement".

APPENDIX B — METHOD 2 FOR PROSPECTUS CERTIFICATES FOR RULE 415 OFFERINGS

Method 2: Non-forward Looking Prospectus Certificates to be Included in Both a MJDS Prospectus and Supplement

Part 1 — MJDS Prospectus for a Rule 415 Offering

1.1 Certificate of Issuer and Promoter — If method 2 is elected by an issuer, a preliminary MJDS prospectus and a MJDS prospectus shall contain a certificate in the following form signed by

(a) the chief executive officer and the chief financial officer of the issuer;

(b) on behalf of the board of directors of the issuer, any two directors of the issuer, other than the chief executive officer or chief financial officer, duly authorized to sign; and

(c) any person or company who is a promoter of the issuer:

This MJDS prospectus, together with the documents incorporated in this prospectus, constitutes full, true and plain disclosure of all material facts relating to the securities as required by the securities laws of [insert name of each jurisdiction in which qualified] [insert if distribution made in Quebec — "and does not contain any misrepresentation likely to affect the value or the market price of the securities to be distributed."].

1.2 Underwriters' Certificates — A preliminary MJDS prospectus and a MJDS prospectus for a rule 415 offering shall contain an underwriter's certificate in the following form signed by each underwriter who

(a) at the time of filing, is, or it is known will be, in a contractual relationship with the issuer or selling securityholder for the securities to be distributed under the MJDS prospectus; and

(b) elects method 2:

> *To the best of our knowledge, information and belief, the MJDS prospectus, together with the documents incorporated in the prospectus, constitutes full, true and plain disclosure of all material facts relating to the securities as required by [insert name of each jurisdiction in which qualified] [insert if distribution made in Quebec — "and does not contain any misrepresentation likely to affect the value or the market price of the securities to be distributed."].*

1.3 Guarantor's Certificate — A MJDS prospectus shall contain a certificate in the form described in section 1.1 signed by a guarantor of the securities to be distributed under the MJDS prospectus, if

(a) this Instrument requires a prospectus certificate of the guarantor; and

(b) method 2 is elected by the guarantor.

1.4 Amendments — (1) An amendment to a MJDS prospectus or an amended and restated MJDS prospectus shall, subject to subsection (2), contain

(a) the certificates required under section 1.1 to be included in a MJDS prospectus, if the issuer has elected method 2;

(b) the certificate described in section 1.2 signed by each underwriter who

(i) at the time of filing the amendment or the amended and restated MJDS prospectus, is, or it is known will be, in a contractual relationship with the issuer or selling securityholder for the securities to be distributed under the MJDS prospectus, and

(ii) has elected method 2; and

(c) the certificate required under section 1.3 to be included in a MJDS prospectus, if the MJDS prospectus contains a guarantor's certificate in the form described in section 1.3.

(2) In each certificate required under subsection (1), the reference to "this MJDS prospectus" shall be omitted and replaced by

(a) in the case of an amendment to a MJDS prospectus, "the MJDS prospectus dated [insert date] as amended by this amendment"; and

(b) in the case of an amended and restated MJDS prospectus, "this amended and restated MJDS prospectus".

Part 2 — MJDS Prospectus Supplement

2.1 Certificate of Issuer and Promoter — If method 2 is elected by an issuer, each MJDS prospectus supplement shall contain a certificate in the following form signed by

(a) the chief executive officer and the chief financial officer of the issuer;

(b) on behalf of the board of directors of the issuer, any two directors of the issuer, other than the chief executive officer or chief financial officer, duly authorized to sign; and

(c) any person or company who is a promoter of the issuer:

> *The MJDS prospectus, together with the documents incorporated in the prospectus, as supplemented by the foregoing, constitutes full, true and plain disclosure of all material facts relating to the securities offered under the MJDS prospectus and this supplement as required by [insert name of each jurisdiction in which qualified] [insert if distribution made in Quebec — "and does not contain any misrepresentation likely to affect the value or the market price of the securities to be distributed."].*

2.2 Underwriters' Certificates — Each MJDS prospectus supplement shall contain a certificate in the following form signed by each underwriter who

(a) is in a contractual relationship with the issuer or selling securityholder for the securities being distributed under the supplement; and

(b) has elected method 2:

> *To the best of our knowledge, information and belief, the MJDS prospectus, together with the documents incorporated in the prospectus, as supplemented by the foregoing, constitutes full, true and plain disclosure of all material facts relating to the securities offered under the MJDS prospectus and this supplement as required by [insert name of each jurisdiction in which qualified] [insert if distribution made in Quebec — "and does not contain any misrepresentation likely to affect the value or the market price of the securities to be distributed."].*

2.3 Guarantor's Certificate — Each MJDS prospectus supplement shall contain a certificate in the form described in section 2.1 signed by a guarantor of the securities being distributed under the MJDS prospectus supplement, if

(a) this Instrument requires a prospectus certificate of the guarantor; and

(b) method 2 is elected by the guarantor.

2.4 Amendments — (1) An amendment to a MJDS prospectus supplement or an amended and restated MJDS prospectus supplement shall, subject to subsection (2), contain

(a) the certificates required under section 2.1 to be included in a MJDS prospectus supplement, if the MJDS prospectus supplement contains an issuer's certificate in the form described in section 2.1;

(b) the certificate described in section 2.2 signed by each underwriter who

(i) at the time of filing the amendment or the amended and restated MJDS prospectus supplement, is in a contractual relationship with the issuer or selling securityholder for the securities being distributed under the MJDS prospectus supplement, and

(ii) has elected method 2; and

(c) the certificate required under section 2.3 to be included in a MJDS prospectus supplement, if the MJDS prospectus supplement contains a guarantor's certificate in the form described in section 2.3.

(2) In each certificate required under subsection (1), the reference to "this MJDS prospectus supplement" shall be omitted and replaced by

(a) in the case of an amendment to a MJDS prospectus supplement, "the MJDS prospectus supplement dated [insert date] as amended by this amendment"; and

(b) in the case of an amended and restated MJDS prospectus supplement, "this amended and restated MJDS prospectus supplement".

Final Rule: (1998) 21 O.S.C.B. 6919; Approval by OSC: (1998) 21 O.S.C.B. 5099; Request for Comments: (1997) 20 O.S.C.B. 6496. Replaced NPS 45 (1991) 14 O.S.C.B. 2899 and a rule which was originally a blanket order (1991) 14 O.S.C.B. 2863 which was deemed to be a rule under s. 143.1(1) of the Act and remade into a rule entitled *In the Matter of Regulation 910, R.R.O. 1980, as amended and In the Matter of The Multijurisdictional Disclosure System* [including National Policy Statement No. 45] (1997) 20 O.S.C.B. 1219.

Rules: Rule 71-801, 13-502, App. C, Item A; NI 71-102.

Policies and Orders: NPS 71-101CP, 71-102CP; OSCN 41-703.

Form 71-101F1 — Forms of Submission to Jurisdiction and Appointment of Agent for Service of Process

1. — MJDS Prospectus Distribution of Securities

1. Name of issuer (the "Issuer"): ....

2. Jurisdiction of incorporation of Issuer: ....

3. Address of principal place of business of Issuer: ....

4. Description of securities (the "Securities"):...

5. Date of MJDS prospectus (the "Prospectus") under which the Securities are offered: ....

6. Name of agent (the "Agent"): ....

7. Address for service of process of Agent in Canada: ....

8. The Issuer designates and appoints the Agent at the address of the Agent stated above as its agent upon whom may be served any notice, pleading, subpoena, summons or other process in any action, investigation or administrative, criminal, quasi-criminal, penal or other proceeding (the "Proceeding") arising out of, relating to or concerning the distribution of the Securities made or purported to be made under the Prospectus or the obligations of the Issuer as a reporting issuer, and irrevocably waives any right to raise as a defence in any such Proceeding any alleged lack of jurisdiction to bring such Proceeding.

9. The Issuer irrevocably and unconditionally submits to the non-exclusive jurisdiction of

(a) the judicial, quasi-judicial and administrative tribunals of each of the provinces [and territories] of Canada in which the Securities are distributed under the Prospectus; and

(b) any administrative proceeding in any such province [or territory],

in any Proceeding arising out of or related to or concerning the distribution of the Securities made or purported to be made under the Prospectus.

10. Until six years after it has ceased to be a reporting issuer in any Canadian province or territory, the Issuer will file a new submission to jurisdiction and appointment of agent for service of process in this form at least 30 days before termination of this submission to jurisdiction and appointment of agent for service of process.

11. Until six years after it has ceased to be a reporting issuer in any Canadian province or territory, the Issuer will file an amended submission to jurisdiction and appointment of agent for service of process at least 30 days before any change in the name or above address of the Agent.

12. This submission to jurisdiction and appointment of agent for service of process will be governed by and construed in accordance with the laws of .... [province of above address of Agent].

Dated: ....

....[Issuer]

By: .... [Name and title]

The undersigned accepts the appointment as agent for service of process of [Issuer] under the terms and conditions of the appointment of agent for service of process stated above.

Dated: ....

....[Agent]

By: .... [Name and title]

2. — Take-over or Issuer Bid

1. Name of offeror (the "Offeror"): ....

2. Jurisdiction of incorporation of Offeror: ....

3. Address of principal place of business of Offeror: ....

4. Description of securities (the "Securities"): ....

5. Date of Bid (the "Bid") for the Securities: ....

6. Name of agent (the "Agent"): ....

7. Address for service of process of Agent in Canada: ....

8. The Offeror designates and appoints the Agent at the address of the Agent stated above as its agent upon whom may be served any notice, pleading, subpoena, summons or other process in any action, investigation or administrative, criminal, quasi-criminal, penal or other proceeding (the "Proceeding") arising out of, relating to or concerning the Bid [insert for securities exchange bids — "or the obligations of the Offeror

as a reporting issuer"], and irrevocably waives any right to raise as a defence in any such Proceeding any alleged lack of jurisdiction to bring such Proceeding.

9. The Offeror irrevocably and unconditionally submits to the non-exclusive jurisdiction of

    (a) the judicial, quasi-judicial and administrative tribunals of each of the provinces [and territories] of Canada in which the Bid is made, and

    (b) any administrative proceeding in any such province [or territory],

in any Proceeding arising out of or related to or concerning the Bid.

10. Until six years from the date of the Bid, the Offeror will file a new submission to jurisdiction and appointment of agent for service of process in this form at least 30 days before termination of this submission to jurisdiction and appointment of agent for service of process.

11. Until six years from the date of the Bid, the Offeror will file an amended submission to jurisdiction and appointment of agent for service of process at least 30 days before any change in the name or above address of the Agent.

12. This submission to jurisdiction and appointment of agent for service of process must be governed by and construed in accordance with the laws of .... [province of above address of Agent].

Dated: ....

................................[Offeror]

    By: .... [Name and title]

The undersigned accepts the appointment as agent for service of process of .... [Offeror] under the terms and conditions of the appointment of agent for service of process stated above.

Dated: ....

................................[Agent]

    By: .... [Name and title]

3. — Trust Indenture

1. Name of trustee (the "Trustee"): ....

2. Jurisdiction of incorporation of Trustee: ....

3. Address of principal place of business of Trustee: ....

4. Description of securities (the "Securities"): ....

5. Date of trust indenture (the "Indenture") under which the Securities are issued: ....

6. Name of agent (the "Agent"): ....

7. Address for service of process of Agent in Canada: ....

8. The Trustee designates and appoints the Agent at the address of the Agent stated above as its agent upon whom may be served any notice, pleading, subpoena, summons or other process in any action, investigation or administrative, criminal, quasi-criminal, penal or other proceeding (the "Proceeding") arising out of or relating to or concerning the Indenture, and irrevocably waives any right to raise as a defence in any such Proceeding any alleged lack of jurisdiction to bring such Proceeding.

9. The Trustee irrevocably and unconditionally submits to the non-exclusive jurisdiction of:

    (a) the judicial, quasi-judicial and administrative tribunals of each of the provinces [and territories] of Canada in which the Securities are issued, and

    (b) any administrative proceeding in any such province [or territory],

in any Proceeding arising out of or related to or concerning the Indenture.

10. Until six years from the termination of the Indenture, the Trustee will file a new Submission to Jurisdiction and Appointment of Agent for Service of Process in this form at least 30 days before termination of this Submission to Jurisdiction and Appointment of Agent for Service of Process.

11. Until six years from the termination of the Indenture, the Trustee will file an amended Submission to Jurisdiction and Appointment of Agent for Service of Process at least 30 days before any change in the name or above address of the Agent.

12. This submission to jurisdiction and appointment of agent for service of process shall be governed by and construed in accordance with the laws of .... [province of above address of Agent].

Dated: ....

................................[Trustee]

    By: .... [Name and title]

The undersigned accepts the appointment as agent for service of process of .... [Issuer] under the terms and conditions of the foregoing Appointment of Agent for Service of Process.

Dated: ....

................................[Agent]

    By: .... [Name and title]

Companion Policy 71-101CP — To National Instrument 71-101 The Multijurisdictional Disclosure System

Table of Contents

PART 1 — INTRODUCTION AND PURPOSE

1.1 Introduction and Purpose — The multijurisdictional disclosure system is a joint initiative by the CSA and the SEC to reduce duplicative regulation in cross-border offerings, issuer bids, take-over bids, business combinations and continuous disclosure and other filings.

The multijurisdictional disclosure system (the "MJDS") was originally implemented in Canada in 1991 by the members of the CSA through National Policy Statement No. 45 ("NP 45"). NP 45 was replaced by National Instrument 71-101 ("NI 71-101") which implements in each Canadian jurisdiction those portions of NP 45 which are of a legislative nature. Companion Policy 71-101CP to NI 71-101 ("this Policy") provides other information including statements relating to the exercise of discretion by the Canadian securities regulatory authorities under NI 71-101 and the manner in which its provisions are intended to be interpreted or applied by them.

NI 71-101 sets out the substantive requirements of the MJDS which apply in all jurisdictions. Each jurisdiction has implemented NI 71-101 by one or more instruments forming part of the law of that jurisdiction ("the implementing law of a jurisdiction"). The implementing law of a jurisdiction can take the form of a regulation, rule, ruling or order. Form 71-101F1 sets out the forms of submission to jurisdiction and appointment of agent for service of process.

Ontario, Alberta, British Columbia, Manitoba and Nova Scotia have adopted NI 71-101 by rule. Saskatchewan has adopted it by regulation. All other jurisdictions have adopted NI 71-101 by Policy Statement. To the extent that any provision of this Policy is inconsistent or conflicts with the applicable provisions of NI 71-101 in those jurisdictions that have adopted NI 71-101 by Policy Statement, the provisions of NI 71-101 prevail over the provisions of this Policy.

PART 2 — OVERVIEW OF THE MJDS

2.1 Purpose — The MJDS is intended to remove unnecessary obstacles to certain offerings of securities of U.S. issuers in Canada, to facilitate take-over and issuer bids and business combinations involving securities of certain U.S. issuers and to facilitate compliance by U.S. issuers with proxy and continuous disclosure requirements, while ensuring that Canadian investors remain adequately protected.

2.2 Application — (1) Offerings — The MJDS permits public offerings of securities of U.S. issuers that meet the eligibility criteria specified in NI 71-101 to be made in Canada on the basis of disclosure documents prepared in accordance with U.S. federal securities law, with certain additional Canadian disclosure. A public offering of securities of a U.S. issuer may be made under the MJDS either in Canada and the United States or in Canada only.

(2) Rights Offerings, Bids and Business Combinations — The MJDS also reduces disincentives to the extension to Canadian securityholders of rights offerings by U.S. issuers by permitting such rights offerings to be made in Canada on the basis of U.S. disclosure documents. Similarly, it facilitates the extension to Canadian securityholders of U.S. issuers of take-over bids, issuer bids and business combinations in the circumstances contemplated by Parts 12 and 13 of NI 71-101. The MJDS permits such transactions to be made in Canada generally in the same manner as in the United States and on the basis of U.S. disclosure documents.

2.3 Regulatory Review — Regulatory review of disclosure documents used under the MJDS for offerings made by a U.S. issuer both in Canada and the United States will be that customary in the United States, with the SEC being responsible for carrying out the review. Whether the offering is made both in Canada and the United States or solely in Canada, Canadian securities regulatory authorities will monitor materials filed under the MJDS to check compliance with the specific disclosure and filing requirements of NI 71-101. In addition, the substance of the disclosure documents will be reviewed in the unusual case if, through monitoring of the materials or otherwise, the Canadian securities regulatory authorities have reason to believe that there may be a problem with a transaction or the related disclosure or other special circumstances exist.

2.4 Liability Unaffected — The MJDS does not change the liability provisions of Canadian securities legislation or the discretionary authority of Canadian securities regulatory authorities to halt a distribution, remove an exemption, cease trade the related securities, or refuse to issue a receipt for a preliminary MJDS Prospectus or a MJDS Prospectus. The securities regulatory authority or, in the case of Ontario, the regulator, may also grant exemptions from the requirements of NI 71-101 in specific cases and also exercise its public interest jurisdiction if it determines that it is necessary to do so in order to preserve the integrity of the Canadian capital markets.

2.5 Compliance with U.S. Law — Use of the MJDS is based on compliance with U.S. federal securities law. Thus, any person or company carrying out a transaction or filing a document in Canada under the MJDS must comply in full with all applicable U.S. requirements. However, a violation of a U.S. requirement will not automatically disqualify a person or company from using the MJDS with respect to a transaction or document. A person or company that violates a U.S. requirement, depending upon the circumstances, may be considered to have violated an equivalent requirement of a jurisdiction in Canada with respect to a transaction or document.

2.6 The U.S. Multijurisdictional Disclosure System — (1) Concurrently with the adoption of NP 45, the SEC adopted rules, forms and schedules for the implementation of a similar multijurisdictional disclosure system in the United States. The U.S. system removes unnecessary impediments to certain offerings of securities of Canadian issuers in the United States and facilitates the extension to U.S. securityholders of Canadian issuers of take-over bids, issuer bids and business combinations in the circumstances contemplated by the U.S. system.

(2) The procedures to be followed in Canada when the U.S. system is used for certain offerings of securities of a Canadian issuer in the U.S. are set out in Part 4 of this Policy.

PART 3 — NI 71-101

3.1 Application of NI 71-101 in each Jurisdiction — The MJDS provided for in NI 71-101 has been implemented in each jurisdiction. Except to the extent specifically provided in NI 71-101 or the implementing law of a jurisdiction, the securities legislation continues to apply. The securities legislation may prescribe additional requirements or procedures in relation to the transactions and filings contemplated in NI 71-101.

3.2 MJDS Prospectus Distributions of Securities of U.S. Issuers — (1) **Election to Use the MJDS** — The use of the MJDS to distribute securities of a U.S. issuer is elective. Persons or companies permitted to distribute securities of a U.S. issuer under NI 71-101 may alternatively make those distributions in accordance with other provisions of the securities legislation, including, if the relevant eligibility criteria are satisfied, case by case exemptive relief under CSA Notice 95-4 Proposed Foreign Issuer Prospectus and Continuous Disclosure System.

(2) **General** — NI 71-101 permits the following securities of a U.S. issuer to be distributed by prospectus in Canada, either by the issuer or by a selling securityholder, on the basis of documentation prepared in accordance with U.S. federal securities law, with certain additional Canadian disclosure:

    (a) non-convertible debt and non-convertible preferred shares that have an investment grade rating;

    (b) convertible debt and preferred shares that have an investment grade rating and may not be converted for at least one year after issuance, if the issuer meets a public float requirement;

    (c) certain rights to acquire securities of the issuer; and

    (d) other securities, if the issuer meets a public float requirement.

The MJDS may also be used for securities exchange bids and business combinations, in each case as described below.

The purpose of the public float requirement is to single out issuers whose size is such that (i) information about them is publicly disseminated and (ii) they have a significant market following. As a result, the marketplace can be expected to set efficiently a price for the securities of these issuers based on publicly available information.

Non-convertible debt and preferred shares that have an investment grade rating are particularly appropriate for the MJDS because these securities trade primarily on the basis of their yield and an assessment of creditworthiness by an independent rating organization. Typically, the four highest rating categories, within which there may be subcategories or gradations indicating relative standing, signify an investment grade rating by an independent rating organization. The investment grade ratings for certain rating organizations currently are:

Rating Organization	Debt	Preferred Shares
CBRS Inc.	A++, A+, A or B++	P-1+, P-1, P-2 or P-3
Dominion Bond Rating Service Limited	AAA, AA, A or BBB	Pfd-1, Pfd-2 or Pfd-3
Moody's Investors Service, Inc.	Aaa, Aa, A or Baa	"aaa", "aa", "a" or "baa"
Standard & Poor's Corporation	AAA, AA, A or BBB	AAA, AA, A or BBB

The lack of a public float requirement for offerings of these securities allows the MJDS to be used by issuers of securities having an investment grade rating, such as finance subsidiaries, that access the market frequently, but do not meet the public float requirements. Debt and preferred shares that have an investment grade rating and are not convertible into other securities for at least one year after issuance can be expected to trade primarily on the basis of their yield and independent rating, but are also priced to some extent on the basis of the anticipated value of the security into which they are convertible. Thus, the MJDS is available for these securities on the basis of their investment grade rating, coupled with a public float requirement.

In the case of offerings of common shares or other securities other than non-convertible debt and preferred shares that have an investment grade rating, the MJDS is available upon satisfaction of a public float requirement. The MJDS generally may not be used for the offering of derivative securities, except in the circumstances set out in subsection 3.3(2) of NI 71-101. Therefore, offerings of derivative securities such as stock index warrants, currency warrants and debt the interest on which is based upon the performance of a stock index may not be made under the MJDS.

Subject to certain limitations, the MJDS permits U.S. issuers to make rights offerings by prospectus to existing securityholders in Canada on the basis of documentation prepared in accordance with U.S. federal securities law, with certain additional Canadian disclosure. There is no public float requirement for rights offerings since existing securityholders can reasonably be expected to be familiar with the issuer and follow publicly available information concerning it.

The MJDS is available for rights offerings primarily to encourage fair treatment of Canadian investors. Previously, a U.S. issuer might not have extended rights offerings to its securityholders in Canada due to the perceived costs and burdens of meeting Canadian regulatory requirements. The MJDS is intended to alter a U.S. issuer's cost-benefit analysis in favour of extending a rights offering to Canadian investors.

Offerings of debt and preferred shares that are not eligible to be made under paragraph 3.1(a) of NI 71-101, rights offerings that are not eligible to be made under paragraph 3.1(b) of NI 71-101, securities exchange bids that are not eligible to be made under section 12.3 of NI 71-101, and business combinations that are not eligible to be made under section 13.1 may be made under paragraph 3.1(c) of NI 71-101, if subparagraphs 3.1(c)(i) and (ii) of NI 71-101 are satisfied.

(3) Public Interest Jurisdiction — All MJDS prospectus distributions remain subject to the fundamental principle that transactions must not be prejudicial to the public interest. The Canadian securities regulatory authorities will continue to exercise their public interest jurisdiction in specific cases if they determine that it is necessary to do so to preserve the integrity of the Canadian capital markets or to protect investors.

(4) Form and Content of MJDS Prospectus — A preliminary MJDS prospectus, MJDS prospectus or amendment or supplement to a preliminary MJDS prospectus or MJDS prospectus need not comply with the prospectus form and content requirements of securities legislation applicable to distributions of securities made other than under NI 71-101 except as specifically provided in NI 71-101 and the implementing law of a jurisdiction.

Each preliminary MJDS prospectus and MJDS prospectus is subject to requirements of securities legislation to provide full, true and plain disclosure of all material facts relating to the securities proposed to be distributed and not to contain an untrue statement of a material fact or omit to state a material fact that is required to be stated or that is necessary to make a statement not misleading in light of the circumstances in which it was made.

(5) Format of MJDS Prospectus — A preliminary MJDS prospectus and a MJDS prospectus may be either a separate Canadian prospectus or a wrap-around prospectus that includes the U.S. prospectus filed with the SEC.

An issuer is required to file a preliminary MJDS prospectus for use in Canada even if the issuer does not prepare a preliminary prospectus for use in the United States.

(6) Reconciliation of Financial Statements — Reconciliation of financial statements to Canadian GAAP is not required for distributions made under NI 71-101 other than those made under paragraph 3.1(c) of NI 71-101.

An issuer eligible under paragraph 3.1(c) of NI 71-101 to file a MJDS prospectus may apply to each applicable Canadian securities regulatory authority for an exemption permitting the issuer to reconcile financial statements in the MJDS prospectus to International Accounting Standards in lieu of Canadian GAAP.

U.S. federal securities law requires that annual financial statements be accompanied by an auditor's report prepared in accordance with U.S. generally accepted auditing standards. Therefore, a MJDS prospectus which by definition, includes a U.S. prospectus, would include audited financial statements with a report prepared in accordance with U.S. generally accepted auditing standards. Unlike section 4.6 of NI 71-101 which imposes a requirement to reconcile financial statements to Canadian GAAP, no additional auditing standard requirement is imposed by NI 71-101.

(7) Underwriters' Certificate in Rights Offerings — A preliminary MJDS prospectus and a MJDS prospectus used for a distribution of rights under NI 71-101 need not contain an underwriters' certificate if (i) there is no soliciting activity in the local jurisdiction other than the dissemination by the issuer of the rights and the preliminary MJDS prospectus and MJDS prospectus and the solicitation of the exercise of those rights by existing securityholders, and (ii) securities acquired under a standby underwriting commitment by a dealer to purchase securities unsubscribed for by other securityholders are not resold in the local jurisdiction.

(8) Distributions made in Quebec — For distributions made in Quebec, both English and French language versions of the preliminary MJDS Prospectus, MJDS Prospectus and each amendment and supplement thereto are required to be filed. Legislation in Quebec requires that French language versions of the documents or portions of documents incorporated by reference into any of those documents be filed in Quebec not later than the time the incorporating document is filed. Thus, French language versions of continuous disclosure documents need not be filed until incorporated by reference. In addition, information contained in a Form 10-K, Form 10-Q or Form 8-K prescribed under the 1934 Act that is not required to be disclosed under Quebec requirements applicable to distributions not made under the MJDS need not be included in the French language versions of those documents.

Despite the foregoing, section 6.15 of NI 71-101 provides that French language versions of the disclosure documents are not required to be filed for rights offerings made under paragraph 3.1(b) of NI 71-101, unless (i) the issuer is a reporting issuer in Quebec other than solely as a result of rights offerings made under paragraph 3.1(b) of NI 71-101, or (ii) 20 percent or more of the class of securities in respect of which the rights are issued is held by persons or companies whose last address as shown on the books of the issuer is in Canada.

(9) Modification or Amendment — Part 7 of NI 71-101 outlines the amendment and supplement procedures for MJDS prospectus distributions.

An amendment to a registration statement that modifies the related U.S. prospectus, other than an amendment that has been made as a result of the occurrence of an adverse material change since the filing of the preliminary MJDS prospectus or an amendment to the preliminary MJDS prospectus, need not be filed as an amendment to the preliminary MJDS prospectus.

(10) Advertising — The provisions of securities legislation relating to the advertising of securities or the making of representations or undertakings in respect of distributions of securities, other than representations as to listing or quotation of securities, including the distribution of material to potential investors and the provision of information to the media before the issuance of a receipt for the MJDS prospectus, apply to distributions made under the MJDS.

(11) Review Procedures — Disclosure documents filed for a distribution under NI 71-101 will be subject to SEC review procedures if the offering is being made both in Canada and the United States. Whether the offering is made both in Canada and the United States or solely in Canada, the Canadian securities regulatory authorities will monitor materials filed under NI 71-101 to check compliance with the specific disclosure and filing requirements of NI 71-101. In addition, the substance of the disclosure documents will be reviewed in the unusual case if, through monitoring of the materials or otherwise, the Canadian securities regulatory authorities have reason to believe that there may be a problem with a transaction or the related disclosure or other special circumstances exist.

An issuer making an offering in Canada and the U.S. using the MJDS must select a principal jurisdiction in Canada. As of the date of this Policy, the Canadian securities regulatory authorities of New Brunswick, Prince Edward Island, Newfoundland, Yukon Territory and the Northwest Territories have indicated that they will not agree to act as principal jurisdiction under section 5.1 of NI 71-101.

(12) Receipt Procedures — The receipt for a preliminary MJDS Prospectus filed under NI 71-101 will be issued by each regulator when the preliminary MJDS Prospectus and all other required documentation have been filed with it in the manner required by NI 71-101.

If a distribution under NI 71-101 is being made concurrently in the United States, the receipt for a MJDS prospectus filed under NI 71-101 will be issued by each regulator when the following conditions have been satisfied, unless the regulator has reason to believe that there may be a problem with the transaction or the related disclosure or other special circumstances exist,

(a) if the regulator is in the principal jurisdiction, the related registration statement has become effective under the SEC rules, as notified in writing by the issuer under section 6.11 of NI 71-101;

(b) in the case of the other jurisdictions, the regulator in the principal jurisdiction has notified each other applicable regulator that the regulator in the principal jurisdiction has issued a receipt for the MJDS Prospectus; and

(c) the MJDS prospectus, all documents incorporated or deemed to be incorporated therein by reference and all other documentation required to be filed under NI 71-101 have been filed with the regulator in the manner required by NI 71-101.

If the offering is being made solely in Canada, the receipt for a MJDS prospectus filed under NI 71-101 will be issued by each applicable regulator when the conditions set out in paragraphs (b) and (c) above have been satisfied, unless it has reason to believe that there may be a problem with the transaction or the related disclosure or other special circumstances exist.

Issuers filing a MJDS Prospectus under NI 71-101 may elect to use the receipt system in the national policy on mutual reliance for prospectuses. Reference should be made to that policy for the procedures, requirements and benefits of the system provided by that policy.

(13) Rule 415 Offerings and Rule 430A Offerings —

(a) The procedures permitted by Rule 415 and Rule 430A under the 1933 Act may be used for offerings of securities under NI 71-101. National Policy Statement No. 44 Rules for Shelf Prospectus Offerings and for Pricing Offerings after the Final Prospectus is Receipted and any successor instrument to that National Policy Statement does not apply to those offerings. A prospectus supplement filed in accordance with the procedures permitted by Rule 415 or Rule 430A will not be subject to the review procedures set out in subsection 3.2(11) or the receipt procedures set out in subsection 3.2(12) of this Policy.

(b) None of a revised U.S. prospectus, a prospectus supplement, a rule 415 prospectus supplement and a rule 430A pricing prospectus is an amendment to a MJDS prospectus.

(14) Certification for Rule 415 Offerings — Method 1 can be substituted for method 2 and vice versa until the filing of the MJDS prospectus. The method chosen for the provision of the issuer's and underwriters' certificates need not be the same.

Method 1 allows the use of prospectus supplements and in the case of MTN programs, pricing supplements (i.e., supplements setting the price and certain variable terms of the securities rather than establishing the program) that do not contain certificates, if a "forward-looking" certificate has been included in the prospectus or in the supplement establishing the program.

Method 2 requires the inclusion of certificates in each prospectus supplement and pricing supplement filed under the MJDS, provided that no certificate is required to be included in a prospectus supplement or pricing supplement filed in the principal jurisdiction if the securities covered by the prospectus supplement or pricing supplement are not offered in Canada.

The text of the certificates for rule 415 offerings is set forth in the appendix to NI 71-101.

(15) Disclosure of Interest of Underwriter — An underwriter of the Canadian distribution named in the preliminary MJDS Prospectus or MJDS Prospectus remains subject to any obligation under Canadian securities legislation to disclose the names of persons or companies having an interest in its capital.

(16) Conflicts of Interest — The provisions of Canadian securities legislation that regulate conflicts of interest in connection with the distribution of securities of a registered dealer, a connected issuer of a registered dealer or a related issuer of a registered dealer, other than disclosure, apply to distributions under NI 71-101. In some jurisdictions, participation of an independent underwriter in these distributions may be required.

(17) Trust Indenture Requirements — Section 19.1 of NI 71-101 provides that any requirement of a jurisdiction applicable to trust indentures for any debt outstanding or guaranteed thereunder, including a requirement that a person or company appointed as a trustee under a trust indenture be resident or authorized to do business in the jurisdiction, does not apply to offerings made under NI 71-101, if the conditions of Section 19.1 are met.

(18) Fees — Canadian securities legislation regarding fees applies to a filing made under NI 71-101.

3.3 Registration Requirements for Rights Offerings — The dealer registration requirement applies to

(a) a dealer that solicits exercise of rights; and

(b) a dealer that resells securities acquired under a standby underwriting commitment by the dealer to purchase securities unsubscribed for by other securityholders

in a rights offering made under NI 71-101.

3.4 Bids for Securities of U.S. Issuers — (1) General — Subject to the provisions of Part 12 of NI 71-101, the MJDS permits eligible take-over bids and issuer bids for securities of a U.S. issuer to be made in accordance with U.S. federal securities law to Canadian residents if Canadian residents hold less than 40 percent of the securities. The MJDS enables offerors generally to comply with applicable U.S. disclosure requirements and requirements governing the conduct of the bid instead of complying with Canadian requirements.

The MJDS is extended to take-over bids and issuer bids primarily to encourage fair treatment of Canadian investors. Securityholders in a particular jurisdiction who are excluded from an offer may be relegated to choosing, without the disclosure and procedural safeguards available under either the Canadian or the U.S. regulatory scheme, either to sell into the secondary market at less than the full bid price and incur additional transactional costs or to remain minority securityholders subject to the possibility of being forced out of their equity position in a subsequent merger. The application of the MJDS to bids is intended to facilitate bids by reducing duplicative regulation and avoiding conflict between the two regulatory schemes. Because the substantive protections and disclosure obligations applicable to bids in the United States are, as a whole, comparable to those prescribed by Canadian securities legislation, Canadian resident holders of securities of U.S. issuers should remain adequately protected by the application of U.S. rather than Canadian rules in the circumstances contemplated by NI 71-101.

Particularly when relatively few securities are held by Canadian residents, there may be a disincentive to extend a bid to them if doing so would require compliance with additional Canadian regulatory requirements. The availability of the MJDS for bids for securities of U.S. issuers is intended to alter the offeror's cost-benefit analysis in favour of extending those bids to Canadian residents.

There are no offeror eligibility requirements except in the case of securities exchange bids. For securities exchange bids made under the MJDS, compliance with U.S. disclosure requirements satisfies Canadian disclosure requirements with respect to the offeror and the offered securities only if the offeror meets certain reporting history, listing and other eligibility requirements and, in the case of securities exchange take-over bids, a public float or investment grade rating requirement. In take-over bids, unlike issuer bids and rights offerings, the investor has not already made an investment decision with respect to the issuer of the securities that are being offered in the exchange.

Bids made under the MJDS must be extended to all holders of the class of securities subject to the bid in Canada and the United States. Further, bids must be made on the same terms and conditions to all securityholders.

The provisions of securities legislation governing the form and content of disclosure documents and the conduct of bids are varied in respect of bids made under the MJDS to the extent provided in NI 71-101 and the implementing law of a jurisdiction. Bids made under the MJDS remain subject to any requirements to file with the Canadian securities regulatory authorities and send a bid circular, a directors' circular or an individual director's or officer's circular and any notice of change or notice of variation to holders of the securities subject to the bid.

The requirement to send bid materials to holders of the securities subject to the bid applies whether those materials are published, sent or given to securityholders resident in the United States of America by the use of stockholder lists and security position listings, or by long form or summary publication.

Each MJDS take-over bid circular, MJDS issuer bid circular, MJDS directors' circular and MJDS director's or officer's circular remains subject to the requirement that it not contain an untrue statement of a material fact or omit to state a material fact that is required to be stated or that is necessary to make a statement not misleading in light of the circumstances in which it was made.

(2) Alternative Exemptions — Provision is made in the Canadian securities legislation of some jurisdictions for exemption from take-over bid and issuer bid requirements if the bid is made in compliance with the laws of a recognized jurisdiction and there are relatively few holders in the jurisdiction holding a relatively small percentage of the class of securities subject to the bid. An offeror may make a bid under the MJDS in certain jurisdictions and under such an exemption in others.

(3) Certain Continuing Requirements —

(a) Early Warning — Provisions of Canadian securities legislation that require disclosure of acquisitions reaching a certain threshold or restrict acquisitions of securities once such a threshold has been reached continue to apply in respect of U.S. offeree issuers that are reporting issuers in a jurisdiction.

(b) Going Private Transactions — Bids made under the MJDS are subject to the requirements of Canadian securities legislation relating to going private transactions, other than the requirement to provide a valuation at the time of a take-over bid if it is anticipated by the offeror that a going private transaction will follow the bid.

(c) Pre-bid Integration — Canadian securities legislation regulating take-over bids includes provisions regarding integration of pre-bid transactions with the bid. These provisions apply to MJDS bids only if 20 percent or more of a class of securities that is the subject of a take-over bid made under the MJDS is held by persons or companies whose last address as shown on the books of the issuer is in Canada.

(d) Valuation Requirements in Issuer and Insider Bids — The valuation requirements of Canadian securities legislation with respect to issuer bids and insider bids apply to issuer bids and insider bids made under the MJDS only if 20 percent or more of a class of securities that is the subject of the bid is held by persons or companies whose last address as shown on the books of the issuer is in Canada.

(e) Public Interest Jurisdiction — All bids remain subject to the fundamental principle that transactions must not be prejudicial to the public interest. The Canadian securities regulatory authorities will continue to exercise their public interest jurisdiction in specific cases if they determine that it is necessary to do so in order to preserve the integrity of the Canadian capital markets or to protect investors.

(4) Directors' and Individual Director's and Officer's Circulars — If a take-over bid is made under the MJDS, the offeree issuer and its directors and officers may elect to comply either with the requirements of Canadian securities legislation or as provided in NI 71-101 with U.S. federal securities law in respect of their response to the bid. In the case of compliance by the directors or by individual directors or officers with Canadian requirements, the requirements set out in NI 71-101 regarding directors' circulars or individual director's or officer's circulars, as the case may be, do not apply. Notwithstanding that a take-over bid was eligible to be made under the MJDS, the offeree issuer and its directors and officers may not use the MJDS in respect of the bid if the offeror did not make the bid under the MJDS.

(5) Bids Made in Quebec — A French language version of a MJDS bid circular, together with French language versions of all documents or parts thereof incorporated by reference into the MJDS bid circular that contain information required to be disclosed in a bid circular not prepared in accordance with NI 71-101, is required to be filed in Quebec.

However, a French language version of a MJDS bid circular is not required to be filed for a bid made under the MJDS, unless (i) the offeree issuer is a reporting issuer in Quebec, or (ii) 20 percent or more of a class of securities that is the subject of the bid is held by persons or companies whose last address as shown on the books of the issuer is in Canada.

(6) Notices of Variation and Notices of Change — The provisions of Canadian securities legislation that prescribe the circumstances in which a bid circular, directors' circular, or individual officer's or director's circular is required to be changed or varied and the form and content of the applicable disclosure documents do not apply to bids made under the MJDS, unless, in respect of the directors' circular or individual officer's or director's circular, the directors or individual officer or director have elected to comply with the requirements of Canadian securities legislation otherwise applicable. Instead, disclosure documents filed under the MJDS should be changed or varied in accordance with the requirements of section 12.15 of NI 71-101.

(7) Fees — Canadian securities legislation regarding fees applies to a bid made under NI 71-101.

3.5 Business Combinations — The MJDS permits securities of a U.S. issuer to be distributed by prospectus in Canada on the basis of documentation prepared in accordance with U.S. federal securities law, with certain additional Canadian disclosure, in connection with a business combination if less than 40 percent of the securities to be distributed by the successor issuer would be held by Canadian residents. As in the case of bids, the MJDS is available for business combinations primarily to encourage fair treatment of Canadian investors. A MJDS prospectus filed for a distribution of securities in connection with a business combination need not contain a reconciliation of the financial statements in the prospectus to Canadian GAAP.

Canadian securities legislation of most of the jurisdictions provides for an exemption from prospectus requirements for certain distributions of securities issued in connection with a statutory amalgamation, merger or arrangement. As a result, an issuer may elect not to use the MJDS, but to distribute securities issued in a business combination under a prospectus exemption. A consequence of using a prospectus exemption instead of the MJDS may be resale restrictions on the distributed securities. However, under rules or blanket rulings or orders issued in certain jurisdictions, the resale of securities acquired under such an exemption is not a distribution for which a prospectus is required if the issuer meets certain eligibility and reporting requirements and the resale is executed through the facilities of a stock exchange or certain other regulated markets outside of the jurisdiction.

A business combination made under the MJDS must comply with the relevant requirements of securities legislation relating to going private transactions and related party transactions. All business combinations remain subject to the fundamental principle that transactions must not be prejudicial to the public interest. The Canadian securities regulatory authorities will continue to exercise their public interest jurisdiction in specific cases if they determine that it is necessary to do so to preserve the integrity of the Canadian capital markets or to protect investors.

Part 7: TRANSAC-TIONS OUTSIDE JURISDICTIONS

3.6 Continuous Disclosure, Proxies and Proxy Solicitation, Insider Reporting and Shareholder Communication — (1) General — An issuer that files a prospectus or a bid circular for a securities exchange take-over bid in certain jurisdictions becomes a reporting issuer in those jurisdictions, thereby becoming subject, among other things, to certain continuous disclosure, proxy and proxy solicitation, and shareholder communication requirements, and its insiders becoming subject to certain insider reporting requirements.

Parts 14 through 18 of NI 71-101 substitute U.S. federal securities law requirements for the requirements of Canadian securities legislation otherwise applicable to U.S. issuers and other persons or companies that satisfy the relevant eligibility criteria, if any, specified in those parts and that elect to comply with the requirements specified in those parts.

Canadian securities legislation in certain jurisdictions requires that issuers

(a) prepare their financial statements in accordance with, or reconcile the financial statements to, Canadian GAAP;

(b) state in the notes to the financial statements which option has been applied in the choice of generally accepted accounting principles; and

(c) include an auditor's report on the financial statements prepared in accordance with Canadian GAAS or include an explanation of the significant differences between U.S. generally accepted auditing standards and Canadian GAAS.

U.S. issuers filing financial statements in accordance with Part 15 of NI 71-101 are exempt from these requirements under rules, blanket rulings or orders issued in those jurisdictions.

(2) Communication with Beneficial Owners of Securities of a Reporting Issuer — If a U.S. issuer elects to comply with section 18.1 of NI 71-101, any Canadian clearing agency (i.e. The Canadian Depositary for Securities Limited) and any intermediary whose last address as shown on the books of the issuer is in the local jurisdiction is required to comply with the requirements of National Policy Statement No. 41 and any successor instrument to that National Policy Statement for such issuer, including, without limitation, responding to search cards and delivering proxy-related materials within the time periods specified in National Policy Statement No. 41 and under any successor instrument to that National Policy Statement.

PART 4 — CERTAIN OFFERINGS BY CANADIAN ISSUERS UNDER THE U.S. MULTIJURISDICTIONAL DISCLOSURE SYSTEM

4.1 U.S. Trust Indenture Exemption — Rule 4d-9 made under the Trust Indenture Act of 1939 grants certain exemptions from the U.S. trust indenture provisions for a trust indenture filed with the SEC in connection with an offering of securities by a Canadian issuer under the U.S. multijurisdictional disclosure system if the trust indenture is subject to the Canada Business Corporations Act, the Bank Act (Canada), the Business Corporations Act (Ontario) or the Company Act (British Columbia). The trust indenture provisions of the Canada Business Corporations Act, the Bank Act (Canada) and the Company Act (British Columbia) apply to issuers incorporated under the respective statute, whether the debt is distributed in Canada or elsewhere. The trust indenture provisions of the Business Corporations Act (Ontario) and the Company Act (British Columbia) apply in certain circumstances to issuers whether or not incorporated under the applicable statute. In order for the trust indenture provisions of the Business Corporations Act (Ontario) to apply to a trust indenture, a prospectus or securities exchange issuer or take-over bid circular must be filed in Ontario in respect of the debt to be issued or guaranteed under the trust indenture. The Company Act (British Columbia) trust indenture provisions apply if the debt is issued (i) by a company incorporated in British Columbia regardless of where the debt is distributed, or (ii) to residents in British Columbia whether the debt is issued by prospectus, private placement or other exemption, subject to certain limited exceptions set out in the Company Act (British Columbia). Therefore, in order for the exemption in Rule 4d-9 to be available, Canadian issuers, other than those incorporated under the Canada Business Corporations Act, the Bank Act (Canada) or the Company Act (British Columbia) must either file a prospectus or securities exchange issuer or take-over bid circular in Ontario in connection with the offering or offer the securities in British Columbia by prospectus, private placement or under another exemption from the prospectus filing requirement other than those specified in the Company Act (British Columbia).

4.2 Prospectus Filing in Canada — (1) General — An issuer distributing securities in the U.S. under the U.S. multijurisdictional disclosure system may be subject to a requirement to file a prospectus with a Canadian securities regulatory authority in a jurisdiction because part of the securities offered may be offered or sold to purchasers in that jurisdiction or as a result of the likelihood that the securities sold in the U.S. will not come to rest outside that jurisdiction and thus the offering constitutes a distribution in that jurisdiction for which a prospectus is required to be filed.

(2) Distribution from British Columbia, Alberta or Quebec —

(a) An issuer located in British Columbia, Alberta or Quebec that is distributing securities in the U.S. under the U.S. multijurisdictional disclosure system is subject to a requirement to file a prospectus with the Canadian securities regulatory authority in British Columbia, Alberta or Quebec, respectively, because the U.S. distribution is being made from British Columbia, Alberta or Quebec, respectively, even if the securities qualified by the prospectus are offered and sold only in the United States of America.

(b) Under British Columbia Rule 71-801 and Alberta Rule 71-801, an issuer filing a prospectus with the British Columbia Securities Commission or Alberta Securities Commission, respectively, in circumstances described in paragraph (a) need not include in the prospectus an underwriter's certificate.

(c) An issuer filing a prospectus with the Commission des valeurs mobilières du Québec in circumstances described in paragraph (a) may apply to the Commission des valeurs mobilières du Québec for an exemption from those requirements that solely would be applicable if the distribution were being made to purchasers in Quebec.

(d) An issuer that files a prospectus in British Columbia or Alberta in circumstances described in paragraph (a) should advise the SEC of the Canadian securities regulatory authority that is the review jurisdiction. The prospectus will be subject to the review procedures applicable to short form prospectuses. The British Columbia Securities Commission or the Alberta Securities Commission will send the issuer the receipt for the prospectus after the comments, if any, on the prospectus have been resolved. If the issuer has filed a registration statement on Form F-9 or F-10 prescribed under the 1933 Act with the SEC in connection with the distribution, the issuer should advise the SEC of the issuance of the receipt for the prospectus in order that the registration statement may become effective before the end of the seven calendar day period in Rule 467(b) under the 1933 Act.

(e) An issuer that files a prospectus in Quebec in circumstances described in paragraph (a) should advise the SEC that the Commission des valeurs mobilières du Québec is the review jurisdiction. The Commission des valeurs mobilières du Québec will complete its review of the prospectus within three business days of filing of the prospectus and will send the issuer the receipt for the prospectus after the comments, if any, on the prospectus have been resolved. If the issuer has filed a registration statement on Form F-9 or F-10 in connection with the distribution, the issuer should advise the SEC of the issuance of the receipt for the prospectus in order that the registration statement may become effective before the end of the seven calendar day period in Rule 467(b) under the 1933 Act.

4.3 Filings in Saskatchewan, Manitoba, Ontario and Nova Scotia For U.S. Only Distributions — (1) Filing Procedures — If an issuer other than an issuer located in British Columbia, Alberta or Quebec, that files a Form F-9 or F-10 in connection with a distribution solely in the United States of America under the multijurisdictional disclosure system adopted by the SEC seeks to have the registration statement become effective before the end of the seven calendar day period in Rule 467(b) under the 1933 Act, the issuer may select Saskatchewan, Manitoba, Ontario or Nova Scotia as review jurisdiction, file the registration statement filed with the SEC with the Canadian securities regulatory authority in the review jurisdiction contemporaneously with the filing of the registration statement with the SEC, obtain a notification of clearance from the regulator and advise the SEC of the issuance of the notification of clearance.

(2) Confirmation of Review Jurisdiction — If the Canadian securities regulatory authority selected under subsection (1) elects not to act as review jurisdiction, the issuer may select another Canadian securities regulatory authority as review jurisdiction and advise the SEC of the Canadian securities regulatory authority selected as review jurisdiction.

(3) Review Procedures —

(a) The Canadian securities regulatory authority in the review jurisdiction will monitor registration statements filed under subsection (1). The substance of a registration statement will be reviewed in the unusual case if, through monitoring of the materials or otherwise, the Canadian securities regulatory authority has reason to believe that there may be a problem with the transaction or the related disclosure or other special circumstances exist.

(b) If the review jurisdiction selects a registration statement for review, it will send its comments to the issuer within three business days of the filing of the registration statement.

(4) Notification of Clearance Procedures — A notification of clearance for the registration statement will be issued by the regulator in the review jurisdiction once any comments have been resolved, unless the Canadian securities regulatory authority in the review jurisdiction has reason to believe that there may be a problem with the transaction or the related disclosure or other special circumstances exist.

(5) Filing of Amendments to Registration Statement — An issuer that files a registration statement under subsection (1) shall also file with the regulator in the review jurisdiction all amendments to the registration statement contemporaneously with the filing of such documents with the SEC.

Adoption by OSC: (1998) 21 O.S.C.B. 5099; Request for Comments: (1997) 20 O.S.C.B. 6496.

National Instrument 71-102 — Continuous Disclosure and Other Exemptions Relating to Foreign Issuers

Date: March 30, 2004, as amended effective June 1, 2005, December 29, 2006, December 31, 2007, January 1, 2011, September 30, 2014 and November 17, 2015

27 O.S.C.B. 3560, 28 O.S.C.B. 4977, 30 O.S.C.B. (Supp-1) 32, 30 O.S.C.B. 10509, 33 O.S.C.B. (Supp. 5) 76, 37 O.S.C.B. 6753 and 38 O.S.C.B. 7563

Table of Contents

PART 1 — DEFINITIONS AND INTERPRETATION

1.1 Definitions and Interpretation — In this Instrument:

"AIF" means a completed Form 51-102F2 *Annual Information Form* or, in the case of an SEC foreign issuer, a completed Form 51-102F2 or an annual report or transition report under the 1934 Act on Form 10-K, or Form 20-F;

"business acquisition report" means a completed Form 51-102F4 *Business Acquisition Report*;

"class" includes a series of a class;

"convertible security" means a security of an issuer that is convertible into, or carries the right of the holder to acquire, or of the issuer to cause the acquisition of, a security of the same issuer;

"designated foreign issuer" means a foreign reporting issuer

 (a) that does not have a class of securities registered under section 12 of the 1934 Act and is not required to file reports under section 15(d) of the 1934 Act;

 (b) that is subject to foreign disclosure requirements in a designated foreign jurisdiction; and

 (c) for which the total number of equity securities owned, directly or indirectly, by residents of Canada does not exceed 10 per cent, on a fully-diluted basis, of the total number of equity securities of the issuer, calculated in accordance with sections 1.2 and 1.3;

"designated foreign jurisdiction" means Australia, France, Germany, Hong Kong, Italy, Japan, Mexico, the Netherlands, New Zealand, Singapore, South Africa, Spain, Sweden, Switzerland or the United Kingdom of Great Britain and Northern Ireland;

"exchangeable security" means a security of an issuer that is exchangeable for, or carries the right of the holder to acquire, or of the issuer to cause the acquisition of, a security of another issuer;

"exchange-traded security" means a security that is listed on a recognized exchange or is quoted on a recognized quotation and trade reporting system or is listed on an exchange or quoted on a quotation and trade reporting system that is recognized for the purposes of National Instrument 21-101 *Marketplace Operation* and National Instrument 23-101 *Trading Rules*;

"executive officer" means, for a reporting issuer, an individual who is

 (a) a chair, vice-chair or president;

 (b) a vice-president in charge of a principal business unit, division or function including sales, finance or production; or

 (c) performing a policy-making function in respect of the issuer;

"financial statements" has the same meaning as in section 1.1 of National Instrument 51-102 *Continuous Disclosure Obligations*;

"foreign disclosure requirements" means the requirements to which a foreign reporting issuer is subject concerning the disclosure made to the public, to securityholders of the issuer or to a foreign regulatory authority

 (a) relating to the foreign reporting issuer and the trading in its securities; and

 (b) that is made publicly available in the foreign jurisdiction under

  (i) the securities laws of the foreign jurisdiction in which the principal trading market of the foreign reporting issuer is located; or

  (ii) the rules of the marketplace that is the principal trading market of the foreign reporting issuer;

"foreign regulatory authority" means a securities commission, exchange or other securities market regulatory authority in a designated foreign jurisdiction;

"foreign reporting issuer" means a reporting issuer, other than an investment fund, that is incorporated or organized under the laws of a foreign jurisdiction, unless

> (a) outstanding voting securities carrying more than 50 per cent of the votes for the election of directors are owned, directly or indirectly, by residents of Canada; and

> (b) any one or more of the following is true:

>> (i) the majority of the executive officers or directors of the issuer are residents of Canada;

>> (ii) more than 50 per cent of the consolidated assets of the issuer are located in Canada; or

>> (iii) the business of the issuer is administered principally in Canada;

"inter-dealer bond broker" means a person or company that is approved by the Investment Industry Regulatory Organization of Canada under its Rule 36 *Inter-Dealer Bond Brokerage Systems*, as amended, and is subject to its Rule 36 and its Rule 2100 *Inter-Dealer Bond Brokerage Systems*, as amended;

"interim period" means,

> (a) in the case of a year other than a non-standard year or a transition year, a period commencing on the first day of the financial year and ending nine, six or three months before the end of the financial year,

> (a.1) in the case of a non-standard year, a period commencing on the first day of the financial year and ending within 22 days of the date that is nine, six or three months before the end of the financial year; or

> (b) in the case of a transition year, a period commencing on the first day of the transition year and ending

>> (i) three, six, nine or twelve months, if applicable, after the end of the old financial year; or

>> (ii) twelve, nine, six or three months, if applicable, before the end of the transition year;

"marketplace" has the same meaning as in National Instrument 21-101 *Marketplace Operation*;

"MD&A" means a completed Form 51-102F1 *Management's Discussion & Analysis* or, in the case of an SEC foreign issuer, a completed Form 51-102F1 or management's discussion and analysis prepared in accordance with Item 303 of Regulation S-K under the 1934 Act;

"multiple convertible security" means a security of an issuer that is convertible into, or exchangeable for, or carries the right of the holder to acquire, or of the issuer to cause the acquisition of, a convertible security, an exchangeable security or another multiple convertible security;

"Nasdaq" means Nasdaq National Market and Nasdaq SmallCap Market;

"NI 52-107" means National Instrument 52-107 *Acceptable Accounting Principles and Auditing Standards*;

"non-standard year" means a financial year, other than a transition year, that does not have 365 days, or 366 days if it includes February 29;

"old financial year" means the financial year of a reporting issuer that immediately precedes its transition year;

"principal trading market" means the published market on which the largest trading volume in the equity securities of the issuer occurred during the issuer's most recent financial year that ended before the date the determination is being made;

"published market" means, for a class of securities, a marketplace on which the securities have traded that discloses regularly in a publication of general and regular paid circulation or in a form that is broadly distributed by electronic means the prices at which those securities have traded;

"recognized exchange" means

> (a) in Ontario, an exchange recognized by the securities regulatory authority to carry on business as a stock exchange;

> (a.1) in Québec, a person or company authorized by the securities regulatory authority to carry on business as an exchange; and

> (b) in every other jurisdiction, an exchange recognized by the securities regulatory authority as an exchange, selfregulatory organization or self-regulatory body;

"recognized quotation and trade reporting system" means

> (a) in every jurisdiction other than British Columbia, a quotation and trade reporting system recognized by the securities regulatory authority under securities legislation to carry on business as a quotation and trade reporting system; and

> (b) in British Columbia, a quotation and trade reporting system recognized by the securities regulatory authority under securities legislation as a quotation and trade reporting system or as an exchange;

"SEC foreign issuer" means a foreign reporting issuer that

> (a) has a class of securities registered under section 12 of the 1934 Act or is required to file reports under section 15(d) of the 1934 Act; and

> (b) is not registered or required to be registered as an investment company under the *Investment Company Act of 1940* of the United States of America, as amended;

"transition year" means the financial year of a reporting issuer in which the issuer changes its financial year-end;

"TSX" means the Toronto Stock Exchange;

"underlying security" means a security issued or transferred, or to be issued or transferred, in accordance with the terms of a convertible security, an exchangeable security or a multiple convertible security;

"U.S. market" means an exchange in the United States of America or Nasdaq; and

"U.S. market requirements" means the requirements of the U.S. market on which the reporting issuer's securities are listed or quoted.

1.2 Determination of Canadian Shareholders — (1) For the purposes of section 4.14 and paragraph (c) of the definition of "designated foreign issuer", a reference to equity securities owned, directly or indirectly, by residents of Canada, includes

> (a) the underlying securities that are equity securities of the foreign reporting issuer; and

> (b) the equity securities of the foreign reporting issuer represented by an American depositary receipt or an American depositary share issued by a depositary holding equity securities of the foreign reporting issuer.

(2) For the purposes of paragraph (a) of the definition of "foreign reporting issuer", securities represented by American depositary receipts or American depositary shares issued by a depositary holding voting securities of the foreign reporting issuer must be included as outstanding in determining both

Part 7: TRANSAC-
TIONS OUTSIDE
JURISDICTIONS

the number of votes attached to securities owned, directly or indirectly, by residents of Canada and the number of votes attached to all of the issuer's outstanding voting securities.

1.3 Timing for Calculation of Designated Foreign Issuer and Foreign Reporting Issuer — For the purposes of paragraph (c) of the definition of "designated foreign issuer", paragraph (a) of the definition of "foreign reporting issuer" and section 4.14, the calculation is made,

(a) if the issuer has not completed a financial year since becoming a reporting issuer, at the date that the issuer became a reporting issuer; and

(b) for all other issuers,

(i) for the purpose of financial statement and MD&A filings under this Instrument, on the first day of the most recent financial year or year-to-date interim period for which financial performance is presented in the financial statements or MD&A; and

(ii) for the purpose of other continuous disclosure filing obligations under this Instrument, on the first day of the issuer's current financial year.

PART 2 — LANGUAGE OF DOCUMENTS

2.1 French or English — (1) A person or company must file a document required to be filed under this Instrument in either French or English.

(2) Notwithstanding subsection (1), if a person or company files a document only in French or only in English but delivers to securityholders of an issuer a version of the document in the other language, the person or company must file that other version not later than when it is first delivered to securityholders.

(3) In Québec, a reporting issuer must comply with linguistic obligations and rights prescribed by Québec law.

2.2 Filings Prepared in a Language other than French or English — (1) If a person or company files a document that is required to be filed under this Instrument that is a translation of a document prepared in a language other than French or English, the person or company must file the document upon which the translation was based.

(2) A foreign reporting issuer filing a document upon which the translation was based under subsection (1) must attach to the document a certificate as to the accuracy of the translation.

PART 3 — FILING AND SENDING OF DOCUMENTS

3.1 Timing of Filing of Documents — A person or company filing a document under this Instrument must file the document at the same time as, or as soon as practicable after, the filing or furnishing of the document to the SEC or to a foreign regulatory authority.

3.2 Sending of Documents to Canadian Securityholders — If a person or company sends a document to holders of securities of any class under U.S. federal securities law, or the laws or requirements of a designated foreign jurisdiction, and that document is required to be filed under this Instrument, then the document must be sent in the same manner and at the same time, or as soon as practicable after, to holders of securities of that class in the local jurisdiction.

PART 4 — SEC FOREIGN ISSUERS

4.1 Amendments and Supplements — Any amendments or supplements to disclosure documents filed by an SEC foreign issuer under this Instrument must also be filed.

4.2 Material Change Reporting — An SEC foreign issuer satisfies securities legislation requirements relating to disclosure of material changes if the issuer

(a) complies with the U.S. market requirements for making public disclosure of material information on a timely basis;

(b) complies with foreign disclosure requirements for making public disclosure of material information on a timely basis, if securities of the issuer are not listed or quoted on a U.S. market;

(c) promptly files each news release issued by it for the purpose of complying with the requirements referred to in paragraph (a) or (b);

(d) complies with the requirements of U.S. federal securities law for filing or furnishing current reports to the SEC; and

(e) files the current reports filed with or furnished to the SEC.

4.3 Financial Statements — An SEC foreign issuer satisfies securities legislation requirements relating to the preparation, approval, filing and delivery of financial statements and auditor's reports on annual financial statements if it

(a) complies with the requirements of U.S. federal securities law relating to financial statements and auditor's reports on annual financial statements;

(b) complies with the U.S. market requirements relating to financial statements, if securities of the issuer are listed or quoted on a U.S. market;

(c) files the financial statements and auditor's reports on annual financial statements required to be filed with or furnished to the SEC or a U.S. market;

(d) complies with section 3.2 of this Instrument;

(e) complies with NI 52-107 as it relates to financial statements of the issuer that are included in any documents specified in paragraph (c); and

(f) complies with NI 52-108 *Auditor Oversight*.

4.4 AIFs and MD&A — An SEC foreign issuer satisfies securities legislation requirements relating to the preparation, approval, filing and delivery of AIFs and MD&A if it

(a) complies with the requirements of U.S. federal securities law relating to annual reports, quarterly reports, current reports and management's discussion and analysis;

(b) files each annual report, quarterly report, current report and management's discussion and analysis filed with or furnished to the SEC;

(c) complies with section 3.2 of this Instrument; and

(d) complies with NI 52-107 as it relates to financial statements of the issuer that are included in any documents specified in paragraph (b).

4.5 Business Acquisition Reports — An SEC foreign issuer satisfies securities legislation requirements relating to the preparation and filing of business acquisition reports if it

(a) complies with the requirements of U.S. federal securities law relating to business acquisition reports;

(b) files each business acquisition report filed with or furnished to the SEC;

(c) complies with section 3.2 of this Instrument; and

(d) complies with NI 52-107 as it relates to financial statements that are included in any documents specified in paragraph (b).

4.6 Proxies and Proxy Solicitation by the Issuer and Information Circulars — An SEC foreign issuer satisfies securities legislation requirements relating to information circulars, proxies and proxy solicitation if it

(a) complies with the requirements of U.S. federal securities law relating to proxy statements, proxies and proxy solicitation;

(b) files all material relating to a meeting of securityholders that is filed with or furnished to the SEC;

(c) sends each document filed under paragraph (b) to securityholders in the local jurisdiction in the manner and at the time required by U.S. federal securities laws and U.S. market requirements; and

(d) complies with NI 52-107 as it relates to financial statements of the issuer that are included in any documents specified in paragraph (b).

4.7 Proxy Solicitation by Another Person or Company — (1) A person or company, other than the SEC foreign issuer, satisfies securities legislation requirements relating to information circulars, proxies and proxy solicitation with respect to an SEC foreign issuer if the person or company complies with the requirements of subsection 4.6.

(2) If a proxy solicitation is made with respect to an SEC foreign issuer by a person or company other than the SEC foreign issuer and the person or company soliciting proxies lacks access to the relevant list of securityholders of the SEC foreign issuer, subsection (1) is not available, if

(a) the aggregate published trading volume of the class on the TSX, Aequitas NEO Exchange Inc., the Canadian Securities Exchange and the TSX Venture Exchange exceeded the aggregate published trading volume of the class on all U.S. markets

(i) for the 12 calendar month period before commencement of the proxy solicitation, if there is no other proxy solicitation for securities of the same class in progress, or

(ii) for the 12 calendar month period before commencement of the first proxy solicitation, if another proxy solicitation for securities of the same class is already in progress;

(b) the information disclosed by the SEC foreign issuer in its most recent Form 10-K or Form 20-F filed with the SEC under the 1934 Act demonstrated that paragraph (a) of the definition of "foreign reporting issuer" applied to the SEC foreign issuer; or

(c) the person or company soliciting proxies reasonably believes that paragraph (a) of the definition of "foreign reporting issuer" applies to the SEC foreign issuer.

4.8 Disclosure of Voting Results — An SEC foreign issuer satisfies securities legislation requirements relating to disclosure of securityholder voting results if the issuer

(a) complies with the requirements of U.S. federal securities law relating to disclosure of securityholder voting results; and

(b) files a copy of all disclosure of securityholder voting results filed with or furnished to the SEC.

4.9 Filing of Certain News Releases — An SEC foreign issuer satisfies securities legislation requirements relating to the filing of news releases that disclose information regarding its financial performance or financial condition if the issuer

(a) complies with the requirements of U.S. federal securities laws relating to the filing of news releases disclosing financial information; and

(b) files a copy of each news release disclosing financial information that is filed with or furnished to the SEC.

4.10 Filing of Certain Documents — Securities legislation requirements relating to the filing of documents affecting the rights of securityholders and the filing of material contracts do not apply to an SEC foreign issuer.

4.11 Early Warning — A person or company satisfies the early warning requirements and acquisition announcement provisions of securities legislation in respect of securities of an SEC foreign issuer that has a class of securities registered under section 12 of the 1934 Act if the person or company

(a) complies with the requirements of U.S. federal securities law relating to the reporting of beneficial ownership of equity securities of the SEC foreign issuer; and

(b) files each report of beneficial ownership that is filed with or furnished to the SEC.

4.12 Insider Reporting — The insider reporting requirement does not apply to an insider of an SEC foreign issuer that has a class of securities registered under section 12 of the 1934 Act if the insider complies with the requirements of U.S. federal securities law relating to insider reporting.

4.13 Communication with Beneficial Owners of Securities — An SEC foreign issuer that has a class of securities registered under section 12 of the 1934 Act satisfies securities legislation requirements relating to communications with, delivery of materials to and conferring voting rights upon nonregistered holders of its securities who hold their interests in the securities through one or more intermediaries if the issuer

(a) complies with the requirements of Rule 14a-13 under the 1934 Act for any depositary and any intermediary whose last address as shown on the books of the issuer is in Canada; and

(b) complies with the requirements of National Instrument 54-101 *Communication with Beneficial Owners of Securities of a Reporting Issuer* with respect to fees payable to intermediaries, for any depositary and any intermediary whose last address as shown on the books of the issuer is in Canada.

4.14 Business Combinations and Related Party Transactions — Securities legislation requirements relating to business combinations and related party transactions in Multilateral Instrument 61-101 *Protection of Minority Security Holders in Special Transactions* do not apply to an SEC foreign issuer carrying out a business combination or related party transaction if the total number of equity securities of the SEC foreign issuer owned, directly or indirectly, by residents of Canada, does not exceed 20 per cent, on a diluted basis, of the total number of equity securities of the SEC foreign issuer.

4.15 **Change of Auditor** — An SEC foreign issuer satisfies securities legislation requirements relating to a change of auditor if the issuer

(a) complies with the requirements of U.S. federal securities laws relating to a change of auditor; and

(b) files a copy of all materials relating to a change of auditor that are filed with or furnished to the SEC.

4.16 **Restricted Securities** — (1) Securities legislation continuous disclosure requirements relating to restricted securities do not apply in respect of SEC foreign issuers.

(2) Securities legislation minority approval requirements relating to restricted securities do not apply in respect of SEC foreign issuers.

PART 5 — DESIGNATED FOREIGN ISSUERS

5.1 **Amendments and Supplements** — Any amendments or supplements to disclosure documents filed by a designated foreign issuer under this Instrument must also be filed.

5.2 **Mandatory Annual Disclosure by Designated Foreign Issuer** — To rely on this Part, a designated foreign issuer must, at least once a year, disclose in, or as an appendix to, a document that it is required by foreign disclosure requirements to send to its securityholders and that it sends to its securityholders in Canada

(a) that it is a designated foreign issuer as defined in this Instrument;

(b) that it is subject to the foreign regulatory requirements of a foreign regulatory authority; and

(c) the name of the foreign regulatory authority referred to in paragraph (b).

5.3 **Material Change Reporting** — A designated foreign issuer satisfies securities legislation requirements relating to disclosure of material changes if the issuer

(a) complies with foreign disclosure requirements for making public disclosure of material information on a timely basis;

(b) promptly files each news release issued by it for the purpose of complying with the requirements referred to in paragraph (a); and

(c) files the documents disclosing the material information filed with or furnished to the foreign regulatory authority or disseminated to the public or securityholders of the issuer.

5.4 **Financial Statements** — A designated foreign issuer satisfies securities legislation requirements relating to the preparation, approval, filing and delivery of financial statements and auditor's reports on annual financial statements if it

(a) complies with the foreign disclosure requirements relating to financial statements and auditor's reports on annual financial statements;

(b) files the financial statements and auditor's reports on annual financial statements required to be filed with or furnished to the foreign regulatory authority;

(c) complies with section 3.2 of this Instrument;

(d) complies with NI 52-107 as it relates to financial statements of the issuer that are included in any documents specified in paragraph (b); and

(e) complies with NI 52-108 *Auditor Oversight*.

5.5 **AIFs & MD&A** — A designated foreign issuer satisfies securities legislation requirements relating to the preparation, approval, filing and delivery of AIFs and MD&A if it

(a) complies with the foreign disclosure requirements relating to annual reports, quarterly reports and management's discussion and analysis;

(b) files each annual report, quarterly report and management's discussion and analysis required to be filed with or furnished to the foreign regulatory authority;

(c) complies with section 3.2 of this Instrument; and

(d) complies with NI 52-107 as it relates to financial statements of the issuer that are included in any documents specified in paragraph (b).

5.6 **Business Acquisition Reports** — A designated foreign issuer satisfies securities legislation requirements relating to the preparation and filing of business acquisition reports if it

(a) complies with the foreign disclosure requirements relating to business acquisitions;

(b) files each report in respect of a business acquisition required to be filed with or furnished to the foreign regulatory authority;

(c) complies with section 3.2 of this Instrument; and

(d) complies with NI 52-107 as it relates to financial statements that are included in any documents specified in paragraph (b).

5.7 **Proxies and Proxy Solicitation by the Issuer and Information Circulars** — A designated foreign issuer satisfies securities legislation requirements relating to information circulars, proxies and proxy solicitation if it

(a) complies with the foreign disclosure requirements relating to proxy statements, proxies and proxy solicitation;

(b) files all material relating to a meeting of securityholders that is filed with or furnished to the foreign regulatory authority;

(c) complies with section 3.2 of this Instrument; and

(d) complies with NI 52-107 as it relates to financial statements of the issuer that are included in any documents specified in paragraph (b).

5.8 **Proxy Solicitation by Another Person or Company** — (1) A person or company, other than the designated foreign issuer, satisfies securities legislation requirements relating to information circulars, proxies and proxy solicitation with respect to a designated foreign issuer if the person or company satisfies the requirements of section 5.7.

(2) If a proxy solicitation is made with respect to a designated foreign issuer by a person or company other than the designated foreign issuer and the person or company soliciting proxies lacks access to the relevant list of securityholders of the designated foreign issuer, subsection (1) is not available, if

(a) the aggregate published trading volume of the class on the TSX, Aequitas NEO Exchange Inc., the Canadian Securities Exchange and the TSX Venture Exchange exceeded the aggregate trading volume on securities marketplaces outside Canada

(i) for the 12 calendar months before commencement of the proxy solicitation, if there is no other proxy solicitation for securities of the same class in progress, or

(ii) for the 12 calendar month period before the commencement of the first proxy solicitation, if another proxy solicitation for securities of the same class is already in progress;

(b) the information disclosed by the designated foreign issuer in a document filed within the previous 12 months with a foreign regulatory authority, demonstrated that paragraph (a) of the definition of "foreign reporting issuer" applied to the designated foreign issuer; or

(c) the person or company soliciting proxies reasonably believes that paragraph (a) of the definition of "foreign reporting issuer" applies to the designated foreign issuer.

5.9 Disclosure of Voting Results — A designated foreign issuer satisfies securities legislation requirements relating to disclosure of securityholder voting results if the issuer

(a) complies with the foreign disclosure requirements relating to disclosure of securityholder voting results; and

(b) files each report disclosing securityholder voting results that is filed with or furnished to a foreign regulatory authority.

5.10 Filing of Certain News Releases — A designated foreign issuer satisfies securities legislation requirements relating to the filing of news releases that disclose information regarding its financial performance or financial condition if the issuer

(a) complies with the foreign disclosure requirements relating to the filing of news releases disclosing financial information; and

(b) files a copy of each news release disclosing financial information that is filed with or furnished to a foreign regulatory authority.

5.11 Filing of Certain Documents — Securities legislation requirements relating to the filing of documents affecting the rights of securityholders and the filing of material contracts do not apply to a designated foreign issuer.

5.12 Early Warning — A person or company satisfies the early warning requirements and acquisition announcement provisions of securities legislation in respect of securities of a designated foreign issuer if the person or company

(a) complies with the foreign disclosure requirements relating to reporting of beneficial ownership of equity securities of the designated foreign issuer; and

(b) files each report of beneficial ownership that is filed with or furnished to the foreign regulatory authority.

5.13 Insider Reporting — The insider reporting requirement does not apply to an insider of a designated foreign issuer if the insider complies with foreign disclosure requirements relating to insider reporting.

5.14 Communication with Beneficial Owners of Securities — A designated foreign issuer satisfies securities legislation requirements relating to communications with, delivery of materials to and conferring voting rights upon non-registered holders of its securities who hold their interests in the securities through one or more intermediaries if the issuer

(a) complies with foreign disclosure requirements relating to communication with beneficial owners of securities; and

(b) complies with the requirements of National Instrument 54-101 *Communication with Beneficial Owners of Securities of a Reporting Issuer* with respect to fees payable to intermediaries, for any depositary and any intermediary whose last address as shown on the books of the issuer is in Canada.

5.15 Business Combinations and Related Party Transactions — Securities legislation requirements relating to business combinations and related party transactions in Multilateral Instrument 61-101 *Protection of Minority Security Holders in Special Transactions* do not apply to a designated foreign issuer carrying out a business combination or related party transaction.

5.16 Change in Year-End — A designated foreign issuer satisfies securities legislation requirements relating to a change in year-end if the issuer

(a) complies with foreign disclosure requirements relating to a change in year-end; and

(b) files a copy of all filings made under foreign disclosure requirements relating to the change in year-end.

5.17 Change of Auditor — A designated foreign issuer satisfies securities legislation requirements relating to a change of auditor if the issuer

(a) complies with foreign disclosure requirements relating to a change of auditor; and

(b) files a copy of all filings made under foreign disclosure requirements relating to the change of auditor.

5.18 Restricted Securities — (1) Securities legislation continuous disclosure requirements relating to restricted securities do not apply in respect of designated foreign issuers.

(2) Securities legislation minority approval requirements relating to restricted securities do not apply in respect of designated foreign issuers.

PART 6 — [REPEALED]

PART 7 — EFFECTIVE DATE

7.1 Effective Date — This Instrument comes into force on March 30, 2004.

Final Rule: (2004) 27 O.S.C.B. 3560; Approval of OSC: (2003) 26 O.S.C.B. (Supp-3) 191 (December 19, 2003); Request for Comments: (2003) 26 O.S.C.B. 4577 and (2002) 25 O.S.C.B. 3701.

Amendment to Rule: (2005) 28 O.S.C.B. 4977; Approval by OSC: (2005) 28 O.S.C.B. (Supp-1) 54.

Amendment to Rule: (2007) 30 O.S.C.B. 32; Approval by OSC: (2006) 29 O.S.C.B. (Supp-2) 1; Request for Comments: (2005) 28 O.S.C.B. 9845.

Amendment to Rule: 30 O.S.C.B. 10509; Approval by OSC: (2007) 30 O.S.C.B. 8570.

Amendment to Rule: (2010) 33 O.S.C.B. (Supp. 5) 76; Approval by OSC: (2010) 33 O.S.C.B. (Supp. 3) 113; Request for Comments: (2009) 32 O.S.C.B. (Supp. 6) 1.

Amendment to Rule: Approval by OSC: (2014) 37 O.S.C.B. 6753; Request for Comments: (2013) O.S.C.B. 10147.

Rules: Rule 71-802.

Policies and Orders: CSAN 51-338.

Companion Policy 71-102CP — Continuous Disclosure and Other Exemptions Relating to Foreign Issuers

PART 1 — GENERAL

1.1 Introduction and Purpose — (1) National Instrument 71-102 *Continuous Disclosure and Other Exemptions Relating to Foreign Issuers* (the "Instrument") provides broad relief from most of the requirements of National Instrument 51-102 *Continuous Disclosure Obligations* ("NI 51-102") for two sub-categories of foreign reporting issuers — SEC foreign issuers and designated foreign issuers — on the condition that they comply with the continuous disclosure ("CD") requirements of the SEC or a designated foreign jurisdiction. SEC foreign issuers and designated foreign issuers are also exempted from certain other requirements of provincial and territorial securities legislation, including insider reporting and early warning, that are not contained in NI 51-102.

(2) This Companion Policy provides information about how the provincial and territorial securities regulatory authorities interpret the Instrument, and should be read in conjunction with it.

1.2 Other Relevant Legislation — In addition to the Instrument, foreign issuers should consult the following non-exhaustive list of legislation to see how it may apply to them:

(1) implementing legislation (the regulation, rule, ruling, order or other instrument that implements the Instrument in each applicable jurisdiction);

(2) NI 51-102;

(3) National Instrument 52-107 *Acceptable Accounting Principles and Auditing Standards* ("NI 52-107"); and

(4) National Instrument 71-101 *The Multijurisdictional Disclosure System* ("NI 71-101").

1.3 Multijurisdictional Disclosure System — NI 71-101 permits certain U.S. incorporated issuers to satisfy specified Canadian CD requirements by using disclosure prepared in accordance with U.S. requirements. The Instrument does not replace or alter NI 71-101. There are instances in which NI 71-101 and the Instrument offer similar relief to a reporting issuer, but other instances in which the relief available to a reporting issuer in one instrument differs from the relief available to the reporting issuer under the other instrument. Many issuers that are eligible for an exemption under the Instrument will be ineligible to rely on NI 71-101 and vice versa. For example, the Instrument defines a class of "SEC foreign issuers". Not all U.S. issuers referred to in NI 71-101 are SEC foreign issuers and not all SEC foreign issuers are U.S. issuers.

1.4 Exemptions May Not Require Disclosure — Most of the exemptions in the Instrument are only available to a person or company that complies with a particular aspect of either U.S. federal securities laws or the laws of a designated foreign jurisdiction. If those laws do not require the issuer to disclose, file or send any information, for example, because the issuer may rely on an exemption under those laws, then the issuer is not required to disclose, file or send any information to rely on the exemption contained in the Instrument.

PART 2 — DEFINITIONS

2.1 Foreign Reporting Issuers — To qualify for any of the exemptions contained in the Instrument the issuer in question must be a "foreign reporting issuer". The definition of foreign reporting issuer is based upon the definition of foreign private issuer in Rule 405 of the 1933 Act and Rule 3b-4 of the 1934 Act. For the purposes of the definition of "foreign reporting issuer", it is the CSA's view that

    (a) in calculating the percentage of assets located in Canada, the issuer should use the book value of the assets recorded in its most recent consolidated financial statements, either annual or interim; and

    (b) in determining the outstanding voting securities that are owned, directly or indirectly, by residents of Canada, an issuer should

        (i) use reasonable efforts to identify securities held by a broker, dealer, bank, trust company or nominee or any of them for the accounts of customers resident in Canada;

        (ii) count securities beneficially owned by residents of Canada as reported on reports of beneficial ownership, including insider reports and early warning reports; and

        (iii) assume that a customer is a resident of the jurisdiction or foreign jurisdiction in which the nominee has its principal place of business if, after reasonable inquiry, information regarding the jurisdiction or foreign jurisdiction of residence of the customer is unavailable.

The determination of the percentage of securities of the foreign issuer owned by residents of Canada should be made in the same manner for the purposes of paragraph (c) of the definition of "designated foreign issuer". This method of calculation differs from that of NI 71-101, which only requires a calculation based on the address of record. Accordingly, some SEC foreign issuers may qualify for exemptive relief under NI 71-101 but not under the Instrument.

2.2 Investment Funds — Generally, the definition of "investment fund" would not include a trust or other entity that issues securities which entitle the holder to substantially all of the net cash flows generated by: (i) an underlying business owned by the trust or other entity, or (ii) the income-producing properties owned by the trust or other entity. Examples of trusts or other entities that are not included in the definition are business income trusts, real estate investment trusts and royalty trusts.

PART 3 — INSIDER REPORTS

3.1 [repealed]

PART 4 — FILING OF DISCLOSURE DOCUMENTS

4.1 Filing of Disclosure Documents on SEDAR — A foreign issuer does not have to file multiple copies of a foreign disclosure document that it is filing to satisfy the conditions of more than one exemption under the Instrument. The issuer need only file the document in one SEDAR category, and under any other applicable SEDAR category may provide an appropriate reference to the location of the filed document. For example, a foreign issuer may wish to file its U.S. Form 20F to satisfy the conditions relating to both the AIF exemption and the MD&A exemption. The foreign issuer could file the Form 20F on SEDAR under either of the AIF category or the MD&A category, and under the other category would file a letter giving the SEDAR project number that the Form 20F is filed under.

PART 5 — ELECTRONIC DELIVERY OF DOCUMENTS

5.1 Electronic Delivery of Documents — Any documents required to be sent under the Instrument may be sent by electronic delivery, as long as such delivery is made in compliance with Québec Notice 11-201 *Relating to the Delivery of Documents by Electronic Means*, in Québec, and National Policy 11-201 *Delivery of Documents by Electronic Means*, in the rest of Canada.

PART 6 — EXEMPTIONS NOT INCLUDED

6.1 Resource Issuers — Standards of Disclosure for Mineral Projects and Oil and Gas Activities — The Instrument does not provide an exemption from National Instrument 43-101 *Standards of Disclosure for Mineral Projects* or National Instrument 51-101 *Standards of Disclosure for Oil and Gas Activities*. Issuers are reminded that those National Instruments apply to SEC foreign issuers and designated foreign issuers.

6.2 SEC Foreign Issuers — NI 51-102 contains exemptions for SEC issuers from the change in year-end requirements in NI 51-102. SEC foreign issuers under the Instrument will also meet the definition of SEC issuers under NI 51-102, and so will be able to rely on the change in year-end exemption in NI 51-102.

6.3 Foreign Reporting Issuers — The Instrument does not provide an exemption for any foreign reporting issuers from the requirement in section 4.9 of NI 51-102. A foreign reporting issuer must deliver a notice if it has been a party to an amalgamation, arrangement, merger, winding-up, reverse takeover, reorganization or other transaction that will have the effect of changing its continuous disclosure obligations under NI 51-102. The Instrument also does not provide an exemption for any foreign reporting issuers from the requirement to file disclosure materials under section 11.1 of NI 51-102 or to file a notice of change of status under section 11.2 of NI 51-102.

6.4 Financial Statements and Auditor's Report Relief — Section 4.3 of the Instrument provides certain relief for an SEC foreign issuer relating to financial statements and auditors' reports on annual financial statements. Section 5.4 provides similar relief for a designated foreign issuer. The relief is available only if the particular foreign issuer meets all of the conditions listed in sections 4.3 and 5.4, respectively, including the requirement to comply with NI 52-107 and NI 52-108 *Auditor Oversight*. Sections 4.3 and 5.4 do not provide relief from

 (a) the certification requirements in National Instrument 52-109 *Certification of Disclosure in Issuers' Annual or Interim Filings*, or

 (b) the audit committee requirements in National Instrument 52-110 *Audit Committees*.

SEC foreign issuers and designated foreign issuers must look to those instruments for any exemptions that may be available to them.

PART 7 — EXEMPTIONS

7.1 Exemptions — (1) The exemptions contained in the Instrument are in addition to any exemptions that may be available to an issuer under any other applicable legislation.

(2) Issuers that have been given an exemption, waiver or approval by a regulator or securities regulatory authority before the Instrument and NI 51-102 came into effect, may be entitled to continue to rely on that exemption, waiver or approval. Issuers should refer to section 13.2 of NI 51-102 to determine in what circumstances the prior exemption, waiver or approval is available and what the reporting issuer must do to continue to rely on it.

(3) If an issuer wishes to seek exemptive relief from NI 51-102 or other requirements of provincial and territorial securities legislation on grounds similar but not identical to those permitted under the Instrument, the issuer should apply for this relief under the exemptive provisions of NI 51-102, or other provincial and territorial securities legislation, as the case may be.

PART 8 — TRANSITION

8.1 Transition — The amendments to the Instrument and this Policy which came into effect on January 1, 2011 only apply to documents required to be prepared, filed, delivered or sent under the Instrument for periods relating to financial years beginning on or after January 1, 2011.

Adoption by OSC: (2004) 27 O.S.C.B. 3574 and (2003) 26 O.S.C.B. (Supp-3) 191 (December 19, 2003); Request for Comments: (2003) 26 O.S.C.B. 4577 and (2002) 25 O.S.C.B. 3701.

Adoption of Amendment by OSC: (2007) 30 O.S.C.B. (Supp-1) 189 and (2006) 29 O.S.C.B. (Supp-2) 1; Request for Comments: (2005) 28 O.S.C.B. 9845.

Adoption of Amendment to OSC: (2008) 31 O.S.C.B. 11350.

Adoption of Amendment to OSC: (2010) 33 O.S.C.B. (Supp. 5) 78 and (Supp. 3) 113; Request for Comments: (2009) 32 O.S.C.B. (Supp. 6) 1.

Adoption of Amendment to OSC: (2014) 37 O.S.C.B. 6753; Request for Comments: (2013) 36 O.S.C.B. 10147.

Rule 71-801 — Implementing the Multijurisdictional Disclosure System

Date: **November 6, 1998, as amended effective February 1, 2008 (by Rule 62-504), March 17, 2008 and May 9, 2016**

21 O.S.C.B. 6919, 31 O.S.C.B. 1289, 31 O.S.C.B. (Supp. 2) 262 and 39 O.S.C.B. 4289

PART 1 — DEFINITIONS

1.1 Definitions — (1) Each term used in this Rule that is defined or interpreted in Part 1 of NI 71-101 has the meaning ascribed to it in that Part.

(2) In this Rule "NI 71-101" means "National Instrument 71-101 The Multijurisdictional Disclosure System".

(3) In this Rule, "NI 62-104" means "National Instrument 62-104 *Take-Over Bids and Issuers Bids*".

PART 2 — MJDS PROSPECTUS DISTRIBUTIONS

2.1 Preliminary MJDS Prospectus and MJDS Prospectus — (1) The following provisions of the Act do not apply to a distribution of securities made by MJDS prospectus in accordance with NI 71-101

    (a) subsection 57(1), insofar as that section concerns the form, content and circumstances of filing of an amendment to a preliminary prospectus or prospectus;

    (b) subsection 57(2), insofar as that subsection specifies the time period that must elapse before the distribution of additional securities may be proceeded with;

    (c) subsections 58(1) and 59(1); and

    (d) section 62, insofar as that section limits the duration of the distribution of securities under a MJDS prospectus in relation to a rule 415 offering.

(2) Despite subsection 65(1) of the Act, the waiting period between the issuance by the Director of a receipt for a preliminary MJDS prospectus and the issuance by the Director of a receipt for a MJDS prospectus may be less than ten days.

(3) National Instrument 41-101 General Prospectus Requirements does not apply to a distribution of securities under NI 71-101.

2.2 Underwriters' Options — Rule 48-502 Over-Allotment Options and Underwriters' Compensation does not apply to an underwriter of securities of a U.S. issuer distributed in Canada and the U.S. in accordance with NI 71-101.

PART 3 — BIDS FOR SECURITIES OF U.S. ISSUERS

3.1 Application of the Act and regulations to bids — (1) The following provisions of NI 62-104 do not apply to a bid made in compliance with Part 12 of NI 71-101:

    (a) sections 1.6, 2.1 to 2.3, and 2.5 to 2.7, clause 2.8(b), subsections 2.10(2), (3) and (4), subsections 2.11(1.1) and (5), subsections 2.12(1.1), (3), (3.1), (4), (5), and (6), sections 2.13 to 2.16, 2.23 to 2.34; and

    (b) section 2.4 unless security holders of the offeree issuer whose last address as shown on the books of the issuer is in Canada, as determined in accordance with subsections 12.1(2) through (4) of NI 71-101, hold 20% or more of a class of securities that is the subject of the bid;

(2) The following provisions of NI 62-104 apply to a bid made in compliance with Part 12 of NI 71-101:

    (a) clause 2.8(a), section 2.9, subsections 2.10(1), 2.11(2), (3) and (4), and subsection 2.12(2);

    (b) subsection 2.11(1), except the requirement to send a notice of change to each holder of securities that, before the expiry of the deposit period referred to in the bid, are convertible into securities of the class that is subject to the bid who are in Ontario; and

    (c) subsection 2.12(1), except the requirement to send a notice of variation to each holder of securities that, before the expiry of the deposit period referred to in the bid, are convertible into securities of the class that is subject to the bid who are in Ontario.

3.2 Application of the Act and regulations to MJDS directors' circulars and MJDS individual director's or officer's circulars — (1) Subsections 2.17(2), and (3), sections 2.18 and 2.19, subsection 2.20(6) and sections 2.21 and 2.22 do not apply to the directors or the individual directors or officers of an offeree issuer who elect to comply with Part 12 of NI 71-101 instead of provisions of NI 62-104 otherwise applicable in preparation of a directors' circular or individual director's or officer's circular for a take-over bid made for securities of the offeree issuer under Part 12 of NI 71-101.

(2) The following provisions of NI 62-104 apply to the directors or the individual directors or officers of an offeree issuer who elect to comply with Part 12 of NI 71-101 instead of provisions of NI 62-104 otherwise applicable in preparation of a directors' circular or individual director's or officer's circular for a take-over bid made for securities of the offeree issuer under Part 12 of NI 71-101:

(a) subsections 2.17(1) and 2.20(1), except the requirement to send a directors' circular or an individual director's or officer's circular to each holder of securities that, before the expiry of the deposit period referred to in the bid, are convertible into securities of the class that is subject to the bid who are in Ontario;

(b) subsections 2.18(1) and 2.20(2), except the requirement to send notice of change to holders of securities that, before the expiry of the deposit period referred to in the bid, are convertible into securities of the class that is subject to the bid who are in Ontario;

(c) subsections 2.20(4) and (5), except the requirement to send a copy of an individual director's or officer's circular and a notice of change to holders of securities that, before the expiry of the deposit period referred to in the bid, are convertible into securities of the class that is subject to the bid who are in Ontario; and

(d) subsections 2.17(4), 2.18(2), 2.20(3) and (7)..

PART 4 — FINANCIAL REPORTING AND PROXIES AND PROXY SOLICITATION

4.1 Certification of Financial Statements — The obligations under sections 77 and 78 of the Act to certify financial statements as required by the regulations do not apply to financial statements filed under section 15.1 of NI 71-101.

4.2 AIF and MD and A — Rule 51-501 AIF and MD&A does not apply to a reporting issuer that files an annual report and quarterly report and sends an annual report in accordance with section 15.2 of NI 71-101.

4.3 Proxies and Proxy Solicitation — Rule 54-501 Prospectus Disclosure in Certain Information Circulars does not apply to materials filed and delivered under section 16.1 or 16.2 of NI 71-101.

PART 5 — FORM

5.1 Submission to Jurisdiction and Appointment of Agent for Service of Process — A submission to jurisdiction and appointment of agent for service of process required under section 6.9, paragraph 12.10(1)(e), or subparagraph 19.1(b)(iii) of NI 71-101 shall be prepared in accordance with Form 71-101F1.

PART 6 — EFFECTIVE DATE

6.1 Effective Date — The Rule comes into force on November 1, 1998

Final Rule: (1998) 21 O.S.C.B. 6919; Approval of OSC: (1998) 21 O.S.C.B. 5099; Request for Comments: (1997) 20 O.S.C.B. 6496.

Amendment to Rule: (2008) 31 O.S.C.B. 1289; Approval by OSC: (2007) 30 O.S.C.B. (Supp 6) 1 (Dec. 14, 2007).

Amendment to Rule: (2008) 31 O.S.C.B. (Supp. 2) 262; Approval by OSC: (2007) 30 O.S.C.B. (Supp 7) 1 (Dec. 21, 2007).

Amendment to Rule: (2016) 39 O.S.C.B. (Supp. 1) 117; Approved by OSC (2016) 39 O.S.C.B. 4289

Part 7: TRANSAC-
TIONS OUTSIDE
JURISDICTIONS

OSC Rule 71-802 — Implementing National Instrument 71-102 Continuous Disclosure and Other Exemptions Relating to Foreign Issuers

Date: March 30, 2004, as amended effective February 1, 2008 (by Rule 61-801) and January 1, 2011
27 O.S.C.B. 3577, 31 O.S.C.B. 1365 and 33 O.S.C.B. (Supp. 5) 80

Table of Contents

PART 1 — DEFINITIONS AND INTERPRETATION

1.1 Definitions and Interpretation — (1) In this Rule

"NI 51-102" means National Instrument 51-102 *Continuous Disclosure Obligations*;

"NI 62-103" means National Instrument 62-103 *The Early Warning System and Related Take-Over Bid and Insider Reporting Issues*;

"NI 62-104" means National Instrument 62-104 *Take-Over Bids and Issuer Bids*;

"NI 71-102" means National Instrument 71-102 *Continuous Disclosure and Other Exemptions Relating to Foreign Issuers*;

"Rule 51-801" means Rule 51-801 *Implementing National Instrument 51-102 Continuous Disclosure Obligations*; and

"Rule 56-501" means Rule 56-501 *Restricted Shares*.

(2) Each term used in this Rule that is defined or interpreted in Part 1 of NI 71-102 has the meaning ascribed to it in that Part.

PART 2 — SEC FOREIGN ISSUERS

2.1 Material Change Reporting — Section 7.1 and paragraph 12.1(1)(b) of NI 51-102 and section 3.6 of Rule 51-801 do not apply to an SEC foreign issuer that complies with section 4.2 of NI 71-102.

2.2 Annual Reports, AIFs, Business Acquisition Reports and MD&A — Subsection 12.1(1) of NI 51-102 does not apply to an SEC foreign issuer that complies with section 4.4 of NI 71-102.

2.3 Early Warning — A person or company is exempt from section 5.2 of NI 62-104 and the requirements of NI 62-103 in respect of securities of an SEC foreign issuer if the person or company complies with section 4.11 of NI 71-102.

2.4 Business Combinations and Related Party Transactions — (1) MI 61-101 *Protection of Minority Security Holders in Special Transactions* does not apply to an SEC foreign issuer carrying out a going private transaction or related party transaction if the total number of equity securities of the SEC foreign issuer owned, directly or indirectly by residents of Canada does not exceed 20 per cent, on a diluted basis, of the total number of equity securities of the SEC foreign issuer as at the first day of its current financial year.

(2) Despite subsection (1), if the SEC foreign issuer has not completed a financial year since becoming a reporting issuer, the calculation in subsection (1) is made at the date that the issuer became a reporting issuer.

2.5 Restricted Shares — Section 10.1 of NI 51-102 and Part 3 of Rule 56-501 do not apply in respect of an SEC foreign issuer.

PART 3 — DESIGNATED FOREIGN ISSUERS

3.1 Material Change Reporting — Section 7.1 and paragraph 12.1(1)(b) of NI 51-102 and section 3.4 of Rule 51-801 do not apply to a designated foreign issuer that complies with section 5.3 of NI 71-102.

3.2 Annual Reports, AIFs, Business Acquisition Reports and MD&A — Subsection 12.1(1) of NI 51-102 does not apply to a designated foreign issuer that complies with section 5.5 of NI 71-102.

3.3 Early Warning — A person or company is exempt from section 5.2 of NI 62-104 and the requirements of NI 62-103 in respect of securities of a designated foreign issuer if the person or company complies with section 5.12 of NI 71-102.

3.4 Restricted Shares — Section 10.1 of NI 51-102 and Part 3 of Rule 56-501 do not apply in respect of a designated foreign issuer.

PART 4 — EFFECTIVE DATE

4.1 Effective Date — This Rule comes into force on the date NI 71-102 comes into force.

Final Rule: (2004) 27 O.S.C.B. 3577; Approval by OSC: (2003) 26 O.S.C.B. (Supp-3) 219 (December 19, 2003); Request for Comments: (2003) 26 O.S.C.B. 4577 and (2002) 25 O.S.C.B. 3701.

Amendment to Rule: (2010) 33 O.S.C.B. (Supp. 5) 80; Approval by OSC: (2010) 33 O.S.C.B. (Supp. 3) 113; Request for Comments: (2009) 32 O.S.C.B. (Supp. 6) 1.

Rules: NI 71-102.

7.2 — Distributions Outside The Jurisdiction

See also OPS 1.5.

OSC Rule 72-501 — Prospectus Exemption For First Trade Over A Market Outside Ontario

Date: **June 12, 1998**

21 O.S.C.B. 3873

[Rescinded: 25 O.S.C.B. 7843]

PART VIII — INVESTMENT FUNDS

8.1 — Investment Fund Distributions

See also NPS 29, OSCN 41.

National Instrument 81-101 — Mutual Fund Prospectus Disclosure

Date: January 28, 2000, as amended effective December 31, 2003, June 1, 2005, November 1, 2006, March 17, 2008, September 8, 2008, June 30, 2010, January 1, 2011, April 30, 2012, May 14, 2013, May 31, 2013, September 1, 2013, January 1, 2014, September 22, 2014, March 30, 2015 and November 17, 2015

23 O.S.C.B. (Supp) 3, 27 O.S.C.B. 752, 28 O.S.C.B. 4965, 29 O.S.C.B. 8842, 31 O.S.C.B. (Supp. 2) 241, 31 O.S.C.B. 8568, 33 O.S.C.B. 5585, 33 O.S.C.B. 11399, 35 O.S.C.B. 3429, 36 O.S.C.B. 4929, 36 O.S.C.B. 2619, 36 O.S.C.B. 7813, 36 O.S.C.B. 9612, 37 O.S.C.B. (Supp. 4), 37 O.S.C.B. 11026, 38 O.S.C.B. 1382 and 38 O.S.C.B. 9336

[Editor's note: in connection with amendments which were published at (2013) 36 O.S.C.B. 7813, a transition provision is as follows:

"Transition

(1) A mutual fund must, on or before May 13, 2014, file a completed Form 81-101F3 Contents of Fund Facts Document for each class or series of securities of the mutual fund that, on that date, are the subject of disclosure under a simplified prospectus.

(2) The date of a fund facts document filed under subsection (1) must be the date on which it was filed.

Any exemption from or waiver of a provision of NI 81-101 Mutual Fund Prospectus Disclosure *in relation to the prospectus delivery requirements for mutual funds, or an approval in relation to those requirements, expires on the date that this Instrument comes into force."]*

[Editor's note: in connection with amendments that were published at (2014) 37 O.S.C.B. 95, the following transition provision was included:

"Transition

(1) If a non-redeemable investment fund filed a prospectus on or before September 22, 2014,

   (a) until September 21, 2015, sections 2.12 to 2.17 of National Instrument 81-102 Mutual Funds *do not apply to the non-redeemable investment fund, and*

   (b) until March 21, 2016, sections 2.2, 2.3 and 2.5 of National Instrument 81-102 Mutual Funds *do not apply to the non-redeemable investment fund.*

(2) If a mutual fund filed a prospectus on or before September 22, 2014, until March 21, 2016, subsection 2.5(2) of National Instrument 81-102 Mutual Funds, *as amended by subsection 11(2) of this Instrument, does not apply to the mutual fund if the mutual fund complies with subsection 2.5(2) of National Instrument 81-102* Mutual Funds *as that provision was in force on September 21, 2014.*

(3) Despite any amendments to the contrary in this Instrument, if a sales communication, other than an advertisement, was printed before September 22, 2014, the sales communication may be used until March 23, 2015.

Table of Contents

PART 1 — DEFINITIONS, INTERPRETATION AND APPLICATION

1.1 Definitions — In this Instrument

"Aequitas personal information form" means a personal information form for an individual prepared pursuant to Aequitas NEO Exchange Inc. Form 3, as amended from time to time;

"business day" means any day other than a Saturday, a Sunday or a statutory holiday;

"commodity pool" means a mutual fund, other than a precious metals fund, that has adopted fundamental investment objectives that permit it to use

(a) specified derivatives other than as permitted by National Instrument 81-102 *Investment Funds*, or

(b) physical commodities other than as permitted by that instrument;

"educational material" means material containing general information about one or more of investing in general, mutual funds, portfolio management, capital markets, retirement savings, income or education saving plans and financial planning, if the material does not promote a particular mutual fund or mutual fund family or the products or services offered by a particular mutual fund or mutual fund family;

"executive officer" means, for a mutual fund, a manager of a mutual fund or a promoter of a mutual fund, an individual who is

(a) a chair, vice-chair or president,

(b) a vice-president in charge of a principal business unit, division or function including sales, finance or product development, or

(c) performing a policy-making function;

"financial statements" includes interim financial reports;

"financial year" includes the first completed financial period of a mutual fund beginning with the inception of the mutual fund and ending on the date of its first financial year end;

"fund facts document" means a completed Form 81-101F3 *Contents of Fund Facts Document*;

"independent review committee" means the independent review committee of the investment fund established under National Instrument 81-107 *Independent Review Committee for Investment Funds*;

"managed account" has the meaning ascribed to that term in National Instrument 31-103 *Registration Requirements, Exemptions and Ongoing Registrant Obligations*;

"material contract" means, for a mutual fund, a contract listed in the annual information form of the mutual fund in response to Item 16 of Form 81-101F2 Contents of Annual Information Form;

"multiple AIF" means a document containing two or more annual information forms that have been consolidated in accordance with section 5.4;

"multiple SP" means a document containing two or more simplified prospectuses that have been consolidated in accordance with subsection 5.1(1);

"Part A section" means the section of a simplified prospectus that contains the disclosure required by Part A of Form 81-101F1 Contents of Simplified Prospectus;

"Part B section" means the section of a simplified prospectus that contains the disclosure required by Part B of Form 81-101F1;

"permitted client" has the meaning ascribed to that term in National Instrument 31-103 *Registration Requirements, Exemptions and Ongoing Registrant Obligations*;

"personal information form" means

    (a) a completed Schedule 1 of Appendix A to National Instrument 41-101 *General Prospectus Requirements*,

    (b) a completed TSX/TSXV personal information form submitted by an individual to the Toronto Stock Exchange or to the TSX Venture Exchange to which is attached a completed certificate and consent in the form set out in Schedule 1 — Part B of Appendix A to National Instrument 41-101 *General Prospectus Requirements*;

    (c) a completed Aequitas personal information form submitted by an individual to Aequitas NEO Exchange Inc., to which is attached a completed certificate and consent in the form set out in Schedule 1 — Part B of Appendix A to National Instrument 41-101 *General Prospectus Requirements*;

"plain language" means language that can be understood by a reasonable person, applying a reasonable effort;

"pre-authorized purchase plan" means a contract or other arrangement for the purchase of securities of a mutual fund, by payments of a specified amount, on a regularly scheduled basis, and which can be terminated at any time;

"precious metals fund" means a mutual fund that has adopted fundamental investment objectives, and received all required regulatory approvals, that permit it to invest in precious metals or in entities that invest in precious metals and that otherwise complies with National Instrument 81-102 *Investment Funds*;

"predecessor personal information form" means

    (a) a completed Schedule 1 of Appendix A to National Instrument 41-101 *General Prospectus Requirements* in the form that was in effect from March 17, 2008 until May 14, 2013, or

    (b) a completed TSX/TSXV personal information form to which is attached a completed certificate and consent in the form that was in effect between March 17, 2008 and May 14, 2013;

"single AIF" means an annual information form that has not been consolidated with another annual information form under section 5.4;

"single SP" means a simplified prospectus that has not been consolidated with another simplified prospectus under subsection 5.1(1),

"statutory right of action" means,

    (a) in Alberta, paragraph 206(a) of the *Securities Act* (Alberta),

    (b) in British Columbia, section 135 of the *Securities Act* (British Columbia),

    (c) in Manitoba, section 141.2 of the *Securities Act* (Manitoba),

    (d) in New Brunswick, section 155 of the *Securities Act* (New Brunswick),

    (e) in Northwest Territories, section 116 of the *Securities Act* (Northwest Territories),

    (f) in Nunavut, section 116 of the *Securities Act* (Nunavut),

    (g) in Saskatchewan, section 141(2) of *The Securities Act, 1988* (Saskatchewan), and

    (h) in Yukon, section 116 of the *Securities Act* (Yukon);

"statutory right of withdrawal" means,

    (a) in Alberta, subsection 130(1) of the *Securities Act* (Alberta),

    (b) in British Columbia, subsections 83(3) and (5) of the *Securities Act* (British Columbia),

    (c) in Manitoba, sections 1.2 and 1.5 of Local Rule 41-502 *Prospectus Delivery Requirement* (Manitoba),

    (d) in New Brunswick, subsection 88(2) of the *Securities Act* (New Brunswick),

    (e) in Northwest Territories, section 101(2) of the *Securities Act* (Northwest Territories),

    (f) in Nunavut, subsection 101(2) of the *Securities Act* (Nunavut),

    (g) in Saskatchewan, section 79(3) of *The Securities Act, 1988* (Saskatchewan), and

    (h) in Yukon, subsection 101(2) of the *Securities Act* (Yukon).

"TSX/TSXV personal information form" means a completed personal information form of an individual in compliance with the requirements of Form 4 for the Toronto Stock Exchange or Form 2A for the TSX Venture Exchange, as applicable, each as amended from time to time.

1.2 Interpretation — Terms defined in National Instrument 81-102 *Investment Funds* or National Instrument 81-105 *Mutual Fund Sales Practices* and used in this Instrument have the respective meanings ascribed to them in those Instruments.

1.3 Application — This Instrument does not apply to mutual funds that are

    (a) labour-sponsored venture capital corporations;

    (b) commodity pools; or

    (c) listed and posted for trading on a stock exchange or quoted on an over-the-counter market.

PART 2 — DISCLOSURE DOCUMENTS

2.1 Filing of Disclosure Documents — (1) A mutual fund

(a) that files a preliminary prospectus must file the preliminary prospectus in the form of a preliminary simplified prospectus prepared in accordance with Form 81-101F1 and concurrently file

(i) a preliminary annual information form prepared and certified in accordance with Form 81-101F2; and

(ii) a preliminary fund facts document for each class or series of securities of the mutual fund prepared in accordance with Form 81-101F3;

(b) that files a *pro forma* prospectus must file the *pro forma* prospectus in the form of a *pro forma* simplified prospectus prepared in accordance with Form 81-101F1 and concurrently file

(i) a *pro forma* annual information form prepared in accordance with Form 81-101F2; and

(ii) a *pro forma* fund facts document for each class or series of securities of the mutual fund prepared in accordance with Form 81-101F3;

(c) that files a prospectus must file the prospectus in the form of a simplified prospectus prepared in accordance with Form 81-101F1 and concurrently file

(i) an annual information form prepared and certified in accordance with Form 81-101F2; and

(ii) a fund facts document for each class or series of securities of the mutual fund prepared in accordance with Form 81-101F3;

(d) that files an amendment to a prospectus must

(i) file an amendment

(A) to the simplified prospectus and concurrently file an amendment to the related annual information form, or

(B) to the related annual information form if changes are made only to the annual information form;

(ii) if the amendment relates to the information contained in a fund facts document, concurrently file an amendment to the fund facts document;

(iii) if the amendment relates to a new class or series of securities of the mutual fund that is referable to the same portfolio of assets, concurrently file a fund facts document for the new class or series; and

(e) must file an amendment to a fund facts document, if a material change occurs that relates to the information contained in the fund facts document, as soon as practicable and, in any event, within 10 days after the day the change occurs.

(2) A mutual fund must not file a prospectus more than 90 days after the date of the receipt for the preliminary prospectus that relates to the prospectus.

2.2 Amendments to Disclosure Documents — (1) An amendment to a simplified prospectus or to an annual information form may consist of either

(a) an amendment that does not fully restate the text of the simplified prospectus or annual information form; or

(b) an amended and restated simplified prospectus or annual information form.

(2) Despite subsection (1), an amendment to the Part B section that is separately bound from the Part A section of a simplified prospectus must be effected only by way of an amended and restated Part B section.

(3) An amendment to a simplified prospectus or to an annual information form must be identified and dated as follows:

1. For an amendment that does not restate the text of a simplified prospectus or annual information form:

Amendment No. [insert amendment number] dated [insert date of amendment] to [identify document] dated [insert date of document being amended].

2. For an amended and restated simplified prospectus, other than an amendment to which subsection (2) applies, or annual information form:

Amended and Restated [identify document] dated [insert date of amendment], amending and restating [identify document] dated [insert date of document being amended].

(4) An amendment to a fund facts document must be prepared in accordance with Form 81-101F3 without any further identification and dated as of the date the fund facts document is being amended.

2.2.1 Amendment to a Preliminary Simplified Prospectus — (1) Except in Ontario, if, after a receipt for a preliminary simplified prospectus is issued but before a receipt for the simplified prospectus is issued, a material adverse change occurs, an amendment to the preliminary simplified prospectus must be filed as soon as practicable, but in any event within 10 days after the change occurs.

[Note: In Ontario, subsection 57(1) of the Securities Act *(Ontario) imposes a similar requirement to file an amendment to a preliminary prospectus.]*[1]

(2) The regulator must issue a receipt for an amendment to a preliminary simplified prospectus as soon as practicable after the amendment is filed.

2.2.2 Delivery of Amendments — Except in Ontario, a mutual fund must deliver an amendment to a preliminary simplified prospectus as soon as practicable to each recipient of the preliminary simplified prospectus according to the record of recipients required to be maintained under securities legislation.

[Note: In Ontario, subsection 57(3) of the Securities Act *(Ontario) imposes similar requirements regarding the delivery of amendments to a preliminary prospectus.]*

2.2.3 Amendment to a Simplified Prospectus — (1) Except in Ontario, if, after a receipt for a simplified prospectus is issued but before the completion of the distribution under the simplified prospectus, a material change occurs, a mutual fund must file an amendment to the simplified prospectus as soon as practicable, but in any event within 10 days after the day the change occurs.

---

[1] In Ontario, a number of prospectus related requirements in this Instrument are set out in the *Securities Act* (Ontario). We have identified carve-outs from the Instrument where a similar requirement is set out in the *Securities Act* (Ontario). Notes included in this Instrument have been inserted for convenience of reference only and do not form part of this Instrument or have any force or effect as a rule or policy.

[Note: In Ontario, subsection 57(1) of the Securities Act (Ontario) imposes a similar obligation to file an amendment to a final prospectus where there has been a material change.]

(2) Except in Ontario, if, after a receipt for a simplified prospectus or an amendment to a simplified prospectus is issued but before the completion of the distribution under the simplified prospectus or the amendment to the simplified prospectus, securities in addition to the securities previously disclosed in the simplified prospectus or the amendment to the simplified prospectus are to be distributed, an amendment to the simplified prospectus disclosing the additional securities must be filed, as soon as practicable, but in any event within 10 days after the decision to increase the number of securities offered.

[Note: In Ontario, subsection 57(2) of the Securities Act (Ontario) imposes a similar requirement to file an amendment to a prospectus any time there is a proposed distribution of securities in addition to that disclosed under the prospectus.]

(3) Except in Ontario, the regulator must issue a receipt for an amendment to a simplified prospectus filed under this section unless the regulator considers that there are grounds set out in securities legislation that would cause the regulator not to issue the receipt for a simplified prospectus.

[Note: In Ontario, subsection 57(2.1) of the Securities Act (Ontario) imposes a similar obligation for the Director to issue a receipt for an amendment to a prospectus unless there are proper grounds for refusing the receipt.]

(4) Except in Ontario, the regulator must not refuse to issue a receipt under subsection (3) without giving the mutual fund that filed the simplified prospectus an opportunity to be heard.

[Note: In Ontario, subsections 57(2.1) and 61(3) of the Securities Act (Ontario) impose a similar restriction on the Director to refuse to issue a receipt for a prospectus without first giving an issuer an opportunity to be heard.]

2.3 Supporting Documents — (1) A mutual fund must

(a) file with a preliminary simplified prospectus, a preliminary annual information form and a preliminary fund facts document for each class or series of securities of the mutual fund

(i) a copy of the preliminary annual information form certified in accordance with Part 5.1,

(ii) a submission to the jurisdiction and appointment of an agent for service of process of the manager of the mutual fund in the form set out in Appendix C to National Instrument 41-101 *General Prospectus Requirements*, if the manager of the mutual fund is incorporated, continued or organized under the laws of a foreign jurisdiction or resides outside of Canada,

(iii) a copy of any material contract and a copy of any amendment to a material contract that have not previously been filed, other than a contract entered into in the ordinary course of business,

(iv) a copy of the following documents and a copy of any amendment to the following documents that have not previously been filed:

(A) by-laws or other corresponding instruments currently in effect,

(B) any securityholder or voting trust agreement that the mutual fund has access to and that can reasonably be regarded as material to an investor in securities of the mutual fund, and

(C) any other contract of the mutual fund that creates or can reasonably be regarded as materially affecting the rights or obligations of the mutual fund's securityholders generally, and

(v) any other supporting documents required to be filed under securities legislation; and

(b) at the time a preliminary simplified prospectus, a preliminary annual information form and a preliminary fund facts document for each class or series of securities of the mutual fund are filed, deliver or send to the securities regulatory authority

(i) for

(A) a new mutual fund, a copy of a draft opening statement of financial position of the mutual fund, and

(B) an existing mutual fund, a copy of the latest audited financial statements of the mutual fund,

(ii) a personal information form for:

(A) each director and executive officer of the mutual fund;

(B) each director and executive officer of the manager of the mutual fund;

(C) each promoter of the mutual fund;

(D) if the promoter is not an individual, each director and executive officer of the promoter,

(iii) a signed letter to the regulator from the auditor of the mutual fund prepared in accordance with the form suggested for this circumstance by the Handbook, if a financial statement of the mutual fund incorporated by reference in the preliminary simplified prospectus is accompanied by an unsigned auditor's report, and

(iv) any other supporting documents required to be delivered or sent to the securities regulatory authority under securities legislation.

(1.1) Despite subparagraph (1)(b)(ii), a mutual fund is not required to deliver to the regulator a personal information form for an individual if the mutual fund, the mutual fund's manager, another issuer or the manager of another investment fund issuer, previously delivered a personal information form for the individual and all of the following are satisfied:

(a) the certificate and consent included in or attached to the personal information form was executed by the individual within three years preceding the date of filing of the preliminary simplified prospectus, preliminary annual information form and preliminary fund facts document for each class or series of securities of the mutual fund;

(b) the responses given by the individual to questions 6 through 10 of the individual's personal information form are correct as at a date that is no earlier than 30 days before the filing of the preliminary simplified prospectus, preliminary annual information form and preliminary fund facts document for each class or series of securities of the mutual fund;

(c) if the personal information form was previously delivered to the regulator by another issuer, the issuer delivers to the regulator, concurrently with the filing of the preliminary simplified prospectus, preliminary annual information form and preliminary fund facts document for each class or series of securities of the mutual fund, a copy of the previously delivered personal information form or alternative information that is satisfactory to the regulator.

(1.2) Until May 14, 2016, subparagraph (1)(b)(ii) does not apply to a mutual fund in respect of the delivery of a personal information form for an individual if the mutual fund, the mutual fund's manager, another issuer or the manager of another investment fund issuer previously delivered to the regulator a predecessor personal information form for the individual and all of the following are satisfied:

(a) the certificate and consent included in or attached to the predecessor personal information form was executed by the individual within three years preceding the date of filing of the preliminary simplified prospectus, preliminary annual information form and preliminary fund facts document for each class or series of securities of the mutual fund;

(b) the responses given by the individual to questions 4(B) and (C) and questions 6 through 9 or, in the case of a TSX/TSXV personal information form in effect after September 8, 2011, questions 6 through 10, of the individual's predecessor personal information form are correct as at a date that is no earlier than 30 days before the filing of the preliminary simplified prospectus, preliminary annual information form and preliminary fund facts document for each class or series of securities of the mutual fund.

(2) A mutual fund must

(a) file with a *pro forma* simplified prospectus, a *pro forma* annual information form and a *pro forma* fund facts document for each class or series of securities of the mutual fund

(i) a copy of any material contract of the mutual fund, and a copy of any amendment to a material contract of the mutual fund, not previously filed,

(ii) a submission to the jurisdiction and appointment of an agent for service of process of the manager of the mutual fund in the form set out in Appendix C to National Instrument 41-101 *General Prospectus Requirements*, if the manager of the mutual fund is incorporated, continued or organized under the laws of a foreign jurisdiction or resides outside of Canada and if that document has not already been filed,

(ii.1) a copy of the following documents and a copy of any amendment to the following documents that have not previously been filed:

(A) by-laws or other corresponding instruments currently in effect,

(B) any securityholder or voting trust agreement that the mutual fund has access to and that can reasonably be regarded as material to an investor in securities of the mutual fund, and

(iii) any other supporting documents required to be filed under securities legislation; and

(b) at the time a *pro forma* simplified prospectus, a *pro forma* annual information form and a *pro forma* fund facts document for each class or series of securities of the mutual fund are filed, deliver or send to the securities regulatory authority

(i) a copy of the *pro forma* simplified prospectus, blacklined to show changes and the text of deletions from the latest simplified prospectus previously filed,

(ii) a copy of the *pro forma* annual information form, blacklined to show changes and the text of deletions from the latest annual information form previously filed,

(ii.1) a copy of the *pro forma* fund facts document for each class or series of securities of the mutual fund, blacklined to show changes, including the text of deletions, from the latest fund facts document previously filed,

(iii) [repealed]

(iv) a personal information form for:

(A) each director and executive officer of the mutual fund;

(B) each director and executive officer of the manager of the mutual fund;

(C) each promoter of the mutual fund;

(D) if the promoter is not an individual, each director and executive officer of the promoter, and

(v) any other supporting documents required to be delivered or sent to the securities regulatory authority under securities legislation.

(2.1) Despite subparagraph (2)(b)(iv), a mutual fund is not required to deliver to the regulator a personal information form for an individual if the mutual fund, the mutual fund's manager, another issuer or the manager of another investment fund issuer previously delivered a personal information form for the individual and all of the following are satisfied:

(a) the certificate and consent included in or attached to the personal information form was executed by the individual within three years preceding the date of filing of the *pro forma* simplified prospectus, *pro forma* annual information form and *pro forma* fund facts document for each class or series of securities of the mutual fund;

(b) the responses given by the individual to questions 6 through 10 of the individual's personal information form are correct as at a date that is no earlier than 30 days before the filing of the *pro forma* simplified prospectus, *pro forma* annual information form and *pro forma* fund facts document for each class or series of securities of the mutual fund;

(c) if the personal information form was previously delivered to the regulator by another issuer, the issuer delivers to the regulator, concurrently with the filing of the *pro forma* simplified prospectus, *pro forma* annual information form and *pro forma* fund facts document for each class or series of securities of the mutual fund, a copy of the previously delivered personal information form or alternative information that is satisfactory to the regulator.

(2.2) Until May 14, 2016, subparagraph (2)(b)(iv) does not apply to a mutual fund in respect of the delivery of a personal information form for an individual if the mutual fund, the mutual fund's manager, another issuer or the manager of another investment fund issuer previously delivered to the regulator a predecessor personal information form for the individual and all of the following are satisfied:

(a) the certificate and consent included in or attached to the predecessor personal information form was executed by the individual within three years preceding the date of filing of the *pro forma* simplified prospectus, *pro forma* annual information form and *pro forma* fund facts document for each class or series of securities of the mutual fund;

(b) the responses given by the individual to questions 4(B) and (C) and questions 6 through 9 or, in the case of a TSX/TSXV personal information form in effect after September 8, 2011, questions 6 through 10, of the individual's predecessor personal information form are correct as at a date that is no earlier than 30 days before the filing of the *pro forma* simplified prospectus, *pro forma* annual information form and *pro forma* fund facts document for each class or series of securities of the mutual fund.

(3) A mutual fund must

    (a) file with a simplified prospectus, an annual information form and a fund facts document for each class or series of securities of the mutual fund

        (i) a copy of any material contract, and a copy of any amendment to a material contract, of the mutual fund and not previously filed,

        (i.1) a copy of the following documents and a copy of any amendment to the following documents that have not previously been filed:

            (A) by-laws or other corresponding instruments currently in effect,

            (B) any securityholder or voting trust agreement that the mutual fund has access to and that can reasonably be regarded as material to an investor in securities of the mutual fund,

        (ii) for a new mutual fund, a copy of the audited statement of financial position of the mutual fund,

        (iii) a copy of the annual information form certified in accordance with Part 5.1,

        (iv) a submission to the jurisdiction and appointment of an agent for service of process of the manager of the mutual fund in the form set out in Appendix C to National Instrument 41-101 *General Prospectus Requirements*, if the manager of the mutual fund is incorporated, continued or organized under the laws of a foreign jurisdiction or resides outside of Canada and if that document has not already been filed,

        (v) any consents required by section 2.6,

        (vi) a copy of each report or valuation referred to in the simplified prospectus, for which a consent is required to be filed under section 2.6 and that has not previously been filed, and

        (vii) any other supporting documents required to be filed under securities legislation; and

    (b) at the time a simplified prospectus is filed, deliver or send to the securities regulatory authority

        (i) a copy of the simplified prospectus, blacklined to show changes and the text of deletions from the preliminary or *pro forma* simplified prospectus,

        (ii) a copy of the annual information form, blacklined to show changes and the text of deletions from the preliminary or *pro forma* annual information form,

        (ii.1) a copy of the fund facts document for each class or series of securities of the mutual fund, blacklined to show changes, including the text of deletions, from the preliminary or *pro forma* fund facts document,

        (iii) details of any changes to the personal information required to be delivered under subparagraph (1)(b)(ii) or (2)(b)(iv), in the form of the Personal Information Form and Authorization, since the delivery of that information in connection with the filing of the simplified prospectus of the mutual fund or another mutual fund managed by the manager, and

        (iv) any other supporting documents required to be delivered or sent to the securities regulatory authority under securities legislation.

(4) A mutual fund must

    (a) file with an amendment to a simplified prospectus and an amendment to the annual information form

        (i) a copy of the amendment to the annual information form certified in accordance with Part 5.1,

        (ii) any consents required by section 2.6,

        (iii) a copy of any material contract of the mutual fund, and a copy of any amendment to a material contract of the mutual fund, not previously filed,

        (iii.1) if the amendment relates to the information contained in a fund facts document, an amendment to the fund facts document, and

        (iv) any other supporting documents required to be filed under securities legislation;

    (b) at the time an amendment to a simplified prospectus is filed, deliver or send to the securities regulatory authority

        (i) if the amendment to the simplified prospectus is in the form of an amended and restated simplified prospectus, a copy of that document blacklined to show changes and the text of deletions from the simplified prospectus,

        (ii) if the amendment to the annual information form is in the form of an amended and restated annual information form, a copy of the amended annual information form, blacklined to show changes and the text of deletions from the annual information form,

        (ii.1) if an amendment to a fund facts document is filed, a copy of the fund facts document, blacklined to show changes, including the text of deletions, from the latest fund facts document previously filed,

        (iii) details of any changes to the personal information required to be delivered under subparagraph (1)(b)(ii), (2)(b)(iv) or (3)(b)(iii), in the form of the Personal Information Form and Authorization, since the delivery of that information in connection with the filing of the simplified prospectus of the mutual fund or another mutual fund managed by the manager, and

        (iv) any other supporting documents required to be delivered or sent to the securities regulatory authority under securities legislation.

(5) A mutual fund must

    (a) file with an amendment to an annual information form in circumstances in which the corresponding simplified prospectus is not amended

        (i) a copy of the amendment to the annual information form certified in accordance with Part 5.1,

        (ii) any consents required by section 2.6,

        (iii) a copy of any material contract of the mutual fund, and a copy of any amendment to a material contract of the mutual fund, not previously filed,

        (iii.1) if the amendment relates to the information contained in a fund facts document, an amendment to the fund facts document, and

        (iv) any other supporting documents required to be filed under securities legislation; and

(b) at the time an amendment to an annual information form is filed, deliver or send to the securities regulatory authority

(i) details of any changes to the personal information required to be delivered under subparagraph (1)(b)(ii), (2)(b)(iv) or (3)(b)(iii), in the form of the Personal Information Form and Authorization, since the delivery of that information in connection with the filing of the simplified prospectus of the mutual fund or another mutual fund managed by the manager,

(ii) if the amendment is in the form of an amended and restated annual information form, a copy of the amended and restated annual information form blacklined to show changes and the text of deletions from the annual information form,

(ii.1) if an amendment to a fund facts document is filed, a copy of the fund facts document, blacklined to show changes, including the text of deletions, from the latest fund facts document previously filed, and

(iii) any other supporting documents required to be delivered or sent to the securities regulatory authority under securities legislation.

(5.1) A mutual fund must

(a) file the following documents with an amendment to a fund facts document unless subsection (4) or (5) applies:

(i) an amendment to the corresponding annual information form, certified in accordance with Part 5.1,

(ii) any other supporting documents required to be filed under securities legislation; and

(b) at the time an amendment to a fund facts document is filed, deliver or send to the securities regulatory authority

(i) details of any changes to the personal information required to be delivered under subparagraph (1)(b)(ii), (2)(b)(iv) or (3)(b)(iii), in the form of the Personal Information Form and Authorization, since the delivery of that information in connection with the filing of the simplified prospectus of the mutual fund or another mutual fund managed by the manager,

(ii) a copy of the amended and restated fund facts document blacklined to show changes, including the text of deletions, from the most recently filed fund facts document; and

(iii) any other supporting documents required to be delivered or sent to the securities regulatory authority under securities legislation.

(6) Despite any other provision of this section, a mutual fund may

(a) omit or mark to be unreadable certain provisions of a material contract or an amendment to a material contract filed under this section

(i) if the manager of the mutual fund reasonably believes that disclosure of those provisions would be seriously prejudicial to the interests of the mutual fund or would violate confidentiality provisions, and

(ii) if a provision is omitted or marked to be unreadable under subparagraph (i), the mutual fund must include a description of the type of information that has been omitted or marked to be unreadable immediately after the provision that is omitted or marked to be unreadable in the copy of the material contract or amendment to the material contract filed by the mutual fund; and

(b) delete commercial or financial information from the copy of an agreement of the mutual fund, its manager or trustee with a portfolio adviser or portfolio advisers of the mutual fund filed under this section if the disclosure of that information could reasonably be expected to

(i) prejudice significantly the competitive position of a party to the agreement, or

(ii) interfere significantly with negotiations in which parties to the agreement are involved.

2.3.1 Websites — (1) If a mutual fund or the mutual fund's family has a website, the mutual fund must post to at least one of those websites a fund facts document filed under this Part as soon as practicable and, in any event, within 10 days after the date that the document is filed.

(2) A fund facts document posted to the website referred to in subsection (1) must

(a) be displayed in a manner that would be considered prominent to a reasonable person; and

(b) not be attached to or bound with another fund facts document.

(3) Subsection (1) does not apply if the fund facts document is posted to a website of the manager of the mutual fund in the manner required under subsection (2).

2.4 Simplified Prospectus — A simplified prospectus is a prospectus for the purposes of securities legislation.

2.5 Lapse Date — (1) This section does not apply in Ontario.

(2) In this section, "lapse date" means, with reference to the distribution of a security that has been qualified under a simplified prospectus, the date that is 12 months after the date of the most recent simplified prospectus relating to the security.

(3) A mutual fund must not continue the distribution of a security to which the prospectus requirement applies after the lapse date unless the mutual fund files a new simplified prospectus that complies with securities legislation and a receipt for that new simplified prospectus is issued by the regulator.

(4) Despite subsection (3), a distribution may be continued for a further 12 months after a lapse date if,

(a) the mutual fund delivers a *pro forma* simplified prospectus not less than 30 days before the lapse date of the previous simplified prospectus;

(b) the mutual fund files a new final simplified prospectus not later than 10 days after the lapse date of the previous simplified prospectus; and

(c) a receipt for the new final simplified prospectus is issued by the regulator within 20 days after the lapse date of the previous simplified prospectus.

(5) The continued distribution of securities after the lapse date does not contravene subsection (3) unless and until any of the conditions of subsection (4) are not complied with.

(6) Subject to any extension granted under subsection (7), if a condition in subsection (4) is not complied with, a purchaser may cancel a purchase made in a distribution after the lapse date in reliance on subsection (4) within 90 days after the purchaser first became aware of the failure to comply with the condition.

(7) The regulator may, on an application of a mutual fund, extend, subject to such terms and conditions as it may impose, the times provided by subsection (4) where in its opinion it would not be prejudicial to the public interest to do so.

[Note: In Ontario, section 62 of the Securities Act *(Ontario) imposes similar requirements regarding refiling of prospectuses.]*

2.6 Consents of Experts — (1) A mutual fund must file the written consent of

(a) any solicitor, auditor, accountant, engineer, or appraiser;

(b) any notary in Québec; and

(c) any person or company whose profession or business gives authority to a statement made by that person or company

if that person or company is named in a simplified prospectus or an amendment to a simplified prospectus, directly or, if applicable, in a document incorporated by reference,

(d) as having prepared or certified any part of the simplified prospectus or the amendment;

(e) as having opined on financial statements from which selected information included in the simplified prospectus has been derived and which audit opinion is referred to in the simplified prospectus directly or in a document incorporated by reference; or

(f) as having prepared or certified a report, valuation, statement or opinion referred to in the simplified prospectus or the amendment, directly or in a document incorporated by reference.

(2) The consent referred to in subsection (1) must

(a) be filed no later than the time the simplified prospectus or the amendment to the simplified prospectus is filed or, for the purposes of future financial statements that have been incorporated by reference in a simplified prospectus, no later than the date that those financial statements are filed;

(b) state that the person or company being named consents

(i) to being named, and

(ii) to the use of that person or company's report, valuation, statement or opinion;

(c) refer to the report, valuation, statement or opinion stating the date of the report, valuation, statement or opinion; and

(d) contain a statement that the person or company being named

(i) has read the simplified prospectus, and

(ii) has no reason to believe that there are any misrepresentations in the information contained in it that are

(A) derived from the report, valuation, statement or opinion, or

(B) within the knowledge of the person or company as a result of the services performed by the person or company in connection with the report, financial statements, valuation, statement or opinion.

(3) In addition to any other requirement of this section, the consent of an auditor or accountant must also state

(a) the dates of the financial statements on which the report of the auditor or accountant is made; and

(b) that the auditor or accountant has no reason to believe that there are any misrepresentations in the information contained in the simplified prospectus that are

(i) derived from the financial statements on which the auditor or accountant has reported, or

(ii) within the knowledge of the auditor or accountant as a result of the audit of the financial statements.

(4) Subsection (1) does not apply to a designated rating organization or its DRO affiliate that issues a rating to the securities being distributed under the simplified prospectus.

2.7 Language of Documents — (1) A mutual fund must file a simplified prospectus and any other document required to be filed under this Instrument in French or in English.

(2) In Québec, a simplified prospectus and any document required to be incorporated by reference into a simplified prospectus must be in French or in French and English.

(3) Despite subsection (1), if a mutual fund files a document only in French or only in English but delivers to a securityholder or prospective securityholder a version of the document in the other language, the mutual fund must file that other version not later than when it is first delivered to the securityholder or prospective securityholder.

2.8 Statement of Rights — Except in Ontario, a simplified prospectus must contain a statement of the rights given to a purchaser under securities legislation in case of a failure to deliver the simplified prospectus or in case of a misrepresentation in the simplified prospectus.

[Note: In Ontario, section 60 of the Securities Act *(Ontario) imposes a similar requirement for the inclusion of a statement of rights in a prospectus.]*

PART 3 — DOCUMENTS INCORPORATED BY REFERENCE AND DELIVERY TO SECURITYHOLDERS

3.1 Documents Incorporated by Reference — The following documents must, by means of a statement to that effect, be incorporated by reference into, and form part of, a simplified prospectus:

1. The annual information form that is filed concurrently with the simplified prospectus.

1.1 The most recently filed fund facts document for each class or series of securities of the mutual fund, filed either concurrently with or after the date of the simplified prospectus.

1.2 If the mutual fund has not yet filed comparative annual financial statements of the mutual fund, the most recently filed interim financial report of the mutual fund that were filed before or after the date of the simplified prospectus.

1.3 If the mutual fund has not yet filed interim financial report or comparative annual financial statements of the mutual fund, the audited statement of financial position that was filed with the simplified prospectus.

1.4 If the mutual fund has not yet filed an annual management report of fund performance of the mutual fund, the most recently filed interim management report of fund performance of the mutual fund that was filed before or after the date of the simplified prospectus.

2. The most recently filed comparative annual financial statements of the mutual fund, together with the accompanying report of the auditor, filed either before or after the date of the simplified prospectus.

3. The most recently filed interim financial report of the mutual fund that were filed before or after the date of the simplified prospectus and that pertain to a period after the period to which the annual financial statements then incorporated by reference in the simplified prospectus pertain.

4. The most recently filed annual management report of fund performance of the mutual fund that was filed before or after the date of the simplified prospectus.

5. The most recently filed interim management report of fund performance of the mutual fund that was filed before or after the date of the simplified prospectus and that pertains to a period after the period to which the annual management report of fund performance then incorporated by reference in the simplified prospectus pertains.

3.1.1 Audit of Financial Statements — Any financial statements, other than interim financial reports, incorporated by reference in a simplified prospectus must meet the audit requirements in Part 2 of National Instrument 81-106 *Investment Fund Continuous Disclosure*.

3.1.2 Review of Unaudited Financial Statements — Any unaudited financial statements incorporated by reference in a simplified prospectus at the date of filing of the simplified prospectus must have been reviewed in accordance with the relevant standards set out in the Handbook for a review of financial statements by the mutual fund's auditor or a review of financial statements by a public accountant.

3.1.3 Approval of Financial Statements and Related Documents — A mutual fund must not file a simplified prospectus unless each financial statement and each management report of fund performance incorporated by reference in the simplified prospectus has been approved in accordance with the requirements in Part 2 and Part 4 of National Instrument 81-106 *Investment Fund Continuous Disclosure*.

3.2 Delivery of Preliminary Simplified Prospectus and Simplified Prospectus — (1) The requirement under securities legislation to deliver or send a preliminary prospectus of a mutual fund to a person or company is satisfied by delivering or sending a preliminary simplified prospectus for the mutual fund filed under this Instrument, prepared in accordance with Form 81-101F1, either with or without the documents incorporated by reference.

(2) If a prospectus is required under securities legislation to be delivered or sent to a person or company, the fund facts document most recently filed under this Instrument for the applicable class or series of securities must be delivered or sent to the person or company at the same time and in the same manner as otherwise required for the prospectus.

(2.1) The requirement under securities legislation to deliver or send a prospectus does not apply if a fund facts document is delivered or sent under subsection (2).

(2.2) In Nova Scotia, a fund facts document is a disclosure document prescribed under subsection 76(1A) of the *Securities Act* (Nova Scotia).

(2.3) In Ontario, a fund facts document is a disclosure document prescribed under subsection 71(1.1) of the *Securities Act* (Ontario).

Amendment

(2)–(2.3) [Repealed.]

To come into force on May 30, 2016

---

(3) Except in Ontario, any dealer distributing a security during the waiting period must

(a) send a copy of the preliminary simplified prospectus to each prospective purchaser who indicates an interest in purchasing the security and requests a copy of such preliminary simplified prospectus; and

(b) maintain a record of the names and addresses of all persons and companies to whom the preliminary simplified prospectus has been forwarded.

[Note: In Ontario, sections 66 and 67 of the Securities Act *(Ontario) impose similar requirements regarding the distribution of a preliminary prospectus and maintaining a distribution list.]*

Addition

3.2.01 Pre-Sale Delivery of Fund Facts Document — **(1)** If securities legislation requires a dealer to deliver or send a prospectus in connection with a purchase of a security of a mutual fund, the dealer must, unless the dealer has previously done so, deliver to the purchaser the fund facts document most recently filed under this Instrument for the applicable class or series of securities of the mutual fund before the dealer accepts an instruction from the purchaser for the purchase of the security.

(2) In Nova Scotia, a fund facts document is a disclosure document prescribed under subsection 76(1A) of the *Securities Act* (Nova Scotia).

(3) In Ontario, a fund facts document is a disclosure document prescribed under subsection 71(1.1) of the *Securities Act* (Ontario).

(4) The requirement under securities legislation to deliver or send a prospectus in connection with a purchase of a security of a mutual fund does not apply if

(a) a fund facts document for the applicable class or series of securities of the mutual fund is

(i) delivered to the purchaser before the dealer accepts an instruction from the purchaser for the purchase of the security, or

(ii) delivered or sent to the purchaser in accordance with section 3.2.02 or 3.2.04 and the conditions set out in the applicable section are satisfied, or

(b) section 3.2.03 applies and the conditions set out in that section are satisfied.

3.2.02 Exception to Pre-Sale Delivery of Fund Facts Document — **(1)** Despite subsection 3.2.01(1), a dealer may deliver or send to the purchaser the most recently filed fund facts document for the applicable class or series of securities of the mutual fund not later than midnight on the second business day after entering into the purchase of a security of the mutual fund, if all of the following apply:

(a) the purchaser instructs the dealer that the purchase must be completed immediately or by a specified time;

(b) it is not reasonably practicable for the dealer to deliver the fund facts document before the time specified by the purchaser under paragraph (a);

(c) before the instruction from the purchaser for the purchase of a security of the mutual fund is accepted,

    (i) the dealer informs the purchaser of the existence and purpose of the fund facts document and explains the dealer's obligation to deliver the fund facts document,

    (ii) the purchaser consents to the dealer delivering or sending the fund facts document after entering into the purchase, and

    (iii) the dealer verbally discloses to the purchaser a summary of all of the following:

        (A) the fundamental features of the mutual fund, and what it primarily invests in, as set out under the heading "What does the fund invest in?" in Item 3 of Part I of the fund facts document;

        (B) the investment risk level of the mutual fund as set out under the heading "How risky is it?" in Item 4 of Part I of the fund facts document;

        (C) the suitability of the mutual fund for particular investors as set out under the heading "Who is this fund for?" in Item 7 of Part I of the fund facts document;

        (D) any costs associated with buying, owning and selling a security of the mutual fund as set out under the heading "How much does it cost?" in Item I of Part II of the fund facts document;

        (E) any applicable withdrawal rights or rescission rights that the purchaser is entitled to under securities legislation, as set out under the heading "What if I change my mind?" in Item 2 of Part II of the fund facts document.

(2) For the purposes of subparagraph (1)(c)(ii), the consent must be given in respect of a specific instruction to purchase a security of a mutual fund and, for greater certainty, cannot be in the form of blanket consent from the purchaser.

3.2.03 Delivery of Fund Facts for Subsequent Purchases Under a Pre-authorized Purchase Plan — Despite subsection 3.2.01(1), a dealer is not required to deliver the fund facts document to a purchaser in connection with a purchase of a security of a mutual fund made pursuant to a pre-authorized purchase plan if all of the following apply:

(a) the purchase is not the first purchase under the plan;

(b) the dealer has provided a notice to the purchaser that states,

    (i) subject to paragraph (c), the purchaser will not receive a fund facts document after the date of the notice, unless the purchaser specifically requests it,

    (ii) the purchaser is entitled to receive upon request, at no cost to the purchaser, the most recently filed fund facts document by calling a specified toll-free number, or by sending a request by mail or e-mail to a specified address or e-mail address,

    (iii) how to access the fund facts document electronically,

    (iv) the purchaser will not have a right of withdrawal under securities legislation for subsequent purchases of a security of a mutual fund under the plan, but will continue to have a right of action if there is a misrepresentation in the prospectus or any document incorporated by reference into the prospectus, and

    (v) the purchaser may terminate the plan at any time;

(c) at least annually during the term of the plan, the dealer notifies the purchaser in writing of how the purchaser can request the most recently filed fund facts document; and

(d) the dealer delivers or sends the most recently filed fund facts document to the purchaser if the purchaser requests it.

3.2.04 Delivery of Fund Facts for Managed Accounts and Permitted Clients — Despite subsection 3.2.01(1), a dealer may deliver or send to the purchaser of a security of a mutual fund the most recently filed fund facts document for the applicable class or series of securities of the mutual fund not later than midnight on the second business day after entering into the purchase of a security of the mutual fund if

(a) the purchase is made in a managed account, or

(b) the purchaser is a permitted client that is not an individual.

3.2.05 Electronic Delivery of the Fund Facts Document — **(1)** If the purchaser of a security of a mutual fund consents, a fund facts document that may be or is required to be delivered or sent under this Part may be delivered or sent electronically.

(2) For the purposes of subsection (1), a fund facts document may be delivered or sent to the purchaser by means of an e-mail that contains

(a) the fund facts document as an attachment, or

(b) a hyperlink that leads directly to the fund facts document.

To come into force on May 30, 2016

3.2.1 Fund facts document — purchaser's right of withdrawal — (1) A purchaser has a right of withdrawal in respect of a fund facts document that was delivered or sent under subsection 3.2(2), as the purchaser would otherwise have when a prospectus is required to be delivered or sent under securities legislation and, for that purpose, a fund facts document is a prescribed document under the statutory right of withdrawal.

Amendment

3.2.1 Fund facts document — purchaser's right of withdrawal — **(1)** A purchaser has a right of withdrawal in respect of a fund facts document that was delivered or sent under sections 3.2.01, 3.2.02 or 3.2.04, as the purchaser would otherwise have when a prospectus is required to be delivered or sent under securities legislation and, for that purpose, a fund facts document is a prescribed document under the statutory right of withdrawal.

To come into force on May 30, 2016

(2) In Nova Scotia, instead of subsection (1), subsection 76(2) of the *Securities Act* (Nova Scotia) applies.

(3) In Ontario, instead of subsection (1), subsection 71(2) of the *Securities Act* (Ontario) applies.

(4) In Québec, instead of subsection (1), section 30 of the *Securities Act* (Québec) applies..

3.2.2 Fund facts document — purchaser's right of action for failure to deliver or send — (1) A purchaser has a right of action if a fund facts document is not delivered or sent as required by subsection 3.2(2), as the purchaser would otherwise have when a prospectus is not delivered or sent as required under securities legislation and, for that purpose, a fund facts document is a prescribed document under the statutory right of action.

Amendment

3.2.2 Fund facts document — purchaser's right of action for failure to deliver or send — **(1)** A purchaser has a right of action if a fund facts document is not delivered or sent as required by sections 3.2.01, 3.2.02 or 3.2.04, as the purchaser would otherwise have when a prospectus is not delivered or sent as required under securities legislation and, for that purpose, a fund facts document is a prescribed document under the statutory right of action.

To come into force on May 30, 2016

(2) In Nova Scotia, instead of subsection (1), subsection 141(1) of the *Securities Act* (Nova Scotia) applies.

(3) In Ontario, instead of subsection (1), section 133 of the *Securities Act* (Ontario) applies.

(4) In Québec, instead of subsection (1), section 214 of the *Securities Act* (Québec) applies.

3.3 Documents to be Delivered or Sent upon Request — (1) A mutual fund must deliver or send to any person or company that requests the simplified prospectus of the mutual fund or any of the documents incorporated by reference into the simplified prospectus, a copy of the simplified prospectus or requested document.

(2) A mutual fund must deliver or send, to any person or company that requests the annual information form of the mutual fund, the current simplified prospectus of the mutual fund with the annual information form, unless the mutual fund has previously delivered or sent that simplified prospectus to that person or company.

(3) A mutual fund must deliver or send all documents requested under this section within three business days of receipt of the request and free of charge.

3.4 Toll-Free Telephone Number or Collect Telephone Calls — A mutual fund must have a toll-free telephone number for, or accept collect telephone calls from, persons or companies that want to receive a copy of the simplified prospectus of the mutual fund and any or all documents incorporated by reference into the simplified prospectus.

3.5 Soliciting Expressions of Interest Prohibited — Neither a multiple SP that includes both a *pro forma* simplified prospectus and a preliminary simplified prospectus nor a multiple AIF that includes both a *pro forma* annual information form and a preliminary annual information form may be used to solicit expressions of interest.

PART 4 — PLAIN LANGUAGE AND PRESENTATION

4.1 Plain Language and Presentation — (1) A simplified prospectus, annual information form and fund facts document must be prepared using plain language and be in a format that assists in readability and comprehension.

(2) A simplified prospectus

(a) must present all information briefly and concisely;

(b) must present the items listed in the Part A section of Form 81-101F1 and the items listed in the Part B section of Form 81-101F1 in the order stipulated in those parts;

(c) may, unless the Part B section is being bound separately from the Part A section as permitted by subsection 5.3(1), place the Part B section of the simplified prospectus in any location in the simplified prospectus;

(d) must use the headings and sub-headings stipulated in Form 81-101F1, and may use sub-headings in items for which no sub-headings are stipulated;

(e) must contain only educational material or the information that is specifically mandated or permitted by Form 81-101F1; and

(f) must not incorporate by reference into the simplified prospectus, from any other document, information that is required to be included in a simplified prospectus.

(3) A fund facts document must

(a) be prepared for each class and each series of securities of a mutual fund in accordance with Form 81-101F3;

(b) present the items listed in the Part I section of Form 81-101F3 and the items listed in the Part II section of Form 81-101F3 in the order stipulated in those parts;

(c) use the headings and sub-headings stipulated in Form 81-101F3;

(d) contain only the information that is specifically required or permitted to be in Form 81-101F3;

(e) not incorporate any information by reference; and

(f) not exceed four pages in length.

4.2 Preparation in the Required Form — Despite provisions in securities legislation relating to the presentation of the content of a prospectus, the simplified prospectus and annual information form and a fund facts document must be prepared in accordance with this Instrument.

PART 5 — PACKAGING

5.1 Combinations of Documents — (1) A simplified prospectus must not be consolidated with one or more other simplified prospectuses to form a multiple SP unless the Part A sections of each simplified prospectus are substantially similar.

(2) A multiple SP must be prepared in accordance with the applicable requirements of Form 81-101F1.

5.2 Combinations of Fund Facts Documents for Delivery Purposes — (1) A fund facts document delivered or sent under section 3.2 must not be attached to or bound with any other materials or documents, except that it may be attached to or bound with one or more of the following:

1. A general front cover pertaining to the package of attached or bound materials and documents.

2. A trade confirmation which discloses the purchase of securities of the mutual fund.

3. A fund facts document of another mutual fund if that fund facts document is being delivered or sent under section 3.2.

4. A simplified prospectus or a multiple SP of the mutual fund.

5. Any document incorporated by reference into the simplified prospectus or the multiple SP.

6. Account application documents.

7. Registered tax plan applications and documents.

(2) If a trade confirmation referred to in subsection (1) is attached to or bound with a fund facts document, any other disclosure document required to be delivered or sent to satisfy a regulatory requirement for purchases listed in the trade confirmation may be attached to or bound with the fund facts document.

(3) If a fund facts document is attached to or bound with any of the materials or documents referred to in subsection (1), a table of contents specifying all documents must be attached to or bound with the fund facts document, except when the only other documents attached to or bound with the fund facts document are the general front cover or the trade confirmation.

(4) If one or more fund facts documents are attached to or bound with any of the materials or documents referred to in subsection (1), only the general front cover, the table of contents and the trade confirmation may be placed in front of those fund facts documents.

Amendment

5.2 Combinations of Fund Facts Documents for Delivery Purposes — (1) If a fund facts document for a particular class or series of securities of a mutual fund is delivered under subsection 3.2.01(1), the fund facts document must not be combined with any other materials or documents.

(2) Despite subsection (1), a fund facts document may be combined with one or more other fund facts documents if the combination of documents is not so extensive as to cause a reasonable person to conclude that the combination of documents prevents the information from being presented in a simple, accessible and comparable format.

(3) Despite subsection (2), if multiple fund facts documents are being delivered electronically at the same time, those fund facts documents cannot be combined into a single e-mail attachment or a single document accessible through a hyperlink.

(4) A fund facts document delivered or sent under section 3.2.02, 3.2.03, or 3.2.04 must not be combined with any other materials or documents including, for greater certainty, another fund facts document, except one or more of the following:

(a) a general front cover pertaining to the package of attached or bound materials and documents;

(b) a trade confirmation which discloses the purchase of securities of the mutual fund;

(c) a fund facts document of another mutual fund if that fund facts document is also being delivered or sent under section 3.2.02, 3.2.03, or 3.2.04;

(d) the simplified prospectus or the multiple SP of the mutual fund;

(e) any material or document incorporated by reference into the simplified prospectus or the multiple SP of the mutual fund;

(f) an account application document;

(g) a registered tax plan application or related document.

(5) If a trade confirmation referred to in paragraph (4)(b) is combined with a fund facts document, any other disclosure documents required to be delivered or sent to satisfy a regulatory requirement for purchases listed in the trade confirmation may be combined with the fund facts document.

(6) If a fund facts document is combined with any of the materials or documents referred to in subsection (4), a table of contents specifying all documents must be combined with the fund facts document, unless the only other documents combined with the fund facts document are the general front cover permitted under paragraph (4)(a) or the trade confirmation permitted under paragraph (4)(b).

(7) If one or more fund facts documents are combined with any of the materials or documents referred to in subsection (4), only the general front cover permitted under paragraph (4)(a), the table of contents required under subsection (6) and the trade confirmation permitted under paragraph (4)(b) may be placed in front of the fund facts documents.

To come into force on May 30, 2016.

5.3 Separate Binding of Part B Sections of a Multiple SP — (1) The Part B sections of a multiple SP may be bound separately from the Part A section of that document.

(2) If a Part B section of a multiple SP is bound separately from the Part A section of the multiple SP

(a) all of the Part B sections of the multiple SP must be bound separately from the Part A section; and

(b) all or some of the Part B sections may be bound together with each other or separately.

5.4 Annual Information Forms — (1) An annual information form must be consolidated with one or more other annual information forms into a multiple AIF if the related simplified prospectuses are consolidated into a multiple SP.

(2) A multiple AIF must be prepared in accordance with the applicable requirements of Form 81-101F2.

5.5 Combinations of Fund Facts Documents for Filing Purposes — For the purposes of section 2.1, a fund facts document may be attached to or bound with another fund facts document of a mutual fund in a simplified prospectus or, if a multiple SP, another fund facts document of a mutual fund combined in the multiple SP.

Part 8: MUTUAL FUNDS

Amendment

5.5 5.5 Combinations of Fund Facts Documents for Filing Purposes — For the purposes of section 2.1, a fund facts document may be combined with another fund facts document of a mutual fund in a simplified prospectus or, if a multiple SP, another fund facts document of a mutual fund combined in the multiple SP.

To come into force on May 30, 2016

PART 5.1 — CERTIFICATES

5.1.1 **Interpretation** — For the purposes of this Part,

"manager certificate form" means a certificate in the form set out in Item 20 of Form 81-101F2 and attached to the annual information form,

"mutual fund certificate form" means a certificate in the form set out in Item 19 of Form 81-101F2 and attached to the annual information form,

"principal distributor certificate form" means a certificate in the form set out in Item 22 of Form 81-101F2 and attached to the annual information form, and

"promoter certificate form" means a certificate in the form set out in Item 21 of Form 81-101F2 and attached to the annual information form.

5.1.2 **Date of Certificates** — The date of the certificates required by this Instrument must be within 3 business days before the filing of the preliminary simplified prospectus, the simplified prospectus, the amendment to the simplified prospectus, the amendment to the annual information form or the amendment to the fund facts document, as applicable.

5.1.3 **Certificate of the Mutual Fund** — (1) Except in Ontario, a simplified prospectus of a mutual fund must be certified by the mutual fund.

[Note: In Ontario, section 58 of the Securities Act *(Ontario) imposes a similar requirement that a prospectus contain a certificate of the issuer.]*

(2) A mutual fund must certify its simplified prospectus in the form of the mutual fund certificate form.

5.1.4 **Certificate of Principal Distributor** — A simplified prospectus of a mutual fund must be certified by each principal distributor in the form of the principal distributor certificate form.

5.1.5 **Certificate of the Manager** — A simplified prospectus of a mutual fund must be certified by the manager of the mutual fund in the form of the manager certificate form.

5.1.6 **Certificate of Promoter** — (1) Except in Ontario, a simplified prospectus of a mutual fund must be certified by each promoter of the mutual fund.

[Note: In Ontario, subsection 58(1) of the Securities Act *(Ontario) imposes a similar requirement that a prospectus contain a certificate signed by each promoter of the issuer.]*

(2) A prospectus certificate required under this Instrument or other securities legislation to be signed by a promoter must be in the form of the promoter certificate form.

(3) Except in Ontario, the regulator may require any person or company who was a promoter of the mutual fund within the two preceding years to sign a certificate in the promoter certificate form.

[Note: In Ontario, subsection 58(6) of the Securities Act *(Ontario) provides the Director with similar discretion to require a person or company who was a promoter of the issuer within the two preceding years to sign a prospectus certificate, subject to such conditions as the Director considers proper.]*

(4) Despite subsection (3), in British Columbia, the powers of the regulator with respect to the matters described in subsection (3) are set out in the *Securities Act* (British Columbia).

(5) Except in Ontario, with the consent of the regulator, a certificate of a promoter for a simplified prospectus may be signed by an agent duly authorized in writing by the person or company required to sign the certificate.

[Note: In Ontario, subsection 58(7) of the Securities Act *(Ontario) provides the Director with similar discretion to permit the certificate to be signed by an agent of a promoter.]*

5.1.7 **Certificates of Corporate Mutual Funds** — (1) Except in Ontario, if the mutual fund is a company, the certificate of the mutual fund required under section 5.1.3 must be signed

    (a) by the chief executive officer and the chief financial officer of the mutual fund; and

    (b) on behalf of the board of directors of the mutual fund, by

        (i) any two directors of the mutual fund, other than the persons referred to in paragraph (a) above, or

        (ii) if the mutual fund has only three directors, two of whom are the persons referred to in paragraph (a) above, all the directors of the mutual fund.

(2) Except in Ontario, if the regulator is satisfied that either or both of the chief executive officer or chief financial officer cannot sign a certificate in a simplified prospectus, the regulator may accept a certificate signed by another officer.

[Note: In Ontario, section 58 of the Securities Act *(Ontario) imposes similar requirements regarding who must sign the issuer certificate.]*

PART 6 — EXEMPTIONS

6.1 **Grant of Exemption** — (1) The regulator or the securities regulatory authority may grant an exemption from the provisions of this Instrument, in whole or in part, subject to such conditions or restrictions as may be imposed in the exemption.

(2) Despite subsection (1), in Ontario, only the regulator may grant such an exemption.

(3) Except in Ontario, an exemption referred to in subsection (1) is granted under the statute referred to in Appendix B of National Instrument 14-101 *Definitions* opposite the name of the local jurisdiction.

6.2 Evidence of exemption — (1) Subject to subsection (2) and without limiting the manner in which an exemption may be evidenced, the granting under this Part of an exemption from any form or content requirements relating to a simplified prospectus, annual information form or fund facts document, may be evidenced by the issuance of a receipt for a simplified prospectus and annual information form, or an amendment to a simplified prospectus or annual information form.

(2) The issuance of a receipt for a simplified prospectus and annual information form or an amendment to a simplified prospectus or annual information form is not evidence that the exemption has been granted unless

(a) the person or company that sought the exemption sent to the regulator or securities regulatory authority a letter or memorandum describing the matters relating to the exemption and indicating why consideration should be given to the granting of the exemption:

(i) on or before the date of the filing of the preliminary or *pro forma* simplified prospectus and annual information form;

(ii) at least 10 days before the issuance of the receipt in the case of an amendment to a simplified prospectus or annual information form; or

(iii) after the date of the filing of the preliminary or *pro forma* simplified prospectus and annual information form and received a written acknowledgement from the regulator or securities regulatory authority that the exemption may be evidenced in the manner set out in subsection (1); and

(b) the regulator or securities regulatory authority has not before, or concurrently with, the issuance of the receipt sent notice to the person or company that sought the exemption, that the exemption sought may not be evidenced in the manner set out in subsection (1).

PART 7 — EFFECTIVE DATE

7.1 Effective Date — This Instrument comes into force on February 1, 2000.

Final Rule: (2000) 23 O.S.C.B. (Supp)1; Approval by OSC: (1999) 22 O.S.C.B. (Supp2) 1; Request for Comments: (1999) 22 O.S.C.B. 2605 and (1998) 21 O.S.C.B. 4817. Replaced NPS 36.

Amendment to Rule: 24 O.S.C.B. 2680 (April 27, 2001); Approval by OSC: 24 O.S.C.B. 1071 (February 16, 2001); Request for Comments: 23 O.S.C.B. 4195 (June 16, 2000) and 23 O.S.C.B. (Supp) 133 (January 28, 2000).

Amendment to Rule: 27 O.S.C.B. 752; Approval of OSC: 26 O.S.C.B. 6837; Request for Comments: (2002) 25 O.S.C.B. 4705.

Amendment to Rule: 28 O.S.C.B. 4965; Approval of OSC: (2005) 28 O.S.C.B. (Supp-1) 42; Request for Comments: (2004) 27 O.S.C.B. 5157 and (2002) 25 O.S.C.B. 6273.

Amendment to Rule: (2006) 29 O.S.C.B. 8842; Approval of OSC: (2006) 29 O.S.C.B. (Supp-1) 1; Request for Comments: (2005) 28 O.S.C.B. (Supp-2) 1 and (2004) 28 O.S.C.B. 465.

Amendment to Rule: 31 O.S.C.B. (Supp. 2) 241 (March 7, 2008); Approval by OSC: 30 O.S.C.B. (Supp 7) 1 (Dec. 21, 2007); Request for Comments: 29 O.S.C.B. (Supp 3) 1 (Dec. 22, 2006).

Amendment to Rule: (2008) 31 O.S.C.B. 8568; Approval by OSC: 31 O.S.C.B. 6275; Request for Comments: (2007) 30 O.S.C.B. 4965.

Amendment to Rule: (2010) 33 O.S.C.B. 11399; Approval by OSC: (2010) 33 O.S.C.B. (Supp. 4) 1; Request for Comments: (2009) 32 O.S.C.B. (Supp. 1), (2008) 31 O.S.C.B. 10479, (2007) 30 O.S.C.B. (Supp. 4) 1 and (2003) 26 O.S.C.B. 1443.

Amendment to Rule: (2012) 35 O.S.C.B. 3429; Approval by OSC: (2012) 35 O.S.C.B. 1375; Request for Comments: (2010) 33 O.S.C.B. 5833.

Amendment to Rule: (2013) 36 O.S.C.B. 4929; Approval by OSC: (2013) 36 O.S.C.B. (Supp. 2) 1; Request for Comments: (2011) 34 O.S.C.B. (Supp. 4) 1.

Amendment to Rule: (2013) 36 O.S.C.B. 2619; Request for Comments: (2012) 35 O.S.C.B. 6887.

Amendment to Rule: (2013) 36 O.S.C.B. 7813; Approval by OSC: (2013) 36 O.S.C.B. 6001; Request for Comments: (2012) 35 O.S.C.B. 5755 and (2011) 34 O.S.C.B. 8561.

Amendment to Rule: Approval by OSC: (2013) 36 O.S.C.B. 9612; Request for Comments: (2009) 32 O.S.C.B. 8381.

Amendment to Rule: (2015) 38 O.S.C.B. 1382.

Rules: Rule 13-502, App. C, Item A; NI 41-101, 81-102, 81-104, 81-106, 81-107.

Policies: NPS 81-101CP, 81-102CP, 81-106CP, 11-202; CSAN 81-321; OSCN 81-708, 81-717, 81-721, 81-722.

Form 81-101F1 — Contents of Simplified Prospectus

Table of Contents

General Instructions

PART A GENERAL DISCLOSURE

General Instructions

General

(1) *This Form describes the disclosure required in a simplified prospectus of a mutual fund. Each Item of this Form outlines disclosure requirements. Instructions to help you provide this disclosure are printed in italic type.*

(2) *Terms defined in National Instrument 81-101 Mutual Fund Prospectus Disclosure, National Instrument 81-102 Investment Funds or National Instrument 81-105 Mutual Fund Sales Practices and used in this Form have the meanings that they have in those national instruments.*

(3) *A simplified prospectus shall state the required information concisely and in plain language. Reference should be made to Part 3 of Companion Policy 81-101CP for a discussion concerning plain language and presentation.*

(4) *Respond as simply and directly as is reasonably possible and include only as much information as is necessary for an understanding of the fundamental and particular characteristics of the mutual fund. Brevity is especially important in describing practices or aspects of a mutual fund's operations that do not differ materially from those of other mutual funds.*

(5) *National Instrument 81-101 requires the simplified prospectus to be presented in a format that assists in readability and comprehension. This Form does not mandate the use of a specific format to achieve these goals. However, mutual funds are encouraged to use, as appropriate, tables, captions, bullet points or other organizational techniques that assist in presenting the required disclosure clearly and concisely.*

(6) *Each Item shall be presented under the heading or sub-heading stipulated in this Form; references to the relevant Item number are optional. If no sub-heading for an Item is stipulated in this Form, a mutual fund may include sub-headings, under the required headings, at its option.*

(7) *A simplified prospectus may contain photographs and artwork only if they are relevant to the business of the mutual fund, mutual fund family or members of the organization of the mutual fund and are not misleading.*

(8) *Any footnotes to tables provided for under any Item in this Form may be deleted if the substance of the footnotes is otherwise provided.*

Contents of a Simplified Prospectus

(9) *A simplified prospectus shall pertain to one mutual fund, and shall consist of two sections, a Part A section and a Part B section.*

(10) *The Part A section of a simplified prospectus contains the response to the Items in Part A of this Form and contains introductory information about the mutual fund, general information about mutual funds and information applicable to the mutual funds managed by the mutual fund organization.*

(11) *The Part B section of a simplified prospectus contains the response to the Items in Part B of this Form and contains specific information about the mutual fund to which the simplified prospectus pertains.*

(12) *Despite securities legislation, a simplified prospectus shall present each Item in the Part A section and each Item in the Part B section in the respective order provided for in this Form. However, the Part B section of the simplified prospectus may be placed in any location in the simplified prospectus. For a single SP, this means that the Part B section may be placed before the Part A section, somewhere in the middle of the Part A section or after the Part A section, except for the covers.*

(13) *Subsection 5.1(3) of National Instrument 81-101 permits certain documents to be attached to, or bound with, a simplified prospectus. Those documents consist of the documents incorporated by reference into the simplified prospectus, educational material, account application documents, registered tax plan applications and documents and any point of sale disclosure documents required by securities legislation. No other documents may be attached to, or bound with, a simplified prospectus.*

Consolidation of Simplified Prospectuses into a Multiple SP

(14) *Subsection 5.1(1) of National Instrument 81-101 states that simplified prospectuses shall not be consolidated to form a multiple SP unless the Part A sections of each simplified prospectus are substantially similar. The Part A sections in a consolidated document need not be repeated. These provisions permit a mutual fund organization to create a document that contains the disclosure for a number of mutual funds in the same family.*

(15) *As with a single SP, a multiple SP will consist of two Parts:*

1. A Part A section that contains general information about the mutual funds, or the mutual fund family, described in the document.

2. A number of Part B sections, each of which will provide specific information about one mutual fund. The Part B sections shall not be consolidated with each other so that, in a multiple SP, information about each of the mutual funds described in the document shall be provided on a fund by fund or catalogue basis and shall set out for each mutual fund separately the information required by Part B of this Form. Each Part B section shall start on a new page.

(16) *For a multiple SP in which the Part A and Part B sections are bound together, the Part B sections may be placed at any location in the document; that is, before the Part A section, somewhere in the middle of the Part A section or after the Part A section, except for the back cover. If the Part B sections are bound with the Part A section, the Part B sections shall be kept together in the document.*

(17) *Section 5.3 of National Instrument 81-101 permits the Part B sections of a multiple SP to be bound separately from the Part A section of the document. If one Part B section is bound separately from the Part A section of the document, all Part B sections must be separate from the Part A section of the document.*

(18) *Subsection 5.3(2) of National Instrument 81-101 permits Part B sections that have been bound separately from the related Part A section to either be bound individually or together, at the option of the mutual fund organization. There is no prohibition against the same Part B section of a multiple SP being bound by itself for distribution to some investors, and also being bound with the Part B section of other mutual funds for distribution to other investors.*

(19) *Section 3.2 of National Instrument 81-101 provides that the requirement under securities legislation to deliver a prospectus for a mutual fund will be satisfied by the delivery of a simplified prospectus, either with or without the documents incorporated by reference. Mutual fund organizations that bind separately the Part B sections of a multiple SP from the Part A section are reminded that, since a simplified prospectus consists of a Part A section and a Part B section, delivery of both sections is necessary in order to satisfy the delivery obligations in connection with the sale of securities of a particular mutual fund.*

(20) *In Items 1 through 4 of Part A of this Form, specific instructions are provided for a single SP and a multiple SP and in some cases for a multiple SP for which the Part A section is either bound with, or separate from, the Part B sections of the document. The remainder of Part A of this Form generally refers to disclosure required for "a mutual fund" in a "simplified prospectus". This disclosure should be modified as appropriate to reflect multiple mutual funds covered by a multiple SP.*

Multi-Class Mutual Funds

(21) *A mutual fund that has more than one class or series that are referable to the same portfolio may treat each class or series as a separate mutual fund for purposes of this Form, or may combine disclosure of one or more of the classes or series in one simplified prospectus. If disclosure pertaining to more than one class or series is combined in one simplified prospectus, separate disclosure in response to each item in this Form must be provided for each class or series unless the responses would be identical for each class or series.*

(22) *As provided in National Instrument 81-102, a section, part, class or series of a class of securities of a mutual fund that is referable to a separate portfolio of assets is considered to be a separate mutual fund. Those principles are applicable to National Instrument 81-101 and this Form.*

Part A — General Disclosure

Item 1 — Front Cover Disclosure

1.1 — For a Single SP

(1) Indicate on the front cover whether the document is a preliminary simplified prospectus, a pro forma simplified prospectus or a simplified prospectus.

(2) Indicate on the front cover the name of the mutual fund to which the simplified prospectus pertains. If the mutual fund has more than one class or series of securities, indicate the name of each of those classes or series covered in the simplified prospectus.

(3) Despite securities legislation, state on the front cover of a preliminary simplified prospectus the following:

A copy of this Simplified Prospectus has been filed with [the securities authority(ies) in each of/certain of the provinces/provinces and territories of Canada] but the Simplified Prospectus has not yet become final for the purpose of a distribution. Information contained in this Simplified Prospectus may not be complete and may have to be amended. The [units/shares] described in this Simplified Prospectus may not be sold to you until a receipt for the Simplified Prospectus is obtained by the mutual fund from the securities regulatory [authority(ies)].

(4) If a commercial copy of the preliminary simplified prospectus is prepared, print the legend referred to in subsection (3) in red ink.

(5) For a preliminary simplified prospectus or simplified prospectus, indicate the date of the document, which shall be the date of the certificates contained in the related annual information form. This date shall be within three business days of the date the document is filed with the securities regulatory authority. Write the date in full, writing the name of the month in words. A *pro forma* simplified prospectus need not be dated, but may reflect the anticipated date of the simplified prospectus.

(6) State, in substantially the following words:

No securities regulatory authority has expressed an opinion about these [units/shares] and it is an offence to claim otherwise.

INSTRUCTION

Complete the bracketed information in subsection (3) above by

(a) inserting the name of each jurisdiction of Canada in which the mutual fund intends to offer securities under the prospectus;

(b) stating that the filing has been made in each of the provinces of Canada or each of the provinces and territories of Canada; or

(c) identifying the filing jurisdictions of Canada by exception (i.e. every province of Canada or every province and territory of Canada, except [excluded jurisdictions]).

1.2 — For a Multiple SP in which the Part A section and the Part B sections are bound together

(1) Indicate on the front cover whether the document is a preliminary simplified prospectus, a *pro forma* simplified prospectus or a simplified prospectus for each of the mutual funds to which the document pertains.

(2) Indicate on the front cover the names of the mutual funds and, at the option of the mutual funds, the name of the mutual fund family, to which the document pertains. If the mutual fund has more than one class or series of securities, indicate the name of each of those classes or series covered in the simplified prospectus.

(3) Despite securities legislation, state on the front cover of a document that contains a preliminary simplified prospectus the following:

A copy of this document has been filed with [the securities authority(ies) in each of/certain of the provinces/provinces and territories of Canada] but has not yet become final for the purpose of a distribution. Information contained in this document may not be complete and may have to be amended. The [units/shares] described in this document may not be sold to you until receipts for this document are obtained by the mutual fund from the securities regulatory [authority(ies)].

(4) If a commercial copy of the document that contains a preliminary simplified prospectus is prepared, print the legend referred to in subsection (3) in red ink.

(5) If the document contains a preliminary simplified prospectus or a simplified prospectus, indicate the date of the document, which shall be the date of the certificates contained in the related multiple AIF. This date shall be within three business days of the date the document is filed with the securities regulatory authority. Write the date in full, writing the name of the month in words. A document that is a *pro forma* multiple SP need not be dated, but may reflect the anticipated date of the multiple SP.

(6) State, in substantially the following words:

No securities regulatory authority has expressed an opinion about these [units/shares] and it is an offence to claim otherwise.

INSTRUCTION

Complete the bracketed information in subsection (3) above by

(a) inserting the name of each jurisdiction of Canada in which the mutual fund intends to offer securities under the prospectus;

(b) stating that the filing has been made in each of the provinces of Canada or each of the provinces and territories of Canada; or

(c) identifying the filing jurisdictions of Canada by exception (i.e. every province of Canada or every province and territory of Canada, except [excluded jurisdictions]).

1.3 — For a Multiple SP in which the Part A section is bound separately from the Part B sections

(1) Comply with Item 1.2.

(2) State prominently, in substantially the following words:

A complete simplified prospectus for the mutual funds listed on this page consists of this document and an additional disclosure document that provides specific information about the mutual funds in which you are investing. This document provides general information applicable to all of the [name of mutual fund family] funds. You must be provided with the additional disclosure document.

Item 2 — Table of Contents

2.1 — For a Single SP

(1) Despite securities legislation, at the option of the mutual fund, include a table of contents.

(2) If a table of contents is included, begin it on a new page, which may be the inside front cover of the document.

2.2 — For a Multiple SP in which the Part A section and the Part B sections are bound together

(1) Include a table of contents.

(2) Include in the table of contents, under the heading "Fund Specific Information", a list of all of the mutual funds to which the document pertains, with the numbers of the pages where information about each mutual fund can be found.

(3) Begin the table of contents on a new page, which may be the inside front cover of the document.

2.3 — For a Multiple SP in which the Part A section is bound separately from the Part B sections

(1) Include a table of contents for the Part A section of the multiple SP.

(2) Begin the table of contents on a new page, which may be the inside front cover of the document.

(3) Include, immediately following the table of contents and on the same page, a list of the mutual funds to which the multiple SP pertains and details on how the Part B disclosure for each mutual fund will be provided.

Item 3 — Introductory Disclosure

3.1 — For a Single SP

Provide, either on a new page or immediately under the table of contents, under the heading "Introduction", the following statement in substantially the following words:

- This Simplified Prospectus contains selected important information to help you make an informed investment decision and to help you understand your rights.

- This Simplified Prospectus contains information about the Fund and the risks of investing in mutual funds generally, as well as the names of the firms responsible for the management of the Fund.

- Additional information about the Fund is available in the following documents:
  - the Annual Information Form;
  - the most recently filed Fund Facts;
  - the most recently filed annual financial statements;
  - any interim financial report filed after those annual financial statements;
  - the most recently filed annual management report of fund performance;
  - any interim management report of fund performance filed after that annual management report of fund performance.

These documents are incorporated by reference into this Simplified Prospectus, which means that they legally form part of this document just as if they were printed as a part of this document. You can get a copy of these documents, at your request, and at no cost, by calling [toll-free/collect] [insert the toll-free telephone number or telephone number where collect calls are accepted, as required by section 3.4 of the Instrument], or from your dealer.

- [If applicable] These documents are available on the [mutual fund's/mutual fund family's] Internet site at [insert mutual fund's Internet site address], or by contacting the [mutual fund/mutual fund family] at [insert mutual fund's/mutual fund family's e-mail address].

- These documents and other information about the Fund are available on the Internet at www.sedar.com.

3.2 — For a Multiple SP

Provide, either on a new page or immediately under the table of contents, under the heading "Introduction" the following statement in substantially the following words:

- This document contains selected important information to help you make an informed investment decision and to help you understand your rights as an investor.

- This document is divided into two parts. The first part, [from pages .... through ....], contains general information applicable to all of the [name of fund family] Funds. The second part, [from pages .... through ....] [which is separately bound], contains specific information about each of the Funds described in this document.

- Additional information about each Fund is available in the following documents:
  - the Annual Information Form;
  - the most recently filed Fund Facts;
  - the most recently filed annual financial statements;
  - any interim financial report filed after those annual financial statements;
  - the most recently filed annual management report of fund performance;
  - any interim management report of fund performance filed after that annual management report of fund performance.

These documents are incorporated by reference into this document, which means that they legally form part of this document just as if they were printed as a part of this document. You can get a copy of these documents, at your request, and at no cost, by calling [toll-free/collect] [insert the toll-free telephone number or telephone number where collect calls are accepted, as required by section 3.4 of the Instrument], or from your dealer.

- [If applicable] These documents are available on the [mutual funds'/mutual fund family's] Internet site at [insert mutual funds'/mutual fund family's Internet site address], or by contacting the [mutual funds/mutual fund family] at [insert e-mail address].

- These documents and other information about the Funds are available at www.sedar.com.

Item 4 — General Investment Risks

(1) Disclose under the heading "What is a Mutual Fund and What are the Risks of Investing in a Mutual Fund?"

(a) a brief general description of the nature of a mutual fund; and

(b) the risk factors or other investment considerations that an investor should take into account that are associated with investing in mutual funds generally.

(2) For a multiple SP, at the option of the mutual fund, disclose the risk factors and investment considerations that are applicable to more than one of those mutual funds.

(3) At a minimum, in response to the requirements of subsection (1), include disclosure in substantially the following words:

- Mutual funds own different types of investments, depending upon their investment objectives. The value of these investments will change from day to day, reflecting changes in interest rates, economic conditions, and market and company news. As a result, the value of a mutual fund's [units/shares] may go up and down, and the value of your investment in a mutual fund may be more or less when you redeem it than when you purchased it.

- [If applicable], The full amount of your investment in any [name of mutual fund family] mutual fund is not guaranteed.

- Unlike bank accounts or GICs, mutual fund [units/shares] are not covered by the Canada Deposit Insurance Corporation or any other government deposit insurer.

(4) State that, under exceptional circumstances, a mutual fund may suspend redemptions. Provide a reference to the disclosure provided in response to Item 6(2) of Part A of this Form.

INSTRUCTIONS:

(1) *Examples of the risks that may be disclosed under subsection (2) are stock market risk, interest rate risk, foreign security risk, foreign currency risk, specialization risk and risk associated with the use of derivatives. If this risk disclosure is provided under this subsection, the fund-specific disclosure about each mutual fund described in the document should contain a reference to the appropriate parts of this risk disclosure.*

(2) *In providing disclosure under subsection (1), follow the instructions under Item 9 of Part B of this Form, as appropriate.*

Item 5 — Organization and Management Details for a Multiple SP

(1) Provide, under the heading "Organization and Management of the [name of mutual fund family]", information about the manager, trustee, portfolio adviser, principal distributor, custodian, registrar, auditor and securities lending agent of the mutual funds to which the document relates in the form of a diagram or table.

(2) For each entity listed in the diagram or table, briefly describe the services provided by that entity and the relationship of that entity to the manager.

(3) For each entity listed in the diagram or table, other than the manager of the mutual funds, provide the municipality and the province or country where it principally provides its services to the mutual funds. Provide the complete municipal address for the manager of the mutual funds.

(3.1) Under a separate sub-heading "Independent Review Committee" in the diagram or table, briefly describe the independent review committee of the mutual funds, including

- an appropriate summary of its mandate,

- its composition, that it prepares at least annually a report of its activities for securityholders which is available on the [mutual fund's/mutual fund family's] Internet site at [insert mutual fund's Internet site address], or at the securityholders request at no cost, by contacting the [mutual fund/mutual fund family] at [insert mutual fund's /mutual fund family's e-mail address], and

- that additional information about the independent review committee, including the names of the members, is available in the mutual fund's Annual Information Form.

(4) At the option of the mutual fund, provide, under a separate sub-heading, details of the manager of the mutual fund, including the history and background of the manager and any overall investment strategy or approach used by the manager in connection with the mutual funds for which it acts as manager.

(4.1) If a mutual fund holds, in accordance with section 2.5 of National Instrument 81-102 *Investment Funds*, securities of another mutual fund that is managed by the same manager or an affiliate or associate of the manager, disclose

(a) that the securities of the other mutual fund held by the mutual fund will not be voted; and

(b) if applicable, that the manager may arrange for the securities of the other mutual fund to be voted by the beneficial holders of the securities of the mutual fund.

(5) Despite subsection (1), if the information required by subsection (1) is not the same for substantially all of the mutual funds described in the document, provide in the diagram or table contemplated by subsection (1) only that information that is the same for substantially all of the mutual funds and provide the remaining disclosure required by that subsection in the diagram or table required by Item 4(1) of Part B of this Form.

(6) Despite subsection (3.1), if the information required by subsection (3.1) is not the same for substantially all of the mutual funds described in the document, provide only that information that is the same for substantially all of the mutual funds and provide the remaining disclosure required by that subsection under Item 4(3.1) of Part B of this Form.

INSTRUCTIONS:

(1) *The information required to be disclosed in this Item shall be presented prominently, using enough space so that it is easy to read.*

(2) *The descriptions of the services provided by the listed entities should be brief. For instance, the manager may be described as "manages the overall business and operations of the funds", a portfolio adviser may be described as "provides investment advice to the manager about the investment portfolio of the funds" or "manages the investment portfolio of the funds", and a "principal distributor" may be described as "markets the securities of the funds and sells securities [through brokers and dealers] [or its own sales force]".*

(3) *The information about the independent review committee should be brief. For instance, its mandate may in part be described as "reviewing, and providing input on, the manager's written policies and procedures which deal with conflict of interest matters for the manager and reviewing such conflict of interest matters." A cross-reference to the annual information form for additional information on the independent review committee and fund governance should be included.*

Item 6 — Purchases, Switches and Redemptions

(1) Briefly describe, under the heading "Purchases, Switches and Redemptions", how an investor can purchase and redeem the securities of the mutual fund or switch them for securities of other mutual funds, how often the mutual fund is valued, and state that the issue and redemption price of those securities is based on the mutual fund's net asset value of a security of that class, or series of a class, next determined after the receipt by the mutual fund of the purchase order or redemption order.

(2) State that, under extraordinary circumstances, the rights of investors to redeem securities may be suspended by the mutual fund, and describe the circumstances when the suspension of redemption rights could occur.

(3) For a new mutual fund that is being sold on a best efforts basis, state whether the issue price will be fixed during the initial distribution period, and state when the mutual fund will begin issuing and redeeming securities based on the net asset value per security of the mutual fund.

(4) Describe all available purchase options and state, if applicable, that the choice of different purchase options requires the investor to pay different fees and expenses and, if applicable, that the choice of different purchase options affects the amount of compensation paid by a member of the organization of the mutual fund to a dealer. Include cross-references to the disclosure provided under Items 8 and 9 of Part A of this Form.

(5) Under the sub-heading "Short-term Trading"

(a) describe the adverse effects, if any, that short-term trades in securities of the mutual fund by an investor may have on other investors in the mutual fund;

(b) describe the restrictions, if any, that may be imposed by the mutual fund to deter short-term trades, including the circumstances, if any, under which such restrictions may not apply;

(c) where the mutual fund does not impose restrictions on short-term trades, state the specific basis for the view of the manager that it is appropriate for the mutual fund not to do so; and

(d) if applicable, state that the annual information form includes a description of all arrangements, whether formal or informal, with any person or company, to permit short-term trades of securities of the mutual fund.

INSTRUCTION:

In the disclosure required by subsection (5), include a brief description of the short-term trading activities in the mutual fund that are considered by the manager to be inappropriate or excessive. Where the manager imposes a short-term trading fee, include a cross-reference to the disclosure provided under Item 8 of Part A of this Form.

Item 7 — Optional Services Provided by the Mutual Fund Organization

If applicable, under the heading "Optional Services", describe the optional services that may be obtained by typical investors from the mutual fund organization.

INSTRUCTION:

Disclosure in this Item should include, for example, any asset allocation services, registered tax plans, foreign content monitoring plans, regular investment and withdrawal plans, U.S. dollar purchase plans, periodic purchase plans, contractual plans, periodic withdrawal plans or switch privileges.

Item 8 — Fees and Expenses

8.1 — General Disclosure

(1) Set out information about the fees and expenses payable by the mutual fund and by investors in the mutual fund under the heading "Fees and Expenses".

(1.1) If the mutual fund holds securities of other mutual funds, disclose that with respect to securities of another mutual fund

(a) there are fees and expenses payable by the other mutual funds in addition to the fees and expenses payable by the mutual fund;

(b) no management fees or incentive fees are payable by the mutual fund that, to a reasonable person, would duplicate a fee payable by the other mutual fund for the same service;

(c) no sales fees or redemption fees are payable by the mutual fund in relation to its purchases or redemptions of the securities of the other mutual fund if the other mutual fund is managed by the manager or an affiliate or associate of the manager of the mutual fund; and

(d) no sales fees or redemption fees are payable by the mutual fund in relation to its purchases or redemptions of securities of the other mutual fund that, to a reasonable person, would duplicate a fee payable by an investor in the mutual fund.

(2) The information required by this Item shall first be a summary of the fees, charges and expenses of the mutual fund and investors presented in the form of the following table, appropriately completed, and introduced using substantially the following words:

> This table lists the fees and expenses that you may have to pay if you invest in the [insert the name of the mutual fund]. You may have to pay some of these fees and expenses directly. The Fund may have to pay some of these fees and expenses, which will therefore reduce the value of your investment in the Fund.

(3) Include the fees for any optional services provided by the mutual fund organization, as described by Item 7 of Part A of this Form, in the table.

(3.1) Under "Operating Expenses" in the table, include a description of the fees and expenses payable in connection with the independent review committee.

(4) If management fees are payable directly by investors, add a line item in the table to disclose the maximum percentage that could be paid by investors.

(5) If the manager permits negotiation of a management fee rebate, provide disclosure of these arrangements. If these arrangements are not available for each mutual fund described in the document, make this disclosure in the description of fees and expenses required for each fund by Item 5 of Part B of this Form and include a cross-reference to that information in the table required by this Item.

Fees and Expenses Payable by the Fund	
Management Fees	*[See Instruction (1)] [disclosure re management fee rebate program]*
Operating Expenses	*[See Instructions (2) and (3)] Fund[s] pay[s] all operating expenses, including ....*
Fees and Expenses Payable Directly by You	
Sales Charges	*[specify percentage, as a percentage of ....]*
Switch Fees	*[specify percentage, as a percentage of ...., or specify amount]*
Redemption Fees	*[specify percentage, as a percentage of ...., or specify amount]*
Short-term Trading Fee	*[specify percentage, as a percentage of ....]*
Registered Tax Plan Fees *[include this disclosure and specify the type of fees if the registered tax plan is sponsored by the mutual fund and is described in the simplified prospectus]*	*[specify amount]*
Other Fees and Expenses *[specify type]*	*[specify amount]*

(6) Despite subsection (3.1), if the information required by subsection (3.1) is not the same for each mutual fund described in the document, make this disclosure in the description of fees and expenses required for each fund by Item 5 of Part B of this Form and include a cross-reference to that information in the table required by this Item.

INSTRUCTIONS:

(1) *If the table pertains to more than one mutual fund and not all of the mutual funds pay the same management fees, under "Management Fees" in the table, either*

> (a) *state that the management fees are unique to each mutual fund, include management fee disclosure for each mutual fund as a separate line item in the table required by Item 5 of Part B of this Form for that mutual fund, and include a cross-reference to that table; or*

> (b) *list the amount of the management fee, including any performance or incentive fee, for each mutual fund separately.*

(2) *If the table pertains to more than one mutual fund and not all of the mutual funds have the same obligations to pay operating expenses, either*

> (a) *state that the operating expenses payable by the mutual funds are unique to each mutual fund, include the description of the operating expenses payable by each mutual fund as a separate line item in the table required by Item 5 of Part B of this Form for that mutual fund, and include a cross-reference to that table; or*

> (b) *provide the disclosure concerning the operating expenses for each mutual fund contemplated by this Item separately.*

(3) *Under "Operating Expenses", state whether the mutual fund pays all of its operating expenses and list the main components of those expenses. If the mutual fund pays only certain operating expenses and is not responsible for payment of all such expenses, adjust the statement in the table to reflect the proper contractual responsibility of the mutual fund.*

(4) *Show all fees or expenses payable by the mutual fund, even if it is expected that the manager of the mutual fund or other member of the organization of the mutual fund will waive or absorb some or all of those fees and expenses.*

(5) *If the management fees of a mutual fund are payable directly by a securityholder and vary so that specific disclosure of the amount of the management fees cannot be disclosed in the simplified prospectus of the mutual fund, or cannot be derived from disclosure in the simplified prospectus, provide as much disclosure as is possible about the management fees to be paid by securityholders, including the highest possible rate or range of those management fees.*

8.2 — Illustrations of Different Purchase Options

(1) Under the sub-heading "Impact of Sales Charges" provide information, substantially in the form of the following table, concerning the amount of fees payable by an investor under the available purchase options and introduced using substantially the following words:

> The following table shows the amount of fees that you would have to pay under the different purchase options available to you if you made an investment of $1,000 in the Fund, if you held that investment for one, three, five or ten years and redeemed immediately before the end of that period.

	At Time of Purchase	1 Year	3 Years	5 Years	10 Years
Sales Charge Option	$..........	—	—	—	—
Redemption Charge Option[1]	—	$..........	$..........	$..........	$..........
No Load Option	—	—			
[Other purchase options]	$..........	$..........	$..........	$..........	$..........

Notes:

(1) *Redemption charges may apply only if you redeem your [units/shares] in a particular year. Redemption charges are shown under "Fees and Expenses" above.*

(2) In preparing the table contemplated by this Item, assume, in determining the fees paid under the sales charge option, that

    (a) the maximum sales commission disclosed in the simplified prospectus is paid by the investor; and

    (b) if the mutual fund has a deferred sales charge option in which the amount paid by an investor at the time of a redemption of securities is based upon the net asset value of those securities at that time, an annual return of five percent since time of purchase, and disclose that assumption in a footnote to the table.

Item 9 — Dealer Compensation

9.1 — General

Provide, under the heading "Dealer Compensation", the disclosure of sales practices and equity interests required by sections 8.1 and 8.2 of National Instrument 81-105.

INSTRUCTIONS:

    (1) Briefly state the compensation paid and the sales practices followed by the members of the organization of the mutual fund in a concise and explicit manner, without explaining the requirements and parameters for permitted compensation contained in National Instrument 81-105.

    (2) For example, if the manager of the mutual fund pays an up-front sales commission to participating dealers, so state and include the range of commissions paid. If the manager permits participating dealers to retain the sales commissions paid by investors as compensation, so state and include the range of commissions that can be retained. If the manager or another member of the mutual fund's organization pays trailing commissions, so state and provide an explanation of the basis of calculation of these commissions and the range of the rates of such commissions. If the mutual fund organization from time to time pays the permitted marketing expenses of participating dealers on a co-operative basis, so state. If the mutual fund organization from time to time holds educational conferences that sales representatives of participating dealers may attend or from time to time pays certain of the expenses incurred by participating dealers in holding educational conferences for sales representatives, so state.

    (3) If the members of the organization of the mutual funds follow any other sales practices permitted by National Instrument 81-105, briefly describe these sales practices.

    (4) Include a brief summary of the equity interests between the members of the organization of the mutual fund and participating dealers and representatives as required by section 8.2 of National Instrument 81-105. This disclosure may be provided by means of a diagram or table.

9.2 — Dealer Compensation from Management Fees

Disclose, under the heading "Dealer Compensation from Management Fees", the approximate percentage obtained from a fraction

    (a) the numerator of which is the aggregate amount of cash paid to registered dealers in the last completed financial year of the manager of the mutual fund, for payments made

        (i) by

            (A) the manager of the mutual fund, or

            (B) an affiliate of the manager,

        (ii) in order to

            (A) pay compensation to registered dealers in connection with the distribution of securities of the mutual fund or mutual funds that are members of the same mutual fund family as the mutual fund, or

            (B) pay for any marketing, fund promotion or educational activity in connection with the mutual fund or mutual funds that are members of the same mutual fund family as the mutual fund; and

    (b) the denominator of which is the aggregate amount of management fees received by the managers of the mutual fund and all other mutual funds in the same mutual fund family as the mutual fund in the last completed financial year of the manager.

Part 8: MUTUAL FUNDS

INSTRUCTION:

(1) The disclosure presented under this Item should be described as information about the approximate percentage of management fees paid by mutual funds in the same family as the mutual fund that were used to fund commissions or other promotional activities of the mutual fund family in the most recently completed financial year of the manager of the mutual fund.

(2) The calculations made under this Item should take into account the payment of sales and trailing commissions and the costs of participation in co-operative marketing, fund promotion and educational conferences.

(3) Amounts paid out by a mutual fund organization as sales commissions should be netted against amounts received from deferred sales charges.

Item 10 — Income Tax Considerations for Investors

(1) Briefly describe under the heading "Income Tax Considerations for Investors" the income tax consequences for investors of income and capital gains distributions made by the mutual fund, as well as of the gains or losses that occur on the disposition of securities of the mutual fund by the investor.

(2) This description shall explain the different tax treatment applicable to mutual fund securities held in a registered tax plan as compared to mutual fund securities held in non-registered accounts.

(3) Describe the impact of the mutual fund's distribution policy on a taxable investor who acquires securities of the mutual fund late in a calendar year.

(4) If material, describe the potential impact of the mutual fund's anticipated portfolio turnover rate on a taxable investor.

(5) Describe how the adjusted cost base of a security of a mutual fund can be calculated by those investors holding outside a registered tax plan.

INSTRUCTION:

(1) If management fees are paid directly by investors, describe generally the income tax consequences to taxable investors of this arrangement.

(2) Subsection (2) is particularly relevant for investors who hold their mutual fund investments through RRSPs, if they have invested in a mutual fund that requires management fees to be paid directly by the investors. Detailed disclosure of the tax consequences of this arrangement on those investors should be made by such mutual funds.

Item 11 — Statement of Rights

Provide a brief explanation, under the heading "What are your Legal Rights?", of an investor's statutory rights of rescission and damages, including the right of action for misrepresentations contained in the simplified prospectus and in any documents incorporated by reference into the simplified prospectus, in substantially the following words:

Securities legislation in some provinces and territories gives you the right to withdraw from an agreement to buy mutual funds within two business days of receiving the Simplified Prospectus or Fund Facts, or to cancel your purchase within 48 hours of receiving confirmation of your order.

Securities legislation in some provinces and territories also allows you to cancel an agreement to buy mutual fund [units/shares] and get your money back, or to make a claim for damages, if the Simplified Prospectus, Annual Information Form, Fund Facts or financial statements misrepresent any facts about the fund. These rights must usually be exercised within certain time limits.

For more information, refer to the securities legislation of your province or territory or consult a lawyer.

.

Item 12 — Additional Information

(1) Provide any specific disclosure required or permitted to be disclosed in a prospectus under securities legislation or by an order or ruling of the securities regulatory authority pertaining to the mutual fund that is not otherwise required to be disclosed by this Form.

(2) This Item does not apply to the requirements of securities legislation that are form requirements for a prospectus.

INSTRUCTIONS:

(1) An example of a provision of securities legislation that may be relevant to this Item is the requirement contained in the conflict of interest provisions of the Canadian securities legislation of a number of jurisdictions to the effect that a mutual fund shall not make an investment in respect of which a related person will receive any fee or compensation except for fees paid pursuant to a contract disclosed in, among other things, a prospectus. Another example is the requirement of some jurisdictions that certain statements be included in a simplified prospectus of a mutual fund with a non-Canadian manager.

(2) For a single SP, provide this disclosure either under this Item or under Item 14 of Part B of this Form, whichever is more appropriate.

(3) For a multiple SP, this disclosure should be provided under this Item if the disclosure pertains to all of the mutual funds described in the document. If the disclosure does not pertain to all of those funds, the disclosure should be provided in the fund-specific disclosure required or permitted under Item 14 of Part B of this Form.

Item 13 — Part B Introduction

(1) For a multiple SP, at the option of the mutual fund, include in a separate section any explanatory information that would otherwise be repeated identically in each Part B section of the document.

(2) Any information included in an introductory section under subsection (1) may be omitted elsewhere in the Part B section of the document.

INSTRUCTION:

(1) *This Item may be used to avoid the need for repetition of standard information in each Part B section of a multiple SP.*

(2) Examples of the type of information that may be moved to an introductory section from other parts of the Part B section are:

(a) *definitions or explanations of terms used in each Part B section, such as "portfolio turnover rate" and "management expense ratio"; and*

(b) *discussion or explanations of the tables or charts that are required in each Part B section of the document.*

(3) *A similar Item is contained in Item 3 of Part B of this Form. A mutual fund organization may include this section either at the end of the Part A section of the multiple SP or at the beginning of the Part B section, at its option.*

Item 14 — Back Cover

(1) State on the back cover the name of the mutual fund or funds included in the document or the mutual fund family, as well as the name, address and telephone number of the manager of the mutual fund or funds.

(2) State, in substantially the following words:

- Additional information about the Fund[s] is available in the Fund['s/s'] Annual Information Form, Fund Facts, management reports of fund performance and financial statements. These documents are incorporated by reference into this Simplified Prospectus, which means that they legally form part of this document just as if they were printed as a part of this document.

- You can get a copy of these documents at your request, and at no cost, by calling [toll-free/collect] [insert toll-free telephone number or telephone number where collect calls are accepted, as required by section 3.4 of the Instrument], or from your dealer or by e-mail at [insert e-mail address].

- These documents and other information about the Fund[s], such as information circulars and material contracts, are also available [on the [insert name of mutual fund manager] internet site at [insert fund's Internet site] or] or at www.sedar.com.

(3) For a multiple SP in which the Part A section is bound separately from the Part B sections, state, in substantially the following words:

A complete simplified prospectus for the mutual funds listed on this cover consists of this document and any additional disclosure document that provides specific information about the mutual funds in which you are investing. This document provides general information applicable to all of the [name of mutual fund family] funds. When you request a simplified prospectus, you must be provided with the additional disclosure document.

Part B — Fund-Specific Information

Item 1 — General

(1) For a multiple SP in which the Part B sections are bound separately from the Part A section, include at the bottom of each page of a Part B section a footer in substantially the following words and in a type size consistent with the rest of the document:

This document provides specific information about [name of Fund]. It should be read in conjunction with the rest of the simplified prospectus of the [name of mutual fund family] dated [insert date]. This document and the document that provides general information about [name of mutual fund family] together constitute the simplified prospectus.

(2) If the Part B section is an amended and restated document, add to the footer required by subsection (1) a statement that the document has been amended and restated on [insert date].

Item 2 — Introductory

2.1 — For a Single SP

Include at the top of the first page of the Part B section of the simplified prospectus, the heading "Specific Information about the [name of Fund]".

2.2 — For a Multiple SP in which the Part A section and the Part B sections are bound together

Include

(a) at the top of the first page of the first Part B section in the document, the heading "Specific Information about Each of the Mutual Funds Described in this Document"; and

(b) at the top of each page of a Part B section of the document, a heading consisting of the name of the mutual fund described on that page.

2.3 — For a Multiple SP in which the Part A section is bound separately from the Part B sections

Include at the top of each page of a Part B section of the document, a heading consisting of the name of the mutual fund described on that page.

Item 3 — General Information

(1) For a multiple SP, at the option of the mutual fund, include in an introductory section any explanatory information that would otherwise be repeated identically in each Part B section of the document.

(2) Any information included in an introductory section under subsection (1) may be omitted elsewhere in the Part B section of the document.

INSTRUCTIONS:

(1) *See the Instruction to Item 13 of Part A of this Form.*

(2) *If the disclosure contemplated by this Item is included in Part A of the multiple SP under Item 13 of Part A of this Form, include in the introduction section of each Part B section of the multiple SP a cross-reference to where this disclosure is located in the Part A section of the multiple SP.*

Item 4 — Organization and Management Details

(1) For a single SP, under the heading "Organization and Management of the [name of mutual fund]", provide information about the manager, trustee, portfolio adviser, principal distributor, custodian, registrar, auditor and securities lending agent of the mutual fund in the form of a diagram or table.

(2) For each entity listed in the diagram or table, briefly describe the services provided by that entity and the relationship of that entity to the manager.

(3) For each entity listed in the diagram or table, other than the manager of the mutual fund, provide the municipality and the province or country where it principally provides its services to the mutual funds. Provide the complete municipal address for the manager of the mutual fund.

(3.1) Under a separate sub-heading "Independent Review Committee" in the diagram or table, briefly describe the independent review committee of the mutual funds, including

- an appropriate summary of its mandate,

- its composition,

- that it prepares at least annually a report of its activities for securityholders which is available on the [mutual fund's/mutual fund family's] Internet site at [insert mutual fund's Internet site address], or at securityholders request at no cost, by contacting the [mutual fund/mutual fund family] at [insert mutual fund's /mutual fund family's e-mail address], and

- that additional information about the independent review committee, including the names of the members, is available in the mutual fund's Annual Information Form.

(4) At the option of the mutual fund, include under a separate sub-heading, details of the manager of the mutual fund, including the history and background of the manager and any overall investment strategy or approach used by the manager in connection with its mutual funds.

(4.1) If a mutual fund holds in accordance with section 2.5 of National Instrument 81-102 *Investment Funds* securities of another mutual fund that is managed by the same manager or an affiliate or associate of the manager, disclose

(a) that the securities of the other mutual fund held by the mutual fund shall not be voted; and

(b) if applicable, that the manager may arrange for the securities of the other mutual fund to be voted by the beneficial holders of the securities of the mutual fund.

(5) Follow the requirements and instructions of Item 5 of Part A of this Form in connection with the diagram or table.

Item 5 — Fund Details

Under the heading "Fund Details", disclose, in a table

    (a) the type of mutual fund that the mutual fund is best characterized as;

    (b) the date on which the mutual fund was started;

    (c) the nature of the securities offered by the simplified prospectus;

    (d) whether the mutual fund is eligible as an investment for registered retirement savings plans, registered retirement income funds or deferred profit sharing plans;

    (e) [repealed]

    (f) if this information is not contained in the table required by Item 8.1 of Part A of this Form

        (i) the amount of the management fee, including any performance or incentive fee, charged to the mutual fund; and

        (ii) details concerning the operating expenses paid by the mutual fund contemplated by Instruction (3) of Item 8.1 of Part A of this Form; and

        (iii) the amount of the fees and expenses payable in connection with the independent review committee, charged to the mutual fund; and

    (g) any information required by subsection (5) of Item 5 of Part A of this Form to be contained in Part B.

INSTRUCTIONS:

(1) *In disclosing the date on which the mutual fund started, use the date on which the securities of the mutual fund first became available to the public, which will be on, or about, the date of the issuance of the first receipt for a prospectus of the mutual fund. For a mutual fund that formerly offered its securities privately, disclose this fact.*

(2) *If the mutual fund pays a fee that is determined by the performance of the mutual fund, the disclosure required by paragraph 7.1(c) of National Instrument 81-102 to be described in a simplified prospectus of the mutual fund should be included in a footnote to the description of the incentive fee in the table.*

(3) *Examples of types of mutual funds that could be listed in response to paragraph (a) are money market, equity, bond or balanced funds related, if appropriate, to a geographical region, or any other description that accurately identifies the type of mutual fund*

(4) *If the rights attached to the securities being offered are materially limited or qualified by those attached to any other class or series of securities of the mutual fund or if another class or series of securities of the mutual fund ranks ahead of or equally with the securities being offered, include, as part of the disclosure provided in response to paragraph (c), information regarding those other securities that will enable investors to understand the rights attaching to the securities being offered.*

(5) *In providing the disclosure contemplated by paragraph (f), provide any disclosure required by, and follow, the Instructions to Item 8.1 of Part A of this Form.*

Item 6 — Fundamental Investment Objectives

(1) Set out under the heading "What Does the Fund Invest In?" and under the sub-heading "Investment Objectives" the fundamental investment objectives of the mutual fund, including information that describes the fundamental nature of the mutual fund, or the fundamental features of the mutual fund, that distinguish it from other mutual funds.

(2) Describe the nature of any securityholder or other approval that may be required in order to change the fundamental investment objectives of the mutual fund and any of the material investment strategies to be used to achieve those investment objectives.

(3) Describe any restrictions on investments adopted by the mutual funds, beyond what is required under securities legislation, that pertain to the fundamental nature of the mutual fund.

(4) If the mutual fund purports to arrange a guarantee or insurance in order to protect all or some of the principal amount of an investment in the mutual fund, include this fact as a fundamental investment objective of the mutual fund and

    (a) identify the person or company providing the guarantee or insurance;

    (b) provide the material terms of the guarantee or insurance, including the maturity date of the guarantee or insurance;

    (c) if applicable, state that the guarantee or insurance does not apply to the amount of any redemptions before the maturity date of the guarantee or before the death of the securityholder and that redemptions before that date would be based on the net asset value of the mutual fund at the time; and

    (d) modify any other disclosure required by this section appropriately.

(5) For an index mutual fund,

    (a) disclose the name or names of the permitted index or permitted indices on which the investments of the index mutual fund are based,

    (b) briefly describe the nature of that permitted index or those permitted indices.

INSTRUCTIONS:

(1) *State the type or types of securities, such as money market instruments, bonds, equity securities or securities of another mutual fund, in which the mutual fund will primarily invest under normal market conditions.*

(2) *If the mutual fund primarily invests, or intends to primarily invest, or if its name implies that it will primarily invest*

    (a) in a particular type of issuer, such as foreign issuers, small capitalization issuers or issuers located in emerging market countries;

    (b) in a particular geographic location or industry segment; or

    (c) in portfolio assets other than securities,

the mutual fund's fundamental investment objectives should so indicate.

(3) *If a particular investment strategy is an essential aspect of the mutual fund, as evidenced by the name of the mutual fund or the manner in which the mutual fund is marketed, disclose this strategy as an investment objective. This instruction would be applicable, for example, to a mutual fund that described itself as an "asset allocation fund" or a "mutual fund that invests primarily through the use of derivatives".*

Item 7 — Investment Strategies

(1) Describe under the heading "What Does The Fund Invest In?" and under the sub-heading "Investment Strategies"

    (a) the principal investment strategies that the mutual fund intends to use in achieving its investment objectives; and

    (b) the process by which the mutual fund's portfolio adviser selects securities for the fund's portfolio, including any investment approach, philosophy, practices or techniques used by the portfolio adviser or any particular style of portfolio management that the portfolio adviser intends to follow.

    (c) if the mutual fund may hold securities of other mutual funds,

        (i) whether the mutual fund intends to purchase securities of, or enter into specified derivative transactions for which the underlying interest is based on the securities of, other mutual funds;

        (ii) whether or not the other mutual funds may be managed by the manager or an affiliate or associate of the manager of the mutual fund;

        (iii) what percentage of the net asset value of the mutual fund is dedicated to the investment in the securities of, or the entering into of specified derivative transactions for which the underlying interest is based on the securities of, other mutual funds; and

        (iv) the process or criteria used to select the other mutual funds.

(2) Indicate what types of securities, other than those held by the mutual fund in accordance with its fundamental investment objectives, may form part of the mutual fund's portfolio assets under normal market conditions.

(3) If the mutual fund intends to use derivatives

    (a) for hedging purposes only, state that the mutual fund may use derivatives for hedging purposes only;

    (b) for non-hedging purposes, or for hedging and non-hedging purposes, briefly describe

        (i) how derivatives are or will be used in conjunction with other securities to achieve the mutual fund's investment objectives,

        (ii) the types of derivatives expected to be used and give a brief description of the nature of each type, and

        (iii) the limits of the mutual fund's use of derivatives.

(4) State whether any, and if so what proportion, of the assets of the mutual fund may or will be invested in foreign securities.

(5) If the mutual fund is not a money market fund, and intends to engage in active and frequent trading of portfolio securities as a principal investment strategy to achieve its investment objectives such that the portfolio turnover rate of the mutual fund is expected to be more than 70 percent, describe

    (a) the tax consequences to securityholders of an active portfolio turnover, and

    (b) how the tax consequences of, or trading costs associated with, the mutual fund's portfolio turnover may affect the mutual fund's performance.

(6) If the mutual fund may depart temporarily from its fundamental investment objectives as a result of adverse market, economic, political or other considerations, disclose any temporary defensive tactics the mutual fund's portfolio adviser may use or intends to use in response to such conditions.

(7) Describe any restrictions on investments adopted by the mutual fund, beyond what is required under securities legislation, that do not pertain to the fundamental nature of the mutual fund.

(8) If the mutual fund intends to enter into securities lending, repurchase or reverse repurchase transactions under sections 2.12, 2.13 or 2.14 of National Instrument 81-102

    (a) state that the mutual fund may enter into securities lending, repurchase or reverse repurchase transactions; and

    (b) briefly describe

        (i) how those transactions are or will be entered into in conjunction with other strategies and investments of the mutual fund to achieve the mutual fund's investment objectives;

        (ii) the types of those transactions to be entered into and give a brief description of the nature of each type, and

        (iii) the limits of the mutual fund's entering into of those transactions.

(9) For an index mutual fund,

    (a) for the 12 month period immediately preceding the date of the simplified prospectus,

        (i) indicate whether one or more securities represented more than 10 percent of the permitted index or premitted indices;

        (ii) identify that security or those securities; and

        (iii) disclose the maximum percentage of the permitted index or permitted indices that the security or securities represented in the 12 month period; and

    (b) disclose the maximum percentage of the permitted index or permitted indices that the security or securities referred to in paragraph (a) represented at the most recent date for which that information is available.

(10) If the mutual fund intends to sell securities short under section 2.6.1 of National Instrument 81-102 *Investment Funds*,

    (a) state that the mutual fund may sell securities short; and

    (b) briefly describe

        (i) the short selling process, and

        (ii) how short sales of securities are or will be entered into in conjunction with other strategies and investments of the mutual fund to achieve the mutual fund's investment objectives.

INSTRUCTION:

A mutual fund may, in responding to this Item, provide a discussion of the general investment approach or philosophy followed by the portfolio adviser of the mutual fund.

Item 8 — [Repealed]

Item 9 — Risks

(1) Set out specific information concerning any material risks associated with an investment in the mutual fund, other than those risks previously discussed in response to Item 4 of Part A of this Form, under the heading "What are the Risks of Investing in the Fund?".

(1.1) If securities of a mutual fund representing more than 10% of the net asset value of the mutual fund are held by a securityholder, including another mutual fund, the mutual fund must disclose

    (a) the percentage of the net asset value of the mutual fund that those securities represent as at a date within 30 days of the date of the simplified prospectus of the mutual fund, and

    (b) the risks associated with a possible redemption requested by the securityholder.

(1.2) If the mutual fund may hold securities of a foreign mutual fund in accordance with subsection 2.5(3)(b) of National Instrument 81-102 *Investment Funds*, disclose the risks associated with that investment.

(2) For a money market fund, include disclosure to the effect that although the mutual fund intends to maintain a constant price for its securities, there is no guarantee that the price will not go up and down.

(3) Include specific cross-references to the risks described in response to paragraph 1(b) of Item 4 of Part A of this Form that are applicable to the mutual fund.

(4) If the mutual fund offers more than one class or series of securities, disclose the risks that the investment performance, expenses or liabilities of one class or series may affect the value of the securities of another class or series, if applicable.

(5) For an index mutual fund, disclose that the mutual fund may, in basing its investment decisions on one or more permitted indices, have more of its net asset value invested in one or more issuers than is usually permitted for mutual funds, and disclose the risks associated with that fact, including the possible effect of that fact on the liquidity and diversification of the mutual fund, its ability to satisfy redemption requests and on the volatility of the mutual fund.

(6) If, at any time during the 12 month period immediately preceding the date that is 30 days before the date of the simplified prospectus, more than 10 percent of the net asset value of a mutual fund were invested in the securities of an issuer, other than a government security or a security issued by a clearing corporation, disclose

(a) the name of the issuer and the securities;

(b) the maximum percentage of the net asset value of the mutual fund that securities of that issuer represented during the 12 month period; and

(c) disclose the risks associated with these matters, including the possible or actual effect of that fact on the liquidity and diversification of the mutual fund, its ability to satisfy redemption requests and on the volatility of the mutual fund.

(7) As applicable, describe the risks associated with the mutual fund entering into

(a) derivative transactions for non-hedging purposes;

(b) securities lending, repurchase or reverse repurchase transactions; and

(c) short sales of securities.

INSTRUCTIONS:

(1) *Consider the mutual fund's portfolio investments as a whole.*

(2) *Provide the disclosure in the context of the mutual fund's fundamental investment objectives and investment strategies, outlining the risks associated with any particular aspect of those fundamental investment objectives and investment strategies.*

(3) *Include a discussion of general market, political, market sector, liquidity, interest rate, foreign currency, diversification, credit, legal and operational risks, as appropriate*

(4) *Include a brief discussion of general investment risks, such as specific company developments, stock market conditions, general economic and financial conditions in those countries where the investments of the mutual fund are listed for trading, applicable to the particular mutual fund.*

(5) [Repealed]

(6) *In responding to subsection (6) above, it is necessary to disclose only that at a time during the 12 month period referred to, more than 10 percent of the net assets of the mutual fund were invested in the securities of an issuer. Other than the maximum percentage required to be disclosed under paragraph (6)(b), the mutual fund is not required to provide particulars or a summary of any such occurrences.*

Item 9.1 — Investment Risk Classification Methodology

(1) Briefly describe the methodology used by the manager for the purpose of identifying the investment risk level of the mutual fund as required by Item 5(2) in Part I of 81-101F3.

(2) State how frequently the investment risk level of the mutual fund is reviewed.

(3) Disclose that the methodology that the manager uses to identify the investment risk level of the mutual fund is available on request, at no cost, by calling [toll-free/collect call telephone number] or by writing to [address].

INSTRUCTION:

Include a brief description of the formulas, methods or criteria used by the manager of the mutual fund in identifying the investment risk level of the mutual fund.

Item 10 — Suitability

Provide a brief statement of the suitability of the mutual fund for particular investors under the heading "Who Should Invest in this Fund?", describing either or both of the characteristics of the investor for whom the mutual fund may or may not be an appropriate investment, and the portfolios for which the mutual fund is suited or for which the mutual fund should not be used.

INSTRUCTIONS:

(1) *In responding to the disclosure required by this Item, indicate the level of investor risk tolerance that would be appropriate for investment in the mutual fund.*

(1.1) Briefly describe how the manager has determined the level of investor risk tolerance that would be appropriate for investment in the mutual fund.

(2) If the mutual fund is particularly unsuitable for certain types of investors or for certain types of investment portfolios, emphasize this aspect of the mutual fund, and disclose both the types of investors who should not invest in the mutual fund, with regard to investments on both a short and long term basis, and the types of portfolios that should not invest in the mutual fund. Conversely, it might be appropriate to discuss whether the mutual fund is particularly suitable for particular investment objectives.

Item 11 — [Repealed]

Item 12 — Distribution Policy

State under the heading "Distribution Policy" whether distributions are made by the mutual fund in cash or reinvested in securities of the mutual fund, and indicate when distributions are made.

Item 13 — Financial Highlights

13.1 — [Repealed]

13.2 — Illustration of Fund Expenses Indirectly Borne by Investors

(1) Under the heading "Fund Expenses Indirectly Borne by Investors", provide an example of the share of the expenses of the mutual fund indirectly borne by investors, containing the information and based on the assumptions described in (2).

(2) The information to be provided under this Item shall be an investor's cumulative proportional share of the fees and expenses paid by the mutual fund, in dollars, over a period of one, three, five and 10 years, assuming

    (a) an initial investment of $1,000;

    (b) a total annual return of the mutual fund of five percent in each year, calculated in accordance with section 15 of National Instrument 81-102;

    (c) a management expense ratio of the mutual fund the same throughout the 10 year period as they were in the last completed financial year of the mutual fund, excluding any performance fees paid in a year which would not have been paid had the mutual fund earned a total return of five percent in that last completed financial year.

(3) Provide an introduction to the disclosure that explains that the disclosure is intended to help an investor compare the cost of investing in the mutual fund with the cost of investing in other mutual funds, shows the amount of fees and expenses paid by the mutual fund that are indirectly borne by an investor, and describes the assumptions used.

(4) The management expense ratio used in calculating the disclosure provided under this Item must be the management expense ratio calculated in accordance with Part 15 of National Instrument 81-106 *Investment Fund Continuous Disclosure*.

(5) Provide a cross-reference to the disclosure provided under Item 8 of Part A of this Form for information about fees and expenses paid directly by the investor which are not included in the calculation of management expense ratio.

Item 14 — Additional Information

(1) Provide any specific disclosure required or permitted to be disclosed in a prospectus under securities legislation or by an order or ruling of the securities regulatory authority pertaining to the mutual fund that is not otherwise required to be disclosed by this Form.

(2) This Item does not apply to requirements of securities legislation that are form requirements for a prospectus.

INSTRUCTIONS:

(1) See Instruction (1) to Item 12 of Part A of this Form for examples of disclosure that might appropriately be made under these Items

(2) For a simplified prospectus that is not part of a multiple SP, provide this disclosure either under this Item or under Item 12 of Part A of this Form, whichever is more appropriate

(3) For a multiple SP, this disclosure should be provided under this Item if the disclosure does not pertain to all of the mutual funds described in the document. If the disclosure pertains to all of those funds, the disclosure should be provided in the fund-specific disclosure required or permitted under Item 12 of Part A of this Form.

Form 81-101F2 — Contents of Annual Information Form

Table of Contents

General Instructions

    Item 1: Front Cover Disclosure
    Item 2: Table of Contents
    Item 3: Name, Formation and History of the Mutual Fund
    Item 4: Investment Restrictions
    Item 5: Description of Securities Offered by the Mutual Fund
    Item 6: Valuation of Portfolio Securities

Item 7: Calculation of Net Asset Value
Item 8: Purchases and Switches
Item 9: Redemption of Securities
Item 10: Responsibility for Mutual Fund Operations
Item 11: Conflicts of Interest
Item 12: Fund Governance
Item 13: Fees and Expenses
Item 14: Income Tax Considerations
Item 15: Remuneration of Directors, Officers and Trustees
Item 16: Material Contracts
Item 17: Legal and Administrative Proceedings
Item 18: Other Material Information
Item 19: Certificate of the Mutual Fund
Item 20: Certificate of the Manager of the Mutual Fund
Item 21: Certificate of Each Promoter of the Mutual Fund
Item 22: Certificate of the Principal Distributor of the Mutual Fund
Item 23: Exemptions and Approvals
Item 24: Back Cover

General Instructions

General

(1) *This Form describes the disclosure that is required in an annual information form of a mutual fund. Each Item of this Form outlines disclosure requirements. Instructions to help you provide this disclosure are printed in italic type.*

(2) *Terms defined in National Instrument 81-101 Mutual Fund Prospectus Disclosure, National Instrument 81-102 Investment Funds or National Instrument 81-105 Mutual Fund Sales Practices and used in this Form have the meanings that they have in those national instruments. However, subsection 1.3(3) of National Instrument 81-102 does not apply to this Form.*

(3) *An annual information form is intended to supplement the information contained in the related simplified prospectus. Information contained in the related simplified prospectus need not be repeated except as required to make the annual information form comprehensible as an independent document. Generally speaking, all of the disclosure required to be provided in connection with a particular requirement of Form 81-101F1 ("the SP Form") in order to satisfy statutory disclosure requirements should be contained in the simplified prospectus. For some Items, it may be appropriate to expand in the annual information form on matters discussed in the simplified prospectus; for instance, a mutual fund organization may wish to describe in an annual information form some of its optional services in more detail than in the simplified prospectus. Generally speaking, however, an annual information form is intended to provide disclosure about different matters than those discussed in the simplified prospectus, which may be of assistance or interest to some investors.*

(4) *Unless otherwise required by this Form, information may be presented in a different format and style in an annual information form than in a simplified prospectus. An annual information form is required by National Instrument 81-101 to be presented in a format that assists in readability and comprehension. This Form generally does not mandate the use of a specific format to achieve this goal and mutual funds are encouraged to use, as appropriate, tables, captions, bullet points or other organizational techniques that assist in presenting the disclosure clearly.*

(5) *An annual information form may contain photographs and artwork only if they are relevant to the business of the mutual fund, mutual fund family or members of the organization of the mutual fund and are not misleading.*

(6) *As with a simplified prospectus, an annual information form is to be prepared using plain language. Reference should be made to Part 3 of Companion Policy 81-101CP for a discussion concerning plain language and presentation.*

(7) *Any footnotes provided for under any Item of this Form may be deleted if the substance of the footnotes is otherwise provided.*

Contents of an Annual Information Form

(8) *An annual information form pertains to one mutual fund but, unlike a simplified prospectus, is not required to be divided into a discrete Part A section, pertaining to general disclosure, and a Part B section, pertaining to fund-specific disclosure.*

(9) *It is not necessary to disclose the Items required by this Form in an annual information form in any particular order or under any particular heading. This is unlike the rule for a simplified prospectus, which provides that information contained in a simplified prospectus must be in the order and under the headings required by the SP Form.*

Consolidation of Annual Information Forms into a Multiple AIF

(10) *Section 5.4 of National Instrument 81-101 requires an annual information form to be consolidated with one or more other annual information forms into a multiple AIF if the related simplified prospectuses are consolidated into a multiple SP. As the Instrument does not prevent the consolidation of annual information forms even if the related simplified prospectuses are not consolidated, a mutual fund organization may prepare one multiple AIF that pertains to all of its mutual funds, even if the simplified prospectuses for those mutual funds are not fully or even partially consolidated.*

(11) *Unlike the situation with a multiple SP, National Instrument 81-101 does not permit parts of a multiple AIF to be bound separately.*

(12) *Unlike the requirements for a multiple SP, there are no requirements that disclosure concerning each mutual fund described in a multiple AIF be organized in any particular manner or order. In particular, it is not necessary to use the catalogue approach required to be used in a*

multiple SP in which disclosure about individual mutual funds is required to be separately presented. Information may be presented separately for each mutual fund, or consolidated, at the option of the mutual fund organization.

(13) *The requirements in this Form generally speak of "a mutual fund". These requirements apply to each mutual fund to which a multiple AIF pertains.*

Multi-Class Mutual Funds

(14) *A mutual fund that has more than one class or series that are referable to the same portfolio may treat each class or series as a separate mutual fund for purposes of this Form, or may combine disclosure of one or more of the classes or series in one annual information form. If disclosure pertaining to more than one class or series is combined in one annual information form, separate disclosure in response to each Item in this Form must be provided for each class or series unless the responses would be identical for each class or series.*

(15) *As provided in National Instrument 81-102, a section, party, class or series of a class of securities of a mutual fund that is referable to a separate portfolio of assets is considered to be a separate mutual fund. Those principles are applicable to National Instrument 81-101 and this Form.*

Item 1 — Front Cover Disclosure

1.1 — For a Single AIF

(1) Indicate on the front cover whether the document is a preliminary annual information form, a *pro forma* annual information form or an annual information form.

(2) Indicate on the front cover the name of the mutual fund to which the annual information form pertains. If the mutual fund has more than one class or series of securities, indicate the name of each of those classes or series covered in the annual information form.

(3) Despite securities legislation, state on the front cover of a preliminary annual information form the following:

> A copy of this annual information form has been filed with [the securities authority(ies) in each of/certain of the provinces/provinces and territories of Canada] but has not yet become final for the purpose of a distribution. Information contained in this annual information form may not be complete and may have to be amended. The securities described in this annual information form may not be sold to you until a receipt for the annual information form is obtained by the mutual fund from the securities regulatory [authority(ies)].

(4) If a commercial copy of the preliminary annual information form is prepared, print the legend referred to in subsection (3) in red ink.

(5) For a preliminary annual information form or annual information form, indicate the date of the document, which shall be the date of the certificates for the document. This date shall be within three business days of the date it is filed with the securities regulatory authority. Write the date of the document in full, writing the name of the month in words. A *pro forma* annual information form need not be dated, but may reflect the anticipated date of the annual information form.

(6) State, in substantially the following words:

> No securities regulatory authority has expressed an opinion about these [units/shares] and it is an offence to claim otherwise.

INSTRUCTION

Complete the bracketed information in subsection (3) above by

> *(a) inserting the name of each jurisdiction of Canada in which the mutual fund intends to offer securities under the prospectus;*
>
> *(b) stating that the filing has been made in each of the provinces of Canada or each of the provinces and territories of Canada; or*
>
> *(c) identifying the filing jurisdictions of Canada by exception (i.e. every province of Canada or every province and territory of Canada, except [excluded jurisdictions]).*

1.2 — For a Multiple AIF

(1) Indicate on the front cover whether the document is a preliminary annual information form, a *pro forma* annual information form or an annual information form for each of the mutual funds to which the document pertains.

(2) Indicate on the front cover the names of the mutual funds and, at the option of the mutual funds, the name of the mutual fund family to which the document pertains. If the mutual fund has more than one class or series of securities, indicate the name of each of those classes or series covered in the document.

(3) Despite securities legislation, state on the front cover of a document that contains a preliminary annual information form the following:

> A copy of this annual information form has been filed with [the securities authority(ies) in each of/certain of the provinces/provinces and territories of Canada] but has not yet become final for the purpose of a distribution. Information contained in this annual information form may not be complete and may have to be amended. The securities described in this annual information form may not be sold to you until a receipt for the annual information form is obtained by the mutual fund from the securities regulatory [authority(ies)].

(4) If a commercial copy of a document that contains a preliminary annual information form is prepared, print the legend referred to in subsection (3) in red ink.

(5) If the document contains a preliminary annual information form or annual information form, indicate the date of the document, which shall be the date of the certificates for the document. This date shall be within three business days of the date it is filed with the securities regulatory authority. Write the date of the document in full, writing the name of the month in words. A document that is a *pro forma* multiple AIF need not be dated, but may reflect the anticipated date of the multiple AIF.

(6) State, in substantially the following words:

> No securities regulatory authority has expressed an opinion about these [units/shares] and it is an offence to claim otherwise.

INSTRUCTION

Complete the bracketed information in subsection (3) above by

 (a) inserting the name of each jurisdiction of Canada in which the mutual fund intends to offer securities under the prospectus;

 (b) stating that the filing has been made in each of the provinces of Canada or each of the provinces and territories of Canada; or

 (c) identifying the filing jurisdictions of Canada by exception (i.e. every province of Canada or every province and territory of Canada, except [excluded jurisdictions]).

Item 2 — Table of Contents

Include a table of contents.

Item 3 — Name, Formation and History of the Mutual Fund

(1) State the full name of the mutual fund and the address of its head or registered office.

(2) State the laws under which the mutual fund was formed and the date and manner of its formation.

(3) Identify the constating documents of the mutual fund and, if material, state whether the constating documents have been amended in the last 10 years and describe the amendments.

(4) If the mutual fund's name has been changed in the last 10 years, state the mutual fund's former name or names and the date on which it was changed.

(5) Disclose, and provide details about, any major events affecting the mutual fund in the last 10 years. Include information, if applicable, about

 (a) the mutual fund having participated in, or been formed from, an amalgamation or merger with one or more other mutual funds;

 (b) the mutual fund having participated in any reorganization or transfer of assets in which the securityholders of another issuer became securityholders of the mutual fund;

 (c) any changes in fundamental investment objectives or material investment strategies;

 (d) any changes in the portfolio adviser or changes in, or of control of, the manager; and

 (e) the mutual fund, before it filed a prospectus as a mutual fund, having existed as a closed-end investment fund, non-public mutual fund or other entity.

Item 4 — Investment Restrictions

(1) Include a statement to the effect that the mutual fund is subject to certain restrictions and practices contained in securities legislation, including National Instrument 81-102, which are designed in part to ensure that the investments of the mutual fund are diversified and relatively liquid and to ensure the proper administration of the mutual fund, and state that the mutual fund is managed in accordance with these restrictions and practices.

(2) If the mutual fund has received the approval of the securities regulatory authorities to vary any of the investment restrictions and practices contained in securities legislation, including National Instrument 81-102, provide details of the permitted variations.

(2.1) If the mutual fund has relied on the approval of the independent review committee and the relevant requirements of NI 81-107 to vary any of the investment restrictions and practices contained in securities legislation, including NI 81-102, provide details of the permitted variations.

(2.2) If the mutual fund has relied on the approval of the independent review committee to implement a reorganization with, or transfer of assets to, another mutual fund or to proceed with a change of auditor of the mutual fund as permitted by NI 81-102, provide details.

(3) Describe the nature of any securityholder or other approval that may be required in order to change the fundamental investment objectives and any of the material investment strategies to be used to achieve the investment objectives.

(4) State the restrictions on the investment objectives and strategies that arise out of any of the following matters:

 1. Whether the securities of the mutual fund are or will be a qualified investment within the meaning of the ITA for retirement savings plans, retirement income funds, education savings plans, deferred profit sharing plans or other plans registered under the ITA.

 2. Whether the securities of the mutual fund are or will be recognized as a registered investment within the meaning of the ITA.

(5) State whether the mutual fund has deviated in the last year from the rules under the ITA that apply to the status of its securities as

 (a) qualified investments within the meaning of the ITA for retirement savings plans, retirement income funds, education savings plans, deferred profit sharing plans or other plans registered under the ITA; or

 (b) registered investments within the meaning of the ITA.

(6) State the consequences of any deviation described in response to subsection (5).

Item 5 — Description of Securities Offered by the Mutual Fund

(1) State the description or the designation of securities, or the series or classes of securities, offered by the mutual fund under the related simplified prospectus and describe the securities or all material attributes and characteristics, including

 (a) dividend or distribution rights;

 (b) voting rights;

(c) liquidation or other rights upon the termination of the mutual fund;

(d) conversion rights;

(e) redemption rights; and

(f) provisions as to amendment of any of these rights or provisions.

(2) Describe the rights of securityholders to approve

(a) the matters set out in section 5.1 of National Instrument 81-102; and

(b) any matters provided for in the constating documents of the mutual fund.

Item 6 — Valuation of Portfolio Securities

(1) Describe the methods used to value the various types or classes of portfolio assets of the mutual fund and its liabilities for the purpose of calculating net asset value.

(1.1) If the valuation principles and practices established by the manager differ from Canadian GAAP, describe the differences.

(2) If the manager has discretion to deviate from the mutual fund's valuation practices described in subsection (1), disclose when and to what extent that discretion may be exercised and, if it has been exercised in the past three years, provide an example of how it has been exercised or, if it has not been exercised in the past three years, so state.

Item 7 — Calculation of Net Asset Value

(1) State that the issue and redemption price of securities of the mutual fund is based on the mutual fund's net asset value next determined after the receipt of a purchase order and a redemption order. Describe the method followed or to be followed by the mutual fund in determining the net asset value.

(2) State the frequency at which the net asset value is determined and the date and time of day at which it is determined.

(2.1) Describe the manner in which the net asset value and net asset value per security of the mutual fund will be made available to the public and state that the information will be available at no cost to the public.

(3) If a money market mutual fund intends to maintain a constant net asset value per security, disclose this intention and disclose how the mutual fund intends to maintain this constant net asset value.

Item 8 — Purchases and Switches

(1) Describe the procedure followed or to be followed by investors who desire to purchase securities of the mutual fund or switch them for securities of other mutual funds.

(2) State that the issue price of securities is based on the net asset value of a security of that class, or series of a class, next determined after the receipt by the mutual fund of the purchase order.

(3) Describe how the securities of the mutual fund are distributed. If sales are effected through a principal distributor, give brief details of any arrangements with the principal distributor.

(4) Describe all available purchase options and state, if applicable, that the choice of different purchase options requires the investor to pay different fees and expenses and, if applicable, that the choice of different purchase options affects the amount of compensation paid by a member of the organization of the mutual fund to the dealer.

(5) Disclose that a dealer may make provision in arrangements that it has with an investor that will require the investor to compensate the dealer for any losses suffered by the dealer in connection with a failed settlement of a purchase of securities of the mutual fund caused by the investor.

(6) For a mutual fund that is being sold on a best efforts basis, state whether the issue price will be fixed during the initial distribution period, and state when the mutual fund will begin issuing securities at the net asset value per security of the mutual fund.

Item 9 — Redemption of Securities

(1) Describe the procedures followed, or to be followed, by an investor who desires to redeem securities of the mutual fund, specifying the procedures to be followed and documents to be delivered before a redemption order pertaining to securities of the mutual fund is accepted by the mutual fund for processing and before payment of the proceeds of redemption is made by the mutual fund.

(2) State that the redemption price of the securities is based on the net asset value of a security of that class, or series of a class, next determined after the receipt by the mutual fund of the redemption order.

(3) Disclose that a dealer may make provision in arrangements that it has with an investor that will require the investor to compensate the dealer for any losses suffered by the dealer in connection with any failure of the investor to satisfy the requirements of the mutual fund or securities legislation for a redemption of securities of the mutual fund.

(4) Discuss the circumstances under which the mutual fund may suspend redemptions of the securities of the mutual fund.

Item 10 — Responsibility for Mutual Fund Operations

10.1 — General

Describe how each of the following aspects of the operations of the mutual fund are administered and who administers those functions:

(a) the management and administration of the mutual fund, including valuation services, fund accounting and securityholder records, other than the management of the portfolio assets;

(b) the management of the portfolio assets, including the provision of investment analysis or investment recommendations and the making of investment decisions;

(c) the purchase and sale of portfolio assets by the mutual fund and the making of brokerage arrangements relating to the portfolio assets;

(d) the distribution of the securities of the mutual fund;

(e) if the mutual fund is a trust, the trusteeship of the mutual fund;

(f) if the mutual fund is a corporation, the oversight of the affairs of the mutual fund by the directors of the mutual fund;

(g) the custodianship of the assets of the mutual fund; and

(h) the oversight of the manager of the mutual fund by the independent review committee.

INSTRUCTION:

The disclosure required under Item 10.1 may be provided separately from, or combined with, the detailed disclosure concerning the persons or companies that provide services to the mutual fund required by Items 10.2 through 10.10.

10.2 — Manager

(1) State the name, address, telephone number, e-mail address and, if applicable, website address of the manager of the mutual fund.

(2) List the names and home addresses in full or, alternatively, solely the municipality of residence or postal address, and the respective positions and offices held with the manager and their respective principal occupations at, and within the five years preceding, the date of the annual information form, of all partners, directors and executive officers of the manager of the mutual fund at the date of the annual information form.

(3) If a partner, director or executive officer of the manager of the mutual fund has held more than one office with the manager of the mutual fund within the past five years, state only the current office held.

(4) If the principal occupation of a director or executive officer of the manager of the mutual fund is with an organization other than the manager of the mutual fund, state the principal business in which the organization is engaged.

(5) Describe the circumstances under which any agreement with the manager of the mutual fund may be terminated, and include a brief description of the essential terms of this agreement.

10.3 — Portfolio Adviser

(1) If the manager of the mutual fund provides the portfolio management services in connection with the mutual fund, so state.

(2) If the manager does not provide portfolio management services, state the names and municipality of the principal or head office for each portfolio adviser of the mutual fund.

(3) State

(a) the extent to which investment decisions are made by certain individuals employed by the manager or a portfolio adviser and whether those decisions are subject to the oversight, approval or ratification of a committee; and

(b) the name, title, and length of time of service of the person or persons employed by or associated with either the manager or a portfolio adviser of the mutual fund who is or are principally responsible for the day-to-day management of a material portion of the portfolio of the mutual fund, implementing a particular material strategy or managing a particular segment of the portfolio of the mutual fund, and each person's business experience in the last five years.

(4) Describe the circumstances under which any agreement with a portfolio adviser of the mutual fund may be terminated, and include a brief description of the essential terms of this agreement.

10.4 — Brokerage Arrangements

(1) If any brokerage transactions involving the client brokerage commissions of the mutual fund have been or might be directed to a dealer in return for the provision of any good or service, by the dealer or a third party, other than order execution, state

(a) the process for, and factors considered in, selecting a dealer to effect securities transactions for the mutual fund, including whether receiving goods or services in addition to order execution is a factor, and whether and how the process may differ for a dealer that is an affiliated entity;

(b) the nature of the arrangements under which order execution goods and services or research goods and services might be provided;

(c) each type of good or service, other than order execution, that might be provided; and

(d) the method by which the portfolio adviser makes a good faith determination that the mutual fund, on whose behalf the portfolio adviser directs any brokerage transactions involving client brokerage commissions to a dealer in return for the provision of any order execution goods and services or research goods and services, by the dealer or a third party, receives reasonable benefit considering both the use of the goods or services and the amount of client brokerage commissions paid.

(2) Since the date of the last annual information form, if any brokerage transactions involving the client brokerage commissions of the mutual fund have been or might be directed to a dealer in return for the provision of any good or service, by the dealer or third party, other than order execution, state

    (a) each type of good or service, other than order execution, that has been provided to the manager or the portfolio adviser of the mutual fund; and

    (b) the name of any affiliated entity that provided any good or service referred to in paragraph (a), separately identifying each affiliated entity and each type of good or service provided by each affiliated entity.

(3) If any brokerage transactions involving the client brokerage commissions of the mutual fund have been or might be directed to a dealer in return for the provision of any good or service, by the dealer or a third party, other than order execution, state that the name of any other dealer or third party that provided a good or service referred to in paragraph (2)(a), that was not disclosed under paragraph (2)(b), will be provided upon request by contacting the mutual fund or mutual fund family at [insert telephone number] or at [insert mutual fund or mutual fund family e-mail address].

INSTRUCTIONS:

Terms defined in NI 23-102 — Use of Client Brokerage Commissions have the same meaning where used in this Item.

10.5 — Principal Distributor

(1) If applicable, state the name and address of the principal distributor of the mutual fund.

(2) Describe the circumstances under which any agreement with the principal distributor of the mutual fund may be terminated, and include a brief description of the essential terms of this agreement.

10.6 — Directors, Executive Officers and Trustees

(1) List the names and home addresses in full or, alternatively, solely the municipality of residence or postal address, and the principal occupations at, or within the five years preceding, the date of the annual information form, of all directors or executive officers of an incorporated mutual fund or of the individual trustee or trustees, if any, of a mutual fund that is a trust.

(2) State, for a mutual fund that is a trust, the names and municipality of residence for each person or company that is responsible for performing the trusteeship function of the mutual fund.

(3) Indicate, for an incorporated mutual fund, all positions and offices with the mutual fund then held by each person named in response to subsection (1).

(4) If the principal occupation of a director, executive officer or trustee is that of a partner, director or executive officer of a company other than the mutual fund, state the business in which the company is engaged.

(5) If a director or executive officer of an incorporated mutual fund has held more than one position in the mutual fund, state only the first and last position held.

(6) For a mutual fund that is a limited partnership, provide the information required by this Item for the general partner of the mutual fund, modified as appropriate.

10.7 — Custodian

(1) State the name, municipality of the principal or head office, and nature of business of the custodian and any principal sub-custodian of the mutual fund.

(2) Describe generally the sub-custodian arrangements of the mutual fund.

INSTRUCTION:

A "principal sub-custodian" is a sub-custodian to whom custodial authority has been delegated in respect of a material portion or segment of the portfolio assets of the mutual fund.

10.8 — Auditor

State the name and municipality of the auditor of the mutual fund.

10.9 — Registrar

If applicable, state the name of the registrar of securities of the mutual fund and the municipalities in which the register of securities of the mutual fund are kept.

10.9.1 — Securities Lending Agent

(1) State the name of each securities lending agent of the mutual fund and the municipality of each securities lending agent's principal or head office.

(2) State whether any securities lending agent of the mutual fund is an affiliate or associate of the manager of the mutual fund.

(3) Briefly describe the essential terms of each agreement with each securities lending agent. Include the amount of collateral required to be delivered in connection with a securities lending transaction as a percentage of the market value of the loaned securities, and briefly describe any indemnities provided in, and the termination provisions of, each such agreement.

10.10 — Other Service Providers

State the name, municipality of the principal or head office, and the nature of business of each other person or company that provides services relating to portfolio valuation, securityholder records, fund accounting, or other material services, in respect of the mutual fund, and describe the material features of the contractual arrangements by which the person or company has been retained.

Item 11 — Conflicts of Interest

11.1 — Principal Holders of Securities

(1) The information required in response to this Item shall be given as of a specified date within 30 days before the date of the annual information form.

(2) Disclose the number and percentage of securities of each class or series of voting securities of the mutual fund and of the manager of the mutual fund owned of record or beneficially, directly or indirectly, by each person or company that owns of record, or is known by the mutual fund or the manager to own beneficially, directly or indirectly, more than 10 percent of any class or series of voting securities, and disclose whether the securities are owned both of record and beneficially, of record only, or beneficially only.

(3) For any entity that is named in response to subsection (2), disclose the name of any person or company of which that entity is a "controlled entity".

(4) If any person or company named in respect of subsection (2) owns of record or beneficially, directly or indirectly, more than 10 percent of any class of voting securities of the principal distributor of the mutual fund, disclose the number and percentage of securities of the class so owned.

(5) Disclose the percentage of securities of each class or series of voting or equity securities beneficially owned, directly or indirectly, in aggregate, by all the directors, senior officers and trustees

    (a) of the mutual fund

        (i) in the mutual fund if the aggregate level of ownership exceeds 10 percent,

        (ii) in the manager, or

        (iii) in any person or company that provides services to the mutual fund or the manager; and

    (b) of the manager

        (i) in the mutual fund if the aggregate level of ownership exceeds 10 percent,

        (ii) in the manager, or

        (iii) in any person or company that provides services to the mutual fund or the manager.

(6) Disclose the percentage of securities of each class or series of voting or equity securities beneficially owned, directly or indirectly, in aggregate, by all the independent review committee members of the mutual fund

    (a) in the mutual fund if the aggregate level of ownership exceeds 10 percent,

    (b) in the manager, or

    (c) in any person or company that provides services to the mutual fund or the manager.

11.2 — Affiliated Entities

(1) State whether any person or company that provides services to the mutual fund or the manager in relation to the mutual fund is an affiliated entity of the manager, and show the relationships of those affiliated entities in the form of an appropriately labelled diagram.

(2) State that disclosure of the amount of fees received from the mutual fund by each person or company described in subsection (1) is contained in the audited financial statements of the mutual fund.

(3) Identify any individual who is a director or senior officer of the mutual fund or partner, director or officer of the manager and also of any affiliated entity of the manager described in response to subsection (1), and give particulars of the relationship.

INSTRUCTIONS:

(1) A person or company is an "affiliated entity" of another person or company if one is a subsidiary entity of the other or if both are subsidiary entities of the same person or company or if each of them is a controlled entity of the same person or company.

(2) A person or company is a "controlled entity" of a person or company if

    (a) in the case of a person or company

        (i) voting securities of the first-mentioned person or company carrying more than 50 percent of the votes for the election of directors are held, otherwise than by way of security only, by or for the benefit of the other person or company, and

        (ii) the votes carried by the securities are entitled, if exercised, to elect a majority of the directors of the first-mentioned person or company;

(b) in the case of a partnership that does not have directors, other than a limited partnership, the second-mentioned person or company holds more than 50 percent of the interests in the partnership; or

(c) in the case of a limited partnership, the general partner is the second-mentioned person or company.

(3) *A person or company is a "subsidiary entity" of another person or company if*

    (a) it is a controlled entity of

        (i) that other,

        (ii) that other and one or more persons or companies, each of which is a controlled entity of that other, or

        (iii) two or more persons or companies, each of which is a controlled entity of that other; or

    (b) it is a subsidiary entity of a person or company that is that other's subsidiary entity.

(4) *For the purposes of subsection (1) of Item 11.2, the provision of services includes the provision of brokerage services in connection with execution of portfolio transactions for the mutual fund.*

11.3 — Dealer Manager Disclosure

If the mutual fund is dealer managed, disclose this fact and that the mutual fund is subject to the restrictions set out in section 4.1 of National Instrument 81-102, and summarize section 4.1 of National Instrument 81-102.

Item 12 — Fund Governance

(1) Provide detailed information concerning the governance of the mutual fund, including information concerning

(a) the mandate and responsibilities of the independent review committee and the reasons for any change in the composition of the independent review committee since the date of the most recently filed annual information form;

(a.1) any other body or group that has responsibility for fund governance and the extent to which its members are independent of the manager of the mutual fund; and

(b) descriptions of the policies, practices or guidelines of the mutual fund or the manager relating to business practices, sales practices, risk management controls and internal conflicts of interest, and if the mutual fund or the manager have no such policies, practices or guidelines, a statement to that effect.

(2) If the mutual fund intends to use derivatives or sell securities short, describe the policies and practices of the mutual fund to manage the risks associated with engaging in those types of transactions.

(3) In the disclosure provided under subsection (2), include disclosure of

(a) whether there are written policies and procedures in place that set out the objectives and goals for derivatives trading and short selling and the risk management procedures applicable to those transactions;

(b) who is responsible for setting and reviewing the policies and procedures referred to in paragraph (a), how often are the policies and procedures reviewed, and the extent and nature of the involvement of the board of directors or trustee in the risk management process;

(c) whether there are trading limits or other controls on derivative trading or short selling in place and who is responsible for authorizing the trading and placing limits or other controls on the trading;

(d) whether there are individuals or groups that monitor the risks independent of those who trade; and

(e) whether risk measurement procedures or simulations are used to test the portfolio under stress conditions.

(4) If the mutual fund intends to enter into securities lending, repurchase or reverse repurchase transactions, describe the policies and practices of the mutual fund to manage the risks associated with those transactions.

(5) In the disclosure provided under subsection (4), include disclosure of

(a) the involvement of an agent to administer the transactions on behalf of the mutual fund, and the details of the instructions provided by the mutual fund to the agent under the agreement between the mutual fund and the agent;

(b) whether there are written policies and procedures in place that set out the objectives and goals for securities lending, repurchase transactions or reverse repurchase transactions, and the risk management procedures applicable to the mutual fund's entering into of those transactions;

(c) who is responsible for setting and reviewing the agreement referred to in paragraph (a) and the policies and procedures referred to in paragraph (b), how often the policies and procedures are reviewed, and the extent and nature of the involvement of the board of directors or trustee in the risk management process;

(d) whether there are limits or other controls in place on the entering into of those transactions by the mutual fund and who is responsible for authorizing those limits or other controls on those transactions;

(e) whether there are individuals or groups that monitor the risks independent of those who enter into those transactions on behalf of the mutual fund; and

(f) whether risk measurement procedures or simulations are used to test the portfolio under stress conditions.

(6) If the mutual fund held securities of other mutual funds during the year, provide details on how the manager of the mutual fund exercised its discretion with regard to the voting rights attached to the securities of the other mutual funds when the securityholders of the other mutual funds were called upon to vote.

(7) Unless the mutual fund invests exclusively in non-voting securities, describe the policies and procedures that the mutual fund follows when voting proxies relating to portfolio securities including

(a) the procedures followed when a vote presents a conflict between the interests of securityholders and those of the mutual fund's manager, portfolio adviser, or any affiliate or associate of the mutual fund, its manager or its portfolio adviser;

(b) any policies and procedures of the mutual fund's portfolio adviser, or any other third party, that the mutual fund follows, or that are followed on the mutual fund's behalf, to determine how to vote proxies relating to portfolio securities.

State that the policies and procedures that the mutual fund follows when voting proxies relating to portfolio securities are available on request, at no cost, by calling [toll-free/collect call telephone number] or by writing to [address].

(8) State that the mutual fund's proxy voting record for the most recent period ended June 30 of each year is available free of charge to any securityholder of the mutual fund upon request at any time after August 31 of that year. If the proxy voting record is available on the mutual fund's website, provide the website address.

(9) Describe the policies and procedures of the mutual fund relating to the monitoring, detection and deterrence of short-term trades of mutual fund securities by investors. If the mutual fund has no such policies and procedures, provide a statement to that effect.

(10) Describe any arrangements, whether formal or informal, with any person or company, to permit short-term trades in securities of the mutual fund, including

(a) the name of such person or company, and

(b) the terms of such arrangements, including

(i) any restrictions imposed on the short-term trades; and

(ii) any compensation or other consideration received by the manager, the mutual fund or any other party pursuant to such arrangements.

INSTRUCTION:

(1) *The disclosure provided under this Item should make appropriate distinctions between the risks associated with the intended use by the mutual fund of derivatives for hedging purposes as against the mutual fund's intended use of derivatives for non-hedging purposes.*

(2) *If the mutual fund has an independent review committee, state in the disclosure provided under paragraph (1)(b) that NI 81-107 requires the manager to have policies and procedures relating to conflicts of interest.*

INSTRUCTION:

The mutual fund's proxy voting policies and procedures must address the requirements of section 10.2 of National Instrument 81-106 Investment Fund Continuous Disclosure.

Item 13 — Fees and Expenses

13.1 — Management Fee Rebate or Distribution Programs

(1) Disclose details of all arrangements that are in effect or will be in effect during the currency of the annual information form that will result, directly or indirectly, in one securityholder in the mutual fund paying as a percentage of the securityholder's investment in the mutual fund a management fee that differs from that payable by another securityholder.

(2) In the disclosure required by subsection (1), describe

(a) who pays the management fee;

(b) whether a reduced fee is paid at the relevant time or whether the full fee is paid at that time with a repayment of a portion of the management fee to follow at a later date;

(c) who funds the reduction or repayment of management fees, when the reduction or repayment is made and whether it is made in cash or in securities of the mutual fund;

(d) whether the differing management fees are negotiable or calculated in accordance with a fixed schedule;

(e) if the management fees are negotiable, the factors or criteria relevant to the negotiations and state who negotiates the fees with the investor;

(f) whether the differing management fees payable are based on the number or value of the securities of the mutual fund purchased during a specified period or the number or value of the securities of the mutual fund held at a particular time; and

(g) any other factors that could affect the amount of the management fees payable.

(3) Disclose the income tax consequences to the mutual fund and its securityholders of a management fee structure that results in one securityholder paying a management fee that differs from another.

Item 14 — Income Tax Considerations

(1) State in general terms the bases upon which the income and capital receipts of the mutual fund are taxed.

(2) State in general terms the income tax consequences to the holders of the securities offered of

(a) any distribution to the holders in the form of dividends or otherwise, including amounts reinvested in securities of the mutual fund;

(b) the redemption of securities;

(c) the issue of securities; and

(d) any transfers between mutual funds.

Item 15 — Remuneration of Directors, Officers and Trustees

(1) If the management functions of the mutual fund are carried out by employees of the mutual fund, provide for those employees the disclosure concerning executive compensation that is required to be provided for executive officers of an issuer under securities legislation.

(2) Describe any arrangements under which compensation was paid or payable by the mutual fund during the most recently completed financial year of the mutual fund, for the services of directors of the mutual fund, members of an independent board of governors or advisory board of the mutual fund and members of the independent review committee of the mutual fund, including the amounts paid, the name of the individual and any expenses reimbursed by the mutual fund to the individual

(a) in that capacity, including any additional amounts payable for committee participation or special assignments; and

(b) as consultant or expert.

(3) For a mutual fund that is a trust, describe the arrangements, including the amounts paid and expenses reimbursed, under which compensation was paid or payable by the mutual fund during the most recently completed financial year of the mutual fund for the services of the trustee or trustees of the mutual fund.

INSTRUCTION:

The disclosure required under Item 15(1) regarding executive compensation for management functions carried out by employees of a mutual fund must be made in accordance with the disclosure requirements of Form 51-102F6 Statement of Executive Compensation.

Item 16 — Material Contracts

(1) List and provide particulars of

(a) the articles of incorporation, continuation or amalgamation, the declaration of trust or trust agreement of the mutual fund, the limited partnership agreement or any other constating or establishing documents of the mutual fund;

(b) any agreement of the mutual fund or trustee with the manager of the mutual fund;

(c) any agreement of the mutual fund, the manager or trustee with the portfolio adviser or portfolio advisers of the mutual fund;

(d) any agreement of the mutual fund, the manager or trustee with the custodian of the mutual fund;

(e) any agreement of the mutual fund, the manager or trustee with the principal distributor of the mutual fund; and

(f) any other contract or agreement that is material to the mutual fund.

(2) State a reasonable time at which and place where the contracts or agreements listed in response to subsection (1) may be inspected by prospective or existing securityholders.

(3) Include, in describing particulars of contracts, the date of, parties to, consideration paid by the mutual fund under, termination provisions of, and general nature of, the contracts.

INSTRUCTION:

This Item does not require disclosure of contracts entered into in the ordinary course of business of the mutual fund.

Item 17 — Legal and Administrative Proceedings

(1) Describe briefly any ongoing legal and administrative proceedings material to the mutual fund, to which the mutual fund, its manager or principal distributor is a party.

(2) For all matters disclosed under subsection (1), disclose

(a) the name of the court or agency having jurisdiction;

(b) the date on which the proceeding was instituted;

(c) the principal parties to the proceeding;

(d) the nature of the proceeding and, if applicable, the amount claimed; and

(e) whether the proceedings are being contested and the present status of the proceedings.

(3) Provide similar disclosure about any proceedings known to be contemplated.

(4) Describe the penalties or sanctions imposed and the grounds on which they were imposed or the terms of any settlement agreement and the circumstances that gave rise to the settlement agreement, if the manager of the mutual fund, or a director or officer of the mutual fund or the partner, director or officer of the manager of the mutual fund has,

(a) in the 10 years before the date of the simplified prospectus, been subject to any penalties or sanctions imposed by a court or securities regulator relating to trading in securities, promotion or management of a publicly-traded mutual fund, or theft of fraud, or been subject to any other penalties or sanctions imposed by a court or regulatory body that would be likely to be considered important to a reasonable investor in determining whether to purchase securities of the mutual fund; or

(b) in the 10 years before the date of the simplified prospectus but after the date that National Instrument 81-101 came into force, entered into a settlement agreement with a court, securities regulatory or other regulatory body, in relation to any of the matters referred to in paragraph (a).

(5) If the manager of the mutual fund, or a director or officer of the mutual fund or the partner, director or officer of the manager of the mutual fund has, within the 10 years before the date of the simplified prospectus, been subject to any penalties or sanctions imposed by a court or securities regulator relating to trading in securities, promotion or management of a publicly traded mutual fund, or theft or fraud, or has entered into a settlement agreement with a regulatory authority in relation to any of these matters, describe the penalties or sanctions imposed and the grounds on which they were imposed or the terms of the settlement agreement.

Item 18 — Other Material Information

(1) Give particulars of any other material facts relating to the securities proposed to be offered that are not otherwise required to be disclosed by this Form or the SP Form.

(2) Provide any specific disclosure required or permitted to be disclosed in a prospectus under securities legislation that is not otherwise required to be disclosed by this Form.

(3) Subsection (2) does not apply to requirements of securities legislation that are form requirements for a prospectus.

INSTRUCTION:

The disclosure provided under subsection (2) may also be provided under Item 12 of Part A or Item 14 of Part B of the SP Form. If the disclosure is provided under one of these Items, it need not be provided under this Item.

Item 19 — Certificate of the Mutual Fund

(1) Include a certificate of the mutual fund that states:

    (a) for a simplified prospectus and annual information form,

        "This annual information form, together with the simplified prospectus and the documents incorporated by reference into the simplified prospectus, constitute full, true and plain disclosure of all material facts relating to the securities offered by the simplified prospectus, as required by the securities legislation of [insert the jurisdictions in which qualified] and do not contain any misrepresentations."

    (b) for an amendment to a simplified prospectus or annual information form that does not restate the simplified prospectus or annual information form,

        "This amendment no. [specify amendment number and date], together with the [amended and restated] annual information form dated [specify], [amending and restating the annual information form dated [specify],] [as amended by (specify prior amendments and dates)] and the [amended and restated] simplified prospectus dated [specify], [amending and restating the simplified prospectus dated [specify],] [as amended by (specify prior amendments and dates)] and the documents incorporated by reference into the [amended and restated] simplified prospectus, [as amended,] constitute full, true and plain disclosure of all material facts relating to the securities offered by the [amended and restated] simplified prospectus, [as amended,] as required by the securities legislation of [insert the jurisdictions in which qualified] and do not contain any misrepresentations.", and

    (c) for an amendment that amends and restates a simplified prospectus or annual information form,

        "This amended and restated annual information form dated [specify], amending and restating the annual information form dated [specify] [, as amended by (specify prior amendments and dates)], together with the [amended and restated] simplified prospectus dated [specify] [, amending and restating the simplified prospectus dated [specify]] [, as amended by (specify prior amendments and dates)] and the documents incorporated by reference into the [amended and restated] simplified prospectus, [as amended,] constitute full, true and plain disclosure of all material facts relating to the securities offered by the [amended and restated] simplified prospectus, [as amended,] as required by the securities legislation of [insert the jurisdictions in which qualified] and do not contain any misrepresentations."

(1.1) For a non-offering prospectus, change "securities offered by the simplified prospectus" to "securities previously issued by the mutual fund" wherever it appears in the statement in Item 19(1)(a).

(2) The certificate required to be signed by the mutual fund shall, if the mutual fund is established as a trust, be signed

    (a) if any trustee of the mutual fund is an individual, by each individual who is a trustee or by a duly authorized attorney of the individual; or

    (b) if any trustee of the mutual fund is a body corporate, by the duly authorized signing officer or officers of the body corporate.

(3) Despite subsection (2), if the declaration of trust or trust agreement establishing the mutual fund delegates the authority to do so, or otherwise authorizes a person to do so, the certificate form required to be signed by the trustee or trustees of the mutual fund may be signed by the person to whom the authority is delegated or who is authorized.

(4) Despite subsections (2) and (3), if the trustee of the mutual fund is also its manager, the certificate shall indicate that it is being signed by the person or company both in its capacity of trustee and in its capacity as manager of the mutual fund and shall be signed in the manner prescribed by Item 20.

Item 20 — Certificate of the Manager of the Mutual Fund

(1) Include a certificate of the manager of the mutual fund in the same form as the certificate signed by the mutual fund.

(2) The certificate shall, if the manager is a company, be signed by the chief executive officer and the chief financial officer of the manager, and on behalf of the board of directors of the manager by any two directors of the manager other than the chief executive officer or chief financial officer, duly authorized to sign.

(3) Despite subsection (2), if the manager has only three directors, two of whom are the chief executive officer and chief financial officer, the certificate required by subsection (2) to be signed on behalf of the board of directors of the manager shall be signed by the remaining director of the manager.

Item 21 — Certificate of Each Promoter of the Mutual Fund

(1) Include a certificate of each promoter of the mutual fund in the same form as the certificate signed by the mutual fund.

(2) The certificate to be signed by the promoter shall be signed by any officer or director of the promoter duly authorized to sign.

Item 22 — Certificate of the Principal Distributor of the Mutual Fund

(1) Include a certificate of the principal distributor of the mutual fund that states:

> "To the best of our knowledge, information and belief, this annual information form, together with the simplified prospectus and the documents incorporated by reference into the simplified prospectus, constitute full, true and plain disclosure of all material facts relating to the securities offered by the simplified prospectus, as required by the securities legislation of [insert the jurisdictions in which qualified] and do not contain any misrepresentations."

(2) The certificate to be signed by the principal distributor shall be signed by any officer or director of the principal distributor duly authorized to sign.

INSTRUCTION:

For a mutual fund that has a principal distributor, the certificate required by this Item is necessary to satisfy the requirements of securities legislation that an underwriter sign a certificate to a prospectus.

Item 23 — Exemptions and Approvals

(1) Describe all exemptions from, or approvals under, this Instrument, National Instrument 81-102, National Instrument 81-105 or National Policy Statement No. 39, obtained by the mutual fund or the manager that continue to be relied upon by the mutual fund or the manager.

(2) Include the disclosure required by subsection (1) in the section of the annual information form that describes the matter to which the exemption pertains.

Item 24 — Back Cover

(1) State on the back cover the name of the mutual fund or funds included in the annual information form or the mutual fund family, as well as the name, address and telephone number of the manager of the mutual fund or funds.

(2) State, in substantially the following words:

- Additional information about the Fund[s] is available in the Fund['s/s'] Fund Facts, management reports of fund performance and financial statements.

- You can get a copy of these documents at no cost by calling [toll-free/collect] [insert toll-free telephone number or telephone number where collect calls are accepted, as required by section 3.4 of the Instrument], or from your dealer or by e-mail at [insert e-mail address].

- These documents and other information about the Fund[s], such as information circulars and material contracts, are also available on the [insert name of mutual fund manager] internet site at [insert fund's Internet site] or at www.sedar.com.

Form 81-101F3 — Contents of Fund Facts Document

General Instructions:

General

(1) This Form describes the disclosure required in a fund facts document for a mutual fund. Each Item of this Form outlines disclosure requirements. Instructions to help you provide this disclosure are in italic type.

(2) Terms defined in National Instrument 81-101 Mutual Fund Prospectus Disclosure, National Instrument 81-102 Investment Funds, National Instrument 81-105 Mutual Fund Sales Practices or National Instrument 81-106 Investment Fund Continuous Disclosure and used in this Form have the meanings that they have in those national instruments.

(3) A fund facts document must state the required information concisely and in plain language.

(4) Respond as simply and directly as is reasonably possible. Include only the information necessary for a reasonable investor to understand the fundamental and particular characteristics of the mutual fund.

(5) National Instrument 81-101 Mutual Fund Prospectus Disclosure requires the fund facts document to be presented in a format that assists in readability and comprehension. This Form does not mandate the use of a specific format or template to achieve these goals. However, mutual funds must use, as appropriate, tables, captions, bullet points or other organizational techniques that assist in presenting the required disclosure clearly and concisely.

(6) This Form does not mandate the use of a specific font size or style but the font must be legible. Where the fund facts document is made available online, information must be presented in a way that enables it to be printed in a readable format.

(7) A fund facts document can be produced in colour or in black and white, and in portrait or landscape orientation.

(8) Except as permitted by subsection (8.1), a fund facts document must contain only the information that is specifically mandated or permitted by this Form. In addition, each Item must be presented in the order and under the heading or sub-heading stipulated in this Form.

(8.1) A fund facts document may contain a brief explanation of a material change or a proposed fundamental change. The disclosure may be included in a textbox before Item 2 of Part I or in the most relevant section of the fund facts document. If necessary, the mutual fund may provide a crossreference to a more detailed explanation at the end of the fund facts document.

(9) A fund facts document must not contain design elements (e.g., graphics, photos, artwork) that detract from the information disclosed in the document.

Contents of a Fund Facts Document

(10) A fund facts document must disclose information about only one class or series of securities of a mutual fund. Mutual funds that have more than one class or series that are referable to the same portfolio of assets must prepare a separate fund facts document for each class or series.

(11) The fund facts document must be prepared on letter-size paper and must consist of two Parts: Part I and Part II.

(12) The fund facts document must begin with the responses to the Items in Part I of this Form.

(13) Part I must be followed by the responses to the Items in Part II of this Form.

(14) Each of Part I and Part II must not exceed one page in length, unless the required information in any section causes the disclosure to exceed this limit. Where this is the case, a fund facts document must not exceed a total of four pages in length.

(15) A mutual fund must not attach or bind other documents to a fund facts document, except those documents permitted under section 5.4 of National Instrument 81-101 Mutual Fund Prospectus Disclosure.

Consolidation of Fund Facts Document into a Multiple Fund Facts Document

(16) Fund facts documents must not be consolidated with each other to form a multiple fund facts document, except as permitted by section 5.4 of National Instrument 81-101 Mutual Fund Prospectus Disclosure. When a multiple fund facts document is permitted under the Instrument, a mutual fund must provide information about each of the mutual funds described in the document on a fund-by-fund or catalogue basis and must set out for each mutual fund separately the information required by this Form. Each fund facts document must start on a new page, and may not share a page with another fund facts document.

Multi-Class Mutual Funds

(17) As provided in National Instrument 81-102 Investment Funds, a section, part, class or series of a class of securities of a mutual fund that is referable to a separate portfolio of assets is considered to be a separate mutual fund. Those principles apply to National Instrument 81-101 Mutual Fund Prospectus Disclosure and this Form.

Part I — Information about the Fund

Item 1 — Introduction

Include at the top of the first page a heading consisting of:

- (a) the title "Fund Facts";
- (b) the name of the manager of the mutual fund;
- (c) the name of the mutual fund to which the fund facts document pertains;
- (c.1) if the mutual fund has more than one class or series of securities, the name of the class or series described in the fund facts document;
- (d) the date of the document;
- (e) a brief introduction to the document using wording substantially similar to the following:

    This document contains key information you should know about [insert name of the mutual fund]. You can find more details in the fund's simplified prospectus. Ask your representative for a copy, contact [insert name of the manager of the mutual fund] at [insert if applicable the toll-free number and email address of the manager of the mutual fund] or visit [insert the website of the mutual fund, the mutual fund's family or the manager of the mutual fund] [as applicable]; and

- (f) state in bold type using wording substantially similar to the following:

    Before you invest in any fund, consider how the fund would work with your other investments and your tolerance for risk.

INSTRUCTION:

The date for a fund facts document that is filed with a preliminary simplified prospectus or simplified prospectus must be the date of the certificate contained in the related annual information form. The date for a fund facts document that is filed with a pro forma simplified prospectus must be the date of the anticipated simplified prospectus. The date for an amended fund facts document must be the date of the certificate contained in the related amended annual information form.

Item 2 — Quick Facts

Under the heading "Quick Facts", include disclosure in the form of the following table:

Fund code: (see instruction 0.1)	**Fund manager:** (see instruction 3.1)
Date [class/series] started: (see instruction 1)	**Portfolio manager:** (see instruction 4)
Total value of the fund on [date]: (see instruction 2)	**Distributions:** (see instruction 5)

Management expense ratio (MER): (see instruction 3)	**Minimum investment:** (see instruction 6)

INSTRUCTIONS:

(0.1) At the option of the mutual fund, include all recognized and publicly available identification codes for the class or series of the mutual fund.

(1) Use the date that the securities of the class or series of the mutual fund described in the fund facts document first became available to the public.

(2) Specify the net asset value of the mutual fund as at a date within 60 days before the date of the fund facts document. The amount disclosed must take into consideration all classes or series that are referable to the same portfolio of assets. For a newly established mutual fund, simply state that this information is not available because it is a new mutual fund.

(3) Use the management expense ratio (MER) disclosed in the most recently filed management report of fund performance (MRFP) for the mutual fund. The MER must be net of fee waivers or absorptions and, despite section 15.1(2) of National Instrument 81-106 Investment Fund Continuous Disclosure, need not include any additional disclosure about the waivers or absorptions. For a newly established mutual fund that has not yet filed a management report of fund performance, state that the MER is not available because it is a new mutual fund.

(3.1) Specify the name of the manager of the mutual fund.

(4) Name the mutual fund's portfolio manager. The mutual fund may also name the specific individual(s) responsible for portfolio selection and if applicable, the name of the sub-advisor(s).

(5) Include disclosure under this element of the "Quick Facts" only if distributions are a fundamental feature of the mutual fund. Disclose the expected frequency and timing of distributions. If there is a targeted amount for distributions, the mutual fund may include this information.

(6) Specify both the minimum amount for an initial investment and for each additional investment. This can include minimum amounts for pre-authorized contribution plans.

Item 3 — Investments of the Fund

(1) Briefly set out under the heading "What does the fund invest in?" a description of the fundamental nature of the mutual fund, or the fundamental features of the mutual fund that distinguish it from other mutual funds.

(2) For an index mutual fund,

(a) disclose the name or names of the permitted index or permitted indices on which the investments of the index mutual fund are based, and

(b) briefly describe the nature of that permitted index or those permitted indices.

(3) Include an introduction to the information provided in response to subsection (4) and subsection (5) using wording similar to the following:

The charts below give you a snapshot of the fund's investments on [insert date]. The fund's investments will change.

(4) Include under the sub-heading "Top 10 investments [date]", a table disclosing the following:

(a) the top 10 positions held by the mutual fund, each expressed as a percentage of the net asset value of the mutual fund;

(b) the percentage of net asset value of the mutual fund represented by the top 10 positions; and

(c) the total number of positions held by the mutual fund.

(5) Under the sub-heading "Investment mix [date]" include at least one, and up to two, charts or tables that illustrate the investment mix of the mutual fund's investment portfolio.

INSTRUCTIONS:

(1) Include in the information under "What does this fund invest in?" a description of what the mutual fund primarily invests in, or intends to primarily invest in, or that its name implies that it will primarily invest in, such as

(a) particular types of issuers, such as foreign issuers, small capitalization issuers or issuers located in emerging market countries;

(b) particular geographic locations or industry segments; or

(c) portfolio assets other than securities.

(2) Include a particular investment strategy only if it is an essential aspect of the mutual fund, as evidenced by the name of the mutual fund or the manner in which the mutual fund is marketed.

(3) If a mutual fund's stated objective is to invest primarily in Canadian securities, specify the maximum exposure to investments in foreign markets.

(4) The information under "Top 10 investments" and "Investment mix" is intended to give a snapshot of the composition of the mutual fund's investment portfolio. The information required to be disclosed under these sub-headings must be as at a date within 60 days before the date of the fund facts document. The date shown must be the same as the one used in Item 2 for the total value of the mutual fund.

(5) If the mutual fund owns more than one class of securities of an issuer, those classes should be aggregated for the purposes of this Item, however, debt and equity securities of an issuer must not be aggregated.

(6) Portfolio assets other than securities should be aggregated if they have substantially similar investment risks and profiles. For instance, gold certificates should be aggregated, even if they are issued by different financial institutions.

(7) Treat cash and cash equivalents as one separate discrete category.

(8) In determining its holdings for purposes of the disclosure required by this Item, a mutual fund must, for each long position in a derivative that is held by the mutual fund for purposes other than hedging and for each index participation unit held by the mutual fund, consider that it holds directly the underlying interest of that derivative or its proportionate share of the securities held by the issuer of the index participation unit.

(9) If a mutual fund invests substantially all of its assets directly or indirectly (through the use of derivatives) in securities of one other mutual fund, list the 10 largest holdings of the other mutual fund and show the percentage of the other mutual fund's net asset value represented by the top 10 positions. If the mutual fund is not able to disclose this information as at a date within 60 days before the date of the fund facts document, the mutual fund must include this information as disclosed by the other mutual fund in the other mutual fund's most recently filed fund facts document, or its most recently filed management report of fund performance, whichever is most recent.

(10) Indicate whether any of the mutual fund's top 10 positions are short positions.

(11) Each investment mix chart or table must show a breakdown of the mutual fund's investment portfolio into appropriate subgroups and the percentage of the aggregate net asset value of the mutual fund constituted by each subgroup. The names of the subgroups are not prescribed and can include security type, industry segment or geographic location. The mutual fund should use the most appropriate categories given the nature of the mutual fund. The choices made must be consistent with disclosure provided under "Summary of Investment Portfolio" in the mutual fund's MRFP.

(12) In presenting the investment mix of the mutual fund, consider the most effective way of conveying the information to investors. All tables or charts must be clear and legible.

(13) For new mutual funds where the information required to be disclosed under "Top 10 investments" and "Investment mix" is not available, include the required sub-headings and provide a brief statement explaining why the required information is not available.

Item 4: — Risks

(1) Under the heading "How risky is it?", state the following:

> The value of the fund can go down as well as up. You could lose money.

> One way to gauge risk is to look at how much a fund's returns change over time. This is called "volatility".

> In general, funds with higher volatility will have returns that change more over time. They typically have a greater chance of losing money and may have a greater chance of higher returns. Funds with lower volatility tend to have returns that change less over time. They typically have lower returns and may have a lower chance of losing money.

(2) Under the sub-heading "Risk rating",

> (a) using the investment risk classification methodology adopted by the manager of the mutual fund, identify the mutual fund's investment risk level on the following risk scale:

Low	Low to medium	Medium	Medium to high	High

> (b) unless the mutual fund is a newly established mutual fund, include an introduction to the risk scale which states the following:

> > [Insert name of manager of the mutual fund] has rated the volatility of this fund as [insert investment risk level identified in paragraph (a) in bold type].

> > This rating is based on how much the fund's returns have changed from year to year. It doesn't tell you how volatile the fund will be in the future. The rating can change over time. A fund with a low risk rating can still lose money.

> (c) for a newly established mutual fund, include an introduction to the risk scale which states the following:

> > [Insert name of manager of the mutual fund] has rated the volatility of this fund as [insert investment risk level identified in paragraph (a) in bold type].

> > Because this is a new fund, the risk rating is only an estimate by [insert name of manager of the mutual fund]. Generally, the rating is based on how much the fund's returns have changed from year to year. It doesn't tell you how volatile the fund will be in the future. The rating can change over time. A fund with a low risk rating can still lose money.

> (d) following the risk scale, state using wording substantially similar to the following:

> > For more information about the risk rating and specific risks that can affect the fund's returns, see the [insert cross-reference to the appropriate section of the mutual fund's simplified prospectus] section of the fund's simplified prospectus.

(3) Under the sub-heading "No guarantees", state using wording substantially similar to the following:

> Like most mutual funds, this fund doesn't have any guarantees. You may not get back the amount of money you invest.

INSTRUCTIONS:

> *(1) Based upon the investment risk classification methodology adopted by the manager of the mutual fund, identify where the mutual fund fits on the continuum of investment risk levels by showing the full investment risk scale set out in Item 4(2)(a) and highlighting the applicable category on the scale. Consideration should be given to ensure that the highlighted investment risk rating is easily identifiable.*

Item 5: — Past Performance

(1) Under the heading "How has the fund performed?", include an introduction using wording substantially similar to the following:

> This section tells you how [name of class/series of securities described in the fund facts document] [units/shares] of the fund have performed over the past [insert number of calendar years shown in the bar chart required under paragraph (2)(a)] years. Returns are after expenses have been deducted. These expenses reduce the fund's returns.

(2) Under the sub-heading "Year-by-year returns",

    (a) provide a bar chart that shows the annual total return of the mutual fund, in chronological order with the most recent year on the right of the bar chart, for the lesser of

        (i) each of the 10 most recently completed calendar years, and

        (ii) each of the completed calendar years in which the mutual fund has been in existence and which the mutual fund was a reporting issuer; and

    (b) include an introduction to the bar chart using wording substantially similar to the following:

> This chart shows how [name of class/series of securities described in the fund facts document] [units/shares] of the fund performed in each of the past [insert number of calendar years shown in the bar chart required under paragraph (a)]. The fund dropped in value in [for the particular years shown in the bar chart required under paragraph (a), insert the number of years in which the value of the mutual fund dropped] of the [insert number of calendar years shown in the bar chart required in paragraph (a)] years. The range of returns and change from year to year can help you assess how risky the fund has been in the past. It does not tell you how the fund will perform in the future.

(3) Under the sub-heading "Best and worst 3-month returns",

    (a) provide information for the period covered in the bar chart required under paragraph (2)(a) in the form of the following table:

	Return	**3 months ending**	**If you invested $1,000 at the beginning of the period**
Best return	(see instruction 8)	(see instruction 10)	Your investment would [rise/drop] to (see instruction 12).
Worst return	(see instruction 9)	(see instruction 11)	Your investment would [rise/drop] to (see instruction 13).

    (b) include an introduction to the table using wording substantially similar to the following:

> This table shows the best and worst returns for the [name of class/series of securities described in the fund facts document] [units/shares] of the fund in a 3-month period over the past [insert number of calendar years shown in the bar chart required under paragraph (2)(a)]. The best and worst 3-month returns could be higher or lower in the future. Consider how much of a loss you could afford to take in a short period of time.

(4) Under the sub-heading "Average return", show the following:

    (a) the final value of a hypothetical $1000 investment in the mutual fund as at the end of the period that ends within 60 days before the date of the fund facts document and consists of the lesser of

        (i) 10 years, or

        (ii) the time since inception of the mutual fund;

    (b) the annual compounded rate of return that equates the hypothetical $1000 investment to the final value.

INSTRUCTIONS

(1) In responding to the requirements of this Item, a mutual fund must comply with the relevant sections of Part 15 of National Instrument 81-102 Investment Funds as if those sections applied to a fund facts document.

(2) Use a linear scale for each axis of the bar chart required by this Item.

(3) The x-axis and y-axis for the bar chart required by this Item must intersect at zero.

(4) A mutual fund that distributes different classes or series of securities that are referable to the same portfolio of assets must show performance data related only to the specific class or series of securities being described in the fund facts document.

(5) If the information required to be disclosed under this Item is not reasonably available, include the required sub-headings and provide a brief statement explaining why the required information is not available. Information relating to year-by-year returns in the bar chart will generally not be available for a mutual fund that has been distributing securities under a simplified prospectus for less than one calendar year. Information under "Best and worst 3-month returns" and "Average return" will generally not be available for a mutual fund that has been distributing securities under a simplified prospectus for less than 12 consecutive months.

(6) The dollar amounts shown under this Item may be rounded up to the nearest dollar.

(7) The percentage amounts shown under this Item may be rounded to one decimal place.

(8) Show the best rolling 3-month return as at the end of the period that ends within 60 days before the date of the fund facts document.

(9) Show the worst rolling 3-month return as at the end of the period that ends within 60 days before the date of the fund facts document.

(10) Insert the end date for the best 3-month return period.

(11) Insert the end date for the worst 3-month return period.

(12) Insert the final value that would equate with a hypothetical $1000 investment for the best 3-month return period shown in the table.

(13) Insert the final value that would equate with a hypothetical $1000 investment for the worst 3-month return period shown in the table.

Item 6 — [deleted]

Item 7 — Suitability

(1) Provide a brief statement of the suitability of the mutual fund for particular investors under the heading "Who is this fund for?". Describe the characteristics of the investor for whom the mutual fund may or may not be an appropriate investment, and the portfolios for which the mutual fund is and is not suited.

INSTRUCTION:

If the mutual fund is particularly unsuitable for certain types of investors or for certain types of investment portfolios, emphasize this aspect of the mutual fund. Disclose both the types of investors who should not invest in the mutual fund, with regard to investments on both a short- and long-term basis, and the types of portfolios that should not invest in the mutual fund. If the mutual fund is particularly suitable for investors who have particular investment objectives, this can also be disclosed.

Item 8 — Impact of Income Taxes on Investor Returns

Under the heading "A word about tax" provide a brief explanation of the income tax consequences for investors using wording similar to the following:

In general, you'll have to pay income tax on any money you make on a fund. How much you pay depends on the tax laws where you live and whether or not you hold the fund in a registered plan such as a Registered Retirement Savings Plan, or a Tax-Free Savings Account.

Keep in mind that if you hold your fund in a non-registered account, fund distributions are included in your taxable income, whether you get them in cash or have them reinvested.

Part II — Costs, Rights and Other Information

Item 1 — Costs of Buying, Owning and Selling the Fund

1.1 — Introduction

Under the heading "How much does it cost?", state the following:

> The following tables show the fees and expenses you could pay to buy, own and sell [name of the class/series of securities described in the fund facts document] [units/shares] of the fund. The fees and expenses — including any commissions — can vary among [classes/series] of a fund and among funds. Higher commissions can influence representatives to recommend one investment over another. Ask about other funds and investments that may be suitable for you at a lower cost.

1.2 — Illustrations of Different Sales Charge Options

(1) For a mutual fund with multiple sales charge options, include an introduction under the sub-heading "Sales charges" using wording similar to the following:

> You have to choose a sales charge option when you buy the fund. Ask about the pros and cons of each option.

(2) Provide information about the sales charges payable by an investor under the available sales charge options in the form of the following table:

Sales charge option	What you pay		How it works
	in per cent (%)	in dollars ($)	
(see instruction 1)	(see instruction 2)	« (see instruction 3) »	(see instruction 4)

(3) If the mutual fund has only one sales charge option, replace the introductory statement required in paragraph (1) above with a statement highlighting the sales charge option applicable to the mutual fund.

(4) If the mutual fund does not have any sales charges, replace the introductory statement and the table required in paragraph (1) and paragraph (2) above with a general statement explaining that no sales charges apply.

INSTRUCTIONS:

(1) The mutual fund must disclose all sales charge options (e.g., initial sales charge, deferred sales charge) that apply to the class or series being described in the fund facts document. It is not necessary to disclose sales charge options that do not apply to the series or class to which the fund facts document relates.

(2) Specify each sales charge option as a percentage. For an initial sales charge, include a range for the amount that can be charged, if applicable. For a deferred sales charge, provide the full sales charge schedule.

(3) Specify each sales charge option in dollar terms. For an initial sales charge, include a range for the amount that can be charged on every $1,000 investment, if applicable. For a deferred sales charge, include a range for the amount that can be charged on every $1,000 redemption.

(4) Provide a brief overview of the key elements of how each sales charge option works including:

- *whether the amount payable is negotiable;*
- *whether the amount payable is deducted from the amount paid at the time of purchase or from the amount received at the time of sale;*
- *who pays and who receives the amount payable under each sales charge option.*

In the case of a deferred sales charge, the disclosure must also briefly state:

- *any amount payable as an upfront sales commission;*
- *who pays and who receives the amount payable as the upfront sales commission;*
- *any free redemption amount and key details about how it works;*
- *whether switches can be made without incurring a sales charge; and*
- *how the amount paid by an investor at the time of a redemption of securities is calculated, for example, whether it is based on the net asset value of those securities at the time of redemption or another time.*

1.3 — Fund expenses

(1) Under the sub-heading "Fund expenses" include an introduction using wording similar to the following:

> You don't pay these expenses directly. They affect you because they reduce the fund's returns.

(2) Unless the mutual fund has not yet filed a management report of fund performance, provide information about the expenses of the mutual fund in the form of the following table:

	Annual rate (as a % of the fund's value)
Management expense ratio (MER) This is the total of the fund's management fee (including the trailing commission) and operating expenses. (see instruction 1)	(see instruction 2)
Trading expense ratio (TER) These are the fund's trading costs.	(see instruction 3)
Fund expenses	(see instruction 4)

(3) Unless the mutual fund has not yet filed a management report of fund performance, above the table required under subsection (2), include a statement using wording similar to the following:

> As of [see instruction 5], the fund's expenses were [insert amount included in table required under subsection (2)]% of its value. This equals $[see instruction 6] for every $1,000 invested.

(4) For a mutual fund that has not yet filed a management report of fund performance, state the following:

> The fund's expenses are made up of the management fee, operating expenses and trading costs. The [class'/series'] annual management fee is [see instruction 7]% of the [class'/series'] value.

> Because this [class/series] is new, operating expenses and trading costs are not yet available.

(5) If the mutual fund pays an incentive fee that is determined by the performance of the mutual fund, provide a brief statement disclosing the amount of the fee and the circumstances in which the mutual fund will pay it.

(6) Under the sub-heading "More about the trailing commission", state whether the manager of the mutual fund or another member of the mutual fund's organization pays trailing commissions. If trailing commissions are paid, include a description using wording substantially similar to the following:

> The trailing commission is an ongoing commission. It is paid for as long as you own the fund. It is for the services and advice that your representative and their firm provide to you.

> [Insert name of fund manager] pays the trailing commission to your representative's firm. It is paid from the fund's management fee and is based on the value of your investment. The rate depends on the sales charge option you choose.

(7) If applicable, disclose the range of the rates of the trailing commission for each sales charge option disclosed under Item 1.2.

INSTRUCTIONS:

(1) If any fees or expenses otherwise payable by the mutual fund were waived or otherwise absorbed by a member of the organization of the mutual fund, despite section 15.1(2) of National Instrument 81-106 Investment Fund Continuous Disclosure, only include a statement in substantially the following words:

> *[Insert name of the manager of the mutual fund] waived some of the fund's expenses. If it had not done so, the MER would have been higher.*

(2) Use the same MER that is disclosed in Item 2 of Part 1 of this Form.

(2.1) If applicable, include a reference to any fixed administration fees in the management expense ratio description required in the table under Item 1.3(2).

(3) Use the trading expense ratio disclosed in the most recently filed management report of fund performance (MRFP) for the mutual fund.

(4) The amount included for fund expenses is the amount arrived at by adding the MER and the trading expense ratio. Use a bold font or other formatting to indicate that fund expenses is the total of all ongoing expenses set out in the chart and is not a separate expense charged to the fund.

(5) Insert the date of the most recently filed management report of fund performance.

(6) Insert the equivalent dollar amount of the ongoing expenses of the fund for each $1,000 investment.

(7) The percentage disclosed for the management fee must correspond to the percentage shown in the fee table in the simplified prospectus.

(7.1) For a mutual fund that is required to include the disclosure under subsection (4), in the description of the items that make up fund fees, include a reference to any fixed administrative fees, if applicable. Also disclose the amount of the fixed administration fee in the same manner as required for the management fee. The percentage disclosed for the fixed administration fee must correspond to the percentage shown in the fee table in the simplified prospectus.

(8) In disclosing the range of rates of trailing commissions for each sales charge option, show both the percentage amount and the equivalent dollar amount for each $1000 investment.

1.4 — Other Fees

(1) Under the sub-heading "Other fees", provide an introduction using wording substantially similar to the following:

You may have to pay other fees when you buy, hold, sell or switch [units/shares] of the fund.

(2) Provide information about the amount of fees, other than sales charges, payable by an investor when they buy, hold, sell or switch units or shares of the mutual fund, substantially in the form of the following table:

Fee	What you pay
(see instruction 1)	(see instruction 2)

INSTRUCTIONS:

(1) Under this Item, it is necessary to include only those fees that apply to the particular class or series of securities of the mutual fund. Examples include management fees and administration fees payable directly by investors, short-term trading fees, switch fees and change fees. This also includes any requirement for an investor to participate in a fee-based arrangement with their dealer in order to be eligible to purchase the particular class or series of securities of the mutual fund. If there are no other fees associated with buying, holding, selling or switching units or shares of the mutual fund, replace the table with a statement to that effect.

(2) Provide a brief description of each fee disclosing the amount to be paid as a percentage (or, if applicable, a fixed dollar amount) and state who charges the fee. If the amount of the fee varies so that specific disclosure of the amount of the fee cannot be disclosed include, where possible, the highest possible rate or range for that fee.

Item 2: — Statement of Rights

Under the heading "What if I change my mind?", state using wording substantially similar to the following:

Under securities law in some provinces and territories, you have the right to:

- withdraw from an agreement to buy mutual funds within two business days after you receive a simplified prospectus or Fund Facts document, or

- cancel your purchase within 48 hours after you receive confirmation of the purchase.

In some provinces and territories, you also have the right to cancel a purchase, or in some jurisdictions, claim damages, if the simplified prospectus, annual information form, Fund Facts document or financial statements contain a misrepresentation. You must act within the time limit set by the securities law in your province or territory. For more information, see the securities law of your province or territory or ask a lawyer.

Item 3 — More Information About the Fund

(1) Under the heading "For more information", state using wording substantially similar to the following:

Contact [insert name of the manager of the mutual fund] or your representative for a copy of the fund's simplified prospectus and other disclosure documents. These documents and the Fund Facts make up the fund's legal documents.

(2) State the name, address and toll-free telephone number of the manager of the mutual fund. If applicable, also state the e-mail address and website of the manager of the mutual fund.

(3) State using wording substantially similar to the following:

To learn more about investing in mutual funds, see the brochure **Understanding mutual funds**, which is available on the website of the Canadian Securities Administrators at www.securitiesadministrators.ca.

Companion Policy 81-101CP — To National Instrument 81-101 Mutual Fund Prospectus Disclosure

Table of Contents

PART 1 — PURPOSE OF THE COMPANION POLICY

1.1 Purpose of the Companion Policy — The purpose of this Companion Policy is to state the views of the Canadian Securities Administrators (CSA or we) on various matters relating to the Instrument, including,

(a) a discussion of the general approach taken by the CSA in, and the general regulatory purpose for, the Instrument;

(b) explanation and discussion of various parts of the Instrument; and

(c) examples of some matters described in the Instrument.

PART 2 — PURPOSE AND GENERAL APPROACH OF THE INSTRUMENT

2.1 Purpose of the Instrument — (1) The purpose of the Instrument is to ensure that the offering disclosure regime for mutual funds provides investors with disclosure documents that clearly and concisely state information that investors should consider in connection with an investment decision about the mutual fund, while recognizing that different investors have differing needs in receiving disclosure.

(2) The disclosure regime for mutual funds is built on two main principles:

- providing investors with key information about a mutual fund; and
- providing the information in a simple, accessible and comparable format.

(3) We use the following approaches in the Instrument to achieve the principles referred to in subsection (2):

1. The Instrument has been designed so that fund companies prepare offering disclosure documents that investors would find helpful in making investment decisions.

2. The Instrument contemplates the use of three disclosure documents by a mutual fund:

- a simplified prospectus;
- an annual information form; and
- a summary document called the 'fund facts', which contains key information about a mutual fund.

Together with the financial statements, the management reports of fund performance and other documents incorporated by reference, these documents contain full, true and plain disclosure about the mutual fund.

3. Subsection 4.1(1) of the Instrument requires that the simplified prospectus, annual information form and fund facts document be prepared using plain language and in a format that assists in readability and comprehension. The Instrument and related forms provide detailed requirements on the content and format of these documents.

(4) Mutual funds, managers and participants in the mutual fund industry should prepare disclosure documents and carry out delivery in a manner that is consistent with the spirit and intent of the Instrument.

2.1.1 Fund Facts Document — (1) The Instrument requires that the fund facts document be in plain language, be no longer than 4 pages in length, and highlight key information important to investors, including performance, risk and cost. The fund facts document is incorporated by reference into the simplified prospectus.

(2) The Instrument and Form 81-101F3 set out detailed requirements on the content and format of a fund facts document, while allowing some flexibility to accommodate different kinds of mutual funds. The requirements are designed to ensure that the information in a fund facts document of a mutual fund is clear, concise, understandable and easily comparable with information in the fund facts document of other mutual funds.

(3) To help write the fund facts document in plain language, mutual fund companies can use the Flesch-Kincaid methodology to assess the readability of a fund facts document. The Flesch-Kincaid grade level scale is a methodology that rates the readability of a text to a corresponding grade level and can be determined by the use of Flesch-Kincaid tests built into commonly used word processing programs. The CSA will generally consider a grade level of 6.0 or less on the Flesch-Kincaid grade level scale to indicate that a fund facts document is written in plain language. For French-language documents, mutual fund companies may wish to consider using other appropriate readability tools.

(4) The Instrument requires delivery of the fund facts document, which satisfies the prospectus delivery requirements under applicable securities legislation. The CSA also encourages the use and distribution of the fund facts document as a key part of the sales process in helping to inform investors about mutual funds they are considering for investment.

(5) The CSA generally consider volatility to be a suitable basis for determining the investment risk rating of a mutual fund. For this reason, Form 81-101F3 prescribes specific disclosure in the fund facts document explaining how volatility can be used as a measure to gauge the risk of an investment. If the disclosure is not compatible with the specific investment risk classification methodology that is used by the manager of the mutual fund, the CSA will consider applications for relief from Item 4 of Form 81-101F3. In making the application, the manager must demonstrate the suitability of using an alternative measure in determining the investment risk rating of its mutual fund. The application must also provide sample disclosure in place of the prescribed disclosure that would assist investors in understanding the investment risk rating of the mutual fund.

2.2 Simplified Prospectus — (1) A simplified prospectus is the prospectus for the purposes of securities legislation. While the Instrument requires delivery of a fund facts document to an investor in connection with a purchase, an investor may also request delivery a copy of the simplified prospectus, or any other documents incorporated by reference into the simplified prospectus.

(2) The Instrument and Form 81-101F1 set out detailed requirements on the content and format of a simplified prospectus. The requirements enable the information about a mutual fund to be clear, concise, understandable, well-organized and to easily compare one mutual fund with another.

2.3 Annual Information Form — (1) The Instrument requires that a supplemental disclosure document, the annual information form, be provided to any person on request. The annual information form is incorporated by reference into the simplified prospectus.

(2) Information contained in the related simplified prospectus will generally not be repeated in an annual information form except as necessary to make the annual information form comprehensible as an independent document. In general, an annual information form is intended to provide disclosure about different matters than those discussed in the fund facts document and simplified prospectus, such as information concerning the internal operations of the manager of the mutual fund, which may be of assistance or interest to some investors.

Part 8: MUTUAL FUNDS

(3) The Instrument and Form 81-101F2 allow for more flexibility in the preparation of an annual information form than is the case with a simplified prospectus and fund facts document. The requirements for the order of disclosing information are less stringent for an annual information form than for a fund facts document or a simplified prospectus. An annual information form may include information not specifically required by Form 81-101F2.

2.4 Financial Statements and Management Reports of Fund Performance — The Instrument requires that the mutual fund's most recently audited financial statements, any interim financial reports filed after those audited statements, the mutual fund's most recently filed annual management report of fund performance and any interim management report of fund performance filed after that annual management report be provided upon request to any person or company requesting them. Like the fund facts document and the annual information form, these financial statements and management reports of fund performance are incorporated by reference into the simplified prospectus. The result is that future filings of these documents will be incorporated by reference into the simplified prospectus, while superseding the financial statements and management reports of fund performance previously filed.

2.5 Filing and Delivery of Documents — (1) Section 2.3 of the Instrument distinguishes between documents that are required by securities legislation to be "filed" with the securities regulatory authority or regulator and those that must be "delivered" or "sent" to the securities regulatory authority or regulator. Documents that are "filed" are on the public record. Documents that are "delivered" or "sent" are not necessarily on the public record. All documents required to be filed under the Instrument must be filed in accordance with National Instrument 13-101 *System for Electronic Document Analysis and Retrieval (SEDAR)*.

(2) Section 1.1 of the Instrument defines "business day" as any day other than a Saturday, Sunday or a statutory holiday. In some cases, a statutory holiday may only be a statutory holiday in one jurisdiction. The definition of business day should be applied in each local jurisdiction in which a prospectus is being filed. For example, section 5.1.2 of the Instrument states that the date of the certificate in a simplified prospectus must be within 3 business days before the filing of the simplified prospectus. The certificates in the simplified prospectus are dated Day 1. Day 2 is a statutory holiday in Québec but not in Alberta. If the simplified prospectus is filed in both Alberta and Québec, it must be filed no later than Day 4 in order to comply with the requirement in section 5.1.2 of the Instrument, despite the fact that Day 2 was not a business day in Québec. If the simplified prospectus is filed only in Québec, it could be filed on Day 5.

2.5.1 Personal Information Forms — (1) If mutual funds are relying upon a previously delivered personal information form or predecessor personal information form, mutual funds are reminded that the responses to certain questions in the form must still be correct. Accordingly, in order to meet these requirements mutual funds should obtain appropriate confirmations from the individual concerned.

(2) Paragraphs 2.3(1.1)(c) and 2.3(2.1)(c) of the Instrument require that in certain circumstances a mutual fund deliver a copy of a previously delivered personal information form, or "alternative information that is satisfactory to the regulator". Our interpretation of what would potentially be alternative information that is satisfactory to the regulator is, with respect to the previous delivery of an individual's personal information form, the System for Electronic Document Analysis and Retrieval (SEDAR) project number and name of issuer. In most cases this information will be sufficient. Staff will contact mutual funds in cases where it is not. Mutual funds wishing to proceed in this manner should provide the information in the cover letter for the preliminary or pro forma simplified prospectus.

(3) If a mutual fund is delivering a copy of a previously delivered personal information form pursuant to paragraphs 2.3(1.1)(c) and 2.3(2.1)(c) of the instrument, the mutual fund should deliver it as a personal information form on SEDAR, in the same way that a new personal information form would be delivered.

2.6 Supporting Documents — (1) [Repealed]

(2) Subsection 2.3(6) of the Instrument permits certain material contracts to be filed with certain commercial or financial information deleted in order to keep this information confidential. For example, specific fees and expenses and non-competition clauses could be kept confidential under this provision. In these cases, the benefits of disclosing the information to the public are outweighed by the potentially adverse consequences to mutual fund managers and portfolio advisers. However, the basic terms of these agreements must be included in the contracts that are filed, such as provisions relating to the term and termination of the agreements and the rights and responsibilities of the parties to the agreements.

2.7 Amendments — (1) Paragraph 2.1(1)(d) of the Instrument requires an amendment to an annual information form to be filed whenever an amendment to a simplified prospectus is filed. Similarly, subsection 2.3(5.1) of the Instrument requires an amendment to an annual information form to be filed whenever an amendment to a fund facts document is filed. If the substance of the amendment to the fund facts document or to the simplified prospectus would not require a change to the text of the annual information form, the amendment to the annual information form would consist only of the certificate page referring to the mutual fund to which the amendment to the fund facts document or the simplified prospectus pertains.

(2.1) General Instruction (8.1) of Form 81-101F3 permits a mutual fund to disclose a material change and proposed fundamental change, such as a proposed merger, in an amended and restated fund facts document. We would permit flexibility in selecting the appropriate section of the amended and restated fund facts document to describe the material change or proposed fundamental change. However, we also expect that the variable sections of the fund facts document, such as the Top 10 investments and investment mix, to be updated within 60 days before the date of the fund facts document. In addition, if a mutual fund completes a calendar year or files a management report of fund performance prior to the filing of the amended and restated fund facts document, we expect the fund facts document to reflect the updated information.

(2) Paragraph 2.1(1)(e) of the Instrument requires a mutual fund to file an amendment to a fund facts document when a material change to the mutual fund occurs that requires a change to the disclosure in the fund facts document. This mirrors the requirement in paragraph 11.2(1)(d) of National Instrument 81-106 Investment Fund Continuous Disclosure. We would not generally consider changes to the top 10 investments, investment mix or year-by-year returns of the mutual fund to be material changes. We would generally consider changes to the mutual fund's investment objective or risk level to be material changes under securities legislation.

(3) A commercial copy of an amended and restated simplified prospectus and annual information form can be created by reprinting the entire document or by putting stickers on an existing document that provide the new text created by the amendment. If stickers are used, one sticker will be required for the substance of the amendments and a separate sticker will be required for the cover page of the document that describes the type and date of the document, as applicable.

(4) Subsection 2.2(4) of the Instrument requires that any amendment to a fund facts document can only take the form of an amended and restated fund facts document. Accordingly, the commercial copy of an amended and restated fund facts document can only be created by reprinting the entire document.

(5) The requirements in section 2.2 of the Instrument apply to an amendment to a full simplified prospectus and to an amendment only to a Part A or Part B section of a simplified prospectus in cases where the Part A and Part B sections are bound separately. Section 2.2 of the Instrument requires amendments to various parts of a multiple SP to be evidenced as follows:

1. Multiple SP with Part A and the Part B sections bound together. An amendment to either or both of the Part A or Part B sections could be in the form of a free standing amending instrument that would be delivered to investors with the rest of the multiple SP. The amending instrument would be identified, in accordance with subsection 2.2(3) of the Instrument, as "Amendment No. [insert number], dated [date of amendment] to the simplified prospectus document for the [name of funds] dated [date of original document]". Or, the amendment could be in the form of a restated and amended multiple SP document, identified as such in accordance with subsection 2.2(3).

2. Multiple SP with Part A and the Part B sections bound separately. If there is an amendment to the Part A section of the document but not to a Part B section, the amendment could be in the form of an amending document or an amended and restated Part A document. An amending document could be identified as "Amendment No. [insert number], dated [date of amendment], to the Part A section of the simplified prospectuses of the [name of funds] dated [original date of multiple SP]", and the amended and restated Part A document could be identified as "Amended and Restated Simplified Prospectuses dated [date of amendment] of the [name of funds], amending and restating the Simplified Prospectuses dated [original date of document].".

3. In the circumstances described in paragraph 2 above, no amendment is required to be made to the Part B sections of the multiple SP. The footer that is required by Item 1 of Part B of Form 81-101F1 to be on the bottom of each page of a Part B section will continue to show the date of the original Part A document. For this reason, the amended Part A document must be identified in a way that shows the date of the amendments and the original date of the document so that investors know that it relates to the corresponding Part B sections.

4. If there is an amendment to a Part B section of a multiple SP with Part A and Part B sections bound separately the amendment must be made by way of an amended and restated Part B document, whether or not an amendment is being made to the Part A section. If no amendment to the Part A section is being made, no amendment is required to the Part A document. The amended and restated Part B document will include a statement in the footer required by Item 1 of Part B of Form 81-101F1 that identifies the document as a document that amends and restates the original Part B document.

(6) Subsection 2.2(4) of the Instrument requires an amendment to a fund facts document to be in the form of an amended and restated fund facts document. An amended fund facts document does not have to be otherwise identified, except for the date of the amendment.

(7) An amendment to a prospectus of a mutual fund, even if it amends and restates the prospectus, does not change the date under Canadian securities legislation by which the mutual fund must renew the prospectus. That date, which is commonly referred to as the "lapse date" for the prospectus, remains that date established under securities legislation. An amendment to a fund facts document will also not change the lapse date for a prospectus.

(8) Securities legislation says that a person or company must not distribute securities, unless a preliminary prospectus and a prospectus have been filed and receipts have been issued by the securities regulatory authority or regulator. This requirement also applies to mutual funds. If a mutual fund adds a new class or series of securities to a simplified prospectus that is referable to a new separate portfolio of assets, a preliminary simplified prospectus must be filed, together with a preliminary annual information form and preliminary fund facts document. However, if the new class or series of securities is referable to an existing portfolio of assets, the new class or series may be added by an amendment to the simplified prospectus. In this case, a preliminary fund facts document for the new class or series must still be filed, as set out in subparagraph 2.1(1)(d)(iii) of the Instrument.

2.8 Websites — Section 2.3.1 of the Instrument requires a mutual fund to post its fund facts document to the website of the mutual fund, the mutual fund's family or the manager of the mutual fund, as applicable. A fund facts document should remain on the website at least until the next fund facts document for the mutual fund is posted. A fund facts document must be displayed in an easily visible and accessible location on the website. It should also be presented in a format that is convenient for both reading online and printing on paper.

PART 3 — PLAIN LANGUAGE AND PRESENTATION

3.1 Plain Language — Subsection 4.1(1) of the Instrument requires that a simplified prospectus, annual information form and fund facts document be written in plain language. The reason for using "plain language" is to communicate in a way that the audience could immediately understand what you tell them. The plain language approach focuses on the needs and abilities of the audience to ensure that the content of a communication is relevant, the organization of the information is logical, the language is appropriate and the presentation is visually appealing.

Mutual funds should consider the following plain language techniques in preparing their documents:

- Organize the document into clear, concise sections, paragraphs and sentences.
- Use:
  - common everyday words
  - technical, legal and business terms only when unavoidable and provide clear and concise explanations for them
  - the active voice
  - short sentences and paragraphs
  - a conversational and personal tone
  - examples and illustrations to explain abstract concepts.
- Avoid:
  - superfluous words
  - unnecessary technical, legal and business jargon
  - vague boilerplate wording
  - glossaries and defined terms unless they aid in understanding the disclosure
  - abstractions by using more concrete terms or examples
  - excessive detail
  - multiple negatives.

3.2 Presentation — (1) Subsection 4.1(1) of the Instrument requires that a simplified prospectus, annual information form and fund facts document be presented in a format that assists in readability and comprehension. The Instrument and related forms also set out certain aspects of a simplified prospectus, annual information form and fund facts document that must be presented in a required format, requiring some information to be presented in the form of tables, charts or diagrams. Within these requirements, mutual funds have flexibility in the format used for simplified prospectuses, annual information forms and fund facts documents.

The formatting of documents can contribute substantially to the ease with which the document can be read and understood. Mutual funds should consider using the following formatting ideas when preparing their documents:

- reasonably-sized, easy-to-read typefaces
- reasonably-sized, easy-to-read typefaces
- headings that are clearly differentiated from the body text
- bulleted or numbered lists
- margins, boxes or shading to highlight information or for supplementary information
- tables, graphs and diagrams for complex information
- "question and answer" format to organize information
- sufficient white space on each page
- images, colour, lines and other graphical elements
- avoiding the use of upper-case, bold, italic or underlining in blocks of text
- avoiding full-justified margins.

(2) We think documents would be easier to read and understand with the use of the design features set out in subsection (1). The use of logos and pictures that accurately depict aspects of the mutual fund industry, the mutual fund or mutual fund family or products and services offered by the mutual fund family may also aid in comprehension and readability. However we think that an excessive use or crowding of design features might make the documents more difficult to read or understand.

(3) On occasion, we have seen amendments to simplified prospectuses prepared in highly legal and technical styles. For example, some amendments merely reference specific lines or sections of a simplified prospectus that are being amended, without providing the reader with a restated section or an explanation for the changes. In addition, some amendments have been presented in the form of photocopies of some other documents, such as meeting materials, with the word "amendment" written on the top of the photocopy. We think that these approaches are inappropriate ways of amending a simplified prospectus or annual information form under the Instrument.

Material changes to mutual funds must be described in a format that assists in readability and comprehension, as required by subsection 4.1(1) of the Instrument. Amendments should be expressed clearly, and in a manner that enables the reader to easily read and understand both the amendment and the revised sections of the relevant document. This manner of expression may require the preparation of either an amended and restated simplified prospectus or annual information form or a clearly worded amendment insert for the existing simplified prospectus or annual information form. Any amendment to a fund facts document must be in the form of an amended and restated fund facts document.

PART 4 — THE MULTIPLE SP

4.1 General Provisions Relating to a Multiple SP — (1) A consolidated "simplified prospectus" pertaining to a number of mutual funds is in law a number of separate simplified prospectuses, one simplified prospectus for each mutual fund. Further, a receipt issued by the securities regulatory authority or regulator in connection with a consolidated "simplified prospectus" in law represents a separate receipt for the simplified prospectus pertaining to each mutual fund. The Instrument and Form 81-101F1 make clear that a simplified prospectus under the Instrument pertains to one mutual fund and use the term "multiple SP" to refer to a document that contains more than one simplified prospectus.

(2) Under the Instrument, a simplified prospectus consists of two sections: a Part A section, which provides introductory information about the mutual fund, general information about mutual funds and information applicable to the mutual funds managed by the mutual fund organization, and a Part B section, which contains specific information about the mutual fund.

(3) The Instrument states that simplified prospectuses must not be consolidated to form a multiple SP unless the Part A section of each simplified prospectus is substantially similar. We think the term "substantially similar" would be applicable in this context if there is a high degree of similarity among the Part A sections of the simplified prospectuses that are proposed to be consolidated. This option would be available generally to mutual funds in the same mutual fund family that are administered by the same entities and operated in the same manner. There may be some deviation between the disclosure that would be provided for some of the mutual funds; those deviations have been largely contemplated by the Form 81-101F1.

(4) In order to maximize flexibility for mutual fund organizations and improve the accessibility of disclosure provided to investors, the Instrument allows the Part B sections of a multiple SP to be bound separately from the Part A section. In addition, the Instrument permits the physical separation of each Part B section that pertains to a different mutual fund. This would permit an investor to be provided with a Part A section that described the mutual fund family and mutual fund organization generally, and only the mutual fund-specific disclosure that relates to the mutual fund or mutual funds in which the investor is interested. This approach could permit a "back pocket" approach in which the Part B sections of a simplified prospectus could be inserted in a pocket of the Part A section of the document.

(5) The Instrument contains no restrictions on how many simplified prospectuses can be consolidated into a multiple SP.

4.2 Adding Additional Funds to a Multiple SP — (1) Mutual funds may create and file a document that contains both a pro forma simplified prospectus and a preliminary simplified prospectus in order to include the disclosure of a new mutual fund in documents that already pertain to existing mutual funds.

(2) A new mutual fund may be added to a multiple SP that contains final simplified prospectuses. In this case, an amended multiple SP and multiple AIF containing disclosure of the new mutual fund, as well as a new fund facts document for each class or series of the new mutual fund would be filed. The preliminary filing would constitute the filing of a preliminary simplified prospectus, annual information form and fund facts document for the new mutual fund, and a draft amended and restated simplified prospectus and annual information form for each existing mutual fund. The final filing of documents would include a simplified prospectus, annual information form and fund facts document for the new mutual fund, and an amended and restated simplified prospectus and annual information form for each previously existing mutual fund. An amendment to an existing fund facts document would generally not be necessary.

(3) An amendment to a prospectus of a mutual fund does not change the "lapse date" of the prospectus under Canadian securities legislation. Mutual funds are encouraged to pay particular attention to this issue when following the procedures described in subsection (2).

PART 4.1 — THE FUND FACTS DOCUMENT

4.1.1 General Purposes — The general purposes of the offering disclosure regime for mutual funds and of the fund facts document are described in section 2.1 of this Policy. This Part provides guidance to preparers of the fund facts document in meeting those purposes.

A sample fund facts document is set out in Appendix A to this Policy. The sample is provided for illustrative purposes only.

4.1.2 Multiple Class Mutual Funds — The purpose for the requirements on the content and format of a fund facts document is to give investors the opportunity to easily compare the key information of one mutual fund to another. For many mutual funds, the class or series may affect not only the management expense ratio and performance, but a number of other considerations as well, such as minimum investment amounts, distributions, suitability, dealer compensation and sales charge options. For this reason, the Instrument requires a fund facts document to be prepared for each class and each series of a mutual fund that is referable to the same portfolio of assets.

4.1.3 Filings — (1) Section 2.1 of the Instrument requires that a fund facts document for each class and series of the securities of a mutual fund be filed concurrently with the mutual fund's simplified prospectus and annual information form.

(2) The most recently filed fund facts document for a mutual fund is incorporated by reference into the simplified prospectus under section 3.1 of the Instrument, with the result that any fund facts document filed under the Instrument after the date of receipt for the simplified prospectus supersedes the fund facts document previously filed.

(3) Section 2.3.1 of the Instrument requires a fund facts document filed under Part 2 of the Instrument to be posted by the mutual fund to the website of the mutual fund, the mutual fund's family or the manager of the mutual fund. Only a final fund facts document filed under the Instrument should be posted to a website. A preliminary or pro forma fund facts document, for example, should not be posted.

4.1.4 Additional Information — Paragraph 4.1(3)(d) of the Instrument requires a fund facts document to include only information that is specifically mandated or permitted by the required Form 81-101F3.

4.1.5 Format — The Instrument requires a mutual fund to use the headings and sub-headings stipulated in the Instrument and Form 81-101F3.

PART 5 — THE SIMPLIFIED PROSPECTUS

5.1 General Purposes — The general purposes of a simplified prospectus are described in section 2.1 of this Policy. This Part provides guidance to preparers of simplified prospectuses in meeting those purposes.

5.2 Catalogue Approach — The Instrument requires that a multiple SP must present the fund-specific, or Part B, disclosure about each fund using a catalogue approach. That is, the disclosure about each mutual fund must be presented separately from the disclosure about each other mutual fund.

5.2.1 Accessibility of a Simplified Prospectus — Mutual funds, managers, and dealers should encourage investors who want more information about a mutual fund to request and read the simplified prospectus and any of the documents incorporated by reference into the simplified prospectus. The Instrument requires that a simplified prospectus or any of the documents incorporated by reference be sent within three business days of a request.

5.3 Additional Information — (1) Paragraph 4.1(2)(a) of the Instrument provides that a simplified prospectus must provide all information briefly and concisely. Paragraph 4.1(2)(e) of the Instrument requires that a simplified prospectus must include only educational material or information that is specifically mandated or permitted by Form 81-101F1.

(2) [repealed]

(3) Item 12 of Part A and Item 14 of Part B of Form 81-101F1 permit disclosure of information required or permitted by securities legislation or by an order or ruling of the securities regulatory authority pertaining to the mutual fund that is not otherwise required to be disclosed by Form 81-101F1. This addition has been made to ensure that such information is not technically prohibited from being included in a simplified prospectus by paragraph 4.1(2)(e) of the Instrument. Instruction (1) to Item 12 of Part A of Form 81-101F1 contains examples of the type of disclosure that may be appropriately included under these Items.

5.4 Inclusion of Educational Material — (1) Paragraph 4.1(2)(e) of the Instrument permits educational material to be included in a simplified prospectus. There are no requirements on the location of any educational material. However, the CSA thinks that educational material will be more useful if placed close to mandated disclosure to which it substantively relates.

(2) Educational material contained in a simplified prospectus is subject to the general requirements of the Instrument and should be presented in a manner consistent with the rest of the simplified prospectus. That is, the educational material should be concise, clear and not detract from the clarity or presentation of the information in the simplified prospectus.

(3) The definition of "educational material" contained in section 1.1 of the Instrument excludes material that promotes a particular mutual fund or mutual fund family, or the products or services offered by the mutual fund or mutual fund family. A mutual fund, mutual fund family or those products or services may be referred to in educational material as an example if the reference does not promote those entities, products or services. Mutual funds should ensure that any material included within, attached to or bound with a simplified prospectus is educational material within the meaning of this definition.

5.5 Format — A simplified prospectus must use the headings and specified sub-headings exactly as they are set out in the Instrument. If no sub-headings are specified, a simplified prospectus may include additional sub-headings under the required headings.

PART 6 — THE ANNUAL INFORMATION FORM

6.1 General Purposes — The general purposes of an annual information form are described in section 2.1 of this Policy. This Part provides guidance to preparers of annual information forms in meeting those purposes.

6.2 [repealed]

6.3 Consolidation of Annual Information Forms — Subsection 5.4(1) of the Instrument requires the consolidation of annual information forms into a multiple AIF if the related simplified prospectuses are consolidated into a multiple SP. It is noted that the Instrument does not prevent the consolidation of annual information forms even if the related simplified prospectuses are not consolidated. Therefore, a mutual fund organization may prepare, for instance, one multiple AIF that pertains to all of its mutual funds, even if the simplified prospectuses for those mutual funds are not fully or even partially consolidated.

6.4 Additional Material — (1) The Instrument and AIF Form do not prohibit the inclusion in an annual information form of information not specifically required by the AIF Form. Among other things, a mutual fund may therefore include educational information in an annual information form. Additional material in an annual information form is, however, subject to the general requirements contained in subsection 4.1(1) of the Instrument that all information must be presented in plain language and in a format that assists in readability and comprehension.

(2) If a mutual fund includes additional information, such as educational material, in an annual information form, that material should not be included primarily for purpose of promotion. An annual information form is designed to be easily understandable to investors and less legalistic in its drafting than traditional prospectuses, but it still constitutes part of a prospectus under securities legislation.

PART 7 — DELIVERY

7.1 Delivery of the Fund Facts Document, Simplified Prospectus and Annual Information Form — (1) The Instrument contemplates delivery to all investors of a fund facts document in accordance with the requirements in securities legislation. It does not require the delivery of the simplified prospectus, or any other documents incorporated by reference into the simplified prospectus, unless requested. Mutual funds or dealers may also provide investors with any of the other disclosure documents incorporated by reference into the simplified prospectus.

(2) The CSA encourage mutual funds, managers, and dealers to make disclosure documents, par-ticularly the fund facts document, available to potential investors as soon as possible in the sales process, in advance of any requirements contained in the Instrument or securities legislation, either directly or through dealers and others involved in selling mutual fund securities to investors.

(2.1) Nothing in the Instrument prevents the simplified prospectus, annual information form or fund facts document from being prepared in other languages, provided that these documents are delivered or sent in addition to any disclosure document filed and required to be delivered in ac-cordance with the Instrument. We would consider such documents to be sales communications.

(3) We do not consider the requirements of section 3.4 of the Instrument to be exclusive. Mutual funds and managers of mutual funds are encouraged to inform investors about using their websites and e-mail addresses to request further information and additional documents.

7.1.1 Electronic Delivery — (1) A simplified prospectus, or any document incorporated by reference into the simplified prospectus, that is required to be delivered or sent under the Instrument may be delivered or sent by means of electronic delivery. Electronic delivery may include sending an electronic copy of the relevant document directly to the investor as an attachment or link, or directing the investor to the specific document on a website.

(2) In addition to the requirements in the Instrument and the guidance in this section, mutual funds, managers and dealers may want to refer to National Policy 11-201 *Delivery of Documents by Electronic Means* and, in Québec, Notice 11-201 relating to the *Delivery of Documents by Electronic Means* for additional guidance.

7.2 Section 3.3 of the Instrument requires that a mutual fund deliver or send to a person or company, upon request, a simplified prospectus or documents incorporated by reference. The CSA are of the view that compliance with this specifically-mandated requirement by an unregistered entity is not a breach of the registration requirements of securities legislation.

7.3 (1) Mutual fund organizations that create physically separate Part B sections are reminded of section 3.2 of the Instrument, which provides that the requirement under securities legislation to deliver or send a prospectus for a mutual fund is satisfied by the delivery or sending of a simplified prospectus for the mutual fund. This obligation would be satisfied only by the delivery of both the Part A and Part B sections of a simplified prospectus. Particularly in the case of a switch by an investor from one mutual fund to another in a mutual fund family, the mutual fund organization must ensure that the investor is provided with the Part B section of the simplified prospectus pertaining to the mutual fund just purchased, even if the Part A section of the simplified prospectus was previously delivered.

(2) Subsection 5.3(2) of the Instrument permits Part B sections that have been bound separately from the related Part A section to either be bound individually or together, at the option of the mutual fund organization. There is no prohibition against the same Part B section of a multiple SP being bound by itself for distribution to some investors, but also being bound with the Part B section of other mutual funds for distribution to other investors.

7.4 Delivery of Non-Educational Material — The Instrument and related forms contain no restrictions on the delivery of non-educational material such as promotional brochures with either of the simplified prospectus and the annual information form. This type of material may, therefore, be delivered with, but cannot be included within, wrapped around, or attached or bound to, the simplified prospectus and the annual information form. The Instrument does not permit the binding of educational and non-educational material with the Fund Facts Document. The intention of the Instrument is not to unreasonably encumber the Fund Facts with additional documents.

Amendment

7.1 Delivery of the Simplified Prospectus and Annual Information Form — The Instrument contemplates delivery to all investors of a fund facts document in accordance with the requirements in securities legislation. It does not require the delivery of the simplified prospectus, or any other documents incorporated by reference into the simplified prospectus, unless requested. Mutual funds or dealers may also provide investors with any of the other disclosure documents incorporated by reference into the simplified prospectus.

7.2 Pre-Sale Delivery of the Fund Facts Document — (1) The Instrument requires a fund facts document to be delivered before a dealer accepts an instruction for the purchase of a security of a mutual fund. The purpose of pre-sale delivery of a fund facts document is to provide a purchaser with key information about the mutual fund that will inform a purchase decision. What constitutes "before" is intended to be flexible, provided it occurs within a reasonable timeframe before the purchaser's instruction to purchase. Accordingly, the Canadian securities regulatory authorities would generally expect that delivery of a fund facts document will occur within a timeframe that provides a purchaser with a reasonable opportunity to consider the information in the fund facts document before proceeding with the transaction. It should not be delivered so far in advance of the purchase of a security of a mutual fund that the delivery cannot be said to have any connection with the purchaser's instruction to purchase the mutual fund.

(2) Where a purchaser has already received a fund facts document for a particular class or series of securities of a mutual fund, it is not necessary to deliver to the purchaser another fund facts document for a subsequent purchase of that same class or series of securities of a mutual fund, unless a more recent version of the fund facts document has been filed.

7.3 Post-Sale Delivery of the Fund Facts Document — **(1)** While the Instrument generally requires pre-sale delivery of the fund facts document, it also sets out specific requirements that would permit post-sale delivery of the fund facts document in circumstances where the purchaser has indicated that they require the purchase of a security of a mutual fund to be completed immediately, or by a specified time, and it is not reasonably practicable for the dealer to effect pre-sale delivery of the fund facts document within the timeframe specified by the purchaser.

(2) The requirements for post-sale delivery of the fund facts document are set out in section 3.2.02 and should be interpreted consistently with the dealer's general duties to act fairly, honestly and in good faith and to establish and maintain a compliance system in accordance with securities legislation. Accordingly, the Canadian securities regulatory authorities expect dealers will adapt their business models to comply with the general requirement for pre-sale delivery of the fund facts document.

(3) Section 3.2.02 requires dealers to provide a summary of the information contained in the fund facts document. This should include describing the purpose of the fund facts document, the type of information it contains, and advising purchasers that they are entitled to receive and review the fund facts document before the purchase of a security of a mutual fund. Where the purchaser consents to post-sale delivery of the fund facts document, dealers are required to provide verbal disclosure of certain information contained in the fund facts document. This would include a description of the fundamental features of the mutual fund and what it primarily invests in, as well as the investment risk level of the mutual fund. The Canadian securities regulatory authorities would not generally consider it necessary to disclose the information included in the fund facts document under "Top 10 investments" or "Investment mix". In disclosing the suitability of the mutual fund for particular investors, dealers would be required to describe the characteristics of the investor for whom the mutual fund may or may not be an appropriate investment, and the portfolios for which the mutual fund is and is not suited. In terms of providing an overview of any costs associated with buying, selling and owning the mutual fund, the information provided should, at a minimum, include a discussion of any applicable sales charges, as well as ongoing fund expenses (e.g., MER and TER), and any applicable trailing commissions. Information related to sales charges and trailing commissions is also required as part of pre-trade disclosure requirements set out in National Instrument 31-103 *Registration Requirements, Exemptions and Ongoing Registrant Obligations*. Finally, dealers would also be required to provide purchasers with a summary of any applicable right to withdraw from a purchase within two days after receipt of the fund facts document and to rescind a purchase within 48 hours after receipt of the trade confirmation for the purchase. This latter requirement is intended to alert purchasers to the fact that they will have an opportunity to consider the information in the fund facts document that will be delivered or sent post-sale and, based on that information, determine whether they want to cancel their purchase of the mutual fund securities at that time.

(4) Where a purchaser consents to receive delivery of the fund facts document after entering into the purchase of a security of a mutual fund, the consent will only be valid for the particular transaction. A dealer cannot rely on a blanket consent from a purchaser to carry out post-sale delivery of the fund facts document for other purchases of mutual fund securities.

(5) In accordance with existing practices, dealers must establish internal policies and procedures to ensure delivery of the fund facts document occurs in accordance with Part 3. Dealers must maintain evidence of delivery of the fund facts document, as well as receipt of purchaser consents to receive delivery of the fund facts document after entering into the purchase of a security of a mutual fund. Dealers must also maintain adequate records to evidence that satisfactory disclosure about the fund facts document has been provided to purchasers in compliance with section 3.2.02. Such records should also indicate why delivery of the fund facts document was impracticable in the circumstances. The Canadian securities regulatory authorities expect that dealers will follow their current practices to maintain evidence of required disclosures to sufficiently document delivery of the fund facts document.

(6) The Instrument does not specify a particular manner of evidencing a purchaser's consent to allow delivery of the fund facts document after entering into the purchase of a security of a mutual fund. In particular, the Instrument does not require dealers to obtain written consent from clients. The Canadian securities regulatory authorities expect that dealers will follow their current policies and procedures for tracking and monitoring client instructions and authorizations.

(7) The Canadian securities regulatory authorities expect that dealers will remain faithful to the overall objective of ensuring that purchasers are provided with a fund facts document prior to accepting instructions to purchase a security of a mutual fund. Although the instrument allows for post-sale delivery of the fund facts document in certain limited circumstances, the Canadian securities regulatory authorities expect that post-sale delivery of the fund facts document will be the exception rather than the norm. The Canadian securities regulatory authorities may examine practices or arrangements that raise the suspicion of being structured to permit dealers to do indirectly what they cannot do directly and that are inconsistent with the overall intent of providing key information to investors at a time that is most relevant to their purchase decision.

(8) Section 3.2.03 sets out an exception from the requirement to deliver a fund facts document for subsequent purchases of a mutual fund made pursuant to a pre-authorized purchase plan provided certain conditions are met. One of these conditions requires investors to be provided with an initial notice indicating, among other things, that they will not receive a fund facts document unless they specifically request it. The notice must also specify how a fund facts document can be obtained. Investors must also be provided with an annual notice reminding them about how they can request a fund facts document. The Canadian securities regulatory authorities expect that both the initial notice and the annual notice will be presented in a clear, comprehensible and prominent manner so that investors can easily ascertain how they can avail themselves of the option to request a fund facts document.

7.4 Methods of Delivery — **(1)** The methods of delivery of a fund facts document are consistent with methods of delivery of a prospectus under securities legislation. A fund facts document required to be delivered or sent under Part 3 of the Instrument may be delivered or sent electronically, subject to the purchaser's consent. Electronic delivery may include providing an electronic copy of a fund facts document to the purchaser in the form of an e-mail attachment or providing a hyperlink to the fund facts document.

(2) The Canadian securities regulatory authorities will not consider the making of a fund facts document available on a website, or referring an investor to a general website address where the fund facts document can be found to constitute delivery under the Instrument, even if the investor consents to that method of delivery.

(3) Where a hyperlink is provided to the purchaser, the link should lead the purchaser directly to the specific fund facts document for the applicable class or series of the mutual fund being purchased. Consideration should be given to ensuring that the hyperlink remains accessible to the purchaser for so long as the purchaser may reasonably need to consult it.

(4) In the case of online transactions conducted through order execution service accounts, there may be a number of ways in which compliance with the requirement for pre-sale delivery of the fund facts document could be achieved. For example, dealers could consider the use of a "pop-up" notice informing the purchaser that a fund fact document is available for review and provide a hyperlink to the relevant fund facts document. Dealers could also consider requiring the purchaser to "click through" the fund facts document prior to accepting their purchase order.

(5) In addition to the requirements in the Instrument and the guidance in this section, dealers may want to refer to National Policy 11-201 *Electronic Delivery of Documents* for additional guidance.

7.5 Consolidation of Fund Facts Documents — **(1)** For the purposes of pre-sale delivery, subsection 5.2(2) of the Instrument allows a fund facts document to be combined with one or more fund facts documents, provided the size of the document does not make the presentation of the information inconsistent with the principles of simplicity, accessibility and comparability. For example, a fund facts document may be combined with fund facts documents of other classes or series of securities of the same mutual fund, other mutual funds from the same fund family, or other mutual funds of a similar type from different fund families. In making this determination, mutual funds, managers and participants in the mutual fund industry should consider the ability of an investor to easily find and use the information that is relevant to the particular mutual funds securities they are considering purchasing, and whether a reasonable person in the circumstances would come to the same conclusion. We think a document combining more than 10 fund facts documents may discourage an investor from finding and reading each fund facts document and obscure key information, which is inconsistent with the principles of simplicity, accessibility and comparability.

(2) Where multiple fund facts documents are being delivered electronically in compliance with the pre-sale delivery requirement, subsection 5.2(3) prohibits those fund facts documents from being combined into a single e-mail attachment. The use of a hyperlink that directs the investor to a single document combining all the relevant fund facts would also be prohibited under the Instrument. Instead, a dealer would be expected to provide individual attachments or hyperlinks for each fund facts document that is required to be delivered.

(3) When delivery of the fund facts document occurs after the purchase transaction, subsections 5.2(4) to (6) of the Instrument permit a fund facts document to be combined with certain other materials or documents. With the exception of a general front cover, a table of contents or a trade confirmation, subsection 5.2(7) requires the fund facts document to be located as the first item in the package of documents or materials.

7.6 Preparation of Disclosure Documents in Other Languages — Nothing in the Instrument prevents the simplified prospectus, annual information form or fund facts document from being prepared in other languages, provided that these documents are delivered or sent in addition to any disclosure document filed and required to be delivered in accordance with the Instrument. The Canadian securities regulatory authorities would consider such documents to be sales communications.

7.7 Delivery of Documents by a Mutual Fund — Section 3.3 of the Instrument requires that a mutual fund deliver or send to a person or company, upon request and free of charge, a simplified prospectus or documents incorporated by reference. The Canadian securities regulatory authorities are of the view that compliance with this specifically-mandated requirement by an unregistered entity is not a breach of the registration requirements of securities legislation.

7.8 Delivery of Separate Part A and Part B Sections — Mutual fund organizations that create physically separate Part B sections are reminded that any obligation to provide the simplified prospectus would be satisfied only by the delivery of both the Part A and Part B sections of a simplified prospectus.

7.9 Delivery of Non-Educational Material — The Instrument and related forms contain no restrictions on the delivery of non-educational material such as promotional brochures with either of the simplified prospectus and the annual information form. This type of material may, therefore, be delivered with, but cannot be included within, or attached to, the simplified prospectus and the annual information form. The Instrument does not permit the binding of educational and non-educational material with the fund facts document. The intention of the Instrument is not to unreasonably encumber the fund facts document with additional documents.

To come into force on May 30, 2016

PART 8 — COMMENTARY ON INVESTMENT AND RELATED DISCLOSURE

8.1 Investment Disclosure — Form 81-101F1 requires detailed disclosure concerning a number of aspects of the investment approach taken by a mutual fund, including disclosure concerning fundamental investment objectives, investment strategies, risk and risk management. Form 81-101F3 also contains a summarized form of this disclosure. For many mutual funds, the best persons to prepare and review the disclosure would be the portfolio advisers of the mutual fund and we think mutual funds should generally involve them in preparing and reviewing this disclosure.

8.2 Portfolio Advisers — Form 81-101F2 requires disclosure concerning the extent to which investment decisions are made by particular individuals employed by a portfolio adviser or by committee. Section 10.3(3)(b) requires certain information about the individuals principally responsible for the investment portfolio of the mutual fund. Part 11 of National Instrument 81-106 *Investment Fund Continuous Disclosure* requires a simplified prospectus to be amended if a material change occurs in the affairs of the mutual fund that results in a change to the disclosure in the simplified prospectus and fund facts document. Section 7.1 of Companion Policy 81-106CP *Investment Fund Continuous Disclosure* discusses when a departure of a high-profile individual from a portfolio adviser of a mutual fund may constitute a material change for the mutual fund. If the departure is not a material change for the mutual fund, there is no requirement to amend a simplified prospectus, as long as the simplified prospectus contains full, true and plain disclosure about the mutual fund.

PART 9 — NEED FOR MULTIPLE OR SEPARATE APPLICATIONS

9.1 Need for Multiple or Separate Applications — (1) The CSA note that a person or company that obtains an exemption from a provision of the Instrument need not apply again for the same exemption at the time of each simplified prospectus, annual information form and fund facts document refiling, unless there has been some change in an important fact relating to the granting of the exemption.

(2) The principle described in subsection (1) does not necessarily apply to applications required to be made under the Regulations to the *Securities Act* (Quebec) for relief from provisions of those Regulations that are substantially similar to those contained in the Instrument. In that case, an application may be required with each refiling of a simplified prospectus, annual information form and fund facts document of a mutual fund.

(3) In Quebec, it may be necessary to apply for exemptions from the equivalent sections in the Act and the Regulations.

PART 10 — EXEMPTIONS

10.1 Applications Involving Novel or Substantive Issues — Section 6.2 of the Instrument allows exemptive relief from form and content requirements for a simplified prospectus, an annual information or a fund facts document to be evidenced by way of issuance of a receipt. In cases where the CSA thinks that an application for exemptive relief raises novel and substantive issues, or raises a novel policy concern, the CSA may request that such applications follow the process set out in National Policy 11-203 *Process for Exemptive Relief Applications in Multiple Jurisdictions*. This will likely be the case for applications seeking exemptive relief from the form and content requirements of the fund facts document.

Appendix A — Sample Fund Facts Document

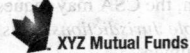 XYZ Mutual Funds

FUND FACTS

XYZ Canadian Equity Fund – Series B

June 30, 20XX

This document contains key information you should know about XYZ Canadian Equity Fund. You can find more details in the fund's simplified prospectus. Ask your representative for a copy, contact XYZ Mutual Funds at 1-800-555-5556 or investing@xyzfunds.com, or visit www.xyzfunds.com.

Before you invest in any fund, consider how the fund would work with your other investments and your tolerance for risk.

Quick facts

Fund code:	XYZ123	Fund manager:	XYZ Mutual Funds
Date series started:	March 31, 2000	Portfolio manager:	Capital Asset Management Ltd.
Total value of fund on June 1, 20XX:	$1 billion	Distributions:	Annually, on December 15
Management expense ratio (MER):	2.25%	Minimum investment:	$500 initial, $50 additional

What does the fund invest in?

The fund invests in a broad range of stocks of Canadian companies. They can be of any size and from any industry.
The charts below give you a snapshot of the fund's investments on June 1, 20XX. The fund's investments will change.

Top 10 investments (June 1, 20XX)

1.	Royal Bank of Canada	7.5%
2.	Toronto-Dominion Bank	7.1%
3.	Canadian Natural Resources	5.8%
4.	The Bank of Nova Scotia	4.1%
5.	Cenovus Energy Inc.	3.7%
6.	Suncor Energy Inc.	3.2%
7.	Enbridge Inc.	3.1%
8.	Canadian Imperial Bank of Commerce	2.9%
9.	Manulife Financial Corporation	2.7%
10.	Canadian National Railway Company	1.9%
Total percentage of top 10 investments		**42.0%**
Total number of investments		**93**

Investment mix (June 1, 20XX)

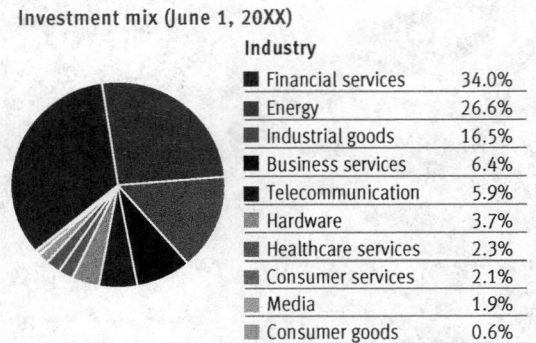

Industry

Financial services	34.0%
Energy	26.6%
Industrial goods	16.5%
Business services	6.4%
Telecommunication	5.9%
Hardware	3.7%
Healthcare services	2.3%
Consumer services	2.1%
Media	1.9%
Consumer goods	0.6%

How risky is it?

The value of the fund can go down as well as up. You could lose money.

One way to gauge risk is to look at how much a fund's returns change over time. This is called "volatility".

In general, funds with higher volatility will have returns that change more over time. They typically have a greater chance of losing money and may have a greater chance of higher returns. Funds with lower volatility tend to have returns that change less over time. They typically have lower returns and may have a lower chance of losing money.

Risk rating

XYZ Mutual Funds has rated the volatility of this fund as **medium**.

This rating is based on how much the fund's returns have changed from year to year. It doesn't tell you how volatile the fund will be in the future. The rating can change over time. A fund with a low risk rating can still lose money.

Low	Low to medium	**Medium**	Medium to high	High

For more information about the risk rating and specific risks that can affect the fund's returns, see the Risk section of the fund's simplified prospectus.

No guarantees

Like most mutual funds, this fund doesn't have any guarantees. You may not get back the amount of money you invest.

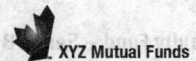 **XYZ Mutual Funds**

XYZ Canadian Equity Fund – Series B

How has the fund performed?

This section tells you how Series B units of the fund have performed over the past 10 years. Returns are after expenses have been deducted. These expenses reduce the fund's returns.

Year-by-year returns

This chart shows how Series B units of the fund performed in each of the past 10 years. The fund dropped in value in 3 of the 10 years. The range of returns and change from year to year can help you assess how risky the fund has been in the past. It does not tell you how the fund will perform in the future.

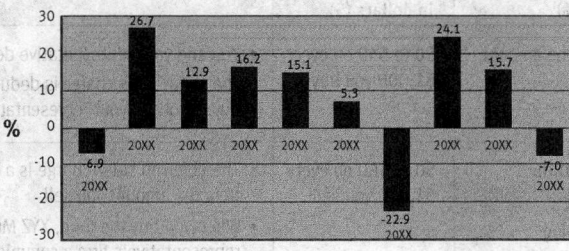

Best and worst 3-month returns

This table shows the best and worst returns for Series B units of the fund in a 3-month period over the past 10 years. The best and worst 3-month returns could be higher or lower in the future. Consider how much of a loss you could afford to take in a short period of time.

	Return	3 months ending	If you invested $1,000 at the beginning of the period
Best return	32.6%	April 30, 2003	Your investment would rise to $1,326.
Worst return	-24.7%	November 30, 2008	Your investment would drop to $753.

Average return

The annual compounded return of Series B units of the fund was 6.8% over the past 10 years. If you had invested $1,000 in the fund 10 years ago, your investment would now be worth $1,930.

Who is this fund for?

Investors who:

- are looking for a long-term investment
- want to invest in a broad range of stocks of Canadian companies
- can handle the ups and downs of the stock market.

❗ Don't buy this fund if you need a steady source of income from your investment.

A word about tax

In general, you'll have to pay income tax on any money you make on a fund. How much you pay depends on the tax laws where you live and whether or not you hold the fund in a registered plan, such as a Registered Retirement Savings Plan or a Tax-Free Savings Account.

Keep in mind that if you hold your fund in a non-registered account, fund distributions are included in your taxable income, whether you get them in cash or have them reinvested.

Part 8: MUTUAL FUNDS

 **XYZ Mutual Funds**

XYZ Canadian Equity Fund – Series B

How much does it cost?

The following tables show the fees and expenses you could pay to buy, own and sell Series B units of the fund. The fees and expenses — including any commissions — can vary among series of a fund and among funds. Higher commissions can influence representatives to recommend one investment over another. Ask about other funds and investments that may be suitable for you at a lower cost.

1. Sales charges

You have to choose a sales charge option when you buy the fund. Ask about the pros and cons of each option.

Sales charge option	What you pay		How it works
	in per cent (%)	**in dollars ($)**	
Initial sales charge	0% to 4% of the amount you buy	$0 to $40 on every $1,000 you buy	• You and your representative decide on the rate. • The initial sales charge is deducted from the amount you buy. It goes to your representative's firm as a commission.
Deferred sales charge	**If you sell within:** 1 year of buying 6.0% 2 years of buying 5.0% 3 years of buying 4.0% 4 years of buying 3.0% 5 years of buying 2.0% 6 years of buying 1.0% After 6 years nothing	$0 to $60 on every $1,000 you sell	• The deferred sales charge is a set rate. It is deducted from the amount you sell. • When you buy the fund, XYZ Mutual Funds pays your representative's firm a commission of 4.9%. Any deferred sales charge you pay goes to XYZ Mutual Funds. • You can sell up to 10% of your units each year without paying a deferred sales charge. • You can switch to Series B units of other XYZ Mutual Funds at any time without paying a deferred sales charge. The deferred sales charge schedule will be based on the date you bought the first fund.

2. Fund expenses

You don't pay these expenses directly. They affect you because they reduce the fund's returns.
As of March 31, 20XX, the fund's expenses were 2.30% of its value. This equals $23 for every $1,000 invested.

	Annual rate (as a % of the fund's value)
Management expense ratio (MER) This is the total of the fund's management fee (which includes the trailing commission) and operating expenses. XYZ Mutual Funds waived some of the fund's expenses. If it had not done so, the MER would have been higher.	2.25%
Trading expense ratio (TER) These are the fund's trading costs.	0.05%
Fund expenses	**2.30%**

More about the trailing commission

The trailing commission is an ongoing commission. It is paid for as long as you own the fund. It is for the services and advice that your representative and their firm provide to you.

XYZ Mutual Funds pays the trailing commission to your representative's firm. It is paid from the fund's management fee and is based on the value of your investment. The rate depends on the sales charge option you choose.

Sales charge option	Amount of trailing commission	
	in per cent (%)	**in dollars ($)**
Initial sales charge	0% to 1% of the value of your investment each year	$0 to $10 each year on every $1,000 invested
Deferred sales charge	0% to 0.50% of the value of your investment each year	$0 to $5 each year on every $1,000 invested

XYZ Mutual Funds

XYZ Canadian Equity Fund – Series B

How much does it cost? cont'd

3. Other fees

You may have to pay other fees when you buy, hold, sell or switch units of the fund.

Fee	What you pay
Short-term trading fee	1% of the value of units you sell or switch within 90 days of buying them. This fee goes to the fund.
Switch fee	Your representative's firm may charge you up to 2% of the value of units you switch to another XYZ Mutual Fund.
Change fee	Your representative's firm may charge you up to 2% of the value of units you switch to another series of the fund.

What if I change my mind?

Under securities law in some provinces and territories, you have the right to:

- withdraw from an agreement to buy mutual fund units within two business days after you receive a simplified prospectus or Fund Facts document, or

- cancel your purchase within 48 hours after you receive confirmation of the purchase.

In some provinces and territories, you also have the right to cancel a purchase, or in some jurisdictions, claim damages, if the simplified prospectus, annual information form, Fund Facts document or financial statements contain a misrepresentation. You must act within the time limit set by the securities law in your province or territory.

For more information, see the securities law of your province or territory or ask a lawyer.

For more information

Contact XYZ Mutual Funds or your representative for a copy of the fund's simplified prospectus and other disclosure documents. These documents and the Fund Facts make up the fund's legal documents.

XYZ Mutual Funds
123 Asset Allocation St.
Toronto, ON M1A 2B3

Phone: (416) 555-5555
Toll-free: 1-800-555-5556
Email: investing@xyzfunds.com
www.xyzfunds.com

To learn more about investing in mutual funds, see the brochure **Understanding mutual funds,** which is available on the website of the Canadian Securities Administrators at **www.securities-administrators.ca.**

® Registered trademark of XYZ Mutual Funds.

Adoption by OSC: (2000) 23 O.S.C.B. (Supp) 11 and (1999) 22 O.S.C.B. (Supp2) 28; Request for Comments: (1999) 22 O.S.C.B. 2605 and (1998) 21 O.S.C.B. 4817.

Adoption of Amendment to Companion Policy by OSC: 24 O.S.C.B. 2680 (April 27, 2001) and 24 O.S.C.B. 1071 (February 16, 2001); Request for Comments: 23 O.S.C.B. 4195 (June 16, 2000).

Adoption of Amendments to Companion Policy by OSC: (2005) 28 O.S.C.B. 4968 and (Supp-1) 45; Request for Comments: (2004) 27 O.S.C.B. 5157 and (2002) 25 O.S.C.B. 6273.

Adoption of Amendments to Companion Policy by OSC: (2008) 31 O.S.C.B. (Supp. 2) 254 and 30 O.S.C.B. (Supp. 7) 1 (Dec. 21, 2007); Request for Comments: 29 O.S.C.B. (Supp. 3) 1 (Dec. 22, 2006).

Adoption of Amendments to Companion Policy: (2010) 33 O.S.C.B. 11417 and (Supp. 4) 1; Request for Comments: (2009) 32 O.S.C.B. (Supp. 1) 1, (2008) 31 O.S.C.B. 10479, (2007) 30 O.S.C.B. (Supp. 4) 1 and (2003) 26 O.S.C.B. 1443.

Adoption of Amendments to Companion Policy: (2013) 36 O.S.C.B. 4934 and (Supp. 2) 1; Request for Comments: (2011) 34 O.S.C.B. (Supp. 4) 1.

Adoption of Amendments to Companion Policy: (2013) 36 O.S.C.B. 7824 and 6001; Request for Comments: (2012) 35 O.S.C.B. 5755 and (2011) 34 O.S.C.B. 8561.

Adoption of Amendments to Companion Policy: (2013) 36 O.S.C.B. 9612; Request for Comments: (2009) 32 O.S.C.B. 8381.

National Instrument 81-102 — Investment Funds

Date: January 28, 2000, amended effective December 31, 2003, June 1, 2005, November 1, 2006, September 8, 2008, September 28, 2009, January 1, 2011, April 30, 2012, May 31, 2013, September 1, 2013, January 1, 2014 and September 22, 2014

23 O.S.C.B. (Supp) 59, 27 O.S.C.B. 745, 28 O.S.C.B. 4969, 29 O.S.C.B. 8845, 31 O.S.C.B. 8569, 32 O.S.C.B. (Supp. 4) 378, 33 O.S.C.B. 11431, 35 O.S.C.B. 3415, 36 O.S.C.B. 7827, 36 O.S.C.B. 9612 and 37 O.S.C.B. (Supp. 4)

Table of Contents

PART 1 — DEFINITIONS AND APPLICATION

1.1 Definitions — In this Instrument

"acceptable clearing corporation" means a clearing corporation that is an acceptable clearing corporation under the Joint Regulatory Financial Questionnaire and Report;

"advertisement" means a sales communication that is published or designed for use on or through a public medium;

"asset allocation service" means an administrative service under which the investment of a person or company is allocated, in whole or in part, among mutual funds to which this Instrument applies and reallocated among those mutual funds and, if applicable, other assets according to an asset allocation strategy;

"book-based system" means a system for the central handling of securities or equivalent book-based entries under which all securities of a class or series deposited within the system are treated as fungible and may be transferred or pledged by bookkeeping entry without physical delivery;

"borrowing agent" means any of the following:

(a) a custodian or sub-custodian that holds assets in connection with a short sale of securities by an investment fund;

(b) a qualified dealer from whom an investment fund borrows securities in order to sell them short;

"cash cover" means any of the following assets of a mutual fund that are held by the mutual fund, have not been allocated for specific purposes and are available to satisfy all or part of the obligations arising from a position in specified derivatives held by the mutual fund or from a short sale of securities made by the mutual fund:

(a) cash;

(b) cash equivalents;

(c) synthetic cash;

(d) receivables of the mutual fund arising from the disposition of portfolio assets, net of payables arising from the acquisition of portfolio assets;

(e) securities purchased by the mutual fund in a reverse repurchase transaction under section 2.14, to the extent of the cash paid for those securities by the mutual fund;

(f) each evidence of indebtedness that has a remaining term to maturity of 365 days or less and a designated rating;

(g) each floating rate evidence of indebtedness if

(i) the floating interest rate of the indebtedness is reset no later than every 185 days, and

(ii) the principal amount of the indebtedness will continue to have a market value of approximately par at the time of each change in the rate to be paid to the holders of the evidence of indebtedness;

(h) securities issued by a money market fund;

"cash equivalent" means an evidence of indebtedness that has a remaining term to maturity of 365 days or less and that is issued, or fully and unconditionally guaranteed as to principal and interest, by

(a) the government of Canada or the government of a jurisdiction,

(b) the government of the United States of America, the government of one of the states of the United States of America, the government of another sovereign state or a permitted supranational agency, if, in each case, the evidence of indebtedness has a designated rating, or

(c) a Canadian financial institution, or a financial institution that is not incorporated or organized under the laws of Canada or of a jurisdiction if, in either case, evidences of indebtedness of that issuer or guarantor that are rated as short term debt by a designated rating organization or its DRO affiliate have a designated rating;

"clearing corporation" means an organization through which trades in options or standardized futures are cleared and settled;

"clearing corporation option" means an option, other than an option on futures, issued by a clearing corporation;

"clone fund" means an investment fund that has adopted a fundamental investment objective to track the performance of another investment fund;

"conventional convertible security" means a security of an issuer that is, according to its terms, convertible into, or exchangeable for, other securities of the issuer, or of an affiliate of the issuer;

"conventional floating rate debt instrument" means an evidence of indebtedness of which the interest obligations are based upon a benchmark commonly used in commercial lending arrangements;

"conventional warrant or right" means a security of an issuer, other than a clearing corporation, that gives the holder the right to purchase securities of the issuer or of an affiliate of the issuer;

"currency cross hedge" means the substitution by an investment fund of a risk to one currency for a risk to another currency, if neither currency is a currency in which the investment fund determines its net asset value per security and the aggregate amount of currency risk to which the investment fund is exposed is not increased by the substitution;

"custodian" means the institution appointed by an investment fund to hold portfolio assets of the investment fund;

"dealer managed investment fund" means an investment fund the portfolio adviser of which is a dealer manager;

"dealer manager" means

(a) a specified dealer that acts as a portfolio adviser,

(b) a portfolio adviser in which a specified dealer, or a partner, director, officer, salesperson or principal shareholder of a specified dealer, directly or indirectly owns of record or beneficially, or exercises control or direction over, securities carrying more than 10 percent of the total votes attaching to securities of the portfolio adviser, or

(c) a partner, director or officer of a portfolio adviser referred to in paragraph (b);

"debt-like security" means a security purchased by a mutual fund, other than a conventional convertible security or a conventional floating rate debt instrument, that evidences an indebtedness of the issuer if

(a) either

(i) the amount of principal, interest or principal and interest to be paid to the holder is linked in whole or in part by a formula to the appreciation or depreciation in the market price, value or level of one or more underlying interests on a predetermined date or dates, or

(ii) the security provides the holder with a right to convert or exchange the security into or for the underlying interest or to purchase the underlying interest, and

(b) on the date of acquisition by the mutual fund, the percentage of the purchase price attributable to the component of the security that is not linked to an underlying interest is less than 80 percent of the purchase price paid by the mutual fund;

"delta" means the positive or negative number that is a measure of the change in market value of an option relative to changes in the value of the underlying interest of the option;

"designated rating" means, for a security or instrument, a rating issued by a designated rating organization, or its DRO affiliate, that is at or above one of the following rating categories, or that is at or above a category that replaces one of the following rating categories, if

(a) there has been no announcement by the designated rating organization or its DRO affiliate of which the investment fund or its manager is or reasonably should be aware that the rating of the security or instrument to which the designated rating was given may be down-graded to a rating category that would not be a designated rating, and

(b) no designated rating organization or any of its DRO affiliates has rated the security or instrument in a rating category that is not a designated rating:

Designated Rating Organization	Commercial Paper/ Short Term Debt	Long Term Debt
DBRS Limited	R-1 (low)	A
Fitch, Inc.	F1	A
Moody's Canada Inc.	P-1	A2
Standard & Poor's Ratings Services (Canada)	A-1 (Low)	A

"designated rating organization" means

(a) each of DBRS Limited, Fitch, Inc., Moody's Canada Inc., Standard & Poor's Ratings Services (Canada), including their DRO affiliates; or

(b) any other credit rating organization that has been designated under securities legislation;

"DRO affiliate" has the same meaning as in section 1 of National Instrument 25-101 *Designated Rating Organizations*;

"equivalent debt" means, in relation to an option, swap, forward contract or debt-like security, an evidence of indebtedness of approximately the same term as, or a longer term than, the remaining term to maturity of the option, swap, contract or debt-like security and that ranks equally with, or subordinate to, the claim for payment that may arise under the option, swap, contract or debt-like security;

"fixed portfolio ETF" means an exchange-traded mutual fund not in continuous distribution that

(a) has fundamental investment objectives which include holding and maintaining a fixed portfolio of publicly traded equity securities of one or more issuers the names of which are disclosed in its prospectus, and

(b) trades the securities referred to in paragraph (a) only in the circumstances disclosed in its prospectus;

"floating rate evidence of indebtedness" means an evidence of indebtedness that has a floating rate of interest determined over the term of the obligation by reference to a commonly used benchmark interest rate and that satisfies any of the following:

(a) if the evidence of indebtedness was issued by a person or company other than a government or a permitted supranational agency, it has a designated rating;

(b) the evidence of indebtedness was issued, or is fully and unconditionally guaranteed as to principal and interest, by any of the following:

(i) the government of Canada or the government of a jurisdiction of Canada;

(ii) the government of the United States of America, the government of one of the states of the United States of America, the government of another sovereign state or a permitted supranational agency, if, in each case, the evidence of indebtedness has a designated rating;

"forward contract" means an agreement, not entered into with, or traded on, a stock exchange or futures exchange or cleared by a clearing corporation, to do one or more of the following on terms or at a price established by or determinable by reference to the agreement and at or by a time in the future established by or determinable by reference to the agreement:

1. Make or take delivery of the underlying interest of the agreement.

2. Settle in cash instead of delivery;

"fundamental investment objectives" means the investment objectives of an investment fund that define both the fundamental nature of the investment fund and the fundamental investment features of the investment fund that distinguish it from other investment funds;

"futures exchange" means an association or organization operated to provide the facilities necessary for the trading of standardized futures;

"government security" means an evidence of indebtedness issued, or fully and unconditionally guaranteed as to principal and interest, by any of the government of Canada, the government of a jurisdiction or the government of the United States of America;

"guaranteed mortgage" means a mortgage fully and unconditionally guaranteed, or insured, by the government of Canada, by the government of a jurisdiction or by an agency of any of those governments or by a corporation approved by the Office of the Superintendent of Financial Institutions to offer its services to the public in Canada as an insurer of mortgages;

"hedging" means the entering into of a transaction, or a series of transactions, and the maintaining of the position or positions resulting from the transaction or series of transactions

(a) if

(i) the intended effect of the transaction, or the intended cumulative effect of the series of transactions, is to offset or reduce a specific risk associated with all or a portion of an existing investment or position or group of investments or positions,

(ii) the transaction or series of transactions results in a high degree of negative correlation between changes in the value of the investment or position, or group of investments or positions, being hedged and changes in the value of the instrument or instruments with which the investment or position is hedged, and

(iii) there are reasonable grounds to believe that the transaction or series of transactions no more than offset the effect of price changes in the investment or position, or group of investments or positions, being hedged, or

(b) if the transaction, or series of transactions, is a currency cross hedge;

"IIROC" means the Investment Industry Regulatory Organization of Canada;

"illiquid asset" means

(a) a portfolio asset that cannot be readily disposed of through market facilities on which public quotations in common use are widely available at an amount that at least approximates the amount at which the portfolio asset is valued in calculating the net asset value per security of the mutual fund, or

(b) a restricted security held by a mutual fund, the resale of which is prohibited by a representation, undertaking or agreement by the mutual fund or by the predecessor in title of the mutual fund;

"independent review committee" means the independent review committee of the investment fund established under National Instrument 81-107 *Independent Review Committee for Investment Funds*

"index mutual fund" means a mutual fund that has adopted fundamental investment objectives that require the mutual fund to

(a) hold the securities that are included in a permitted index or permitted indices of the mutual fund in substantially the same proportion as those securities are reflected in that permitted index or those permitted indices, or

(b) invest in a manner that causes the mutual fund to replicate the performance of that index or those permitted indices;

"index participation unit" means a security traded on a stock exchange in Canada or the United States and issued by an issuer the only purpose of which is to

(a) hold the securities that are included in a specified widely quoted market index in substantially the same proportion as those securities are reflected in that index, or

(b) invest in a manner that causes the issuer to replicate the performance of that index;

"investment fund conflict of interest investment restrictions" means the provisions of securities legislation that are referred to in Appendix D;

"investment fund conflict of interest reporting requirements" means the provisions of securities legislation that are referred to in Appendix E;

"investor fees" means, in connection with the purchase, conversion, holding, transfer or redemption of securities of an investment fund, all fees, charges and expenses that are or may become payable by a securityholder of the investment fund to,

(a) in the case of a mutual fund, a member of the organization of the mutual fund other than a member of the organization acting solely as a participating dealer, and

(b) in the case of a non-redeemable investment fund, the manager of the non-redeemable investment fund;

"Joint Regulatory Financial Questionnaire and Report" means the Joint Regulatory Financial Questionnaire and Report of various Canadian SROs on the date that this Instrument comes into force and every successor to the form that does not materially lessen the criteria for an entity to be recognized as an "acceptable clearing corporation";

"long position" means a position held by an investment fund that, for

(a) an option, entitles the investment fund to elect to purchase, sell, receive or deliver the underlying interest or, instead, pay or receive cash,

(b) a standardized future or forward contract, obliges the investment fund to accept delivery of the underlying interest or, instead, pay or receive cash,

(c) a call option on futures, entitles the investment fund to elect to assume a long position in standardized futures,

(d) a put option on futures, entitles the investment fund to elect to assume a short position in standardized futures, and

(e) a swap, obliges the investment fund to accept delivery of the underlying interest or receive cash;

"management expense ratio" means the ratio, expressed as a percentage, of the expenses of an investment fund to its average net asset value, calculated in accordance with Part 15 of National Instrument 81-106 *Investment Fund Continuous Disclosure*;

"manager" means an investment fund manager;

"manager-prescribed number of units" means, in relation to an exchange-traded mutual fund that is in continuous distribution, the number of units determined by the manager from time to time for the purposes of subscription orders, exchanges, redemptions or for other purposes;

"material change" has the meaning ascribed to that term in National Instrument 81-106 *Investment Fund Continuous Disclosure*;

"member of the organization" has the meaning ascribed to that term in National Instrument 81-105 Mutual Fund Sales Practices;

"MFDA" means the Mutual Fund Dealers Association of Canada;

"money market fund" means a mutual fund that invests its assets in accordance with section 2.18;

"mortgage" includes a hypothec or security that creates a charge on real property in order to secure a debt;

"mutual fund rating entity" means an entity

(a) that rates or ranks the performance of mutual funds or asset allocation services through an objective methodology that is

(i) based on quantitative performance measurements,

(ii) applied consistently to all mutual funds or asset allocation services rated or ranked by it, and

(iii) disclosed on the entity's website,

(b) that is not a member of the organization of any mutual fund, and

(c) whose services to assign a rating or ranking to any mutual fund or asset allocation service are not procured by the promoter, manager, portfolio adviser, principal distributor or participating dealer of any mutual fund or asset allocation service, or any of their affiliates;

"net asset value" means the value of the total assets of the investment fund less the value of the total liabilities, other than net assets attributable to securityholders, of the investment fund, as at a specific date, determined in accordance with Part 14 of National Instrument 81-106 *Investment Fund Continuous Disclosure*;

"NI 81-107" means National Instrument 81-107 *Independent Review Committee for Investment Funds*.

"non-resident sub-adviser" means a person or company providing portfolio management advice

(a) whose principal place of business is outside of Canada,

(b) that advises a portfolio adviser to an investment fund, and

(c) that is not registered under securities legislation in the jurisdiction in which the portfolio adviser that it advises is located;

"option" means an agreement that provides the holder with the right, but not the obligation, to do one or more of the following on terms or at a price established by or determinable by reference to the agreement at or by a time established by the agreement:

1. Receive an amount of cash determinable by reference to a specified quantity of the underlying interest of the option.

2. Purchase a specified quantity of the underlying interest of the option.

3. Sell a specified quantity of the underlying interest of the option;

"option on futures" means an option the underlying interest of which is a standardized future;

"order receipt office" means, for a mutual fund

(a) the principal office of the mutual fund,

(b) the principal office of the principal distributor of the mutual fund, or

(c) a location to which a purchase order or redemption order for securities of the mutual fund is required or permitted by the mutual fund to be delivered by participating dealers or the principal distributor of the mutual fund;

"overall rating or ranking" means a rating or ranking of a mutual fund or asset allocation service that is calculated from standard performance data for one or more performance measurement periods, which includes the longest period for which the mutual fund or asset allocation service is required under securities legislation to calculate standard performance data, other than the period since the inception of the mutual fund;

"participating dealer" means a dealer other than the principal distributor that distributes securities of a mutual fund;

"participating fund" means a mutual fund in which an asset allocation service permits investment;

"performance data" means a rating, ranking, quotation, discussion or analysis regarding an aspect of the investment performance of an investment fund, an asset allocation service, a security, an index or a benchmark;

"permitted gold certificate" means a certificate representing gold if the gold is

(a) available for delivery in Canada, free of charge, to or to the order of the holder of the certificate,

(b) of a minimum fineness of 995 parts per 1,000,

(c) held in Canada,

(d) in the form of either bars or wafers, and

(e) if not purchased from a bank listed in Schedule I, II or III of the *Bank Act (Canada)*, fully insured against loss and bankruptcy by an insurance company licensed under the laws of Canada or a jurisdiction;

"permitted index" means, in relation to a mutual fund, a market index that is

(a) both

(i) administered by an organization that is not affiliated with any of the mutual fund, its manager, its portfolio adviser or its principal distributor, and

(ii) available to persons or companies other than the mutual fund, or

(b) widely recognized and used;

"permitted supranational agency" means the African Development Bank, the Asian Development Bank, the Caribbean Development Bank, the European Bank for Reconstruction and Development, the European Investment Bank, the Inter-American Development Bank, the International Bank for Reconstruction and Development and the International Finance Corporation;

"physical commodity", means, in an original or processed state, an agricultural product, forest product, product of the sea, mineral, metal, hydrocarbon fuel product, precious stone or other gem;

"portfolio adviser" means a person or company that provides investment advice or portfolio management services under a contract with the investment fund or with the manager of the investment fund;

"portfolio asset" means an asset of an investment fund;

"pricing date" means, for the sale of a security of a mutual fund, the date on which the net asset value per security of the mutual fund is calculated for the purpose of determining the price at which that security is to be issued;

"principal distributor" means a person or company through whom securities of a mutual fund are distributed under an arrangement with the mutual fund or its manager that provides

(a) an exclusive right to distribute the securities of the mutual fund in a particular area, or

(b) a feature that gives or is intended to give the person or company a material competitive advantage over others in the distribution of the securities of the mutual fund;

"public quotation" includes, for the purposes of calculating the amount of illiquid assets held by a mutual fund, any quotation of a price for a fixed income security made through the inter-dealer bond market;

"purchase" means, in connection with an acquisition of a portfolio asset by an investment fund, an acquisition that is the result of a decision made and action taken by the investment fund;

"qualified security" means

(a) an evidence of indebtedness that is issued, or fully and unconditionally guaranteed as to principal and interest, by

(i) the government of Canada or the government of a jurisdiction,

(ii) the government of the United States of America, the government of one of the states of the United States of America, the government of another sovereign state, or a permitted supranational agency, if, in each case, the evidence of indebtedness has a designated rating, or

(iii) a Canadian financial institution or a financial institution that is not incorporated or organized under the laws of Canada or of a jurisdiction if, in either case, evidences of indebtedness of that issuer or guarantor that are rated as short term debt by a designated rating organization or its DRO affiliate have a designated rating, or

(b) commercial paper that has a term to maturity of 365 days or less and a designated rating and that was issued by a person or company other than a government or permitted supranational agency;

"report to securityholders" means a report that includes annual financial statements or interim financial reports, or an annual or interim management report of fund performance, and that is delivered to securityholders of an investment fund;

"restricted security" means a security, other than a specified derivative, the resale of which is restricted or limited by a representation, undertaking or agreement by the mutual fund or by the mutual fund's predecessor in title, or by law;

"sales communication" means a communication relating to, and by, an investment fund or asset allocation service, its promoter, manager, portfolio adviser, principal distributor, a participating dealer or a person or company providing services to any of them, that

(a) is made

(i) to a securityholder of the investment fund or participant in the asset allocation service, or

(ii) to a person or company that is not a securityholder of the investment fund or participant in the asset allocation service, to induce the purchase of securities of the investment fund or the use of the asset allocation service, and

(b) in the case of an investment fund, is not contained in any of the following documents of the investment fund:

1. A prospectus or preliminary or *pro forma* prospectus.

2. An annual information form or preliminary or *pro forma* annual information form.

3. A fund facts document or preliminary or *pro forma* fund facts document.

4. Financial statements, including the notes to the financial statements and the auditor's report on the financial statements.

5. A trade confirmation.

6. A statement of account.

7. Annual or interim management report of fund performance;

"scholarship plan" has the meaning ascribed to that term in section 1.1 of National Instrument 81-106 *Investment Fund Continuous Disclosure*;

"short position" means a position held by an investment fund that, for

(a) an option, obliges the investment fund, at the election of another, to purchase, sell, receive or deliver the underlying interest, or, instead, pay or receive cash,

(b) a standardized future or forward contract, obliges the investment fund, at the election of another, to deliver the underlying interest or, instead, pay or receive cash,

(c) a call option on futures, obliges the investment fund, at the election of another, to assume a short position in standardized futures, and

(d) a put option on futures, obliges the investment fund, at the election of another, to assume a long position in standardized futures;

"special warrant" means a security that, by its terms or the terms of an accompanying contractual obligation, entitles or requires the holder to acquire another security without payment of material additional consideration and obliges the issuer of the special warrant or the other security to undertake efforts to file a prospectus to qualify the distribution of the other security;

"specified asset-backed security" means a security that

(a) is primarily serviced by the cash flows of a discrete pool of receivables or other financial assets, either fixed or revolving, that by their terms convert into cash within a finite time, and any rights or assets designed to assure the servicing or timely distribution of proceeds to securityholders, and

(b) by its terms entitles an investor in that security to a return of the investment of that investor at or by a time established by or determinable by reference to an agreement, except as a result of losses incurred on, or the non-performance of, the financial assets;

"specified dealer" means a dealer other than a dealer whose activities as a dealer are restricted by the terms of its registration to one or both of

(a) acting solely in respect of mutual fund securities;

(b) acting solely in respect of transactions in which a person or company registered in the category of exempt market dealer in a jurisdiction is permitted to engage;

"specified derivative" means an instrument, agreement or security, the market price, value or payment obligations of which are derived from, referenced to or based on an underlying interest, other than

(a) a conventional convertible security,

(b) a specified asset-backed security,

(c) an index participation unit,

(d) a government or corporate strip bond,

(e) a capital, equity dividend or income share of a subdivided equity or fixed income security,

(f) a conventional warrant or right, or

(g) a special warrant;

"standardized future" means an agreement traded on a futures exchange pursuant to standardized conditions contained in the by-laws, rules or regulations of the futures exchange, and cleared by a clearing corporation, to do one or more of the following at a price established by or determinable by reference to the agreement and at or by a time established by or determinable by reference to the agreement:

1. Make or take delivery of the underlying interest of the agreement.

2. Settle the obligation in cash instead of delivery of the underlying interest;

"sub-custodian" means, for an investment fund, an entity that has been appointed to hold portfolio assets of the investment fund in accordance with section 6.1 by either the custodian or a sub-custodian of the investment fund;

"swap" means an agreement that provides for

(a) an exchange of principal amounts,

(b) the obligation to make, and the right to receive, cash payments based upon the value, level or price, or on relative changes or movements of the value, level or price, of one or more underlying interests, which payments may be netted against each other, or

(c) the right or obligation to make, and the right or obligation to receive, physical delivery of an underlying interest instead of the cash payments referred to in paragraph (b);

"synthetic cash" means a position that in aggregate provides the holder with the economic equivalent of the return on a banker's acceptance accepted by a bank listed in Schedule I of the Bank Act (Canada) and that consists of

(a) a long position in a portfolio of shares and a short position in a standardized future of which the underlying interest consists of a stock index, if

(i) there is a high degree of positive correlation between changes in the value of the portfolio of shares and changes in the value of the stock index, and

(ii) the ratio between the value of the portfolio of shares and the standardized future is such that, for any change in the value of one, a change of similar magnitude occurs in the value of the other

(b) a long position in the evidences of indebtedness issued, or fully and unconditionally guaranteed as to principal and interest, by any of the government of Canada or the government of a jurisdiction and a short position in a standardized future of which the underlying interest consists of evidences of indebtedness of the same issuer and same term to maturity, if

(i) there is a high degree of positive correlation between changes in the value of the portfolio of evidences of indebtedness and changes in the value of the standardized future, and

(ii) the ratio between the value of the evidences of indebtedness and the standardized future is such that, for any change in the value of one, a change of similar magnitude occurs in the value of the other, or

(c) a long position in securities of an issuer and a short position in a standardized future of which the underlying interest is securities of that issuer, if the ratio between the value of the securities of that issuer and the position in the standardized future is such that, for any change in the value of one, a change of similar magnitude occurs in the value of the other;

Part 8: MUTUAL FUNDS

"underlying interest" means, for a specified derivative, the security, commodity, financial instrument, currency, interest rate, foreign exchange rate, economic indicator, index, basket, agreement, benchmark or any other reference, interest or variable, and, if applicable, the relationship between any of the foregoing, from, to or on which the market price, value or payment obligation of the specified derivative is derived, referenced or based; and

"underlying market exposure" means, for a position of an investment fund in

(a) an option, the quantity of the underlying interest of the option position multiplied by the market value of one unit of the underlying interest, multiplied, in turn, by the delta of the option,

(b) a standardized future or forward contract, the quantity of the underlying interest of the position multiplied by the current market value of one unit of the underlying interest; or

(c) a swap, the underlying market exposure, as calculated under paragraph (b), for the long position of the investment fund in the swap.

1.2 Application — (1) This Instrument applies only to

(a) a mutual fund that offers or has offered securities under a prospectus for so long as the mutual fund remains a reporting issuer,

(a.1) a non-redeemable investment fund that is a reporting issuer, and,

(b) a person or company in respect of activities pertaining to an investment fund referred to in paragraphs (a) and (a.1) or pertaining to the filing of a prospectus to which subsection 3.1(1) applies.

(2) Despite subsection (1), this Instrument does not apply to a scholarship plan.

(3) Despite subsection (1), in Québec, in respect of investment funds organized under an Act to establish the *Fonds de solidarité des travailleurs du Québec (F.T.Q.)* (chapter F-3.2.1), an Act to establish *Fondaction, le Fonds de développement de la Confédération des syndicats nationaux pour la coopération et l'emploi* (chapter F-3.1.2), or an Act constituting *Capital régional et coopératif Desjardins* (chapter C-6.1), the following requirements apply:

(a) sections 2.12 to 2.17;

(b) Part 6;

(c) Part 15, except for paragraph 15.8(2)(b);

(d) Part 19;

(e) Part 20.

(4) For greater certainty, in British Columbia, if a provision of this Instrument conflicts or is inconsistent with a provision of the *Employee Investment Act* (British Columbia) or the *Small Business Venture Capital Act* (British Columbia), the provision of the Employee Investment Act or the Small Business Venture Capital Act, as the case may be, prevails.

1.3 Interpretation — (1) Each section, part, class or series of a class of securities of an investment fund that is referable to a separate portfolio of assets is considered to be a separate investment fund for purposes of this Instrument.

(2) An investment fund that renews or extends a securities lending, repurchase or reverse repurchase transaction is entering into a securities lending, repurchase or reverse repurchase agreement for the purposes of section 2.12, 2.13 or 2.14.

PART 2 — INVESTMENTS

2.1 Concentration Restriction — (1) A mutual fund must not purchase a security of an issuer, enter into a specified derivatives transaction or purchase index participation units if, immediately after the transaction, more than 10 percent of its net asset value would be invested in securities of any issuer.

(2) Subsection (1) does not apply to the purchase of any of the following:

(a) a government security;

(b) a security issued by a clearing corporation;

(c) a security issued by a mutual fund if the purchase is made in accordance with the requirements of section 2.5;

(d) an index participation unit that is a security of a mutual fund;

(e) an equity security if the purchase is made by a fixed portfolio ETF in accordance with its investment objectives.

(3) In determining a mutual fund's compliance with the restrictions contained in this section, the mutual fund must, for each long position in a specified derivative that is held by the mutual fund for purposes other than hedging and for each index participation unit held by the mutual fund, consider that it holds directly the underlying interest of that specified derivative or its proportionate share of the securities held by the issuer of the index participation unit.

(4) Despite subsection (3), the mutual fund must not include in the determination referred to in subsection (3) a security or instrument that is a component of, but that represents less than 10 percent of

(a) a stock or bond index that is the underlying interest of a specified derivative; or

(b) the securities held by the issuer of an index participation unit.

(5) Despite subsection (1), an index mutual fund, the name of which includes the word "index", may, in order to satisfy its fundamental investment objectives, purchase a security, enter into a specified derivatives transaction or purchase index participation units if its prospectus contains the disclosure referred to in subsection (5) of Item 6 and subsection (5) of Item 9 of Part B of Form 81-101F1 Contents of Simplified Prospectus.

2.2 Control Restrictions — (1) An investment fund must not purchase a security of an issuer

(a) if, immediately after the purchase, the investment fund would hold securities representing more than 10% of

(i) the votes attaching to the outstanding voting securities of the issuer; or

(ii) the outstanding equity securities of the issuer; or

(b) for the purpose of exercising control over, or management of, the issuer.

(1.1) Subsection (1) does not apply to the purchase of any of the following:

(a) a security issued by an investment fund if the purchase is made in accordance with section 2.5;

(b) an index participation unit that is a security of an investment fund.

(2) If an investment fund acquires a security of an issuer other than as the result of a purchase, and the acquisition results in the investment fund exceeding the limits described in paragraph (1)(a), the investment fund must as quickly as is commercially reasonable, and in any event no later than 90 days after the acquisition, reduce its holdings of those securities so that it does not hold securities exceeding those limits.

(3) In determining its compliance with the restrictions contained in this section, an investment fund must

(a) assume the conversion of special warrants held by it; and

(b) consider that it holds directly the underlying securities represented by any American depositary receipts held by it.

2.3 Restrictions Concerning Types of Investments — (1) A mutual fund must not

(a) purchase real property;

(b) purchase a mortgage, other than a guaranteed mortgage;

(c) purchase a guaranteed mortgage if, immediately after the purchase, more than 10 percent of its net asset value would be made up of guaranteed mortgages;

(d) purchase a gold certificate, other than a permitted gold certificate;

(e) purchase gold or a permitted gold certificate if, immediately after the purchase, more than 10 percent of its net asset value would be made up of gold and permitted gold certificates;

(f) except to the extent permitted by paragraphs (d) and (e), purchase a physical commodity;

(g) purchase, sell or use a specified derivative other than in compliance with sections 2.7 to 2.11;

(h) purchase, sell or use a specified derivative the underlying interest of which is

(i) a physical commodity other than gold, or

(ii) a specified derivative of which the underlying interest is a physical commodity other than gold; or

(i) purchase an interest in a loan syndication or loan participation if the purchase would require the mutual fund to assume any responsibilities in administering the loan in relation to the borrower.

(2) A non-redeemable investment fund must not do any of the following:

(a) purchase real property;

(b) purchase a mortgage, other than a guaranteed mortgage

(c) purchase an interest in a loan syndication, or loan participation, if the purchase would require the non-redeemable investment fund to assume any responsibilities in administering the loan in relation to the borrower.

2.4 Restrictions Concerning Illiquid Assets — (1) A mutual fund must not purchase an illiquid asset if, immediately after the purchase, more than 10 percent of its net asset value would be made up of illiquid assets.

(2) A mutual fund must not have invested, for a period of 90 days or more, more than 15 percent of its net asset value, in illiquid assets.

(3) If more than 15 percent of the net asset value of a mutual fund is made up of illiquid assets, the mutual fund must, as quickly as is commercially reasonable, take all necessary steps to reduce the percentage of its net asset value made up of illiquid assets to 15 percent or less.

2.5 Investments in Other Investment Funds — (1) For the purposes of this section, an investment fund is considered to be holding a security of another investment fund if

(a) it holds securities issued by the other investment fund, or

(b) it is maintaining a position in a specified derivative for which the underlying interest is a security of the other investment fund.

(2) An investment fund must not purchase or hold a security of another investment fund unless,

(a) if the investment fund is a mutual fund, the other investment fund is a mutual fund that is subject to this Instrument and offers or has offered securities under a simplified prospectus in accordance with National Instrument 81-101 *Mutual Fund Prospectus Disclosure*,

(a.1) if the investment fund is a non-redeemable investment fund, one or both of the following apply:

(i) the other investment fund is subject to this Instrument;

(ii) the other investment fund complies with the provisions of this Instrument applicable to a non-redeemable investment fund,

(b) at the time of the purchase of that security, the other investment fund holds no more than 10% of its net asset value in securities of other investment funds,

(c) if the investment fund is a mutual fund, the investment fund and the other investment fund are reporting issuers in the local jurisdiction,

(c.1) the investment fund is a non-redeemable investment fund, the other investment fund is a reporting issuer in a jurisdiction in which the investment fund is a reporting issuer,

(d) no management fees or incentive fees are payable by the investment fund that, to a reasonable person, would duplicate a fee payable by the other investment fund for the same service,

(e) no sales fees or redemption fees are payable by the investment fund in relation to its purchases or redemptions of the securities of the other investment fund if the other investment fund is managed by the manager or an affiliate or associate of the manager of the investment fund, and

(f) no sales fees or redemption fees are payable by the investment fund in relation to its purchases or redemptions of securities of the other investment fund that, to a reasonable person, would duplicate a fee payable by an investor in the investment fund.

(3) Paragraphs (2)(a), (a.1), (c) and (c.1) do not apply if the security

(a) is an index participation unit issued by an investment fund, or

(b) is issued by another investment fund established with the approval of the government of a foreign jurisdiction and the only means by which the foreign jurisdiction permits investment in the securities of issuers of that foreign jurisdiction is through that type of investment fund.

(4) Paragraph (2)(b) does not apply if the other investment fund

(a) is a clone fund, or

(b) in accordance with this section purchases or holds securities

(i) of a money market fund, or

(ii) that are index participation units issued by an investment fund.

(5) Paragraphs (2)(e) and (f) do not apply to brokerage fees incurred for the purchase or sale of an index participation unit issued by an investment fund.

(6) An investment fund that holds securities of another investment fund that is managed by the same manager or an affiliate or associate of the manager

(a) must not vote any of those securities, and

(b) may, if the manager so chooses, arrange for all of the securities it holds of the other investment fund to be voted by the beneficial holders of securities of the investment fund.

(7) The investment fund conflict of interest investment restrictions and the investment fund conflict of interest reporting requirements do not apply to an investment fund which purchases or holds securities of another investment fund if the purchase or holding is made in accordance with this section.

2.6 Investment Practices — An investment fund must not,

(a) in the case of a mutual fund, borrow cash or provide a security interest over any of its portfolio assets unless

(i) the transaction is a temporary measure to accommodate requests for the redemption of securities of the mutual fund while the mutual fund effects an orderly liquidation of portfolio assets, or to permit the mutual fund to settle portfolio transactions and, after giving effect to all transactions undertaken under this subparagraph, the outstanding amount of all borrowings of the mutual fund does not exceed five percent of its net asset value at the time of the borrowing,

(ii) the security interest is required to enable the mutual fund to effect a specified derivative transaction or short sale of securities under this Instrument, is made in accordance with industry practice for that type of transaction and relates only to obligations arising under the particular specified derivatives transaction or short sale,

(iii) the security interest secures a claim for the fees and expenses of the custodian or a sub-custodian of the mutual fund for services rendered in that capacity as permitted by subsection 6.4(3), or

(iv) in the case of an exchange-traded mutual fund that is not in continuous distribution, the transaction is to finance the acquisition of its portfolio securities and the outstanding amount of all borrowings is repaid on the closing of its initial public offering;

(b) in the case of a mutual fund, purchase securities on margin, unless permitted by section 2.7 or 2.8;

(c) in the case of a mutual fund, sell securities short other than in compliance with section 2.6.1, unless permitted by section 2.7 or 2.8;

(d) purchase a security, other than a specified derivative, that by its terms may require the investment fund to make a contribution in addition to the payment of the purchase price;

(e) engage in the business of underwriting, or marketing to the public, securities of any other issuer;

(f) lend cash or portfolio assets other than cash;

(g) guarantee securities or obligations of a person or company; or

(h) purchase securities other than through market facilities through which these securities are normally bought and sold unless the purchase price approximates the prevailing market price or the parties are at arm's length in connection with the transaction.

2.6.1 Short Sales — (1) A mutual fund may sell a security short if

(a) the security sold short is sold for cash;

(b) the security sold short is not any of the following:

(i) a security that the mutual fund is otherwise not permitted by securities legislation to purchase at the time of the short sale transaction;

(ii) an illiquid asset;

(iii) a security of an investment fund other than an index participation unit; and

(c) at the time the mutual fund sells the security short

(i) the mutual fund has borrowed or arranged to borrow from a borrowing agent the security that is to be sold under the short sale;

(ii) the aggregate market value of all securities of the issuer of the securities sold short by the mutual fund does not exceed 5% of the net asset value of the mutual fund; and

(iii) the aggregate market value of all securities sold short by the mutual fund does not exceed 20% of the net asset value of the mutual fund.

(2) A mutual fund that sells securities short must hold cash cover in an amount that, together with portfolio assets deposited with borrowing agents as security in connection with short sales of securities by the mutual fund, is at least 150% of the aggregate market value of all securities sold short by the mutual fund on a daily mark-to-market basis.

(3) A mutual fund must not use the cash from a short sale to enter into a long position in a security, other than a security that qualifies as cash cover.

2.7 Transactions in Specified Derivatives for Hedging and Non-hedging Purposes — (1) A mutual fund must not purchase an option or a debt-like security or enter into a swap or a forward contract unless, at the time of the transaction, any of the following apply:

(a) in the case of an option, the option is a clearing corporation option;

(b) the option, debt-like security, swap or contract, has a designated rating;

(c) the equivalent debt of the counterparty, or of a person or company that has fully and unconditionally guaranteed the obligations of the counterparty in respect of the option, debt-like security, swap or contract, has a designated rating.

(2) If the credit rating of an option that is not a clearing corporation option, the credit rating of a debt-like security, swap or forward contract, or the credit rating of the equivalent debt of the writer or guarantor of the option, debt-like security, swap or contract, falls below the level of designated rating while the option, debt-like security, swap or contract is held by a mutual fund, the mutual fund must take the steps that are reasonably required to close out its position in the option, debt-like security, swap or contract in an orderly and timely fashion.

(3) Despite any other provisions contained in this Part, a mutual fund may enter into a trade to close out all or part of a position in a specified derivative, in which case the cash cover held to cover the underlying market exposure of the part of the position that is closed out may be released.

(4) The mark-to-market value of the exposure of a mutual fund under its specified derivatives positions with any one counterparty other than an acceptable clearing corporation or a clearing corporation that clears and settles transactions made on a futures exchange listed in Appendix A, calculated in accordance with subsection (5), must not exceed, for a period of 30 days or more, 10 percent of the net asset value of the mutual fund.

(5) The mark-to-market value of specified derivatives positions of a mutual fund with any one counterparty must be, for the purposes of subsection (4),

   (a) if the mutual fund has an agreement with the counterparty that provides for netting or the right of set-off, the net mark-to-market value of the specified derivatives positions of the mutual fund; and

   (b) in all other cases, the aggregated mark-to-market value of the specified derivative positions of the mutual fund.

2.8 Transactions in Specified Derivatives for Purposes Other than Hedging — (1) A mutual fund must not

   (a) purchase a debt-like security that has an options component or an option, unless, immediately after the purchase, not more than 10 percent of its net asset value would be made up of those instruments held for purposes other than hedging;

   (b) write a call option, or have outstanding a written call option, that is not an option on futures unless, as long as the position remains open, the mutual fund holds

      (i) an equivalent quantity of the underlying interest of the option,

      (ii) a right or obligation, exercisable at any time that the option is exercisable, to acquire an equivalent quantity of the underlying interest of the option, and cash cover that, together with margin on account for the position, is not less than the amount, if any, by which the strike price of the right or obligation to acquire the underlying interest exceeds the strike price of the option, or

      (iii) a combination of the positions referred to in subparagraphs (i) and (ii) that is sufficient, without recourse to other assets of the mutual fund, to enable the mutual fund to satisfy its obligations to deliver the underlying interest of the option;

   (c) write a put option, or have outstanding a written put option, that is not an option on futures, unless, as long as the position remains open, the mutual fund holds

      (i) a right or obligation, exercisable at any time that the option is exercisable, to sell an equivalent quantity of the underlying interest of the option, and cash cover in an amount that, together with margin on account for the position, is not less than the amount, if any, by which the strike price of the option exceeds the strike price of the right or obligation to sell the underlying interest,

      (ii) cash cover that, together with margin on account for the option position, is not less than the strike price of the option, or

      (iii) a combination of the positions referred to in subparagraphs (i) and (ii) that is sufficient, without recourse to other assets of the mutual fund, to enable the mutual fund to acquire the underlying interest of the option;

   (d) open or maintain a long position in a debt-like security that has a component that is a long position in a forward contract, or in a standardized future or forward contract, unless the mutual fund holds cash cover in an amount that, together with margin on account for the specified derivative and the market value of the specified derivative, is not less than, on a daily mark-to-market basis, the underlying market exposure of the specified derivative;

   (e) open or maintain a short position in a standardized future or forward contract, unless the mutual fund holds

      (i) an equivalent quantity of the underlying interest of the future or contract,

      (ii) a right or obligation to acquire an equivalent quantity of the underlying interest of the future or contract and cash cover that together with margin on account for the position is not less than the amount, if any, by which the strike price of the right or obligation to acquire the underlying interest exceeds the forward price of the contract, or

      (iii) a combination of the positions referred to in subparagraphs (i) and (ii) that is sufficient, without recourse to other assets of the mutual fund, to enable the mutual fund to deliver the underlying interest of the future or contract; or

   (f) enter into, or maintain, a swap position unless

      (i) for periods when the mutual fund would be entitled to receive payments under the swap, the mutual fund holds cash cover in an amount that, together with margin on account for the swap and the market value of the swap, is not less than, on a daily mark-to-market basis, the underlying market exposure of the swap; and

      (ii) for periods when the mutual fund would be required to make payments under the swap, the mutual fund holds

         (A) an equivalent quantity of the underlying interest of the swap,

         (B) a right or obligation to acquire an equivalent quantity of the underlying interest of the swap and cash cover that, together with margin on account for the position, is not less than the aggregate amount of the obligations of the mutual fund under the swap, or

         (C) a combination of the positions referred to in clauses (A) and (B) that is sufficient, without recourse to other assets of the mutual fund, to enable the mutual fund to satisfy its obligations under the swap.

(2) A mutual fund must treat any synthetic cash position on any date as providing the cash cover equal to the notional principal value of a banker's acceptance then being accepted by a bank listed in Schedule I of the *Bank Act* (Canada) that would produce the same annualized return as the synthetic cash position is then producing.

2.9 Transactions in Specified Derivatives for Hedging Purposes — (1) Sections 2.1, 2.2, 2.4 and 2.8 do not apply to the use of specified derivatives by a mutual fund for hedging purposes.

(2) Section 2.2 does not apply to the use of specified derivatives by a non-redeemable investment fund for hedging purposes.

2.10 Adviser Requirements — (1) If a portfolio adviser of an investment fund receives advice from a non-resident sub-adviser concerning the use of options or standardized futures by the investment fund, the investment fund must not invest in or use options or standardized futures unless

    (a) the obligations and duties of the non-resident sub-adviser are set out in a written agreement with the portfolio adviser; and

    (b) the portfolio adviser contractually agrees with the investment fund to be responsible for any loss that arises out of the failure of the non-resident sub-adviser

        (i) to exercise the powers and discharge the duties of its office honestly, in good faith and in the best interests of the investment fund, and

        (ii) to exercise the degree of care, diligence and skill that a reasonably prudent person would exercise in the circumstances.

(2) An investment fund must not relieve a portfolio adviser of the investment fund from liability for loss for which the portfolio adviser has assumed responsibility under paragraph (1)(b) that arises out of the failure of the relevant non-resident sub-adviser

    (a) to exercise the powers and discharge the duties of its office honestly, in good faith and in the best interests of the investment fund, or

    (b) to exercise the degree of care, diligence and skill that a reasonably prudent person would exercise in the circumstances.

(3) Despite subsection 4.4(3), an investment fund may indemnify a portfolio adviser against legal fees, judgments and amounts paid in settlement, actually and reasonably incurred by that person or company in connection with services provided by a non-resident sub-adviser for which the portfolio adviser has assumed responsibility under paragraph (1)(b), only if

    (a) those fees, judgments and amounts were not incurred as a result of a breach of the standard of care described in subsection (1) or (2); and

    (b) the investment fund has reasonable grounds to believe that the action or inaction that caused the payment of the fees, judgments and amounts paid in settlement was in the best interests of the investment fund.

(4) An investment fund must not incur the cost of any portion of liability insurance that insures a person or company for a liability except to the extent that the person or company may be indemnified for that liability under this section.

2.11 Commencement of Use of Specified Derivatives and Short Selling by an Investment Fund — (1) An investment fund that has not used specified derivatives must not begin using specified derivatives, and an investment fund that has not sold a security short in accordance with section 2.6.1 must not sell a security short unless

    (a) in the case of a mutual fund, other than an exchange-traded mutual fund that is not in continuous distribution, its prospectus contains the disclosure required for a mutual fund intending to engage in the activity;

    (a.1) in the case of an exchange-traded mutual fund that is not in continuous distribution or of a non-redeemable investment fund, the investment fund issues a news release that contains both of the following:

        (i) the disclosure required in a prospectus for an exchange-traded mutual fund that is not in continuous distribution, or a non-redeemable investment fund, intending to engage in the activity;

        (ii) date on which the activity is intended to begin; and

    (b) the investment fund has provided to its securityholders, not less than 60 days before it begins the intended activity, written notice that discloses its intent to engage in the activity and the disclosure referred to in paragraph (a) or (a.1), as applicable.

(2) A mutual fund, other than an exchange-traded mutual fund that is not in continuous distribution, is not required to provide the notice referred to in paragraph (1)(b) if each prospectus of the mutual fund since its inception has contained the disclosure referred to in paragraph (1)(a).

(3) Subsection (1) does not apply to an exchange-traded mutual fund that is not in continuous distribution, or to a non-redeemable investment fund, if each prospectus of the investment fund filed since its inception has contained the disclosure referred to in paragraph (1)(a.1).

2.12 Securities Loans — (1) Despite any other provision of this Instrument, an investment fund may enter into a securities lending transaction as lender if the following conditions are satisfied for the transaction:

1. The transaction is administered and supervised in the manner required by section 2.15 and 2.16.

2. The transaction is made under a written agreement that implements the requirements of this section.

3. Securities are loaned by the investment fund in exchange for collateral.

4. The securities transferred, either by the investment fund or to the investment fund as collateral, as part of the transaction are immediately available for good delivery under applicable legislation.

5. The collateral to be delivered to the investment fund at the beginning of the transaction

    (a) is received by the investment fund either before or at the same time as it delivers the loaned securities; and

    (b) has a market value equal to at least 102 percent of the market value of the loaned securities.

6. The collateral to be delivered to the investment fund is one or more of

    (a) cash;

    (b) qualified securities;

    (c) securities that are immediately convertible into, or exchangeable for, securities of the same issuer, class or type, and the same term, if applicable, as the securities that are being loaned by the investment fund, and in at least the same number as those loaned by the investment fund; or

    (d) irrevocable letters of credit issued by a Canadian financial institution that is not the counterparty, or an affiliate counterparty, of the investment fund in the transaction, if evidences of indebtedness of the Canadian financial institution that are rated as short term debt by a designated rating organization or its DRO affiliate have a designated rating.

7. The collateral and loaned securities are marked to market on each business day, and the amount of collateral in the possession of the investment fund is adjusted on each business day to ensure that the market value of collateral maintained by the investment fund in connection with the transaction is at least 102 percent of the market value of the loaned securities.

8. If an event of default by a borrower occurs, the investment fund, in addition to any other remedy available under the agreement or applicable law, has the right under the agreement to retain and dispose of the collateral to the extent necessary to satisfy its claims under the agreement.

9. The borrower is required to pay promptly to the investment fund amounts equal to and as compensation for all dividends and interest paid, and all distributions made, on the loaned securities during the term of the transaction.

10. The transaction is a "securities lending arrangement" under section 260 of the ITA.

11. The investment fund is entitled to terminate the transaction at any time and recall the loaned securities within the normal and customary settlement period for securities lending transactions in the market in which securities are lent.

12. Immediately after the investment fund enters into the transaction, the aggregate market value of all securities loaned by the investment fund in securities lending transactions and not yet returned to it or sold by the investment fund in repurchase transactions under section 2.13 and not yet repurchased does not exceed 50% of the net asset value of the investment fund.

(2) An investment fund may hold all cash delivered to it as the collateral in a securities lending transaction or may use the cash to purchase

    (a) qualified securities having a remaining term to maturity no longer than 90 days;

    (b) securities under a reverse repurchase agreement permitted by section 2.14; or

    (c) a combination of the securities referred to in paragraphs (a) and (b).

(3) An investment fund, during the term of a securities lending transaction, must hold all, and must not invest or dispose of any, non-cash collateral delivered to it as collateral in the transaction.

2.13 Repurchase Transactions

— (1) Despite any other provision of this Instrument, an investment fund may enter into a repurchase transaction if the following conditions are satisfied for the transaction:

1. The transaction is administered and supervised in the manner required by section 2.15 and 2.16.

2. The transaction is made under a written agreement that implements the requirements of this section.

3. Securities are sold for cash by the investment fund, with the investment fund assuming an obligation to repurchase the securities for cash.

4. The securities transferred by the investment fund as part of the transaction are immediately available for good delivery under applicable legislation.

5. The cash to be delivered to the investment fund at the beginning of the transaction

    (a) is received by the investment fund either before or at the same time as it delivers the sold securities; and

    (b) is in an amount equal to at least 102 percent of the market value of the sold securities.

6. The sold securities are marked to market on each business day, and the amount of sale proceeds in the possession of the investment fund is adjusted on each business day to ensure that the amount of cash maintained by the investment fund in connection with the transaction is at least 102 percent of the market value of the sold securities.

7. If an event of default by a purchaser occurs, the investment fund, in addition to any other remedy available under the agreement or applicable law, has the right under the agreement to retain or dispose of the sale proceeds delivered to it by the purchaser to the extent necessary to satisfy its claims under the agreement.

8. The purchaser of the securities is required to pay promptly to the investment fund amounts equal to and as compensation for all dividends and interest paid, and all distributions made, on the sold securities during the term of the transaction.

9. The transaction is a "securities lending arrangement" under section 260 of the ITA.

10. The term of the repurchase agreement, before any extension or renewal that requires the consent of both the investment fund and the purchaser, is not more than 30 days.

11. Immediately after the investment fund enters into the transaction, the aggregate market value of all securities loaned by the investment fund in securities lending transactions under section 2.12 and not yet returned to it or sold by the investment fund in repurchase transactions and not yet repurchased does not exceed 50% of the net asset value of the investment fund.

(2) An investment fund may hold cash delivered to it as consideration for sold securities in a repurchase transaction or may use the cash to purchase

    (a) qualified securities having a remaining term to maturity no longer than 30 days;

    (b) securities under a reverse repurchase agreement permitted by section 2.14; or

    (c) a combination of the securities referred to in paragraphs (a) and (b).

2.14 Reverse Repurchase Transactions

— (1) Despite any other provision of this Instrument, an investment fund may enter into a reverse repurchase transaction if the following conditions are satisfied for the transaction:

1. The transaction is administered and supervised in the manner required by sections 2.15 and 2.16.

2. The transaction is made under a written agreement that implements the requirements of this section.

3. Qualified securities are purchased for cash by the investment fund, with the investment fund assuming the obligation to resell them for cash.

4. The securities transferred as part of the transaction are immediately available for good delivery under applicable legislation.

5. The securities to be delivered to the investment fund at the beginning of the transaction

    (a) are received by the investment fund either before or at the same time as it delivers the cash used by it to purchase those securities; and

    (b) have a market value equal to at least 102 percent of the cash paid for the securities by the investment fund.

6. The purchased securities are marked to market on each business day, and either the amount of cash paid for the purchased securities or the amount of purchased securities in the possession of the seller or the investment fund is adjusted on each business day to ensure that the market value of purchased securities held by the investment fund in connection with the transaction is not less than 102 percent of the cash paid by the investment fund.

7. If an event of default by a seller occurs, the investment fund, in addition to any other remedy available in the agreement or applicable law, has the right under the agreement to retain or dispose of the purchased securities delivered to it by the seller to the extent necessary to satisfy its claims under the agreement.

8. The transaction is a "securities lending arrangement" under section 260 of the ITA.

9. The term of the reverse repurchase agreement, before any extension or renewal that requires the consent of both the seller and the investment fund, is not more than 30 days.

2.15 Agent for Securities Lending, Repurchase and Reverse Repurchase Transactions — (1) The manager of an investment fund must appoint an agent or agents to act on behalf of the investment fund to administer the securities lending and repurchase transactions entered into by the investment fund.

(2) The manager of the investment fund may appoint an agent or agents to act on behalf of the investment fund to administer the reverse repurchase transactions entered into by the investment fund.

(3) The custodian or a sub-custodian of the investment fund must be the agent appointed under subsection (1) or (2).

(4) The manager of an investment fund must not authorize an agent to enter into a securities lending, repurchase or, if applicable, reverse repurchase transactions on behalf of the investment fund until the agent enters into a written agreement with the manager and the investment fund in which

(a) the investment fund and the manager provide instructions to the agent on the parameters to be followed in entering into the type of transactions to which the agreement pertains;

(b) the agent agrees to comply with this Instrument, accepts the standard of care referred to in subsection (5) and agrees to ensure that all transactions entered into by it on behalf of the investment fund will comply with this Instrument; and

(c) the agent agrees to provide to the investment fund and the manager regular, comprehensive and timely reports summarizing the investment fund's securities lending, repurchase and reverse repurchase transactions, as applicable.

(5) An agent appointed under this section, in administering the securities lending, repurchase and, if applicable, reverse repurchase transactions of the investment fund must exercise the degree of care, diligence and skill that a reasonably prudent person would exercise in the circumstances.

2.16 Controls and Records — (1) An investment fund must not enter into transactions under sections 2.12, 2.13 or 2.14 unless,

(a) for transactions to be entered into through an agent appointed under section 2.15, the manager has reasonable grounds to believe that the agent has established and maintains appropriate internal controls and procedures and records; and

(b) for reverse repurchase transactions directly entered into by the investment fund without an agent, the manager has established and maintains appropriate internal controls, procedures and records.

(2) The internal controls, procedures and records referred to in subsection (1) must include

(a) a list of approved borrowers, purchasers and sellers based on generally accepted creditworthiness standards;

(b) as applicable, transaction and credit limits for each counterparty; and

(c) collateral diversification standards.

(3) The manager of an investment fund must, on a periodic basis not less frequently than annually,

(a) review the agreements with any agent appointed under section 2.15 to determine if the agreements are in compliance with this Instrument;

(b) review the internal controls described in subsection (2) to ensure their continued adequacy and appropriateness;

(c) make reasonable enquiries as to whether the agent is administering the securities lending, repurchase or reverse repurchase transactions of the investment fund in a competent and responsible manner, in conformity with the requirements of this Instrument and in conformity with the agreement between the agent, the manager and the investment fund entered into under subsection 2.15(4);

(d) review the terms of any agreement between the investment fund and an agent entered into under subsection 2.15(4) in order to determine if the instructions provided to the agent in connection with the securities lending, repurchase or reverse repurchase transactions of the investment fund continue to be appropriate; and

(e) make or cause to be made any changes that may be necessary to ensure that

(i) the agreements with agents are in compliance with this Instrument;

(ii) the internal controls described in subsection (2) are adequate and appropriate,

(iii) the securities lending, repurchase or reverse repurchase transactions of the investment fund are administered in the manner described in paragraph (c), and

(iv) the terms of each agreement between the investment fund and an agent entered into under subsection 2.15(4) are appropriate.

2.17 Commencement of Securities Lending, Repurchase and Reverse Repurchase Transactions by an Investment Fund — (1) An investment fund must not enter into securities lending, repurchase or reverse repurchase transactions unless,

(a) in the case of a mutual fund, other than an exchange-traded mutual fund that is not in continuous distribution, its prospectus contains the disclosure required for mutual funds entering into those types of transactions;

(b) in the case of an exchange-traded mutual fund that is not in continuous distribution or of a non-redeemable investment fund, the investment fund issues a news release that contains both of the following:

(i) the disclosure required in a prospectus for an exchange-traded mutual fund that is not in continuous distribution, or a non-redeemable investment fund, entering into those types of transactions;

(ii) the date on which the investment fund intends to begin entering into those types of transactions; and

(c) the investment fund provides to its securityholders, at least 60 days before it begins entering into those types of transactions, written notice that discloses its intent to begin entering into those types of transactions and the disclosure referred to in paragraph (a) or (b), as applicable.

(2) Paragraph (1)(c) does not apply to a mutual fund that has entered into reverse repurchase agreements as permitted by a decision of the securities regulatory authority or regulator.

(3) Paragraph (1)(c) does not apply to a mutual fund, other than an exchange-traded mutual fund that is not in continuous distribution, if each prospectus of the mutual fund filed since its inception contains the disclosure referred to in paragraph (1)(a).

(4) Subsection (1) does not apply to an exchange-traded mutual fund that is not in continuous distribution, or to a non-redeemable investment fund, if each prospectus of the investment fund filed since its inception contains the disclosure referred to in paragraph (1)(b).

2.18 Money Market Fund — (1) A mutual fund must not describe itself as a "money market fund" in its prospectus, a continuous disclosure document or a sales communication unless

> (a) it has all of its assets invested in one or more of the following:

> > (i) cash,

> > (ii) cash equivalents,

> > (iii) an evidence of indebtedness that has a remaining term to maturity of 365 days or less and a designated rating,

> > (iv) a floating rate evidence of indebtedness if

> > > (A) the floating interest rate of the indebtedness is reset no later than every 185 days, and

> > > (B) the principal amount of the indebtedness will continue to have a market value of approximately par at the time of each change in the rate to be paid to the holders of the evidence of indebtedness, or

> > (v) securities issued by one or more money market funds,

> (b) it has a portfolio of assets, excluding a security described in subparagraph (a)(v), with a dollar-weighted average term to maturity not exceeding

> > (i) 180 days, and

> > (ii) 90 days when calculated on the basis that the term of a floating rate obligation is the period remaining to the date of the next rate setting,

> (c) not less than 95% of its assets invested in accordance with paragraph (a) are denominated in a currency in which the net asset value per security of the mutual fund is calculated, and

> (d) it has not less than

> > (i) 5% of its assets invested in cash or readily convertible into cash within one day, and

> > (ii) 15% of its assets invested in cash or readily convertible into cash within one week.

(2) Despite any other provision of this Instrument, a mutual fund that describes itself as a "money market fund" must not use a specified derivative or sell securities short.

(3) A non-redeemable investment fund must not describe itself as a "money market fund".

PART 3 — NEW MUTUAL FUNDS

3.1 Initial Investment in a New Mutual Fund — (1) A person or company must not file a prospectus for a newly established mutual fund unless

> (a) an investment of at least $150,000 in securities of the mutual fund has been made, and those securities are beneficially owned, before the time of filing by

> > (i) the manager, a portfolio adviser, a promoter or a sponsor of the mutual fund,

> > (ii) the partners, directors, officers or securityholders of any of the manager, a portfolio adviser, a promoter or a sponsor of the mutual fund, or

> > (iii) a combination of the persons or companies referred to subparagraphs (i) and (ii); or

> (b) the prospectus of the mutual fund states that the mutual fund will not issue securities other than those referred to in paragraph (a) unless subscriptions aggregating not less than $500,000 have been received by the mutual fund from investors other than the persons and companies referred to in paragraph (a) and accepted by the mutual fund.

(2) A mutual fund must not redeem a security issued upon an investment in the mutual fund referred to in paragraph (1)(a) until $500,000 has been received from persons or companies other than the persons and companies referred to in paragraph (1)(a).

3.2 Prohibition Against Distribution — If a prospectus of a mutual fund contains the disclosure described in paragraph 3.1(1)(b), the mutual fund must not distribute any securities unless the subscriptions described in that disclosure, together with payment for the securities subscribed for, have been received.

3.3 Prohibition Against Reimbursement of Organization Costs — (1) The costs of incorporation, formation or initial organization of a mutual fund, or of the preparation and filing of any of the preliminary prospectus, preliminary annual information form, preliminary fund facts document, initial prospectus, annual information form or fund facts document of the mutual fund must not be borne by the mutual fund or its securityholders.

(2) Subsection (1) does not apply to an exchange-traded mutual fund unless the fund is in continuous distribution.

PART 4 — CONFLICTS OF INTEREST

4.1 Prohibited Investments — (1) A dealer managed investment fund must not knowingly make an investment in a class of securities of an issuer during, or for 60 days after, the period in which the dealer manager of the investment fund, or an associate or affiliate of the dealer manager of the investment fund, acts as an underwriter in the distribution of securities of that class of securities, except as a member of the selling group distributing five percent or less of the securities underwritten.

(2) A dealer managed investment fund must not knowingly make an investment in a class of securities of an issuer of which a partner, director, officer or employee of the dealer manager of the investment fund, or a partner, director, officer or employee of an affiliate or associate of the dealer manager, is a partner, director or officer, unless the partner, director, officer or employee

> (a) does not participate in the formulation of investment decisions made on behalf of the dealer managed investment fund;

> (b) does not have access before implementation to information concerning investment decisions made on behalf of the dealer managed investment fund; and

> (c) does not influence, other than through research, statistical and other reports generally available to clients, the investment decisions made on behalf of the dealer managed investment fund.

(3) Subsections (1) and (2) do not apply to an investment in a class of securities issued or fully and unconditionally guaranteed by the government of Canada or the government of a jurisdiction.

(4) Subsection (1) does not apply to an investment in a class of securities of an issuer if, at the time of each investment

    (a) the independent review committee of the dealer managed investment fund has approved the transaction under subsection 5.2(2) of NI 81-107;

    (b) in a class of debt securities of an issuer other than a class of securities referred to in subsection (3), the security has been given, and continues to have, a designated rating by a designated rating organization or its DRO affiliate;

    (c) in any other class of securities of an issuer,

        (i) the distribution of the class of equity securities is made by prospectus filed with one or more securities regulatory authorities or regulators in Canada, and

        (ii) during the 60 day period referred to in subsection (1) the investment is made on an exchange on which the class of equity securities of the issuer is listed and traded; and

    (d) no later than the time the dealer managed investment fund files its annual financial statements, the manager of the dealer managed investment fund files the particulars of each investment made by the dealer managed investment fund during its most recently completed financial year.

(4.1) In paragraph (4)(b), "designated rating" has the meaning ascribed to it in National Instrument 44-101 — *Short Form Prospectus Distributions*.

(5) The provisions of securities legislation that are referred to in Appendix C do not apply with respect to an investment in a class of securities of an issuer referred to in subsection (4) if the investment is made in accordance with that subsection.

4.2 Self-Dealing — (1) An investment fund must not purchase a security from, sell a security to, or enter into a securities lending, repurchase or reverse repurchase transaction under section 2.12, 2.13 or 2.14 with any of the following persons or companies:

    1. The manager, portfolio adviser or trustee of the investment fund.

    2. A partner, director or officer of the investment fund or of the manager, portfolio adviser or trustee of the investment fund.

    3. An associate or affiliate of a person or company referred to in paragraph 1 or 2.

    4. A person or company, having fewer than 100 securityholders of record, of which a partner, director or officer of the investment fund or a partner, director or officer of the manager or portfolio adviser of the investment fund is a partner, director, officer or securityholder.

(2) Subsection (1) applies in the case of a sale of a security to, or a purchase of a security from, an investment fund only if the person or company that would be selling to, or purchasing from, the investment fund would be doing so as principal.

4.3 Exception — (1) Section 4.2 does not apply to a purchase or sale of a security by an investment fund if the price payable for the security is:

    (a) not more than the ask price of the security as reported by any available public quotation in common use, in the case of a purchase by the investment fund; or

    (b) not less than the bid price of the security as reported by any available public quotation in common use, in the case of a sale by the investment fund.

(2) Section 4.2 does not apply to a purchase or sale of a class of debt securities by an investment fund from, or to, another investment fund managed by the same manager or an affiliate of the manager, if, at the time of the transaction

    (a) the investment fund is purchasing from, or selling to, another investment fund to which NI 81-107 applies;

    (b) the independent review committee of the investment fund has approved the transaction under subsection 5.2(2) of NI 81-107; and

    (c) the transaction complies with subsection 6.1(2) of NI 81-107.

4.4 Liability and Indemnification — (1) An agreement or declaration of trust by which a person or company acts as manager of an investment fund must provide that the manager is responsible for any loss that arises out of the failure of the manager, or of any person or company retained by the manager or the investment fund to discharge any of the manager's responsibilities to the investment fund,

    (a) to exercise the powers and discharge the duties of its office honestly, in good faith and in the best interests of the investment fund, and

    (b) to exercise the degree of care, diligence and skill that a reasonably prudent person would exercise in the circumstances.

(2) An investment fund must not relieve the manager of the investment fund from liability for loss that arises out of the failure of the manager, or of any person retained by the manager or the investment fund to discharge any of the manager's responsibilities to the investment fund,

    (a) to exercise the powers and discharge the duties of its office honestly, in good faith and in the best interests of the investment fund, or

    (b) to exercise the degree of care, diligence and skill that a reasonably prudent person would exercise in the circumstances.

(3) An investment fund may indemnify a person or company providing services to it against legal fees, judgments and amounts paid in settlement, actually and reasonably incurred by that person or company in connection with services provided by that person or company to the investment fund, if

    (a) those fees, judgments and amounts were not incurred as a result of a breach of the standard of care described in subsection (1) or (2); and

    (b) the investment fund has reasonable grounds to believe that the action or inaction that caused the payment of the fees, judgments and amounts paid in settlement was in the best interests of the investment fund.

(4) An investment fund must not incur the cost of any portion of liability insurance that insures a person or company for a liability except to the extent that the person or company may be indemnified for that liability under this section.

(5) This section does not apply to any losses to an investment fund or securityholder arising out of an action or inaction by any of the following:

    (a) a director of the investment fund;

    (b) a custodian or sub-custodian of the investment fund, except as set out in subsection (6).

(6) This section applies to any losses to an investment fund or securityholder arising out of an action or inaction by a custodian or sub-custodian acting as agent of the investment fund in administering the securities lending, repurchase or reverse repurchase transactions of the investment fund.

PART 5 — FUNDAMENTAL CHANGES

5.1 Matters Requiring Securityholder Approval — (1) The prior approval of the securityholders of an investment fund, given as provided in section 5.2, is required before the occurrence of each of the following:

(a) the basis of the calculation of a fee or expense that is charged to the investment fund or directly to its securityholders by the investment fund or its manager in connection with the holding of securities of the investment fund is changed in a way that could result in an increase in charges to the investment fund or to its securityholders;

(a.1) a fee or expense, to be charged to the investment fund or directly to its securityholders by the investment fund or its manager in connection with the holding of securities of the investment fund that could result in an increase in charges to the investment fund or to its securityholders, is introduced;

(b) the manager of the investment fund is changed, unless the new manager is an affiliate of the current manager;

(c) the fundamental investment objectives of the investment fund are changed;

(d) [repealed]

(e) the investment fund decreases the frequency of the calculation of its net asset value per security;

(f) the investment fund undertakes a reorganization with, or transfers its assets to, another issuer, if

(i) the investment fund ceases to continue after the reorganization or transfer of assets, and

(ii) the transaction results in the securityholders of the investment fund becoming securityholders in the other issuer;

(g) the investment fund undertakes a reorganization with, or acquires assets from, another issuer, if

(i) the investment fund continues after the reorganization or transfer of assets, and

(ii) the transaction results in the securityholders of the other issuer becoming securityholders in the investment fund, and

(iii) the transaction would be a material change to the investment fund;

(h) the investment fund implements any of the following:

(i) in the case of a non-redeemable investment fund, a restructuring into a mutual fund;

(ii) in the case of a mutual fund, a restructuring into a non-redeemable investment fund;

(iii) a restructuring into an issuer that is not a investment fund.

(2) An investment fund must not bear any of the costs or expenses associated with a restructuring referred to in paragraph (1)(h).

5.2 Approval of Securityholders — (1) Unless a greater majority is required by the constating documents of the investment fund, the laws applicable to the investment fund or an applicable agreement, the approval of the securityholders of the investment fund to a matter referred to in subsection 5.1(1) must be given by a resolution passed by at least a majority of the votes cast at a meeting of the securityholders of the investment fund duly called and held to consider the matter.

(2) Despite subsection (1), the holders of securities of a class or series of a class of securities of an investment fund must vote separately as a class or series of a class on a matter referred to in subsection 5.1(1) if that class or series of a class is affected by the action referred to in subsection 5.1(1) in a manner different from holders of securities of other classes or series of a class.

(3) Despite subsection 5.1(1) and subsections (1) and (2), if the constating documents of the investment fund so provide, the holders of securities of a class or series of a class of securities of an investment fund must not be entitled to vote on a matter referred to in subsection 5.1(1) if they, as holders of the class or series of a class, are not affected by the action referred to in subsection 5.1(1).

5.3 Circumstances in Which Approval of Securityholders Not Required — (1) Despite subsection 5.1(1), the approval of securityholders of an investment fund is not required to be obtained for a change referred to in paragraphs 5.1(1)(a) and (a.1)

(a) if

(i) the investment fund is at arm's length to the person or company charging the fee or expense to the investment fund referred to in paragraphs 5.1(1)(a) and (a.1),

(ii) the prospectus of the investment fund discloses that, although the approval of securityholders will not be obtained before making the changes, securityholders will be sent a written notice at least 60 days before the effective date of the change that is to be made that could result in an increase in charges to the investment fund, and

(iii) the notice referred to in subparagraph (ii) is actually sent at least 60 days before the effective date of the change; or

(b) if, in the case of a mutual fund,

(i) the mutual fund is permitted by this Instrument to be described as a "no-load" fund,

(ii) the prospectus of the mutual fund discloses that securityholders will be sent a written notice at least 60 days before the effective date of a change that is to be made that could result in an increase in charges to the mutual fund, and

(iii) the notice referred to in subparagraph (ii) is actually sent at least 60 days before the effective date of the change.

(2) Despite subsection 5.1(1), the approval of securityholders of an investment fund is not required to be obtained for a change referred to in paragraph 5.1(1)(f) if either of the following paragraphs apply:

(a) all of the following apply:

(i) the independent review committee of the investment fund has approved the change under subsection 5.2(2) of NI 81-107;

(ii) the investment fund is being reorganized with, or its assets are being transferred to, another investment fund to which this Instrument and NI 81-107 apply and that is managed by the manager, or an affiliate of the manager, of the investment fund;

(iii) the reorganization or transfer of assets of the investment fund complies with the criteria in paragraphs 5.6(1)(a), (b), (c), (d), (g), (h), (i), (j) and (k);

(iv) the prospectus of the investment fund discloses that, although the approval of securityholders may not be obtained before making the change, securityholders will be sent a written notice at least 60 days before the effective date of the change;

(v) the notice referred to in subparagraph (iv) to securityholders is sent at least 60 days before the effective date of the change;

(b) all of the following apply:

(i) the investment fund is a non-redeemable investment fund that is being reorganized with, or its assets are being transferred to, a mutual fund that is

(A) a mutual fund to which this Instrument and NI 81-107 apply,

(B) managed by the manager, or an affiliate of the manager, of the investment fund,

(C) not in default of any requirement of securities legislation, and

(D) a reporting issuer in the local jurisdiction and the mutual fund has a current prospectus in the local jurisdiction;

(ii) the transaction is a tax-deferred transaction under subsection 85(1) of the ITA;

(iii) the securities of the investment fund do not give securityholders of the investment fund the right to request that the investment fund redeem the securities;

(iv) since its inception, there has been no market through which securityholders of the investment fund could sell securities of the investment fund;

(v) every prospectus of the investment fund discloses that

(A) securityholders of the investment fund, other than the manager, promoter or an affiliate of the manager or promoter, will cease to be securityholders of the investment fund within 30 months following the completion of the initial public offering by the investment fund, and

(B) the investment fund will, within 30 months following the completion of the initial public offering of the investment fund, undertake a reorganization with, or transfer its assets to, a mutual fund that is managed by the manager of the investment fund or by an affiliate of the manager of the investment fund;

(vi) the mutual fund bears none of the costs and expenses associated with the transaction;

(vii) the reorganization or transfer of assets of the investment fund complies with subparagraphs 5.3(2)(a)(i), (iv) and (v) and paragraphs 5.6(1)(d) and (k).

5.3.1 Change of Auditor of an Investment Fund — The auditor of an investment fund must not be changed unless

(a) the independent review committee of the investment fund has approved the change of auditor under subsection 5.2(2) of NI 81-107;

(b) the prospectus of the investment fund discloses that, although the approval of securityholders will not be obtained before making the change, securityholders will be sent a written notice at least 60 days before the effective date of the change, and

(c) the notice referred to in paragraph (b) to securityholders is sent 60 days before the effective date of the change.

5.4 Formalities Concerning Meetings of Securityholders — (1) A meeting of securityholders of an investment fund called to consider any matter referred to in subsection 5.1(1) must be called on written notice sent at least 21 days before the date of the meeting.

(2) The notice referred to in subsection (1) must contain or be accompanied by a statement that includes

(a) a description of the change or transaction proposed to be made or entered into and, if the matter is one referred to in paragraphs 5.1(1)(a) and (a.1), the effect that the change would have had on the management expense ratio of the investment fund had the change been in force throughout the investment fund's last completed financial year;

(b) the date of the proposed implementation of the change or transaction; and

(c) all other information and documents necessary to comply with the applicable proxy solicitation requirements of securities legislation for the meeting.

5.5 Approval of Securities Regulatory Authority — (1) The approval of the securities regulatory authority or regulator is required before

(a) the manager of an investment fund is changed, unless the new manager is an affiliate of the current manager;

(a.1) a change of control of the manager of an investment fund occurs;

(b) a reorganization or transfer of assets of an investment fund is implemented, if the transaction will result in the securityholders of the investment fund becoming securityholders in another issuer;

(c) a change of the custodian of an investment fund is implemented, if there has been or will be, in connection with the proposed change, a change of the type referred to in paragraph (a); or

(d) an investment fund suspends, other than under section 10.6, the rights of securityholders to request that the investment fund redeem their securities.

(2) [Repealed.]

(3) Despite subsection (1), in Ontario only the regulator may grant an approval referred to in subsection (1).

5.6 Pre-Approved Reorganizations and Transfers — (1) Despite subsection 5.5(1), the approval of the securities regulatory authority or regulator is not required to implement a transaction referred to in paragraph 5.5(1)(b) if all of the following paragraphs apply:

(a) the investment fund is being reorganized with, or its assets are being transferred to, another investment fund to which this Instrument applies and that

(i) is managed by the manager, or an affiliate of the manager, of the investment fund,

(ii) a reasonable person would consider to have substantially similar fundamental investment objectives, valuation procedures and fee structure as the investment fund,

(iii) is not in default of any requirement of securities legislation, and

(iv) is a reporting issuer in the local jurisdiction and, if it is a mutual fund, also has a current prospectus in the local jurisdiction;

(b) the transaction is a "qualifying exchange" within the meaning of section 132.2 of the ITA or is a tax-deferred transaction under subsection 85(1), 85.1(1), 86(1) or 87(1) of the ITA;

(c) the transaction contemplates the wind-up of the investment fund as soon as reasonably possible following the transaction;

(d) the portfolio assets of the investment fund to be acquired by the other investment fund as part of the transaction

(i) may be acquired by the other investment fund in compliance with this Instrument, and

(ii) are acceptable to the portfolio adviser of the other investment fund and consistent with the other investment fund's fundamental investment objectives;

(e) the transaction is approved

(i) by the securityholders of the investment fund in accordance with paragraph 5.1(1)(f), unless subsection 5.3(2) applies, and

(ii) if required, by the securityholders of the other investment fund in accordance with paragraph 5.1(1)(g);

(f) the materials sent to securityholders of the investment fund in connection with the approval under paragraph 5.1(1)(f) include

(i) a circular that, in addition to other requirements prescribed by law, describes the proposed transaction, the investment fund into which the investment fund will be reorganized, the income tax considerations for the investment funds participating in the transaction and their securityholders, and, if the investment fund is a corporation and the transaction involves its shareholders becoming securityholders of an investment fund that is established as a trust, a description of the material differences between being a shareholder of a corporation and being a securityholder of a trust,

(ii) if the other investment fund is a mutual fund, the most recently filed fund facts document for the other investment fund, and

(iii) a statement that securityholders may, in respect of the reorganized investment fund,

(A) obtain all of the following documents at no cost by contacting the reorganized investment fund at an address or telephone number specified in the statement:

(I) if the reorganized investment fund is a mutual fund, the current prospectus;

(II) the most recently filed annual information form, if one has been filed;

(III) as applicable, the most recently filed fund facts document;

(IV) the most recently filed annual financial statements and interim financial reports;

(V) the most recently filed annual and interim management reports of fund performance, or

(B) access those documents at a website address specified in the statement;

(g) the investment fund has complied with Part 11 of National Instrument 81-106 *Investment Fund Continuous Disclosure* in connection with the making of the decision to proceed with the transaction by the board of directors of the manager of the investment fund or of the investment fund;

(h) the investment funds participating in the transaction bear none of the costs and expenses associated with the transaction;

(i) if the investment fund is a mutual fund, securityholders of the investment fund continue to have the right to redeem securities of the investment fund up to the close of business on the business day immediately before the effective date of the transaction;

(j) if the investment fund is a non-redeemable investment fund, all of the following apply:

(i) the investment fund issues and files a news release that discloses the transaction;

(ii) securityholders of the investment fund may redeem securities of the investment fund at a date that is after the date of the news release referred to in subparagraph (i) and before the effective date of the transaction;

(iii) the securities submitted for redemption in accordance with subparagraph (ii) are redeemed at a price equal to their net asset value per security on the redemption date;

(k) the consideration offered to securityholders of the investment fund for the transaction has a value that is equal to the net asset value of the investment fund calculated on the date of the transaction.

(1.1) Despite subsection 5.5(1), the approval of the securities regulatory authority or regulator is not required to implement a transaction referred to in paragraph 5.5(1)(b) if all the conditions in paragraph 5.3(2)(b) are satisfied and the independent review committee of the mutual fund involved in the transaction has approved the transaction in accordance with subsection 5.2(2) of NI 81-107.

(2) An investment fund that has continued after a transaction described in paragraph 5.5(1)(b) must, if the audit report accompanying its audited financial statements for its first completed financial year after the transaction contains a modified opinion in respect of the value of the portfolio assets acquired by the investment fund in the transaction, send a copy of those financial statements to each person or company that was a securityholder of an investment fund that was terminated as a result of the transaction and that is not a securityholder of the investment fund.

5.7 Applications — (1) An application for an approval required under section 5.5 must contain,

(a) if the application is required by paragraph 5.5(1)(a) or (a.1),

(i) details of the proposed transaction,

(ii) details of the proposed new manager or the person or company proposing to acquire control of the manager,

(iii) as applicable, the names, residence addresses and birthdates of

(A) all proposed new partners, directors or officers of the manager,

(B) all partners, directors or officers of the person or company proposing to acquire control of the manager,

(C) any proposed new individual trustee of the investment fund, and

(D) any new directors or officers of the investment fund,

(iv) all information necessary to permit the securities regulatory authority or regulator to conduct security checks on the individuals referred to in subparagraph (iii),

(v) sufficient information to establish the integrity and experience of the persons or companies referred to in subparagraphs (ii) and (iii), and

(vi) details of how the proposed transaction will affect the management and administration of the investment fund;

(b) if the application is required by paragraph 5.5(1)(b),

    (i) details of the proposed transaction,

    (ii) details of the total annual returns of the investment fund and, if the other issuer is an investment fund, the other issuer for each of the previous five years,

    (iii) a description of the differences between, as applicable, the fundamental investment objectives, investment strategies, valuation procedures and fee structure of the investment fund and the other issuer and any other material differences between the investment fund and the other issuer, and

    (iv) a description of those elements of the proposed transaction that make section 5.6 inapplicable;

(c) if the application is required by paragraph 5.5(1)(c), sufficient information to establish that the proposed custodial arrangements will be in compliance with Part 6;

(d) if the application relates to a matter that would constitute a material change for the investment fund, a draft amendment to the prospectus and, if applicable, to the fund facts document of the investment fund reflecting the change; and

(e) if the matter is one that requires the approval of securityholders, confirmation that the approval has been obtained or will be obtained before the change is implemented.

(2) An investment fund that applies for an approval under paragraph 5.5(1)(d) must

(a) make that application to the securities regulatory authority or regulator in the jurisdiction in which the head office or registered office of the investment fund is situated; and

(b) concurrently file a copy of the application so made with the securities regulatory authority or the regulator in the local jurisdiction if the head office or registered office of the investment fund is not situated in the local jurisdiction.

(3) An investment fund that has complied with subsection (2) in the local jurisdiction may suspend the right of securityholders to request that the investment fund redeem their securities if

(a) the securities regulatory authority or regulator in the jurisdiction in which the head office or registered office of the investment fund is situated has granted approval to the application made under paragraph (2)(a); and

(b) the securities regulatory authority or regulator in the local jurisdiction has not notified the investment fund, by the close of business on the business day immediately following the day on which the copy of the application referred to in paragraph (2)(b) was received, either that

    (i) the securities regulatory authority or regulator has refused to grant approval to the application, or

    (ii) this subsection may not be relied upon by the investment fund in the local jurisdiction.

5.8 Matters Requiring Notice — (1) A person or company must not continue to act as manager of an investment fund following a direct or indirect change of control of the person or company unless

(a) notice of the change of control was given to all securityholders of the investment fund at least 60 days before the change; and

(b) the notice referred to in paragraph (a) contains the information that would be required by law to be provided to securityholders if securityholder approval of the change were required to be obtained.

(2) A mutual fund must not terminate unless notice of the termination is given to all securityholders of the mutual fund at least 60 days before termination.

(3) The manager of a mutual fund that has terminated must give notice of the termination to the securities regulatory authority within 30 days of the termination.

5.8.1 Termination of a Non-Redeemable Investment Fund — (1) A non-redeemable investment fund must not terminate unless the investment fund first issues and files a news release that discloses the termination.

(2) A non-redeemable investment fund must not terminate earlier than 15 days or later than 90 days after the filing of the news release under subsection (1).

(3) Subsections (1) and (2) do not apply in respect of a transaction referred to in paragraph 5.1(1)(f).

5.9 Relief from Certain Regulatory Requirements — (1) The investment fund conflict of interest investment restrictions and the investment fund conflict of interest reporting requirements do not apply to a transaction referred to in paragraph 5.5(1)(b) if the approval of the securities regulatory authority or regulator has been given to the transaction.

(2) The investment fund conflict of interest investment restrictions and the investment fund conflict of interest reporting requirements do not apply to a transaction described in section 5.6.

PART 6 — CUSTODIANSHIP OF PORTFOLIO ASSETS

6.1 General — (1) Except as provided in sections 6.8, 6.8.1 and 6.9, all portfolio assets of an investment fund must be held under the custodianship of one custodian that satisfies the requirements of section 6.2.

(2) Except as provided in subsection 6.5(3) and sections 6.8, 6.8.1 and 6.9, portfolio assets of an investment fund must be held

(a) in Canada by the custodian or a sub-custodian of the investment fund; or

(b) outside Canada by the custodian or a sub-custodian of the investment fund, if appropriate to facilitate portfolio transactions of the investment fund outside Canada.

(3) The custodian or a sub-custodian of an investment fund may appoint one or more sub-custodians to hold portfolio assets of the investment fund, if

(a) in the case of an appointment by the custodian, the investment fund consents in writing to the appointment,

(a.1) in the case of an appointment by a sub-custodian, the investment fund and the custodian of the investment fund consent in writing to the appointment,

(b) the sub-custodian that is to be appointed is an entity described in section 6.2 or 6.3, as applicable,

(c) the arrangements under which a sub-custodian is appointed are such that the investment fund may enforce rights directly, or require the custodian or a sub-custodian to enforce rights on behalf of the investment fund, to the portfolio assets held by the appointed sub-custodian, and

(d) the appointment is otherwise in compliance with this Instrument.

(4) The written consent referred to in paragraphs (3)(a) and (a.1) may be in the form of a general consent, contained in the agreement governing the relationship between the investment fund and the custodian, or the custodian and the sub-custodian, to the appointment of entities that are part of an international network of sub-custodians within the organization of the appointed custodian or sub-custodian.

(5) A custodian or sub-custodian must provide to the investment fund a list of all entities that are appointed sub-custodians under a general consent referred to in subsection (4).

(6) Despite any other provisions of this Part, the manager of an investment fund shall not act as custodian or sub-custodian of the investment fund.

6.2 Entities Qualified to Act as Custodian or Sub-Custodian for Assets Held in Canada — If portfolio assets are held in Canada by a custodian or sub-custodian, the custodian or sub-custodian must be one of the following:

1. a bank listed in Schedule I, II or III of the *Bank Act* (Canada).

2. a trust company that is incorporated under the laws of Canada or a jurisdiction and licensed or registered under the laws of Canada or a jurisdiction, and that has equity, as reported in its most recent audited financial statements, of not less than $10,000,000;

3. a company that is incorporated under the laws of Canada or of a jurisdiction, and that is an affiliate of a bank or trust company referred to in paragraph 1 or 2, if either of the following applies:

    (a) the company has equity, as reported in its most recent audited financial statements that have been made public, of not less than $10,000,000;

    (b) the bank or trust company has assumed responsibility for all of the custodial obligations of the company for that investment fund.

6.3 Entities Qualified to Act as Sub-Custodian for Assets Held outside Canada — If portfolio assets are held outside of Canada by a sub-custodian, the sub-custodian must be one of the following:

1. an entity referred to in section 6.2;

2. an entity that

    (a) is incorporated or organized under the laws of a country, or a political subdivision of a country, other than Canada,

    (b) is regulated as a banking institution or trust company by the government, or an agency of the government, of the country under the laws of which it is incorporated or organized, or a political subdivision of that country, and

    (c) has equity, as reported in its most recent audited financial statements, of not less than the equivalent of $100,000,000;

3. an affiliate of an entity referred to in paragraph 1 or 2 if either of the following applies:

    (a) the affiliate has equity, as reported in its most recent audited financial statements that have been made public, of not less than the equivalent of $100,000,000;

    (b) the entity referred to in paragraph 1 or 2 has assumed responsibility for all of the custodial obligations of the affiliate for that investment fund.

6.4 Contents of Custodian and Sub-Custodian Agreements — (1) All custodian agreements and sub-custodian agreements of an investment fund must provide for

    (a) the location of portfolio assets,

    (b) any appointment of a sub-custodian,

    (c) requirements concerning lists of sub-custodians,

    (d) the method of holding portfolio assets,

    (e) the standard of care and responsibility for loss, and

    (f) requirements concerning review and compliance reports.

(2) A sub-custodian agreement concerning the portfolio assets of an investment fund must provide for the safekeeping of portfolio assets on terms consistent with the custodian agreement of the investment fund.

(2.1) An agreement referred to under subsections (1) and (2) must comply with the requirements of this Part.

(3) A custodian agreement or sub-custodian agreement concerning the portfolio assets of an investment fund must not

    (a) provide for the creation of any security interest on the portfolio assets of the investment fund except for a good faith claim for payment of the fees and expenses of the custodian or a sub-custodian for acting in that capacity or to secure the obligations of the investment fund to repay borrowings by the investment fund from the custodian or a sub-custodian for the purpose of settling portfolio transactions; or

    (b) contain a provision that would require the payment of a fee to the custodian or a sub-custodian for the transfer of the beneficial ownership of portfolio assets of the investment fund, other than for safekeeping and administrative services in connection with acting as custodian or sub-custodian.

6.5 Holding of Portfolio Assets and Payment of Fees — (1) Except as provided in subsections (2) and (3) and sections 6.8, 6.8.1 and 6.9, portfolio assets of an investment fund not registered in the name of the investment fund must be registered in the name of the custodian or a sub-custodian of the investment fund, or any of their respective nominees, with an account number or other designation in the records of the custodian sufficient to show that the beneficial ownership of the portfolio assets is vested in the investment fund.

(2) The custodian or a sub-custodian of an investment fund, or an applicable nominee, must segregate portfolio assets issued in bearer form to show that the beneficial ownership of the property is vested in the investment fund.

(3) The custodian or a sub-custodian of an investment fund may deposit portfolio assets of the investment fund with a depository, or a clearing agency, that operates a book-based system.

(4) The custodian or a sub-custodian of an investment fund arranging for the deposit of portfolio assets of the investment fund with, and their delivery to, a depository, or clearing agency, that operates a book-based system must ensure that the records of any of the applicable participants in that book-based system or of the custodian contain an account number or other designation sufficient to show that the beneficial ownership of the portfolio assets is vested in the investment fund.

(5) An investment fund must not pay a fee to the custodian or a sub-custodian of the investment fund for the transfer of beneficial ownership of portfolio assets of the investment fund other than for safekeeping and administrative services in connection with acting as custodian or sub-custodian.

6.6 Standard of Care — (1) The custodian and each sub-custodian of an investment fund, in carrying out their duties concerning the safekeeping of, and dealing with, the portfolio assets of the investment fund, must exercise

    (a) the degree of care, diligence and skill that a reasonably prudent person would exercise in the circumstances; or

    (b) at least the same degree of care as they exercise with respect to their own property of a similar kind, if this is a higher degree of care than the degree of care referred to in paragraph (a).

(2) An investment fund must not relieve the custodian or a sub-custodian of the investment fund from liability to the investment fund or to a securityholder of the investment fund for loss that arises out of the failure of the custodian or sub-custodian to exercise the standard of care imposed by subsection (1).

(3) An investment fund may indemnify the custodian or a sub-custodian against legal fees, judgments and amounts paid in settlement, actually and reasonably incurred by that entity in connection with custodial or sub-custodial services provided by that entity to the investment fund, if those fees, judgments and amounts were not incurred as a result of a breach of the standard of care imposed by subsection (1).

(4) An investment fund must not incur the cost of any portion of liability insurance that insures the custodian or a sub-custodian for a liability, except to the extent that the custodian or sub-custodian may be indemnified for that liability under this section.

6.7 Review and Compliance Reports — (1) The custodian of an investment fund must, on a periodic basis not less frequently than annually,

    (a) review the custodian agreement and all sub-custodian agreements of the investment fund to determine if those agreements are in compliance with this Part;

    (b) make reasonable enquiries as to whether each sub-custodian satisfies the applicable requirements of section 6.2 or 6.3; and

    (c) make or cause to be made any changes that may be necessary to ensure that

        (i) the custodian and sub-custodian agreements are in compliance with this Part; and

        (ii) all sub-custodians of the investment fund satisfy the applicable requirements of section 6.2 or 6.3.

(2) The custodian of an investment fund must, within 60 days after the end of each financial year of the investment fund, advise the investment fund in writing

    (a) of the names and addresses of all sub-custodians of the investment fund;

    (b) whether the custodian and sub-custodian agreements are in compliance with this Part; and

    (c) whether, to the best of the knowledge and belief of the custodian, each sub-custodian satisfies section 6.2 or 6.3, as applicable.

(3) A copy of the report referred to in subsection (2) must be delivered by or on behalf of the investment fund to the securities regulatory authority within 30 days after the filing of the annual financial statements of the investment fund.

6.8 Custodial Provisions relating to Derivatives and Securities Lending, Repurchase and Reverse Repurchase Agreements — (1) An investment fund may deposit portfolio assets as margin for transactions in Canada involving clearing corporation options, options on futures or standardized futures with a dealer that is a member of an SRO that is a participating member of CIPF if the amount of margin deposited does not, when aggregated with the amount of margin already held by the dealer on behalf of the investment fund, exceed 10 percent of the net asset value of the investment fund as at the time of deposit.

(2) An investment fund may deposit portfolio assets with a dealer as margin for transactions outside Canada involving clearing corporation options, options on futures or standardized futures if

    (a) in the case of standardized futures and options on futures, the dealer is a member of a futures exchange or, in the case of clearing corporation options, is a member of a stock exchange, and, as a result in either case, is subject to a regulatory audit;

    (b) the dealer has a net worth, determined from its most recent audited financial statements that have been made public, in excess of the equivalent of $50 million; and

    (c) the amount of margin deposited does not, when aggregated with the amount of margin already held by the dealer on behalf of the investment fund, exceed 10 percent of the net asset value of the investment fund as at the time of deposit.

(3) An investment fund may deposit with its counterparty portfolio assets over which it has granted a security interest in connection with a particular specified derivatives transaction.

(4) The agreement by which portfolio assets are deposited in accordance with subsection (1), (2) or (3) must require the person or company holding the portfolio assets to ensure that its records show that the investment fund is the beneficial owner of the portfolio assets.

(5) An investment fund may deliver portfolio assets to a person or company in satisfaction of its obligations under a securities lending, repurchase or reverse repurchase agreement that complies with this Instrument if the collateral, cash proceeds or purchased securities that are delivered to the investment fund in connection with the transaction are held under the custodianship of the custodian or a sub-custodian of the investment fund in compliance with this Part.

6.8.1 Custodial Provisions relating to Short Sales — (1) Except where the borrowing agent is the investment fund's custodian or sub-custodian, if an investment fund deposits portfolio assets with a borrowing agent as security in connection with a short sale of securities, the market value of portfolio assets deposited with the borrowing agent must not, when aggregated with the market value of portfolio assets already held by the borrowing agent as security for outstanding short sales of securities by the investment fund, exceed 10% of the net asset value of the investment fund at the time of deposit.

(2) An investment fund must not deposit portfolio assets as security in connection with a short sale of securities with a dealer in Canada unless the dealer is a registered dealer and is a member of IIROC.

(3) An investment fund must not deposit portfolio assets as security in connection with a short sale of securities with a dealer outside of Canada unless that dealer

(a) is a member of a stock exchange and is subject to a regulatory audit; and

(b) has a net worth, determined from its most recent audited financial statements that have been made public, in excess of the equivalent of $50 million.

6.9 Separate Account for Paying Expenses — An investment fund may deposit cash in Canada with an entity referred to in paragraph 1 or 2 of section 6.2 to facilitate the payment of regular operating expenses of the investment fund.

PART 7 — INCENTIVE FEES

7.1 Incentive Fees — A mutual fund must not pay, or enter into arrangements that would require it to pay, and securities of a mutual fund must not be sold on the basis that an investor would be required to pay, a fee that is determined by the performance of the mutual fund, unless

(a) the fee is calculated with reference to a benchmark or index that

(i) reflects the market sectors in which the mutual fund invests according to its fundamental investment objectives,

(ii) is available to persons or companies other than the mutual fund and persons providing services to it, and

(iii) is a total return benchmark or index;

(b) the payment of the fee is based upon a comparison of the cumulative total return of the mutual fund against the cumulative total percentage increase or decrease of the benchmark or index for the period that began immediately after the last period for which the performance fee was paid; and

(c) the method of calculation of the fee and details of the composition of the benchmark or index are described in the prospectus of the mutual fund.

7.2 Multiple Portfolio Advisers — Section 7.1 applies to fees payable to a portfolio adviser of a mutual fund that has more than one portfolio adviser, if the fees are calculated on the basis of the performance of the portfolio assets under management by that portfolio adviser, as if those portfolio assets were a separate mutual fund.

PART 8 — CONTRACTUAL PLANS

8.1 Contractual Plans — A person or company must not sell securities of a mutual fund by way of a contractual plan unless

(a) the contractual plan was established, and its terms described in a prospectus that was filed with the securities regulatory authority, before the date that this Instrument came into force;

(b) there have been no changes made to the contractual plan or the rights of securityholders under the contractual plan since the date that this Instrument came into force; and

(c) the contractual plan has continued to be operated in the same manner after the date that this Instrument came into force as it was on that date.

PART 9 — SALE OF SECURITIES OF AN INVESTMENT FUND

9.0.1 Application — This Part, other than subsection 9.3(2), does not apply to an exchange-traded mutual fund that is not in continuous distribution.

9.1 Transmission and Receipt of Purchase Orders — (0.1) This section does not apply to an exchange-traded mutual fund.

(1) Each purchase order for securities of a mutual fund received by a participating dealer at a location that is not its principal office must, on the day the order is received, be sent by same day or next day courier, same day or next day priority post, telephone or electronic means, without charge to the person or company placing the order or to the mutual fund, to the principal office of the participating dealer or a person or company providing services to the participating dealer.

(2) Each purchase order for securities of a mutual fund received by a participating dealer at its principal office, a person or company providing services to the participating dealer, or by the principal distributor of the mutual fund at a location that is not an order receipt office of the mutual fund must, on the day the order is received, be sent by same day or next day courier, same day or next day priority post, telephone or electronic means, without charge to the person or company placing the order or to the mutual fund, to an order receipt office of the mutual fund.

(3) Despite subsections (1) and (2), a purchase order for securities of a mutual fund received at a location referred to in those subsections after normal business hours on a business day, or on a day that is not a business day, may be sent, in the manner and to the place required by those subsections, on the next business day.

(4) A participating dealer, a principal distributor or a person or company providing services to the participating dealer or principal distributor, that sends purchase orders electronically may

(a) specify a time on a business day by which a purchase order must be received in order that it be sent electronically on that business day; and

(b) despite subsections (1) and (2), send electronically on the next business day a purchase order received after the time specified under paragraph (a).

(5) A mutual fund is deemed to have received a purchase order for securities of the mutual fund when the order is received at an order receipt office of the mutual fund.

(6) Despite subsection (5), a mutual fund may provide that a purchase order for securities of the mutual fund received at an order receipt office of the mutual fund after a specified time on a business day, or on a day that is not a business day, will be considered to be received by the mutual fund on the next business day following the day of actual receipt.

(7) A principal distributor or participating dealer must ensure that a copy of each purchase order received in a jurisdiction is sent, by the time it is sent to the order receipt office of the mutual fund under subsection (2), to a person responsible for the supervision of trades made on behalf of clients for the principal distributor or participating dealer in the jurisdiction.

9.2 Acceptance of Purchase Orders — A mutual fund may reject a purchase order for the purchase of securities of the mutual fund if

(a) the rejection of the order is made no later than one business day after receipt by the mutual fund of the order;

(b) on rejection of the order, all cash received with the order is refunded immediately; and

(c) the prospectus of the mutual fund states that the right to reject a purchase order for securities of the mutual fund is reserved and reflects the requirements of paragraphs (a) and (b).

9.3 Issue Price of Securities — (1) The issue price of a security of a mutual fund to which a purchase order pertains must be the net asset value per security of that class, or series of a class, next determined after the receipt by the mutual fund of the order.

(2) The issue price of a security of an exchange-traded mutual fund that is not in continuous distribution, or of a non-redeemable investment fund, must not,

(a) as far as reasonably practicable, be a price that causes dilution of the net asset value of other outstanding securities of the investment fund at the time the security is issued, and

(b) be a price that is less than the most recent net asset value per security of that class, or series of a class, calculated prior to the pricing of the offering.

9.4 Delivery of Funds and Settlement — (1) A principal distributor, a participating dealer, or a person or company providing services to the principal distributor or participating dealer must forward any cash or securities received for payment of the issue price of securities of a mutual fund to an order receipt office of the mutual fund so that the cash or securities arrive at the order receipt office as soon as practicable and in any event no later than the third business day after the pricing date.

(2) Payment of the issue price of securities of a mutual fund must be made to the mutual fund on or before the third business day after the pricing date for the securities by using any or a combination of the following methods of payment:

(a) by paying cash in a currency in which the net asset value per security of the mutual fund is calculated;

(b) by making good delivery of securities if

(i) the mutual fund would at the time of payment be permitted to purchase those securities,

(ii) the securities are acceptable to the portfolio adviser of the mutual fund and consistent with the mutual fund's investment objectives, and

(iii) the value of the securities is at least equal to the issue price of the securities of the mutual fund for which they are payment, valued as if the securities were portfolio assets of the mutual fund.

(3) [Repealed]

(4) If payment of the issue price of the securities of a mutual fund to which a purchase order pertains is not made on or before the third business day after the pricing date or if the mutual fund has been paid the issue price by a cheque or method of payment that is subsequently not honoured,

(a) the mutual fund must redeem the securities to which the purchase order pertains as if it had received an order for the redemption of the securities on the fourth business day after the pricing date or on the day on which the mutual fund first knows that the method of payment will not be honoured; and

(b) the amount of the redemption proceeds derived from the redemption must be applied to reduce the amount owing to the mutual fund on the purchase of the securities and any banking costs incurred by the mutual fund in connection with the dishonoured cheque.

(5) If the amount of the redemption proceeds referred to in subsection (4) exceeds the aggregate of issue price of the securities and any banking costs incurred by the mutual fund in connection with the dishonoured cheque, the difference must belong to the mutual fund.

(6) If the amount of the redemption proceeds referred to in subsection (4) is less than the issue price of the securities and any banking costs incurred by the mutual fund in connection with the dishonoured cheque,

(a) if the mutual fund has a principal distributor, the principal distributor must pay, immediately upon notification by the mutual fund, to the mutual fund the amount of the deficiency; or

(b) if the mutual fund does not have a principal distributor, the participating dealer that delivered the relevant purchase order to the mutual fund must pay immediately, upon notification by the mutual fund, to the mutual fund the amount of the deficiency.

PART 9.1 — WARRANTS AND SPECIFIED DERIVATIVES

9.1.1 Issuance of Warrants or Specified Derivatives — An investment fund must not

(a) issue a conventional warrant or right, or

(b) enter into a position in a specified derivative the underlying interest of which is a security of the investment fund.

PART 10 — REDEMPTION OF SECURITIES OF AN INVESTMENT FUND

10.1 Requirements for Redemptions — (1) No mutual fund must not pay redemption proceeds unless

(a) if the security of the investment fund to be redeemed is represented by a certificate, the investment fund has received the certificate or appropriate indemnities in connection with a lost certificate; and

(b) either

(i) the investment fund has received a written redemption order, duly completed and executed by or on behalf of the securityholder, or

(ii) the investment fund permits the making of redemption orders by telephone or electronic means by, or on behalf of, a securityholder who has made prior arrangements with the investment fund in that regard and the relevant redemption order is made in compliance with those arrangements.

(2) An investment fund may establish reasonable requirements applicable to securityholders who wish to have the investment fund redeem securities, not contrary to this Instrument, as to procedures to be followed and documents to be delivered by the following times:

(a) in the case of a mutual fund, other than an exchange-traded mutual fund that is not in continuous distribution, by the time of delivery of a redemption order to an order receipt office of the mutual fund;

(a.1) in the case of an exchange-traded mutual fund that is not in continuous distribution or of a non-redeemable investment fund, by the time of delivery of a redemption order;

(b) by the time of payment of redemption proceeds.

(3) A manager of an investment fund must provide to securityholders of the investment fund at least annually a statement containing the following:

(a) a description of the requirements referred to in subsection (1);

(b) a description of the requirements established by the investment fund under subsection (2);

(c) a detailed reference to all documentation required for redemption of securities of the investment fund;

(d) detailed instructions on the manner in which documentation is to be delivered to participating dealers, the investment fund or a person or company providing services to the investment fund to which a redemption order may be made;

(e) a description of all other procedural or communication requirements;

(f) an explanation of the consequences of failing to meet timing requirements .

(4) The statement referred to in subsection (3) is not required to be separately provided, in any year, if the requirements are described in any document that is sent to all securityholders in that year.

10.2 Transmission and Receipt of Redemption Orders — (0.1) This section does not apply to an exchange-traded mutual fund.

(1) Each redemption order for securities of a mutual fund received by a participating dealer at a location that is not its principal office must, on the day the order is received, be sent by same day or next day courier, same day or next day priority post, telephone or electronic means, without charge to the relevant securityholder or to the mutual fund, to the principal office of the participating dealer or a person or company providing services to the participating dealer.

(2) Each redemption order for securities of a mutual fund received by a participating dealer at its principal office, by the principal distributor of the mutual fund at a location that is not an order receipt office of the mutual fund, or a person or company providing services to the participating dealer or principal distributor must, on the day the order is received, be sent by same day or next day courier, same day or next day priority post, telephone or electronic means, without charge to the relevant securityholder or to the mutual fund, to an order receipt office of the mutual fund.

(3) Despite subsections (1) and (2), a redemption order for securities of a mutual fund received at a location referred to in those subsections after normal business hours on a business day, or on a day that is not a business day, may be sent, in the manner and to the place required by those subsections, on the next business day.

(4) A participating dealer, a principal distributor, or a person or company providing services to the participating dealer or principal distributor, that sends redemption orders electronically may

(a) specify a time on a business day by which a redemption order must be received in order that it be sent electronically on that business day; and

(b) despite subsections (1) and (2), send electronically on the next business day a redemption order received after the time specified under paragraph (a).

(5) A mutual fund is deemed to have received a redemption order for securities of the mutual fund when the order is received at an order receipt office of the mutual fund or all requirements of the mutual fund established under paragraph 10.1(2)(a) have been satisfied, whichever is later.

(6) If a mutual fund determines that its requirements established under paragraph 10.1(2)(a) have not been satisfied, the mutual fund must notify the securityholder making the redemption order, by the close of business on the business day after the date of the delivery to the mutual fund of the incomplete redemption order, that its requirements established under paragraph 10.1(2)(a) have not been satisfied and must specify procedures still to be followed or the documents still to be delivered by that securityholder.

(7) Despite subsection (5), a mutual fund may provide that orders for the redemption of securities that are received at an order receipt office of the mutual fund after a specified time on a business day, or on a day that is not a business day, will be considered to be received by the mutual fund on the next business day following the day of actual receipt.

10.3 Redemption Price of Securities — (1) The redemption price of a security of a mutual fund to which a redemption order pertains must be the net asset value per security of that class, or series of a class, next determined after the receipt by the mutual fund of the order.

(2) Despite subsection (1), the redemption price of a security of an exchange-traded mutual fund that is not in continuous distribution may be a price that is less than the net asset value of the security and that is determined on a date specified in the exchange-traded mutual fund's prospectus or annual information form.

(3) Despite subsection (1), the redemption price of a security of an exchange-traded mutual fund that is in continuous distribution may, if a securityholder redeems fewer than the manager-prescribed number of units, be a price that is calculated by reference to the closing price of the security on the stock exchange on which the security is listed and posted for trading, next determined after the receipt by the exchange-traded mutual fund of the redemption order.

(4) The redemption price of a security of a non-redeemable investment fund must not be a price that is more than the net asset value of the security determined on a redemption date specified in the prospectus or annual information form of the investment fund.

10.4 Payment of Redemption Price — (1) Subject to subsection 10.1(1) and to compliance with any requirements established by the mutual fund under paragraph 10.1(2)(b), a mutual fund must pay the redemption proceeds for securities that are the subject of a redemption order

(a) within three business days after the date of calculation of the net asset value per security used in establishing the redemption price; or

(b) if payment of the redemption proceeds was not made at the time referred to in paragraph (a) because a requirement established under paragraph 10.1(2)(b) or a requirement of subsection 10.1(1) had not been satisfied, within three business days of

(i) the satisfaction of the relevant requirement, or

(ii) the decision by the mutual fund to waive the requirement, if the requirement was a requirement established under paragraph 10.1(2)(b).

(1.1) Despite subsection (1), an exchange-traded mutual fund that is not in continuous distribution must pay the redemption proceeds for securities that are the subject of a redemption order no later than 15 business days after the valuation date on which the redemption price was established.

(1.2) A non-redeemable investment fund must pay the redemption proceeds for securities that are the subject of a redemption order no later than 15 business days after the valuation date on which the redemption price was established.

(2) The redemption proceeds for a redeemed security, less any applicable investor fees, must be paid to or to the order of the securityholder of the security.

(3) An investment fund must pay the redemption proceeds for a redeemed security by using any or a combination of the following methods of payment:

    (a) by paying cash in the currency in which the net asset value per security of the redeemed security was calculated;

    (b) with the prior written consent of the securityholder for a redemption other than an exchange of a manager-prescribed number of units, by making good delivery to the securityholder of portfolio assets, the value of which is equal to the amount at which those portfolio assets were valued in calculating the net asset value per security used to establish the redemption price.

(4) [Repealed]

(5) If the redemption proceeds for a redeemed security are paid in currency, an investment fund is deemed to have made payment

    (a) when the investment fund, its manager or principal distributor mails a cheque or transmits funds in the required amount to or to the order of the securityholder of the securities; or

    (b) if the securityholder has requested that redemption proceeds be delivered in a currency other than that permitted in subsection (3), when the investment fund delivers the redemption proceeds to the manager or principal distributor of the investment fund for conversion into that currency and delivery forthwith to the securityholder.

10.5 Failure to Complete Redemption Order — (1) If a requirement of a mutual fund referred to in subsection 10.1(1) or established under paragraph 10.1(2)(b) has not been satisfied on or before the close of business on the tenth business day after the date of the redemption of the relevant securities, and, in the case of a requirement established under paragraph 10.1(2)(b), the mutual fund does not waive satisfaction of the requirement, the mutual fund must

    (a) issue, to the person or company that immediately before the redemption held the securities that were redeemed, a number of securities equal to the number of securities that were redeemed, as if the mutual fund had received from the person or company on the tenth business day after the redemption, and accepted immediately before the close of business on the tenth business day after the redemption, an order for the purchase of that number of securities; and

    (b) apply the amount of the redemption proceeds to the payment of the issue price of the securities.

(2) If the amount of the issue price of the securities referred to in subsection (1) is less than the redemption proceeds, the difference must belong to the mutual fund.

(3) If the amount of the issue price of the securities referred to in subsection (1) exceeds the redemption proceeds

    (a) if the mutual fund has a principal distributor, the principal distributor must pay immediately to the mutual fund the amount of the deficiency;

    (b) if the mutual fund does not have a principal distributor, the participating dealer that delivered the relevant redemption order to the mutual fund must pay immediately to the mutual fund the amount of the deficiency; or

    (c) if the mutual fund has no principal distributor and no dealer delivered the relevant redemption order to the mutual fund, the manager of the mutual fund must pay immediately to the mutual fund the amount of the deficiency.

10.6 Suspension of Redemptions — (1) An investment fund may suspend the right of securityholders to request that the investment fund redeem its securities for the whole or any part of a period during which either of the following occurs:

    (a) normal trading is suspended on a stock exchange, options exchange or futures exchange within or outside Canada on which securities are listed and posted for trading, or on which specified derivatives are traded, if those securities or specified derivatives represent more than 50% by value, or underlying market exposure, of the total assets of the investment fund without allowance for liabilities and if those securities or specified derivatives are not traded on any other exchange that represents a reasonably practical alternative for the investment fund;

    (b) in the case of a clone fund, the investment fund whose performance it tracks has suspended redemptions.

(2) An investment fund that has an obligation to pay the redemption proceeds for securities that have been redeemed in accordance with subsection 10.4(1), (1.1) or (1.2) may postpone payment during a period in which the right of securityholders to request redemption of their securities is suspended, whether that suspension was made under subsection (1) or pursuant to an approval of the securities regulatory authority or regulator.

(3) An investment fund must not accept a purchase order for securities of the investment fund during a period in which it is exercising rights under subsection (1) or at a time in which it is relying on an approval of the securities regulatory authority or regulator contemplated by paragraph 5.5(1)(d).

PART 11 — COMMINGLING OF CASH

11.1 Principal Distributors and Service Providers — (1) Cash received by a principal distributor of a mutual fund, by a person or company providing services to the mutual fund or the principal distributor, or by a person or company providing services to a non-redeemable investment fund, for investment in, or on the redemption of, securities of the investment fund, or on the distribution of assets of the investment fund, until disbursed as permitted by subsection (3),

    (a) must be accounted for separately and be deposited in a trust account or trust accounts established and maintained in accordance with the requirements of section 11.3, and

    (b) may be commingled only with cash received by the principal distributor or service provider for the sale or on the redemption of other investment fund securities.

(2) Except as permitted by subsection (3), the principal distributor, a person or company providing services to the mutual fund or principal distributor, or a person or company providing services to the non-redeemable investment fund, must not use any of the cash referred to in subsection (1) to finance its own or any other operations in any way.

(3) The principal distributor or person or company providing services to an investment fund or principal distributor may withdraw cash from a trust account referred to in paragraph (1)(a) for any of the following purposes:

    (a) remitting to the investment fund the amount or, if subsection (5) applies, the net amount, to be invested in the securities of the investment fund;

    (b) remitting to the relevant persons or companies redemption or distribution proceeds being paid on behalf of the investment fund;

    (c) paying fees, charges and expenses that are payable by an investor in connection with the purchase, conversion, holding, transfer or redemption of securities of the investment fund.

(4) All interest earned on cash held in a trust account referred to in paragraph (1)(a) must be paid to securityholders or to each of the investment funds to which the trust account pertains, pro rata based on cash flow,

(a) no less frequently than monthly if the amount owing to an investment fund or to a securityholder is $10 or more; and

(b) no less frequently than once a year.

(5) When making payments to an investment fund, the principal distributor or service provider may offset the proceeds of redemption of securities of the investment fund or amounts held for distributions to be paid on behalf of the investment fund held in the trust account against amounts held in the trust account for investment in the investment fund.

11.2 Participating Dealers — (1) Cash received by a participating dealer, or by a person or company providing services to a participating dealer, for investment in, or on the redemption of, securities of a mutual fund, or on the distribution of assets of a mutual fund, until disbursed as permitted by subsection (3)

(a) must be accounted for separately and must be deposited in a trust account or trust accounts established and maintained in accordance with section 11.3; and

(b) may be commingled only with cash received by the participating dealer or service provider for the sale or on the redemption of other mutual fund securities.

(2) Except as permitted by subsection (3), the participating dealer or person or company providing services to the participating dealer must not use any of the cash referred to in subsection (1) to finance its own or any other operations in any way.

(3) A participating dealer or person or company providing services to the participating dealer may withdraw cash from a trust account referred to in paragraph (1)(a) for the purpose of

(a) remitting to the mutual fund or the principal distributor of the mutual fund the amount or, if subsection (5) applies, the net amount, to be invested in the securities of the mutual fund;

(b) remitting to the relevant persons or companies redemption or distribution proceeds being paid on behalf of the mutual fund; or

(c) paying fees, charges and expenses that are payable by an investor in connection with the purchase, conversion, holding, transfer or redemption of securities of the mutual fund.

(4) All interest earned on cash held in a trust account referred to in paragraph (1)(a) must be paid to securityholders or to each of the mutual funds to which the trust account pertains, pro rata based on cash flow,

(a) no less frequently than monthly if the amount owing to a mutual fund or to a securityholder is $10 or more; and

(b) no less frequently than once a year.

(5) When making payments to a mutual fund, a participating dealer or service provider may offset the proceeds of redemption of securities of the mutual fund and amounts held for distributions to be paid on behalf of a mutual fund held in the trust account against amounts held in the trust account for investment in the mutual fund.

(6) A participating dealer or person providing services to the participating dealer must permit the mutual fund and the principal distributor, through their respective auditors or other designated representatives, to examine the books and records of the participating dealer to verify the compliance with this section of the participating dealer or person providing services.

11.3 Trust Accounts — A principal distributor or participating dealer, a person or company providing services to the principal distributor or participating dealer, or a person or company providing services to an investment fund, that deposits cash into a trust account in accordance with section 11.1 or 11.2 must

(a) advise, in writing, the financial institution with which the account is opened at the time of the opening of the account and annually thereafter, that

(i) the account is established for the purpose of holding client funds in trust,

(ii) the account is to be labelled by the financial institution as a "trust account",

(iii) the account is not to be accessed by any person other than authorized representatives of the principal distributor or participating dealer, of a person or company providing services to the principal distributor or participating dealer, or of a person or company providing services to the investment fund, and

(iv) the cash in the trust account may not be used to cover shortfalls in any accounts of the principal distributor or participating dealer, of a person or company providing services to the principal distributor or participating dealer, or of a person or company providing services to the investment fund;

(b) ensure that the trust account bears interest at rates equivalent to comparable accounts of the financial institution; and

(c) ensure that any charges against the trust account are not paid or reimbursed out of the trust account.

11.4 Exemption — (1) Sections 11.1 and 11.2 do not apply to a member of IIROC.

(1.1) Except in Québec, sections 11.1 and 11.2 do not apply to a member of the MFDA.

(1.2) In Québec, sections 11.1 and 11.2 do not apply to a mutual fund dealer.

(1.3) Section 11.1 does not apply to CDS Clearing and Depository Services Inc.

(2) A participating dealer that is a member of an SRO referred to in subsection (1) or (1.1) or, in Québec, that is a mutual fund dealer, must permit the mutual fund and the principal distributor, through their respective auditors or other designated representatives, to examine the books and records of the participating dealer to verify the participating dealer's compliance with the requirements of its association or exchange, or the requirements applicable to the mutual fund dealer under the regulations in Québec, that relate to the commingling of cash.

11.5 Right of Inspection — The investment fund, its trustee, manager and principal distributor must ensure that all contractual arrangements made between any of them and any person or company providing services to the investment fund permit the representatives of the investment fund, its manager and trustee to examine the books and records of those persons or companies in order to monitor compliance with this Instrument.

PART 12 — COMPLIANCE REPORTS

12.1 Compliance Reports — (1) A mutual fund, other than an exchange-traded mutual fund that is not in continuous distribution, that does not have a principal distributor must complete and file, within 140 days after the financial year end of the mutual fund

    (a) a report in the form contained in Appendix B-1 describing compliance by the mutual fund during that financial year with the applicable requirements of Parts 9, 10 and 11; and

    (b) a report by the auditor of the mutual fund, in the form contained in Appendix B-1, concerning the report referred to in paragraph (a).

(2) The principal distributor of a mutual fund must complete and file, within 90 days after the financial year end of the principal distributor

    (a) a report in the form contained in Appendix B-2 describing compliance by the principal distributor during that financial year with the applicable requirements of Parts 9, 10 and 11; and

    (b) a report by the auditor of the principal distributor or by the auditor of the mutual fund, in the form contained in Appendix B-2, concerning the report referred to in paragraph (a).

(3) Each participating dealer that distributes securities of a mutual fund in a financial year of the participating dealer must complete and file, within 90 days after the end of that financial year

    (a) a report in the form contained in Appendix B-3 describing compliance by the participating dealer during that financial year with the applicable requirements of Parts 9, 10 and 11 in connection with its distribution of securities of all mutual funds in that financial year; and

    (b) a report by the auditor of the participating dealer, in the form contained in Appendix B-3, concerning the report referred to in paragraph (a).

(4) Subsections (2) and (3) do not apply to a member of IIROC.

(4.1) Except in Québec, subsections (2) and (3) do not apply to a member of the MFDA.

(4.2) In Québec, subsections (2) and (3) do not apply to a mutual fund dealer.

13.3 Sales Communications of Non-Redeemable Investment Funds During the Waiting Period and the Distribution Period — The Canadian securities regulatory authorities remind non-redeemable investment funds of the restrictions contained in securities legislation relating to the distribution of material and advertising and marketing in connection with a prospectus offering during the waiting period and during the distribution period following the issuance of a receipt for the final prospectus. Part 15 of the Instrument does not vary any of the restrictions imposed during these periods.

PART 13 — CALCULATION OF NET ASSET VALUE PER SECURITY [REPEALED]

PART 14 — RECORD DATE

14.0.1 Application — This Part does not apply to an exchange-traded mutual fund.

14.1 Record Date — The record date for determining the right of securityholders of a mutual fund to receive a dividend or distribution by the mutual fund must be one of

    (a) the day on which the net asset value per security is determined for the purpose of calculating the amount of the payment of the dividend or distribution;

    (b) the last day on which the net asset value per security of the mutual fund was calculated before the day referred to in paragraph (a); or

    (c) if the day referred to in paragraph (b) is not a business day, the last day on which the net asset value per security of the mutual fund was calculated before the day referred to in paragraph (b).

PART 15 — SALES COMMUNICATIONS AND PROHIBITED REPRESENTATIONS

15.1 Ability to Make Sales Communications — Sales communications pertaining to an investment fund must be made by a person or company in accordance with this Part.

15.2 Sales Communications — General Requirements — (1) Despite any other provision of this Part, a sales communication must not

    (a) be untrue or misleading; or

    (b) include a statement that conflicts with information that is contained in the preliminary prospectus, the preliminary annual information form, the preliminary fund facts document, the prospectus, the annual information form or the fund facts document, as applicable,

        (i) of an investment fund, or

        (ii) in which an asset allocation service is described.

(2) All performance data or disclosure specifically required by this Instrument and contained in a written sales communication must be at least as large as 10-point type.

15.3 Prohibited Disclosure in Sales Communications — (1) A sales communication must not compare the performance of an investment fund or asset allocation service with the performance or change of any benchmark or investment unless

    (a) it includes all facts that, if disclosed, would be likely to alter materially the conclusions reasonably drawn or implied by the comparison;

    (b) it presents data for each subject of the comparison for the same period or periods;

    (c) it explains clearly any factors necessary to make the comparison fair and not misleading; and

    (d) in the case of a comparison with a benchmark

        (i) the benchmark existed and was widely recognized and available during the period for which the comparison is made, or

        (ii) the benchmark did not exist for all or part of the period, but a reconstruction or calculation of what the benchmark would have been during that period, calculated on a basis consistent with its current basis of calculation, is widely recognized and available.

(2) A sales communication for a mutual fund or asset allocation service that is prohibited by paragraph 15.6(1)(a) from disclosing performance data must not provide performance data for any benchmark or investment other than a mutual fund or asset allocation service under common management with the mutual fund or asset allocation service to which the sales communication pertains.

(2.1) A sales communication for a non-redeemable investment fund that is restricted by paragraph 15.6(1)(a) from disclosing performance data must not provide performance data for any benchmark or investment, other than a non-redeemable investment fund under common management with the non-redeemable investment fund to which the sales communication pertains.

(3) Despite subsection (2), a sales communication for an index mutual fund may provide performance data for the index on which the investments of the mutual fund are based if the index complies with the requirements for benchmarks contained in paragraph (1)(d).

(4) A sales communication must not refer to a performance rating or ranking of a mutual fund or asset allocation service unless

    (a) the rating or ranking is prepared by a mutual fund rating entity;

    (b) standard performance data is provided for any mutual fund or asset allocation service for which a performance rating or ranking is given;

    (c) the rating or ranking is provided for each period for which standard performance data is required to be given, except the period since the inception of the mutual fund;

    (d) the rating or ranking is based on a published category of mutual funds that

        (i) provides a reasonable basis for evaluating the performance of the mutual fund or asset allocation service, and

        (ii) is not established or maintained by a member of the organization of the mutual fund or asset allocation service;

    (e) the sales communication contains the following disclosure:

        (i) the name of the category within which the mutual fund or asset allocation service is rated or ranked, including the name of the organization that maintains the category,

        (ii) the number of mutual funds in the applicable category for each period of standard performance data required under paragraph (c),

        (iii) the name of the mutual fund rating entity that provided the rating or ranking,

        (iv) the length of the period or the first day of the period on which the rating or ranking is based, and its ending date,

        (v) a statement that the rating or ranking is subject to change every month,

        (vi) the criteria on which the rating or ranking is based, and

        (vii) if the rating or ranking consists of a symbol rather than a number, the meaning of the symbol, and

    (f) the rating or ranking is to the same calendar month end that is

        (i) not more than 45 days before the date of the appearance or use of the advertisement in which it is included, and

        (ii) not more than three months before the date of first publication of any other sales communication in which it is included.

(4.1) Despite paragraph (4)(c), a sales communication may refer to an overall rating or ranking of a mutual fund or asset allocation service in addition to each rating or ranking required under paragraph (4)(c) if the sales communication otherwise complies with the requirements of subsection (4).

(5) A sales communication must not refer to a credit rating of securities of an investment fund unless

    (a) the rating is current and was prepared by a designated rating organization or its DRO affiliate;

    (b) there has been no announcement by the designated rating organization or any of its DRO affiliates of which the investment fund or its manager is or ought to be aware that the credit rating of the securities may be down-graded; and

    (c) no designated rating organization or any of its DRO affiliates is currently rating the securities at a lower level.

(6) A sales communication must not refer to a mutual fund as, or imply that it is, a money fund, cash fund or money market fund unless, at the time the sales communication is used and for each period for which money market fund standard performance data is provided, the mutual fund is and was a money market fund under this Instrument.

(7) A sales communication shall not state or imply that a registered retirement savings plan, registered retirement income fund or registered education savings plan in itself, rather than the investment fund to which the sales communication relates, is an investment.

15.4 Required Disclosure and Warnings in Sales Communications — (1) A written sales communication must

    (a) bear the name of the dealer that distributed the sales communication; and

    (b) if the sales communication is not an advertisement, contain the date of first publication of the sales communication.

(2) A sales communication that includes a rate of return or a mathematical table illustrating the potential effect of a compound rate of return must contain a statement in substantially the following words:

    [The rate of return or mathematical table shown] is used only to illustrate the effects of the compound growth rate and is not intended to reflect future values of [the investment fund or asset allocation service] or returns on investment [in the investment fund or from the use of the asset allocation service].

(3) A sales communication, other than a report to securityholders, of a mutual fund that is not a money market fund and that does not contain performance data must contain a warning in substantially the following words:

    Commissions, trailing commissions, management fees and expenses all may be associated with mutual fund investments. Please read the prospectus before investing. Mutual funds are not guaranteed, their values change frequently and past performance may not be repeated.

(3.1) A sales communication, other than a report to securityholders, of a non-redeemable investment fund that does not contain performance data must contain a warning in substantially the following words:

    [*If the securities of the non-redeemable investment fund are listed or quoted on an exchange or other market, state the following:*] "You will usually pay brokerage fees to your dealer if you purchase or sell [units or shares] of the investment fund on [*state the exchange or other market on which the securities of the investment fund are listed or quoted*]. If the [units or shares] are purchased or sold on [*state the exchange or other market*], investors may pay more than the current net asset value when buying [units or shares] of the investment fund and may receive less than the current net asset value when selling them."

    [*State the following in all cases:*] "There are ongoing fees and expenses associated with owning [units or shares] of an investment fund. An investment fund must prepare disclosure documents that contain key information about the fund. You can find more detailed information about the fund in these documents. Investment funds are not guaranteed, their values change frequently and past performance may not be repeated."

(4) A sales communication, other than a report to securityholders, of a money market fund that does not contain performance data must contain a warning in substantially the following words:

> Commissions, trailing commissions, management fees and expenses all may be associated with mutual fund investments. Please read the prospectus before investing. Mutual fund securities are not covered by the Canada Deposit Insurance Corporation or by any other government deposit insurer. There can be no assurances that the fund will be able to maintain its net asset value per security at a constant amount or that the the full amount of your investment in the fund will be returned to you. Past performance may not be repeated.

(5) A sales communication for an asset allocation service that does not contain performance data must contain a warning in substantially the following words:

> Commissions, trailing commissions, management fees and expenses all may be associated with mutual fund investments and the use of an asset allocation service. Please read the prospectus of the mutual funds in which investment may be made under the asset allocation service before investing. Mutual funds are not guaranteed, their values change frequently and past performance may not be repeated.

(6) A sales communication, other than a report to securityholders, of a mutual fund that is not a money market fund and that contains performance data must contain a warning in substantially the following words:

> Commissions, trailing commissions, management fees and expenses all may be associated with mutual fund investments. Please read the prospectus before investing. The indicated rate[s] of return is [are] the historical annual compounded total return[s] including changes in [share or unit] value and reinvestment of all [dividends or distributions] and does [do] not take into account sales, redemption, distribution or optional charges or income taxes payable by any securityholder that would have reduced returns. Mutual funds are not guaranteed, their values change frequently and past performance may not be repeated.

(6.1) A sales communication, other than a report to securityholders, of a non-redeemable investment fund that contains performance data must contain a warning in substantially the following words:

> [*If the securities of the non-redeemable investment fund are listed or quoted on an exchange or other market, state the following:*] "You will usually pay brokerage fees to your dealer if you purchase or sell [units or shares] of the investment fund on [*state the exchange or other market on which the securities of the investment fund are listed or quoted*]. If the [units or shares] are purchased or sold on [*state the exchange or other market*], investors may pay more than the current net asset value when buying [units or shares] of the investment fund and may receive less than the current net asset value when selling them."

> [*State the following in all cases:*] "There are ongoing fees and expenses associated with owning [units or shares] of an investment fund. An investment fund must prepare disclosure documents that contain key information about the fund. You can find more detailed information about the fund in these documents. The indicated rate[s] of return is [are] the historical annual compounded total return[s] including changes in [share or unit] value and reinvestment of all [dividends or distributions] and does [do] not take into account [*state the following, as applicable:*] [certain fees such as redemption fees or optional charges or] income taxes payable by any securityholder that would have reduced returns. Investment funds are not guaranteed, their values change frequently and past performance may not be repeated."

(7) A sales communication, other than a report to securityholders, of a money market fund that contains performance data must contain

> (a) a warning in substantially the following words:

> > Commissions, trailing commissions, management fees and expenses all may be associated with mutual fund investments. Please read the prospectus before investing. The performance data provided assumes reinvestment of distributions only and does not take into account sales, redemption, distribution or optional charges or income taxes payable by any securityholder that would have reduced returns. Mutual fund securities are not covered by the Canada Deposit Insurance Corporation or by any other government deposit insurer. There can be no assurances that the fund will be able to maintain its net asset value per security at a constant amount or that the full amount of your investment in the fund will be returned to you. Past performance may not be repeated.; and

> (b) a statement in substantially the following words, immediately following the performance data:

> > This is an annualized historical yield based on the seven day period ended on [date] [annualized in the case of effective yield by compounding the seven day return] and does not represent an actual one year return.

(8) A sales communication for an asset allocation service that contains performance data must contain a warning in substantially the following words:

> Commissions, trailing commissions, management fees and expenses all may be associated with mutual fund investments and the use of an asset allocation service. Please read the prospectus of the mutual funds in which investment may be made under the asset allocation service before investing. The indicated rate[s] of return is [are] the historical annual compounded total return[s] assuming the investment strategy recommended by the asset allocation service is used and after deduction of the fees and charges in respect of the service. The return[s] is [are] based on the historical annual compounded total returns of the participating funds including changes in [share] [unit] value and reinvestment of all [dividends or distributions] and does [do] not take into account sales, redemption, distribution or optional charges or income taxes payable by any securityholder in respect of a participating fund that would have reduced returns. Mutual funds are not guaranteed, their values change frequently and past performance may not be repeated.

(9) A sales communication distributed after the issue of a receipt for a preliminary prospectus of the mutual fund described in the sales communication but before the issue of a receipt for its prospectus must contain a warning in substantially the following words:

> A preliminary prospectus relating to the fund has been filed with certain Canadian securities commissions or similar authorities. You cannot buy [units] [shares] of the fund until the relevant securities commissions or similar authorities issue receipts for the prospectus of the fund.

(10) A sales communication for an investment fund or asset allocation service that purports to arrange a guarantee or insurance in order to protect all or some of the principal amount of an investment in the investment fund or asset allocation service must

> (a) identify the person or company providing the guarantee or insurance;

> (b) provide the material terms of the guarantee or insurance, including the maturity date of the guarantee or insurance;

> (c) if applicable, state that the guarantee or insurance does not apply to the amount of any redemptions before the maturity date of the guarantee or before the death of the securityholder and that redemptions before that date would be based on the net asset value per security of the investment fund at the time; and

> (d) modify any other disclosure required by this section appropriately.

(11) The warnings referred to in this section must be communicated in a manner that a reasonable person would consider clear and easily understood at the same time as, and through the medium by which, the related sales communication is communicated.

15.5 Disclosure Regarding Distribution Fees — (1) A person or company must not describe a mutual fund in a sales communication as a "no-load fund" or use words of like effect if on a purchase or redemption of securities of the mutual fund investor fees are payable by an investor or if any fees, charges or expenses are payable by an investor to a participating dealer of the mutual fund named in the sales communication, other than

(a) fees and charges related to specific optional services;

(b) for a mutual fund that is not a money market fund, redemption fees on the redemption of securities of the mutual fund that are redeemed within 90 days after the purchase of the securities, if the existence of the fees is disclosed in the sales communication, or in the prospectus of the mutual fund; or

(c) costs that are payable only on the set-up or closing of a securityholder's account and that reflect the administrative costs of establishing or closing the account, if the existence of the costs is disclosed in the sales communication, or in the prospectus of the mutual fund.

(2) If a sales communication describes a mutual fund as "no-load" or uses words to like effect, the sales communication must

(a) indicate the principal distributor or a participating dealer through which an investor may purchase the mutual fund on a no-load basis;

(b) disclose that management fees and operating expenses are paid by the mutual fund; and

(c) disclose the existence of any trailing commissions paid by a member of the organization of the mutual fund.

(3) A sales communication containing a reference to the existence or absence of fees or charges, other than the disclosure required by section 15.4 or a reference to the term "no-load", must disclose the types of fees and charges that exist.

(4) The rate of sales charges or commissions for the sale of securities of a mutual fund or the use of an asset allocation service must be expressed in a sales communication as a percentage of the amount paid by the purchaser and as a percentage of the net amount invested if a reference is made to sales charges or commissions.

15.6 Performance Data — General Requirements — (1) A sales communication pertaining to an investment fund or asset allocation service must not contain performance data of the investment fund or asset allocation service unless all of the following paragraphs apply:

(a) one of the following subparagraphs applies:

(i) in the case of a mutual fund, either of the following applies:

(A) the mutual fund has distributed securities under a prospectus in a jurisdiction for a period of at least 12 consecutive months;

(B) the mutual fund previously existed as a non-redeemable investment fund and has been a reporting issuer in a jurisdiction for a period of at least 12 consecutive months;

(ii) in the case of a non-redeemable investment fund, the non-redeemable investment fund has been a reporting issuer in a jurisdiction for at least 12 consecutive months;

(iii) in the case of an asset allocation service, the asset allocation service has been operated for at least 12 consecutive months and has invested only in participating funds each of which has distributed securities under a prospectus in a jurisdiction for at least 12 consecutive months;

(iv) if the sales communication pertains to an investment fund or asset allocation service that does not satisfy subparagraph (i), (ii) or (iii), the sales communication is sent only to one of the following:

(A) securityholders of the investment fund or participants in the asset allocation service;

(B) securityholders of an investment fund or participants in an asset allocation service under common management with the investment fund or asset allocation service;

(b) the sales communication includes standard performance data of the investment fund or asset allocation service and, in the case of a written sales communication, the standard performance data is presented in type size that is equal to or larger than that used to present the other performance data;

(c) the performance data reflects or includes references to all elements of return;

(d) except as permitted by subsection 15.3(3), the sales communication does not contain performance data for a period that is,

(i) in the case of a mutual fund, before the time when the mutual fund offered its securities under a prospectus;

(ii) in the case of a non-redeemable investment fund, before the non-redeemable investment fund was a reporting issuer;

(iii) in the case of an asset allocation service, before the asset allocation service commenced operation.

(2) Despite subparagraph (1)(d)(i), a sales communication pertaining to a mutual fund referred to in clause (1)(a)(i)(B) that contains performance data of the mutual fund must include performance data for the period that the fund existed as a non-redeemable investment fund and was a reporting issuer.

15.7 Advertisements — An advertisement for a mutual fund or asset allocation service must not compare the performance of the mutual fund or asset allocation service with any benchmark or investment other than

(a) one or more mutual funds or asset allocation services that are under common management or administration with the mutual fund or asset allocation service to which the advertisement pertains;

(b) one or more mutual funds or asset allocation services that have fundamental investment objectives that a reasonable person would consider similar to the mutual fund or asset allocation service to which the advertisement pertains; or

(c) an index.

15.7.1 Advertisements for Non-Redeemable Investment Funds — An advertisement for a non-redeemable investment fund must not compare the performance of the non-redeemable investment fund with any benchmark or investment other than any of the following:

(a) one or more non-redeemable investment funds that are under common management or administration with the non-redeemable investment fund to which the advertisement pertains;

(b) one or more non-redeemable investment funds that have fundamental investment objectives that a reasonable person would consider similar to the non-redeemable investment fund to which the advertisement pertains;

(c) an index.

15.8 Performance Measurement Periods Covered by Performance Data — (1) A sales communication, other than a report to securityholders, that relates to a money market fund may provide standard performance data only if

(a) the standard performance data has been calculated for the most recent seven day period for which it is practicable to calculate, taking into account publication deadlines; and

(b) the seven day period does not start more than 45 days before the date of the appearance, use or publication of the sales communication.

(2) A sales communication, other than a report to securityholders, that relates to an asset allocation service, or to an investment fund other than a money market fund, must not provide standard performance data unless,

(a) to the extent applicable, the standard performance data has been calculated for 10, 5, 3 and one year periods,

(a.1) in the case of a mutual fund that has been offering securities by way of prospectus for more than one and less than 10 years, the standard performance data has been calculated for the period since the inception of the mutual fund,

(a.2) in the case of a non-redeemable investment fund that has been a reporting issuer for more than one and less than 10 years, the standard performance data has been calculated for the period since the inception of the non-redeemable investment fund, and

(b) the periods referred to in paragraphs (a), (a.1) and (a.2) end on the same calendar month end that is

(i) not more than 45 days before the date of the appearance or use of the advertisement in which it is included, and

(ii) not more than three months before the date of first publication of any other sales communication in which it is included.

(3) A report to securityholders must not contain standard performance data unless,

(a) to the extent applicable, the standard performance data has been calculated for 10, 5, 3 and one year periods,

(a.1) in the case of a mutual fund that has been offering securities by way of prospectus for more than one and less than 10 years, the standard performance data has been calculated for the period since the inception of the mutual fund,

(a.2) in the case of a non-redeemable investment fund that has been a reporting issuer for more than one and less than 10 years, the standard performance data has been calculated for the period since the inception of the non-redeemable investment fund, and

(b) the periods referred to in paragraphs (a), (a.1) and (a.2) end on the day as of which the statement of financial position of the financial statements contained in the report to securityholders was prepared.

(4) A sales communication must clearly identify the periods for which performance data is calculated.

15.9 Changes affecting Performance Data — (1) If, during or after a performance measurement period of performance data contained in a sales communication, there have been changes in the business, operations or affairs of the investment fund or asset allocation service to which the sales communication pertains that could have materially affected the performance of the investment fund or asset allocation service, the sales communication must contain

(a) summary disclosure of the changes, and of how those changes could have affected the performance had those changes been in effect throughout the performance measurement period; and

(b) for a money market fund that during the performance measurement period did not pay or accrue the full amount of any fees and charges of the type described under paragraph 15.11(1)1, disclosure of the difference between the full amounts and the amounts actually charged, expressed as an annualized percentage on a basis comparable to current yield.

(2) If an investment fund has, in the last 10 years, undertaken a reorganization with, or acquired assets from, another investment fund in a transaction that was a material change for the investment fund or would have been a material change for the investment fund had this Instrument been in force at the time of the transaction, then, in any sales communication of the investment fund,

(a) the investment fund must provide summary disclosure of the transaction;

(b) the investment fund may include its performance data covering any part of a period before the transaction only if it also includes the performance data for the other fund for the same periods;

(c) the investment fund must not include its performance data for any part of a period after the transaction unless

(i) 12 months have passed since the transaction, or

(ii) the investment fund includes in the sales communication the performance data for itself and the other investment fund referred to in paragraph (b); and

(d) the investment fund must not include any performance data for any period that is composed of both time before and after the transaction.

15.10 Formula for Calculating Standard Performance Data — (1) The standard performance data of an investment fund must be calculated in accordance with this Part.

(2) In this Part

"current yield" means the yield of a money market fund expressed as a percentage and determined by applying the following formula:

$$\text{current yield} = [\text{seven day return} \times 365/7] \times 100;$$

"effective yield" means the yield of a money market fund expressed as a percentage and determined by applying the following formula:

$$\text{effective yield} = [(\text{seven day return} + 1)^{365/7} - 1] \times 100;$$

"seven day return" means the income yield of an account of a securityholder in a money market fund that is calculated by

(a) determining the net change, exclusive of new subscriptions other than from the reinvestment of distributions or proceeds of redemption of securities of the money market fund, in the value of the account,

(b) subtracting all fees and charges of the type referred to in paragraph 15.11(1)3 for the seven day period, and

(c) dividing the result by the value of the account at the beginning of the seven day period;

"standard performance data" means, as calculated in each case in accordance with this Part,

(a) for a money market fund, either of the following:

(i) the current yield;

(ii) the current yield and effective yield, if the effective yield is reported in a type size that is at least equal to that of the current yield, and

(b) for any investment fund other than a money market fund, the total return;

"total return" means the annual compounded rate of return for an investment fund for a period that would equate the initial value to the redeemable value at the end of the period, expressed as a percentage, and determined by applying the following formula:

$$\text{total return} = [(\text{redeemable value}/\text{initial value})^{(1/N)} - 1] \times 100$$

where

N = the length of the performance measurement period in years, with a minimum value of 1.

(3) If there are fees and charges of the type described in paragraph 15.11(1)1 relevant to the calculation of redeemable value and initial value of the securities of an investment fund, the redeemable value and initial value of securities of an investment fund must be the net asset value of one unit or share of the investment fund at the beginning or at the end of the performance measurement period, minus the amount of those fees and charges calculated by applying the assumptions referred to in that paragraph to a hypothetical securityholder account.

(4) If there are no fees and charges of the type described in paragraph 15.11(1)1 relevant to a calculation of total return, the calculation of total return for an investment fund may assume a hypothetical investment of one security of the investment fund and be calculated as follows:

(a) "initial value" means the net asset value of one unit or share of an investment fund at the beginning of the performance measurement period; and

(b) "redeemable value" =

$$R \times (1 + D_1/P_1) \times (1 + D_2/P_2) \times (1 + D_3/P_3) \ldots \times (1 + D_n/P_n)$$

where

R = the net asset value of one unit or security of the investment fund at the end of the performance measurement period,

D = the dividend or distribution amount per security of the investment fund at the time of each distribution,

P = the dividend or distribution reinvestment price per security of the investment fund at the time of each distribution, and

n = the number of dividends or distributions during the performance measurement period.

(5) Standard performance data of an asset allocation service must be based upon the standard performance data of its participating funds.

(6) Performance data

(a) for an investment fund other than a money market fund must be calculated to the nearest one-tenth of one percent; and

(b) for a money market fund must be calculated to the nearest one-hundredth of one percent.

15.11 Assumptions for Calculating Standard Performance Data — (1) The following assumptions must be made in the calculation of standard performance data of an investment fund:

1. Recurring fees and charges that are payable by all securityholders

(a) are accrued or paid in proportion to the length of the performance measurement period;

(b) if structured in a manner that would result in the performance information being dependent on the size of an investment, are calculated on the basis of an investment equal to the greater of $10,000 or the minimum amount that may be invested; and

(c) if fully negotiable, are calculated on the basis of the average fees paid by accounts of the size referred to in paragraph (b).

2. There are no fees and charges related to specific optional services.

3. All fees and charges payable by the investment fund are accrued or paid.

4. Dividends or distributions by the investment fund are reinvested in the investment fund at the net asset value per security of the investment fund on the reinvestment dates during the performance measurement period.

5. There are no non-recurring fees and charges that are payable by some or all securityholders and no recurring fees and charges that are payable by some but not all securityholders.

6. In the case of a mutual fund, a complete redemption occurs at the end of the performance measurement period so that the ending redeemable value includes elements of return that have been accrued but not yet paid to securityholders.

7. In the case of a non-redeemable investment fund, a complete redemption occurs at the net asset value of one security at the end of the performance measurement period so that the ending redeemable value includes elements of return that have been accrued but not yet paid to securityholders.

(2) The following assumptions must be made in the calculation of standard performance data of an asset allocation service:

1. Fees and charges that are payable by participants in the asset allocation service

(a) are accrued or paid in proportion to the length of the performance measurement period;

(b) if structured in a manner that would result in the performance information being dependent on the size of an investment, are calculated on the basis of an investment equal to the greater of $10,000 or the minimum amount that may be invested; and

(c) if fully negotiable, are calculated on the basis of the average fees paid by accounts of the size referred to in paragraph (b).

2. There are no fees and charges related to specific optional services.

3. The investment strategy recommended by the asset allocation service is utilized for the performance measurement period.

4. Transfer fees are

(a) accrued or paid;

(b) if structured in a manner that would result in the performance information being dependent on the size of an investment, calculated on the basis of an account equal to the greater of $10,000 or the minimum amount that may be invested; and

(c) if the fees and charges are fully negotiable, calculated on the basis of the average fees paid by an account of the size referred to in paragraph (b).

5. A complete redemption occurs at the end of the performance measurement period so that the ending redeemable value includes elements of return that have been accrued but not yet paid to securityholders.

(3) The calculation of standard performance data must be based on actual historical performance and the fees and charges payable by the investment fund and securityholders, or the asset allocation service and participants, in effect during the performance measurement period.

15.12 Sales Communications During the Waiting Period — If a sales communication is used after the issue of a receipt for a preliminary prospectus of the mutual fund described in the sales communication but before the issue of a receipt for its prospectus, the sales communication must state only

(a) whether the security represents a share in a corporation or an interest in a non-corporate entity;

(b) the name of the mutual fund and its manager;

(c) the fundamental investment objectives of the mutual fund;

(d) without giving details, whether the security is or will be a qualified investment for a registered retirement savings plan, registered retirement income fund or registered education savings plan or qualifies or will qualify the holder for special tax treatment; and

(e) any additional information permitted by securities legislation.

15.13 Prohibited Representations — (1) Securities issued by an unincorporated investment fund must be described by a term that is not and does not include the word "shares".

(2) A communication by an investment fund or asset allocation service, its promoter, manager, portfolio adviser, principal distributor, participating dealer or a person providing services to the investment fund or asset allocation service must not describe the investment fund as a commodity pool or as a vehicle for investors to participate in the speculative trading of, or leveraged investment in, derivatives, unless the investment fund is a commodity pool as defined in National Instrument 81-104 *Commodity Pools*.

15.14 Sales Communication — Multi-Class Investment Funds — A sales communication for an investment fund that distributes different classes or series of securities that are referable to the same portfolio must not contain performance data unless the sales communication complies with the following requirements:

1. The sales communication clearly specifies the class or series of security to which any performance data contained in the sales communication relates.

2. If the sales communication refers to more than one class or series of security and provides performance data for any one class or series, the sales communication must provide performance data for each class or series of security referred to in the sales communication and must clearly explain the reasons for different performance data among the classes or series.

3. A sales communication for a new class or series of security must not contain performance data for the existing class or series unless the sales communication clearly explains any differences between the new class or series and the existing class or series that could affect performance.

PART 16 — CALCULATION OF MANAGEMENT EXPENSE RATIO [REPEALED]

PART 17 — FINANCIAL STATEMENT REQUIREMENTS [REPEALED]

PART 18 — SECURITYHOLDER RECORDS

18.1 Maintenance of Records — An investment fund that is not a corporation must maintain, or cause to be maintained, up to date records of

(a) the names and latest known addresses of each securityholder of the investment fund;

(b) the number and class or series of a class of securities held by each securityholder of the investment fund; and

(c) the date and details of each issue and redemption of securities, and each distribution, of the investment fund.

18.2 Availability of Records — (1) An investment fund that is not a corporation must make, or cause to be made, the records referred to in section 18.1 available for inspection, free of charge, during normal business hours at its principal or head office by a securityholder or a representative of a securityholder, if the securityholder has agreed in writing that the information contained in the register will not be used by the securityholder for any purpose other than either of the following:

(a) in the case of a mutual fund, attempting to influence the voting of securityholders of the mutual fund or a matter relating to the relationships among the mutual fund, the members of the organization of the mutual fund, and the securityholders, partners, directors and officers of those entities;

(b) in the case of a non-redeemable investment fund, attempting to influence the voting of securityholders of the non-redeemable investment fund or a matter relating to the relationships among the non-redeemable investment fund, the manager and portfolio adviser of the non-redeemable investment fund and any of their affiliates, and the securityholders, partners, directors and officers of those entities.

(2) An investment fund must, upon written request by a securityholder of the investment fund, provide, or cause to be provided, to the securityholder a copy of the records referred to in paragraphs 18.1(a) and (b) if the securityholder

(a) has agreed in writing that the information contained in the register will not be used by the securityholder for any purpose other than attempting to influence the voting of securityholders of the investment fund or a matter relating to the administration of the investment fund; and

(b) has paid a reasonable fee to the investment fund that does not exceed the reasonable costs to the investment fund of providing the copy of the register.

PART 19 — EXEMPTIONS AND APPROVALS

19.1 Exemption — (1) The regulator or securities regulatory authority may grant an exemption from this Instrument, in whole or in part, subject to such conditions or restrictions as may be imposed in the exemption.

(2) Despite subsection (1), in Ontario only the regulator may grant such an exemption.

19.2 Exemption or Approval under Prior Policy — (1) A mutual fund that has obtained, from the regulator or securities regulatory authority, an exemption or waiver from, or approval under, a provision of National Policy Statement No. 39 before this Instrument came into force is exempt from any substantially similar provision of this Instrument, if any, on the same conditions, if any, as are contained in the earlier exemption or approval, unless the regulator or securities regulatory authority has revoked that exemption or waiver under authority provided to it in securities legislation.

(2) Despite Part 7, a mutual fund that has obtained, from the regulator or securities regulatory authority, approval under National Policy Statement No. 39 to pay incentive fees may continue to pay incentive fees on the terms of that approval if disclosure of the method of calculation of the fees and details of the composition of the benchmark or index used in calculating the fees are described in the prospectus of the mutual fund.

(3) A mutual fund that intends to rely upon subsection (1) must, at the time of the first filing of its pro forma prospectus after this Instrument comes into force, send to the regulator a letter or memorandum containing

(a) a brief description of the nature of the exemption from, or approval under, National Policy Statement No. 39 previously obtained; and

(b) the provision in the Instrument that is substantially similar to the provision in National Policy Statement No. 39 from or under which the exemption or approval was previously obtained.

19.3 Revocation of exemptions — (1) A mutual fund that has obtained an exemption or waiver from, or approval under, National Policy Statement No. 39 or this Instrument before December 31, 2003, that relates to a mutual fund investing in other mutual funds, may no longer rely on the exemption, waiver or approval as of December 31, 2004.

(2) In British Columbia, subsection (1) does not apply.

PART 20 — TRANSITIONAL

20.1 Effective Date — This Instrument comes into force on February 1, 2000.

20.2 Sales Communications — Sales communications, other than advertisements, that were printed before December 31, 1999 may be used until August 1, 2000, despite any requirements in this Instrument.

20.3 Reports to Securityholders — This Instrument does not apply to reports to securityholders

(a) printed before February 1, 2000; or

(b) that include only financial statements that relate to financial periods that ended before February 1, 2000.

20.4 Mortgage Funds — (1) Paragraphs 2.3(1)(b) and (c) do not apply to a mutual fund that has adopted fundamental investment objectives to permit it to invest in mortgages in accordance with National Policy Statement No. 29 if

(a) a National Instrument replacing National Policy Statement No. 29 has not come into force;

(b) the mutual fund was established, and has a prospectus for which a receipt was issued, before the date that this Instrument came into force; and

(c) the mutual fund complies with National Policy Statement No. 29.

(2) If a non-redeemable investment fund has adopted fundamental investment objectives to permit it to invest in mortgages, paragraph 2.3(2)(b) does not apply to the non-redeemable investment fund if the non-redeemable investment fund was established, and has a prospectus for which a receipt was issued, on or before September 22, 2014.

20.5 Delayed Coming into Force — (1) Despite section 20.1, subsection 4.4(1) does not come into force until August 1, 2000.

(2) Despite section 20.1, the following provisions of this Instrument do not come into force until February 1, 2001:

1. Subsection 2.4(2).

2. Subsection 2.7(4).

3. Subsection 6.4(1).

4. Subsection 6.8(4).

APPENDIX A — FUTURES EXCHANGES FOR THE PURPOSE OF SUBSECTION 2.7(4) — DERIVATIVE COUNTERPARTY EXPOSURE LIMITS

Futures Exchanges

Australia

Sydney Futures Exchange

Australian Financial Futures Market

Austria

Osterreichische Termin-und Option Borse (OTOB — The Austrian Options and Futures Exchange)

Belgium

Belfox CV (Belgium Futures and Options Exchange)

Brazil

Bolsa Brasileira de Futuros

Bolsa de Mercadorias & Futuros

Bolsa de Valores de Rio de Janeiro

Canada

The Winnipeg Commodity Exchange

The Toronto Futures Exchange

The Montreal Exchange

Denmark

Kobenhavus Fondsbors (Copenhagen Stock Exchange)

Garenti fonden for Dankse Optioner og Futures (Guarantee Fund for Danish Options and Futures)

Futop (Copenhagen Stock Exchange)

Finland

Helsinki Stock Exchange

Oy Suomen Optiopörssi (Finnish Options Exchange)

Suomen Optionmeklarit Oy (Finnish Options Market)

France

Marché à terme international de France S.A. (MATIF S.A.)

Marché des option négociables à Paris (MUNCP)

Germany

DTB Deutsche Terminbörse GmbH

EUREX

Hong Kong

Hong Kong Futures Exchange Limited

Ireland

Irish Futures and Options Exchange

Italy

Milan Italiano Futures Exchange

Japan

Osaka Shoken Torihikisho (Osaka Securities Exchange)

The Tokyo Commodity Exchange for Industry

The Tokyo International Financial Futures Exchange

Tokyo Grain Exchange

Tokyo Stock Exchange

Netherlands

AEX Options & Futures Exchange

EOE-Optiebeurs (European Options Exchange)

Financiele Termijnmarkt Amsterdam N.V.

New Zealand

New Zealand Futures and Options Exchange

Norway

Oslo Stock Exchange

Philippines

Manila International Futures Exchange

Portugal

Bosa de Derivatives de Porto

Singapore

Singapore Commodity Exchange (SICOM)

Singapore International Monetary Exchange Limited (SIMEX)

Spain

Meff Renta Fija

Meff Renta Variable

Sweden

OM Stockholm Fondkommission AB

Switzerland

EUREX

United Kingdom

International Petroleum Exchange (IPE)

London International Financial Futures and Options Exchange (LIFFE)

London Metal Exchange (LME)

OM London

United States

Chicago Board of Options Exchange (CBOE)

Chicago Board of Trade (CBOT)

Chicago Mercantile Exchange (CME)

Commodity Exchange, Inc. (COMEX)

Financial Instrument Exchange (Finex) a division of the New York Cotton Exchange

Board of Trade of Kansas City, Missouri, Inc.

Mid-America Commodity Exchange

Minneapolis Grain Exchange (MGE)

New York Futures Exchange, Inc. (NYFE)

New York Mercantile Exchange (NYMECX)

New York Board of Trade (NYBOT)

Pacific Stock Exchange

Philadelphia Board of Trade (PBOT)

Twin Cities Board of Trade

APPENDIX B-1 — COMPLIANCE REPORT

TO: [The appropriate securities regulatory authorities]

FROM: [Name of mutual fund]

RE: Compliance Report on National Instrument 81-102 For the year ended [insert date]

We hereby confirm that we have complied with the applicable requirements of Parts 9, 10 and 11 of National Instrument 81-102 for the year ended [insert date] [except as follows:] [list exceptions, if any].

[NAME of mutual fund]

.... Signature

.... Name and office of the person executing this report

.... Date

APPENDIX B-1 — AUDIT REPORT

TO: [The appropriate securities regulatory authorities]

RE: Compliance Report on National Instrument 81-102 For the year ended [insert date]

We have audited [name of mutual fund]'s report made under section 12.1 of National Instrument 81-102 regarding its compliance for the year ended [insert date] with the applicable requirements of Parts 9, 10 and 11 of that National Instrument. Compliance with these requirements is the responsibility of the management of [name of mutual fund] (the "Fund"). Our responsibility is to express an opinion on management's compliance report based on our audit.

We conducted our audit in accordance with standards for assurance engagements set out in the CICA Handbook. Those standards require that we plan and perform an audit to obtain reasonable assurance as a basis for our opinion. Such an audit includes examining, on a test basis, evidence supporting the assertions in management's compliance report.

In our opinion, the Fund's statement of compliance for the year ended [insert date] complies, in all material respects, with the applicable requirements of Parts 9, 10 and 11 of National Instrument 81-102.

This report is provided solely for the purpose of assisting the securities regulatory authority [ies] to which it is addressed in discharging its [their] responsibilities and should not be used for any other purpose.

City

Date

Chartered Accountants

APPENDIX B-2 — COMPLIANCE REPORT

TO: [The appropriate securities regulatory authorities]

FROM: [Name of principal distributor] (the "Distributor")

RE: Compliance Report on National Instrument 81-102 For the year ended [insert date]

FOR: [Name(s) of the mutual fund (the "Fund[s]")]

We hereby confirm that we have complied with the applicable requirements of Parts 9, 10 and 11 of National Instrument 81-102 in respect of the Fund[s] for the year ended [insert date] [except as follows:] [list exceptions, if any].

[NAME of the Distributor]

.... Signature

.... Name and office of the person executing this report

.... Date

APPENDIX B-2 — AUDIT REPORT

TO: [The appropriate securities regulatory authorities]

RE: Compliance Report on National Instrument 81-102 For the year ended [insert date]

We have audited [name of principal distributor]'s report made under section 12.1 of National Instrument 81-102 regarding its compliance for the year ended [insert date] with the applicable requirements of Parts 9, 10 and 11 of that National Instrument in respect of the [name of mutual funds] (the "Funds"). Compliance with these requirements is the responsibility of the management of [name of principal distributor] (the "Company"). Our responsibility is to express an opinion on management's compliance report based on our audit.

We conducted our audit in accordance with standards for assurance engagements set out in the CICA Handbook. Those standards require that we plan and perform an audit to obtain reasonable assurance as a basis for our opinion. Such an audit includes examining, on a test basis, evidence supporting the assertions in management's compliance report.

In our opinion, the Company's statement of compliance for the year ended [insert date] complies, in all material respects, with the applicable requirements of Parts 9, 10 and 11 of National Instrument 81-102 in respect of the Funds.

This report is provided solely for the purpose of assisting the securities regulatory authority [ies] to which it is addressed in discharging its [their] responsibilities and should not be used for any other purpose.

City

Date

Chartered Accountants

APPENDIX B-3 — COMPLIANCE REPORT

TO: [The appropriate securities regulatory authorities]

FROM: [Name of participating dealer] (the "Distributor")

RE: Compliance Report on National Instrument 81-102 For the year ended [insert date]

We hereby confirm that we have sold mutual fund securities to which National Instrument 81-102 is applicable. In connection with our activities in distributing these securities, we have complied with the applicable requirements of Parts 9, 10 and 11 of National Instrument 81-102 for the year ended [insert date] [except as follows:] [list exceptions, if any].

[NAME of the Distributor]

.... Signature

.... Name and office of the person executing this report

.... Date

APPENDIX B-3 — AUDIT REPORT

TO: [The appropriate securities regulatory authorities]

RE: Compliance Report on National Instrument 81-102 For the year ended [insert date]

We have audited [name of participating dealer]'s report made under section 12.1 of National Instrument 81-102 regarding its compliance for the year ended [insert date] with the applicable requirements of Parts 9, 10 and 11 of that National Instrument in respect of sales of mutual fund securities. Compliance with these requirements is the responsibility of the management of [name of participating dealer] (the "Company"). Our responsibility is to express an opinion on management's compliance report based on our audit.

We conducted our audit in accordance with standards for assurance engagements set out in the CICA Handbook. Those standards require that we plan and perform an audit to obtain reasonable assurance as a basis for our opinion. Such an audit includes examining, on a test basis, evidence supporting the assertions in management's compliance report.

In our opinion, the Company's statement of compliance for the year ended [insert date] complies, in all material respects, with the applicable requirements of Parts 9, 10 and 11 of National Instrument 81-102 in respect of sales of mutual fund securities.

This report is provided solely for the purpose of assisting the securities regulatory authority [ies] to which it is addressed in discharging its [their] responsibilities and should not be used for any other purpose.

City

Date

Chartered Accountants

APPENDIX C — PROVISIONS CONTAINED IN SECURITIES LEGISLATION FOR THE PURPOSE OF SUBSECTION 4.1(5) — PROHIBITED INVESTMENTS

JURISDICTION	SECURITIES LEGISLATION REFERENCE
All Jurisdictions	s. 13.6 of National Instrument 31-103 *Registration Requirements, Exemptions and Ongoing Registrant Obligations*
Newfoundland and Labrador	s. 191 of Reg 805/96

APPENDIX D — INVESTMENT FUND CONFLICT OF INTEREST INVESTMENT RESTRICTIONS

Jurisdiction	Securities Legislation Reference
All Jurisdictions	ss. 13.5(2)(a) and (b) of National Instrument 31-103 *Registration Requirements, Exemptions and Ongoing Registrant Obligations*
Alberta	ss. 185(2) and (3) of the *Securities Act* (Alberta)
British Columbia	s. 6(2) of BC Instrument 81-513 *Self-Dealing*
New Brunswick	s. 137(2) of the *Securities Act* (New Brunswick)
Newfoundland and Labrador	ss. 112(2), 112(3), 119(2)(a) and 119(2)(b) of the *Securities Act* (Newfoundland and Labrador)
Nova Scotia	ss. 119(2) and (3) of the *Securities Act* (Nova Scotia)
Ontario	ss. 111(2) and (3) of the *Securities Act* (Ontario)
Saskatchewan	ss. 120(2) and (3) of the *The Securities Act, 1988* (Saskatchewan)

APPENDIX E — INVESTMENT FUND CONFLICT OF INTEREST REPORTING REQUIREMENTS

Jurisdiction	Securities Legislation Reference
Alberta	s. 191(1)(a) of the *Securities Act* (Alberta)
British Columbia	s. 9(a) of BC Instrument 81-513 *Self-Dealing*
New Brunswick	s. 143(1)(a) of the *Securities Act* (New Brunswick)
Newfoundland and Labrador	s. 118(1)(a) of the *Securities Act* (Newfoundland and Labrador)
Nova Scotia	s. 125(1)(a) of the *Securities Act* (Nova Scotia)
Ontario	s. 117(1)(a) of the *Securities Act* (Ontario)
Saskatchewan	s. 126(1)(a) of the *The Securities Act, 1988* (Saskatchewan).

Final Rule: (2000) 23 O.S.C.B. (Supp) 57; Approval by OSC: (1999) 22 O.S.C.B. (Supp2) 71; Request for Comments: (1999) 22 O.S.C.B. (Supp) and (1997) 20 O.S.C.B. (Supp2).

Amendment to Rule: 24 O.S.C.B. 2680 (April 27, 2001); Approval by OSC: 24 O.S.C.B. 1071 (February 16, 2001); Request for Comments: 23 O.S.C.B. 4195 (June 16, 2000) and 23 O.S.C.B. (Supp) 133 (January 23, 2000).

Amendment to Rule: 27 O.S.C.B. 752; Approval by OSC: 26 O.S.C.B. 6837; Request for Comments: (2002) 25 O.S.C.B. 4705.

Amendment to Rule: 28 O.S.C.B. 4969; Approval by OSC: 28 O.S.C.B. (Supp-1) 46; Request for Comments: (2004) 27 O.S.C.B. 5157 and (2002) 25 O.S.C.B. 6273.

Amendment to Rule: 29 O.S.C.B. 8845; Approval by OSC: 29 O.S.C.B. (Supp-1) 1; Request for Comments: 28 O.S.C.B. (Supp-2) 1 and 27 O.S.C.B. 465.

Amendment to Rule: 31 O.S.C.B. 8569; Approval by OSC: 31 O.S.C.B. 6275; Request for Comments: 30 O.S.C.B. 4965.

Amendment to Rule: 32 O.S.C.B. (Supp. 4) 378; Approval by OSC: 32 O.S.C.B. (Supp. 2) 1; Request for Comments: 31 O.S.C.B. 2279.

Amendment to Rule: (2010) 33 O.S.C.B. 11431; Approval by OSC: (2010) 33 O.S.C.B. (Supp. 4) 1; Request for Comments: (2009) 32 O.S.C.B. (Supp. 1) 1, (2008) 31 O.S.C.B. 10479, (2007) 30 O.S.C.B. (Supp. 4) 1 and (2003) 26 O.S.C.B. 1443.

Amendment to Rule: (2012) 35 O.S.C.B. 3415; Approval by OSC: (2012) 35 O.S.C.B. 1375; Request for Comments: (2010) 33 O.S.C.B. 5833.

Amendment to Rule: Approval by OSC: (2013) 36 O.S.C.B. 2619; Request for Comments: (2012) 35 O.S.C.B. 6887.

Amendment to Rule: (2013) 36 O.S.C.B. 7827; Approval by OSC: (2013) 36 O.S.C.B. 6001; Request for Comments: (2012) 35 O.S.C.B. 5755 and (2011) 34 O.S.C.B. 8561.

Amendment to Rule: (2013) 36 O.S.C.B. 12197; Approval by OSC: (2013) 36 O.S.C.B. 9612; Request for Comments: (2009) 32 O.S.C.B. 8381.

Amendment to Rule: Approval by OSC: (2014) 37 O.S.C.B. (Supp. 4); Request for Comments: (2013) 36 O.S.C.B. (Supp. 3).

Rules: NI 41-101, 81-101, 81-106, 81-107.

Policies and Orders: NPS 81-102CP, 81-106CP, 81-107CP; CSAN 81-319; OSCN 81-706; 81-708, 81-711, 81-712, 81-715, 81-716, 81-720, 33-733.

Part 8: MUTUAL FUNDS

Companion Policy 81-102CP — To National Instrument 81-102 Investment Funds

PART 1 — PURPOSE

1.1 Purpose — The purpose of this Policy is to state the views of the Canadian securities regulatory authorities on various matters relating to National Instrument 81-102 *Investment Funds* (the "Instrument"), including

(a) the interpretation of various terms used in the Instrument;

(b) recommendations concerning the operating procedures that the Canadian securities regulatory authorities suggest that investment funds, or persons performing services for the investment funds subject to the Instrument, adopt to ensure compliance with the Instrument;

(c) discussions of circumstances in which the Canadian securities regulatory authorities have granted relief from particular requirements of National Policy Statement No. 39 ("NP39"), the predecessor to the Instrument, and the conditions that those authorities imposed in granting that relief; and

(d) recommendations concerning applications for approvals required under, or relief from, provisions of the Instrument.

PART 2 — COMMENTS ON DEFINITIONS CONTAINED IN THE INSTRUMENT

2.1 "asset allocation service" — The definition of "asset allocation service" in the Instrument includes only specific administrative services in which an investment in mutual funds subject to the Instrument is an integral part. The Canadian securities regulatory authorities do not view this definition as including general investment services such as discretionary portfolio management that may, but are not required to, invest in mutual funds subject to this Instrument.

2.2 "cash equivalent" — The definition of "cash equivalent" in the Instrument includes certain evidences of indebtedness of Canadian financial institutions. This includes banker's acceptances.

2.3 "clearing corporation" — The definition of "clearing corporation" in the Instrument includes both incorporated and unincorporated organizations, which may, but need not, be part of an options or futures exchange.

2.4 "debt-like security" — Paragraph (b) of the definition of "debt-like security" in the Instrument provides that the value of the component of an instrument that is not linked to the underlying interest of the instrument must account for less than 80 percent of the aggregate value of the instrument in order that the instrument be considered a debt-like security. The Canadian securities regulatory authorities have structured this provision in this manner to emphasize what they consider the most appropriate manner to value these instruments. That is, one should first value the component of the instrument that is not linked to the underlying interest, as this is often much easier to value than the component that is linked to the underlying interest.

The Canadian securities regulatory authorities recognize the valuation difficulties that can arise if one attempts to value, by itself, the component of an instrument that is linked to the underlying interest.

2.4.1 "designated rating" and "designated rating organization" — The Canadian securities regulatory authorities recognize there are existing contracts that use the predecessor terms "approved credit rating", "approved rating" and "approved credit rating organization". The content of the new definitions "designated rating" and "designated rating organization" is substantially the same as the content of their respective predecessor terms, only the terminology has changed. Therefore, it is reasonable to interpret the predecessor terms as having the same meaning as the definition of "designated rating" and "designated rating organization" in the Instrument, as applicable

2.5 "fundamental investment objectives" — (1) The definition of "fundamental investment objectives" is relevant in connection with paragraph 5.1(c) of the Instrument, which requires that the approval of securityholders of an investment fund be obtained before any change is made to the fundamental investment objectives of the investment fund. The fundamental investment objectives of an investment fund are required to be disclosed in a simplified prospectus under Part B of Form 81-101F1 *Contents of Simplified Prospectus* or under the requirements of Form 41-101F2 *Information Required in an Investment Fund Prospectus*. The definition of "fundamental investment objectives" contained in the Instrument uses the language contained in the disclosure requirements of Form 81-101F1 and Form 41-101F2, and the definition should be read to include the matters that would have to be disclosed under the Item of the applicable form concerning "Fundamental Investment Objectives". Accordingly, any change to the investment fund requiring a change to that disclosure would trigger the requirement for securityholder approval under paragraph 5.1(1)(c) of the Instrument.

(2) Form 41-101F2 and Part B of Form 81-101F1 set out, among other things, the obligation that an investment fund disclose in a prospectus both its fundamental investment objectives and its investment strategies. The matters required to be disclosed under the Item of the applicable form relating to "Investment Strategies" are not "fundamental investment objectives" under the Instrument.

(3) Generally speaking, the "fundamental investment objectives" of an investment fund are those attributes that define its fundamental nature. For example, investment funds that are guaranteed or insured, or that pursue a highly specific investment approach such as index funds or derivative funds, may be defined by those attributes. Often the manner in which an investment fund is marketed will provide evidence as to its fundamental nature; an investment fund whose advertisements emphasize, for instance, that investments are guaranteed likely will have the existence of a guarantee as a "fundamental investment objective".

(4) [Deleted.]

(5) One component of the definition of "fundamental investment objectives" is that those objectives distinguish an investment fund from other investment funds. This component does not imply that the fundamental investment objectives for each investment fund must be unique. Two or more investment funds can have identical fundamental investment objectives.

2.6 "guaranteed mortgage" — A mortgage insured under the *National Housing Act* (Canada) or similar provincial statutes is a "guaranteed mortgage" for the purposes of the Instrument.

2.7 "hedging" — (1) One component of the definition of "hedging" is the requirement that hedging transactions result in a "high degree of negative correlation between changes in the value of the investment or position, or group of investments or positions, being hedged and changes in the value of the instrument or instruments with which the investment or position is hedged". The Canadian securities regulatory authorities are of the view that there need not be complete congruence between the hedging instrument or instruments and the position or positions being hedged if it is reasonable to regard the one as a hedging instrument for the other, taking into account the closeness of the relationship between fluctuations in the price of the two and the availability and pricing of hedging instruments.

(2) The definition of "hedging" includes a reference to the "maintaining" of the position resulting from a hedging transaction or series of hedging transactions. The inclusion of this component in the definition requires an investment fund to ensure that a transaction continues to offset specific risks of the investment fund in order that the transaction be considered a "hedging" transaction under the Instrument; if the "hedging" position ceases to provide an offset to an existing risk of an investment fund, then that position is no longer a hedging position under the Instrument, and can be held by the investment fund only in compliance with the specified derivatives rules of the Instrument that apply to non-hedging positions. The component of the definition that requires the "maintaining" of a hedge position does not mean that an investment fund is locked into a specified derivatives position; it simply means that the specified derivatives position must continue to satisfy the definition of "hedging" in order to receive hedging treatment under the Instrument.

(3) Paragraph (b) of the definition of "hedging" has been included to ensure that currency cross hedging continues to be permitted under the Instrument. Currency cross hedging is the substitution of currency risk associated with one currency for currency risk associated with another currency, if neither currency is a currency in which the investment fund determines its net asset value per security and the aggregate amount of currency risk to which the investment fund is exposed is not increased by the substitution. Currency cross hedging is to be distinguished from currency hedging, as that term is ordinarily used. Ordinary currency hedging, in the context of investment funds, would involve replacing the investment fund's exposure to a "non-net asset value" currency with exposure to a currency in which the investment fund calculates its net asset value per security. That type of currency hedging is subject to paragraph (a) of the definition of "hedging".

2.8 "illiquid asset" — A portfolio asset of a mutual fund that meets the definition of "illiquid asset" will be an illiquid asset even if a person or company, including the manager or the portfolio adviser of a mutual fund or a partner, director or officer of the manager or portfolio adviser of a mutual fund or any of their respective associates or affiliates, has agreed to purchase the asset from the mutual fund. That type of agreement does not affect the words of the definition, which defines "illiquid asset" in terms of whether that asset cannot be readily disposed of through market facilities on which public quotations in common use are widely available.

2.9 "manager" — The definition of "manager" under the Instrument only applies to the person or company that actually directs the business of the investment fund, and does not apply to others, such as trustees, that do not actually carry out this function. Also, a "manager" would not include a person or company whose duties are limited to acting as a service provider to the investment fund, such as a portfolio adviser.

2.10 "option" — The definition of "option" includes warrants, whether or not the warrants are listed on a stock exchange or quoted on an over-the-counter market.

2.11 "performance data" — The term "performance data" includes data on an aspect of the investment performance of an investment fund, an asset allocation service, security, index or benchmark. This could include data concerning return, volatility or yield. The Canadian securities regulatory authorities note that the term "performance data" would not include a rating prepared by an independent organization reflecting the credit quality, rather than the performance, of, for instance, an investment fund's portfolio or the participating funds of an asset allocation service.

2.12 "public medium" — An "advertisement" is defined in the Instrument to mean a sales communication that is published or designed for use on or through a "public medium". The Canadian securities regulatory authorities interpret the term "public medium" to include print, television, radio, tape recordings, video tapes, computer disks, the Internet, displays, signs, billboards, motion pictures and telephones.

2.13 "purchase" — (1) The definition of a "purchase", in connection with the acquisition of a portfolio asset by an investment fund, means an acquisition that is the result of a decision made and action taken by the investment fund.

(2) The Canadian securities regulatory authorities consider that the following types of transactions would generally be purchases of a security by an investment fund under the definition:

1. The investment fund effects an ordinary purchase of the security, or, at its option, exercises, converts or exchanges a convertible security held by it.

2. The investment fund receives the security as consideration for a security tendered by the investment fund into a take-over bid.

3. The investment fund receives the security as the result of a merger, amalgamation, plan of arrangement or other reorganization for which the investment fund voted in favour.

4. The investment fund receives the security as a result of the automatic exercise of an exchange or conversion right attached to another security held by the investment fund in accordance with the terms of that other security or the exercise of that exchange or conversion right at the option of the investment fund.

5.   (a) The investment fund has become legally entitled to dispose of the collateral held by it under a securities loan or repurchase agreement and to apply proceeds of realization to satisfy the obligation of the counterparty of the investment fund under the transaction, and

    (b) sufficient time has passed after the event described in paragraph (a) to enable the investment fund to sell the collateral in a manner that maintains an orderly market and that permits the preservation of the best value for the investment fund.

(3) The Canadian securities regulatory authorities consider that the following types of transactions would generally not be purchases of a security by an investment fund under the definition:

1. The investment fund receives the security as a result of a compulsory acquisition by an issuer following completion of a successful take-over bid.

2. The investment fund receives the security as a result of a merger, amalgamation, plan of arrangement or other reorganization that the investment fund voted against.

3. The investment fund receives the security as the result of the exercise of an exchange or conversion right attached to a security held by the investment fund made at the discretion of the issuer of the security held by the investment fund.

4. The investment fund declines to tender into an issuer bid, even though its decision is likely to result in an increase in its percentage holdings of a security beyond what the the investment fund would be permitted under the Instrument to purchase.

2.14 "restricted security" — A special warrant is a form of restricted security and, accordingly, the provisions of the Instrument applying to restricted securities apply to special warrants.

2.15 "sales communication" — (1) The term "sales communication" includes a communication by an investment fund to (i) a securityholder of the investment fund and (ii) a person or company that is not a securityholder if the purpose of the communication is to induce the purchase of securities of the investment fund. A sales communication therefore does not include a communication solely between an investment fund or its promoter, manager, principal distributor or portfolio adviser and a participating dealer, or between the principal distributor or a participating dealer and its registered salespersons, that is indicated to be internal or confidential and that is not designed to be passed on by any principal distributor, participating dealer or registered salesperson to any securityholder of, or potential investor in, the investment fund. In the view of the Canadian securities regulatory authorities, if a communication of that type were so passed on by the principal distributor, participating dealer or registered salesperson, the communication would be a sales communication made by the party passing on the communication if the recipient of the communication were a securityholder of the investment fund or if the intent of the principal distributor, participating dealer or registered salesperson in passing on the communication were to induce the purchase of securities of the investment fund.

(2) The term "sales communication" is defined in the Instrument such that the communication need not be in writing and includes any oral communication. The Canadian securities regulatory authorities are of the view that the requirements in the Instrument pertaining to sales communications would apply to statements made at an investor conference to securityholders or to others to induce the purchase of securities of the investment fund.

(3) The Canadian securities regulatory authorities are of the view that image advertisements that are intended to promote a corporate identity or the expertise of an investment fund manager fall outside the definition of "sales communication". However, an advertisement or other communication that refers to a specific investment fund or funds or promotes any particular investment portfolio or strategy would be a sales communication and therefore be required to include warnings of the type now described in section 15.4 of the Instrument.

(4) In the case of an investment fund, paragraph (b) of the definition of a "sales communication" in the Instrument excludes sales communications contained in certain documents that the investment fund is required to prepare, including audited or unaudited financial statements, statements of account and confirmations of trade. The Canadian securities regulatory authorities are of the view that if information is contained in these types of documents that is not required to be included by securities legislation, any such additional material is not excluded by paragraph (b) of the definition of sales communication and may, therefore, constitute a sales communication if the additional material otherwise falls within the definition of that term in the Instrument.

2.16 "specified derivative" — (1) The term "specified derivative" is defined to mean an instrument, agreement or security, the market price, value or payment obligations of which are derived from, referenced to or based on an underlying interest. Certain instruments, agreements or securities that would otherwise be specified derivatives within the meaning of the definition are then excluded from the definition for purposes of the Instrument.

(2) Because of the broad ambit of the lead-in language to the definition, it is impossible to list every instrument, agreement or security that might be caught by that lead-in language but that is not considered to be a derivative in any normal commercial sense of that term. The Canadian securities regulatory authorities consider conventional floating rate debt instruments, securities of an investment fund, American depositary receipts and instalment receipts generally to be within this category, and generally will not treat those instruments as specified derivatives in administering the Instrument.

(3) However, the Canadian securities regulatory authorities note that these general exclusions may not be applicable in cases in which a mutual fund invests in one of the vehicles described in subsection (2) with the result that the mutual fund obtains or increases exposure to a particular underlying

interest in excess of the limit set out in section 2.1 of the Instrument. In such circumstances, the Canadian securities regulatory authorities are likely to consider that instrument a specified derivative under the Instrument.

2.17 "standardized future" — The definition of "standardized future" refers to an agreement traded on a futures exchange. This type of agreement is called a "futures contract" in the legislation of some jurisdictions, and an "exchange contract" in the legislation of some other jurisdictions (such as British Columbia and Alberta). The term "standardized future" is used in the Instrument to refer to these types of contracts, to avoid conflict with existing local definitions.

2.18 "swap" — The Canadian securities regulatory authorities are of the view that the definition of a swap in the Instrument would include conventional interest rate and currency swaps, as well as equity swaps.

PART 3 — INVESTMENTS

3.1 Evidences of Indebtedness of Foreign Governments and Supranational Agencies — (1) Section 2.1 of the Instrument prohibits mutual funds from purchasing a security of an issuer, other than a government security or a security issued by a clearing corporation if, immediately after the purchase, more than 10% of their net asset value would be invested in securities of that issuer. The term "government security" is defined in the Instrument as an evidence of indebtedness that is issued, or fully and unconditionally guaranteed as to principal and interest, by any of the government of Canada, the government of a jurisdiction or the government of the United States of America.

(2) Before the Instrument came into force, the Canadian securities regulatory authorities granted relief from the predecessor provision of NP39 to a number of international bond funds in order to permit those mutual funds to pursue their fundamental investment objectives with greater flexibility.

(3) The Canadian securities regulatory authorities will continue to consider applications for relief from section 2.1 of the Instrument if the mutual fund making the application demonstrates that the relief will better enable the mutual fund to meet its fundamental investment objectives. This relief will ordinarily be restricted to international bond funds.

(4) The relief from paragraph 2.04(1)(a) of NP39, which is replaced by section 2.1 of the Instrument, that has been provided to a mutual fund has generally been limited to the following circumstances:

    1. The mutual fund has been permitted to invest up to 20% of its net asset value in evidences of indebtedness of any one issuer if those evidences of indebtedness are issued, or guaranteed fully as to principal and interest, by supranational agencies or governments other than the government of Canada, the government of a jurisdiction or the government of the United States of America and are rated "AA" by Standard & Poor's Rating Services (Canada) or its DRO affiliate, or have an equivalent rating by one or more other designated rating organizations or their DRO affiliates.

    2. The mutual fund has been permitted to invest up to 35% of its net asset value in evidences of indebtedness of any one issuer, if those securities are issued by issuers described in paragraph 1 and are rated "AAA" by Standard & Poor's Rating Services (Canada) or its DRO affiliate, or have an equivalent rating by one or more other designated rating organizations or their DRO affiliates.

(5) It is noted that the relief described in paragraphs 3.1(4)1 and 2 cannot be combined for one issuer.

(6) [deleted]

(7) The relief from paragraph 2.04(1)(a) of NP39, which is replaced by section 2.1 of the Instrument, has generally been provided only if

    (a) the securities that may be purchased under the relief referred to in subsection (4) are traded on a mature and liquid market;

    (b) the acquisition of the evidences of indebtedness by the mutual fund is consistent with its fundamental investment objectives;

    (c) the prospectus or simplified prospectus of the mutual fund disclosed the additional risks associated with the concentration of the net asset value of the mutual fund in securities of fewer issuers, such as the potential additional exposure to the risk of default of the issuer in which the fund has so invested and the risks, including foreign exchange risks, of investing in the country in which that issuer is located; and

    (d) the prospectus or simplified prospectus of the mutual fund gave details of the relief provided by the Canadian securities regulatory authorities, including the conditions imposed and the type of securities covered by the exemption.

3.2 Index Mutual Funds — (1) An "index mutual fund" is defined in section 1.1 of the Instrument as a mutual fund that has adopted fundamental investment objectives that require it to

    (a) hold the securities that are included in a permitted index or permitted indices of the mutual fund in substantially the same proportion as those securities are reflected in that permitted index or those permitted indices; or

    (b) invest in a manner that causes the mutual fund to replicate the performance of that permitted index or those permitted indices.

(2) This definition includes only mutual funds whose entire portfolio is invested in accordance with one or more permitted indices. The Canadian securities regulatory authorities recognize that there may be mutual funds that invest part of their portfolio in accordance with a permitted index or indices, with a remaining part of the portfolio being actively managed. Those mutual funds cannot avail themselves of the relief provided by subsection 2.1(5) of the Instrument, which provides relief from the "10 percent rule" contained in subsection 2.1(1) of the Instrument, because they are not "index mutual funds". The Canadian securities regulatory authorities acknowledge that there may be principles behind the relief contained in subsection 2.1(5) of the Instrument is also applicable to "partially-indexed" mutual funds. Therefore, the Canadian securities regulatory authorities will consider applications from those types of mutual funds for relief analogous to that provided by subsection 2.1(5) of the Instrument.

(3) It is noted that the manager of an index mutual fund may make a decision to base all or some of the investments of the mutual fund on a different permitted index than a permitted index previously used. This decision might be made for investment reasons or because that index no longer satisfies the definition of "permitted index" in the Instrument. It is noted that this decision by the manager will be considered by the Canadian securities regulatory authorities generally to constitute a change of fundamental investment objectives, thereby requiring securityholder approval under paragraph 5.1(1)(c) of the Instrument. In addition, this decision would also constitute a material change for the mutual fund, thereby requiring an amendment to the prospectus of the mutual fund and the issuing of a press release under Part 11 of National Instrument 81-106 *Investment Fund Continuous Disclosure*.

3.2.1 Control Restrictions — An investment fund generally holds a passive stake in the businesses in which it invests; that is, an investment fund generally does not seek to obtain control of, or become involved in, the management of investee companies. This key restriction on the type of investment activities that may be undertaken by an investment fund is codified in section 2.2 of the Instrument. Exceptions to this are labour sponsored or venture capital funds, where some degree of involvement in the management of the investees is generally an integral part of the investment strategy.

In determining whether an investment fund exercises control over, or is involved in the management of, an investee company, for the purposes of compliance with section 2.2 of the Instrument, the Canadian securities regulatory authorities will generally consider indicators, including the following:

(a) any right of the investment fund to appoint directors, or observers, of the board of the investee company;

(b) any right of the investment fund to restrict the management of the investee company, or to approve or veto decisions made by the management of the investee company;

(c) any right of the investment fund to restrict the transfer of securities by other securityholders of the investee company.

The Canadian securities regulatory authorities will take the above factors into consideration when considering the nature of an investment fund's investment in an issuer to determine whether the investment fund is in compliance with section 2.2 of the Instrument. The Canadian securities regulatory authorities will also refer to the applicable accounting standards in determining whether an investment fund is exercising control over an issuer.

3.3 Special Warrants — An investment fund is required by subsection 2.2(3) of the Instrument to assume the conversion of each special warrant it holds. This requirement is imposed because the nature of a special warrant is such that there is a high degree of likelihood that its conversion feature will be exercised shortly after its issuance, once a prospectus relating to the underlying security has been filed.

3.3.1 Illiquid assets — (1) Although section 2.4 of the Instrument does not apply to non-redeemable investment funds, the Canadian securities regulatory authorities expect the manager of an investment fund (whether a mutual fund or a non-redeemable investment fund) to establish an effective liquidity risk management policy that considers the liquidity of the types of assets in which the investment fund will be invested, and the fund's obligations and other liabilities (for example, meeting redemption requests, or margin calls from derivative counterparties). Appropriate internal limits for the investment fund's liquidity needs, in line with its investment strategies, should be established.

(2) As portfolio assets may become illiquid when market conditions change, the Canadian securities regulatory authorities are of the view that the manager should regularly measure, monitor and manage the liquidity of the investment fund's portfolio assets, keeping in mind the time to liquidate each portfolio asset, the price the asset may be sold at and the pattern of redemption requests.

(3) Furthermore, the Canadian securities regulatory authorities are of the view that illiquid assets are generally more difficult to value, for the purposes of calculating an investment fund's net asset value, than assets which are liquid. As a result, where a non-redeemable investment fund has a large proportion of its assets invested in illiquid assets, this raises concerns about the accuracy of the fund's net asset value and the amount of any fees calculated with reference to net asset value. Accordingly, staff of the Canadian securities regulatory authorities may raise comments or questions in the course of their reviews of the prospectuses or continuous disclosure documents of non-redeemable investment funds where such funds have a significant proportion of their assets invested in illiquid assets.

3.4 Investment in Other Investment Funds — (1) [Deleted.]

(2) Subsection 2.5(7) of the Instrument provides that certain investment restrictions and reporting requirements do not apply to investments in other investment funds made in accordance with section 2.5 of the Instrument. In some cases, an investment fund's investments in other investment funds will be exempt from the requirements of section 2.5 of the Instrument because of an exemption granted by the regulator or securities regulatory authority. In these cases, assuming the investment fund complies with the terms of the exemption, its investments in other investmnt funds would be considered to have been made in accordance with section 2.5 of the Instrument. It is also noted that subsection 2.5(7) of the Instrument applies only with respect to an investment fund's investments in other investment funds, and not for any other investment or transaction.

3.5 Instalments of Purchase Price — Paragraph 2.6(d) of the Instrument prohibits an investment fund from purchasing a security, other than a specified derivative, that by its terms may require the investment fund to make a contribution in addition to the payment of the purchase price. This prohibition does not extend to the purchase of securities that are paid for on an instalment basis in which the total purchase price and the amounts of all instalments are fixed at the time the first instalment is made.

3.6 Purchase of Evidences of Indebtedness — Paragraph 2.6(f) of the Instrument prohibits an investment fund from lending either cash or a portfolio asset other than cash. The Canadian securities regulatory authorities are of the view that the purchase of an evidence of indebtedness, such as a bond or debenture, a loan participation or loan syndication as permitted by paragraph 2.3(1)(i) or (2)(c) of the Instrument, or the purchase of a preferred share that is treated as debt for accounting purposes, does not constitute the lending of cash or a portfolio asset.

3.7 Securities Lending, Repurchase and Reverse Repurchase Transactions — (1) Section 2.12, 2.13 and 2.14 of the Instrument each contains a number of conditions that must be satisfied in order that an investment fund may enter into a securities lending, repurchase or reverse repurchase transaction in compliance with the Instrument. It is expected that, in addition to satisfying these conditions, the manager on behalf of the investment fund, in co-ordination with an agent, will ensure that the documentation evidencing these types of transactions contains customary provisions to protect the investment fund and to document the transaction properly. Among other things, these provisions would normally include:

(a) a definition of an "event of default" under the agreement, which would include failure to deliver cash of securities, or to promptly pay to the investment fund amounts equal to dividends and interest paid, and distributions made, on loaned or sold securities, as required by the agreement;

(b) provisions giving non-defaulting parties rights of termination, rights to sell the collateral, rights to purchase identical securities to replace the loaned securities and legal rights of set-off in connection with their obligations if an event of default occurs; and

(c) provisions that deal with, if an event of default occurs, how the value of collateral or securities held by the non-defaulting party that is in excess of the amount owed by the defaulting party will be treated.

(2) Section 2.12, 2.13 and 2.14 of the Instrument each imposes a requirement that an investment fund that has entered into a securities lending, repurchase or reverse repurchase transaction hold cash or securities of at least 102% of the market value of the securities or cash held by the investment fund's counterparty under the transaction. It is noted that the 102% requirement is a minimum requirement, and that it may be appropriate for the manager of an investment fund, or the agent acting on behalf of the investment fund, to negotiate the holding of a greater amount of cash or securities if necessary to protect the interests of the investment fund in particular transaction, having regard to the level of risk for the investment fund in the transaction. In addition, if the recognized best practices for a particular type of transaction in a particular market calls for a higher level of collateralization than 102%, it is expected that, absent special circumstances, the manager or agent would ensure that its arrangements reflect the relevant best practices for that transaction.

(3) Paragraph 3 of subsection 2.12(1) of the Instrument refers to securities lending transactions in terms of securities that are "loaned" by an investment fund in exchange for collateral. Some securities lending transactions are documented so that title to the "loaned" securities is transferred from the "lender" to the "borrower". The Canadian securities regulatory authorities do not consider this fact as sufficient to disqualify those transactions as

Part 8: MUTUAL FUNDS

securities loan transactions within the meaning of the Instrument, so long as the transaction is in fact substantively a loan. References throughout the Instrument to "loaned" securities, and similar references, should be read to include securities "transferred" under a securities lending transaction.

(4) Subparagraph 6(d) of subsection 2.12(1) permits the use of irrevocable letters of credit as collateral in securities lending transactions. The Canadian securities regulatory authorities believe that at a minimum, the prudent use of letters of credit will involve the following arrangments:

(a) the investment fund should be allowed to draw down any amount of the letter of credit at any time by presenting its sight draft and certifying that the borrower is in default of its obligation under the securities lending agreement, and the amount capable of being drawn down would represent the current market value of the outstanding loaned securities or the amount required to cure any other borrower default; and

(b) the letter of credit should be structured so that the lender may draw down, on the date immediately preceding its expiration date, an amount equal to the current market value of all outstanding loaned securities on that date.

(5) Paragraph 9 of subsection 2.12(1) and paragraph 8 of subsection 2.13(1) of the Instrument each provides that the agreement under which an investment fund enters into a securities lending or repurchase transaction include a provision requiring the investment fund's counterparty to promptly pay to the investment fund, among other things, distributions made on the securities loaned or sold in the transaction. In this context, the term "distributions" should be read broadly to include all payments or distributions of any type made on the underlying securities, including without limitation, distributions of property, stock dividends, securities received as the result of splits, all rights to purchase additional securities and full or partial redemption proceeds. This extended meaning conforms to the meaning given the term "distributions" in several standard forms of securities loan agreements widely used in the securities lending and repurchase markets.

(6) Sections 2.12, 2.13 and 2.14 of the Instrument each make reference to the "delivery" and "holding" of securities or collateral by the investment fund. The Canadian securities regulatory authorities note that these terms will include the delivery or holding by an agent for an investment fund. In addition, the Canadian securities regulatory authorities recognize that under ordinary market practice, agents pool collateral for securities lending/repurchase clients; this pooling of itself is not considered a violation of the Instrument.

(7) Sections 2.12, 2.13 and 2.14 of the Instrument each require that the securities involved in a securities lending, repurchase or reverse repurchase transaction be marked to market daily and adjusted as required daily. It is recognized that market practice often involves an agent marking to market a portfolio at the end of a business day, and effecting the necessary adjustments to a portfolio on the next business day. So long as each action occurs on each business day, this market practice is not a breach of the Instrument.

(8) As noted in subsection (7), the Instrument requires the daily marking to market of the securities involved in a securities lending, repurchase or reverse repurchase transaction. The valuation principles used in this marking to market may be those generally used by the agent acting for the investment fund, even if those principles deviate from the principles that are used by the investment fund in valuing its portfolio assets for the purposes of calculating net asset value.

(9) Paragraph 6 of subsection 2.13(1) of the Instrument imposes a requirement concerning the delivery of sales proceeds to the investment fund equal to 102% of the market value of the securities sold in the transaction. It is noted that accrued interest on the sold securities should be included in the calculation of the market value of those securities.

(10) Section 2.15 of the Instrument imposes the obligation on a manager of an investment fund to appoint an agent or agents to administer its securities lending and repurchase transactions, and makes optional the ability of a manager to appoint an agent or agents to administer its reverse repurchase transactions. A manager that appoints more than one agent to carry out these functions may allocate responsibility as it considers best. For instance, it may be appropriate that one agent be responsible for domestic transactions, with one or more agents responsible for off-shore transactions. Managers should ensure that the various requirements of sections 2.15 and 2.16 of the Instrument are satisfied for all agents.

(11) It is noted that the responsibilities of an agent appointed under section 2.15 of the Instrument include all aspects of acting on behalf of an investment fund in connection with securities lending, repurchase or reverse repurchase agreements. This includes acting in connection with the reinvestment of collateral or securities held during the life of a transaction.

(12) Subsection 2.15(3) of the Instrument requires that an agent appointed by an investment fund to administer its securities lending, repurchase or reverse repurchase transactions shall be a custodian or sub-custodian of the investment fund. It is noted that the provisions of Part 6 of the Instrument generally apply to the agent in connection with its activities relating to securities lending, repurchase or reverse repurchase transactions. The agent must have been appointed as custodian or sub-custodian in accordance with section 6.1, and must satisfy the other requirements of Part 6 in carrying out its responsibilities.

(13) Subsection 2.15(4) of the Instrument provides that the manager of an investment fund must not authorize an agent to enter into securities lending, repurchase or, if applicable, reverse repurchase transactions on behalf of the investment fund unless there is a written agreement between the agent, the manager and the investment fund that deals with certain prescribed matters. Subsection (4) requires that the manager and the investment fund, in the agreement, provide instructions to the agent on the parameters to be followed in entering into the type of transaction to which the agreement pertains. The parameters would normally include:

(a) details on the types of transactions that may be entered into by the investment fund;

(b) types of portfolio assets of the investment fund to be used in the transaction;

(c) specification of maximum transaction size, or aggregate amount of assets that may be committed to transactions at any one time;

(d) specification of permitted counterparties;

(e) any specific requirements regarding collateralization, including minimum requirements as to amount and diversification of collateralization, and details on the nature of the collateral that may be accepted by the investment fund;

(f) directions and an outline of responsibilities for the reinvestment of cash collateral received by the investment fund under the program to ensure that proper levels of liquidity are maintained at all times; and

(g) duties and obligations on the agent to take action to obtain payment by a borrower of any amounts owed by the borrower.

(14) The definition of "cash cover" contained in section 1.1 of the Instrument requires that the portfolio assets be used for cash cover not be "allocated for specific purposes". Securities loaned by a mutual fund in a securities lending transaction have been allocated for specific purposes and therefore cannot be used as cash cover by the mutual fund for its specified derivatives obligations.

(15) An investment fund sometimes needs to vote securities held by it in order to protect its interests in connection with corporate transactions or developments relating to the issuers of the securities. The manager and the portfolio adviser of a investment fund, or the agent of the investment fund administering a securities lending program on behalf of the investment fund, should monitor corporate developments relating to securities that are loaned by the investment fund in securities lending transactions, and take all necessary steps to ensure that the investment fund can exercise a right to

vote the securities when necessary. This may be done by way of a termination of a securities lending transaction and recall of loaned securities, as described in paragraph 11 of subsection 2.12(1) of the Instrument.

(16) As part of the prudent management of a securities lending, repurchase or reverse repurchase program, managers of investment funds, together with their agents, should ensure that transfers of securities in connection with those programs are effected in a secure manner over an organized market or settlement system. For foreign securities, this may entail ensuring that securities are cleared through central depositories. Investment funds and their agents should pay close attention to settlement arrangements when entering into securities lending, repurchase and reverse repurchase transactions.

3.7.1 Money Market Funds — Section 2.18 of the Instrument imposes daily and weekly liquidity requirements on money market funds. Specifically, money market funds must keep 5% of their assets invested in cash or readily convertible into cash within one day, and 15% of their assets invested in cash or readily convertible into cash within one week. Assets that are "readily convertible to cash" would generally be short-term, highly liquid investments that are readily convertible to known amounts of cash and which are subject to an insignificant risk of changes in value. Such assets can be sold in the ordinary course of business within one business day (in the case of the daily liquidity requirement) or within five business days (in the case of the weekly liquidity requirement) at approximately the value ascribed to them by the money market fund. The Canadian securities regulatory authorities note that the securities do not have to mature within the one and five business day periods. For example, direct obligations of the Canadian or U.S. government, or of a provincial government, that mature after one or five business days but that can be readily converted to cash within one or five business days, would likely be eligible for the 5% and 15% liquidity requirements.

3.8 Prohibited Investments — (1) Subsection 4.1(4) of the Instrument permits a dealer managed investment fund to make an investment otherwise prohibited by subsection 4.1(1) of the Instrument and the corresponding provisions in securities legislation referred to in Appendix C to the Instrument if the independent review committee of the dealer managed investment fund has approved the transaction under subsection 5.2(2) of National Instrument 81-107 *Independent Review Committee for Investment Funds* ("NI 81-107"). The Canadian securities regulatory authorities expect the independent review committee may contemplate giving its approval as a standing instruction, as contemplated in section 5.4 of NI 81-107.

(2) Subsection 4.3(2) of the Instrument permits an investment fund to purchase a class of debt securities from, or sell a class of debt securities to, another investment fund managed by the same manager or an affiliate of the manager where the price payable for the security is not publicly available, if the independent review committee of the investment fund has approved the transaction under subsection 5.2(2) of NI 81-107 and the requirements in section 6.1 of NI 81-107 have been met. The Canadian securities regulatory authorities expect the independent review committee may contemplate giving its approval as a standing instruction, as contemplated in section 5.4 of NI 81-107.

(3) In providing its approval under paragraph 4.3(2) of the Instrument, the Canadian securities regulatory authorities expect the independent review committee to have satisfied itself that the price of the security is fair. It may do this by considering the price quoted on a marketplace (e.g., CanPx or TRACE), or by obtaining a quote from an independent, arm's-length purchaser or seller, immediately before the purchase or sale.

PART 4 — USE OF SPECIFIED DERIVATIVES

4.1 Exercising Options on Futures — Paragraphs 2.8(1)(d) and (e) of the Instrument prohibit a mutual fund from, among other things, opening and maintaining a position in a standardized future except under the conditions referred to in those paragraphs. Opening and maintaining a position in a standardized future could be effected through the exercise by a mutual fund of an option on futures. Therefore, it should be noted that a mutual fund cannot exercise an option on futures and assume a position in a standardized future unless the applicable provisions of paragraphs 2.8(1)(d) or (e) are satisfied.

4.2 Registration Matters — The Canadian securities regulatory authorities remind industry participants of the following requirements contained in securities legislation:

1. An investment fund may only invest in or use clearing corporation options and over-the-counter options if the portfolio adviser advising with respect to these investments

   (a) is permitted, either by virtue of registration as an adviser under the securities legislation or commodity futures legislation of the jurisdiction in which the portfolio adviser is providing the advice or an exemption from the requirement to be registered, to provide that advice to the investment fund under the laws of that jurisdiction; and

   (b) has satisfied all applicable option proficiency requirements of that jurisdiction.

2. An investment fund may invest in or use futures and options on futures only if the portfolio adviser advising with respect to these investments or uses is registered as an adviser under the securities or commodity futures legislation of the jurisdiction in which the portfolio adviser is providing the advice, if this registration is required in that jurisdiction, and meets the proficiency requirements for advising with respect to futures and options on futures in the jurisdiction.

3. A portfolio adviser of an investment fund that receives advice from a non-resident sub-adviser as contemplated by section 2.10 of the Instrument is not relieved from the registration requirements described in paragraphs 1 and 2.

4. In Ontario, a non-resident sub-adviser is required, under the commodity futures legislation of Ontario, to be registered in Ontario if it provides advice to another portfolio adviser of an investment fund in Ontario concerning the use of standardized futures by the investment fund. Section 2.10 of the Instrument does not exempt the non-resident sub-adviser from this requirement. A non-resident sub-adviser should apply for an exemption in Ontario if it wishes to carry out the arrangements contemplated by section 2.10 without being registered in Ontario under that legislation.

4.3 Leveraging — The Instrument is designed to prevent the use of specified derivatives for the purpose of leveraging the assets of the mutual fund. The definition of "hedging" prohibits leveraging with specified derivatives used for hedging purposes. The provisions of subsection 2.8(1) of the Instrument restrict leveraging with specified derivatives used for non-hedging purposes.

4.4 Cash Cover — The definition of "cash cover" in the Instrument prescribes the securities or other portfolio assets that may be used to satisfy the cash cover requirements relating to specified derivatives positions of mutual funds required by Part 2 of the Instrument. The definition of "cash cover" includes various interest-bearing securities; the definition includes interest accrued on those securities, and so mutual funds are able to include accrued interest for purposes of cash cover calculations.

PART 5 — LIABILITY AND INDEMNIFICATION

5.1 Liability and Indemnification — (1) Subsection 4.4(1) of the Instrument contains provisions that require that any agreement or declaration of trust under which a person or company acts as manager of an investment fund provide that the manager is responsible for any loss that arises out of the failure of it, and of any person or company retained by it or the investment fund to discharge any of the manager's responsibilities to the investment fund, to satisfy the standard of care referred to in that section. Subsection 4.4(2) of the Instrument provides that an investment fund must not relieve the manager from that liability.

(2) The purpose of these provisions is to ensure that the manager remains responsible to the investment fund and therefore indirectly to its securityholders for the duty of care that is imposed by the securities legislation of most jurisdictions, and to clarify that the manager is responsible for ensuring that service providers perform to the level of that standard of care. The Instrument does not regulate the contractual relationships between the manager and service providers; whether a manager can seek indemnification from a service provider that fails to satisfy that standard of care is a contractual issue between those parties.

(3) Subsection 4.4(5) of the Instrument provides that section 4.4 does not apply to any losses to an investment fund or securityholder arising out of an action or inaction by a custodian or sub-custodian or by a director of an investment fund. A separate liability regime is imposed, on custodians or sub-custodians by section 6.6 of the Instrument. Directors are subject to the liability regime imposed by the relevant corporate legislation.

5.2 Securities Lending, Repurchase and Reverse Repurchase Transactions — (1) As described in section 5.1, section 4.4 of the Instrument is designed to ensure that the manager of an investment fund is responsible for any loss that arises out of the failure of it, and of any person or company retained by it or the investment fund to discharge any of the manager's responsibilities to the investment fund, to satisfy the standard of care referred to in that section.

(2) The retention by a manager of an agent under section 2.15 of the Instrument to administer the investment fund's securities lending, repurchase or reverse repurchase transactions does not relieve the manager from ultimate responsibility for the administration of those transactions in accordance with the Instrument and in conformity with the standard of care imposed on the manager by statute and required to be imposed on the agent in the relevant agreement by subsection 2.15(4) of the Instrument.

(3) Under subsection 2.15(3) of the Instrument, the custodian or sub-custodian of an investment fund must be the agent appointed to act on behalf of the investment fund to administer securities lending, repurchase or reverse repurchase transactions of the investment fund. The activities of the agent, as custodian or sub-custodian, are not within the responsibility of the manager of the investment fund, as provided for in subsection 4.4(5) of the Instrument. However, the activities of the agent, in its role as administering the investment funds' securities lending, repurchase or reverse repurchase transactions, are within the ultimate responsbility of the manager, as provided for in subsection 4.4(6) of the Instrument.

PART 6 — SECURITYHOLDER MATTERS

6.1 Meetings of Securityholders — Subsection 5.4(1) of the Instrument imposes a requirement that a meeting of securityholders of an investment fund called for the purpose of considering any of the matters referred to in subsection 5.1(1) of the Instrument must be called on notice sent at least 21 days before the date of the meeting. Industry participants are reminded that the provisions of National Instrument 54-101 *Communication with Beneficial Owners of Securities of a Reporting Issuer*, or a successor instrument, may apply to any meetings of securityholders of investment funds and that those provisions may require that a longer period of notice be given.

6.2 Limited Liability — (1) Investment funds generally are structured in a manner that ensures that investors are not exposed to the risk of loss of an amount more than their original investment. This is a very important and essential attribute of investment funds.

(2) Investment funds that are structured as corporations do not raise pressing liability problems because of the limited liability regime of corporate statutes.

(3) Investment funds that are structured as limited partnerships may raise some concerns about the loss of limited liability if limited partners participate in the management or control of the partnership. The Canadian securities regulatory authorities encourage managers of investment funds that are structured as limited partnerships to consider this issue in connection with the holding of meetings of securityholders, even if required under subsection 5.1(1) of the Instrument. In addition, in the view of the Canadian securities regulatory authorities, all managers of investment funds that are structured as limited partnerships should include a discussion of this issue as a risk factor in prospectuses.

6.3 Calculation of Fees — (1) Paragraph 5.1(1)(a) of the Instrument requires securityholder approval before the basis of the calculation of a fee or expense that is charged to an investment fund is changed in a way that could result in an increase in charges to the investment fund. The Canadian securities regulatory authorities note that the phrase "basis of the calculation" includes any increase in the rate at which a particular fee is charged to the investment fund.

(2) The Canadian securities regulatory authorities are of the view that the requirement of paragraph 5.1(1)(a) of the Instrument would not apply in instances where the change to the basis of the calculation is the result of separate individual agreements between the manager of the investment fund and individual securityholders of the investment fund, and the resulting increase in charges is payable directly or indirectly by those individual securityholders only.

6.4 Fund Conversions — (1) For the purposes of subparagraphs 5.1(1)(h)(i), (ii) and (iii) of the Instrument, the Canadian securities regulatory authorities consider that any change that will restructure an investment fund from its original structure requires the prior approval of the securityholders of the investment fund. For example, a non-redeemable investment fund may be designed to convert into a mutual fund on a specified date, or it may be designed to convert into a mutual fund after a specified date if the securities of the investment fund have traded at a specified discount to their net asset value per security for more than a set period of time. In each case, when the event that triggers the conversion occurs, the redemption feature of the securities of the non-redeemable investment fund changes and the securities of the non-redeemable investment fund will typically become redeemable at their net asset value per security daily. This change in the redemption feature of the securities of the investment fund may not be implemented unless securityholder approval has been obtained under subparagraph 5.1(1)(h)(i) of the Instrument. Another example of a change requiring securityholder approval is where an investment fund seeks to obtain control, or become involved in the management, of companies in which it invests, which is inconsistent with the nature of an investment fund. In such a situation, the investment fund would be required to obtain securityholder approval under subparagraph 5.1(1)(h)(iii) of the Instrument, in order to convert into a non-investment fund issuer, before it could become involved in the management of, or exercise control over, investees.

(2) For the purposes of subsection 5.1(2) of the Instrument, the Canadian securities regulatory authorities consider the costs and expenses associated with a change referred to in paragraph 5.1(1)(h) of the Instrument to include costs associated with the securityholder meeting to obtain approval of the

change, the costs of preparing and filing a prospectus to commence continuous distribution of securities if the investment fund is converting from a non-redeemable investment fund to a mutual fund in continuous distribution, and brokerage commissions payable as a result of any portfolio realignment necessary to carry out the transaction.

PART 7 — CHANGES

7.1 Integrity and Competence of Investment Fund Management Groups — (1) Paragraph 5.5(1)(a) of the Instrument requires that the approval of the securities regulatory authority be obtained before the manager of an investment fund is changed. Paragraph 5.5(1)(a.1) of the Instrument contemplates similar approval to a change in control of a manager.

(2) In connection with each of these approvals, applicants are required by section 5.7 of the Instrument to provide information to the securities regulatory authority concerning the integrity and experience of the persons or companies that are proposed to be involved in, or control, the management of the investment fund after the proposed transaction.

(3) The Canadian securities regulatory authorities would generally consider it helpful in their assessment of the integrity and experience of the proposed new management group that will manage an investment fund after a change in manager if the application set out, among any other information the applicant wishes to provide

    (a) the name, registered address and principal business activity or the name, residential address and occupation or employment of

        (i) if the proposed manager is not a public company, each beneficial owner of securities of each shareholder, partner or limited partner of the proposed manager, and

        (ii) if the proposed manager is a public company, each beneficial owner of securities of each shareholder of the proposed manager that is the beneficial holder, directly or indirectly, of more than 10% of the outstanding securities of the proposed manager; and

    (b) information concerning

        (i) if the proposed manager is not a public company, each shareholder, partner or limited partner of the proposed manager,

        (ii) if the proposed manager is a public company, each shareholder that is the beneficial holder, directly or indirectly, of more than 10% of the outstanding securities of the proposed manager,

        (iii) each director and officer of the proposed manager, and

        (iv) each proposed director, officer or individual trustee of the investment fund.

(4) The Canadian securities regulatory authorities would generally consider it helpful if the information relating to the persons and companies referred to in paragraph (3)(b) included

    (a) for a company

        (i) its name, registered address and principal business activity,

        (ii) the number of securities or partnership units of the proposed manager beneficially owned, directly or indirectly, and

        (iii) particulars of any existing or potential conflicts of interest that may arise as a result of the activities of the company and its relationship with the management group of the investment fund; and

    (b) for an individual

        (i) his or her name, birthdate and residential address,

        (ii) his or her principal occupation or employment,

        (iii) his or her principal occupations or employment during the five years before the date of the application, with a particular emphasis on the individual's experience in the financial services industry,

        (iv) the individual's educational background, including information regarding courses successfully taken that relate to the financial services industry,

        (v) his or her position and responsibilities with the proposed manager or the controlling shareholders of the proposed manager or the investment fund,

        (vi) whether he or she is, or within five years before the date of the application has been, a director, officer or promoter of any reporting issuer other than the investment fund, and if so, disclosing the names of the reporting issuers and their business purpose, with a particular emphasis on relationships between the individual and other investment funds,

        (vii) the number of securities or partnership units of the proposed manager beneficially owned, directly or indirectly,

        (viii) particulars of any existing or potential conflicts of interest that may arise as a result of the individual's outside business interests and his or her relationship with the management group of the investment fund, and

        (ix) a description of the individual's relationships to the proposed manager and other service providers to the investment fund.

(5) The Canadian securities regulatory authorities would generally consider it helpful in their assessment of the integrity and experience of the persons or companies that are proposed to manage an investment fund after a change of control of the manager, if the application set out, among any other information that applicant wishes to provide, a description of

    (a) the proposed corporate ownership of the manager of the investment fund after the proposed transaction, indicating for each proposed direct or indirect shareholder of the manager of the investment fund the information about that shareholder referred to in subsection (4);

    (b) the proposed officers and directors of the manager of the investment fund, of the investment fund and of each of the proposed controlling shareholders of the investment fund, indicating for each individual, the information about that individual referred to in subsection (4);

    (c) any anticipated changes to be made to the officers and directors of the manager of the investment fund, of the investment fund and of each of the proposed controlling shareholders of the investment fund that are not set out in paragraph (b); and

    (d) the relationship of the members of the proposed controlling shareholders and the other members of the management group to the manager and any other service provider to the investment fund.

7.2 Mergers of Investment Funds — Subsection 5.6(1) of the Instrument provides that mergers of investment funds may be carried out on the conditions described in that subsection without prior approval of the securities regulatory authority. The Canadian securities regulatory authorities consider that the types of transactions contemplated by subsection 5.6(1) of the Instrument when carried out in accordance with the conditions of that subsection address the fundamental regulatory concerns raised by mergers of investment funds. Subsection 5.6(1) of the Instrument is designed to facilitate consolidations of investment funds within fund families that have similar fundamental investment objectives and strategies and that are operated in a consistent and similar fashion. Since subsection 5.6(1) will be unavailable unless the investment funds involved in the transaction have substantially similar fundamental investment objectives and strategies and are operated in a substantially similar fashion, the Canadian securities regulatory authorities do not expect that the portfolios of the consolidating funds will be required to be realigned to any great extent before a merger. If realignment is necessary, the Canadian securities regulatory authorities note that paragraph 5.6(1)(h) of the Instrument provides that none of the costs and expenses associated with the transaction may be borne by the investment fund. Brokerage commissions payable as a result of any portfolio realignment necessary to carry out the transaction would, in the view of the Canadian securities regulatory authorities, be costs and expenses associated with the transaction.

7.3 Regulatory Approval for Reorganizations — (1) Paragraph 5.7(1)(b) of the Instrument requires certain details to be provided in respect of an application for regulatory approval required by paragraph 5.5(1)(b) that is not automatically approved under subsection 5.6(1). The Canadian securities regulatory authorities will be reviewing this type of proposed transaction, among other things, to ensure that adequate disclosure of the differences between the issuers participating in the proposed transaction is given to securityholders of the investment fund that will be merged, reorganized or amalgamated with another issuer.

(2) If an investment fund is proposed to be merged, amalgamated or reorganized with an investment fund that has a net asset value that is smaller than the net asset value of the terminating investment fund, the Canadian securities regulatory authorities will consider the implications of the proposed transaction on the smaller continuing investment fund. The Canadian securities regulatory authorities believe that this type of transaction generally would constitute a material change for the smaller continuing investment fund, thereby triggering the requirements of paragraph 5.1(1)(g) of the Instrument and Part 11 of National Instrument 81-106 *Investment Fund Continuous Disclosure*.

7.4 [Deleted.]

7.5 Circumstances in Which Approval of Securityholders Not Required — (1) Subsection 5.3(2) of the Instrument provides that an investment fund's reorganization with, or transfer of assets to, another issuer may be carried out on the conditions described in paragraph 5.3(2)(a) or (b) without the prior approval of the securityholders of the investment fund.

(2) If the manager refers the change contemplated in subsection 5.3(2) of the Instrument to the investment fund's independent review committee, and subsequently seeks the approval of the securityholders of the investment fund, the Canadian securities regulatory authorities expect the manager to include a description of the independent review committee's determination in the written notice to securityholders referred to in section 5.4 of the Instrument.

(3) The Canadian securities regulatory authorities expect the written notice referred to in subparagraph 5.3(2)(a)(iv) and (v) of the Instrument to include, at a minimum, the expected date of the reorganization, the name of the other investment fund with which the investment fund will be reorganized, how a securityholder of the investment fund may obtain a copy of the other investment fund's fund facts, simplified prospectus or annual information form, as applicable, and a description of the determination of the investment fund's independent review committee with respect to the reorganization.

7.6 Change of Auditor — Section 5.3.1 of the Instrument requires that the independent review committee of the investment fund give its prior approval to the manager before the auditor of the investment fund may be changed.

7.7 Connection to NI 81-107 — There may be matters under subsection 5.1(1) of the Instrument that may also be a conflict of interest matter as defined in NI 81-107. The Canadian securities regulatory authorities expect any matter under subsection 5.1(1) of the Instrument subject to review by the independent review committee to be referred by the manager to the independent review committee before seeking the approval of securityholders of the investment fund. The Canadian securities regulatory authorities further expect the manager to include a description of the independent review committee's determination in the written notice to securityholders referred to in subsection 5.4(2) of the Instrument.

7.8 Termination of an Investment Fund — Subsection 5.8(2) of the Instrument requires a mutual fund that is terminating to give notice of the termination to all securityholders of the mutual fund. Section 5.8.1 of the Instrument requires a non-redeemable investment fund that is terminating to issue and file a press release announcing the termination. Investment funds for which the termination is a material change must also comply with the requirements of Part 11 of National Instrument 81-106 *Investment Fund Continuous Disclosure*.

PART 8 — CUSTODIANSHIP OF PORTFOLIO ASSETS

8.1 Standard of Care — The standard of care prescribed by section 6.6 of the Instrument is a minimum standard only. Similarly, the provisions of section 6.5 of the Instrument, designed to protect an investment fund from loss in the event of the insolvency of those holding its portfolio assets, are minimum requirements. The Canadian securities regulatory authorities are of the view that the requirements set out in section 6.5 may require custodians and sub-custodians to take such additional steps as may be necessary or desirable properly to protect the portfolio assets of the investment fund in a foreign jurisdiction and to ensure that those portfolio assets are unavailable to satisfy the claims of creditors of the custodian or sub-custodian, having regard to creditor protection and bankruptcy legislation of any foreign jurisdiction in which portfolio assets of an investment fund may be located.

8.2 Book-Based System — (1) Subsection 6.5(3) of the Instrument provides that a custodian or sub-custodian of an investment fund may arrange for the deposit of portfolio assets of the investment fund with a depository, or clearing agency, that operates a book-based system. Such depositories or clearing agencies include The Canadian Depository For Securities Limited, the Depository Trust Company or any other domestic or foreign depository or clearing agency that is incorporated or organized under the laws of a country or a political subdivision of a country and operates a book-based system in that country or political subdivision or operates a transnational book-based system.

(2) A depository or clearing agency that operates a book-based system used by an investment fund is not considered to be a custodian or sub-custodian of the investment fund.

8.3 Compliance — Paragraph 6.7(1)(c) of the Instrument requires the custodian of an investment fund to make any changes periodically that may be necessary to ensure that the custodian and sub-custodian agreements comply with Part 6, and that there is no sub-custodian of the investment fund that does not satisfy the applicable requirements of sections 6.2 or 6.3. The Canadian securities regulatory authorities note that necessary changes to ensure this compliance could include a change of sub-custodian.

PART 9 — CONTRACTUAL PLANS

9.1 Contractual Plans — Industry participants are reminded that the term "contractual plan" used in Part 8 of the Instrument is a defined term in the securities legislation of most jurisdictions, and that contractual plans as so defined are not the same as automatic or periodic investment plans. The distinguishing feature of a contractual plan is that sales charges are not deducted at a constant rate as investments in mutual fund securities are made under the plan; rather, proportionately higher sales charges are deducted from the investments made during the first year, or in some plans the first two years.

PART 10 — SALES AND REDEMPTIONS OF SECURITIES

10.1 General — The purposes of Parts 9, 10 and 11 of the Instrument include ensuring that

(a) investors' cash is received by an investment fund promptly;

(b) the opportunity for loss of an investors' cash before investment in the investment fund is minimized; and

(c) the investment fund or the appropriate investor receives all interest that accrues on cash during the periods between delivery of the cash by an investor until investment in the investment fund, in the case of the purchase of investment fund securities, or between payment of the cash by the investment fund until receipt by the investor, in the case of redemptions.

10.2 Interpretation — (1) [Deleted.]

(2) The Instrument refers to "securityholders" of an investment fund in several provisions. Investment funds must keep a record of the holders of their securities. An investment fund registers a holder of its securities on this record as requested by the person or company placing a purchase order or as subsequently requested by that registered securityholder. The Canadian securities regulatory authorities are of the view that an investment fund is entitled to rely on its register of holders of securities to determine the names of such holders and in its determination as to whom it is to take instructions from.

(3) Accordingly, when the Instrument refers to "securityholder" of an investment fund, it is referring to the securityholder registered as a holder of securities on the records of the investment fund. If that registered securityholder is a participating dealer acting for its client, the investment fund deals with and takes instructions from that participating dealer. The Instrument does not regulate the relationship between the participating dealer and its client for whom the participating dealer is acting as agent. The Canadian securities regulatory authorities note however, that the participating dealer should, as a matter of prudent business practice, obtain appropriate instructions, in writing, from its client when dealing with the client's beneficial holdings in an investment fund.

10.3 Receipt of Orders — (1) A principal distributor or participating dealer of a mutual fund should endeavour, to the extent possible, to receive cash to be invested in the mutual fund at the time the order to which they pertain is placed.

(2) A dealer receiving an order for redemption should, at the time of receipt of the investor's order, obtain from the investor all relevant documentation required by the mutual fund in respect of the redemption including, without limitation, any written request for redemption that may be required by the mutual fund, duly completed and executed, and any certificates representing the mutual fund securities to be redeemed, so that all required documentation is available at the time the redemption order is transmitted to the mutual fund or to its principal distributor for transmittal to the mutual fund.

10.4 Backward Pricing — Subsections 9.3(1) and 10.3(1) of the Instrument provide that the issue price or the redemption price of a security of a mutual fund to which a purchase order or redemption order pertains shall be the net asset value per security, next determined after the receipt by the mutual fund of the relevant order. For clarification, the Canadian securities regulatory authorities emphasize that the issue price and redemption price cannot be based upon any net asset value per security calculated before receipt by the mutual fund of the relevant order.

10.5 Coverage of Losses — (1) Subsection 9.4(6) of the Instrument provides that certain participating dealers may be required to compensate a mutual fund for a loss suffered as the result of a failed settlement of a purchase of securities of the mutual fund. Similarly, subsection 10.5(3) of the Instrument provides that certain participating dealers may be required to compensate a mutual fund for a loss suffered as the result of a redemption that could not be completed due to the failure to satisfy the requirements of the mutual fund concerning redemptions.

(2) The Canadian securities regulatory authorities have not carried forward into the Instrument the provisions contained in NP39 relating to a participating dealer's ability to recover from their clients or other participating dealers any amounts that they were required to pay to a mutual fund. If participating dealers wish to provide for such rights they should make the appropriate provisions in the contractual arrangements that they enter into with their clients or other participating dealers.

10.6 Issue Price of Securities for Non-Redeemable Investment Funds — (1) Paragraph 9.3(2)(a) of the Instrument provides that the issue price of the securities of a non-redeemable investment fund must not, as far as reasonably practicable, be a price that causes dilution of the net asset value of the other outstanding securities of the investment fund at the time the security is issued. The Canadian securities regulatory authorities consider that, to satisfy this requirement, the issue price of the securities should generally not be a price that is less than the net asset value per security of that class, or series of a class, determined on the date of issuance. However, the Canadian securities regulatory authorities recognize that the determination of what is "reasonably practicable" is fact-specific and will vary depending on the type of offering or issuance.

(2) For example, the Canadian securities regulatory authorities generally expect that any issuances of new securities of a non-redeemable investment fund in connection with a merger of the fund, or any issuances of new securities to the manager of the non-redeemable investment fund as payment of management fees, be issued at a price that is not less than the NAV per security on the date of issuance. However, the Canadian securities regulatory authorities have observed when an existing non-redeemable investment fund issues new securities under a prospectus, the issue price typically exceeds the net asset value per security on the day before the date of the prospectus, such that the net proceeds of the offering on a per unit basis is no less than the net asset value per security on the day before the date of the prospectus. The Canadian securities regulatory authorities do not consider this issue price to cause dilution to the net asset value of other outstanding securities of the investment fund.

PART 11 — COMMINGLING OF CASH

11.1 Commingling of Cash — (1) Part 11 of the Instrument requires principal distributors and participating dealers to account separately for cash they may receive for the purchase of, or upon the redemption of, investment fund securities. Those principal distributors and participating dealers are prohibited from commingling any cash so received with their other assets or with cash held for the purchase or upon the sale of securities of other types of securities. The Canadian securities regulatory authorities are of the view that this means that dealers may not deposit into the trust accounts established under Part 11 cash obtained from the purchase or sale of other types of securities such as guaranteed investment certificates, government treasury bills, segregated funds or bonds.

(2) Subsections 11.1(2) and 11.2(2) of the Instrument state that principal distributors and participating dealers, respectively, may not use any cash received for the investment in investment fund securities to finance their own operations. The Canadian securities regulatory authorities are of the view that any costs associated with returned client cheques that did not have sufficient funds to cover a trade ("NSF cheques") are a cost of doing business and should be borne by the applicable principal distributor or participating dealer and should not be offset by interest income earned on the trust accounts established under Part 11 of the Instrument.

(3) No overdraft positions should arise in these trust accounts.

(4) Subsections 11.1(3) and 11.2(3) of the Instrument prescribe the circumstances under which a principal distributor or participating dealer, respectively, may withdraw funds from the trust accounts established under Part 11 of the Instrument. This would prevent the practice of "lapping". Lapping occurs as a result of the timing differences between trade date and settlement date, when cash of an investment fund client held for a trade which has not yet settled is used to settle a trade for another investment fund client who has not provided adequate cash to cover the settlement of that other trade on the settlement date. The Canadian securities regulatory authorities view this practice as a violation of subsections 11.1(3) and 11.2(3) of the Instrument.

(5) Subsections 11.1(4) and 11.2(4) of the Instrument require that interest earned on cash held in the trust accounts established under Part 11 of the Instrument be paid to the applicable investment fund or its securityholders "pro rata based on cash flow". The Canadian securities regulatory authorities are of the view that this requirement means, in effect, that the applicable investment fund or securityholder should be paid the amount of interest that the investment fund or securityholder would have received had the cash held in trust for that investment fund or securityholder been the only cash held in that trust account.

(6) Paragraph 11.3(b) of the Instrument requires that trust accounts maintained in accordance with sections 11.1 or 11.2 of the Instrument bear interest "at rates equivalent to comparable accounts of the financial institution". A type of account that ordinarily pays zero interest may be used for trust accounts under sections 11.1 or 11.2 of the Instrument so long as zero interest is the rate of interest paid on that type of account for all depositors other than trust accounts.

PART 12 — PUBLICATION OF NET ASSET VALUE PER SECURITY [REPEALED]

PART 13 — PROHIBITED REPRESENTATIONS AND SALES COMMUNICATIONS

13.1 Misleading Sales Communications — (1) Part 15 of the Instrument prohibits misleading sales communications relating to investment funds and asset allocation services. Whether a particular description, representation, illustration or other statement in a sales communication is misleading depends upon an evaluation of the context in which it is made. The following list sets out some of the circumstances, in the view of the Canadian securities regulatory authorities, in which a sales communication would be misleading. No attempt has been made to enumerate all such circumstances since each sales communication must be assessed individually.

    1. A statement would be misleading if it lacks explanations, qualifications, limitations or other statements necessary or appropriate to make the statement not misleading.

    2. A representation about past or future investment performance would be misleading if it is

        (a) a portrayal of past income, gain or growth of assets that conveys an impression of the net investment results achieved by an actual or hypothetical investment that is not justified under the circumstances;

        (b) a representation about security of capital or expenses associated with an investment that is not justified under the circumstances or a representation about possible future gains or income; or

        (c) a representation or presentation of past investment performance that implies that future gains or income may be inferred from or predicted based on past investment performance or portrayals of past performance.

    3. A statement about the characteristics or attributes of an investment fund or an asset allocation service would be misleading if

        (a) it concerns possible benefits connected with or resulting from services to be provided or methods of operation and does not give equal prominence to discussion of any risks or associated limitations;

        (b) it makes exaggerated or unsubstantiated claims about management skill or techniques; characteristics of the investment fund or asset allocation service; an investment in securities issued by the fund or recommended by the service; services offered by the fund, the service or their respective manager; or effects of government supervision; or

        (c) it makes unwarranted or incompletely explained comparisons to other investment vehicles or indices.

    4. A sales communication that quoted a third party source would be misleading if the quote were out of context and proper attribution of the source were not given.

(2) Performance data information may be misleading even if it complies technically with the requirements of the Instrument. For instance, subsections 15.8(1) and (2) of the Instrument contain requirements that the standard performance data for investment funds given in sales communications be for prescribed periods falling within prescribed amounts of time before the date of the appearance or use of the advertisement or first date of publication of any other sales communication. That standard performance data may be misleading if it does not adequately reflect intervening events occurring after the prescribed period. An example of such an intervening event would be, in the case of money market funds, a substantial decline in interest rates after the prescribed period.

(3) An advertisement that presents information in a manner that distorts information contained in the preliminary prospectus or prospectus, or preliminary prospectus, preliminary fund facts document and preliminary annual information form, as applicable, or prospectus, fund facts document and annual information form of an investment fund or that includes a visual image that provides a misleading impression will be considered to be misleading.

(4) Any discussion of the income tax implications of an investment in an investment fund security should be balanced with a discussion of any other material aspects of the offering.

(5) Paragraph 15.2(1)(b) of the Instrument provides that sales communications must not include any statement that conflicts with information that is contained in, among other things and as applicable, a prospectus or fund facts document. The Canadian securities regulatory authorities are of the view that a sales communication that provides performance data in compliance with the requirements of Part 15 of the Instrument for time periods that differ

from those shown in a prospectus, fund facts document or management report of fund performance does not violate the requirements of paragraph 15.2(1)(b) of the Instrument.

(6) Subsection 15.3(1) of the Instrument permits an investment fund or asset allocation service to compare its performance to, among other things, other types of investments or benchmarks on certain conditions. Examples of such other types of investments or benchmarks to which the performance of an investment fund or asset allocation service may be compared include consumer price indices; stock, bond or other types of indices; averages; returns payable on guaranteed investment certificates or other certificates of deposit; and returns from an investment in real estate.

(7) Paragraph 15.3(1)(c) of the Instrument requires that if the performance of an investment fund or asset allocation service is compared to that of another investment or benchmark, the comparison sets out clearly any factors necessary to ensure that the comparison is fair and not misleading. Such factors would include an explanation of any relevant differences between the investment fund or asset allocation service and the investment or benchmark to which it is compared. Examples of such differences include any relevant differences in the guarantees of, or insurance on, the principal of or return from the investment or benchmark; fluctuations in principal, income or total return; any differing tax treatment; and, for a comparison to an index or average, any differences between the composition or calculation of the index or average and the investment portfolio of the investment fund or asset allocation service.

13.2 Other Provisions — (1) Subsection 15.9(1) of the Instrument imposes certain disclosure requirements for sales communications in circumstances in which there was a change in the business, operations or affairs of an investment fund or asset allocation service during or after a performance measurement period of performance data contained in the sales communication that could have materially affected the performance of the investment fund or asset allocation service. Examples of these changes are changes in the management, investment objectives, portfolio adviser, ownership of the manager, fees and charges, or of policies concerning the waiving or absorbing of fees and charges, of the investment fund or asset allocation service; or of a change in the characterization of a mutual fund as a money market fund. A reorganization or restructuring of an investment fund that results in a conversion of a non-redeemable investment fund into a mutual fund, or the conversion of a mutual fund into a non-redeemable investment fund, would also be an example of such a change.

(1.1) Subparagraph 15.6(1)(d)(i) of the Instrument prohibits a sales communication pertaining to a mutual fund from including performance data for a period that is before the time when the mutual fund offered its securities under a prospectus. Where the mutual fund has previously existed as a non-redeemable investment fund and has been a reporting issuer in a jurisdiction for a period of at least 12 consecutive months, either as a mutual fund or a non-redeemable investment fund, subsection 15.6(2) requires any sales communication that contains performance data of the mutual fund to include performance data for the period that the fund existed as a non-redeemable investment fund. The Canadian securities regulatory authorities are of the view that performance data pertaining to a mutual fund that has converted from a non-redeemable investment fund should include both the periods before and after the converting transaction, similar to the past performance information presented in the mutual fund's management report of fund performance. Performance data must not be included for any period before the time the non-redeemable investment fund was a reporting issuer.

(2) Paragraph 15.11(1)5 of the Instrument requires that no non-recurring fees and charges that are payable by some or all securityholders and no recurring fees and charges that are payable by some but not all securityholders be assumed in calculating standard performance data. Examples of non-recurring types of fees and charges are front-end sales commissions and contingent deferred sales charges, and examples of recurring types of fees and charges are the annual fees paid by purchasers who purchased on a contingent deferred charge basis.

(3) Paragraphs 15.11(1)2 and 15.11(2)2 of the Instrument require that no fees and charges related to optional services be assumed in calculating standard performance data. Examples of these fees and charges include transfer fees, except in the case of an asset allocation service, and fees and charges for registered retirement savings plans, registered retirement income funds, registered education savings plans, pre-authorized investment plans and systematic withdrawal plans.

(4) The Canadian securities regulatory authorities are of the view that it is inappropriate and misleading for an investment fund that is continuing following a merger to prepare and use *pro forma* performance information or financial statements that purport to show the combined performance of the two funds during a period before their actual merger. The Canadian securities regulatory authorities are of the view that such *pro forma* information is hypothetical, involving the making of many assumptions that could affect the results.

(5) Subsections 15.8(2) and (3) of the Instrument require disclosure of standard performance data of a mutual fund, in some circumstances, from "the inception of the mutual fund". It is noted that paragraph 15.6(1)((d) generally prohibits disclosure of performance data for a period that is before the time when the mutual fund offered its securities under a prospectus or before an asset allocation service commenced operation. Also, each of Instruction (1) to Item 5 of Part B of Form 81-101F1 *Contents of Simplified Prospectus* and Instruction (1) to Item 2 of Part I of Form 81-101F3 *Contents of Fund Facts Document* requires disclosure of the date on which a mutual fund's securities first became available to the public as the date on which the mutual fund "started". Therefore consistent with these provisions, the words "inception of the mutual fund" in subsections 15.8(2) and (3) of the Instrument should be read as referring to the beginning of the distribution of the securities of the mutual fund under a prospectus of the mutual fund, and not from any previous time in which the mutual fund may have existed but did not offer its securities under a prospectus. If a mutual fund previously existed as a non-redeemable investment fund, the words "inception of the mutual fund" in subsections 15.8(2) and (3) of the Instrument should be read as referring to the date that the non-redeemable investment fund became a reporting issuer.

(6) Paragraph 15.6(1)((a) of the Instrument contains a prohibition against the inclusion of performance data for a mutual fund that has been distributing securities for less than 12 consecutive months. The creation of a new class or series of security of an existing mutual fund does not constitute the creation of a new mutual fund and therefore does not subject the mutual fund to the restrictions of paragraph 15.6(1)((a) unless the new class or series is referable to a new portfolio of assets.

(7) Section 15.14 of the Instrument contains the rules relating to sales communications for multi-class investment funds. Those rules are applicable to an investment fund that has more than one class of securities that are referable to the same portfolio of assets. Section 15.14 does not deal directly with asset allocation services. It is possible that asset allocation services could offer multiple "classes"; the Canadian securities regulatory authorities recommend that any sales communications for those services generally respect the principles of section 15.14 in order to ensure that those sales communications not be misleading.

(8) The Canadian securities regulatory authorities believe that the use of hypothetical or *pro forma* performance data for new classes of securities of a multi-class investment fund would generally be misleading.

13.3 Sales Communications of Non-Redeemable Investment Funds During the Waiting Period and the Distribution Period — The Canadian securities regulatory authorities remind non-redeemable investment funds of the restrictions contained in securities legislation relating to the distribution of material and advertising and marketing in connection with a prospectus offering during the waiting period and during the distribution period following the issuance of a receipt for the final prospectus. Part 15 of the Instrument does not vary any of the restrictions imposed during these periods.

PART 14 — FINANCIAL DISCLOSURE MATTERS [REPEALED]

PART 15 — SECURITYHOLDER RECORDS

15.1 Securityholder Records — (1) Section 18.1 of the Instrument requires the maintenance of securityholder records, including past records, relating to the issue and redemption of securities and distributions of the investment fund. Section 18.1 of the Instrument does not require that these records need be held indefinitely. It is up to the particular investment fund, having regard to prudent business practice and any applicable statutory limitation periods, to decide how long it wishes to retain old records.

(2) The Canadian securities regulatory authorities are of the view that the requirements in section 18.1 to maintain securityholder records may be satisfied if the investment fund maintains up to date records of registered securityholders. Each investment fund may decide whether it wishes to maintain records of beneficial securityholders.

PART 16 — EXEMPTIONS AND APPROVALS

16.1 Need for Multiple or Separate Applications — The Canadian securities regulatory authorities note that a person or company that obtains an exemption from a provision of the Instrument need not apply again for the same exemption at the time of each prospectus or simplified prospectus refiling unless there has been some change in an important fact relating to the granting of the exemption. This also applies to exemptions from NP39 granted before the Instrument; as provided in section 19.2 of the Instrument, it is not necessary to obtain an exemption from the corresponding provision of the Instrument.

16.2 Exemptions under Prior Policies — (1) Subsection 19.2(1) of the Instrument provides that a mutual fund that has obtained, from the regulatory or securities regulatory authority, an exemption from a provision of NP 39 before the Instrument came into force is granted an exemption from any substantially similar provision of the Instrument, if any, on the same conditions, if any, contained in the earlier exemption.

(2) The Canadian securities regulatory authorities are of the view that the fact that a number of small amendments have been made to many of the provisions of the Instrument from the corresponding provision of NP39 should not lead to the conclusion that the provisions are not "substantially similar", if the general purpose of the provisions remain the same. For instance, even though some changes have been made in the Instrument, the Canadian securities regulatory authorities consider paragraph 2.2(1)(a) of the Instrument to be substantially similar to paragraph 2.04(1)(b) of NP39, in that the primary purpose of both provisions is to prohibit mutual funds from acquiring securities of an issuer sufficient to permit the mutual fund to control or significantly influence the control of that issuer.

(3) The Canadian securities regulatory authorities are of the view that the new provisions of the Instrument relating to mutual funds investing in other mutual funds introduced on December 31, 2003 are not "substantially similar" to those of the Instrument which they replace.

16.3 Waivers and Orders concerning "Fund of Funds" — (1) The Canadian securities regulatory authorities in a number of jurisdictions have provided waivers and orders from NP39 and securities legislation to permit "fund of funds" to exist and carry on investment activities not otherwise permitted by NP39 or securities legislation. Some of those waivers and orders contained "sunset" provisions that provided that they expired when legislation or a policy or rule of the Canadian securities regulatory authorities came into force that effectively provided for a new "fund of funds" regime. For greater certainty, the Canadian securities regulatory authorities note that the coming into force of the Instrument will not trigger the "sunset" of those waivers and orders.

(2) For greater certainty, note that the coming into force of the Instrument did not trigger the "sunset" of those waivers and orders. However, the coming into force of section 19.3 of the Instrument will effectively cause those waivers and orders to expire one year after its coming into force.

Adoption by OSC: (2000) 23 O.S.C.B. (Supp) 116 and (1999) 22 O.S.C.B. (Supp2) 153; Request for Comments: (1999) 22 O.S.C.B. (Supp) and (1997) 20 O.S.C.B. (Supp2).

Adoption of Amendment to Companion Policy by OSC: 24 O.S.C.B. 2680 (April 27, 2001) and 24 O.S.C.B. 1071 (February 16, 2001); Request for Comments: 23 O.S.C.B. 4195 (June 16, 2000) and 23 O.S.C.B. (Supp) 133 (January 28, 2000).

Adoption of Amendment to Companion Policy by OSC: (2004) 27 O.S.C.B. 751 and (2003) 26 O.S.C.B. 6837; Request for Comments: (2002) 25 O.S.C.B. 4705.

Adoption of Amendment to Companion Policy by OSC: (2005) 28 O.S.C.B. 4971 and (Supp-1) 46; Request for Comments: (2004) 27 O.S.C.B. 5157 and (2002) 25 O.S.C.B. 6273.

Adoption of Amendment to Companion Policy by OSC: (2006) 29 O.S.C.B. 8848 and (Supp-1) 1; Request for Comments: (2005) 28 O.S.C.B. (Supp-2) 1 and (2004) 27 O.S.C.B. 465.

Adoption of Amendment to Companion Policy by OSC: (2008) 31 O.S.C.B. 8570 and 6275; Request for Comments: (2007) 30 O.S.C.B. 4965.

Adoption of Amendment to Companion Policy: (2010) 33 O.S.C.B. 11432 and (Supp. 4) 1; Request for Comments: (2009) 32 O.S.C.B. (Supp. 1) 1, (2008) 31 O.S.C.B. 10479, (2007) 30 O.S.C.B. (Supp. 4) 1 and (2003) 26 O.S.C.B. 1443.

Adoption of Amendment to Companion Policy: (2012) 35 O.S.C.B. 3426 and 1375; Request for Comments: (2010) 33 O.S.C.B. 5833.

Adoption of Amendment to Companion Policy: (2013) 36 O.S.C.B. 2619; Request for Comments: (2012) 35 O.S.C.B. 6887.

Adoption of Amendment to Companion Policy: (2014) 37 O.S.C.B. (Supp. 4) 96; Request for Comments: (2013) 36 O.S.C.B. (Supp. 3).

National Instrument 81-104 — Commodity Pools

Date: October 25, 2002, as amended effective June 1, 2005, September 19, 2005, November 1, 2006, March 17, 2008, September 28, 2009, January 1, 2014 and September 22, 2014

25 O.S.C.B. 6997, 28 O.S.C.B. 4973, 28 O.S.C.B. 7184, 29 O.S.C.B. 8849, 31 O.S.C.B. 1009 and (Supp. 2) 255, 32 O.S.C.B. (Supp. 4) 378, 36 O.S.C.B. 9612 and 37 O.S.C.B. (Supp. 4)

Table of Contents

PART 1 — DEFINITIONS, APPLICATION AND INTERPRETATION

1.1 Definitions — (1) In this Instrument

"Canadian Securities Course" means a course prepared and conducted by the Canadian Securities Institute and so named by that Institute as of the date on which this Instrument comes into force, every predecessor to that course, and every successor to that course that does not narrow the scope of the significant subject matter of the course;

"Chartered Financial Analyst Program" means the three level program prepared and conducted by the Association for Investment Management and Research, and so named by that Association as of the date on which this Instrument comes into force, every predecessor to that program, and every successor to that program that does not narrow the scope of the significant subject matter of the program;

"commodity pool" means a mutual fund, other than a precious metals fund, that has adopted fundamental investment objectives that permit it to use or invest in

    (a) specified derivatives in a manner that is not permitted by National Instrument 81-102 *Investment Funds*, or

    (b) physical commodities in a manner that is not permitted by National Instrument 81-102;

"Derivatives Fundamentals Course" means a course prepared and conducted by the Canadian Securities Institute and so named by that Institute as of the date that this Instrument comes into force, every predecessor to that course, and every successor to that course that does not narrow the scope of the significant subject matter of the course;

"independent review committee" means the independent review committee of the investment fund established under National Instrument 81-107 *Independent Review Committee for Investment Funds*;

"mutual fund restricted individual" means an individual registered as a dealing representative of a registered dealer, if the activities of that individual are restricted to trading in securities of mutual funds; and

"precious metals fund" means a mutual fund that has adopted fundamental investment objectives, and received all required regulatory approvals, that permit it to invest in precious metals or in entities that invest in precious metals and that otherwise complies with National Instrument 81-102.

(2) Terms defined in National Instrument 81-102 and used in this Instrument have the respective meanings ascribed to them in National Instrument 81-102.

1.2 **Application** — This Instrument applies only to

    (a) a commodity pool that

        (i) offers, or has offered, securities under a prospectus for so long as the commodity pool remains a reporting issuer, or

        (ii) is filing a preliminary prospectus or its first prospectus; and

    (b) a person or company in respect of activities pertaining to a commodity pool referred to in paragraph (a) or pertaining to the filing of a prospectus to which subsection 3.2(1) applies.

1.3 **Interpretation** — (1) Each section, part, class or series of a class of securities of a commodity pool that is referable to a separate portfolio of assets is considered to be a separate commodity pool for purposes of this Instrument.

(2) For the purposes of a commodity pool complying with section 2.3 of National Instrument 81-102, the definition of the term "public quotation" used in the definition of the term "illiquid asset" in section 1.1 of National Instrument 81-102, includes any quotation of a price for foreign currency forwards and foreign currency options in the interbank market.

PART 2 — INVESTMENT RESTRICTIONS AND PRACTICES

2.1 **Investment Restrictions and Practices** — (1) Section 2.1 of National Instrument 81-102 does not apply to restrict the exposure of a commodity pool to a counterparty of the commodity pool in specified derivatives transactions.

(2) The following provisions of National Instrument 81-102 do not apply to a commodity pool:

    1. Paragraphs 2.3(d), (e), (f), (g) and (h).

    2. Paragraph 2.7(1)(a).

    3. Subsections 2.7(3), (4) and (5).

    4. Sections 2.8 and 2.11.

PART 3 — NEW COMMODITY POOLS

3.1 **Non-Application** — Sections 3.1 and 3.2 of National Instrument 81-102 do not apply to a commodity pool.

3.2 **New Commodity Pools** — (1) No person or company shall file a prospectus for a newly established commodity pool unless

    (a) an investment of at least $50,000 in securities of the commodity pool has been made, and those securities are beneficially owned, before the time of filing by

        (i) the manager, a portfolio adviser, a promoter or a sponsor of the commodity pool,

        (ii) the directors, officers or shareholders of any of the manager, a portfolio adviser, a promoter or a sponsor of the commodity pool, or

        (iii) any combination of the persons or companies referred to in subparagraphs (i) and (ii); and

    (b) the prospectus of the commodity pool states that the commodity pool will not issue securities other than those referred to in paragraph (a) unless subscriptions aggregating not less than $500,000 have been received by the commodity pool from investors other than the persons and companies referred to in subparagraphs (i) and (ii) of paragraph (a) and accepted by the commodity pool.

(2) A commodity pool may redeem, repurchase or return any amount invested in, securities issued upon the investment in the commodity pool referred to in paragraph (1)(a) only if

    (a) securities issued under paragraph (1)(a) that had an aggregate issue price of $50,000 remain outstanding and at least $50,000 invested under paragraph (1)(a) remains invested in the commodity pool; or

    (b) the redemption, repurchase or return is effected as part of the dissolution or termination of the commodity pool.

3.3 **Prohibition Against Distribution** — If a prospectus of a commodity pool contains the disclosure described in paragraph 3.2(1)(b), the commodity pool shall not distribute any securities unless the subscriptions described in that disclosure, together with payment for the securities subscribed for, have been received.

PART 4 — PROFICIENCY AND SUPERVISORY REQUIREMENTS

4.1 **Proficiency and Supervisory Requirements** — (1) No mutual fund restricted individual shall trade in a security of a commodity pool unless that individual

    (a) has received at least a passing grade for the Canadian Securities Course;

    (b) has received at least a passing grade for the Derivatives Fundamentals Course;

    (c) has successfully completed the Chartered Financial Analyst Program; or

    (d) meets the proficiency standards applicable to trading in securities of commodity pools required by a self-regulatory organization of which the individual, or his or her organization, is a member if the securities regulatory authority or regulator has completed any required review, approval or non-disapproval of the regulatory instrument of the self-regulatory organization that establishes those proficiency standards.

(2) No principal distributor or participating dealer shall trade in a security of a commodity pool in the local jurisdiction unless the individual designated by the principal distributor or participating dealer to be responsible for the supervision of trades of securities of commodity pools in the local jurisdiction has received at least a passing grade for the Derivatives Fundamentals Course or has successfully completed the Chartered Financial Analyst Program.

(3) Despite subsection (2), but subject to compliance with securities legislation, a principal distributor may agree to act as principal distributor of a commodity pool and may trade in securities of a commodity pool if all trades are effected through a participating dealer that satisfies the requirements of subsection (2).

PART 5 — INCENTIVE FEES

5.1 **Non-Application** — Part 7 of National Instrument 81-102 does not apply to a commodity pool.

5.2 Incentive Fees — A commodity pool shall not pay, or enter into arrangements that would require it to pay, and no securities of a commodity pool shall be sold on the basis that an investor would be required to pay, a fee that is determined by the performance of the commodity pool, unless

(a) the payment of the fee is based on the cumulative total return of the commodity pool for the period that began immediately after the last period for which the performance fee was paid; and

(b) the method of calculation of the fee is described in the prospectus of the commodity pool.

5.3 Multiple Portfolio Advisors — Section 5.2 applies to fees payable to a portfolio adviser of a commodity pool that has more than one portfolio adviser, if the fees are calculated on the basis of the performance of the portfolio assets under management by that portfolio adviser, as if those portfolio assets were a separate commodity pool.

PART 6 — REDEMPTION OF SECURITIES OF A COMMODITY POOL

6.1 Frequency of Redemptions — If disclosed in its prospectus, a commodity pool may include, as part of the requirements established under subsection 10.1(2) of National Instrument 81-102, a provision that securityholders of the commodity pool shall not have the right to redeem their securities for a period up to six months after the date on which the receipt is issued for the initial prospectus of the commodity pool.

6.2 Required Notice of Redemption — Despite section 10.3 of National Instrument 81-102, a commodity pool may implement a policy providing that a person or company making a redemption order for securities shall receive the net asset value for those securities determined, as provided in the policy, on the first or second business day after the date of receipt by the commodity pool of the redemption order.

6.3 Payment of Redemption Proceeds — The references in subsection 10.4(1) of National Instrument 81-102 to "three business days" shall be read as references to "15 days" in relation to commodity pools.

PART 7 — [REPEALED]

PART 8 — CONTINUOUS DISCLOSURE — FINANCIAL STATEMENTS

8.1–8.4 [repealed]

8.5 Leverage Disclosure — (1) A commodity pool shall include in its interim financial reports and its audited financial statements disclosure of the minimum and maximum level of leverage experienced by the commodity pool in the period covered by the financial statements, together with a brief explanation of how the commodity pool uses the term "leverage" and the significance of the maximum and minimum levels of leverage to the commodity pool.

(2) The information required by subsection (1) may be included in the body of the financial statements or in notes to the financial statements.

PART 9 — [REPEALED]

PART 10 — EXEMPTION

10.1 Exemption — (1) The regulator or the securities regulatory authority may grant an exemption from this Instrument, in whole or in part, subject to such conditions or restrictions as may be imposed in the exemption.

(2) Despite subsection (1), in Ontario, only the regulator may grant such an exemption.

PART 11 — EFFECTIVE DATE AND TRANSITIONAL

11.1 Effective Date — this Instrument comes into force on November 1, 2002.

11.2 Prospectus Disclosure — The prospectus of a commodity pool for which a receipt is obtained before the date that this Instrument comes into force is not required to comply with the disclosure requirements of this Instrument.

Final Rule: (2002) 25 O.S.C.B. 6997; Approval of OSC: (2002) 25 O.S.C.B. 5337; Request for Comments: (2001) 24 O.S.C.B. 7419, (2000) 23 O.S.C.B. 3855 and (1997) 20 O.S.C.B. (Supp 2) 109. Replaced OPS 11.4.

Amendment to Rule: (2005) 28 O.S.C.B. 4973; Approval of OSC: (2005) 28 O.S.C.B. (Supp-1) 50; Request for Comments: (2004) 27 O.S.C.B. 5157; (2002) 25 O.S.C.B. 6273.

Approval of amendment to Rule by OSC: (2005) 28 O.S.C.B. 7184.

Amendment to Rule: (2006) 29 O.S.C.B. 8849; Approval of OSC: (2006) 29 O.S.C.B. (Supp-1) 1; Request for Comments: (2005) 28 O.S.C.B. (Supp-2) 1 and (2004) 27 O.S.C.B. 465.

Amendment to Rule and Approval of OSC: 31 O.S.C.B. 1009.

Amendment to Rule: (2008) 31 O.S.C.B. (Supp. 2) 255; Approval of OSC: 30 O.S.C.B. (Supp. 7) 1 (Dec. 21, 2007); Request for Comments: 29 O.S.C.B. (Supp. 3) 1 (Dec. 22, 2006).

Amendment to Rule: (2009) 32 O.S.C.B. (Supp. 4) 378; Approval by OSC: (2009) 32 O.S.C.B. (Supp. 2) 1; Request for Comments: (2008) 31 O.S.C.B. 68.

Amendment to Rule: (2013) 36 O.S.C.B. 12197; Approval by OSC: (2013) 36 O.S.C.B. 9612; Request for Comments: (2009) 32 O.S.C.B. 8381.

Amendment to Rule: Approval by OSC: (2014) 37 O.S.C.B. (Supp. 4) 128; Request for Comments: (2013) 36 O.S.C.B. (Supp. 3).

Rules: NI 81-106, 81-107.

Part 8: MUTUAL FUNDS

Companion Policy 81-104CP — To National Instrument 81-104 Commodity Pools

PART 1 — PURPOSE AND BACKGROUND

1.1 Purpose — This Policy clarifies how National Instrument 81-104 (the "Instrument") integrates with National Instrument 81-102 *Investment Funds*, and brings certain matters relating to the Instrument to the attention of persons or companies involved with the establishment or administration of commodity pools.

1.2 What the Instrument Covers — (1) The Instrument regulates publicly offered mutual funds that use certain alternative investment strategies involving specified derivatives and commodities. The Instrument defines the term "commodity pool" as a mutual fund that is permitted to use or invest in specified derivatives and physical commodities beyond what is permitted by National Instrument 81-102. Industry players refer to these mutual funds as "commodity pools" and the members of the Canadian Securities Administrators that have implemented the Instrument (the "CSA") have retained this term to describe these mutual funds.

(2) The CSA note that the Instrument specifically allows commodity pools liberalized use of derivatives, leverage strategies and commodities so that they can pursue traditional commodity pool investment strategies. By implementing the Instrument, the CSA are not providing relief for all alternative investment strategies that may be adopted by investment funds. In particular, the CSA point out that a number of strategies, including non derivative-related short selling, cannot be followed by commodity pools and other mutual funds due to prohibitions contained in National Instrument 81-102. A person or company that wishes to sell to the public investment funds that use alternative investment strategies not contemplated by the Instrument should consider using available exemptions from prospectus requirements or structuring the fund as a closed end investment fund. The CSA will consider on a case by case basis applications for exemptions from applicable restrictions contained in National Instrument 81-102 if a mutual fund structure is proposed. Any application for exemption should describe how the proposed alternative investment strategy meets the policy goals behind the rules in National Instrument 81-102 and why a mutual fund structure is in the public interest.

1.3 Background to the Instrument — The CSA developed the Instrument in order to create an updated uniform national regulatory regime for commodity pools. Commodity pools have been sold in most jurisdictions in Canada under prospectuses filed with the CSA for over twenty years. The Ontario Securities Commission published a policy statement, OSC Policy Statement 11.4 Commodity Pool Programs, to set parameters for the operation and administration of these investment vehicles. The other members of the CSA regulated commodity pools through exemptive orders giving relief, on conditions, from requirements of applicable securities legislation in their jurisdiction, including National Instrument 81-102 and its predecessor instrument. The exemptive relief orders were largely consistent with the guidelines contained in the Ontario policy statement. The Ontario Securities Commission and the other members of the CSA that have implemented the Instrument recognize that the Ontario policy statement has become outmoded and no longer reflects the regulatory approach now favoured by the CSA.

1.4 Regulatory Principles for Commodity Pools — (1) The CSA considered the following regulatory principles in developing and implementing the Instrument:

    (a) Commodity pools should be regulated in the same manner as conventional mutual funds, except in respect of their use of specified derivatives and leverage strategies. Therefore, commodity pools are defined in the Instrument as a type of mutual fund, so that the rules of National Instrument 81-102, and other applicable securities legislation apply except as provided otherwise in the Instrument.

    (b) Commodity pools should be granted greater freedom in their use of specified derivatives and leverage strategies than conventional mutual funds, in exchange for requirements which, among other things, are aimed at increasing the information available to investors about the investment strategies, risks and on-going performance of commodity pools. Therefore, the Instrument generally exempts commodity pools from the specified derivative rules of National Instrument 81-102.

PART 2 — GENERAL STRUCTURE OF THE INSTRUMENT

2.1 Relationship to Securities Legislation Applicable to Mutual Funds — (1) Since by definition, commodity pools are mutual funds, they are subject to mutual fund rules unless those rules are specifically excluded. The Instrument contains only those provisions that are specific to commodity pools. Provisions applicable to all mutual funds, including commodity pools, are contained in National Instrument 81-102.

(2) Persons involved with the establishment or administration of a commodity pool should review the following rules:

    1. National Instrument 81-102. That National Instrument contains general rules concerning the operation of mutual funds, all of which are applicable to commodity pools unless specifically excluded by the Instrument.

    2. Applicable mutual fund related securities legislation. For example, commodity pools are subject to the financial statement reporting requirements for mutual funds, except as varied or supplemented in the Instrument.

3. Prospectus requirements of the securities legislation of a jurisdiction applicable to long form issuers generally, and mutual funds in particular. National Instrument 81-101 *Mutual Fund Prospectus Disclosure* does not allow commodity pools to use the prospectus disclosure system created by that National Instrument.

4. Securities legislation of a jurisdiction that applies to dealers in securities of a mutual fund. Since commodity pools are mutual funds, dealers registered in a jurisdiction to sell mutual funds can trade in these securities. The Instrument imposes additional proficiency requirements for salespersons who are registered to sell only mutual funds and for the supervisors of trades in commodity pools.

2.2 **Derivatives Use** — (1) The regime implemented by the Instrument is designed to allow commodity pools considerable freedom in entering into derivatives transactions. Commodity pools are not subject to the majority of sections 2.7 and 2.8 of National Instrument 81-102, which contain most of the rules governing specified derivatives used by mutual funds. Commodity pools, however, remain subject to the main investment restrictions and rules governing investment practices contained in National Instrument 81-102 that do not relate directly to derivatives or commodity transactions.

(2) Commodity pools remain generally subject to section 2.1 of National Instrument 81-102 except as provided in subsection 2.1(1) of the Instrument. Section 2.1 of National Instrument 81-102 contains the prohibition against a mutual fund investing more than 10 percent of its net assets in the securities of an issuer. The effect of subsection 2.1(1) of the Instrument is that a commodity pool need not be restricted by this prohibition in relation to its specified derivatives transactions with any one counterparty. That is, a commodity pool may "invest" more than 10 percent of its net assets with any one counterparty in one or more specified derivatives transactions. This exception to the 10 percent rule is designed to allow commodity pools greater flexibility in their specified derivatives transactions. However, a commodity pool remains subject to the 10 percent rule in relation to any securities of any issuers, including counterparties, other than the "securities" acquired from counterparties in specified derivatives transactions. A commodity pool may enter into an unlimited number of specified derivatives transactions with any counterparty without regard to the 10 percent rule, but remains subject to the 10 percent rule in relation to any, for example, common shares of that counterparty acquired by it. In addition, the "look through" rule contained in subsection 2.1(3) of National Instrument 81-102 will still apply to those specified derivatives transactions, requiring a commodity pool to take into account the underlying interests of specified derivatives transactions in order to ensure compliance with section 2.1 of National Instrument 81-102.

(3) Commodity pools, as with other mutual funds, remain subject to paragraphs 2.6(b) and (c) of National Instrument 81-102, which prohibit mutual funds from purchasing securities on margin or selling securities short, unless these strategies are permitted by sections 2.7 or 2.8 of that National Instrument. Commodity pools contemplating purchasing securities on margin or selling securities short in connection with their specified derivatives strategies should review sections 2.7 and 2.8 of National Instrument 81-102 to determine permissible practices. Any other strategy which involves purchasing securities on margin or selling securities short is not permitted for commodity pools, in the same manner as that other strategy is not permitted for conventional mutual funds. The Instrument exempts commodity pools from most of the provisions of sections 2.7 or 2.8 of National Instrument 81-102, but is not intended to remove the permission to purchase securities on margin or sell securities short in specified derivatives transactions provided for in paragraphs 2.6(b) and (c) of National Instrument 81-102.

PART 3 — [REPEALED]

PART 4 — LIMITED LIABILITY

4.1 **Limited Liability** — (1) Mutual funds generally are structured in a manner that ensures that investors are not exposed to the risk of loss of an amount more than their original investment. The CSA consider this a very important and essential attribute of mutual funds. This is especially important in the context of commodity pools. One of the most important rationales for the existence of commodity pools is that they enable investors to invest indirectly in certain types of derivative products, particularly futures and forwards, without putting more than the amount of their investment at risk. A direct investment in some derivative products could expose an investor to losses beyond the original investment.

(2) The CSA expect that commodity pools will be structured in a manner that provides as much assurance as possible to their securityholders that securityholders will not be at risk for more than the amount of their original investment. The CSA recommend that commodity pool promoters and managers consider other ways, apart from the structuring of a pool, to limit the liability of securityholders. For example, commodity pools could enter into contracts only if the other party to the agreement agreed to limit recourse under the agreement to the assets of the pool.

(3) Mutual funds structured as corporations do not raise pressing liability problems because of the limited liability regime of corporate statutes.

(4) Mutual funds structured as limited partnerships may raise some concerns about the loss of limited liability if limited partners are viewed as participating in the management or control of the partnership. The statute and case law concerning when limited partners can lose their limited partner status, including the Quebec Civil Code, varies from province to province. The risks associated with this type of structure in the jurisdictions where the prospectus is filed should be disclosed.

(5) Mutual funds structured as trusts are subject to their constitution and the common and civil law of trusts. A commodity pool operator should consider this law, together with the factual circumstances surrounding the establishment of the commodity pool, including the ability of the investors in the commodity pool to influence the administration and management of the commodity pool, to ensure that investors' liability is limited to the amount they have invested in the commodity pool. If applicable, a commodity pool should disclose in the prospectus the risks associated with the structuring of a commodity pool as a trust in relation to the possibility that purchasers of securities of the commodity pool may become liable to make an additional contribution beyond the price of the securities.

Adoption by OSC: (2002) 25 O.S.C.B. 6997 and 5337; Request for Comments: (2001) 24 O.S.C.B. 7419, (2000) 23 O.S.C.B. 3855 and (1997) 20 O.S.C.B. (Supp 2) 109.

Adoption of Amendment by OSC: (2005) 28 O.S.C.B. 4974 and (2005) 28 O.S.C.B. (Supp-1) 50; Request for Comments: (2004) 27 O.S.C.B. 5157 and (2002) 25 O.S.C.B. 6273.

Adoption of Amendment by OSC: (2008) 31 O.S.C.B. 1009.

Adoption of Amendment by OSC: (2014) 37 O.S.C.B. (Supp. 4) 129.

National Instrument 81-105 — Mutual Fund Sales Practices

Date: **May 1, 1998, as amended effective September 28, 2009 and September 22, 2014**

21 O.S.C.B. 2713, 32 O.S.C.B. (Supp. 4) 378 and 37 O.S.C.B. (Supp. 4)

Table of Contents

PART 1 — DEFINITIONS, INTERPRETATION AND APPLICATION

1.1 Definitions — In this Instrument

"direct costs" means reasonable, out-of-pocket costs and expenses directly attributable to

    (a) the production and presentation of a sales communication referred to in Part 5, or

    (b) the presentation and organization of a conference or seminar referred to in Part 5, other than any travel, accommodation or personal incidental expenses associated with the attendance of an individual at the conference or seminar;

"equity interest" means, in relation to an issuer,

    (a) if the issuer is a reporting issuer in any jurisdiction and its securities are listed on a Canadian stock exchange, the direct or indirect ownership of securities representing more than ten percent of any class of voting securities, equity securities or partnership units of the issuer, or

    (b) for all other issuers, the direct or indirect ownership of a voting security, equity security or partnership unit of the issuer;

"equity security" means a security of an issuer that carries a residual right to participate in the earnings of the issuer and, upon the liquidation or winding up of the issuer, in the distribution of its assets;

"IDA" means the Investment Dealers Association of Canada;

"IFIC" means The Investment Funds institute of Canada;

"member of the organization" means, for a mutual fund

(a) the manager of the mutual fund,

(b) the principal distributor of the mutual fund,

(c) the portfolio adviser of the mutual fund,

(d) an affiliate of any of the persons or companies referred to in paragraph (a), (b) or (c), or

(e) a person or company that is organized by a member of the organization of the mutual fund as a vehicle to fund payment of commissions to participating dealers and that has a right to arrange for the distribution of the securities of the mutual fund;

"mutual fund family" means two or more mutual funds that have

(a) the same manager, or

(b) managers that are affiliates of each other; and

"representative" means, for a participating dealer,

(a) a partner, director, officer or employee of the participating dealer,

(b) an individual who trades securities on behalf of the participating dealer, whether or not the individual is employed by the dealer, and

(c) any company through which a person referred to in paragraphs (a) or (b) carries on activities in connection with services provided to the participating dealer.

1.2 Interpretation — Terms defined in National Instrument 81-102 *Investment Funds* and used in this Instrument have the respective meanings ascribed to them in National Instrument 81-102 *Investment Funds*.

1.3 Application — This Instrument applies to

(a) a distribution of securities of a mutual fund that offers or has offered securities under a prospectus or simplified prospectus for so long as the mutual fund remains a reporting issuer; and

(b) a person or company in respect of activities pertaining to a mutual fund referred to in paragraph (a).

PART 2 — GENERAL

2.1 Restrictions on Payments or Provision of Benefits — (1) No member of the organization of a mutual fund and no mutual fund shall, in connection with the distribution of securities of the mutual fund

(a) make a payment of money to a participating dealer or a representative of a participating dealer;

(b) provide a non-monetary benefit to a participating dealer or a representative of a participating dealer; or

(c) pay for or make reimbursement of a cost or expense incurred or to be incurred by a participating dealer or a representative of a participating dealer.

(2) Despite subsection (1), a member of the organization of a mutual fund may

(a) make a payment of money or provide a non-monetary benefit to a participating dealer, or pay for or make reimbursement of a cost or expense incurred or to be incurred by a participating dealer or its representatives, if permitted by Part 3 or 5; and

(b) provide a non-monetary benefit to a representative of a participating dealer, if permitted by Part 5.

(3) A member of the organization of a mutual fund shall not, and shall not represent that it may, make a payment, provide a non-monetary benefit or pay for or make reimbursement of a cost or expense otherwise permitted by subsection (2) that is conditional on

(a) the sale of a particular amount or value of securities of one or more mutual funds by a participating dealer or a representative; or

(b) a particular amount or value of securities of one or more mutual funds being held in accounts of clients of a participating dealer or a representative.

2.2 Restrictions on Solicitation and Acceptance of Payments or Benefits — (1) No participating dealer and no representative of a participating dealer shall solicit or accept from a mutual fund or a member of the organization of the mutual fund, in connection with the distribution of securities of the mutual fund, the payment of money, the provision of a non-monetary benefit or payment or reimbursement for a cost or expense incurred or to be incurred by the participating dealer or representatives of the participating dealer.

(2) Despite subsection (1),

(a) a participating dealer may solicit and accept a payment of money, provision of a non-monetary benefit or payment or reimbursement for a cost or expense incurred or to be incurred by it or its representatives from a member of the organization of the mutual fund, if the member is permitted by Part 3 or 5 to make the payment, provide the benefit or make the payment or reimbursement; and

(b) a representative of a participating dealer may accept the provision of a non-monetary benefit from a member of the organization of the mutual fund, if the member is permitted by Part 5 to provide the benefit.

2.3 Application of Instrument to Some Participating Dealers or Representatives — (1) Nothing in this Instrument prohibits a person or company that is both a member of the organization of a mutual fund and a participating dealer of a mutual fund in a different mutual fund family from undertaking any activity, if

(a) the activity is undertaken in the person or company's capacity as a participating dealer of the mutual fund of which it is a participating dealer, and not in its capacity as a member of the organization of the mutual fund of which it is a member; and

(b) a participating dealer is not prohibited by this Instrument from undertaking that activity.

(2) Nothing in this Instrument prohibits a representative of a participating dealer that is also a member of the organization of a mutual fund from soliciting or accepting any payment, non-monetary benefit or reimbursement otherwise permitted by this Instrument from the participating dealer, if the payment, provision of the non-monetary benefit or reimbursement is made in the participating dealer's capacity as a participating dealer and not in its capacity as a member of the organization of a mutual fund.

PART 3 — PERMITTED COMPENSATION

3.1 Commissions — A member of the organization of a mutual fund may pay to a participating dealer a commission in money for the distribution of a security of the mutual fund made through the participating dealer, if

(a) the obligation to make the payment arises at the time of the trade;

(b) the prospectus or simplified prospectus of the mutual fund discloses the range of rates of commissions that may be paid and the method of calculation used in determining the amount of those commissions; and

(c) the rate of the commission does not increase

(i) based on increases in the amount or value of securities of the mutual fund sold, or of mutual funds in the same mutual fund family as the mutual fund sold, or of any or all of the foregoing,

(ii) based on increases in the amount or value of securities of the mutual fund, or of mutual funds in the same mutual fund family as the mutual fund, or of any or all of the foregoing, held in accounts of clients of the participating dealer, or

(iii) for a particular period of the year in which the commission is paid or earned.

3.2 Trailing Commissions — (1) A member of the organization of a mutual fund may pay to a participating dealer a trailing commission in money that is based upon the aggregate value of securities of the mutual fund held in accounts of clients of the participating dealer as at a particular time or during a particular period, if

(a) the obligation to make the payment arises after the time of the trade;

(b) the prospectus or simplified prospectus of the mutual fund discloses the range of rates of trailing commissions that may be paid and the method of calculation and relevant times or time periods used in determining the amount of those trailing commissions;

(c) the method and time of calculation of the trailing commission and the relevant times or time periods used in determining the amount of the trailing commission are the same for all participating dealers of the mutual fund; and

(d) the rate of the trailing commission does not increase

(i) based on increases in the amount or value of securities of the mutual fund sold, or of mutual funds in the same mutual fund family as the mutual fund sold, or of any or all of the foregoing,

(ii) based on increases in the amount or value of securities of the mutual fund, or of mutual funds in the same mutual fund family as the mutual fund, or of any or all of the foregoing, held in accounts of clients of the participating dealer, or

(iii) for a particular period of the year in which the trailing commission is paid or earned.

(2) A member of the organization of a mutual fund may establish policies and practices concerning the timing of payments of trailing commissions so long as all trailing commissions are paid within one year from the date earned.

(3) Despite subsection (1), a member of the organization of a mutual fund may decline to pay a trailing commission to a participating dealer in connection with securities of the mutual fund held in the accounts of clients of the participating dealer if

(a) the securities in respect of which no trailing commission is paid were acquired by those clients before the date that this Instrument came into force;

(b) the amount of securities held in the accounts of those clients is below a threshold specified in the policy referred to in paragraph (c); and

(c) the non-payment of the trailing commission is in conformity with a policy of the member of the organization of the mutual fund that was in place and was followed on July 1, 1997.

PART 4 — INTERNAL DEALER INCENTIVE PRACTICES

4.1 Participating Dealers' Practices — (1) No participating dealer shall provide an incentive to any of its representatives to recommend mutual funds of one mutual fund family over mutual funds of another mutual fund family.

(2) Despite subsection (1), the compensation paid to a representative of a participating dealer by the participating dealer may reflect commissions received by the participating dealer from members of the organizations of mutual funds, so long as the compensation paid to a representative for the securities of a mutual fund sold or held, as a percentage of the commission paid to the participating dealer, is the same for all mutual fund families.

4.2 Principal Distributors' Practices — (1) A principal distributor of a mutual fund that is also a participating dealer of another mutual fund shall not provide an incentive for any of its representatives to recommend a mutual fund of which it is a principal distributor over a mutual fund of which it is a participating dealer.

(2) Despite subsection (1), the compensation paid to a representative of a principal distributor by the principal distributor may reflect commissions received by the principal distributor from members of the organization of which it is a member and members of organizations of other mutual funds if

(a) the compensation paid to a representative for the securities of a mutual fund sold or held, as a percentage of the commission paid to the principal distributor, is the same for all mutual fund families, including the mutual fund family of the principal distributor; and

(b) the commissions paid to the principal distributor in connection with the distribution of securities of a mutual fund of which it is a principal distributor are not in excess of the commissions provided to any participating dealer in connection with the distribution of those securities.

PART 5 — MARKETING AND EDUCATIONAL PRACTICES

5.1 Cooperative Marketing Practices — A member of the organization of a mutual fund may pay, to a participating dealer, direct costs incurred by the participating dealer relating to a sales communication, investor conference or investor seminar prepared or presented by the participating dealer, if

(a) the primary purpose of the sales communication, investor conference or investor seminar is to promote, or provide educational information concerning, the mutual fund, the mutual fund family of which the mutual fund is a member or mutual funds generally;

(b) in the case of an investor conference or investor seminar, the conference or seminar is presented by the participating dealer to investors or potential investors of the mutual fund, another mutual fund in the same mutual fund family, or of mutual funds generally;

(c) the participating dealer provides invoices for, or receipts evidencing payment of, the direct costs to be paid by a member of the organization of the mutual fund;

(d) the aggregate direct costs of the sales communication, investor conference or investor seminar paid by all members of organizations of mutual funds do not exceed 50 percent of the total direct costs incurred by the participating dealer; and

(e) the sales communication discloses, or persons attending the investor conference or investor seminar are informed in writing of, the identity of all parties paying for a portion of the costs of the sales communication, investor conference or investor seminar.

5.2 Mutual Fund Sponsored Conferences — A member of the organization of a mutual fund may provide a non-monetary benefit to a representative of a participating dealer by allowing him or her to attend a conference or seminar organized and presented by members of the organization of the mutual fund, if

(a) the primary purpose of the conference or seminar is the provision of educational information about financial planning, investing in securities, mutual fund industry matters, the mutual fund, the mutual fund family of which the mutual fund is a member or mutual funds generally;

(b) the selection of the representatives of the participating dealer to attend the conference or seminar is made exclusively by the participating dealer, uninfluenced by any member of the organization of the mutual fund;

(c) the conference or seminar is held in

(i) Canada,

(ii) the continental United States of America, or

(iii) a location where a portfolio adviser of the mutual fund carries on business, if the primary purpose of the conference or seminar is the provision of educational information about the investments or activities of the mutual fund carried on by that portfolio adviser;

(d) no member of the organization of the mutual fund pays any travel, accommodation or personal incidental expenses associated with the attendance of the representative at the conference or seminar; and

(e) the costs relating to the organization and presentation of the conference or seminar are reasonable having regard to the purpose of the conference or seminar.

5.3 Third Party Sponsored Educational Events — A member of the organization of a mutual fund may, for a conference, seminar or course that is organized and presented by a person or company that is not member of the organization of the mutual fund or a participating dealer, pay the registration fees of a representative of a participating dealer for the conference, seminar or course, if

(a) the primary purpose of the conference, seminar or course is the provision of educational information about financial planning, investing in securities, mutual fund industry matters or mutual funds generally;

(b) the participating dealer provides invoices for or receipts evidencing payment of the registration fees to be paid by a member of the organization of the mutual fund;

(c) the selection of the representatives of the participating dealer to attend the conference, seminar or course is made exclusively by the participating dealer, uninfluenced by any member of the organization of the mutual fund; and

(d) the conference, seminar or course is held in Canada or the continental United States of America.

5.4 Industry Association Sponsored Events — (1) Except as permitted by section 5.3 or subsection (2), no member of the organization of a mutual fund may pay money, provide non-monetary benefits or pay or reimburse costs or expenses relating to a conference, seminar or course that is organized and presented by IFIC, the IDA or another trade or industry association.

(2) A member of the organization of a mutual fund may pay, to IFIC, the IDA or their respective affiliates or associates, direct costs incurred by IFIC, the IDA or their respective affiliates or associates relating to a conference or seminar organized and presented by IFIC, the IDA or their respective affiliates or associates, if

(a) the primary purpose of the conference or seminar is the provision of educational information about financial planning, investing in securities, mutual fund industry matters or mutual funds generally;

(b) the members of the organization of mutual funds in a mutual fund family in aggregate pay not more than 10 percent of the total direct costs incurred by IFIC, the IDA or their respective affiliates or associates for the organization and presentation of the conference or seminar;

(c) the selection of the representatives of a participating dealer to attend the conference or seminar is made exclusively by the participating dealer, uninfluenced by any member of the organization of the mutual fund; and

(d) the conference or seminar is held in Canada or the continental United States of America.

5.5 Participating Dealer Sponsored Events — A member of the organization of a mutual fund may pay, to a participating dealer, direct costs incurred by the participating dealer relating to a conference or seminar that is organized and presented by the participating dealer, and that is not an investor conference or investor seminar referred to in section 5.1, if

(a) the primary purpose of the conference or seminar is the provision of educational information about financial planning, investing in securities, mutual fund industry matters, the mutual fund, the mutual fund family of which the mutual fund is a member or mutual funds generally;

(b) the members of the organization of mutual funds in a mutual fund family in aggregate pay not more than 10 percent of the total direct costs incurred by the participating dealer for the organization and presentation of the conference or seminar;

(c) the aggregate direct costs of the conference or seminar paid by all members of organizations of mutual funds do not exceed 66 percent of the total direct costs incurred by the participating dealer;

(d) the selection of the representatives of the participating dealer to attend the conference or seminar is made exclusively by the participating dealer, uninfluenced by any member of the organization of the mutual fund; and

(e) the conference or seminar is held in

(i) Canada,

(ii) the continental United States of America, or

(iii) a location where a portfolio adviser of the mutual fund carries on business, if the primary purpose of the conference or seminar is the provision of educational information about the investments or activities of the mutual fund carried on by that portfolio adviser.

5.6 Promotional Items and Business Promotion Activities — A member of the organization of a mutual fund may provide to a representative of a participating dealer non-monetary benefits of a promotional nature and of minimal value, and a member of the organization of a mutual fund may engage in business promotion activities that result in a representative of a participating dealer receiving a non-monetary benefit if

(a) the provision of the benefits and activities is neither so extensive nor so frequent as to cause a reasonable person to question whether the provision of the benefits or activities improperly influence the investment advice given by the representative to his or her clients; and

(b) in the case of business promotion activities, no member of the organization of the mutual fund pays the travel, accommodation or personal incidental expenses associated with the attendance of the representative at the activities.

PART 6 — PORTFOLIO TRANSACTIONS

6.1 Reciprocal Commissions and Portfolio Transactions — (1) No member of the organization of a mutual fund shall influence or attempt to influence how, or if, a participating dealer will pay or allocate in a particular manner to any representative all or part of a brokerage commission or of an amount representing the spread on a principal transaction arising from a portfolio transaction of the mutual fund executed by the participating dealer.

(2) No member of the organization of a mutual fund shall direct a portfolio transaction of a mutual fund to a participating dealer or principal distributor of the mutual fund except through individuals designated by the participating dealer or principal distributor as the institutional representatives of the participating dealer or principal distributor.

(3) No member of the organization of a mutual fund shall advise a representative of a participating dealer or a person or company employed by a principal distributor, other than an individual referred to in subsection (2), of a portfolio transaction of the mutual fund to be directed to the participating dealer or principal distributor.

(4) No member of the organization of a mutual fund shall direct, or offer or agree to direct, a portfolio transaction of the mutual fund to a participating dealer or principal distributor as inducement or reward for the participating dealer or principal distributor selling or having sold securities of the mutual fund or maintaining or having maintained particular levels of securities of the mutual fund in accounts of clients.

(5) No participating dealer shall solicit or execute portfolio transactions of a mutual fund as inducement or reward for the participating dealer selling, or having sold, securities of the mutual fund or maintaining, or having maintained, particular levels of securities of the mutual fund in accounts of clients.

6.2 Obligations of Participating Dealers Executing Portfolio Transactions — No participating dealer shall execute a portfolio transaction of a mutual fund unless it has been directed to the participating dealer through an individual designated by the participating dealer as an institutional representative of the participating dealer.

PART 7 — OTHER SALES PRACTICES

7.1 Commission Rebates — (1) A participating dealer or representative of a participating dealer may pay all or part of a fee or commission payable by a securityholder on the redemption of securities of a mutual fund that occurs in connection with the purchase by the securityholder of securities of a mutual fund in a different mutual fund family, only if

(a) the participating dealer, or a representative on behalf of the participating dealer, before taking any steps in connection with the redemption, provides the securityholder with written disclosure of the matters described in subsection (2) and obtains the written consent of the securityholder to the completion of the redemption; and

(b) the participating dealer is not a member of the organization of the mutual fund the securities of which are being acquired.

(2) The written disclosure referred to in subsection (1) shall include

(a) a reasonable estimate of the amount of the fee or commission being paid by the participating dealer on the redemption;

(b) a reasonable estimate of the amount of the redemption charges to which the securityholder will be subject in connection with the securities of the mutual fund being acquired, expressed both as dollar amounts and as percentages of the value of the securities being redeemed, and the times at which those charges would be made; and

(c) the tax consequences of the redemption.

(3) No member of the organization of a mutual fund, other than a member that is also a participating dealer acting in compliance with subsection (1), shall pay to any person or company all or part of a fee or commission payable by a securityholder on the redemption of securities of another mutual fund that is not in the same mutual fund family.

7.2 Financial Assistance — (1) No member of the organization of a mutual fund shall provide financial assistance to a participating dealer of the mutual fund, a representative of the participating dealer or their respective associates or affiliates.

(2) No participating dealer and no representative of a participating dealer of a mutual fund shall solicit or accept financial assistance from a member of the organization of the mutual fund.

(3) Subsections (1) and (2) do not apply to financial assistance provided by

(a) a Canadian financial institution in the ordinary course of its business, if no conditions to the provision of the financial assistance promote the distribution of securities of particular mutual funds; or

(b) affiliates.

7.3 Charitable Donations — (1) No member of the organization of a mutual fund shall make a charitable donation if the tax credit or deduction arising from the donation benefits a participating dealer, a representative of a participating dealer or a person or company that is an associate or affiliate of a participating dealer or of a representative of a participating dealer.

(2) Subsection (1) does not apply to a charitable donation made by a member of the organization of a mutual fund if the tax credit or deduction arising from the donation benefits an affiliate of the member of the organization of the mutual fund.

7.4 Tied Selling — No person or company shall require another person or company

(a) to invest in securities of a particular mutual fund or mutual fund family, either as a condition or on terms that appear to a reasonable person to be a condition, of supplying or continuing to supply products or services; or

(b) to purchase or use any products or services, either as a condition or on terms that appear to a reasonable person to be a condition, of selling securities of a particular mutual fund or mutual fund family.

PART 8 — PROSPECTUS AND POINT OF SALE DISCLOSURE

8.1 Disclosure of Sales Practices — (1) A mutual fund shall provide in its prospectus or simplified prospectus a complete description of

(a) all compensation payable by members of the organization of the mutual fund to all principal distributors and participating dealers of the mutual fund; and

(b) the sales practices followed by the members of the organization of the mutual fund for distribution of securities of the mutual fund.

8.2 Disclosure of Equity Interests — (1) A mutual fund shall disclose in its prospectus or simplified prospectus the amount of any equity interest that

(a) a member of the organization of the mutual fund has in a participating dealer;

(b) a participating dealer and associates of the participating dealer, in aggregate, have in any member of the organization of the mutual fund; and

(c) a representative of a participating dealer and associates of the representative, in aggregate, have in any member of the organization of the mutual fund.

(2) If a member of the organization of a mutual fund is not a reporting issuer and the securities of the member are not listed on a Canadian stock exchange, the mutual fund is not required to provide the disclosure required by paragraph (1)(c) if it discloses

(a) the aggregate equity interests held by all representatives of a participating dealer and their respective associates in the member of the organization of the mutual fund; and

(b) the equity interests held by a representative of a participating dealer and associates of the representative if the representative and his or her associates have direct or indirect ownership of securities representing more than five percent of any class of voting securities, equity securities or partnership units of the member of the organization of the mutual fund.

(3) For each trade of a security of a mutual fund that is required to make any of the disclosure described in this section, a participating dealer shall deliver to the purchaser a document that discloses the amount of any equity interest that

(a) a member of the organization of the mutual fund has in the participating dealer;

(b) the participating dealer and its associates, in aggregate, have in any member of the organization of the mutual fund;

(c) the representatives of the participating dealer and associates of those representatives, in aggregate, have in any member of the organization of the mutual fund; and

(d) the representative of the participating dealer that is acting on the trade, and associates of the representative, in aggregate, have in any member of the organization of the mutual fund.

(4) No participating dealer shall complete a trade to which subsection (3) applies unless the participating dealer obtains the prior written consent of the purchaser to the completion of the trade after the purchaser has received the document required by subsection (3).

(5) A participating dealer is not required to comply with subsections (3) and (4) for a trade if the purchaser in the trade has already been provided with a document under subsection (3) on a previous trade and the information contained in the document has not changed.

8.3 Disclosure Requirements If No Prospectus or Simplified Prospectus — A mutual fund that does not have a current prospectus or simplified prospectus shall prepare a document containing the information required by this Instrument to be provided in a prospectus or simplified prospectus and deliver, or cause to be delivered, a copy of the document to each purchaser of securities of the mutual fund at or before the time of the applicable trade in securities of the mutual fund, other than a trade in connection with a dividend reinvestment plan of the mutual fund.

PART 9 — EXEMPTION

9.1 Exemption — (1) The regulator or securities regulatory authority may grant an exemption to this Instrument, in whole or in part, subject to such conditions or restrictions as may be imposed in the exemption.

(2) Despite subsection (1), in Ontario, only the securities regulatory authority may grant such an exemption.

PART 10 — TRANSITIONAL

10.1 Effective Date — This Instrument comes into force on May 1, 1998.

10.2 Prospectus Disclosure — The prospectus of a mutual fund for which a receipt is obtained before the date that this Instrument comes into force is not required to comply with the disclosure requirements of this Instrument.

Final Rule: (1998) 21 O.S.C.B. 2713; Approval by Minister: (1998) 21 O.S.C.B. 2108; Approval by OSC: (1998) 21 O.S.C.B. 747; Request for Comments: (1997) 20 O.S.C.B 3879 and (1996) 19 O.S.C.B. 4727.

Amendment to Rule: (2009) 32 O.S.C.B. (Supp. 4) 378; Approval by OSC: (2009) 32 O.S.C.B. (Supp. 2) 1.

Amendment to Rule: Approval by OSC: (2014) 37 O.S.C.B. (Supp. 4); Request for Comments: (2013) 36 O.S.C.B. (Supp. 3).

Policies and Orders: OSCN 81-707, 11-760.

Companion Policy 81-105CP — To National Instrument 81-105 Mutual Fund Sales Practices

Table of Contents

PART 1 — PURPOSE

1.1 **Purpose** — The purpose of this Policy is to state the views of the Canadian securities regulatory authorities on various matters relating to National Instrument 81-105 Mutual Fund Sales Practices (the "Instrument"), including

(a) a discussion of the general approach taken by the Canadian securities regulatory authorities in, and the general regulatory purpose for, the Instrument;

(b) the interpretation of various terms used in the Instrument; and

(c) examples of some of the matters described in the Instrument.

PART 2 — GENERAL DISCUSSION OF THE INSTRUMENT

2.1 **Background** — (1) The Instrument has been adopted by the Canadian securities regulatory authorities as a response to the concern of many participants in the mutual fund industry that the pre-existing regulatory strategy of reliance on prospectus disclosure of sales practices, coupled with the discipline imposed by competitive market forces, were not sufficient to discourage sales practices and compensation arrangements that gave rise to questions as to whether participating dealers and their representatives were being induced to sell mutual fund securities on the basis of the incentives they were receiving as opposed to what was suitable for and in the best interests of their clients.

(2) Mutual fund sales practices have been of interest and concern to the Canadian securities regulatory authorities and the mutual fund industry for a number of years. In August 1991, The Investment Funds Institute of Canada ("IFIC") issued its report on mutual fund sales incentives (the "1991 IFIC Report"). The 1991 IFIC Report was followed by the release, in October 1991, of the IFIC Code of Conduct (the "1991 IFIC Code") dealing with sales incentives.

The 1991 IFIC Code required enhanced disclosure of sales incentives offered as compensation for sales of mutual fund securities and also required that investors in mutual funds be provided with a separate "point-of-sale" disclosure statement advising investors of the sales incentives applicable to the purchase.

(3) A substantial review of the investment fund industry was undertaken by Ontario Securities Commission ("OSC") Commissioner Glorianne Stromberg at the request of the OSC in February 1994. Her report *Regulatory Strategies for the Mid-'90s — Recommendations for Regulating Investment Funds in Canada"*, was prepared for the Canadian Securities Administrators ("CSA") and released in January 1995.

(4) Commissioner Stromberg noted in her report that as a result of competitive pressures "questionable sales practices and incentives have become commonplace in the industry". She concluded that the regulatory strategy referred to in subsection (1) above would be an appropriate regulatory strategy if certain recommended fundamental changes were made to the regulation of sales practices.[1]

(5) In response to Commissioner Stromberg's report, IFIC, after extensive industry consultation, released its recommendations for a Code of Sales Practices for the Mutual Fund Industry dated March 29, 1996 (the "IFIC Code").[2] The IFIC Code stated in its preamble:

> The Draft Code is designed to establish the industry standard of conduct and to reflect its concern for investor protection. The sales practices suggested in the Draft Code are designed to align the interests of the principal parties to the transaction, *i.e.* the investor, fund manager and, where applicable, third party fund distributor firm and salesperson, and to encourage long term relationships among them. If implemented, the Draft Code would prohibit many sales practices which could result in conflicts of interest between the interests of an investor and those of the distributor firm, its salespersons and a fund manager. IFIC believes that it is important, in the case of sales practices permitted under the Draft Code, that there be full disclosure of the sales practice in order that an investor is fully informed of the circumstances surrounding investment in mutual funds.

(6) In the absence of a self-regulatory organization which could adopt the IFIC Code as a regulation applicable to all distributors of securities of mutual funds, IFIC recommended that the provisions of the IFIC Code be reflected in rules of the Canadian securities regulatory authorities. This request was endorsed by the Investment Funds Steering Group.[3]

(7) The Instrument is based on, and in Ontario, is an amended version of, a proposed Ontario rule regarding mutual fund sales practices (the "Ontario Draft Rule") published for comment in Ontario on August 30, 1996 at (1996), 19 OSCB 4734. The Ontario Draft Rule reflected the approach taken in the IFIC Code and also reflected certain of the by-laws and rules of the IDA. This Instrument reflects the discussions of the Canadian securities regulatory authorities of comments received in Ontario in respect of the Ontario Draft Rule. The Canadian securities regulatory authorities have made the Instrument in order to make mandatory, on an industry-wide basis across Canada, restrictions on certain sales and business practices followed by participants in the mutual fund industry.

2.2 General Purpose of the Instrument — (1) The purpose of the Instrument is to ensure that the interests of investors remain uppermost in the actions of participants in the mutual fund industry by setting minimum standards of conduct to be followed by industry participants in their activities in distributing mutual fund securities. The minimum standards of conduct established by the Instrument are designed to minimize the conflicts between the legitimate commercial goals of industry participants and the fundamental obligations outlined in subsection (2) that are owed by industry participants towards investors.

(2) The Instrument prohibits certain sales practices and compensation arrangements that have developed and that the Canadian securities regulatory authorities consider undermine, compromise or conflict with the following fundamental obligations of industry participants to their investor clients:

(a) investment recommendations should be made by a representative of a participating dealer to an investor based on the investor's investment objectives and circumstances and must be suitable for that investor;

(b) a participating dealer and its representatives have a primary obligation to act in the best interests of clients;

(c) where an investor is relying on a participating dealer and a representative of a participating dealer to provide him or her with independent expertise and advice regarding options for mutual fund or other investments, the participating dealer and the representative of the participating dealer have a fiduciary obligation not to compromise the provision of this expertise and advice;

(d) a participating dealer, as a registrant under securities legislation, is required to exercise adequate and appropriate supervision of its representatives who are dealing with clients to ensure compliance with all statutory and other legal obligations;

(e) members of the organization of a mutual fund providing management services to a mutual fund have an obligation to act honestly, in good faith and in the best interests of the mutual fund and its securityholders; and

(f) full, true and plain disclosure of all material facts concerning a mutual fund, including the compensation paid to participating dealers and their representatives and other sales practices followed in connection with the distribution of mutual fund securities, is essential to ensure that investors understand the nature of the investments they are making and the impact of fees and charges on them.

(3) The Canadian securities regulatory authorities are aware that other sales practices or compensation arrangements could arise that also undermine or compromise the focus of industry participants in complying with the fundamental obligations outlined in subsection (2). The Canadian securities regulatory authorities expect participants in the mutual fund industry to be and remain faithful to their fundamental obligations to the investing public, and not to allow practices or arrangements to develop that threaten this high standard of conduct. In this context, the restrictions on sales practices articulated by the Instrument should be seen as the minimum standards that should be followed by industry participants in order to fulfil their fundamental obligations.

2.3 Application of the Instrument to Labour-Sponsored Venture Capital Corporations — (1) Labour-sponsored venture capital corporations ("LSVCCs") are investment vehicles existing under the *Income Tax Act* (Canada) and legislation of some jurisdictions. LSVCCs that are structured as mutual funds are regulated as mutual funds in a number of jurisdictions, including Ontario and British Columbia, subject to certain exemptions. LSVCCs are considered not to be mutual funds in Quebec under Quebec securities legislation. LSVCCs are also considered not to be mutual funds in Manitoba; however, the Manitoba Securities Commission has issued a local instrument that makes LSVCCs in Manitoba subject to the Instrument.

(2) The Canadian securities regulatory authorities consider LSVCCs to be subject to the Instrument except in those jurisdictions in which LSVCCs are considered not to be mutual funds, in the case of Quebec, or have specifically been made subject to the Instrument, in the case of Manitoba.

(3) Section 2.1 of the Instrument prohibits a mutual fund from making a payment of money or providing a non-monetary benefit to a participating dealer or a representative of a participating dealer or paying for or making reimbursement of a cost or expense incurred or to be incurred by a

---

[1] *"Regulatory Strategies for the Mid-'90s — Recommendations for Regulating Investment Funds in Canada"* prepared by Glorianne Stromberg for the Canadian Securities Administrators, January 1995, at page 44.

[2] *"Recommendations for a Code of Sales Practices for the Mutual Fund Industry"* released by IFIC on March 29, 1996. The IFIC Code was published in Ontario at (1996), 19 OSCB 2170.

[3] The Investment Funds Steering Group was established in June 1995 by the Canadian Securities Administrators to consider the recommendations contained in Commissioner Stromberg's report. The Investment Funds Steering Group delivered its final report, *"The Stromberg Report — An Industry Perspective"*, to the Canadian Securities Administrators in November 1996.

participating dealer or representative of a participating dealer. Under the Instrument, all such payments or actions must be made by members of the organization of a mutual fund, not the mutual fund itself.

(4) Costs relating to the distribution of securities of LSVCCs are currently paid by the LSVCCs themselves for reasons related to the specialized organizational and legal structure of LSVCCs. Therefore, the applicable Canadian securities regulatory authorities will entertain applications from LSVCCs for relief from the provisions of the Instrument that prohibit mutual funds from making the payments or effecting the actions described in section 2.1 of the Instrument. The relief, if granted by the securities regulatory authority in a jurisdiction for an LSVCC, will permit the LSVCC to make those payments or take those actions, subject to all of the other requirements of the Instrument. Under such relief, the LSVCC, for example, would be permitted to pay trailing commissions directly to participating dealers, but subject to the requirements of section 3.2 of the Instrument and any other condition imposed in connection with such relief.

2.4 Indirect Avoidance of the Instrument — (1) The Canadian securities regulatory authorities have in connection with the IFIC Code, on occasion, encountered creative ways in which arrangements have been structured that permit benefits to be provided by a mutual fund organization to a participating dealer in a manner that the Canadian securities authorities would regard as contrary to the clear spirit and intent of the IFIC Code.

(2) The Canadian securities regulatory authorities may examine arrangements that raise the suspicion of being structured to permit a party to do indirectly what it cannot do directly. The Canadian securities regulatory authorities regard the prohibitions contained in the Instrument as prohibitions against both direct and indirect actions in relation to the subject matter of the prohibition.

(3) For example, Part 2 of the Instrument contains the basic prohibitions of the Instrument against members of the organization of a mutual fund making payments, among other things, to participating dealers or their representatives in connection with the distribution of securities of the mutual fund. This provision prohibits both the direct and indirect payment of money from mutual fund organizations to dealers, and the Canadian securities regulatory authorities will not hesitate to look through an arrangement in which, for example, a mutual fund organization paid money to a third party in connection with the distribution of securities of the mutual fund, knowing that the money would flow back to the participating dealer.

(4) It is noted that the draft of the Instrument that was published for comment contained a prohibition against indirect action. The Canadian securities regulatory authorities note that that provision was deleted from the final version of the Instrument because, as a matter of legislative drafting, it was considered unnecessary to be included in the Instrument. No inference should be taken from the deletion that the principle contained in that provision is inapplicable to the Instrument.

PART 3 — DEFINITION OF "REPRESENTATIVE"

3.1 (1) [Repealed]

(2) Paragraph (b) of the definition of "representative" includes personal holding companies of the persons referred to in paragraph (a) of the definition. The Canadian securities regulatory authorities have included this paragraph to ensure that the provisions of the Instrument apply both to the persons who carry on activities through personal holding companies and to the holding companies themselves.

PART 4 — DISCUSSION OF CERTAIN ASPECTS OF PART 2 OF THE INSTRUMENT

4.1 The phrase "in connection with the distribution of securities" — The prohibitions and restrictions contained in sections 2.1 and 2.2 of the Instrument relate to actions taken "in connection with the distribution of securities" of a mutual fund. The Canadian securities regulatory authorities are of the view that this phrase includes, without limitation, any activity done in furtherance of the sale, distribution or marketing of securities of mutual funds. This would include promotional activities relating to the investment in securities or mutual funds generally, or educational activities concerning financial, investment or retirement planning that could involve a discussion of the advantages and disadvantages of mutual fund investments. Any compensation or non-monetary benefits given to solidify or promote a relationship between a member of the organization of a mutual fund and a participating dealer and its representatives would fall within the scope of these sections. The phrase should not be interpreted restrictively or narrowly.

4.2 Non-Monetary Benefits — (1) Part 2 of the Instrument contains restrictions and prohibitions on the provision of, among other things, non-monetary benefits to participating dealers and their representatives.

(2) The Canadian securities regulatory authorities are of the view that the term "non-monetary benefits" includes any goods, services or other benefits that could be provided to or received by a person or company and that could be perceived by that person as being of benefit, advantage or value to him, her or it. The matters that are included in the term include, without limitation

    (a) domestic or foreign trips, food, beverages and accommodation, regardless of whether these benefits are provided in connection with attendance at a conference or other event sponsored by a member of the organization of a mutual fund;

    (b) entertainment, including the provision of tickets to concerts, theatre or sporting events, or the ability to participate in events such as golf tournaments;

    (c) gifts and non-cash gratuities;

    (d) invitations to educational seminars or conferences organized by members of the organization of a mutual fund;

    (e) attendance at educational seminars, conferences or courses; and

    (f) computer hardware, including networking hardware and general business software systems.

(3) The term "non-monetary benefits" does not include the goods and services that are provided by mutual fund organizations to participating dealers to facilitate the marketing of securities of the mutual fund, such as brochures, educational material, supplies of prospectuses or simplified prospectuses and financial statements.

(4) Some mutual fund organizations provide participating dealers with computer software that is designed to assist in determining which of the mutual funds of the organization are most appropriate for a client of the participating dealer, having regard to the investment objectives and financial condition of the client. The Canadian securities regulatory authorities are of the view that the provision of this type of proprietary software is not a non-monetary benefit to the participating dealer and is in the nature of marketing materials as referred to in subsection (3).

(5) However, the Canadian securities regulatory authorities consider that the provision of financial planning software of a more general nature, whether proprietary to the mutual fund organization or not, would likely constitute a non-monetary benefit. In addition, other non-proprietary software that is provided to the participating dealer would generally be considered to be a non-monetary benefit.

(6) The provision by a member of the organization of a mutual fund to a participating dealer of computer software, the only purpose of which is to facilitate the electronic interface between the participating dealer and the members of the organization of the mutual fund, is not considered to be included in the term "non-monetary benefits".

4.3 The phrase "pay for or make reimbursement of a cost or expense incurred or to be incurred by a participating dealer or a representative of a participating dealer" — Section 2.1 of the Instrument contains restrictions and prohibitions on the ability of a mutual fund and a member of the organization of a mutual fund to "pay for or make reimbursement of a cost or expense incurred or to be incurred by a participating dealer or a representative of a participating dealer". Section 2.2 contains corresponding restrictions and prohibitions on the ability of a participating dealer and its representatives to solicit or accept such payments. The Canadian securities regulatory authorities are of the view that this phrase includes direct or indirect reimbursement of costs or expenses, any payment that compensates a participating dealer or representative for such costs or expenses or any other method whereby the member of the organization of the mutual fund directly or indirectly bears the costs or expenses incurred.

4.4 Exception for Some Participating Dealers and Representatives — (1) Section 2.3 of the Instrument provides that nothing in the Instrument prohibits a person or company that is both a member of the organization of a mutual fund and a participating dealer of a mutual fund in a different mutual fund family from undertaking any activity, if

(a) the activity is undertaken in the person or company's capacity as a participating dealer of the mutual fund of which it is a participating dealer, and not in its capacity as a member of the organization of the mutual fund of which it is a member; and

(b) a participating dealer is not prohibited by the Instrument from undertaking that activity.

(2) That section is designed to respond to the fact that many registrants that are participating dealers will also be members of organizations of mutual funds; for example, a dealer that is owned by a bank will likely be an affiliate of the manager or principal distributor of a mutual fund sponsored by that bank and thus be a member of the organization of that mutual fund.

(3) The Canadian securities regulatory authorities intend that a participating dealer that is also a member of the organization of a mutual fund will have the freedom to operate as a participating dealer without concern over technically breaching the restrictions on members of the organizations of mutual funds contained in the Instrument. Some examples of how section 2.3 of the Instrument would be relevant to certain actions, assuming that the conditions of section 2.3 were satisfied, are as follows:

(a) a participating dealer that is also a member of the organization of a mutual fund would not be constrained in how it compensates its own representatives or employees by the provisions of Part 2 of the Instrument;

(b) a participating dealer that is also a member of the organization of a mutual fund would not be limited by the operation of section 5.1 of the Instrument in presenting an investor conference by the fact that the dealer may also be a member of the organization of the mutual fund;

(c) section 5.2 of the Instrument would not prevent a participating dealer that is also a member of the organization of a mutual fund from paying the travel, accommodation and personal incidental expenses for its own representatives to attend conferences sponsored by the mutual fund organization; and

(d) section 5.5 of the Instrument would not operate to subject a participating dealer to the limitations contained in that section if the dealer was sponsoring a conference for its own representatives; the dealer would be able to pay for its own costs even though technically, the dealer was a member of the organization of a mutual fund.

(4) Similarly, by reason of subsection 2.3(2), the Instrument will not affect the ability of a representative of a participating dealer that is a member of the organization of a mutual fund to receive compensation otherwise permitted by the Instrument from the participating dealer.

(5) The Canadian securities regulatory authorities note they would consider any action in which the relationship between a mutual fund organization and a participating dealer that was a member of the organization was used in an attempt to avoid the Instrument to be offensive to the Instrument.

PART 5 — COMMISSIONS

5.1 Method of Calculation — Paragraphs 3.1(b) and 3.2(b) of the Instrument require the disclosure of the method of calculation used in determining the amount of sales commissions and trailing commissions. The Canadian securities regulatory authorities are of the view that this requirement will be satisfied with disclosure of a general nature as to how those commissions are calculated; the authorities expect that this disclosure would describe, generally, that the amount of a commission is calculated through multiplying a specified rate of commission by some aggregate dollar amount of securities sold or held as at a specified time.

5.2 Bonus Commissions — Subparagraphs 3.1(c)(iii) and 3.2(1)(d)(iii) of the Instrument prevent the payment of "bonus commissions", in which the rates of commissions paid or earned during a particular period of the year are higher than the rates of commissions paid or earned for any other time. This provision should not be read to prevent a mutual fund from changing its general commission rates at some time during a year. It is noted that in such circumstances, the mutual fund should amend its prospectus or simplified prospectus to disclose the change in general commission rates applicable to sales of its securities.

5.3 Trailing Commission Thresholds — (1) The Canadian securities regulatory authorities note that the IFIC Code permits a mutual fund organization to pay, and a participating dealer to accept, trailing commissions based on the assets in an individual representative's client accounts, on a representative by representative basis. The IFIC Code further provides that a mutual fund organization could establish a payment policy whereby no trailing commission would be paid to a participating dealer in respect of a particular representative if the assets in the representative's client accounts did not exceed $100,000.

(2) The Canadian securities regulatory authorities consider that the effect of the rules established by subsection 2.1(3) and section 3.2 of the Instrument mean that mutual fund organizations can no longer establish the minimum asset thresholds referred to in the IFIC Code. These sections require that the percentage that a trailing commission represents of the aggregate value of securities of a mutual fund held in accounts of clients of a participating dealer must be the same for that participating dealer, regardless of the aggregate value of securities of the mutual fund in accounts of clients of the participating dealer at any time or the aggregate level of sales of securities of the mutual fund by the participating dealer.

(3) Subsection 3.2(3) of the Instrument provides a limited transitional exception to the general provisions of section 3.2 concerning minimum thresholds in relation to trailing commissions. Subsection 3.2(3) permits a member of the organization of a mutual fund not to pay a trailing commission in respect of securities of the mutual fund held in accounts of clients of the participating dealer in certain circumstances; namely that the non-payment be consistent with a policy established and followed on July 1, 1997, and that the securities with respect to which no trailing commission is paid must have been acquired by those clients before the date that the Instrument came into force. The rules established by section 3.2 are not intended to

retroactively affect existing arrangements between mutual fund organizations and participating dealers respecting securities acquired before the Instrument came into force.

(4) The following examples are offered to illustrate the operation of subsection 3.2(3) of the Instrument. In each case, assume that a mutual fund organization had in place on July 1, 1997 a policy of not paying trailing commissions in respect of securities held in accounts of clients of a participating dealer, on a representative by representative basis, if the aggregate value of securities in those accounts was less than $100,000.

(a) At some time after the Instrument came into force, securities in client accounts totalled $75,000 in value, of which $50,000 were acquired before the Instrument came into force, and $25,000 were acquired after the Instrument came into force. The mutual fund organization is entitled under the Instrument to decline to pay a trailing commission in respect of the $50,000 value of securities acquired before the Instrument came into force, but must pay a trailing commission on the $25,000 value of securities acquired after the Instrument came into force; and

(b) At some time after the Instrument came into force, securities in client accounts totalled $125,000 in value, of which $50,000 were acquired before the Instrument came into force, and $75,000 were acquired after the Instrument came into force. The mutual fund organization is required to pay trailing commissions on the $75,000 worth of the securities acquired after the Instrument came into force. Also, since the $100,000 threshold established under the policy of the organization in place on July 1, 1997 was exceeded, the mutual fund organization would pay a trailing commission on all $125,000 value of securities held in the accounts.

(5) The Canadian securities regulatory authorities note that mutual fund organizations are not required to continue to maintain those policies of not paying trailing commissions in the circumstances described in subsections (3) and (4). As provided in paragraph 3.2(3)(c) of the Instrument, any non-payment of a trailing commission under section 3.2 must be in conformity with the pre-established policy of the mutual fund organization.

(6) The Instrument is intended to remove the conflicts inherent in representatives seeking to achieve specific asset and sales thresholds in order to receive compensation in respect of mutual fund sales. An internal compensation system of a participating dealer whereby a representative is not paid any portion of a commission that is less than a specified dollar amount could be viewed as imposing indirectly an asset and sales threshold for that representative. The Canadian securities regulatory authorities are concerned that the internal compensation systems of participating dealers not impose, in effect, an asset or sales threshold to be achieved by representatives in order to receive a commission paid by a mutual fund organization in respect of mutual fund sales.

(7) The Canadian securities regulatory authorities have received questions as to whether a mutual fund organization is required to pay the same rate of commission, inclusive of trailing commissions, to all participating dealers that sell the securities of the mutual fund organization's mutual fund family. The Canadian securities regulatory authorities note that the Instrument does not require the same rate of commission to be paid. However, the Canadian securities regulatory authorities would consider that the rules set out in Part 3 of the Instrument prohibiting mutual fund organizations from setting minimum asset and sales thresholds in respect of commission payments would be offended if a mutual fund organization established a practice of only paying participating dealers commissions, or higher rates of commissions, if these dealers met a specified asset or sales threshold.

PART 6 — INTERNAL DEALER INCENTIVE PRACTICES

6.1 Internal Dealer Incentive Practices — Sections 4.1 and 4.2 of the Instrument permit different payments to be made by participating dealers to their representatives for different mutual funds if the difference in payments is a result of the different commissions received by the dealer from mutual fund organizations. The Canadian securities regulatory authorities recognize that different mutual fund organizations may pay different levels of commissions to dealers and that there is no compelling reason to prevent those differentials from flowing through to the representatives.

PART 7 — MARKETING AND EDUCATIONAL PRACTICES

7.1 Definition of "direct costs" — (1) The phrase "out-of-pocket" costs and expenses, used in the definition of "direct costs" contained in section 1.1 of the Instrument, does not include internal salary and overhead costs associated with the efforts of the participating dealer relating to the applicable sales communication or event. The definition of "direct costs" specifically excludes any costs incurred by a participating dealer for travel, accommodation or personal incidental expenses associated with the attendance of individuals at applicable events. The Canadian securities regulatory authorities are of the view that those types of expenses form part of the cost of doing business for the participating dealer and may not be borne by mutual fund organizations.

(2) Part 5 of the Instrument permits a member of the organization of a mutual fund to pay direct costs incurred by a participating dealer relating to certain sales communications or events on the conditions indicated, which include, in some circumstances, a condition that the participating dealer provide invoices or receipts for the costs to be paid by the member. The Canadian securities regulatory authorities expect members of organizations of mutual funds to exercise reasonable diligence to ensure that the direct costs indicated on invoices or receipts received from participating dealers represent direct costs that are reasonable in the circumstances. The Canadian securities regulatory authorities also expect participating dealers to exercise reasonable diligence to ensure that the direct costs indicated on invoices or receipts delivered to members of organizations of mutual funds represent direct costs incurred by the participating dealer.

7.2 Cooperative Marketing Practices — (1) Section 5.1 of the Instrument is designed to permit some cooperative marketing between mutual fund organizations and participating dealers, within the parameters set out in that section. The Canadian securities regulatory authorities are aware that participating dealers conduct certain marketing on behalf of mutual fund organizations and accordingly have permitted a limited sharing of the costs of sales communications and investor conferences and seminars that are organized and presented by participating dealers on the conditions contained in section 5.1. Section 5.1, however, does not permit a participating dealer to receive compensation or reimbursement from a mutual fund organization for its general marketing expenses, such as, for example, costs associated with client appreciation events or general client mailings or sales communications that relate generally to the business or operations of the participating dealer. Those costs may not be borne by mutual fund organizations.

(2) Paragraph 5.1(c) of the Instrument requires a participating dealer to provide invoices for, or receipts evidencing payment of, the direct costs permitted under section 5.1 to be paid by a member of the organization of the mutual fund. The Canadian securities regulatory authorities are of the view that a participating dealer may establish procedures to facilitate the efficient payment or reimbursement of these costs, and note the following in that regard.

(a) It is not necessary that the reimbursement of these costs be processed by the head office of a participating dealer; participating dealers may deal with mutual fund organizations at an appropriately local office level. However, the Canadian securities regulatory authorities emphasize that the Instrument makes a distinction between actions taken by a "participating dealer" and by a "representative". Paragraph 5.1(c) of the Instrument requires a participating dealer to provide the invoices and receipts to the mutual fund organization, and this action cannot be taken directly by representatives of the participating dealer;

(b) The Canadian securities regulatory authorities would not object to participating dealers directing mutual fund organizations to pay suppliers or service providers directly, so long as the payment is otherwise permitted to be made under section 5.1 of the Instrument. There is no need for the mutual fund organization to pay the participating dealer the relevant amount of the costs, who then must pay the supplier.

(3) Paragraph 5.1(e) of the Instrument requires written disclosure of the identity of the parties paying for a portion of the costs of a sales communication, investor conference or investor seminar. The Canadian securities regulatory authorities consider that this disclosure should be in sufficient detail to make clear that a clearly-identified party has paid a portion of the costs. As a result, the mere display of a party's logo would be considered insufficient disclosure both because the display may not adequately identify the party or make clear that the party has paid some of the costs of the event.

7.3 Mutual Fund Sponsored Conferences — (1) Section 5.2 of the Instrument requires that the costs relating to the organization and presentation of a conference or seminar described in that section be reasonable, having regard to the purpose of the conference or seminar. The Canadian securities regulatory authorities are of the view that "reasonable" costs in this context could include the provision of food and beverages for attendees at the conference or seminar, the provision of conference or seminar materials and the payment or waiver of registration fees at the conference or seminar. The term "reasonable" costs would not include gifts or entertainment provided to attendees other than as permitted by section 5.6 of the Instrument.

(2) Section 5.2 of the Instrument requires that the selection of the representatives of a participating dealer to attend a mutual fund sponsored conference or seminar is to be made exclusively by the participating dealer, uninfluenced by the mutual fund organization. The Canadian securities regulatory authorities note that the restriction does not prevent mutual fund organizations from organizing events that are tailored to the interests of particular categories of representatives, and advising the participating dealers of the nature of those events. So, for instance, a mutual fund organization would be free to organize events designed for junior representatives in which entry-level information concerning mutual funds was provided; the organization could advise the participating dealers that it would be appropriate that junior representatives attend. Identifying specific representatives would not constitute compliance with section 5.2 of the Instrument.

7.4 Third Party Sponsored Educational Events — Section 5.3 of the Instrument permits a member of the organization of a mutual fund to pay the registration fees of a representative of a participating dealer for a third party sponsored educational event referred to in that section. The term "registration fees" should be read with its ordinary meaning and should not be read to include travel, accommodation or other incidental costs associated with the attendance of the representative at the event.

7.5 Meaning of "Location" — Subparagraphs 5.2(c)(iii) and 5.5(e)(iii) of the Instrument permit the events to which sections 5.2 and 5.5 apply to take place in a location where a portfolio adviser of a mutual fund carries on business, subject to the condition contained in these subparagraphs. The Canadian securities regulatory authorities note that the term "location" will be interpreted by them to mean the city or immediate locale where the portfolio adviser carries on business. The Canadian securities authorities will regard as abusive any attempt to construe the term "location" in an excessively wide manner. So, for example, for a portfolio adviser carrying on business from an office in London, England, "location" means London or the immediate vicinity; it does not mean England, the British Isles or Europe.

7.6 Promotional Items and Business Promotion Activities — (1) Section 5.6 of the Instrument permits the provision of "non-monetary benefits of a promotional nature" of minimal value. Examples of this type of benefit include reminder advertising such as pens, calendars, t-shirts, hats, coffee mugs, paperweights and golf balls.

(2) Section 5.6 of the Instrument permits a member of the organization of a mutual fund family to engage in reasonable business promotion activities. Examples of such activities include occasional meals or drinks, tickets to sporting events, concerts or the theatre or the ability to participate in events such as golf tournaments and other comparable entertainment.

PART 8 — RECIPROCAL COMMISSIONS AND PORTFOLIO TRANSACTIONS

8.1 Reciprocal Commissions and Portfolio Transactions — (1) Part 6 of the Instrument is designed to ensure that "best execution" practices are followed in making brokerage arrangements for mutual funds. It limits the connection between a participating dealer's distribution activities in respect of a mutual fund and its activities in carrying out portfolio transactions for the mutual fund. In this regard, subsection 6.1(2) and section 6.2 of the Instrument require that portfolio transactions for a mutual fund are to be carried out only through a representative of a participating dealer who has been designated as an institutional representative by that participating dealer. The Canadian securities regulatory authorities expect that industry participants will not attempt to circumvent the intent of the Instrument by designating persons as institutional representatives to undertake portfolio transactions for mutual fund organizations if those persons have little or no other dealings with institutional accounts.

(2) The Canadian securities regulatory authorities recognize that certain types of information sharing between a member of the organization of a mutual fund and a participating dealer or a principal distributor are legitimate. For example, disclosure of trading history to a participating dealer while negotiating commission rates for future trades would not offend subsection 6.1(3) of the Instrument.

PART 9 — OTHER SALES PRACTICES

9.1 Commission Rebates — Subsection 7.1(2) of the Instrument requires disclosure of the tax consequences of a redemption. The Canadian securities regulatory authorities expect that this disclosure will be of a general nature, showing the tax effects of a redemption for taxpayers at different marginal rates.

9.2 Tied Selling — (1) The Canadian securities regulatory authorities note that the "products or services" referred to in paragraph 7.4(b) of the Instrument include the opening of an account.

(2) The Canadian securities regulatory authorities made section 7.4 of the Instrument in response to a similar provision in the IFIC Code, but also as a result of their concern that certain industry participants could use their ability to provide services (such as making loans) to investors and use undue influence to require or otherwise improperly require or coerce such investors to acquire mutual fund securities as a condition of providing these services. The Canadian securities regulatory authorities are aware that certain industry participants offer financial incentives or advantages to certain clients; the practice of offering these financial incentives or advantages is commonly referred to as "relationship pricing". Section 7.4 is not intended to prohibit so-called "relationship pricing" or other beneficial selling arrangements similar to relationship pricing. For example, the Canadian securities regulatory authorities would consider that section 7.4 was not offended if a financial institution offered to make a loan to a customer on more favourable terms or conditions than the financial institution would otherwise offer to the customer, if as a condition to obtaining the favourable terms or conditions, the customer acquired securities of mutual funds sponsored by the financial institution. Section 7.4 would be offended, however, if the financial institution refused to make a loan to that customer unless the customer acquired securities of mutual funds sponsored by the financial institution in circumstances, for example, where the customer otherwise met the financial institution's criteria for making loans.

PART 10 — DISCLOSURE REQUIREMENTS

10.1 Disclosure of Equity Interests — Section 8.2 of the Instrument requires a mutual fund to disclose equity interests held by participating dealers and their representatives in members of the organization of the mutual fund. The Canadian securities regulatory authorities note that the term "equity interest" is a defined term and has a different meaning depending on whether the relevant member of the organization of a mutual fund is a reporting issuer whose securities are listed on a Canadian stock exchange or not. For example, for a member of an organization that is a reporting issuer whose securities are listed on a Canadian stock exchange, the threshold for disclosure of an equity holding by a participating dealer or a representative of a participating dealer is 10 percent of any class of securities of that member. The Canadian securities regulatory authorities expect the mutual fund to use its reasonable best efforts to seek the relevant information from a member of the organization of the mutual fund that is a reporting issuer whose securities are listed on a Canadian stock exchange. The Canadian securities regulatory authorities would not object to a mutual fund organization disclosing that the information disclosed in the prospectus is to the best of its knowledge.

10.2 Disclosure Requirements — Section 8.3 of the Instrument sets out the disclosure requirements for distributions of securities of a mutual fund subject to the Instrument that are made under an exemption from the prospectus requirements of the securities legislation and in circumstances in which the mutual fund does not have a current prospectus or simplified prospectus available to be delivered to the purchaser of the securities of the mutual fund.

PART 11 — EXEMPTIONS

11.1 Exemptions — (1) The procedure to obtain, in more than one jurisdiction, an exemption from the Instrument is as follows:

(a) the applicant should file an application in writing simultaneously in all jurisdictions in which it requires an exemption;

(b) the application should indicate the name of the principal jurisdiction selected by the applicant for the purpose of dealing with the application and, if applicable, any related prospectus filing and of each other jurisdiction where the application and, if applicable, a related prospectus is being filed;

(c) the Canadian securities regulatory authority of the principal jurisdiction or the regulator in the principal jurisdiction will, on behalf of the applicant, contact the Canadian securities regulatory authorities or regulators in the other jurisdictions in which the application has been made for their comments concerning the application and will forward all comments to the issuer; and

(d) the applicant should respond in writing to all comments to the Canadian securities regulatory authority in the principal jurisdiction, which will forward the response to the Canadian securities regulatory authorities in the other jurisdictions and again coordinate comments.

(2) In order to enable the Canadian securities regulatory authorities to deal with applications on a timely basis, issuers are encouraged to file applications simultaneously in all jurisdictions in which they require an approval or an exemption.

Adoption by OSC: (1998) 21 O.S.C.B. 2713 and (1998) 21 O.S.C.B. 779; Request for Comments: (1997) 20 O.S.C.B. 3879 and (1996) 19 O.S.C.B. 4727.

Adoption of Amendment by OSC: (2009) 32 O.S.C.B. (Supp. 4) 379 and 32 O.S.C.B. (Supp. 2) 1.

National Instrument 81-106 — Investment Fund Continuous Disclosure

Date: June 1, 2005, as amended effective November 1, 2006, July 4, 2008, September 8, 2008, January 1, 2011, April 30, 2012, May 31, 2013, January 1, 2014 and September 22, 2014

28 O.S.C.B. 4911, 29 O.S.C.B. 8850, 31 O.S.C.B. 6577, 31 O.S.C.B. 8559, 33 O.S.C.B. 11433, 35 O.S.C.B. 3426, 36 O.S.C.B. 2619, 36 O.S.C.B. 12197 and (2014) 37 O.S.C.B. (Supp. 4).

Table of Contents

Part 8: MUTUAL FUNDS

PART 1 — DEFINITIONS AND APPLICATIONS

1.1 Definitions — In this Instrument

"annual management report of fund performance" means a document prepared in accordance with Part B of Form 81-106F1;

"current value" means, for an asset held by, or a liability of, an investment fund, the value calculated in accordance with Canadian GAAP;

"education savings plan" means an agreement between one or more persons and another person or organization, in which the other person or organization agrees to pay or cause to be paid, to or for one or more beneficiaries designated in connection with the agreement, scholarship awards;

"EVCC" means an employee venture capital corporation that does not have a restricted constitution, and is registered under Part 2 of the *Employee Investment Act* (British Columbia), R.S.B.C. 1996 c. 112, and whose business objective is making multiple investments;

"financial statements" includes interim financial reports;

"independent review committee" means the independent review committee of the investment fund established under National Instrument 81-107 *Independent Review Committee for Investment Funds*;

"independent valuation" means a valuation of the assets and liabilities, or of the venture investments, of a labour sponsored or venture capital fund that contains the opinion of an independent valuator as to the current value of the assets and liabilities, or of the venture investments, and that is prepared in accordance with Part 8;

"independent valuator" means a valuator that is independent of the labour sponsored or venture capital fund and that has appropriate qualifications;

"interim management report of fund performance" means a document prepared in accordance with Part C of Form 81-106F1;

"interim period" means, in relation to an investment fund,

(a) a period of at least three months that ends six months before the end of a financial year of the investment fund, or

(b) in the case of a transition year of the investment fund, a period commencing on the first day of the transition year and ending six months after the end of its old financial year;

"investment fund" means a mutual fund or a non-redeemable investment fund, and, for greater certainty in British Columbia, includes an EVCC and a VCC;

"labour sponsored or venture capital fund" means an investment fund that is

(a) a labour sponsored investment fund corporation or a labour sponsored venture capital corporation under provincial legislation,

(b) a registered or prescribed labour sponsored venture capital corporation as defined in the ITA,

(c) an EVCC, or

(d) a VCC;

"management expense ratio" means the ratio, expressed as a percentage, of the expenses of an investment fund to its average net asset value, calculated in accordance with Part 15;

"management fees" means the total fees paid or payable by an investment fund to its manager or one or more portfolio advisers or sub-advisers, including incentive or performance fees, but excluding operating expenses of the investment fund;

"management report of fund performance" means an annual management report of fund performance or an interim management report of fund performance;

"material change" means, in relation to an investment fund,

(a) a change in the business, operations or affairs of the investment fund that would be considered important by a reasonable investor in determining whether to purchase or continue to hold securities of the investment fund, or

(b) a decision to implement a change referred to in paragraph (a) made

    (i) by the board of directors of the investment fund or the board of directors of the manager of the investment fund or other persons acting in a similar capacity,

    (ii) by senior management of the investment fund who believe that confirmation of the decision by the board of directors or such other persons acting in a similar capacity is probable, or

    (iii) by senior management of the manager of the investment fund who believe that confirmation of the decision by the board of directors of the manager or such other persons acting in a similar capacity is probable;

"material contract" means, for an investment fund, a document that the investment fund would be required to list in an annual information form under Item 16 of Form 81-101F2 if the investment fund filed a simplified prospectus under National Instrument 81-101 *Mutual Fund Prospectus Disclosure*;

"mutual fund in the jurisdiction" means an incorporated or unincorporated mutual fund that is a reporting issuer in, or that is organized under the laws of, the local jurisdiction, but does not include a private mutual fund;

"National Instrument 51-102" means National Instrument 51-102 *Continuous Disclosure Obligations*;

"National Instrument 81-107" means National Instrument 81-107 *Independent Review Committee for Investment Funds*;

"net asset value" means the value of the total assets of the investment fund less the value of the total liabilities, other than assets attributable to securityholders, of the investment fund, as at a specific date, determined in accordance with Part 14;

"non-redeemable investment fund" means an issuer,

    (a) whose primary purpose is to invest money provided by its securityholders,

    (b) that does not invest,

        (i) for the purpose of exercising or seeking to exercise control of an issuer, other than an issuer that is a mutual fund or a non-redeemable investment fund, or

        (ii) for the purpose of being actively involved in the management of any issuer in which it invests, other than an issuer that is a mutual fund or a non-redeemable investment fund, and

    (c) that is not a mutual fund;

"publicly accountable enterprise" means a publicly accountable enterprise as defined in the Handbook;

"quarterly portfolio disclosure" means the disclosure prepared in accordance with Part 6;

"scholarship award" means any amount, other than a refund of contributions, that is paid or payable directly or indirectly to further the education of a beneficiary designated under an education savings plan;

"scholarship plan" means an arrangement under which contributions to education savings plans are pooled to provide scholarship awards to designated beneficiaries;

"statement of changes in financial position" means a statement of changes in equity or a statement of changes in net assets attributable to securityholders;

"transition year" means the financial year of an investment fund in which a change of year end occurs;

"VCC" means a venture capital corporation registered under Part 1 of the *Small Business Venture Capital Act* (British Columbia), R.S.B.C. 1996 c. 429 whose business objective is making multiple investments; and

"venture investment" means an investment in a private company or an investment made in accordance with the requirements of provincial labour sponsored or venture capital fund legislation or the ITA.

1.2 **Application** — (1) Except as otherwise provided in this Instrument, this Instrument applies to

    (a) an investment fund that is a reporting issuer; and

    (b) subject to subsection (2), a mutual fund in the jurisdiction.

(2) Despite paragraph (1)(b), in Alberta, British Columbia, Manitoba and Newfoundland and Labrador, this Instrument does not apply to a mutual fund that is not a reporting issuer.

(3) [Repealed.]

(4) In Québec, this Instrument does not apply to a reporting issuer organized under

    (a) an Act to establish the Fonds de solidarité des travailleurs du Québec (F.T.Q.) R.S.Q., chapter F-3.2.1;

    (b) an Act to establish Fondaction, le Fonds de développement de la Confédération des syndicats nationaux pour la coopération et l'emploi (R.S.Q., chapter F-3.1.2); or

    (c) an Act constituting Capital régional et coopératif Desjardins, Loi constituant Capital régional et coopératif Desjardins (R.S.Q., chapter C-6.1).

1.3 **Interpretation** — (1) Each section, part, class or series of a class of securities of an investment fund that is referable to a separate portfolio of assets is considered to be a separate investment fund for the purposes of this Instrument.

(2) Terms defined in National Instrument 81-102 *Investment Funds* and used in this Instrument have the respective meanings ascribed to them in that Instrument.

(3) Terms defined in National Instrument 81-104 *Commodity Pools* or National Instrument 81-105 *Mutual Fund Sales Practices* and used in this Instrument have the respective meanings ascribed to them in those Instruments except that references in those definitions to "mutual fund" must be read as references to "investment fund".

1.4 **Language of Documents** — (1) A document that is required to be filed under this Instrument must be prepared in French or English.

(2) If an investment fund files a document in French or in English, and a translation of the document into the other language is sent to a securityholder, the investment fund must file the translated document not later than when it is sent to the securityholder.

(3) In Québec, the linguistic obligations and rights prescribed by Québec law must be complied with.

Part 8: MUTUAL FUNDS

PART 2 — FINANCIAL STATEMENTS

2.1 Comparative Annual Financial Statements and Auditor's Report — (1) An investment fund must file annual financial statements for the investment fund's most recently completed financial year that include

(a) a statement of financial position as at the end of that financial year and a statement of financial position as at the end of the immediately preceding financial year;

(b) a statement of comprehensive income for that financial year and a statement of comprehensive income for the immediately preceding financial year;

(c) statement of changes in financial position for that financial year and a statement of changes in financial position for the immediately preceding financial year;

(d) for financial years beginning on or after January 1, 2014, a statement of cash flows for that financial year and a statement of cash flows for the immediately preceding financial year;

(e) a statement of investment portfolio as at the end of that financial year;

(f) a statement of financial position as at the beginning of the immediately preceding financial year if the investment fund discloses in its annual financial statements an unreserved statement of compliance with IFRS and the investment fund:

(i) applies an accounting policy retrospectively in its annual financial statements,

(ii) makes a retrospective restatement of items in its annual financial statements, or

(iii) reclassifies items in its annual financial statements; and

(g) notes to the annual financial statements.

(2) Annual financial statements filed under subsection (1) must be accompanied by an auditor's report.

2.2 Filing Deadline for Annual Financial Statements — The annual financial statements and auditor's report required to be filed under section 2.1 must be filed on or before the 90th day after the investment fund's most recently completed financial year.

2.3 Interim Financial Statements — An investment fund must file an interim financial report for the investment fund's most recently completed interim period that includes

(a) a statement of financial position as at the end of that interim period and a statement of financial position as at the end of the immediately preceding financial year;

(b) a statement of comprehensive income for that interim period and a statement of comprehensive income for the corresponding period in the immediately preceding financial year;

(c) a statement of changes in financial position for that interim period and a statement of changes in financial position for the corresponding period in the immediately preceding financial year;

(d) for financial years beginning on or after January 1, 2014, a statement of cash flows for that interim period and a statement of cash flows for the corresponding period in the immediately preceding financial year;

(e) a statement of investment portfolio as at the end of that interim period; and

(f) a statement of financial position as at the beginning of the immediately preceding financial year if the investment fund discloses in its interim financial report an unreserved statement of compliance with International Accounting Standard 34 *Interim Financial Reporting* and the investment fund

(i) applies an accounting policy retrospectively in its interim financial report,

(ii) makes a retrospective restatement of items in its interim financial report, or

(iii) reclassifies items in its interim financial report; and

(g) notes to the interim financial report.

2.4 Filing Deadline for Interim Financial Report — The interim financial report required to be filed under section 2.3 must be filed on or before the 60th day after the end of the most recent interim period of the investment fund.

2.5 Approval of Financial Statements — (1) The board of directors of an investment fund that is a corporation must approve the financial statements of the investment fund before those financial statements are filed or made available to securityholders or potential purchasers of securities of the investment fund.

(2) The trustee or trustees of an investment fund that is a trust, or another person or company authorized to do so by the constating documents of the investment fund, must approve the financial statements of the investment fund, before those financial statements are filed or made available to securityholders or potential purchasers of securities of the investment fund.

2.6 Acceptable Accounting Principles — (1) For financial years beginning before January 1, 2014, the financial statements of an investment fund must be prepared in accordance with Canadian GAAP applicable to public enterprises.

(2) For financial years beginning on or after January 1, 2014, the financial statements of an investment fund must be prepared in accordance with Canadian GAAP applicable to publicly accountable enterprises.

(3) Financial statements must be prepared in accordance with the same accounting principles for all periods presented in the financial statements.

2.7 Acceptable Auditing Standards — (1) Financial statements that are required to be audited must be audited in accordance with Canadian GAAS.

(2) For financial years beginning before January 1, 2014, audited financial statements must be accompanied by an auditor's report prepared in accordance with Canadian GAAS and the following requirements:

1. The auditor's report must not contain a reservation or express a modified opinion.

2. The auditor's report must identify all financial periods presented for which the auditor has issued an auditor's report.

3. If the investment fund has changed its auditor and a comparative period presented in the financial statements was audited by a different auditor, the auditor's report must refer to the former auditor's report on the comparative period.

4. The auditor's report must identify the auditing standards used to conduct the audit and the accounting principles used to prepare the financial statements.

(3) For financial years beginning on or after January 1, 2014, audited financial statements must be accompanied by an auditor's report prepared in accordance with Canadian GAAS and the following requirements:

1. The auditor's report expresses an unmodified opinion.

2. The auditor's report identifies all financial periods presented for which the auditor has issued an auditor's report.

3. The auditor's report is in the form specified by Canadian GAAS for an audit of financial statements prepared in accordance with a fair presentation framework.

4. The auditor's report refers to IFRS as the applicable fair presentation framework.

5. If the investment fund has changed its auditor and a comparative period presented in the financial statements was audited by a predecessor auditor, the financial statements are accompanied by the predecessor auditor's report on the comparative period or the auditor's report refers to the predecessor auditor's report on the comparative period.

2.8 Acceptable Auditors — An auditor's report must be prepared and signed by a person or company that is authorized to sign an auditor's report by the laws of a jurisdiction of Canada, and that meets the professional standards of that jurisdiction.

2.9 Change in Year End — (1) This section applies to an investment fund that is a reporting issuer.

(2) Section 4.8 of National Instrument 51-102 applies to an investment fund that changes its financial year end, except that

(a) a reference to "interim period" must be read as "interim period" as defined in this Instrument;

(b) a requirement under National Instrument 51-102 to include specified financial statements must be read as a requirement to include the financial statements required under this Part; and

(c) a reference to "filing deadline" in subsection 4.8(2) of National Instrument 51-102 must be read as a reference to the filing deadlines provided for under section 2.2 and 2.4 of this Instrument.

(3) Despite section 2.4, an investment fund is not required to file an interim financial report for any period in a transition year if the transition year is less than nine months in length.

(4) Despite paragraphs 4.8(7)(a) and (b) and (8)(a) and (b) of National Instrument 51-102,

(a) for an interim financial report for an interim period in the transition year, the investment fund must include as comparative information

(i) a statement of financial position as at the end of its old financial year; and

(ii) a statement of comprehensive income, a statement of changes in financial position, and a statement of cash flows, for the interim period of the old financial year;

(b) for an interim financial report for an interim period in a new financial year, the investment fund must include as comparative information

(i) a statement of financial position as at the end of the transition year; and

(ii) a statement of comprehensive income, a statement of changes in financial position, and a statement of cash flows, for the period that is one year earlier than the interim period in the new financial year.

2.10 Change in Legal Structure — If an investment fund that is a reporting issuer is party to an amalgamation, arrangement, merger, winding-up, reorganization or other transaction that will result in

(a) the investment fund terminating or ceasing to be a reporting issuer,

(b) another entity becoming an investment fund,

(c) a change in the investment fund's financial year end, or

(d) a change in the name of the investment fund,

the investment fund must, as soon as practicable, and in any event not later than the deadline for the first filing required by this Instrument following the transaction, file a notice stating:

(e) the names of the parties to the transaction;

(f) a description of the transaction;

(g) the effective date of the transaction;

(h) if applicable, the names of each party that terminated or ceased to be a reporting issuer following the transaction and of each continuing entity;

(i) if applicable, the date of the investment fund's first financial year end following the transaction; and

(j) if applicable, the periods, including the comparative periods, if any, of the interim financial report and annual financial statements required to be filed for the investment fund's first financial year following the transaction.

2.11 Filing Exemption for Mutual Funds that are Non-Reporting Issuers — A mutual fund that is not a reporting issuer is exempt from the filing requirements of section 2.1 for a financial year or section 2.3 for an interim period if

(a) the mutual fund prepares the applicable financial statements in accordance with this Instrument;

(b) the mutual fund delivers the financial statements to its securityholders in accordance with Part 5 within the same time periods as if the financial statements were required to be filed;

(c) the mutual fund has advised the regulator or securities regulatory authority that it is relying on this exemption not to file its financial statements; and

(d) the mutual fund has included in a note to the financial statements that it is relying on this exemption not to file its financial statements.

2.12 Disclosure of Auditor Review of Interim Financial Report — (1) This section applies to an investment fund that is a reporting issuer.

(2) If an auditor has not performed a review of the interim financial report required to be filed, the interim financial report must be accompanied by a notice indicating that the interim financial report has not been reviewed by an auditor.

(3) If an investment fund engaged an auditor to perform a review of the interim financial report required to be filed and the auditor was unable to complete the review, the interim financial report must be accompanied by a notice indicating that the auditor was unable to complete a review of the interim financial report and the reasons why.

(4) If an auditor has performed a review of the interim financial report required to be filed and the auditor has expressed a reservation in the auditor's interim review report, the interim financial report must be accompanied by a written review report from the auditor.

PART 3 — FINANCIAL DISCLOSURE REQUIREMENTS

3.1 Statement of Financial Position — The statement of financial position of an investment fund must disclose the following as separate line items, each shown at current value:

1. cash, term deposits and, if not included in the statement of investment portfolio, short term debt instruments.

2. investments.

3. accounts receivable relating to securities issued.

4. accounts receivable relating to portfolio assets sold.

5. accounts receivable relating to margin paid or deposited on futures or forward contracts.

6. amounts receivable or payable in respect of derivatives transactions, including premiums or discounts received or paid.

7. deposits with brokers for portfolio securities sold short.

8. accrued expenses.

9. accrued incentive arrangements or performance compensation.

10. portfolio securities sold short.

11. liabilities for securities redeemed.

12. liabilities for portfolio assets purchased.

13. income tax payable.

14. total equity or net assets attributable to securityholders and, if applicable, for each class or series.

15. total equity per security or net assets attributable to secutrityholders per security, or if applicable, per security of each class or series.

3.2 Statement of Comprehensive Income — The statement of comprehensive income of an investment fund must disclose the following information as separate line items:

1. dividend revenue.

2. interest revenue.

3. income from derivatives.

4. revenue from securities lending.

5. management fees, excluding incentive or performance fees.

6. incentive or performance fees.

7. audit fees.

8. directors' or trustees' fees.

8.1 independent review committee fees.

9. custodial fees.

10. legal fees.

10.1 commissions and other portfolio transaction costs.

11. securityholder reporting costs.

12. [repealed]

13. amounts that would otherwise have been payable by the investment fund that were waived or paid by the manager or a portfolio adviser of the investment fund.

14. income tax.

15. [repealed]

16. realized gains or losses.

17. unrealized gains or losses.

17.1 if recognized as an expense, distributions, showing separately the amount distributed out of net investment income and out of realized gains on portfolio assets sold.

18. increase or decrease in total equity from operations, or in net assets attributable to secutrityholders from operations, excluding distributions, and, if applicable, for each class or series.

19. increase or decrease in total equity from operations per security, or in net assets attributable to securityholders from operations, excluding distributions, per security or, if applicable, per security of each class or series.

3.3 Statement of Changes in Financial Position — The statement of changes in financial position of an investment fund must disclose, for each class or series, the following as separate line items:

1. total equity or net assets attributable to securityholders at the beginning of the period.

2. [repealed]

3. proceeds from the issuance of securities of the investment fund.

4. aggregate amounts paid on redemption of securities of the investment fund.

5. securities issued on reinvestment of distributions.

6. if not recognized as an expense, distributions, showing seprately the amount distributed out of net investment income and out of realized gains on portfolio assets sold.

6.1 return of capital.

7. total equity or net assets attibutable to secutiryholders at the end of the period.

3.4 Statement of Cash Flows — The statement of cash flows of an investment fund must disclose the following as separate line items:

1. [repealed]

2. proceeds of disposition of portfolio assets.

3. payments for the purchase of portfolio assets.

4. proceeds from the issuance of securities of the investment fund.

5. aggregate amounts paid on redemption of securities of the investment fund.

6. compensation paid in respect of the sale of securities of the investment fund.

3.5 Statement of Investment Portfolio — (1) The statement of investment portfolio of an investment fund must disclose the following for each portfolio asset held or sold short:

1. the name of the issuer of the portfolio asset.

2. a description of the portfolio asset, including

(a) for an equity security, the name of the class of the security.

(b) for a debt instrument not included in paragraph (c), all characteristics commonly used commercially to identify the instrument, including the name of the instrument, the interest rate of the instrument, the maturity date of the instrument, whether the instrument is convertible or exchangeable and, if used to identify the instrument, the priority of the instrument.

(c) for a debt instrument referred to in the definition of "money market fund" in National Instrument 81-102 *Investment Funds*, the name, interest rate and maturity date of the instrument.

(d) for a portfolio asset not referred to in paragraph (a), (b) or (c), the name of the portfolio asset and the material terms and conditions of the portfolio asset commonly used commercially in describing the portfolio asset.

3. the number or aggregate face value of the portfolio asset.

4. the cost of the portfolio asset.

5. the current value of the portfolio asset.

(2) For the purposes of subsection (1), disclosure for a long portfolio must be segregated from the disclosure for a short portfolio.

(3) For the purposes of subsection (1) and subject to subsection (2), disclosure must be aggregated for portfolio assets having the same description and issuer.

(4), (5) [repealed]

(6) If an investment fund holds positions in derivatives, the investment fund must disclose in the statement of investment portfolio or the notes to that statement,

(a) for long and short positions in options,

(i) the quantity of the underlying interest, the number of options, the underlying interest, the strike price, the expiration month and year, the cost and the current value, and

(ii) if the underlying interest is a future, information about the future in accordance with subparagraph (i);

(b) for positions in futures and forwards, the number of futures and forwards, the underlying interest, the price at which the contract was entered into, the delivery month and year and the current value;

(c) for positions in swaps, the number of swap contracts, the underlying interest, the principal or notional amount, the payment dates, and the current value; and

(d) if a rating of a counterparty has fallen below the designated rating level.

(7) If applicable, the statement of investment portfolio included in the financial statements of the investment fund, or the notes to the statement of investment portfolio, must identify the underlying interest that is being hedged by each position taken by the investment fund in a derivative.

(8) An investment fund may omit the information required by subsection (1) about mortgages from a statement of investment portfolio if the statement of investment portfolio discloses

(a) the total number of mortgages held;

(b) the aggregate current value of mortgages held;

(c) a breakdown of mortgages, by reference to number and current value among mortgages insured under the *National Housing Act* (Canada), insured conventional mortgages and uninsured conventional mortgages

(d) a breakdown of mortgages, by reference to number and current value, among mortgages that are pre-payable and those that are not pre-payable; and

Part 8: MUTUAL FUNDS

(e) a breakdown of mortgages, by reference to number, current value, amortized cost and outstanding principal value, among groups of mortgages having contractual interest rates varying by no more than one quarter of one percent.

(9) An investment fund must maintain records of all portfolio transactions undertaken by the investment fund.

3.6 Notes to Financial Statements — (1) The notes to the financial statements of an investment fund must disclose the following:

1. the basis for determining current value and cost of portfolio assets and, if a method of determining cost other than by reference to the average cost of the portfolio assets is used, the method used.

1.1 for financial years beginning on or after January 1, 2014, the basis for classifying the investment fund's outstanding securities, or each class or series of outstanding securities, as either equity instruments or financial liabilities.

2. if the investment fund has outstanding more than one class or series of securities ranking equally against its net assets, but differing in other respects,

    (a) the number of authorized securities of each class or series;

    (b) the number of securities of each class or series that have been issued and are outstanding;

    (c) the differences between the classes or series, including differences in sales charges, and management fees;

    (d) the method used to allocate income and expenses, and realized and unrealized capital gains and losses, to each class;

    (e) the fee arrangements for any class-level expenses paid to affiliates; and

    (f) transactions involving the issue or redemption of securities of the investment fund undertaken in the period for each class of securities to which the financial statements pertain.

3. to the extent the amount is ascertainable, the portion of the total client brokerage commissions, as defined in National Instrument 23-102 — *Use of Client Brokerage Commissions*, paid or payable to dealers by the investment fund for the provision of goods or services by the dealers or third parties, other than order execution.

4. the total cost of distribution of the investment fund's securities recorded in the statement of changes in net assets.

5. the net asset value per security as at the date of the financial statements compared to the total equity per security or net assets attributable to securityholders per security as shown on the statement of financial position, and an explanation of each of the differences between these amounts.

(2) If not disclosed elsewhere in the financial statements, an investment fund that borrows money must, in a note to the financial statements, disclose the minimum and maximum amount borrowed during the period to which the financial statements or management report of fund performance pertain.

(3) For financial years beginning on or after January 1, 2014, the notes to the financial statements must disclose

    (a) in the case of annual financial statements, an unreserved statement of compliance with IFRS; and

    (b) in the case of interim financial reports, an unreserved statement of compliance with International Accounting Standard 34 *Interim Financial Reporting*.

3.7 Inapplicable Line Items — Despite the requirements of this Part, an investment fund may omit a line item from the financial statements for any matter that does not apply to the investment fund or for which the investment fund has nothing to disclose.

3.8 Disclosure of Securities Lending Transactions — (1) An investment fund must disclose, in the statement of investment portfolio included in the financial statements of the investment fund, or in the notes to the financial statements,

    (a) the aggregate dollar value of portfolio securities that were lent in the securities lending transactions of the investment fund that are outstanding as at the date of the financial statements; and

    (b) the type and aggregate amount of collateral received by the investment fund under securities lending transactions of the investment fund that are outstanding as at the date of the financial statements.

(2) The statement of financial position of an investment fund that has received cash collateral from a securities lending transaction that is outstanding as of the date of the financial statements must disclose separately

    (a) the cash collateral received by the investment fund; and

    (b) the obligation to repay the cash collateral.

(3) The statement of comprehensive income of an investment fund must disclose income from a securities lending transaction as revenue.

(4) An investment fund must include, in the notes to the financial statements, a reconciliation of the gross amount generated from the securities lending transactions of the investment fund to the revenue from securities lending disclosed in the statement of comprehensive income of the investment fund under item 4 of section 3.2.

(5) The disclosure referred to in subsection (4) must include each of the following:

    (a) the name of each person or company who was entitled to receive payments out of the gross amount generated from the securities lending transactions of the investment fund;

    (b) the amount each recipient named under paragraph (a) was entitled to receive;

    (c) the aggregate of the amounts disclosed under paragraph (b) as a percentage of the gross amount generated from the securities lending transactions of the investment fund.

3.9 Disclosure of Repurchase Transactions — (1) An investment fund, in the statement of investment portfolio included in the financial statements of the investment fund, or in the notes to that statement, must, for a repurchase transaction of the investment fund that is outstanding as at the date of the statement, disclose

    (a) the date of the transaction;

    (b) the expiration date of the transaction;

    (c) the nature and current value of the portfolio securities sold by the investment fund;

    (d) the amount of cash received and the repurchase price to be paid by the investment fund; and

(e) the current value of the sold portfolio securities as at the date of the statement.

(2) The statement of financial position of an investment fund that has entered into a repurchase transaction that is outstanding as of the date of the statement of financial position must disclose separately the obligation of the investment fund to repay the collateral.

(3) The statement of comprehensive income of an investment fund must disclose income from the use of the cash received on a repurchase transaction as revenue.

(4) The information required by this section may be presented on an aggregate basis.

3.10 Disclosure of Reverse Repurchase Transactions — (1) An investment fund, in the statement of investment portfolio or in the notes to that statement, must, for a reverse repurchase transaction of the investment fund that is outstanding as at the date of the statement, disclose

    (a) the date of the transaction;

    (b) the expiration date of the transaction;

    (c) the total dollar amount paid by the investment fund;

    (d) the nature and current value or principal amount of the portfolio securities received by the investment fund; and

    (e) the current value of the purchased portfolio securities as at the date of the statement.

(2) The statement of financial position of an investment fund that has entered into a reverse repurchase transaction that is outstanding as of the date of the financial statements must disclose separately the reverse repurchase agreement relating to the transaction at current value.

(3) The statement of comprehensive income of an investment fund must disclose income from a reverse repurchase transaction as revenue.

(4) The information required by this section may be presented on an aggregate basis.

3.11 Scholarship Plans — (1) In addition to the requirements of this Part, an investment fund that is a scholarship plan must disclose, as of the end of its most recently completed financial year, a separate statement or schedule to the financial statements that provides

    (a) a summary of education savings plans and units outstanding by year of eligibility, including

        (i) disclosure of the number of units by year of eligibility for the opening units, units purchased, units forfeited and the ending units,

        (ii) disclosure of the principal amounts and the accumulated income per year of eligibility, and their total balances, and

        (iii) a reconciliation of the total balances of the principal amounts and the accumulated income in the statement or schedule to the statement of financial position of the scholarship plan;

    (b) the total number of units outstanding; and

    (c) a statement of scholarship awards paid to beneficiaries, and a reconciliation of the amount of scholarship awards paid with the statement of comprehensive income.

(2) Despite sections 3.1 and 3.2, an investment fund that is a scholarship plan may omit the "total equity per security or net assets attributable to securityholders per security" and "increase or decrease in total equity from operations, excluding distributions, per security" line items from its financial statements.

PART 4 — MANAGEMENT REPORTS OF FUND PERFORMANCE

4.1 Application — This Part applies to an investment fund that is a reporting issuer.

4.2 Filing of Management Reports of Fund Performance — An investment fund, other than an investment fund that is a scholarship plan, must file an annual management report of fund performance for each financial year and an interim management report of fund performance for each interim period at the same time that it files its annual financial statements or its interim financial report for that financial period.

4.3 Filing of Annual Management Report of Fund Performance for an Investment Fund that is a Scholarship Plan — An investment fund that is a scholarship plan must file an annual management report of fund performance for each financial year at the same time that it files its annual financial statements.

4.4 Contents of Management Reports of Fund Performance — A management report of fund performance required by this Part must

    (a) be prepared in accordance with Form 81-106F1; and

    (b) not incorporate by reference information from any other document that is required to be included in a management report of fund performance.

4.5 Approval of Management Reports of Fund Performance — (1) The board of directors of an investment fund that is a corporation must approve the management report of fund performance of the investment fund before the report is filed or made available to a holder or potential purchaser of securities of the investment fund.

(2) The trustee or trustees of an investment fund that is a trust, or another person or company authorized to do so by the constating documents of the investment fund, must approve the management report of fund performance of the investment fund before the report is filed or made available to a holder or potential purchaser of securities of the investment fund.

PART 5 — DELIVERY OF FINANCIAL STATEMENTS AND MANAGEMENT REPORTS OF FUND PERFORMANCE

5.1 Delivery of Certain Continuous Disclosure Documents — (1) In this Part, "securityholder" means a registered holder or beneficial owner of securities issued by an investment fund.

(2) Subject to section 5.2 or section 5.3, an investment fund must send to a securityholder, by the filing deadline for the document, the following:

    (a) annual financial statements;

    (b) interim financial report;

    (c) if required to be prepared by the investment fund, the annual management report of fund performance;

(d) if required to be prepared by the investment fund, the interim management report of fund performance.

(3) An investment fund must apply the procedures set out in National Instrument 54-101 *Communication with Beneficial Owners of Securities of a Reporting Issuer* when complying with this Part.

(4) Despite subsection (3), National Instrument 54-101 *Communication with Beneficial Owners of Securities of a Reporting Issuer* does not apply to an investment fund with respect to a requirement under this Part if the investment fund has the necessary information to communicate directly with a beneficial owner of its securities.

5.2 Sending According to Standing Instructions — (1) Subsection 5.1(2) does not apply to an investment fund that requests standing instructions from a securityholder in accordance with this section and sends the documents listed in subsection 5.1(2) according to those instructions.

(2) An investment fund relying on subsection 5.2(1) must send, to each securityholder, a document that

(a) explains the choices a securityholder has to receive the documents listed in subsection 5.1(2);

(b) solicits instructions from the securityholder about delivery of those documents; and

(c) explains that the instructions provided by the securityholder will continue to be followed by the investment fund until they are changed by the securityholder.

(3) If a person or company becomes a securityholder of an investment fund, the investment fund must solicit instructions in accordance with subsection (2) from the securityholder as soon as reasonably practicable after the investment fund accepts a purchase order from the securityholder.

(4) An investment fund must rely on instructions given under this section until a securityholder changes them.

(5) At least once a year, an investment fund must send each securityholder a reminder that

(a) the securityholder is entitled to receive the documents listed in subsection 5.1(2);

(b) the investment fund is relying on delivery instructions provided by the securityholder;

(c) explains how a securityholder can change the instructions it has given; and

(d) the securityholder can obtain the documents on the SEDAR website and on the investment fund's website, if applicable, and by contacting the investment fund.

5.3 Sending According to Annual Instructions — (1) Subsection 5.1(2) does not apply to an investment fund that requests annual instructions from a securityholder in accordance with this section and sends the documents listed in subsection 5.1(2) according to those instructions.

(2) Subsection (1) does not apply to an investment fund that has previously relied on subsection 5.2(1).

(3) An investment fund relying on subsection 5.3(1) must send annually to each securityholder a request form the securityholder may use to instruct the investment fund as to which of the documents listed in subsection 5.1(2) the securityholder wishes to receive.

(4) The request form described in subsection (3) must be accompanied by a notice explaining that

(a) the securityholder is providing delivery instructions for the current year only; and

(b) the documents are available on the SEDAR website and on the investment fund's website, if applicable, and by contacting the investment fund.

5.4 General — (1) If a securityholder requests any of the documents listed in subsection 5.1(2), an investment fund must send a copy of the requested documents by the later of

(a) the filing deadline for the requested document; and

(b) ten calendar days after the investment fund receives the request.

(2) An investment fund must not charge a fee for sending the documents referred to in this Part and must ensure that securityholders can respond without cost to the solicitations of instructions required by this Part.

(3) Investment funds under common management may solicit one set of delivery instructions from a securityholder that will apply to all of the investment funds under common management held by that securityholder.

(4) Despite subsection 7.1(3), for the purposes of delivery to a securityholder, an investment fund may bind its management report of fund performance with the management report of fund performance for one or more other investment funds if the securityholder holds each investment fund.

5.5 Websites — An investment fund that is a reporting issuer and that has a website must post to the website any documents listed in subsection 5.1(2) no later than the date that those documents are filed.

PART 6 — QUARTERLY PORTFOLIO DISCLOSURE

6.1 Application — This Part applies to an investment fund that is a reporting issuer, other than a scholarship plan or a labour sponsored or venture capital fund.

6.2 Preparation and Dissemination — (1) An investment fund must prepare quarterly portfolio disclosure that includes

(a) a summary of investment portfolio prepared in accordance with Item 5 of Part B of Form 81-106F1 as at the end of

(i) each period of at least three months that ends three or nine months before the end of a financial year of the investment fund; or

(ii) in the case of a transition year of the investment fund, each period commencing on the first day of the transition year and ending either three, nine or twelve months, if applicable, after the end of its old financial year; and

(b) the total net asset value of the investment fund as at the end of the periods specified in (a)(i) or (ii).

(2) An investment fund that has a website must post to the website the quarterly portfolio disclosure within 60 days of the end of the period for which the quarterly portfolio disclosure was prepared.

(3) An investment fund must promptly send the most recent quarterly portfolio disclosure, without charge, to any securityholder of the investment fund, upon a request made by the securityholder 60 days after the end of the period to which the quarterly portfolio disclosure pertains.

PART 7 — BINDING AND PRESENTATION

7.1 Binding of Financial Statements and Management Reports of Fund Performance — (1) An investment fund must not bind its financial statements with the financial statements of another investment fund in a document unless all information relating to the investment fund is presented together and not intermingled with information relating to the other investment fund.

(2) Despite subsection (1), if a document contains the financial statements of more than one investment fund, the notes to the financial statements may be combined and presented in a separate part of the document.

(3) An investment fund must not bind its management report of fund performance with the management report of fund performance for another investment fund.

7.2 Multiple Class Investment Funds — (1) An investment fund that has more than one class or series of securities outstanding that are referable to a single portfolio must prepare financial statements and management reports of fund performance that contain information concerning all of the classes or series.

(2) If an investment fund has more than one class or series of securities outstanding, the distinctions between the classes or series must be disclosed in the financial statements and management reports of fund performance.

PART 8 — INDEPENDENT VALUATIONS FOR LABOUR SPONSORED OR VENTURE CAPITAL FUNDS

8.1 Application — This Part applies to a labour sponsored or venture capital fund that is a reporting issuer.

8.2 Exemption from Requirement to Disclose Individual Current Values for Venture Investments — Despite item 5 of subsection 3.5(1), a labour sponsored or venture capital fund is exempt from the requirement to present separately in a statement of investment portfolio the current value of each venture investment that does not have a market value if

(a) the labour sponsored or venture capital fund discloses in the statement of investment portfolio

(i) the cost amounts for each venture investment,

(ii) the total cost of the venture investments,

(iii) the total adjustment from cost to current value of the venture investments, and

(iv) the total current value of the venture investments;

(b) the labour sponsored or venture capital fund discloses in the statement of investment portfolio tables showing the distribution of venture investments by stage of development and by industry classification including

(i) the number of venture investments in each stage of development and industry class,

(ii) the total cost and aggregate current value of the venture investments for each stage of development and industry class, and

(iii) the total cost and aggregate current value of venture investments for each stage of development and industry class as a percentage of total venture investments;

(c) for a statement of investment portfolio contained in annual financial statements, the labour sponsored or venture capital fund has obtained an independent valuation relating to the value of the venture investments or to the net assets of the fund and has filed the independent valuation concurrently with the filing of the annual financial statements;

(d) for a statement of investment portfolio contained in an interim financial report, the labour sponsored or venture capital fund obtained and filed the independent valuation referred to in paragraph (c) in connection with the preparation of the most recent annual financial statements of the labour sponsored or venture capital fund; and

(e) the labour sponsored or venture capital fund has disclosed in the applicable financial statements that an independent valuation has been obtained as of the end of the applicable financial year.

8.3 Disclosure Concerning Independent Valuator — A labour sponsored or venture capital fund that obtains an independent valuation must include, in the statement of investment portfolio contained in its annual financial statements, or in the notes to the annual financial statements,

(a) a description of the independent valuator's qualifications, and

(b) a description of any past, present or anticipated relationship between the independent valuator and the labour sponsored or venture capital fund, its manager or portfolio adviser.

8.4 Content of Independent Valuation — An independent valuation must provide the aggregate current value of the venture investments or of the total equity or net assets attributable to securityholders of the labour sponsored or venture capital fund as at the fund's financial year end.

8.5 Independent Valuator's Consent — A labour sponsored or venture capital fund obtaining an independent valuation must

(a) obtain the independent valuator's consent to its filing; and

(b) include a statement in the valuation report, signed by the independent valuator, in substantially the following form:

We refer to the independent valuation of the [total equity/net assets attributable to securityholders/venture investments] of [name of labour sponsored or venture capital fund] as of [date of financial year end] dated .... We consent to the filing of the independent valuation with the securities regulatory authorities.

PART 9 — ANNUAL INFORMATION FORM

9.1 Application — This Part applies to an investment fund that is a reporting issuer.

9.2 Requirement to File Annual Information Form — An investment fund must file an annual information form if the investment fund has not obtained a receipt for a prospectus during the last 12 months preceding its financial year end.

9.3 Filing Deadline for Annual Information Form — An investment fund required under section 9.2 to file an annual information form must file the annual information form no later than 90 days after the end of its most recently completed financial year.

9.4 Preparation and Content of Annual Information Form — (1) An annual information form required to be filed under section 9.2 must be prepared as of the end of the most recently completed financial year of the investment fund to which it pertains.

(2) An annual information form required to be filed must be prepared in accordance with Form 81-101F2, except that

(a) a reference to "mutual fund" must be read as a reference to "investment fund";

(b) General Instructions (3), (10) and (14) of Form 81-101F2 do not apply;

(c) subsections (3), (4) and (6) of Item 1.1 of Form 81-101F2 do not apply;

(d) subsections (3), (4) and (6) of Item 1.2 of Form 81-101F2 do not apply;

(e) Item 5 of Form 81-101F2 must be completed in connection with all of the securities of the investment fund;

(f) Item 15 of Form 81-101F2 does not apply to an investment fund that is a corporation, except for the disclosure in connection with the independent review committee; and

(g) Items 19, 20, 21 and 22 of Form 81-101F2 do not apply.

(3) An investment fund required to file an annual information form must at the same time file copies of all material incorporated by reference in the annual information form that it has not previously filed.

PART 10 — PROXY VOTING DISCLOSURE FOR PORTFOLIO SECURITIES HELD

10.1 Application — This Part applies to an investment fund that is a reporting issuer.

10.2 Requirement to Establish Policies and Procedures — (1) An investment fund must establish policies and procedures that it will follow to determine whether, and how, to vote on any matter for which the investment fund receives, in its capacity as securityholder, proxy materials for a meeting of securityholders of an issuer.

(2) The policies and procedures referred to in subsection (1) must include

(a) a standing policy for dealing with routine matters on which the investment fund may vote;

(b) the circumstances under which the investment fund will deviate from the standing policy for routine matters;

(c) the policies under which, and the procedures by which, the investment fund will determine how to vote or refrain from voting on non-routine matters; and

(d) procedures to ensure that portfolio securities held by the investment fund are voted in accordance with the instructions of the investment fund.

(3) An investment fund that has not prepared an annual information form in accordance with Part 9 or in accordance with National Instrument 81-101 *Mutual Fund Prospectus Disclosure* must include a summary of the policies and procedures required by this section in its prospectus.

10.3 Proxy Voting Record — An investment fund must maintain a proxy voting record that includes, for each time that the investment fund receives, in its capacity as securityholder, materials relating to a meeting of securityholders of a reporting issuer or the equivalent of a reporting issuer in a foreign jurisdiction,

(a) the name of the issuer;

(b) the exchange ticker symbol of the portfolio securities, unless not readily available to the investment fund;

(c) the CUSIP number for the portfolio securities;

(d) the meeting date;

(e) a brief identification of the matter or matters to be voted on at the meeting;

(f) whether the matter or matters voted on were proposed by the issuer, its management or another person or company;

(g) whether the investment fund voted on the matter or matters;

(h) if applicable, how the investment fund voted on the matter or matters; and

(i) whether votes cast by the investment fund were for or against the recommendations of management of the issuer.

10.4 Preparation and Availability of Proxy Voting Record — (1) An investment fund must prepare a proxy voting record on an annual basis for the period ending on June 30 of each year.

(2) An investment fund that has a website must post the proxy voting record to the website no later than August 31 of each year.

(3) An investment fund must promptly send the most recent copy of the investment fund's proxy voting policies and procedures and proxy voting record, without charge, to any securityholder upon a request made by the securityholder after August 31.

PART 11 — MATERIAL CHANGE REPORTS

11.1 Application — This Part applies to an investment fund that is a reporting issuer.

11.2 Publication of Material Change — (1) If a material change occurs in the affairs of an investment fund, the investment fund must

(a) promptly issue and file a news release that is authorized by an executive officer of the manager of the investment fund and that discloses the nature and substance of the material change;

(b) post all disclosure made under paragraph (a) on the website of the investment fund or the investment fund manager;

(c) as soon as practicable, but in any event no later than 10 days after the date on which the change occurs, file a report containing the information required by Form 51-102F3, except that a reference in Form 51-102F3 to

(i) the term "material change" must be read as "material change" under this Instrument;

(ii) "section 7.1 of National Instrument 51-102" in Item 3 of Part 2 must be read as a reference to "section 11.2 of National Instrument 81-106";

(iii) "subsection 7.1(2) of National Instrument 51-102" in Item 6 of Part 2 must be read as a reference to "subsection 11.2(2) of National Instrument 81-106";

(iv) "subsection 7.1(5) of National Instrument 51-102" in Items 6 and 7 of Part 2 must be read as a reference to "subsection 11.2(4) of National Instrument 81-106"; and

(v) "executive officer of your company" in Item 8 of Part 2 must be read as a reference to "officer of the investment fund or of the manager of the investment fund"; and

(d) file an amendment to its prospectus, simplified prospectus or fund facts document that discloses the material change in accordance with the requirements of securities legislation.

(2) If

(a) in the opinion of the board of directors or trustee of an investment fund or the manager, and if that opinion is arrived at in a reasonable manner, the disclosure required by subsection (1) would be unduly detrimental to the investment fund's interest; or

(b) the material change

(i) consists of a decision to implement a change made by senior management of the investment fund or senior management of the manager of the investment fund who believe that confirmation of the decision by the board of directors or persons acting in a similar capacity is probable; and

(ii) senior management of the investment fund or senior management of the manager of the investment fund has no reason to believe that persons with knowledge of the material change have made use of that knowledge in purchasing or selling securities of the investment fund,

the investment fund may, instead of complying with subsection (1), immediately file the report required under paragraph (1)(c) marked to indicate that it is confidential, together with written reasons for non-disclosure.

(3) [Repealed]

(4) If a report has been filed under subsection (2), the investment fund must advise the regulator or securities regulatory authority in writing within ten days of the initial filing of the report if it believes the report should continue to remain confidential and every 10 days thereafter until the material change is generally disclosed in the manner referred to in subsection (1) or, if the material change consists of a decision of the type referred to in paragraph (2)(b), until that decision has been rejected by the board of directors of the investment fund or the board of directors of the manager of the investment fund.

(5) Despite filing a report under subsection (2), an investment fund must promptly and generally disclose the material change in the manner referred to in subsection (1) upon the investment fund becoming aware, or having reasonable grounds to believe, that a person or company is purchasing or selling securities of the investment fund with knowledge of the material change that has not been generally disclosed.

PART 12 — PROXY SOLICITATION AND INFORMATION CIRCULARS

12.1 Application — This Part applies to an investment fund that is a reporting issuer.

12.2 Sending of Proxies and Information Circulars — (1) If management of an investment fund or the manager of an investment fund gives or intends to give notice of a meeting to registered holders of the investment fund, management or the manager must, at the same time as or before giving that notice, send to each registered holder who is entitled to notice of the meeting a form of proxy for use at the meeting.

(2) A person or company that solicits proxies from registered holders of an investment fund must

(a) in the case of a solicitation by or on behalf of management of the investment fund, send with the notice of meeting to each registered holder whose proxy is solicited a completed Form 51-102F5; or

(b) in the case of a solicitation by or on behalf of any person or company other than management of the investment fund, at the same time as or before the solicitation, send a completed Form 51-102F5 and a form of proxy to each registered holder whose proxy is solicited.

12.3 Exemption — (1) Subsection 12.2(2) does not apply to a solicitation by a person or company in respect of securities of which the person or company is the beneficial owner.

(2) Paragraph 12.2(2)(b) does not apply to a solicitation if the total number of securityholders whose proxies are solicited is not more than 15.

(3) For the purposes of subsection (2), two or more persons or companies who are joint registered owners of one or more securities are considered to be one securityholder.

12.4 Compliance with National Instrument 51-102 — A person or company that solicits proxies under section 12.2 must comply with sections 9.3 and 9.4 of National Instrument 51-102 as if those sections applied to the person or company.

PART 13 — CHANGE OF AUDITOR DISCLOSURE

13.1 Application — This Part applies to an investment fund that is a reporting issuer.

13.2 Change of Auditor — Section 4.11 of National Instrument 51-102 applies to an investment fund that changes its auditor, except that references in that section to the "board of directors" are to be read as references to,

(a) if the investment fund is a corporation, the "board of directors of the investment fund", or

(b) if the investment fund is a trust, the "trustee or trustees or another person or company authorized by the constating documents of the investment fund".

PART 14 — CALCULATION OF NET ASSET VALUE

14.1 Application — This Part applies to an investment fund that is a reporting issuer.

14.2 Calculation, Frequency and Currency — (1) The net asset value of an investment fund must be calculated using the fair value of the investment fund's assets and liabilities.

(1.1) The net asset value of an investment fund must include the income and expenses of the investment fund accrued up to the date of calculation of the net asset value.

(1.2) For the purposes of subsection (1), fair value means

 (a) the market value based on reported prices and quotations in an active market, or

 (b) if the market value is not available, or the manager of the investment fund believes that it is unreliable, a value that is fair and reasonable in all the relevant circumstances.

(1.3) The manager of an investment fund must

 (a) establish and maintain appropriate written policies and procedures for determining the fair value of the investment fund's assets and liabilities; and

 (b) consistently follow those policies and procedures.

(1.4) The manager of an investment fund must maintain a record of the determination of fair value and the reasons supporting that determination.

(2) For the purposes of calculating net asset value for purchases and redemptions of its securities as required by Parts 9 and 10 of National Instrument 81-102 *Investment Funds*, a labour sponsored or venture capital fund that has included a deferred charge for sales commissions in the calculation may continue to do so, provided that

 (a) the calculation reflects the amortization of this deferred charge over the remaining amortization period, and

 (b) the labour sponsored or venture capital fund ceased adding to this deferred charge by December 31, 2003.

(3) An investment fund must calculate its net asset value at least as frequently as the following:

 (a) if the investment fund does not use specified derivatives or sell securities short, once a week;

 (b) if the investment fund uses specified derivatives or sells securities short, once every business day.

(4) A mutual fund that holds securities of other mutual funds must have dates for the calculation of net asset value that are compatible with those of the other mutual funds.

(5) Despite paragraph (3)(a), an investment fund that, at the date that this Instrument comes into force, calculates net asset value no less frequently than once a month may continue to calculate net asset value at least as frequently as it does at that date.

(6) The net asset value of an investment fund must be calculated in the currency of Canada or in the currency of the United States of America or both.

(6.1) An investment fund must, upon calculating the net asset value of the investment fund under this section, make the following information available to the public at no cost:

 (a) the net asset value of the investment fund;

 (b) the net asset value per security of the investment fund unless the investment fund is a scholarship plan.

(7) An investment fund that arranges for the publication of its net asset value or net asset value per security in the financial press must ensure that its current net asset value or net asset value per security is provided on a timely basis to the financial press.

14.3 Portfolio Transactions — The net asset value of an investment fund must include each purchase or sale of a portfolio asset no later than in the next calculation of the net asset value after the date the purchase or sale becomes binding.

14.4 Capital Transactions — The investment fund must include each issue or redemption of a security of the investment fund in the next calculation of net asset value the investment fund makes after the calculation of net asset value used to establish the issue or redemption price.

PART 15 — CALCULATION OF MANAGEMENT EXPENSE RATIO

15.1 Calculation of Management Expense Ratio — (1) An investment fund may disclose its management expense ratio only if the management expense ratio is calculated for the financial year or interim period of the investment fund and if it is calculated by

 (a) dividing

  (i) the aggregate of

   (A) total expenses of the investment fund, excluding distributions if recognized as an expense, commissions and other portfolio transaction costs, before income taxes, for the financial year or interim period, as shown on its statement of comprehensive income; and

   (B) any other fee, charge or expense of the investment fund that has the effect of reducing the investment fund's net asset value;

  by

  (ii) the average net asset value of the investment fund for the financial year or interim period, obtained by

   (A) adding together the net asset values of the investment fund as at the close of business of the investment fund on each day during the financial year or interim period on which the net asset value of the investment fund has been calculated, and

   (B) dividing the amount obtained under clause (A) by the number of days during the financial year or interim period on which the net asset value of the investment fund has been calculated; and

 (b) multiplying the result obtained under paragraph (a) by 100.

(2) If any fees and expenses otherwise payable by an investment fund in a financial year or interim period were waived or otherwise absorbed by a member of the organization of the investment fund, the investment fund must disclose, in a note to the disclosure of its management expense ratio, details of

 (a) what the management expense ratio would have been without any waivers or absorptions;

 (b) the length of time that the waiver or absorption is expected to continue;

 (c) whether the waiver or absorption can be terminated at any time by the member of the organization of the investment fund; and

 (d) any other arrangements concerning the waiver or absorption.

(3) Investment fund expenses rebated by a manager or an investment fund to a securityholder must not be deducted from total expenses of the investment fund in determining the management expense ratio of the investment fund.

(4) An investment fund that has separate classes or series of securities must calculate a management expense ratio for each class or series, in the manner required by this section, modified as appropriate.

(5) The management expense ratio of an investment fund for a financial period of less than or greater than twelve months must be annualized.

(6) If an investment fund provides its management expense ratio to a service provider that will arrange for public dissemination of the management expense ratio,

(a) the investment fund must provide the management expense ratio calculated in accordance with this Part; and

(b) the requirement to provide note disclosure contained in subsection (2) does not apply if the investment fund indicates, as applicable, that fees have been waived, expenses have been absorbed, or that fees or expenses were paid directly by investors during the period for which the management expense ratio was calculated.

15.2 Fund of Funds Calculation — (1) For the purposes of subparagraph 15.1(1)(a)(i), the total expenses for a financial year or interim period of an investment fund that invests in securities of other investment funds is equal to the sum of

(a) the total expenses incurred by the investment fund that are for the period for which the calculation of the management expense ratio is made and that are attributable to its investment in each underlying investment fund, as calculated by

(i) multiplying the total expenses of each underlying investment fund, excluding distributions if recognized as an expense, commissions and other portfolio transaction costs, before income taxes, for the financial year or interim period, by

(ii) the average proportion of securities of the underlying investment fund held by the investment fund during the financial year or interim period, calculated by

(A) adding together the proportion of securities of the underlying investment fund held by the investment fund on each day in the period, and

(B) dividing the amount obtained under clause (A) by the number of days in the period; and

(b) the total expenses of the investment fund, excluding distributions if recognized as an expense, commissions and other portfolio transaction costs, before income taxes, for the period.

(2) An investment fund that has exposure to one or more other investment funds through the use of derivatives in a financial year or interim period must calculate its management expense ratio for the financial year or interim period in the manner described in subsection (1), treating each investment fund to which it has exposure as an "underlying investment fund" under subsection (1).

(3) Subsection (2) does not apply if the derivatives do not expose the investment fund to expenses that would be incurred by a direct investment in the relevant investment funds.

(4) Management fees rebated by an underlying fund to an investment fund that invests in the underlying fund must be deducted from total expenses of the underlying fund if the rebate is made for the purpose of avoiding duplication of fees between the two investment funds.

PART 16 — ADDITIONAL FILING REQUIREMENTS

16.1 Application — This Part applies to an investment fund that is a reporting issuer.

16.2 Additional Filing Requirements — If an investment fund sends to its securityholders any disclosure document other than those required by this Instrument, the investment fund must file a copy of the document on the same date as, or as soon as practicable after, the date on which the document is sent to its securityholders.

16.3 Voting Result — An investment fund must, promptly following a meeting of securityholders at which a matter was submitted to a vote, file a report that discloses, for each matter voted upon

(a) a brief description of the matter voted upon and the outcome of the vote; and

(b) if the vote was conducted by ballot, the number and percentage of votes cast, which includes votes cast in person and by proxy, for, against, or withheld from, each vote.

16.4 Filing of Material Contracts — An investment fund that is not subject to National Instrument 81-101 *Mutual Fund Prospectus Disclosure*, or securities legislation that imposes a similar requirement, must file a copy of any material contract of the investment fund not previously filed, or any amendment to any material contract of the investment fund not previously filed

(a) with the final prospectus of the investment fund; or

(b) upon the execution of the material contract or amendment.

PART 17 — EXEMPTIONS

17.1 Exemption — (1) The regulator or securities regulatory authority may grant an exemption from this Instrument, in whole or in part, subject to such conditions or restrictions as may be imposed in the exemption.

(2) Despite subsection (1), in Ontario only the regulator may grant an exemption from any part of this Instrument.

PART 18 — EFFECTIVE DATE AND TRANSITION

18.1 Effective Date — This Instrument comes into force on June 1, 2005.

18.2–18.5 [Repealed]

18.5.1 Transition to IFRS — (1) For the first interim period in the financial year beginning on or after January 1, 2014, an investment fund must file, with its interim financial report for that interim period, an opening statement of financial position as at the date of transition to IFRS.

(2) For the first financial year beginning on or after January 1, 2014, an investment fund must file, with its annual financial statements for that financial year, an audited opening statement of financial position as at the date of transition to IFRS.

(3) Despite sections 3.1, 3.2, 3.3, 3.4 and 3.6, for financial years beginning before January 1, 2014, an investment fund may present line items and use terminology in its financial statements consistent with the immediately preceding financial year.

18.5.2 Securities Lending — For financial years beginning before January 1, 2016, an investment fund is not required to comply with subsections 3.8(4) and (5).

18.6 Existing Exemptions — (1) An investment fund that has obtained an exemption or waiver from, or approval under, securities legislation, National Policy 39, National Instrument 81-101 *Mutual Fund Prospectus Disclosure*, National Instrument 81-102 *Investment Funds*, National Instrument 81-104 *Commodity Pools* or National Instrument 81-105 *Mutual Fund Sales Practices* relating to its continuous disclosure obligations is exempt from any substantially similar provision of this Instrument to the same extent and on the same conditions, if any, as contained in the exemption, waiver or approval, unless the regulator or securities regulatory authority has revoked that exemption, waiver or approval under authority provided to it in securities legislation.

(2) An investment fund must, at the time that it first intends to rely on subsection (1) in connection with a filing requirement under this Instrument, inform the securities regulatory authority in writing of

    (a) the general nature of the prior exemption, waiver or approval and the date on which it was granted; and

    (b) the provision in respect of which the prior exemption, waiver or approval applied and the substantially similar provision of this Instrument.

Final Rule: (2005) 28 O.S.C.B. 4911; Approval by OSC: (2005) 28 O.S.C.B. (Supp-1) 1; Request for Comments: (2004) 27 O.S.C.B. 5157; (2002) 25 O.S.C.B. 6273.

Amendment to Rule: (2006) 29 O.S.C.B. 8850; Approval by OSC: (2006) 29 O.S.C.B. (Supp-1) 1; Request for Comments: (2005) 28 O.S.C.B. (Supp-2) 1 and (2004) 27 O.S.C.B. 465.

Amendment to Rule: (2008) 31 O.S.C.B. 8559; Approval by OSC: (2008) 31 O.S.C.B. 6275; Request for Comments: (2007) 30 O.S.C.B. 4965.

Amendment to Rule: (2010) 33 O.S.C.B. 11433; Approval by OSC: (2010) 33 O.S.C.B. (Supp. 4) 1; Request for Comments: (2009) 32 O.S.C.B. (Supp. 1) 1, (2008) 31 O.S.C.B. 10479, (2007) 30 O.S.C.B. (Supp. 4) 1 and (2003) 26 O.S.C.B. 1443.

Amendment to Rule: (2012) 35 O.S.C.B. 3426; Approval by OSC: (2012) 35 O.S.C.B. 1375; Request for Comments: (2010) 33 O.S.C.B. 5833.

Amendment to Rule: (2013) 36 O.S.C.B. 2619; Request for Comments: (2012) 35 O.S.C.B. 6887.

Amendment to Rule: Approval by OSC: (2013) 36 O.S.C.B. 9612; Request for Comments: (2009) 32 O.S.C.B. 8381

Rules: NI 51-102, 81-107; Rule 81-801.

Policies and Orders: NPS 81-106CP, 12-203; OPS 51-601, 81-801CP; CSAN 81-315, 52-320; OSCN 11-763, 81-705, 81-709, 81-717, 81-718, 81-719, 33-733.

Form 81-106F1 — Contents of Annual and Interim Management Report of Fund Performance

Table of Contents

Part A — Instructions and Interpretation

Item 1 — General

(a) — The Form

The Form describes the disclosure required in an annual or interim management report of fund performance (MRFP) of an investment fund. Each item of the Form outlines disclosure or format requirements. Instructions to help you comply with these requirements are printed in italic type.

(b) — Plain Language

An MRFP must state the required information concisely and in plain language (as defined in National Instrument 81-101 *Mutual Fund Prospectus Disclosure*). Refer to Part 1 of Companion Policy 81-106CP for a discussion concerning plain language and presentation.

When preparing an MRFP, respond as simply and directly as is reasonably possible and include only as much information as is necessary for readers to understand the matters for which you are providing disclosure.

(c) — Format

Present the MRFP in a format that assists readability and comprehension. The Form generally does not mandate the use of a specific format to achieve these goals, except in the case of disclosure of financial highlights and past performance as required by Items 3 and 4 of each of Parts B and C of the Form; that disclosure must be presented in the format specified in the Form.

An MRFP must use the headings and sub-headings shown in the Form. Within this framework, investment funds are encouraged to use, as appropriate, tables, captions, bullet points or other organizational techniques that assist in presenting the required disclosure clearly and concisely. Disclosure provided in response to any item does not need to be repeated elsewhere. The interim MRFP must use the same headings as used in the annual MRFP.

The Form does not prohibit including information beyond what the Form requires. An investment fund may include artwork and educational material (as defined in National Instrument 81-101 *Mutual Fund Prospectus Disclosure*) in its annual and interim MRFP. However, an investment fund must take reasonable care to ensure that including such material does not obscure the required information and does not lengthen the MRFP excessively.

(d) — Focus on Material Information

You do not need to disclose information that is not material. You do not need to respond to any item in this Form that is inapplicable and you may omit negative answers.

(e) — What is Material?

Would a reasonable investor's decision to buy, sell or hold securities of an investment fund likely be influenced or changed if the information in question was omitted or misstated? If so, the information is material. This concept of materiality is consistent with the financial reporting notion of materiality contained in the Handbook. In determining whether information is material, take into account both quantitative and qualitative factors.

(f) — Terminology

All references to "net assets" or "net assets per security" in this Form are references to total equity or net assets attributable to securityholders determined in accordance with Canadian GAAP as presented in the financial statements of the investment fund. All references to "net asset value" or "net asset value per security" in this Form are references to net asset value determined in accordance with Part 14 of the Instrument. Investment funds must use net assets as shown on the financial statements in the "The Fund's Net Assets per [Unit/Share]" table. All other calculations for the purposes of the MRFP must be made using net asset value.

Item 2 — Management Discussion of Fund Performance

The management discussion of fund performance is an analysis and explanation that is designed to complement and supplement an investment fund's financial statements. The discussion is the equivalent to the corporate management discussion and analysis (MD&A) with specific modifications for investment funds. It provides the manager of an investment fund with the opportunity to discuss the investment fund's position and financial results for the relevant period. The discussion is intended to give a reader the ability to look at the investment fund through the eyes of management by providing both a historical and prospective analysis of the investment activities and operations of the investment fund. Coupled with the financial highlights, this information should enable readers to better assess the investment fund's performance and future prospects.

Focus the management discussion on material information about the performance of the investment fund, with particular emphasis on known material trends, commitments, events, risks or uncertainties that the manager reasonably expects to have a material effect on the investment fund's future performance or investment activities.

The description of the disclosure requirements is intentionally general. This Form contains a minimum number of specific instructions in order to allow, as well as encourage, investment funds to discuss their activities in the most appropriate manner and to tailor their comments to their individual circumstances.

Part B — Content Requirements for Annual Management Report of Fund Performance

Item 1 — First Page Disclosure

The first page of an annual MRFP must contain disclosure in substantially the following words:

> This annual management report of fund performance contains financial highlights but does not contain the complete annual financial statements of the investment fund. You can get a copy of the annual financial statements at your request, and at no cost, by calling [toll-free/collect call telephone number], by writing to us at [insert address] or by visiting our website at [insert address] or SEDAR at www.sedar.com.
>
> Securityholders may also contact us using one of these methods to request a copy of the investment fund's interim financial report, proxy voting policies and procedures, proxy voting disclosure record, or quarterly portfolio disclosure.

Instruction:

If the MRFP is bound with the financial statements of the investment fund, modify the first page wording appropriately.

Item 2 — Management Discussion of Fund Performance

2.1 — Investment Objective and Strategies

Disclose under the heading "Investment Objective and Strategies" a brief summary of the fundamental investment objective and strategies of the investment fund.

Instruction:

Disclosing the fundamental investment objective provides investors with a reference point for assessing the information contained in the MRFP. It must be a concise summary of the fundamental investment objective and strategies of the investment fund, and not merely copied from the prospectus.

2.2 — Risk

Disclose under the heading "Risk" a discussion of how changes to the investment fund over the financial year affected the overall level of risk associated with an investment in the investment fund.

Instruction:

Ensure that the discussion is not merely a repeat of information contained in the prospectus of the investment fund, but rather a discussion that reflects any changes in risk level of the investment fund over the financial year.

Consider how the changes in the risks associated with an investment in the investment fund affect the suitability or investor risk tolerance stated in the prospectus or offering document. All investment funds should refer to Items 9 and 10 of Part B of Form 81-101F1 as if those sections applied to them.

2.3 — Results of Operations

(1) Under the heading "Results of Operations" provide a summary of the results of operations of the investment fund for the financial year to which the MDFP [Editor's note: should be "*MRFP*"] pertains, including a discussion of

(a) any material changes in investments in specific portfolio assets and overall asset mix from the previous period;

(b) how the composition and changes to the composition of the investment portfolio relate to the investment fund's fundamental investment objective and strategies or to changes in the economy, markets or unusual events;

(c) unusual trends in redemptions or sales and the effect of these on the investment fund;

(d) significant components and changes to the components of revenue and expenses;

(e) risks, events, trends and commitments that had a material effect on past performance; and

(f) unusual or infrequent events or transactions, economic changes and market conditions that affected performance.

(2) An investment fund that borrows money, other than immaterial operating overdrafts, must disclose,

(a) the minimum and maximum amount borrowed during the period;

(b) the percentage of net assets of the investment fund that the borrowing represented as of the end of the period;

(c) how the borrowed money was used; and

(d) the terms of the borrowing arrangements.

Instruction:

Explain the nature of and reasons for changes in your investment fund's performance. Do not simply disclose the amount of change in a financial statement item from period to period. Avoid the use of boilerplate language. Your discussion should assist the reader to understand the significant factors that have affected the performance of the investment fund.

2.4 — Recent Developments

Under the heading "Recent Developments" discuss the developments affecting the investment fund, including

(a) known changes to the strategic position of the investment fund;

(b) known material trends, commitments, events or uncertainties that might reasonably be expected to affect the investment fund;

(c) changes to the manager or portfolio adviser, or change of control of the manager, of the investment fund;

(d) the effects of any actual or planned reorganizations, mergers or similar transactions;

(e) the estimated effects of changes in accounting policies adopted subsequent to year end; and

(f) changes to the composition or members of the independent review committee of the investment fund.

Instruction:

(1) Preparing the management discussion necessarily involves some degree of prediction or projection. The discussion must describe anticipated events, decisions, circumstances, opportunities and risks that management considers reasonably likely to materially impact performance. It must also describe management's vision, strategy and targets.

(2) There is no requirement to provide forward-looking information. If any forward-looking information is provided, it must contain a statement that the information is forward-looking, a description of the factors that may cause actual results to differ materially from the forward-looking information, your material assumptions and appropriate risk disclosure and cautionary language. You must also discuss any forward-looking information disclosed for a prior period which, in light of intervening events and absent further explanations, may be misleading.

2.5 — Related Party Transactions

Under the heading "Related Party Transactions" discuss any transactions involving related parties to the investment fund.

Instructions:

(1) In determining who is a related party, investment funds should look to the Handbook. In addition, related parties include the manager and portfolio adviser (or their affiliates) and a broker or dealer related to any of the investment fund, its manager or portfolio adviser.

(2) When discussing related party transactions, include the identity of the related party, the relationship to the investment fund, the purpose of the transaction, the measurement basis used to determine the recorded amount and any ongoing commitments to the related party.

(3) Related party transactions include portfolio transactions with related parties of the investment fund. When discussing these transactions, include the dollar amount of commission, spread or any other fee that the investment fund paid to any related party in connection with a portfolio transaction.

(4) If the investment fund has an independent review committee, state whether the investment fund has relied on the positive recommendation or approval of the independent review committee to proceed with the transaction, and provide details of any conditions or parameters surrounding the transaction imposed by the independent review committee in its positive recommendation or approval.

Item 3 — Financial Highlights

3.1 — Financial Highlights

(1) Provide selected financial highlights for the investment fund under the heading "Financial Highlights" in the form of the following tables, appropriately completed, and introduced using the following words:

> The following tables show selected key financial information about the Fund and are intended to help you understand the Fund's financial performance for the past [insert number] years.

The Fund's Net Assets per [Unit/Share][1]

	[insert year]	[insert year]	[insert year]	[insert year]	[insert year]
Net Assets, beginning of year	$.........	$.........	$.........	$.........	$.........
Increase (decrease) from operations:					
total revenue	$.........	$.........	$.........	$.........	$.........
total expenses [excluding distributions]	$.........	$.........	$.........	$.........	$.........
realized gains (losses) for the period	$.........	$.........	$.........	$.........	$.........
unrealized gains (losses) for the period	$.........	$.........	$.........	$.........	$.........
Total increase (decrease) from operations[2]	$.........	$.........	$.........	$.........	$.........
Distributions:					
From net investment income (excluding dividends)	$.........	$.........	$.........	$.........	$.........
From dividends	$.........	$.........	$.........	$.........	$.........
From capital gains	$.........	$.........	$.........	$.........	$.........
Return of capital	$.........	$.........	$.........	$.........	$.........
Total Annual Distributions[3]	$.........	$.........	$.........	$.........	$.........
Net assets at [insert last day of financial year] of year shown	$.........	$.........	$.........	$.........	$.........

Notes:

(1) *This information is derived from the Fund's audited annual financial statements. The net assets per security presented in the financial statements differs from the net asset value calculated for fund pricing purposes. [An explanation of these differences can be found in the notes to the financial statements./This difference is due to [explain].]*

(2) *Net assets and distributions are based on the actual number of [units/shares] outstanding at the relevant time. The increase/decrease from operations is based on the weighted average number of [units/shares] outstanding over the financial period.*

(3) *Distributions were [paid in cash/reinvested in additional [units/shares] of the Fund, or both].*

Ratios and Supplemental Data

	[insert year]	[insert year]	[insert year]	[insert year]	[insert year]
Total net asset value (000's)[1]	$..........	$..........	$..........	$..........	$..........
Number of [units/shares] outstanding[1]					
Management expense ratio[2]	%..........	%..........	%..........	%..........	%..........
Management expense ratio before waivers or absorptions	%..........	%..........	%..........	%..........	%..........
Trading expense ratio[3]	%..........	%..........	%..........	%..........	%..........
Portfolio turnover rate[4]	%..........	%..........	%..........	%..........	%..........
Net asset value per [unit/share]	$..........	$..........	$..........	$..........	$..........
Closing market price [if applicable]	$..........	$..........	$..........	$..........	$..........

Notes:

(1) *This information is provided as at [insert date of end of financial year] of the year shown.*

(2) *Management expense ratio is based on total expenses (excluding [distributions], commissions and other portfolio transaction costs) for the stated period and is expressed as an annualized percentage of daily average net asset value during the period.*

(3) *The trading expense ratio represents total commissions and other portfolio transaction costs expressed as an annualized percentage of daily average net asset value during the period.*

(4) *The Fund's portfolio turnover rate indicates how actively the Fund's portfolio adviser manages its portfolio investments. A portfolio turnover rate of 100% is equivalent to the Fund buying and selling all of the securities in its portfolio once in the course of the year. The higher a fund's portfolio turnover rate in a year, the greater the trading costs payable by the fund in the year, and the greater the chance of an investor receiving taxable capital gains in the year. There is not necessarily a relationship between a high turnover rate and the performance of a fund.*

(2) [Repealed]

(3) Modify the table appropriately for corporate investment funds.

(4) Show the financial highlights individually for each class or series, if a multi-class fund.

(5) Provide per unit or per share amounts to the nearest cent, and provide percentage amounts to two decimal places.

(6) Except for net assets, net asset value and distributions, calculate per unit/share values on the basis of the weighted average number of unit/shares outstanding over the financial period.

(7) Provide the selected financial information required by this Item in chronological order for each of the five most recently completed financial years of the investment fund for which audited financial statements have been filed, with the information for the most recent financial year in the first column on the left of the table.

(7.1) (a) For financial years beginning on or after January 1, 2014, the financial highlights may be derived from the investment fund's financial statements prepared in accordance with subsections 2.6(1) of the Instrument.

(b) For financial periods beginning on or after January 1, 2014, derive the financial highlights from the investment fund's financial statements prepared in accordance with subsecion 2.6(2) of the Instrument.

(c) Despite paragraph (a), in an annual MRFP for a financial year beginning on or after January 1, 2014, derive the financial highlights for the immediately preceding financial year from financial statements prepared in accordance with subsection 2.6(2) of the Instrument.

(d) If the financial highlights relate to financial periods beginning both before and on or after January 1, 2014, disclose, in a note to the table, the accounting principles applicable to each period.

(8) If the investment fund has merged with another investment fund, include in the table only the financial information of the continuing investment fund.

(9) Calculate the management expense ratio of the investment fund as required by Part 15 of the Instrument. Include a brief description of the method of calculating the management expense ratio in a note to the table.

(10) If the investment fund,

(a) changed, or proposes to change, the basis of the calculation of the management fees or of the other fees, charges or expenses that are charged to the investment fund; or

(b) introduces or proposes to introduce a new fee,

and if the change would have had an effect on the management expense ratio for the last completed financial year of the investment fund if the change had been in effect throughout that financial year, disclose the effect of the change on the management expense ratio in a note to the "Ratios and Supplemental Data" table.

(11) Do not include disclosure concerning portfolio turnover rate for a money market fund.

(12) (a) Calculate the trading expense ratio by dividing

(i) the total commissions and other portfolio transaction costs disclosed in the statement of operations, by

(ii) the same denominator used to calculate the management expense ratio.

(b) If an investment fund invests in securities of other investment funds, calculate the trading expense ratio using the methodology required for the calculation of the management expense ratio in section 15.2 of the Instrument, making reasonable assumptions or estimates when necessary.

(13) Provide the closing market price only if the investment fund is traded on an exchange.

Instructions:

(1) Calculate the investment fund's portfolio turnover rate by dividing the lesser of the amounts of the cost of purchases and proceeds of sales of portfolio securities for the financial year by the average of the value of the portfolio securities owned by the investment fund in the financial year. Calculate the monthly average by totalling the values of portfolio securities as at the beginning and end of the first month of the financial year and as at the end of each of the succeeding 11 months and dividing the sum by 13. Exclude from both numerator and denominator amounts relating to all portfolio securities having a remaining term to maturity on the date of acquisition by the investment fund of one year or less.

(2) Further to instruction (1), include:

(a) proceeds from a short sale in the value of the portfolio securities sold during the period;

(b) the cost of covering a short sale in the value of portfolio securities purchased during the period;

(c) premiums paid to purchase options in the value of portfolio securities purchased during the period; and

(d) premiums received from the sale of options in the value of the portfolio securities sold during the period.

(3) If the investment fund acquired the assets of another investment fund in exchange for its own shares during the financial year in a purchase-of-assets transaction, exclude from the calculation of portfolio turnover rate the value of securities acquired and sold to realign the fund's portfolio. Adjust the denominator of the portfolio turnover computation to reflect these excluded purchases and sales and disclose them in a footnote.

3.2 — Scholarship Plans

An investment fund that is a scholarship plan must comply with Item 3.1, except that the following table must replace "The Fund's Net Assets per [Unit/Share]" table and the "Ratios and Supplemental Data" table.

Financial & Operating Highlights (with comparative figures)

	[insert year]	[insert year]	[insert year]	[insert year]	[insert year]
Statement of Financial Position					
Total Assets	$	$	$	$	$
Net Assets	$	$	$	$	$
% change of Net Assets	%	%	%	%	%
Statement of Comprehensive Income					
Scholarship Awards	$	$	$	$	$
Canadian Education Savings Grant	$	$	$	$	$
Net investment income	$	$	$	$	$
Other					
Total number of [agreements/units] in plans					
% change in the total number of agreements	%	%	%	%	%

3.3 — Management Fees

Disclose the basis for calculating the management fees paid by the investment fund and a breakdown of the services received in consideration of the management fees, as a percentage of management fees.

Instruction:

The disclosure must list the major services paid for out of the management fees, including portfolio adviser compensation, waived or absorbed expenses, trailing commissions and sales commissions, if applicable. Services may be grouped together so that commercially sensitive information, such as the specific compensation paid to a portfolio adviser or the manager's profit, is not determinable.

Item 4 — Past Performance

4.1 — General

(1) In responding to the requirements of this Item, an investment fund must comply with sections 15.2, 15.3, 15.9, 15.10, 15.11 and 15.14 of National Instrument 81-102 *Investment Funds* as if those sections applied to the annual MRFP.

(2) Despite the specific requirements of this Item, do not provide performance data for any period if the investment fund was not a reporting issuer at all times during the period.

Part 8: MUTUAL FUNDS

(3) Set out in the footnotes to the chart or table required by this Item the assumptions relevant to the calculation of the performance information, including any assumptions or estimates made in order to calculate the return on the short portfolio, if applicable. Include a statement of the significance of the assumption that distributions are reinvested for taxable investments.

(4) In a general introduction to the "Past Performance" section, indicate, as applicable, that

(a) the performance information shown assumes that all distributions made by the investment fund in the periods shown were reinvested in additional securities of the investment fund; and

(b) the performance information does not take into account sales, redemption, distribution or other optional charges that would have reduced returns or performance; and

(c) how the investment fund has performed in the past does not necessarily indicate how it will perform in the future.

(5) Use a linear scale for each axis of the bar chart required by this Item.

(6) The x-axis must intersect the y-axis at 0 for the "Year-by-Year Returns" bar chart.

4.2 — Year-by-Year Returns

(1) Provide a bar chart, under the heading "Past Performance" and under the sub-heading "Year-by-Year Returns", that shows, in chronological order with the most recent year on the right of the bar chart, the annual total return of the investment fund for the lesser of

(a) each of the ten most recently completed financial years; and

(b) each of the completed financial years in which the investment fund has been in existence and which the investment fund was a reporting issuer.

(2) Provide an introduction to the bar chart that

(a) indicates that the bar chart shows the investment fund's annual performance for each of the years shown, and illustrates how the investment fund's performance has changed from year to year; and

(b) indicates that the bar chart shows, in percentage terms, how much an investment made on the first day of each financial year would have grown or decreased by the last day of each financial year.

(3) If the investment fund holds short portfolio positions, show separately the annual total return for both the long portfolio positions and the short portfolio positions in addition to the overall total return.

4.3 — Annual Compound Returns

(1) If the investment fund is not a money market fund, disclose, in the form of a table, under the sub-heading "Annual Compound Returns"

(a) the investment fund's past performance for the ten, five, three and one year periods ended on the last day of the investment fund's financial year; and

(b) if the investment fund was a reporting issuer for more than one and less than ten years, the investment fund's past performance since the inception of the investment fund.

(2) Include in the table, for the same periods for which the annual compound returns of the investment fund are provided, the historical annual compound total returns or changes of

(a) one or more appropriate broad-based securities market indices; and

(b) at the option of the investment fund, one or more non-securities indices or narrowly-based market indices that reflect the market sectors in which the investment fund invests.

(3) Include a brief description of the broad-based securities market index (or indices) and provide a discussion of the relative performance of the investment fund as compared to that index.

(4) If the investment fund includes in the table an index that is different from the one included in the most recently filed MRFP, explain the reasons for the change and include the disclosure required by this Item for both the new and former indices.

(5) Calculate the annual compound return in accordance with the requirements of Part 15 of National Instrument 81-102 *Investment Funds*.

(6) If the investment fund holds short portfolio positions, show separately the annual compound returns for both the long and the short portfolio positions in addition to the overall annual compound returns.

Instructions:

(1) An "appropriate broad-based securities market index" is one that

(a) is administered by an organization that is not affiliated with any of the mutual fund, its manager, portfolio adviser or principal distributor, unless the index is widely recognized and used; and

(b) has been adjusted by its administrator to reflect the reinvestment of dividends on securities in the index or interest on debt.

(2) It may be appropriate for an investment fund that invests in more than one type of security to compare its performance to more than one relevant index. For example, a balanced fund may wish to compare its performance to both a bond index and an equity index.

(3) In addition to the appropriate broad-based securities market index, the investment fund may compare its performance to other financial or narrowly-based securities indices (or a blend of indices) that reflect the market sectors in which the investment fund invests or that provide useful comparatives to the performance of the investment fund. For example, an investment fund could compare its performance to an index that measured the performance of certain sectors of the stock market (e.g. communications companies, financial sector companies, etc.) or to a non-securities index, such as the Consumer Price Index, so long as the comparison is not misleading.

4.4 — Scholarship Plans

An investment fund that is a scholarship plan must comply with this Item, except that year-by-year returns and annual compound returns must be calculated based on the scholarship plan's total portfolio adjusted for cash flows.

Item 5 — *Summary of Investment Portfolio*

(1) Include, under the heading "Summary of Investment Portfolio", a summary of the investment fund's portfolio as at the end of the financial year of the investment fund to which the annual MRFP pertains.

(2) The summary of investment portfolio

(a) must break down the entire portfolio of the investment fund into appropriate subgroups, and must show the percentage of the aggregate net asset value of the investment fund constituted by each subgroup;

(b) must disclose the top 25 positions held by the investment fund, each expressed as a percentage of net asset value of the investment fund;

(c) must disclose long positions separately from short positions; and

(d) must disclose separately the total percentage of net asset value represented by the long positions and by the short positions.

(3) Indicate that the summary of investment portfolio may change due to ongoing portfolio transactions of the investment fund and a quarterly update is available.

Instructions:

(1) The summary of investment portfolio is designed to give the reader an easily accessible snapshot of the portfolio of the investment fund as at the end of the financial year for which the annual MRFP pertains. As with the other components of the annual MRFP, care should be taken to ensure that the information in the summary of investment portfolio is presented in an easily accessible and understandable way.

(2) The Canadian securities regulatory authorities have not prescribed the names of the categories into which the portfolio should be broken down. An investment fund should use the most appropriate categories given the nature of the fund. If appropriate, an investment fund may use more than one breakdown, for instance showing the portfolio of the investment fund broken down according to security type, industry, geographical locations, etc.

(3) Instead of a table, the disclosure required by (2)(a) of this Item may be presented in the form of a pie chart.

(4) If the investment fund owns more than one class of securities of an issuer, those classes should be aggregated for the purposes of this Item, however, debt and equity securities of an issuer must not be aggregated.

(5) Portfolio assets other than securities should be aggregated if they have substantially similar investment risks and profiles. For instance, gold certificates should be aggregated, even if they are issued by different financial institutions.

(6) Treat cash and cash equivalents as one separate discrete category.

(7) In determining its holdings for purposes of the disclosure required by this Item, an investment fund should, for each long position in a derivative that is held by the investment fund for purposes other than hedging and for each index participation unit held by the investment fund, consider that it holds directly the underlying interest of that derivative or its proportionate share of the securities held by the issuer of the index participation unit.

(8) If an investment fund invests substantially all of its assets directly or indirectly (through the use of derivatives) in securities of one other fund, list only the 25 largest holdings of the other investment fund by percentage of net asset value of the other investment fund, as disclosed by the other investment fund as at the most recent quarter end.

(9) If the investment fund invests in other investment funds, include a statement to the effect that the prospectus and other information about the underlying investment funds are available on the internet at www.sedar.com.

(10) A labour sponsored or venture capital fund must disclose its top 25 positions, but is not required to express any of its venture investments as a percentage of the fund's net asset value if it complies with the conditions in Part 8 of the Instrument to be exempt from disclosing the individual current values of venture investments in its statement of investment portfolio.

Item 6 — *Other Material Information*

Provide any other material information relating to the investment fund not otherwise required to be disclosed by this Part, including information required to be disclosed pursuant to an order or exemption received by the investment fund.

Part C — Content Requirements for Interim Management Report of Fund Performance

Item 1 — *First Page Disclosure*

The first page of an interim MRFP must contain disclosure in substantially the following words:

"This interim management report of fund performance contains financial highlights but does not contain either the interim financial report or annual financial statements of the investment fund. You can get a copy of the interim financial report or annual financial statements at your request, and at no cost, by calling [toll-free/collect call telephone number], by writing to us at [insert address] or by visiting our website at [insert address] or SEDAR at www.sedar.com.

Securityholders may also contact us using one of these methods to request a copy of the investment fund's proxy voting policies and procedures, proxy voting disclosure record, or quarterly portfolio disclosure."

Instruction:

If the MRFP is bound with the financial statements of the investment fund, modify the first page wording appropriately.

Item 2 — Management Discussion of Fund Performance

2.1 — Results of Operations

Update the analysis of the investment fund's results of operations provided in the most recent annual MRFP. Discuss any material changes to any of the components listed in Item 2.3 of Part B.

2.2 — Recent Developments

If there have been any significant developments affecting the investment fund since the most recent annual MRFP, discuss those developments and their impact on the investment fund, in accordance with the requirements of Item 2.4 of Part B.

2.3 — Related Party Transactions

Provide the disclosure required by Item 2.5 of Part B.

Instructions:

(1) If the first MRFP you file in this Form is not an annual MRFP, you must provide all the disclosure required by Part B, except for Items 3 and 4, in the first MRFP.

(2) The discussion in an interim MRFP is intended to update the reader on material developments since the date of the most recent annual MRFP. You may assume the reader has access to your annual MRFP, so it is not necessary to restate all of the information contained in the most recent annual discussion.

(3) The discussion in an interim MRFP should deal with the financial period to which the interim MRFP pertains.

Item 3 — Financial Highlights

(1) Provide the disclosure required by Item 3.1 of Part B, with an additional column on the left of the table representing the interim period.

(2) Provide the disclosure required by Item 3.3 of Part B of the form.

Instruction:

If the distributions cannot be allocated by type at the end of the interim period, provide only total distributions by unit/share.

Item 4 — Past Performance

Provide a bar chart prepared in accordance with Item 4.2 of Part B, and include the total return calculated for the interim period.

Item 5 — Summary of Investment Portfolio

(1) Include a summary of investment portfolio as at the end of the financial period to which the interim MRFP pertains.

(2) The summary of investment portfolio must be prepared in accordance with Item 5 of Part B.

Item 6 — Other Material Information

Provide any other material information relating to the investment fund not otherwise required to be disclosed by this Part including information required to be disclosed pursuant to an order or exemption received by the investment fund.

Companion Policy 81-106CP — To National Instrument 81-106 Investment Fund Continuous Disclosure

Table of Contents

PART 1 — PURPOSE AND APPLICATION OF THE COMPANION POLICY

1.1 Purpose — The purpose of this Companion Policy (the Policy) is to help you understand how the Canadian securities regulatory authorities (CSA or we) interpret or apply certain provisions of National Instrument 81-106 *Investment Fund Continuous Disclosure* (the Instrument).

1.2 Application — (1) The Instrument applies to investment funds. The general nature of an investment fund is that the money invested in it is professionally managed on the basis of a stated investment policy, usually expressed in terms of investment objectives and strategies, and is invested in a portfolio of securities. The fund has the discretion to buy and sell investments within the constraints of its investment policy. Investment decisions are made by a manager or portfolio adviser acting on behalf of the fund. An investment fund provides a means whereby investors can have their money professionally managed rather than making their own decisions about investing in individual securities.

(2) An investment fund generally does not seek to obtain control of or become involved in the management of companies in which it invests. Exceptions to this include labour sponsored or venture capital funds, where some degree of involvement in the management of the investees is an integral part of the investment strategy.

Investment funds can be distinguished from holding companies, which generally exert a significant degree of control over the companies in which they invest. They can also be distinguished from the issuers known as "Income Trusts" which generally issue securities that entitle the holder to net cash flows generated by (i) an underlying business owned by the trust or other entity, or (ii) the income-producing property owned by the trust or other entity. Examples of entities that are not investment funds are business income trusts, real estate investment trusts and royalty trusts.

(3) Investment funds that meet the definition of "mutual fund" in securities legislation — generally because their securities are redeemable on demand or within a specified period after demand at net asset value per security — are referred to as mutual funds. Other investment funds are generally referred to as non-redeemable investment funds. The definition of "non-redeemable investment fund" included in this instrument summarises the concepts discussed above. Because of their similarity to mutual funds, they are subject to similar reporting requirements. Examples include closed-end funds, funds traded on exchanges with limited redeemability, certain limited partnerships investing in portfolios of securities such as flow-through shares, and scholarship plans (other than self-directed RESPs as defined in OSC Rule 46-501 *Self-Directed Registered Education Savings Plans*).

(4) Labour sponsored and venture capital funds may or may not be considered to be mutual funds depending on the requirements of the provincial legislation under which they are established (for example, shares of Ontario labour sponsored funds are generally redeemable on demand, while shares of British Columbia employee venture capital corporations are not). Nevertheless, these issuers are investment funds and must comply with the general disclosure rules for investment funds as well as specific requirements for labour sponsored and venture capital funds included in Part 8 of this Instrument.

1.3 Definitions — (1) A term used in the Instrument and defined in the securities statute of a local jurisdiction has the meaning given to it in that statute unless (a) the definition in that statute is restricted to a specific portion of the statute that does not govern continuous disclosure, or (b) the context otherwise requires.

(2) For instance, the term "material change" is defined in local securities legislation of most jurisdictions. The CSA consider the meaning given to this term in securities legislation to be substantially similar to the definition set out in the Instrument.

(3) The Instrument uses accounting terms that may be defined or referred to in Canadian GAAP appliable to publicly accountable enterprises. Some of these terms may be defined differently in securities legislation. National Instrument 14-101 *Definitions* provides that a term used in the Instrument and defined in the securities statute of a local jurisdiction has a meaning given to it in the statute unless the definition in that statute is restricted to a specific portion of the statute, or the context otherwise requires.

1.4 Plain Language Principles — The CSA believe that plain language will help investors understand an investment fund's disclosure documents so that they can make informed investment decisions. You can achieve this by

- using short sentences
- using definite, everyday language
- using the active voice
- avoiding unnecessary words
- organizing the document into clear, concise sections, paragraphs and sentences
- avoiding jargon
- using personal pronouns to speak directly to the reader
- avoiding reliance on glossaries and defined terms unless it helps to understand the disclosure
- using technical terms only where necessary and explaining those terms clearly
- avoiding boilerplate wording
- using concrete terms and examples
- using charts and tables where it makes the disclosure easier to understand.

1.5 Signature and Certificates — The directors, trustee or manager of an investment fund are not required to file signed or certified continuous disclosure documents. They are responsible for the information in the investment fund's disclosure documents whether or not a document is signed or certified, and it is an offence under securities legislation to make a false or misleading statement in any required document.

1.6 Filings on SEDAR — All documents required to be filed under the Instrument must be filed in accordance with National Instrument 13-101 *System for Electronic Document Analysis and Retrieval (SEDAR).*

1.7 Corporate Law Requirements — Some investment funds may be subject to requirements of corporate law that address matters similar to those addressed by the Instrument, and which may impose additional or more onerous requirements. For example, applicable corporate law may require investment funds to deliver annual financial statements to securityholders. This Instrument cannot provide exemptions from these requirements.

PART 2 — FINANCIAL STATEMENTS

2.1 Interrelationship of Financial Statements with Canadian GAAP — (1) [Repealed]

(1.1) Subsection 2.6(2) of the Instrument, applicable to financial years beginning on or after January 1, 2014, refers to Canadian GAAP for publicly accountable enterprises, which is IFRS incorporated into the Handbook, contained in Part I of the Handbook. IFRS is defined in National Instrument 14-401 *Definitions* as the standards and interpretations adopted by the International Accounting Standards Board.

Subsection 2.6(1) of the Instrument, applicable to financial years beginning before January 1, 2014, refers to Canadian GAAP as applicable to public enterprises, which the CSA considers to be the Standards in Part V in the Handbook.

(2) The CSA believe that an investment fund's financial statements must include certain information, at a minimum, in order to provide full disclosure. The Instrument sets out these minimum requirements, but does not mandate all the required disclosure. Canadian GAAP applicable to publicly accountable enterprises also contains minimum requirements relating to the content of financial statements. An investment fund's financial statements must meet these requirements as well.

In some cases, the Instrument prescribes line items that may already be required by Canadian GAAP, but these line items are expressed more specifically for the activities of an investment fund. For example, Canadian GAAP requires a "trade and other receivables" line item on the statement of financial position, but the instrument requires accounts receivable to be broken down into more specific categories. In other instances, the line items prescribed in the Instrument are in addition to those in Canadian GAAP.

While the Instrument prescribes line items, it does not prescribe the order in which those line items are presented. Investment funds should present line items, as well as any subtotals or totals, in a logical order that will contribute to a reader's overall understanding of the financial statements.

Investment funds are responsible for disclosing all material information concering their financial position and financial performance in the financial statements.

2.1.1 Classification of Securities Issued by an Investment Fund — (1) One goal of the Instrument is comparable financial statement presentation between investment funds. However, the adoption of IFRS results in certain changes to this presentation. For example, the presentation is impacted by the classification of an investment fund's securities as either equity instruments or financial liabilities. Certain line items, such as "total equity or net assets attributable to securityholders", acknowledge the difference between an equity and liability presentation, but maintain a comaparable measurement between investment funds regardless of this classification.

(2) If an investment fund's securities are classified as financial liabilities, IFRS requires financing costs to include certain distributions made by the investment fund to those securityholders. However, if an investment fund's securities are classified as equity instruments, distributions to holders of these securities are classified as equity instruments, distributions to holders of these securities are not included in financing costs (and are not recognized as an expense), creating a difference that reduces comparability. To address this, the Instrument requires distributions to be excluded from certain calculations, specifically: (i) increase or decrease in net assets attributable to securityholders from operations as disclosed in the statement of comprehensive income, and (ii) determination of total expenses for the management expense ratio (MER).

(3) For investment funds that classify their own securities as financial liabilities, "net assets attributable to securityholders" represents the equivalent of "total equity" for investment funds that classify their own securities as equity instruments. Net assets atrributable to secutrityholders does not include amounts owed on securities issued by the investment fund that provide leverage to the fund.

2.2 Filing Deadline for Annual Financial Statements and Auditor's Report — Section 2.2 of the Instrument sets out the filing deadline for annual financial statements. While section 2.2 of the Instrument does not address the auditor's report date, investment funds are encouraged to file their annual financial statements as soon as possible after the date of the auditor's report.

2.3 — [repealed]

2.4 Length of Financial Year — For the purposes of the Instrument, unless otherwise expressly provided, references to a financial year apply regardless of the length of that year. The first financial year of an investment fund commences on the date of its incorporation or organization and ends at the close of that year.

2.5 Contents of Statement of Comprehensive Income — The amount of fund expenses waived or paid by the manager or portfolio adviser of the investment fund disclosed in the statement of comprehensive income excludes amounts waived or paid due to an expense cap that would require securityholder approval to change.

2.5.1 Disclosure of Investment Portfolio — (1) The term "statement of investment portfolio" is used to describe the disclosure required by section 3.5 of the Instrument. As this term is not used in the Handbook, preparers may refer to it as a "schedule of investment portfolio" within a complete set of investment fund financial statements. Regardless of how the disclosure is described, sections 2.1 and 2.3 of the Instrument requires it to be included within a complete set of investment fund financial statements, and subsection 2.1(2) of the Instrument requires annual financial statements to be accompanied by an auditor's report, for the purposes of securities legislation.

If financial statements for more than one investment fund are bound together, Part 7 of the Instrument requires all of the information pertaining to each investment fund to be presented together and not intermingled with information relating to another investment fund. The CSA is of the view that this requirement applies equally to the portfolio disclosure, which should be presented together with the other financial information relating to the investment fund.

(2) If an investment fund invests substantially all of its assets directly, or indirectly through the use of derivatives, in securities of one other investment fund, the investment fund should provide in the statement of investment portfolio, or the notes to that statement, additional disclosure concerning the holdings of the other investment fund, as available, in order to assist investors in understanding the actual portfolio to which the investment fund is exposed. The CSA is of the view that such disclosure is consistent with the requirements in the Handbook relating to financial instrument disclosure.

2.6 Disclosure of Soft Dollars — The notes to the financial statements of an investment fund must contain disclosure of soft dollar amounts when such amounts are ascertainable. When calculating these amounts, investment funds should include the quantifiable value of goods and services, beyond the amount attributed to order execution, received directly from the dealer executing the fund's portfolio transactions, or from a third party.

2.7 Securities Lending Transactions — (1) Section 3.8 of the Instrument imposes certain reporting requirements on investment funds in connection with any securities lending transactions entered into by the investment fund. These requirements were included to ensure that certain aspects of securities lending transactions are disclosed in the same manner.

Generally, in a securities ledning transaction, the investment fund is able to call the original securities back at any time, and the securities returned must be the same or substantially the same as the original securities. The investment fund retains substantially all of the risks and rewards of ownership.

(2) [Repealed.]

(3) The Canadian securities regulatory authorities consider that, for the purposes of disclosing the gross amount generated from securities lending transactions in the notes to the financial statements of an investment fund pursuant to subsection 3.8(4) of the Instrument, all amounts generated in relation to the securities lending transactions of the investment fund must be disclosed, prior to the deduction of any amounts paid to securities lending agents or other service providers pursuant to any revenue sharing arrangement. Furthermore, for the purposes of subsection 3.8(4) of the Instrument, the Canadian securities regulatory authorities are of the view that any proceeds generated as a result of investing the collateral delivered to the investment fund in connection with a securities lending transaction form part of the gross amount from the securities lending transaction and must be included in the amount disclosed in the notes to the financial statements under subsection 3.8(4) of the Instrument.

2.8 Change in Year End — (1) The change in year end reporting requirements are adopted from National Instrument 51-102, with appropriate modifications to reflect that investment funds report on a six month interim period.

(2) The definition of "interim period" in the Instrument differs from the definition of this term in National Instrument 51-102. An investment fund cannot have more than one interim period in a transition year.

Part 8: MUTUAL FUNDS

(3) The interim financial report for the new financial year will have comparatives from the corresponding months in the preceding year, whether or not they are from the transition year or from the old financial year, they were previously prepared or not, or they straddle a year-end.

(4) If an investment fund voluntarily reports on a quarterly basis, it should follow the requirements set out in National Instrument 51-102 for a change in year end, with appropriate modifications.

(5) Appendix A to this Policy outlines the financial statement filing requirements under section 2.9 of the Instrument for an investment fund that changes its year end.

2.9 [Repealed]

2.10 Mutual Funds that are Non-Reporting Issuers — The requirement in subsection 2.11(c) to advise the applicable regulator or securities regulatory authority of a mutual fund's reliance on the financial statement filing exemption provided in section 2.11 of the Instrument can be satisfied by a one-time notice.

PART 3 — AUDITORS AND THEIR REPORTS

3.1 Acceptable Auditor — Securities legislation in most jurisdictions prohibits a regulator or securities regulatory authority from issuing a receipt for a prospectus if it appears that a person or company who has prepared any part of the prospectus, or is named as having prepared or certified a report used in connection with a prospectus, is not acceptable.

Investment funds that are reporting issuers, and their auditors, should refer to National Instrument 52-108 *Auditor Oversight* for requirements relating to auditor oversight by the Canadian Public Accountability Board.

3.2 Modification of Opinion — (1) The Instrument prohibits an auditor's report from expressing a modified opinion under Canadian GAAS. A modification of opinion includes a qualification of opinion, an adverse opinion, and a disclaimer of opinion.

(2) Part 17 of the Instrument permits the regulator or securities regulatory authority to grant exemptive relief from the Instrument, including the requirement that an auditor's report express an unmodified opinion or other similar communication that would constitute a modification of opinion under Canadian GAAS. However, we will generally recommend that such exemptive relief should not be granted if the modification of opinion or other similar communication is

    (a) due to a departure from accounting principles permitted by the Instrument, or

    (b) due to a limitation in the scope of the auditor's examination that

        (i) results in the auditor being unable to form an opinion on the financial statements as a whole,

        (ii) is imposed or could reasonably be eliminated by management, or

        (iii) could reasonably be expected to be recurring.

3.3 Auditor's Involvement with Management Reports of Fund Performance — Investment funds' auditors are expected to comply with the Handbook with respect to their involvement with the annual and interim management reports of fund performance required by the Instrument as these reports contain financial information extracted from the financial statements.

3.4 Auditor Involvement with Interim Financial Reports — (1) The board of directors of an investment fund that is a corporation or the trustees of an investment fund that is a trust, in discharging their responsibilities for ensuring a reliable interim financial report, should consider engaging an external auditor to carry out a review of the interim financial report.

(2) Section 2.12 of the Instrument requires an investment fund to disclose if an auditor has not performed a review of the interim financial report, to disclose if an auditor was unable to complete a review and why, and to file a written report from the auditor if the auditor performed a review and expressed a reservation in the auditor's interim review report. No positive statement is required when an auditor performed a review and provided an unqualified communication. If an auditor was engaged to perform a review on an interim financial report applying review standards set out in the Handbook, and the auditor was unable to complete the review, the investment fund's disclosure of the reasons why the auditor was unable to complete the review should normally include a discussion of

    (a) inadequate internal control,

    (b) a limitation on the scope of the auditor's work, or

    (c) a failure of management to provide the auditor with written representations the auditor believes are necessary.

(3) The terms "review" and "written review report" used in section 2.12 of the Instrument refer to the auditor's review of and report on an interim financial report using standards for a review of an interim financial report by the auditor as set out in the Handbook.

(4) The Instrument does not specify the form of notice that should accompany an interim financial report that has not been reviewed by the auditor. The notice accompanies, but does not form part of, the interim financial report. We expect that the notice will normally be provided on a separate page appearing immediately before the interim financial report, in a manner similar to an auditor's report that accompanies annual financial statements.

PART 4 — DELIVERY OF FINANCIAL STATEMENTS AND MANAGEMENT REPORTS OF FUND PERFORMANCE

4.1 Delivery Instructions — (1) The Instrument gives investment funds the following choices for the delivery of financial statements and management reports of fund performance:

    (a) send these documents to all securityholders;

    (b) obtain standing instructions from securityholders with respect to the documents they wish to receive; or

    (c) obtain annual instructions from securityholders by sending them an annual request form they can use to indicate which documents they wish to receive.

The choices are intended to provide some flexibility concerning the delivery of continuous disclosure documents to securityholders. An investment fund can use any combination of the delivery options for its securityholders. However, the Instrument specifies that once an investment fund chooses option (b) for a securityholder, it cannot switch back to option (c) for that securityholder at a later date. The purpose of this requirement is to encourage investment funds to obtain standing instructions and to ensure that if a securityholder provides standing instructions, the investment fund will abide by those instructions unless the securityholder specifically changes them.

(2) When soliciting delivery instructions from a securityholder, an investment fund can deem no response from the securityholder to be a request by the securityholder to receive all, some or none of the documents listed in subsection 5.1(2) of the Instrument. When soliciting delivery instructions, an investment fund should make clear what the consequence of no response will be to its securityholders.

(3) Investment funds should solicit delivery instructions sufficiently ahead of time so that securityholders can receive the requested documents by the relevant filing deadline. Securityholders should also be given a reasonable amount of time to respond to a request for instructions. Investment funds should provide securityholders with complete contact information for the investment fund, including a toll-free telephone number or a number for collect calls.

(4) Investment funds under common management can solicit one set of delivery instructions from a securityholder that will apply to all of the funds in the same fund family that the securityholder owns. If a securityholder has given an investment fund standing delivery instructions and then later acquires the securities of another investment fund managed by the same manager, the newly acquired fund can rely on those standing instructions.

(5) The Instrument requires investment funds to deliver the quarterly portfolio disclosure and the proxy voting record to securityholders upon request, but does not require investment funds to solicit delivery instructions from securityholders with respect to this disclosure. Investment funds are obligated to state on the first page of their management reports of fund performance that this disclosure is available.

4.2 Communication with Beneficial Owners — Generally, investment funds must apply the procedures set out in National Instrument 54-101 *Communication with Beneficial Owners of Securities of a Reporting Issuer* for the purposes of Part 5 of the Instrument, but an exemption from National Instrument 54-101 is available to investment funds that have beneficial owner information.

We recognize that different types of investment funds have different access to beneficial owner information (for example, mutual funds are more likely to have beneficial owner information than exchange-traded funds) and that the procedures in National Instrument 54-101 may not be efficient for every investment fund. We intend the provisions in Part 5 of the Instrument to provide investment funds with flexibility to communicate directly with the beneficial owners of their securities. If an investment fund has the necessary information to communicate directly with one or more beneficial owners of its securities, it can do so, even though it may need to rely on National Instrument 54-101 to communicate with other beneficial owners of its securities.

4.3 Binding — For the purposes of delivery to a securityholder, the Instrument permits more than one management report of fund performance to be bound together if the securityholder owns all of the funds to which the management reports relate. There is no prohibition in the Instrument against binding the management report of fund performance with the financial statements for one investment fund for the purposes of delivering these documents to a securityholder who has requested them.

4.4 Electronic Delivery — Any documents required to be sent under the Instrument may be sent by electronic delivery, as long as such delivery is made in compliance with National Policy 11-201 *Delivery of Documents by Electronic Means* and, in Quebec, Quebec Staff Notice *The Delivery of Documents by Electronic Means*. In particular, the annual reminder required by section 5.2 and the request form required by section 5.3 of the Instrument may be given in electronic form and may be combined with other notices. Request forms and notices may alternatively be sent with account statements or other materials sent to securityholders by an investment fund.

4.5 Website Disclosure — The Instrument does not specify the length of time that continuous disclosure documents must remain on an investment fund's website. In the CSA's view, the documents should stay on the website for a reasonable length of time, and at least until they are replaced by more current versions.

PART 5 — INDEPENDENT VALUATIONS

5.1 Independent Valuations — (1) Part 8 of the Instrument is designed to address the concerns raised by labour sponsored or venture capital funds that disclosing a fair value for their venture investments may disadvantage the private companies in which they invest. Section 8.2 permits alternative disclosure by a labour sponsored or venture capital fund of its statement of investment portfolio. Labour sponsored or venture capital funds must disclose the individual securities in which they invest, but may aggregate all changes from costs of the venture investments, thereby only showing an aggregate adjustment from cost to fair value for these securities. This alternative disclosure is only permitted if the labour sponsored or venture capital fund has obtained an independent valuation in accordance with Part 8 of the Instrument.

(2) The CSA expect the independent valuator's report to provide either a number or a range of values which the independent valuator considers to be a fair and reasonable expression of the value of the venture investments or of the net asset value of the labour sponsored or venture capital fund. The independent valuation should include a critical review of the valuation methodology and an assessment of whether it was properly applied. A report on compliance with stated valuation policies and practices cannot take the place of an independent valuation.

The valuation report should disclose the scope of the review, including any limitations on the scope, and the implications of these limitations on the independent valuator's conclusion.

(3) The independent valuator should refer to the reporting standards of the Canadian Institute of Chartered Business Valuators for guidance.

(4) A labour sponsored or venture capital fund obtaining an independent valuation should furnish the independent valuator with access to its manager, advisers and all material information in its possession relevant to the independent valuation.

5.2 Independent Valuators — (1) It is a question of fact as to whether a valuator is independent of the labour sponsored or venture capital fund. In determining the independence of the valuator, a number of factors may be relevant, including whether

   (a) the valuator or an affiliated entity has a material financial interest in future business in respect of which an agreement, commitment or understanding exists involving the fund or a person or company listed in paragraph (2)(a); or

   (b) the valuator or its affiliated entity is a lender of a material amount of indebtedness to any of the issuers of the fund's illiquid investments.

(2) The CSA would generally consider a valuator not to be independent of a labour sponsored or venture capital fund where

   (a) the valuator or an affiliated entity of the valuator is

      (i) the manager of the fund,

      (ii) a portfolio adviser of the fund,

      (iii) an insider of the fund,

Part 8: MUTUAL FUNDS

(iv) an associate of the fund,

(v) an affiliated entity of the fund, or

(vi) an affiliated entity of any of the persons or companies named in this paragraph (a);

(b) the compensation of the valuator or an affiliated entity of the valuator depends in whole or in part upon an agreement, arrangement or understanding that gives the valuator, or its affiliated entity, a financial incentive in respect of the conclusions reached in the valuation; or

(c) the valuator or an affiliated entity of the valuator has a material investment in the labour sponsored or venture capital fund or in a portfolio asset of the fund.

PART 6 — PROXY VOTING DISCLOSURE FOR PORTFOLIO SECURITIES HELD

6.1 Proxy Voting Disclosure — (1) An investment fund's manager, acting on the investment fund's behalf, has the right and obligation to vote proxies relating to the investment fund's portfolio securities. As a practical matter, the manager may delegate this function to the investment fund's portfolio adviser as part of the adviser's general management of investment fund assets. In either case, the manager or portfolio adviser voting proxies on behalf of an investment fund must do so in a manner consistent with the best interests of the fund and its securityholders.

(2) Because of the substantial institutional voting power held by investment funds, the increasing importance of the exercise of that power to securityholders, and the potential for conflicts of interest with respect to the exercise of proxy voting, we believe that investment funds should disclose their proxy voting policies and procedures, and should make their actual proxy voting records available to securityholders.

(3) The Instrument requires that the investment fund establish policies and procedures for determining whether, and how, to vote on any matter for which the investment fund receives proxy materials for a meeting of securityholders of an issuer. The CSA consider an investment fund to "receive" a document when it is delivered to any service provider or to the investment fund in respect of securities held beneficially by the investment fund. Proxy materials may be delivered to a manager, a portfolio adviser or sub-adviser, or a custodian. All of these deliveries are considered delivered "to" the investment fund.

(4) The Instrument requires an investment fund to maintain an annual proxy voting record as of June 30 and to post this to the fund's website if it has one. However, investment funds may choose to disclose their proxy votes throughout the course of the year, and may also choose to disclose how they intend to vote prior to the shareholder meeting.

6.2 Proxy Voting Policies and Procedures — (1) Section 10.2 of the Instrument sets out, in general terms, what the securities regulatory authorities consider to be minimum policies and procedures for the proxy voting process. Investment funds are responsible for adopting any additional policies relevant to their particular situation. For example, investment funds should consider whether they require any specific policies dealing with shareholder meetings of issuers resident in other countries.

(2) An investment fund sometimes needs to vote securities held by it in order to protect its interests in connection with corporate transactions or developments relating to the issuers of its portfolio securities. The manager and portfolio adviser, or the agent of the investment fund administering a securities lending program on behalf of the investment fund, should monitor corporate developments relating to portfolio securities that are loaned by the investment fund in securities lending transactions, and take all necessary steps to ensure that the investment fund can exercise a right to vote the securities when necessary.

PART 7 — MATERIAL CHANGE

7.1 Material Changes — Determining whether a change is a material change will depend on the specific facts and circumstances surrounding the change. However, the CSA is of the view that

(a) the change of portfolio adviser of an investment fund will generally constitute a material change for the investment fund, and

(b) the departure of a high-profile individual from the employ of a portfolio adviser of an investment fund may constitute a material change for the investment fund, depending on how prominently the investment fund featured that individual in its marketing. An investment fund that emphasized the ability of a particular individual to encourage investors to purchase the fund could not later take the position that the departure of that individual was immaterial to investors and therefore not a material change.

7.2 Confidential Material Change Report — The CSA are of the view that in order for an investment fund to file a confidential material change report under Section 11.2 of the Instrument, the investment fund or its manager should advise insiders of the prohibition against trading during the filing period of a confidential material change report and must also take steps to monitor trading activity.

PART 8 — INFORMATION CIRCULARS

8.1 Sending of Proxies and Information Circulars — Investment funds are reminded that National Instrument 54-101 prescribes certain procedures relating to the delivery of proxy-related materials sent to beneficial owners of securities.

PART 9 — NET ASSET VALUE

9.1 Publication of Net Asset Value Per Security — An investment fund that arranges for the publication of its net asset value per security should calculate its net asset value per security and make the results of that calculation available to the financial press as quickly as is commercially practicable. An investment fund should attempt to meet the deadlines of the financial press for publication in order to ensure that its net asset values per security are publicly available as quickly as possible.

9.2 Fair Value Guidance — Section 14.2 of the Instrument requires an investment fund to calculate its net asset value based on the fair value of the investment fund's assets and liabilities. This may differ from the calculation of "current value" for financial statement purposes. Section 3.6 of the Instrument requires an explanation of this difference.

While investment funds are required to comply with the definition of "fair value" in the Instrument when calculating net asset value, they may also look to the Handbook for guidance on the measurement of fair value. The fair value principles articulated in the Handbook can be applied by investment funds when valuing assets and liabilities.

9.3 — [repealed]

9.4 Determination of Fair Value in Calculating Net Asset Value — (1) A market is generally considered active when quoted prices are readily and regularly available from an exchange, dealer, broker, industry group, pricing service or regulatory agency, and those prices reflect actual and regularly occurring market transactions on an arm's length basis. Accordingly, fair value should not reflect the amount that would be received or paid in a forced transaction, involuntary liquidation or distress sale.

(2) Paragraph 15.1(1)(a) requires the investment fund to use its "total expenses" (other than distributions if these are an expense for the investment fund) before income taxes for the relevant period as the basis for the calculation of MER. Total expenses, before income taxes, include interest charges and taxes, including sales taxes, GST and capital taxes payable by the investment fund. Withholding taxes need not be included in the MER calculation.

The CSA is of the view that if an investment fund issues debt-like securities or securities that otherwise provide leverage to the fund, payments to holders of these securities should be treated as financing costs from the perspective of the investment fund's other classes of securities (the classes that benefit from the financing or leverage). These costs should not be excluded from total expenses when calculating the MER of the investment fund's other classes of securities. Securities that provide leverage generally include preferred shares.

Non-optional fees paid directly by investors in connection with the holding of an investment fund's securities do not have to be included in the MER calculation.

(3) Whether a particular event is a significant event for a security depends on whether the event may affect the value of the security. Generally, significant events fall into one of three categories: (i) issuer specific events — e.g. the resignation of the CEO or an after-hours earnings announcement, (ii) market events — e.g. a natural disaster, a political event, or a significant governmental action like raising interest rates, and (iii) volatility events — e.g. a significant movement in North American equity markets that may directly impact the market prices of securities traded on overseas exchanges.

Whether a market movement is significant is a matter to be determined by the manager through the establishment of tolerance levels which it may choose to base on, for example, a specified intraday and/or interday percentage movement of a specific index, security or basket of securities. In all cases, the appropriate triggers should be determined based on the manager's own due diligence and understanding of the correlations relevant to each investment fund's portfolio.

9.5 Fair Value Techniques — The CSA do not endorse any particular fair value technique as we recognize that this is a constantly evolving process. However, whichever technique is used, it should be applied consistently for a portfolio security throughout the fund complex and reviewed for reasonableness on a regular basis.

9.6 Valuation Policies and Procedures — An investment fund's valuation policy should be approved by the manager's board of directors. The policies and procedures should describe the process for monitoring significant events or other situations that could call into question whether a quoted market price is representative of fair value. They should also describe the methods by which the manager will review and test valuations to evaluate the quality of the prices obtained as well as the general functioning of the valuation process. The manager should also consider whether its valuation process is a conflict of interest matter as defined in NI 81-107.

PART 10 — CALCULATION OF MANAGEMENT EXPENSE RATIO

10.1 Calculation of Management Expense Ratio — (1) Part 15 of the Instrument sets out the method to be used by an investment fund to calculate its management expense ratio (MER). The requirements apply in all circumstances in which an investment fund circulates and discloses an MER. This includes disclosure in a sales communication, a prospectus, a fund facts document, an annual information form, financial statements, a management report of fund performance or a report to securityholders.

(2) Paragraph 15.1(1)(a) requires the investment fund to use its "total expenses" (other than distributions if these are an expense for the investment fund) before income taxes for the relevant period as the basis for the calculation of MER. Total expenses, before income taxes, include interest charges and taxes, including sales taxes, GST and capital taxes payable by the investment fund. Withholding taxes need not be included in the MER calculation.

The CSA is of the view that if an investment fund issues debt-like securities or securities that otherwise provide leverage to the fund, payments to holders of these securities should be treated as financing costs from the perspective of the investment fund's other classes of securities (the classes that benefit from the financing or leverage). These costs should not be excluded from total expenses when calculating the MER of the investment fund's other classes of securities. Securities that provide leverage generally include preferred shares.

Non-optional fees paid directly by investors in connection with the holding of an investment fund's securities do not have to be included in the MER calculation.

(3) The CSA recognize that an investment fund may incur fees and charges that are not included in total expenses, but that reduce the net asset value and the amount of investable assets of the investment fund. Sales commissions paid by an investment fund in connection with the sale of the investment fund's securities are an example of such fees and charges. We believe that these fees and charges should be reflected in the MER of the investment fund.

(4) While brokerage commissions and other portfolio transaction costs are expenses of an investment fund for accounting purposes, they are not included in the MER. These costs are reflected in the trading expense ratio.

(5) In its management report of fund performance, an investment fund must disclose historical MERs for five years calculated in accordance with Part 15. If the investment fund has not calculated the historical MERs in the manner required by the Instrument, we are of the view that the change in the method of calculating the MER should be treated in a manner similar to a change in accounting policy under International Accounting Standard 8 *Accounting Policies, Changes in Accounting Estimates and Errors*. Under Canadian GAAP, a change in accounting policy requires a retrospective application of the change for all periods shown. However, the Handbook acknowledges that there may be circumstances where the data needed to restate the financial information is not reasonably determinable.

If an investment fund restates its MER for any of the five years it is required to show, the investment fund should describe this restatement in the first document released and in the first management report of fund performance in which the restated MERs are reported.

If an investment fund does not restate its MER for prior periods because, based on specific facts and circumstances, the information required to do so is not reasonably determinable, the MER for all financial periods ending after the effective date of the Instrument must be calculated in accordance with Part 15. In this case, the investment fund must also disclose

(i) that the method of calculating MER has changed, specifying for which periods the MER has been calculated in accordance with the change;

(ii) that the investment fund has not restated the MER for specified prior periods;

(iii) the impact that the change would have had if the investment fund had restated the MER for the specified prior periods (for example, would the MER have increased or decreased and an estimate of the increase or decrease); and

(iv) a description of the main differences between an MER calculated in accordance with the Instrument and the previous calculations.

The disclosure outlined above should be provided for all periods presented until such time as all MERs presented are calculated in accordance with the Instrument.

Appendix A — Examples of Filing Requirements for Changes in Year End

The following examples assume the old financial year ended on December 31, 20X0.

Transition Year	Comparative Annual Financial Statements to Transition Year	New Financial Year	Comparative Annual Financial Statements to New Financial Year	Interim Periods for Transition Year	Comparative Interim Periods to Transition Year	Interim Periods for New Financial Year	Comparative Interim Periods to New Financial Year
Up to 3 months							
3 months ended 3/31/X1	12 months ended 12/31/X0	3/31/X2	3 months ended 3/31/X1 and 12 months ended 12/31/X0	Not applicable	Not applicable	6 months ended 9/30/X1	6 months ended 9/30/X0
4 to 6 months							
6 months ended 6/30/X1	12 months ended 12/31/X0	6/30/X2	6 months ended 6/30/X1 and 12 months ended 12/31/X0	Not applicable	Not applicable	6 months ended 12/31/X1	6 months ended 12/31/X0
7 or 8 months							
8 months ended 8/31/X1	12 months ended 12/31/X0	8/31/X2	8 months ended 8/31/X1 and 12 months ended 12/31/X0	Not applicable	Not applicable	6 months ended 2/28/X2	6 months ended 2/28/X1
9 to 11 months							
11 months ended 11/30/X1	12 months ended 12/31/X0	11/30/X2	11 months ended 11/30/X1	6 months ended 6/30/X1	6 months ended 6/30/X0	6 months ended 5/31/X2	6 months ended 5/31/X1
11 to 15 months							
15 months ended 3/31/X2	12 months ended 12/31/X0	3/31/X3	15 months ended 3/31/X2	6 months ended 6/30/X1	6 months ended 6/30/X0	6 months ended 9/30/X2	6 months ended 9/30/X1

Appendix B — Contact Addresses

Alberta Securities Commission

Suite 600

250 - 5th Street SW

Calgary, Alberta

T2P 0R4

Attention: Corporate Finance

British Columbia Securities Commission

P.O. Box 10142, Pacific Centre

701 West Georgia Street

Vancouver, British Columbia

V7Y 1L2

Attention: Financial Reporting

Manitoba Securities Commission

500-400 St. Mary Avenue

Winnipeg, Manitoba

R3C 4K5

Attention: Corporate Finance

Financial and Consumer Services Commission (New Brunswick)

85 Charlotte Street, Suite 300

Saint John, NB

E2L 2J2

Attention: Corporate Finance

Financial Services Regulation Division Department of Government Services

P.O. Box 8700

St. John's, NL

A1B 4J6

Attention: Superintendent of Securities

Department of Justice, Northwest Territories

Securities Office

P.O. Box 1320

1st Floor, 5009-49th Street

Yellowknife, NWT X1A 2L9

Attention: Superintendent of Securities

Nova Scotia Securities Commission

2nd Floor, Joseph Howe Building

1690 Hollis Street

Halifax, Nova Scotia B3J 3J9

Attention: Corporate Finance

Department of Justice, Nunavut

Legal Registries Division

P.O. Box 1000 — Station 570

1st Floor, Brown Building

Iqaluit, NT X0A 0H0

Attention: Superintendent of Securities

Ontario Securities Commission

20 Queen Street West, 22nd Floor

Toronto, ON M5H 3S8

Attention: Continuous Disclosure, Investment Funds

Registrar of Securities, Prince Edward Island

P.O. Box 2000

95 Rochford Street, 5ᵗʰ Floor,

Charlottetown, PEI

C1A 7N8

Attention: Registrar of Securities

Autorité des marchés financiers

800 Square Victoria, 22nd Floor

P.O. Box 246, Tour de la Bourse

Montréal, Québec

H4Z 1G3

Attention: Direction des fonds d'investissement

Financial and Consumer Affairs Authority of Saskatchewan — Securities Division

601-1919 Saskatchewan Drive

Regina, SK

S4P 3V7

Attention: Deputy Director, Corporate Finance

Superintendent of Securities, Government of Yukon

Corporate Affairs J-9

P.O. Box 2703

Whitehorse, Yukon

Y1A 5H3

Attention: Superintendent of Securities

Adoption by OSC: (2005) 28 O.S.C.B. 4949 and (Supp-1) 1; Request for Comments: (2004) 27 O.S.C.B. 5157 and (2002) 24 O.S.C.B. 6273.

Adoption of Amendments by OSC: (2008) 31 O.S.C.B. 8565 and 6275; Request for Comments: (2007) 30 O.S.C.B. 4965.

Adoption of Amendments to Policy: (2010) 33 O.S.C.B. 11434 and (Supp. 4) 1; Request for Comments: (2009) 32 O.S.C.B. (Supp. 1) 1, (2008) 31 O.S.C.B. 10479, (2007) 30 O.S.C.B. (Supp. 4) 1 and (2003) 26 O.S.C.B. 1443.

Adoption of Amendments to Policy: (2013) 36 O.S.C.B. 9612; Request for Comments: (2009) 32 O.S.C.B. 8381.

Rules: NI 81-106; Rule 81-801.

Policies and Orders: OPS 81-801CP.

National Instrument 81-107 — Independent Review Committee for Investment Funds

Date: November 1, 2006, as amended effective September 28, 2009, May 6, 2011, September 22, 2014 and January 11, 2015

29 O.S.C.B. 8807, 32 O.S.C.B. (Supp. 4) 379, 34 O.S.C.B. 5171, 37 O.S.C.B. (Supp. 5) and 38 O.S.C.B. 342.

Table of Contents

Introduction

This National Instrument (the Instrument) contains both rules and accompanying commentary on those rules. The Canadian Securities Administrators (the CSA or we), have made these rules under authority granted by the securities legislation of their jurisdiction.

The commentary may explain the implications of a rule, offer examples or indicate different ways to comply with a rule. It may expand on a particular subject without being exhaustive. The commentary is not legally binding, but it does reflect the views of the CSA. Commentary always appears in italic type and, outside of this introduction, is titled "Commentary".

Part 1 — Definitions and application

1.1 — Investment funds subject to Instrument

(1) This Instrument applies to an investment fund that is a reporting issuer.

(2) In Québec, this Instrument does not apply to a reporting issuer organized under

(a) an Act to establish the Fonds de solidarité des travailleurs du Québec (F.T.Q.) R.S.Q., chapter F-3.2.1;

(b) an Act to establish Fondaction, le Fonds de dévelopement de la Confédération des syndicats nationaux pour la coopération et l'emploi (R.S.Q., chapter F-3.1.2); and

(c) an Act constituting Capital régional et coopératif Desjardins (R.S.Q., chapter C-6.1).

Commentary

1. This Instrument applies to all publicly offered mutual funds and non-redeemable investment funds. Investment funds subject to this Instrument include:

• labour sponsored or venture capital funds;

• scholarship plans;

• mutual funds and closed-end funds listed and posted for trading on a stock exchange or quoted on an over-the-counter market; and

• investment funds not governed by National Instrument 81-101 (NI 81-102) Investment Funds.

2. This Instrument does not regulate mutual funds that are not reporting issuers (commonly referred to as pooled funds), for example, mutual funds that sell securities to the public only under capital raising exemptions in securities legislation.

Part 8: MUTUAL FUNDS

1.2 — Definition of "conflict of interest matter"

In this Instrument, "a conflict of interest matter" means

> (a) a situation where a reasonable person would consider a manager, or an entity related to the manager, to have an interest that may conflict with the manager's ability to act in good faith and in the best interests of the investment fund; or

> (b) a conflict of interest or self-dealing provision listed in Appendix A that restricts or prohibits an investment fund, a manager or an entity related to the manager from proceeding with a proposed action.

Commentary

1. Section 5.1 of this Instrument requires that a manager refer all conflict of interest matters to the independent review committee (IRC).

2. The CSA do not consider the 'reasonable person' test described in paragraph (a) to capture inconsequential matters. It is expected that, among the factors the manager will look to for guidance to identify conflict of interest matters caught by this Instrument, will be industry best practices. The CSA expect, however, each manager to consider the nature of its investment fund operations when making its decisions about which conflict of interest matters it faces for the funds it manages.

3. The types of conflicts of interest faced by the portfolio manager or portfolio adviser (or sub-adviser) or any other entity related to the manager this Instrument captures relate to the decisions made on behalf of the investment fund that may affect or influence the manager's ability to make decisions in good faith and in the best interests of the investment fund. This Instrument is not intended to capture the conflicts of interest at the service provider level generally.

The CSA expect the manager to consider whether a particular portfolio manager or portfolio adviser or any other 'entity related to the manager' would have any conflicts of interest falling within the definition.

For example, paragraph (a) might, depending on the circumstances, capture these conflicts of the portfolio manager or portfolio adviser:

- *portfolio management processes for the investment fund, including allocation of investments among a family of investment funds; and*

- *trading practices for the investment fund, including negotiating soft dollar arrangements with dealers with whom the adviser places portfolio transactions for the investment fund.*

4. The CSA contemplate that an 'entity related to the manager' will have its own policies and procedures to address any conflicts of interest in its operations. It is expected the manager will make reasonable inquiries of these policies and procedures. The conflicts of interest facing these entities, including any third party portfolio manager or portfolio adviser, may affect, or be perceived to affect, the manager's ability to make decisions in the best interests of the investment fund. The manager is expected to refer such conflicts to the IRC under this Instrument.

5. For greater certainty, paragraph (b) requires that a 'conflict of interest matter' includes any course of action that the investment fund, the manager or an entity related to the manager would otherwise be restricted or prohibited from proceeding with because of a conflict of interest or self-dealing prohibition in securities legislation. These include the types of transactions described under subsection 5.2(1) of this Instrument.

1.3 — Definition of "entity related to the manager"

In this Instrument, "entity related to the manager" means

> (a) a person or company that can direct or materially affect the direction of the management and policies of the manager or the investment fund, other than as a member of the independent review committee; or

> (b) an associate, affiliate, partner, director, officer or subsidiary of the manager or of a person or company referred to in paragraph (a).

Commentary

1. The CSA consider an 'entity related to the manager' in paragraph (a) to include:

- *the portfolio manager or portfolio adviser (or sub-adviser) of the investment fund, including any third party portfolio manager or portfolio adviser;*

- *the administrator of a scholarship plan; and*

- *any person or company that can materially direct or affect the manager's management or policies, including through contractual agreements or ownership of voting securities.*

1.4 — Definition of "independent"

(1) In this Instrument, a member of the independent review committee is "independent" if the member has no material relationship with the manager, the investment fund, or an entity related to the manager.

(2) For the purposes of subsection (1), a material relationship means a relationship which could reasonably be perceived to interfere with the member's judgment regarding a conflict of interest matter.

Commentary

1. Under subsection 3.7(3), all members of the IRC must be independent of the manager, the investment fund and entities related to the manager. The CSA believe that all members must be independent because the principal function of the IRC is to review activities and transactions that involve inherent conflicts of interest between an investment fund and its manager. Given this role, it is important that the members of the IRC are free from conflicting loyalties.

2. While the members of the IRC should not themselves be subject to inherent conflicts or divided loyalties, the CSA recognize that there may be inherent conflicts relating to inter-fund issues where a single IRC acts for a family of investment funds. In those cases, this Instrument requires members to conduct themselves in accordance with their written charter and in accordance with the standard of care set out in this Instrument.

The CSA do not consider the IRC's ability to set its own reasonable compensation to be a material relationship with the manager or investment fund under subsection 1.4(1).

3. A material relationship referred to in subsection 1.4(1) may include an ownership, commercial, charitable, industrial, banking, consulting, legal, accounting or familial relationship. The CSA expect managers and IRC members to consider both past and current relationships when determining whether a material relationship exists.

For example, depending on the circumstances, the following individuals may be independent under section 1.4:

- an independent member of an existing advisory board or IRC of an investment fund;
- an independent member or former independent member of the board of directors, or of a special committee of the board of directors, of an investment fund;
- a former independent member of the board of directors, or special committee of the board of directors, of the manager;
- an individual appointed as a trustee for an investment fund; and
- an independent member of the board of directors, or of a special committee of the board of directors, of a registered trust company that acts as trustee for an investment fund.

By way of further example, the CSA consider it unlikely that the following individuals would be independent under section 1.4:

- a person who is or has recently been an employee or executive officer of the manager or investment fund; and
- a person whose immediate family member is or has recently been an executive officer of the manager or investment fund.

The CSA also consider that it would be rare that a member of the board of directors, or special committee of the board of directors, of a manager could be 'independent' within the meaning of this Instrument. One such example of when a member of the board of directors of a manager could be 'independent' may be "owner-operated" investment funds, sold exclusively to defined groups of investors, such as members of a trade or professional association or co-operative organization, who directly or indirectly, own the manager. In the case of these investment funds, the CSA view the interests of the independent members of the board of directors of the manager and investors as aligned.

1.5 — Definition of "inter-fund self-dealing investment prohibitions"

In this Instrument, "inter-fund self-dealing investment prohibitions" means the provisions listed in Appendix B that prohibit

(a) a portfolio manager from knowingly causing any investment portfolio managed by it to purchase or sell, or

(b) an investment fund from purchasing or selling,

the securities of an issuer from or to the account of a responsible person, an associate of a responsible person or the portfolio manager.

1.6 — Definition of "manager"

In this Instrument, "manager" means a person or company that directs the business, operations and affairs of an investment fund.

Commentary

1. The CSA are of the view that the term 'manager' should be interpreted broadly.

The term "manager" is intended to include a group of members on the board of an investment fund or the general partner of an investment fund organized as a limited partnership, where it acts in the capacity of 'manager'/decision-maker.

2. The CSA have, in connection with prospectus reviews, on occasion encountered investment funds structured in unusual ways. The CSA may examine an investment fund if it seems that it was structured to avoid the operation of this Instrument.

1.7 — Definition of "standing instruction"

In this Instrument, "standing instruction" means a written approval or recommendation from the independent review committee that permits the manager to proceed with a proposed action under section 5.2 or 5.3 on an ongoing basis.

Part 2 — Functions of the manager

2.1 — Manager standard of care

A manager in exercising its powers and discharging its duties related to the management of the investment fund must

(a) act honestly and in good faith, and in the best interests of the investment fund; and

(b) exercise the degree of care, diligence and skill that a reasonably prudent person would exercise in comparable circumstances.

Commentary

1. This section introduces a required standard of care for managers in certain jurisdictions and is intended to create a uniform standard of care provision for managers of investment funds subject to this Instrument.

2.2 — Manager to have written policies and procedures

(1) Before proceeding with a conflict of interest matter or any other matter that securities legislation requires the manager to refer to the independent review committee, the manager must

    (a) establish written policies and procedures that it must follow on that matter or on that type of matter, having regard to its duties under securities legislation; and

    (b) refer the policies and procedures to the independent review committee for its review and input.

(2) In establishing the written policies and procedures described in subsection (1), the manager must consider the input of the independent review committee, if any.

(3) The manager may revise its policies and procedures if it provides the independent review committee with a written description of any significant changes for the independent review committee's review and input before implementing the revisions.

Commentary

1. Section 2.2 contemplates that a manager should identify for each investment fund the conflict of interest matters it expects will arise and that will be required to be referred to the IRC under section 5.1, and review its policies and procedures for those matters with the IRC.

Section 2.2 further requires the manager to establish policies and procedures for other matters it expects will arise and that will be required by securities legislation to be referred to the IRC, for example, certain reorganizations and transfers of assets between related mutual funds under Part 5 of NI 81-102.

2. A manager is expected to establish policies and procedures that are consistent with its obligations to the investment fund under securities legislation to make decisions in the best interests of the fund. Paragraph (1)(a) is intended to reinforce this obligation.

A manager that manages more than one investment fund may establish policies and procedures for an action or category of actions for all of the investment funds it manages. Alternatively, the manager may establish separate policies and procedures for the action or category of actions for each of its investment funds, or groups of its investment funds.

However structured, the CSA expect the written policies and procedures the manager establishes to be designed to prevent any violations by the manager and the investment fund of securities legislation in the areas that this Instrument addresses, and to detect and promptly correct any violations that occur.

3. A manager is expected to follow the policies and procedures established under this section. In referring a matter to the IRC under section 5.1, the CSA expect the manager to inform the IRC whether its proposed action follows its written policies and procedures on the matter.

If an unanticipated conflict of interest matter arises for which the manager does not have a policy and procedure, the CSA expect the manager to bring the matter and its proposed action to the IRC for its review and input at the time the matter is referred to the IRC.

4. Small investment fund families may require fewer written policies and procedures than large fund complexes that, for example, have conflicts of interest as a result of affiliations with other financial service firms.

2.3 — Manager to maintain records

A manager must maintain a record of any activity that is subject to the review of the independent review committee, including

    (a) a copy of the policies and procedures that address the matter;

    (b) minutes of its meetings, if any; and

    (c) copies of materials, including any written reports, provided to the independent review committee.

Commentary

1. This section is intended to assist the CSA in determining whether the manager is adhering to this Instrument, and in identifying weaknesses in the manager's policies and procedures if violations do occur. The CSA expect managers to keep records in accordance with existing best practices.

2. A manager is expected under this section to keep minutes only of any material discussions it has at meetings with the IRC or internally on matters subject to the review of the IRC.

The CSA do not view this section or this Instrument as preventing the IRC and manager from sharing record keeping and maintaining joint records of IRC and manager meetings.

3. The CSA expect a manager to keep records of the actions it takes in respect of a matter referred to the IRC. This includes any otherwise restricted or prohibited transactions described in subsection 5.2(1) for which the manager requires the IRC's approval under Part 6 of this Instrument or under Part 4 of NI 81-102.

2.4 — Manager to provide assistance

(1) When a manager refers to the independent review committee a conflict of interest matter or any other matter that securities legislation requires it to refer, or refers its policies and procedures related to such matters, the manager must

    (a) provide the independent review committee with information sufficient for the independent review committee to properly carry out its responsibilities, including

        (i) a description of the facts and circumstances giving rise to the matter;

        (ii) the manager's policies and procedures;

(iii) the manager's proposed course of action, if applicable; and

(iv) all further information the independent review committee reasonably requests;

(b) make its officers who are knowledgeable about the matter available to attend meetings of the independent review committee or respond to inquiries of the independent review committee about the matter; and

(c) provide the independent review committee with any other assistance it reasonably requests in its review of the matter.

(2) A manager must not prevent or attempt to prevent the independent review committee, or a member of the independent review committee, from communicating with the securities regulatory authority or regulator.

Part 3 — Independent review committee

3.1 — Independent review committee for an investment fund

An investment fund must have an independent review committee.

Commentary

1. A manager is expected to establish an IRC using a structure that is appropriate for the investment funds it manages, having regard to the expected workload of that committee. For example, a manager may establish one IRC for each of the investment funds it manages, for several of its investment funds, or for all of its investment funds.

2. This Instrument does not prevent investment funds from sharing an IRC with investment funds managed by another manager. This Instrument also does not prevent a third party from offering IRCs for investment funds. Managers of smaller families of investment funds may find these to be cost-effective ways to establish IRCs for their investment funds.

3.2 — Initial appointments

The manager must appoint each member of an investment fund's first independent review committee.

3.3 — Vacancies and reappointments

(1) An independent review committee must fill a vacancy on the independent review committee as soon as practicable.

(2) A member whose term has expired, or will soon expire, may be reappointed by the other members of the independent review committee.

(3) In filling a vacancy on the independent review committee or reappointing a member of the independent review committee, the independent review committee must consider the manager's recommendations, if any.

(4) A member may not be reappointed for a term or terms of office that, if served, would result in the member serving on the independent review committee for longer than 6 years, unless the manager agrees to the reappointment.

(5) If, for any reason, an independent review committee has no members, the manager must appoint a member to fill each vacancy as soon as practicable.

Commentary

1. Consistent with the manager's role to appoint the first members of an IRC, if at any time the IRC has no members, the manager will also appoint the replacement members. The CSA anticipate that the circumstances contemplated in subsection (5) will occur rarely, such as in the event of a change of manager or change in control of the manager. In these circumstances, managers should consider their timely disclosure obligations under securities legislation.

2. The manager may suggest candidates and may provide assistance to the IRC in the selection and recruitment process when a vacancy arises. Subsection (3) requires the IRC to consider the manager's recommendation, if any, when filling a vacancy or reappointing a member of the IRC.

The CSA believe that allowing the IRC to select its own members and decide the term a member can serve will foster independent-minded committees that will be focussed on the best interests of the investment fund. The CSA also consider the members of the IRC to be best-positioned to judge the manner in which a prospective member can contribute to the effectiveness of the IRC.

3. The maximum term limit of 6 years specified in subsection (4) for a member to serve on an investment fund's IRC is intended to enhance the independence and effectiveness of the IRC. An IRC may reappoint a member beyond the maximum term, but only with the agreement of the manager.

3.4 — Term of office

The term of office of a member of an independent review committee must be not less than 1 year and not more than 3 years, and must be set by the manager or the independent review committee, as the case may be, at the time the member is appointed.

Commentary

1. To ensure continuity and continued independence from the manager, the CSA recommend that the terms of all IRC members be staggered.

Part 8: MUTUAL FUNDS

3.5 — Nominating criteria

Before a member of the independent review committee is appointed, the manager or the independent review committee, as the case may be, must consider

      (a) the competencies and skills the independent review committee, as a whole, should possess;

      (b) the competencies and skills of each other member of the independent review committee; and

      (c) the competencies and skills the prospective member would bring to the independent review committee.

Commentary

1. Section 3.5 sets out the criteria the manager and the IRC must consider before appointing a member of the IRC. Subject to these requirements, the manager and the IRC may establish nominating criteria in addition to those set out in this section.

3.6 — Written charter

(1) The independent review committee must adopt a written charter that includes its mandate, responsibilities and functions, and the policies and procedures it will follow when performing its functions.

(2) If the independent review committee and the manager agree in writing that the independent review committee will perform functions other than those prescribed by securities legislation, the charter must include a description of the functions that are the subject of the agreement.

(3) In adopting the charter, the independent review committee must consider the manager's recommendations, if any.

Commentary

1. The CSA expect the written charter to set out the necessary policies and procedures to ensure the IRC performs its role adequately and effectively and in compliance with this Instrument. An IRC acting for more than one investment fund may choose to establish a separate charter for each fund. Alternatively, an IRC may choose to establish one charter for all of the investment funds it oversees or groups of investment funds.

2. The IRC should consider the specific matters subject to its review when developing the policies and procedures to be set out in its charter.

3. Without discussing all of the policies and procedures that may be set out in the written charter, the CSA expect that the written charter will include the following:

    • *policies and procedures the IRC must follow when reviewing conflict of interest matters,*

    • *criteria for the IRC to consider in setting its compensation and expenses and the compensation and expenses of any advisors employed by the IRC,*

    • *a policy relating to IRC member ownership of securities of the investment fund, manager or in any person or company that provides services to the investment fund or the manager,*

    • *policies and procedures that describe how a member of the IRC is to conduct himself or herself when he or she faces a conflict of interest, or could be perceived to face a conflict of interest, with respect to a matter being considered or to be considered by the IRC,*

    • *policies and procedures that describe how the IRC is to interact with any existing advisory board or board of directors of the investment fund and the manager, and*

    • *policies and procedures that describe how any subcommittee of the IRC to which has been delegated any of the functions of the IRC, is to report to the IRC.*

4. The manager and the IRC may agree that the IRC will perform functions in addition to those prescribed by this Instrument and elsewhere in securities legislation. This Instrument does not preclude those arrangements, nor does this Instrument regulate those arrangements.

3.7 — Composition

(1) An independent review committee must have at least three members.

(2) The size of the independent review committee is to be determined by the manager, with a view to facilitating effective decision-making, and may only be changed by the manager.

(3) Every independent review committee member must be independent.

(4) An independent review committee must appoint a member as Chair.

(5) The Chair of an independent review committee is responsible for managing the mandate, and responsibilities and functions, of the independent review committee.

Commentary

1. To ensure its effectiveness, a manager should consider the workload of the IRC when determining its size. The CSA expect that the manager will seek the input of the IRC prior to changing the size of the IRC.

2. The CSA anticipate that the Chair of the IRC will lead IRC meetings, foster communication among IRC members, and ensure the IRC carries out its responsibilities in a timely and effective manner.

The CSA expect the IRC Chair will be the primary person to interact with the manager on issues relating to the investment fund. An IRC Chair and the manager may agree to have regular communication as a way for the IRC Chair to keep informed of the operations of the investment fund between meetings, and of any significant events relating to the investment fund.

3. The requirement that all members of the IRC be independent does not preclude the IRC from consulting with others who can help the members understand matters that are beyond their specific expertise, or help them understand industry practices or trends, for example.

3.8 — Compensation

(1) The manager may set the initial compensation and expenses of an independent review committee that is appointed under section 3.2 or subsection 3.3(5).

(2) Subject to subsection (1), the independent review committee must set reasonable compensation and proper expenses for its members.

(3) When setting its compensation and expenses under subsection (2), the independent review committee must consider

    (a) the independent review committee's most recent assessment of its compensation under paragraph 4.2(2)(b); and

    (b) the manager's recommendations, if any.

Commentary

1. This section permits the manager to determine the amount and type of compensation and expenses the IRC members will initially receive. To avoid undue influence from the manager, subsection (2) requires that, subsequent to the initial setting of compensation and other than in the unusual circumstance described in subsection 3.3(5), members of the IRC have the sole authority for determining their compensation. The Instrument permits the manager to recommend to the members of the IRC the amount and type of compensation to be paid, and requires the IRC to consider that recommendation.

2. The CSA expect the IRC and the manager to decide the IRC's compensation in a manner consistent with good governance practices. Among the factors the IRC and manager should consider when determining the appropriate level of compensation are the following:

- *the number, nature and complexity of the investment funds and the fund families for which the IRC acts;*
- *the nature and extent of the workload of each member of the IRC, including the commitment of time and energy that is expected from each member;*
- *industry best practices, including industry averages and surveys on IRC compensation; and*
- *the best interests of the investment fund.*

3. The CSA expect that the IRC and the manager will discuss any instance where the IRC disagrees with the manager's recommendations under paragraph (3)(b), in an attempt to reach an agreement that is satisfactory to both the IRC and the manager.

3.9 — Standard of care

(1) Every member of an independent review committee, in exercising his or her powers and discharging his or her duties related to the investment fund, and, for greater certainty, not to any other person, as a member of the independent review committee must

    (a) act honestly and in good faith, with a view to the best interests of the investment fund; and

    (b) exercise the degree of care, diligence and skill that a reasonably prudent person would exercise in comparable circumstances.

(2) Every member of an independent review committee must comply with this Instrument and the written charter of the independent review committee required under section 3.6.

(3) A member of the independent review committee does not breach paragraph (1)(b), if the member exercised the care, diligence and skill that a reasonably prudent person would exercise in comparable circumstances, including reliance in good faith on

    (a) a report or certification represented as full and true to the independent review committee by the manager or an entity related to the manager; or

    (b) a report of a person whose profession lends credibility to a statement made by the person.

(4) A member of the independent review committee has complied with his or her duties under paragraph (1)(a) if the member has relied in good faith on

    (a) a report or certification represented as full and true to the independent review committee by the manager or an entity related to the manager; or

    (b) a report of a person whose profession lends credibility to a statement made by the person.

Commentary

1. The standard of care for IRC members under this section is consistent with the special relationship between the IRC and the investment fund.

The CSA consider the role of the members of the IRC to be similar to corporate directors, though with a much more limited mandate, and therefore we would expect any defences available to corporate directors to also be available to IRC members.

2. The CSA consider the best interests of the investment fund referred to in paragraph (1)(a) to generally be consistent with the interests of the securityholders in the investment fund as a whole.

3. It is not the intention of the CSA to create a duty of care on the part of the IRC to any other person under paragraph (1)(b).

3.10 — Ceasing to be a member

(1) An individual ceases to be a member of an independent review committee when

(a) the investment fund terminates;

(b) the manager of the investment fund changes, unless the new manager is an affiliate of the former manager; or

(c) there is a change of control of the manager of the investment fund.

(2) An individual ceases to be a member of an independent review committee if

(a) the individual resigns;

(b) the individual's term of office expires and the member is not reappointed;

(c) a majority of the other members of the independent review committee vote to remove the individual; or

(d) a majority of the securityholders of the investment fund vote to remove the individual at a special meeting called for that purpose by the manager.

(3) An individual ceases to be a member of the independent review committee if the individual is

(a) no longer independent within the meaning of section 1.4 and the cause of the member's non-independence is not temporary for which the member can recuse himself or herself;

(b) of unsound mind and has been so found by a court in Canada or elsewhere;

(c) bankrupt;

(d) prohibited from acting as a director or officer of any issuer in Canada;

(e) subject to any penalties or sanctions made by a court relating to provincial and territorial securities legislation; or

(f) a party to a settlement agreement with a provincial or territorial securities regulatory authority.

(4) If an individual ceases to be a member of the independent review committee due to a circumstance described in subsection (2), the manager must, as soon as practicable, notify the securities regulatory authority or regulator of the date and the reason the individual ceased to be a member.

(5) The notification referred to in subsection (4) is satisfied if it is made to the investment fund's principal regulator.

(6) The notice of a meeting of securityholders of an investment fund called to consider the removal of a member under paragraph (2)(d) must comply with the notice requirements set out in section 5.4 of National Instrument 81-102 *Investment Funds*.

(7) For any member of the independent review committee who receives notice or otherwise learns of a meeting of securityholders called to consider the removal of the member under paragraph (2)(d),

(a) the member may submit to the manager a written statement giving reasons for opposing the removal; and

(b) the manager must, as soon as practicable, send a copy of the statement referred to in paragraph (a) to every securityholder entitled to receive notice of the meeting and to the member unless the statement is included in or attached to the notice documents required by subsection (6).

Commentary

1. The CSA do not anticipate that the securityholder vote contemplated in paragraph 3.10(2)(d) will be routine. When a manager calls a meeting of securityholders to consider the removal of a member, subsection (7) requires that the member will have an opportunity to respond to the manager's notice.

2. In the circumstances described in paragraphs 3.10(1)(b) and (c), all members of the IRC will cease to be members. This does not preclude the new manager from reappointing the former members of the IRC under subsection 3.3(5).

3. Paragraph 3.10(3)(a) is meant to exclude a situation where a member may face, or be perceived to face, a conflict of interest with respect to a specific conflict of interest matter the IRC is considering.

3.11 — Authority

(1) An independent review committee has authority to

(a) request information it determines useful or necessary from the manager and its officers to carry out its duties;

(b) engage independent counsel and other advisors it determines useful or necessary to carry out its duties;

(c) set reasonable compensation and proper expenses for any independent counsel and other advisors engaged by the independent review committee; and

(d) delegate to a subcommittee of at least three members of the independent review committee any of its functions, except the removal of a member under paragraph 3.10(2)(c).

(2) If the independent review committee delegates to a subcommittee under paragraph (1)(d) any of its functions, the subcommittee must report on its activities to the independent review committee at least annually.

(3) Despite any other provision in this Instrument, an independent review committee may communicate directly with the securities regulatory authority or regulator with respect to any matter.

Commentary

1. The CSA recognize that utilizing the manager's staff and industry experts may be important to help the members of the IRC deal with matters that are beyond the level of their expertise, or help them understand different practices among investment funds.

While this Instrument does not require legal counsel or other advisers for the IRC to be independent of the manager or the investment fund, there may be instances when the members of the IRC believe they need access to counsel or advisers who are free from conflicting loyalties. Paragraph (1)(b) gives the IRC the discretion and authority to hire independent legal counsel and other advisers. The CSA expect that the IRC will use independent advisors selectively and only to assist, not replace, IRC decision-making. The CSA do not anticipate that IRCs will routinely use external counsel and other advisers.

2. Paragraph (1)(d) is intended to allow an IRC of more than three members to delegate any of its functions, except the removal of an IRC member, to a subcommittee of at least three members. The CSA expect in such instances that the written charter of the IRC will include a defined mandate and reporting requirements for any subcommittee.

The CSA do not consider delegation by the IRC of a function to a subcommittee to absolve the IRC from its responsibility for the function.

3. Subsection (3) specifies that the IRC may inform the securities regulatory authority or regulator of any concerns or issues that it may not otherwise be required to report. For example, the IRC may be concerned if very few matters have been referred by the manager for review, or it may have found, or have reasonable grounds to suspect, a breach of securities legislation has occurred. However, the IRC has no obligation to report matters other than those prescribed by this Instrument or elsewhere in securities legislation.

4. The CSA do not consider that this section or this Instrument prevents the manager from communicating with the securities regulatory authorities with respect to any matter.

3.12 — Decisions

(1) A decision by the independent review committee on a conflict of interest matter or any other matter that securities legislation requires the independent review committee to review requires the agreement of a majority of the independent review committee's members.

(2) If, for any reason, an independent review committee has two members, a decision by the independent review committee must be unanimous.

(3) An independent review committee with one member may not make a decision.

Commentary

1. This section requires a decision of the members of the IRC to represent the majority. Should the IRC find itself with two members, subsection (2) permits the IRC to continue to make decisions on conflict of interest matters provided the remaining two members agree.

3.13 — Fees and expenses to be paid by the investment fund

The investment fund must pay from the assets of its fund all reasonable costs and expenses reasonably incurred in the compliance of this Instrument.

Commentary

1. A manager is expected to allocate the costs associated with the IRC on an equitable and reasonable basis amongst the investment funds for which the IRC acts.

This Instrument does not prohibit a manager from reimbursing the investment fund for any of the costs associated with compliance with this Instrument. It is expected that the prospectus will disclose whether or not the manager will reimburse the investment fund.

2. The CSA do not expect costs that the manager or investment fund would ordinarily incur in the operation of the investment fund without the presence of the IRC (for example, rent) to be charged to the investment fund under this section. Among the costs the CSA expect will be charged to the investment fund under this section are the following:

- *the compensation and expenses payable to the members of the IRC and to any independent counsel and other advisers employed by the IRC;*

- *the costs of the orientation and continuing education of the members of the IRC; and*

- *the costs and expenses associated with a special meeting of securityholders called by the manager to remove a member or members of the IRC.*

3.14 — Indemnification and insurance

(1) In this section, "member" means:

   (a) a member of the independent review committee;

   (b) a former member of the independent review committee; and

   (c) the heirs, executors, administrators or other legal representatives of the estate of an individual in (a) or (b).

(2) An investment fund and manager may indemnify a member against all costs, charges and expenses, including an amount paid to settle an action or satisfy a judgment, reasonably incurred by the person in respect of any civil, criminal, administrative, investigative or other proceeding in which the member is involved because of being or having been a member.

(3) An investment fund and manager may advance moneys to a member for the costs, charges and expenses of a proceeding referred to in subsection (2). The member must repay the moneys if the member does not fulfill the conditions of subsection (4).

(4) An investment fund and manager may not indemnify a member under subsection (2) unless

    (a) the member acted honestly and in good faith, with a view to the best interests of the investment fund; and

    (b) in the case of a criminal or administrative action or proceeding that is enforced by a monetary penalty, the member had reasonable grounds for believing that the individual's conduct was lawful.

(5) Despite subsection (2), a member referred to in that subsection is entitled to an indemnity from the investment fund in respect of all costs, charges and expenses reasonably incurred by the member in connection with the defence of any civil, criminal, administrative, investigative or other proceeding to which the member is subject because of the member's association with the investment fund as described in subsection (2), if the member seeking indemnity

    (a) was not judged by the court or other competent authority to have committed any fault or omitted to do anything that ought to have been done; and

    (b) fulfills the conditions set out in subsection (4).

(6) An investment fund and manager may purchase and maintain insurance for the benefit of any member referred to in subsection (2) against any liability incurred by the member in his or her capacity as a member.

Commentary

1. This Instrument requires that members of an IRC be accountable for their actions. At the same time, this section does not prevent an investment fund or a manager from limiting a member's financial exposure through insurance and indemnification.

2. This section permits an investment fund and the manager to indemnify and purchase insurance coverage for the members of the IRC on terms comparable to those applicable to directors of corporations. The broad goals underlying the indemnity provisions are to allow for reimbursement for reasonable good faith behaviour, thereby discouraging the hindsight application of perfection to the IRC's actions.

Under this section, the investment fund is required to indemnify an IRC member who has been sued and has successfully defended the action, subject to certain conditions. If the IRC member does not defend the action successfully, the investment fund and manager may indemnify the member in certain circumstances. The intention of indemnity is to encourage responsible behaviour yet still permit enough leeway to attract strong candidates.

The two conditions which must be satisfied in either instance under this section for an IRC member to be indemnified are:

• the IRC member must have acted in a manner consistent with his or her fiduciary duty with respect to the action or matter for which the IRC member is seeking the indemnification; and

• the IRC member must have had reasonable grounds for believing that his or her conduct was lawful.

The CSA expect any such coverage to be on reasonable commercial terms.

3. It is open to members of the IRC to negotiate contractual indemnities with the manager and the investment fund provided the protection is permissible under this section.

3.15 — Orientation and continuing education

(1) The manager and independent review committee must provide orientation consisting of educational or informational programs that enable a new independent review committee member to understand

    (a) the role of the independent review committee and its members collectively; and

    (b) the role of the individual member.

(2) The manager may provide a member of the independent review committee with educational or informational programs, as the manager considers useful or necessary, that enable the member to understand the nature and operation of the manager's and investment fund's businesses.

(3) The independent review committee may reasonably supplement the educational and informational programs provided to its members under this section.

Commentary

1. The CSA expect members of the IRC to regularly participate in educational or informational programs that may be useful to the members in understanding and fulfilling their duties.

Section 3.15 sets out only the minimum educational programs that a manager and IRC are expected to provide for members of the IRC. Educational activities could include presentations, seminars or discussion groups conducted by:

• personnel of the investment fund or manager,

• outside experts,

• industry groups,

• representatives of the investment fund's various service providers, and

• educational organizations and institutions.

2. The CSA expect a discussion of a member's role referred to in paragraph (1)(b) to include a reference to the commitment of time and energy that is expected from the member.

Part 4 — Functions of independent review committee

4.1 — Review of matters referred by manager

(1) The independent review committee must review and provide its decision under section 5.2 or under section 5.3 to the manager on a conflict of interest matter that the manager refers to the independent review committee for review.

(2) The independent review committee must perform any other function required by securities legislation.

(3) The independent review committee has the authority to choose whether to deliberate and decide on a matter referred to in subsection (1) and (2) in the absence of the manager, any representative of the manager and any entity related to the manager.

(4) Despite subsection (3), an independent review committee must hold at least one meeting annually at which the manager, any representative of the manager or any entity related to the manager are not in attendance.

(5) The independent review committee has no power, authority or responsibility for the operation of the investment fund or the manager except as provided in this section.

Commentary

1. The Instrument requires the IRC only to consider matters referred to it by the manager that involve or may be perceived to involve a conflict of interest for the manager between its own interests and its duty to manage an investment fund.

Securities legislation also requires the IRC to consider other matters. For example, a change in a mutual fund's auditor and certain reorganizations and transfers of assets between related mutual funds under Part 5 of NI 81-102 require the review and prior approval of the IRC for the manager to proceed.

2. The manager and the IRC may agree that the IRC will perform functions in addition to those prescribed by this Instrument and elsewhere in securities legislation. This Instrument does not preclude those arrangements, nor does this Instrument regulate those arrangements.

3. Subsection (3) permits the IRC to decide who, other than IRC members, may attend any IRC meeting other than the meeting referred to in subsection (4). Subsection (3) also does not preclude the IRC from receiving oral or written submissions from the manager or from holding meetings with representatives of the manager or an entity related to the manager or any other person not independent under this Instrument. The CSA believe utilizing the manager's staff and industry experts may be important to help the members of the IRC understand matters that are beyond their specific expertise, or help them understand different practices among investment funds.

4. The requirement that the IRC hold at least one meeting without anyone else present (including management of the investment fund) is intended to give the members of the IRC an opportunity to speak freely about any sensitive issues, including any concerns about the manager.

The CSA are of the view that subsection (4) is satisfied if the IRC holds a portion of any meeting annually without the presence of the manager, any representative of the manager or any entity related to the manager.

4.2 — Regular assessments

(1) At least annually, the independent review committee must review and assess the adequacy and effectiveness of

    (a) the manager's written policies and procedures required under section 2.2;

    (b) any standing instruction it has provided to the manager under section 5.4;

    (c) the manager's and the investment fund's compliance with any conditions imposed by the independent review committee in a recommendation or approval it has provided to the manager; and

    (d) any subcommittee to which the independent review committee has delegated, under paragraph 3.11(1)(d), any of its functions.

(2) At least annually, the independent review committee must review and assess

    (a) the independence of its members; and

    (b) the compensation of its members.

(3) At least annually, the independent review committee must review and assess its effectiveness as a committee, as well as the effectiveness and contribution of each of its members.

(4) The review by the independent review committee required under subsection (3) must include a consideration of

    (a) the independent review committee's written charter referred to in section 3.6;

    (b) the competencies and knowledge each member is expected to bring to the independent review committee;

    (c) the level of complexity of the issues reasonably expected to be raised by members in connection with the matters under review by the independent review committee; and

    (d) the ability of each member to contribute the necessary time required to serve effectively on the independent review committee.

Commentary

1. Section 4.2 sets out the minimum assessments the independent review committee must perform. Subject to these requirements, the IRC may establish a process for (and determine the frequency of) additional assessments as it sees fit.

2. The annual self-assessment by the IRC should improve performance by strengthening each member's understanding of his or her role and fostering better communication and greater cohesiveness among members.

3. When evaluating individual performance, it is expected that the IRC consider factors such as the member's attendance and participation in meetings, continuing education activities and industry knowledge. The manager may also provide IRC members with feedback which the IRC may consider.

It is expected the self-assessment should focus on both substantive and procedural aspects of the IRC's operations. When evaluating the IRC's structure and effectiveness, the IRC should consider factors such as the following:

- the frequency of meetings;

- the substance of meeting agendas;

- the policies and procedures that the manager has established to refer matters to the IRC;

- the usefulness of the materials provided to the members of the IRC;

- the collective experience and background of the members of the IRC;

- the number of funds the IRC oversees; and

- the amount and form of compensation the members receive from an individual investment fund and in aggregate from the fund family.

4. The CSA expect the members of an IRC to respond appropriately to address any weaknesses found in a self-assessment. For example, it may be necessary to improve the IRC members' continuing education, recommend ways to improve the quality and sufficiency of the information provided to them, or recommend to the manager decreasing the number of investment funds under the IRC's oversight.

In rare circumstances, the IRC may consider removing a member of the IRC as contemplated under paragraph 3.10(2)(c) as a result of the self-assessment.

4.3 — Reporting to the manager

The independent review committee must as soon as practicable deliver to the manager a written report of the results of an assessment under subsection 4.2(1) and (2) that includes

(a) a description of each instance of a breach of any of the manager's policies or procedures of which the independent review committee is aware, or that it has reason to believe has occurred;

(b) a description of each instance of a breach of a condition imposed by the independent review committee in a recommendation or approval it has provided to the manager, of which the independent review committee is aware, or that it has reason to believe has occurred; and

(c) recommendations for any changes the independent review committee considers should be made to the manager's policies and procedures.

4.4 — Reporting to securityholders

(1) An independent review committee must prepare, for each financial year of the investment fund and no later than the date the investment fund files its annual financial statements, a report to securityholders of the investment fund that describes the independent review committee and its activities for the financial year and includes

(a) the name of each member of the independent review committee at the date of the report, with

(i) the member's length of service on the independent review committee;

(ii) the name of any other fund family on whose independent review committee the member serves; and

(iii) if applicable, a description of any relationship that may cause a reasonable person to question the member's independence and the basis upon which the independent review committee determined that the member is independent;

(b) the percentage of securities of each class or series of voting or equity securities beneficially owned, directly or indirectly, in aggregate, by all the members of the independent review committee of the investment fund

(i) in the investment fund if the aggregate level of ownership exceeds 10 percent;

(ii) in the manager; or

(iii) in any person or company that provides services to the investment fund or the manager;

(c) the identity of the Chair of the independent review committee;

(d) any changes in the composition or membership of the independent review committee during the period;

(e) the aggregate compensation paid to the independent review committee and any indemnities paid to members of the independent review committee by the investment fund during the period;

(f) a description of the process and criteria used by the independent review committee to determine the appropriate level of compensation of its members and any instance when, in setting the compensation and expenses of its members, the independent review committee did not follow the recommendation of the manager, including

(i) a summary of the manager's recommendation; and

(ii) the independent review committee's reasons for not following the recommendation;

(g) if known, a description of each instance when the manager acted in a conflict of interest matter referred to the independent review committee for which the independent review committee did not give a positive recommendation, including

(i) a summary of the recommendation; and

(ii) if known, the manager's reasons for proceeding without following the recommendation of the independent review committee and the result of proceeding;

(h) if known, a description of each instance when the manager acted in a conflict of interest matter but did not meet a condition imposed by the independent review committee in its recommendation or approval, including

(i) the nature of the condition;

(ii) if known, the manager's reasons for not meeting the condition; and

(iii) whether the independent review committee is of the view that the manager has taken, or proposes to take, appropriate action to deal with the matter; and

(i) a brief summary of any recommendations and approvals the manager relied upon during the period.

(2) The report required under subsection (1) must as soon as practicable

(a) be sent by the investment fund, without charge, to a securityholder of the investment fund, upon the securityholder's request;

(b) be made available and prominently displayed by the manager on the investment fund's, investment fund family's or manager's website, if it has a website;

(c) be filed by the investment fund with the securities regulatory authority or regulator; and

(d) be delivered by the independent review committee to the manager.

Commentary

1. The report to be filed with the securities regulatory authorities should be filed on the SEDAR group profile number of the investment fund as a continuous disclosure document. The CSA expect that the investment fund will pay any reasonable costs associated with the filing of the report.

2. It is expected the report will be displayed in an easily visible location on the home page of the website of the investment fund, the investment fund family or the manager, as applicable. The CSA expect the report to remain on the website at least until the posting of the next report.

3. The disclosure required in subparagraph (1)(a)(iii) is expected to be provided only in instances where a member could reasonably be perceived to not be 'independent' under this Instrument.

4.5 — Reporting to securities regulatory authorities

(1) If the independent review committee is aware of an instance where the manager acted in a conflict of interest matter under subsection 5.2(1) but did not comply with a condition or conditions imposed by securities legislation or the independent review committee in its approval, the independent review committee must, as soon as practicable, notify in writing the securities regulatory authority or regulator.

(2) The notification referred to in subsection (1) is satisfied if it is made to the investment fund's principal regulator.

Commentary

1. Subsection (1) captures a breach of a condition imposed for an otherwise prohibited or restricted transaction described in subsection 5.2(1), for which the manager has acted under Part 6 of this Instrument or under Part 4 of NI 81-102. This includes a breach of a condition imposed by the IRC as part of its approval (including a standing instruction), or, for example, any conditions imposed for inter-fund trading under section 6.1 of this Instrument or section 4.3 of NI 81-102, for transactions in securities of related issuers under section 6.2 of this Instrument, and for purchases of securities underwritten by related underwriters under section 4.1 of NI 81-102.

The CSA consider that a breach of a condition imposed by securities legislation (including this Instrument) or by the IRC in a transaction described in subsection 5.2(1) will result in the transaction having been made in contravention of securities legislation. In such instances, the securities regulatory authorities may consider taking various action, including requiring the manager to unwind the transaction and pay any costs associated with doing so.

2. The CSA expect that the IRC will include in its notification the steps the manager proposes to take, or has taken, to remedy the breach, if known.

3. Notification under this section is not intended to be a mechanism to resolve disputes between an IRC and a manager, or to raise inconsequential matters with the securities regulatory authorities.

4. The CSA do not view this section or this Instrument as preventing the manager from communicating with the securities regulatory authorities with respect to any matter.

4.6 — Independent review committee to maintain records

An independent review committee must maintain records, including

(a) a copy of its current written charter;

(b) minutes of its meetings;

(c) copies of any materials and written reports provided to it;

(d) copies of materials and written reports prepared by it; and

(e) the decisions it makes.

Commentary

1. Section 4.6 sets out the minimum requirements regarding the record keeping by an IRC. The CSA expect IRCs to keep records in accordance with existing best practices.

2. The IRC is expected under paragraph (b) to keep minutes only of any material discussions it has at meetings with the manager or internally on matters subject to its review.

The CSA do not view this section or this Instrument as preventing the IRC and manager from sharing record keeping and maintaining joint records of IRC and manager meetings.

3. The CSA expect the IRC to keep records of any actions it takes in respect of a matter referred to it, in particular any transaction otherwise prohibited or restricted by securities legislation, as described in subsection 5.2(1), for which the manager has sought the approval of the IRC.

Part 5 — Conflict of interest matters

5.1 — Manager to refer conflict of interest matters to independent review committee

(1) Subject to section 5.4, when a conflict of interest matter arises, and before taking any action in the matter, the manager must

    (a) determine what action it proposes to take in respect of the matter, having regard to

        (i) its duties under securities legislation; and

        (ii) its written policies and procedures on the matter; and

    (b) refer the matter, along with its proposed action, to the independent review committee for its review and decision.

(2) If a manager must hold a meeting of securityholders to obtain securityholder approval before taking an action in a conflict of interest matter, the manager must include a summary of the independent review committee's decision under subsection (1) in the notice of the meeting.

Commentary

1. Section 5.1 recognizes that a manager may not be able to objectively determine whether it is acting in the best interests of the investment fund when it has a conflict of interest. This section requires managers to refer all conflict of interest matters — not just those subject to prohibitions or restrictions under securities legislation — to the IRC so that an independent perspective can be brought to bear on the manager's proposed action.

A decision tree for different types of conflict of interest matters is set out in Appendix A to the Commentary.

While the CSA expect the IRC to bring a high degree of rigour and skeptical objectivity to its review of conflict of interest matters, the CSA do not consider it the role of the IRC to second-guess the investment or business decisions of a manager or an entity related to the manager.

2. Section 5.1 sets out how the manager must proceed when faced with a conflict of interest matter.

Referring proposed actions involving conflict of interest matters to the IRC for its review is not considered by the CSA to detract from the manager's obligations to the investment fund under securities legislation to make decisions in the best interests of the fund. Subparagraph (a)(i) is intended to reinforce this obligation.

3. In referring a matter to the IRC, a manager is expected to inform the IRC whether its proposed action follows its written policies and procedures on the matter under section 2.2.

If an unanticipated conflict of interest matter arises for which the manager does not have an existing written policy and procedure, the CSA expect the manager to bring the matter and its proposed action to the IRC for its review and input at the time the matter is referred to the IRC.

4. There may be matters that are subject to a securityholder vote that also involve a "conflict of interest matter" under this Instrument. For example, increases in the charges of the manager to the mutual fund will be a conflict of interest matter as well as a matter subject to a securityholder vote under Part 5 of National Instrument 81-102. For these matters, subsection (2) requires a manager to refer the matter first to the IRC before seeking the approval of securityholders, and to include a summary of the IRC's decision in the written notice to securityholders.

5.2 — Matters requiring independent review committee approval

(1) A manager may not proceed with a proposed action under section 5.1 without the approval of the independent review committee if the action is

    (a) an inter-fund trade as described in subsection 6.1(2) of this Instrument or a transaction as described in subsection 4.2(1) of National Instrument 81-102 *Investment Funds*;

    (b) a transaction in securities of an issuer as described in subsection 6.2(1) of this Instrument; or

    (c) an investment in a class of securities of an issuer underwritten by an entity related to the manager as described in subsection 4.1(1) of National Instrument 81-102 *Investment Funds*.

(2) An independent review committee must not approve an action unless it has determined, after reasonable inquiry, that the action

    (a) is proposed by the manager free from any influence by an entity related to the manager and without taking into account any consideration relevant to an entity related to the manager;

    (b) represents the business judgment of the manager uninfluenced by considerations other than the best interests of the investment fund;

(c) is in compliance with the manager's written policies and procedures relating to the action; and

(d) achieves a fair and reasonable result for the investment fund.

Commentary

1. For the transactions described in subsection (1), provided the manager receives the IRC's approval under this section, and satisfies the additional conditions imposed under the applicable sections of Part 6 of this Instrument or Part 4 of NI 81-102, the manager will be permitted to proceed with the action without obtaining regulatory exemptive relief.

The IRC may give its approval for certain actions or categories of actions in the form of a standing instruction as described in section 5.4. If no standing instruction is in effect, the manager is required to seek the IRC's approval prior to proceeding with any action set out in subsection (1). An IRC may consider as guidance any conditions in prior exemptive relief orders, waivers or approvals obtained from the securities regulatory authorities when contemplating the appropriate terms and conditions in its approval.

2. If the IRC does not approve a proposed action described in subsection (1), the manager is not permitted to proceed without obtaining exemptive relief from the securities regulatory authorities. The CSA consider it in the best interests of the investment fund, and ultimately investors, for the IRC to be able to stop any proposed action which does not meet the test in subsection (2).

3. The CSA would usually expect that, before the IRC approves a proposed action described in subsection (1), it will have requested from the manager or others a report or certification to assist in its determination that the test in subsection (2) has been met.

4. The CSA expect that the manager will discuss with the IRC any instance where the IRC does not approve a proposed action, so that an alternative action satisfactory to both the manager and the IRC can be found, if possible.

5. The CSA consider that the ability of the manager to seek the removal of a member or members of the IRC under paragraph 3.10(2)(d) sufficiently addresses any concern that a manager may have about an IRC's ongoing refusal to approve matters.

5.3 — Matters subject to independent review committee recommendation

(1) Before a manager may proceed with a proposed action under section 5.1 other than those set out in subsection 5.2(1),

(a) the independent review committee must provide a recommendation to the manager as to whether, in the committee's opinion after reasonable inquiry, the proposed action achieves a fair and reasonable result for the investment fund; and

(b) the manager must consider the recommendation of the independent review committee.

(2) If the manager decides to proceed with an action in a conflict of interest matter that, in the opinion of the independent review committee after reasonable inquiry, does not achieve a fair and reasonable result for the investment fund under paragraph (1)(a), the manager must notify in writing the independent review committee before proceeding with the proposed action.

(3) Upon receiving the notification described in subsection (2), the independent review committee may require the manager to notify securityholders of the investment fund of the manager's decision.

(4) A notification to securityholders under subsection (3) must

(a) sufficiently describe the proposed action of the manager, the recommendation of the independent review committee and the manager's reasons for proceeding;

(b) state the date of the proposed implementation of the action; and

(c) be sent by the manager to each securityholder of the investment fund at least thirty days before the effective date of the proposed action.

(5) The investment fund must, as soon as practicable, file the notification referred to in subsection (4) with the securities regulatory authority or regulator upon the notice being sent to securityholders.

Commentary

1. This section captures all conflict of interest matters a manager encounters other than those listed in subsection 5.2(1). This includes conflict of interest matters prohibited or restricted by securities legislation not specified in subsection 5.2(1), and a manager's business and commercial decisions made on behalf of the investment fund that may be motivated, or be perceived to be motivated, by the manager's own interests rather than the best interests of the investment fund. Examples include:

* *increasing charges to the investment fund for costs incurred by the manager in operating the fund;*

* *correcting material errors made by the manager in administering the investment fund;*

* *negotiating soft dollar arrangements with dealers with whom the manager places portfolio transactions for the investment fund; and*

* *choosing to bring services in-house over using third-party service providers.*

The CSA expect that, in seeking guidance in identifying conflict of interest matters caught by this Instrument, among the factors the manager will look to for guidance to identify conflict of interest matters will be industry best practices. However, the CSA also acknowledge that each manager will need to consider the nature of its investment fund operations in determining a conflict of interest matter.

2. The CSA expect the IRC's recommendation to state a positive or negative response as to whether they view the proposed action as achieving a fair and reasonable result for the investment fund.

3. For a proposed action in a conflict of interest matter under this section that is prohibited or restricted by securities legislation (but not specified in subsection 5.2(1)), a manager will still need to seek exemptive relief from the securities regulatory authorities.

4. Subsection (2) recognizes that, in exceptional circumstances, the manager may decide to proceed with a proposed course of action despite a negative recommendation from the IRC. In such instances, subsection (2) requires the manager to notify the IRC before proceeding with the action. If the IRC determines that the proposed action is sufficiently important to warrant notice to securityholders in the investment fund, the IRC has the authority to require the manager to give such notification before proceeding with the action.

The CSA anticipate that the situation of a manager proceeding with a conflict of interest matter, despite a negative recommendation by the IRC, will occur infrequently.

5. The notification referred to in subsection (5) should be filed on the SEDAR group profile number of the investment fund as a continuous disclosure document.

5.4 — *Standing instructions by the independent review committee*

(1) Despite section 5.1, the manager is not required to refer a conflict of interest matter nor its proposed action to the independent review committee if the manager complies with the terms of a standing instruction that is in effect.

(2) For any action for which the independent review committee has provided a standing instruction, at the time of the independent review committee's regular assessment described in subsection 4.2(1),

> (a) the manager must provide a written report to the independent review committee describing each instance that it acted in reliance on a standing instruction; and

> (b) the independent review committee must

>> (i) review and assess the adequacy and effectiveness of the manager's written policies and procedures on the matter or on that type of matter with respect to all actions permitted by each standing instruction;

>> (ii) review and assess the manager's and investment fund's compliance with any conditions imposed by it in each standing instruction;

>> (iii) reaffirm or amend each standing instruction;

>> (iv) establish new standing instructions, if necessary; and

>> (v) advise the manager in writing of all changes to the standing instructions.

(3) A manager may continue to rely on a standing instruction under subsection (1) until such time as the independent review committee notifies the manager that the standing instruction has been amended or is no longer in effect.

Commentary

1. Section 5.4 recognizes that there are certain actions or categories of actions of the manager for which it may be appropriate for the IRC to choose to provide a standing instruction. For example, this may include a manager's ongoing voting of proxies on securities held by the investment fund when the manager has a business relationship with the issuer of the securities, or, a manager's decision to engage in inter-fund trading.

2. The CSA expect that, before providing or continuing a standing instruction to the manager for an action or category of actions, the IRC will have:

> * *reviewed the manager's written policies and procedures with respect to the action or category of actions;*

> * *requested from the manager or other persons a report or certification to assist in deciding whether to give its approval or recommendation for the action or category of actions under subsection 5.2(1) or 5.3(1), as the case may be;*

> * *considered whether a standing instruction for the particular action or category of actions is appropriate for the investment fund; and*

> * *established very clear terms and conditions surrounding the standing instruction for the action or category of actions.*

An IRC may consider including in any standing instruction any terms or conditions in prior exemptive relief orders, waivers or approvals obtained from the securities regulatory authorities.

3. As part of the IRC's review under subparagraph (2)(b)(ii), the IRC is expected to be mindful of its reporting obligation under section 4.5 of this Instrument, which includes notifying the securities regulatory authorities of any instance where the manager, in proceeding with an action, did not meet a condition imposed by the IRC in its approval (this includes a standing instruction).

4. This section is intended to improve the flexibility and timeliness of the manager's decisions concerning a proposed course of action in a conflict of interest matter.

Part 6 — Exempted transactions

6.1 — *Inter-fund trades*

(1) In this section

> (a) "current market price of the security" means,

>> (i) if the security is an exchange-traded security or a foreign exchange-traded security,

>>> (A) the closing sale price on the day of the transaction as reported on the exchange upon which the security is listed or the quotation trade reporting system upon which the security is quoted, or

(B) if there are no reported transactions for the day of the transaction, the average of the highest current bid and lowest current ask for the security as displayed on the exchange upon which the security is listed or the quotation trade reporting system upon which the security is quoted, or

(C) if the closing sale price on the day of the transaction is outside of the closing bid and closing ask, the average of the highest current bid and lowest current ask for the security as displayed on the exchange upon which the security is listed or the quotation trade reporting system upon which the security is quoted; or

(ii) for all other securities, the average of the highest current bid and lowest current ask determined on the basis of reasonable inquiry; and

(b) "market integrity requirements" means

(i) if the security is an exchange-traded security, the purchase or sale

(A) is printed on a marketplace that executes trades of the security; and

(B) complies with the market conduct and display requirements of the marketplace, its regulation services provider and securities regulatory authorities; or

(ii) if the security is a foreign exchange-traded security, the purchase or sale complies with the requirements that govern transparency and trading of foreign exchange-traded securities on the foreign exchange or foreign quotation and trade reporting system; or

(iii) for all other securities, the purchase or sale is through a dealer, if the purchase or sale is required to be reported by a registered dealer under applicable securities legislation.

(2) The portfolio manager of an investment fund may purchase a security of any issuer from, or sell a security of any issuer to, another investment fund managed by the same manager or an affiliate of the manager, if, at the time of the transaction

(a) the investment fund is purchasing from, or selling to, another investment fund to which this Instrument applies;

(b) the independent review committee has approved the transaction under subsection 5.2(2);

(c) the bid and ask price of the security is readily available;

(d) the investment fund receives no consideration and the only cost for the trade is the nominal cost incurred by the investment fund to print or otherwise display the trade;

(e) the transaction is executed at the current market price of the security;

(f) the transaction is subject to market integrity requirements; and

(g) the investment fund keeps written records, including

(i) a record of each purchase and sale of securities;

(ii) the parties to the trade; and

(iii) the terms of the purchase or sale

for five years after the end of the fiscal year in which the trade occurred, the most recent two years in a reasonably accessible place.

(3) The provisions of National Instrument 21-101 *Marketplace Operation*, and Part 6 and Part 8 of National Instrument 23-101 *Trading Rules*, do not apply to a portfolio manager or portfolio adviser of an investment fund, or an investment fund, with respect to a purchase or sale of a security referred to in subsection (2) if the purchase or sale is made in accordance with that subsection.

(4) The inter-fund self-dealing investment prohibitions do not apply to a portfolio manager or portfolio adviser of an investment fund, or an investment fund, with respect to a purchase or sale of a security referred to in subsection (2) if the purchase or sale is made in accordance with that subsection.

(5) The dealer registration requirement does not apply to a portfolio manager of an investment fund, with respect to a purchase or sale of a security referred to in subsection (2) if the purchase or sale is made in accordance with that subsection.

(6) In subsection (5), "dealer registration requirement" has the meaning ascribed to that term in National Instrument 14-101 *Definitions*.

Commentary

1. The term "inter-fund self-dealing investment prohibitions" is defined in section 1.5 of this Instrument. It is intended to capture the prohibitions in the securities legislation and certain regulations of each securities regulatory authority regarding inter-fund trades.

2. This section is intended to exempt investment funds from the prohibitions in the securities legislation and certain regulations that preclude inter-fund trades. It is not intended to apply to securities issued by an investment fund that are purchased by another fund within the same fund family.

The CSA are of the view that this section applies to inter-fund trades between fund families of the same manager provided the purchase or sale is made in accordance with subsection (2).

3. This section is also intended to provide a portfolio manager with a dealer registration exemption, where necessary, for inter-fund trades made in accordance with this section, but will not apply to any other activities of the portfolio manager. The exemption is based on compliance with this Instrument and the limitation of its application to prospectus-qualified investment funds. The CSA note that the Registration Reform project may re-examine this exemption.

4. This section sets out the minimum conditions for inter-fund trades to proceed without regulatory exemptive relief. An IRC may consider including in any approval any terms or conditions in prior exemptive relief orders, waivers or approvals obtained from the securities regulatory authorities.

5. This section does not specify the policies and procedures that a manager must have to effect inter-fund trades. However, the CSA expect the manager's policies to include factors or criteria for

- *allocating securities purchased for or sold by two or more investment funds managed by the manager; and*

- *ensuring that the terms of purchase or sale will be no less beneficial to the investment fund than those generally available to other market participants in arm's-length transactions.*

6. The CSA expect that the IRC may give its approval in the form of a standing instruction under section 5.4, to give the manager greater flexibility to take advantage of perceived market opportunity.

7. Paragraph (2)(c) requires that the market quotations for the transactions be transparent. The CSA expect that if the price information is publicly available from a marketplace, newspaper or through a data vendor, for example, this will be the price. If the price is not publicly available, the CSA expect the investment fund to obtain at least one quote from an independent, arm's-length purchaser or seller, immediately before the purchase or sale.

8. The CSA consider the requirement in paragraph (2)(f) to be a way to facilitate price discovery and integrity. The CSA believe this is essential to well-functioning and efficient capital markets. Subparagraph (1)(b)(iii) is intended to capture, for corporate debt securities, the requirement, if applicable, to report the trade to CanPx, and for illiquid securities, the requirement, if applicable, to report the trade to the Canadian Unlisted Board (CUB).

9. Paragraph (2)(g) sets out the minimum expectations regarding the records an investment fund must keep of its inter-fund trades made in reliance on this section. The records should be detailed, and sufficient to establish a proper audit trail of the transactions.

6.2 — Transactions in securities of related issuers

(1) An investment fund may make or hold an investment in the security of an issuer related to it, its manager, or an entity related to the manager, if

(a) at the time that the investment is made,

(i) the independent review committee has approved the investment under subsection 5.2(2); and

(ii) the purchase is made on an exchange on which the securities of the issuer are listed and traded; and

(b) no later than the time the investment fund files its annual financial statements, the manager of the investment fund files with the securities regulatory authority or regulator the particulars of the investment.

(2) The investment fund conflict of interest investment restrictions do not apply to an investment fund with respect to an investment referred to in subsection (1) if the investment is made in accordance with that subsection.

(3) In subsection (2), "investment fund conflict of interest investment restrictions" has the meaning ascribed to that term in National Instrument 81-102 *Investment Funds*.

Commentary

1. This section is intended to relieve investment funds in Quebec, and mutual funds elsewhere in Canada, from the prohibitions in the securities legislation of each securities regulatory authority that preclude investments in securities of related issuers.

2. This section sets out the minimum conditions for purchases to proceed without regulatory exemptive relief. An IRC may consider including in any approval any terms or conditions in prior exemptive relief orders, waivers or approvals obtained from the securities regulatory authorities.

The CSA expect that the IRC may give its approval in the form of a standing instruction as described in section 5.4 to allow the manager greater flexibility in its decisions.

3. This section contemplates that the manager will comply with the applicable reporting requirements under securities legislation for each purchase. The filing referred to in paragraph (1)(b) should be filed on the SEDAR group profile number of the investment fund, as a continuous disclosure document.

4. If an IRC gives its approval for the investment fund to purchase securities of an issuer described in this section, and then subsequently withdraws its approval for additional purchases, the CSA will not consider the continued holding of the securities to be subject to subsection 1.2(b) of the Instrument. However, we will expect the manager to consider whether continuing to hold those securities is a conflict of interest matter that subsection 1.2(a) of the Instrument would require the manager to refer to the IRC.

Part 7 — Exemptions

7.1 — Exemptions

(1) The securities regulatory authority or regulator may grant an exemption from this Instrument, in whole or in part, subject to such conditions or restrictions as may be imposed in the exemption.

(2) Despite subsection (1), in Ontario only the regulator may grant such an exemption.

7.2 — Existing exemptions, waivers or approvals

Any exemption, waiver or approval under a provision of securities legislation that was effective before this Instrument came into force and that deals with the matters that this Instrument regulates, will expire one year after this Instrument comes into force.

Commentary

1. The CSA have, in a number of jurisdictions, granted exemptions and waivers from the conflict of interest and self-dealing provisions in securities legislation to permit the manager and/or the investment fund to make investments not otherwise permitted by securities legislation. Some of those exemptions and waivers contained "sunset" provisions that provided for the expiry of the exemption or waiver upon the coming into force of legislation or a CSA policy or rule that effectively provides for fund governance.

For greater certainty, the CSA note that the coming into force of section 7.2 of this Instrument will effectively cause all exemptions and waivers that deal with the matters regulated by this Instrument — not just those exemptions and waivers that deal with the matters under subsection 5.2(1) — to expire one year after its coming into force whether or not they contained a "sunset" provision.

Part 8 — Effective date

8.1 — Effective date

This Instrument comes into force on November 1, 2006.

8.2 — Transition

(1) Despite section 8.1, this Instrument does not apply to an investment fund until the earlier of

(a) the date on which the manager provides to the securities regulatory authority or regulator the notification referred to in subsection (4); and

(b) the date one year after this Instrument comes into force.

(2) Despite subsection (1), six months from the date this Instrument comes into force the manager must appoint the first members of the independent review committee under section 3.2 in compliance with this Instrument.

(3) Despite section 4.4, the independent review committee's first report to securityholders must be completed by the 120th day after the end of the first financial year of the investment fund to which this Instrument applies.

(4) A manager of an investment fund must notify the securities regulatory authority or regulator in writing if it intends to comply with this Instrument prior to the expiration of the transition period under subsection (1).

(5) The notification referred to in subsection (4) is satisfied if the notification is made to the investment fund's principal regulator.

Commentary

1. Section 8.2 is intended to address transitional concerns.

The CSA expect that all investment funds will be compliant with this Instrument following the expiry of the transition period under subsection 8.2(1), twelve months after the Instrument is in force. For an investment fund established after the expiry of the transition period, it is expected that the investment fund will be compliant with this Instrument before any purchase order for securities of the investment fund is accepted.

2. Subsection 8.2(2) allows a manager an extra six months from the date this Instrument is in force to appoint the initial members of the IRC.

While a six month transition period exists for the appointment of IRC members, the CSA strongly encourage a timely appointment of the IRC by the manager so that within the twelve month transitional period there is sufficient time for the IRC to adopt its charter, to review the manager's policies and procedures, and to review (subject to manager referral) any existing conflict of interest matters.

The transition period is also intended to give the manager sufficient time to refer existing and new conflict of interest matters to the IRC for its review and determination.

3. The CSA anticipate a manager or investment fund may wish to rely on the Instrument before the expiry of the transition period so that it may proceed with IRC approval for an otherwise prohibited or restricted transaction in securities legislation described in subsection 5.2(1). This may not occur unless there is complete compliance with the Instrument. Subsection (4) is intended to assist the CSA in knowing which managers of investment funds are proceeding in this manner before the expiry of the transition period.

4. For investment funds established before the expiry of the transition period, the CSA expect the manager to establish policies and procedures on any conflict of interest matters (if they do not already have them), and to refer to the IRC these policies and procedures and any decisions related to such matters prior to the end of the transition period.

5. The CSA do not consider a manager's organization of an investment fund (such as the initial setting of fees or the initial choice of service providers) to be subject to IRC review, unless the manager's decisions give rise to a conflict of interest concerning the manager's obligations to existing investment funds within the manager's fund family. However, the CSA expect the manager will establish policies and procedures for any conflict of interest matters arising from the investment fund's organization or otherwise, and refer to the IRC these policies and procedures and any decisions related to such matters.

It is anticipated that the manager will wish to engage the IRC early in the establishment of the investment fund to ensure the IRC is adequately informed of potential new conflicts of interest.

6. An investment fund, whether established before or after the date this Instrument comes into force, has a total transition period of up to twelve months from the date the Instrument comes into force to comply with the Instrument. Only if the manager of an investment fund intends to comply with the Instrument in its entirety before the expiry of the transition period is the notice in subsection (4) required.

7. It is expected that investment funds will incorporate any new disclosure obligations arising out of this Instrument as part of their annual prospectus renewal or continuous disclosure filing following the expiry of the transition period.

8. The CSA do not consider the expenses incurred by existing investment funds in establishing an IRC under this Instrument to be caught by section 5.1 of NI 81-102. We do not view section 5.1 as intending to capture the costs associated with compliance by an investment fund with new regulatory requirements.

Appendix A — Conflict of Interest or Self-Dealing Provisions

JURISDICTION	SECURITIES LEGISLATION REFERENCE
Alberta	Part 15 — Insider Trading and Self-Dealing of the *Securities Act* (Alberta)
British Columbia	BC Instrument 81-513 *Self-Dealing*
Manitoba	Part XI — Insider Trading of the *Securities Act* (Manitoba)
Newfoundland and Labrador	Part XX — Insider Trading and Self-Dealing of the *Securities Act* (Newfoundland and Labrador)
New Brunswick	Part 10 — Insider Trading and Self-Dealing of the *Securities Act* (New Brunswick)
Northwest Territories	Part 11 — Insider Reporting and Early Warning of the *Securities Act* (Northwest Territories)
Nova Scotia	Sections 112 — 128 of the *Securities Act* (Nova Scotia)
Nunavut	Part 11 — Insider Reporting and Early Warning of the *Securities Act* (Nunavut)
Ontario	Part XXI — Insider Trading and Self-Dealing of the *Securities Act* (Ontario)
Prince Edward Island	Part 11 — Insider Reporting and Early Warning of the *Securities Act* (Prince Edward Island)
Quebec	Section 236 of the *Securities Regulation* (Quebec)
Saskatchewan	Part XVII — Insider Trading and Self-Dealing — Mutual Funds of the *Securities Act* (Saskatchewan)
Yukon	Part 11 — Insider Reporting and Early Warning of the *Securities Act* (Yukon)
Alberta, British Columbia, Manitoba, Newfoundland and Labrador, New Brunswick, Northwest Territories, Nova Scotia, Nunavut, Ontario, Prince Edward Island, Quebec, Saskatchewan and Yukon	Part 4 of National Instrument 81-102 *Investment Funds* and section 13.5 of National Instrument 31-103 — *Registration Requirements, Exemptions and Ongoing Registrant Obligations*

Appendix B — Inter-Fund Self-Dealing Conflict of Interest Provisions

JURISDICTION	LEGISLATION REFERENCE
Alberta	Section 13.5(2)(b) of National Instrument 31-103 *Registration Requirements, Exemptions and Ongoing Registrant Obligations*
British Columbia	Section 13.5(2)(b) of National Instrument 31-103 *Registration Requirements, Exemptions and Ongoing Registrant Obligations*
Manitoba	Section 13.5(2)(b) of National Instrument 31-103 *Registration Requirements, Exemptions and Ongoing Registrant Obligations*
New Brunswick	Section 144(1)(b) of the *Securities Act* (New Brunswick) Section 11.7(6) of Local Rule 31-501 Registration Requirements Section 13.5(2)(b) of National Instrument 31-103 *Registration Requirements, Exemptions and Ongoing Registrant Obligations*
Newfoundland and Labrador	Section 119(2)(b) of the *Securities Act* (Newfoundland and Labrador) Section 103(6) of Reg. 805/96 Section 13.5(2)(b) of National Instrument 31-103 *Registration Requirements, Exemptions and Ongoing Registrant Obligations*
Northwest Territories	Section 13.5(2)(b) of National Instrument 31-103 *Registration Requirements, Exemptions and Ongoing Registrant Obligations*
Nova Scotia	Section 126(2)(b) of the *Securities Act* (Nova Scotia) Section 32(6) of the General Securities Rules Section 13.5(2)(b) of National Instrument 31-103 *Registration Requirements, Exemptions and Ongoing Registrant Obligations*
Nunavut	Section 13.5(2)(b) of National Instrument 31-103 *Registration Requirements, Exemptions and Ongoing Registrant Obligations*
Ontario	Section 13.5(2)(b) of National Instrument 31-103 *Registration Requirements, Exemptions and Ongoing Registrant Obligations*
Prince Edward Island	Section 13.5(2)(b) of National Instrument 31-103 *Registration Requirements, Exemptions and Ongoing Registrant Obligations*

JURISDICTION	LEGISLATION REFERENCE
Quebec	Section 13.5(2)(b) of National Instrument 31-103 *Registration Requirements, Exemptions and Ongoing Registrant Obligations*
Saskatchewan	Section 13.5(2)(b) of National Instrument 31-103 *Registration Requirements, Exemptions and Ongoing Registrant Obligations*
Yukon	Section 13.5(2)(b) of National Instrument 31-103 *Registration Requirements, Exemptions and Ongoing Registrant Obligations*

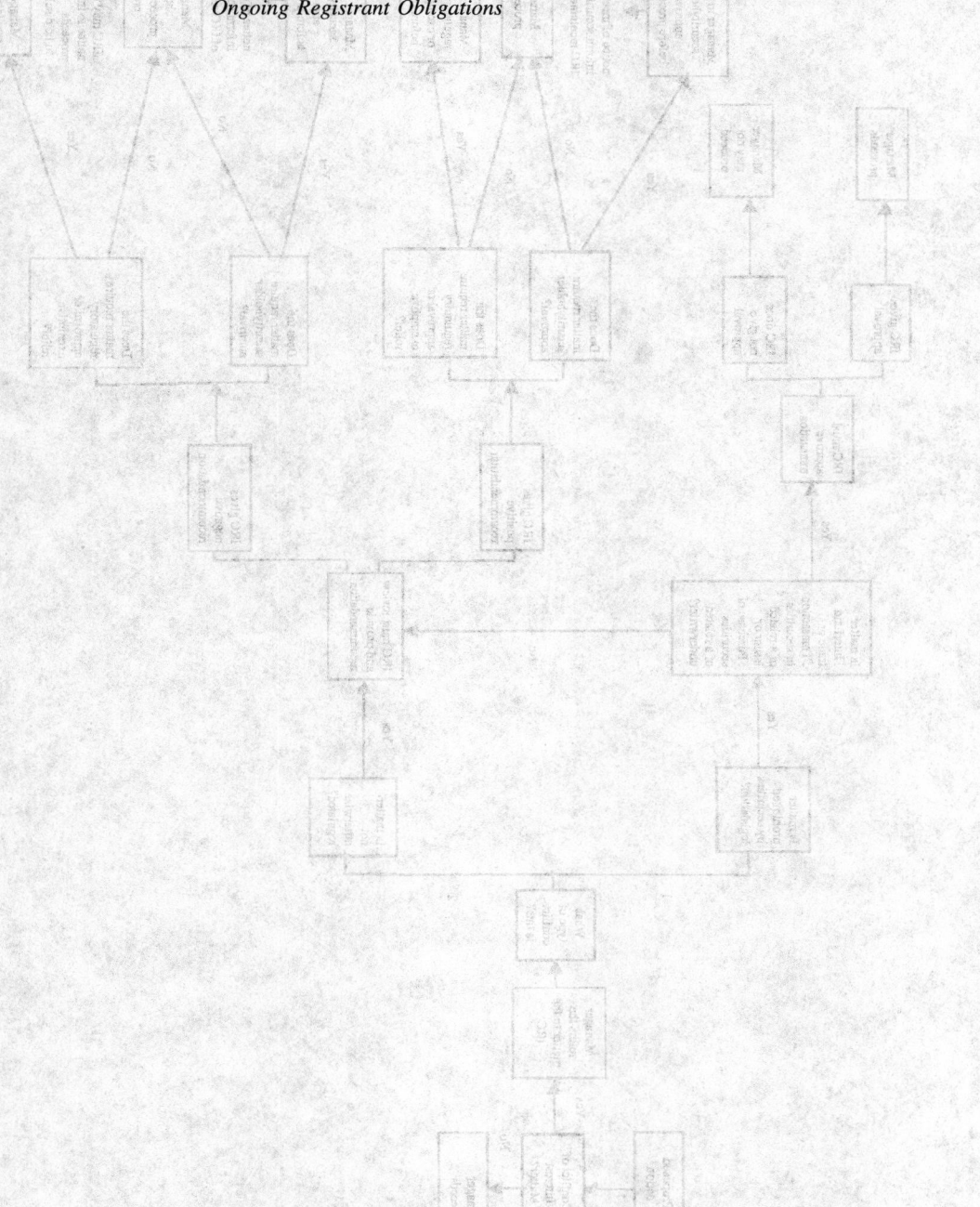

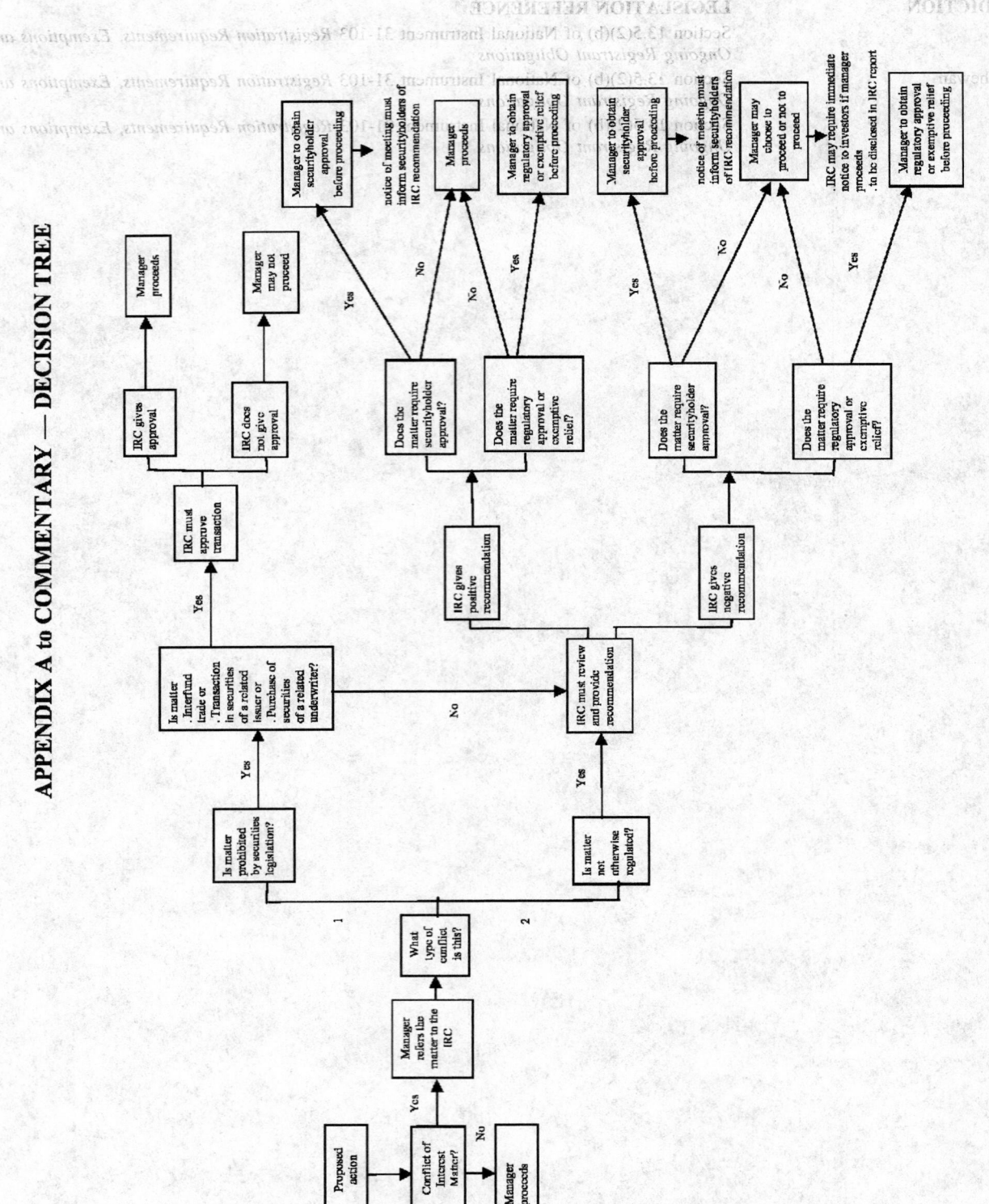

APPENDIX A to COMMENTARY — DECISION TREE

Final Rule: 29 O.S.C.B. 8807; Approval by OSC: 29 O.S.C.B. (Supp-1) 1; Request for Comments: 28 O.S.C.B. (Supp-2) 1 and 27 O.S.C.B. 465.

Amendment to Rule: (2009) 32 O.S.C.B. (Supp. 4) 379; Approval by OSC: 32 O.S.C.B. (Supp. 2) 1; Request for Comments: 31 O.S.C.B. 2279.

Amendment to Rule: (2015) 38 O.S.C.B. 342.

Related Provisions: OSA 121.1, 121.4, Part XXI.

Rules: NI 81-101, 81-102, 81-106, 41-101, Rule 81-802.

Policies and Orders: OPS 81-802CP; CSAN 81-317; OSCN 81-713.

CSA Notice 81-302 — Sales of Mutual Funds in Upcoming RRSP Season

Date: December 12, 1997

20 O.S.C.B. 6732

[Not reproduced]

CSA Staff Notice 81-306 — Disclosure by Mutual Funds of Changes in Calculation of Management Expense Ratio

Date: April 7, 2000

23 O.S.C.B. 2486

Background

On February 1, 2000, National Instrument 81-102 Mutual Funds (the "National Instrument") came into force across Canada. Section 16.1 of the National Instrument changes the method of calculation of management expense ratios (MER) for mutual funds and has the effect of requiring mutual funds to re-calculate MERs for financial periods that ended before the National Instrument came into force. Subsection 17.2(2) of the National Instrument and the prospectus form requirements of National Instrument 81-101 Mutual Fund Prospectus Disclosure require a mutual fund to disclose its MER for the last five completed financial years in its financial statements and its simplified prospectus.

The National Instrument was published in final form in November 1999. After that publication, the staff of the Canadian Securities Administrators (CSA) received submissions from The Investment Funds Institute of Canada (IFIC) and fund companies to the effect that calculating MERs for financial periods that ended before February 1, 2000 in accordance with section 16.1 of the National Instrument would be very difficult, and in some cases, virtually impossible due to the lack of data.

The CSA considered these submissions and determined to amend the National Instrument to provide that restatement of MER in accordance with section 16.1 is not mandatory for financial periods of mutual funds that ended before February 1, 2000. On January 28, 2000[1], the CSA published for comment a series of amendments to the National Instrument, primarily to propose a regime permitting mutual funds to lend their securities and use repurchase agreements, but also to deal with certain issues concerning MERs.

The Proposed Amendments to the National Instrument

The Notice accompanying the publication for comment of the January 28 amendments stated that the CSA propose to add section 16.3 to the National Instrument, along with a revised section 20.3 of the National Instrument.

Proposed section 16.3 of the National Instrument states that the MER calculation in section 16.1 does not apply to the disclosure and calculation of the MER for a financial period that ended before February 1, 2000. Mutual funds will have the option of restating MERs for prior periods in accordance with the National Instrument or disclosing MERs for those periods as calculated in accordance with securities legislation in force as at January 31, 2000. The proposed revisions to section 20.3 of the National Instrument will clarify that the National Instrument does not apply to reports to securityholders (as defined in the National Instrument) that include only financial statements that relate to financial periods that ended before the National Instrument came into force.

Purpose of CSA Staff Notice

The CSA outlined in the January 28 Notice that they are examining the implications of this proposed rule amendment in the context of Canadian generally accepted accounting principles (GAAP) and mutual fund financial statement presentation. The Notice indicated also that the CSA would be reviewing what guidance could be given to mutual funds by the CSA on the need to disclose the effect of a change to the calculation of MER when the MER for prior periods is not restated.

CSA staff propose to recommend that the CSA amend the Companion Policy to provide this guidance, however in the interim, CSA staff are publishing this CSA Staff notice. CSA staff are of the view that mutual funds must provide consistent disclosure concerning changes in the calculation of MERs in order to assist investors in understanding the change and to assist them in comparing the MERs of different mutual funds.

Staff Guidance

Staff are of the view that the change in the method of calculating the MER of a mutual fund required by the National Instrument should be treated in a manner which is similar to a change in accounting policy under section 1506 of the CICA Handbook. Under Canadian GAAP, a change in accounting policy requires a retroactive restatement of the financial information for all periods shown. The CICA Handbook acknowledges however that there may be circumstances where the data needed to restate the financial information is not reasonably determinable. Proposed section 16.3 permits a mutual fund to follow the guidance set out in the CICA Handbook without violating the National Instrument.

---

[1]In Ontario, at (2000) 23 OSCB (Suppl.)

If a mutual fund retroactively restates its MER for the five years required to be shown in its financial statements and simplified prospectus, the mutual fund should describe this restatement in the first such documents released in which the restated amounts are reported.

If a mutual fund does not restate its MER for prior periods because, based on its specific facts and circumstances, the information required to do so is not reasonably determinable, the MER for all financial periods ending after February 1, 2000 must be calculated in accordance with the National Instrument. The mutual fund must also disclose:

- that the method of calculating MER has changed, specifying for which periods the MER has been calculated in accordance with the change;

- that the mutual fund has not restated the MER for specified prior periods;

- the impact the change would have had if the mutual fund had restated the MER for the specified prior periods. For example, would the MER have increased or decreased if the MER had been restated? If possible, provide an estimate of the increase or decrease if the MER had been restated; and

- a description of the main differences between an MER calculated in accordance with the National Instrument and one calculated in accordance with NP 39.

The disclosure outlined above should be provided for all periods presented until such time as all MERs presented are calculated in accordance with the National Instrument.

As outlined in the January 28 Notice, the CSA are seeking comments on the proposed amendments. Mutual fund industry participants should provide comments if they have continuing concerns on the impact of the change in the method of calculating MER.

Income Taxes

CSA staff have considered other inquiries regarding the proper calculation of MER as required by the National Instrument and are outlining their views on the following questions raised.

1. Should the MER include foreign withholding taxes on dividends?

   Section 16.1 of the National Instrument requires a mutual fund to express its "total expenses" for a financial year "as shown on its income statement" as a percentage of its average net assets for that year. Staff are of the view that Canadian GAAP would permit a mutual fund to deduct withholding taxes from the income to which they apply. Accordingly, withholding taxes would not be recorded as "total expenses" on the mutual fund's income statement and need not be included in its MER calculation.

2. Does a mutual fund corporation have to include capital taxes and income taxes in its MER calculation?

   Mutual fund trusts generally distribute all taxable income and sufficient net realized capital gains in order that the trust is not subject to income taxes. However, this tax treatment is not available to mutual fund corporations. Staff accept that the MER calculations for mutual fund trusts and mutual fund corporations should be carried out in a way that causes their MERs to be comparable. This comparability is achieved when a mutual fund corporation excludes income taxes from its calculation of the MER.

   However, staff are of the view that Canadian GAAP would require a mutual fund corporation to include capital taxes as an expense of the mutual fund. Accordingly, capital taxes should be taken into account in that fund's calculation of MER.

CSA Notice 81-311 — Report on Consultation Paper 81-403 Rethinking Point of Sale Disclosure for Mutual Funds and Segregated Funds

Date: April 30, 2004

27 O.S.C.B. 4293

[Not reproduced]

CSA Notice 81-312 — Final Guidelines for Capital Accumulation Plans — Prepared by the Joint Forum of Financial Market Regulators

Date: May 28, 2004

27 O.S.C.B. 5410

Dear Stakeholder:

Re: Guidelines for Capital Accumulation Plans

We are pleased to announce that, with the approval of the Canadian Association of Pension Supervisory Authorities (CAPSA), the Canadian Council of Insurance Regulators (CCIR) and the Canadian Securities Administrators (CSA), the Joint Forum of Financial Market Regulators has released *Guidelines for Capital Accumulation Plans.*

A capital accumulation plan (CAP) is a tax-assisted investment or savings plan that permits the members of the CAP to make investment decisions among two or more options offered within the plan. A CAP may be established by an employer, trade union, association or any combination of these entities for the benefit of employees or members.

The purpose of the guidelines is to:

- Outline and clarify the rights and responsibilities of CAP sponsors, service providers and members.

- Ensure that CAP members have the information and assistance they need to make informed investment decisions in a capital accumulation plan.

- Ensure that there is a similar regulatory result for all CAP products and services regardless of the regulatory regime that applies to them.

In April, 2003, the Joint Forum released for consultation *Proposed Guidelines for Capital Accumulation Plans*. These proposals were developed by the Joint Forum's Committee on Capital Accumulation Plans with the assistance of an industry task force. The Joint Forum is very appreciative of the comments on the proposed guidelines received from all stakeholders through written submissions and through participation in focus group sessions held across Canada with plan sponsors, members and service providers. The final guidelines incorporate changes that address issues raised and suggestions made during the consultations. We are particularly indebted to the work of the members of the industry task force whose expertise was instrumental in the success of this initiative.

During the consultations, a number of stakeholders identified issues related to the differences in investment rules for pension funds, mutual funds, segregated funds and other pooled investment funds. The Joint Forum has asked the Committee on Capital Accumulation Plans to address these issues as part of the implementation of the guidelines.

While the guidelines are being released today, a 19-month transition period has been established for plan sponsors and service providers to make any necessary revisions to the operation of their capital accumulation plans. Regulators expect the guidelines to be followed in full by December 31, 2005. It is hoped that plan sponsors and service providers will take the measures necessary to follow the guidelines as soon as practical during the transition period.

The guidelines will be implemented through the Joint Forum's constituent groups and through industry associations:

- CAPSA has adopted the guidelines for registered defined contribution pension plans.

- The CSA is issuing a request for comment on a proposed securities exemption based on the guidelines.

- The Canadian Life and Health Insurance Association (CLHIA) will initiate a process to have the guidelines adopted by December 31, 2004 and will expect its member companies to follow them by December 31, 2005.

You can obtain a copy of the guidelines, a summary of the comments received during the consultations and responses to the comments, and the CSA's request for comment on a proposed securities exemption rule from the websites of CAPSA (www.capsa-acor.org), CCIR (www.ccir-ccrra.org), CSA (www.csa-acvm.ca) or the Joint Forum (www.jointforum.ca).

CSA Staff Notice 81-314 — Removal of Foreign Content Restrictions for Registered Plans — Eliminating Indirect Foreign Content Exposure in Certain RSP Funds

Date: March 18, 2005

28 O.S.C.B. 2599

Introduction

This Staff Notice applies to RSP Funds, which for the purpose of this Staff Notice are:

(a) an "RSP clone fund" which is a mutual fund that has adopted fundamental investment objectives to link its performance to the performance of another mutual fund whose securities constitute foreign property for registered plans and to ensure that the securities of the mutual fund will not constitute foreign property under the *Income Tax Act*, as defined in National Instrument 81-102 — *Mutual Funds* ("NI 81-102");

(b) a mutual fund which qualifies as an RSP clone fund except that it links its performance to the performance of a group of foreign securities that are similar to the portfolio of the underlying fund; and

(c) a mutual fund which qualifies as an RSP clone fund except that it links its performance to the performance of more than one underlying fund.

The purpose of this Staff Notice is to set out staff's guidance in response to the recent federal government budget proposal to remove foreign content restrictions for registered plans. In particular, this Staff Notice addresses the following:

- RSP Funds closing out their forward contracts, derivatives, or debt-like securities that link the performance of the fund to the performance of either another mutual fund or funds whose securities constitute foreign property for registered plans, or a group of foreign securities that are similar to the portfolio of the underlying fund (the Indirect Foreign Exposure);

- whether RSP Funds require securityholder approval to do so; and

- timely disclosure requirements and requirements to amend prospectuses and annual information forms (collectively, Prospectus Documents) for RSP Funds that: (i) close out their Indirect Foreign Exposure; or (ii) remove references to the pre-budget foreign content restrictions for registered plans in their Prospectus Documents.

Background

On February 23, 2005, the federal government introduced a budget in Parliament that, if implemented, will eliminate the 30% limit on foreign content for registered plans retroactive to the start of 2005. While the related implementing legislation has not been passed yet, industry has asked staff to clarify a number of issues stemming from the change. In particular, we have been asked for guidance on whether closing out the Indirect Foreign Exposure for RSP Funds would under Part 5 of NI 81-102 constitute:

1. a change to the fundamental investment objective of the RSP Funds that would require securityholder approval; and

2. a significant change with respect to the RSP Fund that would require compliance with the timely disclosure requirements under securities legislation and the filing of an amendment to the Prospectus Documents of the RSP Funds.

We have also been asked whether we will expect RSP Funds, whose Prospectus Documents contain disclosure about the foreign content restrictions, to immediately amend their Prospectus Documents to correct this disclosure.

Staff Guidance

We recognize that the legislative process will take time before it is complete and that RSP Fund managers are monitoring this process closely. RSP Fund managers will wish to assess the progress of the adoption of implementing legislation before they decide if and when to close out any Indirect Foreign Exposure. If they decide that to close out the Indirect Foreign Exposure is in the best interests of the fund, then RSP Fund managers will also need to determine whether closing out the Indirect Foreign Exposure would constitute a change to the fundamental investment objectives of their RSP Funds or a significant change with the implications described above.

While not recommending any specific course of action to RSP Fund managers, if RSP Fund managers decide to close out Indirect Foreign Exposure, we offer the following guidance with respect to Part 5 of NI 81-102.

1. — Securityholder Approval

For RSP Fund managers who conclude that closing out the Indirect Foreign Exposure is not a change to the fundamental investment objective of a RSP Fund which requires securityholder approval, we will not look behind the decision if the only change is to discontinue the Indirect Foreign Exposure and replace it with a direct investment in the underlying funds or group of foreign securities.

2. — Timely Disclosure Requirements

For RSP Fund managers who conclude that closing out the Indirect Foreign Exposure is not a significant change requiring compliance with the timely disclosure requirements in securities legislation and requiring the filing of an amendment to the Prospectus Documents of the RSP Funds, we will not look behind the decision if the only change is to discontinue the Indirect Foreign Exposure and replace it with a direct investment in the underlying funds or group of foreign securities.

In making this decision, RSP Fund managers should be alert to the fact that the parameters of "a significant change" are different from those of "a change to the fundamental investment objective".

If RSP Fund managers conclude that closing out the Indirect Foreign Exposure is not a significant change, we encourage RSP Fund managers to consider other forms of communication that would provide securityholders with access to information about this change, but that would not be prohibitively costly to RSP Fund managers. Examples include a message on the RSP Fund's website or a notice in the next scheduled mailing to securityholders.

If RSP Fund managers decide to remove references to the 30% foreign content limit in Prospectus Documents of RSP Funds as a result of the recent budget proposal, in our view, it will generally not be necessary to make such changes until the next renewal of the Prospectus Documents.

Additional Guidance

RSP Fund managers of a RSP Fund, that does not fit within the circumstances set out above but who still think that closing out the RSP Fund's Indirect Foreign Exposure would not be a change to the fundamental investment objective or a significant change, may wish to contact the CSA to seek specific guidance.

We will consider issuing additional CSA Staff Notices in the future if appropriate to address further issues.

CSA Staff Notice 81-315 — Frequently Asked Questions on NI 81-106 Investment Fund Continuous Disclosure

Date: **November 25, 2005**

28 O.S.C.B. 9417

Background

On June 1, 2005, National Instrument 81-106 *Investment Fund Continuous Disclosure* (NI 81-106) came into force. In order to assist issuers subject to NI 81-106, we have compiled a list of frequently asked questions (FAQs) and staff's response to those questions.

FAQs

After reviewing NI 81-106, some readers have questions regarding its application and interpretation. This list of FAQs is not exhaustive, but represents the types of inquiries we have received.

We have divided the FAQs into the following subject categories:

A. Definitions, Application and Transition Issues

B. Financial Statements

C. Management Reports of Fund Performance (MRFPs)

D. Delivery of Continuous Disclosure Documents to Securityholders

E. Binding and Presentation

F. Quarterly Portfolio Disclosure

G. Proxy Voting Disclosure

A. — Definitions, Application and Transition Issues

A-1

Q: Sections 18.3 and 18.4 of NI 81-106 provide a transition year for the filing of annual financial statements and annual information forms. Does this transition year only apply to investment funds in existence on June 1, 2005?

A: Yes, these transition provisions only apply to investment funds that were in existence on June 1, 2005. Investment funds created after that date do not require a "transition" year and must comply with the 90 day annual and 60 day interim filing deadlines.

A-2

Q: The decisions of some regulators granting pooled funds relief from publicly filing their financial statements contain a sunset clause stating that the exemption expires on the date that NI 81-106 comes into force, which was June 1, 2005. However, pursuant to the transition provisions, pooled funds are only obligated to comply with NI 81-106 for financial years ending on or after June 30, 2005. Can pooled funds that previously received relief from filing their financial statements continue to rely on that exemption for interim financial statements relating to periods prior to the application of NI 81-106?

A: Yes. In the jurisdictions where this relief was granted, we did not intend to create a gap between the application of the exemptive relief orders and the application of NI 81-106. Pooled funds that were granted an exemption from filing financial statements can continue to rely on that exemption up until the time when they must begin complying with NI 81-106. NI 81-106 also grants pooled funds an exemption from filing their financial statements, subject to certain conditions.

A-3

Q: Does OSC Rule 51-501 still apply to non-redeemable investment funds?

A: The Ontario Securities Commission extended the revocation date of OSC Rule 51-501 to May 30, 2006 (see (2005) 28 OSCB 4559). Investment funds subject to OSC Rule 51-501 must continue to comply with that rule, up until such time as they are required to begin complying with NI 81-106.

A-4

Q: Must commodity pools subject to NI 81-104 file quarterly financial statements for interim periods ending prior to their first annual period to which NI 81-106 applies?

A: No, we amended NI 81-104 to delete this requirement effective June 1, 2005.

A-5

Q: Must mutual funds subject to NI 81-101 comply with Part 9 (Annual Information Form) of NI 81-106?

A: If a mutual fund has a current simplified prospectus and annual information form as required by NI 81-101, it does not have to file an annual information form in accordance with NI 81-106. Other investment funds that are in continuous distribution and renew their prospectus annually also do not have to file an annual information form in accordance with Part 9 of NI 81-106. Only investment funds without a current prospectus are required to file an annual information form in accordance with NI 81-106.

A-6

Q: Do mutual funds have to include past performance and financial highlights in their simplified prospectus this year?

A: We amended NI 81-101 to indicate that a mutual fund may remove past performance and financial highlights from its simplified prospectus only after the mutual fund has filed its first annual MRFP.

A-7

Q: Some investment funds have received exemptive relief (for example, from the requirement to report transactions between a mutual fund and a related person) on the condition that certain disclosure is provided in the statement of portfolio transactions. However, this statement is no longer required. What happens to the exemptive relief?

A: Investment funds should not rely on this exemptive relief because they cannot comply with the condition requiring disclosure in the statement of portfolio transactions. Investment funds in this situation should contact their principal regulator if they still require the exemptive relief.

B. — Financial Statements

B-1

Q: Is the requirement to disclose that the auditor has not reviewed the interim financial statements fulfilled by clearly marking the interim statements as "unaudited"?

A: No, if the interim statements are not reviewed by the auditor, they must be accompanied by a separate notice as required by section 2.12 of NI 81-106 and as described in section 3.4 of Companion Policy 81-106CP.

B-2

Q: What should be included in "securityholder reporting costs" (statement of operations, line item 11)?

A: While an investment fund must assess in its own circumstances what securityholder reporting costs it has incurred, examples would include the costs associated with the printing and mailing of the financial statements, MRFPs and any other required securityholder document.

B-3

Q: Line item 18 of the statement of operations is "increase or decrease in net assets from operations, and, if applicable, for each class or series". Please clarify how the overall net increase or decrease in net assets should be allocated to each class or series.

A: Investment funds with more than one class or series are currently allocating income and net assets between classes and series, and should generally continue to use the same method.

B-4

Q: Can line item 19 of the statement of operations be called "earnings per share" instead?

A: To provide comparability between investment funds, the prescribed wording for item 19 should be used.

B-5

Q: The notes to the financial statements must disclose the total commissions paid to dealers for portfolio transactions. To the extent the amount is ascertainable, the soft-dollar portion (the amount paid for goods and services other than order execution) of these payments must also be disclosed. What does "to the extent the amount is ascertainable" mean? If an investment fund does not have this information, what must it disclose?

A: Investment funds should make reasonable efforts to determine the soft-dollar portion of commissions paid on portfolio transactions. For mutual funds, Form 81-101F2 already requires funds to disclose the names of entities that provided investment decision-making services to the fund if those services were paid for through brokerage transactions executed on the fund's behalf. To the extent an investment fund can assess the value of these services (either through its own valuation process using reasonable estimates or the entities' pricing), NI 81-106 requires the fund to disclose this amount in the notes to the financial statements. In cases where the investment fund cannot ascertain the value of the soft dollar portion, a statement should be included in the notes that the soft dollar portion is unascertainable.

B-6

Q: Given that mutual funds are subject to NI 81-105, what should be included in the "total cost of distribution of the investment fund's securities recorded in the statement of changes in net assets" required in the notes to the financial statements?

A: This item only applies to investment funds that are permitted to pay distribution costs (for example, funds that are not subject to NI 81-105 or have received an exemption from NI 81-105). If distribution costs are paid out of management fees, they do not have to be disclosed separately in the notes (but may be disclosed in the management fee breakdown provided in the MRFP).

B-7

Q: Subsection 15.1(1) of NI 81-106 requires the numerator of the management expense ratio to include total expenses before income taxes as shown on an investment fund's statement of operations, and any other fee, charge or expense of the investment fund that has the effect of reducing the investment fund's net asset value. Does the management expense ratio have to include sales commissions paid by an investment fund in connection with the offering of its securities (including one-time commissions) and other offering costs paid by the investment fund?

A: Yes, offering costs paid by an investment fund must be included in its management expense ratio. Offering costs are charges that have the effect of reducing the investment fund's net asset value, and the management expense ratio is not limited to recurring charges only. Additional disclosure may be added by the investment fund explaining why the management expense ratio is higher for the year that the investment fund did an offering.

C. — Management Reports of Fund Performance

C-1

Q: Do the MRFPs have to include information about classes or series of securities that are not publicly offered?

A: Yes. Part 7 of NI 81-106 requires an investment fund with more than one class or series of securities outstanding referable to a single portfolio to prepare financial statements and MRFPs that contain information concerning all of the classes or series.

C-2

Q: Can the MRFP be tailored to include only information that is specific to the series or class of a fund that an investor owns?

A: No, the MRFP must contain information concerning all of an investment fund's classes or series. We encourage investment funds to clearly distinguish the information for each class or series.

Form 81-106F1 — Item 3 — Financial Highlights

C-3

Q: The trading expense ratio must be calculated using the total commissions and other portfolio transaction costs disclosed in the notes to the financial statements. What should be included in "other portfolio transaction costs"?

A: The trading expense ratio must be calculated using the number disclosed in the notes to the financial statements in response to item 3(a) of s. 3.6(1) of NI 81-106.

C-4

Q: The trading expense ratio is to be calculated using the same denominator as the management expense ratio. Given that portfolio transactions occur at a fund level, can the trading expense ratio be calculated using fund average net assets (rather than assets at the class or series level)?

A: Yes, the denominator used in calculating the trading expense ratio can be the average net assets of the fund as a whole. The trading expense ratio does not have to be calculated at the class or series level.

C-5

Q: As the financial highlights tables present historical information for the past five years, does the trading expense ratio have to be calculated for years prior to the implementation of NI 81-106?

A: No, you do not have to go back and calculate the trading expense ratio for financial periods ending prior to the implementation of NI 81-106. A footnote may be added to the financial highlights table explaining that the trading expense ratio is a new requirement.

C-6

Q: As there is a new instruction regarding the calculation of the portfolio turnover rate following a purchase-of-assets transaction between two investment funds, does the portfolio turnover rate have to be recalculated for prior years?

A: No, you do not have to recalculate the portfolio turnover rate for prior years. If applicable, the difference in the portfolio turnover rate calculation can be explained in a footnote.

C-7

Q: The financial highlights tables in the MRFPs are slightly different from the statement of financial highlights previously prepared. Can the new tables be constructed using the audited numbers from past statements of financial highlights? Do the numbers have to be recalculated or can a footnote explaining that prior years have not been recalculated be added to the financial highlights tables in the MRFPs?

A: For the financial highlights tables, investment funds should use the audited numbers previously published in their financial statements. Information for prior years does not have to be recalculated.

Form 81-106F1 — Item 3 — Management Fees

C-8

Q: For the breakdown of management fees required by item 3.3 of Form 81-106F1, given that certain information may be commercially sensitive, can services be grouped into categories? Does the breakdown have to add up to 100% of the management fees?

A: The requirement to breakdown management fees is intended to show investors what is included in the fee. The objective of this requirement is to show what portion goes to the distribution channel by way of trailing commissions, etc. This requirement does not necessitate disclosure of commercially sensitive information (such as the specific compensation paid to portfolio advisers or the manager's profit). Services can be grouped together — for example, "general administration, investment advice and profit" could be one category for which a percentage is given.

The breakdown of management fees does not have to add to 100%, as the item requires disclosure of the *major* services paid for out of the management fee, not a complete accounting.

C-9

Q: Does the breakdown of management fees have to be shown separately by series for a multi-class fund?

A: Any differences between classes or series must be disclosed.

C-10

Q: Is it acceptable for the breakdown of management fees to include the percentage of management fees representing waived or absorbed expenses if the manager paid for fund expenses on the securityholders' behalf?

A: Yes, the breakdown of management fees can include the percentage representing waived or absorbed expenses.

Form 81-106F1 — Item 4 — Past Performance

C-11

Q: How should the return on the short portfolio be calculated?

A: NI 81-106 does not set out how to calculate the return on the short portfolio. Generally, we are of the view that it is possible to calculate the return on the long and short portfolio separately, on a dollar-weighted basis. Investment funds may make reasonable assumptions and estimates in order to calculate the return on the short portfolio, as long as these are explained in the MRFP (for example, with note disclosure under the bar chart).

C-12

Q: Can a fund in existence for less than twelve months show past performance?

A: Yes, a young fund can show past performance, if it has completed a financial year (it has audited annual financial statements) and was a reporting issuer at all times during the period for which the performance data is provided. The fund should clearly indicate that the performance shown is for a period of less than one year.

For mutual funds subject to NI 81-102, the "young fund rule" continues to apply to sales communications pursuant to subsection 15.6(a) of NI 81-102.

Form 81-106F1 — Item 5 — Summary of Investment Portfolio

C-13

> *Q:* If an investment fund invests in multiple underlying funds, should the summary of investment portfolio list the underlying funds, or does the investment fund have to "look through" to the portfolio of the underlying funds?

> *A:* An investment fund does not have to "look through" to the portfolio of underlying funds. The "look through" only applies when the investment fund invests substantially all of its assets in one underlying fund.

C-14

> *Q:* Part 8 of NI 81-106 exempts a labour sponsored or venture capital fund from the requirement to disclose the current value of a venture investment, subject to certain conditions. Does this exemption extend to the summary of investment portfolio in the MRFP?

> *A:* Yes, if a labour sponsored or venture capital fund complies with the conditions in Part 8 of NI 81-106 in order to be exempt from disclosing the individual current values of venture investments, this exemption extends to the summary of investment portfolio.

D. — Delivery of Continuous Disclosure Documents to Securityholders

D-1

> *Q:* Can an investment fund use standing instructions for one group of securityholders, annual instructions for another group of securityholders, and choose to deliver the disclosure documents to a third group of securityholders?

> *A:* Yes, an investment fund can use any combination of the delivery options available in Part 5 of NI 81-106. However, if the fund has obtained standing instructions from a securityholder, it cannot obtain annual instructions from that securityholder.

D-2

> *Q:* If an investment fund obtains standing instructions with respect to the delivery of financial statements and MRFPs, can the dealers provide annual generic reminders to clients that they have provided instructions to the investment fund which can be changed by contacting the fund?

> *A:* If an investment fund obtains standing instructions, it is obligated to advise securityholders annually of the documents they are entitled to receive and of how their delivery instructions can be changed. NI 81-106 does not place this obligation on the dealer, but if the investment fund can send the required annual reminder through its dealers, it may do so.

D-3

> *Q:* If an investment fund has information about some, but not all, of its beneficial owners, can it communicate directly with the beneficial owners for which it does have information and rely on NI 54-101 to communicate with its other beneficial owners?

> *A:* Yes, if an investment fund has the necessary information to communicate directly with one or more beneficial owners of its securities, it can do so, even though it may need to rely on NI 54-101 to communicate with other beneficial owners of its securities.

D-4

> *Q:* Do investment funds have to solicit new delivery instructions from securityholders who provided standing instructions prior to NI 81-106 coming into force?

> *A:* NI 81-106 requires investment funds to obtain delivery instructions for each document listed in subsection 5.1(2). It will be necessary to obtain delivery instructions for MRFPs (prior instructions would not have contemplated MRFPs).

D-5

> *Q:* NI 81-106 requires an investment fund to post certain documents on its website. For how long must these documents remain on the website?

> *A:* NI 81-106 does not specify the length of time that continuous disclosure documents must remain on an investment fund's website. In our view, the documents should stay on the website for a reasonable length of time, and at least until they are replaced by updated versions.

E. — Binding and Presentation

E-1

> *Q:* As the financial statements for more than one investment fund can be bound together, can the MRFP for one investment fund be bound with a set of financial statements that includes the statements for the relevant fund as well as the statements for other investment funds?

> *A:* Yes. If the financial statements for a group of investment funds are bound together, this document can be bound to the MRFP for one of the investment funds included in the group.

E-2

> *Q:* How should the MRFPs be filed on SEDAR — individually or as a group?

> *A:* Each MRFP should be filed on SEDAR only under the individual investment fund to which it pertains (and not under a group profile).

F. — Quarterly Portfolio Disclosure

F-1

> *Q:* Does an investment fund with a December 31 year end have to prepare quarterly portfolio disclosure for the period ending June 30?

A: No, the quarterly portfolio disclosure only has to be prepared for the first and third quarters. (An interim MRFP must be prepared and filed for the period ending June 30.)

G. — Proxy Voting Disclosure

G-1

Q: Does an investment fund's proxy voting record only have to report how the fund voted at meetings of Canadian public issuers, or must it include meetings of all publicly traded issuers, Canadian and foreign?

A: The proxy voting record should provide disclosure of all proxies received in connection with meetings of public issuers, both Canadian and foreign.

G-2

Q: If an investment fund delegates proxy voting to a third party portfolio adviser, can it rely on the proxy voting policies of the portfolio adviser?

A: Yes, but the investment fund is still responsible for ensuring that its proxy voting policies and procedures meet the requirements in section 10.2 of NI 81-106.

G-3

Q: How will securityholders know that the proxy voting record and the proxy voting policies and procedures are available to them?

A: The MRFPs must state on the first page that this disclosure is available (see Part B, Item 1 and Part C, Item 1 of Form 81-106F1). Investment funds are obligated to send their first annual MRFP to every securityholder, including an explanation of the new requirements and the availability of quarterly portfolio disclosure and proxy voting disclosure (see section 18.5 of NI 81-106). We also amended the annual information form to require this disclosure (see Item 12 of Form 81-101F2).

G-4

Q: When can securityholders request proxy voting policies and procedures?

A: Securityholders can request a copy of the proxy voting policies and procedures at any time. The transition provision in section 18.2 of NI 81-106 only applies to the proxy voting record.

CSA Staff Notice 81-316 — Hedge Funds

Date: January 12, 2007

30 O.S.C.B. 277

Background

CSA staff conducted a sample-based review of hedge funds in Canada, beginning in early 2005 and continuing into 2006, which involved a combination of compliance reviews of hedge fund managers and advisers, disclosure reviews and industry consultations. We did this review because we recognized the trend of increasing retailization of hedge funds. It was also important to us to examine the issues raised about hedge funds regulation as a result of the failure of certain hedge funds in Canada and globally.

"Hedge funds" can be difficult to define. For the purposes of our review, we used a broad definition of hedge funds: investment pools that use alternative investment strategies not generally available to traditional mutual funds such as taking both long and short positions and using arbitrage, leverage, options, futures, bonds and other financial instruments to capitalize on market conditions.

We also considered the report by the Task Force to Modernize Securities Legislation in Canada issued in October 2006 (the Allen Report) which covered a wide range of topics including hedge funds and principal protected notes (PPNs).[1]

General conclusion

We concluded that our regime contains an appropriate securities regulatory framework for hedge funds, but that certain areas within it could be improved. Those areas are discussed later in this notice under "Areas of Concern".

Two topics identified in our review — PPNs and referral arrangements — we thought needed further in-depth study. On July 7, 2006 the CSA issued Canadian Securities Administrators' Notice 46-303 Principal Protected Notes (the PPN Notice) that outlined the CSA's concerns with the distribution and sale of PPNs and signaled the CSA's intention to do further consultations on PPNs. Referral arrangements are being studied through a separate CSA project the results of which will form part of the CSA Registration Reform Project.

Finally, as discussed in more detail later in this notice, the CSA, through the Registration Reform Project, is proposing to require the registration of fund managers.

---

[1]The Allen Report canvassed several issues relating to hedge funds and made recommendations to address them, including that:

- A regulatory framework for the public offering of hedge funds be established, similar to the framework for mutual funds;
- PPNs linked to hedge funds be regulated according to the nature of the underlying investment rather than the character of the note;
- Financial intermediaries selling hedge funds and other structured products linked to hedge funds meet certain proficiency requirements; and
- Hedge fund managers be registered.

What we covered in our review

1. — Current regulation of hedge funds

Hedge funds are distributed in different ways — under a prospectus, under exemptions in securities legislation that allow them to be sold without a prospectus and, in some cases, through linked products, such as PPNs, that are sold on the basis that they fall outside the scope of provincial securities legislation.[2]

Hedge funds sold under a prospectus or through exemptions in securities legislation are regulated through a range of general securities legislation requirements:

- *Portfolio managers* who manage the fund portfolios must be registered. In this notice, portfolio managers are referred to as "*advisers*", as they provide advice to the funds on the portfolio of securities held by the fund. This is in contrast to the situation in the United States, where most hedge fund advisers are exempt from regulation.[3]

- *Dealers* who sell securities must be registered.

- *Know your client (KYC) and suitability requirements (which include knowing your product)* must be met by registered advisers and dealers advising on or selling hedge funds.

- *Hedge funds sold without a prospectus* can be sold only to:

  - accredited investors who meet certain net income or financial asset tests;

  - investors who can make a minimum purchase in the fund of $150,000;

  - investors in certain jurisdictions[4] who receive a mandated form of disclosure and acknowledge the risk of the investment they are making. Investors have 2 days to change their minds about the investment and have certain rights of action if the disclosure contains a misrepresentation.

- *Disclosure requirements apply, depending on how the hedge fund is sold*:

  - funds of hedge funds sold under a prospectus are required to give full, true and plain disclosure about the fund;

  - hedge funds sold to accredited investors or investors purchasing at least $150,000 are not technically required to provide disclosure, although in our review we found that some form of offering document was usually provided;

  - hedge funds sold under the offering memorandum exemption[5] must provide a specific form of offering memorandum to investors.

- *Continuous disclosure* (such as financial statements) must be provided by prospectus-qualified funds of hedge funds and, in some jurisdictions[6], by hedge funds sold under certain exemptions.

- *Compliance reviews of* advisers, fund managers and dealers are performed by compliance staff of the securities regulatory authorities and the SROs using risk-based approaches.

Investors can also get access to hedge funds through linked products such as PPNs that are sold on the basis that they fall outside the scope of provincial securities legislation. As noted above, the CSA has raised certain concerns with PPNs and is looking into them through the consultation process discussed in the PPN Notice.

2. — Compliance reviews of hedge fund managers and advisers

Certain CSA jurisdictions (Ontario, British Columbia and Quebec) conducted coordinated field examinations of 13 market participants, which included hedge fund advisers and managers. The population covered by the reviews included 37 hedge funds with a total value of $1.25 billion and 9 PPNs with a value of $1.4 billion. Market participants were chosen for a field examination based on their size, the number and types of products offered (hedge funds, funds of hedge funds and PPNs) and also included a random sampling.

The reviews focused on a number of areas, including the safeguarding of client assets, valuation processes, marketing materials and offering documents, the extent and type of fees being charged, product liquidity, the existence of referral arrangements and product distribution.

Generally, our findings across the participating jurisdictions were consistent. Our reviews revealed the following:

- *Custody* — Client assets were held in safekeeping predominantly by large, reputable third parties such as banks, dealers and trust companies.

- *Valuations* — Valuations for hedge funds were performed on a reasonably frequent basis (weekly, bi-weekly, monthly) either in-house or by third party service providers. When valuations were performed in-house, automatic price feeds from various external sources were

---

[2]Or, in Québec, under an applicable exemption (see section 3(9)or 3(14) of the *Securities Act* (Québec)).

[3]The U.S. *Investment Company Act of 1940* exempts from its requirements funds that limit their distribution to private placements with high net-worth individuals or institutions, or that have 100 or fewer beneficial owners. The U.S. *Investment Advisers Act* is interpreted as exempting portfolio managers who act on behalf of 14 or fewer funds.

[4]British Columbia, New Brunswick, Nova Scotia and Newfoundland and Labrador.

[5]See footnote 4, in British Columbia, New Brunswick, Nova Scotia and Newfoundland and Labrador.

[6]Under NI 81-106 *Investment Funds Continuous Disclosure* in Ontario, Quebec, Saskatchewan, Nova Scotia and New Brunswick, hedge funds that are not reporting issuers are still required to provide certain continuous disclosure to investors.

used to minimize the risk of pricing errors. When valuations were outsourced, the only issue noted was that many of the market participants did not maintain evidence of their oversight review of the funds' calculation of net asset value (NAV).

- *Marketing* — We had concerns about the presentation of performance returns and inadequate or inaccurate disclosure in some of the marketing materials we reviewed. In some cases, actual performance returns were presented together with simulated back tested data and disclaimers accompanying these types of performance presentations were weak.

- *Fees* — The reviews revealed that there are multiple layers of fees in hedge funds, including management fees, performance fees, up-front sales fees, trailer fees, and early redemption fees. In the case of funds of hedge funds, there is an additional layer of management and performance fees. While the fees associated with these products were disclosed in the offering documents, we had concerns with the clarity of the disclosure, the fact that the disclosure of various fees often appeared in many unrelated places in the documents and not on a consolidated/summary basis, and with the transparency of the overall levels of fees.

- *Exempt offering disclosure* — While we found that the product disclosure covered information similar to prospectus-level disclosure, there was a lack of consistency in the presentation of information. Given that these are complex products with layered structures and multiple fees, this made the disclosure difficult to understand and compare across products.

- *Liquidity* — The majority of the hedge funds reviewed in our sample that were sold in the exempt market allowed for weekly or monthly redemptions at NAV. Prospectus-qualified funds were traded daily on the exchange.

- *Referral Arrangements* — We noted certain issues relating to referral arrangements in Ontario and British Columbia. In Ontario, there was an instance where a registrant inappropriately delegated its responsibility to supervise trades and assess the suitability of trades for its client to a non-registrant. The written agreement between the registrant and non-registrant did not clearly set out the roles and responsibilities of each party, including who was responsible for disclosure of the referral arrangements to clients. In British Columbia, there was an instance relating to inadequate disclosure of conflicts of interest. These instances were not representative of the population.

- *Distribution* — During the compliance reviews, we found that hedge funds and PPNs were frequently distributed through investment dealers and mutual fund dealers. In British Columbia and Quebec, the majority of hedge funds were distributed by the funds' portfolio managers.

3. — Disclosure reviews

We completed disclosure reviews on a number of hedge funds, funds of hedge funds and PPNs through regular prospectus reviews, focused disclosure reviews and through reviews of hedge fund managers. We looked at hedge fund prospectuses, offering memoranda and sales communications and marketing materials.

4. — Industry consultation

We consulted with a variety of industry professionals on issues relating to hedge fund distribution, disclosure, retailization and regulatory requirements. We discussed the importance of registrants completing adequate due diligence and know-your-product assessments on hedge fund investments before recommending them to clients, along with the equally important obligation of a registrant to meet its KYC and suitability obligations.

Industry representatives told us that investors want more access to hedge funds and that other markets and regulators around the world have moved to support increased retail access to hedge funds. The importance of the PPN market was also discussed, particularly as PPNs are used as a way to give retail investors access to hedge funds.

Areas of concern

While we concluded that the current securities regulatory framework for hedge funds is appropriate, in the course of our review we noted some areas that we should continue to monitor or that could be improved. These areas are described below, along with our views on how we intend to monitor or make improvements to them.

A. — Principal protected notes

In the PPN Notice the CSA outlined a number of concerns with PPNs:

- they give retail investors access to alternative asset classes that are not usually available to retail investors without a prospectus, and that carry different risks;

- investors may not be getting sufficient disclosure about the PPN (for example, on the structure, fees and risks) to make an informed investment decision;

- some PPNs are linked to more complex investments and may pose more investment risk than was contemplated when securities legislation was enacted to exclude financial institution deposits from securities regulation and to exempt guaranteed debt instruments;

- registrants selling PPNs may not be meeting their KYC and suitability obligations.

The CSA is continuing its further consultation on PPNs.

B. — Referral arrangements

Securities legislation in some jurisdictions and some self-regulatory organizations have specific requirements for how registrants handle referrals to and from registrants. Even where specific requirements do not exist, registrants are still bound by their obligations under securities legislation and their general obligation to act in the best interests of their clients.

We see certain risks with referral arrangements. One of the risks is that the roles and responsibilities of the different registrants involved in the referral, including who must disclose the arrangement to the client, may not always be clearly established. Another risk is that registrants will refer clients to someone selling hedge funds or products linked to hedge funds simply because of the fees the registrants will receive, without considering whether the referral is in the best interests of their clients.

There is a separate CSA project on referral arrangements that is examining ways to address concerns relating to referral arrangements and the results of this work will form part of the CSA Registration Reform Project.

C. — Distribution

Dealers should ensure that they and their salespersons have sufficient proficiency and product knowledge of these very complex products to adequately assess suitability of the products for their clients. The dealer SROs should monitor that dealers and their salespersons are performing reasonable KYC and suitability assessments in the distribution of hedge funds.

D. — Registration and oversight of fund managers

Currently, fund managers need not be registered unless they are also managing portfolio assets, in which case they must be registered as advisers. However, recognizing the role fund managers play in establishing, promoting and running investment funds and providing or overseeing a broad range of services (including fund valuation and registrar and transfer agency activities), the CSA is proposing to require the registration of fund managers, including hedge funds, through the Registration Reform Project.

The registration requirements for fund managers would focus on ensuring that they:

- have the resources to carry out their functions, or to properly supervise the functions if they are contracted to a third party, and to provide proper services to investors;

- manage their conflicts of interest;

- have adequate capital and insurance to provide protection for investors and minimize the risk of loss and disruption to them;

- have sufficient proficiency and integrity to carry out their functions.

Also, subject to resource requirements and overall compliance priorities, we will consider continuing our compliance/examination field reviews of the hedge fund industry participants including advisers and fund managers (in the jurisdictions with the statutory ability to do these reviews).

E. — Disclosure

In the course of our review, we found that the non-prospectus offering disclosure (typically an offering memorandum) provided by some of the hedge funds could have been clearer. We will continue to review non-prospectus offering documents in the course of any compliance reviews of hedge fund managers and advisers and note any disclosure concerns to them in the course of those reviews.

Prospectus-qualified funds of hedge funds are reviewed through our established prospectus review program. These products tend to be complex and in our reviews we will continue to concentrate on clear disclosure about the funds including their structures, risks and the fees associated with them.

We will respond to problematic marketing materials that may come to our attention by requiring them to be modified or withdrawn. Some CSA jurisdictions may also review these materials as part of a continuous disclosure review program. In any reviews we may conduct, the following guiding principles[7] will be considered:

- past performance can only be shown if certain standard periods are included and if it is calculated in a standard way;

- past performance of an underlying fund or other funds managed by the same adviser may be shown, but only if it is clear that the disclosure relates to another fund under common management or if the fund being sold is linked to the fund being advertised;

- sales communications must include clear warning language about how data is calculated and that past performance does not indicate future performance;

- performance data must be sufficiently current so as not to be misleading;

- there must be clear and understandable disclosure of other key elements of the product, including fees and costs.

---

[7]These principles are based largely on requirements in mutual fund rules, specifically Part 15 of National Instrument 81-102.

F. — Financial disclosure and valuation

Through our regular prospectus reviews and through discussions of numerous transition questions around National Instrument 81-106 *Investment Funds Continuous Disclosure*, we identified several challenges for hedge funds that may be required to meet the valuation and financial disclosure requirements of NI 81-106, such as:

- for funds linked to offshore hedge funds, completing financial disclosure for the Canadian top fund within 90 days of the fund's year end;

- calculating NAV as frequently as typically required for other investment funds;

- sensitivity around the disclosure of specific underlying hedge fund portfolio assets.

We will continue to look at ways to balance the need for transparency with the recognition that there may be unique financial disclosure issues for some hedge funds.

We will also continue to study hedge fund valuation issues, particularly:

- the role of service providers (offshore fund managers, fund administrators) in providing fund valuations or verifying fund valuations done internally;

- the policies and procedures and internal controls for valuation, for example, segregation of duties within the fund complex to mitigate any conflict of interest between those who value the funds and those who may benefit from how a fund is valued;

- the fund manager's oversight of the valuation process;

- the policies and procedures that Canadian-based funds that invest in offshore hedge funds have in place to verify valuations and other financial disclosure about those hedge funds;

- the work being done at the international level on these issues, for example, through IOSCO.

CSA Staff Notice 81-317 — Frequently Asked Questions on National Instrument 81-107 Independent Review Committee for Investment Funds

Date: **March 30, 2007**

30 O.S.C.B. 2807

Background

On November 1, 2006, National Instrument 81-107 *Independent Review Committee for Investment Funds* (NI 81-107 or the Instrument) came into force[1]. To assist issuers in complying with NI 81-107, we have compiled a list of frequently asked questions (FAQs) and staff's responses to those questions.

FAQs

After reviewing NI 81-107, some readers have raised questions regarding its application and interpretation. This list of FAQs is not exhaustive, but broadly reflects the types of inquiries we have received.

We have divided the FAQs into two categories:

A. application and transition issues, and

B. specific questions on sections of the Instrument.

A. — Application and Transition Issues

Transition Period

A-1

Q. Section 8.2 of the Instrument gives investment funds up to November 1, 2007 to comply with the Instrument. Does this transition period apply only to investment funds in existence on November 1, 2006?

A. No, the transition period applies to all investment funds. Investment funds established after November 1, 2006 may take advantage of the transition period. The transition period expires on November 1, 2007, at which time all investment funds must comply with the Instrument.

An investment fund established after November 1, 2007 must have an independent review committee (IRC) before its prospectus is receipted in accordance with section 3.1. Before the investment fund accepts any purchase order for securities, it must comply with the rest of the Instrument (please see A-2).

A-2

Q. What must a manager do during the transition period?

A. Subsection 8.2(2) of the Instrument requires the manager to appoint the first members of the IRC by May 1, 2007. By November 1, 2007, all investment funds must comply with the rest of the Instrument.

---

[1]In Québec, NI 81-107 came into force November 15, 2006.

The Instrument requires a manager to establish policies and procedures on conflict of interest matters in accordance with section 2.2 and to refer these conflict of interest matters to the IRC for its review as set out in section 5.1 before taking any action. A manager may want to use the transition period to satisfy these requirements for any conflict of interest matter inherent or necessary in the operation of the fund to be ready to comply on November 1, 2007.

The six month period for the appointment of IRC members, and the one year transition period for the Instrument, is intended to provide sufficient time for the manager and IRC to comply with the Instrument. This includes (among other things): the IRC adopting its charter; reviewing the manager's policies and procedures; and reviewing (once referred by the manager) any conflict of interest matters anticipated to exist on November 1, 2007.

A-3

Q. During the transition period, is an investment fund required to amend an existing prospectus to comply with the new prospectus disclosure requirements introduced in the consequential amendments to the Instrument?

A. No. Commentary 7 to section 8.2 of the Instrument indicates an investment fund may incorporate the new disclosure in its first annual prospectus renewal and continuous disclosure filing after the transition period expires. If a manager provides notice under subsection 8.2(4) that it intends to comply with the Instrument before November 1, 2007, the investment fund must incorporate the new disclosure in its next annual prospectus renewal and next interim or annual continuous disclosure filing following the notification.

A-4

Q. May the new exemptions introduced in Part 4 and Part 5 of National Instrument 81-102 *Mutual Funds* (NI 81-102) be relied upon during the transition period?

A. The changes made to Part 4 and Part 5 of NI 81-102 may only be relied upon if there is 'complete compliance' with the Instrument (please see A-8). Although the consequential amendments to NI 81-102 came into force November 1, 2006, the intention was that the new exemptions would apply only when the manager and investment fund have fully complied with the Instrument, which may not be the case during the transition period. An investment fund that provides notice under subsection 8.2(4) that it intends to comply with the Instrument before the transition period expires, may rely on the exemptions in Part 4 and Part 5 of NI 81-102 at the time they provide this notice.

Existing Exemptions, Waivers and Approvals

A-5

Q. Section 7.2 of the Instrument says that all existing exemptions, waivers and approvals that deal with matters regulated by the Instrument will expire November 1, 2007. Does section 7.2 capture all exemptions, waivers and approvals dealing with conflict of interest matters, or does this section apply only to existing relief that falls into a new exemption under either the Instrument or NI 81-102?

A. Section 7.2 captures all exemptions, waivers and approvals that deal with conflict of interest matters, regardless of whether the relief specifically is covered by a new exemption in either NI 81-107 or NI 81-102. Accordingly, all existing exemptions, waivers and approvals that deal with matters regulated by the Instrument will expire on November 1, 2007.

A-6

Q. What happens to existing relief expiring on November 1, 2007, for which there will be no equivalent exemption in either NI 81-107 or NI 81-102?

A. We recognize that there will be some exemptions, waivers and approvals on conflict of interest matters that do not have a corresponding exemption under the Instrument or NI 81-102. If the investment fund still requires that exemption, waiver or approval, the fund will need to apply for the exemptive relief not otherwise addressed in NI 81-107 or NI 81-102. Filers will want to consider what conditions may be appropriate for that relief since the IRC will, under the Instrument, review all conflict of interest matters. We encourage you to make these applications early.

A-7

Q. During the transition period, can a manager or investment fund continue to rely on existing exemptions, waivers and approvals even if the 'sunset provision' states that the relief expires with the coming into force of an instrument dealing with the matter?

A. Yes. Section 7.2 permits a manager and investment fund to continue to rely on any exemption, waiver and approval that deals with matters regulated by NI 81-107 until November 1, 2007, despite any 'sunset provision' in any particular relief.

Exemptions and Applications during the Transition Period

A-8

Q. During the transition period, can an application be made for exemptive relief of the type the CSA has previously granted for conflict of interest matters that the Instrument regulates? Would the CSA grant new exemptive relief before November 1, 2007, equivalent to a new exemption in the Instrument or NI 81-102?

A. We will continue to consider requests for exemptive relief on conflict of interest matters. For similar relief to that granted in the past, we will generally consider imposing terms and conditions that are the same as in the past, including a 'sunset provision' that the relief will expire on November 1, 2007.

Generally, we would not expect to recommend a new type of exemptive relief on a conflict of interest matter before the transition period expires just because that exemption is included in the Instrument or NI 81-102. This is because the new exemptions in the Instrument and NI 81-102 anticipate that the manager and investment fund will be fully compliant with the Instrument, which may not be the case for a fund that requests relief during the transition period.

Early Compliance with the Instrument

A-9

Q. Commentary 3 to section 8.2 of the Instrument states that a manager may not, under subsection 8.2(4), notify the regulator that the manager intends to comply with the Instrument before the transition period expires unless there is "complete compliance" with the Instrument. What is meant by "complete compliance" with the Instrument?

A. The one year transition period (to November 1, 2007) is intended to provide managers and IRCs with sufficient time to comply with the Instrument (please see A-2 above). If a manager decides it wants to have its IRC in operation before November 1, 2007, the manager must give us notice under subsection 8.2(4). Once a manager notifies the regulator under this section, the manager and IRC must comply with all parts of the Instrument.

A-10

Q. If a manager gives notice under subsection 8.2(4) of the Instrument of its intention to comply with the Instrument before November 1, 2007, is the investment fund required to amend its existing prospectus to comply with the new IRC disclosure requirements?

A. No, commentary 7 to section 8.2 of the Instrument says an investment fund may incorporate the new disclosure requirements in its next annual prospectus renewal and continuous disclosure filing after the transition period expires (please see A-3 above).

However, if a manager intends to rely on an exemption in the Instrument or NI 81-102 that requires prospectus disclosure (or if the IRC requires prospectus disclosure as part of its approval), the investment fund must amend its prospectus to add the requisite disclosure before relying on the exemption.

A-11

Q. If a manager gives notice under subsection 8.2(4), when must the IRC complete its first IRC report and subsequent IRC reports to securityholders under section 4.4?

A. Subsection 8.2(3) of the Instrument states that the IRC must complete its first report by the 120th day after the end of the first financial year of the investment fund after the Instrument applies.

Example: An investment fund has a December 31 financial year end. If the manager gave notice under subsection 8.2(4) on December 1, 2006, the IRC must complete its first report by April 29, 2007. If the manager gives notice anytime between January, 1, 2007 and October 31, 2007, the IRC must complete its first report by April 29, 2008. If no notice is given, the transition period for the investment fund will expire November 1, 2007, and the IRC must complete its first report April 29, 2008.

Following the first IRC report, the IRC must complete subsequent reports for each financial year of the investment fund no later than the date the investment fund files its annual financial statements.

Regardless of the timing of the first IRC report to securityholders, the Instrument requires the IRC to carry out all other functions under the Instrument, including its regular assessments under section 4.2 of the Instrument, as soon as the Instrument applies.

B. — Specific Questions on Sections of the Instrument

Part 1 — Definitions and Application

B-1

Q. What are the types of conflicts of interest facing "an entity related to the manager" that are intended to be caught in the definition "conflict of interest matter" in paragraph 1.2(a) of the Instrument?

A. It was not intended that all sub-advisor conflicts of interest be referred to the IRC. The intention of paragraph 1.2(a) was to bring to the attention of the IRC those types of conflicts faced by a service provider when managing/providing services to an investment fund that raise the question of whether the decision being made is in the best interests of the fund. Examples of potential conflict of interest matters under paragraph 1.2(a) are a sub-advisor's allocation of securities among a family of investment funds; and soft dollar arrangements with dealers with whom the sub-advisor places portfolio transactions for the investment fund.

Part 2 — Functions of the Manager

B-2

Q. Section 2.2 of the Instrument requires the manager to establish policies and procedures it must follow for a particular conflict of interest matter and to refer those policies and procedures to the IRC for its review and input before proceeding with a conflict of interest matter. If the conflict of interest (as defined in section 1.2) is that of the advisor/sub-advisor, which policies and procedures should be brought to the IRC, those of the manager or the advisor or sub-advisor?

A. The Instrument requires the manager to refer its own policies and procedures to the IRC. To fulfil a manager's standard of care under securities legislation, a manager must have sufficient policies and procedures to monitor how an advisor/sub-advisor handles its own conflicts of interest when providing services to the investment fund.

Part 3 — Independent Review Committee

B-3

Q. Paragraph 3.10(2)(d) of the Instrument specifies that an individual ceases to be a member of the IRC if a majority of the securityholders of the investment fund vote to remove the individual at a special meeting called for that purpose by the manager. Does 'majority' mean "50% +1", or does it mean 'majority' as set out in subsection 5.2(1) of NI 81-102?

A. The intention of paragraph 3.10(2)(d) was to require the same 'majority' for securityholder votes as required in subsection 5.2(1) of NI 81-102, being a "majority of the votes cast at a meeting of the securityholders". We will revise this section to provide greater clarity when we next propose amendments to the Instrument.

B-4

Q. Section 3.14 of the Instrument sets out the indemnification and insurance an investment fund and manager may provide to a member of an IRC. May an entity related to the manager (as defined in section 1.3), including the parent corporation of the manager, indemnify and/or insure members of the IRC?

A. Yes. Section 3.14 does not preclude IRC members from receiving an indemnity and/or insurance from entities other than the investment fund and manager, including an entity related to the manager.

Part 5 — Manager to Refer Conflict of Interest Matters to IRC

B-5

Q. Subsection 5.2(1) of the Instrument sets out the conflict of interest matters that require IRC approval for the manager to proceed. Paragraph 5.2(1)(a) refers to both inter-fund trades captured by section 6.1 of the Instrument and transactions described in subsection 4.2(1) of NI 81-102. Does this mean all transactions described in subsection 4.2(1) of NI 81-102 require IRC approval to proceed?

A. No, the intention of subsection 5.2(1) was to capture only those conflict of interest matters that are subject to a new exemption under the Instrument or NI 81-102. Accordingly, paragraph 5.2(1)(a) was only intended to refer to inter-fund trades captured by section 6.1 of the Instrument and/or subsection 4.2(1) of NI 81-102. We will revise this section to provide greater clarity when we next propose amendments to the Instrument.

B-6

Q. Paragraph 5.4(2)(a) of the Instrument requires the manager, with respect to each instance it acted in reliance on a standing instruction from the IRC, to provide a written report to the IRC at the time of the IRC's regular assessment under section 4.2. Can 'each instance' be a 'category of instances' for trades or conflict of interest matters that arise repeatedly and are all handled the same way?

A. Yes. The Instrument does not prevent a manager from interpreting, in circumstances where there are recurring transactions or matters, 'each instance' to mean a 'category of instances'. For example, if a manager has received a standing instruction with respect to a category of trades, the manager does not have to provide to the IRC details of each transaction within the category.

However, to comply with this reporting requirement, a manager would need to provide the IRC with enough detail (for example, the number of instances/trades) in the report for the IRC to be able to determine whether the manager has fulfilled any terms of the IRC's standing instruction. Also, paragraph 2.4(1)(c) requires the manager to provide more detailed information to the IRC on request. We will revise this section to provide greater clarity when we next propose amendments to the Instrument.

Part 6 — Exempted Transactions

B-7

Q. The inter-fund trading exemption in section 6.1 of the Instrument requires that trades of exchange-traded securities be at 'closing sale price'. Would the CSA consider applications for exemptive relief to permit inter-fund trades of exchange-traded securities to occur throughout the trading day, at the 'last sale price' immediately prior to the time of the inter-fund trade?

A. Yes, upon appropriate terms and conditions. The conditions in section 6.1 are intended to minimize the possibility that the price of the security is being manipulated. Some additional conditions might be necessary for trades made during the trading day. We intend to revise the section to permit 'last sale price' when we next propose amendments to the Instrument.

B-8

Q. In addition to cross-trades of securities between investment funds, does the inter-fund trading exemption in section 6.1 apply to in-kind transactions between investment funds (i.e., the settlement of a purchase or redemption of units of an investment fund with the securities of an issuer)?

A. Yes, section 6.1 applies to in-kind transactions between investment funds.

Section 6.1 applies to an investment fund's purchase of a security from, or sale of a security to, another investment fund managed by the same manager or an affiliate of the manager, provided the investment funds are subject to NI 81-107. Mutual fund fund-of-fund transactions made in accordance with section 2.5 of NI 81-102 must also comply with the requirements in section 6.1.

The inter-fund trading exemption in section 6.1 does not apply to purchases or sales of securities of an issuer between an investment fund and managed account or pooled fund, nor between managed accounts and pooled funds. We will continue to consider requests for exemptive relief for these types of transactions on the same terms and conditions granted previously.

CSA Staff Notice 81-319 — Status Report on the Implementation of Point of Sale Disclosure for Mutual Funds

Date: June 18, 2010

33 O.S.C.B. 5449

Purpose

This Notice provides an update on the implementation of the Canadian Securities Administrators (CSA) point of sale disclosure project for mutual funds.

Background

On June 19, 2009, the CSA published proposed amendments to National Instrument 81-101 *Mutual Fund Prospectus Disclosure*, its Forms and Companion Policy (collectively, the Instrument), aimed at providing investors with more meaningful and effective disclosure. The Instrument was the first step in implementing the point of sale disclosure framework published in October 2008 by the Joint Forum of Financial Market Regulators (the Joint Forum), which includes the CSA. Under the framework, investors would receive key information about a mutual fund at a time that is relevant to their investment decision.

Central to the new prospectus disclosure regime is the Fund Facts document. It is in plain language, will be no more than two pages and highlights the potential benefits, risks and the costs of investing in a mutual fund. Investors would generally receive a Fund Facts when they buy a fund for the first time (at or before the "point of sale").

The comment period expired on October 17, 2009. We received 54 comment letters on the Instrument. Copies of the comment letters have been posted on the Ontario Securities Commission website at www.osc.gov.on.ca. Copies are also available from any CSA member.

This is a significant investor protection initiative. Canadian investors have approximately $620 billion invested in mutual funds held in over 47 million accounts. We think the disclosure required by the Instrument would provide investors with the opportunity to make more informed investment decisions by giving investors key information about a mutual fund, in language they can easily understand, at a time that is relevant to their investment decision. The Instrument also keeps pace with developing global standards on point of sale disclosure and delivery.

A staged approach to implementation

The comments show that stakeholders generally agree with the benefits of providing investors with a more meaningful and simplified form of disclosure, and support the Fund Facts as a way of providing concise, plain language information that describes key elements of the mutual fund under consideration.

However, we received significant comments related to operational and compliance concerns with point of sale delivery for mutual funds. A large number of commenters also asked the CSA to implement a point of sale disclosure regime for other types of publicly offered investment funds and other securities at the same time.

While the CSA agrees that further review and consideration of issues related to point of sale delivery for mutual funds are necessary, we also think that it would be beneficial for the Fund Facts document to be made available to investors and market participants as soon as possible. This would provide investors with the opportunity to have access to key information about a mutual fund sooner. It would also allow investors and dealers to become familiar with the document and start using the Fund Facts in the decision-making process. Accordingly, the CSA has concluded to proceed with a staged implementation of the project.

The CSA remains committed to implementing point of sale disclosure for mutual funds. A staged implementation will allow us the opportunity to continue to consult with stakeholders and to consider the applicability of the point of sale regime for mutual funds to other types of publicly offered investment funds, with the possible outcome of implementing a point of sale delivery requirement at the same time for all comparable investment fund products. At this time, we are not considering the applicability of point of sale to securities other than publicly offered investment funds.

We anticipate a staged implementation of the project to proceed as follows:

1. — File and post Fund Facts

We will finalize the requirements in the Instrument requiring a mutual fund to prepare and file a Fund Facts document and have it posted to the mutual fund's or its manager's website. As part of these requirements, a Fund Facts would be required to be delivered to an investor upon request.

Since the expiry of the comment period, we have focused on the feedback related to the Fund Facts. In response to the comments received, we have made some non-material revisions to the Fund Facts document published in June 2009. Appendix A to this Notice contains an example of a form of Fund Facts the CSA expects will satisfy the requirements of the final Instrument.

We anticipate publishing the Fund Facts requirements by December 2010, with an effective date in early 2011. The requirements will include a transition period.

2. — Deliver Fund Facts under current requirements

In mid-2011, we expect to publish for comment a proposal to allow delivery of the Fund Facts to satisfy the current prospectus delivery requirements under securities legislation to deliver a prospectus within two days of buying a mutual fund. As part of this proposal, we do not intend to make any changes to a mutual fund's obligation to file its simplified prospectus and annual information form with the CSA, and these documents would continue to be made available to investors on a website and upon request, at no cost.

While this work on delivery within the existing requirements is underway, the CSA will consider applications for exemptive relief to permit the early use by dealers of the Fund Facts to satisfy the current prospectus delivery requirements. We will publish a staff notice in 2011 that sets out the key terms and conditions the CSA anticipate requiring as part of any exemption.

3. — Point of sale delivery

Once the CSA has completed its review and consideration of the issues related to point of sale delivery, including consultations with all stakeholders, we intend to move forward with requirements for point of sale delivery for mutual funds and possibly for other types of publicly offered investment funds. We will publish for further comment any proposed requirements that would implement these delivery requirements.

Appendix A
Sample Fund Facts Document

FUND FACTS

XYZ Mutual Funds

XYZ Canadian Equity Fund – Series A
June 30, 20XX

This document contains key information you should know about XYZ Canadian Equity Fund. You can find more detailed information in the fund's simplified prospectus. Ask your adviser for a copy, contact XYZ Mutual Funds at 1-800-555-5556 or investing@xyzfunds.com, or visit www.xyzfunds.com.

Quick facts

Date fund created:	January 1, 1996	Portfolio manager	Capital Asset Management Ltd.
Total value on June 1, 20XX:	$1 billion	Distributions	Annually, on December 15
Management expense ratio (MER):	2.25%	Minimum investment	$500 initial, $50 additional

What does the fund invest in?

The fund invests in Canadian companies. They can be of any size and from any industry. The charts below give you a snapshot of the fund's investments on June 1, 20XX. The fund's investments will change.

Top 10 Investments (June 1, 20XX)
1. Royal Bank of Canada
2. Encana Corp.
3. Petro-Canada
4. Alcan Inc.
5. Canadian National Railway Company
6. Goldcorp. Inc.
7. Extendicare Inc.
8. Husky Energy
9. Open Text
10. Thomson Reuters Corp.

Total investments   126
The top 10 investments make up 32% of the fund.

Investment mix (June 1, 20XX)

[pie chart]

Industry	
Financial services	34.0%
Energy	26.6%
Industrial goods	16.5%
Business services	6.4%
Telecommunication	5.9%
Hardware	3.7%
Healthcare services	2.3%
Consumer services	2.1%
Media	1.9%
Consumer goods	0.6%

How has the fund performed?

This section tells you how the fund has performed over the past 10 years. Returns are after expenses have been deducted. These expenses reduce the fund's returns.

It's important to note that this doesn't tell you how the fund will perform in the future. Also, your actual after-tax return will depend on your personal tax situation.

Average return
A person who invested $1,000 in the fund 10 years ago now has $2,705. This works out to an annual compound return of 10.5%.

Year-by-year returns
This chart shows how the fund has performed in each of the past 10 years. The fund dropped in value in three of the 10 years.

[bar chart]

How risky is it?

When you invest in a fund, the value of your investment can go down as well as up. XYZ Mutual Funds has rated this fund's risk as medium. For a description of the specific risks of this fund, see the fund's simplified prospectus.

Low	Low to medium	Medium	Medium to high	High

Are there any guarantees?

Like most mutual funds, this fund doesn't have any guarantees. You may not get back the amount of money you invest.

Who is this fund for?

Investors who:
- are looking for a long-term investment
- want to invest in a broad range of Canadian companies
- can handle the ups and downs of the stock market.

! Don't buy this fund if you need a steady source of income from your investment.

Before you invest in any fund, you should consider how it would work with your other investments and your tolerance for risk.

A word about tax

In general, you'll have to pay income tax on any money you make on a fund. How much you pay depends on the tax laws where you live and whether or not you hold the fund in a registered plan, such as a Registered Retirement Savings Plan or a Tax-Free Savings Account.

Keep in mind that if you hold your fund in a non-registered account, fund distributions are included in your taxable income, whether you get them in cash or have them reinvested.

How much does it cost?

The following tables show the fees and expenses you could pay to buy, own and sell Series A units of the fund. The fees and expenses are different for each series. Ask about other series that may be suitable for you.

1. Sales charges

You have to choose a sales charge option when you buy the fund. Ask about the pros and cons of each option.

Sales charge option	What you pay		How it works
	in per cent (%)	in dollars ($)	
Initial sales charge	0% to 4% of the amount you buy	$0 to $40 on every $1,000 you buy	• You and your adviser decide on the rate. • The initial sales charge is deducted from the amount you buy. It goes to your investment firm as a commission.
Deferred sales charge	If you sell within: 1 year of buying 6.0% 2 years of buying 5.0% 3 years of buying 4.0% 4 years of buying 3.0% 5 years of buying 2.0% 6 years of buying 1.0% After 6 years nothing	$0 to $60 on every $1,000 you sell	• The deferred sales charge is a set rate. It is deducted from the amount you sell. • When you buy the fund, XYZ Mutual Funds pays your investment firm a commission of 4.9%. Any deferred sales charge you pay goes to XYZ Mutual Funds. • You can sell up to 10% of your units each year without paying a deferred sales charge. • You can switch to Series A units of other XYZ Mutual Funds at any time without paying a deferred sales charge. The deferred sales charge schedule will be based on the date you bought the first fund.

2. Fund expenses

You don't pay these expenses directly. They affect you because they reduce the fund's returns.

As of March 31, 20XX, the fund's expenses were 2.30% of its value. This equals $23 for every $1,000 invested.

	Annual rate (as a % of the fund's value)
Management expense ratio (MER) This is the total of the fund's management fee and operating expenses. XYZ Mutual Funds waived some of the fund's expenses. If it had not done so, the MER would have been higher.	2.25%
Trading expense ratio (TER) These are the fund's trading costs.	0.05%
Fund expenses	**2.30%**

Trailing commission

XYZ Mutual Funds pays your investment firm a trailing commission for as long as you own the fund. It is for the services and advice your investment firm provides to you. Investment firms may pay part of the trailing commission to their representatives.

The trailing commission is paid out of the management fee. The rate depends on the sales charge option you choose:
- Initial sales charge – up to 1.0% of the value of your investment each year. This equals $10 each year for every $1,000 invested.
- Deferred sales charge – up to 0.50% of the value of your investment each year. This equals $5 each year for $1,000 invested.

3. Other fees

You may have to pay other fees when you sell or switch units of the fund.

Fee	What you pay
Short-term trading fee	1% of the value of units you sell or switch within 90 days of buying them. This fee goes to the fund.
Switch fee	Your investment firm may charge you up to 2% of the value of units you switch to another XYZ Mutual Fund.
Change fee	Your investment firm may charge you up to 2% of the value of units you switch to another series of the fund.

What if I change my mind?

Under securities law in some provinces and territories, you have the right to:
- withdraw from an agreement to buy mutual fund units within two business days after you receive a simplified prospectus, or

For more information

Contact XYZ Mutual Funds or your adviser for a copy of the fund's simplified prospectus and other disclosure documents. These documents and the Fund Facts make up the fund's legal documents.

- cancel your purchase within 48 hours after you receive confirmation of the purchase.

In some provinces and territories, you also have the right to cancel a purchase, or in some jurisdictions, claim damages, if the simplified prospectus, annual information form or financial statements contain a misrepresentation. You must act within the time limit set by the securities law in your province or territory.

For more information, see the securities law of your province or territory or ask a lawyer.

XYZ Mutual Funds
123 Asset Allocation St.
Toronto, ON M1A 2B3

Phone: (416) 555-5555
Toll-free: 1-800-555-5556
Email: investing@xyzfunds.com
www.xyzfunds.com

Part 8: MUTUAL FUNDS

Policies and Orders: CSAN 81-321.

CSA Staff Notice 81-320 (Revised) — Update on International Financial Reporting Standards for Investment Funds

Date: October 8, 2010 as revised March 23, 2011 and March 30, 2012

33 O.S.C.B. 8815, 34 O.S.C.B. 3473 and 35 O.S.C.B. 3005

First published October 8, 2010, revised March 23, 2011 and March 30, 2012

Purpose

This notice updates investment funds and their advisers on the adoption of International Financial Reporting Standards (IFRS) by investment funds in Canada.

The Handbook of the Canadian Institute of Chartered Accountants (Handbook) refers to "investment companies", the majority of which are "investment funds" for the purposes of securities legislation. This notice applies only to those investment companies that are investment funds as defined in securities legislation and are subject to National Instrument 81-106 *Investment Fund Continuous Disclosure* (NI 81-106).[1]

The Canadian Securities Administrators (CSA) previously published proposals relating to the adoption of IFRS by investment funds on October 16, 2009.[2] These proposals were based on the Canadian Accounting Standards Board (AcSB) decision to transition financial reporting for Canadian publicly accountable enterprises to IFRS as issued by the International Accounting Standards Board (IASB) for financial years beginning on or after January 1, 2011.

The AcSB has deferred for a third time the transition to IFRS for investment companies. On February 29, 2012, the AcSB issued amendments to the Handbook extending the deferral to January 1, 2014.[3]

Background

Under existing International Accounting Standard 27 *Consolidated and Separate Financial Statements* (IAS 27) and the recently issued IFRS 10 *Consolidated Financial Statements*, which replaces IAS 27 for financial years beginning on or after January 1, 2013, an entity must consolidate investments that it controls. The IASB published the Exposure Draft *Investment Entities* on August 25, 2011[4] which proposed that an "investment entity" be exempt from consolidating entities that it controls and instead account for controlling interests in other entities at fair value. The IASB has not yet indicated a target date when a final standard for investment entities will be available.[5]

The AcSB amended Part I of the Handbook to require investment companies, as defined in and applying Accounting Guideline 18 *Investment Companies*, to adopt IFRS as issued by the IASB for interim and annual periods beginning on or after January 1, 2014, with earlier adoption permitted. The deferral of the mandatory changeover to January 1, 2014 is intended to allow the IASB's proposed exemption from consolidation for investment entities to be in place prior to the adoption of IFRS by investment entities in Canada.

Move to IFRS by Investment Funds

CSA staff are also of the view that it would be preferable for the IASB's proposed consolidation exemption to be in place when IFRS is adopted by investment funds in Canada. Accordingly, we will be reviewing and revising the proposed amendments to NI 81-106 and related consequential amendments, previously published for comment in 2009, in light of the recent developments at both the IASB and AcSB.

The CSA comment period for the proposed amendments ended on January 14, 2010, and the majority of the comments related to the implications of IAS 27 to Canadian investment funds. Given the proposed exemption that the IASB is now considering, the issues raised by commenters relating to consolidation may no longer exist for the majority of investment funds. As a result, CSA staff anticipate that the proposed amendments to NI 81-106 related to the consolidation requirement may no longer be required.

In order to have more certainty about the scope and impact of the anticipated exemption from consolidation for investment entities that the IASB is considering, CSA staff will take additional time before seeking approval in each CSA jurisdiction to either republish or finalize IFRS-related amendments to NI 81-106 and other instruments related to investment funds, with the goal of having the necessary IFRS-related amendments for investment funds in force by January 1, 2014.

Prior to the mandatory changeover to IFRS set out in the Handbook, CSA staff consider the standards in Part V of the Handbook to be Canadian generally accepted accounting principles (Canadian GAAP) as applicable to public enterprises for securities legislation purposes. CSA staff recognize that some investment funds may want to prepare their financial statements in accordance with IFRS as issued by the IASB for annual periods beginning prior to January 1, 2014. Therefore, an investment fund that wants to use IFRS for interim and annual financial statements relating to annual periods beginning prior to January 1, 2014 must apply for exemptive relief from the current requirement to

---

[1] The IFRS-related amendments to CSA rules for issuers that are not investment funds came into force on January 1, 2011.

[2] These proposals were published in French on March 12, 2010 by the Autorité des marchés financiers and the New Brunswick Securities Commission.

[3] The AcSB Decision Summary regarding the most recent deferral is at http://www.frascanada.ca/accounting-standards-board/meetings/decision-summaries/2011/item59121.aspx

[4] The Exposure Draft Investment Entities and comment letters submitted to the IASB can be found on the Consolidations — Investment Entities project webpage http://www.ifrs.org/Current+Projects/IASB +Projects/Consolidation/IE/investment+entities+ED+Aug+2011/ED+ and+comment+letters.htm.

[5] The IASB work plan and projected timetable for this project can be found in the Standards Development section of the IASB/IFRS website (www.ifrs.org/Current+Projects/IASB+Projects/IASB+Work+Plan.htm).

prepare its financial statements in accordance with Canadian GAAP as applicable to public enterprises.[6] Investment funds filing applications for exemptive relief from NI 81-106 should also identify any issues that early adoption may create with respect to their financial disclosure.

CSA Staff Notice 52-320 *Disclosure of Expected Changes in Accounting Policies Relating to Changeover to International Financial Reporting Standards*[7] sets out the CSA's views on the disclosure that investment funds should be providing in advance of the changeover to IFRS. Investment funds should continue to provide appropriate disclosure about the expected impacts of the changeover to IFRS in accordance with the guidance in CSA Staff Notice 52-320 in their annual and interim filings in advance of the January 1, 2014 changeover date.

CSA Staff Notice 81-321 — Early Use of the Fund Facts to Satisfy Prospectus Delivery Requirements

Date: **February 25, 2011**

34 O.S.C.B. 2252

Purpose

The Canadian Securities Administrators (the CSA or we) anticipate that we may begin receiving applications for exemptive relief to allow the early use of the Fund Facts to satisfy the current prospectus delivery requirements. This Notice provides guidance on key terms and conditions that the CSA will look for when considering these types of applications.

Background

On June 16, 2010, we published CSA Staff Notice 81-319 *Status Report on the Implementation of Point of Sale Disclosure for Mutual Funds* (the Staff Notice). The Staff Notice outlined the CSA's decision to implement the point of sale disclosure framework in three stages. The CSA has begun its work on stage 2 of the implementation.

The Staff Notice specified that while work on stage 2 is underway, the CSA would consider applications for exemptive relief to permit the early use of the Fund Facts to satisfy the current prospectus delivery requirements. It also stated that the CSA would publish a staff notice in early 2011 that sets out the key terms and conditions the CSA anticipates requiring as part of any exemption.

Stage 1 was completed on January 1, 2011 when amendments to National Instrument 81-101 *Mutual Fund Prospectus Disclosure* (the Instrument) came into force. The Instrument, which was published on October 6, 2010, contains the requirements to produce and file the Fund Facts document and for it to be made available on the mutual fund's or mutual fund manager's website. The Fund Facts document must also be delivered or sent to investors free of charge upon request.

The Fund Facts document is a new summary disclosure document and is central to the point of sale disclosure framework. It highlights key information for investors, including fund performance, risk and the costs of buying and owning a fund, in a short, easy-to-read document that is no more than two pages, double-sided, in length.

Stage 2 involves publishing for comment proposed amendments to allow delivery of the Fund Facts to satisfy the current prospectus delivery requirements under securities legislation to deliver a prospectus within two days of buying a mutual fund. The CSA expects to publish the proposed amendments in mid-2011.

In stage 3, after completing our review and consideration of the issues related to point of sale delivery, we will publish for further comment any proposed requirements that would implement point of sale delivery for mutual funds. We will also be considering point of sale delivery for other types of publicly offered investment funds.

Terms and Conditions for Exemptive Relief

Set out below are the key terms and conditions that the CSA anticipates requiring as part of an exemption to allow the early use of the Fund Facts to satisfy the current prospectus delivery requirements. The CSA may also consider other terms and conditions as part of its review of an application.

Filing requirements

- The mutual fund must file a Fund Facts in compliance with Form 81-101F3 *Contents of Fund Facts Document*.

- An amendment to the simplified prospectus (SP) must be filed to specify, under Item 3 of Part A of Form 81-101F1 *Contents of Simplified Prospectus*, that the Fund Facts is incorporated by reference into the SP.

- A mutual fund must continue to file the SP and annual information form (AIF), as required by securities legislation.

Availability of documents

- The Fund Facts must continue to be made available to investors on the mutual fund's or mutual fund manager's website and delivered or sent to investors free of charge upon request.

- A mutual fund's SP and AIF must continue to be delivered or sent to investors free of charge upon request.

---

[6]This requirement is found in section 2.6 of NI 81-106.

[7]This CSA Staff Notice was published May 9, 2008.

Delivery requirements

- A Fund Facts must be delivered in accordance with the current prospectus delivery requirements under securities legislation.

- The current withdrawal and rescission rights under securities legislation that apply to delivery of, and failure to deliver, the prospectus will apply to delivery of, and failure to deliver, the Fund Facts. These rights must be disclosed in or with the Fund Facts.

- A Fund Facts may only be bound with other Fund Facts that are being delivered at the same time within the current prospectus delivery requirements for mutual funds purchased by the investor.

Expiry of exemptive relief

- Any exemptive relief granted will expire upon the coming into force of any legislation or rules relating to delivery of the Fund Facts to satisfy the prospectus delivery requirements under securities legislation. This is commonly referred to as a "sunset clause".

For More Information

Applicants and their counsel are encouraged to contact CSA staff at an early stage in the planning of an application for exemptive relief to discuss the terms and conditions set out in the Notice.

CSA Staff Notice 81-322 — Status Report on the Implementation of the Modernization of Investment Fund Product Regulation Project and Request for Comment on Phase 2 Proposals

Date: May 26, 2011

34 O.S.C.B. 6092

Purpose

This Notice provides an update on the implementation of the Canadian Securities Administrators' (CSA) project to modernize the product regulation of publicly offered investment funds (the Modernization Project). We also seek feedback from investors and industry stakeholders on the CSA's proposal to focus next on developing an operational rule for non-redeemable investment funds, as part of a staged approach to proceeding with the Modernization Project.

Background

The Modernization Project's mandate is to review the product regulation of publicly offered investment funds and to consider whether our current regulatory approach sufficiently addresses product and market developments in the Canadian investment fund industry, and continues to adequately protect investors. The types of investment funds that are within the scope of the Modernization Project include: (i) open-end mutual funds[1], (ii) exchange-traded mutual funds[2] and (iii) non-redeemable investment funds.[3]

Open-end mutual funds rose in popularity subsequent to the passage of changes to the *Income Tax Act* (Canada) in the late 1950's, which enabled them to rapidly flourish as vehicles for registered retirement savings plans. By the late 1960's, assets under management by open-end mutual funds had considerably surpassed those under management by non-redeemable investment funds, which prior to that time had been the most prevalent form of publicly offered investment fund. The quick rise to mass appeal of the open-end mutual fund product led to much of the literature written on the need for regulation of mutual funds in Canada, and subsequent regulatory initiatives which focused on open-end mutual funds. Such initiatives included National Policy 39 — *Mutual Funds* (NP 39), an amalgamation of mutual fund policies from the 1970's and 1980's, which was implemented in November 1987. NP 39 was subsequently reformulated into National Instrument 81-102 *Mutual Funds* (NI 81-102) in January 2000. As a result, the investment fund product regulation we have today was drafted primarily with the traditional open-end mutual fund in mind.

Over the last decade, however, the gamut of publicly-offered investment fund products available to retail investors has expanded. Exchange-traded mutual funds have proliferated, with assets under management growing from approximately $6 billion in December 2000 to approximately $41 billion in March 2011[4]. Non-redeemable investment funds, although not new to the product landscape, have evolved in structure and complexity. In a time of rapid market development and innovation and increasing complexity of investment fund products, we think it is important that we assess the current regulatory framework that applies to different types of publicly offered investment funds to ensure our investor protection, fairness and market efficiency objectives are being met.

---

[1]Open-end mutual funds generally issue an unlimited number of units or shares from treasury on a continuous basis and provide a regular redemption feature, typically daily, at the fund's net asset value (NAV).

[2]Exchange-traded mutual funds are open-end mutual funds whose units trade on an exchange. It is typically only large institutional investors (designated brokers) that purchase or redeem exchange-traded mutual fund units directly from the exchange-traded mutual fund at the fund's NAV, and then only in large blocks, which are usually exchanged in-kind with baskets of the underlying securities. Individual retail investors typically buy and sell units of exchange-traded mutual funds on the exchange at prevailing market prices, which may be at a premium or discount to a fund's NAV.

[3]Non-redeemable investment funds typically issue a finite number of units or shares on an initial public offering, following which the units or shares are generally traded on an exchange at prevailing market prices, which may be at a premium or discount to NAV. They may offer the opportunity to redeem on an infrequent basis at a price based on the fund's NAV. See footnote 8 for details.

[4]Source: Investor Economics.

The Modernization Project is a continuation of the CSA's efforts to regulate comparable publicly offered investment fund products in a similar manner.[5] Most recently, the CSA indicated that as part of the final stage of implementation of the point of sale disclosure proposals, we will consider point of sale disclosure requirements for other types of publicly offered investment funds, not just open-end mutual funds.[6] We anticipate that our work on the Modernization Project may inform this effort.

We are carrying out the Modernization Project in two phases.

Status of Modernization Project — Phase 1

On June 25, 2010, the CSA published amendments to NI 81-102, as well as related consequential amendments (together, the Phase 1 Amendments), for a 90-day comment period.

The Phase 1 Amendments focus primarily on publicly offered "mutual funds", as defined under Canadian securities legislation. Open-end mutual funds and exchange-traded mutual funds are "mutual funds" as each of them have a redemption feature that "*entitles the holder to receive on demand, or within a specified period after demand, an amount computed by reference to the value of a proportionate interest in the whole or in the part of the net assets*"[7]. The Phase 1 Amendments propose to codify exemptive relief that has frequently been granted by the CSA to recognize market and product developments, particularly the proliferation of exchange-traded mutual funds. The Phase 1 Amendments are also intended to keep pace with developing global standards in mutual fund product regulation. This includes updates to the requirements related to money market funds.

The comment period for the Phase 1 Amendments ended on September 24, 2010. We received 24 comment letters. Subject to any material changes being made to the Phase 1 Amendments, the CSA anticipate publishing the amendments in final form by late summer 2011.

Status of Modernization Project — Phase 2

While work is underway to finalize the Phase 1 Amendments, we are beginning work on Phase 2 of the Modernization Project. The CSA's objective in Phase 2 is to identify and address any market efficiency, investor protection or fairness issues that arise out of the differing regulatory regimes that apply to different types of publicly offered investment funds. Our aim in Phase 2 is to reduce the potential for regulatory arbitrage that may exist within the current regulatory framework.

The CSA propose to proceed with Phase 2 of the Modernization Project in stages, as described below. A staged approach will allow us the opportunity to focus first on investor protection and fairness concerns we have identified that arise out of the lack of an operational rule for non-redeemable investment funds.

Phase 2 — Stage 1 Proposal

As securities of non-redeemable investment funds are not redeemable on demand based on net asset value, these funds are generally not considered by the CSA to be "mutual funds" under securities legislation and are accordingly not subject to the operational requirements of NI 81-102.[8] These operational provisions include important self-dealing restrictions intended to protect mutual fund investors from transactions that may place the fund manager's interests ahead of theirs, and voting rights which enable investors to vote on proposed fundamental changes to the fund. In our view, securityholders of non-redeemable investment funds should similarly have these basic protections. While the structure and operations of mutual funds and non-redeemable investment funds may vary, both types of funds are fundamentally the same as they each offer investors the benefits of pooled investing and portfolio management services. We think this common primary purpose of investing money provided by their securityholders necessitates that both types of funds equally follow certain core investor protection and fairness principles.

We have begun to consider adopting certain core restrictions and operational requirements analogous to those in NI 81-102 for non-redeemable investment funds, to address certain investor protection and fairness concerns we have identified. Among these concerns are: protecting investors from transactions that give rise to a conflict of interest; providing investors with the opportunity to vote on important changes that may impact the investment fund and its investors; ensuring the proper safeguarding of the investment fund's assets; and, potentially, some core investment restrictions. We anticipate that a proposed new stand-alone rule will be published for comment in early 2012.

Phase 2 — Stage 2 Proposal

In the second stage of Phase 2 of the Modernization Project, we propose to re-examine the investment restrictions applicable to open-end mutual funds and exchange-traded mutual funds under Part 2 of NI 81-102 to assess what, if any, changes should be made in recognition of market and product developments.

Increasingly, open-end mutual funds and exchange-traded mutual funds have sought more flexibility to make certain investments and employ strategies not currently permitted under NI 81-102, such as investments in physical commodities and new derivatives strategies. We propose to consider in the second stage of Phase 2 whether it would be beneficial to investors if certain investment restrictions in NI 81-102 were

---

[5] National Instrument 81-106 *Investment Fund Continuous Disclosure* (June, 2005) and National Instrument 81-107 *Independent Review Committee for Investment Funds* (November, 2006) apply to all types of retail investment funds.

[6] See CSA Staff Notice 81-319 — *Status Report on the Implementation of Point of Sale Disclosure for Mutual Funds* (2010) 33 OSCB 5449, at page 5450.

[7] See definition of "mutual fund" in s. 1(1) of the *Securities Act* (Ontario) and similar definitions in the respective *Securities Acts* of the CSA jurisdictions.

[8] Non-redeemable investment funds listed on stock exchanges may, on an infrequent basis, offer the ability to redeem at a price based on NAV. The CSA generally take the view that where this redemption opportunity arises more frequently than once per year (e.g. monthly or quarterly), the fund provides a regular redemption feature and is therefore considered to be a "mutual fund" subject to the requirements of NI 81-102. Where however this redemption opportunity arises no more frequently than once per year, the fund is not considered a "mutual fund" and escapes the application of NI 81-102.

loosened. Relaxing certain investment restrictions may also achieve a more fair and consistent regulatory framework across all investment fund products. At the same time, informed by past experience and recent market events, we will also consider whether additional investment restrictions on mutual funds are needed to further reduce product and market risks and to ensure a mutual fund's ability to satisfy redemptions on demand. We anticipate we may also during this stage consider requirements or restrictions for non-redeemable investment funds that are in addition to those we are initially proposing in the first stage of Phase 2. We anticipate publishing for comment any proposed amendments in 2013.

Specific Issues for Consideration on the Modernization Project — Phase 2

In the first stage of Phase 2, we propose to introduce a new stand-alone rule that would apply only to non-redeemable investment funds. We anticipate that the rule will initially impose certain core restrictions and operational requirements on non-redeemable investment funds that will promote the investor protection and fairness principles we think should apply to all types of publicly offered investment funds. Among the requirements the CSA have identified are:

- *Conflict of interest provisions* to prohibit certain self-dealing transactions between the non-redeemable investment fund and its manager, trustee or portfolio advisor, and to restrict certain investments in related persons or companies.

    These could be similar to the restrictions that apply to mutual funds under Part 4 of NI 81-102 and under the mutual fund conflict of interest provisions in the Securities Acts of the various CSA jurisdictions. In some jurisdictions, consideration will be given to recommending amendments to the Securities Acts that would implement, or facilitate the implementation of, these requirements;

- *Securityholder and regulatory approval requirements* for specified fundamental changes to the non-redeemable investment fund (e.g. change of investment objective, merger with another fund, increase in fees, etc.) and to the management of the fund. These could be similar to the requirements for mutual funds in Part 5 of NI 81-102; and

- *Custodianship requirements* designed to ensure that the assets of the non-redeemable investment fund are sufficiently safeguarded.

    Currently, custodianship requirements for non-redeemable investment funds are set out in Part 14 of NI 41-101 — *General Prospectus Requirements* (NI 41-101). The CSA propose to move these requirements out of NI 41-101 and into the stand-alone rule for non-redeemable investment funds.

The introduction of the above minimum requirements for non-redeemable investment funds will extend key protections and rights to investors in these funds that are currently available only to investors in retail open-end mutual funds and exchange-traded mutual funds.

Specifically, restrictions on self-dealing and related-party transactions for non-redeemable investment funds would mandate consistent treatment of these types of transactions under securities legislation by all types of retail investment funds. This would result in fund managers of non-redeemable investment funds being required to seek regulatory and/or independent review committee approval under NI 81-107 *Independent Review Committee for Investment Funds* to engage in these types of transactions, as is already required of fund managers of retail mutual funds.

The requirements would further ensure that investors of non-redeemable investment funds have consistent and guaranteed voting rights on important changes that may impact the investment fund or its management.

Finally, the requirements would ensure that all non-redeemable investment funds comply with the custodianship requirements, not just those who filed a prospectus under NI 41-101 since the coming into force of that rule in 2008.

[Request for Comment portion of notice omitted]

CSA Staff Notice 81-323 — Status Report on Consultation under CSA Discussion Paper and Request for Comment 81-407 — *Mutual Fund Fees*

Date: December 17, 2013

36 O.S.C.B. 11989

[Not reproduced]

CSA Notice and Request for Comment 81-324 — Proposed CSA Mutual Fund Risk Classification Methodology for Use in Fund Facts

Date: December 12, 2013

36 O.S.C.B. 11849

[Not reproduced]

CSA Staff Notice 81-325 — Status Report on Consultation under CSA Notice 81-324 and Request for Comment on Proposed CSA Mutual Fund Risk Classification Methodology for Use in Fund Facts

Date: January 29, 2015

38 O.S.C.B. 767

[Not reproduced]

CSA Staff Notice 81-326 — Update on an Alternative Funds Framework for Investment Funds

Date: **February 12, 2015**

38 O.S.C.B. 1297

[Not reproduced]

OSC Rule 81-501 — Mutual Fund Reinvestment Plans

[Revoked by Rule 45-802]

Final Rule: (1997) 20 O.S.C.B. 5163; Approval by OSC: (1997) 20 O.S.C.B. 4051; Request for Comments: (1996) 19 O.S.C.B. 2795 and (1997) 20 O.S.C.B. 811. Replaced two rules which were originally blanket rulings (1983) 6 O.S.C.B. 1078 and (1985) 8 O.S.C.B. 4308, which were deemed to be rules entitled *In the Matter of the Automatic Reinvestment of Dividends or Distributions in Shares or Units of Mutual Funds* (1997) 20 O.S.C.B. 1220 and *In the Matter of Mandatory Investment of Dividends in Shares or Units of Mutual Funds* (1997) 20 O.S.C.B. 1220.

OSC Staff Notice 81-704 — Limited Powers of Attorney and Letters of Authorization Used in the Sale of Mutual Funds

Date: **August 4, 2000**

23 O.S.C.B. 5269

Introduction

The purpose of this Notice is to communicate the views of the staff of the Ontario Securities Commission (the "staff") on the use of powers of attorney, letters of authorization or trading authorizations (collectively "powers of attorney") by dealers and their sales representatives in the purchase and redemption of mutual fund securities.

Background

A large number of mutual fund securities are registered in the security registers of mutual funds in client name. Mutual fund companies must look to the registered unitholder (i.e. the investor) for instructions to execute a trade. Hence, where a dealer submits an order on behalf of its client, mutual fund companies should require that dealers provide instructions bearing the client's signature for each trade before processing a trade in client name. At the same time, staff understand the impracticalities for dealers in obtaining a client's signature for every trade. Mutual fund companies have informed staff that they will accept a power of attorney signed by a client which authorizes the client's dealer to request trades on behalf of the client.

National Instrument 81-102 — Mutual Funds prohibits a mutual fund from paying redemption proceeds prior to the receipt by the mutual fund of a written request for redemption from the securityholder. A written request is not required, however, if alternative "arrangements" are made between the mutual fund and the securityholder. The mutual fund industry typically accepts powers of attorney signed by clients of dealers. These powers of attorney purport to give dealers authority to purchase and redeem the clients' securities, and as such, many industry participants view them as an acceptable alternative "arrangement".

Issues of Concern

Staff have serious concerns about the scope and form of powers of attorney which dealers and their sales representatives commonly obtain from their clients. Staff compliance examinations of the operations of both dealers and fund managers have revealed that many powers of attorney confer unlimited powers on dealers and their representatives that are not permitted by their category of registration. These unlimited powers of attorney may permit a dealer's representatives to place trades without having received specific prior instructions from the client. Staff concerns about the ability to conduct discretionary trading are heightened where there is little or no supervision by a dealer of its representatives. When dealers fail to supervise the use of powers of attorney carefully, there is a much greater risk that inappropriate uses of such powers of attorney will not be prevented or detected.

Staff are concerned about how these powers of attorney are presented to clients and question whether clients understand the contents of the documents and the inherent risks involved in executing unlimited powers of attorney.

Recommendations

Staff recommend that dealers and their representatives discontinue the use of powers of attorney that confer unlimited authority and discretion over their clients' accounts.

In order to ensure appropriate use of powers of attorney, staff recommend that dealers develop a standard document or form of power of attorney that:

- clearly states the name of the dealer, as well as the name of the specified representative;

- provides for the signature of a designated partner, director, officer or branch manager of the dealer whereby that designated individual indicates approval and acceptance of the power of attorney;

- provides for the dealer representative's signature;

- states that the power of attorney will terminate if and when the specified representative leaves the employment of the dealer;

- clearly states that the power of attorney is limited to trading in mutual funds and that the dealer's representative must obtain prior specific consent from the client for each trade;

- clearly states that the dealer's representative is limited to providing investment recommendations and executing the client's trading orders, and that he or she may not make any decision to buy or sell mutual fund securities on behalf of the client; and

- is labelled in such a way that it clearly conveys the limited scope and power given by the client to the dealer and representative. Acceptable titles include "Limited Power of Attorney" or "Letter of Authorization".

Staff recommend that a dealer have legal counsel review the document to ensure that it does not grant to the dealer and the dealer's representatives discretionary authority over a client's account.

Staff also recommend that a dealer set up control procedures to monitor the use of powers of attorney. Recommended procedures include:

- attaching a copy of the limited power of attorney to each trade order form and indicating the original copy of the power of attorney is on the dealer's file (this will help to ensure that the branch manager, head office and the mutual fund company are aware of the authorization);

- keeping a copy of the power of attorney document on the dealer representative's file and at head office of the dealer;

- appropriate client signature verification procedures;

- procedures to record and retain, whether electronically or manually, specific oral or written trade instructions received from clients and for the dealer to regularly assess the adequacy of documented instructions;

- procedures to identify client accounts where limited powers of attorney have been granted;

- ensuring that branch managers and head office carry out supervision on these accounts on a regular basis prior to executing a trade, or within a reasonable time after executing a trade, to ensure that all transactions are performed according to clients' prior and specific instructions, and in accordance with clients' investment objectives;

- procedures to ensure clients receive a confirmation of every trade directly from the mutual fund company or from the dealer's head office; and

- documenting in writing the control procedures in a policies and procedures manual made available to representatives.

OSC Staff Notice 81-705 — Implementation of a Continuous Disclosure Review Program for Investment Funds — Investment Funds Branch

Date: February 28, 2003

26 O.S.C.B. 1757

The Investment Funds Branch (the "Branch") at the Ontario Securities Commission ("OSC") is responsible for administering regulation of all investment funds. Investment funds include mutual funds, non-redeemable investment funds (defined in OSC Rule 14-501), exchange-traded funds, split share corporations, labour sponsored funds, commodity pools and scholarship plans.

The Branch currently has 14 members including lawyers, accountants, review officers and support staff.

One of the goals of the Branch is to improve continuous disclosure documents for the benefit of investment fund investors. To this end, the Branch published proposed National Instrument 81-106 — Investment Fund Continuous Disclosure on September 20, 2002. As a next step, the Branch will introduce a continuous disclosure review program for all investment funds ("CD Review Program") in March 2003. The purpose of this Notice is to communicate the general features of the CD Review Program.

In addition to monitoring investment funds for timely and complete disclosure of information, the CD Review Program will be used to monitor how investment funds are being managed. This will include checking for compliance with Ontario securities law and how an investment fund is being managed compared to the investment objective and strategies disclosed in the fund's prospectus.

Types of Review

Investment funds will be subject to either a full, issue-oriented or basic review based on selective review criteria. Like the selective review approach to prospectus review, the responsibility for full compliance with applicable securities legislation, policies and practices remains with the investment funds and their managers. The fact that an investment fund has not been selected for review in a given year in no way detracts from such responsibility.

Full Review

A full review would typically include a comprehensive examination of the investment fund's entire disclosure record including financial statements for a minimum of the past two years. In addition to all the prescribed regulatory filings, staff may review other materials that are aimed at investors, such as the fund manager's website and newsletters.

Issue Oriented Review

An issue-oriented review focuses on particular issues. Some of these issues may include valuation, compliance with investment objectives, compliance with conditions of orders (e.g. conflict of interest orders) and incentive fee disclosure.

Basic Review

A basic review ensures all required continuous disclosure documents have been filed in accordance with the requirements of Ontario securities law.

How will investment funds be selected for review?

The CD Review Program will focus on those investment funds whose principal jurisdiction is Ontario.

Investment funds will be selected for review primarily through a risk-based approach. A random selection basis will also be used from time to time to supplement the risk-based selection. Since the selection process is primarily risk-based, some investment funds may be reviewed more frequently than others.

The continuous disclosure review criteria are likely to change frequently as certain disclosure related issues gain greater prominence or as questions are raised about particular accounting issues or disclosure practices.

We do not propose to review all the funds in a fund family unless there is reason to believe that the risks are more widespread. Rather, we intend to select a sample of funds from within a fund family based on our risk assessment.

The following is the current list of continuous disclosure review criteria:

1. Investment Fund's Financial Condition or Results
   - The investment fund is experiencing financial difficulty, as indicated by high net redemptions, few liquid assets, high concentration of assets and other financial indicators.
   - The investment fund has recently restated or corrected prior years' financial results (e.g., due to a NAV correction).
   - The investment fund is not complying with its stated investment objective.
   - The investment objective results in significant exposure to small issuers, high-yield (low-grade) bonds.
   - The investment fund has investment objectives and strategies akin to a hedge fund.

2. Accounting Methods and Practices
   - The investment fund has completed transactions where the accounting treatment is unclear or where staff is aware of divergent views as to accounting practice.

3. Auditor Related Issues
   - The auditors' report includes a qualified opinion, non-standard wording or missing information.
   - The auditor is terminated or resigns, and the investment fund has disclosed a disagreement, unresolved issue or consultation as described in National Policy Statement 31.
   - Previous experience or information available to staff indicates that the investment fund, its auditor or a particular director or officer of the investment fund or the fund manager warrants additional scrutiny.

4. Prior Regulatory Scrutiny
   - The investment fund or the fund complex has not recently been the subject of a CD Review by staff of the OSC or another provincial securities regulator.
   - The investment fund or fund complex has a history of prior defaults or prior non-compliance with securities requirements.
   - Another branch of the Commission, or another regulator, has referred a matter to the attention of the Investment Funds Branch.
   - Public complaints, media reports, staff observations or other credible sources indicate that disclosure issues may exist.

What is a Continuous Disclosure Review process?

The following outlines how a typical review would be performed:
- Each review begins with a "desk review". In a desk review, staff will review all relevant filings to identify potential issues that would require additional investigation. During a desk review, the fund will not usually be contacted. If no issue is identified, the review is completed. Essentially, the CD Review Program will not impose cost or resource demands on investment funds that meet all of their regulatory obligations and are managed according to their prospectus disclosure and other representations.

- If the desk review has identified certain issues, then additional information may be requested for further investigation. A letter would be sent to the investment fund advising that it had been selected for a CD Review. The letter would also outline what information is being requested. We expect the investment funds to provide their response within a specified time frame. Please note that a comprehensive, complete response will allow the Investment Funds Branch to complete the CD review in an effective and timely manner and reduce the amount of follow up work. If necessary, additional comment letters would follow.

How will issues identified in a CD Review be resolved?

Staff will work with the investment fund to resolve issues in a timely manner. Staff will be aggressive in pursuing matters arising from continuous disclosure reviews and in enforcing the requirements of Ontario securities law through all available means. The Investment Funds Branch works closely with the Enforcement Branch when determining the type of regulatory action necessary if staff believes an investment fund has breached Ontario securities law.

What is the impact to the investment funds prospectus review criteria?

The Investment Funds Branch will continue its selective review of prospectus filings. When necessary and appropriate, staff will co-ordinate its work on the two review programs to improve effectiveness and efficiency.

Communication with the industry

At least annually, the Branch will publish the findings of its CD Review Program.

Policies and Orders: OSCN 81-709, 33-733.

OSC Staff Notice 81-706 — Treatment of Sales Commissions in the Calculation of Net Asset Value of Labour Sponsored Investment Funds

Date: September 30, 2003
26 O.S.C.B. 6707

The purpose of this Staff Notice is to set out staff's views on the implications for net asset value calculations for purchases and redemptions of shares (Pricing NAV) by labour sponsored investment funds (LSIFs) of a change in the accounting for sales commissions paid out of an LSIF's assets.

Facts

For the past 10 years LSIFs have been permitted to pay sales commissions out of fund assets. The Commission since 1999 has granted specific exemptive relief from National Instrument 81-105 Mutual Fund Sales Practices to this effect.

The practice of many LSIFs has been to record sales commissions paid out of fund assets as an asset (deferred charge) on a fund's statement of net assets and to amortize this amount to retained earnings on a straight line basis over 8 years. The amortization period matches the period for which an investor is required to hold the related shares in order to avoid being required to repay associated tax credits and to avoid paying a redemption fee.

In July 2003 the Accounting Standards Board of the CICA issued a new Handbook Section, Generally Accepted Accounting Principles, Section 1100, effective for financial years beginning on or after October 1, 2003. This Handbook section clarifies the basis on which an entity determines the appropriate accounting for a transaction in the absence of specific recommendations in the CICA Handbook. In particular, the revised definition of generally accepted accounting principles (GAAP) indicates that accounting practices cannot be considered to comply with GAAP by virtue of their use in similar circumstances by a significant number of entities in Canada. In other words, industry practice on its own will not meet the definition of GAAP. LSIFs have relied on industry practice to treat sales commissions as a deferred charge.

The result of this Handbook change is that, for financial years beginning on or after October 1, 2003, the LSIF industry will no longer be able to treat the sales commissions paid by the fund as an asset on their statement of net assets.

Issue

Generally, the calculation of the Pricing NAV has been set out in each LSIF's prospectus. Without being explicitly stated, the Pricing NAV has typically been determined on a basis that is consistent with GAAP. An LSIF that continues, after this accounting change, to calculate its Pricing NAV in accordance with the basis set out in the prospectus will have a Pricing NAV that is different from the net asset value (NAV) determined by reference to the financial statements.

Staff Position

It is intended that proposed National Instrument 81-106 Investment Fund Continuous Disclosure (NI 81-106), which will be published for a second comment period later this year, will require Pricing NAV for all investment funds, including LSIFs, to be calculated in accordance with GAAP. The expected effective date for proposed NI 81-106 is July 1, 2004.

For transitional purposes only, NI 81-106 will propose limited exemptive relief from the proposed requirement to calculate Pricing NAV in accordance with GAAP to LSIFs that cease adding new sales commissions to the existing deferred charge by December 31, 2003. Relief will be limited to allowing Pricing NAV to be determined on the basis that the deferred charge existing at December 31, 2003 will continue to be amortized over its remaining amortization period. It is expected that all other elements of the calculation of the Pricing NAV will be in accordance with GAAP.

The implication of staff's position is that, for a period of up to 8 years, the Pricing NAV for those LSIFs that are granted exemptive relief will differ from the NAV in the financial statements prepared in accordance with GAAP. However, the relief proposed will limit the amount of that difference. LSIFs that follow this transitional method will be required to provide in the notes to their financial statements a reconciliation between the NAV calculated for financial statement purposes and the Pricing NAV.

Staff expect LSIFs to inform existing and new investors of the changes to the accounting for sales commissions paid out of fund assets and the impact of this change on the fund and investors.

OSC Staff Notice 81-708 — Model Portfolios of Mutual Funds

Date: May 26, 2006
29 O.S.C.B. 4295

Please refer to MRRS Decision Documents *In the Matter of Royal Mutual Funds Inc.*, *In the Matter of RBC Asset Management Inc.*, and *In the Matter of Royal Mutual Funds Inc.* (the *Decision Documents*), which are published in today's bulletin.

Overview

This notice addresses the issues raised in the Decision Documents for certain mutual fund dealers, investment counsels and portfolio managers (*IC/PMs*), and mutual fund managers conducting registerable activity in Ontario.

The intention of this notice is to provide guidance about exemptions required by market participants planning to introduce products and services in situations similar to those described in the Decision Documents.

The relevant fact situations

The Decision Documents provide exemptive relief for two firms: one firm is both an IC/PM and a fund manager (*IC/PM-Fund Manager*). The IC/PM Fund Manager makes decisions about rebalancing changes in model portfolios of mutual funds, including changes within pre-determined parameters as well as replacing existing funds with new funds. It also trades to carry out these rebalancing decisions made in its discretion. The other firm is an affiliated mutual fund dealer that sells these model portfolio products. A mutual fund dealer selling a model portfolio product that involves a separate IC/PM and fund manager would be in a similar situation.

Staff consider that the rebalancing activity undertaken by the IC/PM is discretionary management that affects the client's holdings directly. It is as though the IC/PM is advising the client directly, through its own actions as passed on through the mutual fund dealer. This situation differs from a fund of funds, where discretionary activity carried out in the top fund affects only that fund, and not the actual holdings in a client's account.

The mutual fund dealer through which the model portfolio product is sold to clients is therefore considered to be providing discretionary management to the client. This activity is not permitted for a mutual fund dealer without an exemption from the adviser registration requirement.

The IC/PM-Fund Manager in the Decision Documents carries out trades in units of the funds in each model portfolio that it decides in its discretion are appropriate, as authorised by the account opening agreement between the client and the mutual fund dealer. An IC/PM-Fund Manager in this situation usually holds no mutual fund dealer registration, to comply with MFDA rules.

Similar to the fact situation in the Decision Documents, if an IC/PM-Fund Manager trades to implement decisions made in its discretionary authority, it is required to be registered as a dealer in an appropriate category or obtain exemptive relief from the dealer registration requirements. This particular trading activity is not considered incidental to the IC/PM-Fund Manager's adviser registration.

Disclosure about model portfolio products

Existing disclosure

Model portfolio products are not offered as separately qualified funds under a prospectus, like a fund of funds. Model portfolio products are generally described in a prospectus as a service. More specific details about the model portfolio product are usually found in the account opening documentation.

It is clear that disclosure is an important element in selling model portfolio products. While considering the applications for exemptive relief that resulted in the Decision Documents, staff consulted with members of the mutual fund industry and reviewed the prospectus and account opening documentation for numerous model portfolio products to learn more about products already in the marketplace.

Staff found that direct discretionary management of the client's investment is often involved in these model portfolio products, to varying degrees. The requirement to describe the model portfolio products is not particularly specific, and the result is that descriptions in both prospectuses and account opening documentation vary significantly, from very good to very unclear. Staff also found that some descriptions were quite detailed, while others were not; these differences made it impossible to compare the model portfolio products.

Disclosure expectations

Prospectuses that describe model portfolio products like those in the Decision Documents are expected at a minimum to include the following:

- clear description of the model portfolio product

- clear description of the number of model portfolios, including how many portfolios are offered, the types of portfolios offered (such as growth, income, or balanced), and the fact that the portfolios consist of funds of the fund manager

- clear explanation of how the model portfolios are designed and who is involved in designing them

- clear explanation of the how investment ranges are established, how re-balancing occurs, and whether new funds may be substituted in the model portfolios

- the minimum amount required to invest in the model portfolio product

- the fees associated with the model portfolio product, including the basis on which they are charged and how they are paid

- clear description of reinvestments of distributions

- where to get more information and how to sign up for the model portfolio product

The account opening documentation is typically generated by the fund manager, and it contains details about the model portfolio products such as fees as well as information specific to the client. To help investors better understand model portfolio products, staff expect that fund managers will ensure their account opening documentation fully describes their model portfolio products. In addition to the information included in the prospectus, the account opening documentation should include at a minimum:

- clear description of all fees payable, including the services for which the fees are to be paid, and the compensation received by each of the entities that are involved

- clear description of what discretionary authority is exercised, how it is exercised, and by which entity

- clear description of when client consent is required for an action

- clear description of the entity or entities legally responsible to the investor for any liabilities concerning the model portfolio product

OSC Staff Notice 81-709 — Report on Staff's Continuous Disclosure Review of Investment Funds (2008)

Date: May 29, 2008
31 O.S.C.B. 5381

1. — Purpose

This notice summarizes the findings and comments as at March 31, 2008, arising from the Continuous Disclosure Review Program conducted by the Investment Funds Branch (the Branch) of the Ontario Securities Commission (OSC).

Continuous disclosure review has been an important element of our approach to securities regulation and aims to improve disclosure available to investors. In 2003, the Branch set out a framework for the continuous disclosure review of investment funds in OSC Staff Notice 81-705 *Implementation of a Continuous Disclosure Review Program for Investment Funds — Investment Funds Branch* (Staff Notice 81-705). The purpose of that notice was to communicate general features of the Continuous Disclosure Review Program.

Following the publication of Staff Notice 81-705, the Branch developed continuous disclosure rules specific to investment funds. The result was National Instrument 81-106 *Investment Fund Continuous Disclosure* (NI 81-106) which came into force on June 1, 2005. Subsequently, we conducted an issue-oriented review of general compliance with NI 81-106. This notice focuses on issues identified in the course of the review, aiming to assist preparers of financial statements and management reports of fund performance (MRFP) in improving their future continuous disclosure.

2. — Scope of Review

NI 81-106 sets out the requirements for:

- financial statements and MRFPs;

- quarterly portfolio disclosure;

- annual information forms (for funds not subject to National Instrument 81-101 *Mutual Fund Prospectus Disclosure*); and

- proxy voting records.

Our review focused on these requirements and the investment fund's public disclosure record including the fund manager's website and all prescribed regulatory filings on SEDAR. Our review predominantly covered financial year-ends in 2005 and 2006, but also captured some periods ending in 2007.

We reviewed a sample of investment funds and sent comment letters to fund managers who, in aggregate, manage approximately 45% of the industry's assets under management. We focused on conventional mutual funds because they are the investment vehicle of choice for most Canadian investors. Although our findings are mainly based on the review of disclosure of conventional mutual funds, other investment funds such as closed-end and exchange traded funds will also benefit from this notice, and its guidance can be applied to their continuous disclosure.

3. — Executive Summary

We noted the following areas for improvement which are discussed in more detail in the body of the notice.

Quality of the discussion

- *Results of operations.* Management's discussion of the investment fund's activities in the results of operations section should be more thorough and analyze and explain the nature of and reasons for changes in the fund.

- *Broad-based index.* Discussion of the relative performance of the investment fund as compared to a broad-based securities market index is required and cannot be replaced by a comparison to a narrow index or blended benchmark.

- *Discussion of relative performance.* A more thorough discussion of why the investment fund under- or over-performed the index should be provided.

Overall presentation

- *Plain language.* MRFPs should be written in plain language and avoid the use of jargon and technical language.

- *Investment subgroups.* Management should review the investment portfolio to determine if the most appropriate categories have been used when disclosing the summary of investment portfolio in the MRFP or quarterly portfolio disclosure, and whether the breakdown conveys the nature of the fund to readers.

- *Analytical review of financial statements.* Management should perform an analytical review of the financial statements to ensure that all significant changes have been explained in the results of operations.

- *Financial statement notes presentation.* Notes to the financial statements are part of continuous disclosure and should not be convoluted with inapplicable information.

Regulatory compliance

- *Commissions to related parties.* Unless exemptive relief has been obtained, a monthly report must be filed when a fund pays a fee to a related company on a purchase or sale of portfolio securities.

- *Financial highlights tables.* The format specified in Form 81-106F1 (the Form) for financial highlights and past performance is mandated.

- *Annual compound returns.* Certain information must be discussed including the performance of all series and changes in an index from the prior period. Discussion of past performance should be limited to the standard performance periods.

- *Mandatory notes to financial statements.* Certain information must be disclosed in the notes to the financial statements to provide consistent and comparable financial statements.

4. — Quality of the Discussion

4.1 — Results of Operations

The summary of results of operations in the MRFP is an area that requires more attention. The intent of the summary is to put the financial statements into words and provide context for the financial results. Part B, subsection 2.3(1) of the Form requires that the results of operations include a discussion of changes to an investment fund. The list in subsection 2.3(1) addresses changes in portfolio assets, revenue and expenses, and redemptions or sales which correspond to data in the financial statements and can be found specifically in the statement of net assets, statement of investment portfolio, statement of operations, and statement of changes in net assets. The list also covers changes to the economy and markets, and requires that these factors be related back to changes in the composition of the investment portfolio.

In our review, we found that approximately 40% of investment funds selected had financial statements that revealed significant changes in the fund which were not discussed in the results of operations section of the MRFP. Examples of significant changes over the prior year included: an increase in redemptions by 81%; custodian fees that tripled; and an 11% increase in the holdings of a specific sector. In response to our comment letters, fund managers were able to address our questions with comprehensive and insightful explanations. Most fund managers stated that they did not include such explanations because they did not believe that the information fell within the requirements of subsection 2.3(1), or the discussion was not warranted because it did not add useful information pertaining to the investor's investment.

While discussion and analysis of every financial statement item may not be warranted, we expect that the results of operations will focus on significant changes in the fund over the financial period and discuss the reasons for the changes. We remind preparers to review the list of items in subsection 2.3(1). Generally, these items are material and must be discussed in the summary of the results of operations, as applicable.

We also found that 25% of investment funds disclosed significant changes but provided very little explanation or analysis. For example, we expect a fund to discuss why expenses increased, rather than simply stating that expenses were higher. As explained in the Form, the management discussion of fund performance (which includes the results of operations) "provides the manager of an investment fund with the opportunity to discuss the investment fund's position and financial results for the relevant period. The discussion is intended to give a reader the ability to look at the investment fund through the eyes of management by providing both a historical and prospective analysis of the investment activities and operations of the investment fund. Coupled with the financial highlights, this information should enable readers to better assess the investment fund's performance and future prospects." In response to our comment letters, investment funds provided us with disclosure that should have been included in the results of operations. We expect such information to be discussed in the MRFP, enabling readers to look through the eyes of management.

4.2 — Annual Compound Returns

(a) — Broad-based securities market index

Approximately 65% of fund managers did not compare the relative performance of an investment fund to a broad-based securities market index. We remind preparers that the discussion of the relative performance of an investment fund as compared to a broad-based securities market index is a requirement under Part B, subsection 4.3(3) of the Form. Please note that instruction (3) to section 4.3 states that a narrowly-based securities index or a blended index may be used in addition to a broad-based securities market index. Neither a narrowly-based index or a blended index can be a substitute for the broad-based index.

Some investment funds only provided a discussion of the fund's performance relative to a narrowly-based securities index. One fund manager explained this decision by citing concerns that the comparison of an investment fund's performance to a broad-based index would not be fully appreciated by investors. We believe that investors are more likely to understand the broad-based index as it is more widely recognized than a narrow index. A comparison to the broad-based index will help readers understand the fund's performance relative to the movement of the market more generally. In the MRFP, a fund manager has the opportunity to explain variances between the fund's performance and the general market, which may be caused by factors such as different sector exposure, and there is always the option of expanding the discussion by adding a comparison to a narrowly-based index.

(b) — Discussion of relative performance

Some investment funds should have provided a more thorough discussion of the relative performance of the investment fund as compared to the appropriate index. This issue was raised with 75% of fund managers. We do not believe simply stating that the fund under- or over-performed relative to the index is a suitable discussion. Instead, we expect an explanation as to why the fund under- or over-performed relative to the index.

Often, we saw disclosure that a fund's performance was due to over- and under-weight portfolio allocations. Investment funds should consider using percentages and quantitative measures when discussing over- and under-weight portfolio allocations; otherwise, based on the disclosure provided, the reader has no sense of the magnitude of the over- or under-weight positions in various industry sectors or countries.

(c) — Discussion of past performance

While we have not taken issue with the discussion of an investment fund's performance relative to an index appearing in the results of operations section rather than the annual compound returns section of the MRFP, we remind preparers that all rules relating to past performance in Part B, item 4 of the Form must still be applied. In one example, the results of operations discussed the performance of a narrow index which was not disclosed in the annual compound returns table. If a discussion of past performance is included elsewhere in the MRFP, all rules governing the disclosure of past performance still apply, such as providing disclosure only for standard performance periods.

5. — Overall Presentation

5.1 — Plain Language

We remind investment funds of the requirement to use plain language, which is stated in the beginning of the Form. We noted the use of jargon and technical language in the management discussion of fund performance. Some examples include:

- "off-index allocations"
- "duration positioning"
- "fundamental bottom-up strategy with a top down country overlay".

We believe that plain language will help investors understand an investment fund's disclosure documents so that they can make informed investment decisions. We strongly encourage investment funds to communicate as simply and directly as possible.

5.2 — Summary of Investment Portfolio

In our view, 17% of investment funds did not break down their investment portfolio into appropriate subgroups in the summary of investment portfolio, as required by Part B, paragraph 5(2)(a) of the Form. The instructions in this section state that an investment fund should use the most appropriate categories given the nature of the fund. An investment fund may use more than one breakdown, such as by security type, industry, or geographical locations, so as to provide the most meaningful information.

We reviewed a precious metals fund with the majority of its assets invested in Canada that provided a geographic breakdown of the investment portfolio. A breakdown by precious metals and precious metals activities would have been more meaningful given the nature of the fund, as opposed to a breakdown by geography.

We also raised a comment if we felt that one subgroup was too generic and obvious. For example, we saw over 40% of one fund classified as "Other" and 75% of another fund labelled as "Income Funds". In such cases, we do not believe that the disclosure is meaningful nor does it provide the reader with additional information.

5.3 — Analytical Review

As discussed earlier in this notice, the management discussion of fund performance is an analysis and explanation designed to complement and supplement an investment fund's financial statements. Management should perform an analytical review of the financial statements to ensure that the management discussion of fund performance is complete and explains the significant changes of the fund or any unusual events. In our review of financial statements, we found significant changes that were not addressed in management's discussion. By performing an analytical review, it is likely that most items required to be discussed in the results of operations (Part B, subsection 2.3(1) of the Form) are identified.

5.4 — Financial Statement Notes Presentation

For two fund managers, certain notes to the financial statements were unrelated to the investment funds included in the bound document. One set of notes had been prepared for all the funds managed by the fund manager, but the financial statements were bound in different sets. As a result, some information in the notes related to investment funds that were not included in the particular set of financial statements. For example, the notes contained information on management fee changes, performance and incentive fees, and fund windups for individual funds regardless of whether those funds were included in that set of financial statements.

Inclusion of notes that do not relate to investment funds in the document is confusing. While subsection 7.1(2) of NI 81-106 allows notes to the financial statements to be combined when financial statements of investment funds are bound together in a document, in our view, notes should only be included if they actually relate to the investment funds in the document. Notes to the financial statements are part of continuous disclosure and should not be convoluted. We do not believe that it is appropriate to create one set of notes for the whole fund complex that is then attached to every set of financial statements without being modified for relevance. We remind preparers to review all notes to determine those relevant to the investment funds in the document.

5.5 — Websites

We found that approximately 40% of fund managers did not provide easily accessible links to continuous disclosure documents on their websites. In one example, a link to the fund prospectus was available on the fund manager's website but not given much prominence. In another example, the financial statements, MRFPs, proxy voting records, and quarterly portfolio disclosure were not easily accessible from the fund's webpage as they were posted under a menu option that did not seem to relate to these documents. We also found that in some cases excessive drilling down was required to reach documents. In these situations, we raised comments asking that the fund manager consider adding more intuitive links to the fund's disclosure documents on their website.

Since NI 81-106 removed mandatory delivery of continuous disclosure documents to all unitholders, access to these documents by alternative methods should be made as simple as possible. Unitholders may not wish to receive paper copies of financial statements and MRFPs in the mail because they are opting to find this information online. In our view, funds should ensure that their websites are organized in a way that makes this information relatively easy to find (and is in keeping with the spirit of section 5.5 of NI 81-106).

5.6 — SEDAR Filings

Each MRFP should be filed on SEDAR only under the individual investment fund to which it pertains (and not under a group profile) as stated in item E-2 of CSA Staff Notice 81-315 *Frequently Asked Questions on National Instrument 81-106 Investment Fund Continuous Disclosure* (the FAQs). Further, if the financial statements and the accompanying notes for each fund are in a separate document, the relevant statements should only be filed under the fund to which they pertain (consistent with item E-2 in the FAQs). Please note that only the disclosure relevant to a particular fund should be filed under that fund's profile on SEDAR.

In one example, a fund manager produced stand-alone financial statements for each fund, but filed all the financial statements and MRFPs under every fund's profile. This made it very difficult to find the disclosure applicable to the individual fund. In this case, we requested that future SEDAR filings be corrected.

6. — Regulatory Compliance

6.1 — Commissions to Related Parties

Where commissions were paid to brokerage firms that are affiliates of an investment fund, we asked for confirmation that the fund complied with the reporting requirement in paragraph 117(1)(c) of the *Securities Act* (Ontario). Investment funds must file a monthly report when a fund pays a fee to a related company on a purchase or sale of portfolio securities, unless the fund has obtained exemptive relief from this requirement. Some exemptive relief obtained in the past can no longer be relied upon as it was conditional on certain disclosure being provided in the statement of portfolio transactions, which is no longer required.

6.2 — Financial Highlights Tables

Part A, subsection 1(c) of the Form states that we do not generally mandate the use of a specific format for the MRFP, *except* for financial highlights and past performance as required by items 3 and 4 of Parts B and C of the Form. We found that approximately 40% of fund managers did not follow the set format of the financial highlights tables.

For example, with the implementation of Section 3855 of the CICA Handbook, some funds added a new line in the Fund's Net Asset Value (NAV) per Unit/Share table to represent the effect of the new accounting policy on NAV. We indicated in our comment letters that, while an explanation of the difference can be added to the MRFP, the tables' format must be maintained.

One fund manager added new ratios to the Ratios and Supplemental Data table, such as "MER excluding performance fee". In this manager's opinion, performance fees are not prevalent in the industry and it believes that additional ratios will benefit investors and provide fuller disclosure. Again, while an explanation can be added to the MRFP, additional lines cannot be included in the standard tables. The format of the financial highlights and past performance tables must be adhered to as mandated by the Form to ensure comparability between investment funds.

6.3 — Management Fees

The purpose of the requirement in Part B, section 3.3 of the Form is to promote transparency around the composition of management fees. The FAQs discuss our expectations with respect to management fee breakdown in items C-8 through to C-10. We remind investment funds that the purpose of the breakdown is to explain to investors what services are provided in exchange for the management fee. If services cannot be individually itemized, the nature of those services should at least be described qualitatively. For example, some funds did not indicate that the manager's fee for acting as trustee is included in the management fee. Even if trustee fees are not separately recorded, the management fee breakdown should disclose that these fees form part of the management fee.

Item C-8 in the FAQs states that the breakdown of management fees does not have to add to 100%, as the item requires disclosure of the *major* services paid for out of the management fee. We expect services to be expressed as an actual percentage of management fees, not as an estimate or a range, because the MRFP reports the prior period's activity. We also reiterate that the management fees breakdown must disclose any differences between classes or series.

Reminders

Some of the requirements of our rules were overlooked. Based on our review, we provide the following reminders.

Part 8: MUTUAL FUNDS

MRFP

6.4 — Investment Objective and Strategies

Approximately 40% of fund managers should have provided a more concise summary of the investment objective and strategies of their investment funds. The disclosure must be a concise summary of the fundamental investment objective and strategies of the investment fund, and not merely copied from the prospectus (Part B, section 2.1 of the Form). For some funds, we found that the investment objectives and strategies disclosed in the MRFP and simplified prospectus had exactly the same wording.

6.5 — Risk

Approximately 40% of fund managers did not provide an adequate discussion of risk. A discussion of how changes to the investment fund have affected the overall level of risk associated with an investment in the investment fund is required (Part B, section 2.2 of the Form). We noted that some funds merely repeated the risk information contained in the fund's prospectus or annual information form, while others only examined the impact of the main risk factors during the financial period. In both examples, the disclosure is generally incomplete as the discussion of risk should be focused on explaining how changes to the investment fund have affected the overall level of risk. We expect investment funds to provide a commentary on whether changes in the fund have had an impact on risk, along with a discussion of whether the suitability of the investment has changed from what was previously disclosed in the prospectus.

6.6 — Annual Compound Returns

(a) — Multiple series

Almost all investment funds with multiple series discussed the performance of only one series of the investment fund, typically the retail series. The Form requires a discussion of the performance of the investment fund relative to the broad-based securities market index (Part B, subsection 4.3(3)) and NI 81-106 states that the distinctions between the series must be disclosed in the MRFP (subsection 7.2(2)). At a minimum, investment funds must provide an explanation as to how the performance of all series differs from the specific series discussed.

(b) — Change in index from prior period

If an index is different from the one included in the most recently filed MRFP, the reasons for the change must be explained and the requirements relating to annual compound returns must be disclosed separately for both the new and former indices for the financial year (Part B, subsection 4.3(4) of the Form). This means that both indices must appear in the annual compound returns table in the year of the change to help readers compare the fund's performance to the new and former indices. One investment fund showed a blend of the new and former indices, which does not fulfil the requirement.

(c) — Non-standard performance periods

Part B, item 4 of the Form only allows the disclosure of past performance for the ten, five, three, one year, and since inception periods in the annual MRFP. Part C also allows for the inclusion of the interim period in the bar chart of the interim MRFP. We do not believe that the discussion of past performance should focus on non-standard performance periods such as the six-month return in the annual MRFP, or the quarterly return in the interim MRFP. In our comment letters, we asked that future discussions be limited to the standard performance periods.

6.7 — Interim MRFP

We remind preparers that the interim MRFP was specifically designed as an update to the last annual MRFP and was intended to be a shorter document. Interim MRFPs are not required to repeat all of the annual MRFP disclosure, but only update the required sections in Part C of the Form.

Financial Statements

6.8 — Mandatory Notes to Financial Statements

NI 81-106 lists items which must be disclosed in the notes to the financial statements (subsection 3.6(1)). We found that not all information required was disclosed. For example, the method used to allocate income and expenses, and realized and unrealized capital gains and losses to each class was sometimes not disclosed in the notes (item 2(d)). Also missing was the basis for determining cost of portfolio assets (item (1)). Almost all investment funds only discussed the basis for determining cost in the context that gains and losses on securities sold were determined on the basis of average cost. We remind investment funds to include a more general statement about the basis for determining the cost of portfolio assets.

Other Matters

6.9 — National Instrument 81-102 Mutual Funds Compliance Reports

Some investment funds did not file the compliance report from their custodian to the securities regulatory authority within 30 days after the filing of the annual financial statements (subsection 6.7(3) of National Instrument 81-102 *Mutual Funds* (NI 81-102)). In addition, some investment funds did not file the report describing compliance with Parts 9, 10 and 11 of NI 81-102, along with their auditor's compliance report, within the time limit as required by Part 12 of NI 81-102. We remind investment funds that the above reports must be filed on time.

6.10 — Annual Notification of Unitholders' Rights to Redemption

Fund managers are required to notify securityholders annually of their redemption rights (subsections 10.1(3) and 10.1(4) of NI 81-102). Some investment funds fulfilled this requirement in the past by including a note in the annual financial statements explaining the rights of securityholders with respect to redemption of securities. Under NI 81-106, investment funds are allowed to deliver certain continuous disclosure documents according to standing or annual instructions received from securityholders, which means that financial statements are not required to be sent to all securityholders anymore (sections 5.2 and 5.3 of NI 81-106). We remind investment funds that the requirements of NI 81-102 to provide all securityholders, at least annually, with a statement outlining rights with respect to redemptions may no longer be met by including it in the financial statements if those financial statements are not sent to every unitholder.

7. — Conclusion

Our findings suggest that investment funds can improve the quality of their continuous disclosure. Good disclosure is an opportunity to reach investors and advisors. We expect funds to consider the guidance in this notice when reviewing their continuous disclosure records to ensure their disclosure documents comply with NI 81-106. In future situations where disclosure requirements are not met, we will ask that the disclosure document be revised and refiled.

In some cases, staff is continuing to correspond with investment funds included in this review to obtain additional information and resolve the issues identified. On completion of this review, staff will expand our scope to include other investment funds such as closed-end funds, exchange traded funds, labour sponsored investment funds, limited partnerships, and scholarship plans. We will communicate our findings of the continuous disclosure of those types of investment funds in the future.

Policies and Orders: OSCN 81-705, 33-733.

OSC Staff Notice 81-710 — Approvals for Change in Control of a Mutual Fund Manager and Change of a Mutual Fund Manager under National Instrument 81-102 Mutual Funds

Date: May 14, 2010

33 O.S.C.B. 4288

Purpose

This notice sets out the views of staff of the Ontario Securities Commission (OSC Staff) on circumstances that may cause OSC Staff to view a proposed transaction or relevant series of transactions for which regulatory approval in respect of a mutual fund has been sought under Part 5 of National Instrument 81-102 *Mutual Funds* (NI 81-102) as requiring securityholder approval.

Change in Control of a Manager vs. Change of Manager

A change in control of the manager of a mutual fund requires the prior approval by the securities regulatory authorities under subsection 5.5(2) of NI 81-102. A change in the manager of a mutual fund requires prior approval by the securities regulatory authorities under paragraph 5.5(1)(a) of NI 81-102 and, unless the new manager is an affiliate of the current manager, prior securityholder approval pursuant to paragraph 5.1(b) of NI 81-102.

OSC Staff have seen an increasing number of applications for approval of a change in control of the manager of a mutual fund that, upon further examination of the substance of the proposed transaction or relevant series of transactions and its impact on the securityholders of the mutual fund, appear to OSC Staff to make it appropriate for approval by the securities regulatory authorities to be provided on the basis that there is a change in the manager of the mutual fund requiring securityholder approval.

In our review of applications for regulatory approval for a change in control of the manager of the mutual fund, OSC Staff will consider the intended final outcome for the securityholders of the mutual fund. We may ask the applicant for submissions in order to ascertain whether the result for securityholders of the proposed transaction or relevant series of transactions is effectively a change of the manager, rather than a change in control of the manager. When examining the substance of a proposed transaction or relevant series of transactions, OSC Staff will raise questions where it appears the transaction or series of transactions has been structured to effect a change of manager of the mutual fund without securityholder approval.

Generally, this issue will arise if a proposed transaction or relevant series of transactions is structured in one of the following ways:

   (i) the manager of a mutual fund amalgamates with another investment fund manager; or

   (ii) if, immediately following a change in control of the manager of the mutual fund, a change of manager will occur where the new manager will be the entity that acquired control of the original manager or an affiliate of such entity; or

   (iii) when it is contemplated that within a foreseeable period of time following a change in control of the manager of the mutual fund, a change of manager of the mutual fund will occur where the new manager will be the entity that acquired control of the original manager or an affiliate of such entity.

Further Information

Issuers and their counsel are encouraged to contact OSC Staff at an early stage in the planning of any transaction that may give rise to any questions concerning the issue discussed in this Notice.

OSC Staff Notice 81-711 — Closed-End Investment Fund Conversions to Open-End Mutual Funds

Date: **October 29, 2010**

33 O.S.C.B. 9953

Purpose

This notice sets out the views of staff of the Ontario Securities Commission (OSC staff) on the regulatory issues related to the conversion of closed-end funds into mutual funds, and the types of comments OSC staff will generally raise in the course of a review of a built-in conversion feature or a conversion.

Background

Closed-end funds differ from mutual funds in several key ways.

Mutual funds are typically in continuous distribution, which means that they issue an unlimited number of units or shares from treasury. These funds provide a regular redemption feature, typically daily, at the fund's net asset value (NAV). Mutual funds are regulated by National Instrument 81-102 *Mutual Funds* (NI 81-102), which prescribes product requirements including rules related to investment restrictions, borrowing, organizational costs, incentive fees, conflicts of interest, purchases and redemptions and sales communications.

By contrast, closed-end funds are not in continuous distribution. Rather, they issue a finite number of units or shares from treasury on an initial public offering (or IPO) which may be followed by subsequent offerings. Following issuance, these units or shares are typically traded on a stock exchange, often at a discount to NAV. Closed-end funds may offer an annual redemption at NAV. These funds are not subject to NI 81-102 and often engage in investment strategies, such as borrowing, beyond the limits prescribed for mutual funds.

The differences in structure and features of closed-end funds and mutual funds and in the regulatory regimes that govern them give rise to a number of regulatory issues when a conversion of a closed-end fund into a mutual fund is contemplated or occurs.

Types of closed-end fund conversions

Recently, OSC staff have seen a number of closed-end funds that intend to convert to a mutual fund, often within less than two years of their initial offering. A key objective of conversion is to provide investors in the closed-end fund with enhanced liquidity through a more frequent redemption feature at NAV.

To date, OSC staff have seen a variety of ways a closed-end fund may convert to a mutual fund. The following are among the more common approaches to conversion:

- *Built-in conversion features* — The closed-end fund is structured with an automatic conversion feature that typically will be triggered in one of two ways: (1) as at or before a specified date, usually within two years of the fund's initial offering; or (2) after a specified date, if the fund trades at a certain discount (often 2%) to NAV for more than a set period of time (often 10 days);

- *Securityholder approvals* — At some point after the initial distribution, the fund manager seeks securityholder approval to convert or merge the closed-end fund into a mutual fund; or

- *Mergers* — The closed-end fund is merged with a mutual fund at some point after the initial distribution of the closed-end fund. These mergers are often in accordance with 'permitted merger' provisions of the closed-end fund's declaration of trust. Under these provisions, the requirement for securityholder approval is typically not triggered provided certain conditions are met, such as the merging funds having consistent investment objectives and strategies.

Regulatory issues

To date, OSC staff have reviewed built-in conversion features and conversions as part of our prospectus reviews and in the context of applications for exemptive relief, pre-filings and inquiries. OSC staff have identified a number of key regulatory issues for consideration in the context of a conversion-related review. In the course of such review, the issuer may be asked for submissions to assist staff in determining whether these regulatory issues have been appropriately addressed.

1. — The conversion process

Transparency

OSC staff expect that the key aspects of the conversion process will be clearly disclosed to investors. Disclosure should include a description of the event or events that will trigger the conversion, the expected timing and steps of the conversion, what approvals, if any, will be required to effect the conversion, any expected periods of illiquidity, who will bear the cost of the conversion, what class or series of units or shares investors will hold after the conversion and the investor's ability to redeem after the conversion.

For closed-end funds with a built-in conversion feature, disclosure regarding the conversion should be made prominently in the fund's initial prospectus.

Where closed-end funds do not contain a built-in feature, but it is contemplated that the closed-end fund may convert to a mutual fund within a foreseeable period of time following initial distribution, OSC staff will generally expect disclosure regarding the possible conversion, as well as key aspects of the contemplated conversion process, to be provided in the initial prospectus.

Where closed-end funds do not contain a built-in feature and the decision to convert is made only after the initial distribution of the closed-end fund, OSC staff expect that this decision will trigger the material change reporting requirements. If the fund manager is seeking securityholder approval for the conversion, OSC staff expect appropriate disclosure regarding the conversion to be in the circular sent to investors in connection with the approval.

Notice to investors

OSC staff expect that investors will be provided with sufficient written notice prior to the conversion of the closed-end fund. For closed-end funds with a built-in conversion feature, our view is that the fund's initial prospectus should disclose that prior written notice of the conversion will be provided to investors and the length of the notice period. In instances where securityholder approval is not being sought, OSC staff would generally consider at least 60 days prior written notice to be appropriate. Where securityholder approval is being sought for the conversion, securities legislation sets out the notice requirements for a meeting of securityholders.

Redemption right and periods of no liquidity

Typically, a closed-end fund will cease trading on the exchange and may temporarily suspend redemptions prior to and immediately following conversion to a mutual fund. OSC staff expect that investors will be provided with a redemption right prior to such suspension and conversion. We further expect that the conversion will be structured so that any period of no liquidity (both before and after the conversion), is as short as possible.

2. — Post-conversion compliance with NI 81-102

Compliance with NI 81-102

OSC staff generally expect that a closed-end fund with a built-in conversion feature will comply with NI 81-102 from its inception, particularly if the conversion may, or will, happen within a foreseeable period of time from the initial distribution of the closed-end fund.

If the closed-end fund intends to operate in a manner not permitted by NI 81-102, it may need exemptive relief to continue certain investment strategies or features at the time that it converts to a mutual fund. In these instances, OSC staff recommend that the application for the exemptive relief be filed concurrently with the initial prospectus filing of the closed-end fund. These applications will be evaluated in the context of the regulatory regime and policy concerns currently applicable to conventional mutual funds. If the decision to convert is made only after the initial distribution of the closed-end fund, OSC staff expect the issuer to have considered what modifications, if any, to the features or investment strategies of the fund are necessary to be in compliance with NI 81-102 upon conversion to a mutual fund.

Consistent investment objectives and strategies

For a closed-end fund without a built-in conversion feature that converts after the initial distribution, OSC staff expect the issuer to consider if there will be a fundamental change to the investment objectives, strategies, fees, management and operations of the closed-end fund following its conversion to a mutual fund. If so, OSC staff would generally expect securityholders of the fund to be given the opportunity to vote on these fundamental changes.

Illustration of past performance

OSC staff have observed that, following conversion to a mutual fund, some funds wish to show the past performance of the closed-end fund in sales communications. Section 15.6 of NI 81-102 prohibits a mutual fund from showing in sales communications past performance from a period that is before the time when the mutual fund offered its securities under a simplified prospectus. This would prohibit the display of the past performance of the closed-end fund. However, the form requirements applicable to management reports of fund performance under Form 81-106F1 require that reporting issuers show past performance from inception, including pre-conversion past performance.

When contemplating a built-in conversion feature or conversion, OSC staff expect issuers to consider how they intend to illustrate past performance. If the issuer requests exemptive relief to permit the mutual fund to show the past performance of the closed-end fund in sales communications, OSC staff will consider whether the past performance is relevant and useful for investors and will be appropriately presented and qualified, as necessary.

3. — Costs associated with the conversion

Merger costs

When conversions are structured as a merger between the closed-end fund and a mutual fund, OSC staff expect that the fund manager will absorb the costs of the merger. Costs of the merger are more appropriately borne by the fund manager as opposed to securityholders where it is the fund manager's decision to merge the funds and the manager benefits from the merger. In such instances, OSC staff generally take the view that it is inappropriate for any merger costs to be charged either to the terminating closed-end fund or to the continuing mutual fund.

For Further Information

Issuers and their counsel are encouraged to contact OSC staff at an early stage in the planning of a conversion feature or conversion that may give rise to any questions concerning the issues discussed in this Notice.

OSC Staff Notice 81-712 — 2010 Investment Funds Branch Annual Report

Date: October 15, 2010

33 O.S.C.B. 9429

Table of Contents

Introduction

1. Key Policy Initiatives

    1.1 Point of Sale (POS)

    1.2 Scholarship Plans

    1.3 Modernization of Investment Fund Product Regulation

    1.4 NI 31-103 — Registration Requirements and Exemptions

    1.5 NI 23-102 — Use of Client Brokerage Commissions — Prospectus Form Amendments

    1.6 International Financial Reporting Standards (IFRS)

    1.7 Amendments to Part VI of the TSX Company Manual — Fund Mergers

2. Disclosure and Compliance Reviews

    2.1 Focused Reviews of Investment Funds, September 2008 — September 2009

    2.2 Targeted Reviews of Independent Review Committee (IRC) Disclosure

    2.3 Commodity Based Funds

    2.4 Closed-end Fund Conversions

    2.5 Daily Leveraged Exchange Traded Funds

    2.6 Long-term Warrant Offerings

    2.7 Income Trust Funds — Change in Investment Objectives and Voting Rights

3. Recent Developments in Staff Practices

    3.1 OSC Staff Notice 81-710 — Approvals for Change in Control of a Mutual Fund Manager and Change of a Mutual Fund Manager under National Instrument 81-102 Mutual Funds

    3.2 The Investment Funds Practitioner

4. Further Information

Introduction

This is the first Investment Funds (IF) Branch annual report. This report provides an overview of the key activities and initiatives of the IF Branch for the 2010 fiscal year (April 1, 2009 to March 31, 2010) including:

- key policy initiatives,

- disclosure and compliance reviews, and

- recent developments in staff practices.

The report also provides some updates on the foregoing where there have been new developments since the end of the fiscal year.

The IF Branch of the Ontario Securities Commission (OSC) is responsible for overseeing over 3159 publicly-offered investment funds. Approximately $517 billion of assets are held by publicly-offered investments funds based in Ontario. This represents 80% of the approximately $644 billion in publicly-offered investment fund assets in Canada.

We administer the regulatory framework for investment funds, including:

- reviewing and assessing product disclosure for all types of investment funds, including prospectuses and continuous disclosure filings,

- considering applications for discretionary relief from securities legislation and rules, and

- taking a leadership role in developing new rules and policies to adapt to the changing environment in the investment fund industry.

The investment fund products we oversee include conventional mutual funds, closed-end funds and mutual funds (including index based funds) listed and posted for trading on a stock exchange (ETFs), commodity pools, scholarship plans, labour-sponsored or venture capital funds and flow-through limited partnerships.

We generally distinguish between conventional mutual funds and non-conventional investment funds on the basis of how an investor can obtain liquidity for their investment. Conventional mutual funds provide investors with the right to obtain their proportionate share of a fund's net asset value (NAV) on demand. Non-conventional funds, such as closed-end funds and ETFs, generally provide investors with liquidity by listing their securities on a stock exchange or through an alternative redemption feature that may not permit investors to redeem on demand or that is at a discount to NAV. We discuss the different types of funds further on our website www.osc.gov.on.ca at *Investment Funds — Fund Operations*.

In the last ten years, offerings of non-conventional mutual funds, particularly ETFs, have proliferated. The number of ETFs has grown from 3 in December 2000 to 109 in December 2009 to 146 at the end of June 2010. ETF assets under management have grown at a much faster rate than conventional mutual funds and increased over 500% from approximately $6 billion in December 2000 to over $30 billion in December 2009.

Total Mutual Funds and ETF Assets
In billions of dollars

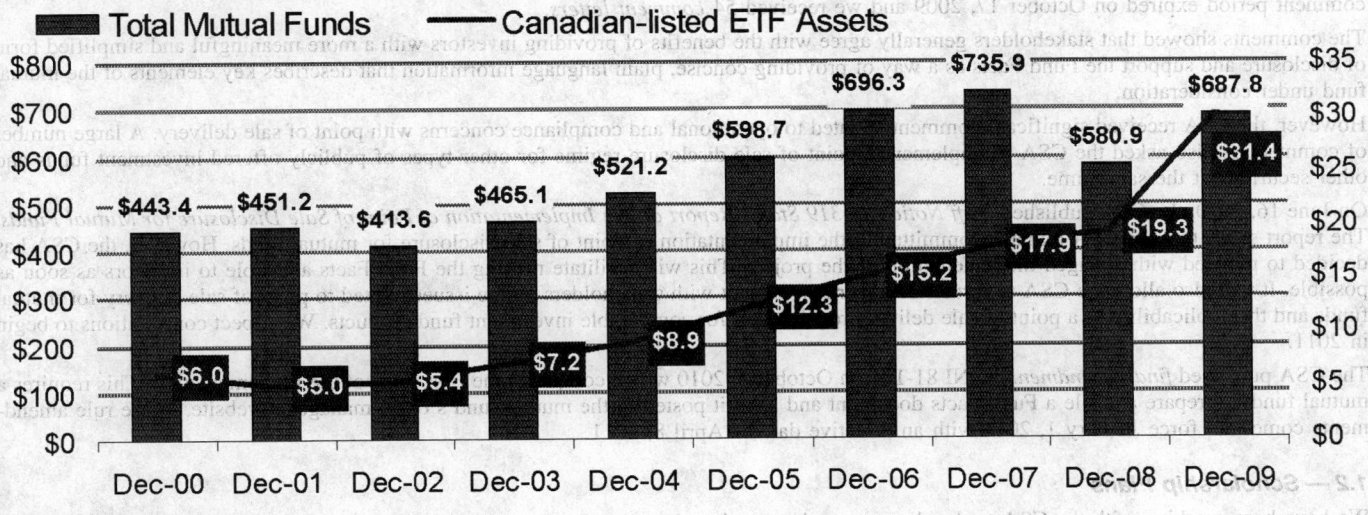

▬ Total Mutual Funds   ── Canadian-listed ETF Assets

$443.4	$451.2	$413.6	$465.1	$521.2	$598.7	$696.3	$735.9	$580.9	$687.8	
$6.0	$5.0	$5.4	$7.2	$8.9	$12.3	$15.2	$17.9	$19.3	$31.4	

Dec-00 Dec-01 Dec-02 Dec-03 Dec-04 Dec-05 Dec-06 Dec-07 Dec-08 Dec-09

Source: Investor Economics

The dynamic nature of the investment funds industry requires IF staff to constantly adapt and respond to rapid product developments and innovations. In all aspects of investment funds regulation, we strive to be effective and responsive and to achieve and enhance investor protection.

This report provides information about some of the initiatives we are undertaking to promote clear and concise disclosure in order to assist investors to make more informed investment decisions and to address the sufficiency of regulatory coverage across all investment fund products. The report also highlights recent product and market developments and our regulatory response to these developments to assist the investment fund industry in understanding and complying with current regulatory requirements.

1. — Key Policy Initiatives

We continue to play a leading role in several significant policy initiatives with other securities regulators in Canada through the Canadian Securities Administrators (the CSA). We also work with colleagues in other OSC branches on various initiatives that impact the fund industry. This section reports on the status of significant policy initiatives including:

- the CSA's point of sale project,
- the CSA's scholarship plan project, and
- the CSA's project to modernize investment fund product regulation.

This section also reports on other projects we have worked on with other OSC branches that impact the fund industry including:

- CSA National Instrument 31-103 *Registration Requirements and Exemptions* (NI 31-103),
- CSA National Instrument 23-102 *Use of Client Brokerage Commissions* (NI 23-102),
- CSA Implementation of International Financial Reporting Standards, and
- Amendments to the TSX Company Manual.

1.1 — Point of Sale (POS)

The CSA POS project is a continuation of the project begun by securities and insurance regulators to harmonize the disclosure regime of mutual funds and segregated funds, as described in the *Framework paper* published by the Joint Forum of Financial Market Regulators (the Joint Forum) on October 24, 2008.

The Joint Forum focussed on three principles:

- providing investors with key information about a fund,
- providing the information in a simple, accessible, and comparable format, and
- providing the information before investors make their decision to buy.

Part 8: MUTUAL FUNDS

This is a significant investor protection initiative. Central to the proposal is the *Fund Facts* document. It is a short and concise document written in plain language that highlights the potential benefits, risks and costs of investing in a mutual fund. Investors would receive a Fund Facts at a time that is relevant to their investment decision, generally before they buy a fund for the first time.

On June 19, 2009, the CSA published *proposed amendments* to National Instrument 81-101 *Mutual Fund Prospectus Disclosure*, its Forms and Companion Policy (collectively, NI 81-101) as a first step in implementing the key concepts and principles set out by the Joint Forum. The comment period expired on October 17, 2009 and we received 54 *comment letters*.

The comments showed that stakeholders generally agree with the benefits of providing investors with a more meaningful and simplified form of disclosure and support the Fund Facts as a way of providing concise, plain language information that describes key elements of the mutual fund under consideration.

However, the CSA received significant comments related to operational and compliance concerns with point of sale delivery. A large number of commenters also asked the CSA to implement a point of sale disclosure regime for other types of publicly offered investment funds and other securities at the same time.

On June 16, 2010, the CSA published *Staff Notice 81-319 Status Report on the Implementation of Point of Sale Disclosure for Mutual Funds*. The report states that the CSA remains committed to the implementation of point of sale disclosure for mutual funds. However, the CSA has decided to proceed with a staged implementation of the project. This will facilitate making the Fund Facts available to investors as soon as possible. It will also allow the CSA to further consider and consult with stakeholders on the issues related to point of sale delivery for mutual funds and the applicability of a point of sale delivery requirement for comparable investment fund products. We expect consultations to begin in 2011.

The CSA published *final amendments* to NI 81-101 on October 6, 2010 which completes the first stage of the implementation. This requires a mutual fund to prepare and file a Fund Facts document and have it posted to the mutual fund's or its manager's website. These rule amendments come into force January 1, 2011 with an effective date of April 8, 2011.

1.2 — Scholarship Plans

We have been working with the CSA to develop proposals to update the rules that govern the formation and operation of scholarship plans, which are a type of investment fund product used by Canadians to save for their children's education.

On March 26, 2010, the CSA published *proposed amendments* to National Instrument 41-101 *General Prospectus Requirements* (NI 41-101) and proposed *new Form 41-101F3 Information Required in a Scholarship Plan Prospectus* that includes a new plan summary document. The proposals set out the first phase of the CSA's initiative to modernize the securities regulation of scholarship plans, which involves providing investors with a new prospectus form specifically tailored for scholarship plans.

This is an important investor-focused initiative. The number of investors in scholarship plans, particularly investors with low to modest incomes, has grown substantially since 1998 when the Government of Canada actively began encouraging saving for post-secondary education through the Canada Education Savings Grant (CESG).

We know that many investors have trouble understanding the unique features and complexity of scholarship plans. Central to the new prospectus form is the Plan Summary document. It is in plain language, will generally be no more than three pages, and highlights the potential benefits, risks and costs of investing in a scholarship plan.

The comment period for the proposed amendments to NI 41-101 expired on June 22, 2010 and 13 *comment letters* were received. The CSA is currently reviewing and considering all of the comments received.

The second phase of the CSA's initiative is to reformulate National Policy 15 *Conditions Precedent to Acceptance of Scholarship or Educational Plan Prospectuses* (NP 15) by replacing it with a new operational rule for scholarship plans. While certain aspects of scholarship plan regulation have been updated (for example, specific disclosure requirements for scholarship plans in their management reports of fund performance), a comprehensive review of NP 15 has not been conducted since the policy was put into place. We are considering issues such as investment restrictions, fees, the calculation and disclosure of performance data, sales communications, and actuarial certification for scholarship plans.

1.3 — Modernization of Investment Fund Product Regulation

On June 25, 2010, the CSA published *proposed amendments* to National Instrument 81-102 *Mutual Funds* (NI 81-102) and National Instrument 81-106 *Investment Fund Continuous Disclosure* (NI 81-106). These amendments focussed on Phase 1 of our proposals to modernize investment fund product regulation.

Phase 1 codifies frequently granted exemptive relief to mutual funds under NI 81-102 and NI 81-106. This includes various technical relief granted to ETFs to facilitate their trading on a stock exchange, relief to engage in short-selling, and relief to allow the commingling of cash received for purchases and redemptions of mutual fund securities with cash received for purchases and sales of other securities sold by a dealer. The codified exemptions are subject to conditions that are designed to address any potential investor protection concerns based on our experience granting the relief on a discretionary basis.

Phase 1 also proposes to introduce additional liquidity and term restrictions on investments by money market funds in short-term debt, including asset backed commercial paper (ABCP). It would also increase the transparency of such portfolio holdings for all investment funds. These proposed new requirements take into account feedback received on *CSA Consultation Paper 11-405 Securities Regulatory Proposals Stemming from the 2007-2008 Credit Market Turmoil and its Effect on the ABCP Market in Canada* and the results of our targeted reviews of money market fund managers discussed below in section 2.1.

The comment period on the Phase 1 amendments expired on September 24, 2010 and 19 *comment letters* were received. The CSA continues to review and consider all of the comments received.

Phase 2 of the initiative, now underway, will assess whether there are any market efficiency, fairness, or investor protection issues that arise out of the differing regulatory regimes that apply to different types of investment funds and other competing retail investment products. Phase 2 will consider what initiatives may be necessary in order to achieve more consistent, fair, and functional regulation across the investment fund product spectrum.

1.4 — NI 31-103 — Registration Requirements and Exemptions

National Instrument 31-103 Registration Requirements and Exemptions (NI 31-103) came into force on September 28, 2009. The OSC's Compliance and Registrant Regulation (CRR) Branch led this significant CSA project, with IF staff providing support on issues that impacted the investment fund industry. Most notably, NI 31-103 created a new category of registration for investment fund managers that direct the business, operations, and affairs of investment funds. Registered investment fund managers are subject to new, on-going requirements on their business operations and client relationships, including capital and insurance requirements. NI 31-103 also contains the conflict of interest prohibitions that previously existed under s. 118 of the *Securities Act* (Ontario).

As part of this CSA registration reform initiative, we drafted *consequential amendments* to the schedules in National Instrument 81-107 *Independent Review Committee for Investment Funds* (NI 81-107). The purpose of these amendments was to preserve the exemptions from the conflict of interest prohibitions codified under NI 81-107. We continue to work with our colleagues in the CRR Branch on various implementation issues related to NI 31-103, such as the interpretation of the investment fund manager registration requirement for non-residents.

1.5 — NI 23-102 — Use of Client Brokerage Commissions — Prospectus Form Amendments

National Instrument 23-102 Use of Client Brokerage Commissions (NI 23-102) came into force on June 30, 2010. The OSC's Market Regulation Branch led this initiative. Our contribution included proposed *consequential amendments* to the investment fund prospectus disclosure forms, Form 81-101F2 and Form 41-101F2 (the Form Amendments), to coincide with the coming into force of NI 23-102.

The Form Amendments harmonize the disclosure requirements related to the use of client brokerage commissions with NI 23-102 by requiring disclosure of the nature and details of any arrangements the fund's adviser has entered into relating to the use of client brokerage commissions. While the Form Amendments replaced similar existing disclosure requirements for conventional mutual funds in Form 81-101F2, the disclosure requirement is new for all other types of investment funds that use Form 41-101F2.

1.6 — International Financial Reporting Standards (IFRS)

The Canadian Accounting Standards Board (AcSB) has adopted a strategic plan to move financial reporting for Canadian publicly accountable enterprises, including investment funds, to International Financial Reporting Standards (IFRS), as issued by the International Accounting Standards Board (IASB). The OSC supports Canada's move to IFRS, a globally accepted, high quality set of accounting principles.

We have been working with the OSC's IFRS Working Group and the Office of the Chief Accountant to address what regulatory changes may be necessary to accommodate the transition to IFRS for investment funds. On October 16, 2009, the CSA published *proposed amendments* to NI 81-106 and related consequential amendments. The amendments include changes to accounting terms and transitional changes in order to assist filers with their conversion to IFRS. The comment period expired on January 14, 2010 and 11 *comment letters* were received.

The majority of the comments related to the IFRS requirement that investment funds consolidate their portfolio holdings for financial reporting purposes. This remains a significant issue for the investment fund industry as it transitions to IFRS, and it is currently a focus of the IASB. The CSA is waiting for the deliberations currently underway by the IASB on this issue to be completed before proceeding with the proposed amendments to NI 81-106.

In the interim, the AcSB issued a decision summary dated June 16, 2010 advising that it was proposing a change to the CICA Handbook so that IFRS will apply to investment companies only for financial years beginning on or after January 1, 2012 (as opposed to January 1, 2011 which is the adoption date for other publicly accountable enterprises), although early adoption would be permitted. On October 1, 2010, the AcSB published amendments to the Introduction to Part I of the CICA Handbook to reflect the foregoing. On October 8, 2010, the CSA published *CSA Staff Notice 81-320 Update on IFRS for Investment Funds*. The notice confirms that the CSA is now working towards the goal of having the necessary IFRS related amendments for investment funds in force by January 12, 2012.

1.7 — Amendments to Part VI of the TSX Company Manual — Fund Mergers

We worked with staff in the Market Regulation Branch in reviewing *amendments* to Part VI of the Toronto Stock Exchange (the TSX) Company Manual. We recommended that the Commission approve the amendments, which came into force on August 16, 2010. The amendments codify a new securityholder voting requirement for investment funds that are listed issuers and that are the target of an acquisition. The amendments also codify two new exemptions from securityholder voting requirements in connection with acquisitions. The exemptions are based on TSX staff practice and are subject to several conditions including IRC approval.

2. — Disclosure and Compliance Reviews

On an ongoing basis, staff in the IF Branch review the prospectus and continuous disclosure filings of Ontario-based investment funds. Risk-based criteria are used to select investment funds for reviews of their disclosure documents. We may also choose to conduct targeted reviews of a particular industry segment or on a particular topic. In addition to our prospectus and continuous disclosure reviews, the IF Branch works closely with staff in the CRR Branch on issues related to fund manager compliance and identifying possible emerging issues. This can sometimes lead to us conducting joint reviews.

This section discusses:

- the findings of the focused reviews that staff in the IF Branch conducted with the CRR Branch in response to the market events of 2008-2009,

- our reviews of disclosure related to NI 81-107, and
- some observations and themes from our on-going prospectus disclosure reviews of certain types of investment funds.

2.1 — Focused Reviews of Investment Funds, September 2008 — September 2009

In response to concerns emerging from the market turmoil experienced by the global financial services industry, we worked with our colleagues in the CRR Branch to conduct extensive reviews of major segments of the Canadian investment fund industry. The reviews focused on Ontario-based money market funds, non-conventional investment funds, and hedge funds. The primary purpose of the reviews was to assess fund managers' compliance with Ontario securities laws.

On January 19, 2010, in conjunction with the CRR Branch, we published *OSC Staff Notice 33-733 Report on Focused Reviews of Investment Funds, September 2008 — September 2009*. The report summarizes the findings from the responses to the questionnaires sent to each category of investment fund and from the on-site visits. It also includes suggested practices. The questionnaires and on-sites visits were used to gather information about the funds' portfolio holdings, exposure to illiquid assets, valuation methodologies, and the approaches used to manage the risk of large redemptions during the market downturn.

The report concludes that, despite the overall market downturn and its impact on the returns of many of these products during our review period, we did not observe any industry-wide compliance issues. During our on-site visits, however, we noted some instances of noncompliance which we addressed separately with each individual fund manager.

2.2 — Targeted Reviews of Independent Review Committee (IRC) Disclosure

NI 81-107, which became fully operational in November, 2007 following a one year transition period, introduced the requirement for every investment fund that is a reporting issuer to have a fully independent body, the Independent Review Committee (the IRC). The IRC's role is to oversee all decisions involving an actual or perceived conflict of interest faced by the fund manager in the operation of the fund.

In developing the instrument, the CSA recognized potential benefits or efficiencies may be derived by permitting investment funds to make limited investments in securities of related issuers or trade portfolio securities with related investment funds. Accordingly, NI 81-107 allows fund managers to engage in a limited number of related-party and self-dealing transactions that are otherwise prohibited or restricted by securities legislation. The IRC, however, must approve these transactions and the instrument also imposes objective pricing and transparency requirements on these transactions.

After NI 81-107 came into effect, the CSA continued to receive a number of applications for discretionary relief to permit related-party and self-dealing transactions beyond the exemptions codified under the rule. Each of these applications represented a subtle policy shift from the CSA's position when NI 81-107 came into force. Before proceeding any further with novel applications on a case-by-case basis, we concluded it was important to evaluate how the IRC approval mechanism is working and report back to our Commission.

Consequently, IF staff conducted a series of informal meetings with IRCs and carried out a targeted review of the continuous disclosure filings related to IRCs and NI 81-107 generally. The purpose of the meetings was to obtain informal feedback from IRC members on their experience working with the rule. The purpose of the reviews was to assess industry compliance and identify areas of the rule that may require greater clarification or oversight.

We reviewed a sample of approximately 141 investment funds from 41 fund managers, including conventional mutual funds, ETFs, scholarship plans, labour-sponsored or venture capital funds and flow-through limited partnerships. The managers varied in size from $46 million to $95 billion in assets under management.

We anticipate publishing an OSC Staff Notice which summarizes our observations and provides guidance by December, 2010.

2.3 — Commodity Based Funds

We saw an increased number of new offerings for investment funds that invest all or primarily all of their assets in physical commodities such as gold, silver, platinum, or copper. This trend emerged in both conventional mutual funds and ETFs and was consistent with a global trend of new commodities-based financial products designed to enable retail investors to tap into the recent commodities boom. Our prospectus reviews of these products focused on ensuring there was proper disclosure to investors. In particular, we raised comments designed to improve disclosure regarding:

- risks associated with investing in a single commodity,
- the potential for increased transaction and custodian costs, and
- the experience of the custodian.

2.4 — Closed-End Fund Conversions

IF staff also noted an increase in the number of closed-end investment funds that trade on an exchange with investment objectives to automatically convert to open-end mutual funds. Typically, the conversion occurs in one of two ways: automatically at a specified date (for example, two years from the fund's inception); or if the fund trades at a certain discount (often 2%) to NAV for a period of time after a specified date. In our prospectus reviews of these products and the conversion feature generally, we have focused on whether the funds continue to have the same or substantially similar investment objectives and strategies before and after the conversion. We have generally taken the view that these products should be compliant with the regulatory requirements applicable to conventional mutual funds from inception if they intend to convert to a mutual fund within a relatively short timeframe. Our reviews of these products also focused on improving key disclosure to investors. The key areas of disclosure are:

- the potential that these products will trade at a discount to NAV up to the time of conversion,

- fees for investors both before and after the fund converts to a mutual fund,

- identification of the objective or value to investors of investing in a closed-end fund that will convert in the short-term to a mutual fund,

- the risks associated with the conversions, including that the closed-end fund may have to amend its investment objective or strategies upon conversion to a mutual fund, and

- performance disclosure for periods before and after conversion.

Our prospectus reviews have helped inform Phase 2 of the CSA's project to modernize investment fund product regulation, by identifying some of the issues that arise from having different regulatory regimes for different types of investment fund products.

We anticipate publishing an OSC Staff Notice shortly which sets out our views on the regulatory issues we have identified related to closed-end investment fund conversions and the types of comments IF staff will generally raise as part of our review.

2.5 — Daily Leveraged Exchange Traded Funds

We continued to see a number of new ETF offerings — daily leveraged ETFs in particular. Daily leveraged ETFs are exchange-traded investment funds that provide daily investment results that correspond to a multiple of an underlying index. For instance, a leveraged ETF's investment objective may be to provide a return that is equal to two times the daily return of the S&P/TSX 60 index or two times the inverse of the daily return of the S&P/TSX 60 index.

A key issue with daily leveraged ETFs is that some investors do not understand that over periods longer than a day, the return of the fund may differ significantly from its underlying index. This effect becomes more pronounced as the amount of leverage, the time period the daily leveraged ETF is held, and the volatility of the underlying index, increase.

We met with manufacturers of daily leveraged ETFs to express the concern that investors may not be adequately informed regarding the unique risks associated with daily leveraged ETFs. In the course of the prospectus renewals for a number of these products, we also requested that a plainly worded, brief warning in bold type be added to the cover page of the prospectus, advising of the risks of investing in daily leveraged ETFs for periods longer than a day.

2.6 — Long-Term Warrant Offerings

We have noted an increased number of long-term warrant offerings. Investment funds typically provide existing investors with a stand-alone right or warrant at no charge under these offerings, but the investor must pay a price to exercise the warrant to obtain another unit of the investment fund. IF staff discussed these types of offerings previously in the *September 2008* publication of the Investment Funds Practitioner.

A distinguishing feature of these offerings is that the exercise period of the warrants can range from 6 months to up to a year or longer. A further distinguishing feature is that the exercise price of the warrant is often higher than the current price at which an investor could obtain a unit of the fund on a stock exchange. Normally, the exercise price in a conventional short-term rights offering is at a discount to the current market price to encourage existing investors to subscribe.

The extended exercise period and pricing terms in long-term warrant offerings increase the possibility that the warrant could be traded to another investor that is not an existing unitholder. Consequently, our prospectus reviews of these offerings have focussed on what disclosure and rights will be provided to investors that exercise warrants under these offerings. We have generally sought confirmation that:

- the prospectus for the offering qualifies the underlying securities that the warrants can be exercised into in addition to the warrants themselves, as required by s 4.2(a) of NI 45-101 — *Rights Offerings*, and

- the filer intends to deliver the prospectus upon exercise of the warrant where it has been traded to another investor and the exercise period is more than 6 months.

2.7 — Income Trust Funds — Change in Investment Objectives and Voting Rights

The federal government has announced changes to the taxation of distributions of publicly-traded income trusts which take effect in 2011. Consequently, many income trusts are converting back to corporations or pursuing other strategic alternatives. This change impacted mutual funds that invest in income trust securities as the number of income trusts in which they could invest continued to shrink.

A number of conventional mutual funds with the objective to invest primarily in income trust securities were created when income trusts were popular. We saw a number of these mutual funds address the decline in available income trusts by changing their investment objectives to broaden their ability to invest in other types of securities. IF staff reviewed prospectus amendments and renewals filed by these funds to confirm that the disclosure indicated that investors would be provided with the right to vote on the proposed change in investment objective as required under NI 81-102.

3. — Recent Developments in Staff Practices

We continue our efforts to be transparent regarding the IF Branch's practices and procedures in as timely a manner as possible. Our intent in doing so is to better enable fund managers and their advisors to avoid potential regulatory issues when they are at the planning stage for a new fund or transaction. Our primary transparency tools are staff notices and the Investment Funds Practitioner newsletter.

3.1 — OSC Staff Notice 81-710 — Approvals for Change in Control of a Mutual Fund Manager and Change of a Mutual Fund Manager under National Instrument 81-102 Mutual Funds

In our review of applications for regulatory approval of a change in control of the manager of a mutual fund, we saw an increasing number of applications that appeared to have been structured to effect a change of manager of the mutual fund without seeking the requisite securityholder approval.

For example, we saw that some fund managers were taking the view that a change of control of manager followed by an amalgamation either immediately after, or within a foreseeable period of time following, the change in control did not trigger the voting rights provided under NI 81-102 for a change of fund manager.

To inform issuers and their counsel of our concerns and the types of questions we may ask in reviewing such applications, we published on May 14, 2010, *OSC Staff Notice 81-710 Approvals for Change in Control of a Mutual Fund Manager and Change of a Mutual Fund Manager under National Instrument 81-102 Mutual Funds*.

3.2 — The Investment Funds Practitioner

The Practitioner is an overview of recent issues arising from applications for discretionary relief, prospectuses, and continuous disclosure documents that investment funds file with the OSC and that are reviewed by IF staff. It is intended to assist investment fund managers and their advisors who regularly prepare public disclosure documents and applications for exemptive relief on behalf of investment funds.

The Practitioner is also intended to make fund managers more broadly aware of some of the issues we have raised in connection with our reviews and how we have resolved them. The Practitioner can be found on our website www.osc.gov.on.ca at Information for *Investment Funds*.

In January, we published the *fourth edition* of the Investment Funds Practitioner. Topics included:

- NI 81-107 and the Conflicts Provisions
- Mergers and Reorganizations
- Timing for Obtaining a Prospectus Receipt
- Two-tiered Structured Products
- Yield Disclosure in Prospectuses
- Prospectus Lapse Dates
- Auditor Consents

We intend to publish the fifth edition of the Investment Funds Practitioner this fiscal year. We welcome suggestions for future topics. Possible topics may include:

- Secondary Managed Account Prospectus Relief
- Custodians and Prime Brokers for Funds using NI 41-101
- Inter-fund Trades of Illiquid Securities
- Deeming to Have Ceased to be a Reporting Issuer Applications and Filing the Last Set of Financial Statements
- ETFs/Index Participation Units and Investment Objectives — Naming the Index

4. — Further Information

If you have any questions regarding, or feedback on, our first IF Branch Report, please send them to investmentfunds@osc.gov.on.ca.

You may find additional information regarding investment funds and the IF Branch on our *website*.

We have also attached a list of IF Branch staff at the end of this report.

[List of Investment Funds Branch staff omitted]

OSC Staff Notice 81-713 — Focussed Disclosure Review — National Instrument 81-107 Independent Review Committee for Investment Funds

Date: March 25, 2011

34 O.S.C.B. 3465

Introduction

In March 2010, staff of the Ontario Securities Commission (OSC) ("Staff" or "we") concluded a series of focussed reviews of independent review committee (IRC) related disclosure and informal discussions with IRC members. We recently compiled and analysed our findings from these reviews and discussions.

The scope of the reviews was limited to disclosure related to National Instrument 81-107 — *Independent Review Committee for Investment Funds* (NI 81-107 or the Rule). Overall, we noted a high level of compliance with the disclosure requirements related to NI 81-107. We also received generally positive feedback from IRC members regarding their experiences with NI 81-107.

This notice summarizes our findings and general observations in the following areas:

- IRC fees and compensation,

- IRC composition and interaction with the fund manager, and

- the use of standing instructions.

The notice concludes with a brief discussion regarding applications for exemptive relief from the conflict of interest prohibitions in securities legislation and next steps for NI 81-107.

1. — Background

1.1 — NI 81-107

NI 81-107 requires every investment fund that is a reporting issuer in Canada to have a fully independent body, the IRC, whose role is to oversee all decisions involving an actual or perceived conflict of interest faced by the fund manager in the operation of the fund.

Prior to NI 81-107, there was no requirement for investment fund managers to have any type of independent oversight over how they manage or monitor conflicts of interest. Several reports on investment funds and fund governance had concluded that the structure of the fund industry — where the investor's ownership of the fund is separate from the fund manager's management and control of the fund — creates the potential for the interests of fund investors to diverge from the pecuniary interests of the fund manager. This structure has the potential to cause a fund manager to act contrary to its fiduciary duty to the investment fund, and ultimately, to investors. NI 81-107 imposed a minimum, consistent standard of independent oversight for all publicly offered investment funds in each of the jurisdictions represented by the Canadian Securities Administrators (the CSA).

The Rule captures two types of conflicts that arise in the operation of an investment fund: (i) 'business' or 'operational' conflicts i.e. those relating to the operation by the fund manager of its funds that are not specifically regulated under securities legislation, except through the general duties of loyalty and care imposed on the fund manager under securities legislation; and (ii) 'structural' conflicts i.e. those resulting from proposed transactions by the fund manager with related entities of the fund manager, fund or portfolio manager currently prohibited or restricted by securities legislation.

The Rule requires the fund manager to establish written policies and procedures that it must follow when making a decision involving a conflict of interest matter and to refer the matter to the IRC for its recommendation or approval, as appropriate, before proceeding.

A decision by the fund manager to engage in certain transactions that comprise 'structural' conflicts must be approved by the IRC before the transaction may proceed. Approval by the IRC of each transaction may be provided on a case-by-case basis or take the form of a standing instruction. For any other course of action not restricted by securities legislation, but which raises an actual or perceived conflict of interest for the fund manager, the fund manager is required to refer the conflict of interest matter to the IRC, which must then provide the fund manager with a recommendation that must be considered by the fund manager before proceeding.

NI 81-107 came into force on November 1, 2006 and its transition period ended on November 1, 2007.

1.2 — Continuous Disclosure Reviews

Between September 2009 and March 2010, staff reviewed NI 81-107 related disclosure of a sample of 141 investment funds managed by 41 different fund managers, covering annual financial periods ending in 2008 and 2009, including: (a) the prospectus (long form or simplified prospectus as applicable to the fund); (b) the annual information form; (c) annual financial statements of the fund; (d) the IRC Report to Securityholders; (e) the annual management report of fund performance; and (f) the website of the fund manager or funds as applicable.

Fund managers included in the sample were selected for review based on criteria designed to reflect a fair representation of fund family size and fund type. Of the 41 fund managers reviewed, 21 were fund managers of conventional mutual funds with assets under management representing approximately 83% of total assets under management of conventional mutual funds. These fund managers had assets under management ranging from $46 million to $95 billion.

Of the remaining managers in the sample, 12 were fund managers of exchange-traded funds (ETFs) representing approximately 66% of the total market capitalization of ETFs listed on the TSX. We also reviewed flow through limited partnerships managed by 3 fund managers, labour-sponsored investment funds managed by 2 fund managers, and scholarship plans managed by 3 fund managers. In total, we reviewed 82 conventional mutual funds, 42 exchange-traded funds, 7 flow through limited partnerships, 6 labour sponsored investment funds and 4 scholarship plans.

1.3 — Meetings with IRCs

During 2009, we also met informally with twelve IRCs of fund managers with assets under management ranging from approximately $950 million to $95 billion. Staff from the *Compliance and Registrant Regulation* branch of the OSC accompanied Investment Funds staff at these meetings.

The purpose of the meetings was to obtain general feedback from IRCs on five broad topics: (i) the IRC's relationship with the fund manager; (ii) the IRC's initial and ongoing orientation to the fund manager's business; (iii) the IRC's involvement in the fund manager's decision to apply for exemptive relief; (iv) the IRC's experience with standing instructions; and (v) general comments from the IRC on NI 81-107.

2. — Findings and Comments

In the course of our disclosure reviews, we gathered information with a view to assessing some of the key concerns expressed by the fund industry when we published the Rule for comment. Specifically, that IRCs would be expensive; it would be difficult to attract and retain IRC members; and the IRCs could undermine the fund managers' ability to effectively manage its funds. Our reviews revealed that:

- IRC fees represent a minimal portion of a fund's total net assets,

- all funds reviewed were able to create and retain an IRC under the Rule, and

- standing instructions on conflict of interest matters enable the fund manager to effectively manage fund operations.

We noted only one recurring disclosure deficiency of significance. In a number of instances, funds failed to disclose IRC fees as a separate line item in the funds' financial statements as required under NI 81-106 — *Investment Fund Continuous Disclosure* (NI 81-106). We discuss this briefly as well as some general observations on other topics below.

All fund managers received notice of our reviews and were advised of any deficiencies specific to the funds they managed that we observed during the course of our review.

2.1 — IRC Fees and Compensation

2.1.1 — IRC Fees

During the course of the comment process in the development of NI 81-107, concern was expressed about the costs associated with establishing and maintaining IRCs. Specifically, we were told that higher costs to investors caused by an IRC would reduce the overall competitiveness of the fund industry.

We found in our reviews that IRC fees and compensation across different sizes and sectors of the investment fund industry generally represent a minimal portion of a fund's total net assets, significantly less than the approximate 1% to 3% of a fund's total net asset value represented by the typical fund manager fee.

For fund managers we reviewed with assets under management of less than $500 million, IRC fees ranged between 0.000033% and 0.27% of total net assets of the fund. For fund managers with assets under management between $500 million and $5 billion, IRC fees ranged between 0.0005% and 0.096% of total net assets of the fund. IRC fees ranged between 0.000067% and 0.041% of total net assets of funds managed by fund managers with assets under management over $5 billion.

2.1.2 — IRC Compensation

IRC Members

Overall annual compensation amongst IRC members we reviewed ranged between $0 and $50,000 per annum. We found that annual compensation of IRC members was highest, on average, for IRCs of fund managers with assets under management over $5 billion (i.e. $26,500 per IRC member).

Annual IRC member compensation for fund managers with between $0 and $500 million in assets under management ranged between $0 and $30,000. For fund managers with assets under management between $500 million and $5 billion, annual IRC member compensation ranged between $2,000 and $40,000. Annual IRC member compensation for fund managers with over $5 billion in assets under management, ranged between $10,000 and $50,000.

IRC Chairs

Overall annual compensation amongst IRC chairs we reviewed ranged between $0 and $75,000 per annum. Similar to IRC members, we observed that annual compensation of IRC chairs was highest, on average, for IRCs of fund managers with assets under management over $5 billion (i.e.$34,117 per IRC chair).

Annual IRC chair compensation for fund managers with between $0 and $500 million in assets under management ranged between $0 and $40,000. For fund managers with assets under management between $500 million and $5 billion, annual IRC chair compensation ranged between $2,000 and $50,000. Annual IRC chair compensation for fund managers with over $5 billion in assets under management ranged between $10,000 and $75,000.

2.1.3 — IRC Fees Disclosure

The majority of fund managers we reviewed disclosed IRC fees as a separate line item in the fund's Statement of Operations. In a number of instances, however, IRC fees were combined in the Statement of Operations with other fees such as directors' fees, administration fees, trustees' fees and administration costs. In a few instances, IRC fees were not disclosed at all in the Statement of Operations.

One explanation given for the absence of this information was the fund manager's view that the IRC fees accrued were not 'material'. We remind fund managers that all IRC fees paid by the fund must be appropriately disclosed in the fund's financial statements as a separate line item from directors' fees, trustees' fees and other expenses, in accordance with section 3.2, Item 8.1 of NI 81-106. This disclosure requirement is intended to provide transparency of the amount of IRC fees that were specifically charged to the investment fund.

2.1.4 — General Comments and Observations Regarding IRC Compensation

We did not find any IRC members who received indemnities from the fund or the fund manager in their capacity as IRC members.

The factors used to assess the level of compensation of IRCs were generally consistent across the IRCs of all funds in our sample and typically included three or more of the following factors:

- the best interests of the funds,
- the number, nature and complexity of the funds,
- the number of funds overseen by the IRC,
- that compensation paid by each fund to the IRC should reflect the benefits accruing to that fund,
- the fund manager's recommendation on compensation,
- comparative compensation amongst other IRCs i.e. industry practice,
- comparative compensation amongst other IRCs that oversee similarly structured investment funds with similar conflicts of interest,
- the results of the IRC's annual self-assessment,
- frequency of meetings of the IRC, time devoted by each IRC member and the workload of each IRC member, and
- the breadth and depth of the relevant experience of each IRC member.

We observed that fund managers used four different methods for allocating IRC fees among the funds they manage: (1) proportionately based on the total net assets of the fund; (2) equally among their funds; (3) based on the average number of securityholders and the average number of transactions per fund and per series for the period; and (4) at least two fund managers used a complexity factor to proportionately allocate IRC fees to their funds i.e. the more complex the fund structure, the greater proportion of total IRC fees allocated to that fund.

We also observed that four fund managers absorbed IRC fees. These fund managers had assets under management of more than $5 billion.

2.2 — IRC Composition and Interaction with the Fund Manager

During the course of the comment process in the development of NI 81-107, concern was expressed about the availability of qualified candidates to serve as IRC members and that fund managers would face significant difficulty in finding qualified candidates. We did not observe any funds that were unable to create and retain an IRC with qualified members as required under the Rule.

2.2.1 — IRC Composition

We found that a significant number of IRC members have expertise in the financial services industry. The size of the IRCs reviewed ranged between three members (the required number under the Rule) and nine members, with most of the IRCs reviewed having three members.

The mandate of almost all of the IRCs reviewed was limited to the Rule's mandate for the IRC to provide oversight of the fund manager's handling of conflict of interest matters. A few IRCs in the sample also act as advisory boards to the fund manager and/or to the funds more generally on a range of topics. In at least three instances, these latter IRCs were associated with fund managers with more than $5 billion in assets under management.

The majority of IRCs consulted had IRC members who sat on only one IRC. A few IRCs had at least one member who sat on two IRCs.

Almost all of the IRCs reviewed had no changes in composition for the fiscal years ending in 2008 and 2009. For the few IRCs that did experience changes in composition, the disclosure indicated that these changes were typically due to one or more of the following factors: (a) a change in control of the fund manager; (b) one or more IRC members ceasing to be independent; (c) expiry of IRC member terms or reduction of IRC size; or (d) change of fund manager.

2.2.2 — IRC Independence

We found only a few instances that caused us to question the independence of IRC members. Fund managers and IRCs are reminded that to be independent, a member of an IRC must not have a material relationship which could be perceived to interfere with the IRC member's judgment regarding a conflict of interest matter (see the definition of "independent" in section 1.4 of NI 81-107). For example, we have questioned whether counsel that acts for the fund manager and/or the funds should act as an IRC member, given the pecuniary relationship that exists. Staff will continue in the normal course of our prospectus and application reviews to monitor the independence of IRC members.

A few IRC Reports to Securityholders provided detailed explanations of instances where IRC member independence could be called into question due to: (a) a specific conflict of interest of an IRC member which arose at the time (in which case the member resigned from the IRC); (b) aggregate ownership of IRC members in a specific fund of the fund manager beyond 10%; or (c) ownership or other involvement by IRC members in companies that provide services to the fund manager or the applicable investment funds.

One IRC Report to Securityholders disclosed that as part of its annual assessment, IRC members are required to complete an annual declaration that the member is "independent" as defined in section 1.4 of NI 81-107. We think the practice of an annual certification of independence by IRC members is beneficial and consistent with section 4.2(2)(a) of NI 81-107. We encourage IRCs to consider this approach.

2.2.3 — Interaction with Fund Manager

The IRCs we met with told us that IRC members generally engage in active, constructive discussions with fund managers. Differences of opinion between IRC members and the fund manager are typically resolved by active debate and ongoing discussion until IRC members are satisfied that a conflict of interest is appropriately addressed and a reasonable result will be achieved for the funds.

IRC members told us that their fund managers support the ongoing education of IRC members by:

- facilitating attendance at seminars sponsored by law firms and private entities,

- making executive officers, portfolio managers, and sub-advisors available as needed to provide more information on a topic,
- providing news articles and press releases of interest on conflict matters, and
- including an education component at regularly scheduled IRC meetings.

We were also told that fund managers typically orient new IRC members to the fund manager's business by:

- providing written materials,
- introducing IRC members to members of each of the fund manager's business units,
- reviewing the IRC charter, and
- reviewing the conditions of any exemptive relief previously granted in connection with structural conflicts.

We did not find any instances where a fund manager proceeded with a conflict of interest matter without the positive recommendation of the fund's IRC.

In our reviews, we noted some inconsistency in disclosure by IRCs in the IRC Report to Securityholders of transactions which did not comply with a term of a standing approval of the IRC. In one case, the IRC Report disclosed a breach of a standing approval which was a transactional error caused by a sub-advisor to the fund. However, staff reviewed a similar instance where an IRC did not disclose a breach of a term of a standing approval in its IRC Report to Securityholders. The explanation given to staff for the lack of disclosure in the IRC Report was the fund manager's view that the transactional error was caused by a sub-advisor, not the fund manager, and was not 'material'. We remind IRCs that any known breach of a term of a standing approval issued by the IRC is required to be disclosed in the IRC Report to Securityholders by section 4.4(1)(h) of NI 81-107.

2.2.4 — Use of Legal Counsel

While the majority of IRCs we met with advised that they have independent external counsel on retainer, most told us that to date there has not been a need for them to obtain advice from external counsel.

A few IRCs specifically mentioned their reliance on independent external counsel only for establishing the IRC charter and issues related to the indemnities of IRC members.

2.3 — Standing Instructions

When we published NI 81-107 for comment, concern was expressed about the IRC potentially undermining the ability of a fund manager to effectively manage its funds by requiring it to constantly seek an IRC recommendation or approval. To address this concern, NI 81-107 permits the IRC to issue standing instructions on specific conflict of interest matters. We observed that standing instructions have been used in a variety of conflict of interest matters.

In our reviews, we found that most fund managers have standing instructions related to the following matters:

- Trading with a Related Broker-Dealer,
- Trading Aggregation and Allocation,
- Client Brokerage Commissions/Soft Dollars/Best Execution,
- Proxy Voting/Voting Procedures,
- Fund Valuation,
- Net Asset Value/Error Correction,
- Trust Accounting,
- Allocation of Fund Expenses,
- Personal Trading,
- Business Entertainment and Gifts,
- Portfolio Management and Investment Decisions,
- Related Issuer Purchases/Inter-Fund Trading,
- Fund Expense Policy (including Related Party Expenses),
- Excessive Trading Policy, and
- Changing Subadvisors or Service Providers.

We further observed standing instructions in some cases on a number of other conflict of interest matters, including:

- Fund on Fund Arrangements,
- Sales Practices,
- Unitholder Activity,

- Custody,
- Launching, Merging or Closing Funds,
- Fundamental Changes,
- Fairness Policy,
- Role of the Head Trader,
- Trade Error Correction,
- Transfer Agency/Error Correction,
- Administration Errors,
- Management Fee Rebates,
- Lending to Affiliate Borrowers,
- Benchmark Selection,
- Seed Capital Withdrawal,
- Commingling of Cash,
- Complaint Management,
- Client Privacy,
- Dissemination of Portfolio Information,
- Dual Employment Policy, and
- Indemnities for Independent Directors.

At least four IRCs we met with indicated that they review standing instructions quarterly in addition to the annual assessment required by section 4.2(1)(b) of NI 81-107. Reporting to the IRC of 'each instance' of the fund manager's reliance on the IRC's standing instructions also occurred quarterly in these cases.

A number of IRC members told us that amendments to existing standing instructions occur as needed, in response to market developments and the fund manager's request.

The IRC Reports to Securityholders reviewed provided a list of standing instructions issued by the IRC, however, only a few of these reports provided a brief summary of the actual or perceived conflict of interest that each particular standing instruction was intended to address. We think this practice is beneficial and encourage IRCs to consider this approach.

3. — Applications for Discretionary Exemptions from the Conflict of Interest Prohibitions

Since the Rule became fully effective in November 2007, we have received a number of applications for discretionary relief from the conflict of interest prohibitions in securities legislation. These applications generally fall into one of three groups:

- reissued relief, which has consisted of revoking and replacing exemptions that were granted by the CSA prior to NI 81-107 coming into force with the terms and conditions updated to reflect NI 81-107 and the role of the IRC;
- relief analogous to the codified exemptions in NI 81-107 and NI 81-102, which has generally consisted of new relief that is granted on the same terms and conditions as the exemptions codified under NI 81-107 and NI 81-102; and
- new requests for discretionary exemptions not previously granted and beyond the scope of the exemptions codified in NI 81-107 and NI 81-102.

In each instance, the applicant has sought to rely upon IRC approval of the transaction as the basis for requesting the exemption. Most IRCs we met with told us that they are advised by the fund manager of its intention to file an exemptive relief application. Staff continue to encourage fund managers to advise their IRCs prior to applying for any exemptive relief. Generally, we expect:

- the IRC has been informed about the fund manager's intention and reasons for applying for relief,
- the application indicates that the IRC has been consulted, and
- the application indicates the IRC's view of the relief requested.

In the limited instances when new exemptive relief has been granted, the fund manager has been able to demonstrate a compelling market need for the exemption. In each instance, the relief has generally been limited in scope, and has included conditions that address objective and transparent pricing.

Next Steps

Overall, we received positive feedback from IRC members regarding their experiences working with fund managers under NI 81-107. We also noted a high level of compliance with disclosure requirements related to NI 81-107. We intend to continue to monitor fund manager and IRC practices under NI 81-107 with a view to providing further guidance and notices as needed.

Staff will continue in the normal course of our prospectus and application reviews to inquire about the process and criteria used by an IRC to arrive at a positive recommendation or approval of a particular conflict of interest matter. Occasionally, this will include requesting the minutes of an IRC's discussion or materials related to a matter subject to its review, or asking to speak with the IRC or IRC Chair to discuss a specific matter.

Finally, Staff will continue to consider new applications for exemptive relief from the conflict of interest prohibitions in securities legislation on a case by case basis. Generally, Staff's view is that fund managers must demonstrate a compelling need or market necessity for the exemptive relief. We encourage fund managers and their counsel to contact us before proceeding with applications for exemptive relief not previously granted and beyond the scope of the exemptions codified under NI 81-107.

OSC Staff Notice 81-714 — Compliance with Form 41-101F2 — Information Required In An Investment Fund Prospectus

Date: March 4, 2011

34 O.S.C.B. 2518

Purpose

This notice sets out the views of staff of the Ontario Securities Commission (Staff) on the disclosure required by Form 41-101F2 — *Information Required in an Investment Fund Prospectus* (the Form or Form 41-101F2) and the types of comments Staff will generally raise in the course of a review of an investment fund prospectus required to be filed in the form of Form 41-101F2.

Background

National Instrument 41-101 *General Prospectus Requirements* (NI 41-101) prescribes the use of Form 41-101F2 by all investment funds filing prospectuses, other than mutual funds that file prospectuses under National Instrument 81-101 — *Mutual Funds*. The Form includes specific disclosure requirements for investment funds that are in addition to the general requirement in securities legislation to provide full, true and plain disclosure of all material facts in the prospectus relating to the securities to be distributed.

Compliance with Form 41-101F2

Compliance with the disclosure requirements of Form 41-101F2 is important because the Form is intended to provide clear and concise information about the investment fund to investors that will assist them in making informed investment decisions. Staff expect the disclosure to comply with the plain language principles listed in section 4.1 of Companion Policy 41-101CP and to be presented in the order and using the headings specified in the Form. This allows the prospectus disclosure to be presented in an easy-to-read format that can be understood by investors and more easily compared to other investment funds.

Recently, Staff have seen a number of prospectuses required to be in the form of Form 41-101F2 that have departed from the general requirements relating to the use of plain language, brevity and the ordering of information and use of headings. In our reviews, Staff have begun to raise specific concerns with cover page and prospectus summary disclosure and disclosure related to the investment objectives of the fund. Staff have also begun to consider whether the requirements and purpose of the Form are being met in a multi-fund prospectus.

Cover Page and Prospectus Summary Disclosure

Increasingly, Staff have observed cover page and prospectus summary disclosure that contain too much detail about the investment fund's strategies, manager, portfolio advisor and distribution policies and the sector(s) that the fund will invest in, as well as information not specifically contemplated by the Form. In some instances, entire disclosure items from other sections of the Form have been included in the cover page and prospectus summary, including performance data, charts and graphs. Staff have also seen the introduction of headings, such as Investment Rationale, as well as an increase in promotional and marketing language in the cover page and prospectus summary. For example, there has been disclosure about the managers' beliefs regarding the economy and why an investment strategy adopted by the fund should be considered attractive by investors.

In our prospectus reviews, Staff will consider the purpose of the Form, and specifically, the intent of the cover page and prospectus summary disclosure, which is to ensure investors are presented with information about the investment fund in a clear, concise and comparable format that assists them in making informed investment decisions.

Generally, Staff's view is that the cover page disclosure should only provide a brief description of the investment fund and the securities to be distributed and be limited to the disclosure specifically mandated by Item 1 of Form 41-101F2. Consequently, in our reviews Staff may ask that cover page disclosure be reduced or request that certain disclosure be removed. Similarly, Staff expect that the prospectus summary disclosure will generally only provide a brief summary of the information that appears elsewhere in the prospectus, as set out by Item 3.3 of Form 41-101F2. In our reviews, Staff may request some disclosure in the prospectus summary be removed and be replaced with cross-references to the more detailed disclosure that appears elsewhere in the prospectus, as mandated by Item 3.3(2), in order to maintain the brevity of the section. Generally, Staff have requested that charts and graphs not mandated by the Form be removed from the prospectus summary.

As part of our reviews, we have reminded filers and their counsel that information not contemplated under any other section of the Form may be disclosed under "Other Material Facts" as specified by Item 35 of the Form.

In instances where the investment fund has complex or unique risks, features or costs, Staff have begun to request that additional, tailored disclosure that is specific to the securities to be distributed be added to the cover page or the prospectus summary disclosure to ensure investors are provided with full, true and plain disclosure of all material facts. This tailored disclosure has included the request by Staff for the inclusion of a plainly worded, brief warning presented in bold type or in text boxes in these sections.

Disclosure About Investment Objectives

Item 5.1 of the Form requires information that describes the fundamental nature of the investment fund, or the fundamental features of the investment fund, that distinguish it from other investment funds. The Instructions to Item 5.1 of the Form specifically require a statement of the type(s) of securities in which the investment fund will primarily invest under normal market conditions.

Staff have observed investment objectives limited to a statement about the nature of the returns that the investment fund seeks to provide to investors. For example, Staff have seen disclosure that states that the objective of the investment fund is to provide shareholders with the opportunity for capital appreciation, without sufficient accompanying detail. Generally, Staff expect that filers will comply with all aspects of Item 5 of Form 41-101F2. In our reviews, Staff have requested that some investment strategies that are an essential aspect of the investment fund, as described in Instruction (3) to Item 5.1 of the Form, be disclosed as an investment objective of the investment fund. Staff may also ask that certain disclosure that does not form part of the investment objective, such as an investment fund's initial indicative yield, be removed.

Prospectuses For Multiple Investment Funds

Recently, exchange traded mutual funds (ETFs) have filed prospectuses that combine disclosure for multiple ETFs in the same document. As the number and types of ETFs have proliferated, Staff have observed multiple ETF prospectuses that combine disclosure for different types of ETFs, including index participation units, actively managed ETFs, inverse and leveraged ETFs and commodity pools.

Generally, Staff's view is that the number of investment funds offered in a prospectus should be limited to investment funds with substantially similar investment objectives, strategies and features. In our reviews of multiple ETF prospectuses, Staff will consider whether the combination of multiple investment funds into one single prospectus impacts the ability of investors to be provided full, true and plain disclosure. When the number of investment funds incorporated into one prospectus interferes with the presentation of key information in a clear, concise and comparable format for investors, Staff will request that the filer separate the investment funds into different prospectus documents.

Further Information

Filers and their counsel are encouraged to contact Staff at an early stage in the planning of any distribution that may give rise to any questions concerning the issues discussed in this Notice.

OSC Staff Notice 81-715 — Cross-Listings by Foreign Exchange-Traded Funds

Date: **August 26, 2011**

34 O.S.C.B. 8819

Purpose

This notice sets out the views of staff of the Ontario Securities Commission (OSC Staff or we) regarding the application of prospectus requirements and investment fund product regulation in connection with cross-listings on an exchange in Ontario by foreign exchange-traded mutual funds.

Background

Exchange-traded mutual funds (ETFs) are open-end mutual funds in continuous distribution whose securities trade over an exchange. We have received several inquiries relating to foreign ETFs that may be interested in cross-listing their securities on an exchange in Ontario.

Regulatory Issues

The increasingly global market for investment products requires balancing the benefits of investor access to potentially high quality foreign products with investor protection and maintaining consistent product regulation between domestic and foreign products. As the ETF industry continues to evolve, its products are becoming more diverse and complex. This requires ensuring that investors fully understand the risks of the products they are purchasing.

Regulatory oversight of investment fund products is achieved primarily through disclosure requirements and product regulation, which arises when an investment fund is either actively selling its securities or conducting a distribution in Ontario.

OSC Staff's view is that a cross-listing of foreign ETF securities would generally be a distribution in Ontario. ETFs differ from other exchange-listed issuers primarily because an ETF's exchange listing functions as the primary distribution channel through which an ETF issues its securities to investors and increases its net assets. As a result, we do not consider the ETF's exchange listing as merely providing a source of secondary market liquidity.

OSC Staff's view is that foreign ETF providers must file a prospectus to qualify their securities and comply with investment fund product regulation in Ontario before applying to cross-list on an exchange in Ontario. Similarly, we take the view that foreign providers of other products that are comparable to ETFs and use a similar distribution structure as ETFs, such as some exchange-traded notes (ETNs), must also file a prospectus before applying to cross-list their securities on an exchange in Ontario.

OSC Staff intend to continue to monitor this issue, as well as developments in the ETF industry generally, with a view to assessing whether a modified approach to cross-listings of foreign investment products may be warranted. We are prepared to discuss whether there may be circumstances in which we are prepared to consider an exception to the approach reflected in this notice.

Further Information

Filers and their counsel are encouraged to contact OSC Staff at an early stage in the planning of any foreign ETF or ETN distribution that may give rise to any questions concerning the issues discussed in this Notice.

OSC Staff Notice 81-716 — 2011 Summary Report for Investment Fund Issuers

Date: November 4, 2011

34 O.S.C.B. 11046

Table of Contents

Introduction

This report provides an overview of the key activities and initiatives of the Ontario Securities Commission for 2010/2011 that impact investment fund issuers and the fund industry, including:

- key policy initiatives,

- disclosure and compliance reviews, and

- recent developments in staff practices.

This report provides information about the status of some of the initiatives the OSC is undertaking to promote clear and concise disclosure in order to assist investors to make more informed investment decisions. The report also provides information about our work to address the sufficiency of regulatory coverage across all investment fund products. It highlights recent product and market developments, as well as our regulatory response to these developments, in order to assist the investment fund industry in understanding and complying with current regulatory requirements.

The OSC is responsible for overseeing over 3000 publicly-offered investment funds. Ontario based publicly-offered investment funds hold approximately 80% of the over $800 billion in publicly-offered investment fund assets in Canada.

We administer the regulatory framework for investment funds, including:

- reviewing and assessing product disclosure for all types of investment funds, including prospectuses and continuous disclosure filings,

- considering applications for discretionary relief from securities legislation and rules, and

- taking a leadership role in developing new rules and policies to adapt to the changing environment in the investment fund industry.

We also monitor and participate in investment fund regulatory developments globally, primarily through our work with the International Organization of Securities Commissions (IOSCO). OSC staff participation on IOSCO SC5 Investment Management technical committee informs both our operational and policy work. We discuss our participation with IOSCO further on our website at www.osc.gov.on.ca at *About the OSC — Co-operation*

The investment fund products we oversee include both conventional mutual funds and non-conventional investment funds. Non-conventional funds include non-redeemable investment funds such as closed-end funds, mutual funds listed and posted for trading on a stock exchange (ETFs), commodity pools, scholarship plans, labour-sponsored or venture capital funds and flow-through limited partnerships. We discuss the different types of funds further on our website at www.osc.gov.on.ca *Investment Funds — Fund Operations*

While non-conventional funds remain small relative to the conventional fund industry in terms of number and assets under management, they continue to grow at a faster rate than conventional funds. Offerings of non-conventional funds, particularly ETFs, continue to proliferate. In 2011, assets under management by ETF providers exceeded $40 billion for the first time.[1] As of June 2011 the number of exchange-traded products listed on the Toronto Stock Exchange (TSX) topped 200.[2] These products include 187 ETFs and 14 exchange-traded notes.[3] The number of listed ETF products on the TSX has more than doubled in the past two years, bringing the total market cap to approximately $49 billion.[4]

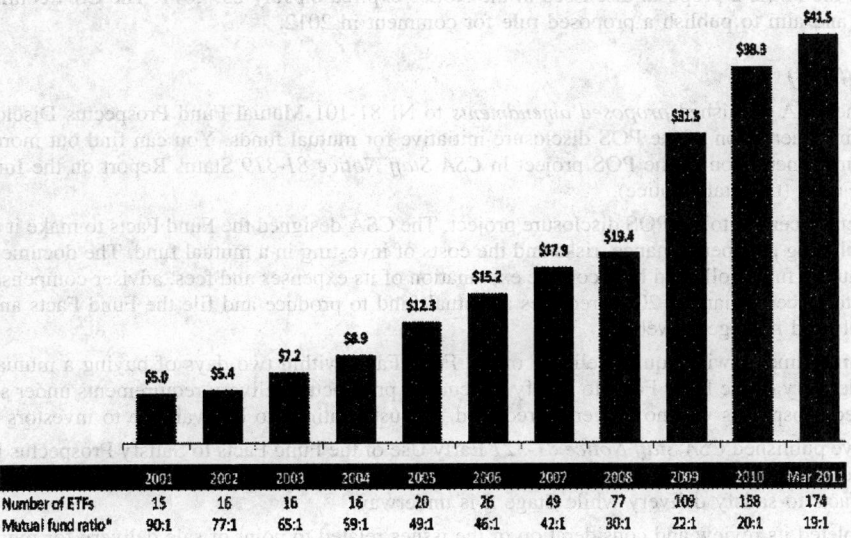

	2001	2002	2003	2004	2005	2006	2007	2008	2009	2010	Mar 2011
Number of ETFs	15	16	16	16	20	26	49	77	109	158	174
Mutual fund ratio*	90:1	77:1	65:1	59:1	49:1	46:1	42:1	30:1	22:1	20:1	19:1

The closed-end fund industry has also recently seen renewed growth exceeding over $30 billion in assets under management for the first time since December 2007.[5]

As these and other non-conventional investment products, such as linked note derivative offerings, increase in number, the OSC will continue to assess and respond to product developments and innovations with a view to promoting investor protection and assessing the sufficiency and consistency of regulatory treatment of different investment fund products.

1. — Key Policy Initiatives

The OSC continues to play a leading role in several significant policy initiatives with other securities regulators in Canada through the Canadian Securities Administrators (the CSA). This section reports on the status of significant policy initiatives including:

- the CSA's project to modernize investment fund product regulation, and
- the point of sale project.

We also report on other projects that impact investment funds and the fund industry including:

- National Instrument 41-101 — General Prospectus Requirements, and
- OSC Staff Notice 81-715 — Cross-listings by Foreign Exchange Traded Funds.

1.1 — Modernization of Investment Fund Product Regulation

The modernization project's mandate is to review the regulation of publicly offered investment funds with a view to developing rules that recognize product developments and trends in the investment fund industry. The project is being carried out in two phases.

The first phase of this CSA initiative is *proposed amendments* to National Instrument 81-102 Mutual Funds (NI 81-102) and National Instrument 81-106 Investment Fund Continuous Disclosure (NI 81-106), which were published for comment on June 25, 2010. Phase 1 involves amending existing rules to update certain regulatory requirements for mutual funds in order to keep pace with market and product developments, particularly with respect to ETFs. The amendments also introduce new liquidity and term restrictions on money market fund holdings. The comment period for these proposals expired on September 24, 2010 and 24 comment letters were received. The CSA have reviewed and considered all of the comments and expect to publish final amendments for this first phase of the project by the end of 2011.

[1]Investor Economics ETF and Index Funds Report First Quarter 2011

[2]TSX News Release June 1, 2011

[3]TSX News Release June 1, 2011

[4]TSX News Release June 1, 2011

[5]Investor Economics Insight Monthly Update May 2011

On May 26, 2011, the CSA published *CSA Staff Notice 81-322 —* Status Report on the Implementation of the Modernization of Investment Fund Product Regulation Project and Request for Comment on Phase 2 Proposals (the Notice). The Notice provides an update on the status of the Modernization project generally, including an anticipated timeline for the stages of the project. It also seeks specific feedback from investors and industry stakeholders on the CSA's proposal to focus next on developing an operational rule for non-redeemable investment funds. This second phase of the initiative aims to introduce certain core investment restrictions and operational requirements for non-redeemable investment funds that are analogous to those applicable to mutual funds under NI 81-102. The purpose of Phase 2 would be to address investor protection and fairness concerns the CSA have identified. The CSA's goal in making these proposals is to achieve more consistent, fair and functional regulation across the investment fund product spectrum.

The comment period on the Phase 2 proposal discussed in the Notice expired on July 25, 2011. The CSA continue to review and consider all the comments received and aim to publish a proposed rule for comment in 2012.

1.2 — Point of Sale (POS)

On August 12, 2011, the CSA published *proposed amendments* to NI 81-101 Mutual Fund Prospectus Disclosure (NI 81-101) that set out Stage 2 of the CSA's implementation of the POS disclosure initiative for mutual funds. You can find out more about the CSA's decision to proceed with a staged implementation of the POS project in *CSA Staff Notice 81-319* Status Report on the Implementation of Point of Sale Disclosure for Mutual Funds (the Staff Notice).

The *Fund Facts* document is central to the POS disclosure project. The CSA designed the Fund Facts to make it easier for investors to find and use key information, including past performance, risks and the costs of investing in a mutual fund. The document provides investors with key information about the mutual fund, followed by a concise explanation of its expenses and fees, adviser compensation and the investor's rights. Stage 1, which came into force January 1, 2011, requires a mutual fund to produce and file the Fund Facts and for it to be available on the mutual fund's or mutual fund manager's website.

The Stage 2 proposed amendments will require delivery of the Fund Facts within two days of buying a mutual fund. The proposed amendments will also permit delivery of the Fund Facts to satisfy the current prospectus delivery requirements under securities legislation. Although delivery of the simplified prospectus will no longer be required, it must continue to be available to investors upon request.

On February 24, 2011, we published *CSA Staff Notice 81-321* Early Use of the Fund Facts to Satisfy Prospectus Delivery Requirements, which provides guidance on the key terms and conditions that the CSA will look for when considering applications for exemptive relief to permit the early use of the Fund Facts to satisfy delivery while Stage 2 is underway.

Once the CSA has completed its review and consideration of the issues related to point of sale delivery for mutual funds, in Stage 3 the CSA will publish for further comment any proposed requirements that would implement point of sale delivery for mutual funds. As part of Stage 3, we will also consider point of sale delivery for other types of publicly offered investment funds.

1.3 — National Instrument 41-101 — General Prospectus Requirements

The CSA published *proposed amendments* to NI 41-101 on July 15, 2011. The purpose of the amendments is to enhance the effectiveness of prospectus disclosure standards, clarify the requirements, address significant identified gaps, and eliminate or modify ineffective or unduly burdensome requirements. The amendments are based on CSA experience with the rule to date, feedback from the public and requests for relief from issuers.

Key amendments that impact investment funds include:

- A specific requirement to describe maximum and minimum amounts of leverage through use of derivatives,

- A new requirement to disclose trading expense ratio,

- Expansion of the disclosure requirement concerning ownership interests in a fund and the manager, and

- A requirement for management to disclose bankruptcies and cease trade orders in respect of all issuers (not just investment fund issuers).

1.4 — OSC Staff Notice 81-715 — Cross-listings by Foreign Exchange Traded Funds

We published *OSC Staff Notice 81-715* on August 26, 2011 in response to inquiries we have received in recent years from U.S. based ETFs. The notice sets out OSC staff's view regarding the applicable securities regulatory requirements in connection with potential cross-listings by U.S. based ETFs.

The notice confirms staff's view that a cross-listing by a foreign based ETF would generally be a distribution in Ontario and, consequently, that foreign ETF providers must file a prospectus to qualify their securities and comply with product regulation in Ontario before applying to cross-list on an exchange in Ontario. The notice further confirms staff's view that foreign providers of other products that are comparable to ETFs and use a similar distribution structure to ETFs, such as some exchange traded notes (ETNs), must also file a prospectus before applying to cross-list their securities on an exchange in Ontario.

2. — Disclosure and Compliance Reviews

On an ongoing basis, OSC staff review the prospectus and continuous disclosure filings of Ontario-based investment funds. Risk-based criteria are used to select investment funds for reviews of their disclosure documents. We may also choose to conduct targeted reviews of a particular industry segment or on a particular topic. In addition to our prospectus and continuous disclosure reviews, the Investment Funds (IF) Branch works closely with staff in the Compliance and Registrant Regulation (CRR) Branch on issues related to fund manager compliance and identifying possible emerging issues. This can sometimes lead to us conducting joint reviews.

This section discusses some observations, findings and themes from:

- our prospectus reviews of non-redeemable investment funds and ETFs,
- our prospectus reviews of hypothetical pro-forma performance data,
- our focused continuous disclosure reviews of money market funds, ETFs and investment portfolio holdings, and
- our focused disclosure reviews of Independent Review Committees.

2.1 — Non-redeemable Investment Funds

We reviewed a high number of prospectuses for non-redeemable investment funds as a result of the renewed growth in this industry segment over the past year. These funds are non-conventional investment funds, and are often referred to as closed-end funds. They are generally not redeemable on demand for net asset value and list their securities for trading on an exchange. In addition, they are generally not in continuous distribution, relying on cash from limited underwritten offerings to acquire their initial assets.

We will continue to monitor developments in this industry through our prospectus reviews with a view to informing what regulatory changes may be appropriate in connection with Phase 2 of our Modernization project discussed above.

2.1.1 — OSC Staff Notice 81-711 Closed-end Investment Fund Conversions to Open-end Mutual Funds

We published *OSC Staff Notice 81-711* on October 29, 2010, in response to the increasing use of a built-in conversion feature by which a closed-end fund converts to an open-end mutual fund.

Closed-end fund securities typically trade on an exchange, but often at a discount to their net asset value (NAV). Historically, the industry has attempted to manage this discount by providing investors with an annual redemption right at NAV. The annual redemption right has resulted in significant redemptions and early fund terminations in some instances. A key objective of the conversion feature is to provide investors in the closed-end fund with enhanced liquidity through a more frequent redemption feature at NAV after the fund converts to an open-end mutual fund.

The notice sets out the views of OSC staff on the regulatory issues related to closed-end fund conversions and the types of comments staff will generally raise in the course of a review of a built-in conversion feature. As discussed in the notice, we have focused on whether the funds continue to have the same or substantially similar investment objectives, strategies and fees before and after the conversion. We have generally taken the view that these products should be compliant with the regulatory requirements applicable to conventional mutual funds from inception if they intend to convert to a mutual fund within a relatively short timeframe. Our prospectus reviews have focused on key areas of disclosure such as:

- the potential that these products will trade at a discount to NAV up to the time of conversion,
- fees payable by investors both before and after the fund converts to a mutual fund,
- the risks associated with the conversion, and
- performance disclosure for periods before and after conversion.

2.1.2 — Long-term Warrant Offerings

We noted a continued resurgence in the use of long-term warrant offerings by closed-end funds. These offerings appear unique to closed-end funds that rely on them to replenish their asset base after experiencing redemptions at an annual redemption date. We discussed these offerings previously in *last year's branch report* and the OSC Investment Funds Practitioner. Our concerns relate primarily to prospectus delivery on exercise of the warrants and dilution.

OSC staff continue to raise comments on long-term warrant offerings with a view to:

- promoting the disclosure of any unique risks, such as dilution,
- confirming that the investor that pays the subscription price receives a prospectus, and
- better understanding the use of this method of capital raising for investment funds.

2.2 — OSC Staff Notice 81-714 Compliance with Form 41-101F2 — Information Required in an Investment Fund Prospectus

We published *OSC Staff Notice 81-714* on March 4, 2011, in response to the increasing number of closed-end fund prospectuses that were not complying with the Form 41-101F2 requirements relating to the use of plain language, brevity and the ordering of information and use of headings. In particular, we noted that closed-end funds were providing increasing amounts of information on the cover page and in the summary of their prospectuses.

The Notice sets out the types of comments staff will generally raise as part of our reviews to encourage presentation to investors of information about the investment fund in a clear, concise and comparable format that assists them in making informed investment decisions. For example, IF staff may ask that cover page disclosure be reduced or request that certain disclosure be removed. In instances where the investment fund has complex or unique risks, features or costs, staff ask for additional, tailored disclosure that is specific to the securities to be distributed. The disclosure should be added to the cover page or the prospectus summary disclosure so that investors are provided with full, true and plain disclosure of all material facts. Staff may also ask the fund or its fund manager to include a plainly worded, brief warning presented in bold type or in text boxes.

The Notice also states that OSC staff will raise comments when the investment objective does not clearly set out the fundamental features of the investment fund that distinguish it from other funds. In addition, it sets out staff's view that the number of investment funds offered in a single long form prospectus should be limited to those investment funds with substantially similar investment objectives, strategies and features, with a view to facilitating full, true and plain disclosure to investors.

2.3 — Exchange-traded Funds and Index Participation Units

We note that over the past few years there has been a proliferation in the number of product offerings from index providers. We also recognize that there is an interest on the part of ETF providers to differentiate themselves in the market by branching out beyond the traditional indices. Staff are of the view that the term "market index" should be interpreted in a manner that is consistent with the investment restrictions set out in NI 81-102.

We have been raising comments on some ETF prospectuses where the ETF describes its securities as being index participation units (IPUs) under NI 81-102 in instances where they did not appear to be tracking a market index as contemplated under NI 81-102 because:

- the index provides exposure to asset classes or strategies that a mutual fund would not be able to engage in directly,

- the index tracks the price of a commodity,

- the index purports to track the performance of hedge funds, real property, or incorporates leverage or shorting strategies,

- the index is designed to terminate at a specified time, and

- the index is overly concentrated in a few issuers.

We also discussed market indices and IPUs in the May, 2011 edition of *the Investment Funds Practitioner*.

2.4 — Hypothetical Pro-forma Performance Data

We continue to raise comments regarding the use of hypothetical pro-forma performance data by all investment funds and other products such as linked notes. We have discussed the use of performance data and yield disclosure in offering documents previously in the November 30, 2007 and January 8, 2010 editions of the *Investment Funds Practitioner*. Our CRR Branch, along with the CSA, also published *CSA Staff Notice 31-325 — Marketing Practices of Portfolio Managers* on July 8, 2011. The notice discusses some of the concerns with the use of hypothetical performance data including that many investors may not have sophisticated investment knowledge sufficient to fully understand its inherent risks and limitations. In order to address this concern, we generally request the removal of hypothetical pro-forma performance data disclosure.

2.5 — Continuous Disclosure Reviews

The IF Branch continued our continuous disclosure review program this year by applying risk based criteria to select investment funds for reviews of their disclosure documents. We also conducted targeted reviews of particular industry segments and topics. This section discusses some of our reviews and findings in connection with:

- money market funds,

- ETFs,

- investment portfolio holdings, and

- fund facts risk rankings.

2.5.1 — Money Market Funds

In response to recent global regulatory developments related to money market funds and to further inform our own CSA proposals (see Modernization of Investment Fund Product Regulation above), we commenced a targeted review of money market funds focused on their risk and liquidity profiles. We anticipate the reviews will provide us with a better understanding of the makeup of the industry's capitalization (i.e. retail vs. institutional), redemption experience, and any differences between the different types of money market funds (e.g. Premium and T-Bill). The reviews will also look at differences in exposure between money market funds offered in Canadian and U.S. currencies.

To this point, the reviews have provided OSC staff with some initial insights on how the Canadian money market industry competes and how money market funds are dealing with various market risks, including sovereign default risks in Greece and their potential effect on short term paper issued by European banks and businesses. We also used the reviews to quickly assess the potential exposure of Canadian and U.S. money market funds to potential U.S. government debt defaults in the event the debt ceiling issue was not resolved in the U.S.

2.5.2 — ETFs

In response to the continued growth of the ETF industry and the growing complexity of ETF products, we completed targeted reviews of ETFs. The reviews were primarily focused on the valuation of illiquid assets and the use of proprietary derivatives, such as forwards. We reviewed a total of 40 ETFs from 11 fund managers, which represent approximately 70% of the ETF industry.

We will continue to monitor developments in this industry through our prospectus reviews with a view to informing what regulatory changes or guidance may be appropriate in connection with the Modernization project discussed above.

2.5.3 — Investment Portfolio Holdings

We are currently engaged in a focused review of the investment portfolio holdings disclosed in the management reports of fund performance (MRFPs), financial statements and in the Fund Facts. As part of this focused review, staff intend to examine: (1) whether the summarized investment portfolio in the MRFP and Fund Facts provides information classified into appropriate sub-groups and provides meaningful information to investors about the fund's portfolio, and (2) whether the investment portfolio in the financial statements provides sufficiently organized information for investors to assess consistency and performance against the fund's stated investment objectives and strategies.

Our review is intended to examine how closely a fund's stated investment objectives and strategies are implemented over time. Following the review, we will consider providing guidance around the presentation of a fund's investment portfolio disclosure and how the fund's discussion of its investment strategy can be updated and improved based on how the fund has been investing. We anticipate completing the review by fall, 2011.

2.5.4 — Fund Facts Risk Ranking Reviews

We also currently have under way a focused review of the investment risk classification methodology in the simplified prospectus. Following amendments to the simplified prospectus form which added a requirement to describe the methodology by which the fund manager identifies the investment risk level of a mutual fund, we have noticed that such disclosure in the simplified prospectus may be overly brief. As part of this focused review, staff are asking for a copy of the methodology which the manager is required to make available to investors, in order to assess: (1) whether the prospectus disclosure is adequate; and (2) whether the investment risk classifications in the simplified prospectus and Fund Facts documents seem to be appropriate.

2.6 — OSC Staff Notice 81-713 Focused Disclosure Review National Instrument 81-107 Independent Review Committee for Investment Funds

As discussed in last year's annual report, the IF Branch completed targeted reviews of NI 81-107 related disclosure. We reported our findings in *OSC Staff Notice 81-713* which we published on March 25, 2011.

3. — Outreach and Consultation

We continue our efforts to be transparent regarding practices and procedures that impact investment fund issuers in as timely a manner as possible. Our intent in doing so is to better enable fund managers and their advisors to avoid potential regulatory issues when they are at the planning stage for a new fund or transaction.

3.1 — Investment Funds Product Advisory Committee (IFPAC)

The OSC announced the members of our first ever Investment Funds Product Advisory Committee on *August 11, 2011*.

In an environment of rapid product growth and increasing complexity of investment fund products, we recognize the unique perspective that market participants, particularly product manufacturers and portfolio advisors, may have in identifying and anticipating market and product trends.

The IFPAC will advise OSC staff specifically on emerging product developments and innovations occurring in the investment fund industry. The committee will discuss the impact of these developments and emerging issues. The IFPAC may also act as one source of feedback to OSC staff on the development of policy and rule-making initiatives to promote investor protection, fairness and market efficiency across all types of publicly offered investment fund products.

The initial IFPAC members are:

Ghassan (Jason) Agaby	Dynamic Funds
Tom Bradley	Steadyhand Investment Funds
Darren Farkas	Fidelity Investments Canada ULC
Adam Felesky	Horizons Exchange Traded Funds (ETFs)
Goshka Folda	Investor Economics
Kevin Gopaul	BMO Asset Management
Ed Jackson	RBC Capital Markets
Oliver McMahon	Blackrock Asset Management Canada
Marian Passmore	Canadian Foundation for Advancement of Investor Rights
Jeff Ray	Manulife Investments
Mary Taylor	Mackenzie Investment
Mark Yamada	PUR Investing Inc.

IFPAC members will serve a two year term. IFPAC will meet quarterly and be chaired initially by Rhonda Goldberg, Director of the Investment Funds Branch.

In addition to IFPAC, OSC staff continue to meet frequently with stakeholders, including investment fund managers and their advisors, investor advocates and subject matter experts on various topics to inform our policy and operational work. For example, in July, 2011 we brought together a range of product specialists, which included ETF manufacturers, asset managers on both the buy and sell side as well as academics to discuss with OSC staff the use of derivatives and synthetic ETFs.

3.2 — The OSC Investment Funds Practitioner

The Practitioner is an overview of recent issues arising from applications for discretionary relief, prospectuses and continuous disclosure documents that investment funds file with the OSC and that are reviewed by the IF Branch. It is intended to assist investment fund managers and their advisors who regularly prepare public disclosure documents and applications for exemptive relief on behalf of investment funds.

Part 8: MUTUAL FUNDS

The Practitioner is also intended to make fund managers more broadly aware of some of the issues we have raised in connection with our reviews and how we have resolved them. The Practitioner can be found on our website www.osc.gov.on.ca at Information for Investment Funds.

In May, we published the fifth edition of the *Investment Funds Practitioner*. Topics included:

- Requirements to Calculate Daily NAV

- Split Shares — Relief from s. 119 of the Act

- Split Shares — Secondary Offerings

- Forward Agreement Fee Disclosure

- PIFs for CCO

- Short Form Prospectus Eligibility

- Relief from 90-Day Prospectus Filing Requirement

- Definition of Index Participation Unit

- Point of Sale FAQs

We intend to publish the sixth edition of the Investment Funds Practitioner this fiscal year. We welcome suggestions for future topics.

4. — Feedback and Contact Information

If you have any questions regarding, or feedback on, our second Annual Report, please send them to investmentfunds@osc.gov.on.ca.

You can find additional information regarding investment funds and the IF Branch on our *website*.

We have also attached a list of IF Branch staff at the end of this report.

[list of IF Branch staff omitted]

OSC Staff Notice 81-717 — Report on Staff's Continuous Disclosure Review of Portfolio Holdings by Investment Funds

Date: **August 2, 2012**

35 O.S.C.B. 7004

Purpose of the Notice

This notice reports the findings and recommendations of staff of the Investment Funds Branch of the Ontario Securities Commission (**Staff** or **we**) arising from a targeted review of portfolio holdings and other related disclosure filed by investment funds. This notice supplements the guidance and interpretations provided in National Instrument 81-106 *Investment Fund Continuous Disclosure* (**NI 81-106**), National Instrument 81-101 *Mutual Fund Prospectus Disclosure* (**NI 81-101**), and Form 81-101F3 *Contents of Fund Facts Document* (**Form 81-101F3**).

Objective and Scope of Review

Disclosure of a fund's investment portfolio provides key information to investors in assessing consistency and performance against the fund's stated investment objectives and strategies. As part of our continuous disclosure review program, we recently sought to assess how effectively the categorization of a fund's investment portfolio in its disclosure reflects the fund's investment objective and to assess regulatory compliance in the fund's on-going disclosure.

Between August 2011 and June 2012, staff reviewed portfolio disclosure of a sample of investment funds as presented in their annual or interim Management Reports of Fund Performance (**MRFPs**), Fund Facts as applicable, and Statements of Investment Portfolio. These items were reviewed against the investment objectives set out in the prospectus of each fund.

We reviewed disclosure of a sample of 203 investment funds managed by 40 different fund managers with a head office in Ontario, covering annual financial periods ending in 2010 and interim periods ending in 2011. Fund managers included in the sample were selected for review based on criteria designed to reflect a fair representation of fund family size and type.

Of the 40 fund managers reviewed,

- 24 were fund managers of conventional mutual funds representing 52.5% of total assets under management of all conventional mutual funds

- 5 were fund managers of exchange-traded funds (**ETFs**) representing approximately 98.7% of the total market capitalization of ETFs listed on the TSX

- 6 were fund managers of closed-end funds

- 3 were fund managers of flow-through limited partnerships; and

- 2 were fund managers of labour sponsored investment funds.

Summary of Findings and Comments

Our findings indicate that the portfolio disclosure presented in a fund's MRFP, Statement of Investment Portfolio and Fund Facts can be improved to provide more meaningful information to investors about the composition of the portfolio and how the fund's investments align with the investment objectives set out in the fund's prospectus. Specifically, we observed three key trends:

- the use of portfolio categories that did not reflect the unique characteristics of the fund as set out in its investment objectives;

- inconsistencies in the categories used across different disclosure documents of the fund to describe the investments in the portfolio; and

- the use of broad, generic categories instead of more discrete, specific categories that would provide more meaningful information on portfolio composition and the alignment of portfolio investments with the fund's investment objectives.

We sent comment letters to all 40 fund managers in our sample. Of the 203 funds we reviewed, we issued comments on 120 funds. No funds were required to refile or restate any disclosure documents as a result of our review. However, the fund managers that received a comment letter committed to improve future disclosure as follows:

- 33% will improve the portfolio listing in their financial statements;

- 36% will improve portfolio categorization in their MRFP; and

- 26% will improve the categorization of the investment mix in their Fund Facts.

Our findings are discussed below.

1. — Statement of Investment Portfolio — Financial Statements

1.1 — Existing Requirements in NI 81-106

NI 81-106 sets out the minimum disclosure requirements for an investment fund's financial statements.[1] For example, section 3.5 of NI 81-106 requires investment funds to separate long and short portfolio holdings and to aggregate disclosure for portfolio assets having the same description and issuer.[2]

Staff take the view that the portfolio holdings disclosed in the fund's financial statements should be presented in a way that is meaningful and understandable to readers and that the statement of investment portfolio should be clearly organized. In our view, subtotals should be provided so that investors can understand their exposure immediately, without having to perform calculations.

In addition, we remind investment funds of the guidance provided by the Canadian Institute of Chartered Accountants (**CICA**)[3] which has indicated that the statement of investment portfolio should provide a profile of securities, summarized by type and/or other groupings considered the most meaningful to users. One of the suggested groupings is classification by investment objective.

1.2 — Choice of Portfolio Classification in view of Investment Objectives

From our review of the statement of investment portfolio in the financial statements, we saw that the majority of fund managers rely on common portfolio breakdowns. As a result, many funds in the same fund family break down their portfolios using the same categories regardless of the type or unique characteristics of the fund.

Staff generally expect the statement of investment portfolio to break down the portfolio into the most discrete, specific categories given the nature and unique characteristics of the fund. For example, we observed one fund focused on investing in equity securities of issuers connected to global financial infrastructure which categorized its portfolio by country. In our view, further classification of the portfolio into specific categories such as sector or company type would have better demonstrated how the fund's investments aligned with its investment objectives.

Staff look to the investment objectives and strategies of an investment fund, as disclosed in the prospectus, to determine its key characteristics. Since the investment objectives and strategies outline what the fund will primarily invest in and how it will distinguish itself from similar funds, we generally expect the objectives to be reflected in the categories selected. This will allow an investor to better understand if the fund holds what it set out to invest in, or whether over time its investments have drifted from the stated objectives.

Some fund managers expressed the view that since the statement of investment portfolio is part of the financial statements, they choose to classify the portfolio by asset class, consistent with the purpose of the financial statements. Other fund managers thought it would be more beneficial to use standard classifications from service providers such as Bloomberg or Standard & Poors, which are widely available and would offer comparability when reviewing financial statements of similar funds across fund families. A number of fund managers expressed the view that groupings based on investment objectives would only detract from the clarity of the existing disclosure.

In Staff's view, it is critical that an investor be provided with disclosure that shows how the investments made by the fund are consistent with the fund's investment objectives. Presenting breakdowns strictly by asset class may be of limited utility to investors. Classification by the categories reflected in a fund's investment objectives is important because it is likely that the fund was sold to the investor based on the distinguishing characteristics described in the fund's investment objectives and strategies.

---

[1] Section 2.1(2) of Companion Policy 81-106CP.

[2] Section 3.5(2) and (3) of NI 81-106.

[3] The Research Report Financial Reporting by Investment Funds in 1997, which was subsequently updated in 2009. The Study Group was comprised primarily of auditors and members of the investment fund industry.

Market Capitalization

Some funds stated in their investment objectives or strategies that they would invest in companies of a certain market capitalization, only to fail to break down their portfolio by issuer size in the financial statements.

Again, we generally expect that if the fund or the name of the fund indicates a focus on market capitalization, a break down by company size should be included to demonstrate to investors that the investment objectives and strategies have been followed. While we recognize that the industry has not standardized definitions for small, medium, and large capitalization, we encourage portfolio managers to consider using their own categories which can be explained in the disclosure. We also encourage fund managers to revisit the wording in the prospectus to ensure clarity and plain meaning.

1.3 — Other Disclosure Documents

Some fund managers stated that the additional classifications we requested in the financial statements were already provided in other parts of the fund's continuous disclosure record, such as in the MRFP, Fund Facts, or the fund's website. We remind issuers that while the MRFP is intended to supplement the financial statements, funds are not required to bind or deliver the two documents together,[4] and that each continuous disclosure document must be considered independent of any other document. In light of this, fund managers should consider whether the specific portfolio categories used in the MRFP should also be mirrored in the financial statements. We note that this approach is consistent with the principles underlying Canadian generally accepted accounting principles (**Canadian GAAP**) which discuss the concepts of reliability, relevance and understandability.[5]

1.4 — Inconsistency in Disclosure Documents

In some cases, we identified inconsistency between the disclosure in the financial statements and the fund's other documents. For example, one fund's results of operations in the MRFP discussed how the fund's performance was affected by sector *and* investments in different countries, yet the portfolio categorization in the financial statements was based only on geography. We generally take the view that classifications in the statement of investment portfolio should provide the same level of insight in the financial statements as is available in the MRFP, especially since investors may not review or receive both documents.

1.5 — Broad Categories

As part of our review, we commented on categories in the statement of investment portfolio we considered to be too broad or generic. For example, we reviewed a fund identified as a gold and precious metals fund by its name, which classified over 96% of its portfolio as "Mining and Precious Metals" without any further classification. While we did not consider the heading Mining and Precious Metals to be incorrect, the presentation of the portfolio would have been enhanced by use of more discrete, specific categories providing a more detailed description of the fund's portfolio investments, for example, by type of precious metal. Staff expect that the categories used will reflect the unique composition of a fund's portfolio. We also generally expect that fund managers will consult with their portfolio managers on how the fund's portfolio should be categorized to effectively demonstrate how the fund's investments are aligned with its investment objectives.

In another case, we observed that a fund's classifications had not been updated to reflect a change in the portfolio mix and, as a result, a number of companies with varying business models were grouped together under the broad heading "Business", which we found to be vague and confusing. Staff expect funds to perform periodic reviews to ensure that the categories initially selected in the Statement of Investment Portfolio remain applicable and relevant to the fund and its investment objectives.

2. — Management Report of Fund Performance

2.1 — Existing Requirements in Form 81-106F1

Form 81-106F1 *Contents of Annual and Interim Management Report of Fund Performance* (**Form 81-106F1**) includes a number of requirements to ensure that the MRFP is in a format that assists readability and comprehension.[6] It also specifies that care should be taken to ensure that the information in the Summary of Investment Portfolio is presented in an easily accessible and understandable way[7].

Form 81-106F1 further requires that an investment fund should use the most appropriate categories to break down its summary of investment portfolio given the nature of the fund. If appropriate, more than one breakdown can be used according to type, industry, geographical locations, etc[8].

2.2 — Summary of Investment Portfolio

In our review of funds' MRFPs, we observed the same trends and raised the same comments discussed above under *Choice of Portfolio Classification in view of Investment Objectives* and *Broad Categories*.

---

[4]Refer to National Instrument 81-106, Part 5 — Delivery of Financial Statements and Management Reports of Fund Performance.

[5]Section 1000 of the CICA Handbook.

[6]Item 1(c) — Part A of Form 81-106F1.

[7]Instruction 1 to Item 5 — Part B of Form 81-106F1.

[8]Instruction 2 to Item 5 — Part B of Form 81-106F1.

2.3 — Top 25 Holdings — Labour Sponsored Investment Funds (LSIFs)

We observed that the two labour-sponsored investment funds we reviewed did not list their top 25 holdings in their MRFPs. One of these LSIFs considered the obligation to disclose the fund's top 25 positions to only apply if the fund held more than 25 positions.

LSIFs are reminded of the requirement in Instruction 10 to Item 5 — Part B of Form 81-106F1 to disclose the fund's top 25 positions. If the LSIF holds fewer than 25 positions, we take the view that these positions should be disclosed in the Summary of Investment Portfolio in the MRFP.

3. — Fund Facts

3.1 — Inconsistency in Portfolio Categorization — Fund Facts versus the MRFP

As part of our review, we compared the categories used to break down fund portfolios in the Fund Facts against those disclosed in the funds' MRFP. In most cases, at least one of the categories used in the MRFP to break down the portfolio was reflected in the Fund Facts.

However, we also observed some inconsistencies. We saw portfolio breakdowns in the Fund Facts of some funds that were based on categories not used in the MRFP. In these instances, we viewed the categories used in the MRFP as more reflective of the investment objectives of the fund as well as more appropriate for use in the Fund Facts. For example, a life sciences and technology mutual fund categorized its Investment Mix in the Fund Facts by generic sectors such as information technology, health care, cash, and telecommunication services among other categories. The fund's MRFP, however, used specific categories more suitable to life sciences and technology such as software, communications equipment, computers and peripherals, internet software and services.

In another example, an asset allocation fund categorized its portfolio in the MRFP by sectors such as Canadian equities, Canadian fixed income, global fixed income, cash and cash equivalents, international equities and U.S. equities. The Investment Mix, however, was categorized by the type of underlying funds in which the fund invested.

We also observed a small number of mutual funds that used two or more categories in their MRFP to break down the fund's portfolio while the Fund Facts used only one of these categories. In Staff's view, the Investment Mix of each fund would have better reflected the fund's investment objective if an additional categorization, consistent with that of the MRFP, had also been included. This approach would have resulted in an Investment Mix composed of two pie charts or tables in the Fund Facts, as permitted by Form 81-101F3[9], instead of one. Fund managers of these funds indicated that they would consider using the mirrored basis for portfolio categorization in the Fund Facts and MRFP. Staff's view is that fund managers should consider using more than one pie chart or table in the Fund Facts when doing so would better display how the fund's investments align with its investment objectives.

We remind fund managers of the requirement in Form 81-101F3 *Contents of Fund Facts Document* (**Form 81-101F3**) to ensure consistency between the basis for portfolio categorization in the Fund Facts and the MRFP[10].

3.2 — Absence of a 'Look-Through' to the Holdings of Related Underlying Funds

In our review of the Fund Facts, we also observed that the Investment Mix disclosure of certain mutual funds which invested in related underlying funds did not "look-through" to the actual holdings of the underlying funds. Instead, the Investment Mix of the top fund specified only the types of related underlying funds. In our view, the Investment Mix of the top fund would have provided more meaningful disclosure to investors if it had used categories based on the actual holdings of its related underlying funds.

Staff remind fund managers that where a top fund is substantially invested in a single underlying fund, Form 81-101F3 requires that there should be a look-through to the holdings of the underlying fund as appropriate[11].

We acknowledge that Form 81-101F3 does not currently require a "look-through" to portfolio holdings where one top fund invests in multiple, related or unrelated, underlying funds. However, where a top fund is invested in underlying funds managed by the same fund manager, we encourage fund managers to consider an Investment Mix that looks through to the holdings of the related underlying funds. Given the common management of top and bottom funds, Staff would expect a fund manager to have access to the portfolio holdings of the underlying funds and, accordingly, be in a position to provide meaningful information to investors in the Investment Mix on the exposure to various securities resulting from the fund-of-funds structure.

3.3 — Broad Categories

Our review of the Fund Facts highlighted the same trends discussed above under *Broad Categories* that were observed with respect to the MRFP and the Statement of Investment Portfolio.

3.4 — General Compliance — Top 10 Holdings

In our review, we found a high level of compliance with Item 3(4) — *Investments of the Fund* of Form 81-101F3 which mandates Fund Facts disclosure of a mutual fund's top 10 investments. We did, however, find one fund that inadvertently provided the top 10 industry sectors in which the fund had invested, instead of the top 10 positions held by the mutual fund. The fund manager agreed to make the appropriate change to the issuer's Fund Facts.

---

[9] Item 3(5) — Part I of Form 81-101F3.

[10] Instruction 11 to Item 3 — Part I of Form 81-101F3.

[11] Instruction 9 to Item 3 — Part I of Form 81-101F3.

Conclusion

Our review indicates that investment funds can further improve the quality of their continuous disclosure relating to portfolio holdings. Useful, relevant disclosure is critical to maintaining and strengthening investor confidence and efficient capital markets. In our view, the categorization of a fund's portfolio should be directly connected to the specific asset classes and unique characteristics of the funds as set out in its investment objectives. Each of the Fund Facts, MRFP and financial statements of the fund should be considered independent of each other and provide investors with meaningful information to assess how closely the investment objectives of the fund are being implemented over time.

We encourage fund managers to consider the guidance in this notice when preparing their continuous disclosure to ensure it complies with securities rules and regulations.

OSC Staff Notice 81-718 — Summary Report for Investment Fund Issuers

Date: January 24, 2013

36 O.S.C.B. 1025

Table of Contents

Introduction

This third annual Summary Report for Investment Fund Issuers provides an overview of the key activities and initiatives of the Ontario Securities Commission for 2012 that impact investment fund issuers and the fund industry, including:

- key policy initiatives,

- emerging issues and trends,

- disclosure and compliance reviews, and

- recent developments in staff practices.

This report provides information about the status of some of the initiatives the OSC is undertaking to promote clear and concise disclosure in order to assist investors to make more informed investment decisions. The report also provides information about our work to address the sufficiency of regulatory coverage across all investment fund products. It highlights recent product and market developments, as well as our regulatory response to these developments, in order to assist the investment fund industry in understanding and complying with current regulatory requirements.

The OSC is responsible for overseeing over 3000 publicly-offered investment funds. Ontario based publicly-offered investment funds hold approximately 80% of the near $900 billion in publicly-offered investment fund assets in Canada.

We administer the regulatory framework for investment funds, including:

- reviewing and assessing product disclosure for all types of investment funds, including prospectuses and continuous disclosure filings,

- considering applications for discretionary relief from securities legislation and rules, and

- taking a leadership role in developing new rules and policies to adapt to the changing environment in the investment fund industry.

We also monitor and participate in investment fund regulatory developments globally, primarily through our work with the International Organization of Securities Commissions (IOSCO). OSC staff participation on the IOSCO C5 Investment Management committee informs our operational and policy work. We discuss our participation with IOSCO further on our website at www.osc.gov.on.ca at *About the OSC — Co-operation*. In this report, we highlight some of the recent work by IOSCO C5 we think will be of interest to investment fund issuers.

The investment fund products we oversee include both conventional mutual funds and non-conventional investment funds. Non-conventional funds include non-redeemable investment funds such as closed-end funds, mutual funds listed and posted for trading on a stock exchange (ETFs), commodity pools, scholarship plans, labour-sponsored or venture capital funds and flow-through limited partnerships. We discuss the different types of funds further on our website at www.osc.gov.on.ca *Investment Funds — Fund Operations*.

The ETF market continues to grow steadily, outpacing the growth of conventional mutual funds and closed-end funds. As at October 2012, there were 260 ETFs with assets of approximately $54.4 billion. In comparison, as at the end of 2011, there were 229 ETFs with assets of approximately $43.2 billion, representing an increase in assets of approximately 26%. In contrast, conventional fund assets increased by approximately 8%, and closed-end funds assets remained flat, over the same period.

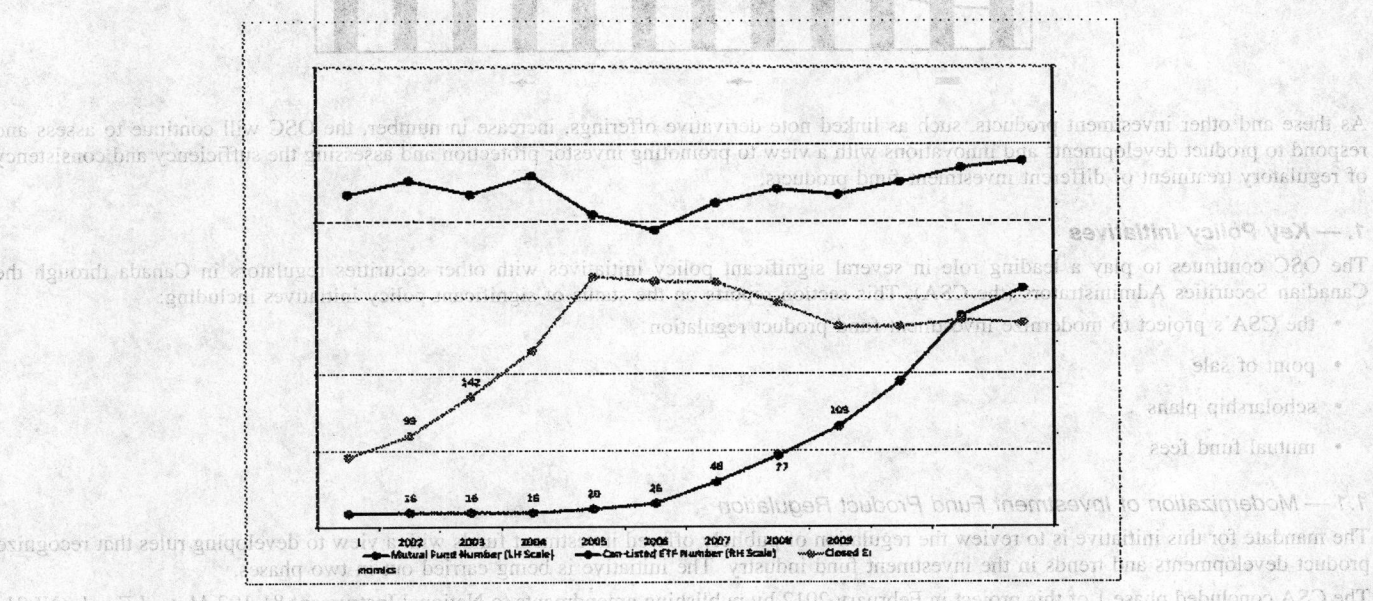

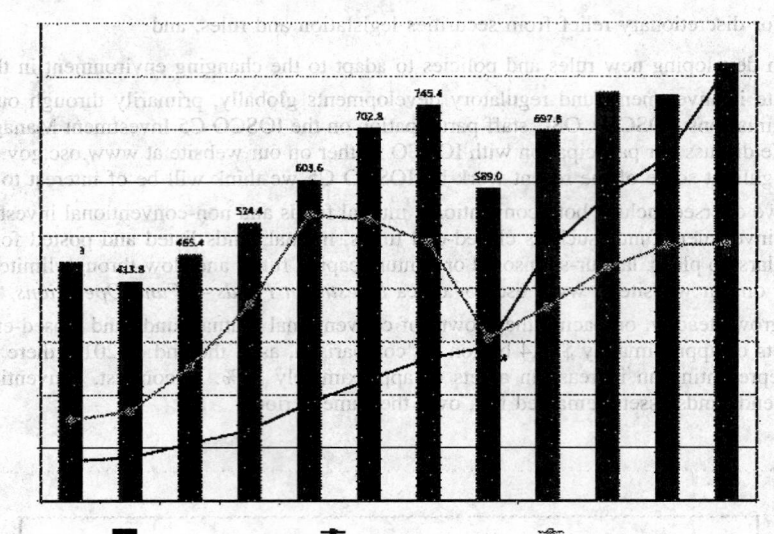

As these and other investment products, such as linked note derivative offerings, increase in number, the OSC will continue to assess and respond to product developments and innovations with a view to promoting investor protection and assessing the sufficiency and consistency of regulatory treatment of different investment fund products.

1. — Key Policy Initiatives

The OSC continues to play a leading role in several significant policy initiatives with other securities regulators in Canada through the Canadian Securities Administrators (the CSA). This section reports on the status of significant policy initiatives including:

- the CSA's project to modernize investment fund product regulation

- point of sale

- scholarship plans

- mutual fund fees

1.1 — Modernization of Investment Fund Product Regulation

The mandate for this initiative is to review the regulation of publicly offered investment funds with a view to developing rules that recognize product developments and trends in the investment fund industry. The initiative is being carried out in two phases.

The CSA concluded phase 1 of this project in February 2012 by publishing amendments to National Instrument 81-102 *Mutual Funds* (NI 81-102) and National Instrument 81-106 *Investment Fund Continuous Disclosure* (NI 81-106). The amendments updated certain regulatory requirements for mutual funds in order to keep pace with market and product developments, particularly with respect to ETFs. The amendments also introduced new liquidity and term restrictions on money market fund holdings. The amendments came into force on April 30, 2012, other than amendments relating to money market funds which had a 6 month transition period and came into force on October 31, 2012.

Phase 2 of this initiative, now underway, focuses on developing core investment restrictions and operational requirements for publicly offered non-redeemable investment funds, as outlined in CSA Staff Notice 81-322. Concurrently with this work, which will consist of amendments to NI 81-102, the CSA are also considering amendments to National Instrument 81-104 *Commodity Pools* (NI 81-104) to create a more comprehensive alternative investment fund framework that will operate in conjunction with the proposed amendments to NI 81-102. We are considering having NI 81-104 apply to both mutual funds and non-redeemable investment funds that invest in assets or use investment strategies that would not be permitted under the proposed amendments to NI 81-102. The CSA's goal is to achieve a more consistent, fair and functional regulatory regime across the investment fund product spectrum. We are also considering ways to help investors better differentiate between investment funds that use alternative investment strategies from those that do not. This may include a naming convention, new prospectus and continuous disclosure requirements and new marketing requirements.

We anticipate that the CSA will be able to finalize some aspects of the proposals for non-redeemable investment funds in advance of others. These include the proposed conflicts of interest provisions, securityholder and regulatory approval requirements, and custodianship requirements. Other aspects, particularly certain proposed investment restrictions that are interrelated with the proposals for NI 81-104, will likely require more time to consider and evaluate. We expect these components will be considered in conjunction with each other and to come into effect at the same time.

As part of this work, we will also be seeking input on proposals to enhance the disclosure requirements for all investment funds related to securities lending, repurchase and reverse repurchase transactions to keep pace with global regulatory developments.

The CSA plans to publish its Phase 2 proposals for comment early in 2013.

1.2 — Point of Sale

The Point of Sale (POS) Project is a continuation of the CSA's participation in the project by the Joint Forum of Financial Market Regulators to develop a more effective disclosure regime for conventional mutual funds and segregated funds.

The Fund Facts is central to the POS project and is designed to make it easier for investors to find and use key information. The Fund Facts is in plain language, no more than two pages double-sided and highlights key information that is important to investors, including past performance, risks and the costs of investing in a mutual fund.

On June 18, 2010, the CSA announced its approach to proceed with a staged implementation of the POS Project in CSA Staff Notice 81-319.

Stage 1, which came into force January 1, 2011, requires mutual funds to produce and file the Fund Facts and for it to be available on the mutual fund's or mutual fund manager's website. The Fund Facts must also be delivered or sent to investors free of charge on request.

On August 12, 2011, the CSA published proposed amendments to NI 81-101 *Mutual Fund Prospectus Disclosure* that set out Stage 2 of the POS Project (2011 Proposal). Stage 2 proposes to allow delivery of the Fund Facts to satisfy the current prospectus delivery requirements to deliver a prospectus within two days of buying a mutual fund. Although delivery of the simplified prospectus will no longer be required, the simplified prospectus must still continue to be made available to investors upon request.

In response to stakeholder feedback, particularly from investor advocates, to the 2011 Proposal, on June 21, 2012, the CSA published for second comment changes to the Fund Facts. These changes focused primarily on the presentation of risk in the Fund Facts document. The comment period expired on September 6, 2012. We received 33 comment letters from stakeholders.

In the June, 2012 publication, we committed that before finalizing any changes to the Fund Facts content, the CSA would test the proposed changes with investors. The results of this testing would inform what changes the CSA would make to the Fund Facts before finalizing Stage 2. This testing was completed in October 2012. The CSA expects to publish final materials for Stage 2 proposals by Summer 2013.

Concurrent with this work, the CSA is working on a CSA risk rating methodology in response to feedback received that we should mandate a risk methodology for use in the Fund Facts. The CSA expects to consult on this methodology and to publish it for comment on a separate timeframe from the Stage 2 proposals.

In stage 3, the CSA will complete its review and consideration of the issues related to point of sale delivery for mutual funds, as well as publish for further comment any proposed rules that would implement point of sale delivery for mutual funds. As part of this work, we will also consider the applicability of a Fund Facts-type document and point of sale delivery for other types of publicly offered investment funds.

1.3 — Scholarship Plans

We have been continuing to work with the CSA to update and improve the disclosure rules that govern scholarship plans, which are a type of investment fund product used by Canadians to save for their children's education.

Amendments to National Instrument 41-101 *General Prospectus Requirements* (NI 41-101) and proposed new Form 41-101F3 *Information Required in a Scholarship Plan Prospectus* were first published for comment on March 24, 2010, and then for a second comment period on *November 25, 2011*. After reviewing the comments received and further considering the proposals, several changes have been made and the CSA published *the new prospectus form in final form* on January 10, 2013.

The proposals aim to improve the prospectus disclosure provided by scholarship plans by introducing a prospectus form tailored to reflect the unique features of this product. This is an important investor-focused initiative. We know that many investors have trouble understanding the features and complexity of scholarship plans. The new Form 41-101F3 will require scholarship plans to provide investors with key information in a simple, accessible and comparable format to assist them in making a more informed investment decision.

Central to the new prospectus form is the Plan Summary document. Similar to the Fund Facts for mutual funds, it is written in plain language, will be no more than four pages, and highlights the potential risks and the costs of investing in a scholarship plan. It will form part of the prospectus, but will be bound separately.

The CSA expect that adoption of the new prospectus form will lead to more understandable and effective disclosure for investors, enabling them to better understand the possible outcomes and risks associated with investing in scholarship plans.

Following final publication in January 2013, we anticipate the *new prospectus form* to come into force in Spring 2013.

1.4 — Mutual Fund Fees

On December 13, 2012, the CSA published for comment Consultation Paper 81-407 *Mutual Fund Fees* which examines the mutual fund fee structure in Canada and identifies potential investor protection and fairness issues arising from that structure. The Consultation Paper further sets out various topics for discussion in order to determine whether any regulatory responses are needed to address the issues identified.

The Consultation Paper is the first step in the CSA's public consultations on this topic. Some of the options discussed would impact mutual funds or mutual fund manufacturers directly, and others would impact those who sell the product.

While the focus of this paper is on mutual funds, the CSA recognize that there are other investment fund products whose fee structure may raise similar investor protection and fairness issues for investors. Accordingly, we anticipate that any regulatory initiative we might ultimately undertake would assess whether the same initiative should also apply to other investment funds and comparable securities products.

Before considering any of these options further, the CSA intend to consult extensively with investors and industry participants, and will continue to closely monitor and assess the effects of existing regulatory reforms in Canada, such as the POS initiative, and around the world.

The comments on the Consultation Paper will help inform a roundtable the CSA plans to hold with investors and industry participants in 2013. The comments and discussions will also help the CSA determine what, if any, regulatory responses might be appropriate.

The comment period on the Consultation Paper closes on April 12, 2013.

2. — Emerging Issues and Trends

2.1 — Pre-Paid Forward Structures in Prospectus Offerings

We continue to consider the use of forward purchase agreements (prepaid forwards) by both mutual funds and non-redeemable investment funds (closed-end funds). We discussed this topic in the *December 2011 edition of the Investment Funds Practitioner*. In the prepaid forward structure, the fund proposes to pay an amount at the outset of the agreement, which could be substantially all of the fund's assets, to a counterparty. The counterparty is obligated to deliver the performance of a reference fund to the fund at a later date.

Staff have expressed concern about the use of prepaid forwards by investment funds because of the fund's exposure to the counterparty and the credit risk of the counterparty. We also view a prepaid forward, which transfers substantially all of the fund's assets to a counterparty, to change the nature of the fund from a portfolio of diversified holdings to a concentrated investment in one asset that is essentially an unsecured obligation of the counterparty.

To date, OSC staff have generally not recommended discretionary relief for mutual funds to use prepaid forwards. For closed-end funds, which do not require relief to use prepaid forwards, we have, through our prospectus reviews, allowed prepaid forwards only if the risks identified above are mitigated. This has included requiring the counterparty to post collateral for the benefit of the fund (subject to the terms described in the *December 2011 Investment Funds Practitioner*), and requiring the fund's prospectus to describe the terms of the prepaid forward and include a textbox on the cover page disclosing the fund's counterparty exposure and related risks.

As part of our re-examination of the use by investment funds of prepaid forwards, we have been meeting with counterparties to these agreements to discuss the parameters which could mitigate the concerns we have identified. The requirements under consideration include providing prospectus disclosure of what happens if there is a default or bankruptcy of the counterparty, daily posting of the collateral on the fund manager's website, and prescribing custodianship requirements for the collateral.

We will continue to consider this issue with a view to providing further guidance on the use of prepaid forwards by both mutual funds and closed-end funds in the Investment Funds Practitioner or an OSC staff notice.

2.2 — Fund Names

We have noted fund names in preliminary prospectus filings that are not consistent with the fund's investment objectives or investment strategies. We discussed this topic in the April 2012 edition of the *Investment Funds Practitioner*.

In naming new funds, staff expects that fund managers will consider selecting names which closely reflect the fund's investment objectives, and which distinguish the fund from other funds.

2.3 — Foreign Index Participation Units

We noted a continued trend in discretionary relief applications by mutual funds for exemptions from the fund on fund provisions in NI 81-102 to permit top funds to invest in foreign ETFs that, but for the fact that they are not listed on a stock exchange in Canada or the United States, would meet the definition of an index participation unit (IPU) in NI 81-102. For the purposes of this discussion, we refer to these foreign ETFs as Foreign IPUs. The Foreign IPUs for which discretionary relief has been sought to date have included ETFs listed on stock exchanges in the U.K., Germany, Ireland, and China.

The concept of an IPU in NI 81-102 was initially created at a time when there was a limited number of ETFs that tracked broad based diversified indices in Canada and the United States. Since this initial concept, we have observed over the past few years a proliferation in the number of product offerings from index providers, particularly ETFs, that track an index that may not qualify as a "market index" as that term is used in the definition of an IPU in NI 81-102. Staff believes that a market index should be one that is constituted in a manner that is consistent with the investment restrictions set out in NI 81-102. We discussed ETFs and IPUs in *last year's branch report*. We also discussed market indices and IPUs in the May 2011 edition of the *Investment Funds Practitioner*.

In considering whether to recommend discretionary relief to allow investments in Foreign IPUs, we have been asking for submissions detailing:

- whether the Foreign IPUs hold the securities that are included in a "widely quoted market index";

- the use, if any, of complex swap-based synthetic index replication strategies in the Foreign IPUs;

- whether the regulatory framework under which the Foreign IPUs operate is substantially similar to the regulatory framework of Canada; and

- the reasons as to why the top fund needs access to the Foreign IPU, and why it cannot meet its investment objectives in a manner that complies with the fund on fund provisions set out in NI 81-102.

To date, staff has been reluctant to recommend discretionary relief in instances where the Foreign IPUs use a synthetic index replication strategy because of its complexity and opacity. Staff has otherwise been prepared to consider recommending discretionary relief to allow investments in Foreign IPUs up to a specified limit in instances where it is demonstrated that the investment in Foreign IPUs is consistent with, and fundamental to, the investment objectives of the fund, and that the regulatory regime of the Foreign IPUs is substantially similar to the regulatory regime in Canada.

2.4 — Exposure to Commodities

We reviewed an increasing number of discretionary relief applications from investment funds with objectives aimed at providing investors with exposure to physical commodities, particularly precious metals. These funds directly hold the underlying commodity, or invest indirectly in the underlying commodity by investing in futures contracts or by investing in an ETF that tracks the price of that underlying commodity or directly holds the underlying commodity.

This trend appears to be driven by a growing acceptance of commodities as a separate asset class that may provide the benefit of diversification for a "traditional" portfolio consisting of stocks, bonds and cash, as well as by the desire of product manufacturers to capitalize on the growing retail demand for commodity-linked investments.

To date, staff have generally been prepared to recommend discretionary relief for mutual funds, other than precious metal mutual funds, to permit investments of up to 10% of the net asset value of the fund in gold and/or silver, to achieve this asset diversification. Staff have also recommended relief to permit funds with objectives to provide exposure to a particular sector or industry to invest up to 10% of their net asset value in physical commodities related to the sector or industry.

However, staff have generally taken the view that investments in physical commodities by conventional mutual funds, other than precious metal funds, in excess of 10% of net asset value are not consistent with the nature of a mutual fund as a diversified portfolio of securities.

2.5 — Increase in Linked Note Offerings

There was an increase in the number of linked note pricing supplements filed during the course of 2012. CSA Staff Notice 44-304 *Linked Notes Distributed Under the Shelf Prospectus System* sets out staff's concerns about disclosure provided in the shelf prospectus relating to the linked notes, as well as the process for requesting the pre-clearance of linked notes under the shelf prospectus system.

We continue to review the supplements filed for pre-clearance that are offering "novel" derivatives. As part of our reviews:

- staff have expressed concerns about some novel underlying interests that consist of actively managed portfolios. In those instances, we have raised comments regarding the transparency of the underlying interest, and whether the linked note or the underlying interest should be subject to some additional requirements similar to those that apply to investment funds.

- staff have expressed concern with structures where discretion could be exercised by the issuer of the linked notes in any material calculations affecting the linked notes. In such instances, staff have asked that an independent calculation agent be used.

- we reviewed some supplements that had not been filed for pre-clearance, and raised comments in instances where the supplement included disclosure such as past performance data that was potentially misleading.

- we asked filers to provide, among other things, continuous disclosure regarding the linked notes on a website and to refer investors to the site in the supplement; and disclosure of all fees payable by holders of the notes, including fees paid to dealers.

We will continue reviewing these supplements with a view to informing what regulatory changes or guidance may be appropriate in connection with novel offerings filed under National Instrument 44-102 *Shelf Distributions*.

3. — Disclosure and Compliance Reviews

On an ongoing basis, OSC staff review the prospectus and continuous disclosure filings of Ontario-based investment funds. Risk-based criteria are used to select investment funds for reviews of their disclosure documents. We may also choose to conduct targeted reviews of a particular industry segment or on a particular topic. In addition to our prospectus and continuous disclosure reviews, the Investment Funds (IF) Branch works closely with staff in the Compliance and Registrant Regulation (CRR) Branch on issues related to fund manager compliance and identifying possible emerging issues. This can sometimes lead to us conducting joint reviews.

3.1 — Continuous Disclosure Reviews

This section discusses some of our reviews and findings in connection with:

- advertising and marketing materials
- yield/income funds
- risk ratings in Fund Facts
- review of portfolio holdings

3.1.1 — Advertising and Marketing materials

We commenced a targeted review of advertising and marketing materials of investment funds. A key objective of this review is to raise awareness for preparers of advertising and marketing materials that staff are monitoring advertising activities and looking beyond technical compliance with the OSC's marketing rules to determine if overall the information presented is potentially misleading to retail investors.

As part of this initiative, in addition to continuing ad hoc reviews of advertising materials based on staff's monitoring, dedicated IF Branch staff have been selecting advertising and marketing materials of 4 to 6 investment fund managers to review on a quarterly basis. These reviews cover conventional mutual funds, closed-end funds, exchange-traded funds, commodity pools, and labor sponsored investment funds.

As part of the review, staff have been asking the selected investment fund manager for all advertisements and marketing materials appearing in newspapers, presentations, brochures, the internet, television and radio ads, social media, fund manager websites, email blasts, and green sheets during the previous quarter. Staff also ask for a description of the policies and procedures relating to the investment fund manager's marketing activities.

A few common or recurring issues that we have noted during our reviews to date include:

- inappropriate use of hypothetical data
- use of unsupportable statements
- failure to provide a balanced message on risk/reward

Part 8: MUTUAL FUNDS

- internet ads without the required appropriate warning language

- lack of adherence to the requirement to provide standard performance

- use of misleading headlines, or headlines that suggest a degree of safety, a lack of risk, or phenomenal skills or results.

Our reviews have resulted in investment fund managers:

- removing certain advertisements that we brought to their attention

- materially changing their sales communications

- reviewing and revising their policies and procedures

- re-training their staff involved in producing and approving their marketing materials.

We expect to publish our observations and guidance arising from this review in Spring 2013.

3.1.2 — Yield/Income Funds

We reviewed the prospectuses of a sample of investment funds that make regular distributions to investors. The scope of this review included the distribution policies and the investment fund manager's decision making process on the form and amount of the distributions.

We identified a number of issues, including:

- Funds paying distributions in excess of the fund's increase in net asset value from operations. In these instances, while such distributions are essentially a return to the investor of their own capital, the use of terminology such as "yield" or "income" in the fund's name implies underlying performance or earnings;

- Funds paying distributions in the form of reinvested units unless, for funds held in non-registered plans, the investor expressly chooses to receive cash distributions. In staff's view, receiving reinvested units may conflict with the funds' stated focus of providing investors with a regular income stream.

You can find further details regarding this review in the *April 2012 Investment Funds Practitioner*. In addition to identifying staff's concerns, the Practitioner communicated OSC staff's expectations regarding disclosure that should be provided in prospectuses and continuous disclosure documents to highlight the nature of the distributions, indicate why distributions were made despite the shortfall in earnings, and what investor action is needed if cash distributions are desired.

We will continue to monitor these offerings through our prospectus reviews with a view to informing what regulatory changes or guidance may be appropriate.

3.1.3 — Risk Ratings In Fund Facts

We continued to carry out a focused review of the risk ratings assigned to mutual funds in the Fund Facts document with a view to identifying outliers, and asking the mutual fund managers to provide submissions to support the determination of the risk rating of the mutual fund. We introduced the scope of this focused review in *last year's summary report*.

We identified mutual funds with risk ratings of "low to medium" or "medium" compared with peer funds with risk ratings of "medium to high" and "high". Where we challenged the risk rating of the mutual fund relative to the risk classification methodology used by the manager, as identified in the simplified prospectus, we relied upon objective data and benchmarks to support our analysis.

As a result of the review, some mutual fund managers changed the fund risk rating, increasing the rating from "medium" to "medium to high". In these instances, staff asked that an amended and restated Fund Facts be filed to reflect the change. OSC staff generally take the view that an increase to a mutual fund's risk rating is a material change under securities legislation.

3.1.4 — Review of Portfolio Holdings

The scope of this review was introduced in last year's summary report. During the year, the IF Branch completed its targeted review of portfolio holdings by investment funds. We reported our findings in OSC Staff Notice 81-717 *Report on Staff's Continuous Disclosure Review of Portfolio Holdings by Investment Funds*, which was published in August, 2012.

3.2 — Compliance and Registrant Regulation Branch and Investment Fund Manager Compliance Reviews

In November 2012, staff of the CRR Branch published OSC Staff Notice 33-738 *OSC Annual Summary Report for Dealers, Advisers and Investment Fund Managers*. The primary purpose of the Staff Notice is to assist registrants, including investment fund managers (IFMs), in complying with their regulatory obligations under Ontario securities law. The Staff Notice summarizes new and proposed rules and initiatives impacting registrants, current trends in deficiencies from compliance reviews of registrants (and suggested practices to address them), and current trends in registration issues.

Section 5.5 of the Staff Notice contains information specifically for IFMs, from the reviews carried out by the CRR Branch. Topics included:

- insufficient oversight of outsourced functions and service providers

- valuation of restricted securities

- inappropriate expenses charged to funds

- inadequate insurance coverage

- marketing practices

Also during the year, the CRR Branch published Multilateral Instrument 32-102 *Registration Exemptions for Non-Resident Investment Fund Managers* (MI 32-102) containing the registration requirements that apply in Ontario, Quebec, and Newfoundland and Labrador to non-resident IFMs, which include international and domestic IFMs who do not have a place of business in the province.

Under MI 32-102, the registration of all non-resident IFMs that have a significant connecting factor to Ontario is required unless they can rely on one of the available exemptions. Existing non-resident IFMs that are acting as an IFM in Ontario must have applied for registration by December 31, 2012.

For more information, see MI 32-102.

4. — Outreach, Consultation and Education

We continue our efforts to be transparent regarding practices and procedures that impact investment fund issuers in as timely a manner as possible. Our intent in doing so is to better enable fund managers and their advisors to avoid potential regulatory issues when they are at the planning stage for a new fund or transaction.

4.1 — Investment Funds Product Advisory Committee (IFPAC)

The OSC's IFPAC was established in August, 2011. The IFPAC, which is currently comprised of 13 members, advises OSC staff specifically on emerging product developments and innovations occurring in the investment fund industry, and discusses the impact of these developments and emerging issues. The IFPAC also acts as one source of feedback to OSC staff on the development of policy and rule-making initiatives to promote investor protection, fairness and market efficiency across all types of publicly offered investment fund products. The IFPAC meets quarterly and is chaired by Rhonda Goldberg, Director of the Investment Funds Branch. The IFPAC members serve a two year term. The initial two year term expires in 2013, and we expect to solicit applications for membership in Spring 2013. You can find a *list of current IFPAC members* on the OSC website.

Topics of discussion with the IFPAC have included the increasing use and complexity of derivatives; trends in structured products; and emerging asset classes (such as commodities) and foreign products/indices.

In addition to the IFPAC, OSC staff continue to meet frequently with stakeholders, including investment fund managers and their advisors, investor advocates and subject matter experts on various topics to inform our policy and operational work. In May, 2012, Som Seif, founder of Claymore Investments Inc., worked with OSC staff in a consultant capacity, to discuss investment fund product trends, and capital market developments generally.

OSC Staff also continue to hold regular meetings with staff of the U.S. Securities and Exchange Commission. These meetings help to ensure that our regulatory approaches to product development are consistent and that opportunities for regulatory arbitrage between our markets are minimized.

4.2 — The Investment Funds Practitioner

The Investment Funds Practitioner is an overview of recent and topical issues arising from applications for discretionary relief, prospectuses and continuous disclosure documents that investment fund issuers file with the OSC and that are reviewed by the IF Branch. It is intended to assist investment fund managers and their advisors who regularly prepare public disclosure documents and applications for discretionary relief on behalf of investment funds.

The Practitioner is also intended to make fund managers more broadly aware of some of the issues we have raised in connection with our reviews and how we have resolved them. The Practitioner can be found on our website www.osc.gov.on.ca at *Information for Investment Funds*.

We have published 3 editions of the Investment Funds Practitioner since last year's summary report: *December 2011*, *April 2012* and *November 2012*. We welcome suggestions for future topics.

4.3 — IFRS Transition Update

In March 2012, we published CSA Staff Notice 81-320 (Revised) *Update on International Financial Reporting Standards* (IFRS) *for Investment Funds* to update the investment fund industry on the deferral of the IFRS mandatory changeover date for investment funds in Canada to January 2014. The deferral was to continue to allow the International Accounting Standards Board (IASB) additional time to consider proposals for an "investment entity" to be exempt from the general IFRS requirement to consolidate entities that the investment entity may control. The Staff Notice reminded investment funds that want to use IFRS for financial statements for periods beginning before January 1, 2014 that they must apply for discretionary relief from the current requirement to prepare financial statements in accordance with Canadian generally accepted accounting principles, and that their discretionary relief application must identify any issues that early adoption may create with respect to their financial disclosure.

In October 2012, the IASB published *Investment Entities*, which introduced the exception, for investment entities, to the general IFRS principle that all subsidiaries must be consolidated.

The direction and clarity provided by this publication will now allow CSA staff to finalize the proposed amendments to NI 81-106 that were originally published in October 2009, in anticipation of the adoption of IFRS by investment funds in Canada. We expect to publish the proposed amendments to NI 81-106 in final form in the Fall of 2013, ahead of the mandatory changeover date of January 1, 2014.

4.4 — IOSCO C5 Investment Management

In 2010, the G20 requested that the Financial Stability Board (FSB), in collaboration with other international standard setting bodies, develop recommendations to strengthen the oversight and regulation of the shadow banking system, which includes money market funds (MMFs). In Fall 2011, the FSB asked IOSCO to undertake a review of potential regulatory reforms of MMFs that would mitigate their susceptibility to runs and other systemic risks, and to develop policy recommendations. OSC staff participated on the IOSCO C5 working group formed to respond to the FSB's request.

In April 2012, IOSCO published a consultation paper providing an analysis of the systemic risks posed by MMFs and outlining potential reform options for their regulation. IOSCO finalized its recommendations to the FSB and published them in October 2012. In November, the FSB endorsed the recommendations as an effective framework for strengthening the resilience of MMFs to risks.

The IOSCO recommendations are intended to provide a common framework for the global regulation of MMFs, while recognizing that the size, features and systemic relevance of MMFs differ across jurisdictions. The recommendations relate to improving the valuation of MMF portfolios, implementing measures for liquidity management in both normal and stressed market conditions, and requiring MMFs that maintain a constant NAV to convert to variable NAV where workable, and if not, to include safeguards to reinforce their resilience and ability to face significant redemptions.

As discussed earlier in this summary report under "Modernization of Investment Fund Product Regulation", the CSA amended NI 81-102 earlier in 2012 to introduce new liquidity and term restrictions on MMF holdings.

Other current initiatives of the IOSCO Investment Management committee include articulating principles for the valuation of collective investment schemes, for liquidity risk management and for the regulation of ETFs. IF Branch staff participated in the smaller working group established for the ETF project. Final publications of these papers are expected shortly. The Committee will also be working on defining criteria to identify "non-bank" systemically important financial institutions (in the area of asset management).

5. — Feedback and Contact Information

If you have any questions regarding, or feedback on, our third annual summary report, please send them to investmentfunds@osc.gov.on.ca.

You can find additional information regarding investment funds and the IF Branch on our *website*.

We have also attached a list of IF Branch staff at the end of this report.

[list of IF Branch staff omitted]

OSC Staff Notice 81-719 — Effect of Proposed *Income Tax Act* Amendments on Investment Funds — Character Conversion Transactions

Date: April 3, 2013

36 O.S.C.B. 3817

Purpose

This notice sets out the views of staff of the Ontario Securities Commission (Staff) on the types of considerations investment fund managers should be contemplating in response to proposed amendments to the *Income Tax Act* (Canada) (the *Tax Act*) that impact investment funds that engage in character conversion transactions (as described below).

Background

On March 21, 2013, the Minister of Finance presented the federal government's 2013 budget. The budget contains proposed amendments to the *Tax Act* (the Budget Amendments), which impact certain investment funds that use specified derivatives (generally a forward agreement) to provide investors with an economic return based on the performance of a reference fund. The Budget Amendments will apply to forward agreements entered into on or after budget day as well as forward agreements entered into before budget day if the term of the agreement is extended on or after budget day.

Through the use of a forward agreement, an investment fund characterizes the economic return of a reference fund, which would otherwise be treated as ordinary income in the hands of its securityholders, as capital gains. Investment funds that employ this structure generally have investment objectives of providing "tax advantaged" returns to securityholders.

The Budget Amendments will effectively prohibit the character conversion described above, meaning that the economic returns provided to investors will be taxable as ordinary income.

Staff's Views

Staff are of the view that investment fund managers should consider the effects of the Budget Amendments on their investment funds that use these investment structures, particularly if the income conversion feature is an essential aspect of the fund, as evidenced by the fund's investment objective, its name or the manner in which the fund is marketed. As such, we ask investment fund managers to consider their disclosure obligations under the *Securities Act* (Ontario) and National Instrument 81-106 *Investment Fund Continuous Disclosure*.

While these considerations are underway, we ask managers to consider the need to cap their affected funds to new and additional investments. Investment fund managers may also wish to consider whether any communication with current securityholders of their funds is appropriate to notify them of the Budget Amendments and their potential impact on the applicable funds.

While investment fund managers and their counsel work to better understand the full impact of the Budget Amendments, Staff are of the view that managers must also consider their longer-term response to the Budget Amendments, including whether changes to their funds' investment objectives and investment strategies will be needed or whether the funds need to be restructured, reorganized or terminated.

Further Information

Filers and their counsel are encouraged to contact Staff to discuss the issues raised in this notice.

OSC Staff Notice 81-720 — Report on Staff's Continuous Disclosure Review of Sales Communications by Investment Funds

Date: **July 18, 2013**
36 O.S.C.B. 7132

Purpose

This notice sets out guidance from staff of the Investment Funds Branch of the Ontario Securities Commission (Staff or we) based on our findings from a targeted continuous disclosure (CD) review of the advertising and marketing materials of publicly offered investment funds.

Objective and Scope of Our Review

Starting May 2012, Staff conducted targeted CD reviews of sales communications from a sample of investment funds. These reviews were in addition to the ad hoc reviews Staff conduct on a regular basis.

Each quarter, we selected 4 or 5 investment fund managers and asked for their sales communications for the previous three months. These included all published and non-print advertising in newspapers, presentations, brochures, internet ads, social media, fund manager websites, television and radio ads, email blasts, green sheets and any other marketing materials.

The fund managers included in our sample offer a range of fund types, including conventional mutual funds, closed-end funds, exchange-traded funds, commodity pools and labour sponsored investment funds. As the advertising of conventional mutual funds is primarily targeted to retail investors, we chose to focus a higher proportion of our CD reviews on this type of investment fund.

Included in our review were 8 medium to large mutual fund groups. Together, these fund groups have assets under management (AUM) of more than $270 billion, or about 30% of the industry total, and offer more than 800 mutual funds to the public. We also selected 4 smaller fund groups, as well as some specialty funds. The ETF providers included in our sample represent approximately 20% of the ETF industry AUM.

Two key objectives of our CD reviews are to raise the awareness of market participants that Staff monitor the advertising and marketing materials of publicly offered investment funds on an ongoing basis, and to provide staff guidance that supplements existing rules and staff publications.[1] We recognise that sales communications play an important role in the business of investment fund issuers. Staff expects the marketing of investment funds to provide clear, accurate and balanced messages, particularly when directed at retail investors.

We worked closely with, and followed similar approaches of staff in the Compliance and Registrant Regulation Branch who regularly conduct reviews of sales communications as part of their oversight of registrants.

Summary of Findings

Overall, we noted general compliance with disclosure requirements related to sales communications. However, we did observe that some basic requirements, such as providing the date of first publication for a written sales communication,[2] were frequently not met. Also, some sales communications did not contain all the information mandated for a sales communication, but rather referred to another source, such as the fund's website or prospectus, for more information.

The targeted CD reviews yielded the following key outcomes:

- Marketing, legal and/or compliance departments of fund managers initiated reviews of their current policies and procedures relating to marketing, and conducted training sessions with their staff on sales communications,

- Fund Managers committed to more frequent reviews of older marketing materials to ensure they remain in compliance with current requirements and ongoing staff guidance.

- Potentially misleading performance charts in sales communications were removed or replaced with more balanced charts.

- Potentially misleading headlines or slogans were removed from advertisements and marketing materials.

- Standard performance data was moved from the general disclaimer and placed in closer proximity to other performance data in the sales communication.

- Potentially misleading statements were removed from sales communications.

Staff guidance based on our observations from the targeted CD reviews is provided below.

---

[1]See Part 15 of National Instrument 81-102 *Mutual Funds* (NI 81-102) and Part 13 of National Instrument 41-101 *General Prospectus Requirements*, as well as Parts 2 and 13 of Companion Policy 81-102CP (CP). See also CSA Staff Notice 31-325 — Marketing Practices of Portfolio Managers, OSC Staff Notice 81-716 — 2011 Summary Report for Investment Fund Issuers and the November, 2007, January, 2010 and April, 2012 editions of the Investment Funds Practitioner.

[2]As required by section 15.4(1) of NI 81-102.

1. — When is a Communication a "Sales Communication"?

A "sales communication" is defined in NI 81-102.[3] The definition is very broad in terms of the content of the sales communication — it applies to communications that "relate to" mutual funds, fund managers, companies providing services to them, or a number of other entities. A sales communication can include a reference to a specific fund or to a family of funds. Short communications, including tweets or internet banners, can also be sales communications, if one of the purposes of the communication is to induce someone to buy one or more investment funds.

When assessing whether a communication with respect to an investment fund is a "sales communication" we encourage fund managers, whether or not the investment fund is a mutual fund, to look to the definition of "sales communication" in NI 81-102 for guidance. When assessing sales communications of mutual funds and non-redeemable investment funds, Staff will look to the parameters in Part 15 of NI 81-102 to inform our reviews. Staff consider the NI 81-102 principles to serve as best-practice standards for the marketing materials of all types of investment funds.

Branding

If a communication is intended to promote a corporate identity or the expertise of a fund manager, it falls outside the definition of a sales communication. Staff will generally take the view, however, that any time marketing material is about one or more investment funds, it becomes a sales communication and no longer falls within the branding exception.[4]

"For Advisor Use Only"

For marketing directed at dealers, Staff are of the view that labelling the document "for advisor use only" may not be sufficient. Staff also expect, in combination with the statement, a more pro-active effort to restrict broad distribution for any document that is intended to be for internal use and is not designed as a sales communication to a potential investor.

In Staff's view, internal or confidential communications, while not generally considered to be sales communications, should nonetheless be guided by the general parameters in Part 15 of NI 81-102. This is particularly important if distribution of the communication to potential investors may occur, or in instances where dealers and their sales representatives may be relying on the communication to convey information about a particular investment fund to investors.

2. — Fairness of Sales Communications

When assessing whether a sales communication is fairly presented, Staff will look at the sales communication from the perspective of the retail investor. In Staff's view, the sales communication should be in plain language, and not rely on the use of industry jargon, defined terms, or acronyms not easily understood by retail investors. We expect important facts and risks associated with the investment fund to be clearly outlined and not buried within the disclaimer or fine print.

Warnings, disclaimers and qualifications

In Staff's view, any warnings, disclaimers or qualifications used in sales communications should be consistent with the content of the sales communication, including any headline claims.

Yield and distributions

We remind fund managers that if a distribution or yield is quantified in a sales communication, the disclosure should specify: the basis of the calculation, the percentage of total distributions comprising reinvested units, whether the yield is calculated based on the net asset value or market price of the fund's securities, the time period covered by the distributions, the key assumptions and the impact of any changes to the key assumptions on the target distribution or yield.[5] In Staff's view, return of capital distributions should not be marketed so as to suggest that they represent investment returns.

3. — Misleading Sales Communications

When assessing whether a sales communication of an investment fund may be misleading, Staff generally will consider whether a particular term, phrase, description, illustration or other statement may create an unrealistic expectation or an unjustified sense of safety, particularly from the perspective of the retail investor.

Commodity Pools

For sales communications regarding commodity pools, Staff are of the view that any sales communication must clearly identify the issuer as a commodity pool, and further, must explain how the commodity pool differs from a conventional mutual fund.

In Staff's view, a commodity pool should not be referred to as a mutual fund in sales communications. Commodity pools are a specialized type of mutual fund that use certain alternative investment strategies involving specified derivatives or physical commodities beyond what is permitted by NI 81-102. As a result, the investment returns and investment risks of commodity pools may be significantly different from those of conventional mutual funds.

---

[3]See section 1.1 of NI 81-102 and section 2.15 of the CP.

[4]See section 2.15(3) of the CP.

[5]See the April, 2012 edition of the Investment Funds Practitioner.

Benchmarks

We remind fund managers of mutual funds and non-redeemable investment funds to look to Part 15.3 of NI 81-102 in assessing whether a sales communication that compares the fund to a benchmark, investment or ranking may create an unrealistic expectation for the retail investor.

Exaggerated and unsubstantiated claims

We remind fund managers that sales communications should not contain statements that are vague or exaggerated, or that cannot otherwise be verified. For example, Staff would consider statements such as "superior proven performance" or "superior risk adjusted performance" to be both vague (superior to what?) and exaggerated (is the performance repeatable or does it imply certain future returns?).

"Bait and switch"

In Staff's view, sales communications for publicly offered investment funds must convey the attributes and performance of the investment fund that is actually being offered for distribution. If the sales communication highlights the attributes and investment returns of a similar fund offered by the fund manager or an affiliate, but that fund is not available for sale in Canada, we would expect key information about the investment fund that is being offered for distribution to be given equal prominence in the sales communication.

If a sales communication includes a comparison to another investment fund not being offered for distribution by the fund manager, we would expect the sales communication to include: all facts that, if disclosed, could materially alter the conclusions reasonably drawn or implied by the comparison, data for each subject of the comparison for the same time periods, and a clear explanation of any factors necessary to make the comparison fair and not misleading.

Presentation of risk disclosure

In marketing, advertisements and other types of communications, Staff expect that the risks associated with the investment fund will be clearly disclosed and easily visible.

It is critical that the risk disclosure in any sales communication be given equal prominence to disclosure about the potential investment returns and benefits of the fund, and that the tone of the sales communication not detract from the significance of the risks. In Staff's view, if a particular benefit is highlighted in the sales communication, any potential risks associated with the investment strategy in achieving the benefit should also be pointed out.

If an investment fund has a high level of risk or special risk factors that may not be immediately apparent to the retail investor, Staff are of the view that the sales communication should clearly disclose the nature of these risks. If the investment fund has a particular feature or investment strategy that makes it significantly different from other similar funds, we would expect the sales communication to convey the unique characteristics of the fund, particularly if specific risks are associated with the unique feature.

Client lists and endorsements

In Staff's view, any representative client list included in a sales communication should only include the clients of the fund manager's asset management business, and should not list the clients the fund manager may deal with in another capacity. There should always be some nexus between the representative clients listed in the sales communication and the investment fund that is being promoted. Staff expect that the clients listed should be investors in the same fund that is the subject of the sales communication or in a similar fund.

4. — Performance Data

When assessing performance data in sales communications, Staff take the view that placing standard performance data in the disclaimer at the end of the sales communication is not consistent with the spirit and intent of Part 15 of NI 81-102. If standard performance data is provided, Staff expect the standard performance data to be given equal prominence to any other performance data disclosed in the sales communication.

We remind fund managers that standard performance data and general market data used in sales communications should be regularly updated, so as to not become stale or misleading.

Performance Awards

We consider performance awards in sales communications, such as the Lipper or Morningstar awards, to be performance ratings or rankings, which must comply with certain disclosure requirements.[6] Fund managers are reminded to comply with the requirements, or to seek discretionary relief, before using such awards in sales communications.

Staff are of the view that only awards that the investment fund has won should be used in sales communications. If the sales communication refers to an award won more than two years ago, the award must still be relevant to the investment fund's current investment objectives and strategies.

Some awards are not based on fund performance, but rather are awards to the fund manager or portfolio manager. Awards to the fund manager can be referred to in the sales communications of the fund manager's family of funds, provided the award was not for a specific investment fund. When used in a fund's sales communication, the type of award should be clearly disclosed so that it is not confused with an award for fund performance. Staff would expect such details as the name of the award provider, the ranking (if any) and where to go for additional information about the award (including the criteria upon which the award is based) to be included in the sales communication.

---

[6]See section 15.3(4) of NI 81-102.

Hypothetical data

In Staff's view, investment funds should refrain from using hypothetical data in sales communications intended for retail investors. Our concerns with hypothetical data include:[7]

- there is often little indication that the performance shown is hypothetical;

- retail investors may not have the investment knowledge to fully understand the risks and limitations of the hypothetical performance data; and

- the disclosure does not or cannot adequately describe the underlying methodology and the risks and limitations of the hypothetical performance data in a manner that is clear and easily accessible to the retail investor within the space limitations of the sales communication.

It can be appropriate to present hypothetical performance data in marketing materials for dealers and their sales representatives. In these instances, we expect there to be clear and meaningful disclosure regarding the methodology and assumptions used to calculate the hypothetical performance data, as well as any other relevant factors.

5. — Alternative Media

Internet advertising can take a variety of forms, including webpages, banner advertisements, video streaming (such as YouTube), discussion forums, social networking and micro-blogging (such as Twitter).

We encourage fund managers to consider the appropriateness of certain new media formats if content limitations prevent the fund manager from providing clear, accurate and balanced messages in the sales communication or insert the required warning language. In Staff's view, warning language must be visible on the same page as the sales communication or within "one click". Some internet sites provide lengthy disclaimers that scroll quickly. Staff expect that all information, including disclaimers, should be easily comprehensible to the retail investor on their first viewing of the advertisement.

Conclusion

We recognize the importance of sales communications to a fund manager's business. While a certain degree of creativity is to be expected, Staff remind fund managers to be mindful of the target audience for marketing and advertisements, particularly when it's the retail investor. In addition to the requirement that sales communications be technically compliant with existing requirements, we expect that they also conform with the spirit and intent of the rules as outlined in this guidance and other staff publications. Staff will continue, in the normal course of our prospectus reviews and on a targeted basis, to review the sales communications of publicly offered investment funds.

We encourage fund managers to consider the guidance in this notice when preparing sales communications for investment funds.

OSC Staff Notice 81-721 — Frequently Asked Questions on The Implementation of Stage 2 of Point of Sale Disclosure for Mutual Funds — *Delivery of Fund Facts*

Date: September 5, 2013

36 O.S.C.B. 8678

Purpose

Final amendments (Amendments) implementing Stage 2 of the Point of Sale disclosure initiative were published by the CSA on June 13, 2013. On September 1, 2013, the Amendments came into force. To assist issuers in complying with the Amendments, we have compiled a list of frequently asked questions (FAQs) and OSC staff's responses to those questions.

Background

The Amendments will allow delivery of the Fund Facts instead of the simplified prospectus to satisfy the prospectus delivery requirements under securities legislation to deliver a prospectus within two days of buying a mutual fund. The Amendments also include changes to the presentation of risk and performance in the Fund Facts.

The Amendments will be phased-in, with transition periods for the amendments to Form 81-101F3 — *Contents of Fund Facts Document* (Form 81-101F3) and the requirement to deliver the Fund Facts to satisfy prospectus delivery obligations under securities legislation. The key dates are as follows:

- January 13, 2014 — the amendments to Form 81-101F3 take effect;

- May 13, 2014 — filing deadline to file Fund Facts in the amended form; and

- June 13, 2014 — the delivery requirement for the Fund Facts takes effect.

FAQs

After reviewing the Amendments, OSC staff have received questions regarding its application and interpretation. This list of FAQs is not exhaustive, but broadly reflects the types of inquiries we have received.

---

[7]See CSA Notice 31-325 — Marketing Practices of Portfolio Managers and OSC Staff Notice 81-716 — 2011 Summary Report for Investment Fund Issuers.

We have divided the FAQs into two categories:

- A. Amendments to Form 81-101F3; and B. Delivery of Fund Facts.

A. — Amendments to Form 81-101F3

A-1

Q. What SEDAR filing category should be used to file the Fund Facts in the amended form?

A. As of January 13, 2014, a mutual fund that files a preliminary or pro forma simplified prospectus and annual information form must concurrently file a Fund Facts in the amended form for each class or series of the mutual fund offered under the simplified prospectus on SEDAR under the applicable filing category, i.e. "Preliminary fund facts" or "Pro forma fund facts".

If a mutual fund has not already done so, the Amendments also require the mutual fund to file a Fund Facts in the amended form for each class or series of the mutual fund by May 13, 2014. In the latter case, the Fund Facts in the amended form should be filed under the SEDAR filing category "Stage 2 Fund Facts". Fund Facts filed under "Stage 2 Fund Facts" will be made public automatically.

A-2

Q. Does a Fund Facts filed under the SEDAR filing category "Stage 2 Fund Facts" need to be filed with a certificate page and/or a blackline of the Fund Facts showing changes from the latest Fund Facts previously filed?

A. A Fund Facts filed under the SEDAR filing category "Stage 2 Fund Facts" does not require a certificate page or a blackline of the Fund Facts showing changes from the latest Fund Facts previously filed.

A-2

Q. Can a Fund Facts in the amended form be filed with a preliminary or pro forma simplified prospectus and annual information form before the amended Form 81-101F3 requirements take effect on January 13, 2014?

A. Exemptive relief from Form 81-101F3 is required to file a Fund Facts in the amended form before January 13, 2014, when the amended form requirements take effect. If filing a preliminary or pro forma simplified prospectus and annual information form before January 13, 2014, filers seeking this relief should file a cover letter on SEDAR under the applicable project number requesting an exemption from Form 81-101F3, along with a brief explanation of the rationale for early compliance with the amended form requirements. An exemption from Form 81-101F3 will be evidenced by the issuance of a receipt for the simplified prospectus and annual information form. Staff will consider recommending that the relief be granted if filers comply with the amended Form 81-101F3 requirements in their entirety.

A-4

Q. We expect to file a preliminary or pro forma simplified prospectus and annual information form after the amendments to Form 81-101F3 take effect on January 13, 2014, but before the deadline for filing Fund Facts in the amended form on May 13, 2014. Do we also need to file Fund Facts in the amended form under the SEDAR filing category "Stage 2 Fund Facts"?

A. If a receipt for the simplified prospectus and annual information form is issued before May 13, 2014, then the mutual fund can concurrently file the Fund Facts in the amended form with its simplified prospectus and annual information form. A separate filing of the Fund Facts under the SEDAR filing category "Stage 2 Fund Facts" is not necessary.

If a receipt for the simplified prospectus and annual information form is not issued until after May 13, 2014, then the mutual fund must (a) file a Fund Facts in the amended form under the SEDAR filing category "Stage 2 Fund Facts" before May 13, 2014, and (b) file a Fund Facts in the amended form with the simplified prospectus and annual information form. The Amendments extended the timeframe for certain information disclosed in the Fund Facts from 30 days to 60 days. Thus, within the 60 day period, the Fund Facts filed with the mutual fund's simplified prospectus and annual information form can be the same Fund Facts previously filed under the SEDAR filing category "Stage 2 Fund Facts" but with a changed date to correspond with the prospectus filing date.

A-5

Q. We expect to file a preliminary or pro forma simplified prospectus and annual information form after May 13, 2014. Should the accompanying blacklined Fund Facts show changes from the Fund Facts previously filed with the 2012 final prospectus or the Fund Facts more recently filed under the SEDAR filing category "Stage 2 Fund Facts"?

A. The blacklined Fund Facts should show changes from the latest Fund Facts previously filed which, in this case, would be the Fund Facts filed under SEDAR filing category "Stage 2 Fund Facts."

B. — Delivery of Fund Facts

B-1

Q. Can a Fund Facts be delivered to satisfy the prospectus delivery requirements in securities legislation before the Fund Facts delivery requirement takes effect on June 13, 2014?

A. Exemptive relief is required to deliver the Fund Facts to satisfy the prospectus delivery requirements before June 13, 2014. CSA Staff Notice 81-321 — *Early Use of the Fund Facts to Satisfy Prospectus Delivery* Requirements provides guidance on the key terms and conditions that the CSA will look for when considering these types of applications for exemptive relief. Filers who were previously granted exemptive relief to permit the early use of Fund Facts can rely on the exemptive relief until it terminates by operation of the sunset clause in the exemptive relief order, which is the date the Fund Facts delivery requirement takes effect, i.e. June 13, 2014.

B-2

Q. Can filers who were previously granted exemptive relief from the prospectus delivery requirements for pre-authorized purchase plans continue to rely on the relief after the Fund Facts delivery requirement takes effect on June 13, 2014?

A. As the sunset clauses in these exemptive relief orders vary, filers should review the sunset clause in their exemptive relief order to determine when the relief terminates.

OSC Staff Notice 81-722 — Mortgage Investment Entities and Investment Funds

Date: September 12, 2013

36 O.S.C.B. 8945

Purpose

This notice sets out guidance from staff of the Ontario Securities Commission (Staff) on the factors that Staff will consider in determining whether an issuer which proposes to invest all or substantially all of its assets in a pool of mortgages (a mortgage investment entity or MIE) is an investment fund.[1] For the purposes of this notice, an MIE is an issuer that invests in mortgages in the manner described below.

For a discussion of the registration requirements applicable to entities that invest their assets in mortgages, please see CSA Staff Notice 31-323 *Guidance Relating to the Registration Obligations of Mortgage Investment Entities* (CSA Staff Notice 31-323).[2]

Background

Recently, Staff have seen an increase in the number of prospectus filings by MIEs. Often, these MIEs describe themselves as non-redeemable investment funds and file a prospectus in the form of a completed Form 41-101F2 *Information Required in an Investment Fund Prospectus* (Form 41-101F2).

Generally, the mortgages[3] purchased by these MIEs are originated and serviced by one or more mortgage originators (each, an Originator), who may or may not act as the MIE's manager. Regardless of whether the Originator is the MIE's manager, the Originator may nonetheless use the MIE as a source of funding for the Originator's mortgage lending business.

Staff are generally of the view that MIEs with the attributes described above are not investment funds for the reasons provided below.

MIEs and Investment Funds

Consistent with the definition of "non-redeemable investment fund" in subsection 1(1) of the *Securities Act* (Ontario) and the discussion in section 1.2 of Companion Policy 81-106CP to National Instrument 81-106 *Investment Fund Continuous Disclosure*, an investment fund does not invest for the purpose of exercising or seeking to exercise control, or being actively involved in the management, of any issuer.[4]

In Staff's view, structuring an offering of an issuer that describes itself as a non-redeemable investment fund, where the issuer is, or is an extension of, an operating business is contrary to the spirit and intent of the definition of a non-redeemable investment fund.

In our reviews of MIE prospectuses, Staff have been carefully examining the role played by the Originator in the public offering, and its relationship to the MIE. Based on our reviews, it appears that MIEs are often an extension of the Originator's business. Essentially, the Originator sources mortgages, which are then funded through the money raised by the MIE in its public offering. The MIE thereby becomes the lender to the mortgagor, which results in the MIE engaging in, or being the source of funding for, a lending business on behalf of the Originator. In Staffs view, this is inconsistent with the nature of an investment fund and is, in essence, an operating business.

Staff are of the view that the Originator plays a vital role for the MIE, such that the performance of the MIE is largely dependent on the Originator's business expertise in originating and servicing mortgages. In fact, this expertise is what the MIE is indirectly offering to the public through its securities. Even though the MIE has been established as a separate legal entity, in our prospectus reviews, Staff are examining the relationship of the MIE and Originator comprehensively, and may regard the MIE as part of the Originator's business.

While MIEs may appear similar to investment funds that invest in debt or equity securities, unlike such funds, which purchase the securities on the secondary market or through primary distributions, MIEs indirectly lend money to individual mortgagors in respect of mortgages that are tailor-made by the Originator for the mortgagor. Accordingly, in Staff's view, an MIE is more akin to a lending business than an investment fund, which generally invests in a portfolio of securities.

Prospectus and Continuous Disclosure Requirements

Staff believe that information regarding the Originator's business and how it decides what mortgages to originate and how to service them is material information for securityholders of the MIE. The MIE's success depends on the Originator and its expertise, which, as stated above, is indirectly what is being offered to the public through the MIE's securities.

---

[1]This notice focuses on those MIEs that describe themselves as non-redeemable investment funds and propose to become reporting issuers. Therefore, the discussion in this notice does not address mutual funds subject to National Policy 29 *Mutual Funds Investing in Mortgages*, which are a particular type of mutual fund established prior to the coming into force of National Instrument 81-102 *Mutual Funds* (NI 81-102).

[2]While the discussion in CSA Staff Notice 31-323 focuses on applicable registration requirements, the current notice focuses on the nature of an MIE and why Staff generally do not consider MIEs to be investment funds.

[3]The mortgages purchased by MIEs are generally not "guaranteed mortgages", as defined in NI 81-102.

[4]For a further discussion of these issues, please see *The Investment Funds Practitioner — November 2012*, (2012) 35 OSCB 9997 at 10000 and 10001.

As, in Staff's view, they are not investment funds, the MIEs described in this notice are required to file an initial prospectus in the form of a completed Form 41-101 F1 *Information Required in* a *Prospectus* (Form 41-101 F1), not Form 41-101 F2. Staff believe that the use of Form 41-101F1 enhances investor protection, as Form 41-101F2 is designed to provide disclosure regarding a passively held portfolio and would not, in Staff's view, provide investors with meaningful disclosure about the MIE's operating business.

This investor protection concern also extends to the continuous disclosure (CD) regime. Consistent with Staff's view outlined above, MIEs are expected to comply with the CD regime applicable to reporting issuers that are not investment funds (National Instrument 51-102 *Continuous Disclosure Obligations*). This will generally provide investors with more meaningful disclosure regarding the MIE and the Originator's role vis-à-vis the MIE than the CD regime applicable to investment funds.[5]

Further Information

The determination of whether an entity is an investment fund is fact-specific. If issuers and their counsel are uncertain regarding whether an MIE is an investment fund, we encourage them to use the pre-filing procedures under Part 8 of National Policy 11-202 *Process for Prospectus Reviews in Multiple Jurisdictions*.

OSC Staff Notice 81-723 — Summary Report for Investment Fund Issuers 2013

Date: **February 13, 2014**

37 O.S.C.B. 1584

Introduction

This, our fourth annual Summary Report for Investment Fund Issuers, provides an overview of the key activities and initiatives of the Ontario Securities Commission for 2013 that impact investment fund issuers and the fund industry, including:

- key policy initiatives,

- emerging issues and trends,

- continuous disclosure and compliance reviews, and

- recent developments in staff practices.

The following pages provide information about the status of some of the initiatives the OSC is undertaking to promote clear and concise disclosure in order to assist investors to make more informed investment decisions. The report also provides information about our work to address the sufficiency of regulatory coverage across all investment fund products. It highlights recent product and market developments, as well as our regulatory response to these developments, in order to assist the investment fund industry in understanding and complying with current regulatory requirements.

The OSC is responsible for overseeing over 3,500 publicly-offered investment funds. Ontario based publicly-offered investment funds hold approximately 80% of the just over $1 trillion in publicly-offered investment fund assets in Canada.

We administer the regulatory framework for investment funds, including:

- reviewing and assessing product disclosure for all types of investment funds, including prospectuses and continuous disclosure filings,

- considering applications for discretionary relief from securities legislation and rules, and

- taking a leadership role in developing new rules and policies to adapt to the changing environment in the investment fund industry.

We also monitor and participate in investment fund regulatory developments globally, primarily through our work with the International Organization of Securities Commissions (IOSCO). OSC staff participation on the IOSCO C5 Investment Management and IOSCO C8 Retail Investors committees informs our operational and policy work. We discuss our *participation with IOSCO* further on our website at www.osc.gov.on.ca. In this report, we highlight some of the recent work by IOSCO C5 and IOSCO C8 that we think will be of interest to investment fund issuers.

The investment fund products we oversee include both conventional mutual funds and non-conventional investment funds. Non-conventional funds include non-redeemable investment funds such as closed-end funds, mutual funds listed and posted for trading on a stock exchange (ETFs), commodity pools, scholarship plans, labour-sponsored or venture capital funds and flow-through limited partnerships. We discuss the different types of funds further on our website at www.osc.gov.on.ca *Investment Funds — Fund Operations*.

The ETF market continued to grow steadily during the course of the year. As at December 2013, there were 284 ETFs with assets of approximately $63.1 billion. In comparison, as at December 2012, there were 265 ETFs with assets of approximately $56.4 billion, representing an increase in assets of almost 12%. Over the same period, conventional fund assets increased by approximately 17%. As at September 2013, closed-end fund assets had declined by approximately $3 billion from the previous December to approximately $30.8 billion.

[5]In addition to other differences between the CD regime for investment funds and for non-investment fund issuers, a reporting issuer that is not an investment fund is currently required to prepare its financial statements in accordance with the International Financial Reporting Standards (IFRS). Investment funds are not required to prepare their financial statements in accordance with IFRS until financial years beginning on or after January 1, 2014.

Part 8: MUTUAL FUNDS

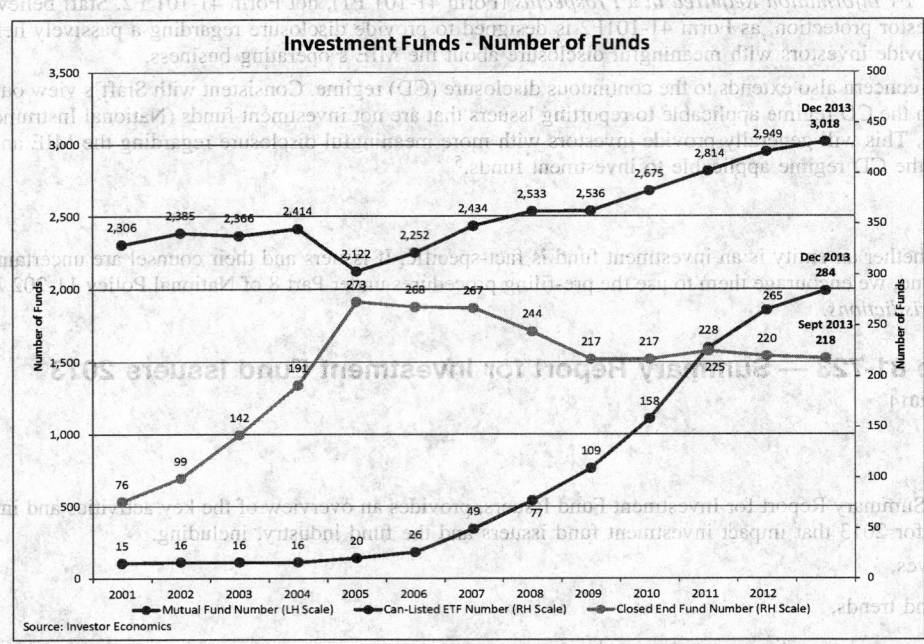

Investment Funds - Number of Funds

Source: Investor Economics

As these and other investment products increase in number, and as the use of ETFs by retail investors continues to grow, the OSC will continue to assess and respond to product developments and innovations with a view to promoting investor protection and assessing the sufficiency and consistency of the regulatory treatment of different investment fund products.

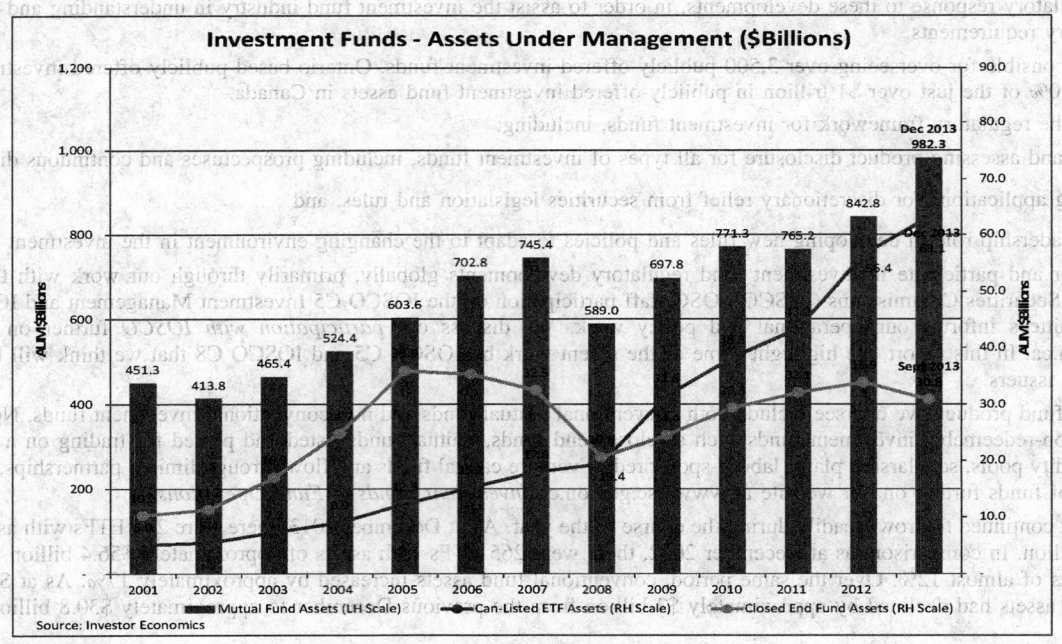

Investment Funds - Assets Under Management ($Billions)

Source: Investor Economics

1. — Key Policy Initiatives

The OSC continues to play a leading role in several significant policy initiatives with other securities regulators in Canada through the Canadian Securities Administrators (the CSA). This section reports on the status of significant policy initiatives including:

- transition to IFRS

- mutual fund fees

- point of sale and risk classification methodology for Fund Facts

- modernization of investment fund product regulation
- exempt market
- electronic delivery of documents
- scholarship plans

1.1 — Transition to IFRS

The CSA completed the final step in the transition to International Financial Reporting Standards (IFRS) for investment funds with the publication of final amendments to *National Instrument 81-106 Investment Fund Continuous Disclosure (NI 81-106), its Companion Policy and related amendments on October 3, 2013*. Initially proposed in 2009, the IFRS-related amendments to NI 81-106 were deferred when the International Accounting Standards Board (IASB) agreed to make revisions to resolve a potentially significant accounting issue for investment funds. The final amendments reflect comments received on the 2009 proposal, additional stakeholder consultations and further IASB developments related to investment funds. The changes impact investment fund requirements relating to the presentation of financial statements and terminology to reflect the transition to IFRS.

In Ontario, the amendments to NI 81-106 and related amendments received ministerial approval on November 21, 2013. Investment funds must apply the changes for financial years beginning on or after January 1, 2014.

1.2 — Mutual Fund Fees

On December 13, 2012 the CSA published for comment *CSA Discussion Paper and Request for Comment 81-407 Mutual Fund Fees* (the Discussion Paper). The Discussion Paper examined a number of investor protection issues that we think arise from the current mutual fund fee structure in Canada, including the potential conflicts of interests that embedded advisor compensation, or trailing commissions, may give rise to. It solicited comments on several potential regulatory options to address the issues identified including, among others, introducing a statutory best interest duty for advisors and capping or banning trailing commissions.

We received 99 comment letters on the Discussion Paper from various industry stakeholders as well as various investor advocates and individual investors.

The OSC and CSA also held various in-person consultations[6] throughout the Summer and Fall of 2013, to probe deeper into some of the themes emerging from the comment letters received in response to the Discussion Paper.

On December 12, 2013 the CSA published *CSA Staff Notice 81-323 Status Report on Consultation under CSA Discussion Paper and Request for Comment 81-407 Mutual Fund Fees*, which provides a summary of the key comments received on the Discussion Paper through the comment process and the subsequent in-person consultations.

1.3 — Point of Sale and Risk Classification Methodology for Fund Facts

The Point of Sale (POS) Project is a continuation of the CSA's participation in the project by the Joint Forum of Financial Market Regulators to develop a more effective disclosure regime for conventional mutual funds and segregated funds. The Fund Facts is central to the POS project and is designed to make it easier for investors to find and use key information.

On June 18, 2010, the CSA announced its approach to proceed with a staged implementation of the POS Project in *CSA Staff Notice 81-319 Status Report on the Implementation of Point of Sale Disclosure for Mutual Funds*.

Stage 1, which came into force January 1, 2011, required that mutual funds produce and file the Fund Facts, and for the Fund Facts to be available on the mutual fund's or mutual fund manager's website. The Fund Facts must also be delivered or sent to investors free of charge on request.

Stage 2, allowing the delivery of the Fund Facts to satisfy the current prospectus delivery requirements to deliver a prospectus within two days of buying a mutual fund, was completed with the publication of final amendments on June 13, 2013. The amendments are phased-in, with the amendments to *Form 81-101F3 Contents of Fund Facts Document*, including enhancements to the presentation of the risk and performance sections of the Fund Facts, effective as of January 13, 2014. The amendments that require delivery of the Fund Facts and allow for the Fund Facts to satisfy the current prospectus delivery requirement under securities legislation to deliver a prospectus within two days of buying a mutual fund take effect on June 13, 2014.

On September 5, 2013, we published *OSC Staff Notice 81-721 — Frequently Asked Questions on the Implementation of Stage 2 of Point of Sale Disclosure for Mutual Funds — Delivery of Fund Facts (FAQs)*. The FAQs were published to respond to implementation questions related to the Stage 2 final amendments.

In Stage 3, the CSA is proceeding with three concurrent work streams: (i) the development of a CSA mutual fund risk classification methodology, (ii) proposed amendments aimed at implementing pre-sale delivery of the Fund Facts, and (iii) the development of a summary disclosure document for exchangetraded mutual funds (ETFs), similar to the Fund Facts, and a requirement to deliver the summary disclosure document within two days of an investor buying an ETF.

On December 12, 2013, the CSA published *CSA Notice 81-324 and Request for Comments Proposed CSA Mutual Fund Risk Classification Methodology for Use in Fund Facts* (the Proposed Methodology), which sets out a proposed risk classification methodology for use by mutual fund managers in the Fund Facts. The CSA developed the Proposed Methodology in response to stakeholder feedback that the CSA has

---

[6]The consultations on the Discussion Paper included a public roundtable held at the OSC on June 7, 2013, followed by non-public consultations carried out by the British Columbia Securities Commission on June 24 and 25 and by the AMF on September 5, September 17 and October 3, 2013.

received throughout the POS Project, notably that a standardized risk classification methodology proposed by the CSA would be more useful to investors as it would provide a consistent and comparable basis for measuring the risk of different mutual funds.

Prior to the publication of the Proposed Methodology, the CSA held consultations with industry representatives, academics and investor advocates to seek their feedback. The comment period for the Proposed Methodology is open until March 12, 2014. We are also seeking feedback on whether the CSA should mandate the Proposed Methodology or, alternatively, adopt it as guidance for investment fund managers.

In relation to the second work stream of Stage 3, the CSA expect to publish for comment in Spring, 2014 proposed amendments aimed at implementing pre-sale delivery of the Fund Facts. The original proposals relating to the pre-sale delivery of Fund Facts were published for comment in June 2009. The CSA are revisiting the original 2009 proposals, informed by the regulatory regimes of other jurisdictions that have implemented pre-sale delivery requirements, by IOSCO principles, and by the comments received from stakeholders.

Finally, as part of the third work stream related to Stage 3, the CSA granted exemptive relief orders introducing an alternative delivery regime for ETFs which requires delivery of a summary disclosure document with the trade confirmations for all ETF purchases as of September 2013. The CSA exemptive relief orders cover all ETF manufacturers and bank-owned dealers, which account for approximately 80% of ETF trades. The codification of these orders encompassing a Fund Facts-type document for ETFs and an accompanying alternative delivery model is expected to be published for comment in Fall, 2014.

1.4 — Modernization of Investment Fund Product Regulation

The mandate for this initiative is to review the regulation of publicly offered investment funds with a view to developing rules that recognize product developments and trends in the investment fund industry. The initiative is being carried out in two phases.

Phase 1 of this initiative, which amended National Instrument 81-102 *Mutual Funds* (NI 81-102) to update certain regulatory requirements for mutual funds, came into force in 2012.

Phase 2 of this initiative, now underway, consists of three parts:

- amendments to NI 81-102 to introduce core investment restrictions and operational requirements for publicly offered non-redeemable investment funds (the NI 81-102 Amendments);

- amendments to National Instrument 81-104 *Commodity Pools* to create a more comprehensive alternative investment fund framework that will operate in conjunction with the proposed amendments to NI 81-102 (the Alternative Fund Proposals); and

- the introduction of new requirements intended to enhance the disclosure provided by all investment funds related to securities lending, repurchase and reverse repurchase transactions and to keep pace with global regulatory developments (the Securities Lending Disclosure Requirements).

The Phase 2 proposals were published for comment on March 27, 2013 for a 90 day comment period. In June, 2013, the CSA received a request from 42 market participants asking for an extension of the comment period on the basis that the Phase 2 proposals represented fundamental changes to the regulatory framework for non-redeemable investment funds, and that market participants required additional time to formulate a constructive response. In light of this request, the CSA published *CSA Staff Notice 11-324 Extension of Comment Period (Staff Notice 11-324)*, which announced that the comment period for the Phase 2 proposals was being extended until August 23, 2013. Staff Notice 11-324 also provided an update prioritizing the proposed amendments that the CSA intended to finalize, and indicated that implementation of the Alternative Fund Proposals would be considered in conjunction with certain investment restriction proposals for NI 81-102, which will be finalized and come into force at a later date.

By the closing of the comment period on August 23, 2013, the CSA had received *49 comment letters* from a wide range of market participants, including investment fund managers, investment dealers, law firms and an investor advocate. The CSA have reviewed all the comments that were received and are currently working on responding to those comments with a view to finalizing the NI 81-102 Amendments and the Securities Lending Disclosure Requirements by Summer, 2014.

1.5 — Exempt Market

As part of the OSC's exempt market initiative, we are pursuing the following efforts for investment funds as articulated in *OSC Notice 45-712 Progress Report on Review of Prospectus Exemptions to Facilitate Capital Raising*:

- Amending the accredited investor exemption to permit fully managed accounts, where the adviser has a fiduciary relationship with the investor, to purchase any securities on an exempt basis, including investment fund securities. Currently, in Ontario only, investment funds are carved out of the managed account category of the accredited investor exemption. Removing the carve-out would harmonize the managed account category of the accredited investor exemption in Canada. We are currently aiming to publish this amendment for comment as part of the CSA's review of the accredited investor and minimum amount exemptions.

- Improving data collection related to exempt market activities. We are currently developing for publication for comment enhanced reporting requirements and a revised form of Report of Exempt Distributions for investment fund issuers in Ontario.

1.6 — Electronic Delivery of Documents

This is a reminder to all investment fund issuers that, effective February 19, 2014, *OSC Rule 11-501 Electronic Delivery of Documents to the Ontario Securities Commission* (OSC Rule 11-501), will make it mandatory for all market participants to electronically file a number of documents that are currently filed in paper format with the OSC.

OSC Rule 11-501 requires a number of documents to be electronically filed or delivered to the OSC, including:

- Form 45-106F1 and Form 45-501F1 *Report of Exempt Distributions*

- Applications for exemptive relief and notice filings

- Pre-files or waiver applications (for prospectuses or applications)
- Forms, notices and other materials required under Ontario's securities rules that are not filed through the System for Electronic Document Analysis and Retrieval (SEDAR), the System for Electronic Disclosure by Insiders (SEDI), or the National Registration Database (NRD).

Filers must electronically transmit the required documents through the electronic filing portal located on the OSC's website starting February 19, 2014, although market participants may elect to electronically file on a voluntary basis in the interim.

1.7 — Scholarship Plans

On May 31, 2013, amendments to *National Instrument 41-101 General Prospectus Requirements (NI 41-101), including new Form 41-101F3 Information Required in a Scholarship Plan Prospectus* came into force (the New Form).

The New Form aims to improve the prospectus disclosure provided by scholarship plans by introducing a prospectus form tailored to reflect the unique features of this product. The New Form requires scholarship plans to provide investors with key information in a simple, accessible and comparable format to assist them in making a more informed investment decision.

Central to the New Form is the Plan Summary document. Similar to the Fund Facts for mutual funds, it is written in plain language, is to be no more than four pages, and highlights the potential risks and the costs of investing in a scholarship plan. It forms part of the prospectus, but is bound separately.

The timing of the coming into force of the New Form was designed to ensure that it was adopted by each scholarship plan provider during their 2013 prospectus renewal cycle. The CSA expect that adoption of the New Form will lead to more understandable and effective disclosure for investors, enabling them to better appreciate the possible outcomes and risks associated with investing in scholarship plans.

2. — Emerging Issues and Trends

2.1 — Investments in Mortgages

Over the course of the last year, we saw an incremental increase in the number of prospectus offerings by issuers, purporting to be investment funds, that proposed to invest substantially all of their assets in a pool of mortgages (a mortgage investment entity or MIE). Generally, the mortgages purchased by these MIEs are originated and serviced by one or more mortgage originators, who may or may not act as the MIE's manager. In most instances, the originator uses the MIE as a source of funding for the originator's mortgage lending business. In staff's view, this type of MIE is not an investment fund.

Staff provided guidance in *OSC Staff Notice 81-722 Mortgage Investment Entities and Investment Funds*, which was published on September 12, 2013, setting out the factors that staff would consider in determining whether an MIE is an investment fund. The notice detailed the reasons for staff's view, and reminded issuers that, since these MIEs are not considered investment funds, any initial prospectus filed by such issuers should be prepared and filed in the form of a completed Form 41-101F1 *Information Required in a Prospectus*, and any continuous disclosure should be filed in accordance with the continuous disclosure regime applicable to reporting issuers that are not investment funds (National Instrument 51-102 *Continuous Disclosure Obligations*).

2.2 — Update on Linked Note Offerings

We continue to review novel linked note supplements filed for pre-clearance under *National Instrument 44-102 Shelf Distributions* and *CSA Staff Notice 44-304 Linked Notes Distributed under Shelf Prospectus System*. We also continue to monitor the development of the industry generally and regulatory developments internationally.

We are becoming increasingly aware of the convergence of some notes with other investment products, particularly where the return on the notes is derived from the return on an investment fund. We are also reviewing the approach followed in other jurisdictions, such as the U.S., regarding disclosure of the fair value of the note on the cover page of the supplement. We are considering publishing guidance regarding the foregoing and as an update to CSA Staff Notice 44-304 in the upcoming fiscal year. We anticipate revising the pre-clearance criteria for notes linked to investment funds such that each offering of notes that is linked to one or more conventional mutual funds may be considered novel and subject to pre-clearance, whether a template was previously pre-cleared or not.

2.3 — Increased Use of Derivatives

We have observed an increase in the use of derivatives by investment funds to offer more efficient investment exposure to areas that are harder to reach through direct investments, as well as to modify investment exposure in response to macro changes in the capital markets.

For example, certain investment funds are using currency derivatives to create fixed income exposure to emerging markets while holding domestic securities, and shorter term fixed income funds are creating exposure through interest rate derivatives while holding longer term debt. Funds are increasingly hedging and modifying their investment exposures in response to the changes in capital market expectations, including expectations relating to the direction of interest rates.

In response to this trend, our focus has been to ensure that there is a sufficient and appropriate level of disclosure so that investors can understand how the investment exposure is modified and created, and the additional risk that accompanies certain derivative transactions. We also focus on whether these exposure adjustments are within the fund's stated investment objectives and strategies.

2.4 — Senior Secured and Floating Rate Loans

Over the course of the year, we observed an increase in offerings of non-investment grade fixed income products. As fixed income offerings move away from investment grade, our focus has been on ensuring that the disclosure by investment funds investing in fixed income securities provides sufficient information about the type, features and risks of the non-investment grade debt that is included in the investment fund portfolio. We note that, generally, the names and description of these investment funds (which include, for example, "senior" or "secured") may preclude investors from being alerted to the higher risks associated with the non-investment grade debt.

2.5 — Character Conversion Transactions

On March 21, 2013, the Minister of Finance presented the federal government's 2013 budget. The budget contained amendments to the *Tax Act* (the Budget Amendments), which impacted investment funds that used specified derivatives (generally forward agreements) to provide investors with an economic return based on the performance of a reference fund.

Through the use of forward agreements, these funds were able to characterize the economic return of a reference fund, which would otherwise be treated as ordinary income in the hands of its securityholders, as capital gains. Investment funds that employed this structure generally have investment objectives of providing "tax advantaged" returns to securityholders. The Budget Amendments effectively prohibited the character conversion described above, meaning that from the effective date of the Budget Amendments, the economic returns provided to investors would be taxable as ordinary income.

Subsequent to the budget announcement, we issued *OSC Staff Notice 81-719 Effect of Proposed Income Tax Act Amendments on Investment Funds — Character Conversion Transactions* (the Conversion Notice). The Conversion Notice stated that investment fund managers should consider the effects of the Budget Amendments on their investment funds, particularly if income conversion was an essential aspect of the fund, as evidenced by the fund's investment objective, name or the manner in which the fund was marketed. The Conversion Notice further advised investment fund managers that they should consider whether affected investment funds should be capped to new and additional investments.

Investment Funds staff took part in several discussions with senior staff from the Ministry of Finance (Canada) and Canada Revenue Agency concerning the Budget Amendments. In these discussions, we provided background information on the use of character conversion transactions by investment funds and the impact of the Budget Amendments.

As a result of the Budget Amendments, we reviewed a number of prospectus amendments for investment funds, as well as applications that were filed in connection with fundamental changes being made by investment funds to alter their investment structures.

3. — Disclosure and Compliance Reviews

On an ongoing basis, OSC staff review the prospectus and continuous disclosure filings of Ontario-based investment funds. Risk-based criteria are used to select investment funds for reviews of their disclosure documents. We may also choose to conduct targeted reviews of a particular industry segment or on a particular topic. In addition to our prospectus and continuous disclosure reviews, the Investment Funds Branch works closely with staff in the Compliance and Registrant Regulation (CRR) Branch on issues related to fund manager compliance and identifying possible emerging issues. This sometimes leads to us conducting joint reviews.

3.1 — Continuous Disclosure Reviews

This section discusses some of our reviews and findings in connection with:

- bullion funds
- risk ratings in Fund Facts
- sales communications/advertising
- fixed income ETFs
- operating expenses

3.1.1 — Bullion Funds

In response to a significant drop in gold bullion prices in April 2013, staff conducted a targeted review of investment funds that hold substantially all of their assets in precious metals bullion. In order to understand how the funds and their managers responded to the market events, we asked about the asset flows in these funds and in bullion markets, as well as the impact of the market events on the premium and discount spread of bullion exchange-traded funds. We also looked into how the fund manager assessed each fund's ability to liquidate bullion to meet redemptions in times of stress. We were informed that physical markets for bullion remained liquid during this period of declining prices. In terms of fulfilling redemption requests, gold bullion funds generally benefit from: (i) the size of the gold bullion markets relative to the funds' holdings, and (ii) the short settlement period for gold bullion transactions relative to redemption transactions which affords the ability to know, with certainty, the required liquidity to support redemption activity.

3.1.2 — Risk Ratings in Fund Facts

During the year, staff completed targeted continuous disclosure reviews of risk ratings of mutual funds disclosed in their Fund Facts. Staff have conducted similar reviews in the past and continue to monitor the risk ratings of mutual funds. As part of the review, staff focused on mutual funds in the same fund family that had both a currency hedged fund and an unhedged fund that provided exposure to the same underlying fund or portfolio. These reviews were initiated since staff noted that fund managers tend to rate both the currency hedged fund and the unhedged fund with the same risk ratings, even though volatility of past returns varied between the two funds. It is staff's view that the risk ratings for currency hedged funds should be determined separate and apart from their unhedged counterparts.

Staff communicated their views to a number of fund managers as part of these continuous disclosure reviews and also reiterated their views on this issue in the most recent *Investment Funds Practitioner published in November 2013*.

3.1.3 — Sales Communications/Advertising

In July 2013, staff of the Investment Funds Branch issued *OSC Staff Notice 81-720 Report on Staff's Continuous Disclosure Review of Sales Communications by Investment Funds* (the Sales Communication Notice). The Sales Communication Notice sets out guidance based on our findings from a targeted continuous disclosure review of the advertising and marketing materials of publicly offered investment funds (the Sales Communication Review).

The Sales Communication Review began in May 2012. During the review, we selected 4 or 5 investment fund managers each quarter and asked for their sales communications for the previous three months. These included all published and non-print advertising in newspapers, presentations, brochures, internet ads, social media, fund manager websites, television and radio ads, email blasts, green sheets and any other marketing materials.

The fund managers included in our sample offered a range of fund types, including conventional mutual funds, closed-end funds, exchange-traded funds, commodity pools and labour sponsored investment funds. As the advertising of conventional mutual funds is primarily targeted to retail investors, we chose to focus a higher proportion of our CD reviews on this type of investment fund.

Included in our review were 8 medium to large mutual fund groups. Together, these fund groups have assets under management of more than $270 billion, or about 30% of the industry total, and offer more than 800 mutual funds to the public. We also selected 4 smaller fund groups, as well as some specialty funds. The ETF providers included in our sample represent approximately 20% of the ETF industry assets under management.

The Sales Communication Review found general compliance with disclosure requirements related to sales communications. However, some sales communications did not contain all the information mandated for a sales communication, but rather referred to another source, such as the fund's website or prospectus, for more information.

Key outcomes from the Sales Communication Review included:

- marketing, legal and/or compliance departments of fund managers initiated reviews of their current policies and procedures relating to marketing, and conducted training sessions with their staff on sales communications;

- potentially misleading performance charts in sales communications were removed or replaced with more balanced charts; and

- potentially misleading headlines and statements were removed from advertisements and marketing materials.

The Sales Communication Notice provided guidance to investment funds based on our observations from the Sales Communication Review. Topics on which we provided guidance included:

- the applicability of the disclosure requirements related to sales communications to materials created for branding purposes or for distribution to dealers;

- examples of features or statements that may cause a sales communication to be potentially misleading by creating an unrealistic expectation or an unjustified sense of safety, particularly from the perspective of the retail investor;

- the use of performance data in sales communications; and

- sales communications transmitted through alternative media.

3.1.4 — Fixed Income ETFs

In response to the increased volatility seen in the fixed income markets, we undertook a review of fixed income ETFs, focusing on the liquidity of underlying assets and the effectiveness of the market making function by designated brokers. We examined how fund managers assessed the liquidity of the underlying assets of the ETFs. We also enquired with the ETF managers regarding the controls in place to ensure effective operation of the designated brokers' market making function, including details and scope of any legal agreements, number and size of market makers, monitoring programs and contingency plans. We wrote to four ETF managers, with head-offices in Ontario, covering more than 90% of ETF assets under management.

We noted that ETF managers generally conduct thorough due diligence when selecting and monitoring the designated brokers for their funds. ETF managers generally also appear to have good controls in place to monitor market quality statistics for their ETFs such as premiums/discounts to NAV or liquidity of underlying holdings. Where required, we have communicated further with individual ETF managers regarding industry best practices. Investment Funds staff will continue to monitor market quality statistics of the Canadian ETF market on an ongoing basis to identify any instances where regulatory action may be required.

3.1.5 — Operating Expenses

During the year, staff highlighted the disclosure of fees and expenses as an area of particular focus for prospectus and continuous disclosure reviews. Subsequently, staff started a targeted review of the allocation of overhead expenses between fund managers and their funds, in particular, how fund managers address conflicts of interest and whether sufficient disclosure is provided to investors in prospectuses, financial statements and the management reports of fund performance relating to these related party transactions.

This targeted review focuses on all types of publicly offered investment funds, including conventional mutual funds, ETFs and closed-end funds, and included fund managers ranging from the largest to the smallest in terms of assets under management, as well as bank-affiliated fund managers. The review is currently ongoing and we intend to publish a staff notice in 2014 with the findings of the review.

3.2 — Compliance and Registrant Regulation Branch and Investment Fund Manager Compliance Reviews

In November 2013, staff of the CRR Branch published OSC Staff Notice 33-742 OSC Annual Summary Report for Dealers, Advisers and Investment Fund Managers. The Staff Notice summarizes new and proposed rules and initiatives impacting registrants, current trends in deficiencies from compliance reviews of registrants (and suggested practices to address them), and current trends in registration issues.

Section 4.4 of OSC Staff Notice 33-742 contains information specifically for investment fund managers derived from the reviews carried out by the CRR Branch. Topics included:

- inappropriate expenses charged to funds,
- inadequate disclosure in offering memoranda,
- inadequate oversight of outsourced functions and service providers, and
- non-delivery of net asset value adjustments.

4. — Outreach, Consultation and Education

We continue our efforts to be transparent regarding practices and procedures that impact investment fund issuers in as timely a manner as possible. Our intent in doing so is to better enable fund managers and their advisors to avoid potential regulatory issues when they are at the planning stage for a new fund or transaction. As indicated at various points earlier in this report, we publish guidance and updates for the investment fund industry periodically.

During the year, we updated stakeholders on the status of the IFRS-related amendments, before and after the publication of those amendments, at three events organized by national accounting firms. After publishing the amendments, we also presented to, and discussed the amendments with, the Investment Funds Standing Committee at CPA Canada. We have also participated in the discussion of on-going implementation issues at the IFRS Discussion Group at CPA Canada.

In our bid to provide responsive regulation, we engage in periodic discussions with, and seek feedback on our various policy initiatives from, other regulators such as the Mutual Fund Dealers Association of Canada and the Investment Industry Regulatory Organization of Canada. We also seek input from the OSC's Investor Advisory Panel, whose mandate is to solicit and represent the views of investors on the Commission's policy and rule-making initiatives.

As in past years, we met with staff from the Investment Management and Derivatives divisions of the Securities and Exchange Commission to discuss investment fund trends, novel products and emerging issues that are common to our respective jurisdictions. These meetings help ensure that our regulatory approaches to product development are consistent and that opportunities for regulatory arbitrage between our markets are minimized.

Finally, in an effort to ensure effective national oversight of the investment fund industry, the CSA's Investment Funds Committee holds monthly conference calls. The Committee provides a forum for discussing novel applications, policy interpretation and initiatives, and operational matters in a timely fashion. It ensures that regulatory requirements are nationally applied consistently, fairly, and effectively, pursuant to the Passport system. In January 2014, Rhonda Goldberg, Director of the Investment Funds Branch, was appointed Chair of the Committee.

4.1 — Investment Funds Product Advisory Committee (IFPAC)

The OSC's IFPAC was established in August, 2011. The IFPAC, which is currently comprised of 12 external members, advises OSC staff specifically on emerging product developments and innovations occurring in the investment fund industry, and discusses the impact of these developments and emerging issues. The IFPAC also acts as one source of feedback to OSC staff on the development of policy and rule-making initiatives to promote investor protection, fairness and market efficiency across all types of investment fund products. The IFPAC meets quarterly and members serve a two year term. The initial two year term expired in Spring, 2013, with 6 members returning and 6 new members joining. You can find a *list of current IFPAC members* on the OSC website.

Topics of discussion with IFPAC this year have included the cost of ownership of investment fund products, the proposed risk classification methodology for use in the Fund Facts, linked notes, the exempt market review and the changes proposed to the Report of Exempt Distribution for investment fund issuers.

4.2 — The Investment Funds Practitioner

The Investment Funds Practitioner is an overview of recent and topical issues arising from applications for discretionary relief, prospectuses and continuous disclosure documents that investment fund issuers file with the OSC and that are reviewed by the Investment Funds Branch. It is intended to assist investment fund managers and their advisors who regularly prepare public disclosure documents and applications for discretionary relief on behalf of investment funds. The Practitioner is also intended to make fund managers more broadly aware of some of the issues we have raised in connection with our reviews and how we have resolved them. The Practitioner can be found on our website www.osc.gov.on.ca at *Information for Investment Funds.*

We have published 2 editions of the Investment Funds Practitioner since last year's summary report: *May 2013* and *November 2013.* We welcome suggestions for future topics.

4.3 — IOSCO Committee 5 — Investment Management

Investment Funds staff continued their participation in IOSCO C5 during 2013. This committee is focussed on investment management issues and is comprised of representatives from almost 30 regulators. The international developments discussed at C5 inform our policy and operational work, which is also guided by the principles and best practices published by IOSCO. During 2013, these included principles related to valuation, liquidity risk management and the regulation of ETFs. On January 8, 2014, IOSCO and the FSB jointly published a consultation document entitled "Assessment Methodologies for Identifying Non-Bank Non-Insurance Global Systemically Important Financial Institutions" for public comment. C5 participated in the development of the methodology for investment funds, including hedge funds, and fund managers. Current C5 initiatives include reviewing reliance on credit ratings and an examination of safe keeping and custody practices.

4.4 — IOSCO Committee 8 — Retail Investors

During the year, Howard Wetston, Chair and CEO of the OSC, was appointed Vice Chair of the Board of IOSCO. In June 2013 he was also appointed Chair of the newly formed IOSCO Committee 8. The Investment Funds Branch, with support from the Office of the Investor, Communications, the Investor Education Fund, and Office of Domestic and International Affairs branches of the OSC, assist the Chair of C8 in carrying out his duties.

The primary mandate for C8, which was approved by the IOSCO Board in June, 2013, is to conduct IOSCO's policy work on retail investor education and financial literacy. A secondary mandate is to advise the IOSCO Board on emerging retail investor protection matters.

C8 is intended to:

- reflect IOSCO's commitment to investor protection through the promotion of investor education and financial literacy and demonstrate a leadership role in developing guidance and policy for IOSCO members on behalf of retail investors

- be a forum to share experiences and develop approaches on investor education and financial literacy; and

- help the IOSCO Board take retail investor perspectives into account in prioritizing, coordinating and driving IOSCO's work.

During the year, OSC staff led C8's effort in the development of a strategic framework document. The purpose of this project is to identify and describe work streams that will establish the strategic direction of IOSCO's investor education and financial literacy efforts. This document sets out IOSCO's niche in investor education and financial literacy, current thinking and research, a strategy for program development, proposed work streams and best practices. It is anticipated that the best practices will be published for consultation by March, 2014.

5. — Feedback and Contact Information

If you have any questions regarding, or feedback on, our third annual summary report, please send them to investmentfunds@osc.gov.on.ca.

You can find additional information regarding investment funds and the Investment Funds Branch on our *website*.

We have also attached a list of Investment Funds Branch staff at the end of this report.

OSC Staff Notice 81-724 — Report on Staff's Continuous Disclosure Review of the Fees and Expenses Disclosure by Investment Funds

Date: May 8, 2014

37 O.S.C.B. 4603

Purpose

This notice sets out recommendations from staff of the Investment Funds Branch of the Ontario Securities Commission (**Staff** or **we**) based on our observations from a targeted continuous disclosure (**CD**) review of the fees and expenses disclosure practices of investment funds.

Objective and Scope of our Review

As part of our broader review of fee disclosure, starting August 2013, Staff conducted targeted CD reviews of the fees and expenses disclosure practices of a sample of fund managers.

Included in our review were 18 fund managers offering various types of investment funds, including conventional mutual funds, exchange-traded funds and closed-end funds. These fund groups have assets under management of approximately $210 billion.

We reviewed their funds' current prospectus and continuous disclosure records, including financial statements, management reports of fund performance (**MRFPs**) and independent review committee reports to examine whether the current disclosure of fees and expenses:

i. provides sufficient information to investors on how the fees and expenses are being charged; and

ii. accurately and fully describes fund managers' allocation of expenses to the funds they manage.

We coordinated our review closely with, and followed similar approaches of, staff in the Compliance and Registrant Regulation Branch (the **CRR Branch**) who regularly conduct reviews of fund expenses as part of their oversight of registrants. Further guidance on expense allocation will be issued by staff in the CRR Branch in their upcoming publication in OSC Staff Notice 33-743 *Guidance on Sales Practices, Expense Allocation and Other Relevant Areas Developed from the Results of the Targeted Review of Large Investment Fund Managers* (**Staff Notice 33-743**).

Background

Funds generally pay management fees and operating expenses to cover the various costs of their operation. These typically include costs for various services such as fund administration, portfolio advisory services, fund distribution, security services, safekeeping and custodial services, fund accounting and valuation, and audit and legal services.

Management fees are generally calculated as a percentage of the net assets of a fund and are paid to the fund manager. Operating expenses are either charged directly to the funds as they are incurred or may be covered by a fixed administration fee charged to the fund. The fixed administration fee is calculated as a percentage of the net assets of a fund and is paid to the fund manager in exchange for the fund manager bearing the operating expenses of the fund.

Part 8: MUTUAL FUNDS

The management agreement or trust agreement between the fund and the fund manager generally sets out which services are covered by the management fees and which services are covered by the operating expenses.

In practice, fund managers have to arrange for their funds' operations to be performed either in-house or by third party service providers. Where a fund manager provides operating services in-house to its funds, and the management agreement does not explicitly stipulate that those services are covered by the management fee, the fund manager may expect to recover the costs of such services, including a portion of its general overhead and administrative expenses, from its funds as operating expenses.

Summary of Observations

Overall, we noted good general compliance with disclosure requirements related to fees and expenses. In some instances, we noted opportunities for fund managers to enhance the disclosure. Our targeted CD review yielded the following observations regarding fees and expenses disclosure practices and expense allocation practices in the fund industry:

1. — Fees and Expenses Disclosure

- We noted varying fee and expense models within the fund industry. While certain fund managers paid for the costs of certain operating services out of their management fees, others charged those costs to their funds as operating expenses. For example, the costs associated with custodians were included in the management fees for some funds, or charged separately as operating expenses for other funds;

- The prospectuses we reviewed generally did not include the detail necessary for investors to know the specific costs and services paid for out of management fees relative to those charged to funds as operating expenses. General "catch-all" wording, such as "general administrative services" or "costs to administer the fund", were often used to describe the costs and services covered by the management fees. Similarly, wording such as "other general operating expenses", "other day-to-day operating expenses", or "general administrative costs" were used to describe operating expenses. Staff frequently needed to refer to the trust agreement or management agreement for greater detail on the services paid for out of management fees; and

- Staff also noted the use of "catch-all" wording in the MRFPs which did not provide sufficient specificity of the services received by the fund in consideration of the management fees paid to the fund manager.[1] Similarly, some funds did not disclose their expenses in the financial statements as separate line items[2] but rather used one catch-all line item, such as "operating costs" or "general operating expenses" to include a variety of fund expenses.

2. — Expense Allocation

- About half of the fund managers in our sample allocated part of their expenses to the funds they manage. While allocation practices varied among them, the expenses they generally allocated included such items as salaries, office rent, utilities, printing and copying, postage, and office supplies. The remaining fund managers either did not allocate their expenses to their funds or charged fixed administration fees;

- Fund managers used different allocation models to allocate expenses. Generally, fund managers charged to their funds the proportionate share of their costs based on the time or resources they dedicated to the funds' day-to-day operations. Those costs were further allocated across the family of funds and among various series of each fund using varying metrics such as number of investors in the funds/series or the assets under management of the funds/series;

- The majority of those fund managers who allocated expenses to their funds relied on general disclosure in the prospectus that the funds pay their own operating expenses as a basis to recover expenses from their funds. Only a few of those reviewed briefly mentioned in the prospectus that the fund manager recovers certain costs from their funds; and

- In our review of the financial statements and MRFPs, we observed that the majority of fund managers who allocated expenses to their funds did not provide related party disclosure.[3] Only a few provided note disclosure with respect to the allocation, but failed to provide details such as the amount or measurement basis of the transactions.

Based on these observations from our CD review, Staff make the following recommendations for fees and expenses disclosure and expenses allocation going forward.

Recommendations

1. — Fees and Expenses Disclosure

a. — Transparency in Disclosure of Management Fees and Expenses

In Staff's view, the prospectus and continuous disclosure documents should disclose the specific services that the fund manager provides to the fund in consideration of the management fees and the types of expenses charged to the fund as operating expenses. The use of general "catch all" terminology should be avoided.

---

[1] As required under part B, item 3.3 of Form 81-106F1 *Contents of Annual and Interim Management Report of Fund Performance* (**Form 81-106F1**).

[2] As required by section 3.2 of National Instrument 81-106 — *Investment Fund Continuous Disclosure* (**NI 81-106**).

[3] As required by International Accounting Standard 24 *Related Party Disclosures*, and by part B, item 2.5 of Form 81-106F1.

To meet the standard of full, true and plain disclosure[4], the prospectus should provide details sufficient for investors to clearly distinguish the types of expenses, in particular the types of administrative and operating expenses, that are covered by management fees from those that are covered by operating expenses. Investors should not have to refer to the management or trust agreement to determine whether a particular cost is covered by management fees or charged as a separate operating expense to the funds. Having all the relevant fees and expenses information disclosed in the prospectus will enable investors to compare the different fee models and structures, and make an informed investment decision.

We also remind fund managers to clearly describe the major services paid for out of the management fees in their funds' MRFPs, as well as to provide the required line items in the funds' financial statements, in accordance with existing requirements.[5] We encourage fund managers to disclose as much information as possible regarding the types of operating expenses that are charged to the funds in the financial statements by using relevant and descriptive line items, in addition to the mandated line items.

b. — Transparency in Disclosure of Expense Allocation

In Staff's view, fund managers should consider enhancing the transparency of their expense allocation as a way to mitigate the actual and perceived conflicts of interest inherent in such practices (as further discussed below). For example, a fund manager should, to the extent possible, ensure that its funds' prospectus specifies the types of costs the fund manager may recover from its funds. We also remind fund managers to disclose the particulars of the material conflicts of interest in the prospectus.[6]

On the continuous disclosure side, we remind fund managers to comply with related party disclosure requirements and provide the relevant details of the transactions in the funds' financial statements and MRFPs.[7] Disclosure should also explain how the conflicts are mitigated by including, for example, information concerning the policies, practices or guidelines of the funds or the manager relating to the allocation practice in the annual information form.[8]

2. — Expense Allocation

a. — Conflict of Interest

Fund managers have an inherent conflict of interest when allocating expenses between themselves and the funds they manage. We remind fund managers of their duty to act honestly, in good faith and in the best interests of the fund[9] when allocating expenses. Managers should be able to demonstrate that the allocation of an expense is not inconsistent with their duty of care and that they are not putting their own interests ahead of those of the fund and its securityholders.

Staff expect the general expenses allocated to the funds to have a direct relationship to the daily operation of the funds and to be fair and reasonable to the funds, as if the result of arm's length bargaining. Fund managers should avoid recovering expenses using opaque or complex methodologies that are not intuitive and not directly linked to the services being performed for the funds.

b. — Compliance with NI 81-107

Given that the allocation of expenses is generally viewed as a conflict of interest matter, it should be referred to the independent review committee.[10] Fund managers should have policies and procedures in place dealing with the allocation of expenses between the fund manager and its funds.[11] We found that the fund managers selected in our review generally complied with these requirements, and reviewed their policies and procedures at least annually.

c. — Appropriate Expense Allocation

Because of the inherent conflict of interest, Staff expect the expenses allocated to the funds to generally be limited to:

- costs and expenses that were necessarily incurred in the daily operation of the funds;

- reasonable costs and expenses that are reasonably incurred in the operation of the funds;

- expenses that are closely linked to the specific operation of the funds; and

- the proportionate share of the allocated expenses can be accurately and readily determined.

Certain costs must be incurred by fund managers to carry out their business as fund managers. Staff are generally of the view that it is not appropriate for funds to pay for the:

- costs and expenses that the fund manager would normally incur in the ordinary course of their operations as fund manager, such as, the compensation paid to their executive officers and directors; or

---

[4]As required by section 56(1) of the *Securities Act* (Ontario).

[5]See notes 1 and 2.

[6]As required by Item 19.3 of Form 41-101F2 *Information Required in an Investment Fund Prospectus*.

[7]See note 3.

[8]As required by Item 12(1)(b) of Form 81-101F2 *Contents of Annual Information Form*.

[9]As required by section 116 of the *Securities Act* (Ontario).

[10]As required by section 5.1 of National Instrument 81-107 *Independent Review Committee for Investment Funds* (**NI 81-107**).

[11]As required by section 2.2 of NI 81-107.

Part 8: MUTUAL FUNDS

- costs that are driven by the fund manager's business and organizational initiatives, such as, restructuring and rationalizing funds line-up.[12]

We encourage fund managers to exercise sound judgement in their expense allocation. In situations where it is uncertain whether certain expenses may be appropriately allocated to the funds, fund managers should make their decision having regard to the best interests of securityholders, and avoid any allocation that gives rise to a material conflict of interest for the fund managers.

Please refer to Staff Notice 33-743 for further examples and guidance on this topic to be issued by staff in the CRR Branch.

Conclusion

The fees and expenses of a fund are an important consideration for investors. We encourage fund managers to clearly disclose fees and expenses to provide more transparency and clarity, where possible, on what services are paid for out of the management fees, which services are charged as operating expenses and how all the fees and expenses are being allocated. Staff remind fund managers of their duty of care when allocating expenses.

We encourage fund managers to consider the recommendations in the notice when preparing disclosure so as to promote investors' understanding of fees and expenses.

Questions may be referred to:

[Omitted.]

OSC Staff Notice 81-725 — Recent Amendments to Part XXI Insider Trading and Self-Dealing of the *Securities Act* (Ontario) — Transition Issues

Date: August 7, 2014

37 O.S.C.B. 7255

Purpose

This notice provides the views of Ontario Securities Commission staff on questions that have been raised regarding certain amendments to the *Securities Act* (Ontario) (the Act) included in the 2014 Ontario Budget Bill which received Royal Assent on July 24, 2014 (the Amendments).

Background

Part XXI of the Act, *Insider Trading and Self-Dealing*, contains conflict of interest investment restrictions which, until July 24, 2014, only applied to mutual funds. The Amendments extend the conflict of interest investment restrictions to all investment funds, so that they apply to non-redeemable investment funds and mutual funds. While there are certain structural differences between different types of investment funds, in staff's view these differences do not support differential treatment with respect to the conflict of interest investment restrictions.

Some questions have been raised about the application of Part XXI to non-redeemable investment funds and about the impact of the Amendments on the existing requirements for mutual funds in Ontario.

Staff's Views on Transition Issues

Grandfathering Provisions

One question that has been raised is whether the Amendments require mutual funds to divest investments previously made in compliance with section 111 of the Act as it read prior to July 24, 2014. With respect to mutual funds that have always been subject to Part XXI of the Act, the Amendments were not, in staff's view, intended to have any effect. The Amendments include grandfathering provisions in subsections 111(3) and (4) which staff read as intending to allow mutual funds to not have to divest any investments made prior to July 24, 2014. The grandfathering provisions also permit investment funds newly caught by Part XXI of the Act to continue to hold any investments made prior to July 24, 2014. However, going forward, related investment funds will have to consider their combined aggregate position in a particular investment when determining whether any further investment is permitted.

Another question staff have been asked is how an existing non-redeemable investment fund can comply with section 115. This provision prohibits an investment fund from engaging in certain related-party transactions unless specific disclosure is made in the investment fund's prospectus. However, most existing non-redeemable investment funds will not have made the prospectus disclosure and are unable to do so since they no longer have a current prospectus. In staff's view, the Amendments are forward-looking from July 24, 2014 and intended to apply only to non-redeemable investment funds that file a preliminary prospectus, a prospectus or an amendment to a prospectus on or after July 24, 2014.

Connection to NI 81-102

Staff have received inquiries about the connection between the Amendments and National Instrument 81-102 *Mutual Funds* (NI 81-102). NI 81-102 currently applies to mutual funds only, but, pursuant to final amendments published June 19, 2014 (the Modernization Rules), effective September 22, 2014, NI 81-102 will also apply to non-redeemable investment funds. Where a provision of NI 81-102 impacts a provision of the Amendments, staff's intention was that the Amendments be read in conjunction with NI 81-102, including the transition periods provided in NI 81-102.

---

[12]See OSC Staff Notice *Issues Arising Out Of Mutual Fund Mergers and Similar Reorganizations* dated September 15, 1995.

Some of the conflict of interest investment restrictions that have been extended to all investment funds by the Amendments are also contemplated in NI 81-102. "Fund on fund" investing is one example. The conflict of interest investment restrictions in the Act have been extended to restrict a non-redeemable investment fund from investing in a related investment fund in certain situations. Section 2.5 of NI 81-102, which also governs fund on fund investing, provides an exemption from those restrictions. However, pursuant to the Modernization Rules, section 2.5 of NI 81-102 will not apply to non-redeemable investment funds that filed a prospectus on or before September 22, 2014 until March 21, 2016. Staff are of the view that, with respect to fund on fund investing, existing non-redeemable investment funds may avail themselves of this transition period provided in the Modernization Rules.

Staff remind investment fund issuers that the Amendments do, however, prohibit certain types of investments by all investment funds after July 24, 2014, and create new conflict of interest reporting requirements for non-redeemable investment funds. The application of the Amendments to related-party or self-dealing transactions involving investment funds should be carefully considered. In some cases, the transactions may be contemplated by National Instrument 81-107 *Independent Review Committee for Investment Funds*, so the requirements and exemptions in this rule should also be considered.

Further Information

Investment funds and their counsel are encouraged to contact staff in the Investment Funds and Structured Products Branch with any further questions relating to the application of the Amendments.

Questions may be referred to:

[Omitted.]

OSC Staff Notice 81-726 — 2014 Summary Report for Investment Fund and Structured Product Issuers

Date: February 26, 2015

38 O.S.C.B. 1841

[Not reproduced]

OSC Staff Notice 81-727 — Report on Staff's Continuous Disclosure Review of Mutual Fund Practices Relating to Portfolio Liquidity

Date: June 25, 2015

38 O.S.C.B. 5678

Purpose of This Notice

Staff of the Investment Funds and Structured Products Branch (*Staff* or *we*) of the Ontario Securities Commission (*OSC*) recently conducted targeted reviews focused on mutual fund practices relating to i) liquidity assessments of fund holdings, ii) liquidity stress testing, and iii) liquidity valuation considerations. This notice provides a summary of our findings and related guidance.

Objectives and Scope of Our Review

Units of mutual funds, including exchange-traded mutual funds (*ETFs*) (together, *funds*), are redeemable on demand, and funds generally offer their securities on a continuous basis. To facilitate purchases and redemptions of funds' units on a daily basis, funds are required to invest primarily in liquid investments in accordance with National Instrument 81-102 — *Investment Funds* (*NI 81-102*). When holding primarily liquid investments, funds are able to provide reliable and objective valuations of the fund's net asset value (*NAV*); which in turn enables the fund to meet investor redemption requests without significant disruption to the portfolio.

In late 2014, we commenced a series of targeted reviews of funds investing in asset classes that may be more susceptible to liquidity concerns. Staff focused on the following three fund categories:

1. High yield debt funds, including funds that focus on senior loans investments;

2. Emerging market funds; and

3. Small capitalization equity funds.

Our review focused on the following three areas:

1. Liquidity assessments of fund holdings: Staff assessed whether funds have appropriate policies and procedures to identify potential illiquid assets.

2. Liquidity stress testing: Staff assessed whether funds have appropriate policies and procedures to manage higher levels of redemption requests in an orderly manner under various stress scenarios.

3. Liquidity valuation considerations: Staff assessed whether funds' valuation processes have appropriately taken liquidity into consideration.

In total, we reviewed 22 funds, consisting of conventional mutual funds and ETFs managed by 16 investment fund managers (*IFMs*). The 16 IFMs manage approximately $391 billion in assets under management (*AUM*).

We did not find any practices or disclosures that resulted in a referral to either OSC's Compliance and Registrant Regulation or Enforcement branches.

Background

While the mutual fund industry consists largely of funds focused on traditional asset classes, such as equities and investment grade debt, staff have noted an increase in fund offerings with asset classes that may have higher liquidity risks.

The mutual fund industry has approximately $1.3 trillion in AUM, while ETF AUM is approximately $81 billion. As of February 2015, approximately 7% of total industry AUM was held in high yield global fixed income funds, 4% in Canadian, U.S. or global small/mid cap funds and 1% in emerging market equity funds.

Review Observations and Recommendations

Liquidity Assessments of Fund Holdings

Observations

Liquidity metrics

We found IFMs monitor varying metrics across asset classes in assessing the liquidity of their funds' holdings. As fixed income and debt holdings are not generally traded on exchanges, IFMs utilize a number of market quality metrics to determine the level of liquidity for these assets. These metrics include the number of dealers making a market, frequency of quotes, bid-ask spreads, outstanding issue size and frequency of price movements.

For listed equity investments, most IFMs use liquidity metrics, such as trading volume and bid-ask spreads. We found that some IFMs have the view that equity investments are liquid as long as the investments are listed on an exchange, without further consideration of market activity and conditions.

Many IFMs have established assessment or review committees to determine whether a security is illiquid. In addition to representations from the fund manager, these committees often consist of technical experts, such as portfolio advisors and fund accountants. Once a security is flagged as an illiquid asset, the review committee determines what actions need to be taken to ensure compliance with securities laws and the fund's investment policies.

Staff recognizes there is considerable judgment involved in liquidity assessments. Review committees can add objectivity and expertise into the assessment process for IFMs.

Monitoring of Liquidity

During our review we found instances, in particular funds focused on small capitalization issuers, where investment holdings have not exhibited trading volume or market activity needed to support the disposal of investments in a short period of time. These funds took corrective action and decreased their illiquid holdings to an appropriate level to ensure compliance with NI 81-102. To ensure compliance with securities laws, the IFMs for these funds developed policies and procedures to monitor a holdings' liquidity on a frequent and timely basis.

Illiquid investments, by their nature, can be difficult to dispose of. As a result, corrective actions can potentially cause significant disruption to a fund's portfolio. Staff supports ongoing liquidity monitoring as an important preventive tool.

Recommendations

1. — Written policies and procedures

Funds should have robust written policies and procedures on liquidity assessments at the time of an investment purchase and on an ongoing basis. The liquidity assessments should be based on objective and relevant quantitative metrics on an ongoing basis as market activity and conditions can vary and decline over time.

We expect funds to tailor their policies and procedures, as well as liquidity metrics, for different asset classes. While not an exhaustive list, they should consider the following metrics noted from the review that were used in making liquidity assessments:

- Volume metrics (e.g. average daily or weekly trading volume)
- Bid-ask spreads
- Number of participants making a market for the holding
- Outstanding issue size

2. — Market activity and conditions

The definition of "illiquid asset" in NI 81-102 refers to the ability to readily dispose of a portfolio asset through a market facility on which public quotations are available at a price that approximates the amount at which the portfolio asset is valued. Being listed on a stock exchange with a quoted price alone, in staff's view, is not generally sufficient to conclude that a particular holding is liquid. A stock listing does not necessarily mean that an equity investment could be readily disposed at a price that approximates the last market transaction or is within the current bid-ask spread.

Based on the redemption requirements set out in NI 81-102, specifically the requirement that redemption requests must be settled in 3 business days, IFMs should consider whether the funds' investment holdings can be readily disposed of in this period without a significant adverse impact to the portfolio. In considering market activity, IFMs can compare the size of a particular investment holding with the trading volume of such investment.

Liquidity Stress Testing

Observations

Current Practices

We found most IFMs engaged in some type of stress testing on an ongoing basis to assess the ability of a fund to meet unexpected large redemptions. However, some did not. We noted others conducted scenario analysis to assess the ability of the portfolio to meet redemptions, but this analysis incorporated only historical redemption rates without consideration of higher levels.

IFMs of funds investing in emerging market securities were generally more rigorous in stress testing their portfolios on an ongoing basis. Emerging market portfolios were typically subject to bi-weekly or ad-hoc discussions and analysis regarding their geographical and country specific exposure, geopolitical events and currency exposures.

Further, we found that funds investing in asset classes that have higher liquidity risks generally had investment parameters designed to mitigate such risks. For example, funds that invest in senior loans typically held higher cash levels and had higher degrees of diversification in the fund's holdings.

We see stress testing as a prudent way for IFMs to ensure funds can manage unexpected large redemption requests together with stressed market conditions.

Recommendations

1. — Standalone stress testing

Funds should have written stress testing policies and procedures in place to ensure the fund can effectively execute redemptions in stressed market conditions. Written procedures can speak to the order in which assets may be liquidated to minimize the negative impact to the portfolio and the remaining unitholders.

2. — Scenario analysis

When performing stress testing, IFMs should build into the scenario analysis redemption rates that exceed their past redemption experience. Together with liquidity stress testing, IFMs should consider stress testing for portfolio performance. As liquidity of underlying investments, large redemption requests and stressed market conditions tend to correlate with each other, effective stress testing should take into consideration different market conditions that would affect the performance of the funds. For example, for fixed income funds, consider the impact on the portfolio should interest rates change. Emerging market funds could consider the impact of a particular geopolitical uncertainty.

3. — Risk discussion and investment parameters

Funds with higher exposure to potentially illiquid assets should provide additional disclosure and ongoing discussion of the risk management policies and investment restrictions in place designed to mitigate liquidity risk. Funds can provide risk management discussion in the investment strategies section of the prospectus or management discussion and analysis in the management report of fund performance (*MRFP*). We think better risk management discussion provides clarity of the fund's investment policies and can enhance investor understanding and expectations. Staff found that some funds investing in senior loans, for example, have disclosed more defined investment restrictions around cash and marketable investment holding levels, and use of liquidity metrics, such as minimum tranche size and credit quality, as part of their strategies to mitigate liquidity risk.

To enhance investors' understanding and expectation of the investment risk, funds should disclose material risks that would significantly impact their funds' performance. For example, a potential increase in interest rates may negatively impact performance for fixed income funds.

Liquidity Valuation Considerations Observations

Valuation Practices

With respect to valuation, we found that closing market values were generally used for equity investments, including small capitalization issuers, without any further consideration of market activity and conditions.

For fixed income investments, we found IFMs accessed information helpful in assessing market activity and conditions. This included third party vendors providing over the counter broker quotes, and service providers who produce supplemental pricing information such as data freshness reports, quote sizes, and number of broker quotes. We found IFMs typically consider approximate price adjustments as a result of this supplemental information in the fair valuing of their fixed income holdings.

Recommendations

1. — Fair value determination for NAV calculation purposes

Fair value is defined in National Instrument 81-106 *Investment Fund Continuous Disclosure* (*NI 81-106*) to mean (a) the market value based on reported prices and quotations in an active market, or (b) if the market value is not available, or the manager of the investment fund believes that it is unreliable, a value that is fair and reasonable in all the relevant circumstances.

We refer funds to International Financial Reporting Standards 13 (*IFRS 13*) *Fair Value Measurements* which sets out guidance for determining fair value, as well as the accompanying disclosure requirements.

IFRS has established a three level fair value hierarchy, based on the type of inputs used to measure fair value. For investment valuation purposes;

- Level 1 inputs are quoted prices (unadjusted) in an active market for identical investments.

- Level 2 inputs are inputs other than quoted prices included within Level 1 that are observable for the investment either directly or indirectly.

- Level 3 inputs are unobservable inputs for the investment.

In order to measure an investment solely based on a quoted price, the fund must conclude that there is an 'active market' for the investment. IFRS 13 defines a market as active if transactions for the asset or liability occur with sufficient frequency and volume to provide pricing information on an ongoing basis. IFRS 13 also provides some guidance on when the volume or level of activity on a market may indicate that a transaction price or quoted price does not represent fair value.

Staff takes the view that a fund's determination of whether an investment is quoted in an active market under IFRS 13 must be a consideration in determining whether the investment meets the illiquid asset restrictions under NI 81-102.

2. — Disclosure

If an investment is not quoted in an active market, then fair value is determined based on a consideration of other inputs, and additional disclosure with respect to those investments is required in the funds' financial statements in accordance with IFRS 13. We refer funds to IFRS 13 which sets out relevant disclosure requirements.

We encourage funds to provide additional information when fair valuing fixed income and debt instruments, as level 2 inputs are often used.

To the extent that the valuation procedures are different between NAV calculation and for financial statement purposes, item 5 of subsection 3.6(1) of NI 81-106 requires notes disclosure detailing and explaining the differences.

3. — Independent Review Committee (IRC) input on valuation of illiquid assets

Given the actual and/or perceived conflict of interest that arises when IFMs value illiquid assets (such as when the IFM overrides valuations provided by external pricing sources), we expect IFMs to obtain standing instructions from the funds' IRC in regard to their valuation policies and procedures to ensure that any conflicts of interest are appropriately identified and mitigated.

Conclusion

We found that IFMs are generally aware of liquidity risks, and have taken liquidity risks into consideration in their day-to-day management of the funds. We did not find any practices or disclosures that resulted in a referral to either OSC's Compliance and Registrant Regulation or Enforcement branches.

We expect IFMs to use the guidance provided in this notice. Asset classes that may be more susceptible to liquidity concerns will remain a focus for Staff. We continue to monitor the development in this area, and will publish more guidance or take other regulatory action as needed.

Questions may be referred to:

Ritu Kalra

Senior Accountant

Investment Funds and Structured Products Branch

(416) 593-8063

rkalra@osc.gov.on.ca

Abid Zaman

Accountant

Investment Funds and Structured Products Branch

(416) 204-4955

azaman@osc.gov.on.ca

Sovener Yu

Accountant

Investment Funds and Structured Products Branch

(416) 593-2395

syu@osc.gov.on.ca

Raymond Chan

Manager

Investment Funds and Structured Products Branch

(416) 593-8128

rchan@osc.gov.on.ca

OSC Staff Notice 81-728 — Use of "Index" in Investment Fund Names and Objectives

Date: July 9, 2015

38 O.S.C.B. 6141

Purpose

This notice sets out guidance from staff of the Ontario Securities Commission (Staff) regarding the factors that Staff will consider in our prospectus reviews of investment funds whose investment objectives are to replicate the performance of an index, and which include the word "index" in their names (Index Tracking Funds).

Background

Staff have seen an increasing trend of prospectus filings by funds that purport to be Index Tracking Funds. In Staff's view, the index whose performance an Index Tracking Fund seeks to replicate should generally satisfy two conditions: (i) absence of discretion and (ii) transparency, as outlined below. Where these conditions are not satisfied, in the course of our prospectus reviews, we will ask that references to the purported index in the fund's investment objectives and name be removed.

Further, Staff note that an index that satisfies the conditions described in this notice may nonetheless not satisfy the definition of "index mutual fund" or "index participation unit" in National Instrument 81-102 *Investment Funds* (NI 81-102). In such a situation, even though the fund may include "index" in its name and investment objectives, the exemptions provided to index mutual funds or index participation units under NI 81-102 may not be relied on.

Absence of Discretion

An Index Tracking Fund seeks to replicate the performance of an identified index, which is generally considered a passive investment strategy. Accordingly, in Staff's view, in order to be an Index Tracking Fund, the methodology governing the index whose performance is being replicated (the Methodology) should generally not allow for the application of material discretion on the part of the index provider or any other party involved in the administration of the index. This means that the index should use objective and verifiable data as inputs, and the Methodology should specify the rules by which the material aspects of the index, such as index value, weighting and constituents, are determined given such inputs.

If material discretion may be employed in administering the index, Staff will generally view the Methodology as being more akin to an active investment strategy. While an investment fund may employ such a strategy (provided it is otherwise permissible under NI 81-102), we think that it is misleading to investors to refer to such a strategy as an "index" in the fund's name and investment objectives, or to market the fund in a way that suggests that it is an Index Tracking Fund.

Transparency of Index

Staff also expect the index whose performance an Index Tracking Fund seeks to replicate to be transparent. In our view, transparency can be achieved by making either the Methodology or the constituents of the index available to the public, by posting the Methodology or list of constituents on the website of the Index Tracking Fund or the index provider. Staff also expect the list of constituents to be updated as the index is rebalanced or reconstituted.

We would further expect an Index Tracking Fund's prospectus to sufficiently describe the applicable index, including the key factors in determining the constituents of the index and how often the index is rebalanced and reconstituted,[1] and to include a link to the website where the Methodology or list of index constituents can be found. The Index Tracking Fund's prospectus should also disclose how the Index Tracking Fund replicates the index (e.g., by direct investment in the constituents of the index, by stratified sampling, or by synthetic exposure through a derivative).

Transparency of the index assists investors in understanding the index to assess whether the Index Tracking Fund is an appropriate investment for the investor. Generally, Staff will expect the Methodology to include sufficient detail to assist in making such a judgment.

In instances where a fund manager does not wish to disclose the Methodology or the constituents of the index, Staff have taken the view that the purported index is a proprietary quantitative model and, while the fund may employ that model as an investment strategy, it is generally inappropriate for the fund to market itself as an Index Tracking Fund. Accordingly, we have asked that such funds remove any reference to "index" from their names and investment objectives.

Further Information

Investment fund managers and their counsel are encouraged to contact Staff at an early stage in the structuring of an Index Tracking Fund that may give rise to any questions concerning the issues discussed in this notice.

Questions

If you have any questions, please refer them to:

Mostafa Asadi

Senior Legal Counsel, Investment Funds and Structured Products Branch

---

[1]This position is consistent with previous guidance published by Staff on exchange-traded funds that replicate the performance of indices. See *Investment Funds Practitioner*, OSC, (2012) 35 OSCB 3597 at 3598.

Ontario Securities Commission

Tel: 416-593-8171

E-mail: masadi@osc.gov.on.ca

Pei-Ching Huang

Senior Legal Counsel, Investment Funds and Structured Products Branch

Ontario Securities Commission

Tel: 416-593-8264

E-mail: phuang@osc.gov.on.ca

OSC Staff Notice 81-729 — 2015 Summary Report for Investment Fund and Structured Product Issuers

Date: February 18, 2016

(2016), 39 OSCB 1459

[Not reproduced]

OSC Rule 81-801 — Implementing National Instrument 81-106 Investment Fund Continuous Disclosure

Date: June 1, 2005 as amended effective January 1, 2014

28 O.S.C.B. 4962 and 36 O.S.C.B. 9612

PART 1 — DEFINITIONS

1.1 Definitions — (1) In this Rule, "NI 81-106" means "National Instrument 81-106 *Investment Fund Continuous Disclosure*".

(2) Each term used in this Rule that is defined or interpreted in Part 1 of NI 81-106 has the meaning ascribed to it in that Part.

PART 2 — APPLICATION

2.1 Application — Except as specifically provided otherwise in this Rule, this Rule applies to

(a) an investment fund that is a reporting issuer; and

(b) a mutual fund in Ontario.

PART 3 — INTERRELATIONSHIP WITH LEGISLATION

3.1 Annual Financial Statements — Content — (1) The financial statements required under section 78 of the Act must include the statements and notes described in subsection 2.1(1) of NI 81-106.

(2) Sections 2.2, 2.5, 2.6, 2.7, 2.8, 2.9 and 2.11 of NI 81-106 apply to financial statements and auditor's reports required under section 78 of the Act as if any reference to financial statements or auditor's reports in those sections is a reference to section 78 of the Act.

(3) This section applies for financial years ending on or after June 30, 2005.

3.2 Interim Financial Reports — Content — (1) The financial statements required under section 77 of the Act must include the statements and notes described in section 2.3 of NI 81-106.

(2) Sections 2.4, 2.5, 2.6, 2.9, 2.11 and 2.12 of NI 81-106 apply to financial statements required under section 77 of the Act as if any reference to financial statements in those sections is a reference to section 77 of the Act.

(3) This section applies for interim periods ending after the period determined in subsection 3.1(3).

3.3 Filing Annual Financial Statements — Exemption — Section 78 of the Act does not apply to an investment fund that is a reporting issuer, or to a mutual fund in Ontario, that complies with sections 2.1, 2.2, 2.5, 2.6, 2.7, 2.8, 2.9 and 2.11 of NI 81-106 for financial years ending on or after June 30, 2005.

3.4 Filing Interim Financial Reports — Exemption — Section 77 of the Act does not apply to an investment fund that is a reporting issuer, or to a mutual fund in Ontario, that complies with sections 2.3, 2.4, 2.5, 2.6, 2.9, 2.11 and 2.12 of NI 81-106 for interim periods ending after the period determined in section 3.3.

3.5 Delivering Financial Statements — Exemption — Section 79 of the Act does not apply to an investment fund that is a reporting issuer, or to a mutual fund in Ontario, that complies with Part 5 of NI 81-106 in the case of

(a) annual financial statements for financial years ending on or after June 30, 2005; and

(b) interim financial reports for interim periods ending after the period determined in subsection (a).

3.6 Material Change Reports — Form — Every report required under subsection 75(2) of the Act must be a completed Form 51-102F3, as modified by s. 11.2(1)(c) of NI 81-106, except that the reference in Part 2, Item 3 of Form 51-102F3 to section 11.2 of NI 81-106 shall be read as referring to subsection 75(1) of the Act and references in Part 2, Items 6 and 7 of Form 51-102F3 to subsections 11.2(2), 11.2(4) or 11.2(5) of NI 81-106 shall be read as referring to subsections 75(3), 75(4) or 75(5), respectively, of the Act.

3.7 Issuance of Material Change News Release — Exemption — Subsection 75(1) of the Act does not apply to an investment fund that is a reporting issuer that complies with subsection 11.2(1)(a) of NI 81-106.

3.8 Filing Material Change Report — Exemption — Subsection 75(2) of the Act does not apply to an investment fund that is a reporting issuer that complies with subsection 11.2(1)(c) of NI 81-106.

3.9 Annual Filing — Exemption — Investment funds that are reporting issuers are exempt from subsection 81(2) of the Act.

3.10 Information Circulars — Form — An information circular referred to in clause (a) or (b) of subsection 86(1) of the Act must be a completed Form 51-102F5 from and after July 1, 2005.

3.11 Filing Information Circular — Exemption — Subsection 81(1) of the Act does not apply to an investment fund that is a reporting issuer that complies with section 12.4 of NI 81-106, from and after July 1, 2005.

3.12 Solicitation of Proxies — Exemption — Section 85 of the Act does not apply to an investment fund that is a reporting issuer that complies with subsection 12.2(1) of NI 81-106, from and after July 1, 2005.

3.13 Sending Information Circular — Exemption — Section 86 of the Act does not apply to an investment fund that is a reporting issuer that complies with subsection 12.2(2) of NI 81-106, from and after July 1, 2005.

PART 4 — EFFECTIVE DATE

4.1 Effective Date — (1) This rule comes into force on June 1, 2005.

(2) Despite subsection (1), the amendments to this Rule which came into force on January 1, 2014 only apply to financial periods relating to financial years beginning on or after January 1, 2014.

Final Rule: (2005) 28 O.S.C.B. 4962; Approval by OSC: (2005) 28 O.S.C.B. (Supp-1) 1; Request for Comments: (2004) 27 O.S.C.B. 5157 and (2002) 25 O.S.C.B. 6273.

Rules: NI 81-106, 51-102.

Policies and Orders: NPS 81-106CP; OPS 81-801CP.

Companion Policy 81-801CP — To Ontario Securities Commission Rule 81-801 Implementing National Instrument 81-106 Investment Fund Continuous Disclosure

1.1 Introduction — The purpose of this Companion Policy is to provide information relating to the manner in which the Ontario Securities Commission interprets or applies certain provisions of OSC Rule 81-801 *Implementing National Instrument 81-106 Investment Fund Continuous Disclosure* (the Implementing Rule) and National Instrument 81-106 *Investment Fund Continuous Disclosure* (NI 81-106).

1.2 Interrelationship between NI 81-106 and the Securities Act (Ontario) (the Act) — NI 81-106 is intended to provide a single source of harmonized continuous disclosure obligations for investment funds. As a result, NI 81-106 sometimes repeats (without any substantive change) certain requirements that are also dealt with in the Act under Part XVIII *Continuous Disclosure* and Part XIX *Proxies and Proxy Solicitation*. In addition, NI 81-106, through the Implementing Rule, varies or adds to some of the requirements contained in Parts XVIII and XIX of the Act. The cumulative effect of NI 81-106 and the Implementing Rule is that NI 81-106 supersedes the requirements found in Parts XVIII and XIX of the Act (other than sections 76 and 87, the subject matter of which are not dealt with in NI 81-106). Investment funds that are reporting issuers and mutual funds in Ontario can and should therefore refer to NI 1-106 in place of the continuous disclosure and proxy solicitation requirements contained in Parts XVIII and XIX of the Act (other than sections 76 and 87).

Adoption by OSC: (2005) 28 O.S.C.B. 4964 and (Supp-1) 1; Request for Comments: (2004) 27 O.S.C.B. 5157 and (2002) 25 O.S.C.B. 6273.

Rules: NI 81-106; Rule 81-801.

OSC Rule 81-802 — Implementing National Instrument 81-107 Independent Review Committee for Investment Funds

Date: November 1, 2006

29 O.S.C.B. 8840

PART 1 — DEFINITIONS AND INTERPRETATION

1.1 Definition — In this Rule, "NI 81-107" means National Instrument 81-107 *Independent Review Committee for Investment Funds*.

1.2 Interpretation — A term used in this Rule that is defined or interpreted in NI 81-107 has the meaning ascribed to it in NI 81-107.

PART 2 — APPLICATION

2.1 Application — This Rule applies to an investment fund that is a reporting issuer.

PART 3 — INTERRELATIONSHIP WITH LEGISLATION

3.1 Designation as market participant — (1) An independent review committee is designated as a market participant for the purposes of the Act.

(2) A manager of a non-redeemable investment fund is designated as a market participant for the purposes of the Act.

3.3 Definition of manager — In NI 81-107 "manager" means an "investment fund manager" under the Act.

3.4 Standard of care for manager — In NI 81-107, the standard of care and fiduciary duty required of a manager of a mutual fund in order to meet its obligation under NI 81-107 is the same standard of care and fiduciary duty imposed under section 116 of the Act.

PART 4 — EFFECTIVE DATE

4.1 Effective Date — (1) This Rule comes into force on November 1, 2006.

(2) Despite subsection (1), the amendments to this Rule which came into force on January 1, 2014 only apply to financial periods relating to financial years beginning on or after January 1, 2014.

Final Rule: 29 O.S.C.B. 8840; Approval by O.S.C.: 29 O.S.C.B. (Supp-1) 1; Request for Comments: 28 O.S.C.B. (Supp-2) 1 and 27 O.S.C.B. 465.

Definitions: OSA 1(1) "market participant"; 1(1) investment fund manager.

Companion Policy 81-802CP — To Ontario Securities Commission Rule 81-802 Implementing National Instrument 81-107 Independent Review Committee for Investment Funds

1.1 Introduction — The purpose of this Companion Policy is to provide information relating to the manner in which the Ontario Securities Commission (the Commission) interprets or applies certain provisions of Commission Rule 81-802 *Implementing National Instrument 81-107 Independent Review Committee for Investment Funds* (the Implementing Rule) and National Instrument 81-107 *Independent Review Committee for Investment Funds* (NI 81-107).

1.2 Interrelationship between NI 81-107 and the *Securities Act* (Ontario) (the Act) — NI 81-107 is intended to impose a minimum, consistent standard of governance for all publicly offered investment funds by introducing the requirement for a fully independent advisory body, the independent review committee (the IRC), charged with overseeing all conflict of interest matters faced by the manager in the operation of an investment fund. As a result, NI 81-107 sometimes repeats (without any substantive change) certain requirements that are also dealt with in the Act under Part XXI *Insider Trading and Self Dealing.*

The cumulative effect of NI 81-107 and the Implementing Rule is that the standard of care and fiduciary duty required under section 2.1 of NI 81-107 is the same standard of care and fiduciary duty imposed under section 116 of the Act for a manager of a mutual fund, and sections 6.1 and 6.2 of NI 81-107 provide for exemptions from some of the prohibitions in Part XXI of the Act, as permitted under sections 121.1 and 121.4 of the Act. A manager of a mutual fund that is a reporting issuer can and should therefore refer to section 2.1 of NI 81-107 in place of section 116 of the Act, and investment funds or mutual funds, respectively, should refer to sections 6.1 and 6.2 of NI 81-107 to see if the exemptions from the prohibitions contained in Part XXI of the Act are met.

Adoption by OSC: (2006) 29 O.S.C.B. 8841 and (Supp-1) 1; Request for Comments: 28 O.S.C.B. (Supp-2) 1 and 27 O.S.C.B. 465.

Approval 81-901 — Approval of Trustees of Mutual Fund Trusts

Approval: dated January 14, 1997: (1997) 20 O.S.C.B. 200; Replaced Interim OSC Policy 11.1 which was rescinded effective January 14, 1997.

Mutual Fund Trusts: Approval of Trustees Under Clause 213(3)(b) of the Loan and Trust Corporations Act

WHEREAS:

Clause 213(2)(b) of the *Loan and Trust Corporations Act* (the "LTCA") provides that no body corporate, other than a registered trust company under the LTCA, shall act as a trustee in respect of any service it provides to the public. Clause 213(3)(b) of the LTCA provides that clause 213(2)(b) does not apply to a body corporate that manages a mutual fund trust and that is approved by the Commission to act as trustee of the mutual fund trust.

The term **"mutual fund trust"** is defined in the *Income Tax Act* (Canada) (the "ITA"), but not in the LTCA or the *Securities Act* (the "Act"). In this Approval, the term means a trust that is one or more of (i) a mutual fund, as defined in the Act, (ii) a mutual fund trust, as defined in the ITA, or (iii) a trust that expects to be in a position to elect to be deemed to have been a mutual fund trust, as defined in the ITA, from the date of its inception.

In 1988, the Commission published Interim Policy Statement No. 11.1 entitled "Mutual Fund Trusts; Interim Ontario Securities Commission Approval of Mutual Fund Trustees pursuant to Clause 213(3)(b) of the *Loan and Trust Corporations Act*, 1987 (formerly Bill 116)" ("Interim Policy 11.1"). In Interim Policy 11.1, the Commission approved all bodies corporate that manage mutual fund trusts to act as trustee of a mutual fund trust in Ontario if the securities of the mutual fund are distributed by means of a prospectus or simplified prospectus for which a receipt has been issued by the Director under the Act. The Commission reserved the right to revoke its approval in appropriate circumstances and specified that the interim approval conferred under Interim Policy 11.1 would terminate upon the effective date of a final version of Policy Statement No. 11.1, whereupon the approval of bodies corporate to act as a trustee of a mutual fund would be governed by, and subject to, the terms of such policy statement.

The Commission stated that it was not intended that bodies corporate that met the criteria specified in Interim Policy 11.1, but did not meet the criteria specified in the final version of the policy statement, would be exempted from the criteria specified in that final version.

As part of its review of all of its policy statements, the Commission has decided to replace the approval contained in Interim Policy 11.1 with the approval contained in this document (the "Approval"). The Commission is, concurrently with the adoption of the Approval, rescinding Interim Policy 11.1.

NOW THEREFORE, the Commission hereby grants approval to any body corporate that manages a mutual fund trust to act as the trustee of the mutual fund trust in Ontario if

(a) the body corporate is the manager, within the meaning of National Policy Statement No. 39 or any rule replacing National Policy Statement No. 39, of the mutual trust fund; and

(b) securities of the mutual fund trust are distributed by means of a prospectus or simplified prospectus for which a receipt has been issued by the Director under the Act.

This Approval, unless earlier revoked or amended by the Commission, is effective until it is superseded by a regulation or rule made under the Act.

Recognition Order 81-902 — Recognized Rating Agencies

Recognition Order: dated February 25, 1997: (1997) 20 O.S.C.B. 1034. Replaced OSC Policy 11.2 which was repealed effective March 1, 1997.

[Not reproduced, as no longer relevant]

PART IX — DERIVATIVES

9.1 — Trades in Derivatives

OSC Rule 91-501 — Strip Bonds

Date: May 1, 1998, as amended effective September 14, 2005, September 28, 2009, January 11, 2015 and May 5, 2015

21 O.S.C.B. 2746, 28 O.S.C.B. (Supp-4) 141, 32 O.S.C.B. (Supp. 4) 392, 37 O.S.C.B. (Supp. 5), and 38 O.S.C.B. 4161

Table of Contents

PART 1 — DEFINITIONS AND INTERPRETATION

1.1 Definitions — In this Rule

"specified purchaser" means, at any specific time, a purchaser of a strip bond to whom a copy of a then-current strip bond information statement has not been delivered;

"qualified market intermediary" means, for a trade of a strip bond, a market intermediary that, absent this Rule, would be permitted under Ontario securities legislation to make the trade if the strip bond is a security described in paragraphs 2.34(2)(a) or (b) of National Instrument 45-106 *Prospectus Exemptions*;

"specified strip bond" means a strip bond other than a debt security issued by or guaranteed by the Government of Canada or the government of a province or territory of Canada;

"strip bond" means

    (a) an interest in an amount of principal or interest payable under an underlying bond, or in a pool of amounts of principal or interest payable under one or more underlying bonds, in either case in which the sole entitlement of the holder of the interest is to receive, at a specific future date, a sum certain in money that is fixed at the date of issue of the interest,

    (b) a security that consists of at least two or more of the interests referred to in paragraph (a) and that is not an underlying bond, or

    (c) a certificate or receipt representing an interest referred to in paragraph (a) or security referred to in paragraph (b);

"strip bond information statement" means an information statement that

    (a) has been accepted by the Director, if that acceptance has not been revoked,

    (b) contains the information referred to in section 4.1, and

    (c) does not, in a material respect, contain any information that is misleading or untrue or omit to include any information that is necessary to make other information in the information statement not misleading in the light of the circumstances in which it is made; and

"underlying bond" means a bond, debenture or other evidence of indebtedness of or guaranteed by the Government of Canada or any province or territory of Canada or by any foreign country or any political division of a foreign country.

1.2 Interpretation — (1) For the purpose of the definition of "specified purchaser", a purchaser of a strip bond includes a beneficiary of a defined contribution pension plan for whose benefit a strip bond is purchased, and who made the investment decision to purchase the strip bond.

(2) References in this Rule to "entering into an agreement of purchase and sale with a specified purchaser", or words to like effect, shall be read with reference to a purchaser referred to in subsection (1) to refer to entering into an agreement of purchase and sale with the defined contribution pension plan of which the purchaser is a beneficiary.

PART 2 — REGISTRATION AND PROSPECTUS EXEMPTIONS

2.1 Removal of Exemptions — (1) The exemptions from the dealer registration requirement contained in paragraph 8.20(2)(b) [*Specified debt*] of National Instrument 31-103 *Registration Requirements, Exemptions and Ongoing Registrant Obligations* and paragraph 3.34(2)(b) [*Specified debt*] of National Instrument 45-106 *Prospectus Exemptions* are not available for a trade in a specified strip bond.

(2) The exemption from the prospectus requirement contained in paragraph 2.34(2)(b) [*Specified debt*] of National Instrument 45-106 *Prospectus Exemptions* is not available for a distribution of a specified strip bond.

2.2 Registration Exemption — The registration requirement does not apply to a trade in a specified strip bond made by

    (a) a person or company that is not a market intermediary;

    (b) a qualified market intermediary to a person or company that is not a specified purchaser; or

    (c) a qualified market intermediary to a specified purchaser if the qualified market intermediary delivers a strip bond information statement to the specified purchaser before the specified purchaser enters into an agreement of purchase and sale relating to the trade.

2.3 Prospectus Exemption — The prospectus requirement does not apply to a distribution

    (a) of a type referred to in section 2.2;

    (b) by a qualified market intermediary to a person or company that is not a specified purchaser; or

    (c) by a registrant in accordance with section 3.1.

PART 3 — DELIVERY OBLIGATION

3.1 Delivery Obligation — Every registrant, before entering into an agreement of purchase and sale relating to a trade in a strip bond with a specified purchaser, shall deliver a strip bond information statement to the specified purchaser.

PART 4 — STRIP BOND INFORMATION STATEMENT

4.1 Contents of Strip Bond Information Statement — A strip bond information statement shall clearly describe

    (a) the nature of strip bonds, the rights of holders of strip bonds and how strip bonds differ from conventional interest-bearing debt securities;

    (b) the fluctuations, and volatility of fluctuations, in the market price and value of strip bonds resulting from fluctuations in interest rates;

    (c) the effect on the volatility of fluctuations referred to in paragraph (b) associated with the time to maturity of strip bonds;

    (d) the secondary market for strip bonds and underlying bonds;

    (e) custodial arrangements for strip bonds and underlying bonds;

    (f) the Canadian federal income tax consequences of buying, selling and holding strip bonds; and

    (g) the existence of dealer mark-ups or commissions on the purchase and sale of strip bonds and the impact, illustrated in tabular form, of different mark-ups or commissions on the yield to maturity of a strip bond, and shall include a statement inviting the prospective purchaser or seller of a strip bond to compare the yield to maturity of the strip bond, calculated after giving effect to any applicable dealer mark-up or commission, against the similarly calculated yield to maturity of a conventional interest-bearing debt security, and to inquire about the dealer's bid and ask prices for the subject strip bond.

4.2 Acceptance of Strip Bond Information Statement — (1) The Director shall accept a proposed strip bond information statement if the strip bond information statement complies with section 4.1.

(2) The Director shall not refuse to accept a strip bond information statement without giving the person or company who submitted the strip bond information statement for acceptance an opportunity to be heard.

(3) The person or company that submits a proposed strip bond information statement to the Director for acceptance shall file the strip bond information statement within seven days after its acceptance.

4.3 Revocation of Acceptance — (1) The Director may revoke an acceptance of a strip bond information statement if the strip bond information statement does not comply with section 4.1.

(2) The Director shall not revoke an acceptance of a strip bond information statement without giving the person or company who filed the strip bond information statement an opportunity to be heard.

PART 5 — EXEMPTION

5.1 Exemption — The Director may grant an exemption to this Rule, in whole or in part, subject to such conditions or restrictions as may be imposed in the exemption.

PART 6 — EFFECTIVE DATE

6.1 Effective Date — This Rule comes into force on May 1, 1998.

Final Rule: (1998) 21 O.S.C.B. 2746; Approval by Minister: (1998) 21 O.S.C.B. 75; Request for Comments: (1996) 19 O.S.C.B. 3467. Replaced a rule which was originally a blanket ruling (1984) 7 O.S.C.B. 4085 which was deemed to be a rule under s. 143.1(1) of the Act and remade into a rule entitled *In the Matter of Zero Coupon Strip Bonds*.

Amendments to Rule: (2005) 28 O.S.C.B. (Supp-4) 141; Approval by OSC: (2005) 28 O.S.C.B. (Supp-3) 223; Request for Comments: (2004) 27 O.S.C.B. (Supp-3) 1.

Amendments to Rule: (2009) 32 O.S.C.B. (Supp. 4) 392; Approval by OSC: (2009) 32 O.S.C.B. (Supp. 2) 1; Request for Comments: (2008) 31 O.S.C.B. 2279.

Amendments to Rule: (2015) 38 O.S.C.B. 4161.

Part 9:
DERIVATIVES

Companion Policy 91-501CP — To Rule 91-501 Strip Bonds

Table of Contents

PART 1 — INTRODUCTION

1.1 Introduction — The purpose of this Policy is to state the Commission's interpretation of certain provisions of Rule 91-501 Strip Bonds (the "Rule"), and to bring certain matters relating to the Rule to the attention of participants in the strip bond market.

PART 2 — DEFINITION OF STRIP BONDS

2.1 Interests in Pools — The definition of strip bonds includes interests in pools of amounts described in paragraph (a) of the definition. An interest in a pool, in this context, would include an interest in strip bonds held through deposit receipts that represent a non-traceable interest in underlying physical coupons or bonds. The effect of including pools of this nature in the Rule is to permit a depository to hold physical coupons or bonds en bloc, and to issue deposit receipts in various principal amounts that do not necessarily correspond to specific coupons or bonds. Interests in pools can appropriately be treated as strip bonds as long as it is clear that holding an interest in a pool represents a right to receive a sum certain in money at a specific future date rather than amounts determined on the basis of the performance of a portfolio of securities.

2.2 Strip Bond Packages — The definition of strip bond includes strip bond packages, which are defined to mean a security, other than an underlying bond, consisting of two or more of the interests described in paragraph (a) of the definition of strip bonds. This inclusion has been made to ensure that strip bond information statements contain disclosure about strip bond packages as well as ordinary strip bonds. The Investment Dealers Association of Canada information statement accepted by the Director for use under the predecessor policy to the Rule treats strip bond packages separately from strip bonds in several respects. For instance, the statement discloses that the payment characteristics of strip bond packages may more closely resemble conventional debt than strip bonds. In contrast to strip bonds, the income stream received on a strip bond package prior to maturity or the final payment date may be reinvested at the then prevailing interest rates. Therefore, the market price of a strip bond package will not be as volatile as the market price of a strip bond with the same credit risk and term to maturity or final payment date. However, it may be more volatile than the market price of a conventional interest-bearing debt security with the same credit risk and term to maturity. Also, strip bond packages are treated differently for tax purposes than strip bonds.

PART 3 — REGISTRATION EXEMPTIONS

3.1 Removal of Registration Exemptions — Section 2.1 of the Rule provides that the exemption from the dealer registration requirement and the exemption from the prospectus requirement referred to in that section are not available for a trade in a specified strip bond (as defined in section 1.1 of the Rule). Specified strip bonds are those strip bonds for which a registration or prospectus exemption is not provided in the Act (e.g., foreign government strip bonds).

3.2 Provision of Registration Exemptions — (1) The Rule provides registration exemptions for trades of specified strip bonds in three situations.

(2) First, a registration exemption is provided by paragraph 2.2(a) of the Rule for trades of specified strip bonds by non-market intermediaries; this exemption ensures that persons who are not market intermediaries may trade in specified strip bonds without compliance with the Rule on the same basis as they could trade in other exempt securities under the Act.

(3) Second, a registration exemption is provided by paragraph 2.2(b) of the Rule for trades of specified strip bonds by a "qualified market intermediary" to a person or company that is not a specified purchaser. A qualified market intermediary is defined in the Rule to be a market intermediary that, in effect, is permitted to trade in government bonds; the effect of this exemption, therefore, is to make available a registration exemption for specified strip bonds to those persons or companies who are permitted to trade in the underlying government bonds.

(4) The Commission notes that the term "qualified market intermediaries" includes both those market intermediaries that are permitted to trade in government securities pursuant to their registration, or pursuant to an exemption from registration that has not been made unavailable to the intermediary.

(5) Third, a registration exemption is provided by paragraph 2.2(c) of the Rule for trades of specified strip bonds by a qualified market intermediary to a person or company that is a specified purchaser if that purchaser receives the specified strip bond information statement before the specified purchaser enters into an agreement of purchase and sale relating to the trade.

PART 4 — DELIVERY OBLIGATION

4.1 Delivery Obligation — Paragraph 2.2(c) and section 3.1 of the Rule impose an obligation for the delivery of a strip bond information statement before an agreement of purchase and sale relating to a trade in a strip bond is entered into. The Commission notes that this obligation may be satisfied in a number of ways, so long as delivery of a current strip bond information statement has been made to a specified purchaser by that time. For instance, a registrant could satisfy the obligation by effecting a mass mailing of the statement to all of its clients, or by routinely delivering the statement to each client when the client opens an account with the registrant.

4.2 Beneficiaries of Defined Contribution Pension Plans — Section 1.2 of the Rule includes in the definition of "specified purchaser" a beneficiary of a defined contribution pension plan for whose benefit a strip bond is purchased, and who made the investment decision to purchase the strip bond. The effect of section 1.2 of the Rule is to ensure that defined contribution pension plan members who make investment decisions to purchase strip bonds are treated as purchasers under the Rule, even though those members likely will not directly enter into an agreement of purchase and sale for the strip bonds with the seller of the strip bonds. Under section 1.2, a seller of strip bonds must provide the pension plan member with a strip bond information statement if a copy of that statement has not been previously delivered to him or her (i.e., if that member is a "specified purchaser"), and that delivery must take place before the seller enters into the agreement of purchase and sale in respect of that sale, even if the agreement of purchase and sale is with the pension plan rather than the pension plan member.

PART 5 — STRIP BOND INFORMATION STATEMENTS

5.1 Strip Bond Information Statements — (1) A strip bond information statement is defined in the Rule as an information statement that has been accepted by the Director, if that acceptance has not been revoked, and satisfies the information requirements of the definition.

(2) The effect of this definition is that a strip bond information statement is not a strip bond information statement for the purposes of the Rule if it does not include information required to be included, or, in a material respect, contains any information that is misleading or untrue or omits to include any information in the information statement that is necessary to make other information in the information statement not misleading in the light of the circumstances in which it is made, even if the Director has accepted the information statement and has not taken the step of revoking his or her acceptance of the statement. The onus is on the person or company using a strip bond information statement to ensure that it satisfies the information requirements of the definition.

PART 6 — FEES

6.1 Fees — A submission of a proposed strip bond statement to the Director for acceptance should be accompanied by the fee referred to in item E1 of Appendix C of OSC Rule 13-502 *Fees*.

Adoption by OSC: (1998) 21 O.S.C.B. 2479 and (1998) 21 O.S.C.B. 75; Request for Comments: (1996) 19 O.S.C.B. 3467.

Adoption of Amendment by OSC: (2009) 32 O.S.C.B. (Supp. 4) 393 and 32 O.S.C.B. (Supp. 2) 1; Request for Comments: (2008) 31 O.S.C.B. 2279.

OSC Rule 91-502 — Trades in Recognized Options — Rule Under the Securities Act

Date: April 4, 1997, as amended effective September 14, 2005, September 28, 2009, January 11, 2015, May 5, 2015 and May 9, 2016.
20 O.S.C.B. 1731, 28 O.S.C.B. (Supp-4) 142, 32 O.S.C.B. (Supp. 4) 393, 37 O.S.C.B. (Supp. 5), 38 O.S.C.B. (Supp. 1) and 39 O.S.C.B. 4292

Table of Contents

Part 9:
DERIVATIVES

APPENDIX B RISK DISCLOSURE STATEMENT

PART 1 — DEFINITIONS

1.1 Definitions — In this Rule

"Canadian Options Course" means the course prepared and conducted by The Canadian Securities Institute and so named by that Institute on the date that this Rule comes into force and every predecessor to that course and every successor to that course that does not significantly narrow a subject matter;

"CFA" means the *Commodity Futures Act*;

"clearing corporation" means an association or organization through which trades in options or futures contracts are cleared and settled.

"commodity" has the meaning ascribed to that term in the CFA;

"equity option" means an option that is issued by a clearing corporation the underlying interest of which is one or more equity securities;

"equity security" means a security of an issuer that carries a residual right to participate in the earnings of the issuer and, on liquidation or winding up of the issuer, in its assets;

"non-equity accepted option" means

    (a) an option that is issued by a clearing corporation, other than a commodity futures option within the meaning of the CFA, the underlying interest of which consists only of one or more evidences of indebtedness, interest rates, stock market indices, precious metals or commodities, or

    (b) an option that is issued by a clearing corporation and that is included in an additional category of options accepted by the Director under section 4.1, the underlying interest of which is not an equity security;

"option" means an agreement that provides the holder with the right, but not the obligation, to do one or more of the following on terms or at a price established by or determinable by reference to the agreement at or by a time established by the agreement:

1. receive an amount of cash determinable by reference to a specified quantity of the underlying interest of the option.

2. purchase a specified quantity of the underlying interest of the option.

3. sell a specified quantity of the underlying interest of the option;

"options hedger" means a person or company trading in a recognized option the underlying interest of which relates to a risk to which a business carried on by the person or company is exposed, if

    (a) the risk arises as a necessary part of the business carried on by the person or company, and relates to fluctuations in

        (i) the price of a commodity related to the business,

        (ii) the value of liabilities which the person or company has incurred in connection with the business, or

        (iii) the value of a portfolio of investments which the person or company owns in connection with the business, and

    (b) the person or company offsets or attempts to offset all or a portion of the risk through trading in recognized options, whether or not any particular trade is effected for that purpose;

"recognized dealer" means a person or company

    (a) registered under the Act as a dealer in the category of broker or investment dealer,

    (b) registered under the CFA as a dealer in the category of futures commission merchant and that is a member of The Alberta Stock Exchange, The Toronto Stock Exchange, the TFE, The Montreal Exchange, the Vancouver Stock Exchange, The Winnipeg Commodity Exchange or the Investment Dealers Association of Canada,

    (c) who is a member of The Alberta Stock Exchange, The Toronto Stock Exchange, the TFE, The Montreal Exchange, the Vancouver Stock Exchange, The Winnipeg Commodity Exchange or the Investment Dealers Association of Canada only as to a trade in a recognized option on behalf of an options hedger, or

    (d) who, with respect to an option traded on the TFE, is an Unrestricted Trader Member of the TFE, acting in accordance with the By-laws of the TFE;

"recognized market" means a stock exchange recognized under section 21 of the Act on which options are traded;

"recognized market clearing corporation" means a clearing corporation through which trades in options entered into on or through a recognized market are cleared and settled;

"recognized option" means an equity option or a non-equity accepted option

    (a) traded on an exchange or market and cleared at the time this Rule comes into force or thereafter through a clearing corporation that is not a recognized market clearing corporation,

    (b) traded on an exchange or market and cleared at the time this Rule comes into force through a recognized market clearing corporation, or

    (c) recognized under section 4.2;

"risk disclosure statement" means

    (a) on or before January 1, 1999, either the statement attached to this Rule as Appendix A or the statement attached to the Rule as Appendix B, and

    (b) after January 1, 1999, the statement attached to this Rule as Appendix B;

"TFE" means The Toronto Futures Exchange, or any successor organization to The Toronto Futures Exchange; and

"underlying interest" means for an option, the security, commodity, financial instrument, currency, interest rate, foreign exchanges rate, economic indicator, index, basket, agreement or benchmark, and, if applicable, the relationship between any of the foregoing, from or on which the market price, value or payment obligations of the option are derived or based.

PART 2 — PROSPECTUS AND REGISTRATION EXEMPTIONS

2.1 Prospectus Exemptions — Section 53 of the Act does not apply to a trade in a recognized option entered into by

(a) a recognized dealer acting as principal; or

(b) a person or company trading through a recognized dealer if the person or company has been provided with the risk disclosure statement by the recognized dealer.

2.2 Registration Exemptions — (1) The dealer registration exemptions referred to in section 8.5(a) of NI 31-101 *Registration Requirements, Exemptions and Ongoing Registrant Obligations* are not available for a trade in a recognized option that is a non-equity accepted option.

(2) The dealer registration requirement does not apply to a trade in a recognized option that is an non-equity accepted option entered into by

(a) a recognized dealer acting as principal; or

(b) a person or company trading through a recognized dealer.

(3) The adviser registration requirement does not apply to advice given with respect to a recognized option that is a non-equity accepted option by a person registered as adviser under the CFA or a person or company exempt from the requirement to be so registered.

PART 3 — PROFICIENCY REQUIREMENTS

3.1 Proficiency Requirements — No person shall trade as agent in, or give advice in respect of, a recognized option unless he or she has successfully completed the Canadian Options Course.

PART 4 — ADDITIONAL OR AMENDED OPTIONS

4.1 Additional Non-Equity Accepted Options — The Director shall accept an additional category of option as a non-equity accepted option if

(a) each condition of the proposed additional category of option would be in conformity with normal commercial practices having regard to, among other things, the trading, exercise and settlement of the option or, if not so in conformity, that there would be reasonable justification for the divergence; and

(b) the risks resulting for investors in the proposed additional category of option are adequately described by the risk disclosure statement.

4.2 Recognition of Additional Non-Equity Accepted Options Traded on Recognized Markets — (1) A recognized market or a recognized market clearing corporation shall deliver to the Director the contract specifications for any option before the introduction for trading of the option on the market.

(2) If the additional option is a non-equity accepted option, the additional option becomes a recognized option unless the Director informs the recognized market within 10 business days after the filing that the Director refuses to accept the additional option as a recognized option.

(3) The Director shall not refuse to accept an additional option as a recognized option unless

(a) any condition of the proposed additional option would not be in conformity with normal commercial practices having regard to, among other things, the trading, exercise and settlement of the option without there being reasonable justification for the divergence; or

(b) the risks resulting for investors in the proposed additional option are not adequately described by the risk disclosure statement.

4.3 Changes to Recognized Options Traded on Recognized Markets — (1) No change to the contract specifications of any recognized option traded on a recognized market that is material shall be implemented without the prior approval of the Director.

(2) A recognized market may apply for the prior approval of the Director by delivering to the Director the details of the proposed change.

(3) The recognized market may implement the proposed change unless the Director informs the recognized market, within 10 business days after the filing, that he or she has refused to accept the proposed change.

(4) The Director shall not refuse to accept a proposed change to a recognized option unless

(a) the proposed change would result in the option not being in conformity with normal commercial practices having regard to, among other things, the trading, exercise and settlement of the option without there being reasonable justification for the divergence; or

(b) the risks resulting for investors from the proposed change are not adequately described by the risk disclosure statement.

PART 5 — RECOGNIZED MARKET CLEARING CORPORATIONS

5.1 Filing Requirements — Every recognized market clearing corporation shall deliver to the Commission each by-law, rule, regulation and policy approved by the board of directors of the recognized market clearing corporation within five days after the date on which it is approved and before its approval by the membership of the recognized market clearing corporation.

5.2 Approval by Commission — (1) No by-law, rule, regulation or policy of a recognized market clearing corporation shall come into force without the approval of the Commission.

(2) A by-law, rule, regulation or policy of a recognized market clearing corporation that has not been approved by the Commission within 30 days after the delivery referred to in section 5.1 shall be deemed to be approved by the Commission on the thirtieth day after the delivery unless the Commission or its staff has notified the recognized market clearing corporation that approval of the Commission will not be forthcoming within the 30 day period for any reason, including that further information is required in connection with the by-law, rule, regulation or policy.

(3) The Commission shall not fail to approve a by-law, rule, regulation or policy of a recognized market clearing corporation unless the by-law, rule, regulation or policy

(a) may adversely affect the likelihood that obligations arising out of options cleared through the recognized market clearing corporation would be met in accordance with normal commercial practices;

(b) may adversely expose investors to unfair, improper or fraudulent practices;

(c) may adversely affect the fostering of fair and efficient capital markets and confidence in the capital markets; or

(d) may be prejudicial to the public interest.

5.3 Reporting Requirements — Each recognized market clearing corporation shall deliver to the Commission

    (a) within 150 days after the end of each of its fiscal years, its audited financial information for the fiscal year; and

    (b) within five days after the occurrence of a change that is material to information provided to the Commission respecting incorporation, principal or registered office, officers, directors or shareholders, details of the change.

PART 6 — EXEMPTION

6.1 Exemption — The Director may grant an exemption to this Rule, in whole or in part, subject to such conditions or restrictions as may be imposed in the exemption.

PART 7 — REVOCATION OF BLANKET RULINGS

7.1 Revocation of Blanket Rulings — The following Blanket Rulings of the Commission are revoked:

1. *In the Mater of The Recognized Options Rationalization Order and In The Matter of the Options Clearing Corporation* (1992), 15 OSCB 3817.

2. *In the Matter of the Recognized Options Rationalization Order and In the matter of The Montreal Exchange* (1993), 16 OSCB 4916.

PART 8 — EFFECTIVE DATE

8.1 Effective Date — This Rule comes into force on the later of March 2, 1997 and the date determined under section 143.4 of the Act.

Appendix A

No securities commission or similar authority in Canada has in any way passed upon the merits of Options referred to herein and any representation to the contrary is an offence. This document contains condensed information respecting the Options referred to herein. Additional information may be obtained from your broker.

Disclosure Statement for Recognized Market Options

A high degree of risk may be involved in the purchase and sale of Options, depending to a large measure on how and why Options are used. Options may not be suitable for every investor. See "Risks in Options Trading" and "Additional Information".

Introduction

This Disclosure Statement sets forth general information relevant to the purchase and sale of Put and Call Options traded on a recognized market and cleared through a clearing corporation. Information concerning the underlying interests on which Options are traded, the terms and conditions of these Options, the recognized markets on which they trade and the applicable clearing corporations may be obtained from your broker. Information on investment strategies and possible uses of Options may also be obtained from your broker.

This Disclosure Statement refers only to Options and clearing corporations which have been recognized or qualified for purposes of this Disclosure Statement by provincial securities administrators where required. The Options discussed herein trade on markets which, for the purposes of this Disclosure Statement only, are referred to as "recognized markets".

Nature of an Option

An Option is a contract entered into on a recognized market between a seller (sometimes known as a writer) and a purchaser where all the terms and conditions of the contract (called the "specifications"), other than the consideration (called the "premium") for the Option, are standardized and predetermined by the recognized market. The premium, paid by the purchaser to the seller, is determined in the market on the basis of supply and demand, reflecting such factors as the duration of the Option, the difference between the exercise price of the Option and the market price of the underlying interest, the price volatility and other characteristics of the underlying interest.

There are two types of Options: Calls and Puts. A Call gives the purchaser a right to buy, and a Put the right to sell, a specific underlying interest at a stated exercise price and within a specified period of time or on a specific date. An Option subjects the seller to an obligation to honour the right granted to the purchaser if exercised by the purchaser. Underlying interests can be shares of a specific corporation, bonds, notes, bills, certificates of deposit, commodities, foreign currency, the cash value of an interest in a stock index or any other interest provided for in the specifications.

An Option transaction is entered into on a recognized market by a purchaser and a seller represented by their respective brokers. When the transaction is concluded it is cleared by a clearing corporation affiliated with the recognized market on which the Option is traded. When an Option transaction is cleared by the clearing corporation it is divided into two contracts with the clearing corporation becoming the seller to the purchaser in the transaction and the purchaser to the seller. Thus on every outstanding Option, the purchaser may exercise the Option against the clearing corporation and the seller may be called upon to perform his obligation through exercise of the Option by the clearing corporation.

Options may also be classified according to delivery requirements: actual delivery and cash delivery. An actual delivery Option requires the physical delivery of the underlying interest if the Option is exercised. A cash delivery Option requires a cash payment of the difference between the aggregate exercise price and the value of the underlying interest at a specified time prior or subsequent to the time the Option is exercised.

Options are issued in series designated by an expiration month, an exercise price, an underlying interest and a unit of trading. At the time trading is introduced in Options with a new expiration month, the recognized market on which the Option is traded establishes exercise prices that reflect the current spot prices of the underlying interest. Generally, three series of Options are introduced with exercise prices at, below and above the current spot price. When the spot price of the underlying interest moves, additional Options may be added with different exercise prices. Options having the same underlying interest and expiration month, but having different exercise prices, may trade at the same time.

Specifications of Options

Specifications of Options are fixed by the recognized market on which they are traded. These specifications may include such items as trading units, exercise prices, expiration dates, last day of trading, and the time for determining settlement values.

An Option may be bought or sold only on the recognized market on which the Option is traded. The recognized market and the clearing corporation may each impose restrictions on certain types of transactions, and under certain circumstances may modify the specifications of outstanding Options. In addition, a recognized market or a clearing corporation may limit the number of Options which may be held by an investor, and may limit the exercise of Options under prescribed circumstances.

Exercising Options

An Option may have either an American style exercise or European style exercise irrespective of where the recognized market is located. An American style Option can be exercised by the purchaser at any time before the expiration. To do this, the purchaser notifies the broker through whom the Option was purchased. A purchaser should ascertain in advance from his broker the latest date on which he may give such notice to his broker. A European style Option may only be exercised by the purchaser on a specified date. Upon receiving an exercise notice from the purchaser's broker, the clearing corporation assigns it to a member which may re-assign it to a client on a random or other predetermined selection basis.

Upon assignment, the seller must make delivery of (in the case of a Call) or take delivery of and pay for (in the case of a Put) the underlying interest. In the case of a cash delivery Option, the seller must, in lieu of delivery, pay the positive difference between the aggregate exercise price and the settlement value of the underlying interest (in the case of both a Call and a Put).

A purchaser of an Option which expires loses the premium paid for the Option and his transaction costs. The seller of an Option which expires will have as his gain the premium received for the Option less his transaction costs.

Trading of Options

Each recognized market permits secondary market trading of its Options. This enables purchasers and sellers of Options to close out their positions by offsetting sales and purchases. By selling an Option with the same terms as the one purchased, or buying an Option with the same terms as the one sold, an investor can liquidate his position (called an "offsetting transaction"). Offsetting transactions must be made prior to expiration of an Option or by a specified date prior to expiration. Offsetting transactions must be effected through the broker through whom the Option was initially sold or purchased.

Price movements in the underlying interest of an Option will generally be reflected to some extent in the secondary market value of the Option and the purchaser who wishes to realize a profit will have to sell or exercise his Option during the life of the Option or on the specified date for exercise, as the case may be.

Costs of Options Trading

Margin Requirements

Prior to trading Options, a seller must deposit with his broker cash or securities as collateral (called "margin") for the obligation to buy (in the case of a Put) or sell (in the case of a Call) the underlying interest if the Option should be exercised. Minimum margin rates are set by the recognized market on which the Option trades. Higher rates of margin may be required by the seller's broker.

Margin requirements of various recognized markets may differ. In addition, they are subject to change at any time and such changes may apply retroactively to Option positions previously established.

Commission Charges

Commissions are charged by brokers on the purchase or sale of Options as well as on the exercise of Options and the delivery of underlying interests.

Risks in Options Trading

Options can be employed to serve a number of investment strategies including those concerning investments in or related to underlying interests. SOME STRATEGIES FOR BUYING AND SELLING OPTIONS INVOLVE GREATER RISK THAN OTHERS.

The following is a brief summary of some of the risks connected with trading in Options:

(i) Because an Option has a limited life, the purchaser runs the risk of losing his entire investment in a relatively short period of time. If the price of the underlying interest does not rise above (in the case of a Call) or fall below (in the case of a Put) the exercise price of the Option plus premium and transaction costs during the life of the Option, or by the specified date for exercise, as the case may be, the Option may be of little or no value and if allowed to expire will be worthless.

(ii) The seller of a Call who does not own the underlying interest is subject to a risk of loss should the price of the underlying interest increase. If the Call is exercised and the seller is required to purchase the underlying interest at a market price above the exercise price in order to make delivery, he will suffer a loss.

(iii) The seller of a Put who does not have a corresponding short position (that is an obligation to deliver what he does not own) in the underlying interest will suffer a loss if the price of the underlying interest decreases below the exercise price, plus transaction costs minus the premium received. Under such circumstances, the seller of the Put will be required to purchase the underlying interest at a price above the market price, with the result that any immediate sale will give rise to a loss.

(iv) The seller of a Call who owns the underlying interest is subject to the full risk of his investment position should the market price of the underlying interest decline during the life of the Call, or by the specified date for exercise, as the case may be, but will not share in any gain above the exercise price.

(v) The seller of a Put who has a corresponding short position in the underlying interest is subject to the full risk of his investment position should the market price of the underlying interest rise during the life of the Put, or by the specified date for exercise, as the case may be, but will not share in any gain resulting from a decrease in price below the exercise price.

(vi) Transactions for certain Options may be carried out in a foreign currency. Accordingly, purchasers and sellers of these Options using Canadian dollars will be exposed to risks from fluctuations in the foreign exchange market as well as to risks from fluctuations in the price of the underlying interest.

(vii) There can be no assurance that a liquid market will exist for a particular Option to permit an offsetting transaction. For example, there may be insufficient trading interest in the particular Option; or trading halts, suspensions or other restrictions may be imposed on the Option or the underlying interest; or some event may interrupt normal market operations; or a recognized market could for regulatory or other reasons decide or be compelled to discontinue or restrict trading in the Option. In such circumstances the purchaser of the Option would only have the alternative of exercising his Option in order to realize any profit, and the seller would be unable to terminate his obligation until the Option expired or until he performed his obligation upon being assigned an exercise notice.

(viii) The seller of an American style Option has no control over when he might be assigned an exercise notice. He should assume that an exercise notice will be assigned to him in circumstances where the seller may incur a loss.

(ix) In unforeseen circumstances there may be a shortage of underlying interests available for delivery upon exercise of actual delivery Options, which could increase the cost of or make impossible the acquisition of the underlying interests and cause the clearing corporation to impose special exercise settlement procedures.

(x) In addition to the risks described above which apply generally to the buying and selling of Options, there are timing risks unique to Options that are settled by the payment of cash.

The exercise of Options settled in cash results in a cash payment from the seller to the purchaser based on the difference between the exercise price of the Option and the settlement value. The settlement value is based on the value of the underlying interest at a specified time determined by the rules of the recognized market. This specified time could vary with the Option. For example, the specified time could be the time for establishing the closing value of the underlying interest on the day of exercise or in the case of some Options based on a stock index the time for establishing the value of the underlying interest which is based on the opening prices of constituent stocks on the day following the last day of trading. Options for which the settlement value is based on opening prices may not, unless the applicable recognized market announces a rule change to the contrary, trade on that day.

The settlement value for Options, futures contracts and futures options may not be calculated in the same manner even though each may be based on the same underlying interest.

Where the settlement value of a cash delivery Option is determined after the exercise period, the purchaser who exercises such Option will suffer from any unfavourable change in the value of the underlying interest from the time of his decision to exercise to the time settlement value is determined. With actual delivery Options, this risk can be covered by a complementary transaction in the actual market for the underlying interest.

The seller of a cash delivery Option is not informed that he has been assigned an exercise notice until the business day following exercise, at the earliest, and the seller will suffer from any unfavourable change in the value of the underlying interest from the time of determination of the settlement value to the time he learns that he has been assigned. Unlike the seller of an actual delivery Option, the seller of a cash delivery Option cannot satisfy his assignment obligations by delivery of the lower valued underlying interest, but must pay cash in an amount determined by the settlement value.

The type of risk discussed above makes spreads and other complex option strategies involving cash delivery Options substantially more risky than similar strategies involving actual delivery Options.

Tax Consequences

The income tax consequences of trading in Options are dependent upon the nature of the business activities of the investor and the transaction in question. Investors are urged to consult their own professional advisers to determine the consequences applicable to their particular circumstances.

Additional Information

Before buying or selling an Option an investor should discuss with his broker:

- His investment needs and objectives
- The risks he is prepared to take
- The specifications of Options he may wish to trade
- Commission rates
- Margin requirements
- Any other matter of possible concern

Specifications for each Option are available on request from your broker and from the recognized market on which the Option is traded. Should there be any difference in interpretation between this document and the specifications for a given Option, the specifications shall prevail.

Appendix B — Risk Disclosure Statement

Risk Disclosure Statement for Futures and Options

This brief statement does not disclose all of the risks and other significant aspects of trading in futures and options. In light of the risks, you should undertake such transactions only if you understand the nature of the contracts (and contractual relationships) into which you are entering and the extent of your exposure to risk. Trading in futures and options is not suitable for many members of the public. You should carefully consider whether trading is appropriate for you in light of your experience, objectives, financial resources and other relevant circumstances.

Futures

1. — Effect of "Leverage" or "Gearing"

Transactions in futures carry a high degree of risk. The amount of initial margin is small relative to the value of the futures contract so that transactions are "leveraged" or "geared". A relatively small market movement will have a proportionately larger impact on the funds you have deposited or will have to deposit: this may work against you as well as for you. You may sustain a total loss of initial margin funds and any additional funds deposited with the firm to maintain your position. If the market moves against your position or margin levels are increased, you may be called upon to pay substantial additional funds on short notice to maintain your position. If you fail to comply with a request for additional funds within the time prescribed, your position may be liquidated at a loss and you will be liable for any resulting deficit.

2. — Risk-reducing Orders or Strategies

The placing of certain orders (e.g. "stop-loss" order, where permitted under local law, or "stop-limit" orders) which are intended to limit losses to certain amounts may not be effective because market conditions may make it impossible to execute such orders. Strategies using combinations of positions, such as "spread" and "straddle" positions may be as risky as taking simple "long" or "short" positions.

Options

3. — Variable Degree of Risk

Transactions in options carry a high degree of risk. Purchasers and sellers of options should familiarize themselves with the type of option (i.e. put or call) which they contemplate trading and the associated risks. You should calculate the extent to which the value of the options must increase for your position to become profitable, taking into account the premium and all transaction costs.

The purchaser of options may offset or exercise the options or allow the options to expire. The exercise of an option results either in a cash settlement or in the purchaser acquiring or delivering the underlying interest. If the option is on a future, the purchaser will acquire a futures position with associated liabilities for margin (see the section on Futures above). If the purchased options expire worthless, you will suffer a total loss of your investment which will consist of the option premium plus transaction costs. If you are contemplating purchasing deep-out-of-the-money options, you should be aware that the chance of such options becoming profitable ordinarily is remote.

Selling ("writing" or "granting") an option generally entails considerably greater risk than purchasing options. Although the premium received by the seller is fixed, the seller may sustain a loss well in excess of that amount. The seller will be liable for additional margin to maintain the position if the market moves unfavourably. The seller will also be exposed to the risk of the purchaser exercising the option and the seller will be obligated to either settle the option in cash or to acquire or deliver the underlying interest. If the option is on a future, the seller will acquire a position in a future with associated liabilities for margin (see the section on Futures above). If the option is "covered" by the seller holding a corresponding position in the underlying interest or a future or another option, the risk may be reduced. If the option is not covered, the risk of loss can be unlimited.

Certain exchanges in some jurisdictions permit deferred payment of the option premium, exposing the purchaser to liability for margin payments not exceeding the amount of the premium. The purchaser is still subject to the risk of losing the premium and transaction costs. When the option is exercised or expires, the purchaser is responsible for any unpaid premium outstanding at that time.

Additional Risks Common to Futures and Options

4. — Terms and Conditions of Contracts

You should ask the firm with which you deal about the terms and conditions of the specific futures or options which you are trading and associated obligations (e.g., the circumstances under which you may become obligated to make or take delivery of the underlying interest of a futures contract and, in respect of options, expiration dates and restrictions on the time for exercise). Under certain circumstances the specifications of outstanding contracts (including the exercise price of an option) may be modified by the exchange or clearing house to reflect changes in the underlying interest.

5. — Suspension or Restriction of Trading and Pricing Relationships

Market conditions (e.g. illiquidity) and/or the operation of the rules of certain markets (e.g. the suspension of trading in any contract or contract month because of price limits or "circuit breakers") may increase the risk of loss by making it difficult or impossible to effect transactions or liquidate/offset positions. If you have sold options, this may increase the risk of loss.

Further, normal pricing relationships between the underlying interest and the future, and the underlying interest and the option may not exist. This can occur when, for example, the futures contract underlying the option is subject to price limits while the option is not. The absence of an underlying reference price may make it difficult to judge "fair" value.

6. — Deposited Cash and Property

You should familiarize yourself with the protections accorded money or other property you deposit for domestic and foreign transactions, particularly in the event of a firm insolvency or bankruptcy. The extent to which you may recover your money or property may be governed by specific legislation or local rules. In some jurisdictions, property which had been specifically identifiable as your own will be prorated in the same manner as cash for purposes of distribution in the event of a shortfall.

7. — Commission and Other Charges

Before you begin to trade, you should obtain a clear explanation of all commission, fees and other charges for which you will be liable. These charges will affect your net profit (if any) or increase your loss.

8. — Transactions in Other Jurisdictions

Transactions on markets in other jurisdictions, including markets formally linked to a domestic market, may expose you to additional risk. Such markets may be subject to regulation which may offer different or diminished investor protection. Before you trade you should enquire about any rules relevant to your particular transactions. Your local regulatory authority will be unable to compel the enforcement of the rules of regulatory authorities or markets in other jurisdictions where your transactions have been effected. You should ask the firm with which you deal for details about the types of redress available in both your home jurisdiction and other relevant jurisdictions before you start to trade.

9. — Currency Risks

The profit or loss in transactions in foreign currency-denominated contracts (whether they are traded in your own or another jurisdiction) will be affected by fluctuations in currency rates where there is a need to convert from the currency denomination of the contract to another currency.

10. — Trading Facilities

Most open-outcry and electronic trading facilities are supported by computer-based component systems for the order-routing, execution, matching, registration or clearing of trades. As with all facilities and systems, they are vulnerable to temporary disruption or failure. Your ability to recover certain losses may be subject to limits on liability imposed by the system provider, the market, the clearing house and/or member firms. Such limits may vary; you should ask the firm with which you deal for details in this respect.

11. — Electronic Trading

Trading on an electronic trading system may differ not only from trading in an open-outcry market but also from trading on other electronic trading systems. If you undertake transactions on an electronic trading system, you will be exposed to risks associated with the system including the failure of hardware and software. The result of any system failure may be that your order is either not executed according to your instructions or is not executed at all. Your ability to recover certain losses which are particularly attributable to trading on a market using an electronic trading system may be limited to less than the amount of your total loss.

12. — Off-exchange Transactions

In some jurisdictions, and only then in restricted circumstances, firms are permitted to effect off-exchange transactions. The firm with which you deal may be acting as your counterparty to the transaction. It may be difficult or impossible to liquidate an existing position, to assess the value, to determine a fair price or to assess the exposure to risk. For these reasons, these transactions may involve increased risks.

Off-exchange transactions may be less regulated or subject to a separate regulatory regime. Before you undertake such transactions, you should familiarize yourself with applicable rules.

Final Rule: (1997) 20 O.S.C.B. 1731; Approval by OSC: (1997) 20 O.S.C.B. 361; Request for Comments: (1995) 18 O.S.C.B. 4921.

Amendment to Rule: (2005) 28 O.S.C.B. (Supp-4) 142; Approval by OSC: (2005) 28 O.S.C.B. (Supp-3) 224; Request for Comments: (2004) 27 O.S.C.B. (Supp-3) 1.

Amendment to Rule: (2009) 32 O.S.C.B. (Supp. 4) 393; Approval by OSC: 32 O.S.C.B. (Supp. 2) 1.

Amendment to Rule: (2015) 38 O.S.C.B. 4160.

Amendment to Rule: (2016) 39 O.S.C.B. (Supp. 1) 120; Approved by OSC: (2016) 39 O.S.C.B. 4292

OSC Rule 91-503 — Trades in Commodity Futures Contracts and Commodity Futures Options Entered into on Commodity Futures Exchanges Situate Outside of Ontario — Rule Under the Securities Act

Date:　　　April 4, 1997
20 O.S.C.B. 1739

PART I — DEFINITIONS

A. Definitions — In this Rule

"CFA means "the *Commodity Futures Act*";

"commodity futures contract", "commodity futures exchange" and "commodity futures option" have the respective meanings ascribed to them in the CFA;

"exempt exchange" means a commodity futures exchange that is not registered with or recognized by the Commission under the CFA and the forms of contracts of which are not accepted by the Director under the CFA; and

"exempt exchange contract" means a commodity futures contract or a commodity futures option entered into on an exempt exchange.

PART II — REGISTRATION AND PROSPECTUS EXEMPTIONS

A. Registration Exemption — Section 25 of the Act does not apply to a trade in, or advice given in respect of, an exempt exchange contract.

B. Prospectus Exemption — Section 53 of the Act does not apply to a trade in an exempt exchange contract.

PART II — REVOCATION OF BLANKET RULINGS

A. Revocation of Blanket Rulings — The following Blanket Rulings of the Commission are revoked only in respect of the relief provided under the Act:

1. *In the Matter of Trading in Commodity Futures Contracts and Commodity Futures Options Entered Into On Commodity Futures Exchanges Situate Outside Canada Other than Commodity Futures Exchanges in the United States of America* (1980), 15 OSCB 7, as varied by (1984), 7 OSCB 995.

2. *In the Matter of Trading in Commodity Futures Contracts Entered into on the Montreal Stock Exchange* (August 25, 1980) OSCWS 15A, as varied by *In the Matter of Trading in Commodity Futures Contracts and Commodity Futures Options Entered into on The Montreal Exchange* (1989), 12 OSCB 3392.

3. *In the Matter of Trading in Commodity Futures Contracts and Commodity Futures Options Entered into on Commodity Futures Exchanges in the United States of America* (1984), 7 OSCB 4576.

Final Rule: (1997) 20 O.S.C.B. 1739; Approval by OSC: (1997) 20 O.S.C.B. 374; Request for Comments: (1995) 18 O.S.C.B. 4929.

OSC Rule 91-506 — Derivatives: Product Determination

Date: **December 31, 2013, amended effective April 30, 2015**

36 O.S.C.B. 11015 and 38 O.S.C.B. 1375

1. Application — This Rule applies to Ontario Securities Commission Rule 91-507 — *Trade Repositories and Derivatives Data Reporting.*

2. Excluded derivatives — (1) A contract or instrument is prescribed not to be a derivative if it is

    (a) regulated by,

        (i) gaming control legislation of Canada or a jurisdiction of Canada, or

        (ii) gaming control legislation of a foreign jurisdiction, if the contract or instrument

            (A) is entered into outside of Canada,

            (B) is not in violation of legislation of Canada or Ontario, and

            (C) would be regulated under gaming control legislation of Canada or Ontario if it had been entered into in Ontario;

    (b) an insurance or annuity contract entered into,

        (i) with an insurer holding a licence under insurance legislation of Canada or a jurisdiction of Canada and regulated as insurance under that legislation, or

        (ii) outside of Canada with an insurer holding a licence under insurance legislation of a foreign jurisdiction, if it would be regulated as insurance under insurance legislation of Canada or Ontario if it had been entered into in Ontario;

    (c) a contract or instrument for the purchase and sale of currency that,

        (i) except where all or part of the delivery of the currency referenced in the contract or instrument is rendered impossible or commercially unreasonable by an intervening event or occurrence not reasonably within the control of the parties, their affiliates or their agents, requires settlement by the delivery of the currency referenced in the contract or instrument,

            (A) within two business days, or

            (B) after two business days provided that the contract or instrument was entered into contemporaneously with a related security trade and the contract or instrument requires settlement on or before the relevant security trade settlement deadline,

        (ii) is intended by the counterparties, at the time of the execution of the transaction, to be settled by the delivery of the currency referenced in the contract within the time periods set out in subparagraph (i), and

        (iii) does not allow for the contract or instrument to be rolled over;

    (d) a contract or instrument for delivery of a commodity other than cash or currency that,

        (i) is intended by the counterparties, at the time of execution of the transaction, to be settled by delivery of the commodity, and

        (ii) does not allow for cash settlement in place of delivery except where all or part of the delivery is rendered impossible or commercially unreasonable by an intervening event or occurrence not reasonably within the control of the counterparties, their affiliates, or their agents;

    (e) evidence of a deposit issued by a bank listed in Schedule I, II or III to the *Bank Act* (Canada), by an association to which the *Cooperative Credit Associations Act* (Canada) applies or by a company to which the *Trust and Loan Companies Act* (Canada) applies;

Part 9: DERIVATIVES

(f) evidence of a deposit issued by a credit union or league to which the *Credit Unions and Caisses Populaires Act, 1994* or a similar statute of Canada or a jurisdiction of Canada (other than Ontario) applies or by a loan corporation or trust corporation registered under the *Loan and Trust Corporations Act* or a similar statute of a jurisdiction of Canada (other than Ontario); or

(g) traded on an exchange recognized by a securities regulatory authority, an exchange exempt from recognition by a securities regulatory authority or an exchange that is regulated in a foreign jurisdiction by a signatory to the International Organization of Securities Commissions' Multilateral Memorandum of Understanding.

(2) For the purposes of paragraph (1)(g), an exchange does not include a derivatives trading facility.

3. Investment contracts and over-the-counter options — A contract or instrument, other than a contract or instrument to which section 2 applies, that is a derivative, and that is otherwise a security solely by reason of being an investment contract under paragraph (n) of the definition of "security" in subsection 1(1) of the Act, or being an option described in paragraph (d) of that definition, that is not described in section 5, is prescribed not to be a security.

4. Derivatives that are securities — A contract or instrument, other than a contract or instrument to which any of sections 2 and 3 apply, that is a security and would otherwise be a derivative is prescribed not to be a derivative.

5. Derivatives prescribed to be securities — A contract or instrument that is a security and would otherwise be a derivative, other than a contract or instrument to which any of sections 2 to 4 apply, is prescribed not to be a derivative if such contract or instrument is used by an issuer or affiliate of an issuer solely to compensate an employee or service provider or as a financing instrument and whose underlying interest is a share or stock of that issuer or its affiliate.

Final Rule: Approval by OSC: (2013) 36 O.S.C.B. 11015; Request for Comments: (2013) 36 O.S.C.B. 5737.

Amendment to Rule: (2015) 38 O.S.C.B. 1375

Companion Policy 91-506CP — To Ontario Securities Commission Rule 91-506 Derivatives: Product Determination

Part 1 — General Comments

Introduction

This Companion Policy (the "Policy") sets out the views of the Commission ("our" or "we") on various matters relating to Ontario Securities Commission Rule 91-506 *Derivatives: Product Determination* (the "Rule").

Except for Part 1, the numbering and headings in this Companion Policy correspond to the numbering and headings in the Rule. Any general guidance for a Section appears immediately after the Section name. Any specific guidance on sections in the Rule follows any general guidance.

The Rule applies only to the Ontario Securities Commission Rule 91-507 *Trade Repositories and Derivatives Data Reporting*.

Unless defined in the Rule or this Companion Policy, terms used in the Rule and in this Companion Policy have the meaning given to them in securities legislation, including, for greater certainty, in National Instrument 14-101 *Definitions* and Ontario Securities Commission Rule 14-501 *Definitions*.

In this Companion Policy, the term "contract" is interpreted to mean "contract or instrument".

Part 2 — Guidance

Excluded derivatives

2. (1)(a) — Gaming contracts

Paragraph 2(1)(a) of the Rule prescribes certain domestic and foreign gaming contracts not to be "derivatives". While a gaming contract may come within the definition of "derivative", it is generally not recognized as being a financial derivative and typically does not pose the same potential risk to the financial system as other derivatives products. In addition, the Commission does not believe that the derivatives regulatory regime will be appropriate for this type of contract. Further, gaming control legislation of Canada (or a jurisdiction of Canada), or equivalent gaming control legislation of a foreign jurisdiction, generally has consumer protection as an objective and is therefore aligned with the objective of securities legislation to provide protection to investors from unfair, improper or fraudulent practices.

With respect to subparagraph 2(1)(a)(ii), a contract that is regulated by gaming control legislation of a foreign jurisdiction would only qualify for this exclusion if: (1) its execution does not violate legislation of Canada or Ontario, and (2) it would be considered a gaming contract under domestic legislation. If a contract would be treated as a derivative if entered into in Ontario, but would be considered a gaming contract in a foreign jurisdiction, the contract does not qualify for this exclusion, irrespective of its characterization in the foreign jurisdiction.

(b) — Insurance and annuity contracts

Paragraph 2(1)(b) of the Rule prescribes qualifying insurance or annuity contracts not to be "derivatives". A reinsurance contract would be considered to be an insurance or annuity contract.

While an insurance contract may come within the definition of "derivative", it is generally not recognized as a financial derivative and typically does not pose the same potential risk to the financial system as other derivatives products. The Commission does not believe that the derivatives regulatory regime will be appropriate for this type of contract. Further, a comprehensive regime is already in place that regulates the insurance industry in Canada and the insurance legislation of Canada (or a jurisdiction of Canada), or equivalent insurance legislation of a foreign jurisdiction, has consumer protection as an objective and is therefore aligned with the objective of securities legislation to provide protection to investors from unfair, improper or fraudulent practices.

Certain derivatives that have characteristics similar to insurance contracts, including credit derivatives and climate-based derivatives, will be treated as derivatives and not insurance or annuity contracts.

Subparagraph 2(1)(b)(i) requires an insurance or annuity contract to be entered into with a domestically licensed insurer and that the contract be regulated as an insurance or annuity contract under Canadian insurance legislation. Therefore, for example, an interest rate derivative entered into by a licensed insurance company would not be an excluded derivative.

With respect to subparagraph 2(1)(b)(ii), an insurance or annuity contract that is made outside of Canada would only qualify for this exclusion if it would be regulated under insurance legislation of Canada or Ontario if made in Ontario. Where a contract would otherwise be treated as a derivative if entered into in Canada, but is considered an insurance contract in a foreign jurisdiction, the contract does not qualify for this exclusion, irrespective of its characterization in the foreign jurisdiction. Subparagraph 2(1)(b)(ii) is included to address the situation where a local counterparty purchases insurance for an interest that is located outside of Canada and the insurer is not required to be licensed in Canada.

(c) — Currency exchange contracts

Paragraph 2(1)(c) of the Rule prescribes a short-term contract for the purchase and sale of a currency not to be a "derivative" if it is settled within the time limits set out in subparagraph 2(1)(c)(i). This provision is intended to apply exclusively to contracts that facilitate the conversion of one currency into another currency specified in the contract. These currency exchange services are often provided by financial institutions or other businesses that exchange one currency for another for clients' personal or business use (e.g., for purposes of travel or to make payment of an obligation denominated in a foreign currency).

Timing of delivery (subparagraph 2(1)(c)(i))

To qualify for this exclusion the contract must require physical delivery of the currency referenced in the contract within the time periods prescribed in subparagraph 2(1)(c)(i). If a contract does not have a fixed settlement date or otherwise allows for settlement beyond the prescribed periods or permits settlement by delivery of a currency other than the currency referenced in the contract, it will not qualify for this exclusion.

Clause 2(1)(c)(i)(A) applies to a transaction that settles by delivery of the referenced currency within two business days — being the industry standard maximum settlement period for a spot foreign exchange transaction.

Clause 2(1)(c)(i)(B) allows for a longer settlement period if the foreign exchange transaction is entered into contemporaneously with a related securities trade. This exclusion reflects the fact that the settlement period for certain securities trades can be three or more days. In order for the provision to apply, the securities trade and foreign exchange transaction must be related, meaning that the currency to which the foreign exchange transaction pertains was used to facilitate the settlement of the related security purchase.

Where a contract for the purchase or sale of a currency provides for multiple exchanges of cash flows, all such exchanges must occur within the timelines prescribed in subparagraph 2(1)(c)(i) in order for the exclusion in paragraph 2(1)(c) to apply.

Settlement by delivery except where impossible or commercially unreasonable (subparagraph 2(1)(c)(i))

Subparagraph 2(1)(c)(i) requires that a contract must not permit settlement in a currency other than what is referenced in the contract unless delivery is rendered impossible or commercially unreasonable as a result of events not reasonably within the control of the counterparties.

Settlement by delivery of the currency referenced in the contract requires the currency contracted for to be delivered and not an equivalent amount in a different currency. For example, where a contract references Japanese Yen, such currency must be delivered in order for this exclusion to apply. We consider delivery to mean actual delivery of the original currency contracted for either in cash or through electronic funds transfer. In situations where settlement takes place through the delivery of an alternate currency or account notation without actual currency transfer, there is no settlement by delivery and therefore the exclusion in paragraph 2(1)(c) would not apply.

We consider events that are not reasonably within the control of the counterparties to include events that cannot be reasonably anticipated, avoided or remedied. An example of an intervening event that would render delivery to be commercially unreasonable would include a situation where a government in a foreign jurisdiction imposes capital controls that restrict the flow of the currency required to be delivered. A change in the market value of the currency itself will not render delivery commercially unreasonable.

Intention requirement (subparagraph 2(1)(c)(ii))

Subparagraph 2(1)(c)(ii) excludes from the reporting requirement a contract for the purchase and sale of a currency that is intended to be settled through the delivery of the currency referenced in such contract. The intention to settle a contract by delivery may be inferred from the terms of the relevant contract as well as from the surrounding facts and circumstances.

When examining the specific terms of a contract for evidence of intention to deliver, we take the position that the contract must create an obligation on the counterparties to make or take delivery of the currency and not merely an option to make or take delivery. Any agreement, arrangement or understanding between the parties, including a side agreement, standard account terms or operational procedures that allow for the settlement in a currency other than the referenced currency or on a date after the time period specified in subparagraph 2(1)(c)(i) is an indication that the parties do not intend to settle the transaction by delivery of the prescribed currency within the specified time periods.

We are generally of the view that certain provisions, including standard industry provisions, the effect of which may result in a transaction not being physically settled, will not necessarily negate the intention to deliver. The contract as a whole needs to be reviewed in order to determine whether the counterparties' intention was to actually deliver the contracted currency. Examples of provisions that may be consistent with the intention requirement under subparagraph 2(1)(c)(ii) include:

- a netting provision that allows two counterparties who are party to multiple contracts that require delivery of a currency to net offsetting obligations, provided that the counterparties intended to settle through delivery at the time the contract was created and the netted settlement is physically settled in the currency prescribed by the contract, and

- a provision where cash settlement is triggered by a termination right that arises as a result of a breach of the terms of the contract.

Although these types of provisions permit settlement by means other than the delivery of the relevant currency, they are included in the contract for practical and efficiency reasons.

In addition to the contract itself, intention may also be inferred from the conduct of the counterparties. Where a counterparty's conduct indicates an intention not to settle by delivery, the contract will not qualify for the exclusion in paragraph 2(1)(c). For example, where it could be inferred from the conduct that counterparties intend to rely on breach or frustration provisions in the contract in order to achieve an economic outcome that is, or is akin to, settlement by means other than delivery of the relevant currency, the contract will not qualify for this exclusion. Similarly, a contract would not qualify for this exclusion where it can be inferred from their conduct that the counterparties intend to enter into collateral or amending agreements which, together with the original contract, achieve an economic outcome that is, or is akin to, settlement by means other than delivery of the relevant currency.

Rolling over (subparagraph 2(1)(c)(iii))

Subparagraph 2(1)(c)(iii) provides that, in order to qualify for the reporting exclusion in paragraph 2(1)(c), a currency exchange contract must not permit a rollover of the contract. Therefore, physical delivery of the relevant currencies must occur in the time periods prescribed in subparagraph 2(1)(c)(i). To the extent that a contract does not have a fixed settlement date or otherwise allows for the settlement date to be extended beyond the periods prescribed in subparagraph 2(1)(c)(i), the Commission would consider it to permit a rollover of the contract. Similarly, any terms or practice that permits the settlement date of the contract to be extended by simultaneously closing the contract and entering into a new contract without delivery of the relevant currencies would also not qualify for the exclusion in paragraph 2(1)(c).

The Commission does not intend that the exclusion in paragraph 2(1)(c) will apply to contracts entered into through platforms that facilitate investment or speculation based on the relative value of currencies. These platforms typically do not provide for physical delivery of the currency referenced in the contract, but instead close out the positions by crediting client accounts held by the person operating the platform, often applying the credit using a standard currency.

(d) — Commodities

Paragraph 2(1)(d) of the Rule prescribes a contract for the delivery of a commodity not to be a "derivative" if it meets the criteria in subparagraphs 2(1)(d)(i) and (ii).

Commodity

The exclusion available under paragraph 2(1)(d) is limited to commercial transactions in goods that can be delivered either in a physical form or by delivery of the instrument evidencing ownership of the commodity. We take the position that commodities include goods such as agricultural products, forest products, products of the sea, minerals, metals, hydrocarbon fuel, precious stones or other gems, electricity, oil and natural gas (and by-products, and associated refined products, thereof), and water. We also consider certain intangible commodities, such as carbon credits and emission allowances, to be commodities. In contrast, this exclusion will not apply to financial commodities such as currencies, interest rates, securities and indexes.

Intention requirement (subparagraph 2(1)(d)(i))

Subparagraph 2(1)(d)(i) of the Rule requires that counterparties *intend* to settle the contract by delivering the commodity. Intention can be inferred from the terms of the relevant contract as well as from the surrounding facts and circumstances.

When examining the specific terms of a contract for evidence of an intention to deliver, we take the position that the contract must create an obligation on the counterparties to make or take delivery of the commodity and not merely an option to make or take delivery. Subject to the comments below on subparagraph 2(1)(d)(ii), we are of the view that a contract containing a provision that permits the contract to be settled by means other than delivery of the commodity, or that includes an option or has the effect of creating an option to settle the contract by a method other than through the delivery of the commodity, would not satisfy the intention requirement and therefore does not qualify for this exclusion.

We are generally of the view that certain provisions, including standard industry provisions, the effect of which may result in a transaction not being physically settled, may not necessarily negate the intention to deliver. The contract as a whole needs to be reviewed in order to determine whether the counterparties' intention was to actually deliver the commodity. Examples of provisions that may be consistent with the intention requirement under subparagraph 2(1)(d)(i) include:

- an option to change the volume or quantity, or the timing or manner of delivery, of the commodity to be delivered;

- a netting provision that allows two counterparties who are party to multiple contracts that require delivery of a commodity to net offsetting obligations provided that the counterparties intended to settle each contract through delivery at the time the contract was created;

- an option that allows the counterparty that is to accept delivery of a commodity to assign the obligation to accept delivery of the commodity to a third-party; and

- a provision where cash settlement is triggered by a termination right arising as a result of the breach of the terms of the contract or an event of default thereunder.

Although these types of provisions permit some form of cash settlement, they are included in the contract for practical and efficiency reasons.

In addition to the contract itself, intention may also be inferred from the conduct of the counterparties. For example, where it could be inferred from the conduct that counterparties intend to rely on breach or frustration provisions in the contract in order to achieve an economic outcome that is, or is akin to, cash settlement, the contract will not qualify for this exclusion. Similarly, a contract will not qualify for this exclusion where it can be inferred from their conduct that the counterparties intend to enter into collateral or amending agreements which, together with the original contract, achieve an economic outcome that is, or is akin to, cash settlement of the original contract.

When determining the intention of the counterparties, we will examine their conduct at execution and throughout the duration of the contract. Factors that we will consider include whether a counterparty is in the business of producing, delivering or using the commodity in question and whether the counterparties regularly make or take delivery of the commodity relative to the frequency with which they enter into such contracts in relation to the commodity.

Situations may exist where, after entering into the contract for delivery of the commodity, the counterparties enter into an agreement that terminates their obligation to deliver or accept delivery of the commodity (often referred to as a "book-out" agreement). Book-out agreements are typically separately negotiated, new agreements where the counterparties have no obligation to enter into such agreements and such book-out agreements are not provided for by the terms of the contract as initially entered into. We will generally not consider a book-out to be a "derivative" provided that, at the time of execution of the original contract, the counterparties intended that the commodity would be delivered.

Settlement by delivery except where impossible or commercially unreasonable (subparagraph 2(1)(d)(ii))

Subparagraph 2(1)(d)(ii) requires that a contract not permit cash settlement in place of delivery unless physical settlement is rendered impossible or commercially unreasonable as a result of an intervening event or occurrence not reasonably within the control of the counterparties, their affiliates or their agents. A change in the market value of the commodity itself will not render delivery commercially unreasonable. In general, we consider examples of events not reasonably within the control of the counterparties would include:

- events to which typical *force majeure* clauses would apply,

- problems in delivery systems such as the unavailability of transmission lines for electricity or a pipeline for oil or gas where an alternative method of delivery is not reasonably available, and

- problems incurred by a counterparty in producing the commodity that they are obliged to deliver such as a fire at an oil refinery or a drought preventing crops from growing where an alternative source for the commodity is not reasonably available.

In our view, cash settlement in these circumstances would not preclude the requisite intention under subparagraph 2(1)(d)(i) from being satisfied.

(e) and (f) — Evidence of a deposit

Paragraphs 2(1)(e) and (f) of the Rule prescribe certain evidence of deposits not to be a "derivative".

Paragraph 2(1)(f) refers to "similar statutes of Canada or a jurisdiction of Canada". While the *Credit Unions and Caisses Populaires Act, 1994* (Ontario) is Ontario legislation, it is intended that all federal or province-specific statutes will receive the same treatment in every province or territory. For example, if a credit union to which the Ontario *Credit Unions and Caisses Populaires Act, 1994* (Ontario) applies issues an evidence of deposit to a market participant that is located in a different province, that province would apply the same treatment under its equivalent legislation.

(g) — Exchange-traded derivatives

Paragraph 2(1)(g) of the Rule prescribes a contract not to be a derivative if it is traded on certain prescribed exchanges. Exchange-traded derivatives provide a measure of transparency to regulators and to the public, and for this reason are not required to be reported. We note that where a transaction is cleared through a clearing agency, but not traded on an exchange, it will not be considered to be exchange-traded and will be required to be reported.

Subsection 2(2) of the Rule excludes derivatives trading facilities from the meaning of exchange as it is used in paragraph 2(1)(g). A derivatives trading facility means a person or company that constitutes, maintains, or provides a facility or market that brings together buyers and sellers of over-the-counter derivatives, brings together the orders of multiple buyers and multiple sellers, and uses methods under which the orders interact with each other and the buyers and sellers agree to the terms of trades.

For example, the following would not be considered an exchange for purposes of paragraph 2(1)(g): a "swap execution facility" as defined in the *Commodity Exchange Act* 7 U.S.C. §(1a)(50); a "security-based swap execution facility" as defined in the *Securities Exchange Act of 1934* 15 U.S.C. §78c(a)(77); and a "multilateral trading facility" as defined in Directive 2014/65/EU Article 4(1)(22) of the European Parliament; and an "organized trading facility" as defined in Directive 2014/65/EU Article 4(1)(23) of the European Parliament. Therefore derivatives traded on the foregoing facilities that would otherwise be considered derivatives for the purposes of this Rule are required to be reported.

(h) — Additional contracts not considered to be derivatives

Apart from the contracts expressly prescribed not to be derivatives in section 2 of the Rule, there are other contracts that we do not consider to be "derivatives" for the purposes of securities or derivatives legislation. A feature common to these contracts is that they are entered into for consumer, business or non-profit purposes that do not involve investment, speculation or hedging. Typically, they provide for the transfer of ownership of a good or the provision of a service. In most cases, they are not traded on a market.

These contracts include, but are not limited to:

- a consumer or commercial contract to acquire, or lease real or personal property, to provide personal services, to sell or assign rights, equipment, receivables or inventory, or to obtain a loan or mortgage, including a loan or mortgage with a variable rate of interest, interest rate cap, interest rate lock or embedded interest rate option;

- a consumer contract to purchase non-financial products or services at a fixed, capped or collared price;

- an employment contract or retirement benefit arrangement;

- a guarantee;

- a performance bond;

- a commercial sale, servicing, or distribution arrangement;

- a contract for the purpose of effecting a business purchase and sale or combination transaction;

- a contract representing a lending arrangement in connection with building an inventory of assets in anticipation of a securitization of such assets; and

- a commercial contract containing mechanisms indexing the purchase price or payment terms for inflation such as via reference to an interest rate or consumer price index.

Investment contracts and over-the-counter options

3. Section 3 of the Rule prescribes a contract (to which section 2 of the Rule does not apply) that is a derivative and a security solely by reason of being an investment contract under paragraph (n) of the definition of "security" in subsection 1(1) of the Act, not to be a security. Some types of contracts traded over-the-counter, such as foreign exchange contracts and contracts for difference meet the definition of "derivative" (because their market price, value, delivery obligations, payment obligations or settlement obligations are derived from, referenced to or based on an underlying interest) but also meet the definition of "security" (because they are investment contracts). This section prescribes that such instruments will be treated as derivatives and therefore be required to be reported to a designated trade repository.

Similarly, options fall within both the definition of "derivative" and the definition of "security". Section 3 of the Rule prescribes an option that is only a security by virtue of paragraph (d) of the definition of "security" in subsection 1(1) of the Act (and not described in section 5 of the Rule), not to be a security. This section prescribes that such instruments will be treated as derivatives and therefore will be required to be reported to a designated trade repository. This treatment will only apply to options that are traded over-the-counter. Under paragraph 2(g), exchange-traded options will not be required to be reported to a designated trade repository. Further, options that are entered into on a commodity futures exchange pursuant to standardized terms and conditions are commodity futures options and therefore regulated under the *Commodity Futures Act* (Ontario) and excluded from the definition of "derivative".

Derivatives that are securities

4. Section 4 of the Rule prescribes a contract (to which sections 2 and 3 of the Rule do not apply) that is a security and a derivative, not to be a derivative. Derivatives that are securities and which are contemplated as falling within this section include structured notes, asset-backed securities, exchange-traded notes, capital trust units, exchangeable securities, income trust units, securities of investment funds and warrants. This section ensures that such instruments will continue to be subject to applicable prospectus disclosure and continuous disclosure requirements in securities legislation as well as applicable registration requirements for dealers and advisers. The Commission anticipates that it will again review the categorization of instruments as securities and derivatives once the comprehensive derivatives regime has been implemented.

Derivatives prescribed to be securities

5. Section 5 of the Rule prescribes a security-based derivative that is used by an issuer or its affiliate to compensate an officer, director, employee or service provider, or as a financing instrument, not to be a derivative. Examples of the compensation instruments that are contemplated as falling within section 5 include stock options, phantom stock units, restricted share units, deferred share units, restricted share awards, performance share units, stock appreciation rights and compensation instruments provided to service providers, such as broker options. Securities treatment would also apply to the aforementioned instruments when used as a financing instrument, for example, rights, warrants and special warrants, or subscription rights/receipts or convertible instruments issued to raise capital for any purpose. The Commission takes the view that an instrument would only be considered a financing instrument if it is used for capital-raising purposes. An equity swap, for example, would generally not be considered a financing instrument. The classes of derivatives referred to in section 5 can have similar or the same economic effect as a securities issuance and are therefore subject to requirements generally applicable to securities. As they are prescribed not to be derivatives they are not subject to the derivatives reporting requirements.

Adoption of Policy by OSC: (2013) 36 O.S.C.B. 110115; Request for Comments: (2013) 36 O.S.C.B. 5737

Amendment to Rule: (2015) 38 O.S.C.B. 1375

OSC Rule 91-507 — Trade Repositories and Derivatives Data Reporting

Date: December 31, 2013 as amended effective July 2, 2014, September 9, 2014 and April 30, 2015

36 O.S.C.B. 11015, 37 O.S.C.B. 6313, 37 O.S.C.B. 7559 and 38 O.S.C.B. 1352

PART 1 — DEFINITIONS AND INTERPRETATION

1. Definitions — (1) In this Rule

"asset class" means the asset category underlying a derivative and includes interest rate, foreign exchange, credit, equity and commodity;

"board of directors" means, in the case of a designated trade repository that does not have a board of directors, a group of individuals that acts in a capacity similar to a board of directors;

"creation data" means the data in the fields listed in Appendix A;

"derivatives dealer" means a person or company engaging in or holding himself, herself or itself out as engaging in the business of trading in derivatives in Ontario as principal or agent;

"derivatives data" means all data related to a transaction that is required to be reported pursuant to Part 3;

"Global Legal Entity Identifier System" means the system for unique identification of parties to financial transactions developed by the Legal Entity Identifier System Regulatory Oversight Committee;

"Legal Entity Identifier System Regulatory Oversight Committee" means the international working group established by the Finance Ministers and the Central Bank Governors of the Group of Twenty nations and the Financial Stability Board, under the Charter of the Regulatory Oversight Committee for the Global Legal Entity Identifier System dated November 5, 2012;

"life-cycle event" means an event that results in a change to derivatives data previously reported to a designated trade repository in respect of a transaction;

"life-cycle event data" means changes to creation data resulting from a life-cycle event;

"local counterparty" means a counterparty to a transaction if, at the time of the transaction, one or more of the following apply:

> (a) the counterparty is a person or company, other than an individual, organized under the laws of Ontario or that has its head office or principal place of business in Ontario;

> (b) the counterparty is registered under Ontario securities law as a derivatives dealer or in an alternative category as a consequence of trading in derivatives;

> (c) the counterparty is an affiliate of a person or company described in paragraph (a), and such person or company is responsible for the liabilities of that affiliated party;

"participant" means a person or company that has entered into an agreement with a designated trade repository to access the services of the designated trade repository;

"reporting counterparty" means the counterparty to a transaction as determined under section 25 that is required to report derivatives data under section 26;

"transaction" means entering into, assigning, selling or otherwise acquiring or disposing of a derivative or the novation of a derivative;

"user" means, in respect of a designated trade repository, a counterparty (or delegate of a counterparty) to a transaction reported to that designated trade repository pursuant to this Rule; and

"valuation data" means data that reflects the current value of the transaction and includes the data in the applicable fields listed in Appendix A under the heading "Valuation Data".

(2) In this Rule, each of the following terms has the same meaning as in National Instrument 52-107 *Acceptable Accounting Principles and Auditing Standards*: "accounting principles"; "auditing standards"; "publicly accountable enterprise"; "U.S. AICPA GAAS"; "U.S. GAAP"; and "U.S. PCAOB GAAS".

(3) In this Rule, "interim period" has the same meaning as in section 1.1 of National Instrument 51-102 *Continuous Disclosure Obligations*.

PART 2 — TRADE REPOSITORY DESIGNATION AND ONGOING REQUIREMENTS

2. Trade repository initial filing of information and designation — (1) An applicant for designation under section 21.2.2 of the Act must file a completed Form 91-507F1 — *Application For Designation and Trade Repository Information Statement*.

(2) In addition to the requirement set out in subsection (1), an applicant for designation under section 21.2.2 of the Act whose head office or principal place of business is located outside of Ontario must

> (a) certify on Form 91-507F1 that it will provide the Commission with access to its books and records and will submit to onsite inspection and examination by the Commission,

> (b) certify on Form 91-507F1 that it will provide the Commission with an opinion of legal counsel that

>> (i) the applicant has the power and authority to provide the Commission with access to its books and records, and

>> (ii) the applicant has the power and authority to submit to onsite inspection and examination by the Commission.

(3) In addition to the requirements set out in subsections (1) and (2), an applicant for designation under section 21.2.2 of the Act whose head office or principal place of business is located in a foreign jurisdiction must file a completed Form 91-507F2 — *Submission to Jurisdiction and Appointment of Agent for Service of Process*.

(4) Within 7 days of becoming aware of an inaccuracy in or making a change to the information provided in Form 91-507F1, an applicant must file an amendment to Form 91-507F1 in the manner set out in that Form.

3. Change in information — (1) Subject to subsection (2), a designated trade repository must not implement a significant change to a matter set out in Form 91-507F1 unless it has filed an amendment to Form 91-507F1 in the manner set out in that Form at least 45 days before implementing the change.

(2) A designated trade repository must file an amendment to the information provided in Exhibit I (Fees) of Form 91-507F1 in the manner set out in the Form at least 15 days before implementing a change to the information provided in the Exhibit.

(3) For a change to a matter set out in Form 91-507F1 other than a change referred to in subsection (1) or (2), a designated trade repository must file an amendment to Form 91-507F1 in the manner set out in that Form by the earlier of

> (a) the close of business of the designated trade repository on the 10th day after the end of the month in which the change was made, and

> (b) the time the designated trade repository publicly discloses the change.

4. Filing of initial audited financial statements — (1) An applicant must file audited financial statements for its most recently completed financial year with the Commission as part of its application for designation under section 21.2.2 of the Act.

(2) The financial statements referred to in subsection (1) must

> (a) be prepared in accordance with one of the following

>> (i) Canadian GAAP applicable to a publicly accountable enterprise,

>> (ii) IFRS, or

>> (iii) U.S. GAAP, if the person or company is incorporated or organized under the laws of the United States of America,

Part 9:
DERIVATIVES

(b) identify in the notes to the financial statements the accounting principles used to prepare the financial statements,

(c) disclose the presentation currency, and

(d) be audited in accordance with

    (i) Canadian GAAS,

    (ii) International Standards on Auditing, or

    (iii) U.S. AICPA GAAS or U.S. PCAOB GAAS if the person or company is incorporated or organized under the laws of the United States of America.

(3) The financial statements referred to in subsection (1) must be accompanied by an auditor's report that

(a) expresses an unmodified opinion if the financial statements are audited in accordance with Canadian GAAS or International Standards on Auditing,

(b) expresses an unqualified opinion if the financial statements are audited in accordance with U.S. AICPA GAAS or U.S. PCAOB GAAS,

(c) identifies all financial periods presented for which the auditor's report applies,

(d) identifies the auditing standards used to conduct the audit,

(e) identifies the accounting principles used to prepare the financial statements,

(f) is prepared in accordance with the same auditing standards used to conduct the audit, and

(g) is prepared and signed by a person or company that is authorized to sign an auditor's report under the laws of a jurisdiction of Canada or a foreign jurisdiction, and that meets the professional standards of that jurisdiction.

5. Filing of annual audited and interim financial statements — (1) A designated trade repository must file annual audited financial statements that comply with the requirements in subsections 4(2) and 4(3) with the Commission no later than the 90th day after the end of its financial year.

(2) A designated trade repository must file interim financial statements with the Commission no later than the 45th day after the end of each interim period.

(3) The interim financial statements referred to in subsection (2) must

(a) be prepared in accordance with one of the following

    (i) Canadian GAAP applicable to a publicly accountable enterprise,

    (ii) IFRS, or

    (iii) U.S. GAAP, if the person or company is incorporated or organized under the laws of the United States of America, and

(b) identify in the notes to the financial statements the accounting principles used to prepare the financial statements.

6. Ceasing to carry on business — (1) A designated trade repository that intends to cease carrying on business in Ontario as a trade repository must make an application and file a report on Form 91-507F3 — *Cessation of Operations Report For Trade Repository* at least 180 days before the date on which it intends to cease carrying on that business.

(2) A designated trade repository that involuntarily ceases to carry on business in Ontario as a trade repository must file a report on Form 91-507F3 as soon as practicable after it ceases to carry on that business.

7. Legal framework — (1) A designated trade repository must establish, implement, maintain and enforce written rules, policies and procedures reasonably designed to ensure a well-founded, clear, transparent, and enforceable legal basis for each material aspect of its activities.

(2) Without limiting the generality of subsection (1), a designated trade repository must establish, implement, maintain and enforce written rules, policies and procedures that are not contrary to the public interest and that are reasonably designed to ensure that

(a) such rules, policies and procedures and the contractual arrangements are supported by the laws applicable to those rules, policies, procedures and contractual arrangements,

(b) the rights and obligations of a user, owner and regulator with respect to the use of the designated trade repository's information are clear and transparent,

(c) the contractual arrangements that it enters into and supporting documentation clearly state service levels, rights of access, protection of confidential information, intellectual property rights and operational reliability, and

(d) the status of records of contracts in its repository and whether those records of contracts are the legal contracts of record are clearly established.

8. Governance — (1) A designated trade repository must establish, implement and maintain written governance arrangements that

(a) are well-defined, clear and transparent,

(b) set out a clear organizational structure with consistent lines of responsibility,

(c) provide for effective internal controls,

(d) promote the safety and efficiency of the designated trade repository,

(e) ensure effective oversight of the designated trade repository,

(f) support the stability of the broader financial system and other relevant public interest considerations, and

(g) properly balance the interests of relevant stakeholders.

(2) A designated trade repository must establish, implement, maintain and enforce written rules, policies and procedures reasonably designed to identify and manage existing and potential conflicts of interest.

(3) A designated trade repository must publicly disclose on its website

(a) the governance arrangements established in accordance with subsection (1), and

(b) the rules, policies and procedures established in accordance with subsection (2).

9. Board of directors — (1) A designated trade repository must have a board of directors.

(2) The board of directors of a designated trade repository must include

(a) individuals who have an appropriate level of skill and experience to effectively and efficiently oversee the management of its operations in accordance with all relevant laws, and

(b) appropriate representation by individuals who are independent of the designated trade repository.

(3) The board of directors of a designated trade repository must, in consultation with the chief compliance officer of the designated trade repository, resolve conflicts of interest identified by the chief compliance officer.

(4) The board of directors of a designated trade repository must meet with the chief compliance officer of the designated trade repository on a regular basis.

10. Management — (1) A designated trade repository must establish, implement, maintain and enforce written rules, policies and procedures that

(a) specify the roles and responsibilities of management, and

(b) ensure that management has the experience, competencies, integrity and mix of skills necessary to discharge its roles and responsibilities.

(2) A designated trade repository must notify the Commission no later than the 5th business day after appointing or replacing its chief compliance officer, chief executive officer or chief risk officer.

11. Chief compliance officer — (1) The board of directors of a designated trade repository must appoint a chief compliance officer with the appropriate experience, competencies, integrity and mix of skills necessary to serve in that capacity.

(2) The chief compliance officer of a designated trade repository must report directly to the board of directors of the designated trade repository or, if so directed by the board of directors, to the chief executive officer of the designated trade repository.

(3) The chief compliance officer of a designated trade repository must

(a) establish, implement, maintain and enforce written rules, policies and procedures to identify and resolve conflicts of interest,

(b) establish, implement, maintain and enforce written rules, policies and procedures to ensure that the designated trade repository complies with securities legislation,

(c) monitor compliance with the rules, policies and procedures required under paragraphs (a) and (b) on an ongoing basis,

(d) report to the board of directors of the designated trade repository as soon as practicable upon becoming aware of a circumstance indicating that the designated trade repository, or an individual acting on its behalf, is not in compliance with the securities laws of a jurisdiction in which it operates and one or more of the following apply:

(i) the non-compliance creates a risk of harm to a user;

(ii) the non-compliance creates a risk of harm to the capital markets;

(iii) the non-compliance is part of a pattern of non-compliance;

(iv) the non-compliance may have an impact on the ability of the designated trade repository to carry on business as a trade repository in compliance with securities legislation,

(e) report to the designated trade repository's board of directors as soon as practicable upon becoming aware of a conflict of interest that creates a risk of harm to a user or to the capital markets, and

(f) prepare and certify an annual report assessing compliance by the designated trade repository, and individuals acting on its behalf, with securities legislation and submit the report to the board of directors.

(4) Concurrently with submitting a report under paragraph (3)(d), (3)(e) or (3)(f), the chief compliance officer must file a copy of the report with the Commission.

12. Fees — All fees and other material costs imposed by a designated trade repository on its participants must be

(a) fairly and equitably allocated among participants, and

(b) publicly disclosed on its website for each service it offers with respect to the collection and maintenance of derivatives data.

13. Access to designated trade repository services — (1) A designated trade repository must establish, implement, maintain and enforce written rules, policies and procedures that establish objective, risk-based criteria for participation that permit fair and open access to the services it provides.

(2) A designated trade repository must publicly disclose on its website the rules, policies and procedures referred to in subsection (1).

(3) A designated trade repository must not do any of the following:

(a) unreasonably prohibit, condition or limit access by a person or company to the services offered by the designated trade repository;

(b) permit unreasonable discrimination among the participants of the designated trade repository;

(c) impose a burden on competition that is not reasonably necessary and appropriate;

(d) require the use or purchase of another service for a person or company to utilize the trade reporting service offered by the designated trade repository.

14. Acceptance of reporting — A designated trade repository must accept derivatives data from a participant for a transaction in a derivative of the asset class or classes set out in the designated trade repository's designation order.

15. Communication policies, procedures and standards — A designated trade repository must use or accommodate relevant internationally accepted communication procedures and standards in order to facilitate the efficient exchange of data between its systems and those of

(a) its participants,

(b) other trade repositories,

(c) exchanges, clearing agencies, alternative trading systems, and other marketplaces, and

(d) other service providers.

16. Due process — For a decision made by a designated trade repository that directly adversely affects a participant or an applicant that applies to become a participant, the designated trade repository must ensure that

(a) the participant or applicant is given an opportunity to be heard or make representations, and

(b) it keeps records of, gives reasons for, and provides for reviews of its decisions, including, for each applicant, the reasons for granting, denying or limiting access.

17. Rules, policies and procedures — (1) The rules, policies and procedures of a designated trade repository must

(a) be clear and comprehensive and provide sufficient information to enable a participant to have an accurate understanding of its rights and obligations in accessing the services of the designated trade repository and the risks, fees, and other material costs they incur by using the services of the designated trade repository,

(b) be reasonably designed to govern all aspects of the services offered by the designated trade repository with respect to the collection and maintenance of derivatives data and other information on a completed transaction, and

(c) not be inconsistent with securities legislation.

(2) A designated trade repository must monitor compliance with its rules, policies and procedures on an ongoing basis.

(3) A designated trade repository must establish, implement, maintain and enforce written rules, policies and procedures for sanctioning non-compliance with its rules, policies and procedures.

(4) A designated trade repository must publicly disclose on its website

(a) its rules, policies and procedures referred to in this section, and

(b) its procedures for adopting new rules, policies and procedures or amending existing rules, policies and procedures.

(5) A designated trade repository must file its proposed new or amended rules, policies and procedures for approval in accordance with the terms and conditions of its designation order, unless the order explicitly exempts the designated trade repository from this requirement.

18. Records of data reported — (1) A designated trade repository must design its recordkeeping procedures to ensure that it records derivatives data accurately, completely and on a timely basis.

(2) A designated trade repository must keep, in a safe location and in a durable form, records of derivatives data in relation to a transaction for the life of the transaction and for a further 7 years after the date on which the transaction expires or terminates.

(3) Throughout the period described in subsection (2), a designated trade repository must create and maintain at least one copy of each record of derivatives data required to be kept under subsection (2), in a safe location and in a durable form, separate from the location of the original record.

19. Comprehensive risk-management framework — A designated trade repository must establish, implement and maintain a written risk-management framework for comprehensively managing risks including business, legal, and operational risks.

20. General business risk — (1) A designated trade repository must establish, implement and maintain appropriate systems, controls and procedures to identify, monitor, and manage its general business risk.

(2) Without limiting the generality of subsection (1), a designated trade repository must hold sufficient insurance coverage and liquid net assets funded by equity to cover potential general business losses in order that it can continue operations and services as a going concern in order to achieve a recovery or an orderly wind down if those losses materialize.

(3) For the purposes of subsection (2), a designated trade repository must hold, at a minimum, liquid net assets funded by equity equal to six months of current operating expenses.

(4) A designated trade repository must identify scenarios that may potentially prevent it from being able to provide its critical operations and services as a going concern and assess the effectiveness of a full range of options for an orderly wind-down.

(5) A designated trade repository must establish, implement, maintain and enforce written rules, policies and procedures reasonably designed to facilitate its orderly wind-down based on the results of the assessment required by subsection (4).

(6) A designated trade repository must establish, implement, maintain and enforce written rules, policies and procedures to ensure that it or a successor entity, insolvency administrator or other legal representative, will continue to comply with the requirements of subsection 6(2) and section 37 in the event of the bankruptcy or insolvency of the designated trade repository or the wind-down of the designated trade repository's operations.

21. System and other operational risk requirements — (1) A designated trade repository must establish, implement, maintain and enforce appropriate systems, controls and procedures to identify and minimize the impact of all plausible sources of operational risk, both internal and external, including risks to data integrity, data security, business continuity and capacity and performance management.

(2) The systems, controls and procedures established pursuant to subsection (1) must be approved by the board of directors of the designated trade repository.

(3) Without limiting the generality of subsection (1), a designated trade repository must

(a) develop and maintain

(i) an adequate system of internal controls over its systems, and

(ii) adequate information technology general controls, including without limitation, controls relating to information systems operations, information security and integrity, change management, problem management, network support and system software support,

(b) in accordance with prudent business practice, on a reasonably frequent basis and, in any event, at least annually

(i) make reasonable current and future capacity estimates, and

(ii) conduct capacity stress tests to determine the ability of those systems to process transactions in an accurate, timely and efficient manner, and

(c) promptly notify the Commission of a material systems failure, malfunction, delay or other disruptive incident, or a breach of data security, integrity or confidentiality, and provide a post-incident report that includes a root-cause analysis as soon as practicable.

(4) Without limiting the generality of subsection (1), a designated trade repository must establish, implement, maintain and enforce business continuity plans, including disaster recovery plans reasonably designed to

(a) achieve prompt recovery of its operations following a disruption,

(b) allow for the timely recovery of information, including derivatives data, in the event of a disruption, and

(c) provide for the exercise of authority in the event of an emergency.

(5) A designated trade repository must test its business continuity plans, including disaster recovery plans, at least annually.

(6) For each of its systems for collecting and maintaining reports of derivatives data, a designated trade repository must annually engage a qualified party to conduct an independent review and prepare a report in accordance with established audit standards to ensure that it is in compliance with paragraphs (3)(a) and (b) and subsections (4) and (5).

(7) A designated trade repository must provide the report prepared in accordance with subsection (6) to

(a) its board of directors or audit committee promptly upon the completion of the report, and

(b) the Commission not later than the 30th day after providing the report to its board of directors or audit committee.

(8) A designated trade repository must publicly disclose on its website all technology requirements regarding interfacing with or accessing the services provided by the designated trade repository,

(a) if operations have not begun, sufficiently in advance of operations to allow a reasonable period for testing and system modification by participants, and

(b) if operations have begun, sufficiently in advance of implementing a material change to technology requirements to allow a reasonable period for testing and system modification by participants.

(9) A designated trade repository must make available testing facilities for interfacing with or accessing the services provided by the designated trade repository,

(a) if operations have not begun, sufficiently in advance of operations to allow a reasonable period for testing and system modification by participants, and

(b) if operations have begun, sufficiently in advance of implementing a material change to technology requirements to allow a reasonable period for testing and system modification by participants.

(10) A designated trade repository must not begin operations in Ontario unless it has complied with paragraphs (8)(a) and (9)(a).

(11) Paragraphs (8)(b) and (9)(b) do not apply to a designated trade repository if

(a) the change to its technology requirements must be made immediately to address a failure, malfunction or material delay of its systems or equipment,

(b) the designated trade repository immediately notifies the Commission of its intention to make the change to its technology requirements, and

(c) the designated trade repository publicly discloses on its website the changed technology requirements as soon as practicable.

22. Data security and confidentiality — (1) A designated trade repository must establish, implement, maintain and enforce written rules, policies and procedures reasonably designed to ensure the safety, privacy and confidentiality of the derivatives data.

(2) A designated trade repository must not release derivatives data for commercial or business purposes unless

(a) the derivatives data has otherwise been disclosed pursuant to section 39, or

(b) the counterparties to the transaction have provided the designated trade repository with their express written consent to use or release the derivatives data.

23. Confirmation of data and information — (1) A designated trade repository must establish, implement, maintain and enforce written rules, policies and procedures to confirm with each counterparty to a transaction, or agent acting on behalf of such counterparty, that the derivatives data that the designated trade repository receives from a reporting counterparty, or from a party to whom a reporting counterparty has delegated its reporting obligation under this Rule, is accurate.

(2) Despite subsection (1), a designated trade repository need only confirm the accuracy of the derivatives data it receives with those counterparties that are participants of the designated trade repository.

24. Outsourcing — If a designated trade repository outsources a material service or system to a service provider, including to an associate or affiliate of the designated trade repository, the designated trade repository must

(a) establish, implement, maintain and enforce written rules, policies and procedures for the selection of a service provider to which a material service or system may be outsourced and for the evaluation and approval of such an outsourcing arrangement,

(b) identify any conflicts of interest between the designated trade repository and a service provider to which a material service or system is outsourced, and establish, implement, maintain and enforce written rules, policies and procedures to mitigate and manage those conflicts of interest,

(c) enter into a written contract with the service provider that is appropriate for the materiality and nature of the outsourced activity and that provides for adequate termination procedures,

(d) maintain access to the books and records of the service provider relating to the outsourced activity,

(e) ensure that the Commission has the same access to all data, information and systems maintained by the service provider on behalf of the designated trade repository that it would have absent the outsourcing arrangement,

(f) ensure that all persons conducting audits or independent reviews of the designated trade repository under this Rule have appropriate access to all data, information and systems maintained by the service provider on behalf of the designated trade repository that such persons would have absent the outsourcing arrangement,

(g) take appropriate measures to determine that a service provider to which a material service or system is outsourced establishes, maintains and periodically tests an appropriate business continuity plan, including a disaster recovery plan in accordance with the requirements under section 21,

(h) take appropriate measures to ensure that the service provider protects the safety, privacy and confidentiality of derivatives data and of users' confidential information in accordance with the requirements under section 22, and

(i) establish, implement, maintain and enforce written rules, policies and procedures to regularly review the performance of the service provider under the outsourcing arrangement.

PART 3 — DATA REPORTING

25. Reporting counterparty — (1) The reporting counterparty with respect to a transaction involving a local counterparty is

(a) if the transaction is cleared through a recognized or exempt clearing agency, the recognized or exempt clearing agency,

(b) if the transaction is not cleared through a recognized or exempt clearing agency and is between two derivatives dealers, the derivatives dealer determined to be the reporting counterparty under the ISDA methodology,

(c) if paragraphs (a) and (b) do not apply to the transaction and the transaction is between two derivatives dealers, each derivatives dealer,

(d) if the transaction is not cleared through a recognized or exempt clearing agency and is between a derivatives dealer and a counterparty that is not a derivatives dealer, the derivatives dealer,

(e) if paragraphs (a) to (d) do not apply to the transaction, the counterparty determined to be the reporting counterparty under the ISDA methodology, and

(f) in any other case, each local counterparty to the transaction.

(2) A party that would not be the reporting counterparty under the ISDA methodology with regard to a transaction required to be reported under this Rule may rely on paragraph (1)(b) or (e) in respect of that transaction only if

(a) each party to the transaction has agreed to the terms of a multilateral agreement

(i) that is administered by and delivered to the International Swaps and Derivatives Association, Inc., and

(ii) under which the process set out in the ISDA methodology is required to be followed by it with respect to each transaction required to be reported under this Rule,

(b) the ISDA methodology process is followed in determining the reporting counterparty in respect of that transaction, and

(c) each party to the transaction consents to the release to the Commission by the International Swaps and Derivatives Association, Inc. of information relevant in determining the applicability of paragraphs (a) and (b) to it.

(3) For the purposes of this section, "ISDA methodology" means the methodology described in the Canadian Transaction Reporting Party Requirements (issued by the International Swaps and Derivatives Association, Inc. and dated April 4, 2014).

26. Duty to report — (1) A reporting counterparty to a transaction involving a local counterparty must report, or cause to be reported, the data required to be reported under this Part to a designated trade repository.

(2) A reporting counterparty in respect of a transaction is responsible for ensuring that all reporting obligations in respect of that transaction have been fulfilled.

(3) A reporting counterparty may delegate its reporting obligations under this Rule, but remains responsible for ensuring the timely and accurate reporting of derivatives data required by this Rule.

(4) Despite subsection (1), if no designated trade repository accepts the data required to be reported by this Part, the reporting counterparty must electronically report the data required to be reported by this Part to the Commission.

(5) A reporting counterparty satisfies the reporting obligation in respect of a transaction required to be reported under subsection (1) if

(a) the transaction is required to be reported solely because a counterparty to the transaction is a local counterparty pursuant to paragraph (b) or (c) of the definition of "local counterparty",

(b) the transaction is reported to a designated trade repository pursuant to

(i) the securities legislation of a province of Canada other than Ontario, or

(ii) the laws of a foreign jurisdiction listed in Appendix B; and

(c) the reporting counterparty instructs the designated trade repository referred to in paragraph (b) to provide the Commission with access to the derivatives data that it is required to report pursuant to this Rule and otherwise uses its best efforts to provide the Commission with access to such derivatives data.

(6) A reporting counterparty must ensure that all reported derivatives data relating to a transaction

(a) is reported to the same designated trade repository to which the initial report was made or, if the initial report was made to the Commission under subsection (4), to the Commission, and

(b) is accurate and contains no misrepresentation.

(7) A reporting counterparty must report an error or omission in the derivatives data as soon as technologically practicable upon discovery of the error or omission, and in no event later than the end of the business day following the day of discovery of the error or omission.

(8) A local counterparty, other than the reporting counterparty, must notify the reporting counterparty of an error or omission with respect to derivatives data relating to a transaction to which it is a counterparty as soon as technologically practicable upon discovery of the error or omission, and in no event later than the end of the business day following the day of discovery of the error or omission.

(9) A recognized or exempt clearing agency must report derivatives data to the designated trade repository specified by a local counterparty and may not report derivatives data to another trade repository without the consent of the local counterparty where

(a) the reporting counterparty to a transaction is the recognized or exempt clearing agency, and

(b) the local counterparty to the transaction that is not a recognized or exempt clearing agency has specified a designated trade repository to which derivatives data in respect of that transaction is to be reported.

27. Identifiers, general — A reporting counterparty must include the following in every report required by this Part:

(a) the legal entity identifier of each counterparty to the transaction as set out in section 28;

(b) the unique transaction identifier for the transaction as set out in section 29;

(c) the unique product identifier for the transaction as set out in section 30.

28. **Legal entity identifiers** — (1) A designated trade repository must identify each counterparty to a transaction that is required to be reported under this Rule in all recordkeeping and all reporting required under this Rule by means of a single legal entity identifier.

(2) Each of the following rules apply to legal entity identifiers

(a) a legal entity identifier must be a unique identification code assigned to a counterparty in accordance with the standards set by the Global Legal Entity Identifier System, and

(b) a local counterparty must comply with all applicable requirements imposed by the Global Legal Entity Identifier System.

(3) Despite subsection (2), if the Global Legal Entity Identifier System is unavailable to a counterparty to a transaction at the time when a report under this Rule is required to be made, all of the following rules apply

(a) each counterparty to the transaction must obtain a substitute legal entity identifier which complies with the standards established March 8, 2013 by the Legal Entity Identifier Regulatory Oversight Committee for pre-legal entity identifiers,

(b) a local counterparty must use the substitute legal entity identifier until a legal entity identifier is assigned to the counterparty in accordance with the standards set by the Global Legal Entity Identifier System as required under paragraph (2)(a), and

(c) after the holder of a substitute legal entity identifier is assigned a legal entity identifier in accordance with the standards set by the Global Legal Entity Identifier System as required under paragraph (2)(a), the local counterparty must ensure that it is identified only by the assigned legal entity identifier in all derivatives data reported pursuant to this Rule in respect of transactions to which it is a counterparty.

29.1 Each local counterparty to a transaction that is required to be reported under this Rule must obtain a legal entity identifier, if eligible to receive one, assigned to the counterparty in accordance with the standards set by the Global Legal Entity Identifier System.

29. **Unique transaction identifiers** — (1) A designated trade repository must identify each transaction that is required to be reported under this Rule in all recordkeeping and all reporting required under this Rule by means of a unique transaction identifier.

(2) A designated trade repository must assign a unique transaction identifier to a transaction, using its own methodology or incorporating a unique transaction identifier previously assigned to the transaction.

(3) A designated trade repository must not assign more than one unique transaction identifier to a transaction.

30. **Unique product identifiers** — (1) For the purposes of this section, a unique product identifier means a code that uniquely identifies a derivative and is assigned in accordance with international or industry standards.

(2) A reporting counterparty must identify each transaction that is required to be reported under this Rule in all recordkeeping and all reporting required under this Rule by means of a unique product identifier.

(3) A reporting counterparty must not assign more than one unique product identifier to a transaction.

(4) If international or industry standards for a unique product identifier are unavailable for a particular derivative when a report is required to be made to a designated trade repository under this Rule, a reporting counterparty must assign a unique product identifier to the transaction using its own methodology.

31. **Creation data** — (1) Upon execution of a transaction that is required to be reported under this Rule, a reporting counterparty must report the creation data relating to that transaction to a designated trade repository.

(2) A reporting counterparty in respect of a transaction must report creation data in real time.

(3) If it is not technologically practicable to report creation data in real time, a reporting counterparty must report creation data as soon as technologically practicable and in no event later than the end of the business day following the day on which the data would otherwise be required to be reported.

32. **Life-cycle event data** — (1) For a transaction that is required to be reported under this Rule, the reporting counterparty must report all life-cycle event data to a designated trade repository by the end of the business day on which the life-cycle event occurs.

(2) If it is not technologically practicable to report life-cycle event data by the end of the business day on which the life-cycle event occurs, the reporting counterparty must report life-cycle event data no later than the end of the business day following the day on which the life-cycle event occurs.

33. **Valuation data** — (1) For a transaction that is required to be reported under this Rule, a reporting counterparty must report valuation data, based on industry accepted valuation standards, to a designated trade repository

(a) daily, based on relevant closing market data from the previous business day, if the reporting counterparty is a derivatives dealer or a recognized or exempt clearing agency, or

(b) quarterly, as of the last day of each calendar quarter, if the reporting counterparty is not a derivatives dealer or a recognized or exempt clearing agency.

(2) Valuation data required to be reported pursuant to paragraph 1(b) must be reported to the designated trade repository no later than 30 days after the end of the calendar quarter.

34. **Pre-existing transactions** — (1) Despite section 31 and subject to subsection 43(5), a reporting counterparty (as determined under subsection 25(1)) to a transaction required to be reported under subsection 26(1) is required to report only the creation data indicated in the column in Appendix A entitled "Required for Pre-existing Transactions" on or before April 30, 2015 if

(a) the reporting counterparty is a derivatives dealer or a recognized or exempt clearing agency,

(b) the transaction was entered into before October 31, 2014, and

(c) there were outstanding contractual obligations with respect to the transaction on October 31, 2014.

(1.1) Despite section 31 and subject to subsection 43(6), a reporting counterparty (as determined under subsection 25(1)) to a transaction required to be reported under subsection 26(1) is required to report only the creation data indicated in the column in Appendix A entitled "Required for Pre-existing Transactions" on or before December 31, 2015 if

(a) the reporting counterparty is neither a derivatives dealer nor a recognized or exempt clearing agency,

(b) the transaction was entered into before June 30, 2015, and

(c) there were outstanding contractual obligations with respect to the transaction on June 30, 2015.

(2) Despite section 32, for a transaction to which subsection (1) or (1.1) applies, a reporting counterparty's obligation to report life-cycle event data under section 32 commences only after it has reported creation data in accordance with subsection (1) or (1.1).

(3) Despite section 33, for a transaction to which subsection (1) or (1.1) applies, a reporting counterparty's obligation to report valuation data under section 33 commences only after it has reported creation data in accordance with subsection (1) or (1.1).

35. **Timing requirements for reporting data to another designated trade repository** — Despite the data reporting timing requirements in sections 31, 32, 33 and 34, where a designated trade repository ceases operations or stops accepting derivatives data for a certain asset class of derivatives, the reporting counterparty may fulfill its reporting obligations under this Rule by reporting the derivatives data to another designated trade repository, or the Commission if there is not an available designated trade repository, within a reasonable period of time.

36. **Records of data reported** — (1) A reporting counterparty must keep transaction records for the life of each transaction and for a further 7 years after the date on which the transaction expires or terminates.

(2) A reporting counterparty must keep records referred to in subsection (1) in a safe location and in a durable form.

PART 4 — DATA DISSEMINATION AND ACCESS TO DATA

37. **Data available to regulators** — (1) A designated trade repository must, at no cost

(a) provide to the Commission direct, continuous and timely electronic access to such data in the designated trade repository's possession as is required by the Commission in order to carry out the Commission's mandate,

(b) accept and promptly fulfil any data requests from the Commission in order to carry out the Commission's mandate,

(c) create and make available to the Commission aggregate data derived from data in the designated trade repository's possession as required by the Commission in order to carry out the Commission's mandate, and

(d) disclose to the Commission the manner in which the derivatives data provided under paragraph (c) has been aggregated.

(2) A designated trade repository must conform to internationally accepted regulatory access standards applicable to trade repositories.

(3) A reporting counterparty must use its best efforts to provide the Commission with access to all derivatives data that it is required to report pursuant to this Rule, including instructing a trade repository to provide the Commission with access to such data.

38. **Data available to counterparties** — (1) A designated trade repository must provide counterparties to a transaction with timely access to all derivatives data relevant to that transaction which is submitted to the designated trade repository.

(2) A designated trade repository must have appropriate verification and authorization procedures in place to deal with access pursuant to subsection (1) by non-reporting counterparties or a party acting on behalf of a non-reporting counterparty.

(3) Each counterparty to a transaction is deemed to have consented to the release of all derivatives data required to be reported or disclosed under this Rule.

(4) Subsection (3) applies despite any agreement to the contrary between the counterparties to a transaction.

39. **Data available to public** — (1) A designated trade repository must, on a periodic basis, create and make available to the public, at no cost, aggregate data on open positions, volume, number and, where applicable, price, relating to the transactions reported to it pursuant to this Rule.

(2) The periodic aggregate data made available to the public pursuant to subsection (1) must be complemented at a minimum by breakdowns, where applicable, by currency of denomination, geographic location of reference entity or asset, asset class, contract type, maturity and whether the transaction is cleared.

(3) A designated trade repository must make transaction level reports of the data indicated in the column entitled "Required for Public Dissemination" in Appendix A for each transaction reported pursuant to this Rule available to the public at no cost not later than

(4) In disclosing transaction level reports required by subsection (3), a designated trade repository must not disclose the identity of either counterparty to the transaction.

(5) A designated trade repository must make the data required to be made available to the public under this section available in a usable form through a publicly accessible website or other publicly accessible technology or medium.

(6) Despite subsections (1) to (5), a designated trade repository is not required to make public any derivatives data for transactions entered into between affiliated companies as defined under subsection 1(2) of the Act.

PART 5 — EXCLUSIONS

40. Despite any other section of this Rule, a local counterparty is under no obligation to report derivatives data for a transaction if,

(a) the transaction relates to a derivative the asset class of which is a commodity other than cash or currency,

(b) the local counterparty is not a derivatives dealer, and

(c) the local counterparty has less than $500,000 aggregate notional value, without netting, under all its outstanding transactions at the time of the transaction including the additional notional value related to that transaction.

41. Despite any other section of this Rule, a counterparty is under no obligation to report derivatives data in relation to a transaction if it is entered into between

(a) Her Majesty in right of Ontario or the Ontario Financing Authority when acting as agent for Her Majesty in right of Ontario, and

(b) an Ontario crown corporation or crown agency that forms part of a consolidated entity with Her Majesty in right of Ontario for accounting purposes.

PART 6 — EXEMPTIONS

42. A Director may grant an exemption to this Rule, in whole or in part, subject to such conditions or restrictions as may be imposed in the exemption.

PART 7 — EFFECTIVE DATE

43. **Effective date** — (1) Parts 1, 2, 4, and 6 come into force on December 31, 2013.

(2) Despite subsection (1), subsection 39(3) does not apply until July 29, 2016.

(3) Parts 3 and 5 come into force October 31, 2014.

(4) Despite subsection (3), Part 3 does not apply so as to require a reporting counterparty that is not a derivatives dealer or a recognized or exempt clearing agency to make any reports under that Part until June 30, 2015.

(5) Despite subsection (3) and section 34, Part 3 does not apply to a transaction entered into before October 31, 2014 that expires or terminates on or before April 30, 2015 if the reporting counterparty to the transaction is a derivatives dealer or a recognized or exempt clearing agency.

(6) Despite subsection (3) and section 34, Part 3 does not apply to a transaction entered into before June 30, 2015 that expires or terminates on or before December 31, 2015 if the reporting counterparty to the transaction is neither a derivatives dealer nor a recognized or exempt clearing agency.

APPENDIX A — TO OSC RULE 91-507 — TRADE REPOSITORIES AND DERIVATIVES DATA REPORTING MINIMUM DATA FIELDS REQUIRED TO BE REPORTED TO A DESIGNATED TRADE REPOSITORY

Instructions:

The reporting counterparty is required to provide a response for each of the fields unless the field is not applicable to the transaction.

Data field	Description	Required for Public Dissemination	Required for Pre-existing Transactions
Transaction identifier	The unique transaction identifier as provided by the designated trade repository or the identifier as identified by the two counterparties, electronic trading venue of execution or clearing agency.	N	Y
Master agreement type	The type of master agreement, if used for the reported transaction.	N	N
Master agreement version	Date of the master agreement version (e.g., 2002, 2006).	N	N
Cleared	Indicate whether the transaction has been cleared by a clearing agency.	Y	Y
Clearing agency	LEI of the clearing agency where the transaction is or will be cleared.	N	Y
Clearing member	LEI of the clearing member, if the clearing member is not a counterparty.	N	N
Clearing exemption	Indicate whether one or more of the counterparties to the transaction are exempted from a mandatory clearing requirement.	Y	N
Broker/Clearing intermediary	LEI of the broker acting as an intermediary for the reporting counterparty without becoming a counterparty.	N	N
Electronic trading venue identifier	LEI of the electronic trading venue where the transaction was executed.	Y (Only "Yes" or "No" shall be publicly disseminated)	Y
Inter-affiliate	Indicate whether the transaction is between two affiliated entities. (This field is only required to be reported as of April 30, 2015.)	N	N
Collateralization	Indicate whether the transaction is collateralized. Field Values: • Fully (initial and variation margin required to be posted by both parties), • Partially (variation only required to be posted by both parties),		

Part 9: DERIVATIVES

Data field	Description	Required for Public Dissemination	Required for Pre-existing Transactions
	• One-way (one party will be required to post some form of collateral),	Y	N
	• Uncollateralized.		
Identifier of reporting counterparty	LEI of the reporting counterparty or, in case of an individual, its client code.	N	Y
Identifier of non-reporting counterparty	LEI of the non-reporting counterparty or, in case of an individual, its client code.	N	Y
Counterparty side	Indicate whether the reporting counterparty was the buyer or seller. In the case of swaps, other than credit default, the buyer will represent the payer of leg 1 and the seller will be the payer of leg 2.	N	Y
Identifier of agent reporting the transaction	LEI of the agent reporting the transaction if reporting of the transaction has been delegated by the reporting counterparty.	N	N
Jurisdiction of reporting counterparty	If the reporting counterparty is a local counterparty under the derivatives data reporting rules of one or more provinces of Canada, indicate all of the jurisdictions in which it is a local counterparty.	N	N
Jurisdiction of non-reporting counterparty	If the non-reporting counterparty is a local counterparty under the derivatives data reporting rules of one or more provinces of Canada, indicate all of the jurisdictions in which it is a local counterparty.	N	N
A. Common Data	• These fields are required to be reported for all derivative transactions even if the information may be entered in an Asset field below.		
	• Fields do not have to be reported if the unique product identifier adequately describes those fields.		
Unique product identifier	Unique product identification code based on the taxonomy of the product.	Y	N
Transaction type	The name of the transaction type (e.g., swap, swaption, forwards, options, basis swap, index swap, basket swap, other).	Y	Y
Underlying asset identifier 1	The unique identifier of the asset referenced in the transaction.	Y	Y
Underlying asset identifier 2	The unique identifier of the second asset referenced in the transaction, if more than one. If more than two assets identified in the transaction, report the unique identifiers for those additional underlying assets.	Y	Y
Asset class	Major asset class of the product (e.g., interest rate, credit, commodity, foreign exchange, equity, etc.).	Y	N
Effective date or start date	The date the transaction becomes effective or starts.	Y	Y
Maturity, termination or end date	The date the transaction expires.	Y	Y
Payment frequency or dates	The dates or frequency the transaction requires payments to be made (e.g., quarterly, monthly).	Y	Y
Reset frequency or dates	The dates or frequency at which the price resets (e.g., quarterly, semi-annually, annually).	Y	Y
Day count convention	Factor used to calculate the payments (e.g., 30/360, actual/360).	Y	Y
Delivery type	Indicate whether transaction is settled physically or in cash.	N	Y

Data field	Description	Required for Public Dissemination	Required for Pre-existing Transactions
Price 1	The price, yield, spread, coupon, etc., of the derivative. The price/rate should not include any premiums such as commissions, collateral premiums, accrued interest, etc.	Y	Y
Price 2	The price, yield, spread, coupon, etc., of the derivative. The price/rate should not include any premiums such as commissions, collateral premiums, accrued interest, etc.	Y	Y
Price notation type 1	The manner in which the price is expressed (e.g., percent, basis points, etc.).	Y	Y
Price notation type 2	The manner in which the price is expressed (e.g., percent, basis points, etc.).	Y	Y
Price multiplier	The number of units of the underlying reference entity represented by 1 unit of the contract.	N	N
Notional amount leg 1	Total notional amount(s) of leg 1 of the contract.	Y	Y
Notional amount leg 2	Total notional amount(s) of leg 2 of the contract.	Y	Y
Currency leg 1	Currency(ies) of leg 1.	Y	Y
Currency leg 2	Currency(ies) of leg 2.	Y	Y
Settlement currency	The currency used to determine the cash settlement amount.	Y	Y
Up-front payment	Amount of any up-front payment.	N	N
Currency or currencies of up-front payment	The currency in which any up-front payment is made by one counterparty to another.	N	N
Embedded option	Indicate whether the option is an embedded option.	Y	N
B. Additional Asset Information	These additional fields are required to be reported for transactions in the respective types of derivatives set out below, even if the information is entered in a Common Data field above.		
i) Interest rate derivatives			
Fixed rate leg 1	The rate used to determine the payment amount for leg 1 of the transaction.	N	Y
Fixed rate leg 2	The rate used to determine the payment amount for leg 2 of the transaction.	N	Y
Floating rate leg 1	The floating rate used to determine the payment amount for leg 1 of the transaction.	N	Y
Floating rate leg 2	The floating rate used to determine the payment amount for leg 2 of the transaction.	N	Y
Fixed rate day count convention	Factor used to calculate the fixed payer payments (e.g., 30/360, actual/360).	N	Y
Fixed leg payment frequency or dates	Frequency or dates of payments for the fixed rate leg of the transaction (e.g., quarterly, semi-annually, annually).	N	Y
Floating leg payment frequency or dates	Frequency or dates of payments for the floating rate leg of the transaction (e.g., quarterly, semi-annually, annually).	N	Y
Floating rate reset frequency or dates	The dates or frequency at which the floating leg of the transaction resets (e.g., quarterly, semi-annually, annually).	N	Y

Data field	Description	Required for Public Dissemination	Required for Pre-existing Transactions
ii) Currency derivatives			
Exchange rate	Contractual rate(s) of exchange of the currencies.	N	Y
iii) Commodity derivatives			
Sub-asset class	Specific information to identify the type of commodity derivative (e.g., Agriculture, Power, Oil, Natural Gas, Freights, Metals, Index, Environmental, Exotic).	Y	Y
Quantity	Total quantity in the unit of measure of an underlying commodity.	Y	Y
Unit of measure	Unit of measure for the quantity of each side of the transaction (e.g., barrels, bushels, etc.).	Y	Y
Grade	Grade of product being delivered (e.g., grade of oil).	N	Y
Delivery point	The delivery location.	N	N
Load type	For power, load profile for the delivery.	N	Y
Transmission days	For power, the delivery days of the week.	N	Y
Transmission duration	For power, the hours of day transmission starts and ends.	N	Y
C. Options	These additional fields are required to be reported for options transactions set out below, even if the information is entered in a Common Data field above.		
Option exercise date	The date(s) on which the option may be exercised.	Y	Y
Option premium	Fixed premium paid by the buyer to the seller.	Y	Y
Strike price (cap/floor rate)	The strike price of the option.	Y	Y
Option style	Indicate whether the option can be exercised on a fixed date or anytime during the life of the contract (e.g., American, European, Bermudan, Asian).	Y	Y
Option type	Put/call.	Y	Y
D. Event Data			
Action	Describes the type of event to the transaction (e.g., new transaction, modification or cancellation of existing transaction, etc.).	Y	N
Execution timestamp	Where the transaction was executed on a trading venue, the time and date of execution, expressed using Coordinated Universal Time (UTC).	Y	Y (If available)
Post-transaction events	Indicate whether the transaction resulted from a post-transaction service (e.g. compression, reconciliation, etc.) or from a lifecycle event (e.g. novation, amendment, etc.).	N	N
Reporting date	The time and date the transaction was submitted to the trade repository, expressed using UTC.	N	N
E. Valuation data	These additional fields are required to be reported on a continuing basis for all reported derivative transactions, including reported pre-existing transactions.		

Data field	Description	Required for Public Dissemination	Required for Pre-existing Transactions
Value of transaction calculated by the reporting counterparty	Mark-to-market valuation of the transaction, or mark-to-model valuation	N	N
Valuation currency	Indicate the currency used when reporting the value of the transaction.	N	N
Valuation date	Date of the latest mark-to-market or mark-to-model valuation.	N	N
F. Other details	Where the terms of the transaction cannot be effectively reported in the above prescribed fields, provide any additional information that may be necessary.	N	Y

APPENDIX B — TO OSC RULE 91-507 — TRADE REPOSITORIES AND DERIVATIVES DATA REPORTING EQUIVALENT TRADE REPORTING LAWS OF FOREIGN JURISDICTIONS SUBJECT TO DEEMED COMPLIANCE PURSUANT TO SUBSECTION 26(5)

The Commission has determined that the laws and regulations of the following jurisdictions outside of Ontario are equivalent for the purposes of the deemed compliance provision in subsection 26(5).

Jurisdiction	Law, Regulation and/or Instrument
United States of America	*CFTC Real-Time Public Reporting of Swap Transaction Data*, 17 C.F.R. pt. 43 (2013). *CFTC Swap Data Recordkeeping and Reporting Requirements*, 17 C.F.R. pt. 45 (2013). *CFTC Swap Data Recordkeeping and Reporting Requirements: Pre-Enactment and Transition Swaps*, 17 C.F.R. pt. 46 (2013).
European Union	Regulation (EU) 648/2012 of the European Parliament and Council of 4 July 2012 on OTC derivatives, central counterparties and trade repositories.
	Commission Delegated Regulation (EU) No 148/2013 of 19 December 2012 supplementing Regulation (EU) No 648/2012 of the European Parliament and of the Council on OTC derivatives, central counterparties and trade repositories with regard to regulatory technical standards on the minimum details of the data to be reported to trade repositories.
	Commission Delegated Regulation (EU) No 151/2013 of 19 December 2012 supplementing Regulation (EU) No 648/2012 of the European Parliament and of the Council on OTC derivatives, central counterparties and trade repositories, with regard to regulatory technical standards specifying the data to be published and made available by trade repositories and operational standards for aggregating, comparing and accessing the data.
	Commission Implementing Regulation (EU) No 1247/2012 of 19 December 2012 laying down implementing technical standards with regard to the format and frequency of trade reports to trade repositories according to Regulation (EU) No 648/2012 of the European Parliament and of the Council on OTC derivatives, central counterparties and trade repositories.

Final Rule: Approval by OSC: (2013) 36 O.S.C.B. 11015; Request for Comments: (2013) 36 O.S.C.B. 5737.

Amendment to Rule: (2014) 37 O.S.C.B. 6313; Approval by OSC: (2014) 37 O.S.C.B. 3949

Amendment to Rule: (2014) 37 O.S.C.B. 7559; Approval by OSC: (2014) 37 O.S.C.B. 6069

Amendment to Rule: (2015) 38 O.S.C.B. 1352

Form 91-507F1 — Application for Designation Trade Repository Information Statement

Filer: [ ] *TRADE REPOSITORY*

Type of Filing: *[ ] INITIAL*   *[ ] AMENDMENT*

1. Full name of trade repository:

2. Name(s) under which business is conducted, if different from item 1:

3. If this filing makes a name change on behalf of the trade repository in respect of the name set out in item 1 or item 2, enter the previous name and the new name.

       Previous name:

       New name:

4. Head office

       Address:

       Telephone:

       Facsimile:

5. Mailing address (if different):

6. Other offices

       Address:

       Telephone:

       Facsimile:

7. Website address:

8. Contact employee

       Name and title:

       Telephone number:

       Facsimile:

       E-mail address:

9. Counsel

       Firm name:

       Contact name:

       Telephone number:

       Facsimile:

       E-mail address:

10. Canadian counsel (if applicable)

       Firm name:

       Contact name:

       Telephone number:

       Facsimile:

       E-mail address:

Exhibits

File all Exhibits with the Filing. For each Exhibit, include the name of the trade repository, the date of filing of the Exhibit and the date as of which the information is accurate (if different from the date of the filing). If any Exhibit required is inapplicable, a statement to that effect shall be furnished instead of such Exhibit.

Except as provided below, if the filer files an amendment to the information provided in its Filing and the information relates to an Exhibit filed with the Filing or a subsequent amendment, the filer must, in order to comply with section 3 of OSC Rule 91-507 Trade Repositories and Derivatives Data Reporting (the "TR Rule"), provide a description of the change, the expected date of the implementation of the change, and file a complete and updated Exhibit. The filer must provide a clean and blacklined version showing changes from the previous filing.

If the filer has otherwise filed the information required by the previous paragraph pursuant to section 17 of the TR Rule, it is not required to file the information again as an amendment to an Exhibit. However, if supplementary material relating to a filed rule is contained in an Exhibit, an amendment to the Exhibit must also be filed.

Exhibit A — Corporate Governance

1. Legal status:

       [ ] Corporation

       [ ] Partnership

       [ ] Other (specify):

2. Indicate the following:

    1. Date (DD/MM/YYYY) of formation.

    2. Place of formation.

    3. Statute under which trade repository was organized.

    4. Regulatory status in other jurisdictions.

3. Provide a copy of the constating documents (including corporate by-laws), shareholder agreements, partnership agreements and other similar documents, and all subsequent amendments.

4. Provide the policies and procedures to address potential conflicts of interest arising from the operation of the trade repository or the services it provides, including those related to the commercial interest of the trade repository, the interests of its owners and its operators, the responsibilities and sound functioning of the trade repository, and those between the operations of the trade repository and its regulatory responsibilities.

5. An applicant that is located outside of Ontario that is applying for designation as a trade repository under section 21.2.2(1) of the Act must additionally provide the following:

    1. An opinion of legal counsel that, as a matter of law the applicant has the power and authority to provide the Commission with prompt access to the applicant's books and records, and submit to onsite inspection and examination by the Commission, and

    2. A completed Form 91-507F2, Submission to Jurisdiction and Appointment of Agent for Service.

Exhibit B — Ownership

A list of the registered or beneficial holders of securities of, partnership interests in, or other ownership interests in, the trade repository. For each of the persons listed in the Exhibit, please provide the following:

    1. Name.

    2. Principal business or occupation and title.

    3. Ownership interest.

    4. Nature of the ownership interest, including a description of the type of security, partnership interest or other ownership interest.

In the case of a trade repository that is publicly traded, if the trade repository is a corporation, please only provide a list of each shareholder that directly owns five percent or more of a class of a security with voting rights.

Exhibit C — Organization

1. A list of partners, officers, governors, and members of the board of directors and any standing committees of the board, or persons performing similar functions, who presently hold or have held their offices or positions during the previous year, indicating the following for each:

    1. Name.

    2. Principal business or occupation and title.

    3. Dates of commencement and expiry of present term of office or position.

    4. Type of business in which each is primarily engaged and current employer.

    5. Type of business in which each was primarily engaged in the preceding five years, if different from that set out in item 4.

    6. Whether the person is considered to be an independent director.

2. A list of the committees of the board, including their mandates.

3. The name of the trade repository's Chief Compliance Officer.

Exhibit D — Affiliates

1. For each affiliated entity of the trade repository provide the name and head office address and describe the principal business of the affiliate.

2. For each affiliated entity of the trade repository

    (i) to which the trade repository has outsourced any of its key services or systems described in Exhibit E — Operations of the Trade Repository, including business recordkeeping, recordkeeping of trade data, trade data reporting, trade data comparison, data feed, or

    (ii) with which the trade repository has any other material business relationship, including loans, cross-guarantees, etc.,

provide the following information:

    1. Name and address of the affiliate.

    2. The name and title of the directors and officers, or persons performing similar functions, of the affiliate.

    3. A description of the nature and extent of the contractual and other agreements with the trade repository, and the roles and responsibilities of the affiliate under the arrangement.

    4. A copy of each material contract relating to any outsourced functions or other material relationship.

    5. Copies of constating documents (including corporate by-laws), shareholder agreements, partnership agreements and other similar documents.

6. For the latest financial year of any affiliated entity that has any outstanding loans or cross-guarantee arrangements with the trade repository, financial statements, which may be unaudited, prepared in accordance with:

    a. Canadian GAAP applicable to publicly accountable enterprises;

    b. IFRS; or

    c. U.S. GAAP where the affiliated entity is incorporated or organized under the laws of the U.S.

Exhibit E — Operations of the Trade Repository

Describe in detail the manner of operation of the trade repository and its associated functions. This should include, but not be limited to, a description of the following:

1. The structure of the trade repository.

2. Means of access by the trade repository's participants and, if applicable, their clients to the trade repository's facilities and services.

3. The hours of operation.

4. A description of the facilities and services offered by the trade repository including, but not limited to, collection and maintenance of derivatives data.

5. A list of the types of derivatives instruments for which data recordkeeping is offered, including, but not limited to, a description of the features and characteristics of the instruments.

6. Procedures regarding the entry, display and reporting of derivatives data.

7. Description of recordkeeping procedures that ensure derivatives data is recorded accurately, completely and on a timely basis.

8. The safeguards and procedures to protect derivatives data of the trade repository's participants, including required policies and procedures reasonably designed to protect the privacy and confidentiality of the data.

9. Training provided to participants and a copy of any materials provided with respect to systems and rules and other requirements of the trade repository.

10. Steps taken to ensure that the trade repository's participants have knowledge of and comply with the requirements of the trade repository.

11. A description of the trade repository's risk management framework for comprehensively managing risks including business, legal, and operational risks.

The filer must provide all policies, procedures and manuals related to the operation of the trade repository.

Exhibit F — Outsourcing

Where the trade repository has outsourced the operation of key services or systems described in Exhibit E — Operations of the Trade Repository to an arms-length third party, including any function associated with the collection and maintenance of derivatives data, provide the following information:

1. Name and address of person or company (including any affiliates of the trade repository) to which the function has been outsourced.

2. A description of the nature and extent of the contractual or other agreement with the trade repository and the roles and responsibilities of the arms-length party under the arrangement.

3. A copy of each material contract relating to any outsourced function.

Exhibit G — Systems and Contingency Planning

For each of the systems for collecting and maintaining reports of derivatives data, describe:

1. Current and future capacity estimates.

2. Procedures for reviewing system capacity.

3. Procedures for reviewing system security.

4. Procedures to conduct stress tests.

5. A description of the filer's business continuity and disaster recovery plans, including any relevant documentation.

6. Procedures to test business continuity and disaster recovery plans.

7. The list of data to be reported by all types of participants.

8. A description of the data format or formats that will be available to the Commission and other persons receiving trade reporting data.

Exhibit H — Access to Services

1. A complete set of all forms, agreements or other materials pertaining to access to the services of the trade repository described in Exhibit E.4.

2. Describe the types of trade repository participants.

3. Describe the trade repository's criteria for access to the services of the trade repository.

4. Describe any differences in access to the services offered by the trade repository to different groups or types of participants.

5. Describe conditions under which the trade repository's participants may be subject to suspension or termination with regard to access to the services of the trade repository.

6. Describe any procedures that will be involved in the suspension or termination of a participant.

7. Describe the trade repository's arrangements for permitting clients of participants to have access to the trade repository. Provide a copy of any agreements or documentation relating to these arrangements.

Exhibit I — Fees

A description of the fee model and all fees charged by the trade repository, or by a party to which services have been directly or indirectly outsourced, including, but not limited to, fees relating to access and the collection and maintenance of derivatives data, how such fees are set, and any fee rebates or discounts and how the rebates and discounts are set.

Certificate of Trade Repository

The undersigned certifies that the information given in this report is true and correct.

DATED at .... this .... day of ...., 20..........

.... (Name of trade repository)

.... (Name of director, officer or partner — please type or print)

.... (Signature of director, officer or partner)

.... (Official capacity — please type or print)

If Applicable, Additional Certificate of Trade Repository that is Located Outside of Ontario

The undersigned certifies that

   (a) it will provide the Commission with access to its books and records and will submit to onsite inspection and examination by the Commission;

   (b) as a matter of law, it has the power and authority to

       i. provide the Commission with access to its books and records, and

       ii. submit to onsite inspection and examination by the Commission.

DATED at .... this .... day of ...., 20..........

.... (Name of trade repository)

.... (Name of director, officer or partner — please type or print)

.... (Signature of director, officer or partner)

.... (Official capacity — please type or print)

Form 91-507F2 — Trade Repository Submission to Jurisdiction and Appointment of Agent for Service of Process

1. Name of trade repository (the "Trade Repository"):

....

2. Jurisdiction of incorporation, or equivalent, of Trade Repository:

....

3. Address of principal place of business of Trade Repository:

....

4. Name of the agent for service of process for the Trade Repository (the "Agent"):

....

5. Address of Agent for service of process in Ontario:

....

6. The Trade Repository designates and appoints the Agent as its agent upon whom may be served a notice, pleading, subpoena, summons or other process in any action, investigation or administrative, criminal, quasi-criminal, penal or other proceeding arising out of or relating to or concerning the activities of the Trade Repository in Ontario. The Trade Repository hereby irrevocably waives any right to challenge service upon its Agent as not binding upon the Trade Repository.

7. The Trade Repository agrees to unconditionally and irrevocably attorn to the non-exclusive jurisdiction of (i) the courts and administrative tribunals of Ontario and (ii) any proceeding in any province or territory arising out of, related to, concerning or in any other manner connected with the regulation and oversight of the activities of the Trade Repository in Ontario.

8. The Trade Repository shall file a new submission to jurisdiction and appointment of agent for service of process in this form at least 30 days before the Trade Repository ceases to be designated or exempted by the Commission, to be in effect for six years from the date it ceases to be designated or exempted unless otherwise amended in accordance with section 9.

9. Until six years after it has ceased to be a designated or exempted by the Commission from the recognition requirement under subsection 21.2.2(1) of the Act, the Trade Repository shall file an amended submission to jurisdiction and appointment of agent for service of process at least 30 days before any change in the name or above address of the Agent.

10. This submission to jurisdiction and appointment of agent for service of process shall be governed by and construed in accordance with the laws of Ontario.

Dated: ....

....

Signature of the Trade Repository

....

Print name and title of signing officer of the Trade Repository

Agent — Consent to Act as Agent for Service

I, ... (name of Agent in full; if Corporation, full Corporate name) of ....(business address), hereby accept the appointment as agent for service of process of ....(insert name of Trade Repository) and hereby consent to act as agent for service pursuant to the terms of the appointment executed by .... (insert name of Trade Repository) on .... (insert date).

Dated: ....

....

Signature of Agent

....

Print name of person signing and, if Agent is not an individual, the title of the person

Form 91-507F3 — Cessation of Operations Report for Trade Repository

1. Identification:

    A. Full name of the designated trade repository:

    B. Name(s) under which business is conducted, if different from item 1A:

2. Date designated trade repository proposes to cease carrying on business as a trade repository:

3. If cessation of business was involuntary, date trade repository has ceased to carry on business as a trade repository:

Exhibits

File all Exhibits with the Cessation of Operations Report. For each exhibit, include the name of the trade repository, the date of filing of the exhibit and the date as of which the information is accurate (if different from the date of the filing). If any Exhibit required is inapplicable, a statement to that effect shall be furnished instead of such Exhibit.

Exhibit A

The reasons for the designated trade repository ceasing to carry on business as a trade repository.

Exhibit B

A list of all derivatives instruments for which data recordkeeping is offered during the last 30 days prior to ceasing business as a trade repository.

Exhibit C

A list of all participants who are counterparties to a transaction whose derivatives data is required to be reported pursuant to OSC Rule 91-507 — Trade Repositories and Derivatives Data Reporting and for whom the trade repository provided services during the last 30 days prior to ceasing business as a trade repository.

Certificate of Trade Repository

The undersigned certifies that the information given in this report is true and correct.

DATED at .... this .... day of .... 20 ....

.... (Name of trade repository)

.... (Name of director, officer or partner — please type or print)

.... (Signature of director, officer or partner)

.... (Official capacity — please type or print)

Companion Policy 91-507CP — To Ontario Securities Commission Rule 91-507 Trade Repositories and Derivatives Data Reporting

Part 1 — General Comments

Introduction

This companion policy (the "Policy") sets out the views of the Commission ("our" or "we") on various matters relating to Ontario Securities Commission Rule 91-507 *Trade Repositories and Derivatives Data Reporting* (the "Rule") and related securities legislation.

The numbering of Parts, sections and subsections from Part 2 on in this Policy generally corresponds to the numbering in the Rule. Any general guidance for a Part appears immediately after the Part's name. Any specific guidance on a section or subsection follows any general guidance. If there is no guidance for a Part, section or subsection, the numbering in this Policy will skip to the next provision that does have guidance.

Unless defined in the Rule or this Policy, terms used in the Rule and in this Policy have the meaning given to them in securities legislation, including, for greater certainty, in National Instrument 14-101 *Definitions* and OSC Rule 14-501 *Definitions*.

Definitions and interpretation

1. (1) In this Policy,

"CPSS" means the Committee on Payment and Settlement Systems,

"FMI" means a financial market infrastructure, as described in the PFMI Report,

"Global LEI System" means the Global Legal Entity Identifier System,

"IOSCO" means the Technical Committee of the International Organization of Securities Commissions,

"LEI" means a legal entity identifier,

"LEI ROC" means the LEI Regulatory Oversight Committee,

"PFMI Report" means the April 2012 final report entitled *Principles for financial market infrastructures* published by CPSS and IOSCO, as amended from time to time,[1] and

"principle" means, unless the context otherwise indicates, a principle set out in the PFMI Report.

(2) A "life-cycle event" is defined in the Rule as an event that results in a change to derivatives data previously reported to a designated trade repository. Where a life-cycle event occurs, the corresponding life-cycle event data must be reported under section 32 of the Rule by the end of the business day on which the life-cycle event occurs. When reporting a life-cycle event, there is no obligation to re-report derivatives data that has not changed — only new data and changes to previously reported data need to be reported. Examples of a life-cycle event would include

- a change to the termination date for the transaction,

- a change in the cash flows, payment frequency, currency, numbering convention, spread, benchmark, reference entity or rates originally reported,

- the availability of a legal entity identifier for a counterparty previously identified by name or by some other identifier,

- a corporate action affecting a security or securities on which the transaction is based (e.g., a merger, dividend, stock split, or bankruptcy),

- a change to the notional amount of a transaction including contractually agreed upon changes (e.g., amortization schedule),

- the exercise of a right or option that is an element of the expired transaction, and

- the satisfaction of a level, event, barrier or other condition contained in the original transaction.

(3) Paragraph (c) of the definition of "local counterparty" captures affiliates of parties mentioned in paragraph (a) of the "local counterparty" definition, provided that such party guarantees the liabilities of the affiliate. It is our view that the guarantee must be for all or substantially all of the affiliate's liabilities.

(4) The term "transaction" is defined in the Rule and used instead of the term "trade", as defined in the Act, in order to reflect the types of activities that require a unique transaction report, as opposed to the modification of an existing transaction report. The primary difference between the two definitions is that unlike the term "transaction", the term "trade" includes material amendments and terminations.

A material amendment is not referred to in the definition of "transaction" but is required to be reported as a life-cycle event in connection with an existing transaction under section 32. A termination is not referred to in the definition of "transaction", as the expiry or termination of a transaction would be reported to a trade repository as a life-cycle event without the requirement for a new transaction record.

[1]The PFMI Report is available on the Bank for International Settlements' website (www.bis.org) and the IOSCO website (www.iosco.org).

In addition, unlike the definition of "trade", the definition of "transaction" includes a novation to a clearing agency. Each transaction resulting from a novation of a bi-lateral transaction to a clearing agency is required to be reported as a separate, new transaction with reporting links to the original transaction.

(5) The term "valuation data" is defined in the Rule as data that reflects the current value of a transaction. It is the Commission's view that valuation data can be calculated based upon the use of an industry-accepted methodology such as mark-to-market or mark-to-model, or another valuation method that is in accordance with accounting principles and will result in a reasonable valuation of a transaction.[2] The valuation methodology should be consistent over the entire life of a transaction.

Part 2 — Trade Repository Designation and Ongoing Requirements

Part 2 contains rules for designation of a trade repository and ongoing requirements for a designated trade repository. To obtain and maintain a designation as a trade repository, a person or entity must comply with these rules and requirements in addition to all of the terms and conditions in the designation order made by the Commission. In order to comply with the reporting obligations contained in Part 3, counterparties must report to a designated trade repository. While there is no prohibition on an undesignated trade repository operating in Ontario, a counterparty that reports a transaction to an undesignated trade repository would not be in compliance with its reporting obligations under this Rule with respect to that transaction.

The legal entity that applies to be a designated trade repository will typically be the entity that operates the facility and collects and maintains records of completed transactions reported to the trade repository by other persons or companies. In some cases, the applicant may operate more than one trade repository facility. In such cases, the trade repository may file separate forms in respect of each trade repository facility, or it may choose to file one form to cover all of the different trade repository facilities. If the latter alternative is chosen, the trade repository must clearly identify the facility to which the information or changes submitted under this Part apply.

Trade repository initial filing of information and designation

2. (1) In determining whether to designate an applicant as a trade repository under section 21.2.2 of the Act, it is anticipated that the Commission will consider a number of factors, including

- whether it is in the public interest to designate the applicant,
- the manner in which the trade repository proposes to comply with the Rule,
- whether the trade repository has meaningful representation on its governing body,
- whether the trade repository has sufficient financial and operational resources for the proper performance of its functions,
- whether the rules and procedures of the trade repository ensure that its business is conducted in an orderly manner that fosters both fair and efficient capital markets, and improves transparency in the derivatives market,
- whether the trade repository has policies and procedures to effectively identify and manage conflicts of interest arising from its operation or the services it provides,
- whether the requirements of the trade repository relating to access to its services are fair and reasonable,
- whether the trade repository's process for setting fees is fair, transparent and appropriate,
- whether the trade repository's fees are inequitably allocated among the participants, have the effect of creating barriers to access or place an undue burden on any participant or class of participants,
- the manner and process for the Commission and other applicable regulatory agencies to receive or access derivatives data, including the timing, type of reports, and any confidentiality restrictions,
- whether the trade repository has robust and comprehensive policies, procedures, processes and systems to ensure the security and confidentiality of derivatives data, and
- whether the trade repository has entered into a memorandum of understanding with its local securities regulator.

The Commission will examine whether the trade repository has been, or will be, in compliance with securities legislation. This includes compliance with the Rule and any terms and conditions attached to the Commission's designation order in respect of a designated trade repository.

A trade repository that is applying for designation must demonstrate that it has established, implemented, maintained and enforced appropriate written rules, policies and procedures that are in accordance with standards applicable to trade repositories. We consider that these rules, policies and procedures include, but are not limited to, the principles and key considerations and explanatory notes applicable to trade repositories in the PFMI Report. These principles are set out in the following chart, along with the corresponding sections of the Rule the interpretation of which we consider ought to be consistent with the principles:

Principle in the PFMI Report applicable to a trade repository	Relevant section(s) of the Rule
Principle 1: Legal Basis	Section 7 — Legal framework

---

[2]For example, see International Financial Reporting Standard 13, *Fair Value Measurement.*

Principle in the PFMI Report applicable to a trade repository	Relevant section(s) of the Rule
	Section 17 — Rules (in part)
Principle 2: Governance	Section 8 — Governance
	Section 9 — Board of directors
	Section 10 — Management
Principle 3: Framework for the comprehensive management of risks	Section 19 — Comprehensive risk management framework
	Section 20 — General business risk (in part)
Principle 15: General business risk	Section 20 — General business risk
Principle 17: Operational risk	Section 21 — System and other operational risk requirements
	Section 22 — Data security and confidentiality
	Section 24 — Outsourcing
Principle 18: Access and participation requirements	Section 13 — Access to designated trade repository services
	Section 16 — Due process (in part)
	Section 17 — Rules (in part)
Principle 19: Tiered participation arrangements	No equivalent provisions in the Rule; however, the trade repository may be expected to observe or broadly observe the principle, where applicable.
Principle 20: FMI links	No equivalent provisions in the Rule; however, the trade repository may be expected to observe or broadly observe the principle, where applicable.
Principle 21: Efficiency and effectiveness	No equivalent provisions in the Rule; however, the trade repository may be expected to observe or broadly observe the principle, where applicable.
Principle 22: Communication procedures and standards	Section 15 — Communication policies, procedures and standards
Principle 23: Disclosure of rules, key procedures, and market data	Section 17 — Rules (in part)
Principle 24: Disclosure of market data by trade repositories	Sections in Part 4 — Data Dissemination and Access to Data

It is anticipated that the Commission will apply the principles in its oversight activities of designated trade repositories. Therefore, in complying with the Rule, designated trade repositories will be expected to observe the principles.

The forms filed by an applicant or designated trade repository under the Rule will be kept confidential in accordance with the provisions of securities legislation. The Commission is of the view that the forms generally contain proprietary financial, commercial and technical information, and that the cost and potential risks to the filers of disclosure outweigh the benefit of the principle requiring that forms be made available for public inspection. However, the Commission would expect a designated trade repository to publicly disclose its responses to the CPSS-IOSCO consultative report entitled *Disclosure framework for financial market infrastructures*, which is a supplement to the PFMI Report.[3] In

---

[3]Publication available on the BIS website (www.bis.org) and the IOSCO website (www.iosco.org).

addition, much of the information that will be included in the forms that are filed will be required to be made publicly available by a designated trade repository pursuant to the Rule or the terms and conditions of the designation order imposed by the Commission.

While Form 91-507F1 — *Application for Designation and Trade Repository Information Statement* and any amendments to it will be kept generally confidential, if the Commission considers that it is in the public interest to do so, it may require the applicant or designated trade repository to publicly disclose a summary of the information contained in such form, or amendments to it.

Notwithstanding the confidential nature of the forms, an applicant's application itself (excluding forms) will be published for comment for a minimum period of 30 days.

Change in information

3. (1) Under subsection 3(1), a designated trade repository is required to file an amendment to the information provided in Form 91-507F1 at least 45 days prior to implementing a significant change. The Commission considers a change to be significant when it could impact a designated trade repository, its users, participants, market participants, investors, or the capital markets (including derivatives markets and the markets for assets underlying a derivative). The Commission would consider a significant change to include, but not be limited to,

- a change in the structure of the designated trade repository, including procedures governing how derivatives data is collected and maintained (included in any back-up sites), that has or may have a direct impact on users in Ontario,

- a change to the services provided by the designated trade repository, or a change that affects the services provided, including the hours of operation, that has or may have a direct impact on users in Ontario,

- a change to means of access to the designated trade repository's facility and its services, including changes to data formats or protocols, that has or may have a direct impact on users in Ontario,

- a change to the types of derivative asset classes or categories of derivatives that may be reported to the designated trade repository,

- a change to the systems and technology used by the designated trade repository that collect, maintain and disseminate derivatives data, including matters affecting capacity,

- a change to the governance of the designated trade repository, including changes to the structure of its board of directors or board committees and their related mandates,

- a change in control of the designated trade repository,

- a change in affiliates that provide key services or systems to, or on behalf of, the designated trade repository,

- a change to outsourcing arrangements for key services or systems of the designated trade repository,

- a change to fees or the fee structure of the designated trade repository,

- a change in the designated trade repository's policies and procedures relating to risk-management, including relating to business continuity and data security, that has or may have an impact on the designated trade repository's provision of services to its participants,

- the commencement of a new type of business activity, either directly or indirectly through an affiliate, and

- a change in the location of the designated trade repository's head office or primary place of business or the location where the main data servers or contingency sites are housed.

(2) The Commission generally considers a change in a designated trade repository's fees or fee structure to be a significant change. However, the Commission recognizes that designated trade repositories may frequently change their fees or fee structure and may need to implement fee changes within timeframes that are shorter than the 45-day notice period contemplated in subsection (1). To facilitate this process, subsection 3(2) provides that a designated trade repository may provide information that describes the change to fees or fee structure in a shorter timeframe (at least 15 days before the expected implementation date of the change to fees or fee structure). See section 12 of this Policy for guidance with respect to fee requirements applicable to designated trade repositories.

The Commission will make best efforts to review amendments to Form 91-507F1 filed in accordance with subsections 3(1) and 3(2) before the proposed date of implementation of the change. However, where the changes are complex, raise regulatory concerns, or when additional information is required, the Commission's review may exceed these timeframes.

(3) Subsection 3(3) sets out the filing requirements for changes to information provided in a filed Form 91-507F1 other than those described in subsections 3(1) or (2). Such changes to information are not considered significant and include changes that:

- would not have an impact on the designated trade repository's structure or participants, or more broadly on market participants, investors or the capital markets; or

- are administrative changes, such as

  - changes in the routine processes, policies, practices, or administration of the designated trade repository that would not impact participants,

  - changes due to standardization of terminology,

  - corrections of spelling or typographical errors,

  - changes to the types of designated trade repository participants in Ontario,

  - necessary changes to conform to applicable regulatory or other legal requirements of Ontario or Canada, and

- minor system or technology changes that would not significantly impact the system or its capacity.

For the changes referred to in subsection 3(3), the Commission may review these filings to ascertain whether they have been categorized appropriately. If the Commission disagrees with the categorization, the designated trade repository will be notified in writing. Where the Commission determines that changes reported under subsection 3(3) are in fact significant changes under subsection 3(1), the designated trade repository will be required to file an amended Form 91-507F1 that will be subject to review by the Commission.

Ceasing to carry on business

6. (1) In addition to filing a completed Form 91-507F3 — *Cessation of Operations Report for Trade Repository*, a designated trade repository that intends to cease carrying on business in Ontario as a designated trade repository must make an application to voluntarily surrender its designation to the Commission pursuant to securities legislation. The Commission may accept the voluntary surrender subject to terms and conditions.[4]

Legal framework

7. (1) Designated trade repositories are required to have rules, policies, and procedures in place that provide a legal basis for their activities in all relevant jurisdictions, whether within Canada or any foreign jurisdiction, where they have activities.

Governance

8. Designated trade repositories are required to have in place governance arrangements that meet the minimum requirements and policy objectives set out in subsections 8(1) and 8(2).

(3) Under subsection 8(3), a designated trade repository is required to make the written governance arrangements required under subsections 8(1) and (2) available to the public on its website. The Commission expects that this information will be posted on the trade repository's publicly accessible website and that interested parties will be able to locate the information through a web search or through clearly identified links on the designated trade repository's website.

Board of directors

9. The board of directors of a designated trade repository is subject to various requirements, such as requirements pertaining to board composition and conflicts of interest. To the extent that a designated trade repository is not organized as a corporation, the requirements relating to the board of directors may be fulfilled by a body that performs functions that are equivalent to the functions of a board of directors.

(2) Paragraph 9(2)(a) requires individuals who comprise the board of directors of a designated trade repository to have an appropriate level of skill and experience to effectively and efficiently oversee the management of its operations. This would include individuals with experience and skills in areas such as business recovery, contingency planning, financial market systems and data management.

Under paragraph 9(2)(b), the board of directors of a designated trade repository must include individuals who are independent of the designated trade repository. The Commission would view individuals who have no direct or indirect material relationship with the designated trade repository as independent. The Commission would expect that independent directors of a designated trade repository would represent the public interest by ensuring that regulatory and public transparency objectives are fulfilled, and that the interests of participants who are not derivatives dealers are considered.

Chief compliance officer

11. (3) References to harm to the capital markets in subsection 11(3) may be in relation to domestic or international capital markets.

Fees

12. A designated trade repository is responsible for ensuring that the fees it sets are in compliance with section 12. In assessing whether a designated trade repository's fees and costs are fairly and equitably allocated among participants as required under paragraph 12(a), the Commission will consider a number of factors, including

- the number and complexity of the transactions being reported,

- the amount of the fee or cost imposed relative to the cost of providing the services,

- the amount of fees or costs charged by other comparable trade repositories, where relevant, to report similar transactions in the market,

- with respect to market data fees and costs, the amount of market data fees charged relative to the market share of the designated trade repository, and

- whether the fees or costs represent a barrier to accessing the services of the designated trade repository for any category of participant.

A designated trade repository should provide clear descriptions of priced services for comparability purposes. Other than fees for individual services, a designated trade repository should also disclose other fees and costs related to connecting to or accessing the trade repository. For example, a designated trade repository should disclose information on the system design, as well as technology and communication proce-

---

[4]Section 21.4 of the Act provides that the Commission may impose terms and conditions on an application for voluntary surrender. The transfer of derivatives data/information can be addressed through the terms and conditions imposed by the Commission on such application.

dures, that influence the costs of using the designated trade repository. A designated trade repository is also expected to provide timely notice to participants and the public of any changes to services and fees.

Access to designated trade repository services

13. (3) Under subsection 13(3), a designated trade repository is prohibited from unreasonably limiting access to its services, permitting unreasonable discrimination among its participants, imposing unreasonable burdens on competition or requiring the use or purchase of another service in order for a person or company to utilize its trade reporting service. For example, a designated trade repository should not engage in anti-competitive practices such as setting overly restrictive terms of use or engaging in anti-competitive price discrimination. A designated trade repository should not develop closed, proprietary interfaces that result in vendor lock-in or barriers to entry with respect to competing service providers that rely on the data maintained by the designated trade repository.

Acceptance of reporting

14. Section 14 requires that a designated trade repository accept derivatives data for all derivatives of the asset class or classes set out in its designation order. For example, if the designation order of a designated trade repository includes interest rate derivatives, the designated trade repository is required to accept transaction data for all types of interest rate derivatives that are entered into by a local counterparty. It is possible that a designated trade repository may accept derivatives data for only a subset of a class of derivatives if this is indicated in its designation order. For example, there may be designated trade repositories that accept derivatives data for only certain types of commodity derivatives such as energy derivatives.

Communication policies, procedures and standards

15. Section 15 sets out the communication standard required to be used by a designated trade repository in communications with other specified entities. The reference in paragraph 15(d) to "other service providers" could include persons or companies who offer technological or transaction processing or post-transaction services.

Rules, policies and procedures

17. Section 17 requires that the publicly disclosed written rules and procedures of a designated trade repository be clear and comprehensive, and include explanatory material written in plain language so that participants can fully understand the system's design and operations, their rights and obligations, and the risks of participating in the system. Moreover, a designated trade repository should disclose to its participants and to the public, basic operational information and responses to the CPSS-IOSCO *Disclosure framework for financial market infrastructures*.

(2) Subsection 17(2) requires that a designated trade repository monitor compliance with its rules and procedures. The methodology of monitoring such compliance should be fully documented.

(3) Subsection 17(3) requires a designated trade repository to implement processes for dealing with non-compliance with its rules and procedures. This subsection does not preclude enforcement action by any other person or company, including the Commission or other regulatory body.

(5) Subsection 17(5) requires a designated trade repository to file its rules and procedures with the Commission for approval, in accordance with the terms and conditions of the designation order. Upon designation, the Commission may develop and implement a protocol with the designated trade repository that will set out the procedures to be followed with respect to the review and approval of rules and procedures and any amendments thereto. Generally, such a rule protocol will be appended to and form part of the designation order. Depending on the nature of the changes to the designated trade repository's rules and procedures, such changes may also impact the information contained in Form 91-507F1. In such cases, the designated trade repository will be required to file a revised Form 91-507F1 with the Commission. See section 3 of this Policy for a discussion of the filing requirements.

Records of data reported

18. A designated trade repository is a market participant under securities legislation and therefore subject to the record-keeping requirements under securities legislation. The record-keeping requirements under section 18 are in addition to the requirements under securities legislation.

(2) Subsection 18(2) requires that records be maintained for 7 years after the expiration or termination of a transaction. The requirement to maintain records for 7 years after the expiration or termination of a transaction, rather than from the date the transaction was entered into, reflects the fact that transactions create on-going obligations and information is subject to change throughout the life of a transaction.

Comprehensive risk-management framework

19. Requirements for a comprehensive risk-management framework of a designated trade repository are set out in section 19.

Features of framework

A designated trade repository should have a written risk-management framework (including policies, procedures, and systems) that enable it to identify, measure, monitor, and manage effectively the range of risks that arise in, or are borne by, a designated trade repository. A designated trade repository's framework should include the identification and management of risks that could materially affect its ability to perform or to provide services as expected, such as interdependencies.

Establishing a framework

A designated trade repository should have comprehensive internal processes to help its board of directors and senior management monitor and assess the adequacy and effectiveness of its risk-management policies, procedures, systems, and controls. These processes should be fully documented and readily available to the designated trade repository's personnel who are responsible for implementing them.

Maintaining a framework

A designated trade repository should regularly review the material risks it bears from, and poses to, other entities (such as other FMIs, settlement banks, liquidity providers, or service providers) as a result of interdependencies, and develop appropriate risk-management tools to address these risks. These tools should include business continuity arrangements that allow for rapid recovery and resumption of critical operations and services in the event of operational disruptions and recovery or orderly wind-down plans should the trade repository become non-viable.

General business risk

20. (1) Subsection 20(1) requires a designated trade repository to manage its general business risk effectively. General business risk includes any potential impairment of the designated trade repository's financial position (as a business concern) as a consequence of a decline in its revenues or an increase in its expenses, such that expenses exceed revenues and result in a loss that must be charged against capital or an inadequacy of resources necessary to carry on business as a designated trade repository.

(2) For the purposes of subsection 20(2), the amount of liquid net assets funded by equity that a designated trade repository should hold is to be determined by its general business risk profile and the length of time required to achieve a recovery or orderly wind-down, as appropriate, of its critical operations and services, if such action is taken.

(3) Subsection (3) requires a designated trade repository, for the purposes of subsection (2), to hold liquid net assets funded by equity equal to no less than six months of current operating expenses.

(4) For the purposes of subsections 20(4) and (5), and in connection with developing a comprehensive risk-management framework under section 19, a designated trade repository should identify scenarios that may potentially prevent it from being able to provide its critical operations and services as a going concern, and assess the effectiveness of a full range of options for recovery or orderly wind-down. These scenarios should take into account the various independent and related risks to which the designated trade repository is exposed.

Based on the required assessment of scenarios under subsection 20(4) (and taking into account any constraints potentially imposed by legislation), the designated trade repository should prepare appropriate written plans for its recovery or orderly wind-down. The plan should contain, among other elements, a substantive summary of the key recovery or orderly wind-down strategies, the identification of the designated trade repository's critical operations and services, and a description of the measures needed to implement the key strategies. The designated trade repository should maintain the plan on an ongoing basis, to achieve recovery and orderly wind-down, and should hold sufficient liquid net assets funded by equity to implement this plan (see also subsections 20(2) and (3) above). A designated trade repository should also take into consideration the operational, technological, and legal requirements for participants to establish and move to an alternative arrangement in the event of an orderly wind-down.

Systems and other operational risk requirements

21. (1) Subsection 21(1) sets out a general principle concerning the management of operational risk. In interpreting subsection 21(1), the following key considerations should be applied:

- a designated trade repository should establish a robust operational risk-management framework with appropriate systems, policies, procedures, and controls to identify, monitor, and manage operational risks;

- a designated trade repository should review, audit, and test systems, operational policies, procedures, and controls, periodically and after any significant changes; and

- a designated trade repository should have clearly defined operational-reliability objectives and policies in place that are designed to achieve those objectives.

(2) The board of directors of a designated trade repository should clearly define the roles and responsibilities for addressing operational risk and approve the designated trade repository's operational risk-management framework.

(3) Paragraph 21(3)(a) requires a designated trade repository to develop and maintain an adequate system of internal control over its systems as well as adequate general information-technology controls. The latter controls are implemented to support information technology planning, acquisition, development and maintenance, computer operations, information systems support, and security. Recommended Canadian guides as to what constitutes adequate information technology controls include "*Information Technology Control Guidelines*" from the Canadian Institute of Chartered Accountants and "*COBIT*" from the IT Governance Institute. A designated trade repository should ensure that its information-technology controls address the integrity of the data that it maintains, by protecting all derivatives data submitted from corruption, loss, improper disclosure, unauthorized access and other processing risks.

Paragraph 21(3)(b) requires a designated trade repository to thoroughly assess future needs and make systems capacity and performance estimates in a method consistent with prudent business practice at least once a year. The paragraph also imposes an annual requirement for designated trade repositories to conduct periodic capacity stress tests. Continual changes in technology, risk management requirements and competitive pressures will often result in these activities or tests being carried out more frequently.

Paragraph 21(3)(c) requires a designated trade repository to notify the Commission of any material systems failure. The Commission would consider a failure, malfunction, delay or other disruptive incident to be "material" if the designated trade repository would in the normal course of its operations escalate the incident to, or inform, its senior management that is responsible for technology, or the incident would have an impact on participants. The Commission also expects that, as part of this notification, the designated trade repository will provide updates on the status of the failure, the resumption of service, and the results of its internal review of the failure.

(4) Subsection 21(4) requires that a designated trade repository establish, implement, maintain and enforce business continuity plans, including disaster recovery plans. The Commission believes that these plans should allow the designated trade repository to provide continuous and undisrupted service, as back-up systems ideally should commence processing immediately. Where a disruption is unavoidable, a designated trade repository is expected to provide prompt recovery of operations, meaning that it resumes operations within 2 hours following the disruptive event. Under paragraph 21(4)(c), an emergency event could include any external sources of operational risk, such as the failure of critical service providers or utilities or events affecting a wide metropolitan area, such as natural disasters, terrorism, and pandemics. Business continuity planning should encompass all policies and procedures to ensure uninterrupted provision of key services regardless of the cause of potential disruption.

(5) Subsection 21(5) requires a designated trade repository to test its business continuity plans at least once a year. The expectation is that the designated trade repository would engage relevant industry participants, as necessary, in tests of its business continuity plans, including testing of back-up facilities for both the designated trade repository and its participants.

(6) Subsection 21(6) requires a designated trade repository to engage a qualified party to conduct an annual independent assessment of the internal controls referred to in paragraphs 21(3)(a) and (b) and subsections 21(4) and (5). A qualified party is a person or company or a group of persons or companies with relevant experience in both information technology and in the evaluation of related internal controls in a complex information technology environment, such as external auditors or third party information system consultants. The Commission is of the view that this obligation may also be satisfied by an independent assessment by an internal audit department that is compliant with the International Standards for the Professional Practice of Internal Auditing published by the Institute of Internal Audit. Before engaging a qualified party, the designated trade repository should notify the Commission.

(8) Subsection 21(8) requires designated trade repositories to make public all material changes to technology requirements to allow participants a reasonable period to make system modifications and test their modified systems. In determining what a reasonable period is, the Commission of the view that the designated trade repository should consult with participants and that a reasonable period would allow all participants a reasonable opportunity to develop, implement and test systems changes. We expect that the needs of all types of participants would be considered, including those of smaller and less sophisticated participants.

(9) Subsection 21(9) requires designated trade repositories to make available testing facilities in advance of material changes to technology requirements to allow participants a reasonable period to test their modified systems and interfaces with the designated trade repository. In determining what a reasonable period is, the Commission of the view that the designated trade repository should consult with participants and that a reasonable period would allow all participants a reasonable opportunity to develop, implement and test systems changes. We expect that the needs of all types of participants would be considered, including those of smaller and less sophisticated participants.

Data security and confidentiality

22. (1) Subsection 22(1) provides that a designated trade repository must establish policies and procedures to ensure the safety, privacy and confidentiality of derivatives data to be reported to it under the Rule. The policies must include limitations on access to confidential trade repository data and safeguards to protect against persons and companies affiliated with the designated trade repository from using trade repository data for their personal benefit or the benefit of others.

(2) Subsection 22(2) prohibits a designated trade repository from releasing reported derivatives data, for a commercial or business purpose, that is not required to be publicly disclosed under section 39 without the express written consent of the counterparties to the transaction or transactions to which the derivatives data relates. The purpose of this provision is to ensure that users of the designated trade repository have some measure of control over their derivatives data.

Confirmation of data and information

23. Subsection 23(1) requires a designated trade repository to have and follow written policies and procedures for confirming the accuracy of the derivatives data received from a reporting counterparty. A designated trade repository must confirm the accuracy of the derivatives data with each counterparty to a reported transaction provided that the non-reporting counterparty is a participant of the trade repository. Where the non-reporting counterparty is not a participant of the trade repository, there is no obligation to confirm with such non-reporting counterparty.

The purpose of the confirmation requirement in subsection 23(1) is to ensure that the reported information is agreed to by both counterparties. However, in cases where a non-reporting counterparty is not a participant of the relevant designated trade repository, the designated trade repository would not be in a position to confirm the accuracy of the derivatives data with such counterparty. As such, under subsection 23(2) a designated trade repository will not be obligated to confirm the accuracy of the derivatives data with a counterparty that is not a participant of the designated trade repository. Additionally, similar to the reporting obligations in section 26, confirmation under subsection 23(1) can be delegated under section 26(3) to a third-party representative.

A trade repository may satisfy its obligation under section 23 to confirm the derivatives data reported for a transaction by notice to each counterparty to the transaction that is a participant of the designated trade repository, or its delegated third-party representative where applicable, that a report has been made naming the participant as a counterparty to a transaction, accompanied by a means of accessing a report of the derivatives data submitted. The policies and procedures of the designated trade repository may provide that if the designated trade repository does not receive a response from a counterparty within 48 hours, the counterparty is deemed to confirm the derivatives data as reported.

Outsourcing

24. Section 24 sets out requirements applicable to a designated trade repository that outsources any of its key services or systems to a service provider. Generally, a designated trade repository must establish policies and procedures to evaluate and approve these outsourcing arrangements. Such policies and procedures include assessing the suitability of potential service providers and the ability of the designated trade repository to continue to comply with securities legislation in the event of bankruptcy, insolvency or the termination of business of the service provider. A designated trade repository is also required to monitor the ongoing performance of a service provider to which it outsources a key service, system or facility. The requirements under section 24 apply regardless of whether the outsourcing arrangements are with third-party service providers or affiliates of the designated trade repository. A designated trade repository that outsources its services or systems remains responsible for those services or systems and for compliance with securities legislation.

Part 3 — Data Reporting

Part 3 deals with reporting obligations for transactions and includes a description of the counterparties that will be subject to the duty to report, requirements as to the timing of reports and a description of the data that is required to be reported.

Reporting counterparty

25. Section 25 outlines how the counterparty required to report derivatives data and fulfil the ongoing reporting obligations under the Rule is determined. Reporting obligations on derivatives dealers apply irrespective of whether the derivatives dealer is a registrant.

(1) Subsection 25(1) outlines a hierarchy for determining which counterparty to a transaction will be required to report the transaction based on the counterparty to the transaction that is best suited to fulfill the reporting obligation. For example, for transactions that are cleared through a recognized or exempt clearing agency, the clearing agency is best positioned to report derivatives data and is therefore required to act as reporting counterparty

Although there may be situations in which the reporting obligation falls on both counterparties to a transaction, it is the Commission's view that in such cases the counterparties should select one counterparty to fulfill the reporting obligation to avoid duplicative reporting. For example, if a transaction required to be reported is between two dealers, each dealer has an obligation to report under paragraph 25(1)(b). Similarly, if a transaction is between two local counterparties that are not dealers, both local counterparties have an obligation to report under paragraph 25(1)(d). However, because a reporting counterparty may delegate its reporting obligations under subsection 26(3), the Commission expects that the practical outcome is that one counterparty will delegate its reporting obligation to the other (or a mutually agreed upon third party) and only one report will be filed in respect of the transaction. Therefore, although both counterparties to the transaction examples described above ultimately have the reporting obligation, they may institute contracts, systems and practices to agree to delegate the reporting function to one party. The intention of these provisions is to facilitate one counterparty reporting through delegation while requiring both counterparties to have procedures or contractual arrangements in place to ensure that reporting occurs.

Subsections 25(1)(b) and (e) also provide for an alternate reporting option for situations in which the reporting obligation falls on both counterparties to a transaction. For example, pursuant to subsection 25(1)(b) the reporting counterparty for a transaction involving two derivatives dealers may, subject to certain preconditions, be determined in accordance with the ISDA methodology. This option is also available for two non-dealers pursuant to 25(1)(e). The ISDA methodology is publically available at www.ISDA.com. It has been developed in order to facilitate one-sided transaction reporting and provides a consistent method for determining the party required to act as reporting counterparty. The non-reporting counterparty as determined under the ISDA Methodology is not a reporting counterparty for the purposes of the TR Rule in respect of a transaction in which the parties have chosen to use the ISDA Methodology. There is no requirement for counterparties to a transaction to use the ISDA Methodology. Further, the ISDA Methodology is not available in respect of transactions between a dealer and non-dealer; such transactions are always required to be reported by the dealer.

(2) Subsection 25(2) prescribes the conditions under which the ISDA Methodology can be used. Paragraphs 25(1)(b) and (e) are only available where both counterparties to the transaction have agreed in advance to the terms of the multilateral ISDA agreement which incorporates the process for determining a reporting counterparty in accordance with ISDA methodology. This is done through the execution and delivery to ISDA of the ISDA Representation Letter that includes an agreement to follow the ISDA Methodology for determining the reporting counterparty. The ISDA Representation Letter is available at www.ISDA.com.

Paragraphs 25(1)(b) and (e) are only available in respect of a reportable transaction if the parties to the transaction have executed and delivered the ISDA Representation Letter to ISDA and have agreed to follow the ISDA Methodology for that transaction. In situations where both counterparties to a transaction have executed and delivered the ISDA Representation Letter but agree to report using a different method, paragraphs 25(1)(b) and (e) would not be applicable. Further, paragraphs 25(1)(b) and (e) are only available in respect of a reportable transaction where the parties to that transaction have consented to ISDA's release to the Commission of information which indicates that the parties have signed the ISDA Representation Letter.

Duty to report

26. Section 26 outlines the duty to report derivatives data.

(1) Subsection 26(1) requires that, subject to sections 40, 41, 42 and 43, derivatives data for each transaction to which one or more counterparties is a local counterparty be reported to a designated trade repository. The counterparty required to report the derivatives data is the reporting counterparty as determined under section 25.

(2) Under subsection 26(2), the reporting counterparty for a transaction must ensure that all reporting obligations are fulfilled. This includes ongoing requirements such as the reporting of life-cycle event data and valuation data.

(3) Subsection 26(3) permits the delegation of all reporting obligations of a reporting counterparty. This includes reporting of initial creation data, life-cycle event data and valuation data. For example, some or all of the reporting obligations may be delegated to a third-party service provider. However, the reporting counterparty remains responsible for ensuring that the derivatives data is accurate and reported within the timeframes required under the Rule.

Part 9: DERIVATIVES

(4) With respect to subsection 26(4), prior to the reporting rules in Part 3 coming into force, the Commission will provide public guidance on how reports for transactions that are not accepted for reporting by any designated trade repository should be electronically submitted to the Commission.

(5) Subsection 26(5) provides for limited substituted compliance with this Rule where a transaction has been reported to a designated trade repository pursuant to the law of a province of Canada other than Ontario or of a foreign jurisdiction listed in Appendix B, provided that the additional conditions set out in paragraphs (a) and (c) are satisfied.

(6) Paragraph 26(6)(a) requires that all derivatives data reported for a given transaction be reported to the same designated trade repository to which the initial report is submitted or, with respect to transactions reported under section 26(4), to the Commission. For a bi-lateral transaction that is assumed by a clearing agency (novation), the designated trade repository to which all derivatives data for the assumed transactions must be reported is the designated trade repository to which the original bi-lateral transaction was reported.

The purpose of this requirement is to ensure the Commission has access to all reported derivatives data for a particular transaction from the same entity. It is not intended to restrict counterparties' ability to report to multiple trade repositories. Where the entity to which the transaction was originally reported is no longer a designated trade repository, all data relevant to that transaction should be reported to another designated trade repository as otherwise required by the Rule.

(7) The Commission interprets the requirement in subsection 26(7) to report errors or omissions in derivatives data "as soon as technologically practicable" after it is discovered, to mean upon discovery and in any case no later than the end of the business day on which the error or omission is discovered.

(8) Under subsection 26(8), where a local counterparty that is not a reporting counterparty discovers an error or omission in respect of derivatives data that is reported to a designated trade repository, such local counterparty has an obligation to report the error or omission to the reporting counterparty. Once the error or omission is reported to the reporting counterparty, the reporting counterparty then has an obligation under subsection 26(7) to report the error or omission to the designated trade repository or to the Commission in accordance with subsection 26(6). The Commission interprets the requirement in subsection 26(8) to notify the reporting counterparty of errors or omissions in derivatives data to mean upon discovery and in any case no later than the end of the business day on which the error or omission is discovered.

Legal entity identifiers

28. (1) Subsection 28(1) requires that a designated trade repository identify all counterparties to a transaction by a legal entity identifier. It is envisioned that this identifier be a LEI under the Global LEI System. The Global LEI System is a G20 endorsed initiative[5] that will uniquely identify parties to transactions. It is currently being designed and implemented under the direction of the LEI ROC, a governance body endorsed by the G20.

(2) The "Global Legal Entity Identifier System" referred to in subsection 28(2) means the G20 endorsed system that will serve as a public-good utility responsible for overseeing the issuance of legal entity identifiers globally to counterparties who enter into transactions.

(3) If the Global LEI System is not available at the time counterparties are required to report their LEI under the Rule, they must use a substitute legal entity identifier. The substitute legal entity identifier must be in accordance with the standards established by the LEI ROC for pre-LEI identifiers. At the time the Global LEI System is operational; counterparties must cease using their substitute LEI and commence reporting their LEI. The substitute LEI and LEI could be identical.

Unique transaction identifier

29. A unique transaction identifier will be assigned by the designated trade repository to each transaction which has been submitted to it. The designated trade repository may utilize its own methodology or incorporate a previously assigned identifier that has been assigned by, for example, a clearing agency, trading platform, or third-party service provider. However, the designated trade repository must ensure that no other transaction shares the same identifier.

A transaction in this context means a transaction from the perspective of all counterparties to the transaction. For example, both counterparties to a single swap transaction would identify the transaction by the same single identifier. For a bi-lateral transaction that is novated to a clearing agency, the reporting of the novated transactions should reference the unique transaction identifier of the original bi-lateral transaction.

Unique product identifier

30. Section 30 requires that a reporting counterparty identify each transaction that is subject to the reporting obligation under the Rule by means of a unique product identifier. There is currently a system of product taxonomy that may be used for this purpose.[6] To the extent that a unique product identifier is not available for a particular transaction type, a reporting counterparty would be required to create one using an alternative methodology.

Creation data

31. Subsection 31(2) requires that reporting of creation data be made in real time, which means that creation data should be reported as soon as technologically practicable after the execution of a transaction. In evaluating what will be considered to be "technological practicable", the Commission will take into account the prevalence of implementation and use of technology by comparable counterparties located in Canada and in foreign jurisdictions. The Commission may also conduct independent reviews to determine the state of reporting technology.

---

[5]See http://www.financialstabilityboard.org/list/fsb_publications/tid_156/index.htm for more information.

[6]See http://www2.isda.org/identifiers-and-otc-taxonomies/ for more information.

(3) Subsection 31(3) is intended to take into account the fact that not all counterparties will have the same technological capabilities. For example, counterparties that do not regularly engage in transactions would, at least in the near term, likely not be as well situated to achieve real-time reporting. Further, for certain post-transaction operations, such as trade compressions involving numerous transactions, real time reporting may not currently be practicable. In all cases, the outside limit for reporting is the end of the business day following execution of the transaction.

Life-cycle event data

32. The Commission notes that, in accordance with subsection 26(6), all reported derivatives data relating to a particular transaction must be reported to the same designated trade repository to which the initial report was made, or to the Commission for transactions for which derivatives data was reported to the Commission in accordance with subsection 26(4).

(1) Life-cycle event data is not required to be reported in real time but rather at the end of the business day on which the life-cycle event occurs. The end of business day report may include multiple life-cycle events that occurred on that day.

Valuation data

33. Valuation data with respect to a transaction that is subject to the reporting obligations under the Rule is required to be reported by the reporting counterparty. For both cleared and uncleared transactions, counterparties may, as described in subsection 26(3), delegate the reporting of valuation data to a third party, but such counterparties remain ultimately responsible for ensuring the timely and accurate reporting of this data. The Commission notes that, in accordance with subsection 26(6), all reported derivatives data relating to a particular transaction must be reported to the same designated trade repository to which the initial report was made, or to the Commission for transactions for which the initial report was made to the Commission in accordance with subsection 26(4).

(1) Subsection 33(1) provides for differing frequency of valuation data reporting based on the type of entity that is the reporting counterparty.

Pre-existing derivatives

34. Section 34 outlines reporting obligations in relation to transactions that were entered into prior to the commencement of the reporting obligations. Where the reporting counterparty is a derivatives dealer or a recognized or exempt clearing agency, subsection 34(1) requires that pre-existing transactions that were entered into before October 31, 2014 and that will not expire or terminate on or before April 30, 2015 to be reported to a designated trade repository no later than April 30, 2015. Similarly, where the reporting counterparty is neither a derivatives dealer nor a recognized or exempt clearing agency, subsection 34(1.1) requires that pre-existing transactions that were entered into before June 30, 2015 and that will not expire or terminate on or before December 31, 2015 to be reported to a designated trade repository no later than December 31, 2015. In addition, only the data indicated in the column entitled "Required for Pre-existing Transactions" in Appendix A will be required to be reported for pre-existing transactions.

Transactions that are entered into before October 31, 2014 and that expire or terminate on or before April 30, 2015 will not be subject to the reporting obligation, if the reporting counterparty to the transaction is a derivatives dealer or a recognized or exempt clearing agency. Similarly, transactions for which the reporting counterparty is neither a derivatives dealer nor a recognized or exempt clearing agency will not be subject to the reporting obligation if they are entered into before June 30, 2015 but will expire or terminate on or before December 31, 2015. These transactions are exempted from the reporting obligation in the Rule, to relieve some of the reporting burden for counterparties and because they would provide marginal utility to the Commission due to their imminent termination or expiry.

The derivatives data required to be reported for pre-existing transactions under section 34 is substantively the same as the requirement under CFTC Rule 17 CFR Part 46 — *Swap Data Recordkeeping and Reporting Requirements: Pre-Enactment and Transition Swaps.* Therefore, to the extent that a reporting counterparty has reported pre-existing transaction derivatives data required by the CFTC rule, this would meet the derivatives data reporting requirements under section 34. This interpretation applies only to pre-existing transactions.

Part 4 — Data Dissemination and Access to Data

Data available to regulators

37. (1) Subsection 37(1) requires designated trade repositories to, at no cost to the Commission: (a) provide to the Commission continuous and timely electronic access to derivatives data; (b) promptly fulfill data requests from the Commission; (c) provide aggregate derivatives data; and (d) disclose how data has been aggregated. Electronic access includes the ability of the Commission to access, download, or receive a direct real-time feed of derivatives data maintained by the designated trade repository.

The derivatives data covered by this subsection are data necessary to carry out the Commission's mandate to protect against unfair, improper or fraudulent practices, to foster fair and efficient capital markets, to promote confidence in the capital markets, and to address systemic risk. This includes derivatives data with respect to any transaction or transactions that may impact Ontario's capital markets.

Transactions that reference an underlying asset or class of assets with a nexus to Ontario or Canada can impact Ontario's capital markets even if the counterparties to the transaction are not local counterparties. Therefore, the Commission has a regulatory interest in transactions involving such underlying interests even if such data is not submitted pursuant to the reporting obligations in the Rule, but is held by a designated trade repository.

(2) Subsection 37(2) requires a designated trade repository to conform to internationally accepted regulatory access standards applicable to trade repositories. Trade repository regulatory access standards have been developed by CPSS and IOSCO. It is expected that all designated trade repositories will comply with the access recommendations in CPSS-IOSCO's final report.[7]

---

[7]See report entitled "Authorities' Access to TR Data" available at http://www.bis.org/publ/cpss110.htm.

(3) The Commission interprets the requirement for a reporting counterparty to use best efforts to provide the Commission with access to derivatives data to mean, at a minimum, instructing the designated trade repository to release derivative data to the Commission.

Data available to counterparties

38. Section 38 is intended to ensure that each counterparty, and any person acting on behalf of a counterparty, has access to all derivatives data relating to its transaction(s) in a timely manner. The Commission is of the view that where a counterparty has provided consent to a trade repository to grant access to data to a third-party service provider, the trade repository shall grant such access on the terms consented to.

Data available to public

39. (1) Subsection 39(1) requires a designated trade repository to make available to the public, free of charge, certain aggregate data for all transactions reported to it under the Rule (including open positions, volume, number of transactions, and price). It is expected that a designated trade repository will provide aggregate data by notional amounts outstanding and level of activity. Such aggregate data is expected to be available on the designated trade repository's website.

(2) Subsection 39(2) requires that the aggregate data that is disclosed under subsection 39(1), be broken down into various categories of information. The following are examples of the aggregate data required under subsection 39(2):

- currency of denomination (the currency in which the derivative is denominated);

- geographic location of the underlying reference entity (e.g., Canada for derivatives which reference the TSX60 index);

- asset class of reference entity (e.g., fixed income, credit, or equity);

- product type (e.g., options, forwards, or swaps);

- cleared or uncleared;

- maturity (broken down into maturity ranges, such as less than one year, 1-2 years, 2-3 years).

(3) Subsection 39(3) requires a designated trade repository to publicly report the data indicated in the column entitled "Required for public dissemination" in Appendix A of the Rule. For transactions where at least one counterparty is a derivatives dealer, paragraph 39(3)(a) requires that such data be publicly disseminated by the end of the day following the day on which the designated trade repository receives the data. For transactions where neither counterparty is a derivatives dealer, paragraph 39(3)(b) requires that such data be publicly disseminated by the end of the second day following the day on which the designated trade repository receives the data. The purpose of the public reporting delays is to ensure that counterparties have adequate time to enter into any offsetting transaction that may be necessary to hedge their positions. These time delays apply to all transactions, regardless of transaction size.

(4) Subsection 39(4) provides that a designated trade repository must not disclose the identity of either counterparty to the transaction. This means that published data must be anonymized and the names or legal entity identifiers of counterparties must not be published. This provision is not intended to create a requirement for a designated trade repository to determine whether anonymized published data could reveal the identity of a counterparty based on the terms of the transaction.

Part 5 — Exclusions

40. Section 40 provides that the reporting obligation for a physical commodity transaction entered into between two non-derivatives dealers does not apply in certain limited circumstances. This exclusion only applies if a local counterparty to a transaction has less than $500,000 aggregate notional value under all outstanding derivatives transactions, including the additional notional value related to that transaction. In calculating this exposure, the notional value of all outstanding transactions, including transactions from all asset classes and with all counterparties, domestic and foreign, should be included. The notional value of a physical commodity transaction would be calculated by multiplying the quantity of the physical commodity by the price for that commodity. A counterparty that is above the $500,000 threshold is required to act as reporting counterparty for a transaction involving a party that is exempt from the reporting obligation under section 40. In a situation where both counterparties to a transaction qualify for this exclusion, it would not be necessary to determine a reporting counterparty in accordance with section 25.

This relief applies to physical commodity transactions that are not excluded derivatives for the purpose of the reporting obligation in paragraph 2(d) of OSC Rule 91-506 *Derivatives: Product Determination*. An example of a physical commodity transaction that is required to be reported (and therefore could benefit from this relief) is a physical commodity contract that allows for cash settlement in place of delivery.

Part 7 — Effective Date

Effective date

43. (2) The requirement under subsection 39(3) to make transaction level data reports available to the public does not apply until April 30, 2015.

(3) Where the counterparty is a derivatives dealer or recognized or exempted clearing agency, subsection 42(3) provides that no reporting is required until October 31, 2014.

(4) Where neither of the counterparties is a derivatives dealer or a recognized or exempted clearing agency, subsection 42(4) provides that no reporting is required until June 30, 2015. This provision only applies where the reporting counterparty is a neither a derivatives dealer nor a clearing agency. For example, where the counterparties to a transaction are a dealer and a non-dealer, the derivatives dealer will be required to report according to the timing outlined in subsection 42(3).

(5) Subsection 43(5) provides that, if the reporting counterparty to the transaction is a derivatives dealer or a recognized or exempt clearing agency, no reporting is required for pre-existing transactions that terminate or expire on or before April 30, 2015.

(6) Subsection 43(6) provides that, if the reporting counterparty to the transaction is neither a derivatives dealer nor a recognized or exempt clearing agency, no reporting is required for pre-existing transactions that terminate or expire on or before December 31, 2015.

Adoption of Policy by OSC: (2013) 36 O.S.C.B. 11015; Request for Comments: (2013) 36 O.S.C.B. 5737

Adoption of Amendment by OSC: (2014) 37 O.S.C.B. 3949

Adoption of Amendment by OSC: (2014) 37 O.S.C.B. 6069

OSC Staff Notice 91-701 — Debt-Like Derivative Securities

Date: 1996/06/21
19 O.S.C.B. 3427

The Commission staff, by this notice, is withdrawing its notice on Debt-like Derivative Securities issued July 5, 1991 ((1991), 14 OSCB 3316, Carswell, 1995, p. 1420). That notice stated, among other things, that issuers proposing to distribute certain debt-like securities should not rely upon the prospectus exemption contained in clause 72(1)(a) [now 73(1)(a)] of the *Securities Act* (the "Act") as it relates to the issue of securities described in clause 35(2)(1) of the Act without the prior approval of the Director, Corporate Finance.

Staff is aware that there has been some confusion in the market concerning the availability of the exemption described above to debt-like derivatives. For instance, staff has received, on occasion, inconsistent legal opinions from practitioners with respect to substantially similar transactions. In order to attempt to address this confusion, a Task Force consisting of an industry representative, legal practitioners, a member of the Commission and Commission staff has been formed to review the regulation of debt-like derivatives in Ontario. The members of the Task Force are Kirby C. Gavelin, RBC Dominion Securities Inc.; Stephen R. Ashbourne, Blake, Cassels & Graydon; Philip J. Henderson, Stikeman, Elliott; Paul M. Moore, Tory, Tory, Deslauriers & Binnington; Robert P. Wildeboer, Wildeboer Rand Thomson Apps; and John A. Geller, Susan Wolburgh Jenah, Tanis J. MacLaren, Margo L. Paul and M. Cecilia Williams of the Ontario Securities Commission.

The Task Force is expected to make written recommendations to the Commission and the Canadian Securities Administrators concerning the regulation of debt-like derivatives. It is anticipated that these recommendations will be published for comment to inform any further policy development in this area.

Whether the prospectus exemption described above is available for distributions of debt-like derivatives depends upon the nature and structure of the instruments proposed to be issued. Staff encourages persons contemplating a distribution of debt-like derivatives to confer with staff before proceeding with the distribution in reliance upon the above-noted exemption.

Questions or comments concerning this notice should be provided to: Market Operations

OSC Staff Notice 91-702 — Offerings of Contracts for Difference and Foreign Exchange Contracts to Investors in Ontario

Date: October 27, 2009
32 O.S.C.B. 9003

I. — Purpose

Staff of the Ontario Securities Commission have issued this notice

- to respond to enquiries from issuers, dealers and other market participants requesting a staff position on the applicability of Ontario securities law to offerings of Contracts for Difference (CFDs), foreign exchange contracts (forex or FX contracts), and similar "over-the-counter" derivative products (OTC derivatives) to investors in Ontario;

- to highlight certain investor protection concerns we have with some of these products, particularly where the products are being offered to retail investors by unregistered, offshore entities through the internet; and

- to outline the securities law and other regulatory requirements applicable when offering these products and to indicate circumstances in which staff may be prepared to recommend limited exemptive relief on terms and conditions.

This notice will primarily focus on CFDs. However, the guidance in this notice should also be considered generally in the context of offerings of forex contracts and similar OTC derivatives to investors in Ontario, whether through the internet or otherwise. This notice is not intended to address direct or intermediated trading between institutions. We note that Canadian financial institutions are exempt from the registration requirements under the *Securities Act* (Ontario) (the Act).[1]

II. — Interim Nature of Guidance

This notice reflects the views of OSC staff and is intended to provide interim guidance pending the development by the Canadian Securities Administrators (the CSA) of a harmonized CSA approach to the regulation of OTC derivatives and/or the introduction of new or revised derivatives legislation in Ontario. In this regard, CSA staff are closely reviewing a number of developments in this area, including the recent

[1] Please refer to section 35.1 of the Act.

adoption of a new *Derivatives Act* in Québec (the QDA), the recommendations relating to OTC derivatives made in the CFA Advisory Committee's final report,[2] and other developments in jurisdictions outside of Canada.

We anticipate that this notice will be amended or withdrawn if the CSA adopts a harmonized approach to the regulation of OTC derivatives and/or new or revised derivatives legislation is introduced in Ontario and/or federal derivatives legislation is introduced as part of the mandate of a Canadian Securities Commission.

We remind issuers, dealers and other market participants that there may be important differences in the regulatory treatment of CFDs across the CSA and that market participants should review the specific requirements of securities legislation (and, where applicable, commodity futures legislation and derivatives legislation) in these jurisdictions prior to offering CFDs to investors in these jurisdictions.

III. — Background

Staff have recently received a number of enquiries from issuers, dealers and other market participants relating to the potential application of Ontario securities law to offerings of CFDs, forex contracts, and similar OTC derivative products to investors in Ontario.

These enquiries have generally focused on the question whether the issuance of a CFD to an investor in Ontario involves a "trade" and a "distribution" in a "security" to that investor for the purposes of Ontario securities law.

As a result of these enquiries, OSC staff, in consultation with staff in the other Canadian jurisdictions and staff of the Investment Industry Regulatory Organization of Canada (IIROC), have conducted a review of the issuance and the distribution of CFDs to investors. We have set out below our initial conclusions from this review and our views on the application of Ontario securities law to offerings of CFDs to investors, and particularly retail investors.

We would also like to take this opportunity to highlight some of the investor protection concerns we have with offerings of CFDs to investors in circumstances where such offerings are made without the protections of dealer involvement. We understand that, in some cases, CFDs are being offered to investors directly through the internet rather than through an appropriately registered dealer. In these circumstances, we believe the investor protection concerns with such offerings may be significant.

IV. — Discussion

1. — What are CFDs?

A CFD is a derivative product that allows an investor to obtain economic exposure (for speculative, investment or hedging purposes) to an underlying asset (the underlying asset), such as a share, index, market sector, currency or commodity, without acquiring ownership of the underlying asset. CFDs are generally cash-settled although in some cases investors may also have the option of requesting physical delivery of the underlying asset.

A CFD typically involves a contract between two parties, a seller and a buyer, that creates payment rights and obligations based on the price movements of the underlying asset. CFDs allow investors to take long or short positions in relation to the underlying asset but, unlike futures contracts, have no fixed expiry date or contract size. For example, a holder of a long contract will benefit from an upward movement in the price of the underlying asset and would receive as payment the difference in price of the underlying asset from the initial contract price to the price at the time the contract is closed (hence a "contract for difference").

CFDs are generally based on a "market maker model" and not the "intermediated trade model". That is to say that the original seller of the CFD is also the only possible buyer for an investor.

CFDs are currently being offered to investors in a number of foreign jurisdictions. CFDs are also being offered to investors, including retail investors, in Canada through internet platforms being operated by CFD providers.

For more information about CFDs, please refer to the IIROC position paper "Regulatory Analysis of Contracts for Differences (CFDs)" (the IIROC Position Paper).[3]

2. — Investor protection concerns

CFDs are a relatively new product in Canada which raise a variety of investor protection concerns, including concerns relating to:

- complexity of the product and the offering model;
- use of margin or leverage;
- in the case of certain offerings, highly promotional and potentially misleading selling materials;
- lack of product suitability determination;
- in some cases, lack of available information relating to the underlying asset;
- potential volatility of the underlying asset (for example, currency fluctuations);
- embedded fees and lack of price transparency; and

---

[2]The CFA Advisory Committee's final report may be found on the website of the Ministry of Government Services of Ontario. See: http://www.gov.on.ca/MGS/en/AbtMin/121808.html.

[3]The IIROC Position Paper is available on the IIROC website. http://docs.iiroc.ca/DisplayDocument.aspx?DocumentID=CF983987B0A449C881DFCF5EDC640E99&Language=en

- counterparty risk (including risks associated with the counterparty being situated out of jurisdiction).

In some cases, CFDs are being offered to investors directly through the internet by unregistered dealers rather than through a registered dealer. To the extent CFDs are being offered without the protections of dealer involvement, we believe these investor protection concerns may be significant.

Members of the CSA have previously highlighted some of the risks associated with forex contracts in a number of publications.[4]

V. — Application of Ontario securities law

In view of the investor protection concerns and enquiries related to the application of securities laws to CFDs, we have considered the question of whether the issuance of a CFD to an investor in Ontario involves a "trade" and a "distribution" in a "security" to that investor for the purposes of Ontario securities law.

Staff's view is that CFDs, when offered to investors in Ontario, engage the purposes of the Act and constitute "investment contracts" and "securities" for the purposes of Ontario securities law. In our view, CFDs are also "derivatives"[5] for the purposes of Ontario securities law.

In arriving at this conclusion, we have considered the decision of the Supreme Court of Canada in *Pacific Coast Coin Exchange v. Ontario (Securities Commission)*[6] and the various judicial and administrative decisions that have been issued subsequent to that case.[7]

We believe there are a number of important parallels between the facts of the *Pacific Coast* case and the current trend towards offerings of CFDs to investors through the internet. These parallels include the fact that the products involve contracts that are marketed as a form of investment, the contracts involve similar forms of underlying interest, the contracts make extensive use of margin in order to magnify profits and losses, and there is significant reliance by the investor on the CFD provider to act as a counterparty, design and operate the internet platforms, and hedge risk appropriately in order to ensure the CFD provider is able to satisfy its payment and performance obligations.

We note further that the *Pacific Coast* line of cases emphasizes the need to consider the economic realities of the transaction and to focus on the substance rather than the form of a transaction.

It is important to note that the case law generally endorses a purposive interpretation of "security" that would include considering the objective of investor protection. In view of the investor protection concerns we have identified with offerings of CFDs, and the regulatory protections provided by the Act, we believe a purposive interpretation of "security" leads to the conclusion that such offerings involve a trade and a distribution of a security.

CFDs may also be securities under one or more alternative branches of the definition of "security" or may be a "security" that is not covered by the non-exclusive list of enumerated categories of securities.

VI. — Implications of conclusion for market participants

Since we consider CFDs to be securities under the Act, we are of the view that CFD providers that wish to offer CFDs to investors in Ontario, absent statutory exemptions or exemptive relief, are required to comply with the registration and prospectus requirements of Ontario securities law. Additional details regarding certain of the registration and prospectus requirements are set out below.

It should also be noted that investors may also have civil remedies against CFD providers that fail to comply with Ontario securities law, including a right to withdraw from the transaction and/or damages for losses, on the grounds that such transactions were conducted in breach of securities law.

1. — Registration Requirement

General. Any person or company that acts as a dealer or adviser with respect to securities must register under the Act as either a dealer or adviser, respectively. As such, engaging in or holding oneself out as engaging in the business of trading or advising with respect to CFDs triggers the dealer and adviser registration requirements in the Act.

With respect to institutional and very high net worth investors, it should be noted that National Instrument 31-103 *Registration Requirements and Exemptions* (NI 31-103) provides international dealers and advisers with an exemption from the registration requirements in the Act.[8] These exemptions are only available in limited circumstances, including, trading with or advising "permitted clients"[9].

---

[4]See, for example,

- Ontario Securities Commission News Release dated August 15, 2004 — *"If you're playing the FOREX market, make sure you can handle the risk"*
- British Columbia Securities Commission Investor Alert dated April 19, 2007 *"InvestorWatch: FOREX"*
- British Columbia Securities Commission News Release dated November 6, 2003 — *"Securities watchdog says be wary of foreign currency trading"*

See also the investor awareness publication issued by the Australian Securities and Investments Commission *"Contracts for difference: complex and high risk?"* available at http://www.fido.asic.gov.au/fido/fido.nsf/byid/2B97220FCC6D5BB6CA2571EF007C9751?opendocument

[5]See section 1.1 of the Act and the definition of "derivative" in subsection 1.1(3) of OSC Rule 14-501 *Definitions*.

[6][1978] 2 S.C.R. 112.

[7]For an overview of cases that have considered the "investment contract" branch of the definition of "security", please see the decision and reasons *In the Matter of Universal Settlements International Inc.* dated September 29, 2006 (former Vice-Chair Paul Moore and Commissioners Harold Hands and Wendell Wigle) and the decisions cited therein.

[8]Please refer to sections 8.18 and 8.26 of NI 31-103.

[9]"Permitted client" is defined in section 1.1 and 8.26 of NI 31-103.

Dealer Registration. Where the trade of a CFD is with a retail investor, the appropriate dealer category of registration is "investment dealer". The investment dealer category of registration requires, among other things, IIROC membership.

Where a person or company is in the business of trading in securities to "accredited investors"[10], the dealer category of registration most often used is exempt market dealer (EMD). However, NI 31-103 prohibits any registrant that is not an IIROC member from lending money, extending credit or providing margin to a client. We believe that the investor protection concerns are greatest where the CFD provider is not a member of IIROC and is not complying with IIROC rules, including rules relating to proficiency, capital adequacy and margin requirements. Accordingly, given the use of margin, the appropriate category of registration for a dealer who trades CFDs is the investment dealer category, which requires IIROC membership, regardless of whether such trades are made to retail investors or accredited investors.

Margin. IIROC has prescribed minimum margin rates for CFDs that are significantly higher (i.e., more restrictive) than the rates offered by many unregistered CFD providers. As a result of the lower margin rates offered by unregistered CFD providers, investors who purchase CFDs through these entities are able to take significantly larger positions and become significantly more exposed to gains and losses based on movement in the price of the underlying asset.

We have been advised that IIROC staff are currently reviewing the margin rates it has prescribed for certain over-the-counter derivative products, including CFDs and spot forex contracts, and may propose rules prescribing higher minimum margin rates for such products in the future. Any such rule proposals would be subject to the ordinary public notice and comment process and regulatory approval process for rules by a self-regulatory organization.

KYC and Suitability. Know your client (KYC) due diligence and suitability determinations are essential elements of the investor protection regime imposed through the registration requirement.[11] KYC and *initial* suitability determination — whether access to the CFD trading platform is appropriate for a given client — must be performed by CFD providers. However, we appreciate the difficulty in reviewing individual trades for suitability, given that these are internet platforms analogous to day trading platforms or discount brokerage accounts. IIROC rules[12] exempt member firms that provide execution-only services such as discount brokerage from the obligation to determine whether each *trade* is suitable for the client. However, IIROC has also communicated the following expectations for any member proposing to sell CFDs or forex contracts:[13]

- applicable risk disclosure documents and client suitability waivers provided must be in a form acceptable to IIROC;

- the firm's policies and procedures, amongst other things, should assess the depth of investment knowledge and trading experience of the client before an account is approved to be opened;

- the relationship and responsibilities, including conflicts of interest between the issuer and broker/dealer should be fully disclosed to the client and acknowledged in writing; and

- cumulative loss limits for each client's account should be established.

For more information about IIROC's requirements and views relating to CFDs and similar products, including requirements and views relating to proficiency of salespeople, please refer to the IIROC Position Paper and contact information for IIROC staff in the Paper.

2. — Prospectus Requirement — Applications by investment dealers for exemptive relief

In view of our conclusion that the issuance of a CFD to an investor in Ontario involves a distribution of a security to that investor for the purposes of Ontario securities law, we take the view that the issuer of such product must, absent exemptive relief, comply with the prospectus requirements of Ontario securities law.

We acknowledge that the prospectus requirement may not be well-suited to offerings of certain types of OTC derivative products, including CFDs and forex contracts, to investors and that modified requirements, focused on ensuring appropriate transparency as to the nature of the product and investor risk, imposed as terms and conditions of an exemptive relief order exempting an issuer from the prospectus requirement, may be better suited for these products. However, OSC staff will consider exemption applications on a case-by-case basis.

OSC staff may be prepared to recommend relief from the prospectus requirement in section 53 of the Act that would otherwise apply to a "distribution" of a CFD to an investor in Ontario provided that:

- the distribution is made through a registrant that is in compliance with its terms of registration under the Act and with the rules and expectations of IIROC applicable to such transaction (including minimum margin rates acceptable to IIROC)

- prior to entering into the CFD transaction, the investor is provided with a risk disclosure statement that clearly explains, in plain language, the product and the risks associated with an investment in the product

- in circumstances where the CFD counterparty is a separate entity from the registrant, and is not itself a registrant and member of IIROC, the counterparty is subject to meaningful capital adequacy requirements in its home jurisdiction that are reasonably comparable to the requirements applicable to investment dealers in Canada and the investor is provided with meaningful financial disclosure about the counterparty that is acceptable to staff and that allows the investor to make a meaningful assessment as to the ability of the CFD counterparty to satisfy its performance and payment obligations

---

[10]As defined in section 1.1 of National Instrument 45-106 — *Prospectus and Registration Exemptions.*

[11]Please refer to sections 13.2 and 13.3 of NI 31-103 and CSA Staff Notice 33-315 — *Suitability Obligation and Know Your Product.*

[12]Please refer to Rule 3200 of IIROC's Dealer Member Rules.

[13]Please refer to page 22 of the IIROC Position Paper.

- the requested relief includes a sunset provision that provides that the relief will expire on or shortly after the earlier of the introduction of legislation or a rule governing the issuance of CFDs to investors and four years from the date of the order

We expect this exemptive relief to apply only to offerings of CFDs to investors in Ontario. Market participants seeking to offer such products to investors in other jurisdictions in Canada should consult with the appropriate regulatory authorities in these other jurisdictions.

3. — Insider reporting of CFD transactions

Staff wish to take this opportunity to remind market participants that the insider reporting obligations contained in Part XXI of the *Securities Act* (Ontario) and related rules, including Multilateral Instrument 55-103 *Insider Reporting of Certain Derivative Transactions (Equity Monetization)* (MI 55-103),[14] will generally require an insider of a reporting issuer to file insider reports about transactions in CFDs that involve, directly or indirectly, securities of the insider's reporting issuer in a similar manner to transactions in other securities of the insider's reporting issuer.

4. — Insider trading involving CFDs

Similarly, we wish to take this opportunity to remind insiders and other persons in a special relationship with a reporting issuer (collectively, special relationship persons) that the prohibitions on trading and tipping contained in Ontario securities law will generally apply to transactions in CFDs that involve, directly or indirectly, securities of the special relationship person's reporting issuer in a similar manner to transactions in other securities of the insider's reporting issuer.

For more information relating to the CSA's views on the insider trading and tipping prohibitions, please refer to National Policy 51-201 *Disclosure Standards*.

OSC Staff Notice 91-703 — Staff Recommendation on the Reporting of Inter-Affiliate Transactions by End-Users under OSC Rule 91-507 Trade Repositories and Derivatives Date Reporting

Date: June 4, 2015

38 O.S.C.B. 5036

[Not reproduced]

OSC Staff Notice 91-704 — Compliance Review Plan for OSC Rule 91-507 Trade Repositories and Derivatives Data Reporting

Date: July 2, 2015

38 O.S.C.B. 5933

[Not reproduced]

Part 9: DERIVATIVES

---

[14]In December 2008, the CSA published proposed NI 55-104 *Insider Reporting Requirements and Exemptions* (NI 55-104) for comment. Proposed NI 55-104 will, if adopted, repeal and replace MI 55-103.

Dated: June 4, 2015
38 O.S.C.B. 5032

Dated: July 2, 2015
38 O.S.C.B. 5833

[Not reproduced]

ONTARIO SECURITIES COMMISSION RULES OF PROCEDURE

made under Made under the
Statutory Powers Procedure Act
R.S.O. 1990, c. S.22, as amended

[Editor's note: The OSC Rules of Procedure, as amended and consolidated as of April 8, 2014, apply to all proceedings before the OSC commenced on or after April 1, 2009. The OSC Rules of Practice ((1997) 20 O.S.C.B. 1947), which were published in the 47th edition of Carswell's Consolidated Securities Act, Regulations and Rules, *apply to all proceedings commenced on or prior to March 31, 2009. The OSC has adopted Practice Guidelines dated April 24, 2012, December 4, 2012 and April 8, 2014, which are not reproduced herein.]*

Table of Contents

APPENDIX A – PRE-HEARING CONFERENCE FORM

GENERAL RULES

Rule 1 — General

(See also the SPPA.)

1.1 Interpretation — In these Rules:

"Act" means the *Securities Act*, R.S.O. 1990, c. S.5, as amended;

"address" includes a valid address for electronic transmission;

"application" includes an application:

(a) by Staff pursuant to section 127 of the Act;

(b) for review of a decision of the Director pursuant to section 8 of the Act;

(c) for review of a decision of a stock exchange, a self-regulatory organization, a quotation and trade reporting system or a clearing agency pursuant to section 21.7 of the Act;

(d) for a further decision pursuant to subsection 9(6) of the Act;

(e) for a revocation or a variation of a decision pursuant to section 144 of the Act;

(f) pursuant to section 104 and/or section 127 of the Act in connection with take-over bids, issuer bids and mergers and acquisitions transactions; and

(g) for an order authorizing disclosure pursuant to section 17 of the Act.

"Bulletin" means the Commission Bulletin;

"Commission" means the Ontario Securities Commission;

"company" means a company as defined in subsection 1(1) of the Act;

"decision" means a decision as defined in subsection 1(1) of the Act;

"Director" means a Director as defined in subsection 1(1) of the Act;

"electronic hearing" means an electronic hearing as defined in subsection 1(1) of the SPPA;

"electronic transmission" means transmission by facsimile or electronic mail (e-mail);

"file" means to file with the Office of the Secretary to the Commission in accordance with Rule 1.5.4;

"holiday" means:

(a) any Saturday or Sunday,

(b) New Year's Day,

(c) Family Day,

(d) Good Friday,

(e) Easter Monday,

(f) Victoria Day,

(g) Canada Day,

(h) Civic Holiday,

(i) Labour Day,

(j) Thanksgiving Day,

(k) Remembrance Day,

(l) Christmas Day,

(m) Boxing Day,

(n) any special holiday proclaimed by the Governor General or the Lieutenant Governor, and

(o) where New Year's Day, Canada Day or Remembrance Day falls on a Saturday or Sunday, the following Monday is a holiday, where Christmas Day falls on a Saturday or Sunday, the following Monday and Tuesday are holidays, and where Christmas Day falls on a Friday, the following Monday is a holiday;

"intervenor" means a person who has applied to intervene pursuant to the Rules and who has been granted intervenor status by order of a Panel;

"oral hearing" means an oral hearing as defined in subsection 1(1) of the SPPA;

"Panel" means a quorum of at least 2 members of the Commission pursuant to subsection 3(11) of the Act or a single member of the Commission authorized by order of the Commission pursuant to subsection 3.5(3) of the Act;

"party" may include:

(a) a person recognized as a party by the Act;

(b) a person entitled by law to be a party to the proceeding;

(c) a person granted party status by order of a Panel; and

(d) Staff;

"person" means a person as defined in subsection 1(1) of the Act, and where applicable, includes a company as defined in subsection 1(1) of the Act;

"representative" means, in respect of a proceeding to which the Rules apply, a person authorized under the *Law Society Act*, R.S.O. 1990, c. L.8, as amended, to represent a person in a proceeding;

"Rules" means the *Ontario Securities Commission Rules of Procedure*;

"Secretary" means the Secretary to the Commission appointed pursuant to section 7 of the Act;

"service" means the delivery of a document to a party in accordance with the Rules;

"SPPA" means the *Statutory Powers Procedure Act*, R.S.O. 1990, c. S.22, as amended;

"Staff" means Staff of the Commission;

"Website" means the Commission's Website; and

"written hearing" means a hearing conducted in writing as defined in subsection 1(1) of the SPPA.

1.2 General Principles — **(1)** Unless otherwise provided in the Rules, the Rules apply to all proceedings before a Panel where the Commission is authorized under the Act or the *Commodity Futures Act*, R.S.O. 1990, c. C.20, as amended, or otherwise by law to hold a hearing.

(2) Except where otherwise specifically provided in the SPPA, if there is a conflict between the SPPA and the Rules, the SPPA shall prevail over the Rules.

(3) The Rules shall be construed to secure the most expeditious and least expensive determination of every proceeding before the Commission on its merits, consistent with the requirements of natural justice.

(4) Effect of Irregularity in Form — No proceeding, document or order in a proceeding is invalid by reason of a defect or other irregularity in form.

1.3 General Powers of a Panel under the Rules — **(1)** The Commission may, from time to time, issue procedural directions or practice guidelines with respect to the application of the Rules as may be appropriate. The Commission shall give notice of these procedural directions or practice guidelines by issuing a notice from the Office of the Secretary, which shall be posted on the Website and published in the Bulletin.

1.4 Procedural Directions or Orders by a Panel — **(1)** A Panel may exercise any of its powers under the Rules on its own initiative or at the request of a party.

(2) A Panel may issue procedural directions or orders with respect to the application of the Rules in respect of any proceeding before it, and may impose any conditions in the direction or order as it considers appropriate.

(3) A Panel may waive or vary any of the Rules in respect of any proceeding before it, if it is of the opinion that to do so would be in the public interest or that it would otherwise be advisable to secure the just and expeditious determination of the matters in issue.

(4) In considering a request to waive or vary any of the Rules or to hold a hearing on an expedited basis, a Panel may consider factors including:

(a) the nature of the matters in issue;

(b) whether adherence to the time periods set out in the Rules would be likely to cause undue delay or prejudice to any of the parties;

(c) costs; and

(d) any other factors a Panel considers relevant in the public interest.

(5) When granting a request for an expedited hearing, a Panel may, as a condition, require that the parties file documents electronically.

1.5 Service and Filing

1.5.1 Service of Documents on Parties — **(1)** All documents required to be served under the Rules shall be served by one of the following methods:

(a) by personal delivery to the party;

(b) by delivery to the representative of the party;

(c) by delivery to an adult person at the premises where the party resides, is employed or carries on business, or where the representative of the party carries on business;

(d) by delivery to a company, by leaving a copy with an officer, director or agent of the company, or a person at any place of business of the company who appears to be in control or management of the place of business;

(e) regular, registered or certified mail to the last known address of the party or the representative of the party;

(f) electronically to the facsimile number or e-mail address of the party or the representative of the party;

(g) by courier to the last known address of the party or the representative of the party; or

(h) by any other means authorized by a Panel.

(2) Date on Which Service is Effective — Service is deemed to be effective, when delivered:

(a) by personal delivery, on the day of delivery;

(b) by mail, on the fifth day after the day of mailing;

(c) electronically, on the same day;

(d) by courier, on the earlier of the date on the delivery receipt or the second day after it was sent; or

(e) by any other means authorized by a Panel, on the date specified by the Panel.

(3) Service After 4:30 p.m. — Documents served after 4:30 p.m. shall be deemed to have been served on the next day that is not a holiday.

1.5.2 Information on Documents Served or Filed — **(1)** A person who serves or files a document should include with it the following information:

(a) the person's name, address, telephone number, facsimile number and e-mail address, as applicable; or

(b) if the person is represented by a representative, the name, address, telephone number, facsimile number and e-mail address of the representative, as applicable; and

(c) the name of the proceeding to which the document relates; and

(d) the name of the person or representative being served.

(2) If any information referred to in subrule 1.5.2(1) changes, the person who provided the information shall notify the person to whom the information was provided and the Secretary of the change and any new information.

1.5.3 Inability to Effect Service — **(1)** If a person required to serve a document is unable to serve it by one of the methods described in Rule 1.5.1, the person may apply to a Panel for an order for substituted, validated or waived service.

(2) Application for an Order for Substituted, Validated or Waived Service — The application shall be filed with an affidavit setting out the efforts already made to serve the person and stating:

(a) why the proposed method of substituted service is likely to be successful; or

(b) why a Panel should validate or waive service on that person.

(3) Substituted, Validated or Waived Service — A Panel may give directions for substituted service or, where necessary, may validate or waive service if it considers it appropriate.

1.5.4 Filing — **(1)** A document required under the Rules to be filed shall be filed by personal delivery, mail, facsimile transmission or courier to the offices of the Commission, marked to the attention of the Secretary, or, alternatively if the Secretary consents, by e-mail to the Secretary.

(2) The filing of a document with the Secretary pursuant to these Rules does not constitute service of the document on any party to the proceeding, including Staff or any other person.

(3) Unless otherwise specified in the Rules or otherwise directed by the Secretary, when a document is filed, 5 copies shall be filed. The Secretary may require that a greater number of copies be filed.

(4) Filing After 4:30 p.m. — Documents filed after 4:30 p.m. shall be deemed to have been filed on the next day that is not a holiday.

1.5.5 Binding of Documents — **(1)** A record for a motion and an application should have a light blue backsheet.

(2) A factum or case book filed by an applicant or a moving party should be bound front and back in white covers. A factum or case book of a respondent or responding party should be bound front and back in green covers.

1.5.6. Electronic Transmission — If a document is filed with the Secretary by electronic transmission, the required number of print copies of the document shall be filed forthwith.

1.5.7 Lengthy Facsimile Transmissions — Documents filed by facsimile transmission shall not exceed 25 pages, including the cover sheet, except with the consent of the Secretary.

1.5.8 Requirement to File Electronically — The Secretary may require a party to file an electronic version of any or all documents.

1.6 Time — **(1)** When computing time under the Rules, except where a contrary intention appears:

(a) if there is a reference to a number of days between 2 events, they are counted by excluding the day on which the first event occurs and including the day on which the second event occurs;

(b) if a period of less than 7 days is prescribed, holidays are not counted; and

(c) if the time for doing an act under the Rules expires on a holiday, the act may be done on the next day that is not a holiday.

(2) Extension or Abridgement — A Panel may extend or abridge any time period prescribed under the Rules, before or after the time period expires and on any conditions that the Panel considers advisable. Prior to the commencement of a hearing, a Panel may authorize the Secretary to extend or abridge any time period under the Rules with respect to a hearing.

1.7 Parties —

1.7.1 Appearance and Representation — In any proceeding a party may be self-represented or may be represented by a representative.

1.7.2 Self-Representation — **(1)** When a party first appears before a Panel in a proceeding, the party shall file or otherwise state on the record, and keep current during the proceeding, the party's address, telephone number, facsimile number and e-mail address, as applicable.

(2) Representation by a Representative — When a person first appears as representative for a party in a proceeding before a Panel, the person shall file or otherwise state on the record, and keep current during the proceeding, the person's address, telephone number, facsimile number and e-mail address, as applicable, and the name and address of the party being represented.

1.7.3 Change in Representation by a Party — **(1)** A party who is represented by a representative may change the representative by serving on the representative and on every other party, and filing a notice of the change, giving the name, address, telephone number, facsimile number and e-mail address of the new representative, as applicable.

(2) A party who is represented by a representative may elect to act in person by serving on the representative and on every other party and filing a notice of the intention to act in person, giving the party's address, telephone number, facsimile number and e-mail address, as applicable.

1.7.4. Withdrawal by a Representative — **(1)** A representative for a party in a proceeding may withdraw as representative for the party only with leave of the Panel.

(2) A notice of motion seeking leave to withdraw as representative must be served on the party and filed, and must state all facts material to a determination of the motion, including a statement of the reasons why leave should be given. The notice must not disclose any solicitor client communication in which solicitor client privilege has not been waived.

(3) The notice of motion shall include:

(a) the client's last known address or the address for service, if different; and

(b) the client's telephone number, facsimile number and e-mail address, as applicable, unless the Panel orders otherwise.

1.8 Intervenors —

1.8.1 Motion for Leave to Intervene — **(1)** A motion for leave to intervene in a proceeding shall be made pursuant to Rule 3.

(2) A motion for leave to intervene shall set out:

(a) the title of the proceeding in which the person making the request wishes to intervene;

(b) the name and address of the person making the request;

(c) a concise statement of the scope of the proposed intervention, the issue that directly affects that person and the extent to which that person wishes to intervene; and

(d) the reasons why intervenor status should be granted.

(3) A Panel may grant leave to intervene or refuse the request on any terms and conditions that it deems appropriate.

(4) Factors — In considering a motion for leave to intervene, a Panel may consider factors such as:

(a) the nature of the matter;

(b) the issues;

(c) whether the person or company is directly affected;

(d) the likelihood that the person or company will be able to make a useful and unique contribution to the Panel's understanding of the issues;

(e) any delay or prejudice to the parties; and

(f) any other factor the Panel considers relevant.

RULES OF PROCEDURE

1.8.2 Application of the Rules — Once a person has been granted intervenor status, the Rules, including those with respect to the service and filing of documents, apply to the intervenor as if it were a party, subject to the order of a Panel.

COMMENCEMENT OF PROCEEDINGS

Rule 2 — Application and Notice of Hearing

2.1 Application by Staff — **(1)** Subject to Rule 2.4, an application by Staff pursuant to section 127 of the Act shall be made by filing a Statement of Allegations.

(2) Issuance and Service of a Notice of Hearing — Once a Statement of Allegations has been filed by Staff, the Secretary shall issue a Notice of Hearing forthwith.

(3) Staff shall serve the Statement of Allegations and the Notice of Hearing forthwith on all the parties.

2.2 Application for Review of a Decision of the Director, a Stock Exchange, a Self-Regulatory Organization or a Clearing Agency — **(1)** An application for review of a decision of the Director, a stock exchange, a self-regulatory organization or a clearing agency pursuant to section 8 or 21.7 of the Act shall be made in accordance with Rule 14.

(2) Issuance of a Notice of Hearing — In the case of an application referred to in subrule 2.2(1), the Secretary shall issue a Notice of Hearing only after all the documents required to be filed and served pursuant to Rule 14 have been filed and served.

(3) The Secretary shall issue the Notice of Hearing and the applicant shall serve it on all the parties and on any other persons as the Secretary considers necessary.

2.3 Application for a Further Decision pursuant to Subsection 9(6) of the Act or for a Revocation or Variation of a Decision pursuant to Section 144 of the Act — **(1)** An application for a further decision pursuant to subsection 9(6) of the Act or an application pursuant to section 144 of the Act for a revocation or a variation of a decision made by a Panel shall be made in accordance with Rule 15.

(2) In the case of an application referred to in subrule 2.3(1), the Secretary shall issue a Notice of Hearing only after all the documents required to be filed and served pursuant to Rule 15 have been filed and served.

(3) The applicant shall serve the Notice of Hearing on all the parties and on any other persons as the Secretary considers necessary.

2.4 Application pursuant to Section 104 and/or Section 127 of the Act — **(1)** An application made pursuant to section 104 of the Act in connection with a take-over bid or an issuer bid by an interested person as defined in subsection 89(1) of the Act, or an application pursuant to section 127 of the Act in connection with a take-over bid or an issuer bid, shall be made in accordance with Rule 16, with any modifications as the circumstances require.

(2) Issuance of a Notice of Hearing — The Secretary shall issue a Notice of Hearing for an application referred to in subrule 2.4(1) only after all the documents required to be filed and served pursuant to Rule 16 have been filed and served.

(3) The applicant shall serve the Notice of Hearing on all the parties and on any other persons or companies as the Secretary considers necessary.

2.5 Effect of a Notice of Hearing — **(1)** A proceeding commences upon the issuance of a Notice of Hearing by the Secretary.

(2) Publication on the Website and in the Bulletin — A Notice of Hearing, together with the Statement of Allegations or any other document required to be filed in connection with an application under Rule 2, shall be posted on the Website upon confirmation of service on the parties or, in any event, no later than 2 days following the issuance of the Notice of Hearing, and shall be published as soon as possible in the Bulletin.

2.6 Request for a Written Hearing — Any request to have an application heard by way of a written hearing pursuant to Rule 11 shall be specified in the application.

2.7 Notice of a Constitutional Question — If a party intends to raise a question about the constitutional validity or applicability of legislation, a regulation or a by-law made under legislation, or a common law rule, the party shall serve a notice of the constitutional question on the Attorneys General of Canada and Ontario and on the other parties, and file it as soon as the circumstances requiring a notice become known and in any event, at least 15 days before the question is to be argued.

PROCEDURES BEFORE HEARINGS

Rule 3 — Motions

3.1 Time and Date — A person who wishes to make a motion shall contact the Secretary, who may set a time and date for the hearing of the motion by a Panel.

3.2 Notice — **(1)** A motion shall be made by filing a notice of motion accompanied by a motion record, including any affidavit(s) setting out the facts to be relied upon.

(2) The person making the motion shall serve the motion on each party and file the motion, at least 10 days before the day on which the motion is to be heard.

3.3 Request for a Written Hearing — Any request to have a motion heard by way of a written hearing pursuant to Rule 11 shall be specified in the notice of motion.

3.4 Response — **(1)** A party served with a notice of motion may serve on the person making the motion and on each other party an affidavit(s) in response, at least 6 days before the day on which the motion is to be heard.

(2) The party serving any affidavit(s) in response shall file the affidavit(s) in response, within the period set out in subrule 3.4(1).

3.5 Reply — **(1)** A party served with any affidavit(s) in response to a motion may serve on the person making the response and on each other party an affidavit(s) in reply, at least 4 days before the day on which the motion is to be heard.

(2) The party serving any affidavit(s) in reply shall file the affidavit(s) in reply, within the period set out in subrule 3.5(1).

3.6 Memorandum of Fact and Law — **(1)** The party making the motion shall serve a memorandum of fact and law on each party and file it, at least 4 days before the day on which the motion is to be heard.

(2) A party served with a notice of motion and affidavit(s) shall serve a memorandum of fact and law on each party and file it, at least 2 days before the day on which the motion is to be heard.

3.7 Affidavit(s) — **(1)** Subject to subrule 3.7(2), evidence on a motion may be made by affidavit(s).

(2) Where a party files an affidavit in respect of a motion, the party shall make the deponent reasonably available for cross-examination by any adverse party.

(3) If the circumstances require, the Panel may, before the hearing, grant leave on any terms and conditions that it deems appropriate for:

    (a) oral testimony in relation to an issue raised in the notice of motion; and

    (b) the cross-examination of a deponent to an affidavit.

3.8 Where No Notice Required — The Panel may permit a party to make a motion without notice if:

    (a) the nature of the motion or the circumstances render service of a notice of motion impractical or unnecessary; or

    (b) the delay necessary to effect service might entail serious consequences.

3.9 Filing Motion Materials — If the party bringing a motion fails to comply with the time limits for the filing of motion materials set out in the Rules or directed by the Secretary, the Panel may dispose of the motion as it considers appropriate.

Rule 4 — Disclosure

(See also sections 5.4 and 8 of the SPPA and Part VI of the Act.)

4.1 Interpretation — **(1)** In Rule 4, "**document**" includes a sound recording, video-tape, film, photograph, chart, graph, map, plan, survey, book of account, and information recorded or stored by means of any device.

(2) "**Particulars**" includes:

    (a) the grounds upon which any remedy or order is being sought or opposed in the proceeding; and

    (b) a general statement of the alleged material facts upon which the party relies in the proceeding.

4.2 Disclosure Order — At any stage in a proceeding, the Panel may order that a party:

    (a) provide to another party and to the Panel any particulars that the Panel considers necessary for a full and satisfactory understanding of the subject of the proceeding; and

    (b) make any other disclosure required by this Rule, within the time limits and on any conditions that the Panel may specify.

4.3 Disclosure of Documents or Things — **(1) Requirement to Disclose** — Each party to a proceeding shall deliver to every other party copies of all documents that the party intends to produce or enter as evidence at the hearing, as soon as is reasonably practicable after the Notice of Hearing is served, and in any case, at least 20 days before the commencement of the hearing on the merits or as determined by a Panel as the circumstances require.

(2) In the case of a hearing under section 127 of the Act and subject to Rule 4.7, Staff shall make available for inspection by every other party all other documents and things that are in the possession or control of Staff that are relevant to the hearing. Staff shall provide copies, or permit the inspecting party to make copies, of these documents at the inspecting party's expense, as soon as is reasonably practicable after the Notice of Hearing is served, and in any case at least 20 days before the commencement of the hearing.

(3) Non-disclosure of a Document or Thing — A party who does not disclose a document or thing in compliance with subrule 4.3(1) may not refer to the document or thing or introduce it in evidence at the hearing without leave of the Panel, which may be on any conditions that the Panel considers just.

4.4 Disclosure Where Section 8 of the SPPA Applies — Subject to Rule 4.7, if the good character, propriety of conduct or competence of a party is an issue in a proceeding, Staff shall provide particulars of the allegations and disclose to the party against whom the allegations are made all documents and things in Staff's possession or control relevant to the allegations, as soon as is reasonably practicable after the Notice of Hearing is served, and in any case at least 20 days before the commencement of the hearing on the merits.

4.5 Witness Lists and Summaries — (1) Provision of a Witness List — A party to a proceeding shall serve every other party and file with the Secretary a list of the witnesses the party intends to call to testify on the party's behalf at the hearing, at least 10 days before the commencement of the hearing.

(2) Provision of Witness Summaries — If material matters to which a witness is to testify have not otherwise been disclosed, a party to a proceeding shall provide to every other party a summary of the evidence that the witness is expected to give at the hearing, at least 10 days before the commencement of the hearing.

(3) Content of the Witness Summary — A witness summary shall contain:

(a) the substance of the evidence of the witness;

(b) reference to any documents that the witness will refer to; and

(c) the witness's name and address or, if the witness's address is not provided, the name and address of a person through whom the witness can be contacted.

(4) Failure to Provide a Witness List or a Summary — A party who does not include a witness in the witness list or provide a summary of the evidence a witness is expected to give in accordance with subrules 4.5(1), 4.5(2) and 4.5(3), may not call that person as a witness without leave of the Panel, which may be on any conditions as the Panel considers just.

(5) Incomplete Witness Summary — A witness may not testify to material matters that were not previously disclosed without leave of the Panel, which may be on any conditions that the Panel considers just.

4.6 Expert Witness — (1) Intent to Call an Expert — A party who intends to call an expert to give evidence at a hearing shall inform the other parties of the intent to call the expert and state the issue on which the expert will be giving evidence, at least 90 days before the commencement of the hearing.

(2) Provision of an Expert's Affidavit or an Expert's Report — A party who intends to introduce evidence of an expert witness at the hearing shall either:

(a) serve the expert's report on each other party at least 60 days before the commencement of the hearing; or

(b) if granted leave by a Panel, serve an affidavit of the expert witness on each other party, at least 60 days before the commencement of the hearing. Where an affidavit of an expert witness is used, and the deponent is cross-examined prior to the hearing, the Panel reserves the right to call the expert to testify at the hearing if necessary.

(3) Provision of an Expert's Affidavit or an Expert's Report in Response — A party on whom an expert's affidavit or expert's report referred to in subrule 4.6(2) has been served and who wishes to respond with expert evidence to a matter set out in the affidavit or report, shall serve an expert's affidavit or expert's report in response on each other party, at least 30 days before the commencement of the hearing.

(4) Provision of an Expert's Affidavit or an Expert's Report in Reply — A party on whom a responding expert's affidavit or responding expert's report has been served and who wishes to reply with expert evidence to a matter set out in that affidavit or report, shall serve an expert's affidavit or expert's report in reply on each other party, at least 15 days before the commencement of the hearing.

(5) An affidavit or report referred to in subrules 4.6(2), 4.6(3) and 4.6(4) shall include:

(a) the name, address and qualifications of the expert;

(b) the substance of the expert's evidence; and

(c) a list of any documents that the expert will refer to.

(6) Failure to Advise of Intent to Call an Expert — A party who fails to comply with subrule 4.6(1) may not call the expert as a witness without leave of the Panel, which may be on any conditions that the Panel considers just.

(7) Failure to Provide an Expert's Affidavit or Expert's Report — A party who fails to comply with subrules 4.6(2), 4.6(3) and 4.6(4) may not file the expert's affidavit or report without leave of the Panel, which may be on any conditions that the Panel considers just.

4.7 Request to Issue a Summons — (1) At the request of a party, a summons to a witness may be issued pursuant to section 12 of the SPPA.

(2) The issuance of or a refusal to issue a summons may be reviewed by a Panel by motion filed in accordance with Rule 3.

(3) Once a summons is served, it is effective for the duration of the hearing as long as the witness is advised of the adjourned dates.

Rule 5 — Public Access to Documents

5.1 Public Documents — Subject to Rule 5.2 and subrule 10.9(3), documents required to be filed or received in evidence in proceedings shall be available to the public.

5.2 Request Regarding Confidentiality — **(1)** At the request of a party or person, the Panel may order that any document filed with the Secretary or any document received in evidence or transcript of the proceeding be kept confidential pursuant to section 9 of the SPPA.

(2) A party or person who makes a request pursuant to subrule 5.2(1) shall advise the Panel of the reasons for the request.

(3) The Panel may, if it is of the opinion that there are valid reasons for restricting access to a document, declare the document confidential and make such other orders as it deems appropriate.

Rule 6 — Pre-Hearing Conferences

(See also section 5.3 of the SPPA.)

6.1 Requesting a Pre-Hearing Conference — **(1)** A Panel may direct the parties in a proceeding to participate in a pre-hearing conference at any stage of the proceeding.

(2) Any party may request a pre-hearing conference by filing a request.

6.2 Issues at a Pre-Hearing Conference — At a pre-hearing conference, a Panel may:

(a) create a timetable for the scheduling of the hearing;

(b) create a timetable for any pre-hearing matters, including the disclosure of documents or things and the delivery of witness lists and summaries and experts' affidavits or reports;

(c) amend an existing timetable;

(d) schedule any preliminary motions;

(e) consider with the parties:

(i) agreed upon facts or evidence; and

(ii) the resolution of any or all of the allegations in the proceeding, subject to Rule 6.8;

(f) make procedural orders with respect to:

(i) the simplification or clarification of issues in the proceeding;

(ii) the disclosure of documents or things; and

(iii) any other matter that may assist in the just and most expeditious disposition of the proceeding.

6.3 Notice — **(1)** The Secretary shall give notice of a pre-hearing conference to the parties and to any other persons as the Panel directs.

(2) The notice shall include:

(a) the date, time, place and purpose of the pre-hearing conference;

(b) any direction of the Panel regarding the exchange or filing of documents or pre-hearing submissions as prescribed by Rule 6.4 and, if so, the issues to be addressed and the date or dates on or before which the documents or pre-hearing submissions must be exchanged and filed;

(c) a direction as to whether parties are required to attend in person and,

(i) if so, that they may be accompanied by a representative; or

(ii) if not, that they may be represented by a representative who has the authority to make agreements and undertakings on their behalf;

(d) a statement that if a party does not attend (in person or by a representative, as required) at the pre-hearing conference, the Panel may proceed in the absence of that party; and

(e) a statement that any order made by the Panel at the pre-hearing conference will be binding on all the parties.

6.4 Filing and Exchange of Documents for a Pre-Hearing Conference — The parties shall serve and file a pre-hearing conference form (see Appendix A of the Rules). All documents intended to be used at the pre-hearing conference that may be of assistance shall be exchanged among the parties and be made available to the Panel.

6.5 Oral or Electronic — A pre-hearing conference may be held in person or by way of an electronic hearing, as the Panel may direct.

6.6 Public Access — **(1)** In order to encourage a full and frank exchange of views, a pre-hearing conference shall be confidential and conducted in private.

(2) Any pre-hearing submissions referred to in Rule 6.4 shall not be made available to the public.

6.7 Orders — A Panel that presides at a pre-hearing conference may make such order as it considers necessary or advisable with respect to the conduct of the proceeding, including an order relating to the matters set out in subrule 6.2(f).

6.8 Disqualification — A Panel that presides at a pre-hearing conference at which the parties attempt to settle any or all of the allegations, as contemplated in subrule 6.2(e)(ii), shall not preside at the hearing on the merits unless the parties consent.

HEARINGS

Rule 7 — Failure to Participate at the Hearing and Withdrawal

(See also sections 6 and 7 of the SPPA.)

7.1 Failure to Participate — If a Notice of Hearing has been served on any party and the party does not attend the hearing, the Panel may proceed in the party's absence and that party is not entitled to any further notice in the proceeding.

7.2 Withdrawal — **(1)** A person or company that has filed an application under Rule 2 or a request for leave to intervene under Rule 1.8.1 may withdraw the application or request at any time before a final determination of the application or request by a Panel.

(2) The person or company referred to in subrule 7.2(1) shall serve a notice of withdrawal on each party and on each intervenor and file the notice.

(3) In the case of a withdrawal of a Statement of Allegations or of an application under Rule 2, the notice of withdrawal shall be posted on the Website and published in the Bulletin.

7.3 Discontinuance of Intervention — **(1)** An intervenor may discontinue the intervention at any time before a final determination of the application by the Panel on any terms that the Panel deems appropriate.

(2) The intervenor referred to in subrule 7.3(1) shall serve a notice of discontinuance on each party and on each intervenor and file the notice.

Rule 8 — Public Access to Hearings

8.1 Open to the Public Except under Certain Conditions — Subject to Rule 8.2, a hearing shall be open to the public, except when having regard to the circumstances, the Panel is of the opinion that intimate financial, personal or other matters may be disclosed at the hearing and that the desirability of avoiding that disclosure in the interests of any person affected or in the public interest outweighs the desirability of adhering to the principle that hearings be open to the public pursuant to section 9 of the SPPA.

8.2 In Camera Hearing — If a party wishes to have a hearing held in camera, the party shall make a request at the commencement of the hearing before the Panel pursuant to section 9 of the SPPA. The Panel will make a decision on whether or not to hold the hearing or a portion of the hearing in camera, based on the facts and circumstances of each case.

8.3 Request to Make a Visual or Audio Recording — **(1)** Any request to make a visual or audio recording of a hearing should be made in writing to the Secretary at least 5 days before the day of the hearing on which the audio or visual recording is to be made.

(2) Media personnel or any person permitted to make a visual or audio recording under subrule 8.3(1) will be subject to the direction of the chair of the Panel.

(3) Media personnel shall not engage in any activity at the hearing that may disrupt the hearing. Disruptive activities include:

(a) interviewing persons in the hearing room at any time or in the vicinity of the hearing room;

(b) television lights, cables and other equipment which, when in use, could distract the persons in the hearing room;

(c) electronic flash for still photography;

(d) movement of persons or equipment while the hearing is in session; and

(e) any other behaviour that disrupts or detracts from the process of the hearing.

Rule 9 — Adjournments

9.1 How and When to Request an Adjournment — **(1)** As soon as a party decides to request an adjournment, the party shall advise the other parties and the Secretary.

(2) With Consent — If the other parties consent to the adjournment and the requesting party files a written request certifying that it is made on consent, the Panel may:

(a) refuse the request;

(b) reschedule the hearing without a hearing on the request; or

(c) require a hearing on the request.

(3) Without Consent — If the parties do not consent to a request for adjournment, the requesting party shall serve and file a notice of motion on the other parties as soon as possible. The notice of motion shall set out:

(a) the reasons for the adjournment;

(b) the length of time requested for the adjournment; and

(c) the earliest available dates for that party to make submissions on the motion.

(4) If the parties do not consent, the requesting party and/or the party's representative shall appear before the Panel to request the adjournment orally and shall be prepared to proceed if the adjournment is denied.

(5) After considering the submissions of the parties, the Panel may grant or deny the adjournment on any terms that it considers appropriate.

9.2 Factors Considered — In deciding whether to grant an adjournment, the Panel shall consider all relevant factors, including, but not restricted to, the following:

(a) whether an adjournment would be in the public interest;

(b) whether all parties consent to the request;

(c) whether granting or denying the adjournment would prejudice any party;

(d) the amount of notice of the hearing date that the requesting party received;

(e) the number of any previous adjournment requests made and by whom;

(f) the reasons provided to support the adjournment request;

(g) the cost to the Commission and to the other parties for rescheduling the hearing;

(h) evidence that the party made reasonable efforts to avoid the need for the adjournment; and

(i) whether the adjournment is necessary to provide an opportunity for a fair hearing.

Rule 10 — Conduct of Oral Hearings

(See also the French Language Services Act and sections 5.2 and 15 of the SPPA.)

10.1 Oral Hearings — An oral hearing shall be conducted in accordance with the provisions set out in the SPPA.

10.2 Electronic Hearings — A hearing may be conducted by way of an electronic hearing, unless a party objects as provided by subsection 5.2(2) of the SPPA.

10.3 Video-Conferencing — A hearing may be conducted by video-conferencing or by other similar means approved by the Secretary.

10.4 Hearings Conducted in French and in English — **(1)** A hearing may be conducted in English or in French or in both English and French.

(2) A party or intervenor requesting a proceeding to be conducted in French or in both English and French must notify the Secretary's Office in writing of their choice as soon as possible, and in any event, at least thirty (30) days before a hearing.

(3) Hearings held in French or in both English and French are conducted in accordance with the Commission's Practice Guideline for French Hearings.

10.5 Interpreters for Other Languages — If a party requires an interpreter for a language other than English or French, the party shall notify the Secretary as soon as possible, and in any event, at least 30 days before the hearing, and the Secretary will arrange for an interpreter at the requesting party's expense.

10.6 Special Needs of Parties or Witnesses — Parties should notify the Secretary as soon as possible, and in any event at least 30 days before the hearing, of any special needs of parties or their witnesses for the hearing.

10.7 Affirmation of a Witness — Oral examination of witnesses shall be conducted under affirmation or oath that their evidence will be true.

10.8 Transcripts of Proceedings — Official transcripts of proceedings are prepared by a court reporting services agency retained by the Commission. Parties who wish to obtain a copy of the transcripts may do so directly from the court reporting services agency at their own expense.

10.9 Final Arguments and Submissions — **(1)** Except in the case of a written hearing where parties shall file final written submissions pursuant to Rule 11.6, a party may file and serve on every other party a factum consisting of a concise argument stating the facts and law relied upon by the party.

(2) Final submissions may include:

(a) facts or quotations from the oral evidence, referenced to the transcript volume and page number if a transcript is available; or

(b) facts or quotations from documentation filed as exhibits, referenced to the exhibit and page number; and

(c) a concise summary of the law.

(3) Final arguments and submissions shall not be made public until the commencement of the hearing of the submissions.

(4) A party referring to any court decision, legal article or authority shall provide a copy for each member of the Panel and each party.

(5) Parties may include in their argument the details of the specific order that they request.

(6) Any party may file a draft order within the time permitted by the Panel, but shall do so only if they serve a copy on all other parties.

Rule 11 — Written Hearings

(See also subsections 5.1(1), 6(4), 7(2) and 9(1.1) of the SPPA.)

11.1 Application — **(1)** This Rule does not apply to the admissibility, at an oral hearing, of written evidence admissible under section 15 of the SPPA.

(2) Nothing in this Rule precludes a Panel from directing that further submissions be filed in respect of a matter arising in a hearing. If the Panel so directs, the parties may also be given an opportunity to make oral submissions on a matter, which may be time-limited by the Panel.

11.2 Filing — Where this Rule requires that documentation be filed with the Secretary, 5 copies shall be filed, except in the case of a notice of an objection to a written hearing which shall be filed in duplicate.

11.3 Definition of an Applicant — In this Rule, **"applicant"** means the party who instituted the proceeding or the person or company who is bringing a motion.

11.4 When to Hold a Written Hearing — **(1)** A Panel may conduct any proceeding or part of a proceeding, including motions, by means of a written hearing.

(2) Written hearings may be held in the following circumstances unless a party objects, as provided by subsection 5.1(2) of the SPPA:

(a) motions relating to procedural issues;

(b) hearings on agreed facts; and

(c) any other motions or applications that the Panel considers are appropriate for a written hearing.

11.5 Converting From or to a Written Hearing — **(1)** A Panel may:

(a) continue a written hearing as an oral hearing;

(b) subject to subsection 5.2(2) of the SPPA, continue a written hearing as an electronic hearing; or

(c) subject to subsection 5.1(2) of the SPPA, continue an oral hearing or an electronic hearing as a written hearing.

(2) If a Panel decides to continue a written hearing as an oral or electronic hearing or an oral or electronic hearing as a written hearing, it shall notify the parties of its decision and may provide directions as to the holding of that hearing. Any procedures set down in the Rules for such a hearing shall apply.

11.6 Submissions and Supporting Documents — **(1)** Within 10 days after receiving notice that a hearing will be in writing, the applicant shall serve on all other parties and file written submissions setting out:

(a) the grounds on which the request for the remedy or order is made;

(b) a statement of the facts and evidence relied on in support of the remedy or order requested; and

(c) any law relied on in support of the remedy or order requested.

(2) A Panel may require the applicant to provide further information, which the applicant shall serve on every other party.

11.7 Objection to a Written Hearing — **(1)** A party who objects to a hearing being held as a written hearing shall file and serve a notice of objection setting out the reasons for the objection, within 5 days after receiving notice of the written hearing.

(2) A notice of objection shall set out the reasons for the objection in the submissions relating to the matter and be accompanied by a statement of the facts, any evidence and any law relied on in support of the objection.

11.8 Response to an Objection — **(1)** If a party wishes to respond, the party shall do so by serving the written response on every other party and filing it within 7 days after the notice of objection has been served on the party.

(2) The response shall set out the party's submissions and be accompanied by a statement of the facts, any evidence and any law relied on in support of the response.

11.9 Decision — **(1)** Upon consideration of the written record, the Panel may render a decision as to whether the matter shall be heard at an oral or a written hearing.

Rule 12 — Settlement Agreements

12.1 Purpose of Settlement Conference — **(1)** The purpose of a settlement conference is to provide the parties with the opportunity, prior to proceeding to a hearing under this Rule to approve a settlement agreement, to make confidential submissions on a proposed settlement to a Panel in order to obtain guidance on whether the terms of the proposed settlement would, in the view of the Panel, be in the public interest.

(2) At least one settlement conference shall be held before a hearing to approve the settlement agreement.

12.2 Application for a Settlement Conference — **(1)** An application for a settlement conference shall be filed jointly by the parties to the proposed settlement no later than 5 days before the settlement conference.

(2) The application shall be accompanied by:

(a) the consent in writing of the parties to participate in the settlement conference;

(b) an agreement concerning the confidentiality of the settlement discussions and any document or thing presented at the settlement conference; and

(c) a draft of the proposed settlement agreement or a joint memorandum setting out the terms of the proposed settlement between the parties.

12.3 Notice of Settlement Conference — **(1)** The Secretary shall issue a Notice of Settlement Conference for an application referred to in subrule 12.2(1) only after all the documents required to be filed pursuant to subrule 12.2(2) have been filed.

(2) The Notice of Settlement Conference shall be issued only to the parties to the settlement conference and shall not be published or otherwise made available to the public.

12.4 Oral or Electronic — A settlement conference may be held in person or by way of electronic hearing, as the Panel may direct.

12.5 In Camera Proceeding — **(1)** The settlement conference shall be held in camera and no transcript or other record of the proceeding shall be made unless the parties to the settlement request otherwise, except that the Panel may make such record of the conference as it deems necessary for its own record and use.

(2) Rule 5.1 shall not apply to any document or thing filed under Rule 12.1 or presented at a settlement conference or any record made by the Panel pursuant to subrule 12.5(1), and any such document or thing shall be kept confidential pursuant to Rule 9 of the SPPA and shall not be made available to the public.

12.6 No Communication to Panel Hearing the Merits — In the event that the matter subject to the settlement conference proceeds to a hearing on the merits, the Panel presiding at the settlement conference shall not participate in the hearing on the merits and no communication made at the settlement conference shall be disclosed to the Panel hearing the matter on the merits.

12.7 Application for a Hearing to Approve the Settlement — **(1)** An application for a hearing to approve a settlement shall be filed jointly by the parties to the settlement no later than 2 days before the hearing.

(2) The application shall be accompanied by:

(a) a draft order;

(b) the respondent's consent to the order; and

(c) the settlement agreement signed by the settling parties.

12.8 Notice of Settlement Hearing — The Secretary shall issue a Notice of Hearing for an application referred to in subrule 12.7(1) only after all the documents required to be filed pursuant to subrule 12.7(2) have been filed.

12.9 Settlement Hearing Panel — The Panel presiding at the hearing to approve the settlement shall be one or more of the members of the Panel that presided at the settlement conference.

12.10 Public Settlement Hearing — **(1)** A hearing to approve an application under subrule 12.7(1) shall be open to the public.

(2) The Panel may issue oral or written reasons if it deems it appropriate to do so.

12.11 Publication of Settlement Agreement When Approved — The order approving the settlement agreement, the settlement agreement, and the Panel's reasons, if any, shall be posted on the Commission's website and in the *Bulletin* forthwith following approval of the settlement agreement by the Panel, unless otherwise ordered by the Panel.

Rule 13 — Simultaneous Hearing with Other Securities Administrators

(See also subsection 2(5) of the Act.)

13.1 Request for Simultaneous Hearing — **(1)** At the request of a party to a proceeding or on the Commission's own initiative, the Commission may hold a hearing in or outside Ontario in conjunction with any other body empowered by statute to administer or regulate trading in securities.

(2) A request for a simultaneous hearing shall be made in writing and state the reasons for a simultaneous hearing.

(3) Invitation to Federal Corporations Branch — If the issue that is the subject of the simultaneous hearing is also of interest to the Director, Corporations Branch, of the Federal Department of Consumer and Corporate Affairs in administering the *Canada Business Corporations Act*, R.S.C. 1985, c. C-44, as amended, the applicant may also request that the federal officer be invited to join the hearing.

(4) Factors in Deciding Whether to Hold a Simultaneous Hearing — When deciding whether to hold a simultaneous hearing, the Commission may take into account any circumstances it considers relevant, which may include whether:

(a) the issues raised through the application and the evidence and arguments to be presented are likely to be substantially the same, notwithstanding any apparent difference in the form of the several applications or the specific legislation in each jurisdiction;

(b) there is an urgent business reason for holding one simultaneous hearing rather than multiple hearings; or

(c) the matter in issue is a novel one and it is in the public interest that securities administrators strive to achieve consistency in their decision-making on the matter.

(5) Factors in Deciding Where to Hold a Simultaneous Hearing — When deciding where to hold a simultaneous hearing, the Commission may take into account any circumstances it considers relevant, which may include:

(a) the preponderance of convenience to the majority of interested parties, taking into account where the majority of the parties reside or have their principal places of business and where witnesses reside; and

(b) where it can be determined that it is in the public interest to do so.

13.2 Payment of Expenses — **(1)** If a party requests that a simultaneous hearing be held outside Ontario, the Commission may, despite any general public interest perceived in the holding of a simultaneous hearing, before and as a condition precedent to its granting the request, require that party to undertake to pay the additional costs incurred by the Commission.

(2) These costs include travel and related expenses incurred by the Panel, Staff, witness fees and expenses.

Rule 14 — Review of a Decision of the Director, a Stock Exchange, a Self-Regulatory Organization or a Clearing Agency

(See also sections 8 and 21.7 of the Act.)

14.1 Application — In Rule 14, **"decision"** means any direction, decision, order, ruling or other requirement made by the Director, a stock exchange, a self-regulatory organization or a clearing agency.

14.2 Application for a Hearing and Review — **(1)** An application for a hearing and review of a decision pursuant to section 8 or 21.7 of the Act shall:

(a) identify the decision in respect of which the hearing and review is being sought;

(b) state the interest in the decision of the party filing the request;

(c) state in summary form the alleged errors in the decision and the reasons for requesting the hearing and review; and

(d) state the desired outcome.

14.3 Record — **(1)** The party requesting a hearing and review of a decision shall obtain from the Director, stock exchange, self-regulatory organization or clearing agency a record of the subject proceeding and file it.

(2) The record of the proceeding shall include:

(a) the application or other document by which the proceeding was commenced;

(b) the Notice of Hearing;

(c) any interim orders made in the proceeding;

(d) any documentary evidence filed in the proceeding, subject to any limitation expressly imposed by any statute, regulation or rules on the extent to which, or the purpose for which, any such documents may be used in any proceeding;

(e) a copy of any other documents relevant in the proceeding that are referred to in the party's statement of fact and law;

(f) any transcript of the oral evidence given at the hearing; and

(g) the decision that is the subject of the request for a hearing and review and the reasons therefore, if reasons were given.

(3) Omission of Documents from Record — Despite subrule 14.3(1), any of the documents may be omitted from the record if all parties consent, and the Panel agrees or the Panel otherwise directs.

(4) Where Record Unavailable — In the circumstance where no record is available, the parties shall advise the Panel.

14.4 Service and Filing — **(1)** An application for a hearing and review of a decision shall be served by the applicant on every other party to the original proceeding and filed.

(2) The party requesting a hearing and review shall provide a copy of the record of the proceeding to any other party that requests a copy of the record.

(3) The party requesting a hearing and review shall perfect the application by complying with Rule 14.3 and subrules 14.4(1) and 14.4(2):

    (a) if no transcript of evidence is required for the review, within 30 days after filing the request; or

    (b) if a transcript of evidence is required for the review, within 60 days after receiving notice that the evidence has been transcribed.

(4) If the party requesting a hearing and review has not complied with subrule 14.4(3), the Secretary may serve a notice on the requester that the request may be dismissed for delay unless it is perfected within 10 days after service of the notice.

(5) Dismissal Where Default not Cured — If the party requesting a hearing and review does not cure the default within 10 days after the service of the notice under subrule 14.4(4), or within a longer period allowed by a Panel, a Panel may make an order dismissing the request and serve the order on the requester.

(6) Record in Response — A party served with an application for a hearing and review and record may serve a record in response on the person making the application and on each other party, at least 15 days before the day on which the application is to be heard.

(7) Record in Reply — A party served with a record in response to an application for hearing and review may serve a record in reply on the person making the response and on each other party an affidavit(s) in reply, at least 5 days before the day on which the application is to be heard.

14.5 New Evidence — If a party proposes to introduce new evidence at the hearing and review, that party shall, at least 10 days before the hearing and review, advise every other party as to the substance of the new evidence and shall deliver to every other party copies of all new documents that the party will rely on at the hearing and review.

14.6 Order Dispensing with Transcripts — The Panel may direct that a transcript of the oral evidence be dispensed with, if the Panel is of the opinion that a transcript of the oral evidence taken at the original hearing is unnecessary to deal effectively with the hearing and review, or for any reason the Panel considers appropriate.

14.7 Stay of a Decision — **(1)** Before the hearing and review, the party requesting the hearing and review may apply to the Panel for an order staying the original decision until the hearing and review is concluded.

(2) The party shall make the application in writing on notice to all the parties and the application shall state the reasons why a stay is required.

14.8 Setting Down for a Hearing — Once the record of the proceeding is perfected in accordance with subrule 14.4(3), the Secretary shall give notice of the time and place for the hearing and review.

14.9 Statement of Fact and Law in an Oral Hearing — **(1)** The party requesting a hearing and review shall, if an oral hearing is to be held, serve on every other party and file the memorandum of fact and law being relied upon, at least 30 days before the date of the hearing and review.

(2) Each other party to the hearing and review shall serve on every other party and file a statement of the points to be argued and the memorandum of fact and law being relied upon by it at least 15 days before the date of the hearing and review.

Rule 15 — Further Decision pursuant to Subsection 9(6) of the Act or Revocation or Variation of a Decision pursuant to Section 144 of the Act

15.1 Application — **(1)** An application for a further decision pursuant to subsection 9(6) of the Act or an application pursuant to section 144 of the Act for a revocation or a variation of a decision made by a Panel shall:

    (a) identify the decision in respect of which the request is being made;

    (b) state the interest in the decision of the party filing the request;

    (c) state the factual and legal grounds for the request; and

    (d) state the desired outcome.

(2) An application for a further decision or an application for a revocation or variation of a decision made by a Panel shall be served by the applicant on every other party to the original proceeding and filed.

15.2 New Evidence — If a party proposes to introduce new evidence at the hearing of the application for a further decision or for a revocation or variation of a decision, the party shall, at least 10 days before the hearing, advise every other party as to the substance of the new evidence and shall deliver to every other party copies of all new documents that the party will rely on at the hearing.

15.3 Whether or Not to Hold an Oral Hearing — **(1)** UUpon reviewing the application, a Panel may, on the basis of the written record:

    (a) decide to grant the application;

RULES OF PROCEDURE

(b) refuse to grant the application; or

(c) decide to hold an oral hearing to consider the application.

15.4 Statement of Fact and Law in an Oral Hearing — **(1)** The party requesting a further decision or a revocation or a variation of a decision made by a Panel shall, if an oral hearing is to be held, serve on every other party and file a statement of the points to be argued and the memorandum of fact and law being relied upon by it at least 10 days before the date of the hearing.

(2) Each other party to a hearing shall, if an oral hearing is to be held, serve on every other party and file a statement of the points to be argued and the memorandum of fact and law being relied upon by it at least 5 days before the date of the hearing.

15.5 Written Hearing — If the parties consent to a further decision, revocation or variation of a decision made by a Panel, the matter may be heard in writing.

Rule 16 — Application pursuant to Section 104 and/or Section 127 of the Act

16.1 Application — **(1)** An application made pursuant to section 104 of the Act in connection with a take-over bid or an issuer bid by an interested person as defined in subsection 89(1) of the Act, or an application made pursuant to section 127 of the Act in connection with a take-over bid or an issuer bid, shall be made by serving it on every other party and on the Manager of Take-Over Bids, Issuer Bids and Mergers and Acquisitions Transactions and filing it.

(2) An application shall be accompanied by a memorandum of fact and law and any affidavit(s) as appropriate setting out the facts to be relied upon.

16.2 Setting Down for a Hearing — Once all the documents for the application have been filed in accordance with Rule 16.1, the Secretary shall establish the schedule for the filing of a response and a reply and give notice of the time and place for the hearing of the application.

16.3 Response — A party served with an application may serve on the person making the application and on each other party a memorandum of fact and law and any affidavit(s), and file them in accordance with the schedule established by the Secretary.

16.4 Reply — A party served with a memorandum of fact and law and any affidavit(s) in response to an application may serve on the person making the response and on each other party a memorandum of fact and law and any affidavit(s) in reply, and file them in accordance with the schedule established by the Secretary.

16.5 Request for Leave to Intervene — A request for leave to intervene in an application relating to a take-over bid or an issuer bid shall be made by serving it on each of the parties and filing it in accordance with Rule 1.8.1.

DECISIONS

Rule 17 — Oral and Written Decisions

(See also section 17 of the SPPA.)

17.1 Issuance of Decisions — **(1)** A Panel may reserve its decision or may give its decision orally at the end of the hearing.

(2) Written Final Decisions — A Panel shall issue a final written decision, which shall be the official decision.

(3) Discrepancy — If there is a discrepancy between an oral decision rendered at the hearing and the written decision, the written decision shall prevail.

17.2 Service of Decisions and Reasons — **(1)** The Secretary shall send to all parties to the proceeding a copy of the Panel's final decision, including any reasons that have been given.

(2) Publication — A decision shall be published on the Website and in the Bulletin, unless a Panel orders that it shall remain confidential.

17.3 Sanctions Hearing — **(1)** Unless the parties to a proceeding agree to the contrary, a separate hearing shall be held to determine the matter of sanctions and costs.

(2) Following the issuance of the reasons for the decision on the merits, the Secretary shall set a date for the sanctions hearing if such a hearing is necessary.

(3) Submissions by Staff — Staff shall file submissions regarding the matter of sanctions and costs at least 10 days before the sanctions hearing, unless the Panel provides otherwise.

(4) Responding Submissions — A respondent shall file submissions regarding the matter of sanctions and costs at least 5 days before the sanctions hearing, unless the Panel provides otherwise.

(5) Reply Submissions — Staff shall file any reply submissions regarding the matter of sanctions and costs at least 2 days before the sanctions hearing, unless the Panel provides otherwise.

COSTS AWARDS

Rule 18 — Costs

(See also section 127.1 of the Act.)

18.1 Request for an Award of Costs — **(1)** A Panel may award costs against a respondent at the request of Staff after having considered any submissions from the parties.

(2) Content of a Request for an Award of Costs — A request for costs by Staff shall be made in a written motion and served on the respondent and it shall contain the following information:

(a) an explanation of the basis of the claim;

(b) a summary statement of hours and fees for each lawyer and each professional that worked on the file, supported by time dockets setting out the hourly wage for the individual and a description of the work performed;

(c) a summary statement of disbursements for each lawyer or professional, supported by corresponding invoices and receipts. If invoices or receipts are not obtainable, the Commission may accept a written record of disbursements and associated dates; and

(d) an affidavit declaring that all the information contained in the dockets and the summary statement of disbursements are true and accurate, and all disbursements were incurred directly and necessarily as a result of the investigation or proceeding.

(3) Time Limit for Making a Request for an Award of Costs — A request for an award of costs on a motion or on the main proceeding shall be served by Staff on the respondent no later than 30 days after the issuance of a final order or decision of a Panel on the main proceeding.

(4) Response — The respondent served with a request for an award of costs may serve on Staff a response setting out any objections to the request, within 15 days of the request.

(5) Reply — After receiving a response, Staff may serve a reply to the respondent's objections within 5 days of receiving the response.

(6) General Principle — A Panel has the discretion to shorten or extend any of these time limits, and may consider the timeliness of any request for costs in determining the amount to be awarded.

18.2 Factors Considered When Awarding Costs — In exercising its discretion under section 127.1 of the Act to award costs against a person or company, a Panel may consider the following factors:

(a) whether the respondent failed to comply with a procedural order or direction of the Panel;

(b) the complexity of the proceeding;

(c) the importance of the issues;

(d) the conduct of Staff during the investigation and during the proceeding, and how Staff's conduct contributed to the costs of the investigation and the proceeding;

(e) whether the respondent contributed to a shorter, more efficient, and more effective hearing, or whether the conduct of the respondent unnecessarily lengthened the duration of the proceeding;

(f) whether any step in the proceeding was taken in an improper, vexatious, unreasonable, or negligent fashion or in error;

(g) whether the respondent participated in the proceeding in a way that helped the Commission understand the issues before it;

(h) whether the respondent participated in a responsible, informed and well-prepared manner;

(i) whether the respondent co-operated with Staff and disclosed all relevant information;

(j) whether the respondent denied or refused to admit anything that should have been admitted; or

(k) any other factors the Panel considers relevant.

18.3 Payment of Investigation Costs — **(1)** If the Panel orders under subsection 127.1(1) of the Act that the costs of the investigation be paid by a person or company whose affairs were the subject of an investigation, the costs awarded may include the following:

(a) the costs of Staff involved in the investigation, based on the time spent on the investigation by each member of Staff and the applicable hourly rate as prescribed by subrule 18.3(3);

(b) the actual amount of the fees and disbursements paid to a person appointed or engaged under sections 5, 11 or 12 of the Act;

(c) the actual amount of the witness examination costs;

(d) the actual amount of the court reporter's fees;

(e) the actual cost of the transcripts of examinations of individuals during the course of the investigation;

(f) the actual costs of experts;

(g) the disbursements and the incidental costs incurred in respect of the investigation; and

(h) any other costs the Panel considers relevant.

RULES OF PROCEDURE

(2) Payment of Hearing Costs — If the Panel orders under subsection 127.1(2) of the Act that the costs of, or related to, a hearing be paid by a person or company whose affairs were the subject of a hearing, the costs awarded may include the following:

(a) the costs of Staff involved in the hearing, based on the time spent on the hearing by each member of Staff and the applicable hourly rate as prescribed by subrule 18.3(3);

(b) the actual amount of the fees and disbursements paid to a person appointed or engaged under sections 5, 11 or 12 of the Act;

(c) the reasonable costs of witnesses, other than a witness referred to in sub-paragraph (b) required to attend at the hearing;

(d) the reasonable costs for the services of a lawyer acting as counsel with or for Staff;

(e) the costs to the Commission to administer the hearing, including fees paid to the court reporter, fees for transcripts, and disbursements required to conduct a hearing;

(f) the reasonable costs incurred for each expert or person engaged by Staff; and

(g) any other costs the Panel considers relevant.

(3) Publication of Costs in Staff Notice — The specific hourly rates for the costs categories, which can be determined a priori, set out in subrules 18.3(1) and 18.3(2) shall be published from time to time as a Staff Notice and will be posted on the Website and published in the Bulletin.

Appendix A — Pre-Hearing Conference Form

The parties may submit this form pursuant to Rule 6.4. In the alternative, the parties may submit such other written submissions as they deem appropriate.

In the Matter of the Securities Act R.S.O. 1990, c. S.5, as Amended
and
In the Matter of [Insert Style of Cause]
DATE OF PRE-HEARING:
PRE-HEARING CONFERENCE SUBMISSIONS OF:
(insert name of Party)
REPRESENTATIVE:

I. — Introductory Matters

A. — Procedural History

1. Notice of Hearing and Statement of Allegations — Date of Issue:

2. Date(s) of Alleged Conduct:

3. Date of Hearing:

4. Interim Orders:

    a) Temporary Cease Trade Order: (Date of Order)

      Provide Details:

    b) Freeze Order: (Date of Order)

      Provide Details:

B. — Unrepresented Respondents

1. Are any of the Respondents in this proceeding unrepresented?

2. Has Staff provided any unrepresented Respondent(s) with a copy of the *OSC Guide to Enforcement Proceedings and OSC Frequently Asked Questions About Hearings*?

    Provide Details:

3. Has Staff informed any unrepresented Respondent(s) about the OSC Litigation Assistance Program?

    Provide Details:

4. Does the Respondent intend to apply for the OSC Litigation Assistance Program?

C. — Settlement Discussions

1. Have the parties discussed settlement?

    Provide Details:

2. Is there a reasonable prospect of this matter settling?

    Provide Details:

D. — Disclosure (Rule 4)

1. Has Staff made disclosure to the Respondent in accordance with subrules 4.3(1) and (2)?

    Provide Details:

2. Has the Respondent made disclosure to Staff in accordance with subrule 4.3(1)?

    Provide Details:

3. Is further disclosure requested?

    Provide Details:

4. Are there any issues in respect of a third party and disclosure?

    Provide Details:

II. — Pre-Hearing Matters

A. — Severance

1. Do you expect to bring a motion to sever the hearing of certain Respondents?

    Provide Details:

B. — Disclosure

1. Do you expect to bring a motion respecting disclosure?

   Provide Details:

C. — Other

1. Do you expect to bring any other motions?

   Provide Details:

III. — The Hearing

A. — Procedure on Hearing

1. Will you be requesting that the hearing, or any part of the hearing, be conducted electronically? (Rule 10.2)

   Provide Details:

2. Will you be requesting that the hearing, or any part of the hearing, be conducted in writing? (Rule 11)

   Provide Details:

B. — Hearing Brief re: Documents

1. Have you prepared or will you be preparing a Hearing Brief?

   Provide Details:

The Hearing Brief has been delivered to the other parties:

   Provide Details:

OR

The Hearing Brief will be delivered by: ....

   Provide Details:

IV. — Evidentiary Matters

A. — Expert Evidence

1. Will you be tendering the opinion evidence of a duly qualified expert for admission?

By Staff:

By the Respondent:

2. Upon what issue(s) will you be tendering such evidence?

   Provide Details:

3. Will you be challenging the qualification of the expert?

   Provide Details:

4. Will you be filing an expert's report? When?

   Provide Details:

5. Will you be challenging the admissibility of the report?

   Provide Details:

B. — Privilege

1. Will you be asserting any claim of privilege in respect of any evidence proposed for introduction:

   Provide Details:

C. — Procedural Issues

1. Will you be asking the Commission to rule on any procedural matters?

   Provide Details:

2. Are you making any admissions?

   Provide Details:

D. — Documents

1. Has Staff prepared a brief of documents?

   Provide Details:

2. Does the Respondent object to the admissibility of any of the documents?

   Provide Details:

3. Has the Respondent prepared a brief of documents?

    Provide Details:

4. Does Staff object to the admissibility of any of the documents?

    Provide Details:

V. — Length and Scheduling of Proceedings

1. — Length of Hearing and Scheduling of Proceeding

Has the hearing been scheduled? If so, when?

If not, what is the anticipated length of time needed to deal with pre-hearing matters?

For Staff:

For the Respondent:

2. — Witnesses

Please list the witnesses you will be calling:

Witness Name	Estimated Time for Examination — in-Chief	Estimated Time for Cross-Examination (to be completed at pre-hearing)

Dated: At Toronto this .... day of ...., 2009

Final Rules: (2009) 32 O.S.C.B. 1991; Request for Comments: (2007) 30 O.S.C.B. 4339.

Amendment to Rules: (2010) 33 O.S.C.B. 6653 and 8017; Request for Comments: (2010) 33 O.S.C.B. 2096.

Amendment to Rules: (2012) 35 O.S.C.B. 10071.

Amendment to Rules: (2014) 37 O.S.C.B. 4168

RULES OF PROCEDURE

PROCEDURES FOR OPPORTUNITIES TO BE HEARD BEFORE DIRECTOR'S DECISIONS ON REGISTRATION MATTERS

1. — When These Procedures Are Used

These Procedures apply wherever section 31 of the *Securities Act* gives an applicant the right to an opportunity to be heard by the Director before the Director makes a decision concerning the applicant's registration status.

2. — Who Is Involved

(a) In these Procedures,

the **"applicant"** is the individual or entity that has the right to an opportunity to be heard;

the **"Director"** is the senior employee of the Ontario Securities Commission who has been authorized to act as decision-maker for purposes of section 31 of the *Securities Act*; and

"staff" refers to employees of the Ontario Securities Commission other than the Director.

(b) The applicant may choose to be represented by a lawyer or an agent, but is not required to do so. These Procedures are intended to ensure that opportunities to be heard by the Director are handled in a way that is not unnecessarily formal, while ensuring a fair hearing. If the applicant chooses to be represented by a lawyer or an agent, staff will communicate with the applicant through the lawyer or agent.

3. — Extension of Time Periods

The Director may extend any time period set out in these Procedures. If either staff or the applicant wishes to request the extension of a time period, they should send their request to the Director in writing, and copy the other party. Their request should include the reason that the extension is required.

4. — Staff's Notice to Applicant

If staff recommends that the Director refuse to grant, renew, reinstate or amend the applicant's registration or if staff recommends that the Director impose terms and conditions on the applicant's registration, staff must send a letter giving the applicant notice of the recommendation and brief reasons for it. Staff must include a copy of these Procedures in the letter to the applicant.

5. — Applicant's Response

(a) If the applicant wishes to be heard by the Director before a decision is made on staff's recommendation, the applicant must inform staff by letter or by e-mail. Normally, the applicant's response must be delivered within two weeks after receiving staff's letter. However, in exceptional circumstances, staff may require the applicant to respond more quickly. The time period for response will be set out in staff's letter to the applicant.

(b) If the applicant does not respond within the time set out in staff's letter, the Director will proceed to make a decision.

The rest of these Procedures describe the process to be followed if the applicant chooses to be heard by the Director.

6. — Choice of Written Submissions or Appearance

(a) The opportunity to be heard will normally be conducted as an exchange of written submissions. However, either the applicant or staff may request that the opportunity to be heard be conducted as an appearance. Written submissions may be made by letter or by e-mail. An appearance means an appearance in the presence of the Director or by telephone conference or other interactive electronic means acceptable to both the applicant and staff.

(b) A request that the opportunity to be heard be conducted as an appearance must be made in writing to the Director with a brief statement of the reasons for making the request. The Director will give the other party an opportunity to object to the request before deciding whether to grant a request for an appearance.

(c) The Director may also decide on his or her own initiative that the opportunity to be heard will be conducted as an appearance, in which case the Director must promptly inform the applicant and staff of his or her decision.

7. — Exchange of Written Submissions

This paragraph describes the process to be followed if the opportunity to be heard is to be conducted by exchange of written submissions.

(a) Staff must provide the applicant and the Director with a written submission setting out the facts and law supporting staff's recommendation. Normally, staff's submission must be delivered to the applicant and the Director within two weeks after staff receives notice that the applicant wishes to exercise the right to be heard. However, in exceptional circumstances, the Director may require staff's submissions to be delivered more quickly.

(b) The applicant must then provide the Director and staff with a written submission responding to staff's submissions. Normally, the applicant's submissions must be delivered within two weeks after the applicant receives staff's submission. However, in exceptional circumstances, the Director may require the applicant's submissions to be delivered more quickly.

(c) In most cases, there will only be one exchange of written submissions so that the Director is able to render a decision without unnecessary delay. However, the applicant and staff may agree to make further submissions or either of them may request that the Director allow further submissions. Any such request or agreement must be made within one week after the delivery of the applicant's submissions under (b), above.

8. — Appearance Before the Director

This paragraph describes the process to be followed if the opportunity to be heard is to be conducted as an appearance.

(a) An appearance before the Director will generally be an informal proceeding. The Ontario Securities Commission Rules of Practice and the Rules of Civil Procedure do not apply to such proceedings.

(b) At the appearance, the Director may ask any question and admit any evidence which he or she sees fit, except where the evidence is subject to a legal privilege. Witnesses may be called, examined and cross-examined with the consent of the Director. The applicant and any witnesses may give evidence under oath or affirmation.

(c) The proceedings will be open to the public unless intimate financial, personal or other matters may be disclosed that, in the opinion of the Director, would outweigh the public benefit of openness in Ontario Securities Commission proceedings.

9. — Director's Decision

(a) Where an opportunity to be heard has been conducted by exchange of written submissions, the Director will normally make a decision concerning staff's recommendation no more than thirty days after delivery of the final submissions of the applicant and staff. If either the applicant or staff fails to meet the deadlines for delivery of their submissions, the Director may make a decision concerning staff's recommendation without further notice or delay.

(b) Where an opportunity to be heard has been conducted as an appearance, the Director must make a decision concerning staff's recommendation no more than thirty days after the end of the appearance.

(c) The Director must provide written reasons for his or her decision to the applicant and staff as soon as reasonably possible, but need not do so at the same time as the decision is first communicated to the applicant and staff.

10. — Public Record

(a) All written submissions and transcripts of appearances will be available to the public upon request, unless intimate financial, personal or other matters may be disclosed that, in the opinion of the Director, would outweigh the public benefit of openness in Ontario Securities Commission proceedings.

(b) The decision of the Director and his or her reasons for decision will be published in the *Ontario Securities Commission Bulletin* and posted on the Ontario Securities Commission's website.

11. — Right of Review

(a) The applicant has the right under subsection 8(2) of the *Securities Act* to ask the Ontario Securities Commission to review the Director's decision.

(b) A request for a review must be made by registered mail sent to the Secretary of the Ontario Securities Commission and copied to the Director within thirty days after the later of the making of the Director's decision or the issuing of reasons for the Director's decision.

(c) Applications for review are governed by Rule 9 of the *Ontario Securities Commission's Rules of Practice*. A copy of the *Rules of Practice* can be obtained from the Secretary's office or from the Ontario Securities Commission's website.

(d) If the applicant requests a review, the Director's decision will still take effect immediately after it is made unless the Commission grants the applicant a stay of the decision.

PRACTICE GUIDELINE — ELECTRONIC COPIES OF WRITTEN SUBMISSIONS

Practice Guideline — June 16, 2015 Electronic Copies of Written Submissions (Ontario Securities Commission Rules of Procedure (2014), 37 O.S.C.B. 4168 and *Statutory Powers Procedure Act*, R.S.O. 1990, c. S.22, as amended)

Preamble

Pursuant to Rules 1.2(3), 1.3, 1.4, 1.5.4 and 1.5.8 of the Ontario Securities Commission *Rules of Procedure* (2014), 37 O.S.C.B. 4168, the Ontario Securities Commission (the "Commission") is issuing this practice guideline relating to the filing of written submissions in electronic format (this "Practice Guideline").

This Practice Guideline will, effective July 1, 2015, apply to all proceedings before the Commission ("OSC Proceedings"), including proceedings commenced prior to such effective date.

1. — General Principles and Application

The purpose of this Practice Guideline is to establish a uniform approach to the filing of written submissions in electronic format by the parties to OSC Proceedings to facilitate the review of such submissions by the Panel.

2. — Electronic Written Submissions

All written submissions (including text and image/picture documents) that are filed with the Commission in connection with OSC Proceedings shall, on the same day, also be filed electronically as multi-page Portable Document Formatted (PDF) documents that will allow full text searching. Electronic written submissions shall be filed by e-mailing them to the Registrar of the Commission at registrar@osc.gov.on.ca. The e-mail must include the title of the proceeding, the party's name and that of counsel, if applicable, and a list of the attachments to the e-mail.

3. — Consequences of Non-Compliance

A party which fails to comply with this Practice Guideline may be considered by the Panel, in its discretion, to have failed to file its written submissions within the prescribed period of time.

4. — Power of the Panel

This Practice Guideline does not restrict in any way the discretion of the Panel to make rulings as it deems appropriate in the circumstances, including rulings permitting the filing of electronic copies of submissions in other formats.

OPPORTUNITIES TO BE HEARD

NATIONAL POLICY STATEMENTS (OLD NUMBERING SYSTEM)

Status of National Policy Statements (Old Numbering System)

No.	Name	Status
1	Clearance of National Issues	Replaced by NPS 43-201
2A	Guide for Mining Engineers, Geologists and Prospectors	Replaced by NI 43-101
2B	Guide for Engineers and Geologists Submitting Oil and Gas Reports to Canadian Provincial Securities Administrators	Replaced by NI 51-101
3	Unacceptable Auditors	Withdrawn: (2006) 29 O.S.C.B. (Supp-2) 4
4	Conditions for Dealer Sub-Underwritings	Rescinded: (1999) 22 O.S.C.B. 1895
5	Recognition of Profits in Real Estate Transactions	Repealed
6	Mutual Funds: Sales Charges	Repealed
7	Mutual Funds: Management Fees	Repealed
8	Mutual Funds: Computation of Net Asset Value per Share	Repealed
9	Mutual Funds: Forward Pricing, Sales and Redemptions Charges	Repealed
10	Mutual Funds: Redemption of Securities	Repealed
11	Mutual Funds: Changes of Management — Change in Investment Policies	Repealed
12	Disclosure of "Market Out" Clauses in Underwriting Agreements in Prospectuses	Replaced by NI 41-101
13	Disclaimer Clause on Prospectus	Replaced by NI 41-101
14	Acceptability of Currencies in Material Filed with Securities Regulatory Authorities	Repealed: (2007) 30 O.S.C.B. (Supp. 7) 3
15	Conditions Precedent to Acceptance of Scholarship or Educational Plan Prospectuses	Remains in force
16	Maintenance of Provincial Trading Records	Rescinded: (1999) 22 O.S.C.B. 1895
17	Violations of Securities Laws of Other Jurisdictions — Conduct Affecting Fitness for Continued Registration	Replaced by NPS 34-201
18	Conflict of Interest — Registrants Acting as Corporate Directors	Replaced by NPS 34-202
19	Mutual Funds Sales Companies: Commingling of Funds and Securities	Repealed
20	Trading in Unqualified Securities — Securities in Primary Distribution in Other Jurisdictions	Rescinded: (1999) 22 O.S.C.B. 1895
21	National Advertising — Warnings	Repealed: (2007) 30 O.S.C.B. (Supp. 7) 3
22	Use of Information and Opinion Re Mining and Oil Properties by Registrants and Others	Repealed: (2007) 30 O.S.C.B. (Supp-5) 2
23	Mutual Funds: "In-House" Funds	Repealed
24	Mutual Funds: Contractual Plans	Repealed
25	Registrants: Advertising: Disclosure of Interest	Rescinded: (2003) 26 O.S.C.B. 6350
26	Mutual Funds: Acceptance or Rejection of Subscriptions for Fund Shares or Units	Repealed
27	Canadian Generally Accepted Accounting Principles	Rescinded and replaced by NI 52-107 and NI 81-106
28	Mutual Funds: Investment Restrictions — Options	Repealed
29	Mutual Funds Investing in Mortgages	Remains in force
30	Processing of "Seasoned Prospectuses"	Rescinded; see NPS 43-201
31	Change of Auditor of a Reporting Issuer	Rescinded and replaced by NI 51-102 and NI 81-106
32	Prospectus Warning Re: Scope of Distribution	Replaced by NI 41-101
33	Financing of Film Productions	Repealed: (1997) 20 O.S.C.B. 1877
34	Unincorporated Issuers Requirement to Maintain a Register of Security Holders	Rescinded; see NI 81-102
35	Purchaser's Statutory Rights	Replaced by NI 41-101
36	Mutual Funds: Simplified Prospectus Qualification System	Replaced by NI 81-101
37	Take-Over Bids: Reciprocal Cease Trading Orders	Rescinded and replaced by NPS 62-201
38	Take-Over Bids — Defensive Tactics	Rescinded and replaced by NPS 62-202

No.	Name	Status
39	Mutual Funds	Replaced by NI 81-102
40	Timely Disclosure	Replaced by NPS 51-201
41	Shareholder Communication	Replaced by NI 54-101 and 54-102
42	Advertising of Securities on Radio or Television	Remains in force
44	Rules for Shelf Prospectus Offerings and for Pricing Offerings After the Final Prospectus is Receipted	Replaced by NI 44-102 and NI 44-103
45	Multijurisdictional Disclosure System	Replaced by NI 71-101
47	Prompt Offering Qualification System	Replaced by NI 44-101
48	Future-Oriented Financial Information	Revoked: (2007) 30 O.S.C.B. 10512
49	Self-Regulatory Organization Membership	Rescinded: (2003) 26 O.S.C.B. 6350
50	Reservations in an Auditor's Report	Rescinded and replaced by NI 52-107 and NI 81-106
51	Changes in the Ending Date of a Financial Year and in Reporting Status	Rescinded and replaced by NI 51-102 and NI 81-106

National Policy Statement 15 — Conditions Precedent to Acceptance of Scholarship or Educational Plan Prospectuses

[Editor's Note: In the process of being reformulated as National Instrument 46-102; See also OSCN 31-702]

The sale of contracts or plans commonly referred to as "university scholarship plans" or "scholarship agreements" must be subject to the following conditions before the prospectus will be acceptable for filing:

(1) A very clear distinction must be drawn between the "foundation" (which is described as a body without any profit motive or desire for pecuniary gain) and the distributor (the registered distribution agency who sell the plan under a commission arrangement often described as an "enrolment fee") in order that the public will not be induced into the error of believing that there are no sales charges or other commissions.

(2) The scholarship plan distributors and salesmen, of course, must hold registration under the specific provincial acts. The use of such expressions as "education counsellors", "scholarship counsellors or advisers", "enrolment counsellors" is viewed as misleading and should not be used.

(3) The funds received from the subscribers must be deposited with a Canadian chartered bank or a provincially licensed trust company or other similar financial institution whose accounts are normally insured by the Canada Deposit Insurance Corporation or La Régie de l'assurance-depôts du Québec. Where a subscriber's account is not afforded the protection of insurance by the Canada Deposit Insurance Corporation or La Régie de l'assurance-depôts du Québec, the fund administrator must ensure that such subscriber's account is considered to be assets under administration in the hands of the depository.

(4) The fund administrator, which is usually the "foundation", will secure the best interest rate possible on the deposits, and the interest paid on the subscriber's capital shall be transferred to a trust fund held by the same depository which in turn will be administered for the benefit of the beneficiaries of the plans. In securing the best interest rate possible the fund administrator may, where not contrary to the scholarship agreement, cause the subscriber's deposits to be invested in mortgages provided that such mortgages are:

   (a) first mortgages on residential properties of 8 units or less located in Canada and having a maturity not exceeding 5 years, provided that first mortgages may be on residential properties of more than 8 units when the following conditions are met:

   (i) the scholarship plans under administration have total net assets of at least $50,000,000;

   (ii) the mortgages are insured under the National Housing Act (Canada) or any similar provincial statute or are insured by an insurance company registered or licensed under the Canadian and British Insurance Companies Act (Canada), the Foreign Insurance Companies Act (Canada), or any similar statute of a Canadian province or territory; and

   (iii) not more than 20 percent of the funds from sources described in 4(h)(i) and 4(h)(ii) below are invested in such mortgages on residential properties of more than 8 units;

   (b) an amount which is not more than 75% of the fair market value of the property securing the mortgage, except when:

   (i) such a mortgage is insured under the National Housing Act (Canada) or any similar act of a province; or

   (ii) the excess over 75% is insured by an insurance company registered or licensed under the Canadian and British Insurance Companies Act (Canada), the Foreign Insurance Companies Act (Canada) or insurance acts or similar acts of a Canadian province or territory;

   (c) acquired from a lending institution with which the fund, the administrator of the fund, the trustee(s) and the distributor of the fund are dealing at arm's length;

   (d) purchased and sold at fair market value, i.e. that principal amount which produces at least the yield prevailing for the sale of comparable fully serviced mortgages as established by major mortgage lenders under similar conditions;

   (e) fully funded, serviced and not in arrears at the date of acquisition;

(f)   not on a property in which:

   (i)   the administrator, the trustee or the distributor of the fund or any senior officer or director thereof, or

   (ii)   any person or company who is a substantial security-holder of the administrator, a trustee or the distributor of the fund, or

   (iii) any associate or affiliate of persons or institutions mentioned in subparagraphs (i) and (ii),

   has an interest as mortgagor or as an associate of a mortgagor;

(g)   limited in amount, in respect of any one mortgage, to $75,000 for funds having less than $5,000,000 in net assets; and to the lesser of $500,000 or 2.5 per cent of its net assets where they exceed $5,000,000 but are less than $50,000,000; and to the amount not exceeding 1.0 percent of its net assets for funds having $50,000,000 or more in net assets, and for the purpose of this paragraph, a series of mortgages on one condominium development shall be considered as one mortgage;

(h)   restricted in total to an amount not greater than 75% of

   (i)   funds arising from new contracts sold to subscribers pursuant to a prospectus which contains disclosure of the arrangements in respect of mortgage investment and which has been accepted for filing by the Administrator; and

   (ii)   funds held on behalf of subscribers who, after receipt of an information circular which has first been filed with and accepted by the Administrator, have agreed in writing to permit their plan contracts to be included in the mortgage investment arrangement;

(i)   on properties appraised by a qualified appraiser such as a bank, trust company, loan company or insurance company, or other person or company which makes appraisals and whose opinions are relied upon in connection with lending or servicing activities, and who in the judgment of the management company or trustee of the specific fund is properly qualified to make such a determination;

(j)   not on raw land or undeveloped land.

(5)   The depository must maintain an accounting system which will permit it to determine the total amount of deposits made by each subscriber, all deductions from such deposits and the amount of interest produced by the deposits of each subscriber.

(6)   The trust funds shall be administered pursuant to a trust indenture or deed in accordance with the terms detailed in the prospectus, and must contain a provision under which a licensed trust company agrees to act in the place of the foundation in the event that the foundation refuses to or is unable to act.

(7)   The fees charged, including the commissions of the distributor and its salesmen, must not exceed $200 per plan. The first $100 paid under the plan may be applied against this fee and the balance may be deducted at a maximum rate of 50% of each of the further contributions.

(8)   From these fees sufficient funds must be set aside in trust to pay the future costs of administering the trusts established under 6. These funds shall not be used directly or indirectly for any other purpose. The costs of distribution must be borne fully by the distribution company. Any additional sums rebated or otherwise paid by the depository to assist in the payment of the charges for administration of the funds shall be held in trust by the foundation solely for this purpose and shall not be paid directly or indirectly for any other purpose.

(9)   The plan must grant the subscriber the right to withdraw from the plan without any cost to the subscriber within 60 days from the execution of the contract.

(10)   Where the subscriber wishes to withdraw from a plan after 60 days from the date of the execution of the contract, the subscriber shall not be obliged to pay any fees in addition to those already paid, but may lose the total amount of fees paid to that point.

(11)   It is considered contrary to the public interest to accept for filing a scholarship plan which calls for the complete forfeiture of the capital and accumulated interest in cases where the plan is abandoned before its maturity. The same shall apply to so-called "special" plans which consist of the simple deposit by the subscriber of an amount equivalent to the interest, without any right to reimbursement.

(12)   The schedule of instalment payments must be equitable for all children enrolled. In the setting of the schedules, accounts must be kept of the age of the children and the number of instalments foreseen so that there is an actuarial equivalent between the instalments foreseen for each age and each plan. Accordingly the so-called "family plans" are not acceptable.

(13)   All beneficiaries must participate equally in the advantages of the plan. The foundation or trustee must make provision in the trust indenture for the payment of equivalent scholarships for each of the eligible participants.

(14)   Scholarship plan agreements must be filed with the preliminary prospectus (or prospectus as the case may be) as part of the supporting material together with a copy of the trust agreement.

(15)   The prospectus shall clearly indicate on its front page the speculative nature of the scholarship plans and the real cost of participation in the plan to the subscriber.

National Policy Statement 29 — Mutual Funds Investing in Mortgages

[Editor's Note: Under consideration to be reformulated as National Instrument 81-103.]

Section I
Applicability

I.

    (1)   This policy applies to any mutual fund having 10% or more of its portfolio invested in mortgages or hypothecs, except that sub-section III(1) applies only to a mutual fund having 50% or more of its portfolio invested in mortgages or hypothecs.

    (2)   Except where in conflict with this policy, all relevant mutual fund policies apply.

Section II
Definitions

II.   For the purpose of this policy:

    (1)   "qualified appraiser" means a bank, trust company, loan company or insurance company, or other person or company which makes appraisals and whose opinions are relied upon in connection with lending or servicing activities, and who in the judgment of the management company or trustee of the specific fund is properly qualified to make such a determination;

    (2)   "substantial security holder" means any person, company or combination of persons or companies that beneficially owns directly or indirectly more than 10% of the voting rights attached to all outstanding equity shares;

    (3)   "liquid assets" means cash or deposits with a Canadian chartered bank or with any trust company registered under the laws of any province of Canada which are cashable or saleable prior to maturity, debt securities valued at market issued or guaranteed by the governments of Canada or any of the Canadian provinces, and money market instruments maturing prior to one year from the date of issue.

Section III
Investment Policy

III.

    (1)   Liquidity:

        (a)   The prospectus of a mutual fund investing in mortgages shall include a provision that the fund will not invest in mortgages if such acquisition would have the effect of reducing the fund's liquid assets to an amount less than the amount established by the following formula:

Net assets of the fund (market value)

$ 1,000,00 or less	$ 100,000
$ 1,000,000	$ 100,000 + 10% on next $ 1,000,000
$ 2,000,000	$ 200,000 + 9% on next $ 3,000,000
$ 5,000,000	$ 470,000 + 8% on next $ 5,000,000
$10,000,000	$ 870,000 + 7% on next $10,000,000
$20,000,000	$1,570,000 + 6% on next $10,000,000
$30,000,000 or over	$2,170,000 + 5% on excess

        (b)   To provide liquidity for redemption purposes only, a fund may borrow an amount not exceeding 10% of its net assets.

    (2)   Restrictions:

        (2.1) A fund may not invest in mortgages:

        (a)   more than 10% of its net assets until its net assets have reached and continue to be maintained at a minimum of $350,000;

        (b)   on raw land or undeveloped land;

        (c)   other than first mortgages on properties located in Canada;

        (d)   on residential properties of more than 8 units and on commercial and industrial properties, until the fund has net assets of at least $15,000,000. In any event, the total amount of such mortgages must never exceed 40% of the net assets of the fund provided that those mortgages constituting the excess of 20% of the net assets of the fund that are invested in such mortgages must be insured either by an agency of the Government of Canada or of a Province of Canada;

        (e)   unless the property securing the mortgage has been appraised by a qualified appraiser;

        (f)   an amount which is more than 75% of the fair market value of the property securing the mortgage, except when:

            (i)   such mortgage is insured under the National Housing Act (Canada) or any similar act of a province, or

            (ii)   the excess over 75% is insured by an insurance company registered or licensed under the Canadian and British Insurance Companies Act (Canada), the Foreign Insurance Companies Act (Canada) or insurance acts or similar acts of a Canadian province or territory;

        (g)   with a maturity exceeding 10 years for mortgages on the types of properties referred to in subsection 2.1(d) and 5 years in all other cases except that up to 10% of the net assets of the fund may be invested in residential mortgages with a maturity not exceeding 10 years; the amortization period of each mortgage must not exceed 30 years, except for mortgages insured under the National Housing Act (Canada) or any similar act of a province;

(h) an amount exceeding $75,000 for funds having less than $1,500,000 in net assets; and the lesser of $1,000,000 or 5% of its net assets when they exceed $1,500,000, but are less than $50,000,000; and an amount exceeding 2% of its net assets for funds having $50,000,000 or more in net assets, for any one mortgage, and for the purpose of this paragraph, a series of mortgages on one condominium development shall be considered as one mortgage;

(i) on a property in which:

(i) any senior officer, director or trustee of the mutual fund, its management company or distribution or

(ii) any person or company who is a substantial security holder of the mutual fund, its management company or its distribution company, or

(iii) any associate or affiliate of persons or institutions mentioned in subparagraphs (i) or (ii), except in the case of a mortgage on a family dwelling for less than $75,000,

has an interest as mortgagor.

(2.2) Neither the fund nor the management company on behalf of the fund shall enter into forward commitments binding on the fund with regard to mortgages to be acquired by it if, at the time moneys are to be disbursed by the fund as a result of such commitments, the liquidity requirements established under sub-section III.(1)(a) would be violated by such a disbursement.

ARM'S LENGTH TRANSACTIONS
INVESTOR'S YIELD

(2.3) Where a fund acquires mortgages from a lending institution with which the fund, its management company and/or the insiders of either of them are dealing at arm's length, such mortgages shall be acquired at that principal amount which produces at least the yield prevailing for the sale of comparable unserviced mortgages by major mortgage lenders under similar conditions.

NOT AT ARM'S LENGTH TRANSACTIONS

(2.4) In all cases not covered by sub-section (2.3), mortgages shall be acquired by the fund according to only one of the following three methods:

LENDER'S RATE

(a) at that principal amount which will produce a yield to the fund equal to the interest rate at which the lending institution is making commitments to loan on the security of comparable mortgages at the time of purchase by the fund;

FORWARD COMMITMENT RATE

(b) at that principal amount which will produce the same yield to the fund as the interest rate charged by the lending institution to the mortgagor on the date of commitment provided that the date of commitment is not more than 120 days prior to the date of acquisition of the mortgage by the fund, and the interest rate is equal to the rate at which the lending institution made commitments to loan mortgages on the date of commitment; or

MODIFIED LENDER'S RATE

(c) at that principal amount which will produce a yield to the fund of not more than a quarter of one per cent less than the interest rate at which the lending institution is making commitments, at the time of purchase, to loan on the security of comparable mortgages provided that the lending institution which sells mortgages to the fund has entered into an agreement to repurchase the mortgages from the fund in circumstances benefiting the fund and that such an agreement is considered by the administrators to justify the difference in yield to the fund.

(2.5) For the purpose of determining the net asset value of mortgages in the portfolio:

(a) the value of conventional mortgages shall be calculated on a consistent basis, to produce a principal amount which will produce a yield,

(i) equal to the yield prevailing for the sale of comparable conventional mortgages by major lending if ascertainable on the date of valuation; or

(ii) equal to or not less than one quarter of one per cent below the interest rate at which major lending institutions are making commitments on the date of valuation.

(b) in the case of mortgages guaranteed under the National Housing Act such mortgages shall be valued at market value.

(2.6) Any change by a fund from one of the methods of acquisition described in subsection (2.4) to another of these methods, or in the method of valuation of mortgages included in its portfolio, shall be subject to the prior approval of the Administrators.

Section IV
Disclosure

IV. The prospectus of the fund shall include:

(a)

    (i)   A statement of the various methods used by mutual funds generally for determining the price at which mortgages are acquired in the terms of subsection III(2.3) and (2.4), and a brief comparison of the effects these methods may have on the yield to the fund under the assumptions of increasing, decreasing and stable interest rates;

    (ii)   A designation of which of the methods outlined in paragraph IV(a)(i) is used by the fund;

    (iii)   The method used for determining the price at which mortgages have been sold by the fund during the preceding financial year, if any;

(b)   A description of the methods used to value all portfolio holdings (including mortgages in arrears) in determining the net asset value of the fund;

(c)   A statement of the benefits or advantages derived by the management company or an affiliate or associate of the management company, from managing the fund and the sale or purchase of mortgages to or from the fund;

(d)

    (i)   The origin of the mortgages acquired by the fund during the preceding financial year;

    (ii)   The distribution of mortgages between mortgages insured under the National Housing Act (Canada) insured and uninsured conventional mortgages;

    (iii)   The fund's policy concerning the origin and distribution of mortgages to be acquired by the fund in the future;

(e)   A table showing the distribution of the mortgage portfolio according to the type of property securing the mortgage (single family dwelling, condominium, multi-unit dwelling of up to 8 units, multi-unit dwelling of more than 8 units, commercial, industrial);

(f)   A table showing the contractual interest rate in groups of not more than one quarter per cent for the mortgages in the portfolio;

(g)   A table showing, with one year intervals, the date at which mortgages included in the portfolio reach maturity;

(h)   A table showing the geographical distribution of the mortgage portfolio;

(i)   A table showing the status of mortgages having instalments 90 days or more in arrears;

(j)   In each of the tables required under this Section, the number of mortgages and market value shall be shown. Furthermore, in the case of the tables required under subsections IV(e) and (f) the amortized cost and outstanding principal value shall be shown.

Effective September 1, 1977

Revised October 28, 1987

National Policy Statement 42 — Advertising of Securities on Radio or Television

Part I — Background

Until September 1986, the regulations established by the Canadian Radio and Television Commission (the "C.R.T.C.") prohibited the advertising of securities on radio or television, except for certain exempt securities. These restrictions were removed by the C.R.T.C. for radio as of September 19, 1986, and for television as of September 1, 1988.

In its public notice dated September 19, 1986, announcing amendments to regulations respecting radio broadcasting the C.R.T.C. stated:

> "The Commission has also eliminated provisions dealing with the advertising of bonds, shares and other securities as it considers that those matters do not fall within its mandate under the Broadcasting Act."

In response to the repeal of the restrictions on advertising of securities by the C.R.T.C., the Canadian Securities Administrators issued a Draft Policy Statement No. 42 in April of 1988, and invited public comment. The effect of the Draft Policy was essentially to replace the C.R.T.C. restrictions with similar restrictions. The Draft Policy was intended to be an interim measure while a thorough study of the issues involved in the advertising of securities generally was undertaken.

Such a study involves the consideration of, among other matters, the report of the private sector committee given to the Ontario Securities Commission in October 1987, the registration requirements under securities legislation, and recent decisions of the courts, and will involve consultation with the broadcast industry.

In the meantime, in view of the September 1, 1988, repeal of the C.R.T.C. regulations in respect of the advertising of securities on television, the Canadian Securities Administrators are of the view that an Interim Policy should be finalized to restrict advertising before problems occur and economic interests arise that might be prejudiced by future restrictions.

Part II — Purpose of the Interim Policy

Provincial securities regulation serves to protect investors within the province by regulating the conduct of persons involved in the sale of securities, and by regulating disclosure in respect of both new issues and securities traded on the secondary market.

It is appropriate that securities regulation restrict the advertising of securities on the basis of investor protection, so long as the restrictions are reasonable and not unduly restrictive in the light of their objective.

The Canadian Securities Administrators are of the view that the most effective way of ensuring that advertising of securities is not false, misleading or deceptive is to restrict such advertising to the period of a distribution by way of prospectus, and to require that the advertising be placed either by registrants, who have a direct responsibility to both their clients and the securities administrators, or by the issuers that are making the distribution.

A brief advertisement of securities may have a high impact but nonetheless be misleading, although it may not be intentionally false or deceptive, as it cannot by its nature give appropriate cautions or address the issue of suitability. Accordingly, only very basic information specifically as set out in the Policy Statement may be included in advertisements of securities other than exempted securities.

Securities exempted from the Policy are those in respect to which investors have historically been viewed as not requiring registration and prospectus protections under securities legislation.

Part III — Statement of Policy

No person or company shall promote, by radio or television broadcast, investment in specific securities other than those exempted securities listed in Part IV below, except in accordance with this Policy Statement.

Advertisements of specific securities, other than exempted securities, the contents of which are restricted in accordance with Part V below, may be placed on radio or television only during a distribution of the securities pursuant to a prospectus or preliminary prospectus for which a receipt has been issued by the securities administrator in the jurisdiction in which the advertisement is placed. Advertising of such securities may be placed only by a person or company who is registered as a dealer in the jurisdiction in which the advertisement is placed and who is authorized to sell such securities, or by the issuer of the securities.

Issuers placing advertisements directly rather than through a registrant are reminded that the advertising of specific securities is considered under provincial securities legislation to be trading in securities and, accordingly, registration as a securities issuer or an exemption from registration must be obtained from the jurisdiction in which the advertisement is placed.

Where any person contravenes this Policy Statement, it may, in the discretion of the securities administrator having jurisdiction, result in the issuance of a cease trade order in respect of the security in question, the suspension or revocation of the registration of any registrant involved, or such other action as is warranted in the circumstances.

This Policy Statement is not intended to affect advertisements by issuers in respect to publicity campaigns that are aimed at either selling products or raising public awareness in respect to the issuer, provided that they are not accompanied by an advertisement for the sale of securities. In this context, a reference to a listing on an exchange is not appropriate. Further, nothing in this Policy Statement prohibits corporate or generally informative advertising by registrants.

Part IV — Exempted Securities

The following securities are exempted from this Policy Statement:

1. Bonds, debentures or other evidences of indebtedness,

    (a) of or guaranteed by the Government of Canada or any province of Canada;

    (b) of any municipal corporation in Canada, including debentures issued for public, separate, secondary or vocational school purposes, or guaranteed by any municipal corporation in Canada, or secured by or payable out of rates or taxes levied under the law of any province of Canada on property in such province and collectable by or through the municipality in which such property is situated; or

    (c) of or guaranteed by a bank to which the Bank Act (Canada) applies, or by a trust company or loan corporation licensed or registered under provincial or federal regulatory statutes.

2. Certificates or receipts issued by a loan or trust company registered under a provincial or federal regulatory statute for moneys received for guaranteed investment.

Part V — Permitted Advertisements

Advertising of specific securities as permitted in Part III, other than exempted securities, is restricted to giving the following information:

(a) the name of the issuer of the securities;

(b) a concise statement of the nature of the business of the issuer;

(c) the specific type of securities offered (e.g., common shares, subordinated shares, bonds, etc.), the number offered for subscription and their price;

(d) a concise statement of whether the securities are qualified for special tax treatment;

(e) the name of the registrant, if any, placing the advertisement; and

(f) instructions for obtaining a copy of the prospectus or preliminary prospectus.

Notwithstanding section 15.02 of National Policy Statement No. 39, advertising of specific mutual funds is permitted on the same restricted basis.

Part VI — Duration of Policy

This Policy will expire on the date a comprehensive National Policy on the advertisement of securities in all media is adopted in final form.

UNIFORM ACT POLICIES

Status — Uniform Act Policies

No.	Name	Status
2-01	"Undertakings" — Extra-Provincial Companies	Rescinded: (1998) 21 O.S.C.B. 7753
2-02	Prospectuses — Annual Re-Filings	Rescinded: (1998) 21 O.S.C.B. 7753
2-03	Prospectuses and Amendments — Certification (Section 52) Supporting Documentation	Rescinded: (1998) 21 O.S.C.B. 7753
2-04	Consent of Solicitors — Disclosure of Interest	Rescinded: (1998) 21 O.S.C.B. 7753
2-05	Applications Under Sections 34(1)14 and 71(1)(h) of the Securities Act, R.S.O. 1980, c.466 by a Company Wishing to Sell Additional Securities to its Security Holders	Replaced by NI 45-101
2-06	Use of Shareholders' Lists by Registrants	Rescinded: (1998) 21 O.S.C.B. 7753
2-07	Surrender of Registration — Other than Salesman	Replaced by Rule 33-501
2-08	Declaration as to Short Position — Listed and Unlisted Securities	Rescinded: (1998) 21 O.S.C.B. 7753
2-09	Insider Trading Reports — Loan and Trust Companies	Rescinded: (1998) 21 O.S.C.B. 7753
2-10	Insider Trading Reports — Persons Required to Report in More than One Capacity	Rescinded: (1998) 21 O.S.C.B. 2745
2-11	Policy Statement in Connection with Applications to the Commission for an Order Under Section 121(3) of the Securities Act, 1966 (now Section 79(a) of the new Act or section 173(3) of the Business Corporations Act, 1970 (Ontario))	Rescinded: (1998) 21 O.S.C.B. 2155
2-12	Timely Disclosure	Replaced by NPS 40
2-13	Advertising During Waiting Period Between Preliminary and Final Prospectuses	Renumbered as OSC Policy 47-601

UNIFORM ACT POLICIES

UNIFORM ACT POLICIES

Status — Uniform Act Policies

No.	Name	Status
2-01	Undertakings — Extra-Provincial Companies	Rescinded (1998) 21 O.S.C.B. 7753
2-02	Prospectuses — Annual Re Filings	Rescinded (1999) 21 O.S.C.B. 7753
2-03	Prospectuses and Amendments — Certification (Section 72) Supporting Documentation	Rescinded (1999) 21 O.S.C.B. 7753
2-04	Consent of Solicitors — Disclosure of Interest	Rescinded (1998) 21 O.S.C.B. 7753
2-05	Applications Under Sections 94(1)14 and 71(1)(b) of the Securities Act, R.S.O. 1980 Whereby a Company Wishing to Sell Additional Securities to its Security Holder	Replaced by NI 45-101
2-06	Use of Shareholders' Lists by Registrants	Rescinded (1998) 21 O.S.C.B. 7753
2-07	Surrender of Registration — Other than Salesman	Replaced by Rule 33-501
2-08	Declaration as to Short Position — Listed and Unlisted Securities	Rescinded (1999) 21 O.S.C.B. 7753
2-09	Insider Trading Reports — Loan and Trust Companies	Rescinded (1999) 21 O.S.C.B. 7753
2-10	Insider Trading Reports — Persons Required to Report in More than One Capacity	Rescinded (1998) 21 O.S.C.B. 7745
2-11	Policy Statement in Connection with Applications to the Commission for an Order Under Section 12(3) of the Securities Act, 1966 (now Section 79187 of the new Act or section 173(3) of the Business Corporations Act, 1970 (Ontario))	Rescinded (1998) 21 O.S.C.B. 7753
2-12	Timely Disclosure	Replaced by NP51-49
2-13	Advertising During Waiting Period Between Preliminary and Final Prospectuses	Renumbered as OSC Policy 47-601

O.S.C. POLICIES

Status — O.S.C. Policies (Old Numbering System)

No.	Name	Status
1.	*General*	
1.1	O.S.C. Policy Statements — General	Rescinded: (1999) 22 O.S.C.B. 1335
1.2	Publication of Unlisted or Over-the-Counter Quotations	Repealed
1.3	Restricted Shares	Replaced by NI 56-501
1.4	Reciprocal Enforcement of Cease Trading Orders	Withdrawn Sept. 1, 2008 (according to the OSC's Policy Reformulation Table of Concordance)
1.5	Distribution of Securities outside Ontario	Replaced by Interpretation Note
1.6	Strip Bonds	Replaced by Rule 91-501
1.7	The Securities Advisory Committee to the OSC	Amended and renumbered as OPS 11-601
1.8	Canadian Over-the-Counter Automated Trading System (COATS)	Repealed
1.9	Use by Dealers of Brokerage Commission as Payment for Goods or Services other than Order Execution Services — ("Soft Dollar" Deals)	Replaced by NI 23-102
2.	*Ontario Securities Commission Procedure and Related Matters*	
2.1	Applications to the Ontario Securities Commission	Remains in force
2.2	Public Availability of Material Filed Under the Securities Act	Renumbered as OPS 13-601
2.3	Joint Hearings With Other Provincial Administrators — Conditions Precedent and Costs	Replaced by Rules of Practice
2.4	Conflict of Interest Guidelines for Members of the Ontario Securities Commission and its Staff	Replaced by By-law No. 2 (2003) 26 O.S.C.B. 293
2.5	Certificates of No Default under section 71(8) [72(8)] and List of Defaulting Issuers under Section 71(9) [72(9)] of the Securities Act	Replaced by OPS 51-601
2.6	Applications for Exemption from Preparation and Mailing of Interim Financial Statements, Annual Financial Statements and Proxy Solicitation Material	Renumbered as OPS 52-601
2.7	Appeals to the Ontario Securities Commission by Way of Hearing and Review	Replaced by Rules of Practice
2.8	Application for Ontario Securities Commission Consent to Obtain Transcripts of Evidence Taken During Investigations or Hearings	Replaced by Rules of Practice
2.9	Cease Trading Order — Applications for Partial Revocation to Permit a Securityholder to Establish a Tax Loss for Income Tax Purposes	Replaced by OPS 57-602
2.10	Restrictions on Practice Before the Commission and its Staff Upon Termination of the Appointments of Members of the Commission and its Staff	Replaced by By-law No. 2; (2003) 26 O.S.C.B. 293
2.11	Conflicts of Interest of Members of the Ontario Securities Commission	Replaced by By-law No. 2; (2003) 26 O.S.C.B. 293
2.12	Televising of Ontario Securities Commission Hearing	Replaced by Rules of Practice
3.	*Self-Regulatory Organizations*	
3.1	Recognition by the Commission of Stock Exchanges, etc.	Replaced in part by BOR 21-901 and 62-904 and by Rules 45-501 and 45-502
4.	*Registration*	
4.1	Public Ownership of Dealers, Conditions of Registration and Institutional Ownership	Rescinded: (1999) 22 O.S.C.B. 1335
4.2	Suspension of Registration — Criminal Charges Pending	Renumbered as OSC Policy 34-602
4.3	Self-directed RRSPs and Other Plans Recognized by the Commission for Purposes of this Policy Statement and Administered by Brokers or Investment Dealers on Behalf of Authorized Trustees	Remains in force
4.4	Dual Registration Under the Securities Act	Replaced by Rule 31-501 and Companion Policy 31-501CP
4.5	Dual Licensing of Life Insurance Agents	Repealed (1994) 17 O.S.C.B. 6073
4.6	Registration — Declaration of Personal Bankruptcy	Renumbered as OSC Policy 34-601

SECTION 1 — GENERAL

O.S.C. Policy 1.5 — Distribution of Securities outside Ontario

[Repealed]

Notice

O.S.C. Policy 1.5 (formerly Draft Policy 3-47) entitled "Distributions of Securities Outside Ontario" primarily addresses the policy concern that securities distributed prospectus-free abroad not be illegally distributed or redistributed into Ontario or to Ontario residents.

Policy 1.5 adopts a broad construction of the definitions of "trade" and "distribution" in the *Securities Act* (Ontario) (the "Act") and states that in light of the breadth of these terms, a distribution of securities by an issuer outside Ontario may also be considered to be a distribution of securities in Ontario requiring compliance with the prospectus provisions of the Act or an exemption therefrom. The subject matter of Policy 1.5 is thus relevant both to distributions by issuers incorporated or continued under the laws of Ontario or whose head office is situate in Ontario ("Ontario issuers") and to distributions by all other issuers ("non- Ontario issuers") regardless of their connection, if any, with Ontario.

Policy 1.5 does not apply to issuers who satisfied the criteria for eligible reporting issuers set forth in O.S.C. Policy 5.6 entitled "Prompt Offering Qualification System" whether or not such issuers intended to effect distributions outside Ontario in accordance with Policy 5.6.

The Commission has received a considerable number of comments with respect to Policy 1.5. Some commentators have expressed the concern that Policy 1.5 will seriously interfere with the capital formation process for issuers effecting financings outside Ontario where it is manifest that there is no intention that the securities distributed abroad will find their way into Ontario and where no question arises of bringing the Ontario capital markets into disrepute.

The Commission is of the view that Policy 1.5 may have unduly interfered with legitimate distributions outside of Ontario. Therefore, as of the publication of this Bulletin, the Commission has repealed Policy 1.5. At the same time the Commission wants to make known its views on the application of the Act to distributions of securities outside of Ontario. The Commission is therefore publishing, in place and stead of Policy 1.5, the following Interpretation Note.

Interpretation Note

[Editor's Note: This Interpretation Note was to be reformulated as OSC Rule 72-101: 23 O.S.C.B. 6260 (September 8, 2000) but this is not proceeding according to OSCN 11-739]

Distributions of Securities Outside Ontario

1. The Provisions of the Act

The basic prospectus requirement of the Act is contained in subsection 52(1) [53(1)] which provides, in part, as follows:

"No person or company shall *trade* in a security on his own account or on behalf of any other person or company,

. . . . .

(b)   ... where such trade would be a *distribution* of such security,

unless a preliminary prospectus and a prospectus have been filed and receipts therefor obtained from the Director." (emphasis added)

The term "trade" is defined in paragraph 1(1)42 [1(1)] of the Act, in part, as follows:

"'trade' ... includes,

i.   any sale or disposition of a security for valuable consideration, whether the terms of payment be on margin, instalment or otherwise, but does not include a purchase of a security or, except as provided in subparagraph iv, a transfer, pledge or encumbrance of securities for the purpose of giving collateral for a bona fide debt,

v.   any act, advertisement, solicitation, conduct or negotiation directly or indirectly in furtherance of any of the foregoing;"

The term "distribution" is defined in paragraph 1(1)11 [1(1)] of the Act, in part, as follows:

"'distribution', where used in relation to trading and securities means,

i.   a trade in securities of an issuer *that have not been previously issued*,

. . . . .

iii.   a trade in previously issued securities of an issuer from the holdings of any person, company or combination of persons or companies holding a sufficient number of any securities of that issuer to affect materially the control of that issuer, but any holding of any person, company or combination of persons or companies holding more than 20 per cent of the outstanding voting securities of an issuer shall, in the absence of evidence to the contrary, be deemed to affect materially the control of that issuer,

. . . . .

(emphasis added)

A "distribution" thus includes a sale by an issuer of its previously unissued securities to a purchaser, whether or not such purchaser is an underwriter of the securities. While a sale by an issuer to an underwriter acting as purchaser is exempt from the prospectus requirements of the Act by paragraph 71(1)(r) [72(1)(r)], the sale by the underwriter of such securities constitutes a distribution pursuant to subsection 71(6) [72(6)] of the Act.

The term "underwriter" is defined in paragraph 1(1)43 [1(1)] of the Act, in part, as follows:

> "'underwriter' means a person or company who, as principal, agrees to purchase securities with a view to distribution or who, as agent, offers for sale or sells securities in connection with a distribution and includes a person or company who has a direct or indirect participation in any such distribution, but does not include, ..."

2. Statement of Principle

In light of the outlined provisions of the Act, including the broad definition of "trade", *and depending on the connecting factors with Ontario*, a distribution of securities outside Ontario by Ontario or non-Ontario issuers might also be considered to be a distribution of securities in Ontario requiring compliance with the prospectus provisions of the Act or an exemption therefrom.

However, where a distribution of securities is effected outside of Ontario by Ontario or non-Ontario issuers and where reasonable steps are taken by the issuer, underwriter and other participants effecting such distribution to ensure that such securities come to rest outside of Ontario, the Commission takes the view that a prospectus is not required under the Act, nor is an exemption from the prospectus requirements necessary. Reasonable precaution and restrictions should be implemented by the issuer, underwriters and other participants in the distribution to ensure that the securities are not distributed, or redistributed, into Ontario or to Ontario residents and that such securities come to rest outside Ontario. Such precaution and restrictions should be designed to ensure that the entire distribution process results in the securities being held by or for the benefit of non-residents, as opposed to intermediaries in the distribution chain holding securities for resale to Ontario residents.

3. The Operation of the Principle

The number and nature of the restrictions that should be implemented, and precautions taken, in connection with the distribution of securities outside Ontario to ensure that such securities come to rest outside Ontario will, of necessity, vary with the circumstances surrounding each distribution.

In some financings, some of the following restrictions or precautions might be advisable:

(1)   A restriction in the underwriting agreement against the underwriters selling the securities being offered to any Ontario resident;

(2)   A similar restriction in the banking group or selling group agreements requiring banking group members or selling group members not to offer securities to Ontario residents;

(3)   An "all-sold" certificate by the underwriters that they have not, to the best of their knowledge, sold any securities to Ontario residents;

(4)   A statement provided in the confirmation slip sent by underwriters to purchasers of the offered securities that it is the underwriters' understanding that the purchaser is not a resident of Ontario; or

(5)   A provision in the transfer agency agreement between the transfer agent and the issuer requiring the transfer agent not to register securities in the name of any Ontario resident for a period of time (e.g. ninety days) from the date of closing.

In Eurobond or Eurodollar financings sufficient precaution will generally have been taken where:

(1)   the offering circular contains a legend stating that the securities are not qualified for sale in Ontario or Canada and may not be offered or sold directly or indirectly in Ontario or Canada;

(2)   the underwriters contractually agree that they will observe this restriction regarding the prohibition of offering in Ontario or Canada; and

(3)   the securities to be distributed are initially issued in temporary form exchangeable for definitive securities 90 days after completion of the distribution upon certification that the definitive securities are not beneficially owned by Ontario or Canadian residents.

In other cases other factors will be relevant, including the class and nature of the securities being distributed, the attractiveness to Ontario investors of such securities, the likelihood that, absent such restrictions or precautions, the securities would come to rest in Ontario, whether a market for the class of securities being distributed or any other securities of the issuer already exists in Ontario, the likelihood of the development in the future of a market in Ontario for the securities being distributed, the way in which the distribution is proposed to be effected, the relationship between the capital markets of Ontario and the jurisdictions in which the securities are being distributed and the ease of access of one to the other, whether or not the underwriters and other participants in the distribution are, or are affiliated with, investment dealers that conduct substantial activities in Ontario and the presence of the issuer in Ontario (whether through the conduct of business in Ontario, a number of shareholders resident in Ontario, the issuer being closely followed by Ontario investors or otherwise).

In cases of private placements outside of Ontario, where hold periods would have been applicable if the placement had taken place in Ontario, the Commission takes the view that the restrictions made or precautions taken to ensure that the securities come to rest outside Ontario need not be effective beyond the time for the hold period which would have applied had the placement been made in Ontario.

The onus is on the issuer, underwriters and other participants in the distribution to determine the number and nature of the restrictions to be implemented and precaution to be taken.

4. Ontario Registrants

Each Ontario registrant has the duty to take reasonable steps to ensure that trades in securities effected by or through such registrant do not involve trades of securities into Ontario or to Ontario residents without compliance with the prospectus requirements of the Act or in reliance on an exemption therefrom. More particularly, a registrant who sells, on behalf of one of his clients, securities in Ontario or who purchases securities outside Ontario must take reasonable steps to ensure that the transaction does not involve the distribution of securities not qualified in Ontario coming to rest in Ontario or with Ontario residents.

All Ontario registrants should establish standard procedures to prevent unlawful distributions of securities into Ontario and to ensure that the registrant meets its continuing responsibility to know both its clients and the securities being sold by or to its clients.

See also National Policy 20.

5. *The Integrity of the Ontario Capital Markets and the Jurisdiction of the O.S.C.*

Needless to say, the Commission will not hesitate to intervene, to the extent of its powers, in distributions of securities outside of Ontario which negatively impact upon the integrity of Ontario capital markets.

Where the Commission becomes aware of distributions abroad by Ontario issuers that bring the reputation of Ontario's capital markets into disrepute, the Commission is of the view that it has the jurisdiction, for the due administration of the Act and in order to preserve the integrity of the Ontario capital markets, to exercise its cease trade powers or to take other appropriate action against issuers, underwriters and other participants so distributing securities abroad.

SECTION 2 — ONTARIO SECURITIES COMMISSION PROCEDURE AND RELATED MATTERS

O.S.C. Policy 2.1 — Applications to the Ontario Securities Commission

[Editor's note: Under consideration to be reformulated as OPS 12-601.]

A. Types of Applications and Fees

1. The procedures set forth in this Policy Statement apply to all applications made to the Ontario Securities Commission under appropriate sections of the *Securities Act* (Ontario) (the "Act"), the regulations made under the Act (the "Regulation"), O.S.C. Policy Statements and the *Business Corporations Act* (Ontario) (the "OBCA"). Applications for registration as an adviser, dealer or underwriter are not dealt with here. In addition, there are other, more informal decisions made by the Commission (such as under National Policy No. 11), the Director of the Commission or the Deputy-Director under the Act, the Regulation or some of the Policy Statements that do not require the formal application contemplated by this Policy Statement.

2. The following sections of the Act, the Regulation and the OBCA provide for applications to the Commission. Applications made otherwise than to the Commission are not dealt with here. Generally speaking, such sections contemplate orders by the Commission granting relief from various statutory requirements. The fee payable to the Commission when an application under one of these sections of the Act or the OBCA is found in Schedule 1 to the Regulation and the Schedule to the regulations made under the OBCA, respectively:

Section of the Act	Section of the Regulation*
61(5) [62(5)]	2(4)(b)
73 [74]	12(5) [Revoked]
73 [74] (supplementary	133(3) [Revoked]
application)	136(4) [Revoked]
79 [80]	138 [Revoked]
79 [80] (b)(iii)	
(in conjunction with	
Policy Statement 2.6 [52-601])	**Section of the OBCA**
82 [83]	1(8)
87 [88]	117(2)
99 [100]	
109 [113]	
111(2) [115(2)]	
113(2) [117(2)]	
114(3) [118(3)]	
117(2) [121(2)]	
140 [144]	

Notes:

* See also Reg. secs. 104, 211, 217 and 233.

B. Submission of Applications

1. All applications shall be addressed to:

    The Secretary to the Commission,

    Ontario Securities Commission,

    Suite 1800, Box 55

    20 Queen Street West,

    Toronto, Ontario,

    M5H 3S8.

    TDX #76

2.   Cheques in the amounts of the appropriate fees should be submitted with the application and made payable to the Treasurer of Ontario.

C. Number of Copies and Confidentiality

1.   The original executed application and two copies should be submitted. If Commission staff determine that the application should be heard by the full Commission, nine additional copies will be requested from the applicant. Additional copies should be made available on request of the Secretary for the use of the financial press. If the supporting material appended to the application is bulky, only one copy of the supporting material need be filed unless the Commission requests further copies.

2.   Upon receipt by the Commission of an application, one copy of the application shall be placed immediately in the public file unless confidentiality is specifically requested. Where confidentiality is requested, applicants should be prepared to demonstrate that such confidentiality is reasonable in the circumstances and would not be contrary to the public interest. Reference may be made in this regard to section 137(2) [140(2)] of the Act.

D. Contents and Format

There is no prescribed form for applications but they are often prepared in letter form. Applications should be divided into parts dealing with each of the following headings, as applicable, including the information, where relevant, indicated below:

(a) Summary

Include the name of the issuer, the name of the applicant (if different from the issuer), the statute, regulation or policy statement pursuant to which the application is made and the nature of the relief sought.

(b) The Issuer

(i)   the name of the issuer;

(ii)   jurisdiction and date of incorporation or (in the case of unincorporated entities) organization;

(iii)   (if relevant (such as in most applications under section 73 [74] of the Act) and where not otherwise dealt with in an exhibit such as financial statements or an annual report) capital structure — authorized and issued capital and debt obligations;

(iv)   whether the issuer is a reporting issuer;

(v)   listing status — whether listed on the TSE or any other stock exchange or trading over-the-counter, and recent price and volume trading data, if relevant;

(vi)   a statement that the issuer is not on the list of defaulting reporting issuers maintained pursuant to section 71(9) [72(9)];

(c) The Applicant

If the applicant is a person or company other than the issuer, include those items in clause (b) which are relevant to the applicant and explain the applicant's relationship to the issuer.

(d) Order or Decision Sought

(i)   the facts on which the application is based;

(ii)   the reasons for making the application;

(iii)   relevant considerations including case law, prior Commission decisions, policies and argument regarding the foregoing;

(iv)   other relevant circumstances including regulatory decisions, applications pending, conditions or recommendations;

(v)   supporting documents — such documents may be included as schedules or exhibits to the application and references in the application may be made to such supporting documents; and

(vi)   where thought appropriate, a draft form of order for the consideration of the Commission staff.

        Where more than one order or decision is sought, so indicate and remit the necessary fees.

(e) Verification

Each application must be signed by the party submitting the application and must contain a statement certifying the truth of the facts contained therein. If the application is not signed by the applicant and is made by an agent for the applicant such statement may be omitted if the application is accompanied by a statement made by the applicant confirming the authority of the agent to prepare and file the application and confirming also the truth of the facts contained in the application. Sample language might include:

      We authorize the making and filing of the attached application by _____ and confirm the truth of the facts contained therein.

      DATED at _____ this _____ day of _____, 19

                                             _____
                                                authorized officer"

E. Commission Procedure

1.   Upon receipt of an application with the correct fee, a member of the Commission staff will be assigned to review the application and recommend disposition. The staff member may contact the applicant if further information or clarification is required. Where the additional information or clarification sought is not provided with reasonable dispatch, the Commission on its own motion or on the recom-

mendation of the staff member may decide that the application should be treated as abandoned. No application will be treated as abandoned simply because a staff member has not had an opportunity to review it. The staff member may recommend that a quorum of the Commission make a certain decision on an ad hoc basis without a hearing. If such a recommendation is accepted, an order will be prepared and signed by two members of the Commission without a hearing. No application will be refused without the applicant being afforded the opportunity of a hearing.

2. Where the staff member recommends denial of an application or where a matter is contentious or of general importance or of a non-routine nature, the application will be set down for hearing before the Commission. The staff memorandum respecting the application will be forwarded to the applicant. The Commission meets regularly on Thursdays and hears such applications. The applicant is afforded an opportunity to present the application and the staff member who dealt with the application will generally be present at the hearing.

3. The application and all relevant supporting material and the staff memorandum must be delivered to the Commission no later than the Wednesday, eight days prior to the regular Commission meeting at which the application will be heard.

4. In those cases where a clear and compelling situation exists, requests may be made to the Secretary to the Commission or to the staff member dealing with the application to expedite the hearing.

5. The hearing itself is generally conducted on an informal basis with the decision being rendered orally by the Commission. In the normal course, the Commission will have reviewed the material prior to the meeting, will ask questions of the applicant with respect thereto and will not expect the application to be set forth again. In some cases a more formal hearing may be required. Hearings are open to the public unless the Commission is satisfied that there is sufficient reason to hear the matter, or part of the matter, in camera. Hearings are usually transcribed, although an applicant should specifically request transcription if it is believed necessary. Hearings under section 73 [74] of the Act are seldom transcribed as section 73 [74] rulings are not subject to appeal.

6. Although section 73 [74] of the Act provides for rulings with respect to trades or intended trades, the Commission is generally reluctant to issue rulings which have retroactive effect. As an alternative, the Commission may in appropriate circumstances determine that no action will be taken with respect to a particular transaction.

7. An application may be withdrawn at any time before the Commission has reached a decision on the matter without prejudice to the right of the applicant to re-apply. Decisions of the Commission, except rulings made under section 73 [74] of the Act, are subject to appeal to the Divisional Court of the Supreme Court of Ontario.

(Former Policy 3-18: First published (1968) O.S.C.B. 237; amended (1969) O.S.C.B. 71, (1969) 185, (1974) O.S.C.B. 2; policy further amplified in *Re Warren Explorations Ltd.*, (1976) O.S.C.B. 111. Former Policy 3-18A: First published (1974) O.S.C.B. 84. Former Policy 3-19: First published (1968) O.S.C.B. 15; amended (1968) O.S.C.B. 235, (1969) O.S.C.B. 16, (1971) O.S.C.B. 203, (1973) O.S.C.B. 77. Former Policy 3-49. First published (1980) O.S.C.B. 461; published as 2.1 (1984) 2 O.S.C.B. 360E.)

Policies and Orders: OSCN 12-704, NPS 11-203.

Section 4 — Registration

O.S.C. Policy 4.3 — Self-directed RRSP's and Other Plans Recognized by the Commission for Purposes of this Policy Statement and Administered by Brokers or Investment Dealers on Behalf of Authorized Trustees

[Editor's Note: To be reformulated as National Instrument 33-101 "Administration of Self-Directed RRSPs, RESPs, and RRIFs by Dealers"; Request for Comments 21 O.S.C.B. 965 (February 13, 1998); currently on hold according to OSCN 11-739]

The Ontario Securities Commission will not object to arrangements between brokers or investment dealers and authorized trustees concerning the administration of self-directed registered retirement savings plans and other plans recognized by the Commission for the purpose of Policy Statement 4.3, the terms of which allow brokers or investment dealers to retain possession of any assets of a trust, (the "Plans") provided that:

1.

   (a) the authorized trustee is a financial institution as defined in the by-laws and regulations of the self-regulatory organizations of which the broker or investment dealer is a member unless the Commission and the self-regulatory organizations rule otherwise; and

   (b) primary liability to planholders for any breach of trust remains that of the authorized trustee;

2. physical control over plan securities on hand is maintained by designated employees of the broker or investment dealer;

3. subject to any additional requirements of the authorized trustee:

   (a) securities held by a broker or investment dealer for the authorized trustee on behalf of its individual planholders are held in safekeeping for the authorized trustee in a location reserved solely for those securities. Such securities may only be released on instruction of the authorized trustee or the planholder;

   (b) while such securities are held in safekeeping for the authorized trustee within such safekeeping system, they may be held in bulk segregation on behalf of its individual planholders and identified as being so held in the broker's or investment dealer's security position record, customers' ledger and the statement of account provided to the planholder and to the authorized trustee. Securities that are held by a depository approved by the self-regulatory organization of which the broker or investment dealer is a member should be held in a separate plan segregation account (by security). Where a broker or investment dealer is a member of a recognized depository, the use of that depository for lodging of securities held for plan accounts is recommended; and

(c)   the securities required to be segregated be determined at least twice each week;

4.   the means, be it numerical code or otherwise, by which accounts of planholders for self-directed plans are identified is clearly distinguishable from the manner of identifying other types of accounts and each account is itself identified as being that of the authorized trustee for the planholders as beneficial owner, each being named. All such accounts should be kept in a separate section of the customer account records specifically reserved for such plan accounts;

5.   all cash received by the dealer for or on behalf of plan accounts is transferred to the authorized trustee by the next business day except that cash required or received in connection with the settlement of securities transactions shall be transferred from the dealer to the authorized trustee or from the authorized trustee to the dealer as the case may be, on the settlement or value date specified in the confirmation of trade;

6.   the agreement between the broker or investment dealer and the authorized trustee incorporates the protection afforded planholders by clause 3(a) above and prohibits the broker or investment dealer from using assets from the authorized trustee's plan account for the planholders to pay claims the broker or investment dealer may have against that particular planholder's non-plan accounts other than claims in respect of administration fees or administration expenses relating to the plan account;

7.   where the terms and conditions of the plan contain investment restrictions required under the *Income Tax Act* (Canada), the broker or investment dealer shall advise each planholder (i) that there are consequences pursuant to the *Income Tax Act* (Canada) on the acquisition or holding by the account of non-qualified investments or excess foreign property and (ii) on a monthly basis, if non-qualified investments or excess foreign properties have been acquired for the account or if previously acquired qualified investments have become unqualified;

8.   all of the regulatory authorities under which the authorized trustee operates have acknowledged that they have received all legal opinions, tax rulings or other documentation the authority has requested from the authorized trustee;

9.   approval of the self-regulatory organization of which the broker or investment dealer is a member has been obtained prior to the arrangement being implemented and the National Examiner of the National Contingency Fund has been notified;

10.

(a)   a report is prepared by the broker or investment dealer on a monthly basis identifying, by security, the quantity required to be segregated but which is not so segregated. The report shall be in a form acceptable to the Commission. Such report shall be filed with the examiners of the self-regulatory organization in duplicate within 10 business days of the last business day of each month. The examiners shall file a copy of this report with the National Examiner of the National Contingency Fund. The frequency of this report will be reviewed periodically by the Commission;

(b)   the foregoing report will not be required by a broker or investment dealer where the self-regulatory organization has reviewed the systems and procedures pertaining to the operation of the plan and is satisfied that such systems and procedures are operating in accordance with the requirements of this policy. Such review shall be conducted as part of every regular examination of the broker or investment dealer carried out by the self-regulatory organization.

(Former Policy 3-55: (Interim) first published (1981) 1 O.S.C.B. 22E; final (1982) 3 O.S.C.B. 47E; published as 4.3 (1982) 4 O.S.C.B. 408E; revised (1984) 7 O.S.C.B. 3879.)

1.0 — PROCEDURE AND RELATED MATTERS

1.1 — Powers of OSC Secretary

Order: dated January 27, 1987.

Summary: Secretary of the Commission is vested with various powers.

In the Matter of the Securities Act, R.S.O. 1980, Chapter 466, as Amended
and
In the Matter of the Secretary to the Ontario Securities Commission

Order (Section 10(1)(d))

WHEREAS section 10(1)(d) [7(1)(e)] of the *Securities Act*, R.S.O. 1980, Chapter 466, as amended (the "Act") empowers the Secretary to the Ontario Securities Commission (the "Commission") to exercise such powers as are vested in him by the Commission;

AND WHEREAS the Commission considers it expedient for the due administration of the Act;

IT IS THEREFORE ORDERED, pursuant to subsection 10(1)(d) [7(1)(e)] of the Act, that the Secretary be and is hereby vested with the power to certify:

    (a) as to the dates upon which any hearing took place before the Commission;

    (b) as to the commissioners who sat on a panel hearing any matter and the date of the appointment and expiry of such appointment to the Commission of each commissioner;

    (c) as to the issuance of any Notice of Hearing, Order or Decision by the Commission and the dates thereof without appending such Notice of Hearing, Order or Decision to such certificate;

    (d) as to the exhibits filed at any hearing before the Commission without appending the exhibits to such certificate; and

    (e) as to the transcripts of any hearing before the Commission, without appending such transcripts to the certificate.

1.2 — Assignment of Certain Powers and Duties of the Ontario Securities Commission

Assignment: dated October 25, 2013: 36 O.S.C.B. 10876; amended and restated assignment dated July 3, 2012: 35 O.S.C.B. 6846; amended and restated assignment dated February 2, 2010: 33 O.S.C.B. 1165 as amended June 22, 2012: 35 O.S.C.B. 6845; replaced assignment dated March 16, 2007: 30 O.S.C.B. 2527; replaced assignment dated May 8, 2006: 29 O.S.C.B. 4505; replaced assignment dated March 27, 2006: 29 O.S.C.B. 4510; replaced assignment dated June 30, 2005: 28 O.S.C.B. 6893; replaced assignment dated April 12, 1999: 20 O.S.C.B. 2399, as amended September 7, 1999: 22 O.S.C.B. 5693, February 15, 2000: 23 O.S.C.B. 1312, January 23, 2001: 24 O.S.C.B. 874, April 27, 2001: 24 O.S.C.B. 2776, October 3, 2001: 24 O.S.C.B. 6026, April 15, 2003: 26 O.S.C.B. 3106 and February 3, 2004: 27 O.S.C.B. 2308; replaced assignment dated March 10, 1995: 18 O.S.C.B. 1156; as amended by amendment of assignment dated November 9, 1995: 18 O.S.C.B. 5423; June 27, 1997: 20 O.S.C.B. 3473 and May 22, 1998: 21 O.S.C.B. 3795.

In the Matter of
the Securities Act,
R.S.O. 1990, Chapter S. 5, as Amended
and
In the Matter of
the Assignment of Certain Powers and Duties of the
Ontario Securities Commission

Assignment
Subsection 6(3)

WHEREAS:

A. On July 3, 2012, pursuant to subsection 6(3) of the Act, the Ontario Securities Commission (the "Commission") issued an assignment (the "July 3, 2012 Assignment") assigning certain of its powers and duties under the *Securities Act* (Ontario) (the "Act") to each "Director" as that term is defined in subsection 1(1) of the Act, acting individually;

B. The Commission considers it desirable to amend and restate the July 3, 2012 Assignment by adding a new paragraph 2(b.1) where the Commission assigns its powers and duties under clauses 21(5)(a) and 21.2(3) 2 of the Act but only in certain limited circumstances as described in that paragraph;

NOW THEREFORE:

1. Effective July 26, 2012, the February 2, 2010 Assignment is revoked, without prejudice to the effectiveness of any lawful exercise prior to the date of this revocation of the powers and duties assigned thereby, and is hereby replaced with the following amended and restated assignment (the "Assignment").

2. Pursuant to subsection 6(3) of the Act, the Commission assigns to each Director, acting individually, the powers and duties vested in or imposed on the Commission by:

    (a) clauses 21(5)(a), 21(5)(b), 21.0.1(a) and 21.0.1(b) of the Act but only:

        (i) with respect to the review and decision regarding information filed in Form 21-101F1 or Form 21-101F2 or the exhibits thereto, and

        (ii) where such information relates to matters that do not raise significant regulatory or public interest concerns and do not introduce a novel feature to the capital markets;

    (b) clauses 21(5)(e), 21.0.1(c) and subsections 21.1(4), 21.2(3) and 21.2.1(3) of the Act, but only in respect of by-laws, rules, regulations, policies, procedures, interpretations or practices that

        (i) do not raise significant regulatory or public interest concerns and,

        (ii) where they relate to an exchange, a quotation and trade reporting system, an alternative trading system or a clearing agency, do not introduce a novel feature to the capital markets;

    (b.1) clauses 21(5)(a) and 21.2(3) 2 of the Act, but only in respect of matters requiring approval under the terms and conditions of a Commission order recognizing an exchange or a clearing agency that

        (i) do not raise significant regulatory or public interest concerns and,

        (ii) do not introduce a novel feature to the capital markets;

    (c) subsection 62(5) of the Act;

        (i) do not raise significant regulatory or public interest concerns and,

        (ii) do not introduce a novel feature to the capital markets;

    (d) section 74 of the Act, but only in respect of orders that a person or company is not subject to section 53 of the Act in connection with solicitations of expressions of interest before the filing of a preliminary short form prospectus in accordance with National Instrument 44-101 *Short Form Prospectus Distributions* for securities to be issued pursuant to an over-allotment option granted to an underwriter by an issuer or a selling securityholder of an issuer;

    (e) subclause 1(10)(a)(ii) of the Act but only in respect of a reporting issuer:

        (i) whose outstanding securities, including debt securities, are beneficially owned, directly or indirectly, by fewer than 15 securityholders in Ontario and fewer than 51 securityholders in total worldwide,

        (ii) whose securities, including debt securities, are not traded in Canada or another country on a marketplace as defined in National Instrument 21-101*Marketplace Operation* or any other facility for bringing together buyers and sellers of securities where trading data is publicly reported,

        (iii) that is not in default of any of its obligations as a reporting issuer, and

        (iv) that will not be a reporting issuer in any jurisdiction of Canada immediately following the Director making an order that the reporting issuer is not a reporting issuer;

    (f) clause 1(11)(b) of the Act, in the circumstances described in Parts 2 and 3 of Ontario Securities Commission Policy 12-602 *Designating an Issuer in Certain Other Canadian Jurisdictions as a Reporting Issuer in Ontario*;

    (g) paragraph 1 of subsection 127(1) of the Act, provided the making of the order under subsection 127(1) of the Act is not contested on its merits and is only in respect of suspending the registration of:

        (i) a registrant that has, in the opinion of the Director, acted contrary to the public interest and consents to such suspension; and

        (ii) a registrant that has filed an application to surrender the registrant's registration pursuant to section 30 of the Act and has also consented to the suspension of the registrant's registration;

    (h) paragraph 2 and paragraph 2.1 of subsection 127(1) of the Act and subsections 127(2), (3), (5), (7), (8) and (9) of the Act, provided that the making of the order under subsections 127(1), (7) or (8) of the Act is not contested on its merits and is only in respect of

        (i) trading, generally or by a person or company identified in the cease trade order, or acquisition, by a particular person or company identified in the cease trade order, in or of securities of a reporting issuer that has failed to file, as applicable,

            (A) comparative annual financial statements or interim financial reports containing the statements and the notes required by National Instrument 51-102 *Continuous Disclosure Obligations* ("NI 51-102") or by National Instrument 71-102 *Continuous Disclosure and Other Exemptions Relating to Foreign Issuers* ("NI 71-102"),

            (B) an auditor's report issued in connection with comparative annual financial statements required by NI 51-102, and NI 71-102,

(C) an AIF, MD&A, information circular, or business acquisition report (all as defined by NI 51-102 and by NI 71-102) containing information for each of the content items required by NI 51-102 and the applicable form, by Part 5 of National Instrument 52-110 *Audit Committees*, or by NI 71-102;

(D) a report on reserves data and other oil and gas information as required by National Instrument 51-101 *Standards of Disclosure for Oil and Gas Activities* ("NI 51-101") containing information for each of the content items required by NI 51-101 and Form 51-101F2,

(E) a technical report as required by National Instrument 43-101 *Standards of Disclosure for Mineral Projects* ("NI 43-101") containing information for each of the content items required by NI 43-101 and Form 43-101F1, or

(F) certification of filings as required by National Instrument 52-109 *Certification of Disclosure in Issuers' Annual and Interim Filings*

within the time period prescribed by Ontario securities law;

(ii) trading, generally or by a person or company identified in the cease trade order, or acquisition, by a particular person or company identified in the cease trade order, in or of securities of a reporting issuer that has acknowledged in writing that comparative annual financial statements or interim financial reports filed with the Commission were not prepared in accordance with generally accepted accounting principles, including, but not limited to, where an issuer has advised the Commission or staff in writing, or has publicly announced, that it intends to restate such financial statements;

(iii) trading, generally or by a person or company identified in the cease trade order, or acquisition, by a particular person or company identified in the cease trade order, in or of securities of a reporting issuer that has filed its financial statements accompanied by an auditor's report prepared by a public accounting firm that is, as of the date of the auditor's report, not a participating audit firm as defined by National Instrument 52-108 *Auditor Oversight*, or is not in compliance with any restrictions or sanctions imposed by the Canadian Public Accountability Board;

(i) subsection 140(2) of the Act in the circumstances described in clauses (b), (c) and (j) of section C of Ontario Securities Commission Policy 13-601 *Public Availability of Material Filed Under the Securities Act*;

(j) section 144 of the Act to:

(i) revoke or vary any decision made by a Director under authority assigned to him or her by the Commission pursuant to this Assignment or a predecessor Assignment, including another decision made under section 144 of the Act, but only if at the time of revoking or varying such decision the Director would have been authorized to make the decision being varied or revoked, or

(ii) vary any order made by the Commission under section 127 of the Act to the extent necessary to permit transfers of securities as contemplated by Section 3.2 of National Policy 12-202 *Revocation of a Compliance-related Cease Trade Order*,

provided that a person or company directly affected by a decision of a Director made pursuant to this Assignment may, by notice in writing sent by registered mail to the Secretary of the Commission within 30 days after the mailing of the notice of the decision, request and be entitled to a hearing and review of such decision by the Commission.

3. The Executive Director of the Commission shall from time to time determine which one or more other Directors, in each case acting alone, should, as an administrative matter, exercise each of the powers or perform each of the duties assigned by the Commission in paragraph 2 above, each of which powers may also be exercised and performed by the Executive Director, acting alone.

4. No person or company shall be required to inquire as to the authority of a member of the staff of the Commission to sign a decision pursuant to this Assignment in the capacity of a Director, and a decision purporting to be signed pursuant to this Assignment by a member of the staff of the Commission in the capacity of a Director shall be conclusively deemed to have been signed by a Director authorized by this Assignment without proof of such authority.

5. This Assignment does not preclude the Commission from itself exercising or performing any of the assigned powers or duties.

[Editor's note: see also BOR 1.3.]

1.3 — Designation by the Executive Director of Positions for the Purposes of the Definition of Director

Designation and Determination: dated March 4, 2010: 33 O.S.C.B. 2069; replaced a Designation and Determination dated August 16, 2007: 30 O.S.C.B. 7301; replaced a Designation and Determination dated August 17, 2005: 28 O.S.C.B. 7478, which replaced a Designation and Determination dated February 15, 2000: 23 O.S.C.B. 1311, as amended: 23 O.S.C.B. 7088: 23 O.S.C.B. 7087, 24 O.S.C.B. 4859, 26 O.S.C.B. 1569 and 26 O.S.C.B. 2635; which replaced a Designation and Determination dated April 12, 1999: 22 O.S.C.B. 2399 as amended September 7, 1999 [not published] which replaced a Designation and Determination dated May 10, 1996: (1996), 19 O.S.C.B. 2617 which revoked a Determination and Designation dated March 10, 1995: (1995), 18 O.S.C.B. 1154 as amended by Amendment of Determination and Designation dated November 9, 1995: (1995), 18 O.S.C.B. 5423.

**In the Matter of
the Securities Act,
R.S.O. 1990, Chapter S.5, as Amended (the "Act")
and
In the Matter
of the Designation by the Executive Director of Positions for the Purposes of the Definition of Director in the Act
and
In the Matter of
the Assignment of Certain Powers and Duties of the
Ontario Securities Commission**

Executive Director's Designation and Determination

WHEREAS:

A. On March 16, 2007, the Commission issued an amended and restated Assignment (the **March 2007 Assignment**) pursuant to subsection 6(3) of the Act, assigning certain of its powers and duties under the Act to each "Director" as that term is defined in subsection 1(1) of the Act, acting individually.

B. On February 2, 2010, the Commission revoked the March 2007 Assignment and replaced it with an amended and restated assignment (the **February 2010 Assignment**).

C. Under subsection 1(1) of the Act, "Director" means the Executive Director of the Commission, a Director or Deputy Director of the Commission, or a person employed by the Commission in a position designated by the Executive Director.

D. The February 2010 Assignment provides that the Executive Director of the Commission shall from time to time determine which one or more other Directors, in each case acting alone, should, as an administrative matter, exercise each of the powers or perform each of the duties assigned by the Commission in paragraph 2 of the Assignment, each of which powers may also be exercised and performed by the Executive Director alone.

E. On August 16, 2007, the Executive Director issued a designation and determination (the **August 2007 Designation**) whereby the Executive Director, among other things: (i) revoked the previous existing designation and determination, (ii) designated certain positions, whether or not in an acting capacity, for the purposes of the definition of "Director" contained in subsection 1(1) of the Act, and (iii) determined that, in addition to the Executive Director acting alone, each Director (other than certain specified Directors) may exercise the powers and perform the duties assigned by the Commission to Directors in the March 2007 Assignment an any other successor assignment in effect from time to time, until otherwise determined by the Executive Director.

F. The Compliance and Registrant Regulation Branch of the Commission is implementing a new organizational structure (the **Reorganized CRR**) with four multi-functional, integrated teams reporting to two new Deputy Director positions.

G. Under the Reorganized CRR, the positions of Assistant Manager, Registrant Regulation will not be continued and many activities which were previously the responsibility of these Assistant Managers will become the responsibility of the new positions of Senior Registration Supervisor or Registration Supervisor for three of the four teams.

NOW THEREFORE, the Executive Director:

1. revokes the August 2007 Designation;

2. designates each of the following positions, whether or not in an acting capacity, for the purposes of the definition of "Director" contained in subsection 1(1) of the Act:

(a) each Manager and Assistant Manager in the Corporate Finance Branch of the Commission,

(b) each Manager, Assistant Manager, Senior Registration Supervisor and Registration Supervisor in the Compliance and Registrant Regulation Branch of the Commission,

(c) each Manager and Assistant Manager in the Market Regulation Branch of the Commission,

(d) each Manager and Assistant Manager in the Enforcement Branch of the Commission,

(e) each Manager and Assistant Manager in the Investment Funds Branch of the Commission,

(f) the Chief Accountant of the Commission, and

(g) the General Counsel of the Commission;

3. designates the Supervisor-Insider Reporting Group and each Senior Legal Counsel and Senior Accountant in the Corporate Finance Branch of the Commission for the purposes of the definition of "Director" contained in subsection 1(1) of the Act, but solely for the purpose of granting exemptions from fees for the late filing of insider reports on Form 55-102F2 under Commission Rule 13-502 Fees; and

4. determines that, in addition to the Executive Director acting alone, each Director, other than the Supervisor-Insider Reporting Group, and each Senior Legal Counsel and Senior Accountant in the Corporate Finance Branch of the Commission, may exercise the powers and perform the duties assigned by the Commission to Directors in the February 2010 Assignment and any successor assignment in effect from time to time, until otherwise determined by the Executive Director.

[Editor's note: See also BOR 1.2.]

1.4 — Authorization by Commission Pursuant to Subsection 3.5(3) of Certain Powers Respecting Hearings

Authorization Order: April 12, 2013 [not published in the O.S.C.B.]

In the Matter of
the Securities Act,
R.S.O. 1990, Chapter S.5, as Amended (the "Act")
and
In the Matter of
an Authorization Pursuant to Subsection 3.5(3) of the Act

Authorization Order
Subsection 3.5(3)

WHEREAS a quorum of the Ontario Securities Commission (the "Commission") may, pursuant to subsection 3.5(3) of the Act, in writing authorize any member of the Commission to exercise any of the powers and perform any of the duties of the Commission, except the power to conduct contested hearings on the merits.

AND WHEREAS, by an authorization order made on February 14, 2013 pursuant to subsection 3.5(3) of the Act each of HOWARD I. WETSTON, JAMES E.A. TURNER, JAMES D. CARNWATH, MARY G. CONDON, PAULETTE L. KENNEDY, VERN KRISHNA, CHRISTOPHER PORTNER, EDWARD P. KERWIN, AND ALAN J. LENCZNER, acting alone, to exercise, subject to subsection 3.5(4) of the Act, the powers of the Commission to grant adjournments and set dates for hearings, to hear and determine procedural matters, and to make and give any orders, directions, appointments, applications and consents under sections 5, 11, 12, 17, 19, 20, 122, 126, 127, 128, 129, 144, 146 and 152 of the Act that the Commission is authorized to make and give, except the power to conduct contested hearings on the merits.

NOW, THEREFORE, IT IS ORDERED that the Authorization is hereby revoked as of 12:00 a.m. on April 12, 2013; and

THE COMMISSION HEREBY AUTHORIZES, pursuant to subsection 3.5(3) of the Act, each of HOWARD I. WETSTON, JAMES E.A. TURNER, MARY G. CONDON, JAMES D. CARNWATH, EDWIN P. KERWIN, VERN KRISHNA, ALAN J. LENCZNER, CHRISTOPHER PORTNER AND C. WESLEY M. SCOTT, acting alone, to exercise, subject to subsection 3.5(4) of the Act, the powers of the Commission to grant adjournments and set dates for hearings, to hear and determine procedural matters, and to make and give any orders, directions, appointments, applications and consents under sections 5, 11, 12, 17, 19, 20, 122, 126, 127, 128, 129, 144, 146 and 152 of the Act that the Commission is authorized to make and give, including the power to conduct contested hearings on the merits; and

THE COMMISSION FURTHER ORDERS that this Authorization Order shall have full force and effect as of 12:01 a.m. of April 12, 2013 until revoked or such further amendment may be made.

1.5 — Appointment of Acting Secretary

Order: dated June 10, 2005: 28 O.S.C.B. 5363.

In the Matter of
the Securities Act, R.S.O. 1990, Chapter S.5, as Amended (the "Act")
and
In the Matter of
the Secretary to the Commission

Order
Subsections 3.5(3) and 7(3)

WHEREAS a quorum of the Ontario Securities Commission (the "Commission") may, pursuant to subsection 3.5(3) of the Act, in writing authorize any member of the Commission to exercise any of the powers and perform any of the duties of the Commission, except the power to conduct contested hearings on the merits.

AND WHEREAS, the Secretary to the Commission may from time to time be absent from the Commission and unable to exercise the powers vested in the Secretary under the Act;

AND WHEREAS by order made on November 1, 2004, pursuant to subsection 7(3) of the Act (the "Order") the Commission designated Daisy Aranha to act in the capacity of Secretary in the absence of the Secretary.

NOW, THEREFORE, IT IS ORDERED that the Order is hereby revoked; and

THE COMMISSION HEREBY AUTHORIZES, pursuant to subsection 3.5(3) and subsection 7(3) of the Act, that any one of Josee Turcotts, Christos Grivas and Daisy Aranha is hereby designated to act in the capacity of Secretary and may alone, in the absence of the Secretary, exercise the powers vested in the Secretary under the Act of the Regulation thereto.

BLANKET ORDERS

2.0 — CERTAIN CAPITAL MARKET PARTICIPANTS

2.1 — Recognition of Certain Stock Exchanges — s. 154(1) of the Regulation

Recognition: dated October 6, 2000: (2000), 23 O.S.C.B. 6985

In the Matter of Regulation Made Under the Securities Act, R.S.O. 1990, Chapter S. 5, as Amended, R.R.O. 1990, Reg. 1015 as Amended (The "Regulation")
and
In the Matter of the Recognition of Certain Stock Exchanges

Order (Section 154(1) of the Regulation)

WHEREAS the Commission appointed the Canadian Unlisted Board ("CUB") an agent to operate an over-the-counter trade reporting facility pursuant to section 153 of the Regulation;

AND WHEREAS CUB operates a facility for the reporting of over-the-counter trading as contemplated by Part VI of the Regulation;

AND WHEREAS Part VI of the Regulation requires that every purchase or sale of a security made by a registered dealer must be reported to the trade reporting facility except those trades made through a Canadian stock exchange or a stock exchange or organized market recognized by the Commission;

AND UPON the Commission being satisfied that to do so would not be prejudicial to the public interest;

THE COMMISSION HEREBY RECOGNIZES, pursuant to s. 154(1) of the Regulation, the following stock exchanges and organized markets for the purpose of excluding trades executed on such stock exchanges and organized markets from the trade reporting requirements of Part VI;

    (a) NASDAQ;

    (b) The International Stock Exchange of the United Kingdom and the Republic of Ireland Limited; and

    (c) all stock exchanges outside of Canada that require participants to report details of transactions and publish such details.

2.2 — Assignment of Certain Powers of the Director to IIROC

Assignment: dated September 22, 2009
32 O.S.C.B. 8658

In the Matter of the Securities Act, R.S.O. 1990, c. S.5, as amended (the OSA)
and the Commodity Futures Act, R.S.O. 1990, C.20, as amended (the CFA)
and
In the Matter of the Revocation of the Assignment of Certain Powers and Duties of the Director to the Investment Industry Regulatory Organization of Canada (IIROC) and The Assignment of Certain Powers and Duties of the Director to IIROC

Revocation
(Subsection 21.5(3) OSA and Subsection 20(3) of the CFA)

Assignment
(Subsection 21.5(2) of the OSA and Subsection 20(2) CFA)

1. IIROC is a "recognized self-regulatory organization", as defined in subsection 1(1) of the OSA and subsection 1(1) of the CFA.

2. Subsection 21.5(2) of the OSA provides that the Executive Director may, with the approval of the Ontario Securities Commission (the **Commission**), assign to a recognized self-regulatory organization any of the powers and duties of the Director under Part XI of the OSA or the regulations related to that Part.

3. Subsection 20(2) of the CFA provides that the Executive Director may, with the approval of the Commission, assign to a recognized self-regulatory organization any of the powers and duties of the Director under Part VIII of the CFA or the regulations related to that Part.

4. Subsection 21.5(3) of the OSA provides that, with the approval of the Commission, the Executive Director may at any time revoke, in whole or in part, an assignment of powers and duties made under section 21.5 of the OSA.

5. Subsection 20(3) of the CFA provides that, with the approval of the Commission, the Executive Director may at any time revoke, in whole or in part, an assignment of powers and duties made under section 20 of the CFA.

6. In an Assignment dated June 1, 2008 (the **Existing Assignment**), with the approval of the Commission, the Executive Director assigned to IIROC certain powers and duties of the Director under:

    (a) Part XI of the OSA and the regulations related to that Part (including -- subsection 127(1) and clauses 127(2)(b), (d), (e), (g) and (h) of the OSA Regulation (defined below) and Parts 2 and 4 of OSC Rule 31-502 *Proficiency Requirements for Registrants (OSC Rule 31-502)*, pursuant to subsection 21.5(2) of the OSA; and

    (b) Part VIII of the CFA and the regulations related to that Part, pursuant to subsection 20(2) of the CFA.

7. A copy of the Existing Assignment is attached hereto as Schedule A.

8. Schedule 26 (the **OSA Schedule**) of the *Budget Measures Act, 2009* provides for amendments to the OSA, including section 4 of the Schedule (the **OSA Part XI Amendments**) which provides for the repeal of the current Part XI and substitution of a new Part XI.

9. On June 5, 2009, the *Budget Measures Act, 2009* received Royal Assent.

10. Subsection 21(2) of the OSA Schedule provides that the OSA Part XI Amendments will come into force on a day to be named by proclamation of the Lieutenant Governor.

11. On July 14, 2009, the Commission revoked OSC Rule 31-502. The making and revoking of this rule was subject to the approval of the Minister, which occurred on August 28, 2009. The making and revoking of this rule is effective on September 28, 2009, assuming that the proclamation described in paragraph 10 and the proclamation by the Lieutenant Governor of other specified sections of the OSA Schedule occurs by September 28, 2009.

12. On July 20, 2009, the Commission revoked section 127 of R.R.O. 1990, Regulation 1015, as amended, made under the OSA (the "**OSA Regulation**"). The revocation of this section is also effective on September 28, 2009, assuming the proclamations described in paragraph 11 occur by September 28, 2009.

13. The Executive Director and the Commission consider it now desirable for the Existing Assignment to be replaced by this new Assignment.

NOW THEREFORE:

Subject to the proclamations described in paragraph 11 occurring by September 28, 2009,

1. Under subsection 21.5(3) of the OSA and subsection 20(3) of the CFA, the Executive Director revokes the Existing Assignment, effective on September 28, 2009, without prejudice to the effectiveness of any exercise, prior to such revocation, of the powers and duties that were assigned by the Existing Assignment.

2. Under subsection 21.5(2) of the OSA and subsection 20(2) of the CFA, effective on September 28, 2009, the Executive Director assigns to IIROC:

(A) with respect to applications for registration, applications for reinstatement of registration and applications for amendment of registration from individuals who are approved persons of members of IIROC and individuals who are applying to become approved persons of members of IIROC, the powers and duties vested in or imposed on the Director by:

(a) sections 27 and 31 of the OSA,

(b) section 23 of the CFA, and

(c) subsections 37(7) and 38(2) of R.R.O. 1990, Regulation 90, made under the CFA; and

(B) with respect to the registration of individuals who are approved persons of IIROC, the powers and duties vested in or imposed upon the Director by:

(a) section 28 of the OSA, but only in respect of the power to impose terms and conditions at any time during the period of registration, and paragraph 5 of section 31 of the OSA, and

(b) subsections 23(2) of the CFA, but only in respect of the power to impose terms and conditions at any time during the period of registration, and subsection 23(3) of the CFA.

DATED at Toronto, this 22nd day of September, 2009.

Schedule A

[not reproduced]

BLANKET ORDERS

ONTARIO SECURITIES COMMISSION NOTICES

The notices contained in this section have been published in the O.S.C. Bulletin. They consist of Ontario Securities Commission notices that have not been allocated a 5-digit number in accordance with the current numbering system which can be found under "Rules (including National Instruments) and Policies, Recognition and Designation Orders and Notices with the Numbering System for the Policy Reformulation Project".

Ontario Securities Commission Notices

Notice 41 — Adviser Registration, Disclosure and Other Issues Relating to Labour Sponsored Investment Funds

Date: 1995/11/17

18 O.S.C.B. 5420

[Not reproduced.]

Notice 44 — Viatical Settlements

Date: 1996/08/30

19 O.S.C.B. 4680

A viatical settlement is a relatively new investment product originating in the United States, whereby an individual with a terminal illness transfers the right to receive death benefits due under his or her life insurance policy to a third party in return for a cash payment, typically discounted from the face value of the policy. The investor expects to collect the benefits under the policy upon the death of the insured. Viatical settlements are generally arranged by a promoter who performs a number of pre-settlement and post-settlement services.

It has been brought to the attention of Commission staff that viatical settlements are being marketed in Ontario to retail investors and that registrants are being approached as potential sales agents. There appears to be considerable uncertainty as to the application of the *Securities Act* (Ontario) to these investments. Commission staff is publishing this notice in response to requests for clarification of the question.

The *Securities Act* (Ontario) (the "Act") applies to all trades in "securities" within the meaning of subsection 1(1) of the Act. The definition of "security" includes any "investment contract". The meaning of this term is not set out in the Act, but has been elaborated in a series of court decisions in Canada and in the United States, where federal securities laws employ a similar definition of a "security".

Viatical settlements can take a variety of legal forms. If the viatical settlement takes the form of a fractional interest in a pool of benefit payments, the settlement is simply an asset-backed security, and as such is a security for purposes of the Act. If an investor is matched with a particular policy holder, the settlement may constitute an investment contract and therefore a "security" for purposes of the Act. This would be determined by the collateral contractual arrangements and circumstances surrounding the settlement. One of the circumstances where a viatical settlement would, in staff's view, constitute an investment contract rather than a commercial contract is, for example, where the investor relies on the intermediary to select and evaluate the policy(ies), to monitor the health of the insured and to collect the benefits.

Commission staff's position as to what constitutes an investment contract in the context of viatical settlements is unchanged by the recent opinion of the majority of a three person panel of the United States Court of Appeals for the District of Columbia in *Securities and Exchange Commission v. Life Partners Incorporated and Brian D. Pardo*, decided July 5, 1996. In the view of Commission staff, the majority conclusion that certain viatical settlements were not investment contracts was based on a narrow, technical, interpretive approach. As the strongly worded dissent in the *Life Partners* case points out, this is not characteristic of the leading case law in the area. Canadian courts (and most U.S. courts) have traditionally taken a broad remedial approach to interpreting the definition of a security under securities legislation, particularly in respect of the "investment contract" branch of the definition.

Commission staff encourages all those considering engaging in the sale of viatical settlements to discuss securities regulatory issues with staff at an early stage.

For further information please contact: Advisory Services

IFRS No. 1 — Investment Funds and Structured Products Branch — IFRS Release No. 1

Date: September 30, 2014

  37 O.S.C.B. 9053

[Not reproduced]

IFRS No. 2 — Investment Funds and Structured Products Branch — IFRS Release No. 2

Date: November 27, 2014

  37 O.S.C.B. 10341

[Not reproduced]

IFRS No. 3 — Investment Funds and Structured Products Branch — IFRS Release No. 3

Date: December 30, 2014

  37 O.S.C.B. 11429

[Not reproduced]

IFRS No. 4 — Ontario Securities Commission, Investment Funds and Structured Products Branch — IFRS Release No. 4

Date: January 29, 2015

  38 O.S.C.B. 830

[Not reproduced]

2015 — The Investment Funds Practitioner — Topical Reference Guide

Date: As of July 2015

Table of Contents

1. — ANNOUNCEMENTS

2. — APPLICATIONS FOR RELIEF

NOTICES

5. — INDEPENDENT REVIEW COMMITTEES (IRC)

6. — MARKETING PRACTICES

7. — PROCESS MATTERS

8. — PROSPECTUSES

NOTICES

December 2015 — OSC the Investment Funds Practitioner

Date: December 17, 2015

38 O.S.C.B. 10486

From the Investment Funds and Structured Products Branch, Ontario Securities Commission

What is the Investment Funds Practitioner?

The Practitioner is an overview of recent issues arising from applications for discretionary relief, prospectuses, and continuous disclosure documents that investment funds file with the OSC. It is intended to assist investment fund managers and their staff or advisors who regularly prepare public disclosure documents and applications for exemptive relief on behalf of investment funds.

The Practitioner is also intended to make you more broadly aware of some of the issues we have raised in connection with our reviews of documents filed with us and how we have resolved them. We hope that fund managers and their advisors will find this information useful and that the Practitioner can serve as a useful resource when preparing applications and disclosure documents.

The information contained in the Practitioner is based on particular factual circumstances. Outcomes may differ as facts change or as regulatory approaches evolve. We will continue to assess each case on its own merits.

The Practitioner has been prepared by staff of the Investment Funds and Structured Products Branch and the views it expresses do not necessarily reflect the views of the Commission or the Canadian Securities Administrators.

Request for Feedback

This is the 16th edition of the Practitioner. Previous editions of the Practitioner are available on the OSC website www.osc.gov.on.ca under *Investment Funds & Structured Products* on the *Industry* tab. We welcome your feedback and any suggestions for topics that you would like us to cover in future editions. Please forward your comments by email to *investmentfunds@osc.gov.on.ca*.

Prospectuses

New Scholarship Plans — Up-Front Commission Structure

Staff have previously raised comments in respect of group scholarship plans that require subscribers to pay up-front commissions to sales representatives. We have recently observed that some plan providers appear to be shifting their focus towards the development of new individual plans with similar features.

Group scholarship plans (**GSPs**) have historically required the up-front payment of sales commissions to sales representatives who sell them. Currently, most plan providers require 100% of a subscriber's initial contributions to a GSP to be directed to the payment of the sales commission until half of the commission is paid. Subsequently, 50% of the subscriber's contributions are directed to the payment of the sales commission until it is paid in full. This practice only allows for a small portion of a subscriber's initial contributions, if any, to be invested in the plan's actual portfolio investments. Depending on the circumstances, it can take two years or longer before the sales commission is fully paid. Staff have determined to no longer recommend prospectus receipts for new scholarship plans with similar up-front commission structures that lack the ability of a subscriber to receive a refund, in whole or in part, for paid sales commissions in appropriate circumstances.

We recently received a prospectus which proposed to establish a new individual scholarship plan. The plan, however, required subscribers to pay an up-front sales commission without the possibility of any refund should the subscriber withdraw from the plan. Staff indicated that we would not be willing to recommend a prospectus receipt for this plan on the basis that receipting it, without a mechanism to provide for a refund, in whole or in part, of any sales charges to subscribers, would not, in our view, be in the public interest. The prospectus was subsequently withdrawn.

We encourage any scholarship plan providers that are contemplating the creation of new scholarship plans to consult with staff prior to developing new compensation models for their sales representatives.

Applications

Relief from Fund Facts Delivery Requirement for Automatic Switching Programs that Facilitate Fee Reductions Based on Client Asset Thresholds

Staff have recently recommended exemptive relief from the Fund Facts delivery requirement in order to facilitate a new automatic switching program. The automatic switching program involves the fund manager, on behalf of investors, initiating automatic switches between a new set of series of funds, with each series offering a different tier of management and administration fees based on the size of an investor's investment, in order to enable investors to immediately benefit from fee discounts for which they become eligible. Each automatic switch involves the redemption of units of one series, immediately followed by the purchase of units of a different series. Each such purchase would be considered a "distribution" as defined in the *Securities Act* (Ontario), which would trigger the fund facts delivery requirement.

The conditions of the decision include (a) prospectus and Fund Facts disclosure of, among other things, (i) the eligibility requirements for the various series and (ii) the rates of the fees applicable, or the fee discounts applicable, to the various series and (b) notification provided to existing and new investors in the relevant series of funds[1].

Issuers and their counsel contemplating the launch of similar automatic switching programs are encouraged to contact staff if there are any questions about the conditions of such relief.

Relief from Financial Statement Filing and Delivery Requirements of NI 81-106 for Pooled Fund on Funds

We continue to receive some applications on behalf of pooled funds (i.e. mutual funds that are not reporting issuers) that act as top funds in fund on fund structures, for exemptive relief from the financial statement filing and delivery deadlines under National Instrument 81-106 *Investment Fund Continuous Disclosure* (**NI 81-106**). Although there are some past decisions granting this relief, no recent decisions granting similar relief have been issued.

In the past decisions, filers requested relief to accommodate fund on fund arrangements where the bottom fund was established in a foreign jurisdiction and had a different financial statement reporting deadline than the top fund. While there is an exemption in section 2.11 of NI 81-106 available to pooled funds from the requirement to file financial statements, the filers generally submitted that the top funds were unable to comply with the financial statement delivery deadlines in NI 81-106 because the top funds' auditors could not complete their audit until they received audited financial statements of the bottom funds. The decisions granted an extension of the annual financial statement due date to align the top funds' reporting deadlines with those of the bottom funds.

Staff have further considered the issue and hold the view that top fund pooled funds should structure their affairs and set their financial year ends so that they can comply with their obligations under NI 81-106. As a result, going forward, staff are not generally prepared to recommend this type of relief.

Continuous Disclosure

IFRS for Investment Funds

Last year, staff commenced an issue-oriented continuous disclosure review focusing on the transition to International Financial Reporting Standards (**IFRS**). We reviewed the first IFRS financial statements required to be filed under NI 81-106, which consisted of the interim financial reports of investment funds with calendar year-end reporting periods. In Fall 2014, we issued a number of IFRS Releases, outlining the most common issues identified during the review. IFRS Release No. 4 — *First IFRS Annual Financial Statements — Tips for Year End* published on January 23, 2015 was a tip sheet listing key elements that are required in the first IFRS annual financial statements.

---

[1]See *In the Matter of Fidelity Investments Canada ULC* dated October 28, 2015.

NOTICES

In 2015, we expanded our review by examining a sample of the IFRS audited annual financial statements for investment funds with the financial year ended March 31, 2015. As part of our review, we checked for compliance with the IFRS transition requirements found in NI 81-106. We identified one issue relating to the presentation of financial highlights in the annual management report of fund performance (**MRFP**).

For the first annual MRFP after the transition to IFRS, both the current and immediately preceding financial years in the financial highlights table must present information derived from IFRS because these periods are derived from audited financial statements prepared in accordance with IFRS (see Part B, Item 3.1(7.1)(c) of Form 81-106F1 *Contents of Annual and Interim Management Report of Fund Performance* (the **Form**)). In our review, we noted that one fund manager presented information for the current financial year in IFRS, but used Part V of the CPA Canada Handbook (pre-changeover Canadian GAAP) to prepare information for the immediately preceding financial year. In addition, the same manager did not include a footnote to the financial highlights table disclosing the accounting principles applicable to each period (see Part B, Item 3.1(7.1)(d) of the Form).

MRFPs for the next few years will contain financial highlights tables that present information derived from both financial statements prepared in accordance with IFRS and pre-changeover Canadian GAAP. As an example, for investment funds with calendar year-end reporting periods, information in the financial highlights table will be derived from financial statements prepared in accordance with IFRS for 2013, 2014 and all subsequent financial years. For as long as the 2012 financial year is included in the table, both IFRS and pre-changeover Canadian GAAP information will be presented in the table. Accordingly, an explanation of the accounting principles applicable to each period must appear as a footnote to the table until 2017, at which point all financial highlights in the table will be based on the same accounting principle.

For the vast majority of investment funds selected during our review, we did not identify any issues in the IFRS audited annual financial statements and related MRFPs. Given the level of compliance that we have observed in respect of the transition requirements in NI 81-106, staff's view is that the review of the IFRS annual financial statements does not need to be extended.

Process Matters

Transition of Investment Funds to Corporate Issuer Status

We have recently seen closed-end investment funds seeking to transition to corporate issuers for various reasons, one of which is to change the investment strategy of the fund to focus on obtaining control of, or becoming involved in, the management of underlying investee companies.

Staff generally take the view that a fund manager's decision to change a fund's operation from investment fund to corporate issuer constitutes a "restructuring" that triggers the requirement for a securityholder vote as contemplated by subparagraph 5.1(1)(h)(iii) of NI 81-102.

Staff's view is that the following disclosure should be provided in the management information circular[2] for the securityholder meeting:

- financial statements and management's discussion & analysis for the issuer's two most recently completed financial years and most recent interim period prepared in accordance with applicable Canadian securities legislation as if the issuer were a corporate issuer instead of an investment fund;

- a discussion of the key differences between the requirements in securities legislation that apply to an investment fund versus a corporate issuer, for example, the differences in the disclosure requirements; and

- a statement of executive compensation prepared in compliance with Form 51-102F6 *Statement of Executive Compensation*.

Fund managers considering the transition of investment funds they manage to corporate issuers should be mindful of the above requirements and are encouraged to engage staff in the Corporate Finance Branch of the Commission prior to transitioning if their framework for transition raises novel issues outside of the above-noted parameters.

July 2015 — The Investment Funds Practitioner

Date: July 23, 2015
38 O.S.C.B. 6584

OSC the Investment Funds Practitioner From the Investment Funds and Structured Products Branch, Ontario Securities Commission

What is the Investment Funds Practitioner?

The Practitioner is an overview of recent issues arising from applications for discretionary relief, prospectuses, and continuous disclosure documents that investment funds file with the OSC. It is intended to assist investment fund managers and their staff or advisors who regularly prepare public disclosure documents and applications for exemptive relief on behalf of investment funds.

The Practitioner is also intended to make you more broadly aware of some of the issues we have raised in connection with our reviews of documents filed with us and how we have resolved them. We hope that fund managers and their advisors will find this information useful and that the Practitioner can serve as a useful resource when preparing applications and disclosure documents.

The information contained in the Practitioner is based on particular factual circumstances. Outcomes may differ as facts change or as regulatory approaches evolve. We will continue to assess each case on its own merits.

---

[2]Refer to section 5.4 of NI 81-102 and Part 12 of NI 81-106 for requirements relevant to the management information circular required for securityholder meetings pursuant to section 5.1 of NI 81-102.

The Practitioner has been prepared by staff of the Investment Funds and Structured Products Branch and the views it expresses do not necessarily reflect the views of the Commission or the Canadian Securities Administrators.

Request for Feedback

This is the 15th edition of the Practitioner. Previous editions of the Practitioner are available on the OSC website www.osc.gov.on.ca under *Investment Funds & Structured Products* on the *Industry* tab. We welcome your feedback and any suggestions for topics that you would like us to cover in future editions. Please forward your comments by email to investmentfunds@osc.gov.on.ca.

Prospectuses

Prospectus Review Priorities

Staff continue to see investment funds offering an increasing number of classes or series of securities, each with slightly different attributes or features. For full reviews of prospectus filings, staff will now focus on disclosure relating to the different classes or series offered by investment funds. As set out in the November 2013 edition of the *Investment Funds Practitioner*, staff will also continue to focus on fees and expenses disclosure and on the clear articulation of investment objectives and strategies.

Staff's current prospectus review priorities are intended to achieve the following objectives:

- encourage more consistent disclosure by investment funds to enhance comparability of the three noted themes;

- promote the disclosure of all relevant information to investors in a clear, understandable and accurate manner and challenge "boiler plate disclosure"; and

- provide more focused comments to filers on issues of particular importance to investors to assist them in making more informed investment decisions.

Staff will consider, among other things, the scope of the following disclosure in the prospectus:

Classes or Series Offered by an Investment Fund:

- sufficient clarity to assist investors in distinguishing the differences between and purpose of each class or series, including the type of investor and fee model each class or series is intended for, if applicable;

- disclosure of the differences in dealer compensation for each class or series;

- explanations of the differences in fees, in addition to dealer compensation, that are in plain language and clear for each class or series; and

- sufficient disclosure regarding switches between classes or series, including automatic and default switches.

Fees and Expenses:

- a summary of all applicable fees and expenses;

- explanations of fees and expenses that are in plain language and clear so that investors can understand what each fee is for and what services or activities the fee covers; and

- sufficient clarity to allow staff to determine that there is no duplication of fees and expenses and whether the overall cost of the fund is comparable to similar investment funds and not contrary to the public interest.

Investment Objectives and Strategies:

- investment objectives and strategies of the fund that provide meaningful information to investors, namely, a clear and accurate picture of the fund and the asset classes the fund will invest in;

- identification of all material risks associated with the fund's objectives and strategies; and

- sufficient differentiation in the disclosure to assist investors in distinguishing between multiple funds within a prospectus or fund family and understanding the difference between funds that appear similar in name and/or investment strategies.

Staff remind investment fund issuers and their counsel that staff's increased focus on these areas in our prospectus reviews does not take away from the issuer's responsibility to comply with all applicable securities legislation, policies and practices. Staff will continue to raise general comments in the course of a prospectus review as appropriate.

Default Mutual Fund Distributions — Fixed Rate Distribution Series

As noted in the April 2015 edition of the *Investment Funds Practitioner*, staff continue to review and examine distribution policies generally, with a particular emphasis on funds or series that seek to make regular distributions.

In the course of our prospectus reviews, staff have been raising comments on the distribution policies of funds offering fixed rate distribution securities (FRDS), often referred to as "T-series". Generally, FRDS are marketed to investors seeking consistent monthly cashflow. Annual distribution rates are often set above the level of income expected to be generated by the fund, resulting in distributions comprised of return of capital, potentially providing investors with more tax efficient distributions. For many FRDS, distributions are reinvested rather than paid in cash, unless the investor specifically requests cash distributions.

Generally, staff's view is that when investors have the option to receive distributions in the form of reinvested securities or cash, having a "default" feature of reinvestment of FRDS distributions can cause investor confusion because such reinvestment appears to be inconsistent with the purpose of these securities, which is to provide monthly cashflow. As a result, staff have been asking fund managers to explain why a default feature of reinvestment of distributions is appropriate given the purpose of these securities and to consider changing the distribution policy so that FRDS distributions default to cash, rather than reinvestment.

To date, a number of fund managers have either changed their distribution policies for FRDS to default to cash distributions or have committed to doing so within a reasonable time period. We generally expect that this change will be made on a going forward basis to new purchases, with the exception of purchases made pursuant to an existing pre-authorized plan.

Going forward, staff will be contacting fund managers with FRDS to bring this issue to their attention and to communicate staff's concerns and expectations. We will continue to work with issuers and their counsel for a consistent approach to the implementation of distribution policies for FRDS.

Mutual Funds Currently Investing in Closed-End Funds

Recent amendments to National Instrument 81-102 *Investment Funds* (NI 81-102), which became effective on September 22, 2014 (the Modernization Amendments) prohibit a mutual fund from investing in, or holding, securities of a non-redeemable investment fund (NRIF).[3] Mutual funds that filed a prospectus on or before September 22, 2014 have until March 21, 2016 (the Transition Date) to comply with this requirement.

As staff continue to review pro forma renewal prospectuses for these mutual funds, we are reminding such issuers and their counsel that the mutual funds' investments in NRIFs, often referred to as 'closed-end funds', will need to cease by the Transition Date, unless the mutual fund has obtained exemptive relief to continue with these investments. Mutual funds invested in NRIFs with renewal prospectuses receipted between March 2015 and March 2016 will be eligible to distribute their securities beyond the Transition Date but cannot be invested in NRIFs beyond the Transition Date. We remind fund managers that obtaining a prospectus receipt during this period should not be considered as an indication of staff's willingness to allow these mutual funds to continue to invest in an NRIF beyond the Transition Date or to recommend exemptive relief to permit these investments beyond the Transition Date. Any applications for exemptive relief to permit such investments beyond the Transition Date will be considered on a case-by-case basis.

Staff encourage issuers and their counsel to contact staff as early as possible to discuss any plans to seek exemptive relief.

Disclosure of IRC Compensation

We have recently seen variations in the prospectus disclosure of annual compensation paid to members of a fund's Independent Review Committee (IRC) established pursuant to National Instrument 81-107 *Independent Review Committee for Investment Funds* (NI 81-107). Disclosure of the compensation paid by a fund to each member of a fund's IRC is required in the fund's most recently completed financial year.[4] In certain cases, we have seen only the aggregate compensation paid to all IRC members be disclosed, and in other cases, only the retainer payable to IRC members in the normal course is disclosed.

Staff remind issuers that these sections require disclosure of the name of the individual IRC member and the specific amount of compensation, including any expenses reimbursed by the fund, actually paid to the individual IRC member during the fund's most recently completed financial year.

Use of "Index" in Investment Fund Names and Objectives

On July 9, 2015, staff published OSC Staff Notice 81-728 *Use of "Index" in Investment Fund Names and Objectives* (Staff Notice 81-728)[5] which provides guidance on the issues that staff will consider in reviewing the prospectuses of investment funds that describe themselves, in their names and investment objectives, as tracking an index. Staff Notice 81-728 was drafted in response to an increasing trend in investment funds that track indices.

Applications

IRC Notification Requirements — Inter-Fund Trades Involving Pooled Funds

Relief to permit inter-fund trades between investment funds that are reporting issuers and pooled funds has been routinely granted on conditions similar to those set out in section 6.1 of NI 81-107. Among other items, the conditions have included the requirement for each pooled fund to establish an Independent Review Committee (IRC) to oversee such trades on behalf of the pooled funds.

Section 4.5 of NI 81-107 requires the IRC of an investment fund that is a reporting issuer to notify the fund's principal regulator when the IRC becomes aware of an instance where the manager acted in a conflict of interest matter under subsection 5.2(1)[6] of NI 81-107 but did not comply with a condition or conditions imposed by securities legislation or the IRC in its approval. This reporting requirement has also been included in exemptive relief decisions to permit inter-fund trades involving investment funds not covered by NI 81-107, for example, pooled funds.[7]

---

[3] Subsection 2.5(2) of NI 81-102.

[4] Item 15(2) of Form 81-101F2 *Annual Information Form*, Item 19.1(12) of Form 41-101F2 *Information Required in an Investment Fund Prospectus*, and Part D, Item 2.7(2) of Form 41-101F3 *Information Required in a Scholarship Plan Prospectus*.

[5] Staff Notice 81-728 can be found on the OSC website at http://www.osc.gov.on.ca/en/SecuritiesLaw_sn_20150709_81-728_use-of-index.htm.

[6] Section 5.2(1) of NI 81-107 refers to three types of conflict of interest matters i.e. inter-fund trading, related party underwriting and purchases of securities of a related issuer over an exchange.

[7] See *In the Matter of PIMCO Canada Corp.* dated October 7, 2014, *In the Matter of Manulife Asset Management* dated July 5, 2013, and *In the Matter of Deans Knight Capital Management Ltd.* dated January 25, 2012.

Staff wish to remind filers that we will continue to require the inclusion of this notification requirement as a representation in decisions granting relief to permit inter-fund trades between pooled funds or between pooled funds and other investment funds that are reporting issuers.

Scope of Future-Oriented Relief for Pooled Funds Investing in Related Pooled Funds

Staff have recently reviewed a number of applications for relief from the conflict of interest investment restrictions in securities legislation to permit pooled funds to invest in related pooled funds. These applications have often included requests for relief for future fund-on-fund structures (future-oriented relief) that are not yet actually planned and that may not be substantially similar in features and purposes, to those structures described in the application. In these applications, the scope of future-oriented relief requested has often been much broader than the scope needed for the fund-on-fund structures described in the application.

Staff are prepared to consider recommending future-oriented relief for future fund-on-fund structures that are substantially similar in features and purposes, to fund structures that a Filer expects to implement in the near future. While we appreciate that prior decisions may have been framed more broadly, staff are increasingly taking the view that future-oriented relief should generally be limited to the specific facts (i.e. structures) that trigger the need for the relief. Accordingly, in recent decisions, staff have only recommended future-oriented relief limited to structures substantially similar to the planned structures described in the application.[8]

Staff also note that the terms and conditions of a decision are contemplated to address the conflicts in the particular planned fund-on-fund structures described in an application but may not address the conflicts in a different structure. Consequently, staff also require that each planned structure be described in sufficient detail, as to its features and purpose, to permit staff to consider any potential conflicts of interest, so as to propose conditions appropriate, in staff's view, for the specific structure.

Continuous Disclosure

Awards in Sales Communications

As part of staff's ongoing continuous disclosure review of sales communications, we have reviewed selected investment fund managers (IFMs) with advertising and marketing materials that reference various industry awards. It is staff's view that awards are, in substance, performance based ratings, and that sales communications that contain references to such ratings or rankings should comply with the requirements set out in National Instrument 81-102 *Investment Funds* (NI 81-102).[9] Based on staff's review of the criteria and methodology applied to the selection of award winners, while the quantitative considerations are performance based, criteria generally also includes a subjective component.

The sales communication requirements for mutual funds in Part 15 of NI 81-102 do not permit the use of a performance rating or ranking of a mutual fund that is based partially on a subjective component. NI 81-102 permits the use of a performance rating or ranking in a sales communication where it meets certain requirements, including the requirement that the performance rating or ranking be prepared by a mutual fund rating entity. While other methodologies employed may fall within the definition of "mutual fund rating entity", in staff's view, given the subjective component of industry awards generally, these awards are typically not a rating or ranking permitted to be used in a sales communication for a mutual fund.

While staff note that the references to industry awards in sales communications appear to be a wide-spread practice among mutual funds and exchange-traded funds in the marketplace, staff's view is that this practice should be discontinued. Staff recognize the importance of sales communications and strongly encourage IFMs and their counsel to contact staff regarding sales communications that may give rise to questions concerning this issue.

[8]Recent decisions reflecting more limited future-oriented relief for pooled funds investing in related pooled funds include: *In the Matter of East West Investment Management Corporation* dated May 19, 2015, *In the Matter of BloombergSen Inc.* dated April 17, 2015 and *In the Matter of MacDougall Investment Counsel Inc.* dated January 29, 2015.

[9]Subsection 15.3(4) of NI 81-102.

Staff are prepared to consider accommodating future-oriented relief for future fund-on-fund structures that are substantially similar in features and purposes to those structures that a filer expects to implement in the near future. While we appreciate that prior decisions may have been framed more broadly, staff are increasingly taking the view that future-oriented relief should generally be limited to those specific facts (i.e. structures substantially similar to the planned structures) that trigger the need for the relief. Accordingly, in recent decisions staff have only recommended future-oriented relief limited to structures substantially similar to the planned structures described in the application.

INTERGOVERNMENTAL AGREEMENTS

Intergovernmental Agreement IA-1 — Hockin-Kwinter Accord Securities Act (Ontario) Accord
Date: 1987/04/28

Tom Hockin, Minister of State (Finance) for Canada, and Monte Kwinter, Minister of Financial Institutions for the Province of Ontario, reached the following understanding with respect to the implementation of their respective regimes for the regulation of securities-related activities of federal financial institutions (banks, federal trust and loan companies, and federal insurance companies) and their subsidiaries or affiliates:

1. There is a clear interest across Canada in the efficient functioning of the Canadian capital markets. It is essential that comparable activities be regulated in a comparable manner. The Office of the Superintendent of Financial Institutions ("OSFI") will regulate federal financial institutions. The Ontario Securities Commission ("OSC") will regulate in Ontario the subsidiaries or affiliates of federal financial institutions which are engaged in securities-related activities. The OSFI will work in consultation with the OSC and other provincial regulators in order to harmonize the standards to which the securities-related activities of the institutions under their respective jurisdictions are subject.

2. Both levels of government recognize the importance of having an integrated regulatory regime take effect on June 30, 1987.

3. The OSFI will regulate the securities-related activities of federal financial institutions carried on directly by the institution, which activities may comprise:

(a)   all activities relating to sovereign debt of or guaranteed by federal, provincial and municipal governments, foreign countries and any political divisions thereof, and certain recognized international agencies;

(b)   all money market activities;

(c)   all activities relating to debt securities of the institution (including bankers' acceptances, GIC's, and variable insurance contracts) and debt securities of an affiliated company that are guaranteed by the institution;

(d)   all secondary market trades in corporate debt securities;

(e)   all capital market activities in syndicated or consortium loans, whether or not issued in the form of securitized debt instruments;

(f)   unsolicited participation in secondary trading of equity securities, provided that execution is effected through a registered dealer or broker;

(g)   portfolio management and investment counselling to the extent permitted by the federal legislation applicable to the institution;

(h)   dealings in mutual fund shares or units each in relation to corporate sponsored accounts for pension plans, deferred profit sharing plans, retirement plans, and other similar capital accumulation plans; and

(i)   trades for fully managed accounts.

4. Other than as specifically set out in 3 above, the following securities-related activities of a federal financial institution shall be carried on in a subsidiary or an affiliate, which activities, together with any additional securities-related activities that the institution chooses to carry on in the subsidiary or affiliate, shall be regulated at the provincial level:

(a)   all activities relating to the primary distribution of equity securities including acting as a selling agent in connection with the distribution of mutual funds;

(b)   all activities relating to the primary distribution of corporate debt securities;

(c)   secondary market trading in equity securities; and

(d)   portfolio management and investment counselling.

5. Registration of employees of federal financial institutions will be implemented in such a manner that such employees may also be employees of the institution's securities subsidiary or affiliate, and vice-versa, and may work in both capacities from the same premises.

6. The federal government has responsibility for the entry of non-residents into the Canadian capital markets.

7. Both levels of government will continue to consult on all matters set out in this document.

[Released April 28, 1987]

Office of the Superintendent of Financial Institutions Canada	Bureau du surintendant des institutions financières Canada
Superintendent	Surintendant
Ottawa, Canada	
K1A 0H2	

March 25, 1988

Mr. Stanley M. Beck, Q.C.
Chairman

Ontario Securities Commission

Suite 1800

20 Queen Street

Toronto, Ontario

M5H 3S8

Dear Mr. Beck:

Further to our agreement to exchange certain information regarding securities dealers held by federal financial institutions and those federal financial institutions, I would like to confirm the following additional matters.

1.   Guideline 17(a) relating to Canadian banks is spent. Notice to that effect will be given in the normal course as holders of our guideline publication are advised of modifications thereto.

2.   Guideline 17(b) relating to foreign banks will be modified shortly. It will continue to prohibit the undertaking of banking, trust and insurance business by foreign banks directly or through their related securities dealers. The prohibition with respect to trust and insurance business will be revoked when federal financial institutions are permitted to undertake such business.

    As this guideline is widely distributed for information purposes, it will contain more information than the contents of the undertaking to be signed by a foreign bank. I will, however, review the guideline with you prior to releasing it.

3.   Undertakings as set out in Annex A will be required from foreign banks. Existing undertakings will be modified in accordance with our agreement and guideline 17(b), where applicable. All undertakings will be immediately treated as modified, notwithstanding any delay in their execution.

Yours sincerely,

Michael A. Mackenzie

Annex A

APPLICATION FOR AN ORDER OF GOVERNOR IN COUNCIL, PURSUANT TO SUBSECTION 307(3) OF THE BANK ACT (THE "ACT"), CONSENTING TO THE ACQUISITION OF SHARES BY FOREIGN BANK ("BANK") IN CANADIAN DEALER ("DEALER")

WHEREAS Bank, a foreign bank within the meaning of the Act, has applied to the Minister of Finance (the "Minister"), pursuant to subsection 307(3) of the Act, for an Order of the Governor in Council, consenting to the acquisition by Bank of shares of Dealer in such a number as to cause Dealer to become a non-bank affiliate of Bank;

NOW THEREFORE, in consideration of the issuance of the said Order by Governor in Council, Bank hereby agrees with Her Majesty the Queen in right of Canada, as follows:

(1)   Bank undertakes not to engage in Canada in any banking, trust or insurance activities, either directly or through Dealer, provided that Dealer may provide margin facilities to its clients and may carry credit balances, in the ordinary course of business, as services ancillary to those set out in subparagraph 307(1)(c)(iii) of the Act and may make loans to employees for the purpose of purchasing residences, furnishings therefor and automobiles.

(2)   Bank will cause Dealer to be registered if required under the securities laws, regulations or policies of any province or territory in Canada in which Dealer shall undertake any securities activities;

(3)

(a)   If Bank is, at any time or times, in breach of or in default under any provision of this Agreement, and such breach or default is not remedied within 90 days from the date of receipt by Bank of notice by the Superintendent of such breach, the Minister may, by direction in writing, require Bank to dispose of such of its direct or indirect holdings in Dealer as to cause Dealer to cease to be a non-bank affiliate (within the meaning of subsection 303(1) of the *Bank Act*) of Bank within the period of time specified by him.

(b)   Bank agrees to comply with a direction given to it under paragraph (a) by the Minister.

(4)   This Agreement shall become effective upon the issuance by the Governor in Council of an Order under subsection 307(3) of the *Bank Act* consenting to the acquisition by Bank of shares of Dealer.

IN WITNESS WHEREOF Foreign Bank has executed this Agreement and affixed its corporate seal under the hands of its proper signing officers duly authorized in that behalf.

DATED at _____, this _____ day of _____, 1988.

Foreign Bank

Per:

_____ c/s

Intergovernmental Agreement IA-2 — Memorandum of Understanding with the Office of the Superintendent of Financial Institutions

Date: **1988/03/28**

The Office of the Superintendent of Financial Institutions ("OSFI") and the Ontario Securities Commission (the "OSC") have reached the following understanding.

1. — Definitions

1.01 In this Memorandum of Understanding:

(a) "Accord" means the accord of April 28, 1987, reached between the Minister of State (Finance) for Canada and the Minister of Financial Institutions for the Province of Ontario with respect to the regulation of the securities-related activities of FFIs and FFI-related dealers;

(b) "capital adequacy rules" means sections 95 to 100, inclusive, of the Regulation to the *Securities Act*, including the minimum free capital, bonding, insurance, contingency trust fund and audit requirements provided by those sections, and the corresponding provisions of the by-laws of the self-regulatory organizations;

(c) "FFI" means a federal financial institution, being a bank, trust company, loan corporation, insurance company or cooperative credit association the governing legislation of which is an Act of Parliament, which has or is seeking approval to have an interest in an FFI-related dealer;

(d) "FFI-related dealer" means a dealer in securities or adviser with respect to securities that is or will be a registrant under the *Securities Act* and in which an FFI has or is seeking approval to have an interest, the purchase or acquisition of which requires the prior approval of the Minister of Finance for Canada;

(e) "Securities Act" means the *Securities Act* (Ontario) and the Regulation thereunder; and

(f) "self-regulatory organization" means The Toronto Stock Exchange, the Ontario District of the Investment Dealers' Association of Canada or any other comparable organization recognized from time to time by the OSC for purposes of the self-regulation of dealers or advisers under the *Securities Act*.

2. — General Principles

2.01 OSFI and the OSC acknowledge that the Accord provides that OSFI will regulate FFIs and the OSC will regulate in Ontario FFI-related dealers. This Memorandum of Understanding sets forth a statement of intent of OSFI and the OSC with respect to coordination of certain policies for the regulation of FFI-related dealers by OSC and FFIs by OSFI.

3. — SRO Membership and Capital Adequacy Rules

3.01 The OSC acknowledges that OSFI, in recommending that Ministerial approval be given to the acquisition by FFIs of interests in FFI-related dealers, is relying on the system of regulation currently applicable under the *Securities Act* and the by-laws of the self-regulatory organizations and, in particular, the capital adequacy rules.

3.02 The OSC will require that an FFI-related dealer be a member of a self-regulatory organization or be registered in an appropriate category of registrant under the *Securities Act*. Prior to any granting of the necessary approval of the Minister of Finance to the purchase of an interest by an FFI in an FFI-related dealer, the OSC will inform OSFI of the category in which the FFI-related dealer is or will be registered, its conditions of registration, the self-regulatory organization, if any, that is or will be responsible for its audit and any other relevant details with respect to regulation of it.

3.03 The OSC will not allow an FFI-related dealer to cease to be a member of a self-regulatory organization or to change its category of registration unless:

(a) the OSC requires the FFI-related dealer to be registered in an appropriate category of registration under the *Securities Act* having capital adequacy rules that are substantially equivalent to the capital adequacy rules of its former category of registration; or

(b) in the case of ceasing to be a member of a self-regulatory organization, the FFI-related dealer continues to be a member of another self-regulatory organization having capital adequacy rules that are substantially equivalent to the capital adequacy rules of the former self-regulatory organization.

3.04 Before making, approving or determining not to object to any material change to the capital adequacy rules, the OSC will consult with OSFI and give it a reasonable opportunity to review and to comment upon the proposed change. If OSFI considers that the proposed change would materially weaken the capital adequacy rules, the OSC and OSFI will use their best efforts to reach agreement on an appropriate change, if any. If, within a reasonable period of time, no agreement is reached, the OSC will not permit the proposed change to be implemented earlier than 180 days thereafter.

4. — Activities of FFI-Related Dealers

4.01 The OSC acknowledges that the OSFI has legitimate policy concerns as to the scope of the business carried on by FFI-related dealers, including the concern that an FFI not make use of an FFI-related dealer to carry on a business that the FFI is not itself permitted to carry on.

4.02 The OSC will ensure that an FFI-related dealer does not carry on the business of a bank, trust company, loan corporation or insurance company if the related FFI is not then permitted to carry on that business.

5. — Sharing of Information

5.01 Each of OSFI and the OSC acknowledges that the other, in the ordinary course of carrying out its regulatory responsibilities, has the right to obtain certain information about, or access to books and records of, FFI-related dealers or FFIs, respectively.

Notwithstanding any legal right to do so, neither OSFI nor the OSC will seek information about, nor access to the books and records of, an FFI-related dealer or an FFI, respectively, from the FFI-related dealer or FFI or cause to seek to cause the related FFI or FFI-related dealer, respectively, to provide such information or access to the books and records without first making a request in accordance with this paragraph.

Subject to applicable law, each of OSFI and the OSC will cooperate with all reasonable requests of the other for such information or access.

5.02 Each of OSFI and the OSC will use its best efforts to provide the other with information it has that an FFI-related dealer or an FFI, respectively, has or appears to have breached, or is expected to breach, in any material way the *Securities Act* or the by-laws of a self regulatory organization of which the FFI-related dealer is a member or the governing legislation of the FFI, respectively.

5.03 If OSFI or the OSC receives a request made in accordance with paragraph 5.01 and the information or books and records requested are not in its possession or subject to its control and direction, it will use its best efforts to obtain the information or books and records.

5.04 All requests made under paragraph 5.01 shall be made in writing and addressed to the contact officer listed in Annex "A". Each request shall specify:

(a)   a general description of the information or books and records being sought;

(b)   a general description of the regulatory concern that forms the basis for the request and the purpose for which the request is made; and

(c)   the desired time period for reply.

In the case of an urgent matter, a request may be made orally, provided that the request is subsequently confirmed in writing.

Where certain information of a routine nature is requested to be provided from time to time, one specific request for the information pursuant to paragraph 5.01 will suffice as a request for the information to be provided on the basis set forth in the request.

5.05 OSFI and the OSC will use any information or books and records furnished in response to a request made in accordance with paragraph 5.01 solely for the purpose stated in connection with the making of the request.

5.06 Each of OSFI and the OSC will keep confidential any request made to it in accordance with paragraph 5.01 and any information or books and records furnished to it in accordance with this Memorandum of Understanding.

6. — Ongoing Regulation

6.01 OSFI will regulate FFIs and the OSC will regulate FFI-related dealers in accordance with the terms and underlying principles of this Memorandum of Understanding and the Accord. Without limiting the generality of the foregoing, OSFI will not:

(a)   require or request any undertaking from any FFI that is inconsistent with this Memorandum of Understanding;

(b)   require or request any undertaking from any FFI in respect of an FFI-related dealer, other than in the form agreed upon and attached hereto as Annex B, or publish or establish any guideline, policy, or rule or recommend any regulation that prescribes the manner in which FFI-related dealers are to carry on business or is otherwise directed at FFI-related dealers, without first giving the OSC a reasonable opportunity to review and to comment upon it. If, within a reasonable period of time not to exceed 180 days after the date upon which the guideline, policy, or rule was first released for review, no agreement is reached, the guideline, policy, or rule will not be implemented earlier than 180 days thereafter.

   For greater certainty, nothing in this Memorandum of Understanding restricts in any fashion OSFI's ability to set capital rules for FFIs.

6.02 Promptly after the OSC receives notice of any change of control of any FFI-related dealer, the OSC will give notice of the change to OSFI and will permit OSFI to review and to comment upon the change during the period which the OSC has to review it.

7. — Effective Date and Termination

7.01 This Memorandum of Understanding will be effective from the date of its execution by OSFI and the OSC.

7.02 This Memorandum of Understanding may be terminated by OSFI or the OSC by giving 180 days notice to the other. Neither OSFI nor the OSC will give notice of termination on the basis of a dispute between them without first using its best efforts to resolve the dispute.

DATED this 28th day of March, 1988

Office of the Superintendent of Financial Institutions

Ontario Securities Commission

Michael A. Mackenzie
Superintendent

Stanley M. Beck, Q.C.
Chairman

[Annex A and B omitted]

IA-3 — Memorandum of Understanding — Mutual Reliance Review System

Date: 1999/10/14

22 O.S.C.B. 6813

[Editor's Note: The MRRS has been replaced by the Passport System: see NPS 11-202 and 11-203.]

Minister of Finance Approval: Not published; Request for Comments: 21 O.S.C.B. 3882 (June 19, 1998); Replaced a Memorandum of Understanding for Expedited Review of Short Form Prospectuses and Renewal AIFs: 19 O.S.C.B. 6863 (December 20, 1996).

IA-4 — OSC Oversight of TSE Rule Proposals

Date: 1997/10/23

20 O.S.C.B. 5682

John A. Geller, Acting Chairman

Ontario Securities Commission

20 Queen Street West

Suite 800

Toronto, Ontario

M5H 3S8

Dear Mr. Geller:

Re: Protocol for Commission Oversight of Toronto Stock Exchange Rule Proposals ("Protocol")

This letter details a new Protocol for the approval of rule proposals of the Exchange and of the Canadian Dealing Network. This Protocol supplants the existing Commission-Exchange protocol dated December 18, 1984. For the sake of simplicity, separate references to CDN have not been added to the Protocol. When reviewing a CDN rule proposal all references in the Protocol to the "Exchange" and the "Board of Governors of the Exchange" should be read as "CDN" and its governing body.

1. — Scope of the Protocol

The Exchange shall file all by-laws, rules, regulations and policy statements of general application, and amendments thereto, adopted by the Board of Governors of the Exchange ("Rules") with the Commission for approval. The manner in which a Rule is approved by the Commission shall be determined by whether or not the Exchange has characterized the Rule as "public interest" or "non-public interest".

2. — "Public Interest" v. "Non-public Interest"

A "public interest" Rule would be any Rule that, in the opinion of the Exchange;

a) impinges upon the application of Ontario securities law; or

b) could have a material impact (either positive or negative) on public investors, listed or unlisted companies or non-member registrants.

Any Rule falling outside of this definition would be categorized as a "non-public interest" Rule.

Prior to proposing a Rule that is of a "public interest" nature, as defined above, the Board of Governors shall have determined that the entry into force of such "public interest" Rule would be in the best interests of the capital markets of Ontario. The material filed with the Commission in relation to "public interest" Rules shall be accompanied by a statement to that effect.

3. — Prior Notice of Significant "Public Interest" Rules

Where the Exchange is developing a "public interest" Rule that the Exchange anticipates will result in a significant change in Exchange policy, amendments to a significant number of Exchange Rules or may be the subject of significant public comment as a result of publication, the Exchange shall notify Commission staff in advance in writing. The purpose of such prior notification is to prepare Commission staff so that they can react in a timely way to the proposal upon filing. Prior notification shall not be interpreted by Commission staff as an opportunity to participate in Exchange policy development.

4. — Publication of "Public Interest" Rules for Comment

All "public interest" Rules approved by the Exchange's Board of Governors shall be published for comment in the OSC Bulletin for a 30-day comment period. Commission staff shall use their best efforts to ensure publication of "public interest" Rules in the issue of the OSC Bulletin immediately following filing of the "public interest" Rule with the Commission. The Exchange shall also publish a Regulatory Notice regarding the "public interest" Rule.

Responses to all requests for comments shall be directed to the Exchange, with copies to the Commission. The Exchange shall provide the Commission with a summary of all comments and the Exchange's responses to same, which summary shall be published in accordance with sections 5 and 6.

5. — Material Revisions to "Public Interest" Rules

Any "public interest" Rule which is revised subsequent to its publication for comment in a way that has a material effect on the Rule's substance and/or effect shall be published in the OSC Bulletin and in an Exchange Regulatory Notice for a second 30-day comment period. The request for comment shall include the Exchange's summary of comments and responses thereto together with an explanation of the revision to the Rule and the supporting rationale for the amendment.

INTERGOVERN-MENTAL AGREEMENTS

6. — Publication of Notice of Approval

Notice of Approval of both "public interest" and "non-public interest" Rules shall be published in the OSC Bulletin, in addition to Exchange Notices. The Notice of Approval shall provide a short summary of the essence of the Rule prepared by the Exchange. All such notices relating to "public interest" Rules shall also include the Exchange's summary of comments and responses thereto.

7. — Timing of Commission Staff Review of "Public Interest" Rules

Commission staff shall use their best efforts to conduct their initial internal review of all "public interest" Rules during the 30-day request for comment period. (This section does not, in any way, restrict the amount of time that may be necessary for Commission staff to consider any comments received during the comment period or effect the effective date of "public interest" Rules under subsection 8.2)

8. — Effective Date of Rules

The provisions of this section are subject to section 10.

8.1 — Effective Date — "Non-Public Interest" Rules

"Non-public interest" Rules shall be filed with the Commission and, without Commission staff review, shall be deemed to have been approved upon being so filed and will be effective upon the date indicated by the Exchange in the filing letter.

Commission staff may periodically review "non-public interest" filings of the Exchange to audit the appropriateness of the categorization of such filings. The Exchange shall be notified in writing of the Commission's findings on any such audit.

8.2 — Effective Date — "Public Interest"

(1) "Public interest" Rules shall be effective upon the earlier of:

    (a) notification from the Commission that the Rule has been approved; and

    (b)

    (i)   if no comments are received, 20 business days after the end of the public comment period,

    (ii)   if comments are received, 30 business days after delivery to the Commission of the Exchange's summary of comments and responses thereto, or

    (iii)   if a Rule is published for further comments under section 5, 30 business days after delivery to the Commission of the Exchange's summary of those further comments and responses thereto,

unless the responsible staff person at the Commission has notified the Exchange within that period that further information regarding the nature, purpose or effect of the Rule is required in order for the Commission to form a reasoned judgment concerning the matter.

(2) The Exchange may make "public interest" Rules effective immediately upon adoption by the Board of Governors where the Board determines that:

    (a) confidentiality prior to introduction is necessary to protect proprietary commercial information such as new product or service design; or

    (b) there is an urgent need to implement the Rule forthwith because of a substantial risk of material harm to investors, members, the Canadian Investor Protection Fund or the Exchange itself.

Should the Exchange believe that immediate implementation is appropriate, Exchange staff shall so advise Commission staff in advance of the Exchange publishing the Rule and filing it with the Commission. Such notice shall be in writing and shall include analysis in support of the need for immediate implementation.

Any such Rules shall be effective until such time as the Commission makes its decision with respect to approval. Although effective immediately, such "public interest" Rules shall still be published for comment, and subsequently be reviewed and considered for approval by the Commission. If the Commission decides not to approve any such Rule in a form agreeable to the Exchange, the Exchange shall forthwith amend the Rule, in a manner satisfactory to the Commission, or repeal it.

9. — Material to be Filed with the Commission

The filing of each "public interest" Exchange Rule shall be accompanied by a concise statement, together with supporting analysis where appropriate, of its nature, purposes and effects including the possible effects of the Rule on market structure, competition and the costs of compliance. The supporting analysis shall, where appropriate, include a description of the context in which the Rule was developed, the process followed, the issues considered, the alternative approaches considered and rejected (including reasons) and a review of the policy implications. The Exchange shall also advise the Commission if another Canadian exchange or SRO is making a simultaneous filing in another jurisdiction relating to the "public interest" matter that is the subject of an Exchange Rule. Where the Exchange is aware that another major SRO in Canada, the U.S. or other jurisdiction has a counterpart to any proposed Rule, the Exchange shall compare the Rule to such counterpart, noting and explaining any differences between the proposed Rule and any such counterpart.

The filing of each "non-public interest" Exchange Rule shall also be accompanied by a supporting analysis which may be less detailed, but which shall include the reason(s) that it is considered not to be a "public interest" Rule.

With respect to "public interest" Rules, it is the intention of the Exchange to make available to the public on request all comments received unless a writer specifically requests confidentiality. This shall be noted in the request for comments, as shall the caveat that access to confidential comments shall not be permitted except as may be required by law.

10. — Application of Section 21 of the Securities Act (Ontario)

It is understood that the Commission shall not be constrained in any way from exercising its power under paragraph 21(5)(e) of the *Securities Act (Ontario)* with respect to any Rule notwithstanding its having been approved.

If this Protocol meets with the Commission's approval, please so indicate by your signature on the following page.

Yours truly,

Rowland Fleming

President and Chief Executive Officer

As Acting Chairman of the Ontario Securities Commission, I concur with the foregoing Protocol for consideration of Exchange Rules

John A. Geller

Acting Chairman

Ontario Securities Commission

cc: John W. Carson

[Minister of Finance approval received December 18, 1997 (21 O.S.C.B. 904)]

IA-5 — Memorandum of Understanding Respecting the Oversight of Exchanges and Quotation and Trade Reporting Systems

Date: September 13, 2002; amended October 2, 2009 and December 17, 2010

25 O.S.C.B. 6021, 32 O.S.C.B. 7764 and 33 O.S.C.B. 11658

Memorandum of Understanding respecting the Oversight of Exchanges and Quotation and Trade Reporting Systems among: Alberta Securities Commission (ASC) Autorité des marchés financiers (AMF) British Columbia Securities Commission (BCSC) Manitoba Securities Commission (MSC) Ontario Securities Commission (OSC) Saskatchewan Financial Services Commission (SFSC) (each a Party, collectively the Parties)

The Parties agree as follows:

1. — Underlying Principles

(a) — Lead Regulator Model

(i) Each recognized exchange (Exchange) and recognized quotation and trade reporting system (QTRS) subject to this Memorandum of Understanding (MOU) has a lead regulator (Lead Regulator) responsible for its oversight and one or more exempting regulators (Exempting Regulator).

(ii) The Exempting Regulator of an Exchange or QTRS exempts it from recognition as an Exchange or QTRS on the basis that:

    (A) the Exchange or QTRS is and will continue to be recognized by the Lead Regulator as an Exchange or QTRS;

    (B) the Lead Regulator is responsible for conducting the regulatory oversight of the Exchange or QTRS; and

    (C) the Lead Regulator will inform the Exempting Regulator of its oversight activities and the Exempting Regulator will have the opportunity to raise issues concerning the oversight of the Exchange or QTRS with the Lead Regulator in accordance with this MOU.

(iii) The Lead Regulator is responsible for conducting an oversight program (the Oversight Program) of the Exchange or QTRS that will include the purpose and matters described in section 3.

(iv) The Parties will act in good faith to resolve issues raised by any Exempting Regulator in connection with the Oversight Program carried out by the Lead Regulator.

(b) — Scope

The terms of this MOU are applied by the Parties in respect of the oversight of an Exchange or QTRS identified on a list entitled "List of Exchanges, Lead Regulators and Exempting Regulators in relation to the Memorandum of Understanding respecting the Oversight of Exchanges and Quotation and Trade Reporting Systems" ("List of Exchanges"), published concurrently with this MOU by each Party. The List of Exchanges does not form part of this MOU. It may be amended from time to time and will be published by each Party after any such amendment.

(c) — Previous Memorandum of Understanding

This MOU supersedes any prior Memorandum of Understanding about the Oversight of Exchanges and Quotation and Trade Reporting Systems among the ASC, Commission des valeurs mobilières du Québec, now the AMF, BCSC, MSC and OSC.

2. — Definition

"Lead Regulator" means the Party that is designated on the List of Exchanges from time to time as being the Lead Regulator responsible for the oversight of a particular Exchange or QTRS by consensus of the Parties that have either recognized or exempted from recognition this Exchange or QTRS or are in the process of doing so.

3. — Oversight Program

(a) The purpose of the Oversight Program[1] is to ensure that each Exchange and QTRS meets appropriate standards for market operation and regulation based on the type of activities carried out by the Exchange or QTRS. Where applicable, those standards will include:

    (i) fair representation in corporate governance and rule-making;

    (ii) effective management of conflicts of interests;

    (ii) adequate ownership/control structure;

    (iv) financial viability;

    (v) sufficient resources to carry out market and regulatory functions;

    (vi) fair access for market participants and issuers;

    (vii) orderly markets through appropriate review of traded products, trading rules and financial requirements for market participants;

    (viii) transparency through timely access to accurate information on orders and trades;

    (ix) market integrity through the adoption of rules that are not contrary to the public interest, prohibit unfair trading practices, prevent market manipulation and customer and market abuses and promote just and equitable principles of trades;

    (x) monitoring of the conduct of the market participants and enforcement of the rules and requirements governing such conduct;

    (xi) proper identification and management of risks;

    (xii) effective clearing and settlement arrangements and systems;

    (xiii) information sharing and regulatory cooperation;

    (xiv) appropriate listed or quoted company regulation;

    (xv) adequate financial products and instruments development process;

    (xvi) specific trading and position limits;

    (xvii) appropriate inventory and stock delivery management procedures; and

    (xviii) appropriate coordination regarding the market surveillance of the underlying securities.

(b) The Lead Regulator will establish and conduct the Oversight Program. At a minimum, the Oversight Program will include the following:

    (i) Review of information filed by the Exchange or QTRS on critical financial and operational matters, risk management and significant changes to operations, including information filed under National Instrument 21-101 — Marketplace Operation, related to:

        (A) corporate governance;

        (B) rules;

        (C) systems and operations;

        (D) access;

        (E) listing criteria and/ or financial instrument development;

        (F) fees;

        (G) financial viability; and

        (H) regulation.

    (ii) Review and approval, where applicable, of changes to Exchange or QTRS bylaws, rules, policies, and other similar instruments (Rules) under the procedures established by the Lead Regulator from time to time.

    (iii) Periodic oversight review of Exchange or QTRS functions, including to the extent applicable:

        (A) corporate finance policies: policies relating to minimum listing or quoting requirements, continuing listing or quoting requirements or tier maintenance requirements, sponsorship and continuous disclosure;

        (B) trading halts, suspensions and de-listing procedures;

        (C) co-ordination with the markets of the underlying securities;

        (D) monitoring of trading and position limits;

        (E) surveillance and enforcement: procedures for detection of non-compliance and resolution of outstanding issues;

        (F) access: requirements for access to the facilities of the Exchange or QTRS and fair application of those requirements;

        (G) information transparency: procedures for the dissemination of market information;

        (H) corporate governance: corporate governance procedures, including policy and rule making process;

        (I) risk management; and

        (J) systems and technology.

(c) The Lead Regulator will retain sole discretion regarding the manner in which the Oversight Program is carried out, including determining the order and timing of its oversight review of the functions under section 3(b)(iii). However, the Lead Regulator will perform the oversight reviews of these functions at least once every three years. Once it has obtained the necessary internal approval and when the final report of the oversight review performed under section 3(b)(iii) is sent to the Exchange or QTRS, the Lead Regulator will also provide a copy of the final report and any responses of the Exchange or QTRS to the report to each Exempting Regulator.

---

[1]The matters outlined in the Oversight Program are intended to set out the minimum level of oversight exercised in respect of an Exchange or QTRS. The Lead Regulator may conduct additional review procedures.

(d) If issuers or parties that are directly affected by a decision of the Exchange or QTRS in the jurisdiction of an Exempting Regulator appeal that decision to the Lead Regulator or request a hearing and review of that decision by the Lead Regulator, the Lead Regulator will provide videoconferencing facilities or other electronic equipment as necessary and appropriate to permit and facilitate the participation of the parties in the proceedings in the jurisdiction of the Exempting Regulator. The Lead Regulator will also provide simultaneous translation facilities or other facilities necessary and appropriate to permit the participation of the parties in the proceedings in French or English, at their request.

(e) The Lead Regulator will inform each Exempting Regulator in writing of any material changes in how it performs its obligations under this MOU.

4. — Involvement of an Exempting Regulator

(a) The Lead Regulator acknowledges that an Exempting Regulator may require that the Exchange or QTRS provide to that Exempting Regulator:

(i) copies of information filed by the Exchange or QTRS pursuant to section 3(b)(i) at the same time that the Exchange or QTRS files the information with the Lead Regulator; and

(ii) copies of all Rules that the Exchange or QTRS files with the Lead Regulator under the Lead Regulator's procedures referred to in section 3(b)(ii) at the same time that the Exchange or QTRS files the Rules with the Lead Regulator,

(iii) copies of all final Rules once approved by the Lead Regulator under the Lead Regulator's procedures referred to in section 3(b)(ii);

(iv) in the specific context of an investigation by an Exempting Regulator and upon a specific request from that Exempting Regulator, information in writing about the marketplace participants, the shareholders or the market operations of the Exchange or QTRS.

(b) If an Exempting Regulator advises the Lead Regulator that it has specific concerns regarding the operations of the Exchange or QTRS in the jurisdiction of the Exempting Regulator and requests that the Lead Regulator perform an oversight review of the Exchange or QTRS in that jurisdiction, the Lead Regulator may determine to conduct an oversight review of:

(i) the office of the Exchange or QTRS in the jurisdiction of the Exempting Regulator; or

(ii) a function performed by an Exchange or QTRS office in that jurisdiction.

The Exempting Regulator may, as part of its request, ask that the Lead Regulator include staff of the Exempting Regulator in the Lead Regulator's oversight review. The Lead Regulator may, as a condition of performing the oversight review, request the assistance of staff of the Exempting Regulator in which case the Exempting Regulator will use its best efforts to provide this assistance.

(c) If the Lead Regulator advises the Exempting Regulator that it cannot or will not conduct the oversight review referred to in section 4(b), the Exempting Regulator may conduct the oversight review without the participation of the Lead Regulator. In that case, the Exempting Regulator will provide copies of the results of the oversight review to the Lead Regulator at the same time it sends the results to the Exchange or QTRS.

5. — Information Sharing

(a) The Lead Regulator will, upon written request from an Exempting Regulator, provide or request the Exchange or QTRS to provide to the Exempting Regulator any information about the marketplace participants, the shareholders and the market operations of the Exchange or QTRS. This would include shareholder and participating organization lists, product and trading information and disciplinary decisions.

(b) In addition, to the extent practicable and as appropriate in the particular circumstances, the Lead Regulator will inform the Exempting Regulators in advance of any material events, or material decisions taken either by the Lead Regulator or the Exchange or QTRS, that may have a significant impact on the operations or activities of the Exchange or QTRS.

6. — Oversight Committee

(a) An oversight committee will continue to have the mandate to act as a forum and venue for the discussion of issues, concerns and proposals related to the oversight of marketplaces by the Parties (Oversight Committee).

(b) The Oversight Committee will include staff representatives from each of the Parties who have responsibility and/or expertise in the areas of marketplace oversight and market regulation.

(c) The Oversight Committee will meet at least once annually in person and will conduct conference calls at least quarterly.

(d) At least quarterly, the Parties will provide to the Oversight Committee a summary report on their oversight activities conducted during the period that will include a summary description of any material changes made to their oversight program, including the procedures for the review and approval of Exchange or QTRS Rules.

(e) At least annually, the Oversight Committee will provide to the Canadian Securities Administrators a written report of the oversight activities of the committee members during the previous period.

7. — Issues Forum

(a) The Parties acknowledge that:

(i) more than one Exchange or QTRS may file the same Rules to different Lead Regulators for review and approval at the same time;

(ii) one Exchange or QTRS may file a Rule to its Lead Regulator for review and approval that is the same as an existing Rule adopted by a different Exchange or QTRS with a different Lead Regulator; or

(iii) an Exempting Regulator may have material concerns regarding a Rule that the Exchange or QTRS has filed for review and approval with the Lead Regulator under the Lead Regulator's procedures referred to in section 3(b)(ii).

(b) In the event the circumstances set out in section 7(a) arise, the Lead Regulators will act in good faith to resolve the issues or concerns raised by any of the parties involved in a dispute or disagreement in order to either achieve consistent results among the Lead Regulators or to address the concerns of the Exempting Regulator.

(c) The Parties to this MOU will establish a committee of the Chairs or other senior executives of the parties involved (the "Issues Forum") that will attempt to reach a consensus between the parties on any issue in dispute or disagreement under section 7(a). The Issues Forum will make recommendations to the various parties. Staff of any of the parties involved in a dispute or disagreement may submit the issue in dispute or the matter causing the disagreement to the Issues Forum.

INTERGOVERN-
MENTAL
AGREEMENTS

(d) The Issues Forum will include the Chair or another senior executive of each Party involved in a dispute or disagreement under 7(a). For purposes of this section and if there are joint Lead Regulators of an Exchange or QTRS, the joint Lead Regulators of the Exchange or QTRS will be considered to be separate parties.

8. — Waiver and Termination

(a) The provisions of this MOU may be waived by mutual agreement of the Parties.

(b) If the Lead Regulator or an Exempting Regulator of an Exchange or QTRS believes that another Party is not satisfactorily performing its obligations under this MOU, it may give written notice to the other Party stating that belief and providing particulars in reasonable detail of the alleged failure to perform. If the Party receiving the notice has not satisfied the notifying Party within two months of the delivery of the notice either that its performance is satisfactory or that it has taken or will take acceptable steps to rectify its performance, the notifying Party may by written notice to the other Party terminate this MOU as it relates to that Exchange or QTRS on a date not less than six months following delivery of the notice of termination. In that case, the notifying Party will send to the Exchange or QTRS a copy of its notice of termination at the same time it sends the notice to all the other Parties.

(c) In the event any significant change to the ownership, structure or operations of an Exchange or QTRS affects the oversight of the Exchange or QTRS, a Lead Regulator or any Exempting Regulator may give written notice to the other Parties stating its concerns. If a resolution cannot be reached within two months of the delivery of the notice, the notifying Party may by written notice to the other Parties terminate this MOU as it relates to the Exchange or QTRS on a date not less than six months following delivery of the notice of termination. In that case, the notifying Party will send to the Exchange or QTRS a copy of its notice of termination at the same time it sends the notice to all the other Parties.

(d) For purposes of this section and if applicable, the joint Lead Regulators of the Exchange or QTRS will be considered one party.

9. — Amendments to and Withdrawal from this MOU

(a) This MOU may be amended from time to time as mutually agreed upon by the Parties. Any amendments must be in writing and approved by the duly authorized representatives of each Party. Any amendment of this MOU is subject to Ministerial approval in Ontario and to Governmental approval in Québec. For clarity, the List of Exchanges does not form part of this MOU.

(b) The Parties acknowledge that the securities regulators of any other jurisdiction where an Exchange or QTRS is recognized or exempted from recognition may become a Party to this MOU.

(c) Each Party can, at any time, withdraw from this MOU on at least 90 days written notice to all other Parties.

10. — Effective Date

This MOU comes into effect on January 1, 2010.

List of Exchanges, Lead Regulators and Exempting Regulators in relation to the Memorandum of Understanding respecting the Oversight of Exchanges and Quotation and Trade Reporting Systems As of January 1, 2011

EXCHANGE QTRS	LEAD REGULATOR(S)	EXEMPTING REGULATOR(S)
Bourse de Montréal Inc.	Autorité des marchés financiers	Ontario Securities Commission
CNSX Markets Inc.	Ontario Securities Commission	Alberta Securities Commission Autorité des marchés financiers British Columbia Securities Commission Manitoba Securities Commission
ICE Futures Canada Inc.	Manitoba Securities Commission	Autorité des marchés financiers
Natural Gas Exchange Inc.	Alberta Securities Commission	Autorité des marchés financiers Manitoba Securities Commission Ontario Securities Commission
TSX Inc.	Ontario Securities Commission	Alberta Securities Commission Autorité des marchés financiers British Columbia Securities Commission
TSX Venture Exchange Inc.	Alberta Securities Commission British Columbia Securities Commission	Autorité des marchés financiers Manitoba Securities Commission Ontario Securities Commission

[Minister of Finance Approval given November 27, 2009: 32 O.S.C.B. 10452]

IA-6 — OTC Agreement

Date: 2000/10/06

23 O.S.C.B. 8447

THIS AGREEMENT made as of the 6th day of October, 2000,

AMONG:

CANADIAN UNLISTED BOARD INC.

("CUB")

-and-

CANADIAN VENTURE EXCHANGE INC.

("CDNX")

-and-

THE ONTARIO SECURITIES COMMISSION

("OSC")

Whereas:

A. By an agreement made as of February 28, 1991 among The Toronto Stock Exchange (the "TSE"), the OSC and the Canadian Dealing Network Inc. ("CDN"), CDN (a wholly-owned subsidiary of the TSE) took on assignment from the OSC and has been operating a trade reporting system (the "CDN Reporting System") and a quotation system (the "CDN Quotation System") (collectively, the "CDN System") to provide visibility for over-the-counter ("OTC") trading- of equity securities in the Province of Ontario;

B. By an agreement made as of September 29, 2000 among CDNX, the TSE and CDN (the "CDN Agreement"), the TSE and CDN have agreed to cease operating the CDN System;

C. The OSC wishes to ensure that a system continues to exist in the Province of Ontario through which OSC registered dealers can continue their mandatory reporting of all OTC trading in unlisted and unquoted equity securities in the Province of Ontario not specifically excluded from the reporting requirements of the *Securities Act, R.S.O. 1990, Chapter S. 5* and the regulations thereto (collectively, the "Act");

D. Subject to the terms and conditions of this Agreement, CUB, a wholly owned subsidiary of CDNX, is prepared to operate an internet web-based reporting system for the reporting by registered dealers of OTC trading in unlisted and unquoted equity securities in the Province of Ontario (the "OTC System") and to provide certain services to the OSC with respect thereto; and

E. Subject to the terms and conditions of this Agreement, CDNX has agreed to ensure that CUB fulfils its obligations hereunder and has adequate resources (including those made available to it by CDNX) to operate the OTC System and to provide to the OSC those services called for by this Agreement;

NOW THEREFORE in consideration of the premises and the mutual covenants, terms and conditions herein contained, the parties hereto do hereby mutually covenant and agree as follows:

1. — The OTC System

1.1 The OTC System to be operated by CUB pursuant to this Agreement shall possess the characteristics and functionality described in Schedule "A" which is attached hereto and forms a part of this Agreement; provided, however, and the parties further agree that for greater certainty the OTC System will not provide for visible trade reporting.

1.2 The OTC System shall commence operation as at 5:00 p.m. EST on October 6, 2000 such that mandatory reporting by OSC registered dealers of all OTC trading in unlisted and unquoted equity securities in the Province of Ontario not specifically excluded from the reporting requirements of the Act (hereinafter referred to as "Ontario OTC trading") via the OTC System will commence on October 10, 2000.

1.3 All right, title and interest in and to the OTC System shall be owned solely by CUB, its successors and permitted assigns. For greater certainty, the right, title and interest in and to all registered and unregistered trademarks, trade names, service marks, copyrights, designs, inventions, patents, patent applications, patent rights, licenses, franchises, processes, technology, trade secrets and other industrial property pertaining to the OTC System developed by CUB (or on behalf of CUB by CDNX) or to any developments or enhancements of the OTC System implemented by CUB shall be owned solely by CUB, its successors and permitted assigns and, subject as herein otherwise provided, the OSC, OSC registered dealers who report trades on the OTC System ("Users") and any other parties shall acquire no rights in or license to use the OTC System except as may be necessary for the due implementation of this Agreement.

2. — Administration/Operation of The OTC System

2.1 Subject to the terms and conditions of this Agreement, CUB shall administer and operate the OTC System by providing:

(i)   trade reporting services in respect of Ontario OTC trading by Users;

(ii)   surveillance services as referred to in Part 4 of this Agreement in respect of Ontario OTC trading by Users; and

(iii)   such services as may be required to record and account for the fees referred to in subsection 2.3 below and charged by CUB for use of the OTC System.

2.2 CUB will provide such staff as are necessary to operate the OTC System with the functionality described In Schedule "A".

2.3 CUB may establish and from time to time amend a schedule of fees that it will be entitled to charge for use of the OTC System. Such fees shall be established at a level which, in the aggregate, will permit CUB to be reimbursed for all costs associated with the development and ongoing operation of the OTC System, including all operating, capital and related costs. All fees charged by CUB will be consistent with CUB's status as a not-for-profit entity and, though not subject to prior approval by the OSC, may be reviewed by the OSC.

2.4 All fees and other revenue derived from the operation of the OTC System will be retained by CUB.

2.5 CUB will ensure that each User shall, as a condition of using the OTC System, enter into an agreement with CUB (the "User Agreement") in the form and upon substantially the terms attached hereto as Schedule "B".

3. — Regulation of the OTC System

3.1 In the event that the OTC System is implemented prior to the implementation of the OSC's rules governing alternative trading systems (the "ATS Rules") and unless otherwise agreed, the parties agree that the OTC System will be regulated in two phases as follows:

(i)   for the period commencing on the date of implementation of the OTC System and ending on the date of implementation in Ontario of a local rule relating to Ontario OTC trading which will be implemented concurrently with the ATS Rules or such other rules as the OSC may apply to Ontario OTC trading (the "Ontario Local Rule"), the OTC System will be regulated in accordance with the OTC Terms and Conditions which are attached as Schedule "A" to the User Agreement (the "User Obligations"); and

(ii)   commencing on the date of implementation of the Ontario Local Rule and ending on the date of the termination of this Agreement, the OTC System will be regulated in accordance with the Ontario Local Rule.

3.2 In the event that the OTC System is implemented after implementation of the Ontario Local Rule, the OTC System will be regulated in accordance with the Ontario Local Rule.

3.3 It is recognized and agreed that CUB shall not make any rules or regulations regarding Ontario OTC trading and that until such time as the Ontario Local Rule is implemented the OTC System will be operated and governed in accordance with the User Obligations.

4. — Surveillance Services in Respect of The OTC System

4.1 CUB will provide surveillance services as described in confidential Schedule "C" which is attached hereto and forms a part of this Agreement in respect of Ontario OTC trading that is reported to the OTC System; provided, however, and it is further understood and agreed, that the responsibility for enforcement regulatory activity pertaining to Ontario OTC trading will rest exclusively with the OSC and CUB will not provide enforcement services in respect of the market participants using the OTC System.

4.2 The surveillance services described in confidential Schedule "C" and provided by CUB in respect of Ontario OTC trading that is reported to the OTC System will be comprised generally of and limited to the following:

(i)   exception monitoring for Ontario OTC trading activity in violation of the terms of any User Agreement, applicable trading rules or applicable securities laws; and

(ii)   press release monitoring for issuer disclosure in respect of Ontario OTC trading in violation of applicable securities laws.

4.3 All matters requiring enforcement action will be referred to the applicable securities regulatory body which it is anticipated will be the OSC in most cases involving the OTC System.

4.4 CUB will impose no trading halts in respect of any Ontario OTC trading reported to the OTC System.

4.5 CUB will provide to the OSC on request all such Ontario OTC trading and surveillance data respectively reported to the OTC System and collected by CUB as the OSC may require for its investigative and enforcement purposes.

5. — Maintenance of Trading Data

5.1 Ontario OTC reporting and surveillance data respectively reported to the OTC System and collected by CUB will be maintained by CUB for its surveillance and the OSC's enforcement purposes only, and will not be published. For greater certainty, CUB shall ensure that such data is retained for a period of at least seven (7) years and accessible to OSC staff for investigative and enforcement purposes.

5.2 CUB recognizes its obligation to provide the OSC access (via the OTC System) to data collected by CUB in respect of Ontario OTC trading reported to the OTC System so as to assist the OSC in carrying out its regulatory responsibilities.

6. — Acknowledgments of the OSC

6.1 Effective as at 5:00 p.m. EST on October 6, 2000, the OSC by separate instrument has appointed CUB as the OSC's agent as contemplated in, Part VI of the *Regulation*, for the purpose of operating the OTC System.

6.2 In order to assist CUB in its operation of the OTC System, the OSC may obtain and provide to CUB such information as the OSC deems appropriate, including information:

(i)   on disciplinary or other action the OSC determines to take against a User which, in the OSC's view, will have a material impact on the User's participation in the OTC System; and

(ii)   relating to issuers of OTC Securities (being the same as "COATS Securities" as defined in section 152 of Part VI of the Regulation), OSC registered dealers or any other Persons (as such latter term is defined in the Act) that leads the OSC to believe that there has been or will be a breach of the terms and conditions of Part VI of the Regulation.

7. — Covenants of CDNX

7.1 CDNX agrees to ensure that CUB fulfils its obligations under this Agreement and has adequate resources (including those made available to it by CDNX) to operate the OTC System and to provide to the OSC those services called for by this Agreement.

8. — CUB to Limit The Liability of CDNX

8.1 CUB agrees that it will, in connection with the performance by it of its obligations under this Agreement, take reasonable precautions to limit the liability, if any, of CDNX to any third party in connection with the operation of the OTC System, such precautions to include, where possible, the use of disclaimers in connection with the supply of information and the insertion of appropriate limiting conditions in contracts entered into by CUB.

9. — Term and Termination

9.1 This Agreement shall come into force and effect as at 5:00 p.m. EST on October 6, 2000 (the "Effective Date") such that the reporting of Ontario OTC trading via the OTC System will commence on October 10, 2000 and (provided that it is not terminated due to termination of the CDN Agreement pursuant to the terms thereof) shall survive from such date until the earlier of the day upon which it is terminated pursuant to subsection 9.2 hereof or the day upon which this Agreement is replaced by a new agreement entered into amongst the parties by reason of implementation by the OSC of the Ontario Local Rule; provided, however, that if this Agreement is so replaced the replacement agreement will not itself be able to be terminated before the earliest date that this Agreement can be terminated pursuant to subsection 9.2 hereof.

9.2 At any time at least three (3) years after the Effective Date, any of the parties may give one (1) year's written notice to the others of its decision to terminate its obligations hereunder, and this Agreement shall thereafter terminate on the expiry of such notice.

10. — Non Performance

10.1 If a party to this Agreement believes that another party is not performing satisfactorily its obligations under this Agreement, it may give written notice to the other party stating that belief accompanied by particulars in reasonable detail of the alleged failure to perform. If the party receiving such notice has not satisfied the notifying party within one (1) month of the delivery of the notice either that its performance is satisfactory or that it has taken or will take acceptable steps to rectify its performance, the notifying party may by written notice to the other parties terminate this Agreement on a date not less than three (3) months following delivery of such notice.

11. — Notice

Any notice or other communication required or permitted to be given hereunder shall be sufficiently given if delivered in person or if sent by facsimile transmission:

11.1 in the case of CUB, both for itself and on behalf of CDNX, at the following address:

Canadian Unlisted Board Inc.
c/o Canadian Venture Exchange Inc.
10th Floor, 300 Fifth Avenue S.W.
Calgary, Alberta T2P 3C4

Attention:

CDNX Vice President, Regulatory Affairs
& Corporate Secretary
Facsimile No: (403) 237-0450

11.2 in the case of the OSC, at the following address:

The Ontario Securities Commission
Suite 1800, P.O. Box 55
20 Queen Street West
Toronto, Ontario M5H 3S8

Attention: Manager, Market Regulation
Facsimile No: (416) 593-8240

or at such other address as the party to which such notice or other communication is to be given has last notified to the other parties in the manner provided in this section, and if so given the same shall be deemed to have been received on the date of such delivery or sending.

12. — Further Assurances, Amendments and Waivers

12.1 Each party hereto covenants and agrees that it shall from time to time and at all times execute and deliver all such further documents and assurances as shall be reasonably required in order to fully perform and carry out the intent of this Agreement. This Agreement can only be amended with the consent in writing of both parties and no party shall be deemed to have waived any provision of this Agreement unless such waiver is in writing.

13. — Applicable Law

13.1 This Agreement shall be governed by and construed in accordance with the laws of the Province of Ontario and the laws of Canada applicable therein.

14. — Counterparts and Facsimile Signature

14.1 This Agreement may be executed in separate counterparts and all such counterparts shall together constitute one and the same instrument.

14.2 The parties agree that executed copies of this Agreement may be delivered by fax or similar device and that the signatures appearing on the copies so delivered will be as binding as if copies bearing original signatures had been delivered; each party undertakes to deliver to the other party a copy of this Agreement bearing original signatures, forthwith upon demand.

15. — Force Majeure

15.1 No party shall be responsible for delays or failures in performance resulting from acts beyond the control of such party. Such acts shall include, but not be limited to, acts of God, the operation of any law, regulation or order of government or other similar Authority, any labour disparity or dispute, strike, lockout, riot, explosion, war, invasion, epidemic, fire, earthquake or other natural disaster, power failure or system failure including network failures.

16. — Successors and Assigns

16.1 Neither CUB, CDNX nor the OSC shall assign this Agreement or any of their respective rights or obligations hereunder without the prior written consent of the others. This Agreement shall enure to the benefit of and be binding upon the respective successors and permitted assigns of the parties hereto.

IN WITNESS WHEREOF, the parties have hereunto duly executed this Agreement as of the day and year first above written.

CANADIAN UNLISTED BOARD INC.

Per: _____
              Authorized Signatory
Per: _____
              Authorized Signatory

CANADIAN VENTURE EXCHANGE INC.

Per: _____
              Authorized Signatory
Per: _____
              Authorized Signatory

THE ONTARIO SECURITIES COMMISSION

Per: _____
              Authorized Signatory
Per: _____
              Authorized Signatory

This is Schedule "A" to that certain Agreement made as of the 6th day of October, 2000, among Canadian Unlisted Board Inc., Canadian Venture Exchange Inc. and The Ontario Securities Commission

OTC System Characteristics and Functionality

1.1 — Characteristics

— Included Characteristics

The OTC System will be a CUB-developed internet web-based system solution for the reporting of Ontario OTC trading the general characteristics of which will be a system:

1. providing a secure, reliable environment to enable registered dealers to report trades in securities according to the *Securities Act (Ontario)*.

2. providing a basic reporting, surveillance, and administrative functionality with unexplained trading and disclosure anomalies being forwarded to the OSC for enforcement and further investigation.

3. providing a separation of Ontario OTC trading from CDNX and the CDNX brand.

4. separable from CDNX technology operations and deployable to other technical environments should the OSC choose to change service providers.

5. extendable to other provincial jurisdictions in support of possible national trade reporting.

6. possessing a separate logical billing system within CDNX's Oracle Financials to generate invoices and statements for CUB that are distinct from those of CDNX.

7. possessing a backup OTC System application server (existing disaster recovery hardware at CDNX Business Continuity Planning ("BCP") recovery sites having sufficient capacity to accommodate the OTC System application).

1.2 — Functionality

1.2.1 — *Included Functionality*

The OTC System will possess the following functionality:

1.2.1.1 — *Registered Dealer Functionality:*

1. Registered Dealer administrative functions

1.1 Provide the ability for the registered dealer (who may or may not be TSE or CDNX members) to logon, logoff and change their passwords

2. Report a trade

2.1 Report a trade done today (typically reported by the selling registered dealer)

  2.1.1 Data includes: symbol, volume, price, contra-broker, time-stamp, identification of which side reported the trade.

2.2 Limit or restrict the registered dealer from reporting a trade that was executed prior to the current day. 'As of reporting to be handled by the administrative or market regulation function of CUB (see *Administrative Functionality below*).

3. Report a trade cancellation

4. Inquire on trading activity for an issue

4.1 The reporting functions proposed with respect to Ontario OTC trading are purposely limited.

4.2 Data attributes to be displayed are:

  4.2.1 For today: high price, low price, last price, net change, volume, value, # trades and list of all trades

  4.2.2 For historical periods: high price, low price, last price, net change, volume, value, # trades

5. View Administrative Notice Board

5.1 Contains textual information posted by CUB administrative and market regulation staff

6. Online Help

6.1 Display of "How To" information explaining the operation of the OTG System

6.2 Inquiries to list:

  6.2.1 Securities on the system that have reported activity (stock list) that would include the issue name, symbol, and Cusip number (if applicable)

  6.2.2 Yesterday's and today's add's, delete's and changes to the stock list

  6.2.3 A directory of registered dealer users Ids and names

1.2.1.2 — *Administrative Functionality:*

Administrative functionality will be used by CUB staff to administer the OTC System.

1. UserID administration

1.1 Setup new UserID

1.2 Maintain UserID (change, delete, force password changes)

2. Security Master maintenance

2.1 Add, change, delete issues that can be reported. This functionality can be done in real-time.

2.2 Update Trading status to restrict the reporting of trades

3. Report trade (on behalf of a registered dealer)

3.1 Similar to the registered dealer function to report a trade.

3.2 This functionality can also serve as a short-term backup service should operational problems arise with accessing the system.

4. Report a trade done up to 364 days ago ("as of")

4.1 'As of' reporting is done by CUB staff on behalf of the registered dealer. The registered dealer would send (via fax) to CUB the particulars of the delayed trade report.

4.2 Historical information to be updated to reflect the reported trade.

5. Report trade cancellation (on behalf of a registered dealer)

5.1 Similar to the registered dealer function to report a trade cancellation.

5.2 This functionality can also serve as a short-term backup service should operational problems arise with accessing the system.

5.3 Historical information would be updated to reflect the cancelled trade.

6. Post and clear notices and other textual information to Administrative Notice Board

6.1   The transaction is logged to an audit trail file

7. Online Help maintenance

7.1   Update static "How To" information

1.2.1.3 — Regulatory Functionality:

Regulatory functionality will be that employed by CUB staff to provide regulatory oversight or surveillance of Ontario OTC trading (it being understood that all enforcement action arising from CUB's surveillance activities in respect of Ontario OTC trading that is reported to the OTC System will be undertaken by the OSO). Due to the nature of Ontario OTC trading, all such regulatory functionality will be of a post-trade nature.

1. Alerts of reported trades that cause exceptions to price change and volume tolerance parameters.

2. OSC access to the OTC System to perform specified inquiry functions:

2.1   Today and historical trading inquiries (see *Registered Dealer Functionality* above)

2.2   Generate reports on trading activity per Registered Dealer firm, per security, and for all securities per specified (flexible) date range.

2.3   Access to Online Help inquiries (see *Registered Dealer Functionality* above)

3. Ad hoc reports for investigations forwarded to the OSC.

4. Data extracts for investigations forwarded to the OSC.

1.2.1.4 — Operational Functionality:

Operational functionality will be global in nature and apply to the entire OTC System.

- Implement a standalone OTC System application server (NT operating system), separate from CDNX systems.
- Establish recovery procedures to transfer the application to an existing CDNX NT server on an interim basis in the event of a CUB/OTC System server failure.
- Store trade summaries for surveillance purposes (history)
- Store detail trade records for investigative purposes (history)
- Conduct daily backup of files and databases
- Include OTC System in CDNX BCP and provide 48 hour recovery time for the CUB OTC System at the CDNX BCP recovery site(s)
- Generate billing reports
- Generate monthly reports of trading activity for invoice preparation.

1.3 — Excluded Functionality

The OTC System will NOT possess the following functionality:

- Capability regarding investigation and enforcement of trading and disclosure- anomalies generated by the system.
- Capability to prioritize price/volume exceptions.
- Capability to generate real time data feeds-or press reports.
- Capability to transfer historical trade information from the TSE/CATS system.

This is Schedule "B" to that certain Agreement made as of the 6th day of October, 2000, among Canadian Unlisted Board Inc., Canadian Venture Exchange Inc. and The Ontario Securities Commission

Canadian Unlisted Board Inc. User Agreement
(the "Agreement")

WHEREAS the Canadian Venture Exchange Inc. ("CDNX" or the "Exchange") has entered into an agreement with the Toronto Stock Exchange Inc. ("TSE") and the Canadian Dealing Network Inc. ("CDN") whereby:

(i)   as at 5:00 p.m. EST on September 29, 2000, the TSE and CDN shall cease operating the CDN Quotation System such that eligible CDN quoted issuers that have filed complete applications as determined by CDNX shall commence trading on CDNX Tier 3 as at the start of business on October 2, 2000; and

(ii)   as at 5:00 p.m. EST on October 6, 2000, the TSE and CDN shall cease operating the CDN Reporting System such that as of the start of business on October 10, 2000, OSC registered dealers can continue their mandatory reporting of all OTC trading in unlisted and un-quoted equity securities in the province of Ontario not specifically excluded from the reporting requirements of the Act and the regulations thereto via the OTC System;

WHEREAS the Canadian Unlisted Board Inc., a wholly owned subsidiary of CDNX ("CUB"), CDNX and the Ontario Securities Commission (the "Commission") have entered into an agreement pursuant to which CUB will operate an Internet web-based reporting system for the reporting by dealers of trading in unlisted and unquoted equity securities in Ontario (the "OTC System") for the purposes of Part VI of Regulation 1015 ("Part VI");

WHEREAS CUB has been appointed as an agent of the Commission for the purposes of developing computer software and providing and operating computer facilities for the reporting of trading in unlisted and unquoted equity securities in Ontario pursuant to section 153 of Part VI;

WHEREAS for the purposes of this agreement the following definitions shall apply:

"Act" means the Securities Act, R.S.O. 1990, c. S.5 as amended;

"CDN Policy" means that policy which has been adopted by CDN board of directors respecting trading in unlisted and unquoted equity securities in Ontario;

"OTC security" shall have the same meaning as 'COATS security' as defined in section 152 of Part VI;

"Person" means a "person" as that term is defined in the Act;

"User" means a registrant under the Act and who reports trades on the OTC System;

WHEREAS in order to assist CUB in its operation of the OTC System, the Commission may obtain and provide to CUB such information as the Commission deems appropriate, including information:

(i) on disciplinary or other action the Commission determines to take against a User which, in the Commission's view, will have a material impact on the User's participation in the OTC System; and

(ii) relating to issuers of OTC Securities, registrants under the Act or any other Persons that leads the Commission to believe that there has been or will be a breach of the terms and conditions of Part VI.

WHEREAS the Commission and CUB have agreed that in the event that the OTC system is implemented prior to the implementation of the OSC's rules governing alternative trading systems (the "ATS Rules") the OTC System shall be regulated in the following two phases:

(i) for the period commencing on the date of implementation of the OTC System and ending on the date of the implementation of a local Ontario rule relating to Ontario OTC trading which will be implemented concurrently with the ATS Rules or such other rules as the OSC may apply to Ontario OTC trading (the "Ontario Local Rule"), the OTC System will be regulated in accordance with Part VI and those portions of the CDN Policy pertaining to trade reporting of unlisted and unquoted equity securities in Ontario as in effect at 5:00 p.m. EST October 6, 2000; and

(ii) commencing on the date of the implementation of the Ontario Local Rule and ending on the date of the termination of the Agreement, the OTC System will be regulated in accordance with the Ontario Local Rule.

WHEREAS CUB will provide monitoring and surveillance services to the OSC in respect of trading in securities reported through the OTC System CUB will not provide enforcement services in respect of the market participants using the OTC System.

WHEREAS CUB will refer any matters relating to a suspected violation of applicable trading rules or securities laws to the OSC or other applicable securities regulatory body.

WHEREAS CUB has agreed to provide to the OSC on request all such trading and surveillance data collected by CUB in respect of the OTC System as the OSC may require.

WHEREAS the OSC requires registered dealers to act in accordance with applicable securities legislation including but not limited to the obligation to deal fairly, honestly and in good faith with its customers.

WHEREAS the OSC expects registered dealers, as part of their general obligations, to have policies and procedures which enable them to operate in a manner which is consistent with the requirements set out in the OTC Terms and Conditions (as defined below);

NOW, THEREFORE, in consideration of CUB permitting the undersigned User to utilize the OTC System, the User agrees with CUB as follows:

1. The User is a registered dealer within the meaning of the Act and shall at all times act in accordance with applicable securities legislation including but not limited to the obligation to deal fairly, honestly and in good faith with its customers and shall have policies and procedures which enable them to operate in a manner which is consistent with the requirements set out in the OTC Terms and Conditions (as defined below);

2. Until such time as the Ontario Local Rule is implemented, the User agrees that the OTC System will be operated and governed in accordance with:

(i) Part VI and those portions of the CDN Policy pertaining to trade reporting of unlisted and unquoted equity securities in Ontario as in effect at 5:00 p.m. EST on October 6, 2000; and

(ii) such directives as may be issued by authority of the Board of Directors of CUB in respect of the use of the OTC System;

(collectively, the "OTC Terms and Conditions" which are attached as Schedule "A" to this Agreement) and the User shall comply with the OTC Terms and Conditions.

3. The User shall promptly communicate to CUB transaction reports with respect to OTC securities in accordance with the OTC Terms and Conditions;

4. The User shall comply with all requirements of the OTC Terms and Conditions and without limiting the generality of the foregoing, all Users acknowledge and agree:

(i)   that they will provide to CUB any and all records, reports, and information required or requested by CUB in order for CUB to satisfy its regulatory obligations, in such manner and form, including electronically, as may be required by CUB from time to time;

(ii) that they will permit CUB or its designate to inspect their records at any time;

(iii) that CUB may suspend the User's access to the OTC System pending a determination of the OSC in respect of any referral by CUB to the OSC of any suspected violation of the User's obligation to comply with section 1 above; and

INTERGOVERN-
MENTAL
AGREEMENTS

(iv) that CUB may terminate the User's access to the OTC System upon notification to CUB by the OSC that the User has violated the OTC Terms and Conditions.

5. The User shall pay, when due, any applicable fees or charges established by CUB from time to time and which current fees and charges are attached as Schedule "B" to this Agreement.

6. The User acknowledges that it is possible that from time to time the OTC System may be disrupted, contain inaccurate information, omit required information or may otherwise operate in an unsatisfactory manner (such events being hereinafter referred to as "Errors") whether through malfunction of equipment, power failure, human error or other reason. The causes of such Errors may be attributable to CUB, the Exchange, negligent or wilful acts or omissions of current or former directors, governors, officers, employees or committee members of CUB or the Exchange (hereinafter collectively referred to as "Personnel") or persons or companies who have supplied goods or services to either CUB or the Exchange in connection with the OTC System (hereinafter referred to as "Contractors").

7. It is acknowledged that neither CUB nor the Exchange assumes any responsibility with respect to the use to which the User, its employees or agents puts the facilities, services or the information obtained therefrom or with respect to the results of such use. It is further acknowledged that the information, services and facilities provided hereunder are provided on the express condition that Users making use of them assent that no liability whatsoever in relation thereto shall be incurred by CUB, the Exchange or Personnel.

8. The User agrees that none of CUB, the Exchange or Personnel shall have any liability whatsoever to the User with respect to any loss, damage, cost, expense or other liability or claim suffered or incurred by or made against the User, directly or indirectly, by reason of Errors, or arising from any negligent, reckless or wilful act or omission or out of the use, operation or regulation of the OTC System by CUB, the Exchange, Personnel or Contractors, or otherwise as a result of the use by the User of the facilities, services or information provided by CUB or the Exchange. By making use of the facilities, services or information provided by CUB or the Exchange the User expressly agrees to accept all liability arising from such use.

9. It is acknowledged by the User that the sole remedy for any wilful or negligent actor omission of any Personnel or Contractors shall be appropriate action, of a disciplinary nature or otherwise, instituted solely at the discretion of CUB or the Exchange.

10. CUB may terminate or amend this Agreement, subject to the approval of its Board of Directors and upon notice to the User, and any subsequent participation of the User in the OTC System shall constitute acceptance by the User of any such amendment.

11. It is acknowledged that neither CUB nor the Exchange shall incur any liability to the User with respect to any loss or damage whatsoever that the User may suffer, directly or indirectly, by reason of any termination of this Agreement.

12. In the event that any legal proceeding is brought or threatened against CUB, the Exchange, Personnel or Contractors to impose liability which arises directly or indirectly from the use by the-User of the OTC System or from the use by the User of the facilities, services or information provided by CUB or the Exchange, the User agrees to indemnify and save CUB and the Exchange harmless from and against:

(i) all liabilities, damages, losses, costs, charges and expenses of every nature and kind (including, without limitation, legal and professional fees) incurred by CUB or the Exchange in connection with the proceeding, including costs incurred to indemnify Personnel;

(ii) any recovery adjudged against CUB, the Exchange or Personnel in the event that any of them is found to be liable; and

(iii) any payment by CUB or the Exchange, made with the consent of the User, in settlement of such proceeding.

13. Except as otherwise expressly provided herein, all of the terms used in this Agreement which are defined in OTC Terms and Conditions are used herein as so defined.

14. This Agreement shall be governed by and construed in accordance with the laws of the Province of Ontario.

15. The Agreement shall not be binding until accepted in writing by CUB.

16. The Agreement shall be effective as of the date accepted in writing by CUB.

.... [Insert Name of User]

By: .... Authorized Signatory

.... Name and Title of Authorized Signatory (Please Print Name and Title)

By: .... Authorized Signatory

.... Name and Title of Authorized Signatory (Please Print Name and Title)

Accepted this .... day of.........., 200.........

CANADIAN UNLISTED BOARD INC.

By:.....................................

Schedule "A" to User Agreement
OTC Terms and Conditions

A. — Transaction Reporting

1. — Operation and Administration of OTC System

1.1. All Users shall comply with the Terms and Conditions governing the operation and administration of the OTC System, which Terms and Conditions- shall include:

1.2. those matters set forth in Part VI applicable to trade reporting in respect of over-the-counter equity securities in Ontario;

1.3. those portions of the former CDN Policy pertaining to trade reporting of unlisted and unquoted equity securities in Ontario as in effect at 5:00 p.m. EST on October 6, 2000 and incorporated herein, and

1.4. such directives as may be issued by authority of the Board of Directors of CUB in respect of the use of the OTC System.

2. — Trades to be Reported

2.1. Pursuant to Part VI, every purchase or sale in Ontario of an OTC security made by a registered dealer, as principal or agent, must be reported through the OTC System, with the following exceptions (which shall not be reported through the OTC System):

2.1.1 a trade made through the facilities of a stock exchange or other organized market recognized and identified in this section A-2;

2.1.2 a distribution effected in accordance with the Act by or on behalf of an issuer; or

2.1.3 a secondary trade made in reliance on the exemptions in clauses 72(1)(a), (c) or (d) of the Act.

2.2 Where a security that is listed on one or more of the Canadian stock exchanges becomes suspended (i.e., it is no longer posted for trading) on all such exchanges, then any trade in that security by a registered dealer shall become reportable through the OTC System if that security and trade is otherwise required to be reported through the OTC System.

2.3 The obligation to report a trade in an OTC security - applies only with respect to purchases and sales in Ontario of such security. A purchase or sale in Ontario for the purpose of these OTC Terms and Conditions is one in which either:

2.3.1 the person to whom the trade is confirmed (other than a User) is a resident of Ontario; or

2.3.2 the User's trader or sales representative handling the trade is acting from an Ontario office (irrespective of whether the User is acting as principal or agent).

2.4. Transactions that are merely booked through a User's inventory for purposes of adding a usual mark-up or commission in respect of trades which, for all intents and purposes, are agency trades on NASDAQ or a foreign stock exchange, need not be reported through the OTC System. Such transactions are considered to be trades made through the facilities of a foreign stock exchange or NASDAQ.

2.5. With respect to clause 2.1.1 above, CUB recognizes NASDAQ, The International Stock Exchange of the United Kingdom and the Republic of Ireland Limited, and all stock exchanges outside of Canada that require participants to report details of transactions and publish such details.

2.6. Trades may not be aggregated for reporting purposes except that trades from orders received prior to the opening of the OTC System and simultaneously reported at the opening may be aggregated into a single transaction report.

3. — Who Reports Trades

3.1. Every purchase or sale in an OTC security that is required to be reported under subsection A-2 above shall be reported on the OTC System in accordance with the following provisions:

3.1.1 Where the transaction involves only one User, that User shall report the trade.

3.1.2 Where the transaction involves two Users, the User by or through whom the sale is made shall report the trade.

3.1.3 Where the transaction is not a trade in Ontario for the seller, the User by or through whom the purchase is made must report the trade.

4. — Method, Timing and Content of Trade Reports

4.1. For reporting purposes, a trade is a transaction between a User and a given client, or another User, In a specific OTC security, at a given price, and executed at a certain time.

4.2 For the purposes of this section A4, "Reportable Trades" shall mean every purchase or sale in an OTC security that is required to be reported under subsection A-3.

4.3 All trade tickets for Reportable Trades shall be time stamped at the time of execution.

4.4 All Reportable Trades taking place at or between 9:30 A.M. and 5:00 P.M. on a business day shall be reported through the OTC System within three minutes after execution.

4.5. All Reportable Trades taking place after 5:00 P.M. on a business day and prior to 9:30 A.M. the next business day shall be reported through the OTC System between 8:30 A.M. and 9:30 A.M. the next business day and shall form part of the trading statistics for the next business day.

4.6 .All reports of Reportable Trades shall contain the following information:

4.6.1 symbol of the OTC security traded;

4.6.2 number of shares traded;

4.6.3 price of the trade as required by section A-5;

4.6.4 the identities of the purchasing and selling Users;

4.6.5 the time of execution of the transaction; and

4.6.6 any trade marker required by these OTC Terms and Conditions.

5. — Price to be Reported

5.1. The price to be reported is the price at which the User actually traded with its customer, adjusted by the amount that would be customary as a commission or spread in such transaction.

5.2. A trade with another User is to be reported at the actual price agreed upon. This applies to a trade in which the reporting User is acting as agent for a customer, as well as to a trade in which the User acts as principal vis-a-vis the other User.

B. — Dealers' Obligations

1. — Prices to Customers

1.1 Spread or Mark-Up: Where a trade is substantially an agency transaction, the size of any spread or "mark-up" should reflect the riskless nature of the transaction.

1.2 Interpositioning: Users shall not arrange or otherwise participate in any transaction which interpositions an intermediary or other third party in a way that will result in an unfavourable price for a customer of any User.

1.3 Users shall not enter into any transaction with a customer for any OTC security at any price that is not reasonably related to the then current market price of that security or charge a customer a commission or service charge that is not fair and reasonable in all the circumstances.

2. — Fair Dealings

2.1. Users shall transact business openly and fairly and in accordance with just and equitable principles of trade. No fictitious sale or contract shall be made in an OTC security.

3. — Customer Priority

3.1 No User Shall:

3.1.1 buy or initiate the purchase of a OTC security for its own account or for any account in which it or any person associated with it is directly or indirectly interested, while such User holds or has knowledge that any person associated with it holds an unexecuted market order or limit price order to buy such security for a customer,

3.1.2 sell or initiate the sale of any OTC security for its own account or for any account in which it or any person associated with it is directly or indirectly interested, while it holds or has knowledge that any person associated with it holds an unexecuted market order or limit price order to sell such security for a customer.

3.2 The provisions of this section shall not apply:

3.2.1 to any purchase or sale of any OTC security in an amount less than the customary unit of trading made by a User to offset odd-lot orders for customers;

3.2.2 to any purchase or sale of any OTC security upon terms for delivery other than those specified in such unexecuted market or limit price order; or

3.2.3 to any unexecuted order that la subject to a condition that has not been satisfied.

3.3 For purposes of this section a User may include a reasonable commission charge in determining whether its customers order is at the same price as a principal order.

4. — Best Market Price

4.1. Where a User executes a trade with or for its client for an OTC security that is posted for trading on a foreign market recognized under this subsection, the User shall execute the trade. on behalf of the client at a price equal to or better than the market price in the foreign market (taking exchange rates into account), plus or minus (as the case may be) a reasonable commission and any added cost of executing the order in the foreign market.

4.2. For the purpose of this subsection, CUB presently recognizes any foreign stock exchange or organized market that provides real time public dissemination of information, including firm market quotations and trading statistics.

5. — Manipulative or Deceptive Trading

5.1. A User shall not use or knowingly participate in the use of any manipulative or deceptive method of trading in connection with the purchase or sale of an OTC security that creates or may create a false or misleading appearance of trading activity or an artificial price for the said security. Without in any way limiting the generality of the foregoing, the following shall be deemed manipulative or deceptive methods of trading:

5.1.1 making a fictitious trade or giving or accepting an order which involves no change in the beneficial ownership of an OTC security;

5.1.2 entering an order or orders for the purchase of an OTC security with the knowledge that an order or orders of substantially the same size, at substantially the same time and at substantially the same price for the sale of any such security, has been or will be entered by or for the same or different persons and with the intention of creating a false or misleading appearance of active public trading in a security or with respect to the market price of an OTC security;

5.1.3 entering an order or orders for the sale of an OTC security with the knowledge that an order or orders of substantially the same size, at substantially the same time and at substantially the same price for the purchase of such security, has been or will be entered by or for the same or different person and with the intention of creating a false or misleading appearance of active public trading in a security or with respect to the market price of an OTC security;

5.1.4 making purchases of, or offers to purchase an OTC security at successively higher prices, or sales of or offers to sell any such security at successively lower prices for the purpose of creating or inducing a false or misleading appearance of trading in such security or for the purpose of unduly or improperly influencing the market price of such security; or

5.1.5 effecting, alone or with one or more persons, a series of trades in an OTC security, for the purpose of inducing the purchase or sale of such security, which creates actual or apparent trading in such security or raises or depresses the price of such security.

6. — Restrictions on Trading During Distributions

Restricted Users

6.1. The restrictions on trading during a distribution set out in this part 6.1 entitled "Restricted Users" apply to a User (a "restricted User") involved in a distribution by prospectus of an OTC security or a distribution by prospectus, Exchange Offering Prospectus, Statement of Material Facts or "wide distribution" of a security that is related to an OTC security. The restrictions do not apply to a User involved in a distribution only as a selling group member that is not obligated to purchase any unsold securities

6.1.1 Two securities are "related" if they have substantially the same characteristics, or

(a)   one is immediately convertible, exercisable or exchangeable into the other, and

(b)   the conversion, exercise or exchange price at the beginning of the restricted period (as defined below) is less than 110% of the offer price of the underlying security on the principal market where the underlying security is traded.

6.1.2 A "wide distribution" means a series of distribution principal trades to not less than 25 separate and unrelated client accounts, no one of which participate to the extent of more than 50% of the total value of the distribution.

Restrictions

6.1.3 During the restricted period, a restricted User shall not bid for or purchase an OTC security that is being distributed or that is related to a security being distributed except as follows:

Distributed Securities

6.1.4 Restricted User Not Short. A restricted User that is not short the OTC security being distributed may bid for or purchase it at or below the lower of the highest independent bid price at the time of the bid or purchase and the distribution price.

(a) A restricted User may bid for or purchase the OTC security being distributed at or below the distribution price.

(b) A restricted User that makesan initial bid below the distribution price shall not raise that bid price during the restricted period.

6.1.5 Restricted User Short. A restricted User that is short the OTC security being distributed may bid for or purchase it at or below the distribution price.

Related Securities

6.1.6 A restricted User may bid for or purchase a related OTC security at or below the highest independent bid price.

6.1.7 If there is no independent bid price for a related OTC security, a restricted User shall not bid for or purchase that security without the prior consent of CUB.

(a) A bid price is "independent" if it is for the account of a User that is not involved in the distribution or is involved only as a member of a selling group.

(b) A restricted User shall not solicit purchase orders for the OTC security being distributed or any related OTC security during the restricted period except orders to purchase OTC securities being sold pursuant to the distribution.

(c) The above restrictions do not affect sales by restricted Users to unsolicited client buy orders, In the case of an OTC security that will be listed on the Toronto Stock Exchange ("TSE") or the Canadian Venture Exchange Inc. ("CDNX") and until such time as the OTC security is actually listed and posted for trading on the TSE or CDNX and the TSE's or CDNX's market stabilization rules apply, Users must comply with the above market stabilization restrictions.

All Users

6.2   The restrictions on trading during a distribution set out in this part 6.2 entitled "All Users" apply to all Users

Restrictions

6.2.1 During the restricted period, no User shall participate in a trade of an OTC security that is being distributed or that is related to an OTC security being distributed involving a purchase by or on behalf of:

(a)   the issuer of the OTC security;

(b)   a selling OTC security holder whose securities are being distributed

(c)   an affiliate of the issuer or selling OTC security holder; or

(d)   a person acting jointly or in concert with any of the foregoing.

6.3   The "restricted period" begins on the later of;

6.3.1 the ninth trading day (or, in the case of a OTC security that is related to a TSE or CDNX-listed security, the second trading day) prior to the date on which the offering price of the OTC securities to be distributed is determined; and

6.3.2 the date on which the restricted User agrees to participate in a distribution, whether or not the terms and conditions of such participation have been agreed upon.

6.3.3 The restricted period ends on the earlier of:

(a) the ninth trading day (or, in the case of a OTC security that is related to a TSE or CDNX listed security, the second trading day) prior to the date on which the offering price of the OTC securities to be distributed is determined; and

(b) the date on which the restricted User has sold all of the OTC securities allotted to it (including all securities acquired by it in connection with the distribution) and any stabilization- arrangements to which it is a party have been terminated; and

(c) the date on which the distribution has been terminated pursuant to applicable securities legislation,

provided that, if purchasers of 5% or more of the OTC securities allotted to or acquired by a restricted User in connection with a distribution give notice that they intend to exercise their statutory rights of withdrawal, the restricted period shall again apply to that User until the OTC security, are resold or the distribution ends, as provided above. Securities are not considered "sold" before the receipt for the final prospectus has been issued.

7. — Disclosure of Interest or Control

7.1. Any User that is an insider (as that term is defined in the Act) or is controlled by, directly or indirectly, controls, or is under common control of any issuer must disclose to its customers prior to, and confirm, in writing, at the time of buying or selling any OTC security of such an issuer, the nature and existence of any such relationship.

8. — System Failures

8.1. Trades made during an OTC system power failure- or any other event that would fully or partially disable the system or cause it to malfunction must be reported on the system immediately upon the system being available to accept such data.

9. — Settlement Rules

9.1. The settlement of transactions shall conform to the rules and practices of the TSE, CDNX and The Canadian Depository for Securities Limited.

C. — Fees And Charges

1. Every User shall pay the applicable OTC System fees.

2. All fees and charges of CUB, including, but not limited to. the fees charged for transaction reports shall be determined by CUB's board of directors.

D. — Access

1. Where the Commission has provided CUB with information relating to;

1.1 disciplinary or other action the Commission determines to take against a User which, in the Commission's view will have a material impact on the User's participation in the OTC System; or

1.2 the issuers of OTC Securities, registrants under the Act or any other persons that leads the Commission to believe that there has been or will be a breach of the terms and conditions of Part VI.

2. CUB may suspend the Users access to the OTC System pending a determination by the Commission in respect of such matters.

3. Where CUB has referred any matter relating to a suspected violation by a User of the OTC Terms and Conditions, CUB may suspend the Users access to the OTC System pending a determination by the Commission in respect of such matters.

4. Where the Commission has notified CUB that a User has violated the OTC Terms and Conditions, CUB may terminate the User's access to the OTC System

E. — Miscellaneous

1. All references to a "business day" in this Schedule "A" shall mean any day from Monday to Friday inclusive.

2. All references to a time of day in the Schedule "A" shall mean Eastern Standard Time.

Schedule "B" to User Agreement
Canadian Unlisted Board Inc. User and Transaction Fees

1. USER TRANSACTION FEE

$1.95/trade (each side)

2. USER FEE:

Monthly Fee of $150.00

per Employee CUB access ID granted,

up to a maximum of $500.00/month per User

IA-7 — Oversight of IIROC by the CSA

Date: June 1, 2008
31 O.S.C.B. 5630

Memorandum of Understanding Regarding

Oversight of Investment Industry Regulatory Organization of Canada among:
British Columbia Securities Commission
Alberta Securities Commission
Saskatchewan Financial Services Commission
Manitoba Securities Commission
Ontario Securities Commission
Autorité Des Marchés Financiers
Newfoundland and Labrador, Securities Division, Department of Government Services and Lands
Nova Scotia Securities Commission
New Brunswick Securities Commission
(each a Recognizing Regulator, collectively Parties)

The Parties agree as follows:

1. — Underlying Principles

a. — Recognition

Investment Industry Regulatory Organization of Canada (IIROC) is recognized as a self-regulatory organization under applicable legislation by each of the Recognizing Regulators and is a regulation services provider pursuant to National Instrument 23-101 *Trading Rules*.

b. — Oversight Program

To ensure effective oversight of IIROC's performance of its self-regulatory activities and regulation services, the Parties to this Memorandum of Understanding (MOU) have developed an oversight program (the Oversight Program) which includes:

(i) reviewing information filed by IIROC, as set out in section 4;

(ii) reviewing and approving new and amended rules, policies and other similar instruments (Rules) and by-laws of IIROC, as set out in Appendix "A"; and

(iii) performing periodic reviews of IIROC's self-regulatory activities and regulation services.

The purpose of the Oversight Program is to ensure that IIROC is acting in accordance with its public interest mandate, specifically by complying with its terms and conditions of recognition.

c. — Previous Memoranda of Understanding

This MOU supersedes the letter agreement dated June 5, 2001 between the Investment Dealers Association of Canada (IDA) and the recognizing regulators of the IDA regarding the coordination of oversight of the IDA by the Canadian Securities Administrators and the Memorandum of Understanding Regarding Oversight of Market Regulation Services Inc. (RS) dated May 1, 2002 among the recognizing regulators of RS.

2. — Definitions

"Approved Person" has the meaning attributed to that term in IIROC's Rules, as amended from time to time.

"Member" has the meaning attributed to that term in IIROC's By-law No. 1, as amended from time to time.

"Principal Regulator" means the Recognizing Regulator that is designated as such from time to time by consensus of all the Recognizing Regulators.

3. — General Provisions

a. — Oversight Committee

An oversight committee will be established (the Oversight Committee) which will act as a forum and venue for the discussion of issues, concerns and proposals related to the oversight of IIROC.

The Oversight Committee will include staff representatives from each of the Recognizing Regulators.

The Oversight Committee will provide to the CSA Chairs an annual written report that will include a summary of all oversight activities during the previous period.

b. — Staff Contact

The Principal Regulator will provide IIROC with key staff contacts in each jurisdiction for the purposes of matters arising under this MOU or relating to oversight in general.

INTERGOVERN-MENTAL AGREEMENTS

c. — *Status Meetings*

The Principal Regulator will organize quarterly conference calls and an annual in-person meeting of the Oversight Committee and IIROC staff. The purpose is to discuss matters relating to the oversight of IIROC, issues relating to the regulation of IIROC's Members and other matters that are of interest to the Recognizing Regulators and IIROC. The Principal Regulator is also responsible for taking minutes of these calls and in-person meetings.

4. — Review of Information Filed

Any comments of the staff of the Recognizing Regulators on information filed by IIROC will be sent to the Principal Regulator. The Principal Regulator will request that IIROC respond to comments raised by the Recognizing Regulators and forward any response to the Recognizing Regulators.

5. — Review of By-laws and Rules

The Recognizing Regulators have developed a Joint Rule Review Protocol (the Protocol) for coordinating the review and approval of IIROC by-laws and Rules, as sets out in Appendix "A".

6. — Oversight Reviews

a. — *Coordination of Oversight Reviews*

(i) The Recognizing Regulators will use their best efforts to carry out reviews of IIROC offices at least once every three years. A Recognizing Regulator may choose to participate in the review of an IIROC office depending on the functions carried out in that office, or may choose to rely on another Recognizing Regulator for the review of an IIROC office. In cases where a Recognizing Regulator chooses not to review the IIROC office in its jurisdiction, the other Recognizing Regulators may conduct a review of that IIROC office. Those Recognizing Regulators who participate in a review are considered to be "Reviewing Regulators" for the purpose of oversight reviews.

(ii) The Reviewing Regulators agree to coordinate their reviews of IIROC's offices by conducting their reviews at the same time and evaluating IIROC using a uniform review program and uniform performance benchmarks.

(iii) The Principal Regulator will develop a review program in consultation with the Reviewing Regulators.

(iv) For each IIROC office, a Reviewing Regulator will be designated as the Responsible Regulator who has overall responsibility for the review of that office. In particular, the Responsible Regulator will ensure that the review is appropriately staffed, will draft the review report for that office taking into account findings and comments of the Reviewing Regulators of that office, and will report on the status and results of the review of that office.

(v) The Principal Regulator will also arrange periodic conference calls of the Reviewing Regulators during the course of a review, the purpose of which is to discuss the findings at different IIROC offices and to ensure consistent recommendations for similar findings.

b. — *Review of Draft Reports and Issuance of Final Reports and Follow-Up Plans*

At the conclusion of a review, staff of the Principal Regulator and the Reviewing Regulators will use their best efforts to follow the procedures set out below, taking into account language translation needs, when applicable:

(i) Each Responsible Regulator will provide to all Reviewing Regulators a draft report on the results of the review of its IIROC office. The Reviewing Regulators will agree in advance on the date on which the draft reports should be completed.

(ii) The Principal Regulator will review the draft reports for consistency of findings and recommendations and provide any needed comments to the Responsible Regulators within 10 business days of receipt of all the draft reports.

(iii) The Responsible Regulators will review the comments and make appropriate revisions to their reports, taking into consideration comments from the relevant Reviewing Regulators, and forward their revised draft reports to the Principal Regulator within 10 business days of receipt of the Principal Regulator's comments.

(iv) Within 10 business days of receipt of all the revised draft reports, the Principal Regulator will forward the draft reports on each office to IIROC for it to confirm factual accuracy.

(v) IIROC will review the draft reports for factual accuracy and respond to all the Reviewing Regulators with comments within 15 business days of receipt of the draft reports.

(vi) The Responsible Regulators will consider IIROC's comments and revise their reports as necessary, and will forward a copy of their final reports to the Principal Regulator within 20 business days of receiving IIROC's comments.

(vii) The Principal Regulator will combine the final reports on each IIROC office into a consolidated report and prepare an executive summary to the consolidated report. The Principal Regulator will forward the consolidated report to the Reviewing Regulators for their review within 20 business days of receipt of all the final reports.

(viii) The Reviewing Regulators will provide to the Principal Regulator any comments on the consolidated report within 10 business days of receipt of the consolidated report.

(ix) The Principal Regulator will review the comments, make any appropriate changes to the consolidated report, and forward the consolidated report to IIROC for a formal response with copies to the Reviewing Regulators, within 10 business days of receipt of the Reviewing Regulators' comments.

(x) IIROC will use its best efforts to respond to the consolidated report within 20 business days of receipt of the report. A copy of its response will be sent to all the Reviewing Regulators.

(xi) The Responsible Regulator will review IIROC's response, develop a follow-up plan for the applicable IIROC office, and forward its follow-up plan to the Principal Regulator, within 20 business days of receipt of IIROC's response.

(xii) The Principal Regulator will provide the final consolidated report, together with IIROC's response and the follow-up plan for each IIROC office, to the CSA Chairs and IIROC once each Reviewing Regulator has obtained the necessary internal approval.

c. — Interim Reviews

Although the Principal Regulator will co-ordinate periodic reviews as described above, each Recognizing Regulator retains the ability to perform a review of IIROC to deal with significant and/or local issues that require immediate attention and that would be best dealt with through a review of an IIROC office. The Recognizing Regulator desiring to perform an interim review of IIROC will provide prior notice of the interim review to the Oversight Committee.

7. — Appendix

Appendix "A" to this MOU is an integral part of this MOU.

8. — Amendments to and Withdrawal from this MOU

This MOU may be amended from time to time as mutually agreed upon by the Recognizing Regulators. Any amendments must be in writing and approved by the duly authorized representatives of each Recognizing Regulator.

Each Recognizing Regulator can, at any time, withdraw from this MOU on at least 90 days written notice to the Principal Regulator and to each Recognizing Regulator.

9. — Effective Date

This MOU comes into effect on June 1, 2008 in Alberta, British Columbia, Manitoba, New Brunswick, Newfoundland and Labrador, Nova Scotia and Saskatchewan, and on September 1, 2008 in Ontario. In Quebec, this MOU comes into effect on the date it is signed by the AMF and by the Minister responsible for Canadian Intergovernmental Affairs or by a person authorized by the Minister.

British Columbia Securities Commission

Alberta Securities Commission

Saskatchewan Financial Services Commission

Manitoba Securities Commission

Ontario Securities Commission

Autorité des marchés financiers

Minister Responsible for Canadian Intergovernmental Affairs

Newfoundland and Labrador, Securities Division, Department of Government Services and Lands

Nova Scotia Securities Commission

New Brunswick Securities Commission

Appendix A — Joint Rule Review Protocol for IIROC

1. — Scope and Purpose

a. "Rules" includes any new rule or amendment to a rule, policy or other similar instrument.

b. Any new or amended by-law will follow the process for rule review and approval set out in this Protocol.

c. The Recognizing Regulators have entered into this Protocol to establish uniform procedures for their review and approval of Rules proposed by IIROC.

2. — Classification of Rules

a. — Classification of Rules by IIROC

IIROC will classify each proposed Rule as a "Housekeeping" Rule or a "Public Comment" Rule and will provide notice of classification in the materials filed with each Recognizing Regulator.

b. — Criteria for Classification of Rules

(i) A "Housekeeping" Rule is a proposed Rule that has no material impact on investors, issuers, members, registrants or the capital markets in any province or territory of Canada and that:

(A) corrects spelling, punctuation, typographical or grammatical mistakes or inaccurate cross-referencing;

(B) makes stylistic or formatting changes to headings or paragraph numbers;

(C) makes other necessary changes of an editorial nature (such as standardization of terminology);

(D) establishes or changes a due, fee or other charge imposed by IIROC pursuant to a Rule or fee model that has been previously approved by the Recognizing Regulators;

(E) changes the routine internal processes, practice, or administration of IIROC; or

(F) is reasonably necessary to conform IIROC's Rules to applicable securities legislation, statutory or legal requirements; and

(ii) A "Public Comment" Rule is any proposed Rule that is not a Housekeeping Rule.

c. — Disagreements Regarding Classification

(i) If staff of a Recognizing Regulator believe that a proposed Rule is incorrectly classified as a Housekeeping Rule, they will, within 10 days of the date of filing by IIROC, inform staff of the Principal Regulator of their intention to disagree with the classification, with an analysis of their reasons for disagreeing with the classification. Within 5 days of receiving a notice of disagreement from staff of one of the Recognizing Regulators, staff of the Principal Regulator will arrange a conference call among staff of the Recognizing Regulators to discuss the disagreement with the classification. If the disagreement still exists after the conference call, staff of the Principal Regulator will promptly notify IIROC.

(ii) If a notice of disagreement is sent to IIROC under paragraph 2(c)(I), IIROC will reclassify the proposed Rule as a Public Comment Rule.

3. — Required Materials

a. IIROC will file the information required under this section concurrently in both English and French, accompanied with a translation certificate, with the applicable Recognizing Regulators.

b. IIROC will file the following information with each Housekeeping Rule:

(i) a cover letter that indicates the classification of the Rule and the rationale for the classification;

(ii) the text of the proposed Rule, and, where applicable, a blacklined version of the Rule indicating changes to an existing rule; and

(iii) a notice for publication that contains the following:

(A) a brief description of the Rule,

(B) the reasons for the Housekeeping classification,

(C) the date that the Rule was approved by the IIROC Board and the Board Resolution, and

(D) the anticipated effective date of the Rule.

c. IIROC will file the following information with each Public Comment Rule:

(i) a cover letter that indicates the classification of the Rule, how IIROC has taken the public interest into account when developing the Rule and why the Rule is in the public interest;

(ii) the text of the proposed Rule, and, where applicable, a blacklined version of the Rule indicating changes to an existing rule; and

(iii) a notice of publication including:

(A) a concise statement, together with supporting analysis, of the nature, purpose and effect of the proposed Rule;

(B) the possible effects of the proposed Rule on market structure, Members, non-Members, competition and the costs of compliance;

(C) a description of the Rule and the Rule-making process, including a description of the context in which the proposed Rule was developed, the date that the Rule was approved by the IIROC Board and the Board Resolution, the process followed, the issues considered, the consultation process undertaken and alternative approaches considered and the reasons for rejecting those alternatives;

(D) where the proposed Rule requires technological systems changes to be made by IIROC, Members or other market participants, a description of the implications of the proposed Rule and, where possible, a discussion of material implementation issues and plans;

(E) where relevant, a reference to other jurisdictions including an indication as to whether another regulator in Canada, the United States or another jurisdiction has a comparable rule or has made or is contemplating making a comparable rule and, if applicable, a comparison of the proposed Rule to the rule of the other jurisdiction;

(F) the anticipated date on which IIROC proposes that the proposed Rule be effective;

(G) a statement that the IIROC Board has determined that the proposed Rule is not contrary to the public interest; and

(H) a request for public comment together with details on how to submit comments with the comment period deadline, and a statement that IIROC would make available to the public all comments received during the comment period.

4. — Review Criteria

Without limiting the discretion of the Recognizing Regulators, the Recognizing Regulators agree that the following are factors that should be considered by the Recognizing Regulators in reviewing IIROC Rule proposals:

a. whether IIROC followed its established internal governance practices in approving the proposed Rule;

b. whether IIROC followed the requirements of this Protocol and has provided sufficient analysis of the nature, purpose and effect of a proposed Rule;

c. whether IIROC has considered consequential amendments; and

d. whether the proposed Rule conflicts with applicable laws or the terms and conditions of a Recognizing Regulator's recognition order.

5. — Rule Review and Approval Process — Housekeeping Rules

a. IIROC will file each proposed Housekeeping Rule and the materials described in subsection 3(b) of this Protocol with each Recognizing Regulator.

b. Upon receipt of IIROC's notice of publication, staff of the Principal Regulator will immediately send confirmation of receipt of the proposed Housekeeping Rule to IIROC, with copies to the other Recognizing Regulators.

c. If none of the Recognizing Regulators objects to the classification of the proposed Rule as a Housekeeping Rule within the time limit set out in paragraph 2(c)(I), the proposed Rule will be deemed to be approved and will be effective on the date designated by IIROC in its filing.

6. — Rule Review and Approval Process — Public Comment Rules

a. IIROC will file each proposed Public Comment Rule and the materials described in subsection 3(c) of this Protocol with each Recognizing Regulator.

b. Upon receipt of IIROC's notice of publication, staff of the Principal Regulator will immediately send confirmation of receipt of the proposed Public Comment Rule to IIROC, with copies to the other Recognizing Regulators.

c. As soon as practicable and in any event within 14 days of receipt of IIROC's notice of publication, the Principal Regulator will, and the other Recognizing Regulators may, publish for a 30-day comment period (commencing on the date the proposed Public Comment Rule appears in the bulletin or on the website of the Principal Regulator) in its bulletin or on its website the text of the proposed Public Comment Rule and the notice of publication filed by IIROC. The Principal Regulator and the other Recognizing Regulators that publish the Rule will coordinate the publication date.

d. During the 30-day comment period, staff of each of the Recognizing Regulators will provide significant comments to staff of the Principal Regulator in writing, with copies to the other Recognizing Regulators. If staff of the Principal Regulator do not receive any such comments within the 30-day period, the other Recognizing Regulators will be deemed to not have any comments.

e. Promptly following the 30-day comment period, IIROC will confirm with staff of the Principal Regulator whether any public comments were received and, if so, IIROC will forward the public comments to each of the Recognizing Regulators.

f. If comments from staff of the Recognizing Regulators and the public comments do not raise any significant issues, staff of the Recognizing Regulators will proceed immediately to the approval of the proposed Rule following the steps outlined insubparagraphs (j)–(n) below.

g. If comments from staff of the Recognizing Regulators or the public comments received raise significant issues, staff of the Principal Regulator will send IIROC written notice, within 7 days of the end of the 30-day comment period, that the Public Comment Rule will be subject to a full review as set out in subparagraph 6(h) below.

h. For a full review of a Public Comment Rule, the Recognizing Regulators will use best efforts to adhere to the following process:

(i) Staff of the Principal Regulator will prepare and deliver to staff of the other Recognizing Regulators, within 7 days of receiving from IIROC confirmation that no public comments were received or a summary of public comments and IIROC's response to the public comments, a draft comment letter that incorporates the comments raised by staff of the Recognizing Regulators;

(ii) within 7 days of receipt, staff of each of the Recognizing Regulators will provide comments on the draft comment letter prepared by staff of the Principal Regulator, with copies to the other Recognizing Regulators; if staff of the Principal Regulator does not receive any comments within the 7-day period, the other Recognizing Regulators will be deemed not to have any comments;

(iii) Staff of the Principal Regulator will consolidate all comments received, and may identify different views from staff of the Recognizing Regulators; in the event that comments received conflict, staff of the Recognizing Regulators will try to reach an agreement to deal with the conflict; if the conflict cannot be resolved, the Principal Regulator will use its best efforts to arrange, within 14 days of becoming aware of the conflict, for the Chair or another senior executive of each of the Recognizing Regulators to discuss the issues and attempt to establish a consensus;

(iv) within 3 days of the other Recognizing Regulators' response (or deemed response) or of the resolution of conflicts by the Chairs or senior executives of the Recognizing Regulators, staff of the Principal Regulator will send the comment letter to IIROC, with a copy to each of the other Recognizing Regulators;

(v) within 14 days of receipt, IIROC will respond in writing to the comment letter sent by staff of the Principal Regulator, with a copy to staff of each of the other Recognizing Regulators; and

(vi) each of the other Recognizing Regulators will provide material comments to the Principal Regulator in writing within 10 days of IIROC's response, and the Principal Regulator will provide its comments to the other Recognizing Regulators within the same period; if the Principal Regulator does not receive any comments within the 10-day period, the other Recognizing Regulators will be deemed not to have any comments.

i. IIROC and the Recognizing Regulators will discuss and attempt to resolve the concerns raised by any of the Recognizing Regulators within 30 days of receiving comments from staff of the other Recognizing Regulators regarding IIROC's response referred to in subparagraph 6(h)(V), but if the concerns are not resolved to the satisfaction of all Recognizing Regulators, review of the proposed Rule will be escalated to be discussed among the Chairs or other senior executives of the Recognizing Regulators as described below:

(i) the Principal Regulator will use its best efforts to schedule a meeting of the chairs or other senior executives of the Recognizing Regulators within 14 days of the end of the 30-day period noted in paragraph 6(i) above; and

(ii) the chairs or other senior executives of the Recognizing Regulators will discuss the issues and attempt to establish a consensus among the Recognizing Regulators. If, after the consultations, the Chairs or other senior executives of the Recognizing Regulators are unable to agree on the appropriate outcome for the proposed Rule, IIROC will not be able to adopt the Rule.

j. Staff of the Principal Regulator will prepare documentation for approval of the proposed Rule by the Principal Regulator within 14 days of resolving comments under paragraph 6(i).

k. After a proposed rule is approved by the Principal Regulator, staff of the Principal Regulator will promptly circulate to the other Recognizing Regulators the documentation.

l. Staff of the other Recognizing Regulators will seek the necessary approval within 30 days of receipt of the documentation from the Principal Regulator, or such later time as is mutually agreed by staff of the Recognizing Regulators.

m. Staff of each Recognizing Regulator will inform staff of the Principal Regulator in writing of the decision concerning the proposed Rule immediately following the decision.

n. Staff of the Principal Regulator will communicate in writing the approval of a proposed Rule to IIROC promptly upon receipt of notification from all of the other Recognizing Regulators of their decision.

7. — Immediate Implementation

a. If IIROC reasonably believes that there is an urgent need to implement a proposed Rule because of a substantial risk of material harm to investors, Members, marketplace participants or the Canadian Investor Protection Fund, IIROC may make the proposed Rule effective immediately upon approval by IIROC's Board, provided that:

(i) IIROC provides each Recognizing Regulator with written notice of its intention to rely upon this procedure at least 10 days before the proposed Rule is considered for approval by IIROC's Board; and

(ii) IIROC's written notice includes:

(A) the date on which IIROC intends the proposed Rule to be effective, and

(B) an analysis in support of the need for immediate implementation of the proposed Rule.

b. If a Recognizing Regulator does not agree that immediate implementation is necessary, that Recognizing Regulator will, within 5 days after IIROC provides notice to the Principal Regulator, advise the Principal Regulator in writing that it disagrees and provide the reasons for its disagreement, with copies to the other Recognizing Regulators. Staff of the Principal Regulator will promptly notify IIROC of the disagreement.

c. IIROC and the Recognizing Regulators will discuss and attempt to resolve the concerns raised by the Recognizing Regulators on a timely basis, but if the concerns are not resolved to the satisfaction of all Recognizing Regulators, the proposed Rule cannot be immediately implemented.

d. If no notice is received by IIROC by the end of the tenth day following the day on which IIROC provided the notification to the Principal Regulator, the Recognizing Regulators will be deemed to have approved the immediate implementation of the proposed Rule.

e. Proposed Rules approved (or deemed to have been approved) for immediate implementation will be effective on the later of:

(i) the date on which each Recognizing Regulator has approved (or is deemed to have approved) the immediate implementation; and

(ii) the date designated by IIROC in its written notice to the Principal Regulator.

f. A Rule that is implemented immediately will be published (if it is a Public Comment Rule), reviewed, and approved in accordance with this Protocol.

g. Where the Recognizing Regulators subsequently disapprove a Rule that was implemented immediately, IIROC will promptly repeal the Rule.

8. — Effective Date of Rules

a. Public Comment Rules (other than Rules implemented under Section 7 (Immediate Implementation) of this Protocol) will be effective on the later of:

(i) the date of publication of notice of approval, and

(ii) the date designated by IIROC under paragraph 3(c)(III)(6) of this Protocol.

b. Housekeeping Rules will be effective on the date designated by IIROC under paragraph 3(b)(III)(3) of this Protocol.

9. — Revisions and Republication

a. If, subsequent to its publication for comment, IIROC revises a Public Comment Rule in a manner that results in a material change in the proposed Rule's substance and/or effect, the Principal Regulator will, in consultation with IIROC and staff of the other Recognizing Regulators determine whether or not the revised Rule should be published for an additional 30-day comment period.

b. If a Public Comment Rule is republished under subsection (a), the request for comments will include a blacklined version marked to the original published version, the date of Board approval (if different from the original published version), IIROC's summary of comments submitted and responses in respect of the previous request for comments, together with an explanation of the revisions to the proposed Rule and the supporting rationale for the revisions.

10. — Publication of Notice of Approval

a. The Principal Regulator will prepare a notice of approval of each Public Comment Rule and publish the notice, together with the summary of the proposed Rule prepared by IIROC and IIROC's summary of comments submitted and responses, if applicable, and will coordinate with staff of the other Recognizing Regulators.

b. For any Housekeeping Rule, the Principal Regulator will publish the text of the proposed Rule and the notice for publication referred to in subparagraph 3(b)(III).

c. Recognizing Regulators other than the Principal Regulator may publish any notice of approval.

11. — Review of Protocol

IIROC and staff of the Recognizing Regulators will, once every three years, conduct a joint review of the operation of this Protocol in order to identify issues that have arisen since the last review relating to compliance with this Protocol, the continuing appropriateness of the timelines and other requirements set out in this Protocol, and necessary or desirable amendments to this Protocol to address identified issues.

12. — Waiving or Varying of the Rule Review Protocol

a. IIROC may file a written request with the Principal Regulator, with copies to the other Recognizing Regulators, to waive or vary any part of this Protocol.

b. Within 7 days of receipt of IIROC's request, a Recognizing Regulator who objects to the granting of the waiver or variation will notify the Principal Regulator of its objection, together with its reason(s) for the objection. If the Principal Regulator does not receive any notices of objection, the other Recognizing Regulators are deemed to not object to the waiver or variation.

c. The Principal Regulator will provide to IIROC on the eighth day of receipt of IIROC's request either:

    (i) written notice that a Recognizing Regulator objects to granting the waiver or variation; or

    (ii) written notice that the waiver or variation has been granted by the Principal Regulator on behalf of all the Recognizing Regulators.

d. A waiver or variation may be specific or general and may be made for a time or for all time as mutually agreed by staff of the Recognizing Regulators.

[Minister of Finance approval received July 24, 2008 (31 O.S.C.B. 7589).]

IA-8 — Memorandum of Understanding Regarding Canadian Investor Protection Fund

Date: September 30, 2008

31 O.S.C.B. 7556

Memorandum of Understanding
BETWEEN:
Alberta Securities Commission;
Autorité des marchés financiers (Québec);
British Columbia Securities Commission;
Manitoba Securities Commission;
New Brunswick Securities Commission;
Financial Services Regulation Division, Department of Government Services, Consumer & Commercial Affairs Branch (Newfoundland and Labrador);
Legal Registries Division, Department of Justice (Northwest Territories);
Nova Scotia Securities Commission;
Legal Registries Division, Department of Justice (Nunavut);
Ontario Securities Commission;
Securities Office, Consumer, Corporate and Insurance Services Division, Office of the Attorney General (Prince Edward Island);
Saskatchewan Financial Services Commission;
Superintendent of Securities, Community Services (Yukon)
(each, a "Regulator")
(collectively, the "Canadian Securities Administrators")
and
Canadian Investor Protection Fund,
a corporation incorporated under the laws of Canada

The parties agree as follows:

1. — Underlying Principles

1.1 — Participation in a Compensation or Contingency Fund

The Canadian Securities Administrators (the "CSA") consist of the authority in each Canadian province and territory that, under statute, regulates the securities industry within its jurisdiction. Each Regulator is responsible for promoting both investor protection and fair and efficient capital markets in its jurisdiction.

Securities laws and regulations in each Canadian province and territory may require registered dealers to participate in a compensation fund or contingency trust fund approved by the Regulator or a contingency fund deemed acceptable by the Regulator (collectively, "compensation or contingency fund") and established by, among others, a self-regulatory organization ("SRO").

INTERGOVERN-MENTAL AGREEMENTS

Certain Regulators have issued Approvals of or a Deemed Acceptable Decision for the Canadian Investor Protection Fund (the "CIPF") as a compensation or contingency fund.

1.2 — The Canadian Investor Protection Fund

The CIPF was established by its sponsoring SROs to protect Customers who have suffered financial loss due to the insolvency of a Member Firm of any one of the sponsoring SROs. As of the effective date of this Memorandum of Understanding ("MOU"), the Investment Dealers Association of Canada ("IDA"), or its successor, is the CIPF's only sponsoring SRO.

The CIPF will enter into an Industry Agreement with the IDA, or its successor, which contemplates that other SROs may become parties to the agreement.

The CIPF acts, for the purpose of this MOU, as a compensation or contingency fund. It provides protection on a discretionary basis to prescribed limits to eligible Customers of Participating SRO Member Firms suffering losses if Customer property comprising securities, cash and other property held by such Member Firms is unavailable as a result of the insolvency of a Member Firm and, in connection with such coverage, will engage in risk management activities to minimize the likelihood of such losses.

The CIPF is financed by Member Firms through its Participating SROs.

1.3 — The Memorandum of Understanding

On July 2, 1991, the CIPF entered into a MOU with the Regulators existing at the time, with the exception of the former Commission des valeurs mobilières du Québec ("CVMQ"), which MOU was subsequently amended. On June 20, 1997, the CIPF entered into a MOU with the CVMQ, which MOU was subsequently amended.

The parties to the 1991 MOU, as amended, wish to amend and restate the MOU to reflect changes in the nature of the CIPF's role and responsibilities and to enhance the protection of investors and maintain investor confidence in the Canadian capital markets.

The Autorité des marchés financiers ("Autorité") is rescinding the MOU entered into in 1997, as amended, between the CVMQ and the CIPF, with the unanimous consent of the parties thereto, and is becoming a party to this MOU.

The Approvals or Deemed Acceptable Decision issued by certain Regulators regarding the CIPF are subject to the CIPF complying with this MOU.

2. — Definitions

"Applicable Regulator" means each Regulator in the jurisdiction in which a Member Firm is registered.

"Approval" means the approval of the CIPF by a Regulator required pursuant to the securities laws and regulations in a Canadian province or territory which may stipulate that registered dealers must participate in a compensation fund or contingency trust fund approved by the Regulator and established by, among others, an SRO.

"Approving Regulator" means a Regulator that has issued an Approval or a Deemed Acceptable Decision regarding the CIPF.

"By-law Number 1" means the By-law Number 1 of the CIPF.

"Coverage Policies" means policies established from time to time by the CIPF's Board of Directors pursuant to the section of the Approval and Deemed Acceptable Decision regarding Customer Protection.

"Customer" has the meaning ascribed to that term in the Coverage Policies.

"Deemed Acceptable Decision" means the decision regarding the CIPF by a Regulator pursuant to the securities laws and regulations in a Canadian province or territory which may stipulate that a dealer with an unrestricted practice or a discount broker must participate in a contingency fund deemed acceptable by the Regulator.

"Fund" means the liquid assets of the CIPF available for protection of Customers of Member Firms.

"Industry Agreement" means an agreement, as amended from time to time, between the CIPF and any Participating SRO regarding the basis on which the CIPF provides protection to Customers of Member Firms.

"Member Firm" means a member or participant of any of the Participating SROs that is a registered dealer in Canada.

"Participating Regulator" means a Regulator, other than the Principal Regulator, that is participating in an oversight review of the CIPF.

"Participating SRO" means an SRO that is a party to or that becomes a party to the Industry Agreement.

"Principal Regulator" means the Regulator that is designated as such from time to time by consensus of the Regulators.

"Reportable Condition" means any condition which could give rise to payments being made out of the Fund, including, without limitation, the suspension, expulsion or appointment of a monitor in respect of a Member Firm or similar action by a Participating SRO and any condition which has contributed substantially to or, if appropriate corrective action is not taken, could reasonably be expected to:

> (a) inhibit a Member Firm from promptly completing securities transactions, promptly segregating Customers' securities as required or promptly discharging its responsibilities to Customers, other Member Firms and other creditors;
>
> (b) result in material financial loss;
>
> (c) result in material misstatements of the Member Firm's financial statements; or
>
> (d) result in violations of the minimum record requirements of a Participating SRO to an extent that could reasonably be expected to result in the conditions described in parts (a), (b), or (c) above.

3. — Approval and Deemed Acceptable Decision

The CIPF will abide by the terms and conditions of any Approval or Deemed Acceptable Decision made by a Regulator.

4. — Member Reviews

The CIPF will review, in accordance with the Industry Agreement, the business and operations of any Member Firm, or designated groups of Member Firms, where a situation has occurred that in the opinion of the CIPF constitutes a Reportable Condition.

5. — Oversight Program

5.1 — *Purposes of the Oversight Program*

The CSA have developed a program of oversight for the CIPF to ensure that the CIPF is appropriately discharging its responsibilities as a compensation or contingency fund for Customers of Member Firms. The purposes of this oversight program include but are not limited to:

 (i) determining compliance with this MOU and the terms and conditions of any Approvals or Deemed Acceptable Decision made by the Regulators regarding the CIPF;

 (ii) ensuring that the CIPF continues to have the appropriate governance structure to fulfill its obligations;

 (iii) ensuring that the CIPF is appropriately discharging its core functions;

 (iv) ensuring that the CIPF is managing its risks adequately;

 (v) identifying and addressing any deficiencies in the CIPF's functioning as a compensation or contingency fund for Customers of Member Firms and ensuring the effective resolution of these deficiencies; and

 (vi) ensuring that the CIPF has established and maintains transparent, fair and reasonable Coverage Policies.

5.2 — *Oversight Reviews*

As part of this oversight program, the CSA will carry out reviews of the CIPF on a periodic basis.

The Principal Regulator will solicit interest from the other Regulators with respect to participating in the oversight review. The Regulators that choose to participate will be considered to be Participating Regulators for the purpose of the CIPF oversight review.

The Principal Regulator will develop the review program in consultation with the Participating Regulators. The Principal Regulator will be responsible for adequate staffing of the review and co-ordinating the review and resulting report of the Participating Regulators.

At the conclusion of a CIPF review, the Principal Regulator and the Participating Regulators will finalize the review report. In finalizing the review report, the Principal Regulator and the Participating Regulators will use their best efforts to follow the procedures set out in Schedule A to this MOU, or such other procedures as agreed upon by the Principal Regulator and the Participating Regulators, taking into account language translation needs, where applicable.

5.3 — *Reporting to the CSA*

5.3.1 — *Reporting Obligations*

The CIPF will report to each Regulator in accordance with the provisions of Schedule B to this MOU.

Any comments from the Regulators on any report, document or information provided by the CIPF will be sent to the Principal Regulator. The Principal Regulator will request that the CIPF respond to comments raised by the Regulators and will forward any response to the Regulators.

5.3.2 — *CIPF Actions in Respect of Member Firms*

The CIPF will prepare and provide to the Applicable Regulators a report detailing any action taken with respect to a Member Firm. For Member Firm insolvencies, the report will describe the circumstances of the insolvency, including a summary of the actions taken by the Member Firm, the Participating SRO and the CIPF and any committee or person acting on behalf of such parties. These reports will be delivered within 90 days of the action taken by the CIPF or Participating SRO or the liquidation of the Member Firm or at such other time as agreed to between the parties hereto.

5.4 — *Review and Approval of By-law Number 1*

The CIPF will file with the Approving Regulators any proposed changes to the CIPF's By-law Number 1 for prior approval. The Approving Regulators will review and approve any proposed changes to the CIPF's By-law Number 1 according to the process set out in Schedule C to this MOU.

6. — Miscellaneous Provisions

6.1 — *Confidentiality*

All notices, reports, documents and any other information provided pursuant to this MOU are being provided for regulatory purposes and will be supplied and maintained in confidence, except as required for regulatory purposes.

6.2 — *Authority*

Nothing in this MOU is intended to limit the powers of any of the Regulators under applicable securities laws to take any measures authorized under such laws.

6.3 — Legal Action Against the CIPF

Nothing in this MOU will be interpreted to prevent a Customer from taking legal action against the CIPF in a court of competent jurisdiction in Canada, nor will the CIPF contest the jurisdiction of such a court to consider a claim where the claimant has exhausted the CIPF's internal claim review process.

6.4 — Schedules

The Schedules to the MOU are an integral part of this MOU.

6.5 — Amendments and withdrawal from the MOU

This MOU may be amended from time to time as mutually agreed upon by the Regulators and the CIPF. Any amendments must be in writing and approved by the duly authorized representatives of each Regulator in accordance with the applicable legislation of each province or territory.

Each Regulator can, at any time, withdraw from this MOU on at least 90 days written notice to the Regulators and to the CIPF.

6.6 — Effective Date

This MOU comes into effect on September 30, 2008.

IN WITNESS WHEREOF the duly authorized signatories of the parties below have signed this MOU as of the Effective Date of the MOU stated above.

CANADIAN INVESTOR PROTECTION FUND   ALBERTA SECURITIES COMMISSION

AUTORITÉ DES MARCHÉS FINANCIERS   BRITISH COLUMBIA SECURITIES COMMISSION

For purposes of An Act respecting the Ministère du Conseil exécutif (R.S.Q., c. M-30),

Title: Secrétaire général associé aux affaires intergouvernementales canadiennes

MANITOBA SECURITIES COMMISSION   NEW BRUNSWICK SECURITIES COMMISSION

FINANCIAL SERVICES REGULATION DIVISION, DEPARTMENT OF GOVERNMENT SERVICES, CONSUMER & COMMERCIAL AFFAIRS BRANCH (NEWFOUNDLAND AND LABRADOR)   LEGAL REGISTRIES DIVISION, DEPARTMENT OF JUSTICE (NORTHWEST TERRITORIES)

NOVA SCOTIA SECURITIES COMMISSION   LEGAL REGISTRIES DIVISION, DEPARTMENT OF JUSTICE (NUNAVUT)

ONTARIO SECURITIES COMMISSION   SECURITIES OFFICE, CONSUMER, CORPORATE AND INSURANCE SERVICES DIVISION, OFFICE OF THE ATTORNEY GENERAL (PRINCE EDWARD ISLAND)

SASKATCHEWAN FINANCIAL SERVICES COMMISSION   SUPERINTENDENT OF SECURITIES, COMMUNITY SERVICES (YUKON)

Schedule A — Oversight Reviews

1) Each Participating Regulator will provide to the Principal Regulator their report points on the results of the review;

2) Within 20 business days of receipt of all report points, the Principal Regulator will prepare a draft report combining the report points of the Participating Regulators and send it to the Participating Regulators for comment;

3) Any Participating Regulator that has comments on the draft report will send its comments to the Principal Regulator within 10 business days of receiving the draft report, with copies to the other Participating Regulators;

4) The Principal Regulator will consolidate the comments of the Participating Regulators and revise the draft report, as necessary, within 15 business days of receiving the comments;

5) The Principal Regulator will forward a copy of the revised draft report to the Participating Regulators for their approval and the Participating Regulators will provide their approval to the Principal Regulator within 10 business days of receiving the revised draft report;

6) The Principal Regulator will forward a copy of the revised draft report to the CIPF for it to confirm the factual accuracy of the draft report;

7) The CIPF will review the draft report for factual accuracy and respond with comments within 15 business days of receipt;

8) Within 15 business days of receiving the CIPF's comments, the Principal Regulator will take into account the CIPF's comments, revise the draft report, as necessary, and forward a copy of the draft report and the CIPF's comments to the Participating Regulators for comment;

9) Within 10 business days of receipt, the Participating Regulators will review the draft report and the CIPF's comments and respond with comments;

10) Within 15 business days of receiving the Participating Regulators' comments, the Principal Regulator will consolidate these comments, revise the draft report, as necessary, and forward a copy of the revised draft report to the Participating Regulators for their approval;

11) The Participating Regulators will provide their approval to the Principal Regulator within 10 business days of receiving the revised draft report;

12) The Principal Regulator will forward a copy of the final report to the CIPF for formal response;

13) The CIPF will use its best efforts to respond to the final report to the Principal Regulator within 20 business days of receipt;

14) The Principal Regulator will review the CIPF's response, develop a follow-up plan and forward a copy of the follow-up plan and the CIPF's response to the Participating Regulators for comments, within 15 business days of receiving the CIPF's response;

15) The Participating Regulators will review the follow-up plan and respond with comments within 10 business days of receipt, with copies to the other Participating Regulators;

16) The Principal Regulator will consolidate these comments and revise the follow-up plan, as necessary;

17) The Principal Regulator and the Participating Regulators will seek any necessary internal approvals of the follow-up plan; and

18) The Principal Regulator will provide the final report, including the CIPF's response and the follow-up plan, to the staff of the Regulators, the CSA Chairs and the CIPF.

Schedule B — Reporting to the CSA

1) — Requested Information

a) A Regulator may, at any time, request any reports, documents, or information from the CIPF and the CIPF will comply with that request for information.

2) — Prior Notification

a) The CIPF will provide to the CSA, at least 60 days prior notice before:

    i) Implementing any changes to its Coverage Policies;

    ii) Implementing any changes to its method of assessing Member Firms;

    iii) Implementing any changes to the Industry Agreement; and

    iv) Adding an SRO as a party to the Industry Agreement.

b) In emergency situations where, in the opinion of the CIPF, 60 days prior notice is considered unreasonable, the CIPF will inform the CSA with as much advance notice as possible in the circumstances. Such notice will include an explanation of why the 60-day period is considered to be unreasonable.

3) — Ad Hoc Reporting

a) The CIPF will immediately report to the Applicable Regulators any Reportable Conditions with respect to a Member Firm of which the CIPF has been notified;

b) The CIPF will immediately report to the CSA where a Participating SRO has withdrawn or has been expelled from participation in the CIPF. The CIPF will include in its report the reasons for the SRO's withdrawal or expulsion.

c) The CIPF will immediately report to the CSA any actual or potential material adverse change in the level of the CIPF assets, together with the CIPF's plan to deal with the situation.

d) The CIPF will report to the CSA any changes to its investment policies within 30 days of such changes.

4) — Annual Reporting

a) The CIPF will file with the CSA its annual audited financial statements, together with the report of the auditor, within 90 days after the end of each fiscal year.

b) The CIPF will provide the following information to the CSA, within 90 days after the end of each fiscal year:

    i) Description of any changes in the composition of the CIPF's Board of Directors in the previous fiscal year, including the names and terms of any incoming directors, the names of any outgoing directors, and whether any incoming directors are public directors as defined in the CIPF's By-law Number 1;

    ii) Description of any changes to the CIPF's By-law Number 1;

    iii) Any suggestions that the CIPF has made to any Participating SROs in the previous fiscal year regarding the Participating SROs' making new rules or amending existing rules, and the Participating SROs' response to those suggestions; and

iv) Where the CIPF has directed a Participating SRO to take certain actions about Member Firms that are in financial difficulty pursuant to the Industry Agreement, details about the CIPF's direction and comment on whether the CIPF is satisfied with the Participating SRO's response.

c) The CIPF will provide a written report to the CSA staff and meet with the CSA Chairs at least once a year to report on the CIPF's operations and activities, including but not limited to:

i) The Board of Directors' annual review of the adequacy of the level of assets in the Fund, assessment amounts, and assessment methodology;

ii) The CIPF resources, including whether the CIPF is fully staffed;

iii) Member Firm insolvencies and any resulting Customer claims;

iv) Risk management issues, including how the CIPF evaluated risks, what risk management issues were identified and how the CIPF dealt with these issues;

v) The Board of Directors' assessment of the need for additional risk management tools; and

vi) The extent and results of any Member Firm reviews conducted pursuant to the Industry Agreement.

Schedule C — Review and Approval of By-law Number 1 Amendments

In reviewing and approving changes to the CIPF's By-law Number 1, the Approving Regulators will use their best efforts to adhere to the following process:

1) The CIPF will file each proposed change to the CIPF's By-law Number 1 ("Amendment") with each Approving Regulator;

2) Upon receipt of an Amendment, the Principal Regulator will immediately send confirmation of receipt of the Amendment to the CIPF, with copies to the other Approving Regulators;

3) If, in the opinion of the Approving Regulators, the Amendment raises public interest issues or concerns, the Approving Regulators may publish the Amendment for a 30-day comment period;

4) Within 20 business days of receiving the Amendment, each of the Approving Regulators will provide significant comments to the Principal Regulator in writing, with copies to the other Approving Regulators. If the Principal Regulator does not receive any such comments within the 20-business-day period, the other Approving Regulators will be deemed to not have any comments;

5) Within 7 business days of the end of the 20-business-day period, the Principal Regulator will consolidate all comments received and send a comment letter to the CIPF. In the event that any comments of the Approving Regulators conflict, the Approving Regulators will try to resolve the conflict before the comment letter is sent to the CIPF;

6) Within 14 business days of receipt of the comment letter of the Approving Regulators, the CIPF will respond in writing to the Principal Regulator, with a copy to each of the other Approving Regulators;

7) Each of the other Approving Regulators will provide material comments to the Principal Regulator in writing within 10 business days of the CIPF's response, and the Principal Regulator will provide its comments to the other Approving Regulators within the same period. If the Principal Regulator does not receive any comments within the 10-business-day period, the other Approving Regulators will be deemed to not have any comments;

8) If applicable, the CIPF and the Approving Regulators will discuss and attempt to resolve the concerns raised by any of the Approving Regulators within 20 business days of receiving comments from the other Approving Regulators regarding the CIPF's response. If the concerns are not resolved to the satisfaction of all Approving Regulators, review of the Amendment will be escalated to be discussed among the Chairs or other senior executives of the Approving Regulators. If the Chairs or other senior executives of the Approving Regulators are unable to agree on the appropriate outcome of the Amendment, the CIPF will not be able to adopt the Amendment;

9) The Principal Regulator will prepare documentation for approval of the Amendment by the Principal Regulator within 14 business days of resolving comments under paragraph (8);

10) After an Amendment is approved by the Principal Regulator, the Principal Regulator will promptly circulate the approval documentation to the other Approving Regulators;

11) The other Approving Regulators will seek the necessary approval within 20 business days of receipt of the documentation from the Principal Regulator, or such later time as is mutually agreed by the Approving Regulators;

12) Each Approving Regulator will inform the Principal Regulator in writing of the decision concerning the Amendment immediately following the decision;

13) The Principal Regulator will communicate in writing the approval of an Amendment to the CIPF and to all Regulators promptly upon receipt of notification from all of the other Approving Regulators of their decision.

[Minister of Finance Approval: September 19, 2008: 31 O.S.C.B. 9460.]

IA-9 — Memorandum of Understanding Between the Minister of Finance of Ontario and the OSC

Date: **May 26, 2003; replaced November 5, 2009**
26 O.S.C.B. 4125; 32 O.S.C.B. 9983

Memorandum of Understanding Dated November 5, 2009 Between the Minister of Finance of Ontario (herein called the "Minister") and The Ontario Securities Commission (herein called the "Commission")

A — Introduction

1. The Commission is a statutory corporation without share capital and is comprised of members appointed by the Lieutenant Governor in Council. The Commission is an agent of Her Majesty in right of Ontario (section 3(12) of the *Securities Act*) and is classified by the Management Board of Cabinet (Management Board) as a Regulatory Agency with a governing board, and, for purposes of the Procurement Directive, as a "Other Included Entity".

2. Under the *Securities Act* and the *Commodity Futures Act* (the "Statutes"), the Commission is responsible for the administration of the Statutes and for discharging the powers and duties assigned to it under the Statutes and any other relevant legislation.

3. The mandate of the Commission under section 1.1 of the *Securities Act* and section 1.1 of the *Commodity Futures Act* is to provide protection to investors from unfair, improper or fraudulent practices and to foster fair and efficient capital markets and confidence in their integrity.

4. The *Securities Act* requires that every five years the Commission and the Minister shall enter into a memorandum of understanding setting out:

    a. the respective roles and responsibilities of the Minister and the Chair of the Commission (the "Chief Executive Officer" or "Chair");

    b. the accountability relationship between the Commission and the Minister;

    c. the responsibility of the Commission to provide to the Minister business plans, operational budgets and plans for proposed significant changes in the operations or activities of the Commission; and

    d. any other matters that the Minister may require.

5. The *Securities Act* further requires that the Commission shall promptly give the Minister or his/her designate (the "Minister") such information about its activities, operations and financial affairs as the Minister requests.

6. The Minister and the Chair are committed to a strong and independent Commission that is empowered to fulfill its statutory mandate efficiently and effectively and share the goal of establishing and maintaining a co-operative relationship that facilitates the efficient administration of the Commission and fulfilment of its statutory responsibilities.

7. The purpose of this Memorandum of Understanding ("Memorandum") is to clarify the operational roles, responsibilities and relationship between the Commission and the Minister and record their mutual understanding in respect of these matters.

8. The Memorandum does not affect, modify, limit or interfere with the responsibilities of the Minister, the Commission or the Chair under the Statutes or any other legislation. In the event of a conflict between the provisions of the Memorandum and the Statutes or such other legislation, the Statutes or such other legislation shall prevail.

B — Guiding Principles

9. The parties agree that they will adhere to the principles set out below in their relationship.

10. The Minister recognizes that the Commission is a statutory entity and that the Commission, the Chair and the Executive Director of the Commission (the "Executive Director" or "Chief Administrative Officer") exercise powers and perform duties in accordance with their respective mandates under the Statutes and other relevant legislation. The Commission's regulatory and adjudicative decisions must be made and be seen by the public to be made in an independent and impartial manner.

11. The Commission shall operate as an arm's-length agency of the Government of Ontario.

12. Commission staff are employees of the Commission and are accountable to the Chair and the Chief Administrative Officer ("CAO"). The Commission is a public body for purposes of the *Public Service of Ontario Act, 2006* (PSOA) and is subject to those parts of the PSOA that establish a conflict of interest framework, provisions relating to political activity, and the mechanisms for disclosures of wrongdoing in the public service. Employees of the Commission are public servants under the PSOA and are subject only to those provisions described above.

13. The Commission acknowledges that it is accountable to the Minister as set out in the Statutes in exercising its statutory mandate. The fundamental principle of accountability will be observed in the management, administration and operations of the Commission.

14. As an agency of the Government, the Commission agrees to abide by the management principles established by the Government of Ontario. These principles include ethical behaviour, accountability, excellence in management, wise use of public funds, high quality service to the public and fairness in the marketplace.

15. All members and employees will be subject to the Commission's Code of Conduct relating to conflicts of interest in connection with the conduct of the affairs of the Commission.

16. The parties to this Memorandum are committed to avoiding duplication of work or services.

17. The parties to this Memorandum recognize that the timely exchange of information and effective consultation when necessary are essential to discharging their respective responsibilities.

18. The Commission undertakes to report to, and share information with, the Minister as required by the Statutes and this Memorandum.

C — Roles and Responsibilities

The Minister

The Minister is accountable to the Legislature for the Commission's fulfilment of its mandate and its compliance with government policies, and for reporting to the Legislature on the affairs of the Commission. In addition to the rights and duties of the Minister as set out in the Statutes, the Minister is responsible for:

19. monitoring the activities of the Commission to ensure that its mandate is being fulfilled. To this end, the Minister may designate a person to examine any financial or accounting procedures, activities or practices of the Commission, as provided in section 3.8(2) of the *Securities Act*;

20. reporting to Cabinet and the Legislature on the affairs of the Commission, including tabling reports in the Legislature as required. This includes the requirement that the Minister shall lay the Commission's annual report before the Assembly within one month of receiving the Commission's report;

21. reviewing the Commission's annual business plan and submitting the plan to Management Board, as required by the Agency Establishment and Accountability Directive, including pursuant to a request at any time by the Chair of Management Board to submit the Commission's business plan to Management Board for review;

22. as may be permitted, ensuring that the Commission is advised and consulted when significant new directions for the Commission are contemplated or when initiatives are taken to amend any legislation or regulations that affect the Commission;

23. ensuring that the Commission is aware of policy directions or decisions of the Government that may impact the Commission's business plan;

24. meeting with the Chair as necessary (at a minimum, once every quarter) to discuss issues relating to the effective discharge of the Commission's mandate and the need for services or support to be provided by the Ministry to the Commission;

25. making recommendations to Cabinet relating to the appointment and reappointment of the Chair, Vice-Chair(s) and Commission members pursuant to the process established by legislation or by Management Board, as applicable, following consultation with the Chair, as appropriate;

26. ensuring that members appointed to the Commission are aware of all policies, directives, guidelines and procedures for Cabinet appointees as applicable;

27. ensuring that the Commission is aware of all applicable Management Board Directives;

28. ensuring that the Commission receives such information and assistance as required or as requested to meet its responsibilities under the Statutes, other relevant legislation, applicable Management Board Directives and this Memorandum;

29. appointing an advisory committee under section 143.12 of the *Securities Act*;

30. directing that a periodic review of the Commission be conducted and making subsequent recommendations to Management Board;

31. following consultations with the Chair, recommending to Management Board the elimination, consolidation or acquisition of the Commission and any change to the Commission's mandate that needs corresponding change to the Commission's constituting instrument; and

32. recommending to Management Board the powers to be given to the Commission when a change in the mandate of the Commission is being proposed.

The Chair and Board of Directors

The Chair acknowledges that accountability to the government means direct accountability to the Minister. The Board of Directors of the Commission (the "Board") acknowledges that accountability to the government means accountability to the Minister through the Chair. In addition to the rights and duties as set out in the Statutes, the Chair and the Board are responsible and accountable to the Minister for:

33. overseeing the management of the financial and other affairs of the Commission in accordance with its statutory mandate and business plan;

34. overseeing the provision of high quality regulatory services that protect the public interest and enhance public confidence in the regulated sectors;

35. overseeing management's identification of principal risks to the Commission's operations and the implementation of appropriate processes to manage these risks and ensuring that the Commission otherwise conducts itself in accordance with good governance practices; and

36. ensuring that stakeholders are consulted, as appropriate, on the Commission's goals, objectives and strategic direction.

Furthermore, the Chair is responsible and accountable to the Minister for:

37. providing any necessary orientation of new members of the Commission, ensuring that new members are made aware of the provisions on conflict of interest, ethical conduct and political activities set out in the Commission's Code of Conduct, and developing and maintaining an effective performance measurement system for evaluating Commission members in a manner consistent with best practices;

38. reviewing with the Minister the Commission's performance based results included in the Commission's statement of priorities on an annual basis;

39. ensuring that a report describing the performance achieved as against the objectives and targets set out in the Commission's statement of priorities is published on an annual basis;

40. ensuring that significant policy initiatives undertaken by the Commission, and other matters relating to its operations, that would be of importance to the Minister are brought to the attention of the Minister in a timely fashion, as well as being addressed at the next scheduled monthly work-in-progress meeting;

41. ensuring the Commission's compliance with applicable Management Board Directives;

42. ensuring the Commission's compliance with the *Archives and Recordkeeping Act, 2006*, S.O. 2006, chapter 34, Schedule A;

43. causing the Commission to prepare and deliver to the Minister the Commission's statement of priorities, annual report including financial statements and any other information about the Commission's activities, operations and financial affairs as the Minister requests;

44. causing the Commission to prepare, submit and review with the Minister its business plan for the current year and at least two years beyond following its adoption by the Commission;

45. ensuring that the Commission's business plan includes a system of performance measures and a report on the achievement of the objectives set out in the business plan;

46. acting as the Commission's primary spokesperson;

47. at the request of the Minister, preparing material, attending and/or making a presentation before Cabinet, the Legislature or Committees of either, on matters affecting or pertaining to the Commission;

48. notifying the Minister of upcoming vacancies in order-in-council appointments to the Commission and making recommendations to the Minister on persons appropriate to fill such vacancies;

49. providing the Commission with such information, assistance and advice as the Commission requires to meet its responsibilities under the Statutes and other relevant legislation;

50. reviewing board members' expenses and ensuring procedures are established for reviewing and approving board members' per diem claims; and

51. evaluating the performance of the CAO in consultation with the Board.

The Board of Directors

Furthermore, the Board is responsible and accountable to the Minister for:

52. subject to the approval of the Minister, making by-laws governing a variety of corporate matters, including:

    a. the administration, management and conduct of the affairs of the Commission;

    b. the appointment of an auditor;

    c. the powers, functions and duties of the Chair, each Vice-Chair and officers employed by the Commission;

    d. the remuneration and benefits of the Chair, each Vice-Chair and the other members of the Commission; and

    e. the appointment, operation or dissolution of committees of the Board and the delegation of duties of the Board to such committees.

    (For example, the Board has established the following standing committees: Audit and Finance Committee, Governance and Nominating Committee, and Human Resources and Compensation Committee.)

The Deputy Minister

The Deputy Minister is accountable to the Minister for the performance of the Ministry in providing administrative support to the Commission and for carrying out the roles and responsibilities assigned to him by the Minister, Management Board Directives and this Memorandum. In accordance with the PSOA (and applicable Government directives), the Deputy Minister may delegate any of the powers and duties assigned to him by law. The Deputy Minister is responsible for:

53. advising and assisting the Minister in discharging assigned ministerial responsibility with respect to the Commission;

54. monitoring the activities of the Commission on behalf of the Minister to ensure that its mandate is being fulfilled and that it is acting in accordance with applicable Government policies;

55. meeting with the Chair at least quarterly to discuss issues relating to the effective discharge of the Commission's mandate;

56. informing the Commission of all directives, guidelines, policies and decisions of the Ministry and Government that apply to or may affect the Commission;

57. ensuring that the Commission receives such information and assistance as required or requested to meet its responsibilities under the Statutes, other relevant legislation, applicable Management Board Directives, and this Memorandum; and

58. undertaking on behalf of the Minister assessments of whether or not the Commission is fulfilling its legislative mandate, identifying any need for corrective action and recommending to the Minister ways to resolve issues that have been identified.

The Chief Administrative Officer

The CAO of the Commission is responsible and accountable to the Chair for:

59. the development, implementation and ongoing monitoring of an effective performance measurement and management system for the Commission under the direction of the Chair. The performance measures relating to the Commission's goals and priorities once approved by the Commission and prior to June 30 each year, will be forwarded to the Minister for approval;

60. ensuring that the Commission provides high quality service to the public in carrying out its responsibilities and establishes a process for responding to and resolving complaints from the public. The Commission's process for responding to complaints about the quality of services is separate from any statutory provisions about re-consideration, appeals, etc. of the Commission's adjudicative or regulatory decisions;

61. ensuring the development and maintenance of the necessary information and reporting systems in support of the efficient functioning of the Commission;

62. keeping the Chair and the Board informed and up-to-date on program operations;

63. ensuring that documents and reports are prepared as requested by the Board including corporate plans and budgets, annual business plans and quarterly reports; and

64. ensuring that documentation and proper controls are maintained to support expenditures and keep track of material variances between projected and actual expenditures.

D — Financial Arrangements

65. The operations of the Commission are funded by fees collected from market participants and details regarding the Commission's authority with respect to the fees and revenue it collects are set out in section 3.4 of the *Securities Act*.

66. The Commission acknowledges that property and/or services ordered/purchased by the Commission are purchased by it for the use of the Crown in right of Ontario, and are not subject to the goods and services tax.

E — Reporting Requirements

67. The Commission shall forward for the Minister's approval an annual business plan by July of each year.

68. The business plan shall meet the requirements set out in Schedule D of the Agency Establishment and Accountability Directive.

69. Within six months after the end of each fiscal year, the Commission shall deliver to the Minister an annual report on the affairs of the Commission for that fiscal year. Within one month of receiving the Commission's annual report, the Minister shall lay the report before the Assembly.

70. The annual report shall include the Commission's audited financial statements for the most recently completed financial year and the auditor's report thereon; a description of activities during the financial year reported on; a discussion of significant variances between actual and planned results and an explanation of actions to be taken, if any, to address these variances; a description of the Commission's corporate governance structure; and the names of the appointees to the Commission, including when each was first appointed and when the current term of appointment expires.

71. The Commission will ensure that all reports and other material set out in Appendix A, required to be submitted to the Minister are submitted in a timely manner, as outlined in the Appendix.

F — Audit Arrangements

72. Pursuant to the *Securities Act*, the Commission shall prepare financial statements according to generally accepted accounting principles. The financial statements must present the financial position, results of operations and changes in the financial position of the Commission for its most recently completed financial year.

73. The Commission shall appoint one or more auditors licensed under the *Public Accountancy Act* or the Auditor General of Ontario to audit the financial statements of the Commission for each financial year.

74. The Chair shall provide the Minister with a copy of any report from an audit of the Commission conducted pursuant to paragraph 73 of this Memorandum. The Chair shall have an opportunity to comment on any audit report that is submitted to the Minister or Management Board prior to such submission.

75. The Commission shall advise the Minister annually of any outstanding audit recommendations.

G — Administrative Arrangements

76. The Commission may participate in government-wide shared services or arrangements, where applicable.

77. The Commission shall respond to access requests and privacy investigations and shall fulfill all requirements under the Freedom of Information and Protection of Privacy Act (FOIPPA) with support from the Ministry of Finance FOIPPA Co-ordinator.

78. The Commission will be subject to the following Management Board Directives, Operational Policy and Guidelines:

     Agency Establishment and Accountability;

     Enhancing Privacy: Computer Matching of Personal Information;

     Freedom of Information and Privacy;

     Government Appointees;

     Management of Recorded Information;

     Procurement;

     Travel, Meal and Hospitality Expenses; and

     Visual Identity.

79. Where the same matters dealt with in these Directives are the subject of provisions in the *Securities Act*, the regulations and the rules thereunder, the latter provisions will govern. For greater clarity, the provision under the heading "Remuneration" in the "Government Appointees" Directive that provides for remuneration of appointees is not applicable to the Commission by virtue of section 3.2 of the *Securities Act*.

H — Time Period and Process for Review and Amendment

80. This Memorandum, to be executed by the Minister and the Chair on behalf of the Commission, becomes effective when executed by the parties. It shall remain in effect for a period of five years from the date of signature unless earlier amended or replaced. If not earlier amended

or replaced, this Memorandum must be reviewed before expiry and renewed or revised. It shall remain in effect until superseded by a new Memorandum of Understanding approved by Management Board and executed by the parties.

81. This Memorandum shall be reviewed upon the request of either party to it. This Memorandum must be either affirmed for continuance or revised upon the appointment of a new Minister or Chair.

82. The Minister is responsible for recommending to Management Board the approval of this Memorandum prior to execution by the parties. If this Memorandum is amended, the Minister shall submit a copy of the amended Memorandum to Management Board for approval.

IN WITNESS WHEREOF this Memorandum has been signed by the Minister and by the Chair of the Commission on behalf of the Commission.

"Dwight Duncan"	November 5, 2009
The Honourable Dwight Duncan	Date
Minister of Finance	

"W. David Wilson"	November 4, 2009
W. David Wilson	Date
Chair	
Ontario Securities Commission	

Appendix "A" — Ontario Securities Commission — Statutory Reporting Requirements and Communications with the Minister of Finance

Reporting Required under the Securities Act and Commodity Futures Act (CFA)

The following is a list of statutory reporting requirements (Commission to the Minister):

- **Memorandum of Understanding with the Minister:** The Commission and the Minister shall enter into an Memorandum of Understanding every five years, beginning with the 1998-99 fiscal year. (*Securities Act*, s. 3.7(1))

- **Provision of Information to the Minister:** The Commission shall promptly give the Minister such information about its activities, operations and financial affairs as the Minister requests. (*Securities Act*, s. 3.8(1))

- **Annual Report and Audited Financial Statements:** Within six months after the end of each fiscal year (i.e. by September 30), the Commission shall deliver to the Minister an annual report, including the Commission's audited financial statements, on the affairs of the Commission for that fiscal year. (*Securities Act*, s. 3.10(1))

- **Statement of Priorities:** The Commission is to deliver its statement of priorities to the Minister within 90 days after the end of its financial year (i.e. by June 30). (*Securities Act*, s. 143.9(1))

Statutory Requirements for Ministerial Approval

- **Ministerial Approval of By-laws:** The Commission must deliver to the Minister a copy of every by-law passed by it for Ministerial approval. (*Securities Act*, s. 3.2(4))

- **Ministerial Approval of Short-term Borrowing:** The Minister must approve terms and conditions of any short-term (up to two years) borrowing by the Commission. (*Securities Act*, s. 3.3(2))

- **Ministerial Approval of Commission Regulations:** Concurrently with making a rule and subject to the approval of the Minister, the Commission may make a regulation that amends or revokes any provision of a regulation made by the LGIC under the *Securities Act* or by the Commission under subsection 143(3) of the *Securities Act* or subsection 65(3) of the CFA, that in the opinion of the Commission is necessary or advisable to effectively implement the rule. (*Securities Act*, s. 143(3)) (CFA, s. 65(3))

- **Ministerial Approval of Non-publication of Notice of Urgent Rule:** The Commission is not required to publish notice of a proposed rule if it believes there is an urgent need for the rule and without it there is substantial risk of material harm to investors or to the integrity of the capital markets, and if the Minister approves. (*Securities Act*, s. 143.2(5)) (CFA, s. 67(5))

- **Ministerial Approval of Rules:** The Commission must deliver to the Minister a copy of every rule made by it together with the following:

   (1) A copy of the notices published under section 143.2, unless publication of notice was not required, and copies of all documents referred to in the notices.

   (2) A summary of the representations made and other documents submitted in respect of the rule as proposed.

   (3) All other material information that was considered by the Commission in connection with the making of the rule. (*Securities Act*, s. 143.3(1)) (CFA, s. 68(1))

- **Ministerial Approval of Agreements, Memoranda of Understanding, Arrangements:** The Commission must deliver to the Minister for approval every agreement, memorandum of understanding or arrangement between the Commission and,

   (1) another securities or financial regulatory authority;

   (2) any self-regulatory body or organization; or

(3) any jurisdiction. (*Securities Act*, s. 143.10(1)) (CFA, s. 74(1))

Other Communications

- **Business Plan:** The practice is to forward the Plan to the Ministry following Board approval in accordance with the Memorandum and the Agency Establishment and Accountability Directive.

- **Information Sharing:** The Ministry of Finance and the Commission have established an information sharing protocol under which the Commission does not share information relating to securities regulatory investigations or proceedings except in accordance with the protocol and the *Securities Act*. In addition to the protocol, inquiries received by the Minister's office regarding a case in progress at the Commission are re-directed to the Commission. Any response made by the Minister's office to the inquiring party will indicate that the inquiry has been forwarded to the Commission and that the Minister cannot interfere with an enforcement investigation or proceeding.

Current Communications Protocol — Rules, Policies, Agreements, Memoranda of Understanding or Arrangements

1. — Ministerial Approval of Rules

- The Commission must approve a proposed rule for publication for comment, following which the proposed rule will be published in the Bulletin. The minimum comment period is 90 days. (Note: Publication of notice of a proposed rule is not required in certain circumstances (see *Securities Act*, s. 143.2(5) and CFA, s. 67(5)). One of these is where the Commission believes there is an urgent need for the proposed rule and that, without it, there is a substantial risk of material harm to investors or the integrity of the capital markets. In these circumstances, the Commission must have prior approval of the Minister to make the rule without publication of notice.)

- If the Commission does not propose any material changes to the proposed rule after the comment period, the rule must go back to the Commission to be approved/made. It must then be delivered to the Minister for approval. A notice of the final rule must be published in the Bulletin.

- If material changes are made to the rule, then the Commission must approve its re-publication for further comment. The Ministry will be notified prior to any re-publication and provided with a copy of the changes to rule and the notice.

- Following any further comment period, the rule must be approved/made by the Commission. Once approved by the Commission, it will be sent to the Minister for approval and published in the Bulletin.

- Within 60 days after a rule is delivered to the Minister, the Minister may,
  - approve the rule,
  - reject the rule, or
  - return it to the Commission for further consideration.

- A rule that is approved by the Minister comes into force 15 days after it is approved unless there is a later day specified in the rule, in which case it comes into force on that later day.

- If the Minister does not approve a rule, reject it or return it to the Commission for further consideration, the rule comes into force:
  - if a day is specified in the rule that is at least 75 days after the rule is delivered to the Minister, then on that date;
  - if no date is specified, then on the 75th day after the rule is delivered to the Minister; or
  - if the date specified is within 75 days after the rule is delivered to the Minister, then on the 75th day after the rule is delivered to the Minister.

2. — Policies

- There is no statutory requirement that policies be approved by the Minister. However, the Commission has adopted an informal practice of sending to the Ministry (for information purposes) a copy of every proposed and final policy.

3. — Ministerial Approval of Agreements, Memoranda of Understanding or Arrangements

- The Commission must deliver to the Minister for approval and publish, subject to subsection 143.10(1.1), every agreement, memorandum of understanding or arrangement (MOU) between the Commission and,
  - another securities or financial regulatory authority;
  - any self-regulatory body or organization; or
  - any jurisdiction.

- If an MOU is required to be published, the Commission will provide the Minister with a copy of the proposed MOU together with a copy of the notice that will be published in the Bulletin.

- The Minister may approve or reject the MOU within 60 days after it is published in the Bulletin.

- If the Minister approves the MOU, it comes into effect on the date specified in the MOU, or if no date is specified, on the date approved. If the Minister does not approve or reject the MOU before the expiration of 60 days, the MOU comes into effect on the date specified in the MOU, or if no date is specified, on the expiry of the 60-day period.

4. — Commission Regulations

- Concurrently with making a rule, and subject to the approval of the Minister, the Commission may make a regulation that amends or revokes any provision of a regulation made by the LGIC or by the Commission under section 143(3) of the *Securities Act* or section 65(2) of the CFA that in the opinion of the Commission is necessary or advisable to effectively implement the rule.

- The proposed regulation must be made by the Commission and sent to the Minister for final approval.

5. — Other

- The Commission provides the Ministry with an overview of rule-making and MOU activity at the Commission on a regular basis.

- WIP meetings are scheduled on a regular basis.

IA-10 — Memorandum of Understanding between certain provincial securities regulators and the Investment Industry Regulatory Organization of Canada (IIROC) and the Mutual Fund Dealers Association of Canada (MFDA) concerning MFDA access to the National Registration Database (NRD)

Date: **January 21, 2011**

34 O.S.C.B. 711

August 3, 2010

Mr. Larry Waite

President and Chief Executive Officer

Mutual Fund Dealers Association of Canada

Suite 1600, 121 King Street West,

Toronto, Ontario

M5H 3T9

Dear Mr. Waite:

Re: Access to the National Registration Database system by Mutual Fund Dealers Association of Canada

This letter agreement ("**Agreement**") is between the British Columbia Securities Commission ("**BCSC**"), Alberta Securities Commission ("**ASC**"), Ontario Securities Commission ("**OSC**"), Autorité des marchés financiers ("**AMF**"), and the Investment Industry Regulatory Organization of Canada ("collectively, the "**Regulators**"), on the one hand, and the Mutual Fund Dealers Association of Canada ("**MFDA**"), on the other. In this Agreement, the Regulators, together with the securities regulatory authorities of Saskatchewan, Manitoba, Newfoundland and Labrador, New Brunswick, Nova Scotia, Prince Edward Island, Yukon, the Northwest Territories and Nunavut, are collectively referred to as the "**Securities Administrators**".

This Agreement confirms the terms and conditions under which the Regulators have authorized the MFDA to access and use the National Registration Database system ("**NRD**"). Such access and use is subject to approval by CDS Inc. in accordance with the NRD Operations Agreement between the Regulators and CDS Inc. Subject to the foregoing, the MFDA is authorized by the Regulators to access and use NRD on the following terms and conditions:

1. The MFDA's access to and use of NRD is limited to:

    (a) viewing information and adding regulatory notes concerning current and former MFDA Members or Approved Persons (as defined in MFDA By-Law No. 1) and applicants for MFDA membership or approval (collectively, "**MFDA Members and Approved Persons**") for the purpose of ensuring compliance with and enforcement of MFDA By-laws, Rules, Policies and other requirements prescribed by the MFDA; and

    (b) viewing information concerning non-MFDA Members and non-Approved Persons ("**Other Persons**") for the purpose of identifying the appropriate regulatory authority to which complaints about such Other Persons may be referred.

2. The MFDA may add regulatory notes to NRD concerning current and former MFDA Members and Approved Persons in accordance with the Canadian Securities Administrators' Regulatory Procedures Manual. These regulatory notes may be for early warnings, terms and conditions, compliance and enforcement issues. The MFDA is not authorized to add any other information to NRD.

3. The MFDA is not permitted to collect, use or disclose the information which it views on NRD for any commercial or other non-regulatory purpose or in the course of a commercial or other non-regulatory activity. The MFDA acknowledges the necessity to respect the privacy of individuals and will comply with privacy legislation where applicable.

4. The MFDA is not permitted to disclose the information which it obtains from or views on NRD to any other person, except the authorities identified in section 23 of MFDA By-law No. 1 or where required by law.

5. The MFDA will ensure that access to NRD by staff of the MFDA will be in compliance with the MFDA's Internal Procedure — NRD Access by MFDA Staff, a copy of which is attached as Schedule A.

6. MFDA staff located in British Columbia, Alberta or Ontario will be granted access to NRD through the use of user names and passwords created by the BCSC, ASC or OSC, as applicable. Requests for granting or terminating NRD access will be made through the MFDA's Director, Membership Services and Communications, who will make such requests to the securities regulatory authority in whose jurisdiction

the relevant MFDA staff member is located. Immediately upon request, the MFDA will cease use of any user names and passwords, and will surrender and provide the details thereof, to the securities regulatory authority which created the user name and password.

7. The MFDA agrees to defend, indemnify and hold each of the Securities Administrators and their respective commissioners, commission members, directors, employees and agents harmless from and against any and all damages, liabilities, losses, demands, claims, actions, suits, costs, charges or expenses (including all legal and advisor's fees, costs and expenses) suffered or incurred by any of them in connection with, or arising or resulting from, the MFDA's access to or use of NRD. This indemnity, and paragraphs 3, 4 and 6 above, shall survive the termination of this Agreement.

The Regulators may at any time, in their sole discretion, modify or amend the above terms and conditions governing the MFDA's access to and use of NRD, upon written notification to the MFDA. The MFDA may request a change to the above terms and conditions by submitting a request in writing to the Regulators. The acceptance of any such requested change shall be in the sole discretion of the Regulators.

The Regulators, on the one hand, or the MFDA, on the other hand, may terminate this Agreement at any time, upon the provision of written notification to the other party.

The parties may send any request or give notice in respect of this Agreement (other than as contemplated in paragraph 6 above) by fax, email or courier, to the other party at the following address:

To the Regulators:

CSA IT Systems Office

c/o Ontario Securities Commission

20 Queen Street West

19th Floor, Box 55

Toronto, Ontario, M5H 3S8

Attention: Ian Campbell

Chief Information Officer

Economic Analysis, Strategy and Project Planning Branch
Email: icampbell@osc.gov.on.ca
Tel.: (416) 593-8306
Fax: (416) 593-8218

To the MFDA:

Mutual Fund Dealers Association of Canada

Suite 1600, 121 King Street West

Toronto, ON, M5H 3T9

Attention: Ken Woodard

Director, Membership Services and Communications
Email: kwoodard@mfda.ca
Tel.: (416) 943-4602
Fax: (416) 943-1218

This Agreement constitutes the entire agreement between the parties pertaining to the subject matter hereof and supersedes any prior agreements, understandings, negotiations and discussions, whether written or oral, pertaining to the subject matter hereof.

This Agreement may be executed simultaneously in two or more counterparts, each of which shall be deemed an original, including any fax counterpart, and it shall not be necessary when making proof of this Agreement to account for more than one counterpart.

The execution of this Agreement by the AMF may be subject to any approval or consent required by the AMF under any law to which the AMF is subject.

Please indicate your acknowledgement, confirmation and acceptance of the foregoing by signing the enclosed copy of this letter where indicated and returning one (1) original signed copy to the attention of the CSA IT Systems Office, c/o Deputy Director, Policy and Project Office — Economic Analysis, Strategy and Project Planning Branch of the Ontario Securities Commission at 20 Queen Street West, 19th Floor, Toronto, Ontario M5H 3S8.

Yours truly,

ALBERTA SECURITIES COMMISSION

Per: "David Linder", Executive Director

AUTORITÉ DES MARCHÉS FINANCIERS

Per: "Jean St. Gelais", Chair

For purposes of An Act respecting the Ministère du Conseil exécutif (R.S.Q., c. M-30), Secrétaire général associé aux affaires intergouvernementales canadiennes

Per: "Yves Castonguay", Secrétaire général associé aux Affaires intergouvernementales canadiennes

BRITISH COLUMBIA SECURITIES COMMISSION

Per: "Paul Bourque", Executive Director

ONTARIO SECURITIES COMMISSION

Per: "Peggy Dowdall-Logie", Executive Director and Chief Administrative Officer

INVESTMENT INDUSTRY REGULATORY ORGANIZATION OF CANADA

Per: "Paul Riccardi", Senior Vice President,

Enforcement, Policy and Registration

"Rossana DiLieto", Vice President,

Registrations and Complaints

c. Saskatchewan Financial Services Commission

Manitoba Securities Commission

New Brunswick Securities Commission

Superintendent of Securities of Prince Edward Island

Nova Scotia Securities Commission

Newfoundland and Labrador Securities Commission

Superintendent of Securities of the Yukon

Registrar of Securities of the Northwest Territories

Registrar of Securities of Nunavut

Acknowledged, confirmed and accepted this 21st day of October, 2010.

MUTUAL FUND DEALERS ASSOCIATION OF CANADA

"Mark T. Gordon", Executive Vice President

Schedule A — Mutual Fund Dealers Association of Canada — MFDA Internal Procedure — NRD Access by MFDA Staff

A. — Introduction

Many of the securities regulatory authorities in Canada use a database for registrations called the National Registration Database ("NRD"). Registrants are required to update and submit changes to their registration using NRD. Such updates and changes would include termination of a Registrant sponsored by them ("Approved Person"), transfer of an Approved Person, new sponsorship of a proposed Approved Person and registration of corporate changes such as branch opening and closings.

The MFDA requires certain registration information for conducting reviews of Members, Membership applications and enforcement of our rules, by-laws and policies. The CSA and IIROC have granted NRD access to the MFDA to facilitate this activity. *It is important to note that the CSA and IIROC have placed strict terms and limitations on our access, which are reflected in this procedure, and it is essential that all staff ensure that they fully comply with this procedure.*

The MFDA is authorized only to view information about MFDA Members, applicants, and Approved Persons and to add regulatory notes about such firms and individuals. The MFDA also has limited authority to identify individuals who are the subject of complaints. For further details, see section D of this procedure below. Access to NRD within the MFDA is strictly-controlled and limited to a few specifically-designated individuals.

This procedure is an important MFDA policy. An employee's failure to comply with this procedure may be considered to be a violation of the terms of their employment agreement.

The procedure is set forth below.

B. — Restriction of Access to Authorized Staff Members

NRD access will be restricted to the following authorized staff members:

- For the Enforcement Department access will be restricted to the Director and Managers of Case Assessment, the Case Assessment Analysts, the Case Assessment Officers, Director and Managers of Investigations and the Administrative Assistant, Investigations.

- For the Membership Services Department, access will be restricted to the Director, Membership Services and the Membership Services Coordinators.

- For Compliance, access will be restricted to the Vice-President, Directors, Managers and Senior Compliance Officers.

- For the Prairie Region, access will be restricted to the Regional Director, the Compliance Manager, Senior Compliance Officers, the Investigations Manager and the Administrative Assistant.

- For the Pacific Region, access will be restricted to the Regional Director, the Compliance Manager, Senior Compliance Officers, the Investigations Manager and the Administrative Assistant.

- All of the above positions will have access to view information on NRD, however, only the following positions will be permitted to add regulatory notes:

  - Director and Managers of Case Assessment

  - Prairie and Pacific Region Investigations Managers

- Case Assessment Analysts
- Case Assessment Officers
- Administrative Assistant, Investigations
- Director, Membership Services

The Director, Membership Services and Communications will maintain on a current basis a list of the individuals who currently have NRD access. Individuals in the above positions will not have access until it has been authorized by the British Columbia Securities Commission (in the case of the Pacific Region), Alberta Securities Commission (in the case of the Prairie Region) or the Ontario Securities Commission in accordance with the procedures noted below. Only designated staff will be allowed access to NRD.

Requests for granting or terminating access will be made through the Director, Membership Services and Communications, who will deal with the applicable securities regulatory authority. MFDA management must ensure that they provide immediate notification of the resignation, suspension or termination of authorized individuals to the Director, Membership Services and Communications, as it is imperative that the MFDA provide immediate notification of such events to the applicable securities regulatory authority so that that the individual's NRD authorization may be revoked. No other MFDA departments or staff members will have access to NRD.

C. — Process for Accessing NRD Information

Any requests from departmental staff members for NRD information will be required to be made via Email to an authorized staff member. The Email should specify the following:

a. The individual or firm name that you are requesting information for;

b. The reason for the request; and

c. The file number to which the request is associated, where appropriate.

Any information obtained from NRD may only be used in accordance with section D below.

D. — Use of Registration Information

Authorized staff may access NRD:

- to view information concerning current and former MFDA Members or Approved Persons (as defined in MFDA By-Law No. 1) and applicants for MFDA membership or approval for the purpose of ensuring compliance with and enforcement of MFDA By-laws, Rules, Policies and other requirements prescribed by the MFDA. Certain authorized staff, as set out in Part B of the procedure, may also access NRD to add regulatory notes. Any regulatory notes must be added in accordance with the Canadian Securities Administrators' Regulatory Procedures Manual. These regulatory notes may be for early warnings, terms and conditions, compliance and enforcement issues. No other information may be added to NRD; or

- to view information concerning non-MFDA Members and non-Approved Persons ("Other Persons") for the purpose of identifying the appropriate regulatory authority to which complaints about such Other Persons may be referred.

Bear in mind that you must comply with all applicable privacy laws. Information obtained from or viewed on NRD may not be disclosed to any entity or individual other than the authorities permitted by MFDA By-law 1, section 23 or where required by law. Such information may not be collected, used or disclosed for, or in the course of, any commercial or non-regulatory purpose or activity.

E. — Questions

Any questions regarding this procedure should be directed to the Director, Membership Services and Communications.

IA-11 — Memorandum of Understanding Concerning Consultation, Cooperation and the Exchange of Information between the Ontario Securities Commission and the Canadian Public Accountability Board

Date: December 5, 2013

36 O.S.C.B. 11538

The Parties agree as follows

Article One — Underlying Principles

1. The Ontario Securities Commission (the "OSC") is responsible for the regulation of the capital markets in Ontario. It has a dual mandate to provide protection to investors and to foster fair and efficient capital markets and confidence in capital markets. The OSC has developed requirements for timely and accurate public disclosure of information by Reporting Issuers who raise money from Ontario investors. These requirements obligate Reporting Issuers to have their financial statements audited by a Public Accounting Firm that is a member of, and subject to inspection by, the Canadian Public Accountability Board ("CPAB").

2. The mandate of CPAB is to contribute to public confidence in the integrity of financial reporting by public companies by maintaining a register of Public Accounting Firms that audit Reporting Issuers and to oversee the audit of the financial statements of Reporting Issuers. CPAB's authority to carry out its inspection and audit oversight program in Ontario, is set out in the *Canadian Public Accountability Board Act (Ontario), 2006* (the "CPAB Act").

3. The OSC and CPAB recognize the overlap between their respective mandates and acknowledge the significance of working with each other to promote higher quality auditing and investor confidence in the financial reporting of Reporting Issuers in Ontario.

4. In order to carry out their mandates effectively, the OSC and CPAB require access to highly confidential information from Public Accounting Firms and Reporting Issuers.

5. The OSC and CPAB recognise that it is in the public interest that they have access to such confidential information and, that the confidentiality of that information be maintained.

6. CPAB recognizes that the obligations of the OSC under this Memorandum of Understanding ("MOU") to keep information confidential do not in any way restrict the OSC's ability to use the information in connection with a confidential investigation, including disclosure to a person being examined who is under a confidentiality obligation, and CPAB recognizes further that the OSC's confidentiality obligations are subject to the legal duty of the OSC to make disclosure in connection with a proceeding commenced or proposed to be commenced by the OSC under the *Securities Act* or an examination of a witness, including a witness summoned as part of an investigation under the *Securities Act*.

7. The OSC and CPAB have therefore entered into this MOU regarding mutual assistance and the exchange of information on a confidential basis to assist each organization in fulfilling its respective mandate.

Article Two — Definitions

8. For the purpose of this MOU:

"Accounting Principles" has the same meaning as in National Instrument 52-107 *Acceptable Accounting Principles and Auditing Standards*;

"Authority" means:

(a) The Canadian Public Accountability Board (CPAB), a corporation without share capital incorporated under the Canada *Corporations Act* by letters patent dated April 15, 2003; or

(b) The Ontario Securities Commission (OSC), a corporation continued under the *Securities Act*, R.S.O. 1990; (collectively, the "Authorities")

"Confidential Information" means information that has been reasonably identified as confidential by the supplying Authority, and

(a) is not information that is, at the time of disclosure, or has become, part of the public domain, or

(b) is not the same information that the receiving Authority obtained from a party other than the supplying Authority,

"CPAB's Rules" means the rules governing CPAB's inspections of Participating Audit Firms as prescribed by CPAB under its by-laws;

"Law" means any law, regulation, order, or regulatory rules or requirement applicable in Canada;

"Non-Confidential Information" means information in the possession of either Authority that is not Confidential Information or has ceased to be Confidential Information;

"Person" or *"Persons"* means a natural person, legal entity, partnership or unincorporated association;

"Public Accounting Firm" means a sole proprietorship, partnership, corporation, or other legal entity engaged in the business of providing services as public accountants;

"Ontario Securities Law" and *"Reporting Issuer"* each have the same meaning as in the *Securities Act* (Ontario), (the "Securities Act");

"Designated Professional", *"Generally Accepted Auditing Standards"* or *"GAAS"*, *"Participating Audit Firm"* and *"Professional Standards"* each have the same meaning as in the CPAB Act.

Article Three — Intent of MOU

9. This MOU is a statement of intent to consult, cooperate and exchange information in connection with the inspection, supervision, investigation and oversight of Public Accounting Firms and Reporting Issuers in a manner consistent with and permitted by the Law that governs the Authorities. This cooperation has been and will continue to be primarily achieved through ongoing informal discussions and consultation, supplemented when necessary, by more in-depth cooperation. The provisions of this MOU are intended to support such informal communication, as well as to facilitate the exchange of information where desirable, subject to applicable Law.

10. The Authorities recognise that it is in the public interest that the OSC and CPAB obtain access to confidential information from the other Authority in a timely manner and that, subject to Section 6, the confidentiality of information provided by the Authorities be maintained.

Article Four — Scope of Consultation, Cooperation and Exchange of Information

11. The Authorities will, within the framework of this MOU, cooperate to promote compliance with their respective missions and mandates.

12. CPAB will share Non-Confidential Information and, subject to Article Six, Confidential Information, and provide assistance to the OSC in obtaining and interpreting such information, which includes, without limitation:

a. Notice and particulars of a situation where CPAB has identified, or becomes aware of a violation, or a series of violations, of Professional Standards or CPAB's Rules at a Participating Audit Firm, relating to an audit or audits of one or more Reporting Issuers performed by a Participating Audit Firm, which violation, or series of violations, creates a heightened risk to the investing public.

b. Notice and particulars of any restriction or sanction CPAB has imposed on, or removed from, any Participating Audit Firm.

c. Notice and particulars of any requirement CPAB has imposed on, or removed from, any Participating Audit Firm.

d. Notice of situations in which CPAB has required a Reporting Issuer to seek the views of the Commission regarding a matter in question.

e. Information, if it becomes known to CPAB in the course of its inspection or investigation activities, that a Reporting Issuer will be:

    i. re-filing annual or interim financial statements,

    ii. re-stating or potentially restating financial information for comparative periods in annual or interim financial statements for reasons other than the retrospective application of a change in accounting standard or policy or a new accounting standard.

f. Notice CPAB has terminated the status of any audit firm as a Participating Audit Firm because of the failure of such firm to comply with the provisions of CPAB's Participation Agreement and the particulars of the failure.

g. Any anonymous tip received by CPAB that, in CPAB's judgement, suggests a Reporting Issuer may have materially misstated its financial statements, or otherwise breached Ontario Securities Law.

h. Information CPAB may have about a Participating Audit Firm or Firms, or a Reporting Issuer or Issuers, which CPAB, in its judgment believes should be brought to the attention of the OSC.

13. CPAB will share Non-Confidential Information and, subject to Article Six, Confidential Information, and provide assistance to the OSC in obtaining and interpreting such information, regarding CPAB's general strategic plans for inspections, the general results of inspecting Participating Audit Firms or Reporting Issuer audit files, and related issues that may be relevant to assessing compliance with Ontario Securities Law. Such information includes, without limitation, notice of any targeted reviews of Participating Audit Firms or Reporting Issuer audit files resulting from CPAB's risk analysis; a targeted review being a review which is not part of CPAB's annual review process.

14. The Authorities will consult regularly at the staff level regarding the following areas of common interest relating to risk issues and day to day regulatory matters, subject to Article Six:

a. Risk assessment processes;

b. Analyzing areas of high risk relating to particular industries, or Reporting Issuers, with significant operations in foreign jurisdictions;

c. Analyzing and sharing information on the OSC's continuous disclosure review focus areas relating to the application of Generally Accepted Auditing Standards or the application of International Financial Reporting Standards (IFRS) in the financial statements of Reporting Issuers;

d. Analyzing and sharing information relating to the OSC's results of the continuous disclosure review focus areas described in (c);

e. International developments in accounting and auditing standards; and

f. Any other areas of mutual interest.

15. To supplement informal consultations, the OSC will share Non-Confidential and, subject to Article Six, Confidential Information, and provide assistance to CPAB in interpreting such information, relevant to CPAB's mandate. Such information includes without limitation:

a. Notice and particulars of a situation where the OSC has identified, or becomes aware of a potential violation of Professional Standards or CPAB's Rules at a Participating Audit Firm, relating to an audit of a Reporting Issuer performed by a Participating Audit Firm, which potential violation creates a heightened risk to the investing public;

b. Particulars of any restatement of the annual financial statements of a Reporting Issuer as a result of a continuous disclosure, or issue-oriented, review by the OSC;

c. Advance notice of issue-oriented continuous disclosure reviews that may result in the request of information from Participating Audit Firms; and

d. Any anonymous tip received by the OSC that suggests a Designated Professional or Participating Audit Firm has not performed sufficient procedures to support an opinion in an auditor's report that accompanies a Reporting Issuer's financial statements filed in accordance with Ontario Securities Law.

e. Information the OSC may have about a Participating Audit Firm or Firms, or a Reporting Issuer or Issuers, which the OSC, in its judgment believes should be brought to the attention of CPAB.

16. If the OSC provides CPAB with information under Section 15 of the MOU, CPAB will inform the OSC whether any review or examination of a Designated Professional or Participating Audit Firm is being or will be performed by CPAB in light of the information provided. If a review or examination is performed, CPAB will advise the OSC, if it identifies any potential breach of Ontario Securities Law.

Article Five — Permissible Uses of Information

17. Either Authority may use Confidential Information or Non-Confidential Information obtained under this MOU for the purpose of carrying out their respective mandates.

Article Six — Confidentiality of Information and Onward Sharing

18. Except for disclosures in accordance with this MOU, including disclosures in the course of permissible uses of information under Article Five, and except as provided in Section 6, each Authority will maintain the confidentiality of Confidential Information shared under this MOU, requests made under this MOU, the contents of such requests, and any other matters arising under this MOU.

19. To the fullest extent permitted by Law, one Authority will notify the other Authority of any legally enforceable demand for Confidential Information furnished under this MOU and prior to compliance with the demand, the Authority from which the information was demanded will assert all appropriate legal exemptions or privileges with respect to such information as may be available.

20. Except as otherwise provided under this Article and subject to Section 6, Confidential Information may not be disclosed by either Authority to third parties unless each Authority has provided the other with its written consent to such disclosure. Third parties shall include foreign securities or financial regulatory authorities. If consent is not obtained from the Authority, the Authorities will consult to discuss the reasons for withholding approval of such use and the circumstances, if any, under which the intended use by the Authority might be allowed.

21. Subject to section 22, when either Authority intends to share Confidential Information under this MOU, the other Authority will confirm that it will treat this information as highly confidential and that it will protect it to the fullest extent permitted by Law.

22. The OSC has made a determination under section 153 of the *Securities Act* that information received by the OSC from CPAB under paragraph 12(a) of this agreement shall be maintained in confidence. This determination shall not apply to information received under paragraph 12(a) after the date that is three years following the date the MOU becomes effective, unless the OSC makes another determination with respect to such information.

23. Where the OSC intends to share Confidential Information with another securities or financial regulatory authority in Canada, the OSC shall provide that authority with CPAB's general description of the nature of the Confidential Information and particulars of the prejudice that could arise from its release. The OSC will not share the information unless, prior to receiving the Confidential Information from the OSC, the receiving authority shall provide the OSC and CPAB with its written assurance that:

    a. it has taken appropriate steps to protect the Confidential Information from disclosure under that jurisdiction's access to information legislation;

    b. without restricting the receiving authority's ability to use or constraining its ability to disclose the information as described in Section 6 (if the section were read by substituting the OSC with the name of the receiving authority), the receiving authority will maintain the confidentiality of the Confidential Information and will not disclose the Confidential Information to third parties unless CPAB has provided the receiving authority with its written consent to such disclosure; and

    c. it will notify the OSC and CPAB of any legally enforceable demand for Confidential Information prior to compliance with the demand, and shall assert all appropriate legal exemptions or privileges with respect to such information as may be available.

Article Seven — Costs

24. The Authorities will consult with one another in matters relating to specific requests made under this MOU that may involve substantial cost. If it appears that responding to a request for assistance will involve substantial costs being incurred by the requested Authority, the Authorities will consider the establishment of a cost-sharing arrangement before responding to the request.

Article Eight

25. The Authorities will review after 3 years following the date of execution of the MOU, and may at any other time agree to review, the functioning and effectiveness of this MOU with a view, among other things, to modifying it as appropriate should that be considered necessary or helpful to the fulfillment of each Authority's respective mandate. This MOU may not be amended without the written consent of each of the Authorities.

Article Nine — Termination

26. Unless otherwise agreed to by the Authorities in advance of termination, this MOU will terminate on the earlier of (a) the expiration of 30 days after the date either Authority gives written notice to the other Authority of its intention to terminate same, and (b) 3 years following the date of execution of the MOU. Cooperation will continue with respect to all matters on which assistance was sought under the MOU, until the date of termination, unless the Authority seeking assistance terminates the matter for which assistance was requested. Article Six will survive the termination of the MOU.

Executed by the Authorities and effective as of this 27th day of November, 2013:

Canadian Public Accountability Board   Ontario Securities Commission

"Brian Hunt"   *"James Turner"*

Brian Hunt   **James Turner**

Chief Executive Officer   Vice-Chair

Canadian Public Accountability Board   Ontario Securities Commission

150 York Street, Suite 900, Box 90   20 Queen Street West, 22nd Floor

Toronto, Ontario M5H 3S5   Toronto, Ontario M5H 3S8

Appendix A — Contacts

The Authorities may send any communication, request or give notice under this MOU by fax, email or courier to the other Authority at the following address:

ONTARIO SECURITIES COMMISSION (OSC)

    20 Queen Street West, 19th Floor

    Toronto, Ontario

    M5H 3S8

Attention: Cameron McInnis or the Chief Accountant

                    Office of the Chief Accountant

Telephone: (416) 593 3675

Fax: (416) 593 8177

Email: cmcinnis@osc.gov.on.ca

CANADIAN PUBLIC ACCOUNTABILITY BOARD (CPAB)

Canadian Public Accountability Board
150 York Street, Suite 900, Box 90
Toronto, Ontario
M5H 3S5

Attention: J. Neil St. John
                    General Counsel
Telephone: (416) 840 2571
Fax: (416) 850 9235
Email: neil.stjohn@cpab-ccrc.ca

IA-12 — Notice of Memorandum of Understanding Concerning Cooperation and the Exchange of Information Related to the Supervision of Cross-Border Covered Entities

Date: March 27, 2014
38 O.S.C.B. 3034

[Not reproduced]

IA-13 — Notice of Memorandum of Understanding Concerning Monitoring of the Ongoing Compliance with Recognition Conditions by CCPs Established in Canada

Date: January 7, 2016
(2016), 39 OSCB 11

[Not reproduced]

IA — Other Intergovernmental Agreements

(not comprehensive)

Description	Date/Citation	Minister of Finance Approval/Citation
MOU-United States Securities and Exchange Commission	1988/01/07 11 O.S.C.B. 114	
MOU-Commission des opérations de bourse (France)	1992/01/31 15 O.S.C.B. 1173	
MOU-Commodity Futures Trading Commission (U.S.)	1992/07/07 15 O.S.C.B. 3199	
MOU-Commissione Nazionale per la Societa e la Borsa (Italy)	1994/10/20 not published	
MOU-Australian Securities Commission	1995/07/05 18 O.S.C.B. 3109	1995/08/29 18 O.S.C.B. 4171
MOU-Securities Enforcement Review Committee	1996/06/01 19 O.S.C.B. 3427	
Information Sharing Arrangement with the SEC	1996/08/28 19 O.S.C.B. 5090	
MOU-Investment Advisers and Investment Adviser Representatives (NASAA)	1997/04/27 20 O.S.C.B. 2774	1997/07/07 20 O.S.C.B. 3712
MOU-Hong Kong Securities and Futures Commission	1997/02/25 20 O.S.C.B. 1026	1997/04/23 20 O.S.C.B. 2275
The Declaration on Cooperation and Supervision of International Futures Markets and Clearing Organizations	1999/11/30 23 O.S.C.B. 3	2000/03/02 23 O.S.C.B. 1731
Capital Pool Companies Operating Agreement	2002/04/12 25 O.S.C.B. 2079	2002/06/14 25 O.S.C.B. 3315
MOU — International Organization of Securities Commissions (IOSCO)	2002/10/16 25 O.S.C.B. 7157	2002/12/05 25 O.S.C.B. 8409
MOU — China Securities Regulatory Commission	2003/03/21 26 O.S.C.B. 2636	2003/05/05 26 O.S.C.B. 3711

Description	Date/Citation	Minister of Finance Approval/Citation
MOU — Autorité des marchés financiers regarding Co-ordination and Information Sharing relating to TMX Group Inc., TSX Inc. and Bourse de Montréal Inc.	2008/10/17 31 O.S.C.B. 9957	2008/12/16 32 O.S.C.B. 2453
MOU — seven other provincial securities regulatory authorities and China Banking Regulatory Commission	2010/04/23 33 O.S.C.B. 3608	2010/06/17 33 O.S.C.B. 5774
MOU — Autorité des marchés financiers and the Securities and Exchange Commission concerning Consultation, Cooperation and the Exchange of Information Related to the Supervision of Cross-Border Regulated Entities	2010/06/18 33 O.S.C.B. 5457	2010/08/11 33 O.S.C.B. 7324
Exchange of Letters between certain provincial securities regulators and the China Insurance Regulatory Commission concerning regulatory co-operation related to the overseas investment operations of Chinese insurance firms	2010/11/12 33 O.S.C.B. 10355	2010/12/17 33 O.S.C.B. 11611
MOU between certain provincial securities regulators and IIROC with respect to the administration and application of surplus finds generated by the operation of NRD	2011/04/22 34 O.S.C.B. 4846	2011/03/14 34 O.S.C.B. 5427
MOU between the OSC and the Financial Industry Regulatory Authority, Inc.	2011/11/10 34 O.S.C.B. 11500	2011/12/13 34 O.S.C.B. 12674
MOU between ASC, AMF, BCSC, OSC and Australian Securities and Investments Commission	2012/01/25 35 O.S.C.B. 1660	2012/03/23 35 O.S.C.B. 3297
MOU on the Cooperation of Competent Authorities for the Supervision of the Credit Rating Agencies	2012/03/07 35 O.S.C.B. 2556	2012/03/23 35 O.S.C.B. 3295
Letter Agreement between OSC and Association of Professional Geoscientists of Ontario	2012/08/20 35 O.S.C.B. 8383	2012/11/12 35 O.S.C.B. 10476
Agreement in Support of the Outsourcing and Management of the CSA National Systems among BCSC, ASC, OSC and AMF	2013/04/02 36 O.S.C.B. 4148	2013/06/13 36 O.S.C.B. 6210
CSA National Systems Intellectual Property and Ownership Agreement among BCSC, ASC, OSC and AMF	2013/04/02 36 O.S.C.B. 4163	2013/06/13 36 O.S.C.B. 6211
Amended and restated NRD Surplus Application Agreement among IIROC, BCSC, ASC, OSC and AMF	2013/04/02 36 O.S.C.B. 4174	2013/06/13 36 O.S.C.B. 6212
Amended and restated SEDAR and SEDI Surplus Application Agreement among BCSC, ASC, OSC and AMF	2013/04/02 36 O.S.C.B. 4178	2013/06/13 36 O.S.C.B. 6213
MOU concerning Consultation, Cooperation and the Exchange of Information Related to the Supervision of Cross-Border Regulated Entities with the Bank of England	2013/06/26 36 O.S.C.B. 6926	2013/08/21 36 O.S.C.B. 9112
MOU concerning Consultation, Cooperation and the Exchange of Information Related to the Supervision of Cross-Border Regulated Entities with Financial Conduct Authorities	2013/06/26 36 O.S.C.B. 6926	2013/08/21 36 O.S.C.B. 9112
MOU concerning Consultation, Cooperation and the Exchange of Information Related to the Supervision of Cross-Border Alternative Investment Fund Managers with 29 European regulatory authorities	2013/08/22 36 O.S.C.B. (Supp. 5) 1	2013/08/21 36 O.S.C.B. 9110
MOU concerning the oversight of the MFDA	2013/10/07 36 O.S.C.B. 7909	2013/10/02 36 O.S.C.B. 10005
MOU concerning Concerning Cooperation and the Exchange of Information Related to the Supervision of Cross-Border Covered Entities	2014/03/25 37 O.S.C.B. 3035	2014/05/26 37 O.S.C.B. 5248
Exchange of Letters Concerning Cooperation between Members of the Canadian Securities Administrators and the Superintendencia de Valores y Seguros of Chile	2014/04/08 37 O.S.C.B. 3592	2014//06/09 37 O.S.C.B. 5550
MOU Respecting the Oversight of Certain Clearing and Settlement Systems	2014/04/08 37 O.S.C.B. 3592, amended 2014/07/03	2014/06/09 37 O.S.C.B. 5981
Letter of Arrangement between the Office of Superintendent of Financial Institutions (OSFI) and the Ontario Securities Commission	2015/05/27 38 O.S.C.B. 4887	2015/06/18 38 O.S.C.B. 5449

INTERGOVERN-
MENTAL
AGREEMENTS

Description	Date/Citation	Minister of Finance Approval/Citation
MOU — Autorité des marchés financiers regarding Co-ordination and Information Sharing relating to TMX Group Inc., TSX Inc. and Bourse de Montréal Inc.	2009/10/17 31 O.S.C.B. 9957	2008/12/16 32 O.S.C.B. 2458
MOU — seven other provincial securities regulators and China Banking Regulatory Commission	2010/04/23 33 O.S.C.B. 5608	2010/06/17 35 O.S.C.B. 5774
MOU — Autorité des marchés financiers and the Securities and Exchange Commission concerning Consultation, Cooperation and the Exchange of Information Related to the Supervision of Cross-Border Regulated Entities	2010/06/18 35 O.S.C.B. 5437	2010/08/11 33 O.S.C.B. 7324
Exchange of Letters between certain provincial securities regulators and the China Insurance Regulatory Commission concerning regulatory co-operation related to the overseas investment operations of Chinese insurance firms	2010/11/12 33 O.S.C.B. 10835	2010/12/17 33 O.S.C.B. 11611
MOU between certain provincial securities regulators and HROC with respect to the administration and application of surplus funds generated by the operation of NRD	2011/04/22 34 O.S.C.B. 4846	2011/03/18 34 O.S.C.B. 5427
MOU between the OSC and the Financial Industry Regulatory Authority, Inc.	2011/11/10 34 O.S.C.B. 11500	2011/12/13 34 O.S.C.B. 12614
MOU between ASC, AMF, BCSC, OSC and Australian Securities and Investments Commission	2012/01/25 35 O.S.C.B. 1660	2012/03/23 35 O.S.C.B. 3327
MOU on the Cooperation of Competent Authorities for the Supervision of the Credit Rating Agencies	2012/03/07 35 O.S.C.B. 2566	2012/04/23 35 O.S.C.B. 3295
Letter Agreement between OSC and Association of Professional Geoscientists of Ontario	2012/08/29 35 O.S.C.B. 8383	2012/11/14 35 O.S.C.B. 10410
Agreement in Support of the Outsourcing and Management of the CSA National Systems among BCSC, ASC, OSC and AMF	2013/04/02 36 O.S.C.B. 4148	2013/06/13 36 O.S.C.B. 6210
CSA National Systems Intellectual Property and Ownership Agreement among BCSC, ASC, OSC and AMF	2013/04/02 36 O.S.C.B. 4161	2013/06/13 36 O.S.C.B. 6211
Amended and restated NRD Surplus Application Agreement among IIROC, BCSC, ASC, OSC and AMF	2013/04/02 36 O.S.C.B. 4174	2013/06/13 36 O.S.C.B. 6212
Amended and restated SEDAR and SEDI Surplus Application Agreement among BCSC, ASC, OSC and AMF	2013/04/02 36 O.S.C.B. 4178	2013/06/13 36 O.S.C.B. 6213
MOU concerning Consultation, Cooperation and the Exchange of Information Related to the Supervision of Cross-Border Regulated Entities with the Bank of England	2013/06/26 36 O.S.C.B. 6926	2014/03/21 36 O.S.C.B. 9112
MOU concerning Consultation, Cooperation and the Exchange of Information Related to the Supervision of Cross-Border Regulated Entities with Financial Conduct Authority	2013/06/26 36 O.S.C.B. 6926	2013/08/21 36 O.S.C.B. 9112
MOU concerning Consultation, Cooperation and the Exchange of Information Related to the Supervision of Cross-Border Alternative Investment Fund Managers with 29 European regulatory authorities	2013/05/22 36 O.S.C.B. (Supp 5) 1	2013/08/21 36 O.S.C.B. 9116
MOU concerning the oversight of the MFDA	2013/10/17 36 O.S.C.B. 7909	2013/10/02 36 O.S.C.B. 10005
MOU concerning Cooperation and the Exchange of Information Related to the Supervision of Cross-Border Covered Entities	2014/07/25 37 O.S.C.B. 8035	2014/07/26 37 O.S.C.B. 3248
Exchange of Letters Concerning Cooperation between Members of the Canadian Securities Administrators and the Superintendencia de Valores y Seguros of Chile	2014/04/08 37 O.S.C.B. 3592	2014/09/09 37 O.S.C.B. 5550
MOU Respecting the Oversight of Certain Clearing and Settlement Systems	2014/04/08 37 O.S.C.B. 3592, amended 2014/07/03	2014/06/09 37 O.S.C.B. 5981
Letter of Arrangement between the Office of Superintendent of Financial Institutions (OSFI) and the Ontario Securities Commission	2015/05/27 38 O.S.C.B. 4587	2015/06/18 38 O.S.C.B. 5149

INDEX

Throughout this Index, the Ontario Securities Commission is referred to as the "OSC".

A

Accredited investor
- defined, NI 45-106, s. 1.1; NPS 45-106CP, s. 3.5
- exemption from prospectus requirement for, NI 45-106, s. 2.3
- sale of exempt securities to, OSCN 33-735

Advertising
- distribution on the Internet, NPS 47-201
- during waiting period between preliminary and final prospectuses, NPS 41-101CP, s. 6.5
- exempt transactions, NPS 45-106CP, s. 3.3
- issuers using mass, CSAN 51-336
- mutual funds, NI 81-102, Part 15
- OSC prior approval, OSA 50
- prospectus offering, NPS 41-101CP, Part 6
- prohibitions
- • OSC endorsement, OSA 46
- • using another registrant's name, OSA 43
- securities on radio or television, NPS 42

Adviser, *see also Registrants*
- categories, OSA 26(6); NI 31-103, s. 7.2
- defined, OSA 1(1)
- exemptions from registration, OSA 34, 35.1; NI 33-103, ss. 8.23–8.26
- international, NI 33-103, s. 8.26; Rule 35-502
- marketing practices, CSAN 31-325; OSCN 33-729
- model portfolios, OSCN 81-708
- national compliance review, OSCN 33-720
- non-resident, OSA 35.2; Rule 35-502
- registration requirement, OSA 25(3), *see also Registration*

Alternative trading systems, *see also Marketplace*
- clearing and settlement, NI 21-101, Part 13
- defined, OSA 1(1); NI 21-101, 1.1; NPS 21-101CP, 3.3
- initial operations, OSCN 21-706
- making decision respecting, OSA 20.0.1
- monitoring and enforcement, NI 23-101, Part 8; OSCN 21-704
- participation fees, Rule 13-502, Part 3.1
- process for filing, OSCN 81-705
- requirements, NI 21-101 Part 6; NPS 21-101CP, 3.4
- system changes, OSCN 21-706

Amalgamations
- as business combination, MI 61-101, s. 1.1
- change in financial year end, NI 51-102, s. 4.8
- disclosure in information circular, Form 51-102F5

- eligibility requirement for short form prospectus system, NI 44-101, 2.8
- insider trading reports after, NI 55-101, Part 7
- notice re accounting treatment, NI 51-102, s. 4.9
- prospectus exemption, NI 45-106, s. 2.11; NPS 45-106CP, s. 4.2
- restructuring transaction, NI 51-102
- trading of securities pending, Rule 48-501
- under MJDS, NI 71-101, Part 13

Annual information form (AIF)
- AIF defined, Rule 14-501; NI 51-102
- form, Form 51-102F2, 81-101F2
- investment fund issuers
- • disclosure re soft dollars, OPS 1.9, Part IIIC
- • Form, Form 81-101F2
- • general, NI 81-101, NI 81-106, Part 9
- mineral projects, NI 43-101
- non-investment fund issuers
- • form, Form 51-102F2
- • frequently asked questions, CSAN 51-311, Part D
- • requirement to file, NI 51-102, Part 6
- • under the short form prospectus system, NI 44-101, Part 3

Applications
- accredited investor recognition, OPS 45-106CP, s. 3.5
- authorization to search, OSA 13(4)
- cease to be reporting issuer, OSA 1(10); OSCN 12-703, CSAN 12-307
- declaration of non-compliance, OSA 128
- deem to be reporting issuer, OSA 1(11); OPS 12-602; CSAN 12-307
- exemption from, for
- • continuous and timely disclosure obligations, OSA 80; NI 51-102, Part 13; NI 81-106, Part 17
- • insider trading reporting, OSA 121(2); NI 55-104, Part 10
- • MJDS, NI 71-101, Part 21
- • mutual fund sales practices, NPS 81-105CP, Part 11
- • OPS 61-501, OSCN 61-701
- • prospectus requirements, OSA 74; NI 45-106, s. 7.1
- • proxy solicitation, OSA 88
- • registration requirements, OSA 74; NI 31-103, s. 15.1
- • SEDAR, NI 13-101, 3.2
- • self-dealing restrictions, OSA 113, 115(2), 117(2), 121(2); NI 31-103, s. 13.5
- • take-over bid requirements, OSA 104(2)
- • where application not otherwise provided for, OSA 147

INDEX